W9-DDO-390

A Concordance of the Ugaritic Literature

A Concordance of the Ugaritic Literature

Richard E. Whitaker

Harvard University Press, Cambridge, Massachusetts, 1972

Library of Congress Catalog Card Number 74–184104

SBN 674–15915–2

Printed in the United States of America

Introduction

The present volume contains a concordance of all of the Ugaritic alphabetic texts published in *Corpus des tablettes en cunéiformes alphabétiques,*[1] *Le Palais royal d'Ugarit* II,[2] *Le Palais royal d'Ugarit* V,[3] *Ugaritica* V,[4] *Ugaritica* VI,[5] and *Ugaritic Textbook*.[6] UT was consulted on all texts it contains and served as the source for texts not included in the other publications. Where discrepancies were found between hand copies or photographs of the cuneiform and the transliterated texts, the cuneiform was followed. The transliteration system is that used in CTCA and UT.

Many of the texts from Ugarit are in fragmentary condition. A few were omitted because they contained only scattered letters. For the sake of usefulness it seemed best to include as many texts as possible; therefore proposed reconstructions have been freely included. These are clearly indicated by inclusion in brackets and should be taken into account in computing any word frequencies based on this concordance. There has been no attempt made to indicate the precise number of letters missing in a break. Three dashes indicates that there appears to be at least a full word missing, while five dashes represents a full line or nearly a full line of missing text. Less than three dashes approximates the number of letters missing.

The assembly of the concordance and the make-up of pages were done on the IBM 360/91 computer at the University of California at Los Angeles. The camera-ready copy was prepared on an RCA Videocomp at the Los Angeles *Times*. The programs for this work were developed by the compiler and Dr. David W. Packard of the Classics Department, UCLA.

The order of the alphabet used in the concordance is as follows: a, i, u, b, g, d, ḏ, h, w, z, ḥ, ḫ, ṭ, ẓ, y, k, l, m, n, s, s̀, ʿ, ǵ, p, ṣ, q, r, š, t, ṯ (the order of the Ugaritic alphabet found in the glossary of UT). Words are arranged according to base form rather than actual form. Since there is no general agreement on the analysis of many forms, there will inevitably be disagreements over the judgments that were made in analyzing the texts for this concordance. Where it appeared to the compiler that there were no clear grounds for making decisions, words are included under more than one root. Double or triple listing, however, is kept to a minimum. Variant spellings of words, particularly when these involved interchanged letters such as *ssw* and *s̀sw*, are also given double listing.

The forms under which roots should be listed have presented a number of problems for which the following conventions have been established. No attempt is made to distinguish between homographs. The radical aleph is represented by "a" so that "i" and "u" are used only to list base forms in which these letters consistently occur. Nouns are normally listed according to the singular form, with masculine and feminine nouns from the same verbal root listed separately. The exception to this is found in nouns which occur very frequently and for which the distinction between singular and plural has more than a numerical significance: for example, *il* and *ilm*.

When the form occurring in the text is clearly the result of a scribal error, the actual form is retained in the concordance, but the word is listed under its corrected base form. Since all of the above problems introduce a subjective element into the analysis of where forms will be listed in the concordance, the index beginning on page 653 gives all the forms, other than the actual form, under which words may be listed.

The scribes at Ugarit were not consistent in their use of word dividers. All actual word dividers in the text as well as ends of lines which served as word dividers in the text are represented by periods in the concordance. All places where the compiler supplied word dividers or made divisions for the sake of constructing a concordance are represented by small spaces between the letters in the concordance. The scribes occasionally inserted word dividers where they do not belong. These have been re-

[1] Andrée Herdner (Paris: Imprimerie Nationale, 1963), hereafter cited CTCA.

[2] Charles Virolleaud (Paris: Imprimerie Nationale, 1957), hereafter cited PRU II.

[3] Charles Virolleaud (Paris: Imprimerie Nationale, 1965), hereafter cited PRU V.

[4] Jean Nongayrol, Emmanuel Laroche, Charles Virolleaud, and Claude F. A. Schaeffer (Paris: Imprimerie Nationale, 1968), hereafter cited UG V.

[5] André Parrot et al. (Paris: Mission Archéologique de Ras Shamra, 1969), hereafter cited UG VI.

[6] Cyrus H. Gordon (Rome: Pontifical Biblical Institute, 1965), hereafter cited UT.

tained, but the words have been listed under the corrected base form. The section of the word preceding the word divider is also listed under its actual form; thus *bn.š* is listed under both *bn* and *bnš*.

The words listed under each base form are further subalphabetized on the basis of their following context, again using the base forms of the context rather than actual forms. This allows the user of the concordance to see at a glance what words are used together in the language, even though the actual forms may vary slightly.

There is no single, generally accepted system for the citation of Ugaritic texts. The system of citation used in the present work includes the numbers used in both CTCA and UT, the two most readily available collections of Ugaritic texts. The form of the citation is CCC(UUU)ccc, where CCC is the unique portion of the CTCA citation, UUU is the corresponding portion of the UT citation, and ccc is the portion of the citation common to both; thus 1 (^{c}NT.IX).3.26 is in CTCA 1.3.26 and in UT ^{c}NT.IX.3.26. Periods are used to divide sections of the citations. Texts appearing in UT but not in CTCA are simply cited by their UT number. Texts included in CTCA have a hyphen in parentheses after the text number if they are not included in UT. There are two texts in CTCA that are appendices without any standard numbers. These are cited as APP.I and APP.II. Since UT includes the texts from PRU II and PRU V and cites them by their publication number with a 1000 to 2000 series number (the first text in PRU II is 1001, the first in PRU V, 2001, and so on), the UT numbers have been used for these. They can easily be translated into the PRU numbers by scholars using those volumes. Texts from UG V, which are in neither UT nor CTCA, are cited as UG5. The "liver" texts from UG VI are cited by their excavation numbers, RS61(24).

All notices of errors, criticisms, and proposals for other analyses of words will be gladly received by the compiler and given careful consideration when further publication of texts brings the need for a new edition of the concordance.

The number of people and institutions who have made this work possible have also contributed greatly to my pleasure in carrying it out. Primary thanks go to Dr. David W. Packard, Department of Classics, University of California at Los Angeles, who originally suggested the possibility of a computer concordance of Ugaritic, wrote the first concordancing programs for Ugaritic, taught me to program, and assisted in innumerable ways at every step of development. Thanks also must go to his wife, Pam, who shared his time so willingly and provided quarters and meals for me on several occasions.

Thanks are also due Dr. Lamia Shehadeh and Mr. Gary Midkiff, who offered help in proofreading and encouragement in the early stages of the project, and Professor Frank M. Cross, who suggested and encouraged the publication of the concordance.

Funds for this project have come from a number of sources. The Harvard University Computing Center provided the support for the initial development of a concordance of the literary texts. The American Philosophical Society supported the expansion of this into a concordance of all of the texts from Ugarit and the development of a printing system using an upper/lower case print chain that provided a usable copy for proofreading and research.

The American Philological Association in its 1969 Summer Institute in Computer Applications to Classical Studies under grants from IBM and the National Endowment for the Humanities provided the much appreciated opportunity for me to become seriously involved in programming and to begin work on the photocomposition stage of the concordance.

Central College, where I teach, has been generous in its allocation of research time on the computer and provided a research grant for the summer of 1971 which allowed me to run the final stage of the project at UCLA and the Los Angeles *Times*.

Every programmer knows the odd and late hours that are spent at the computer center. Only a patient and resourceful wife and family can endure these, and their moral support in spite of these hardships was a continuing encouragement.

R.E.W.
Central College
Summer 1971

A Concordance of the Ugaritic Literature

a

aupš

.b.bt.iwrpzn.|ṯt.aṯtm.w.pǵt.aḥt.b bt.[-]r[-].|[aṯ]t.b.bt.aupš.|[aṯ]t.b.bt.ṯpṭb'l.|[---.]n[--.mḏ]rǵlm.|[---.]b.bt[.---]l.|[ṯ 80[119].12

snry.|[b]n.sdy.bn.ṯty.|bn.ḥyn.bn.ǵlm.|bn.yyn.w.bn.au[pš].|bn.kdrn.|'rgzy.w.bn.'dy.|bn.gmḥn.w.ḥgbt.|bn.tgḏ 131[309].25

arty.|tlmu.zlyy.|pdu.qmnzy.|bdl.qrṭy.|trgn.bn.tǵh.|aupš.qmnzy.|ṯrry.mṣbty.|prn.nǵṯy.|ṯrḏn.zlyy. 89[312].8

ubdy.mdm.|šd.b d.'bdmlk.|šd.b d.yšn.ḥrš.|šd.b d.aupš.|šd.b d.ršpab.aḫ.ubn.|šd.b d.bn.uṯryn.|[ubd]y.mryn 82[300].1.4

[tḥṣ.ml]k.brr.|'lm.š.š[--].l[--.]'rb.šp|š.w ḥl[.ml]k.|bn.aup[š.--].bsbn hzpḫ ṯlṯt.|kṯr[.---.--]trt ḫmšt.bn gda[.-.]mḏ'.| APP.II[173].58

[-----].|ǵnbn[.---].|pdn[.---].|ṯr[--.---].|nn[-.---].|au[pš.---].|i[---.---].|pgl[--.---].|šy[.---].|bn.uḫn.|ybru.i[---]. 2161.6

aupṯ

ll.krm.aḥ[d.---].|krm.uḫn.b.šdmy.ṯlṯ.bzl[.d]prn[.---].|aupṯ.krm.aḥd.nšpin.kr[m.]aḥd[.---].|dmt.lḫsn.krm.aḥd.ann 1081.14

ab

'q h.ib.iqni.|'p'p h.sp.ṯrml.|d b ḥlm y.il.ytn.|b ḏrt y.ab.adm.|w ld.špḥ.l krk|t.w ǵlm.l 'bd.|il.ttb'.mlakm.|l yṯb.i 14[KRT].6.297

rn.[-]dm[.-].|ašlw.b ṣp.'n h.|d b ḥlm y.il.ytn.|b ḏrt y.ab.adm.|w ld.špḥ.l krt.|w ǵlm.l 'bd.il.|krt.yhṯ.w ḥlm.|'bd. 14[KRT].3.151

w yškb.nhmmt.|w yqmṣ.w b ḥlm h.|il.yrd.b ḏhrt h.|ab adm.w yqrb.|b šal.krt.m at.|krt.k ybky.|ydm'.n'mn.ǵl 14[KRT].1.37

ẓr y.al.tṣr.|udm.rbt.w udm ṯrrt.|udm.ytnt.il w ušn.|ab.adm.w ṯṯb.|mlakm.l h.lm.ank.|ksp.w yrq.ḫrṣ.|yd.mqm 14[KRT].3.136

.t[ṣr].|udm[.r]bt.w u[dm].|[ṯ]rrt.udm.y[t]n[t].|il.ušn.ab[.ad]m.|rḥq.mlk.l bt y.|n[g.]krt.l ḥẓ[r y].|w y'n[y.k]rt[.ṯ] 14[KRT].6.278

.al.tṣr].|[udm.rbt.w udm].|[ṯrrt.udm.ytnt].|[il.w ušn.ab.adm].|[rḥq.mlk.l bt y].|[ng.kr]t.l ḥ[ẓ]r y.|[-----].|[---.ttb 14[KRT].5.259

|ydm'.n'mn.ǵlm.|il.mlk[.ṯ]r ab h.|yarš.hm.drk[t].|k ab.adm.|[-----]. 14[KRT].1.43

[l]krt.|k [k]lb.b bt k.n'tq.k inr.|ap.ḫšt k.ap.ab.ik mtm.|tmtn.u ḫšt k.l ntn.|'tq.b d.aṯt.ab ṣrry.|tbky k.a 16.1[125].3

ḥm.]w l ṯ' dbḥ n.|ndbḥ.hw.ṯ' n[ṯ'y.hw.nkt.nk]t.ytši.l ab bn il.|ytši.l d[r.bn il.l]mpḥrt.bn il.|l ṯkm[n.w šnm.]hn '[32[2].1.33

m.w l ṯ'.d[bḥ n.ndbḥ].|hw.ṯ'.nṯ'y.hw.nkt.n[k]t.ytši[.l ab.bn.il].|ytši.l dr.bn.il.l mpḫrt.bn.i[l.l ṯkmn.w š]nm hn š.| 32[2].1.16

ḥm.w l.ṯ'.dbḥ n.ndbḥ.hw.ṯ' |nṯ'y.|hw.nkt.nkt.y[t]ši.l ab.bn.il.ytši.l dr.|bn il.l mpḫrt.bn.il.l ṯkmn[.w]šnm.hn.'r.| 32[2].1.25

[---.hw.ṯ'.nṯ']y.|[hw.nkt.nkt.ytši.l ab.bn.il.ytši.l d]r.bn[.il].|[l mpḫrt.bn.il.l ṯkmn.w šnm.hn š]. 32[2].1.2

m.w l.ṯ'.dbḥ n.ndb]ḥ.|[hw.ṯ'.nṯ'y.hw.nkt.nkt.]yt[ši.l ab.bn.il].|[ytši.l dr.bn.il.l mpḫ]rt.[bn.il.l ṯkmn.w šn]m hn š. 32[2].1.9A

].|[---].ksp[.---].|[---.--]ir[.---].|[---].'l.ynḥ[m].|[---.]'l.ab.b[---].|[---.]'l.'[--].|[---.']l.'[--]. 1144.14

-].|ltm.mrqdm.d š[-]l[-].|w t'n.pǵt.ṯkmt.mym.|qrym.ab.dbḥ.l ilm.|š'ly.dǵṯ h.b šmym.|dǵṯ.hrnmy.d kbkbm.|l tb 19[1AQHT].4.191

qẓ.tn nkl y|rḫ ytrḫ.ib t'rb m b bh|t h.w atn mhr h l a|b h.alp ksp w rbt ḫ|rṣ.išlḥ ẓhrm iq|nim.atn šd h krm[m] 24[77].19

šal.krt.m at.|krt.k ybky.|ydm'.n'mn.ǵlm.|il.mlk[.ṯ]r ab h.|yarš.hm.drk[t].|k ab.adm.|[-----]. 14[KRT].1.41

ṣ bn.amt.|[tn.b]nm.aqny.|[tn.ṯa]rm.amid.|[w y'n].ṯr.ab h.il.|d[--].b bk.krt.|b dm'.n'mn.ǵlm.|il.trḥṣ.w tadm.|rḥ 14[KRT].2.59

ẓr.mgdl.rkb.|ṯkmm.ḥmt.nša.|[y]d h.šmmh.dbḥ.|l ṯr.ab h.il.šrd.|[b'l].b dbḥ h.bn dgn.|[b m]ṣd h.yrd.krt.|[l g]gt. 14[KRT].4.169

ln h.klny y.qš h.|nbln.klny y.nbł.ks h.|any.l yṣḥ.ṯr.il.ab h.il.|mlk.d yknn h.yṣḥ.aṯrt.|w bn h.ilt.w ṣbrt.arḫ h.|wn 3['NT.VI].5.43

ny n.q[š] h.n[bln].|klny n[.n]bl.ks h.|[an]y.l yṣḥ.ṯr il.ab h.|[i]l.mlk.d yknn h.yṣḥ.|aṯrt.w bn h.ilt.w ṣbrt.|ary h.w 4[51].4.47

[-----].|[---.--]y.|[-----].|[any.l yṣ]ḥ.ṯr.|[il.ab h.i]l.mlk.|[d yknn h.yṣ]ḥ.aṯ|[rt.w bn h.]ilt.|[w ṣbrt.ary] 4[51].1.5

.|[hml]t.tn.b'l.w 'nn h.bn.dgn.arṯ m.pḏ h.|[w y'n.]ṯr.ab h.il.'bd k.b'l.y ym m.'bd k.b'l.|[--.--]m.bn.dgn.a[s]r km. 2.1[137].36

[ṯn]y.d't hm.išt.ištm.yitmr.ḥrb.ltšt.|[--]n hm.rgm.l ṯr.ab h.il.tḥm.ym.b'l km.|[adn]km.ṯpṭ.nhr.tn.il m.d tq h.d tq 2.1[137].33

yd h].|š[g]r h bm ymn.t[--.---].|[--.]l b'l.'bd[.---].|ṯr ab h il.ṯtrm[.---].|tšlḥm yrḫ.ggn[.---].|k[.---.ḫ]mš.ḫssm[.---]. 2001.1.15

ẓ [l].|n'mn.ilm l ḫt[n].|m.b'l trḫ pdry b[t h].|aqrb k ab h b'[l].|yǵtr.'ṯtr t|rḫ l k ybrdmy.b[t.a]|b h lb[u] y'rr.w y 24[77].27

r.ṯǵr.|bt.il.pn.l mgr lb.t'dbn.|nšb.l inr.t'dbn.ktp.|b il ab h.g'r.yṯb.il.kb[-].|aṯ[rt.]il.yṯb.b mrzḥ h.|yšt[.il.y]n.'d šb'. UG5.1.1.14

--.-]llm.trtḥṣ.|btlt.'n[t].tptr' ṯd[h].|limm.w t'l.'m.il.|ab h.ḥpr.p'l k.y[--].|šm' k.l arḫ.w bn.[--].|limm.ql.b udn.k 13[6].21

ab

[---.]ktb nǵr krm.|[---].ab h.krm ar.|[---.]h.mḫtrt.pṯtm.|[---.-]t h.ušpǵt tišr.|[---.šm 2001.2.2
n.k ṯrm.|[--]b b[ht].|[zbl.]ym.b hkl.ṯpṭ.nh[r].yṯir.ṯr.il.ab h l pn[.zb]l y[m].|[l pn.ṯp]ṭ[.nhr.]mlkt.[--]pm.l mlkt.wn. 2.3[129].21
[t h].|aqrb k ab h b'[l].|yǵtr.'ṯtr t|rẖ l k ybrdmy.b[t.a]|b h lb[u] y'rr.w y'[n].|yrẖ nyr šmm.w n'[n].|'ma nkl ẖt 24[77].29
w tphn.[---].|b grn.yẖrb[.---].|yǵly.yẖsp.ib[.---].|'l.bt.ab h.nšrm.trẖ[p]n.|ybṣr.ḥbl.diym.|tbky.pǵt.bm.lb.|tdm'.b 19[1AQHT].1.32
r.ḥl.|rḥb.mknpt.ap.|[k]rt.bnm.il.špḥ.|lṭpn.w qdš.'l.|ab h.y'rb.ybky.|w yšnn.ytn.g h.|bky.b ḥy k.ab n.ašmẖ.|b l. 16.1[125].12
[npt].|ap.krt bn[m.il].|špḥ.lṭpn[.w qdš].|bkm.t'r[b.'l.ab h].|t'rb.ḥ[--].|b ṯtm.t[---].|šknt.[---].|bkym[.---].|ǵr.y[--- 16.2[125].112
bln.|rd.l mlk.amlk.|l drkt.k aṯb.an.|ytb'.yṣb ǵlm.'l.|ab h.y'rb.yšu g h.|w yṣḥ.šm' m'.l krt.|ṯ'.ištm'.w tqǵ udn.|k 16.6[127].40
m.ṣpn.b alp.šd.rbt.kmn.|hlk.aẖt h.b'l.y'n.tdrq.|ybnt.ab h.šrḥq.aṯt.l pnn h.|št.alp.qdm h.mria.w tk.|pn h.tḥspn. 3['NT].4.84
.hlk.kbkbm.|bkm.tmdln.'r.|bkm.tṣmd.pḥl.bkm.|tšu.ab h.tštnn.l[b]mt 'r.|l ysmsm.bmt.pḥl.|y dnil.ysb.palt h.|b 19[1AQHT].2.59
.l [p'n.il.yhbr.w yql].|yštḥwy.[w ykbdn h.---].|ṯr.il[.ab h.---].|ḥš b[ht m.tbnn.ḥš.trmmn.hkl m].|b tk.[---].|bn.[- 1['NT.IX].3.26
nm.]mṣr.|[t]bu.ḏdm.qn[-.-]n[-.-]lt.|ql h.yš[m'].ṯr.[il].ab h.[---]l.|b šb't.ḥdrm.[b ṯ]mn[t.ap].|sgrt.g[-].[-]ẓ[.---] h[.-- 3['NT.VI].5.18
.'rbt.|l pn.špš.|w pn.špš.nr.|b y.mid.w um.|tšmẖ.m ab.|w al.trḥln.|'tn.ẖrd.ank.|'m ny.šlm.|kll.|w mnm.|šlm ' 1015.11
[--.]ab.w il[--].|[--] šlm.šlm i[l].|[š]lm.il.šr.|dgn.w b'l.|'ṭ w kmṯ UG5.10.1.1
.l yṯbr.ẖṭ.mṯpṭ k.w y'n[.'ṯtr].dm[-]k[-].|[--]ḥ.b y.ṯr.il.ab y.ank.in.bt[.l] y[.km.]ilm[.w] ḥẓr[.k bn].|[qd]š.lbum.trd. 2.3[129].19
rmt.al m.qḥn y.š y.qḥn y.|[--.]šir.b krm.nṭṭt.dm.'lt.b ab y.|u---].'lt.b k.lk.l pn y.yrk.b'l.[--].|[---.]'nt.šzrm.tštšḥ.k 1001.1.9
h.uzrm.ilm.ylḥm.|uzrm.yšqy.bn.qdš.|l tbrknn l ṯr.il ab y.|tmrnn.l bny.bnwt.|w ykn.bn h b bt.šrš.b qrb.|hkl h.n 17[2AQHT].1.24
|[qht.ǵ]zr.at.aẖ.w an.a[ẖt k].|[---].šb'.ṯir k.[---].|[---.]ab y.ndt.ank[.---].|[---.--]l.mlk.tlk.b ṣd[.---].|[---.]mt.išryt[.- 18[3AQHT].1.26
ank.|'m mlakt h šm' h.|w b.'ly skn.yd' rgm h.|w ht ab y ǵm[--].|t[--.---].|ls[--.---].|ṣḥ[.---].|ky.m[--.---].|w pr[-- 1021.9
q.b irt.lbnn.mk.b šb'.|[ymm.---]k.aliyn.b'l.|[---].r' h ab y.|[---.]'[---]. 22.2[124].27
bt.y'bdr[.mṯb.klt].|knyt.w t'n[.btlt.'nt].|yṯb l y.ṯr.il[.ab y.---].|yṯb.l y.w l h.[---].|[--.i]mṣẖ.nn.k imr.l arṣ.|[ašhlk] 3['NT.VI].4.7
l ẓr.[mg]dl.rkb.|ṯkmm.ḥm[t].ša.yd k.|šmm.dbḥ.l ṯr.|ab k.il.šrd.b'l.|b dbḥ k.bn.dgn.|b mṣd k.w yrd.|krt.l ggt.'d 14[KRT].2.77
k.l ttn.pnm.|'m.nrt.ilm.špš.|tšu.g h.w tṣḥ.|tḥm.ṯr.il.ab k.|hwt.lṭpn.ḥtk k.|pl.'nt.šdm.y špš.|pl.'nt.šdm.il.yš[t k]. 6[49].4.34
yql.yšt]ḥwyn.w y|[kbdn h.yšu.g h.w y]ṣḥ.tḥm.|[ṯr.il.ab k.hwt.l]ṭpn.ḥtk k.|[qryy.b arṣ.mlḥ]mt.št b 'p|[r m.ddym 1['NT.IX].2.18
.|w rgm l k[ṯr.w ẖss.ṯny.l hyn].|d ḥrš.y[dm.tḥm.ṯr.il.ab k.]|hwt.lṭpn[.ḥtk k.---].|yh.kṯr.b[---].|št.lskt.n[--.---].|'d 1['NT.IX].3.5
p.yṣb.yṯb.b hkl.|w ywsrnn.ggn h.|lk.l ab k.yṣb.lk.|l[ab]k.w rgm.'ny.|l k[rt.adn k.]ištm['].|w tqǵ[.udn.k ǵz.ǵzm 16.6[127].28
t.l kḥṯ.drkt.|ap.yṣb.yṯb.b hkl.|w ywsrnn.ggn h.|lk.l ab k.yṣb.lk.|l[ab]k.w rgm.'ny.|l k[rt.adn k.]ištm['].|w tqǵ 16.6[127].27
ab k.l pn.zbl.ym.l pn[.ṯ]pṭ[.n]hr.|[ik.a]l.yšm' k.ṯr.[i]l.ab k.l ys'.[alt.]ṯ[bt |k.l y]hpk.|[ksa.]mlk k.l yṯbr.ẖṭ.mṯpṭ k. 2.3[129].17
n.ilm.mt.ik.tmt[ẖ]|ṣ.'m.aliyn.b'l.|ik.al.yšm['] k.ṯr.|il.ab k.l ys'.alt.|ṯbt k.l yhpk.ksa.mlk k.|l yṯbr.ẖṭ.mṯpṭ k.|yru. 6[49].6.27
--.-]nn.nrt.ilm.špš.tšu.g h.w t[ṣḥ.šm]'.m'.|[-.yṯ]ir ṯr.il.ab k.l pn.zbl.ym.l pn[.ṯ]pṭ[.n]hr.|[ik.a]l.yšm' k.ṯr.[i]l.ab k.l 2.3[129].16
ẖ.|b l.mt k.ngln.k klb.|b bt k.n'tq.k inr.|ap.ẖšt k.ap.ab.k mtm.|tmtn.u ẖšt k.l ntn.|'tq.b d.aṯt.ab.ṣrry.|ik m.yrg 16.1[125].17
l.mt k.ngln.|k klb.[b]bt k.n'tq.|k inr[.ap.]ẖšt k.|ap.ab.k mtm.tmtn.|u ẖšt k.l bky.'tq.|b d.aṯt ab.ṣrry.|u ilm.tm 16.2[125].102
lṯmg.|kdrl.|wql.|adrdn.|prn.|'bdil.|ušy.šbn[-].|aẖt.ab.|krwn.|nnḏ.|mkl.|kzǵb.|iyrḏ. 1069.13
n.|[---.]hr n.km.šḥr.|[---.y]lt n.km.qdm.|[-.k]bd n.il.ab n.|kbd k iš.tikln.|ṯd n.km.mrm.tqrṣn.|il.yẓḥq.bm.|lb.w 12[75].1.9
qdš.'l.|ab h.y'rb.ybky.|w yšnn.ytn.g h.|bky.b ḥy k.ab n.ašmẖ.|b l.mt k.ngln.k klb.|b bt k.n'tq.k inr.|ap.ẖšt k. 16.1[125].14
trm.tṣr.trm[.']tqt.|tbky.w tšnn.[tt]n.|g h.bky.b ḥ[y k.a]b n.|nšmẖ.b l.mt k.ngln.|k klb.[b]bt k.n'tq.|k inr[.ap.]ẖš 16.2[125].98
.diy hmt nšrm.|tpr.w du.b nši.'n h.w ypn.|yḥd.hrgb.ab.nšrm.|yšu.g h.w yṣḥ.knp.hr[g]b.|b'l.yṯb.b'l.y[ṯb]r.diy[.h 19[1AQHT].3.121
mtm.|tmtn.u ẖšt k.l ntn.|'tq.b d.aṯt.ab ṣrry.|tbky k.ab.ǵr.b'l.|ṣpn.ḥlm.qdš.|any.ḥlm.adr.ḥl.|rḥb.mknpt.ap.|[k] 16.1[125].6
b d.aṯt ab.ṣrry.|u ilm.tmtn.špḥ.|[l]ṭpn.l yḥ.t[b]ky k.|ab.ǵr.b'l.ṣ[p]n.ḥlm.|qdš.nny.ḥ[l]m.adr.|ḥl.rḥb.mk[npt].|ap 16.2[125].107
ap.ẖšt k.ap.ab.k mtm.|tmtn.u ẖšt k.l ntn.|'tq.b d.aṯt.ab.ṣrry.|ik m.yrgm.bn.il.|krt.špḥ.lṭpn.|w qdš.u ilm.tmtn.| 16.1[125].19
.]ẖšt k.|ap.ab.k mtm.tmtn.|u ẖšt k.l bky.'tq.|b d.aṯt ab.ṣrry.|u ilm.tmtn.špḥ.|[l]ṭpn.l yḥ.t[b]ky k.|ab.ǵr.b'l.ṣ[p] 16.2[125].104
p.ẖšt k.ap.ab.ik mtm.|tmtn.u ẖšt k.l ntn.|'tq.b d.aṯt.ab ṣrry.|tbky k.ab.ǵr.b'l.|ṣpn.ḥlm.qdš.|any.ḥlm.adr.ḥl.|rḥ 16.1[125].5
hrm.qrb.apq.thmtm].|[ygly.]ḏl i[l].w ybu[.q]rš.mlk[.ab.šnm.l p'n.il.]|[yhbr.]w yql[.y]štḥw[y.]w ykb[dn h.--]r y[- 2.3[129].5
pid.tk ẖrš[n.---.tk.ǵr.ks].|ygly ḏd.i[l.w ybu.qrš.mlk].|ab.šnm.l [p'n.il.yhbr.w yql].|yštḥwy.[w ykbdn h.---].|ṯr.il[. 1['NT.IX].3.24
.nhrm.|[qrb.ap]q.thmtm tgly.ḏd il.|[w tbu.qr]š.mlk.ab.šnm.|[l p'n.il.t]hbr.w tql.tštḥ|[wy.w tkbd]n h.tlšn.aqht. 17[2AQHT].6.49
nhrm.qrb.|[a]pq.thmtm.tgly.ḏd.|il.w tbu.qrš..|mlk.ab.šnm.l p'n.|il.thbr.w tql.|tštḥwy.w tkbdn h.|tšu.g h.w tṣ 6:1.36[49.1.8]
bk.nhrm.|qrb.apq.thmtm.|tgly.ḏd.il.w tbu.|qrš.mlk.ab.šnm.|l p'n.il.thbr.w tql.|tštḥwy.w tkbd h.|hlm.il.k yphn 4[51].4.24
.qr]b.[ap]q.|[thm]tm.tgl.ḏ[d.]i[l.]w tbu.|[qr]š.m[l]k.ab[.šnm.]mṣr.|[t]bu.ḏdm.qn[-.-]n[-.-]lt.|ql h.yš[m'].ṯr.[il].a 3['NT.VI].5.16
rm].|[qrb.apq.thmtm].|[tgly.ḏd.il.w]tb[a].|[qrš.mlk.ab.]šnm.|[tša.g hm.w tṣ]ḥ.sbn.|[---]l[.---.]'d.|ksm.mhyt[.m] 5[67].6.2
tḥwy.pẖr [m'd.qmm.a--.am]|r ṯny.d't km.w rgm.l ṯr.a[b.-.il.ṯny.l pẖr].|m'd.tḥm.ym.b'l km.adn km.ṯ[pṭ.nhr].|tn 2.1[137].16
ṯr[.il.ab -.w t'n.rbt].|aṯr[t.ym.šm'.l qdš].|w am[rr.l dgy.rbt].|aṯrt 4[51].4.1
ṯb[-.---].|ab[.---].|ḥyi[l.---].|iẖy[.---].|ar[.---].|'ṯtr[.---].|bn.[---].|yly[. 2131.2

abb

---.-]pṭ.|[---.]knys.[---].|[---.--]by.|[---.-]ṯby[.---].|[---].abb[.---].|[---.-]k[-.-]n[-].|[---.--]m.šr.d.yṯ[b].|[---.--]y.d.ẖbṯ. 2134.7

abbly

.|brqd.|bnn.|kbln.ṣ[md].|bn gmrt.|bn.il.ṣm[d].|bn abbly.|yṯ'd.ṣm[d].|bn.liy.|'šrm.ṣ[md].|ṯṯ kbd.b ḥ[--].|w.ar 2113.20

abg

ils.|bn ḥšbn.|bn uryy.|bn kṯl.|bn army.|bn gln.|bn abg.|bn.nǵry.|bn.srwd.|mtnn.|bn gš[-].|bn gbrn.|bn uldy. 1064.12

abd

[--.]ḥy[--.--.]l ašṣi.hm.ap.amr[--].|[---].w b ym.mnẖ l abd.b ym.irtm.m[--].|[ṯpṭ].nhr.tl'm.ṯm.ḥrbm.its.anšq.|[-]ht 2.4[68].3
aṯt.|ddy.[a]ḏddy.|bn.mlkr[šp].|bn.y[k]n.|ynḥm.|bn.abd.b'[l].|mnḥm.bn[.---].|krmn[py].|bn.[--]m.|bn.asr[-].|b 2014.48

-].|[---]m.il[.---].|[---]d nhr.umt.|[---.]rpat.bt.|[m]lk.itdb.d šbʻ.|[a]ẖm.l h.ṯmnt.bn um.|krt.ḥtk n.rš.|krt.grdš.m 14[KRT].1.8
k h.|krt yʻn.ḥtk h.rš.|mid.grdš.ṯbt h.|w b tm hn.špḥ.yitbd.|w b.pẖyr h.yrṯ.|yʻrb.b ḥdr h.ybky.|b ṯn.[-]gmm.w y 14[KRT].1.24
-]q.n[ṯ]k.l ydʻ.l bn.l pq ḥmt.|[---.--]n h.ḥmt.w tʻbtn h.abd y.|[---.ǵ]r.šrǵzz.ybky.km.nʻr.|[w ydmʻ.k]m.ṣǵr.špš.b š UG5.8.36
adt y.[---].|lb.ab[d k].al[.---].|[-]tm.iph.adt y.w.[---].|tšṣḥq.hn.aṯt.l.ʻbd.|š 1017.2
kḥ.w yiẖd.b qrb[.-].|[--.t]ṯkḥ.w tiẖd.b uš[k.--].|[-.b]ʻl.yabd.l alp.|[---.bt]lt.ʻnt.|[---]q.hry.w yld.|[---]m.ḥbl.kṯ[r]t.| 11[132].1.3
m ḥrn.mṣd h.mnt.nṯk nḥš.|šmrr.nḥš.ʻq šr.ln h.mlẖš.|abd.ln h.ydy.ḥmt.|b ḥrn.pnm.trǵnw.w ṯtkl.|bnwt h.ykr.ʻr. UG5.7.60
šlm šmm h mnt.nṯk.nḥš.|šmrr.nḥš ʻq šr.ln h.mlẖš.|abd.ln h.ydy ḥmt.hlm.ytq šqy.|nḥš.yšlḥm.nḥš.ʻq šr.yʻdb.|k UG5.7.54
ql b.ʻm.|ršp.bbt h.mnt.nḥš.šmrr.|nḥš.ʻq šr.ln h.mlẖš.abd.ln h.ydy.|ḥmt.hlm.ytq.nḥš.yšlḥm.nḥš ʻq.|š.yʻdb.ksa w UG5.7.32
.w kmṯ.ḥryt h.mnt.nṯk.nḥš.šm|rr.nḥš.ʻq šr.ln h.mlẖš abd.ln h.|ydy.ḥmt.hlm.ytq nḥš yšlḥm.nḥš.|ʻq.šr.yʻdb.ksa.w UG5.7.37
.|yrẖ.lrgt h.mnt.nṯk.n[ḥš].šmrr.|nḥš.ʻq šr.ln h.mlẖš.abd.ln h.ydy.|ḥmt.hlm.ytq.nḥš.yšlḥm.nḥš.|ʻq šr.yʻdb.ksa.w UG5.7.27
.|mlk.ʻṯtrt h.mnt.nṯk.nḥš.šmrr.|nḥš.ʻq šr.ln h.mlẖš abd.ln h.ydy.|ḥmt.hlm.ytq.nḥš.yšlḥm.nḥš.|ʻq šr.yʻdb.ksa.w UG5.7.42
.mrym.ṣpn.mnt y.nṯk.|nḥš.šmrr.nḥš.ʻq šr ln h.|mlẖš.abd.ln h.ydy.ḥmt.hlm.ytq.|nḥš.yšlḥm.nḥš.ʻq šr.ydb.ksa.|w UG5.7.11
r.w ẖss.kptr h.mnt.nṯk.nḥš.|šmrr.nḥš.ʻq šr.ln h.mlẖš.abd.|ln h.ydy.ḥmt.hlm ytq.nḥš.|yšlḥm.nḥš.ʻq šr.yʻdb ksa.| UG5.7.47
m.nḥš.ʻq šr[.yʻ]db.ksa.|nḥš.šmrr.nḥš.ʻq šr.ln h.ml|ẖš.abd.ln h.ydy.ḥmt.hlm.ytq.|w ytb.|tqru.l špš.um h.špš.[um. UG5.7.22
.b ʻdt.thmtm.|mnt.nṯk.nḥš.šmrr.nḥš.|ʻq šr.ln h.mlẖš abd.ln h.ydy.|ḥmt.hlm.ytq ytqšqy.nḥš.yšlḥm.ʻq šr.|yʻdb.ks UG5.7.5
.ʻm.|dgn.ttl h.mnt.nṯk.nḥš.šmrr.|nḥš.ʻq šr.ln h.mlẖš.abd.ln h.|ydy.ḥmt.hlm.ytq.nḥš.yšlḥm.|nḥš.ʻq šr.yʻdb.ksa.w UG5.7.16
-.ḥ]mt.|[---.šp]š.l [hrm.ǵ]rpl.ʻl.arṣ.|[---.]ḥmt.l p[.nṯ]k.abd.l p.ak[l].|[ṯm.dl.]isp.ḥ[mt.---.-]hm.yasp.ḥmt.|[---.š]pš.l UG5.8.10
]p.ḥmt.isp.[šp]š l hrm.ǵrpl.ʻl arṣ.|[l a]n ḥmt.l p[.n]ṯk.abd.l p.akl ṯm.dl.|[---.q]l.bl.tbḥ[n.l]azd.ʻr.qdm.|[---].ʻẓ q[d UG5.8.20
mit.ʻ[šr.---].|[ṯ]lṯ.abd[.---].|[---.]anyt[.---].|[-----].|ʻšrm.l.umdym.|ʻšr.l.ktl. 2110.2

abdg

rqd.|bn.abdg.|ilyn.|bn.tan.|bn.arm.|bn.bʻl.ṣdq.|bn.army.|bn.rpiy 1046.1.2

abdḥr

.ilštmʻy.|bn.ʻn.rqdy.|bn.gʻyn.|bn.ǵrn.|bn.agynt.|bn.abdḥr.snry.|dqn.šlmn.|prdn.ndb[--].|[-]rn.ẖbty.|abmn.bn. 87[64].36
|ṣbu.any[t].|bn.kṯan.|ǵr.tšʻ[.ʻšr.b]nš.|ṣbu.any[t].|bn abdḥ[r].|pdym.|ẖmš.bnšm.|snrym.|tšʻ.bnš[m].|gbʻlym.|a 79[83].11

abdʻn

.|bn.ypy.gbʻly.|bn.grgs.ilštmʻy.|bn.ẖran.ilštmʻy.|bn.abdʻn.ilštmʻy.|bn.ʻn.rqdy.|bn.gʻyn.|bn.ǵrn.|bn.agynt.|bn. 87[64].31
[---].rb.|[-]lpl.|bn.asrn.|bn.šẖyn.|bn.abdʻn.|bn.ẖnqn.|bn.nmq.|bn.amdn.|bn.špšn. 1067.5
n agmn.|bn [-]ln.bn.ṯbil.|bn is.bn tbdn.|bn uryy.|bn abdʻn.|bn prkl.|bn štn.|bn annyn.|b[n] slg.|u[--] dit.|bn p 101[10].9

abḏr

nb.|[--.--]n.|[--.--]n.|bn.[---].|bn.ʻr[--].|bn.nkt[-].|bn.abḏr.|bn.ḥrẓn.|bn.ḏqnt.|bn.gmrš.|bn.nmq.|bn.špš[yn].|b 2023.3.9
--]ḥy.|[---.--]t.|[-----].|[---.]l[--].|[bn.]ubn.|kbšm.|bn.abḏr.|bn.kpltn.|bn.prn.|ʻbdm.|bn.kḏǵbr.|bn.mṣrn.|bn.[-] 114[324].2.6
.|[l.--]ḥl.|[l.--.]mgmr.|[l.-.]qdšt.|l.ʻṯtrt.ndrgd.|l.ʻṯtrt.abḏr.|l.dml.|l.ilt[.-]pn.|l.uš[ẖr]y.|[---.-]mrn.|l ṯwl.|[--]ḏ[-- 1001.1.13

aby

mšu.|ẖṯpy.|ǵldy.|iẖǵl.|aby.|abmn.|ynḥm.|npl.|ynḥm.|mtbʻl.|bn ǵlmn.|bn sgld. 1065.5
bʻln.|yrmn.|ʻnil.|pmlk.|aby.|ʻdyn.|aǵlyn.|[--]rd.|[--]qrd.|[--]r. 1066.5
šbn.|iyʻdm.w bʻl h.|ddy.|ʻmy.|iwrnr.|alnr.|maẖdt.|aby.|[-----].|[-]nt.|ydn.|mnn.w bn h.|ṯkn. 107[15].8

abyy

|[šd.]bn.ṯqdy.b d.gmrd.|[š]d bn.synn.b d.gmrd.|[šd.]abyy.b d.ibrmḏ.|[šd.]bn.ṯṯrn.b d.bnš.aǵlkz.|[šd.b]d.b[n].tk 82[300].2.19

abyn

yn.|[--]tn.|[--]tn.bn.aḏmṯn.|[-]tn bn.agyn.|ullym.bn.abynm.|antn.bn.iwr[n]r.|pwn.ṯmry.|ksyn.bn.lḥsn.|[-]kyn.ṯ 94[313].6
[yd.]mizrt.p yln.mk.b šbʻ.ymm.|[w]yqrb.bʻl.b ḥnt h.abynt.|[d]nil.mt.rpi anẖ.ǵzr.|[mt.]hrnmy.d in.bn.l h.|km.a 17[2AQHT].1.17

abyt

miẖdym.|bn.ḥṭb.|bn abyt.|bn ẖdl.|bn ṣdqn.|bn ayy.|bn dbb.|w nḥl h.|bn nʻmy 2016.1.3

abl

[n.ʻr]my.|[--]ṯy.|bn.ǵdʻ.|bn.ʻyn.|bn.grb[n].|yṯtn.|bn.ab[l].|kry.|psš.|ilṯḥm.|ḥrm.|bn.bty.|ʻby.|šm[n].bn.apn.|k 2078.10

ablḥ

[---].|bn.a[--].|w.nḥl h.|bn.alz.|w.nḥl h.|bn.sny.|bn.ablḥ.|[-----].|w [---].|bn.[---].|bn.yr[--].|bn.kṯr[t].|bn.šml.| 2163.1.15

ablm

m].|ʻm.yṭpn.mhr.š[t.tšu.g h].|w tṣḥ.yṯb.yṭp.[---].|qrt.ablm.ablm.[qrt.zbl.yrẖ].|ik.al.yḥdṯ.yrẖ.b[---].|b qrn.ymn h. 18[3AQHT].4.8
.---].|[---.]mt.išryt[.---].|[---.--]r.almd k.[---].|[---.]qrt.ablm.a[blm].|[qrt.zbl.]yrẖ.d mgdl.š[---].|[---.]mn.ʻr hm[.---] 18[3AQHT].1.30
.brḥ.p ʻlm h.|ʻnt.p dr.dr.ʻdb.uẖry mṭ yd h.|ymǵ.l qrt.ablm.abl[m].|qrt.zbl.yrẖ.yšu g h.|w yṣḥ.y l k.qrt.ablm.|d ʻl 19[1AQHT].4.163
qrt.ablm.abl[m].|qrt.zbl.yrẖ.yšu g h.|w yṣḥ.y l k.qrt.ablm.|d ʻl k.mḫṣ.aqht.ǵzr.|ʻwrt.yšt k.bʻl.l ht.|w ʻlm h.l ʻnt. 19[1AQHT].4.165
.yṭpn.mhr.š[t.tšu.g h].|w tṣḥ.yṯb.yṭp.[---].|qrt.ablm.ablm.[qrt.zbl.yrẖ].|ik.al.yḥdṯ.yrẖ.b[---].|b qrn.ymn h.b anš 18[3AQHT].4.8
[---.]mt.išryt[.---].|[---.--]r.almd k.[---].|[---.]qrt.ablm.a[blm].|[qrt.zbl.]yrẖ.d mgdl.š[---].|[---.]mn.ʻr hm[.---].|[---. 18[3AQHT].1.30
ʻlm h.|ʻnt.p dr.dr.ʻdb.uẖry mṭ yd h.|ymǵ.l qrt.ablm.abl[m].|qrt.zbl.yrẖ.yšu g h.|w yṣḥ.y l k.qrt.ablm.|d ʻl k.m 19[1AQHT].4.163

abm

rpr.qšt. | ugry.qšt. | bn.ṣrptn.qšt. | bn.mṣry.qšt. | arny. | abm.qšt. | ḥdṯn.ql‘. | yṯpṭ.qšt. | ilṯḥm.qšt.w.ql‘. | ṣdqm.qšt.w.ql 119[321].2.2
| ymy.bn[.---]. | ‘bd‘n.p[--.---]. | [-]d[-]l.bn.ḥrn. | aḫty.bt.abm. | [-]rbn.‘dd.nryn. | [ab]r[p]u.bn.kbd. | [-]m[-].bn.ṣmrt. | li 102[322].6.2

abmlk

]ḫrpn. | gmrš[.bn].mrnn. | ‘bdmlk.bn.‘myn. | agyn.r‘y. | abmlk.bn.ilrš. | iḫyn.bn.ḫryn. | [ab]ǵl.bn.gdn. | [---].bn.bqš. | [- 102[323].4.10
-]. | dnn.bn.yṣr[.---]. | sln.bn.‘ṯt[-.---]. | pdy.bn.nr[-.---]. | abmlk.bn.un[-.---]. | nrn.bn.mtn[-.---]. | aḫyn.bn.nbk[-.---]. | r 90[314].1.8

abmn

n. | rbil. | plsy. | ygmr. | mnṯ. | prḫ. | ‘dršp. | ršpab. | ṯnw. | abmn. | abǵl. | b‘ldn. | yp‘. 1032.11
. | bn.aḫdy.‘šrt. | ṯṯn.‘ṣrt. | bn.pnmn.‘šrt. | ‘bdadt.ḫmšt. | abmn.ilštm‘y.ḫmš[t]. | ‘zn.bn.brn.ḫmšt. | m‘rt.ḫmšt. | arṯṯb.b 1062.25
ṯn.b gt.mzln. | ṯn.b ulm. | abmn.b gt.m‘rb. | atn. | ḫryn. | bn.‘nt. | llwn. | agdṯb. | aǵltn. | [-] 1061.3
[---.n]ḥl h. | [---].bn.mryn. | [---].bn.ṯyl. | annmt.nḥl h. | abmn.bn.‘bd. | liy.bn.rqdy. | bn.ršp. 1036.13
bn.abdḫr.snry. | dqn.šlmn. | prdn.ndb[--]. | [-]rn.ḫbty. | abmn.bn.qdmn. | n‘mn.bn.‘bdilm. 87[64].40
brq. | [--.]qtn bn.drṣy. | [--]kn bn.pri. | [r]špab bn.pni. | [ab]mn bn.qṣy. | [‘]pṯrm bn.agmz. | [-]n bn.iln. | [--]nn bn.ibm. 2087.9
].py[-.d.]yṯb.b.gt.aǵld. | šgn.bn b[--.---].d.yṯb.b.ilštm‘. | abmn.bn.r[---].b.syn. | bn.irṣ[-.---.]h. | šdyn.b[n.---.--]n. 2015.2.7
mšu. | ḫṯpy. | ǵldy. | iḫǵl. | aby. | abmn. | ynḥm. | npl. | ynḥm. | mtb‘l. | bn ǵlmn. | bn sgld. 1065.6
d‘l.q[š]t.w.ql‘. | b[n].ilyn.qšt.w.ql‘. | šmrm.ql‘. | ubr‘y. | abmn.qšt.w.ṯn.ql‘m. | qdmn.ṯṯ.qštm.w.ṯlṯ.ql‘m. | bn.ṣdqil.ṯṯ.q 119[321].3.2
bn.ṯ‘ln.qš[t.w.q]l‘. | ‘ṯqbt.qšt. | [-]ll.qšt.w.ql‘. | ḫlb.rpš. | abmn.qšt. | ẓẓn.qšt. | dqry.qš[t]. | rkby. | bn.knn.qšt. | pbyn.qšt 119[321].2.31
[---]. | ṯlṯ.‘l.gmrš[.---]. | kd.‘l.‘bd[--]. | kd.‘l.aǵlt[n]. | ṯlṯ.‘l.a[b]m[n]. | arb‘.‘l[.--]ly. | kd.[‘l.--]ẓ. | kd.[‘l.---]. | [--.--]ḫ.bn.ag[1082.1.21
irm.šd.šd.‘šy. | w.šir.šd.krm. | d.krwn. | šir.šd.šd.‘šy. | d.abmn. | šir.šd.krm. | d.yrmn. | šir.[š]d.mlṯḥ.šd.‘šy. | d.ynḥm. | t 1079.11
aǵltn. | urtn. | annṯb. | ubn. | špšyn. | abmn. | [--]dn. | [t]b‘m. | [--]mlk. | [--]ty. | mtnb‘l. | bn.ndbn. | b 1072.6

abn

.]b km.y‘n. | [---.yd‘.l] yd‘t. | [---.t]asrn. | [---.]trks. | [---.]abnm.upqt. | [---.]l w ǵr mtn y. | [---.]rq.gb. | [---.--]kl.tǵr.mtn 1[‘NT.X].5.11
-]. | bn[.---.ušk]ny. | bn.kdrn.uškny. | bn.lgn.uškny. | bn.abn.uškny. | bn.arz.š‘rty. | bn.ibrd.m‘rby. | ṣdqn.gb‘ly. | bn.yp 87[64].24
yn.b‘l. | w ymlk.b arṣ.il.kl h. | [---] š abn.b rḥbt. | [---] š abn.b kknt. 6.1.67[49.1.39]
tr.‘rẓ.yrd. | l kḥṯ.aliyn.b‘l. | w ymlk.b arṣ.il.kl h. | [---] š abn.b rḥbt. | [---] š abn.b kknt. 6.1.66[49.1.38]
-]. | bn.y[---]. | [-----]. | [bn.a]mdy. | bn.ḫlln. | bn.kṯn. | bn.abn. | bn.nskn. | bn.gmrn. | bn[.-]škn. | [---.--]n. | [---.--]n. | [--.]‘ 2021.2.5
um.pḥl.pḥlt.bt.abn.bt šmm w thm. | qrit.l špš.um h.špš.um.ql.bl.‘m. | il.mbk UG5.7.1
r. | un.l riš h.‘pr.plṯt. | l qdqd h.lpš.yks. | mizrtm.ǵr.b abn. | ydy.psltm.b y‘r. | yhdy.lḥm.w dqn. | yṯlṯ.qn.ḏr‘ h.yḥrṯ. | 5[67].6.17
l b‘l. | ǵr.b ab.td[.ps]ltm[.b y‘r]. | thdy.lḥm.w dqn[.ṯṯlṯ]. | qn.ḏr‘ h.tḥrṯ.k 6[62].1.2
n y.aṯt.itrḫ. | y bn.ašld.šu.‘db.tk.mdbr qdš. | ṯm tgrgr.l abnm.w l.‘ṣm.šb‘.šnt. | tmt.ṯmn.nqpt.‘d.ilm.n‘mm.ttlkn. | šd. 23[52].66
.ym.w ṯn. | ṯlṯ.rb‘.ym.ymš. | ṯdṯ.ym.ḥẓ k.al.tš‘l. | qrt h.abn.yd k. | mšdpt.w hn.špšm. | b šb‘.w l.yšn.pbl. | mlk.l qr.ṯig 14[KRT].3.117
. | [---.]mlkr[-] h.b.nṯk. | [---.]šb‘m. | [---.]ḫrg.‘šrm. | [---.]abn.ksp.ṯlṯ. | [---].bty.ksp.‘šr[t]. | [---.-]mb‘l.[---].‘šrt. | [---.]ḥg 2153.6
--].aǵwyn.‘n k.ẓẓ.w k mǵ.ilm. | [--.]k ‘ṣm.k ‘šm.l ttn.k abnm.l thggn. 1001.2.13
mṣb.mznm.um h. | kp mznm.iḫ h yṯ‘r. | mšrrm.aḫt h l a | bn mznm.nkl w ib. | d ašr.ar yrḫ.w y | rḫ yar k. | [ašr ilht k 24[77].36
| ṯṯb.[---.--]ša. | tlm.km[.---.]yd h.k šr. | knr.uṣb‘t h ḫrṣ.abn. | p h.tiḥd.šnt h.w akl.bqmm. | tšt ḫrṣ.k lb ilnm. | w ṯn.gp 19[1AQHT].1.8
]pšg.iqni.mit.pṯtm. | [---].mitm.kslm. | [---].pwt.ṯlṯ.mat.abn.ṣrp. | [---.-]qt.l.ṯrmnm. | [---].ṯlṯm.iqnu. | [---.l.]ṯrmn.mlk. 1106.10
r.---]. | [---.p]ṯtm.l.ip[--.---]. | [---.]ksl.ṯlṯ.m[at.---]. | [---].abn.ṣr[p.---]. | [---.-]rt.ṯlṯm[.---]. | [--]l.ṯrmn.m[lk.---]. | [---.--]r 1106.27
d. | pwt. | ṯmn.mat.pṯtm. | kkrm.alpm. | ḫmš.mat.kbd. | abn.ṣrp. 2051.10
| ‘šr.rṭm. | kkr[.-].ḫt. | mitm[.p]ṯtm. | ṯlṯm[.---].kst. | alp.a[bn.ṣ]rp. 1114.6
rgm.iṯ.l y.]w argm k.hwt. | [w aṯny k.rgm.]‘ṣ.w lḫšt. | [abn.rgm.l td]‘.nš[m.w l t]bn. | [hmlt.a]rṣ.[tant.šmm.‘m.ar]ṣ. 3[‘NT].4.59
spr.bnš.mlk. | d taršn.‘msn. | bṣr.abn.špšyn. | dqn. | aǵlmn. | kn‘m. | aḫršp. | anntn. | b‘lrm. | [-]ra 2067.1.3
.iṯ.l y.d argmn k]. | [h]wt.d aṯ[ny k.---.rgm.‘ṣ]. | w lḫšt.abn[.tant.šmm.‘m.arṣ.thmt]. | ‘m kbkbm[.abn.brq.d l td‘.šm 7.2[130].19
.rgm. | iṯ.l y.w argm k. | hwt.w aṯny k.rgm. | ‘ṣ.w lḫšt.abn. | tant.šmm.‘m.arṣ. | thmt.‘mn.kbkbm. | abn.brq.d l.td‘.š 3[‘NT].3.20
.r[gm.iṯ.l y.w argm k]. | hwt.w aṯny k[.rgm.‘ṣ.w lḫšt.abn]. | tunt.šmm.‘m[.arṣ.thmt.‘mn.kbkbm]. | rgm.l td‘.nš[m. 1[‘NT.IX].3.13
[-----]. | l abn[.---]. | aḫdt.plk h[.b yd h]. | plk.qlt.b ymn h. | npyn h.mk 4[51].2.2
b km.y‘n. | [---].yd‘.l yd‘t. | [---.]tasrn.ṯr il. | [---.]rks.bn.abnm. | [---.]upqt.‘rb. | [---.w ẓ]r.mtn y at.zd. | [---.]t‘rb.bši. | [- 1[‘NT.X].5.23

abǵl

nḥm.aḏddy. | ykny.aḏddy. | m[--].aḏddy. | yp‘.aḏddy. | abǵl.aḏ[ddy]. | abǵl.a[---]. | rbil.[---]. | kḏyn.[---.-]gṯ. | šmrm.a[2014.25
kny.aḏddy. | m[--].aḏddy. | yp‘.aḏddy. | abǵl.aḏ[ddy]. | abǵl.a[---]. | rbil.[---]. | kḏyn.[---.-]gṯ. | šmrm.a[ḏdd]y.tb[--]. | y 2014.26
lk.bn.‘myn. | agyn.r‘y. | abmlk.bn.ilrš. | iḫyn.bn.ḫryn. | [ab]ǵl.bn.gdn. | [---].bn.bqš. | [---].bn.pdn. | [---.bn.-]ky. | [---.bn 102[323].4.12
. | plsy. | ygmr. | mnṯ. | prḫ. | ‘dršp. | ršpab. | ṯnw. | abmn. | abǵl. | b‘ldn. | yp‘. 1032.12
n.[-]r[-.]ḫmšt. | bn.ḥdṯ.‘šrt. | bn.ḫnyn.‘šrt. | rpan.ḫmšt. | abǵl.ḫmšt. | bn.aḫdy.‘šrt. | ṯṯn.‘ṣrt. | bn.pnmn.‘šrt. | ‘bdadt.ḫm 1062.20
ḫmš ‘l.bn[.---]. | ḫmš ‘l r‘l[-]. | ḫmš ‘l ykn[.--]. | ḫ[mš] ‘l abǵ[l]. | ḫmš ‘l ilb[‘l]. | ‘šr ‘l [---]. 2034.2.7
n.ḫpn. | l.k[-]w.ḫpn. | l.ṣ[--].š‘[rt]. | l.‘dy.š[‘]r[t]. | ṯlṯ.l.‘d.ab[ǵ]l. | l.ydln.š‘rt. | l.kṯrmlk.ḫpn. | l.‘bdil[m].ḫpn. | tmrtn.š‘rt 1117.7
[-----]. | w.[-----]. | w.abǵl.nḥ[l h.--]. | w.unṯ.aḥd.l h[.---]. | dnn.bn.yṣr[.---]. | sln.bn. 90[314].1.3
.‘bdadt.b‘ln.yp‘mlk. | ṯǵrm.mnḥm.klyn.‘dršp.ǵlmn. | [a]bǵl.ṣṣn.ǵrn. | šib.mqdšt.‘b[dml]k.ṯṯpḥ.mrṯn. | ḫdǵlm.i[---]n. 2011.14
r[-.---]. | špš[yn.---]. | [--]b[.---]. | ‘bd‘ṯ[tr.---]. | bdil[.---]. | abǵl.[---]. | [.---]. | ḏmrb‘[l.---]. | iḫyn.[---]. | ‘bdb‘[l.---]. | uwil[.- 102[322].2.3

abṣdq

bd'nt. | [---.-]šn. | [---.']bdilt. | [---.-]lgn. | [---.--]gbn. | [---.a]bṣdq. | [---.--]š. | [---.ṣ]dq. | tgmr. | yṣḥm. | ṯlṯm. | aḥd. | kbd. | b 1055.1.11

abṣn

n.ilb'l.krwn.lbn.'dn. | ḫyrn.md'. | šm'n.rb 'šrt.kkln.'bd.abṣn. | šdyn.unn.dqn. | 'bd'nt.rb 'šrt.mnḥm.ṯb'm.sḫr.'zn.ilhd. 2011.5

abrḫṭ

iytlm. | bn ayln. | bn.kln. | bn.'lln. | bn.liy. | bn.nqṯn. | bn abrḫṭ. | bn.grdy. | bn.ṣlpn. | bn ǵlmn. | bn sgld. 1064.27

abrm

ṯṯ.mat.ṯṯm.kbd šmn. | l.abrm.alṯyy. | [m]it.ṯlṯm.kbd.šmn. | [l.]abrm.mšrm. | [mi]tm.ar 2095.2
.ṯṯm.kbd šmn. | l.abrm.alṯyy. | [m]it.ṯlṯm.kbd.šmn. | [l.]abrm.mšrm. | [mi]tm.arb'm.ṯmn.kbd. | [l.]sbrdnm. | m[i]t.l.b 2095.4

abrpu

y. | n'mn.mṣry. | y'l.kn'ny. | gdn.bn.umy. | kn'm.š'rty. | abrpu.ubr'y. | b.gt.bn.ṯlṯ. | ilḏ.b.gt.psḫn. 91[311].10
.---]. | [-]d[-]l.bn.ḥrn. | aḫty.bt.abm. | [-]rbn.'dd.nryn. | [ab]r[p]u.bn.kbd. | [-]m[-].bn.ṣmrt. | liy.bn.yṣi. | ḏmrhd.bn.srt. 102[322].6.4
y[---]. | bn.ǵlyn. | bdl.ar. | bn.šyn. | bn.ubrš. | bn.d[--]b. | abrpu. | bn.k[n]y. | bn.klyn. | bn.gmḫn. | ḥnn. | ayab. | bn.gm[-- 1035.3.5

abršn

ṯk. | bn.arwdn. | tmrtn. | šd'l.bn aḫyn. | m'rbym. | rpan. | abršn. | atlgy. | šršn. 95[91].8
'šrt.ksp.'l.[-]lpy. | bn.ady.kkr.š'rt. | nṯk h. | kb[d.]mn.'l.abršn. | b[n.---].kršu.nṯk h. | [---.--]mm.b.krsi. 1146.11
.---]. | bn.nṣdn[.ḫm]št. | bn.arsw '[šr]m. | 'šdyn.ḫmš[t]. | abršn.'šr[t]. | b'ln.ḫmšt. | w.nḥl h.ḫm[š]t. | bn.unp.arb't. | 'bdb 1062.7
šd.snrym.dt.'qb. | b.ayly. | šd.abršn. | šd.kkn.[bn].ubyn. | šd.bn.li[y]. | šd.bn.š[--]y. | šd.bn.ṯ[- 2026.3

abršp

l[--.---]. | ar[--.---.--]l. | aty[n.bn.]šm'nt. | ḥnn[.bn].pls. | abrš[p.bn.]ḫrpn. | gmrš[.bn].mrnn. | 'bdmlk.bn.'myn. | agyn.r 102[323].4.6
.tlmyn.ṯt.qštm.w.ql'. | bn.ysd.qšt. | [ǵ]mrm. | ilgn.qšt. | abršp.qšt. | ssg.qšt. | ynḥm.qšt. | pprn.qšt. | uln.qšt. | bn.nkl qšt 105[86].2

abškn

ḥ. | artn. | ybnil. | brqn. | adr[dn]. | krwn. | arkḏn. | ilmn. | abškn. | ykn. | ršpab. | klyn. | ḥgbn. | ḥṯṯn. | 'bdmlk. | y[--]k. | [--- 1024.1.14
]'.yn. | [---].ṯmn.yn. | [---.-]ṯr.kdm.yn. | [-]dyn.arb'.yn. | abškn.kdm.yn. | šbn.kdm.yn. | 'bdiltp.ṯm[n].y[n]. | qṣn.ḫ[---]. 1085.7

abšr

n.qṣn. | 'lpy. | kṯy. | bn.ẓmn. | bn.trdn. | ypq. | 'bd. | qrḥ. | abšr. | bn.bdn. | ḏmry. | bn.pndr. | bn.aḫt. | bn.'dn. | bn.išb'[l]. 2117.4.28

agbṯr

ksdm. | ṣdqn. | nwrḏr. | ṯrin. | 'dršp. | pqr. | agbṯr. | 'bd. | ksd. 1044.7

agdn

l ym hnd. | iwr[k]l.pdy. | agdn.bn.nrgn. | w ynḥm.aḫ h. | w.b'ln aḫ h. | w.ḥṯṯn bn h. | w. 1006.3

agdṯb

ṯn.b ulm. | abmn.b gt.m'rb. | atn. | ḫryn. | bn.'nt. | llwn. | agdṯb. | aǵltn. | [-]wn. | bldn. | [-]ln. | [-]ldn. | [i]wryn. | ḫbsn. | ul 1061.8
[---]n[.---]. | [ag]dṯb.bn[.---]. | 'bdil.bn.[---]. | 'pṯn.bn.ṯṣq[-]. | mnn.bn.krmn. 85[80].1.2
ḫmšt.'š[rt]. | ksp.'l.agd[ṯb]. | w nit w m'ṣd. | w ḫrmṯt. | 'šrt.ksp. | 'l.ḫ[z]rn. | w.nit. 2053.2
n.'šrm. | d.bn.šb'l.uḫnpy.ḫmšm. | b.bn.ṯṯm.ṯlṯm. | b.bn.agdṯb.'šrm. | b.bn.ibn.arb't.'šrt. | b.bn.mnn.ṯṯm. | b.rpan.bn.y 2054.1.12

agzr

pamt.šb'. | iqnu.šmt[.---]. | [b]n.šrm. | iqran.ilm.n'mm[.agzry ym.bn]ym. | ynqm.b ap zd.aṯrt.[---]. | špš.mṣprt dlt h 23[52].23

agzrt

mlk. | šmm.tlak.ṭl.amr.. | bn km k bk[r.z]bl.am.. | rkm.agzrt[.--].arḫ.. | b'l.azrt.'nt.[-]ld. | kbd h.l yd' hr h.[---]d[-]. | t 13[6].29

agyn

rwn.b.yny.iytlm. | šgryn.ary.b.yny. | bn.yddn.b.rkby. | agyn.agny. | ṯqbn.mldy. 2071.8
b'l. | [---]n.bn.agyn. | [--]ṯn. | [--]tn.bn.aḏmṯn. | [-]tn bn.agyn. | ullym.bn.abynm. | antn.bn.iwr[n]r. | pwn.ṯmry. | ksyn. 94[313].5
[.---]. | šd.pll.b d.qrt. | š[d].anndr.b d.bdn.nḥ[l h]. | [šd.]agyn.b d.kmrn.n[ḥl] h. | [š]d.nbzn.[-]l.qrt. | [š]d.agpṯr.b d.sḫr 2029.8
n.qln.mtn.ydln. | b'ltdtt.tlgn.ytn. | b'ltǵpṯm.krwn.ilšn.agyn. | mnn.šr.ugrt.ḏkr.yṣr. | tǵǵln.ḫmš.ddm. | [---].ḫmš.ddm 2011.36
abrš[p.bn.]ḫrpn. | gmrš[.bn].mrnn. | 'bdmlk.bn.'myn. | agyn.r'y. | abmlk.bn.ilrš. | iḫyn.bn.ḫryn. | [ab]ǵl.bn.gdn. | [---]. 102[323].4.9
[---]ym.mddb'l. | [---]n.bn.agyn. | [--]ṯn. | [--]tn.bn.aḏmṯn. | [-]tn bn.agyn. | ullym.bn.aby 94[313].2
]. | [b]n.g'yn.ḫr[-]. | lbnym. | grgš.[---]. | bn.ǵrn.[---]. | bn.agyn[.---]. | iyṯ[-.---]. 93[328].16
[b]n 'ntn.[---]. | bn agyn[.---]. | b[n] 'ṯlṯ[.---]. | bn qṭy[.---]. | bn yp'[.---]. | [---]b'm[. 105[86].2
ḥny.yd[.---]. | yd.ṯlṯ.kl[t h.---]. | w.ṯṯm.ṣi[n.---]. | tn[--]. | agyn.[---]. | [w].ṯn.[---]. 81[329].21

agynt

. | bn.abd'n.ilštm'y. | bn.'n.rqdy. | bn.g'yn. | bn.ǵrn. | bn.agynt. | bn.abdḥr.snry. | dqn.šlmn. | prdn.ndb[--]. | [-]rn.ḫbty. 87[64].35

agytn

[-]n.y‘rtym.|gmm.w.bn.p[--].|trn.w.p[-]y.|bn.b‘yn.w.agytn.|[---] gnym.|[--]ry.w ary.|[---]ǵrbtym.|[---.]w šb‘l.|[- 131[309].12

aglby

bn.al[--].|bn.nb[dg].|bn.ild[-].|[-----].|[bn.]nnr.|[bn.]aglby.|[bn.]b‘ly.|[md̠]rǵlm.|[bn.]kdgdl.|[b]n.qṭn.|[b]n.ǵrg 104[316].5
[l]k ‘šrm.|ṣṣ abš[-] mit [‘š]r kbd.|ṣṣ yd̠rd ‘šrm.|ṣṣ bn aglby t̠lt̠[m].|ṣṣ bn.šrš‘m.[---].|ṣṣ mlkn‘m.a[rb‘m].|ṣṣ mlk 2097.13

agm

kn.|‘nqpat.|ilštm‘.|šbn.|ṭbq.|rqd.|šrš.|gn‘y.|m‘qb.|agm.|bir.|ypr.|hzp.|šql.|m‘rḥ[-].|sl[h̠].|snr.|‘rgz.|ykn‘m. 2074.28
g[z].|y‘r[t].|amd̠[y].|atl[g].|bṣr[y].|[---].|[---]y.|ar.|agm.w.h̠pty.|h̠lb.ṣpn.|mril.|‘nmky.|‘nqpat.|ṭbq.|hzp.|gn‘ 71[113].49
|[h̠l]bkrd.|[h̠l]b‘prm.|[q]dš.|[a]md̠y.|[gn]‘y.|m‘qb.|agm.|h̠pty.|ypr.|h̠rṣb‘.|uh̠np.|art.|[--]n.|[-----].|[-----].|nn 2058.2.2
.yn.|hzp.tš‘.yn.|[b]ir.‘šr[.---]m ḥsp.|h̠pty.kdm[.---].|[a]gm.arb‘[.---].|šrš.šb‘.mṣb.|rqd.t̠lt̠.mṣb.w.[---].|uh̠np.t̠t̠.mṣ 2004.31

agmz

p[r] ušknym.dt.[b d.---].|bn.btr.|bn.‘ms.|bn.pṣn.|bn.agmz.|bn.[--]n.|bn.a[--].|[------].|[------].|[------].|[------].|[- 2021.1.5
n bn.pri.|[r]špab bn.pni.|[ab]mn bn.qṣy.|[‘]pt̠rm bn.agmz.|[-]n bn.iln.|[--]nn bn.ibm.|[-]n bn.ḥrn.|[š]mmn bn. 2087.10

agmy

ǵpt̠m.|[k]rwn.|ḥrš.mrkbt.|mnḥm.|mṣrn.|md̠rǵlm.|agmy.|‘dyn.|‘bdb‘l.|‘bdkt̠r.‘bd.|tdǵl.|b‘lṣn.|nsk.ksp.|iwrt 1039.2.17
|arb‘.bnšm.b[.---].|‘šrm.bnšm.[b.]‘d[--].|arb‘.bnšm.b.ag[m]y.|arb‘.bnšm.b.h̠pty.|t̠t̠.bnšm.b.bir.|t̠t̠.bnšm b.uh̠np.| 2076.11
[sp]r.k[--].|t̠[t̠.bn]šm[.b.a]gmy.|t̠t̠.bn[šm.---].|‘šr.b[nšm.---].|arb‘[.bnšm.---].|t̠t̠.‘šr. 2076.2
[-----].|bn.t[--.---].|agmy[.---].|bn.dlq[-.---].|tǵyn.bn.ubn.t̠ql[m].|yšn.ḥrš.mrkb 122[308].1.3

agmn

[-----].|[bn.]ibln.|ysd.|bn.t̠mq.|bn.agmn.|bn.uṣb.|bn.yzg.|bn.anntn.|bn.kwn.|ǵmšd.|bn.‘bdḥ 115[301].4.4
l h.|bn ksln.t̠lth̠.|bn yṣmh̠.bn.t̠rn w nḥl h.|bn srd.bn agmn.|bn [-]ln.bn.t̠bil.|bn is.bn tbdn.|bn uryy.|bn abd‘n.| 101[10].5
ršp.bn[.---].|kd.šmn.‘l.yddn.|kd.‘l.ššy.|kd.‘l.nd̠bn.bn.agmn.|[k]d.‘l.brq.|[kd]m.[‘l].kt̠r.|[kd]m[.---].ḥ[--].|[-----].| 1082.1.8

agn

gp ym.w yṣǵd.gp..thm.|[yqḥ.]il.mšt‘ltm.mšt‘ltm.l riš.agn.|hl h.[t]špl.hl h.trm.hl h.tṣḥ.ad ad.|w hl h.tṣḥ.um.um.t 23[52].31
.il.k ym.|w yd.il.k mdb.yqḥ.il.mšt‘ltm.|mšt‘ltm.l riš.agn.yqḥ.tš.b bt h.|il.h̠ṭ h.nḥt.il.ymnn.mṭ.yd h.yšu.|yr.šmm 23[52].36
ḥm.|‘l.išt.šb‘ d.ǵzrm.ṭb.[g]d.b ḥlb.annh̠ b h̠mat.|w ‘l.agn.šb‘ d m.dǵ[t̠.---]t.|tlk m.rḥmy.w tṣd[.---].|tḥgrn.ǵzr.n‘ 23[52].15
|[---.]arb‘t[.---].|[---.]qdš[.---].|[---.k]su.p[--.---].|[---.]agn[.---].|[---.b‘lt.b]htm[.---].|[---.--]by.ṭ[--.---].|[---.--]n[.---] 45[45].5

agny

b.yny.iytlm.|s̀gryn.ary.b.yny.|bn.yddn.b.rkby.|agyn.agny.|t̠qbn.mldy. 2071.8

agpt̠

---].|bn.[---].ar.|bn.[---].b.ar.|špšyn[.---.]yt̠b.b.ar.|bn.ag[p]t̠.h̠pt̠.d[.yt̠b.b].š‘rt.|yly.bn.t̠rnq.[-]r.d.yt̠b.b.ilštm‘.|ilšl 2015.1.25

agpt̠n

šd knn.bn.ann.‘db.|šd.iln[-].bn.irt̠r.l.sh̠rn.nḥl h.|šd[.ag]pt̠n.b[n.]brrn.l.qrt.|šd[.--]dy.bn.brzn.|l.qrt. 2029.21
spr.ubdy.art.|šd.prn.b d.agpt̠n.nḥl h.|šd.s̀wn.b d.ttyn.nḥl [h].|šd.tt̠yn[.b]n.arkšt.|l‘q 2029.2
[--]ǵyn.b[n.---].|krwn.b[n.---].|tgyn.m‘[---].|w.agpt̠n[.---].|t̠ynd̠r[-.---].|gt.tg[yn.---].|pwn[.---]. 103[334].4

agpt̠r

.|[šd.]agyn.b d.kmrn.n[ḥl] h.|[š]d.nbzn.[-]l.qrt.|[š]d.agpt̠r.b d.sh̠rn.nḥl h.|šd.annmn.b d.tyn.nḥl h.|šd.pǵyn[.b] 2029.10
r‘ym.dt.b d.iytlm.|h̠yrn.w.s̀ǵr h.|s̀ǵr.bn.prsn.|agpt̠r.w.s̀ǵ[r h].|t̠‘ln.|mztn.w.s̀ǵr [h].|s̀ǵr.plṭ.|s[d]rn [w].t̠n 2072.4
bdl.gt.bn.tbšn.|bn.mnyy.š‘rty.|aryn.ad̠ddy.|agpt̠r.|šb‘l.mlky.|n‘mn.mṣry.|y‘l.kn‘ny.|gdn.bn.umy.|kn‘ 91[311].4

agr

rb].|nrt.ilm.špš.mǵy[t].|pǵt.l ahlm.rgm.l yṭ[pn.y]|bl.agrtn.bat.b d̠d k.[pǵt].|bat.b hlm w y‘n.yṭpn[.mhr].|št.qḥn. 19[1AQHT].4.213
lm.|w.rgm.t̠t̠b.l y.|w.mnd‘.k.ank.|aḥš.mǵy.mnd‘.|k.igr.w.u.[--].|‘m.špš.[---].|nšlḥ[.---].|[---.m]at.|[---.]mat.|š[-- 2009.1.12
.t̠lt̠m.dd.[---.]n[---.---].|w.a[r]b‘[.---].bnš[.š]dyn[.---].|agr.[---.--]n.t̠n.‘šr h.d[--.---].|[---.]ḥdt̠n.‘šr.dd[.---].|[---.]yd.s 1098.33

agtt̠p

bdy.|[b]‘ln.|[-]šdm.|iwryn.|n‘mn.|[-----].|b gt.yny.|agtt̠p.|bn.‘nt.|ǵzldn.|t̠rn.|h̠dbt̠.|[-]ḥl.aǵltn.|[-]n.|[-]mt̠.|[- 1043.11

ad

št‘ltm.mšt‘ltm.l riš.agn.|hl h.[t]špl.hl h.trm.hl h.tṣḥ.ad ad.|w hl h.tṣḥ.um.um.tirk m.yd.il.k ym.|w yd il.k mdb. 23[52].32
ḥmm.|a[t̠]tm.at̠t.il.at̠t.il.w ‘lm h.w hm.|at̠tm.tṣḥn y.ad ad.nḥtm.h̠ṭ k.|mmnnm.mṭ yd k.hl.‘ṣr.tḥrr.l išt.|w ṣḥrrt. 23[52].43
ltm.mšt‘ltm.l riš.agn.|hl h.[t]špl.hl h.trm.hl h.tṣḥ.ad ad.|w hl h.tṣḥ.um.um.tirk m.yd.il.k ym.|w yd il.k mdb.ark 23[52].32
m.|a[t̠]tm.at̠t.il.at̠t.il.w ‘lm h.w hm.|at̠tm.tṣḥn y.ad ad.nḥtm.h̠ṭ k.|mmnnm.mṭ yd k.hl.‘ṣr.tḥrr.l išt.|w ṣḥrrt.l p 23[52].43
špš.|l.‘mrpi.rgm.|‘m špš.kll.mid m.|šlm.|l.[--]n.špš.|ad[.‘]bd h.uk.škn.|k.[---.]sglt h.hw.|w.b[.---.]uk.nǵr.|w.[---] 2060.6

adad

.|w.t̠n.‘l.|mlk.|w.aḥd.|‘l atlg.|w l.‘ṣm.|tspr.|nrn.al.tud|ad.at.l hm.|t̠t̠m.ksp. 1010.19

adb'l

.sbd. | šrm.[---].ḫpn. | ḥrš[bhtm.--]n.'bdyrḫ.ḥdṯn.y'r. | adb'l[.---].ḥdṯn.yḥmn.bnil. | 'dn.w.ildgn.ḥṭbm. | tdǵlm.iln.b'[2011.19

add

rmn w šnm. | il w aṯrt. | ḫnn il. | nṣbt il. | šlm il. | il ḥš il add. | b'l ṣpn b'l. | ugrt. | b mrḥ il. | b nit il. | b ṣmd il. | b dṯn il. 30[107].9

ady

spr.ytnm. | bn.ḫlbym. | bn.ady. | bn.'ṯtry. | bn.ḫrẓn. | ady. | bn.birtn. | bn.ḥrẓn. | bn.bddn. | bn.anny. | ytršp. | bn.szn. 115[301].1.6
spr.ytnm. | bn.ḫlbym. | bn.ady. | bn.'ṯtry. | bn.ḫrẓn. | ady. | bn.birtn. | bn.ḥrẓn. | bn.bddn. | 115[301].1.3
ḥrtm[.---]. | bn.ṯmq[-.---]. | bn.ntp.[---]. | bn.lbnn.[----]. | ady.ḥ[--.---]. | [-]b[-]n.[---]. | bn.atnb.mr[--.---]. | bn.sḫr.mr[-.-- 88[304].5
---].bn.ṯdnyn. | ddm.ḥ[ṭm].'l.šrn. | 'šrt.ksp.'l.[-]lpy. | bn.ady.kkr.š'rt. | nṯk h. | kb[d.]mn.'l.abršn. | b[n.---].kršu.nṯk h. | 1146.9
t. | ssg.qšt. | ynḥm.qšt. | pprn.qšt. | uln.qšt. | bn.nkl qšt. | ady.qšt. | bn.srn.qšt. | bn.gdrn.qšt. | prpr.qšt. | ugry.qšt. | bn.ṣr 119[321].1.41

adldn

| w.nḥl h. | w.nḥl hm. | bn.ḥrm. | bn.brzn. | w.nḥl h. | bn.adldn. | bn.šbl. | bn.ḫnzr. | bn.arwṭ. | bn.ṯbtnq. | bn.pṭdn. | bn.n 113[400].1.12
.krwn.l bn.'myn. | šd.bn.prmn.l aḫny. | šd.bn ḥnn.l bn.adldn. | šd.bn.nṣdn.l bn.'mlbi. | šd.ṯpḫln.l bn.ǵl. | w dṯn.nḥl h. 2089.7
-]. | [-----]. | [ṣṣ].b[n].ṣd[-.---]. | [ṣṣ].bn.npr.ḫmšm. | ṣṣ.bn.adldn.ṯlṯm. | ṣṣ.bn.'glt.ṯlṯm. | ṣṣ.bn.'bd.'šrm. | ṣṣ.bn.mṣḥ[n].'šr 2096.16

adm

]. | tkl.m[k]ly.'l.umt[k.--]. | d ttql.b ym.trtḥ[ṣ.--]. | [----.a]dm.tium.b ǵlp y[m.--]. | d alp šd.ẓu h.b ym.t[---]. | tlbš.npṣ. 19[1AQHT].4.204
m[k]ly.'l.umt[k.--]. | d ttql.b ym.trtḥ[ṣ.--]. | [----.a]dm.tium.b ǵlp y[m.--]. | d alp šd.ẓu h.b ym.t[---]. | tlbš.npṣ.ǵzr.tš 19[1AQHT].4.204
[-]dm[.-]. | ašlw.b ṣp.'n h. | d b ḥlm y.il.ytn. | b ḏrt y.ab.adm. | w ld.šph.l krt. | w ǵlm.l 'bd.il. | krt.yḫṭ.w ḥlm. | 'bd.il. 14[KRT].3.151
h.ib.iqni. | 'p'p h.sp.ṯrml. | d b ḥlm y.il.ytn. | b ḏrt y.ab.adm. | w ld.šph.l krk | t.w ǵlm.l 'bd. | il.ttb'.mlakm. | l ytb.idk 14[KRT].6.297
škb.nhmmt. | w yqmṣ.w b ḥlm h. | il.yrd.b ḏhrt h. | ab adm.w yqrb. | b šal.krt.m at. | krt.k ybky. | ydm'.n'mn.ǵlm. | i 14[KRT].1.37
y.al.tṣr. | udm.rbt.w udm ṯrrt. | udm.ytnt.il w ušn. | ab.adm.w ṯtb. | mlakm.l h.lm.ank. | ksp.w yrq.ḫrṣ. | yd.mqm h. 14[KRT].3.136
| ṯḫṣ.b 'mq.tḫtṣb.bn. | qrytm tmḫṣ.lim.ḫp y[m]. | tṣmt.adm.ṣat.š[p]š. | tḥt h.k kdrt.ri[š]. | 'l h.k irbym.kp.k.qṣm. | ǵr 3['NT].2.8
w ǵlm.l 'bd.il. | krt.yḫṭ.w ḥlm. | 'bd.il.w hdrt. | yrtḥṣ.w yadm. | yrḥṣ.yd h.amt h. | uṣb't h.'d.ṯkm. | 'rb.b ẓl.ḫmt.lqḥ. | i 14[KRT].3.156
].ṯr.ab h.il. | d[--].b bk.krt. | b dm'.n'mn.ǵlm. | il.trḥṣ.w tadm. | rḥṣ[.y]d k.amt. | uṣb['t k.]'d[.ṯ]km. | 'rb[.b ẓl.ḫmt]. | q 14[KRT].2.62
tṣr]. | [udm.rbt.w udm]. | [ṯrrt.udm.ytnt]. | [il.w ušn.ab.adm]. | [rḥq.mlk.l bt y]. | [ng.kr]t.l ḥ[ẓ]r y. | [-----]. | [---.ttb']. | 14[KRT].5.259
]. | udm[.r]bt.w u[dm]. | [ṯ]rrt.udm.y[t]n[t]. | il.ušn.ab[.ad]m. | rḥq.mlk.l bt y. | n[g.]krt.l ḥẓ[r y]. | w y'n[y.k]rt[.ṯ]'. | l 14[KRT].6.278
| [---.-]r[-.il]m.rbm.n'l[.-]gr. | [---.]'ṣ.b d h.ydrm[.]pi[-.]adm. | [---.]iṯ[-].yšql.yṯk[.--]np bl.hn. | [---].ḥ[m]t.pṭr.w.p nḥš UG5.8.32
m'.n'mn.ǵlm. | il.mlk[.ṯ]r ab h. | yarš.hm.drk[t]. | k ab.adm. | [-----]. 14[KRT].1.43

admn

[---.]unṯ[.---]. | [---.]šrq[-.---]. | [---.]'d 'lm[.---]. | [---.]'d.admn[.---]. | [---.--]d.ytr.mṯ[--]. | [-----]. | [-----]. | [---].ḫmš[.---]. 2156.4

adn

k ymǵy.adn. | ilm.rbm 'm dtn. | w yšal.mṭpṭ.yld. | w y'ny.nn[.--]. | t'ny UG5.6.1
šd.bn.adn. | [b] d.armwl. | [šd].mrnn. | b d.[-]tw[-]. | šd.bn[.---]. | b d. 2028.1
bn.ḫran. | bn.srt. | bn.adn. | bn.'gw. | bn.urt. | aḫdbu. | pḥ[-]. | bn.'b . | bn.uḏn[-]. | bn. 121[307].3
nyr šmm.w n'[n]. | 'ma nkl ḫtn y.a[ḫ]r. | nkl yrḫ ytrḫ.adn h. | yšt mṣb.mznm.um h. | kp mznm.iḫ h yt'r. | mšrrm.a 24[77].33
[.---]h. | šm' ilht kṯr[t.--]mm. | nh l yd h tzdn[.---]n. | l ad[n h.---]. | dgn tt[--.---.-]l | '.l kṯrt hl[l.sn]nt. | ylak yrḫ ny[r] 24[77].13
bn.b'ln.biry. | ṯlṯ.b'lm. | w.adn hm.ṯr.w.arb'.bnt h. | yrḫm.yd.ṯn.bn h. | b'lm.w.ṯlṯ.n'rm. 2080.3
[---.]b[--]. | [---].šḫr.[---]. | [---].al ytb'[.--]. | [---.]l adn.ḥwt[.--]. | [--]h.w yššil[.--]. | [---.]lp[--]. 1023.4
l.ybnn. | adn y. | rgm. | tḥm.t[g]yn. | bn k. | l.p['n.adn y]. | q[lt.---]. | l.yb[nn]. | b'l y.r[gm]. | tḥm.'bd[--]. | 'bd k. | 2115.1.6
l.ybnn. | adn y. | rgm. | tḥm.t[g]yn. | bn k. | l.p['n.adn y]. | q[lt.---]. | l.yb 2115.1.2
d.atn.prln.rb. | khnm rb.nqdm. | ṯ'y.nqmd.mlk ugr[t]. | adn.yrgb.b'l.ṯrmn. 6.6[62.2].57
sl]h.l arṣ.ṯtbr. | [---.]aḫ h.tbky. | [--.m]rṣ.mlk. | [---.]krt.adn k. | [w y'ny.]ǵzr.ilḥu. | [---.]mrṣ.mlk. | [--.k]rt.adn k. | [--. 16.1[125].57
. | 'šrt.qḥ.tp k.b yd. | [-]r[-]k.bm.ymn. | tlk.škn.'l.ṣrrt. | adn k.šqrb.[---]. | b mgn k.w ḫrṣ.l kl. | apnk.ǵzr.ilḥu. | [m]rḥ 16.1[125].44
nn.ggn h. | lk.l ab k.yṣb.lk. | l[ab]k.w rgm.'ny. | l k[rt.adn k.]ištm[']. | w tqǵ[.udn.k ǵz.ǵzm]. | tdbr.w[ǵ]rm[.ṯtwy]. 16.6[127].29
.]krt.adn k. | [w y'ny.]ǵzr.ilḥu. | [---.]mr̃ṣ.mlk. | [--.k]rt.adn k. | [--.d]bḥ.dbḥ. | [--.']šr.'šrt. | '[---.---]. | b[---.---]. | t[--.---] 16.1[125].60
y. | w l h[-] y'l m. | bn y.yšal. | ṯryl.w rgm. | ṯtb.l aḫ k. | l adn k. 138.19
. | w h[t] aḫ y. | bn y.yšal. | ṯryl.w rgm[.-]. | ṯtb.l aḫ k. | l adn k. 138.19
tšty. | w t'n.mṯt ḥry. | l l[ḥ]m.l š[ty].ṣḥt km. | db[ḥ.l krt.a]dn km. | 'l.krt.tbun.km. | rgm.ṯ[rm.]rgm hm. | b ḏrt[.---.]krt 15[128].6.5
r.ḥrb.ltšt. | [--]n hm.rgm.l ṯr.ab h.il.tḥm.ym.b'l km. | [adn]km.ṯpṭ.nhr.tn.il m.d tq h.d tqyn h. | [hml]t.tn.b'l.w 'nn 2.1[137].34
km.w rgm.l ṯr.a[b.-.il.tny.l pḫr]. | m'd.tḥm.ym.b'l km.adn km.ṯ[pṭ.nhr]. | tn.il m.d tq h.d tqyn.hmlt.tn.b'l.[w 'nn h 2.1[137].17
.mlak.ym.t'dt.ṯpṭ.nh[r.---]. | [---].an.rgmt.l ym.b'l km.ad[n km.ṯpṭ]. | [nhr.---.]hwt.gmr.hd.l wny[-.---]. | [---.]iyr h.g 2.1[137].45
h.uk.škn. | k.[---.]sglt h.hw. | w.b[.---.]uk.nǵr. | w.[---].adny.l.yḫsr. | w.[ank.yd]'.l.yd't. | h[t.---.]l.špš.b'l k. | '[--.s]glt 2060.9
.yw.ilt.[---]. | w p'r.šm.ym[-.---]. | t'nyn.l zn.tn[.---]. | at.adn.tp'r[.---]. | ank.lṭpn.il[.d pid.---]. | 'l.ydm.p'rt[.---]. | šm k. 1['NT.X].4.17
.]ḫdmn. | [bn.]nklb. | [---]dn. | [---]y. | [-----]. | [-----]. | bn.adn. | prtn. | bn.btry. 1073.3.3
d. | sǵr.awldn.aḥd. | sǵr.idṯn.aḥd. | sǵr.sndrn.aḥd. | sǵr.adn.ṣdq.aḥd. | sǵr.irgn.aḥd. | sǵr.ršpab.aḥd. | sǵr.arwṭ.aḥd. | s 1140.8
sny. | nsk.ks[p.--]mrtn.kṭrmlk. | yḥmn.aḫm[l]k.'bdrpu.adn.ṯ[--]. | bdn.qln.mtn.ydln. | b'ltdtt.tlgn.ytn. | b'ltǵpṭm.krw 2011.33

adnn‘m

ṯlṯ.mat.ṯlṯm. | kbd.šmn. | l kny. | ṯmnym.šmn. | b d.adnn‘m. 1094.5

adn‘m

. | b‘ln. | ytršp. | ḥmšm.ṯmn.kbd. | tgmr.bnš.mlk. | d.b d.adn‘m. | [š]b‘.b.ḥrṯm. | [ṯ]lṯ.b.ṯǵrm. | rb qrt.aḥd. | ṯmn.ḫzr. | w. 1024.2.27
[sp]r.bnš.ml[k.d.b] d adn[‘m]. | [---].riš[.---].kt. | [y]nḥm. | ilb‘l. | ‘bdyr[ḫ]. | ṯtpḥ. | art 1024.1.1

ad‘y

ydn.bn.ilrpi. | w.ṯb‘m.‘rb.b.‘[d]n. | ḏmry.bn.yrm. | ‘rb.b.ad‘y. 2079.10

ad‘l

l‘. | bn.znan.qšt. | bn.arz.[ar]b‘.qšt.w.arb[‘.]ql‘m. | b[n.]ad‘l.q[š]t.w.ql‘. | b[n].ilyn.qšt.w.ql‘. | šmrm.ql‘. | ubr‘y. | abmn 119[321].2.46

adr

t.l.‘šrm.ksp hm. | šstm.b.šb‘m. | ṯlṯ.mat.trm.b.‘šrt. | mit.adrm.b.‘šrt. | ‘šr.ydt.b.‘šrt. | ḫmš.kkrm.ṣml. | ‘šrt.ksp h. | ḫmš. 1127.8
n.adr.gdm.b rumm. | adr.qrnt.b y‘lm.mtnm. | b ‘qbt.ṯr.adr.b ǵlil.qnm. | tn.l kṯr.w ḫss.yb‘l.qšt l ‘nt. | qṣ‘t.l ybmt.lim 17[2AQHT].6.23
mlkt[.---]. | kd.yn.l.[---]. | armwl w [--]. | arb‘.yn.[--]. | l adrm.b[--]. | šqym. 1092.7
]ṣ‘t k.ybmt.limm. | w y‘n.aqht.ǵzr.adr.ṯqbm. | [d]lbnn.adr.gdm.b rumm. | adr.qrnt.b y‘lm.mtnm. | b ‘qbt.ṯr.adr.b ǵl 17[2AQHT].6.21
i.ap[h]n.ǵzr. | [mt.hrn]my.ytšu. | [yṯb.b ap.ṯ]ǵr[.ṯ]ḥt. | [adrm.d b grn.y]dn. | [dn.almnt.y]ṯpṭ. | [ṯpṭ.ytm.---] h. | [---.--- 19[1AQHT].1.23
.mt. | rpi.a hn.ǵzr.mt.hrnm[y]. | ytšu.yṯb.b ap.ṯǵr.tḥt. | adrm.d b grn.ydn. | dn.almnt.yṯpṭ.ṯpṭ.ytm. | b nši ‘n h.w yph 17[2AQHT].5.7
ṯn pǵn.[-]dr | m.ṯn kndwm adrm. | w knd pnṯ.dq. | ṯn ḫpnm.ṯn pldm ǵlmm. | kpld.b[-.-]r[140[98].2
.aṯt.ab ṣrry. | tbky k.ab.ǵr.b‘l. | ṣpn.ḥlm.qdš. | any.ḥlm.adr.ḥl. | rḥb.mknpt.ap. | [k]rt.bnm.il.špḥ. | lṯpn.w qdš.‘l. | ab h 16.1[125].8
ṭpn.l yḥ.t[b]ky k. | ab.ǵr.b‘l.ṣ[p]n.ḥlm. | qdš.nny.ḥ[l]m.adr. | ḥl.rḥb.mk[npt]. | ap.krt bn[m.il]. | špḥ.lṭpn[.w qdš]. | bk 16.2[125].108
y‘n.aqht.ǵzr.adr.ṯqbm. | [d]lbnn.adr.gdm.b rumm. | adr.qrnt.b y‘lm.mtnm. | b ‘qbt.ṯr.adr.b ǵlil.qnm. | tn.l kṯr.w 17[2AQHT].6.22
ṯ[b]. | any kn.dt. | likt.mṣrm. | hn dt.b.ṣr. | mtt.by. | gšm.adr. | nškḥ.w. | rb.tmtt. | lqḥ.kl.ḏr‘. | b d a[-]m.w.ank. | k[l.]ḏr‘ 2059.14
št k.[l]. | [‘nt.tq]ḥ[.q]ṣ‘t k.ybmt.limm. | w y‘n.aqht.ǵzr.adr.ṯqbm. | [d]lbnn.adr.gdm.b rumm. | adr.qrnt.b y‘lm.mtn 17[2AQHT].6.20
[.---]. | ‘ḏbm.[---]. | uḫry.l[---]. | mṣt.ks h.t[--.---]. | idm.adr[.---]. | idm.‘rẓ.t‘r[ẓ.---]. | ‘n.b‘l.a[ḫ]ḏ[.---]. | ẓr h.aḫḏ.qš[t.-- 12[75].2.30
mš[.---]t.ḥdrm. | w.[---.a]ḥd.d.sgrm. | w p[tḥ.---.]l.aḥd.adr. | [---.--]t.b[ḥd]r.mškb. | ṯl[l.---.--]ḥ. | b lṯk.bt. | [pt]ḥ.aḥd.l 1151.5

adrdn

‘bdyrḫ. | ubn.ḫyrn. | ybnil.adrdn. | klyn.kkln. | ‘dmlk.tdn. | ‘zn.pǵdn. | [a]nndn. | [r]špab. 1070.3
t. | [y]nḥm. | ilb‘l. | ‘bdyr[ḫ]. | ṯtpḥ. | artn. | ybnil. | brqn. | adr[dn]. | krwn. | arkdn. | ilmn. | abškn. | ykn. | ršpab. | klyn. | ḥ 1024.1.10
spr.updt. | d b d.mlkytn. | kdrl. | slṯmg. | adrdn. | l[l]wn. | ydln. | ldn. | tdǵl. | ibrkyṯ. 1034.5
‘d[rš]p. | pqr. | ṯǵr. | ttǵl. | ṯn.yṣḥm. | slṯmg. | kdrl. | wql. | adrdn. | prn. | ‘bdil. | ušy.šbn[-]. | aḫt.ab. | krwn. | nnḏ. | mkl. | k 1069.9
[ḫrš].bhtm.b‘l.šd. | [---d]nil. | [a]drdn. | [---]n. | pǵdn. | ṯtpḥ. | ḥgbn. | šrm. | bn.ymil. | bn.kḏǵdl 1039.1.22

adrt

drtm.w.pǵt.aḥt.b[.bt.---]. | aṯt.w ṯn.n‘rm.b.bt.ilsk. | aṯt.ad[r]t.b.bt.armwl. | aṯt.aḥt.b.bt.iwrpzn. | ṯt.aṯtm.w.pǵt.aḥt.b 80[119].9
t.krz. | [aṯt.]w.pǵt.b.bt.gg. | [ǵz]r.aḥd.b.bt.nwrḏ. | [aṯ]t.adrt.b.bt.artṯb. | aṯt.w.ṯn.bn h.b.bt.iwwpzn. | aṯt.w.pǵt.b.bt.y 80[119].4
aṯt.w.]pǵt.aḥt.b.bt.tt. | [aṯt.w.]bt h.b.bt.trǵds. | [---.]aṯt.adrt.w.pǵt.a[ḥt.b.bt.---]. | [---.‘]šrm.npš.b.bt.[---]. | [---.]w.pǵt 80[119].28
w.ṯn.bn h.b.bt.iwwpzn. | aṯt.w.pǵt.b.bt.ydrm. | ṯt.aṯtm.adrtm.w.pǵt.aḥt.b[.bt.---]. | aṯt.w ṯn.n‘rm.b.bt.ilsk. | aṯt.ad[r] 80[119].7
.aṯt.adrt.w.ṯlṯ.ǵzr[m]. | w.ḫmš.n‘rt.b.bt.sk[n]. | ṯt.aṯtm.adrtm.w.pǵt.w ǵzr[.aḥd.b.bt.---]. | aṯt.w.ṯt.pǵtm.w.ǵzr.aḥd.b 80[119].18
.bt.ṯpṭb‘l. | [---.]n[--.mḏ]rǵlm. | [---.]b.bt[.---]l. | [ṯ]lṯ.aṯt.adrt.w.ṯlṯ.ǵzr[m]. | w.ḫmš.n‘rt.b.bt.sk[n]. | ṯt.aṯtm.adrtm.w.p 80[119].16
[---].yryt. | [---.a]drt. | [--.ṯt]m.ṯmn.k[bd]. | [---.yr]yt.dq[-]. | [--.ṯ]lṯm.l.mi[t]. | 2170.2
--]. | w tglṯ thmt.‘[--.---]. | yṣi.ǵl h tḥm b[.---]. | mrḥ h l adrt[.---]. | ṯtb ‘ṯrt b ǵl[.---]. | qrẓ tšt.l šmal[.---]. | arbḥ.‘n h tš 2001.1.7

adt

adt y.[---]. | lb.ab[d k].al[.---]. | [-]tm.iph.adt y.w.[---]. | tšṣḥq.hn.aṯt.l.‘bd. | šb‘t.w.nṣp.ksp. | [-]tm.rb[.-- 1017.3
p.ank. | [---].l.ǵr.amn. | [---.-]ktt.hn.ib. | [---.]mlk. | [---.]adt y.td‘. | w.ap.mlk.uḏ[r]. | [-]d‘.k.iḫd.[---]. | w.mlk.b‘l y. | lm 1012.19
bd k. | l.p‘n. | adt y. | šb‘ d. | w.šb‘ id. | mrḥqtm. | qlt. | ‘m.adt y. | mnm.šlm. | rgm.ṯṯb. | l.‘bd h. 52[89].12
l.mlkt. | adt y.rgm. | tḥm.illdr. | ‘bd k.. | l.p‘n a[dt y]. | šb‘ d[.w šb‘ d]. | 1014.2
l.mlkt. | adt y. | rgm. | tḥm.tlmyn. | ‘bd k. | l.p‘n. | adt y. | šb‘ d. | w.šb‘ id 52[89].2
[---.a]dt y. | [---].irrṯwm.‘bd k. | [---.a]dt y.mrḥqm. | [---].adt y.yšlm. | [---.]mlk n.amṣ. | [.---].nn. | [1012.3
l.mlkt. | adt y. | rgm. | tḥm.tlmyn. | ‘bd k. | l.p‘n. | adt y. | šb‘ d. | w.šb‘ id. | mrḥqtm. | qlt. | ‘m.adt y. | mnm.šlm. | 52[89].7
l.mlkt. | adt y.rgm. | tḥm.illdr. | ‘bd k.. | l.p‘n a[dt y]. | šb‘ d[.w šb‘ d]. | mrḥq[tm.qlt]. | mn[m.šlm]. 1014.5
--.a]dt y. | [---].irrṯwm.‘bd k. | [---.a]dt y.mrḥqm. | [---].adt y.yšlm. | [---.]mlk n.amṣ. | [.---].nn. | [---.]qrt.dt. | [---.--]s‘. 1012.4
[---.a]dt y. | [---].irrṯwm.‘bd k. | [---.a]dt y.mrḥqm. | [---].adt y.yšl 1012.1
adt y.[---]. | lb.ab[d k].al[.---]. | [-]tm.iph.adt y.w.[---]. | tšṣḥq. 1017.1
n ny.‘m ny. | kll.mid. | šlm. | w.ap.ank. | nḫt.ṯm ny. | ‘m.adt ny. | mnm.šlm. | rgm.ṯṯb. | l.‘bd k. 51[95].15
l um y.adt ny. | rgm. | tḥm.tlmyn. | w.aḫtmlk ‘bd k. | l.p‘n.adt ny. | m 51[95].1
m y.adt ny. | rgm. | tḥm.tlmyn. | w.aḫtmlk ‘bd k. | l.p‘n.adt ny. | mrḥqtm. | qlny.ilm. | tǵr k. | tšlm k. | hn ny.‘m ny. | kl 51[95].5

adty

bnšm.dt.iṯ.alpm.l hm. | bn.niršn. | bn.adty. | bn.alz. | bn.birtn. | bn.mlṣ. | bn.q[--]. | bn.[---]. | bn.ṯ[-]r. 2023.1.3
.ṣqn. | bn.šyn. | bn.prtn. | bn.ypr. | mrum. | bn.‘[--]t. | bn.adty. | bn.krwn. | bn.ngsk. | bn.qnḏ. | bn.pity. | w.nḥl h. | bn.rt. 113[400].3.13
tmn.ḫmšm. | [ṣṣ] ‘mtḏl ṯlṯm. | ṣṣ ‘mlbi ṯṯ l ‘šrm. | ṣṣ bn adty ḫmšm. | ṣṣ amtrn arb‘m. | ṣṣ iytlm mit ṯlṯm kbd. | ṣṣ m[l] 2097.7

b ṯlṯ. | ilmlk.ʻšr.ṣin. | mlknʻm.ʻšr. | bn.adty.ʻšr. | [ṣ]dqšlm ḫmš. | krzn.ḫmš. | ubrʻym.ḫmš. | [----]. | [bn 2039.4
lḥn. | [---.ṯ]lḥ[n]. | [---.--ṯ]lḥn. | [---.]ṯlḥn. | [---.]ṯlḥn. | bn adty ṯlḥn.bn qrwl ṯlḥn. 98[11].36

ad̲ddy

d̲ddy. | ynḥm.ad̲ddy. | ykny.ad̲ddy. | m[--].ad̲ddy. | ypʻ.ad̲ddy. | abǵl.ad̲[ddy]. | abǵl.a[---]. | rbil.[---]. | kd̲yn.[---.-]gṯ. | š 2014.24
.ad̲ddy. | ykny.ad̲ddy. | m[--].ad̲ddy. | ypʻ.ad̲ddy. | abǵl.ad̲[ddy]. | abǵl.a[---]. | rbil.[---]. | kd̲yn.[---.-]gṯ. | šmrm.a[d̲dd] 2014.25
bdl.gt.bn.tbšn. | bn.mnyy.šʻrty. | aryn.ad̲ddy. | agpṯr. | šbʻl.mlky. | nʻmn.mṣry. | yʻl.knʻny. | gdn.bn.u 91[311].3
.knn. | iwrḫz.b d.skn. | škny.ad̲ddy. | mšu.ad̲ddy. | plsy.ad̲ddy. | aḫyn. | ygmr.ad̲ddy. | gln.aṯṯ. | ddy.[a]d̲ddy. | bn.mlkr 2014.40
šmrm.a[d̲dd]y.tb[--]. | ynḥm.ad̲ddy. | ǵd̲ǵd.ad̲ddy. | sw.ad̲ddy. | ildy.ad̲ddy. | grʻ.ad̲ddy. | ʻbd.ršp ad̲ddy. | ʻdn.bn.knn. 2014.32
ddy. | plsy.ad̲ddy. | aḫyn. | ygmr.ad̲ddy. | gln.aṯṯ. | ddy.[a]d̲ddy. | bn.mlkr[šp]. | bn.y[k]n. | ynḥm. | bn.abd.bʻ[l]. | mnḥ 2014.44
uḫd. | [---.-]luḫ. | [---.-]tn.b d.mlkt. | [---.]l.mḫṣ. | ab[---.]ad̲ddy.bn.skn. | bn.[---.]uḫd. | bn.n[---.]hbṭn. | bn.m[--.]skn. | b 2014.8
.ur[-.---]. | bn.knn[.---]y. | bn.ymlk[.b]d.skn. | bn.yḥnn.ad̲ddy. | bn.pdǵy.mḫdy. | bn.yyn.md̲rǵl. | bn.ʻlr. | ḫṯpy.ad̲ddy. 2014.16
| škny.ad̲ddy. | mšu.ad̲ddy. | plsy.ad̲ddy. | aḫyn. | ygmr.ad̲ddy. | gln.aṯṯ. | ddy.[a]d̲ddy. | bn.mlkr[šp]. | bn.y[k]n. | ynḥ 2014.42
]y.tb[--]. | ynḥm.ad̲ddy. | ǵd̲ǵd.ad̲ddy. | sw.ad̲ddy. | ildy.ad̲ddy. | grʻ.ad̲ddy. | ʻbd.ršp ad̲ddy. | ʻdn.bn.knn. | iwrḫz.b d.s 2014.33
ǵy.mḫdy. | bn.yyn.md̲rǵl. | bn.ʻlr. | ḫṯpy.ad̲ddy. | ynḥm.ad̲ddy. | ykny.ad̲ddy. | m[--].ad̲ddy. | ypʻ.ad̲ddy. | abǵl.ad̲[ddy 2014.21
.ad̲ddy. | bn.pdǵy.mḫdy. | bn.yyn.md̲rǵl. | bn.ʻlr. | ḫṯpy.ad̲ddy. | ynḥm.ad̲ddy. | ykny.ad̲ddy. | m[--].ad̲ddy. | ypʻ.ad̲dd 2014.20
n.ʻlr. | ḫṯpy.ad̲ddy. | ynḥm.ad̲ddy. | ykny.ad̲ddy. | m[--].ad̲ddy. | ypʻ.ad̲ddy. | abǵl.ad̲[ddy]. | abǵl.a[---]. | rbil.[---]. | kd̲y 2014.23
dy. | ʻbd.ršp ad̲ddy. | ʻdn.bn.knn. | iwrḫz.b d.skn. | škny.ad̲ddy. | mšu.ad̲ddy. | plsy.ad̲ddy. | aḫyn. | ygmr.ad̲ddy. | gln.a 2014.38
.yyn.md̲rǵl. | bn.ʻlr. | ḫṯpy.ad̲ddy. | ynḥm.ad̲ddy. | ykny.ad̲ddy. | m[--].ad̲ddy. | ypʻ.ad̲ddy. | abǵl.ad̲[ddy]. | abǵl.a[---]. 2014.22
n.[---.-]gṯ. | šmrm.a[d̲dd]y.tb[--]. | ynḥm.ad̲ddy. | ǵd̲ǵd.ad̲ddy. | sw.ad̲ddy. | ildy.ad̲ddy. | grʻ.ad̲ddy. | ʻbd.ršp ad̲ddy. | ʻ 2014.31
ḥm.ad̲ddy. | ǵd̲ǵd.ad̲ddy. | sw.ad̲ddy. | ildy.ad̲ddy. | grʻ.ad̲ddy. | ʻbd.ršp ad̲ddy. | ʻdn.bn.knn. | iwrḫz.b d.skn. | škny.ad̲ 2014.34
d.ad̲ddy. | sw.ad̲ddy. | ildy.ad̲ddy. | grʻ.ad̲ddy. | ʻbd.ršp ad̲ddy. | ʻdn.bn.knn. | iwrḫz.b d.skn. | škny.ad̲ddy. | mšu.ad̲dd 2014.35
rbil.[---]. | kd̲yn.[---.-]gṯ. | šmrm.a[d̲dd]y.tb[--]. | ynḥm.ad̲ddy. | ǵd̲ǵd.ad̲ddy. | sw.ad̲ddy. | ildy.ad̲ddy. | grʻ.ad̲ddy. | ʻb 2014.30
d̲ddy. | ʻdn.bn.knn. | iwrḫz.b d.skn. | škny.ad̲ddy. | mšu.ad̲ddy. | plsy.ad̲ddy. | aḫyn. | ygmr.ad̲ddy. | gln.aṯṯ. | ddy.[a]d̲d 2014.39
.ad̲[ddy]. | abǵl.a[---]. | rbil.[---]. | kd̲yn.[---.-]gṯ. | šmrm.a[d̲dd]y.tb[--]. | ynḥm.ad̲ddy. | ǵd̲ǵd.ad̲ddy. | sw.ad̲ddy. | ildy. 2014.29
dnm. | m[i]t.l.bn.ʻẓmt.rišy. | mit.l.tlmyn.bn.ʻdy. | [---.]l.ad̲ddy. | [--.]l.kkln. 2095.9

ad̲ddn

š. | b[n.]tlš. | d̲mr. | mkrm. | ʻzn. | ypltׂ. | ʻbdmlk. | ynḥm. | ad̲ddn. | mtn. | plsy. | qṭn. | ypr. | bn.ymy. | bn.ʻrd. | [-]b.da[-]. | [1035.4.7

ad̲dt

[---]rn. | [--]ṣb. | [--]ps. | [--]ṯb. | [--]ln. | [---]r. | [---]y. | bn.ad̲dt. | bn.atnb. | bn.yšd. | bn.bršm. | bn.gṯprg. | gṯpbn. | bn.b[-- 1057.8

ad̲mny

bt.il. | bʻl.bt.ad̲mny. | bʻl.bt.pdy. | bʻl.bt.nqly. | bʻl.bt.ʻlr. | bʻl.bt.ssl. | bʻl.bt.ṯ 31[14].2

ad̲mṯn

[---]ym.mddbʻl. | [---]n.bn.agyn. | [--]ṯn. | [--]tn.bn.ad̲mṯn. | [-]tn bn.agyn. | ullym.bn.abynm. | antn.bn.iwr[n]r. | 94[313].4

ahb

tšt[.r]imt.[l irt h.tšr.l dd.aliyn.bʻl]. | [ahb]t pdr[y.bt.ar.ahbt.ṭly.bt.rb.dd]. | arṣy bt.y[ʻbdr.---]. | rgm l btl[t.ʻnt.ṯny.l y 7.2[130].11
---.t]št.rimt. | l irt h.mšr.l.dd.aliyn. | bʻl.yd.pdry.bt.ar. | ahbt.ṭly.bt.rb.dd.arṣy. | bt.yʻbdr.km ǵlmm. | w ʻrb n.l pʻn.ʻnt. 3[ʻNT].3.4
--]dyn.bʻd.[--]d̲yn.w l. | [--]k bʻlt bhtm[.--]tn k. | [--]y.l ihbt.yb[--].rgm y. | [---.]škb.w m[--.]mlakt. | [---.]ʻl.w tš[ʻd]n. 1002.46
arṣ.tspr b y | rdm.arṣ.w td' ilm. | k mtt.yšmʻ.aliyn.bʻl. | yuhb.ʻglt.b dbr.prt. | b šd.šḥlmmt.škb. | ʻmn h.šbʻ.l šbʻm. | tš[ʻ 5[67].5.18
--.]yṣt d̲m[r.---]. | tšt[.r]imt.[l irt h.tšr.l dd.aliyn.bʻl]. | [ahb]t pdr[y.bt.ar.ahbt.ṭly.bt.rb.dd]. | arṣy bt.y[ʻbdr.---]. | rgm 7.2[130].11
t. | b krpnm.yn.b k.ḫrṣ. | dm.ʻṣm.hm.yd.il mlk. | yḫss k.ahbt.ṯr.tʻrr k. | w tʻn.rbt.aṯrt ym. | tḥm k.il.ḥkm.ḥkmt. | ʻm ʻl 4[51].4.39
.tiḫd.knr h.b yd[h.tšt]. | rimt.l irt h.tšr.dd.al[iyn]. | bʻl.ahbt. UG5.3.2.8

ahl

.tššqy ilm. | tsad.tkbd.hmt.bʻl. | ḥkpt il.kl h.tbʻ.kṯr. | l ahl h.hyn.tbʻ.l mš | knt h.apnk.dnil.m[t]. | rpi.aphn.ǵzr.m[t]. 17[2AQHT].5.32
pḫr.qbṣ.dtn. | ṣǵrt hn.abkrn. | tbrk.ilm.tity. | tity.ilm.l ahl hm. | dr il.l mšknt hm. | w tqrb.w ld.bn.l h. | w tqrb.w ld. 15[128].3.18
ahlm.rgm.l yṯ[pn.y] | bl.agrtn.bat.b d̲d k.[pǵt]. | bat.b hlm w yʻn.yṯpn[.mhr]. | št.qḥn.w tšqyn.yn.qḥ. | ks.b d y.qbʻt. 19[1AQHT].4.214
dm.yd.mḫṣt.a[qh]t.ǵ | zr.tmḫṣ.alpm.ib.št[-.]št. | ḥršm l ahlm p[---.]km. | [-]bl lb h.km.bṯn.y[--.-]ah. | ṯnm.tšqy msk.h 19[1AQHT].4.222
--]. | pǵt.minš.šdm l mʻ[rb]. | nrt.ilm.špš.mǵy[t]. | pǵt.l ahlm.rgm.l yṯ[pn.y] | bl.agrtn.bat.b d̲d k.[pǵt]. | bat.b hlm w 19[1AQHT].4.212

awl

m ṯr.w tkms.hd.p[.-]. | km.ibr.b tk.mšmš d[--]. | ittpq.l awl. | išttk.lm.ttkn. | štk.mlk.dn. | štk.šibt.ʻn. | štk.qr.bt.il. | w 12[75].2.57

awldn

m. | sǵr.bn.ḫpsry.aḥd. | sǵr.artn.aḥd. | sǵr.ʻdn.aḥd. | sǵr.awldn.aḥd. | sǵr.idṯn.aḥd. | sǵr.sndrn.aḥd. | sǵr.adn.ṣdq.aḥd. | 1140.5
. | dqn. | ṯlṯ.klbm. | ḫmn. | [---.-]rsd. | bn[.-]pṭ. | bn kdrn. | awldn. | arswn.yʻr[ty.--]. | bn.ugr. | gny. | ṯn.mdm. 86[305].9

awpn

iḫyn.uṯpt.ḥẓm. | anšrm.uṯpt.ḥẓm. | w uṯpt.srdnnm. | awpn.uṯpt.ḥẓm. | w uṯpt.srdnnm. | rpan.uṯpt.srdnnm. | šbʻm. 1124.4

awr

| w.bn h.n[--.---]. | ḥnil.[---]. | aršmg.mru. | b‘l.šlm.‘bd. | awr.ṯǵrn.‘bd. | ‘bd.ḫmn.šm‘.rgm. | s̀dn.[k]bs̀. | šdyn.mḫ[ṣ]. | aṯ 2084.11

az

gr.rq. | ṯṭ.prqt. | w.mrdt.prqt.pṯt. | lbš.psm.rq. | ṯn.mrdt.az. | ṯlṯ.pld.š‘rt. | ṯ[---].kbm. | p[---]r.aḥd. | [-----]. | [-----]. | [---.-- 1112.6

azd

a]n ḥmt.l p[.n]ṯk.abd.l p.akl ṯm.dl. | [---.q]l.bl.tbḥ[n.l]azd.‘r.qdm. | [---].‘ẓ q[dm.--.šp]š. | [---.šm]n.mšḥt.kṯpm.a[-]ṯ[UG5.8.21

azzlt

trt.šd. | [---.-]rt.mḫṣ.bnš.mlk.yb‘l hm. | [---.--]t.w.ḫpn.l.azzlt. | [---.]l.‘ṯtrt.šd. | [---].yb‘lnn. | [---.--]n.b.ṯlṯ.šnt.l.nṣd. | [-- 1106.54

azr

b. | l arṣ.yṣq.‘mr. | un.l riš h.‘pr.plṯt. | l qdqd h.lpš.yks. | mizrtm.ǵr.b abn. | ydy.psltm.b y‘r. | yhdy.lḥm.w dqn. | yṯlṯ.q 5[67].6.17
.ylḥm. | [uzr.yšqy.]bn.qdš.yd. | [ṣt h.y‘l.]w yškb.yd. | [mizrt.]p ynl.hn.ym. | [w ṯn.uzr.]ilm.dnil. | [uzr.ilm.]ylḥm.uz 17[2AQHT].1.6
.]yšqy.bn qdš.yd.ṣt h. | [dn]il.yd.ṣt h.y‘l.w yškb. | [yd.]mizrt.p yln.mk.b šb‘.ymm. | [w]yqrb.b‘l.b ḥnt h.abynt. | [d] 17[2AQHT].1.16
r.ysmt.šd. | [šḥl]mmt.t[mǵ.]l b‘l.np[l]. | [l a]rṣ[.lpš].tks.miz[rtm]. 5[67].6.31

azrt

mr.. | bn km k bk[r.z]bl.am.. | rkm.agzrt[.--].arḫ.. | b‘l.azrt.‘nt.[-]ld. | kbd h.l yd‘ hr h.[---]d[-]. | tnq[.---.]in[b]b.p‘r. | 13[6].30

aḥd

-]. | ḫmš[.---]t.ḥdrm. | w.[---.a]ḥd.d.sgrm. | w p[tḥ.---.]l.aḥd.adr. | [---.--]t.b[ḥd]r.mškb. | ṯl[l.---.--]ḥ. | b lṯk.bt. | [pt]ḥ.a 1151.5
.b.‘nqpat. | [aḥd.al]p.d aǵlmn. | [d aḫd b.g]t gbry. | [---].aḥd.aḫd.b.y‘ny. | [---.-]ḥm.b.aḫd.ḥrṯ. | [---.]aḫd.b.grn.uškn. | [1129.14
| ḥrṯ h.aḥd.b gt.nḫl. | aḥd.b gt.knpy.w.aḥd.b gt.ṯrmn. | aḥd.alp.idṯn.d aḫd.b.‘nqpat. | [aḥd.al]p.d aǵlmn. | [d aḫd b.g 1129.11
npy.w.aḥd.b gt.ṯrmn. | aḥd.alp.idṯn.d aḫd.b.‘nqpat. | [aḥd.al]p.d aǵlmn. | [d aḫd b.g]t gbry. | [---].aḥd.aḫd.b.y‘ny. | [1129.12
. | aupṯ.krm.aḥd.nšpin.kr[m.]aḥd[.---]. | dmt.lḫsn.krm.aḥd.annḏr.kr[m.---]. | aǵt.mryn.ary[.]yukl.krm.[---]. | gdn.kr 1081.15
h]. | wšṯn.bn h. | ṯmgdl.ykn‘my.w.aṯt h. | w.bn h.w.alp.aḥ[d]. | aǵltn.[--]y.w[.aṯt h]. | w.bn h.w.alp.w.[---]. | [-]ln.[---]. 1080.6
y]bnn.ṣmdm. | ṯp[ṭ]b‘l.ṣmdm. | [---.ṣ]mdm.w.ḥrṣ. | [---].aḥdm. | [iwr]pzn.aḥdm. | [i]lšpš.aḥd. 2033.2.6
[ṭ]b‘l.ṣmdm. | [---.ṣ]mdm.w.ḥrṣ. | [---].aḥdm. | [iwr]pzn.aḥdm. | [i]lšpš.aḥd. 2033.2.7
tš‘.ṣmdm. | ṯlṯm.b d. | ibrtlm. | w.pat.aḥt. | in.b hm. 1141.4
mr.w.bnš. | rqd arb‘. | šbn aḥd. | ṭbq aḥd. | šrš aḥd. | bir aḥd. | uḫnp. | hzp ṯn. | m‘qb arb‘. 2040.31
[---].‘šr. | [---].ṯlṯ. | [---].ṯmn. | [---].ṯlṯ. | [---].aḥd. | u[--].ṯn. | hz[p].ṯṯ. | ḫrṣb‘.aḥd. | ypr.arb. | m[-]qb.‘šr. | ṯn‘ 70[112].5
dr‘.b ym.tn.aḥd. | b aḫ k.ispa.w yṯb. | ap.d anšt.im[-]. | aḥd.b aḫ k.l[--]n. | hn[-.]aḥẓ[.---]l[-]. | [‘]nt.akl[y.nšm]. | akly. 6[49].5.22
]y.b kbrt. | ‘l k.pht.[-]l[-]. | b šdm.‘l k.pht. | dr‘.b ym.tn.aḥd. | b aḫ k.ispa.w yṯb. | ap.d anšt.im[-]. | aḥd.b aḫ k.l[--]n. | 6[49].5.19
ṯn.ṣbrm. | b.uškn. | ṣbr.aḥd. | b.ar. | ṣbr.aḥd. | b.mlk. | ṣbr.aḥd. | b.m‘rby. | ṣbr.aḥd. | b.u 2073.3
.aḥd. | b.mlk. | ṣbr.aḥd. | b.m‘rby. | ṣbr.aḥd. | b.ulm. | ṣbr.aḥd. | b.ubr‘y. 2073.11
r.aḥd. | b.ar. | ṣbr.aḥd. | b.mlk. | ṣbr.aḥd. | b.m‘rby. | ṣbr.aḥd. | b.ulm. | ṣbr.aḥd. | b.ubr‘y. 2073.9
. | arṣ.gm.yṣḥ il. | l rbt.aṯrt ym.šm‘. | l rbt.aṯr[t] ym.tn. | aḥd.b bn k.amlkn. | w t‘n.rbt.aṯrt ym. | bl.nmlk.yd‘.ylḥn. | w 6.1.46[49.1.18]
-]. | aṯt.w ṯn.n‘rm.b.bt.ilsk. | aṯt.ad[r]t.b.bt.armwl. | aṯt.aḥt.b.bt.iwrpzn. | ṯt.aṯtm.w.pǵt.aḥt.b bt.[-]r[-]. | [aṯ]t.b.bt.au 80[119].10
. | ṯt.aṯtm.w.pǵt.w.ǵzr.aḥd.b.[bt.---]. | aṯt.w.bn h.w.pǵt.aḥt.b.bt.m[--]. | aṯt.w.ṯt.bt h.b.bt.ḫḏmrd. | aṯt.w.ṯn.ǵzrm.b.bt 80[119].21
[aṯt.w].bn h.b.bt.krz. | [aṯt.]w.pǵt.b.bt.gg. | [ǵz]r.aḥd.b.bt.nwrḏ. | [aṯ]t.adrt.b.bt.artṯb. | aṯt.w.ṯn.bn h.b.bt.iww 80[119].3
t.bt h.b.bt.ḫḏmrd. | aṯt.w.ṯn.ǵzrm.b.bt.ṣdqš[lm]. | [a]ṯt.aḥt.b.bt.rpi[--]. | [aṯt.]w.bt h.b.bt.alḫn. | [aṯt.w.]pǵt.aḥt.b.bt.t 80[119].24
]ṯt.aḥt.b.bt.rpi[--]. | [aṯt.]w.bt h.b.bt.alḫn. | [aṯt.w.]pǵt.aḥt.b.bt.tt. | [aṯt.w.]bt h.b.bt.trǵds. | [---.]aṯt.adrt.w.pǵt.a[ḥt. 80[119].26
ad[r]t.b.bt.armwl. | aṯt.aḥt.b.bt.iwrpzn. | ṯt.aṯtm.w.pǵt.aḥt.b bt.[-]r[-]. | [aṯ]t.b.bt.aupš. | [aṯ]t.b.bt.ṯpṭb‘l. | [---.]n[--.m 80[119].11
ṯt.w.ṯt.pǵtm.w.ǵzr.aḥd.b.[bt.---]. | ṯt.aṯtm.w.pǵt.w.ǵzr.aḥd.b.[bt.---]. | aṯt.w.bn h.w.pǵt.aḥt.b.bt.m[--]. | aṯt.w.ṯt.bt h. 80[119].20
]. | w.ḫmš.n‘rt.b.bt.sk[n]. | ṯt.aṯtm.adrtm.w.pǵt.w ǵzr[.aḥd.b.bt.---]. | aṯt.w.ṯt.pǵtm.w.ǵzr.aḥd.b.[bt.---]. | ṯt.aṯtm.w.p 80[119].18
t.iwwpzn. | aṯt.w.pǵt.b.bt.ydrm. | ṯt.aṯtm.adrtm.w.pǵt.aḥt.b[.bt.---]. | aṯt.w ṯn.n‘rm.b.bt.ilsk. | aṯt.ad[r]t.b.bt.armwl. 80[119].7
drtm.w.pǵt.w ǵzr[.aḥd.b.bt.---]. | aṯt.w.ṯt.pǵtm.w.ǵzr.aḥd.b.[bt.---]. | ṯt.aṯtm.w.pǵt.w.ǵzr.aḥd.b.[bt.---]. | aṯt.w.bn h 80[119].19
ḥt.b.bt.tt. | [aṯt.w.]bt h.b.bt.trǵds. | [---.]aṯt.adrt.w.pǵt.a[ḥt.b.bt.---]. | [---.‘]šrm.npš.b.bt.[---]. | [---.]w.pǵt.aḥt.b.bt.[-- 80[119].28
.pǵt.a[ḥt.b.bt.---]. | [---.‘]šrm.npš.b.bt.[---]. | [---.]w.pǵt.aḥt.b.bt.[---]. 80[119].30
ṯlṯ.ṣmdm. | b.nḫry. | ṣmdm.b.ṯp[--]. | aḥdm.b.gm[--]. 144[317].4
t. | arb‘m.kbd. | ṯlṯ.alp.ṣpr.dt.aḫd. | ḥrṯ h.aḥd.b gt.nḫl. | aḥd.b gt.knpy.w.aḥd.b gt.ṯrmn. | aḥd.alp.idṯn.d aḫd.b.‘nqpa 1129.10
aḫmn.arb‘.mat. | arb‘m.kbd. | ṯlṯ.alp.ṣpr.dt.aḫd. | ḥrṯ h.aḥd.b gt.nḫl. | aḥd.b gt.knpy.w.aḥd.b gt.ṯrmn. | aḥd.alp.idṯn. 1129.9
.alp.ṣpr.dt.aḫd. | ḥrṯ h.aḥd.b gt.nḫl. | aḥd.b gt.knpy.w.aḥd.b gt.ṯrmn. | aḥd.alp.idṯn.d aḫd.b.‘nqpat. | [aḥd.al]p.d aǵl 1129.10
.yr[š]. | lmd.aḥd.b d.yḥ[--]. | ṯlṯ.lmdm.b d.nḥ[--]. | lmd.aḥd.b d.ar[--]. | ṯlṯ.lmdm.b d.[---]. | ṯlṯ.lmdm.b d.[---]. 1050.7
d.[---]. | šb‘.lmdm.b d.s[n]rn. | lmd.aḥd.b d.yr[š]. | lmd.aḥd.b d.yḥ[--]. | ṯlṯ.lmdm.b d.nḥ[--]. | lmd.aḥd.b d.ar[--]. | ṯlṯ.l 1050.5
nšm[.---]. | ḫḏǵlm.b d.[---]. | šb‘.lmdm.b d.s[n]rn. | lmd.aḥd.b d.yr[š]. | lmd.aḥd.b d.yḥ[--]. | ṯlṯ.lmdm.b d.nḥ[--]. | lmd 1050.4
dm.b d.snrn. | [---.lm]dm.b d.nrn. | [---.ḫ]ḏǵlm. | [lmd.]aḥd.b d.yrš. 1051.6
]. | [---.]bn.a[--.---]. | [---.]bn.i[--.---]. | [---].ṯp[--.---]. | [---.a]ḥt.b d[.---]. | [---.]b d.rb.[m]dlm. | [---.l i]ytlm. | [---].gmn. | [2162.B.1
ṯn.ṣbrm. | b.uškn. | ṣbr.aḥd. | b.ar. | ṣbr.aḥd. | b.mlk. | ṣbr.aḥd. | b.m‘rby. | ṣbr.aḥd. | b.ulm. | ṣbr.aḥd. | b 2073.5
n.ṣbrm. | b.uškn. | ṣbr.aḥd. | b.ar. | ṣbr.aḥd. | b.mlk. | ṣbr.aḥd. | b.m‘rby. | ṣbr.aḥd. | b.ulm. | ṣbr.aḥd. | b.ubr‘y. 2073.7
.ulm.ṯṯ.‘šr h.ḫrmṯt. | ṯt.nitm.ṯn.m‘ṣdm.ṯn.mqbm. | krk.aḥt. | b.sǵy.ḫmš.ḫrmṯt.nit. | krk.m‘ṣd.mqb. | b.gt.‘mq.ḫmš.ḫr 2048.6
lbš.aḥd. | b.‘šrt. | w.ṯn.b.ḫmšt. | ṯprt.b.ṯlṯt. | mṯyn.b.ṯṯt. | ṯn.lbšm.b. 1108.1
h. | kkr.š‘rt. | šb‘t.ksp h. | ḫmš.mqdm.dnyn. | b.ṯql.dprn.aḥd. | b.ṯql. | ḫmšm.‘rgz.b.ḫmšt. 1127.20

[-----]. | [ḫ]pn.aḫd.b.ṯqlm. | lbš.aḫd.b.ṯqlm. | ḫpn.pṯtm.b ʿšr. | tgmr.ksp.ṯlṯm. | ṯqlm.kbd. 1115.3
[-----]. | [ḫ]pn.aḫd.b.ṯqlm. | lbš.aḫd.b.ṯqlm. | ḫpn.pṯtm.b ʿšr. | tgmr.ksp.ṯlṯm. 1115.2
| ʿnmky.ḥmr.w.bnš. | rqd arbʿ. | šbn aḫd. | ṯbq aḫd. | šrš aḫd. | bir aḫd. | uḫnp. | hzp ṯn. | mʿqb arbʿ. 2040.30
w.arbʿ.bnt h. | yrḫm.yd.ṯn.bn h. | bʿlm.w.ṯlṯ.nʿrm.w.bt.aḫt. | bn.lwn.ṯlṯtm.bʿlm. | bn.bʿly.ṯlṯtm.bʿlm. | w.aḫd.ḫbṯ. | w.a 2080.5
lpm.ḫḏḏ. | w l.rbt.kmyr. | aṯr.ṯn.ṯn.hlk. | aṯr.ṯlṯ.kl hm. | aḫd.bt h.ysgr. | almnt.škr. | tškr.zbl.ʿršm. | yšu.ʿwr. | mzl.ymzl 14[KRT].4.184
lp. | nṯq.ṯn.qlʿm. | ḫmš.ṣmdm.w ḥrṣ. | ṯryn.sswm. | ṯryn.aḫd.d bnš. | arbʿ.ṣmdm.apnt. | w ḥrṣ. | tšʿm.mrḫ.aḫd. | kbd. 1123.6
[---.--]t ḫ[dr]. | [-----]. | ḫmš[.---]t.ḫdrm. | w.[---.a]ḫd.d.sgrm. | w p[tḥ.---.]l.aḫd.adr. | [---.--]t.b[ḫd]r.mškb. | ṯl 1151.4
khp mid. | dblt yṯnt w ṣmqm yṯn[m]. | w qmḥ bql yṣq aḫd h. | b ap h. 160[55].25
.hn nʿr. | d yšt.l.lṣb h ḫšʿr klb. | [w]riš.pqq.w šr h. | yšt.aḫd h.dm zt.ḫrpnt. UG5.1.2.6
]yṣq b a[p h]. | [k ḫr s]sw mġmġ w b[ṣql ʿrgz]. | [ydk aḫ]d h w yṣq b ap h. | [k ḫr]ssw ḫndrṯ w ṯ[qd m]r. | [ydk aḫ 160[55].5
k [ḫr ssw mġmġ]. | w [bṣql.ʿrgz.ydk]. | a[ḫd h.w.yṣq.b.ap h]. | k.[ḫr.ssw.ḫndrṯ]. | w.ṯ[qd.mr.ydk.aḫd 161[56].4
ap h. | [k l yḫru w]l yṯtn mss št qlql. | [w št ʿrgz y]dk aḫd h w yṣq b ap h. | [k.yiḫd akl s]sw št mkšr grn. | [w št ašk 160[55].9
l.ssw]. | št.mkš[r.grn]. | w.št.ašk[rr]. | w.pr.ḫdr[t.ydk]. | aḫd h.w.yṣq[.b.ap h]. | k.yiḫd.akl.s[sw]. | št.nni.št.mk[št.grn]. 161[56].16
. | k.l.ḫ[ru.w.l.yṯtn.ssw]. | mss.[št.qlql.w.št]. | ʿrgz[.ydk.aḫd h]. | w.yṣq[.b.ap h]. | k.yiḫd[.akl.ssw]. | št.mkš[r.grn]. | w. 161[56].10
d.akl.s[sw]. | št.nni.št.mk[št.grn]. | št.irġn.ḥmr[.ydk]. | aḫd h.w.yṣq.b[.ap h]. | k.yraš.ssw.[št]. | bln.qṭ.yṣq.b.a[p h]. | k 161[56].20
.š[t.nni.w.pr.ʿbk]. | w.pr[.ḫdrt.w.št]. | irġ[n.ḥmr.ydk]. | aḫd[h.w.yṣq.b.ap h]. | k yr[a]š.ss[w.w.ykhp]. | mid.dblt.yṯ[nt 161[56].31
ḫd h.w.yṣq.b.ap h]. | k.[ḫr.ssw.ḫndrṯ]. | w.ṯ[qd.mr.ydk.aḫd h]. | w.y[ṣq.b.ap h]. | k.l.ḫ[ru.w.l.yṯtn.ssw]. | mss.[št.qlql. 161[56].6
d h w yṣq b ap h. | [k ḫr]ssw ḫndrṯ w ṯ[qd m]r. | [ydk aḫd h w yṣq b ap h. | [k l yḫru w]l yṯtn mss št qlql. | [w št ʿr 160[55].7
mid.dblt.yṯ[nt.w]. | ṣmq[m].yṯnm.w[.qmḥ.bql]. | tdkn.aḫd h.w[.yṣq]. | b.ap h. 161[56].35
[---.--]t.š l i[l.---]. | [--.aṯ]rt.š[.---]. | [---.]l pdr[-.---]. | ṣin aḫd h[.---]. | l ʿṯtrt[.---]. | ʿlm.kmm[.---]. | w b ṯlṯ.ṣ[in.---]. | l ll. 37[22].5
arbʿ.ʿšr.ġzrm. | arbʿ.aṯt. | pġt.aḫt. | w.pġy.aḫ. 2081.3
[---.ṣ]mdm[.---]. | [ul]l.aḫdm.w[.---]. | [mʿq]b.aḫdm.w[.---]. | [ʿr]gz.ṯlṯ.ṣmd[m.---]. | [1179.2
[---.ṣ]mdm[.---]. | [ul]l.aḫdm.w[.---]. | [mʿq]b.aḫdm.w[.---]. | [ʿr]gz.ṯlṯ.ṣmd[m.---]. | [m]ṣbt.ṣmdm.[---]. | [--] 1179.3
.w.bt.aḫt. | bn.lwn.ṯlṯtm.bʿlm. | bn.bʿly.ṯlṯtm.bʿlm. | w.aḫd.ḫbṯ. | w.arbʿ.aṯt. | bn.lg.ṯn.bn h. | bʿlm.w.aḫt h. | b.šrt. | šty 2080.8
.---]. | [---.-]rt.l.dml[.---]. | [b.yrḫ].nql.ṯn.ḫpn[.---]. | [---].aḫd.ḫmš.am[--.---]. | [---.--]m.qmṣ.ṯlṯm.i[qnu.---]. | [b.yr]ḫ.m 1106.36
[--]. | ṯ[-]r.b iš[-]. | bʿl h.š[-]rt. | ḫqr.[--.ṯq]l rb. | ṯl[ṯ.---]. | aḫt.ḫm[-.---]. | b ym.dbḥ.ṯp[-]. | aḫt.l mzy.bn[--]. | aḫt.l mkt.ġ 39[19].12
y.ḥmr.w.bnš. | ṯbil. | ʿnmky.ḥmr.w.bnš. | rqd arbʿ. | šbn aḫd. | ṯbq aḫd. | šrš aḫd. | bir aḫd. | uḫnp. | hzp ṯn. | mʿqb arbʿ. 2040.28
d.l ydd. | il.ġzr.yqra.mt. | b npš h.ystrn ydd. | b gngn h.aḫd y.d ym | lk.ʿl.ilm.l ymru. | ilm.w nšm.d yšb | [ʿ].hmlt.arṣ. 4[51].7.49
[---].ṯmn. | [---].ṯlṯ. | [---].aḫd. | u[--].ṯn. | hz[p].ṯṯ. | ḫrṣbʿ.aḫd. | ypr.arb. | m[-]qb.ʿšr. | ṯnʿy.ṯlṯ. | ḫlb ʿprm.ṯn. | tmḏy.ṯlṯ. | [70[112].8
. | [---.a]bṣdq. | [---.--]š. | [---.ṣ]dq. | tgmr. | yṣḥm. | ṯlṯm. | aḫd. | kbd. | bnš.mlk. 1055.2.4
nm. | ʿšr.mrum. | šbʿ.ḫsnm. | tšʿm.ṯṯ.kbd.mdrġlm. | ʿšrm.aḫd.kbd.ḫsnm. | ubnyn. | ṯṯm[.l.]mit.ṯlṯ. | kbd[.tg]mr.bnš. | l.b. 1028.10
aḫd.kbd. | arbʿm.b ḫzr. | lqḥ šʿrt. | ṯṯ ʿšr h.lqḥ. | ḫlpnt. | ṯṯ.ḥrṯm 2052.1
. | ṯryn.aḫd.d bnš. | arbʿ.ṣmdm.apnt. | w ḥrṣ. | tšʿm.mrḫ.aḫd. | kbd. 1123.9
dr. | [---.--]t.b[ḫd]r.mškb. | ṯl[l.---.--]ḥ. | b lṯk.bt. | [pt]ḥ.aḫd.l.bt.ʿbdm. | [ṯ]n.ptḥ msb.bt.tu. | w.ptḥ[.aḫ]d.mmt. | ṯṯ.pt[1151.9
qr.[--.ṯq]l rb. | ṯl[ṯ.---]. | aḫt.ḫm[-.---]. | b ym.dbḥ.ṯp[-]. | aḫt.l mzy.bn[--]. | aḫt.l mkt.ġr. | aḫt.l ʿṯtrt. | arbʿ.ʿṣrm. | gt.ṯrm 39[19].14
---]. | aḫt.ḫm[-.---]. | b ym.dbḥ.ṯp[-]. | aḫt.l mzy.bn[--]. | aḫt.l mkt.ġr. | aḫt.l ʿṯtrt. | arbʿ.ʿṣrm. | gt.ṯrmn. | aḫt.slḫu. 39[19].15
.---]. | b ym.dbḥ.ṯp[-]. | aḫt.l mzy.bn[--]. | aḫt.l mkt.ġr. | aḫt.l ʿṯtrt. | arbʿ.ʿṣrm. | gt.ṯrmn. | aḫt.slḫu. 39[19].16
k.bt. | [pt]ḥ.aḫd.l.bt.ʿbdm. | [ṯ]n.ptḥ msb.bt.tu. | w.ptḥ[.aḫ]d.mmt. | ṯṯ.pt[ḥ.---]. | ṯn.pt[ḥ.---]. | w.pt[ḥ.--]r.ṭġr. | ṯmn.ḥl 1151.11
d.---]. | krm.uḫn.b.šdmy.ṯlṯ.bzl[.d]prn[.---]. | aupṯ.krm.aḫd.nšpin.kr[m.]aḫd[.---]. | dmt.lḫsn.krm.aḫd.anndr.kr[m.-- 1081.14
.bn[--]. | aḫt.l mkt.ġr. | aḫt.l ʿṯtrt. | arbʿ.ʿṣrm. | gt.ṯrmn. | aḫt.slḫu. 39[19].19
sġr.ʿdn.aḫd. | sġr.awldn.aḫd. | sġr.idṯn.aḫd. | sġr.sndrn.aḫd. | sġr.adn.ṣdq.aḫd. | sġr.irgn.aḫd. | sġr.ršpab.aḫd. | sġr.ar 1140.7
ṯn.rʿy.uzm. | sġr.bn.ḫpsry.aḫd. | sġr.artn.aḫd. | sġr.ʿdn.aḫd. | sġr.awldn.aḫd. | sġr.idṯn.aḫd. | sġr.sndrn.aḫd. | sġr.adn. 1140.4
sndrn.aḫd. | sġr.adn.ṣdq.aḫd. | sġr.irgn.aḫd. | sġr.ršpab.aḫd. | sġr.arwṯ.aḫd. | sġr.bn.mġln. | aḫd. 1140.10
ṯn.rʿy.uzm. | sġr.bn.ḫpsry.aḫd. | sġr.artn.aḫd. | sġr.ʿdn.aḫd. | sġr.awldn.aḫd. | sġr.idṯn.aḫ 1140.2
.bn.ḫpsry.aḫd. | sġr.artn.aḫd. | sġr.ʿdn.aḫd. | sġr.awldn.aḫd. | sġr.idṯn.aḫd. | sġr.sndrn.aḫd. | sġr.adn.ṣdq.aḫd. | sġr.irg 1140.5
wldn.aḫd. | sġr.idṯn.aḫd. | sġr.sndrn.aḫd. | sġr.adn.ṣdq.aḫd. | sġr.irgn.aḫd. | sġr.ršpab.aḫd. | sġr.arwṯ.aḫd. | sġr.bn.mġ 1140.8
.adn.ṣdq.aḫd. | sġr.irgn.aḫd. | sġr.ršpab.aḫd. | sġr.arwṯ.aḫd. | sġr.bn.mġln. | aḫd. 1140.11
. | sġr.artn.aḫd. | sġr.ʿdn.aḫd. | sġr.awldn.aḫd. | sġr.idṯn.aḫd. | sġr.sndrn.aḫd. | sġr.adn.ṣdq.aḫd. | sġr.irgn.aḫd. | sġr.ršp 1140.6
ṯn.rʿy.uzm. | sġr.bn.ḫpsry.aḫd. | sġr.artn.aḫd. | sġr.ʿdn.aḫd. | sġr.awldn.aḫd. | sġr.idṯn.aḫd. | sġr.sndrn. 1140.3
r.idṯn.aḫd. | sġr.sndrn.aḫd. | sġr.adn.ṣdq.aḫd. | sġr.irgn.aḫd. | sġr.ršpab.aḫd. | sġr.arwṯ.aḫd. | sġr.bn.mġln. | aḫd. 1140.9
.l k. | arbʿ.ʿṣm. | ʿl.ar. | w.ṯlṯ. | ʿl.ubrʿy. | w.ṯn.ʿl. | mlk. | w.aḫd. | ʿl atlg. | w l.ʿṣm. | tspr. | nrn.al.tud | ad.at.l hm. | ṯṯm.ksp. 1010.15
[---.--]n.aḫd. | [p]dr.ḫsyn.aḫd. | pdr.mlk.aḫd. 130[29].1
[---.--]n.aḫd. | [p]dr.ḫsyn.aḫd. | pdr.mlk.aḫd. 130[29].2
ṯlt mrkb[t]. | ṣpyt b ḫrṣ[.w] ṣmdm trm.d [ṣ]py. | w.trm.aḫdm. | ṣpym. | ṯlt mrkbt mlk. | d.l.ṣpy. | [---.t]r hm. | [---].ššb. 1122.3
bnš. | ṯbil. | ʿnmky.ḥmr.w.bnš. | rqd arbʿ. | šbn aḫd. | ṯbq aḫd. | šrš aḫd. | bir aḫd. | uḫnp. | hzp ṯn. | mʿqb arbʿ. 2040.29
[---.-]ḫ[-]. | [---.--]r. | [---.--]ṣ. | [-----]. | [--]lm.aḫd. | [--]l.l ḫr[-.---]. | [--]m.dt nšu. | [---.]d[--.---]. | [---.--]m aḫ 156[-].5
ḏr.kr[m.---]. | aġt.mryn.ary[.]yukl.krm.[---]. | gdn.krm.aḫ[d.--]r.krm.[---]. | ary.ʿšr.arbʿ.kbd.[---]. | [--]yy.ṯṯ.krmm.šl[- 1081.17
.šdmy.ṯlṯ.bzl[.d]prn[.---]. | aupṯ.krm.aḫd.nšpin.kr[m.]aḫd[.---]. | dmt.lḫsn.krm.aḫd.anndr.kr[m.---]. | aġt.mryn.ary 1081.14
ry.ʿšr.ṯn.k[rmm.---]. | liy.krm.aḫd[.---]. | ʿbdmlk.krm.aḫ[d.---]. | krm.ubdy.b d.ġ[--.---]. | krm.pyn.arty[.---]. | ṯlṯ.kr 1081.6
ṯ.krm.yknʿm.ṯmn.krm[.---]. | krm.nʿmn.b.ḫly.ull.krm.aḫ[d.---]. | krm.uḫn.b.šdmy.ṯlṯ.bzl[.d]prn[.---]. | aupṯ.krm.aḫ 1081.12
.---]. | ʿnmky.ʿšr.[---]. | ṯmry.ʿšr.ṯn.k[rmm.---]. | liy.krm.aḫd[.---]. | ʿbdmlk.krm.aḫ[d.---]. | krm.ubdy.b d.ġ[--.---]. | kr 1081.5
d[--.---]. | [---.]ḫdṯn.ʿšr.dd[.---]. | [---.]yd.sġr[.---.--]r h. | aḫ[d.---.ʿ]šrm.d[d.---]. | ʿš[r.---.--]r h. | my y[--.---.--]d. | ʿšrm[.- 1098.36
]ʿgltn. | [---.šr]t.aḫt. | [---].šrt.aḫt. | [---].šrt.aḫt. | [---.]šrt.aḫt. | [---.]šrt.aḫ. | [---.]šr.aḫt. | [---].šr[t]. | [---.k]hnm. | [---.š]rt. 2162.c.3

aḥd

[---.ʿg]ltn. | [---].ʿgltn. | [---.]ʿg̱ltn. | [---.šr]t.aḥt. | [---].šrt.aḥt. | [---].šrt.aḥt. | [---.]šrt.aḥt. | [---.]šrt.aḥ. | [---.]šr.aḥt. | [---]. 2162.c.1
-].ʿgltn. | [---.]ʿgltn. | [---.šr]t.aḥt. | [---].šrt.aḥt. | [---].šrt.aḥt. | [---.]šrt.aḥt. | [---.]šrt.aḥ. | [---.]šr.aḥt. | [---].šr[t]. | [---.k]h 2162.c.2
n. | [---].skn. | [---.ʿg]ltn. | [---].ʿgltn. | [---.]ʿgltn. | [---.šr]t.aḥt. | [---].šrt.aḥt. | [---].šrt.aḥt. | [---.]šrt.aḥt. | [---.]šrt.aḥ. | [---. 2162.b.12
t.aḥt. | [---].šrt.aḥt. | [---].šrt.aḥt. | [---.]šrt.aḥt. | [---.]šrt.aḥ. | [---.]šr.aḥt. | [---].šr[t]. | [---.k]hnm. | [---.š]rt.aḥt. | [---.šr]t 2162.c.4
šrt.aḥt. | [---].šrt.aḥt. | [---.]šrt.aḥt. | [---.]šrt.aḥ. | [---.]šr.aḥt. | [---].šr[t]. | [---.k]hnm. | [---.š]rt.aḥt. | [---.šr]tm. | [---.]šrt 2162.c.5
--.]šrt.aḥ. | [---.]šr.aḥt. | [---].šr[t]. | [---.k]hnm. | [---.š]rt.aḥt. | [---.šr]tm. | [---.]šrtm. | [---.šrt.]aḥt. 2162.c.8
[---.--]ǵz. | [---.]qrt. | [---].aṯt. | [---.]w arbʿ.nʿr[m]. | [---.a]ḥd. | [---.]ṯlṯ.aṯt. 2142.5
--.]m[--]. | [---].bn[.---]. | [-----]. | [---].ḫ[mr]. | [---.]w.bnš.aḥd. | [---.--]m. | [---].ʿtgrm. | [---.-]ṣbm. | [---.]nrn.mʿry. | [---.-- 2043.5
.[---]. | tšṣḥq.hn.aṯt.l.ʿbd. | šbʿt.w.nṣp.ksp. | [-]tm.rb[.--.a]ḥd. | [---.--]t.b[-]. | [---.-]y[-]. 1017.6
. | [--]l.l ḫr[-.---]. | [--]m.dt nšu. | [---.]d[--.---]. | [---.--]m aḥ[d]. | [-----]. | [---.--]m. 156[-].9
š.psm.rq. | ṯn.mrdt.az. | ṯlṯ.pld.šʿrt. | ṯ[---].kbm. | p[---]r.aḥd. | [-----]. | [-----]. | [---.--]y. | [---.-]ṯt. | [---.]w.sbsg. | [-----]. | [- 1112.9
r.ḥmr. | ḥmr.ḥmr. | ḥmr.ḥmr. | ḥmr.ḥmr. | ḥmr.w izml.aḥt. 146[87].7
[---.--]n.aḥd. | [p]dr.ḫsyn.aḥd. | pdr.mlk.aḥd. 130[29].3
lḥm b h. | w l bbt šqym. | š l uḫr ḫlmṭ. | w tr l qlḥ. | ym aḥd. ug5.11.14
rgn.aḥd. | sǵr.ršpab.aḥd. | sǵr.arwṯ.aḥd. | sǵr.bn.mǵln. | aḥd. 1140.13
---.ṣ]mdm.w.ḥrṣ. | [---].aḥdm. | [iwr]pzn.aḥdm. | [i]lšpš.aḥd. 2033.2.8
arbʿ.ʿšr.ǵzrm. | arbʿ.aṯt. | pǵt.aḥt. | w.pǵy.aḥ. 2081.4
--.k]hnm. | [---.š]rt.aḥt. | [---.šr]tm. | [---.]šrtm. | [---.šrt.]aḥt. 2162.c.11
[--.--]š.aḥd. 128[-].1
npš. | [---].npš. | [---.ḫm]š.npš. | [---].npš. | [---].npš. | [---.a]ḥd. 1142.8

aḥẓ

.ispa.w yṯb. | ap.d anšt.im[-]. | aḥd.b aḫ k.l[--]n. | hn[-.]aḥẓ[.---]l[-]. | [ʿ]nt.akl[y.nšm]. | akly.hml[t.arṣ]. | w y[-]l.a[---] 6[49].5.23

aḥl

ql.yph.b palt.bṣ[q]l. | yph.b yǵlm.bṣql.y[ḥb]q. | w ynšq.aḥl.an bṣ[ql]. | ynpʿ.b palt.bṣql ypʿ b yǵlm. | ur.tisp k.yd.aqht 19[1aqht].2.64
ph. | šblt.b akt.šblt.ypʿ. | b ḥmdrt.šblt.yḥ[bq]. | w ynšq.aḥl.an.šblt. | tpʿ.b aklt.šblt.tpʿ[.b ḥm]drt. | ur.tisp k.yd.aqht.ǵ 19[1aqht].2.71

aḥrṯp

kbln.ʿbdyrǵ.ilgt. | ǵyrn.ybnn qrwn. | ypltn.ʿbdnt. | klby.aḥrṯp. | ilyn.ʿlby.ṣdkn. | gmrt.ṯlmyn. | ʿbdnt. | bdy.ḥrš arkd. | bl 1045.5

aḫ

d.ʿbdmlk. | šd.b d.yšn.ḥrš. | šd.b d.aupš. | šd.b d.ršpab.aḫ.ubn. | šd.b d.bn.uṯryn. | [ubd]y.mrynm. | [š]d.bn.ṣnrn.b d. 82[300].1.5
ql.ṯrm[.w]m | ria.il.ʿglm.d[t]. | šnt.imr.qmṣ.l[l]im. | ṣḥ.aḫ h.b bht h.a[r]y h. | b qrb hkl h.ṣḥ. | šbʿm.bn.aṯrt. | špq.ilm. 4[51].6.44
b.pn h.ṯǵr. | yṣu.hlm.aḫ h.tph. | [ksl]h.l arṣ.ṯṯbr. | [---.]aḫ h.tbky. | [--.m]rṣ.mlk. | [---.]krt.adn k. | [w yʿny.]ǵzr.ilḥu. | 16.1[125].55
l ym hnd. | iwr[k]l.pdy. | agdn.bn.nrgn. | w ynḥm.aḫ h. | w.bʿln aḫ h. | w.ḥṯṯn bn h. | w.btšy.bt h. | w.ištrmy. | bt. 1006.4
d. | iwr[k]l.pdy. | agdn.bn.nrgn. | w ynḥm.aḫ h. | w.bʿln aḫ h. | w.ḥṯṯn bn h. | w.btšy.bt h. | w.ištrmy. | bt.ʿbd mlk. | w.s 1006.5
--]. | w.ṯn.bn h.w.b[---.---]. | b tn[--.---]. | swn.qrty[.---]. | uḫ h.w.ʿšr[.---]. | klyn.apsn[y.---]. | plzn.qrty[.---]. | w.klt h.b.t 81[329].9
tṣḥ[.---]. | tšqy[.---]. | tr.ḥt[-.---]. | w msk.tr[.---]. | tqrb.aḫ[h.w tṣḥ]. | lm.tbʿrn[.---]. | mn.yrḫ.k m[rṣ.---]. | mn.k dw.k 16.2[125].79
.d in.bn.l h. | km.aḫ h.w šrš.km.ary h. | bl.iṯ.bn.l h.km aḫ h.w šrš. | km.ary h.uzrm.ilm.ylḥm. | uzrm.yšqy.bn.qdš. | l 17[2aqht].1.21
t. | [d]nil.mt.rpi anḫ.ǵzr. | [mt.]hrnmy.d in.bn.l h. | km.aḫ h.w šrš.km.ary h. | bl.iṯ.bn.l h.km aḫ h.w šrš. | km.ary h.u 17[2aqht].1.20
lbš.km.lpš.dm a[ḫ h]. | km.all.dm.ary h. | k šbʿt.l šbʿm.aḫ h.ym[.--]. | w ṯmnt.l ṯmnym. | šr.aḫy h.mẓa h. | w mẓa h.š 12[75].2.49
ʿnt.hlkt.w.šnwt. | tp.aḫ.h.k.ysmsm. | tspi.šir.h.l.bl.ḥrb. | tšt.dm.h.l.bl.ks. | tpnn.ʿn. rs225.2
. | šbʿ.šnt.il.mla.[-]. | w ṯmn.nqpnt.ʿd. | k lbš.km.lpš.dm a[ḫ h]. | km.all.dm.ary h. | k šbʿt.l šbʿm.aḫ h.ym[.--]. | w ṯmnt 12[75].2.47
t. | b ʿd ʿlm...gnʿ. | iršt.aršt. | l aḫ y.l rʿ y.dt. | w ytnnn. | l aḫ h.l rʿ h. | rʿ ʿlm. | ttn.w tn. | w l ttn. | w al ttn. | tn ks yn. | w i 1019.1.10
ry h. | k šbʿt.l šbʿm.aḫ h.ym[.--]. | w ṯmnt.l ṯmnym. | šr.aḫy h.mẓa h. | w mẓa h.šr.yly h. | b skn.sknm.b ʿdn. | ʿdnm.k 12[75].2.51
m. | [a]ḫt h.šib.yṣat.mrḥ h. | l tl.yṣb.pn h.ṯǵr. | yṣu.hlm.aḫ h.tph. | [ksl]h.l arṣ.ṯṯbr. | [---.]aḫ h.tbky. | [--.m]rṣ.mlk. | [- 16.1[125].53
nkl yrḫ ytrḫ.adn h. | yšt mṣb.mznm.um h. | kp mznm.iḫ h ytʿr. | mšrrm.aḫt h l a | bn mznm.nkl w ib. | d ašr.ar yrḫ. 24[77].35
pt.w.mqḥm. | w.ṯlṯm.yn šbʿ.kbd d ṯbṯ. | w.ḫmšm.yn.d iḫ h. 1103.23
ḥq.btlt.[ʿnt]. | [tšu.]g h.w tṣḥ.šmʿ.m[ʿ.l a] | [qht.ǵ]zr.at.aḫ.w an.a[ḫt k]. | [---].šbʿ.ṯir k.[---]. | [---.]ab y.ndt.ank[.---]. | [18[3aqht].1.24
y. | w.ap.ank.mnm. | [ḫ]s[r]t.w.uḫ y. | [y]ʿmsn.ṯmn. | w.[u]ḫ y.al ybʿrn. 2065.21
ʿlm k.šmḫ.bn.ilm.mt. | [---.]g h.w aṣḥ.ik.yṣḥn. | [bʿl.ʿm.aḫ y.ik].yqrun.hd. | [ʿm.ary y.---.--]p.mlḥm y. | [---.---]lt.qẓb. 5[67].2.22
n y.yšal. | ṯryl.p rgm. | l mlk.šm y. | w l h.yʿl m. | w h[t] aḫ y. | bn y.yšal. | ṯryl.w rgm[.-]. | ṯṯb.l aḫ k. | l adn k. 138.15
šlm k. | iky.lḥt. | spr.d likt. | ʿm.ṯryl. | mh y.rgmt. | w ht.aḫ y. | bn y.yšal. | ṯryl.p rgm. | l mlk.šm y. | w l h.yʿl m. | w h[t 138.10
šlm k. | ik y.lḥt. | spr.d likt. | ʿm.ṯryl. | mh y.rgmt. | w ht.aḫ y. | bn y.yšal. | ṯryl.p rgm. | l mlk.šm y. | w l h[-] yʿl m. | bn 138.10
k hwt. | [y]rš.ʿm y. | mnm.iršt k. | d ḫsrt.w.ank. | aštn..l.iḫ y. | w.ap.ank.mnm. | [ḫ]s[r]t.w.uḫ y. | [y]ʿmsn.ṯmn. | w.[u]ḫ 2065.17
ṯḥm.hl[--]. | l pḫry.a[ḫ y]. | w l g.p[-]r[--]. | yšlm[.l k]. | [i]lm[.ṯǵr k]. | [t]š[lm k.--- 56[21].2
| b sin.lpš.tšṣq[n h]. | b qṣ.all.tšu.g h.w[tṣ] | ḥ.at.mt.tn.aḫ y. | w ʿn.bn.ilm.mt.mh. | taršn.l btlt.ʿnt. | an.itlk.w aṣd.kl. | 6[49].2.12
ṯbn.ank. | w anḫn.w tnḫ.b irt y. | npš.k yld.bn.l y.km. | aḫ y.w šrš.km ary y. | nṣb.skn.ilib y.b qdš. | ztr.ʿm y.l ʿpr.ḏm 17[2aqht].2.15
kbm. | l tbrkn.alk brkt. | tmrn.alk.nmr[rt]. | imḫṣ.mḫṣ.aḫ y.akl[.m] | kly[.ʿ]l.umt y.w yʿn[.dn] | il.mt.rpi npš ṯḥ[.pǵt] 19[1aqht].4.196
-.š]d.gṯr. | [--]ḫ[d].šd.hwt. | [--.]iḫd.šd.gṯr. | [w]ht.yšmʿ.uḫ y. | l g y.w yhbṭ.bnš. | w ytn.ilm.b d hm. | b d.iḫqm.gṯr. | w 55[18].17
tʿzz k.alp ymm. | w rbt.šnt. | b ʿd ʿlm...gnʿ. | iršt.aršt. | l aḫ y.l rʿ y.dt. | w ytnnn. | l aḫ h.l rʿ h. | rʿ ʿlm. | ttn.w tn. | w l tt 1019.1.8
k[--].ṣḥn.bʿl.ʿm. | aḫ y.qran.hd.ʿm.ary y. | w lḥm m ʿm aḫ y.lḥm. | w št m.ʿm.a[ḫ] yn. | p nšt.bʿl.[ṭ]ʿn.iṭʿn k. | [---.]ma[5[67].1.24
bn m.um y.kly y. | yṯb.ʿm.bʿl.ṣrrt. | ṣpn.yšu g h.w yṣḥ. | aḫ y m.ytnt.bʿl. | spu y.bn m.um y.kl | y y.ytʿn.k gmrm. | mt.ʿ 6[49].6.14

--.]bn.ilm.mt. | [--]u.šbʿt.ǵlm h. | [---].bn.ilm.mt. | p[-]n.aẖ y m.ytn.bʿl. | [s]pu y.bn m.um y.kly y. | ytb.ʿm.bʿl.ṣrrt. | ṣp 6[49].6.10
mtt.lqḥt. | w.ṯṯb.ank.l hm. | w.any k.ṯt. | by.ʿky.ʿryt. | w.aẖ y.mhk. | b lb h.al.yšt. 2059.26
ẖsrt.w.ank. | aštn..l.iẖ y. | w.ap.ank.mnm. | [ẖ]s[r]t.w.uẖ y. | [y]ʿmsn.ṯmn. | w.[u]ẖ y.al ybʿrn. 2065.19
hm.šbʿ. | ydt y.b ṣʿ.hm.ks.ymsk. | nhr.k[--].ṣḥn.bʿl.ʿm. | aẖ y.qran.hd.ʿm.ary y. | w lḥm m ʿm aẖ y.lḥm. | w št m.ʿm.a[5[67].1.23
ṯḥm iwrḏr. | l iwrpẖn. | bn y.aẖ y.rgm. | ilm.tǵr k. | tšlm k. | ik y.lḥt. | spr.d likt. | ʿm.ṯryl. | 138.3
ṯḥm.iwrḏr. | l iwrpẖn. | bn y.aẖ y.rgm. | ilm.tǵr k. | tšlm k. | iky.lḥt. | spr.d likt. | ʿm.ṯryl. | m 138.3
l.mlk.ugrt. | aẖ y.rgm. | ṯḥm.mlk.ṣr.aẖ k. | y[š]lm.l k.ilm. | tǵr k.tšlm k. | h 2059.2
l.mlk[.u]grt. | iẖ y.rgm. | [ṯḥ]m.m[lk.-]bl[-]. | yšlm.l[k].ilm. | tǵr.tšl[m] k. | [- 2159.2
iy.q | [rdm.]bht y.bnt. | [dt.ksp.dtm]. | [ẖrṣ.hk]l y. | [---.]aẖ y. | [---.]aẖ y. | [----]y. | [---.]rb. | [---].ṣḥt. | [---.--]t. | [---.]il 4[51].8.38
[t]ḥm.uṯryn[.---]. | [g]rgš ʿbdy[--]. | [--.]l mlk [---]. | [---].aẖ y[.---]. | [--]q lpš[.---]. | [---] y št k[.---]. | [---.]l m[lk]. 2130.1.4
]bht y.bnt. | [dt.ksp.dtm]. | [ẖrṣ.hk]l y. | [---.]aẖ y. | [---.]aẖ y. | [----]y. | [---.]rb. | [---].ṣḥt. | [---.--]t. | [---.]ilm. | [---.--]u. 4[51].8.39
.qran.hd.ʿm.ary y. | w lḥm m ʿm aẖ y.lḥm. | w št m.ʿm.a[ẖ] yn. | p nšt.bʿl.[t]ʿn.itʿn k. | [---.]ma[---] k.k tmẖṣ. | [ltn.bṯ 5[67].1.25
t.tšu. | g h.w tṣḥ.tbšr bʿl. | bšrt k.yblt.y[b]n. | bt.l k.km.aẖ k.w ḥẓr. | km.ary k.ṣḥ.ẖrn. | b bht k.ʿḏbt.b qrb. | hkl k.tbl 4[51].5.90
ymšẖ. | bʿl.ymšẖ.hm.b ʿp. | nṭʿn.b arṣ.ib y. | w b ʿpr.qm.aẖ k. | w tšu.ʿn h.btlt.ʿnt. | w tšu.ʿn h.w tʿn. | w tʿn.arẖ.w tr.b 10[76].2.25
spt.l šʿr. | ṯl.ydʿt.hlk.kbkbm. | a[-]ẖ.hy.mẖ.tmẖṣ.mẖṣ[.aẖ k]. | tkl.m[k]ly.ʿl.umt[k.--]. | d ttql.b ym.trtḥ[ṣ.--]. | [----.a] 19[1AQHT].4.201
lk.šm y. | w l h[-] yʿl m. | bn y.yšal. | ṯryl.w rgm. | ṯṯb.l aẖ k. | l adn k. 138.18
h.yʿl m. | w h[t] aẖ y. | bn y.yšal. | ṯryl.w rgm[.-]. | ṯṯb.l aẖ k. | l adn k. 138.18
m.tn.aḥd. | b aẖ k.ispa.w ytb. | ap.d anšt.im[-]. | aḥd.b aẖ k.l[--]n. | hn[-.]aẖẓ[.---]l[-]. | [ʾ]nt.akl[y.nšm]. | akly.hml[t. 6[49].5.22
t. | ʿl k.pht.[-]l[-]. | b šdm.ʿl k.pht. | drʿ.b ym.tn.aḥd. | b aẖ k.ispa.w ytb. | ap.d anšt.im[-]. | aḥd.b aẖ k.l[--]n. | hn[-.]aẖ 6[49].5.20
l.mlk.ugrt. | aẖ y.rgm. | ṯḥm.mlk.ṣr.aẖ k. | y[š]lm.l k.ilm. | tǵr k.tšlm k. | hn ny.ʿm n. | šlm.ṯm ny. | 2059.3
--]. | lk[.---]. | ki[--.---]. | w ẖ[--.---]. | my[.---]. | aṯ[t.---]. | aẖ k[.---]. | tr.ḥ[---]. | w tṣḥ[.---]. | tšqy[.---]. | tr.ḥt[-.---]. | w ms 16.2[125].73
.---]. | [---]d nhr.umt. | [---.]rpat.bt. | [m]lk.itdb.d šbʿ. | [a]ẖm.l h.ṯmnt.bn um. | krt.ḥtk n.rš. | krt.grdš.mknt. | aṯt.ṣdq 14[KRT].1.9
| [--]in.b.trzy. | [--]yn.b.glltky. | ṯd[y]n.b.glltky. | lbw[-].uẖ.pdm.b.yʿrt. | pǵyn.b.tpḥ. | amri[l].b.šrš. | aǵltn.b.midẖ. | [-- 2118.10
n.aṯr k.hn[.---]. | yd k.ṣǵr.tnšq.špt k.ṯm. | ṯkm.bm ṯkm.aẖm.qym.il. | b lsmt.ṯm.yṯbš.šm.il.mt m. | yʿbš.brk n.šm.il.ǵz 22.2[124].5
la[t.r]umm. | tšu knp.btlt.ʿn[t]. | tšu.knp.w tr.b ʿp. | tk.aẖ šmk.mlat rumm. | w yšu.ʿn h.aliyn.bʿl. | w yšu.ʿn h.w yʿn. 10[76].2.12
n.aẖd.b yd h. | w qṣʿt h.bm.ymn h. | idk.l ytn pnm. | tk.aẖ.šmk.mla[t.r]umm. | tšu knp.btlt.ʿn[t]. | tšu.knp.w tr.b ʿp. | 10[76].2.9

aẖd

ẓr h.aẖḏ.qš[t.---]. | p ʿn.bʿl.aẖḏ[.---]. | w ṣmt.ǵllm[.---]. | aẖḏ.aklm.k [---]. | npl.b mšmš[.---]. | anp n m yẖr[r.---]. | bmt 12[75].2.36
n mss št qlql. | [w št ʿrgz y]dk aḥd h w yṣq b ap h. | [k.yiḥd akl s]šw št mkšr grn. | [w št aškrr w p]r ḥḏrt. | [-----]. | [- 160[55].10
ss.[št.qlql.w.št]. | ʿrgz[.ydk.aḥd h]. | w.yṣq[.b.ap h]. | k.yiḥd[.akl.ššw]. | št.mkš[r.grn]. | w.št.ašk[rr]. | w.pr.ḥḏr[t.ydk] 161[56].12
.št.ašk[rr]. | w.pr.ḥḏr[t.ydk]. | aḥd h.w.yṣq[.b.ap h]. | k.yiḥd.akl.s[šw]. | št.nni.št.mk[št.grn]. | št.irǵn.ḥmr[.ydk]. | aḥd 161[56].17
lṭpn. | [il.d]pid.l tbrk. | [krt.]ṯʿ.l tmr.nʿmn. | [ǵlm.]il.ks.yiḥd. | [il.b]yd.krpn.bm. | [ymn.]brkm.ybrk. | [ʿbd h.]ybrk.il. 15[128].2.16
m]nt h bt.il.ṯḥ.gg h.b ym. | [ti]ṯ.rḥṣ.npṣ h.b ym.rṯ. | [--.y]iḥd.il.ʿbd h.ybrk. | [dni]l mt rpi.ymr.ǵzr. | [mt.hr]nmy npš. 17[2AQHT].1.35
bdr. | w yʿn lṭpn il d pid. | p ʿbd.an.ʿnn.aṯrt. | p.ʿbd.ank.aẖḏ.ulṯ. | hm.amt.aṯrt.tlbn. | lbnt.ybn.bt.l bʿl. | km ilm.w ḥẓr. 4[51].4.60
[--].ytkḥ.w yiḥd.b qrb[.-]. | [--.t]ṯkḥ.w tiḥd.b uš[k.--]. | [-.b]ʿl.yabd.l alp. | [---.bt]lt.ʿnt. | [---]q.hry.w 11[132].1.2
gbry. | [---].aẖḏ.aẖḏ.b.yʿny. | [---.-]ḥm.b.aẖḏ.ḥrṯ. | [---.]aẖḏ.b.grn.uškn. | [---.]aẖḏ.ḥrṯ. 1129.16
. | aẖḏ.alp.idṯn.d aẖḏ.b.ʿnqpat. | [aẖḏ.al]p.d aǵlmn. | [d aẖḏ b.g]t gbry. | [---].aẖḏ.aẖḏ.b.yʿny. | [---.-]ḥm.b.aẖḏ.ḥrṯ. | [- 1129.13
qrb.[---]. | b mgn k.w ẖrṣ.l kl. | apnk.ǵzr.ilhu. | [m]rḥ h.yiḥd.b yd. | [g]rgr h.bm.ymn. | [w]yqrb.trẓẓ h. | [---].mǵy h. 16.1[125].47
yn.ǵlm.bʿl. | in.bʿl.b bht ht. | il hd.b qrb.hkl h. | qšt hn.aẖd.b yd h. | w qṣʿt h.bm.ymn h. | idk.l ytn pnm. | tk.aẖ.šmk. 10[76].2.6
rbẖ.ʿn h tšu w[.---]. | aylt tǵpy tr.ʿn[.---]. | b[b]r.mrḥ h.ti[ẖd.b yd h]. | š[g]r h bm ymn.t[--.---]. | [--.]l bʿl.ʿbd[.---]. | tr 2001.1.12
k.k ilm. | [---.]ybl.k bn.qdš.mnḥy k.ap.anš.zbl.bʿ[l]. | [-.yuẖ]d.b yd.mšẖṭ.bm.ymn.mẖṣ.ǵlmm.yš[--]. | [ymn h.ʿn]t.tu 2.1[137].39
qpat. | [aẖḏ.al]p.d aǵlmn. | [d aẖḏ b.g]t gbry. | [---].aẖḏ.aẖḏ.b.yʿny. | [---.-]ḥm.b.aẖḏ.ḥrṯ. | [---.]aẖḏ.b.grn.uškn. | [---.] 1129.14
.nẖl. | aẖḏ.b gt.knpy.w.aẖḏ.b gt.ṯrmn. | aẖḏ.alp.idṯn.d aẖḏ.b.ʿnqpat. | [aẖḏ.al]p.d aǵlmn. | [d aẖḏ b.g]t gbry. | [---].a 1129.11
[--].ytkḥ.w yiḥd.b qrb[.-]. | [--.t]ṯkḥ.w tiḥd.b uš[k.--]. | [-.b]ʿl.yabd.l alp. | 11[132].1.1
ṯ h. | k lb.arẖ.l ʿgl h.k lb. | ṯat.l imr h.km.lb. | ʿnt.aṯr.bʿl.tiḥd. | bn.ilm.mt.b ḥrb. | tbqʿnn.b ẖṯr.tdry | nn.b išt.tšrpnn. | b 6[49].2.30
yiḥd.bʿl.bn.aṯrt. | rbm.ymẖṣ.b ktp. | dk ym.ymẖṣ.b ṣmd. | ṣḥr 6[49].5.1
| [---].ʿpr.bt k.ygr[š k.---]. | [---.]y.ḥr.ḥr.bnt.ḥ[---]. | [--.]uẖd.[bʿ]l m.ʿ[--].yd k.amṣ.yd[.--]. | [---.]ḥš[.-]nm[.--.]k.[--].w 1001.1.14
.hm.tqrm.l mt.b rn k. | [--]ẖp.an.arnn.ql.špš.ḥw.bṯnm.uẖd.bʿlm. | [--.a]ṯm.prṯl.l riš h.ḥmṯ.ṯmṯ. | [--.]ydbr.ṯrmt.al m. 1001.1.6
š.w amrr. | yštn.aṯrt.l bmt.ʿr. | l ysmsmt.bmt.pḥl. | qdš.yuẖdm.šbʿr. | amrr.k kbkb.l pnm. | aṯr.btlt.ʿnt. | w bʿl.tbʿ.mry 4[51].4.16
anyt.miẖd[t]. | br.ṯpṯbʿ[l.---]. | br.dmty[.---]. | ṯkt.ydln[.---]. | ṯkt.ṯry 84[319].1.1
t m.tbn[n]. | ḥš.trmmn.hk[l m]. | b tk.ṣrrt.ṣpn. | alp.šd.aẖḏ bt. | rbt.kmn.hkl. | w yʿn.kṯr.w ẖss. | šmʿ.l aliyn bʿl. | bn.l 4[51].5.118
l pn mlk. | šin k itn. | rʿ y šṣa idn l y. | l šmn iṯr hw. | p iẖdn gnryn. | im mlkytn yrgm. | aẖnnn. | w iẖd. 1020.7
ydʿt k.bt.k anšt.w i[n.b ilht]. | qlṣ k.tbʿ.bt.ḥnp.lb[k.--.ti] | ẖd.d iṯ.b kbd k.tšt.b [---]. | irt k.dṯ.ydṯ.mʿqb k.[ttbʿ]. | [bt] 18[3AQHT].1.17
ilm.bnt.bh[t k].a[l.tš]mẖ. | al.tšmẖ.b r[m.h]kl[k]. | al.aẖd.hm.b y[--] y.[---]b[-]. | b gdlt.arkt y.am[---]. | qdqd k.ašhl 3[ʿNT.VI].5.30
ḥ[--]. | ṯ[--]. | [--] aṯt yqḥ ʿz. | [---]ḏ. | [---]. | [---]. | hm qrt tuẖd.hm mt yʿl bnš. | bt bn bnš yqḥ ʿz. | w yḥdy mrḥqm. RS61[24.277.29]
m[.bnt.bht k.--]. | [al.tšmẖ.]al.tš[mẖ.b rm.h] | [kl k.al.]aẖd hm.[---]. | [---.b]gdlt.ar[kt y.am--]. | [---.qdq]d k.ašhlk[.š 18[3AQHT].1.9
t. | tgmr.uz.aẖmn.arbʿ.mat. | arbʿm.kbd. | ṯlṯ.alp.ṣpr.dt.aẖḏ. | ḥrṯ h.aẖḏ.b gt.nẖl. | aẖḏ.b gt.knpy.w.aẖḏ.b gt.ṯrmn. | a 1129.8
. | [d aẖḏ b.g]t gbry. | [---].aẖḏ.aẖḏ.b.yʿny. | [---.-]ḥm.b.aẖḏ.ḥrṯ. | [---.]aẖḏ.b.grn.uškn. | [---.]aẖḏ.ḥrṯ. 1129.15
.yʿny. | [---.-]ḥm.b.aẖḏ.ḥrṯ. | [---.]aẖḏ.b.grn.uškn. | [---.]aẖḏ.ḥrṯ. 1129.17
ṣu.qṭr h. | l ʿpr.ḏmr.aṯr h.ṭbq.lḥt. | niṣ h.grš d.ʿšy.ln h. | aẖd.yd h.b škrn.mʿms h. | [k]šbʿ yn.spu.ksm h.bt.bʿl. | [w m] 17[2AQHT].1.31
. | ẓtr.ʿm y.l ʿpr.ḏmr.aṯr[y]. | ṭbq lḥt.niṣ y.grš. | d ʿšy.ln.aẖd.yd y.b š | krn mʿms y k šbʿt yn. | spu.ksm y.bt.bʿl.[w]mn 17[2AQHT].2.19
iṣ k.gr[š.d ʿšy.ln k]. | spu.ksm k.bt.[bʿl.w mnt k]. | bt il.aẖd.yd k.b [škrn]. | mʿms k.k šbʿt.yn.ṭ[ẖ]. | gg k.b ym.ṭiṭ.rḥṣ. 17[2AQHT].2.5

aḫd

[.t]ḫšn.|rḥq[.---.td‘].|qdm ym.bmt.[nhr].|tṭṭn.ib.b‘l.tiḫd.|y‘rm.šnu.hd.gpt.|ǵr.w y‘n.aliyn.|b‘l.ib.hdt.lm.tḥš.|l 4[51].7.35
pḥ.|l ydn.‘bd.mlk.|d št.‘l.ḫrd h.|špḥ.al.thbṭ.|ḫrd.‘ps.aḫd.kw|sgt.|ḫrd ksp.[--]r.|ymm.w[.---].|[-----].|w[.-----].|[- 2062.2.6
n.šlm.b ṣ[‘.trḥṣ].|yd h.btlt.‘nt.uṣb‘t[h.ybmt].|limm.tiḫd.knr h.b yd[h.tšt].|rimt.l irt h.tšr.dd.al[iyn].|b‘l.ahbt. UG5.3.2.6
.lm.qd[.---].|šmn.prst[.---].|ydr.hm.ym[.---].|‘l amr.yu[ḫd.ksa.mlk h].|nḫt.kḥṭ.d[rkt h.b bt y].|aṣḥ.rpi[m.iqra.il 22.1[123].17
.l bnš klnmw.|l yarš ḫswn.|ḫmš ‘šr.sp.|l bnš tpnr d yaḫd l g ynm.|ṯṯ spm l tgyn.|arb‘ spm l ll[-].|ṯn spm.l slyy. 137.2[93].11
[-----].|w.[-----].|w.abǵl.nḥ[l h.--].|w.unṯ.aḫd.l h[.---].|dnn.bn.yṣr[.---].|sln.bn.‘ṯt[-.---].|pdy.bn.nr[-.- 90[314].1.4
lb.a[rḫ].|l ‘gl h.k lb.ṯa[t].|l imr h.km.lb.‘n[t].|aṯr.b‘l.tiḫd.m[t].|b sin.lpš.tšṣq[n h].|b qṣ.all.tšu.g h.w[tṣ]|ḥ.at.mt 6[49].2.9
[--.]ilm.b ṣpn.|‘dr.l[‘r].‘rm.|ṯb.l pd[r.]pdrm.|ṯṯ.l ṯṯm.aḫd.‘r.|šb‘m.šb‘.pdr.|ṯmnym.b‘l.[----].|tš‘m.b‘l.mr[-].|bt[.-- 4[51].7.9
ṭ.bm.ymn.mḫṣ.ǵlmm.yš[--].|[ymn h.‘n]t.tuḫd.šmal h.tuḫd.‘ṯtrt.ik.m[ḫṣt.ml]|[ak.ym.t‘]dt.ṯpṭ.nhr.mlak.mṯḫr.yḥb[2.1[137].40
[-----].|l abn[.---].|aḫdt.plk h[.b yd h].|plk.qlt.b ymn h.|npyn h.mks.bšr h.|t 4[51].2.3
dm.adr[.---].|idm.‘rẓ.t‘r[ẓ.---].|‘n.b‘l.a[ḫ]ḏ[.---].|ẓr h.aḫḏ.qš[t.---].|p ‘n.b‘l.aḫḏ[.---].|w ṣmt.ǵllm[.---].|aḫḏ.aklm. 12[75].2.33
]d.b yd.mšḫṭ.bm.ymn.mḫṣ.ǵlmm.yš[--].|[ymn h.‘n]t.tuḫd.šmal h.tuḫd.‘ṯtrt.ik.m[ḫṣt.ml]|[ak.ym.t‘]dt.ṯpṭ.nhr.ml 2.1[137].40
-]ša.|tlm.km[.---.]yd h.k šr.|knr.uṣb‘t h ḫrṣ.abn.|p h.tiḫd.šnt h.w akl.bqmm.|tšt ḫrṣ.k lb ilnm.|w ṯn.gprm.mn g 19[1AQHT].1.9
.mlk.|d.b d.adn‘m.|[š]b‘.b.ḥrṯm.|[ṯ]lṯ.b.ṯǵrm.|rb qrt.aḫd.|ṯmn.ḫzr.|w.arb‘.ḥršm.|dt.tb‘ln.b.pḫn.|ṯṯtm.ḫzr.w.‘št. 1024.3.3
[-].š[--]m.|[----]r[.---]š[.--]qm.|id.u [---]t.|lḥn š[-]‘[--.]aḫd[.-].|tšm‘.mṯt.[ḥ]ry.|ṭṭbḫ.šmn.[m]ri h.|t[p]ṯḥ.rḥbt.yn.|‘ 15[128].4.13
[---.]ydm ym.|[---.]ydm nhr.|[---.]trǵt.|[---.]h aḫd[.--].|[---.]iln[-.---].|[---.--]ḫ[.---].|[---.]dt[-.---].|[---.]ksḥ[49[73].1.4
.ib.|[---.]mlk.|[---.]adt y.td‘.|w.ap.mlk.uḏ[r].|[-]d‘.k.iḫd.[---].|w.mlk.b‘l y.|lm.škn.hnk.|l ‘bd h.alpm.š[šw]m.|rg 1012.21
t‘r[ẓ.---].|‘n.b‘l.a[ḫ]ḏ[.---].|ẓr h.aḫḏ.qš[t.---].|p ‘n.b‘l.aḫḏ[.---].|w ṣmt.ǵllm[.---].|aḫḏ.aklm.k [---].|npl.b mšmš[.-- 12[75].2.34
ṣt.ks h.t[--.---].|idm.adr[.---].|idm.‘rẓ.t‘r[ẓ.---].|‘n.b‘l.a[ḫ]ḏ[.---].|ẓr h.aḫḏ.qš[t.---].|p ‘n.b‘l.aḫḏ[.---].|w ṣmt.ǵllm[12[75].2.32
n iṯr hw.|p iḫdn gnryn.|im mlkytn yrgm.|aḫnnn.|w iḫd. 1020.10

aḫdbu

bn.ḫran.|bn.srt.|bn.adn.|bn.‘gw.|bn.urt.|aḫdbu.|pḥ[-].|bn.‘b .|bn.uḏn[-].|bn.yṣr. 121[307].6

aḫdy

bn.ḥdṯ.‘šrt.|bn.ḫnyn.‘šrt.|rpan.ḫmšt.|abǵl.ḫmšt.|bn.aḫdy.‘šrt.|ṯṯn.‘ṣrt.|bn.pnmn.‘šrt.|‘bdadt.ḫmšt.|abmn.ilštm 1062.21

aḫyn

y.bn.nr[-.---].|abmlk.bn.un[-.---].|nrn.bn.mtn[-.---].|aḫyn.bn.nbk[-.---].|ršpn.bn.b‘ly[.---].|bnil.bn.yṣr[.---].|‘dyn 90[314].1.10
rḫz.b d.skn.|škny.aḏddy.|mšu.aḏddy.|plsy.aḏddy.|aḫyn.|ygmr.aḏddy.|gln.aṭṭ.|ddy.[a]ḏddy.|bn.mlkr[šp].|bn 2014.41
.|[-]ǵl.|bn.b‘ltǵpṯ.|ḥrš.btm.|ršpab.|[r]ṣn.|[a]ǵlmn.|[a]ḫyn.|[k]rwn.|[k]l[by].|[--]ṭn.|[---]d.|a[ǵ]ltn.|[-----].|[--]n 2060.13
i[l]štm‘ym.|bn.ṯk.|bn.arwdn.|tmrtn.|šd‘l.bn aḫyn.|m‘rbym.|rpan.|abršn.|atlgy.|šršn. 95[91].5

aḫmlk

lm.ṯṯ mat.|šmmn.bn.‘dš.ṯṯ mat.|ušknym.|yp‘.alpm.|aḫ[m]lk.bn.nskn.alpm.|krw.šlmy.|alpm.|atn.bṣry.alpm.|lb 1060.2.3
ymd.šr.b d ansny.|nsk.ks[p.--]mrtn.kṯrmlk.|yḥmn.aḫm[l]k.‘bdrpu.adn.ṯ[--].|bdn.qln.mtn.ydln.|b‘ltdtt.tlgn.yt 2011.33

aḫmn

].|[-----].|[---.-]y[-.---].|w bn ‘ṭl.[---].|ypḫ kn‘m[.---].|aḫmn bt[.---].|b ḫmṯ ‘ṯr ṯmn[.---]. 207[57].10
.mat.|šb‘m[.t]š‘.kbd.|tgmr.uz.ǵrn.arb‘.mat.|tgmr.uz.aḫmn.arb‘.mat.|arb‘m.kbd.|ṯlṯ.alp.ṣpr.dt.aḫd.|ḥrṯ h.aḥd.b 1129.6

aḫn

.l bn.ǵl.|w dṯn.nḥl h.l bn.pl.|šd.krwn.l aḫn.|šd.‘yy.l aḫn.|šd.brdn.l bn.bly.|šd gzl.l.bn.ṭbr[n].|šd.ḫzmyn.l a[--].| 2089.12
lbi.|šd.ṯpḫln.l bn.ǵl.|w dṯn.nḥl h.l bn.pl.|šd.krwn.l aḫn.|šd.‘yy.l aḫn.|šd.brdn.l bn.bly.|šd gzl.l.bn.ṭbr[n].|šd.ḫ 2089.11

aḫny

n‘m.l.bn.‘mnr.|šd.bn.krwn.l bn.‘myn.|šd.bn.prmn.l aḫny.|šd.bn ḥnn.l bn.adlḏn.|šd.bn.nṣdn.l bn.‘mlbi.|šd.ṯpḫl 2089.6
.|[šd.b]d.b[n].tkwn.|[ubdy.mḏ]rǵlm.|[šd.bn.--]n.b d.aḫny.|[šd.bn.--]rt.b d.ṯpṭb‘l.|[ubdy.]mḫ[ṣ]m.|[šd.bn.]uzpy. 82[300].2.23

aḫqm

.---].|[---.]‘ḏr[.---].|str[-.---].|bdlm.d[t.---].|‘dn.[---].|aḫqm bir[-.---].|kṯrmlk.ns[--.---].|bn.tbd.ilšt[m‘y.---].|mty.i 90[314].2.4

aḫr

.bl.at.[---].|yisp hm.b[‘l.---].|bn.dgn[.---].|‘ḏbm.[---].|uḫry.l[---].|mṣt.ks h.t[--.---].|idm.adr[.---].|idm.‘rẓ.t‘r[ẓ.--- 12[75].2.28
n.aqht.ǵzr.|al.tšrgn.y btlt m.dm.l ǵzr.|šrg k.ḫḫm.mt.uḫryt.mh.yqḥ.|mh.yqḥ.mt.aṯryt.spsg.ysk.|[l]riš.ḥrṣ.l ẓr.qd 17[2AQHT].6.35
qht.ǵzr.|‘wrt.yšt k.b‘l.l ht.|w ‘lm h.l ‘nt.p dr.dr.|‘db.uḫry.mṭ.yd h.|dnil.bt h.ymǵyn.yšt|ql.dnil.l hkl h.‘rb.b|kyt 19[1AQHT].4.169
ht.ǵzr.amd.gr bt il.|‘nt.brḥ.p ‘lm h.‘nt.p dr[.dr].|‘db.uḫry mṭ.yd h.|ymǵ.l mrrt.tǵll.b nr.|yšu.g h.w yṣḥ.y l k.mrr 19[1AQHT].3.155
|yp‘.riš.ǵly.b d.ns‘ k.|‘nt.brḥ.p ‘lm h.|‘nt.p dr.dr.‘db.uḫry mṭ yd h.|ymǵ.l qrt.ablm.abl[m].|qrt.zbl.yrḫ.yšu g h.| 19[1AQHT].3.162
bḥ.tdmm.|amht.k b h.bṯt.l tbṭ.|w b h.tdmmt.amht.|aḫr.mǵy.aliyn.b‘l.|mǵyt.btlt.‘nt.|tmgnn.rbt[.a]ṯrt ym.|tǵẓy 4[51].3.23
db.imr.|b pḫd.l npš.kṯr.w ḫss.|l brlt.hyn.d ḥrš.|ydm.aḫr.ymǵy.kṯr.|w ḫss.b d.dnil.ytnn.|qšt.l brk h.y‘db.|qṣ‘t.a 17[2AQHT].5.25
ilqṣm.|yak.l kṯr.w ḫss.|w ṯb l mspr..k tlakn.|ǵlmm.|aḫr.mǵy.kṯr.w ḫss.|št.alp.qdm h.mra.|w tk.pn h.t‘db.ksu.| 4[51].5.106
ṯpṭ.nhr.|tšu ilm rašt hm.l ẓr.brkt hm.ln.kḥṯ.zbl hm.|aḫr.tmǵyn.mlak ym.t‘dt.ṯpṭ.nhr.l p‘n.il.|[l t]pl.l tšthwy.pḫr 2.1[137].30
rt.ṯ‘.‘[-]r.|[--.]b bt h.yšt.‘rb.|[--] h.ytn.w [--]u.l ytn.|[aḫ]r.mǵy.‘[d]t.ilm.|[w]y‘n.aliy[n.]b‘l.|[---.]tb‘.l lṭpn.|[il.d] 15[128].2.11
[u] y‘rr.w y‘[n].|yrḫ nyr šmm.w n‘[n].|‘ma nkl ḫtn y.a[ḫ]r.|nkl yrḫ ytrḫ.adn h.|yšt mṣb.mznm.um h.|kp mznm. 24[77].32
h.wspm.|atn.w ṯlṯ h.ḫrṣm.|ylk ym.w ṯn.|ṯlṯ.rb‘.ym.|aḫr.špšm.b rb‘.|ymǵy.l udm.rbt.|w udm[.ṯr]rt.|grnn.‘rm.| 14[KRT].4.209
dt.|km irby.tškn.|šd.k ḥsn.pat.|mdbr.tlkn.|ym.w ṯn.aḫr.|šp[š]m.b [ṯ]lṯ.|ym[ǵy.]l qdš.|a[ṯrt.]ṣrm.w l ilt.|ṣd[yn] 14[KRT].4.195

kbt.---].|t'ln.l mr[kbt hm.tity.l] |'r hm.tl[kn.ym.w tn.aḫr.špšm].|b ṯlṯ.mġy[.rpum.l grnt].|i[ln]y[m].l mṯ't[.---].|[- 22.1[123].24
dg[-.---].|t'ln.l mrkbt hm.ti[ty.l 'r hm].|tlkn.ym.w ṯa aḫr.š[pšm.b ṯlṯ].|mġy.rpum.l grnt.i[lnym.l] |mṯ't.w y'n.dni 20[121].2.5

aḫrm

br[-].|yrpu.|kdn.|p'ṣ.|bn.liy.|yd'.|šmn.|'dy.|'nbr.|aḫrm.|bn.qrdy.|bn.šm'n.|bn.ġlmy.|ġly.|bn.dnn.|bn.rmy.| 2117.3.30

aḫršp

.|d taršn.'msn.|bṣr.abn.špšyn.|dqn.|aġlmn.|kn'm.|aḫršp.|anntn.|b'lrm.|[-]ral.|šḏn.|[-]ġl.|bn.b'ltġpṯ.|ḥrš.bt 2067.1.7

aḫt

.|slṯmg.|kdrl.|wql.|adrdn.|prn.|'bdil.|ušy.šbn[-].|aḫt.ab.|krwn.|nnḏ.|mkl.|kzġb.|iyrḏ. 1069.13
.|ypq.|'bd.|qrḥ.|abšr.|bn.bdn.|ḏmry.|bn.pndr.|bn.aḫt.|bn.'dn.|bn.išb'[l]. 2117.4.32
h.aliyn.b'l.|w yšu.'n h.w y'n.|w y'n.btlt.'nt.|n'mt.bn.aḫt.b'l.|l pnn h.ydd.w yqm.|l p'n h.ykr'.w yql.|w yšu.g h. 10[76].2.16
.mli[.--].|il hd.mla.u[--.--].|blt.p btlt.'n[t].|w p.n'mt.aḫt[.b'l].|y'l.b'l.b ġ[r.---].|w bn.dgn.b š[---].|b'l.yṯb.l ks[i.m 10[76].3.11
.b'lm.|w.aḥd.ḫbṯ.|w.arb'.aṯt.|bn.lg.ṯn.bn h.|b'lm.w.aḫt h.|b.šrt.|šty.w.bn h. 2080.11
k.l ttn pnm.'m.b'l.|mrym.ṣpn.b alp.šd.rbt.kmn.|hlk.aḫt h.b'l.y'n.tdrq.|ybnt.ab h.šrḥq.aṯt.l pnn h.|št.alp.qdm h. 3['NT].4.83
h.|yšt mṣb.mznm.um h.|kp mznm.iḫ h yṯ'r.|mšrrm.aḫt h l a|bn mznm.nkl w ib.|d ašr.ar yrḫ.w y|rḫ yar k.|[aš 24[77].36
m.|[---.]dyn.ḫmšt.'šrt.|[---.-]til.ḫmšt.l 'šrm.|[--.-]n.w.aḫt h.arb'm.|[--.-]dn.'šrm.|[--.-]dwn.ṯlṯm.w.šb'.alpm.|[kṯ]r 2054.2.21
rgr h.bm.ymn.|[w]yqrb.trẓẓ h.|[---].mġy h.w ġlm.|[a]ḫt h.šib.yṣat.mrḥ h.|l tl.yṣb.pn h.tġr.|yṣu.hlm.aḫ h.tph.|[16.1[125].51
dd.w yqm.|l p'n h.ykr'.w yql.|w yšu.g h.w yṣḥ.|hwt.aḫt.w nar[-].|qrn.d bat k.btlt.'nt.|qrn.d bat k b'l.ymšḥ.|b'l. 10[76].2.20
[tḥm.---].|[l.---].|[a]ḫt y.rgm.|[y]šlm.l k.|[il]m.tšlm k.|[tġ]r k.|[--]y.ibr[-].|[- 1016.3
.tbkn.w tdm.l y.[--].|[---].al.trgm.l aḫt k.|[---.]l [ ]dm.aḫt k.|yd't.k rḥmt.|al.tšt.b šdm.mm h.|b smkt.ṣat.npš h.|[16.1[125].32
bkn.al.|tdm.l y.al tkl.bn.|qr.'n k.mḫ.riš k.|udm't.ṣḥ.aḫt k.|ṯtmnt.bt.ḥmḥ h.|d[-]n.tbkn.w tdm.l y.[--].|[---].al.tr 16.1[125].28
t.npš h.|[-]mt[-].ṣba.rbt.|špš.w tgh.nyr.|rbt.w rgm.l aḫt k.|ṯtmnt.krt n.dbḥ.|dbḥ.mlk.'šr.|'šrt.qḥ.tp k.b yd.|[-]r 16.1[125].38
nt.bt.ḥmḥ h.|d[-]n.tbkn.w tdm.l y.[--].|[---].al.trgm.l aḫt k.|[---.]l [ ]dm.aḫt k.|yd't.k rḥmt.|al.tšt.b šdm.mm h.| 16.1[125].31
'nt].|[tšu.]g h.w tṣḥ.šm'.m['.l a]|[qht.ġ]zr.at.aḫ.w an.a[ḫt k].|[---].šb'.tir k.[---].|[---.]ab y.ndt.ank[.---].|[---.--]l.m 18[3AQHT].1.24
qlt.b ġlt.yd k.|l tdn.dn.almnt.|l ṯpṭ.ṯpṭ.qṣr.npš.|km.aḫt.'rš.mdw.|anšt.'rš.zbln.|rd.l mlk.amlk.|l drkt.k aṯb.an.| 16.6[127].35
.|ṯšm.'l.dl.l pn k.|l tšlḥm.ytm.b'd.|ksl k.almnt.km.|aḫt.'rš.mdw.anšt.|'rš.zbln.rd.l mlk.|amlk.l drkt k.aṯb.|an. 16.6[127].51
ṭbt.n[--].|[---.b]ṯnm w ttb.'l.bṯnt.trtḥ[ṣ.---].|[---.t]ṯb h.aḫt.ppšr.w ppšrt[.---].|[---.]k.drḫm.w aṯb.l ntbt.k.'ṣm l t[--]. 1001.2.6

aḫty

bn[.---].|ymy.bn[.---].|'bd'n.p[--.---].|[-]d[-]l.bn.ḥrn.|aḫty.bt.abm.|[-]rbn.'dd.nryn.|[ab]r[p]u.bn.kbd.|[-]m[-].bn. 102[322].6.2

aḫtmlk

l um y.adt ny.|rgm.|tḥm.tlmyn.|w.aḫtmlk 'bd k.|l.p'n.adt ny.|mrḥqtm.|qlny.ilm.|tġr k.|tšlm 51[95].4

aṯṯ

y.|mšu.aḏddy.|plsy.aḏddy.|aḫyn.|ygmr.aḏddy.|gln.aṯṯ.|ddy.[a]ḏddy.|bn.mlkr[šp].|bn.y[k]n.|ynḥm.|bn.abd.b' 2014.43

aṭm

.b rn k.|[--]ḫp.an.arnn.ql.špš.ḥw.bṯnm.uḫd.b'lm.|[--.a]ṭm.prṯl.l riš h.ḥmṭ.ṭmṭ.|[--.]ydbr.ṯrmt.al m.qḥn y.š y.qḥn 1001.1.7
[.--].b g[--].|[---.]ḫ[--.]bnt.ṣ'ṣ.bnt.ḫkp[.---].|[---].aḥw.aṭm.prṯl[.---].|[---.]mnt.[l]p'n[.-.-]bd h.aqšr[.---].|[---].ptḥ y 1001.1.19

ay

br.špm.yd[.---.---]r.|l riš hm.w yš[--.--]m.|lḥm.b lḥm ay.w šty.b ḫmr yn ay.|šlm.mlk.šlm.mlkt.'rbm m.ṯnnm.|mt 23[52].6
.|l riš hm.w yš[--.--]m.|lḥm.b lḥm ay.w šty.b ḫmr yn ay.|šlm.mlk.šlm.mlkt.'rbm m.ṯnnm.|mt.w šr.yṯb.b d h.ḫṭ.ṯ 23[52].6
pr['.--].|ṣd.b hkl h[.---].|[------].|[---.l]ḫm[.---].|[---].ay š[---].|[---.b ḥ]rb.mlḥ[t.qṣ].|[mri.tšty.krpnm].yn.b ks.ḫ[r 17[2AQHT].6.3

ayab

n.d[--]b.|abrpu.|bn.k[n]y.|bn.klyn.|bn.gmḫn.|ḥnn.|ayab.|bn.gm[--].|bn.[---].|g[---].|p[---].|b[---].|[---].|[---].| 1035.3.10
ilk.r[--].|aršm.b'l [aṯt].|ttḫ.b'l aṯt.|ayab.b'l aṯt.|iyṯr.b'l aṯt.|ptm.b'l ššlmt.|'dršp.b'l ššlmt.|ṯtrn 1077.4

ayaḫ

spr.'rbnm.|dt.'rb.|b.mtn.bn.ayaḫ.|b.ḫbṯ h.ḥwt.ṯt h.|w.mnm.šalm.|dt.tknn.|'l.'rbnm.|h 1161.3
.d.|'rb.bt.mlk.|w.b.spr.l.št.|yrm'l.|ṣry.|iršy.|y'ḏrd.|ayaḫ.|bn.aylt.|ḫmš.mat.arb'm.|kbd.ksp.anyt.|d.'rb.b.anyt. 2106.8
m].|yddt[.---].|ilšn.[---].|ṣdqn.[----].|pndḏn.b[n.---].|ayaḫ.b[n.---]. 96[333].6

ayiḫ

t[m'y.---].|mty.ilšt[m'y.---].|bn.pynq.'nqp[a]t[y.---].|ayiḫ.ilšt[m'y.---].|[b]dlm.dt.yṯb[.---].|[-]y[--].'nqp[aty.---].|' 90[314].2.9

ayḫ

-].|bn.ḥyl.|bn.g'yn.|ḥyn.|bn.armg[-].|b'lmṯpṭ.|[bn].ayḫ.|[---]rn.|ill.|ġlmn.|bn.ytrm.|bn.ḫgbt.|mtn.|mḫtn.|[p] 1035.2.6

ayy

miḫdym.|bn.ḥṭb.|bn abyt.|bn ḫdl.|bn ṣdqn.|bn ayy.|bn dbb.|w nḥl h.|bn n'myn.|bn aṯtyy.|bn ḫlp.|bn.ẓll. 2016.1.6

ayl

n.bʻl. | [tṯ]bḫ.šbʻm.ṣin. | [k gm]n.aliyn.bʻl. | [tṯb]ḫ.šbʻm.aylm. | [k gmn.]aliyn.bʻl. | [tṯbḫ.š]bʻm.yʻlm. | [k gmn.al]iyn.bʻ 6[62].1.24
y. | bn.il[-]šy. | bn.ybšr. | bn.sly. | bn.ḥlbt. | bn.brzt. | bn.ayl. | [-----]. | ʻbd[--]. | bn.i[--]. | ʻd[--]. | ild[--]. | bn.qṣn. | ʻlpy. | kṯ 2117.2.14

ayly

šd.snrym.dt.ʻqb. | b.ayly. | šd.abršn. | šd.kkn.[bn].ubyn. | šd.bn.li[y]. | šd.bn.š[--]y. 2026.2
ʻrt. | pǵyn.b.tpḥ. | amri[l].b.šrš. | aǵltn.b.midḫ. | [--]n.b.ayly. | [-]lyn.b.nǵḥt. | [---.]b.nh[-]t. | [---.]almš. | [---.--]ty. | [---. 2118.14

ayln

gbrn. | bn uldy. | synn.bn knʻm. | bn kbr. | bn iytlm. | bn ayln. | bn.kln. | bn.ʻlln. | bn.liy. | bn.nqṯn. | bn abrḫṯ. | bn.grdy. 1064.22
nntn.yṣr. | annmn.w.ṯlṯ.nʻ[r] h. | rpan.w.ṯ[n.]bn h. | bn.ayln.w.ṯn.bn h. | yt. 2068.27

aylt

w.hm.brlt.anḫr. | b ym.hm.brk y.tkšd. | rumm.ʻn.kḏd.aylt. | hm.imt.imt.npš.blt. | ḥmr.p imt.b klt. | yd y.ilḥm.hm.š 5[67].1.17
mlk. | w.b.spr.l.št. | yrmʻl. | ṣry. | iršy. | yʻḏrd. | ayaḫ. | bn.aylt. | ḫmš.mat.arbʻm. | kbd.ksp.anyt. | d.ʻrb.b.anyt. | l.mlk.gb 2106.9
.w npš. | anḫr.b ym. | brkt.šbšt. | k rumm.hm. | ʻn.kḏd.aylt. | mt hm.ks.ym | sk.nhr hm. | šbʻ.ydt y.b ṣʻ. | [--.]šbʻ.rbt. | [UG5.4.8
rt b ǵl[.---]. | qrẓ tšt.l šmal[.---]. | arbḫ.ʻn h tšu w[.---]. | aylt tǵpy ṯr.ʻn[.---]. | b[b]r.mrḥ h.ti[ḫd.b yd h]. | š[g]r h bm 2001.1.11
npš. | [---.--]t.hd.tngṯm h. | [---.-]ḥm k b ṣpn. | [---.]išqb.aylt. | [---.--]m.b km.yʻn. | [---].ydʻ.l ydʻt. | [---.]tasrn.ṯr il. | [---. 1[ʻNT.X].5.19

aymr

ydlp. | tmn h.kṯr.ṣmdm.ynḥt.w ypʻr.šmt hm. | šm k.at.aymr.aymr.mr.ym.mr.ym. | l ksi h.nhr l kḥṯ.drkt h.trtqṣ. | b 2.4[68].19
tmn h.kṯr.ṣmdm.ynḥt.w ypʻr.šmt hm. | šm k.at.aymr.aymr.mr.ym.mr.ym. | l ksi h.nhr l kḥṯ.drkt h.trtqṣ. | b d bʻl.k 2.4[68].19
.ypʻt.b[--.---]. | aliyn.bʻl[.---]. | drkt k.mšl[-.---]. | b riš k.aymr[.---]. | ṯpṭ.nhr.yṯb[r.ḥrn.y ym.yṯbr.ḥrn]. | riš k.ʻṯtrt.[šm. 2.1[137].6

akdṯb

ḫbsn. | ulmk. | ʻdršp. | bn.knn. | pdyn. | bn.aṯtl.ṯn. | kdln.akdṯb. | ṯn.b gt yknʻm. 1061.21

aky

sn. | bn.ṣpr. | kmn. | bn.ršp. | tmn. | šmmn. | bn.rmy. | bn.aky. | ʻbdḫmn. | bn.ʻdṯ. | kṯy. | bn.ḫny. | bn.ssm. | bn.ḫnn. | [--]n 1047.13

akl

m.w ṯn.tikl. | išt.b bht m.nblat. | b hk[l] m.ṯlṯ.kbʻ ym. | tikl[.i]št.b bht m. | nbla[t.]b hkl m. | ḫmš.ṯ[d]ṯ.ym.tikl. | išt.[b 4[51].6.27
.arz h. | tšt.išt.b bht m. | nb[l]at.b hkl m. | hn.ym.w ṯn.tikl. | išt.b bht m.nblat. | b hk[l] m.ṯlṯ.kbʻ ym. | tikl[.i]št.b bht 4[51].6.24
m. | tikl[.i]št.b bht m. | nbla[t.]b hkl m. | ḫmš.ṯ[d]ṯ.ym.tikl. | išt.[b]bht m.nblat. | b[qrb.hk]l m.mk. | b šb[ʻ.]y[mm].t 4[51].6.29
[sp]r.akl[.---].ṯryn. | [tg]mr.akl.b.g[t.b]ir.alp. | [ʻ]šrm.l.mit.ḫ[p]r.ʻbdm. | mitm.drt.ṯmnym 2013.2
[ʻ]šrm.l.mit.ḫ[p]r.ʻbdm. | mitm.drt.ṯmnym.drt. | tgmr.akl.b.gt[.b]ʻln. | ṯlṯ.mat.ṯṯm.kbd. | ṯṯm.ṯṯ.kbd.ḫpr.ʻbdm. | šbʻm 2013.5
.kbd.ḫpr.ʻbdm. | šbʻm.drt.arbʻm.drt. | l.a[--.---]. | tgm[r.ak]l.b.gt.ḥldy. | ṯlṯ.ma[t].ʻšr.kbd. | šbʻ m[at].kbd.ḫpr.ʻbdm. 2013.10
t].kbd.ḫpr.ʻbdm. | mit[.d]rt.arbʻm.drt. | [---]m. | t[gm]r.akl.b.gt.ǵ[l]. | ṯlṯ.mat.ʻšrm[.---]. | ṯmnym.drt.a[--]. | drt.l.alpm 2013.15
šnt.šntm.lm.l.tlk. | w.lḥt.akl.ky. | likt.ʻm.špš. | bʻl k.ky.akl. | b.ḫwt k.inn. | špš n.[---]. | hm.al[k.--]. | ytnt[.---]. | ṯn[.---] 2060.19
. | tštyn.ṯlṯ.rbʻ.ym.ḫmš. | ṯdṯ.ym.tlḥmn.rpum. | tštyn.bt.ikl.b prʻ. | yṣq.b irt.lbnn.mk.b šbʻ. | [ymm.---]k.aliyn.bʻl. | [--- 22.2[124].24
[.---.]yd h.k šr. | knr.uṣbʻt h ḥrṣ.abn. | p h.tiḫd.šnt h.w akl.bqmm. | tšt ḥrṣ.k lb ilnm. | w ṯn.gprm.mn gpr h.šr. | aqht. 19[1AQHT].1.9
. | b tk.mlbr. | ilšiy. | kry amt. | ʻpr.ʻẓm yd. | ugrm.ḫl.ld. | aklm.tbrk k. | w ld ʻqqm. | ilm.ypʻr. | šmt hm. | b hm.qrnm. | k 12[75].1.26
| ur.tisp k.yd.aqht. | ǵzr.tšt k.b qrb m.asm. | y.dnh.ysb.aklt h.yph. | šblt.b akt.šblt.ypʻ. | b ḥmdrt.šblt.yḫ[bq]. | w ynšq 19[1AQHT].2.68
[--].w rbb. | š[---]npš išt. | w.l.tikl w l tš[t]. 2003.3
b hm.pn.bʻl. | bʻl.ytlk.w yṣd. | yḥ pat.mlbr. | wn.ymǵy.aklm. | w ymẓa.ʻqqm. | bʻl.ḥmd m.yḥmd m. | bn.dgn.yhrr m. 12[75].1.36
šlmym.lqḥ.akl. | yḥmn.ṯlṯ.šmn. | a[---.]kdm. | ʻ[---]ʻm.kd. | a[----]ḥr.ṯlṯ. | y[136[84].1
aḫd.qš[t.---]. | p ʻn.bʻl.aḫd[.---]. | w ṣmt.ǵllm[.---]. | aḫd.aklm.k [---]. | npl.b mšmš[.---]. | anp n m yḥr[r.---]. | bmt n m 12[75].2.36
| ydʻm.l.ydʻt. | ʻm y.špš.bʻl k. | šnt.šntm.lm.l.tlk. | w.lḥt.akl.ky. | likt.ʻm.špš. | bʻl k.ky.akl. | b.ḫwt k.inn. | špš n.[---]. | h 2060.17
d.bʻl. | b dbḥ k.bn.dgn. | b mṣd k.w yrd. | krt.l ggt.ʻdb. | akl.l qryt. | ḥṭt.l bt.ḫbr. | yip.lḥm.d ḫmš. | mǵd.ṯdṯ.yrḫm. | ʻdn 14[KRT].2.81
. | [bʻl].b dbḥ h.bn dgn. | [b m]ṣd h.yrd.krt. | [l g]gt.ʻdb.akl.l qryt. | ḥṭt.l bt.ḫbr. | yip.lḥm.d ḫmš. | [mǵ]d.ṯdṯ.yr[ḫm]. | 14[KRT].4.172
y.rgm. | bn.ḫrn k. | mǵy. | hbṭ.hw. | ḫrd.w.šl hw. | qr[-]. | akl n.b.grnt. | l.bʻr. | ap.krmm. | ḫlq. | qrt n.ḫlq. | w.dʻ.dʻ. 2114.8
.qlql.w.št]. | ʻrgz[.ydk.aḥd h]. | w.yṣq[.b.ap h]. | k.yiḫd[.akl.ššw]. | št.mkš[r.grn]. | w.št.ašk[rr]. | w.pr.ḥḏr[t.ydk]. | aḥd 161[56].12
s št qlql. | [w št ʻrgz y]dk aḥd h w yṣq b ap h. | [k.yiḫd akl s]šw št mkšr grn. | [w št aškrr w p]r ḥḏrt. | [-----]. | [---.-]n 160[55].10
k[rr]. | w.pr.ḥḏr[t.ydk]. | aḥd h.w.yṣq[.b.ap h]. | k.yiḫd.akl.š[šw]. | št.nni.št.mk[št.grn]. | št.irǵn.ḥmr[.ydk]. | aḥd h.w. 161[56].17
.bʻlt.šmm.rmm. | [bʻl]t.kpṯ.w ʻnt.di.dit.rḫpt. | [---.-]rm.aklt.ʻgl.ʻl.mšt. | [---.--]r.špr.w yšt.il. | [---.--]n.il ǵnṯ.ʻgl il. | [---. UG5.2.1.9
y.ʻ[m.]bn y. | mnm.[šl]m[.r]gm[.ṯṯb]. | ky.lik.bn y. | lḥt.akl.ʻm y. | mid y w ǵbn y. | w.bn y.hn kt. | yškn.anyt. | ym.yšr 2061.10
dry | nn.b išt.tšrpnn. | b rḥm.tṭḥnn.b šd. | tdrʻnn.šir h.l tikl. | ʻṣrm.mnt h.l tkly. | npr[m.]šir.l šir.yṣḥ. 6[49].2.35
t.ypʻ. | b ḥmdrt.šblt.yḫ[bq]. | w ynšq.aḥl.an.šblt. | tpʻ.b aklt.šblt.tpʻ[.b ḥm]drt. | ur.tisp k.yd.aqht.ǵz[r]. | tšt k.bm.qr 19[1AQHT].2.72
| ǵzr.tšt k.b qrb m.asm. | y.dnh.ysb.aklt h.yph. | šblt.b akt.šblt.ypʻ. | b ḥmdrt.šblt.yḫ[bq]. | w ynšq.aḥl.an.šblt. | tpʻ.b 19[1AQHT].2.69
m.šḥr. | [---.y]lt n.km.qdm. | [-.k]bd n.il.ab n. | kbd k iš.tikln. | ṯd n.km.mrm.tqrṣn. | il.yzḥq.bm. | lb.w ygmḏ.bm kbd. 12[75].1.10
ṯlṯm.ktn. | ḫmšm.izml. | ḫmš.kbd.arbʻm. | dd.akl. | ṯṯ.ʻšr h.yn. | kd.šmn.l.nr.ilm. | kdm.dǵm. | ṯṯ.kdm.ztm. 1126.4
-]. | w[.-----]. | l[.-----]. | h[--.---]. | šp[š.---]. | ʻm.k[--.lḥt]. | akl.yṯ[ṯb.--]pt. | ib.ʻltn.a[--.--]y. | w.spr.in[.-.]ʻd m. | spr n.ṯhr[. 2060.30
[---.šp]š.l [hrm.ǵ]rpl.ʻl.arṣ. | [---.]ḥmt.l p[.nṯ]k.abd.l p.ak[l]. | [ṯm.dl.]isp.ḥ[mt.---.-]hm.yasp.ḥmt. | [---.š]pš.l [hrm.ǵ UG5.8.10
isp.[šp]š l hrm.ǵrpl.ʻl arṣ. | [l a]n ḥmt.l p[.n]ṯk.abd.l p.akl ṯm.dl. | [---.q]l.bl.tbḥ[n.l]azd.ʻr.qdm. | [---].ʻẓ q[dm.--.šp] UG5.8.20
md m.[---]. | il.hr[r.---]. | kb[-.---]. | ym.[---]. | yšḥr[.---]. | yikl[.---]. | km.s[--.---]. | tš[.---]. | t[---.---]. | [-----]. | [-----]. | b [-- 12[75].2.14

[sp]r.akl[.---].ṯryn. | [tg]mr.akl.b.g[t.b]ir.alp. | [‘]šrm.l.mit.ḥ[p]r.‘b 2013.1

id y w ǵbn y. | w.bn y.hn kt. | yškn.anyt. | ym.yšrr. | w.ak[l.---]. | [--].š[--.--]. 2061.15

rb[m.--]š[-]. | [---].nš.b [---]. | [---].tm[--.--]at[.---]. | [---.]akl[.---]. | [---.-]l[-.-]hg[.---]. | [---.-]r[-.il]m.rbm.n‘l[.-]gr. | [---.] UG5.8.29

aktmy

[w.]qšt.w ql‘. | ḥd[t]n.qšt.w.ql‘. | bn.bb.qšt.w[.ql]‘. | bn.aktmy.qšt. | šdyn.qšt. | bdn.qšt.w.ql‘. | bn.šmlbi.qšt.w.ql‘. | bn. 119[321].4.10

al

r‘y. | w.ṯn.‘l. | mlk. | w.aḥd. | ‘l atlg. | w l.‘ṣm. | tspr. | nrn.al.tud | ad.at.l hm. | ṯṯm.ksp. 1010.19

k.y ilm.bnt.bh[t k].a[l.tš]mḫ. | al.tšmḫ.b r[m.h]kl[k]. | al.aḫd.hm.b y[--] y.[---]b[-]. | b gdlt.arkt y.am[---]. | qdqd k.a 3['NT.VI].5.30

.y ilm[.bnt.bht k.--]. | [al.tšmḫ.]al.tš[mḫ.b rm.h] | [kl k.al.]aḫd hm.[---]. | [---.b]gdlt.ar[kt y.am--]. | [---.qdq]d k.ašhl 18[3AQHT].1.9

y.b d[-.--]y.[---]. | [---.]‘m.w hm[.--]yt.w.[---]. | [---.ṯ]y.al.an[k.--.]il[m.--]y. | [--.m]ṣlm.pn y[.-.]tlkn. | [---.]rḫbn.hm.[- 1002.58

n.ṯrnq.[-]r.d.yṯb.b.ilštm‘. | ilšlm.bn.gs[-.--]r.d.yṯb.b.gt.al. | ilmlk.[--]kt.[--.d.]yṯb.b.šb[n]. | bn.pr[-.]d.y[ṯb.b].šlmy. | tl 2015.1.27

. | w qdš.u ilm.tmtn. | špḥ.lṭpn.l yḥ. | w y‘ny.krt.ṯ‘. | bn.al.tbkn.al. | tdm.l y.al tkl.bn. | qr.‘n k.mḫ.riš k. | udm‘t.ṣḥ.aḫt 16.1[125].25

p.ank.mnm. | [ḫ]s[r]t.w.uḫ y. | [y]‘msn.ṯmn. | w.[u]ḫ y.al yb‘rn. 2065.21

t. | ‘l.w.likt. | ‘m k.w.hm. | l.‘l.w.lakm. | ilak.w.at. | um y.al.tdḥṣ. | w.ap.mhkm. | b.lb k.al. | tšt. 1013.21

.u ilm.tmtn. | špḥ.lṭpn.l yḥ. | w y‘ny.krt.ṯ‘. | bn.al.tbkn.al. | tdm.l y.al tkl.bn. | qr.‘n k.mḫ.riš k. | udm‘t.ṣḥ.aḫt k. | ṯtm 16.1[125].25

.d mlk. | b ḥwt.špḥ. | l ydn.‘bd.mlk. | d št.‘l.ḫrd h. | špḥ.al.thbṭ. | ḫrd.‘ps.aḥd.kw | sgt. | ḫrd ksp.[--]r. | ymm.w[.---]. | [-- 2062.2.5

. | w tṣḥ.yṯb.ytp.[---]. | qrt.ablm.ablm.[qrt.zbl.yrḫ]. | ik.al.yḫdṯ.yrḫ.b[---]. | b qrn.ymn h.b anšt[.---]. | qdqd h.w y‘n.y 18[3AQHT].4.9

.idk.pnm]. | al.ttn.‘m.pḫr.m‘d.t[k.ǵr.ll.l p‘n.il]. | al.tpl.al.tštḥwy.pḫr [m‘d.qmm.a--.am]] | r ṯny.d‘t km.w rgm.l ṯr.a[2.1[137].15

. | w ytnnn. | l aḫ h.l r‘ h. | r‘ ‘lm. | ttn.w tn. | w l ttn. | w al ttn. | tn ks yn. | w ištn. | ‘bd.prṭ.ṯhm. | qrq.pt.ḏmn. | l iṯtl. 1019.1.14

. | [---]w yrmy[.q]rn h. | [---.-]ny h pdr.ttǵr. | [---.n]šr k.al ttn.l n. | [---.]tn l rbd. | [---.]b‘lt h w yn. | [---.rk]b ‘rpt. | [---. 2001.2.12

]bb. | [----.]lm y. | [---.--]p. | [---.d]bḥ. | t[---.id]k. | pn[m.al.ttn]. | ‘m.[krt.msw]n. | w r[gm.l krt.]ṯ‘. | ṯḥm[.pbl.mlk]. | qḥ 14[KRT].5.246

pr.š[--.---]. | uṭ.ṯbr.ap hm.tb‘.ǵlm[m.al.ṯṯb.idk.pnm]. | al.ttn.‘m.pḫr.m‘d.t[k.ǵr.ll.l p‘n.il]. | al.tpl.al.tštḥwy.pḫr [m‘d 2.1[137].14

idk.al.ttn.pnm. | ‘m.ǵr.trǵzz. | ‘m.ǵr.ṯrmg. | ‘m.tlm.ǵṣr.arṣ. | ša.ǵr. 4[51].8.1

r.iht. | np šmm.šmšr. | l dgy.aṯrt. | mǵ.l qdš.amrr. | idk.al.tnn. | pnm.tk.ḥqkpt. | il.kl h.kptr. | ksu.ṯbt h.ḥkpt. | arṣ.nḥlt 3['NT.VI].6.12

[idk.al.ttn.pnm.tk.ḥkpt.il.kl h]. | [kptr.]ks[u.ṯbt h.ḥkpt.arṣ.nḥlt h 1['NT.IX].3.01

lb.l ẓr.rḥtm. | w rd.bt ḫptt. | arṣ.tspr.b y | rdm.arṣ. | idk.al.ttn. | pnm.tk.qrt h. | hmry.mk.ksu. | ṯbt h.ḫḫ.arṣ. | nḥlt h.w 4[51].8.10

n.ḫnzr k. | ‘m k.pdry.bt.ar. | ‘m k.ṭṭly.bt.rb.idk. | pn k.al ttn.tk.ǵr. | knkny.ša.ǵr.‘l ydm. | ḫlb.l ẓr.rḥtm w rd. | bt ḫpṯ 5[67].5.12

.nhr]. | b ‘lṣ.‘lṣm.npr.š[--.---]. | uṭ.ṯbr.ap hm.tb‘.ǵlm[m.al.ṯṯb.idk.pnm]. | al.ttn.‘m.pḫr.m‘d.t[k.ǵr.ll.l p‘n.il]. | al.tpl.al 2.1[137].13

. | špḥ.lṭpn.l yḥ. | w y‘ny.krt.ṯ‘. | bn.al.tbkn.al. | tdm.l y.al tkl.bn. | qr.‘n k.mḫ.riš k. | udm‘t.ṣḥ.aḫt k. | ṯtmnt.bt.ḥmḥ h 16.1[125].26

.yṯb.b‘l.l bht h. | u mlk.u bl mlk. | arṣ.drkt.yštkn. | dll.al.ilak.l bn. | ilm.mt.‘dd.l ydd. | il.ǵzr.yqra.mt. | b npš h.ystrn 4[51].7.45

ḫd.b‘lm. | [--.a]ṯm.prṯl.l riš h.ḥmṯ.ṯmṯ. | [--.]ydbr.ṯrmt.al m.qḥn y.š y.qḥn y. | [--.]šir.b krm.nṭṭt.dm.‘lt.b ab y. | u---]. 1001.1.8

[-----]. | [---.--]dn. | [---.--]dd. | [---.--]n.kb | [--.---.]al.yns. | [---.]ysd k. | [---.--]r.dr.dr. | [---.--]y k.w rḥd. | [---]y il 4[51].3.5

.al.ṯṯb.idk.pnm]. | al.ttn.‘m.pḫr.m‘d.t[k.ǵr.ll.l p‘n.il]. | al.tpl.al.tštḥwy.pḫr [m‘d.qmm.a--.am]] | r ṯny.d‘t km.w rgm. 2.1[137].15

.y l k.mrrt. | tǵll.b nr.d ‘l k.mḫṣ.aqht. | ǵzr.šrš k.b arṣ.al. | yp‘.riš.ǵly.b d.ns‘ k. | ‘nt.brḥ.p ‘lm h. | ‘nt.p dr.dr.‘db.uḫr 19[1AQHT].3.159

.ḫḫ.arṣ. | nḥlt h.w ngr. | ‘nn.ilm.al. | tqrb.l bn.ilm. | mt.al.y‘db km. | k imr.b p h. | k lli.b ṯbrn. | qn h.ṯḫtan. | nrt.ilm.š 4[51].8.17

qr. | mmlat.dm.ym.w ṯn. | ṯlṯ.rb‘.ym.ymš. | ṯdṯ.ym.ḥẓ k.al.tš‘l. | qrt h.abn.yd k. | mšdpt.w hn.špšm. | b šb‘.w l.yšn.pbl. 14[KRT].3.116

al.ṯǵl[.---]. | prdmn.‘bd.ali[yn]. | b‘l.sid.zbl.b‘l. | arṣ.qm.yṯ‘r. | 3['NT].1.1

.m[rkbt]. | b trbṣ.[bn.amt]. | q[ḥ.kr]t[.šlmm]. | š[lmm.]al.t[ṣr]. | udm[.r]bt.w u[dm]. | [ṯ]rrt.udm.y[t]n[t]. | il.ušn.ab[. 14[KRT].6.275

qḥ.krt.šlmm. | šlmm.w ng.mlk. | l bt y.rḥq.krt. | l ḥẓr y.al.tṣr. | udm.rbt.w udm ṯrrt. | udm.ytnt.il w ušn. | ab.adm.w ṯ 14[KRT].3.133

[wm.mrkbt]. | b[trbṣ.bn.amt]. | [qḥ.krt.šlmm]. | [šlmm.al.tṣr]. | [udm.rbt.w udm]. | [ṯrrt.udm.ytnt]. | [il.w ušn.ab.ad 14[KRT].5.256

. | hmry.mk.ksu. | ṯbt h.ḫḫ.arṣ. | nḥlt h.w ngr. | ‘nn.ilm.al. | tqrb.l bn.ilm. | mt.al.y‘db km. | k imr.b p h. | k lli.b ṯbrn. | 4[51].8.15

t k. | ṯtmnt.bt.ḥmḥ h. | d[-]n.tbkn.w tdm.l y.[--]. | [---].al.trgm.l aḫt k. | [---.]l [ ]dm.aḫt k. | yd‘t.k rḥmt. | al.tšt.b šd 16.1[125].31

l pn.špš. | w pn.špš.nr. | b y.mid.w um. | tšmḫ.m ab. | w al.trḫln. | ‘tn.ḫrd.ank. | ‘m ny.šlm. | kll. | w mnm. | šlm ‘m. | u 1015.12

ašt.urbt.b bh[t] m. | ḥln.b qrb.hkl m. | w y‘n.aliyn b‘l. | al.tšt.urbt.b[bhtm]. | [ḥln].b qrb.hk[l m]. 4[51].5.126

t.ur[bt.]b bht m. | ḥln.b qr[b.hk]l m. | w ‘n.ali[yn.]b‘l. | al.tšt.u[rb]t.b bht m. | ḥln.b q[rb.hk]l m. | al td[.pdr]y.bt ar. | 4[51].6.8

[---].al.trgm.l aḫt k. | [---.]l [ ]dm.aḫt k. | yd‘t.k rḥmt. | al.tšt.b šdm.mm h. | b smkt.ṣat.npš h. | [-]mt[-].ṣba.rbt. | špš. 16.1[125].34

-]. | dk k.kbkb[.---]. | dm.mt.aṣḫ[.---]. | ydd.b qr[b.---]. | al.ašt.b[---]. | ahpk k.l[--.---]. | ṯmm.w lk[.---]. | w lk.ilm[.---]. 5[67].3.11

.lakm. | ilak.w.at. | um y.al.tdḥṣ. | w.ap.mhkm. | b.lb k.al. | tšt. 1013.23

k.l hm. | w.any k.ṯt. | by.‘ky.‘ryt. | w.aḫ y.mhk. | b lb h.al.yšt. 2059.27

.ilm.m]t. | w t‘n.btlt.‘n[t.bnt.]bht | k.y ilm.bnt.bh[t k].a[l.tš]mḫ. | al.tšmḫ.b r[m.h]kl[k]. | al.aḫd.hm.b y[--] y.[---]b[3['NT.VI].5.28

].w t‘n.[btlt.‘nt.---]. | [bnt.bht]k.y ilm[.bnt.bht k.--]. | [al.tšmḫ.]al.tš[mḫ.b rm.h] | [kl k.al.]aḫd hm.[---]. | [---.b]gdlt 18[3AQHT].1.8

tlt.‘nt.---]. | [bnt.bht]k.y ilm[.bnt.bht k.--]. | [al.tšmḫ.]al.tš[mḫ.b rm.h] | [kl k.al.]aḫd hm.[---]. | [---.b]gdlt.ar[kt y.a 18[3AQHT].1.8

t‘n.btlt.‘n[t.bnt.]bht | k.y ilm.bnt.bh[t k].a[l.tš]mḫ. | al.tšmḫ.b r[m.h]kl[k]. | al.aḫd.hm.b y[--] y.[---]b[-]. | b gdlt. 3['NT.VI].5.29

.l mt.šm‘.m‘. | l bn.ilm.mt.ik.tmt[ḫ] | ṣ.‘m.aliyn.b‘l. | ik.al.yšm[‘] k.ṯr. | il.ab k.l ys‘.alt. | ṯbt k.l yhpk.ksa.mlk k. | l yṯb 6[49].6.26

.m‘. | [-.yṯ]ir ṯr.il.ab k.l pn.zbl.ym.l pn[.ṯ]pṭ[.n]hr. | [ik.a]l.yšm‘ k.ṯr.[i]l.ab k.l ys‘.[alt.]ṯ[bt | k.l y]hpk. | [ksa.]mlk k.l 2.3[129].17

.w t]‘nynn.ap ank.aḥwy. | aqht[.ǵz]r.w y‘n.aqht.ǵzr. | al.tšrgn.y btlt m.dm.l ǵzr. | šrg k.ḫḫm.mt.uḫryt.mh.yqḥ. | m 17[2AQHT].6.34

[---.]b[--]. | [---].šḥr.[---]. | [---].al yṯb‘[.--]. | [---.]l adn.ḥwt[.--]. | [--]h.w yššil[.--]. | [---.]lp[--]. 1023.3

.ali[yn.]b‘l. | al.tšt.u[rb]t.b bht m. | ḥln.b q[rb.hk]l m. | al td[.pdr]y.bt ar. | [---.ṭ]l]y.bt.rb. | [---.m]dd.il ym. | [---.-]qlṣn 4[51].6.10

]pp h.w[.---]. | [---.]l k[.---]. | [-----]. | [-----]. | [-----]. | [---].al.tš[--.---]. | [---.]l ksi y.w pr[‘]. | [---].pr‘.ank.[---]. | [---.]ank. 1002.12

adt y.[---]. | lb.ab[d k].al[.---]. | [-]tm.iph.adt y.w.[---]. | tšṣḥq.hn.aṯt.l.‘bd. | šb‘t.w.nṣ 1017.2

aliy

.ḫḫ.arṣ.nḥlt h.tša. | g hm.w tṣḥ.tḥm.aliyn. | bn.b'l.hwt.aliy.qrdm. | bhṯ.bn.ilm.mt.'bd k.an. | w d 'lm k.šmḫ.bn.ilm. 5[67].2.18
.rgm.l bn.ilm.mt. | ṯny.l ydd.il ǵzr. | tḥm.aliyn.b'l.hwt.aliy. | qrdm.bhṯ.l bn.ilm mt. | 'bd k.an.w d.'lm k. | tb'.w l.yṯb. 5[67].2.10
. | l bn.ilm.mt. | ṯny.l ydd. | il.ǵzr.tḥm. | aliyn.b'l. | [hw]t.aliy.q | [rdm.]bht y.bnt. | [dt.ksp.dtm]. | [ḫrṣ.hk]l y. | [---.]aḫ y 4[51].8.34
rgm.l btlt.'nt. | ṯny.l ymmt.limm. | tḥm.aliyn.b'l.hwt. | aliy.qrdm.qry.b arṣ. | mlḥmt št.b 'pr m.ddym. | sk.šlm.l kbd. 3['NT].3.11
.y'nyn.l ib.yp'. | l b'l.ṣrt.l rkb.'rpt. | tḥm.aliyn.b'l.hwt.aliy. | qrdm.qry.b arṣ.mlḥmt. | št.b 'p[r] m.ddym.sk.šlm. | l k 3['NT].4.51
| rgm l btl[t.'nt.ṯny.l ybmt.limm.tḥm.aliyn.b'l]. | hw[t.aliy.qrdm.qryy.b arṣ.mlḥmt.št]. | [b ']pr[m.ddym.sk.šlm.l k 7.2[130].14
r. | w ḫss.ṯny.l h | yn.d ḥrš.ydm. | tḥm.al[iyn.b'l]. | h[wt.aliy.qrdm]. 3['NT.VI].6.25

aliyn

hmry.mk.ksu. | ṯbt.ḫḫ.arṣ.nḥlt h.tša. | g hm.w tṣḥ.tḥm.aliyn. | bn.b'l.hwt.aliy.qrdm. | bhṯ.bn.ilm.mt.'bd k.an. | w d 'l 5[67].2.17
. | bt ḫpṯt.arṣ.tspr b y | rdm.arṣ.w td' ilm. | k mtt.yšm'.aliyn.b'l. | yuhb.'glt.b dbr.prt. | b šd.šḫlmmt.škb. | 'mn h.šb'.l 5[67].5.17
yd[h.---]. | [--.]yṣt ḏm[r.---]. | tšt[.r]imt.[l irt h.tšr.l dd.aliyn.b'l]. | [ahb]t pdr[y.bt.ar.ahbt.ṭly.bt.rb.dd]. | arṣy bt.y['b 7.2[130].10
mt]. | limm.tiḫd.knr h.b yd[h.tšt]. | rimt.l irt h.tšr.dd.al[iyn]. | b'l.ahbt. UG5.3.2.7
b.'rpt. | bl.ašt.urbt.b bh[t] m. | ḥln.b qrb.hkl m. | w y'n.aliyn b'l. | al.tšt.urbt.b[bhtm]. | [ḥln].b qrb.hk[l m]. 4[51].5.125
]n b'l. | bl.ašt.ur[bt.]b bht m. | ḥln.b qr[b.hk]l m. | w 'n.ali[yn.]b'l. | al.tšt.u[rb]t.b bht m. | ḥln.b q[rb.hk]l m. | al td[.p 4[51].6.7
mt.[nhr]. | ṯṯn.ib.b'l.tiḫd. | y'rm.šnu.hd.gpt. | ǵr.w y'n.aliyn. | b'l.ib.hdt.lm.tḫš. | lm.tḫš.nṯq.dmrn. | 'n.b'l.qdm.yd h. 4[51].7.37
nt.šdm.y špš. | pl.'nt.šdm.il.yš[t k]. | b'l.'nt.mḥrṯ[-]. | iy.aliyn.b'l. | iy.zbl.b'l.arṣ. | w t'n.nrt.ilm.š[p]š. | šd yn.'n.b qbt[.t 6[49].4.39
.'nt.šdm.y špš. | pl.'nt.šdm.il.yšt k. | [b]'l.'nt.mḥrṯt. | iy.aliyn.b'l. | iy.zbl.b'l.arṣ. | ttb'.btlt.'nt. | idk.l ttn.pnm. | 'm.nrt.i 6[49].4.28
l.'ln.špš. | tṣḥ.l mt.šm'.m'. | l bn.ilm.mt.ik.tmt[ḫ] | ṣ.'m.aliyn.b'l. | ik.al.yšm['] k.ṯr. | il.ab k.l ys'.alt. | ṯbt k.l yhpk.ksa. 6[49].6.25
tǵṣ[.pnt.ks]l h. | anš.dt.ẓr.[h]. | tšu.g h.w tṣḥ[.i]k. | mǵy.aliy[n.b]'l. | ik.mǵyt.b[t]lt. | 'nt.mḫṣ y hm[.m]ḫṣ. | bn y.hm[. 4[51].2.22
. | alp.šd.aḫd bt. | rbt.kmn.hkl. | w y'n.kṯr.w ḫss. | šm'.l aliyn b'l. | bn.l rkb.'rpt. | bl.ašt.urbt.b bh[t] m. | ḥln.b qrb.hkl 4[51].5.121
ḫs]s. | ṯṯb.b'l.l[hwt y]. | ṯn.rgm.k[ṯr.w]ḫss. | šm'.m'.l al[iy]n b'l. | bl.ašt.ur[bt.]b bht m. | ḥln.b qr[b.hk]l m. | w 'n.al 4[51].6.4
m.n[bl]at.b hkl m. | sb.ksp.l rqm.ḫrṣ. | nṣb.l lbnt.šmḫ. | aliyn.b'l.ht y.bnt. | dt.ksp.hkl y.dtm. | ḫrṣ.'dbt.bht[h.b']l. | y' 4[51].6.36
. | yqṯ b'l.w yšt.ym.ykly.ṯpṭ.nhr. | b šm.tg'r m.'ṯtrt.bṯ l aliyn.[b'l.] | bṯ.l rkb.'rpt.k šby n.zb[l.ym.k] | šby n.ṯpṭ.nhr.w 2.4[68].28
y.kbd hyt. | w rgm.l btlt.'nt. | ṯny.l ymmt.limm. | tḥm.aliyn.b'l.hwt. | aliy.qrdm.qry.b arṣ. | mlḥmt št.b 'pr m.ddym. 3['NT].3.10
pt. | [-]'n.ǵlmm.y'nyn.l ib.yp'. | l b'l.ṣrt.l rkb.'rpt. | tḥm.aliyn.b'l.hwt.aliy. | qrdm.qry.b arṣ.mlḥmt. | št.b 'p[r] m.ddy 3['NT].4.51
hwt. | w rgm.l kṯr. | w ḫss.ṯny.l h | yn.d ḥrš.ydm. | tḥm.al[iyn.b'l]. | h[wt.aliy.qrdm]. 3['NT.VI].6.24
.rkb.'rpt. | tb'.rgm.l bn.ilm.mt. | ṯny.l ydd.il ǵzr. | tḥm.aliyn.b'l.hwt.aliy. | qrdm.bhṯ.l bn.ilm mt. | 'bd k.an.w d.'lm 5[67].2.10
| bd hwt.w rgm. | l bn.ilm.mt. | ṯny.l ydd. | il.ǵzr.tḥm. | aliyn.b'l. | [hw]t.aliy.q | [rdm.]bht y.bnt. | [dt.ksp.dtm]. | [ḫrṣ. 4[51].8.33
ṣy bt.y['bdr.---]. | rgm l btl[t.'nt.ṯny.l ybmt.limm.tḥm.aliyn.b'l]. | hw[t.aliy.qrdm.qryy.b arṣ.mlḥmt.št]. | [b ']pr[m. 7.2[130].13
[k mt.aliyn.b'l]. | k ḫlq.z[bl.b'l.arṣ]. | w hm.ḥy.a[liyn.b'l]. | w hm.iṯ.zbl.b'[l.arṣ]. | b ḥlm.lṭpn.il.d pid. | b ḏrt. 6[49].3.2
y'n.'ṯtr.'rẓ. | l amlk.b ṣrrt.ṣpn. | yrd.'ṯtr.'rẓ.yrd. | l kḥṯ.aliyn.b'l. | w ymlk.b arṣ.il.kl h. | [---] š abn.b rḥbt. | [---] š abn 6.1.64[49.1.36]
tšu.knp.w tr.b 'p. | tk.aḫ šmk.mlat rumm. | w yšu.'n h.aliyn.b'l. | w yšu.'n h.w y'n. | w y'n.btlt.'nt. | n'mt.bn.aḫt.b'l. 10[76].2.13
t.ilm.š[p]š. | šd yn.'n.b qbt[.t] | bl lyt.'l.umt k. | w abqṯ.aliyn.b'l. | w t'n.btlt.'nt. | an.l an.y špš. | an.l an.il.yǵr[.-]. | tǵr 6[49].4.44
šby n.zb[l.ym.k] | šby n.ṯpṭ.nhr.w yṣa b[.--]. | ybṯ.nn.aliyn.b'l.w [---]. | ym.l mt.b'l m.ym l[--.---]. | ḥm.l šrr.w [---]. 2.4[68].31
.arṣ.dbr. | l ysmt.šd.šḫlmmt. | mǵny.l b'l.npl.l a | rṣ.mt.aliyn.b'l. | ḫlq.zbl.b'l.arṣ. | apnk.lṭpn.il. | d pid.yrd.l ksi.yṯb. | l 5[67].6.9
'm.alpm. | [k g]mn.aliyn.b'l. | [ṭṭ]bḫ.šb'm.ṣin. | [k gm]n.aliyn.b'l. | [ṭṭb]ḫ.šb'm.aylm. | [k gmn.]aliyn.b'l. | [ṭṭbḫ.š]b'm. 6[62].1.23
tqbrn h.tštnn.b ḫrt. | ilm.arṣ.ṭṭbḫ.šb'm. | rumm.k gmn.aliyn. | [b]'l.ṭṭbḫ.šb'm.alpm. | [k g]mn.aliyn.b'l. | [ṭṭ]bḫ.šb'm.ṣ 6[62].1.19
.aylm. | [k gmn.]aliyn.b'l. | [ṭṭbḫ.š]b'm.y'lm. | [k gmn.al]iyn.b'l. | [ṭṭbḫ.šb'm.]ḥmrm. | [k gm]n.al[i]yn.b['l]. | [---]ḥ h 6[62].1.27
'm.ṣin. | [k gm]n.aliyn.b'l. | [ṭṭb]ḫ.šb'm.aylm. | [k gmn.]aliyn.b'l. | [ṭṭbḫ.š]b'm.y'lm. | [k gmn.al]iyn.b'l. | [ṭṭbḫ.šb'm.]ḥ 6[62].1.25
. | rumm.k gmn.aliyn. | [b]'l.ṭṭbḫ.šb'm.alpm. | [k g]mn.aliyn.b'l. | [ṭṭ]bḫ.šb'm.ṣin. | [k gm]n.aliyn.b'l. | [ṭṭb]ḫ.šb'm.ayl 6[62].1.21
[---.t]št.rimt. | l irt h.mšr.l.dd.aliyn. | b'l.yd.pdry.bt.ar. | ahbt.ṭly.bt.rb.dd.arṣy. | bt.y'bdr.k 3['NT].3.2
.bnwt. | šmm.šmn.tmṭrn. | nḫlm.tlk.nbtm. | w id'.k ḥy.aliyn.b'l. | k iṯ.zbl.b'l.arṣ. | b ḥlm.lṭpn.il d pid. | b ḏrt.bny.bn 6[49].3.8
h.w yṣḥ. | aṯbn.ank.w anḫn. | w tnḫ.b irt y.npš. | k ḥy.aliyn.b'l. | k iṯ.zbl.b'l.arṣ. | gm.yṣḥ.il.l btlt. | 'nt.šm'.l btlt.'n[t] 6[49].3.20
g h.w tṣḥ.tšmḫ ht. | aṯrt.w bn h.ilt.w ṣb | rt.ary h.k mt.aliyn. | b'l.k ḫlq.zbl.b'l. | arṣ.gm.yṣḥ il. | l rbt.aṯrt ym.šm'. | l r 6.1.41[49.1.13]
[k mt.aliyn.b'l]. | k ḫlq.z[bl.b'l.arṣ]. | w hm.ḥy.a[liyn.b'l]. | w hm.iṯ. 6[49].3.01
rt.ilm.špš. | 'ms m'.l y.aliyn.b'l. | tšm'.nrt.ilm.špš. | tšu.aliyn.b'l.l ktp. | 'nt.k tšt h.tš'lyn h. | b ṣrrt.ṣpn.tbkyn h. | w tq 6[62].1.14
šb'.l šb'm. | tš[']ly.ṯmn.l ṯmnym. | w [th]rn.w tldn mṯ. | al[iyn.b']l šlbšn. | i[---.---.--]l h.mǵẓ. | y[--.---.]l irt h. | n[--.---]. 5[67].5.23
t.tld[n]. | a[lp].l btlt.'nt. | w ypt l ybmt.li[mm]. | w y'ny.aliyn[.b'l]. | lm.k qnym.'l[m.--]. | k dr d.d yknn[.--]. | b'l.yṣǵd. 10[76].3.5
. | amht.k b h.bṯt.l tbṯ. | w b h.tdmmt.amht. | aḫr.mǵy.aliyn.b'l. | mǵyt.btlt.'nt. | tmgnn.rbt[.a]ṯrt ym. | tǵẓyn.qnyt.il 4[51].3.23
m.l yrḫm. | l šnt.[m]k.b šb'. | šnt.w [--].bn.ilm.mt. | 'm.aliyn.b'l.yšu. | g h.w yṣḥ.'l k.b[']l m. | pht.qlt.'l k.pht. | dry.b 6[49].5.10
al.tǵl[.---]. | prdmn.'bd.ali[yn]. | b'l.sid.zbl.b'l. | arṣ.qm.yṯ'r. | w yšlḥmn h. | ybrd.ṯd.l 3['NT].1.2
št.alp.qdm h.mra. | w tk.pn h.t'db.ksu. | w yṯṯb.l ymn.aliyn. | b'l.'d.lḥm.št[y.ilm]. | [w]y'n.aliy[n.b'l]. | [--]b[.---]. | ḥš 4[51].5.109
. | arṣ.mǵt.l n'm y.arṣ. | dbr.ysmt.šd.šḫlmmt. | ngš.ank.aliyn b'l. | 'dbnn ank.imr.b p y. | k lli.b ṯbrn q y.ḫtu hw. | nrt. 6[49].2.21
--.--]r.dr.dr. | [---.--]y k.w rḥd. | [---]y ilm.d mlk. | y[ṯ]b.aliyn.b'l. | yt'dd.rkb.'rpt. | [--].ydd.w yqlṣn. | yqm.w ywpṯn.b 4[51].3.10
. | ymlk.'ṯtr.'rẓ. | apnk.'ṯtr.'rẓ. | y'l.b ṣrrt.ṣpn. | yṯb.l kḥṯ.aliyn. | b'l.p'n h.l tmǵyn. | hdm.riš h.l ymǵy. | aps h.w y'n.'ṯtr 6.1.58[49.1.30]
md.. | ḫrṣ.w bn.bht.ksp. | w ḫrṣ.bht.ṭhrm. | iqnim.šmḫ.aliyn. | b'l.ṣḥ.ḫrn.b bht h. | 'ḏbt.b qrb hkl h. | yblnn ǵrm.mid. 4[51].5.97
rqm. | bt.arzm.ykllnn h. | hm.bt.lbnt.y'msn h. | l yrgm.l aliyn b'l. | ṣḥ.ḫrn.b bhm k. | 'ḏbt.b qrb.hkl k. | tbl k.ǵrm.mid. 4[51].5.74
.b'l.[----]. | tš'm.b'l.mr[-]. | bt[.--]b b'l.b qrb. | bt.w y'n.aliyn. | b'l.ašt m.kṯr bn. | ym.kṯr.bnm.'dt. | ypth.ḥln.b bht m. 4[51].7.14
'.bk. | tšt.k yn.udm't.gm. | tṣḥ.l nrt.ilm.špš. | 'ms m'.l y.aliyn.b'l. | tšm'.nrt.ilm.špš. | tšu.aliyn.b'l.l ktp. | 'nt.k tšt h.tš'l 6[62].1.12
.kṯr.w ḫss. | ṣḥq.kṯr.w ḫss. | yšu.g h.w yṣḥ. | l rgmt.l k.l ali | yn.b'l.ṯṯbn.b'l. | l hwt y.ypth.ḥ | ln.b bht m.urbt. | b qrb.h 4[51].7.23
. | tḥm k.il.ḥkm.ḥkm k. | 'm.'lm.ḥyt.ḥẓt.tḥm k. | mlk n.aliyn.b'l.ṯpṭ n. | in.d 'ln h.klny y.qš h. | nbln.klny y.nbl.ks h. 3['NT.VI].5.40

.|ṯḥm k.il.ḥkm.ḥkmt.|ʻm ʻlm.ḥyt.ḥẓt.|ṯḥm k.mlk n.aliy[n.]bʻl.|ṯpṭ n.w in.d ʻln h.|klny n.q[š] h.n[bln].|klny n[. 4[51].4.43
l.b kbd h.b p h yrd.|k ḥrr.zt.ybl.arṣ.w pr.|ʻṣm.yraun.aliyn.bʻl.|ṯtʻ.nn.rkb.ʻrpt.|tbʻ.rgm.l bn.ilm.mt.|ṯny.l ydd.il ǵ 5[67].2.6
-]m.rbt.aṯrt.ym.|[nǵ]ẓ.qnyt.ilm.|[---].nmgn.hwt.|[--].aliyn.bʻl.|[--.]rbt.aṯrt.ym.|[---.]btlt.ʻnt.|[--.tl]ḥm.tšty.|[ilm. 4[51].3.37
su.|w yṯṯb.l ymn.aliyn.|bʻl.ʻd.lḥm.št[y.ilm].|[w]yʻn.aliy[n.bʻl].|[--]b[.---].|ḥš.bht m.k[ṯr].|ḥš.rmm.hk[l m].|ḥš.b 4[51].5.111
-].|b mdd.il.y[--.---].|b ym.il.d[--.---.n]|hr.il.y[--.---].|aliyn.[bʻl.---].|btlt.[ʻnt.---].|mh.k[--.---].|w at[--.---].|aṯr[t.-- 4[51].2.37
ʻnt.ttnn.|[---].bʻl m.d ip[---].|[il.]hd.d ʻnn.n[--].|[----.]aliyn.b[ʻl].|[---.btl]t.ʻn[t.-.]p h.|[---.---]n.|[-----].|[-----].|[---. 10[76].2.34
at.ypʻt.b[--.---].|aliyn.bʻl[.---].|drkt k.mšl[-.---].|b riš k.aymr[.---].|ṯpṭ.nhr.y 2.1[137].4
m.pʻrt[.---].|šm k.mdd.i[l.---].|bt ksp y.d[--.---].|b d.aliyn b[ʻl.---].|kd.ynaṣn[.---].|gršnn.l k[si.mlk h.l nḫt.l kḥṯ]. 1[ʻNT.X].4.22
.|[---]q.hry.w yld.|[---]m.ḥbl.kṯ[r]t.|[---.bt]lt.ʻnt.|[---.ali]yn.bʻl.|[---.]mʻn.|[-----].|[-----].|[---.--]r.|[---.--]qk.|[---.- 11[132].1.8
--].d l ydʻ bn il.|[---.]pḫr kkbm.|[---.]dr dt.šmm.|[---.al]iyn bʻl.|[---].rkb.ʻrpt.|[---.]ǵš.l limm.|[---.]l yṯb.l arṣ.|[-- 10[76].1.6
]bʻlt h w yn.|[---.rk]b ʻrpt.|[---.--]n.w mnu dg.|[---.]l aliyn bʻl.|[---].rkb ʻrpt. 2001.2.17
tyn.bt.ikl.b prʻ.|yṣq.b irt.lbnn.mk.b šbʻ.|[ymm.---]k.aliyn.bʻl.|[---].rʻ h ab y.|[---.]ʻ[---]. 22.2[124].26
.|[--] h.ytn.w [--]u.l ytn.|[aḫ]r.mǵy.ʻ[d]t.ilm.|[w]yʻn.aliy[n.]bʻl.|[---.]tbʻ.l lṯpn.|[il.d]pid.l tbrk.|[krt.]ṯʻ.l tmr.nʻ 15[128].2.12
[---].aliyn.|[bʻl.---.-]ip.dpr k.|[---.-]mn k.ššrt.|[---.--]t.npš.ʻgl.|[-- 5[67].5.1
[------.i]qnim.[--].|[---.]aliyn.bʻl.|[---.--]k.mdd il.|y[m.---.]l ṯr.qdqd h.|il[.--.]rḥq.b 4[51].7.2
yʻlm.|[k gmn.al]iyn.bʻl.|[ṭtbḫ.šbʻm.]ḥmrm.|[k gm]n.al[i]yn.b[ʻl].|[---]ḫ h.tšt bm.ʻ[--].|[---.]zr h.ybm.l ilm.|[id]k. 6.1.29[49.1.1]
[-----].|[------.]ṯr.|[---.aliy]n.bʻl.|[------.]yrḫ.zbl.|[--.kṯ]r w ḫss.|[---]n.rḥm y.ršp z 15[128].2.3
šr.ḥtk.dgn.|k.ibr.l bʻl[.yl]d.|w rum.l rkb.ʻrpt.|yšmḫ.aliyn.bʻl. 10[76].3.38

algbṯ

ʻšrt.ksp h.|ḫmš.kkr.qnm.|ṯlṯt.w.ṯlṯt.ksp h.|arbʻ.kkr.|algbṯ.arbʻt.|ksp h.|kkr.šʻrt.|šbʻt.ksp h.|ḫmš.mqdm.dnyn.| 1127.15

alḏy

.ḥdṯn.yḥmn.bnil.|ʻdn.w.ildgn.ḥṯbm.|tdǵlm.iln.bʻ[l]n.alḏy.|tdn.ṣr[--.--]t.ʻzn.mtn.n[bd]g.|ḥrš qṯn[.---.]dqn.bʻln.|ǵ 2011.21

alz

].|bn.qnḏ.|ṣmq[-].|bn.anny.|bn.ʻmtdl.|bn.ʻmyn.|bn.alz.|bn.birtn.|[bn.]ylkn.|[bn.]krwn.|[bn.-]ty.|[bn.]iršn.|bn 117[325].1.12
bnšm.dt.iṯ.alpm.l hm.|bn.niršn.|bn.adty.|bn.alz.|bn.birtn.|bn.mlṣ.|bn.q[--].|bn.[---].|bn.ṯ[-]r.|bn.grdn. 2023.1.4
n.|mʻqb.|ṯpn.|mʻr.|lbnm.|nḫl.|yʻny.|atn.|utly.|bn.alz.|bn ḫlm.|bn.ḏmr.|bn.ʻyn.|ubnyn.|rpš d ydy.|ǵbl.|mlk 2075.15
.mlk.|bn.alṯn.|bn.ṯmyr.|ẓbr.|bn.ṯdṯb.|bn.ʻrmn.|bn.alz.|bn.mṣrn.|bn.ʻdy.|bn.ršpy.|[---.]mn.|[--.-]sn.|[bn.-]ny. 115[301].2.14
---].|b[n.---].|b[n.---].|bn.[---].|bn.a[--].|w.nḥl h.|bn.alz.|w.nḥl h.|bn.sny.|bn.ablḥ.|[-----].|w [---].|bn.[---].|bn. 2163.1.12

alzy

mit.šmn.d.nm[-.]b d.mzy.alzy.|ḫmš.kkr.ḥlb.|ḫmš.kkr.brr.|kkr.ḫmš.mat.kbd.ṯlṯ.šm[n 1135.1

alḫb

t.drʻ.w.tšʻm.drt.|[w].ṯmnym.l.mit.dd.ḥpr.bnšm.|b.gt.alḫb.ṯṯm.drʻ.w.ḫmšm.drt.w.ṯṯm.dd.|ḥpr.bnšm.|b.gt.knpy. 1098.16

alḫn

.b.bt.ṣdqš[lm].|[a]ṯt.aḥt.b.bt.rpi[--].|[aṯt.]w.bt h.b.bt.alḫn.|[aṯt.w.]pǵt.aḥt.b.bt.tt.|[aṯt.w.]bt h.b.bt.trǵds.|[---.]aṯ 80[119].25
ksp.|kkrm.šʻrt.štt.b d.gg[ʻt].|b.ʻšrt.ksp.|ṯlṯ.uṯbm.b d.alḫn.b.ʻšrt[.k]sp.|rṯ.l.ql.d.ybl.prd.|b.ṯql.w.nṣp.ksp.|ṯmn.lbš 2101.11
kbt.ḫmš.ʻšr h.prs.|bt.mrkbt.w l šant.ṯṯ.|l bt.ʻšrm.|bt alḫnm.ṯlṯm ṯṯ kbd. 2105.4

aly

t.l.mlk.|ʻbdyrḫ.bn.ṯyl.|ʻbdn.w.aṯt h.w.bn h.|gpn.bn[.a]ly.|bn.rqd[y].ṯbg.|iḫmlk.|ypʻn w.aṯt h.|anntn.yṣr.|annm 2068.20
ʻl.bn.n[--].|ḥy bn.dnn.ṯkt.|ilthm.bn.dnn.ṯkt.|šbʻl.bn.aly.ṯkt.|klby.bn.iḫy.ṯkt.|pss.bn.buly.ṯkt.|ʻpṣpn.bn.ʻdy.ṯkt.| 2085.6

alkbl

r.|atlg.|mit.ksp.d mkr.|ilštmʻ.|ʻšrm.l mit.ksp.|ʻl.bn.alkbl.šb[ny].|ʻšrm ksp.ʻl.|wrt.mtny.w ʻl.|prdny.aṯt h. 2107.16

all

mlbš.ṯrmnm.|[---]h.lbš.allm.lbnm.|[---].all.šmt.|[---].all.iqni.arbʻm.kbl.|[---].iqni.ʻšrm.ǵprt.|[---.š]pšg.iqni.mit.pṯ 1106.6
la.[-].|w ṯmn.nqpnt.ʻd.|k lbš.km.lpš.dm a[ḫ h].|km.all.dm.ary h.|k šbʻt.l šbʻm.aḫ h.ym[.--].|w ṯmnt.l ṯmnym.| 12[75].2.48
ṯrmnm.|k.ytn.w.b.bt.|mlk.mlbš.|ytn.l hm.|šbʻ.lbšm.allm.|l ušḫry.|ṯlṯ.mat.pṯtm.|l.mgmr.b.ṯlṯ.|šnt. 1107.9
at.šʻrt.ḫmšm.kbd.|[---.-]nd.l.mlbš.ṯrmnm.|[---]h.lbš.allm.lbnm.|[---].all.šmt.|[---].all.iqni.arbʻm.kbl.|[---].iqni.ʻš 1106.4
m.lb.ʻn[t].|aṯr.bʻl.tiḫd.m[t].|b sin.lpš.tšṣq[n h].|b qṣ.all.tšu.g h.w[ṣ]|ḥ.at.mt.tn.aḫ y.|w ʻn.bn.ilm.mt.mh.|taršn 6[49].2.11
tbky.pǵt.bm.lb.|tdmʻ.bm.kbd.|tmzʻ.kst.dnil.mt.|rpi.al.ǵzr.mt.hrnmy.|apnk.dnil.mt.|rpi.yṣly.ʻrpt.b |ḥm.un.yr.ʻ 19[1AQHT].1.37
.|bl.šrʻ.thmtm.bl.|ṭbn.ql.bʻl.k tmzʻ.|kst.dnil.mt.rpi.|all.ǵzr.m[t.]hr[nmy].|gm.l bt[h.dnil.k yṣḥ].|šmʻ.pǵt.ṯkmt[. 19[1AQHT].1.48
d.|[---.-]nd.l.mlbš.ṯrmnm.|[---]h.lbš.allm.lbnm.|[---].all.šmt.|[---].all.iqni.arbʻm.kbl.|[---].iqni.ʻšrm.ǵprt.|[---.š]p 1106.5
š[bʻ].mat.šʻrt.|[---.]iqnu.[---.]lbš.ṯrmnm.|[---.iqn]i.lbš.al[l.---].|[---].ṯṯ.lbš[.---].|[---.]kbd.ṯṯ.i[qnu.---].|[---.]ǵprt.ʻš[r 1106.21

almg

.|nḥ.ṯṯ.mat.|šm[n].rqḥ.|kkrm.brdl.|mit.tišrm.|ṯlṯm.almg.|ḫmšm.kkr.|qnm.|ʻšrm.kk[r].|brr.|[ʻ]šrm.npš.|ʻšrm. 141[120].8

almnt

qṣr.npš.l tdy.|ṯšm.ʻl.dl.l pn k.|l tšlḥm.ytm.bʻd.|ksl k.almnt.km.|aḫt.ʻrš.mdw.anšt.|ʻrš.zbln.rd.l mlk.|amlk.l drkt 16.6[127].50
.ǵzm].|tdbr.w[ǵ]rm[.ṯṯwy].|šqlt.b ǵlt.yd k.|l tdn.dn.almnt.|l ṯṯpṭ.ṯpṭ.qṣr.npš.|km.aḫt.ʻrš.mdw.|anšt.ʻrš.zbln.|r 16.6[127].33

k ǵz.ǵzm.tdbr. | w ǵrm.ṯṯwy.šqlt. | b ǵlt.yd k.l tdn. | dn.almnt.l ṯṯpṭ. | ṯpṭ qṣr.npš.l tdy. | ṯšm.ʿl.dl.l pn k. | l tšlḥm.ytm 16.6[127].46
bt.kmyr. | aṯr.ṯn.ṯn.hlk. | aṯr.ṯlṯ.kl hm. | aḥd.bt h.ysgr. | almnt.škr. | tškr.zbl.ʿršm. | yšu.ʿwr. | mzl.ymzl. | w ybl.trḫ.ḥdṯ 14[KRT].4.185
bt.kmyr. | [a]ṯr.ṯn.ṯn.hlk. | aṯr.ṯlṯ.kl hm̃. | yḥd.bt h.sgr. | almnt.škr. | tškr.zbl.ʿršm. | yšu.ʿwr.mzl. | ymzl.w yṣi.trḫ. | ḥdṯ 14[KRT].2.97
rnm[y]. | ytšu.ytb.b ap.ṯǵr.tḥt. | adrm.d b grn.ydn. | dn.almnt.yṯpṭ.ṯpṭ.ytm. | b nši ʿn h.w yphn.b alp. | šd.rbt.kmn.hl 17[2AQHT].5.8
y.ytšu. | [ytb.b ap.ṯ]ǵr[.t]ḥt. | [adrm.d b grn.y]dn. | [dn.almnt.y]ṯpṭ. | [ṯpṭ.ytm.---] h. | [---.---]n. | [-----]. | hlk.[---.b n]ši 19[1AQHT].1.24

almš

.midḫ. | [--]n.b.ayly. | [-]lyn.b.nġḥt. | [---.]b.nh[-]t. | [---.]almš. | [---.--]ty. | [---.-]i[-.--]. | [-----]. | [---.--]y. | [---.--]lm. | ḫḏ 2118.17

aln

ḫ. | l dmgy.amt. | aṯrt.qḥ. | ksan k.ḥdg k. | ḥtl k.w ẓi. | b aln.tk m. | b tk.mlbr. | ilšiy. | kry amt. | ʿpr.ʿẓm yd. | ugrm.ḫl.l 12[75].1.20

alnr

bt šbn. | iyʿdm.w bʿl h. | ddy. | ʿmy. | iwrnr. | alnr. | maḫdt. | aby. | [-----]. | [-]nt. | ydn. | mnn.w bn h. | ṯkn. 107[15].6

alp

tnt. | ʿšr.rṯm. | kkr[.-].ḫt. | mitm[.p]ṯtm. | ṯlṯm[.---].kst. | alp.a[bn.ṣ]rp. 1114.6
a[ṯt h]. | wšṯn.bn h. | ṯmgdl.yknʿmy.w.aṯt h. | w.bn h.w.alp.aḫ[d]. | aǵltn.[--]y.w[.aṯt h]. | w.bn h.w.alp.w.[---]. | [-]ln.[1080.6
t. | ʿbdilm.ṯṯ mat. | šmmn.bn.ʿdš.ṯṯ mat. | ušknym. | ypʿ.alpm. | aḫ[m]lk.bn.nskn.alpm. | krw.šlmy. | alpm. | atn.bṣry.al 1060.2.2
it.dnn. | mitm.iqnu. | ḫmš.ʿšr.qn.nʿm.ʿn[m]. | ṯn.ḥblm.alp.alp.am[-]. | ṯmn.ḥblm.šbʿ.šbʿ.ma[-]. | ʿšr.kkr.rtn. | b d.šmʿ 1128.30
rat.bqʿ. | ṯlṯ.[-]ṯt.aš[ʿ]t.šmn.uz. | mi[t].ygb.bqʿ. | a[--].ʿṯ. | a[l]pm.alpnm. | ṯlṯ.m[a]t.art.ḥkpt. | mit.dnn. | mitm.iqnu. | ḫ 1128.25
dnn. | mitm.iqnu. | ḫmš.ʿšr.qn.nʿm.ʿn[m]. | ṯn.ḥblm.alp.alp.am[-]. | ṯmn.ḥblm.šbʿ.šbʿ.ma[-]. | ʿšr.kkr.rtn. | b d.šmʿy.bn 1128.30
yl | y.zbl.mlk.ʿllm y.km.tdd. | ʿnt.ṣd.tštr.ʿpt.šmm. | ṭbḫ.alpm.ap ṣin.šql.ṯrm. | w mri ilm.ʿglm.dt.šnt. | imr.qmṣ.llim.k 22.2[124].12
--.---]. | ymḫṣ k.k[--.---]. | il.dbḥ.[---]. | pʿr.b[--.---]. | ṭbḫ.alp[m.ap.ṣin.šql]. | ṯrm.w [mri.ilm.ʿglm.dt.šnt]. | imr.[qmṣ.lli 1[ʿNT.X].4.30
m. | ḫrṣ.ʿdbt.bht[h.bʿ]l. | yʿdb.hd.ʿdb[.ʿd]bt. | hkl h.ṭbḫ.alpm[.ap]. | ṣin.šql.ṯrm[.w]m | ria.il.ʿglm.d[t]. | šnt.imr.qmṣ.l 4[51].6.40
ṯ.w.ytn.hm.l k. | w.lḥt.alpm.ḫršm. | k.rgmt.l y.bly m. | alpm.aršt.l k.w.l y. | mn.bnš.d.l.i[--].ʿ[m k]. | l.alpm.w.l.y[n.-- 2064.23
knym. | ypʿ.alpm. | aḫ[m]lk.bn.nskn.alpm. | krw.šlmy. | alpm. | atn.bṣry.alpm. | lbnym. | ṯm[n.]alp mitm. | ilbʿl ḫmš m 1060.2.5
t.ila.il š[--.]il. | d yqny.ḏdm.yd.mḫṣt.a[qh]t.ǵ | zr.tmḫṣ.alpm.ib.št[-.]št. | ḥršm l ahlm p[---.]km. | [-]bl lb h.km.bṯn.y[19[1AQHT].4.221
h.aḥd.b gt.nḫl. | aḥd.b gt.knpy.w.aḥd.b gt.ṯrmn. | aḥd.alp.idṯn.d aḥd.b.ʿnqpat. | [aḥd.al]p.d aǵlmn. | [d aḥd b.g]t gb 1129.11
lṯ. | ṯmn.kkr.brr. | arbʿ.alpm.pḥm. | ḫmš.mat.kbd. | arbʿ.alpm.iqni. | ḫmš.mat.kbd. | ṯlṯm.ḫmš kbd ktn. | ḫmš.rṯm. | ḫm 1130.5
| ṣlʿt.alp.mri. | ʿšr.bmt.alp.mri. | ṯn.nšbm. | ṯmnym.tbṯḫ.alp. | uz.mrat.mlḥt. | arbʿ.uzm.mrat.bqʿ. | ṯlṯ.[-]ṯt.aš[ʿ]t.šmn.u 1128.19
. | b.ʿšrt.ksp.b.a[--]. | ṯqlm.ḫr[ṣ.]b.ṯmnt.ksp. | ʿšrt.ksp.b.alp.[b d].bn.[---]. | tšʿ.ṣin.b.tšʿt.ksp. | mšlt.b.ṯql.ksp. | kdwṯ.l.g 2101.21
spr.irgmn. | ṯlṯ.ḫmš.alpm. | b d.brq.maḫdy. | kkr.ṯlṯ. | b d.bn.by.ar[y]. | alpm.ṯlṯ. | b 1134.2
[n.]alp mitm. | ilbʿl ḫmš m[at]. | ʿdn.ḫmš.mat. | bn.[-]d.alp. | bn.[-]pn.ṯṯ mat. 1060.2.11
ʿl.alpm.bnš.yd. | tiṯm[n].w.ʿl.[---]. | [-]rym.t[i]ṯṯmn. | šnl.bn.ṣ[q] 2104.1
.d mit. | ḫmš.ṯnt.d ṯl | ṯ mat. | ṯt.ṯnt.d alp | alpm.ṯlṯ ktt. | alp.brr. | kkr.tznt. | ḫmšt.kkr tyt. 1130.15
nš. | šrp.w ṣp ḫršḫ. | ʿlm b ǵb ḫyr. | ṯmn l ṯlṯm ṣin. | šbʿ.alpm. | bt bʿl.ugrt.ṯn šm. | ʿlm.l ršp.mlk. | alp w.š.l bʿlt. | bwrm UG5.12.B.5
.w.aḥd.b gt.ṯrmn. | aḥd.alp.idṯn.d aḥd.b.ʿnqpat. | [aḥd.al]p.d aǵlmn. | [d aḥd b.g]t gbry. | [---].aḥd.aḥd.b.yʿny. | [---.- 1129.12
[---.]ḫlmt.alp.šnt.w[.---]. | šntm.alp.d krr[.---]. | alp.pr.bʿl.[---]. | w prt.tkt.[---]. | šnt.[---]. | ššw. 2158.1.2
n.ṯn[.---]. | w.ṯlṯ.alp h.[---]. | swn.qrty.w.[b]n h[.---]. | w.alp h.w.a[r]bʿ.l.arbʿ[m.---]. | pln.ṯmry.w.ṯn.bn h.w[.---]. | ymr 2044.7
--]. | am[-]n.[---]. | w.a[ṯt] h.[---]. | ḫḏmtn.ṯn[.---]. | w.ṯlṯ.alp h.[---]. | swn.qrty.w.[b]n h[.---]. | w.alp h.w.a[r]bʿ.l.arbʿ[2044.5
m. | w šnpt.il š. | l ʿnt.ḥl š.ṯn šm. | l gṯrm.ǵṣ b šmal. | d alpm.w alp w š. | šrp.w šlmm kmm. | l bʿl.ṣpn b ʿrʿr. | pamt ṯlṯ UG5.13.27
.bly m. | alpm.aršt.l k.w.l y. | mn.bnš.d.l.i[--].ʿ[m k]. | l.alpm.w.l.y[n.--]t. | w.bl.bnš.hw[-.--]y. | w.k.at.trg[m.--]. | w.[-- 2064.25
lhm.[ṯkmn.w šnm]. | dqt.ršp.šrp.w š[lmm.dqtm]. | ilh[.a]lp.w š[.il]hm.[gdlt.ilhm]. | bʿ[l.š].aṯrt[.š.ṯkm]n w [šnm.š]. | ʿ 35[3].14
m.ṯkmn.w šnm dqt. | ršp.dqt.šrp w šlmm.dqtm. | [i]lh.alp w š ilhm.gdl[t.]ilhm. | [b]ʿl š.aṯrt.š.ṯkmn w šnm.š. | ʿnt.š.r 34[1].5
ilhm]. | ṯkmn.w [šnm.dqt.ršp.šrp]. | w šlmm.[dqtm.ilh.alp.w š]. | ilhm.gd[lt.ilhm.bʿl.š.aṯrt.š]. | ṯkmn.w š[nm.š.ʿnt.š.r APP.II[173].15
]. | il.ḫyr.ilib.š. | arṣ w šmm.š. | il.š.kṯrt.š. | dgn.š.bʿl.ḫlb alp w š. | bʿl ṣpn alp.w.š. | ṯrty.alp.w.š. | yrḫ.š.ṣpn.š. | kṯr š ʿṯtr. UG5.9.2.4
š.ʿnt ṣpn.alp. | w š.pdry š.ddmš š. | w b urbt.ilib š. | bʿl alp w š. | dgn.š.il tʿḏr.š. | bʿl š.ʿnt š.ršp š. | šlmm. | w šnpt.il š. | UG5.13.20
il.š.kṯrt.š. | dgn.š.bʿl.ḫlb alp w š. | bʿl ṣpn alp.w.š. | ṯrty.alp.w.š. | yrḫ.š.ṣpn.š. | kṯr š ʿṯtr.š. | [ʿṯt]rt.š.šgr w iṯm š. | [---.]š. UG5.9.2.6
.w ynt.qr[t]. | w mtntm.š l rmš. | w kbd.w š.l šlm kbd. | alp.w š.l bʿl ṣpn. | dqt l ṣpn.šrp.w šlmm. | kmm.w bbt.bʿl.ugr UG5.13.9
y[nt] qrt. | [w mtmt]m.[š.l] rm[š.]kbd.w š. | [l šlm.kbd.al]p.w š.[l] bʿl.ṣpn. | [dqt.l.ṣpn.šrp].w š[l]mm.kmm. | [w bbt. 36[9].1.14
yrḫ ḫyr.b ym ḥdṯ. | alp.w š.l bʿlt bhtm. | b arbʿt ʿšrt.bʿl. | ʿrkm. | b ṯmnt.ʿšrt.yr | tḫ UG5.12.A.2
ṯlṯm ṣin. | šbʿ.alpm. | bt bʿl.ugrt.ṯn šm. | ʿlm.l ršp.mlk. | alp w.š.l bʿlt. | bwrm š.iṯtqb. | w š.nbk m w.š. | gt mlk š.ʿlm. | l UG5.12.B.8
. | šrp.w šlmm ilib š. | bʿl ugrt š.bʿl ḫlb š. | yrḫ š.ʿnt ṣpn.alp. | w š.pdry š.ddmš š. | w b urbt.ilib š. | bʿl alp w š. | dgn.š.il UG5.13.17
bt.bʿl.ugrt. | w kdm.w npš ilib. | gdlt.il š.bʿl š.ʿnt. | ṣpn.alp.w š.pdry.š. | šrp.w šlmm ilib š. | bʿl ugrt š.bʿl ḫlb š. | yrḫ š. UG5.13.14
lk.l.prgl.ṣqrn.b.gg. | ar[bʿ.]arbʿ.mṯbt.azmr.b h.š.šr[-]. | al[p.w].š.šlmm.pamt.šbʿ.klb h. | yr[--.]mlk.ṣbu.špš.w.ḥl.mlk. 35[3].52
rr. | ʿlm.tzǵ.b ǵb.ṣpn. | nḥkt.ksp.w ḫrṣ ṭʿ ṯn šm l btbt. | alp.w š šrp.alp šlmm. | l bʿl.ʿṣr l ṣpn. | npš.w.š.l ršp bbt. | [ʿ]ṣr UG5.12.A.9
npt.il š. | l ʿnt.ḥl š.ṯn šm. | l gṯrm.ǵṣ b šmal. | d alpm.w alp w š. | šrp.w šlmm kmm. | l bʿl.ṣpn b ʿrʿr. | pamt ṯlṯm š l qr UG5.13.27
rṣ w šmm.š. | il.š.kṯrt.š. | dgn.š.bʿl.ḫlb alp w š. | bʿl ṣpn alp.w.š. | ṯrty.alp.w.š. | yrḫ.š.ṣpn.š. | kṯr š ʿṯtr.š. | [ʿṯt]rt.š.šgr w UG5.9.2.5
dbḥ.ṣp[n.---]. | il.alp.w š[.---]. | bʿlm.alp.w š[.---]. | bʿlm.alp.w š[.---]. | arṣ.w šmm.š.kṯr[t] š.yrḫ[.---]. | ṣpn.š.kṯr.š.pdry UG5.9.1.4
dbḥ.ṣp[n.---]. | il.alp.w š[.---]. | bʿlm.alp.w š[.---]. | bʿlm.alp.w š[.---]. | arṣ.w šmm.š.kṯr[t] š.yrḫ[.--- UG5.9.1.3
dbḥ.ṣp[n.---]. | il.alp.w š[.---]. | bʿlm.alp.w š[.---]. | bʿlm.alp.w š[.---]. | arṣ.w šm UG5.9.1.2
. | l špš[.w y]rḫ.l gṯr.ṯn. | [ṯql.ksp].ṯb.ap.w npš. | [---].bt.alp w š. | [---.--]m.l gṯrm. | [---.]l ʿnt m. | [---.--]rm.d krm. | [--- 33[5].16
pm. | [w.]ṯlṯm.ṣin. | anndr.yknʿmy. | w.aṯt h.w.bn h. | w.alp.w.tš[ʿ.]ṣin. 1080.17

kkr.w.[ml]tḫ.tyt.[---].|[b]šbʻ[m.w.n]ṣp.ksp.|[tgm]r.[alp.w.]tlt.mat. 2101.28
.|[--]d mʻqby[.---].|swn.qrty.w[.att h].|[w].bn h.w.tn.alpm.|[w.]tltm.ṣin.|anndr.yknʻmy.|w.att h.w.bn h.|w.alp. 1080.13
r[-]m.[-]trmt.|lbš.w [-]tn.ušpġt.|ḫr[-].tltt.mzn.|drk.š.alp.w tlt.|ṣin.šlm[m.]šbʻ pamt.|l ilm.šb[ʻ.]l ktr.|ʻlm.tʻrbn.gt 33[5].6
[-]dmu.apsty.b[--].|w.bn h.w att h.w.alp.w tmn.ṣin.|[-]dln.qmnzy.w.a[tt h].|wštn.bn h.|tmgdl.y 1080.2
.|w.bn h.w.alp.aḫ[d].|aġltn.[--]y.w[.att h].|w.bn h.w.alp.w.[---].|[-]ln.[---].|w.tn.bn [h.---].|[--]d mʻqby[.---].|sw 1080.8
arbʻm.qšt.|alp ḥzm.w alp.|ntq.tn.qlʻm.|ḫmš.ṣmdm.w ḫrṣ.|tryn.sswm. 1123.2
.ʻdb.|[---].tʻtqn.|[---.-]ʻb.idk.|[l ytn.pnm.tk.]in.bb.b alp ḥzr.|[rbt.kmn.l pʻ]n.ʻnt.|[yhbr.w yql.yšt]ḥwyn.w y|[kb 1[ʻNT.IX].2.14
.sswm.|nʻmm.[--].ttm.w.at.|ngt.w.ytn.hm.l k.|w.lḥt.alpm.ḫršm.|k.rgmt.l y.bly m.|alpm.aršt.l k.w.l y.|mn.bnš. 2064.21
l.yšn.pbl.|mlk.l qr.tigt.ibr h.|l ql.nhqt.ḥmr h.|l gʻt.alp.ḥrt.zġt.|klb.ṣpr.w ylak.|mlakm.l k.ʻm.krt.|mswn h.tḥ 14[KRT].3.122
n.pbl.|mlk.l [qr.]tiqt.|ibr h[.l]ql.nhqt.|ḥmr[h.l gʻt.]alp.|ḥrt[.l z]ġt.klb.|[ṣ]pr[.apn]k.|[pb]l[.mlk.g]m.l att |[h.k 14[KRT].5.225
.ul.mad.|tlt.mat.rbt.|ḫpt.d bl.spr.|tnn.d bl.hg.|hlk.l alpm.ḫdd.|w l rbt.kmyr.|[a]tr.tn.tn.hlk.|atr.tlt.kl hm.|yḥd 14[KRT].2.92
[b.w ysi.ʻdn].|mʻ[.ṣ]bu h.u[l.mad].|tlt.mat.rbt.|hlk.l alpm.ḫdd.|w l.rbt.kmyr.|atr.tn.tn.hlk.|atr.tlt.kl hm.|aḥd.b 14[KRT].4.180
rbʻ.kkrm.|tmn.mat.kbd.|pwt.|tmn.mat.pttm.|kkrm.alpm.|ḫmš.mat.kbd.|abn.ṣrp. 2051.8
alpm.arbʻ.mat.k[bd].|mit.b d.yd[r]m.|alp ḫmš mat.kbd.d[--]. 2109.3
[---].dt.it.|[---].tlt.kbd.|[---].alpm.ḫmš.mat.|šbʻm[.t]šʻ.kbd.|tgmr.uz.ġrn.arbʻ.mat.|tgmr 1129.3
mpḫm.|b d.ḫss.mṣbtm.|yṣq.ksp.yšl|ḥ.ḫrṣ.yṣq.ksp.|l alpm.ḫrṣ.yṣq|m.l rbbt.|yṣq-ḫym.w tbtḫ.|kt.il.dt.rbtm.|kt.i 4[51].1.28
nt.|hll.snnt.apnk.dnil.|mt.rpi.ap.hn.ġzr.mt.|hrnmy.alp.ytbḫ.l kt|rt.yšlḥm.ktrt.w y|ššq.bnt.[hl]l.snnt.|hn.ym.w 17[2AQHT].2.29
[t]ḫm.ittl.|l mnn.ilm.|tġr k.tšlm k.|tʻzz k.alp ymm.|w rbt.šnt.|b ʻd ʻlm...gnʻ.|iršt.aršt.|l aḫ y.l rʻ y.dt 1019.1.4
n.atrt.|špq.ilm.krm.y[n].|špq.ilht.ḫprt[.yn].|špq.ilm.alpm.y[n].|špq.ilht.arḫt[.yn].|špq.ilm.kḥtm.yn.|špq.ilht.ks 4[51].6.49
b arbʻt.ʻšr[t].|yrtḥṣ.mlk.b[rr].|b ym.mlat.|tqln.alpm.|yrḫ.ʻšrt.l bʻ[l].|dqtm.w ynt.qr[t].|w mtntm.š l rmš.| UG5.13.4
[mlk.b ar]bʻt.ʻ[š]rt.yrtḥṣ.mlk.brr.|[b ym.ml]at.y[ql]n.al[p]m.yrḫ.ʻšrt.|[l bʻl.ṣ]pn.[dq]tm.w y[nt] qrt.|[w mtmt]m.[36[9].1.11
m.arṣ.ttbḫ.šbʻm.|rumm.k gmn.aliyn.|[b]ʻl.ttbḫ.šbʻm.alpm.|[k g]mn.aliyn.bʻl.|[tt]bḫ.šbʻm.ṣin.|[k gm]n.aliyn.bʻl. 6[62].1.20
tlt.d yṣa.|b d.šmmn.|l argmn.|l nskm.|tmn.kkrm.|alp.kbd.|[m]itm.kbd. 147[90].6
spr.ḥtbn.sbrdnm.|ḫmš.kkrm.alp kb[d].|tlt.l.nskm.birtym.|b d.urtn.w.tt.mat.brr.|b.tmn 2101.2
m.ridn.|mt.šmm.ks.qdš.|l tphn h.att.krpn.|l tʻn.atrt.alp.|kd.yqḥ.b ḫmr.|rbt.ymsk.b msk h.|qm.ybd.w yšr.|mṣlt 3[ʻNT].1.15
mš[m.ḥm]r.škm.|[---.tt.dd.]gdl.tt.dd.šʻrm.|[---.hn.w.al]p.kd.nbt.kd.šmn.mr.|[---].kmn.ltḥ.sbbyn.|[---.-]ʻt.ltḥ.šš 142[12].8
[---.]tt.dd.gdl.tt.dd.šʻrm.|[---.-]hn.w.alp.kd.nbt.kd.šmn.mr.|[---.]arbʻ.mat.ḫswn.ltḥ.aqhr.|[---.ltḥ 142[12].2
nkl y|rḫ ytrḫ.ib tʻrb m b bh|t h.w atn mhr h l a|b h.alp ksp w rbt ḫ|rṣ.išlḥ zhrm iq|nim.atn šd h krm[m].|šd d 24[77].20
šny.|ʻrb[.---].|w.b.p[.--].|apš[ny].|b.yṣi h.|ḥwt.[---].|alp.k[sp].|tšʻn.|w.hm.al[-].|l.tšʻn.|mṣrm.|tmkrn.|ypḥ.ʻbdi 2116.11
.bn.ʻdš.tt mat.|ušknym.|ypʻ.alpm.|aḫ[m]lk.bn.nskn.alpm.|krw.šlmy.|alpm.|atn.bṣry.alpm.|lbnym.|tm[n.]alp 1060.2.3
-]n.w.aḫt h.arbʻm.|[--.-]dn.ʻšrm.|[--.-]dwn.tltm.w.šbʻ.alpm.|[kt]rmlk.ʻšrm.|[--]ny.ʻšrt.trbyt.|[--.]ʻbd.tltm.|[---].tlt 2054.2.23
]lm.yʻ[--.---].|[--.-]g[-.-]s w [---].|w yn[t.q]rt.y[---].|w al[p.l]il.w bu[rm.---].|ytk.gdlt.ilhm.[tkmn.w šnm].|dqt.ršp 35[3].11
--.---].|t.k[-]ml.[---].|l[---].w y[nt.qrt.---].|[---.--]n[.w alp.l il.w bu]|[rm.---.ytk.gdlt.ilhm].|tkmn.w [šnm.dqt.ršp.š APP.II[173].12
š.ym š.[bʻ]l knp.|[---.g]dlt.ṣpn.dqt.šrp.w [š]lmm.|[---.a]lp.l bʻl.w atrt.ʻṣr[m] l inš.|[ilm.---].lbbmm.gdlt.ʻrb špš w 36[9].1.8
[---.]arḫt.tld[n].|a[lp].l btlt.ʻnt.|w ypt l ybmt.li[mm].|w yʻny.aliyn[.bʻl].|lm. 10[76].3.3
bnšm.dt.it.alpm.l hm.|bn.niršn.|bn.adty.|bn.alz.|bn.birtn.|bn.mlṣ.|b 2023.1.1
.|aḫ[m]lk.bn.nskn.alpm.|krw.šlmy.|alpm.|atn.bṣry.alpm.|lbnym.|tm[n.]alp mitm.|ilbʻl ḫmš m[at].|ʻdn.ḫmš.m 1060.2.6
[---.--]t.slḫ.npš.tʻ w[.--.k]bdm.|[---.--]mm.tn.šm.w alp.l[--]n.|[---.]š.il š.bʻl š.dgn š.|[---.--]r.w tt pl.gdlt.[ṣ]pn.dq 36[9].1.2
pm.|krw.šlmy.|alpm.|atn.bṣry.alpm.|lbnym.|tm[n.]alp mitm.|ilbʻl ḫmš m[at].|ʻdn.ḫmš.mat.|bn.[-]d.alp.|bn.[- 1060.2.8
š.kkr.ḥlb.|ḫmš.kkr.brr.|kkr.ḫmš.mat.kbd.tlt.šm[n].|alp.mitm.kbd.tlt.ḥlb.|šbʻ.l.ʻšrm.kkr.tlt.|d.ybl.blym. 1135.5
iršt.yṣḥm.|arbʻ.alpm.|mitm.kbd.tlt.|arbʻ.kkrm.|tmn.mat.kbd.|pwt.|tmn. 2051.2
-].|[-----].|[-----].|alp[.---.--]r.|mit.lḥ[m.---.-]dyt.|ṣlʻt.alp.mri.|ʻšr.bmt.alp.mri.|tn.nšbm.|tmnym.tbtḫ.alp.|uz.mr 1128.16
ʻšrm ddm kbd[.-] l alpm mrim.|tt ddm l ṣin mrat.|ʻšr ddm.l šmʻrgm.|ʻšr ddm. 1100.1
|alp[.---.--]r.|mit.lḥ[m.---.-]dyt.|ṣlʻt.alp.mri.|ʻšr.bmt.alp.mri.|tn.nšbm.|tmnym.tbtḫ.alp.|uz.mrat.mlḥt.|arbʻ.uz 1128.17
arbʻm.qšt.|alp ḥzm.w alp.|ntq.tn.qlʻm.|ḫmš.ṣmdm.w ḫrṣ.|tryn.sswm.|tryn.aḥd. 1123.2
.|nʻr y.tḥ.l pn.ib.|hn.hm.yrgm.mlk.|bʻl y.tmġyy.hn.|alpm.sswm.hnd.|w.mlk.bʻl y.bnš.|bnny.ʻmn.|mlakty.hnd.| 1012.32
nš.|bnny.ʻmn.|mlakty.hnd.|ylak ʻm y.|w.tʻl.tḥ.hn.|[a]lpm.sswm.|[---].w.tb. 1012.38
r].|[-]dʻ.k.iḫd.[---].|w.mlk.bʻl y.|lm.škn.hnk.|l ʻbd h.alpm.s[sw]m.|rgmt.ʻly.tḥ.lm.|l.ytn.hm.mlk.[b]ʻl y.|w.hn.ib 1012.24
-.]š.il š.bʻl š.dgn š.|[---.--]r.w tt pl.gdlt.[ṣ]pn.dqt.|[---.al]p ʻnt.gdlt.b tltt mrm.|[---.i]l š.bʻl š.atrt.š.ym š.[bʻ]l knp.|[36[9].1.5
bt.alpm.|ʻšr.bnšm.|ḫmš.bnši.tt[---].|ʻšr.b gt.[---].|tn.ʻšr.b.gt.ir 2103.1
ḫmšm.dd.|nʻr.|ḫmšm.tišr.|ḫmš.ktnt.|ḫmš.tnt.alpm.|ʻšrm.hbn.|tlt.mat.dd.|šʻrm.|mit.šmn.|ʻšr.kat.|zrw. 2102.5
[sp]r.akl[.---].tryn.|[tg]mr.akl.b.g[t.b]ir.alp.|[ʻ]šrm.l.mit.ḥ[p]r.ʻbdm.|mitm.drt.tmnym.drt.|tgmr.a 2013.2
alpm.pḥm.ḫm[š].mat.kbd.|b d.tt.w.tlt.ktnt.b dm.tt.|w.tmn 1110.1
tmn.kkr.tlt.|tmn.kkr.brr.|arbʻ.alpm.pḥm.|ḫmš.mat.kbd.|arbʻ.alpm.iqni.|ḫmš.mat.kbd.|tl 1130.3
dr.bʻl.š.ršp.š.ddmš.š.|w šlmm.ilib.š.i[l.--]m d gbl.ṣpn.al[p].|pḫr.ilm.š.ym.š[.k]nr.š.[--.]ʻṣrm gdlt.|bʻlm.kmm.bʻlm. UG5.9.1.10
[---.]ḫlmt.alp.šnt.w[.---].|šntm.alp.d krr[.---].|alp.pr.bʻl.[---].|w prt.tkt.[---].|šnt.[---].|ššw.ʻttrt.w ššw.ʻ[nt. 2158.1.3
-]zn.a[--.---].|[---.--]y.ns[--.---].|[---.]trgm[.-----].|[---.]alp.p[--.---].|[--.]ht.ap[.---].|[---.]iln[--.---]. 63[26].2.3
rn.arbʻ.mat.|tgmr.uz.aḫmn.arbʻ.mat.|arbʻm.kbd.|tlt.alp.ṣpr.dt.aḥd.|ḥrt h.aḥd.b gt.nḫl.|aḥd.b gt.knpy.w.aḥd.b 1129.8
hlk.aḫt h.bʻl.yʻn.tdrq.|ybnt.ab h.šrḥq.att.l pnn h.|št.alp.qdm h.mria.w tk.|pn h.tḥspn.m h.w trḥṣ.|tl.šmm.šmn. 3[ʻNT].4.85
.|w tb l mspr..k tlakn.|ġlmm.|aḥr.mġy.ktr.w ḫss.|št.alp.qdm h.mra.|w tk.pn h.tʻdb.ksu.|w yttb.l ymn.aliyn.|bʻl 4[51].5.107
b š[---].|bʻl.ytb.l ks[i.mlk h].|bn.dgn.l kḥ[t.drkt h].|l alp.ql.z[--.---].|l np ql.nd.[----].|tlk.w tr.b[ḫl].|b nʻmm.b ys 10[76].3.16
ks[i.mlk h].|bn.dgn.l kḥ[t.drkt h].|l alp.ql.z[--.---].|l np ql.nd.[----].|tlk.w.tr.b[ḫl].|b nʻmm.b ys[mm.---].|arḫ.ar 10[76].3.17
t[.mat.a]rbʻ.kbd.|w.[---.-]mʻt.|tlt[m.---.-]rm.|ʻšr[.---].alpm.|arbʻ.ddm.l.k[-]ḫ.|tmnym.dd.dd.kbd.|[l].mdr[ġ]lm.| 2012.17

alpm.arb‘.mat.k[bd]. | mit.b d.yd[r]m. | alp ḫmš mat.kbd.d[- 2109.1
. | [---].ḫmšm.ḥmr.škm. | [tt.dd.]gdl.ṯṯ.dd.š‘rm. | [---.a]lp.arb‘.mat.tyt. | [---.kd.]nbt.k[d.]šmn.mr. | [---.l]ṯḥ.sb[by]n 142[12].14
dqt.ṯ‘.ynt.ṯ m.dqt.ṯ‘m. | mtntm nkbd.alp.š.l il. | gdlt.ilhm.ṯkmn.w šnm dqt. | ršp.dqt.šrp w šlmm.d 34[1].2
. | ḥš.bht m.tbn[n]. | ḥš.trmmn.hk[l m]. | b tk.ṣrrt.ṣpn. | alp.šd.aḫd bt. | rbt.kmn.hkl. | w y‘n.kṯr.w ḫss. | šm‘.l aliyn b‘l 4[51].5.118
.arṣ.ṯl.šm[m.t]sk h. | rbb.nsk h.kbkbm. | ttpp.anhbm.d alp.šd[.ẓu h.b ym]. | ṯl[.---]. 3['NT].4.89
ttql.b ym.trtḥ[ṣ.--]. | [----.a]dm.tium.b ǵlp y[m.--]. | d alp šd.ẓu h.b ym.t[---]. | tlbš.npṣ.ǵzr.tšt.ḫ[---.b] | nšg h.ḥrb.t 19[1AQHT].4.205
ttpp.anhb[m.d alp.šd]. | ẓu h.b ym[.---]. | [--]rn.l [---]. 3['NT].3.03
.arṣ.ṯlṯ.mtḥ.ǵyrm. | idk.l ttn pnm.‘m.b‘l. | mrym.ṣpn.b alp.šd.rbt.kmn. | hlk.aḫt h.b‘l.y‘n.tdrq. | ybnt.ab h.šrḥq.aṯt.l 3['NT].4.82
grn.ydn. | dn.almnt.yṯpṭ.ṯpṭ.ytm. | b nši ‘n h.w yphn.b alp. | šd.rbt.kmn.hlk.kṯr. | k y‘n.w y‘n.tdrq.ḫss. | hlk.qšt.ybln. 17[2AQHT].5.9
qb k.[ttb‘]. | [bt]lt.‘nt.idk.l ttn.[pnm]. | ['m.a]qht.ǵzr.b alp.š[d]. | [rbt.]kmn.w ṣḥq.btlt.['nt]. | [tšu.]g h.w tṣḥ.šm‘.m['. 18[3AQHT].1.21
.tk.ḫqkpt. | il.kl h.kptr. | ksu.ṯbt h.ḫkpt. | arṣ.nḥlt h. | b alp.šd.rbt. | kmn.l p‘n.kṯ. | hbr.w ql.tšth | wy.w kbd hwt. | w r 3['NT.VI].6.17
.tk.ḫkpt.il.kl h]. | [kptr.]ks[u.ṯbt h.ḫkpt.arṣ.nḥlt h]. | b alp.šd.r[bt.kmn.l p‘n.kṯr]. | hbr.w ql.t[šthwy.w kbd.hwt]. | w 1['NT.IX].3.2
tan. | nrt.ilm.špš. | ṣḥrrt.la. | šmm.b yd.md | d.ilm.mt.b a | lp.šd.rbt.k | mn.l p‘n.mt. | hbr.w ql. | tšthwy.w k | bd hwt.w 4[51].8.24
ṣ. | p‘nm.w tr.arṣ. | idk.l ttn.pnm. | ‘m.b‘l.mrym.ṣpn. | b alp.šd.rbt.kmn. | ṣḥq.btlt.‘nt.tšu. | g h.w tṣḥ.tbšr b‘l. | bšrt k.y 4[51].5.86
.b ǵb.ṣpn. | nḥkt.ksp.w ḫrṣ ṯ‘ ṯn šm l btbt. | alp.w š šrp.alp šlmm. | l b‘l.‘ṣr l ṣpn. | npš.w.š.l ršp bbt. | [‘]ṣrm l h.ršp [-] UG5.12.A.9
mnḥ.b d.ybnn. | arb‘.mat. | l.alp.šmn. | nḥ.ṯṯ.mat. | šm[n].rqḥ. | kkrm.brdl. | mit.tišrm. | ṯlṯ 141[120].3
[---.]ḫlmt.alp.šnt.w[.---]. | šntm.alp.d krr[.---]. | alp.pr.b‘l.[---]. | w prt.tk 2158.1.1
ṣ igy.ḫmšm. | ṣṣ yrpi m[it.---]. | ṣṣ bn.š[m]mn ‘[šr.---]. | alp.ṯṯm. | kbd.mlḥt. 2097.20
‘šrm.kkr.kkrm. | alp.ṯṯ.mat.kbd. 2111.2
ḫmš.alpm. | b d.brq.maḫdy. | kkr.ṯlṯ. | b d.bn.by.ar[y]. | alpm.ṯlṯ. | b d.šim.il[š]tm‘y. 1134.6
mšm w. | ḫmš.ṯnt.d mit. | ḫmš.ṯnt.d ṯl | ṯ mat. | ṯt.ṯnt.d alp | alpm.ṯlṯ ktt. | alp.brr. | kkr.tznt. | ḫmšt.kkr tyt. 1130.13
. | b d.urtn.w.ṯṯ.mat.brr. | b.ṯmnym.ksp.ṯlṯt.kbd. | ḫmš.alp.ṯlṯ.l.ḫlby. | b d.tlmi.b.‘šrm.ḫmšt. | kbd.ksp. | kkrm.š‘rt.štt. 2101.6
. | arb‘m.ṯlṯ.mḫsrn. | mtb‘l.rišy. | ṯlṯm.ṯlṯ.‘l.nsk. | arym. | alp.ṯlṯ.‘l. | nsk.art. | ḫmš.mat.ṯlṯ. | ‘l.mtn.rišy. 1137.7
r[b‘]. | [---.-]aḥ.mqḥ mqḥm. | [---.--]t.‘šr rmǵt.[--]. | [---].alp.[---].alp. | [---.-]rbd.kbd.ṯnm kbd. | [---.-]nnm ṯrm. | [---.]ṯl 1145.1.6
w b[--.---]. | ilib[.---]. | alp.[---]. | ili[b.---]. | t‘r[.---]. | dq[t.---]. | nb[--.---]. 44[44].3
ḥr[š.---]. | [---.ṯ]lṯ.[---.]dpm. | [---.]bnšn. | [---.ḫ]mšm.ṣmd.alpm. | [---.bn]šm. | [---.]ḫmš.ṣmd.alpm. | [---.bnš]m. | [---.]‘šr. 2038.15
bnšn. | [---.ḫ]mšm.ṣmd.alpm. | [---.bn]šm. | [---.]ḫmš.ṣmd.alpm. | [---.bnš]m. | [---.]‘šr.ṣmd.alpm. | [---.bn]šm. | [---.--]m.ḫ 2038.17
bn]šm. | [---.]ḫmš.ṣmd.alpm. | [---.bnš]m. | [---.]‘šr.ṣmd.alpm. | [---.bn]šm. | [---.--]m.ḫmš.ṣmdm. | [---.bnš]m. 2038.19
iḫd.b qrb[.-]. | [--.t]ṯkḥ.w tiḫd.b uš[k.--]. | [-.b]‘l.yabd.l alp. | [---.bt]lt.‘nt. | [---]q.hry.w yld. | [---]m.ḥbl.kṯ[r]t. | [---.bt] 11[132].1.3
--]. | [-]m.m[--.---]. | [m]itm.dr[t.---]. | ['š]r.[k]bd[.---]. | [a]lpm[.---]. | tg[m]r.[---]. | ṯlṯ ma[t.---]. | ṯmnym[.---]. | [ṯ]mny[2013.24
[---.--]b. | [---.r]iš k. | [---.]bn ‘n km. | [---.]alp. | [---.]ym.rbt. | [---.]b nhrm. | ['b]r.gbl.‘br. | q‘l.‘br.iht. | np 3['NT.VI].6.4
alp[.---]. | mat[.---]. | ḫrṣ[.---]. | ṯlṯ.k[---]. | ṯlṯ.a[--.---]. | ḫmš[.---] 148[96].1
kl.b.gt.ǵ[l]. | ṯlṯ.mat.‘šrm[.---]. | ṯmnym.drt.a[--]. | drt.l.alpm[.---]. | šb‘m.ṯn.kbd[.ḥpr.‘b]dm. | tg[mr.---]. | [-]m.m[--.-- 2013.18
. | [---.]šdm. | [---.-]nm.prš.glbm. | [---.]‘gd.dqr. | [---.]ṯn.alpm. | [---.ṯ]n alpm. | [---.--]r[.‘]šr.ṣin. | [---.]klkl. 1142.8
-.-]aḥ.mqḥ mqḥm. | [---.--]t.‘šr rmǵt.[--]. | [---].alp.[---].alp. | [---.-]rbd.kbd.ṯnm kbd. | [---.-]nnm ṯrm. | [---.]ṯlṯ kbd.ṣi 1145.1.6
---]. | [-----]. | [---.--]r. | [---.--]qk. | [---.--]ik. | [-----]. | [---.]alp. | [---.--]ḫ. | [---.--]d[-]. | [---.--]t. 11[132].1.16
]. | [-----]. | [-----]. | [-----]. | [-----]. | [-----]. | [-----]. | [-----]. | alp[.---.--]r. | mit.lḥ[m.---.-]dyt. | ṣl‘t.alp.mri. | ‘šr.bmt.alp.mri 1128.14
--.-]nm.prš.glbm. | [---.]‘gd.dqr. | [---.]ṯn.alpm. | [---.ṯ]n alpm. | [---.--]r[.‘]šr.ṣin. | [---.]klkl. 1142.8
] il. | [---]ṯ. | klṯṯb. | gsn. | arm[w]l. | bn.ṣdqn. | ḫlbn. | tbq.alp. 2039.17
im[-.---]. | [---.]š.s[--.---]. | [---.-]lb[.--].š[.---]. | [---.]b‘lm al[p]. UG5.9.2.21
iwrḫz.[n]‘rm. | yṣr[.-]qb. | w.ṯn.bnš.iytlm. | w.‘šrm.ṣmd.alpm. 2066.2.7

alpy

n.s[-]p[-]. | bn.nrpd. | bn.ḥ[-]y. | b‘lskn. | bn.‘bd. | ḫyrn. | alpy. | bn.plsy. | bn.qrr[-]. | bn.ḥyl. | bn.g‘yn. | ḥyn. | bn.armg[-] 1035.1.18

alpn

| ṯlṯ.[-]ṯt.aš[‘]t.šmn.uz. | mi[t].ygb.bq‘. | a[--].‘ṭ. | a[l]pm.alpnm. | ṯlṯ.m[a]t.art.ḥkpt. | mit.dnn. | mitm.iqnu. | ḫmš.‘šr.q 1128.25

alt

-]y.tnn.w ygl.w ynsk.‘[-]. | [--]y.l arṣ[.id]y.alt.l aḥš.idy.alt.in l y. | [--]t.b‘l.ḥẓ.ršp.b[n].km.yr.klyt h.w lb h. | [ṯ]n.p k. 1001.1.2
k.tmt[ḫ] | ṣ.‘m.aliyn.b‘l. | ik.al.yšm[‘] k.ṯr. | il.ab k.l ys‘.alt. | ṯbt k.l yhpk.ksa.mlk k. | l yṯbr.ḫṭ.mṯpṭ k. | yru.bn ilm t.ṯ 6[49].6.27
bl.ym.l pn[.ṯ]pṭ[.n]hr. | [ik.a]l.yšm‘ k.ṯr.[i]l.ab k.l ys‘.[alt.]ṯ[bt | k.l y]hpk. | [ksa.]mlk k.l yṯbr.ḫṭ.mṯpṭ k.w y‘n[.‘ṯtr] 2.3[129].17
]ḥṣ.b‘l m[.--]y.tnn.w ygl.w ynsk.‘[-]. | [--]y.l arṣ[.id]y.alt.l aḥš.idy.alt.in l y. | [--]t.b‘l.ḥẓ.ršp.b[n].km.yr.klyt h.w lb 1001.1.2

alṯy

.ušn.yp km.ulp.]qṯy. | [ulp.ddmy.ulp.ḫry.ulp.ḫty.u]lp.alṯy. | [ulp.ǵbr.ulp.ḫbt km.ulp.mdll km.ulp]. | [qr zbl.ušn.yp APP.I[-].1.15
. | [---.u ṯḫṭu.ulp.qṯy.ulp.ddm]y. | [ulp.ḫry.ulp.ḫty.ulp.alṯy.ulp.ǵbr]. | [ulp.ḫbt km.ulp.mdll km.ulp.qr zbl]. | [u ṯḫṭu. 32[2].1.7
ušn.yp km.ulp.q[ṯy.ulp.ddm]y. | ulp.ḫry.ulp.ḫ[t]y.ulp.alṯy.ul[p.ǵbr.]ulp. | ḫbt km.ulp.m[dl]l km.ulp.qr zbl.u[š]n y 32[2].1.21
ṯt.ušn.yp kn.ulp qṯy. | ulp.ddmy.ul[p.ḫ]ry.ulp.ḫty.ulp.alṯy. | ulp.ǵbr.ulp.[ḫbt] kn[.u]lp.mdll kn.ulp qr z[bl]. | lšn yp 32[2].1.29
--].u ṯḫṭi[n.ulp.qṯy]. | ulp.ddmy.ul[p.ḫry.u]lp.ḫty.ulp[.alṯy.ulp.]ǵbr. | ulp.ḫbt kn.ulp.md[ll k]n.ulp.q[r zbl]. | u ṯḫṭin 32[2].1.12
. | [ušn.yp kn.ulp.qṯy.ulp.]ddmy.ulp ḫry. | [ulp.ḫty.ulp.alṯy.ulp.ǵbr.ul]p.ḫbt kn. | [ulp.mdll kn.ulp.qr zbl.ušn.y]p kn APP.I[-].1.5
--.ušn.yp kn.ulp.q]ṯy. | [ulp.ddmy.ulp.ḫry.ulp.ḫty.ulp.alṯy]. | [ulp.ǵbr.ulp.ḫbt kn.ulp.mdll kn.ulp.]qr zbl. | [ušn.yp APP.I[-].2.13
any.al[ṯy]. | d b atlg[.---]. | ḫmš ‘š[r]. | kkr.ṯ[lṯ]. | ṯt hrt[m]. | ṯn mq[2056.1
l ištnm. | kd l ḫty. | maḫdh. | kd l kblbn. | kdm.mṯḫ. | l.alṯy. | kd.l mrynm. | šb‘ yn. | l mrynm. | b yṯbmlk. | kdm.ǵbiš ḫ 1090.8

d.qlt].|ankn.rgmt.l.b'l y.|l.špš.'lm.l.'ttrt.|l.'nt.l.kl.il.alṯ[y].|nmry.mlk.'lm.|mlk n.b'l y.ḥw[t.--].|yšhr k.w.'m.ṣ[-- 2008.1.8
[s]ǵr.bn.bdn.|[sǵ]r.bn.psḥn.|alty.|sǵr.npr.|bn.ḫty.|ṯn.bnš ibrdr.|bnš tlmi.|sǵr.ḥryn.|'d 2082.3
spr.ḥršm.|liy.bn.qqln.|[---.a]lty.|[-----].|[---]tl.|[---]'bl.|[---]bln.|[---]dy.|[---.n]ḥl h.|[- 1036.3

alṯyy

ṯṯ.mat.ṯṯm.kbd šmn.|l.abrm.alṯyy.|[m]it.ṯlṯm.kbd.šmn.|[l.]abrm.mšrm.|[mi]tm.arb'm.ṯ 2095.2

alṯn

.|bn.army.|bn.krmn.|bn.ykn.|bn.'ṯtrab.|uṣn[-].|bn.alṯn.|bn.aš[-]š.|bn.štn.|bn.ilš.|bn.tnabn.|bn.ḥṣn.|ṣprn.|bn 1046.1.14
nqdm.|bn.alṯn.|bn.dly.|bn.btry.|bn.ḫdmn.|[bn].šty.|[bn].kdgdl.|[---. 2018.2
n.ṯbrn.|bn.ḫgby.|bn.pity.|bn.slgyn.|'zn.bn.mlk.|bn.alṯn.|bn.ṯmyr.|ẓbr.|bn.ṯdṯb.|bn.'rmn.|bn.alz.|bn.mṣrn.|b 115[301].2.9

alṯt

] šmḥ[.---].|ddm gt dprnm.|l ḥršm.|ddm l 'nqt.|dd l alṯt.w l lmdt h.|dd l iḫyn.|dd l [---]. 1101.11

am

m.tmr.zbl.mlk.|šmm.tlak.ṭl.amr..|bn km k bk[r.z]bl.am..|rkm.agzrt[.--].arḫ..|b'l.azrt.'nt.[-]ld.|kbd h.l yd' hr h. 13[6].28

amd

ym].|mlk.yṣm.y l km.qr.mym.d '[l k].|mḫṣ.aqht.ǵzr.amd.gr bt il.|'nt.brḥ.p 'lm h.'nt.p dr[.dr].|'db.uḫry mṭ.yd h 19[1AQHT].3.153

amdy

bn.nz'n.|bn.slmz[-].|bn.k'[--].|bn.y[---].|[-----].|[bn.a]mdy.|bn.ḫlln.|bn.kṯn.|bn.abn.|bn.nskn.|bn.gmrn.|bn[.- 2021.2.2

amdn

[ly].|bn.snr[n].|bn.pzn[y].|bn.mg[lb].|bn.db[--].|bn.amd[n].|annš[-]. 2020.13
bn.asrn.|bn.šḫyn.|bn.abd'n.|bn.ḫnqn.|bn.nmq.|bn.amdn.|bn.špšn. 1067.8
.|w.nḥl hm.|bn.nqly.|bn.snrn.|bn.tgd.|bn.d[-]n.|bn.amdn.|bn.ṯmrn.|bn.pzny.|bn.mglb.|bn.[--]b.|bn.[---].|bn.[105[86].4

amḏy

.|[---].|mid[-].|ubš.|mṣb[t].|ḥl.y[---].|'rg[z].|y'r[t].|amḏ[y].|atl[g].|bṣr[y].|[---].|[---]y.|ar.|agm.w.ḫpty.|ḫlb.ṣ 71[113].43
].|[-----].|[-----].|[-----].|[ḫl]bkrd.|[ḫl]b'prm.|[q]dš.|[a]mdy.|[gn]'y.|m'qb.|agm.|ḫpty.|ypr.|ḫrṣb'.|uḫnp.|art.| 2058.1.29
d.ḥ[mr.---].|ṣ'.ḥmr.w[.---].|ṣ'q.ḥmr.w.[---].|ḫlb 'prm.amḏy.[ḥm]r.w bn[š].|gn'y.[---.bn]š.|uškn[.---].'šr.bnšm.|'n 2040.16
rkby.|šḥq.|ǵn.|ṣ'.|mld.|amḏy.|ḫlb'prm.|ḫpty.|[ḫr]ṣb'.|[m']rb. 2077.6
'.kbd.|ḫlb rpš arb'.'šr.|bq't ṯṯ.|irab ṯn.'šr.|ḫbš.ṯmn.|amḏy.arb'.'šr.|[-]n'y.ṯṯ.'šr. 67[110].11
rṣb'.aḥd.|ypr.arb.|m[-]qb.'šr.|ṯn'y.ṯlṯ.|ḫlb 'prm.ṯn.|tmḏy.ṯlṯ.|[--]rt.arb'.|[---].'šr. 70[112].13

amn

np[š.a]rš.|l.pn.b'[l y.l].pn.b'l y.|w.urk.ym.b'l y.|l.pn.amn.w.l.pn.|il.mṣrm.dt.ṭǵrn.|npš.špš.mlk.|rb.b'l y. 1018.21
|[---].amr k.|[---].k.ybt.mlk.|[---].w.ap.ank.|[---].l.ǵr.amn.|[---.-]ktt.hn.ib.|[---.]mlk.|[---.]adt y.td'.|w.ap.mlk.uḏ 1012.16

amṣ

bd k.|[---.a]dt y.mrḥqm.|[---].adt y.yšlm.|[---.]mlk n.amṣ.|[.---].nn.|[---.]qrt.dt.|[---.--]s'.hn.mlk.|[---.l]qḥ.hn.l.ḥ 1012.5
.---].|[---.]y.ḥr.ḥr.bnt.ḥ[---].|[--.]uḫd.[b']l m.'[--].yd k.amṣ.yd[.--].|[---.]ḥš[.-]nm[.--.]k.[--].w yḫnp[.---].|[---.]ylm.b 1001.1.14

amr

-].|k d lbšt.bir.mlak.|šmm.tmr.zbl.mlk.|šmm.tlak.ṭl.amr..|bn km k bk[r.z]bl.am..|rkm.agzrt[.--].arḫ..|b'l.azrt.' 13[6].27
.|ym.lm.qd[.---].|šmn.prst[.---].|ydr.hm.ym[.---].|'l amr.yu[ḫd.ksa.mlk h].|nḫt.kḥṯ.d[rkt h.b bt y].|aṣḥ.rpi[m.i 22.1[123].17
w yšr.|mṣltm.bd.n'm.|yšr.ǵzr.ṭb.ql.|'l.b'l.b ṣrrt.|ṣpn.ytmr.b'l.|bnt h.y'n.pdry.|bt.ar.apn.ṭly.|[bt.r]b.pdr.yd'.|[--- 3['NT].1.22
tšṯḥwy.pḫr.m'd.qmm.a[--].amr.|[ṯn]y.d't hm.išt.ištm.yitmr.ḥrb.ltšt.|[--]n hm.rgm.l ṯr.ab h.il.ṯḥm.ym.b'l km.|[ad 2.1[137].32
[-----].|[-----].|il.šm'.amr k.ph[.-].|k il.ḥkmt.k ṯr.lṭpn.|ṣḥ.ngr.il.ilš.il[š].|w aṯt h. 16[126].4.2
ṣ.|ṯlḥn.il.d mla.|mnm.dbbm.d |msdt.arṣ.|s'.il.dqt.k amr.|sknt.k ḥwt.yman.|d b h.rumm.l rbbt. 4[51].1.42
rp]um.tštyn.|[---.]il.d 'rgzm.|[---.]dt.'l.lty.|[---.]tdbḥ.amr.|ṯmn b qrb.hkl y.[aṯr h.rpum].|tdd.aṯr h.tdd.iln[ym.--- 20[121].1.10
dt.ṭpṭ.nhr.l p'n.il.|[l t]pl.l tšṯḥwy.pḫr.m'd.qmm.a[--].amr.|[ṯn]y.d't hm.išt.ištm.yitmr.ḥrb.ltšt.|[--]n hm.rgm.l ṯr. 2.1[137].31
d.t[k.ǵr.ll.l p'n.il].|al.tpl.al.tšṯḥwy.pḫr [m'd.qmm.a--.am]|r ṯny.d't km.w rgm.l ṯr.a[b.-.il.ṯny.l pḫr].|m'd.ṯḥm.ym 2.1[137].15
km.r[--].|amr [---].|ḫṯ.ṯk[l.---].|[-]l[--.---]. 2002.2

amril

.|ṯd[y]n.b.gllṯky.|lbw[-].uḫ.pdm.b.y'rt.|pǵyn.b.tpḥ.|amri[l].b.šrš.|aǵltn.b.midḫ.|[--]n.b.ayly.|[-]lyn.b.ngḥt.|[---. 2118.12

amrb'l

.|ykr.|bly.|ṯb'm.|ḥdṯn.|rpty.|ilym.|bn.'br.|mnip'l.|amrb'l.|dqry.|ṯdy.|yp'b'l.|bdlm.|bn.pḏ[-].|bn.[---]. 1058.16

amry

---]'m.kd.|a[----]ḥr.ṯlṯ.|y[---.bn.]kran.ḫmš.|'[---].kd.|amry.kdm.|mnn.bn.gṯtn.kdm.|ynḥm.bn[.-]r[-]t.ṯlṯ.|plwn.k 136[84].8
l tgyn.|arb' spm l ll[-].|ṯn spm.l slyy.|ṯlṯ spm l dlšpš amry. 137.2[93].15

amrr

l.‘br.|q‘l.‘br.iht.|np.šmm.šmšr.|l dgy.aṯrt.|mǵ.l qdš.amrr.|idk.al.tnn.|pnm.tk.ḥqkpt.|il.kl h.kptr.|ksu.ṯbt h.ḥk 3[‘NT.VI].6.11
tn.aṯrt.l bmt.‘r.|l ysmsmt.bmt.pḥl.|qdš.yuḫdm.šb‘r.|amrr.k kbkb.l pnm.|aṯr.btlt.‘nt.|w b‘l.tb‘.mrym.ṣpn.|idk.l 4[51].4.17
ṯr[.il.ab -.w t‘n.rbt].|aṯr[t.ym.šm‘.l qdš].|w am[rr.l dgy.rbt].|aṯrt.ym[.mdl.‘r].|ṣmd.pḥl[.št.gpnm.dt].|k 4[51].4.3
t].|ksp.dt.yr[q.nqbnm].|‘db.gpn.atnt[y].|yšm‘.qd.w amr[r].|mdl.‘r.ṣmd.pḥl.|št.gpnm.dt.ksp.|dt.yrq.nqbnm.|‘d 4[51].4.8
.dt.ksp.|dt.yrq.nqbnm.|‘db.gpn.atnt h.|yḥbq.qdš.w amrr.|yštn.aṯrt.l bmt.‘r.|l ysmsmt.bmt.pḥl.|qdš.yuḫdm.šb‘ 4[51].4.13
mrmnmn.|brrn aryn.|a[-]ḥn tlyn.|atdb w ‘r.|qdš w amrr.|ṯḫr w bd.|[k]ṯr ḫss šlm.|šlm il bt.|šlm il ḫš[t].|ršp i UG5.7.71

amt

dnt.w dbḥ.tdmm.|amht.k b h.bṯt.l tbṯ.|w b h.tdmmt.amht.|aḫr.mǵy.aliyn.b‘l.|mǵyt.btlt.‘nt.|tmgnn.rbt[.a]ṯrt y 4[51].3.22
pn il d pid.|p ‘bd.an.‘nn.aṯrt.|p.‘bd.ank.aḫd.ulṯ.|hm.amt.aṯrt.tlbn.|lbnt.ybn.bt.l b‘l.|km ilm.w ḥẓr.k bn.aṯrt.|w 4[51].4.61
m.|lb.w ygmd.bm kbd.|ẓi.at.l tlš.|amt.yrḫ.|l dmgy.amt.|aṯrt.qḥ.|ksan k.ḥdg k.|ḥtl k.w ẓi.|b aln.tk m.|b tk.m 12[75].1.16
dy.|‘bdil[.b]n ṣdqn.|bnšm.h[-]mt.yphm.|kbby.yd.bt.amt.|ilmlk. 2045.7
bk.krt.|b dm‘.n‘mn.ǵlm.|il.trḥṣ.w tadm.|rḥṣ[.y]d k.amt.|uṣb[‘t k.]‘d[.ṯ]km.|‘rb[.b ẓl.ḫmt].|qḥ im[r.b yd k].|im 14[KRT].2.63
t.yḫṭ.w ḥlm.|‘bd.il.w hdrt.|yrtḥṣ.w yadm.|yrḥṣ.yd h.amt h.|uṣb‘t h.‘d.ṯkm.|‘rb.b ẓl.ḫmt.lqḥ.|imr.dbḥ.b yd h.|ll 14[KRT].3.157
m.tqrṣn.|il.yẓḥq.bm.|lb.w ygmd.bm kbd.|ẓi.at.l tlš.|amt.yrḫ.|l dmgy.amt.|aṯrt.qḥ.|ksan k.ḥdg k.|ḥtl k.w ẓi.|b 12[75].1.15
.]yd.mqm h.|[w ‘b]d.‘lm.ṯlṯ.|[ssw]m.mrkbt b trbṣ bn.amt.|[tn.b]nm.aqny.|[tn.ṯa]rm.amid.|[w y‘n].ṯr.ab h.il.|d[- 14[KRT].2.56
.|rkb.‘rpt.dbḥ.|bṯt.w dbḥ.w dbḥ.|dnt.w dbḥ.tdmm.|amht.k b h.bṯt.l tbṯ.|w b h.tdmmt.amht.|aḫr.mǵy.aliyn.b‘l. 4[51].3.21
d.mqm h].|w ‘bd[.‘lm.ṯlṯ].|sswm.m[rkbt].|b trbṣ.[bn.amt].|q[ḥ.kr]t[.šlmm].|š[lmm.]al.t[ṣr].|udm[.r]bt.w u[dm]. 14[KRT].6.273
.yd.mqm] h.|‘bd[.‘lm.ṯlṯ].|ss[wm.mrkbt].|b[trbṣ.bn.amt].|[qḥ.krt.šlmm].|[šlmm.al.tṣr].|[udm.rbt.w udm].|[ṯrr 14[KRT].5.254
rṣ.|yd.mqm h.w ‘bd.‘lm.|ṯlṯ.sswm.mrkbt.|b trbṣ.bn.amt.|qḥ.krt.šlmm.|šlmm.w ng.mlk.|l bt y.rḥq.krt.|l ḥẓr y. 14[KRT].3.129
h.---].|d bnšm.yd.grbs hm.|w.tn.‘šr h.ḫpnt.|[s]šwm.amtm.‘kyt.|yd.llḫ hm.|w.ṯlṯ.l.‘šrm.|ḫpnt.sšwm.ṯn.|pddm. 2049.4
.ḥdg k.|ḥtl k.w ẓi.|b aln.tk m.|b tk.mlbr.|ilšiy.|kry amt.|‘pr.‘ẓm yd.|ugrm.ḫl.ld.|aklm.tbrk k.|w ld ‘qqm.|ilm 12[75].1.23
ṣ].|yd.mqm h.w ‘bd.|‘lm.ṯlṯ.sswm.|mrkbt.b trbṣ.|bn.amt.p d.[i]n.|b bt y.ttn.tn.|l y.mṯt.ḥry.|n‘mt.šbḥ.bkr k.|d 14[KRT].6.287
rṣ.|yd.mqm h.w ‘bd.|‘lm.ṯlṯ.sswm.mrkbt.|b trbṣt.bn.amt.|p d.in.b bt y.ttn.|tn.l y.mṯt.ḥry.|n‘mt.špḥ.bkr k.|d k. 14[KRT].3.141
n.|kdm.l.mdrǵlm.|kd.l.mṣrym.|kd.mštt.mlk.|kd.bn.amht [-]t.|w.bn.mṣrym.|arb‘m.yn.|l.ḫrd.|ḫmšm.ḫmš.|kbd 1089.9

amtm

b.|ydn.|il‘nt.|bn.urt.|ydn.|qṭn.|bn.asr.|bn.‘dy.|bn.amt[m].|myn.|šr.|bn.zql.|bn.iḫy.|bn.iyṯr.|bn.‘yn.|bn.ǵzl. 2117.3.49

amtrn

] ‘mtdl ṯlṯm.|ṣṣ ‘mlbi ṯṯ l ‘šrm.|ṣṣ bn adty ḫmšm.|ṣṣ amtrn arb‘m.|ṣṣ iytlm mit ṯlṯm kbd.|ṣṣ m[l]k ‘šrm.|ṣṣ abš[- 2097.8
kl.|šd.b d.klb.|šd.b d.klby.|šd.b d.iytlm.|ṯn.šdm.b d.amtrn.|šd.b d.iwrm[--].|šd.b d.yṯpr.|šd.b d.krb[-].|šd.b d.b 2090.12
.bn.‘yn.|ṯn.šdm.b d.klṯṯb.|šd.b d.krz[n].|ṯlṯ.šdm.b d.amtr[n].|ṯn.šdm.b d.skn.|šd.b d[.‘b]dyrḫ.|šd.b [d.--]ṯṯb. 2090.22

an

lt.[‘nt].|[tšu.]g h.w tṣḥ.šm‘.m[‘.l a]|[qht.ǵ]zr.at.aḫ.w an.a[ḫt k].|[---].šb‘.ṯir k.[---].|[---.]ab y.ndt.ank[.---].|[---.--] 18[3AQHT].1.24
k.|w abqṯ.aliyn.b‘l.|w t‘n.btlt.‘nt.|an.l an.y špš.|an.l an.il.yǵr[.-].|tǵr k.š[---.---].|yštd[.---].|dr[.---].|r[---.---]. 6[49].4.47
ph.b palt.bṣ[q]l.|yph.b yǵlm.bṣql.y[ḥb]q.|w ynšq.aḥl.an bṣ[ql].|ynp‘.b palt.bṣql yp‘ b yǵlm.|ur.tisp k.yd.aqht.|ǵ 19[1AQHT].2.64
ḥ.at.mt.tn.aḫ y.|w ‘n.bn.ilm.mt.mh.|taršn.l btlt.‘nt.|an.itlk.w aṣd.kl.|ǵr.l kbd.arṣ.kl.gb‘.|l kbd.šdm.npš.ḫsrt.|b 6[49].2.15
ḥm.aliyn.|bn.b‘l.hwt.aliy.qrdm.|bhṯ.bn.ilm.mt.‘bd k.an.|w d ‘lm k.šmḫ.bn.ilm.mt.|[---.]g h.w aṣḥ.ik.yṣḥn.|[b‘l.‘ 5[67].2.19
|tḥm.aliyn.b‘l.hwt.aliy.|qrdm.bhṯ.l bn.ilm mt.|‘bd k.an.w d.‘lm k.|tb‘.w l.ytb.ilm.idk.|l ytn.pn.‘m.bn.ilm.mt.|tk 5[67].2.12
t.‘rš.mdw.anšt.|‘rš.zbln.rd.l mlk.|amlk.l drkt k.aṯb.|an.w y‘ny.krt ṯ‘.yṯbr.|ḥrn.y bn.yṯbr.ḥrn.|riš k.‘ṯrt.šm.b‘l.| 16.6[127].54
.ḥ[mt.---.-]hm.yasp.ḥmt.|[---.š]pš.l [hrm.ǵrpl].‘l.arṣ.l an.|[ḥ]mt.i[l.w] ḥrn.yisp.ḥmt.|[b‘l.w]dgn[.yi]sp.ḥmt.‘nt.w UG5.8.12
t.šḥr.w šlm.|[yis]p.ḥmt.isp.[šp]š l hrm.ǵrpl.‘l arṣ.|[l a]n ḥmt.l p[.n]ṯk.abd.l p.akl ṯm.dl.|[---.q]l.bl.tbḥ[n.l]azd.‘r UG5.8.20
|bl lyt.‘l.umt k.|w abqṯ.aliyn.b‘l.|w t‘n.btlt.‘nt.|an.l an.y špš.|an.l an.il.yǵr[.-].|tǵr k.š[---.---].|yštd[.---].|dr[.-- 6[49].4.46
mt k.|w abqṯ.aliyn.b‘l.|w t‘n.btlt.‘nt.|an.l an.y špš.|an.l an.il.yǵr[.-].|tǵr k.š[---.---].|yštd[.---].|dr[.---].|r[---.-- 6[49].4.47
bt[.t]|bl lyt.‘l.umt k.|w abqṯ.aliyn.b‘l.|w t‘n.btlt.‘nt.|an.l an.y špš.|an.l an.il.yǵr[.-].|tǵr k.š[---.---].|yštd[.---].|d 6[49].4.46
bt.aṯrt ym.|bl.nmlk.yd‘.ylḥn.|w y‘n.lṭpn.il d pi|d dq.anm.l yrẓ.|‘m.b‘l.l y‘db.mrḥ.|‘m.bn.dgn.k tms m.|w ‘n.rbt. 6.1.50[49.1.22]
ryt.spsg.ysk.|[l]riš.ḥrṣ.l ẓr.qdqd y.|[--.]mt.kl.amt.w an.mtm.amt.|[ap.m]ṯn.rgmm.argm.qštm.|[----.]mhrm.ht.tṣ 17[2AQHT].6.38
ṯly.bt rb.|mṯb.arṣ.bt y‘bdr.|w y‘n lṭpn il d pid.|p ‘bd.an.‘nn.aṯrt.|p. bd.ank.aḫd.ulṯ.|hm.amt.aṯrt.tlbn.|lbnt.ybn. 4[51].4.59
q[dš.b ǵr.nḥ]lt y.|w t[‘n].btlt.[‘]nt.ṯṯb.|[ybmt.]limm.[a]n.aqry.|[b arṣ].mlḥmt.[aš]t.b ‘pr m.|ddym.ask[.šlm.]l kb 3[‘NT].4.66
t.bg[--.---].|[---.-]dm.mlak.ym.t‘dt.ṯpṭ.nh[r.---].|[---].an.rgmt.l ym.b‘l km.ad[n km.ṯpṭ].|[nhr.---.]hwt.gmr.hd.l w 2.1[137].45
.šnt k.|[--.]w špt k.l tššy.hm.tqrm.l mt.b rn k.|[--]ḫp.an.arnn.ql.špš.ḥw.bṭnm.uḫd.b‘lm.|[--.a]ṯm.prṯl.l riš h.ḥmt.ṯ 1001.1.6
|šblt.b akt.šblt.yp‘.|b ḥmdrt.šblt.yḥ[bq].|w ynšq.aḥl.an.šblt.|tp‘.b aklt.šblt.tp‘[.b ḥm]drt.|ur.tisp k.yd.aqht.ǵz[r] 19[1AQHT].2.71
]m.ap.mṯn.rgmm.|argmn.lk.lk.‘nn.ilm.|atm.bštm.w an.šnt.|uǵr.l rḥq.ilm.inbb.|l rḥq.ilnym.ṯn.mṯpdm.|tḥt.‘nt.a 3[‘NT].4.77
y h.---].|w y‘n.kṯr.w ḫss[.lk.lk.‘nn.ilm.]|atm.bštm.w an[.šnt.kptr].|l rḥq.ilm.ḥkp[t.l rḥq.ilnym].|ṯn.mṯpdm.tḥt.[‘ 1[‘NT.IX].3.18
t.‘rš.mdw.|anšt.‘rš.zbln.|rd.l mlk.amlk.|l drkt.k aṯb.an.|ytb‘.yṣb ǵlm.‘l.|ab h.y‘rb.yšu g h.|w yṣḥ.šm‘ m‘.l krt.|ṯ 16.6[127].38

anan

d]mt qdš.|[---].b.dmt qdš.|[---].b.dmt qdš.|[---.--]n.b.anan.|[--]yl.b.bq‘t.b.gt.tgyn.|[--]in.b.trzy.|[--]yn.b.glltky.|ṯ 2118.5

ands

|[-]lkynt.nsk.ṯlṯ.|[-]by.nsk.ṯlṯ.|šmny.|ḫršn.|ldn.|bn.ands.|bn.ann.|bn.‘bdpdr.|šd.iyry.l.‘bdb‘l.|šd.šmmn.l.bn.št 1102.14

anhb

ttpp.anhb[m.d alp.šd]. | ẓu h.b ym[.---]. | [--]rn.l [---]. 3[ʻNT].3.03
šmm.šmn.arṣ.ṭl.šm[m.t]sk h. | rbb.nsk h.kbkbm. | ttpp.anhbm.d alp.šd[.ẓu h.b ym]. | ṭl[.---]. 3[ʻNT].4.89
[-]p[-]l[.---]. | k lli.[---]. | kpr.[šbʻ.bnt.rḥ.gdm.w anhbm]. | w tqr[y.ǵlmm.b št.ǵr.---]. | [ʻ]d tš[bʻ.tmtḫṣ.---]. | kly 7.2[130].3
ǵy h.---]. | [-].l yʻmdn.i[---.---]. | kpr.šbʻ bn[t.rḥ.gdm.w anhbm]. | kla[t.ṯǵ]r[t.bht.ʻnt.w tqry.ǵlmm.b št.ǵr]. | ap ʻnt t 7.2[130].23
n[--.---.-]š[--]. | kpr.šbʻ.bnt.rḥ.gdm. | w anhbm.klat.ṯǵrt. | bht.ʻnt.w tqry.ǵlmm. | b št.ǵr.w hln.ʻnt.tm 3[ʻNT].2.3

anḫ

.b šbʻ.ymm. | [w]yqrb.bʻl.b ḥnt h.abynt. | [d]nil.mt.rpi anḫ.ǵzr. | [mt.]hrnmy.d in.bn.l h. | km.aḫ h.w šrš.km.ary h. | 17[2AQHT].1.18

anḫr

w yʻny.bn. | ilm.mt.npš[.-]. | npš.lbun. | thw.w npš. | anḫr.b ym. | brkt.šbšt. | k rumm.hm. | ʻn.kd̲d.aylt. | mt hm.ks. UG5.4.5
| mt.hwt.ydd.bn.il. | ǵzr.p np.š.npš.lbim. | thw.hm.brlt.anḫr. | b ym.hm.brk y.tkšd. | rumm.ʻn.kd̲d.aylt. | hm.imt.imt. 5[67].1.15

any

anyt.miḫd[t]. | br.ṯpṭbʻ[l.---]. | br.dmty[.---]. | ṯkt.ydln[.---]. | ṯ 84[319].1.1
any.al[ty]. | d b atlg[.---]. | ḫmš ʻš[r]. | kkr.ṯ[lṯ]. | ṯt hrt[m]. | ṯn 2056.1
ǵr.ṯ[--.---]. | ṣbu.any[t]. | bn.kṯan. | ǵr.tšʻ[.ʻšr.b]nš. | ṣbu.any[t]. | bn abdḫ[r]. | pdym. | ḫmš.bnšm. | snrym. | tšʻ.bnš[m]. 79[83].10
n. | ṭbq[ym]. | mʻq[bym]. | tšʻ.ʻ[šr.bnš]. | ǵr.ṯ[--.---]. | ṣbu.any[t]. | bn.kṯan. | ǵr.tšʻ[.ʻšr.b]nš. | ṣbu.any[t]. | bn abdḫ[r]. | p 79[83].7
ḥrš.anyt. | bnš.gt.glʻd. | bnš.gt.ngr. | rʻym. | bn.ḫri[-]. | bnš.gt.ʻṯtrt. 1040.1
. | yry[.---.]br. | ydn[.---].kry. | bn.ydd[.---.b]r. | prkl.bʻl.any.d.b d.abr[-]. 2123.7
ršy. | yʻd̲rd. | ayaḫ. | bn.aylt. | ḫmš.mat.arbʻm. | kbd.ksp.anyt. | d.ʻrb.b.anyt. | l.mlk.gbl. | w.ḫmšm.ksp. | lqḥ.mlk.gbl. | l 2106.11
rb.b.anyt. | l.mlk.gbl. | w.ḫmšm.ksp. | lqḥ.mlk.gbl. | lbš.anyt h. | bʻrm.ksp. | mḫr.hn. 2106.16
lk. | ht.lik[t.--.]mlk[.--]. | w.mlk.yštal.b.hn[--]. | hmt.w.anyt.hm.tʻ[rb]. | mkr.hn d.w.rgm.ank[.--]. | mlkt.ybqš.anyt.w 2008.2.11
.anyt.hm.tʻ[rb]. | mkr.hn d.w.rgm.ank[.--]. | mlkt.ybqš.anyt.w.at[--]. | w mkr n.mlk[.---]. 2008.2.13
n. | ʻtq.b d.aṯt.ab ṣrry. | tbky k.ab.ǵr.bʻl. | ṣpn.ḥlm.qdš. | any.ḥlm.adr.ḥl. | rḥb.mknpt.ap. | [k]rt.bnm.il.špḥ. | lṭpn.w qd 16.1[125].8
tn.špḥ. | [l]ṭpn.l yḥ.t[b]ky k. | ab.ǵr.bʻl.ṣ[p]n.ḥlm. | qdš.nny.ḥ[l]m.adr. | ḥl.rḥb.mk[npt]. | ap.krt bn[m.il]. | špḥ.lṭpn[. 16.2[125].108
y. | lḥt.akl.ʻm y. | mid y w ǵbn y. | w.bn y.hn kt. | yškn.anyt. | ym.yšrr. | w.ak[l.---]. | [--].š[--.--]. 2061.13
[.-]. | w [k]l hm.b d. | rb.tmtt.lqḥt. | w.ṯṯb.ank.l hm. | w.any k.ṯt. | by.ʻky.ʻryt. | w.aḫ y.mhk. | b lb h.al.yšt. 2059.24
mlk. | bʻl h.ngr.ḥwt k. | w l.a[--]t.tšknn. | ḫmšm.l mi[t].any. | tškn[n.--]h.k[--]. | w šnm[.--.]w[.--]. | w ʻprm.a[--.--]n. | [2062.1.4
hn ny.ʻm n. | šlm.ṯm ny. | ʻm k.mnm[.š]lm. | rgm.ṯṯ[b]. | any kn.dt. | likt.mṣrm. | hn dt.b.ṣr. | mtt.by. | gšm.adr. | nškḥ. 2059.10
yaḫ. | bn.aylt. | ḫmš.mat.arbʻm. | kbd.ksp.anyt. | d.ʻrb.b.anyt. | l.mlk.gbl. | w.ḫmšm.ksp. | lqḥ.mlk.gbl. | lbš.anyt h. | bʻr 2106.12
[-----]. | [---.--]y. | [-----]. | [any.l yṣ]ḥ.ṯr. | [il.ab h.i]l.mlk. | [d yknn h.yṣ]ḥ.aṯ | [rt.w bn h. 4[51].1.4
in.d ʻln h. | klny n.q[š] h.n[bln]. | klny n[.n]bl.ks h. | [an]y.l yṣḥ.ṯr il.ab h. | [i]l.mlk.d yknn h.yṣḥ. | aṯrt.w bn h.ilt. 4[51].4.47
ʻl.ṭpṭ n. | in.d ʻln h.klny y.qš h. | nbln.klny y.nbl.ks h. | any.l yṣḥ.ṯr.il.ab h.il. | mlk.d yknn h.yṣḥ.aṯrt. | w bn h.ilt.w ṣ 3[ʻNT.VI].5.43
an[y]t.mlk[.---]. | w.[ṯ]lṯ.brm.[---]. | arbʻ ʻtkm[.---]. 2057.1
ṣb[u.anyt]. | ʻdn. | ṭbq[ym]. | mʻq[bym]. | tšʻ.ʻ[šr.bnš]. | ǵr.ṯ[--.---]. | ṣ 79[83].1
mit.ʻ[šr.---]. | [ṯ]lṯ.abd[.---]. | [---.]anyt[.---]. | [-----]. | ʻšrm.l.umdym. | ʻšr.l.ktl. 2110.3

ank

bt yʻbdr. | w yʻn lṭpn il d pid. | p ʻbd.an.ʻnn.aṯrt. | p.ʻbd.ank.aḫd.ulṯ. | hm.amt.aṯrt.tlbn. | lbnt.ybn.bt.l bʻl. | km ilm.w 4[51].4.60
hmlt. | arṣ.mǵt.l nʻm y.arṣ. | dbr.ysmt.šd.šḥlmmt. | ngš.ank.aliyn bʻl. | ʻdbnn ank.imr.b p y. | k lli.b ṯbrn q y.ḫtu hw. 6[49].2.21
y.arṣ. | dbr.ysmt.šd.šḥlmmt. | ngš.ank.aliyn bʻl. | ʻdbnn ank.imr.b p y. | k lli.b ṯbrn q y.ḫtu hw. | nrt.ilm.špš.ṣḥrrt. | la 6[49].2.22
br.ḫt.mṯpṭ k.w yʻn[.ʻṯtr].dm[-]k[-]. | [--]ḥ.b y.ṯr.il.ab y.ank.in.bt[.l] y[.km.]ilm[.w] ḥẓr[.k bn]. | [qd]š.lbum.trd.b n[p 2.3[129].19
-]. | [---.--]dy.w.prʻ[.---]. | [---.]ytn.ml[--].ank.iphn. | [---.a]nk.i[--.--]slm.w.ytb. | [----.--]t.hw[-]y.h[--]r.w rgm.ank. | [-- 1002.37
rt.w ht.a[--]. | w hm.at.trg[m.---]. | w sip.u hw[.---]. | w ank.u šbt[--.---]. | ank.n[--]n[.---]. | kst.l[--.---]. | w.hw.uy.ʻn[--. 54.1.10[13.1.7]
| [---].ibʻr.a[--.]d̲mr. | [---.]w mlk.w rg[m.---]. | [--.rg]m.ank.[b]ʻr.[--]ny. | [--]n.bt k.[---.]bʻ[r.---]. | [--]my.b d[-.--]y.[--- 1002.54
.d l.tdʻ.šmm. | rgm l tdʻ.nšm.w l tbn. | hmlt.arṣ.at m.w ank. | ibǵy h.b tk.ǵr y.il.ṣpn. | b qdš.b ǵr.nḥlt y. | b nʻm.b gbʻ. 3[ʻNT].3.25
]ṣ. | thmt.[ʻmn.kbkbm.abn.brq]. | d l t[dʻ.šmm.at m.w ank]. | ibǵ[y h.b tk.ǵ]r y.il.ṣpn. | b q[dš.b ǵr.nḥ]lt y. | w t[ʻn].b 3[ʻNT].4.62
.ʻmn.kbkbm]. | rgm.l tdʻ.nš[m.w l tbn.hmlt.arṣ]. | at.w ank.ib[ǵy h.---]. | w yʻn.kṯr.w ḫss[.lk.lk.ʻnn.ilm.] | atm.bštm. 1[ʻNT.IX].3.16
.arṣ.thmt]. | ʻm kbkbm[.abn.brq.d l tdʻ.šmm.at m]. | w ank.ib[ǵy h.---]. | [-].l yʻmdn.i[---.---]. | kpr.šbʻ bn[t.rḥ.gdm.w 7.2[130].21
l hdm.yṯpd. | w yprq.lṣb w yṣḥq. | yšu.g h.w yṣḥ. | aṯbn.ank.w anḫn. | w tnḫ.b irt y.npš. | k ḥy.aliyn.bʻl. | k iṯ.zbl.bʻl.a 6[49].3.18
prq.lṣb.w yṣḥq. | pʻn.l hdm.yṯpd.yšu. | g h.w yṣḥ.aṯbn.ank. | w anḫn.w tnḫ.b irt y. | npš.k yld.bn.l y.km. | aḫ y.w šrš 17[2AQHT].2.12
.---]. | ʻnt.b ṣmt.mhr h.[---]. | aqht.w tbk.y[---.---]. | abn.ank.w ʻl.[qšt k.---.ʻl]. | qṣʻt k.at.l ḥ[---.---]. | w ḫlq.ʻpmm[.---]. 18[3AQHT].4.40
.yʻš. | r.w yšqyn h.ybd.w yšr.ʻl h. | nʻm[n.w t]ʻnynn.ap ank.aḥwy. | aqht[.ǵz]r.w yʻn.aqht.ǵzr. | al.tšrgn.y btlt m.dm. 17[2AQHT].6.32
yʻn.lṭpn.il.b pid. | ṯb.bn y.lm ṯb[t] km. | l kḥṯ.zbl k[m.a]nk. | iḥtrš.w [a]škn. | aškn.ydt.[m]rṣ gršt. | zbln.r[---].ymlu. 16[126].5.25
ṯm ny. | ʻm.um y.mnm.šlm. | w.rgm.ṯṯb.l y. | w.mndʻ.k.ank. | aḥš.mǵy.mndʻ. | k.igr.w.u.[--]. | ʻm.špš.[---]. | nšlḥ[.---]. | 2009.1.10
-.]sglt h.hw. | w.b[.---.]uk.ngr. | w.[---].adny.l.yḫsr. | w.[ank.yd]ʻ.l.ydʻt. | h[t.---.]l.špš.bʻl k. | ʻ[--.s]glt h.at. | ht[.---.]špš. 2060.10
l mhr k. | w ʻp.l dr[ʻ].nšr k. | w rbṣ.l ǵr k.inbb. | kt ǵr k.ank.ydʻt. | [-]n.atn.at.mṯb k[.---]. | [š]mm.rm.lk.prẓ kt. | [k]bk 13[6].10
rgm[.---]. | w yrdnn.an[--.---]. | [---].ank.l km[.---]. | l y.ank.ašṣu[.---.]w[.---]. | w hm.at.tr[gm.---]. | w.drm.ʻtr[--.---]. | 54.1.17[13.2.2]
mlk. | l ḥyil. | lm.tlik.ʻm y. | ik y.aškn. | ʻṣm.l bt.dml. | p ank.atn. | ʻṣm.l k. | arbʻ.ʻṣm. | ʻl.ar. | w.ṯlṯ. | ʻl.ubrʻy. | w.ṯn.ʻl. | m 1010.7
. | gšm.adr. | nškḥ.w. | rb.tmtt. | lqḥ.kl.d̲rʻ. | b d a[-]m.w.ank. | k[l.]d̲rʻ hm. | [--.n]pš[.-]. | w [k]l hm.b d. | rb.tmtt.lqḥt. | 2059.18
[-----]. | [-----]. | [-----.lm]. | [ank.ksp.w yrq]. | [ḫrṣ.]yd.mqm h. | [w ʻb]d.ʻlm.ṯlṯ. | [ssw]m.m 14[KRT].1.53
ḥq.mlk.l bt y. | n[g.]krt.l ḥẓ[r y]. | w yʻn[y.k]rt[.ṯ]ʻ. | lm.ank.ksp. | w yr[q.ḫrṣ]. | yd.mqm h.w ʻbd. | ʻlm.ṯlṯ.sswm. | mrk 14[KRT].6.282

rrt.|udm.ytnt.il w ušn.|ab.adm.w tṯb.|mlakm.l h.lm.ank.|ksp.w yrq.ẖrṣ.|yd.mqm h.w ʻbd.|ʻlm.ṯlṯ.sswm.mrkbt. 14[KRT].3.137
ʻ hm.|[--.n]pš[.-].|w [k]l hm.b d.|rb.tmtt.lqḥt.|w.ṯtb.ank.l hm.|w.any k.ṯt.|by.ʻky.ʻryt.|w.aẖ y.mhk.|b lb h.al.yš 2059.23
m.|rḥ.npš h.km.iṯl.brlt h.km.|qṭr.b ap h.b ap.mhr h.ank.|l aḥwy.tqḥ.yṭpn.mhr.št.|tštn.k nšr.b ḥbš h.km.diy.|b 18[3AQHT].4.26
y.ʻn[--.---].|l ytn.w rgm[.---].|w yrdnn.an[--.---].|[---].ank.l km[.---].|l y.ank.ašṣu[.---.]w[.---].|w hm.at.tr[gm.---]. 54.1.16[13.2.1]
[d]n.npṣ h.|[---.]rgm.hn.[--]n.w aspt.[q]l h.|[---.rg]m.ank l[.--.--]rny.|[---.]ṯm.hw.i[--]ty.|[---].ibʻr.a[--.]ḏmr.|[---.] 1002.50
pʻr.šm.ym[-.---].|tʻnyn.l zn.tn[.---].|at.adn.tpʻr[.---].|ank.lṭpn.il[.d pid.---].|ʻl.ydm.pʻrt[.---].|šm k.mdd.i[l.---].|b 1[ʻNT.X].4.18
š.ʻm y.|mnm.iršt k.|d ẖsrt.w.ank.|aštn..l.iẖ y.|w.ap.ank.mnm.|[ẖ]s[r]t.w.uẖ y.|[y]ʻmsn.ṯmn.|w.[u]ẖ y.al ybʻrn. 2065.18
lm.|ṯǵr k.|tšlm k.|hn ny.ʻm ny.|kll.mid.|šlm.|w.ap.ank.|nḫt.ṯm ny.|ʻm.adt ny.|mnm.šlm.|rgm.ṯṯb.|l.ʻbd k. 51[95].13
.l aqry k.b ntb.pšʻ.|[---].b ntb.gan.ašql k.tḥt.|[pʻn y.a]nk.nʻmn.ʻmq.nšm.|[tdʻṣ.pʻn]m.w tr.arṣ.idk.|[l ttn.pn]m.ʻ 17[2AQHT].6.45
l.tš[--.---].|[---.]l ksi y.w pr[ʻ].|[---].prʻ.ank.[---].|[---.]ank.nši[.---].|[---.ṯ]br.ẖss.[---].|[---.--]št.b [---].|[---.--]b.|[--- 1002.15
m.at.trg[m.---].|w sip.u hw[.---].|w ank.u šbt[--.---].|ank.n[--]n[.---].|kst.l[--.---].|w.hw.uy.ʻn[--.---].|l ytn.w rgm 54.1.11[13.1.8]
ṯn.ʻqltn.|šlyṭ.d šbʻy.rašm.|ṯṯkḥ.ttrp.šmm.k rs.|ipd k.ank.ispi.uṭm.|ḏrqm.amt m.l yrt.|b npš.bn ilm.mt.b mh|mr 5[67].1.5
m[.ʻl h].|nšrm.trḫpn.ybṣr.[ḥbl.d]|iym.bn.nšrm.arḫp.an[k.ʻ]l.|aqht.ʻdb k.hlmn.ṯnm.qdqd.|ṯlṯ id.ʻl.udn.špk.km.ši 18[3AQHT].4.21
hm.|l yblt.|w ht.luk ʻm ml[kt].|ṯǵsdb.šmlšn.|w tbʻ ank.|ʻm mlakt h šmʻ h.|w b.ʻly skn.ydʻ rgm h.|w ht ab y ǵ 1021.6
š.nr.|b y.mid.w um.|tšmẖ.m ab.|w al.trḥln.|ʻtn.ḥrd.ank.|ʻm ny.šlm.|kll.|w mnm.|šlm ʻm.|um y.|ʻm y.ṯṯb.|rg 1015.13
ṭ.nhr.|šu.ilm.rašt km.l ẓr.brkt km.ln.kḥṯ.|zbl km.w ank.ʻny.mlak.ym.tʻdt.ṯpṭ.nhr.|tšu ilm rašt hm.l ẓr.brkt hm. 2.1[137].28
-.--]k yṣunn[.---].|[---.--]dy.w.prʻ[.---].|[---.]ytn.ml[--].ank.iphn.|[---.a]nk.i[--.--]slm.w.yṯb.|[----.--]t.hw[-]y.h[--]r. 1002.36
i[--.ʻ]bd k.|l.pʻn.bʻl y[.mrḥqtm].|šbʻ d.w.šbʻ[d.qlt].|ankn.rgmt.l.bʻl y.|l.špš.ʻlm.l.ʻṯtrt.|l.ʻnt.l.kl.il.alṯ[y].|nmry. 2008.1.6
y.|in m.ʻbd k hwt.|[y]rš.ʻm y.|mnm.iršt k.|d ẖsrt.w.ank.|aštn..l.iẖ y.|w.ap.ank.mnm.|[ẖ]s[r]t.w.uẖ y.|[y]ʻmsn. 2065.16
.b d[-.--]y.[---].|[---.]ʻm.w hm[.--]yt.w.[---].|[---.ṯ]y.al.an[k.--.]il[m.--]y.|[--.m]ṣlm.pn y[.-.]tlkn.|[---.]rḫbn.hm.[-.] 1002.58
tal.b.hn[--].|hmt.w.anyt.hm.tʻ[rb].|mkr.hn d.w.rgm.ank[.--].|mlkt.ybqš.anyt.w.at[--].|w mkr n.mlk[.---]. 2008.2.12
[---.--]št.b [---].|[---.--]b.|[---.--]k.|[---.--]an.|[---.--]m.ank.|[---.]asrm.|[---.]dbḥm.|[---.y]rẖ.w šqr.|[---.--]b.b y[--.- 1002.21
[ʻl y.---].|[-----].|r[--.---].|b.[---.mlk].|rb[.bʻl y.---].|w.an[k.---].|arš[.---].|mlk.r[b.bʻ]l y.p.l.|ḥy.np[š.a]rš.|l.pn.bʻ[l 1018.15
--.a]nk.i[--.--]slm.w.yṯb.|[----.--]t.hw[-]y.h[--]r.w rgm.ank.|[---.]hdd tr[--.--]l.aṯrt y.|[--]ptm.ṣḥq.|[---.]rgm.hy.[-]ẖ 1002.38
--]š[-.--].w.ašt.|[---].amr k.|[---].k.ybt.mlk.|[---].w.ap.ank.|[---].l.ǵr.amn.|[---.-]ktt.hn.ib.|[---.]mlk.|[---.]adt y.tdʻ 1012.15
[---.--]l y.ʻm.|[---.]ʻm.|[---.--]y.w.lm.|[---.]il.šlm.|[---.]ank.|[---].mly. 2128.2.6
-]dm.ṯn id.|[--]m.d.l.nʻmm.|[lm.]l.likt.ʻm y.|[---.]ʻbd.ank.|[---.ʻb]d k.|[---.--]l y.ʻm.|[---.]ʻm.|[---.--]y.w.lm.|[---.]i 2128.1.8
tšlm k.|lm[.l.]likt.|ši[l.š]lm y.|[ʻ]d.r[-]š.|[-]ly.l.likt.|[a]nk.[---].|šil.[šlm y].|[l]m.li[kt].|[-]t.ʻ[--]. 2010.11
n.l.ḥwt h.|[---.--]p.hn.ib.d.b.mgšẖ.|[---.i]b.hn[.w.]ht.ank.|[---.--]š[-.--].w.ašt.|[---].amr k.|[---].k.ybt.mlk.|[---].w 1012.11
.|[-----].|[---].al.tš[--.---].|[---.]l ksi y.w pr[ʻ].|[---].prʻ.ank.[---].|[---.]ank.nši[.---].|[---.ṯ]br.ẖss.[---].|[---.--]št.b [---] 1002.14
m.l y[--.---].|[---].mṣrm[.---].|[---.--]n mkr[.---].|[---].ank.[---].|[---.]tny.[---].|[---.]mlk[.---].|[---.--]m.ʻ[--.---]. 2126.6
-.--]ẖ.an[--.---].|[---.]ʻly k[.---].|[---.]at.bt k[.---].|[---.]ank[.---].|[---.-]hn.[---].|[---.--]pp h.w[.---].|[---.]l k[.---].|[-- 1002.5
r.at.aẖ.w an.a[ẖt k].|[---].šbʻ.ṯir k.[---].|[---.]ab y.ndt.ank[.---].|[---.--]l.mlk.tlk.b ṣd[.---].|[---.]mt.išryt[.---].|[---.-- 18[3AQHT].1.26

ann

nsk.ṯlṯ.|[-]by.nsk.ṯlṯ.|šmny.|ḫršn.|ldn.|bn.ands.|bn.ann.|bn.ʻbdpdr.|šd.iyry.l.ʻbdbʻl.|šd.šmmn.l.bn.šty.|šd.bn.a 1102.15
bn.l.qr[t].|šd.pln.bn.tiyn.b d.ilmhr nḥl h.|šd knn.bn.ann.ʻdb.|šd.iln[-].bn.irṯr.l.šḫrn.nḥl h.|šd[.ag]pṯn.b[n.]brrn.l 2029.19
.nḥl h.|šd.pǵyn[.b] d.krmn.l.ty[n.n]ḥl h.|šd.krz.[b]n.ann.ʻ[db].|šd.ṯ[r]yn.bn.tkn.b d.qrt.|šd[.-].dyn.b d.pln.nḥl h. 2029.13
t.|[---.--]m.|[---.--]ṯm.|[---.]ʻšrt.|[-----].|b.[---.---]r.|b.ann[.---.-]ny[-].|b.ḫqn.[---]m.ṣ[-]n.|[b].bn.ay[--.---].l.ʻšrm.|[2054.2.15

annd

dgdl.|bn.smyy.|bn.lbn.|bn.šlmn.|bn.mly.|pslm.|bn.annd.|bn.glʻd.|w.nḥl h.|bn.mlkyy.|[bn].bm[--].|[ʻš]rm.|[-- 2163.3.10

anndn

yrn.|ybnil.adrdn.|klyn.kkln.|ʻdmlk.tdn.|ʻzn.pǵdn.|[a]nndn.|[r]špab.|[-]glm. 1070.7

annḏy

lb]š.bn.sgryn.b[.ṯ]qlm.|[---.]bn.ully.b.ṯ[qlm].|[---.]bn.annḏy.b[.---].|[---.]bn.pd[--.---]. 135[330].6

annḏr

l [h].|šd.ṯṯyn[.b]n.arkšt.|lʻq[.---].|šd.pll.b d.qrt.|š[d].annḏr.b d.bdn.nḥ[l h].|[šd.]agyn.b d.kmrn.n[ḥl] h.|[š]d.nb 2029.7
l ym.hnd.|ʻmṯmr.|bn.nqmpʻ.|mlk.ugrt.|ytn.bt.annḏr.|bn.ytn.bnš.|[ml]k.d.b riš.|[--.-]nt.|[l.ʻb]dmlk.|[--.-] 1009.5
].|ttn.|md.ʻṯt[rt].|kṯkt.|bn.ṯtn[--].|[m]d.m[--].|[b]n.annḏ[r].|bn.ṯdyy.|bn.grbn.|[--.]ully.|[--]ṯiy. 1054.2.2
wn.qrty.w[.aṯt h].|[w].bn h.w.ṯn.alpm.|[w.]ṯlṯm.ṣin.|annḏr.yknʻmy.|w.aṯt h.w.bn h.|w.alp.w.tš[ʻ.]ṣin. 1080.15
pṭ.krm.aḥd.nšpin.kr[m.]aḥd[.---].|dmt.lḥsn.krm.aḥd.annḏr.kr[m.---].|aǵt.mryn.ary[.]yukl.krm.[---].|gdn.krm.aḥ 1081.15
ṯn[.---].|ybni[l.---].|ikrn[.---].|tlmyn[.---].|tldn[.---].|annḏr[.---].|[-]m[--.---]. 106[332].9

annẖ

d.šd ilm.šd aṯrt.w rḥm.|ʻl.išt.šbʻ d.ǵzrm.ṭb.[g]d.b ḥlb.annẖ b ẖmat.|w ʻl.agn.šbʻ d m.dǵ[ṯ.---]t.|tlk m.rḥmy.w tṣd[23[52].14

anny

spr.ḫrš.|qštipṯl.|bn.anny.|ilṣdq.|yplṭn.bn iln.|špšm.nsl h.|[-----]. 1037.3
l h].|ʻbd[--].|bn.s[---].|bn.at[--].|bn.qnḏ.|ṣmq[-].|bn.anny.|bn.ʻmtḏl.|bn.ʻmyn.|bn.alz.|bn.birtn.|[bn.]ylkn.|[bn 117[325].1.9
ṯtry.|bn.ḫrẓn.|ady.|bn.birtn.|bn.ḫrẓn.|bn.bddn.|bn.anny.|ytršp.|bn.szn.|bn.kdgdl.|bn.glʻd.|bn.ktln.|[bn].ǵrg 115[301].1.10
bn.nṣ.|[b]n.ʻṣr.|[---]m.|[bn.]ulnhr.|[bn.p]rn.|[bn.a]nny.|[---]n.|bn.kbln.|bn.pdy.|bn.ṯpdn. 1075.1.6

annyn

is.bn tbdn. | bn uryy. | bn abd‘n. | bn prkl. | bn štn. | bn annyn. | b[n] slg. | u[--] dit. | bn p[-]n. | bn nẓġil. 101[10].12

annmn

l] h. | [š]d.nbzn.[-]l.qrt. | [š]d.agpṯr.b d.šḫrn.nḥl h. | šd.annmn.b d.tyn.nḥl h. | šd.pġyn[.b] d.krmn.l.ty[n.n]ḥl h. | šd. 2029.11
]ly. | bn.rqd[y].ṯbg. | iḫmlk. | yp‘n w.aṯt h. | anntn.yṣr. | annmn.w.ṯlṯ.n‘[r] h. | rpan.w.ṯ[n.]bn h. | bn.ayln.w.ṯn.bn h. | 2068.25
n.b‘ln. | ġltn.‘bd.[---]. | nsk.ḥdm.klyn[.ṣd]qn.‘bdilt.b‘l. | annmn.‘dy.klby.dqn. | ḥrṯm.ḥgbn.‘dn.ynḥm[.---]. | ḥrš.mrkbt 2011.26

annmt

-]bln. | [---]dy. | [---.n]ḥl h. | [---].bn.mryn. | [---].bn.ṯyl. | annmt.nḥl h. | abmn.bn.‘bd. | liy.bn.rqdy. | bn.ršp. 1036.12

annpdgl

-.--]t ugrt. | [---.w n]py.yman. | [w npy.‘rmt.---.w]npy.annpdgl. | [ušn.yp kn.ulp.qṭy.ulp.]ddmy.ulp ḫry. | [ulp.ḫty.u APP.I[-].1.3

anntn

n.]ibln. | ysd. | bn.ṯmq. | bn.agmn. | bn.uṣb. | bn.yzg. | bn.anntn. | bn.kwn. | ġmšd. | bn.‘bdḥy. | bn.ubyn. | slpd. | bn.atnb. 115[301].4.7
mry[n]m. | bn rmy[y]. | yšril[.---]. | anntn bn[.---]. | bn.brzn [---]. | bnil.bn.tl[--]. | bn.brzn.ṯn. | bn.i 2069.4
šn.‘msn. | bṣr.abn.špšyn. | dqn. | aġlmn. | kn‘m. | aḫršp. | anntn. | b‘lrm. | [-]ral. | šdn. | [-]ġl. | bn.b‘ltġpṯ. | ḥrš.btm. | ršpa 2067.1.8
.]aṯ[t h]. | ‘dyn[.---]. | w.ṯn[.bn h.---]. | iwrm[-.]b[n.---]. | annt[n.]w[.---]. | w.ṯn.bn h.[---]. | aġltn.ypr[y.---]. | w.šb‘.ṣin h 2044.15
. | gpn.bn[.a]ly. | bn.rqd[y].ṯbg. | iḫmlk. | yp‘n w.aṯt h. | anntn.yṣr. | annmn.w.ṯlṯ.n‘[r] h. | rpan.w.ṯ[n.]bn h. | bn.ayln. 2068.24
spr.r‘ym. | lqḥ.š‘rt. | anntn. | ‘dn. | sdwn. | mztn. | ḫyrn. | šdn. | [‘š]rm.ṯn kbd. | šġrm. 2098.3
[-----]. | ubyn[.---]. | annt[n.---]. | ipṯn[.---]. | ybni[l.---]. | ikrn[.---]. | tlmyn[.---]. | tld 106[332].3

annṯb

aġltn. | urtn. | annṯb. | ubn. | špšyn. | abmn. | [--]dn. | [ṯ]b‘m. | [--]mlk. | [--]ty. | 1072.3
[ṯl]ṯm.ksp.‘[l]. | [b]n.bly.gb‘ly. | [šp]ḥ.a[n]nṯb. | w.m[--.u]škny. | [‘]š[r.---]t.ksp. | [‘l.---]b bn[.--]. | [-]ḥ 2055.3
annṯb.ḫmšm.ksp ṯlṯm.šl[m.---]. | iwrpzn.‘šrm ‘šrm š[lm.---]. 1131.1
. | arb‘.b d.b[n].ušryn. | kdm.l.urtn. | kdm.l.ilšpš. | kd.l.annṯb. | kd.l.iwrmḏ. | kd.l.ydn. | [---.y]rḫ.ḫyr. | [---.]yn.l.mlkt. 1088.7

ansny

qn[.---]. | [-]ntn.artn.b d[.--]nr[.---]. | ‘zn.w ymd.šr.b d ansny. | nsk.ks[p.--]mrtn.kṯrmlk. | yḥmn.aḫm[l]k.‘bdrpu.adn 2011.31

anġn

[---].bn.anġn. 2141.1

anrmy

‘m.lbš.d.‘rb.bt.mlk. | b.mit.ḫmšt.kbd.ksp. | ṯlṯ.ktnt.b d.an[r]my. | b.‘šrt.ksp.b.a[--]. | ṯqlm.ḫr[ṣ.]b.ṯmnt.ksp. | ‘šrt.ksp. 2101.18
]n.gg‘t. | [‘]dy. | armwl. | uwaḫ. | ypln.w.ṯn.bn h. | ydln. | anr[my]. | mld. | krmp[y]. | bṣmn. 2086.10
mš. | kbd.w lpš. | ḫmš.mispt. | mṯ. | w lpš.d sgr b h. | b d.anrmy. 1109.7

anš

m.‘l k.pht. | dr‘.b ym.tn.aḥd. | b aḫ k.ispa.w ytb. | ap.d anšt.im[-]. | aḥd.b aḫ k.l[--]n. | hn[-.]aḥẓ[.---]l[-]. | [‘]nt.akl[y. 6[49].5.21
nm]. | ṯṯṯ.‘l[n.pn h.td‘.b ‘dn]. | ksl.y[ṯbr.yġṣ.pnt.ksl h]. | anš.[dt.ẓr h.yšu.g h]. | w yṣ[ḥ.---]. | mḫṣ[.---]. | š[--.---]. 19[1AQHT].2.96
h.p‘nm. | ṯṯṯ.b‘d n.ksl.ṯṯbr. | ‘ln.pn h.td‘.ṯġṣ.pnt. | ksl h.anš.dt.ẓr h.tšu. | g h.w tṣḥ.ik.mġy.gpn.w ugr. | mn.ib.yp‘.l b‘l 3[‘NT].3.32
. | [ṯṯṯ.b ‘]dn.ksl. | [ṯṯbr.‘ln.p]n h.td[‘]. | ṯġṣ[.pnt.ks]l h. | anš.dt.ẓr.[h]. | tšu.g h.w tṣḥ[.i]k. | mġy.aliy[n.b]‘l. | ik.mġyt.b[4[51].2.20
‘dr k.b yd.btlt.[‘nt]. | w y‘n.lṭpn.il d p[id]. | yd‘t k.bt.k anšt.w i[n.b ilht]. | qlṣ k.tb‘.bt.ḫnp.lb[k.--.ti] | ḫd.d iṯ.b kbd 18[3AQHT].1.16
---.] | [---].mlak.bn.ktpm.rgm.b‘l h.w y[--.---]. | [---].ap.anš.zbl.b‘l.šdmt.bg[--.---]. | [---.-]dm.mlak.ym.t‘dt.ṯpṭ.nh[r.-- 2.1[137].43
.hw ybl.argmn k.k ilm. | [---.]ybl.k bn.qdš.mnḥy k.ap.anš.zbl.b‘[l]. | [-.yuḫ]d.b yd.mšḫṭ.bm.ymn.mḫṣ.ġlmm.yš[--]. 2.1[137].38
‘m.]y‘ny. | il.b šb‘t.ḥdrm.b ṯmnt. | ap.sgrt.yd‘[t k.]bt.k an[št]. | k in.b ilht.ql[ṣ] k.mh.tarš[n]. | l btlt.‘nt.w t[‘]n.btlt.‘n 3[‘NT.VI].5.35
| l tdn.dn.almnt. | l ṯpṭ.ṯpṭ.qṣr.npš. | km.aḫt.‘rš.mdw. | anšt.‘rš.zbln. | rd.l mlk.amlk. | l drkt.k aṯb.an. | ytb‘.yṣb ġlm.‘ 16.6[127].36
pn k. | l tšlḥm.ytm.b‘d. | ksl k.almnt.km. | aḫt.‘rš.mdw.anšt. | ‘rš.zbln.rd.l mlk. | amlk.l drkt k.aṯb. | an.w y‘ny.krt ṯ‘. 16.6[127].51
t h]. | w ‘l.tlbš.npṣ.aṯt.[--]. | ṣbi nrt.ilm.špš.[-]r[--]. | pġt.minš.šdm l m‘[rb]. | nrt.ilm.špš.mġy[t]. | pġt.l ahlm.rgm.l yṯ[19[1AQHT].4.210
‘l. | [---] k.yšṣi. | [---.]ḫbr.rbt. | [ḫbr.ṯrr]t.il d. | [pid.---].b anšt. | [---.]mlu. | [---.--]tm. 15[128].5.27
lm.[qrt.zbl.yrḫ]. | ik.al.yḥdṯ.yrḫ.b[---]. | b qrn.ymn h.b anšt[.---]. | qdqd h.w y‘n.yṭpn.[mhr.št]. | šm‘.l btlt.‘nt.at.‘[l.q 18[3AQHT].4.10

anšrm

iḫyn.uṯpt.ḥẓm. | anšrm.uṯpt.ḥẓm. | w uṯpt.srdnnm. | awpn.uṯpt.ḥẓm. | w uṯpt. 1124.2

antn

. | [--]tn.bn.aḏmṯn. | [-]tn bn.agyn. | ullym.bn.abynm. | antn.bn.iwr[n]r. | pwn.ṯmry. | ksyn.bn.lḫsn. | [-]kyn.ṯmry. 94[313].7

anṯ

r. | ap.ḫšt k.ap.ab.k mtm. | tmtn.u ḫšt k.l ntn. | ‘tq.b d.aṯt.ab.ṣrry. | ik m.yrgm.bn.il. | krt.špḥ.lṭpn. | w qdš.u ilm.tmt 16.1[125].19
[.ap.]ḫšt k. | ap.ab.k mtm.tmtn. | u ḫšt k.l bky.‘tq. | b d.aṯt ab.ṣrry. | u ilm.tmtn.špḥ. | [l]ṭpn.l yḥ.t[b]ky k. | ab.ġr.b‘l.ṣ 16.2[125].104
r. | ap.ḫšt k.ap.ab.ik mtm. | tmtn.u ḫšt k.l ntn. | ‘tq.b d.aṯt.ab ṣrry. | tbky k.ab.ġr.b‘l. | ṣpn.ḥlm.qdš. | any.ḥlm.adr.ḥl. 16.1[125].5
m.adrtm.w.pġt.aḥt.b[.bt.---]. | aṯt.w tn.n‘rm.b.bt.ilsk. | aṯt.ad[r]t.b.bt.armwl. | aṯt.aḥt.b.bt.iwrpzn. | ṯt.aṯtm.w.pġt.aḥ 80[119].9
.b.bt.krz. | [aṯt.]w.pġt.b.bt.gg. | [ġz]r.aḥd.b.bt.nwrḏ. | [at]t.adrt.b.bt.arttb. | aṯt.w.ṯn.bn h.b.bt.iwwpzn. | aṯt.w.pġt.b. 80[119].4

. | [aṯt.w.]pǵt.aḥt.b.bt.tt. | [aṯt.w.]bt h.b.bt.trǵds. | [---.]aṯt.adrt.w.pǵt.a[ḥt.b.bt.---]. | [---.ʿ]šrm.npš.b.bt.[---]. | [---.]w. 80[119].28
. | aṯt.w.ṯn.bn h.b.bt.iwwpzn. | aṯt.w.pǵt.b.bt.ydrm. | ṯt.aṯtm.adrtm.w.pǵt.aḥt.b[.bt.---]. | aṯt.w ṯn.nʿrm.b.bt.ilsk. | aṯt. 80[119].7
. | [ṯ]lṯ.aṯt.adrt.w.ṯlṯ.ǵzr[m]. | w.ḫmš.nʿrt.b.bt.sk[n]. | ṯt.aṯtm.adrtm.w.pǵt.w ǵzr[.aḥd.b.bt.---]. | aṯt.w.ṯt.pǵtm.w.ǵzr. 80[119].18
]t.b.bt.ṯpṭbʿl. | [---.]n[--.mḏ]rǵlm. | [---.]b.bt[.---]l. | [ṯ]lṯ.aṯt.adrt.w.ṯlṯ.ǵzr[m]. | w.ḫmš.nʿrt.b.bt.sk[n]. | ṯt.aṯtm.adrtm. 80[119].16
t.---]. | aṯt.w ṯn.nʿrm.b.bt.ilsk. | aṯt.ad[r]t.b.bt.armwl. | aṯt.aḥt.b.bt.iwrpzn. | ṯt.aṯtm.w.pǵt.aḥt.b bt.[-]r[-]. | [aṯ]t.b.bt. 80[119].10
.w.ṯt.bt h.b.bt.ḫḏmrd. | aṯt.w.ṯn.ǵzrm.b.bt.ṣdqš[lm]. | [a]ṯt.aḥt.b.bt.rpi[--]. | [aṯt.]w.bt h.b.bt.alḫn. | [aṯt.w.]pǵt.aḥt.b 80[119].24
ilk.r[--]. | aršm.bʿl [aṯt]. | ttḫ.bʿl aṯt. | ayab.bʿl aṯt. | iyṯr.bʿl aṯt. | ptm.bʿl ššlmt. | ʿdršp.bʿl ššlmt. 1077.3
ḫṭ k.mmnnm.mṭ yd k.hl.ʿṣr. | ṯḥrr.l išt.w ṣḥrt.l pḥmm.aṯtm.a[ṯt.il]. | aṯt.il.w ʿlm h.yhbr.špt hm.yš[q]. | hn.špt hm.m 23[52].48
ṭ k.mmnnm.mṭ.yd k. | h[l.]ʿṣr.ṯḥrr.l išt.ṣḥrrt.l pḥmm. | a[ṯ]tm.aṯt.il.aṯt.il.w ʿlm h.w hm. | aṯtm.tṣḥn y.ad ad.nḥtm.ḫṭ 23[52].42
ilk.r[--]. | aršm.bʿl [aṯt]. | ttḫ.bʿl aṯt. | ayab.bʿl aṯt. | iyṯr.bʿl aṯt. | ptm.bʿl ššlmt. | ʿdršp.bʿl ššlmt. | ṯtrn.bʿl ššlm 1077.4
nnm.mṭ.yd k. | h[l.]ʿṣr.ṯḥrr.l išt.ṣḥrrt.l pḥmm. | a[ṯ]tm.aṯt.il.aṯt.il.w ʿlm h.w hm. | aṯtm.tṣḥn y.ad ad.nḥtm.ḫṭ k. | m 23[52].42
mnnm.mṭ yd k.hl.ʿṣr. | ṯḥrr.l išt.w ṣḥrt.l pḥmm.aṯtm.a[ṯt.il]. | aṯt.il.w ʿlm h.yhbr.špt hm.yš[q]. | hn.špt hm.mtqtm. 23[52].48
mṭ yd k.hl.ʿṣr. | ṯḥrr.l išt.w ṣḥrt.l pḥmm.aṯtm.a[ṯt.il]. | aṯt.il.w ʿlm h.yhbr.špt hm.yš[q]. | hn.špt hm.mtqtm.mtqtm. 23[52].49
mṭ.yd k. | h[l.]ʿṣr.ṯḥrr.l išt.ṣḥrrt.l pḥmm. | a[ṯ]tm.aṯt.il.aṯt.il.w ʿlm h.w hm. | aṯtm.tṣḥn y.ad ad.nḥtm.ḫṭ k. | mmnnm 23[52].42
l. | aṯt.aḥt.b.bt.iwrpzn. | ṯt.aṯtm.w.pǵt.aḥt.b bt.[-]r[-]. | [aṯ]t.b.bt.aupš. | [aṯ]t.b.bt.ṯpṭbʿl. | [---.]n[--.mḏ]rǵlm. | [---.]b.bt 80[119].12
rpzn. | ṯt.aṯtm.w.pǵt.aḥt.b bt.[-]r[-]. | [aṯ]t.b.bt.aupš. | [aṯ]t.b.bt.ṯpṭbʿl. | [---.]n[--.mḏ]rǵlm. | [---.]b.bt[.---]l. | [ṯ]lṯ.aṯt.a 80[119].13
n.ṯlṯtm.bʿlm. | bn.bʿly.ṯlṯtm.bʿlm. | w.aḥd.ḫbṭ. | w.arbʿ.aṯt. | bn.lg.ṯn.bn h. | bʿlm.w.aḫt h. | b.šrt. | šty.w.bn h. 2080.9
bʿ[m.---]. | pln.ṯmry.w.ṯn.bn h.w[.---]. | ymrn.apsny.w.aṯt h..b[n.---]. | prd.mʿqby[.w.---.a]ṯt h[.---]. | prṯ.mgd[ly.---.] 2044.9
.w.bn h. | gpn.bn[.a]ly. | bn.rqd[y].ṯbg. | iḫmlk. | ypʿn w.aṯt h. | anntn.yṣr. | annmn.w.ṯlṯ.nʿ[r] h. | rpan.w.ṯ[n.]bn h. | bn 2068.23
aṯt h. | [--]r.w.aṯt h. | ʿbdyrḫ.ṯn ǵlyt h. | aršmg. | ršpy.w.aṯt h. | bn.glgl.uškny. | bn.ṯny.uškny. | mnn.w.aṯt h. | slmu.ḫrš 2068.12
[-]ḏmu.apsty.b[--]. | w.bn h.w aṯt h.w.alp.w ṯmn.ṣin. | [-]dln.qmnzy.w.a[ṯt h]. | wšṯn.bn h. | 1080.2
u.ḫrš.mrkbt. | bnšm.dt.l.mlk. | ʿbdyrḫ.bn.ṯyl. | ʿbdn.w.aṯt h.w.bn h. | gpn.bn[.a]ly. | bn.rqd[y].ṯbg. | iḫmlk. | ypʿn w.a 2068.19
[-]dln.qmnzy.w.a[ṯt h]. | wšṯn.bn h. | ṯmgdl.yknʿmy.w.aṯt h. | w.bn h.w.alp.aḫ[d]. | aǵltn.[--]y.w[.aṯt h]. | w.bn h.w.a 1080.5
[w].bn h.w.ṯn.alpm. | [w.]ṯlṯm.ṣin. | annḏr.yknʿmy. | w.aṯt h.w.bn h. | w.alp.w.tš[ʿ.]ṣin. 1080.16
l.yknʿmy.w.aṯt h. | w.bn h.w.alp.aḫ[d]. | aǵltn.[--]y.w[.aṯt h]. | w.bn h.w.alp.w.[---]. | [-]ln.[---]. | w.ṯn.bn [h.---]. | [--] 1080.7
.[---]. | w.ṯn.bn [h.---]. | [--]d mʿqby[.---]. | swn.qrty.w[.aṯt h]. | [w].bn h.w.ṯn.alpm. | [w.]ṯlṯm.ṣin. | annḏr.yknʿmy. | w 1080.12
aṯt h.w.nʿr h. | bn.ḫby.w.[a]ṯt h. | ynḥm.ulmy. | [--]q.w.aṯt h.w.bn h. | [--]an.w.aṯt h. | [--]y.w.aṯt h. | [--]r.w.aṯt h. | ʿbd 2068.6
bl.ʿršm. | yšu.ʿwr. | mzl.ymzl. | w ybl.trḫ.ḥdṯ. | ybʿr.l ṯn.aṯt h. | w l nkr.mddt. | km irby.tškn. | šd.k ḥsn.pat. | mdbr.tlk 14[KRT].4.190
[š.---]. | [n]it.krk.mʿṣ[d.---]. | b.ḫrbǵlm.ǵlm[n]. | w.trhy.aṯt h. | w.mlky.b[n] h. | ily.mrily.tdgr. 2048.20
bnšm.dt.l.u[--]ṯṯb. | kṯ[r]n. | w.aṯt h.w.nʿr h. | bn.ḫby.w.[a]ṯt h. | ynḥm.ulmy. | [--]q.w.aṯt h. 2068.3
nšm.dt.l.u[--]ṯṯb. | kṯ[r]n. | w.aṯt h.w.nʿr h. | bn.ḫby.w.[a]ṯt h. | ynḥm.ulmy. | [--]q.w.aṯt h.w.bn h. | [--]an.w.aṯt h. | [-- 2068.4
.mʿṣd]. | w ḫrmṯt. | ṯlṯm.ar[bʿ]. | kbd.ksp. | ʿl.tgyn. | w ʿl.aṯt h. | ypḥ.mʿnt. | bn.lbn. 2053.21
p[----]. | gm.l[aṯt h k.yṣḥ]. | šmʿ[.l mṯt.ḥry]. | ṭbḫ.š[mn].mri k. | ptḥ.[rḥ]bt.y 15[128].4.2
ʿt.]alp. | ḥrṭ[.l z]ǵt.klb. | [ṣ]pr[.apn]k. | [pb]l[.mlk.g]m.l aṯt | [h.k]y[ṣḥ.]šmʿ.mʿ. | [--.]ʿm[.-.]aṯt y[.-]. | [---.]ṯḥm. | [---]t. 14[KRT].5.228
rbʿ.qṣʿt.apnk.dnil. | mt.rpi.aphn.ǵzr.mt. | hrnmy.gm.l aṯt h.k yṣḥ. | šmʿ.mṯt.dnty.ʿd[b]. | imr.b pḫd.l npš.kṯr. | w ḫss. 17[2AQHT].5.15
bl.ʿršm. | yšu.ʿwr.mzl. | ymzl.w yṣi.trḫ. | ḥdṯ.ybʿr.l ṯn. | aṯt h.lm.nkr. | mddt h.k irby. | [t]škn.šd. | km.ḥsn.pat.mdbr. | 14[KRT].2.102
.i]lht. | kḥṣ.k mʿr[.---]. | yṣḥ.ngr il.ilš. | ilš.ngr.bt.bʿl. | w aṯt h.ngrt.ilht. | w yʿn.lṭpn.il d pi[d]. | šmʿ.l ngr.il il[š]. | ilš.ng 16[126].4.9
mr k.ph[.-]. | k il.ḥkmt.k ṯr.lṭpn. | ṣḥ.ngr.il.ilš.il[š]. | w aṯt h.ngrt[.i]lht. | kḥṣ.k mʿr[.---]. | yṣḥ.ngr il.ilš. | ilš.ngr.bt.bʿl 16[126].4.5
. | ršpy.w.aṯt h. | bn.glgl.uškny. | bn.ṯny.uškny. | mnn.w.aṯt h. | slmu.ḫrš.mrkbt. | bnšm.dt.l.mlk. | ʿbdyrḫ.bn.ṯyl. | ʿbdn. 2068.15
.w.aṯt h.w.bn h. | [--]an.w.aṯt h. | [--]y.w.aṯt h. | [--]r.w.aṯt h. | ʿbdyrḫ.ṯn ǵlyt h. | aršmg. | ršpy.w.aṯt h. | bn.glgl.uškny 2068.9
.b[n.---]. | prd.mʿqby[.w.---.a]ṯt h[.---]. | prṯ.mgd[ly.---.]aṯ[t h]. | ʿdyn[.---]. | w.ṯn[.bn h.---]. | iwrm[-.]b[n.---]. | annt[n. 2044.11
--]. | w.bn h.w aṯt h.w.alp.w ṯmn.ṣin. | [-]dln.qmnzy.w.a[ṯt h]. | wšṯn.bn h. | ṯmgdl.yknʿmy.w.aṯt h. | w.bn h.w.alp.aḫ 1080.3
.[a]ṯt h. | ynḥm.ulmy. | [--]q.w.aṯt h.w.bn h. | [--]an.w.aṯt h. | [--]y.w.aṯt h. | [--]r.w.aṯt h. | ʿbdyrḫ.ṯn ǵlyt h. | aršmg. | 2068.7
m.ulmy. | [--]q.w.aṯt h.w.bn h. | [--]an.w.aṯt h. | [--]y.w.aṯt h. | [--]r.w.aṯt h. | ʿbdyrḫ.ṯn ǵlyt h. | aršmg. | ršpy.w.aṯt h. | 2068.8
lṯ.ǵzr.mt hrnmy. | [---].hw.mḫ.l ʿrš h.yʿl. | [---].bm.nšq.aṯt h. | [---.]b ḥbq h.ḥmḥmt. | [---.--] n.ylt.ḥmḥmt. | [---.mt.r]p 17[2AQHT].1.40
yd.[---]. | am[-]n.[---]. | w.a[ṯt] h.[---]. | ḥḏmtn.ṯn[.---]. | w.ṯlṯ.alp h.[---]. | swn.qrty.w.[b] 2044.3
[.---]. | ymrn.apsny.w.aṯt h..b[n.---]. | prd.mʿqby[.w.---.a]ṯt h[.---]. | prṯ.mgd[ly.---.]aṯ[t h]. | ʿdyn[.---]. | w.ṯn[.bn h.---] 2044.10
ʿl.bn.alkbl.šb[ny]. | ʿšrm ksp.ʿl. | wrt.mtny.w ʿl. | prdny.aṯt h. 2107.19
[aṯt.w].bn h.b.bt.krz. | [aṯt.]w.pǵt.b.bt.gg. | [ǵz]r.aḥd.b.bt.nwr 80[119].1
ǵzr.aḥd.b.[bt.---]. | ṯt.aṯtm.w.pǵt.w.ǵzr.aḥd.b.[bt.---]. | aṯt.w.bn h.w.pǵt.aḥt.b.bt.m[--]. | aṯt.w.ṯt.bt h.b.bt.ḫḏmrd. | a 80[119].21
. | aṯt.w.ṯn.ǵzrm.b.bt.ṣdqš[lm]. | [a]ṯt.aḥt.b.bt.rpi[--]. | [aṯt.]w.bt h.b.bt.alḫn. | [aṯt.w.]pǵt.aḥt.b.bt.tt. | [aṯt.w.]bt h.b. 80[119].25
pi[--]. | [aṯt.]w.bt h.b.bt.alḫn. | [aṯt.w.]pǵt.aḥt.b.bt.tt. | [aṯt.w.]bt h.b.bt.trǵds. | [---.]aṯt.adrt.w.pǵt.a[ḥt.b.bt.---]. | [---. 80[119].27
qš[lm]. | [a]ṯt.aḥt.b.bt.rpi[--]. | [aṯt.]w.bt h.b.bt.alḫn. | [aṯt.w.]pǵt.aḥt.b.bt.tt. | [aṯt.w.]bt h.b.bt.trǵds. | [---.]aṯt.adrt. 80[119].26
bt.ilsk. | aṯt.ad[r]t.b.bt.armwl. | aṯt.aḥt.b.bt.iwrpzn. | ṯt.aṯtm.w.pǵt.aḥt.b bt.[-]r[-]. | [aṯ]t.b.bt.aupš. | [aṯ]t.b.bt.ṯpṭbʿl. 80[119].11
[aṯt.w].bn h.b.bt.krz. | [aṯt.]w.pǵt.b.bt.gg. | [ǵz]r.aḥd.b.bt.nwrḏ. | [aṯ]t.adrt.b.bt.arttb 80[119].2
rḏ. | [aṯ]t.adrt.b.bt.arttb. | aṯt.w.ṯn.bn h.b.bt.iwwpzn. | aṯt.w.pǵt.b.bt.ydrm. | ṯt.aṯtm.adrtm.w.pǵt.aḥt.b[.bt.---]. | aṯt. 80[119].6
r[.aḥd.b.bt.---]. | aṯt.w.ṯt.pǵtm.w.ǵzr.aḥd.b.[bt.---]. | ṯt.aṯtm.w.pǵt.w.ǵzr.aḥd.b.[bt.---]. | aṯt.w.bn h.w.pǵt.aḥt.b.bt. 80[119].20
t.b.bt.gg. | [ǵz]r.aḥd.b.bt.nwrḏ. | [aṯ]t.adrt.b.bt.arttb. | aṯt.w.ṯn.bn h.b.bt.iwwpzn. | aṯt.w.pǵt.b.bt.ydrm. | ṯt.aṯtm.ad 80[119].5
w.ǵzr.aḥd.b.[bt.---]. | aṯt.w.bn h.w.pǵt.aḥt.b.bt.m[--]. | aṯt.w.ṯt.bt h.b.bt.ḫḏmrd. | aṯt.w.ṯn.ǵzrm.b.bt.ṣdqš[lm]. | [a]ṯt 80[119].22
.w.pǵt.b.bt.ydrm. | ṯt.aṯtm.adrtm.w.pǵt.aḥt.b[.bt.---]. | aṯt.w ṯn.nʿrm.b.bt.ilsk. | aṯt.ad[r]t.b.bt.armwl. | aṯt.aḥt.b.bt.i 80[119].8
.bn h.w.pǵt.aḥt.b.bt.m[--]. | aṯt.w.ṯt.bt h.b.bt.ḫḏmrd. | aṯt.w.ṯn.ǵzrm.b.bt.ṣdqš[lm]. | [a]ṯt.aḥt.b.bt.rpi[--]. | [aṯt.]w.bt 80[119].23
.b.bt.sk[n]. | ṯt.aṯtm.adrtm.w.pǵt.w ǵzr[.aḥd.b.bt.---]. | aṯt.w.ṯt.pǵtm.w.ǵzr.aḥd.b.[bt.---]. | ṯt.aṯtm.w.pǵt.w.ǵzr.aḥd. 80[119].19
ʿmm.agzr ym. | bn.ym.ynqm.b a[p.]ḏ[d.r]gm.l il.ybl. | aṯt y.il.ylt.mh.ylt.ilmy nʿmm. | agzr ym.bn ym.ynqm.b ap.ḏ 23[52].60

r.b ḥbq.ḥmḥmt.tqt[nṣn]. | tldn.šḥr.w šlm.rgm.l il.ybl.a[tt y]. | il.ylt.mh.ylt.yld y.šḥr.w šl[m]. | šu.ʻdb.l špš.rbt.w l k 23[52].52
ṯh.lm. | l.ytn.hm.mlk.[b]ʻl y. | w.hn.ibm.šṣq l y. | p.l.ašt.aṯt y. | nʻr y.ṯh.l pn.ib. | hn.hm.yrgm.mlk. | bʻl y.tmǵyy.hn. | a 1012.28
. | [pb]l[.mlk.g]m.l aṯt | [h.k]y[ṣḥ.]šmʻ.mʻ. | [--.]ʻm[.-.]aṯt y[.-]. | [---.]ṯḥm. | [---]t.[ ]r. | [---.--]n. | [---] h.l ʻdb. | [---]n.y 14[KRT].5.230
yʻn.lṭpn.il d pi[d]. | šmʻ.l ngr.il il[š]. | ilš.ngr bt bʻl. | w aṯt k.ngrt.il[ht]. | ʻl.l ṯkm.bnw n. | l nḫnpt.mšpy. | ṯlṯ.kmm.ṯrr 16[126].4.13
bʻl ny.w ymlk. | [y]ṣb.ʻln.w y[-]y. | [kr]t.ṯʻ.ʻln.bḫr. | [---].aṯt k.ʻl. | [---] k.yšṣi. | [---.]ḫbr.rbt. | [ḫbr.ṯrr]t.il d. | [pid.---].b 15[128].5.23
ṯ.yd h.yšu. | yr.šmm h.yr.b šmm.ʻṣr.yḫrṯ yšt. | l pḥm.il.aṯtm.k ypt.hm.aṯtm.tṣḥn. | y mt.mt.nḥtm.ḫṭ k.mmnnm.mṭ.y 23[52].39
klat.yd h. | b krb.ʻẓm.ridn. | mt.šmm.ks.qdš. | l tphn h.aṯt.krpn. | l tʻn.aṯrt.alp. | kd.yqḥ.b ḫmr. | rbt.ymsk.b msk h. | 3[ʻNT].1.14
[.zb]l y[m]. | [l pn.ṯp]ṭ[.nhr.]mlkt.[--]pm.l mlkt.wn.in.aṯt. | [l]k.k[m.ilm]. | [w ǵlmt.k bn.qdš.]w y[--.]zbl.ym.yʻ[--.]t 2.3[129].22
]. | lb.ab[d k].al[.---]. | [-]tm.iph.adt y.w.[---]. | tšṣḥq.hn.aṯt.l.ʻbd. | šbʻt.w.nṣp.ksp. | [-]tm.rb[.--.a]ḫd. | [---.--]t.b[-]. | [--- 1017.4
lp.šd.rbt.kmn. | hlk.aḫt h.bʻl.yʻn.tdrq. | ybnt.ab h.šrḥq.aṯt.l pnn h. | št.alp.qdm h.mria.w tk. | pn h.ṯḫspn.m h.w trḥṣ 3[ʻNT].4.84
]ybrk.il.krt. | [ṯʻ.ymr]m.nʻm[n.]ǵlm.il. | a[ṯt.tq]ḥ.y krt.aṯt. | tqḥ.bt k.ǵlmt.tšʻrb. | ḥqr k.tld.šbʻ.bnm.l k. | w ṯmn.tṯtm 15[128].2.21
.ybrk. | [ʻbd h.]ybrk.il.krt. | [ṯʻ.ymr]m.nʻm[n.]ǵlm.il. | a[ṯt.tq]ḥ.y krt.aṯt. | tqḥ.bt k.ǵlmt.tšʻrb. | ḥqr k.tld.šbʻ.bnm.l k 15[128].2.21
[---]. | qrd ga[n.--]. | b bt k.[--]. | w l dbḥ[--]. | ṯ[--]. | [--] aṯt yqḥ ʻz. | [---]ḏ. | [---]. | [---]. | hm qrt tuḫd.hm mt yʻl bnš. | b RS61[24.277.25]
| [---.]mdbm.l ḥrn.ḥr[n.---]. | [---.--]m.ql.hm[.---]. | [---].aṯt n.r[---]. | [---.]ḥr[-.--]. | [---.]plnt.[---]. | [---.]ʻmt.l ql.rpi[.---] 1001.1.29
arbʻ.ʻšr.ǵzrm. | arbʻ.aṯt. | pǵt.aḫt. | w.pǵy.aḫ. 2081.2
.r[--]. | aršm.bʻl [aṯt]. | ttḫ.bʻl aṯt. | ayab.bʻl aṯt. | iyṯr.bʻl aṯt. | ptm.bʻl ššlmt. | ʻdršp.bʻl ššlmt. | ṯtrn.bʻl ššlmt. | aršwn.bʻl 1077.5
[a]ḫm.l h.ṯmnt.bn um. | krt.ḥtk n.rš. | krt.grdš.mknt. | aṯt.ṣdq h.l ypq. | mtrḫt.yšr h. | aṯt.trḫ.w tbʻt. | ṯar um.tkn l h. 14[KRT].1.12
.l išt.ṣḥrrt.l pḥmm. | a[ṯ]tm.aṯt.il.aṯt.il.w ʻlm h.w hm. | aṯtm.tṣḥn y.ad ad.nḥtm.ḫṭ k. | mmnnm.mṭ yd k.hl.ʻṣr.ṯḥrr.l 23[52].43
mm h.yr.b šmm.ʻṣr.yḫrṯ yšt. | l pḥm.il.aṯtm.k ypt.hm.aṯtm.tṣḥn. | y mt.mt.nḥtm.ḫṭ k.mmnnm.mṭ.yd k. | h[l.]ʻṣr.ṯḥ 23[52].39
rr.l išt. | w ṣḥrrt.l pḥmm.btm.bt.il.bt.il. | w ʻlm h.w hn.aṯtm.tṣḥn y.mt mt. | nḥtm.ḫṭ k.mmnnm.mṭ yd k.hl.ʻṣr. | ṯḥrr 23[52].46
l ḫlmṭ. | w tr l qlḥ. | w š ḥll ydm. | b qdš il bt. | w tlḥm aṯt. | š l ilbt.šlmm. | kll ylḥm b h. | w l bbt šqym. | š l uḫr ḫlmṭ UG5.11.8
k n.rš. | krt.grdš.mknt. | aṯt.ṣdq h.l ypq. | mtrḫt.yšr h. | aṯt.trḫ.w tbʻt. | ṯar um.tkn l h. | mṯltt.kṯrm.tmt. | mrbʻt.zblnm 14[KRT].1.14
ndd.gzr.l zr.yʻdb.u ymn. | u šmal.b p hm.w l.tšbʻn y.aṯt.itrḫ. | y bn.ašld.šu.ʻdb.tk.mdbr qdš. | ṯm tgrgr.l abnm.w l. 23[52].64
ilk.r[--]. | aršm.bʻl [aṯt]. | ttḫ.bʻl aṯt. | ayab.bʻl aṯt. | iyṯr.bʻl aṯt. | ptm.bʻl ššlmt. | ʻdr 1077.2
bʻl.qdqd k.---]. | [--]t.mṭ.tpln.b g[bl.šnt k.---]. | [--]šnm.aṯtm.t[--.---]. | [m]lakm.ylak.ym.[tʻdt.ṯpṭ.nhr]. | b ʻlṣ.ʻlṣm.npr 2.1[137].10
y[.---] h. | [-]kt[.---.]nrn. | [b]n.nmq[.---]. | [ḫm]št.ksp.ʻl.aṯt. | [-]ṯd[.bn.]štn. 2055.19
.ǵzr.tšt.ḫ[---.b] | nšg h.ḥrb.tšt.b tʻr[t h]. | w ʻl.tlbš.npṣ.aṯt.[--]. | ṣbi nrt.ilm.špš.[-]r[--]. | pǵt.minš.šdm l mʻ[rb]. | nrt.i 19[1AQHT].4.208
--]. | pǵ[t.---]. | lk[.---]. | ki[--.---]. | w ḫ[--.---]. | my[.---]. | aṯ[t.---]. | aḫ k[.---]. | tr.ḫ[---]. | w tṣḥ[.---]. | tšqy[.---]. | tr.ḥt[-.-- 16.2[125].72
[---.--]ǵz. | [---.]qrt. | [---].aṯt. | [---.]w arbʻ.nʻr[m]. | [---.a]ḫd. | [---.]ṯlṯ.aṯt. 2142.3
mt. | [ap.m]ṯn.rgmm.argm.qštm. | [----.]mhrm.ht.tṣdn.tintt. | [---]m.tṣḥq.ʻnt.w b lb.tqny. | [---.]ṯb l y.l aqht.ǵzr.ṯb l 17[2AQHT].6.40
-.]qrt. | [---].aṯt. | [---.]w arbʻ.nʻr[m]. | [---.a]ḫd. | [---.]ṯlṯ.aṯt. 2142.6

asyy

n ḫnn. | b[n.-]n. | bn.ṣṣb. | bn.bʻltn ḫlq. | bn.mlkbn. | bn.asyy ḫlq. | bn.kṯly. | bn.kyn. | bn.ʻbdḫr. | [-]prm ḫlq. | [---]n ḫlq 2016.2.4

asm

pʻ[.b ḥm]drt. | ur.tisp k.yd.aqht.ǵz[r]. | tšt k.bm.qrb m.asm. | b p h.rgm.l yṣa.b špt h[.hwt h]. | b nši ʻn h.w tphn.in.[19[1AQHT].2.74
bṣql ypʻ b yǵlm. | ur.tisp k.yd.aqht. | ǵzr.tšt k.b qrb m.asm. | y.dnh.ysb.aklt h.yph. | šblt.b akt.šblt.ypʻ. | b ḥmdrt.šbl 19[1AQHT].2.67

ass

.bn.qldn. | gld.bt.klb. | l[---].bt.ḫzli. | bn.iḫyn. | ṣdqn.bn.ass. | bʻlyskn.bn.ss. | ṣdqn.bn.imrt. | mnḥm.bn.ḫyrn. | [-]yn.bn 102[323].3.8

asp

| b [----]. | w [----]. | bʻl.[---]. | il hd.b[---]. | at.bl.at.[---]. | yisp hm.b[ʻl.---]. | bn.dgn[.---]. | ʻḏbm.[---]. | uḫry.l[---]. | mṣt. 12[75].2.25
k.b ʻṯtrt.yisp.ḥmt. | [kṯ]r w ḫss.y[i]sp.ḥmt.šḥr.w šlm. | [yis]p.ḥmt.isp.[šp]š l hrm.ǵrpl.ʻl arṣ. | [l a]n ḥmt.l p[.n]ṯk.abd UG5.8.19
mt. | [---.š]pš.l [hrm.ǵrpl].ʻl.arṣ.l an. | [ḥ]mt.i[l.w] ḥrn.yisp.ḥmt. | [bʻl.w]dgn[.yi]sp.ḥmt.ʻnt.w ʻṯtrt. | [ti]sp.ḥmt.y[r] UG5.8.13
ʻṯtrt. | [ti]sp.ḥmt.y[r]ḫ.w.ršp.yisp.ḥmt. | [ʻṯt]r.w ʻṯpr.yisp.ḥmt.ṯṯ.w kṯṯ. | [yus]p.ḥmt.mlk.b ʻṯtrt.yisp.ḥmt. | [kṯ]r w UG5.8.16
.w] ḥrn.yisp.ḥmt. | [bʻl.w]dgn[.yi]sp.ḥmt.ʻnt.w ʻṯtrt. | [ti]sp.ḥmt.y[r]ḫ.w.ršp.yisp.ḥmt. | [ʻṯt]r.w ʻṯpr.yisp.ḥmt.ṯṯ.w UG5.8.15
ʻṯt]r.w ʻṯpr.yisp.ḥmt.ṯṯ.w kṯṯ. | [yus]p.ḥmt.mlk.b ʻṯtrt.yisp.ḥmt. | [kṯ]r w ḫss.y[i]sp.ḥmt.šḥr.w šlm. | [yis]p.ḥmt.isp.[UG5.8.17
[r]ḫ.w.ršp.yisp.ḥmt. | [ʻṯt]r.w ʻṯpr.yisp.ḥmt.ṯṯ.w kṯṯ. | [yus]p.ḥmt.mlk.b ʻṯtrt.yisp.ḥmt. | [kṯ]r w ḫss.y[i]sp.ḥmt.šḥr. UG5.8.17
l].ʻl.arṣ.l an. | [ḥ]mt.i[l.w] ḥrn.yisp.ḥmt. | [bʻl.w]dgn[.yi]sp.ḥmt.ʻnt.w ʻṯtrt. | [ti]sp.ḥmt.y[r]ḫ.w.ršp.yisp.ḥmt. | [ʻṯt]r UG5.8.14
.w]dgn[.yi]sp.ḥmt.ʻnt.w ʻṯtrt. | [ti]sp.ḥmt.y[r]ḫ.w.ršp.yisp.ḥmt. | [ʻṯt]r.w ʻṯpr.yisp.ḥmt.ṯṯ.w kṯṯ. | [yus]p.ḥmt.mlk.b UG5.8.15
ṯ.w kṯṯ. | [yus]p.ḥmt.mlk.b ʻṯtrt.yisp.ḥmt. | [kṯ]r w ḫss.y[i]sp.ḥmt.šḥr.w šlm. | [yis]p.ḥmt.isp.[šp]š l hrm.ǵrpl.ʻl arṣ. UG5.8.18
]ḥmt.l p[.nṯ]k.abd.l p.ak[l]. | [ṯm.dl.]isp.ḥ[mt.---.-]hm.yasp.ḥmt. | [---.š]pš.l [hrm.ǵrpl].ʻl.arṣ.l an. | [ḥ]mt.i[l.w] ḥrn. UG5.8.11
.ǵ]rpl.ʻl.arṣ. | [---.]ḥmt.l p[.nṯ]k.abd.l p.ak[l]. | [ṯm.dl.]isp.ḥ[mt.---.-]hm.yasp.ḥmt. | [---.š]pš.l [hrm.ǵrpl].ʻl.arṣ.l an. UG5.8.11
w ynšq.aḫl.an bṣ[ql]. | ynpʻ.b palt.bṣql ypʻ b yǵlm. | ur.tisp k.yd.aqht. | ǵzr.tšt k.b qrb m.asm. | y.dnh.ysb.aklt h.yph 19[1AQHT].2.66
. | w ynšq.aḫl.an.šblt. | tpʻ.b aklt.šblt.tpʻ[.b ḥm]drt. | ur.tisp k.yd.aqht.ǵz[r]. | tšt k.bm.qrb m.asm. | b p h.rgm.l yṣa.b 19[1AQHT].2.73
-.]mlakt. | [---.]ʻl.w tšʻ[d]n.npṣ h. | [---.]rgm.hn.[--]n.w aspt.[q]l h. | [---.rg]m.ank l[.--.--]rny. | [---.]ṯm.hw.i[--]ty. | [--- 1002.49
r um.tkn l h. | mṯltt.kṯrm.tmt. | mrbʻt.zblnm. | mḫmšt.yitsp. | ršp.nṯdṯt.ǵlm. | ym.mšbʻt hn.b šlḥ. | ṯtpl.yʻn.ḥtk h. | krt 14[KRT].1.18
sp.ḥmt. | [kṯ]r w ḫss.y[i]sp.ḥmt.šḥr.w šlm. | [yis]p.ḥmt.isp.[šp]š l hrm.ǵrpl.ʻl arṣ. | [l a]n ḥmt.l p[.n]ṯk.abd.l p.akl ṯ UG5.8.19
a.tnm y.ytn.[ks.b yd]. | krpn.b klat yd.[---]. | km ll.kḥṣ.tusp[.---]. | tgr.il.bn h.ṯr[.---]. | w yʻn.lṭpn.il.d p[id.---]. | šm.bn 1[ʻNT.X].4.11

asr

. | bn.ʻbṣ. | bn.argb. | ydn. | ilʻnt. | bn.urt. | ydn. | qṭn. | bn.asr. | bn.ʻdy. | bn.amt[m]. | myn. | šr. | bn.zql. | bn.iḫy. | bn.iyṯr. 2117.3.47
.]ṯr.ab h.il.ʻbd k.bʻl.y ym m.ʻbd k.bʻl. | [--.--]m.bn.dgn.a[s]r km.hw ybl.argmn k.k ilm. | [---.]ybl.k bn.qdš.mnḥy k.a 2.1[137].37

. | b qrb.h[kl y.aṯr h.rpum.l] | tdd.aṯr[h.l tdd.ilnym]. | asr.mr[kbt.---]. | t'ln.l mr[kbt hm.tity.l] | 'r hm.tl[kn.ym.w ṯ 22.1[123].22
n.b qrb.hkl y.[aṯr h.rpum]. | tdd.aṯr h.tdd.iln[ym.---]. | asr.sswm.tṣmd.dg[-.---]. | t'ln.l mrkbt hm.ti[ty.l 'r hm]. | tlkn 20[121].2.3
---.]išqb.aylt. | [---.--]m.b km.y'n. | [---].yd'.l yd't. | [---.]tasrn.ṯr il. | [---.]rks.bn.abnm. | [---.]upqt.'rb. | [---.w ẓ]r.mtn 1['NT.X].5.22
[q]dqd.ṯlṯ id.'l.ud[n]. | [---.-]sr.pdm.ṟiš h[m.---]. | 'l.pd.asr.[---.]l[.---]. | mẖlpt.w l.ytk.[d]m['t.]km. | rb't.ṯqlm.ṯṯp[.---. 19[1AQHT].2.81
pn. | [---].nšb.b 'n. | [---.]b km.y'n. | [---.yd'.l] yd't. | [---.t]asrn. | [---.]trks. | [---.]abnm.upqt. | [---.]l w ǵr mtn y. | [---.]r 1['NT.X].5.9
.mlkt. | [---].b d.mršp. | [---.m]rbṣ. | [---.r]b.ṯnnm. | [---.]asrm. | [---.--]kn. | [-----]. | [-----]. | [-----.-]l[-]. | [-----]. | [---.--]k. | 2015.1.6
št. | [---.]ẓ[--.-]rdy k. | [---.i]qnim. | [---.-]šu.b qrb. | [---].asr. | [---.--]m.ymt m. | [---].k iṯl. | [---.--]m.'db.l arṣ. | [---.]špm 1['NT.IX].2.7

asrm

š. | 'ṯr h.mlun.šnpt.ẖṣt h.b'l.ṣpn š. | [--]ṯ š.ilt.mgdl š.ilt.asrm š. | w l ll.šp. pgr.w ṯrmnm.bt mlk. | il[bt].gdlt.ušẖry.gdl 34[1].11
[---]. | [---.--]b. | [---.--]k. | [---.--]an. | [---.--]m.ank. | [---.]asrm. | [---.]dbḥm. | [---.y]rẖ.w šqr. | [---.--]b.b y[--.---]. | [-----]. 1002.22

asrn

t.srdnnm. | šb'm.uṯpt.srdnnm. | bn.aǵli.uṯpt.srdnnm. | asrn.uṯpt.srdnnm. | bn.qṣn.uṯpt.srdnnm. | yly.uṯpt.srdnnm. | 1124.9
[---].rb. | [-]lpl. | bn.asrn. | bn.šẖyn. | bn.abd'n. | bn.ẖnqn. | bn.nmq. | bn.amdn. | bn 1067.3

aǵzt

ašr nkl w ib[.bt]. | ẖrẖb.mlk qẓ ẖrẖb m | lk aǵzt.b sǵ[--.]špš. | yrẖ yṯkḥ yḥ[bq] [-]. | tld bt.[--]t.ẖ[--.l k] | ṯr 24[77].3

aǵli

t.srdnnm. | rpan.uṯpt.srdnnm. | šb'm.uṯpt.srdnnm. | bn.aǵli.uṯpt.srdnnm. | asrn.uṯpt.srdnnm. | bn.qṣn.uṯpt.srdnnm. | 1124.8

aǵld

. | bn.mṣrn. | bn.[-]dr[-]. | [---]l[-]. | [--]ym. | [--]rm. | [bn.]aǵld. | [w.nḥ]l h. | [w.nḥ]l h[.-]. 114[324].3.4
d.mrum. | bt.[-]b[-.-]sy[-]h. | nn[-].b[n].py[-.d.]yṯb.b.gt.aǵld. | šgn.bn b[--.---].d.yṯb.b.ilštm'. | abmn.bn.r[---].b.syn. | b 2015.2.5

aǵlyn

qštm.w.ql'. | bn.ṯ'l.qšt. | bn.[ẖ]dpṯr.ṯt.qštm.[w].ql'. | bn.aǵlyn.ṯt.qštm[.w.ṯl]ṯ.ql'm. | bn.'gw.qšt.w ql'. | bn.tbšn.ṯlṯ.qšt. 119[321].3.19
b'ln. | yrmn. | 'nil. | pmlk. | aby. | 'dyn. | aǵlyn. | [--]rd. | [--]qrd. | [--]r. 1066.7

aǵlkz

.b d.gmrd. | [šd.]abyy.b d.ibrmd. | [šd.]bn.ṯṯrn.b d.bnš.aǵlkz. | [šd.b]d.b[n].tkwn. | [ubdy.md]rǵlm. | [šd.bn.--]n.b d. 82[300].2.20
k[bd.---]. | tgmr k[--.---]. | ẖmšm a[--.---]. | kbd [---]. | d[.a]ǵlkz[.---]. 2120.12

aǵlmn

-]ral. | šdn. | [-]ǵl. | bn.b'ltǵpṯ. | ḥrš.btm. | ršpab. | [r]ṣn. | [a]ǵlmn. | [a]ẖyn. | [k]rwn. | [k]l[by]. | [--]ṯn. | [---]d. | a[ǵ]ltn. | [- 2060.13
.b gt.ṯrmn. | aḥd.alp.idṯn.d aḥd.b.'nqpat. | [aḥd.al]p.d aǵlmn. | [d aḥd b.g]t gbry. | [---].aḥd.aḥd.b.y'ny. | [---.-]ḥm.b. 1129.12
spr.bnš.mlk. | d taršn.'msn. | bṣr.abn.špšyn. | dqn. | aǵlmn. | kn'm. | aḥršp. | anntn. | b'lrm. | [-]ral. | šdn. | [-]ǵl. | bn. 2067.1.5
d.lqḥt.ṯlǵdy. | w.kd.ištir.'m.qrt. | 'št.'šr h.šmn. | 'mn.bn.aǵlmn. | arb'm.ksp.'l.qrt. | b.šd.bn.[u]brš. | ẖmšt.'šrt. | b.šd.bn. 1083.5

aǵltn

aǵltn. | urtn. | annṯb. | ubn. | špšyn. | abmn. | [--]dn. | [ṯ]b'm. | [-- 1072.1
ky. | lbw[-].uẖ.pdm.b.y'rt. | pǵyn.b.tpḥ. | amri[l].b.šrš. | aǵltn.b.midẖ. | [--]n.b.ayly. | [-]lyn.b.nghṯ. | [---.]b.nh[-]t. | [---. 2118.13
[b]n.qṯn. | [b]n.ǵrgn. | [b]n.tgdn. | bn.ẖdyn. | bn.sgr. | bn.aǵltn. | bn.ktln. | bn.'gwn. | bn.yšm'. | bdl.mdrǵlm. | bn.mmy. | 104[316].9
n.kdm.yn. | 'bdiltp.ṯm[n].y[n]. | qṣn.ẖ[---]. | arny.[---]. | aǵltn.ẖmš[.yn]. 1085.12
--]. | iwrm[-.]b[n.---]. | annt[n.]w[.---]. | w.ṯn.bn h.[---]. | aǵltn.ypr[y.---]. | w.šb'.ṣin h[.---]. 2044.17
spr.mdr[ǵlm]. | lt.hlk.b[.---]. | bn.b'yn.š[-.---]. | aǵltn.mid[-.---]. | bn.lṣn.'rm[y]. | aršw.bṣry. | arpṯr.y'rty. | bn. 87[64].4
[---.]ṯlṯm.d.nlqḥt. | [bn.ẖ]tyn.yd.bt h. | [aǵ]ltn. | tdn.bn.ddy. | 'bdil[.b]n ṣdqn. | bnšm.h[-]mt.ypḥm. | k 2045.3
.'l.[---]. | kd.'l.[---]. | ṯlṯ.'l.gmrš[.---]. | kd.'l.'bd[--]. | kd.'l.aǵlt[n]. | ṯlṯ.'l.a[b]m[n]. | arb'.'l[.--]ly. | kd.['l.--]ẓ. | kd.['l.---]. | 1082.1.20
. | abmn.b gt.m'rb. | atn. | ẖryn. | bn.'nt. | llwn. | agdṯb. | aǵltn. | [-]wn. | bldn. | [-]ln. | [-]ldn. | [i]wryn. | ẖbsn. | ulmk. | 'd 1061.9
---]. | b gt.yny. | agttp. | bn.'nt. | ǵzldn. | ṯrn. | ẖdbṯ. | [-]ḥl.aǵltn. | [-]n. | [-]mṯ. | [--.]bn.[']zn. | [--]yn. 1043.16
ṯn.bn h. | ṯmgdl.ykn'my.w.aṯt h. | w.bn h.w.alp.aḥ[d]. | aǵltn.[--]y.w[.aṯt h]. | w.bn h.w.alp.w.[---]. | [-]ln.[---]. | w.ṯn.b 1080.7
[aǵ]ltn. | [--]ṯm.b.gt.irbṣ. | [--]šmyn. | [w.]nḥl h. | bn.qṣn. | bn.ks 1073.1.1
n. | [a]ǵlmn. | [a]ẖyn. | [k]rwn. | [k]l[by]. | [--]ṯn. | [---]d. | a[ǵ]ltn. | [-----]. | [--]ny. | kn'm. | [-]p[-]. | 'pṯn. | pslm.ṣnr. 2060.13

aǵlṯr

[---.]ṯrd. | [---.]qpḥn. | [---.a]ǵlṯr. | [---.]ṯml. | [---.]bn.ḥṣqt. | [---.]bn.udr[-]. 2132.3

aǵt

. | šlmy. | [-----]. | [-----]. | q[---]. | t[---]. | ṯl[rby]. | ṯmr[y]. | aǵ[t]. | dm[t]. | šl[-]. | [---]m. | [-]rm. | [-]dm. | [-]m. | [--]m. | [m]r 2058.2.38
mlk. | gb'ly. | ypr. | ary. | ẓrn. | art. | ṯlḥny. | ṯlrby. | dmt. | aǵt. | w.qmnz. | slẖ. | ykn'm. | šlmy. | w.ull. | ṯmry. | qrt. | 'rm. | n 71[113].14
.kr[m.]aḥd[.---]. | dmt.lẖsn.krm.aḥd.anndr.kr[m.---]. | aǵt.mryn.ary[.]yukl.krm.[---]. | gdn.krm.aḥ[d.--]r.krm.[---]. | 1081.16
qrt ṯqlm.w nṣp. | šlmy.ṯql. | ary ṯql. | ṯmry ṯql.w.nṣp. | aǵt nṣp. | dmt ṯql. | ykn'm ṯql. 69[111].5
'. | [---].ẖbt. | [---].qmy. | [---.]qmy. | [---.--]b. | bn.t[--.---.a]ǵt. | špš[yn.---.u]br'y. | iln.[---]. | bn.[---].ar. | bn.[---].b.ar. | šp 2015.1.19

[l]krt. | k [k]lb.b bt k.nʻtq.k inr. | ap.h̠št k.ap.ab.ik mtm. | tmtn.u h̠št k.l ntn. | ʻtq.b d.at̠t.ab ṣrry. | tbky 16.1[125].3

šmh̠. | b l.mt k.ngln.k klb. | b bt k.nʻtq.k inr. | ap.h̠št k.ap.ab.k mtm. | tmtn.u h̠št k.l ntn. | ʻtq.b d.at̠t.ab.ṣrry. | ik m.y 16.1[125].17

h̠.b l.mt k.ngln. | k klb.[b]bt k.nʻtq. | k inr[.ap.]h̠št k. | ap.ab.k mtm.tmtn. | u h̠št k.l bky.ʻtq. | b d.at̠t ab.ṣrry. | u ilm. 16.2[125].102

wy.yʻš. | r.w yšqyn h.ybd.w yšr.ʻl h. | nʻm[n.w t]ʻnynn.ap ank.ah̠wy. | aqht[.ǵz]r.w yʻn.aqht.ǵzr. | al.tšrgn.y btlt m.d 17[2AQHT].6.32

[y]rš.ʻm y. | mnm.iršt k. | d h̠srt.w.ank. | aštn..l.ih̠ y. | w.ap.ank.mnm. | [h̠]s[r]t.w.uh̠ y. | [y]ʻmsn.t̠mn. | w.[u]h̠ y.al ybʻ 2065.18

y.ilm. | tǵr k. | tšlm k. | hn ny.ʻm ny. | kll.mid. | šlm. | w.ap.ank. | nh̠t.t̠m ny. | ʻm.adt ny. | mnm.šlm. | rgm.t̠t̠b. | l.ʻbd k. 51[95].13

---.--]š[-.--].w.ašt. | [---].amr k. | [---].k.ybt.mlk. | [---].w.ap.ank. | [---].l.ǵr.amn. | [---.-]ktt.hn.ib. | [---.]mlk. | [---.]adt y. 1012.15

b[-.---.]] [---].mlak.bn.ktpm.rgm.bʻl h.w y[--.---]. | [---].ap.anš.zbl.bʻl.šdmt.bg[--.---]. | [---.-]dm.mlak.ym.tʻdt.t̠pṭ.nh[2.1[137].43

km.hw ybl.argmn k.k ilm. | [---.]ybl.k bn.qdš.mnh̠y k.ap.anš.zbl.bʻ[l]. | [-.yuh̠]d.b yd.mšh̠t.bm.ymn.mh̠ṣ.ǵlmm.yš[2.1[137].38

h.tbʻ.ǵlmm.l t̠t̠b.[idk.pnm]. | l ytn.tk.ǵr.ll.ʻm.phr.mʻd.ap.ilm.l lh̠[m]. | yt̠b.bn qdš.l t̠rm.bʻl.qm.ʻl.il.hlm. | ilm.tph h 2.1[137].20

tqrb.w ld.bnt.l h. | mk.b šbʻ.šnt. | bn.krt.km hm.tdr. | ap.bnt.h̠ry. | km hm.w t̠h̠ss.at̠rt. | ndr h.w ilt.p[--]. | w tšu.g h 15[128].3.24

l t̠lb.[---]. | mit.rh̠[.---]. | t̠t̠lb.a[--.---]. | yšu.g h[.---]. | i.ap.bʻ[l.---]. | i.hd.d[---.---]. | ynpʻ.bʻ[l.---]. | b t̠mnt.[---]. | yqrb.[5[67].4.6

.h̠wt[.---]. | [---].nzdt.qr[t]. | [---.]dt nzdt.m[lk]. | [---.]w.ap.bt̠n[.---]. | [---.]bʻl y.y[--]. | [---.-]l[-.---]. 2127.2.6

| b šdm.ʻl k.pht. | drʻ.b ym.tn.ah̠d. | b ah̠ k.ispa.w ytb. | ap.d anšt.im[-]. | ah̠d.b ah̠ k.l[--]n. | hn[-.]ah̠ẓ[.---]l[-]. | [ʻ]nt.a 6[49].5.21

tnṣn.w tldn.tld.[ilm.]nʻmm.agzr ym. | bn.ym.ynqm.b a[p.]d̠[d.r]gm.l il.ybl. | at̠t y.il.ylt.mh.ylt.ilmy nʻmm. | agzr y 23[52].59

.šh̠t.l brk h.tṣi.km. | rh̠.npš h.km.it̠l.brlt h.km. | qt̠r.b ap h.b ap.mhr h.ank. | l ah̠wy.tqh̠.ytpn.mhr.št. | tštn.k nšr.b 18[3AQHT].4.26

u w]l yttn mss št qlql. | [w št ʻrgz y]dk ah̠d h w yṣq b ap h. | [k.yih̠d akl s]šw št mkšr grn. | [w št aškrr w p]r h̠drt. | 160[55].9

.ššw]. | mss.[št.qlql.w.št]. | ʻrgz[.ydk.ah̠d h]. | w.yṣq[.b.ap h]. | k.yih̠d[.akl.ššw]. | št.mkš[r.grn]. | w.št.ašk[rr]. | w.pr.h̠ 161[56].11

r.grn]. | w.št.ašk[rr]. | w.pr.h̠dr[t.ydk]. | ah̠d h.w.yṣq[.b.ap h]. | k.yih̠d.akl.š[šw]. | št.nni.št.mk[št.grn]. | št.irǵn.h̠mr[.y 161[56].16

]. | ah̠d h.w.yṣq.b[.ap h]. | k.yraš.ššw.[št]. | bln.qt.yṣq.b.a[p h]. | k ygʻr[.ššw.---]. | dprn[.---]. | drʻ.[---]. | tmt̠l[.---]. | mǵ 161[56].22

| [k h̠r s]šw mǵmǵ w b[ṣql ʻrgz]. | [ydk ah̠]d h w yṣq b ap h. | [k h̠r]ššw h̠ndrt̠ w t̠[qd m]r. | [ydk ah̠d h w yṣq b ap 160[55].5

k [h̠r ššw mǵmǵ]. | w [bṣql.ʻrgz.ydk]. | a[h̠d h.w.yṣq.b.ap h]. | k.[h̠r.ššw.h̠ndrt̠]. | w.t̠[qd.mr.ydk.ah̠d h]. | w.y[ṣq.b.a 161[56].4

[k.---.]šš[w.---]. | [---.w]yṣq b a[p h]. | [k h̠r s]šw mǵmǵ w b[ṣql ʻrgz]. | [ydk ah̠]d h w yṣq b 160[55].3

h. | [k h̠r]ššw h̠ndrt̠ w t̠[qd m]r. | [ydk ah̠d h w yṣq b ap h. | [k l yh̠ru w]l yttn mss št qlql. | [w št ʻrgz y]dk ah̠d h 160[55].7

]. | k.[h̠r.ššw.h̠ndrt̠]. | w.t̠[qd.mr.ydk.ah̠d h]. | w.y[ṣq.b.ap h]. | k.l.h̠[ru.w.l.yttn.ššw]. | mss.[št.qlql.w.št]. | ʻrgz[.ydk.a 161[56].7

]. | w.pr[.h̠drt.w.št]. | irǵ[n.h̠mr.ydk]. | ah̠d[h.w.yṣq.b.ap h]. | k yr[a]š.šš[w.w.ykhp]. | mid.dblt.yt̠[nt.w]. | ṣmq[m].yt̠ 161[56].31

nni.št.mk[št.grn]. | št.irǵn.h̠mr[.ydk]. | ah̠d h.w.yṣq.b[.ap h]. | k.yraš.ššw.[št]. | bln.qt.yṣq.b.a[p h]. | k ygʻr[.ššw.---]. | 161[56].20

.l brk h]. | yṣat.km.rh̠.npš[h.km.it̠l]. | brlt h.km.qt̠r.[b ap h.---]. | ʻnt.b ṣmt.mhr h.[---]. | aqht.w tbk.y[---.---]. | abn.a 18[3AQHT].4.37

-----]. | [---.-]n[-]. | [k yraš ššw št bln q]t̠ ydk. | [w yṣq b ap h]. | [-----]. | [-----]. | [-----]. | [---.-]rb. | [-----]. | [-----]. | [-----]. | 160[55].15

| dblt ytnt w ṣmqm ytn[m]. | w qmh̠ bql yṣq ah̠d h. | b ap h. 160[55].26

]. | ṣmq[m].ytnm.w[.qmh̠.bql]. | tdkn.ah̠d h.w[.yṣq]. | b.ap h. 161[56].36

.ylak.ym.[tʻdt.t̠pṭ.nhr]. | b ʻlṣ.ʻlṣm.npr.š[--.---]. | ut̠.t̠br.ap hm.tbʻ.ǵlm[m.al.t̠t̠b.idk.pnm]. | al.ttn.ʻm.ph̠r.mʻd.t[k.ǵr.l 2.1[137].13

hkl h. | ʻrb.b bt h.kt̠rt.bnt. | hll.snnt.apnk.dnil. | mt.rpi.ap.hn.ǵzr.mt. | hrnmy.alp.ytbh̠.l kt̠ | rt.yšlh̠m.kt̠rt.w y | ššq.b 17[2AQHT].2.28

t̠mn. | ašrbʻ.qṣʻt.w hn šb[ʻ]. | b ymm.apnk.dnil.mt. | rpi.a hn.ǵzr.mt.hrnm[y]. | ytšu.ytb.b ap.t̠ǵr.t̠ht̠. | adrm.d b grn.y 17[2AQHT].5.5

[.---.]w[.---]. | w hm.at.tr[gm.---]. | w.drm.ʻtr[--.---]. | w ap.ht.k[--.]škn. | w.mtnn[.---.]ʻmn k. | [-]štš.[---.]rgm y. | [-]w 54.1.20[13.2.5]

id.yph.mlk. | r[š]p.h̠gb.ap. | w[.n]pš.ksp. | w h̠rṣ.km[-]. | w.h̠[--.-]lp. | w.š.l[--]p. | w[.--. 2005.1.2

bn.gt̠rm. | bt.mlk.t̠ql.h̠rṣ. | l špš.w yrh̠.l gt̠r. | t̠ql.ksp.t̠b.ap w np[š]. | l ʻnt h.t̠ql.h̠rṣ. | l špš[.w y]rh̠.l gt̠r.t̠n. | [t̠ql.ksp].t̠ 33[5].12

[š]. | l ʻnt h.t̠ql.h̠rṣ. | l špš[.w y]rh̠.l gt̠r.t̠n. | [t̠ql.ksp].t̠b.ap.w npš. | [---].bt.alp w š. | [---.--]m.l gt̠rm. | [---.]l ʻnt m. | [--- 33[5].15

]n.šrm. | iqran.ilm.nʻmm[.agzry ym.bn]ym. | ynqm.b ap zd.at̠rt.[---]. | špš.mṣprt dlt hm[.---]. | w ǵnbm.šlm.ʻrbm.t̠n 23[52].24

[l]krt. | k [k]lb.b bt k.nʻtq.k inr. | ap.h̠št k.ap.ab.ik mtm. | tmtn.u h̠št k.l ntn. | ʻtq.b d.at̠t.ab ṣrr 16.1[125].3

a]b n. | nšmh̠.b l.mt k.ngln. | k klb.[b]bt k.nʻtq. | k inr[.ap.]h̠št k. | ap.ab.k mtm.tmtn. | u h̠št k.l bky.ʻtq. | b d.at̠t ab.ṣ 16.2[125].101

k.ab n.ašmh̠. | b l.mt k.ngln.k klb. | b bt k.nʻtq.k inr. | ap.h̠št k.ap.ab.k mtm. | tmtn.u h̠št k.l ntn. | ʻtq.b d.at̠t.ab.ṣrr 16.1[125].17

. | w t̠n.ytb.krt.l ʻd h. | ytb.l ksi mlk. | l nh̠t.l kh̠t.drkt. | ap.yṣb.ytb.b hkl. | w ywsrnn.ggn h. | lk.l ab k.yṣb.lk. | l[ab]k 16.6[127].25

bš[-.]t[-].ǵlm.l šdt[.-.]ymm. | [---.]b ym.ym.y[--].yš[ ]n.ap k.ʻt̠tr.dm[.---.]] [---.]h̠rh̠rtm.w[--.]n[--.]iš[--.]h[---.]išt. | [-- 2.3[129].12

r]. | [ulp.h̠bt km.ulp.mdll km.ulp.qr zbl]. | [u t̠h̠t̠u.u b ap km.u b qṣrt.npš km.u b qtt]. | [tqt̠t.u t̠h̠t̠u.l dbh̠m.w l.tʻ.d 32[2].1.8A

p. | h̠bt km.ulp.m[dl]l km.ulp.qr zbl.u[š]n yp km. | u b ap km.u b q[ṣ]rt.npš km.u b qtt.tqt̠t. | ušn yp km.l d[b]h̠m.w 32[2].1.23

r.ulp.h̠bt km.ulp.mdll km.ulp]. | [qr zbl.ušn.yp km.b ap km.u b qṣrt.np]št km. | [u b qtt.tqt̠t.ušn.yp km.---.-]yt k APP.I[-].1.17

br.ulp.h̠bt kn.ulp.mdll kn.ulp.]qr zbl. | [ušn.yp kn.u b ap kn.u b qṣrt.npš kn.u b]qtt. | [tqt̠tn.ušn.yp kn.---.-]gym. | [APP.I[-].2.15

ul]p.h̠bt kn. | [ulp.mdll kn.ulp.qr zbl.ušn.y]p kn. | [u b ap kn.u b qṣrt.npšt kn.u b qt]t tqt̠t. | [ušn.yp kn.---.--]l.il.tʻd̠r APP.I[-].1.7

r.ulp.[h̠bt] kn[.u]lp.mdll kn.ulp qr z[bl]. | lšn yp kn.b ap [kn.u b qṣ]rt.npš kn.u b qtt. | tqt̠tn.ušn y[p kn.l dbh̠m.]w 32[2].1.31

]ǵbr. | ulp.h̠bt kn.ulp.md[ll k]n.ulp.q[r zbl]. | u t̠h̠t̠in.b ap kn.u b [q]ṣrt.npš[kn.u b qtt]. | tqt̠tn u t̠h̠t̠in.l bh̠m.w l tʻ. 32[2].1.14

l yblt.h̠btm. | ap ksp hm. | l yblt. | w ht.luk ʻm ml[kt]. | tǵsdb.šmlšn. | w tbʻ 1021.2

ǵy. | hbt.hw. | h̠rd.w.šl hw. | qr[-]. | akl n.b.grnt. | l.bʻr. | ap.krmm. | h̠lq. | qrt n.h̠lq. | w.dʻ.dʻ. 2114.10

r.bʻl.ṣ[p]n.h̠lm. | qdš.nny.h̠[l]m.adr. | h̠l.rh̠b.mk[npt]. | ap.krt bn[m.il]. | šph̠.ltpn[.w qdš]. | bkm.tʻr[b.ʻl.ab h]. | tʻrb.h̠ 16.2[125].110

.ab.ǵr.bʻl. | ṣpn.h̠lm.qdš. | any.h̠lm.adr.h̠l. | rh̠b.mknpt.ap. | [k]rt.bnm.il.šph̠. | ltpn.w qdš.ʻl. | ab h.yʻrb.ybky. | w yšnn 16.1[125].9

t̠h̠ss.at̠rt. | ndr h.w ilt.p[--]. | w tšu.g h.w [tṣh̠]. | ph mʻ.ap.k[rt.--]. | u t̠n.ndr[.---]. | apr.[---]. | [-----]. 15[128].3.28

]. | [---].pit. | [---.]qbat. | [---.]inšt. | [--]u.l tštql. | [---].t̠ry.ap.l tlh̠m. | [l]h̠m.trmmt.l tšt. | yn.tǵẓyt.špš. | rpim.t̠ht̠k. | špš.t 6.6[62.2].42

m l t[--]. | [---.]drk.brh̠.arṣ.lk pn h.yrk.bʻ[l]. | [---.]bt k.ap.l ph̠r k ʻnt tqm.ʻnt.tqm. | [---.p]h̠r k.ygrš k.qr.bt k.ygrš k. 1001.2.9

[.b yʻr]. | thdy.lh̠m.w dqn[.t̠t̠lt̠]. | qn.d̠rʻ h.t̠h̠rt̠.km.gn. | ap lb.k ʻmq.t̠t̠lt̠.bmt. | bʻl.mt.my.lim.bn dgn. | my.hmlt.at̠r.bʻ 6[62].1.5

ltm.b yʻr. | yhdy.lh̠m.w dqn. | yt̠lt̠.qn.d̠rʻ h.yh̠rt̠. | k gn.ap lb.k ʻmq.yt̠lt̠. | bmt.yšu.g h.w yṣh̠. | bʻl.mt.my.lim.bn. | dg 5[67].6.21

| gršnn.l k[si.mlk h.l nh̠t.l kh̠t]. | drkt h.š[--.--]. | w hm.ap.l[--.---]. | ymh̠ṣ k.k[--.---]. | il.dbh̠.[---]. | pʻr.b[--.---]. | t̠bh̠.al 1[ʻNT.X].4.26

|'m k.w.hm.|l.'l.w.lakm.|ilak.w.at.|um y.al.tdḥṣ.|w.ap.mhkm.|b.lb k.al.|tšt. 1013.22
brk h.tṣi.km.|rḥ.npš h.km.iṯl.brlt h.km.|qṭr.b ap h.b ap.mhr h.ank.|l aḥwy.tqḥ.yṭpn.mhr.št.|tštn.k nšr.b ḥbš h.k 18[3AQHT].4.26
l.ǵr.amn.|[---.-]ktt.hn.ib.|[---.]mlk.|[---.]adt y.td'.|w.ap.mlk.ud[r].|[-]d'.k.iḫd.[---].|w.mlk.b'l y.|lm.škn.hnk.|l ' 1012.20
[---.]y[--].ḫtt.mtt[--].|[--.]ḥy[--.--.]l ašṣi.hm.ap.amr[--].|[---].w b ym.mnḫ l abd.b ym.irtm.m[--].|[ṯpṭ].n 2.4[68].2
w ṣmt.ǵllm[.---].|aḫḏ.aklm.k [---].|npl.b mšmš[.---].|anp n m yḥr[r.---].|bmt n m.yšḫn.[---].|qrn h.km.ǵb[-.---].| 12[75].2.38
t.|ql h.yš[m'].ṯr.[il].ab h.[---]l.|b šb't.ḥdrm.[b ṯ]mn[t.ap].|sgrt.g[-].[-]ẓ[.---] h[.---].|'n.ṯk[.---].|'ln.ṯ[--.---].|l p'n.ǵ 3['NT.VI].5.19
m].|[šbt.dqn k.mm'm.]y'ny.|il.b šb't.ḥdrm.b ṯmnt.|ap.sgrt.yd'[t k.]bt.k an[št].|k in.b ilht.ql[ṣ] k.mh.tarš[n].|l 3['NT.VI].5.35
-].|k[--.---].|'šrm[.---].|tšt.tb'[.---].|qrt.mlk[.---].|w.'l.ap.s[--.---].|b hm.w.rgm.hw.al[--].|atn.ksp.l hm.'d.|ilak.'m. 2008.2.5
t.ilm.l ḥkmt.|šbt.dqn k.l tsr k.|rḥntt.d[-].l irt k.|wn ap.'dn.mṭr h.|b'l.y'dn.'dn.ṯkt.b glṯ.|w tn.ql h.b 'rpt.|šrh.l a 4[51].5.68
ḫ.|b'l.mt.my.lim.bn.|dgn.my.hmlt.aṯr.|b'l.ard.b arṣ.ap.|'nt.ttlk.w tṣd.kl.ǵr.|l kbd.arṣ.kl.gb'.|l [k]bd.šdm.tmǵ.l 5[67].6.25
w anhbm].|kla[t.ṯǵ]r[t.bht.'nt.w tqry.ǵlmm.b št.ǵr].|ap 'nt tm[ṯḫṣ.b 'mq.ṯḫtṣb.bn.qrytm.tmḫṣ].|lim ḫ[p.ym.---]. 7.2[130].25
ap.|pd.|mlk.|ar.|atlg.|gb'ly.|ulm.|m'rby.|m'r.|arny.|š'rt 2074.1
ap.|pd.|mlk.arb'.ḫm[rm.w.arb]'.bnšm.|ar.ḫmš.ḥmr[m.w.ḫ 2040.1
.'dbt.bht[h.b']l.|y'db.hd.'db[.'d]bt.|hkl h.ṭbḫ.alpm[.ap].|ṣin.šql.ṯrm[.w]m|ria.il.'glm.d[t].|šnt.imr.qmṣ.l[l]im.| 4[51].6.40
|ymḫṣ k.k[--.---].|il.dbḥ.[---].|p'r.b[--.---].|ṭbḫ.alp[m.ap.ṣin.šql].|ṯrm.w [mri.ilm.'glm.dt.šnt].|imr.[qmṣ.llim.---]. 1['NT.X].4.30
bl.mlk.'llm y.km.tdd.|'nt.ṣd.tštr.'pt.šmm.|ṭbḫ.alpm.ap ṣin.šql.ṯrm.|w mri ilm.'glm.dt.šnt.|imr.qmṣ.llim.k ksp.| 22.2[124].12
|ḫṭ h.imḫṣ h.k d.'l.qšt h.|imḫṣ h.'l.qṣ't h.hwt.|l aḥw.ap.qšt h.l ttn.|l y.w b mt[.-]ḥ.mṣṣ[-]t[.--].|pr'.qẓ.y[bl].šblt.| 19[1AQHT].1.16
spr.ḫrd.arr.|ap arb'm[.--].|pd[.---.ḫm]šm.kb[d].|ǵb[-.---.]kbd.|m[--.---.k 2042.2
.|ḫrṣ.šmḫ.rbt.a[ṯrt].|ym.gm.l ǵlm h.k [tṣḥ].|'n.mkṯr.ap.t[---].|dgy.rbt.aṯr[t.ym].|qḥ.rṯt.b d k t[---].|rbt.'l.ydm[.- 4[51].2.30
ṯt y.il.ylt.mh.ylt.ilmy n'mm.|agzr ym.bn ym.ynqm.b ap.ḏd.št.špt.|l arṣ.špt l šmm.w 'rb.b p hm.'ṣr.šmm.|w dg b 23[52].61
[r] m.ddym.ask.|šlm.l kb[d].awṣ.arbdd.|l kbd.š[d]m.ap.mṯn.rgmm.|argmn.lk.lk.'nn.ilm.|atm.bštm.w an.šnt.|u 3['NT].4.75
t.|mṯb.pdry.b ar.|mẓll.ṭly.bt rb.|mṯb.arṣy.bt.y'bdr.|ap.mṯn.rgmm.|argm k.šskn m'.|mgn.rbt.aṯrt ym.|mǵẓ.qny 4[51].1.20
l]riš.ḥrṣ.l ẓr.qdqd y.|[--.]mt.kl.amt.w an.mtm.amt.|[ap.m]ṯn.rgmm.argm.qštm.|[----.]mhrm.ht.tṣdn.tinṯt.|[---]m 17[2AQHT].6.39
k.dnil.|[m]t.rpi.ap[h]n.ǵzr.|[mt.hrn]my.ytšu.|[yṯb.b ap.ṯ]ǵr[.t]ḫt.|[adrm.d b grn.y]dn.|[dn.almnt.y]ṯpṭ.|[ṯpṭ.yt 19[1AQHT].1.22
.apnk.dnil.mt.|rpi.a hn.ǵzr.mt.hrnm[y].|ytšu.yṯb.b ap.ṯǵr.tḥt.|adrm.d b grn.ydn.|dn.almnt.yṯpṭ.ṯpṭ.ytm.|b nši 17[2AQHT].5.6
--]y[.---.-]nt.[š]ṣat[k.]rḥ.npš.hm.|k.iṯl.brlt n[-.k qṭr.b ap -].|tmǵyn.tša.g h[m.w tṣḥn].|šm'.l dnil.[mt.rpi].|mt.aqh 19[1AQHT].2.88
y.ns[--.---].|[---.]trgm[.-----].|[---.]alp.p[--.---].|[--.]ht.ap[.---].|[---.]iln[--.---]. 63[26].2.4
[-----].|[---].at[--.---].|[---] h.ap.[---].|[---].w t'n.[btlt.'nt.---].|[bnt.bht]k.y ilm[.bnt.bht k 18[3AQHT].1.5
[---].ap[.---].|[---].l y.l [---].|[---] ny.ṯp[--.---].|[---.--]zn.a[--.---].|[63[26].1.1

aphn

drq.ḫss.|hlk.qšt.ybln.hl.yš|rb'.qṣ't.apnk.dnil.|mt.rpi.aphn.ǵzr.mt.|hrnmy.gm.l aṯt h.k yṣḥ.|šm'.mtt.dnty.'d[b].| 17[2AQHT].5.14
[-]t[.--].|pr'.qẓ.y[bl].šblt.|b ǵlp h.apnk.dnil.|[m]t.rpi.ap[h]n.ǵzr.|[mt.hrn]my.ytšu.|[yṯb.b ap.ṯ]ǵr[.t]ḫt.|[adrm.d 19[1AQHT].1.20
b'.kṯr.|l ahl h.hyn.tb'.l mš|knt h.apnk.dnil.m[t].|rpi.aphn.ǵzr.m[t].|hrnmy.qšt.yqb.[--]|rk.'l.aqht.k yq[--.---].|pr 17[2AQHT].5.34

apy

]m.|'šr.ksdm.yd.lmd hm.lqḥ.|'šr.mḫṣm.yd.lmd hm.|apym.|[bn]š gt.iptl.|[---]ym.|[----]m.|[-----].|[bnš.g]t.ir.|bn 1040.10
mṣd k.w yrd.|krt.l ggt.'db.|akl.l qryt.|ḥṭt.l bt.ḫbr.|yip.lḥm.d ḫmš.|mǵd.ṯdṯ.yrḫm.|'dn.ngb.w yṣi.|ṣbu.ṣbi.ngb. 14[KRT].2.83
[b m]ṣd h.yrd.krt.|[l g]gt.'db.akl.l qryt.|ḥṭt.l bt.ḫbr.|yip.lḥm.d ḫmš.|[mǵ]d.ṯdṯ.yr[ḫm].|'dn.ngb.w [yṣi.ṣbu].|ṣbi. 14[KRT].4.174
[-.]l ks[p.-]m.|l.mri[.--].|ṯmn kbd[.--]i.|arb'm[.--].|l apy.mr[i.--].|[---.--]d.|[-----]. 1133.5
d.zlb[n.--].|arb'.'š[r.]dd.n'r.|d.apy[.--].|w.arb['.--]d.apy.'bd h.|w.mrb'[t.l ']bdm. 2094.5
ḥ.d.kly.k ṣḥ.illdrm.|b d.zlb[n.--].|arb'.'š[r.]dd.n'r.|d.apy[.--].|w.arb['.--]d.apy.'bd h.|w.mrb'[t.l ']bdm. 2094.4

apln

l.|bn.arnbt.|qdšm.|b[-.--]t.|[---.-]l[--].|[---.]pr[--].|[-.a]pln.|bn.mzt.|bn.ṯrn.|w.nḥl h.|[--.-]hs.|[--.--]nyn.|[-----]. 2163.2.12

apn

.tr hn.|w.l.ṯt.mrkbtm.|inn.uṯpt.|w.ṯlṯ.ṣmdm.w.ḥrṣ.|apnt.b d.rb.ḥršm.|d.ššа.ḥwy h. 1121.9
ṯmn.mrkbt.dt.|'rb.bt.mlk.|yd.apnt hn.|yd.ḥẓ hn.|yd.tr hn.|w.l.ṯt.mrkbtm.|inn.uṯpt.|w.ṯ 1121.3
mdm.w ḥrṣ.|ṯryn.sśwm.|ṯryn.aḥd.d bnš.|arb'.ṣmdm.apnt.|w ḥrṣ.|tš'm.mrḥ.aḥd.|kbd. 1123.7
.ql.|'l.b'l.b ṣrrt.|ṣpn.ytmr.b'l.|bnt h.y'n.pdry.|bt.ar.apn.ṭly.|[bt.r]b.pdr.yd'.|[---]t.im[-]lt.|[-----].|[---.--]rt. 3['NT].1.24
.--]ṯ.'bd.l.kyn.|k[rm.--.]l.i[w]rtḏl.|ḥl.d[--.'bd]yrḫ.b d.apn.|krm.i[--].l.[---.]a[-]bn. 2027.2.11
.ab[l].|kry.|pss.|ilṯḥm.|ḥrm.|bn.bty.|'by.|šm[n].bn.apn.|krty.|bn.ubr.|[bn] mdḫl.|bn.sy[n]n.|bn.šrn. 2078.17
m.l.'[--].|apnm.l.[---].|apnm.l.d[--].|apnm.l.bn[.---].|apnm.l.[b]n[.---].|apnm.l.bn[.---].|ṯlṯ.ṣmdm[.---].|mṣ[r]n[.-- 145[318].7
d.prḫ[-.---].|apnm.l.'[--].|apnm.l.[---].|apnm.l.d[--].|apnm.l.bn[.---].|apnm.l.[b]n[.---].|apnm.l.bn[.---].|ṯlṯ.ṣmd 145[318].6
---].|apnm.l.d[--].|apnm.l.bn[.---].|apnm.l.[b]n[.---].|apnm.l.bn[.---].|ṯlṯ.ṣmdm[.---].|mṣ[r]n[.---]. 145[318].8
m.a[--.---].|b d.prḫ[-.---].|apnm.l.'[--].|apnm.l.[---].|apnm.l.d[--].|apnm.l.bn[.---].|apnm.l.[b]n[.---].|apnm.l.bn[145[318].5
ṣmdm.a[--.---].|b d.prḫ[-.---].|apnm.l.'[--].|apnm.l.[---].|apnm.l.d[--].|apnm.l.bn[.---].|ap 145[318].3
ṣmdm.a[--.---].|b d.prḫ[-.---].|apnm.l.'[--].|apnm.l.[---].|apnm.l.d[--].|apnm.l.bn[.---].|apnm.l.[b]n[.--- 145[318].4
[-----.apnk].|[dnil.mt.rp]i.apn.ǵz[r].|[mt.hrnmy.]uzr.ilm.ylḥm.|[uzr.yšqy.]bn.qdš.yd. 17[2AQHT].1.2
[---.--]ql.|[---.--]bn.|ap[n.---].|ap[n.---].|ap[n.---].|ap[n.---].|tgmr[.---]ṯm.|ṯṯ.'[-- 152[-].3
[---.--]ql.|[---.--]bn.|ap[n.---].|ap[n.---].|ap[n.---].|ap[n.---].|tgmr[.---]ṯm.|ṯṯ.'[--.---]. 152[-].4
[---.--]ql.|[---.--]bn.|ap[n.---].|ap[n.---].|ap[n.---].|ap[n.---].|tgmr[.---]ṯm.|ṯṯ.'[--.---]. 152[-].5
[---.--]ql.|[---.--]bn.|ap[n.---].|ap[n.---].|ap[n.---].|ap[n.---].|tgmr[.---]ṯm.|ṯṯ.'[--.---]. 152[-].6

m.t[---].|šknt.[---].|bkym[.---].|ġr.y[----].|ydm.[---].|apn.[---].|[--.]b[.---]. 16.2[125].119

apnk

-----].|[---.]abl.qšt ṯmn.|ašrb‘.qṣ‘t.w hn šb[‘].|b ymm.apnk.dnil.mt.|rpi.a hn.ġzr.mt.hrnm[y].|ytšu.yṯb.b ap.ṯġr.t 17[2AQHT].5.4
ġyn.|yštql.dnil.l hkl h.|‘rb.b bt h.kṯrt.bnt.|hll.snnt.apnk.dnil.|mt.rpi.ap.hn.ġzr.mt.|hrnmy.alp.yṯbḫ.l kṯ|rt.yšl 17[2AQHT].2.27
t.b‘l.|ḥkpt il.kl h.tb‘.kṯr.|l ahl h.hyn.tb‘.l mš|knt h.apnk.dnil.m[t].|rpi.aphn.ġzr.m[t].|hrnmy.qšt.yqb.[--]|rk.‘l 17[2AQHT].5.33
.kṯr.|k y‘n.w y‘n.tdrq.ḫss.|hlk.qšt.ybln.hl.yš|rb‘.qṣ‘t.apnk.dnil.|mt.rpi.aphn.ġzr.mt.|hrnmy.gm.l aṯt h.k yṣḥ.|š 17[2AQHT].5.13
|l y.w b mt[.-]ḫ.mṣṣ[-]t[.--].|pr‘.qẓ.y[bl].šblt.|b ġlp h.apnk.dnil.|[m]t.rpi.ap[h]n.ġzr.|[mt.hrn]my.ytšu.|[yṯb.b ap 19[1AQHT].1.19
[-----.apnk].|[dnil.mt.rp]i.apn.ġz[r].|[mt.hrnmy.]uzr.ilm.ylḥm.|[17[2AQHT].1.1
m‘.bm.kbd.|tmz‘.kst.dnil.mt.|rpi.al.ġzr.mt.hrnmy.|apnk.dnil.mt.|rpi.yṣly.‘rpt.b |ḥm.un.yr.‘rpt.|tmṭr.b qẓ.ṭl.yṭ 19[1AQHT].1.38
--.kṯ]r w ḫss.|[---]n.rḥm y.ršp zbl.|[w ‘d]t.ilm.ṯlṯ h.|[ap]nk.krt.ṯ‘.‘[-]r.|[--.]b bt h.yšt.‘rb.|[--] h.ytn.w [--]u.l ytn.| 15[128].2.8
t.|mġny.l b‘l.npl.l a|rṣ.mt.aliyn.b‘l.|ḫlq.zbl.b‘l.arṣ.|apnk.lṭpn.il.|d pid.yrd.l ksi.ytb.|l hdm[.w] l.hdm.yṯb.|l arṣ 5[67].6.11
ymġy.kṯr.|w ḫss.b d.dnil.ytnn.|qšt.l brk h.y‘db.|qṣ‘t.apnk.mṯt.dnty.|tšlḥm.tššqy ilm.|tsad.tkbd.hmt.b‘l.|ḥkpt il 17[2AQHT].5.28
m.|w ‘n.rbt.aṯrt ym.|blt.nmlk.‘ṯtr.‘rẓ.|ymlk.‘ṯtr.‘rẓ.|apnk.‘ṯtr.‘rẓ.|y‘l.b ṣrrt.ṣpn.|yṯb.l kḥṯ.aliyn.|b‘l.p‘n h.l tmġ 6.1.56[49.1.28]
|tlk.škn.‘l.ṣrrt.|adn k.šqrb.[---].|b mgn k.w ḫrṣ.l kl.|apnk.ġzr.ilḥu.|[m]rḥ h.yiḫd.b yd.|[g]rgr h.bm.ymn.|[w]y 16.1[125].46
h[.l]ql.nhqt.|ḥmr[h.l g‘t.]alp.|ḥrṯ[.l z]ġt.klb.|[ṣ]pr[.apn]k.|[pb]l[.mlk.g]m.l aṯt |[h.k]y[ṣḥ.]šm‘.m‘.|[--.]‘m[.-.]a 14[KRT].5.227

apnnk

kl y.aṯr h.rpum.|[l tdd.aṯr h].l tdd.ilnym.|[---.m]rz‘y.apnnk.yrp.|[---.]km.r‘y.ht.alk.|[---.]ṯlṯt.amġy.l bt.|[y.---.b q 21[122].1.5

aps

yṯb.l kḥṯ.aliyn.|b‘l.p‘n h.l tmġyn.|hdm.riš h.l ymġy.|aps h.w y‘n.‘ṯtr.‘rẓ.|l amlk.b ṣrrt.ṣpn.|yrd.‘ṯtr.‘rẓ.yrd.|l kḥ 6.1.61[49.1.33]

apsn

[‘]bdm.|[bn].mṣrn.|[a]ršwn.|‘b[d].|w nḥl h.|atn.bn.ap[s]n.|nsk.ṯlṯ.|bn.[--.]m[-]ḫr.|bn.šmrm.|ṯnnm.|[ar]swn.b 85[80].3.7

apsny

tldn.|ṯrkn.|kli.|plġn.|apŝny.|‘rb[.---].|w.b.p[.--].|apŝ[ny].|b.yṣi h.|ḥwt.[---].|alp.k[sp].|tš‘n.|w.hm.al[-].|l.tš‘ 2116.8
a[r]b‘.l.arb‘[m.---].|pln.ṯmry.w.ṯn.bn h.w[.---].|ymrn.apsny.w.aṯt h..b[n.---].|prd.m‘qby[.w.---.a]ṯt h[.---].|prṯ.mg 2044.9
tldn.|ṯrkn.|kli.|plġn.|apŝny.|‘rb[.---].|w.b.p[.--].|apŝ[ny].|b.yṣi h.|ḥwt.[---].|alp. 2116.5
---].|b tn[--.---].|swn.qrty[.---].|uḫ h.w.‘šr[.---].|klyn.apsn[y.---].|plzn.qrty[.---].|w.klt h.b.t[--.---].|b‘l y.mlk[y.-- 81[329].10

apsty

[-]ḏmu.apsty.b[--].|w.bn h.w aṯt h.w.alp.w ṯmn.ṣin.|[-]dln.qmnzy. 1080.1

apŝny

tldn.|ṯrkn.|kli.|plġn.|apŝny.|‘rb[.---].|w.b.p[.--].|apŝ[ny].|b.yṣi h.|ḥwt.[---].|alp.k[sp].|tš‘n.|w.hm.al[-].|l.tš‘ 2116.8
tldn.|ṯrkn.|kli.|plġn.|apŝny.|‘rb[.---].|w.b.p[.--].|apŝ[ny].|b.yṣi h.|ḥwt.[---].|alp. 2116.5

apq

lṯ.mtḫ.ġyrm].|[idk.]l ytn.pnm.‘m.[i]l.mbk.[nhrm.qrb.apq.thmtm].|[ygly.]ḏl i[l].w ybu[.q]rš.mlk[.ab.šnm.l p‘n.il.] 2.3[129].4
.ybm.l ilm.|[id]k.l ttn.pnm.‘m.|[il.]mbk nhrm.qrb.|[a]pq.thmtm.tgly.ḏd.|il.w tbu.qrš..|mlk.ab.šnm.l p‘n.|il.thb 6.1.34[49.1.6]
.|[w tr.a]rṣ.id[k.l ttn.p]nm.|[‘m.i]l.mbk.nhr[m.qr]b.[ap]q.|[thm]tm.tgl.ḏ[d.]i[l.]w tbu.|[qr]š.m[l]k.ab[.šnm.]mṣr. 3[‘NT.VI].5.14
l.tb‘.mrym.ṣpn.|idk.l ttn.pnm.|‘m.il.mbk.nhrm.|qrb.apq.thmtm.|tgly.ḏd.il.w tbu.|qrš.mlk.ab.šnm.|l p‘n.il.thbr. 4[51].4.22
[idk.l ttn.pnm].|[‘m.il.mbk.nhrm].|[qrb.apq.thmtm].|[tgly.ḏd.il.w]tb[a].|[qrš.mlk.ab.]šnm.|[tša.g 5[67].6.01
‘n]m.w tr.arṣ.idk.|[l ttn.pn]m.‘m il.mbk.nhrm.|[qrb.ap]q.thmtm tgly.ḏd il.|[w tbu.qr]š.mlk.ab.šnm.|[l p‘n.il.t]h 17[2AQHT].6.48

apṯ

n.ṣmd.w.ḥrṣ.|bn.ilb‘l.|bn.idrm.|bn.grgš.|bn.bly.|bn.apṯ.|bn.ysd.|bn.pl[-].|bn.ṯb‘nq.|brqd.|bnn.|kbln.ṣ[md].|b 2113.11
ubn.|dqn.|ḥṯṯn.|[--]n.|[---].|tsn.|rpiy.|mrṯn.|ṯnyn.|apṯ.|šbn.|gbrn.|ṯb‘m.|kyn.|b‘ln.|ytršp.|ḥmšm.ṯmn.kbd.|t 1024.2.18

aṣn

.mdd.i[l.---].|bt ksp y.d[--.---].|b d.aliyn b[‘l.---].|kd.ynaṣn[.---].|gršnn.l k[si.mlk h.l nḫt.l kḥṯ].|drkt h.š[--.--].| 1[‘NT.X].4.23

aqhr

m]itm.nṣ.l bn[.---].|[-]l[-.---].|[-]ṯ.[---].|mṣb[-.---].|kṯ.aqh[r.---].|l bn[.---].|[ṯ]lṯ.[---].|[---.--]yn.š.aḫ[--].|[---.]š.nṣ[. 143[-].2.4
]hn.w.alp.kd.nbt.kd.šmn.mr.|[---.]arb‘.mat.ḫswn.lṯḥ.aqhr.|[---.lṯḥ.]sbbyn.lṯḥ.ššmn.lṯḥ.šḥlt.|[---.lṯḥ.]ṣmqm.[ṯ]ṯ.m 142[12].3

aqht

iṯl].|brlt h.km.qṭr.[b ap h.---].|‘nt.b ṣmt.mhr h.[---].|aqht.w tbk.y[---.---].|abn.ank.w ‘l.[qšt k.---.‘l].|qṣ‘t k.at.l ḥ[18[3AQHT].4.39
q]d k.ašhlk[.šbt k.dmm].|[šbt.dq]n k.mm‘m.w[---].|aqht.w yplṭ k.bn[.dnil.---].|w y‘ḏr k.b yd.btlt.[‘nt].|w y‘n.lṯ 18[3AQHT].1.13
.|p‘n h.ybq‘.kbd h.w yḥd.|iṯ.šmt.iṯ.‘ẓm.w yqḥ b hm.|aqht.ybl.l qẓ.ybky.w yqbr.|yqbr.nn.b mdgt.b knk[-].|w yšu 19[1AQHT].3.146
.dn]il.mt.rpi.w t‘n.|[btlt.‘nt.tšu.g]h.w tṣḥ.hwt.|[---.]aqht.yḏ[--].|[---.--]n.ṣ[---].|[spr.ilmlk.šbny.lmd.atn.]prln. 17[2AQHT].6.54
nil.m[t].|rpi.aphn.ġzr.m[t].|hrnmy.qšt.yqb.[--]|rk.‘l.aqht.k yq[--.---].|pr‘m.ṣd k.y bn[.---].|pr‘m.ṣd k.hn pr[‘.--]. 17[2AQHT].5.36
.tqḥ.ytpn.mhr.št.|tštn.k nšr.b ḥbš h.km.diy.|b t‘rt h.aqht.km.ytb.l lḥ[m].|bn.dnil.l ṯrm.‘l h.nšr[m].|trḫpn.ybṣr. 18[3AQHT].4.29
ṭp.w[---].|l k.ašt k.km.nšr.b ḥb[š y].|km.diy.b t‘rt y.aqht.[km.ytb].|l lḥm.w bn.dnil.l ṯrm[.‘l h].|nšrm.trḫpn.ybṣ 18[3AQHT].4.18
[l a]q[h]t.|[t]krb.[---.]l qrb.mym.|tql.[---.]lb.tt[b]r.|qšt[.---]r.y 19[1AQHT].1.1

.nšr[m].|trẖpn.ybṣr.ḥbl.diy[m.bn].|nšrm.trẖp.‘nt.‘l[.aqht].|t‘dbn h.hlmn.ṯnm[.qdqd].|ṯlṯ id.‘l.udn.š[pk.km].|šiy 18[3AQHT].4.32
nšrm.trẖpn.ybṣr.[ḥbl.d]|iym.bn.nšrm.arẖp.an[k.‘]l.|aqht.‘db k.hlmn.ṯnm.qdqd.|ṯlṯ id.‘l.udn.špk.km.šiy.|dm.k 18[3AQHT].4.22
kl.bqmm.|tšt ḥrṣ.k lb ilnm.|w ṯn.gprm.mn gpr h.šr.|aqht.y‘n.kmr.kmr[.--].|k ap‘.il.b gdrt.k lb.l |ẖṯ h.imẖṣ h.k 19[1AQHT].1.12
k.w tn.qšt k.[l].|[‘nt.tq]ḥ[.q]ṣ‘t k.ybmt.limm.|w y‘n.aqht.ǵzr.adr.ṯqbm.|[d]lbnn.adr.gdm.b rumm.|adr.qrnt.b y 17[2AQHT].6.20
‘l h.|n‘m[n.w t]‘nynn.ap ank.aḥwy.|aqht[.ǵz]r.w y‘n.aqht.ǵzr.|al.tšrgn.y btlt m.dm.l ǵzr.|šrg k.ẖẖm.mt.uẖryt.m 17[2AQHT].6.33
t h.qr.[mym].|mlk.yṣm.y l km.qr.mym.d ‘[l k].|mẖṣ.aqht.ǵzr.amd.gr bt il.|‘nt.brḥ.p ‘lm h.‘nt.p dr[.dr].|‘db.uẖr 19[1AQHT].3.153
‘l.qšt l ‘nt.|qṣ‘t.l ybmt.limm.w t‘n.btlt.|‘nt.irš ḥym.l aqht.ǵzr.|irš ḥym.w atn k.bl mt.|w ašlḥ k.aššpr k.‘m.b‘l.|š 17[2AQHT].6.26
h.-.l]arṣ.ks h.tšpk m.|[l ‘pr.tšu.g h.]w tṣḥ.šm‘.m‘.|[l aqht.ǵzr.i]rš.ksp.w atn k.|[ẖrṣ.w aš]lḥ k.w tn.qšt k.[l].|[‘nt. 17[2AQHT].6.17
.|[rbt.]kmn.w ṣḥq.btlt.[‘nt].|[tšu.]g h.w tṣḥ.šm‘.m[‘.l a]|[qht.ǵ]zr.at.aẖ.w an.a[ẖt k].|[---].šb‘.ṯir k.[---].|[---.]ab y 18[3AQHT].1.23
k.dṯ.ydṯ.m‘qb k.[ttb‘].|[bt]lt.‘nt.idk.l ttn.[pnm].|[‘m.a]qht.ǵzr.b alp.š[d].|[rbt.]kmn.w ṣḥq.btlt.[‘nt].|[tšu.]g h.w 18[3AQHT].1.21
kl h.‘rb.b|kyt.b hkl h.mšspdt.b ḥẓr h.|pẓǵm.ǵr.ybk.l aqht.|ǵzr.ydm‘.l kdd.dnil.|mt.rpi.l ymm.l yrẖm.|l yrẖm.l š 19[1AQHT].4.173
|mt.rpi.l ymm.l yrẖm.|l yrẖm.l šnt.‘d.|šb‘t.šnt.ybk.l aq|ht.ǵzr.yd[m‘.]l kdd.|dnil.mt.r[pi.mk].b šb‘.|šnt.w y‘n[.d 19[1AQHT].4.177
qyn h.ybd.w yšr.‘l h.|n‘m[n.w t]‘nynn.ap ank.aḥwy.|aqht[.ǵz]r.w y‘n.aqht.ǵzr.|al.tšrgn.y btlt m.dm.l ǵzr.|šrg k. 17[2AQHT].6.33
-].|tmǵyn.tša.g h[m.w tṣḥn].|šm‘.l dnil.[mt.rpi].|mt.aqht.ǵzr.[šṣat].|btlt.‘nt.k [rḥ.npš h].|k iṯl.brlt h.[b h.p‘nm]. 19[1AQHT].2.91
[.mh]r.|št.b yn.yšt.ila.il š[--.]il.|d yqny.ḏdm.yd.mẖṣt.a[qh]t.ǵ|zr.tmẖṣ.alpm.ib.št[-.]št.|ḥršm l ahlm p[---.]km.|[- 19[1AQHT].4.220
qrt.zbl.yrẖ.yšu g h.|w yṣḥ.y l k.qrt.ablm.|d ‘l k.mẖṣ.aqht.ǵzr.|‘wrt.yšt k.b‘l.l ht.|w ‘lm h.l ‘nt.p dr.dr.|‘db.uẖry. 19[1AQHT].4.166
l.an bṣ[ql].|ynp‘.b palt.bṣql yp‘ b yǵlm.|ur.tisp k.yd.aqht.|ǵzr.tšt k.b qrb m.asm.|y.dnh.ysb.aklt h.yph.|šblt.b a 19[1AQHT].2.66
aḥl.an.šblt.|tp‘.b aklt.šblt.tp‘[.b ḥm]drt.|ur.tisp k.yd.aqht.ǵz[r].|tšt k.bm.qrb m.asm.|b p h.rgm.l yṣa.b špt h[.h 19[1AQHT].2.73
ll.b nr.|yšu.g h.w yṣḥ.y l k.mrrt.|tǵll.b nr.d ‘l k.mẖṣ.aqht.|ǵzr.šrš k.b arṣ.al.|yp‘.riš.ǵly.b d.ns‘ k.|‘nt.brḥ.p ‘lm 19[1AQHT].3.158
ht.tṣdn.tinṯt.|[---]m.tṣḥq.‘nt.w b lb.tqny.|[---.]ṯb l y.l aqht.ǵzr.ṯb l y w l k.|[---]m.l aqry k.b ntb.pš‘.|[---].b ntb.ga 17[2AQHT].6.42
b.šnm.|[l p‘n.il.t]hbr.w tql.tšth|[wy.w tkbd]n h.tlšn.aqht.ǵzr.|[---.kdd.dn]il.mt.rpi.w t‘n.|[btlt.‘nt.tšu.g]h.w tṣḥ 17[2AQHT].6.51

ar

].|‘rg[z].|y‘r[t].|amḏ[y].|atl[g].|bṣr[y].|[---].|[---]y.|ar.|agm.w.ẖpty.|ẖlb.ṣpn.|mril.|‘nmky.|‘nqpat.|ṭbq.|hzp. 71[113].48
[---.t]št.rimt.|l irt h.mšr.l.dd.aliyn.|b‘l.yd.pdry.bt.ar.|ahbt.ṭly.bt.rb.dd.arṣy.|bt.y‘bdr.km ǵlmm.|w ‘rb n.l p‘n 3[‘NT].3.3
].|tšt[.r]imt.[l irt h.tšr.l dd.aliyn.b‘l].|[ahb]t pdr[y.bt.ar.ahbt.ṭly.bt.rb.dd].|arṣy bt.y[‘bdr.---].|rgm l btl[t.‘nt.ṯny. 7.2[130].11
r.ṭb.ql.|‘l.b‘l.b ṣrrt.|ṣpn.ytmr.b‘l.|bnt h.y‘n.pdry.|bt.ar.apn.ṭly.|[bt.r]b.pdr.yd‘.|[---]t.im[-]lt.|[-----].|[---.--]rt. 3[‘NT].1.24
ap.|pd.|mlk.|ar.|atlg.|gb‘ly.|ulm.|m‘rby.|m‘r.|arny.|š‘rt.|ẖlbrpš.|hry. 2074.4
y.|iln.[---].|bn.[---].ar.|bn.[---].b.ar.|špšyn[.---.]yṯb.b.ar.|bn.ag[p]ṯ.ẖpṯ.d[.yṯb.b].š‘rt.|yly.bn.ṯrnq.[-]r.d.yṯb.b.ilšt 2015.1.24
.|[p]lsy.|bn.ḥrš.|[--.]kbd.|[---].|y[---].|bn.ǵlyn.|bdl.ar.|bn.šyn.|bn.ubrš.|bn.d[--]b.|abrpu.|bn.k[n]y.|bn.klyn. 1035.3.1
b.|bn.t[--.---.a]ǵt.|špš[yn.---.u]br‘y.|iln.[---].|bn.[---].ar.|bn.[---].b.ar.|špšyn[.---.]yṯb.b.ar.|bn.ag[p]ṯ.ẖpṯ.d[.yṯb.b 2015.1.22
bn.qrrn.|bn.dnt.|bn.ṯ‘l[-].|bdl.ar.dt.inn.|mhr l ht.|artyn.|‘dmlk.|bn.alt[-].|iẖy[-].|‘bdgṯr. 1035.1.4
.aškn.|‘ṣm.l bt.dml.|p ank.atn.|‘ṣm.l k.|arb‘.‘ṣm.|‘l.ar.|w.ṯlṯ.|‘l.ubr‘y.|w.ṯn.‘l.|mlk.|w.aḥd.|‘l atlg.|w l.‘ṣm.|ts 1010.10
ap.|pd.|mlk.arb‘.ḥm[rm.w.arb]‘.bnšm.|ar.ẖmš.ḥmr[m.w.ẖm]š.bnšm.|atlg.ḥmr[.---.]bnšm.|gb‘ly.ḥ 2040.4
rt.mṯb.il.mẓll].|bn h.m[ṯb.rbt.aṯrt.ym].|mṯb.pdr[y.bt.ar.mẓll].|ṭly.bt.r[b.mṯb.arṣy].|bt.y‘bdr[.mṯb.klt].|knyt.w t‘ 3[‘NT.VI].4.3
ll.bn h.|mṯb rbt.aṯrt.ym.|mṯb.klt.knyt.|mṯb.pdry.bt.ar.|mẓll.ṭly.bt rb.|mṯb.arṣ.bt y‘bdr.|w y‘n lṭpn il d pid.|p ‘ 4[51].4.55
ll.|bn h.mṯb.rbt.|aṯrt.ym.mṯb.|klt.knyt.|mṯb.pdry.b ar.|mẓll.ṭly.bt rb.|mṯb.arṣy.bt.y‘bdr.|ap.mṯn.rgmm.|argm 4[51].1.17
rt.mṯb.il.|mṯll.b[n h.m]ṯb.rbt.aṯrt.|ym.mṯb.[pdr]y.bt.ar.|[mẓll.]ṭly[.bt.]rb.mṯb.|[arṣy.bt.y‘bdr.mṯb].|[klt.knyt]. 3[‘NT.VI].5.49
.iẖ h yṯ‘r.|mšrrm.aẖt h l a|bn mznm.nkl w ib.|d ašr.ar yrẖ.w y|rẖ yar k.|[ašr ilht kṯrt bn]|t hll.snnt.bnt h|ll b‘l 24[77].38
rm.aẖt h l a|bn mznm.nkl w ib.|d ašr.ar yrẖ.w y|rẖ yar k.|[ašr ilht kṯrt bn]|t hll.snnt.bnt h|ll b‘l gml.yrdt.|b ‘r 24[77].39
k.|mṭrt k.‘m k.šb‘t.|ǵlm k.ṯmn.ẖnzr k.|‘m k.pdry.bt.ar.|‘m k.ṭṭly.bt.rb.idk.|pn k.al ttn.tk.ǵr.|knkny.ša.ǵr.‘l yd 5[67].5.10
ṯn.ṣbrm.|b.uškn.|ṣbr.aḥd.|b.ar.|ṣbr.aḥd.|b.mlk.|ṣbr.aḥd.|b.m‘rby.|ṣbr.aḥd.|b.ulm.|ṣb 2073.4
m.arb‘t.|kbd.ksp.|d.nqdm.|ẖmšm.l mit.|ksp.d.mkr.ar.|arb‘m ksp d mkr.|atlg.|mit.ksp.d mkr.|ilštm‘.|‘šrm.l 2107.10
a]ǵt.|špš[yn.---.u]br‘y.|iln.[---].|bn.[---].ar.|bn.[---].b.ar.|špšyn[.---.]yṯb.b.ar.|bn.ag[p]ṯ.ẖpṯ.d[.yṯb.b].š‘rt.|yly.bn. 2015.1.23
[--.]wmrkm.|bir.ẖmš.|uškn.arb‘.|ubr‘y.ṯlṯ.|ar.ṯmn ‘šr h.|mlk.arb‘.|ǵbl.ẖmš.|atlg.ẖmš ‘šr[h].|ulm ṯ[ṯ]. 68[65].1.5
[š]šw[.i]ryn.arr.|[š]dm.b.mlk.|[--.š]dm.b.ar.|[--.š]dm.b.ulm.|[--.š]dm.b.m‘rby.|[--.šd]m.b.uškn.|[---. 2033.1.3
[---.]ktb nǵr krm.|[---].ab h.krm ar.|[---.]h.mḥtrt.pṭtm.|[---.-]t h.ušpǵt tišr.|[---.šm]m h.nšat 2001.2.2
tšt.u[rb]t.b bht m.|ḥln.b q[rb.hk]l m.|al td[.pdr]y.bt ar.|[---.ṭl]y.bt.rb.|[---.m]dd.il ym.|[---.-]qlṣn.wpṯ m.|[---.]w 4[51].6.10
bq.arb‘.|tkm[.---].|uẖnp[.---].|ušk[n.---].|ubr[‘y.---].|ar[.---].|mlk[.---].|ǵbl[.---].|atl[g.---].|u[lm.---].|m[‘rby.---]. 68[65].2.5
ṯb[-.---].|ab[.---].|ḥyi[l.---].|iẖy[.---].|ar[.---].|‘ṯtr[.---].|bn.[---].|yly[.---].|ykn[.---].|rp[--].|ṯṯw.[-- 2131.5

arbdd

]ṣ.mlḥmt.|ašt[.b ‘]p[r] m.ddym.ask.|šlm.l kb[d].awṣ.arbdd.|l kbd.š[d]m.ap.mṯn.rgmm.|argmn.lk.lk.‘nn.ilm.|at 3[‘NT].4.74
qry.b arṣ.|mlḥmt št.b ‘pr m.ddym.|sk.šlm.l kbd.arṣ.|arbdd.l kbd.šdm.|ḥš k.‘ṣ k.‘bṣ k.|‘m y.p‘n k.tlsmn.‘m y.|tw 3[‘NT].3.14
ry.b arṣ.mlḥmt.|št.b ‘p[r] m.ddym.sk.šlm.|l kbd.arṣ.arbdd.l kbd.šdm.|[ḥ]š k.[‘]ṣ k.‘bṣ k.‘m y.p‘n k.|[tls]mn.[‘]m 3[‘NT].4.54
y.b arṣ.mlḥ]mt.št b ‘p|[r m.ddym.sk.šlm].l kbd.arṣ.|[arbdd.l kbd.š]dm.ḥš k.|[‘ṣ k.‘bṣ k.‘m y.p‘]n k.tlsmn.|[‘m y.t 1[‘NT.IX].2.21
yy.b arṣ.mlḥmt.št].|[b ‘]pr[m.ddym.sk.šlm.l kbd.arṣ.arbdd].|l kbd.š[dm.ḥš k.‘ṣ k.‘bṣ k.‘m y.p‘n k.tls]|[m]n ‘m y 7.2[130].15
arṣ].mlḥmt.[aš]t.b ‘pr m.|ddym.ask[.šlm.]l kbd.arṣ.|ar[bdd.]l kb[d.š]dm.yšt.|[----.]b‘l.mdl h.yb‘r.|[---.]rn h.aqr 3[‘NT].4.69

arbẖ

ḥ h l adrt[.---].|ṯṯb ‘ṯtrt b ǵl[.---].|qrẓ tšt.l šmal[.---].|arbẖ.‘n h tšu w[.---].|aylt tǵpy ṯr.‘n[.---].|b[b]r.mrḥ h.ti[ẖd 2001.1.10

arbn

y'dd.tẖt.bn arbn. | 'bdil.tẖt.ilmlk. | qly.tẖt b'ln.nsk. 1053.1

arb'yn

--]l[-.-]p 'l [---.-]b'm arny. | w 'l [---.]rb'm t̲qlm.w [---] arb'yn. | w 'l.mnḥm.arb' š[mn]. | w 'l bn a[--.-]yn t̲qlm. | [--] k 1103.8

argb

. | ǵly. | bn.dnn. | bn.rmy. | dll. | mny. | krty. | bn.'bṣ. | bn.argb. | ydn. | il'nt. | bn.urt. | ydn. | qt̲n. | bn.asr. | bn.'dy. | bn.am 2117.3.41

argd̲d̲

b ym ḥdt̲. | b.yrẖ.pgrm. | lqḥ.iwrpzn. | argd̲d̲. | tt̲kn. | ybrk. | ntbt. | b.mitm. | 'šrm. | kbd.ẖrṣ. 2006.4

argmn

y. | w t̲pllm.mlk.r[b.--]. | mṣmt.l nqmd.[---.-]št. | hl ny.argmn.d [ybl.n]qmd. | l špš.arn.t̲n[.'šr h.]mn. | 'ṣrm.t̲ql.kbd[. 64[118].18
.l il.šlmm]. | b t̲lt̲t '[šrt.yrtḥṣ.mlk.brr]. | b arb'[t.'šrt.riš.argmn]. | w t̲n šm.l [b'lt.bhtm.'ṣrm.l inš]. | ilm.w š d[d.ilš.š.-- 35[3].4
l.šlmm. | b [t̲lt̲t].'šrt.yrtḥṣ.mlk. | br[r.]b a[r]b't.'šrt.riš. | arg[mn.w t̲n.]šm.l b'lt. | bhtm.'ṣ[rm.l in]š ilm.w š. | dd ilš.š[.- APP.II[173].5
b'l.y ym m.'bd k.b'l. | [--.--]m.bn.dgn.a[s]r km.hw ybl.argmn k.k ilm. | [---.]ybl.k bn.qdš.mnḥy k.ap.anš.zbl.b'[l]. | [2.1[137].37
t̲lt̲.d yṣa. | b d.šmmn. | l argmn. | l nskm. | t̲mn.kkrm. | alp.kbd. | [m]itm.kbd. 147[90].3
spr.argmn.nskm. | rqdym. | šṭšm.t̲t̲ mat. | ṣprn.t̲t̲ mat. | d̲kry.t̲t̲ m 1060.1.1
b'.ktnt.w [---]b. | [ẖm]š.mat pḥm. | [ẖm]š[.m]at.iqnu. | argmn.nqmd.mlk. | ugrt.d ybl.l špš. | mlk.rb.b'l h. | ks.ẖrṣ.kt 64[118].24
spr.argmnm. | 'šrm.ksp.d mkr. | mlk. | t̲lt̲.mat.ksp.d.šb[n]. | mit.k 2107.1
[---.a]rgmn.špš. | [-----]. | [-----]. | [-----]. | [----] h. | [-----]. | [-]b'l. | [-- 2058.1.1

argnd

[-]p[-.---.-]ny. | [-]ẖ[-.---.-]dn. | arb'[m.ksp.]'l. | il[m]l[k.a]rgnd. | uškny[.w]mit. | zt.b d hm.rib. | w [---]. | [-----]. | [-]šy[2055.11

arwdn

ẖ. | [---]ty. | [b]n.ypy.gb'ly. | b[n].ḥyn. | d̲mn.š'rty. | bn.arwdn.ilšt'y. | bn grgs. | bn.ẖran. | bn.arš[w.b]ṣry. | bn.ykn. | b 99[327].1.8
[---.]dd. | [---]n.dd. | [---.]dd. | bn.arwdn.dd. | mnḥm.w.kbln. | bn.ǵlm.dd. | bn.tbšn.dd. | bn.ẖra 131[309].4
i[l]štm'ym. | bn.t̲k. | bn.arwdn. | tmrtn. | šd'l.bn aẖyn. | m'rbym. | rpan. | abršn. | atlgy. 95[91].3

arws

bn.'bdpdr. | šd.iyry.l.'bdb'l. | šd.šmmn.l.bn.šty. | šd.bn.arws.l.bn.ẖlan. | šd.bn.ibryn.l.bn.'mnr. 1102.19

arwt̲

. | sǵr.adn.ṣdq.aḥd. | sǵr.irgn.aḥd. | sǵr.ršpab.aḥd. | sǵr.arwt̲.aḥd. | sǵr.bn.mǵln. | aḥd. 1140.11
. | bn.brzn. | w.nḥl h. | bn.adld̲n. | bn.šbl. | bn.ẖnzr. | bn.arwt̲. | bn.t̲btnq. | bn.pt̲d̲n. | bn.nbdg. | bn.ḥgbn. | bn.tmr. | bn.p 113[400].1.15

arz

hdt.lm.tḥš. | lm.tḥš.nt̲q.dmrn. | 'n.b'l.qdm.yd h. | k tǵd̲.arz.b ymn h. | bkm.yt̲b.b'l.l bht h. | u mlk.u bl mlk. | arṣ.drkt 4[51].7.41
[ḥš.]trmm.hkl h. | y[tl]k.l lbnn.w 'ṣ h. | l[šr]yn.mḥmd.arz h. | h[n.l]bnn.w 'ṣ h. | š[r]yn.mḥmd.arz h. | tšt.išt.b bht m 4[51].6.19
l[šr]yn.mḥmd.arz h. | h[n.l]bnn.w 'ṣ h. | š[r]yn.mḥmd.arz h. | tšt.išt.b bht m. | nb[l]at.b hkl m. | hn.ym.w t̲n.tikl. | išt 4[51].6.21
n. | [-]zǵm. | [i]lib. | [i]lbldn. | [p]dry.bt.mlk. | [-]lp.izr. | [a]rz. | k.t'rb.'t̲trt.šd.bt[.m]lk. | k.t'rbn.ršp m.bt.mlk. | ẖlu.dg. 2004.9
'dn.'dn.t̲kt.b glt̲. | w tn.ql h.b 'rpt. | šrh.l arṣ.brqm. | bt.arzm.yklln h. | hm.bt.lbnt.y'msn h. | l yrgm.l aliyn b'l. | ṣḥ.ẖr 4[51].5.72
. | ark.qšt.w.ql'. | bn.'bdnkl.qšt.w.ql'. | bn.znan.qšt. | bn.arz.[ar]b'.qšt.w.arb['.]ql'm. | b[n.]ad'l.q[š]t.w.ql'. | b[n].ilyn.q 119[321].2.45
y. | bn.kdrn.uškny. | bn.lgn.uškny. | bn.abn.uškny. | bn.arz.š'rty. | bn.ibrd.m'rby. | ṣdqn.gb'ly. | bn.ypy.gb'ly. | bn.grgs 87[64].25

arẖ

.tlak.t̲l.amr.. | bn km k bk[r.z]bl.am.. | rkm.agzrt[.--].arẖ.. | b'l.azrt.'nt.[-]ld. | kbd h.l yd' hr h.[---]d[-]. | tnq[.---.]in 13[6].29
np ql.nd.[----]. | tlk.w tr.b[ẖl]. | b n'mm.b ys[mm.---]. | arẖ.arẖ.[---.tld]. | ibr.tld[.l b'l]. | w rum.l[rkb.'rpt]. | tḥbq.[--- 10[76].3.20
t̲d[h]. | limm.w t'l.'m.il. | ab h.ḥpr.p'l k.y[--]. | šm' k.l arẖ.w bn.[--]. | limm.ql.b udn.k w[-]. | k rtqt mr[.---]. | k d lb 13[6].22
.qm.aẖ k. | w tšu.'n h.btlt.'nt. | w tšu.'n h.w t'n. | w t'n.arẖ.w tr.b lkt. | tr.b lkt.w tr.b ẖl. | [b]n'mm.b ysmm.ẖ[--]k. 10[76].2.28
[t̲kt]. | mẓma.yd.mt̲kt. | tt̲tkr.[--]dn. | 'm.krt.mswn h. | arẖ.tzǵ.l 'gl h. | bn.ḥpt̲.l umht hm. | k tnḥn.udmm. | w y'ny.k 15[128].1.5
[---.]arẖt.tld[n]. | a[lp].l btlt.'nt. | w ypt l ybmt.li[mm]. | w y'ny.ali 10[76].3.2
.y[n]. | špq.ilht.ẖprt[.yn]. | špq.ilm.alpm.y[n]. | špq.ilht.arẖt[.yn]. | špq.ilm.kḥtm.yn. | špq.ilht.ksat[.yn]. | špq.ilm.rḥb 4[51].6.50
. | ym.ymm.y'tqn.l ymm. | l yrẖm.rḥm.'nt.tngt̲ h. | k lb.arẖ.l 'gl h.k lb. | t̲at.l imr h.km.lb. | 'nt.at̲r.b'l.tiẖd. | bn.ilm.m 6[49].2.28
-]. | kd.t[---.ym.ymm]. | y'tqn.w[rḥm.'nt]. | tngt̲ h.k lb.a[rẖ]. | l 'gl h.k lb.t̲a[t]. | l imr h.km.lb.'n[t]. | at̲r.b'l.tiẖd.m[t] 6[49].2.6
arẖ.td.rgm.b ǵr. | b p y.t'lgt.b lšn[y]. | ǵr[.---]b.b pš y.t[--]. | h 2124.1
l.nd.[----]. | tlk.w tr.b[ẖl]. | b n'mm.b ys[mm.---]. | arẖ.arẖ.[---.tld]. | ibr.tld[.l b'l]. | w rum.l[rkb.'rpt]. | tḥbq.[---]. | t 10[76].3.20

ary

n. | t̲lt̲.ẖmš.alpm. | b d.brq.maẖdy. | kkr.t̲lt̲. | b d.bn.by.ar[y]. | alpm.t̲lt̲. | b d.šim.il[š]tm'y. 1134.5
.kt̲tǵlm. | arb'm.t̲lt̲.mẖsrn. | mtb'l.rišy. | t̲ltm.t̲lt̲.'l.nsk. | arym. | alp.t̲lt̲.'l. | nsk.art. | ẖmš.mat.t̲lt̲. | 'l.mtn.rišy. 1137.6
b d.gln.ary. | tgyn.y'rty. | bn.krwn.b.yny.iytlm. | šgryn.ary.b.yny. | bn.yddn.b.rkby. | agyn.agny. | t̲qbn.mldy. 2071.6
grty. | tgyn.arty. | bn.nryn.arty. | bn.ršp.ary. | bn.ǵlmn ary. | bn.ḥṣbn ary. | bn.šdy ary. | bn.ktkt.m'qby. | bn.[---.]t̲lḥn 87[64].13
.arty. | bn.ršp.ary. | bn.ǵlmn ary. | bn.ḥṣbn ary. | bn.šdy ary. | bn.ktkt.m'qby. | bn.[---.]t̲lḥny. | b[n.---.ub]r'y. | [bn.---.u 87[64].15
ty. | bn.nryn.arty. | bn.ršp.ary. | bn.ǵlmn ary. | bn.ḥṣbn ary. | bn.šdy ary. | bn.ktkt.m'qby. | bn.[---.]t̲lḥny. | b[n.---.ub]r 87[64].14

bn.ǵlmn.ary. | [bn].šdy. | [bn].gmḥ. | [---]ty. | [b]n.ypy.gb‘ly. | b[n].ḥyn. 99[327].1.1
rty. | bn.tgd̠n.ugrty. | tgyn.arty. | bn.nryn.arty. | bn.ršp.ary. | bn.ǵlmn ary. | bn.ḥṣbn ary. | bn.šdy ary. | bn.ktkt.m‘qby 87[64].12
yn.ary. | brqn.ṯlḥy. | bn.aryn. | bn.lgn. | bn.b‘yn. | šdyn. | ary. | brqn. | bn.ḫlln. | bn.mṣry. | ṯmn.qšt. | w ‘šr.uṯpt. | upšt irš 118[306].10
md̠rǵlm.d inn. | msgm.l hm. | p‘ṣ.ḫbty. | artyn.ary. | brqn.ṯlḥy. | bn.aryn. | bn.lgn. | bn.b‘yn. | šdyn. | ary. | brq 118[306].4
.aḫ h.w šrš.km.ary h. | bl.iṯ.bn.l h.km aḫ h.w šrš. | km.ary h.uzrm.ilm.ylḥm. | uzrm.yšqy.bn.qdš. | l tbrknn l ṯr.il ab 17[2AQHT].1.22
| ria.il.‘glm.d[t]. | šnt.imr.qmṣ.l[l]im. | ṣḥ.aḫ h.b bht h.a[r]y h. | b qrb hkl h.ṣḥ. | šb‘m.bn.aṯrt. | špq.ilm.krm.y[n]. | šp 4[51].6.44
anḫ.ǵzr. | [mt.]hrnmy.d in.bn.l h. | km.aḫ h.w šrš.km.ary h. | bl.iṯ.bn.l h.km aḫ h.w šrš. | km.ary h.uzrm.ilm.ylḥm. 17[2AQHT].1.20
l.ab h. | [i]l.mlk.d yknn h.yṣḥ. | aṯrt.w bn h.ilt.w ṣbrt. | ary h.wn.in.bt.l b‘l. | km.ilm.w ḥẓr.k bn.aṯrt. | mṯb il.mẓll.bn 4[51].4.50
h.i]l.mlk. | [d yknn h.yṣ]ḥ.aṯ | [rt.w bn h.]ilt. | [w ṣbrt.ary]h. | [wn.in.bt.l b‘l.] | [km.ilm.w ḥẓr]. | [k bn.aṯ]r[t]. | m[ṯ] 4[51].1.9
ṯr.il.ab h.il. | mlk.d yknn h.yṣḥ.aṯrt. | w bn h.ilt.w ṣbrt.arḫ h. | wn.in.bt.l b‘l.km.ilm. | ḥẓr.k b[n.a]ṯrt.mṯb.il. | mṯll.b[3[‘NT.VI].5.45
bdn h. | tšu.g h.w tṣḥ.tšmḫ ht. | aṯrt.w bn h.ilt.w ṣb | rt.ary h.k mt.aliyn. | b‘l.k ḫlq.zbl.b‘l. | arṣ.gm.yṣḥ il. | l rbt.aṯrt 6.1.41[49.1.13]
w ṯmn.nqpnt.‘d. | k lbš.km.lpš.dm a[ḫ h]. | km.all.dm.ary h. | k šb‘t.l šb‘m.aḫ h.ym[.--]. | w ṯmnt.l ṯmnym. | šr.aḫy 12[75].2.48
]m.w[.---.]bnšm. | ilštm‘.arb‘.ḥm[r]m.ḫmš.bnšm. | ǵr. | ary.ḥmr w.bnš. | qmy.ḥmr.w.bnš. | ṯbil. | ‘nmky.ḥmr.w.bnš. | r 2040.23
dmt ṯlṯ. | qmnz ṯql. | zlyy ṯql. | ary ḫmšt. | ykn‘m ḫmšt. | ‘nmky ṯqlm. | [-]kt ‘šrt. | qrn šb‘t. 1176.4
šrš. | lbnm. | ḫlb.krd. | ṣ‘. | mlk. | gb‘ly. | ypr. | ary. | ẓrn. | art. | ṯlḥny. | ṯlrby. | dmt. | aǵt. | w.qmnz. | slḫ. | ykn‘ 71[113].8
‘.hm.ks.ymsk. | nhr.k[--].ṣḥn.b‘l.‘m. | aḫ y.qran.hd.‘m.ary y. | w lḥm m ‘m aḫ y.lḥm. | w št m.‘m.a[ḫ] yn. | p nšt.b‘l.[5[67].1.23
yt.b[t]lt. | ‘nt.mḫṣ y hm[.m]ḫṣ. | bn y.hm[.mkly.ṣ]brt. | ary y[.ẓl].ksp.[a]ṯrt. | k t‘n.ẓl.ksp.w n[-]t. | ḫrṣ.šmḫ.rbt.a[ṯrt]. 4[51].2.26
ḫn.w tnḫ.b irt y. | npš.k yld.bn.l y.km. | aḫ y.w šrš.km ary y. | nṣb.skn.ilib y.b qdš. | ẓtr.‘m y.l ‘pr.d̠mr.aṯr[y]. | ṯbq l 17[2AQHT].2.15
---.]g h.w aṣḥ.ik.yṣḥn. | [b‘l.‘m.aḫ y.ik].yqrun.hd. | [‘m.ary y.---.--]p.mlḥm y. | [---.---]lt.qẓb. | [---.]šmḫ y. | [---.]tb‘. | [- 5[67].2.23
d[.---]. | dmt.lḫsn.krm.aḥd.annd̠r.kr[m.---]. | aǵt.mryn.ary[.]yukl.krm.[---]. | gdn.krm.aḫ[d.--]r.krm.[---]. | ary.‘šr.ar 1081.16
| w.klt h.b.t[--.---]. | b‘l y.mlk[y.---]. | yd.bt h.yd[.---]. | ary.yd.t[--.---]. | ḫtn h.šb‘l[.---]. | ṯlḥny.yd[.---]. | yd.ṯlṯ.kl[t h.- 81[329].15
tbšr b‘l. | bšrt k.yblt.y[b]n. | bt.l k.km.aḫ k.w ḥẓr. | km.ary k.ṣḥ.ḫrn. | b bht k.‘d̠bt.b qrb. | hkl k.tbl k.ǵrm. | mid.ksp. 4[51].5.91
ḥdd.ar[y.---]. | b‘lsip.a[ry.---]. | klt h.[---]. | ṯty.ary.m[--.---]. | nrn.arny[.---]. | w.ṯn.bn h.w.b[---.---]. | b tn[--.-- 81[329].4
yn.ary[.]yukl.krm.[---]. | gdn.krm.aḫ[d.--]r.krm.[---]. | ary.‘šr.arb‘.kbd.[---]. | [--]yy.ṯṯ.krmm.šl[-.---]. | [---.]‘šrm.krm 1081.18
md̠rǵlm.dt.inn. | b d.tlmyn. | b d.gln.ary. | tgyn.y‘rty. | bn.krwn.b.yny.iytlm. | šgryn.ary.b.yny. | bn 2071.3
qrt ṯqlm.w nṣp. | šlmy.ṯql. | ary ṯql. | ṯmry ṯql.w.nṣp. | aǵt nṣp. | dmt ṯql. | ykn‘m ṯql. 69[111].3
ḥdd.ar[y.---]. | b‘lsip.a[ry.---]. | klt h.[---]. | ṯty.ary.m[--.---]. | nrn.ar 81[329].1
ḥdd.ar[y.---]. | b‘lsip.a[ry.---]. | klt h.[---]. | ṯty.ary.m[--.---]. | nrn.arny[.---]. | w.ṯn.b 81[329].2
]. | trn.w.p[-]y. | bn.b‘yn.w.agytn. | [---] gnym. | [--]ry.w ary. | [---]ǵrbtym. | [---.]w šb‘l. | [---.-]ym. | [---.--]ḫm. | [---.--]m 131[309].14

aryn

bdl.gt.bn.tbšn. | bn.mnyy.š‘rty. | aryn.ad̠ddy. | agpṯr. | šb‘l.mlky. | n‘mn.mṣry. | y‘l.kn‘ny. | gdn. 91[311].3
mr[b-]. | qdš mlk [---]. | kbd d ilgb[-]. | mrmnmn. | brrn aryn. | a[-]ḫn tlyn. | atdb w ‘r. | qdš w amrr. | ṯhr w bd. | [k]ṯr UG5.7.71
inn. | msgm.l hm. | p‘ṣ.ḫbty. | artyn.ary. | brqn.ṯlḥy. | bn.aryn. | bn.lgn. | bn.b‘yn. | šdyn. | ary. | brqn. | bn.ḫlln. | bn.mṣry 118[306].6

ark

.]al.tš[mḫ.b rm.h] | [kl k.al.]aḫd hm.[---]. | [---.b]gdlt.ar[kt y.am--]. | [---.qdq]d k.ašhlk[.šbt k.dmm]. | [šbt.dq]n k. 18[3AQHT].1.10
ḫ.b r[m.h]kl[k]. | al.aḫd.hm.b y[--] y.[---]b[-]. | b gdlt.arkt y.am[---]. | qdqd k.ašhlk.šbt[k.dmm]. | [šbt.dqn k.mm‘ 3[‘NT.VI].5.31
| w hl h.tṣḥ.um.um.tirk m.yd.il.k ym. | w yd il.k mdb.ark.yd.il.k ym. | w yd.il.k mdb.yqḥ.il.mšt‘ltm. | mšt‘ltm.l riš. 23[52].34
k.r[b.b‘]l y.p.l. | ḥy.np[š.a]rš. | l.pn.b‘[l y.l].pn.b‘l y. | w.urk.ym.b‘l y. | l.pn.amn.w.l.pn. | il.mṣrm.dt.ṯǵrn. | npš.špš.ml 1018.20
hl h.[t]špl.hl h.trm.hl h.tṣḥ.ad ad. | w hl h.tṣḥ.um.um.tirk m.yd.il.k ym. | w yd il.k mdb.ark.yd.il.k ym. | w yd.il.k 23[52].33
.qšt. | pbyn.qšt. | yddn.qšt.w.ql‘. | š‘rt. | bn.il.qšt.w.ql‘. | ark.qšt.w.ql‘. | bn.‘bdnkl.qšt.w.ql‘. | bn.znan.qšt. | bn.arz.[ar] 119[321].2.42

arkbt

lyskn.bn.ss. | ṣdqn.bn.imrt. | mnḥm.bn.ḫyrn. | [-]yn.bn.arkbt. | [--]zbl.bt.mrnn. | a[--.---.-]‘n. | ml[--.---]. | ar[--.---.--]l. | 102[323].3.12

arkd

y.aḥrṯp. | ilyn.‘lby.ṣdkn. | gmrt.ṯlmyn. | ‘bdnt. | bdy.ḥrš arkd. | blšš lmd. | ḥṯṯn.tqn. | ydd.idṯn. | šǵr.ilgdn. 1045.9

arkd̠n

| ‘bdyr[ḫ]. | ṯṯpḥ. | artn. | ybnil. | brqn. | adr[dn]. | krwn. | arkd̠n. | ilmn. | abškn. | ykn. | ršpab. | klyn. | ḥgbn. | ḥṯṯn. | ‘bdm 1024.1.12

arkšt

d.agpṯn.nḥl h. | šd.šwn.b d.ttyn.nḥl [h]. | šd.ṯṯyn[.b]n.arkšt. | l‘q[.---]. | šd.pll.b d.qrt. | š[d].annd̠r.b d.bdn.nḥ[l h]. | [2029.4

arm

rqd. | bn.abdg. | ilyn. | bn.tan. | bn.arm. | bn.b‘l.ṣdq. | bn.army. | bn.rpiyn. | bn.army. | bn.krmn. | 1046.1.5

armwl

t.aḥt.b[.bt.---]. | aṯt.w ṯn.n‘rm.b.bt.ilsk. | aṯt.ad[r]t.b.bt.armwl. | aṯt.aḥt.b.bt.iwrpzn. | ṯt.aṯṯm.w.pǵt.aḥt.b bt.[-]r[-]. | [80[119].9
ṯn.bn.klby. | bn.iytr. | [‘]bdyrḫ. | [b]n.gg‘t. | [‘]dy. | armwl. | uwaḫ. | ypln.w.ṯn.bn h. | ydln. | anr[my]. | mld. | krmp 2086.6
r‘ym.ḫmš. | [----]. | [bn] itn. | [bn] il. | [---]ṯ. | klṯṯb. | gsn. | arm[w]l. | bn.ṣdqn. | ḫlbn. | tbq.alp. 2039.14
b yrḫ.[---]. | šb‘.yn[.---]. | mlkt[.---]. | kd.yn.l.[---]. | armwl w [--]. | arb‘.yn.[--]. | l adrm.b[--]. | šqym. 1092.5
šd.bn.adn. | [b] d.armwl. | [šd].mrnn. | b d.[-]tw[-]. | šd.bn[.---]. | b d.dd[--]. | šd. 2028.2

army

bn bl. | bn dkn. | bn ils. | bn ḫšbn. | bn uryy. | bn kṯl. | bn army. | bn gln. | bn abg. | bn.nǵry. | bn.srwd. | mtnn. | bn gš[-]. 1064.10
bn.tan. | bn.arm. | bn.b‘l.ṣdq. | bn.army. | bn.rpiyn. | bn.army. | bn.krmn. | bn.ykn. | bn.‘ṯtrab. | uṣn[-]. | bn.alṯn. | bn.aš[1046.1.9
rqd. | bn.abdg. | ilyn. | bn.tan. | bn.arm. | bn.b‘l.ṣdq. | bn.army. | bn.rpiyn. | bn.army. | bn.krmn. | bn.ykn. | bn.‘ṯtrab. | uṣ 1046.1.7
‘m. | bn.‘gw.qšt.w ql‘. | bn.tbšn.ṯlṯ.qšt.w.[ṯlṯ.]ql‘m. | bn.army.ṯt.qštm.w[.]q[l‘]. | bn.rpš.qšt.w.ql‘. | bn.ǵb.qšt. | bn.ytr 119[321].3.22

armsǵ

]. | [bnš.g]t.ir. | bnš.gt.rb[--]. | gpny. | bnš.mǵrt. | kbsm. | armsǵ. 1040.20

arn

pṣ.krw. | ṯt.ḫṯrm.ṯn.kst. | spl.mšlt.w.mqḥm. | w md h. | arn.w mznm. | ṯn.ḫlpnm. | ṯt.mrḥm. | drb. | mrbd. | mškbt. 2050.5
mt.l nqmd.[---.-]št. | hl ny.argmn.d [ybl.n]qmd. | l špš.arn.ṯn[.‘šr h.]mn. | ‘ṣrm.ṯql.kbd[.ks].mn.ḫrṣ. | w arb‘.ktnt.w [64[118].19

arnbt

--]. | w [---]. | bn.[---]. | bn.yr[--]. | bn.kṯr[t]. | bn.šml. | bn.arnbt. | qdšm. | b[-.--]t. | [---.-]l[--]. | [---.]pr[--]. | [-.a]pln. | bn.m 2163.2.7

arny

.qšt. | prpr.qšt. | ugry.qšt. | bn.ṣrptn.qšt. | bn.mṣry.qšt. | arny. | abm.qšt. | ḥdṯn.ql‘. | yṯpṭ.qšt. | ilṯḥm.qšt.w.ql‘. | ṣdqm.q 119[321].2.1
| šlmy. | w.ull. | ṯmry. | qrt. | ‘rm. | nnu. | [--]. | [---]. | m‘r. | arny. | ubr‘y. | ilštm‘. | bir. | m‘qb. | uškn. | snr. | rq[d]. | [---]. | [-- 71[113].27
ryn. | ḫm[š]m l ‘šr ksp ‘l bn llit. | [--]l[-.-]p ‘l [---.-]b‘m arny. | w ‘l [---.]rb‘m ṯqlm.w [---] arb‘yn. | w ‘l.mnḥm.arb‘ š[1103.7
ubr‘y. | arny. | m‘r. | š‘rt. | ḫlb rpš. | bq‘t. | šḥq. | y‘by. | mḫr. 65[108].2
. | [-----]. | [----] h. | [-----]. | [-]b‘l. | [--]m. | [m‘]rby. | m‘r. | arny. | ‘nqpat. | š‘rt. | ubr‘y. | ilštm‘. | šbn. | tbq. | rqd. | [š]rš. | [--- 2058.1.11
ap. | pd. | mlk. | ar. | atlg. | gb‘ly. | ulm. | m‘rby. | m‘r. | arny. | š‘rt. | ḫlbrpš. | hry. | qmṣ. | ṣ‘q. | qmy. | ḫlbkrd. | y‘rt. | ušk 2074.10
kdm.yn. | šbn.kdm.yn. | ‘bdiltp.ṯm[n].y[n]. | qṣn.ḫ[---]. | arny.[---]. | aǵltn.ḫmš[.yn]. 1085.11
.---]. | b‘lsip.a[ry.---]. | klt h.[---]. | ṯty.ary.m[--.---]. | nrn.arny[.---]. | w.ṯn.bn h.w.b[---.---]. | b tn[--.---]. | swn.qrty[.---]. 81[329].5
ulm.ṯn.[---.]bnšm. | m‘rby.[---.--]m.ṯn[.---]. | m‘r.[---]. | arny.[---]. | š‘rt.ṯn[.---]. | bq‘t.[--].ḥ[mr.---]. | ḫlb krd.ḥ[mr.---]. 2040.10

arsw

| b[n.]dtn. | w.nḥl h. | w.nḥl hm. | bn.iršyn. | bn.‘zn. | bn.arŝw. | bn.ḫzrn. | bn.iǵyn. | w.nḥl h. | bn.ksd. | bn.bršm. | bn.kz 113[400].2.14
---]. | bn.b‘yn.š[--.---]. | aǵltn.mid[-.---]. | bn.lṣn.‘rm[y]. | arŝw.bṣry. | arpṯr.y‘rty. | bn.ḫdyn.ugrty. | bn.tgḏn.ugrty. | tgy 87[64].6
. | ḏmn.š‘rty. | bn.arwdn.ilšt‘y. | bn grgs. | bn.ḫran. | bn.arŝ[w.b]ṣry. | bn.ykn. | bn.lṣn.‘rmy. | bn.b‘yn.šly. | bn.ynḥn. | b 99[327].2.1
mdrǵlm.d.b.i[-]‘lt.mlk. | arsw. | dqn. | ṯlṯ.klbm. | ḫmn. | [---.-]rsd. | bn[.-]pṯ. | bn kdrn. | a 86[305].2
[-----]. | ḏ[----]. | ab[--.---]. | bn.nṣdn[.ḫm]št. | bn.arsw ‘[šr]m. | ‘šdyn.ḫmš[t]. | abršn.‘šr[t]. | b‘ln.ḫmšt. | w.nḥl h 1062.5

arswn

bn.ap[s]n. | nsk.ṯlṯ. | bn.[--.]m[-]ḫr. | bn.šmrm. | ṯnnm. | [ar]swn.bn.qqln. | m[--].bn.qqln. | ‘bdil[-].bn.qqln. | liy.bn.qql 85[80].4.2
b‘l aṯt. | ptm.b‘l ššlmt. | ‘dršp.b‘l ššlmt. | ṯtrn.b‘l ššlmt. | arŝwn.b‘l ššlmt. | ḥdṯn.b‘l ššlmt. | ssn.b‘l ššlmt. 1077.9
lṯ.klbm. | ḫmn. | [---.-]rsd. | bn[.-]pṯ. | bn kdrn. | awldn. | arswn.y‘r[ty.--]. | bn.ugr. | gny. | ṯn.mdm. 86[305].10
-----]. | [---.n]ḥ[l h]. | [-]ntm[.---]. | [‘]bdm. | [bn].mṣrn. | [a]rŝwn. | ‘b[d]. | w nḥl h. | atn.bn.ap[s]n. | nsk.ṯlṯ. | bn.[--.]m[-] 85[80].3.4

arspy

nḥm.msg. | bn.ugr.msg. | bn.ǵlṣ msg. | arb‘ l ṯkṣ[-]. | nn.arspy.ms[g]. | [---.ms]g. | bn.[gr]gs.msg. | bn[.--]an.msg. | bn[.- 133[-].1.11

arŝw

| b[n.]dtn. | w.nḥl h. | w.nḥl hm. | bn.iršyn. | bn.‘zn. | bn.arŝw. | bn.ḫzrn. | bn.iǵyn. | w.nḥl h. | bn.ksd. | bn.bršm. | bn.kz 113[400].2.14
---]. | bn.b‘yn.š[--.---]. | aǵltn.mid[-.---]. | bn.lṣn.‘rm[y]. | arŝw.bṣry. | arpṯr.y‘rty. | bn.ḫdyn.ugrty. | bn.tgḏn.ugrty. | tgy 87[64].6
. | ḏmn.š‘rty. | bn.arwdn.ilšt‘y. | bn grgs. | bn.ḫran. | bn.arŝ[w.b]ṣry. | bn.ykn. | bn.lṣn.‘rmy. | bn.b‘yn.šly. | bn.ynḥn. | b 99[327].2.1

arŝwn

b‘l aṯt. | ptm.b‘l ššlmt. | ‘dršp.b‘l ššlmt. | ṯtrn.b‘l ššlmt. | arŝwn.b‘l ššlmt. | ḥdṯn.b‘l ššlmt. | ssn.b‘l ššlmt. 1077.9
-----]. | [---.n]ḥ[l h]. | [-]ntm[.---]. | [‘]bdm. | [bn].mṣrn. | [a]rŝwn. | ‘b[d]. | w nḥl h. | atn.bn.ap[s]n. | nsk.ṯlṯ. | bn.[--.]m[-] 85[80].3.4

arpḫn

bn.irgy. | w.nḥl h. | w.nḥl hm. | [bn].pmn. | bn.gṯrn. | bn.arpḫn. | bn.ṯryn. | bn.dll. | bn.ḫswn. | mrynm. | ‘zn. | ḥyn. | ‘my 1046.3.29

arpṯr

.š[--.---]. | aǵltn.mid[-.---]. | bn.lṣn.‘rm[y]. | arŝw.bṣry. | arpṯr.y‘rty. | bn.ḫdyn.ugrty. | bn.tgḏn.ugrty. | tgyn.arty. | bn.n 87[64].7

arṣ

yṣḥ.y l k.mrrt. | tǵll.b nr.d ‘l k.mḫṣ.aqht. | ǵzr.šrš k.b arṣ.al. | yp‘.riš.ǵly.b d.ns‘ k. | ‘nt.brḥ.p ‘lm h. | ‘nt.p dr.dr.‘db. 19[1AQHT].3.159
yṣḥ. | b‘l.mt.my.lim.bn. | dgn.my.hmlt.aṯr. | b‘l.ard.b arṣ.ap. | ‘nt.ttlk.w tṣd.kl.ǵr. | l kbd.arṣ.kl.gb‘. | l [k]bd.šdm.tm 5[67].6.25
ḫlmmt. | mǵny.l b‘l.npl.l a | rṣ.mt.aliyn.b‘l. | ḫlq.zbl.b‘l.arṣ. | apnk.lṭpn.il. | d pid.yrd.l ksi.ytb. | l hdm[.w] l.hdm.yṯb. 5[67].6.10
b a[r]ṣ.mlḥmt. | ašt[.b ‘]p[r] m.ddym.ask. | šlm.l kb[d].awṣ.arbdd. | l kbd.š[d]m.ap.mṯn.rgmm. | argmn.lk.lk.‘nn.ilm 3[‘NT].4.74
rdm.qry.b arṣ. | mlḥmt št.b ‘pr m.ddym. | sk.šlm.l kbd.arṣ. | arbdd.l kbd.šdm. | ḥš k.‘ṣ k.‘bṣ k. | ‘m y.p‘n k.tlsmn.‘m 3[‘NT].3.13
| [qryy.b arṣ.mlḥ]mt.št b ‘p | [r m.ddym.sk.šlm].l kbd.arṣ. | [arbdd.l kbd.š]dm.ḥš k. | [‘ṣ k.‘bṣ k.‘m y.p‘]n k.tlsmn. | [1[‘NT.IX].2.20
m.qry.b arṣ.mlḥmt. | št.b ‘p[r] m.ddym.sk.šlm. | l kbd.arṣ.arbdd.l kbd.šdm. | [ḥ]š k.[‘]ṣ k.‘bṣ k.‘m y.p‘n k. | [tls]mn. 3[‘NT].4.54
.qryy.b arṣ.mlḥmt.št]. | [b ‘]pr[m.ddym.sk.šlm.l kbd.arṣ.arbdd]. | l kbd.š[dm.ḥš k.‘ṣ k.‘bṣ k.‘m y.p‘n k.tls] | [m]n ‘ 7.2[130].15

y. | [b arṣ].mlḥmt.[aš]t.b ʻpr m. | ddym.ask[.šlm.]l kbd.arṣ. | ar[bdd.]l kb[d.š]dm.yšt. | [----.]bʻl.mdl h.ybʻr. | [---.]rn 3[ʻNT].4.68
. | abn.brq.d l.tdʻ.šmm. | rgm l tdʻ.nšm.w l tbn. | hmlt.arṣ.at m.w ank. | ibǵy h.b tk.ǵr y.il.ṣpn. | b qdš.b ǵr.nḥlt y. | b 3[ʻNT].3.25
[.arṣ.thmt.ʻmn.kbkbm]. | rgm.l tdʻ.nš[m.w l tbn.hmlt.arṣ]. | at.w ank.ib[ǵy h.---]. | w yʻn.kṯr.w ḫss[.lk.lk.ʻnn.ilm.] | 1[ʻNT.IX].3.15
t.ʻnt. | qrn.d bat k bʻl.ymšḥ. | bʻl.ymšḥ.ḥm.b ʻp. | nṭʻn.b arṣ.ib y. | w b ʻpr.qm.aḫ k. | w tšu.ʻn h.btlt.ʻnt. | w tšu.ʻn h.w 10[76].2.24
[k.ym]ḫṣ.bʻl m[.--]y.tnn.w ygl.w ynsk.ʻ[-]. | [--]y.l arṣ[.id]y.alt.l aḥš.idy.alt.in l y. | [--]t.bʻl.ḥẓ.ršp.b[n].km.yr.kl 1001.1.2
l.ydm. | ḫlb.l ẓr.rḥtm. | w rd.bt ḫpṯt. | arṣ.tspr.b y | rdm.arṣ. | idk.al.ttn. | pnm.tk.qrt h. | hmry.mk.ksu. | ṯbt h.ḫḫ.arṣ. | 4[51].8.9
l ytn.bt.l bʻl.k ilm. | [w ḥẓ]r.k bn.aṯrt[.tdʻṣ.]pʻn. | [w tr.a]rṣ.id[k.l ttn.p]nm. | [ʻm.i]l.mbk.nhr[m.qr]b.[ap]q. | [thm]t 3[ʻNT.VI].5.13
ql k.tḥt. | [pʻn y.a]nk.nʻmn.ʻmq.nšm. | [tdʻṣ.pʻn]m.w tr.arṣ.idk. | [l ttn.pn]m.ʻm il.mbk.nhrm. | [qrb.ap]q.thmtm tgly 17[2AQHT].6.46
w ḫrṣ. | bht.ṯhrm.iqnim. | šmḫ.btlt.ʻnt.tdʻṣ. | pʻnm.w tr.arṣ. | idk.l ttn.pnm. | ʻm.bʻl.mrym.ṣpn. | b alp.šd.rbt.kmn. | ṣḥ 4[51].5.83
b ṣrrt.ṣpn. | yrd.ʻṯtr.ʻrẓ.yrd. | l kḥṯ.aliyn.bʻl. | w ymlk.b arṣ.il.kl h. | [---] š abn.b rḥbt. | [---] š abn.b kknt. 6.1.65[49.1.37]
ʻ]lm. | [bʻ]lm. | [bʻ]lm. | [bʻl]m. | [arṣ] w šm[m]. | [-----]. | [a]rṣ. | [u]šḫr[y]. | [ʻ]ṯtrt. | i[l t]ʻḏr bʻl. | ršp. | ddmš. | pḫr ilm. | y 29[17].2.1
ṭrn. | nḫlm.tlk.nbtm. | w idʻ.k ḥy.aliyn.bʻl. | k iṯ.zbl.bʻl.arṣ. | b ḥlm.lṭpn.il d pid. | b ḏrt.bny.bnwt. | šmm.šmn.tmṭrn. | 6[49].3.9
lq.z[bl.bʻl.arṣ]. | w hm.ḥy.a[liyn.bʻl]. | w hm.iṯ.zbl.bʻ[l.arṣ]. | b ḥlm.lṭpn.il.d pid. | b ḏrt.bny.bnwt. | šmm.šmn.tmṭrn. 6[49].3.3
.hm.iṯ.šmt.hm.iṯ[.ʻẓm]. | abky.w aqbrn.ašt.b ḫrt. | i[lm.arṣ.b p h.rgm.l yṣa.b šp] | t h.hwt h.knp.hrgb.bʻl.ṯbr. | bʻl.ṯbr. 19[1AQHT].3.127
m.iṯ.šmt.hm.i[ṯ]. | ʻẓm.abky.w aqbrn h. | ašt.b ḫrt.ilm.arṣ. | b p h.rgm.l yṣa.b špt h.hwt[h]. | knp.nšrm.bʻl.yṯbr. | bʻl. 19[1AQHT].3.112
ḥd.hm.iṯ.šmt.iṯ. | ʻẓm.abky w aqbrn h.aštn. | b ḫrt.ilm.arṣ.b p h.rgm.l[yṣ]a. | b špt h.hwt h.knp.ṣml.bʻ[l]. | bʻl.ṯbr.di 19[1AQHT].3.141
[-----]. | [---.mid.rm.]krt. | [b tk.rpi.]arṣ. | [b pḫr].qbṣ.dtn. | [w t]qrb.w ld. | bn.tl k. | tld.pǵt.t[--]t. | t 15[128].3.3
---]. | tld.pǵ[t.---]. | tld.p[ǵt.---]. | mid.rm[.krt]. | b tk.rpi.ar[ṣ]. | b pḫr.qbṣ.dtn. | ṣǵrt hn.abkrn. | tbrk.ilm.tity. | tity.ilm. 15[128].3.14
n.mṭr h. | bʻl.yʻdn.ʻdn.ṯkt.b glṯ. | w tn.ql h.b ʻrpt. | šrh.l arṣ.brqm. | bt.arzm.yklln h. | hm.bt.lbnt.yʻmsn h. | l yrgm.l al 4[51].5.71
d y.d ym | lk.ʻl.ilm.l ymru. | ilm.w nšm.d yšb | [ʻ].hmlt.arṣ.gm.l ǵ | [lm] h.bʻl k.yṣḥ.ʻn. | [gpn].w ugr.b ǵlmt. | [ʻmm.]y 4[51].7.52
w anḫn. | w tnḫ.b irt y.npš. | k ḥy.aliyn.bʻl. | k iṯ.zbl.bʻl.arṣ. | gm.yṣḥ.il.l btlt. | ʻnt.šmʻ.l btlt.ʻn[t]. | rgm.l nrt.il.šp[š]. | p 6[49].3.21
w bn h.ilt.w ṣb | rt.ary h.k mt.aliyn. | bʻl.k ḫlq.zbl.bʻl. | arṣ.gm.yṣḥ il. | l rbt.aṯrt ym.šmʻ. | l rbt.aṯr[t] ym.tn. | aḥd.b b 6.1.43[49.1.15]
bd.šdm.npš.ḫsrt. | bn.nšm.npš.hmlt. | arṣ.mǵt.l nʻm y.arṣ. | dbr.ysmt.šd.šḥlmmt. | ngš.ank.aliyn bʻl. | ʻdbnn ank.imr 6[49].2.19
d.kl.ǵr. | l kbd.arṣ.kl.gbʻ. | l [k]bd.šdm.tmǵ.l nʻm[y]. | [arṣ.]dbr.ysmt.šd. | [šḥl]mmt.t[mǵ.]l bʻl.np[l]. | [l a]rṣ[.lpš].tks 5[67].6.29
.w tṣ]ḥ.sbn. | [---]l[.---.]ʻd. | ksm.mhyt[.m]ǵny. | l nʻm y.arṣ.dbr. | l ysmt.šd.šḥlmmt. | mǵny.l bʻl.npl.l a | rṣ.mt.aliyn.bʻ 5[67].6.6
ḏ.arz.b ymn h. | bkm.yṯb.bʻl.l bht h. | u mlk.u bl mlk. | arṣ.drkt.yštkn. | dll.al.ilak.l bn. | ilm.mt.ʻdd.l ydd. | il.ǵzr.yqr 4[51].7.44
bky. | b ṯn.[-]gmm.w ydmʻ. | tntkn.udmʻt h. | km.ṯqlm.arṣ h. | km ḫmšt.mṭt h. | bm.bky h.w yšn. | b dmʻ h.nhmmt. | 14[KRT].1.29
]. | [---.]k.drḫm.w aṯb.l ntbt.k.ʻṣm l t[--]. | [---.]drk.brḥ.arṣ.lk pn h.yrk.bʻ[l]. | [---.]bt k.ap.l pḫr k ʻnt tqm.ʻnt.tqm. | [- 1001.2.8
ṯr.il[.ab y.---]. | yṯb.l y.w l h.[---]. | [--.i]mṣḫ.nn.k imr.l arṣ. | [ašhlk].šbt h.dmm.šbt.dqn h. | [mmʻm.-]d.l ytn.bt.l bʻl. 3[ʻNT.VI].5.9
.-]mn k.ššrt. | [---.--]t.npš.ʻgl. | [---.-]nk.aštn.b ḫrt. | ilm.arṣ.w at.qḥ. | ʻrpt k.rḥ k.mdl k. | mṭrt k.ʻm k.šbʻt. | ǵlm k.ṯmn 5[67].5.6
.ʻl ydm. | ḫlb.l ẓr.rḥtm w rd. | bt ḫpṯt.arṣ.tspr b y | rdm.arṣ.w tdʻ ilm. | k mtt.yšmʻ.aliyn.bʻl. | yuhb.ʻglt.b dbr.prt. | b š 5[67].5.16
[k mt.aliyn.bʻl]. | k ḫlq.z[bl.bʻl.arṣ]. | w hm.ḥy.a[liyn.bʻl]. | w hm.iṯ.zbl.bʻ[l.arṣ]. | b ḥlm.lṭpn. 6[49].3.1
[--]n. | hn[-.]aḥẓ[.---]l[-]. | [ʻ]nt.akl[y.nšm]. | akly.hml[t.arṣ]. | w y[-]l.a[---]. | š[--.---]. | bl[.---]. 6[49].5.25
.šdm.il.yš[t k]. | bʻl.ʻnt.mḥrṯ[-]. | iy.aliyn.bʻl. | iy.zbl.bʻl.arṣ. | w tʻn.nrt.ilm.š[p]š. | šd yn.ʻn.b qbt[.t] | bl lyt.ʻl.umt k. | 6[49].4.40
šn.l kbkbm.yʻrb. | [bʻ]l.b kbd h.b p h yrd. | k ḥrr.zt.ybl.arṣ.w pr. | ʻṣm.yraun.aliyn.bʻl. | ṯtʻ.nn.rkb.ʻrpt. | tbʻ.rgm.l bn.i 5[67].2.5
hlm.qdq | d zbl ym.bn.ʻnm.ṯpṭ.nhr.yprsḥ ym. | w yql.l arṣ.w trtqṣ.ṣmd.b d bʻl. | [km.]nšr.b uṣbʻt h.ylm.qdqd.zbl. | [2.4[68].23
[-----]. | yṣq.šm[n.---]. | ʻn.tr.arṣ.w šmm. | sb.l qṣm.arṣ. | l ksm.mhyt.ʻn. | l arṣ.m[ṭ]r.bʻl. | w 16[126].3.2
.p[--.---]. | kṯ.ẓrw.kṯ.nbt.ḏnt.w [-]n[-.---]. | il.ḫyr.ilib.š. | arṣ w šmm.š. | il.š.kṯrt.š. | dgn.š.bʻl.ḫlb alp w š. | bʻl ṣpn alp.w UG5.9.2.2
| il.alp.w š[.---]. | bʻlm.alp.w š[.---]. | bʻlm.alp.w š[.---]. | arṣ.w šmm.š.kṯr[t] š.yrḫ[.---]. | ṣpn.š.kṯr.š.pdry.š.ǵrm.š[.---]. UG5.9.1.5
ṣ]pn. | bʻlm. | [bʻ]lm. | [bʻ]lm. | [bʻ]lm. | [bʻ]lm. | [bʻl]m. | [arṣ] w šm[m]. | [-----]. | [a]rṣ. | [u]šḫr[y]. | [ʻ]ṯtrt. | i[l t]ʻḏr bʻl. | r 29[17].1.12
[---.--]m[.---]. | [-.]rbt.ṯbt.[---]. | rbt.ṯbt.ḥš[n.---]. | y.arṣ.ḥšn[.---]. | tʻtd.tkl.[---]. | tkn.lbn[.---]. | dt.lbn k[.---]. | dk k. 5[67].3.4
yn h. | b ṣrrt.ṣpn.tbkyn h. | w tqbrn h.tštnn.b ḫrt. | ilm.arṣ.ṭṭbḫ.šbʻm. | rumm.k gmn.aliyn. | [b]ʻl.ṭṭbḫ.šbʻm.alpm. | [k 6[62].1.18
m h.mria.w tk. | pn h.tḥspn.m h.w trḥṣ. | ṭl.šmm.šmn.arṣ.ṭl.šm[m.t]sk h. | rbb.nsk h.kbkbm. | ttpp.anhbm.d alp.šd[3[ʻNT].4.87
b bt.šrš.b qrb. | hkl h.nṣb.skn.ilib h.b qdš. | ẓtr.ʻm h.l arṣ.mšṣu.qṭr h. | l ʻpr.ḏmr.aṯr h.ṭbq.lḥt. | niṣ h.grš d.ʻšy.ln h. 17[2AQHT].1.28
bt.šrš.]b qrb.hkl h. | [nṣb.skn.i]lib h.b qdš. | [ẓtr.ʻm h.l a]rṣ.mšṣu. | [qṭr h.l ʻpr.ḏ]mr.a[ṯ]r h. | [ṭbq.lḥt.niṣ h.gr]š.d ʻšy. 17[2AQHT].1.46
[ṯ]r h. | [ṭbq.lḥt.niṣ h.gr]š.d ʻšy. | [ln h.---]. | z[tr.ʻm k.l arṣ.mšṣu.qṭr k]. | l ʻpr.ḏm[r.aṯr k.ṭbq]. | lḥt.niṣ k.gr[š.d ʻšy.ln 17[2AQHT].2.1
k.lṭpn.il. | d pid.yrd.l ksi.yṯb. | l hdm[.w] l.hdm.yṯb. | l arṣ.yṣq.ʻmr. | un.l riš h.ʻpr.plṯt. | l qdqd h.lpš.yks. | mizrtm.ǵr 5[67].6.14
rbm.ymḫṣ.b ktp. | dk ym.ymḫṣ.b ṣmd. | ṣḥr mt.ymṣḫ.l arṣ. | [yṯb.]b[ʻ]l.l ksi.mlk h. | [---].l kḥṯ.drkt h. | l [ym]m.l yrḫ 6[49].5.4
.hmlt.aṯr. | bʻl.ard.b arṣ.ap. | ʻnt.ttlk.w tṣd.kl.ǵr. | l kbd.arṣ.kl.gbʻ. | l [k]bd.šdm.tmǵ.l nʻm[y]. | [arṣ.]dbr.ysmt.šd. | [š 5[67].6.27
lm.mt.mh. | taršn.l btlt.ʻnt. | an.itlk.w aṣd.kl. | ǵr.l kbd.arṣ.kl.gbʻ. | l kbd.šdm.npš.ḫsrt. | bn.nšm.npš.hmlt. | arṣ.mǵt.l 6[49].2.16
q. | [---].tṣb.qšt.bnt. | [---.ʻ]n h.km.bṯn.yqr. | [krpn h.-.l]arṣ.ks h.tšpk m. | [l ʻpr.tšu.g h.]w tṣḥ.šmʻ.mʻ. | [l aqht.ǵzr.i]r 17[2AQHT].6.15
l.]isp.ḥ[mt.---.-]hm.yasp.ḥmt. | [---.š]pš.l [hrm.ǵrpl].ʻl.arṣ.l an. | [ḥ]mt.i[l.w] ḥrn.yisp.ḥmt. | [bʻl.w]dgn[.yi]sp.ḥmt.ʻ UG5.8.12
i]sp.ḥmt.šḥr.w šlm. | [yis]p.ḥmt.isp.[šp]š l hrm.ǵrpl.ʻl arṣ. | [l a]n ḥmt.l p[.n]ṯk.abd.l p.akl ṯm.dl. | [---.q]l.bl.tbḥ[n.l UG5.8.19
[-----]. | yṣq.šm[n.---]. | ʻn.tr.arṣ.w šmm. | sb.l qṣm.arṣ. | l ksm.mhyt.ʻn. | l arṣ.m[ṭ]r.bʻl. | w l šd.mṭr.ʻly. | nʻm.l ar 16[126].3.3
[y]. | [arṣ.]dbr.ysmt.šd. | [šḥl]mmt.t[mǵ.]l bʻl.np[l]. | [l a]rṣ[.lpš].tks.miz[rtm]. 5[67].6.31
. | l nʻm y.arṣ.dbr. | l ysmt.šd.šḥlmmt. | mǵny.l bʻl.npl.l a | rṣ.mt.aliyn.bʻl. | ḫlq.zbl.bʻl.arṣ. | apnk.lṭpn.il. | d pid.yrd.l k 5[67].6.8
[--]r.[---]. | [---.]il.[---]. | [tṣ]un.b arṣ. | mḫnm.ṯrp ym. | lšnm.tlḥk. | šmm.tṯrp. | ym.ḏnbtm. | tnn. 1003.3
---]. | ʻn.tr.arṣ.w šmm. | sb.l qṣm.arṣ. | l ksm.mhyt.ʻn. | l arṣ.m[ṭ]r.bʻl. | w l šd.mṭr.ʻly. | nʻm.l arṣ.mṭr.bʻl. | w l šd.mṭr.ʻl 16[126].3.5
| l ksm.mhyt.ʻn. | l arṣ.m[ṭ]r.bʻl. | w l šd.mṭr.ʻly. | nʻm.l arṣ.mṭr.bʻl. | w l šd.mṭr.ʻly. | nʻm.l ḥṭt.b gn. | bm.nrt.ksmm. | ʻ 16[126].3.7
y.l ybmt.limm.tḥm.aliyn.bʻl]. | hw[t.aliy.qrdm.qryy.b arṣ.mlḥmt.št]. | [b ʻ]pr[m.ddym.sk.šlm.l kbd.arṣ.arbdd]. | l k 7.2[130].14
bʻl.ṣrt.l rkb.ʻrpt. | tḥm.aliyn.bʻl.hwt.aliy. | qrdm.qry.b arṣ.mlḥmt. | št.b ʻp[r] m.ddym.sk.šlm. | l kbd.arṣ.arbdd.l kbd 3[ʻNT].4.52
]dm.yšt. | [----.]bʻl.mdl h.ybʻr. | [---.]rn h.aqry. | [---.]b a[r]ṣ.mlḥmt. | ašt[.b ʻ]p[r] m.ddym.ask. | šlm.l kb[d].awṣ.arb 3[ʻNT].4.72
ny.l ymmt.limm. | tḥm.aliyn.bʻl.hwt. | aliy.qrdm.qry.b arṣ. | mlḥmt št.b ʻpr m.ddym. | sk.šlm.l kbd.arṣ. | arbdd.l kbd 3[ʻNT].3.11

.g h.w y]ṣḥ.tḥm.|[tr.il.ab k.hwt.l]ṭpn.ḥtk k.|[qryy.b arṣ.mlḥ]mt.št b ʻp|[r m.ddym.sk.šlm].l kbd.arṣ.|[arbdd.l k 1[ʻNT.IX].2.19
lt y.|w t[ʻn].btlt.[ʻ]nt.ṯṯb.|[ybmt.]limm.[a]n.aqry.|[b arṣ].mlḥmt.[aš]t.b ʻpr m.|ddym.ask[.šlm.]l kbd.arṣ.|ar[bdd 3[ʻNT].4.67
bd.arṣ.kl.gbʻ.|l kbd.šdm.npš.ḫsrt.|bn.nšm.npš.hmlt.|arṣ.mǵt.l nʻm y.arṣ.|dbr.ysmt.šd.šḥlmmt.|ngš.ank.aliyn bʻl 6[49].2.19
idk.al.ttn.pnm.tk.ḥkpt.il.kl h].|[kptr.]ks[u.ṯbt h.ḥkpt.arṣ.nḥlt h].|b alp.šd.r[bt.kmn.l pʻn.kṯr].|hbr.w ql.t[šṯḥwy. 1[ʻNT.IX].3.1
.al.tnn.|pnm.tk.ḥqkpt.|il.kl h.kptr.|ksu.ṯbt h.ḥkpt.|arṣ.nḥlt h.|b alp.šd.rbt.|kmn.l pʻn.kṯ.|hbr.w ql.tšṯḥ|wy.w 3[ʻNT.VI].6.16
rṣ.|idk.al.ttn.|pnm.tk.qrt h.|hmry.mk.ksu.|ṯbt h.ḫḫ.arṣ.|nḥlt h.w nǵr.|ʻnn.ilm.al.|tqrb.l bn.ilm.|mt.al.yʻdb km. 4[51].8.13
ytn.pn.ʻm.bn.ilm.mt.|tk.qrt h.hmry.mk.ksu.|ṯbt.ḫḫ.arṣ.nḥlt h.tša.|g hm.w tṣḥ.tḥm.aliyn.|bn.bʻl.hwt.aliy.qrdm. 5[67].2.16
.ylm.qdqd.zbl.|[ym.]bn.ʻnm.ṭpṭ.nhr.yprsḥ.ym.yql.|l arṣ.tnǵṣn.pnt h.w ydlp.tmn h.|yqṯ bʻl.w yšt.ym.ykly.ṭpṭ.nh 2.4[68].26
irtm.m[--].|[ṭpṭ].nhr.tlʻm.ṯm.ḥrbm.its.anšq.|[-]htm.l arṣ.ypl.ul ny.w l.ʻpr.ʻẓm ny.|l bʻl[-.---].|ṯḥt.ksi.zbl.ym.w ʻn. 2.4[68].5
idk.al.ttn.pnm.|ʻm.ǵr.trǵzz.|ʻm.ǵr.ṯrmg.|ʻm.tlm.ǵṣr.arṣ.|ša.ǵr.ʻl.ydm.|ḫlb.l ẓr.rḥtm.|w rd.bt ḫpṯt.|arṣ.tspr.b y| 4[51].8.4
.|ʻln.ybl hm.ḫrṣ.|ṯlḥn.il.d mla.|mnm.dbbm.d |msdt.arṣ.|sʻ.il.dqt.k amr.|sknt.k ḥwt.yman.|d b h.rumm.l rbbt. 4[51].1.41
m.ǵṣr.arṣ.|ša.ǵr.ʻl.ydm.|ḫlb.l ẓr.rḥtm.|w rd.bt ḫpṯt.|arṣ.tspr.b y|rdm.arṣ.|idk.al.ttn.|pnm.tk.qrt h.|hmry.mk.k 4[51].8.8
.ǵr.|knkny.ša.ǵr.ʻl ydm.|ḫlb.l ẓr.rḥtm w rd.|bt ḫpṯt.arṣ.tspr b y|rdm.arṣ.w tdʻ ilm.|k mtt.yšmʻ.aliyn.bʻl.|yuhb.ʻ 5[67].5.15
u.m]lk.ʻlm.b ḏmr h.bl.|[---].b ḥtk h.b nmrt h.l r|[--.]arṣ.ʻz k.ḏmr k.l[-]|n k.ḥtk k.nmrt k.b tk.|ugrt.l ymt.špš.w UG5.2.2.9
ṯ.bmt.|bʻl.mt.my.lim.bn dgn.|my.hmlt.aṯr.bʻl.nrd.|b arṣ.ʻm h.trd.nrt.|ilm.špš.ʻd.tšbʻ.bk.|tšt.k yn.udmʻt.gm.|tṣḥ. 6[62].1.8
qrnm w ḏnb.ylšn.|b ḫri h.w ṯnt h.ql.il.[--].|il.k yrdm.arṣ.ʻnt.|w ʻṯtrt.tṣdn.[---].|[---.-]b[-.---].|[ʻṯ]trt w ʻnt[.---].|w UG5.1.1.22
al.tǵl[.---].|prdmn.ʻbd.ali[yn].|bʻl.sid.zbl.bʻl.|arṣ.qm.yṯʻr.|w yšlḥmn h.|ybrd.ṯd.l pnw h.|b ḥrb.mlḥt.|qṣ. 3[ʻNT].1.4
mm.tṯʻr.l hdmm.|[t]ḥspn.m h.w trḥṣ.|[ṭ]l.šmm.šmn.arṣ.rbb.|[r]kb ʻrpt.ṭl.šmm.tsk h.|[rb]b.nsk h.kbkbm. 3[ʻNT].2.39
t.ilmy nʻmm.|agzr ym.bn ym.ynqm.b ap.ḏd.št.špt.|l arṣ.špt l šmm.w ʻrb.b p hm.ʻṣr.šmm.|w dg b ym.w ndd.gzr. 23[52].62
[-----].|[špt.l a]rṣ.špt.l šmm.|[---.l]šn.l kbkbm.yʻrb.|[bʻ]l.b kbd h.b p h yr 5[67].2.2
.rgm.]ʻṣ.w lḫšt.|[abn.rgm.l td]ʻ.nš[m.w l t]bn.|[hmlt.a]rṣ.[tant.šmm.ʻm.ar]ṣ.|thmt.[ʻmn.kbkbm.abn.brq].|d l t[dʻ 3[ʻNT].4.60
t.šdm.il.yšt k.|[b]ʻl.ʻnt.mḥrṯt.|iy.aliyn.bʻl.|iy.zbl.bʻl.arṣ.|ttbʻ.btlt.ʻnt.|idk.l ttn.pnm.|ʻm.nrt.ilm.špš.|tšu.g h.w t 6[49].4.29
[h]wt.d aṯ[ny k.---.rgm.ʻṣ].|w lḫšt.abn[.tant.šmm.ʻm.arṣ.thmt].|ʻm kbkbm[.abn.brq.d l tdʻ.šmm.at m].|w ank.ib[7.2[130].19
m k.|hwt.w aṯny k.rgm.|ʻṣ.w lḫšt.abn.|tant.šmm.ʻm.arṣ.|thmt.ʻmn.kbkbm.|abn.brq.d l.tdʻ.šmm.|rgm l tdʻ.nšm. 3[ʻNT].3.21
bn.rgm.l td]ʻ.nš[m.w l t]bn.|[hmlt.a]rṣ.[tant.šmm.ʻm.ar]ṣ.|thmt.[ʻmn.kbkbm.abn.brq].|d l t[dʻ.šmm.at m.w ank] 3[ʻNT].4.60
k].|hwt.w aṯny k[.rgm.ʻṣ.w lḫšt.abn].|tunt.šmm.ʻm[.arṣ.thmt.ʻmn.kbkbm].|rgm.l tdʻ.nš[m.w l tbn.hmlt.arṣ].|at. 1[ʻNT.IX].3.14
.mrḥ h.|l tl.yṣb.pn h.tǵr.|yṣu.hlm.aḫ h.tph.|[ksl]h.l arṣ.ṯṯbr.|[---.]aḫ h.tbky.|[--.m]rṣ.mlk.|[---.]krt.adn k.|[w yʻ 16.1[125].54
ptr].|l rḥq.ilm.ḥkp[t.l rḥq.ilnym].|ṯn.mṯpdm.tḥt.[ʻnt.arṣ.ṯlṯ.mtḥ].|ǵyrm.idk.l yt[n.pnm.ʻm.lṭpn].|il d pid.tk ḫrš[1[ʻNT.IX].3.20
t.|uǵr.l rḥq.ilm.inbb.|l rḥq.ilnym.ṯn.mṯpdm.|tḥt.ʻnt.arṣ.ṯlṯ.mtḥ.ǵyrm.|idk.l ttn pnm.ʻm.bʻl.|mrym.ṣpn.b alp.šd. 3[ʻNT].4.80
t]r.l r[ḥq.ilm.ḥkpt.l rḥq].|[ilnym.ṯn.mṯpd]m.t[ḥt.ʻnt.arṣ.ṯlṯ.mtḥ.ǵyrm].|[idk.]l ytn.pnm.ʻm.[i]l.mbk.[nhrm.qrb.a 2.3[129].3
[---.--]m.|[-----].|[---.]d arṣ.|[---.]ln.|[---.]nb hm.|[---.-]kn.|[---.]hr n.km.šḥr.|[---. 12[75].1.3
zḥ.---].|bṯt.ʻllm n.[---].|ilm.bt.bʻl k.[---].|dl.ylkn.ḥš.b a[rṣ.---].|b ʻpr.ḫbl ṭtm.[---.]|šqy.rṭa.tnm y.ytn.[ks.b yd].|kr 1[ʻNT.X].4.7
.l hrm.|[ǵrpl.]ʻl.ar[ṣ.---.ḥ]mt.|[---.šp]š.l [hrm.ǵ]rpl.ʻl.arṣ.|[---.]ḥmt.l p[.nṯ]k.abd.l p.ak[l].|[ṯm.dl.]isp.ḥ[mt.---.-]h UG5.8.9
sr.n[--.---.]ḥrn.|[--]p.ḫp h.ḫ[--.---.šp]š.l hrm.|[ǵrpl.]ʻl.ar[ṣ.---.ḥ]mt.|[---.šp]š.l [hrm.ǵ]rpl.ʻl.arṣ.|[---.]ḥmt.l p[.nṯ]k. UG5.8.8
-.al]iyn bʻl.|[---].rkb.ʻrpt.|[---.]ǵš.l limm.|[---.]l yṯb.l arṣ.|[---].mtm.|[---.--]d mhr.ur.|[---.]yḥnnn.|[---.--]t.ytn.|[- 10[76].1.9
ql h.qdš.b[ʻl.y]tn.|ytny.bʻl.ṣ[---.-]pt h.|ql h.q[dš.ṯb]r.arṣ.|[---.]ǵrm[.t]ḫšn.|rḥq[.---.tdʻ].|qdm ym.bmt.[nhr].|ṯṭṯn 4[51].7.31
b.|[---].asr.|[---.--]m.ymt m.|[---].k iṯl.|[---.--]m.ʻdb.l arṣ.|[---.]špm.ʻdb.|[---].tʻtqn.|[---.-]ʻb.idk.|[l ytn.pnm.tk.]in 1[ʻNT.IX].2.10
-.btlt.]ʻnt.|[---.ybmt.]limm.|[---.---]l.limm.|[---.yṯ]b.l arṣ.|[---.--]l.šir.|[---.-]tm.|[---.]yd y.|[----]y.|[---.-]lm.|[---.r 10[76].1.17
[---.--]r.pn[.---].|[---.-]ḏi.u[--.---].|[---].l.ar[ṣ.---].|[---.--]g.irb[-.---].|[---.-]rd.pn.[---].|[---.--]r.ṯṯ d.[---] 2157.3
tn y at zd.|[---.]tʻrb.bši.|[---.]l tzd.l tptq.|[---].g[--.]l arṣ. 1[ʻNT.X].5.28
m.|[l tdd.aṯr]h.l tdd.i[lnym].|[---.]r[--.---].|[---.yṯ]b.l arṣ. 21[122].2.1

arṣy

.mṯb.|klt.knyt.|mṯb.pdry.b ar.|mẓll.ṭly.bt rb.|mṯb.arṣy.bt.yʻbdr.|ap.mtn.rgmm.|argm k.šskn mʻ.|mgn.rbt.aṯr 4[51].1.19
.|mṯb.klt.knyt.|mṯb.pdry.bt.ar.|mẓll.ṭly.bt rb.|mṯb.arṣ.bt yʻbdr.|w yʻn lṭpn il d pid.|p ʻbd.an.ʻnn.aṯrt.|p.ʻbd.an 4[51].4.57
bt.aṯrt.|ym.mṯb.[pdr]y.bt.ar.|[mẓll.]ṭly[.bt.]rb.mṯb.|[arṣy.bt.yʻbdr.mṯb].|[klt.knyt]. 3[ʻNT.VI].5.51
b.rbt.aṯrt.ym].|mṯb.pdr[y.bt.ar.mẓll].|ṭly.bt.r[b.mṯb.arṣy].|bt.yʻbdr[.mṯb.klt].|knyt.w tʻn[.btlt.ʻnt].|yṯb l y.ṯr.il[. 3[ʻNT.VI].4.4
h.mšr.l.dd.aliyn.|bʻl.yd.pdry.bt.ar.|ahbt.ṭly.bt.rb.dd.arṣy.|bt.yʻbdr.km ǵlmm.|w ʻrb n.l pʻn.ʻnt.hbr.|w ql.tšṯḥwy 3[ʻNT].3.4
.l dd.aliyn.bʻl].|[ahb]t pdr[y.bt.ar.ahbt.ṭly.bt.rb.dd].|arṣy bt.y[ʻbdr.---].|rgm l btl[t.ʻnt.ṯny.l ybmt.limm.tḥm.aliy 7.2[130].12
---].|l.ršp[.---].|[l].ršp.[---.--]g.kbd.|[l.i]lt.qb[-.---].|[l.a]rṣy.|[l.--]r[-.---].|[l.--]ḫl.|[l.--.]mgmr.|[l.-.]qdšt.|l.ʻṯtrt.nd 1001.1.11
ḫ[.---].|ṣpn.š.kṯr.š.pdry.š.ǵrm.š[.---].|aṯrt.š.ʻnt.š.špš.š.arṣy.š.ʻṯtrt.š.|ušḫry.š.il.tʻḏr.bʻl.š.ršp.š.ddmš.š.|w šlmm.ilib. UG5.9.1.7

arr

spr.ḫrd.arr.|ap arbʻm[.--].|pd[.---.ḫm]šm.kb[d].|ǵb[-.---.]kbd.|m[-- 2042.1
ḫp.ṣǵrt h.|yrk.tʻl.b ǵr.|mslmt.b ǵr.tliyt.|w tʻl.bkm.b arr.|bm.arr.w b ṣpn.|b nʻm.b ǵr.t[l]iyt.|ql.l bʻl.ttnn.|bšrt.il 10[76].3.30
mṣmt.ʻbs.|arr.d.qr|ht. 1173.2
.|yrk.tʻl.b ǵr.|mslmt.b ǵr.tliyt.|w tʻl.bkm.b arr.|bm.arr.w b ṣpn.|b nʻm.b ǵr.t[l]iyt.|ql.l bʻl.ttnn.|bšrt.il.bš[r.bʻ]l. 10[76].3.31
|[---.b]nšm.b.ugrt.|[---.bn]šm.b.ǵbl.|[---.b]nšm.b.mʻr.arr.|arbʻ.bnšm.b.mnt.|arbʻ.bnšm.b.irbn.|ṯn.bnšm.b.yʻrt.|ṯ 2076.32
[š]šw[.i]ryn.arr.|[š]dm.b.mlk.|[--.š]dm.b.ar.|[--.š]dm.b.ulm.|[--.š]dm.b. 2033.1.1

arš

k.tšlm k.|tʻzz k.alp ymm.|w rbt.šnt.|b ʻd ʻlm...gnʻ.|iršt.aršt.|l aḫ y.l rʻ y.dt.|w ytnnn.|l aḫ h.l rʻ h.|rʻ ʻlm.|ttn. 1019.1.7
.m at.|krt.k ybky.|ydmʻ.nʻmn.ǵlm.|il.mlk[.ṯ]r ab h.|yarš.hm.drk[t].|k ab.adm.|[-----]. 14[KRT].1.42
k.ilm.hn.mtm.|ʻd k.kṯr m.ḫbr k.|w ḫss.dʻt k.|b ym.arš.w tnn.|kṯr.w ḫss.yd.|ytr.kṯr.w ḫss.|spr.ilmlk šbny.|lm 6.6[62.2].50

.|qṣ‘t.l ybmt.limm.w t‘n.btlt.|‘nt.irš ḥym.l aqht.ǵzr.|irš ḥym.w atn k.bl mt.|w ašlḥ k.ašspr k.‘m.b‘l.|šnt.‘m.bn il 17[2AQHT].6.27

r.w ḫss.yb‘l.qšt l ‘nt.|qṣ‘t.l ybmt.limm.w t‘n.btlt.|‘nt.irš ḥym.l aqht.ǵzr.|irš ḥym.w atn k.bl mt.|w ašlḥ k.ašspr k 17[2AQHT].6.26

iršt.yṣḥm.|arb‘.alpm.|mitm.kbd.ṯlṯ.|arb‘.kkrm.|ṯmn.mat.k 2051.1

[--.---].|[-]r[--.--]y.|in m.‘bd k hwt.|[y]rš.‘m y.|mnm.iršt k.|d ḫsrt.w.ank.|aštn..l.iḫ y.|w.ap.ank.mnm.|[ḫ]s[r]t. 2065.15

.ks h.tšpk m.|[l ‘pr.tšu.g h.]w tṣḥ.šm‘.m‘.|[l aqht.ǵzr.i]rš.ksp.w atn k.|[ḫrṣ.w aš]lḥ k.w tn.qšt k.[l].|[‘nt.tq]ḥ[.q]ṣ‘ 17[2AQHT].6.17

šlm k.|t‘zz k.alp ymm.|w rbt.šnt.|b ‘d ‘lm...gn‘.|iršt.aršt.|l aḫ y.l r‘ y.dt.|w ytnnn.|l aḫ h.l r‘ h.|r‘ ‘lm.|ttn.w tn 1019.1.7

ll.tšu.g h.w[tṣ]|ḥ.at.mt.tn.aḫ y.|w ‘n.bn.ilm.mt.mh.|taršn.l btlt.‘nt.|an.itlk.w aṣd.kl.|ǵr.l kbd.arṣ.kl.gb‘.|l kbd.š 6[49].2.14

nt.|ap.sgrt.yd‘[t k.]bt.k an[št].|k in.b ilht.ql[ṣ] k.mh.tarš[n].|l btlt.‘nt.w t[‘]n.btlt.‘n[t].|tḥm k.il.ḥkm.ḥkm k.|‘m 3[‘NT.VI].5.36

tn.hm.l k.|w.lḥt.alpm.ḥršm.|k.rgmt.l y.bly m.|alpm.aršt.l k.w.l y.|mn.bnš.d.l.i[--].‘[m k].|l.alpm.w.l.y[n.--]t.|w. 2064.23

---].|w.an[k.---].|arš[.---].|mlk.r[b.b‘]l y.p.l.|ḥy.np[š.a]rš.|l.pn.b‘[l y.l].pn.b‘l y.|w.urk.ym.b‘l y.|l.pn.amn.w.l.pn 1018.18

.|[---.-]rš.l b‘l.|[---.-]ǵk.rpu mlk.|[‘lm.---.--]k.l tšt k.l iršt.|[‘lm.---.--]k.l tšt k.liršt.|[---.]rpi.mlk ‘lm.b ‘z.|[rpu.m]l UG5.2.2.5

l h.|mḫšt.btn.‘qltn.|šlyṭ.d šb‘t.rašm.|mḫšt.mdd ilm.ar[š].|ṣmt.‘gl.il.‘tk.|mḫšt.klbt.ilm išt.|klt.bt.il.ḏbb.imtḫṣ.ks 3[‘NT].3.40

-----].|r[--.---].|b.[---.mlk].|rb[.b‘l y.---].|w.an[k.---].|arš[.---].|mlk.r[b.b‘]l y.p.l.|ḥy.np[š.a]rš.|l.pn.b‘[l y.l].pn.b‘l 1018.16

.rpu mlk.|[‘lm.---.--]k.l tšt k.l iršt.|[‘lm.---.--]k.l tšt k.liršt.|[---.]rpi.mlk ‘lm.b ‘z.|[rpu.m]lk.‘lm.b ḏmr h.bl.|[---]. UG5.2.2.5

[---.]irš[-.---].|[---.]bn.n[--.---].|[---.]bn.mṣ[--.---].|[---.]b‘lš[-.---]. 2139.1

[---.]h.yb[--].|[---.--]n.irš[.---].|[---.--]mr.ph.|[---.--]mm.hlkt.|[---.]b qrb.‘r.|[---.m] 26[135].2

justify aršḫ

trǵnw.w tṯkl.|bnwt h.ykr.‘r.d qdm.|idk.pnm.l ytn.tk aršḫ.rbt.|w aršḫ.ṯrrt.ydy.b ‘ṣm.‘r‘r.|w b šḥt.‘s.mt.‘r‘rm.yn‘r UG5.7.63

.|bnwt h.ykr.‘r.d qdm.|idk.pnm.l ytn.tk aršḫ.rbt.|w aršḫ.ṯrrt.ydy.b ‘ṣm.‘r‘r.|w b šḥt.‘s.mt.‘r‘rm.yn‘rn h.|ssnm.y UG5.7.64

aršm

ilk.r[--].|aršm.b‘l [aṯt].|ttḫ.b‘l aṯt.|ayab.b‘l aṯt.|iyṯr.b‘l aṯt.|ptm.b‘l 1077.2

aršmg

grgš.|w.lmd h.|aršmg.|w.lmd h.|iyṯr.|[w].lmd h.|[yn]ḥm.|[w.]lmd h.|[i] 1048.3

--].|bqrt[.---].|ṯnǵrn.[---].|w.bn h.n[--.---].|ḥnil.[---].|aršmg.mru.|b‘l.šlm.‘bd.|awr.ṯǵrn.‘bd.|‘bd.ḫmn.šm‘.rgm.|s̀ 2084.9

.aṯt h.|[--]y.w.aṯt h.|[--]r.w.aṯt h.|‘bdyrḫ.ṯn ǵlyt h.|aršmg.|ršpy.w.aṯt h.|bn.glgl.uškny.|bn.ṯny.uškny.|mnn.w. 2068.11

[-]ay[.---].|[a]rš[mg.---].|urt[n.---].|‘dn[.---].|bqrt[.---].|ṯnǵrn.[---].|w.b 2084.2

[---.‘ṯt]rab.|[---.ar]šmg.|[---.‘]bdkṯr.|[---.‘]bdgṯr.|[---.--]n.|[---.‘]bd‘nt.|[---.- 1055.1.2

art

n.uz.|mi[t].ygb.bq‘.|a[--].‘ṭ.|a[l]pm.alpnm.|ṯlṯ.m[a]t.art.ḥkpt.|mit.dnn.|mitm.iqnu.|ḫmš.‘šr.qn.n‘m.‘n[m].|ṯn.ḥ 1128.26

srn.|mtb‘l.rišy.|ṯlṯm.ṯlṯ.‘l.nsk.|arym.|alp.ṯlṯ.‘l.|nsk.art.|ḫmš.mat.ṯlṯ.|‘l.mtn.rišy. 1137.8

spr.ubdy.art.|šd.prn.b d.agpṯn.nḥl h.|šd.s̀wn.b d.ttyn.nḥl [h].|šd.ṯṭy 2029.1

šrš.|lbnm.|ḫlb.krd.|ṣ‘.|mlk.|gb‘ly.|ypr.|ary.|ẓrn.|art.|ṯlḥny.|ṯlrby.|dmt.|aǵt.|w.qmnz.|slḫ.|ykn‘m.|šlmy.| 71[113].10

qrht.d.tššlmn.|ṯlrb h.|art.ṯn.yrḫm.|ṯlrby.yrḫ.w.ḫm[š.ym]m.|ṯlḥny.yrḫ.w.ḫm[š.y 66[109].3

]mḏy.|[gn]‘y.|m‘qb.|agm.|ḫpty.|ypr.|ḫrṣb‘.|uḫnp.|art.|[--]n.|[-----].|[-----].|nnu.|šmg.|šmn.|lbnm.|ṯrm.|bṣr. 2058.2.7

-]l.ṯrmn.m[lk.---].|[---.--]rt.š‘rt[.---].|[---.i]qni.l.ṯr[mn.art.---].|[b.yr]ḫ.riš.yn.[---].|[---.b‘]lt.bhtm.š[--.---].|[---.-]rt.l 1106.31

qrht.b[--.---].|ksp.iš[-.---].|art.[---].|[-----].|[-----].|l [----].|b[--.---].|ḫl[--.---].|ḫp[ty.---] 1147.3

arty

ry.|arpṯr.y‘rty.|bn.ḫdyn.ugrty.|bn.tgḏn.ugrty.|tgyn.arty.|bn.nryn.arty.|bn.ršp.ary.|bn.ǵlmn ary.|bn.ḥṣbn ary. 87[64].10

.|bn.ḫdyn.ugrty.|bn.tgḏn.ugrty.|tgyn.arty.|bn.nryn.arty.|bn.ršp.ary.|bn.ǵlmn ary.|bn.ḥṣbn ary.|bn.s̀dy ary.|b 87[64].11

qrṭym.mddb‘l.|kdn.zlyy.|krwn.arty.|tlmu.zlyy.|pdu.qmnzy.|bdl.qrṭy.|trgn.bn.tǵh.|aupš. 89[312].3

dmlk.krm.aḥ[d.---].|krm.ubdy.b d.ǵ[--.---].|krm.pyn.arty[.---].|ṯlṯ.krm.ubdym.l mlkt.b.‘nmky[.---].|mgdly.ǵlpṯr. 1081.8

artyn

mḏrǵlm.d inn.|msgm.l hm.|p‘ṣ.ḫbty.|artyn.ary.|brqn.ṯlḥy.|bn.aryn.|bn.lgn.|bn.b‘yn.|šdyn.|ary 118[306].4

bn.qrrn.|bn.dnt.|bn.ṯ‘l[-].|bdl.ar.dt.inn.|mhr l ht.|artyn.|‘dmlk.|bn.alt[-].|iḫy[-].|‘bdgṯr.|ḥrr.|bn.s[-]p[-].|bn 1035.1.6

artn

ṯn.r‘y.uzm.|sǵr.bn.ḫpsry.aḥd.|sǵr.artn.aḥd.|sǵr.‘dn.aḥd.|sǵr.awldn.aḥd.|sǵr.idṯn.aḥd.|sǵr.sn 1140.3

ln.ṯb[--.-]nb.trtn.|[---]mm.klby.kl[--].dqn[.---].|[-]ntn.artn.b d[.--]nr[.---].|‘zn.w ymd.šr.b d ansny.|nsk.ks[p.--]mr 2011.30

[‘m].|[---].riš[.---].kt.|[y]nḥm.|ilb‘l.|‘bdyr[ḫ].|ṯtpḥ.|artn.|ybnil.|brqn.|adr[dn].|krwn.|arkḏn.|ilmn.|abškn.|y 1024.1.7

artṯb

ṯt.]w.pǵt.b.bt.gg.|[ǵz]r.aḥd.b.bt.nwrḏ.|[aṯ]t.adrt.b.bt.artṯb.|aṯt.w.ṯn.bn h.b.bt.iwwpzn.|aṯt.w.pǵt.b.bt.ydrm.|ṯt.a 80[119].4

ṯpt.srdnnm.|bn.qṣn.uṯpt.srdnnm.|yly.uṯpt.srdnnm.|artṯb.uṯpt.srdnnm. 1124.12

.|abmn.ilštm‘y.ḫmš[t].|‘zn.bn.brn.ḫmšt.|m‘rt.ḫmšt.|artṯb.bn.ḫmšt.|bn.ysr[.ḫmš]t.|ṣ[-]r.ḫ[mšt].|‘zn.ḫ[mšt]. 1062.28

ašbḥ

n.aš[-]š.|bn.štn.|bn.ilš.|bn.tnabn.|bn.ḥṣn.|ṣprn.|bn.ašbḥ.|bn.qṭnn.|bn.ǵlmn.|[bn].ṣwy.|[bn].ḫnq[n].|[-----].|[-- 1046.1.21

aškrr

w.yṣq[.b.ap h].|k.yiḫd[.akl.s̀s̀w].|št.mkš[r.grn].|w.št.ašk[rr].|w.pr.ḥḏr[t.ydk].|aḥd h.w.yṣq[.b.ap h].|k.yiḫd.akl. 161[56].14

d h w yṣq b ap h.|[k.yiḫd akl s̀]s̀w št mkšr grn.|[w št aškrr w p]r ḥḏrt.|[-----].|[---.-]n[-].|[k yraš s̀s̀w št bln q]ṭ y 160[55].11

aš't

.tbtẖ.alp. | uz.mrat.mlḥt. | arb'.uzm.mrat.bq'. | ṯlṯ.[-]ṯt.aš[']t.šmn.uz. | mi[t].ygb.bq'. | a[--].'ṭ. | a[l]pm.alpnm. | ṯlṯ.m[1128.22

at

y.yw.ilt.[---]. | w p'r.šm.ym[-.---]. | t'nyn.l zn.tn[.---]. | at.adn.tp'r[.---]. | ank.lṭpn.il[.d pid.---]. | 'l.ydm.p'rt[.---]. | šm 1['NT.X].4.17
ṣḥq.btlt.['nt]. | [tšu.]g h.w tṣḥ.šm'.m['.l a] | [qht.ǵ]zr.at.aḫ.w an.a[ḫt k]. | [---].šb'.ṯir k.[---]. | [---.]ab y.ndt.ank[.---] 18[3AQHT].1.24
.l ydlp. | tmn h.kṯr.ṣmdm.ynḥt.w yp'r.šmt hm. | šm k.at.aymr.aymr.mr.ym.mr.ym. | l ksi h.nhr l kḥṯ.drkt h.trtqṣ. 2.4[68].19
. | w.hm.ḫt. | 'l.w.likt. | 'm k.w.hm. | l.'l.w.lakm. | ilak.w.at. | um y.al.tdḥṣ. | w.ap.mhkm. | b.lb k.al. | tšt. 1013.20
[-----]. | [-----]. | b [----]. | w [----]. | b'l.[---]. | il hd.b[---]. | at.bl.at.[---]. | yisp hm.b['l.---]. | bn.dgn[.---]. | 'ḏbm.[---]. | uḫr 12[75].2.24
.[---]. | [---.]'n[.---]. | pnm[.---]. | b'l.n[--.---]. | il.hd[.---]. | at.bl[.at.---]. | ḥmd m.[---]. | il.hr[r.---]. | kb[-.---]. | ym.[---]. | yš 12[75].2.8
[--].nk.[---]. | [---.--]ḥ.an[--.---]. | [---.]'ly k[.---]. | [---.]at.bt k[.---]. | [---.]ank[.---]. | [---.-]hn.[---]. | [---.--]pp h.w[.---]. 1002.4
ḫsr. | w.[ank.yd]'.l.yd't. | h[t.---.]l.špš.b'l k. | '[--.s]glt h.at. | ht[.---.]špš.b'l k. | yd'm.l.yd't. | 'm y.špš.b'l k. | šnt.šntm.l 2060.12
il. | [---.]rks.bn.abnm. | [---.]upqt.'rb. | [---.w ẓ]r.mtn y at zd. | [---.]t'rb.bši. | [---.]l tzd.l tptq. | [---].g[--.]l arṣ. 1['NT.X].5.25
.drkt.dt dr dr k. | kṯr ṣmdm.ynḥt.w yp'r.šmt hm.šm k at. | ygrš.ygrš.grš ym grš ym.l ksi h. | [n]hr l kḥṯ drkt h.trtqṣ. 2.4[68].11
at.yp't.b[--.---]. | aliyn.b'l[.---]. | drkt k.mšl[-.---]. | b riš k.aym 2.1[137].3
['].nšr k. | w rbṣ.l ǵr k.inbb. | kt ǵr k.ank.yd't. | [-]n.atn.at.mṯb k[.---]. | [š]mm.rm.lk.prẓ kt. | [k]bkbm.ṯm.tpl k.lbnt. | 13[6].11
ḥlm h. | il.yrd.b ḏhrt h. | ab adm.w yqrb. | b šal.krt.m at. | krt.k ybky. | ydm'.n'mn.ǵlm. | il.mlk[.ṯ]r ab h. | yarš.hm. 14[KRT].1.38
'l. | mlk. | w.aḥd. | 'l atlg. | w l.'ṣm. | tspr. | nrn.al.tud | ad.at.l hm. | ṯṯm.ksp. 1010.20
aqht.w tbk.y[---.---]. | abn.ank.w 'l.[qšt k.---.'l]. | qṣ't k.at.l ḥ[---.---]. | w ḫlq.'pmm[.---]. 18[3AQHT].4.41
.km.mrm.tqrṣn. | il.yẓḥq.bm. | lb.w ygmḏ.bm kbd. | ẓi.at.l tlš. | amt.yrḫ. | l dmgy.amt. | aṯrt.qḥ. | ksan k.ḥdg k. | ḥtl k 12[75].1.14
k.ššrt. | [---.--]t.npš.'gl. | [---.-]nk.aštn.b ḫrt. | ilm.arṣ.w at.qḥ. | 'rpt k.rḥ k.mdl k. | mṭrt k.'m k.šb't. | ǵlm k.ṯmn.ḥnzr 5[67].5.6
bn.brq.d l.td'.šmm. | rgm l td'.nšm.w l tbn. | hmlt.arṣ.at m.w ank. | ibǵy h.b tk.ǵr y.il.ṣpn. | b qdš.b ǵr.nḥlt y. | b n' 3['NT].3.25
m.'m.ar]ṣ. | thmt.['mn.kbkbm.abn.brq]. | d l t[d'.šmm.at m.w ank]. | ibǵ[y h.b tk.ǵ]r y.il.ṣpn. | b q[dš.b ǵr.nḥ]lt y. | 3['NT].4.62
t.šmm.'m.arṣ.thmt]. | 'm kbkbm[.abn.brq.d l td'.šmm.at m]. | w ank.ib[ǵy h.---]. | [-].l y'mdn.i[---.---]. | kpr.šb' bn[t. 7.2[130].20
iḫd.m[t]. | b sin.lpš.tšṣq[n h]. | b qṣ.all.tšu.g h.w[tṣ] | ḥ.at.mt.tn.aḫ y. | w 'n.bn.ilm.mt.mh. | taršn.l btlt.'nt. | an.itlk. 6[49].2.12
ytn.l.'bdyrḫ. | w.mlk.z[--.--]n.ššwm. | n'mm.[--].ṯṯm.w.at. | nǵt.w.ytn.hm.l k. | w.lḥt.alpm.ḫršm. | k.rgmt.l y.bly m. | 2064.19
anšt[.---]. | qdqd h.w y'n.yṭpn.[mhr.št]. | šm'.l btlt.'nt.at.'[l.qšt h]. | tmḫṣ h.qṣ't h.hwt.l t[ḥwy]. | n'mn.ǵzr.št.ṯrm.w[18[3AQHT].4.12
-].'[m k]. | l.alpm.w.l.y[n.--]t. | w.bl.bnš.hw[-.--]y. | w.k.at.trg[m.--]. | w.[---]n.w.s[--]. | [--]m.m[---]. | [---.m]nd'[.--]. 2064.27
]. | [---].ank.l km[.---]. | l y.ank.ašṣu[.---.]w[.---]. | w hm.at.tr[gm.---]. | w.drm.'tr[--.---]. | w ap.ht.k[--.]škn. | w.mtnn[.- 54.1.18[13.2.3]
lb[--.---]. | u[-]šhr.nuš[-.---]. | b [u]grt.w ht.a[--]. | w hm.at.trg[m.---]. | w sip.u hw[.---]. | w ank.u šbt[--.---]. | ank.n[--] 54.1.8[13.1.5]
b i[--.---]. | l ṯ[--.---]. | ks[.---]. | kr[pn.---]. | at.š['tqt.---]. | š'd[.---]. | rt.[---]. | 'tr[.---]. | b p.š[---]. | il.p.d[---] 16[126].5.42
. | [-----]. | b [----]. | w [----]. | b'l.[---]. | il hd.b[---]. | at.bl.at.[---]. | yisp hm.b['l.---]. | bn.dgn[.---]. | 'ḏbm.[---]. | uḫry.l[-- 12[75].2.24
[---.]'n[.---]. | pnm[.---]. | b'l.n[--.---]. | il.hd[.---]. | at.bl[.at.---]. | ḥmd m.[---]. | il.hr[r.---]. | kb[-.---]. | ym.[---]. | yšḫr[.--- 12[75].2.8

atdb

-]. | kbd d ilgb[-]. | mrmnmn. | brrn aryn. | a[-]ḥn tlyn. | atdb w 'r. | qdš w amrr. | ṯḫr w bd. | [k]ṯr ḫss šlm. | šlm il bt. | UG5.7.71

atw

y.yw.ilt.[---]. | w p'r.šm.ym[-.---]. | t'nyn.l zn.tn[.---]. | at.adn.tp'r[.---]. | ank.lṭpn.il[.d pid.---]. | 'l.ydm.p'rt[.---]. | šm 1['NT.X].4.17
tk.rpi.ar[ṣ]. | b pḫr.qbṣ.dtn. | ṣǵrt hn.abkrn. | tbrk.ilm.tity. | tity.ilm.l ahl hm. | dr il.l mšknt hm. | w tqrb.w ld.bn.l h 15[128].3.17
i.ar[ṣ]. | b pḫr.qbṣ.dtn. | ṣǵrt hn.abkrn. | tbrk.ilm.tity. | tity.ilm.l ahl hm. | dr il.l mšknt hm. | w tqrb.w ld.bn.l h. | w t 15[128].3.18
thmt.'mn.kbkbm]. | rgm.l td'.nš[m.w l tbn.hmlt.arṣ]. | at.w ank.ib[ǵy h.---]. | w y'n.kṯr.w ḫss[.lk.lk.'nn.ilm.] | atm.b 1['NT.IX].3.16
iln[ym.---]. | asr.sswm.ṭṣmd.dg[-.---]. | t'ln.l mrkbt hm.ti[ty.l 'r hm]. | tlkn.ym.w ta aḫr.š[pšm.b ṯlṯ]. | mǵy.rpum.l gr 20[121].2.4
aṯr[h.l tdd.ilnym]. | asr.mr[kbt.---]. | t'ln.l mr[kbt hm.tity.l] | 'r hm.tl[kn.ym.w ṯn.aḫr.špšm]. | b ṯlṯ.mǵy[.rpum.l gr 22.1[123].23
m.'m.ar]ṣ. | thmt.['mn.kbkbm.abn.brq]. | d l t[d'.šmm.at m.w ank]. | ibǵ[y h.b tk.ǵ]r y.il.ṣpn. | b q[dš.b ǵr.nḥ]lt y. | 3['NT].4.62
bn.brq.d l.td'.šmm. | rgm l td'.nšm.w l tbn. | hmlt.arṣ.at m.w ank. | ibǵy h.b tk.ǵr y.il.ṣpn. | b qdš.b ǵr.nḥlt y. | b n' 3['NT].3.25
t.šmm.'m.arṣ.thmt]. | 'm kbkbm[.abn.brq.d l td'.šmm.at m]. | w ank.ib[ǵy h.---]. | [-].l y'mdn.i[---.---]. | kpr.šb' bn[t. 7.2[130].20
.ǵzr.mt hrnmy[.---]. | b grnt.ilm.b qrb.m[ṭ't.ilnym]. | d tit.yspi.spu.q[--.---]. | tpḥ.ṯṣr.shr[.---]. | mr[.---]. 20[121].2.10
r. | uṣb't h.yšu.g h.w y[ṣḥ]. | ik.mǵyt.rbt.aṯr[t.y]m. | ik.atwt.qnyt.i[lm]. | rǵb.rǵbt.w tǵt[--]. | hm.ǵmu.ǵmit.w 's[--]. | l 4[51].4.32

atyn

| [--]zbl.bt.mrnn. | a[--.---.-]'n. | ml[--.---]. | ar[--.---.--]l. | aty[n.bn.]šm'nt. | ḥnn[.bn].pls. | abrš[p.bn.]ḫrpn. | gmrš[.bn]. 102[323].4.4
.nḥl h. | w.nḥl hm. | w.[n]ḥl hm. | b[n.---]. | bn.gzry. | bn.atyn. | bn.ttn. | bn.rwy. | bn.'myn. | bdl.mrynm. | bn.ṣqn. | bn.š 113[400].3.2
ḥrm.b[n].ng[-]n. | atyn.š[r]šy. | 'bdḫmn[.bn.-]bdn. | ḥṣmn.[bn.---]ln. | [--]dm.[bn 102[322].1.2

atlg

spr.rpš d l y[dy]. | atlg. | ulm. | izly. | uḫnp. | bn sḫrn. | m'qb. | ṯpn. | m'r. | lbnm. | n 2075.2
id[-]. | ubš. | mṣb[t]. | ḥl.y[---]. | 'rg[z]. | y'r[t]. | amd[y]. | atl[g]. | bṣr[y]. | [---]. | [---]y. | ar. | agm.w.ḫpty. | ḫlb.ṣpn. | mril. 71[113].44
ap. | pd. | mlk. | ar. | atlg. | gb'ly. | ulm. | m'rby. | m'r. | arny. | š'rt. | ḫlbrpš. | hry. | qm 2074.5
b'.'ṣm. | 'l.ar. | w.ṯlṯ. | 'l.ubr'y. | w.ṯn.'l. | mlk. | w.aḥd. | 'l atlg. | w l.'ṣm. | tspr. | nrn.al.tud | ad.at.l hm. | ṯṯm.ksp. 1010.16
ḥm[rm.w.arb]'.bnšm. | ar.ḫmš.ḥmr[m.w.ḫm]š.bnšm. | atlg.ḥmr[.---.]bnšm. | gb'ly.ḥmr š[--.b]nšm. | ulm.ṯn.[---.]bnš 2040.5
kn.arb'. | ubr'y.ṯlṯ. | ar.ṯmn 'šr h. | mlk.arb'. | ǵbl.ḫmš. | atlg.ḫmš 'šr[h]. | ulm ṯ[ṯ]. | m'rby.ḫmš. | ṯbq.arb'. | tkm[.---]. | 68[65].1.8
qdm. | ḫmšm.l mit. | ksp.d.mkr.ar. | arb'm ksp d mkr. | atlg. | mit.ksp.d mkr. | ilštm'. | 'šrm.l mit.ksp. | 'l.bn.alkbl.šb[2107.12
b.atlg.ṯlṯ.ḫrmṯt.ṯṯm. | mḫrhn.nit.mit.krk.mit. | m'šd.ḫmšm.mq 2048.1

]. | ušk[n.---]. | ubr[‘y.---]. | ar[.---]. | mlk[.---]. | ǵbl[.---]. | atl[g.---]. | u[lm.---]. | m[‘rby.---]. | ṭ[bq.---]. 68[65].2.8

any.al[ṯy]. | d b atlg[.---]. | ẖmš ‘š[r]. | kkr.ṯ[lṯ]. | ṯt hrt[m]. | ṯn mq[pm]. | ulṯ.ṯl[2056.2

atlgy

rwdn. | tmrtn. | šd‘l.bn aẖyn. | m‘rbym. | rpan. | abršn. | atlgy. | šršn. 95[91].9

atlgn

[---.]l mitm.ksp. | [---.]skn. | [---.-]im.bṯd. | [---.b]šḥr.atlgn. | [---].b šḥr. | [---.]bn h. | [-]k[--]g hn.ksp. 2167.4

atm

dd. | l kbd.š[d]m.ap.mṯn.rgmm. | argmn.lk.lk.‘nn.ilm. | atm.bštm.w an.šnt. | uǵr.l rḥq.ilm.inbb. | l rḥq.ilnym.ṯn.mṯp 3[‘NT].4.77

at.w ank.ib[ǵy h.---]. | w y‘n.kṯr.w ẖss[.lk.lk.‘nn.ilm.] | atm.bštm.w an[.šnt.kptr]. | l rḥq.ilm.ḥkp[t.l rḥq.ilnym]. | ṯn. 1[‘NT.IX].3.18

h.l t[dd.ilnym.ṯm]. | yḥpn.ḥy[ly.zbl.mlk.‘llm y]. | šm‘.atm[.---]. | ym.lm.qd[.---]. | šmn.prst[.---]. | ydr.hm.ym[.---]. | 22.1[123].13

atn

| uẖnp. | bn sẖrn. | m‘qb. | ṯpn. | m‘r. | lbnm. | nẖl. | y‘ny. | atn. | utly. | bn.alz. | bn ẖlm. | bn.ḏmr. | bn.‘yn. | ubnyn. | rpš d 2075.13

[.---]. | [‘]bdm. | [bn].mṣrn. | [a]rśwn. | ‘b[d]. | w nḥl h. | atn.bn.ap[s]n. | nsk.ṯlṯ. | bn.[--.]m[-]ẖr. | bn.šmrm. | ṯnnm. | [ar 85[80].3.7

[---]. | bn.[---]. | bn.[---]. | [-----]. | bn[---]. | bn.mlkyy. | bn.atn. | bn.bly. | bn.ṯbrn. | bn.ḥgby. | bn.pity. | bn.slgyn. | ‘zn.bn. 115[301].2.2

yp‘.alpm. | aẖ[m]lk.bn.nskn.alpm. | krw.šlmy. | alpm. | atn.bṣry.alpm. | lbnym. | ṯm[n.]alp mitm. | ilb‘l ẖmš m[at]. | ‘d 1060.2.6

ṯn.b gt.mzln. | ṯn.b ulm. | abmn.b gt.m‘rb. | atn. | ẖryn. | bn.‘nt. | llwn. | agdṯb. | aǵltn. | [-]wn. | bldn. | [-]ln. | 1061.4

n. | kṯr.w ẖss.yd. | ytr.kṯr.w ẖss. | spr.ilmlk šbny. | lmd.atn.prln.rb. | khnm rb.nqdm. | ṯ‘y.nqmd.mlk ugr[t]. | adn.yrg 6.6[62.2].54

| [---.]aqht.yḏ[--]. | [---.--]n.ṣ[---]. | [spr.ilmlk.šbny.lmd.atn.]prln. 17[2AQHT].7.1

lk[.---]. | ṯn.skm.šb‘.mšlt.arb‘.ẖpnt.[---]. | ẖmšm.ṯlṯ.rkb.ntn.ṯlṯ.mat.[---]. | lg.šmn.rqḥ.šr‘m.ušpǵtm.p[--.---]. | kṯ.ẓrw.k UG5.9.1.20

atnb

--]ṣb. | [--]ps. | [--]ṯb. | [--]ln. | [---]r. | [---]y. | bn.aḏdt. | bn.atnb. | bn.yśd. | bn.brśm. | bn.gṯprg. | gṯpbn. | bn.b[--]. | [b]n.[-- 1057.9

nntn. | bn.kwn. | ǵmšd. | bn.‘bdḥy. | bn.ubyn. | slpd. | bn.atnb. | bn.ktmn. | bn.pity. | bn.iryn. | bn.‘bl. | bn.grbn. | bn.iršy 115[301].4.13

t. | ‘pṯn.š‘rt. | ‘bd.yrẖ š‘rt. | ẖbd.ṯr yṣr š‘r. | pdy.yṣr š‘rt. | atnb.ḥr. | š‘rt.š‘rt. 97[315].13

tp.[---]. | bn.lbnn.[----]. | ady.ḥ[--.---]. | [-]b[-]n.[---]. | bn.atnb.mr[--.---]. | bn.sẖr.mr[-.---]. | bn.idrn.‘š[-.---]. | bn.bly.mr 88[304].7

atnt

.‘r.ṣmd.pḥl. | št.gpnm.dt.ksp. | dt.yrq.nqbnm. | ‘db.gpn.atnt h. | yḥbq.qdš.w amrr. | yštn.aṯrt.l bmt.‘r. | l ysmsmt.bmt. 4[51].4.12

| ṣmd.pḥl[.št.gpnm.dt]. | ksp.dt.yr[q.nqbnm]. | ‘db.gpn.atnt[y]. | yšm‘.qd.w amr[r]. | mdl.‘r.ṣmd.pḥl. | št.gpnm.dt.ks 4[51].4.7

aṯm

.il ǵnṯ.‘gl il. | [---.--]d.il.šd yṣd mlk. | [---].yšt.il h. | [---.]iṯm h. | [---.y]mǵy. | [---.]dr h. | [---.-]rš.l b‘l. | [---.-]ǵk.rpu mlk UG5.2.1.14

tiṯṯm[n].w.‘l.[---]. | [-]rym.t[i]ṯṯmn. | šnl.bn.ṣ[q]n.š[--]. | yiṯṯm.w.b[--]. | yšlm. | [‘]šrm.ks[p].yš[lm]. | [il]ṯḥm.b d[.---]. | [2104.5

‘l.alpm.bnš.yd. | tiṯṯm[n].w.‘l.[---]. | [-]rym.t[i]ṯṯmn. | šnl.bn.ṣ[q]n.š[--]. | yiṯṯm. 2104.2

m.[---]. | w rgm.l [---]. | b mud.ṣin[.---]. | mud.ṣin[.---]. | iṯm.mui[-.---]. | dm.mt.aṣ[ḥ.---]. | ydd.b qr[b.---]. | ṯmm.w lk[. 5[67].3.24

‘l.alpm.bnš.yd. | tiṯṯm[n].w.‘l.[---]. | [-]rym.t[i]ṯṯmn. | šnl.bn.ṣ[q]n.š[--]. | yiṯṯm.w.b[--]. | yšlm. | [‘]šrm.ks[2104.3

aṯr

.ṯmnt. | nblu h.špš.ymp. | hlkt.tdr[--]. | špš.b‘d h.t[--]. | aṯr.aṯrm[.---]. | aṯr.aṯrm[.---]. | išdym.t[---]. | b k.mla[.---]. | ud 27[8].7

.špš.ymp. | hlkt.tdr[--]. | špš.b‘d h.t[--]. | aṯr.aṯrm[.---]. | aṯr.aṯrm[.---]. | išdym.t[---]. | b k.mla[.---]. | udm‘t.d[m‘.---]. | [27[8].8

.l ‘nt m. | [---.]l šlm. | [-]l[-.-]ry.ylbš. | mlk.ylk.lqḥ.ilm. | aṯr.ilm.ylk.p‘nm. | mlk.p‘nm.yl[k]. | šb‘.pamt.l kl hm. 33[5].24

]pt. | ib.‘ltn.a[--.--]y. | w.spr.in[.-.]‘d m. | spr n.ṭhr[.--]. | aṯr.iṯ.bqṯ. | w.štn.l y. 2060.34

‘nt.tngṯ h. | k lb.arẖ.l ‘gl h.k lb. | ṯat.l imr h.km.lb. | ‘nt.aṯr.b‘l.tiẖd. | bn.ilm.mt.b ḥrb. | tbq‘nn.b ẖṯr.tdry | nn.b išt.tšr 6[49].2.30

gṯ h.k lb.a[rẖ]. | l ‘gl h.k lb.ṯa[t]. | l imr h.km.lb.‘n[t]. | aṯr.b‘l.tiẖd.m[t]. | b sin.lpš.tšṣq[n h]. | b qṣ.all.tšu.g h.w[tṣ] | 6[49].2.9

| bmt.yšu.g h.w yṣḥ. | b‘l.mt.my.lim.bn. | dgn.my.hmlt.aṯr. | b‘l.ard.b arṣ.ap. | ‘nt.ttlk.w tṣd.kl.ǵr. | l kbd.arṣ.kl.gb‘. | l 5[67].6.24

p lb.k ‘mq.tṯlṯ.bmt. | b‘l.mt.my.lim.bn dgn. | my.hmlt.aṯr.b‘l.nrd. | b arṣ.‘m h.trd.nrt. | ilm.špš.‘d.tšb‘.bk. | tšt.k yn.u 6[62].1.7

smt.bmt.pḥl. | qdš.yuẖdm.šb‘r. | amrr.k kbkb.l pnm. | aṯr.btlt.‘nt. | w b‘l.tb‘.mrym.ṣpn. | idk.l ttn.pnm. | ‘m.il.mbk.n 4[51].4.18

.i]lib h.b qdš. | [ztr.‘m h.l a]rṣ.mšṣu. | [qṭr h.l ‘pr.ḏ]mr.a[ṯ]r h. | [ṭbq.lḥt.niṣ h.gr]š.d ‘šy. | [ln h.---]. | z[tr.‘m k.l arṣ.m 17[2AQHT].1.47

.skn.ilib h.b qdš. | ztr.‘m h.l arṣ.mšṣu.qṭr h. | l ‘pr.ḏmr.aṯr h.ṭbq.lḥt. | niṣ h.grš d.‘šy.ln h. | aẖd.yd h.b škrn.m‘ms h. 17[2AQHT].1.29

ṣḥ.rpi[m.iqra.ilnym]. | b qrb.h[kl y.aṯr h.rpum.l] | tdd.aṯr[h.l tdd.ilnym]. | asr.mr[kbt.---]. | t‘ln.l mr[kbt hm.tity.l] 22.1[123].21

aṣḥ.km.[iqra km.ilnym.b] | hkl y.aṯr[h.rpum.l tdd]. | aṯr h.l t[dd.ilnym.ṯm]. | yḥpn.ḥy[ly.zbl.mlk.‘llm y]. | šm‘.atm 22.1[123].11

.aṣḥ]. | km.iqr[a km.ilnym.b hkl y]. | aṯr h.r[pum.l tdd.aṯr h]. | l tdd.il[nym.---]. | mhr.b‘l[.---.mhr]. | ‘nt.lk b[t y.rpim 22.1[123].5

.aṣḥ km.iqra. | [km.ilnym.b h]kl y.aṯr h.rpum. | [l tdd.aṯr h].l tdd.ilnym. | [---.m]rz‘y.apnnk.yrp. | [---.]km.r‘y.ht.al 21[122].1.4

.aṣ]ḥ km.iqra km. | [ilnym.b hkl]y.aṯr h.rpum. | [l tdd.aṯr]h.l tdd.i[lnym]. | [---.]r[--.---]. | [---.yṯ]b.l arṣ. 21[122].1.12

y. | [---.]tdbḥ.amr. | ṯmn.b qrb.hkl y.[aṯr h.rpum]. | tdd.aṯr h.tdd.iln[ym.---]. | asr.sswm.tṣmd.dg[-.---]. | t‘ln.l mrkbt 20[121].2.2

y. | [rpim.rpim.b]t y.aṣḥ km.iqra. | [km.ilnym.b h]kl y.aṯr h.rpum. | [l tdd.aṯr h].l tdd.ilnym. | [---.m]rz‘y.apnnk.yrp 21[122].1.3

.rpim.rpim.b bt y]. | aṣḥ.km.[iqra km.ilnym.b] | hkl y.aṯr[h.rpum.l tdd]. | aṯr h.l t[dd.ilnym.ṯm]. | yḥpn.ḥy[ly.zbl. 22.1[123].10

r[pim.rpim.b bt y.aṣḥ]. | km.iqr[a km.ilnym.b hkl y]. | aṯr h.r[pum.l tdd.aṯr h]. | l tdd.il[nym.---]. | mhr.b‘l[.---.mhr] 22.1[123].5

y.rpim. | [rpim.bt y.aṣ]ḥ km.iqra km. | [ilnym.b hkl]y.aṯr h.rpum. | [l tdd.aṯr]h.l tdd.i[lnym]. | [---.]r[--.---]. | [---.yṯ] 21[122].1.11

ṯ.d[rkt h.b bt y]. | aṣḥ.rpi[m.iqra.ilnym]. | b qrb.h[kl y.aṯr h.rpum.l] | tdd.aṯr[h.l tdd.ilnym]. | asr.mr[kbt.---]. | t‘ln.l 22.1[123].20

rgzm. | [---.]dt.‘l.lty. | [---.]tdbḥ.amr. | ṯmn.b qrb.hkl y.[aṯr h.rpum]. | tdd.aṯr h.tdd.iln[ym.---]. | asr.sswm.tṣmd.dg[-. 20[121].2.1

qḥ.mṯpṭ. | w y‘ny.nn. | dtn.bt n.mḥ[-]. | l dg.w [-]kl. | w aṯr.hn.mr[-]. UG5.6.16

šrš.km ary y. | nṣb.skn.ilib y.b qdš. | ztr.ʿm y.l ʿpr.ḏmr.aṯr[y]. | ṯbq lḥt.niṣ y.grš. | d ʿšy.ln.aḫd.yd y.b š | krn mʿms y 17[2AQHT].2.17
y[m].l mṯʿt[.---]. | [-]m[.---]. | h.hn bn k.hn[.---]. | bn bn.aṯr k.hn[.---]. | yd k.ṣǵr.tnšq.špt k.ṯm. | ṯkm.bm ṯkm.aḫm.qy 22.2[124].3
ʿšy. | [ln h.---]. | z[tr.ʿm k.l arṣ.mšṣu.qṭr k]. | l ʿpr.ḏm[r.aṯr k.ṯbq]. | lḥt.niṣ k.gr[š.d ʿšy.ln k]. | spu.ksm k.bt.[bʿl.w mn 17[2AQHT].2.2
.dm.l ǵzr. | šrg k.ḫḫm.mt.uḫryt.mh.yqḥ. | mh.yqḥ.mt.aṯryt.spsg.ysk. | [l]riš.ḥrṣ.l ẓr.qdqd y. | [--.]mt.kl.amt.w an. 17[2AQHT].6.36
r y.w bn.bṯn.itnn y. | ytt.nḫšm.mhr k.bn bṯn. | itnn k. | aṯr ršp.ʿṯtrt. | ʿm ʿṯtrt.mr h. | mnt.nṯk.nḫš. UG5.7.TR1
at.rbt. | hlk.l alpm.ḫḏḏ. | w l.rbt.kmyr. | aṯr.ṯn.ṯn.hlk. | aṯr.ṯlṯ.kl hm. | aḥd.bt h.ysgr. | almnt.škr. | tškr.zbl.ʿršm. | yšu. 14[KRT].4.183
l.hg. | hlk.l alpm.ḫḏḏ. | w l rbt.kmyr. | [a]ṯr.ṯn.ṯn.hlk. | aṯr.ṯlṯ.kl hm. | yḥd.bt h.sgr. | almnt.škr. | tškr.zbl.ʿršm. | yšu.ʿ 14[KRT].2.95
bl.spr. | ṯnn.d bl.hg. | hlk.l alpm.ḫḏḏ. | w l rbt.kmyr. | [a]ṯr.ṯn.ṯn.hlk. | aṯr.ṯlṯ.kl hm. | yḥd.bt h.sgr. | almnt.škr. | tškr. 14[KRT].2.94
[l.mad]. | ṯlṯ.mat.rbt. | hlk.l alpm.ḫḏḏ. | w l.rbt.kmyr. | aṯr.ṯn.ṯn.hlk. | aṯr.ṯlṯ.kl hm. | aḥd.bt h.ysgr. | almnt.škr. | tškr. 14[KRT].4.182
[--.]a[--.---]. | [--.-]bt.np[-.---]. | [-] l šd.ql.[---.---].aṯr. | [--.]ǵrm.y[--.---.ḫ]rn. | [-]rk.ḫ[--.---.-]lk. | [-]sr.n[--.---.]ḫr UG5.8.3
nt. | nblu h.špš.ymp. | hlkt.tdr[--]. | špš.bʿd h.t[--]. | aṯr.aṯrm[.---]. | aṯr.aṯrm[.---]. | išdym.t[---]. | b k.mla[.---]. | udmʿt. 27[8].7
.ymp. | hlkt.tdr[--]. | špš.bʿd h.t[--]. | aṯr.aṯrm[.---]. | aṯr.aṯrm[.---]. | išdym.t[---]. | b k.mla[.---]. | udmʿt.d[mʿ.---]. | [---]. 27[8].8
[-----]. | ʿr[.---]. | ʿr[.---]. | ʿr[.---]. | w y[---]. | bʿd[.---]. | yaṯr[.---]. | b d k.[---]. | ṯnnt h[.---]. | ṯlṯt h[.-.w yʿn]. | lṭpn.[il.d 16[126].5.6
[---.--]i[-.]a[--.---]. | [---.]ilm.w ilht.dt. | [---.]šbʿ.l šbʿm.aṯr. | [---.--]ldm.dt ymtm. | [--.--]r.l ẓpn. | [---.]pn.ym.y[--]. | [-- 25[136].3
--.]il[m.--]y. | [--.m]ṣlm.pn y[.-.]tlkn. | [---.]rḥbn.hm.[-.]aṯr[.---]. | [--]šy.w ydn.bʿ[l.---]n. | [--]ʿ.k yn.hm.l.atn.bt y.l h. 1002.60

aṯry

arbʿ.yn.l.mrynm.ḫ[--].kl h. | kdm.l.zn[-.---]. | kd.l.aṯr[y]m. | kdm.ʿm.[--]n. | kd.mštt.[---]n. | kdm.l.mḏrǵlm. | kd.l 1089.3
.ṯǵrn.ʿbd. | ʿbd.ḫmn.šmʿ.rgm. | šdn.[k]bš. | šdyn.mḫ[ṣ]. | aṯry.mḫṣ. | bʿln.mḫṣ. | y[ḥ]ṣdq.mḫṣ. | ṣp[r].ks[d]. | bʿl.š[lm]. | ḫ 2084.15
[--.--]u[-]. | [--.-]rḏ. | [--.-]dn. | [--.]aṯry. 125[-].4

aṯrn

.pdn. | [---.bn.-]ky. | [---.bn.--]r. | [-----]. | [---.--]yn. | [---.]aṯrn. | [---.--]ḫt. | [---.]bʿly. | [---.]nʿmy. | [---.-]ml. | [---.-]mn. | [- 102.5B[323.5].3

aṯrt

rb.ʿẓm.ridn. | mt.šmm.ks.qdš. | l tphn h.aṯt.krpn. | l tʿn.aṯrt.alp. | kd.yqḥ.b ḫmr. | rbt.ymsk.b msk h. | qm.ybd.w yšr. | 3[ʿNT].1.15
b.tʿdbn. | nšb.l inr.tʿdbn.ktp. | b il ab h.gʿr.yṯb.il.kb[-]. | aṯ[rt.]il.yṯb.b mrzḥ h. | yšt[.il.y]n.ʿd šbʿ.trṯ.ʿd škr. | il.hlk.l bt UG5.1.1.15
].mǵẓ.qnyt.ilm. | w tn.bt.l bʿl.km. | [i]lm.w ḥẓr.k bn. | [a]ṯrt.gm.l ǵlm h. | bʿl.yṣḥ.ʿn.gpn. | w ugr.bn.ǵlmt. | ʿmm ym.b 8[51FRAG].5
t.dqn h. | [mmʿm.-]d.l ytn.bt.l bʿl.k ilm. | [w ḥẓ]r.k bn.aṯrt[.tdʿṣ.]pʿn. | [w tr.a]rṣ.id[k.l ttn.p]nm. | [ʿm.i]l.mbk.nhr[3[ʿNT.VI].5.12
bl.ks h. | [an]y.l yṣḥ.ṯr il.ab h. | [i]l.mlk.d yknn h.yṣḥ. | aṯrt.w bn h.ilt.w ṣbrt. | ary h.wn.in.bt.l bʿl. | km.ilm.w ḥẓr.k 4[51].4.49
hbr.w tql. | tštḥwy.w tkbdn h. | tšu.g h.w tṣḥ.tšmḫ ht. | aṯrt.w bn h.ilt.w ṣb | rt.ary h.k mt.aliyn. | bʿl.k ḫlq.zbl.bʿl. | ar 6.1.40[49.1.12]
y.nbl.ks h. | any.l yṣḥ.ṯr.il.ab h.il. | mlk.d yknn h.yṣḥ.aṯrt. | w bn h.ilt.w ṣbrt.arḫ h. | wn.in.bt.l bʿl.km.ilm. | ḥẓr.k b 3[ʿNT.VI].5.44
[-----]. | [any.l yṣ]ḥ.ṯr. | [il.ab h.i]l.mlk. | [d yknn h.yṣ]ḥ.aṯ | [rt.w bn h.]ilt. | [w ṣbrt.ary]h. | [wn.in.bt.l bʿl.] | [km.ilm. 4[51].1.7
.amt.aṯrt.tlbn. | lbnt.ybn.bt.l bʿl. | km ilm.w ḥẓr.k bn.aṯrt. | w tʿn.rbt.aṯrt ym. | rbt.ilm.l ḥkmt. | šbt.dqn k.l tsr k. | r 4[51].5.63
gpn. | šbʿ d.yrgm.ʿl.ʿd.w ʿrbm.tʿnyn. | w šd.šd ilm.šd aṯrt.w rḥm. | ʿl.išt.šbʿ d.ǵzrm.ṭb.[g]d.b ḥlb.annḫ b ḫmat. | w ʿ 23[52].13
nbm.šlm.ʿrbm.ṯn[nm]. | hlkm.b dbḥ nʿmt. | šd[.i]lm.šd.aṯrt.w rḥmy. | [---].y[ṯ]b. | [---]p.gp ym.w yṣǵd.gp..thm. | [yqḥ 23[52].28
il b[n] il. | dr bn il. | mpḫrt bn il. | ṯrmn w šnm. | il w aṯrt. | ḫnn il. | nṣbt il. | šlm il. | il ḥš il add. | bʿl ṣpn bʿl. | ugrt. | 30[107].5
. | [----.--]t.hw[-]y.h[--]r.w rgm.ank. | [---.]hdd tr[--.--]l.aṯrt y. | [--]ptm.ṣḥq. | [---.]rgm.hy.[-]ḫ[-]y.ilak k. | [---.--]g k.y 1002.39
.yṯpd.w ykrkr. | uṣbʿt h.yšu.g h.w y[ṣḥ]. | ik.mǵyt.rbt.aṯr[t.y]m. | ik.atwt.qnyt.i[lm]. | rǵb.rǵbt.w tǵt[--]. | hm.ǵmu.ǵ 4[51].4.31
t.ʿnt. | tmgnn.rbt[.a]ṯrt ym. | tǵẓyn.qnyt.ilm. | w tʿn.rbt.aṯrt ym. | ik.tmgnn.rbt. | aṯrt.ym.tǵẓyn. | qnyt.ilm.mgntm. | ṯr 4[51].3.27
.šmʿ. | l rbt.aṯr[t] ym.tn. | aḥd.b bn k.amlkn. | w tʿn.rbt.aṯrt ym. | bl.nmlk.ydʿ.ylḥn. | w yʿn.lṭpn.il d pi | d dq.anm.l yr 6.1.47[49.1.19]
yrẓ. | ʿm.bʿl.l ydʿ.mrḥ. | ʿm.bn.dgn.k tms m. | w ʿn.rbt.aṯrt ym. | blt.nmlk.ʿṯtr.ʿrẓ. | ymlk.ʿṯtr.ʿrẓ. | apnk.ʿṯtr.ʿrẓ. | yʿl.b 6.1.53[49.1.25]
ary y[.ẓl].ksp.[a]ṯrt. | k tʿn.ẓl.ksp.w n[-]t. | ḫrṣ.šmḫ.rbt.a[ṯrt]. | ym.gm.l ǵlm h.k [tṣḥ]. | ʿn.mkṯr.ap.t[---]. | dgy.rbt.aṯr 4[51].2.28
l.k ḫlq.zbl.bʿl. | arṣ.gm.yṣḥ il. | l rbt.aṯrt ym.šmʿ. | l rbt.aṯr[t] ym.tn. | aḥd.b bn k.amlkn. | w tʿn.rbt.aṯrt ym. | bl.nmlk 6.1.45[49.1.17]
m.w ḥẓr]. | [k bn.aṯ]r[t]. | m[ṯ]b.il.mẓll. | bn h.mṯb.rbt. | aṯrt.ym.mṯb. | klt.knyt. | mṯb.pdry.b ar. | mẓll.ṭly.bt rb. | mṯb. 4[51].1.15
l. | km.ilm.w ḥẓr.k bn.aṯrt. | mṯb il.mẓll.bn h. | mṯb rbt.aṯrt.ym. | mṯb.klt.knyt. | mṯb.pdry.bt.ar. | mẓll.ṭly.bt rb. | mṯb 4[51].4.53
ʿl.km.ilm. | ḥẓr.k b[n.a]ṯrt.mṯb.il. | mṯll.b[n h.m]ṯb.rbt.aṯrt. | ym.mṯb.[pdr]y.bt.ar. | [mẓll.]ṭly[.bt.]rb.mṯb. | [arṣy.bt.y 3[ʿNT.VI].5.48
m.ilm.w ḥẓr]. | k bn.[aṯrt.mṯb.il.mẓll]. | bn h.m[ṯb.rbt.aṯrt.ym]. | mṯb.pdr[y.bt.ar.mẓll]. | ṭly.bt.r[b.mṯb.arṣy]. | bt.yʿ 3[ʿNT.VI].4.2
rt]. | ym.gm.l ǵlm h.k [tṣḥ]. | ʿn.mkṯr.ap.t[---]. | dgy.rbt.aṯr[t.ym]. | qḥ.rṯt.b d k t[---]. | rbt.ʿl.ydm[.---]. | b mdd.il.y[--.- 4[51].2.31
-.w tʿn.rbt]. | aṯr[t.ym.šmʿ.l qdš]. | w am[rr.l dgy.rbt]. | aṯrt.ym[.mdl.ʿr]. | ṣmd.pḥl[.št.gpnm.dt]. | ksp.dt.yr[q.nqbnm 4[51].4.4
y.bt.yʿbdr. | ap.mtn.rgmm. | argm k.šskn mʿ. | mgn.rbt.aṯrt ym. | mǵẓ.qnyt.ilm. | hyn.ʿly.l mpḫm. | b d.ḫss.mṣbṭm. | y 4[51].1.22
t.amht. | aḫr.mǵy.aliyn.bʿl. | mǵyt.btlt.ʿnt. | tmgnn.rbt[.a]ṯrt ym. | tǵẓyn.qnyt.ilm. | w tʿn.rbt.aṯrt ym. | ik.tmgnn.rbt. 4[51].3.25
[i]k.mgn.rbt.aṯrt. | [ym].mǵẓ.qnyt.ilm. | w tn.bt.l bʿl.km. | [i]lm.w ḥẓr.k bn 8[51FRAG].1
m. | tǵẓyn.qnyt.ilm. | w tʿn.rbt.aṯrt ym. | ik.tmgnn.rbt. | aṯrt.ym.tǵẓyn. | qnyt.ilm.mgntm. | ṯr.il.d pid.hm.ǵẓtm. | bny. 4[51].3.29
d.hm.ǵẓtm. | bny.bnwt w tʿn. | btlt.ʿnt.nmgn. | [-]m.rbt.aṯrt.ym. | [nǵ]ẓ.qnyt.ilm. | [---].nmgn.hwt. | [--].aliyn.bʿl. | [--.] 4[51].3.34
. | lbnt.ybn.bt.l bʿl. | km ilm.w ḥẓr.k bn.aṯrt. | w tʿn.rbt.aṯrt ym. | rbt.ilm.l ḥkmt. | šbt.dqn k.l tsr k. | rḫntt.d[-].l irt k. 4[51].5.64
ṯr[.il.ab -.w tʿn.rbt]. | aṯr[t.ym.šmʿ.l qdš]. | w am[rr.l dgy.rbt]. | aṯrt.ym[.mdl.ʿr]. | ṣ 4[51].4.2
ry h.k mt.aliyn. | bʿl.k ḫlq.zbl.bʿl. | arṣ.gm.yṣḥ il. | l rbt.aṯrt ym.šmʿ. | l rbt.aṯr[t] ym.tn. | aḥd.b bn k.amlkn. | w tʿn.rb 6.1.44[49.1.16]
dm.ʿṣm.hm.yd.il mlk. | yḫss k.ahbt.ṯr.tʿrr k. | w tʿn.rbt.aṯrt ym. | tḥm k.il.ḥkm.ḥkmt. | ʿm ʿlm.ḥyt.ḥẓt. | tḥm k.mlk n. 4[51].4.40
nǵ]ẓ.qnyt.ilm. | [---].nmgn.hwt. | [--].aliyn.bʿl. | [--.]rbt.aṯrt.ym. | [---.]btlt.ʿnt. | [--.tl]ḥm.tšty. | [ilm.w tp]q.mrǵtm. | [ṯ 4[51].3.38
w ṣbrt.ary]h. | [wn.in.bt.l bʿl.] | [km.ilm.w ḥẓr]. | [k bn.aṯ]r[t]. | m[ṯ]b.il.mẓll. | bn h.mṯb.rbt. | aṯrt.ym.mṯb. | klt.knyt. 4[51].1.12
h.ilt.w ṣbrt. | ary h.wn.in.bt.l bʿl. | km.ilm.w ḥẓr.k bn.aṯrt. | mṯb il.mẓll.bn h. | mṯb rbt.aṯrt.ym. | mṯb.klt.knyt. | mṯb 4[51].4.51
n h.ilt.w ṣbrt.arḫ h. | wn.in.bt.l bʿl.km.ilm. | ḥẓr.k b[n.a]ṯrt.mṯb.il. | mṯll.b[n h.m]ṯb.rbt.aṯrt. | ym.mṯb.[pdr]y.bt.ar. 3[ʿNT.VI].5.47
[---.wn.in]. | [bt].l [bʿl.km.ilm.w ḥẓr]. | k bn.[aṯrt.mṯb.il.mẓll]. | bn h.m[ṯb.rbt.aṯrt.ym]. | mṯb.pdr[y.bt.ar. 3[ʿNT.VI].4.1

aṯrt

ṯr.il.d pid. | tǵẓy.bny.bnwt. | b nši.ʻn h.w tphn. | hlk.bʻl.aṯtrt. | k tʻn.hlk.btlt. | ʻnt.tdrq.ybmt. | [limm].b h.pʻnm. | [tṭṭ.b 4[51].2.13
ḫṣ y hm[.m]ḫṣ. | bn y.hm[.mkly.ṣ]brt. | ary y[.ẓl].ksp.[a]ṯrt. | k tʻn.ẓl.ksp.w n[-]t. | ḫrṣ.šmḫ.rbt.a[ṯrt]. | ym.gm.l ǵlm 4[51].2.26
.yrq.nqbnm. | ʻdb.gpn.atnt h. | yḥbq.qdš.w amrr. | yštn.aṯrt.l bmt.ʻr. | l ysmsmt.bmt.pḥl. | qdš.yuḫdm.šbʻr. | amrr.k k 4[51].4.14
d pid. | p ʻbd.an.ʻnn.aṯrt. | p.ʻbd.ank.aḫd.ulṯ. | hm.amt.aṯrt.tlbn. | lbnt.ybn.bt.l bʻl. | km ilm.w ḥẓr.k bn.aṯrt. | w tʻn.r 4[51].4.61
.w ygmḏ.bm kbd. | ẓi.at.l tlš. | amt.yrḫ. | l dmgy.amt. | aṯrt.qḥ. | ksan k.ḥdg k. | ḥtl k.w ẓi. | b aln.tk m. | b tk.mlbr. | il 12[75].1.17
nhrm. | [ʻb]r.gbl.ʻbr. | qʻl.ʻbr.iht. | np šmm.šmšr. | l dgy.aṯrt. | mǵ.l qdš.amrr. | idk.al.tnn. | pnm.tk.ḥqkpt. | il.kl h.kptr 3[ʻNT.VI].6.10
bʻ.bnm.l k. | w ṯmn.tṯtmnm. | l k.tld.yṣb.ǵlm. | ynq.ḥlb.a[ṯ]rt. | mṣṣ.ṯd.btlt.[ʻnt]. | mšnq.[---]. 15[128].2.26
ʻ.šnt. | bn.krt.km hm.tdr. | ap.bnt.ḥry. | km hm.w tḫss.aṯrt. | ndr h.w ilt.p[--]. | w tšu.g h.w [tṣḥ]. | ph mʻ.ap.k[rt.--]. | 15[128].3.25
bt[.---]. | [md]bḥt.b.ḫmš[.---]. | [-.]kbd.w.db[ḥ.---]. | [--].aṯrt.ʻṣr[m.l inš.ilm]. | [ṯ]ṯb.mdbḥ.bʻl.g[dlt.---]. | dqt.l.ṣpn.w.d 35[3].40
knp. | [---.g]dlt.ṣpn.dqt.šrp.w [š]lmm. | [---.a]lp.l bʻl.w aṯrt.ʻṣr[m] l inš. | [ilm.---].lbbmm.gdlt.ʻrb špš w ḥl. | [mlk.b a 36[9].1.8
b. | mṯb.arṣ.bt yʻbdr. | w yʻn lṭpn il d pid. | p ʻbd.an.ʻnn.aṯrt. | p.ʻbd.ank.aḫd.ulṯ. | hm.amt.aṯrt.tlbn. | lbnt.ybn.bt.l bʻl. 4[51].4.59
im. | ṣḥ.aḫ h.b bht h.a[r]y h. | b qrb hkl h.ṣḥ. | šbʻm.bn.aṯrt. | špq.ilm.krm.y[n]. | špq.ilht.ḫprt[.yn]. | špq.ilm.alpm.y[4[51].6.46
qdš. | a[ṯrt.]ṣrm.w l ilt. | ṣd[yn]m.ṯm. | yd[r.k]rt.ṯʻ. | i.iṯt.aṯrt.ṣrm. | w ilt.ṣdynm. | hm.ḥry.bt y. | iqḥ.ašʻrb.ǵlmt. | ḥẓr y. 14[KRT].4.201
dbr.tlkn. | ym.w ṯn.aḫr. | šp[š]m.b [ṯ]lṯ. | ym[ǵy.]l qdš. | a[ṯrt.]ṣrm.w l ilt. | ṣd[yn]m.ṯm. | yd[r.k]rt.ṯʻ. | i.iṯt.aṯrt.ṣrm. | 14[KRT].4.198
yiḫd.bʻl.bn.aṯrt. | rbm.ymḫṣ.b ktp. | dk ym.ymḫṣ.b ṣmd. | ṣḥr mt.ymṣḫ.l 6[49].5.1
t.[ṣ]pn.dqt. | [---.al]p ʻnt.gdlt.b ṯlṯt mrm. | [---.i]l š.bʻl š.aṯrt.š.ym š.[bʻ]l knp. | [---.g]dlt.ṣpn.dqt.šrp.w [š]lmm. | [---.a] 36[9].1.6
mm.š.kṯr[t] š.yrḫ[.---]. | ṣpn.š.kṯr.š.pdry.š.ǵrm.š[.---]. | aṯrt.š.ʻnt.š.špš.š.arṣy.š.ʻṯtrt.š. | ušḫry.š.il.tʻḏr.bʻl.š.ršp.š.ddmš UG5.9.1.7
š[lmm.dqtm]. | ilh[.a]lp.w š[.il]hm.[gdlt.ilhm]. | bʻ[l.š].aṯrt[.š.ṯkm]n w [šnm.š]. | ʻnt š ršp š[.dr.il.w pḫr.bʻl]. | gdlt.šl 35[3].15
w šlmm.dqtm. | [i]lh.alp w š ilhm.gdl[t.]ilhm. | [b]ʻl š.aṯrt.š.ṯkmn w šnm.š. | ʻnt.š.ršp.š.dr il w p[ḫ]r bʻl. | gdlt.šlm.g 34[1].6
rp]. | w šlmm.[dqtm.ilh.alp.w š]. | ilhm.gd[lt.ilhm.bʻl.š.aṯrt.š]. | ṯkmn.w š[nm.š.ʻnt.š.ršp.š.dr]. | il.w pḫr[.bʻl.gdlt.šlm. APP.II[173].16
[-----]. | [---.--]t.š l i[l.---]. | [--.aṯ]rt.š[.---]. | [---.]l pdr[-.---]. | ṣin aḥd h[.---]. | l ʻṯtrt[.---]. | ʻlm. 37[22].3
aliyn.[bʻl.---]. | btlt.[ʻnt.---]. | mh.k[--.---]. | w at[--.---]. | aṯr[t.---]. | b im[--.---]. | bl.l[---.---]. | mlk.[---]. | dt [---]. | b ṭ[--.- 4[51].2.41
. | iqran.ilm.nʻmm[.agzry ym.bn]ym. | ynqm.b ap zd.aṯrt.[---]. | špš.mṣprt dlt hm[.---]. | w ǵnbm.šlm.ʻrbm.ṯn[nm]. 23[52].24

aṯtyy

l. | bn ṣdqn. | bn ayy. | bn dbb. | w nḥl h. | bn nʻmyn. | bn aṯtyy. | bn ḫlp. | bn.ẓll. | bn ydy. | bn lzn. | bn.ṯyn. | bn gʻr. | bn. 2016.1.10

aṯtl

dn. | [i]wryn. | ḫbsn. | ulmk. | ʻdršp. | bn.knn. | pdyn. | bn.aṯtl.ṯn. | kdln.akdṯb. | ṯn.b gt yknʻm. 1061.20

i

i

w l ṭlb.[---].|mit.rḥ[.---].|tṭlb.a[--.---].|yšu.g h[.---].|i.ap.b‘[l.---].|i.hd.d[---.---].|ynp‘.b‘[l.---].|b ṯmnt.[---].|yqrb 5[67].4.6

y.]l qdš.|a[ṯrt.]ṣrm.w l ilt.|ṣd[yn]m.ṯm.|yd[r.k]rt.ṯ‘.|i.iṯt.aṯrt.ṣrm.|w ilt.ṣdynm.|hm.ḥry.bt y.|iqḥ.aš‘rb.ǵlmt.|ḥẓ 14[KRT].4.201

mit.rḥ[.---].|tṭlb.a[--.---].|yšu.g h[.---].|i.ap.b‘[l.---].|i.hd.d[---.---].|ynp‘.b‘[l.---].|b ṯmnt.[---].|yqrb.[---].|lḥm.m[5[67].4.7

ib

kr k.|d k.n‘m.‘nt.n‘m h.|km.tsm.‘ṯtrt.ts[m h].|d ‘q h.ib.iqni.‘p[‘p] h.|sp.ṯrml.tḥgrn.[-]dm[.-].|ašlw.b ṣp.‘n h.|d b 14[KRT].3.147

kr k.|d k n‘m.‘nt.|n‘m h.km.tsm.|‘ṯtrt.tsm h.|d ‘q h.ib.iqni.|‘p‘p h.sp.ṯrml.|d b ḥlm y.il.ytn.|b ḏrt y.ab.adm.|w 14[KRT].6.294

ašr nkl w ib[.bt].|ẖrẖb.mlk qẓ ẖrẖb m|lk aǵzt.b sǵ[--.]špš.|yrẖ yṯkḥ 24[77].1

--.]ǵrm[.t]ẖšn.|rḥq[.---.td‘].|qdm ym.bmt.[nhr].|tṭṯn.ib.b‘l.tiẖd.|y‘rm.šnu.hd.gpt.|ǵr.w y‘n.aliyn.|b‘l.ib.hdt.lm.t 4[51].7.35

.dt.|[---.--]s‘.hn.mlk.|[---.l]qḥ.hn.l.ḥwt h.|[---.--]p.hn.ib.d.b.mgšẖ.|[---.i]b.hn[.w.]ht.ank.|[---.--]š[-.--].w.ašt.|[---]. 1012.10

kp mznm.iẖ h yṯ‘r.|mšrrm.aẖt h l a|bn mznm.nkl w ib.|d ašr.ar yrẖ.w y|rẖ yar k.|[ašr ilht kṯrt bn]|t hll.snnt.b 24[77].37

n.‘ṯtrt.---].|b‘l m.hmt.[---].|l šrr.št[.---].|b riš h.[---].|ib h.mš[--.---].|[b]n.‘n h[.---]. 2.4[68].39

tṭṯn.ib.b‘l.tiẖd.|y‘rm.šnu.hd.gpt.|ǵr.w y‘n.aliyn.|b‘l.ib.hdt.lm.tḥš.|lm.tḥš.nṯq.dmrn.|‘n.b‘l.qdm.yd h.|k tǵḏ.arz 4[51].7.38

k.[b]‘l y.|w.hn.ibm.šṣq l y.|p.l.ašt.aṯt y.|n‘r y.ṯh.l pn.ib.|hn.hm.yrgm.mlk.|b‘l y.tmǵyy.hn.|alpm.šŝwm.hnd.|w. 1012.29

lk.|[---.l]qḥ.hn.l.ḥwt h.|[---.--]p.hn.ib.d.b.mgšẖ.|[---.i]b.hn[.w.]ht.ank.|[---.--]š[-.--].w.ašt.|[---].amr k.|[---].k.ybt 1012.11

.|qrn.d bat k b‘l.ymšḥ.|b‘l.ymšḥ.hm.b ‘p.|nṭ‘n.b arṣ.ib y.|w b ‘pr.qm.aẖ k.|w tšu.‘n h.btlt.‘nt.|w tšu.‘n h.w t‘n. 10[76].2.24

-].|udn h.grš h.l ksi.mlk h.|l nẖt.l kḥṯ.drkt h.|mn m.ib.yp‘.l b‘l.ṣrt.l rkb.‘rpt.|[-]‘n.ǵlmm.y‘nyn.l ib.yp‘.|l b‘l.ṣrt.l 3[‘NT].4.48

h.|mn m.ib.yp‘.l b‘l.ṣrt.l rkb.‘rpt.|[-]‘n.ǵlmm.y‘nyn.l ib.yp‘.|l b‘l.ṣrt.l rkb.‘rpt.|tḥm.aliyn.b‘l.hwt.aliy.|qrdm.qry. 3[‘NT].4.49

l h.anš.dt.ẓr h.tšu.|g h.w tṣḥ.ik.mǵy.gpn.w ugr.|mn.ib.yp‘.l b‘l.ṣrt.|l rkb.‘rpt.l mẖšt.mdd.|il ym.l klt.nhr.il.rbm. 3[‘NT].3.34

m.w ‘n.kṯr.w ẖss.l rgmt.|l k.l zbl.b‘l.ṯnt.l rkb.‘rpt.ht.ib k.|b‘l m.ht.ib k.tmẖṣ.ht.tṣmt.ṣrt k.|tqḥ.mlk.‘lm k.drkt.d 2.4[68].8

ẖss.l rgmt.|l k.l zbl.b‘l.ṯnt.l rkb.‘rpt.ht.ib k.|b‘l m.ht.ib k.tmẖṣ.ht.tṣmt.ṣrt k.|tqḥ.mlk.‘lm k.drkt.dt dr dr k.|kṯr 2.4[68].9

-----].|h[--.---].|šp[š.---].|‘m.k[--.lḥt].|akl.yṯ[ṯb.--]pt.|ib.‘ltn.a[--.--]y.|w.spr.in[.-.]‘d m.|spr n.ṯhr[.--].|aṯr.iṯ.bqṯ.| 2060.31

k yrẖ ny[r] šmm.‘m.|ẖr[ẖ]b mlk qẓ.tn nkl y|rẖ ytrẖ.ib t‘rb m b bh|t h.w atn mhr h l a|b h.alp ksp w rbt ẖ|rṣ.iš 24[77].18

.ŝ[ŝw]m.|rgmt.‘ly.ṯh.lm.|l.ytn.hm.mlk.[b]‘l y.|w.hn.ibm.šṣq l y.|p.l.ašt.aṯt y.|n‘r y.ṯh.l pn.ib.|hn.hm.yrgm.mlk. 1012.27

š[--.]il.|d yqny.ḏdm.yd.mẖṣt.a[qh]t.ǵ|zr.tmẖṣ.alpm.ib.št[-.]št.|ḥršm l ahlm p[---.]km.|[-]bl lb h.km.bṯn.y[--.-]ah 19[1AQHT].4.221

.ybt.mlk.|[---].w.ap.ank.|[---].l.ǵr.amn.|[---.-]ktt.hn.ib.|[---.]mlk.|[---.]adt y.td‘.|w.ap.mlk.uḏ[r].|[-]d‘.k.iẖd.[--- 1012.17

.b n]ši.|‘n h.w tphn.[---].|b grn.yẖrb[.---].|yǵly.yẖsp.ib[.---].|‘l.bt.ab h.nšrm.trẖ[p]n.|ybṣr.ḥbl.diym.|tbky.pǵt.b 19[1AQHT].1.31

--]y.|šk[--.--.]kll.|šk[--.--.]hm.|w.k[b--.---].|‘m[.---]m ib.|[---.--]m.|[-----].|[-]š[--.---].|[-]r[--.--]y.|in m.‘bd k hwt. 2065.8

ibyn

lṣ[--].|il[---].|il[---].|ilmlk.|ildgn.|ilyn.|ilrm.|ibrm.|ibyn.|illḏrm.|iǵlkḏ.|[i]ly[-]n.|[-----].|m[--.---].|[-]n.qrqr.|[2022.18

dnn.ṯlṯ.ṣmdm.|bn.‘mnr.|bn.kmn.|bn.ibyn.|bn.mryn.ṣmd.w.ḥrṣ.|bn.prsn.ṣmd.w.ḥrṣ.|bn.ilb‘l.|bn 2113.4

iblbl

|mndym.|bdnh.|l[q]ḥt.|[--]km.‘m.mlk.|[b]ǵl hm.w.iblbl hm.|w.b.ṯb h.[---].|spr ḥ[--.---].|w.‘m[.---].|yqḥ[.---].| 2129.10

ibln

ln.|bn.tnn.|bn.pndr.|bn.nqq.|ḥrš.bhtm.|bn.izl.|bn.ibln.|bn.ilt.|špšyn.nḥl h.|n‘mn.bn.iryn.|nrn.nḥl h.|bn.ẖsn. 85[80].2.4

[-----].|[bn.]ibln.|ysd.|bn.ṯmq.|bn.agmn.|bn.uṣb.|bn.yzg.|bn.anntn.|b 115[301].4.1

ibm

]mn bn.qṣy.|[‘]pṯrm bn.agmz.|[-]n bn.iln.|[--]nn bn.ibm.|[-]n bn.ḥrn.|[š]mmn bn.gmz.|[yn]ḥm bn.ilmd. 2087.12

ibn

.uẖnpy.ẖmšm.|b.bn.ṯtm.ṯlṯm.|b.bn.agdṯb.‘šrm.|b.bn.ibn.arb‘t.‘šrt.|b.bn.mnn.ṯṯm.|b.rpan.bn.yyn.‘šrt.|b.yp‘r.‘šr 2054.1.13

ibr

.b ‘dn.|‘dnm.kn.npl.b‘l.|km ṯr.w tkms.hd.p[.-].|km.ibr.b tk.mšmš d[--].|ittpq.l awl.|išttk.lm.ttkn.|štk.mlk.dn.| 12[75].2.56

.ṯdṯ.ym.|mk.špšm.b šb‘.|w l.yšn.pbl.|mlk.l [qr.]ṯiqt.|ibr h[.l]ql.nhqt.|ḥmr[h.l g‘t.]alp.|ḥrṯ[.l z]ǵt.klb.|[ṣ]pr[.ap 14[KRT].5.224

k.|mšdpt.w hn.špšm.|b šb‘.w l.yšn.pbl.|mlk.l qr.ṯigt.ibr h.|l ql.nhqt.ḥmr h.|l g‘t.alp.ḥrṯ.zǵt.|klb.ṣpr.w ylak.|ml 14[KRT].3.120

ilm.yp‘r.|šmt hm.|b hm.qrnm.|km.ṯrm.w gbṯt.|km.ibrm.|w b hm.pn.b‘l.|b‘l.ytlk.w yṣd.|yḥ pat.mlbr.|wn.ymǵ 12[75].1.32

.w tr.b[ẖl].|b n‘mm.b ys[mm.---].|arẖ.arẖ.[---.tld].|ibr.tld[.l b‘l].|w rum.l[rkb.‘rpt].|tḥbq.[---].|tḥbq[.---].|w t 10[76].3.21

--].|hyrm.h[--.---].|yrmm h[--.---].|mlk.gb‘ h d [---].|ibr.k l hm.d l h q[--.---].|l ytn.l hm.tḥt b‘l[.---].|h.u qšt pn 9[33].2.4

[l]iyt.|ql.l b‘l.ttnn.|bšrt.il.bš[r.b‘]l.|w bšr.ḥtk.dgn.|k.ibr.l b‘l[.yl]d.|w rum.l rkb.‘rpt.|yšmẖ.aliyn.b‘l. 10[76].3.36

.‘n.gpn.|w ugr.bn.ǵlmt.|‘mm ym.bn.ẓlm[t].|rmt.pr‘t.ibr[.mnt].|ṣḥrrm.ḥbl[.--].|‘rpt.tḥt.[---]|m ‘ṣrm.ḥ[---].|glṯ.is 8[51FRAG].9

.|[gpn].w ugr.b ǵlmt.|[‘mm.]ym.bn.ẓlmt.r|[mt.pr‘]t.ibr.mnt.|[ṣḥrrm.ḥbl.‘]rpt.|[---.---.-]ḥt.|[---.---]m.|[----] h. 4[51].7.56

b ym b‘l ysy ym[.---].|rmm.ẖnpm.mẖl[.---].|mlk.nhr.ibr[.---].|zbl b‘l.ǵlm.[---].|ṣǵr hd w r[---.---].|w l nhr nd[-.-- 9[33].2.9

ibrd

škny.|bn.lgn.uškny.|bn.abn.uškny.|bn.arz.š‘rty.|bn.ibrd.m‘rby.|ṣdqn.gb‘ly.|bn.ypy.gb‘ly.|bn.grgs.ilštm‘y.|bn. 87[64].26

‘lytn.bn.ulb.|ytr‘m.bn.swy.|ṣḥrn.bn.qrtm.|bn.špš.bn.ibrd.|‘pṯrm.bn.‘bdy.|n[--.]bn.ŝnd.|[---].bn.[---]. 2024.5

ibrḏr

n.bdn. | [sǵ]r.bn.psḫn. | alṯy. | sǵr.npr. | bn.ḫty. | ṯn.bnš ibrḏr. | bnš tlmi. | sǵr.ḫryn. | ʻdn.w sǵr h. | bn.ḥgbn. 2082.6

ibryn

dbʻl. | šd.šmmn.l.bn.šty. | šd.bn.arws.l.bn.ḫlan. | šd.bn.ibryn.l.bn.ʻmnr. 1102.20

ibrkyṯ

lkytn. | kdrl. | slṯmg. | adrdn. | l[l]wn. | ydln. | ldn. | tdǵl. | ibrkyṯ. 1034.10

ibrm

r[--]. | ilṣ[--]. | il[---]. | il[---]. | ilmlk. | ildgn. | ilyn. | ilrm. | ibrm. | ibyn. | illḏrm. | iǵlkḏ. | [i]ly[-]n. | [-----]. | m[--.---]. | [-]n. 2022.17

ibrmḏ

bn.ṣnrn.b d.nrn. | [š]d.bn.rwy.b d.ydln. | [š].bn.trn.b d.ibrmḏ. | [š]d.bn.ilṯtmr.b d.tbbr. | [w.]šd.nḥl h.b d.ṯṯmd. | [š]d. 82[300].1.10
qdy.b d.gmrd. | [š]d bn.synn.b d.gmrd. | [šd.]abyy.b d.ibrmḏ. | [šd.]bn.ṯṯrn.b d.bnš.aǵlkz. | [šd.b]d.b[n].tkwn. | [ubd 82[300].2.19

ibrn

bn.qdšt. | bn.nṯǵ[-]. | bn.gr[--]. | bn.[---]. | bn.[---]. | mr[u.ibrn]. | bn.i[---]. | bn.n[---]. | bn.b[---]. | bn.iš[--]. | bn.ab[--]. | bn. 113[400].5.17
ṯ. | gt.mlkym. | tmrym. | ṯnqym. | ṯǵrm. | mru.skn. | mru.ibrn. | yqšm. | trrm. | kkrdnm. | yṣrm. | ktrm. | mṣlm. | tkn[m]. | 1026.2.7
qd[šm]. | mru s[kn]. | mru ib[rn]. | mdm. | inšt. | nsk ksp. | yṣḥm. | ḫrš mrkbt. | ḫrš qṭn. | ḥ 73[114].3
ym. | yqšm. | kbšm. | trrm. | khnm. | kzym. | yṣrm. | mru.ibrn. | mru.skn. | nsk.ksp | mḫṣm. | ksdm. | mdrǵlm. | pslm. | yṣ 74[115].12
| [ṣ]ʻq. | [š]ḥq. | nʻrm. | mḫrǵlm. | kzym. | mru.skn. | mru.ibrn. | pslm. | šrm. | yṣḥm. | ʻšrm. | mrum. | ṯnnm. | mqdm. | khn 71[113].64
pṭbʻl. | [šd.---.]b d.ymz. | [šd.b d].klby.psl. | [ub]dy.mri.ibrn. | [š]d.bn.bri.b d.bn.ydln. | [u]bdy.ṯǵrm. | [š]d.ṯǵr.mṯpit.b 82[300].2.5
[---.]mru ib[rn.---]. | [---.]yṣḥm[.---]. | [---.]ʻbd[m.---]. | [---.-]ḫy[-.---]. | [- 1027.1

ibrtlm

tšʻ.ṣmdm. | ṯlṯm.b d. | ibrtlm. | w.pat.aḥt. | in.b hm. 1141.3

igy

n.šršʻm.[---]. | ṣṣ mlknʻm.a[rbʻm]. | ṣṣ mlk mit[.---]. | ṣṣ igy.ḫmšm. | ṣṣ yrpi m[it.---]. | ṣṣ bn.š[m]mn ʻ[šr.---]. | alp.ṯṯm. 2097.17

id

r[.rb]t. | ḫbr[.ṯrrt]. | [-]ʻb[-].š[--]m. | [----]r[.---]š[.--]qm. | id.u [---]t. | lḥn š[-]ʻ[--.]aḫd[.-]. | tšmʻ.mṯt.[ḥ]ry. | ṭṭbḫ.šmn.[m 15[128].4.12
t.il.nbt.b ksp. | šmrgt.b dm.ḫrṣ. | kḥṯ.il.nḫt. | b ẓr.hdm.id. | d pršа.b br. | nʻl.il.d qblbl. | ʻln.ybl hm.ḫrṣ. | ṯlḥn.il.d mla. 4[51].1.35
id ydbḥ mlk. | l ušḫ[r] ḫlmṭ. | l bbt il bt. | š l ḫlmṭ. | w tr l qlḥ. UG5.7.TR3
.ʻ[r]b[.š]p[š]. | w [ḥl.]mlk.[w.]b.ym.ḥdṯ.ṯn.šm. | l.[---]t. | i[d.yd]bḥ.mlk.l.prgl.ṣqrn.b.gg. | ar[bʻ.]arbʻ.mṯbt.azmr.b h.š.š 35[3].50
n.nšrm.arḫp.an[k.ʻ]l. | aqht.ʻdb k.hlmn.ṯnm.qdqd. | ṯlṯ id.ʻl.udn.špk.km.šiy. | dm.km.šḫṭ.l brk h.tṣi.km. | rḥ.npš h.k 18[3AQHT].4.23
šrm.trḫp.ʻnt.ʻl[.aqht]. | tʻdbn h.hlmn.ṯnm[.qdqd]. | ṯlṯ id.ʻl.udn.š[pk.km]. | šiy.dm h.km.šḫ[ṭ.l brk h]. | yṣat.km.rḥ.n 18[3AQHT].4.34
m b dd y.yṣ[--]. | [-.]yṣa.w l.yṣa.hlm.[ṯnm]. | [q]dqd.ṯlṯ id.ʻl.ud[n]. | [---.-]sr.pdm.riš h[m.---]. | ʻl.pd.asr.[---.]l[.---]. | m 19[1AQHT].2.79
id.yph.mlk. | r[š]p.ḥgb.ap. | w[.n]pš.ksp. | w ḫrṣ.km[-]. | w.ḥ[-- 2005.1.1
. | rgm. | ṯḥm.tlmyn. | ʻbd k. | l.pʻn. | adt y. | šbʻ d. | w.šbʻ id. | mrḥqtm. | qlt. | ʻm.adt y. | mnm.šlm. | rgm.ṯṯb. | l.ʻbd h. 52[89].9
b[nn]. | bʻl y.r[gm]. | ṯḥm.ʻbd[--]. | ʻbd k. | l pʻn.bʻl y. | ṯn id.šbʻ d. | mrḥqtm. | qlt.ʻm. | bʻl y.mnm. | šlm. | [r]gm[.ṯṯb]. | [l 2115.2.6
br. | [---] y.ʻm k. | [-]tn.l.stn. | [--.]d.nʻm.lbš k. | [-]dm.ṯn id. | [--]m.d.l.nʻmm. | [lm.]l.likt.ʻm y. | [---.]ʻbd.ank. | [---.ʻb]d 2128.1.5

idy

[.--]y.tnn.w ygl.w ynsk.ʻ[-]. | [--]y.l arṣ[.id]y.alt.l aḥš.idy.alt.in l y. | [--]t.bʻl.ḥẓ.ršp.b[n].km.yr.klyt h.w lb h. | [ṯ]n. 1001.1.2
[k.ym]ḫṣ.bʻl m[.--]y.tnn.w ygl.w ynsk.ʻ[-]. | [--]y.l arṣ[.id]y.alt.l aḥš.idy.alt.in l y. | [--]t.bʻl.ḥẓ.ršp.b[n].km.yr.klyt h. 1001.1.2

idk

idk.al.ttn.pnm. | ʻm.ǵr.trǵzz. | ʻm.ǵr.ṯrmg. | ʻm.tlm.ǵṣr.arṣ. | ša 4[51].8.1
ʻl.ʻbr.iht. | np šmm.šmšr. | l dgy.aṯrt. | mǵ.l qdš.amrr. | idk.al.tnn. | pnm.tk.ḥqkpt. | il.kl h.kptr. | ksu.ṯbt h.ḥkpt. | arṣ. 3[ʻNT.VI].6.12
[idk.al.ttn.pnm.tk.ḥkpt.il.kl h]. | [kptr.]ks[u.ṯbt h.ḥkpt.arṣ.n 1[ʻNT.IX].3.01
. | ḫlb.l ẓr.rḥtm. | w rd.bt ḫpṯt. | arṣ.tspr.b y | rdm.arṣ. | idk.al.ttn. | pnm.tk.qrt h. | hmry.mk.ksu. | ṯbt h.ḫḫ.arṣ. | nḫlt 4[51].8.10
kbd k.tšt.b [---]. | irt k.dṯ.ydṯ.mʻqb k.[ttbʻ]. | [bt]lt.ʻnt.idk.l ttn.[pnm]. | [ʻm.a]qht.ǵzr.b alp.š[d]. | [rbt.]kmn.w ṣḥq.b 18[3AQHT].1.20
.ṯḥt. | [pʻn y.a]nk.nʻmn.ʻmq.nšm. | [tdʻṣ.pʻn]m.w tr.arṣ.idk. | [l ttn.pn]m.ʻm il.mbk.nhrm. | [qrb.ap]q.thmtm tgly.ḏd 17[2AQHT].6.46
[idk.l ttn.pnm]. | [ʻm.il.mbk.nhrm]. | [qrb.apq.thmtm]. | [tgly. 5[67].6.03
mrr.k kbkb.l pnm. | aṯr.btlt.ʻnt. | w bʻl.tbʻ.mrym.ṣpn. | idk.l ttn.pnm. | ʻm.il.mbk.nhrm. | qrb.apq.thmtm. | tgly.ḏd.il. 4[51].4.20
l[i]yn.b[ʻl]. | [---]ḥ h.tšt bm.ʻ[--]. | [---.]zr h.ybm.l ilm. | [id]k.l ttn.pnm.ʻm. | [il.]mbk nhrm.qrb. | [a]pq.thmtm.tgly.ḏd 6.1.32[49.1.4]
rḥq]. | [ilnym.ṯn.mṯpd]m.t[ḥt.ʻnt.arṣ.ṯlṯ.mtḥ.ǵyrm]. | [idk.]l ytn.pnm.ʻm.[i]l.mbk.[nhrm.qrb.apq.thmtm]. | [ygly.]ḏ 2.3[129].4
.bt.l bʻl.k ilm. | [w ḥẓ]r.k bn.aṯrt[.tdʻṣ.]pʻn. | [w tr.a]rṣ.id[k.l ttn.p]nm. | [ʻm.i]l.mbk.nhr[m.qr]b.[ap]q. | [thm]tm.tgl. 3[ʻNT.VI].5.13
.bhṯ.l bn.ilm mt. | ʻbd k.an.w d.ʻlm k. | tbʻ.w l.yṯb.ilm.idk. | l ytn.pn.ʻm.bn.ilm.mt. | tk.qrt h.hmry.mk.ksu. | ṯbt.ḫḫ. 5[67].2.13
ṣ. | bht.ṯhrm.iqnim. | šmḫ.btlt.ʻnt.tdʻṣ. | pʻnm.w tr.arṣ. | idk.l ttn.pnm. | ʻm.bʻl.mrym.ṣpn. | b alp.šd.rbt.kmn. | ṣḥq.btlt 4[51].5.84
b npš.bn ilm.mt.b mh | mrt.ydd.il.ǵzr. | tbʻ.w l.yṯb ilm.idk. | l ytn.pnm.ʻm.bʻl. | mrym.ṣpn.w yʻn. | gpn.w ugr.ṯḥm.bn 5[67].1.9
bb. | l rḥq.ilnym.ṯn.mṯpdm. | ṯḥt.ʻnt.arṣ.ṯlṯ.mtḥ.ǵyrm. | idk.l ttn pnm.ʻm.bʻl. | mrym.ṣpn.b alp.šd.rbt.kmn. | hlk.aḫt 3[ʻNT].4.81
[---.]uṭm.ḏr[qm.---]. | [btl]t.ʻnt.l kl.[---]. | [tt]bʻ.btlt.ʻnt[.idk.l ttn.pnm]. | ʻm.ytpn.mhr.š[t.tšu.g h]. | w tṣḥ.yṯb.ytp.[---] 18[3AQHT].4.5
[t.l rḥq.ilnym]. | ṯn.mṯpdm.ṯḥt.[ʻnt.arṣ.ṯlṯ.mtḥ]. | ǵyrm.idk.l yt[n.pnm.ʻm.lṭpn]. | il d pid.tk ḫrš[n.---.tk.ǵr.ks]. | ygly 1[ʻNT.IX].3.21

]‘l.‘nt.mḥrṯt.|iy.aliyn.b‘l.|iy.zbl.b‘l.arṣ.|ttb‘.btlt.‘nt.|idk.l ttn.pnm.|‘m.nrt.ilm.špš.|tšu.g h.w tṣḥ.|tḥm.ṯr.il.ab k. 6[49].4.31
b qrb.hkl h.|qšt hn.aẖd.b yd h.|w qṣ‘t h.bm.ymn h.|idk.l ytn pnm.|tk.aẖ.šmk.mla[t.r]umm.|tšu knp.btlt.‘n[t].| 10[76].2.8
.|[---.--]m.‘db.l arṣ.|[---.]špm.‘db.|[---].t‘tqn.|[---.-]‘b.idk.|[l ytn.pnm.tk.]in.bb.b alp ḥẓr.|[rbt.kmn.l p‘]n.‘nt.|[yh 1[‘NT.IX].2.13
-]d.‘r.|[----.-]bb.|[----.]lm y.|[---.--]p.|[---.d]bḥ.|t[---.id]k.|pn[m.al.ttn].|‘m.[krt.msw]n.|w r[gm.l krt.]ṯ‘.|tḥm[.p 14[KRT].5.244
|b ‘lṣ.‘lṣm.npr.š[--.---].|uṯ.ṯbr.ap hm.tb‘.ǵlm[m.al.ṯṯb.idk.pnm].|al.ttn.‘m.pḫr.m‘d.t[k.ǵr.ll.l p‘n.il].|al.tpl.al.tštḥ 2.1[137].13
.|ǵlm k.ṯmn.ẖnzr k.|‘m k.pdry.bt.ar.|‘m k.ṭṭly.bt.rb.idk.|pn k.al ttn.tk.ǵr.|knkny.ša.ǵr.‘l ydm.|ẖlb.l ẓr.rḥtm w 5[67].5.11
.|[ng.kr]t.l ḥ[ẓ]r y.|[-----].|[---.ttb‘].|[mlakm.l yṯb].|[idk.pnm.l ytn].|[‘]m[.krt.mswn h].|tš[an.g hm.w tṣḥn].|tḥ[14[KRT].6.265
m.|w ld.špḥ.l krk|t.w ǵlm.l ‘bd.|il.ttb‘.mlakm.|l yṯb.idk.pnm.|l ytn.‘mm.pbl.|mlk.tšan.|g hm.w tṣḥn.|tḥm.krt.ṯ 14[KRT].6.301
mt.|b ḥrn.pnm.trǵnw.w ṯtkl.|bnwt h.ykr.‘r.d qdm.|idk.pnm.l ytn.tk aršẖ.rbt.|w aršẖ.ṯrrt.ydy.b ‘ṣm.‘r‘r.|w b š UG5.7.63
lt.tn.b‘l.[w ‘nn h].|bn.dgn.arṯ m.pḏ h.tb‘.ǵlmm.l ṯṯb.[idk.pnm].|l ytn.tk.ǵr.ll.‘m.phr.m‘d.ap.ilm.l lḥ[m].|yṯb.bn q 2.1[137].19
llu.bn[š.---].|imr.ẖ[--.---].|[--]n.b‘[l.---].|w [--]d.[---].|idk[.-]it[.---].|trgm[.-]dk[.---].|m‘bd[.-]r[-.-]š[-.---].|w kšt.[-- 2158.2.2
[---.--]‘.|[---.]idk.|[---.--]ty.|[---.--]hr.|[---.--]ẖdn.|[---.]bšr y.|[---.--]b.|[-- 28[-].2

idm

.dgn[.---].|‘ḏbm.[---].|uẖry.l[---].|mṣt.ks h.t[--.---].|idm.adr[.---].|idm.‘rẓ.t‘r[ẓ.---].|‘n.b‘l.a[ẖ]d[.---].|ẓr h.aẖḏ.q 12[75].2.30
m.[---].|uẖry.l[---].|mṣt.ks h.t[--.---].|idm.adr[.---].|idm.‘rẓ.t‘r[ẓ.---].|‘n.b‘l.a[ẖ]d[.---].|ẓr h.aẖḏ.qš[t.---].|p ‘n.b‘ 12[75].2.31

idmt

[---.--]n.d[--.]bnš[.---].|[---.]idmt.n[--.]t[--].|[---.--]r.dlt.tḥt n.|[---.]dlt.|[---.b]nš.|[---.]yp 2158B.2

idn

gnryn.|l mlkytn.|ḥnn y l pn mlk.|šin k itn.|r‘ y šṣa idn l y.|l šmn iṯr hw.|p iẖdn gnryn.|im mlkytn yrgm.|aẖn 1020.5

idrm

n.mryn.ṣmd.w.ḥrṣ.|bn.prsn.ṣmd.w.ḥrṣ.|bn.ilb‘l.|bn.idrm.|bn.grgš.|bn.bly.|bn.apṯ.|bn.ysd.|bn.pl[-].|bn.ṯb‘nq. 2113.8
lby.|[-]ḥmn.|[š]pšyn.|[‘b]dmlk.|[---]yn.|bn.ṯ[--].|bn.idrm.|bn.ymn.|bn.ṣry.|bn.mztn.|bn.šlgyn.|bn.[-]gštn.|bn[113[400].2.2

idrn

[-]b[-]n.[---].|bn.atnb.mr[--.---].|bn.sẖr.mr[-.---].|bn.idrn.‘š[-.---].|bn.bly.mr[-.---].|w.nḥl h.mr[-.---].|ilšpš.[---].| 88[304].9

idrp

rẖ.š.ṣpn.š.|kṯr š ‘ṯtr.š.|[‘ṯ]rt.š.šgr w iṯm š.|[---.]š.ršp.idrp.š.|[---.il.t‘]ḏr.š.|[---.-]mt.š.|[-----].|[-----].|[-----].|[---.]i UG5.9.2.10

idṯn

.aḥd.|sǵr.artn.aḥd.|sǵr.‘dn.aḥd.|sǵr.awldn.aḥd.|sǵr.idṯn.aḥd.|sǵr.sndrn.aḥd.|sǵr.adn.ṣdq.aḥd.|sǵr.irgn.aḥd.|sǵ 1140.6
ḥd.b gt.nẖl.|aḥd.b gt.knpy.w.aḥd.b gt.ṯrmn.|aḥd.alp.idṯn.d aḥd.b.‘nqpat.|[aḥd.al]p.d aǵlmn.|[d aẖd b.g]t gbry.| 1129.11
lmyn.|‘bdnt.|bdy.ḥrš arkd.|blšš lmd.|ḥṯṯn.tqn.|ydd.idṯn.|šǵr.ilgdn. 1045.12

iḏrn

|[bn.-]dn.|bn.ummt.|bn.ṯb[-].|bn.[-]r[-].|bn.tgn.|bn.iḏrn.|mnn.|b[n].skn.|bn.p‘ṣ.|bn.ḏrm.|[bn.-]ln.|[bn.-]ḏprḏ. 124[-].6.8

iht

.]alp.|[---.]ym.rbt.|[---.]b nhrm.|[‘b]r.gbl.‘br.|q‘l.‘br.iht.|np šmm.šmšr.|l dgy.aṯrt.|mǵ.l qdš.amrr.|idk.al.tnn.| 3[‘NT.VI].6.8

iwrḏn

bnšm.|b.‘nmky.‘šrm.dr‘[.---.d]rt.|w.ṯn.‘šr h.dd.[---].|iwrḏn.ẖ[--.---].|w.ṯlṯm.dd.[---.]n[---.---].|w.a[r]b‘[.---].bnš[.š 1098.30

iwrḏr

tḥm iwrḏr.|l iwrpẖn.|bn y.aẖ y.rgm.|ilm.tǵr k.|tšlm k.|ik y.lḥt 138.1
tḥm.iwrḏr.|l iwrpẖn.|bn y.aẖ y.rgm.|ilm.tǵr k.|tšlm k.|iky.lḥt. 138.1
tḥm.iwrḏr.|l.plsy.|rgm.|yšlm.l k.|l.trǵds.|w.l.klby.|šm‘t.ẖti.|n 53[54].1

iwrẖz

|ildy.aḏddy.|gr‘.aḏddy.|‘bd.ršp aḏddy.|‘dn.bn.knn.|iwrẖz.b d.skn.|škny.aḏddy.|mšu.aḏddy.|plsy.aḏddy.|aẖyn 2014.37
[s]pr.bnš.mlk.d.b.tbq.|[kr]wn.|[--]n.|[q]ṣy.|ṯn.bn.iwrẖz.[n]‘rm.|yṣr[.-]qb.|w.ṯn.bnš.iytlm.|w.‘šrm.ṣmd.alpm. 2066.2.4

iwrẖṯ

gzḥn.b d.gmrd.|[šd.bn].pll.b d.gmrd.|[šd.bn.-]ll.b d.iwrẖṯ.|[šd.bn.-]nn.b d.bn.šmrm.|[šd.bn.-]ṯtayy.b d.ṯtmd.|[š 82[300].1.25
]d.bn.ilṯtmr.b d.tbbr.|[w.]šd.nḥl h.b d.ṯtmd.|[š]d.b d.iwrẖṯ.|[ṯn].šdm.b d.gmrd.|[šd.]lbny.b d.tbṯtb.|[š]d.bn.ṯ[-]r 82[300].1.13

iwryn

‘nt.|llwn.|agdṯb.|aǵltn.|[-]wn.|bldn.|[-]ln.|[-]ldn.|[i]wryn.|ẖbsn.|ulmk.|‘dršp.|bn.knn.|pdyn.|bn.aṯtl.ṯn.|kdl 1061.14
btwm.|[-]bln.|[-]bldn.|[-]bdy.|[b]‘ln.|[-]šdm.|iwryn.|n‘mn.|[-----].|b gt.yny.|agtṯp.|bn.‘nt.|ǵzldn.|trn.| 1043.7
.nḥl h.|[-]by.w.nḥl h.|[--]ilt.w.nḥl h.|[---]n.|[--]ly.|[iw]ryn.|[--.w.n]ḥl h.|[-]ibln.|bn.nḏbn.|bn.‘bl.|bn.tlšn.|bn. 1063.8

iwrkl

.|ksp.b y[d].|birtym.|[un]ṯ inn.|l [h]m ‘d ṯṯbn.|ksp.iwrkl.|w ṯb.l unṯ hm. 1006.18
|w.ištrmy.|bt.‘bd mlk.|w.snt.|bt.ugrt.|w.pdy h[m].|iwrkl.mit.|ksp.b y[d].|birtym.|[un]ṯ inn.|l [h]m ‘d ṯṯbn.|k 1006.13
l ym hnd.|iwr[k]l.pdy.|agdn.bn.nrgn.|w ynḥm.aẖ h.|w.b‘ln aẖ h.|w. 1006.2

-].|šd.b d.[---].|šd.b d[.---]im.|šd.b d[.bn.--]n.|šd.b d.iwrkl.|šd.b d.klb.|šd.b d.klby.|šd.b d.iytlm.|ṯn.šdm.b d.a 2090.8
arbʻ.ʻšr h.šd.|w.kmsk.d.iwrkl.|ṯlṯ.šd.d.bn.mlkyy.|kmsk.šd.iḫmn.|širm.šd.khn.|ṯlṯ.š 1079.2

iwrmḏ

[n].ušryn.|kdm.l.urtn.|kdm.l.ilšpš.|kd.l.annṯb.|kd.l.iwrmḏ.|kd.l.ydn.|[---.y]rḫ.ḫyr.|[---.]yn.l.mlkt.|[---.yrḫ.]ḫlt 1088.8

iwrmḫ

g.|w.lmd h.|iyṯr.|[w].lmd h.|[yn]ḥm.|[w.]lmd h.|[i]wrmḫ.|[w.]lmd h. 1048.9

iwrnr

bt šbn.|iyʻdm.w bʻl h.|ddy.|ʻmy.|iwrnr.|alnr.|maḫdt.|aby.|[-----].|[-]nt.|ydn.|mnn.w bn h. 107[15].5
bn.aḏmṯn.|[-]tn bn.agyn.|ullym.bn.abynm.|antn.bn.iwr[n]r.|pwn.ṯmry.|ksyn.bn.lḫsn.|[-]kyn.ṯmry. 94[313].7

iwrǵl

].|krm.ilyy.b.m[--.---].|kd.šbʻ.krmm.[---].|ṯn.krm[m.i]wrǵl[.---].|ṯn.krm.[-]myn.[---].|ṯn.krm[.---].|krm.[---].|[-- 1081.26

iwrpzn

dm.|ṯp[ṯ]bʻl.ṣmdm.|[---.ṣ]mdm.w.ḥrṣ.|[---].aḥdm.|[iwr]pzn.aḥdm.|[i]lšpš.aḥd. 2033.2.7
d.b.bt.nwrḏ.|[aṯ]t.adrt.b.bt.arttb.|aṯt.w.ṯn.bn h.b.bt.iwwpzn.|aṯt.w.pǵt.b.bt.ydrm.|ṯt.aṯtm.adrtm.w.pǵt.aḥt.b[.b 80[119].5
b ym ḥdṯ.|b.yrḫ.pgrm.|lqḥ.iwrpzn.|argḏḏ.|ṯṯkn.|ybrk.|ntbt.|b.mitm.|ʻšrm.|kbd.ḫrṣ. 2006.3
[----]lm.|[iwr]pzn.|[i]wrṯǵrn.|iwrṯǵrn.|iwr[--]l.|iw[r--].|iw[r--]ǵt.|iw 2022.2
annṯb.ḫmšm.ksp ṯlṯm.šl[m.---].|iwrpzn.ʻšrm ʻšrm š[lm.---].|ilabn.ʻšrt ṯqlm kbd.ḫmš.šl[m.--- 1131.2
ṯn.nʻrm.b.bt.ilsk.|aṯt.ad[r]t.b.bt.armwl.|aṯt.aḥt.b.bt.iwrpzn.|ṯt.aṯtm.w.pǵt.aḥt.b bt.[-]r[-].|[aṯ]t.b.bt.aupš.|[aṯ]t. 80[119].10

iwrpḫn

tḥm iwrḏr.|l iwrpḫn.|bn y.aḫ y.rgm.|ilm.tǵr k.|tšlm k.|ik y.lḥt.|spr.d li 138.2
tḥm.iwrḏr.|l iwrpḫn.|bn y.aḫ y.rgm.|ilm.tǵr k.|tšlm k.|iky.lḥt.|spr.d li 138.2

iwrtḏl

qn.|[---.--]ʻ.šdyn.l ytršn.|[---.--]ṯ.ʻbd.l.kyn.|k[rm.--.]l.i[w]rtḏl.|ḥl.d[--.ʻbd]yrḫ.b d.apn.|krm.i[--].l.[---.]a[-]bn. 2027.2.10

iwrtn

gmy.|ʻdyn.|ʻbdbʻl.|ʻbdkṯr.ʻbd.|tdǵl.|bʻlṣn.|nsk.ksp.|iwrtn.|ydln.|ʻbdilm.|dqn.|nsk.ṯlṯ.|ʻbdadt.|bṣmn.spr. 1039.2.24

iwrṯǵrn

[----]lm.|[iwr]pzn.|[i]wrṯǵrn.|iwrṯǵrn.|iwr[--]l.|iw[r--].|iw[r--]ǵt.|iw[r---].|iwr 2022.3
[----]lm.|[iwr]pzn.|[i]wrṯǵrn.|iwrṯǵrn.|iwr[--]l.|iw[r--].|iw[r--]ǵt.|iw[r---].|iwr[--].|ilṣ[--] 2022.4

iwrṯrn

[---.a]dt y.|[---].irrṯwm.ʻbd k.|[---.a]dt y.mrḥqm.|[---].adt y.yšlm.|[---.]mlk 1012.2

izl

b]n.ḫrmln.|bn.tnn.|bn.pndr.|bn.nqq.|ḥrš.bhtm.|bn.izl.|bn.ibln.|bn.ilt.|špšyn.nḥl h.|nʻmn.bn.iryn.|nrn.nḥl h. 85[80].2.3

izly

spr.rpš d l y[dy].|atlg.|ulm.|izly.|uḫnp.|bn sḫrn.|mʻqb.|ṯpn.|mʻr.|lbnm.|nḫl.|yʻny.|a 2075.4

izml

.|ḥmr.ḥmr.|ḥmr.ḥmr.|ḥmr.ḥmr.|ḥmr.ḥmr.|ḥmr.w izml.aḥt. 146[87].7
ṯlṯm.ktn.|ḫmšm.izml.|ḫmš.kbd.arbʻm.|dd.akl.|ṯṯ.ʻšr h.yn.|kd.šmn.l.nr.ilm. 1126.2

izr

bḥ ṣpn.|[-]zǵm.|[i]lib.|[i]lbldn.|[p]dry.bt.mlk.|[-]lp.izr.|[a]rz.|k.tʻrb.ʻṯtrt.šd.bt[.m]lk.|k.tʻrbn.ršp m.bt.mlk.|ḫl 2004.8

iḥd

--.š]ilt.|[---.--]m.lm.|[---.š]d.gṯr.|[--]ḥ[d].šd.hwt.|[--.]iḥd.šd.gṯr.|[w]ht.yšmʻ.uḫ y.|l g y.w yhbṭ.bnš.|w ytn.ilm.b 55[18].16

iḫy

n.|bn.asr.|bn.ʻdy.|bn.amt[m].|myn.|šr.|bn.zql.|bn.iḫy.|bn.iyṯr.|bn.ʻyn.|bn.ǵzl.|bn.ṣmy.|bn.il[-]šy.|bn.ybšr.| 2117.2.4
[-----].|[-----].|ynḥm.|iḫy.|bn.mšt.|ʻpsn.|bn.ṣpr.|kmn.|bn.ršp.|tmn.|šmmn.|bn. 1047.4
.bn.qqln.|ʻbdil[-].bn.qqln.|liy.bn.qqln.|mnn.bn.ṣnr.|iḫy.[b]n[.--]l[-].|ʻbdy[rḫ].bn.gttn.|yrmn.bn.ʻn.|krwn.nḥl h. 85[80].4.7
n.dnn.ṯkt.|ilthm.bn.dnn.ṯkt.|šbʻl.bn.aly.ṯkt.|klby.bn.iḫy.ṯkt.|psš.bn.buly.ṯkt.|ʻpṣpn.bn.ʻdy.ṯkt.|nʻmn.bn.ʻyn.ṯkt. 2085.7
ṯb[-.---].|ab[.---].|ḥyi[l.---].|iḫy[.---].|ar[.---].|ʻṯtr[.---].|bn.[---].|yly[.---].|ykn[.---].|rp[- 2131.4

iḫyn

iḫyn.uṯpt.ḥẓm.|anšrm.uṯpt.ḥẓm.|w uṯpt.srdnnm.|awpn.uṯ 1124.1
n].mrnn.|ʻbdmlk.bn.ʻmyn.|agyn.rʻy.|abmlk.bn.ilrš.|iḫyn.bn.ḫryn.|[ab]ǵl.bn.gdn.|[---].bn.bqš.|[---].bn.pdn.|[--- 102[323].4.11
prnm.|l ḫršm.|ddm l ʻnqt.|dd l alṯt.w l lmdt h.|dd l iḫyn.|dd l [---]. 1101.12
bʻl.bn.kdn.|gzl.bn.qldn.|gld.bt.klb.|l[---].bt.ḫzli.|bn.iḫyn.|ṣdqn.bn.ass.|bʻlyskn.bn.ss.|ṣdqn.bn.imrt.|mnḥm.bn. 102[323].3.7

ʻbdʻṯ[tr.---]. | bdil[.---]. | abǵl.[---]. | [.---]. | ḏmrbʻ[l.---]. | iḫyn.[---]. | ʻbdbʻ[l.---]. | uwil[.---]. | ušry[n.---]. | yʻḏrn[.---]. | [ʻ] 102[322].2.6

iḫmlk

l. | ʻbdn.w.aṯt h.w.bn h. | gpn.bn[.a]ly. | bn.rqd[y].ṯbg. | iḫmlk. | ypʻn w.aṯt h. | anntn.yṣr. | annmn.w.ṯlṯ.nʻ[r] h. | rpan. 2068.22

iḫmn

r h.šd. | w.kmsk.d.iwrkl. | ṯlṯ.šd.d.bn.mlkyy. | kmsk.šd.iḫmn. | širm.šd.khn. | ṯlṯ.šd.w.krm.šir.d.ḫli. | širm.šd.šd.ʻšy. | 1079.4

iḫny

[-.---]. | bn.bly.mr[-.---]. | w.nḥl h.mr[-.---]. | ilšpš.[---]. | iḫny.[---]. | bn.[---]. 88[304].13

iḫǵl

mšu. | ḫṯpy. | ǵldy. | iḫǵl. | aby. | abmn. | ynḥm. | npl. | ynḥm. | mtbʻl. | bn ǵlmn. | bn 1065.4

iḫqm

.yšmʻ.uḫ y. | l g y.w yhbṭ.bnš. | w ytn.ilm.b d hm. | b d.iḫqm.gṯr. | w b d.ytrhd. | bʻl. 55[18].20

iy

l.ʻnt.šdm.y špš. | pl.ʻnt.šdm.il.yš[t k]. | bʻl.ʻnt.mḥrṯ[-]. | iy.aliyn.bʻl. | iy.zbl.bʻl.arṣ. | w tʻn.nrt.ilm.š[p]š. | šd yn.ʻn.b qb 6[49].4.39
pl.ʻnt.šdm.y špš. | pl.ʻnt.šdm.il.yšt k. | [b]ʻl.ʻnt.mḥrṯt. | iy.aliyn.bʻl. | iy.zbl.bʻl.arṣ. | ttbʻ.btlt.ʻnt. | idk.l ttn.pnm. | ʻm.n 6[49].4.28
pš. | pl.ʻnt.šdm.il.yš[t k]. | bʻl.ʻnt.mḥrṯ[-]. | iy.aliyn.bʻl. | iy.zbl.bʻl.arṣ. | w tʻn.nrt.ilm.š[p]š. | šd yn.ʻn.b qbt[.t] | bl lyt.ʻl. 6[49].4.40
špš. | pl.ʻnt.šdm.il.yšt k. | [b]ʻl.ʻnt.mḥrṯt. | iy.aliyn.bʻl. | iy.zbl.bʻl.arṣ. | ttbʻ.btlt.ʻnt. | idk.l ttn.pnm. | ʻm.nrt.ilm.špš. | tš 6[49].4.29

iybʻl

ḫpn.d.iqni.w.šmt. | l.iybʻl. | ṯlṯm.l.mit.šʻrt. | l.šr.ʻṯtrt. | mlbš.ṯrmnm. | k.yṯn.w.b.bt. | 1107.2

iyʻdm

bt šbn. | iyʻdm.w bʻl h. | ddy. | ʻmy. | iwrnr. | alnr. | maḫdt. | aby. | [-----]. 107[15].2

iyr

.ad[n km.ṯpṭ]. | [nhr.---.]hwt.gmr.hd.l wny[-.---]. | [---.]iyr h.g[-.]thbr[.---]. 2.1[137].47

iyrḏ

. | ʻbdil. | ušy.šbn[-]. | aḫt.ab. | krwn. | nnḏ. | mkl. | kzǵb. | iyrḏ. 1069.18

iyry

. | šmny. | ḫršn. | ldn. | bn.ands. | bn.ann. | bn.ʻbdpdr. | šd.iyry.l.ʻbdbʻl. | šd.šmmn.l.bn.šty. | šd.bn.arws.l.bn.ḫlan. | šd.b 1102.17

iytlm

gš[-]. | bn gbrn. | bn uldy. | synn.bn knʻm. | bn kbr. | bn iytlm. | bn ayln. | bn.kln. | bn.ʻlln. | bn.liy. | bn.nqṭn. | bn abrḫṭ. 1064.21
[--]n. | [q]ṣy. | ṯn.bn.iwrḫz.[n]ʻrm. | yṣr[.-]qb. | w.ṯn.bnš.iytlm. | w.ʻšrm.ṣmd.alpm. 2066.2.6
rʻym.dt.b d.iytlm. | ḫyrn.w.šǵr h. | šǵr.bn.prsn. | agpṯr.w.šǵ[r h]. | ṯʻln. | m 2072.1
mlbi ṯṯ l ʻšrm. | ṣṣ bn adty ḫmšm. | ṣṣ amtrn arbʻm. | ṣṣ iytlm mit ṯlṯm kbd. | ṣṣ m[l]k ʻšrm. | ṣṣ abš[-] mit [ʻš]r kbd. | ṣ 2097.9
. | b d.tlmyn. | b d.gln.ary. | tgyn.yʻrty. | bn.krwn.b.yny.iytlm. | šgryn.ary.b.yny. | bn.yddn.b.rkby. | agyn.agny. | ṯqbn. 2071.5
[--.-]d[-.---]. | [--.šd]m.b d.iyt[lm]. | [šd.b]d.s[--]. | š[d.b]d.u[--]. | šd.b d.[---]. | šd.b d[.--- 2090.2
[-----]. | šd.prsn.l.[---]. | šd.bddn.l.iytlm. | šd.bn.nbʻm.l.ṯpṭbʻl. | šd.bn mšrn.l.ilšpš. | [šd.bn].kbr.l. 2030.1.3
skn.ṯlṯm. | iytlm.ṯlṯm. | ḫyml.ṯlṯm. | ǵlkz.ṯlṯm. | mlknʻm.ʻšrm. | mrʻm.ʻšr 1116.2
bn.--]n. | šd.b d.iwrkl. | šd.b d.klb. | šd.b d.klby. | šd.b d.iytlm. | ṯn.šdm.b d.amtrn. | šd.b d.iwrm[--]. | šd.b d.ytpr. | šd. 2090.11
ṯp[--.---]. | [---.a]ḥt.b d[.---]. | [---.]b d.rb.[m]dlm. | [---.l i]ytlm. | [---].gmn. | [---].l.urǵttb. | [---.]l.ʻṯtrum. | [---.]l.brqn. | [2162.в.3
ḏm[r.---].br. | bn.i[ytlm.---]. | wr[t.---.]b d.yḥmn. | yry[.---.]br. | ydn[.---.]kry. | b 2123.2
spr.[---]. | iytlm[.---]. | ybnn[.---]. | ilšp[š.---]. 2140.2
[--]n.bu[-]bd.ubln. | [---].l.ubl[n]. | [--.]ṯbq.l.iytlm. | [---].l.iytlm. | [---.]ʻbdilm.l.iytlm. | [---.n]ḥl h.lm.iytlm. 1076.3
-].l.ubl[n]. | [--.]ṯbq.l.iytlm. | [---].l.iytlm. | [---.]ʻbdilm.l.iytlm. | [---.n]ḥl h.lm.iytlm. 1076.5
-]n.bu[-]bd.ubln. | [---].l.ubl[n]. | [--.]ṯbq.l.iytlm. | [---].l.iytlm. | [---.]ʻbdilm.l.iytlm. | [---.n]ḥl h.lm.iytlm. 1076.4
[---].i[y]tl[m]. | [---.--]y. | [-----]. | [---.k]d. | [---.]b gt.ḥgb[-]. | [--.]b g 2166.1
ytlm. | [---].l.iytlm. | [---.]ʻbdilm.l.iytlm. | [---.n]ḥl h.lm.iytlm. 1076.6

iyṯr

r. | bn.ʻdy. | bn.amt[m]. | myn. | šr. | bn.zql. | bn.iḫy. | bn.iyṯr. | bn.ʻyn. | bn.ǵzl. | bn.ṣmy. | bn.il[-]šy. | bn.ybšr. | bn.sly. | b 2117.2.5
ilk.r[--]. | aršm.bʻl [aṯt]. | ttḫ.bʻl aṯt. | ayab.bʻl aṯt. | iyṯr.bʻl aṯt. | ptm.bʻl ššlmt. | ʻdršp.bʻl ššlmt. | ṯtrn.bʻl ššlmt. | ar 1077.5
grgš. | w.lmd h. | aršmg. | w.lmd h. | iyṯr. | [w].lmd h. | [yn]ḫm. | [w.]lmd h. | [i]wrmḫ. | [w.]lmd h. 1048.5
ṯn.bn.klby. | bn.iyṯr. | [ʻ]bdyrḫ. | [b]n.ggʻt. | [ʻ]dy. | armwl. | uwaḫ. | ypln.w.ṯn.b 2086.2
[---.]iy[ṯ]r. | [---.ʻbd.y]rḫ. | [---.b]n.mšrn. | [---].bn.lnn. | [-----]. | [---.- 2135.1

ik

h]. | w ṯṣḥ.yṯb.yṯp.[---]. | qrt.ablm.ablm.[qrt.zbl.yrḫ]. | ik.al.yḥdṯ.yrḫ.b[---]. | b qrn.ymn h.b anšt[.---]. | qdqd h.w yʻ 18[3AQHT].4.9
]ʻ.mʻ. | [-.yṯ]ir ṯr.il.ab k.l pn.zbl.ym.l pn[.ṯ]pṭ[.n]hr. | [ik.a]l.yšmʻ k.ṯr.[i]l.ab k.l ysʻ.[alt.]ṯ[bt | k.l y]hpk. | [ksa.]mlk 2.3[129].17
ṣḥ.l mt.šmʻ.mʻ. | l bn.ilm.mt.ik.tmt[ḫ] | ṣ.ʻm.aliyn.bʻl. | ik.al.yšm[ʻ] k.ṯr. | il.ab k.l ysʻ.alt. | ṯbt k.l yhpk.ksa.mlk k. | l 6[49].6.26

ik

krkr. | uṣb‘t h.yšu.g h.w y[ṣḥ]. | ik.mǵyt.rbt.aṯr[t.y]m. | ik.atwt.qnyt.i[lm]. | rǵb.rǵbt.w tǵt[--]. | hm.ǵmu.ǵmit.w ‘s[--] 4[51].4.32
iwrḏr. | l iwrpḫn. | bn y.aḫ y.rgm. | ilm.tǵr k. | tšlm k. | ik y.lḥt. | spr.d likt. | ‘m.ṯryl. | mh y.rgmt. | w ht.aḫ y. | bn y.yš 138.6
tḥm.rgm. | mlk. | l ḥyil. | lm.tlik.‘m y. | ik y.aškn. | ‘ṣm.l bt.dml. | p ank.atn. | ‘ṣm.l k. | arb‘.‘ṣm. | ‘l.ar. 1010.5
[š.---]. | ql.[---]. | w mlk[.nhš.w mlk.mg]šḫ. | ‘mn.[---]. | ik y.[---]. | w l n[qmd.---]. | [w]nqmd.[---]. | [-.]‘mn.šp[š.mlk.r 64[118].8
-.---]. | b ql[.-----]. | w tštqdn[.-----]. | hm. | w yḥ.mlk. | w ik m.kn.w [---]. | tšknnnn[.---]. 62[26].10
ap.ab.k mtm. | tmtn.u ḫšt k.l ntn. | ‘tq.b d.aṯt.ab.ṣrry. | ik m.yrgm.bn.il. | krt.špḥ.lṭpn. | w qdš.u ilm.tmtn. | špḥ.lṭpn.l 16.1[125].20
[i]k.mgn.rbt.aṯrt. | [ym].mǵẓ.qnyt.ilm. | w tn.bt.l b‘l.km. | [i]l 8[51FRAG].1
nn.rbt[.a]ṯrt ym. | tǵẓyn.qnyt.ilm. | w t‘n.rbt.aṯrt ym. | ik.tmgnn.rbt. | aṯrt.ym.tǵẓyn. | qnyt.ilm.mgntm. | ṯr.il.d pid.h 4[51].3.28
[l]krt. | k [k]lb.b bt k.n‘tq.k inr. | ap.ḫšt k.ap.ab.ik mtm. | tmtn.u ḫšt k.l ntn. | ‘tq.b d.aṯt.ab ṣrry. | tbky k.ab.ǵ 16.1[125].3
.mḫṣ.ǵlmm.yš[--]. | [ymn h.‘n]t.tuḫd.šmal h.tuḫd.‘ṯtrt.ik.m[ḫṣt.ml]] | [ak.ym.t‘]dt.ṯpṭ.nhr.mlak.mṯḫr.yḥb[-.---.]] | [--- 2.1[137].40
m.mt.ql. | b‘l.ql.‘ln.špš. | tṣḥ.l mt.šm‘.m‘. | l bn.ilm.mt.ik.tmt[ḫ] | ṣ.‘m.aliyn.b‘l. | ik.al.yšm[‘] k.ṯr. | il.ab k.l ys‘.alt. | ṯ 6[49].6.24
h.td[‘]. | tǵṣ[.pnt.ks]l h. | anš.dt.ẓr.[h]. | tšu.g h.w tṣḥ[.i]k. | mǵy.aliy[n.b]‘l. | ik.mǵyt.b[t]lt. | ‘nt.mḫṣ y hm[.m]ḫṣ. | b 4[51].2.21
h. | anš.dt.ẓr.[h]. | tšu.g h.w tṣḥ[.i]k. | mǵy.aliy[n.b]‘l. | ik.mǵyt.b[t]lt. | ‘nt.mḫṣ y hm[.m]ḫṣ. | bn y.hm[.mkly.ṣ]brt. | 4[51].2.23
| ‘ln.pn h.td‘.tǵṣ.pnt. | ksl h.anš.dt.ẓr h.tšu. | g h.w tṣḥ.ik.mǵy.gpn.w ugr. | mn.ib.yp‘.l b‘l.ṣrt. | l rkb.‘rpt.l mḫšt.md 3[‘NT].3.33
| p‘n h.l hdm.yṯpd.w ykrkr. | uṣb‘t h.yšu.g h.w y[ṣḥ]. | ik.mǵyt.rbt.aṯr[t.y]m. | ik.atwt.qnyt.i[lm]. | rǵb.rǵbt.w tǵt[--] 4[51].4.31
t.‘bd k.an. | w d ‘lm k.šmḫ.bn.ilm.mt. | [---.]g h.w aṣḥ.ik.yṣḥn. | [b‘l.‘m.aḫ y.ik].yqrun.hd. | [‘m.ary y.---.--]p.mlḥm 5[67].2.21
.šmḫ.bn.ilm.mt. | [---.]g h.w aṣḥ.ik.yṣḥn. | [b‘l.‘m.aḫ y.ik].yqrun.hd. | [‘m.ary y.---.--]p.mlḥm y. | [---.---]lt.qẓb. | [---. 5[67].2.22

iky

.iwrḏr. | l iwrpḫn. | bn y.aḫ y.rgm. | ilm.tǵr k. | tšlm k. | iky.lḥt. | spr.d likt. | ‘m.ṯryl. | mh y.rgmt. | w ht.aḫ y. | bn y.yš 138.6

ikrn

[-----]. | ubyn[.---]. | annt[n.---]. | ipṯn[.---]. | ybni[l.---]. | ikrn[.---]. | tlmyn[.---]. | tldn[.---]. | annḏr[.---]. | [-]m[--.---]. 106[332].6

il

[l k]rt. | [--].ml[k.---]. | [---]m.k[---]. | [-----]. | [---]m.il[.---]. | [---]d nhr.umt. | [---.]rpat.bt. | [m]lk.itdb.d šb‘. | [a]ḫ 14[KRT].1.5
[-----]. | [---.--]y. | [-----]. | [any.l yṣ]ḥ.ṯr. | [il.ab h.i]l.mlk. | [d yknn h.yṣ]ḥ.aṯ | [rt.w bn h.]ilt. | [w ṣbrt.ar 4[51].1.5
klny n.q[š] h.n[bln]. | klny n[.n]bl.ks h. | [an]y.l yṣḥ.ṯr il.ab h. | [i]l.mlk.d yknn h.yṣḥ. | aṯrt.w bn h.ilt.w ṣbrt. | ary h. 4[51].4.47
‘ln h.klny y.qš h. | nbln.klny y.nbl.ks h. | any.l yṣḥ.ṯr.il.ab h.il. | mlk.d yknn h.yṣḥ.aṯrt. | w bn h.ilt.w ṣbrt.arḫ h. | 3[‘NT.VI].5.43
g‘r.ṯǵr. | bt.il.pn.l mgr lb.t‘dbn. | nšb.l inr.t‘dbn.ktp. | b il ab h.g‘r.ytb.il.kb[-]. | aṯ[rt.]il.ytb.b mrzḥ h. | yšt[.il.y]n.‘d š UG5.1.1.14
m.[--.-]llm.trtḥṣ. | btlt.‘n[t].tptr‘ ṭd[h]. | limm.w t‘l.‘m.il. | ab h.ḥpr.p‘l k.y[--]. | šm‘ k.l arḫ.w bn.[--]. | limm.ql.b udn 13[6].20
ṣn.k ṯrm. | [--]b b[ht]. | [zbl.]ym.b hkl.ṯpṭ.nh[r].ytir.ṯr.il.ab h l pn[.zb]l y[m]. | [l pn.ṯp]ṭ[.nhr.]mlkt.[--]pm.l mlkt.w 2.3[129].21
šnm.l [p‘n.il.yhbr.w yql]. | yšṯḥwy.[w ykbdn h.---]. | ṯr.il[.ab h.---]. | ḥš b[ht m.tbnn.ḥš.trmmn.hkl m]. | b tk.[---]. | b 1[‘NT.IX].3.26
[.šnm.]mṣr. | [t]bu.ḏdm.qn[-.-]n[-.-]lt. | ql h.yš[m‘].ṯr.[il].ab h.[---]l. | b šb‘t.ḥdrm.[b ṯ]mn[t.ap]. | sgrt.g[-].[-]ẓ[.---] h 3[‘NT.VI].5.18
k.l ytbr.ḥṭ.mṯpṭ k.w y‘n[.‘ṯtr].dm[-]k[-]. | [--]ḥ.b y.ṯr.il.ab y.ank.in.bt[.l] y[.km.]ilm[.w] ḥẓr[.k bn]. | [qd]š.lbum.tr 2.3[129].19
y h.uzrm.ilm.ylḥm. | uzrm.yšqy.bn.qdš. | l tbrknn l ṯr.il ab y. | tmrnn.l bny.bnwt. | w ykn.bn h b bt.šrš.b qrb. | hkl h 17[2AQHT].1.24
]. | bt.y‘bdr[.mṯb.klt]. | knyt.w t‘n[.btlt.‘nt]. | ytb l y.ṯr.il[.ab y.---]. | ytb.l y.w l h.[---]. | [--.i]mṣḫ.nn.k imr.l arṣ. | [ašh 3[‘NT.VI].4.7
w yql.yšt]ḥwyn.w y | [kbdn h.yšu.g h.w y]ṣḥ.tḥm. | [ṯr.il.ab k.hwt.l]ṭpn.ḥtk k. | [qryy.b arṣ.mlḥ]mt.št b ‘p | [r m.ddy 1[‘NT.IX].2.18
t]. | w rgm l k[ṯr.w ḫss.ṯny.l hyn]. | d ḥrš.y[dm.tḥm.ṯr.il.ab k.] | hwt.lṭpn[.ḥtk k.---]. | yh.kṯr.b[---]. | št.lskt.n[--.---]. 1[‘NT.IX].3.5
idk.l ttn.pnm. | ‘m.nrt.ilm.špš. | tšu.g h.w tṣḥ. | tḥm.ṯr.il.ab k. | hwt.lṭpn.ḥtk k. | pl.‘nt.šdm.y špš. | pl.‘nt.šdm.il.yš[t 6[49].4.34
bn.ilm.mt.ik.tmt[ḫ] | ṣ.‘m.aliyn.b‘l. | ik.al.yšm[‘] k.ṯr. | il.ab k.l ys‘.alt. | ṯbt k.l yhpk.ksa.mlk k. | l ytbr.ḥṭ.mṯpṭ k. | yr 6[49].6.27
.il.ab k.l pn.zbl.ym.l pn[.ṯ]pṭ[.n]hr. | [ik.a]l.yšm‘ k.ṯr.[i]l.ab k.l ys‘.[alt.]ṯ[bt | k.l y]hpk. | [ksa.]mlk k.l ytbr.ḥṭ.mṯpṭ 2.3[129].17
[---.-]nn.nrt.ilm.špš.tšu.g h.w t[ṣḥ.šm]‘.m‘. | [-.yṯ]ir ṯr.il.ab k.l pn.zbl.ym.l pn[.ṯ]pṭ[.n]hr. | [ik.a]l.yšm‘ k.ṯr.[i]l.ab k 2.3[129].16
-]kn. | [---.]hr n.km.šḥr. | [---.y]lt n.km.qdm. | [-.k]bd n.il.ab n. | kbd k iš.tikln. | ṯd n.km.mrm.tqrṣn. | il.yẓḥq.bm. | lb. 12[75].1.9
tr[.il.ab -.w t‘n.rbt]. | aṯr[t.ym.šm‘.l qdš]. | w am[rr.l dgy.rbt]. | a 4[51].4.1
| ṯrmn w šnm. | il w aṯrt. | ḫnn il. | nṣbt il. | šlm il. | il ḥš il add. | b‘l ṣpn b‘l. | ugrt. | b mrḥ il. | b nit il. | b ṣmd il. | b dṯn 30[107].9
.niṣ k.gr[š.d ‘šy.ln k]. | spu.ksm k.bt.[b‘l.w mnt k]. | bt il.aḥd.yd k.b [škrn]. | m‘ms k.k šb‘t.yn.ṯ[ḫ]. | gg k.b ym.ṭiṭ.rḥ 17[2AQHT].2.5
m[m.al.ttb.idk.pnm]. | al.ttn.‘m.pḫr.m‘d.t[k.ǵr.ll.l p‘n.il]. | al.tpl.al.tšṯḥwy.pḫr [m‘d.qmm.a--.am] | r ṯny.d‘t km.w r 2.1[137].14
dbḥ.ṣp[n.---]. | il.alp.w š[.---]. | b‘lm.alp.w š[.---]. | b‘lm.alp.w š[.---]. | arṣ.w š UG5.9.1.2
‘[d.qlt]. | ankn.rgmt.l.b‘l y. | l.špš.‘lm.l.‘ṯtrt. | l.‘nt.l.kl.il.alṯ[y]. | nmry.mlk.‘lm. | mlk n.b‘l y.ḥw[t.--]. | yšhr k.w.‘m.ṣ 2008.1.8
nm.mṯ yd k.hl.‘ṣr. | ṯḥrr.l išt.w ṣḥrt.l pḥmm.aṯtm.a[ṯt.il]. | aṯt.il.w ‘lm h.yhbr.špt hm.yš[q]. | hn.špt hm.mtqtm.mtq 23[52].48
.mṯ.yd k. | h[l.]‘ṣr.tḥrr.l išt.ṣḥrrt.l pḥmm. | a[ṯ]tm.aṯt.il.aṯt.il.w ‘lm h.w hm. | aṯtm.tṣḥn y.ad ad.nḥtm.ḥṭ k. | mmnn 23[52].42
mṯ.yd h.yšu. | yr.šmm h.yr.b šmm.‘ṣr.yḫrṭ yšt. | l pḥm.il.aṯtm.k ypt.hm.aṯtm.tṣḥn. | y mt.mt.nḥtm.ḥṭ k.mmnnm.m 23[52].39
rkm.ybrk. | [‘bd h.]ybrk.il.krt. | [ṯ‘.ymr]m.n‘m[n.]ǵlm.il. | a[ṯt.tq]ḥ.y krt.aṯt. | tqḥ.bt k.ǵlmt.tš‘rb. | ḥqr k.tld.šb‘.bnm 15[128].2.20
rt bn il. | ṯrmn w šnm. | il w aṯrt. | ḫnn il. | nṣbt il. | šlm il. | il ḥš il add. | b‘l ṣpn b‘l. | ugrt. | b mrḥ il. | b nit il. | b ṣmd il 30[107].8
-----]. | il.šm‘.amr k.ph[-]. | k il.ḥkmt.k ṯr.lṭpn. | ṣḥ.ngr.il.ilš.il[š]. | w aṯt h.ngrt[.i]lht. | kḥṣ.k m‘r[.---]. | yṣḥ.ngr il.ilš. 16[126].4.4
.b‘l. | w aṯt h.ngrt.ilht. | w y‘n.lṭpn.il d pi[d]. | šm‘.l ngr.il il[š]. | ilš.ngr bt b‘l. | w aṯt k.ngrt.il[ht]. | ‘l.l ṯkm.bnw n. | l n 16[126].4.11
l.ilš.il[š]. | w aṯt h.ngrt[.i]lht. | kḥṣ.k m‘r[.---]. | yṣḥ.ngr il.ilš. | ilš.ngr.bt.b‘l. | w aṯt h.ngrt.ilht. | w y‘n.lṭpn.il d pi[d]. | 16[126].4.7
m.]al.t[ṣr]. | udm[.r]bt.w u[dm]. | [ṯ]rrt.udm.y[ṯ]n[t]. | il.ušn.ab[.ad]m. | rḥq.mlk.l bt y. | n[g.]krt.l ḥẓ[r y]. | w y‘n[y. 14[KRT].6.278
ṯn.gprm.mn gpr h.šr. | aqht.y‘n.kmr.kmr[.--]. | k ap‘.il.b gdrt.k lb.l | ḥṭ h.imḫṣ h.k d.‘l.qšt h. | imḫṣ h.‘l.qṣ‘t h.hwt 19[1AQHT].1.13
ḥš il add. | b‘l ṣpn b‘l. | ugrt. | b mrḥ il. | b nit il. | b ṣmd il. | b dṯn il. | b šrp il. | b knt il. | b ǵdyn il. | [b]n [---]. 30[107].14
b]dym.ṯlṯ.kkr š‘rt. | iqn[i]m.ṯṯt.‘šrt.ksp h. | ḫmšt.ḥrṣ.bt.il. | b.ḫmšt.‘šrt.ksp. | ḫmš.mat.šmt. | b.‘šrt.ksp. | ‘šr.ṣin.b.ṯṯt.w. 2100.5
l.d]pid.l tbrk. | [krt.]ṯ‘.l tmr.n‘mn. | [ǵlm.]il.ks.yiḫd. | [il.b]yd.krpn.bm. | [ymn.]brkm.ybrk. | [‘bd h.]ybrk.il.krt. | [ṯ‘. 15[128].2.17
b‘l. | ugrt. | b mrḥ il. | b nit il. | b ṣmd il. | b dṯn il. | b šrp il. | b knt il. | b ǵdyn il. | [b]n [---]. 30[107].16

[.---].|yd k.ṣǵr.tnšq.špt k.ṯm.|ṯkm.bm ṯkm.aẖm.qym.il.|b lsmt.ṯm.yṯbš.šm.il.mt m.|y‘bš.brk n.šm.il.ǵzrm.|ṯm.ṯ 22.2[124].5
|nṣbt il.|šlm il.|il ḥš il add.|b‘l ṣpn b‘l.|ugrt.|b mrḥ il.|b nit il.|b ṣmd il.|b dṯn il.|b šrp il.|b knt il.|b ǵdyn il.|[30[107].12
|b mrḥ il.|b nit il.|b ṣmd il.|b dṯn il.|b šrp il.|b knt il.|b ǵdyn il.|[b]n [---]. 30[107].17
šlm il.|il ḥš il add.|b‘l ṣpn b‘l.|ugrt.|b mrḥ il.|b nit il.|b ṣmd il.|b dṯn il.|b šrp il.|b knt il.|b ǵdyn il.|[b]n [---]. 30[107].13
qdqd k.ašhlk.šbt[k.dmm].|[šbt.dqn k.mm‘m.]y‘ny.|il.b šb‘t.ḥdrm.b ṯmnt.|ap.sgrt.yd‘[t k.]bt.k an[št].|k in.b ilh 3['NT.VI].5.34
.|b‘l ṣpn b‘l.|ugrt.|b mrḥ il.|b nit il.|b ṣmd il.|b dṯn il.|b šrp il.|b knt il.|b ǵdyn il.|[b]n [---]. 30[107].15
il b[n] il.|dr bn il.|mpẖrt bn il.|ṯrmn w šnm.|il w aṯrt.|ẖn 30[107].1
s.b yd].|krpn.b klat yd.[---].|km ll.kḥṣ.tusp[.---].|tgr.il.bn h.ṯr[.---].|w y‘n.lṭpn.il.d p[id.---].|šm.bn y.yw.ilt.[---]. 1['NT.X].4.12
b nit il.|b ṣmd il.|b dṯn il.|b šrp il.|b knt il.|b ǵdyn il.|[b]n [---]. 30[107].18
nnm.mṭ yd k.hl.‘ṣr.tḥrr.l išt.|w ṣḥrrt.l pḥmm.btm.bt.il.bt.il.|w ‘lm h.w hn.aṯtm.tṣḥn y.mt mt.|nḥtm.ẖṭ k.mmnn 23[52].45
bt.il.|b‘l.bt.aḏmny.|b‘l.bt.pdy.|b‘l.bt.nqly.|b‘l.bt.‘lr.|b‘l.bt.ssl 31[14].1
bm.arr.w b ṣpn.|b n‘m.b ǵr.t[l]iyt.|ql.l b‘l.ttnn.|bšrt.il.bš[r.b‘]l.|w bšr.ḥtk.dgn.|k.ibr.l b‘l[.yl]d.|w rum.l rkb.‘rp 10[76].3.34
[---.]tṯṯbn.ilm.w.[---].|[---.]w.ksu.b‘lt.b[htm.---].|[---.]il.bt.gdlt.[---].|[---.]hkl[.---]. 47[33].8
mn[t].|y.bt.il.ṯẖ.gg y.b ym.ṭiṭ.|rḥṣ.npṣ y.b ym.rṯ.|dn.il.bt h.ymǵyn.|yštql.dnil.l hkl h.|‘rb.b bt h.kṯrt.bnt.|hll.sn 17[2AQHT].2.24
.|l bbt il bt.|š l ẖlmṭ.|w tr l qlḥ.|w š ḥll ydm.|b qdš il bt.|w tlḥm aṯt.|š l ilbt.šlmm.|kll ylḥm b h.|w l bbt šqym UG5.7.TR3
id ydbḥ mlk.|l ušẖ[r] ẖlmṭ.|l bbt il bt.|š l ẖlmṭ.|w tr l qlḥ.|w š ḥll ydm.|b qdš il bt.|w tlḥm UG5.7.TR3
atdb w ‘r.|qdš w amrr.|ṯẖr w bd.|[k]ṯr ẖss šlm.|šlm il bt.|šlm il ẖš[t].|ršp inšt.|[--]rm il [---].|[---.--]m šlm [---]. UG5.7.72
l.[----].|l.‘ṯ[trt.---].|l.mš[--.---].|l.ilt[.---].|l.b‘lt[.---].|l.il.bt[.---].|l.ilt.[---].|l.ḥtk[.---].|l.ršp[.---].|[l].ršp.[---.--]g.kb 1004.7
dqt.ṯ‘.ynt.ṯ‘m.dqt.ṯ‘m.|mtntm nkbd.alp.š.l il.|gdlt.ilhm.ṯkmn.w šnm dqt.|ršp.dqt.šrp w šlmm.dqtm.|[34[1].2
b‘.|trṯ.‘d.škr.y‘db.yrẖ.|gb h.km.[---.]yqṭqṭ.tḥt.|ṯlḥnt.il.d yd‘nn.|y‘db.lḥm.l h.w d l yd‘nn.|d.mṣd.|ylmn.ẖṭ.tḥt.ṯl UG5.1.1.6
.id.|d prša.b br.|n‘l.il.d qblbl.|‘ln.ybl hm.ẖrṣ.|ṯlḥn.il.d mla.|mnm.dbbm.d |msdt.arṣ.|s‘.il.dqt.k amr.|sknt.k ḥ 4[51].1.39
.--]n b ym.qẓ.|[---.]ym.tlḥmn.|[---.rp]um.tštyn.|[---.]il.d ‘rgzm.|[---.]dt.‘l.lty.|[---.]tdbḥ.amr.|ṯmn.b qrb.hkl y.[a 20[121].1.8
hm.ḥy.a[liyn.b‘l].|w hm.iṯ.zbl.b‘[l.arṣ].|b ḥlm.lṭpn.il.d pid.|b ḏrt.bny.bnwt.|šmm.šmn.tmṭrn.|nẖlm.tlk.nbtm. 6[49].3.4
btm.|w id‘.k ḥy.aliyn.b‘l.|k iṯ.zbl.b‘l.arṣ.|b ḥlm.lṭpn.il d pid.|b ḏrt.bny.bnwt.|šmm.šmn.tmṭrn.|nẖlm.tlk.nbtm. 6[49].3.10
lkn.|w t‘n.rbt.aṯrt ym.|bl.nmlk.yd‘.ylḥn.|w y‘n.lṭpn.il d pi|d dq.anm.l yrẓ.|‘m.b‘l.l y‘db.mrḥ.|‘m.bn.dgn.k tms 6.1.49[49.1.21]
.|ik.tmgnn.rbt.|aṯrt.ym.tǵẓyn.|qnyt.ilm.mgntm.|ṯr.il.d pid.hm.ǵẓtm.|bny.bnwt w t‘n.|btlt.‘nt.nmgn.|[-]m.rbt. 4[51].3.31
nt h|ll b‘l gml.yrdt.|b ‘rgzm.b bz tdm.|lla y.‘m lẓpn i|l ḏ.pid.hn b p y sp|r hn.b špt y mn|t hn ṯlẖ h w mlg h y| 24[77].44
lṭ k.bn[.dnil.---].|w y‘ḏr k.b yd.btlt.[‘nt].|w y‘n.lṭpn.il d p[id].|yd‘t k.bt.k anšt.w i[n.b ilht].|qlṣ k.tb‘.bt.ẖnp.lb[18[3AQHT].1.15
b‘l.npl.l a|rṣ.mt.aliyn.b‘l.|ẖlq.zbl.b‘l.arṣ.|apnk.lṭpn.il.|d pid.yrd.l ksi.yṯb.|l hdm[.w] l.hdm.yṯb.|l arṣ.yṣq.‘mr.| 5[67].6.11
ilm.|ydy.mrṣ.gršm zbln.|in.b ilm.‘ny h.|w y‘n.lṭpn.il.b pid.|ṯb.bn y.lm ṯb[t] km.|l kḥṯ.zbl k[m.a]nk.|iḥtrš.w [a 16[126].5.23
ẖ]r.mǵy.‘[d]t.ilm.|[w]y‘n.aliy[n.]b‘l.|[---.]tb‘.l lṭpn.|[il.d]pid.l tbrk.|[krt.]ṯ‘.l tmr.n‘mn.|[ǵlm.]il.ks.yiẖd.|[il.b]y 15[128].2.14
ṯr[.---].|b d k.[---].|ṯnnt h[.---].|ṯlṯt h[.-.w y‘n].|lṭpn.[il.d pid.my].|b ilm.[ydy.mrṣ].|gršm.z[bln.in.b ilm].|‘ny h.y 16[126].5.10
pyn h.b nhrm.|štt.ẖptr.l išt.|ẖbrṯ.l ẓr.pḥmm.|t‘pp.ṯr.il.d pid.|tǵẓy.bny.bnwt.|b nši.‘n h.w tphn.|hlk.b‘l.aṯtrt.|k 4[51].2.10
ry.bt.ar.|mẓll.ṭly.bt rb.|mṯb.arṣ.bt y‘bdr.|w y‘n lṭpn il d pid.|p ‘bd.an.‘nn.aṯrt.|p.‘bd.ank.aẖd.ulṯ.|hm.amt.aṯrt.t 4[51].4.58
y.bnwt.|šmm.šmn.tmṭrn.|nẖlm.tlk.nbtm.|šmẖ.lṭpn.il.d pid.|p‘n h.l hdm.yṯpd.|w yprq.lṣb w yṣḥq.|yšu.g h.w y 6[49].3.14
.ngr il.ilš.|ilš.ngr.bt.b‘l.|w aṯt h.ngrt.ilht.|w y‘n.lṭpn.il d pi[d].|šm‘.l ngr.il il[š].|ilš.ngr bt b‘l.|w aṯt k.ngrt.il[ht]. 16[126].4.10
.tḥt.[‘nt.arṣ.ṯlṯ.mtḥ].|ǵyrm.idk.l yt[n.pnm.‘m.lṭpn].|il d pid.tk ẖrš[n.---.tk.ǵr.ks].|ygly ḏd.i[l.w ybu.qrš.mlk].|ab 1['NT.IX].3.22
bẖr.|[---].aṯt k.‘l.|[---] k.yšṣi.|[---.]ẖbr.rbt.|[ẖbr.ṯrr]t.il d.|[pid.---].b anšt.|[---.]mlu.|[---.--]tm. 15[128].5.26
m[-.---].|t‘nyn.l zn.tn[.---].|at.adn.tp‘r[.---].|ank.lṭpn.il[.d pid.---].|‘l.ydm.p‘rt[.---].|šm k.mdd.i[l.---].|bt ksp y.d[1['NT.X].4.18
-].|km ll.kḥṣ.tusp[.---].|tgr.il.bn h.ṯr[.---].|w y‘n.lṭpn.il.d p[id.---].|šm.bn y.yw.ilt.[---].|w p‘r.šm.ym[-.---].|t‘nyn. 1['NT.X].4.13
t.b dm.ẖrṣ.|kḥṯ.il.nẖt.|b ẓr.hdm.id.|d prša.b br.|n‘l.il.d qblbl.|‘ln.ybl hm.ẖrṣ.|ṯlḥn.il.d mla.|mnm.dbbm.d |ms 4[51].1.37
b‘t.b ymn h.w y‘n.yṭ[p]n[.mh]r.|št.b yn.yšt.ila.il š[--.]il.|d yqny.ḏdm.yd.mẖṣt.a[qh]t.ǵ|zr.tmẖṣ.alpm.ib.št[-.]št.| 19[1AQHT].4.219
q.ksp.|l alpm.ẖrṣ.yṣq|m.l rbbt.|yṣq-ẖym.w tbṯẖ.|kt.il.dt.rbtm.|kt.il.nbt.b ksp.|šmrgt.b dm.ẖrṣ.|kḥṯ.il.nẖt.|b ẓr 4[51].1.31
il dbḥ.b bt h.mṣd.ṣd.b qrb|hkl [h].ṣḥ.l qṣ.ilm.tlḥmn.|ilm.w UG5.1.1.1
ṯ].|drkt h.š[--.--].|w hm.ap.l[--.---].|ymẖṣ k.k[--.---].|il.dbḥ.[---].|p‘r.b[--.---].|ṭbẖ.alp[m.ap.ṣin.šql].|ṯrm.w [mri.i 1['NT.X].4.28
il ṣpn.|il[i]b.|i[l].|dgn.|b‘[l ṣ]pn.|b‘lm.|[b‘]lm.|[b‘]lm.|[b‘]lm.|[b‘]lm.|[29[17].1.3
‘ṯtpr.|šḥr w šlm.|ngh w srr.|‘dw šr.|ṣdqm šr.|ḥnbn il d[n].|[-]bd w [---].|[--].p il[.---].|[i]l mt mr[b-].|qdš mlk [UG5.10.1.15
l hm.ẖrṣ.|ṯlḥn.il.d mla.|mnm.dbbm.d |msdt.arṣ.|s‘.il.dqt.k amr.|sknt.k ḥwt.yman.|d b h.rumm.l rbbt. 4[51].1.42
[.---.rš]|[p.š]rp.w šl[mm.--.dqt].|[i]lh.gdlt[.ilhm.gdlt.il].|[d]qt.ṯkmn.w [šnm.dqt.--].|[--]t.dqtm.[b nbk.---].|[--.k] 35[3].30
m.---].dq[t.ilh.gdlt].|n.w šnm.dqt[.---].|[i]lh[m.gd]lt.i[l.dqt.ṯkm]|n.w šnm.dqt[.---].|bqtm.b nbk.[---].|kmm.gdlt APP.II[173].33
il b[n] il.|dr bn il.|mpẖrt bn il.|ṯrmn w šnm.|il w aṯrt.|ẖnn il.|nṣ 30[107].1
amt.|[tn.b]nm.aqny.|[tn.ṯa]rm.amid.|[w y‘n].ṯr.ab h.il.|d[--].b bk.krt.|b dm‘.n‘mn.ǵlm.|il.trḥṣ.w tadm.|rḥṣ[.y]d 14[KRT].2.59
.b d k t[---].|rbt.‘l.ydm[.---].|b mdd.il.y[--.---].|b ym.il.d[--.---.n]|hr.il.y[--.---].|aliyn.[b‘l.---].|btlt.[‘nt.---].|mh.k 4[51].2.35
dd ilm.ar[š].|ṣmt.‘gl.il.‘tk.|mẖšt.klbt.ilm išt.|klt.bt.il.ḏbb.imtẖṣ.ksp.|itrṯ.ẖrṣ.ṭrd.b‘l.|b mrym.ṣpn.mšṣṣ.[-]k‘[-]. 3['NT].3.43
l.|[---.--]n.il ǵnṯ.‘gl il.|[---.--]d.il.šd yṣd mlk.|[---].yšt.il h.|[---.]iṯm h.|[---.y]mǵy.|[---.]dr h.|[---.-]rš.l b‘l.|[---.-]ǵ UG5.2.1.13
-.tk.ǵr.ks].|ygly ḏd.i[l.w ybu.qrš.mlk].|ab.šnm.l [p‘n.il.yhbr.w yql].|yštḥwy.[w ykbdn h.---].|ṯr.il[.ab h.---].|ḥš b 1['NT.IX].3.24
.thmtm].|[ygly.]ḏl i[l].w ybu[.q]rš.mlk[.ab.šnm.l p‘n.il.]|[yhbr.]w yql[.y]štḥw[y.]w ykb[dn h.--]r y[---].|[---.k]ṯr. 2.3[129].5
.apq.thmtm.|tgly.ḏd.il.w tbu.|qrš.mlk.ab.šnm.|l p‘n.il.thbr.w tql.|tštḥwy.w tkbd h.|hlm.il.k yphn h.|yprq.lṣb. 4[51].4.25
]pq.thmtm.tgly.ḏd.|il.w tbu.qrš..|mlk.ab.šnm.l p‘n.|il.thbr.w tql.|tštḥwy.w tkbdn h.|tšu.g h.w tṣḥ.tšmẖ ht.|aṯr 6.1.37[49.1.9]
p]q.thmtm tgly.ḏd il.|[w tbu.qr]š.mlk.ab.šnm.|[l p‘n.il.t]hbr.w tql.tštḥ|[wy.w tkbd]n h.tlšn.aqht.ǵzr.|[---.kdd.dn 17[2AQHT].6.50
d m.yḥmd m.|bn.dgn.yhrr m.|b‘l.ngṯ hm.b p‘n h.|w il hd.b ẖrẓ‘ h.|[-----].|[--]t.[---].|[---.]‘n[.---].|pnm[.---].|b‘l. 12[75].1.41
[---.b‘l.b bht h].|[il.hd.b qr]b.hkl h.|w t‘nyn.ǵlm.b‘l.|in.b‘l.b bht ht.|il hd.b 10[76].2.2
|[il.hd.b qr]b.hkl h.|w t‘nyn.ǵlm.b‘l.|in.b‘l.b bht ht.|il hd.b qrb.hkl h.|qšt hn.aẖd.b yd h.|w qṣ‘t h.bm.ymn h.|i 10[76].2.5

-].|t[---.---].|[-----].|[-----].|b [----].|w [----].|b‘l.[---].|il hd.b[---].|at.bl.at.[---].|yisp hm.b[‘l.---].|bn.dgn[.---].|‘ḏ 12[75].2.23
m.ḥ[--]k.ǵrt.|[ql].l b‘l.‘nt.ttnn.|[---].b‘l m.d ip[---].|[il.]hd.d ‘nn.n[--].|[----.]aliyn.b[‘l].|[---.btl]t.‘n[t.-.]p h.|[---.- 10[76].2.33
qnym.‘l[m.--].|k dr d.d yknn[.--].|b‘l.yṣǵd.mli[.--].|il hd.mla.u[--.--].|blt.p btlt.‘n[t].|w p.n‘mt.aẖt[.b‘l].|y‘l.b‘l. 10[76].3.9
[-----].|[--]t.[---].|[---.]‘n[.---].|pnm[.---].|b‘l.n[--. --].|il.hd[.---].|at.bl[.at.---].|ḥmd m.[---].|il.hr[r.---].|kb[-.---].| 12[75].2.6
-].|aṯ[rt.]il.yṯb.b mrzḥ h.|yšt[.il.y]n.‘d šb‘.trṯ.‘d škr.|il.hlk.l bt h.yštql.|l ḥṭr h.y‘msn.nn.ṯkmn.|w šnm.w ngšnn. UG5.1.1.17
‘m.phr.m‘d.ap.ilm.l lḥ[m].|yṯb.bn qdš.l ṯrm.b‘l.qm.‘l.il.hlm.|ilm.tph hm.tphn.mlak.ym.t‘dt.ṯpṭ[.nhr].|t[ǵ]ly.hlm. 2.1[137].21
.srnm.yn.bld.|ǵll.yn.išryt.‘nq.smd.|lbnn.ṭl mrṯ.yḥrṯ.il.|hn.ym.w ṯn.tlḥmn.rpum.|tštyn.ṯlṯ.rb‘.ym.ẖmš.|ṯdṯ.ym.t 22.2[124].20
-].|b‘l.n[--.---].|il.hd[.---].|at.bl[.at.---].|ḥmd m.[---].|il.hr[r.---].|kb[-.---].|ym.[---].|yšḥr[.---].|yikl[.---].|km.s[--. 12[75].2.10
il b[n] il.|dr bn il.|mpẖrt bn il.|ṯrmn w šnm.|il w aṯrt.|ẖnn il.|nṣbt il.|šlm il.|il ḥš il add.|b‘l ṣpn b‘l.|ug 30[107].5
q.krt.|l ḥẓr y.al.tṣr.|udm.rbt.w udm ṯrrt.|udm.ytnt.il w ušn.|ab.adm.w ṯṯb.|mlakm.l h.lm.ank.|ksp.w yrq.ẖrṣ. 14[KRT].3.135
.|[šlmm.al.tṣr].|[udm.rbt.w udm].|[ṯrrt.udm.ytnt].|[il.w ušn.ab.adm].|[rḥq.mlk.l bt y].|[ng.kr]t.l ḥ[ẓ]r y.|[-----] 14[KRT].5.259
--.---].|[--.-]g[-.-]s w [---].|w yn[t.q]rt.y[---].|w al[p.l]il.w bu[rm.---].|ytk.gdlt.ilhm.[ṯkmn.w šnm].|dqt.ršp.šrp.w 35[3].11
].|t.k[-]ml.[---].|l[---].w y[nt.qrt.---].|[---.--]n[.w alp.l il.w bu]|[rm.---.ytk.gdlt.ilhm].|ṯkmn.w [šnm.dqt.ršp.šrp].| APP.II[173].12
.pnm.‘m.|[il.]mbk nhrm.qrb.|[a]pq.thmtm.tgly.ḏd.|il.w tbu.qrš..|mlk.ab.šnm.l p‘n.|il.thbr.w tql.|tštḥwy.w tkb 6.1.35[49.1.7]
ttn.pnm.|‘m.il.mbk.nhrm.|qrb.apq.thmtm.|tgly.ḏd.il.w tbu.|qrš.mlk.ab.šnm.|l p‘n.il.thbr.w tql.|tštḥwy.w tkb 4[51].4.23
pnm].|[‘m.il.mbk.nhrm].|[qrb.apq.thmtm].|[tgly.ḏd.il.w]tb[a].|[qrš.mlk.ab.]šnm.|[tša.g hm.w tṣ]ḥ.sbn.|[---]l[.- 5[67].6.1
tn.pnm.‘m.[i]l.mbk.[nhrm.qrb.apq.thmtm].|[ygly.]ḏl i[l].w ybu[.q]rš.mlk[.ab.šnm.l p‘n.il.]|[yhbr.]w yql[.y]štḥw[2.3[129].5
.pnm.‘m.lṭpn].|il d pid.tk ẖrš[n.---.tk.ǵr.ks].|ygly ḏd.i[l.w ybu.qrš.mlk].|ab.šnm.l [p‘n.il.yhbr.w yql].|yštḥwy.[w 1[‘NT.IX].3.23
nm.|[‘m.i]l.mbk.nhr[m.qr]b.[ap]q.|[thm]tm.tgl.ḏ[d.]i[l.]w tbu.|[qr]š.m[l]k.ab[.šnm.]mṣr.|[t]bu.ḏdm.qn[-.-]n[-.-] 3[‘NT.VI].5.15
l ttn.pn]m.‘m il.mbk.nhrm.|[qrb.ap]q.thmtm tgly.ḏd il.|[w tbu.qr]š.mlk.ab.šnm.|[l p‘n.il.t]hbr.w tql.tštḥ|[wy.w 17[2AQHT].6.48
.|w ld.špḥ.l krt.|w ǵlm.l ‘bd.il.|krt.yẖṭ.w ḥlm.|‘bd.il.w hdrt.|yrtḥṣ.w yadm.|yrḥṣ.yd h.amt h.|uṣb‘t h.‘d.ṯkm. 14[KRT].3.155
hm.yasp.ḥmt.|[---.š]pš.l [hrm.ǵrpl].‘l.arṣ.l an.|[ḥ]mt.i[l.w] ḥrn.yisp.ḥmt.|[b‘l.w]dgn[.yi]sp.ḥmt.‘nt.w ‘ṯtrt.|[ti]s UG5.8.13
yd k.hl.‘ṣr.|tḥrr.l išt.w ṣḥrt.l pḥmm.aṯtm.a[ṯt.il].|aṯt.il.w ‘lm h.yhbr.špt hm.yš[q].|hn.špt hm.mtqtm.mtqtm.k lr 23[52].49
yd k.|h[l.]‘ṣr.tḥrr.l išt.ṣḥrrt.l pḥmm.|a[ṯ]tm.aṯt.il.aṯt.il.w ‘lm h.w hm.|aṯtm.tṣḥn y.ad ad.nḥtm.ẖṭ k.|mmnnm.m 23[52].42
.mṭ yd k.hl.‘ṣr.tḥrr.l išt.|w ṣḥrrt.l pḥmm.btm.bt.il.bt.il.|w ‘lm h.w hn.aṯtm.tṣḥn y.mt mt.|nḥtm.ẖṭ k.mmnnm.m 23[52].45
dl[t.]ilhm.|[b]‘l š.aṯrt.š.ṯkmn w šnm.š.|‘nt.š.ršp.š.dr il w p[ẖ]r b‘l.|gdlt.šlm.gdlt.w burm.[l]b.|rmṣt.ilhm.b‘lm.dṯ 34[1].7
t.ilhm].|b‘[l.š].aṯrt[.š.ṯkm]n w [šnm.š].|‘nt š ršp š[.dr.il.w pẖr.b‘l].|gdlt.šlm[.gdlt.w burm.lb].|rmṣt.ilh[m.b‘lm.--- 35[3].16
d[lt.ilhm.b‘l.š.aṯrt.š].|ṯkmn.w š[nm.š.‘nt.š.ršp.š.dr].|il.w pẖr[.b‘l.gdlt.šlm.gdlt].|w burm.l[b.rmṣt.ilhm].|b‘lm.w APP.II[173].18
awl.|išttk.lm.ttkn.|štk.mlk.dn.|štk.šibt.‘n.|štk.qr.bt.il.|w mṣlt.bt.ḥr[š]. 12[75].2.61
.ql[ṣ] k.mh.tarš[n].|l btlt.‘nt.w t[‘]n.btlt.‘n[t].|tḥm k.il.ḥkm.ḥkm k.|‘m.‘lm.ḥyt.ḥẓt.tḥm k.|mlk n.aliyn.b‘l.ṯpṭ n. 3[‘NT.VI].5.38
mlk.|yẖss k.ahbt.ṯr.t‘rr k.|w t‘n.rbt.aṯrt ym.|tḥm k.il.ḥkm.ḥkmt.|‘m ‘lm.ḥyt.ḥẓt.|tḥm k.mlk n.aliy[n.]b‘l.|ṯpṭ 4[51].4.41
[-----].|[-----].|il.šm‘.amr k.ph[.-].|k il.ḥkmt.k ṯr.lṭpn.|ṣḥ.ngr.il.ilš.il[š].|w aṯt h.ngrt[.i]lht.|kḥṣ. 16[126].4.3
bn il.|ṯrmn w šnm.|il w aṯrt.|ẖnn il.|nṣbt il.|šlm il.|il ḥš il add.|b‘l ṣpn b‘l.|ugrt.|b mrḥ il.|b nit il.|b ṣmd il.|b 30[107].9
mdb.yqḥ.il.mšt‘ltm.|mšt‘ltm.l riš.agn.yqḥ.tš.b bt h.|il.ẖṭ h.nḥt.il.ymnn.mṭ.yd h.yšu.|yr.šmm h.yr.b šmm.‘ṣr.yẖ 23[52].37
šr‘m.ušpǵtm.p[--.---].|kṯ.ẓrw.kṯ.nbt.ḏnt.w [-]n[-.---].|il.ẖyr.ilib.š.|arṣ w šmm.š.|il.š.kṯrt.š.|dgn.š.b‘l.ẖlb alp w š.| UG5.9.2.1
|qdš w amrr.|ṯẖr w bd.|[k]ṯr ẖss šlm.|šlm il bt.|šlm il ẖš[t].|ršp inšt.|[--]rm il [---].|[---.--]m šlm [---]. UG5.7.72
rn.m‘ms h.|[k]šb‘ yn.spu.ksm h.bt.b‘l.|[w m]nt h bt.il.ṭẖ.gg h.b ym.|[ṭi]ṭ.rḥṣ.npṣ h.b ym.rṯ.|[--.y]iẖd.il.‘bd h.yb 17[2AQHT].1.33
n m‘ms y k šb‘t yn.|spu.ksm y.bt.b‘l.[w]mn[t].|y.bt.il.ṭẖ.gg y.b ym.ṭiṭ.|rḥṣ.npṣ y.b ym.rṯ.|dn.il.bt h.ymǵyn.|yšt 17[2AQHT].2.22
[wn.in.bt.l b‘l.]|[km.ilm.w ḥẓr].|[k bn.aṯ]r[t].|m[ṯ]b.il.mẓll.|bn h.mṯb.rbt.|aṯrt.ym.mṯb.|klt.knyt.|mṯb.pdry.b a 4[51].1.13
rt.|ary h.wn.in.bt.l b‘l.|km.ilm.w ḥẓr.k bn.aṯrt.|mṯb il.mẓll.bn h.|mṯb rbt.aṯrt.ym.|mṯb.klt.knyt.|mṯb.pdry.bt.a 4[51].4.52
brt.arẖ h.|wn.in.bt.l b‘l.km.ilm.|ḥẓr.k b[n.a]ṯrt.mṯb.il.|mṯll.b[n h.m]ṯb.rbt.aṯrt.|ym.mṯb.[pdr]y.bt.ar.|[mẓll.]ṭly 3[‘NT.VI].5.47
[---.wn.in].|[bt].l [b‘l.km.ilm.w ḥẓr].|k bn.[aṯrt.mṯb.il.mẓll].|bn h.m[ṯb.rbt.aṯrt.ym].|mṯb.pdr[y.bt.ar.mẓll].|ṭly. 3[‘NT.VI].4.1
pš pgr.|iltm ẖnqtm.|yrẖ kṯy.|ygb hd.|yrgb b‘l.|ydb il.|yarš il.|yrǵm il.|‘mtr.|ydb il.|yrgb lim.|‘mtr.|yarš il.|y UG5.14.B.3
šq.w hr.b ḥbq.ḥmḥmt.tqt[nṣn].|tldn.šḥr.w šlm.rgm.l il.ybl.a[ṯt y].|il.ylt.mh.ylt.yld y.šḥr.w šl[m].|šu.‘db.l špš.rbt 23[52].52
.[ilm.]n‘mm.agzr ym.|bn.ym.ynqm.b a[p.]ḏ[d.r]gm.l il.ybl.|aṯt y.il.ylt.mh.ylt.ilmy n‘mm.|agzr ym.bn ym.ynqm. 23[52].59
|yarš il.|yrǵm il.|‘mtr.|ydb il.|yrgb lim.|‘mtr.|yarš il.|ydb b‘l.|yrǵm b‘l.|‘z b‘l.|ydb hd. UG5.14.B.10
.agzr ym.|bn.ym.ynqm.b a[p.]ḏ[d.r]gm.l il.ybl.|aṯt y.il.ylt.mh.ylt.ilmy n‘mm.|agzr ym.bn ym.ynqm.b ap.ḏd.št.š 23[52].60
.ḥmḥmt.tqt[nṣn].|tldn.šḥr.w šlm.rgm.l il.ybl.a[ṯt y].|il.ylt.mh.ylt.yld y.šḥr.w šl[m].|šu.‘db.l špš.rbt.w l kbkbm.k 23[52].53
pn.w ugr.|mn.ib.yp‘.l b‘l.ṣrt.|l rkb.‘rpt.l mẖšt.mdd.|il ym.l klt.nhr.il.rbm.|l ištbm.tnn.ištml h.|mẖšt.bṯn.‘qltn.| 3[‘NT].3.36
[------.i]qnim.[--].|[---.]aliyn.b‘l.|[---.--]k.mdd il.|y[m.---.]l ṯr.qdqd h.|il[.--.]rḥq.b ǵr.|km.y[--.]ilm.b ṣpn.| 4[51].7.3
b.hk]l m.|al td[.pdr]y.bt ar.|[---.ṭl]y.bt.rb.|[---.m]dd.il ym.|[---.-]qlṣn.wpṯ m.|[---.]w y‘n.kṯr.|[w ẖss.]ṯṯb.b‘l.l hw 4[51].6.12
.|b il ab h.g‘r.yṯb.il.kb[-].|aṯ[rt.]il.yṯb.b mrzḥ h.|yšt[.il.y]n.‘d šb‘.trṯ.‘d škr.|il.hlk.l bt h.yštql.|l ḥṭr h.y‘msn.nn.ṯ UG5.1.1.16
ygb hd.|yrgb b‘l.|ydb il.|yarš il.|yrǵm il.|‘mtr.|ydb il.|yrgb lim.|‘mtr.|yarš il.|ydb b‘l.|yrǵm b‘l.|‘z b‘l.|ydb h UG5.14.B.7
mt.|šnt.tluan.|w yškb.nhmmt.|w yqmṣ.w b ḥlm h.|il.yrd.b ḏhrt h.|ab adm.w yqrb.|b šal.krt.m at.|krt.k ybky. 14[KRT].1.36
gdl.rkb.|ṯkmm.ḥmt.nša.|[y]d h.šmmh.dbḥ.|l ṯr.ab h.il.šrd.|[b‘l].b dbḥ h.bn dgn.|[b m]ṣd h.yrd.krt.|[l g]gt.‘db.a 14[KRT].4.169
mg]dl.rkb.|ṯkmm.ḥm[t].ša.yd k.|šmm.dbḥ.l ṯr.|ab k.il.šrd.b‘l.|b dbḥ k.bn.dgn.|b mṣd k.w yrd.|krt.l ggt.‘db.|ak 14[KRT].2.77
iltm ẖnqtm.|yrẖ kṯy.|ygb hd.|yrgb b‘l.|ydb il.|yarš il.|yrǵm il.|‘mtr.|ydb il.|yrgb lim.|‘mtr.|yarš il.|ydb b‘l.| UG5.14.B.4
|‘ṯtrt.tsm h.|d ‘q h.ib.iqni.|‘p‘p h.sp.ṯrml.|d b ḥlm y.il.ytn.|b ḏrt y.ab.adm.|w ld.špḥ.l krk|t.w ǵlm.l ‘bd.|il.ttb‘. 14[KRT].6.296
h.|sp.ṯrml.tḥgrn.[-]dm[.-].|ašlw.b ṣp.‘n h.|d b ḥlm y.il.ytn.|b ḏrt y.ab.adm.|w ld.špḥ.l krt.|w ǵlm.l ‘bd.il.|krt.y 14[KRT].3.150
n.|nšb.l inr.t‘dbn.ktp.|b il ab h.g‘r.yṯb.il.kb[-].|aṯ[rt.]il.yṯb.b mrzḥ h.|yšt[.il.y]n.‘d šb‘.trṯ.‘d škr.|il.hlk.l bt h.yštq UG5.1.1.15
[--]m.[---.]|gm.ṣḥ.l q[ṣ.ilm.---].|l rḥqm.l p[-.---].|ṣḥ.il.yṯb.b[mrzḥ.---].|bṯt.‘llm n.[---].|ilm.bt.b‘l k.[---].|dl.ylkn 1[‘NT.X].4.4
[---]n.yšt.rpu.mlk.‘lm.w yšt.|[--.]gṯr.w yqr.il.yṯb.b.‘ṯtrt.|il.ṯpṭ.b hd r‘y.d yšr.w yḏmr.|b knr.w ṯlb.b tp. UG5.2.1.2
t.‘l.ydm[.---].|b mdd.il.y[--.---].|b ym.il.d[--.---.n]|hr.il.y[--.---].|aliyn.[b‘l.---].|btlt.[‘nt.---].|mh.k[--.---].|w at[--.- 4[51].2.36

.atr[t.ym]. | qḥ.rtt.b d k t[---]. | rbt.ʿl.ydm[.---]. | b mdd.il.y[--.---]. | b ym.il.d[--.---.n] | hr.il.y[--.---]. | aliyn.[bʿl.---]. | bt 4[51].2.34

.hl h.trm.hl h.tṣḥ.ad ad. | w hl h.tṣḥ.um.um.tirk m.yd.il.k ym. | w yd il.k mdb.ark.yd.il.k ym. | w yd.il.k mdb.yqḥ.il 23[52].33

.tṣḥ.um.um.tirk m.yd.il.k ym. | w yd il.k mdb.ark.yd.il.k ym. | w yd.il.k mdb.yqḥ.il.mštʿltm. | mštʿltm.l riš.agn.yq 23[52].34

.ḥby. | bʿl.qrnm w d̲nb.ylšn. | b ḫri h.w t̲nt h.ql.il.[--]. | il.k yrdm.arṣ.ʿnt. | w ʿt̲trt.tṣdn.[---]. | [---.-]b[-.---]. | [ʿt̲]trt w ʿn UG5.1.1.22

ṣḥ.ad ad. | w hl h.tṣḥ.um.um.tirk m.yd.il.k ym. | w yd il.k mdb.ark.yd.il.k ym. | w yd.il.k mdb.yqḥ.il.mštʿltm. | mšt 23[52].34

rk m.yd.il.k ym. | w yd il.k mdb.ark.yd.il.k ym. | w yd.il.k mdb.yqḥ.il.mštʿltm. | mštʿltm.l riš.agn.yqḥ.tš.b bt h. | il.ḫ 23[52].35

lk.ab.šnm. | l pʿn.il.thbr.w tql. | tštḥwy.w tkbd h. | hlm.il.k yphn h. | yprq.lṣb.w yṣḥq. | pʿn h.l hdm.yt̲pd.w ykrkr. | u 4[51].4.27

n.l mgr lb.tʿdbn. | nšb.l inr.tʿdbn.ktp. | b il ab h.gʿr.yt̲b.il.kb[-]. | at̲[rt.]il.yt̲b.b mrzḥ h. | yšt[.il.y]n.ʿd šbʿ.trt̲.ʿd škr. | il UG5.1.1.14

dgy.at̲rt. | mǵ.l qdš.amrr. | idk.al.tnn. | pnm.tk.ḥqkpt. | il.kl h.kptr. | ksu.t̲bt h.ḥkpt. | arṣ.nḥlt h. | b alp.šd.rbt. | kmn.l 3[ʿNT.VI].6.14

[idk.al.ttn.pnm.tk.ḥkpt.il.kl h]. | [kptr.]ks[u.t̲bt h.ḥkpt.arṣ.nḥlt h]. | b alp.šd.r[bt.km 1[ʿNT.IX].3.01

.hyn d. | ḥrš yd.šlḥm.ššqy. | ilm sad.kbd.hmt.bʿl. | ḥkpt.il.kl h.tšmʿ. | mt̲t.dnty.tʿdb.imr. | b pḏd.l npš.kt̲r.w ḫss. | l brl 17[2AQHT].5.21

.mt̲t.dnty. | tšlḥm.tššqy ilm. | tsad.tkbd.hmt.bʿl. | ḥkpt il.kl h.tbʿ.kt̲r. | l ahl h.hyn.tbʿ.l mš | knt h.apnk.dnil.m[t]. | rp 17[2AQHT].5.31

rt.ṣpn. | yrd.ʿt̲tr.ʿrẓ.yrd. | l kḥt̲.aliyn.bʿl. | w ymlk.b arṣ.il.kl h. | [---] š abn.b rḥbt. | [---] š abn.b kknt. 6.1.65[49.1.37]

tbʿ.l ltpn. | [il.d]pid.l tbrk. | [krt.]t̲ʿ.l tmr.nʿmn. | [ǵlm.]il.ks.yiḫd. | [il.b]yd.krpn.bm. | [ymn.]brkm.ybrk. | [ʿbd h.]yb 15[128].2.16

y.il.ytn. | b d̲rt y.ab.adm. | w ld.špḥ.l krt. | w ǵlm.l ʿbd.il. | krt.yḥt̲.w ḥlm. | ʿbd.il.w hdrt. | yrtḥṣ.w yadm. | yrḥṣ.yd h. 14[KRT].3.153

tmtn.u ḫšt k.l ntn. | ʿtq.b d.at̲t.ab.ṣrry. | ik m.yrgm.bn.il. | krt.špḥ.ltpn. | w qdš.u ilm.tmtn. | špḥ.ltpn.l yḥ. | w yʿny.k 16.1[125].20

. | [il.b]yd.krpn.bm. | [ymn.]brkm.ybrk. | [ʿbd h.]ybrk.il.krt. | [t̲ʿ.ymr]m.nʿm[n.]ǵlm.il. | a[t̲t.tq]ḥ.y krt.at̲t. | tqḥ.bt k 15[128].2.19

ḫ.b irt y.npš. | k ḥy.aliyn.bʿl. | k it̲.zbl.bʿl.arṣ. | gm.yṣḥ.il.l btlt. | ʿnt.šmʿ.l btlt.ʿn[t]. | rgm.l nrt.il.šp[š]. | pl.ʿnt.šdm.y š 6[49].3.22

. | ṣǵrt hn.abkrn. | tbrk.ilm.tity. | tity.ilm.l ahl hm. | dr il.l mšknt hm. | w tqrb.w ld.bn.l h. | w tqrb.w ld.bnt.l h. | mk. 15[128].3.19

ln.kḥt̲.zbl hm. | aḫr.tmǵyn.mlak ym.tʿdt.t̲pt̲.nhr.l pʿn.il. | [l t]pl.l tštḥwy.pḫr.mʿd.qmm.a[--].amr. | [tn]y.dʿt hm.išt. 2.1[137].30

ḥ.hw.t̲ʿ n[t̲ʿy.hw.nkt.nk]t.ytši.l ab bn il. | ytši.l d[r.bn il.l]mpḥrt.bn il. | l t̲km[n.w šnm.]hn ʿ[r]. | [---.]w npy[.---]. | [32[2].1.34

| [hw.t̲ʿ.nt̲ʿy.hw.nkt.nkt.]yt[ši.l ab.bn.il]. | [ytši.l dr.bn.il.l mpḫ]rt.[bn.il.l t̲kmn.w šn]m hn š. | [---.w n]py.gr[.ḥmyt. 32[2].1.9B

.hw.t̲ʿ | nt̲ʿy. | hw.nkt.nkt.y[t]ši.l ab.bn.il.ytši.l dr. | bn il.l mpḫrt.bn.il.l t̲kmn[.w]šnm.hn.ʿr. | w.t̲b.l mspr.m[šr] mš 32[2].1.26

--.hw.t̲ʿ.nt̲ʿ]y. | [hw.nkt.nkt.ytši.l ab.bn.il.ytši.l d]r.bn[.il]. | [l mpḫrt.bn.il.l t̲kmn.w šnm.hn š]. | [w šqrb.š.mšr mšr.b 32[2].1.2

. | hw.t̲ʿ.nt̲ʿy.hw.nkt.n[k]t.ytši[.l ab.bn.il]. | ytši.l dr.bn.il.l mpḫrt.bn.i[l.l t̲kmn.w š]nm hn š. | w šqrb.ʿr.mšr mšr bn. 32[2].1.17

ṣb | rt.ary h.k mt.aliyn. | bʿl.k ḫlq.zbl.bʿl. | arṣ.gm.yṣḥ il. | l rbt.at̲rt ym.šmʿ. | l rbt.at̲r[t] ym.tn. | aḥd.b bn k.amlkn. | 6.1.43[49.1.15]

hw.nkt.nkt.y[t]ši.l ab.bn.il.ytši.l dr. | bn il.l mpḫrt.bn.il.l t̲kmn[.w]šnm.hn.ʿr. | w.t̲b.l mspr.m[šr] mšr.bt.ugrt.w np 32[2].1.26

w.nkt.nk]t.ytši.l ab bn il. | ytši.l d[r.bn il.l]mpḥrt.bn il. | l t̲km[n.w šnm.]hn ʿ[r]. | [---.]w npy[.---]. | [---.]w npy.u[g 32[2].1.34

w.nkt.n[k]t.ytši[.l ab.bn.il]. | ytši.l dr.bn.il.l mpḫrt.bn.i[l.l t̲kmn.w š]nm hn š. | w šqrb.ʿr.mšr mšr bn.ugrt.w [npy.-- 32[2].1.17

w.nkt.nkt.ytši.l ab.bn.il.ytši.l d]r.bn[.il]. | [l mpḫrt.bn.il.l t̲kmn.w šnm.hn š]. | [w šqrb.š.mšr mšr.bn.ugrt.w npy.---. 32[2].1.3

.nkt.nkt.]yt[ši.l ab.bn.il]. | [ytši.l dr.bn.il.l mpḫ]rt.[bn.il.l t̲kmn.w šn]m hn š. | [---.w n]py.gr[.ḥmyt.ugrt.w np]y. | [- 32[2].1.9B

[t.---]. | w ʿsrm[.---]. | ṣlyh šr[-.---]. | [t̲]ltm.w b[--.---]. | l il limm[.---]. | w t̲t.npš[.---]. | kbd.w [---]. | l ṣp[n.---]. | š.[---]. | 40[134].8

]. | ks.ksp[.---]. | krpn.[---]. | w t̲t̲n.[---]. | tʿ.l.tr[-.---]. | bt.il.li[mm.---]. | ʿl.ḥbš.[---]. | mn.lik.[---]. | lik.tl[ak.---]. | tʿddn[.- 5[67].4.21

.rgm.l t̲r.ab h.il.t̲ḥm.ym.bʿl km. | [adn]km.t̲pt̲.nhr.tn.il m.d tq h.d tqyn h. | [hml]t.tn.bʿl.w ʿnn h.bn.dgn.art̲ m.pḏ 2.1[137].34

.t̲ny.l pḫr]. | mʿd.t̲ḥm.ym.bʿl km.adn km.t̲[pt̲.nhr]. | tn.il m.d tq h.d tqyn.hmlt.tn.bʿl.[w ʿnn h]. | bn.dgn.art̲ m.pḏ h. 2.1[137].18

abn.bt šmm w thm. | qrit.l špš.um h.špš.um.ql.bl.ʿm. | il.mbk nhrm.b ʿdt.thmtm. | mnt.nt̲k.nḥš.šmrr.nḥš. | ʿq šr.ln h UG5.7.3

]r.k bn.at̲rt[.tdʿṣ.]pʿn. | [w tr.a]rṣ.id[k.l ttn.p]nm. | [ʿm.i]l.mbk.nhr[m.qr]b.[ap]q. | [thm]tm.tgl.ḏ[d.]i[l.]w tbu. | [qr]š 3[ʿNT.VI].5.14

t̲pd]m.t[ḫt.ʿnt.arṣ.t̲lt̲.mtḥ.ǵyrm]. | [idk.]l ytn.pnm.ʿm.[i]l.mbk.[nhrm.qrb.apq.thmtm]. | [ygly.]ḏl i[l].w ybu[.q]rš.m 2.3[129].4

[idk.l ttn.pnm]. | [ʿm.il.mbk.nhrm]. | [qrb.apq.thmtm]. | [tgly.ḏd.il.w]tb[a]. | [qrš. 5[67].6.02

. | at̲r.btlt.ʿnt. | w bʿl.tbʿ.mrym.ṣpn. | idk.l ttn.pnm. | ʿm.il.mbk.nhrm. | qrb.apq.thmtm. | tgly.ḏd.il.w tbu. | qrš.mlk.ab 4[51].4.21

št bm.ʿ[--]. | [---.]zr h.ybm.l ilm. | [id]k.l ttn.pnm.ʿm. | [il.]mbk nhrm.qrb. | [a]pq.thmtm.tgly.ḏd. | il.w tbu.qrš.. | mlk 6.1.33[49.1.5]

n.ʿmq.nšm. | [tdʿṣ.pʿn]m.w tr.arṣ.idk. | [l ttn.pn]m.ʿm il.mbk.nhrm. | [qrb.ap]q.thmtm tgly.ḏd il. | [w tbu.qr]š.mlk. 17[2AQHT].6.47

.dbt[.---]. | trʿ.trʿn.a[--.---]. | bnt.šdm.ṣḥr[.---]. | šbʿ.šnt.il.mla.[-]. | w t̲mn.nqpnt.ʿd. | k lbš.km.lpš.dm a[ḫ h]. | km.all. 12[75].2.45

š] h.n[bln]. | klny n[.n]bl.ks h. | [an]y.l yṣḥ.t̲r il.ab h. | [i]l.mlk.d yknn h.yṣḥ. | at̲rt.w bn h.ilt.w ṣbrt. | ary h.wn.in.bt. 4[51].4.48

lny y.qš h. | nbln.klny y.nbl.ks h. | any.l yṣḥ.t̲r.il.ab h.il. | mlk.d yknn h.yṣḥ.at̲rt. | w bn h.ilt.w ṣbrt.arḫ h. | wn.in.bt 3[ʿNT.VI].5.43

[-----]. | [---.--]y. | [-----]. | [any.l yṣ]ḥ.t̲r. | [il.ab h.i]l.mlk. | [d yknn h.yṣ]ḥ.at̲ | [rt.w bn h.]ilt. | [w ṣbrt.ary]h. | [4[51].1.5

| b t̲lḥnt.lḥm št. | b krpnm.yn.b k.ḫrṣ. | dm.ʿṣm.hm.yd.il mlk. | yḫss k.ahbt.t̲r.tʿrr k. | w tʿn.rbt.at̲rt ym. | t̲ḥm k.il.ḥk 4[51].4.38

w yqrb. | b šal.krt.m at. | krt.k ybky. | ydmʿ.nʿmn.ǵlm. | il.mlk[.t̲]r ab h. | yarš.hm.drk[t]. | k ab.adm. | [-----]. 14[KRT].1.41

l.mštʿltm. | mštʿltm.l riš.agn.yqḥ.tš.b bt h. | il.ḥt̲ h.nḥt.il.ymnn.mt̲.yd h.yšu. | yr.šmm h.yr.b šmm.ʿṣr.yḥrt̲ yšt. | l pḥ 23[52].37

n.bʿ[l y.l].pn.bʿl y. | w.urk.ym.bʿl y. | l.pn.amn.w.l.pn. | il.mṣrm.dt.tǵrn. | npš.špš.mlk. | rb.bʿl y. 1018.22

t k.t̲m. | t̲km.bm t̲km.aḥm.qym.il. | b lsmt.t̲m.yt̲bš.šm.il.mt m. | yʿbš.brk n.šm.il.ǵzrm. | t̲m.t̲mq.rpu.bʿl.mhr bʿl. | w 22.2[124].6

. | ṣdqm šr. | ḥnbn il d[n]. | [-]bd w [---]. | [--].p il[.---]. | [i]l mt mr[b-]. | qdš mlk [---]. | kbd d ilgb[-]. | mrmnmn. | brrn UG5.10.2.2

.ḫrṣ.yṣq | m.l rbbt. | yṣq-ḥym.w tbt̲ḫ. | kt.il.dt.rbtm. | kt.il.nbt.b ksp. | šmrgt.b dm.ḫrṣ. | kḥt̲.il.nḥt. | b ẓr.hdm.id. | d pr 4[51].1.32

. | kt.il.dt.rbtm. | kt.il.nbt.b ksp. | šmrgt.b dm.ḫrṣ. | kḥt̲.il.nḥt. | b ẓr.hdm.id. | d pršа.b br. | nʿl.il.d qblbl. | ʿln.ybl hm.ḫ 4[51].1.34

w abqt.aliyn.bʿl. | w tʿn.btlt.ʿnt. | an.l an.y špš. | an.l an.il.yǵr[.-]. | tǵr k.š[---.---]. | yštd[.---]. | dr[.---]. | r[---.---]. 6[49].4.47

l. | dr bn il. | mpḫrt bn il. | t̲rmn w šnm. | il w at̲rt. | ḫnn il. | nṣbt il. | šlm il. | il ḥš il add. | bʿl ṣpn bʿl. | ugrt. | b mrḥ il. | b 30[107].6

l t̲ʿ dbḥ n. | ndbḥ.hw.t̲ʿ n[t̲ʿy.hw.nkt.nk]t.ytši.l ab bn il. | ytši.l d[r.bn il.l]mpḥrt.bn il. | l t̲km[n.w šnm.]hn ʿ[r]. | [-- 32[2].1.33

t̲ʿ.d[bḥ n.ndbḥ]. | hw.t̲ʿ.nt̲ʿy.hw.nkt.n[k]t.ytši[.l ab.bn.il]. | ytši.l dr.bn.il.l mpḫrt.bn.i[l.l t̲kmn.w š]nm hn š. | w šqrb 32[2].1.16

l.t̲ʿ.dbḥ n.ndb]ḥ. | [hw.t̲ʿ.nt̲ʿy.hw.nkt.nkt.]yt[ši.l ab.bn.il]. | [ytši.l dr.bn.il.l mpḫ]rt.[bn.il.l t̲kmn.w šn]m hn š. | [---. 32[2].1.9A

l.t̲ʿ.dbḥ n.ndbḥ.hw.t̲ʿ | nt̲ʿy. | hw.nkt.nkt.y[t]ši.l ab.bn.il.ytši.l dr. | bn il.l mpḫrt.bn.il.l t̲kmn[.w]šnm.hn.ʿr. | w.t̲b.l 32[2].1.25

[---.hw.t̲ʿ.nt̲ʿ]y. | [hw.nkt.nkt.ytši.l ab.bn.il.ytši.l d]r.bn[.il]. | [l mpḫrt.bn.il.l t̲kmn.w šnm.hn š]. | [w šq 32[2].1.2

ym.w atn k.bl mt. | w ašlḥ k.ašspr k.ʿm.bʿl. | šnt.ʿm.bn il.tspr.yrḫm. | k bʿl.k yḥwy.yʿšr.ḥwy.yʿš. | r.w yšqyn h.ybd.w 17[2AQHT].6.29

h bt.il.t̲ḥ.gg h.b ym. | [ti]t̲.rḥṣ.npṣ h.b ym.rt̲. | [--.y]iḫd.il.ʿbd h.ybrk. | [dni]l mt rpi.ymr.ǵzr. | [mt.hr]nmy npš.yḥ.dn 17[2AQHT].1.35

l]t.tn.b'l.w 'nn h.bn.dgn.arṯ m.pḏ h.|[w y'n.]ṯr.ab h.il.'bd k.b'l.y ym m.'bd k.b'l.|[--.--]m.bn.dgn.a[s]r km.hw yb 2.1[137].36
tm.|yrẖ kṯy.|ygb hd.|yrgb b'l.|ydb il.|yarš il.|yrǵm il.|'mtr.|ydb il.|yrgb lim.|'mtr.|yarš il.|ydb b'l.|yrǵm b'l. UG5.14.B.5
yṣm.y l km.qr.mym.d '[l k].|mẖṣ.aqht.ǵzr.amd.gr bt il.|'nt.brḥ.p 'lm h.'nt.p dr[.dr].|'db.uẖry mṭ.yd h.|ymǵ.l m 19[1AQHT].3.153
kn.|[--]t.w b lb.tqb[-].|[--]m[-].mtm.uṣb'[t].|[-]tr.šrk.il.|'rb.špš.l ymǵ.|krt.ṣbia.špš.|b'l ny.w ymlk.|[y]ṣb.'ln.w y[15[128].5.17
.'qltn.|šlyṭ.d šb't.rašm.|mẖšt.mdd ilm.ar[š].|ṣmt.'gl.il.'tk.|mẖšt.klbt.ilm išt.|klt.bt.il.ḏbb.imtẖṣ.ksp.|itrṯ.ẖrṣ.ṭrd 3['NT].3.41
-.]šb'.rbt.|[---.]qbṭ.ṯm.|[---.]bn.ilm.|[m]t.šmḥ.p ydd.|il[.ǵ]zr.|b [-]dn.'.z.w.|rgbt.zbl. UG5.4.16
pk.ksa.mlk k.|l yṯbr.ẖṭ.mṯpṭ k.|yru.bn ilm t.ṯt'.y|dd.il.ǵzr.y'r.mt.|b ql h.y[---.---].|b'l.yṯṯbn[.l ksi].|mlk h.l[nẖt. 6[49].6.31
m.ṣpn.w y'n.|gpn.w ugr.tḥm.bn ilm.|mt.hwt.ydd.bn.il.|ǵzr.p np.š.npš.lbim.|thw.hm.brlt.anẖr.|b ym.hm.brk y.t 5[67].1.13
lk.|arṣ.drkt.yštkn.|dll.al.ilak.l bn.|ilm.mt.'dd.l ydd.|il.ǵzr.yqra.mt.|b npš h.ystrn ydd.|b gngn h.aḥd y.d ym|lk. 4[51].7.47
.|ḏrqm.amt m.l yrt.|b npš.bn ilm.mt.b mh|mrt.ydd.il.ǵzr.|tb'.w l.yṯb ilm.idk.|l ytn.pnm.'m.b'l.|mrym.ṣpn.w y 5[67].1.8
n.b'l.|ṯt'.nn.rkb.'rpt.|tb'.rgm.l bn.ilm.mt.|ṯny.l ydd.il ǵzr.|tḥm.aliyn.b'l.hwt.aliy.|qrdm.bhṯ.l bn.ilm mt.|'bd k. 5[67].2.9
|tštḥwy.w k|bd hwt.w rgm.|l bn.ilm.mt.|ṯny.l ydd.|il.ǵzr.tḥm.|aliyn.b'l.|[hw]t.aliy.q|[rdm.]bht y.bnt.|[dt.ksp. 4[51].8.32
m.qym.il.|b lsmt.ṯm.yṯbš.šm.il.mt m.|y'bš.brk n.šm.il.ǵzrm.|ṯm.ṯmq.rpu.b'l.mhr b'l.|w mhr.'nt.ṯm.yḥpn.ḥyl|y. 22.2[124].7
|[---.-]rm.aklt.'gl.'l.mšt.|[---.--]r.špr.w yšt.il.|[---.--]n.il ǵnṯ.'gl il.|[---.--]d.il.šd yṣd mlk.|[---].yšt.il h.|[---.]iṯm h.| UG5.2.1.11
-].|at.š['tqt.---].|š'd[.---].|rt.[---].|'ṭr[.---].|b p.š[---].|il.p.d[---].|'rm.[di.mh.pdrm].|di.š[rr.---].|mr[ṣ.---].|zb[ln.- 16[126].5.47
il b[n] il.|dr bn il.|mpẖrt bn il.|ṯrmn w šnm.|il w aṯrt.|ẖnn il.|nṣbt il.|šlm 30[107].2
.ymǵy.|'ṯtrt.t'db.nšb l h.|w 'nt.ktp.b hm.yg'r.ṯǵr.|bt.il.pn.l mgr lb.t'dbn.|nšb.l inr.t'dbn.ktp.|b il ab h.g'r.yṯb.il. UG5.1.1.12
[-.k]bd n.il.ab n.|kbd k iš.tikln.|ṯd n.km.mrm.tqrṣn.|il.yẓḥq.bm.|lb.w ygmḏ.bm kbd.|ẓi.at.l tlš.|amt.yrẖ.|l dmg 12[75].1.12
l[-].|bn.ṯb'nq.|brqd.|bnn.|kbln.ṣ[md].|bn gmrt.|bn.il.ṣm[d].|bn abbly.|yṯ'd.ṣm[d].|bn.liy.|'šrm.ṣ[md].|ṯṯ kbd. 2113.19
il ṣpn.|il[i]b.|i[l].|dgn.|b'[l ṣ]pn.|b'lm.|[b']lm.|[b']lm.|[b'] 29[17].1.1
'.nšm.w l tbn.|hmlt.arṣ.at m.w ank.|ibǵy h.b tk.ǵr y.il.ṣpn.|b qdš.b ǵr.nḥlt y.|b n'm.b gb'.tliyt.|hlm.'nt.tph.ilm. 3['NT].3.26
bn.brq].|d l t[d'.šmm.at m.w ank].|ibǵ[y h.b tk.ǵ]r y.il.ṣpn.|b q[dš.b ǵr.nḥ]lt y.|w t['n].btlt.[']nt.ṯṯb.|[ybmt.]lim 3['NT].4.63
b'l.yṯb.k ṯbt.ǵr.hd.r['y].|k mdb.b tk.ǵr h.il ṣpn.b [tk].|ǵr.tliyt.šb't.brqm.[---].|ṯmnt.iṣr r't.'ṣ brq y.|ri UG5.3.1.2
kby.|bn.knn.qšt.|pbyn.qšt.|yddn.qšt.w.ql'.|š'rt.|bn.il.qšt.w.ql'.|ark.qšt.w.ql'.|bn.'bdnkl.qšt.w.ql'.|bn.znan.qšt. 119[321].2.41
.ib.yp'.l b'l.ṣrt.|l rkb.'rpt.l mẖšt.mdd.|il ym.l klt.nhr.il.rbm.|l ištbm.tnn.ištml h.|mẖšt.bṯn.'qltn.|šlyṭ.d šb't.rašm 3['NT].3.36
.|[w y'n].ṯr.ab h.il.|d[--].b bk.krt.|b dm'.n'mn.ǵlm.|il.trḥṣ.w tadm.|rḥṣ[.y]d k.amt.|uṣb['t k.]'d[.ṯ]km.|'rb[.b ẓl. 14[KRT].2.62
ṯt pl.gdlt.[ṣ]pn.dqt.|[---.al]p 'nt.gdlt.b ṯlṯt mrm.|[---.i]l š.b'l š.aṯrt.š.ym š.[b']l knp.|[---.g]dlt.ṣpn.dqt.šrp.w [š]lm 36[9].1.6
š.ṯ' w[.--.k]bdm.|[---.--]mm.ṯn.šm.w alp.l[--]n.|[---.]š.il š.b'l š.dgn š.|[---.--]r.w ṯt pl.gdlt.[ṣ]pn.dqt.|[---.al]p 'nt.gd 36[9].1.3
šlmm.|kmm.w bbt.b'l.ugrt.|w kdm.w npš ilib.|gdlt.il š.b'l š.'nt.|ṣpn.alp.w š.pdry.š.|šrp.w šlmm ilib š.|b'l ugrt UG5.13.13
š[l]mm.kmm.|[w bbt.b'l.ugrt.]kdm.w npš.|[ilib.gdlt.il.š.b]'[l.]š.'nt ṣpn.|[---.]w [n]p[š.---].|[---.--]t.w[.---].|[---.--] 36[9].1.17
w.kṯ.nbt.ḏnt.w [-]n[-.---].|il.ẖyr.ilib.š.|arṣ w šmm.š.|il.š.kṯrt.š.|dgn.š.b'l.ẖlb alp w š.|b'l ṣpn alp.w.š.|ṯrṯy.alp.w. UG5.9.2.3
lp w š.|dgn.š.il t'ḏr.š.|b'l š.'nt š.ršp š.|šlmm.|w šnpt.il š.|l 'nt.ḥl š.ṯn šm.|l gṯrm.ǵṣ b šmal.|d alpm.w alp w š.|šr UG5.13.24
št.|[---.--]r.špr.w yšt.il.|[---.--]n.il ǵnṯ.'gl il.|[---.--]d.il.šd yṣd mlk.|[---].yšt.il h.|[---.]iṯm h.|[---.y]mǵy.|[---.]dr UG5.2.1.12
.il.ab k.|hwt.lṭpn.ḥtk k.|pl.'nt.šdm.y špš.|pl.'nt.šdm.il.yš[t k].|b'l.'nt.mḥrṯ[-].|iy.aliyn.b'l.|iy.zbl.b'l.arṣ.|w t'n.n 6[49].4.37
.'n[t].|rgm.l nrt.il.šp[š].|pl.'nt.šdm.y špš.|pl.'nt.šdm.il.yšt k.|[b]'l.'nt.mḥrṯt.|iy.aliyn.b'l.|iy.zbl.b'l.arṣ.|ttb'.btlt.' 6[49].4.26
il.|mpẖrt bn il.|ṯrmn w šnm.|il w aṯrt.|ẖnn il.|nṣbt il.|šlm il.|il ḥš il add.|b'l ṣpn b'l.|ugrt.|b mrḥ il.|b nit il.| 30[107].7
[--.]ab.w il[--].|[--] šlm.šlm i[l].|[š]lm.il.šr.|dgn.w b'l.|'ṯ w kmṯ.|yrẖ w ksa.|yrẖ mkṯy. UG5.10.1.2
b yrẖ.[rišyn.b ym.ḥdṯ].|šmtr.[uṯkl.l il.šlmm].|b ṯlṯt '[šrt.yrtḥṣ.mlk.brr].|b arb'[t.'šrt.riš.argmn]. 35[3].2
[b yr]ẖ[.r]išyn.b ym.ḥdṯ.|[šmtr].uṯkl.l il.šlmm.|b [ṯlṯt].'šrt.yrtḥṣ.mlk.|br[r.]b a[r]b't.'šrt.riš.|arg[APP.II[173].2
[---.'b]d k.|[---.--]l y.'m.|[---.]'m.|[---.--]y.w.lm.|[---.]il.šlm.|[---.]ank.|[---].mly. 2128.2.5
[-----].|[-----].|il.šm'.amr k.ph[.-].|k il.ḥkmt.k ṯr.lṭpn.|ṣḥ.ngr.il.ilš.il[š].|w 16[126].4.2
ḥmy.|[---].y[ṯ]b.|[---]p.gp ym.w yṣǵd.gp..thm.|[yqḥ.]il.mšt'ltm.mšt'ltm.l riš.agn.|hl h.[t]špl.hl h.trm.hl h.tṣḥ.ad 23[52].31
m.|w yd il.k mdb.ark.yd.il.k ym.|w yd.il.k mdb.yqḥ.il.mšt'ltm.|mšt'ltm.l riš.agn.yqḥ.tš.b bt h.|il.ẖṭ h.nḥt.il.ym 23[52].35
m.|qdš.nny.ḥ[l]m.adr.|ḥl.rḥb.mk[npt].|ap.krt bn[m.il].|špḥ.lṭpn[.w qdš].|bkm.t'r[b.'l.ab h].|t'rb.ḥ[--].|b ṯtm.t[16.2[125].110
.ḥlm.qdš.|any.ḥlm.adr.ḥl.|rḥb.mknpt.ap.|[k]rt.bnm.il.špḥ.|lṭpn.w qdš.'l.|ab h.y'rb.ybky.|w yšnn.ytn.g h.|bky. 16.1[125].10
[--.]ab.w il[--].|[--] šlm.šlm i[l].|[š]lm.il.šr.|dgn.w b'l.|'ṯ w kmṯ.|yrẖ w ksa.|yrẖ mkṯy.|ṯkmn w š UG5.10.1.3
d h.|qb't.b ymn h.w y'n.yṭ[p]n[.mh]r.|št.b yn.yšt.ila.il š[--.]il.|d yqny.ḏdm.yd.mẖṣt.a[qh]t.ǵ|zr.tmẖṣ.alpm.ib.št[19[1AQHT].4.219
il.ytn.|b ḏrt y.ab.adm.|w ld.špḥ.l krk|t.w ǵlm.l 'bd.|il.ttb'.mlakm.|l yṯb.idk.pnm.|l ytn.'mm.pbl.|mlk.tšan.|g h 14[KRT].6.300
.d't hm.išt.ištm.yitmr.ḥrb.ltšt.|[--]n hm.rgm.l ṯr.ab h.il.tḥm.ym.b'l km.|[adn]km.ṯpṭ.nhr.tn.il m.d tq h.d tqyn h. 2.1[137].33
'l]m.|[arṣ] w šm[m].|[-----].|[a]rṣ.|[u]šẖr[y].|[']ṯtrt.|i[l t]'ḏr b'l.|ršp.|ddmš.|pẖr ilm.|ym.|uṯẖt.|knr.|mlkm.|šl 29[17].2.4
y.š.ǵrm.š[.---].|aṯrt.š.'nt.š.špš.š.arṣy.š.'ṯtrt.š.|ušẖry.š.il.t'ḏr.b'l.š.ršp.š.ddmš.š.|w šlmm.ilib.š.i[l.--]m d gbl.ṣpn.al[UG5.9.1.8
p kn.u b qṣrt.npšt kn.u b qṭ]t tqṭṭ.|[ušn.yp kn.---.--]l.il.t'ḏr b'l.|[-----.]lšnt.|[---.--]yp.tḥt.|[-----].|[---.]w npy gr.|[APP.I[-].1.8
w š.pdry š.ddmš š.|w b urbt.ilib š.|b'l alp w š.|dgn.š.il t'ḏr.š.|b'l š.'nt š.ršp š.|šlmm.|w šnpt.il š.|l 'nt.ḥl š.ṯn šm. UG5.13.21
kṯr š 'ṯtr.š.|['ṯt]rt.š.šgr w iṯm š.|[---.]š.ršp.idrp.š.|[---.il.t']ḏr.š.|[---.-]mt.š.|[-----].|[-----].|[-----].|[---.]im[-.---].|[-- UG5.9.2.11
il b[n] il.|dr bn il.|mpẖrt bn il.|ṯrmn w šnm.|il w aṯrt.|ẖnn il.|nṣbt il.|šlm il.|il ḥš il ad 30[107].3
.pẖr [m'd.qmm.a--.am]|r ṯny.d't km.w rgm.l ṯr.a[b.-.il.ṯny.l pẖr].|m'd.tḥm.ym.b'l km.adn km.ṯ[pṭ.nhr].|tn.il m. 2.1[137].16
]n.yšt.rpu.mlk.'lm.w yšt.|[--.]gṯr.w yqr.il.yṯb.b.'ṯtrt.|il.ṯpṭ.b hd r'y.d yšr.w yḏmr.|b knr.w ṯlb.b tp.w mṣltm.b m UG5.2.1.3
rt.w 'ṣrm.l[.---].|pamt.w bt.[---].|rmm.w 'l[y.---].|bt.il.ṯq[l.---.kbd].|w bdḥ.k[--.---].|'ṣrm.l i[nš.ilm.ṯb.md]|bḥ.b'l APP.II[173].42
'rt.tmll.išd h.qrn[m].|dt.'l h.riš h.b glṯ.b šm[m].|[---.i]l.ṯr.iṯ.p h.k ṯt.ǵlt[.--].|[---.--] k yn.ddm.l b[--.---].|[---.-]yt š UG5.3.1.8
].|š[g]r h bm ymn.t[--.---].|[--.]l b'l.'bd[.---].|ṯr ab h il.ttrm[.---].|tšlḥm yrẖ.ggn[.---].|k[.---.ẖ]mš.ẖssm[.---].|[---. 2001.1.15
ngšnn.ḥby.|b'l.qrnm w ḏnb.ylšn.|b ẖri h.w ṯnt h.ql.il.[--].|il.k yrdm.arṣ.'nt.|w 'ṯtrt.tṣdn.[---].|[---.-]b[-.---].|['ṯ] UG5.1.1.21
.|[---.]aliyn.b'l.|[---.--]k.mdd il.|y[m.---.]l ṯr.qdqd h.|il[.--.]rḥq.b ǵr.|km.y[--.]ilm.b ṣpn.|'dr.l['r].'rm.|ṯb.l pd[r.] 4[51].7.5
trt.š.|ušẖry.š.il.t'ḏr.b'l.š.ršp.š.ddmš.š.|w šlmm.ilib.š.i[l.--]m d gbl.ṣpn.al[p].|pẖr.ilm.š.ym.š[.k]nr.š.[--.]'ṣrm gdlt. UG5.9.1.10

r. | ʿdw šr. | ṣdqm šr. | ḥnbn il d[n]. | [-]bd w [---]. | [--].p il[.---]. | [i]l mt mr[b-]. | qdš mlk [---]. | kbd d ilgb[-]. | mrmnm UG5.10.2.1
b y[--.---]. | il[.---]. | bʿl[.---]. | [---.--]l.[---]. | [---.g]dlt[.---]. | [---].p[--.---]. | [- 46[-].1.2
-]. | ank.lṯpn.il[.d pid.---]. | ʿl.ydm.pʿrt[.---]. | šm k.mdd.i[l.---]. | bt ksp y.d[--.---]. | b d.aliyn b[ʿl.---]. | kd.ynaṣn[.---]. | 1[ʿNT.X].4.20
[--]r.[---]. | [---.]il.[---]. | [tṣ]un.b arṣ. | mḫnm.ṯrp ym. | lšnm.tlḥk. | šmm.ṯṯrp. | 1003.2
y.ht.alk. | [---.]ṯlṯt.amǵy.l bt. | [y.---.b qrb].hkl y.w yʿn.il. | [---.mrzʿ]y.lk.bt y.rpim. | [rpim.bt y.aṣ]ḥ km.iqra km. | [il 21[122].1.8
[---.]btlt.ʿnt. | [---.]pp.hrm. | [---].d l ydʿ bn il. | [---.]pḫr kkbm. | [---.]dr dt.šmm. | [---.al]iyn bʿl. | [---].rkb. 10[76].1.3
.aylt. | [---.--]m.b km.yʿn. | [---].ydʿ.l ydʿt. | [---.]tasrn.ṯr il. | [---.]rks.bn.abnm. | [---.]upqt.ʿrb. | [---.w ẓ]r.mtn y at zd. | 1[ʿNT.X].5.22
[-----]. | [---.--]t.š l i[l.---]. | [--.aṯ]rt.š[.---]. | [---.]l pdr[-.---]. | ṣin aḥd h[.---]. | l ʿṯtr 37[22].2
-.--]mm.hlkt. | [---.]b qrb.ʿr. | [---.m]lakm l h. | [---.]l.bn.il. | [---.--]a.ʿd h. | [---.--]rh. | [---.--]y.špš. | [---.--]h. | [---.--]th. 26[135].7
.aklt.ʿgl.ʿl.mšt. | [---.--]r.špr.w yšt.il. | [---.--]n.il ǵnṯ.ʿgl il. | [---.--]d.il.šd yṣd mlk. | [---].yšt.il h. | [---.]iṯm h. | [---.y]mǵ UG5.2.1.11
di.dit.rḫpt. | [---.-]rm.aklt.ʿgl.ʿl.mšt. | [---.--]r.špr.w yšt.il. | [---.--]n.il ǵnṯ.ʿgl il. | [---.--]d.il.šd yṣd mlk. | [---].yšt.il h. | [UG5.2.1.10
[---].ybšr.qdš[.---]. | [---.--]t btm.qdš.il[.---]. | [---.b]n.qdš.k[--.---]. | [---.]ʿsb.[-]ḥ[-.---]. | [---.]b[-.]mṯt 2125.2
[k]ṯr ḫss šlm. | šlm il bt. | šlm il ḫš[t]. | ršp inšt. | [--]rm il [---]. | [---.--]m šlm [---]. UG5.7.73
ḫmš. | krzn.ḫmš. | ubrʿym.ḫmš. | [----]. | [bn] itn. | [bn] il. | [---]ṯ. | klṯṯb. | gsn. | arm[w]l. | bn.ṣdqn. | ḫlbn. | tbq.alp. 2039.10
ilib.il. | [-----]. 48[72].1
lk.tšan. | g hm.w tṣḥn. | tḥm.krt.ṯ[ʿ]. | hwt.[n]ʿmn.[ǵlm.il]. 14[KRT].6.306
.ḥtk k.nmrt k.b tk. | ugrt.l ymt.špš.w yrḫ. | w nʿmt.šnt.il. UG5.2.2.12

ilabn

ḫmšm.ksp ṯlṯm.šl[m.---]. | iwrpzn.ʿšrm ʿšrm š[lm.---]. | ilabn.ʿšrt ṯqlm kbd.ḫmš.šl[m.---]. | tlmyn.šbʿt.ʿšrt ʿšrt[.šlm.-- 1131.3

ilann

| kdm.ǵbiš ḫry. | ḫmš yn.b d. | bḥ mlkt. | b mdrʿ. | ṯlṯ bt.il | ann. | kd.bt.ilann. 1090.17
. | ḫmš yn.b d. | bḥ mlkt. | b mdrʿ. | ṯlṯ bt.il | ann. | kd.bt.ilann. 1090.19

ilib

il ṣpn. | il[i]b. | i[l]. | dgn. | bʿ[l ṣ]pn. | bʿlm. | [bʿ]lm. | [bʿ]lm. | [bʿ]lm. | [bʿ 29[17].1.2
ilib.il. | [-----]. 48[72].1
yn.d.ykl.b d.[---]. | b.dbḥ.mlk. | dbḥ ṣpn. | [-]zǵm. | [i]lib. | [i]lbldn. | [p]dry.bt.mlk. | [-]lp.izr. | [a]rz. | k.tʿrb.ʿṯtrt.šd 2004.5
n.šrp].w š[l]mm.kmm. | [w bbt.bʿl.ugrt.]kdm.w npš. | [ilib.gdlt.il.š.b]ʿ[l.]š.ʿnt ṣpn. | [---.]w [n]p[š.---]. | [---.--]t.w[.---] 36[9].1.17
ṣpn.šrp.w šlmm. | kmm.w bbt.bʿl.ugrt. | w kdm.w npš ilib. | gdlt.il š.bʿl š.ʿnt. | ṣpn.alp.w š.pdry.š. | šrp.w šlmm ilib š UG5.13.12
-.mt.r]pi.w ykn.bn h. | [b bt.šrš.]b qrb.hkl h. | [nṣb.skn.i]lib h.b qdš. | [ztr.ʿm h.l a]rṣ.mšṣu. | [qṭr h.l ʿpr.d]mr.a[ṯ]r h. 17[2AQHT].1.45
l bny.bnwt. | w ykn.bn h b bt.šrš.b qrb. | hkl h.nṣb.skn.ilib h.b qdš. | ztr.ʿm h.l arṣ.mšṣu.qṭr h. | l ʿpr.ḏmr.aṯr h.ṭbq.l 17[2AQHT].1.27
. | npš.k yld.bn.l y.km. | aḫ y.w šrš.km ary y. | nṣb.skn.ilib y.b qdš. | ztr.ʿm y.l ʿpr.ḏmr.aṯr[y]. | ṭbq lḥt.niṣ y.grš. | d ʿ 17[2AQHT].2.16
]mm.gdlt.l.b[ʿl.---]. | [dq]t.l.ṣpn.gdlt.l[.---]. | u[gr]t.š.l.[il]ib.ǵ[--.--rt]. | w [ʿṣrm.]l.ri[--.---]. | [--]t.bʿlt.bt[.---]. | [md]bḥt 35[3].35
špǵtm.p[--.---]. | kṯ.ẓrw.kṯ.nbt.ḏnt.w [-]n[-.---]. | il.ḫyr.ilib.š. | arṣ w šmm.š. | il.š.kṯrt.š. | dgn.š.bʿl.ḫlb alp w š. | bʿl ṣp UG5.9.2.1
ṣy.š.ʿṯtrt.š. | ušḫry.š.il.tʿḏr.bʿl.š.ršp.š.ddmš.š. | w šlmm.ilib.š.i[l.--]m d gbl.ṣpn.al[p]. | pḫr.ilm.š.ym.š[.k]nr.š.[--.]ʿṣrm UG5.9.1.10
ḫlb š. | yrḫ š.ʿnt ṣpn.alp. | w š.pdry š.ddmš š. | w b urbt.ilib š. | bʿl alp w š. | dgn.š.il tʿḏr.š. | bʿl š.ʿnt š.ršp š. | šlmm. | w UG5.13.19
ib. | gdlt.il š.bʿl š.ʿnt. | ṣpn.alp.w š.pdry.š. | šrp.w šlmm ilib š. | bʿl ugrt š.bʿl ḫlb š. | yrḫ š.ʿnt ṣpn.alp. | w š.pdry š.ddm UG5.13.15
w b[--.---]. | ilib[.---]. | alp.[---]. | ili[b.---]. | tʿr[.---]. | dq[t.---]. | nb[--.---]. 44[44].2
. | ʿlm.ʿlm.gdlt l bʿl. | ṣpn.ilbt[.---.]d[--]. | l ṣpn[.---.-]lu. | ilib[.---.b]ʿl. | ugrt[.---.--]n. | [w] š l [---]. UG5.13.35
---]. | kmm.gdlt.l b[ʿl.--.dqt]. | l ṣpn.gdlt.[l.---]. | ugrt.š l ili[b.---]. | rt.w ʿṣrm.l[.---]. | pamt.w bt.[---]. | rmm.w ʿl[y.---]. | APP.II[173].38
w b[--.---]. | ilib[.---]. | alp.[---]. | ili[b.---]. | tʿr[.---]. | dq[t.---]. | nb[--.---]. 44[44].4

ilbldn

.d.ykl.b d.[---]. | b.dbḥ.mlk. | dbḥ ṣpn. | [-]zǵm. | [i]lib. | [i]lbldn. | [p]dry.bt.mlk. | [-]lp.izr. | [a]rz. | k.tʿrb.ʿṯtrt.šd.bt[.m] 2004.6

ilbʿl

n.ibyn. | bn.mryn.ṣmd.w.ḥrṣ. | bn.prsn.ṣmd.w.ḥrṣ. | bn.ilbʿl. | bn.idrm. | bn.grgš. | bn.bly. | bn.apṯ. | bn.ysd. | bn.pl[-]. | 2113.7
my. | alpm. | atn.bṣry.alpm. | lbnym. | ṯm[n.]alp mitm. | ilbʿl ḫmš m[at]. | ʿdn.ḫmš.mat. | bn.[-]d.alp. | bn.[-]pn.ṯṯ mat. 1060.2.9
.bnš mlk.b yrḫ iṯt[bnm]. | ršpab.rb ʿšrt.m[r]yn. | pǵdn.ilbʿl.krwn.lbn.ʿdn. | ḫyrn.mdʿ. | šmʿn.rb ʿšrt.kkln.ʿbd.abṣn. | š 2011.3
]r.bnš.ml[k.d.b] d adn[ʿm]. | [---].riš[.---].kt. | [y]nḥm. | ilbʿl. | ʿbdyr[ḫ]. | ṯtpḥ. | artn. | ybnil. | brqn. | adr[dn]. | krwn. | ar 1024.1.4
| ḫmš ʿl rʿl[-]. | ḫmš ʿl ykn[.--]. | ḫ[mš] ʿl abǵ[l]. | ḫmš ʿl ilb[ʿl]. | ʿšr ʿl [---]. 2034.2.8
yn.ʿšrm. | ṣṣ.bn.krwn.ʿš[rm]. | ṣṣ.bn.iršyn.[---]. | [ṣṣ].bn.ilbʿl.ṯl[ṯ]m. | ṣṣ.bn.pṯdn.[--]m. | ṣṣ.[bn].gyn.[---]. | [-----]. | [-----] 2096.6
.---]. | yʿḏrn[.---]. | [ʿ]bdyr[ḫ.---]. | [---]mlk[.---]. | [-----]. | ilbʿl[.---]. | ḫluy.bn[.---]. | ymil.bn.[---]. | dly.bn[.---]. | ynḥm.b 102[322].5.2

ilbt

ilbt. | ušḫry. | ym.bʿl. | yrḫ. | kṯr. | ṯrmn. | pdry. | dqt. | trṯ. | ršp. | ʿ UG5.14.A.1
.ilt.mgdl š.ilt.asrm š. | w l ll.šp. pgr.w ṯrmnm.bt mlk. | il[bt].gdlt.ušḫry.gdlt.ym gdlt. | bʿl gdlt.yrḫ.gdlt. | gdlt.ṯrmn.g 34[1].13
. | w tr l qlḥ. | w š ḥll ydm. | b qdš il bt. | w tlḥm aṯt. | š l ilbt.šlmm. | kll ylḥm b h. | w l bbt šqym. | š l uḫr ḫlmṭ. | w tr l UG5.11.9
t ṯlṯm š l qrnt. | ṯlḥn.bʿlt.bhtm. | ʿlm.ʿlm.gdlt l bʿl. | ṣpn.ilbt[.---.]d[--]. | l ṣpn[.---.-]lu. | ilib[.---.b]ʿl. | ugrt[.---.--]n. | [w] UG5.13.33

ilgdn

nt. | bdy.ḥrš arkd. | blšš lmd. | ḥtṯn.tqn. | ydd.idṯn. | šǵr.ilgdn. 1045.13

ilgn

.w.ql‘.|bn.tlmyn.ṯt.qšṯm.w.ql‘.|bn.ysd.qšt.|[ǵ]mrm.|ilgn.qšt.|abršp.qšt.|ssg.qšt.|ynḥm.qšt.|pprn.qšt.|uln.qšt.| 105[86].1

ilgt

bnš.kld.|kbln.‘bdyrǵ.ilgt.|ǵyrn.ybnn qrwn.|ypltn.‘bdnt.|klby.aḥrṯp.|ilyn.‘lby.ṣd 1045.2

ildgn

[r--]ǵt.|iw[r---].|iwr[--].|ilṣ[--].|il[---].|il[---].|ilmlk.|ildgn.|ilyn.|ilrm.|ibrm.|ibyn.|illḏrm.|iǵlkḏ.|[i]ly[-]n.|[--- 2022.14
n.‘bdyrẖ.ḥdṯn.y‘r.|adb‘l[.---].ḥdṯn.yḥmn.bnil.|‘dn.w.ildgn.ḥṭbm.|tdǵlm.iln.b‘[l]n.alḏy.|tdn.ṣr[--.--]t.‘zn.mtn.n[b 2011.20
qšṯm.w.ql‘.|bn.gṯrn.q[š]t.|bn.ẖdi.ṯt.qšṯm.w.ṯn.ql‘m.|ildgn.qšt.|bn.y‘rn.ṯt.qšṯm w.ql‘.|bn.ḥṣn.qšt.w.ql‘.|bn.gdn.ṯ 119[321].3.9

ildy

ḏdd]y.tb[--].|ynḥm.aḏddy.|ǵdǵd.aḏddy.|sw.aḏddy.|ildy.aḏddy.|gr‘.aḏddy.|‘bd.ršp aḏddy.|‘dn.bn.knn.|iwrẖz. 2014.33

ilḏ

.|gdn.bn.umy.|kn‘m.š‘rty.|abrpu.ubr‘y.|b.gt.bn.ṯlṭ.|ilḏ.b.gt.psḥn. 91[311].12

ilh

dlt.ilhm.[ṯkmn.w šnm].|dqt.ršp.šrp.w š[lmm.dqtm].|ilh[.a]lp.w š[.il]hm.[gdlt.ilhm].|b‘[l.š].aṯrt[.š.ṯkm]n w [šnm. 35[3].14
t.ilhm.ṯkmn.w šnm dqt.|ršp.dqt.šrp w šlmm.dqtm.|[i]lh.alp w š ilhm.gdl[t.]ilhm.|[b]‘l š.aṯrt.š.ṯkmn w šnm.š.|‘n 34[1].5
dlt.ilhm].|ṯkmn.w [šnm.dqt.ršp.šrp].|w šlmm.[dqtm.ilh.alp.w š].|ilhm.gd[lt.ilhm.b‘l.š.aṯrt.š].|ṯkmn.w š[nm.š.‘nt APP.II[173].15
lm.---].|il[hm.]dqt.š[.---.rš]|[p.š]rp.w šl[mm.--.dqt].|[i]lh.gdlt[.ilhm.gdlt.il].|[d]qt.ṯkmn.w [šnm.dqt.--].|[--]t.dqt 35[3].30
-.]ilh[m.dqt.š.--].|[---.--]t.r[šp.šrp.w šl]|[mm.---].dq[t.ilh.gdlt].|n.w šnm.dqt[.---].|[i]lh[m.gd]lt.i[l.dqt.ṯkm]|n.w š APP.II[173].32
mṣry.d.‘rb.b.unṯ.|bn.qrrn.mḏrǵl.|bn.tran.mḏrǵl|bn.ilh.mḏrǵl|špšyn.b.ulm.|bn.qṭn.b.ulm.|bn.gdrn.b.m‘r[by].|[2046.1.4

ilhd

ṣn.|šdyn.unn.dqn.|‘bd‘nt.rb ‘šrt.mnḥm.ṯb‘m.sẖr.‘zn.ilhd.|bnil.rb ‘šrt.lkn.yp‘n.ṯ[--].|yṣḥm.b d.ubn.krwn.tǵd.[m] 2011.7
n.[q]l‘m.|ǵdyn.qšt.w.ql‘.|bn.gzl.qšt.w.ql‘.|[---]n.qšt.|ilhd.qšt.|‘dn.qšt.w.ql‘.|ilmhr.qšt.w.ql‘.|bn.gmrt.qšt.|ǵmrm 119[321].1.7

ilhm

p.š.dr il w p[ẖ]r b‘l.|gdlt.šlm.gdlt.w burm.[l]b.|rmṣt.ilhm.b‘lm.dṯt.w kšm.ẖmš.|‘ṯr h.mlun.šnpt.ẖṣt h.b‘l.ṣpn š.|[34[1].9
p.š.dr].|il.w pẖr[.b‘l.gdlt.šlm.gdlt].|w burm.l[b.rmṣt.ilhm].|b‘lm.w mlu[.---.ksm].|ṯlṯm.w m‘rb[.---].|dbḥ šmn m APP.II[173].19
.dqt.ršp.šrp].|w šlmm.[dqtm.ilh.alp.w š].|ilhm.gd[lt.ilhm.b‘l.š.aṯrt.š].|ṯkmn.w š[nm.š.‘nt.š.ršp.š.dr].|il.w pẖr[.b‘ APP.II[173].16
dqt.ršp.šrp.w š[lmm.dqtm].|ilh[.a]lp.w š[.il]hm.[gdlt.ilhm].|b‘[l.š].aṯrt[.š.ṯkm]n w [šnm.š].|‘nt š ršp š[.dr.il.w pẖ 35[3].14
.|ršp.dqt.šrp w šlmm.dqtm.|[i]lh.alp w š ilhm.gdl[t.]ilhm.|[b]‘l š.aṯrt.š.ṯkmn w šnm.š.|‘nt.š.ršp.š.dr il w p[ẖ]r b‘ 34[1].5
p š[.dr.il.w pẖr.b‘l].|gdlt.šlm[.gdlt.w burm.lb].|rmṣt.ilh[m.b‘lm.---].|ksm.ṯlṯm.[---].|d yqḥ bt[.--]r.dbḥ[.šmn.mr]. 35[3].18
[hm.]dqt.š[.---.rš]|[p.š]rp.w šl[mm.--.dqt].|[i]lh.gdlt[.ilhm.gdlt.il].|[d]qt.ṯkmn.w [šnm.dqt.--].|[--]t.dqtm.[b nbk.- 35[3].30
.šrp.w šl]|[mm.---].dq[t.ilh.gdlt].|n.w šnm.dqt[.---].|[i]lh[m.gd]lt.i[l.dqt.ṯkm]|n.w šnm.dqt[.---].|bqtm.b nbk.[---] APP.II[173].33
mn.w [šnm.dqt.ršp.šrp].|w šlmm.[dqtm.ilh.alp.w š].|ilhm.gd[lt.ilhm.b‘l.š.aṯrt.š].|ṯkmn.w š[nm.š.‘nt.š.ršp.š.dr].|i APP.II[173].16
.w šnm dqt.|ršp.dqt.šrp w šlmm.dqtm.|[i]lh.alp w š ilhm.gdl[t.]ilhm.|[b]‘l š.aṯrt.š.ṯkmn w šnm.š.|‘nt.š.ršp.š.dr i 34[1].5
n.w šnm].|dqt.ršp.šrp.w š[lmm.dqtm].|ilh[.a]lp.w š[.il]hm.[gdlt.ilhm].|b‘[l.š].aṯrt[.š.ṯkm]n w [šnm.š].|‘nt š ršp š 35[3].14
dlt.l [nkl.gdlt.l b‘]|[lt].bht[m].[‘]ṣrm l [inš.ilm].|[---.]ilh[m.dqt.š.--].|[---.--]t.r[šp.šrp.w šl]|[mm.---].dq[t.ilh.gdlt] APP.II[173].30
].|gd[lt].l nkl[.gdlt.l b‘lt.bhtm].|‘š[rm.]l inš[.ilm.---].|il[hm.]dqt.š[.---.rš]|[p.š]rp.w šl[mm.--.dqt].|[i]lh.gdlt[.ilhm 35[3].28
|w yn[t.q]rt.y[---].|w al[p.l]il.w bu[rm.---].|ytk.gdlt.ilhm.[ṯkmn.w šnm].|dqt.ršp.šrp.w š[lmm.dqtm].|ilh[.a]lp. 35[3].12
dqt.ṯ‘.ynt.ṯ‘m.dqt.ṯ‘m.|mtntm nkbd.alp.š.l il.|gdlt.ilhm.ṯkmn.w šnm dqt.|ršp.dqt.šrp w šlmm.dqtm.|[i]lh.alp 34[1].3
[nt.qrt.---].|[---.--]n[.w alp.l il.w bu]|[rm.---.ytk.gdlt.ilhm].|ṯkmn.w [šnm.dqt.ršp.šrp].|w šlmm.[dqtm.ilh.alp.w APP.II[173].13

ilhnm

[--]t.ilhnm.b šnt.|[---.]šb‘.mat.š‘rt.ẖmšm.kbd.|[---.-]nd.l.mlbš.ṯr 1106.1

ilht

krm.y[n].|špq.ilht.ẖprt[.yn].|špq.ilm.alpm.y[n].|špq.ilht.arẖt[.yn].|špq.ilm.kḥṯm.yn.|špq.ilht.ksat[.yn].|špq.ilm 4[51].6.50
[---.--]i[-.]a[--.---].|[---.]ilm.w ilht.dt.|[---.]šb‘.l šb‘m.aṯr.|[---.--]ldm.dt ymtm.|[--.--]r.l ẓp 25[136].2
m.kḥṯm.yn.|špq.ilht.ksat[.yn].|špq.ilm.rḥbt yn.|špq.ilht.dkrt[.yn].|‘d.lḥm.šty.ilm.|w pq mrǵṯm.ṯd.|b ḥrb.mlḥt. 4[51].6.54
.k m‘r[.---].|yṣḥ.ngr il.ilš.|ilš.ngr.bt.b‘l.|w aṯt h.ngrt.ilht.|w y‘n.lṭpn.il d pi[d].|šm‘.l ngr.il il[š].|ilš.ngr bt b‘l.|w 16[126].4.9
b qrb hkl h.ṣḥ.|šb‘m.bn.aṯrt.|špq.ilm.krm.y[n].|špq.ilht.ẖprt[.yn].|špq.ilm.alpm.y[n].|špq.ilht.arẖt[.yn].|špq.il 4[51].6.48
].|k il.ḥkmt.k ṯr.lṭpn.|ṣḥ.ngr.il.ilš.il[š].|w aṯt h.ngrt[.i]lht.|kḥṣ.k m‘r[.---].|yṣḥ.ngr il.ilš.|ilš.ngr.bt.b‘l.|w aṯt h.n 16[126].4.5
.alpm.y[n].|špq.ilht.arẖt[.yn].|špq.ilm.kḥṯm.yn.|špq.ilht.ksat[.yn].|špq.ilm.rḥbt yn.|špq.ilht.dkrt[.yn].|‘d.lḥm.š 4[51].6.52
|bn mznm.nkl w ib.|d ašr.ar yrẖ.w y|rẖ yar k.|[ašr ilht kṯrt bn]|t hll.snnt.bnt h|ll b‘l gml.yrdt.|b ‘rgzm.b bz t 24[77].40
.--].|pt l bšr h.dm a[--.--]ḥ.|w yn.k mtrẖt[.---]h.|šm‘ ilht kṯr[t.--]mm.|nh l yd h tzdn[.---]n.|l ad[n h.---].|dgn tt[24[77].11
l d pi[d].|šm‘.l ngr.il il[š].|ilš.ngr bt b‘l.|w aṯt k.ngrt.il[ht].|‘l.l ṯkm.bnw n.|l nẖnpt.mšpy.|ṯlṯ.kmm.ṯrr y.|[---.]l 16[126].4.13
šb‘t.ḥdrm.b ṯmnt.|ap.sgrt.yd‘[t k.]bt.k an[št].|k in.b ilht.ql[ṣ] k.mh.tarš[n].|l btlt.‘nt.w t[‘]n.btlt.‘n[t].|tḥm k.il.ḥ 3[‘NT.VI].5.36
lt.[‘nt].|w y‘n.lṭpn.il d p[id].|yd‘t k.bt.k anšt.w i[n.b ilht].|qlṣ k.tb‘.bt.ẖnp.lb[k.--.ti]|ẖd.d iṯ.b kbd k.tšt.b [---].|i 18[3AQHT].1.16

ilwn

adml[--.---]. | tlbr[-.---]. | isg.[---]. | ilwn.[---]. | ṯrn.d[d]. | tg d[d]. | ḥdyn.d[d]. | [-]d̲dn.d[d]. | qṯn.d[132[331].4

ilḥu

l.ṣrrt. | adn k.šqrb.[---]. | b mgn k.w ḥrṣ.l kl. | apnk.ǵzr.ilḥu. | [m]rḥ h.yiḫd.b yd. | [g]rgr h.bm.ymn. | [w]yqrb.trẓẓ h. 16.1[125].46
]. | b[---.]ny[.--]. | l bl.sk.w [---] h. | ybm h.šbʻ[.---]. | ǵzr.ilḥu.t[---]l. | trm.tṣr.trm[.ʻ]tqt. | tbky.w tšnn.[tt]n. | g h.bky.b 16.2[125].95
.---]. | mn.yrḫ.k m[rṣ.---]. | mn.k dw.kr[t]. | w yʻny.ǵzr[.ilḥu]. | ṯlṯ.yrḫm.k m[rṣ]. | arbʻ.k dw.k[rt]. | mndʻ.krt.mǵ[y.---] 16.2[125].83
ḫ h.tbky. | [--.m]rṣ.mlk. | [---.]krt.adn k. | [w yʻny.]ǵzr.ilḥu. | [---.]mrṣ.mlk. | [--.k]rt.adn k. | [--.d]bḥ.dbḥ. | [--.ʻ]šr.ʻšrt 16.1[125].58

ilḥbn

n.qšt.w.qlʻ. | ilrb.qšt.w.qlʻ. | psḥn.qšt. | bn.kmy.qšt. | bn.ilḥbn.qšt.w.q[lʻ]. | ršpab.qšt.w.qlʻ. | pdrn.qšt.w.qlʻ. | bn.pǵm[-. 119[321].3.44

ilḫr

[i]ly[-]n. | [-----]. | m[--.---]. | [-]n.qrqr. | [--]n.ymn.y[--]. | ilḫr.ṣdqn[.--]. 2022.26

ily

rišym.dt.ʻrb. | b bnš hm. | d̲mry.w.pṯpṯ.ʻrb. | b.yrm. | [ily.w].d̲mry.ʻrb. | b.ṯbʻm. | ydn.bn.ilrpi. | w.ṯbʻm.ʻrb.b.ʻ[d]n. | d̲ 2079.5
---]. | b.ḫrbǵlm.ǵlm[n]. | w.trhy.aṯt h. | w.mlky.b[n] h. | ily.mrily.tdgr. 2048.22
| u[l]n.qšt.w.qlʻ. | yʻrn.qšt.w.qlʻ. | klby.qšt.w.qlʻ. | bqʻt. | ily.qšt.w.qlʻ. | bn.ḥrẓn.qšt.w.qlʻ. | tgrš.qšt.w.qlʻ. | špšyn.qšt.w. 119[321].2.22

ilyy

.---]. | ḫmrm.ṯṯ.krm[m.---]. | krm.ǵlkz.b.p[--.---]. | krm.ilyy.b.m[--.---]. | kd.šbʻ.krmm.[---]. | ṯn.krm[m.i]wrǵl[.---]. | ṯ 1081.24

ilym

| ʻpṯrm. | bn.ʻbd. | šmbʻl. | ykr. | bly. | ṯbʻm. | ḥdṯn. | rpty. | ilym. | bn.ʻbr. | mnipʻl. | amrbʻl. | dqry. | ṯdy. | ypʻbʻl. | bdlm. | bn 1058.13

ilyn

iw[r---]. | iwr[--]. | ilṣ[--]. | il[---]. | il[---]. | ilmlk. | ildgn. | ilyn. | ilrm. | ibrm. | ibyn. | illd̲rm. | iǵlkd̲. | [i]ly[-]n. | [-----]. | m[2022.15
rqd. | bn.abdg. | ilyn. | bn.tan. | bn.arm. | bn.bʻl.ṣdq. | bn.army. | bn.rpiyn. | bn.a 1046.1.3
n.ṯryn. | bn.dll. | bn.ḫswn. | mrynm. | ʻzn. | ḥyn. | ʻmyn. | ilyn. | yrbʻm. | nʻmn. | bn.kbl. | knʻm. | bdlm. | bn.ṣǵr. | klb. | bn. 1046.3.37
nn. | ʻl.ʻrbnm. | hn hmt. | tknn. | mtn.bn.ʻbdym. | ilrb.bn.ilyn. | ʻbdadt.bn ʻbdkb. | gnʻym. 1161.11
yrǵ.ilgt. | ǵyrn.ybnn qrwn. | ypltn.ʻbdnt. | klby.aḥrṯp. | ilyn.ʻlby.ṣdkn. | gmrt.ṯlmyn. | ʻbdnt. | bdy.ḥrš arkd. | blšš lmd. 1045.6
rz.[ar]bʻ.qšt.w.arb[ʻ.]qlʻm. | b[n.]adʻl.q[š]t.w.qlʻ. | b[n].ilyn.qšt.w.qlʻ. | šmrm.qlʻ. | ubrʻy. | abmn.qšt.w.ṯn.qlʻm. | qdm 119[321].2.47
ṣṣ.bn.ilyn.ṯlṯm. | ṣṣ.bn.kzn.ṯlṯm. | ṣṣ.bn.tlmyn.ʻšrm. | ṣṣ.bn.krwn.ʻš[2096.1
.ṯbil. | bn.iryn. | ṯṯl. | bn.nṣdn. | bn.ydln. | [bn].ʻdy. | [bn].ilyn. 1071.11

ilk

ilk.r[--]. | aršm.bʻl [aṯt]. | ttḫ.bʻl aṯt. | ayab.bʻl aṯt. | iyṯr.bʻl aṯt. 1077.1

ill

.gʻyn. | ḥyn. | bn.armg[-]. | bʻlmṯpṭ. | [bn].ayḫ. | [---]rn. | ill. | ǵlmn. | bn.ytrm. | bn.ḫgbt. | mtn. | mḫtn. | [p]lsy. | bn.ḥrš. | 1035.2.8

illd̲r

l.mlkt. | adt y.rgm. | tḥm.illd̲r. | ʻbd k.. | l.pʻn a[dt y]. | šbʻ d[.w šbʻ d]. | mrḥq[tm.qlt]. | 1014.3

illd̲rm

il[---]. | il[---]. | ilmlk. | ildgn. | ilyn. | ilrm. | ibrm. | ibyn. | illd̲rm. | iǵlkd̲. | [i]ly[-]n. | [-----]. | m[--.---]. | [-]n.qrqr. | [--]n.y 2022.19
qmḥ.d.kly.k ṣḥ.illd̲rm. | b d.zlb[n.--]. | arbʻ.ʻš[r.]dd.nʻr. | d.apy[.--]. | w.arb[ʻ.-- 2094.1
qmḥ.d.kly.b bt.skn. | l.illd̲rm. | ltḥ.ḫṣr.b.šbʻ.ddm. 2093.2

ilm

rt h. | hmry.mk.ksu. | ṯbt h.ḫḫ.arṣ. | nḫlt h.w nǵr. | ʻnn.ilm.al. | tqrb.l bn.ilm. | mt.al.yʻdb km. | k imr.b p h. | k lli.b ṯb 4[51].8.15
m.bn.aṯrt. | špq.ilm.krm.y[n]. | špq.ilht.ḫprt[.yn]. | špq.ilm.alpm.y[n]. | špq.ilht.arḫt[.yn]. | špq.ilm.kḥṯm.yn. | špq.ilh 4[51].6.49
aḥd.hm.iṯ.šmt.hm.iṯ[.ʻẓm]. | abky.w aqbrn.ašt.b ḫrt. | i[lm.arṣ.b p h.rgm.l yṣa.b šp] | t h.hwt h.knp.hrgb.bʻl.ṯbr. | bʻ 19[1AQHT].3.127
.w aḥd.hm.iṯ.šmt.iṯ. | ʻẓm.abky w aqbrn h.aštn. | b ḫrt.ilm.arṣ.b p h.rgm.l[yṣ]a. | b špt h.hwt h.knp.ṣml.bʻ[l]. | bʻl.ṯb 19[1AQHT].3.141
ḥd.hm.iṯ.šmt.hm.i[ṯ]. | ʻẓm.abky.w aqbrn h. | ašt.b ḫrt.ilm.arṣ. | b p h.rgm.l yṣa.b špt h.hwt[h]. | knp.nšrm.bʻl.yṯbr. 19[1AQHT].3.112
| [---.-]mn k.ššrt. | [---.--]t.npš.ʻgl. | [---.-]nk.aštn.b ḫrt. | ilm.arṣ.w at.qḥ. | ʻrpt k.rḥ k.mdl k. | mṭrt k.ʻm k.šbʻt. | ǵlm k. 5[67].5.6
.tšʻlyn h. | b ṣrrt.ṣpn.tbkyn h. | w tqbrn h.tštnn.b ḫrt. | ilm.arṣ.ttbḫ.šbʻm. | rumm.k gmn.aliyn. | [b]ʻl.ṭṭbḫ.šbʻm.alpm 6[62].1.18
.ištml h. | mḫšt.bṯn.ʻqltn. | šlyṭ.d šbʻt.rašm. | mḫšt.mdd ilm.ar[š]. | ṣmt.ʻgl.il.ʻtk. | mḫšt.klbt.ilm išt. | klt.bt.il.d̲bb.imtḫ 3[ʻNT].3.40
t]. | b tk.rpi.ar[ṣ]. | b pḫr.qbṣ.dtn. | ṣǵrt hn.abkrn. | tbrk.ilm.tity. | tity.ilm.l ahl hm. | dr il.l mšknt hm. | w tqrb.w ld.b 15[128].3.17
ṣ.arbdd. | l kbd.š[d]m.ap.mṯn.rgmm. | argmn.lk.lk.ʻnn.ilm. | atm.bštm.w an.šnt. | uǵr.l rḥq.ilm.inbb. | l rḥq.ilnym.ṯn 3[ʻNT].4.76
arṣ]. | at.w ank.ib[ǵy h.---]. | w yʻn.kṯr.w ḫss[.lk.lk.ʻnn.ilm.] | atm.bštm.w an[.šnt.kptr]. | l rḥq.ilm.ḥkp[t.l rḥq.ilnym 1[ʻNT.IX].3.17
. | [---].l ʻnt m. | [---.]l šlm. | [-]l[-.-]ry.ylbš. | mlk.ylk.lqḥ.ilm. | aṯr.ilm.ylk.pʻnm. | mlk.pʻnm.yl[k]. | šbʻ.pamt.l kl hm. 33[5].23
m]n.al[i]yn.b[ʻl]. | [---]ḥ h.tšt bm.ʻ[--]. | [---.]zr h.ybm.l ilm. | [id]k.l ttn.pnm.ʻm. | [il.]mbk nhrm.qrb. | [a]pq.thmtm.t 6.1.31[49.1.3]
rdm.bhṯ.l bn.ilm mt. | ʻbd k.an.w d.ʻlm k. | tbʻ.w l.ytb.ilm.idk. | l ytn.pn.ʻm.bn.ilm.mt. | tk.qrt h.hmry.mk.ksu. | ṯbt. 5[67].2.13
rt. | b npš.bn ilm.mt.b mh | mrt.ydd.il.ǵzr. | tbʻ.w l.yṯb ilm.idk. | l ytn.pnm.ʻm.bʻl. | mrym.ṣpn.w yʻn. | gpn.w ugr.tḥ 5[67].1.9
. | argmn.lk.lk.ʻnn.ilm. | atm.bštm.w an.šnt. | uǵr.l rḥq.ilm.inbb. | l rḥq.ilnym.ṯn.mṯpdm. | tḥt.ʻnt.arṣ.ṯlṯ.mtḥ.ǵyrm. | 3[ʻNT].4.78

t.rašm.|mh̲št.mdd ilm.ar[š].|ṣmt.‘gl.il.‘tk.|mh̲št.klbt.ilm išt.|klt.bt.il.d̲bb.imth̲ṣ.ksp.|itrt̲.h̲rṣ.t̲rd.b‘l.|b mrym.ṣp 3[‘NT].3.42

ṣpn.|b qdš.b ǵr.nh̲lt y.|b n‘m.b gb‘.tliyt.|hlm.‘nt.tph.ilm.b h.p‘nm.|tt̲t.b‘d n.ksl.tt̲br.|‘ln.pn h.td‘.tǵṣ.pnt.|ksl h.a 3[‘NT].3.29

ḥd.šd.gt̲r.|[w]ht.yšm‘.uh̲ y.|l g y.w yhbt̲.bnš.|w ytn.ilm.b d hm.|b d.ih̲qm.gt̲r.|w b d.ytrhd.|b‘l. 55[18].19

dd il.|y[m.---.]l t̲r.qdqd h.|il[.--.]rḥq.b ǵr.|km.y[--.]ilm.b ṣpn.|‘dr.l[‘r].‘rm.|t̲b.l pd[r.]pdrm.|t̲t.l t̲t̲m.ah̲d.‘r.|šb 4[51].7.6

‘t.w y‘n.dnil.[mt.rpi].|yt̲b.ǵzr.mt hrnmy[.---].|b grnt.ilm.b qrb.m[t̲‘t.ilnym].|d tit.yspi.spu.q[--.---].|tpḥ.t̲sr.shr[.- 20[121].2.9

a.šmm.b y[d.bn.ilm.m]t.|w t‘n.btlt.‘n[t.bnt.]bht |k.y ilm.bnt.bh[t k].a[l.tš]mh̲.|al.tšmh̲.b r[m.h]kl[k].|al.ah̲d.h 3[‘NT.VI].5.28

.|[---] h.ap.[---].|[---].w t‘n.[btlt.‘nt.---].|[bnt.bht]k.y ilm[.bnt.bht k.--].|[al.tšmh̲.]al.tš[mh̲.b rm.h]|[kl k.al.]ah̲d 18[3AQHT].1.7

ḥqm.l p[-.---].|ṣḥ.il.yt̲b.b[mrzḥ.---].|bt̲t.‘llm n.[---].|ilm.bt.b‘l k.[---].|dl.ylkn.ḥš.b a[rṣ.---].|b ‘pr.h̲bl t̲tm.[---.]|š 1[‘NT.X].4.6

ns.|[---.]ysd k.|[---.--]r.dr.dr.|[---.--]y k.w rḥd.|[---]y ilm.d mlk.|y[t̲]b.aliyn.b‘l.|yt‘dd.rkb.‘rpt.|[--].ydd.w yqlṣn. 4[51].3.9

[ṣt h.y‘l.]w yškb.yd.|[mizrt.]p ynl.hn.ym.|[w t̲n.uzr.]ilm.dnil.|[uzr.ilm.]ylḥm.uzr.|[yšqy.b]n.qdš t̲lt̲ rb‘ ym.|[uzr 17[2AQHT].1.7

zr.|[ilm.y]lḥm.uzr.yšqy bn.|[qdš.h̲]mš.t̲dt̲.ym.uzr.|[ilm].dnil.uzr.ilm.ylḥm.|[uzr.]yšqy.bn qdš.yd.ṣt h.|[dn]il.yd 17[2AQHT].1.13

l.|[uzr.ilm.]ylḥm.uzr.|[yšqy.b]n.qdš t̲lt̲ rb‘ ym.|[uzr.i]lm.dnil.uzr.|[ilm.y]lḥm.uzr.yšqy bn.|[qdš.h̲]mš.t̲dt̲.ym.uz 17[2AQHT].1.10

rgmm.|argm k.šskn m‘.|mgn.rbt.at̲rt ym.|mǵẓ.qnyt.ilm.|hyn.‘ly.l mpḥm.|b d.h̲ss.mṣbṭm.|yṣq.ksp.yšl|ḥ.h̲rṣ.yṣ 4[51].1.23

t m.|[---.]l šlm.|[-]l[-.-]ry.ylbš.|mlk.ylk.lqḥ.ilm.|at̲r.ilm.ylk.p‘nm.|mlk.p‘nm.yl[k].|šb‘.pamt.l kl hm. 33[5].24

t.l tšt.|yn.tǵẓyt.špš.|rpim.tḥtk.|špš.tḥtk.ilnym.|‘d k.ilm.hn.mtm.|‘d k.kt̲r m.ḥbr k.|w h̲ss.d‘t k.|b ym.arš.w tnn 6.6[62.2].47

[---.--]i[-.]a[--.---].|[---.]ilm.w ilht.dt.|[---.]šb‘.l šb‘m.at̲r.|[---.---]ldm.dt ymtm.|[--.-- 25[136].2

[---].|[---].mr[--.---].|[---].mr[--.]ydm[.---].|[---.]mtbt.ilm.w.b.[---].|[---.]tt̲tbn.ilm.w.[---].|[---.]w.ksu.b‘lt.b[htm.-- 47[33].5

.mgn.rbt.at̲rt.|[ym].mǵẓ.qnyt.ilm.|w tn.bt.l b‘l.km.|[i]lm.w ḥẓr.k bn.|[a]t̲rt.gm.l ǵlm h.|b‘l.yṣḥ.‘n.gpn.|w ugr.b 8[51FRAG].4

ank.ah̲d.ult̲.|hm.amt.at̲rt.tlbn.|lbnt.ybn.bt.l b‘l.|km ilm.w ḥẓr.k bn.at̲rt.|w t‘n.rbt.at̲rt ym.|rbt.ilm.l ḥkmt.|šbt. 4[51].5.63

.yṣḥ.|at̲rt.w bn h.ilt.w ṣbrt.|ary h.wn.in.bt.l b‘l.|km.ilm.w ḥẓr.k bn.at̲rt.|mtb il.mẓll.bn h.|mtb rbt.at̲rt.ym.|mt̲ 4[51].4.51

t̲|[rt.w bn h.]ilt.|[w ṣbrt.ary]h.|[wn.in.bt.l b‘l.]|[km.ilm.w ḥẓr].|[k bn.at̲]r[t].|m[t̲]b.il.mẓll.|bn h.mtb.rbt.|at̲rt. 4[51].1.11

[---.wn.in].|[bt].l [b‘l.km.ilm.w ḥẓr].|k bn.[at̲rt.mtb.il.mẓll].|bn h.m[t̲b.rbt.at̲rt.ym]. 3[‘NT.VI].4.01

hlk].šbt h.dmm.šbt.dqn h.|[mm‘m.-]d.l ytn.bt.l b‘l.k ilm.|[w ḥẓ]r.k bn.at̲rt[.td‘ṣ.]p‘n.|[w tr.a]rṣ.id[k.l ttn.p]nm. 3[‘NT.VI].5.11

‘t̲tr].dm[-]k[-].|[--]ḥ.b y.t̲r.il.ab y.ank.in.bt[.l] y[.km.]ilm[.w] ḥẓr[.k bn].|[qd]š.lbum.trd.b n[p]šn y.trḥṣn.k t̲rm.|[2.3[129].19

[i]k.mgn.rbt.at̲rt.|[ym].mǵẓ.qnyt.ilm.|w tn.bt.l b‘l.km.|[i]lm.w ḥẓr.k bn.|[a]t̲rt.gm.l ǵlm h.| 8[51FRAG].2

h.ystrn ydd.|b gngn h.ah̲d y.d ym|lk.‘l.ilm.l ymru.|ilm.w nšm.d yšb|[‘].hmlt.arṣ.gm.l ǵ|[lm] h.b‘l k.yṣḥ.‘n.|[g 4[51].7.51

tk.pn h.t‘db.ksu.|w yt̲b.l ymn.aliyn.|b‘l.‘d.lḥm.št[y.ilm].|[w]y‘n.aliy[n.b‘l].|[--]b[.---].|ḥš.bht m.k[t̲r].|ḥš.rmm 4[51].5.110

b bt h.yšt.‘rb.|[--] h.ytn.w [--]u.l ytn.|[ah̲]r.mǵy.‘[d]t.ilm.|[w]y‘n.aliy[n.]b‘l.|[---.]tb‘.l lt̲pn.|[il.d]pid.l tbrk.|[krt 15[128].2.11

.b‘l.|mǵyt.btlt.‘nt.|tmgnn.rbt[.a]t̲rt ym.|tǵẓyn.qnyt.ilm.|w t‘n.rbt.at̲rt ym.|ik.tmgnn.rbt.|at̲rt.ym.tǵẓyn.|qnyt.i 4[51].3.26

pn.t̲p]t̲[.nhr.]mlkt.[--]pm.l mlkt.wn.in.at̲t.|[l]k.k[m.ilm].|[w ǵlmt.k bn.qdš.]w y[--.]zbl.ym.y‘[--.]t̲pt̲.nhr.|[-------

[.yn].|špq.ilm.rḥbt yn.|špq.ilht.dkrt[.yn].|‘d.lḥm.šty.ilm.|w pq mrǵtm.t̲d.|b ḥrb.mlḥt.qṣ[.m]r|i.tšty.krp[nm.y]n. 4[51].6.55

iyn.b‘l.|[--.]rbt.at̲rt.ym.|[---.]btlt.‘nt.|[--.tl]ḥm.tšty.|[ilm.w tp]q.mrǵtm.|[t̲d.b ḥrb.m]lḥt.qṣ.|[mri.tšty.k]rpnm yn 4[51].3.41

|b tmnt.[---].|yqrb.[---].|lḥm.m[---.---].|[‘]d.lḥm[.šty.ilm].|w pq.mr[ǵtm.t̲d.---].|b ḥrb.[mlḥt.qṣ.mri].|šty.kr[pnm 5[67].4.12

b‘[t.‘šrt.riš.argmn].|w t̲n šm.l [b‘lt.bhtm.‘ṣrm.l inš].|ilm.w š d[d.ilš.š.--.mlk].|yt̲b.brr[.w mḥ-.---].|ym.[‘]lm.y‘[--. 35[3].6

]b‘t.‘šrt.riš.|arg[mn.w t̲n.]šm.l b‘lt.|bhtm.‘ṣ[rm.l in]š ilm.w š.|dd ilš.š[.---.]mlk.yt̲b br|r.w mḥ[--.---.]w q[--].|ym. APP.II[173].6

il dbḥ.b bt h.mṣd.ṣd.b qrb|hkl [h].ṣḥ.l qṣ.ilm.tlḥmn.|ilm.w tštn.tštn y[n] ‘d šb‘.|trt̲.‘d.škr.y‘db.yrḫ.|gb h.km.[---. UG5.1.1.3

-].mr[--.]ydm[.---].|[---.]mtbt.ilm.w.b.[---].|[---.]tt̲tbn.ilm.w.[---].|[---.]w.ksu.b‘lt.b[htm.---].|[---.]il.bt.gdlt.[---].|[- 47[33].6

h.yṣḥ.at̲rt.|w bn h.ilt.w ṣbrt.arh̲ h.|wn.in.bt.l b‘l.km.ilm.|ḥẓr.k b[n.a]t̲rt.mtb.il.|mt̲ll.b[n h.m]t̲b.rbt.at̲rt.|ym.mt̲ 3[‘NT.VI].5.46

h̲ss[.lk.lk.‘nn.ilm.]|atm.bštm.w an[.šnt.kptr].|l rḥq.ilm.ḥkp[t.l rḥq.ilnym].|t̲n.mt̲pdm.tḥt.[‘nt.arṣ.t̲lt̲.mtḥ].|ǵyr 1[‘NT.IX].3.19

[---.]n[--.---].|[---.kpt]r.l r[ḥq.ilm.ḥkpt.l rḥq].|[ilnym.t̲n.mt̲pd]m.t[ḥt.‘nt.arṣ.t̲lt̲.mtḥ.ǵyrm 2.3[129].2

].|gršm.z[bln.in.b ilm].|‘ny h.y[t̲ny.yt̲lt̲].|rgm.my.b[ilm.ydy].|mrṣ.grš[m.zbln].|in.b ilm.‘[ny h.yrb‘].|yh̲mš.rgm 16[126].5.14

--].|t̲nnt h[.---].|t̲lt̲ h[.-.w y‘n].|lt̲pn.[il.d pid.my].|b ilm.[ydy.mrṣ].|gršm.z[bln.in.b ilm].|‘ny h.y[t̲ny.yt̲lt̲].|rgm. 16[126].5.11

ṣ.g[ršm.zbln].|in.b ilm.‘n[y h.]yt̲dt̲.|yšb‘.rgm.[my.]b ilm.|ydy.mrṣ.gršm zbln.|in.b ilm.‘ny h.|w y‘n.lt̲pn.il.b pid. 16[126].5.20

ṣ.grš[m.zbln].|in.b ilm.‘[ny h.yrb‘].|yh̲mš.rgm.[my.b ilm].|ydy.mrṣ.g[ršm.zbln].|in.b ilm.‘n[y h.]yt̲dt̲.|yšb‘.rgm.[16[126].5.17

[a]rṣ.|[u]šh̲r[y].|[‘]t̲trt.|i[l t]‘d̲r b‘l.|ršp.|ddmš.|pḫr ilm.|ym.|ut̲ht̲.|knr.|mlkm.|šlm. 29[17].2.7

lb.l ẓr.rḥtm w rd.|bt h̲pt̲t.arṣ.tspr b y|rdm.arṣ.w td‘ ilm.|k mtt.yšm‘.aliyn.b‘l.|yuhb.‘glt.b dbr.prt.|b šd.šḥlmmt 5[67].5.16

k t‘rb.‘t̲trt.h̲r[-].|bt mlk.‘šr.‘šr.[--].bt ilm.|kbr[-]m.[-]trmt.|lbš.w [-]tn.ušpǵt.|h̲r[-].t̲lt̲.mzn.|drk. 33[5].2

ml.|h̲mš.kbd.arb‘m.|dd.akl.|t̲t.‘šr h.yn.|kd.šmn.l.nr.ilm.|kdm.dǵm.|t̲t.kdm.ztm. 1126.6

h̲prt[.yn].|špq.ilm.alpm.y[n].|špq.ilht.arh̲t[.yn].|špq.ilm.kḥtm.yn.|špq.ilht.ksat[.yn].|špq.ilm.rḥbt yn.|špq.ilht. 4[51].6.51

h.b bht h.a[r]y h.|b qrb hkl h.ṣḥ.|šb‘m.bn.at̲rt.|špq.ilm.krm.y[n].|špq.ilht.h̲prt[.yn].|špq.ilm.alpm.y[n].|špq.il 4[51].6.47

[ṣ].|b pḫr.qbṣ.dtn.|ṣǵrt hn.abkrn.|tbrk.ilm.tity.|tity.ilm.l ahl hm.|dr il.l mšknt hm.|w tqrb.w ld.bn.l h.|w tqrb. 15[128].3.18

.l b‘l.|km ilm.w ḥẓr.k bn.at̲rt.|w t‘n.rbt.at̲rt ym.|rbt.ilm.l ḥkmt.|šbt.dqn k.l tsr k.|rh̲ntt.d[-].l irt k.|wn ap.‘dn. 4[51].5.65

m[m].|šd dd h ḥrnqm.w |y‘n h̲rh̲b mlk qẓ [l].|n‘mn.ilm l h̲t[n].|m.b‘l trh̲ pdry b[t h].|aqrb k ab h b‘[l].|ygtr.‘t̲t 24[77].25

b‘.ǵlmm.l t̲tb.[idk.pnm].|l ytn.tk.ǵr.ll.‘m.phr.m‘d.ap.ilm.l lḥ[m].|yt̲b.bn qdš.l t̲rm.b‘l.qm.‘l.il.hlm.|ilm.tph hm.t 2.1[137].20

ra.mt.|b npš h.ystrn ydd.|b gngn h.ah̲d y.d ym|lk.‘l.ilm.l ymru.|ilm.w nšm.d yšb|[‘].hmlt.arṣ.gm.l ǵ|[lm] h.b‘l 4[51].7.50

il dbḥ.b bt h.mṣd.ṣd.b qrb|hkl [h].ṣḥ.l qṣ.ilm.tlḥmn.|ilm.w tštn.tštn y[n] ‘d šb‘.|trt̲.‘d.škr.y‘db.yrḫ.| UG5.1.1.2

m.uzr.yšqy bn.|[qdš.h̲]mš.t̲dt̲.ym.uzr.|[ilm].dnil.uzr.ilm.ylḥm.|[uzr.]yšqy.bn qdš.yd.ṣt h.|[dn]il.yd.ṣt h.y‘l.w yš 17[2AQHT].1.13

b.yd.|[mizrt.]p ynl.hn.ym.|[w t̲n.uzr.]ilm.dnil.|[uzr.ilm.]ylḥm.uzr.|[yšqy.b]n.qdš t̲lt̲ rb‘ ym.|[uzr.i]lm.dnil.uzr. 17[2AQHT].1.8

km.ary h.|bl.it̲.bn.l h.km ah̲ h.w šrš.|km.ary h.uzrm.ilm.ylḥm.|uzrm.yšqy.bn.qdš.|l tbrknn l t̲r.il ab y.|tmrnn.l 17[2AQHT].1.22

[-----.apnk].|[dnil.mt.rp]i.apn.ǵz[r].|[mt.hrnmy.]uzr.ilm.ylḥm.|[uzr.yšqy.]bn.qdš.yd.|[ṣt h.y‘l.]w yškb.yd.|[mizr 17[2AQHT].1.3

m.uzr.|[yšqy.b]n.qdš t̲lt̲ rb‘ ym.|[uzr.i]lm.dnil.uzr.|[ilm.y]lḥm.uzr.yšqy bn.|[qdš.h̲]mš.t̲dt̲.ym.uzr.|[ilm].dnil.uz 17[2AQHT].1.11

t‘n.rbt.at̲rt ym.|ik.tmgnn.rbt.|at̲rt.ym.tǵẓyn.|qnyt.ilm.mgntm.|t̲r.il.d pid.hm.ǵẓtm.|bny.bnwt w t‘n.|btlt.‘nt.n 4[51].3.30

d.at̲t.ab.ṣrry.|ik m.yrgm.bn.il.|krt.špḥ.lt̲pn.|w qdš.u ilm.tmtn.|špḥ.lt̲pn.l yḥ.|w y‘ny.krt.t̲‘.|bn.al.tbkn.al.|tdm.l 16.1[125].22

.ab.k mtm.tmtn. | u ẖšt k.l bky.‘tq. | b d.at̠t ab.ṣrry. | u ilm.tmtn.špḥ. | [l]t̠pn.l yḥ.t[b]ky k. | ab.ǵr.b‘l.ṣ[p]n.ḥlm. | qdš. 16.2[125].105
su. | t̠bt h.ẖẖ.arṣ. | nḥlt h.w nǵr. | ‘nn.ilm.al. | tqrb.l bn.ilm. | mt.al.y‘db km. | k imr.b p h. | k lli.b t̠brn. | qn h.t̠ḫtan. | 4[51].8.16
. | k lsmm.mt.ql. | b‘l.ql.‘ln.špš. | tṣḥ.l mt.šm‘.m‘. | l bn.ilm.mt.ik.tmt[ẖ] | ṣ.‘m.aliyn.b‘l. | ik.al.yšm[‘] k.t̠r. | il.ab k.l y 6[49].6.24
. | qn h.t̠ḫtan. | nrt.ilm.špš. | ṣḥrrt.la. | šmm.b yd.md | d.ilm.mt.b a | lp.šd.rbt.k | mn.l p‘n.mt. | hbr.w ql. | tšt̠ḥwy.w k | 4[51].8.24
rs. | ipd k.ank.ispi.uṭm. | d̠rqm.amt m.l yrt. | b npš.bn ilm.mt.b mh | mrt.ydd.il.ǵzr. | tb‘.w l.yt̠b ilm.idk. | l ytn.pnm. 5[67].1.7
arẖ.l ‘gl h.k lb. | t̠at.l imr h.km.lb. | ‘nt.at̠r.b‘l.tiẖd. | bn.ilm.mt.b ḥrb. | tbq‘nn.b ẖt̠r.tdry | nn.b išt.tšrpnn. | b rḥm.tṭḥ 6[49].2.31
ytn.pnm.‘m.b‘l. | mrym.ṣpn.w y‘n. | gpn.w ugr.t̠ḥm.bn ilm. | mt.hwt.ydd.bn.il. | ǵzr.p np.š.npš.lbim. | thw.hm.brlt.a 5[67].1.12
id.an[--.]ṣn[--]. | nrt.ilm.špš[.ṣḥrr]t. | la.šmm.b y[d.bn.ilm.m]t. | w t‘n.btlt.‘n[t.bnt.]bht | k.y ilm.bnt.bh[t k].a[l.tš] 3[‘NT.VI].5.26
b t̠brn q y.ẖtu hw. | nrt.ilm.špš.ṣḥrrt. | la.šmm.b yd.bn ilm.mt. | ym.ymm.y‘tqn.l ymm. | l yrẖm.rḥm.‘nt.tngt̠ h. | k lb 6[49].2.25
[n h]. | b qṣ.all.tšu.g h.w[tṣ] | ḥ.at.mt.tn.aẖ y. | w ‘n.bn.ilm.mt.mh. | taršn.l btlt.‘nt. | an.itlk.w aṣd.kl. | ǵr.l kbd.arṣ.kl 6[49].2.13
w y‘ny.bn. | ilm.mt.npš[.-]. | npš.lbun. | thw.w npš. | anḫr.b ym. | brkt.šbšt UG5.4.2
y.l ydd.il ǵzr. | t̠ḥm.aliyn.b‘l.hwt.aliy. | qrdm.bht̠.l bn.ilm mt. | ‘bd k.an.w d.‘lm k. | tb‘.w l.yt̠b.ilm.idk. | l ytn.pn.‘m 5[67].2.11
g hm.w tṣḥ.t̠ḥm.aliyn. | bn.b‘l.hwt.aliy.qrdm. | bht̠.bn.ilm.mt.‘bd k.an. | w d ‘lm k.šmẖ.bn.ilm.mt. | [---.]g h.w aṣḥ.i 5[67].2.19
t h. | u mlk.u bl mlk. | arṣ.drkt.yštkn. | dll.al.ilak.l bn. | ilm.mt.‘dd.l ydd. | il.ǵzr.yqra.mt. | b npš h.ystrn ydd. | b gng 4[51].7.46
[ym]m.l yrẖm.l yrẖm. | l šnt.[m]k.b šb‘. | šnt.w [--].bn.ilm.mt. | ‘m.aliyn.b‘l.yšu. | g h.w yṣḥ.‘l k.b[‘]l m. | pht.qlt.‘l k. 6[49].5.9
-]mr.limm. | [---.]bn.ilm.mt. | [--]u.šb‘t.ǵlm h. | [---].bn.ilm.mt. | p[-]n.aẖ y m.ytn.b‘l. | [s]pu y.bn m.um y.kly y. | yt̠b. 6[49].6.9
hm. | šb‘.ydt y.b ṣ‘. | [--.]šb‘.rbt. | [---.]qbṭ.t̠m. | [---.]bn.ilm. | [m]t.šmẖ.p ydd. | il[.ǵ]zr. | b [-]dn.‘.z.w. | rgbt.zbl. UG5.4.14
d k.an.w d.‘lm k. | tb‘.w l.yt̠b.ilm.idk. | l ytn.pn.‘m.bn.ilm.mt. | tk.qrt h.hmry.mk.ksu. | t̠bt.ẖẖ.arṣ.nḥlt h.tša. | g hm. 5[67].2.14
.l p‘n.mt. | hbr.w ql. | tšt̠ḥwy.w k | bd hwt.w rgm. | l bn.ilm.mt. | t̠ny.l ydd. | il.ǵzr.t̠ḥm. | aliyn.b‘l. | [hw]t.aliy.q | [rdm. 4[51].8.30
pr. | ‘ṣm.yraun.aliyn.b‘l. | t̠t‘.nn.rkb.‘rpt. | tb‘.rgm.l bn.ilm.mt. | t̠ny.l ydd.il ǵzr. | t̠ḥm.aliyn.b‘l.hwt.aliy. | qrdm.bht̠.l 5[67].2.8
alt. | t̠bt k.l yhpk.ksa.mlk k. | l ytbr.ḥt̠.mt̠pṭ k. | yru.bn ilm t.t̠t‘.y | dd.il.ǵzr.y‘r.mt. | b ql h.y[---.---]. | b‘l.yt̠tbn[.l ksi]. 6[49].6.30
[---.]ru. | [----] h. | [---.--]mt. | [---.--]mr.limm. | [---.]bn.ilm.mt. | [--]u.šb‘t.ǵlm h. | [---].bn.ilm.mt. | p[-]n.aẖ y m.ytn. 6[49].6.7
liy.qrdm. | bht̠.bn.ilm.mt.‘bd k.an. | w d ‘lm k.šmẖ.bn.ilm.mt. | [---.]g h.w aṣḥ.ik.yṣḥn. | [b‘l.‘m.aẖ y.ik].yqrun.hd. | [5[67].2.20
n.t[--.--]. | pamt.šb‘. | iqnu.šmt[.---]. | [b]n.šrm. | iqran.ilm.n‘mm[.agzry ym.bn]ym. | ynqm.b ap zd.at̠rt.[---]. | špš. 23[52].23
n]. | yspr.l ḫmš.l ṣ[---.]šr.pḫr.klat. | tqtnṣn.w tldn.tld.[ilm.]n‘mm.agzr ym. | bn.ym.ynqm.b a[p.]d̠[d.r]gm.l il.ybl. | 23[52].58
.ym.ynqm.b a[p.]d̠[d.r]gm.l il.ybl. | at̠t y.il.ylt.mh.ylt.ilmy n‘mm. | agzr ym.bn ym.ynqm.b ap.d̠d.št.špt. | l arṣ.špt l 23[52].60
dš. | t̠m tgrgr.l abnm.w l.‘ṣm.šb‘.šnt. | tmt.t̠mn.nqpt.‘d.ilm.n‘mm.ttlkn. | šd.tṣdn.pat.mdbr.w ngš.hm.nǵr. | mdr‘.w ṣ 23[52].67
iqra.ilm.n[‘mm.---]. | w ysmm.bn.š[---]. | ytnm.qrt.l ‘ly[.---]. | b m 23[52].1
t̠ḥm iwrd̠r. | l iwrpẖn. | bn y.aẖ y.rgm. | ilm.tǵr k. | tšlm k. | ik y.lḥt. | spr.d likt. | ‘m.t̠ryl. | mh y.rgmt. 138.4
.rgm. | t̠ḥm.mlk. | bn k. | l.p‘n.um y. | qlt.l.um y. | yšlm.ilm. | tǵr k.tšlm k. | hl ny.‘m n[y]. | kll.šlm. | t̠m ny.‘m.um y. | 50[117].7
t[ḥm]. | mlk.bn [k]. | [l].p‘n.um [y]. | qlt[.l um] y. | yšlm.il[m]. | tǵ[r] k.tš[lm] k. | [h]l ny.‘m n[.š]lm. | w.t̠m [ny.‘m.mlk 1013.6
[yš]lm[.ilm]. | tǵr k[.tšlm k]. | hl ny.[---]. | w.pdr[--.---]. | tmǵyn[.---]. | 57[101].1
tlmyn. | w.aẖtmlk ‘bd k. | l.p‘n.adt ny. | mrḥqtm. | qlny.ilm. | tǵr k. | tšlm k. | hn ny.‘m ny. | kll.mid. | šlm. | w.ap.ank. | 51[95].7
t̠ḥm.pgn. | l.mlk.ugrt. | rgm. | yšlm.l k.[il]m. | tǵr k.tšlm k. | hn ny.‘m n.š[l]m. | t̠m ny.‘[m.]bn y. | mn 2061.4
l.mlk.ugrt. | aẖ y.rgm. | t̠ḥm.mlk.ṣr.aẖ k. | y[š]lm.l k.ilm. | tǵr k.tšlm k. | hn ny.‘m n. | šlm.t̠m ny. | ‘m k.mnm[.š]lm 2059.4
t̠ḥm.mlk. | l.t̠ryl.um y.rgm. | yšlm.l k.ilm. | tǵr k.tšlm k. | lḥt.šlm.k.lik[t]. | um y.‘m y.ht.‘m[ny]. | kl 2009.1.3
[l.ml]k.[b‘l y]. | rg[m]. | t̠ḥm.wr[--]. | yšlm.[l] k. | ilm.t[ǵ]r k. | tšlm k. | lm[.l.]likt. | ši[l.š]lm y. | [‘]d.r[-]š. | [-]ly.l. 2010.5
y[šlm.l k.ilm]. | tǵ[r k.tšlm k]. | ‘bd[.---]y. | ‘m[.---]y. | šk[--.--.]kll. | šk[--. 2065.1
[t]ḥm.it̠tl. | l mnn.ilm. | tǵr k.tšlm k. | t‘zz k.alp ymm. | w rbt.šnt. | b ‘d ‘lm...gn‘. 1019.1.2
t̠ḥm.hl[--]. | l pḫry.a[ẖ y]. | w l g.p[-]r[--]. | yšlm[.l k]. | [i]lm[.tǵr k]. | [t]š[lm k.---]. | [-----]. | [-----]. | h[--.---]. | [-----]. | w 56[21].5
l.mlk[.u]grt. | iẖ y.rgm. | [t̠ḥ]m.m[lk.-]bl[-]. | yšlm.l[k].ilm. | tǵr.tšl[m] k. | [-----]. | [-----]. | [--].bt.gb[-.--]. | [--]k[-].w.š 2159.4
pẖd.l npš.kt̠r. | w ẖss.l brlt.hyn d. | ḥrš yd.šlḥm.ššqy. | ilm sad.kbd.hmt.b‘l. | ḥkpt.il.kl h.tšm‘. | mt̠t.dnty.t‘db.imr. | 17[2AQHT].5.20
n. | qšt.l brk h.y‘db. | qṣ‘t.apnk.mt̠t.dnty. | tšlḥm.tššqy ilm. | tsad.tkbd.hmt.b‘l. | ḥkpt il.kl h.tb‘.kt̠r. | l ahl h.hyn.tb‘.l 17[2AQHT].5.29
| ‘nt.ṣd.tštr.‘pt.šmm. | t̠bẖ.alpm.ap ṣin.šql.t̠rm. | w mri ilm.‘glm.dt.šnt. | imr.qmṣ.llim.k ksp. | l ‘brm.zt.ḫrṣ.l ‘brm.kš 22.2[124].13
db[.‘d]bt. | hkl h.t̠bẖ.alpm[.ap]. | ṣin.šql.t̠rm[.w]m | ria.il.‘glm.d[t]. | šnt.imr.qmṣ.l[l]im. | ṣḥ.aẖ h.b bht h.a[r]y h. | b 4[51].6.42
.[---]. | p‘r.b[--.---]. | t̠bẖ.alp[m.ap.ṣin.šql]. | t̠rm.w [mri.ilm.‘glm.dt.šnt]. | imr.[qmṣ.llim.---]. 1[‘NT.X].4.31
rqdm.d š[-]l[-]. | w t‘n.pǵt.t̠kmt.mym. | qrym.ab.dbḥ.l ilm. | š‘ly.dǵt h.b šmym. | dǵt.hrnmy.d kbkbm. | l tbrkn.alk b 19[1AQHT].4.191
. | bkyt.b hk[l]y.mšspdt. | b ḥzr y pzǵm.ǵr.w yq. | dbḥ.ilm.yš‘ly.dǵt h. | b šmym.dǵt hrnmy[.d k] | bkbm.‘[l.---]. | [-]l 19[1AQHT].4.185
]ytdt̠. | yšb‘.rgm.[my.]b ilm. | ydy.mrṣ.gršm zbln. | in.b ilm.‘ny h. | w y‘n.ltpn.il.b pid. | t̠b.bn y.lm t̠b[t] km. | l kḥt̠.zb 16[126].5.22
ny.yt̠lt̠]. | rgm.my.b[ilm.ydy]. | mrṣ.grš[m.zbln]. | in.b ilm.‘[ny h.yrb‘]. | yẖmš.rgm.[my.b ilm]. | ydy.mrṣ.g[ršm.zbln 16[126].5.16
‘]. | yẖmš.rgm.[my.b ilm]. | ydy.mrṣ.g[ršm.zbln]. | in.b ilm.‘n[y h.]ytdt̠. | yšb‘.rgm.[my.]b ilm. | ydy.mrṣ.gršm zbln. | 16[126].5.19
| ltpn.[il.d pid.my]. | b ilm.[ydy.mrṣ]. | gršm.z[bln.in.b ilm]. | ‘ny h.y[t̠ny.yt̠lt̠]. | rgm.my.b[ilm.ydy]. | mrṣ.grš[m.zbl 16[126].5.12
ǵltm.ilm.rišt. | km l ẓr brkt km.w ln.kḥt̠.zbl km.aḥd. | ilm.t‘ny lḥt.mlak.ym.t‘dt.t̠pṭ.nhr. | šu.ilm.rašt km.l ẓr.brkt k 2.1[137].26
t̠ḥm.iwrd̠r. | l iwrpẖn. | bn y.aẖ y.rgm. | ilm.tǵr k. | tšlm k. | iky.lḥt. | spr.d likt. | ‘m.t̠ryl. | mh y.rgmt. | 138.4
‘t.ẖti. | nḥtu.ht. | hm.in mm. | nḥtu.w.lak. | ‘m y.w.yd. | ilm.p.k mtm. | ‘z.mid. | hm.nt̠kp. | m‘n k. | w.mnm. | rgm.d.tš 53[54].12
‘d.ap.ilm.l lḥ[m]. | ytb.bn qdš.l t̠rm.b‘l.qm.‘l.il.hlm. | ilm.tph hm.tphn.mlak.ym.t‘dt.t̠pṭ[.nhr]. | t[ǵ]ly.hlm.rišt hm 2.1[137].22
t. | ‘pr.‘ẓm yd. | ugrm.ẖl.ld. | aklm.tbrk k. | w ld ‘qqm. | ilm.yp‘r. | šmt hm. | b hm.qrnm. | km.t̠rm.w gbtt. | km.ibrm. | 12[75].1.28
hlm. | ilm.tph hm.tphn.mlak.ym.t‘dt.t̠pṭ[.nhr]. | t[ǵ]ly.hlm.rišt hm.l ẓr.brkt hm.w l kḥt̠. | zbl hm.b hm.yg‘r.b‘l.lm.ǵ 2.1[137].23
.ln.kḥt̠. | zbl km.w ank.‘ny.mlak.ym.t‘dt.t̠pṭ.nhr. | tšu ilm rašt hm.l ẓr.brkt hm.ln.kḥt̠.zbl hm. | aẖr.tmǵyn.mlak y 2.1[137].29
ḥt̠.zbl km.aḥd. | ilm.t‘ny lḥt.mlak.ym.t‘dt.t̠pṭ.nhr. | šu.ilm.rašt km.l ẓr.brkt km.ln.kḥt̠. | zbl km.w ank.‘ny.mlak.ym 2.1[137].27
.l ẓr.brkt hm.w l kḥt̠. | zbl hm.b hm.yg‘r.b‘l.lm.ǵltm.ilm.rišt. | km l ẓr brkt km.w ln.kḥt̠.zbl km.aḥd. | ilm.t‘ny lḥt. 2.1[137].24
kd.bt ilm. | rbm. | kd l ištnm. | kd l ḥty. | mahdh. | kd l kblbn. | kdm. 1090.1
--.--]at̠[.---]. | [---.]akl[.---]. | [---.-]l[-.-]hg[.---]. | [---.-]r[-.il]m.rbm.n‘l[.-]gr. | [---.]‘ṣ.b d h.ydrm[.]pi[-.]adm. | [---.]it̠[-]. UG5.8.31

k ymǵy.adn. | ilm.rbm ʿm dtn. | w yšal.mṯpṭ.yld. | w yʿny.nn[.--]. | tʿny.n[---. UG5.6.2

.kṯpm.a[-]ṯ[-]. | [---.--]ḫ b ym.tld[---.]b[-.]y[--.---]. | [---.il]m.rb[m.--]š[-]. | [---].nš.b [---]. | [---].tm[--.--]aṯ[.---]. | [---.]a UG5.8.26

t.arḫt[.yn]. | špq.ilm.kḥṯm.yn. | špq.ilht.ksat[.yn]. | špq.ilm.rḥbt yn. | špq.ilht.dkrt[.yn]. | ʿd.lḥm.šty.ilm. | w pq mrǵṯ 4[51].6.53

.yšu.g h.w y[ṣḥ]. | ik.mǵyt.rbt.aṯr[t.y]m. | ik.atwt.qnyt.i[lm]. | rǵb.rǵbt.w tǵt[--]. | hm.ǵmu.ǵmit.w ʿs[--]. | lḥm.hm.št 4[51].4.32

.š.ddmš.š. | w šlmm.ilib.š.i[l.--]m d gbl.ṣpn.al[p]. | pḫr.ilm.š.ym.š[.k]nr.š.[--.]ʿṣrm gdlt. | bʿlm.kmm.bʿlm.kmm[.bʿl UG5.9.1.9

r[-].ṯlṯt.mzn. | drk.š.alp.w ṯlṯ. | ṣin.šlm[m.]šbʿ pamt. | l ilm.šb[ʿ.]l kṯr. | ʿlm.tʿrbn.gṯrm. | bt.mlk.ṯql.ḫrṣ. | l špš.w yrḫ.l 33[5].8

t h. | km gpn. | šbʿ d.yrgm.ʿl.ʿd.w ʿrbm.tʿnyn. | w šd.šd ilm.šd aṯrt.w rḥm. | ʿl.išt.šbʿ d.ǵzrm.ṭb.[g]d.b ḥlb.annḫ b ḫm 23[52].13

--]. | w ǵnbm.šlm.ʿrbm.ṯn[nm]. | hlkm.b dbḥ nʿmt. | šd[.i]lm.šd.aṯrt.w rḥmy. | [---].y[ṯ]b. | [---]p.gp ym.w yṣǵd.gp..th 23[52].28

l.rb.khnm. | rgm. | ṯḥm.[---]. | yšlm[.l k.ilm]. | tšlm[k.tǵr] k. | tʿzz[k.---.]lm. | w t[--.--]ṣm k. | [-----]. | [55[18].4

[ṯḥm.---]. | [l.---]. | [a]ḫt y.rgm. | [y]šlm.l k. | [il]m.tšlm k. | [tǵ]r k. | [--]y.ibr[-]. | [--]wy.rgm l. | mlkt.ugrt. | [- 1016.5

]. | ṣbi nrt.ilm.špš.[-]r[--]. | pǵt.minš.šdm l mʿ[rb]. | nrt.ilm.špš.mǵy[t]. | pǵt.l ahlm.rgm.l yṯ[pn.y] | bl.agrtn.bat.b ḏd 19[1AQHT].4.211

t.gm. | tṣḥ.l nrt.ilm.špš. | ʿms mʿ.l y.aliyn.bʿl. | tšmʿ.nrt.ilm.špš. | tšu.aliyn.bʿl.l ktp. | ʿnt.k tšt h.tšʿlyn h. | b ṣrrt.ṣpn.tb 6[62].1.13

[---]y.yblmm.u[---]k.yrd[.--.]i[---]n.bn. | [---.-]nn.nrt.ilm.špš.tšu.g h.w t[ṣḥ.šm]ʿ.mʿ. | [-.yṯ]ir ṯr.il.ab k.l pn.zbl.ym. 2.3[129].15

bʿl. | iy.zbl.bʿl.arṣ. | ttbʿ.btlt.ʿnt. | idk.l ttn.pnm. | ʿm.nrt.ilm.špš. | tšu.g h.w tṣḥ. | ṯḥm.ṯr.il.ab k. | hwt.lṭpn.ḥtk k. | pl.ʿn 6[49].4.32

lim.bn dgn. | my.hmlt.aṯr.bʿl.nrd. | b arṣ.ʿm h.trd.nrt. | ilm.špš.ʿd.tšbʿ.bk. | tšt.k yn.udmʿt.gm. | tṣḥ.l nrt.ilm.špš. | ʿms 6[62].1.9

.nrt. | ilm.špš.ʿd.tšbʿ.bk. | tšt.k yn.udmʿt.gm. | tṣḥ.l nrt.ilm.špš. | ʿms mʿ.l y.aliyn.bʿl. | tšmʿ.nrt.ilm.špš. | tšu.aliyn.bʿl. 6[62].1.11

bʿl.arṣ. | gm.yṣḥ.il.l btlt. | ʿnt.šmʿ.l btlt.ʿn[t]. | rgm.l nrt.il.šp[š]. | pl.ʿnt.šdm.y špš. | pl.ʿnt.šdm.il.yšt k. | [b]ʿl.ʿnt.mḥrṯt 6[49].3.24

ʿl. | ʿdbnn ank.imr.b p y. | k lli.b ṯbrn q y.ḫtu hw. | nrt.ilm.špš.ṣḫrrt. | la.šmm.b yd.bn ilm.mt. | ym.ymm.yʿtqn.l ym 6[49].2.24

l.yʿdb km. | k imr.b p h. | k lli.b ṯbrn. | qn h.ṯḫtan. | nrt.ilm.špš. | ṣḫrrt.la. | šmm.b yd.md | d.ilm.mt.b a | lp.šd.rbt.k | 4[51].8.21

| ʿln.ṯ[--.---]. | l pʿn.ǵl[m]m[.---]. | mid.an[--.]ṣn[--]. | nrt.ilm.špš[.ṣḫrr]t. | la.šmm.b y[d.bn.ilm.m]t. | w tʿn.btlt.ʿn[t.bnt 3[ʿNT.VI].5.25

. | bʿl.ʿnt.mḥrṯ[-]. | iy.aliyn.bʿl. | iy.zbl.bʿl.arṣ. | w tʿn.nrt.ilm.š[p]š. | šd yn.ʿn.b qbt[.t] | bl lyt.ʿl.umt k. | w abqṯ.aliyn.bʿl 6[49].4.41

| nšg h.ḥrb.tšt.b tʿr[t h]. | w ʿl.tlbš.npṣ.aṯt.[--]. | ṣbi nrt.ilm.špš.[-]r[--]. | pǵt.minš.šdm l mʿ[rb]. | nrt.ilm.špš.mǵy[t]. | 19[1AQHT].4.209

.ʿrpt. | [--].ydd.w yqlṣn. | yqm.w ywpṯn.b tk. | p[ḫ]r.bn.ilm.štt. | p[--].b ṯlḥn y.qlt. | b ks.ištyn h. | dm.ṯn.dbḥm.šna.bʿl 4[51].3.14

t.b.ḫmš[.---]. | [-.]kbd.w.db[ḥ.---]. | [--].aṯrt.ʿṣr[m.l inš.ilm]. | [ṯ]ṭb.mdbḥ.bʿl.g[dlt.---]. | dqt.l.ṣpn.w.dqt[.---]. | ṯn.l.ʿšr 35[3].40

ʿl[y.---]. | bt.il.ṯq[l.---.kbd]. | w bdḥ.k[--.---]. | ʿṣrm.l i[nš.ilm.ṯb.md] | bḥ.bʿl.[gdlt.---.dqt]. | l ṣpn.w [dqt.---.ṯn.l ʿš] | rm. APP.II[173].44

.]yrḫ.zbl. | [--.kṯ]r w ḫss. | [---]n.rḥm y.ršp zbl. | [w ʿd]t.ilm.ṯlṯ h. | [ap]nk.krt.ṯʿ.ʿ[-]r. | [--.]b bt h.yšt.ʿrb. | [--] h.ytn.w [15[128].2.7

[.---]. | ṯhgrn.ǵzr.nʿm.[---]. | w šm.ʿrbm.yr[.---]. | mṯbt.ilm.ṯmn.ṯ[--.--]. | pamt.šbʿ. | iqnu.šmt[.---]. | [b]n.šrm. | iqran.il 23[52].19

ṣ.bnt.mʿmʿ.ʿbd.ḥrn.[--.]k. | [---].aǵwyn.ʿn k.ẓẓ.w k mǵ.ilm. | [--.]k ʿṣm.k ʿšm.l ttn.k abnm.l thggn. 1001.2.12

y.[---]. | [---.]ʿm.w hm[.--]yt.w.[---]. | [---.ṯ]y.al.an[k.--.]il[m.--]y. | [--.m]ṣlm.pn y[.-.]tlkn. | [---.]rḥbn.hm.[-.]aṯr[.---]. 1002.58

--]. | l yrḫ.gdlt.l [nkl.gdlt.l bʿ] | [lt].bht[m].[ʿ]ṣrm l [inš.ilm]. | [---.]ilh[m.dqt.š.--]. | [---.--]t.r[šp.šrp.w šl] | [mm.---].dq APP.II[173].29

[---.l yrḫ]. | gd[lt].l nkl[.gdlt.l bʿlt.bhtm]. | ʿš[rm.]l inš[.ilm.---]. | il[hm.]dqt.š[.---.rš] | [p.š]rp.w šl[mm.--.dqt]. | [i]lh.g 35[3].27

. | šgr.mud[.---]. | dm.mt.aṣ[ḫ.---]. | yd.b qrb[.---]. | w lk.ilm.[---]. | w rgm.l [---]. | b mud.ṣin[.---]. | mud.ṣin[.---]. | iṯm. 5[67].3.20

.ʿbd k.bʿl. | [--.--]m.bn.dgn.a[s]r km.hw ybl.argmn k.k ilm. | [---.]ybl.k bn.qdš.mnḥy k.ap.anš.zbl.bʿ[l]. | [-.yuḫ]d.b y 2.1[137].37

[--]m.[---.] | gm.ṣḥ.l q[ṣ.ilm.---]. | l rḥqm.l p[-.---]. | ṣḥ.il.ytb.b[mrzḥ.---]. | bṯt.ʿllm n.[- 1[ʿNT.X].4.2

.dqt.šrp.w [š]lmm. | [---.a]lp.l bʿl.w aṯrt.ʿṣr[m] l inš. | [ilm.---].lbbmm.gdlt.ʿrb špš w ḥl. | [mlk.b ar]bʿt.ʿ[š]rt.yrtḥṣ. 36[9].1.9

t w tʿn. | btlt.ʿnt.nmgn. | [-]m.rbt.aṯrt.ym. | [nǵ]ẓ.qnyt.ilm. | [---].nmgn.hwt. | [--].aliyn.bʿl. | [--.]rbt.aṯrt.ym. | [---.]btl 4[51].3.35

]. | al.ašt.b[---]. | ahpk k.l[--.---]. | ṯmm.w lk[.---]. | w lk.ilm[.---]. | nʿm.ilm[.---]. | šgr.mu[d.---]. | šgr.mud[.---]. | dm.mt 5[67].3.14

. | ahpk k.l[--.---]. | ṯmm.w lk[.---]. | w lk.ilm[.---]. | nʿm.ilm[.---]. | šgr.mu[d.---]. | šgr.mud[.---]. | dm.mt.aṣ[ḫ.---]. | yd. 5[67].3.15

ilm[.---]. | tšʿ.ʿš[r.---]. | bn ʿdr[.---]. | ḫmš ʿl.bn[.---]. | ḫmš ʿl rʿl[2034.2.1

y. | [---.]aḫ y. | [----]y. | [---.]rb. | [---].ṣḥt. | [---.--]t. | [---.]ilm. | [---.--]u.yd. | [---.--]k. | [---.gpn.]w ugr. | [---.---]t. 4[51].8.44

. | [---.--]g k.yritn.mǵy.hy.w kn. | [---].ḥln.d b.dmt.um.il[m.---]. | [--]ḏyn.bʿd.[--]ḏyn.w l. | [--]k bʿlt bhtm[.--]tn k. | [-- 1002.43

[---.]š[---]. | [---.]ʿbd.ilm[.---]. 110[-].2

amt ṯlṯm.w yrdt.[m]dbḥt. | gdlt.l bʿlt bhtm.ʿṣrm. | l inš ilm. 34[1].22

arbʿm.kbd. | l.liy.bn.ʿmyn. | mit.ḫmšm.kbd. | d.škn.l.ks.ilm. 1143.14

ilmd

[b]n[.---]. | bn [-]ʿy. | [b]n [i]lmd. | bn [t]bdn. | bn štn. | b[n] kdn. | bn dwn. | bn ḏrn. 2088.3

n bn.ibm. | [-]n bn.ḥrn. | [š]mmn bn.gmz. | [yn]ḥm bn.ilmd. 2087.15

ilmhr

š[-].l.qrt. | šd.iǵlyn.bn.kzbn.l.qr[t]. | šd.pln.bn.tiyn.b d.ilmhr nḥl h. | šd knn.bn.ann.ʿdb. | šd.iln[-].bn.irṯr.l.sḫrn.nḥl 2029.18

. | bn.gzl.qšt.w.qlʿ. | [---]n.qšt. | ilhd.qšt. | ʿdn.qšt.w.qlʿ. | ilmhr.qšt.w.qlʿ. | bn.gmrt.qšt. | ǵmrm. | bn.qṭn.qšt.w.qlʿ. | mrṯ 119[321].1.9

ilmlk

ḫ[-.---]. | [-]p[-.---.-]ny. | [-]ḫ[-.---.-]dn. | arbʿ[m.ksp.]ʿl. | il[m]l[k.a]rgnd. | uškny[.w]mit. | zt.b d hm.rib. | w [---]. | [---- 2055.11

--]. | iw[r--]ǵt. | iw[r---]. | iwr[--]. | ilṣ[--]. | il[---]. | il[---]. | ilmlk. | ildgn. | ilyn. | ilrm. | ibrm. | ibyn. | illḏrm. | iǵlkḏ. | [i]ly[- 2022.13

n.arbʿt. | [b]n.ṯrk.ṯqlm. | [b]n.pdrn.ṯq[lm]. | pdy.[----]. | [i]lmlk.bn.[---]. | [--]ʿ[-.---]. | [---.k]kr. | [-----]. | [---.k]kr. 122[308].1.24

| yʿḏrd.ʿšrm. | gmrd.ʿšrm. | ṣdqšlm.ʿšr[m]. | yknil.ḫmš. | ilmlk.ḫmš. | prṯ.ʿšr. | ubn.ʿšr. 1116.13

b ṯlṯ. | ilmlk.ʿšr.ṣin. | mlknʿm.ʿšr. | bn.adty.ʿšr. | [ṣ]dqšlm ḫmš. | krzn. 2039.2

yʿdd.ṯḥt.bn arbn. | ʿbdil.ṯḥt.ilmlk. | qly.ṯḥt bʿln.nsk. 1053.2

.g]h.w tṣḥ.hwt. | [---.]aqht.ydḏ[--]. | [---.--]n.ṣ[---]. | [spr.ilmlk.šbny.lmd.atn.]prln. 17[2AQHT].7.1

k. | b ym.arš.w tnn. | kṯr.w ḫss.yd. | ytr.kṯr.w ḫss. | spr.ilmlk šbny. | lmd.atn.prln.rb. | khnm rb.nqdm. | ṯʿy.nqmd.ml 6.6[62.2].53

]lsy.ṯṯ mat. | ʿdn.ḫmš [m]at. | [--]kbʿl ṯṯ [mat]. | [-----]. | ilmlk ṯṯ mat. | ʿbdilm.ṯṯ mat. | šmmn.bn.ʿdš.ṯṯ mat. | uškny m. 1060.1.10

[spr.ilmlk.ṯʿ]y.nqmd.mlk.ugrt. 4[51].9.1

t.šm.b'l. | qdqd k.tqln.b gbl. | šnt k.b ḥpn k.w t'n. | spr ilmlk t̠'y. 16[127]EDGE
nq.[-]r.d.yṯb.b.ilštm'. | ilšlm.bn.gs[-.--]r.d.yṯb.b.gt.al. | ilmlk.[--]kt.[--.d.]yṯb.b.šb[n]. | bn.pr[-.]d.y[ṯb.b].šlmy. | tlš.w[2015.2.1
dil[.b]n ṣdqn. | bnšm.h[-]mt.ypḥm. | kbby.yd.bt.amt. | ilmlk. 2045.8

ilmn

]. | ṯṯpḥ. | artn. | ybnil. | brqn. | adr[dn]. | krwn. | arkd̠n. | ilmn. | abškn. | ykn. | ršpab. | klyn. | ḥgbn. | ḥṯṯn. | 'bdmlk. | y[--] 1024.1.13

ilmškl

' h. | trm[-].w[.r' h]. | [']ṯtr[-].w.[r' h]. | ḫlly[-].w.r'[h]. | ilmškl.w.r'[h]. | ššw[.--].w.r[' h]. | kr[mn.--.]w.r[' h]. | šd.[--. 2083.2.2

iln

.]b d h. | qb't.b ymn h.w y'n.yṯ[p]n[.mh]r. | št.b yn.yšt.ila.il š[--.]il. | d yqny.d̠dm.yd.mḫṣt.a[qh]t.ǵ | zr.tmḫṣ.alpm.ib 19[1AQHT].4.219
adb'l[.---].ḥdtn.yḥmn.bnil. | 'dn.w.ildgn.ḥṯbm. | tdǵlm.iln.b'[l]n.aldy. | tdn.ṣr[--.--]t.'zn.mtn.n[bd]g. | ḥrš qṯn[.---.]dq 2011.21
[---.--]r. | [--.]iln. | y'rtym. | bn.gṯrn. | bq'ty. 100[66].2
spr.ḥrš. | qštiptl. | bn.anny. | ilṣdq. | ypltn.bn iln. | špšm.nsl h. | [-----]. 1037.5
ab bn.pni. | [ab]mn bn.qṣy. | [']ptrm bn.agmz. | [-]n bn.iln. | [--]nn bn.ibm. | [-]n bn.ḥrn. | [š]mmn bn.gmz. | [yn]ḥm b 2087.11
[---.]qmy. | [---.--]b. | bn.t[--.---.a]ǵt. | špš[yn.---.u]br'y. | iln.[---]. | bn.[---].ar. | bn.[---].b.ar. | špšyn[.---.]yṯb.b.ar. | bn.ag 2015.1.21

ilnym

a.ilnym]. | b qrb.h[kl y.aṯr h.rpum.l] | tdd.aṯr[h.l tdd.ilnym]. | asr.mr[kbt.---]. | t'ln.l mr[kbt hm.tity.l] | 'r hm.tl[k 22.1[123].21
l y.[---]. | lk bt y.r[pim.rpim.b bt y.aṣḥ]. | km.iqr[a km.ilnym.b hkl y]. | aṯr h.r[pum.l tdd.aṯr h]. | l tdd.il[nym.---]. | 22.1[123].4
--.m]rz'y.lk.bt y. | [rpim.rpim.b]t y.aṣḥ km.iqra. | [km.ilnym.b h]kl y.aṯr h.rpum. | [l tdd.aṯr h].l tdd.ilnym. | [---.m] 21[122].1.3
--.mrz']y.lk.bt y.rpim. | [rpim.bt y.aṣ]ḥ km.iqra km. | [ilnym.b hkl]y.aṯr h.rpum. | [l tdd.aṯr]h.l tdd.i[lnym]. | [---.] 21[122].1.11
hr]. | 'nt.lk b[t y.rpim.rpim.b bt y]. | aṣḥ.km.[iqra km.ilnym.b] | hkl y.aṯr[h.rpum.l tdd]. | aṯr h.l t[dd.ilnym.ṯm]. | 22.1[123].9
d.ksa.mlk h]. | nḫt.kḥṯ.d[rkt h.b bt y]. | aṣḥ.rpi[m.iqra.ilnym]. | b qrb.h[kl y.aṯr h.rpum.l] | tdd.aṯr[h.l tdd.ilnym]. | 22.1[123].19
t.rpi]. | yṯb.ǵzr.mt hrnmy[.---]. | b grnt.ilm.b qrb.m[ṯ't.ilnym]. | d tit.yspi.spu.q[--.---]. | tpḥ.ṯṣr.shr[.---]. | mr[.---]. 20[121].2.9
m]. | tlkn.ym.w ṯa aḫr.š[pšm.b ṯlṯ]. | mǵy.rpum.l grnt.i[lnym.l] | mṯ't.w y'n.dnil.[mt.rpi]. | yṯb.ǵzr.mt hrnmy[.---]. 20[121].2.6
m.tl[kn.ym.w ṯn.aḫr.špšm]. | b ṯlṯ.mǵy[.rpum.l grnt]. | i[ln]y[m].l mṯ't[.---]. | [-]m[.---]. | h.hn bn k.hn[.---]. | bn bn.aṯ 22.1[123].26
[l]ḥm.trmmt.l tšt. | yn.tǵẓyt.špš. | rpim.tḥtk. | špš.tḥtk.ilnym. | 'd k.ilm.hn.mtm. | 'd k.kṯr m.ḥbr k. | w ḫss.d't k. | b y 6.6[62.2].46
a km.ilnym.b] | hkl y.aṯr[h.rpum.l tdd]. | aṯr h.l t[dd.ilnym.ṯm]. | yḥpn.ḥy[ly.zbl.mlk.'llm y]. | šm'.atm[.---]. | ym.l 22.1[123].11
[---.]n[--.---]. | [---.kpt]r.l r[ḥq.ilm.ḥkpt.l rḥq]. | [ilnym.ṯn.mṯpd]m.t[ḥt.'nt.arṣ.ṯlṯ.mtḥ.ǵyrm]. | [idk.]l ytn.pn 2.3[129].3
n.ilm. | atm.bštm.w an.šnt. | uǵr.l rḥq.ilm.inbb. | l rḥq.ilnym.ṯn.mṯpdm. | tḥt.'nt.arṣ.ṯlṯ.mtḥ.ǵyrm. | idk.l ttn pnm.' 3['NT].4.79
lm.] | atm.bštm.w an[.šnt.kptr]. | l rḥq.ilm.ḥkp[t.l rḥq.ilnym]. | ṯn.mṯpdm.tḥt.['nt.arṣ.ṯlṯ.mtḥ]. | ǵyrm.idk.l yt[n.pn 1['NT.IX].3.19
bḥ.amr. | ṯmn.b qrb.hkl y.[aṯr h.rpum]. | tdd.aṯr h.tdd.iln[ym.---]. | asr.sswm.tṣmd.dg[-.---]. | t'ln.l mrkbt hm.ti[ty.l 20[121].2.2
[a km.ilnym.b hkl y]. | aṯr h.r[pum.l tdd.aṯr h]. | l tdd.il[nym.---]. | mhr.b'l[.---.mhr]. | 'nt.lk b[t y.rpim.rpim.b bt y] 22.1[123].6
a. | [km.ilnym.b h]kl y.aṯr h.rpum. | [l tdd.aṯr h].l tdd.ilnym. | [---.m]rz'y.apnnk.yrp. | [---.]km.r'y.ht.alk. | [---.]ṯlṯt.a 21[122].1.4
a km. | [ilnym.b hkl]y.aṯr h.rpum. | [l tdd.aṯr]h.l tdd.i[lnym]. | [---.]r[--.---]. | [---.yṯ]b.l arṣ. 21[122].1.12
[---.rp]um.tdbḥn. | [----.]'d.ilnym. | [---.--]l km amt m. | [---.]b w t'rb.sd. | [---.--]n b ym.q 20[121].1.2

ilnm

't h ḥrṣ.abn. | p h.tiḫd.šnt h.w akl.bqmm. | tšt ḥrṣ.k lb ilnm. | w ṯn.gprm.mn gpr h.šr. | aqht.y'n.kmr.kmr[.--]. | k ap' 19[1AQHT].1.10

ils

ubdym.b.uškn. | [---]lby. | [--]nbbl. | bn bl. | bn dkn. | bn ils. | bn ḥšbn. | bn uryy. | bn kṯl. | bn army. | bn gln. | bn abg. | b 1064.6

ilsk

ṯt.aṯtm.adrtm.w.pǵt.aḫt.b[.bt.---]. | aṯt.w ṯn.n'rm.b.bt.ilsk. | aṯt.ad[r]t.b.bt.armwl. | aṯt.aḫt.b.bt.iwrpzn. | ṯt.aṯtm.w.p 80[119].8
]m. | [bn].ḥrp[-]. | [bn].ḫdpṯr. | [bn.-]dn. | [bn.-]lyn. | [bn.i]lsk. | [bn.---]n. | bn[.---]. | bn[.---]. | bn[.---]. | bn[.---]. | bn[.---]. 124[-].2.10

il'nt

nn. | bn.rmy. | dll. | mny. | krty. | bn.'bṣ. | bn.argb. | ydn. | il'nt. | bn.urt. | ydn. | qṯn. | bn.asr. | bn.'dy. | bn.amt[m]. | myn. | 2117.3.43

ilṣdq

ilṣdq.bn.zry. | b'lytn.bn.ulb. | ytr'm.bn.swy. | ṣḥrn.bn.qrtm. | b 2024.1
spr.ḥrš. | qštiptl. | bn.anny. | ilṣdq. | ypltn.bn iln. | špšm.nsl h. | [-----]. 1037.4
rt.ṯṯt šlm.'šrt. | bn.ḥgby.ṯmnt.l 'šrm.'šrt.ḫmš.kbd. | bn.ilṣdq.šb't ṯlṯt šlm. | bn.ṯmq.arb't ṯqlm šlmm. 1131.9

ilṣy

m. | [ṯlṯ].šdm.d.n'rb.gt.npk. | [š]d.rpan.b d.klṯṯb. | [š]d.ilṣy.b d.'bdym. | [ub]dy.trrm. | [šd.]bn.ṯqdy.b d.gmrd. | [š]d b 82[300].2.15

ilqṣm

kl k. | tbl k.ǵrm.mid.ksp. | gb'm.mḥmd.ḫrṣ. | ybl k.udr.ilqṣm. | w bn.bht.ksp.w ḫrṣ. | bht.ṭhrm.iqnim. | šmḫ.btlt.'nt.t 4[51].5.79
l h. | yblnn ǵrm.mid.ksp. | gb'm lḥmd.ḫrṣ. | yblnn.udr.ilqṣm. | yak.l kṯr.w ḫss. | w ṯb l mspr..k tlakn. | ǵlmm. | aḫr.m 4[51].5.102

ilrb

. | dt.tknn. | 'l.'rbnm. | hn hmt. | tknn. | mtn.bn.'bdym. | ilrb.bn.ilyn. | 'bdadt.bn 'bdkb. | gn'ym. 1161.11
yn.qšt. | bdn.qšt.w.ql'. | bn.šmlbi.qšt.w.ql'. | bn.yy.qšt. | ilrb.qšt. | bn.nmš.ṯt.qšt.w.ql'. | b'l.qšt.w.ql'. 119[321].4.15

'ky.qšt. | 'bdlbit.qšt. | kṭy.qšt.w.ql'. | bn.ḫršn.qšt.w.ql'. | ilrb.qšt.w.ql'. | psḥn.qšt. | bn.kmy.qšt. | bn.ilḥbn.qšt.w.q[l']. | r 119[321].3.41

ilrm

--]. | iwr[--]. | ilṣ[--]. | il[---]. | il[---]. | ilmlk. | ildgn. | ilyn. | ilrm. | ibrm. | ibyn. | illḏrm. | iǵlkḏ. | [i]ly[-]n. | [-----]. | m[--.---]. 2022.16

ilrpi

w.pṯpṯ.'rb. | b.yrm. | [ily.w].ḏmry.'rb. | b.ṯb'm. | ydn.bn.ilrpi. | w.ṯb'm.'rb.b.'[d]n. | ḏmry.bn.yrm. | 'rb.b.ad'y. 2079.7

ilrš

rš[.bn].mrnn. | 'bdmlk.bn.'myn. | agyn.r'y. | abmlk.bn.ilrš. | iḫyn.bn.ḫryn. | [ab]ǵl.bn.gdn. | [---].bn.bqš. | [---].bn.pdn 102[323].4.10
rišym.qnum. | bn.ilrš. | '[p]ṯn. | b[n.'r]my. | [--]ṭy. | bn.ǵd'. | bn.'yn. | bn.grb[n]. | y 2078.2
.buly.ṯkt. | 'pṣpn.bn.'dy.ṯkt. | n'mn.bn.'yn.ṯkt. | 'pṯn.bn.ilrš.ṯkt. | ilṯḥm.bn.šrn.ṯkt. | šmlbu.bn.grb.ṯkt. | šmlbu.bn.yp'.ṯ 2085.11

ilršp

| kd.šmn.ymtšr. | arb'.šmn.'l.'bdn.w.[---]. | kdm.šmn.'l.ilršp.bn[.---]. | kd.šmn.'l.yddn. | kd.'l.ššy. | kd.'l.nḏbn.bn.agm 1082.1.5

ilš

--]. | il.šm'.amr k.ph[.-]. | k il.ḥkmt.k ṯr.lṭpn. | ṣḥ.ngr.il.ilš.il[š]. | w aṯt h.ngrt[.i]lht. | kḥṣ.k m'r[.---]. | yṣḥ.ngr il.ilš. | il 16[126].4.4
l. | w aṯt h.ngrt.ilht. | w y'n.lṭpn.il d pi[d]. | šm'.l ngr.il il[š]. | ilš.ngr bt b'l. | w aṯt k.ngrt.il[ht]. | 'l.l ṯkm.bnw n. | l nḫ 16[126].4.11
lš.il[š]. | w aṯt h.ngrt[.i]lht. | kḥṣ.k m'r[.---]. | yṣḥ.ngr il.ilš. | ilš.ngr.bt.b'l. | w aṯt h.ngrt.ilht. | w y'n.lṭpn.il d pi[d]. | š 16[126].4.7
kn. | bn.'ṯtrab. | uṣn[-]. | bn.alṯn. | bn.aš[-]š. | bn.štn. | bn.ilš. | bn.tnabn. | bn.ḥṣn. | ṣprn. | bn.ašbḥ. | bn.qṭnn. | bn.ǵlmn. | 1046.1.17
| il.šm'.amr k.ph[.-]. | k il.ḥkmt.k ṯr.lṭpn. | ṣḥ.ngr.il.ilš.il[š]. | w aṯt h.ngrt[.i]lht. | kḥṣ.k m'r[.---]. | yṣḥ.ngr il.ilš. | ilš.n 16[126].4.4
š]. | w aṯt h.ngrt[.i]lht. | kḥṣ.k m'r[.---]. | yṣḥ.ngr il.ilš. | ilš.ngr.bt.b'l. | w aṯt h.ngrt.ilht. | w y'n.lṭpn.il d pi[d]. | šm'.l 16[126].4.8
ṯt h.ngrt.ilht. | w y'n.lṭpn.il d pi[d]. | šm'.l ngr.il il[š]. | ilš.ngr bt b'l. | w aṯt k.ngrt.il[ht]. | 'l.l ṯkm.bnw n. | l nḫnpt.m 16[126].4.12
argmn]. | w ṯn šm.l [b'lt.bhtm.'ṣrm.l inš]. | ilm.w š d[d.ilš.š.--.mlk]. | yṯb.brr[.w mḫ-.---]. | ym.[']lm.y'[--.---]. | [--.-]g[- 35[3].6
arg[mn.w ṯn.]šm.l b'lt. | bhtm.'ṣ[rm.l in]š ilm.w š. | dd ilš.š[.---.]mlk.yṯb br | r.w mḫ[--.---.]w q[--]. | ym.'lm.y[---.---]. APP.II[173].7

ilšiy

ḥ. | ksan k.ḥdg k. | ḥtl k.w ẓi. | b aln.tk m. | b tk.mlbr. | ilšiy. | kry amt. | 'pr.'ẓm yd. | ugrm.ḫl.ld. | aklm.tbrk k. | w ld ' 12[75].1.22

ilšḥr

t.prn. | [šd.---.]gt.prn. | [š]d.bn.š[p]šn l gt pr[n]. | šd bn.ilšḥr. | l.gt.mzln. | šd.gldy. | l.gt.mzln. | šd.glln.l.gt.mz[l]n. | šd. 1104.15

ilšlm

[p]ṯ.ḫpṯ.d[.yṯb.b].š'rt. | yly.bn.ṯrnq.[-]r.d.yṯb.b.ilštm'. | ilšlm.bn.gs[-.--]r.d.yṯb.b.gt.al. | ilmlk.[--]kt.[--.d.]yṯb.b.šb[n]. 2015.1.27
.al[-]. | l.tš'n. | mṣrm. | tmkrn. | ypḥ.'bdilt. | bn.m. | ypḥ.ilšlm. | bn.prqdš. | ypḥ.mnḥm. | bn.ḥnn. | brqn.spr. 2116.19

ilšn

]. | bdn.qln.mtn.ydln. | b'ltdtt.tlgn.ytn. | b'ltǵpṯm.krwn.ilšn.agyn. | mnn.šr.ugrt.ḏkr.yṣr. | tǵǵln.ḫmš.ddm. | [---].ḫmš. 2011.36
ilšt[m'ym]. | yddt[.---]. | ilšn.[---]. | ṣdqn.[----]. | pndḏn.b[n.---]. | ayaḫ.b[n.---]. 96[333].3

ilšpš

dm. | [---.ṣ]mdm.w.ḥrṣ. | [---].aḥdm. | [iwr]pzn.aḥdm. | [i]lšpš.aḥd. 2033.2.8
t. | bn kbdy. | bn krk. | bn srty. | bn lth ḫlq. | bn ytr. | bn ilšpš. | ubrš. | bn gmš ḫlq. | bn 'gy. | bn zlbn. | bn.aḫ[--]. | bn[.--- 2016.2.16
.[b]t.ršp.gn. | arb'.b d.b[n].ušryn. | kdm.l.urtn. | kdm.l.ilšpš. | kd.l.anntb. | kd.l.iwrmḏ. | kd.l.ydn. | [---.y]rḫ.ḫyr. | [---. 1088.6
| kkr.lqḥ.ršpy. | tmtrn.bn.pnmn. | kkr. | bn.sgttn. | kkr. | ilšpš.kkr. | bn.ḏltn. | kkr.w[.--]. | ḫ[--.---]. 1118.11
]. | šd.bddn.l.iytlm. | šd.bn.nb'm.l.ṯpṭb'l. | šd.bn mšrn.l.ilšpš. | [šd.bn].kbr.l.snrn. | [---.--]k.l.gmrd. | [---.--]ṭ.l.yšn. | [šd. 2030.1.5
| bn.idrn.'š[-.---]. | bn.bly.mr[-.---]. | w.nḥl h.mr[-.---]. | ilšpš.[---]. | iḫny.[---]. | bn.[---]. 88[304].12
spr.[---]. | iytlm[.---]. | ybnn[.---]. | ilšp[š.---]. 2140.4

ilštm'

n[-].b[n].py[-.d.]yṯb.b.gt.aǵld. | šgn.bn b[--.---].d.yṯb.b.ilštm'. | abmn.bn.r[---].b.syn. | bn.irṣ[-.---.]h. | šdyn.b[n.---.--] 2015.2.6
. | bn.ag[p]ṯ.ḫpṯ.d[.yṯb.b].š'rt. | yly.bn.ṯrnq.[-]r.d.yṯb.b.ilštm'. | ilšlm.bn.gs[-.--]r.d.yṯb.b.gt.al. | ilmlk.[--]kt.[--.d.]yṯb. 2015.1.26
| ṯmry. | qrt. | 'rm. | nnu. | [--]. | [---]. | m'r. | arny. | ubr'y. | ilštm'. | bir. | m'qb. | uškn. | snr. | rq[d]. | [---]. | [---]. | mid[-]. | ub 71[113].29
b gt ilštm'. | bt ubnyn š h d.ytn.ṣṭqn. | ṯut ṭbḫ ṣṭq[n]. | b bz 'zm ṭb 1153.1
šd.ubdy.ilštm'. | dt b d.skn. | šd.bn.ubr'n b gt prn. | šd.bn.gby.gt.prn. | 1104.1
r. | um r[-] gtn ṯṯ ḫsn l ytn. | l rḥt lqḥ ṣṭqn. | bt qbṣ urt ilštm' dbḥ ṣṭqn l. | ršp. 1154.7
p.d.mkr.ar. | arb'm ksp d mkr. | atlg. | mit.ksp.d mkr. | ilštm'. | 'šrm.l mit.ksp. | 'l.bn.alkbl.šb[ny]. | 'šrm ksp.'l. | wrt. 2107.14
. | 'nqpat[.---].bnš. | ubr'y.ar[b'.]ḥm[r]m.w[.---.]bnšm. | ilštm'.arb'.ḥm[r]m.ḫmš.bnšm. | ǵr. | ary.ḥmr w.bnš. | qmy.ḥ 2040.21
il[štm']. | šbn. | ṭbq. | rqd. | uškn. | ḫbt. | [ḫlb].kr[d]. 1177.1
. | hry. | qmṣ. | ṣ'q. | qmy. | ḫlbkrd. | y'rt. | uškn. | 'nqpat. | ilštm'. | šbn. | ṭbq. | rqd. | šrš. | gn'y. | m'qb. | agm. | bir. | ypr. | hz 2074.21
ṣ'[-.---]. | ṣ'q[.---]. | ḫlb.k[rd]. | uškn. | 'nqp[at]. | ubr'[y]. | ilšt[m']. | šbn. | ṭbq. 2146.8
b'l. | [--]m. | [m']rby. | m'r. | arny. | 'nqpat. | š'rt. | ubr'y. | ilštm'. | šbn. | tbq. | rqd. | [š]rš. | [-----]. | [-----]. | [-----]. | [-----]. | [2058.1.15

ilštm'y

. | ṣdqn.gb'ly. | bn.ypy.gb'ly. | bn.grgs.ilštm'y. | bn.ḫran.ilštm'y. | bn.abd'n.ilštm'y. | bn.'n.rqdy. | bn.g'yn. | bn.ǵrn. | bn 87[64].30
-]ty. | [b]n.ypy.gb'ly. | b[n].ḥyn. | ḏmn.š'rty. | bn.arwdn.ilšt'y. | bn grgs. | bn.ḫran. | bn.arš[w.b]ṣry. | bn.ykn. | bn.lṣn.'r 99[327].1.8

y. | bn.ibrd.m'rby. | ṣdqn.gb'ly. | bn.ypy.gb'ly. | bn.grgs.ilštm'y. | bn.ẖran.ilštm'y. | bn.abd'n.ilštm'y. | bn.'n.rqdy. | bn. 87[64].29

py.gb'ly. | bn.grgs.ilštm'y. | bn.ẖran.ilštm'y. | bn.abd'n.ilštm'y. | bn.'n.rqdy. | bn.g'yn. | bn.ǵrn. | bn.agynt. | bn.abdḥr. 87[64].31

i[l]štm'ym. | bn.ṯk. | bn.arwdn. | tmrtn. | šd'l.bn aẖyn. | m'rby 95[91].1

ẖdy.'šrt. | ṯṯn.'ṣrt. | bn.pnmn.'šrt. | 'bdadt.ẖmšt. | abmn.ilštm'y.ẖmš[t]. | 'zn.bn.brn.ẖmšt. | m'rt.ẖmšt. | arṯtb.bn.ẖmšt 1062.25

ilšt[m'ym]. | yddt[.---]. | ilšn.[---]. | ṣdqn.[----]. | pndd̠n.b[n.---]. 96[333].1

spr.mẖṣm. | bn.ẖpšry.b.šbn. | ilštm'ym. | y[---.]bn.'šq. | [---.]bn.tqy. | [---.]bn.šlmy. | [-----]. | [1041.3

.---]. | mty.ilšt[m'y.---]. | bn.pynq.'nqp[a]t[y.---]. | ayiẖ.ilšt[m'y.---]. | [b]dlm.dt.yṯb[.---]. | [-]y[--].'nqp[aty.---]. | 'ṯt[r] 90[314].2.9

bir[-.---]. | kṯrmlk.ns[--.---]. | bn.tbd.ilšt[m'y.---]. | mty.ilšt[m'y.---]. | bn.pynq.'nqp[a]t[y.---]. | ayiẖ.ilšt[m'y.---]. | [b]d 90[314].2.7

]. | 'dn.[---]. | aẖqm bir[-.---]. | kṯrmlk.ns[--.---]. | bn.tbd.ilšt[m'y.---]. | mty.ilšt[m'y.---]. | bn.pynq.'nqp[a]t[y.---]. | ayiẖ 90[314].2.6

q.maẖdy. | kkr.ṯlṯ. | b d.bn.by.ar[y]. | alpm.ṯlṯ. | b d.šim.il[š]tm'y. 1134.7

ilt

ẖmš. | 'ṯr h.mlun.šnpt.ẖṣt h.b'l.ṣpn š. | [--]ṯ š.ilt.mgdl š.ilt.asrm š. | w l ll.šp. pgr.w ṯrmnm.bt mlk. | il[bt].gdlt.ušẖry. 34[1].11

ṯt.w kšm.ẖmš. | 'ṯr h.mlun.šnpt.ẖṣt h.b'l.ṣpn š. | [--]ṯ š.ilt.mgdl š.ilt.asrm š. | w l ll.šp. pgr.w ṯrmnm.bt mlk. | il[bt].g 34[1].11

]y.l yṣḥ.ṯr il.ab h. | [i]l.mlk.d yknn h.yṣḥ. | aṯrt.w bn h.ilt.w ṣbrt. | ary h.wn.in.bt.l b'l. | km.ilm.w ḥẓr.k bn.aṯrt. | mṯ 4[51].4.49

any.l yṣḥ.ṯr.il.ab h.il. | mlk.d yknn h.yṣḥ.aṯrt. | w bn h.ilt.w ṣbrt.arẖ h. | wn.in.bt.l b'l.km.ilm. | ḥẓr.k b[n.a]ṯrt.mṯb.i 3['NT.VI].5.45

ṣ]ḥ.ṯr. | [il.ab h.i]l.mlk. | [d yknn h.yṣ]ḥ.aṯ | [rt.w bn h.]ilt. | [w ṣbrt.ary]h. | [wn.in.bt.l b'l.] | [km.ilm.w ḥẓr]. | [k bn.a 4[51].1.8

šṯḥwy.w tkbdn h. | tšu.g h.w tṣḥ.tšmẖ ht. | aṯrt.w bn h.ilt.w ṣb | rt.ary h.k mt.aliyn. | b'l.k ẖlq.zbl.b'l. | arṣ.gm.yṣḥ il. 6.1.40[49.1.12]

qt. | dqt.trṯ.dqt. | [rš]p.'nt.ẖbly.dbḥn š[p]š pgr. | [g]dlt iltm ẖnqtm.d[q]tm. | [yr]ẖ.kṯy gdlt.w l ǵlmt š. | [w]pamt ṯlṯ 34[1].18

. | kṯr. | ṯrmn. | pdry. | dqt. | trṯ. | ršp. | 'nt ẖbly. | špš pgr. | iltm ẖnqtm. | yrẖ kṯy. | ygb hd. | yrgb b'l. | ydb il. | yarš il. | yrǵ UG5.14.A.13

| šbm.b ksl.qšt h.mdnt. | w hln.'nt.l bt h.tmǵyn. | tštql.ilt.l hkl h. | w l.šb't.tmtẖṣ h.b 'mq. | tẖtṣb.bn.qrtm.tṯ'r. | ksat. 3['NT].2.18

ṯm.w bǵr.arb['.---]. | kdm.yn.prs.qmḥ.[---]. | mdbḥt.bt.ilt.'ṣr[m.l ṣpn.š]. | l ǵlmt.š.w l [---.l yrẖ]. | gd[lt].l nkl[.gdlt.l b 35[3].24

bǵr.arb'.[---.kdm.yn]. | prs.qmḥ.m'[--.---]. | mdbḥt.bt.i[lt.'ṣrm.l]. | ṣpn š.l ǵlm[t.š.w l.---]. | l yrẖ.gdlt.l [nkl.gdlt.l b'] APP.II[173].26

m hm.tdr. | ap.bnt.ḥry. | km hm.w tẖss.aṯrt. | ndr h.w ilt.p[--]. | w tšu.g h.w [tṣḥ]. | ph m'.ap.k[rt.--]. | u ṯn.ndr[.---]. 15[128].3.26

m.w l ilt. | ṣd[yn]m.ṯm. | yd[r.k]rt.ṯ'. | i.iṯt.aṯrt.ṣrm. | w ilt.ṣdynm. | hm.ḥry.bt y. | iqḥ.aš'rb.ǵlmt. | ḥẓr y.ṯn h.wspm. | 14[KRT].4.202

w ṯn.aẖr. | šp[š]m.b [ṯ]lṯ. | ym[ǵy.]l qdš. | a[ṯrt.]ṣrm.w l ilt. | ṣd[yn]m.ṯm. | yd[r.k]rt.ṯ'. | i.iṯt.aṯrt.ṣrm. | w ilt.ṣdynm. | h 14[KRT].4.198

.ilt.[---]. | l.ḥtk[.---]. | l.ršp[.---]. | [l].ršp.[---.--]g.kbd. | [l.i]lt.qb[-.---]. | [l.a]rṣy. | [l.--]r[-.---]. | [l.--]ḥl. | [l.--.]mgmr. | [l.-. 1004.1.10

[---.]'ṯ[trt.---]. | [-.k]su.ilt[.---]. | [ṯl]ṯ.l 'ṯtrt[.---]. | [--.]l ilt.š l 'ṯt[rt.---]. | [']ṣr.l pdr ṯṯ.ṣ[in.---]. | tšnpn.'lm.km[m.---]. | 38[23].4

nn. | bn.pndr. | bn.nqq. | ḥrš.bhtm. | bn.izl. | bn.ibln. | bn.ilt. | špšyn.nḥl h. | n'mn.bn.iryn. | nrn.nḥl h. | bn.ẖsn. | bn.'bd. 85[80].2.5

]mgmr. | [l.-.]qdšt. | l.'ṯtrt.ndrgd. | l.'ṯtrt.abd̠r. | l.dml. | l.ilt[.-]pn. | l.uš[ẖr]y. | [---.-]mrn. | l ṯwl. | [--]d̠[--]. 1001.1.13

r.il.bn h.ṯr[.---]. | w y'n.lṭpn.il.d p[id.---]. | šm.bn y.yw.ilt.[---]. | w p'r.šm.ym[-.---]. | t'nyn.l zn.tn[.---]. | at.adn.tp'r[.- 1['NT.X].4.14

l.[----]. | l.[----]. | l.'ṯ[trt.---]. | l.mš[--.---]. | l.ilt[.---]. | l.b'lt[.---]. | l.il.bt[.---]. | l.ilt.[---]. | l.ḥtk[.---]. | l.ršp[.-- 1004.5

rt.---]. | l.mš[--.---]. | l.ilt[.---]. | l.b'lt[.---]. | l.il.bt[.---]. | l.ilt.[---]. | l.ḥtk[.---]. | l.ršp[.---]. | [l].ršp.[---.--]g.kbd. | [l.i]lt.qb[1004.8

[---.]'ṯ[trt.---]. | [-.k]su.ilt[.---]. | [ṯl]ṯ.l 'ṯtrt[.---]. | [--.]l ilt.š l 'ṯt[rt.---]. | [']ṣr.l pdr ṯṯ.ṣ[38[23].2

ilṯḥm

[q]n.š[--]. | yiṯṯm.w.b[--]. | yšlm. | [']šrm.ks[p].yš[lm]. | [il]ṯḥm.b d[.---]. | [---].ṯl[l]m.[---]. | [--].r[-]y[.---]. | 'l.[--]l[-] h. | ' 2104.8

[---]. | kn'm.bn.[---]. | plšb'l.bn.n[--]. | ḥy bn.dnn.ṯkt. | ilṯḥm.bn.dnn.ṯkt. | šb'l.bn.aly.ṯkt. | klby.bn.iẖy.ṯkt. | pss.bn.b 2085.5

. | 'pṣpn.bn.'dy.ṯkt. | n'mn.bn.'yn.ṯkt. | 'pṯn.bn.ilrš.ṯkt. | ilṯḥm.bn.srn.ṯkt. | šmlbu.bn.grb.ṯkt. | šmlbu.bn.yp'.ṯkt. | [---.- 2085.12

.in ḥẓm.l hm. | [---.--]d̠n. | mrkbt.mtrt. | ngršp. | ngǵln. | ilṯḥm. | b'lṣdq. 1125.2.4

--]. | ds[-.---]. | t[--.---]. | a[--.---]. | [---].ksp.'m[.---]. | [---.]ilṯḥm.w.[---]. | šm't.ḥwt[.---]. | [---].nzdt.qr[t]. | [---.]dt nzdt.m 2127.2.2

bn.ǵd'. | bn.'yn. | bn.grb[n]. | yṯtn. | bn.ab[l]. | kry. | pss. | ilṯḥm. | ḥrm. | bn.bty. | 'by. | šm[n].bn.apn. | krty. | bn.ubr. | [bn 2078.13

št. | bn.mṣry.qšt. | arny. | abm.qšt. | ḥdṯn.ql'. | yṯpṭ.qšt. | ilṯḥm.qšt.w.ql'. | ṣdqm.qšt.w.ql'. | uln.qšt.w.ql'. | uln.qšt. | bn. 119[321].2.5

iltm

.bn.ud̠r[-.---]. | w.'d'.nḥl h[.---]. | w.yknil.nḥl h[.---]. | w.iltm.nḥl h[.---]. | w.unṯm.nḥ[l h.---]. | [---.]'d̠r[.---]. | str[-.---]. | 90[314].1.16

ilṯtmr

. | [š]d.bn.rwy.b d.ydln. | [š].bn.trn.b d.ibrmd̠. | [š]d.bn.ilṯtmr.b d.tbbr. | [w.]šd.nḥl h.b d.ṯṯmd. | [š]d.b d.iwrẖṭ. | [ṯn]. 82[300].1.11

im

n k itn. | r' y šṣa idn l y. | l šmn iṯr hw. | p iẖdn gnryn. | im mlkytn yrgm. | aẖnnn. | w iẖd. 1020.8

imr

rḥṣ[.y]d k.amt. | uṣb['t k.]'d[.ṯ]km. | 'rb[.b ẓl.ẖmt]. | qḥ im[r.b yd k]. | imr.d[bḥ.bm].ymn. | lla.kl[atn]m. | klt.l[ḥm k. 14[KRT].2.66

h.w nǵr. | 'nn.ilm.al. | tqrb.l bn.ilm. | mt.al.y'db km. | k imr.b p h. | k lli.b ṯbrn. | qn h.ṯẖtan. | nrt.ilm.špš. | ṣḥrrt.la. | š 4[51].8.18

. | dbr.ysmt.šd.šḥlmmt. | ngš.ank.aliyn b'l. | 'dbnn ank.imr.b p y. | k lli.b ṯbrn q y.ẖtu hw. | nrt.ilm.špš.ṣḥrrt. | la.šm 6[49].2.22

ǵzr.mt. | hrnmy.gm.l aṯt h.k yṣḥ. | šm'.mṯt.dnty.'d[b]. | imr.b pẖd.l npš.kṯr. | w ẖss.l brlt.hyn d. | ḥrš yd.šlḥm.ššqy. | i 17[2AQHT].5.17

ilm sad.kbd.hmt.b'l. | ḥkpt.il.kl h.tšm'. | mṯt.dnty.t'db.imr. | b pẖd.l npš.kṯr.w ẖss. | l brlt.hyn.d ḥrš. | ydm.aẖr.ymǵ 17[2AQHT].5.22

. | yrḥṣ.yd h.amt h. | uṣb't h.'d.ṯkm. | 'rb.b ẓl.ẖmt.lqḥ. | imr.dbḥ.b yd h. | lla.klatnm. | klt.lḥm h.d nzl. | lqḥ.msrr.'ṣr.d 14[KRT].3.160

. | uṣb['t k.]'d[.ṯ]km. | 'rb[.b ẓl.ẖmt]. | qḥ im[r.b yd k]. | imr.d[bḥ.bm].ymn. | lla.kl[atn]m. | klt.l[ḥm k.d]nzl. | qḥ.ms[14[KRT].2.67

tqn.w[rḥm.'nt]. | tngṯ h.k lb.a[rẖ]. | l 'gl h.k lb.ṯa[t]. | l imr h.km.lb.'n[t]. | aṯr.b'l.tiẖd.m[t]. | b sin.lpš.tššq[n h]. | b qṣ 6[49].2.8

m. | l yrẖm.rḥm.'nt.tngṯ h. | k lb.arẖ.l 'gl h.k lb. | ṯat.l imr h.km.lb. | 'nt.aṯr.b'l.tiẖd. | bn.ilm.mt.b ḥrb. | tbq'nn.b ẖṯr 6[49].2.29

ḥry.ṭbẖ.imr. | w ilḥm.mgṯ.w iṯrm. | tšm'.mṯt.ḥry. | tṭbẖ.imr.w lḥm. | mgṯ.w yṯrm.hn.ym. | w ṯn.yṯb.krt.l 'd h. | yṯb.l k 16.6[127].20

lan.w ypqd. | krt.ṯ'.yšu.g h. | w yṣḥ.šm'.l mṯt. | ḥry.ṭbẖ.imr. | w ilḥm.mgṯ.w iṯrm. | tšm'.mṯt.ḥry. | tṭbẖ.imr.w lḥm. | m 16.6[127].17

--]. | w d.l mdl.r[--.---]. | w ṣin.ʻz.b[ʻl.---]. | llu.bn[š.---]. | imr.ḫ[--.---]. | [--]n.bʻ[l.---]. | w [--]d.[---]. | idk[.-]it[.---]. | trgm 2158.1.16

ṯb l y.ṯr.il[.ab y.---]. | yṯb.l y.w l h.[---]. | [--.i]mṣḫ.nn.k imr.l arṣ. | [ašhlk].šbt h.dmm.šbt.dqn h. | [mmʻm.-]d.l ytn.bt 3[ʻNT.VI].5.9

m. | ṭbḫ.alpm.ap ṣin.šql.ṯrm. | w mri ilm.ʻglm.dt.šnt. | imr.qmṣ.llim.k ksp. | l ʻbrm.zt.ḫrṣ.l ʻbrm.kš. | dpr.ṯlḥn.b qʻl.b 22.2[124].14

ṭbḫ.alpm[.ap]. | ṣin.šql.ṯrm[.w]m | ria.il.ʻglm.d[t]. | šnt.imr.qmṣ.l[l]im. | ṣḥ.aḫ h.b bht h.a[r]y h. | b qrb hkl h.ṣḥ. | šbʻ 4[51].6.43

. | ṭbḫ.alp[m.ap.ṣin.šql]. | ṯrm.w [mri.ilm.ʻglm.dt.šnt]. | imr.[qmṣ.llim.---]. 1[ʻNT.X].4.32

imrt

t.ḫzli. | bn.iḫyn. | ṣdqn.bn.ass. | bʻlyskn.bn.ss. | ṣdqn.bn.imrt. | mnḥm.bn.ḫyrn. | [-]yn.bn.arkbt. | [--]zbl.bt.mrnn. | a[-- 102[323].3.10

imt

t.anḫr. | b ym.hm.brk y.tkšd. | rumm.ʻn.kdd.aylt. | hm.imt.imt.npš.blt. | ḥmr.p imt.b klt. | yd y.ilḥm.hm.šbʻ. | ydt y. 5[67].1.18

tkšd. | rumm.ʻn.kdd.aylt. | hm.imt.imt.npš.blt. | ḥmr.p imt.b klt. | yd y.ilḥm.hm.šbʻ. | ydt y.b ṣʻ.hm.ks.ymsk. | nhr.k[5[67].1.19

ḫr. | b ym.hm.brk y.tkšd. | rumm.ʻn.kdd.aylt. | hm.imt.imt.npš.blt. | ḥmr.p imt.b klt. | yd y.ilḥm.hm.šbʻ. | ydt y.b ṣʻ. 5[67].1.18

in

pn[.zb]l y[m]. | [l pn.ṯp]ṭ[.nhr.]mlkt.[--]pm.l mlkt.wn.in.aṯt. | [l]k.k[m.ilm]. | [w ġlmt.k bn.qdš.]w y[--.]zbl.ym.yʻ[-- 2.3[129].22

[---.]špm.ʻdb. | [---].tʻtqn. | [---.-]ʻb.idk. | [l ytn.pnm.tk.]in.bb.b alp ḥẓr. | [rbt.kmn.l pʻ]n.ʻnt. | [yhbr.w yql.yšt]ḥwyn. 1[ʻNT.IX].2.14

| il.b šbʻt.ḥdrm.b ṯmnt. | ap.sgrt.ydʻ[t k.]bt.k an[št]. | k in.b ilht.ql[ṣ] k.mh.taršʻ[n]. | l btlt.ʻnt.w t[ʻ]n.btlt.ʻn[t]. | ṯḥm 3[ʻNT.VI].5.36

yd.btlt.[ʻnt]. | w yʻn.lṭpn.il d p[id]. | ydʻt k.bt.k anšt.w i[n.b ilht]. | qlṣ k.tbʻ.bt.ḫnp.lb[k.--.ti] | ḫd.d iṯ.b kbd k.tšt.b [18[3AQHT].1.16

[y h.]ytdṯ. | yšbʻ.rgm.[my.]b ilm. | ydy.mrṣ.gršm zbln. | in.b ilm.ʻny h. | w yʻn.lṭpn.il.b pid. | ṯb.bn y.lm ṯb[t] km. | l k 16[126].5.22

h.y[ṯny.ytlṯ]. | rgm.my.b[ilm.ydy]. | mrṣ.grš[m.zbln]. | in.b ilm.ʻ[ny h.yrbʻ]. | yḫmš.rgm.[my.b ilm]. | ydy.mrṣ.g[ršm 16[126].5.16

.yrbʻ]. | yḫmš.rgm.[my.b ilm]. | ydy.mrṣ.g[ršm.zbln]. | in.b ilm.ʻn[y h.]ytdṯ. | yšbʻ.rgm.[my.]b ilm. | ydy.mrṣ.gršm z 16[126].5.19

yʻn]. | lṭpn.[il.d pid.my]. | b ilm.[ydy.mrṣ]. | gršm.z[bln.in.b ilm]. | ʻny h.y[ṯny.ytlṯ]. | rgm.my.b[ilm.ydy]. | mrṣ.grš[m 16[126].5.12

m h.w ʻbd. | ʻlm.ṯlṯ.sswm. | mrkbt.b trbṣ. | bn.amt.p d.[i]n. | b bt y.ttn.tn. | l y.mṯt.ḥry. | nʻmt.šbḥ.bkr k. | d k nʻm.ʻnt. 14[KRT].6.287

m h.w ʻbd. | ʻlm.ṯlṯ.sswm.mrkbt. | b trbṣt.bn.amt. | p d.in.b bt y.ttn. | tn.l y.mṯt.ḥry. | nʻmt.špḥ.bkr k. | d k.nʻm.ʻnt.nʻ 14[KRT].3.142

[ʻb]dmlk. | [-]k.am[ʻ--]. | [w.b] d.bn h[.ʻ]d ʻlm. | [w.un]ṯ.in[n.]b h. | [---.]nʻm[-]. 1009.18

l.yqḥnn.b d. | bʻln.bn.kltn. | w.b d.bn h.ʻd. | ʻlm.w unṯ. | in.b h. 1008.21

tšʻ.ṣmdm. | ṯlṯm.b d. | ibrtlm. | w.pat.aḥt. | in.b hm. 1141.5

l.b ḥnt h.abynt. | [d]nil.mt.rpi anḫ.ġzr. | [mt.]hrnmy.d in.bn.l h. | km.aḫ h.w šrš.km.ary h. | bl.iṯ.bn.l h.km aḫ h.w š 17[2AQHT].1.19

[---.bʻl.b bht h]. | [il.hd.b qr]b.hkl h. | w tʻnyn.ġlm.bʻl. | in.bʻl.b bht ht. | il hd.b qrb.hkl h. | qšt hn.aḫd.b yd h. | w qṣʻt 10[76].2.4

d yknn h.yṣ]ḥ.aṯ | [rt.w bn h.]ilt. | [w ṣbrt.ary]h. | [wn.in.bt.l bʻl.] | [km.ilm.w ḥẓr]. | [k bn.aṯ]r[t]. | m[ṯ]b.il.mẓll. | bn 4[51].1.10

[---.wn.in]. | [bt].l [bʻl.km.ilm.w ḥẓr]. | k bn.[aṯrt.mṯb.il.mẓll]. | bn h. 3[ʻNT.VI].4.02

l.mlk.d yknn h.yṣḥ. | aṯrt.w bn h.ilt.w ṣbrt. | ary h.wn.in.bt.l bʻl. | km.ilm.w ḥẓr.k bn.aṯrt. | mṯb il.mẓll.bn h. | mṯb r 4[51].4.50

. | mlk.d yknn h.yṣḥ.aṯrt. | w bn h.ilt.w ṣbrt.arḫ h. | wn.in.bt.l bʻl.km.ilm. | ḥẓr.k b[n.a]ṯrt.mṯb.il. | mṯll.b[n h.m]ṯb.rb 3[ʻNT.VI].5.46

ṯ.mṯpṭ k.w yʻn[.ʻṯtr].dm[-]k[-]. | [--]ḥ.b y.ṯr.il.ab y.ank.in.bt[.l] y[.km.]ilm[.w] ḥẓr[.k bn]. | [qd]š.lbum.trd.b n[p]šn 2.3[129].19

ḥkm k. | ʻm.ʻlm.ḥyt.ḥẓt.ṯḥm k. | mlk n.aliyn.bʻl.ṯpṭ n. | in.d ʻln h.klny y.qš h. | nbln.klny y.nbl.ks h. | any.l yṣḥ.ṯr.il.a 3[ʻNT.VI].5.41

mt. | ʻm ʻlm.ḥyt.ḥẓt. | ṯḥm k.mlk n.aliy[n.]bʻl. | ṯpṭ n.w in.d ʻln h. | klny n.q[š] h.n[bln]. | klny n[.n]bl.ks h. | [an]y.l yṣ 4[51].4.44

[---].in ḥẓm.l hm. | [---.--]ḏn. | mrkbt.mtrt. | ngršp. | ngġln. | ilṯḥm. 1125.1.1

t. | w.pdy h[m]. | iwrkl.mit. | ksp.b y[d]. | birtym. | [un]ṯ inn. | l [h]m ʻd ṯṯbn. | ksp.iwrkl. | w ṯb.l unṯ hm. 1006.16

tnn.w ygl.w ynsk.ʻ[-]. | [--]y.l arṣ[.id]y.alt.l aḥš.idy.alt.in l y. | [--]t.bʻl.ḥẓ.ršp.b[n].km.yr.klyt h.w lb h. | [ṯ]n.p k.b ġr 1001.1.2

ʻm[.---]m ib. | [---.--]m. | [-----]. | [-]š[--.---]. | [-]r[--.--]y. | in m.ʻbd k hwt. | [y]rš.ʻm y. | mnm.iršt k. | d ḫsrt.w.ank. | aštn 2065.13

bn.qrrn. | bn.dnt. | bn.ṯʻl[-]. | bdl.ar.dt.inn. | mhr l ht. | artyn. | ʻdmlk. | bn.alt[-]. | iḫy[-]. | ʻbdgtr. | ḥrr. 1035.1.4

. | yšlm.l k. | l.trġds. | w.l.klby. | šmʻt.ḫti. | nḫtu.ht. | hm.in mm. | nḫtu.w.lak. | ʻm y.w.yd. | ilm.p.k mtm. | ʻz.mid. | hm. 53[54].9

.diy.hwt.w yql. | ṯḥt.pʻn h.ybqʻ.kbd h.w yḥd. | [i]n.šmt.in.ʻẓm.yšu.g[h]. | w yṣḥ.knp.hrgb.bʻl.ybn. | [b]ʻl.ybn.diy.hwt 19[1AQHT].3.131

iy hmt.tqln. | ṯḥt.pʻn h.ybqʻ.kbdt hm.w[yḥd]. | in.šmt.in.ʻẓm.yšu.g h. | w yṣḥ.knp.nšrm.ybn. | bʻl.ybn.diy hmt nšrm 19[1AQHT].3.117

--]. | tšnpn.ʻlm.km[m.---]. | w.l ll.ʻṣrm.w [---]. | kmm.w.in.ʻṣr[.---]. | w mit.šʻrt.[-]y[-.---]. | w.kdr.w.npt t[--.---]. | w.ksp 38[23].8

| bʻl.ṯbr.diy.hwt.w yql. | ṯḥt.pʻn h.ybqʻ.kbd h.w yḥd. | [i]n.šmt.in.ʻẓm.yšu.g[h]. | w yṣḥ.knp.hrgb.bʻl.ybn. | [b]ʻl.ybn. 19[1AQHT].3.131

ʻl.ṯbr.diy hmt.tqln. | ṯḥt.pʻn h.ybqʻ.kbdt hm.w[yḥd]. | in.šmt.in.ʻẓm.yšu.g h. | w yṣḥ.knp.nšrm.ybn. | bʻl.ybn.diy hm 19[1AQHT].3.117

l.tlk. | w.lḥt.akl.ky. | likt.ʻm.špš. | bʻl k.ky.akl. | b.ḫwt k.inn. | špš n.[---]. | hm.al[k.--]. | ytnt[.---]. | ṯn[.---]. | w[.-----]. | l[. 2060.20

]. | ʻm.k[--.lḥt]. | akl.yt[ṯb.--]pt. | ib.ʻltn.a[--.--]y. | w.spr.in[.-.]ʻd m. | spr n.ṯhr[.--]. | aṯr.iṯ.bqṯ. | w.štn.l y. 2060.32

. | b p h.rgm.l yṣa.b špt h[.hwt h]. | b nši ʻn h.w tphn.in.[---]. | [-.]hlk.ġlmm b dd y.yṣ[--]. | [-.]yṣa.w l.yṣa.hlm.[ṯnm 19[1AQHT].2.76

---.--]l y. | [---.--]r. | [--.]wk[--.---]. | [--].lm.l[--.---]. | [-]m.in[.---]. | [--.]sʻ.[---]. | [---.]n[--.---]. | [--.]aw[--.---]. | [---.]ʻl.y[--.- 45[45].2

inbb

-.]špm.ʻdb. | [---].tʻtqn. | [---.-]ʻb.idk. | [l ytn.pnm.tk.]in.bb.b alp ḥẓr. | [rbt.kmn.l pʻ]n.ʻnt. | [yhbr.w yql.yšt]ḥwyn.w y 1[ʻNT.IX].2.14

sa.w yṯb. | tqru l špš.um h.špš.um.ql.bl.ʻm. | ʻnt w ʻṯtrt inbb h.mnt.nṯk. | nḥš.šlḥm.nḥš.ʻq šr[.yʻ]db.ksa. | nḥš.šmrr.nḥ UG5.7.20

bš k. | ʻtk.ri[š.]l mhr k. | w ʻp.l dr[ʻ].nšr k. | w rbṣ.l ġr k.inbb. | kt ġr k.ank.ydʻt. | [-]n.atn.at.mṯb k[.---]. | [š]mm.rm.lk 13[6].9

gmn.lk.lk.ʻnn.ilm. | atm.bštm.w an.šnt. | uġr.l rḥq.ilm.inbb. | l rḥq.ilnym.ṯn.mṯpdm. | ṯḥt.ʻnt.arṣ.ṯlṯ.mtḥ.ġyrm. | idk. 3[ʻNT].4.78

. | bʻl.azrt.ʻnt.[-]ld. | kbd h.l ydʻ hr h.[---]d[-]. | tnq[.---.]in[b]b.pʻr. | yd h[.--.]ṣʻr.glgl. | a[---]m.rḥ.ḥḏ ʻ[r]pt. | gl[.---.]yh 13[6].32

inn

lk. | yd.apnt hn. | yd.ḥẓ hn. | yd.tr hn. | w.l.ṯt.mrkbtm. | inn.uṯpt. | w.ṯlṯ.ṣmdm.w.ḥrṣ. | apnt.b d.rb.ḥršm. | d.šṣa.ḥwy 1121.7

mḏrġlm.dt.inn. | b d.tlmyn. | b d.gln.ary. | tgyn.yʻrty. | bn.krwn.b.yny.iytl 2071.1

mḏrġlm.d inn. | msgm.l hm. | pʻṣ.ḫbty. | artyn.ary. | brqn.ṯlḥy. | bn.aryn. 118[306].1

inr

[l]krt. | k [k]lb.b bt k.n'tq.k inr. | ap.ẖšt k.ap.ab.ik mtm. | tmtn.u ẖšt k.l ntn. | 'tq.b d.aṯt.a 16.1[125].2

.b ḥy k.ab n.ašmẖ. | b l.mt k.ngln.k klb. | b bt k.n'tq.k inr. | ap.ẖšt k.ap.ab.k mtm. | tmtn.u ẖšt k.l ntn. | 'tq.b d.aṯt.a 16.1[125].16

y k.a]b n. | nšmẖ.b l.mt k.ngln. | k klb.[b]bt k.n'tq. | k inr[.ap.]ẖšt k. | ap.ab.k mtm.tmtn. | u ẖšt k.l bky.'tq. | b d.aṯt 16.2[125].101

'nt.ktp.b hm.yg'r.ṯǵr. | bt.il.pn.l mgr lb.t'dbn. | nšb.l inr.t'dbn.ktp. | b il ab h.g'r.yṯb.il.kb[-]. | aṯ[rt.]il.yṯb.b mrzḥ UG5.1.1.13

inš

. | b arb'[t.'šrt.riš.argmn]. | w ṯn šm.l [b'lt.bhtm.'ṣrm.l inš]. | ilm.w š d[d.ilš.š.--.mlk]. | yṯb.brr[.w mḥ-.---]. | ym.[']lm 35[3].5

a[r]b't.'šrt.riš. | arg[mn.w ṯn.]šm.l b'lt. | bhtm.'ṣ[rm.l in]š ilm.w š. | dd ilš.š[.---.]mlk.yṯb br | r.w mḥ[--.---.]w q[--]. | APP.II[173].6

.w 'l[y.---]. | bt.il.ṯq[l.---.kbd]. | w bdḥ.k[--.---]. | 'ṣrm.l i[nš.ilm.ṯb.md] | bḥ.b'l.[gdlt.---.dqt]. | l ṣpn.w [dqt.---.ṯn.l 'š] | APP.II[173].44

d]bḥt.b.ẖmš[.---]. | [-.]kbd.w.db[ḥ.---]. | [--].aṯrt.'ṣr[m.l inš.ilm]. | [ṯ]ṯb.mdbḥ.b'l.g[dlt.---]. | dqt.l.ṣpn.w.dqt[.---]. | ṯn.l 35[3].40

.w l [---.l yrẖ]. | gd[lt].l nkl[.gdlt.l b'lt.bhtm]. | 'š[rm.]l inš[.ilm.---]. | il[hm.]dqt.š[.---.rš] | [p.š]rp.w šl[mm.--.dqt]. | [i 35[3].27

l.---]. | l yrẖ.gdlt.l [nkl.gdlt.l b'] | [lt].bht[m].[']ṣrm l [inš.ilm]. | [---.]ilh[m.dqt.š.--]. | [---.--]t.r[šp.šrp.w šl] | [mm.---] APP.II[173].29

lt.ṣpn.dqt.šrp.w [š]lmm. | [---.a]lp.l b'l.w aṯrt.'ṣr[m] l inš. | [ilm.---].lbbmm.gdlt.'rb špš w ḥl. | [mlk.b ar]b't.'[š]rt.yr 36[9].1.8

]pamt ṯlṯm.w yrdt.[m]dbḥt. | gdlt.l b'lt bhtm.'ṣrm. | l inš ilm. 34[1].22

khnm. | qdšm. | mkrm. | mdm. | inšt. | ḥrš.bhtm. 75[81].5

[']b[dm]. | 'šrm. | inšt. | mdm. | gt.mlkym. | yqšm. | kbšm. | trrm. | khnm. | kzym. 74[115].3

qd[šm]. | mru s[kn]. | mru ib[rn]. | mdm. | inšt. | nsk ksp. | yṣḥm. | ḥrš mrkbt. | ḥrš qṯn. | ḥrš bhtm. 73[114].5

| [---].hn[.---]. | [---.]šn[.---]. | [---].pit. | [---.]qbat. | [---.]inšt. | [--]u.l tštql. | [---].ṯry.ap.l tlḥm. | [l]ḥm.trmmt.l tšt. | yn. 6.6[62.2].40

. | ṯhr w bd. | [k]tr ẖss šlm. | šlm il bt. | šlm il ẖš[t]. | ršp inšt. | [--]rm il [---]. | [---.--]m šlm [---]. UG5.7.72

mrynm. | mrum. | 'šrm. | ṯnnm. | nq[dm]. | kh[nm]. | inšt. 2019.7

[-]rm. | [-]dm. | [-]m. | [--]m. | [m]ru skn. | šrm. | [--]m. | [i]nšt. 2058.4.4

inšr

d.hwil.gt.prn. | šd.ḥr.gt.prn. | šd.bn.ṯbǵl.gt.prn. | šd.bn.inšr.gt.prn. | šd.[---.]gt.prn. | [šd.---.]gt.prn. | [šd.---.]gt.prn. | [1104.10

ṯdpṯn[.--]. | tny[.--]. | sll[.--]. | mld[.--]. | yqš[.--]. | [-----]. | inš[r.---]. | ršp[.---]. | iẖy[-.--]. | iwr[--.--]. | 'd[--.--]. | pl[--.--]. | gr 1074.10

is

bn.ṯrn w nḥl h. | bn srd.bn agmn. | bn [-]ln.bn.ṯbil. | bn is.bn tbdn. | bn uryy. | bn abd'n. | bn prkl. | bn štn. | bn annyn. 101[10].7

isg

adml[--.---]. | tlbr[-.---]. | isg.[---]. | ilwn.[---]. | ṯrn.d[d]. | tg d[d]. | ḥdyn.d[d]. | [-]ddn.d[132[331].3

isr

nt]. | ṣḥrrm.ḥbl[.--]. | 'rpt.ṯḥt.[---] | m 'ṣrm.ḥ[---]. | glṯ.isr[.---] | m.brt[.---]. | ymt m.[---]. | ši[.---]. | m[---.---]. 8[51FRAG].13

iǵyn

| w.nḥl hm. | bn.iršyn. | bn.'zn. | bn.aršw. | bn.ẖzrn. | bn.iǵyn. | w.nḥl h. | bn.ksd. | bn.bršm. | bn.kzn. | w.nḥl h. | w.nḥl 113[400].2.16

iǵlyn

šd[.-].dyn.b d.pln.nḥl h. | šd.irdyn.bn.ẖrǵš[-].l.qrt. | šd.iǵlyn.bn.kzbn.l.qr[t]. | šd.pln.bn.tiyn.b d.ilmhr nḥl h. | šd kn 2029.17

iǵlkḏ

l[---]. | ilmlk. | ildgn. | ilyn. | ilrm. | ibrm. | ibyn. | illḏrm. | iǵlkḏ. | [i]ly[-]n. | [-----]. | m[--.---]. | [-]n.qrqr. | [--]n.ymn.y[--]. 2022.20

ipd

tkly.bṯn.'qltn. | šlyṭ.d šb'y.rašm. | ṯṯkḥ.ttrp.šmm.k rs. | ipd k.ank.ispi.uṯm. | ḏrqm.amt m.l yrt. | b npš.bn ilm.mt.b 5[67].1.5

| [bṯn.'qltn.]šlyṭ. | [d šb't.rašm].ṯṯkḥ. | [ttrp.šmm.k rks.ipd]k. | [-----]. 5[67].1.31

[---].ydm. | [---].ṯdr. | [---.]mdṯn.ipd. | [---.]m[---.]d.mškbt. | [---.--]m. | [---].ṯlḥn. | [---].ṯnn. | [---. 1152.1.3

ipṯl

d.mqb. | b.gwl.ṯmn.ẖrmṯt.[nit]. | krk.m'ṣd.mqb. | [b] gt.ipṯl.ṯṯ.ẖrmṯ[t.nit]. | [k]rk.m'ṣd.mqb. | [b.g]t.bir.'š[r.---]. | [---]. 2048.13

.ṣmdm. | w.arb'.'šr.bnš. | yd.nǵr.mdr'.yd.š[--]m. | [b.]gt.ipṯl.ṯṯ.ṣmdm. | [w.']šr.bn[š]m.y[d].š[--]. | [-]lm.b d.r[-]m.l[-]m 2038.7

kbd.yn.d.l.ṭb. | b.gt.gwl. | ṯlṯm.tš'[.kbd.yn].d.l[.ṭb].b.gt.ipṯl. | ṯmnym.[yn].ṭb.b.gt.š[---]. | tš'm.[ẖ]mš[.kbd].yn.b gt[.-] 1084.19

.lmd hm.lqḥ. | 'šr.mḥsm.yd.lmd hm. | apym. | [bn]š gt.ipṯl. | [---]ym. | [---]m. | [-----]. | [bnš.g]t.ir. | bnš.gt.rb[--]. | gpn 1040.11

ipṯn

[-----]. | ubyn[.---]. | annt[n.---]. | ipṯn[.---]. | ybni[l.---]. | ikrn[.---]. | tlmyn[.---]. | tldn[.---]. | ann 106[332].4

iṣr

b.b tk.ǵr h.il ṣpn.b [tk]. | ǵr.tliyt.šb't.brqm.[---]. | ṯmnt.iṣr r't.'ṣ brq y. | riš h.tply.ṭly.bn.'n h. | uz'rt.tmll.išd h.qrn[m UG5.3.1.4

iqni

ṣ. | w arb'.ktnt.w [---]b. | [ẖm]š.mat pḥm. | [ẖm]š[.m]at.iqnu. | argmn.nqmd.mlk. | ugrt.d ybl.l špš. | mlk.rb.b'l h. | ks. 64[118].23

ẖpn.d.iqni.w.šmt. | l.iyb'l. | ṯlṯm.l.mit.š'rt. | l.šr.'ttrt. | mlbš.ṯrmnm. | 1107.1

n.kkr.brr. | arb'.alpm.pḥm. | ẖmš.mat.kbd. | arb'.alpm.iqni. | ẖmš.mat.kbd. | ṯlṯm.ẖmš kbd ktn. | ẖmš.rṭm. | ẖmš.ṯnt. 1130.5

'ṭ. | a[l]pm.alpnm. | ṯlṯ.m[a]t.art.ḥkpt. | mit.dnn. | mitm.iqnu. | ẖmš.'šr.qn.n'm.'n[m]. | ṯn.ḥblm.alp.alp.am[-]. | ṯmn.ḥ 1128.28

]m.qmṣ.ṯlṯm.i[qnu.---]. | [b.yr]ẖ.mgmr.mš[--.---]. | [---].iqnu.ẖmš[.---]. | [b.yr]ẖ.pgrm[.---]. 1106.39

t h.w atn mhr h l a|b h.alp ksp w rbt ḫ|rṣ.išlḥ ẓhrm iq|nim.atn šd h krm[m].|šd dd h ḥrnqm.w |y‘n ḫrḫb mlk 24[77].21
.mit.pḥm.|mit.iqni.l mlkt.|ks.ḫrṣ.ktn.mit.pḥm.|mit.iqni.l uṯryn.|ks.ksp.ktn.mit.pḥm.|mit.iqni.l tpnr.|[ks.ksp.k 64[118].30
t.pḥm.|mit.iqni.l tpnr.|[ks.ksp.kt]n.mit.pḥ[m].|[mit.iqni.l]ḫbrtn[r].|[ks.ksp.ktn.mit.pḥ]m.|[mit.iqni.l ḫbrtn]r ṯ 64[118].34
].|[mit.iqni.l]ḫbrtn[r].|[ks.ksp.ktn.mit.pḥ]m.|[mit.iqni.l ḫbrtn]r ṯn.|[ks.ksp.ktn.mit.pḥm].|[mit.iqn]i.l skl.[--]. 64[118].36
rt.d ybl.l špš.|mlk.rb.b‘l h.|ks.ḫrṣ.ktn.mit.pḥm.|mit.iqni.l mlkt.|ks.ḫrṣ.ktn.mit.pḥm.|mit.iqni.l uṯryn.|ks.ksp.kt 64[118].28
.|[mit.iqni.l ḫbrtn]r ṯn.|[ks.ksp.ktn.mit.pḥm].|[mit.iqn]i.l skl.[--].|[---.m]it pḥm.l š[--].|[---.]a[--.--.]hn[--]. 64[118].38
mit.pḥm.|mit.iqni.l uṯryn.|ks.ksp.ktn.mit.pḥm.|mit.iqni.l tpnr.|[ks.ksp.kt]n.mit.pḥ[m].|[mit.iqni.l]ḫbrtn[r].|[64[118].32
.ṯlṯm[.---].|[--]l.ṯrmn.m[lk.---].|[---.--]rt.š‘rt[.---].|[---.i]qni.l.ṯr[mn.art.---].|[b.yr]ḫ.riš.yn.[---].|[---.b‘]lt.bhtm.š[--. 1106.31
--].ṯlṯm.iqnu.|[---.l.]ṯrmn.mlk.|[---.]š‘rt.šb‘.‘šr h.|[---.iqn]i.l.ṯrmn.qrt.|[---.]lbš.ḫmšm.iqnu.|[---].šmt.ḫmšt.ḫndlt. 1106.15
n.qrt.|[---.]lbš.ḫmšm.iqnu.|[---].šmt.ḫmšt.ḫndlt.|[---.iqn]i.l.[-]k.btbt.|[---.l.ṯrm]nm.š[b‘].mat.š‘rt.|[---.]iqnu.[---.]l 1106.18
ṯrm]nm.š[b‘].mat.š‘rt.|[---.]iqnu.[---.]lbš.ṯrmnm.|[---.iqn]i.lbš.al[l.---].|[---].ṯṯ.lbš[.---].|[---.]kbd.ṯṯ.i[qnu.---].|[---. 1106.21
[---].all.iqni.arb‘m.kbl.|[---].iqni.‘šrm.ǵprt.|[---.š]pšg.iqni.mit.pṯtm.|[---].mitm.kslm.|[---].pwt.ṯlṯ.mat.abn.ṣrp.|[- 1106.8
k.|d k n‘m.‘nt.|n‘m h.km.tsm.|‘ṯtrt.tsm h.|d ‘q h.ib.iqni.|‘p‘p h.sp.ṯrml.|d b ḥlm y.il.ytn.|b ḏrt y.ab.adm.|w ld 14[KRT].6.294
k.|d k.n‘m.‘nt.n‘m h.|km.tsm.‘ṯtrt.ts[m h].|d ‘q h.ib.iqni.‘p[‘p] h.|sp.ṯrml.thgrn.[-]dm[.-].|ašlw.b ṣp.‘n h.|d b ḥl 14[KRT].3.147
allm.lbnm.|[---].all.šmt.|[---].all.iqni.arb‘m.kbl.|[---].iqni.‘šrm.ǵprt.|[---.š]pšg.iqni.mit.pṯtm.|[---].mitm.kslm.|[-- 1106.7
š.ṯrmnm.|[---]h.lbš.allm.lbnm.|[---].all.šmt.|[---].all.iqni.arb‘m.kbl.|[---].iqni.‘šrm.ǵprt.|[---.š]pšg.iqni.mit.pṯtm. 1106.6
sp.gb‘m.mḥmd..|ḫrṣ.w bn.bht.ksp.|w ḫrṣ.bht.ṯhrm.|iqnim.šmḫ.aliyn.|b‘l.ṣḥ.ḥrn.b bht h.|‘dbt.b qrb hkl h.|ybln 4[51].5.97
.ḫrṣ.|ybl k.udr.ilqṣm.|w bn.bht.ksp.w ḫrṣ.|bht.ṯhrm.iqnim.|šmḫ.btlt.‘nt.td‘ṣ.|p‘nm.w tr.arṣ.|idk.l ttn.pnm.|‘m. 4[51].5.81
.‘šrt.mzn h.|b [ar]b‘m.ksp.|b d[.‘b]dym.ṯlṯ.kkr š‘rt.|iqn[i]m.ṯṯt.‘šrt.ksp h.|ḫmšt.ḫrṣ.bt.il.|b.ḫmšt.‘šrt.ksp.|ḫmš. 2100.4
[------.i]qnim.[--].|[---.]aliyn.b‘l.|[---.--]k.mdd il.|y[m.---.]l ṯr.qdq 4[51].7.1
ḫpn[.---].|[---].aḥd.ḫmš.am[--.---].|[---.--]m.qmṣ.ṯlṯm.i[qnu.---].|[b.yr]ḫ.mgmr.mš[--.---].|[---].iqnu.ḫmš[.---].|[b. 1106.37
[---].pwt.ṯlṯ.mat.abn.ṣrp.|[---.-]qt.l.ṯrmnm.|[---].ṯlṯm.iqnu.|[---.l.]ṯrmn.mlk.|[---.]š‘rt.šb‘.‘šr h.|[---.iqn]i.l.ṯrmn.qr 1106.12
[---.iqn]i.l.[-]k.btbt.|[---.l.ṯrm]nm.š[b‘].mat.š‘rt.|[---.]iqnu.[---.]lbš.ṯrmnm.|[---.iqn]i.lbš.al[l.---].|[---].ṯṯ.lbš[.---].|[1106.20
[---.]š‘rt.šb‘.‘šr h.|[---.iqn]i.l.ṯrmn.qrt.|[---.]lbš.ḫmšm.iqnu.|[---].šmt.ḫmšt.ḫndlt.|[---.iqn]i.l.[-]k.btbt.|[---.l.ṯrm]n 1106.16
d k.|[tk.ḫršn.---]r.[-]ḫm k.w št.|[---.]ẓ[--.-]rdy k.|[---.i]qnim.|[---.-]šu.b qrb.|[---].asr.|[---.--]m.ymt m.|[---].k iṯl. 1[‘NT.IX].2.5
nm.|[---.iqn]i.lbš.al[l.---].|[---].ṯṯ.lbš[.---].|[---.]kbd.ṯṯ.i[qnu.---].|[---.]ǵprt.‘š[r.---].|[---.p]ṯtm.l.ip[--.---].|[---.]ksl.ṯl 1106.23

ir

pym.|[bn]š gt.ipṯl.|[---]ym.|[----]m.|[-----].|[bnš.g]t.ir.|bnš.gt.rb[--].|gpny.|bnš.mǵrt.|kbsm.|armsǵ. 1040.15

irab

|ṣ‘.ṯmn.|šḥq.‘šrm.arb‘.kbd.|ḫlb rpš arb‘.‘šr.|bq‘t ṯṯ.|irab ṯn.‘šr.|ḥbš.ṯmn.|amḏy.arb‘.‘šr.|[-]n‘y.ṯṯ.‘šr. 67[110].9

irby

p y[m].|ṯṣmt.adm.ṣat.š[p]š.|ṯḥt h.k kdrt.ri[š].|‘l h.k irbym.kp.k.qṣm.|ǵrmn.kp.mhr.‘tkt.|rišt.l bmt h.šnst.|kpt. 3[‘NT].2.10
lu.lb h.|[b šmḫt.kbd.‘nt.tšyt.ṯḥt h.k]kdrt.riš.|[‘l h.k irbym.kp.---.k br]k.tǵll.b dm.|[ḏmr.---.]td[-.]rǵb.|[----]k.|[7.1[131].9
zl.|w ybl.trḫ.ḥdṯ.|yb‘r.l ṯn.aṯt h.|w l nkr.mddt.|km irby.tškn.|šd.k ḥsn.pat.|mdbr.tlkn.|ym.w ṯn.aḫr.|šp[š]m.b 14[KRT].4.192
mzl.w yṣi.trḫ.|ḥdṯ.yb‘r.l ṯn.|aṯt h.lm.nkr.|mddt h.k irby.|[t]škn.šd.|km.ḥsn.pat.mdbr.|lk.ym.w ṯn.ṯlṯ.rb‘ ym.|ḫ 14[KRT].2.103

irbn

‘zn.bn.irbn.|bn.mglb.|bn.ntp.|‘myn.bn ǵḥpn.|bn.kbln.|bn.bly.|b 104[316].1
|[---.b]nšm.b.m‘r.arr.|arb‘.bnšm.b.mnt.|arb‘.bnšm.b.irbn.|ṯn.bnšm.b.y‘rt.|ṯn.bnšm.b.‘rmt.|arb‘.bnšm.b.šrš.|ṯṯ.b 2076.34

irbṣ

.|‘šr.bnšm.|ḫmš.bnši.ṯt[---].|‘šr.b gt.[---].|ṯn.‘šr.b.gt.ir[bṣ].|arb‘.b.gt.b‘ln.|‘št.‘šr.b.gpn.|yd.‘dnm.|arb‘.ǵzlm.|ṯn. 2103.5
[aǵ]ltn.|[--]ṯm.b.gt.irbṣ.|[--]šmyn.|[w.]nḥl h.|bn.qṣn.|bn.ksln.|bn.ṣrym.|bn.ṯ 1073.1.2

irgy

--].|n[----].|bn.[---].|bn.[---].|bn.yk[--].|bn.šmm.|bn.irgy.|w.nḥl h.|w.nḥl hm.|[bn].pmn.|bn.gṯrn.|bn.arpḫn.|b 1046.2.10

irgmn

spr.irgmn.|ṯlṯ.ḫmš.alpm.|b d.brq.maḫdy.|kkr.ṯlṯ.|b d.bn.by.ar 1134.1
l[ṯ].|krk.kly[.--].|ḫmš.mr[kbt].|ṯṯ [-]az[-].|‘št[--.---].|irg[mn.---].|krk[.---]. 2056.12

irgn

.|sǵr.idṯn.aḥd.|sǵr.sndrn.aḥd.|sǵr.adn.ṣdq.aḥd.|sǵr.irgn.aḥd.|sǵr.ršpab.aḥd.|sǵr.arwṯ.aḥd.|sǵr.bn.mǵln.|aḥd. 1140.9
[--]dn.|[ṯ]b‘m.|[--]mlk.|[--]ty.|mtnb‘l.|bn.ndbn.|bn irgn. 1072.13

irdyn

šd.ṯ[r]yn.bn.tkn.b d.qrt.|šd[.-].dyn.b d.pln.nḥl h.|šd.irdyn.bn.ḫrǵš[-].l.qrt.|šd.iǵlyn.bn.kzbn.l.qr[t].|šd.pln.bn.ti 2029.16

iryn

[š]šw[.i]ryn.arr.|[š]dm.b.mlk.|[--.š]dm.b.ar.|[--.š]dm.b.ulm.|[--.š] 2033.1.1
n.bri.b d.bn.ydln.|[u]bdy.ṯǵrm.|[š]d.ṯǵr.mṯpit.b d.bn.iryn.|[u]bdy.šrm.|[š]d.bn.ḫrmln.b d.bn.tnn.|[š]d.bn.ḫrmln 82[300].2.8
dḫy.|bn.ubyn.|slpd.|bn.atnb.|bn.ktmn.|bn.pity.|bn.iryn.|bn.‘bl.|bn.grbn.|bn.iršyn.|bn.nklb.|bn.mryn.|[bn.]b[115[301].4.16
.bhtm.|bn.izl.|bn.ibln.|bn.ilt.|špšyn.nḥl h.|n‘mn.bn.iryn.|nrn.nḥl h.|bn.ḫsn.|bn.‘bd.|[-----].|[---.n]ḥ[l h].|[-]nt 85[80].2.7
bdlḥn[-].|bn.mqwṭ.|bn.bsn.|bn.inr[-].|bn.ṯbil.|bn.iryn.|ṯṯl.|bn.nṣdn.|bn.ydln.|[bn].‘dy.|[bn].ilyn. 1071.6

irǵn

ṣq[.b.ap h]. | k.yiḫd.akl.ś[św]. | št.nni.št.mk[št.grn]. | št.irǵn.ḥmr[.ydk]. | aḥd h.w.yṣq.b[.ap h]. | k.yraš.ššw.[št]. | bln. 161[56].19
]. | mǵm[ǵ.---]. | w.š[t.nni.w.pr.'bk]. | w.pr[.ḥḏrt.w.št]. | irǵ[n.ḥmr.ydk]. | aḥd[h.w.yṣq.b.ap h]. | k yr[a]š.šš[w.w.ykhp 161[56].30

irp

ṯlṯ mat. | w spl ṯlṯ.mat. | w mmskn. | w.ṯt.mqrtm. | w.ṯn.irpm.w.ṯn.trqm. | w.qpt.w.mqḥm. | w.ṯlṯm.yn šb'.kbd d ṭbṭ. | 1103.20

irpbn

mḫṣm. | irpbn. | grgš. | [--]yn. | [---]n. | [--]mrt. 1042.2

iršy

spr.npš.d. | 'rb.bt.mlk. | w.b.spr.l.št. | yrm'l. | ṣry. | iršy. | y'ḏrd. | ayaḫ. | bn.aylt. | ḫmš.mat.arb'm. | kbd.ksp.anyt. 2106.6

iršyn

nb. | bn.ktmn. | bn.pity. | bn.iryn. | bn.'bl. | bn.grbn. | bn.iršyn. | bn.nklb. | bn.mryn. | [bn.]b[--]. | bn.ẓrl. | bn.illm[-]. | bn 115[301].4.19
[-]gštn. | bn[.n]klb. | b[n.]dtn. | w.nḥl h. | w.nḥl hm. | bn.iršyn. | bn.'zn. | bn.arśw. | bn.ḫzrn. | bn.iǵyn. | w.nḥl h. | bn.ksd 113[400].2.12
zn.ṯlṯm. | ṣṣ.bn.tlmyn.'šrm. | ṣṣ.bn.krwn.'š[rm]. | ṣṣ.bn.iršyn.[---]. | [ṣṣ].bn.ilb'l.ṯl[ṯ]m. | ṣṣ.bn.pṯḏn.[--]m. | ṣṣ.[bn].gyn 2096.5

iršn

n.alz. | bn.birtn. | [bn.]ylkn. | [bn.]krwn. | [bn.-]ty. | [bn.]iršn. | bn.[---]. | bn.b[--]. | bn.š[--]. | bn.a[---]. | bn.prsn. | bn.mty 117[325].1.17

irt

dn mṯ. | al[iyn.b']l šlbšn. | i[---.---.--]l h.mǵẓ. | y[--.---.]l irt h. | n[--.---]. 5[67].5.25
t.uṣb't[h.ybmt]. | limm.tiḫd.knr h.b yd[h.tšt]. | rimt.l irt h.tšr.dd.al[iyn]. | b'l.ahbt. UG5.3.2.7
.l[---]. | trḥṣ.yd[h.---]. | [--.]yṣt ḏm[r.---]. | tšt[.r]imt.[l irt h.tšr.l dd.aliyn.b'l]. | [ahb]t pdr[y.bt.ar.ahbt.ṭly.bt.rb.dd]. 7.2[130].10
[---.t]št.rimt. | l irt h.mšr.l.dd.aliyn. | b'l.yd.pdry.bt.ar. | ahbt.ṭly.bt.rb.dd.arṣ 3['NT].3.2
b w yṣḥq. | yšu.g h.w yṣḥ. | aṯbn.ank.w anḫn. | w tnḫ.b irt y.npš. | k ḥy.aliyn.b'l. | k iṯ.zbl.b'l.arṣ. | gm.yṣḥ.il.l btlt. | 'n 6[49].3.19
hdm.yṯpd.yšu. | g h.w yṣḥ.aṯbn.ank. | w anḫn.w tnḫ.b irt y. | npš.k yld.bn.l y.km. | aḫ y.w šrš.km ary y. | nṣb.skn.ili 17[2AQHT].2.13
qlṣ k.tb'.bt.ḫnp.lb[k.--.ti] | ḫd.d iṯ.b kbd k.tšt.b [---]. | irt k.dṯ.ydṯ.m'qb k.[ttb']. | [bt]lt.'nt.idk.l ttn.[pnm]. | ['m.a]q 18[3AQHT].1.19
ṭrt ym. | rbt.ilm.l ḥkmt. | šbt.dqn k.l tsr k. | rḫntt.d[-].l irt k. | wn ap.'dn.mṭr h. | b'l.y'dn.'dn.ṯkt.b glṯ. | w tn.ql h.b 'r 4[51].5.67
.ḫmš. | ṯdṯ.ym.tlḥmn.rpum. | tštyn.bt.ikl.b pr'. | yṣq.b irt.lbnn.mk.b šb'. | [ymm.---]k.aliyn.b'l. | [---].r' h ab y. | [---. 22.2[124].25
--.]l aššı.hm.ap.amr[--]. | [---].w b ym.mnḫ l abd.b ym.irtm.m[--]. | [ṯpṭ].nhr.tl'm.ṯm.ḥrbm.its.anšq. | [-]htm.l arṣ.yp 2.4[68].3

irṯr

tiyn.b d.ilmhr nḥl h. | šd knn.bn.ann.'db. | šd.iln[-].bn.irṯr.l.sḫrn.nḥl h. | šd[.ag]pṯn.b[n.]brrn.l.qrt. | šd[.--]dy.bn.brz 2029.20

išb'l

bn[.---]. | bn.brzn [---]. | bnil.bn.tl[--]. | bn.brzn.ṯn. | bn.išb'l[.---]. | bn.s[---]. | dnn.[bn.---]. | bn[.--]'nt. 2069.8
. | abšr. | bn.bdn. | ḏmry. | bn.pndr. | bn.aḫt. | bn.'dn. | bn.išb'[l]. 2117.4.34

išd

ṯmnt.iṣr r't.'ṣ brq y. | riš h.tply.ṭly.bn.'n h. | uz'rt.tmll.išd h.qrn[m]. | dt.'l h.riš h.b glṯ.b šm[m]. | [---.i]l.ṯr.iṯ.p h.k ṯt UG5.3.1.6
d.š[dm.ḥš k.'ṣ k.'bṣ k.'m y.p'n k.tls] | [m]n 'm y t[wtḥ.išd k.dm.rgm.iṯ.l y.d argmn k]. | [h]wt.d aṯ[ny k.---.rgm.'ṣ]. | 7.2[130].17
bd.šdm. | ḥš k.'ṣ k.'bṣ k. | 'm y.p'n k.tlsmn.'m y. | twtḥ.išd k.dm.rgm. | iṯ.l y.w argm k. | hwt.w aṯny k.rgm. | 'ṣ.w lḫš 3['NT].3.17
m. | [ḥ]š k.[']ṣ k.'bṣ k.'m y.p'n k. | [tls]mn.[']m y.twtḥ.išd k. | [dm.rgm.iṯ.l y.]w argm k.hwt. | [w aṯny k.rgm.]'ṣ.w l 3['NT].4.56
.š]dm.ḥš k. | ['ṣ k.'bṣ k.'m y.p']n k.tlsmn. | ['m y.twtḥ.išd] k.tk.ḫršn. | [---.-]bd k.spr. | [---.-]nk. 1['NT.IX].2.23
[ḥš k.'ṣ k.'bṣ k.']m y.p['n k. | [tlsmn.'m y.twt]ḥ.išd k. | [tk.ḫršn.---]r.[-]ḫm k.w št. | [---.]ẓ[--.-]rdy k. | [---.i]qni 1['NT.IX].2.2
.ṯ[--. --]. | ḥš k.'ṣ k.'[bṣ k.'m y.p'n k.tlsmn]. | 'm y twtḥ.i[šd k.tk.ḫršn.-------------]. | ǵr.ks.dm.r[gm.iṯ.l y.w argm k]. | 1['NT.IX].3.11

išdym

.tdr[--]. | špš.b'd h.t[--]. | aṯr.aṯrm[.---]. | aṯr.aṯrm[.---]. | išdym.t[---]. | b k.mla[.---]. | udm't.d[m'.---]. | [---].bn.[---]. | [-- 27[8].9

išryt

lkm.hn.ym.yṣq.yn.ṯmk. | mrṯ.yn.srnm.yn.bld. | ǵll.yn.išryt.'nq.smd. | lbnn.ṭl mrṯ.yḫrṯ.il. | hn.ym.w ṯn.tlḥmn.rpum. 22.2[124].19
yn.iš[ryt.-]lnr. | spr.[--]ḥ[-] k.šb't. | ghl.ph.ṯmnt. | nblu h.špš.ymp 27[8].1
]ab y.ndt.ank[.---]. | [---.--]l.mlk.tlk.b ṣd[.---]. | [---.]mt.išryt[.---]. | [---.--]r.almd k.[---]. | [---.]qrt.ablm.a[blm]. | [qrt.z 18[3AQHT].1.28

išt

.km.šḥr. | [---.y]lt n.km.qdm. | [-.k]bd n.il.ab n. | kbd k iš.tikln. | ṯd n.km.mrm.tqrṣn. | il.yẓḥq.bm. | lb.w ygmḏ.bm k 12[75].1.10
]pl.l tšthwy.pḫr.m'd.qmm.a[--].amr. | [ṯn]y.d't hm.išt.ištm.yitmr.ḥrb.ltšt. | [--]n hm.rgm.l ṯr.ab h.il.ṯḥm.ym.b'l km 2.1[137].32
[l t]pl.l tšthwy.pḫr.m'd.qmm.a[--].amr. | [ṯn]y.d't hm.išt.ištm.yitmr.ḥrb.ltšt. | [--]n hm.rgm.l ṯr.ab h.il.ṯḥm.ym.b'l 2.1[137].32
h. | tšt.išt.b bht m. | nb[l]at.b hkl m. | hn.ym.w ṯn.tikl. | išt.b bht m.nblat. | b hk[l] m.ṯlṯ.kb' ym. | tikl[.i]št.b bht m. | n 4[51].6.25
md.arz h. | h[n.l]bnn.w 'ṣ h. | š[r]yn.mḥmd.arz h. | tšt.išt.b bht m. | nb[l]at.b hkl m. | hn.ym.w ṯn.tikl. | išt.b bht m.n 4[51].6.22
.[b]bht m.nblat. | b[qrb.hk]l m.mk. | b šb['.]y[mm].td.išt. | b bht m.n[bl]at.b hkl m. | sb.ksp.l rqm.ḫrṣ. | nṣb.l lbnt.š 4[51].6.32
ṯn.tikl. | išt.b bht m.nblat. | b hk[l] m.ṯlṯ.kb' ym. | tikl[.i]št.b bht m. | nbla[t.]b hkl m. | ḫmš.ṯ[d]ṯ.ym.tikl. | išt.[b]bht 4[51].6.27
ikl[.i]št.b bht m. | nbla[t.]b hkl m. | ḫmš.ṯ[d]ṯ.ym.tikl. | išt.[b]bht m.nblat. | b[qrb.hk]l m.mk. | b šb['.]y[mm].td.išt. 4[51].6.30
[--].w rbb. | š[---]npš išt. | w.l.tikl w l tš[t]. 2003.2

n y.mt mt.|nḥtm.ḫṭ k.mmnnm.mṭ yd k.hl.ʿṣr.|tḥrr.l išt.w ṣḥrt.l pḥmm.aṯtm.a[ṯt.il].|aṯt.il.w ʿlm h.yhbr.špt hm.y 23[52].48
ṣḥn y.ad ad.nḥtm.ḫṭ k.|mmnnm.mṭ yd k.hl.ʿṣr.tḥrr.l išt.|w ṣḥrrt.l pḥmm.btm.bt.il.bt.il.|w ʿlm h.w hn.aṯtm.tṣḥn 23[52].44
bšr h.|tmtʿ.md h.b ym.ṯn.|npyn h.b nhrm.|štt.ḫptr.l išt.|ḫbrṯ.l ẓr.pḥmm.|tʿpp.ṯr.il.d pid.|tǵẓy.bny.bnwt.|b nši.ʿ 4[51].2.8
m.|mḫšt.mdd ilm.ar[š].|ṣmt.ʿgl.il.ʿtk.|mḫšt.klbt.ilm išt.|klt.bt.il.ḏbb.imtḫṣ.ksp.|itrṯ.ḫrṣ.ṭrd.bʿl.|b mrym.ṣpn.mš 3[ʿNT].3.42
ʿl k.b[ʿ]l m.|pht.qlt.ʿl k.pht.|dry.b ḥrb.ʿl k.|pht.šrp.b išt.|ʿl k.[pht.ṭḥ]n.b rḥ|m.ʿ[l k.]pht[.dr]y.b kbrt.|ʿl k.pht.[-]l 6[49].5.14
.|y mt.mt.nḥtm.ḫṭ k.mmnnm.mṭ.yd k.|h[l.]ʿṣr.tḥrr.l išt.ṣḥrrt.l pḥmm.|a[ṯ]tm.aṯt.il.aṯt.il.w ʿlm h.w hm.|aṯtm.tṣ 23[52].41
rgm.ʿl.ʿd.w ʿrbm.tʿnyn.|w šd.šd ilm.šd aṯrt.w rḥm.|ʿl.išt.šbʿ d.ǵzrm.ṭb.[g]d.b ḥlb.annḫ b ḫmat.|w ʿl.agn.šbʿ d m.d 23[52].14
aṯr.bʿl.tiḫd.|bn.ilm.mt.b ḥrb.|tbqʿnn.b ḫṯr.tdry|nn.b išt.tšrpnn.|b rḥm.tṭḥnn.b šd.|tdrʿnn.šir h.l tikl.|ʿṣrm.mnt 6[49].2.33
.ap k.ʿṯtr.dm[.---.]|[---.]ḥrḥrtm.w[--.]n[--.]iš[--.]h[---.]išt.|[---]y.yblmm.u[---]k.yrd[.--.]i[---]n.bn.|[---.-]nn.nrt.il 2.3[129].13

ištir

tmḫṣ h.qṣʿt h.hwt.l t[ḥwy].|nʿmn.ǵzr.št.ṯrm.w[---].|ištir.b ddm.w nʿrs[.---].|w tʿn.btlt.ʿnt.ṯb.yṭp.w[---].|l k.ašt 18[3AQHT].4.15
arbʿ.ʿšr h.šmn.|d.lqḥt.ṯlǵdy.|w.kd.ištir.ʿm.qrt.|ʿšt.ʿšr h.šmn.|ʿmn.bn.aǵlmn.|arbʿm.ksp.ʿl.qrt. 1083.3

ištn

kd.bt ilm.|rbm.|kd l ištnm.|kd l ḫty.|maḫdh.|kd l kblbn.|kdm.mṭḫ.|l.alṯy.|kd. 1090.3

ištql

.sgrt.|bʿd h.ʿdbt.ṯlṯ.ptḥ.bt.mnt.|ptḥ.bt.w ubn.hkl.w ištql šql.|tn.km.nḥšm.yḥr.tn.km.|mhr y.w bn.bṯn.itnn y.|y UG5.7.72

ištrmy

nḥm.aḫ h.|w.bʿln aḫ h.|w.ḥṯṯn bn h.|w.btšy.bt h.|w.ištrmy.|bt.ʿbd mlk.|w.snt.|bt.ugrt.|w.pdy h[m].|iwrkl.mit 1006.8

it

|[qrt.zbl.]yrḫ.d mgdl.š[---].|[---.]mn.ʿr hm[.---].|[---.]it[.---].|[---.]ʿp[.---]. 18[3AQHT].1.33

ity

w.[---].|ity[.---].|tlby[.---].|ir[--.---].|pndyn[.---].|w.idṯ[-.---].|b.gt.b 1078.2

itn

.|[ṣ]dqšlm ḫmš.|krzn.ḫmš.|ubrʿym.ḫmš.|[----].|[bn] itn.|[bn] il.|[---]ṯ.|klṯṯb.|gsn.|arm[w]l.|bn.ṣdqn.|ḫlbn.|tb 2039.9

iṯ

bnšm.dt.iṯ.alpm.l hm.|bn.niršn.|bn.adty.|bn.alz.|bn.birtn.|bn.mlṣ. 2023.1.1
.]l qdš.|a[ṯrt.]ṣrm.w l ilt.|ṣd[yn]m.ṯm.|yd[r.k]rt.ṯʿ.|i.iṯt.aṯrt.ṣrm.|w ilt.ṣdynm.|hm.ḥry.bt y.|iqḥ.ašʿrb.ǵlmt.|ḥẓr 14[KRT].4.201
t.k anšt.w i[n.b ilht].|qlṣ k.tbʿ.bt.ḫnp.lb[k.--.ti]|ḫd.d iṯ.b kbd k.tšt.b [---].|irt k.dṯ.ydṯ.mʿqb k.[ttbʿ].|[bt]lt.ʿnt.idk 18[3AQHT].1.18
[mt.]hrnmy.d in.bn.l h.|km.aḫ h.w šrš.km.ary h.|bl.iṯ.bn.l h.km aḫ h.w šrš.|km.ary h.uzrm.ilm.ylḥm.|uzrm.yš 17[2AQHT].1.21
|ib.ʿltn.a[--.--]y.|w.spr.in[.-.]ʿd m.|spr n.ṯhr[.--].|aṯr.iṯ.bqṯ.|w.štn.l y. 2060.34
.šmn.tmṭrn.|nḫlm.tlk.nbtm.|w idʿ.k ḥy.aliyn.bʿl.|k iṯ.zbl.bʿl.arṣ.|b ḥlm.lṭpn.il d pid.|b ḏrt.bny.bnwt.|šmm.šm 6[49].3.9
n.bʿl].|k ḫlq.z[bl.bʿl.arṣ].|w hm.ḥy.a[liyn.bʿl].|w hm.iṯ.zbl.bʿ[l.arṣ].|b ḥlm.lṭpn.il.d pid.|b ḏrt.bny.bnwt.|šmm.š 6[49].3.3
ṯbn.ank.w anḫn.|w tnḫ.b irt y.npš.|k ḥy.aliyn.bʿl.|k iṯ.zbl.bʿl.arṣ.|gm.yṣḥ.il.l btlt.|ʿnt.šmʿ.l btlt.ʿn[t].|rgm.l nrt.i 6[49].3.21
.iṯ[.--.yn.w t]n.w nšt.|w ʿn hm.nǵr mdrʿ[.iṯ.lḥm.---].|iṯ.yn.d ʿrb.bṯk[.---].|mǵ hw.l hn.lg yn h[.---].|w ḥbr h.mla y 23[52].74
.ḥl.mlk.|w.[---].ypm.w.mḫ[--].t[ṯ]tbn.[-].|b.[--].w.km.iṯ.y[--.]šqm.yd[-]. 35[3].55
k.ʿbṣ k.ʿm y.pʿn k.tls]|[m]n ʿm y t[wtḥ.išd k.dm.rgm.iṯ.l y.d argmn k].|[h]wt.d aṯ[ny k.---.rgm.ʿṣ].|w lḫšt.abn[.ta 7.2[130].17
k.ʿbṣ k.|ʿm y.pʿn k.tlsmn.ʿm y.|twtḥ.išd k.dm.rgm.|iṯ.l y.w argm k.|hwt.w aṯny k.rgm.|ʿṣ.w lḫšt.abn.|tant.šm 3[ʿNT].3.18
ʿbṣ k.ʿm y.pʿn k.|[tls]mn.[ʿ]m y.twtḥ.išd k.|[dm.rgm.iṯ.l y.]w argm k.hwt.|[w aṯny k.rgm.]ʿṣ.w lḫšt.|[abn.rgm.l t 3[ʿNT].4.57
|ʿm y twtḥ.i[šd k.tk.ḫršn.-------------].|ǵr.ks.dm.r[gm.iṯ.l y.w argm k].|hwt.w aṯny k[.rgm.ʿṣ.w lḫšt.abn].|tunt.šm 1[ʿNT.IX].3.12
w nlḥm.hm.iṯ[.--.yn.w t]n.w nšt.|w ʿn hm.nǵr mdrʿ[.iṯ.lḥm.---].|iṯ.yn.d ʿrb.bṯk[.---].|mǵ hw.l hn.lg yn h[.---].|w 23[52].73
t].|tqln.tḥ pʿn y.ibq[ʿ.kbd hm.w] |aḥd.hm.iṯ.šmt.hm.i[ṯ].|ʿẓm.abky.w aqbrn h.|ašt.b ḫrt.ilm.arṣ.|b p h.rgm.l yṣa 19[1AQHT].3.110
br.diy.|hyt.tql.tḥt.pʿn y.ibqʿ.|kbd h.w aḥd.hm.iṯ.šmt.iṯ.|ʿẓm.abky w aqbrn h.aštn.|b ḫrt.ilm.arṣ.b p h.rgm.l[yṣ]a 19[1AQHT].3.139
t.|w yql.tḥt.pʿn y.ibq[ʿ.kbd[h].|w aḥd.hm.iṯ.šmt.hm.iṯ[.ʿẓm].|abky.w aqbrn.ašt.b ḫrt.|i[lm.arṣ.b p h.rgm.l yṣa.b 19[1AQHT].3.125
.ṯbr.diy.hyt.tq[l.tḥt].|pʿn h.ybqʿ.kbd h.w yḥd.|iṯ.šmt.iṯ.ʿẓm.w yqḥ b hm.|aqht.ybl.l qẓ.ybky.w yqbr.|yqbr.nn.b 19[1AQHT].3.145
ll.išd h.qrn[m].|dt.ʿl h.riš h.b glṯ.b šm[m].|[---.i]l.ṯr.iṯ.p h.k ṯt.ǵlt[.--].|[---.--] k yn.ddm.l b[--.---].|[---.-]yt š[--.--- UG5.3.1.8
.bʿl.yṯbr.diy.|hyt.tql.tḥt.pʿn y.ibqʿ.|kbd h.w aḥd.hm.iṯ.šmt.iṯ.|ʿẓm.abky w aqbrn h.aštn.|b ḫrt.ilm.arṣ.b p h.rgm 19[1AQHT].3.139
[l].|bʿl.ṯbr.diy.hyt.tq[l.tḥt].|pʿn h.ybqʿ.kbd h.w yḥd.|iṯ.šmt.iṯ.ʿẓm.w yqḥ b hm.|aqht.ybl.l qẓ.ybky.w yqbr.|yqbr. 19[1AQHT].3.145
b[r.diy.hmt].|tqln.tḥ pʿn y.ibq[ʿ.kbd hm.w] |aḥd.hm.iṯ.šmt.hm.i[ṯ].|ʿẓm.abky.w aqbrn h.|ašt.b ḫrt.ilm.arṣ.|b p 19[1AQHT].3.110
]r.diy[.h]wt.|w yql.tḥt.pʿn y.ibq[ʿ.kbd[h].|w aḥd.hm.iṯ.šmt.hm.iṯ[.ʿẓm].|abky.w aqbrn.ašt.b ḫrt.|i[lm.arṣ.b p h.r 19[1AQHT].3.125
bʿd hm.|w ʿrb.hm.hm[.iṯ.--.l]ḥm.w t[n].|w nlḥm.hm.iṯ[.--.yn.w t]n.w nšt.|w ʿn hm.nǵr mdrʿ[.iṯ.lḥm.---].|iṯ.yn.d ʿ 23[52].72
y.nǵr.|nǵr.ptḥ.w ptḥ hw.prṣ.bʿd hm.|w ʿrb.hm.hm[.iṯ.--.l]ḥm.w t[n].|w nlḥm.hm.iṯ[.--.yn.w t]n.w nšt.|w ʿn hm. 23[52].71
[---].dt.iṯ.|[---].ṯlṯ.kbd.|[---].alpm.ḫmš.mat.|šbʿm[.t]šʿ.kbd.|tgmr.u 1129.1

iṯb

--.yrḫ.]ḫlt.šbʿ.[---].mlkt.|[---.yrḫ.]gn.šbʿ[.--].|[---.yrḫ.]iṯb.šb[ʿ.---].|[-----]. 1088.15
yr[.---].|[---].yrḫ.ḫl[t.---].|[---].yrḫ.gn[-.---].|[---.]yrḫ.iṯ[b.---]. 1088.A.5

iṯl

l.[mt.rpi].|mt.aqht.ǵzr.[šṣat].|btlt.ʿnt.k [rḥ.npš h].|k iṯl.brlt h.[b h.pʿnm].|tṭṭ.ʿl[n.pn h.tdʿ.b ʿdn].|ksl.y[ṯbr.ygṣ.p 19[1AQHT].2.93
.špk.km.šiy.|dm.km.šḫṭ.l brk h.tṣi.km.|rḥ.npš h.km.iṯl.brlt h.km.|qṭr.b ap h.b ap.mhr h.ank.|l aḥwy.tqḥ.ytpn. 18[3AQHT].4.25
].|šiy.dm h.km.šḫ[ṭ.l brk h].|yṣat.km.rḥ.npš[h.km.iṯl].|brlt h.km.qṭr.[b ap h.---].|ʿnt.b ṣmt.mhr h.[---].|aqht. 18[3AQHT].4.36
---].|riš.r[--.--]ḥ[.---]y[.---.-]nt.[š]ṣat[k.]rḥ.npš.hm.|k.iṯl.brlt n[-.k qṭr.b ap -].|tmǵyn.tša.g h[m.w tṣḥn].|šmʿ.l dni 19[1AQHT].2.88
im.|[---.-]šu.b qrb.|[---].asr.|[---.--]m.ymt m.|[---].k iṯl.|[---.--]m.ʿdb.l arṣ.|[---.]špm.ʿdb.|[---].tʿtqn.|[---.-]ʿb.idk. 1[ʿNT.IX].2.9

iṯm

.|ṯrṯy.alp.w.š.|yrḫ.š.ṣpn.š.|kṯr š ʿṯtr.š.|[ʿṯt]rt.š.šgr w iṯm š.|[---.]š.ršp.idrp.š.|[---.il.tʿ]ḏr.š.|[---.-]mt.š.|[-----].|[--- UG5.9.2.9

iṯr

tn.|ḥnn y l pn mlk.|šin k itn.|rʿ y šṣa idn l y.|l šmn iṯr hw.|p iḫdn gnryn.|im mlkytn yrgm.|aḫnnn.|w iḫd. 1020.6

iṯt

nm[.šlm].|w.rgm[.ṯṯb.l] y.|hl ny.ʿmn.|mlk.b.ṯy ndr.|iṯt.w.ht.|[-]sny.uḏr h.|w.hm.ḫt.|ʿl.w.likt.|ʿm k.w.hm.|l.ʿl. 1013.14
ny.ʿm.um y.|mnm.šlm.|w.rgm.ṯṯb.l y.|bm.ṯy.ndr.|iṯt.ʿmn.mlkt.|w.rgm y.l[--].|lqt.w.pn.|mlk.nr b n. 50[117].15

iṯtbnm

spr.ḥpr.bnš mlk.b yrḫ iṯt[bnm].|ršpab.rb ʿšrt.m[r]yn.|pǵḏn.ilbʿl.krwn.lbn.ʿdn.|ḫy 2011.1
.l.ḫḏǵb.w.kd.ḥmṣ.|prš.glbm.l.bt.|tgmǵ.ksmm.b.yrḫ.iṯtbnm.|šbʿm.dd.ṯn.kbd.|tgmr.ḥṭm.šbʿ.ddm.|ḫmš.dd.šʿrm. 1099.30
lm[.---].|ṯlṯ.mat.ḫmšm.kb[d].|ḫmš.kbd.l.mdʿ.|b yr[ḫ.iṯtb]nm.|ṯlṯ[.mat.a]rbʿ.kbd.|w.[---.-]mʿt.|ṯlṯ[m.---.-]rm.|ʿšr[2012.13

iṯtl

[t]ḥm.iṯtl.|l mnn.ilm.|tǵr k.tšlm k.|tʿzz k.alp ymm.|w rbt.šnt.|b 1019.1.1
al ttn.|tn ks yn.|w ištn.|ʿbd.prṯ.ṯḥm.|qrq.pṯ.ḏmn.|l iṯtl. 1019.2.3

iṯtqb

bʿl.ugrt.ṯn šm.|ʿlm.l ršp.mlk.|alp w.š.l bʿlt.|bwrm š.iṯtqb.|w š.nbk m w.š.|gt mlk š.ʿlm.|l kṯr.ṯn.ʿlm.|tzǵ[.---.]nš UG5.12.B.9

u

u

p.ab.k mtm.tmtn. | u ḫšt k.l bky.ʻtq. | b d.aṯt ab.ṣrry. | u ilm.tmtn.šph̩. | [l]ṯpn.l yḥ.t[b]ky k. | ab.ǵr.bʻl.ṣ[p]n.ḥlm. | q 16.2[125].105
b d.aṯt.ab.ṣrry. | ik m.yrgm.bn.il. | krt.špḥ.lṭpn. | w qdš.u ilm.tmtn. | špḥ.lṭpn.l yḥ. | w yʻny.krt.ṯʻ. | bn.al.tbkn.al. | td 16.1[125].22
.]ulp. | ḫbt km.ulp.m[dl]l km.ulp.qr zbl.u[š]n yp km. | u b ap km.u b q[ṣ]rt.npš km.u b qṭṭ.tqṭṭ. | ušn yp km.l d[b]ḥ 32[2].1.23
p.ǵbr]. | [ulp.ḫbt km.ulp.mdll km.ulp.qr zbl]. | [u ṯḫṭu.u b ap km.u b qṣrt.npš km.u b qṭt]. | [tqṭṭ.u ṯḫṭu.l dbḥm.w l. 32[2].1.8A
lp.ǵbr.ulp.ḫbt kn.ulp.mdll kn.ulp.]qr zbl. | [ušn.yp kn.u b ap kn.u b qṣrt.npš kn.u b]qṭt. | [tqṭṭn.ušn.yp kn.---.-]gy APP.I[-].2.15
br.ul]p.ḫbt kn. | [ulp.mdll kn.ulp.qr zbl.ušn.y]p kn. | [u b ap kn.u b qṣrt.npšt kn.u b qṭ]t tqṭṭ. | [ušn.yp kn.---.--]l.il. APP.I[-].1.7
ll km.ulp.qr zbl]. | [u ṯḫṭu.u b ap km.u b qṣrt.npš km.u b qṭt]. | [tqṭṭ.u ṯḫṭu.l dbḥm.w l.ṯʻ.dbḥ n.ndb]ḥ. | [hw.ṯʻ.nṯʻy 32[2].1.8A
[ll k]n.ulp.q[r zbl]. | u ṯḫṭin.b ap kn.u b [q]ṣrt.npš[kn.u b qṭt]. | tqṭṭn u ṯḫṭin.l bḥm.w l ṯʻ.d[bḥ n.ndbḥ]. | hw.ṯʻ.nṯʻy. 32[2].1.14
.ulp.qr zbl.u[š]n yp km. | u b ap km.u b q[ṣ]rt.npš km.u b qṭt.tqṭṭ. | ušn yp km.l d[b]ḥm.w l.ṯʻ.dbḥ n.ndbḥ.hw.ṯʻ | n 32[2].1.23
.ulp]. | [qr zbl.ušn.yp km.b ap km.u b qṣrt.np]št km. | [u b qṭt.tqṭṭ.ušn.yp km.---.-]yt km. | [---.]km. | [-----]. | [---.]ugr APP.I[-].1.18
ll kn.ulp qr z[bl]. | lšn yp kn.b ap [kn.u b qṣ]rt.npš kn.u b qṭt. | tqṭṭn.ušn y[p kn.l dbḥm.]w l ṯʻ dbḥ n. | ndbḥ.hw.ṯʻ 32[2].1.31
kn.ulp.]qr zbl. | [ušn.yp kn.u b ap kn.u b qṣrt.npš kn.u b]qṭt. | [tqṭṭn.ušn.yp kn.---.-]gym. | [---.]l kbkb. | [-----]. APP.I[-].2.15
kn.ulp.qr zbl.ušn.y]p kn. | [u b ap kn.u b qṣrt.npšt kn.u b qṭ]t tqṭṭ. | [ušn.yp kn.---.--]l.il.tʻḏr bʻl. | [-----.]lšnt. | [---.--] APP.I[-].1.7
bt km.ulp.mdll km.ulp]. | [qr zbl.ušn.yp km.b ap km.u b qṣrt.np]št km. | [u b qṭt.tqṭṭ.ušn.yp km.---.-]yt km. | [---.] APP.I[-].1.17
km.ulp.m[dl]l km.ulp.qr zbl.u[š]n yp km. | u b ap km.u b q[ṣ]rt.npš km.u b qṭt.tqṭṭ. | ušn yp km.l d[b]ḥm.w l.ṯʻ.db 32[2].1.23
p.ḫbt km.ulp.mdll km.ulp.qr zbl]. | [u ṯḫṭu.u b ap km.u b qṣrt.npš km.u b qṭt]. | [tqṭṭ.u ṯḫṭu.l dbḥm.w l.ṯʻ.dbḥ n.n 32[2].1.8A
ulp.ḫbt kn.ulp.md[ll k]n.ulp.q[r zbl]. | u ṯḫṭin.b ap kn.u b [q]ṣrt.npš[kn.u b qṭt]. | tqṭṭn u ṯḫṭin.l bḥm.w l ṯʻ.d[bḥ n. 32[2].1.14
bt] kn[.u]lp.mdll kn.ulp qr z[bl]. | lšn yp kn.b ap [kn.u b qṣ]rt.npš kn.u b qṭt. | tqṭṭn.ušn y[p kn.l dbḥm.]w l ṯʻ db 32[2].1.31
t kn. | [ulp.mdll kn.ulp.qr zbl.ušn.y]p kn. | [u b ap kn.u b qṣrt.npšt kn.u b qṭ]t tqṭṭ. | [ušn.yp kn.---.--]l.il.tʻḏr bʻl. | [APP.I[-].1.7
ḫbt kn.ulp.mdll kn.ulp.]qr zbl. | [ušn.yp kn.u b ap kn.u b qṣrt.npš kn.u b]qṭt. | [tqṭṭn.ušn.yp kn.---.-]gym. | [---.]l k APP.I[-].2.15
yd h. | k tǵd.arz.b ymn h. | bkm.yṯb.bʻl.l bht h. | u mlk.u bl mlk. | arṣ.drkt.yštkn. | dll.al.ilak.l bn. | ilm.mt.ʻdd.l ydd. 4[51].7.43
š[-.---]. | b [u]grt.w ht.a[--]. | w hm.at.trg[m.---]. | w sip.u hw[.---]. | w ank.u šbt[--.---]. | ank.n[--]n[.---]. | kst.l[--.---]. | 54.1.9[13.1.6]
.alṯy.ulp.ǵbr]. | [ulp.ḫbt km.ulp.mdll km.ulp.qr zbl]. | [u ṯḫṭu.u b ap km.u b qṣrt.npš km.u b qṭt]. | [tqṭṭ.u ṯḫṭu.l db 32[2].1.8A
r mšr.bn.ugrt.w npy.---.]w npy. | [---.w np]y.ugrt. | [---.u ṯḫṭu.ulp.qṭy.ulp.ddm]y. | [ulp.ḫry.ulp.ḫty.ulp.alṯy.ulp.ǵbr] 32[2].1.6
š. | [---.w n]py.gr[.ḥmyt.ugrt.w np]y. | [---].w n[py.---].u ṯḫṭi[n.ulp.qṭy]. | ulp.ddmy.ul[p.ḫry.u]lp.ḫty.ulp[.alṯy.ulp.] 32[2].1.11
.alṯy.ulp.]ǵbr. | ulp.ḫbt kn.ulp.md[ll k]n.ulp.q[r zbl]. | u ṯḫṭin.b ap kn.u b [q]ṣrt.npš[kn.u b qṭt]. | tqṭṭn u ṯḫṭin.l bḥ 32[2].1.14
bl]. | u ṯḫṭin.b ap kn.u b [q]ṣrt.npš[kn.u b qṭt]. | tqṭṭn u ṯḫṭin.l bḥm.w l ṯʻ.d[bḥ n.ndbḥ]. | hw.ṯʻ.nṯʻy.hw.nkt.n[k]t.y 32[2].1.15
bl]. | [u ṯḫṭu.u b ap km.u b qṣrt.npš km.u b qṭt]. | [tqṭṭ.u ṯḫṭu.l dbḥm.w l.ṯʻ.dbḥ n.ndb]ḥ. | [hw.ṯʻ.nṯʻy.hw.nkt.nkt.]y 32[2].1.9
lb.[b]bt k.nʻtq. | k inr[.ap.]ḫšt k. | ap.ab.k mtm.tmtn. | u ḫšt k.l bky.ʻtq. | b d.aṯt ab.ṣrry. | u ilm.tmtn.špḥ. | [l]ṯpn.l y 16.2[125].103
[k]lb.b bt k.nʻtq.k inr. | ap.ḫšt k.ap.ab.ik mtm. | tmtn.u ḫšt k.l ntn. | ʻtq.b d.aṯt.ab ṣrry. | tbky k.ab.ǵr.bʻl. | ṣpn.ḥlm. 16.1[125].4
k klb. | b bt k.nʻtq.k inr. | ap.ḫšt k.ap.ab.k mtm. | tmtn.u ḫšt k.l ntn. | ʻtq.b d.aṯt.ab.ṣrry. | ik m.yrgm.bn.il. | krt.špḥ.l 16.1[125].18
ʻrb.b p hm.ʻṣr.šmm. | w dg b ym.w ndd.gzr.l zr.yʻdb.u ymn. | u šmal.b p hm.w l.tšbʻn y.aṯt.itrḫ. | y bn.ašld.šu.ʻdb. 23[52].63
.bʻl y.u. | ʻ[--.]mlakt.ʻbd h. | [---.]bʻl k.yḫpn. | [---.]ʻm h.u ky. | [---.--]d k.k.tmǵy. | ml[--.--]š[.ml]k.rb. | b[ʻl y.---]. | yd[- 1018.5
l.qdm.yd h. | k tǵd.arz.b ymn h. | bkm.yṯb.bʻl.l bht h. | u mlk.u bl mlk. | arṣ.drkt.yštkn. | dll.al.ilak.l bn. | ilm.mt.ʻdd. 4[51].7.43
w.k.rgm.špš. | mlk.rb.bʻl y.u. | ʻ[--.]mlakt.ʻbd h. | [---.]bʻl k.yḫpn. | [---.]ʻm h.u ky. | [---.--] 1018.2
-]. | ibr.k l hm.d l h q[--.---]. | l ytn.l hm.ṯḥt bʻl[.---]. | h.u qšt pn hdd.b y[.----]. | ʻm.b ym bʻl ysy ym[.---]. | rmm.ḫnp 9[33].2.6
ht.a[--]. | w hm.at.trg[m.---]. | w sip.u hw[.---]. | w ank.u šbt[--.---]. | ank.n[--]n[.---]. | kst.l[--.---]. | w.hw.uy.ʻn[--.---]. 54.1.10[13.1.7]
hm.ʻṣr.šmm. | w dg b ym.w ndd.gzr.l zr.yʻdb.u ymn. | u šmal.b p hm.w l.tšbʻn y.aṯt.itrḫ. | y bn.ašld.šu.ʻdb.tk.mdbr 23[52].64
dr h.w ilt.p[--]. | w tšu.g h.w [tṣḥ]. | ph mʻ.ap.k[rt.--]. | u ṯn.ndr[.---]. | apr.[---]. | [-----]. 15[128].3.29
.rgm.ṯṯb.l y. | w.mndʻ.k.ank. | aḥš.mǵy.mndʻ. | k.igr.w.u.[--]. | ʻm.špš.[---]. | nšlḥ[.---]. | [---.m]at. | [---.]mat. | š[--].išal. 2009.1.12
b]t. | ḫbr[.ṯrrt]. | [-]ʻb[-].š[--]m. | [----]r[.---]š[.--]qm. | id.u [---]t. | lḥn š[-]ʻ[--.]aḫd[.-]. | tšmʻ.mṯt.[ḥ]ry. | ṭṭbḫ.šmn.[m]ri 15[128].4.12

ubdy

spr.ubdy.art. | šd.prn.b d.agpṯn.nḥl h. | šd.šwn.b d.ttyn.nḥl [h]. | 2029.1
šd.ubdy.ilštmʻ. | dt b d.skn. | šd.bn.ubrʻn b gt prn. | šd.bn.gby.gt. 1104.1
[--.]ubdym.b.uškn. | [---]lby. | [--]nbbl. | bn bl. | bn dkn. | bn ils. | b 1064.1
m.---]. | liy.krm.aḥd[.---]. | ʻbdmlk.krm.aḥ[d.---]. | krm.ubdy.b d.ǵ[--.---]. | krm.pyn.arty[.---]. | ṯlṯ.krm.ubdym.l mlkt 1081.7
ṯlṯ.mat. | šbʻm kbd. | zt.ubdym. | b mlk. 1095.3
]. | krm.ubdy.b d.ǵ[--.---]. | krm.pyn.arty[.---]. | ṯlṯ.krm.ubdym.l mlkt.b.ʻnmky[.---]. | mgdly.ǵlpṯr.ṯn.krmm.w.ṯlṯ.ub[1081.9
ubdy.mdm. | šd.b d.ʻbdmlk. | šd.b d.yšn.ḥrš. | šd.b d.aupš. | šd 82[300].1.1
mḏ. | [šd.]bn.ṯṯrn.b d.bnš.aǵlkz. | [šd.b]d.b[n].tkwn. | [ubdy.mḏ]rǵlm. | [šd.bn.--]n.b d.aḫny. | [šd.bn.--]rt.b d.ṯpṯbʻl. 82[300].2.22
ḏ]rǵlm. | [šd.bn.--]n.b d.aḫny. | [šd.bn.--]rt.b d.ṯpṯbʻl. | [ubdy.]mḫ[ṣ]m. | [šd.bn.]uzpy.b d.yšn.ḥrš. | [-----]. | [-----]. | [šd 82[300].2.25
šd.---.b d.]ṯpṯbʻl. | [šd.---.]b d.ymz. | [šd.b d].klby.psl. | [ub]dy.mri.ibrn. | [š]d.bn.bri.b d.bn.ydln. | [u]bdy.ṯǵrm. | [š]d. 82[300].2.5
d.nwrḏ. | [šd.]bn.nḥbl.b d.ʻdbym. | [šd.b]n.qṭy.b d.tt. | [ubd]y.mrim. | [šd.b]n.ṯpdn.b d.bn.gʻr. | [šd.b]n.ṯqrn.b d.ḥby. 82[300].1.20
šd.b d.aupš. | šd.b d.ršpab.aḫ.ubn. | šd.b d.bn.uṯryn. | [ubd]y.mrynm. | [š]d.bn.ṣnrn.b d.nrn. | [š]d.bn.rwy.b d.ydln. | 82[300].1.7
n.ḫrmln.b d.bn.tnn. | [š]d.bn.ḫrmln.ṯn.b d.bn.ḫdmn. | [u]bdy.nqdm. | [ṯlṯ].šdm.d.nʻrb.gt.npk. | [š]d.rpan.b d.klṯṯb. | [82[300].2.12
y.b d.ṯṯmd. | [šd.bn.-]rn.b d.ṣdqšlm. | [šd.b d.]bn.pʻṣ. | [ubdy.ʻ]šrm. | [šd.---]n.b d.brdd. | [---.--]m. | [šd.---.b d.]ṯpṯbʻl. 82[300].1.30
d.bn.ydln. | [u]bdy.ṯǵrm. | [š]d.ṯǵr.mṯpit.b d.bn.iryn. | [u]bdy.šrm. | [š]d.bn.ḫrmln.b d.bn.tnn. | [š]d.bn.ḫrmln.ṯn.b d. 82[300].2.9

‘rb.gt.npk. | [š]d.rpan.b d.klttb. | [š]d.ilṣy.b d.‘bdym. | [ub]dy.trrm. | [šd.]bn.ṯqdy.b d.gmrd. | [š]d bn.synn.b d.gmrd. 82[300].2.16
].klby.psl. | [ub]dy.mri.ibrn. | [š]d.bn.bri.b d.bn.ydln. | [u]bdy.ṯǵrm. | [š]d.ṯǵr.mṯpit.b d.bn.iryn. | [u]bdy.šrm. | [š]d.b 82[300].2.7
. | [---.]bn.[---]. | [---].šd ubdy. | [---.šd] u[b]dy. | [---.]šd.ubdy. | [---.]bn.k[--.]ṯ[l]ṯm ksp b[---]. | [---.]šd b‘ly. | [---.]šd ub 2031.5
dym.l mlkt.b.‘nmky[.---]. | mgdly.ǵlpṯr.ṯn.krmm.w.ṯlṯ.ub[dym.---]. | qmnz.ṯṯ.krm.ykn‘m.ṯmn.krm[.---]. | krm.n‘mn. 1081.10
[---.--]my. | [---.]bn.[---]. | [---].šd ubdy. | [---.šd] u[b]dy. | [---.]šd.ubdy. | [---.]bn.k[--.]ṯ[l]ṯm ksp b[---]. | [---.]šd 2031.4
.]ṯ[l]ṯm ksp b[---]. | [---.]šd b‘ly. | [---.]šd ubdy. | [---.š]d ubdy. | [---.šd] ubdy. | [---.š]d.bn.ṣin. | [---].bn.dly. | [---.]ṯty[-.- 2031.9
y. | [---.]bn.k[--.]ṯ[l]ṯm ksp b[---]. | [---.]šd b‘ly. | [---.]šd ubdy. | [---.š]d ubdy. | [---.šd] ubdy. | [---.š]d.bn.ṣin. | [---].bn.d 2031.8
[---.--]my. | [---.]bn.[---]. | [---].šd ubdy. | [---.šd] u[b]dy. | [---.]šd.ubdy. | [---.]bn.k[--.]ṯ[l]ṯm ksp 2031.3
šd.ubdy[.---]. | šd.bn.ḫb[--.---]. | šd.srn[.---]. | šd.y‘ḏr[.---]. | šd.sw 83[85].1
---]. | [---.]šd b‘ly. | [---.]šd ubdy. | [---.š]d ubdy. | [---.šd] ubdy. | [---.š]d.bn.ṣin. | [---].bn.dly. | [---.]ṯty[-.--]. 2031.10

ubyn

b. | bn.yzg. | bn.anntn. | bn.kwn. | ǵmšd. | bn.‘bdḫy. | bn.ubyn. | slpd. | bn.atnb. | bn.ktmn. | bn.pity. | bn.iryn. | bn.‘bl. | b 115[301].4.11
šd.snrym.dt.‘qb. | b.ayly. | šd.abršn. | šd.kkn.[bn].ubyn. | šd.bn.li[y]. | šd.bn.š[--]y. | šd.bn.ṯ[---]. | šd.‘dmn[.bn.]y 2026.4
[-----]. | ubyn[.---]. | annt[n.---]. | ipṯn[.---]. | ybni[l.---]. | ikrn[.---]. | tlm 106[332].2

ubln

[--]n.bu[-]bd.ubln. | [---].l.ubl[n]. | [--.]ṯbq.l.iytlm. | [---].l.iytlm. | [---.]‘bdilm.l.iytlm. | [-- 1076.2
[---.]ybnn. | [---.]mlkn‘m. | [---.]tǵpṯn. | [--.]ubln. | [--.-]ḫ[-]. | [--.-]s[-]n. | [--.-]nyn. | [---].[-]ǵtyn. | [---].[-]ty 123[326].1.4
[--]n.bu[-]bd.ubln. | [---].l.ubl[n]. | [--.]ṯbq.l.iytlm. | [---].l.iytlm. | [---.]‘bdil 1076.1

ubn

. | y[--]k. | [-----]. | pǵḏn. | [--]n. | [--]ntn. | ‘dn. | lkn. | ktr. | ubn. | dqn. | ḥttn. | [--]n. | [---]. | tsn. | rpiy. | mrṯn. | ṯnyn. | apṯ. | š 1024.2.9
.b‘d h.bhtm.sgrt. | b‘d h.‘dbt.ṯlṯ.ptḥ.bt.mnt. | ptḥ.bt.w ubn.hkl.w ištql šql. | tn.km.nḥšm.yḥr.tn.km. | mhr y.w bn.bṯ UG5.7.72
‘bdyrḫ. | ubn.ḫyrn. | ybnil.adrdn. | klyn.kkln. | ‘dmlk.tdn. | ‘zn.pǵḏn. | [1070.2
ṣṣ mr‘m ḫmšm ḫmš kbd. | ṣṣ ubn ḫmš ‘šr h. | ṣṣ ‘myd ḫmšm. | ṣṣ tmn.ḫmšm. | [ṣṣ] ‘mtḏl ṯlṯ 2097.2
lqḥ.š‘rt. | urḫ.ln.kkrm. | w.rḥd.kd.šmn. | drt.b.kkr. | ubn.ḫṣḥ.kkr. | kkr.lqḥ.ršpy. | tmtrn.bn.pnmn. | kkr. | bn.sgttn. 1118.5
[---.--]ḫy. | [---.--]t. | [-----]. | [---.]l[--]. | [bn.]ubn. | kbšm. | bn.abḏr. | bn.kpltn. | bn.prn. | ‘bdm. | bn.kḏǵbr. | 114[324].2.3
b‘m.sḫr.‘zn.ilhd. | bnil.rb ‘šrt.lkn.yp‘n.ṯ[--]. | yṣḥm.b d.ubn.krwn.tǵd.[m]nḥm. | ‘pṯrm.šm‘rgm.skn.qrt. | ḥgbn.šm‘.sk 2011.9
‘šrm. | ṣdqšlm.‘šr[m]. | yknil.ḫmš. | ilmlk.ḫmš. | prṯ.‘šr. | ubn.‘šr. 1116.15
‘bdmlk. | šd.b d.yšn.ḥrš. | šd.b d.aupš. | šd.b d.ršpab.aḫ.ubn. | šd.b d.bn.uṯryn. | [ubd]y.mrynm. | [š]d.bn.ṣnrn.b d.nrn 82[300].1.5
aǵltn. | urtn. | anntb. | ubn. | špšyn. | abmn. | [--]dn. | [t]b‘m. | [--]mlk. | [--]ty. | mtnb‘l. 1072.4
[-----]. | bn.t[--.---]. | agmy[.---]. | bn.dlq[-.---]. | tǵyn.bn.ubn.ṯql[m]. | yšn.ḥrš.mrkbt.ṯq[lm]. | bn.p‘ṣ.ṯqlm. | mṣrn.ḥrš. 122[308].1.5
[ḫm]š l ‘šrm. | [-]dmm. | b.ubn. 1167.3

ubnyn

. | y‘ny. | atn. | utly. | bn.alz. | bn ḫlm. | bn.ḏmr. | bn.‘yn. | ubnyn. | rpš d ydy. | ǵbl. | mlk. | gwl. | rqd. | ḫlby. | ‘n[q]pat. | m[2075.19
b gt ilštm‘. | bt ubnyn š h d.ytn.ṣtqn. | ṯut ṯbḫ ṣtq[n]. | b bz ‘zm ṯbḫ š[h]. | b 1153.2
šb‘.ḫsnm. | tš‘m.ṯṯ.kbd.mḏrǵlm. | ‘šrm.aḥd.kbd.ḫsnm. | ubnyn. | ṯṯm[.l.]mit.ṯlṯ. | kbd[.tg]mr.bnš. | l.b.bt.mlk. 1028.11

ubš

l[b]nm. | nnu. | ‘rm. | bṣr. | m‘r. | ḫlby. | mṣbt. | snr. | ṯm. | ubš. | glbt. | mi[d]ḫ. | mr[i]l. | ḫlb. | šld. | ‘rgz. | [-----]. 2041.10
‘. | bir. | m‘qb. | uškn. | snr. | rq[d]. | [---]. | [---]. | mid[-]. | ubš. | mṣb[t]. | ḫl.y[---]. | ‘rg[z]. | y‘r[t]. | amḏ[y]. | atl[g]. | bṣr[y] 71[113].38
m]ṣbt.ṣmdm.[---]. | [--]nr.arb‘.[---]. | [--]idḫ.ṣmd[.---]. | [u]bš.[---]. 1179.8

ubr

š. | ilṯḥm. | ḥrm. | bn.bty. | ‘by. | šm[n].bn.apn. | krty. | bn.ubr. | [bn] mdḫl. | bn.sy[n]n. | bn.šrn. 2078.19
]. | bn.by[--]. | bn.a[--]. | bn.iy[--]. | bn.ḫ[---]. | bn.plš. | bn.ubr. | bn.‘pṯb. | ṯbry. | bn.ymn. | krty. | bn.abr[-]. | yrpu. | kdn. | 2117.1.16

ubr‘

spr.blblm. | skn uškn. | skn šbn. | skn ubr‘. | skn ḫrṣb‘. | rb.ntbtš. | [---].‘bd.r[--]. | arb‘.k[--]. | ṯlṯ.ktt. 1033.4

ubr‘y

. | b[n.]ad‘l.q[š]t.w.ql‘. | b[n].ilyn.qšt.w.ql‘. | šmrm.ql‘. | ubr‘y. | abmn.qšt.w.ṯn.ql‘m. | qdmn.ṯṯ.qštm.w.ṯlṯ.ql‘m. | bn.ṣd 119[321].3.1
ubr‘y. | arny. | m‘r. | š‘rt. | ḫlb rpš. | bq‘t. | šḥq. | y‘by. | mḫr. 65[108].1
].qmy. | [---.]qmy. | [---.--]b. | bn.t[--.---.a]ǵt.⌊špš[yn.---.u]br‘y. | iln.[---]. | bn.[---].ar. | bn.[---].b.ar. | špšyn[.---.]yṯb.b.a 2015.1.20
| w.ull. | ṯmry. | qrt. | ‘rm. | nnu. | [--]. | [---]. | m‘r. | arny. | ubr‘y. | ilštm‘. | bir. | m‘qb. | uškn. | snr. | rq[d]. | [---]. | [---]. | mi 71[113].28
[--.---]. | ṣ‘[-.---]. | ṣ‘q[.---]. | ḫlb.k[rd]. | uškn. | ‘nqp[at]. | ubr‘[y]. | ilšt[m‘]. | šbn. | ṯbq. 2146.7
---]. | [-]b‘l. | [--]m. | [m‘]rby. | m‘r. | arny. | ‘nqpat. | š‘rt. | ubr‘y. | ilštm‘. | šbn. | ṯbq. | rqd. | [š]rš. | [-----]. | [-----]. | [-----]. | [- 2058.1.14
n.mṣry. | y‘l.kn‘ny. | gdn.bn.umy. | kn‘m.š‘rty. | abrpu.ubr‘y. | b.gt.bn.ṯlṯ. | ilḏ.b.gt.psḥn. 91[311].10
y. | bn.šdy ary. | bn.ktkt.m‘qby. | bn.[---.]ṯlḫny. | b[n.---.ub]r‘y. | [bn.---.ubr]‘y. | b[n.---]. | bn[.---.ušk]ny. | bn.kdrn.ušk 87[64].18
bn.ktkt.m‘qby. | bn.[---.]ṯlḫny. | b[n.---.ub]r‘y. | [bn.---.ubr]‘y. | b[n.---]. | bn[.---.ušk]ny. | bn.kdrn.uškny. | bn.lgn.ušk 87[64].19
bt.dml. | p ank.atn. | ‘ṣm.l k. | arb‘.‘ṣm. | ‘l.ar. | w.ṯlṯ. | ‘l.ubr‘y. | w.ṯn.‘l. | mlk. | w.aḥd. | ‘l atlg. | w l.‘ṣm. | tspr. | nrn.al.t 1010.12
| mlkn‘m.‘šr. | bn.adty.‘šr. | [ṣ]dqšlm ḫmš. | krzn.ḫmš. | ubr‘ym.ḫmš. | [----]. | [bn] itn. | [bn] il. | [---]ṯ. | klttb. | gsn. | ar 2039.7
| gn‘y.[---.bn]š. | uškn[.---].‘šr.bnšm. | ‘nqpat[.---].bnš. | ubr‘y.ar[b‘.]ḥm[r]m.w[.---.]bnšm. | ilštm‘.arb‘.ḥm[r]m.ḫmš. 2040.20
[--.]wmrkm. | bir.ḫmš. | uškn.arb‘. | ubr‘y.ṯlṯ. | ar.ṯmn ‘šr h. | mlk.arb‘. | ǵbl.ḫmš. | atlg.ḫmš ‘šr[h]. 68[65].1.4

‘rby.ḫmš. | ṯbq.arb‘. | tkm[.---]. | uḫnp[.---]. | ušk[n.---]. | ubr[‘y.---]. | ar[.---]. | mlk[.---]. | ǵbl[.---]. | atl[g.---]. | u[lm.---]. 68[65].2.4

| y[---.]bn.‘šq. | [---.]bn.tqy. | [---.]bn.šlmy. | [-----]. | [---].ubr‘y. | [---].gwl. | [---]ady. | [---]ṣry. | miḫ[-]m. | ṣdqm. | dnn. | ‘ 1041.8

mr[il.---]. | ub[r‘y.---]. | mi[ḫd.---]. | snr[.---]. | ṯm[--.---]. 2144.2

bn[.---]. | ubr[‘ym.---]. | qdm[n.---]. | b‘l[--.---]. | šm[---.---]. | yšr[-.---]. | b 93[328].2

.mlk. | ṣbr.aḥd. | b.m‘rby. | ṣbr.aḥd. | b.ulm. | ṣbr.aḥd. | b.ubr‘y. 2073.12

ubr‘n

šd.ubdy.ilštm‘. | dt b d.skn. | šd.bn.ubr‘n b gt prn. | šd.bn.gby.gt.prn. | šd.bn.kryn.gt.prn. | šd.bn. 1104.3

ubrš

kbdy. | bn krk. | bn srty. | bn ltḥ ḫlq. | bn ytr. | bn ilšpš. | ubrš. | bn gmš ḫlq. | bn ‘gy. | bn zlbn. | bn.aḫ[--]. | bn[.---]. | [---- 2016.2.17

š. | [--.]kbd. | [---]. | y[---]. | bn.ǵlyn. | bdl.ar. | bn.šyn. | bn.ubrš. | bn.d[--]b. | abrpu. | bn.k[n]y. | bn.klyn. | bn.gmḥn. | ḥnn. 1035.3.3

.‘šr h.šmn. | ‘mn.bn.aǵlmn. | arb‘m.ksp.‘l.qrt. | b.šd.bn.[u]brš. | ḫmšt.‘šrt. | b.šd.bn.[-]n. | tl[ṯt].‘šr[t]. | b.š[d].bn.‘myn. | 1083.7

.gṯtn.kdm. | ynḥm.bn[.-]r[-]t.ṯlṯ. | plwn.kdm. | tmyn.bn.ubrš.kd. 136[84].12

ugr

]lm.w ḥẓr.k bn. | [a]ṯrt.gm.l ǵlm h. | b‘l.yṣḥ.‘n.gpn. | w ugr.bn.ǵlmt. | ‘mm ym.bn.ẓlm[t]. | rmt.pr‘t.ibr[.mnt]. | ṣḥrrm 8[51FRAG].7

yšb | [‘].hmlt.arṣ.gm.l ǵ | [lm] h.b‘l k.yṣḥ.‘n. | [gpn].w ugr.b ǵlmt. | [‘mm.]ym.bn.ẓlmt.r | [mt.pr‘]t.ibr.mnt. | [ṣḥrrm. 4[51].7.54

]rsd. | bn[.-]pṯ. | bn kdrn. | awldn. | arswn.y‘r[ty.--]. | bn.ugr. | gny. | ṯn.mdm. 86[305].11

.w š]nm hn š. | w šqrb.‘r.mšr mšr bn.ugrt.w [npy.---.]ugr. | w npy.yman.w npy.‘rmt.w npy.[---]. | w npy.nqmd.ušn 32[2].1.18

. | b aln.tk m. | b tk.mlbr. | ilšiy. | kry amt. | ‘pr.‘ẓm yd. | ugrm.ḫl.ld. | aklm.tbrk k. | w ld ‘qqm. | ilm.yp‘r. | šmt hm. | b 12[75].1.25

ṣ.pnt. | ksl h.anš.dt.ẓr h.tšu. | g h.w tṣḥ.ik.mǵy.gpn.w ugr. | mn.ib.yp‘.l b‘l.ṣrt. | l rkb.‘rpt.l mḫšt.mdd. | il ym.l klt.n 3[‘NT].3.33

ny.[msg]. | bn.mṣrn m[sg]. | yky msg. | ynḥm.msg. | bn.ugr.msg. | bn.ǵlṣ msg. | arb‘ l ṯkṣ[-]. | nn.arspy.ms[g]. | [---.ms] 133[-].1.8

ilm.idk. | l ytn.pnm.‘m.b‘l. | mrym.ṣpn.w y‘n. | gpn.w ugr.ṯḥm.bn ilm. | mt.hwt.ydd.bn.il. | ǵzr.p np.š.npš.lbim. | th 5[67].1.12

ug[r.---]. | ‘nt[.---]. | tmm l bt[.---]. | b[‘]l.ugr[t.---]. | w ‘ṣrm[.--- 40[134].1

t. | [---.--]t. | [---.]ilm. | [---.--]u.yd. | [---.--]k. | [---.gpn.]w ugr. | [---.---]t. 4[51].8.47

ugry

.nkl qšt. | ady.qšt. | bn.srn.qšt. | bn.gdrn.qšt. | prpr.qšt. | ugry.qšt. | bn.ṣrptn.qšt. | bn.mṣry.qšt. | arny. | abm.qšt. | ḥdṯn. 119[321].1.45

ugrt

ny. | lmd.atn.prln.rb. | khnm rb.nqdm. | ṯ‘y.nqmd.mlk ugr[t]. | adn.yrgb.b‘l.ṯrmn. 6.6[62.2].56

l.mlk.ugrt. | aḫ y.rgm. | ṯḥm.mlk.ṣr.aḫ k. | y[š]lm.l k.ilm. | tǵr k.tšl 2059.1

l.mlk[.u]grt. | iḫ y.rgm. | [ṯḥ]m.m[lk.-]bl[-]. | yšlm.l[k].ilm. | tǵr.tšl[2159.1

aṯrt. | ḫnn il. | nṣbt il. | šlm il. | il ḥš il add. | b‘l ṣpn b‘l. | ugrt. | b mrḥ il. | b nit il. | b ṣmd il. | b dṯn il. | b šrp il. | b knt il 30[107].11

[šmt.n]qmp‘. | [bn.nq]md. | [mlk.]ugrt. | b‘l ṣdq. | skn.bt. | mlk.ṯǵr. | [m]lk.bny. | [--].lb.mlk. | [---. 1007.3

m]š.mat pḥm. | [ḫm]š[.m]at.iqnu. | argmn.nqmd.mlk. | ugrt.d ybl.l špš. | mlk.rb.b‘l h. | ks.ḫrṣ.ktn.mit.pḥm. | mit.iqni 64[118].25

n. | b‘ltdtt.tlgn.ytn. | b‘ltǵpṯm.krwn.ilšn.agyn. | mnn.šr.ugrt.ḏkr.yṣr. | tǵǵln.ḫmš.ddm. | [---].ḫmš.ddm. | ṯṯ.l.‘šrm.bn[š 2011.37

kl.hw[.---]. | w [--].brt.lb[--.---]. | u[-]šhr.nuš[-.---]. | b [u]grt.w ht.a[--]. | w hm.at.trg[m.---]. | w sip.u hw[.---]. | w an 54.1.7[13.1.4]

.w š.l b‘l ṣpn. | dqt l ṣpn.šrp.w šlmm. | kmm.w bbt.b‘l.ugrt. | w kdm.w npš ilib. | gdlt.il š.b‘l š.‘nt. | ṣpn.alp.w š.pdry. UG5.13.11

.bn.il.l ṯkmn[.w]šnm.hn.‘r. | w.ṯb.l mspr.m[šr] mšr.bt.ugrt.w npy.gr. | ḥmyt.ugrt.w [np]y.nṯt.ušn.yp kn.ulp qṭy. | ul 32[2].1.27

----.]lšnt. | [---.--]yp.ṯḥt. | [-----]. | [---.]w npy gr. | [ḥmyt.ugrt.w npy.yman.w npy.‘r]mt.w npy. | [---.ušn.yp km.ulp.]q APP.I[-].1.13

hn.‘r. | w.ṯb.l mspr.m[šr] mšr.bt.ugrt.w npy.gr. | ḥmyt.ugrt.w [np]y.nṯt.ušn.yp kn.ulp qṭy. | ulp.ddmy.ul[p.ḫ]ry.ulp 32[2].1.28

ḫrt.bn.i[l.l ṯkmn.w š]nm hn š. | w šqrb.‘r.mšr mšr bn.ugrt.w [npy.---.]ugr. | w npy.yman.w npy.‘rmt.w npy.[---]. | 32[2].1.18

pḫrt.bn.il.l ṯkmn.w šnm.hn š]. | [w šqrb.š.mšr mšr.bn.ugrt.w npy.---.]w npy. | [---.w np]y.ugrt. | [---.u ṯḫṯu.ulp.qṭy. 32[2].1.4

pḫ]rt.[bn.il.l ṯkmn.w šn]m hn š. | [---.w n]py.gr[.ḥmyt.ugrt.w np]y. | [---].w n[py.---].u ṯḫṯi[n.ulp.qṭy]. | ulp.ddmy.ul 32[2].1.10

bn h. | w.btšy.bt h. | w.ištrmy. | bt.‘bd mlk. | w.snt. | bt.ugrt. | w.pdy h[m]. | iwrkl.mit. | ksp.b y[d]. | birtym. | [un]ṯ in 1006.11

l ym.hnd. | ‘mṯtmr. | bn.nqmp‘. | mlk.ugrt. | ytn.bt.anndr. | bn.ytn.bnš. | [ml]k.d.b riš. | [--.-]nt. | [l.‘b 1009.4

l ym hnd. | ‘mṯtmr.bn. | nqmp‘.ml[k]. | ugrt.ytn. | šd.kdǵdl[.bn]. | [-]š[-]y.d.b š[-]y. | [---.y]d gt h[.--]. | 1008.4

[l] b‘l.ṣpn. | [dqt.l.ṣpn.šrp].w š[l]mm.kmm. | [w bbt.b‘l.ugrt.]kdm.w npš. | [ilib.gdlt.il.š.b]‘[l.]š.‘nt ṣpn. | [---.]w [n]p[š 36[9].1.16

. | b unṯ.‘d ‘lm. | mišmn.nqmd. | mlk ugrt. | nqmd.mlk.ugrt. | ktb.spr hnd. | dt brrt.ṣṭqšlm. | ‘bd h.hnd. | w mn km.l y 1005.8

rt h.l r | [--.]arṣ.‘z k.ḏmr k.l[-] | n k.ḥtk k.nmrt k.b tk. | ugrt.l ymt.špš.w yrḫ. | w n‘mt.šnt.il. UG5.2.2.11

ṯḥm[.t]lm[yn]. | l ṯryl.um y. | rgm. | ugrt.tǵr k. | ugrt.tǵr k. | tšlm k.um y. | td‘.ky.‘rbt. | l pn.špš. | 1015.5

rt.kmt. | br.ṣṭqšlm. | b unṯ.‘d ‘lm. | mišmn.nqmd. | mlk ugrt. | nqmd.mlk.ugrt. | ktb.spr hnd. | dt brrt.ṣṭqšlm. | ‘bd h.h 1005.7

ṯḥm[.t]lm[yn]. | l ṯryl.um y. | rgm. | ugrt.tǵr k. | ugrt.tǵr k. | tšlm k.um y. | td‘.ky.‘rbt. | l pn.špš. | w pn.špš.nr. 1015.5

ṯḥm.pgn. | l.mlk.ugrt. | rgm. | yšlm.l k.[il]m. | tǵr k.tšlm k. | hn ny.‘m n.š[l]m. | 2061.2

[---.k]rgmš. | [l.m]lk.ugrt.rgm[.-]y. | [---.--]m.rgm. | [---.]šknt. | [---.--]dy. 1011.2

š.b‘l š.‘nt. | ṣpn.alp.w š.pdry.š. | šrp.w šlmm ilib š. | b‘l ugrt š.b‘l ḫlb š. | yrḫ š.‘nt ṣpn.alp. | w š.pdry š.ddmš š. | w b u UG5.13.16

.---]. | [--.k]mm.gdlt.l.b[‘l.---]. | [dq]t.l.ṣpn.gdlt.l[.---]. | u[gr]t.š.l.[il]ib.ǵ[--.--rt]. | w [‘ṣrm.]l.ri[--.---]. | [--]t.b‘lt.bt[.---] 35[3].35

.b nbk.[---]. | kmm.gdlt.l b[‘l.--.dqt]. | l ṣpn.gdlt.[l.---]. | ugrt.š l ili[b.---]. | rt.w ‘ṣrm.l[.---]. | pamt.w bt.[---]. | rmm.w ‘l APP.II[173].38

ršm. | dt.tb‘ln.b.pḫn. | ṯṯm.ḫzr.w.‘št.‘šr.ḫrš. | dt.tb‘ln.b.ugrt. | ṯṯm.ḫzr. | dt.tb‘ln. | b.gt.ḥršm. | ṯn.ḥršm. | [-]nbkm. | ṯn. 1024.3.8

ḫršḫ. | ‘lm b ǵb ḫyr. | ṯmn l ṯlṯm ṣin. | šb‘.alpm. | bt b‘l.ugrt.ṯn šm. | ‘lm.l ršp.mlk. | alp w.š.l b‘lt. | bwrm š.iṯtqb. | w š. UG5.12.B.6

.rb]. | b‘l h.šlm.[w spš]. | mlk.rb.b‘l h.[---]. | nqmd.mlk.ugr[t.--]. | phy. | w ṯpllm.mlk.r[b.--]. | mṣmt.l nqmd.[---.-]št. | 64[118].14

[il]m.tšlm k. | [tǵ]r k. | [--]y.ibr[-]. | [--]wy.rgm l. | mlkt.ugrt. | [--]kt.rgmt. | [--]y.l.ilak. | [---].‘m y. | [---]m.w.lm. | [---.] 1016.9

šqrb.š.mšr mšr.bn.ugrt.w npy.---.]w npy. | [---.w np]y.ugrt. | [---.u ṯḫṯu.ulp.qṭy.ulp.ddm]y. | [ulp.ḫry.ulp.ḫty.ulp.alṯ 32[2].1.5

n. | [---.bn]šm.b.tmrm. | [---.bn]šm.b.ṯnq. | [---.b]nšm.b.ugrt. | [---.bn]šm.b.ǵbl. | [---.b]nšm.b.m'r.arr. | arb'.bnšm.b.m 2076.30
[---.--]t ugrt. | [---.w n]py.yman. | [w npy.'rmt.---.w]npy.annpdgl. | [APP.I[-].1.1
ug[r.---]. | 'nt[.---]. | tmm l bt[.---]. | b['']l.ugr[t.---]. | w 'ṣrm[.---]. | ṣlyh šr[-.---]. | [ṯ]lṯm.w b[--.---]. | l il l 40[134].4
qṯt.tqṯṯ.ušn.yp km.---.-]yt km. | [---.]km. | [-----]. | [---.]ugrt. | [---].l.lim. | [---.mšr m]šr. | [bn.ugrt.---.--]y. | [---.np]y n APP.I[-].1.21
]km. | [-----]. | [---.]ugrt. | [---].l.lim. | [---.mšr m]šr. | [bn.ugrt.---.--]y. | [---.np]y nqmd. | [---.]pẖr. | [-----]. | [-----]. | [---.t' APP.I[-].2.2
t l b'l. | ṣpn.ilbt[.---.]d[--]. | l ṣpn[.---.-]lu. | ilib[.---.b]'l. | ugrt[.---.--]n. | [w] š l [---]. UG5.13.36
l ṯkm[n.w šnm.]hn '[r]. | [---.]w npy[.---]. | [---.]w npy.u[grt.---]. | [---.--]y.ulp.[---]. | [---.]ǵbr.u[lp.---]. | [---.--]n[.---]. 32[2].2.2
spr 'psm. | dt.št. | uryn. | l mlk.ugrt. 1171.4
[spr.ilmlk.ṯ']y.nqmd.mlk.ugrt. 4[51].9.1

ugrty

.---]. | bn.lṣn.'rm[y]. | aršw.bṣry. | arpṯr.y'rty. | bn.ḫdyn.ugrty. | bn.tgd̲n.ugrty. | tgyn.arty. | bn.nryn.arty. | bn.ršp.ary. 87[64].8
[y]. | aršw.bṣry. | arpṯr.y'rty. | bn.ḫdyn.ugrty. | bn.tgd̲n.ugrty. | tgyn.arty. | bn.nryn.arty. | bn.ršp.ary. | bn.ǵlmn ary. | 87[64].9

udbr

npṣ.'[--.---]. | d.b d.a[--.---]. | w.b d.b[--.---]. | udbr[.---]. | 'rš[.---]. | ṯl[ḥn.---]. | a[--.---]. | ṯn[.---]. | ptr[-.---]. | y 1120.4

udm

t.mswn h. | arḫ.tzǵ.l 'gl h. | bn.ḫpṯ.l umht hm. | k tnḥn.udmm. | w y'ny.krt.ṯ'. 15[128].1.7
t[.šlmm]. | š[lmm.]al.t[ṣr]. | udm[.r]bt.w u[dm]. | [ṯ]rrt.udm.y[t]n[t]. | il.ušn.ab[.ad]m. | rḥq.mlk.l bt y. | n[g.]krt.l ḥẓ[14[KRT].6.277
. | l bt y.rḥq.krt. | l ḥẓr y.al.tṣr. | udm.rbt.w udm ṯrrt. | udm.ytnt.il w ušn. | ab.adm.w ṯṯb. | mlakm.l h.lm.ank. | ksp. 14[KRT].3.135
ḥ.krt.šlmm]. | [šlmm.al.tṣr]. | [udm.rbt.w udm]. | [ṯrrt.udm.ytnt]. | [il.w ušn.ab.adm]. | [rḥq.mlk.l bt y]. | [ng.kr]t.l ḥ 14[KRT].5.258
bt]. | b[trbṣ.bn.amt]. | [qḥ.krt.šlmm]. | [šlmm.al.tṣr]. | [udm.rbt.w udm]. | [ṯrrt.udm.ytnt]. | [il.w ušn.ab.adm]. | [rḥq. 14[KRT].5.257
]. | b trbṣ.[bn.amt]. | q[ḥ.kr]t[.šlmm]. | š[lmm.]al.t[ṣr]. | udm[.r]bt.w u[dm]. | [ṯ]rrt.udm.y[t]n[t]. | il.ušn.ab[.ad]m. | rḥ 14[KRT].6.276
lmm. | šlmm.w ng.mlk. | l bt y.rḥq.krt. | l ḥẓr y.al.tṣr. | udm.rbt.w udm ṯrrt. | udm.ytnt.il w ušn. | ab.adm.w ṯṯb. | ml 14[KRT].3.134
m. | ylk ym.w ṯn. | ṯlṯ.rb'.ym. | aḫr.špšm.b rb'. | ymǵy.l udm.rbt. | w udm[.ṯr]rt. | grnn.'rm. | šrnn.pdrm. | s't.b šdm.ḥṭ 14[KRT].4.210
ṯn.ṯlṯ.rb' ym. | ḫmš.ṯdṯ.ym.mk.špšm. | b šb'.w tmǵy.l udm. | rbm.w l.udm.ṯrrt. | w gr.nn.'rm.šrn. | pdrm.s't.b šdm. 14[KRT].3.108
.amt]. | q[ḥ.kr]t[.šlmm]. | š[lmm.]al.t[ṣr]. | udm[.r]bt.w u[dm]. | [ṯ]rrt.udm.y[t]n[t]. | il.ušn.ab[.ad]m. | rḥq.mlk.l bt y. 14[KRT].6.276
.w ng.mlk. | l bt y.rḥq.krt. | l ḥẓr y.al.tṣr. | udm.rbt.w udm ṯrrt. | udm.ytnt.il w ušn. | ab.adm.w ṯṯb. | mlakm.l h.lm. 14[KRT].3.134
ṣ.bn.amt]. | [qḥ.krt.šlmm]. | [šlmm.al.tṣr]. | [udm.rbt.w udm]. | [ṯrrt.udm.ytnt]. | [il.w ušn.ab.adm]. | [rḥq.mlk.l bt y]. 14[KRT].5.257
ṯn. | ṯlṯ.rb'.ym. | aḫr.špšm.b rb'. | ymǵy.l udm.rbt. | w udm[.ṯr]rt. | grnn.'rm. | šrnn.pdrm. | s't.b šdm.ḥṭb. | w b grnt. 14[KRT].4.211
ḫmš.ṯdṯ.ym.mk.špšm. | b šb'.w tmǵy.l udm. | rbm.w l.udm.ṯrrt. | w gr.nn.'rm.šrn. | pdrm.s't.b šdm. | ḥṭb h.b grnt.ḥ 14[KRT].3.109

udmy

ṭ.l.ql.d.ybl.prd. | b.ṯql.w.nṣp.ksp. | ṯmn.lbšm.w.mšlt. | l.udmym.b.ṯmnt.'šrt.ksp. | šb'm.lbš.d.'rb.bt.mlk. | b.mit.ḫmšt. 2101.15

udm't

'l.nrd. | b arṣ.'m h.trd.nrt. | ilm.špš.'d.tšb'.bk. | tšt.k yn.udm't.gm. | tṣḥ.l nrt.ilm.špš. | 'ms m'.l y.aliyn.b'l. | tšm'.nrt.il 6[62].1.10
.aṯrm[.---]. | aṯr.aṯrm[.---]. | išdym.t[---]. | b k.mla[.---]. | udm't.d[m'.---]. | [---].bn.[---]. | [-----]. 27[8].11
.yrṯ. | y'rb.b ḥdr h.ybky. | b ṯn.[-]gmm.w ydm'. | tntkn.udm't h. | km.ṯqlm.arṣ h. | km ḫmšt.mṭt h. | bm.bky h.w yšn. 14[KRT].1.28
ṯ'. | bn.al.tbkn.al. | tdm.l y.al tkl.bn. | qr.'n k.mḫ.riš k. | udm't.ṣḥ.aḫt k. | ṯtmnt.bt.ḥmḥ h. | d[-]n.tbkn.w tdm.l y.[--]. 16.1[125].28

udn

mṯḥṣ.ksp. | itrṯ.ḫrṣ.ṭrd.b'l. | b mrym.ṣpn.mšṣṣ.[-]k'[-]. | udn h.grš h.l ksi.mlk h. | l nḫt.l kḥṯ.drkt h. | mn m.ib.yp'.l b' 3['NT].4.46
ab h.ḥpr.p'l k.y[--]. | šm' k.l arḫ.w bn.[--]. | limm.ql.b udn.k w[-]. | k rtqt mr[.---]. | k d lbšt.bir.mlak. | šmm.tmr.zb 13[6].23
b.lk. | l[ab]k.w rgm.'ny. | l k[rt.adn k.]ištm['']. | w tqǵ[.udn.k ǵz.ǵzm]. | tdbr.w[ǵ]rm[.ṯṯwy]. | šqlt.b ǵlt.yd k. | l tdn. 16.6[127].30
ab h.y'rb.yšu g h. | w yṣḥ.šm' m'.l krt. | ṯ'.ištm'.w tqǵ udn. | k ǵz.ǵzm.tdbr. | w ǵrm.ṯṯwy.šqlt. | b ǵlt.yd k.l tdn. | dn. 16.6[127].42
.trḫp.'nt.'l[.aqht]. | t'dbn h.hlmn.ṯnm[.qdqd]. | ṯlṯ id.'l.udn.š[pk.km]. | šiy.dm h.km.šḫ[ṭ.l brk h]. | yṣat.km.rḥ.npš[18[3AQHT].4.34
m.arḫp.an[k.']l. | aqht.'db k.hlmn.ṯnm.qdqd. | ṯlṯ id.'l.udn.špk.km.šiy. | dm.km.šḫṭ.l brk h.tṣi.km. | rḥ.npš h.km.iṯl. 18[3AQHT].4.23
dd y.yṣ[--]. | [-.]yṣa.w l.yṣa.hlm.[ṯnm]. | [q]dqd.ṯlṯ id.'l.ud[n]. | [---.-]sr.pdm.riš h[m.---]. | 'l.pd.asr.[---.]l[.---]. | mḫlpt 19[1AQHT].2.79

udr

rb.hkl k. | tbl k.ǵrm.mid.ksp. | gb'm.mḥmd.ḫrṣ. | ybl k.udr.ilqṣm. | w bn.bht.ksp.w ḫrṣ. | bht.ṯhrm.iqnim. | šmḫ.btlt.' 4[51].5.79
b hkl h. | yblnn ǵrm.mid.ksp. | gb'm lḥmd.ḫrṣ. | yblnn.udr.ilqṣm. | yak.l ktr.w ḫss. | w ṯb l mspr..k tlakn. | ǵlmm. | aḫ 4[51].5.102

ud̲r

m[.ṯṯb.l] y. | hl ny.'mn. | mlk.b.ṯy ndr. | iṯt.w.ht. | [-]sny.ud̲r h. | w.hm.ḫt. | 'l.w.likt. | 'm k.w.hm. | l.'l.w.lakm. | ilak.w. 1013.15
. | [---.-]ktt.hn.ib. | [---.]mlk. | [---.]adt y.td'. | w.ap.mlk.ud̲[r]. | [-]d'.k.iḫd.[---]. | w.mlk.b'l y. | lm.škn.hnk. | l 'bd h.alp 1012.20

uwaḫ

bn.klby. | bn.iyṯr. | [']bdyrḫ. | [b]n.gg't. | [']dy. | armwl. | uwaḫ. | ypln.w.ṯn.bn h. | ydln. | anr[my]. | mld. | krmp[y]. | bṣ 2086.7

uwil

abǵl.[---]. | [.---]. | d̲mrb'[l.---]. | iḫyn.[---]. | 'bdb'[l.---]. | uwil[.---]. | ušry[n.---]. | y'd̲rn[.---]. | [']bdyr[ḫ.---]. | [---]mlk[.-- 102[322].2.8

uz

mš.mat. | šb'm[.t]š'.kbd. | tgmr.uz.ǵrn.arb'.mat. | tgmr.uz.aẖmn.arb'.mat. | arb'm.kbd. | ṯlṯ.alp.ṣpr.dt.aḫd. | ḥrṯ h.aḥ 1129.6
uz.mrat.mlḥt. | arb'.uzm.mrat.bq'. | ṯlṯ.[-]ṯt.aš[']t.šmn.uz. | mi[t].ygb.bq'. | a[--].'ṭ. | a[l]pm.alpnm. | ṯlṯ.m[a]t.art.ḥkpt 1128.22
.mri. | ṯn.nšbm. | ṯmnym.tbṯḫ.alp. | uz.mrat.mlḥt. | arb'.uzm.mrat.bq'. | ṯlṯ.[-]ṯt.aš[']t.šmn.uz. | mi[t].ygb.bq'. | a[--].'ṭ. 1128.21
alp.mri. | 'šr.bmt.alp.mri. | ṯn.nšbm. | ṯmnym.tbṯḫ.alp. | uz.mrat.mlḥt. | arb'.uzm.mrat.bq'. | ṯlṯ.[-]ṯt.aš[']t.šmn.uz. | m 1128.20
ṯn.r'y.uzm. | sǵr.bn.ḫpsry.aḥd. | sǵr.artn.aḥd. | sǵr.'dn.aḥd. | sǵr.awl 1140.1
--].ṯlṯ.kbd. | [---].alpm.ḫmš.mat. | šb'm[.t]š'.kbd. | tgmr.uz.ǵrn.arb'.mat. | tgmr.uz.aẖmn.arb'.mat. | arb'm.kbd. | ṯlṯ.al 1129.5

uz'rt

rqm.[---]. | ṯmnt.iṣr r't.'ṣ brq y. | riš h.tply.ṭly.bn.'n h. | uz'rt.tmll.išd h.qrn[m]. | dt.'l h.riš h.b glṯ.b šm[m]. | [---.i]l.ṯr UG5.3.1.6

uzpy

ḫny. | [šd.bn.--]rt.b d.ṯpṭb'l. | [ubdy.]mḫ[ṣ]m. | [šd.bn.]uzpy.b d.yšn.ḥrš. | [-----]. | [-----]. | [šd.b d.--]n. | [šd.b d.--]n. | [82[300].2.26

uzr

.dnil.uzr. | [ilm.y]lḥm.uzr.yšqy bn. | [qdš.ḫ]mš.ṯdṯ.ym.uzr. | [ilm].dnil.uzr.ilm.ylḥm. | [uzr.]yšqy.bn qdš.yd.ṣt h. | [d 17[2AQHT].1.12
.yd. | [ṣt h.y'l.]w yškb.yd. | [mizrt.]p ynl.hn.ym. | [w ṯn.uzr.]ilm.dnil. | [uzr.ilm.]ylḥm.uzr. | [yšqy.b]n.qdš ṯlṯ rb' ym. 17[2AQHT].1.7
.dnil. | [uzr.ilm.]ylḥm.uzr. | [yšqy.b]n.qdš ṯlṯ rb' ym. | [uzr.i]lm.dnil.uzr. | [ilm.y]lḥm.uzr.yšqy bn. | [qdš.ḫ]mš.ṯdṯ.y 17[2AQHT].1.10
y]lḥm.uzr.yšqy bn. | [qdš.ḫ]mš.ṯdṯ.ym.uzr. | [ilm].dnil.uzr.ilm.ylḥm. | [uzr.]yšqy.bn qdš.yd.ṣt h. | [dn]il.yd.ṣt h.y'l. 17[2AQHT].1.13
w šrš.km.ary h. | bl.iṯ.bn.l h.km aḫ h.w šrš. | km.ary h.uzrm.ilm.ylḥm. | uzrm.yšqy.bn.qdš. | l tbrknn l ṯr.il ab y. | tm 17[2AQHT].1.22
.]ylḥm.uzr. | [yšqy.b]n.qdš ṯlṯ rb' ym. | [uzr.i]lm.dnil.uzr. | [ilm.y]lḥm.uzr.yšqy bn. | [qdš.ḫ]mš.ṯdṯ.ym.uzr. | [ilm]. 17[2AQHT].1.10
[-----.apnk]. | [dnil.mt.rp]i.apn.ǵz[r]. | [mt.hrnmy.]uzr.ilm.ylḥm. | [uzr.yšqy.]bn.qdš.yd. | [ṣt h.y'l.]w yškb.yd. | [17[2AQHT].1.3
yškb.yd. | [mizrt.]p ynl.hn.ym. | [w ṯn.uzr.]ilm.dnil. | [uzr.ilm.]ylḥm.uzr. | [yšqy.b]n.qdš ṯlṯ rb' ym. | [uzr.i]lm.dnil. 17[2AQHT].1.8
| [dnil.mt.rp]i.apn.ǵz[r]. | [mt.hrnmy.]uzr.ilm.ylḥm. | [uzr.yšqy.]bn.qdš.yd. | [ṣt h.y'l.]w yškb.yd. | [mizrt.]p ynl.hn. 17[2AQHT].1.4
bn. | [qdš.ḫ]mš.ṯdṯ.ym.uzr. | [ilm].dnil.uzr.ilm.ylḥm. | [uzr.]yšqy.bn qdš.yd.ṣt h. | [dn]il.yd.ṣt h.y'l.w yškb. | [yd.]mi 17[2AQHT].1.14
qy.b]n.qdš ṯlṯ rb' ym. | [uzr.i]lm.dnil.uzr. | [ilm.y]lḥm.uzr.yšqy bn. | [qdš.ḫ]mš.ṯdṯ.ym.uzr. | [ilm].dnil.uzr.ilm.ylḥm 17[2AQHT].1.11
bl.iṯ.bn.l h.km aḫ h.w šrš. | km.ary h.uzrm.ilm.ylḥm. | uzrm.yšqy.bn.qdš. | l tbrknn l ṯr.il ab y. | tmrnn.l bny.bnwt. | 17[2AQHT].1.23
rt.]p ynl.hn.ym. | [w ṯn.uzr.]ilm.dnil. | [uzr.ilm.]ylḥm.uzr. | [yšqy.b]n.qdš ṯlṯ rb' ym. | [uzr.i]lm.dnil.uzr. | [ilm.y]lḥ 17[2AQHT].1.8

uḫd

.b d.mlkt. | [---.]l.mḫṣ. | ab[---.]adddy.bn.skn. | bn.[---.]uḫd. | bn.n[---.]hbṭn. | bn.m[--.]skn. | bn.s[--.b]d.skn. | bn.ur[- 2014.9
šm.dt.]b d.mlk. | [---.b]d.mlkt. | [---.b]d.mlk. | [---.--]ḫ.uḫd. | [---.-]luḫ. | [---.-]tn.b d.mlkt. | [---.]l.mḫṣ. | ab[---.]adddy 2014.4

uḫn

n.krm[.---]. | krm.n'mn.b.ḫly.ull.krm.aḫ[d.---]. | krm.uḫn.b.šdmy.ṯlṯ.bzl[.d]prn[.---]. | aupṯ.krm.aḥd.nšpin.kr[m.]a 1081.13
nn[-.---]. | au[pš.---]. | i[---.---]. | pgl[--.---]. | šy[.---]. | bn.uḫn. | ybru.i[---]. | [p]dyn.[---]. | bnšm.d.b [d.---]. | spḫy.[---]. | [2161.10
--]. | šd.y'ḏr[.---]. | šd.swr.[---]. | šd.bn ppn[-.---]. | šd.bn.uḫn[.---]. 83[85].7

uḫnp

]dš. | [a]mdy. | [gn]'y. | m'qb. | agm. | ḫpty. | ypr. | ḫrṣb'. | uḫnp. | art. | [--]n. | [-----]. | [-----]. | nnu. | šmg. | šmn. | lbnm. | ṯr 2058.2.6
spr.rpš d l y[dy]. | atlg. | ulm. | izly. | uḫnp. | bn sḫrn. | m'qb. | ṯpn. | m'r. | lbnm. | nḫl. | y'ny. | atn. | ut 2075.5
.bnš. | rqd arb'. | šbn aḥd. | ṯbq aḥd. | šrš aḥd. | bir aḥd. | uḫnp. | hzp ṯn. | m'qb arb'. 2040.32
--]. | [a]gm.arb'[.---]. | šrš.šb'.mṣb. | rqd.ṯlṯ.mṣb.w.[---]. | uḫnp.ṯṯ.mṣb. | tgmr.[y]n.mṣb š[b']. | w ḥs[p] ṯn.k[dm]. 2004.34
.ag[m]y. | arb'.bnšm.b.ḫpty. | ṯṯ.bnšm.b.bir. | ṯṯ.bnšm b.uḫnp. | ṯn.bnšm.b.ḫrṣb'. | arb'.bnšm.b.hzp. | arb'.bnšm.b.šql. | 2076.14
mš 'šr[h]. | ulm ṯ[ṯ]. | m'rby.ḫmš. | ṯbq.arb'. | tkm[.---]. | uḫnp[.---]. | ušk[n.---]. | ubr['y.---]. | ar[.---]. | mlk[.---]. | ǵbl[.--- 68[65].2.2
[-]dn[.---]. | [-]bq[.---]. | [r]qd[.---]. | šrš[.---]. | uḫnp[.---]. | [-]tn[--.---]. | km[-.---]. | lm[--.---]. 2165.5

uḫnpy

mšt.l.'šrt. | b.[---].šb't.'šrt. | b.bn.pdrn.'šrm. | d.bn.šb'l.uḫnpy.ḫmšm. | b.bn.ṯtm.ṯlṯm. | b.bn.agdṯb.'šrm. | b.bn.ibn.ar 2054.1.10

uṭ

]lakm.ylak.ym.[t'dt.ṯpṭ.nhr]. | b 'lṣ.'lṣm.npr.š[--.---]. | uṭ.ṯbr.ap hm.tb'.ǵlm[m.al.ṯṯb.idk.pnm]. | al.ttn.'m.pḫr.m'd.t 2.1[137].13

uṭb

mšt. | kbd.ksp. | kkrm.š'rt.štt.b d.gg['t]. | b.'šrt.ksp. | ṯlṯ.uṭbm.b d.alḫn.b.'šrt[.k]sp. | rṭ.l.ql.d.ybl.prd. | b.ṯql.w.nṣp.ks 2101.11

uṭm

| šlyṭ.d šb'y.rašm. | ṯṯkḥ.ttrp.šmm.k rs. | ipd k.ank.ispi.uṭm. | ḏrqm.amt m.l yrt. | b npš.bn ilm.mt.b mh | mrt.ydd.il. 5[67].1.5
[---.]ps[.---]. | [---].yṯbr[.---]. | [---.]uṭm.ḏr[qm.---]. | [btl]t.'nt.l kl.[---]. | [ṯt]b'.btlt.'nt[.idk.l ttn.p 18[3AQHT].4.3

uy

ank.u šbt[--.---]. | ank.n[--]n[.---]. | kst.l[--.---]. | w.hw.uy.'n[--.---]. | l ytn.w rgm[.---]. | w yrdnn.an[--.---]. | [---].ank. 54.1.13[13.1.10]

uk

-]n.špš. | ad[.']bd h.uk.škn. | k.[---.]sglt h.hw. | w.b[.---.]uk.nǵr. | w.[---].adny.l.yḫsr. | w.[ank.yd]'.l.yd't. | h[t.---.]l.špš 2060.8
i.rgm. | 'm špš.kll.mid m. | šlm. | l.[--]n.špš. | ad[.']bd h.uk.škn. | k.[---.]sglt h.hw. | w.b[.---.]uk.nǵr. | w.[---].adny.l.yḫ 2060.6

ul

. | ʿdn.ngb.w [yṣi.ṣbu]. | ṣbi.ng[b.w yṣi.ʿdn]. | mʿ[.ṣ]bu h.u[l.mad]. | ṯlṯ.mat.rbt. | hlk.l alpm.ḫḏḏ. | w l.rbt.kmyr. | aṯr.ṯn 14[KRT].4.178
ḫm. | ʿdn.ngb.w yṣi. | ṣbu.ṣbi.ngb. | w yṣi.ʿdn.mʿ. | ṣbu k.ul.mad. | ṯlṯ.mat.rbt. | ḫpṯ.d bl.spr. | ṯnn.d bl.hg. | hlk.l alpm.ḫ 14[KRT].2.88
[--]. | [ṯpṭ].nhr.tlʿm.ṯm.ḥrbm.its.anšq. | [-]htm.l arṣ.ypl.ul ny.w l.ʿpr.ʿẓm ny. | l bʿl[-.---]. | tḥt.ksi.zbl.ym.w ʿn.kṯr.w ḫ 2.4[68].5

ulb

m[š]t. | bn.unp.arbʿt. | ʿbdbn.ytrš ḫmšt. | krwn.ʿšrt. | bn.ulb ḫmšt. | bn.ḥry.ḫmšt. | swn.ḫmšt. | bn.[-]r[-.]ḫmšt. | bn.ḥdṯ. 1062.13
ilṣdq.bn.zry. | bʿlytn.bn.ulb. | ytrʿm.bn.swy. | ṣḥrn.bn.qrtm. | bn.špš.bn.ibrd. | ʿpṯrm.b 2024.2

ulbtyn

tm.ksp.ʿmn.b[n].ṣdqn. | w.kkrm.ṯlṯ. | mit.ksp.ʿmn. | bn.ulbtyn. | w.kkr.ṯlṯ. | ksp.d.nkly.b.šd. | mit.ḫmšt.kbd. | [l.]gmn. 1143.4

uldy

bg. | bn.nǵry. | bn.srwd. | mtnn. | bn gš[-]. | bn gbrn. | bn uldy. | synn.bn knʿm. | bn kbr. | bn iytlm. | bn ayln. | bn.kln. | b 1064.18

ull

[---.ṣ]mdm[.---]. | [ul]l.aḥdm.w[.---]. | [mʿq]b.aḥdm.w[.---]. | [ʿr]gz.ṯlṯ.ṣmd[m.---] 1179.2
| qmnz.ṯṯ.krm.yknʿm.ṯmn.krm[.---]. | krm.nʿmn.b.ḫly.ull.krm.aḫ[d.---]. | krm.uḫn.b.šdmy.ṯlṯ.bzl[.d]prn[.---]. | aupṯ 1081.12
y. | ṯlrby. | dmt. | aǵt. | w.qmnz. | slḫ. | yknʿm. | šlmy. | w.ull. | ṯmry. | qrt. | ʿrm. | nnu. | [--]. | [---]. | mʿr. | arny. | ubrʿy. | ilš 71[113].19

ully

š.bn.grbn.b.ṯqlm. | [--.lb]š.bn.sgryn.b[.ṯ]qlm. | [---.]bn.ully.b.ṯ[qlm]. | [---.]bn.annḏy.b[.---]. | [---.]bn.pd[--.---]. 135[330].5
--]n.bn.agyn. | [--]ṯn. | [--]ṯn.bn.aḏmṯn. | [-]ṯn bn.agyn. | ullym.bn.abynm. | antn.bn.iwr[n]r. | pwn.ṯmry. | ksyn.bn.lḫs 94[313].6
--]. | [m]d.m[--]. | [b]n.annḏ[r]. | bn.ṯḏyy. | bn.grbn. | [--.]ully. | [--]ṯiy. 1054.2.5

ulm

ṯn.b gt.mzln. | ṯn.b ulm. | abmn.b gt.mʿrb. | atn. | ḫryn. | bn.ʿnt. | llwn. | agdṯb. | aǵl 1061.2
spr.rpš d l y[dy]. | atlg. | ulm. | izly. | uḫnp. | bn sḫrn. | mʿqb. | ṯpn. | mʿr. | lbnm. | nḫl. | yʿ 2075.3
| bn.tran.mḏrǵl | bn.ilh.mḏrǵl | špšyn.b.ulm. | bn.qṯn.b.ulm. | bn.gdrn.b.mʿr[by]. | [w].bn.dʿm[-]. | bn.ppṯ.b[--]. | b[n.-- 2046.1.6
bn.qrrn.mḏrǵl. | bn.tran.mḏrǵl | bn.ilh.mḏrǵl | špšyn.b.ulm. | bn.qṯn.b.ulm. | bn.gdrn.b.mʿr[by]. | [w].bn.dʿm[-]. | bn. 2046.1.5
l.ṭb. | b.gt.mʿrby. | ṯṯm.yn.ṭb.w.ḫmš.l.ʿšrm. | yn.d.l.ṭb.b.ulm. | mit.yn.ṭb.w.ṯṯm.ṯṯ.kbd. | yn.d.l.ṭb.b.gt.ḥḏṯt. | tšʿm.yn.d. 1084.10
ap. | pd. | mlk. | ar. | atlg. | gbʿly. | ulm. | mʿrby. | mʿr. | arny. | šʿrt. | ḫlbrpš. | hry. | qmṣ. | ṣʿq. | qmy. 2074.7
[u]lm. | mṯpṯ.ṯt.qštm.w.ṯn.q[l]ʿm. | kmrṯn.ṯt.qštm.ṯn.[q]lʿm. | ǵ 119[321].1.1
b.ar. | ṣbr.aḥd. | b.mlk. | ṣbr.aḥd. | b.mʿrby. | ṣbr.aḥd. | b.ulm. | ṣbr.aḥd. | b.ubrʿy. 2073.10
ṯ. | ar.ṯmn ʿšr h. | mlk.arbʿ. | ǵbl.ḫmš. | atlg.ḫmš ʿšr[h]. | ulm ṯ[ṯ]. | mʿrby.ḫmš. | ṯbq.arbʿ. | tkm[.---]. | uḫnp[.---]. | ušk[n 68[65].1.9
. | mḫrhn.nit.mit.krk.mit. | mʿṣd.ḫmšm.mqb.[ʿ]šrm. | b.ulm.ṯṯ.ʿšr h.ḫrmṯt. | ṯt.nitm.ṯn.mʿṣdm.ṯn.mqbm. | krk.aḥt. | b. 2048.4
[---.]gtn ṯṯ. | [---.]ṯḥr l ytn ḫs[n]. | ʿbd ulm ṯn un ḫsn. | gdy lqḥ ṣtqn gt bn ndr. | um r[-] gtn ṯṯ ḫsn l 1154.3
]š.bnšm. | atlg.ḥmr[.---.]bnšm. | gbʿly.ḥmr š[--.b]nšm. | ulm.ṯn.[---.]bnšm. | mʿrby.[---.--]m.ṯn[.---]. | mʿr.[---]. | arny.[- 2040.7
šw[.i]ryn.arr. | [š]dm.b.mlk. | [--.š]dm.b.ar. | [--.š]dm.b.ulm. | [--.š]dm.b.mʿrby. | [--.šd]m.b.uškn. | [---.--]n. | [---].tlmd 2033.1.4
[---.b] d.ʿbdḫmn. | [---.b] d.ṯbq. | [---.b] d.šbn. | [---.b] d.ulm. | [---.b] d.ǵbl. | [---.b] d.ʿbdkṯr. | [---.b] d.urǵnr. 1052.6
-]. | ubr[ʿy.---]. | ar[.---]. | mlk[.---]. | ǵbl[.---]. | atl[g.---]. | u[lm.---]. | m[ʿrby.---]. | ṯ[bq.---]. 68[65].2.9
yn.w š. | spr.m[--]. | spr d[---]b.w š. | tt.ḫmš.[---]. | skn.ul[m.---]. | [---]š.[---]. | [---]y[.---]. | sk[n.---]. | u[---.]w š. | [---].w 1093.6
šm[-.---]. | tkn[.---]. | knn.b.ḫ[lb]. | bn mṯ.b.qmy. | nʿr.b.ulm. 2046.2.6

ulmy

sw.qšt. | knn.qšt. | bn.ṯlln.qšt. | bn.šyn.qšt. | ʿbd.qšt. | bn.ulmy.qšt. | ṯqbn.qšt. | bn.qnmlk.qšt. | ytḥm.qšt. | grp.qšt. | mʿr 104[316].5
ṯṯb. | kṯ[r]n. | w.aṯt h.w.nʿr h. | bn.ḫby.w.[a]ṯt h. | ynḥm.ulmy. | [--]q.w.aṯt h.w.bn h. | [--]an.w.aṯt h. | [--]y.w.aṯt h. | [-- 2068.5

ulmk

b. | aǵltn. | [-]wn. | bldn. | [-]ln. | [-]ldn. | [i]wryn. | ḫbsn. | ulmk. | ʿdršp. | bn.knn. | pdyn. | bn.aṯtl.ṯn. | kdln.akdṯb. | ṯn.b g 1061.16

ulmn

lkt.ʿrbm m.ṯnnm. | mt.w šr.yṯb.b d h.ḫṭ.ṯkl.b d h. | ḫṭ.ulmn.yzbrnn.zbrm.gpn. | yṣmdnn.ṣmdm.gpn.yšql.šdmt h. | k 23[52].9

uln

ṭ.qšt. | ilṯḥm.qšt.w.qlʿ. | ṣdqm.qšt.w.qlʿ. | uln.qšt.w.qlʿ. | uln.qšt. | bn.blẓn.qšt.w.qlʿ. | gbʿ.qšt.w.qlʿ. | nṣsn.qšt. | mʿr. | [ʿ] 119[321].2.8
. | ilgn.qšt. | abršp.qšt. | ssg.qšt. | ynḥm.qšt. | pprn.qšt. | uln.qšt. | bn.nkl qšt. | ady.qšt. | bn.srn.qšt. | bn.gdrn.qšt. | prpr. 105[86].4
| ḥdṯn.qlʿ. | ytpṭ.qšt. | ilṯḥm.qšt.w.qlʿ. | ṣdqm.qšt.w.qlʿ. | uln.qšt.w.qlʿ. | uln.qšt. | bn.blẓn.qšt.w.qlʿ. | gbʿ.qšt.w.qlʿ. | nṣṣ 119[321].2.7
| [ʿ]dyn.ṯt.qštm.w.qlʿ. | [-]lrš.qšt.w.qlʿ. | ṯ[ṯ]n.qšt.w.qlʿ. | u[l]n.qšt.w.qlʿ. | yʿrn.qšt.w.qlʿ. | klby.qšt.w.qlʿ. | bqʿt. | ily.qšt. 119[321].2.17

ulnhr

bn.nṣ. | [b]n.ʿṣr. | [---]m. | [bn.]ulnhr. | [bn.p]rn. | [bn.a]nny. | [---]n. | bn.kbln. | bn.pdy. | bn.ṯp 1075.1.4

ulp

. | [---.ušn.yp kn.ulp.q]ṭy. | [ulp.ddmy.ulp.ḫry.ulp.ḫty.ulp.alṯy]. | [ulp.ǵbr.ulp.ḫbt kn.ulp.mdll kn.ulp.]qr zbl. | [ušn. APP.I[-].2.13
. | [---.ušn.yp km.ulp.]qṭy. | [ulp.ddmy.ulp.ḫry.ulp.ḫty.u]lp.alṯy. | [ulp.ǵbr.ulp.ḫbt km.ulp.mdll km.ulp]. | [qr zbl.uš APP.I[-].1.15
dgl. | [ušn.yp kn.ulp.qṭy.ulp.]ddmy.ulp ḫry. | [ulp.ḫty.ulp.alṯy.ulp.ǵbr.ul]p.ḫbt kn. | [ulp.mdll kn.ulp.qr zbl.ušn.y] APP.I[-].1.5

ulp

md.ušn.yp km.ulp.q[ṭy.ulp.ddm]y. | ulp.ḫry.ulp.ḫ[t]y.ulp.alṯy.ul[p.ǵbr.]ulp. | ḫbt km.ulp.m[dl]l km.ulp.qr zbl.u[š] 32[2].1.21
]y.nṯt.ušn.yp kn.ulp qṭy. | ulp.ddmy.ul[p.ḫ]ry.ulp.ḫty.ulp.alṯy. | ulp.ǵbr.ulp.[ḫbt] kn[.u]lp.mdll kn.ulp qr z[bl]. | lš 32[2].1.29
ugrt. | [---.u ṯḫṭu.ulp.qṭy.ulp.ddm]y. | [ulp.ḫry.ulp.ḫty.ulp.alṯy.ulp.ǵbr]. | [ulp.ḫbt km.ulp.mdll km.ulp.qr zbl]. | [u t 32[2].1.7
[py.---].u ṯḫṭi[n.ulp.qṭy]. | ulp.ddmy.ul[p.ḫry.u]lp.ḫty.ulp[.alṯy.ulp.]ǵbr. | ulp.ḫbt kn.ulp.md[ll k]n.ulp.q[r zbl]. | u t 32[2].1.12
npy.---.]w npy. | [---.w np]y.ugrt. | [---.u ṯḫṭu.ulp.qṭy.ulp.ddm]y. | [ulp.ḫry.ulp.ḫty.ulp.alṯy.ulp.ǵbr]. | [ulp.ḫbt km. 32[2].1.6
ḥmyt.ugrt.w np]y. | [---].w n[py.---].u ṯḫṭi[n.ulp.qṭy]. | ulp.ddmy.ul[p.ḫry.u]lp.ḫty.ulp[.alṯy.ulp.]ǵbr. | ulp.ḫbt kn.ul 32[2].1.12
.w npy.gr. | ḥmyt.ugrt.w [np]y.nṯt.ušn.yp kn.ulp qṭy. | ulp.ddmy.ul[p.ḫ]ry.ulp.ḫty.ulp.alṯy. | ulp.ǵbr.ulp.[ḫbt] kn[.u 32[2].1.29
py.ʿrmt.w npy.[---]. | w npy.nqmd.ušn.yp km.ulp.q[ṭy.ulp.ddm]y. | ulp.ḫry.ulp.ḫ[t]y.ulp.alṯy.ul[p.ǵbr.]ulp. | ḫbt km 32[2].1.20
| [w npy.ʿrmt.---.w]npy.annpdgl. | [ušn.yp kn.ulp.qṭy.ulp.]ddmy.ulp ḫry. | [ulp.ḫty.ulp.alṯy.ulp.ǵbr.ul]p.ḫbt kn. | [APP.I[-].1.4
.yman.w npy.ʿr]mt.w npy. | [---.ušn.yp km.ulp.]qṭy. | [ulp.ddmy.ulp.ḫry.ulp.ḫty.u]lp.alṯy. | [ulp.ǵbr.ulp.ḫbt km.ul APP.I[-].1.15
]. | [-----]. | [---.--]r. | [---.]npy. | [---.ušn.yp kn.ulp.q]ṭy. | [ulp.ddmy.ulp.ḫry.ulp.ḫty.ulp.alṯy]. | [ulp.ǵbr.ulp.ḫbt kn.ulp APP.I[-].2.13
.ddmy.ulp.ḫry.ulp.ḫty.u]lp.alṯy. | [ulp.ǵbr.ulp.ḫbt km.ulp.mdll km.ulp]. | [qr zbl.ušn.yp km.b ap km.u b qṣrt.np]št APP.I[-].1.16
m]y. | [ulp.ḫry.ulp.ḫty.ulp.alṯy.ulp.ǵbr]. | [ulp.ḫbt km.ulp.mdll km.ulp.qr zbl]. | [u ṯḫṭu.u b ap km.u b qṣrt.npš km 32[2].1.8
]y. | ulp.ḫry.ulp.ḫ[t]y.ulp.alṯy.ul[p.ǵbr.]ulp. | ḫbt km.ulp.m[dl]l km.ulp.qr zbl.u[š]n yp km. | u b ap km.u b q[ṣ]rt. 32[2].1.22
dmy.ul[p.ḫry.u]lp.ḫty.ulp[.alṯy.ulp.]ǵbr. | ulp.ḫbt kn.ulp.md[ll k]n.ulp.q[r zbl]. | u ṯḫṭin.b ap kn.u b [q]ṣrt.npš[k 32[2].1.13
dmy.ulp ḫry. | [ulp.ḫty.ulp.alṯy.ulp.ǵbr.ul]p.ḫbt kn. | [ulp.mdll kn.ulp.qr zbl.ušn.y]p kn. | [u b ap kn.u b qṣrt.npšt APP.I[-].1.6
.ddmy.ulp.ḫry.ulp.ḫty.ulp.alṯy]. | [ulp.ǵbr.ulp.ḫbt kn.ulp.mdll kn.ulp.]qr zbl. | [ušn.yp kn.u b ap kn.u b qṣrt.npš k APP.I[-].2.14
dmy.ul[p.ḫ]ry.ulp.ḫty.ulp.alṯy. | ulp.ǵbr.ulp.[ḫbt] kn[.u]lp.mdll kn.ulp qr z[bl]. | lšn yp kn.b ap [kn.u b qṣ]rt.npš k 32[2].1.30
p.qṭy.ulp.ddm]y. | [ulp.ḫry.ulp.ḫty.ulp.alṯy.ulp.ǵbr]. | [ulp.ḫbt km.ulp.mdll km.ulp.qr zbl]. | [u ṯḫṭu.u b ap km.u b 32[2].1.8
.q[ṭy.ulp.ddm]y. | ulp.ḫry.ulp.ḫ[t]y.ulp.alṯy.ul[p.ǵbr.]ulp. | ḫbt km.ulp.m[dl]l km.ulp.qr zbl.u[š]n yp km. | u b ap 32[2].1.21
p.]qṭy. | [ulp.ddmy.ulp.ḫry.ulp.ḫty.u]lp.alṯy. | [ulp.ǵbr.ulp.ḫbt km.ulp.mdll km.ulp]. | [qr zbl.ušn.yp km.b ap km.u APP.I[-].1.16
.ulp.qṭy.ulp.]ddmy.ulp ḫry. | [ulp.ḫty.ulp.alṯy.ulp.ǵbr.ul]p.ḫbt kn. | [ulp.mdll kn.ulp.qr zbl.ušn.y]p kn. | [u b ap kn APP.I[-].1.5
p.q]ṭy. | [ulp.ddmy.ulp.ḫry.ulp.ḫty.ulp.alṯy]. | [ulp.ǵbr.ulp.ḫbt kn.ulp.mdll kn.ulp.]qr zbl. | [ušn.yp kn.u b ap kn.u APP.I[-].2.14
lp qṭy. | ulp.ddmy.ul[p.ḫ]ry.ulp.ḫty.ulp.alṯy. | ulp.ǵbr.ulp.[ḫbt] kn[.u]lp.mdll kn.ulp qr z[bl]. | lšn yp kn.b ap [kn.u 32[2].1.30
.qṭy]. | ulp.ddmy.ul[p.ḫry.u]lp.ḫty.ulp[.alṯy.ulp.]ǵbr. | ulp.ḫbt kn.ulp.md[ll k]n.ulp.q[r zbl]. | u ṯḫṭin.b ap kn.u b [q 32[2].1.13
| ḥmyt.ugrt.w [np]y.nṯt.ušn.yp kn.ulp qṭy. | ulp.ddmy.ul[p.ḫ]ry.ulp.ḫty.ulp.alṯy. | ulp.ǵbr.ulp.[ḫbt] kn[.u]lp.mdll k 32[2].1.29
y.[---]. | w npy.nqmd.ušn.yp km.ulp.q[ṭy.ulp.ddm]y. | ulp.ḫry.ulp.ḫ[t]y.ulp.alṯy.ul[p.ǵbr.]ulp. | ḫbt km.ulp.m[dl]l 32[2].1.21
.w np]y. | [---].w n[py.---].u ṯḫṭi[n.ulp.qṭy]. | ulp.ddmy.ul[p.ḫry.u]lp.ḫty.ulp[.alṯy.ulp.]ǵbr. | ulp.ḫbt kn.ulp.md[ll k] 32[2].1.12
py. | [---.w np]y.ugrt. | [---.u ṯḫṭu.ulp.qṭy.ulp.ddm]y. | [ulp.ḫry.ulp.ḫty.ulp.alṯy.ulp.ǵbr]. | [ulp.ḫbt km.ulp.mdll km. 32[2].1.7
py.ʿr]mt.w npy. | [---.ušn.yp km.ulp.]qṭy. | [ulp.ddmy.ulp.ḫry.ulp.ḫty.u]lp.alṯy. | [ulp.ǵbr.ulp.ḫbt km.ulp.mdll km. APP.I[-].1.15
---.--]r. | [---.]npy. | [---.ušn.yp kn.ulp.q]ṭy. | [ulp.ddmy.ulp.ḫry.ulp.ḫty.ulp.alṯy]. | [ulp.ǵbr.ulp.ḫbt kn.ulp.mdll kn.u APP.I[-].2.13
t.---.w]npy.annpdgl. | [ušn.yp kn.ulp.qṭy.ulp.]ddmy.ulp ḫry. | [ulp.ḫty.ulp.alṯy.ulp.ǵbr.ul]p.ḫbt kn. | [ulp.mdll kn APP.I[-].1.4
py.annpdgl. | [ušn.yp kn.ulp.qṭy.ulp.]ddmy.ulp ḫry. | [ulp.ḫty.ulp.alṯy.ulp.ǵbr.ul]p.ḫbt kn. | [ulp.mdll kn.ulp.qr zb APP.I[-].1.5
[---.]npy. | [---.ušn.yp kn.ulp.q]ṭy. | [ulp.ddmy.ulp.ḫry.ulp.ḫty.ulp.alṯy]. | [ulp.ǵbr.ulp.ḫbt kn.ulp.mdll kn.ulp.]qr z APP.I[-].2.13
t.w npy. | [---.ušn.yp km.ulp.]qṭy. | [ulp.ddmy.ulp.ḫry.ulp.ḫty.u]lp.alṯy. | [ulp.ǵbr.ulp.ḫbt km.ulp.mdll km.ulp]. | [q APP.I[-].1.15
w npy.nqmd.ušn.yp km.ulp.q[ṭy.ulp.ddm]y. | ulp.ḫry.ulp.ḫ[t]y.ulp.alṯy.ul[p.ǵbr.]ulp. | ḫbt km.ulp.m[dl]l km.ulp. 32[2].1.21
[---].w n[py.---].u ṯḫṭi[n.ulp.qṭy]. | ulp.ddmy.ul[p.ḫry.u]lp.ḫty.ulp[.alṯy.ulp.]ǵbr. | ulp.ḫbt kn.ulp.md[ll k]n.ulp.q[r 32[2].1.12
.w np]y.ugrt. | [---.u ṯḫṭu.ulp.qṭy.ulp.ddm]y. | [ulp.ḫry.ulp.ḫty.ulp.alṯy.ulp.ǵbr]. | [ulp.ḫbt km.ulp.mdll km.ulp.qr z 32[2].1.7
rt.w [np]y.nṯt.ušn.yp kn.ulp qṭy. | ulp.ddmy.ul[p.ḫ]ry.ulp.ḫty.ulp.alṯy. | ulp.ǵbr.ulp.[ḫbt] kn[.u]lp.mdll kn.ulp qr z 32[2].1.29
-.u ṯḫṭu.ulp.qṭy.ulp.ddm]y. | [ulp.ḫry.ulp.ḫty.ulp.alṯy.ulp.ǵbr]. | [ulp.ḫbt km.ulp.mdll km.ulp.qr zbl]. | [u ṯḫṭu.u b 32[2].1.7
yp km.ulp.q[ṭy.ulp.ddm]y. | ulp.ḫry.ulp.ḫ[t]y.ulp.alṯy.ul[p.ǵbr.]ulp. | ḫbt km.ulp.m[dl]l km.ulp.qr zbl.u[š]n yp km 32[2].1.21
p km.ulp.]qṭy. | [ulp.ddmy.ulp.ḫry.ulp.ḫty.u]lp.alṯy. | [ulp.ǵbr.ulp.ḫbt km.ulp.mdll km.ulp]. | [qr zbl.ušn.yp km.b APP.I[-].1.16
n.yp kn.ulp.qṭy.ulp.]ddmy.ulp ḫry. | [ulp.ḫty.ulp.alṯy.ulp.ǵbr.ul]p.ḫbt kn. | [ulp.mdll kn.ulp.qr zbl.ušn.y]p kn. | [u APP.I[-].1.5
p kn.ulp.q]ṭy. | [ulp.ddmy.ulp.ḫry.ulp.ḫty.ulp.alṯy]. | [ulp.ǵbr.ulp.ḫbt kn.ulp.mdll kn.ulp.]qr zbl. | [ušn.yp kn.u b APP.I[-].2.14
.yp kn.ulp qṭy. | ulp.ddmy.ul[p.ḫ]ry.ulp.ḫty.ulp.alṯy. | ulp.ǵbr.ulp.[ḫbt] kn[.u]lp.mdll kn.ulp qr z[bl]. | lšn yp kn.b 32[2].1.30
ṯḫṭi[n.ulp.qṭy]. | ulp.ddmy.ul[p.ḫry.u]lp.ḫty.ulp[.alṯy.ulp.]ǵbr. | ulp.ḫbt kn.ulp.md[ll k]n.ulp.q[r zbl]. | u ṯḫṭin.b ap 32[2].1.12
r.bt.ugrt.w npy.gr. | ḥmyt.ugrt.w [np]y.nṯt.ušn.yp kn.ulp qṭy. | ulp.ddmy.ul[p.ḫ]ry.ulp.ḫty.ulp.alṯy. | ulp.ǵbr.ulp.[32[2].1.28
n.ugrt.w npy.---.]w npy. | [---.w np]y.ugrt. | [---.u ṯḫṭu.ulp.qṭy.ulp.ddm]y. | [ulp.ḫry.ulp.ḫty.ulp.alṯy.ulp.ǵbr]. | [ulp. 32[2].1.6
an.w npy.ʿrmt.w npy.[---]. | w npy.nqmd.ušn.yp km.ulp.q[ṭy.ulp.ddm]y. | ulp.ḫry.ulp.ḫ[t]y.ulp.alṯy.ul[p.ǵbr.]ulp 32[2].1.20
n]py.gr[.ḥmyt.ugrt.w np]y. | [---].w n[py.---].u ṯḫṭi[n.ulp.qṭy]. | ulp.ddmy.ul[p.ḫry.u]lp.ḫty.ulp[.alṯy.ulp.]ǵbr. | ulp 32[2].1.11
y.yman. | [w npy.ʿrmt.---.w]npy.annpdgl. | [ušn.yp kn.ulp.qṭy.ulp.]ddmy.ulp ḫry. | [ulp.ḫty.ulp.alṯy.ulp.ǵbr.ul]p.ḫ APP.I[-].1.4
ugrt.w npy.yman.w npy.ʿr]mt.w npy. | [---.ušn.yp km.ulp.]qṭy. | [ulp.ddmy.ulp.ḫry.ulp.ḫty.u]lp.alṯy. | [ulp.ǵbr.ulp. APP.I[-].1.14
r bʿl. | [-----]. | [-----]. | [---.--]r. | [---.]npy. | [---.ušn.yp kn.ulp.q]ṭy. | [ulp.ddmy.ulp.ḫry.ulp.ḫty.ulp.alṯy]. | [ulp.ǵbr.ulp. APP.I[-].2.12
y.ulp.ḫty.ulp.alṯy.ulp.ǵbr]. | [ulp.ḫbt km.ulp.mdll km.ulp.qr zbl]. | [u ṯḫṭu.u b ap km.u b qṣrt.npš km.u b qṭt]. | [tq 32[2].1.8
.u]lp.ḫty.ulp[.alṯy.ulp.]ǵbr. | ulp.ḫbt kn.ulp.md[ll k]n.ulp.q[r zbl]. | u ṯḫṭin.b ap kn.u b [q]ṣrt.npš[kn.u b qṭt]. | tqṭṭ 32[2].1.13
lp.ḫ[t]y.ulp.alṯy.ul[p.ǵbr.]ulp. | ḫbt km.ulp.m[dl]l km.ulp.qr zbl.u[š]n yp km. | u b ap km.u b q[ṣ]rt.npš km.u b qṭt 32[2].1.22
y.ulp.ḫty.u]lp.alṯy. | [ulp.ǵbr.ulp.ḫbt km.ulp.mdll km.ulp]. | [qr zbl.ušn.yp km.b ap km.u b qṣrt.np]št km. | [u b qṭt APP.I[-].1.16
. | [ulp.ḫty.ulp.alṯy.ulp.ǵbr.ul]p.ḫbt kn. | [ulp.mdll kn.ulp.qr zbl.ušn.y]p kn. | [u b ap kn.u b qṣrt.npšt kn.u b qṭ]t t APP.I[-].1.6
ry.ulp.ḫty.ulp.alṯy]. | [ulp.ǵbr.ulp.ḫbt kn.ulp.mdll kn.ulp.]qr zbl. | [ušn.yp kn.u b ap kn.u b qṣrt.npš kn.u b]qṭt. | [APP.I[-].2.14
y.ulp.ḫty.ulp.alṯy. | ulp.ǵbr.ulp.[ḫbt] kn[.u]lp.mdll kn.ulp qr z[bl]. | lšn yp kn.b ap [kn.u b qṣ]rt.npš kn.u b qṭt. | tqṭ 32[2].1.30
n ʿ[r]. | [---.]w npy[.---]. | [---.]w npy.u[grt.---]. | [---.--]y.ulp.[---]. | [---.]ǵbr.u[lp.---]. | [---.--]n[.---]. 32[2].2.3
.---]. | [---.]w npy.u[grt.---]. | [---.--]y.ulp.[---]. | [---.]ǵbr.u[lp.---]. | [---.--]n[.---]. 32[2].2.4

ulpm

----]. | bn.‘dy. | w.nḥl h. | bn.‘bl. | bn.[-]rṯn. | bn[.---]. | bn u[l]pm. | bn ‘[p]ty. | bn.kdgdl. | bn.smyy. | bn.lbn. | bn.šlmn. | b 2163.3.2

ulšn

dn.qšt. | bn.pls.qšt. | ǵmrm. | [-]lhd.ṯt.qštm.w.ṯn.ql‘m. | ulšn.ṯt.qšm.w.ql‘. | bn.ml‘n.qšt.w.ql‘. | bn.tmy.qšt.w.ql‘. | ‘ky. 119[321].3.34

ulṯ

| w y‘n lṭpn il d pid. | p ‘bd.an.‘nn.aṯrt. | p.‘bd.ank.aḫd.ulṯ. | hm.amt.aṯrt.tlbn. | lbnt.yḇn.bt.l b‘l. | km ilm.w ḥẓr.k bn 4[51].4.60

tlg[.---]. | ḫmš ‘š[r]. | kkr.ṯ[lṯ]. | ṯt hrt[m]. | ṯn mq[pm]. | ulṯ.ṯl[ṯ]. | krk.kly[.--]. | ḫmš.mr[kbt]. | ṯṯ [-]az[-]. | ‘šṯ[--.---]. | ir 2056.7

um

n. | hl h.[t]špl.hl h.trm.hl h.tṣḥ.ad ad. | w hl h.tṣḥ.um.um.tirk m.yd.il.k ym. | w yd il.k mdb.ark.yd.il.k ym. | w yd.i 23[52].33

ak k. | [---.--]g k.yritn.mǵy.hy.w kn. | [---].ḥln.d b.dmt.um.il[m.---]. | [--]ḏyn.b‘d.[--]ḏyn.w l. | [--]k b‘lt bhtm[.--]tn k 1002.43

iš.agn. | hl h.[t]špl.hl h.trm.hl h.tṣḥ.ad ad. | w hl h.tṣḥ.um.um.tirk m.yd.il.k ym. | w yd il.k mdb.ark.yd.il.k ym. | w 23[52].33

nkl ḫtn y.a[ḫ]r. | nkl yrḫ ytrḫ.adn h. | yšt mṣb.mznm.um h. | kp mznm.iḫ h yṯ‘r. | mšrrm.aḫt h l a | bn mznm.nkl 24[77].34

um.pḫl.pḫlt.bt.abn.bt šmm w thm. | qrit.l špš.um h.špš.um.ql.bl.‘m. | il.mbk nhrm.b ‘dt.thmtm. | mnt.nṯk. UG5.7.2

ṯq ytqšqy.nḥš.yšlḥm.‘q šr. | y‘db.ksa.w.yṯb. | tqru.l špš.um h.špš.um.ql bl. | ‘m b‘l.mrym.ṣpn.mnt y.nṯk. | nḥš.šmrr.n UG5.7.8

.ytq. | nḥš.yšlḥm.nḥš.‘q šr.ydb.ksa. | w yṯb. | tqru.l špš.u h.špš.um.ql.bl.‘m. | dgn.ttl h.mnt.nṯk.nḥš.šmrr. | nḥš.‘q šr.l UG5.7.14

šqy. | nḥš.yšlḥm.nḥš.‘q šr.y‘db. | ksa.w yṯb. | tqru l špš.um h.špš.um.ql bl. | ‘m ḥrn.mṣd h.mnt.nṯk nḥš. | šmrr.nḥš.‘q UG5.7.57

m.ytq.nḥš.yšlḥm.nḥš ‘q. | š.y‘db.ksa w yṯb. | tqru l špš.um h.špš.um.ql bl ‘m. | ṯṯ.w kmṯ.ḥryt h.mnt.nṯk.nḥš.šm | rr. UG5.7.35

.ml | ḫš.abd.ln h.ydy.ḥmt.hlm.ytq. | w yṯb. | tqru.l špš.um h.špš.[um.q]l bl.‘m. | yrḫ.lrgt h.mnt.nṯk.n[ḥš].šmrr. | nḥš UG5.7.25

.ytq nḥš yšlḥm.nḥš. | ‘q.šr.y‘db.ksa.w yṯb. | tqru l špš um h.špš um ql.bl.‘m. | mlk.‘ṯtrt h.mnt.nṯk.nḥš.šmrr. | nḥš.‘q UG5.7.40

.ytq.nḥš.yšlḥm. | nḥš.‘q šr.y‘db.ksa.w yṯb. | tqru l špš.um h.špš.um.ql.bl.‘m. | ‘nt w ‘ṯtrt inbb h.mnt.nṯk. | nḥš.šlḥm UG5.7.19

.ytq.nḥš.yšlḥm.nḥš. | ‘q šr.y‘db.ksa.w yṯb. | tqru.l špš.um h.špš.um.ql b.‘m. | ršp.bbt h.mnt.nḥš.šmrr. | nḥš.‘q šr.ln UG5.7.30

ytq.nḥš. | yšlḥm.nḥš.‘q šr.y‘db ksa. | w yṯb. | tqru l špš.um h.špš.um.ql bl ‘m. | šḥr.w šlm šmm h mnt.nṯk.nḥš. | šmrr UG5.7.51

ṯṯkr.[--]dn. | ‘m.krt.mswn h. | arḫ.tzǵ.l ‘gl h. | bn.ḫpṯ.l umht hm. | k tnḥn.udmm. | w y‘ny.krt.ṯ‘. 15[128].1.6

l um y.adt ny. | rgm. | tḥm.tlmyn. | w.aḫtmlk ‘bd k. | l.p‘n.adt 51[95].1

hm.ḫt. | ‘l.w.likt. | ‘m k.w.hm. | l.‘l.w.lakm. | ilak.w.at. | um y.al.tdḥṣ. | w.ap.mhkm. | b.lb k.al. | tšt. 1013.21

yn]. | l ṯryl.um y. | rgm. | ugrt.tǵr k. | ugrt.tǵr k. | tšlm k.um y. | td‘.ky.‘rbt. | l pn.špš. | w pn.špš.nr. | b y.mid.w um. | tš 1015.6

ṣrrt. | ṣpn.yšu g h.w yṣḥ. | aḫ y m.ytnt.b‘l. | spu y.bn m.um y.kl | y y.yt‘n.k gmrm. | mt.‘z.b‘l.‘z.ynghn. | k rumm.mt.‘ 6[49].6.15

. | [---].bn.ilm.mt. | p[-]n.aḫ y m.ytn.b‘l. | [s]pu y.bn m.um y.kly y. | yṯb.‘m.b‘l.ṣrrt. | ṣpn.yšu g h.w yṣḥ. | aḫ y m.ytnt 6[49].6.11

ǵ[r] k.tš[lm] k. | [h]l ny.‘m n[.š]lm. | w.ṯm [ny.‘m.mlkt.u]m y. | mnm[.šlm]. | w.rgm[.ṯṯb.l] y. | hl ny.‘mn. | mlk.b.ṯy n 1013.9

lm.k.lik[t]. | um y.‘m y.ht.‘m[ny]. | kll.šlm.ṯm ny. | ‘m.um y.mnm.šlm. | w.rgm.ṯṯb.l y. | w.mnd‘.k.ank. | aḫš.mǵy.m 2009.1.8

.ilm. | tǵr k.tšlm k. | hl ny.‘m n[y]. | kll.šlm. | ṯm ny.‘m.um y. | mnm.šlm. | w.rgm.ṯṯb.l y. | bm.ṯy.ndr. | iṯ.‘mn.mlkt. | 50[117].11

y.rgm. | yšlm.l k.ilm. | tǵr k.tšlm k. | lḥt.šlm.k.lik[t]. | um y.‘m y.ht.‘m[ny]. | kll.šlm.ṯm ny. | ‘m.um y.mnm.šlm. | 2009.1.6

rḥln. | ‘tn.ḫrd.ank. | ‘m ny.šlm. | kll. | w mnm. | šlm ‘m. | um y. | ‘m y.tṯṯb. | rgm. 1015.18

l mlkt.u[m] y. | [rg]m[.]t[ḥm]. | mlk.bn [k]. | [l].p‘n.um [y]. | qlt[.l um] y. | yšlm.il[m]. | tǵ[r] k.tš[lm] k. | [h]l ny.‘ 1013.4

l.mlkt. | um y.rgm. | tḥm.mlk. | bn k. | l.p‘n.um y. | qlt.l.um y. | yšlm.ilm. | tǵr k.tšlm k. | hl ny.‘m n[y]. | kl 50[117].5

tḥm[.t]lm[yn]. | l ṯryl.um y. | rgm. | ugrt.tǵr k. | ugrt.tǵr k. | tšlm k.um y. | td‘.ky.‘rb 1015.2

tḥm.mlk. | l.ṯryl.um y.rgm. | yšlm.l k.ilm. | tǵr k.tšlm k. | lḥt.šlm.k.lik[t]. | um 2009.1.2

l mlkt.u[m] y. | [rg]m[.]t[ḥm]. | mlk.bn [k]. | [l].p‘n.um [y]. | qlt[.l u 1013.1

l.mlkt. | um y.rgm. | tḥm.mlk. | bn k. | l.p‘n.um y. | qlt.l.um y. | yšlm.il 50[117].2

l.mlkt. | um y.rgm. | tḥm.mlk. | bn k. | l.p‘n.um y. | qlt.l.um y. | yšlm.ilm. | tǵr k.tšlm k. | hl ny.‘m n[y]. | kll.šlm. | ṯm n 50[117].6

] y. | [rg]m[.]t[ḥm]. | mlk.bn [k]. | [l].p‘n.um [y]. | qlt[.l um] y. | yšlm.il[m]. | tǵ[r] k.tš[lm] k. | [h]l ny.‘m n[.š]lm. | w.ṯ 1013.5

knt. | aṯt.ṣdq h.l ypq. | mtrḫt.yšr h. | aṯt.trḫ.w tb‘t. | ṯar um.tkn l h. | mṯlṯt.kṯrm.tmt. | mrb‘t.zblnm. | mḫmšt.yitsp. | rš 14[KRT].1.15

mt. | [---.]rpat.bt. | [m]lk.itdb.d šb‘. | [a]ḫm.l h.ṯmnt.bn um. | krt.ḥtk n.rš. | krt.grdš.mknt. | aṯt.ṣdq h.l ypq. | mtrḫt.yš 14[KRT].1.9

y.hwt.hrg[b]. | tpr.w du.b nši.‘n h. | [w]yphn.yḥd.ṣml.um.nšrm. | yšu.g h.w yṣḥ.knp.ṣml. | b‘l.yṯbr.b‘l.yṯbr.diy. | hyt 19[1AQHT].3.135

um.pḫl.pḫlt.bt.abn.bt šmm w thm. | qrit.l špš.um h.špš.um. UG5.7.1

m.pḫl.pḫlt.bt.abn.bt šmm w thm. | qrit.l špš.um h.špš.um.ql.bl.‘m. | il.mbk nhrm.b ‘dt.thmtm. | mnt.nṯk.nḥš.šmrr. UG5.7.2

nḥš.yšlḥm.‘q šr. | y‘db.ksa.w.yṯb. | tqru.l špš.um h.špš.um.ql bl. | ‘m b‘l.mrym.ṣpn.mnt y.nṯk. | nḥš.šmrr.nḥš.‘q šr l UG5.7.8

ḥš.yšlḥm.nḥš.‘q šr.ydb.ksa. | w yṯb. | tqru.l špš.u h.špš.um.ql.bl.‘m. | dgn.ttl h.mnt.nṯk.nḥš.šmrr. | nḥš.‘q šr.ln h.ml UG5.7.14

yšlḥm.nḥš.‘q šr.y‘db. | ksa.w yṯb. | tqru l špš.um h.špš.um.ql bl. | ‘m ḥrn.mṣd h.mnt.nṯk nḥš. | šmrr.nḥš.‘q šr.ln h.m UG5.7.57

.yšlḥm.nḥš ‘q. | š.y‘db.ksa w yṯb. | tqru l špš.um h.špš.um.ql bl ‘m. | ṯṯ.w kmṯ.ḥryt h.mnt.nṯk.nḥš.šm | rr.nḥš.‘q šr.l UG5.7.35

d.ln h.ydy.ḥmt.hlm.ytq. | w yṯb. | tqru.l špš.um h.špš.[um.q]l bl.‘m. | yrḫ.lrgt h.mnt.nṯk.n[ḥš].šmrr. | nḥš.‘q šr.ln h. UG5.7.25

yšlḥm.nḥš. | ‘q.šr.y‘db.ksa.w yṯb. | tqru l špš um h.špš um ql.bl.‘m. | mlk.‘ṯtrt h.mnt.nṯk.nḥš.šmrr. | nḥš.‘q šr.ln h.m UG5.7.40

yšlḥm. | nḥš.‘q šr.y‘db.ksa.w yṯb. | tqru l špš.um h.špš.um.ql.bl.‘m. | ‘nt w ‘ṯtrt inbb h.mnt.nṯk. | nḥš.šlḥm.nḥš.‘q šr[UG5.7.19

yšlḥm.nḥš. | ‘q šr.y‘db.ksa.w yṯb. | tqru.l špš.um h.špš.um.ql b.‘m. | ršp.bbt h.mnt.nḥš.šmrr. | nḥš.‘q šr.ln h.mlḫš.ab UG5.7.30

yšlḥm.nḥš.‘q šr.y‘db ksa. | w yṯb. | tqru l špš.um h.špš.um.ql bl ‘m. | šḥr.w šlm šmm h mnt.nṯk.nḥš. | šmrr.nḥš ‘q šr UG5.7.51

.ytq.nḥš.yšlḥm.nḥš. | ‘q šr.y‘db.ksa.w yṯb. | tqru.l špš.um h.špš.um.ql bl.‘m | kṯr.w ḫss.kptr h.mnt.nṯk.nḥš. | šmrr.nḥš.‘q šr.l UG5.7.45

tn ḫs[n]. | ‘bd ulm ṯn un ḫsn. | gdy lqḥ šṭqn gt bn ndr. | um r[-] gtn ṯṯ ḫsn l ytn. | l rḥt lqḥ šṭqn. | bt qbṣ urt ilštm‘ db 1154.5

.um y. | td‘.ky.‘rbt. | l pn.špš. | w pn.špš.nr. | b y.mid.w um. | tšmḫ.m ab. | w al.trḥln. | ‘tn.ḫrd.ank. | ‘m ny.šlm. | kll. | 1015.10

umdy

t.ʿ[šr.---].|[t]lṯ.abd[.---].|[---.]anyt[.---].|[-----].|ʿšrm.l.umdym.|ʿšr.l.ktl. 2110.5

umẖ

.---].|ʿbdil.bn.[---].|ʿpṯn.bn.ṯṣq[-].|mnn.bn.krmn.|bn.umẖ.|yky.bn.slyn.|ypln.bn.ylḥn.|ʿzn.bn.mll.|šrm.|[b]n.šp 85[80].1.6

umy

dy.|agpṯr.|šbʿl.mlky.|nʿmn.mṣry.|yʿl.knʿny.|gdn.bn.umy.|knʿm.šʿrty.|abrpu.ubrʿy.|b.gt.bn.ṯlṯ.|ilḏ.b.gt.psḥn. 91[311].8

ummt

|[-----].|[---.-]l[-].|[bn.-]dt[-].|[bn.-]nn.|[bn.-]dn.|bn.ummt.|bn.ṯb[-].|bn.[-]r[-].|bn.tgn.|bn.iḏrn.|mnn.|b[n].sk 124[-].6.4

umt

kt.|tmrn.alk.nmr[rt].|imẖṣ.mẖṣ.aẖ y.akl[.m]|kly[.ʿ]l.umt y.w yʿn[.dn]|il.mt.rpi npš tḥ[.pǵt].|ṯ[km]t.mym.ḥspt.l 19[1AQHT].4.197
bʿl.arṣ.|w tʿn.nrt.ilm.š[p]š.|šd yn.ʿn.b qbt[.t]|bl lyt.ʿl.umt k.|w abqṯ.aliyn.bʿl.|w tʿn.btlt.ʿnt.|an.l an.y špš.|an.l a 6[49].4.43
.kbkbm.|a[-]ḥ.hy.mẖ.tmẖṣ.mẖṣ[.aẖ k].|tkl.m[k]ly.ʿl.umt[k.--].|d ttql.b ym.trtḥ[ṣ.--].|[----.a]dm.tium.b ǵlp y[m. 19[1AQHT].4.202
--]ẖdn.|[---.]bšr y.|[---.--]b.|[---.--]a h.|[---.--]d.|[---].umt n.|[---.--]yh.wn l.|[---].bt bʿl.|[---.--]y.|[---.--]nt. 28[-].10
[k.---].|[---]m.k[---].|[-----].|[---]m.il[.---].|[---]d nhr.umt.|[---.]rpat.bt.|[m]lk.itdb.d šbʿ.|[a]ẖm.l h.ṯmnt.bn um. 14[KRT].1.6

un

[---.]gtn ṯṯ.|[---.]tḥr l ytn ẖs[n].|ʿbd ulm ṯn un ẖsn.|gdy lqḥ ṣtqn gt bn ndr.|um r[-] gtn ṯṯ ẖsn l ytn.|l r 1154.3
.al.ǵzr.mt.hrnmy.|apnk.dnil.mt.|rpi.yṣly.ʿrpt.b |ḥm.un.yr.ʿrpt.|tmṭr.b qẓ.ṭl.yṭll.|l ǵnbm.šbʿ.šnt.|yṣr k.bʿl.ṯmn.r 19[1AQHT].1.40
id.yrd.l ksi.yṯb.|l hdm[.w] l.hdm.yṯb.|l arṣ.yṣq.ʿmr.|un.l riš h.ʿpr.plṯt.|l qdqd h.lpš.yks.|mizrtm.ǵr.b abn.|ydy. 5[67].6.15

unn

.lbn.ʿdn.|ẖyrn.mdʿ.|šmʿn.rb ʿšrt.kkln.ʿbd.abṣn.|šdyn.unn.dqn.|ʿbdʿnt.rb ʿšrt.mnḥm.ṯbʿm.sẖr.ʿzn.ilhd.|bnil.rb ʿšrt 2011.6

unp

.ẖmš[t].|abršn.ʿšr[t].|bʿln.ẖmšt.|w.nḥl h.ẖm[š]t.|bn.unp.arbʿt.|ʿbdbn.ytrš ẖmšt.|krwn.ʿšrt.|bn.ulb ẖmšt.|bn.ḥr 1062.10

unṯ

[-----].|w.[-----].|w.abǵl.nḥ[l h.--].|w.unṯ.aẖd.l h[.---].|dnn.bn.yṣr[.---].|sln.bn.ʿṯṯ[-.---].|pdy.bn.n 90[314].1.4
b d.|[ʿb]dmlk.|[-]k.am[ʿ--].|[w.b] d.bn h[.ʿ]d ʿlm.|[w.un]ṯ.in[n.]b h.|[---.]nʿm[-]. 1009.18
šm.|l.yqḥnn.b d.|bʿln.bn.kltn.|w.b d.bn h.ʿd.|ʿlm.w unṯ.|in.b h. 1008.20
t.ugrt.|w.pdy h[m].|iwrkl.mit.|ksp.b y[d].|birtym.|[un]ṯ inn.|l [h]m ʿd ṯṯṯbn.|ksp.iwrkl.|w ṯb.l unṯ hm. 1006.16
mṣry.d.ʿrb.b.unṯ.|bn.qrrn.mḏrǵl.|bn.tran.mḏrǵl|bn.ilh.mḏrǵl|špšyn.b.u 2046.1.1
birtym.|[un]ṯ inn.|l [h]m ʿd ṯṯṯbn.|ksp.iwrkl.|w ṯb.l unṯ hm. 1006.19
l.yi[--.-]m[---].|b unṯ.km.špš.|d brt.kmt.|br.ṣṯqšlm.|b unṯ.ʿd ʿlm.|mišmn.nq 1001.1.19
yi[--.-]m[---].|b unṯ.km.špš.|d brt.kmt.|br.ṣṯqšlm.|b unṯ.ʿd ʿlm.|mišmn.nqmd.|mlk ugrt.|nqmd.mlk.ugrt.|ktb.s 1005.5
[---.]unṯ[.---].|[---.]šrq[-.---].|[---.]ʿd ʿlm[.---].|[---.]ʿd.admn[.---]. 2156.1

unṯm

ʿ.nḥl h[.---].|w.yknil.nḥl h[.---].|w.iltm.nḥl h[.---].|w.unṯm.nḥ[l h.---].|[---.]ʿḏr[.---].|str[-.---].|bdlm.d[t.---].|ʿdn. 90[314].1.17

usyy

.kkr.ṯlṯ.|ksp.d.nkly.b.šd.|mit.ẖmšt.kbd.|[l.]gmn.bn.usyy.|mit.ṯṯm.kbd.|l.bn.yšmʿ.|mit.arbʿm.kbd.|l.liy.bn.ʿmy 1143.8

uss

t.|b.ypʿr.ʿšrm.|b.nʿmn.bn.ply.ẖmšt.l.ʿšrm.|b.gdn.bn.uss.ʿšrm.|b.ʿdn.bn.ṯṯ.ʿšrt.|b.bn.qrdmn.ṯlṯm.|b.bṣmn[.bn].ḥr 2054.1.18

uǵr

ṯn.rgmm.|argmn.lk.lk.ʿnn.ilm.|atm.bštm.w an.šnt.|uǵr.l rḥq.ilm.inbb.|l rḥq.ilnym.ṯn.mṯpdm.|tḥt.ʿnt.arṣ.ṯlṯ.mt 3[ʿNT].4.78

upd

spr.updt.|d b d.mlkytn.|kdrl.|slṯmg.|adrdn.|l[l]wn.|ydln.|ld 1034.1

upqt

--].ydʿ.l ydʿt.|[---.]tasrn.ṯr il.|[---.]rks.bn.abnm.|[---.]upqt.ʿrb.|[---.w ẓ]r.mtn y at zd.|[---.]tʿrb.bši.|[---.]l tzd.l tp 1[ʿNT.X].5.24
.yʿn.|[---.ydʿ.l] ydʿt.|[---.t]asrn.|[---.]trks.|[---.]abnm.upqt.|[---.]l w ǵr mtn y.|[---.]rq.gb.|[---.--]kl.tǵr.mtn h.|[-- 1[ʿNT.X].5.11

upšt

.|ary.|brqn.|bn.ẖlln.|bn.mṣry.|ṯmn.qšt.|w ʿšr.uṯpt.|upšt irš[-]. 118[306].16

uṣb

[-----].|[bn.]ibln.|ysd.|bn.ṯmq.|bn.agmn.|bn.uṣb.|bn.yzg.|bn.anntn.|bn.kwn.|ǵmšd.|bn.ʿbdḥy.|bn.uby 115[301].4.5

uṣbʿ

t|[l]t.ʿnt.uṣbʿt h.ybmt.limm.|[t]rḥṣ.yd h.b dm.ḏmr.|[u]ṣbʿt h.b mmʿ.mhrm.|[ṯ]ʿr.ksat.l ksat.ṯlḥnt.|[l]ṯlḥn.hdmm 3[ʿNT].2.35
ym.l ksi h.|[n]hr l kḥṯ drkt h.trtqṣ.b d bʿl km nš|r.b uṣbʿt h.hlm.ktp.zbl ym.bn ydm.|[ṯp]ṭ nhr.yrtqṣ.ṣmd.b d bʿl. 2.4[68].14

l ym.bn ydm.|[ṯp]ṭ nhr.yrtqṣ.ṣmd.b d bʻl.km.nšr.|b[u]ṣbʻt h.ylm.ktp.zbl ym.bn ydm.ṯpṭ.|nhr.ʻz.ym.l ymk.l tnǵṣ 2.4[68].16
r.ym.|l ksi h.nhr l kḥṯ.drkt h.trtqṣ.|b d bʻl.km.nšr b uṣbʻt h.hlm.qdq|d zbl ym.bn.ʻnm.ṯpṭ.nhr.yprsḥ ym.|w yql. 2.4[68].21
prsḥ ym.|w yql.l arṣ.w trtqṣ.ṣmd.b d bʻl.|[km.]nšr.b uṣbʻt h.ylm.qdqd.zbl.|[ym.]bn.ʻnm.ṯpṭ.nhr.yprsḥ.ym.yql.|l 2.4[68].24
-.]btlt.[ʻ]nt.|ṯtb.[---.--]ša.|tlm.km[.---.]yd h.k šr.|knr.uṣbʻt h ḫrṣ.abn.|p h.tiḫd.šnt h.w akl.bqmm.|tšt ḫrṣ.k lb iln 19[1AQHT].1.8
n.nbl[.---].|[--.]yṣq šmn.šlm.b ṣ[ʻ.trḥṣ].|yd h.btlt.ʻnt.uṣbʻt[h.ybmt].|limm.tiḫd.knr h.b yd[h.tšt].|rimt.l irt h.tšr UG5.3.2.5
[b]bt.dm.ḏmr.yṣq.šmn.|šlm.b ṣʻ.trḥṣ.yd h.bt|[l]t.ʻnt.uṣbʻt h.ybmt.limm.|[t]rḥṣ.yd h.b dm.ḏmr.|[u]ṣbʻt h.b mmʻ. 3[ʻNT].2.33
phn h.|yprq.lṣb.w yṣḥq.|pʻn h.l hdm.yṯpd.w ykrkr.|uṣbʻt h.yšu.g h.w y[ṣḥ].|ik.mǵyt.rbt.aṯr[t.y]m.|ik.atwt.qnyt 4[51].4.30
ḥlm.|ʻbd.il.w hdrt.|yrtḥṣ.w yadm.|yrḥṣ.yd h.amt h.|uṣbʻt h.ʻd.ṯkm.|ʻrb.b ẓl.ḫmt.lqḥ.|imr.dbḥ.b yd h.|lla.klatn 14[KRT].3.158
rt.|b dmʻ.nʻmn.ǵlm.|il.trḥṣ.w tadm.|rḥṣ[.y]d k.amt.|uṣb[ʻt k.]ʻd[.ṯ]km.|ʻrb[.b ẓl.ḫmt].|qḥ im[r.b yd k].|imr.d[b 14[KRT].2.64
ṯrm.|[--.]mtm.tbkn.|[--]t.w b lb.tqb[-].|[--]m[-].mtm.uṣbʻ[t].|[-]tr.šrk.il.|ʻrb.špš.l ymǵ.|krt.ṣbia.špš.|bʻl ny.w ym 15[128].5.16

ur

q].|w ynšq.aḫl.an.šblt.|tpʻ.b aklt.šblt.tpʻ[.b ḥm]drt.|ur.tisp k.yd.aqht.ǵz[r].|tšt k.bm.qrb m.asm.|b p h.rgm.l yṣ 19[1AQHT].2.73
.|w ynšq.aḫl.an bṣ[ql].|ynpʻ.b palt.bṣql ypʻ b yǵlm.|ur.tisp k.yd.aqht.|ǵzr.tšt k.b qrb m.asm.|y.dnh.ysb.aklt h. 19[1AQHT].2.66
.]ǵš.l limm.|[---.]l yṯb.l arṣ.|[---].mtm.|[---.--]d mhr.ur.|[---.]yḥnnn.|[---.--]t.ytn.|[---.btlt.]ʻnt.|[---.ybmt.]limm. 10[76].1.11

urbt

š.bʻl ḫlb š.|yrḫ š.ʻnt ṣpn.alp.|w š.pdry š.ddmš š.|w b urbt.ilib š.|bʻl alp w š.|dgn.š.il tʻḏr.š.|bʻl š.ʻnt š.ršp š.|šlm UG5.13.19
bt.b bh[t] m.|ḥln.b qrb.hkl m.|w yʻn.aliyn bʻl.|al.tšt.urbt.b[bhtm].|[ḥln].b qrb.hk[l m]. 4[51].5.126
wt y].|ṯn.rgm.k[ṯr.w]ḫss.|šmʻ.mʻ.l al[iy]n bʻl.|bl.ašt.ur[bt.]b bht m.|ḥln.b qr[b.hk]l m.|w ʻn.ali[yn.]bʻl.|al.tšt.u[4[51].6.5
w yʻn.kṯr.w ḫss.|šmʻ.l aliyn bʻl.|bn.l rkb.ʻrpt.|bl.ašt.urbt.b bh[t] m.|ḥln.b qrb.hkl m.|w yʻn.aliyn bʻl.|al.tšt.urbt 4[51].5.123
t.]b bht m.|ḥln.b qr[b.hk]l m.|w ʻn.ali[yn.]bʻl.|al.tšt.u[rb]t.b bht m.|ḥln.b q[rb.hk]l m.|al td[.pdr]y.bt ar.|[---.ṯ]l 4[51].6.8
bʻl.ašt m.kṯr bn.|ym.kṯr.bnm.ʻdt.|ypṯḥ.ḥln.b bht m.|urbt.b qrb.[h]kl |m.w y[p]tḥ.b dqt.ʻrpt.|ʻl h[wt].kṯr.w ḫss.| 4[51].7.18
mt.l k.l ali|yn.bʻl.ṯṯbn.bʻl.|l hwt y.ypṯḥ.ḥ|ln.b bht m.urbt.|b qrb.hk[l m.yp]tḥ.|bʻl.b dqt[.ʻrp]t.|ql h.qdš.b[ʻl.y]tn 4[51].7.26

urḫ

lqḥ.šʻrt.|urḫ.ln.kkrm.|w.rḥd.kd.šmn.|drt.b.kkr.|ubn.ḫṣḥ.kkr.|kkr.l 1118.2

uryy

|bn srd.bn agmn.|bn [-]ln.bn.ṯbil.|bn is.bn tbdn.|bn uryy.|bn abdʻn.|bn prkl.|bn štn.|bn annyn.|b[n] slg.|u[--] 101[10].8
---]lby.|[--]nbbl.|bn bl.|bn dkn.|bn ils.|bn ḫšbn.|bn uryy.|bn kṯl.|bn army.|bn gln.|bn abg.|bn.nǵry.|bn.srwd. 1064.8

uryn

spr ʻpsm.|dt.št.|uryn.|l mlk.ugrt. 1171.3

urm

.|ḫgbn.ltḥ.|spr.mkrm.|bn.slʻn.prs.|bn.ṯpdn.ltḥ.|bn.urm.ltḥ. 1059.9

urǵnr

|[---.b] d.ulm.|[---.b] d.ǵbl.|[---.b] d.ʻbdkṯr.|[---.b] d.urǵnr. 1052.9

urǵṯṯb

-].|[---.]b d.rb.[m]dlm.|[---.l i]ytlm.|[---].gmn.|[---].l.urǵṯṯb.|[---.]l.ʻṯtrum.|[---.]l.brqn.|[---].skn.|[---.ʻg]ltn.|[---]. 2162.B.5

urt

bn.ḫran.|bn.srt.|bn.adn.|bn.ʻgw.|bn.urt.|aḫdbu.|pḥ[-].|bn.ʻb .|bn.udn[-].|bn.yṣr. 121[307].5
n ndr.|um r[-] gtn ṯṯ ḫsn l ytn.|l rḥt lqḥ ṣtqn.|bt qbṣ urt ilštmʻ dbḥ ṣtqn l.|ršp. 1154.7
y.|dll.|mny.|krty.|bn.ʻbṣ.|bn.argb.|ydn.|ilʻnt.|bn.urt.|ydn.|qṭn.|bn.asr.|bn.ʻdy.|bn.amt[m].|myn.|šr.|bn.z 2117.3.44

urtn

aǵltn.|urtn.|annṯb.|ubn.|špšyn.|abmn.|[--]dn.|[ṯ]bʻm.|[--]mlk.|[1072.2
sp.|ḫmš.kkr.ṣml.|b.ʻšrt.b d.bn.kyn.|ʻšr.kkr.šʻrt.|b d.urtn.b.arbʻm.|arbʻt.ʻšrt.ḫrṣ.|b.ṯqlm.kbd.arbʻm.|ʻšrt.ḫrṣ.b.a 2100.15
brdnm.|ḫmš.kkrm.alp kb[d].|ṯlṯ.l.nskm.birtym.|b d.urtn.w.ṯṯ.mat.brr.|b.ṯmnym.ksp.ṯlṯt.kbd.|ḫmš.alp.ṯlṯ.l.ḫlby 2101.4
trt.|[ṯ]lṯ.ʻšr h.[b]t.ršp.gn.|arbʻ.b d.b[n].ušryn.|kdm.l.urtn.|kdm.l.ilšpš.|kd.l.annṯb.|kd.l.iwrmḏ.|kd.l.ydn.|[---.y 1088.5
[-]ay[.---].|[a]rš[mg.---].|urt[n.---].|ʻdn[.---].|bqrt[.---].|ṯnǵrn.[---].|w.bn h.n[--.---].| 2084.3

uš

rt.|l ḥẓr y.al.tṣr.|udm.rbt.w udm ṯrrt.|udm.ytnt.il w ušn.|ab.adm.w ṯṯb.|mlakm.l h.lm.ank.|ksp.w yrq.ḫrṣ.|yd. 14[KRT].3.135
.]al.t[ṣr].|udm[.r]bt.w u[dm].|[ṯ]rrt.udm.y[t]n[t].|il.ušn.ab[.ad]m.|rḥq.mlk.l bt y.|n[g.]krt.l ḥẓ[r y].|w yʻn[y.k] 14[KRT].6.278
mm.al.tṣr].|[udm.rbt.w udm].|[ṯrrt.udm.ytnt].|[il.w ušn.ab.adm].|[rḥq.mlk.l bt y].|[ng.kr]t.l ḥ[ẓ]r y.|[-----].|[-- 14[KRT].5.259

uš̱ḫr

m aṯt.|š l ilbt.šlmm.|kll ylḥm b h.|w l bbt šqym.|š l uḫr ḫlmṭ.|w tr l qlḥ.|ym aḥd. UG5.11.12
id ydbḥ mlk.|l ušḫ[r] ḫlmṭ.|l bbt il bt.|š l ḫlmṭ.|w tr l qlḥ.|w š ḥll ydm.|b UG5.7.TR3

uš̱ḫry

.ilt.asrm š.|w l ll.šp. pgr.w ṯrmnm.bt mlk.|il[bt].gdlt.ušḫry.gdlt.ym gdlt.|bʻl gdlt.yrḫ.gdlt.|gdlt.ṯrmn.gdlt.pdry.g 34[1].13
ilbt.|ušḫry.|ym.bʻl.|yrḫ.|kṯr.|ṯ1mn.|pdry.|dqt.|trt.|ršp.|ʻnt ḫb UG5.14.A.2

ušẖry

b‘]lm. | [b‘]lm. | [b‘l]m. | [arṣ] w šm[m̂]. | [-----]. | [a]rṣ. | [u]šẖr[y]. | [‘]ṯtrt. | i[l t]‘ḏr b‘l. | ršp. | ddmš. | pẖr ilm. | ym. | uṯẖ 29[17].2.2
ṯr.š.pdry.š.ǵrm.š[.---]. | aṯrt.š.‘nt.š.špš.š.arṣy.š.‘ṯtrt.š. | ušẖry.š.il.t‘ḏr.b‘l.š.ršp.š.ddmš.š. | w šlmm.ilib.š.i[l.--]m d gbl UG5.9.1.8
| k.yṯn.w.b.bt. | mlk.mlbš. | ytn.l hm. | šb‘.lbšm.allm. | l ušẖry. | ṯlṯ.mat.pṯtm. | l.mgmr.b.ṯlṯ. | šnt. 1107.10
-.]qdšt. | l.‘ṯtrt.ndrgd. | l.‘ṯtrt.abḏr. | l.dml. | l.ilt[.-]pn. | l.uš[ẖr]y. | [---.-]mrn. | l ṯwl. | [--]ḏ[--]. 1001.1.14

ušy

tǵl. | ṯn.yṣḥm. | slṯmg. | kdrl. | wql. | adrdn. | prn. | ‘bdil. | ušy.šbn[-]. | aẖt.ab. | krwn. | nnḏ. | mkl. | kzǵb. | iyrḏ. 1069.12

ušk

[--].yṯkḥ.w yiẖd.b qrb[.-]. | [--.t]ṯkḥ.w tiẖd.b uš[k.--]. | [-.b]‘l.yabd.l alp. | [---.bt]lt.‘nt. | [---]q.hry.w yld. | [-- 11[132].1.2

uškn

il[štm‘]. | šbn. | ṭbq. | rqd. | uškn. | ẖbt. | [ẖlb].kr[d]. 1177.5
spr.blblm. | skn uškn. | skn šbn. | skn ubr‘. | skn ẖrṣb‘. | rb.ntbtš. | [---].‘bd.r[--]. 1033.2
nu. | [--]. | [---]. | m‘r. | arny. | ubr‘y. | ilštm‘. | bir. | m‘qb. | uškn. | snr. | rq[d]. | [---]. | [---]. | mid[-]. | ubš. | mṣb[t]. | ḥl.y[---] 71[113].32
y. | š‘rt. | ẖlbrpš. | hry. | qmṣ. | ṣ‘q. | qmy. | ẖlbkrd. | y‘rt. | uškn. | ‘nqpat. | ilštm‘. | šbn. | ṭbq. | rqd. | šrš. | gn‘y. | m‘qb. | ag 2074.19
š[--.---]. | ṣ‘[-.---]. | ṣ‘q[.---]. | ẖlb.k[rd]. | uškn. | ‘nqp[at]. | ubr‘[y]. | ilšt[m‘]. | šbn. | ṭbq. 2146.5
ṯn.ṣbrm. | b.uškn. | ṣbr.aḥd. | b.ar. | ṣbr.aḥd. | b.mlk. | ṣbr.aḥd. | b.m‘rby. | ṣ 2073.2
[--.]wmrkm. | bir.ẖmš. | uškn.arb‘. | ubr‘y.ṯlṯ. | ar.ṯmn ‘šr h. | mlk.arb‘. | ǵbl.ẖmš. | atlg. 68[65].1.3
].aḥd.aẖd.b.y‘ny. | [---.-]ḥm.b.aḥd.ḥrṯ. | [---.]aẖd.b.grn.uškn. | [---.]aẖd.ḥrṯ. 1129.16
lm ṯ[ṯ]. | m‘rby.ẖmš. | ṭbq.arb‘. | tkm[.---]. | uẖnp[.---]. | ušk[n.---]. | ubr[‘y.---]. | ar[.---]. | mlk[.---]. | ǵbl[.---]. | atl[g.---]. 68[65].2.3
.[---]. | ẖlb ‘prm.amḏy.[ḥm]r.w bn[š]. | gn‘y.[---.bn]š. | uškn[.---].‘šr.bnšm. | ‘nqpat[.---].bnš. | ubr‘y.ar[b‘.]ḥm[r]m.w 2040.18
m.b.ar. | [--.š]dm.b.ulm. | [--.š]dm.b.m‘rby. | [--.šd]m.b.uškn. | [---.--]n. | [---].tlmdm. | [y]bnn.ṣmdm. | ṯp[ṭ]b‘l.ṣmdm. | 2033.1.6
[--.]ubdym.b.uškn. | [---]lby. | [--]nbbl. | bn bl. | bn dkn. | bn ils. | bn ḥšbn. | b 1064.1
n.bly. | šd gzl.l.bn.ṭbr[n]. | šd.ẖzmyn.l a[--]. | ṯn šdm b uš[kn]. 2089.16

uškny

r]‘y. | b[n.---]. | bn[.---.ušk]ny. | bn.kdrn.uškny. | bn.lgn.uškny. | bn.abn.uškny. | bn.arz.š‘rty. | bn.ibrd.m‘rby. | ṣdqn.g 87[64].23
n[.---.ušk]ny. | bn.kdrn.uškny. | bn.lgn.uškny. | bn.abn.uškny. | bn.arz.š‘rty. | bn.ibrd.m‘rby. | ṣdqn.gb‘ly. | bn.ypy.gb‘ 87[64].24
]ṯlḥny. | b[n.---.ub]r‘y. | [bn.---.ubr]‘y. | b[n.---]. | bn[.---.ušk]ny. | bn.kdrn.uškny. | bn.lgn.uškny. | bn.abn.uškny. | bn.a 87[64].21
[------]. | [------]. | [------]. | [------]. | [bn.]kblbn[.---]. | [bn] uškny. | bn.krny[-]. | bn.mt. | bn.nz‘n. | bn.slmz[-]. | bn.k‘[--]. | 2021.1.14
]r‘y. | [bn.---.ubr]‘y. | b[n.---]. | bn[.---.ušk]ny. | bn.kdrn.uškny. | bn.lgn.uškny. | bn.abn.uškny. | bn.arz.š‘rty. | bn.ibrd. 87[64].22
aṯt h. | ‘bdyrẖ.ṯn ǵlyt h. | aršmg. | ršpy.w.aṯt h. | bn.glgl.uškny. | bn.ṯny.uškny. | mnn.w.aṯt h. | slmu.ḥrš.mrkbt. | bnšm 2068.13
mẖsrn.d.[--.]ušknym. | brq.ṯlṯ.[mat.ṯ]lṯ. | bsn.mi[t.--]. | ar[--.---]. | k[--.---]. 1136.1
[s]p[r] ušknym.dt.[b d.---]. | bn.btr. | bn.‘ms. | bn.pṣn. | bn.agmz. | bn. 2021.1.1
.-]ny. | [-]ḥ[-.---.-]dn. | arb‘[m.ksp.]‘l. | il[m]l[k.a]rgnd. | uškny[.w]mit. | zt.b d hm.rib. | w [---]. | [-----]. | [-]šy[.---] h. | [2055.12
]. | ilmlk ṯṯ mat. | ‘bdilm.ṯṯ mat. | šmmn.bn.‘dš.ṯṯ mat. | ušknym. | yp‘.alpm. | aẖ[m]lk.bn.nskn.alpm. | krw.šlmy. | alp 1060.2.1
ǵlyt h. | aršmg. | ršpy.w.aṯt h. | bn.glgl.uškny. | bn.ṯny.uškny. | mnn.w.aṯt h. | slmu.ḥrš.mrkbt. | bnšm.dt.l.mlk. | ‘bdy 2068.14
[ṯl]ṯm.ksp.‘[l]. | [b]n.bly.gb‘ly. | [šp]ḥ.a[n]nṯb. | w.m[--.u]škny. | [‘]š[r.---]t.ksp. | [‘l.---]b bn[.--]. | [-]ḥ[-.---]. | [-]p[-.---. 2055.4

ušn

.alṯy.ul[p.ǵbr.]ulp. | ẖbt km.ulp.m[dl]l km.ulp.qr zbl.u[š]n yp km. | u b ap km.u b q[ṣ]rt.npš km.u b qṭt.tqṭṭ. | ušn 32[2].1.22
r. | w npy.yman.w npy.‘rmt.w npy.[---]. | w npy.nqmd.ušn.yp km.ulp.q[ṭy.ulp.ddm]y. | ulp.ẖry.ulp.ẖ[t]y.ulp.alṯy.ul 32[2].1.20
gr. | [ḥmyt.ugrt.w npy.yman.w npy.‘r]mt.w npy. | [---.ušn.yp km.ulp.]qṭy. | [ulp.ddmy.ulp.ẖry.ulp.ẖty.u]lp.alṯy. | [APP.I[-].1.14
.alṯy. | [ulp.ǵbr.ulp.ẖbt km.ulp.mdll km.ulp]. | [qr zbl.ušn.yp km.b ap km.u b qṣrt.np]št km. | [u b qṭt.tqṭṭ.ušn.yp APP.I[-].1.17
š]n yp km. | u b ap km.u b q[ṣ]rt.npš km.u b qṭt.tqṭṭ. | ušn yp km.l d[b]ḥm.w l.ṯ‘.dbḥ n.ndbḥ.hw.ṯ‘ | nṯ‘y. | hw.nkt. 32[2].1.24
l.ušn.yp km.b ap km.u b qṣrt.np]št km. | [u b qṭt.tqṭṭ.ušn.yp km.---.-]yt km. | [---.]km. | [-----]. | [---.]ugrt. | [---].l.li APP.I[-].1.18
.ulp.alṯy.ulp.ǵbr.ul]p.ẖbt kn. | [ulp.mdll kn.ulp.qr zbl.ušn.y]p kn. | [u b ap kn.u b qṣrt.npšt kn.u b qṭ]t tqṭṭ. | [ušn.y APP.I[-].1.6
p.alṯy]. | [ulp.ǵbr.ulp.ẖbt kn.ulp.mdll kn.ulp.]qr zbl. | [ušn.yp kn.u b ap kn.u b qṣrt.npš kn.u b]qṭt. | [tqṭṭn.ušn.yp APP.I[-].2.15
]. | [---.t‘ḏ]r b‘l. | [-----]. | [-----]. | [---.--]r. | [---.]npy. | [---.ušn.yp kn.ulp.q]ṭy. | [ulp.ddmy.ulp.ẖry.ulp.ẖty.ulp.alṯy]. | [u APP.I[-].2.12
[---.w n]py.yman. | [w npy.‘rmt.---.w]npy.annpdgl. | [ušn.yp kn.ulp.qṭy.ulp.]ddmy.ulp ẖry. | [ulp.ẖty.ulp.alṯy.ulp. APP.I[-].1.4
r.m[šr] mšr.bt.ugrt.w npy.gr. | ḥmyt.ugrt.w [np]y.nṯt.ušn.yp kn.ulp qṭy. | ulp.ddmy.ul[p.ẖ]ry.ulp.ẖty.ulp.alṯy. | ul 32[2].1.28
alṯy. | ulp.ǵbr.ulp.[ẖbt] kn[.u]lp.mdll kn.ulp qr z[bl]. | lšn yp kn.b ap [kn.u b qṣ]rt.npš kn.u b qṭt. | tqṭṭn.ušn y[p k 32[2].1.31
l]. | lšn yp kn.b ap [kn.u b qṣ]rt.npš kn.u b qṭt. | tqṭṭn.ušn y[p kn.l dbḥm.]w l ṯ‘ dbḥ n. | ndbḥ.hw.ṯ‘ n[ṯ‘y.hw.nkt.n 32[2].1.32
[ušn.yp kn.u b ap kn.u b qṣrt.npš kn.u b]qṭt. | [tqṭṭn.ušn.yp kn.---.-]gym. | [---.]l kbkb. | [-----]. APP.I[-].2.16
šn.y]p kn. | [u b ap kn.u b qṣrt.npšt kn.u b qṭ]t tqṭṭ. | [ušn.yp kn.---.--]l.il.t‘ḏr b‘l. | [-----.]lšnt. | [---.--]yp.tḥt. | [-----]. APP.I[-].1.8

ušpǵt

bt mlk.‘šr.‘šr.[--].bt ilm. | kbr[-]m.[-]trmt. | lbš.w [-]tn.ušpǵt. | ẖr[-].ṯlṯt.mzn. | drk.š.alp.w ṯlṯ. | ṣin.šlm[m.]šb‘ pamt. 33[5].4
[---]. | ẖmšm.ṯlṯ.rkb.ntn.ṯlṯ.mat.[---]. | lg.šmn.rqḥ.šr‘m.ušpǵtm.p[--.---]. | kṯ.ẓrw.kṯ.nbt.ḏnt.w [-]n[-.---]. | il.ẖyr.ilib.š. UG5.9.1.21
krm. | [---].ab h.krm ar. | [---.]h.mḥtrt.pṯtm. | [---.-]t h.ušpǵt tišr. | [---.šm]m h.nšat ẓl h kbkbm. | [---.]b km kbkbt k 2001.2.4

ušryn

.l.‘šrm[.l.b]t.‘ṯtrt. | [ṯ]lṯ.‘šr h.[b]t.ršp.gn. | arb‘.b d.b[n].ušryn. | kdm.l.urtn. | kdm.l.ilšpš. | kd.l.annṯb. | kd.l.iwrmḏ. | k 1088.4
[.---]. | ḏmrb‘[l.---]. | iẖyn.[---]. | ‘bdb‘[l.---]. | uwil[.---]. | ušry[n.---]. | y‘ḏrn[.---]. | [‘]bdyr[ẖ.---]. | [---]mlk[.---]. | [-----]. | 102[322].2.9

utly

p. | bn sḫrn. | m'qb. | ṯpn. | m'r. | lbnm. | nḫl. | y'ny. | atn. | utly. | bn.alz. | bn ḫlm. | bn.ḏmr. | bn.'yn. | ubnyn. | rpš d ydy. | 2075.14

uṯḫt

ḫr[y]. | [']ṯtrt. | i[l t]'ḏr b'l. | ršp. | ddmš. | pḫr ilm. | ym. | uṯḫt. | knr. | mlkm. | šlm. 29[17].2.9

uṯkl

b yrḫ.[rišyn.b ym.ḥdṯ]. | šmtr.[uṯkl.l il.šlmm]. | b ṯlṯt '[šrt.yrtḥṣ.mlk.brr]. | b arb'[t.'šrt.riš.ar 35[3].2
[b yr]ḫ[.r]išyn.b ym.ḥdṯ. | [šmtr].uṯkl.l il.šlmm. | b [ṯlṯt].'šrt.yrtḥṣ.mlk. | br[r.]b a[r]b'ṯ.'šrt.riš. APP.II[173].2

uṯpt

| šdyn. | ary. | brqn. | bn.ḫlln. | bn.mṣry. | ṯmn.qšt. | w 'šr.uṯpt. | upšt irš[-]. 118[306].15
qšt.w.ar[b']. | [u]ṯpt.ql'.w.ṯt.mr[ḫ]m. | [bn].smyy.qšt.w.u[ṯpt]. | [w.q]l'.w.ṯt.mrḥm. | [bn].šlmn.ql'.w.ṯ[t.---]. | [bn].mlṣ 2047.4
yd.apnt hn. | yd.ḥẓ hn. | yd.tr hn. | w.l.ṯt.mrkbtm. | inn.uṯpt. | w.ṯlṯ.ṣmdm.w.ḥrṣ. | apnt.b d.rb.ḥršm. | d.šṣa.ḥwy h. 1121.7
iḫyn.uṯpt.ḥẓm. | anšrm.uṯpt.ḥẓm. | w uṯpt.srdnnm. | awpn.uṯpt.ḥẓ 1124.1
iḫyn.uṯpt.ḥẓm. | anšrm.uṯpt.ḥẓm. | w uṯpt.srdnnm. | awpn.uṯpt.ḥẓm. | w uṯpt.srdnn 1124.2
.uṯpt.ḥẓm. | anšrm.uṯpt.ḥẓm. | w uṯpt.srdnnm. | awpn.uṯpt.ḥẓm. | w uṯpt.srdnnm. | rpan.uṯpt.srdnnm. | šb'm.uṯpt.sr 1124.4
iḫyn.uṯpt.ḥẓm. | anšrm.uṯpt.ḥẓm. | w uṯpt.srdnnm. | awpn.uṯpt.ḥẓm. | w uṯpt.srdnnm. | rpan.uṯpt.s 1124.3
nnm. | rpan.uṯpt.srdnnm. | šb'm.uṯpt.srdnnm. | bn.aǵli.uṯpt.srdnnm. | asrn.uṯpt.srdnnm. | bn.qṣn.uṯpt.srdnnm. | yly. 1124.8
rdnnm. | asrn.uṯpt.srdnnm. | bn.qṣn.uṯpt.srdnnm. | yly.uṯpt.srdnnm. | artṯb.uṯpt.srdnnm. 1124.11
.uṯpt.ḥẓm. | w uṯpt.srdnnm. | rpan.uṯpt.srdnnm. | šb'm.uṯpt.srdnnm. | bn.aǵli.uṯpt.srdnnm. | asrn.uṯpt.srdnnm. | bn. 1124.7
nnm. | šb'm.uṯpt.srdnnm. | bn.aǵli.uṯpt.srdnnm. | asrn.uṯpt.srdnnm. | bn.qṣn.uṯpt.srdnnm. | yly.uṯpt.srdnnm. | artṯb. 1124.9
nm. | bn.aǵli.uṯpt.srdnnm. | asrn.uṯpt.srdnnm. | bn.qṣn.uṯpt.srdnnm. | yly.uṯpt.srdnnm. | artṯb.uṯpt.srdnnm. 1124.10
nšrm.uṯpt.ḥẓm. | w uṯpt.srdnnm. | awpn.uṯpt.ḥẓm. | w uṯpt.srdnnm. | rpan.uṯpt.srdnnm. | šb'm.uṯpt.srdnnm. | bn.aǵ 1124.5
uṯpt.srdnnm. | awpn.uṯpt.ḥẓm. | w uṯpt.srdnnm. | rpan.uṯpt.srdnnm. | šb'm.uṯpt.srdnnm. | bn.aǵli.uṯpt.srdnnm. | asr 1124.6
dnnm. | bn.qṣn.uṯpt.srdnnm. | yly.uṯpt.srdnnm. | artṯb.uṯpt.srdnnm. 1124.12
[nq]dm.dt.kn.npṣ hm. | [bn].lbn.arb'.qšt.w.ar[b']. | [u]ṯpt.ql'.w.ṯt.mr[ḫ]m. | [bn].smyy.qšt.w.u[ṯpt]. | [w.q]l'.w.ṯt. 2047.3
tm.w.uṯp[t]. | [--.q]l'.w[.---.m]rḥm. | [bn].ḫdmn.qšt.[w.u]ṯp[t].ṯ[--]. | [---].arb'.[---]. | [---].kdl[.---.mr]ḥm.w.ṯ[t.---]. | [- 2047.9
w.ṯt.mrḥm. | [bn].šlmn.ql'.w.ṯ[t.---]. | [bn].mlṣ.qštm.w.uṯp[t]. | [--.q]l'.w[.---.m]rḥm. | [bn].ḫdmn.qšt.[w.u]ṯp[t].ṯ[--]. 2047.7

uṯryn

yšn.ḥrš. | šd.b d.aupš. | šd.b d.ršpab.aḫ.ubn. | šd.b d.bn.uṯryn. | [ubd]y.mrynm. | [š]d.bn.ṣnrn.b d.nrn. | [š]d.bn.rwy.b 82[300].1.6
ḥm. | mit.iqni.l mlkt. | ks.ḫrṣ.ktn.mit.pḥm. | mit.iqni.l uṯryn. | ks.ksp.ktn.mit.pḥm. | mit.iqni.l tpnr. | [ks.ksp.kt]n.m 64[118].30
[t]ḥm.uṯryn[.---]. | [g]rgš 'bdy[--]. | [--.]l mlk [---]. | [---].aḫ y[.---]. | [- 2130.1.1

b

b

|bṯ.l rkb.ʿrpt.k šby n.zb[l.ym.k] |šby n.ṯpṭ.nhr.w yṣa b[.--].|ybṯ.nn.aliyn.bʿl.w [---].|ym.l mt.bʿl m.ym l[--.---].|ḥ 2.4[68].30
r.ṯrmt.al m.qḥn y.š y.qḥn y.|[--.]šir.b krm.nṭṭt.dm.ʿlt.b ab y.|u---].ʿlt.b k.lk.l pn y.yrk.bʿl.[--].|[---.]ʿnt.šzrm.tštšḥ. 1001.1.9
.ʿmr.|un.l riš h.ʿpr.plṯt.|l qdqd h.lpš.yks.|mizrtm.ǵr.b abn.|ydy.psltm.b yʿr.|yhdy.lḥm.w dqn.|yṯlṯ.qn.ḏrʿ h.yḥr 5[67].6.17
l bʿl.|ǵr.b ab.td[.ps]ltm[.b yʿr].|thdy.lḥm.w dqn[.ṯṯlṯ].|qn.ḏrʿ h.tḥrṯ. 6[62].1.2
-].|arbʿ.bnšm.b[.---].|ʿšrm.bnšm.[b.]ʿd[--].|arbʿ.bnšm.b.ag[m]y.|arbʿ.bnšm.b.ḫpty.|ṯṯ.bnšm.b.bir.|ṯṯ.bnšm b.uḫn 2076.11
[sp]r.k[--].|ṯ[ṯ.bn]šm[.b.a]gmy.|ṯṯ.bn[šm.---].|ʿšr.b[nšm.---].|arbʿ[.bnšm.---].|ṯṯ.ʿš 2076.2
.|ydn.bn.ilrpi.|w.ṯbʿm.ʿrb.b.ʿ[d]n.|ḏmry.bn.yrm.|ʿrb.b.adʿy. 2079.10
t.l ahlm.rgm.l yṯ[pn.y]|bl.agrtn.bat.b ḏd k.[pǵt].|bat.b hlm w yʿn.yṭpn[.mhr].|št.qḥn.w tšqyn.yn.qḥ.|ks.b d y.qb 19[1AQHT].4.214
ym.tn.aḥd.|b aḫ k.ispa.w yṯb.|ap.d anšt.im[-].|aḥd.b aḫ k.l[--]n.|hn[-.]aḫẓ[.---]l[-].|[ʿ]nt.akl[y.nšm].|akly.hml[6[49].5.22
brt.|ʿl k.pht.[-]l[-].|b šdm.ʿl k.pht.|drʿ.b ym.tn.aḥd.|b aḫ k.ispa.w yṯb.|ap.d anšt.im[-].|aḥd.b aḫ k.l[--]n.|hn[-.] 6[49].5.20
n.|[d aḫd b.g]t gbry.|[---].aḥd.aḫd.b.yʿny.|[---.-]ḫm.b.aḫd.ḥrṯ.|[---.]aḫd.b.grn.uškn.|[---.]aḫd.ḥrṯ. 1129.15
šd.snrym.dt.ʿqb.|b.ayly.|šd.abršn.|šd.kkn.[bn].ubyn.|šd.bn.li[y].|šd.bn.š[--] 2026.2
.yʿrt.|pǵyn.b.tpḫ.|amri[l].b.šrš.|aǵltn.b.midḫ.|[--]n.b.ayly.|[-]lyn.b.nghṯ.|[---.]b.nh[-]t.|[---.]almš.|[---.--]ty.|[-- 2118.14
t.|ǵzr.tšt k.b qrb m.asm.|y.dnh.ysb.aklt h.yph.|šblt.b akt.šblt.ypʿ.|b ḥmdrt.šblt.yḫ[bq].|w ynšq.aḫl.an.šblt.|tpʿ. 19[1AQHT].2.69
blt.ypʿ.|b ḥmdrt.šblt.yḫ[bq].|w ynšq.aḫl.an.šblt.|tpʿ.b aklt.šblt.tpʿ[.b ḥm]drt.|ur.tisp k.yd.aqht.ǵz[r].|tšt k.bm.q 19[1AQHT].2.72
yrḫ.|l dmgy.amt.|aṯrt.qḥ.|ksan k.ḥdg k.|ḥtl k.w ẓi.|b aln.tk m.|b tk.mlbr.|ilšiy.|kry amt.|ʿpr.ʿẓm yd.|ugrm.ḫl 12[75].1.20
y.|b.ʿšrt.ksp.b.a[--].|ṯqlm.ḫr[ṣ.]b.ṯmnt.ksp.|ʿšrt.ksp.b.alp.[b d].bn.[---].|tšʿ.ṣin.b.tšʿt.ksp.|mšlt.b.ṯql.ksp.|kdwṯ.l. 2101.21
pm.ʿdb.|[---].tʿtqn.|[---.-]ʿb.idk.|[l ytn.pnm.tk.]in.bb.b alp ḥẓr.|[rbt.kmn.l pʿ]n.ʿnt.|[yhbr.w yql.yšt]ḥwyn.w y|[k 1[ʿNT.IX].2.14
nt.arṣ.ṯlṯ.mtḥ.ǵyrm.|idk.l ttn pnm.ʿm.bʿl.|mrym.ṣpn.b alp.šd.rbt.kmn.|hlk.aḫt h.bʿl.yʿn.tdrq.|ybnt.ab h.šrḥq.aṯt. 3[ʿNT].4.82
b grn.ydn.|dn.almnt.yṯpṭ.ṯpṭ.ytm.|b nši ʿn h.w yphn.b alp.|šd.rbt.kmn.hlk.kṯr.|k yʿn.w yʿn.tdrq.ḫss.|hlk.qšt.ybl 17[2AQHT].5.9
ʿqb k.[ttbʿ].|[bt]lt.ʿnt.idk.l ttn.[pnm].|[ʿm.a]qht.ǵzr.b alp.š[d].|[rbt.]kmn.w ṣḥq.btlt.[ʿnt].|[tšu.]g h.w tṣḥ.šmʿ.m 18[3AQHT].1.21
m.tk.ḫkpt.il.kl h].|[kptr.]ks[u.ṯbt h.ḫkpt.arṣ.nḥlt h].|b alp.šd.r[bt.kmn.l pʿn.kṯr].|hbr.w ql.t[štḥwy.w kbd.hwt].| 1[ʿNT.IX].3.2
m.tk.ḫqkpt.|il.kl h.kptr.|ksu.ṯbt h.ḫkpt.|arṣ.nḥlt h.|b alp.šd.rbt.|kmn.l pʿn.kṯ.|hbr.w ql.tštḥ|wy.w kbd hwt.|w 3[ʿNT.VI].6.17
ṯḫtan.|nrt.ilm.špš.|ṣḥrrt.la.|šmm.b yd.md|d.ilm.mt.b a|lp.šd.rbt.k|mn.l pʿn.mt.|hbr.w ql.|tštḥwy.w k|bd hwt. 4[51].8.24
dʿṣ.|pʿnm.w tr.arṣ.|idk.l ttn.pnm.|ʿm.bʿl.mrym.ṣpn.|b alp.šd.rbt.kmn.|ṣḥq.btlt.ʿnt.tšu.|g h.w tṣḥ.tbšr bʿl.|bšrt k 4[51].5.86
-.d]mt qdš.|[---].b.dmt qdš.|[---].b.dmt qdš.|[---.--]n.b.anan.|[--]yl.b.bqʿt.b.gt.tgyn.|[--]in.b.trzy.|[--]yn.b.glltky. 2118.5
ayaḫ.|bn.aylt.|ḥmš.mat.arbʿm.|kbd.ksp.anyt.|d.ʿrb.b.anyt.|l.mlk.gbl.|w.ḫmšm.ksp.|lqḥ.mlk.gbl.|lbš.anyt h.|b 2106.12
šrt.|[---.--]m.|[---.--]tm.|[---.]ʿšrt.|[-----].|b.[---.---]r.|b.ann[.---.-]ny[-].|b.ḫqn.[---]m.ṣ[-]n.|[b].bn.ay[--.---].l.ʿšrm. 2054.2.15
k.ʿl.|[---] k.yšṣi.|[---.]ḫbr.rbt.|[ḫbr.ṯrr]t.il d.|[pid.---].b anšt.|[---.]mlu.|[---.--]tm. 15[128].5.27
blm.[qrt.zbl.yrḫ].|ik.al.yḥdṯ.yrḫ.b[---].|b qrn.ymn h.b anšt[.---].|qdqd h.w yʿn.yṭpn.[mhr.št].|šmʿ.l btlt.ʿnt.at.ʿ[l. 18[3AQHT].4.10
tqtnṣn.w tldn.tld.[ilm.]nʿmm.agzr ym.|bn.ym.ynqm.b a[p.]ḏ[d.r]gm.l il.ybl.|aṯt y.il.ylt.mh.ylt.ilmy nʿmm.|agzr 23[52].59
km.šḫṯ.l brk h.tṣi.km.|rḥ.npš h.km.iṯl.brlt h.km.|qṭr.b ap h.b ap.mhr h.ank.|l aḥwy.tqḥ.ytpn.mhr.št.|tštn.k nšr. 18[3AQHT].4.26
š[r.grn].|w.št.ašk[rr].|w.pr.ḥḏr[t.ydk].|aḥd h.w.yṣq[.b.ap h].|k.yiḫd.akl.š[šw].|št.nni.št.mk[št.grn].|št.irǵn.ḥmr[161[56].16
ṯtn.ššw].|mss.[št.qlql.w.št].|ʿrgz[.ydk.aḥd h].|w.yṣq[.b.ap h].|k.yiḫd[.akl.ššw].|št.mkš[r.grn].|w.št.ašk[rr].|w.pr 161[56].11
ru w]l yttn mss št qlql.|[w št ʿrgz y]dk aḥd h w yṣq b ap h.|[k.yiḫd akl š]šw št mkšr grn.|[w št aškrr w p]r ḥḏrt 160[55].9
k].|aḥd h.w.yṣq.b[.ap h].|k.yraš.ššw.[št].|bln.qṭ.yṣq.b.a[p h].|k ygʿr[.ššw.---].|dprn[.---].|drʿ.[---].|tmṯl[.---].|m 161[56].22
].|[k ḫr š]šw mǵmǵ w b[ṣql ʿrgz].|[ydk aḫ]d h w yṣq b ap h.|[k ḫr]ššw ḫndrṯ w ṯ[qd m]r.|[ydk aḥd h w yṣq b ap 160[55].5
k [ḫr ššw mǵmǵ].|w [bṣql.ʿrgz.ydk].|a[ḥd h.w.yṣq.b.ap h].|k.[ḫr.ššw.ḫndrṯ].|w.ṯ[qd.mr.ydk.aḥd h].|w.y[ṣq.b. 161[56].4
[k.---.]šš[w.---].|[---.w]yṣq b a[p h].|[k ḫr š]šw mǵmǵ w b[ṣql ʿrgz].|[ydk aḫ]d h w yṣq 160[55].3
ap h.|[k ḫr]ššw ḫndrṯ w ṯ[qd m]r.|[ydk aḥd h w yṣq b ap h.|[k l yḫru w]l yttn mss št qlql.|[w št ʿrgz y]dk aḥd 160[55].7
h].|k.[ḫr.ššw.ḫndrṯ].|w.ṯ[qd.mr.ydk.aḥd h].|w.y[ṣq.b.ap h].|k.l.ḫ[ru.w.l.yttn.ššw].|mss.[št.qlql.w.št].|ʿrgz[.ydk 161[56].7
bk].|w.pr[.ḥḏrt.w.št].|irǵ[n.ḥmr.ydk].|aḥd[h.w.yṣq.b.ap h].|k yr[a]š.šš[w.w.ykhp].|mid.dblt.yṯ[nt.w].|ṣmq[m]. 161[56].31
št.nni.št.mk[št.grn].|št.irǵn.ḥmr[.ydk].|aḥd h.w.yṣq.b[.ap h].|k.yraš.ššw.[št].|bln.qṭ.yṣq.b.a[p h].|k ygʿr[.ššw.--- 161[56].20
[t.l brk h].|yṣat.km.rḥ.npš[h.km.iṯl].|brlt h.km.qṭr.[b ap h.---].|ʿnt.b ṣmt.mhr h.[---].|aqht.w tbk.y[---.---].|abn. 18[3AQHT].4.37
|[-----].|[---.-]n[-].|[k yraš ššw št bln q]ṭ ydk.|[w yṣq b ap h].|[-----].|[-----].|[-----].|[---.-]rb.|[-----].|[-----].|[-----] 160[55].15
d.|dblt ytnt w ṣmqm ytn[m].|w qmḥ bql yṣq aḥd h.|b ap h. 160[55].26
w].|ṣmq[m].ytnm.w[.qmḥ.bql].|tdkn.aḥd h.w[.yṣq].|b.ap h. 161[56].36
[b]n.šrm.|iqran.ilm.nʿmm[.agzry ym.bn]ym.|ynqm.b ap zd.aṯrt.[---].|špš.mṣprt dlt hm[.---].|w ǵnbm.šlm.ʿrbm. 23[52].24
lp.|ḫbt km.ulp.m[dl]l km.ulp.qr zbl.u[š]n yp km.|u b ap km.u b q[ṣ]rt.npš km.u b qṭt.tqṭṭ.|ušn yp km.l d[b]ḥm 32[2].1.23
ǵbr].|[ulp.ḫbt km.ulp.mdll km.ulp.qr zbl].|[u ṯḫṭu.u b ap km.u b qṣrt.npš km.u b qṭt].|[tqṭṭ.u ṯḫṭu.l dbḥm.w l.ṯʿ. 32[2].1.8A
ǵbr.ulp.ḫbt km.ulp.mdll km.ulp].|[qr zbl.ušn.yp km.b ap km.u b qṣrt.np]š km.|[u b qṭt.tqṭṭ.ušn.yp km.---.-]yt k APP.I[-].1.17
.ǵbr.ulp.ḫbt kn.ulp.mdll kn.ulp.]qr zbl.|[ušn.yp kn.u b ap kn.u b qṣrt.npš kn.u b]qṭt.|[tqṭṭn.ušn.yp kn.---.-]gym. APP.I[-].2.15
r.ul]p.ḫbt kn.|[ulp.mdll kn.ulp.qr zbl.ušn.y]p kn.|[u b ap kn.u b qṣrt.npšt kn.u b qṭ]t tqṭṭ.|[ušn.yp kn.---.--]l.il.tʿ APP.I[-].1.7
p.]ǵbr.|ulp.ḫbt kn.ulp.md[ll k]n.ulp.q[r zbl].|u ṯḫṭin.b ap kn.u b [q]ṣrt.npš[kn.u b qṭt].|tqṭṭn u ṯḫṭin.l bḥm.w l ṯ 32[2].1.14
ǵbr.ulp.[ḫbt] kn[.u]lp.mdll kn.ulp qr z[bl].|lšn yp kn.b ap [kn.u b qṣ]rt.npš kn.u b qṭt.|tqṭṭn.ušn y[p kn.l dbḥm.] 32[2].1.31
.l brk h.tṣi.km.|rḥ.npš h.km.iṯl.brlt h.km.|qṭr.b ap h.b ap.mhr h.ank.|l aḥwy.tqḥ.ytpn.mhr.št.|tštn.k nšr.b ḥbš h 18[3AQHT].4.26
aṯt y.il.ylt.mh.ylt.ilmy nʿmm.|agzr ym.bn ym.ynqm.b ap.ḏd.št.špt.|l arṣ.špt l šmm.w ʿrb.b p hm.ʿṣr.šmm.|w dg 23[52].61
nk.dnil.|[m]t.rpi.ap[h]n.ǵzr.|[mt.hrn]my.ytšu.|[yṯb.b ap.ṯ]ǵr[.ṭ]ḥt.|[adrm.d b grn.y]dn.|[dn.almnt.y]ṯpṭ.|[ṯpṭ.y 19[1AQHT].1.22

m.apnk.dnil.mt. | rpi.a hn.ǵzr.mt.hrnm[y]. | ytšu.yṯb.b ap.ṯǵr.tḥt. | adrm.d b grn.ydn. | dn.almnt.yṯpṭ.ṯpṭ.ytm. | b n 17[2AQHT].5.6
.---]y[.---.-]nt.[š]ṣat[k.]rḥ.npš.hm. | k.iṯl.brlt n[-.k qṭr.b ap -]. | tmǵyn.tša.g h[m.w tṣḥn]. | šm'.l dnil.[mt.rpi]. | mt.a 19[1AQHT].2.88
r'y. | iln.[---]. | bn.[---].ar. | bn.[---].b.ar. | špšyn[.---.]yṯb.b.ar. | bn.ag[p]ṯ.ḫpṯ.d[.yṯb.b].š'rt. | yly.bn.ṯrnq.[-]r.d.yṯb.b.ilš 2015.1.24
ṯn.ṣbrm. | b.uškn. | ṣbr.aḥd. | b.ar. | ṣbr.aḥd. | b.mlk. | ṣbr.aḥd. | b.m'rby. | ṣbr.aḥd. | b.ulm. | ṣ 2073.4
-.a]ǵt. | špš[yn.---.u]br'y. | iln.[---]. | bn.[---].ar. | bn.[---].b.ar. | špšyn[.---.]yṯb.b.ar. | bn.ag[p]ṯ.ḫpṯ.d[.yṯb.b].š'rt. | yly.b 2015.1.23
[ŝ]ŝw[.i]ryn.arr. | [š]dm.b.mlk. | [--.š]dm.b.ar. | [--.š]dm.b.ulm. | [--.š]dm.b.m'rby. | [--.šd]m.b.uškn. | [-- 2033.1.3
.w yṣḥ.y l k.mrrt. | tǵll.b nr.d 'l k.mḫṣ.aqht. | ǵzr.šrš k.b arṣ.al. | yp'.riš.ǵly.b d.ns' k. | 'nt.brḥ.p 'lm h. | 'nt.p dr.dr.'d 19[1AQHT].3.159
.w yṣḥ. | b'l.mt.my.lim.bn. | dgn.my.hmlt.aṯr. | b'l.ard.b arṣ.ap. | 'nt.ttlk.w tṣd.kl.ǵr. | l kbd.arṣ.kl.gb'. | l [k]bd.šdm.t 5[67].6.25
tlt.'nt. | qrn.d bat k b'l.ymšḥ. | b'l.ymšḥ.hm.b 'p. | nṭ'n.b arṣ.ib y. | w b 'pr.qm.aḫ k. | w tšu.'n h.btlt.'nt. | w tšu.'n h. 10[76].2.24
k.b ṣrrt.ṣpn. | yrd.'ṯtr.'rẓ.yrd. | l kḥṯ.aliyn.b'l. | w ymlk.b arṣ.il.kl h. | [---] š abn.b rḥbt. ¦ [---] š abn.b kknt. 6.1.65[49.1.37]
[--]r.[---]. | [---.]il.[---]. | [tṣ]un.b arṣ. | mḫnm.ṯrp ym. | lšnm.tlḥk. | šmm.tṯrp. | ym.ḏnbtm. | tn 1003.3
ṯny.l ybmt.limm.tḥm.aliyn.b'l]. | hw[t.aliy.qrdm.qryy.b arṣ.mlḥmt.št]. | [b ']pr[m.ddym.sk.šlm.l kbd.arṣ.arbdd]. | l 7.2[130].14
ḥ]lt y. | w t['n].btlt.[']nt.tṯb. | [ybmt.]limm.[a]n.aqry. | [b arṣ].mlḥmt.[aš]t.b 'pr m. | ddym.ask[.šlm.]l kbd.arṣ. | ar[b 3['NT].4.67
šu.g h.w y]ṣḥ.tḥm. | [ṯr.il.ab k.hwt.l]ṭpn.ḥtk k. | [qryy.b arṣ.mlḥ]mt.št b 'p | [r m.ddym.sk.šlm].l kbd.arṣ. | [arbdd.l 1['NT.IX].2.19
ṯny.l ymmt.limm. | tḥm.aliyn.b'l.hwt. | aliy.qrdm.qry.b arṣ. | mlḥmt št.b 'pr m.ddym. | sk.šlm.l kbd.arṣ. | arbdd.l k 3['NT].3.11
.š]dm.yšt. | [----.]b'l.mdl h.yb'r. | [---.]rn h.aqry. | [---.]b a[r]ṣ.mlḥmt. | ašt[.b ']p[r] m.ddym.ask. | šlm.l kb[d].awṣ.ar 3['NT].4.72
| l b'l.ṣrt.l rkb.'rpt. | tḥm.aliyn.b'l.hwt.aliy. | qrdm.qry.b arṣ.mlḥmt. | št.b 'p[r] m.ddym.sk.šlm. | l kbd.arṣ.arbdd.l k 3['NT].4.52
ṯlṯ.bmt. | b'l.mt.my.lim.bn dgn. | my.hmlt.aṯr.b'l.nrd. | b arṣ.'m h.trd.nrt. | ilm.špš.'d.tšb'.bk. | tšt.k yn.udm't.gm. | tṣ 6[62].1.8
rzḥ.---]. | bṯt.'llm n.[---]. | ilm.bt.b'l k.[---]. | dl.ylkn.ḥš.b a[rṣ.---]. | b 'pr.ḫbl ṭtm.[---.] | šqy.rṯa.tnm y.ytn.[ks.b yd]. | 1['NT.X].4.7
.]šḫp.ṣǵrt h. | yrk.t'l.b ǵr. | mslmt.b ǵr.tliyt. | w t'l.bkm.b arr. | bm.arr.w b ṣpn. | b n'm.b ǵr.t[l]iyt. | ql.l b'l.ttnn. | bšrt 10[76].3.30
rt h. | yrk.t'l.b ǵr. | mslmt.b ǵr.tliyt. | w t'l.bkm.b arr. | bm.arr.w b ṣpn. | b n'm.b ǵr.t[l]iyt. | ql.l b'l.ttnn. | bšrt.il.bš[r. 10[76].3.31
b.atlg.ṯlṯ.ḫrmṯt.ṯṯm. | mḫrhn.nit.mit.krk.mit. | m'ṣd.ḫmšm.m 2048.1
any.al[ṯy]. | d b atlg[.---]. | ḫmš 'š[r]. | kkr.ṯ[lṯ]. | ṯt hrt[m]. | ṯn mq[pm]. | ulṯ. 2056.2
b.mit.ḫmšt.kbd.ksp. | ṯlṯ.ktnt.b d.an[r]my. | b.'šrt.ksp.b.a[--]. | ṯqlm.ḫr[ṣ.]b.ṯmnt.ksp. | 'šrt.ksp.b.alp.[b d].bn.[---]. | 2101.19
.yg'r.ṯǵr. | bt.il.pn.l mgr lb.t'dbn. | nšb.l inr.t'dbn.ktp. | b il ab h.g'r.yṯb.il.kb[-]. | aṯ[rt.]il.yṯb.b mrzḥ h. | yšt[.il.y]n.'d UG5.1.1.14
.b šb't.ḥdrm.b ṯmnt. | ap.sgrt.yd'[t k.]bt.k an[št]. | k in.b ilht.ql[ṣ] k.mh.tarš[n]. | l btlt.'nt.w t[']n.btlt.'n[t]. | tḥm k.il 3['NT.VI].5.36
btlt.['nt]. | w y'n.lṭpn.il d p[id]. | yd't k.bt.k anšt.w i[n.b ilht]. | qlṣ k.tb'.bt.ḫnp.lb[k.--.ti] | ḫd.d iṯ.b kbd k.tšt.b [---]. 18[3AQHT].1.16
[---]. | ṯnnt h[.---]. | ṯlṯt h[.-.w y'n]. | lṭpn.[il.d pid.my]. | b ilm.[ydy.mrṣ]. | gršm.z[bln.in.b ilm]. | 'ny h.y[ṯny.yṯlṯ]. | rg 16[126].5.11
rṣ.grš[m.zbln]. | in.b ilm.'[ny h.yrb']. | yḫmš.rgm.[my.b ilm]. | ydy.mrṣ.g[ršm.zbln]. | in.b ilm.'n[y h.]yṯdṯ. | yšb'.rg 16[126].5.17
rṣ.g[ršm.zbln]. | in.b ilm.'n[y h.]yṯdṯ. | yšb'.rgm.[my.]b ilm. | ydy.mrṣ.gršm zbln. | in.b ilm.'ny h. | w y'n.lṭpn.il.b pi 16[126].5.20
rṣ]. | gršm.z[bln.in.b ilm]. | 'ny h.y[ṯny.yṯlṯ]. | rgm.my.b[ilm.ydy]. | mrṣ.grš[m.zbln]. | in.b ilm.'[ny h.yrb']. | yḫmš.r 16[126].5.14
h.]yṯdṯ. | yšb'.rgm.[my.]b ilm. | ydy.mrṣ.gršm zbln. | in.b ilm.'ny h. | w y'n.lṭpn.il.b pid. | ṯb.bn y.lm ṯb[t] km. | l kḥṯ. 16[126].5.22
[ṯny.yṯlṯ]. | rgm.my.b[ilm.ydy]. | mrṣ.grš[m.zbln]. | in.b ilm.'[ny h.yrb']. | yḫmš.rgm.[my.b ilm]. | ydy.mrṣ.g[ršm.zb 16[126].5.16
rb']. | yḫmš.rgm.[my.b ilm]. | ydy.mrṣ.g[ršm.zbln]. | in.b ilm.'n[y h.]yṯdṯ. | yšb'.rgm.[my.]b ilm. | ydy.mrṣ.gršm zbln 16[126].5.19
]. | lṭpn.[il.d pid.my]. | b ilm.[ydy.mrṣ]. | gršm.z[bln.in.b ilm]. | 'ny h.y[ṯny.yṯlṯ]. | rgm.my.b[ilm.ydy]. | mrṣ.grš[m.z 16[126].5.12
nn[-].b[n].py[-.d.]yṯb.b.gt.aǵld. | ŝgn.bn b[--.---].d.yṯb.b.ilštm'. | abmn.bn.r[---].b.syn. | bn.irṣ[-.---.]h. | šdyn.b[n.---.- 2015.2.6
ar. | bn.ag[p]ṯ.ḫpṯ.d[.yṯb.b].š'rt. | yly.bn.ṯrnq.[-]r.d.yṯb.b.ilštm'. | ilšlm.bn.gs[-.--]r.d.yṯb.b.gt.al. | ilmlk.[--]kt.[--.d.]yṯ 2015.1.26
---]. | btlt.['nt.---]. | mh.k[--.---]. | w at[--.---]. | aṯr[t.---]. | b im[--.---]. | bl.l[---.---]. | mlk.[---]. | dt [---]. | b ṭ[--.---]. | gm[.-- 4[51].2.42
l. | [---.b]nšm.b.m'r.arr. | arb'.bnšm.b.mnt. | arb'.bnšm.b.irbn. | ṯn.bnšm.b.y'rt. | ṯn.bnšm.b.'rmt. | arb'.bnšm.b.šrš. | ṯṯ 2076.34
.lṣb w yṣḥq. | yšu.g h.w yṣḥ. | aṯbn.ank.w anḫn. | w tnḫ.b irt y.npš. | k ḥy.aliyn.b'l. | k iṯ.zbl.b'l.arṣ. | gm.yṣḥ.il.l btlt. | ' 6[49].3.19
.l hdm.yṯpd.yšu. | g h.w yṣḥ.aṯbn.ank. | w anḫn.w tnḫ.b irt y. | npš.k yld.bn.l y.km. | aḫ y.w šrš.km ary y. | nṣb.skn.i 17[2AQHT].2.13
ym.ḫmš. | ṯdṯ.ym.tlḥmn.rpum. | tštyn.bt.ikl.b pr'. | yṣq.b irt.lbnn.mk.b šb'. | [ymm.---]k.aliyn.b'l. | [---].r' h ab y. | [-- 22.2[124].25
.'l k.b[']l m. | pht.qlt.'l k.pht. | dry.b ḥrb.'l k. | pht.šrp.b išt. | 'l k.[pht.ṭḥ]n.b rḥ | m.'[l k.]pht[.dr]y.b kbrt. | 'l k.pht.[6[49].5.14
t.aṯr.b'l.tiḫd. | bn.ilm.mt.b ḥrb. | tbq'nn.b ḫṯr.tdry | nn.b išt.tšrpnn. | b rḥm.tṭḥnn.b šd. | tdr'nn.šir h.l tikl. | 'ṣrm.mnt 6[49].2.33
]ṣn.l.dgn. | [---.--]m. | [---].pi[--.-]qš. | [--]pš.šn[--]. | ṯ[-]r.b iš[-]. | b'l h.š'[-]rt. | ḫqr.[--.ṯq]l rb. | ṯl[ṯ.---]. | aḥt.ḫm[-.---]. | b 39[19].8
mḏrǵlm.d.b.i[-]'lt.mlk. | arsw. | dqn. | ṯlṯ.klbm. | ḫmn. | [---.-]rsd. | bn[.-]pṯ 86[305].1
b i[--.---]. | l ṯ[--.---]. | ks[.---]. | kr[pn.---]. | at.š['tqt.---]. | š'd[.-- 16[126].5.38
[ḫm]š l 'šrm. | [-]dmm. | b.ubn. 1167.3
b.mlk. | ṣbr.aḥd. | b.m'rby. | ṣbr.aḥd. | b.ulm. | ṣbr.aḥd. | b.ubr'y. 2073.12
].w kl.hw[.---]. | w [--].brt.lb[--.---]. | u[-]šhr.nuš[-.---]. | b [u]grt.w ht.a[--]. | w hm.at.trg[m.---]. | w sip.u hw[.---]. | w 54.1.7[13.1.4]
ḥršm. | dt.tb'ln.b.pḫn. | ṯṯtm.ḫzr.w.'št.'šr.ḥrš. | dt.tb'ln.b.ugrt. | ṯṯtm.ḫzr. | dt.tb'ln. | b.gt.ḥršm. | ṯn.ḥršm. | [-]nbkm. | ṯ 1024.3.8
tkn. | [---.bn]šm.b.tmrm. | [---.bn]šm.b.ṯnq. | [---.b]nšm.b.ugrt. | [---.bn]šm.b.ǵbl. | [---.b]nšm.b.m'r.arr. | arb'.bnšm.b. 2076.30
l. | ab h.ḥpr.p'l k.y[--]. | šm' k.l arḫ.w bn.[--]. | limm.ql.b udn.k w[-]. | k rtqt mr[.---]. | k d lbšt.bir.mlak. | šmm.tmr.z 13[6].23
.b.ag[m]y. | arb'.bnšm.b.ḫpty. | ṯṯ.bnšm.b.bir. | ṯṯ.bnšm b.uḫnp. | ṯn.bnšm.b.ḫrṣb'. | arb'.bnšm.b.hzp. | arb'.bnšm.b.šql 2076.14
ṯn.b gt.mzln. | ṯn.b ulm. | abmn.b gt.m'rb. | atn. | ḫryn. | bn.'nt. | llwn. | agdṯb. | a 1061.2
l. | bn.tran.mḏrǵl | bn.ilh.mḏrǵl | špšyn.b.ulm. | bn.qṭn.b.ulm. | bn.gdrn.b.m'r[by]. | [w].bn.d'm[-]. | bn.ppṯ.b[--]. | b[n. 2046.1.6
. | bn.qrrn.mḏrǵl. | bn.tran.mḏrǵl | bn.ilh.mḏrǵl | špšyn.b.ulm. | bn.qṭn.b.ulm. | bn.gdrn.b.m'r[by]. | [w].bn.d'm[-]. | b 2046.1.5
d.l.ṭb. | b.gt.m'rby. | ṯṯm.yn.ṭb.w.ḫmš.l.'šrm. | yn.d.l.ṭb.b.ulm. | mit.yn.ṭb.w.ṯṯm.ṯṯ.kbd. | yn.d.l.ṭb.b.gt.ḥdṯt. | tš'm.yn. 1084.10
. | b.ar. | ṣbr.aḥd. | b.mlk. | ṣbr.aḥd. | b.m'rby. | ṣbr.aḥd. | b.ulm. | ṣbr.aḥd. | b.ubr'y. 2073.10
m. | mḫrhn.nit.mit.krk.mit. | m'ṣd.ḫmšm.mqb.[']šrm. | b.ulm.ṯṯ.'šr h.ḫrmṯt. | ṯt.nitm.ṯn.m'ṣdm.ṯn.mqbm. | krk.aḥt. | 2048.4
ŝ]ŝw[.i]ryn.arr. | [š]dm.b.mlk. | [--.š]dm.b.ar. | [--.š]dm.b.ulm. | [--.š]dm.b.m'rby. | [--.šd]m.b.uškn. | [---.--]n. | [---].tl 2033.1.4
]. | šm[-.---]. | tkn[.---]. | knn.b.ḫ[lb]. | bn mṯ.b.qmy. | n'r.b.ulm. 2046.2.6
mṣry.d.'rb.b.unṯ. | bn.qrrn.mḏrǵl. | bn.tran.mḏrǵl | bn.ilh.mḏrǵl | špšyn.b 2046.1.1

l.yi[--.-]m[---].|b unṯ.km.špš.|d brt.kmt.|br.ṣtqšlm.|b unṯ.ʻd ʻlm.|mišmn.n 1001.1.19
l.yi[--.-]m[---].|b unṯ.km.špš.|d brt.kmt.|br.ṣtqšlm.|b unṯ.ʻd ʻlm.|mišmn.nqmd.|mlk ugrt.|nqmd.mlk.ugrt.|ktb 1005.5
.zbl ym.bn ydm.|[tp]ṭ nhr.yrtqṣ.ṣmd.b d bʻl.km.nšr.|b[u]ṣbʻt h.ylm.ktp.zbl ym.bn ydm.ṯpṭ.|nhr.ʻz.ym.l ymk.l t 2.4[68].16
rš ym.l ksi h.|[n]hr l kḥṯ drkt h.trtqṣ.b d bʻl km nš|r.b uṣbʻt h.hlm.ktp.zbl ym.bn ydm.|[ṯp]ṭ nhr.yrtqṣ.ṣmd.b d b 2.4[68].14
.mr.ym.|l ksi h.nhr l kḥṯ.drkt h.trtqṣ.|b d bʻl.km.nšr b uṣbʻt h.hlm.qdq|d zbl ym.bn.ʻnm.ṯpṭ.nhr.yprsḥ ym.|w y 2.4[68].21
.yprsḥ ym.|w yql.l arṣ.w trtqṣ.ṣmd.b d bʻl.|[km.]nšr.b uṣbʻt h.ylm.qdqd.zbl.|[ym.]bn.ʻnm.ṯpṭ.nhr.yprsḥ.ym.yql. 2.4[68].24
t š.bʻl ḫlb š.|yrḫ š.ʻnt ṣpn.alp.|w š.pdry š.ddmš š.|w b urbt.ilib š.|bʻl alp w š.|dgn.š.il tʻḏr.š.|bʻl š.ʻnt š.ršp š.|šl UG5.13.19
[--].yṯkḥ.w yiḫd.b qrb[.-].|[--.t]ṯkḥ.w tiḫd.b uš[k.--].|[-.b]ʻl.yabd.l alp.|[---.bt]lt.ʻnt.|[---]q.hry.w yld.| 11[132].1.2
ṯn.ṣbrm.|b.uškn.|ṣbr.aḥd.|b.ar.|ṣbr.aḥd.|b.mlk.|ṣbr.aḥd.|b.mʻrby.| 2073.2
]dm.b.ar.|[--.š]dm.b.ulm.|[--.š]dm.b.mʻrby.|[--.šd]m.b.uškn.|[---.--]n.|[---].tlmdm.|[y]bnn.ṣmdm.|ṯp[ṭ]bʻl.ṣmdm 2033.1.6
[--.]ubdym.b.uškn.|[---]lby.|[--]nbbl.|bn bl.|bn dkn.|bn ils.|bn ḫšbn.| 1064.1
l bn.bly.|šd gzl.l.bn.ṭbr[n].|šd.ḫzmyn.l a[--].|ṯn šdm b uš[kn]. 2089.16
[--].|arbʻ.bnšm.b.ag[m]y.|arbʻ.bnšm.b.ḫpty.|ṯṯ.bnšm.b.bir.|ṯṯ.bnšm b.uḫnp.|ṯn.bnšm.b.ḫrṣbʻ.|arbʻ.bnšm.b.hzp.| 2076.13
ilht kṯrt bn]|t hll.snnt.bnt h|ll bʻl gml.yrdt.|b ʻrgzm.b bz tdm.|lla y.ʻm lẓpn i|l ḏ.pid.hn b p y sp|r hn.b špt y m 24[77].43
b gt ilštmʻ.|bt ubnyn š h d.ytn.ṣtqn.|ṭut ṭbḫ ṣtq[n].|b bz ʻzm ṭbḫ š[h].|b kl ygz ḥḫ š h. 1153.4
mʻ.|tntkn.udmʻt h.|km.ṯqlm.arṣ h.|km ḫmšt.mṭt h.|bm.bky h.w yšn.|b dmʻ h.nhmmt.|šnt.tluan.|w yškb.nhm 14[KRT].1.31
.b]nm.aqny.|[ṯn.ṯa]rm.amid.|[w yʻn].ṯr.ab h.il.|d[--].b bk.krt.|b dmʻ.nʻmn.ǵlm.|il.trḥṣ.w tadm.|rḥṣ[.y]d k.amt. 14[KRT].2.60
n.pdrn.ʻšrm.|d.bn.šbʻl.uḫnpy.ḫmšm.|b.bn.ṯtm.ṯlṯm.|b.bn.agdṯb.ʻšrm.|b.bn.ibn.arbʻt.ʻšrt.|b.bn.mnn.ṯtm.|b.rpan. 2054.1.12
-].|b.[---.---]r.|b.ann[.---.-]ny[-].|b.ḫqn.[---]m.ṣ[-]n.|[b].bn.ay[--.---].l.ʻšrm.|[-]gp[.---.]ʻrny.ṯtm.|[---.]dyn.ḫmšt.ʻšr 2054.2.17
.šbʻl.uḫnpy.ḫmšm.|b.bn.ṯtm.ṯlṯm.|b.bn.agdṯb.ʻšrm.|b.bn.ibn.arbʻt.ʻšrt.|b.bn.mnn.ṯtm.|b.rpan.bn.yyn.ʻšrt.|b.ypʻ 2054.1.13
.gm.yṣḥ il.|l rbt.aṯrt ym.šmʻ.|l rbt.aṯr[t] ym.tn.|aḥd.b bn k.amlkn.|w tʻn.rbt.aṯrt ym.|bl.nmlk.ydʻ.ylḥn.|w yʻn.l 6.1.46[49.1.18]
|b.bn.ṯtm.ṯlṯm.|b.bn.agdṯb.ʻšrm.|b.bn.ibn.arbʻt.ʻšrt.|b.bn.mnn.ṯtm.|b.rpan.bn.yyn.ʻšrt.|b.ypʻr.ʻšrm.|b.nʻmn.bn. 2054.1.14
.ksp.|[--.--]n.šbʻt.l ṯlṯm.|[---].šbʻt.ʻšrt.|[---.-]kyn.ʻšrt.|b.bn.ʻsl.ʻšrm.ṯqlm kbd.|b.ṯmq.ḫmšt.l.ʻšrt.|b.[---].šbʻt.ʻšrt.|b 2054.1.14
ʻsl.ʻšrm.ṯqlm kbd.|b.ṯmq.ḫmšt.l.ʻšrt.|b.[---].šbʻt.ʻšrt.|b.bn.pdrn.ʻšrm.|d.bn.šbʻl.uḫnpy.ḫmšm.|b.bn.ṯtm.ṯlṯm.|b.b 2054.1.6
.ply.ḫmšt.l.ʻšrm.|b.gdn.bn.uss.ʻšrm.|b.ʻdn.bn.ṯṯ.ʻšrt.|b.bn.qrdmn.ṯlṯm.|b.bṣmn[.bn].ḥrtn.ʻ[--].|b.t[--.---] h.[---].|[2054.1.9
--].šbʻt.ʻšrt.|b.bn.pdrn.ʻšrm.|d.bn.šbʻl.uḫnpy.ḫmšm.|b.bn.ṯtm.ṯlṯm.|b.bn.agdṯb.ʻšrm.|b.bn.ibn.arbʻt.ʻšrt.|b.bn.m 2054.1.20
rišym.dt.ʻrb.|b bnš hm.|ḏmry.w.pṯpṭ.ʻrb.|b.yrm.|[ily.w].ḏmry.ʻrb.|b.ṯbʻ 2054.1.11
[---.]nnd[-].|[-]gbt.|[--]y bnš kb[š]y.|krmpy.b.bṣm.|[-]mrn.ṣd.b gl[-]. 2079.2
.gdn.bn.uss.ʻšrm.|b.ʻdn.bn.ṯṯ.ʻšrt.|b.bn.qrdmn.ṯlṯm.|b.bṣmn[.bn].ḥrtn.ʻ[--].|b.t[--.---] h.[---].|[-----].|[--]ly.ḫmšm 2169.4
.b.ʻrmt.|arbʻ.bnšm.b.šrš.|ṯṯ.bnšm.b.mlk.|arbʻ.bnšm.b.bṣr.|ṯn.bnšm.[b.]rqd.|ṯn.b[nšm.b.---]y.|[---].b[nšm.b.--]nl 2054.1.21
--].b.dmt qdš.|[---].b.dmt qdš.|[---.--]n.b.anan.|[--]yl.b.bqʻt.b.gt.tgyn.|[--]in.b.trzy.|[--]yn.b.glltky.|ṯd[y]n.b.glltk 2076.39
šmal[.---].|arbḫ.ʻn h tšu w[.---].|aylt ṭǵpy ṭr.ʻn[.---].|b[b]r.mrḫ h.ti[ḫd.b yd h].|š[g]r h bm ymn.t[--.---].|[--.]l bʻl 2118.6
sp.|šmrgt.b dm.ḫrṣ.|kḥṯ.il.nḫt.|b ẓr.hdm.id.|d pršа.b br.|nʻl.il.d qblbl.|ʻln.ybl hm.ḫrṣ.|ṯlḥn.il.d mla.|mnm.dbb 2001.1.12
--]t[.----].|l mṭb[.--]t[.---].|[tqdm.]yd.b ṣʻ.t[šl]ḥ.|[ḥrb.b]bš[r].tštn.|[w tʻn].mṯt.ḥry.|[l lḥ]m.l šty.ṣḥt k[m].|[---.]br 4[51].1.36
un.|lm.mṭb[.---].|w lḥm mr.tqdm.|yd.b ṣʻ.tšlḥ.|ḥrb.b bšr.tštn.|[w t]ʻn.mṯt.ḥry.|[l lḥ]m.l šty.ṣḥt km.|[--.dbḥ.l] 15[128].5.8
t.aḥt.b.bt.iwrpzn.|ṯt.aṯtm.w.pǵt.aḥt.b bt.[-]r[-].|[aṯ]t.b.bt.aupš.|[aṯ]t.b.bt.ṯpṯbʻl.|[---.]n[--.mḏ]rǵlm.|[---.]b.bt[.--- 15[128].4.25
zrm.b.bt.ṣdqš[lm].|[a]ṯt.aḥt.b.bt.rpi[--].|[aṯt.]w.bt h.b.bt.alḫn.|[aṯt.w.]pǵt.aḥt.b.bt.tt.|[aṯt.w.]bt h.b.bt.trǵds.|[-- 80[119].12
.pǵt.aḥt.b[.bt.---].|aṯt.w ṯn.nʻrm.b.bt.ilsk.|aṯt.ad[r]t.b.bt.armwl.|aṯt.aḥt.b.bt.iwrpzn.|ṯt.aṯtm.w.pǵt.aḥt.b bt.[-]r[80[119].25
.|[aṯt.]w.pǵt.b.bt.gg.|[ǵz]r.aḥd.b.bt.nwrḏ.|[aṯ]t.adrt.b.bt.arṯṯb.|aṯt.w.ṯn.bn h.b.bt.iwwpzn.|aṯt.w.pǵt.b.bt.ydrm.| 80[119].9
]r.aḥd.b.bt.nwrḏ.|[aṯ]t.adrt.b.bt.arṯṯb.|aṯt.w.ṯn.bn h.b.bt.iwwpzn.|aṯt.w.pǵt.b.bt.ydrm.|ṯt.aṯtm.adrtm.w.pǵt.aḥt 80[119].4
aṯt.w ṯn.nʻrm.b.bt.ilsk.|aṯt.ad[r]t.b.bt.armwl.|aṯt.aḥt.b.bt.iwrpzn.|ṯt.aṯtm.w.pǵt.aḥt.b bt.[-]r[-].|[aṯ]t.b.bt.aupš.|[80[119].5
rm.|ṯt.aṯtm.adrtm.w.pǵt.aḥt.b[.bt.---].|aṯt.w ṯn.nʻrm.b.bt.ilsk.|aṯt.ad[r]t.b.bt.armwl.|aṯt.aḥt.b.bt.iwrpzn.|ṯt.aṯt 80[119].10
[aṯt.w].bn h.b.bt.krz.|[aṯt.]w.pǵt.b.bt.gg.|[ǵz]r.aḥd.b.bt.nwrḏ.|[aṯ]t.adrt.b.bt.arṯṯb.|aṯt.w.ṯn. 80[119].8
mʻ.mhrm.|ʻd.tšbʻ.tmtḫṣ.b bt.|tḫṣb.bn.ṯlḥnm.ymḥ.|[b]bt.dm.ḏmr.yṣq.šmn.|šlm.b ṣʻ.trḥṣ.yd h.bt|[l]t.ʻnt.uṣbʻt h. 80[119].2
m[.w]m|ria.il.ʻglm.d[t].|šnt.imr.qmṣ.l[l]im.|ṣḥ.aḫ h.b bht h.a[r]y h.|b qrb hkl h.ṣḥ.|šbʻm.bn.aṯrt.|špq.ilm.krm. 3[ʻNT].2.31
[---.bʻl.b bht h].|[il.hd.b qr]b.hkl h.|w tʻnyn.ǵlm.bʻl.|in.bʻl.b bht h 4[51].6.44
l.b bht h].|[il.hd.b qr]b.hkl h.|w tʻnyn.ǵlm.bʻl.|in.bʻl.b bht ht.|il hd.b qrb.hkl h.|qšt hn.aḥd.b yd h.|w qṣʻt h.bm. 10[76].2.1
yd.il.k mdb.yqḥ.il.mštʻltm.|mštʻltm.l riš.agn.yqḥ.tš.b bt h.|il.ḥṭ h.nḥt.il.ymnn.mṭ.yd h.yšu.|yr.šmm h.yr.b šm 10[76].2.4
r] šmm.ʻm.|ḫr[ḫ]b mlk qẓ.tn nkl y|rḫ ytrḫ.ib tʻrb m b bh|t h.w atn mhr h l a|b h.alp ksp w rbt ḫ|rṣ.išlḥ ẓhrm i 23[52].36
ṣ y.b ym.rṯ.|dn.il.bt h.ymǵyn.|yštql.dnil.l hkl h.|ʻrb.b bt h.kṯrt.bnt.|hll.snnt.apnk.dnil.|mt.rpi.ap.hn.ǵzr.mt.|hr 24[77].18
ḥm.k[ṯ]rt.|w y[ššq].bnt.hll.snnt.|mk.b šb[ʻ.]ymm.tbʻ.b bt h.|kṯrt.bnt.hll.snnt.|[-]d[-]t.nʻm y.ʻrš.h[--]m.|ysmsmt.ʻ 17[2AQHT].2.26
ht.ksp.|w ḫrṣ.bht.ṭhrm.|iqnim.šmḫ.aliyn.|bʻl.ṣḥ.ḫrn.b bht h.|ʻdbt.b qrb hkl h.|yblnn ǵrm.mid.ksp.|gbʻm lḥmd. 17[2AQHT].2.39
il dbḥ.b bt h.mṣd.ṣd.b qrb|hkl [h].ṣḥ.l qṣ.ilm.tlḥmn.|ilm.w tštn.tš 4[51].5.98
m y.ršp zbl.|[w ʻd]t.ilm.ṯlṯ h.|[ap]nk.krt.ṯʻ.ʻ[-]r.|[--.]b bt h.yšt.ʻrb.|[--] h.ytn.w [--]u.l ytn.|[aḫ]r.mǵy.ʻ[d]t.ilm.|[UG5.1.1.1
bh[t] m.|ḥln.b qrb.hkl m.|w yʻn.aliyn bʻl.|al.tšt.urbt.b[bhtm].|[ḥln].b qrb.hk[l m]. 15[128].2.9
[bt.---].|aṯt.w.bn h.w.pǵt.aḥt.b.bt.m[--].|aṯt.w.ṯt.bt h.b.bt.ḫdmrd.|aṯt.w.ṯn.ǵzrm.b.bt.ṣdqš[lm].|[a]ṯt.aḥt.b.bt.rpi[4[51].5.126
m.tǵll b dm.|ḏmr.ḥlqm.b mmʻ.mhrm.|ʻd.tšbʻ.tmtḫṣ.b bt.|tḫṣb.bn.ṯlḥnm.ymḥ.|[b]bt.dm.ḏmr.yṣq.šmn.|šlm.b ṣʻ 80[119].22
.w ʻbd.|ʻlm.ṯlṯ.sswm.|mrkbt.b trbṣ.|bn.amt.p d.[i]n.|b bt y.ttn.tn.|l y.mṯt.ḥry.|nʻmt.šbḥ.bkr k.|d k nʻm.ʻnt.|nʻ 3[ʻNT].2.29
h.w ʻbd.|ʻlm.ṯlṯ.sswm.mrkbt.|b trbṣt.bn.amt.|p d.in.b bt y.ttn.|tn.l y.mṯt.ḥry.|nʻmt.špḥ.bkr k.|d k.nʻm.ʻnt.nʻm 14[KRT].6.288
[--].[-]l[--.b qr]|b hkl y.[---].|lk bt y.r[pim.rpim.b bt y.aṣḥ].|km.iqr[a km.ilnym.b hkl y].|aṯr h.r[pum.l tdd. 14[KRT].3.142
.il[nym.---].|mhr.bʻl[.---.mhr].|ʻnt.lk b[t y.rpim.rpim.b bt y].|aṣḥ.km.[iqra km.ilnym.b] |hkl y.aṯr[h.rpum.l tdd] 22.1[123].3
m.ym[.---].|ʻl amr.yu[ḫd.ksa.mlk h].|nḫt.kḥṯ.d[rkt h.b bt y].|aṣḥ.rpi[m.iqra.ilnym].|b qrb.h[kl y.aṯr h.rpum.l] |t 22.1[123].8
adrt.b.bt.arṯṯb.|aṯt.w.ṯn.bn h.b.bt.iwwpzn.|aṯt.w.pǵt.b.bt.ydrm.|ṯt.aṯtm.adrtm.w.pǵt.aḥt.b[.bt.---].|aṯt.w ṯn.nʻrm 22.1[123].18

lln h.|hm.bt.lbnt.y‘msn h.|l yrgm.l aliyn b‘l.|ṣḥ.ḫrn.b bhm k.|‘ḏbt.b qrb.hkl k.|tbl k.ǵrm.mid.ksp.|gb‘m.mḥmd 4[51].5.75
.yblt.y[b]n.|bt.l k.km.aḫ k.w ḥẓr.|km.ary k.ṣḥ.ḫrn.|b bht k.‘ḏbt.b qrb.|hkl k.tbl k.ǵrm.|mid.ksp.gb‘m.mḥmd.. 4[51].5.92
.ytn.g h.|bky.b ḥy k.ab n.ašmḫ.|b l.mt k.ngln.k klb.|b bt k.n‘tq.k inr.|ap.ḫšt k.ap.ab.k mtm.|tmtn.u ḫšt k.l ntn. 16.1[125].16
[l]krt.|k [k]lb.b bt k.n‘tq.k inr.|ap.ḫšt k.ap.ab.ik mtm.|tmtn.u ḫšt k.l ntn 16.1[125].2
n.|g h.bky.b ḥ[y k.a]b n.|nšmḫ.b l.mt k.ngln.|k klb.[b]bt k.n‘tq.|k inr[.ap.]ḫšt k.|ap.ab.k mtm.tmtn.|u ḫšt k.l 16.2[125].100
].|w [--].|d [--].|ypḫ[--].|w s[--].|[---].|qrd ga[n.--].|b bt k.[--].|w l dbḥ[--].|ṭ[--].|[--] aṯt yqḥ ‘z.|[---]ḏ.|[---].|[- RS61[24.277.22]
[aṯt.w].bn h.b.bt.krz.|[aṯt.]w.pǵt.b.bt.gg.|[ǵz]r.aḥd.b.bt.nwrḏ.|[aṯ]t.adr 80[119].1
‘n.aliyn.|b‘l.ašt m.kṯr bn.|ym.kṯr.bnm.‘dt.|ypth.ḥln.b bht m.|urbt.b qrb.[h]kl |m.w y[p]tḥ.b dqt.‘rpt.|‘l h[wt].k 4[51].7.17
ṣḥ.|l rgmt.l k.l ali|yn.b‘l.ṯṯbn.b‘l.|l hwt y.yptḥ.ḥ|ln.b bht m.urbt.|b qrb.hk[l m.yp]tḥ.|b‘l.b dqt[.‘rp]t.|ql h.qdš. 4[51].7.26
ṯn.rgm.k[ṯr.w]ḫss.|šm‘.m‘.l al[iy]n b‘l.|bl.ašt.ur[bt.]b bht m.|ḥln.b qr[b.hk]l m.|w ‘n.ali[yn.]b‘l.|al.tšt.u[rb]t.b 4[51].6.5
n.kṯr.w ḫss.|šm‘.l aliyn b‘l.|bn.l rkb.‘rpt.|bl.ašt.urbt.b bh[t] m.|ḥln.b qrb.hkl m.|w y‘n.aliyn b‘l.|al.tšt.urbt.b[b 4[51].5.123
t m.|ḥln.b qr[b.hk]l m.|w ‘n.ali[yn.]b‘l.|al.tšt.u[rb]t.b bht m.|ḥln.b q[rb.hk]l m.|al td[.pdr]y.bt ar.|[---.ṭl]y.bt.r 4[51].6.8
d.arz h.|h[n.l]bnn.w ‘ṣ h.|š[r]yn.mḥmd.arz h.|tšt.išt.b bht m.|nb[l]at.b hkl m.|hn.ym.w ṯn.tikl.|išt.b bht m.nbla 4[51].6.22
ikl.|išt.b bht m.nblat.|b hk[l] m.ṯlṯ.kb‘ ym.|tikl[.i]št.b bht m.|nbla[t.]b hkl m.|ḫmš.ṯ[d]ṯ.ym.tikl.|išt.[b]bht m. 4[51].6.27
ht m.nblat.|b[qrb.hk]l m.mk.|b šb[‘.]y[mm].td.išt.|b bht m.n[bl]at.b hkl m.|sb.ksp.l rqm.ḫrṣ.|nṣb.l lbnt.šmḫ.| 4[51].6.33
tšt.išt.b bht m.|nb[l]at.b hkl m.|hn.ym.w ṯn.tikl.|išt.b bht m.nblat.|b hk[l] m.ṯlṯ.kb‘ ym.|tikl[.i]št.b bht m.|nbla 4[51].6.25
i]št.b bht m.|nbla[t.]b hkl m.|ḫmš.ṯ[d]ṯ.ym.tikl.|išt.[b]bht m.nblat.|b[qrb.hk]l m.mk.|b šb[‘.]y[mm].td.išt.|b b 4[51].6.30
iyb‘l.|ṯlṯm.l.mit.š‘rt.|l.šr.‘ṯtrt.|mlbš.ṯrmnm.|k.ytn.w.b.bt.|mlk.mlbš.|ytn.l hm.|šb‘.lbšm.allm.|l ušḫry.|ṯlṯ.mat. 1107.6
ḏrǵlm.|w.šb‘.‘šr.ḫsnm.|ḫmšm.l.mit.|bnš.l.d.|yškb.l.b.bt.mlk. 1029.16
kbd.ḫsnm.|ubnyn.|ṯṯm[.l.]mit.ṯlṯ.|kbd[.tg]mr.bnš.|l.b.bt.mlk. 1028.14
aṯtm.w.pǵt.w.ǵzr.aḥd.b.[bt.---].|aṯt.w.bn h.w.pǵt.aḥt.b.bt.m[--].|aṯt.w.ṯt.bt h.b.bt.ḫḏmrd.|aṯt.w.ṯn.ǵzrm.b.bt.ṣdq 80[119].21
[aṯt.w].bn h.b.bt.krz.|[aṯt.]w.pǵt.b.bt.gg.|[ǵz]r.aḥd.b.bt.nwrḏ.|[aṯ]t.adrt.b.bt.artṯb.|aṯt.w.ṯn.bn h.b.bt.iwwpzn. 80[119].3
qmḥ.d.kly.b bt.skn.|l.illḏrm.|lṯḥ.ḫṣr.b.šb‘.ddm. 2093.1
[---.]b.bt[.---]l.|[ṯ]lṯ.aṯt.adrt.w.ṯlṯ.ǵzr[m].|w.ḫmš.n‘rt.b.bt.sk[n].|ṯt.aṯtm.adrtm.w.pǵt.w ǵzr[.aḥd.b.bt.---].|aṯt.w.ṯ 80[119].17
t.b.bt.m[--].|aṯt.w.ṯt.bt h.b.bt.ḫḏmrd.|aṯt.w.ṯn.ǵzrm.b.bt.ṣdqš[lm].|[a]ṯt.aḥt.b.bt.rpi[--].|[aṯt.]w.bt h.b.bt.alḫn.|[80[119].23
h.b.bt.ḫḏmrd.|aṯt.w.ṯn.ǵzrm.b.bt.ṣdqš[lm].|[a]ṯt.aḥt.b.bt.rpi[--].|[aṯt.]w.bt h.b.bt.alḫn.|[aṯt.w.]pǵt.aḥt.b.bt.tt.|[80[119].24
ḥmt.|[---.--] n.ylt.ḥmḥmt.|[---.mt.r]pi.w ykn.bn h.|[b bt.šrš.]b qrb.hkl h.|[nṣb.skn.i]lib h.b qdš.|[ztr.‘m h.l a]rṣ. 17[2AQHT].1.44
|l tbrknn l ṯr.il ab y.|tmrnn.l bny.bnwt.|w ykn.bn h b bt.šrš.b qrb.|hkl h.nṣb.skn.ilib h.b qdš.|ztr.‘m h.l arṣ.mšṣ 17[2AQHT].1.26
]w.bt h.b.bt.alḫn.|[aṯt.w.]pǵt.aḥt.b.bt.tt.|[aṯt.w.]bt h.b.bt.trǵds.|[---.]aṯt.adrt.w.pǵt.a[ḥt.b.bt.---].|[---.‘]šrm.npš.b 80[119].27
ḥt.b.bt.rpi[--].|[aṯt.]w.bt h.b.bt.alḫn.|[aṯt.w.]pǵt.aḥt.b.bt.tt.|[aṯt.w.]bt h.b.bt.trǵds.|[---.]aṯt.adrt.w.pǵt.a[ḥt.b.bt. 80[119].26
]ṯq.|w š[--.---].|ḥdṯ[.---.]ḥ[--].|b bt.[-.]l bnt.q[-].|w št.b bt.ṯap[.--].|hy.yd h.w ym[ǵ].|mlak k.‘m dt[n].|lqḥ.mṯpṭ. UG5.6.9
n.|ṯt.aṯtm.w.pǵt.aḥt.b bt.[-]r[-].|[aṯ]t.b.bt.aupš.|[aṯ]t.b.bt.ṯpṭb‘l.|[---.]n[--.mḏ]rǵlm.|[---.]b.bt[.---]l.|[ṯ]lṯ.aṯt.adrt. 80[119].13
[-].|[---.--]m.šr.d.yṯ[b].|[---.--]y.d.ḫbṯ.sy[--].|[---.--]y.b.bt.ṯr[--]. 2134.11
‘ny.nn[.--].|t‘ny.n[---.-]ṯq.|w š[--.---].|ḥdṯ[.---.]ḥ[--].|b bt.[-.]l bnt.q[-].|w št.b bt.ṯap[.--].|hy.yd h.w ym[ǵ].|mlak UG5.6.8
]t.b.bt.armwl.|aṯt.aḥt.b.bt.iwrpzn.|ṯt.aṯtm.w.pǵt.aḥt.b bt.[-]r[-].|[aṯ]t.b.bt.aupš.|[aṯ]t.b.bt.ṯpṭb‘l.|[---.]n[--.mḏ]rǵ 80[119].11
ṯt.pǵtm.w.ǵzr.aḥd.b.[bt.---].|ṯt.aṯtm.w.pǵt.w.ǵzr.aḥd.b.[bt.---].|aṯt.w.bn h.w.pǵt.aḥt.b.bt.m[--].|aṯt.w.ṯt.bt h.b.bt. 80[119].20
wpzn.|aṯt.w.pǵt.b.bt.ydrm.|ṯt.aṯtm.adrtm.w.pǵt.aḥt.b[.bt.---].|aṯt.w ṯn.n‘rm.b.bt.ilsk.|aṯt.ad[r]t.b.bt.armwl.|aṯt 80[119].7
.ḫmš.n‘rt.b.bt.sk[n].|ṯt.aṯtm.adrtm.w.pǵt.w ǵzr[.aḥd.b.bt.---].|aṯt.w.ṯt.pǵtm.w.ǵzr.aḥd.b.[bt.---].|ṯt.aṯtm.w.pǵt.w 80[119].18
.w.pǵt.w ǵzr[.aḥd.b.bt.---].|aṯt.w.ṯt.pǵtm.w.ǵzr.aḥd.b.[bt.---].|ṯt.aṯtm.w.pǵt.w.ǵzr.aḥd.b.[bt.---].|aṯt.w.bn h.w.p 80[119].19
rǵds.|[---.]aṯt.adrt.w.pǵt.a[ḥt.b.bt.---].|[---.‘]šrm.npš.b.bt.[---].|[---.]w.pǵt.aḥt.b.bt.[---]. 80[119].29
.bt.tt.|[aṯt.w.]bt h.b.bt.trǵds.|[---.]aṯt.adrt.w.pǵt.a[ḥt.b.bt.---].|[---.‘]šrm.npš.b.bt.[---].|[---.]w.pǵt.aḥt.b.bt.[---]. 80[119].28
.a[ḥt.b.bt.---].|[---.‘]šrm.npš.b.bt.[---].|[---.]w.pǵt.aḥt.b.bt.[---]. 80[119].30
t.b.bt.aupš.|[aṯ]t.b.bt.ṯpṭb‘l.|[---.]n[--.mḏ]rǵlm.|[---.]b.bt[.---]l.|[ṯ]lṯ.aṯt.adrt.w.ṯlṯ.ǵzr[m].|w.ḫmš.n‘rt.b.bt.sk[n]. 80[119].15
[-----].|[--.]l tṣi.b b[--].bm.k[--].|[--]tb.‘ryt k.k qlt[.---].|[--]at.brt.lb k.‘nn.[-- 60[32].2
br.|ḥrn.y bn.yṯbr.ḥrn.|riš k.‘ṯtrt.šm.b‘l.|qdqd k.tqln.b gbl.|šnt k.b ḥpn k.w t‘n.|spr ilmlk ṯ‘y. 16.6[127].57
yṯbr.ḥrn].|riš k.‘ṯtrt.[šm.b‘l.qdqd k.---].|[--]t.mṭ.tpln.b g[bl.šnt k.---].|[--]šnm.aṯtm.t[--.---].|[m]lakm.ylak.ym.[t‘ 2.1[137].9
ank.|ibǵy h.b tk.ǵr y.il.ṣpn.|b qdš.b ǵr.nḥlt y.|b n‘m.b gb‘.tliyt.|hlm.‘nt.tph.ilm.b h.p‘nm.|tṭṭ.b‘d n.ksl.ṯṯbr.|‘ln. 3[‘NT].3.28
w.]b.ym.ḥdṯ.ṯn.šm.|l.[---]t.|i[d.yd]bḥ.mlk.l.prgl.ṣqrn.b.gg.|ar[b‘.]arb‘.mṯbt.azmr.b h.š.šr[-].|al[p.w].š.šlmm.pam 35[3].50
[al.tšmḫ.]al.tš[mḫ.b rm.h]|[kl k.al.]aḫd hm.[---].|[---.b]gdlt.ar[kt y.am--].|[---.qdq]d k.ašhlk[.šbt k.dmm].|[šbt.d 18[3AQHT].1.10
|al.tšmḫ.b r[m.h]kl[k].|al.aḫd.hm.b y[--] y.[---]b[-].|b gdlt.arkt y.am[---].|qdqd k.ašhlk.šbt[k.dmm].|[šbt.dqn k 3[‘NT.VI].5.31
bn.yyn.‘šrt.|b.yp‘r.‘šrm.|b.n‘mn.bn.ply.ḫmšt.l.‘šrm.|b.gdn.bn.uss.‘šrm.|b.‘dn.bn.ṯṯ.‘šrt.|b.bn.qrdmn.ṯlṯm.|b.bṣ 2054.1.18
ṯn.gprm.mn gpr h.šr.|aqht.y‘n.kmr.kmr[.--].|k ap‘.il.b gdrt.k lb.l |ḫṯ h.imḫṣ h.k d.‘l.qšt h.|imḫṣ h.‘l.qṣ‘t h.hwt.| 19[1AQHT].1.13
‘ṣd.mqb.|b.gt.‘mq.ḫmš.ḫrmṯt.n[it].|krk.m‘ṣd.mqb.|b.gwl.ṯmn.ḫrmṯt.[nit].|krk.m‘ṣd.mqb.|[b] gt.ipṯl.ṯṯ.ḫrmṯ[t. 2048.11
lla.klatnm.|klt.lḥm h.d nzl.|lqḥ.msrr.‘ṣr.db[ḥ].|yṣq.b gl.ḥṯt.yn.|b gl.ḫrṣ.nbt.w ‘ly.|l ẓr.mgdl.rkb.|ṯkmm.ḥmt.nš 14[KRT].4.164
a.kl[atn]m.|klt.l[ḥm k.d]nzl.|qḥ.ms[rr.]‘ṣr.|dbḥ.ṣ[q.b g]l.ḥṯt.|yn.b gl[.ḫ]rṣ.nbt.|‘l.l ẓr.[mg]dl.|w ‘l.l ẓr.[mg]dl.r 14[KRT].2.71
klt.lḥm h.d nzl.|lqḥ.msrr.‘ṣr.db[ḥ].|yṣq.b gl.ḥṯt.yn.|b gl.ḫrṣ.nbt.w ‘ly.|l ẓr.mgdl.rkb.|ṯkmm.ḥmt.nša.|[y]d h.š 14[KRT].4.165
lt.l[ḥm k.d]nzl.|qḥ.ms[rr.]‘ṣr.|dbḥ.ṣ[q.b g]l.ḥṯt.|yn.b gl[.ḫ]rṣ.nbt.|‘l.l ẓr.[mg]dl.|w ‘l.l ẓr.[mg]dl.rkb.|ṯkmm.ḥ 14[KRT].2.72
i[--.---].|d.[---].|bnš[-] mdy[-].|w.b.glb.|phnn.w.|mndym.|bdnh.|l[q]ḥt.|[--]km.‘m.mlk.|[b] 2129.4
b.bq‘t.b.gt.tgyn.|[--]in.b.trzy.|[--]yn.b.glltky.|ṯd[y]n.b.glltky.|lbw[-].uḫ.pdm.b.y‘rt.|pǵyn.b.tpḥ.|amri[l].b.šrš.|a 2118.9
n.b.anan.|[--]yl.b.bq‘t.b.gt.tgyn.|[--]in.b.trzy.|[--]yn.b.glltky.|ṯd[y]n.b.glltky.|lbw[-].uḫ.pdm.b.y‘rt.|pǵyn.b.tpḥ. 2118.8
.tply.ṭly.bn.‘n h.|uz‘rt.tmll.išd h.qrn[m].|dt.‘l h.riš h.b glṯ.b šm[m].|[---.i]l.ṯr.iṯ.p h.k ṯt.ǵlt[.--].|[---.--] k yn.ddm. UG5.3.1.7
.|rḫntt.d[-].l irt k.|wn ap.‘dn.mṭr h.|b‘l.y‘dn.‘dn.ṯkt.b glṯ.|w tn.ql h.b ‘rpt.|šrh.l arṣ.brqm.|bt.arzm.yklln h.|h 4[51].5.69
-].|[-]gbt.|[--]y bnš kb[š]y.|krmpy.b.bṣm.|[-]mrn.ṣd.b gl[-]. 2169.5

b

ṯlṯ.ṣmdm. | b.nḫry. | ṣmdm.b.ṯp[--]. | aḥdm.b.gm[--]. 144[317].4
d.mṯr.ʿly. | nʿm.l arṣ.mṭr.bʿl. | w l šd.mṭr.ʿly. | nʿm.l ḥṭt.b gn. | bm.nrt.ksmm. | ʿl.tl[-]k.ʿṭrṭrm. | nšu.[r]iš.ḥrṯm. | l ẓr.ʿd 16[126].3.9
ilm.mt.ʿdd.l ydd. | il.ġzr.yqra.mt. | b npš h.ystrn ydd. | b gngn h.aḥd y.d ym | lk.ʿl.ilm.l ymru. | ilm.w nšm.d yšb | [ʿ]. 4[51].7.49
[-----]. | [-----.-]l[-]. | [-----]. | [---.--]k. | [---.q]rt. | [---.--]d.b.gnʿ. | [---].ḫbt. | [---].qmy. | [---.]qmy. | [---.--]b. | bn.t[--.---.a] 2015.1.14
.b gt[.-]n. | arbʿm.kbd.yn.ṭb.w.[--]. | ṯmn.kbd.yn.d.l.ṭb.b.gnʿ[y]. | mitm.yn.ḥsp.d.nkly.b.db[ḫ.--]. | mit.arbʿm.kbd.yn. 1084.23
. | ʿšr.b gt.[---]. | ṯn.ʿšr.b.gt.ir[bṣ]. | arbʿ.b.gt.bʿln. | ʿšt.ʿšr.b.gpn. | yd.ʿdnm. | arbʿ.ġzlm. | ṯn.yṣrm. 2103.7
.l] | mṯʿt.w yʿn.dnil.[mt.rpi]. | yṯb.ġzr.mt hrnmy[.---]. | b grnt.ilm.b qrb.m[ṭʿt.ilnym]. | d tit.yspi.spu.q[--.---]. | tpḥ.ṯṣ 20[121].2.9
y. | [---].aḥd.aḥd.b.yʿny. | [---.-]ḫm.b.aḫd.ḥrṯ. | [---.]aḫd.b.grn.uškn. | [---.]aḫd.ḥrṯ. 1129.16
i.a hn.ġzr.mt.hrnm[y]. | ytšu.yṯb.b ap.ṯġr.ṯḥt. | adrm.d b grn.ydn. | dn.almnt.yṯpṭ.ṯpṭ.ytm. | b nši ʿn h.w yphn.b alp. 17[2AQHT].5.7
.ġzr. | [mt.hrn]my.ytšu. | [yṯb.b ap.ṯ]ġr[.t]ḥt. | [adrm.d b grn.y]dn. | [dn.almnt.y]ṯpṭ. | [ṯpṭ.ytm.---] h. | [---.---]n. | [---- 19[1AQHT].1.23
l.udm.ṯrrt. | w gr.nn.ʿrm.šrn. | pdrm.sʿt.b šdm. | ḥṭb h.b grnt.ḥpšt. | sʿt.b nk.šibt.b bqr. | mmlat.dm.ym.w ṯn. | ṯlṯ.rbʿ. 14[KRT].3.112
udm[.ṯr]rt. | grnn.ʿrm. | šrnn.pdrm. | sʿt.b šdm.ḥṭb. | w b grnt.ḥpšt. | sʿt.b npk.šibt.w b | mqr.mmlat. | d[m].ym.w ṯn. 14[KRT].4.215
h. | [---.---]n. | [-----]. | hlk.[---.b n]ši. | ʿn h.w tphn.[---]. | b grn.yḫrb[.---]. | yġly.yḫsp.ib[.---]. | ʿl.bt.ab h.nšrm.trḫ[p]n. | 19[1AQHT].1.30
. | bn.ḫrn k. | mġy. | hbṭ.hw. | ḫrd.w.šl hw. | qr[-]. | akl n.b.grnt. | l.bʿr. | ap.krmm. | ḫlq. | qrt n.ḫlq. | w.dʿ.dʿ. 2114.8
yly.bn.ṯrnq.[-]r.d.yṯb.b.ilštmʿ. | ilšlm.bn.gs[-.--]r.d.yṯb.b.gt.al. | ilmlk.[--]kt.[--.d.]yṯb.b.šb[n]. | bn.pr[-.]d.y[ṯb.b].šlm 2015.1.27
.l.mit.drʿ.w.tšʿm.drt. | [w].ṯmnym.l.mit.dd.ḥpr.bnšm. | b.gt.alḫb.ṯṯm.drʿ.w.ḫmšm.drt.w.ṯṯm.dd. | ḥpr.bnšm. | b.gt.kn 1098.16
-].ṯgd.mrum. | bt.[-]b[-.-]sy[-]h. | nn[-].b[n].py[-.d.]yṯb.b.gt.aġld. | šgn.bn b[--.---].d.yṯb.b.ilštmʿ. | abmn.bn.r[---].b.sy 2015.2.5
b gt ilštmʿ. | bt ubnyn š h d.ytn.ṣṭqn. | ṭut ṭbḫ ṣtq[n]. | b bz ʿz 1153.1
.mʿṣd.mqb. | b.gwl.ṯmn.ḫrmṯt.[nit]. | krk.mʿṣd.mqb. | [b] gt.iptl.ṯṯ.ḫrmṯ[t.nit]. | [k]rk.mʿṣd.mqb. | [b.g]t.bir.ʿš[r.---]. | 2048.13
.ṯmn.ṣmdm. | w.arbʿ.ʿšr.bnš. | yd.nġr.mdrʿ.yd.š[--]m. | [b.]gt.iptl.ṯṯ.ṣmdm. | [w.ʿ]šr.bn[š]m.y[d].š[--]. | [-]lm.b d.r[-]m 2038.7
m.]kbd.yn.d.l.ṭb. | b.gt.gwl. | ṯlṯm.tšʿ[.kbd.yn].d.l[.ṭb].b.gt.iptl. | ṯmnym.[yn].ṭb.b.gt.š[---]. | tšʿm.[ḫ]mš[.kbd].yn.b g 1084.19
alpm. | ʿšr.bnšm. | ḫmš.bnši.ṯt[---]. | ʿšr.b gt.[---]. | ṯn.ʿšr.b.gt.ir[bṣ]. | arbʿ.b.gt.bʿln. | ʿšt.ʿšr.b.gpn. | yd.ʿdnm. | arbʿ.ġzlm 2103.5
[aġ]ltn. | [--]ṯm.b.gt.irbṣ. | [--]šmyn. | [w.]nḫl h. | bn.qṣn. | bn.ksln. | bn.ṣrym. | 1073.1.2
[sp]r.akl[.---].ṯryn. | [tg]mr.akl.b.g[t.b]ir.alp. | [ʿ]šrm.l.mit.ḫ[p]r.ʿbdm. | mitm.drt.ṯmnym.drt 2013.2
ʿṣd.mqb. | [b] gt.iptl.ṯṯ.ḫrmṯ[t.nit]. | [k]rk.mʿṣd.mqb. | [b.g]t.bir.ʿš[r.---]. | [---].krk.mʿ[ṣd.---]. | [b.]gt.ḥrṯm.ḫm[š.---]. | 2048.15
t[.---.]kbd. | ṯṯ.ddm.k[--.b]rqd. | mit.tšʿm.[kb]d.ddm. | b.gt.bir. 2168.4
y. | yʿl.knʿny. | gdn.bn.umy. | knʿm.šʿrty. | abrpu.ubrʿy. | b.gt.bn.ṯlṯ. | ilḏ.b.gt.psḫn. 91[311].11
ity[.---]. | tlby[.---]. | ir[--.---]. | pndyn[.---]. | w.idṯ[-.---]. | b.gt.b[n.---]. | yḫl[.---]. | b.gt.[---]. | [---.]k[--]. 1078.7
| ḫmš.bnši.ṯt[---]. | ʿšr.b gt.[---]. | ṯn.ʿšr.b.gt.ir[bṣ]. | arbʿ.b.gt.bʿln. | ʿšt.ʿšr.b.gpn. | yd.ʿdnm. | arbʿ.ġzlm. | ṯn.yṣrm. 2103.6
rm.l.mit.ḫ[p]r.ʿbdm. | mitm.drt.ṯmnym.drt. | tgmr.akl.b.gt[.b]ʿln. | ṯlṯ.mat.ṯṯm.kbd. | ṯṯm.ṯṯ.kbd.ḥpr.ʿbdm. | šbʿm.drt 2013.5
d.alp.idṯn.d aḥd.b.ʿnqpat. | [aḥd.al]p.d aġlmn. | [d aḫd b.g]t gbry. | [---].aḥd.aḫd.b.yʿny. | [---.-]ḫm.b.aḫd.ḥrṯ. | [---.]a 1129.13
rbʿm.kdm.kbd.yn.ṭb. | w.ḫmšm.k[dm.]kbd.yn.d.l.ṭb. | b.gt.gwl. | ṯlṯm.tšʿ[.kbd.yn].d.l[.ṭb].b.gt.iptl. | ṯmnym.[yn].ṭb. 1084.18
t.ṯpn.ʿšr.ṣmdm. | w.ṯlṯ.ʿšr.bnš. | yd.ytm.yd.rʿy.ḥmrm. | b.gt.gwl.ṯmn.ṣmdm. | w.arbʿ.ʿšr.bnš. | yd.nġr.mdrʿ.yd.š[--]m. 2038.4
[---].i[y]tl[m]. | [---.--]y. | [-----]. | [---.k]d. | [---.]b gt.ḥgb[-]. | [--.]b gt.nṯt[-]. 2166.5
n.arbʿm.drʿ.w.ʿšrm.drt. | w.ṯlṯm.dd.ṯṯ.kbd.ḥpr.bnšm. | b.gt.ḥdṯt.arbʿm.drʿ.w.ṯlṯm.drt. | [w].šbʿm.dd.ṯn.kbd.ḥpr.bnš 1098.22
. | yn.d.l.ṭb.b.ulm. | mit.yn.ṭb.w.ṯṯm.ṯṯ.kbd. | yn.d.l.ṭb.b.gt.ḥdṯt. | tšʿm.yn.d.l.ṭb.b.zbl. | ʿšrm.yn.ṭb.w.ṯṯm.ḫmš.k[b]d. 1084.12
.ḫzr.w.ʿšt.ʿšr.ḫrš. | dt.tbʿln.b.ugrt. | ṯṯm.ḫzr. | dt.tbʿln. | b.gt.ḥršm. | ṯn.ḥršm. | [-]nbkm. | ṯn.ḥršm. | b.gt.ġl. | [-.]nġr.md 1024.3.11
rk.mʿṣd.mqb. | [b.g]t.bir.ʿš[r.---]. | [---].krk.mʿ[ṣd.---]. | [b.]gt.ḥrṯm.ḫm[š.---]. | [n]it.krk.mʿṣ[d.---]. | b.ḫrbġlm.ġlm[n]. 2048.17
.ḥpr.ʿbdm. | šbʿm.drt.arbʿm.drt. | l.a[--.---]. | tgm[r.ak]l.b.gt.ḫldy. | ṯlṯ.ma[t].ʿšr.kbd. | šbʿ m[at].kbd.ḥpr.ʿbdm. | mit[.d 2013.10
k. | ʿdršp. | bn.knn. | pdyn. | bn.aṯtl.ṯn. | kdln.akdṯb. | ṯn.b gt yknʿm. 1061.22
-]bldn. | [-]bdy. | [b]ʿln. | [-]šdm. | iwryn. | nʿmn. | [-----]. | b gt.yny. | agttp. | bn.ʿnt. | ġzldn. | ṯrn. | ḫdbṯ. | [-]ḫl.aġltn. | [-]n. 1043.10
bʿm.kbd. | ṯlṯ.alp.ṣpr.dt.aḥd. | ḥrṯ h.aḥd.b gt.nḫl. | aḥd.b gt.knpy.w.aḥd.b gt.ṯrmn. | aḥd.alp.idṯn.d aḫd.b.ʿnqpat. | [a 1129.10
b.gt.alḫb.ṯṯm.drʿ.w.ḫmšm.drt.w.ṯṯm.dd. | ḥpr.bnšm. | b.gt.knpy.mit.drʿ.ṯṯm.drt.w.šbʿm.dd.arbʿ. | kbd.ḥpr.bnšm. | b 1098.18
ṯn.b gt.mzln. | ṯn.b ulm. | abmn.b gt.mʿrb. | atn. | ḫryn. | bn.ʿnt. | l 1061.1
b.gt.mlkt.b.rḥbn. | ḫmšm.l.mitm.zt. | w.b d.krd. | ḫmšm.l.mit 1096.1
ʿm.drʿ.w.ʿšr.dd.drt. | w[.a]rbʿ.l.ʿšrm.dd.l.yḥšr.bl.bn h. | b.gt.mʿbr.arbʿm.l.mit.drʿ.w.ṯmnym[.drt]. | w.ʿšrm.l.mit.dd.ḥ 1098.12
ṯn.b gt.mzln. | ṯn.b ulm. | abmn.b gt.mʿrb. | atn. | ḫryn. | bn.ʿnt. | llwn. | agdṯb. | aġltn. | [-]wn. | b 1061.3
.gt.ṭbq. | mit.ʿšr.kbd.yn.ṭb. | w.ṯṯm.arbʿ.kbd.yn.d.l.ṭb. | b.gt.mʿrby. | ṯṯm.yn.ṭb.w.ḫmš.l.ʿšrm. | yn.d.l.ṭb.b.ulm. | mit.y 1084.8
. | w.lmd h. | ʿbdrpu. | w.lmd h. | ʿdršp. | w.lmd h. | krwn b.gt.nbk. | ddm.kšmm.l.ḫtn. | ddm.l.trbnn. | ddm.šʿrm.l.trbnn 1099.19
n.arbʿ.mat. | arbʿm.kbd. | ṯlṯ.alp.ṣpr.dt.aḥd. | ḥrṯ h.aḥd.b gt.nḫl. | aḥd.b gt.knpy.w.aḥd.b gt.ṯrmn. | aḥd.alp.idṯn.d aḫ 1129.9
]tl[m]. | [---.--]y. | [-----]. | [---.k]d. | [---.]b gt.ḥgb[-]. | [--.]b gt.nṯt[-]. 2166.6
ʿšr.yn.ṭb. | w.tšʿm.kdm.kbd.yn.d.l.ṭb. | w.arbʿm.yn.ḫlq.b.gt.sknm. | ʿšr.yn.ṭb.w.arbʿm.ḫmš.kbd. | yn.d.l.ṭb.gt.ṭbq. | mi 1084.3
n.d.l.ṭb.b.zbl. | ʿšrm.yn.ṭb.w.ṯṯm.ḫmš.k[b]d. | yn.d.l.ṭb.b.gt.sġy. | arbʿm.kdm.kbd.yn.ṭb. | w.ḫmšm.k[dm.]kbd.yn.d.l. 1084.15
qbm. | krk.aḥt. | b.sġy.ḫmš.ḫrmṯt.nit. | krk.mʿṣd.mqb. | b.gt.ʿmq.ḫmš.ḫrmṯt.n[it]. | krk.mʿṣd.mqb. | b.gwl.ṯmn.ḫrmṯt. 2048.9
mit.drʿ.w.ṯmnym[.drt]. | w.ʿšrm.l.mit.dd.ḥp[r.]bnšm. | b.gt.ġl.ʿšrm.l.mit.drʿ.w.tšʿm.drt. | [w].ṯmnym.l.mit.dd.ḥpr.b 1098.14
bd.ḥpr.ʿbdm. | mit[.d]rt.arbʿm.drt. | [---]m. | t[gm]r.akl.b.gt.ġ[l]. | ṯlṯ.mat.ʿšrm[.---]. | ṯmnym.drt.a[--]. | drt.l.alpm[.--- 2013.15
r. | dt.tbʿln. | b.gt.ḥršm. | ṯn.ḥršm. | [-]nbkm. | ṯn.ḥršm. | b.gt.ġl. | [-.]nġr.mdrʿ. | [-].nġr[.--]m. | [--.]psl.qšt. | [ṯl]ṯ.psl.ḥẓ 1024.3.15
dn.bn.umy. | knʿm.šʿrty. | abrpu.ubrʿy. | b.gt.bn.ṯlṯ. | ilḏ.b.gt.psḫn. 91[311].12
šd.ubdy.ilštmʿ. | dt b d.skn. | šd.bn.ubrʿn b gt prn. | šd.bn.gby.gt.prn. | šd.bn.kryn.gt.prn. | šd.bn.ky.gt. 1104.3
ṯlṯm.dd[.---]. | b.gt.ṣb[-.---]. | mit.ʿšr.[---.]dd[.--]. | tšʿ.dd.ḥ[ṭm.w].ḫm[šm]. | k 2092.2
wl. | ṯlṯm.tšʿ[.kbd.yn].d.l[.ṭb].b.gt.iptl. | ṯmnym.[yn].ṭb.b.gt.š[---]. | tšʿm.[ḫ]mš[.kbd].yn.b gt[.-]n. | arbʿm.kbd.yn.ṭb. 1084.20
mt qdš. | [---].b.dmt qdš. | [---.--]n.b.anan. | [--]yl.b.bqʿt.b.gt.tgyn. | [--]in.b.trzy. | [--]yn.b.glltky. | ṯd[y]n.b.glltky. | lb 2118.6
d.--]m.šbʿ.[---]. | [---].ʿšr.dd[.---]. | [---]mn.arbʿm.y[n]. | b.gt.trġnds. | tšʿ.ʿšr.[dd].kšmm. | ṯn.ʿšr[.dd.ḥ]ṭm. | w.šb[ʿ.---]. 2092.15

spr šd.ri[šym].|kr[-].šdm.ʿ[--].|b gt tm[--] yn[.--].|[---].krm.b ypʿl.yʿdd.|[---.]krm.b [-]dn.l. 2027.1.3
[b.]gt.tpn.ʿšr.ṣmdm.|w.ṯlṯ.ʿšr.bnš.|yd.ytm.yd.rʿy.ḥmrm.|b.g 2038.1
ṣpr.dt.aḫd.|ḥrṯ h.aḥd.b gt.nḫl.|aḥd.b gt.knpy.w.aḥd.b gt.ṯrmn.|aḥd.alp.idṯn.d aḫd.b.ʿnqpat.|[aḥd.al]p.d aǵlmn. 1129.10
npy.mit.drʿ.ṯṯm.drt.w.šbʿm.dd.arbʿ.|kbd.ḥpr.bnšm.|b.gt.ṯrmn.arbʿm.drʿ.w.ʿšrm.drt.|w.ṯlṯm.dd.ṯṯ.kbd.ḥpr.bnšm 1098.20
t.ipṯl.|ṯmnym.[yn].ṭb.b.gt.š[---].|tšʿm.[ḫ]mš[.kbd].yn.b gt[.-]n.|arbʿm.kbd.yn.ṭb.w.[--].|ṯmn.kbd.yn.d.l.ṭb.b.gnʿ[y 1084.21
[---.--]l.|[---.--]ḏ.|[---.--]ḏ.|[---.--]aṣ.|[---.]b gt.[--].|[---.--]n.[--].|[--.--]ǵm.rm[-].|[---.-]ʿm.|[---.k]sp.[--] 1148.8
.ʿšr.[---.]dd[.--].|tšʿ.dd.ḥ[ṭm.w].ḫm[šm].|kdm.kbd.yn.b.gt.[---].|[mi]tm.ḫmšm.ḫmš.k[bd].|[dd].kšmm.tšʿ[.---].|[š] 2092.5
---].|[š]ʿrm.ṯṯ.ʿ[šr].|[dd].ḥṭm.w.ḫ[mšm].|[ṯ]lṯ kbd.yn.b [gt.---].|mit.[---].ṯlṯ.kb[d].|[dd.--]m.šbʿ.[---].|[---].ʿšr.dd[.- 2092.10
bt.alpm.|ʿšr.bnšm.|ḫmš.bnši.ṯt[---].|ʿšr.b gt.[---].|ṯn.ʿšr.b.gt.ir[bṣ].|arbʿ.b.gt.bʿln.|ʿšt.ʿšr.b.gpn.|yd.ʿ 2103.4
.---].|pndyn[.---].|w.idṯ[-.---].|b.gt.b[n.---].|yḫl[.---].|b.gt.[---].|[---.]k[--]. 1078.9
m.b[n.ʿ]n k.ṣmdm.špk[.---].|[---.]nt[-.]mbk kpt.w[.--].b g[--].|[---.]ḥ[--.]bnt.ṣʿṣ.bnt.ḫkp[.---].|[---].aḥw.aṯm.prṯl[.-- 1001.1.17
[---.-]l[-.-]hg[.---].|[---.-]r[-.il]m.rbm.nʿl[.-]gr.|[---.]ʿṣ.b d h.ydrm[.]pi[-.]adm.|[---.]iṯ[-].yšql.yṯk[.--]np bl.hn.|[---]. UG5.8.32
m.ḥmt.nša.|[y]d h.šmmh.dbḥ.|l ṯr.ab h.il.šrd.|[bʿl].b dbḥ h.bn dgn.|[b m]ṣd h.yrd.krt.|[l g]gt.ʿdb.akl.l qryt.|ḥ 14[KRT].4.170
.|ṯkmm.ḥm[t].ša.yd k.|šmm.dbḥ.l ṯr.|ab k.il.šrd.bʿl.|b dbḥ k.bn.dgn.|b mṣd k.w yrd.|krt.l ggt.ʿdb.|akl.l qryt.|ḥ 14[KRT].2.78
yn.d.ykl.b d.[---].|b.dbḥ.mlk.|dbḥ ṣpn.|[-]zǵm.|[i]lib.|[i]lbldn.|[p]dry.bt.mlk 2004.2
.mṣprt dlt hm[.---].|w ǵnbm.šlm.ʿrbm.ṯn[nm].|hlkm.b dbḥ nʿmt.|šd[.i]lm.šd.aṯrt.w rḥmy.|[---].y[ṯ]b.|[---]p.gp y 23[52].27
.[--].|ṯmn.kbd.yn.d.l.ṭb.b.gnʿ[y].|mitm.yn.ḥsp.d.nkly.b.db[ḥ.--].|mit.arbʿm.kbd.yn.ḥsp.l.m[--].|mit.ʿšrm.[k]bd.yn 1084.24
y|rdm.arṣ.w tdʿ ilm.|k mtt.yšmʿ.aliyn.bʿl.|yuhb.ʿglt.b dbr.prt.|b šd.šḥlmmt.škb.|ʿmn h.šbʿ.l šbʿm.|tš[ʿ]ly.ṯmn.l 5[67].5.18
pt h[.hwt h].|b nši ʿn h.w tphn.in.[---].|[-.]hlk.ǵlmm b dd y.yṣ[--].|[-.]yṣa.w l.yṣa.hlm.[ṯnm].|[q]dqd.ṯlṯ id.ʿl.ud[19[1AQHT].2.77
ʿ.trḥṣ.yd h.bt|[l]t.ʿnt.uṣbʿt h.ybmt.limm.|[t]rḥṣ.yd h.b dm.ḏmr.|[u]ṣbʿt h.b mmʿ.mhrm.|[ṯ]ʿr.ksat.l ksat.ṯlḥnt.|[l 3[ʿNT].2.34
h.b ṣḥq.ymlu.|lb h.b šmḫt.kbd.ʿnt.|tšyt.k brkm.tǵll b dm.|ḏmr.ḥlqm.b mmʿ.mhrm.|ʿd.tšbʿ.tmtḫṣ.b bt.|ṯḫṣb.bn 3[ʿNT].2.27
.mhr.ʿtkt.|rišt.l bmt h.šnst.|kpt.b ḥbš h.brkm.tǵl[l].|b dm.ḏmr.ḥlqm.b mm[ʿ].|mhrm.mṭm.tgrš.|šbm.b ksl.qšt h 3[ʿNT].2.14
t.tšyt.tḥt h.k]kdrt.riš.|[ʿl h.k irbym.kp.---.k br]k.tǵll.b dm.|[ḏmr.---.]td[-.]rǵb.|[----]k.|[----] h. 7.1[131].9
.|km.ṯqlm.arṣ h.|km ḫmšt.mtt h.|bm.bky h.w yšn.|b dmʿ h.nhmmt.|šnt.tluan.|w yškb.nhmmt.|w yqmṣ.w b ḥl 14[KRT].1.32
y.|[tn.ṯa]rm.amid.|[w yʿn].ṯr.ab h.il.|d[--].b bk.krt.|b dmʿ.nʿmn.ǵlm.|il.trḥṣ.w tadm.|rḥṣ[.y]d k.amt.|uṣb[ʿt k.]ʿ 14[KRT].2.61
ḫ[-]y.ilak k.|[---.--]g k.yritn.mǵy.hy.w kn.|[---].ḥln.d b.dmt.um.il[m.---].|[--]dyn.bʿd.[--]dyn.w l.|[--]k bʿlt bhtm[. 1002.43
[---.dmt q]dš.|[---.d]mt qdš.|[---].b.dmt qdš.|[---].b.dmt qdš.|[---.--]n.b.anan.|[--]yl.b.bqʿt.b. 2118.3
[---.dmt q]dš.|[---.d]mt qdš.|[---].b.dmt qdš.|[---].b.dmt qdš.|[---.--]n.b.anan.|[--]yl.b.bqʿt.b.gt.tgyn.|[--]in.b.t 2118.4
mlk.d.y[mlk].|[--.]ʿbdyrḫ.l.ml[k].|[--]t.w.lqḥ.|yn[.--].b dn h.|w.ml[k].šswm.nʿmm.|ytn.l.ʿbdyrḫ.|w.mlk.z[--.--]n. 2064.15
ʿms k.k šbʿt.yn.ṯ[ḫ].|gg k.b ym.ṯiṭ.rḥṣ.|npṣ k.b ym rṯ.b uni[l].|pnm.tšmḫ.w ʿl yṣhl pi[t].|yprq.lṣb.w yṣḥq.|pʿn.l h 17[2AQHT].2.8
.šrr.|ḥt m.tʿmt.[ʾ]ṭr.[k]m.|zbln.ʿl.riš h.|w ttb.trḥṣ.nn.b dʿt.|npš h.l lḥm.tpth.|brlt h.l trm.|mt.dm.ḥt.šʿtqt.|dm.la 16.6[127].10
.ʿdt.|ypth.ḥln.b bht m.|urbt.b qrb.[h]kl |m.w y[p]tḥ.b dqt.ʿrpt.|ʿl h[wt].kṯr.w ḫss.|ṣḥq.kṯr.w ḫss.|yšu.g h.w yṣḥ. 4[51].7.19
wt y.yptḥ.ḥ|ln.b bht m.urbt.|b qrb.hk[l m.yp]tḥ.|bʿl.b dqt[.ʿrp]t.|ql h.qdš.b[ʿl.y]tn.|ytny.bʿl.ṣ[---.-]pt h.|ql h.q[d 4[51].7.28
il add.|bʿl ṣpn bʿl.|ugrt.|b mrḥ il.|b nit il.|b ṣmd il.|b dṯn il.|b šrp il.|b knt il.|b ǵdyn il.|[b]n [---]. 30[107].15
.rg]m.ank.[b]ʿr.[--]ny.|[--]n.bt k.[---.]bʿ[r.---].|[--]my.b d[-.--]y.[---].|[---.]ʿm.w hm[.--]yt.w.[---].|[---.ṯ]y.al.an[k.-- 1002.56
ṣ h.qṣʿt h.hwt.l ṯ[hwy].|nʿmn.ǵzr.št.ṯrm.w[---].|ištir.b ḏdm.w nʿrs[.---].|w tʿn.btlt.ʿnt.ṭb.ytp.w[---].|l k.ašt k.km 18[3AQHT].4.15
m.špš.mǵy[t].|pǵt.l ahlm.rgm.l yṯ[pn.y]|bl.agrtn.bat.b ḏd k.[pǵt].|bat.b hlm w yʿn.yṯpn[.mhr].|št.qḥn.w tšqyn.y 19[1AQHT].4.213
.--]k.l tšt k.liršt.|[---.]rpi.mlk ʿlm.b ʿz.|[rpu.m]lk.ʿlm.b ḏmr h.bl.|[---].b ḥtk h.b nmrt h.l r|[--.]arṣ.ʿz k.ḏmr k.l[-] UG5.2.2.7
dʿ.k ḥy.aliyn.bʿl.|k iṯ.zbl.bʿl.arṣ.|b ḥlm.ltpn.il d pid.|b ḏrt.bny.bnwt.|šmm.šmn.tmṭrn.|nḫlm.tlk.nbtm.|šmḫ.ltp 6[49].3.11
a[liyn.bʿl].|w hm.iṯ.zbl.bʿ[l.arṣ].|b ḥlm.ltpn.il.d pid.|b ḏrt.bny.bnwt.|šmm.šmn.tmṭrn.|nḫlm.tlk.nbtm.|w idʿ.k 6[49].3.5
nt.tluan.|w yškb.nhmmt.|w yqmṣ.w b ḥlm h.|il.yrd.b ḏhrt h.|ab adm.w yqrb.|b šal.krt.m at.|krt.k ybky.|ydmʿ 14[KRT].1.36
m h.|d ʿq h.ib.iqni.|ʿpʿp h.sp.ṯrml.|d b ḥlm y.il.ytn.|b ḏrt y.ab.adm.|w ld.špḥ.l krk|t.w ǵlm.l ʿbd.|il.ttbʿ.mlakm 14[KRT].6.297
rml.tḫgrn.[-]dm[.-].|ašlw.b ṣp.ʿn h.|d b ḥlm y.il.ytn.|b ḏrt y.ab.adm.|w ld.špḥ.l krt.|w ǵlm.l ʿbd.il.|krt.yḫṭ.w ḥl 14[KRT].3.151
ḥ.l krt.a]dn km.|ʿl.krt.tbun.km.|rgm.ṯ[rm.]rgm hm.|b ḏrt[.---.]krt.|[----]. 15[128].6.8
m.ḫpn.ḫmš.|kbd.w lpš.|ḫmš.mispt.|mṯ.|w lpš.d sgr b h.|b d.anrmy. 1109.6
pt.dbḥ.|bṯt.w dbḥ.w dbḥ.|dnt.w dbḥ.tdmm.|amht.k b h.bṯt.l tbṯ.|w b h.tdmmt.amht.|aḫr.mǵy.aliyn.bʿl.|mǵyt. 4[51].3.21
bḥ.w dbḥ.|dnt.w dbḥ.tdmm.|amht.k b h.bṯt.l tbṯ.|w b h.tdmmt.amht.|aḫr.mǵy.aliyn.bʿl.|mǵyt.btlt.ʿnt.|tmgnn. 4[51].3.22
dm.|b qdš il bt.|w tlḥm aṯt.|š l ilbt.šlmm.|kll ylḥm b h.|w l bbt šqym.|š l uḫr ḥlmṭ.|w tr l qlḥ.|ym aḥd. UG5.11.10
d.tt.w.ṯlṯ.ktnt.b dm.tt.|w.ṯmnt.ksp.hn.|ktn.d.ṣr.pḥm.b h.w.ṯqlm.|ksp h.mitm.pḥm.b d.skn.|w.ṯt.ktnm.ḫmšt.w.n 1110.4
.|hlk.bʿl.aṯtrt.|k tʿn.hlk.btlt.|ʿnt.tdrq.ybmt.|[limm].b h.pʿnm.|[ṯṭt.b ʿ]dn.ksl.|[ṯṯbr.ʿln.p]n h.td[ʿ].|tǵṣ[.pnt.ks]l 4[51].2.16
|b qdš.b ǵr.nḥlt y.|b nʿm.b gbʿ.tliyt.|hlm.ʿnt.tph.ilm.b h.pʿnm.|ṯṭṭ.bʿd n.ksl.ṯṯbr.|ʿln.pn h.tdʿ.tǵṣ.pnt.|ksl h.anš. 3[ʿNT].3.29
|mt.aqht.ǵzr.[šṣat].|btlt.ʿnt.k [rḥ.npš h].|k iṯl.brlt h.[b h.pʿnm].|ṯṭṭ.ʿl[n.pn h.tdʿ.b ʿdn].|ksl.y[ṯbr.yǵṣ.pnt.ksl h].| 19[1AQHT].2.93
m.d |msdt.arṣ.|sʿ.il.dqt.k amr.|sknt.k ḥwt.yman.|d b h.rumm.l rbbt. 4[51].1.44
i[d.yd]bḥ.mlk.l.prgl.ṣqrn.b.gg.|ar[bʿ.]arbʿ.mṯbt.azmr.b h.š.šr[-].|al[p.w].š.šlmm.pamt.šbʿ.klb h.|yr[--.]mlk.ṣbu.šp 35[3].51
lk.|[-]k.am[ʿ--].|[w.b] d.bn h[.ʿ]d ʿlm.|[w.un]ṯ.in[n.]b h.|[---.]nʿm[-]. 1009.18
qḥnn.b d.|bʿln.bn.kltn.|w.b d.bn h.ʿd.|ʿlm.w unṯ.|in.b h. 1008.21
.rpu.mlk.ʿlm.w yšt.|[--.]gṯr.w yqr.il.ytb.b.ʿṯtrt.|il.ṯpṭ.b hd rʿy.d yšr.w yḏmr.|b knr.w ṯlb.b tp.w mṣltm.b m|rqd UG5.2.1.3
.b.bir.|ṯṯ.bnšm b.uḫnp.|ṯn.bnšm.b.ḫrṣbʿ.|arbʿ.bnšm.b.hzp.|arbʿ.bnšm.b.šql.|arbʿ.bnšm.b.nni.|ṯn.bnšm.b.slḫ.|[- 2076.16
ṭ.yd h.|dnil.bt h.ymǵyn.yšt|ql.dnil.l hkl h.ʿrb.b|kyt.b hkl h.mšspdt.b ḥẓr h.|pẓǵm.ǵr.ybk.l aqht.|ǵzr.ydmʿ.l kd 19[1AQHT].4.172
[--.---].|prʿm.ṣd k.y bn[.---].|prʿm.ṣd k.hn pr[ʿ.--].|ṣd.b hkl h[.---].|[------].|[---.l]ḥm[.---].|[---].ay š[---].|[---.b ḥ]r 17[2AQHT].5.39
.krt.l ʿd h.|ytb.l ksi mlk.|l nḫt.l kḥṯ.drkt.|ap.yṣb.ytb.b hkl.|w ywsrnn.ggn h.|lk.l ab k.yṣb.lk.|l[ab]k.w rgm.ʿny 16.6[127].25
].|lk bt y.r[pim.rpim.b bt y.aṣḥ].|km.iqr[a km.ılnym.b hkl y].|aṯr h.r[pum.l tdd.aṯr h].|l tdd.il[nym.---].|mhr.bʿl 22.1[123].4
ʿy.lk.bt y.|[rpim.rpim.b]t y.aṣḥ km.iqra.|[km.ilnym.b h]kl y.aṯr h.rpum.|[l tdd.aṯr h].l tdd.ilnym.|[---.m]rzʿy.a 21[122].1.3

'[y.lk.bt y.rpim.|[rpim.bt y.aṣ]ḥ km.iqra km.|[ilnym.b hkl]y.aṯr h.rpum.|[l tdd.aṯr]h.l tdd.i[lnym].|[---.]r[--.---] 21[122].1.11
nt.lk b[t y.rpim.rpim.b bt y].|aṣḥ.km.[iqra km.ilnym.b] |hkl y.aṯr[h.rpum.l tdd].|aṯr h.l t[dd.ilnym.ṯm].|yḥpn.ḥ 22.1[123].9
pi.|yṯb.ǵzr.m[t.hrnmy.y]šu.|g h.w yṣḥ.t[b'.---].|bkyt.b hk[l]y.mšspdt.|b ḥẓr y pẓǵm.ǵr.w yq.|dbḥ.ilm.yš'ly.dǵṯ 19[1AQHT].4.183
n.w 'ṣ h.|š[r]yn.mḥmd.arz h.|tšt.išt.b bht m.|nb[l]at.b hkl m.|hn.ym.w ṯn.tikl.|išt.b bht m.nblat.|b hk[l] m.ṯlṯ.k 4[51].6.23
blat.|b hk[l] m.ṯlṯ.kb' ym.|tikl[.i]št.b bht m.|nbla[t.]b hkl m.|ḫmš.ṯ[d]ṯ.ym.tikl.|išt.[b]bht m.nblat.|b[qrb.hk]l 4[51].6.28
qrb.hk]l m.mk.|b šb['.]y[mm].td.išt.|b bht m.n[bl]at.b hkl m.|sb.ksp.l rqm.ḫrṣ.|nṣb.l lbnt.šmḫ.|aliyn.b'l.ht y.bn 4[51].6.33
nb[l]at.b hkl m.|hn.ym.w ṯn.tikl.|išt.b bht m.nblat.|b hk[l] m.ṯlṯ.kb' ym.|tikl[.i]št.b bht m.|nbla[t.]b hkl m.|ḫ 4[51].6.26
bum.trd.b n[p]šn y.trḥṣn.k ṯrm.|[--]b b[ht].|[zbl.]ym.b hkl.ṯpṭ.nh[r].yṯir.ṯr.il.ab h l pn[.zb]l y[m].|[l pn.ṯp]ṭ[.nhr. 2.3[129].21
n h.btlt.'nt.|w tšu.'n h.w t'n.|w t'n.arḫ.w tr.b lkt.|tr.b lkt.w tr.b ḫl.|[b]n'mm.b ysmm.ḥ[--]k.ǵrt.|[ql].l b'l.'nt.tt 10[76].2.29
.|w tšu.'n h.btlt.'nt.|w tšu.'n h.w t'n.|w t'n.arḫ.w tr.b lkt.|tr.b lkt.w tr.b ḫl.|[b]n'mm.b ysmm.ḥ[--]k.ǵrt.|[ql].l 10[76].2.28
q[l.tḥt].|p'n h.ybq'.kbd h.w yḥd.|iṯ.šmt.iṯ.'ẓm.w yqḥ b hm.|aqht.ybl.l qẓ.ybky.w yqbr.|yqbr.nn.b mdgt.b knk[-]. 19[1AQHT].3.145
hr].|t[ǵ]ly.hlm.rišt hm.l ẓr.brkt hm.w l kḥṯ.|zbl hm.b hm.yg'r.b'l.lm.ǵltm.ilm.rišt.|km l ẓr brkt km.w ln.kḥṯ.zb 2.1[137].24
.|b qr'.|'ṯtrt.w 'nt.ymǵy.|'ṯtrt.t'db.nšb l h.|w 'nt.ktp.b hm.yg'r.ṯǵr.|bt.il.pn.l mgr lb.t'dbn.|nšb.l inr.t'dbn.ktp.| UG5.1.1.11
'šrm[.---].|tšt.tb'[.---].|qrt.mlk[.---].|w.'l.ap.s[--.---].|b hm.w.rgm.hw.al[--].|atn.ksp.l hm.'d.|ilak.'m.mlk.|ht.lik[2008.2.6
|šmt hm.|b hm.qrnm.|km.ṯrm.w gbṯt.|km.ibrm.|w b hm.pn.b'l.|b'l.ytlk.w yṣd.|yḥ pat.mlbr.|wn.ymǵy.aklm.| 12[75].1.33
.ḫl.ld.|aklm.tbrk k.|w ld 'qqm.|ilm.yp'r.|šmt hm.|b hm.qrnm.|km.ṯrm.w gbṯt.|km.ibrm.|w b hm.pn.b'l.|b'l. 12[75].1.30
.|w 'ṯtrt.tṣdn.[---].|[---.-]b[-.---].|['ṯ]trt w 'nt[.---].|w b hm.tṯṯb[.--]d h.|km trpa.hn n'r.|d yšt.l.lṣb h ḫš'r klb.|[w UG5.1.2.2
tš'.ṣmdm.|ṯlṯm.b d.|ibrtlm.|w.pat.aḥt.|in.b hm. 1141.5
k.ank.ispi.uṭm.|ḏrqm.amt m.l yrt.|b npš.bn ilm.mt.b mh|mrt.ydd.il.ǵzr.|tb'.w l.yṯb ilm.idk.|l ytn.pnm.'m.b'l. 5[67].1.7
hm.'d.|ilak.'m.mlk.|ht.lik[t.--.]mlk[.--].|w.mlk.yštal.b.hn[--].|hmt.w.anyt.hm.t'[rb].|mkr.hn d.w.rgm.ank[.--].| 2008.2.10
[---].b.hr[-.---]. 2143.1
p]um.tdbḥn.|[----.]'d.ilnym.|[---.--]l km amt m.|[---.]b w t'rb.sd.|[---.--]n b ym.qẓ.|[---.]ym.tlḥmn.|[---.rp]um.tšt 20[121].1.4
n.ṭb.w.ṯṯm.ṯṯ.kbd.|yn.d.l.ṭb.b.gt.ḥdṯt.|tš'm.yn.d.l.ṭb.b.zbl.|'šrm.yn.ṭb.w.ṯṯm.ḫmš.k[b]d.|yn.d.l.ṭb.b.gt.sǵy.|arb' 1084.13
rnmy.|[---].hw.mḫ.l 'rš h.y'l.|[---].bm.nšq.aṯt h.|[---.]b ḥbq h.ḥmḥmt.|[---.--] n.ylt.ḥmḥmt.|[---.mt.r]pi.w ykn.bn 17[2AQHT].1.41
|yhbr.špt hm.yšq.hn.[š]pt hm.mtqtm.|bm.nšq.w hr.[b]ḥbq.w ḥ[m]ḥmt.yṯb[n].|yspr.l ḫmš.l ṣ[---.]šr.pḫr.klat.|t 23[52].56
.|hn.špt hm.mtqtm.mtqtm.k lrmn[.--].|bm.nšq.w hr.b ḥbq.ḥmḥmt.tqt[nṣn].|tldn.šḥr.w šlm.rgm.l il.ybl.a[ṯt y].|i 23[52].51
šr.w yḏmr.|b knr.w ṯlb.b tp.w mṣltm.b m|rqdm.dšn.b.ḥbr.kṯr.ṭbm.|w tšt.'nt.gṯr.b'lt.mlk.b'|lt.drkt.b'lt.šmm.rm UG5.2.1.5
.kp.k.qṣm.|ǵrmn.kp.mhr.'tkt.|rišt.l bmt h.šnst.|kpt.b ḥbš h.brkm.tǵl[l].|b dm.ḏmr.ḥlqm.b mm['].|mhrm.mṭm. 3['NT].2.13
.b ap.mhr h.ank.|l aḥwy.tqḥ.yṭpn.mhr.št.|tštn.k nšr.b ḥbš h.km.diy.|b t'rt h.aqht.km.yṯb.l lḥ[m].|bn.dnil.l ṯrm. 18[3AQHT].4.28
[---.šnst.kpt.b ḥb]š h.'tkt r[išt].|[l bmt h.---.]hy bt h t'rb.|[---.tm]ṯḥṣ b ' 7.1[131].2
'rs[.---].|w t'n.btlt.'nt.ṯb.yṭp.w[---].|l k.ašt k.km.nšr.b ḥb[š y].|km.diy.b t'rt y.aqht.[km.yṯb].|l lḥm.w bn.dnil.l ṯ 18[3AQHT].4.17
rdš.ṯbt h.|w b tm hn.špḥ.yitbd.|w b.pḫyr h.yrṯ.|y'rb.b ḥdr h.ybky.|b ṯn.[-]gmm.w ydm'.|tntkn.udm't h.|km.ṯql 14[KRT].1.26
m.|w.[---.a]ḥd.d.sgrm.|w p[tḥ.---.]l.aḥd.adr.|[---.--]t.b[ḥd]r.mškb.|ṯl[l.---.--]ḥ.|b lṯk.bt.|[pt]ḥ.aḥd.l.bt.'bdm.|[ṯ] 1151.6
h.ymǵyn.yšt|ql.dnil.l hkl h.'rb.b|kyt.b hkl h.mšspdt.b ḥẓr h.|pẓǵm.ǵr.ybk.l aqht.|ǵzr.ydm'.l kdd.dnil.|mt.rpi.l 19[1AQHT].4.172
my.y]šu.|g h.w yṣḥ.t[b'.---].|bkyt.b hk[l]y.mšspdt.|b ḥẓr y pẓǵm.ǵr.w yq.|dbḥ.ilm.yš'ly.dǵṯ h.|b šmym.dǵṯ hr 19[1AQHT].4.184
.t[---]l.|trm.tṣr.trm[.']tqt.|tbky.w tšnn.[tt]n.|g h.bky.b ḥ[y k.a]b n.|nšmḫ.b l.mt k.ngln.|k klb.[b]bt k.n'tq.|k in 16.2[125].98
.|lṭpn.w qdš.'l.|ab h.y'rb.ybky.|w yšnn.ytn.g h.|bky.b ḥy k.ab n.ašmḫ.|b l.mt k.ngln.k klb.|b bt k.n'tq.k inr.|ap 16.1[125].14
ntm.lm.l.tlk.|w.lḥt.akl.ky.|likt.'m.špš.|b'l k.ky.akl.|b.ḥwt k.inn.|špš n.[---].|hm.al[k.--].|ytnt[.---].|ṯn[.---].|w[. 2060.20
.]ḥw[t.---].|[---.]š[--].|w ym ym.yš|al.|w mlk.d mlk.|b ḥwt.špḥ.|l ydn.'bd.mlk.|d št.'l.ḫrd h.|špḥ.al.thbṭ.|ḫrd.'p 2062.2.2
sb[--].|yqḥ.mi[t].|b.ḥwt. 1174.3
.|w šd.šd ilm.šd aṯrt.w rḥm.|'l.išt.šb' d.ǵzrm.ṭb.[g]d.b ḥlb.annḫ b ḫmat.|w 'l.agn.šb' d m.dǵ[ṯ.---]t.|tlk m.rḥmy. 23[52].14
m' h.nhmmt.|šnt.tluan.|w yškb.nhmmt.|w yqmṣ.w b ḥlm h.|il.yrd.b ḏhrt h.|ab adm.w yqrb.|b šal.krt.m at.|k 14[KRT].1.35
ni.'p['p] h.|sp.ṯrml.ṯhgrn.[-]dm[.-].|ašlw.b ṣp.'n h.|d b ḥlm y.il.ytn.|b ḏrt y.ab.adm.|w ld.špḥ.l krt.|w ǵlm.l 'bd. 14[KRT].3.150
km.tsm.|'ṯtrt.tsm h.|d 'q h.ib.iqni.|'p'p h.sp.ṯrml.|d b ḥlm y.il.ytn.|b ḏrt y.ab.adm.|w ld.špḥ.l krk|t.w ǵlm.l 'b 14[KRT].6.296
l.b'l.arṣ].|w hm.ḥy.a[liyn.b'l].|w hm.iṯ.zbl.b'[l.arṣ].|b ḥlm.lṭpn.il.d pid.|b ḏrt.bny.bnwt.|šmm.šmn.tmṭrn.|nḫl 6[49].3.4
nḫlm.tlk.nbtm.|w id'.k ḥy.aliyn.b'l.|k iṯ.zbl.b'l.arṣ.|b ḥlm.lṭpn.il d pid.|b ḏrt.bny.bnwt.|šmm.šmn.tmṭrn.|nḫl 6[49].3.10
.[--]šq h[.---].|bnš r'ym.[---].|kbdt.bnš[.---].|šin.[---].|b ḥlm.[---].|pnt[.---]. 2158.2.9
mt.|rpi.al.ǵzr.mt.hrnmy.|apnk.dnil.mt.|rpi.yṣly.'rpt.b |ḥm.un.yr.'rpt.|tmṭr.b qẓ.ṭl.yṭll.|l ǵnbm.šb'.šnt.|yṣr k.b'l 19[1AQHT].1.39
rt.šblt.yḫ[bq].|w ynšq.aḥl.an.šblt.|tp'.b aklt.šblt.tp'[.b ḥm]drt.|ur.tisp k.yd.aqht.ǵz[r].|tšt k.bm.qrb m.asm.|b p 19[1AQHT].2.72
rb m.asm.|y.dnh.ysb.aklt h.yph.|šblt.b akt.šblt.yp'.|b ḥmdrt.šblt.yḫ[bq].|w ynšq.aḥl.an.šblt.|tp'.b aklt.šblt.tp'[. 19[1AQHT].2.70
.[r]iš.ḥrṯm.|l ẓr.'db.dgn kly.|lḥm.[b]'dn hm.kly.|yn.b ḥmt hm.k[l]y.|šmn.b q[b't hm.---].|bt.krt.t[--]. 16[126].3.15
yškb.|[yd.]mizrt.p yln.mk.b šb'.ymm.|[w]yqrb.b'l.b ḥnt h.abynt.|[d]nil.mt.rpi anḫ.ǵzr.|[mt.]hrnmy.d in.bn.l 17[2AQHT].1.17
.yṯbr.ḥrn.|riš k.'ṯtrt.šm.b'l.|qdqd k.tqln.b gbl.|šnt k.b ḥpn k.w t'n.|spr ilmlk ṯ'y. 16.6[127].58
h.k lb.|ṯat.l imr h.km.lb.|'nt.aṯr.b'l.tiḫd.|bn.ilm.mt.b ḥrb.|tbq'nn.b ḫṯr.tdry|nn.b išt.tšrpnn.|b rḥm.tṭḥnn.b šd. 6[49].2.31
.zbl.b'l.|arṣ.qm.yṯ'r.|w yšlḥmn h.|ybrd.ṯd.l pnw h.|b ḥrb.mlḥt.|qṣ.mri.ndd.|y'šr.w yšqyn h.|ytn.ks.b d h.|krp 3['NT].1.7
m.m[---.---].|[']d.lḥm[.šty.ilm].|w pq.mr[ǵṯm.ṯd.---].|b ḥrb.[mlḥt.qṣ.mri].|šty.kr[pnm.yn.---].|b ks.ḫr[ṣ.dm.'ṣm.- 5[67].4.14
|špq.ilht.dkrt[.yn].|'d.lḥm.šty.ilm.|w pq mrǵṯm.ṯd.|b ḥrb.mlḥt.qṣ[.m]r|i.tšty.krp[nm.y]n.|[b k]s.ḫrṣ.d[m.'ṣm].| 4[51].6.57
hkl h[.---].|[------].|[---.l]ḥm[.---].|[---].ay š[---].|[---.b ḥ]rb.mlḥ[t.qṣ].|[mri.tšty.krpnm].yn.b ks.ḫ[rṣ].|[dm.'ṣm.- 17[2AQHT].6.4
|[---.]btlt.'nt.|[--.tl]ḥm.tšty.|[ilm.w tp]q.mrǵṯm.|[ṯd.b ḥrb.m]lḥt.qṣ.|[mri.tšty.k]rpnm yn.|[b ks.ḫrṣ.dm].'ṣm. 4[51].3.42
n.b'l.yšu.|g h.w yṣḥ.'l k.b[']l m.|pht.qlt.'l k.pht.|dry.b ḥrb.'l k.|pht.šrp.b išt.|'l k.[pht.ṭḥ]n.b rḥ|m.'[l k.]pht[.dr] 6[49].5.13
ṯk nḥš.|šmrr.nḥš.'q šr.ln h.mlḫš.|abd.ln h.ydy.ḥmt.|b ḥrn.pnm.trǵnw.w ṯṯkl.|bnwt h.ykr.'r.d qdm.|idk.pnm.l y UG5.7.61
.|ḥmšm.ṯmn.kbd.|tgmr.bnš.mlk.|d.b d.adn'm.|[š]b'.b.ḥrṯm.|[ṯ]lṯ.b.ṯǵrm.|rb qrt.aḫd.|ṯmn.ḫzr.|w.arb'.ḥršm.|dt 1024.3.1
[---.]rpi.mlk 'lm.b 'z.|[rpu.m]lk.'lm.b ḏmr h.bl.|[---].b ḥtk h.b nmrt h.l r|[--.]arṣ.'z k.ḏmr k.l[-]|n k.ḥtk k.nmrt UG5.2.2.8

d]. | bn abbly. | yṯʿd.ṣm[d]. | bn.liy. | ʿšrm.ṣ[md]. | ṯṯ kbd.b ḥ[--]. | w.arbʿ.ḥ[mrm]. | b m[ʿ]rby. | ṯmn.ṣmd.[---]. | b d.bʿlsr 2113.28

spr.ʿrbnm. | dt.ʿrb. | b.mtn.bn.ayaḫ. | b.ḫbṯ h.ḥwt.ṯt h. | w.mnm.šalm. | dt.tknn. | ʿl.ʿrbnm. | hn hmt. 1161.4

aḥd.kbd. | arbʿm.b ḫzr. | lqḥ šʿrt. | ṯṯ ʿšr h.lqḥ. | ḫlpnt. | ṯṯ.ḥrṯm. | lqḥ.šʿrt. | ʿšr.ḥr 2052.2

ʿm[-]. | bn.ppṯ.b[--]. | b[n.---]. | šm[-.---]. | tkn[.---]. | knn.b.ḫ[lb]. | bn mṯ.b.qmy. | nʿr.b.ulm. 2046.2.4

l.ḥẓ.ršp.b[n].km.yr.klyt h.w lb h. | [ṯ]n.p k.b ǵr.ṯn.p k.b ḫlb.k tgwln.šnt k. | [--.]w špt k.l tššy.hm.tqrm.l mt.b rn k. 1001.1.4

.---]. | qmnz.ṯṯ.krm.yknʿm.ṯmn.krm[.---]. | krm.nʿmn.b.ḫly.ull.krm.aḫ[d.---]. | krm.uḫn.b.šdmy.ṯlṯ.bzl[.d]prn[.---]. 1081.12

t. | w tšu.ʿn h.w tʿn. | w tʿn.arḫ.w tr.b lkt. | tr.b lkt.w tr.b ḫl. | [b]nʿmm.b ysmm.ḥ[--]k.ǵrt. | [ql].l bʿl.ʿnt.ttnn. | [---].b 10[76].2.29

[ṯ.drkt h]. | l alp.ql.ẓ[--.---]. | l np ql.nd.[----]. | tlk.w tr.b[ḫl]. | b nʿmm.b ys[mm.---]. | arḫ.arḫ.[---.tld]. | ibr.tld[.l bʿl] 10[76].3.18

m.šd aṯrt.w rḥm. | ʿl.išt.šbʿ d.ǵzrm.ṭb.[g]d.b ḥlb.annḫ b ḫmat. | w ʿl.agn.šbʿ d m.dǵ[ṯ.---]t. | tlk m.rḥmy.w tṣd[.---]. | 23[52].14

d[.---.---]r. | l riš hm.w yš[--.--]m. | lḥm.b lḥm ay.w šty.b ḫmr yn ay. | šlm.mlk.šlm.mlkt.ʿrbm m.ṯnnm. | mt.w šr.yṯb. 23[52].6

mm.ks.qdš. | l tphn h.aṯt.krpn. | l tʿn.aṯrt.alp. | kd.yqḥ.b ḫmr. | rbt.ymsk.b msk h. | qm.ybd.w yšr. | mṣltm.bd.nʿm. | 3[ʿNT].1.16

m kdm. | w b ṯlṯ.kd yn w krsnm. | w b rbʿ kdm yn. | w b ḫmš kd yn. 1086.5

ym.ṯlṯ.kkr šʿrt. | iqn[i]m.ṯṯt.ʿšrt.ksp h. | ḫmšt.ḥrṣ.bt.il. | b.ḫmšt.ʿšrt.ksp. | ḫmš.mat.šmt. | b.ʿšrt.ksp. | ʿšr.ṣin.b.ṯṯt.w.k 2100.6

ʿbdrt[b.---]. | b ṯṯ ʿr ṯmn.r[qḥ.---]. | p bn btb[-.---]. | b ḫmṯ ʿr k[--.---]. | b ḫmṯ ʿr[.---]. | [-----]. | [---.-]y[-.---]. | w bn 207[57].4

y[-.---]. | w bn ʿṭl.[---]. | ypḫ knʿm[.---]. | aḫmn bt[.---]. | b ḫmṯ ʿr ṯmn[.---]. 207[57].11

ṯ ʿr ṯmn.r[qḥ.---]. | p bn btb[-.---]. | b ḫmṯ ʿr k[--.---]. | b ḫmṯ ʿr[.---]. | [-----]. | [---.-]y[-.---]. | w bn ʿṭl.[---]. | ypḫ knʿm 207[57].5

ʿšr šṭpm. | b ḫmš.šmn. | ʿšrm.gdy. | b ḫmš.šmn. | w ḫmš ṯʿdt. 1097.4

ʿšr šṭpm. | b ḫmš.šmn. | ʿšrm.gdy. | b ḫmš.šmn. | w ḫmš ṯʿdt. 1097.2

lbš.aḥd. | b.ʿšrt. | w.ṯn.b.ḫmšt. | tprt.b.ṯlṯt. | mṯyn.b.ṯṯt. | ṯn.lbšm.b.ʿšrt. | pld.b.arbʿt. | 1108.3

--.--rt]. | w [ʿṣrm.]l.ri[--.---]. | [--]t.bʿlt.bt[.---]. | [md]bḥt.b.ḫmš[.---]. | [-.]kbd.w.db[ḥ.---]. | [--].aṯrt.ʿṣr[m.l inš.ilm]. | [ṯ] 35[3].38

ḫmš.mqdm.dnyn. | b.ṯql.dprn.aḥd. | b.ṯql. | ḫmšm.ʿrgz.b.ḫmšt. 1127.22

ʿšrm.bnšm.[b.]ʿd[--]. | arbʿ.bnšm.b.ag[m]y. | arbʿ.bnšm.b.ḫpty. | ṯṯ.bnšm.b.bir. | ṯṯ.bnšm b.uḫnp. | ṯn.bnšm.b.ḫrṣbʿ. | a 2076.12

--]ṯm. | [---.]ʿšrt. | [-----]. | b.[---.---]r. | b.ann[.---.-]ny[-]. | b.ḫqn.[---]m.ṣ[-]n. | [b].bn.ay[--.---].l.ʿšrm. | [-]gp[.---.]ʿrny.ṯṯ 2054.2.16

n.ṯkmn. | w šnm.w ngšnn.ḫby. | bʿl.qrnm w ḏnb.ylšn. | b ḫri h.w ṯnt h.ql.il.[--]. | il.k yrdm.arṣ.ʿnt. | w ʿṯtrt.tṣdn.[---]. UG5.1.1.21

mʿ[ṣd.---]. | [b.]gt.ḥrṯm.ḫm[š.---]. | [n]it.krk.mʿṣ[d.---]. | b.ḫrbǵlm.ǵlm[n]. | w.trhy.aṯt h. | w.mlky.b[n] h. | ily.mrily.td 2048.19

ḥmd m. | bn.dgn.yhrr m. | bʿl.ngṯ hm.b pʿn h. | w il hd.b ḫrẓʿ h. | [-----]. | [--]t.[---]. | [---.]ʿn[.---]. | pnm[.---]. | bʿl.n[--.-- 12[75].1.41

ṯlṯ mrkb[t]. | ṣpyt b ḫrṣ[.w] ṣmdm trm.d [ṣ]py. | w.trm.aḥdm. | ṣpym. | ṯlṯ mrkb 1122.2

šm.b.ḫpty. | ṯṯ.bnšm.b.bir. | ṯṯ.bnšm b.uḫnp. | ṯn.bnšm.b.ḫrṣbʿ. | arbʿ.bnšm.b.hzp. | arbʿ.bnšm.b.šql. | arbʿ.bnšm.b.nni 2076.15

[h]. | w aḥd.hm.iṯ.šmt.hm.iṯ[.ʿẓm]. | abky.w aqbrn.ašt.b ḫrt. | i[lm.arṣ.b p h.rgm.l yṣa.b šp] | t h.hwt h.knp.hrgb.bʿl. 19[1AQHT].3.126

kbd h.w aḥd.hm.iṯ.šmt.iṯ. | ʿẓm.abky w aqbrn h.aštn. | b ḫrt.ilm.arṣ.b p h.rgm.l[yṣ]a. | b špt h.hwt h.knp.ṣml.bʿ[l]. 19[1AQHT].3.141

w] | aḥd.hm.iṯ.šmt.hm.i[ṯ]. | ʿẓm.abky.w aqbrn h. | ašt.b ḫrt.ilm.arṣ. | b p h.rgm.l yṣa.b špt h.hwt[h]. | knp.nšrm.bʿl 19[1AQHT].3.112

.dpr k. | [---.-]mn k.ššrt. | [---.--]t.npš.ʿgl. | [---.-]nk.aštn.b ḫrt. | ilm.arṣ.w at.qḥ. | ʿrpt k.rḥ k.mdl k. | mṭrt k.ʿm k.šbʿt. 5[67].5.5

.k tšt h.tšʿlyn h. | b ṣrrt.ṣpn.tbkyn h. | w tqbrn h.tštnn.b ḫrt. | ilm.arṣ.ṯṭbḫ.šbʿm. | rumm.k gmn.aliyn. | [b]ʿl.ṯṭbḫ.šbʿ 6[62].1.17

r h.km.lb. | ʿnt.aṯr.bʿl.tiḫd. | bn.ilm.mt.b ḥrb. | tbqʿnn.b ḫṯr.tdry | nn.b išt.tšrpnn. | b rḥm.ṯṭḥnn.b šd. | tdrʿnn.šir h.l 6[49].2.32

--.]ʿm.l.mit.dd.ṯn.kbd.ḫpr.bnšm.ṯmnym.dd. | l u[-]m. | b.tbq.arbʿm.drʿ.w.ʿšr.dd.drt. | w[.a]rbʿ.l.ʿšrm.dd.l.yḫšr.bl.bn 1098.10

aṯr[t.---]. | b im[--.---]. | bl.l[---.---]. | mlk.[---]. | dt [---]. | b ṯ[--.---]. | gm[.---]. | y[--.---]. 4[51].2.46

trḥṣ.w tadm. | rḥṣ[.y]d k.amt. | uṣb[ʿt k.]ʿd[.ṯ]km. | ʿrb[.b ẓl.ḫmt]. | qḥ im[r.b yd k]. | imr.d[bḥ.bm].ymn. | lla.kl[atn] 14[KRT].2.65

yrtḥṣ.w yadm. | yrḥṣ.yd h.amt h. | uṣbʿt h.ʿd.ṯkm. | ʿrb.b ẓl.ḫmt.lqḥ. | imr.dbḥ.b yd h. | lla.klatnm. | klt.lḥm h.d nzl. 14[KRT].3.159

t.rbtm. | kt.il.nbt.b ksp. | šmrgt.b dm.ḫrṣ. | kḥṯ.il.nḥṯ. | b ẓr.hdm.id. | d pršа.b br. | nʿl.il.d qblbl. | ʿln.ybl hm.ḫrṣ. | ṯlḥ 4[51].1.35

.d l h q[--.---]. | l ytn.l hm.ṯḥt bʿl[.---]. | h.u qšt pn hdd.b y[.----]. | ʿm.b ym bʿl ysy ym[.---]. | rmm.ḫnpm.mḫl[.---]. | 9[33].2.6

r k. | tšlm k.um y. | tdʿ.ky.ʿrbt. | l pn.špš. | w pn.špš.nr. | b y.mid.w um. | tšmḫ.m ab. | w al.trḥln. | ʿtn.ḫrd.ank. | ʿm ny. 1015.10

a.]mlk k.l yṯbr.ḫṯ.mṯpṭ k.w yʿn[.ʿṯtr].dm[-]k[-]. | [--]ḥ.b y.ṯr.il.ab y.ank.in.bt[.l] y[.km.]ilm[.w] ḥẓr[.k bn]. | [qd]š.lb 2.3[129].19

ubdy.mdm. | šd.b d.ʿbdmlk. | šd.b d.yšn.ḥrš. | šd.b d.aupš. | šd.b d.ršpab.aḫ.ubn. | šd.b d.bn.uṯryn. | [ubd]y.mr 82[300].1.4

[.---.]br. | ydn[.---].kry. | bn.ydd[.---.b]r. | prkl.bʿl.any.d.b d.abr[-]. 2123.7

spr.ubdy.art. | šd.prn.b d.agptn.nḥl h. | šd.šwn.b d.ttyn.nḥl [h]. | šd.ṯtyn[.b]n.arkšt. 2029.2

ṯlṯ.mat.ṯlṯm. | kbd.šmn. | l kny. | ṯmnym.šmn. | b d.adnnʿm. 1094.5

kyn. | bʿln. | ytršp. | ḥmšm.ṯmn.kbd. | tgmr.bnš.mlk. | d.b d.adnʿm. | [š]bʿ.b.ḥrṯm. | [ṯ]lṯ.b.ṯǵrm. | rb qrt.aḥd. | ṯmn.ḫzr. 1024.2.27

[sp]r.bnš.ml[k.d.b] d adn[ʿm]. | [---].riš[.---].kt. | [y]nḥm. | ilbʿl. | ʿbdyr[ḫ]. | ṯtpḥ 1024.1.1

lkz. | [šd.b]d.b[n].tkwn. | [ubdy.md]rǵlm. | [šd.bn.--]n.b d.aḫny. | [šd.bn.--]rt.b d.ṯptbʿl. | [ubdy.]mḫ[ṣ]m. | [šd.bn.]u 82[300].2.23

ʿl.ydm.pʿrt[.---]. | šm k.mdd.i[l.---]. | bt ksp y.d[--.---]. | b d.aliyn b[ʿl.---]. | kd.ynaṣn[.---]. | gršnn.l k[si.mlk h.l nḫt.l 1[ʿNT.X].4.22

bd.ksp. | kkrm.šʿrt.štt.b d.gg[ʿt]. | b.ʿšrt.ksp. | ṯlṯ.uṯbm.b d.alḫn.b.ʿšrt[.k]sp. | rṯ.l.ql.d.ybl.prd. | b.ṯql.w.nṣp.ksp. | ṯm 2101.11

.iwrkl. | šd.b d.klb. | šd.b d.klby. | šd.b d.iytlm. | ṯn.šdm.b d.amtrn. | šd.b d.iwrm[--]. | šd.b d.yṯpr. | šd.b d.krb[-]. | šd.b 2090.12

.b d.bn.ʿyn. | ṯn.šdm.b d.klṯtb. | šd.b d.krz[n]. | ṯlṯ.šdm.b d.amtr[n]. | ṯn.šdm.b d.skn. | šd.b d[.ʿb]dyrḫ. | šd.b [d.--]ṯtb 2090.22

--].dqn[.---]. | [-]ntn.artn.b d[.--]nr[.---]. | ʿzn.w ymd.šr.b d ansny. | nsk.ks[p.--]mrtn.kṯrmlk. | yḥmn.aḫm[l]k.ʿbdrpu. 2011.31

. | šbʿm.lbš.d.ʿrb.bt.mlk. | b.mit.ḫmšt.kbd.ksp. | ṯlṯ.ktnt.b d.an[r]my. | b.ʿšrt.ksp.b.a[--]. | ṯqlm.ḫr[ṣ.]b.ṯmnt.ksp. | ʿšrt. 2101.18

n.ḫmš. | kbd.w lpš. | ḫmš.mispt. | mṯ. | w lpš.d sgr b h. | b d.anrmy. 1109.7

.k inr. | ap.ḫšt k.ap.ab.k mtm. | tmtn.u ḫšt k.l ntn. | ʿtq.b d.aṯt.ab.ṣrry. | ik m.yrgm.bn.il. | krt.špḥ.lṭpn. | w qdš.u ilm. 16.1[125].19

inr[.ap.]ḫšt k. | ap.ab.k mtm.tmtn. | u ḫšt k.l bky.ʿtq. | b d.aṯt ab.ṣrry. | u ilm.tmtn.špḥ. | [l]ṭpn.l yḥ.t[b]ky k. | ab.ǵr. 16.2[125].104

k inr. | ap.ḫšt k.ap.ab.ik mtm. | tmtn.u ḫšt k.l ntn. | ʿtq.b d.aṯt.ab ṣrry. | tbky k.ab.ǵr.bʿl. | ṣpn.ḥlm.qdš. | any.ḥlm.adr 16.1[125].5

| [---.--]ṯ.ʿbd.l.kyn. | k[rm.--.]l.i[w]rtḏl. | ḥl.d[--.ʿbd]yrḫ.b d.apn. | krm.i[--].l.[---.]a[-]bn. 2027.2.11

šd.bn.adn. | [b] d.armwl. | [šd].mrnn. | b d.[-]tw[-]. | šd.bn[.---]. | b d.dd[--]. 2028.2

š]. | lmd.aḥd.b d.yḫ[--]. | ṯlṯ.lmdm.b d.nḫ[--]. | lmd.aḥd.b d.ar[--]. | ṯlṯ.lmdm.b d.[---]. | ṯlṯ.lmdm.b d.[---]. 1050.7

b.ṣr. | mtt.by. | gšm.adr. | nškḥ.w. | rb.tmtt. | lqḥ.kl.ḏrʿ. | b d a[-]m.w.ank. | k[l.]ḏrʿ hm. | [--.n]pš[.-]. | w [k]l hm.b d. | r 2059.18

npṣ.ʿ[--.---].|d.b d.a[--.---].|w.b d.b[--.---].|udbr[.---].|ʿrš[.---].|ṯl[ḫn.---].|a 1120.2
š]d.bn.ṣnrn.b d.nrn.|[š]d.bn.rwy.b d.ydln.|[š].bn.trn.b d.ibrmḏ.|[š]d.bn.ilṯtmr.b d.tbbr.|[w.]šd.nḥl h.b d.ṯtmd.|[82[300].1.10
bn.ṯqdy.b d.gmrd.|[š]d bn.synn.b d.gmrd.|[šd.]abyy.b d.ibrmḏ.|[šd.]bn.ṯtrn.b d.bnš.aǵlkz.|[šd.b]d.b[n].tkwn.|[82[300].2.19
tšʿ.ṣmdm.|ṯlṯm.b d.|ibrtlm.|w.pat.aḫt.|in.b hm. 1141.2
bn.ngzḫn.b d.gmrd.|[šd.bn].pll.b d.gmrd.|[šd.bn.-]ll.b d.iwrḫṭ.|[šd.bn.-]nn.b d.bn.šmrm.|[šd.bn.-]ṯtayy.b d.ṯtm 82[300].1.25
.|[š]d.bn.ilṯtmr.b d.tbbr.|[w.]šd.nḥl h.b d.ṯtmd.|[š]d.b d.iwrḫṭ.|[ṯn].šdm.b d.gmrd.|[šd.]lbny.b d.tbṯtb.|[š]d.bn.ṭ 82[300].1.13
.u[--].|šd.b d.[---].|šd.b d[.---]im.|šd.b d[.bn.--]n.|šd.b d.iwrkl.|šd.b d.klb.|šd.b d.klby.|šd.b d.iytlm.|ṯn.šdm.b 2090.8
lb.|šd.b d.klby.|šd.b d.iytlm.|ṯn.šdm.b d.amtrn.|šd.b d.iwrm[--].|šd.b d.yṯpr.|šd.b d.krb[-].|šd.b d.bn.pṭḏ.|šd. 2090.13
]ht.yšmʿ.uḫ y.|l g y.w yhbṭ.bnš.|w ytn.ilm.b d hm.|b d.iḫqm.gṯr.|w b d.ytrhd.|bʿl. 55[18].20
rʿym.dt.b d.iytlm.|ḫyrn.w.šǵr h.|šǵr.bn.prsn.|agpṯr.w.šǵ[r h].|ṯʿln. 2072.1
[--.-]d[-.---].|[--.šd]m.b d.iyt[lm].|[šd.b]d.s[--].|š[d.b]d.u[--].|šd.b d.[---].|šd.b d 2090.2
d[.bn.--]n.|šd.b d.iwrkl.|šd.b d.klb.|šd.b d.klby.|šd.b d.iytlm.|ṯn.šdm.b d.amtrn.|šd.b d.iwrm[--].|šd.b d.yṯpr. 2090.11
.ḫrǵš[-].l.qrt.|šd.iǵlyn.bn.kzbn.l.qr[t].|šd.pln.bn.tiyn.b d.ilmhr nḥl h.|šd knn.bn.ann.ʿdb.|šd.iln[-].bn.irṯr.l.šḫrn. 2029.18
m.ṯbʿm.šḫr.ʿzn.ilhd.|bnil.rb ʿšrt.lkn.ypʿn.ṯ[--].|yṣḥm.b d.ubn.krwn.ṯǵd.[m]nḥm.|ʿpṯrm.šmʿrgm.skn.qrt.|ḫgbn.š 2011.9
ʿly.|[---.b] d.ʿbdḫmn.|[---.b] d.ṯbq.|[---.b] d.šbn.|[---.b] d.ulm.|[---.b] d.ǵbl.|[---.b] d.ʿbdkṯr.|[---.b] d.urǵnr. 1052.6
.šbn.|[---.b] d.ulm.|[---.b] d.ǵbl.|[---.b] d.ʿbdkṯr.|[---.b] d.urǵnr. 1052.9
.]ksp.|ḫmš.kkr.ṣml.|b.ʿšrt.b d.bn.kyn.|ʿšr.kkr.šʿrt.|b d.urtn.b.arbʿm.|arbʿt.ʿšrt.ḫrṣ.|b.ṯqlm.kbd.arbʿm.|ʿšrt.ḫrṣ. 2100.15
bn.sbrdnm.|ḫmš.kkrm.alp kb[d].|ṯlṯ.l.nskm.birtym.|b d.urtn.w.ṯṯ.mat.brr.|b.ṯmnym.ksp.ṯlṯt.kbd.|ḫmš.alp.ṯlṯ.l. 2101.4
[--.-]d[-.---].|[--.šd]m.b d.iyt[lm].|[šd.b]d.s[--].|š[d.b]d.u[--].|šd.b d.[---].|šd.b d[.---]im.|šd.b d[.bn.--]n.|šd.b 2090.4
bd mlk.|w.snt.|bt.ugrt.|w.pdy h[m].|iwrkl.mit.|ksp.b y[d].|birtym.|[un]ṯ inn.|l [h]m ʿd ṯṯbn.|ksp.iwrkl.|w ṯb. 1006.14
d.ṯtyn[.b]n.arkšt.|lʿq[.---].|šd.pll.b d.qrt.|š[d].anndr.b d.bdn.nḥ[l h].|[šd.]agyn.b d.kmrn.n[ḥl] h.|[š]d.nbzn.[-]l. 2029.7
|šbʿ yn.|l mrynm.|b yṯbmlk.|kdm.ǵbiš ḫry.|ḫmš yn.b d.|bḫ mlkt.|b mdrʿ.|ṯlṯ bt.il|ann.|kd.bt.ilann. 1090.14
[.---].|mid.an[--.]ṣn[--].|nrt.ilm.špš[.ṣḫrr]t.|la.šmm.b y[d.bn.ilm.m]t.|w tʿn.btlt.ʿn[t.bnt.]bht |k.y ilm.bnt.bh[t 3[ʿNT.VI].5.26
y.|k lli.b ṯbrn q y.ḫtu hw.|nrt.ilm.špš.ṣḫrrt.|la.šmm.b yd.bn ilm.mt.|ym.ymm.yʿtqn.l ymm.|l yrḫm.rḫm.ʿnt.tng 6[49].2.25
|[š]d.bn.bri.b d.bn.ydln.|[u]bdy.ṯǵrm.|[š]d.ṯǵr.mṯpit.b d.bn.iryn.|[u]bdy.šrm.|[š]d.bn.ḫrmln.b d.bn.tnn.|[š]d.bn 82[300].2.8
p.|[ṯ]mn.l.ʿšrm[.l.b]t.ʿṯtrt.|[ṯ]lṯ.ʿšr h.[b]t.ršp.gn.|arbʿ.b d.b[n].ušryn.|kdm.l.urtn.|kdm.l.ilšpš.|kd.l.anntb.|kd.l.i 1088.4
šd.b d.yšn.ḥrš.|šd.b d.aupš.|šd.b d.ršpab.aḫ.ubn.|šd.b d.bn.uṯryn.|[ubd]y.mrynm.|[š]d.bn.ṣnrn.b d.nrn.|[š]d.bn 82[300].1.6
spr.irgmn.|ṯlṯ.ḫmš.alpm.|b d.brq.maḫdy.|kkr.ṯlṯ.|b d.bn.by.ar[y].|alpm.ṯlṯ.|b d.šim.il[š]tmʿy. 1134.5
bym.|[šd.b]n.qty.b d.ṯt.|[ubd]y.mrim.|[šd.b]n.ṯpdn.b d.bn.gʿr.|[šd.b]n.ṯqrn.b d.ḫby.|[ṯn.š]d.bn.ngzḫn.b d.gmrd 82[300].1.21
.|šḫr.ʿlmt.|bnš bnšm.|l.yqḫnn.b d.|bʿln.bn.kltn.|w.b d.bn h.ʿd.|ʿlm.w unṯ.|in.b h. 1008.19
mn km l.yqḫ.|bt.hnd.b d.|[ʿb]dmlk.|[-]k.amʿ[--].|[w.b] d.bn h[.ʿ]d ʿlm.|[w.un]ṯ.in[.n]b h.|[---.]nʿm[-]. 1009.17
dy.šrm.|[š]d.bn.ḫrmln.b d.bn.tnn.|[š]d.bn.ḫrmln.ṯn.b d.bn.ḫdmn.|[u]bdy.nqdm.|[ṯlṯ].šdm.d.nʿrb.gt.npk.|[š]d.r 82[300].2.11
.ymz.|[šd.b d].klby.psl.|[ub]dy.mri.ibrn.|[š]d.bn.bri.b d.bn.ydln.|[u]bdy.ṯǵrm.|[š]d.ṯǵr.mṯpit.b d.bn.iryn.|[u]bd 82[300].2.6
]dwṯm.w.ṯt.ṯprtm.|b.ʿšr[m.]ksp.|ḫmš.kkr.ṣml.|b.ʿšrt.b d.bn.kyn.|ʿšr.kkr.šʿrt.|b d.urtn.b.arbʿm.|arbʿt.ʿšrt.ḫrṣ.|b. 2100.13
].|šd.b d.bn.pṭḏ.|šd.b d.dr.khnm.|šd.b d.bn.ʿmy.|šd.b d.bn.ʿyn.|ṯn.šdm.b d.klṯtb.|šd.b d.krz[n].|ṯlṯ.šdm.b d.am 2090.19
pr.|šd.b d.krb[-].|šd.b d.bn.pṭḏ.|šd.b d.dr.khnm.|šd.b d.bn.ʿmy.|šd.b d.bn.ʿyn.|ṯn.šdm.b d.klṯtb.|šd.b d.krz[n]. 2090.18
mtrn.|šd.b d.iwrm[--].|šd.b d.yṯpr.|šd.b d.krb[-].|šd.b d.bn.pṭḏ.|šd.b d.dr.khnm.|šd.b d.bn.ʿmy.|šd.b d.bn.ʿyn.| 2090.16
k.l.gmrd.|[---.--]ṯ.l.yšn.|[šd.--]ln.|b d.trǵds.|šd.ṯʿlb.|b d.bn.pl.|šd.bn.kt.|b d.pdy.|šd.ḫzr.|[b d].d[---]. 2030.2.4
|[šd.bn.-]ṯtayy.b d.ṯtmd.|[šd.bn.-]rn.b d.ṣdqšlm.|[šd.b d.]bn.pʿṣ.|[ubdy.ʿ]šrm.|[šd.---]n.b d.brdd.|[---.--]m.|[šd.- 82[300].1.29
d.bn].pll.b d.gmrd.|[šd.bn.-]ll.b d.iwrḫṭ.|[šd.bn.-]nn.b d.bn.šmrm.|[šd.bn.-]ṯtayy.b d.ṯtmd.|[šd.bn.-]rn.b d.ṣdqšl 82[300].1.26
|[šd.]abyy.b d.ibrmḏ.|[šd.]bn.ṯtrn.b d.bnš.aǵlkz.|[šd.b]d.b[n].tkwn.|[ubdy.mḏ]rǵlm.|[šd.bn.--]n.b d.aḫny.|[šd. 82[300].2.21
š]d.ṯǵr.mṯpit.b d.bn.iryn.|[u]bdy.šrm.|[š]d.bn.ḫrmln.b d.bn.tnn.|[š]d.bn.ḫrmln.ṯn.b d.bn.ḫdmn.|[u]bdy.nqdm.|[82[300].2.10
]d.s[--].|š[d.b]d.u[--].|šd.b d.[---].|šd.b d[.---]im.|šd.b d[.bn.--]n.|šd.b d.iwrkl.|šd.b d.klb.|šd.b d.klby.|šd.b d.i 2090.7
šrt.ksp.b.a[--].|ṯqlm.ḫr[ṣ.]b.ṯmnt.ksp.|ʿšrt.ksp.b.alp.[b d].bn.[---].|tšʿ.ṣin.b.tšʿt.ksp.|mšlt.b.ṯql.ksp.|kdwṯ.l.grgyn 2101.21
bn.synn.b d.gmrd.|[šd.]abyy.b d.ibrmḏ.|[šd.]bn.ṯtrn.b d.bnš.aǵlkz.|[šd.b]d.b[n].tkwn.|[ubdy.mḏ]rǵlm.|[šd.bn.- 82[300].2.20
uṣbʿt h.hlm.ktp.zbl ym.bn ydm.|[ṯp]ṭ nhr.yrtqṣ.ṣmd.b d bʿl.km.nšr.|b[u]ṣbʿt h.ylm.ktp.zbl ym.bn ydm.ṯpṭ.|nhr 2.4[68].15
r.aymr.mr.ym.mr.ym.|l ksi h.nhr l kḥṯ.drkt h.trtqṣ.|b d bʿl.km.nšr b uṣbʿt h.hlm.qdq|d zbl ym.bn.ʿnm.ṯpṭ.nhr.y 2.4[68].21
rš.ygrš.grš ym grš ym.l ksi h.|[n]hr l kḥṯ drkt h.trtqṣ.b d bʿl km nš|r.b uṣbʿt h.hlm.ktp.zbl ym.bn ydm.|[ṯp]ṭ nhr 2.4[68].13
m.bn.ʿnm.ṯpṭ.nhr.yprsḥ ym.|w yql.l arṣ.w trtqṣ.ṣmd.b d bʿl.|[km.]nšr.b uṣbʿt h.ylm.qdqd.zbl.|[ym.]bn.ʿnm.ṯpṭ.n 2.4[68].23
.|kltn.w l.|bn h.ʿd.ʿlm.|šḫr.ʿlmt.|bnš bnšm.|l.yqḫnn.b d.|bʿln.bn.kltn.|w.b d.bn h.ʿd.|ʿlm.w unṯ.|in.b h. 1008.17
d.b ḥ[--].|w.arbʿ.ḥ[mrm].|b m[ʾ]rby.|ṯmn.ṣmd.[---].|b d.bʿlsr.|yd.ṯdn.ʿšr.|[ḥ]mrm.|ddm.l.ybr[k].|bdmr.prs.l.u[- 2102.3
n.b d.ṣdqšlm.|[šd.b d.]bn.pʿṣ.|[ubdy.ʿ]šrm.|[šd.---]n.b d.brdd.|[---.--]m.|[šd.---.b d.]ṯpṭbʿl.|[šd.---.]b d.ymz.|[šd. 82[300].1.31
spr.irgmn.|ṯlṯ.ḫmš.alpm.|b d.brq.maḫdy.|kkr.ṯlṯ.|b d.bn.by.ar[y].|alpm.ṯlṯ.|b d.šim. 1134.3
k.mmʿm.w[---].|aqht.w yplṭ k.bn[.dnil.---].|w yʿḏr k.b yd.btlt.[ʿnt].|w yʿn.lṯpn.il d p[id].|ydʿt k.bt.k anšt.w i[n.b 18[3AQHT].1.14
npṣ.ʿ[--.---].|d.b d.a[--.---].|w.b d.b[--.---].|udbr[.---].|ʿrš[.---].|ṯl[ḫn.---].|a[--.---].|ṯn[.---]. 1120.3
[---].b d.š[--]mlk.|[---.b] d.gbʿly.|[---.b] d.ʿbdḫmn.|[---.b] d.ṯbq.|[---.b] d.šbn.|[--- 1052.2
.l.ḫlby.|b d.tlmi.b.ʿšrm.ḫmšt.|kbd.ksp.|kkrm.šʿrt.šṯt.b d.gg[ʿt].|b.ʿšrt.ksp.|ṯlṯ.uṯbm.b d.alḫn.b.ʿšrt[.k]sp.|rṯ.l.ql. 2101.9
mḏrǵlm.dt.inn.|b d.tlmyn.|b d.gln.ary.|tgyn.yʿrty.|bn.krwn.b.yny.iytlm.|šgryn.ary.b. 2071.3
.|[ub]dy.trrm.|[šd.]bn.ṯqdy.b d.gmrd.|[š]d bn.synn.b d.gmrd.|[šd.]abyy.b d.ibrmḏ.|[šd.]bn.ṯtrn.b d.bnš.aǵlkz.| 82[300].2.18
klṯtb.|[š]d.ilṣy.b d.ʿbdym.|[ub]dy.trrm.|[šd.]bn.ṯqdy.b d.gmrd.|[š]d bn.synn.b d.gmrd.|[šd.]abyy.b d.ibrmḏ.|[šd 82[300].2.17
n.b d.bn.gʿr.|[šd.b]n.ṯqrn.b d.ḫby.|[ṯn.š]d.bn.ngzḫn.b d.gmrd.|[šd.bn].pll.b d.gmrd.|[šd.bn.-]ll.b d.iwrḫṭ.|[šd.b 82[300].1.23
ṯqrn.b d.ḫby.|[ṯn.š]d.bn.ngzḫn.b d.gmrd.|[šd.bn].pll.b d.gmrd.|[šd.bn.-]ll.b d.iwrḫṭ.|[šd.bn.-]nn.b d.bn.šmrm.|[82[300].1.24
bbr.|[w.]šd.nḥl h.b d.ṯtmd.|[š]d.b d.iwrḫṭ.|[ṯn].šdm.b d.gmrd.|[šd.]lbny.b d.tbṯtb.|[š]d.bn.ṯ[-]rn.b d.ʿdbmlk.|[š 82[300].1.14

--].|b mgn k.w ḫrṣ.l kl.|apnk.ǵzr.ilḥu.|[m]rḥ h.yiḫd.b yd.|[g]rgr h.bm.ymn.|[w]yqrb.trẓẓ h.|[---].mǵy h.w ǵlm 16.1[125].47
b[---].|b d.[---].|šd.[---].|b d.[---].|[-----].|šd.bn.gdy.|b d.ddl. 2028.23
n.|[b] d.armwl.|[šd].mrnn.|b d.[-]tw[-].|šd.bn[.---].|b d.dd[--].|šd.d[---].|b d.d[---].|šd.b[---].|b d.[---].|šd[.---].| 2028.6
ṯr.w ḫss.|l brlt.hyn.d ḥrš.|ydm.aḫr.ymǵy.kṯr.|w ḫss.b d.dnil.ytnn.|qšt.l brk h.y'db.|qṣ't.apnk.mṯt.dnty.|tšlḥm.t 17[2AQHT].5.26
rm[--].|šd.b d.yṯpr.|šd.b d.krb[-].|šd.b d.bn.pṯḏ.|šd.b d.dr.khnm.|šd.b d.bn.'my.|šd.b d.bn.'yn.|ṯn.šdm.b d.klṯṯ 2090.17
mrnn.|b d.[-]tw[-].|šd.bn[.---].|b d.dd[--].|šd.d[---].|b d.d[---].|šd.b[---].|b d.[---].|šd[.---].|b d[.---].|š[d.---].|b d 2028.8
rǵds.|šd.ṯ'lb.|b d.bn.pl.|šd.bn.kt.|b d.pdy.|šd.ḫzr.|[b d].d[---]. 2030.2.8
lm.b'l.|in.b'l.b bht ht.|il hd.b qrb.hkl h.|qšt hn.aḫd.b yd h.|w qṣ't h.bm.ymn h.|idk.l ytn pnm.|tk.aḫ.šmk.mla[10[76].2.6
mlk.šlm.mlkt.'rbm m.ṯnnm.|mt.w šr.yṯb.b d h.ḫṭ.ṯkl.b d h.|ḫṭ.ulmn.yzbrnn.zbrm.gpn.|yṣmdnn.ṣmdm.gpn.yšql. 23[52].8
yn ay.|šlm.mlk.šlm.mlkt.'rbm m.ṯnnm.|mt.w šr.yṯb.b d h.ḫṭ.ṯkl.b d h.|ḫṭ.ulmn.yzbrnn.zbrm.gpn.|yṣmdnn.ṣmd 23[52].8
h.|b ḥrb.mlḥt.|qṣ.mri.ndd.|y'šr.w yšqyn h.|ytn.ks.b d h.|krpn.b klat.yd h.|b krb.'ẓm.ridn.|mt.šmm.ks.qdš.|l 3['NT].1.10
h.amt h.|uṣb't h.'d.ṯkm.|'rb.b ẓl.ḫmt.lqḥ.|imr.dbḥ.b yd h.|lla.klatnm.|klt.lḥm h.d nzl.|lqḥ.msrr.'ṣr.db[ḥ].|yṣ 14[KRT].3.160
[-----].|l abn[.---].|aḫdt.plk h[.b yd h].|plk.qlt.b ymn h.|npyn h.mks.bšr h.|tmt'.md h.b y 4[51].2.3
.|ks.b d y.qb't.b ymn y[.t]q|ḥ.pǵt.w tšqyn h.tq[ḥ.ks.]b d h.|qb't.b ymn h.w y'n.yt[p]n[.mh]r.|št.b yn.yšt.ila.il š[- 19[1AQHT].4.217
h tšu w[.---].|aylt tǵpy ṯr.'n[.---].|b[b]r.mrḥ h.ti[ḫd.b yd h].|š[g]r h bm ymn.t[--.---].|[--.]l b'l.'bd[.---].|ṯr ab h i 2001.1.12
'.trḥṣ].|yd h.btlt.'nt.uṣb't[h.ybmt].|limm.tiḫd.knr h.b yd[h.tšt].|rimt.l irt h.tšr.dd.al[iyn].|b'l.ahbt. UG5.3.2.6
d.gṯr.|[w]ht.yšm'.uḫ y.|l g y.w yhbṭ.bnš.|w ytn.ilm.b d hm.|b d.iḫqm.gṯr.|w b d.ytrhd.|b'l. 55[18].19
n.|arb'[m.ksp.]'l.|il[m]l[k.a]rgnd.|uškny[.w]mit.|zt.b d hm.rib.|w [---].|[-----].|[-]šy[.---] h.|[-]kt[.---.]nrn.|[b]n 2055.13
rḫ.n[ql.---].|[---.]m[---].|[---.yr]ḫ.mgm[r.---].|[---.--]š.b d.h[--.---].|[---.y]rḫ.dbḥ[.---].|[---.-]pn.b d.[---].|[---.]b d.[- 1160.4
qmḥ.d.kly.k ṣḥ.illdrm.|b d.zlb[n.--].|arb'.'š[r.]dd.n'r.|d.apy[.--].|w.arb['.--]d.apy.' 2094.2
.|[ubd]y.mrim.|[šd.b]n.ṯpdn.b d.bn.g'r.|[šd.b]n.ṯqrn.b d.ḫby.|[ṯn.š]d.bn.ngzḥn.b d.gmrd.|[šd.bn].pll.b d.gmrd.| 82[300].1.22
'.|mgn.rbt.aṯrt ym.|mǵẓ.qnyt.ilm.|hyn.'ly.l mpḫm.|b d.ḫss.mṣbṭm.|yṣq.ksp.yšl|ḥ.ḫrṣ.yṣq.ksp.|l alpm.ḫrṣ.yṣq| 4[51].1.25
ṣq-ḫym.w tbṯḫ.|kt.il.dt.rbtm.|kt.il.nbt.b ksp.|šmrgt.b dm.ḫrṣ.|kḥṯ.il.nḫt.|b ẓr.hdm.id.|d prša.b br.|n'l.il.d qbl 4[51].1.33
t.b hlm w y'n.ytpn[.mhr].|št.qḥn.w tšqyn.yn.qḥ.|ks.b d y.qb't.b ymn y[.t]q|ḥ.pǵt.w tšqyn h.tq[ḥ.ks.]b d h.|qb't 19[1AQHT].4.216
mnḥ.b d.ybnn.|arb'.mat.|l.alp.šmn.|nḥ.ṯṯ.mat.|šm[n].rqḥ.|kkr 141[120].1
|k lli.b ṯbrn.|qn h.ṯṯan.|nrt.ilm.špš.|ṣḥrrt.la.|šmm.b yd.md|d.ilm.mt.b a|lp.šd.rbt.k|mn.l p'n.mt.|hbr.w ql.|t 4[51].8.23
n.|[ubd]y.mrynm.|[š]d.bn.ṣnrn.b d.nrn.|[š]d.bn.rwy.b d.ydln.|[š].bn.trn.b d.ibrmḏ.|[š]d.bn.ilṯtmr.b d.tbbr.|[w.] 82[300].1.9
alpm.arb'.mat.k[bd].|mit.b d.yd[r]m.|alp ḫmš mat.kbd.d[--]. 2109.2
ḏm[r.---].br.|bn.i[ytlm.---].|wr[t.---.]b d.yḥmn.|yry[.---.]br.|ydn[.---].kry.|bn.ydd[.---.b]r.|prkl. 2123.3
-].|šb'.lmdm.b d.s[n]rn.|lmd.aḥd.b d.yr[š].|lmd.aḥd.b d.yḥ[--].|ṯlṯ.lmdm.b d.nḥ[--].|lmd.aḥd.b d.ar[--].|ṯlṯ.lmd 1050.5
d.---]n.b d.brdd.|[---.--]m.|[šd.---.b d.]ṯpṭb'l.|[šd.---.]b d.ymz.|[šd.b d].klby.psl.|[ub]dy.mri.ibrn.|[š]d.bn.bri.b d 82[300].2.3
[.---].|ḫdǵlm.b d.[---].|šb'.lmdm.b d.s[n]rn.|lmd.aḥd.b d.yr[š].|lmd.aḥd.b d.yḥ[--].|ṯlṯ.lmdm.b d.nḥ[--].|lmd.aḥd 1050.4
b d.snrn.|[---.lm]dm.b d.nrn.|[---.ḫ]dǵlm.|[lmd.]aḥd.b d.yrš. 1051.6
ubdy.mdm.|šd.b d.'bdmlk.|šd.b d.yšn.ḥrš.|šd.b d.aupš.|šd.b d.ršpab.aḫ.ubn.|šd.b d.bn.uṯ 82[300].1.3
|[šd.bn.--]rt.b d.ṯpṭb'l.|[ubdy.]mḫ[ṣ]m.|[šd.bn.]uzpy.b d.yšn.ḥrš.|[-----].|[-----].|[šd.b d.--]n.|[šd.b d.--]n.|[šd.b 82[300].2.26
g y.w yhbṭ.bnš.|w ytn.ilm.b d hm.|b d.iḫqm.gṯr.|w b d.ytrhd.|b'l. 55[18].21
šd.b d.iytlm.|ṯn.šdm.b d.amtrn.|šd.b d.iwrm[--].|šd.b d.yṯpr.|šd.b d.krb[-].|šd.b d.bn.pṯḏ.|šd.b d.dr.khnm.|šd. 2090.14
]d k.amt.|uṣb['t k.]'d[.ṯ]km.|'rb[.b ẓl.ḫmt].|qḥ im[r.b yd k].|imr.d[bḥ.bm].ymn.|lla.kl[atn]m.|klt.l[ḥm k.d]nzl 14[KRT].2.66
h.k [tšḥ].|'n.mkṯr.ap.t[---].|dgy.rbt.aṯr[t.ym].|qḥ.rṯt.b d k t[---].|rbt.'l.ydm[.---].|b mdd.il.y[--.---].|b ym.il.d[--.- 4[51].2.32
'r[.---].|'r[.---].|'r[.---].|w y[---].|b'd[.---].|yatr[.---].|b d k.[---].|ṯnnt h[.---].|ṯlṯt h[.-.w y'n].|lṯpn.[il.d pid.my].| 16[126].5.7
[---].|šd.b d[.---]im.|šd.b d[.bn.--]n.|šd.b d.iwrkl.|šd.b d.klb.|šd.b d.klby.|šd.b d.iytlm.|ṯn.šdm.b d.amtrn.|šd.b 2090.9
dd.|[---.--]m.|[šd.---.b d.]ṯpṭb'l.|[šd.---.]b d.ymz.|[šd.b d].klby.psl.|[ub]dy.mri.ibrn.|[š]d.bn.bri.b d.bn.ydln.|[u] 82[300].2.4
[.---]im.|šd.b d[.bn.--]n.|šd.b d.iwrkl.|šd.b d.klb.|šd.b d.klby.|šd.b d.iytlm.|ṯn.šdm.b d.amtrn.|šd.b d.iwrm[--]. 2090.10
n.|[u]bdy.nqdm.|[ṯlṯ].šdm.d.n'rb.gt.npk.|[š]d.rpan.b d.klṯṯb.|[š]d.ilṣy.b d.'bdym.|[ub]dy.trrm.|[šd.]bn.ṯqdy.b 82[300].2.14
.b d.dr.khnm.|šd.b d.bn.'my.|šd.b d.bn.'yn.|ṯn.šdm.b d.klṯṯb.|šd.b d.krz[n].|ṯlṯ.šdm.b d.amtr[n].|ṯn.šdm.b d.sk 2090.20
šd.pll.b d.qrt.|š[d].annḏr.b d.bdn.nḥ[l h].|[šd.]agyn.b d.kmrn.n[ḥl] h.|[š]d.nbzn.[-]l.qrt.|[š]d.agpṯr.b d.sḫrn.nḥl 2029.8
.|ṯn.šdm.b d.amtrn.|šd.b d.iwrm[--].|šd.b d.yṯpr.|šd.b d.krb[-].|šd.b d.bn.pṯḏ.|šd.b d.dr.khnm.|šd.b d.bn.'my.| 2090.15
b.gt.mlkt.b.rḫbn.|ḫmšm.l.mitm.zt.|w.b d.krd.|ḫmšm.l.mit.|arb'.kbd. 1096.3
.|šd.b d.bn.'my.|šd.b d.bn.'yn.|ṯn.šdm.b d.klṯṯb.|šd.b d.krz[n].|ṯlṯ.šdm.b d.amtr[n].|ṯn.šdm.b d.skn.|šd.b d[.'b] 2090.21
ṯr.b d.sḫrn.nḥl h.|šd.annmn.b d.tyn.nḥl h.|šd.pǵyn[.b] d.krmn.l.ty[n.n]ḥl h.|šd.krz.[b]n.ann.'[db].|šd.ṯ[r]yn.bn. 2029.12
]pid.l tbrk.|[krt.]ṯ'.l tmr.n'mn.|[ǵlm.]il.ks.yiḫd.|[il.b]yd.krpn.bm.|[ymn.]brkm.ybrk.|['bd h.]ybrk.il.krt.|[ṯ'.y 15[128].2.17
š.b a[rṣ.---].|b 'pr.ḫbl ṯtm.[---.]|šqy.rṯa.tnm y.ytn.[ks.b yd].|krpn.b klat yd.[---].|km ll.kḥṣ.tusp[.---].|tgr.il.bn h.ṯ 1['NT.X].4.9
mit.šmn.d.nm[-.]b d.mzy.alzy.|ḫmš.kkr.ḥlb.|ḫmš.kkr.brr.|kkr.ḫmš.mat.kb 1135.1
[bnšm.dt.]b d.mlk.|[---.b]d.mlkt.|[---.b]d.mlk.|[---.--]ḥ.uḫd.|[---.-]lu 2014.1
[bnšm.dt.]b d.mlk.|[---.b]d.mlkt.|[---.b]d.mlk.|[---.--]ḥ.uḫd.|[---.-]luḫ.|[---.-]tn.b d.mlkt.|[---.]l. 2014.3
spr.updt.|d b d.mlkytn.|kdrl.|slṯmg.|adrdn.|l[l]wn.|ydln.|ldn.|tdǵl.|i 1034.2
[bnšm.dt.]b d.mlk.|[---.b]d.mlkt.|[---.b]d.mlk.|[---.--]ḥ.uḫd.|[---.-]luḫ.|[---.-]tn.b 2014.2
[---.--]y.bṯr.b d.mlkt.|[---.]bṯr.b d.mlkt.|[---].b d.mršp.|[---.m]rbṣ.|[---.r]b.ṯnnm.|[---.]asr 2015.1.2
[---.--]y.bṯr.b d.mlkt.|[---.]bṯr.b d.mlkt.|[---].b d.mršp.|[---.m]rbṣ.|[---. 2015.1.1
.mlkt.|[---.b]d.mlk.|[---.--]ḥ.uḫd.|[---.-]luḫ.|[---.-]tn.b d.mlkt.|[---.]l.mḥṣ.|ab[---.]aḏddy.bn.skn.|bn.[---.]uḫd.|b 2014.6
d.[---].|šd[.---].|b d[.---].|š[d.---].|b d[.---].|šd[.---].|b d.ml[--].|šd.b[---].|b d.[---].|šd.[---].|b d.[---].|[-----].|šd. 2028.16
npšm.|b d.mri.|skn.|'šrm.|ḫmš.|kbd. 157[116].2
ddm.l.ybr[k].|bdmr.prs.l.u[-]m[-].|ṯmn.l.'šrm.|dmd.b d.mry[n]m. 2102.11

[---.--]y.bṯr.b d.mlkt. | [---.]bṯr.b d.mlkt. | [---].b d.mršp. | [---.m]rbṣ. | [---.r]b.ṯnnm. | [---.]asrm. | [---.--]kn. | [2015.1.3
. | [---.]ybl.k bn.qdš.mnḥy k.ap.anš.zbl.bʿ[l]. | [-.yuḫ]d.b yd.mšḫṭ.bm.ymn.mḫṣ.ǵlmm.yš[--]. | [ymn h.ʿn]t.tuḫd.šma 2.1[137].39
šrn.ṯlṯ.ʿš[r.kkr]. | bn.šw.šbʿ.kk[r.---]. | arbʿm.kkr.[---]. | b d.mtn.[l].šlm. 2108.5
ny.b d.tbṯṯb. | [š]d.bn.ṯ[-]rn.b d.ʿdbmlk. | [šd.]bn.brzn.b d.nwrḏ. | [šd.]bn.nḥbl.b d.ʿdbym. | [šd.b]n.qṭy.b d.tt. | [ubd] 82[300].1.17
rn. | lmd.aḥd.b d.yr[š]. | lmd.aḥd.b d.yḫ[--]. | ṯlṯ.lmdm.b d.nḫ[--]. | lmd.aḥd.b d.ar[--]. | ṯlṯ.lmdm.b d.[---]. | ṯlṯ.lmdm. 1050.6
ll.b nr.d ʿl k.mḫṣ.aqht. | ǵzr.šrš k.b arṣ.al. | ypʿ.riš.ǵly.b d.nsʿ k. | ʿnt.brḥ.p ʿlm h. | ʿnt.p dr.dr.ʿdb.uḫry mṭ yd h. | y 19[1AQHT].3.160
.ubn. | šd.b d.bn.uṯryn. | [ubd]y.mrynm. | [š]d.bn.ṣnrn.b d.nrn. | [š]d.bn.rwy.b d.ydln. | [š].bn.trn.b d.ibrmḏ. | [š]d.b 82[300].1.8
-]ʿ.lmdm. | [---.b]ʿln. | [---.]lmdm.b d.snrn. | [---.lm]dm.b d.nrn. | [---.ḫ]ḏǵlm. | [lmd.]aḥd.b d.yrš. 1051.4
]agyn.b d.kmrn.n[ḫl] h. | [š]d.nbzn.[-]l.qrt. | [š]d.agpṯr.b d.sḫrn.nḫl h. | šd.annmn.b d.tyn.nḫl h. | šd.pǵyn[.b] d.krm 2029.10
n. | bn.[---.]uḫd. | bn.n[---.]hbṯn. | bn.m[--.]skn. | bn.s[--.b]d.skn. | bn.ur[-.---]. | bn.knn[.---]y. | bn.ymlk[.b]d.skn. | bn. 2014.12
n.s[--.b]d.skn. | bn.ur[-.---]. | bn.knn[.---]y. | bn.ymlk[.b]d.skn. | bn.yḫnn.aḏddy. | bn.pdǵy.mḫdy. | bn.yyn.mdrǵl. | 2014.15
.ksp.hn. | ktn.d.ṣr.pḥm.b h.w.ṯqlm. | ksp h.mitm.pḥm.b d.skn. | w.ṯt.ktnm.ḫmšt.w.nṣp.ksp.hn. 1110.5
d.klṯtb. | šd.b d.krz[n]. | ṯlṯ.šdm.b d.amtr[n]. | ṯn.šdm.b d.skn. | šd.b d[.ʿb]dyrḫ. | šd.b [d.--]ṯtb. 2090.23
šd.ubdy.ilštmʿ. | dt b d.skn. | šd.bn.ubrʿn b gt prn. | šd.bn.gby.gt.prn. | šd.bn.kry 1104.2
ḏddy. | grʿ.aḏddy. | ʿbd.ršp aḏddy. | ʿdn.bn.knn. | iwrḫz.b d.skn. | škny.aḏddy. | mšu.aḏddy. | plsy.aḏddy. | aḫyn. | ygm 2014.37
ḫmš.bnšm[.---]. | ḫḏǵlm.b d.[---]. | šbʿ.lmdm.b d.s[n]rn. | lmd.aḥd.b d.yr[š]. | lmd.aḥd.b d.yḫ[--]. | ṯlṯ.lmd 1050.3
[---]ʿ.lmdm. | [---.b]ʿln. | [---.]lmdm.b d.snrn. | [---.lm]dm.b d.nrn. | [---.ḫ]ḏǵlm. | [lmd.]aḥd.b d.yr 1051.3
[--.-]d[-.---]. | [--.šd]m.b d.iyt[lm]. | [šd.b]d.s[--]. | š[d.b]d.u[--]. | šd.b d.[---]. | šd.b d[.---]im. | šd.b d[. 2090.3
[---].b d.š[--]mlk. | [---.b] d.gbʿly. | [---.b] d.ʿbdḫmn. | [---.b] d.ṯbq. | [---.b] d.šbn. | [---.b] d.ulm. | [---. 1052.3
[ṯlṯ].šdm.d.nʿrb.gt.npk. | [š]d.rpan.b d.klṯtb. | [š]d.ilṣy.b d.ʿbdym. | [ub]dy.trrm. | [šd.]bn.ṯqdy.b d.gmrd. | [š]d bn.sy 82[300].2.15
šš[r]t.ḫrṣ.ṯqlm.kbd.ʿšrt.mzn h. | b [ar]bʿm.ksp. | b d[.ʿb]dym.ṯlṯ.kkr šʿrt. | iqn[i]m.ṯṯt.ʿšrt.ksp h. | ḫmšt.ḫrṣ.bt.i 2100.3
.b d.krz[n]. | ṯlṯ.šdm.b d.amtr[n]. | ṯn.šdm.b d.skn. | šd.b d[.ʿb]dyrḫ. | šd.b [d.--]ṯtb. 2090.24
] d.ṯbq. | [---.b] d.šbn. | [---.b] d.ulm. | [---.b] d.ǵbl. | [---.b] d.ʿbdkṯr. | [---.b] d.urǵnr. 1052.8
ubdy.mdm. | šd.b d.ʿbdmlk. | šd.b d.yšn.ḥrš. | šd.b d.aupš. | šd.b d.ršpab.aḫ.u 82[300].1.2
[-]r. | [w.l.]bn h.ʿd. | [ʿl]m.mn k. | mn km l.yqḥ. | bt.hnd.b d. | [ʿb]dmlk. | [-]k.amʿ[--]. | [w.b] d.bn h[.ʿ]d ʿlm. | [w.un]ṯ.i 1009.14
-]rn.b d.ʿdbmlk. | [šd.]bn.brzn.b d.nwrḏ. | [šd.]bn.nḥbl.b d.ʿdbym. | [šd.b]n.qṭy.b d.tt. | [ubd]y.mrim. | [šd.b]n.ṯpdn.b 82[300].1.18
[ṯn].šdm.b d.gmrd. | [šd.]lbny.b d.tbṯṯb. | [š]d.bn.ṯ[-]rn.b d.ʿdbmlk. | [šd.]bn.brzn.b d.nwrḏ. | [šd.]bn.nḥbl.b d.ʿdbym 82[300].1.16
bsg. | [-----]. | [-----]. | [---.--]ṯ. | [---.-]b.m.lk. | kdwṯ.ḥdṯ. | b d ʿlpy. 1112.20
dḫmn. | [---.b] d.ṯbq. | [---.b] d.šbn. | [---.b] d.ulm. | [---.b] d.ǵbl. | [---.b] d.ʿbdkṯr. ¦ [---.b] d.urǵnr. 1052.7
. | liy.krm.aḥd[.---]. | ʿbdmlk.krm.aḥ[d.---]. | krm.ubdy.b d.ǵ[--.---]. | krm.pyn.arty[.---]. | ṯlṯ.krm.ubdym.l mlkt.b.ʿn 1081.7
šn. | [šd.--]ln. | b d.trǵds. | šd.ṯʿlb. | b d.bn.pl. | šd.bn.kt. | b d.pdy. | šd.ḫzr. | [b d].d[---]. 2030.2.6
rz.[b]n.ann.ʿ[db]. | šd.ṯ[r]yn.bn.tkn.b d.qrt. | šd[.-].dyn.b d.pln.nḥl h. | šd.irdyn.bn.ḫrǵš[-].l.qrt. | šd.iǵlyn.bn.kzbn.l. 2029.15
ṣmdm.a[--.---]. | b d.prḫ[-.---]. | apnm.l.ʿ[--]. | apnm.l.[---]. | apnm.l.d[--]. | apn 145[318].2
spr.bnš.mlk. | d.b d.prṭ. | tšʿ.l.ʿšrm. | lqḥ.ššlmt. | ṯmn.l.arbʿm. | lqḥ.šʿrt. 1025.2
nn.b d.bn.šmrm. | [šd.bn.-]ṯtayy.b d.ṯtmd. | [šd.bn.-]rn.b d.ṣdqšlm. | [šd.b d.]bn.pʿṣ. | [ubdy.ʿ]šrm. | [šd.---]n.b d.brdd 82[300].1.28
rt.ṣṯqšlm. | ʿbd h.hnd. | w mn km.l yqḥ. | spr.mlk.hnd. | b yd.ṣṯqšlm. | ʿd ʿlm. 1005.14
]l[.---]. | mḫlpt.w l.ytk.[d]m[ʿt.]km. | rbʿt.ṯqlm.ṯtp[.---.]bm. | yd.ṣpn hm.tliy m[.--.ṣ]pn hm. | nṣḥy.šrr.m[---.--]ay. | nb 19[1AQHT].2.83
n.b d.ttyn.nḥl [h]. | šd.ttyn[.b]n.arkšt. | lʿq[.---]. | šd.pll.b d.qrt. | š[d].anndr.b d.bdn.nḥ[l h]. | [šd.]agyn.b d.kmrn.n[ḥ 2029.6
.l.ty[n.n]ḥl h. | šd.krz.[b]n.ann.ʿ[db]. | šd.ṯ[r]yn.bn.tkn.b d.qrt. | šd[.-].dyn.b d.pln.nḥl h. | šd.irdyn.bn.ḫrǵš[-].l.qrt. | 2029.14
n. | w.l.ṯt.mrkbtm. | inn.uṯpt. | w.ṯlṯ.ṣmdm.w.ḥrṣ. | apnt.b d.rb.ḥršm. | d.šṣa.ḥwy h. 1121.9
[---.]bn.i[--.---]. | [---].ṯp[--.---]. | [---.a]ḥt.b d[.---]. | [---.]b d.rb.[m]dlm. | [---.l i]ytlm. | [---].gmn. | [---].l.urǵṯtb. | [---.]l. 2162.B.2
b d a[-]m.w.ank. | k[l.]ḏrʿ hm. | [--.n]pš[.-]. | w [k]l hm.b d. | rb.tmtt.lqḥt. | w.ṯtb.ank.l hm. | w.any k.ṯt. | by.ʿky.ʿryt. | 2059.21
dm. | šd.b d.ʿbdmlk. | šd.b d.yšn.ḥrš. | šd.b d.aupš. | šd.b d.ršpab.aḫ.ubn. | šd.b d.bn.uṯryn. | [ubd]y.mrynm. | [š]d.bn 82[300].1.5
. | [b.]gt.iptl.ṯt.ṣmdm. | [w.ʿ]šr.bn[š]m.y[d].š[--]. | [-]lm.b d.r[-]m.l[-]m. | ṯt.ʿšr.ṣ[mdm]. | w.tšʿ.ʿ[šr.--]m.ḥr[š]. | [---].ḥr[2038.9
. | b d.brq.maḫdy. | kkr.ṯlṯ. | b d.bn.by.ar[y]. | alpm.ṯlṯ. | b d.šim.il[š]tmʿy. 1134.7
k. | [---.b] d.gbʿly. | [---.b] d.ʿbdḫmn. | [---.b] d.ṯbq. | [---.b] d.šbn. | [---.b] d.ulm. | [---.b] d.ǵbl. | [---.b] d.ʿbdkṯr. | [---.b] 1052.5
ṯlṯ.d yṣa. | b d.šmmn. | l argmn. | l nskm. | ṯmn.kkrm. | alp.kbd. | [m]itm. 147[90].2
.alp.alp.am[-]. | ṯmn.ḥblm.šbʿ.šbʿ.ma[-]. | ʿšr.kkr.rtn. | b d.šmʿy.bn.bdn. 1128.33
[---].b d.š[--]mlk. | [---.b] d.gbʿly. | [---.b] d.ʿbdḫmn. | [---.b] d.ṯbq. 1052.1
bn.rwy.b d.ydln. | [š].bn.trn.b d.ibrmḏ. | [š]d.bn.ilṯtmr.b d.tbbr. | [w.]šd.nḥl h.b d.ṯtmd. | [š]d.b d.iwrḫṭ. | [ṯn].šdm.b 82[300].1.11
.ṯtmd. | [š]d.b d.iwrḫṭ. | [ṯn].šdm.b d.gmrd. | [šd.]lbny.b d.tbṯṯb. | [š]d.bn.ṯ[-]rn.b d.ʿdbmlk. | [šd.]bn.brzn.b d.nwrḏ. 82[300].1.15
]d.nbzn.[-]l.qrt. | [š]d.agpṯr.b d.sḫrn.nḫl h. | šd.annmn.b d.tyn.nḫl h. | šd.pǵyn[.b] d.krmn.l.ty[n.n]ḥl h. | šd.krz.[b]n 2029.11
ṯ.mat.brr. | b.ṯmnym.ksp.ṯlṯt.kbd. | ḫmš.alp.ṯlṯ.l.ḥlby. | b d.tlmi.b.ʿšrm.ḫmšt. | kbd.ksp. | kkrm.šʿrt.štt.b d.gg[ʿt]. | b.ʿš 2101.7
mdrǵlm.dt.inn. | b d.tlmyn. | b d.gln.ary. | tgyn.yʿrty. | bn.krwn.b.yny.iytlm. | š 2071.2
].kbr.l.snrn. | [---.--]k.l.gmrd. | [---.--]ṯ.l.yšn. | [šd.--]ln. | b d.trǵds. | šd.ṯʿlb. | b d.bn.pl. | šd.bn.kt. | b d.pdy. | šd.ḫzr. | [b 2030.2.2
.brzn.b d.nwrḏ. | [šd.]bn.nḥbl.b d.ʿdbym. | [šd.b]n.qṭy.b d.tt. | [ubd]y.mrim. | [šd.b]n.ṯpdn.b d.bn.gʿr. | [šd.b]n.ṯqrn. 82[300].1.19
alpm.pḥm.ḫm[š].mat.kbd. | b d.tt.w.ṯlṯ.ktnt.b dm.tt. | w.ṯmnt.ksp.hn. | ktn.d.ṣr.pḥm.b h. 1110.2
alpm.pḥm.ḫm[š].mat.kbd. | b d.tt.w.ṯlṯ.ktnt.b dm.tt. | w.ṯmnt.ksp.hn. | ktn.d.ṣr.pḥm.b h.w.ṯqlm. | ksp h. 1110.2
spr.ubdy.art. | šd.prn.b d.agpṯn.nḫl h. | šd.šwn.b d.ttyn.nḫl [h]. | šd.ttyn[.b]n.arkšt. | lʿq[.---]. | šd.pll.b d.qrt. 2029.3
.trn.b d.ibrmḏ. | [š]d.bn.ilṯtmr.b d.tbbr. | [w.]šd.nḥl h.b d.ṯtmd. | [š]d.b d.iwrḫṭ. | [ṯn].šdm.b d.gmrd. | [šd.]lbny.b d. 82[300].1.12
ll.b d.iwrḫṭ. | [šd.bn.-]nn.b d.bn.šmrm. | [šd.bn.-]ṯtayy.b d.ṯtmd. | [šd.bn.-]rn.b d.ṣdqšlm. | [šd.b d.]bn.pʿṣ. | [ubdy.ʿ]š 82[300].1.27
--].b d.š[--]mlk. | [---.b] d.gbʿly. | [---.b] d.ʿbdḫmn. | [---.b] d.ṯbq. | [---.b] d.šbn. | [---.b] d.ulm. | [---.b] d.ǵbl. | [---.b] d.ʿ 1052.4
n. | [ubdy.md]rǵlm. | [šd.bn.--]n.b d.aḫny. | [šd.bn.--]rt.b d.ṯpṭbʿl. | [ubdy.]mḫ[ṣ]m. | [šd.bn.]uzpy.b d.yšn.ḥrš. | [-----] 82[300].2.24

p‘ṣ. | [ubdy.‘]šrm. | [šd.---]n.b d.brdd. | [---.--]m. | [šd.---.b d.]ṯpṯb‘l. | [šd.---.]b d.ymz. | [šd.b d].klby.psl. | [ub]dy.mri.i 82[300].2.2
m.l aḫt k. | ṯtmnt.krt n.dbḥ. | dbḥ.mlk.‘šr. | ‘šrt.qḥ.tp k.b yd. | [-]r[-]k.bm.ymn. | tlk.škn.‘l.ṣrrt. | adn k.šqrb.[---]. | b 16.1[125].41
šd.bn.adn. | [b] d.armwl. | [šd].mrnn. | b d.[-]tw[-]. | šd.bn[.---]. | b d.dd[--]. | šd.d[---]. | b d.d[---]. | šd. 2028.4
mḫ[ṣ]m. | [šd.bn.]uzpy.b d.yšn.ḥrš. | [-----]. | [-----]. | [šd.b d.--]n. | [šd.b d.--]n. | [šd.b d.--]ǵl. | [šd.b d.--]pšm.šyr. 82[300].2.29
bn.]uzpy.b d.yšn.ḥrš. | [-----]. | [-----]. | [šd.b d.--]n. | [šd.b d.--]n. | [šd.b d.--]ǵl. | [šd.b d.--]pšm.šyr. 82[300].2.30
--.-]nb.trtn. | [---]mm.klby.kl[--].dqn[.---]. | [-]ntn.artn.b d[.--]nr[.---]. | ‘zn.w ymd.šr.b d ansny. | nsk.ks[p.--]mrtn.kṯ 2011.30
.yšn.ḥrš. | [-----]. | [-----]. | [šd.b d.--]n. | [šd.b d.--]n. | [šd.b d.--]ǵl. | [šd.b d.--]pšm.šyr. 82[300].2.31
-]. | [-----]. | [šd.b d.--]n. | [šd.b d.--]n. | [šd.b d.--]ǵl. | [šd.b d.--]pšm.šyr. 82[300].2.32
dm.b d.amtr[n]. | ṯn.šdm.b d.skn. | šd.b d[.‘b]dyrḫ. | šd.b [d.--]ṯṯb. 2090.25
yn.d.ykl.b d.[---]. | b.dbḥ.mlk. | dbḥ ṣpn. | [-]zǵm. | [i]lib. | [i]lbldn. | [p]d 2004.1
[s]p[r] uškny m.dt.[b d.---]. | bn.btr. | bn.‘ms. | bn.pṣn. | bn.agmz. | bn.[--]n. | bn.a[- 2021.1.1
-]. | šy[.---]. | bn.uḫn. | ybru.i[---]. | [p]dyn.[---]. | bnšm.d.b [d.---]. | spḫy.[---]. | [-----]. | b[--.---]. | n‘[--.---]. | [-----]. | ḫn[--. 2161.13
ḫmš.bnšm[.---]. | ḥdǵlm.b d.[---]. | šb‘.lmdm.b d.s[n]rn. | lmd.aḥd.b d.yr[š]. | lmd.aḥd. 1050.2
| [--.šd]m.b d.iyt[lm]. | [šd.b]d.s[--]. | š[d.b]d.u[--]. | šd.b d.[---]. | šd.b d[.---]im. | šd.b d[.bn.--]n. | šd.b d.iwrkl. | šd.b 2090.5
.d[---]. | šd.b[---]. | b d.[---]. | šd[.---]. | b d[.---]. | š[d.---]. | b d[.---]. | šd[.---]. | b d.ml[--]. | šd.b[---]. | b d.[---]. | šd.[---]. | b 2028.14
šd.bn[.---]. | b d.dd[--]. | šd.d[---]. | b d.d[---]. | šd.b[---]. | b d.[---]. | šd[.---]. | b d[.---]. | š[d.---]. | b d[.---]. | šd[.---]. | b d. 2028.10
[--]. | šd.d[---]. | b d.d[---]. | šd.b[---]. | b d.[---]. | šd[.---]. | b d[.---]. | š[d.---]. | b d[.---]. | šd[.---]. | b d.ml[--]. | šd.b[---]. | b 2028.12
.---]. | š[d.---]. | b d[.---]. | šd[.---]. | b d.ml[--]. | šd.b[---]. | b d.[---]. | šd.[---]. | b d.[---]. | [-----]. | šd.bn.gdy. | b d.ddl. 2028.18
-]. | ṯlṯ.lmdm.b d.nḫ[--]. | lmd.aḥd.b d.ar[--]. | ṯlṯ.lmdm.b d.[---]. | ṯlṯ.lmdm.b d.[---]. 1050.8
-.]bn.a[--.---]. | [---.]bn.i[--.---]. | [---].ṯp[--.---]. | [---.a]ḫt.b d[.---]. | [---.]b d.rb.[m]dlm. | [---.l i]ytlm. | [---].gmn. | [---].l. 2162.B.1
.---]. | [---.--]š.b d.h[--.---]. | [---.y]rḫ.dbḥ[.---]. | [---.-]pn.b d.[---]. | [---.]b d.[---]. 1160.6
--]. | yiṯtm.w.b[--]. | yšlm. | [‘]šrm.ks[p].yš[lm]. | [il]ṯḥm.b d[.---]. | [---].ṯl[l]m.[---]. | [--].r[-]y[.---]. | ‘l.[--]l[-] h. | ‘dn.[--- 2104.8
.---]. | šd[.---]. | b d.ml[--]. | šd.b[---]. | b d.[---]. | šd.[---]. | b d.[---]. | [-----]. | šd.bn.gdy. | b d.ddl. 2028.20
[--]. | lmd.aḥd.b d.ar[--]. | ṯlṯ.lmdm.b d.[---]. | ṯlṯ.lmdm.b d.[---]. 1050.9
šr[-]. | [-]b.m[--]. | b y[rḫ]. | pgr[m]. | yṣa[.---]. | lb[-.---]. | b d[.---]. 1158.2.5
d.h[--.---]. | [---.y]rḫ.dbḥ[.---]. | [---.-]pn.b d.[---]. | [---.]b d.[---]. 1160.7
.iyt[lm]. | [šd.b]d.s[--]. | š[d.b]d.u[--]. | šd.b d.[---]. | šd.b d[.---]im. | šd.b d[.bn.--]n. | šd.b d.iwrkl. | šd.b d.klb. | šd.b d 2090.6
m[r.---]. | yṣu.ḫlpn[.---]. | ṯlṯ.dt.p[--.---]. | dt.ṯgmi.[---]. | b d [---]t.[---]. 1159.5
gy.rbt.aṯr[t.ym]. | qḥ.rṯt.b d k t[---]. | rbt.‘l.ydm[.---]. | b mdd.il.y[--.---]. | b ym.il.d[--.---.n] | hr.il.y[--.---]. | aliyn.[b‘l. 4[51].2.34
. | ‘m k.ybl.šd. | a[--].d‘.k. | šld.ašld. | hn.mrṯ.d.štt. | ašld b ldt k. 2009.3.2
[-----]. | [---.]abl.qšt ṯmn. | ašrb‘.qṣ‘t.w hn šb[‘]. | b ymm.apnk.dnil.mt. | rpi.a hn.ǵzr.mt.hrnm[y]. | ytšu.ytb.b 17[2AQHT].5.4
m. | ‘d k.ilm.hn.mtm. | ‘d k.kṯr m.ḥbr k. | w ḫss.d‘t k. | b ym.arš.w tnn. | kṯr.w ḫss.yd. | ytr.kṯr.w ḫss. | spr.ilmlk šbn 6.6[62.2].50
qḥ.rṯt.b d k t[---]. | rbt.‘l.ydm[.---]. | b mdd.il.y[--.---]. | b ym.il.d[--.---.n] | hr.il.y[--.---]. | aliyn.[b‘l.---]. | btlt.[‘nt.---]. | 4[51].2.35
ḥy[--.--.]l aṣṣi.hm.ap.amr[--]. | [---].w b ym.mnḫ l abd.b ym.irtm.m[--]. | [ṯpṭ].nhr.tl‘m.ṯm.ḥrbm.its.anšq. | [-]htm.l 2.4[68].3
| l ytn.l hm.ṯḥt b‘l[.---]. | h.u qšt pn hdd.b y[.----]. | ‘m.b ym b‘l ysy ym[.---]. | rmm.ḫnpm.mḫl[.---]. | mlk.nhr.ibr[.-- 9[33].2.7
y‘ny.bn. | ilm.mt.npš[.-]. | npš.lbun. | thw.w npš. | anḫr.b ym. | brkt.šbšt. | k rumm.hm. | ‘n.kḏd.aylt. | mt hm.ks.ym | s UG5.4.5
]. | b‘l h.š‘[-]rt. | ḫqr.[--.ṯq]l rb. | ṯl[ṯ.---]. | aḥt.ḫm[-.---]. | b ym.dbḥ.ṯp[-]. | aḥt.l mzy.bn[--]. | aḥt.l mkt.ǵr. | aḥt.l ‘ṯtrt. | 39[19].13
t.ydd.bn.il. | ǵzr.p np.š.npš.lbim. | thw.hm.brlt.anḫr. | b ym.hm.brk y.tkšd. | rumm.‘n.kḏd.aylt. | hm.imt.imt.npš.bl 5[67].1.16
d.št.špt. | l arṣ.špt l šmm.w ‘rb.b p hm.‘ṣr.šmm. | w dg b ym.w ndd.gzr.l zr.y‘db.u ymn. | u šmal.b p hm.w l.tšb‘n y. 23[52].63
yrḫ ḫyr.b ym ḥdṯ. | alp.w š.l b‘lt bhtm. | b arb‘t ‘šrt.b‘l. | ‘rkm. | b ṯmn UG5.12.A.1
b.ym.ḥdṯ. | b.yr.pgrm. | lqḥ.b‘lmdr. | w.bn.ḫlp. | miḫd. | b.arb‘. 1156.1
b.ym.ḥdṯ. | b.yrḫ.pgrm. | lqḥ.b‘lm‘dr. | w bn.ḫlp. | w[--]y.d.b‘l 1155.1
b ym ḥdṯ. | b.yrḫ.pgrm. | lqḥ.iwrpzn. | argḏd. | ṯṯkn. | ybrk. | nt 2006.1
[b yr]ḫ[.r]išyn.b ym.ḥdṯ. | [šmtr].uṯkl.l il.šlmm. | b [ṯlṯt].‘šrt.yrtḥṣ.mlk. | br[r APP.II[173].1
b yrḫ.[rišyn.b ym.ḥdṯ]. | šmtr.[uṯkl.l il.šlmm]. | b ṯlṯt ‘[šrt.yrtḥṣ.mlk.brr]. 35[3].1
b.[šb]‘.ṣbu.[š]pš.w.ḥly[t].‘[r]b[.š]p[š]. | w [ḥl.]mlk.[w.]b.ym.ḥdṯ.ṯn.šm. | l.[---]t. | i[d.yd]bḥ.mlk.l.prgl.ṣqrn.b.gg. | ar[35[3].48
yṯṯb]. | brr.b šb‘[.ṣbu.špš.w ḥl] | yt.‘rb špš[.w ḥl.mlk.w.b y] | m.ḥdṯ.ṯn šm[.---.--]t. | b yrḫ.ši[-.b ar]b‘t.‘š | rt.yr[tḥṣ.ml] APP.II[173].52
t]sk h. | rbb.nsk h.kbkbm. | ttpp.anhbm.d alp.šd[.ẓu h.b ym]. | ṯl[.---]. 3['NT].4.89
‘ẓ q[dm.--.šp]š. | [---.šm]n.mšḥt.ktpm.a[-]ṯ[-]. | [---.--]ḫ b ym.tld[---.]b[-.]y[--.---]. | [---.il]m.rb[m.--]š[-]. | [---].nš.b [-- UG5.8.24
[---.-]k.mnḫ[-.---.-]š bš[-.]t[-].ǵlm.l šdt[.-.]ymm. | [---.]b ym.ym.y[--].yš[ ]n.ap k.‘ṯtr.dm[.---.] | [---.]ḥrḥrtm.w[--.]n[2.3[129].12
.]pht[.dr]y.b kbrt. | ‘l k.pht.[-]l[-]. | b šdm.‘l k.pht. | dr‘.b ym.tn.aḥd. | b aḫ k.ispa.w ytb. | ap.d anšt.im[-]. | aḥd.b aḫ 6[49].5.19
b arb‘t.‘šr[t]. | yrtḥṣ.mlk.b[rr]. | b ym.mlat. | tqln.alpm. | yrḫ.‘šrt.l b‘[l]. | dqtm.w ynt.qr[t]. | w UG5.13.3
.gdlt.‘rb špš w ḥl. | [mlk.b ar]b‘t.‘[š]rt.yrtḥṣ.mlk.brr. | [b ym.ml]at.y[ql]n.al[p]m.yrḫ.‘šrt. | [l b‘l.ṣ]pn.[dq]tm.w y[nt] 36[9].1.11
.ḥtt.mtt[--]. | [--.]ḥy[--.--.]l aṣṣi.hm.ap.amr[--]. | [---].w b ym.mnḫ l abd.b ym.irtm.m[--]. | [ṯpṭ].nhr.tl‘m.ṯm.ḥrbm.it 2.4[68].3
.ilnym. | [---.--]l km amt m. | [---.]b w t‘rb.sd. | [---.--]n b ym.qẓ. | [---.]ym.tlḥmn. | [---.rp]um.tštyn. | [---.]il.d ‘rgzm. | 20[121].1.5
.mḫ.tmḫṣ.mḫṣ[.aḫ k]. | tkl.m[k]ly.‘l.umt[k.--]. | d ttql.b ym.trtḥ[ṣ.--]. | [----.a]dm.tium.b ǵlp y[m.--]. | d alp šd.ẓu h. 19[1AQHT].4.203
krn]. | m‘ms k.k šb‘t.yn.ṭ[ḫ]. | gg k.b ym.ṭiṭ.rḥṣ. | npṣ k.b ym rṭ.b uni[l]. | pnm.tšmḫ.w ‘l yṣhl pi[t]. | yprq.lṣb.w yṣḥq. 17[2AQHT].2.8
y.bt.b‘l.[w]mn[t]. | y.bt.il.ṯḥ.gg y.b ym.ṭiṭ. | rḥṣ.npṣ y.b ym.rṭ. | dn.il.bt h.ymǵyn. | yštql.dnil.l hkl h. | ‘rb.b bt h.kṯr 17[2AQHT].2.23
h.bt.b‘l. | [w m]nt h bt.il.ṯḥ.gg h.b ym. | [ṭi]ṭ.rḥṣ.npṣ h.b ym.rṭ. | [--.y]iḫd.il.‘bd h.ybrk. | [dni]l mt rpi.ymr.ǵzr. | [mt. 17[2AQHT].1.34
rtḥ[ṣ.--]. | [----.a]dm.tium.b ǵlp y[m.--]. | d alp šd.ẓu h.b ym.t[---]. | tlbš.npṣ.ǵzr.tšt.ḫ[---.b] | nšg h.ḥrb.tšt.b t‘r[t h]. 19[1AQHT].4.205
. | [k]šb‘ yn.spu.ksm h.bt.b‘l. | [w m]nt h bt.il.ṯḥ.gg h.b ym. | [ṭi]ṭ.rḥṣ.npṣ h.b ym.rṭ. | [--.y]iḫd.il.‘bd h.ybrk. | [dni]l 17[2AQHT].1.33
k šb‘ yn. | spu.ksm y.bt.b‘l.[w]mn[t]. | y.bt.il.ṯḥ.gg y.b ym.ṭiṭ. | rḥṣ.npṣ y.b ym.rṭ. | dn.il.bt h.ymǵyn. | yštql.dnil.l 17[2AQHT].2.22
. | bt il.aḫd.yd k.b [škrn]. | m‘ms k.k šb‘t.yn.ṭ[ḫ]. | gg k.b ym.ṭiṭ.rḥṣ. | npṣ k.b ym rṭ.b uni[l]. | pnm.tšmḫ.w ‘l yṣhl pi[17[2AQHT].2.7

d h]. | plk.qlṯ.b ymn h. | npyn h.mks.bšr h. | tmtʿ.md h.b ym.ṯn. | npyn h.b nhrm. | štt.ḫptr.l išt. | ḫbrṯ.l ẓr.pḥmm. | tʿ 4[51].2.6
ttpp.anhb[m.d alp.šd]. | ẓu h.b ym[.---]. | [--]rn.l [---]. 3[ʿNT].3.02
. | [krt.]ṯʿ.l tmr.nʿmn. | [ǵlm.]il.ks.yiḫd. | [il.b]yd.krpn.bm. | [ymn.]brkm.ybrk. | [ʿbd h.]ybrk.il.krt. | [ṯʿ.ymr]m.nʿm[15[128].2.17
ht ht. | il hd.b qrb.hkl h. | qšt hn.aḫd.b yd h. | w qṣʿt h.bm.ymn h. | idk.l ytn pnm. | tk.aḫ.šmk.mla[t.r]umm. | tšu kn 10[76].2.7
lm.tḥš. | lm.tḥš.nṯq.dmrn. | ʿn.bʿl.qdm.yd h. | k tǵd.arz.b ymn h. | bkm.yṯb.bʿl.l bht h. | u mlk.u bl mlk. | arṣ.drkt.yšt 4[51].7.41
bʿt.b ymn y[.t]q | ḥ.pǵt.w tšqyn h.tq[ḥ.ks.]b d h. | qbʿt.b ymn h.w yʿn.yṯ[p]n[.mh]r. | št.b yn.yšt.ila.il š[--.]il. | d yqn 19[1AQHT].4.218
[-----]. | l abn[.---]. | aḫdt.plk h[.b yd h]. | plk.qlṯ.b ymn h. | npyn h.mks.bšr h. | tmtʿ.md h.b ym.ṯn. | npyn h.b 4[51].2.4
nt.krt n.dbḥ. | dbḥ.mlk.ʿšr. | ʿšrt.qḥ.tp k.b yd. | [-]r[-]k.bm.ymn. | tlk.škn.ʿl.ṣrrt. | adn k.šqrb.[---]. | b mgn k.w ḫrṣ.l k 16.1[125].42
ḫrṣ.l kl. | apnk.ǵzr.ilḥu. | [m]rḥ h.yiḫd.b yd. | [g]rgr h.bm.ymn. | [w]yqrb.trẓẓ h. | [---].mǵy h.w ǵlm. | [a]ḫt h.šib.yṣ 16.1[125].48
yʿn.ytpn[.mhr]. | št.qḥn.w tšqyn.yn.qḥ. | ks.b d y.qbʿt.b ymn y[.t]q | ḥ.pǵt.w tšqyn h.tq[ḥ.ks.]b d h. | qbʿt.b ymn h. 19[1AQHT].4.216
.]ʿd[.ṯ]km. | ʿrb[.b ẓl.ḫmt]. | qḥ im[r.b yd k]. | imr.d[bḥ.bm].ymn. | lla.kl[atn]m. | klt.l[ḥm k.d]nzl. | qḥ.ms[rr.]ʿṣr. | d 14[KRT].2.67
k bn.qdš.mnḥy k.ap.anš.zbl.bʿ[l]. | [-.yuḫ]d.b yd.mšḫṭ.bm.ymn.mḫṣ.ǵlmm.yš[--]. | [ymn h.ʿn]t.tuḫd.šmal h.tuḫd.ʿṯt 2.1[137].39
ylt tǵpy ṯr.ʿn[.---]. | b[b]r.mrḥ h.ti[ḫd.b yd h]. | š[g]r h bm ymn.t[--.---]. | [--.]l bʿl.ʿbd[.---]. | ṯr ab h il.ṯṯrm[.---]. | tšlḥ 2001.1.13
h.tq[ḥ.ks.]b d h. | qbʿt.b ymn h.w yʿn.yṯ[p]n[.mh]r. | št.b yn.yšt.ila.il š[--.]il. | d yqny.ḏdm.yd.mḫṣt.a[qh]t.ǵ | zr.tmḫṣ 19[1AQHT].4.219
.dt.inn. | b d.tlmyn. | b d.gln.ary. | tgyn.yʿrty. | bn.krwn.b.yny.iytlm. | šgryn.ary.b.yny. | bn.yddn.b.rkby. | agyn.agny. 2071.5
gln.ary. | tgyn.yʿrty. | bn.krwn.b.yny.iytlm. | šgryn.ary.b.yny. | bn.yddn.b.rkby. | agyn.agny. | ṯqbn.mldy. 2071.6
šm.b.šql. | arbʿ.bnšm.b.nni. | ṯn.bnšm.b.slḫ. | [---].bnšm.b.yny. | [--.]bnšm.b.lbnm. | arbʿ.bnšm.b.ypr. | [---.]bnšm.b.šbn 2076.20
tʿn. | w tʿn.arḫ.w tr.b lkt. | tr.b lkt.w tr.b ḫl. | [b]nʿmm.b ysmm.ḥ[--]k.ǵrt. | [ql].l bʿl.ʿnt.ttnn. | [---].bʿl m.d ip[---]. | [i 10[76].2.30
.ql.ẓ[--.---]. | l np ql.nd.[----]. | tlk.w tr.b[ḫl]. | b nʿmm.b ys[mm.---]. | arḫ.arḫ.[---.tld]. | ibr.tld[.l bʿl]. | w rum.l[rkb.ʿ 10[76].3.19
ṯ.ǵzr.adr.ṯqbm. | [d]lbnn.adr.gdm.b rumm. | adr.qrnt.b yʿlm.mtnm. | b ʿqbt.ṯr.adr.b ǵlil.qnm. | tn.l kṯr.w ḫss.ybʿl.q 17[2AQHT].6.22
šrm.l.mit.drʿ.w.šbʿm.drt. | w.ʿšrm.l.mit.dd.ḥpr.bnšm. | b.yʿny.arbʿm.drʿ.w.ʿšrm.drt. | w.ṯlṯm.dd.ṯṯ.kbd.ḥpr.bnšm. | b. 1098.26
. | [aḥd.al]p.d aǵlmn. | [d aḥd b.g]t gbry. | [---].aḥd.aḥd.b.yʿny. | [---.-]ḥm.b.aḥd.ḥrṯ. | [---.]aḥd.b.grn.uškn. | [---.]aḥd. 1129.14
r.plṭt. | l qdqd h.lpš.yks. | mizrtm.ǵr.b abn. | ydy.psltm.b yʿr. | yhdy.lḥm.w dqn. | ytlṯ.qn.ḏrʿ h.yḥrṯ. | k gn.ap lb.k ʿm 5[67].6.18
l bʿl. | ǵr.b ab.td[.ps]ltm[.b yʿr]. | thdy.lḥm.w dqn[.ṯṯlṯ]. | qn.ḏrʿ h.tḥrṯ.km.gn. | ap lb.k 6[62].1.2
.trzy. | [--]yn.b.glltky. | ṯd[y]n.b.glltky. | lbw[-].uḫ.pdm.b.yʿrt. | pǵyn.b.tpḫ. | amri[l].b.šrš. | aǵltn.b.midḫ. | [--]n.b.ayly 2118.10
ʿr.arr. | arbʿ.bnšm.b.mnt. | arbʿ.bnšm.b.irbn. | ṯn.bnšm.b.yʿrt. | ṯn.bnšm.b.ʿrmt. | arbʿ.bnšm.b.šrš. | ṯṯ.bnšm.b.mlk. | ar 2076.35
ql.y[ḫb]q. | w ynšq.aḥl.an bṣ[ql]. | ynpʿ.b palt.bṣql ypʿ b yǵlm. | ur.tisp k.yd.aqht. | ǵzr.tšt k.b qrb m.asm. | y.dnh.ys 19[1AQHT].2.65
t.pḥl. | y dnil.ysb.palt h. | bṣql.yph.b palt.bṣ[q]l. | yph.b yǵlm.bṣql.y[ḫb]q. | w ynšq.aḥl.an bṣ[ql]. | ynpʿ.b palt.bṣql 19[1AQHT].2.63
.ri[šym]. | kr[-].šdm.ʿ[--]. | b gt ṯm[--] yn[.--]. | [---].krm.b ypʿl.yʿdd. | [---.]krm.b [-]dn.l.bn.[-]kn. | šd[.---.-]ʿn. | šd[.---.- 2027.1.4
.bn.ibn.arbʿt.ʿšrt. | b.bn.mnn.ṯṯm. | b.rpan.bn.yyn.ʿšrt. | b.ypʿr.ʿšrm. | b.nʿmn.bn.ply.ḫmšt.l.ʿšrm. | b.gdn.bn.uss.ʿšrm. 2054.1.16
.slḫ. | [---].bnšm.b.yny. | [--.]bnšm.b.lbnm. | arbʿ.bnšm.b.ypr. | [---.]bnšm.b.šbn. | [---.b]nšm.b.šmny. | [---.b]nšm.b.šm 2076.22
rkn. | kli. | plǵn. | apšny. | ʿrb[.---]. | w.b.p[.--]. | apš[ny]. | b.yṣi h. | ḥwt.[---]. | alp.k[sp]. | tšʿn. | w.hm.al[-]. | l.tšʿn. | mṣrm 2116.9
ṣ. | ša.ǵr.ʿl.ydm. | ḫlb.l ẓr.rḥtm. | w rd.bt ḫpṯt. | arṣ.tspr.b y | rdm.arṣ. | idk.al.ttn. | pnm.tk.qrt h. | hmry.mk.ksu. | ṯbt h 4[51].8.8
ny.ša.ǵr.ʿl ydm. | ḫlb.l ẓr.rḥtm w rd. | bt ḫpṯt.arṣ.tspr b y | rdm.arṣ.w tdʿ ilm. | k mtt.yšmʿ.aliyn.bʿl. | yuhb.ʿglt.b db 5[67].5.15
spr.ḥpr.bnš mlk.b yrḫ iṯt[bnm]. | ršpab.rb ʿšrt.m[r]yn. | pǵdn.ilbʿl.krwn.lbn.ʿd 2011.1
| kd yn.l.ḫḏǵb.w.kd.ḥmṣ. | prš.glbm.l.bt. | tgmǵ.kšmm.b.yrḫ.iṯtbnm. | šbʿm.dd.ṯn.kbd. | tgmr.ḥṭm.šbʿ.ddm. | ḫmš.dd. 1099.30
l.mḏrǵlm[.---]. | ṯlṯ.mat.ḫmšm.kb[d]. | ḫmš.kbd.l.mdʿ. | b yr[ḫ.iṯtb]nm. | ṯlṯ[.mat.a]rbʿ.kbd. | w.[---.-]mʿt. | ṯlṯ[m.---.-]r 2012.13
--].aḥd.ḫmš.am[--.---]. | [---.--]m.qmṣ.ṯlṯm.i[qnu.---]. | [b.yr]ḫ.mgmr.mš[--.---]. | [---].iqnu.ḫmš[.---]. | [b.yr]ḫ.pgrm[.- 1106.38
b yrḫ.mgm[r.---]. | yṣu.ḫlpn[.---]. | ṯlṯ.dt.p[--.---]. | dt.ṯgmi.[--- 1159.1
š.yn.[---]. | [---.bʿ]lt.bhtm.š[--.---]. | [---.-]rt.l.dml[.---]. | [b.yrḫ].nql.ṯn.ḫpn[.---]. | [---].aḥd.ḫmš.am[--.---]. | [---.--]m.q 1106.35
b yr[ḫ]. | pgr[m]. | yṣa[.---]. | mšr[-]. | [-]b.m[--]. | b y[rḫ]. | pgr[m]. | yṣa[.---]. | lb[-.---]. | b d[.---]. 1158.2.1
b yr[ḫ]. | pgr[m]. | yṣa[.---]. | mšr[-]. | [-]b.m[--]. | b y[rḫ]. | pgr[1158.1.1
b ym ḥdṯ. | b.yrḫ.pgrm. | lqḥ.iwrpzn. | argḏḏ. | ṯṯkn. | ybrk. | ntbt. | b.mitm 2006.2
b.ym.ḥdṯ. | b.yr.pgrm. | lqḥ.bʿlmḏr. | w.bn.ḫlp. | miḫd. | b.arbʿ. | mat.ḫrṣ. 1156.2
b.ym.ḥdṯ. | b.yrḫ.pgrm. | lqḥ.bʿlmʿdr. | w bn.ḫlp. | w[--]y.d.bʿl. | miḫd.b. | 1155.2
u.---]. | [b.yr]ḫ.mgmr.mš[--.---]. | [---].iqnu.ḫmš[.---]. | [b.yr]ḫ.pgrm[.---]. 1106.40
[lk.---]. | [---.--]rt.šʿrt[.---]. | [---.i]qni.l.ṯr[mn.art.---]. | [b.yr]ḫ.riš.yn.[---]. | [---.bʿ]lt.bhtm.š[--.---]. | [---.-]rt.l.dml[.---] 1106.32
| arbʿ.ddm.l.k[-]ḫ. | ṯmnym.dd.dd.kbd. | [l].mḏr[ǵ]lm. | b yrḫ[ri]šyn. | šb[ʿ.--]n.[k]bd. | w[.---.]qmʿt. | [---.]mḏrǵlm. | [- 2012.21
[b yr]ḫ[.r]išyn.b ym.ḥdṯ. | [šmtr].uṯkl.l il.šlmm. | b [ṯlṯt].ʿšrt.y APP.II[173].1
b yrḫ.[rišyn.b ym.ḥdṯ]. | šmtr.[uṯkl.l il.šlmm]. | b ṯlṯt ʿ[šrt.yrt 35[3].1
ḥl] | yt.ʿrb špš[.w ḥl.mlk.w.b y] | m.ḥdṯ.ṯn šm[.---.--]t. | b yrḫ.ši[-.b ar]bʿt.ʿš | rt.yr[tḥṣ.ml]k.brr. | ʿlm.š.š[--].l[--.]ʿrb.šp APP.II[173].54
b y[rḫ.---]. | ʿš[r.---]. | ḫm[š.---]. | b[yrḫ.---]. | [---.]prš. | [-----]. | 2012.1
b yrḫ.[---]. | šbʿ.yn[.---]. | mlkt[.---]. | kd.yn.l.[---]. | armwl w [- 1092.1
b y[rḫ.---]. | ʿš[r.---]. | ḫm[š.---]. | b[yrḫ.---]. | [---.]prš. | [-----]. | l.mšḥ[.---]. | ʿšr.d[d.---]. | ṯṯm.dd. 2012.4
rišym.dt.ʿrb. | b bnš hm. | ḏmry.w.pṭpṭ.ʿrb. | b.yrm. | [ily.w].ḏmry.ʿrb. | b.ṯbʿm. | ydn.bn.ilrpi. | w.ṯbʿm.ʿrb. 2079.4
b. | [---].b.ndb. | [---].b.kmkty. | [---.]yrmly.qrtym. | [---].b.yrml. | [---.]b.yrml. | [---.]b.yrml. | [---.]b.yrml. | [---.]b.yrml. 2119.18
. | [---].b.kmkty. | [---.]yrmly.qrtym. | [---].b.yrml. | [---.]b.yrml. | [---.]b.yrml. | [---.]b.yrml. | [---.]b.yrml. | [---.--]n.b.yr 2119.19
ty. | [---.]yrmly.qrtym. | [---].b.yrml. | [---.]b.yrml. | [---.]b.yrml. | [---.]b.yrml. | [---.]b.yrml. | [---.--]n.b.yrml. | [---.--]ny 2119.20
y.qrtym. | [---].b.yrml. | [---.]b.yrml. | [---.]b.yrml. | [---.]b.yrml. | [---.]b.yrml. | [---.--]n.b.yrml. | [---.--]ny.yrml. | šwn.q 2119.21
].b.yrml. | [---.]b.yrml. | [---.]b.yrml. | [---.]b.yrml. | [---.]b.yrml. | [---.--]n.b.yrml. | [---.--]ny.yrml. | šwn.qrty. | b.šlmy. 2119.22
yrml. | [---.]b.yrml. | [---.]b.yrml. | [---.]b.yrml. | [---.--]n.b.yrml. | [---.--]ny.yrml. | šwn.qrty. | b.šlmy. 2119.23
n. | kdm.mṯḫ. | l.alṯy. | kd.l mrynm. | šbʿ yn. | l mrynm. | b yṯbmlk. | kdm.ǵbiš ḫry. | ḫmš yn.b d. | bḥ mlkt. | b mdrʿ. | ṯlṯ 1090.12
.bh[t k].a[l.tš]mḫ. | al.tšmḫ.b r[m.h]kl[k]. | al.aḫd.hm.b y[--] y.[---]b[-]. | b gdlt.arkt y.am[---]. | qdqd k.ašhlk.šbt[k. 3[ʿNT.VI].5.30

b y[--.---].|il[.---].|b'l[.---].|[---.--]l.[---].|[---.g]dlt[.---].|[---]. 46[-].1.1
.ank.|[---.]asrm.|[---.]dbḥm.|[---.y]rḫ.w šqr.|[---.--]b.b y[--.---].|[-----].|[-----].|[-----].|[---.]mrkbt.|[---.--]a.nrm.| 1002.25
y.š y.qḥn y.|[--.]šir.b krm.nṭṭt.dm.'lt.b ab y.|u---].'lt.b k.lk.l pn y.yrk.b'l.[--].|[---.]'nt.šzrm.tštšḥ.km.ḥ[--].|[---].' 1001.1.10
'd h.t[--].|aṯr.aṯrm[.---].|aṯr.aṯrm[.---].|išdym.t[---].|b k.mla[.---].|udm't.d[m'.---].|[---].bn.[---].|[-----]. 27[8].10
--].|[špt.l a]rṣ.špt.l šmm.|[---.l]šn.l kbkbm.y'rb.|[b']l.b kbd h.b p h yrd.|k ḥrr.zt.ybl.arṣ.w pr.|'ṣm.yraun.aliyn.b' 5[67].2.4
iš.tikln.|ṯd n.km.mrm.tqrṣn.|il.yẓḥq.bm.|lb.w ygmḏ.bm kbd.|ẓi.at.l tlš.|amt.yrḫ.|l dmgy.amt.|aṯrt.qḥ.|ksan k. 12[75].1.13
anšt.w i[n.b ilht].|qlṣ k.tb'.bt.ḫnp.lb[k.--.ti]|ḫd.d iṯ.b kbd k.tšt.b [---].|irt k.dṯ.ydṯ.m'qb k.[ttb'].|[bt]lt.'nt.idk.l 18[3AQHT].1.18
.nšrm.trḫ[p]n.|ybṣr.ḥbl.diym.|tbky.pǵt.bm.lb.|tdm'.bm.kbd.|tmz'.kst.dnil.mt.|rpi.al.ǵzr.mt.hrnmy.|apnk.dnil. 19[1AQHT].1.35
k.|pht.šrp.b išt.|'l k.[pht.ṯḥ]n.b rḥ|m.'[l k.]pht[.dr]y.b kbrt.|'l k.pht.[-]l[-].|b šdm.'l k.pht.|dr'.b ym.tn.aḥd.|b a 6[49].5.16
'l.|w ymlk.b arṣ.il.kl h.|[---] š abn.b rḥbt.|[---] š abn.b kknt. 6.1.67[49.1.39]
lqḥ.š'rt.|urḫ.ln.kkrm.|w.rḥd.kd.šmn.|drt.b.kkr.|ubn.ḫṣḥ.kkr.|kkr.lqḥ.ršpy.|tmtrn.bn.pnmn.|kkr.|b 1118.4
.dlt.tlk.km.p[---].|[---.]bt.tḥbṭ.km.ṣq.ṣdr[.---].|[---.]kl.b kl.l pgm.pgm.l.b[---].|[---.]mdbm.l ḥrn.ḥr[n.---].|[---.--]m. 1001.1.26
lḥt.|qṣ.mri.ndd.|y'šr.w yšqyn h.|ytn.ks.b d h.|krpn.b klat.yd h.|b krb.'ẓm.ridn.|mt.šmm.ks.qdš.|l tphn h.aṯt.k 3['NT].1.11
.|rumm.'n.kḏd.aylt.|hm.imt.imt.npš.blt.|ḥmr.p imt.b klt.|yd y.ilḥm.hm.šb'.|ydt y.b ṣ'.hm.ks.ymsk.|nhr.k[--].ṣ 5[67].1.19
b 'pr.ḫbl ṭtm.[---.]|šqy.rṯa.tnm y.ytn.[ks.b yd].|krpn.b klat yd.[---].|km ll.kḥṣ.tusp[.---].|tgr.il.bn h.ṯr[.---].|w y' 1['NT.X].4.10
yn š h d.ytn.ṣṭqn.|ṭut ṭbḫ ṣtq[n].|b bz 'zm ṭbḫ š[h].|b kl ygz ḥḫ š h. 1153.5
--.-]t h.ušpǵt tišr.|[---.šm]m h.nšat ẓl h kbkbm.|[---.]b km kbkbt k ṯn.|[---.]b'l yḥmdn h.yrṯ y.|[---.]dmrn.l pn h 2001.2.6
d.tngṯm h.|[---.-]ḥm k b ṣpn.|[---.]išqb.aylt.|[---.--]m.b km.y'n.|[---].yd'.l yd't.|[---.]tasrn.ṯr il.|[---.]rks.bn.abnm. 1['NT.X].5.20
]npš.|[---.h]d.tngṯn h.|[---].b ṣpn.|[---].nšb.b 'n.|[---.]b km.y'n.|[---.yd'.l] yd't.|[---.t]asrn.|[---.]trks.|[---.]abnm.u 1['NT.X].5.7
ml.|[---.--]y.|[---.yr]ml.|[---.y]rml.|[---.]kmkty.|[---].b.kmkty.|[---].b.ndb.|[---].b.ndb.|[---].b.ndb.|[---].b.kmkty 2119.12
-].b.kmkty.|[---].b.ndb.|[---].b.ndb.|[---].b.ndb.|[---].b.kmkty.|[---.]yrmly.qrtym.|[---].b.yrml.|[---.]b.yrml.|[---. 2119.16
ḥ b hm.|aqht.ybl.l qẓ.ybky.w yqbr.|yqbr.nn.b mdgt.b knk[-].|w yšu.g h.w yṣḥ.knp.nšrm.|b'l.yṯbr.b'l.yṯbr.diy.| 19[1AQHT].3.147
]gṯr.w yqr.il.yṯb.b.'ṯtrt.|il.ṯpṭ.b hd r'y.d yšr.w yḏmr.|b knr.w ṯlb.b tp.w mṣltm.b m|rqdm.dšn.b.ḥbr.kṯr.ṭbm.|w t UG5.2.1.4
|ugrt.|b mrḥ il.|b nit il.|b ṣmd il.|b dṯn il.|b šrp il.|b knt il.|b ǵdyn il.|[b]n [---]. 30[107].17
--].|lḥm.hm.štym.lḥ[m].|b ṯlḥnt.lḥm št.|b krpnm.yn.b k.ḫrṣ.|dm.'ṣm.hm.yd.il mlk.|yḫss k.ahbt.ṯr.t'rr k.|w t'n.r 4[51].4.37
ǵtm.ṯd.---].|b ḥrb.[mlḥt.qṣ.mri].|šty.kr[pnm.yn.---].|b ks.ḫr[ṣ.dm.'ṣm.---].|ks.ksp[.---].|krpn.[---].|w tṯtn.[---].|t 5[67].4.16
q mrǵtm.ṯd.|b ḥrb.mlḥt.qṣ[.m]r|i.tšty.krp[nm.y]n.|[b k]s.ḫrṣ.d[m.'ṣm].|[---.--]n.|[---.---]t.|[---.--]t.|[---.--]n. 4[51].6.59
].ay š[---].|[---.b ḥ]rb.mlḥ[t.qṣ].|[mri.tšty.krpnm].yn.b ks.ḫ[rṣ].|[dm.'ṣm.---]n.krpn.'l.[k]rpn.|[---.]ym.w t'l.trṯ.|[17[2AQHT].6.5
q.mrǵtm.|[ṯd.b ḥrb.m]lḥt.qṣ.|[mri.tšty.k]rpnm yn.|[b ks.ḫrṣ.dm].'ṣm. 4[51].3.44
m.w ywpṯn.b tk.|p[ḫ]r.bn.ilm.štt.|p[--].b ṯlḥn y.qlt.|b ks.ištyn h.|dm.ṯn.dbḥm.šna.b'l.ṯlṯ.|rkb.'rpt.dbḥ.|bṯt.w d 4[51].3.16
[l].|b dm.ḏmr.ḥlqm.b mm['].|mhrm.mṭm.tgrš.|šbm.b ksl.qšt h.mdnt.|w hln.'nt.l bt h.tmǵyn.|tštql.ilt.l hkl h.| 3['NT].2.16
q|m.l rbbt.|yṣq-ḥym.w tbṯḫ.|kt.il.dt.rbtm.|kt.il.nbt.b ksp.|šmrgt.b dm.ḫrṣ.|kḥṯ.il.nḥt.|b ẓr.hdm.id.|d pršа.b b 4[51].1.32
----].|[-----].|[---.]mrkbt.|[---.--]a.nrm.|[---.--]y.lm[.-.]b k[p].|[---].tr[--.]gpn lk.|[---].km[-.---].|[---.--]k yṣunn[.---] 1002.31
dd.|y'šr.w yšqyn h.|ytn.ks.b d h.|krpn.b klat.yd h.|b krb.'ẓm.ridn.|mt.šmm.ks.qdš.|l tphn h.aṯt.krpn.|l t'n.aṯr 3['NT].1.12
ḥmṯ.ṯmṯ.|[--.]ydbr.ṯrmt.al m.qḥn y.š y.qḥn y.|[--.]šir.b krm.nṭṭt.dm.'lt.b ab y.|u---].'lt.b k.lk.l pn y.yrk.b'l.[--].|[- 1001.1.9
h.|kb[d.]mn.'l.abršn.|b[n.---].kršu.nṯk h.|[---.--]mm.b.krsi. 1146.13
u.ǵmit.w 's[--].|lḥm.hm.štym.lḥ[m].|b ṯlḥnt.lḥm št.|b krpnm.yn.b k.ḫrṣ.|dm.'ṣm.hm.yd.il mlk.|yḫss k.ahbt.ṯr.t 4[51].4.37
yiḥd.b'l.bn.aṯrt.|rbm.ymḫṣ.b ktp.|dk ym.ymḫṣ.b ṣmd.|ṣḥr mt.ymṣḥ.l arṣ.|[yṯb.]b[']l.l 6[49].5.2
.--]ty.|[---.-]i[-.--].|[-----].|[---.--]y.|[---.--]lm.|ḫdmḏr.b.kṯ[t]ǵlm.|mḏl.b.kṯtǵlm. 2118.23
].|[-----].|[---.--]y.|[---.--]lm.|ḫdmḏr.b.kṯ[t]ǵlm.|mḏl.b.kṯtǵlm. 2118.24
[-----].|[--.]l tṣi.b b[--].bm.k[--].|[--]ṯb.'ryt k.k qlt[.---].|[--]at.brt.lb k.'nn.[---].|[--. 60[32].2
h.y'rb.ybky.|w yšnn.ytn.g h.|bky.b ḥy k.ab n.ašmḫ.|b l.mt k.ngln.k klb.|b bt k.n'tq.k inr.|ap.ḫšt k.ap.ab.k mtm 16.1[125].15
]tqt.|tbky.w tšnn.[tt]n.|g h.bky.b ḥ[y k.a]b n.|nšmḫ.b l.mt k.ngln.|k klb.[b]bt k.n'tq.|k inr[.ap.]ḫšt k.|ap.ab.k 16.2[125].99
--].|'l.bt.ab h.nšrm.trḫ[p]n.|ybṣr.ḥbl.diym.|tbky.pǵt.bm.lb.|tdm'.bm.kbd.|tmz'.kst.dnil.mt.|rpi.al.ǵzr.mt.hrnm 19[1AQHT].1.34
.ṯṯb.ank.l hm.|w.any k.ṯt.|by.'ky.'ryt.|w.aḫ y.mhk.|b lb h.al.yšt. 2059.27
.il.ab n.|kbd k iš.tikln.|ṯd n.km.mrm.tqrṣn.|il.yẓḥq.bm.|lb.w ygmḏ.bm kbd.|ẓi.at.l tlš.|amt.yrḫ.|l dmgy.amt.| 12[75].1.12
.|l.'l.w.lakm.|ilak.w.at.|um y.al.tdḥṣ.|w.ap.mhkm.|b.lb k.al.|tšt. 1013.23
m.qštm.|[----.]mhrm.ht.tṣdn.tintt.|[---]m.tṣḥq.'nt.w b lb.tqny.|[---.]tb l y.l aqht.ǵzr.ṯb l y w l k.|[---]m.l aqry k. 17[2AQHT].6.41
-].|['l.]krt.tbkn.|[--.]rgm.ṯrm.|[--.]mtm.tbkn.|[--]t.w b lb.tqb[-].|[--]m[-].mtm.uṣb'[t].|[-]tr.šrk.il.|'rb.špš.l ymǵ.| 15[128].5.15
šm.b.nni.|ṯn.bnšm.b.slḫ.|[---].bnšm.b.yny.|[--.]bnšm.b.lbnm.|arb'.bnšm.b.ypr.|[---.]bnšm.b.šbn.|[---.b]nšm.b.šm 2076.21
k.|[l.p]'n.b'l y.|[šb'] d.šb' [d].|[mr]ḥqtm.|qlt.|'bd k.b.|lwsnd.|[w] b ṣr.|'m.mlk.|w.ht.|mlk.syr.|ns.w.ṯm.|ydb 2063.9
|b mdbr.špm.yd[.---.---]r.|l riš hm.w yš[--.--]m.|lḥm.b lḥm ay.w šty.b ḫmr yn ay.|šlm.mlk.šlm.mlkt.'rbm m.ṯnn 23[52].6
-].|yd k.ṣǵr.tnšq.špt k.ṯm.|ṯkm.bm ṯkm.aḫm.qym.il.|b lsmt.ṯm.yṯbš.šm.il.mt m.|y'bš.brk n.šm.il.ǵzrm.|ṯm.ṯmq. 22.2[124].6
arḫ.td.rgm.b ǵr.|b p y.t'lgt.b lšn[y].|ǵr[.---]b.b pš y.t[--].|hwt.b'l.iš[--].|šm' l y.ypš.[--- 2124.2
[tḥ.---.]l.aḥd.adr.|[---.--]t.b[ḥd]r.mškb.|tl[l.---.--]ḥ.|b lṯk.bt.|[pt]ḥ.aḥd.l.bt.'bdm.|[t]n.ptḥ msb.bt.tu.|w.ptḥ[.aḥ 1151.8
w[-].uḫ.pdm.b.y'rt.|pǵyn.b.tpḫ.|amri[l].b.šrš.|aǵltn.b.midḫ.|[--]n.b.ayly.|[-]lyn.b.nght.|[---.]b.nh[-]t.|[---.]almš 2118.13
spr.npṣm.d yṣa.b milḫ.|'šrm.ḫpn.ḫmš.|kbd.w lpš.|ḫmš.mispt.|mṯ.|w lpš.d 1109.1
šlt.|l.udmym.b.ṯmnt.'šrt.ksp.|šb'm.lbš.d.'rb.bt.mlk.|b.mit.ḫmšt.kbd.ksp.|ṯlṯ.ktnt.b d.an[r]my.|b.'šrt.ksp.b.a[--]. 2101.17
|b.yrḫ.pgrm.|lqḥ.iwrpzn.|argḏḏ.|ṯtkn.|ybrk.|ntbt.|b.mitm.|'šrm.|kbd.ḫrṣ. 2006.8
aṣ[ḫ.---].|yd.b qrb[.---].|w lk.ilm.[---].|w rgm.l [---].|b mud.ṣin[.---].|mud.ṣin[.---].|iṯm.mui[-.---].|dm.mt.aṣ[ḫ.-- 5[67].3.22
d.|[-]r[-]k.bm.ymn.|tlk.škn.'l.ṣrrt.|adn k.šqrb.[---].|b mgn k.w ḫrṣ.l kl.|apnk.ǵzr.ilḥu.|[m]rḥ h.yiḫd.b yd.|[g]r 16.1[125].45
[---.--]s'.hn.mlk.|[---.l]qḥ.hn.l.ḥwt h.|[---.--]p.hn.ib.d.b.mgšḫ.|[---.i]b.hn[.w.]ht.ank.|[---.--]š[-.--].w.ašt.|[---].amr 1012.10
m.n['mm.---].|w ysmm.bn.š[---].|ytnm.qrt.l 'ly[.---].|b mdbr.špm.yd[.---.---]r.|l riš hm.w yš[--.--]m.|lḥm.b lḥm a 23[52].4

d ṯbil. | ʿṯtrt ṣwd[t.---]. | tlk b mdb[r.---]. | ṯḥdṯn w hl[.---]. | w tglṯ thmt.ʿ[--.---]. | yṣi.ǵl h t 2001.1.3
ẓm.w yqḥ b hm. | aqht.ybl.l qẓ.ybky.w yqbr. | yqbr.nn.b mdgt.b knk[-]. | w yšu.g h.w yṣḥ.knp.nšrm. | bʿl.yṯbr.bʿl.yṯ 19[1AQHT].3.147
m. | b yṯbmlk. | kdm.ǵbiš ḫry. | ḫmš yn.b d. | bḥ mlkt. | b mdrʿ. | ṯlṯ bt.il | ann. | kd.bt.ilann. 1090.16
št h. | imḫṣ h.ʿl.qṣʿt h.hwt. | l aḥw.ap.qšt h.l ttn. | l y.w b mt[.-]ḥ.mṣṣ[-]t[.--]. | prʿ.qẓ.y[bl].šblt. | b ǵlp h.apnk.dnil. | [19[1AQHT].1.17
ṯn.ṣbrm. | b.uškn. | ṣbr.aḥd. | b.ar. | ṣbr.aḥd. | b.mlk. | ṣbr.aḥd. | b.mʿrby. | ṣbr.aḥd. | b.ulm. | ṣbr.aḥd. | b.ubrʿ 2073.6
šm.b.yʿrt. | ṯn.bnšm.b.ʿrmt. | arbʿ.bnšm.b.šrš. | ṯṯ.bnšm.b.mlk. | arbʿ.bnšm.b.bṣr. | ṯn.bnšm.[b.]rqd. | ṯn.b[nšm.b.---]y. 2076.38
[š]šw[.i]ryn.arr. | [š]dm.b.mlk. | [--.š]dm.b.ar. | [--.š]dm.b.ulm. | [--.š]dm.b.mʿrby. | [--. 2033.1.2
ṯlṯ.mat. | šbʿm kbd. | zt.ubdym. | b mlk. 1095.4
bmt h.šnst. | kpt.b ḥbš h.brkm.tǵl[l]. | b dm.ḏmr.ḫlqm.b mm[ʿ]. | mhrm.mṭm.tgrš. | šbm.b ksl.qšt h.mdnt. | w hln.ʿnt 3[ʿNT].2.14
h.b šmḫt.kbd.ʿnt. | tšyt.k brkm.tǵll b dm. | ḏmr.ḫlqm.b mmʿ.mhrm. | ʿd.tšbʿ.tmtḫṣ.b bt. | tḫṣb.bn.ṯlḥnm.ymḫ. | [b] 3[ʿNT].2.28
.uṣbʿt h.ybmt.limm. | [t]rḥṣ.yd h.b dm.ḏmr. | [u]ṣbʿt h.b mmʿ.mhrm. | [t]ʿr.ksat.l ksat.ṯlḥnt. | [l]ṯlḥn.hdmm.ṯṯʿr.l hd 3[ʿNT].2.35
rt. | [---.bn]šm.b.ǵbl. | [---.b]nšm.b.mʿr.arr. | arbʿ.bnšm.b.mnt. | arbʿ.bnšm.b.irbn. | ṯn.bnšm.b.yʿrt. | ṯn.bnšm.b.ʿrmt. | 2076.33
n h.aṯt.krpn. | l tʿn.aṯrt.alp. | kd.yqḥ.b ḫmr. | rbt.ymsk.b msk h. | qm.ybd.w yšr. | mṣltm.bd.nʿm. | yšr.ǵzr.ṭb.ql. | ʿl.bʿl 3[ʿNT].1.17
b.ṯnq. | [---.b]nšm.b.ugrt. | [---.bn]šm.b.ǵbl. | [---.b]nšm.b.mʿr.arr. | arbʿ.bnšm.b.mnt. | arbʿ.bnšm.b.irbn. | ṯn.bnšm.b.y 2076.32
l | bn.ilh.mdrǵl | špšyn.b.ulm. | bn.qṭn.b.ulm. | bn.gdrn.b.mʿr[by]. | [w].bn.dʿm[-]. | bn.ppṯ.b[--]. | b[n.---]. | šm[-.---]. | t 2046.1.7
. | b.uškn. | ṣbr.aḥd. | b.ar. | ṣbr.aḥd. | b.mlk. | ṣbr.aḥd. | b.mʿrby. | ṣbr.aḥd. | b.ulm. | ṣbr.aḥd. | b.ubrʿy. 2073.8
. | bn.liy. | ʿšrm.ṣ[md]. | ṯṯ kbd.b ḥ[--]. | w.arbʿ.ḥ[mrm]. | b m[ʿ]rby. | ṯmn.ṣmd.[---]. | b d.bʿlsr. | yd.ṯdn.ʿšr. | [ḥ]mrm. | d 2102.1
[š]dm.b.mlk. | [--.š]dm.b.ar. | [--.š]dm.b.ulm. | [--.š]dm.b.mʿrby. | [--.šd]m.b.uškn. | [---.--]n. | [---].tlmdm. | [y]bnn.ṣm 2033.1.5
mitm.ʿšr kbd. | kšmm.b.mṣbt. | mit.ʿšrm.ṯn kbd. | [kš]mm. | [ʿ]š[r]m.ṯn.kbd.ḥṭm. | [-] 2091.2
---.]ṯlṯm. | [---.n]ḫl. | [---.ṯ]lṯ.mat.šbʿm[.---]. | [---.--]mm.b.mṣbt[.---]. | [---.ṯl]ṯ.mat.ṯmny[m.---]. 2149.4
pdrm. | sʿt.b šdm.ḥṭb. | w b grnt.ḥpšt. | sʿt.b npk.šibt.w b | mqr.mmlat. | d[m].ym.w ṯn. | ṯlṯ.rbʿ.ym. | ḫmš.ṯdṯ.ym. | m 14[KRT].5.216
šrn. | pdrm.sʿt.b šdm. | ḥṭb h.b grnt.ḥpšt. | sʿt.b nk.šibt.b bqr. | mmlat.dm.ym.w ṯn. | ṯlṯ.rbʿ.ym.ymš. | ṯdṯ.ym.ḥẓ k.al. 14[KRT].3.113
.-.]ʿ[-.-]ag šʿrm. | [---.--]mi. | [--.]ṯṯ[m] šbʿ.k[bd]. | [---]m.b.mril. 2091.9
.l inr.tʿdbn.ktp. | b il ab h.gʿr.yṯb.il.kb[-]. | aṯ[rt.]il.yṯb.b mrzḥ h. | yšt[.il.y]n.ʿd šbʿ.trṯ.ʿd škr. | il.hlk.l bt h.yštql. | l ḥṭ UG5.1.1.15
.[---.] | gm.ṣḥ.l q[ṣ.ilm.---]. | l rḥqm.l p[-.---]. | ṣḥ.il.yṯb.b[mrzḥ.---]. | bṯt.ʿllm n.[---]. | ilm.bt.bʿl k.[---]. | dl.ylkn.ḥš.b 1[ʿNT.X].4.4
ḫnn il. | nṣbt il. | šlm il. | il ḥš il add. | bʿl ṣpn bʿl. | ugrt. | b mrḥ il. | b nit il. | b ṣmd il. | b dṯn il. | b šrp il. | b knt il. | b ǵd 30[107].12
.mlk ʿlm.b ʿz. | [rpu.m]lk.ʿlm.b ḏmr h.bl. | [---].b ḥtk h.b nmrt h.l r | [--.]arṣ.ʿz k.ḏmr k.l[-] | n k.ḥtk k.nmrt k.b tk. | UG5.2.2.8
.bʿl.aḫd[.---]. | w ṣmt.ǵllm[.---]. | aḫd.aklm.k [---]. | npl.b mšmš[.---]. | anp n m yḥr[r.---]. | bmt n m.yšḫn.[---]. | qrn h 12[75].2.37
spr.ʿrbnm. | dt.ʿrb. | b.mtn.bn.ayaḫ. | b.ḫbṭ h.hwt.ṯt h. | w.mnm.šalm. | dt.tknn. | ʿl 1161.3
. | ḫmrm.ṯṯ.krm[m.---]. | krm.ǵlkz.b.p[--.---]. | krm.ilyy.b.m[--.---]. | kd.šbʿ.krmm.[---]. | ṯn.krm[m.i]wrǵl[.---]. | ṯn.kr 1081.24
y.ndr. | iṯt.ʿmn.mlkt. | w.rgm y.l[--]. | lqt.w.pn. | mlk.nr b n. 50[117].18
bt il. | šlm il. | il ḥš il add. | bʿl ṣpn bʿl. | ugrt. | b mrḥ il. | b nit il. | b ṣmd il. | b dṯn il. | b šrp il. | b knt il. | b ǵdyn il. | [b] 30[107].13
]. | [i]lh[m.gd]lt.i[l.dqt.ṯkm] | n.w šnm.dqt[.---]. | bqtm.b nbk.[---]. | kmm.gdlt.l b[ʿl.--.dqt]. | l ṣpn.gdlt.[l.---]. | ugrt.š APP.II[173].35
.ilhm.gdlt.il]. | [d]qt.ṯkmn.w [šnm.dqt.--]. | [--]t.dqtm.[b nbk.---]. | [--.k]mm.gdlt.l.b[ʿl.---]. | [dq]t.l.ṣpn.gdlt.l[.---]. | u 35[3].32
.tpḥ. | amri[l].b.šrš. | aǵltn.b.midḫ. | [--]n.b.ayly. | [-]lyn.b.ngḫt. | [---.]b.nh[-]t. | [---.]almš. | [---.--]ty. | [---.-]i[-.--]. | [---- 2118.15
.]kmkty. | [---].b.kmkty. | [---].b.ndb. | [---].b.ndb. | [---].b.ndb. | [---].b.kmkty. | [---.]yrmly.qrtym. | [---].b.yrml. | [---.] 2119.15
-.y]rml. | [---.]kmkty. | [---].b.kmkty. | [---].b.ndb. | [---].b.ndb. | [---].b.ndb. | [---].b.kmkty. | [---.]yrmly.qrtym. | [---].b. 2119.14
---.yr]ml. | [---.y]rml. | [---.]kmkty. | [---].b.kmkty. | [---].b.ndb. | [---].b.ndb. | [---].b.ndb. | [---].b.kmkty. | [---.]yrmly.qr 2119.13
[---.r]iš k. | [---.]bn ʿn km. | [---.]alp. | [---.]ym.rbt. | [---.]b nhrm. | [ʿb]r.gbl.ʿbr. | qʿl.ʿbr.iht. | np šmm.šmšr. | l dgy.aṯrt. 3[ʿNT.VI].6.6
n h. | npyn h.mks.bšr h. | tmtʿ.md h.b ym.ṯn. | npyn h.b nhrm. | štt.ḫptr.l išt. | ḫbrṯ.l zr.pḥmm. | tʿpp.ṯr.il.d pid. | tǵẓ 4[51].2.7
.b.šrš. | aǵltn.b.midḫ. | [--]n.b.ayly. | [-]lyn.b.ngḫt. | [---.]b.nh[-]t. | [---.]almš. | [---.--]ty. | [---.-]i[-.--]. | [-----]. | [---.--]y. | [2118.16
arbʿm.drʿ.w.ṯlṯm.drt. | [w].šbʿm.dd.ṯn.kbd.ḥpr.bnšm. | b.nzl.ʿšrm.l.mit.drʿ.w.šbʿm.drt. | w.ʿšrm.l.mit.dd.ḥpr.bnšm. | 1098.24
ṯlṯ.ṣmdm. | b.nḫry. | ṣmdm.b.ṯp[--]. | aḥdm.b.gm[--]. 144[317].2
.ḫrṣbʿ. | arbʿ.bnšm.b.hzp. | arbʿ.bnšm.b.šql. | arbʿ.bnšm.b.nni. | ṯn.bnšm.b.slḫ. | [---].bnšm.b.yny. | [--.]bnšm.b.lbnm. | 2076.18
t m.w ank. | ibǵy h.b tk.ǵr y.il.ṣpn. | b qdš.b ǵr.nḥlt y. | b nʿm.b gbʿ.tliyt. | hlm.ʿnt.tph.ilm.b h.pʿnm. | ṯṭṭ.bʿd n.ksl.ṯṯb 3[ʿNT].3.28
u.ʿn h.w tʿn. | w tʿn.arḫ.w tr.b lkt. | tr.b lkt.w tr.b ḫl. | [b]nʿmm.b ysmm.ḥ[--]k.ǵrt. | [ql].l bʿl.ʿnt.ttnn. | [---].bʿl m.d 10[76].2.30
h]. | l alp.ql.ẓ[--.---]. | l np ql.nd.[----]. | tlk.w tr.b[ḫl]. | b nʿmm.b ys[mm.---]. | arḫ.arḫ.[---.tld]. | ibr.tld[.l bʿl]. | w ru 10[76].3.19
. | mslmt.b ǵr.tliyt. | w tʿl.bkm.b arr. | bm.arr.w b ṣpn. | b nʿm.b ǵr.t[l]iyt. | ql.l bʿl.ttnn. | bšrt.il.bš[r.bʿ]l. | w bšr.ḥtk.d 10[76].3.32
ʿšrt. | b.bn.mnn.ṯṯm. | b.rpan.bn.yyn.ʿšrt. | b.ypʿr.ʿšrm. | b.nʿmn.bn.ply.ḫmšt.l.ʿšrm. | b.gdn.bn.uss.ʿšrm. | b.ʿdn.bn.ṯṯ.ʿ 2054.1.17
r.nn.ʿrm.šrn. | pdrm.sʿt.b šdm. | ḥṭb h.b grnt.ḥpšt. | sʿt.b nk.šibt.b bqr. | mmlat.dm.ym.w ṯn. | ṯlṯ.rbʿ.ym.ymš. | ṯdṯ.y 14[KRT].3.113
n.ʿrm. | šrnn.pdrm. | sʿt.b šdm.ḥṭb. | w b grnt.ḥpšt. | sʿt.b npk.šibt.w b | mqr.mmlat. | d[m].ym.w ṯn. | ṯlṯ.rbʿ.ym. | ḫm 14[KRT].5.216
rp.šmm.k rs. | ipd k.ank.ispi.uṭm. | ḏrqm.amt m.l yrt. | b npš.bn ilm.mt.b mh | mrt.ydd.il.ǵzr. | tbʿ.w l.yṯb ilm.idk. | l 5[67].1.7
n. | dll.al.ilak.l bn. | ilm.mt.ʿdd.l ydd. | il.ǵzr.yqra.mt. | b npš h.ystrn ydd. | b gngn h.aḥd y.d ym | lk.ʿl.ilm.l ymru. | il 4[51].7.48
nk.in.bt[.l] y[.km.]ilm[.w] ḥẓr[.k bn]. | [qd]š.lbum.trd.b n[p]šn y.trḥṣn.k ṯrm. | [--]b b[ht]. | [zbl.]ym.b hkl.ṭpṭ.nh[r]. 2.3[129].20
. | ymǵ.l mrrt.tǵll.b nr. | yšu.g h.w yṣḥ.y l k.mrrt. | tǵll.b nr.d ʿl k.mḫṣ.aqht. | ǵzr.šrš k.b arṣ.al. | ypʿ.riš.ǵly.b d.nsʿ k. 19[1AQHT].3.158
lm h.ʿnt.p dr[.dr]. | ʿdb.uḫry mṭ.yd h. | ymǵ.l mrrt.tǵll.b nr. | yšu.g h.w yṣḥ.y l k.mrrt. | tǵll.b nr.d ʿl k.mḫṣ.aqht. | ǵz 19[1AQHT].3.156
ʿly. | nʿm.l arṣ.mṭr.bʿl. | w l šd.mṭr.ʿly. | nʿm.l ḥṭt.b gn. | bm.nrt.ksmm. | ʿl.tl[-]k.ʿṭrṭrm. | nšu.[r]iš.ḥrṯm. | l ẓr.ʿdb.dgn 16[126].3.10
št k.bm.qrb m.asm. | b p h.rgm.l yṣa.b špt h[.hwt h]. | b nši ʿn h.w tphn.in.[---]. | [-.]hlk.ǵlmm b dd y.yṣ[--]. | [-.]yṣa 19[1AQHT].2.76
p.ṯǵr.ṯḥt. | adrm.d b grn.ydn. | dn.almnt.yṯpṭ.ṯpṭ.ytm. | b nši ʿn h.w yphn.b alp. | šd.rbt.kmn.hlk.kṯr. | k yʿn.w yʿn.td 17[2AQHT].5.9
išt. | ḫbrṯ.l ẓr.pḥmm. | tʿpp.ṯr.il.d pid. | tǵẓy.bny.bnwt. | b nši.ʿn h.w tphn. | hlk.bʿl.aṯtrt. | k tʿn.hlk.btlt. | ʿnt.tdrq.ybm 4[51].2.12
b nši[.ʿn h.w yphn.yḥd]. | b ʿrpt[.nšrm.yšu]. | [g h.]w yṣḥ[.kn 19[1AQHT].2.105
yṣḥ.knp.nšrm.ybn. | bʿl.ybn.diy hmt nšrm. | tpr.w du.b nši.ʿn h.w ypn. | yḥd.hrgb.ab.nšrm. | yšu.g h.w yṣḥ.knp.hr[19[1AQHT].3.120
knp.hrgb.bʿl.ybn. | [b]ʿl.ybn.diy.hwt.hrg[b]. | tpr.w du.b nši.ʿn h. | [w]yphn.yḥd.ṣml.um.nšrm. | yšu.g h.w yṣḥ.knp. 19[1AQHT].3.134

lmnt.y]ṯpṭ.|[ṯpṭ.ytm.---] h.|[---.---]n.|[-----].|hlk.[---.b n]ši.|ʿn h.w tphn.[---].|b grn.yḫrb[.---].|yǵly.yḫsp.ib[.---]. 19[1AQHT].1.28
w tʿl.trṯ.|[---].yn.ʿšy l ḥbš.|[---.]ḥtn.qn.yṣbt.|[---.--]m.b nši.ʿn h.w tphn.|[---.--]ml.ksl h.k b[r]q.|[---.]m[-]ǵ[-].thm 17[2AQHT].6.10
[m.--].|d alp šd.ẓu h.b ym.t[---].|tlbš.npṣ.ǵzr.tšt.ḫ[---.b] |nšg h.ḥrb.tšt.b tʿr[t h].|w ʿl.tlbš.npṣ.aṯt.[--].|ṣbi nrt.ilm. 19[1AQHT].4.206
t.rp]i.brlt.ǵzr.mt hrnmy.|[---].hw.mḫ.l ʿrš h.yʿl.|[---].bm.nšq.aṯt h.|[---.]b ḥbq h.ḥmḥmt.|[---.--] n.ylt.ḥmḥmt.|[- 17[2AQHT].1.40
l kbkbm.kn[-].|yhbr.špt hm.yšq.hn.[š]pt hm.mtqtm.|bm.nšq.w hr.[b]ḥbq.w ḥ[m]ḥmt.ytb[n].|yspr.l ḫmš.l ṣ[---.] 23[52].56
.špt hm.yš[q].|hn.špt hm.mtqtm.mtqtm.k lrmn[.--].|bm.nšq.w hr.b ḥbq.ḥmḥmt.tqt[nṣn].|tldn.šḥr.w šlm.rgm.l il 23[52].51
.l aqht.ǵzr.ṯb l y w l k.|[---]m.l aqry k.b ntb.pšʿ.|[---].b ntb.gan.ašql k.tḥt.|[pʿn y.a]nk.nʿmn.ʿmq.nšm.|[tdʿṣ.pʿn] 17[2AQHT].6.44
qny.|[---.]ṯb l y.l aqht.ǵzr.ṯb l y w l k.|[---]m.l aqry k.b ntb.pšʿ.|[---].b ntb.gan.ašql k.tḥt.|[pʿn y.a]nk.nʿmn.ʿmq.n 17[2AQHT].6.43
[---.-]bʿm.|[---.b]n.yšm[ʿ].|[---.]mlkr[-] h.b.nṯk.|[---.]šbʿm.|[---.]ḫrg.ʿšrm.|[---.]abn.ksp.ṯlṯ.|[---].bty.k 2153.3
ʿgl h.k lb.ṯa[t].|l imr h.km.lb.ʿn[t].|aṯr.bʿl.tiḫd.m[t].|b sin.lpš.tššq[n h].|b qṣ.all.tšu.g h.w[tṣ]|ḥ.at.mt.tn.aḫ y.| 6[49].2.10
t.aǵld.|šgn.bn b[--.---].d.yṯb.b.ilštmʿ.|abmn.bn.r[---].b.syn.|bn.irṣ[-.---.]h.|šdyn.b[n.---.--]n. 2015.2.7
w ṯmnt.l ṯmnym.|šr.aḫy h.mẓa h.|w mẓa h.šr.yly h.|b skn.sknm.b ʿdn.|ʿdnm.kn.npl.bʿl.|km ṯr.w tkms.hd.p[.-]. 12[75].2.53
m.b.hzp.|arbʿ.bnšm.b.šql.|arbʿ.bnšm.b.nni.|ṯn.bnšm.b.slḫ.|[---].bnšm.b.yny.|[--.]bnšm.b.lbnm.|arbʿ.bnšm.b.ypr. 2076.19
|[---.]l [ ]dm.aḫt k.|ydʿt.k rḥmt.|al.tšt.b šdm.mm h.|b smkt.ṣat.npš h.|[-]mt[-].ṣba.rbt.|špš.w tgh.nyr.|rbt.w rg 16.1[125].35
.|[---.b]nšm.b.šmny.|[---.b]nšm.b.šmngy.|[---.]bnšm.b.snr.mid.|[---.bn]šm.b.tkn.|[---.bn]šm.b.tmrm.|[---.bn]šm. 2076.26
.ṯṯ.ʿšr h.ḫrmṯt.|ṯt.nitm.ṯn.mʿṣdm.ṯn.mqbm.|krk.aḥt.|b.sǵy.ḫmš.ḫrmṯt.nit.|krk.mʿṣd.mqb.|b.gt.ʿmq.ḫmš.ḫrmṯt.n 2048.7
ašr nkl w ib[.bt].|ḫrḫb.mlk qẓ ḫrḫb m|lk aǵzt.b sǵ[--.]špš.|yrḫ ytkḥ yḥ[bq] [-].|tld bt.[--]t.ḫ[--.l k]|ṯrt.l bn 24[77].3
spr.npš.d.|ʿrb.bt.mlk.|w.b.spr.l.št.|yrmʿl.|ṣry.|iršy.|yʿḏrd.|ayaḫ.|bn.aylt.|ḫmš.mat 2106.3
d.|hm.nṯkp.|mʿn k.|w.mnm.|rgm.d.tšmʿ.|ṯmt.w.št.|b.spr.ʿm y. 53[54].19
[.bn].ḥrtn.ʿ[--].|b.t[--.---] h.[---].|[-----].|[--]ly.ḫmšm.b.ʿbdyr[ḫ].|[---].ʿšrm.|[-----].|[---.ʿ]šr[.---].|[---.-]ʿrm.|[---.-- 2054.1.24
l mnn.ilm.|tǵr k.tšlm k.|tʿzz k.alp ymm.|w rbt.šnt.|b ʿd ʿlm...gnʿ.|iršt.aršt.|l aḫ y.l rʿ y.dt.|w ytnnn.|l aḫ h.l rʿ 1019.1.6
šrm.|b.nʿmn.bn.ply.ḫmšt.l.ʿšrm.|b.gdn.bn.uss.ʿšrm.|b.ʿdn.bn.ṯṯ.ʿšrt.|b.bn.qrdmn.ṯlṯm.|b.bṣmn[.bn].ḥrtn.ʿ[--].|b. 2054.1.19
.|[ily.w].ḏmry.ʿrb.|b.ṯbʿm.|ydn.bn.ilrpi.|w.ṯbʿm.ʿrb.b.ʿ[d]n.|ḏmry.bn.yrm.|ʿrb.b.adʿy. 2079.8
l.tl[-]k.ʿṭrṭrm.|nšu.[r]iš.ḥrṯm.|l ẓr.ʿdb.dgn kly.|lḥm.[b]ʿdn hm.kly.|yn.b ḥmt hm.k[l]y.|šmn.b q[bʿt hm.---].|bt. 16[126].3.14
.k [rḥ.npš h].|k iṯl.brlt h.[b h.pʿnm].|ṭṭṭ.ʿl[n.pn h.tdʿ.b ʿdn].|ksl.y[ṯbr.yǵṣ.pnt.ksl h].|anš.[dt.ẓr h.yšu.g h].|w yṣ[19[1AQHT].2.94
|k tʿn.hlk.btlt.|ʿnt.tdrq.ybmt.|[limm].b h.pʿnm.|[ṭṭṭ.b ʿ]dn.ksl.|[ṯṯbr.ʿln.p]n h.td[ʿ].|tǵṣ[.pnt.ks]l h.|anš.dt.ẓr.[h] 4[51].2.17
ym.|šr.aḫy h.mẓa h.|w mẓa h.šr.yly h.|b skn.sknm.b ʿdn.|ʿdnm.kn.npl.bʿl.|km ṯr.w tkms.hd.p[.-].|km.ibr.b tk. 12[75].2.53
thm.|qrit.l špš.um h.špš.um.ql.bl.ʿm.|il.mbk nhrm.b ʿdt.thmtm.|mnt.nṯk.nḥš.šmrr.nḥš.|ʿq šr.ln h.mlḫš abd.ln UG5.7.3
[.---].|ṯn.bnšm.b.š[--].|arbʿ.bnšm.b[.---].|ʿšrm.bnšm.[b.]ʿd[--].|arbʿ.bnšm.b.ag[m]y.|arbʿ.bnšm.b.ḫpty.|ṯṯ.bnšm.b 2076.10
l tšt k.l iršt.|[ʿlm.---.--]k.l tšt k.liršt.|[---.]rpi.mlk ʿlm.b ʿz.|[rpu.m]lk.ʿlm.b ḏmr h.bl.|[---].b ḥtk h.b nmrt h.l r|[-- UG5.2.2.6
l[kt].|tǵsdb.šmlšn.|w tbʿ ank.|ʿm mlakt h šmʿ h.|w b.ʿly skn.ydʿ rgm h.|w ht ab y ǵm[--].|t[--.---].|ls[--.---].|ṣḥ 1021.8
-]šnm.aṯtm.t[--.---].|[m]lakm.ylak.ym.[tʿdt.ṯpṭ.nhr].|b ʿlṣ.ʿlṣm.npr.š[--.---].|uṭ.ṯbr.ap hm.tbʿ.ǵlm[m.al.ṯṯb.idk.pn 2.1[137].12
t.ṯǵrt.|bht.ʿnt.w tqry.ǵlmm.|b št.ǵr.w hln.ʿnt.tm|tḫṣ.b ʿmq.tḫtṣb.bn.|qrytm tmḫṣ.lim.ḫp y[m].|tṣmt.adm.ṣat.š[p 3[ʿNT].2.6
la[t.ṯǵ]r[t.bht.ʿnt.w tqry.ǵlmm.b št.ǵr].|ap ʿnt tm[tḫṣ.b ʿmq.tḫtṣb.bn.qrytm.tmḫṣ].|lim ḫ[p.ym.---].|[--]m.t[-]t[.--- 7.2[130].25
ln.ʿnt.l bt h.tmǵyn.|tštql.ilt.l hkl h.|w l.šbʿt.tmtḫṣ h.b ʿmq.|tḫtṣb.bn.qrtm.tṯʿr.|ksat.l mhr.ṯʿr.ṯlḥnt.|l ṣbim.hdm 3[ʿNT].2.19
b]š h.ʿtkt r[išt].|[l bmt h.---.]hy bt h tʿrb.|[---.tm]tḫṣ b ʿmq.|[tḫtṣb.bn.qrtm.tṯʿr.ṯlḥnt.]l ṣbim.|[hdmm.l ǵzrm.mi 7.1[131].4
.---.ymǵy.]npš.|[---.h]d.tngṯn h.|[---].b ṣpn.|[---].nšb.b ʿn.|[---.]b km.yʿn.|[---.ydʿ.l] ydʿt.|[---.t]asrn.|[---.]trks.|[- 1[ʿNT.X].5.6
y.arbʿm.drʿ.w.ʿšrm.drt.|w.ṯlṯm.dd.ṯṯ.kbd.ḥpr.bnšm.|b.ʿnmky.ʿšrm.drʿ[.---.d]rt.|w.ṯn.ʿšr h.dd.[---].|iwrḏn.ḥ[--.--- 1098.28
d.ǵ[--.---].|krm.pyn.arty[.---].|ṯlṯ.krm.ubdym.l mlkt.b.ʿnmky[.---].|mgdly.ǵlpṯr.ṯn.krmm.w.ṯlṯ.ub[dym.---].|qmn 1081.9
.|aḥd.b gt.knpy.w.aḥd.b gt.ṯrmn.|aḥd.alp.idṯn.d aḫd.b.ʿnqpat.|[aḥd.al]p.d aǵlmn.|[d aḫd b.g]t gbry.|[---].aḥd.a 1129.11
n.d bat k.btlt.ʿnt.|qrn.d bat k bʿl.ymšḥ.|bʿl.ymšḥ.hm.b ʿp.|nṭʿn.b arṣ.ib y.|w b ʿpr.qm.aḫ k.|w tšu.ʿn h.btlt.ʿnt.| 10[76].2.23
ḫ.šmk.mla[t.r]umm.|tšu knp.btlt.ʿn[t].|tšu.knp.w tr.b ʿp.|tk.aḫ šmk.mlat rumm.|w yšu.ʿn h.aliyn.bʿl.|w yšu.ʿn 10[76].2.11
ṯt.ʿllm n.[---].|ilm.bt.bʿl k.[---].|dl.ylkn.ḥš.b a[rṣ.---].|b ʿpr.ḫbl ṭtm.[---.]|šqy.rṯa.tnm y.ytn.[ks.b yd].|krpn.b klat 1[ʿNT.X].4.8
.|tḥm.aliyn.bʿl.hwt.|aliy.qrdm.qry.b arṣ.|mlḥmt št.b ʿpr m.ddym.|sk.šlm.l kbd.arṣ.|arbdd.l kbd.šdm.|ḥš k.ʿṣ k 3[ʿNT].3.12
mdl h.ybʿr.|[---.]rn h.aqry.|[---.]b a[r]ṣ.mlḥmt.|ašt[.b ʿ]p[r] m.ddym.ask.|šlm.l kb[d].awṣ.arbdd.|l kbd.š[d]m.a 3[ʿNT].4.73
t.|tḥm.aliyn.bʿl.hwt.aliy.|qrdm.qry.b arṣ.mlḥmt.|št.b ʿp[r] m.ddym.sk.šlm.|l kbd.arṣ.arbdd.l kbd.šdm.|[ḥ]š k.[ʿ 3[ʿNT].4.53
[ʿ]nt.ṯṯb.|[ybmt.]limm.[a]n.aqry.|[b arṣ].mlḥmt.[aš]t.b ʿpr m.|ddym.ask[.šlm.]l kbd.arṣ.|ar[bdd.]l kb[d.š]dm.yšt. 3[ʿNT].4.67
m.|[ṯr.il.ab k.hwt.l]ṭpn.ḥtk k.|[qryy.b arṣ.mlḥ]mt.št b ʿp|[r m.ddym.sk.šlm].l kbd.arṣ.|[arbdd.l kbd.š]dm.ḥš k.| 1[ʿNT.IX].2.19
ḥm.aliyn.bʿl].|hw[t.aliy.qrdm.qryy.b arṣ.mlḥmt.št].|[b ʿ]pr[m.ddym.sk.šlm.l kbd.arṣ.arbdd].|l kbd.š[dm.ḥš k.ʿṣ 7.2[130].15
bat k bʿl.ymšḥ.|bʿl.ymšḥ.hm.b ʿp.|nṭʿn.b arṣ.ib y.|w b ʿpr.qm.aḫ k.|w tšu.ʿn h.btlt.ʿnt.|w tšu.ʿn h.w tʿn.|w tʿn.a 10[76].2.25
.ʿr.d qdm.|idk.pnm.l ytn.tk aršḫ.rbt.|w aršḫ.ṯrrt.ydy.b ʿṣm.ʿrʿr.|w b šḥt.ʿs.mt.ʿrʿrm.ynʿrn h.|ssnm.ysyn h.ʿdtm.yʿ UG5.7.64
.|[d]lbnn.adr.gdm.b rumm.|adr.qrnt.b yʿlm.mtnm.|b ʿqbt.ṯr.adr.b ǵlil.qnm.|tn.l kṯr.w ḫss.ybʿl.qšt l ʿnt.|qṣʿt.l y 17[2AQHT].6.23
k.|[ašr ilht kṯrt bn]|t hll.snnt.bnt h|ll bʿl gml.yrdt.|b ʿrgzm.b bz tdm.|lla y.ʿm lẓpn i|l ḏ.pid.hn b p y sp|r hn.b 24[77].43
.b.mnt.|arbʿ.bnšm.b.irbn.|ṯn.bnšm.b.yʿrt.|ṯn.bnšm.b.ʿrmt.|arbʿ.bnšm.b.šrš.|ṯṯ.bnšm.b.mlk.|arbʿ.bnšm.b.bṣr.|ṯ 2076.36
šmal.|d alpm.w alp w š.|šrp.w šlmm kmm.|l bʿl.ṣpn b ʿrʿr.|pamt ṯlṯm š l qrnt.|ṯlḥn.bʿlt.bhtm.|ʿlm.ʿlm.gdlt l bʿl. UG5.13.29
b nši[.ʿn h.w yphn.yḥd].|b ʿrpt[.nšrm.yšu].|[g h.]w yṣḥ[.knp.nšrm].|bʿl.yṯb.bʿl.yṯb[r. 19[1AQHT].2.106
k.|wn ap.ʿdn.mṭr h.|bʿl.yʿdn.ʿdn.ṯkt.b glṯ.|w tn.ql h.b ʿrpt.|šrh.l arṣ.brqm.|bt.arzm.yklln h.|hm.bt.lbnt.yʿmsn 4[51].5.70
rbʿ[.k]dwṯm.w.ṯṯ.ṯprtm.|b.ʿšr[m.]ksp.|ḫmš.kkr.ṣml.|b.ʿšrt.b d.bn.kyn.|ʿšr.kkr.šʿrt.|b d.urtn.b.arbʿm.|arbʿt.ʿšrt.ḫ 2100.13
[-----].|[ḫ]pn.aḥd.b.ṯqlm.|lbš.aḥd.b.ṯqlm.|ḫpn.pṯtm.b ʿšr.|tgmr.ksp.ṯlṯm.|ṯqlm.kbd. 1115.4
lbš.aḥd.|b.ʿšrt.|w.ṯn.b.ḫmšt.|ṯprt.b.ṯlṯt.|mṯyn.b.ṯṯt.|ṯn.lbšm.b.ʿšrt.| 1108.2
r.|b.ṯmnym.ksp.ṯlṯt.kbd.|ḫmš.alp.ṯlṯ.l.ḫlby.|b d.tlmi.b.ʿšrm.ḫmšt.|kbd.ksp.|kkrm.šʿrt.štt.b d.gg[ʿt].|b.ʿšrt.ksp.|ṯ 2101.7
.b.šbʿm.|ṯlṯ.mat.trm.b.ʿšrt.|mit.adrm.b.ʿšrt.|ʿšr.ydt.b.ʿšrt.|ḫmš.kkrm.ṣml.|ʿšrt.ksp h.|ḫmš.kkr.qnm.|ṯlṯt.w.ṯlṯt. 1127.9
b.bt.mlk.|b.mit.ḫmšt.kbd.ksp.|ṯlṯ.ktnt.b d.an[r]my.|b.ʿšrt.ksp.b.a[--].|ṯqlm.ḫr[ṣ.]b.ṯmnt.ksp.|ʿšrt.ksp.b.alp.[b d] 2101.19

.ksp.|‘šr.ṣin.b.ṯṯt.w.kmsk.|arb‘[.k]dwṯm.w.ṯt.ṯprtm.|b.‘šr[m.]ksp.|ḫmš.kkr.ṣml.|b.‘šrt.b d.bn.kyn.|‘šr.kkr.š‘rt.| 2100.11
sp h.|ḫmšt.ḫrṣ.bt.il.|b.ḫmšt.‘šrt.ksp.|ḫmš.mat.šmt.|b.‘šrt.ksp.|‘šr.ṣin.b.ṯṯt.w.kmsk.|arb‘[.k]dwṯm.w.ṯt.ṯprtm.|b 2100.8
kkrm.š‘rt.štt.b d.gg[‘t].|b.‘šrt.ksp.|ṯlṯ.uṭbm.b d.alḫn.b.‘šrt[.k]sp.|rṭ.l.ql.d.ybl.prd.|b.ṯql.w.nṣp.ksp.|ṯmn.lbšm.w. 2101.11
.tlmi.b.‘šrm.ḫmšt.|kbd.ksp.|kkrm.š‘rt.štt.b d.gg[‘t].|b.‘šrt.ksp.|ṯlṯ.uṭbm.b d.alḫn.b.‘šrt[.k]sp.|rṭ.l.ql.d.ybl.prd.| 2101.10
ṯ.b [ṯ]ql.ṯlṯt.l.‘šrm.ksp hm.|sstm.b.šb‘m.|ṯlṯ.mat.trm.b.‘šrt.|mit.adrm.b.‘šrt.|‘šr.ydt.b.‘šrt.|ḫmš.kkrm.ṣml.|‘šrt.k 1127.7
.ksp hm.|sstm.b.šb‘m.|ṯlṯ.mat.trm.b.‘šrt.|mit.adrm.b.‘šrt.|‘šr.ydt.b.‘šrt.|ḫmš.kkrm.ṣml.|‘šrt.ksp h.|ḫmš.kkr.q 1127.8
|b.‘šrt.|w.ṯn.b.ḫmšt.|ṯprt.b.ṯlṯt.|mṯyn.b.ṯṯt.|ṯn.lbšm.b.‘šrt.|pld.b.arb‘t.|lbš.ṯn.b.ṯnt.‘šrt. 1108.6
[ṯ]n.prm.b ‘šrm.|arb‘.prm.b.‘š[r]m.|arb‘.b.arb‘m.|ṯṯm.[---.p]rm.|[-]l.b[--.---].|[---].kbd 1138.2
[ṯ]n.prm.b ‘šrm.|arb‘.prm.b.‘š[r]m.|arb‘.b.arb‘m.|ṯṯm.[---.p]rm.|[-]l. 1138.1
ḥmt.|[‘ṯt]r.w ‘ṯtpr.yisp.ḥmt.ṯṭ.w kṯṯ.|[yus]p.ḥmt.mlk.b ‘ṯtrt.yisp.ḥmt.|[kṯ]r w ḫss.y[i]sp.ḥmt.šḥr.w šlm.|[yis]p.ḥ UG5.8.17
[---]n.yšt.rpu.mlk.‘lm.w yšt.|[--.]gṯr.w yqr.il.yṯb.b.‘ṯtrt.|il.ṯpṭ.b hd r‘y.d yšr.w yḏmr.|b knr.w ṯlb.b tp.w mṣl UG5.2.1.2
|[ṭṭbḫ.šb‘m.]ḥmrm.|[k gm]n.al[i]yn.b[‘l].|[---]ḥ h.tšt bm.‘[--].|[---.]zr h.ybm.l ilm.|[id]k.l ttn.pnm.‘m.|[il.]mbk n 6.1.30[49.1.2]
.|[---.]bqt[-].|[b] ǵb.ršp mh bnš.|šrp.w ṣp ḫršḫ.|‘lm b ǵb ḫyr.|ṯmn l ṯlṯm ṣin.|šb‘.alpm.|bt b‘l.ugrt.ṯn šm.|‘lm.l UG5.12.B.3
‘t ‘šrt.b‘l.|‘rkm.|b ṯmnt.‘šrt.yr|ṯḥṣ.mlk.brr.|‘lm.tzǵ.b ǵb.ṣpn.|nḥkt.ksp.w ḫrṣ ṯ‘ ṯn šm l btbt.|alp.w š šrp.alp šl UG5.12.A.7
.|npš.w.š.l ršp bbt.|[‘]ṣrm l h.ršp [-]m.|[---.]bqt[-].|[b] ǵb.ršp mh bnš.|šrp.w ṣp ḫršḫ.|‘lm b ǵb ḫyr.|ṯmn l ṯlṯm UG5.12.B.1
mrm.|[---.bn]šm.b.ṯnq.|[---.b]nšm.b.ugrt.|[---.bn]šm.b.ǵbl.|[---.b]nšm.b.m‘r.arr.|arb‘.bnšm.b.mnt.|arb‘.bnšm.b.i 2076.31
mrḫ il.|b nit il.|b ṣmd il.|b dṯn il.|b šrp il.|b knt il.|b ǵdyn il.|[b]n [---]. 30[107].18
b.|phnn.w.|mndym.|bdnh.|l[q]ḥt.|[--]km.‘m.mlk.|[b]ǵl hm.w.iblbl hm.|w.b.ṯb h.[---].|spr ḥ[--.---].|w.‘m[.---]. 2129.10
-.---].|yṣi.ǵl h tḥm b[.---].|mrḥ h l adrt[.---].|ṯṯb ‘ṯtrt b ǵl[.---].|qrẓ tšt.l šmal[.---].|arbḫ.‘n h tšu w[.---].|aylt tǵp 2001.1.8
r.gdm.b rumm.|adr.qrnt.b y‘lm.mtnm.|b ‘qbt.ṯr.adr.b ǵlil.qnm.|tn.l kṯr.w ḫss.yb‘l.qšt l ‘nt.|qṣ‘t.l ybmt.limm.w 17[2AQHT].6.23
h.l ttn.|l y.w b mt[.-]ḥ.mṣṣ[-]t[.--].|pr‘.qẓ.y[bl].šblt.|b ǵlp h.apnk.dnil.|[m]t.rpi.ap[h]n.ǵzr.|[mt.hrn]my.ytšu.|[19[1AQHT].1.19
y.‘l.umt[k.--].|d ttql.b ym.trtḥ[ṣ.--].|[----.a]dm.tium.b ǵlp y[m.--].|d alp šd.ẓu h.b ym.t[---].|tlbš.npṣ.ǵzr.tšt.ḫ[-- 19[1AQHT].4.204
ṯ‘.ištm‘.w tqǵ udn.|k ǵz.ǵzm.tdbr.|w ǵrm.ṯṯwy.šqlt.|b ǵlt.yd k.l tdn.|dn.almnt.l ṯṯpṭ.|ṯpṭ qṣr.npš.l tdy.|ṯšm.‘l.dl 16.6[127].45
[‘].|w tqǵ[.udn.k ǵz.ǵzm].|tdbr.w[ǵ]rm[.ṯṯwy].|šqlt.b ǵlt.yd k.|l tdn.dn.almnt.|l ṯṯpṭ.ṯpṭ.qṣr.npš.|km.aḫt.‘rš.m 16.6[127].32
arḫ.td.rgm.b ǵr.|b p y.t‘lgt.b lšn[y].|ǵr[.---]b.b pš y.t[--].|hwt.b‘l.iš[--]. 2124.1
n.b‘l.|[---.--]k.mdd il.|y[m.---.]l ṯr.qdqd h.|il[.--.]rḥq.b ǵr.|km.y[--.]ilm.b ṣpn.|‘dr.l[‘r].‘rm.|ṯb.l pd[r.]pdrm.|ṯṯ.l 4[51].7.5
.|hmlt.arṣ.at m.w ank.|ibǵy h.b tk.ǵr y.il.ṣpn.|b qdš.b ǵr.nḥlt y.|b n‘m.b gb‘.tliyt.|hlm.‘nt.tph.ilm.b h.p‘nm.|ṭṭṭ 3[‘NT].3.27
d‘.šmm.at m.w ank].|ibǵ[y h.b tk.ǵ]r y.il.ṣpn.|b q[dš.b ǵr.nḥ]lt y.|w t[‘n].btlt.[‘]nt.ṯṯb.|[ybmt.]limm.[a]n.aqry.|[3[‘NT].4.64
ynn.btn[-.]|y[--.]šr h.w šḫp h.|[--.]šḫp.ṣǵrt h.|yrk.t‘l.b ǵr.|mslmt.b ǵr.tliyt.|w t‘l.bkm.b arr.|bm.arr.w b ṣpn.|b 10[76].3.28
[--.]šr h.w šḫp h.|[--.]šḫp.ṣǵrt h.|yrk.t‘l.b ǵr.|mslmt.b ǵr.tliyt.|w t‘l.bkm.b arr.|bm.arr.w b ṣpn.|b n‘m.b ǵr.t[l]i 10[76].3.29
t.b ǵr.tliyt.|w t‘l.bkm.b arr.|bm.arr.w b ṣpn.|b n‘m.b ǵr.t[l]iyt.|ql.l b‘l.ttnn.|bšrt.il.bš[r.b‘]l.|w bšr.ḥtk.dgn.|k.i 10[76].3.32
l y.|[--]t.b‘l.ḥẓ.ršp.b[n].km.yr.klyt h.w lb h.|[ṯ]n.p k.b ǵr.ṯn.p k.b ḫlb.k tgwln.šnt k.|[--.]w špt k.l tššy.hm.tqrm.l 1001.1.4
la.u[--.--].|blt.p btlt.‘n[t].|w p.n‘mt.aḫt[.b‘l].|y‘l.b‘l.b ǵ[r.---].|w bn.dgn.b š[---].|b‘l.yṯb.l ks[i.mlk h].|bn.dgn.l 10[76].3.12
l a]rṣ.špt.l šmm.|[---.l]šn.l kbkbm.y‘rb.|[b‘]l.b kbd h.b p h yrd.|k ḥrr.zt.ybl.arṣ.w pr.|‘ṣm.yraun.aliyn.b‘l.|ṯt‘.nn. 5[67].2.4
nǵr.|‘nn.ilm.al.|tqrb.l bn.ilm.|mt.al.y‘db km.|k imr.b p h.|k lli.b ṯbrn.|qn h.tḫtan.|nrt.ilm.špš.|ṣḥrrt.la.|šmm. 4[51].8.18
m]drt.|ur.tisp k.yd.aqht.ǵz[r].|tšt k.bm.qrb m.asm.|b p h.rgm.l yṣa.b špt h[.hwt h].|b nši ‘n h.w tphn.in.[---].|[- 19[1AQHT].2.75
hm.iṯ.šmt.iṯ.|‘ẓm.abky w aqbrn h.aštn.|b ḫrt.ilm.arṣ.b p h.rgm.l[yṣ]a.|b špt h.hwt h.knp.ṣml.b‘[l].|b‘l.ṯbr.diy.h 19[1AQHT].3.141
.šmt.hm.i[ṯ].|‘ẓm.abky.w aqbrn h.|ašt.b ḫrt.ilm.arṣ.|b p h.rgm.l yṣa.b špt h.hwt[h].|knp.nšrm.b‘l.yṯbr.|b‘l.ṯbr.d 19[1AQHT].3.113
.iṯ.šmt.hm.iṯ[.‘ẓm].|abky.w aqbrn.ašt.b ḫrt.|i[lm.arṣ.b p h.rgm.l yṣa.b šp]|t h.hwt h.knp.hrgb.b‘l.ṯbr.|b‘l.ṯbr.diy 19[1AQHT].3.127
šmm.|w dg b ym.w ndd.gzr.l zr.y‘db.u ymn.|u šmal.b p hm.w l.tšb‘n y.aṯt.itrḫ.|y bn.ašld.šu.‘db.tk.mdbr qdš.|ṯ 23[52].64
ym.bn ym.ynqm.b ap.ḏd.št.špt.|l arṣ.špt l šmm.w ‘rb.b p hm.‘ṣr.šmm.|w dg b ym.w ndd.gzr.l zr.y‘db.u ymn.|u š 23[52].62
r.ysmt.šd.šḥlmmt.|ngš.ank.aliyn b‘l.|‘dbnn ank.imr.b p y.|k lli.b ṯbrn q y.ḫtu hw.|nrt.ilm.špš.ṣḥrrt.|la.šmm.b 6[49].2.22
l.yrdt.|b ‘rgzm.b bz tdm.|lla y.‘m lẓpn i|l ḏ.pid.hn b p y sp|r hn.b špt y mn|t hn ṯlḫ h w mlg h y|ṯtqt ‘m h b q 24[77].45
arḫ.td.rgm.b ǵr.|b p y.t‘lgt.b lšn[y].|ǵr[.---]b.b pš y.t[--].|hwt.b‘l.iš[--].|šm‘ 2124.2
].|kr[pn.---].|at.š[‘tqt.---].|š‘d[.---].|rt.[---].|‘ṭr[.---].|b p.š[---].|il.p.d[---].|‘rm.[di.mh.pdrm].|di.š[rr.---].|mr[ṣ.- 16[126].5.46
tldn.|ṯrkn.|kli.|plǵn.|apšny.|‘rb[.---].|w.b.p[.--].|apš[ny].|b.yṣi h.|ḥwt.[---].|alp.k[sp].|tš‘n.|w.hm. 2116.7
|yph.b yǵlm.bṣql.y[ḥb]q.|w ynšq.aḥl.an bṣ[ql].|ynp‘.b palt.bṣql yp‘ b yǵlm.|ur.tisp k.yd.aqht.|ǵzr.tšt k.b qrb m. 19[1AQHT].2.65
]mt ‘r.|l ysmsm.bmt.pḫl.|y dnil.ysb.palt h.|bṣql.yph.b palt.bṣ[q]l.|yph.b yǵlm.bṣql.y[ḥb]q.|w ynšq.aḥl.an bṣ[ql]. 19[1AQHT].2.62
d.kbd.hmt.b‘l.|ḥkpt.il.kl h.tšm‘.|mṯt.dnty.t‘db.imr.|b pḫd.l npš.kṯr.w ḫss.|l brlt.hyn.d ḥrš.|ydm.aḫr.ymǵy.kṯr. 17[2AQHT].5.23
t.|hrnmy.gm.l aṯt h.k yṣḥ.|šm‘.mṯt.dnty.‘d[b].|imr.b pḫd.l npš.kṯr.|w ḫss.l brlt.hyn d.|ḥrš yd.šlḥm.ššqy.|ilm s 17[2AQHT].5.17
.b.ṯǵrm.|rb qrt.aḫd.|ṯmn.ḫzr.|w.arb‘.ḥršm.|dt.tb‘ln.b.pḫn.|ṯṯtm.ḫzr.w.‘št.‘šr.ḥrš.|dt.tb‘ln.b.ugrt.|ṯṯtm.ḫzr.|dt.t 1024.3.6
‘n.ḥtk h.rš.|mid.grdš.ṯbt h.|w b tm hn.špḥ.yitbd.|w b.pḫyr h.yrṯ.|y‘rb.b ḥdr h.ybky.|b ṯn.[-]gmm.w ydm‘.|tntk 14[KRT].1.25
[-----].|[---.mid.rm.]krt.|[b tk.rpi.]arṣ.|[b pḫr].qbṣ.dtn.|[w t]qrb.w ld.|bn.tl k.|tld.pǵt.t[--]t.|tld.pǵ 15[128].3.4
d.pǵ[t.---].|tld.p[ǵt.---].|mid.rm[.krt].|b tk.rpi.ar[ṣ].|b pḫr.qbṣ.dtn.|ṣǵrt hn.abkrn.|tbrk.ilm.tity.|tity.ilm.l ahl h 15[128].3.15
.[m]rṣ gršt.|zbln.r[---].ymlu.|n‘m.[-]ṯ[-.--.]yqrṣ.|d[-] b pḫ[-.--.]mḫt.|[---.]tnn.|[---.]tnn. 16[126].5.30
m.|b‘l.ḥmd m.yḥmd m.|bn.dgn.yhrr m.|b‘l.ngṯ hm.b p‘n h.|w il hd.b ḫrẓ‘ h.|[-----].|[--]t.[---].|[---.]‘n[.---].|pn 12[75].1.40
tyn.ṯlṯ.rb‘.ym.ḫmš.|ṯdṯ.ym.tlḥmn.rpum.|tštyn.bt.ikl.b pr‘.|yṣq.b irt.lbnn.mk.b šb‘.|[ymm.---]k.aliyn.b‘l.|[---].r‘ 22.2[124].24
arḫ.td.rgm.b ǵr.|b p y.t‘lgt.b lšn[y].|ǵr[.---]b.b pš y.t[--].|hwt.b‘l.iš[--].|šm‘ l y.ypš.[---].|ḥkr[.---].|‘ṣr[.--. 2124.3
ṯ]lrby.‘šr.ṯn.kb[d.---].|ḫmrm.ṯṯ.krm[m.---].|krm.ǵlkz.b.p[--.---].|krm.ilyy.b.m[--.---].|kd.šb‘.krmm.[---].|ṯn.krm[1081.23
h.šmmh.dbḥ.|l ṯr.ab h.il.šrd.|[b‘l].b dbḥ h.bn dgn.|[b m]ṣd h.yrd.krt.|[l g]gt.‘db.akl.l qryt.|ḥṭt.l bt.ḫbr.|yip.lḥ 14[KRT].4.171
yd k.|šmm.dbḥ.l ṯr.|ab k.il.šrd.b‘l.|b dbḥ k.bn.dgn.|b mṣd k.w yrd.|krt.l ggt.‘db.|akl.l qryt.|ḥṭt.l bt.ḫbr.|yip.lḥ 14[KRT].2.79
.šb‘.ṯir k.[---].|[---.]ab y.ndt.ank[.---].|[---.--]l.mlk.tlk.b ṣd[.---].|[---.]mt.išryt[.---].|[---.--]r.almd k.[---].|[---.]qrt.a 18[3AQHT].1.27
rm.mid.tmtḫṣn.w t]‘n.tḫtṣb.|[w tḥdy.‘nt.tǵdd.kbd h.b ṣḥ]q.ymlu.lb h.|[b šmḫt.kbd.‘nt.tšyt.tḥt h.k]kdrt.riš.|[‘l 7.1[131].7

rm.|mid.tmtḫṣn.w tʻn.|tḫtṣb.w tḥdy.ʻnt.|tǵdd.kbd h.b ṣḥq.ymlu.|lb h.b šmḫt.kbd.ʻnt.|tšyt.k brkm.tǵll b dm.|d̲ 3[ʻNT].2.25
il.|il ḥš il add.|bʻl ṣpn bʻl.|ugrt.|b mrḥ il.|b nit il.|b ṣmd il.|b dt̲n il.|b šrp il.|b knt il.|b ǵdyn il.|[b]n [---]. 30[107].14
yiḫd.bʻl.bn.at̲rt.|rbm.ymḫṣ.b ktp.|dk ym.ymḫṣ.b ṣmd.|ṣḥr mt.ymṣḫ.l arṣ.|[yt̲b.]b[ʻ]l.l ksi.mlk h.|[---].l kḥt̲. 6[49].5.3
t.km.rḥ.npš[h.km.it̲l].|brlt h.km.qt̲r.[b ap h.---].|ʻnt.b ṣmt.mhr h.[---].|aqht.w tbk.y[---.---].|abn.ank.w ʻl.[qšt k. 18[3AQHT].4.38
t.npš.blt.|ḥmr.p imt.b klt.|yd y.ilḥm.hm.šbʻ.|ydt y.b ṣʻ.hm.ks.ymsk.|nhr.k[--].ṣḥn.bʻl.ʻm.|aḫ y.qran.hd.ʻm.ary 5[67].1.21
t.|tḫṣb.bn.t̲lḥnm.ymḥ.|[b]bt.dm.d̲mr.yṣq.šmn.|šlm.b ṣʻ.trḥṣ.yd h.bt|[l]t.ʻnt.uṣbʻt h.ybmt.limm.|[t]rḥṣ.yd h.b d 3[ʻNT].2.32
r.ur[--.---].|[---.n]skt.nʻmn.nbl[.---].|[--.]yṣq šmn.šlm.b ṣ[ʻ.trḥṣ].|yd h.btlt.ʻnt.uṣbʻt[h.ybmt].|limm.tiḫd.knr h.b UG5.3.2.4
.ḫ]br[.---].|bḫr[.--]t[.----].|l mt̲b[.--]t[.---].|[tqdm.]yd.b ṣʻ.t[šl]ḥ.|[ḥrb.b]bš[r].tštn.|[w tʻn].mt̲t.ḥry.|[l lḥ]m.l šty.ṣ 15[128].5.7
.t̲rrt.|bt.krt.tbun.|lm.mt̲b[.---].|w lḥm mr.tqdm.|yd.b ṣʻ.tšlḥ.|ḥrb.b bšr.tštn.|[w t]ʻn.mt̲t.ḥry.|[l lḥ]m.l šty.ṣḥt k 15[128].4.24
m.|ʻn.kd̲d.aylt.|mt hm.ks.ym|sk.nhr hm.|šbʻ.ydt y.b ṣʻ.|[--.]šbʻ.rbt.|[---.]qbṭ.t̲m.|[---.]bn.ilm.|[m]t.šmḥ.p ydd. UG5.4.11
|d ʻq h.ib.iqni.ʻp[ʻp] h.|sp.t̲rml.tḥgrn.[-]dm[.-].|ašlw.b ṣp.ʻn h.|d b ḥlm y.il.ytn.|b d̲rt y.ab.adm.|w ld.špḥ.l krt.| 14[KRT].3.149
.tʻl.b ǵr.|mslmt.b ǵr.tliyt.|w tʻl.bkm.b arr.|bm.arr.w b ṣpn.|b nʻm.b ǵr.t[l]iyt.|ql.l bʻl.ttnn.|bšrt.il.bš[r.bʻ]l.|w bš 10[76].3.31
il.|y[m.---.]l t̲r.qdqd h.|il[.--.]rḥq.b ǵr.|km.y[--.]ilm.b ṣpn.|ʻdr.l[ʻr].ʻrm.|t̲b.l pd[r.]pdrm.|t̲t̲.l t̲t̲m.aḫd.ʻr.|šbʻm. 4[51].7.6
m.ym]m.|[yʻtqn.---.ymǵy.]npš.|[---.h]d.tngt̲n h.|[---].b ṣpn.|[---].nšb.b ʻn.|[---.]b km.yʻn.|[---.ydʻ.l] ydʻt.|[---.t]as 1[ʻNT.X].5.5
[yʻtqn.---].ymǵy.npš.|[---.--]t.hd.tngt̲m h.|[---.-]ḥm k b ṣpn.|[---.]išqb.aylt.|[---.--]m.b km.yʻn.|[---].ydʻ.l ydʻt.|[--- 1[ʻNT.X].5.18
] k.|[-----].|[-----].|[--].bt.gb[-.--].|[--]k[-].w.špš.|[---.b].ṣp[n].|[---.]š[--].|[-----].|[-----].|[---.]t̲ty.|[---.-]rd y.|[---.] 2159.10
.mnm[.š]lm.|rgm.t̲t̲[b].|any kn.dt.|likt.mṣrm.|hn dt.b.ṣr.|mtt.by.|gšm.adr.|nškḥ.w.|rb.tmtt.|lqḥ.kl.d̲rʻ.|b d a[- 2059.12
.|[šbʻ] d.šbʻ [d].|[mr]ḥqtm.|qlt.|ʻbd k.b.|lwsnd.|[w] b ṣr.|ʻm.mlk.|w.ht.|mlk.syr.|ns.w.t̲m.|ydbḥ.|mlǵ[.---].|w. 2063.11
h.|qm.ybd.w yšr.|mṣltm.bd.nʻm.|yšr.ǵzr.ṭb.ql.|ʻl.bʻl.b ṣrrt.|ṣpn.ytmr.bʻl.|bnt h.yʻn.pdry.|bt.ar.apn.ṭly.|[bt.r]b. 3[ʻNT].1.21
ʻ.nrt.ilm.špš.|tšu.aliyn.bʻl.l ktp.|ʻnt.k tšt h.tšʻlyn h.|b ṣrrt.ṣpn.tbkyn h.|w tqbrn h.tštnn.b ḫrt.|ilm.arṣ.tṭbḫ.šbʻ 6[62].1.16
ǵyn.|hdm.riš h.l ymǵy.|aps h.w yʻn.ʻt̲tr.ʻrẓ.|l amlk.b ṣrrt.ṣpn.|yrd.ʻt̲tr.ʻrẓ.yrd.|l kḥt̲.aliyn.bʻl.|w ymlk.b arṣ.il. 6.1.62[49.1.34]
m.|blt.nmlk.ʻt̲tr.ʻrẓ.|ymlk.ʻt̲tr.ʻrẓ.|apnk.ʻt̲tr.ʻrẓ.|yʻl.b ṣrrt.ṣpn.|yt̲b.l kḥt̲.aliyn.|bʻl.pʻn h.l tmǵyn.|hdm.riš h.l y 6.1.57[49.1.29]
n kly.|lḥm.[b]ʻdn hm.kly.|yn.b ḥmt hm.k[l]y.|šmn.b q[bʻt hm.---].|bt.krt.t[--]. 16[126].3.16
.aliyn.bʻl.|iy.zbl.bʻl.arṣ.|w tʻn.nrt.ilm.š[p]š.|šd yn.ʻn.b qbt[.t]|bl lyt.ʻl.umt k.|w abqt̲.aliyn.bʻl.|w tʻn.btlt.ʻnt.|an. 6[49].4.42
] ḫlmṭ.|l bbt il bt.|š l ḫlmṭ.|w tr l qlḥ.|w š ḥll ydm.|b qdš il bt.|w tlḥm at̲t.|š l ilbt.šlmm.|kll ylḥm b h.|w l bbt UG5.7.TR3
l tbn.|hmlt.arṣ.at m.w ank.|ibǵy h.b tk.ǵr y.il.ṣpn.|b qdš.b ǵr.nḥlt y.|b nʻm.b gbʻ.tliyt.|hlm.ʻnt.tph.ilm.b h.pʻn 3[ʻNT].3.27
.|d l t[dʻ.šmm.at m.w ank].|ibǵ[y h.b tk.ǵ]r y.il.ṣpn.|b q[dš.b ǵr.nḥ]lt y.|w t[ʻn].btlt.[ʻ]nt.t̲t̲b.|[ybmt.]limm.[a]n. 3[ʻNT].4.64
nwt.|w ykn.bn h b bt.šrš.b qrb.|hkl h.nṣb.skn.ilib h.b qdš.|ztr.ʻm h.l arṣ.mšṣu.qṭr h.|l ʻpr.d̲mr.at̲r h.ṭbq.lḥt.|niṣ 17[2AQHT].1.27
i.w ykn.bn h.|[b bt.šrš.]b qrb.hkl h.|[nṣb.skn.i]lib h.b qdš.|[ztr.ʻm h.l a]rṣ.mšṣu.|[qṭr h.l ʻpr.d̲]mr.a[t̲]r h.|[ṭbq.l 17[2AQHT].1.45
.k yld.bn.l y.km.|aḫ y.w šrš.km ary y.|nṣb.skn.ilib y.b qdš.|ztr.ʻm y.l ʻpr.d̲mr.at̲r[y].|ṭbq lḥt.niṣ y.grš.|d ʻšy.ln. 17[2AQHT].2.16
k]n.ulp.q[r zbl].|u tḫṭin.b ap kn.u b [q]ṣrt.npš[kn.u b qṭt].|tqṭṭn u tḫṭin.l bḥm.w l t̲ʻ.d[bḥ n.ndbḥ].|hw.t̲ʻ.nt̲ʻy.h 32[2].1.14
km.ulp.qr zbl].|[u tḫṭu.u b ap km.u b qṣrt.npš km.u b qṭt].|[tqṭṭ.u tḫṭu.l dbḥm.w l.t̲ʻ.dbḥ n.ndb]ḥ.|[hw.t̲ʻ.nt̲ʻy.h 32[2].1.8A
lp.qr zbl.u[š]n yp km.|u b ap km.u b q[ṣ]rt.npš km.u b qṭt.tqṭṭ.|ušn yp km.l d[b]ḥm.w l.t̲ʻ.dbḥ n.ndbḥ.hw.t̲ʻ |nt̲ʻ 32[2].1.23
lp].|[qr zbl.ušn.yp km.b ap km.u b qṣrt.np]št km.|[u b qṭt.tqṭṭ.ušn.yp km.---.-]yt km.|[---.]km.|[-----].|[---.]ugrt. APP.I[-].1.18
kn.ulp qr z[bl].|lšn yp kn.b ap [kn.u b qṣ]rt.npš kn.u b qṭt.|tqṭṭn.ušn y[p kn.l dbḥm.]w l t̲ʻ dbḥ n.|ndbḥ.hw.t̲ʻ n[t̲ 32[2].1.31
.ulp.qr zbl.ušn.y]p kn.|[u b ap kn.u b qṣrt.npšt kn.u b qṭ]t tqṭṭ.|[ušn.yp kn.---.--]l.il.tʻd̲r bʻl.|[-----.]lšnt.|[---.--]y APP.I[-].1.7
n.ulp.]qr zbl.|[ušn.yp kn.u b ap kn.u b qṣrt.npš kn.u b]qṭt.|[tqṭṭn.ušn.yp kn.---.-]gym.|[---.]l kbkb.|[-----]. APP.I[-].2.15
.|apnk.dnil.mt.|rpi.yṣly.ʻrpt.b |ḥm.un.yr.ʻrpt.|tmṭr.b qẓ.ṭl.yṭll.|l ǵnbm.šbʻ.šnt.|yṣr k.bʻl.t̲mn.rkb.|ʻrpt.bl.ṭl.bl r 19[1AQHT].1.41
---].|bk[--.--].yq[--.--].|w [---.]rkb[.---].|[---].d[--.---].|b ql[.-----].|w tštqdn[.-----].|hm.|w yḥ.mlk.|w ik m.kn.w [- 62[26].6
|l yt̲br.ḫṭ.mt̲pṭ k.|yru.bn ilm t.t̲tʻ.y|dd.il.ǵzr.yʻr.mt.|b ql h.y[---.---].|bʻl.yt̲t̲bn[.l ksi].|mlk h.l[nḫt.l kḥt̲].|drkt h 6[49].6.32
[--].|b[n.---].|šm[-.---].|tkn[.---].|knn.b.ḫ[lb].|bn mt̲.b.qmy.|nʻr.b.ulm. 2046.2.5
imr.qmṣ.llim.k ksp.|l ʻbrm.zt.ḫrṣ.l ʻbrm.kš.|dpr.t̲lḥn.b qʻl.b qʻl.|mlkm.hn.ym.yṣq.yn.t̲mk.|mrt̲.yn.srnm.yn.bld.| 22.2[124].16
mṣ.llim.k ksp.|l ʻbrm.zt.ḫrṣ.l ʻbrm.kš.|dpr.t̲lḥn.b qʻl.b qʻl.|mlkm.hn.ym.yṣq.yn.t̲mk.|mrt̲.yn.srnm.yn.bld.|ǵll.y 22.2[124].16
y sp|r hn.b špt y mn|t hn t̲lḫ h w mlg h y|t̲tqt ʻm h b qʻt.|tqʻt ʻm prbḫt̲.|dmqt ṣǵrt kt̲rt. 24[77].48
r h.km.lb.ʻn[t].|at̲r.bʻl.tiḫd.m[t].|b sin.lpš.tšṣq[n h].|b qṣ.all.tšu.g h.w[tṣ]|ḥ.at.mt.tn.aḫ y.|w ʻn.bn.ilm.mt.mh.| 6[49].2.11
.ulp.m[dl]l km.ulp.qr zbl.u[š]n yp km.|u b ap km.u b q[ṣ]rt.npš km.u b qṭt.tqṭṭ.|ušn yp km.l d[b]ḥm.w l.t̲ʻ.dbḥ 32[2].1.23
ḫbt km.ulp.mdll km.ulp.qr zbl].|[u tḫṭu.u b ap km.u b qṣrt.npš km.u b qṭt].|[tqṭṭ.u tḫṭu.l dbḥm.w l.t̲ʻ.dbḥ n.ndb 32[2].1.8A
t km.ulp.mdll km.ulp].|[qr zbl.ušn.yp km.b ap km.u b qṣrt.np]št km.|[u b qṭt.tqṭṭ.ušn.yp km.---.-]yt km.|[---.]k APP.I[-].1.17
t kn.ulp.mdll kn.ulp.]qr zbl.|[ušn.yp kn.u b ap kn.u b qṣrt.npš kn.u b]qṭt.|[tqṭṭn.ušn.yp kn.---.-]gym.|[---.]l kb APP.I[-].2.15
kn.|[ulp.mdll kn.ulp.qr zbl.ušn.y]p kn.|[u b ap kn.u b qṣrt.npšt kn.u b qṭ]t tqṭṭ.|[ušn.yp kn.---.--]l.il.tʻd̲r bʻl.|[--- APP.I[-].1.7
t] kn[.u]lp.mdll kn.ulp qr z[bl].|lšn yp kn.b ap [kn.u b qṣ]rt.npš kn.u b qṭt.|tqṭṭn.ušn y[p kn.l dbḥm.]w l t̲ʻ dbḥ 32[2].1.31
p.ḫbt kn.ulp.md[ll k]n.ulp.q[r zbl].|u tḫṭin.b ap kn.u b [q]ṣrt.npš[kn.u b qṭt].|tqṭṭn u tḫṭin.l bḥm.w l t̲ʻ.d[bḥ n.n 32[2].1.14
.šbʻ.pdr.|t̲mnym.bʻl.[----].|tšʻm.bʻl.mr[-].|bt[.--]b bʻl.b qrb.|bt.w yʻn.aliyn.|bʻl.ašt m.kt̲r bn.|ym.kt̲r.bnm.ʻdt.|yp 4[51].7.13
[---.bʻl.b bht h].|[il.hd.b qr]b.hkl h.|w tʻnyn.ǵlm.bʻl.|in.bʻl.b bht ht.|il hd.b qrb.h 10[76].2.2
.bht.ṭhrm.|iqnim.šmḫ.aliyn.|bʻl.ṣḥ.ḫrn.b bht h.|ʻd̲bt.b qrb hkl h.|yblnn ǵrm.mid.ksp.|gbʻm lḥmd.ḫrṣ.|yblnn.ud 4[51].5.99
--.--] n.ylt.ḥmḥmt.|[---.mt.r]pi.w ykn.bn h.|[b bt.šrš.]b qrb.hkl h.|[nṣb.skn.i]lib h.b qdš.|[ztr.ʻm h.l a]rṣ.mšṣu.|[17[2AQHT].1.44
n l t̲r.il ab y.|tmrnn.l bny.bnwt.|w ykn.bn h b bt.šrš.b qrb.|hkl h.nṣb.skn.ilib h.b qdš.|ztr.ʻm h.l arṣ.mšṣu.qṭr h. 17[2AQHT].1.26
lm.d[t].|šnt.imr.qmṣ.l[l]im.|ṣḥ.aḫ h.b bht h.a[r]y h.|b qrb hkl h.ṣḥ.|šbʻm.bn.at̲rt.|špq.ilm.krm.y[n].|špq.ilht.ḫp 4[51].6.45
d.b qr]b.hkl h.|w tʻnyn.ǵlm.bʻl.|in.bʻl.b bht ht.|il hd.b qrb.hkl h.|qšt hn.aḫd.b yd h.|w qṣʻt h.bm.ymn h.|idk.l y 10[76].2.5
k h].|nḫt.kḥt̲.d[rkt h.b bt y].|aṣḥ.rpi[m.iqra.ilnym].|b qrb.h[kl y.at̲r h.rpum.l] |tdd.at̲r[h.l tdd.ilnym].|asr.mr[22.1[123].20
n.|[---.]il.d ʻrgzm.|[---.]dt.ʻl.lty.|[---.]tdbḥ.amr.|t̲mn.b qrb.hkl y.[at̲r h.rpum].|tdd.at̲r h.tdd.iln[ym.---].|asr.ssw 20[121].2.1
nk.yrp.|[---.]km.rʻy.ht.alk.|[---.]t̲lt̲t.amǵy.l bt.|[y.---.b qrb].hkl y.w yʻn.il.|[---.mrzʻ]y.lk.bt y.rpim.|[rpim.bt y.aṣ 21[122].1.8
[--].[-]l[--.b qr]|b hkl y.[---].|lk bt y.r[pim.rpim.b bt y.aṣḥ].|km.iqr[a 22.1[123].1

bt.l k.km.aẖ k.w ḥẓr.|km.ary k.ṣḥ.ẖrn.|b bht k.'ḏbt.b qrb.|hkl k.tbl k.ġrm.|mid.ksp.gb'm.mḥmd..|ẖrṣ.w bn.bh 4[51].5.92
nt.y'msn h.|l yrgm.l aliyn b'l.|ṣḥ.ẖrn.b bhm k.|'ḏbt.b qrb.hkl k.|tbl k.ġrm.mid.ksp.|gb'm.mḥmd.ẖrṣ.|ybl k.ud 4[51].5.76
[b.hk]l m.|w 'n.ali[yn.]b'l.|al.tšt.u[rb]t.b bht m.|ḥln.b q[rb.hk]l m.|al td[.pdr]y.bt ar.|[---.ṯl]y.bt.rb.|[---.m]dd.il 4[51].6.9
]ḫss.|šm'.m'.l al[iy]n b'l.|bl.ašt.ur[bt.]b bht m.|ḥln.b qr[b.hk]l m.|w 'n.ali[yn.]b'l.|al.tšt.u[rb]t.b bht m.|ḥln.b 4[51].6.6
'.l aliyn b'l.|bn.l rkb.'rpt.|bl.ašt.urbt.b bh[t] m.|ḥln.b qrb.hkl m.|w y'n.aliyn b'l.|al.tšt.urbt.b[bhtm].|[ḥln].b q 4[51].5.124
t m.kṯr bn.|ym.kṯr.bnm.'dt.|ypth.ḥln.b bht m.|urbt.b qrb.[h]kl |m.w y[p]tḥ.b dqt.'rpt.|'l h[wt].kṯr.w ḫss.|ṣḥq. 4[51].7.18
la[t.]b hkl m.|ẖmš.ṯ[d]ṯ.ym.tikl.|išt.[b]bht m.nblat.|b[qrb.hk]l m.mk.|b šb['.]y[mm].td.išt.|b bht m.n[bl]at.b h 4[51].6.31
.l ali|yn.b'l.ṯṯbn.b'l.|l hwt y.yptḥ.ḥ|ln.b bht m.urbt.|b qrb.hk[l m.yp]tḥ.|b'l.b dqt[.'rp]t.|ql h.qdš.b['l.y]tn.|yṯny 4[51].7.27
rb.hkl m.|w y'n.aliyn b'l.|al.tšt.urbt.b[bhtm].|[ḥln].b qrb.hk[l m]. 4[51].5.127
aklt.šblt.tp'[.b ḥm]drt.|ur.tisp k.yd.aqht.ġz[r].|tšt k.bm.qrb m.asm.|b p h.rgm.l yṣa.b špt h[.hwt h].|b nši 'n h. 19[1AQHT].2.74
p'.b palt.bṣql yp' b yġlm.|ur.tisp k.yd.aqht.|ġzr.tšt k.b qrb m.asm.|y.dnh.ysb.aklt h.yph.|šblt.b akt.šblt.yp'.|b ḥ 19[1AQHT].2.67
y'n.dnil.[mt.rpi].|yṯb.ġzr.mt hrnmy[.---].|b grnt.ilm.b qrb.m[ṭ'].ilnym].|d tit.yspi.spu.q[--.---].|tpḥ.ṯṣr.shr[.---].| 20[121].2.9
|[---.--]n.irš[.---].|[---.--]mr.ph.|[---.--]mm.hlkt.|[---.]b qrb.'r.|[---.m]lakm l h.|[---.]l.bn.il.|[---.--]a.'d h.|[---.--]r 26[135].5
[--].yṯkḥ.w yiḥd.b qrb[.-].|[--.t]ṯkḥ.w tiḥd.b uš[k.--].|[-.b]'l.yabd.l alp.|[---.b 11[132].1.1
|dt.lbn k[.---].|dk k.kbkb[.---].|dm.mt.aṣḥ[.---].|ydd.b qr[b.---].|al.ašt.b[---].|ahpk k.l[--.---].|ṯmm.w lk[.---].|w 5[67].3.10
r.[-]ḥm k.w št.|[---.]ẓ[--.-]rdy k.|[---.i]qnim.|[---.-]šu.b qrb.|[---].asr.|[---.--]m.ymt m.|[---].k iṯl.|[---.--]m.'db.l ar 1['NT.IX].2.6
--].|šgr.mu[d.---].|šgr.mud[.---].|dm.mt.aṣ[ḥ.---].|yd.b qrb[.---].|w lk.ilm.[---].|w rgm.l [---].|b mud.ṣin[.---].|m 5[67].3.19
].|mud.ṣin[.---].|iṯm.mui[-.---].|dm.mt.aṣ[ḥ.---].|ydd.b qr[b.---].|ṯmm.w lk[.---].|[--]ṯ.lk[.---].|[--]kṯ.il[--.---].|p.š 5[67].3.26
il dbḥ.b bt h.mṣd.ṣd.b qrb|hkl [h].ṣḥ.l qṣ.ilm.tlḥmn.|ilm.w tštn.tštn y[n] 'd šb'.| UG5.1.1.1
].|qrt.ablm.ablm.[qrt.zbl.yrẖ].|ik.al.yḥdṯ.yrẖ.b[---].|b qrn.ymn h.b anšt[.---].|qdqd h.w y'n.yṭpn.[mhr.št].|šm'.l 18[3AQHT].4.10
|y'db.lḥm.l h.w d l yd'nn.|d.mṣd.|ylmn.ẖṯ.tḥt.ṯlḥn.|b qr'.|'ṯtrt.w 'nt.ymġy.|'ṯtrt.t'db.nšb l h.|w 'nt.ktp.b hm.y UG5.1.1.8B
-].|l šrr.w t'[n.'ṯtrt.---].|b'l m.hmt.[---].|l šrr.šṯ[.---].|b riš h.[---].|ib h.mš[--.---].|[b]n.'n h[.---]. 2.4[68].38
at.yp't.b[--.---].|aliyn.b'l[.---].|drkt k.mšl[-.---].|b riš k.aymr[.---].|ṯpṭ.nhr.yṯb[r.ḥrn.y ym.yṯbr.ḥrn].|riš k.'ṯ 2.1[137].6
qmp'.|mlk.ugrt.|ytn.bt.anndr.|bn.ytn.bnš.|[ml]k.d.b riš.|[--.-]nt.|[l.'b]dmlk.|[--.-]m[-]r.|[w.l.]bn h.'d.|['l]m.m 1009.7
t.limm.|w y'n.aqht.ġzr.adr.ṯqbm.|[d]lbnn.adr.gdm.b rumm.|adr.qrnt.b y'lm.mtnm.|b 'qbt.ṯr.adr.b ġlil.qnm.|t 17[2AQHT].6.21
n kd w kd.|w 'l ym kdm.|w b ṯlṯ.kd yn w krsnm.|w b rb' kdm yn.|w b ẖmš kd yn. 1086.4
šš[r]t.ẖrṣ.ṯqlm.kbd.'šrt.mzn h.|b [ar]b'm.ksp.|b d[.'b]dym.ṯlṯ.kkr š'rt.|iqn[i]m.ṯṯt.'šrt.ksp 2100.2
n.b.ẖmšt.|ṯprt.b.ṯlṯt.|mṯyn.b.ṯṯt.|ṯn.lbšm.b.'šrt.|pld.b.arb't.|lbš.ṯn.b.ṯnt.'šrt. 1108.7
b.ym.ḥdṯ.|b.yr.pgrm.|lqḥ.b'lmḏr.|w.bn.ẖlp.|miḥd.|b.arb'.|mat.ẖrṣ. 1156.6
rẖ.pgrm.|lqḥ.b'lm'ḏr.|w bn.ẖlp.|w[--]y.d.b'l.|miḥd.b.|arb'.mat.|ẖrṣ. 1155.6
--].|bn[.---].|bn[.---].|w.yn[.---].|bn.'dr[.---].|ntb[t].|b.arb['].|mat.ẖr[ṣ]. 2007.11
n.b.arb'm.|arb't.'šrt.ẖrṣ.|b.ṯqlm.kbd.arb'm.|'šrt.ẖrṣ.b.arb'm.|mit.ẖršḥ.b.ṯqlm.|w.šb'.'šr.šmn.|d.l.yṣa.bt.mlk.|tg 2100.18
atn.w ṯlṯ h.ẖrṣm.|ylk ym.w ṯn.|ṯlṯ.rb'.ym.|aẖr.špšm.b rb'.|ymġy.l udm.rbt.|w udm[.ṯr]rt.|grnn.'rm.|šrnn.pdrm 14[KRT].4.209
yrẖ ḥyr.b ym ḥdṯ.|alp.w š.l b'lt bhtm.|b arb't 'šrt.b'l.|'rkm.|b ṯmnt.'šrt.yr|tḥṣ.mlk.brr.|'lm.tzġ.b UG5.12.A.3
ṯ.|[šmtr].uṯkl.l il.šlmm.|b [ṯlṯt].'šrt.yrtḥṣ.mlk.|br[r.]b a[r]b't.'šrt.riš.|arg[mn.w ṯn.]šm.l b'lt.|bhtm.'ṣ[rm.l in]š il APP.II[173].4
dṯ].|šmtr.[uṯkl.l il.šlmm].|b ṯlṯt '[šrt.yrtḥṣ.mlk.brr].|b arb'[t.'šrt.riš.argmn].|w ṯn šm.l [b'lt.bhtm.'ṣrm.l inš].|il 35[3].4
t.'ṣr[m] l inš.|[ilm.---].lbbmm.gdlt.'rb špš w ḥl.|[mlk.b ar]b't.'[š]rt.yrtḥṣ.mlk.brr.|[b ym.ml]at.y[ql]n.al[p]m.yrẖ.' 36[9].1.10
b arb't.'šr[t].|yrtḥṣ.mlk.b[rr].|b ym.mlat.|tqln.alpm.|yrẖ.' UG5.13.1
špš[.w ḥl.mlk.w.b y]|m.ḥdṯ.ṯn šm[.---.--]t.|b yrẖ.ši[-.b ar]b't.'š|rt.yr[tḥṣ.ml]k.brr.|'lm.š.š[--].l[--.]'rb.šp|š.w ḥl[. APP.II[173].54
mš.kkr.šml.|b.'šrt.b d.bn.kyn.|'šr.kkr.š'rt.|b d.urtn.b.arb'm.|arb't.'šrt.ẖrṣ.|b.ṯqlm.kbd.arb'm.|'šrt.ẖrṣ.b.arb'm. 2100.15
[ṯ]n.prm.b 'šrm.|arb'.prm.b.'š[r]m.|arb'.b.arb'm.|ṯṯm.[---.p]rm.|[-]l.b[--.---].|[---].kbd.|[---].kb[d.--- 1138.3
[--.l]bš.mtn.b.ar't.|[--.l]bš.bn.ykn'.b.ar't.|[--.l]bš.bn.grbn.b.ṯqlm.|[--.lb]š.bn.sgryn.b[.ṯ]qlm.|[- 135[330].2
[--.l]bš.mtn.b.ar't.|[--.l]bš.bn.ykn'.b.ar't.|[--.l]bš.bn.grbn.b.ṯqlm.|[--.lb] 135[330].1
rq].|[ẖrṣ.]yd.mqm h.|[w 'b]d.'lm.ṯlṯ.|[ssw]m.mrkbt b trbṣ bn.amt.|[ṯn.b]nm.aqny.|[ṯn.ṯa]rm.amid.|[w y'n].ṯr.a 14[KRT].2.56
yr]q.|ẖrṣ[.yd.mqm] h.|'bd[.'lm.ṯlṯ].|ss[wm.mrkbt].|b[trbṣ.bn.amt].|[qḥ.krt.šlmm].|[šlmm.al.tṣr].|[udm.rbt.w 14[KRT].5.254
q].|ẖrṣ.[yd.mqm h].|w 'bd[.'lm.ṯlṯ].|sswm.m[rkbt].|b trbṣ.[bn.amt].|q[ḥ.kr]t[.šlmm].|š[lmm.]al.t[ṣr].|udm[.r]b 14[KRT].6.273
sp.w yrq.ẖrṣ.|yd.mqm h.w 'bd.'lm.|ṯlṯ.sswm.mrkbt.|b trbṣ.bn.amt.|qḥ.krt.šlmm.|šlmm.w ng.mlk.|l bt y.rḥq.kr 14[KRT].3.129
|w yr[q.ẖrṣ].|yd.mqm h.w 'bd.|'lm.ṯlṯ.sswm.|mrkbt.b trbṣ.|bn.amt.p d.[i]n.|b bt y.ttn.tn.|l y.mṯt.ḥry.|n'mt.šbḥ 14[KRT].6.286
sp.w yrq.ẖrṣ.|yd.mqm h.w 'bd.|'lm.ṯlṯ.sswm.mrkbt.|b trbṣt.bn.amt.|p d.in.b bt y.ttn.|tn.l y.mṯt.ḥry.|n'mt.špḥ.b 14[KRT].3.141
t.'n[t.bnt.]bht |k.y ilm.bnt.bh[t k].a[l.tš]mḫ.|al.tšmḫ.b r[m.h]kl[k].|al.aḫd.hm.b y[--] y.[---]b[-].|b gdlt.arkt y.a 3['NT.VI].5.29
].|[bnt.bht]k.y ilm[.bnt.bht k.--].|[al.tšmḫ.]al.tš[mḫ.b rm.h]|[kl k.al.]aḫd hm.[---].|[---.b]gdlt.ar[kt y.am--].|[-- 18[3AQHT].1.8
.klbt.ilm išt.|klt.bt.il.ḏbb.imtḫṣ.ksp.|itrṯ.ẖrṣ.ṯrd.b'l.|b mrym.ṣpn.mšṣṣ.[-]k'[-].|udn h.grš h.l ksi.mlk h.|l nḥt.l k 3['NT].4.45
b.gt.mlkt.b.rḥbn.|ẖmšm.l.mitm.zt.|w.b d.krd.|ẖmšm.l.mit.|arb'.kbd 1096.1
.yrd.|l kḥṯ.aliyn.b'l.|w ymlk.b arṣ.il.kl h.|[---] š abn.b rḥbt.|[---] š abn.b kknt. 6.1.66[49.1.38]
|bn.ilm.mt.b ḥrb.|tbq'nn.b ḫṯr.tdry|nn.b išt.tšrpnn.|b rḥm.ttḥnn.b šd.|tdr'nn.šir h.l tikl.|'ṣrm.mnt h.l tkly.|npr 6[49].2.34
lt.'l k.pht.|dry.b ḥrb.'l k.|pht.šrp.b išt.|'l k.[pht.ṯḥ]n.b rḥ|m.'[l k.]pht[.dr]y.b kbrt.|'l k.pht.[-]l[-].|b šdm.'l k.ph 6[49].5.15
rty.|bn.krwn.b.yny.iytlm.|šgryn.ary.b.yny.|bn.yddn.b.rkby.|agyn.agny.|ṯqbn.mldy. 2071.7
.b ḫlb.k tgwln.šnt k.|[--.]w špt k.l tššy.hm.tqrm.l mt.b rn k.|[--]ḫp.an.arnn.ql.špš.ḥw.bṯnm.uḫd.b'lm.|[--.a]ṯm.p 1001.1.5
b.bn.agdṯb.'šrm.|b.bn.ibn.arb't.'šrt.|b.bn.mnn.ṯṯm.|b.rpan.bn.yyn.'šrt.|b.yp'r.'šrm.|b.n'mn.bn.ply.ẖmšt.l.'šrm. 2054.1.15
.ṯpṭ.b hd r'y.d yšr.w yḏmr.|b knr.w ṯlb.b tp.w mṣltm.b m|rqdm.dšn.b.ḥbr.kṯr.ṭbm.|w tšt.'nt.gṯr.b'lt.mlk.b'|lt.dr UG5.2.1.4
ṯlṯ.mat[.---.]kbd.|ṯṯ.ddm.k[--.b]rqd.|mit.tš'm.[kb]d.ddm.|b.gt.bir. 2168.2
šm.b.šrš.|ṯṯ.bnšm.b.mlk.|arb'.bnšm.b.bṣr.|ṯn.bnšm.[b.]rqd.|ṯn.b[nšm.b.---]y.|[---].b[nšm.b.--]nl.|[---.--]by. 2076.40
w yqmṣ.w b ḥlm h.|il.yrd.b ḏhrt h.|ab adm.w yqrb.|b šal.krt.m at.|krt.k ybky.|ydm'.n'mn.ġlm.|il.mlk[.ṯ]r ab h 14[KRT].1.38

spr.mḫṣm.|bn.ḫpṡry.b.šbn.|ilštm‘ym.|y[---.]bn.‘šq.|[---.]bn.tqy.|[---.]bn.šlmy.|[1041.2
|ilšlm.bn.gs[-.--]r.d.yṯb.b.gt.al.|ilmlk.[--]kt.[--.d.]yṯb.b.šb[n].|bn.pr[-.]d.y[ṯb.b].šlmy.|tlš.w[.n]ḥl h[.-].ṯgd.mrum. 2015.2.1
.yny.|[--.]bnšm.b.lbnm.|arb‘.bnšm.b.ypr.|[---.]bnšm.b.šbn.|[---.b]nšm.b.šmny.|[---.b]nšm.b.šmngy.|[---.]bnšm.b 2076.23
qmḥ.d.kly.b bt.skn.|l.illdrm.|ltḥ.ḫsr.b.šb‘.ddm. 2093.3
t.|d[m].ym.w ṯn.|ṯlṯ.rb‘.ym.|ḫmš.ṯdṯ.ym.|mk.špšm.b šb‘.|w l.yšn.pbl.|mlk.l [qr.]ṯiqt.|ibr h[.l]ql.nhqt.|ḥmr[h. 14[KRT].5.221
ṯ.ym.ḥẓ k.al.tš‘l.|qrt h.abn.yd k.|mšdpt.w hn.špšm.|b šb‘.w l.yšn.pbl.|mlk.l qr.ṯigt.ibr h.|l ql.nhqt.ḥmr h.|l g‘t. 14[KRT].3.119
mdbr.|lk.ym.w ṯn.ṯlṯ.rb‘ ym.|ḫmš.ṯdṯ.ym.mk.špšm.|b šb‘.w tmǵy.l udm.|rbm.w l.udm.ṯrrt.|w gr.nn.‘rm.šrn.|p 14[KRT].3.108
gyn.b.ṯq[l].|ḫmšm.šmt.b.ṯql.|kkr.w.[ml]tḥ.tyt.[---].|[b]šb‘[m.w.n]ṣp.ksp.|[tgm]r.[alp.w.]ṯlṯ.mat. 2101.27
dqd k.ašhlk.šbt[k.dmm].|[šbt.dqn k.mm‘m.]y‘ny.|il.b šb‘t.ḥdrm.b ṯmnt.|ap.sgrt.yd‘[t k.]bt.k an[št].|k in.b ilht. 3[‘NT.VI].5.34
t]bu.ḏdm.qn[-.-]n[-.-]lt.|ql h.yš[m‘].ṯr.[il].ab h.[---]l.|b šb‘t.ḥdrm.[b ṯ]mn[t.ap].|sgrt.g[-].[-]ẓ[.---] h[.---].|‘n.ṯk[.- 3[‘NT.VI].5.19
d.ṣt h.|[dn]il.yd.ṣt h.y‘l.w yškb.|[yd.]mizrt.p yln.mk.b šb‘.ymm.|[w]yqrb.b‘l.b ḥnt h.abynt.|[d]nil.mt.rpi anḫ.ǵz 17[2AQHT].1.16
ṯ[d]ṯ.ym.tikl.|išt.[b]bht m.nblat.|b[qrb.hk]l m.mk.|b šb[‘.]y[mm].td.išt.|b bht m.n[bl]at.b hkl m.|sb.ksp.l rqm. 4[51].6.32
ḫmš.|ṯdṯ.ym.yšlḥm.k[ṯ]rt.|w y[ššq].bnt.hll.snnt.|mk.b šb[‘.]ymm.tb‘.b bt h.|kṯrt.bnt.hll.snnt.|[-]d[-]t.n‘m y.‘rš.h 17[2AQHT].2.39
m.tlḥmn.rpum.|tštyn.bt.ikl.b pr‘.|yṣq.b irt.lbnn.mk.b šb‘.|[ymm.---]k.aliyn.b‘l.|[---].r‘ h ab y.|[---.]‘[---]. 22.2[124].25
rgm.yṯṯb.b.ṯdṯ.ṯn[.--.šmn].|‘ly h.gdlt.rgm.yṯ[ṯb.brr].|b.[šb]‘.ṣbu.[š]pš.w.ḥly[t].‘[r]b[.š]p[š].|w [ḥl.]mlk.[w.]b.ym.ḥ 35[3].47
r.r[gm.yṯṯb.b ṯdṯ.ṯn].|l šmn.‘[ly h.gdlt.rgm.yṯṯb].|brr.b šb‘[.ṣbu.špš.w ḥl]|yt.‘rb špš[.w ḥl.mlk.w.b y]|m.ḥdṯ.ṯn š APP.II[173].51
knt hm.|w tqrb.w ld.bn.l h.|w tqrb.w ld.bnt.l h.|mk.b šb‘.šnt.|bn.krt.km hm.tdr.|ap.bnt.ḥry.|km hm.w tḫss.aṯr 15[128].3.22
‘t.šnt.ybk.l aq|ht.ǵzr.yd[m‘.]l kdd.|dnil.mt.r[pi.mk].b šb‘.|šnt.w y‘n[.dnil.mt.]rpi.|yṯb.ǵzr.m[t.hrnmy.y]šu.|g h. 19[1AQHT].4.179
[---].l kḥṯ.drkt h.|l [ym]m.l yrḫm.l yrḫm.|l šnt.[m]k.b šb‘.|šnt.w [--].bn.ilm.mt.|‘m.aliyn.b‘l.yšu.|g h.w yṣḥ.‘l k. 6[49].5.8
arb‘m.l.mit.tišr.|ṯṯ.ṯṯ.b [ṯ]ql.ṯlṯt.l.‘šrm.ksp hm.|ṡstm.b.šb‘m.|ṯlṯ.mat.trm.b.‘šrt.|mit.adrm.b.‘šrt.|‘šr.ydt.b.‘šrt.|ḫ 1127.6
.qrt.|‘št.‘šr h.šmn.|‘mn.bn.aǵlmn.|arb‘m.ksp.‘l.qrt.|b.šd.bn.[u]brš.|ḫmšt.‘šrt.|b.šd.bn.[-]n.|ṯl[ṯt].‘šr[t].|b.š[d].b 1083.7
.|b.šd.bn.[u]brš.|ḫmšt.‘šrt.|b.šd.bn.[-]n.|ṯl[ṯt].‘šr[t].|b.š[d].bn.‘myn.|ḫmšt.|b.[šd.--]n.|ḫ[m]št[.‘]šrt.|[ar]b‘m.ksp 1083.11
.aǵlmn.|arb‘m.ksp.‘l.qrt.|b.šd.bn.[u]brš.|ḫmšt.‘šrt.|b.šd.bn.[-]n.|ṯl[ṯt].‘šr[t].|b.š[d].bn.‘myn.|ḫmšt.|b.[šd.--]n.| 1083.9
ḥrb.|tbq‘nn.b ḫṯr.tdry|nn.b išt.tšrpnn.|b rḥm.tṭḥnn.b šd.|tdr‘nn.šir h.l tikl.|‘ṣrm.mnt h.l tkly.|npr[m.]šir.l šir.y 6[49].2.34
l udm.|rbm.w l.udm.ṯrrt.|w gr.nn.‘rm.šrn.|pdrm.s‘t.b šdm.|ḥṭb h.b grnt.ḥpšt.|s‘t.b nk.šibt.b bqr.|mmlat.dm.y 14[KRT].3.111
.l udm.rbt.|w udm[.ṯr]rt.|grnn.‘rm.|šrnn.pdrm.|s‘t.b šdm.ḥṭb.|w b grnt.ḥpšt.|s‘t.b npk.šibt.w b |mqr.mmlat.| 14[KRT].4.214
.ṯlṯ.|mit.ksp.‘mn.|bn.ulbtyn.|w.kkr.ṯlṯ.|ksp.d.nkly.b.šd.|mit.ḫmšt.kbd.|[l.]gmn.bn.usyy.|mit.ṯṯm.kbd.|l.bn.yš 1143.6
l.trgm.l aḫt k.|[---.]l [ ]dm.aḫt k.|yd‘t.k rḥmt.|al.tšt.b šdm.mm h.|b smkt.ṣat.npš h.|[-]mt[-].ṣba.rbt.|špš.w tgh. 16.1[125].34
ht.ṭḥ]n.b rḥ|m.‘[l k.]pht[.dr]y.b kbrt.|‘l k.pht.[-]l[-].|b šdm.‘l k.pht.|dr‘.b ym.tn.aḥd.|b aḫ k.ispa.w yṯb.|ap.d an 6[49].5.18
.w td‘ ilm.|k mtt.yšm‘.aliyn.b‘l.|yuhb.‘glt.b dbr.prt.|b šd.šḥlmmt.škb.|‘mn h.šb‘.l šb‘m.|tš[‘]ly.ṯmn.l ṯmnym.|w 5[67].5.19
‘šrt.|b.šd.bn.[-]n.|ṯl[ṯt].‘šr[t].|b.š[d].bn.‘myn.|ḫmšt.|b.[šd.--]n.|ḫ[m]št[.‘]šrt.|[ar]b‘m.ksp.|[---]yn.|[---.]ksp.|[--- 1083.13
rm[.---].|krm.n‘mn.b.ḫly.ull.krm.aḥ[d.---].|krm.uḫn.b.šdmy.ṯlṯ.bzl[.d]prn[.---].|aupṯ.krm.aḥd.nšpin.kr[m.]aḥd[. 1081.13
[---.]l mitm.ksp.|[---.]skn.|[---.-]im.bṯd.|[---.b]šḥr.atlgn.|[---].b šḥr.|[---.]bn h.|[-]k[--]g hn.ksp. 2167.4
m.ksp.|[---.]skn.|[---.-]im.bṯd.|[---.b]šḥr.atlgn.|[---].b šḥr.|[---.]bn h.|[-]k[--]g hn.ksp. 2167.5
.pnm.l ytn.tk aršḫ.rbt.|w aršḫ.ṯrrt.ydy.b ‘ṣm.‘r‘r.|w b šḥt.‘s.mt.‘r‘rm.yn‘rn h.|ssnm.ysyn h.‘dtm.y‘dyn h.yb|ltm UG5.7.65
l ‘pr.ḏmr.aṯr h.ṭbq.lḥt.|niṣ h.grš d.‘šy.ln h.|aḫd.yd h.b škrn.m‘ms h.|[k]šb‘ yn.spu.ksm h.bt.b‘l.|[w m]nt h bt.il. 17[2AQHT].1.31
.l ‘pr.ḏmr.aṯr[y].|ṭbq lḥt.niṣ y.grš.|d ‘šy.ln.aḫd.yd y.b š|krn m‘ms y k šb‘t yn.|spu.ksm y.bt.b‘l.[w]mn[t].|y.bt.i 17[2AQHT].2.19
‘šy.ln k].|spu.ksm k.bt.[b‘l.w mnt k].|bt il.aḫd.yd k.b [škrn].|m‘ms k.k šb‘t.yn.ṭ[ḫ].|gg k.b ym.ṭiṭ.rḥṣ.|npṣ k.b 17[2AQHT].2.5
‘t.zblnm.|mḫmšt.yitsp.|ršp.nṯdṯt.ǵlm.|ym.mšb‘t hn.b šlḥ.|ttpl.y‘n.ḥtk h.|krt y‘n.ḥtk h.rš.|mid.grdš.ṯbt h.|w b 14[KRT].1.20
.b.gt.al.|ilmlk.[--]kt.[--.d.]yṯb.b.šb[n].|bn.pr[-.]d.y[ṯb.b].šlmy.|tlš.w[.n]ḥl h[.-].ṯgd.mrum.|bt.[-]b[-.-]sy[-]h.|nn[-] 2015.2.2
-.]b.yrml.|[---.--]n.b.yrml.|[---.--]ny.yrml.|ṡwn.qrty.|b.šlmy. 2119.26
.pnt h.w ydlp.tmn h.|yqṯ b‘l.w yšt.ym.ykly.ṯpṭ.nhr.|b šm.tg‘r m.‘ṯtrt.bṯ l aliyn.[b‘l.]|bṯ.l rkb.‘rpt.k šby n.zb[l.y 2.4[68].28
š.ršp š.|šlmm.|w šnpt.il š.|l ‘nt.ḥl š.ṯn šm.|l gṯrm.ǵṣ b šmal.|d alpm.w alp w š.|šrp.w šlmm kmm.|l b‘l.ṣpn b ‘r‘ UG5.13.26
t‘n.|tḫtṣb.w tḥdy.‘nt.|tǵdd.kbd h.b ṣḥq.ymlu.|lb h.b šmḫt.kbd.‘nt.|tšyt.k brkm.tǵll b dm.|ḏmr.ḥlqm.b mm‘.m 3[‘NT].2.26
t]‘n.tḫtṣb.|[w tḥdy.‘nt.tǵdd.kbd h.b ṣḥ]q.ymlu.lb h.|[b šmḫt.kbd.‘nt.tšyt.tḥt h.k]kdrt.riš.|[‘l h.k irbym.kp.---.k b 7.1[131].8
|w t‘n.pǵt.ṯkmt.mym.|qrym.ab.dbḥ.l ilm.|š‘ly.dǵṯ h.b šmym.|dǵṯ.hrnmy.d kbkbm.|l tbrkn.alk brkt.|tmrn.alk.n 19[1AQHT].4.192
mššpdt.|b ḥẓr y pẓǵm.ǵr.w yq.|dbḥ.ilm.yš‘ly.dǵṯ h.|b šmym.dǵṯ hrnmy[.d k]|bkbm.‘[l.---].|[-]l h.yd ‘d[.---].|lt 19[1AQHT].4.186
b bt h.|il.ḥṯ h.nḥt.il.ymnn.mṭ.yd h.yšu.|yr.šmm h.yr.b šmm.‘ṣr.yḫrṭ yšt.|l pḥm.il.aṯtm.k ypt.hm.aṯtm.tṣḥn.|y m 23[52].38
d y.|[---.ǵ]r.šrǵzz.ybky.km.n‘r.|[w ydm‘.k]m.ṣǵr.špš.b šmm.tqru.|[---.]nplt.y[--].md‘.nplt.bšr.|[---].w tpky.k[m.] UG5.8.38
wt h.|[--]nn.bnt yš[--.---.-]lk.|[--]b.kmm.l k[--].|[šp]š.b šmm.tq[ru.---.-]rt.|[---.]mn mn[-.---.--]n.nmr.|[--.]l ytk.bl UG5.8.44
ṭly.bn.‘n h.|uz‘rt.tmll.išd h.qrn[m].|dt.‘l h.riš h.b glṯ.b šm[m].|[---.i]l.ṯr.iṯ.p h.k ṯt.ǵlt[.--].|[---.--] k yn.ddm.l b[--. UG5.3.1.7
ypr.|[---.]bnšm.b.šbn.|[---.b]nšm.b.šmny.|[---.b]nšm.b.šmngy.|[---.]bnšm.b.snr.mid.|[---.bn]šm.b.tkn.|[---.bn]šm 2076.25
.lbnm.|arb‘.bnšm.b.ypr.|[---.]bnšm.b.šbn.|[---.b]nšm.b.šmny.|[---.b]nšm.b.šmngy.|[---.]bnšm.b.snr.mid.|[---.bn] 2076.24
[--]t.ilhnm.b šnt.|[---.]šb‘.mat.š‘rt.ḫmšm.kbd.|[---.-]nd.l.mlbš.ṯrmnm.| 1106.1
‘l.yṯbr.b‘l.yṯbr.diy.|hmt.hm.t‘pn.‘l.qbr.bn y.|tšḫṭann.b šnt h.qr.[mym].|mlk.yṣm.y l km.qr.mym.d ‘[l k].|mḫṣ.aq 19[1AQHT].3.151
n.[---].b.ar.|špšyn[.---.]yṯb.b.ar.|bn.ag[p]ṯ.ḫpṯ.d[.yṯb.b].š‘rt.|yly.bn.ṯrnq.[-]r.d.yṯb.b.ilštm‘.|ilšlm.bn.gs[-.--]r.d.yṯ 2015.1.25
.yd.aqht.ǵz[r].|tšt k.bm.qrb m.asm.|b p h.rgm.l yṣa.b špt h[.hwt h].|b nši ‘n h.w tphn.in.[---].|[-.]hlk.ǵlmm b d 19[1AQHT].2.75
m].|abky.w aqbrn.ašt.b ḫrt.|i[lm.arṣ.b p h.rgm.l yṣa.b šp]|t h.hwt h.knp.hrgb.b‘l.ṯbr.|b‘l.ṯbr.diy.hwt.w yql.|tḥt. 19[1AQHT].3.127
m.abky.w aqbrn h.|ašt.b ḫrt.ilm.arṣ.|b p h.rgm.l yṣa.b špt h.hwt[h].|knp.nšrm.b‘l.yṯbr.|b‘l.ṯbr.diy hmt.tqln.|tḥ 19[1AQHT].3.113
bky w aqbrn h.aštn.|b ḫrt.ilm.arṣ.b p h.rgm.l[yṣ]a.|b špt h.hwt h.knp.ṣml.b‘[l].|b‘l.ṯbr.diy.hyt.tq[l.tḥt].|p‘n h.y 19[1AQHT].3.142
m.b bz tdm.|lla y.‘m lẓpn i|l ḏ.pid.hn b p y sp|r hn.b špt y mn|t hn ṯlḫ h w mlg h y|ṯtqt ‘m h b q‘t.|tq‘t ‘m prb 24[77].46
uḫnp.|ṯn.bnšm.b.ḫrṣb‘.|arb‘.bnšm.b.hzp.|arb‘.bnšm.b.šql.|arb‘.bnšm.b.nni.|ṯn.bnšm.b.slḫ.|[---].bnšm.b.yny.|[-- 2076.17
l ṣpn b‘l.|ugrt.|b mrḥ il.|b nit il.|b ṣmd il.|b dṯn il.|b šrp il.|b knt il.|b ǵdyn il.|[b]n [---]. 30[107].16

.b.glltky. | lbw[-].uẖ.pdm.b.y‘rt. | pǵyn.b.tpḫ. | amri[l].b.šrš. | aǵltn.b.midẖ. | [--]n.b.ayly. | [-]lyn.b.ngẖt. | [---.]b.nh[- 2118.12
.b.irbn. | t̠n.bnšm.b.y‘rt. | t̠n.bnšm.b.‘rmt. | arb‘.bnšm.b.šrš. | t̠t̠.bnšm.b.mlk. | arb‘.bnšm.b.bṣr. | t̠n.bnšm.[b.]rqd. | t̠n 2076.37
w.aḥd.ẖbt̠. | w.arb‘.at̠t̠. | bn.lg.t̠n.bn h. | b‘lm.w.aẖt h. | b.šrt. | šty.w.bn h. 2080.12
t.rḥ.gdm.w anhbm]. | kla[t.t̠ǵ]r[t.bẖt.‘nt.w tqry.ǵlmm.b št.ǵr]. | ap ‘nt tm[tḫṣ.b ‘mq.tḫtṣb.bn.qrytm.tmḫṣ]. | lim ẖ[p 7.2[130].24
t.rḥ.gdm. | w anhbm.klat.t̠ǵrt. | bht.‘nt.w tqry.ǵlmm. | b št.ǵr.w hln.‘nt.tm | tḫṣ.b ‘mq.tḫtṣb.bn. | qrytm tmḫṣ.lim.ẖp 3[‘NT].2.5
i.[---]. | kpr.[šb‘.bnt.rḥ.gdm.w anhbm]. | w tqr[y.ǵlmm.b št.ǵr.---]. | [‘]d tš[b‘.tmtḫṣ.---]. | klyn[.---]. | špk.l[---]. | trḥṣ. 7.2[130].4
bn. | nqmp‘.ml[k]. | ugrt.ytn. | šd.kd̠ǵdl[.bn]. | [-]š[-]y.d.b š[-]y. | [---.y]d gt h[.--]. | [---.]yd. | [k]rm h.yd. | [k]lkl h. | [w] 1008.6
bnšm.---]. | t̠t̠.‘šr.bnš[m.---]. | ‘šr[.bn]šm[.---]. | t̠n.bnšm.b.š[--]. | arb‘.bnšm.b[.---]. | ‘šrm.bnšm.[b.]‘d[--]. | arb‘.bnšm.b. 2076.8
t.‘n[t]. | w p.n‘mt.aẖt[.b‘l]. | y‘l.b‘l.b ǵ[r.---]. | w bn.dgn.b š[---]. | b‘l.yt̠b.l ks[i.mlk h]. | bn.dgn.l kḫ[t̠.drkt h]. | l alp.ql. 10[76].3.13
[s]pr.bnš.mlk.d.b.tbq. | [kr]wn. | [--]n. | [q]ṣy. | t̠n.bn.iwrẖz.[n]‘rm. | yṣr[.-]qb. | 2066.1.1
.b nmrt h.l r | [--.]arṣ.‘z k.d̠mr k.l[-] | n k.ḥtk k.nmrt k.b tk. | ugrt.l ymt.špš.w yrẖ. | w n‘mt.šnt.il. UG5.2.2.10
.amt. | at̠rt.qḫ. | ksan k.ḥdg k. | ḥtl k.w ẓi. | b aln.tk m. | b tk.mlbr. | ilšiy. | kry amt. | ‘pr.‘ẓm yd. | ugrm.ẖl.ld. | aklm.tb 12[75].1.21
‘dn. | ‘dnm.kn.npl.b‘l. | km t̠r.w tkms.hd.p[.-]. | km.ibr.b tk.mšmš d[--]. | ittpq.l awl. | išttk.lm.ttkn. | štk.mlk.dn. | štk 12[75].2.56
b‘l.yt̠b.k t̠bt.ǵr.hd.r[‘y]. | k mdb.b tk.ǵr h.il ṣpn.b [tk]. | ǵr.tliyt.šb‘t.brqm.[---]. | t̠mnt.iṣr r‘t.‘ṣ UG5.3.1.2
| rgm l td‘.nšm.w l tbn. | hmlt.arṣ.at m.w ank. | ibǵy h.b tk.ǵr y.il.ṣpn. | b qdš.b ǵr.nḥlt y. | b n‘m.b gb‘.tliyt. | hlm.‘n 3[‘NT].3.26
.kbkbm.abn.brq]. | d l t[d‘.šmm.at m.w ank]. | ibǵ[y h.b tk.ǵ]r y.il.ṣpn. | b q[dš.b ǵr.nḥ]lt y. | w t[‘n].btlt.[‘]nt.t̠t̠b. | [3[‘NT].4.63
b‘l.yt̠b.k t̠bt.ǵr.hd.r[‘y]. | k mdb.b tk.ǵr h.il ṣpn.b [tk]. | ǵr.tliyt.šb‘t.brqm.[---]. | t̠mnt.iṣr r‘t.‘ṣ brq y. | riš h.tpl UG5.3.1.2
.b‘l. | yt‘dd.rkb.‘rpt. | [--].ydd.w yqlṣn. | yqm.w ywpt̠n.b tk. | p[ẖ]r.bn.ilm.štt. | p[--].b t̠lḥn y.qlt. | b ks.ištyn h. | dm.t̠ 4[51].3.13
š.rmm.hk[l m]. | ḥš.bht m.tbn[n]. | ḥš.trmmn.hk[l m]. | b tk.ṣrrt.ṣpn. | alp.šd.aḥd bt. | rbt.kmn.hkl. | w y‘n.kt̠r.w ẖss. 4[51].5.117
[-----]. | [---.mid.rm.]krt. | [b tk.rpi.]arṣ. | [b pẖr].qbṣ.dtn. | [w t]qrb.w ld. | bn.tl k. | tld.pǵ 15[128].3.3
tld.pǵ[t.---]. | tld.pǵ[t.---]. | tld.p[ǵt.---]. | mid.rm[.krt]. | b tk.rpi.ar[ṣ]. | b pẖr.qbṣ.dtn. | ṣǵrt hn.abkrn. | tbrk.ilm.tity. | 15[128].3.14
--]. | t̠r.il[.ab h.---]. | ḥš b[ht m.tbnn.ḥš.trmmn.hkl m]. | b tk.[---]. | bn.[---]. | a[--.---.] 1[‘NT.IX].3.28
[---.b]nšm.b.šmngy. | [---.]bnšm.b.snr.mid. | [---.bn]šm.b.tkn. | [---.bn]šm.b.tmrm. | [---.bn]šm.b.t̠nq. | [---.b]nšm.b.ug 2076.27
. | ttpl.y‘n.ḥtk h. | krt y‘n.ḥtk h.rš. | mid.grdš.t̠bt h. | w b tm hn.šph.yitbd. | w b.pẖyr h.yrt̠. | y‘rb.b ḥdr h.ybky. | b t̠n 14[KRT].1.24
y. | [---.]bnšm.b.snr.mid. | [---.bn]šm.b.tkn. | [---.bn]šm.b.tmrm. | [---.bn]šm.b.t̠nq. | [---.b]nšm.b.ugrt. | [---.bn]šm.b.ǵ 2076.28
y.ary.m[--.---]. | nrn.arny[.---]. | w.t̠n.bn h.w.b[---.---]. | b tn[--.---]. | swn.qrty[.---]. | uẖ h.w.‘šr[.---]. | klyn.apsn[y.---]. 81[329].7
| l aḥwy.tqḥ.yt̠pn.mhr.št. | tštn.k nšr.b ḥbš h.km.diy. | b t‘rt h.aqht.km.yt̠b.l lḥ[m]. | bn.dnil.l t̠rm.‘l h.nšr[m]. | trḥp 18[3AQHT].4.29
u h.b ym.t[---]. | tlbš.npṣ.ǵzr.tšt.ẖ[---.b] | nšǵ h.ḥrb.tšt.b t‘r[t h]. | w ‘l.tlbš.npṣ.at̠t̠.[--]. | ṣbi nrt.ilm.špš.[-]r[--]. | pǵt. 19[1AQHT].4.207
.‘nt.t̠b.yt̠p.w[---]. | l k.ašt k.km.nšr.b ḥb[š y]. | km.diy.b t‘rt y.aqht.[km.yt̠b]. | l lḥm.w bn.dnil.l t̠rm[.‘l h]. | nšrm.tr 18[3AQHT].4.18
.yt̠b.b.‘t̠trt. | il.t̠pt̠.b hd r‘y.d yšr.w yd̠mr. | b knr.w t̠lb.b tp.w mṣltm.b m | rqdm.dšn.b.ḥbr.kt̠r.t̠bm. | w tšt.‘nt.gt̠r.b‘l UG5.2.1.4
.glltky. | td[y]n.b.glltky. | lbw[-].uẖ.pdm.b.y‘rt. | pǵyn.b.tpḫ. | amri[l].b.šrš. | aǵltn.b.midẖ. | [--]n.b.ayly. | [-]lyn.b.ng 2118.11
t qdš. | [---.--]n.b.anan. | [--]yl.b.bq‘t.b.gt.tgyn. | [--]in.b.trzy. | [--]yn.b.glltky. | td[y]n.b.glltky. | lbw[-].uẖ.pdm.b.y‘r 2118.7
.ẖr[ṣ.]b.t̠mnt.ksp. | ‘šrt.ksp.b.alp.[b d].bn.[---]. | tš‘.ṣin.b.tš‘t.ksp. | mšlt.b.t̠ql.ksp. | kdwt.l.grgyn.b.t̠q[l]. | ẖmšm.šmt. 2101.22
h.w.‘šr[.---]. | klyn.apsn[y.---]. | plzn.qrty[.---]. | w.klt h.b.t[--.---]. | b‘l y.mlk[y.---]. | yd.bt h.yd[.---]. | ary.yd.t[--.---]. 81[329].12
.bn.t̠t̠.‘šrt. | b.bn.qrdmn.t̠lt̠m. | b.bṣmn[.bn].ḥrtn.‘[--]. | b.t[--.---] h.[---]. | [-----]. | [--]ly.ẖmšm.b.‘bdyr[ẖ]. | [---].‘šrm. | 2054.1.22
bnš hm. | d̠mry.w.pt̠pt̠.‘rb. | b.yrm. | [ily.w].d̠mry.‘rb. | b.t̠b‘m. | ydn.bn.ilrpi. | w.t̠b‘m.‘rb.b.‘[d]n. | d̠mry.bn.yrm. | ‘rb 2079.6
.al. | tqrb.l bn.ilm. | mt.al.y‘db km. | k imr.b p h. | k lli.b t̠brn. | qn h.tḫtan. | nrt.ilm.špš. | ṣḥrrt.la. | šmm.b yd.md | d.i 4[51].8.19
ḥlmmt. | ngš.ank.aliyn b‘l. | ‘dbnn ank.imr.b p y. | k lli.b t̠brn q y.ḫtu hw. | nrt.ilm.špš.ṣḥrrt. | la.šmm.b yd.bn ilm.m 6[49].2.23
.il. | b.ẖmšt.‘šrt.ksp. | ẖmš.mat.šmt. | b.‘šrt.ksp. | ‘šr.ṣin.b.t̠t̠t.w.kmsk. | arb‘[.k]dwt̠m.w.t̠t.tprtm. | b.‘šr[m.]ksp. | ẖmš. 2100.9
b t̠t̠ ym ḥdt̠. | ḫyr.‘rbt. | špš t̠ǵr h. | ršp. | w ‘bdm tbqrn. | skn. 1162.1
‘bdrt̠[b.---]. | b t̠t̠ ‘tr t̠mn.r[qḥ.---]. | p bn btb[-.---]. | b ẖmt̠ ‘tr k[--.---]. | b ẖ 207[57].2
] | rm.pam[t.---]. | š dd šmn[.gdlt.w.---]. | brr.r[gm.yt̠t̠b.b t̠dt̠.t̠n]. | l šmn.‘[ly h.gdlt.rgm.yt̠t̠b]. | brr.b šb‘[.ṣbu.špš.w ḥ APP.II[173].49
lbš.aḥd. | b.‘šrt. | w.t̠n.b.ẖmšt. | tprt.b.t̠lt̠t. | mtyn.b.t̠t̠t. | t̠n.lbšm.b.‘šrt. | pld.b.arb‘t. | lbš.t̠n.b.t̠nt.‘šrt. 1108.5
l.‘šrm.pamt.[---]. | š.dd.šmn.gdlt.w.[---.brr]. | rgm.yt̠t̠b.b.t̠dt̠.t̠n[.--.šmn]. | ‘ly h.gdlt.rgm.yt̠[t̠b.brr]. | b.[šb]‘.ṣbu.[š]pš. 35[3].45
nh. | l[q]ḥt. | [--]km.‘m.mlk. | [b]ǵl hm.w.iblbl hm. | w.b.t̠b h.[---]. | spr ḥ[---.---]. | w.‘m[.---]. | yqḥ[.---]. | w.n[--.---]. 2129.11
u]m y. | mnm[.šlm]. | w.rgm[.t̠t̠b.l] y. | hl ny.‘mn. | mlk.b.t̠y ndr. | it̠t̠.w.ht. | [-]sny.ud̠r h. | w.hm.ẖt. | ‘l.w.likt. | ‘m k.w 1013.13
. | kll.šlm. | t̠m ny.‘m.um y. | mnm.šlm. | w.rgm.t̠t̠b.l y. | bm.t̠y.ndr. | it̠t̠.‘mn.mlkt. | w.rgm y.l[--]. | lqt.w.pn. | mlk.nr b 50[117].14
[t̠]mnym.dd. | š‘rm.b.t̠ydr. 1166.2
--]. | bn bn.at̠r k.hn[.---]. | yd k.ṣǵr.tnšq.špt k.t̠m. | t̠km.bm t̠km.aḥm.qym.il. | b lsmt.t̠m.yt̠bš.šm.il.mt m. | y‘bš.brk n 22.2[124].5
.w yqlṣn. | yqm.w ywpt̠n.b tk. | p[ẖ]r.bn.ilm.štt. | p[--].b t̠lḥn y.qlt. | b ks.ištyn h. | dm.t̠n.dbḥm.šna.b‘l.t̠lt̠. | rkb.‘rpt. 4[51].3.15
tǵt[--]. | hm.ǵmu.ǵmit.w ‘s[--]. | lḥm.hm.štym.lḥ[m]. | b t̠lḥnt.lḥm št. | b krpnm.yn.b k.ẖrṣ. | dm.‘ṣm.hm.yd.il mlk. | 4[51].4.36
b t̠lt̠. | ilmlk.‘šr.ṣin. | mlkn‘m.‘šr. | bn.adty.‘šr. | [ṣ]dqšlm ẖmš. 2039.1
[-] ym.pr‘ d nkly yn kd w kd. | w ‘l ym kdm. | w b t̠lt̠.kd yn w krsnm. | w b rb‘ kdm yn. | w b ẖmš kd yn. 1086.3
tškn. | šd.k ḥsn.pat. | mdbr.tlkn. | ym.w t̠n.aḥr. | šp[š]m.b [t̠]lt̠. | ym[ǵy.]l qdš. | a[t̠rt.]ṣrm.w l ilt. | ṣd[yn]m.t̠m. | yd[r.k 14[KRT].4.196
.l mr[kbt hm.tity.l] | ‘r hm.tl[kn.ym.w t̠n.aḥr.špšm]. | b t̠lt̠.mǵy[.rpum.l grnt]. | i[ln]y[m].l mt‘t[.---]. | [-]m[.---]. | h. 22.1[123].25
‘ln.l mrkbt hm.ti[ty.l ‘r hm]. | tlkn.ym.w t̠a aḥr.š[pšm.b t̠lt̠]. | mǵy.rpum.l grnt.i[lnym.l] | mt‘t.w y‘n.dnil.[mt.rpi]. | 20[121].2.5
lbš.aḥd. | b.‘šrt. | w.t̠n.b.ẖmšt. | tprt.b.t̠lt̠t. | mtyn.b.t̠t̠t. | t̠n.lbšm.b.‘šrt. | pld.b.arb‘t. | lbš.t̠n.b.t̠nt.‘š 1108.4
[b yr]ẖ[.r]išyn.b ym.ḥdt̠. | [šmtr].ut̠kl.l il.šlmm. | b [t̠lt̠].‘šrt.yrtḥṣ.mlk. | br[r.]b a[r]b‘t.‘šrt.riš. | arg[mn.w t̠n.]š APP.II[173].3
b yrẖ.[rišyn.b ym.ḥdt̠]. | šmtr.[ut̠kl.l il.šlmm]. | b t̠lt̠ ‘[šrt.yrtḥṣ.mlk.brr]. | b arb‘[t.‘šrt.riš.argmn]. | w t̠n šm. 35[3].3
r[-.---]. | ṣin aḥd h[.---]. | l ‘t̠trt[.---]. | ‘lm.kmm[.---]. | w b t̠lt̠.ṣ[in.---]. | l ll.pr[-.---]. | mit š‘[rt.---]. | ptr.k[--.---]. | [-]yu[- 37[22].8
dgn š. | [---.--]r.w t̠t pl.gdlt.[ṣ]pn.dqt. | [---.al]p ‘nt.gdlt.b t̠lt̠ mrm. | [---.i]l š.b‘l š.at̠rt.š.ym š.[b‘]l knp. | [---.g]dlt.ṣpn. 36[9].1.5
-]t.w.ẖpn.l.azzlt. | [---.]l.‘t̠trt.šd. | [---].yb‘lnn. | [---.--]n.b.t̠lt̠.šnt.l.nṣd. | [---.--]ršp.mlk.k.ypdd.mlbš. | u---].mlk.ytn.m 1106.57
.l hm. | šb‘.lbšm.allm. | l ušẖry. | t̠lt̠.mat.pt̠tm. | l.mgmr.b.t̠lt̠. | šnt. 1107.12

-.-]n[-.-]lt. | ql h.yš[m'].tr.[il].ab h.[---]l. | b šb't.ḫdrm.[b t]mn[t.ap]. | sgrt.g[-].[-]ẓ[.---] h[.---]. | 'n.tk[.---]. | 'ln.t[--.--- 3['NT.VI].5.19

šbt[k.dmm]. | [šbt.dqn k.mm'm.]y'ny. | il.b šb't.ḫdrm.b ṯmnt. | ap.sgrt.yd'[t k.]bt.k an[št]. | k in.b ilht.ql[ṣ] k.mh.ta 3['NT.VI].5.34

p. | ṯlṯ.ktnt.b d.an[r]my. | b.'šrt.ksp.b.a[--]. | ṯqlm.ḫr[ṣ.]b.ṯmnt.ksp. | 'šrt.ksp.b.alp.[b d].bn.[---]. | tš'.ṣin.b.tš't.ksp. | 2101.20

.alp kb[d]. | ṯlṯ.l.nskm.birtym. | b d.urtn.w.ṯṯ.mat.brr. | b.ṯmnym.ksp.ṯlṯt.kbd. | ḫmš.alp.ṯlṯ.l.ḥlby. | b d.tlmi.b.'šrm.ḫ 2101.5

bl.prd. | b.ṯql.w.nṣp.ksp. | ṯmn.lbšm.w.mšlt. | l.udmym.b.ṯmnt.'šrt.ksp. | šb'm.lbš.d.'rb.bt.mlk. | b.mit.ḫmšt.kbd.ksp. 2101.15

b ym ḥdṯ. | alp.w š.l b'lt bhtm. | b arb't 'šrt.b'l. | 'rkm. | b ṯmnt.'šrt.yr | ṯḥṣ.mlk.brr. | 'lm.tzǵ.b ǵb.ṣpn. | nḥkt.ksp.w ḫr UG5.12.A.5

.b.ṯlṯt. | mṯyn.b.ṯṯt. | ṯn.lbšm.b.'šrt. | pld.b.arb't. | lbš.ṯn.b.ṯnt.'šrt. 1108.8

u.g h[.---]. | i.ap.b'[l.---]. | i.hd.d[---.---]. | ynp'.b'[l.---]. | b ṯmnt.[---]. | yqrb.[---]. | lḥm.m[---.---]. | [']d.lḥm[.šty.ilm]. | 5[67].4.9

[---].šb't.'šrt. | [---.-]kyn.'šrt. | b.bn.'sl.'šrm.ṯqlm kbd. | b.ṯmq.ḫmšt.l.'šrt. | b.[---].šb't.'šrt. | b.bn.pdrn.'šrm. | d.bn.šb'l 2054.1.7

.il]. | špḥ.lṯpn[.w qdš]. | bkm.t'r[b.'l.ab h]. | t'rb.ḥ[--]. | b ttm.t[---]. | šknt.[---]. | bkym[.---]. | ǵr.y[----]. | ydm.[---]. | ap 16.2[125].114

tm hn.špḥ.yitbd. | w b.pḫyr h.yrṯ. | y'rb.b ḥdr h.ybky. | b ṯn.[-]gmm.w ydm'. | tntkn.udm't h. | km.ṯqlm.arṣ h. | km ḫ 14[KRT].1.27

id. | [---.bn]šm.b.tkn. | [---.bn]šm.b.tmrm. | [---.bn]šm.b.ṯnq. | [---.b]nšm.b.ugrt. | [---.bn]šm.b.ǵbl. | [---.b]nšm.b.m'r. 2076.29

kbd. | tgmr.bnš.mlk. | d.b d.adn'm. | [š]b'.b.ḫrṯm. | [ṯ]lṯ.b.ṯǵrm. | rb qrt.aḥd. | ṯmn.ḫzr. | w.arb'.ḥršm. | dt.tb'ln.b.pḫn. 1024.3.2

ṯlṯ.ṣmdm. | b.nḫry. | ṣmdm.b.ṯp[--]. | aḥdm.b.gm[--]. 144[317].3

arb't. | ksp h. | kkr.š'rt. | šb't.ksp h. | ḫmš.mqdm.dnyn. | b.ṯql.dprn.aḥd. | b.ṯql. | ḫmšm.'rgz.b.ḫmšt. 1127.20

.ksp. | ṯlṯ.uṭbm.b d.alḫn.b.'šrt[.k]sp. | rṯ.l.ql.d.ybl.prd. | b.ṯql.w.nṣp.ksp. | ṯmn.lbšm.w.mšlt. | l.udmym.b.ṯmnt.'šrt.ks 2101.13

rt.ḫrṣ. | b.ṯqlm.kbd.arb'm. | 'šrt.ḫrṣ.b.arb'm. | mit.ḫršḫ.b.ṯqlm. | w.šb'.'šr.šmn. | d.l.yṣa.bt.mlk. | tgmr.ksp.mitm. | ḥm 2100.19

r.š'rt. | šb't.ksp h. | ḫmš.mqdm.dnyn. | b.ṯql.dprn.aḥd. | b.ṯql. | ḫmšm.'rgz.b.ḫmšt. 1127.21

.[---]. | tš'.ṣin.b.tš't.ksp. | mšlt.b.ṯql.ksp. | kdwṯ.l.grgyn.b.ṯq[l]. | ḫmšm.šmt.b.ṯql. | kkr.w.[ml]tḫ.tyt.[---]. | [b]šb'[m.w 2101.24

[-----]. | [ḫ]pn.aḥd.b.ṯqlm. | lbš.aḥd.b.ṯqlm. | ḫpn.pṯtm.b 'šr. | tgmr.ksp.ṯlṯm. | ṯqlm.kbd. 1115.3

n.kyn. | 'šr.kkr.š'rt. | b d.urtn.b.arb'm. | arb't.'šrt.ḫrṣ. | b.ṯqlm.kbd.arb'm. | 'šrt.ḫrṣ.b.arb'm. | mit.ḫršḫ.b.ṯqlm. | w.šb' 2100.17

ksp. | mšlt.b.ṯql.ksp. | kdwṯ.l.grgyn.b.ṯq[l]. | ḫmšm.šmt.b.ṯql. | kkr.w.[ml]tḫ.tyt.[---]. | [b]šb'[m.w.n]ṣp.ksp. | [tgm]r.[2101.25

p. | 'šrt.ksp.b.alp.[b d].bn.[---]. | tš'.ṣin.b.tš't.ksp. | mšlt.b.ṯql.ksp. | kdwṯ.l.grgyn.b.ṯq[l]. | ḫmšm.šmt.b.ṯql. | kkr.w.[ml 2101.23

[-----]. | [ḫ]pn.aḥd.b.ṯqlm. | lbš.aḥd.b.ṯqlm. | ḫpn.pṯtm.b 'šr. | tgmr.ksp.ṯlṯm. | ṯql 1115.2

. | ḥṯbn.ybnn. | arb'm.l.mit.šmn. | arb'm.l.mit.tišr. | ṯṯ.ṯṯ.b [ṯ]ql.ṯlṯt.l.'šrm.ksp hm. | sstm.b.šb'm. | ṯlṯ.mat.trm.b.'šrt. | 1127.5

]bš.mtn.b.ar't. | [--.l]bš.bn.ykn'.b.ar't. | [--.l]bš.bn.grbn.b.ṯqlm. | [--.lb]š.bn.sgryn.b[.ṯ]qlm. | [---.]bn.ully.b.ṯ[qlm]. | [-- 135[330].3

.grbn.b.ṯqlm. | [--.lb]š.bn.sgryn.b[.ṯ]qlm. | [---.]bn.ully.b.ṯ[qlm]. | [---.]bn.anndy.b[.---]. | [---.]bn.pd[--.---]. 135[330].5

.ykn'.b.ar't. | [--.l]bš.bn.grbn.b.ṯqlm. | [--.lb]š.bn.sgryn.b[.ṯ]qlm. | [---.]bn.ully.b.ṯ[qlm]. | [---.]bn.anndy.b[.---]. | [---.] 135[330].4

-]. | b gt ṯm[--] yn[.--]. | [---].krm.b yp'l.y'dd. | [---.]krm.b [-]dn.l.bn.[-]kn. | šd[.---.-]'n. | šd[.---.-]ṣm.l.dqn. | š[d.---.--]d 2027.1.5

. | [---.]qbṯ.ṯm. | [---.]bn.ilm. | [m]t.šmḫ.p ydd. | il[.ǵ]zr. | b [-]dn.'.z.w. | rgbt.zbl. UG5.4.17

p m.bt.mlk. | ḫlu.dg. | ḥdtm. | dbḥ.b'l.k.tdd.b'lt.bhtm. | b.[-]ǵb.ršp.ṣbi. | [---.--]m. | [---.]piln. | [---].ṣmd[.---.]pd[ry]. | [- 2004.15

k.ṣbu.špš.w.ḥl.mlk. | w.[---].ypm.w.mḫ[--].t[t]tbn.[-]. | b.[--].w.km.iṯ.y[--.]šqm.yd[-]. 35[3].55

b.bṣr. | ṯn.bnšm.[b.]rqd. | ṯn.b[nšm.b.---]y. | [---].b[nšm.b.--]nl. | [---.--]by. 2076.42

---.---]. | [-----]. | [-----]. | b [----]. | w [----]. | b'l.[---]. | il hd.b[---]. | at.bl.at.[---]. | yisp hm.b['l.---]. | bn.dgn[.---]. | 'ḏbm.[-- 12[75].2.23

b ilht]. | qlṣ k.tb'.bt.ḫnp.lb[k.--.ti]. | ḫd.d iṯ.b kbd k.tšt.b [---]. | irt k.dṯ.ydṯ.m'qb k.[ttb']. | [bt]lt.'nt.idk.l ttn.[pnm]. | 18[3AQHT].1.18

. | l.[--]n.špš. | ad[.']bd h.uk.škn. | k.[---.]sglt h.hw. | w.b[.---.]uk.nǵr. | w.[---].adny.l.yḫsr. | w.[ank.yd]'.l.yd't. | h[t.--- 2060.8

spr.mdr[ǵlm]. | lt.hlk.b[.---]. | bn.b'yn.š[--.---]. | aǵltn.mid[-.---]. | bn.lṣn.'rm[y]. | arš 87[64].2

k.kbkb[.---]. | dm.mt.aṣḥ[.---]. | ydd.b qr[b.---]. | al.ašt.b[---]. | ahpk k.l[--.---]. | ṯmm.w lk[.---]. | w lk.ilm[.---]. | n'm.i 5[67].3.11

. | [---.]šb'm.dr'.w.arb'm.drt.mit.dd. | [---].ḫpr.bn.šm. | [b.---.]knm.ṯṯm.l.mit.dr'.w.mit.drt. | w[.---.]'m.l.mit.dd.ṯn.kb 1098.7

| b['l y.---]. | yd[--.]mlk. | rb.b['l y.---]. | [-----]. | r[--.---]. | b.[---.mlk]. | rb[.b'l y.---]. | w.an[k.---]. | arš[.---]. | mlk.r[b.b']l 1018.13

-]. | ṯḥdṯn w hl[.---]. | w tglṯ thmt.'[--.---]. | yṣi.ǵl h tḥm b[.---]. | mrḥ h l adrt[.---]. | ṯtb 'ṯrt b ǵl[.---]. | qrẓ tšt.l šmal[.- 2001.1.6

š[m.---]. | 'šr[.bn]šm[.---]. | ṯn.bnšm.b.š[--]. | arb'.bnšm.b[.---]. | 'šrm.bnšm.[b.]'d[--]. | arb'.bnšm.b.ag[m]y. | arb'.bnš 2076.9

-]kyn.'šrt. | b.bn.'sl.'šrm.ṯqlm kbd. | b.ṯmq.ḫmšt.l.'šrt. | b.[---].šb't.'šrt. | b.bn.pdrn.'šrm. | d.bn.šb'l.uḫnpy.ḫmšm. | b.b 2054.1.8

ḥrš.y[dm.tḥm.ṯr.il.ab k.] | hwt.lṭpn[.ḥtk k.---]. | yh.kṯr.b[---]. | št.lskt.n[--.---]. | 'db.bǵrt.ṯ[--. --]. | ḥš k.'ṣ k.'[bṣ k.'m 1['NT.IX].3.7

.sgryn.b[.ṯ]qlm. | [---.]bn.ully.b.ṯ[qlm]. | [---.]bn.anndy.b[.---]. | [---.]bn.pd[--.---]. 135[330].6

ym.tld[---.]b[-.]y[--.---]. | [---.il]m.rb[m.--]š[-]. | [---].nš.b [---]. | [---].tm[--.--]aṯ[.---]. | [---.]akl[.---]. | [---.-]l[-.-]hg[.---]. UG5.8.27

[---].mr[--.---]. | [---].mr[--.]ydm[.---]. | [---.]mṯbt.ilm.w.b[.---]. | [---.]ṯṯtbn.ilm.w.[---]. | [---.]w.ksu.b'lt.b[htm.---]. | [--- 47[33].5

nk.[---]. | [---.]ank.nši[.---]. | [---.ṯ]br.ḫss.[---]. | [---.--]št.b [---]. | [---.--]b. | [---.--]k. | [---.--]an. | [---.--]m.ank. | [---.]asrm 1002.17

. | [---.--]št.'šrt. | [---.--]m. | [---.--]ṯm. | [---.]'šrt. | [-----]. | b.[---.---]r. | b.ann[.---.-]ny[-]. | b.ḫqn.[---]m.ṣ[-]n. | [b].bn.ay[- 2054.2.14

.[---]. | bkym[.---]. | ǵr.y[----]. | ydm.[---]. | apn.[---]. | [--.]b[.---]. 16.2[125].120

.b.mlk. | arb'.bnšm.b.bṣr. | ṯn.bnšm.[b.]rqd. | ṯn.b[nšm.b.---]y. | [---].b[nšm.b.--]nl. | [---.--]by. 2076.41

kl[.---]. | km.s[--.---]. | tš[.---]. | t[---.---]. | [-----]. | [-----]. | b [----]. | w [----]. | b'l.[---]. | il hd.b[---]. | at.bl.at.[---]. | yisp h 12[75].2.20

bir

y.ḥmr.w.bnš. | rqd arb'. | šbn aḥd. | ṯbq aḥd. | šrš aḥd. | bir aḥd. | uḫnp. | hzp ṯn. | m'qb arb'. 2040.31

[sp]r.akl[.---].tryn. | [tg]mr.akl.b.g[t.b]ir.alp. | [']šrm.l.mit.ḥ[p]r.'bdm. | mitm.drt.ṯmnym.drt. | tg 2013.2

[--.]wmrkm. | bir.ḫmš. | uškn.arb'. | ubr'y.ṯlṯ. | ar.ṯmn 'šr h. | mlk.arb'. | ǵbl. 68[65].1.2

qpat. | ilštm'. | šbn. | ṯbq. | rqd. | šrš. | gn'y. | m'qb. | agm. | bir. | ypr. | hzp. | šql. | m'rḫ[-]. | sl[ḫ]. | snr. | 'rgz. | ykn'm. | 'nmk 2074.29

.[--]. | limm.ql.b udn.k w[-]. | k rtqt mr[.---]. | k d lbšt.bir.mlak. | šmm.tmr.zbl.mlk. | šmm.tlak.ṭl.amr.. | bn km k bk 13[6].25

qrt. | 'rm. | nnu. | [--]. | [---]. | m'r. | arny. | ubr'y. | ilštm'. | bir. | m'qb. | uškn. | snr. | rq[d]. | [---]. | [---]. | mid[-]. | ubš. | mṣb[71[113].30

qb. | [b] gt.iptl.ṯṯ.ḫrmt[t.nit]. | [k]rk.m'šd.mqb. | [b.g]t.bir.'š[r.---]. | [---].krk.m'[šd.---]. | [b.]gt.ḥrtm.ḥm[š.---]. | [n]it. 2048.15

| šql ṯlṯ.yn. | šmny.kdm.yn. | šmgy.kd.yn. | hzp.tš'.yn. | [b]ir.'šr[.---]m ḥsp. | ḫpty.kdm[.---]. | [a]gm.arb'[.---]. | šrš.šb'. 2004.29

]. | arb'.bnšm.b.ag[m]y. | arb'.bnšm.b.ḫpty. | ṯṯ.bnšm.b.bir. | ṯṯ.bnšm b.uḫnp. | ṯn.bnšm.b.ḫrṣb'. | arb'.bnšm.b.hzp. | ar 2076.13

r[-.---]. | m'r[-.---]. | bq't.[---]. | šḥq[.---]. | rkby ar[b'm]. | bir ṯ[--]. | 'nqpat [---]. | m[--.---]. | [-----]. | k[--.---]. | [-----]. | ḫmr 2042.16
-.]kbd. | ṯṯ.ddm.k[--.b]rqd. | mit.tš'm.[kb]d.ddm. | b.gt.bir. 2168.4

biry

bn.b'ln.biry. | ṯlṯ.b'lm. | w.adn hm.ṯr.w.arb'.bnt h. | yrḫm.yd.ṯn.bn h. 2080.1

birty

| w.snt. | bt.ugrt. | w.pdy h[m]. | iwrkl.mit. | ksp.b y[d]. | birtym. | [un]ṯ inn. | l [h]m 'd tṯtbn. | ksp.iwrkl. | w ṯb.l unṯ h 1006.15
spr.ḥṯbn.sbrdnm. | ḫmš.kkrm.alp kb[d]. | ṯlṯ.l.nskm.birtym. | b d.urtn.w.ṯṯ.mat.brr. | b.ṯmnym.ksp.ṯlṯt.kbd. | ḫmš. 2101.3

birtn

nm. | bn.ḫlbym. | bn.ady. | bn.'ṯtry. | bn.ḫrẓn. | ady. | bn.birtn. | bn.ḥrẓn. | bn.bddn. | bn.anny. | ytršp. | bn.szn. | bn.kdg 115[301].1.7
d. | ṣmq[-]. | bn.anny. | bn.'mtdl. | bn.'myn. | bn.alz. | bn.birtn. | [bn.]ylkn. | [bn.]krwn. | [bn.-]ty. | [bn.]iršn. | bn.[---]. | b 117[325].1.13
bnšm.dt.iṯ.alpm.l hm. | bn.niršn. | bn.adty. | bn.alz. | bn.birtn. | bn.mlṣ. | bn.q[--]. | bn.[---]. | bn.ṯ[-]r. | bn.grdn. | [bn.-]ḫ 2023.1.5

buly

.bn.dnn.ṯkt. | šb'l.bn.aly.ṯkt. | klby.bn.iḫy.ṯkt. | psš.bn.buly.ṯkt. | 'pṣpn.bn.'dy.ṯkt. | n'mn.bn.'yn.ṯkt. | 'pṯn.bn.ilrš.ṯkt 2085.8

burm

w šnm.š. | 'nt.š.ršp.š.dr il w p[ḫ]r b'l. | gdlt.šlm.gdlt.w burm.[l]b. | rmṣt.ilhm.b'lm.dṯt.w kšm.ḫmš. | 'ṯr h.mlun.šnpt. 34[1].8
š[nm.š.'nt.š.ršp.š.dr]. | il.w pḫr[.b'l.gdlt.šlm.gdlt]. | w burm.l[b.rmṣt.ilhm]. | b'lm.w mlu[.---.ksm]. | ṯlṯm.w m'rb[.-- APP.II[173].19
[šnm.š]. | 'nt š ršp š[.dr.il.w pḫr.b'l]. | gdlt.šlm[.gdlt.w burm.lb]. | rmṣt.ilh[m.b'lm.---]. | ksm.ṯlṯm.[---]. | d yqḥ bt[.--] 35[3].17
]. | [--.-]g[-.-]s w [---]. | w yn[t.q]rt.y[---]. | w al[p.l]il.w bu[rm.---]. | ytk.gdlt.ilhm.[ṯkmn.w šnm]. | dqt.ršp.šrp.w š[lm 35[3].11
[-]ml.[---]. | l[---].w y[nt.qrt.---]. | [---.--]n[.w alp.l il.w bu] | [rm.---.ytk.gdlt.ilhm]. | ṯkmn.w [šnm.dqt.ršp.šrp]. | w šl APP.II[173].12

bb

-.]špm.'db. | [---].t'tqn. | [---.-]'b.idk. | [l ytn.pnm.tk.]in.bb.b alp ḥẓr. | [rbt.kmn.l p']n.'nt. | [yhbr.w yql.yšt]ḥwyn.w y 1['NT.IX].2.14
bn.šp[š.]qšt. | bn.'g[w.]qšt.w ql'. | ḥd[ṯ]n.qšt.w.ql'. | bn.bb.qšt.w[.ql]'. | bn.aktmy.qšt. | šdyn.qšt. | bdn.qšt.w.ql'. | bn.š 119[321].4.9

bbt

id ydbḥ mlk. | l ušḫ[r] ḫlmṭ. | l bbt il bt. | š l ḫlmṭ. | w tr l qlḥ. | w š ḥll ydm. | b qdš il bt. | w tl UG5.7.TR3
bd. | alp.w š.l b'l ṣpn. | dqt l ṣpn.šrp.w šlmm. | kmm.w bbt.b'l.ugrt. | w kdm.w npš ilib. | gdlt.il š.b'l š.'nt. | ṣpn.alp.w UG5.13.11
l]p.w š.[l] b'l.ṣpn. | [dqt.l.ṣpn.šrp].w š[l]mm.kmm. | [w bbt.b'l.ugrt.]kdm.w npš. | [ilib.gdlt.il.š.b]'[l.]š.'nt ṣpn. | [---.] 36[9].1.16
.y'db.ksa.w yṯb. | tqru.l špš.um h.špš.um.ql b.'m. | ršp.bbt h.mnt.nḥš.šmrr. | nḥš.'q šr.ln h.mlḫš.abd.ln h.ydy. | ḥmt. UG5.7.31
t. | alp.w š šrp.alp šlmm. | l b'l.'ṣr l ṣpn. | npš.w.š.l ršp bbt. | [']ṣrm l h.ršp [-]m. | [---.]bqt[-]. | [b] ǵb.ršp mh bnš. | šrp UG5.12.A.11
dš il bt. | w tlḥm aṯt. | š l ilbt.šlmm. | kll ylḥm b h. | w l bbt šqym. | š l uḫr ḫlmṭ. | w tr l qlḥ. | ym aḥd. UG5.11.11

bd

il.tspr.yrḫm. | k b'l.k yḥwy.y'šr.ḥwy.y'š. | r.w yšqyn h.ybd.w yšr.'l h. | n'm[n.w t]'nynn.ap ank.aḥwy. | aqht[.ǵz]r.w 17[2AQHT].6.31
l t'n.aṯrt.alp. | kd.yqḥ.b ḫmr. | rbt.ymsk.b msk h. | qm.ybd.w yšr. | mṣltm.bd.n'm. | yšr.ǵzr.ṭb.ql. | 'l.b'l.b ṣrrt. | ṣpn.y 3['NT].1.18
rrn aryn. | a[-]ḥn tlyn. | atdb w 'r. | qdš w amrr. | ṯḫr w bd. | [k]ṯr ḫss šlm. | šlm il bt. | šlm il ḥš[t]. | ršp inšt. | [--]rm il UG5.7.71
qḥ.b ḫmr. | rbt.ymsk.b msk h. | qm.ybd.w yšr. | mṣltm.bd.n'm. | yšr.ǵzr.ṭb.ql. | 'l.b'l.b ṣrrt. | ṣpn.ytmr.b'l. | bnt h.y'n. 3['NT].1.19

bdil

.---]n. | krr[-.---]. | špš[yn.---]. | [--]b[.---]. | 'bd'ṯ[tr.---]. | bdil[.---]. | abǵl.[---]. | [.---]. | ḏmrb'[l.---]. | iḫyn.[---]. | 'bdb'[l.-- 102[322].2.2

bddn

.ady. | bn.'ṯtry. | bn.ḫrẓn. | ady. | bn.birtn. | bn.ḥrẓn. | bn.bddn. | bn.anny. | ytršp. | bn.szn. | bn.kdgdl. | bn.gl'd. | bn.ktln. 115[301].1.9
. | bn.[---]. | bn.[---]. | w.nḥ[l h]. | bn.ẓr[-]. | mru.skn. | bn.bddn. | bn.ǵrgn. | bn.tgtn. | bn.ḥrẓn. | bn.qdšt. | bn.nṯǵ[-]. | bn.g 113[400].5.7
[-----]. | šd.prsn.l.[---]. | šd.bddn.l.iytlm. | šd.bn.nb'm.l.ṯpṭb'l. | šd.bn mšrn.l.ilšpš. | [šd.b 2030.1.3

bdḥ

amt.w bt.[---]. | rmm.w 'l[y.---]. | bt.il.ṯq[l.---.kbd]. | w bdḥ.k[--.---]. | 'ṣrm.l i[nš.ilm.ṭb.md] | bḥ.b'l.[gdlt.---.dqt]. | l ṣ APP.II[173].43

bdy

dnt. | klby.aḥrṭp. | ilyn.'lby.ṣdkn. | gmrt.ṯlmyn. | 'bdnt. | bdy.ḥrš arkd. | blšš lmd. | ḥṯtn.tqn. | ydd.idṯn. | šǵr.ilgdn. 1045.9

bdl

ḫtn. | [p]lsy. | bn.ḥrš. | [--.]kbd. | [---]. | y[---]. | bn.ǵlyn. | bdl.ar. | bn.šyn. | bn.ubrš. | bn.d[--]b. | abrpu. | bn.k[n]y. | bn.kl 1035.3.1
bn.qrrn. | bn.dnt. | bn.ṯ'l[-]. | bdl.ar.dt.inn. | mhr l ht. | artyn. | 'dmlk. | bn.alt[-]. | iḫy[-]. | 'b 1035.1.4
y. | ilym. | bn.'br. | mnip'l. | amrb'l. | dqry. | ṯdy. | yp'b'l. | bdlm. | bn.pḏ[-]. | bn.[---]. 1058.20
'zn. | ḥyn. | 'myn. | ilyn. | yrb'm. | n'mn. | bn.kbl. | kn'm. | bdlm. | bn.ṣǵr. | klb. | bn.mnḥm. | bn.brqn. | bn.'n. | bn.'bdy. | 'b 1046.3.42
bdl.gt.bn.tbšn. | bn.mnyy.š'rty. | aryn.adddy. | agpṯr. | šb'l.ml 91[311].1
[m'y.---]. | bn.pynq.'nqp[a]t[y.---]. | ayiḫ.ilšt[m'y.---]. | [b]dlm.dt.yṯb[.---]. | [-]y[--].'nqp[aty.---]. | 'ṯt[r]n.[-]bṯ[-.---]. | [- 90[314].2.10
l h[.---]. | w.unṯm.nḥ[l h.---]. | [---.]'ḏr[.---]. | str[-.---]. | bdlm.d[t.---]. | 'dn.[---]. | aḫqm bir[-.---]. | kṯrmlk.ns[--.---]. | b 90[314].2.2
dyn. | bn.sgr. | bn.aǵltn. | bn.ktln. | bn.'gwn. | bn.yšm'. | bdl.mḏrǵlm. | bn.mmy. | bn.ḫnyn. | bn.knn. | khnm. | bn.ṯ'y. | 104[316].9
[n.---]. | bn.gzry. | bn.atyn. | bn.ttn. | bn.rwy. | bn.'myn. | bdl.mrynm. | bn.ṣqn. | bn.šyn. | bn.prtn. | bn.ypr. | mrum. | bn.' 113[400].3.6
spr.bdlm. | n'mn. | rbil. | plsy. | ygmr. | mnṯ. | prḫ. | 'dršp. | ršpab. | ṯ 1032.1

db'l. | kdn.zlyy. | krwn.arty. | tlmu.zlyy. | pdu.qmnzy. | bdl.qrṭy. | trgn.bn.tǵh. | aupš.qmnzy. | ṯrry.mṣbty. | prn.nǵṯy. 89[312].6

bdmr

d.[---]. | b d.b'lsr. | yd.ṯdn.'šr. | [ḥ]mrm. | ddm.l.ybr[k]. | bdmr.prs.l.u[-]m[-]. | ṯmn.l.'šrm. | dmd.b d.mry[n]m. 2102.7

bdn

py. | kṯy. | bn.ẓmn. | bn.trdn. | ypq. | 'bd. | qrḥ. | abšr. | bn.bdn. | ḏmry. | bn.pndr. | bn.aḫt. | bn.'dn. | bn.išb'[l]. 2117.4.29
yn[.b]n.arkšt. | l'q[.---]. | šd.pll.b d.qrt. | š[d].anndr.b d.bdn.nḫ[l h]. | [šd.]agyn.b d.kmrn.n[ḥl] h. | [š]d.nbzn.[-]l.qrt. 2029.7
[s]ǵr.bn.bdn. | [sǵ]r.bn.psḫn. | alṯy. | sǵr.npr. | bn.ḫty. | ṯn.bnš ibrḏr. | b 2082.1
s[p.--]mrtn.kṯrmlk. | yḥmn.aḫm[l]k.'bdrpu.adn.ṯ[--]. | bdn.qln.mtn.ydln. | b'ltdtt.tlgn.ytn. | b'ltǵpṯm.krwn.ilšn.agy 2011.34
n.lky.qšt. | bn.dll.qšt.w.ql[']. | bn.pǵyn.qšt.w[.q]l'. | bn.bdn.qšt. | bn.pls.qšt. | ǵmrm. | [-]lhd.ṯt.qštm.w.ṯn.ql'm. | ulšn.ṯ 119[321].3.30
št.w.ql'. | bn.bb.qšt.w[.ql]'. | bn.aktmy.qšt. | šdyn.qšt. | bdn.qšt.w.ql'. | bn.šmlbi.qšt.w.ql'. | bn.yy.qšt. | ilrb.qšt. | bn.n 119[321].4.12
| šdyn.ššlmt. | prtwn.š'rt. | ṯṯn.š'rt. | 'dn.š'rt. | mnn.š'rt. | bdn.š'rt. | 'pṯn.š'rt. | 'bd.yrḫ š'rt. | ḫbd.ṯr yṣr š'r. | pdy.yṣr š'rt. 97[315].8
[-]. | ṯmn.ḥblm.šb'.šb'.ma[-]. | 'šr.kkr.rtn. | b d.šm'y.bn.bdn. 1128.33

bdnh

]. | d.[---]. | bnš[-] mdy[-]. | w.b.glb. | phnn.w. | mndym. | bdnh. | l[q]ḥt. | [--]km.'m.mlk. | [b]ǵl hm.w.iblbl hm. | w.b.ṯb 2129.7

bhṯ

h.tša. | g hm.w tṣḥ.ṯḥm.aliyn. | bn.b'l.hwt.aliy.qrdm. | bhṯ.bn.ilm.mt.'bd k.an. | w d 'lm k.šmḫ.bn.ilm.mt. | [---.]g h. 5[67].2.19
m.mt. | ṯny.l ydd.il ǵzr. | ṯḥm.aliyn.b'l.hwt.aliy. | qrdm.bhṯ.l bn.ilm mt. | 'bd k.an.w d.'lm k. | tb'.w l.yṯb.ilm.idk. | l y 5[67].2.11

bwa

| pǵt.l ahlm.rgm.l yṯ[pn.y] | bl.agrtn.bat.b ḏd k.[pǵt]. | bat.b hlm w y'n.yṯpn[.mhr]. | št.qḫn.w tšqyn.yn.qḫ. | ks.b d 19[1AQHT].4.214
rt.ilm.špš.mǵy[t]. | pǵt.l ahlm.rgm.l yṯ[pn.y] | bl.agrtn.bat.b ḏd k.[pǵt]. | bat.b hlm w y'n.yṯpn[.mhr]. | št.qḫn.w tšq 19[1AQHT].4.213
[m]t.dm.ḫt.š'tqt dm. | li.w ttb'.š'tqt. | bt.krt.bu.tbu. | bkt.tgly.w tbu. | nṣrt.tbu.pnm. | 'rm.tdu.mh. | pdrm.t 16.6[127].3
[m]t.dm.ḫt.š'tqt dm. | li.w ttb'.š'tqt. | bt.krt.bu.tbu. | bkt.tgly.w tbu. | nṣrt.tbu.pnm. | 'rm.tdu.mh. | pdrm.tdu. 16.6[127].3
bu.b'd y[.---]. 1169.1
m]tm.tgl.ḏ[d.]i[l.]w tbu. | [qr]š.m[l]k.ab[.šnm.]mṣr. | [t]bu.ḏdm.qn[-.-]n[-.-]lt. | ql h.yš[m'].ṯr.[il].ab h.[---]l. | b šb't. 3['NT.VI].5.17
.w yṣḥ. | ḥwt.aḫt.w nar[-]. | qrn.d bat k.btlt.'nt. | qrn.d bat k b'l.ymšḥ. | b'l.ymšḥ.hm.b 'p. | nṭ'n.b arṣ.ib y. | w b 'pr.q 10[76].2.22
kr'.w yql. | w yšu.g h.w yṣḥ. | ḥwt.aḫt.w nar[-]. | qrn.d bat k.btlt.'nt. | qrn.d bat k b'l.ymšḥ. | b'l.ymšḥ.hm.b 'p. | nṭ'n 10[76].2.21
ry. | l l[ḥ]m.l š[ty].ṣḥt km. | db[ḥ.l krt.a]dn km. | 'l.krt.tbun.km. | rgm.ṯ[rm.]rgm hm. | b ḏrt[.---.]krt. | [----]. 15[128].6.6
r h.tš'rb. | 'l h.tš'rb.ẓby h. | ṯr.ḫbr.rbt. | ḫbr.ṯrrt. | bt.krt.tbun. | lm.mṯb[.---]. | w lḥm mr.tqdm. | yd.b ṣ'.tšlḥ. | ḥrb.b bšr 15[128].4.21
.ḫt.š'tqt dm. | li.w ttb'.š'tqt. | bt.krt.bu.tbu. | bkt.tgly.w tbu. | nṣrt.tbu.pnm. | 'rm.tdu.mh. | pdrm.tdu.šrr. | ḫṭ m.t'mt.[16.6[127].4
m. | li.w ttb'.š'tqt. | bt.krt.bu.tbu. | bkt.tgly.w tbu. | nṣrt.tbu.pnm. | 'rm.tdu.mh. | pdrm.tdu.šrr. | ḫṭ m.t'mt.[']ṯr.[k]m. 16.6[127].5
.'m. | [il.]mbk nhrm.qrb. | [a]pq.thmtm.tgly.ḏd. | il.w tbu.qrš.. | mlk.ab.šnm.l p'n. | il.thbr.w tql. | tšthwy.w tkbdn h 6.1.35[49.1.7]
.'m.[i]l.mbk.[nhrm.qrb.apq.thmtm]. | [ygly.]ḏl i[l].w ybu[.q]rš.mlk[.ab.šnm.l p'n.il.] | [yhbr.]w yql[.y]šthw[y.]w y 2.3[129].5
.'m.lṯpn]. | il d pid.tk ḥrš[n.---.tk.ǵr.ks]. | ygly ḏd.i[l.w ybu.qrš.mlk]. | ab.šnm.l [p'n.il.yhbr.w yql]. | yšthwy.[w ykbd 1['NT.IX].3.23
pnm. | 'm.il.mbk.nhrm. | qrb.apq.thmtm. | tgly.ḏd.il.w tbu. | qrš.mlk.ab.šnm. | l p'n.il.thbr.w tql. | tšthwy.w tkbd h. | 4[51].4.23
]m.'m il.mbk.nhrm. | [qrb.ap]q.thmtm tgly.ḏd il. | [w tbu.qr]š.mlk.ab.šnm. | [l p'n.il.t]hbr.w tql.tštḥ | [wy.w tkbd]n 17[2AQHT].6.49
'm.i]l.mbk.nhr[m.qr]b.[ap]q. | [thm]tm.tgl.ḏ[d.]i[l.]w tbu. | [qr]š.m[l]k.ab[.šnm.]mṣr. | [t]bu.ḏdm.qn[-.-]n[-.-]lt. | ql 3['NT.VI].5.15
. | ['m.il.mbk.nhrm]. | [qrb.apq.thmtm]. | [tgly.ḏd.il.w]tb[a]. | [qrš.mlk.ab.]šnm. | [tša.g hm.w tṣ]ḥ.sbn. | [---]l[.---.]'d. 5[67].6.1
bnšm.d.bu. | tš'.dt.tq[ḥn]. | š'rt. | šb' dt tqḥn. | ššlmt. 2099.1

bz

t kṯrt bn] | t hll.snnt.bnt h | ll b'l gml.yrdt. | b 'rgzm.b bz tdm. | lla y.'m lẓpn i | l ḏ.pid.hn b p y sp | r hn.b špt y mn 24[77].43
gt ilštm'. | bt ubnyn š h d.ytn.ṣṭqn. | ṭut ṭbḫ ṣtq[n]. | b bz 'zm ṭbḫ š[h]. | b kl ygz ḥḫ š h. 1153.4

bzl

rm.n'mn.b.ḫly.ull.krm.aḥ[d.---]. | krm.uḫn.b.šdmy.ṯlṯ.bzl[.d]prn[.---]. | aupṯ.krm.aḥd.nšpin.kr[m.]aḥd[.---]. | dmt.l 1081.13

bḥ

n. | l mrynm. | b yṯbmlk. | kdm.ǵbiš ḫry. | ḫmš yn.b d. | bḥ mlkt. | b mdr'. | ṯlṯ bt.il | ann. | kd.bt.ilann. 1090.15

bḥn

l arṣ. | [l a]n ḥmt.l p[.n]ṯk.abd.l p.akl ṯm.dl. | [---.q]l.bl.tbḥ[n.l]azd.'r.qdm. | [---].'ẓ q[dm.--.šp]š. | [---.šm]n.mšḥt.kṯ UG5.8.21

bḫr

mri h]. | [tpṯḥ.rḥ]bt.[yn]. | [---.]rp[.---]. | [---.ḫ]br[.---]. | bḫr[.--]t[.----]. | l mṯb[.--]t[.---]. | [tqdm.]yd.b ṣ'.t[šl]ḥ. | [ḥrb.b 15[128].5.5
ṣbia.špš. | b'l ny.w ymlk. | [y]ṣb.'ln.w y[-]y. | [kr]t.ṯ'.'ln.bḫr. | [---].aṯt k.'l. | [---] k.yšṣi. | [---.]ḫbr.rbt. | [ḫbr.ṯrr]t.il d. | [15[128].5.22

bṭy

bṯt.w dbḥ.w dbḥ. | dnt.w dbḥ.tdmm. | amht.k b h.bṯt.l tbṭ. | w b h.tdmmt.amht. | aḫr.mǵy.aliyn.b'l. | mǵyt.btlt.'nt. | t 4[51].3.21

bṭr

[---.--]y.bṭr.b d.mlkt. | [---.]bṭr.b d.mlkt. | [---].b d.mršp. | [---.m]rbṣ. | [---.r]b.ṯnnm. | [---.] 2015.1.2
[---.--]y.bṭr.b d.mlkt. | [---.]bṭr.b d.mlkt. | [---].b d.mršp. | [---.m]rbṣ. | [2015.1.1

by

gmn. | t̲lt̲.ḫmš.alpm. | b d.brq.maḫdy. | kkr.t̲lt̲. | b d.bn.by.ar[y]. | alpm.t̲lt̲. | b d.šim.il[š]tm‘y. 1134.5
m. | rgm.t̲t̲[b]. | any kn.dt. | likt.mṣrm. | hn dt.b.ṣr. | mtt.by. | gšm.adr. | nškḥ.w. | rb.tmtt. | lqḥ.kl.d̲r‘. | b d a[-]m.w.ank 2059.13
]l hm.b d. | rb.tmtt.lqḥt. | w.t̲t̲b.ank.l hm. | w.any k.t̲t̲. | by.‘ky.‘ryt. | w.aḫ y.mhk. | b lb h.al.yšt. 2059.25

byy

bn a[---]. | bn.byy. | bn.ily[-]. | bn.iy[--]. | bn.t̲y[--]. | bn.p[---]. | gyn[.---]. | bn. 2025.2
dbḥt.byy.bn. | šry.l ‘t̲t. RS61[24.323.1]
| [--]ny. | [bn].t̲rdnt. | [bn].hyadt. | [--]lt. | šmrm. | p‘ṣ.bn.byy.‘šrt. 1047.25

byn

.‘n h.aliyn.b‘l. | w yšu.‘n h.w y‘n. | w y‘n.btlt.‘nt. | n‘mt.bn.aḫt.b‘l. | l pnn h.ydd.w yqm. | l p‘n h.ykr‘.w yql. | w yšu.g 10[76].2.16
.‘ṣ]. | w lḫšt.abn[.tant.šmm.‘m.arṣ.thmt]. | ‘m kbkbm[.abn.brq.d l td‘.šmm.at m]. | w ank.ib[ǵy h.---]. | [-].l y‘mdn.i[7.2[130].20
bn. | [hmlt.a]rṣ.[tant.šmm.‘m.ar]ṣ. | thmt.[‘mn.kbkbm.abn.brq]. | d l t[d‘.šmm.at m.w ank]. | ibǵ[y h.b tk.ǵ]r y.il.ṣp 3[‘NT].4.61
. | ‘ṣ.w lḫšt.abn. | tant.šmm.‘m.arṣ. | thmt.‘mn.kbkbm. | abn.brq.d l.td‘.šmm. | rgm l td‘.nšm.w l tbn. | hmlt.arṣ.at m. 3[‘NT].3.23
.‘mn.kbkbm. | abn.brq.d l.td‘.šmm. | rgm l td‘.nšm.w l tbn. | hmlt.arṣ.at m.w ank. | ibǵy h.b tk.ǵr y.il.ṣpn. | b qdš.b ǵ 3[‘NT].3.24
t.šmm.‘m[.arṣ.thmt.‘mn.kbkbm]. | rgm.l td‘.nš[m.w l tbn.hmlt.arṣ]. | at.w ank.ib[ǵy h.---]. | w y‘n.kt̲r.w ḫss[.lk.lk.‘ 1[‘NT.IX].3.15
t. | [w at̲ny k.rgm.]‘ṣ.w lḫšt. | [abn.rgm.l td]‘.nš[m.w l t]bn. | [hmlt.a]rṣ.[tant.šmm.‘m.ar]ṣ. | thmt.[‘mn.kbkbm.abn. 3[‘NT].4.59
yrtqṣ.ṣmd.b d b‘l.km.nšr. | b[u]ṣb‘t h.ylm.ktp.zbl ym.bn ydm.t̲pṭ. | nhr.‘z.ym.l ymk.l tnǵṣn.pnt h.l ydlp. | tmn h.kt̲ 2.4[68].16
drkt h.trtqṣ.b d b‘l km nš | r.b uṣb‘t h.hlm.ktp.zbl ym.bn ydm. | [t̲p]ṭ nhr.yrtqṣ.ṣmd.b d b‘l.km.nšr. | b[u]ṣb‘t h.yl 2.4[68].14
[ak.ym.t‘]dt.t̲pṭ.nhr.mlak.mt̲ḫr.yḥb[-.---.]] | [---].mlak.bn.ktpm.rgm.b‘l h.w y[--.---]. | [---].ap.anš.zbl.b‘l.šdmt.bg[--. 2.1[137].42
ḫd bt. | rbt.kmn.hkl. | w y‘n.kt̲r.w ḫss. | šm‘.l aliyn b‘l. | bn.l rkb.‘rpt. | bl.ašt.urbt.b bh[t] m. | ḥln.b qrb.hkl m. | w y‘n 4[51].5.122
tlk.w aṣd.kl. | ǵr.l kbd.arṣ.kl.gb‘. | l kbd.šdm.npš.ḫsrt. | bn.nšm.npš.hmlt. | arṣ.mǵt.l n‘m y.arṣ. | dbr.ysmt.šd.šḥlmmt 6[49].2.18
.w bn.dnil.l t̲rm[.‘l h]. | nšrm.trḫpn.ybṣr.[ḥbl.d] | iym.bn.nšrm.arḫp.an[k.‘]l. | aqht.‘db k.hlmn.t̲nm.qdqd. | t̲lt̲ id.‘l. 18[3AQHT].4.21
[m]. | bn.dnil.l t̲rm.‘l h.nšr[m]. | trḫpn.ybṣr.ḥbl.diy[m.bn]. | nšrm.trḫp.‘nt.‘l[.aqht]. | t‘dbn h.hlmn.t̲nm[.qdqd]. | t̲lt̲ i 18[3AQHT].4.31
iyt.šb‘t.brqm.[---]. | t̲mnt.iṣr r‘t.‘ṣ brq y. | riš h.tply.t̲ly.bn.‘n h. | uz‘rt.tmll.išd h.qrn[m]. | dt.‘l h.riš h.b glt̲.b šm[m]. UG5.3.1.5
.hmt.[---]. | l šrr.št[.---]. | b riš h.[---]. | ib h.mš[--.---]. | [b]n.‘n h[.---]. 2.4[68].40
d[.--]. | [---.]ḥš[.-]nm[.--.]k.[--].w yḫnp[.---]. | [---.]ylm.b[n.‘]n k.ṣmdm.špk[.---]. | [---.]nt[-.]mbk kpt.w[.--].b g[--]. | [1001.1.16
[---.--]b. | [---.r]iš k. | [---.]bn ‘n km. | [---.]alp. | [---.]ym.rbt. | [---.]b nhrm. | [‘b]r.gbl.‘br. 3[‘NT.VI].6.3
ṣ.ṣmd.b d b‘l. | [km.]nšr.b uṣb‘t h.ylm.qdqd.zbl. | [ym.]bn.‘nm.t̲pṭ.nhr.yprsḥ.ym.yql. | l arṣ.tnǵṣn.pnt h.w ydlp.tmn 2.4[68].25
t h.trtqṣ. | b d b‘l.km.nšr b uṣb‘t h.hlm.qdq | d zbl ym.bn.‘nm.t̲pṭ.nhr.yprsḥ ym. | w yql.l arṣ.w trtqṣ.ṣmd.b d b‘l. | [2.4[68].22
t.w tqry.ǵlmm. | b št.ǵr.w hln.‘nt.tm | t̲ḫṣ.b ‘mq.t̲ḫtṣb.bn. | qrytm tmḫṣ.lim.ḫp y[m]. | tṣmt.adm.ṣat.š[p]š. | t̲ḥt h.k k 3[‘NT].2.6
t.‘nt.w tqry.ǵlmm.b št.ǵr]. | ap ‘nt tm[t̲ḫṣ.b ‘mq.t̲ḫtṣb.bn.qrytm.tmḫṣ]. | lim ḫ[p.ym.---]. | [--]m.t[-]t[.---]. | m[-]mt[.- 7.2[130].25
mǵyn. | tštql.ilt.l hkl h. | w l.šb‘t.tmt̲ḫṣ h.b ‘mq. | t̲ḫtṣb.bn.qrtm.t̲t̲‘r. | ksat.l mhr.t̲‘r.t̲lḥnt. | l ṣbim.hdmm.l ǵzrm. | mi 3[‘NT].2.20
. | [l bmt h.---.]hy bt h t‘rb. | [---.tm]t̲ḫṣ b ‘mq. | [t̲ḫtṣb.bn.qrtm.t̲t̲‘r.t̲lḥnt.]l ṣbim. | [hdmm.l ǵzrm.mid.tmt̲ḫṣn.w t]‘ 7.1[131].5
[--]at.brt.lb k.‘nn.[---]. | [--.]šdq.k ttn.l y.šn[.---]. | [---.]bn.rgm.w yd‘[.---]. 60[32].6
m. | d̲mr.ḥlqm.b mm‘.mhrm. | ‘d.tšb‘.tmt̲ḫṣ.b bt. | t̲ḫṣb.bn.t̲lḥnm.ymḥ. | [b]bt.dm.d̲mr.yṣq.šmn. | šlm.b ṣ‘.trḥṣ.yd h. 3[‘NT].2.30

bky

w qdš.u ilm.tmtn. | špḥ.lt̲pn.l yḥ. | w y‘ny.krt.t̲‘. | bn.al.tbkn.al. | tdm.l y.al tkl.bn. | qr.‘n k.mḫ.riš k. | udm‘t.ṣḥ.aḫt k. 16.1[125].25
. | [--.]šḫp.ṣǵrt h. | yrk.t‘l.b ǵr. | mslmt.b ǵr.tliyt. | w t‘l.bkm.b arr. | bm.arr.w b ṣpn. | b n‘m.b ǵr.t[l]iyt. | ql.l b‘l.ttnn. 10[76].3.30
uḫry.mṭ.yd h. | dnil.bt h.ymǵyn.yšt | ql.dnil.l hkl h.‘rb.b | kyt.b hkl h.mšspdt.b ḥzr h. | pẓǵm.ǵr.ybk.l aqht. | ǵzr.yd 19[1AQHT].4.171
mt.]rpi. | yt̲b.ǵzr.m[t.hrnmy.y]šu. | g h.w yṣḥ.t[b‘.---]. | bkyt.b hk[l]y.mšspdt. | b ḥzr y pẓǵm.ǵr.w yq. | dbḥ.ilm.yš‘ly 19[1AQHT].4.183
ilḥu.t[---]l. | trm.tṣr.trm[.‘]tqt. | tbky.w tšnn.[tt]n. | g h.bky.b ḥ[y k.a]b n. | nšmḫ.b l.mt k.ngln. | k klb.[b]bt k.n‘tq. | 16.2[125].98
.špḥ. | lt̲pn.w qdš.‘l. | ab h.y‘rb.ybky. | w yšnn.ytn.g h. | bky.b ḥy k.ab n.ašmḫ. | b l.mt k.ngln.k klb. | b bt k.n‘tq.k inr 16.1[125].14
. | w b tm hn.špḥ.yitbd. | w b.pḫyr h.yrt̲. | y‘rb.b ḥdr h.ybky. | b t̲n.[-]gmm.w ydm‘. | tntkn.udm‘t h. | km.t̲qlm.arṣ h. 14[KRT].1.26
[m]t.dm.ḫt.š‘tqt dm. | li.w ttb‘.š‘tqt. | bt.krt.bu.tbu. | bkt.tgly.w tbu. | nṣrt.tbu.pnm. | ‘rm.tdu.mh. | pdrm.tdu.šrr. | 16.6[127].4
l.yrd.b d̲hrt h. | ab adm.w yqrb. | b šal.krt.m at. | krt.k ybky. | ydm‘.n‘mn.ǵlm. | il.mlk[.t̲]r ab h. | yarš.hm.drk[t]. | k 14[KRT].1.39
tntkn.udm‘t h. | km.t̲qlm.arṣ h. | km ḫmšt.mt̲t h. | bm.bky h.w yšn. | b dm‘ h.nhmmt. | šnt.tluan. | w yškb.nhmmt. | 14[KRT].1.31
pš. | tšu.aliyn.b‘l.l ktp. | ‘nt.k tšt h.tš‘lyn h. | b ṣrrt.ṣpn.tbkyn h. | w tqbrn h.tštnn.b ḫrt. | ilm.arṣ.tt̲bḫ.šb‘m. | rumm.k 6[62].1.16
n k.mḫ.riš k. | udm‘t.ṣḥ.aḫt k. | t̲tmnt.bt.ḥmḥ h. | d[-]n.tbkn.w tdm.l y.[--]. | [---].al.trgm.l aḫt k. | [---.]l [ ]dm.aḫt k. 16.1[125].30
ḥ p‘n y.ibq[‘.kbd hm.w] | aḥd.hm.it̲.šmt.hm.i[t̲]. | ‘ẓm.abky.w aqbrn h. | ašt.b ḫrt.ilm.arṣ. | b p h.rgm.l yṣa.b špt h.h 19[1AQHT].3.111
hyt.tql.tḥt.p‘n y.ibq‘. | kbd h.w aḥd.hm.it̲.šmt.it̲. | ‘ẓm.abky w aqbrn h.aštn. | b ḫrt.ilm.arṣ.b p h.rgm.l[yṣ]a. | b špt 19[1AQHT].3.140
bd h.w yḥd. | it̲.šmt.it̲.‘ẓm.w yqḫ b hm. | aqht.ybl.l qẓ.ybky.w yqbr. | yqbr.nn.b mdgt.b knk[-]. | w yšu.g h.w yṣḥ.kn 19[1AQHT].3.146
.tḥt.p‘n y.ibq‘.kbd[h]. | w aḥd.hm.it̲.šmt.hm.it̲[.‘ẓm]. | abky.w aqbrn.ašt.b ḫrt. | i[lm.arṣ.b p h.rgm.l yṣa.b šp] | t h.h 19[1AQHT].3.126
mknpt.ap. | [k]rt.bnm.il.špḥ. | lt̲pn.w qdš.‘l. | ab h.y‘rb.ybky. | w yšnn.ytn.g h. | bky.b ḥy k.ab n.ašmḫ. | b l.mt k.ngln 16.1[125].12
. | ybm h.šb‘[.---]. | ǵzr.ilḥu.t[---]l. | trm.tṣr.trm[.‘]tqt. | tbky.w tšnn.[tt]n. | g h.bky.b ḥ[y k.a]b n. | nšmḫ.b l.mt k.ngl 16.2[125].97
t h.km.qtr.[b ap h.---]. | ‘nt.b ṣmt.mhr h.[---]. | aqht.w tbk.y[---.---]. | abn.ank.w ‘l.[qšt k.---.‘l]. | qṣ‘t k.at.l ḥ[---.---]. 18[3AQHT].4.39
p.ab.ik mtm. | tmtn.u ḫšt k.l ntn. | ‘tq.b d.at̲t.ab ṣrry. | tbky k.ab.ǵr.b‘l. | ṣpn.ḥlm.qdš. | any.ḥlm.adr.ḥl. | rḥb.mknpt. 16.1[125].6
l bky.‘tq. | b d.at̲t ab.ṣrry. | u ilm.tmtn.špḥ. | [l]t̲pn.l yḥ.t[b]ky k. | ab.ǵr.b‘l.ṣ[p]n.ḥlm. | qdš.nny.ḥ[l]m.adr. | ḥl.rḥb.m 16.2[125].106
.špš.b šmm.tqru. | [---.]nplt.y[--].md‘.nplt.bšr. | [---].w tpky.k[m.]n‘r.tdm‘.km. | [ṣǵ]r.bkm.y‘ny[.---.bn]wt h. | [--]nn. UG5.8.40
q ḥmt. | [---.--]n h.ḥmt.w t‘btn h.abd y. | [---.ǵ]r.šrǵzz.ybky.km.n‘r. | [w ydm‘.k]m.ṣǵr.špš.b šmm.tqru. | [---.]nplt.y[UG5.8.37
]nm.aqny. | [tn.t̲a]rm.amid. | [w y‘n].t̲r.ab h.il. | d[--].b bk.krt. | b dm‘.n‘mn.ǵlm. | il.trḥṣ.w tadm. | rḥṣ[.y]d k.amt. | u 14[KRT].2.60
il.l hkl h.‘rb.b | kyt.b hkl h.mšspdt.b ḥzr h. | pẓǵm.ǵr.ybk.l aqht. | ǵzr.ydm‘.l kdd.dnil. | mt.rpi.l ymm.l yrḫm. | l yr 19[1AQHT].4.173

.dnil. | mt.rpi.l ymm.l yrḫm. | l yrḫm.l šnt.ʿd. | šbʿt.šnt.ybk.l aq | ht.ǵzr.yd[mʿ.]l kdd. | dnil.mt.r[pi.mk].b šbʿ. | šnt.w 19[1AQHT].4.177
.tš[mʿ]. | pǵt.ṯkmt.my.ḥspt.l[šʿ]r.ṭl. | ydʿt.hlk.kbkbm. | bkm.tmdln.ʿr. | bkm.tṣmd.pḥl.bkm. | tšu.ab h.tštnn.l[b]mt ʿr 19[1AQHT].2.57
ʿ]r.ṭl. | ydʿt.hlk.kbkbm. | bkm.tmdln.ʿr. | bkm.tṣmd.pḥl.bkm. | tšu.ab h.tštnn.l[b]mt ʿr. | l ysmsm.bmt.pḥl. | y dnil.ys 19[1AQHT].2.58
-].mdʿ.nplt.bšr. | [---].w tpky.k[m.]nʿr.tdmʿ.km. | [ṣǵ]r.bkm.yʿny[.---.bn]wt h. | [--]nn.bnt yš[--.---.-]lk. | [--]b.kmm.l UG5.8.41
. | ḥl.rḫb.mk[npt]. | ap.krt bn[m.il]. | špḥ.lṭpn[.w qdš]. | bkm.tʿr[b.ʿl.ab h]. | tʿrb.ḥ[--]. | b ṯtm.t[---]. | šknt.[---]. | bkym[. 16.2[125].112
k.nʿtq. | k inr[.ap.]ḫšt k. | ap.ab.k mtm.tmtn. | u ḫšt k.l bky.ʿtq. | b d.aṯt ab.ṣrry. | u ilm.tmtn.špḥ. | [l]ṭpn.l yḥ.t[b]ky 16.2[125].103
ḫsp.ib[.---]. | ʿl.bt.ab h.nšrm.trḫ[p]n. | ybṣr.ḥbl.diym. | tbky.pǵt.bm.lb. | tdmʿ.bm.kbd. | tmzʿ.kst.dnil.mt. | rpi.al.ǵzr. 19[1AQHT].1.34
t.my.ḥspt.l[šʿ]r.ṭl. | ydʿt.hlk.kbkbm. | bkm.tmdln.ʿr. | bkm.tṣmd.pḥl.bkm. | tšu.ab h.tštnn.l[b]mt ʿr. | l ysmsm.bmt. 19[1AQHT].2.58
y.hmlt.aṯr.bʿl.nrd. | b arṣ.ʿm h.trd.nrt. | ilm.špš.ʿd.tšbʿ.bk. | tšt.k yn.udmʿt.gm. | tṣḥ.l nrt.ilm.špš. | ʿms mʿ.l y.aliyn.bʿ 6[62].1.9
.ṯḥš.nṯq.dmrn. | ʿn.bʿl.qdm.yd h. | k tǵd.arz.b ymn h. | bkm.yṯb.bʿl.l bht h. | u mlk.u bl mlk. | arṣ.drkt.yštkn. | dll.al.i 4[51].7.42
h.ṯǵr. | yṣu.hlm.aḫ h.tph. | [ksl]h.l arṣ.ṯṯbr. | [---.]aḫ h.tbky. | [--.m]rṣ.mlk. | [---.]krt.adn k. | [w yʿny.]ǵzr.ilḥu. | [---.] 16.1[125].55
ṯt.ḥry. | [l lḥ]m.l šty.ṣḥt k[m]. | [---.]brk.t[---]. | [ʿl.]krt.tbkn. | [--.]rgm.ṯrm. | [--.]mtm.tbkn. | [--]t.w b lb.tqb[-]. | [--]m 15[128].5.12
. | [---.]brk.t[---]. | [ʿl.]krt.tbkn. | [--.]rgm.ṯrm. | [--.]mtm.tbkn. | [--]t.w b lb.tqb[-]. | [--]m[-].mtm.uṣbʿ[t]. | [-]tr.šrk.il. | ʿ 15[128].5.14
bkm.tʿr[b.ʿl.ab h]. | tʿrb.ḥ[--]. | b ṯtm.t[---]. | šknt.[---]. | bkym[.---]. | ǵr.y[----]. | ydm.[---]. | apn.[---]. | [--.]b[.---]. 16.2[125].116

bkr

| mid.rm[.krt]. | b tk.rpi.ar[ṣ]. | b pḫr.qbṣ.dtn. | ṣǵrt hn.abkrn. | tbrk.ilm.tity. | tity.ilm.l ahl hm. | dr il.l mšknt hm. | 15[128].3.16
lak. | šmm.tmr.zbl.mlk. | šmm.tlak.ṭl.amr.. | bn km k bk[r.z]bl.am.. | rkm.agzrt[.--].arḫ.. | bʿl.azrt.ʿnt.[-]ld. | kbd h.l 13[6].28
ṣt.bn.amt. | p d.in.b bt y.ttn. | tn.l y.mṯt.ḥry. | nʿmt.špḥ.bkr k. | d k.nʿm.ʿnt.nʿm h. | km.tsm.ʿṯtrt.ts[m h]. | d ʿq h.ib.iq 14[KRT].3.144
bn.amt.p d.[i]n. | b bt y.ttn.tn. | l y.mṯt.ḥry. | nʿmt.šbḥ.bkr k. | d k nʿm.ʿnt. | nʿm h.km.tsm. | ʿṯtrt.tsm h. | d ʿq h.ib.iq 14[KRT].6.290

bl

t.akl[y.nšm]. | akly.hml[t.arṣ]. | w y[-]l.a[---]. | š[--.---]. | bl[.---]. 6[49].5.28
---]. | [-----]. | b [----]. | w [----]. | bʿl.[---]. | il hd.b[---]. | at.bl.at.[---]. | yisp hm.b[ʿl.---]. | bn.dgn[.---]. | ʿdbm.[---]. | uḫry.l 12[75].2.24
--]. | [---.]ʿn[.---]. | pnm[.---]. | bʿl.n[--.---]. | il.hd[.---]. | at.bl[.at.---]. | ḥmd m.[---]. | il.hr[r.---]. | kb[-.---]. | ym.[---]. | yšḫr 12[75].2.8
r. | [mt.]hrnmy.d in.bn.l h. | km.aḫ h.w šrš.km.ary h. | bl.iṯ.bn.l h.km aḫ h.w šrš. | km.ary h.uzrm.ilm.ylḥm. | uzrm. 17[2AQHT].1.21
l.ʿl arṣ. | [l a]n ḥmt.l p[.n]ṯk.abd.l p.akl ṯm.dl. | [---.q]l.bl.tbḥ[n.l]azd.ʿr.qdm. | [---].ʿẓ q[dm.--.šp]š. | [---.šm]n.mšḥt. UG5.8.21
[--.]ubdym.b.uškn. | [---]lby. | [--]nbbl. | bn bl. | bn dkn. | bn ils. | bn ḫšbn. | bn uryy. | bn kṯl. | bn army. | b 1064.4
.ṯbq.arbʿm.drʿ.w.ʿšr.dd.drt. | w[.a]rbʿ.l.ʿšrm.dd.l.yḫšr.bl.bn h. | b.gt.mʿbr.arbʿm.l.mit.drʿ.w.ṯmnym[.drt]. | w.ʿšrm.l. 1098.11
.w.l y. | mn.bnš.d.l.i[--].ʿ[m k]. | l.alpm.w.l.y[n.--]t. | w.bl.bnš.hw[-.--]y. | w.k.at.trg[m.--].| w.[---]n.w.s[--]. | [--]m.m[2064.26
n.mʿ. | ṣbu k.ul.mad. | ṯlṯ.mat.rbt. | ḫpṯ.d bl.spr. | ṯnn.d bl.hg. | hlk.l alpm.ḫdd. | w l rbt.kmyr. | [a]ṯr.ṯn.ṯn.hlk. | aṯr.ṯlṯ 14[KRT].2.91
--.]ʿṣ.b d h.ydrm[.]pi[-.]adm. | [---.]iṯ[-].yšql.ytk[.--]np bl.hn. | [---].ḥ[m]t.pṭr.w.p nḥš. | [---.--]q.n[ṯ]k.l ydʿ.l bn.l pq UG5.8.33
ʿnt.hlkt.w.šnwt. | tp.aḫ.h.k.ysmsm. | tspi.šir.h.l.bl.ḥrb. | tšt.dm.h.l.bl.ks. | tpnn.ʿn.bṯy.ʿn.bṯt.tpnn. | ʿn.mḫr.ʿn. RS225.3
šnt. | yṣr k.bʿl.ṯmn.rkb. | ʿrpt.bl.ṭl.bl rbb. | bl.šrʿ.thmtm.bl. | ṭbn.ql.bʿl.k tmzʿ. | kst.dnil.mt.rpi. | all.ǵzr.m[t.]hr[nmy]. 19[1AQHT].1.45
ṯr.b qẓ.ṭl.yṭll. | l ǵnbm.šbʿ.šnt. | yṣr k.bʿl.ṯmn.rkb. | ʿrpt.bl.ṭl.bl rbb. | bl.šrʿ.thmtm.bl. | ṭbn.ql.bʿl.k tmzʿ. | kst.dnil.mt.r 19[1AQHT].1.44
nwt. | tp.aḫ.h.k.ysmsm. | tspi.šir.h.l.bl.ḥrb. | tšt.dm.h.l.bl.ks. | tpnn.ʿn.bṯy.ʿn.bṯt.tpnn. | ʿn.mḫr.ʿn.pḫr.ʿn.ṯǵr. | ʿn.ṯǵr.l. RS225.4
.---]. | mh.k[--.---]. | w at[--.---]. | aṯr[t.---]. | b im[--.---]. | bl.l[---.---]. | mlk.[---]. | dt [---]. | b ṯ[--.---]. | gm[.---]. | y[--.---]. 4[51].2.43
m.w tʿn.btlt. | ʿnt.irš ḥym.l aqht.ǵzr. | irš ḥym.w atn k.bl mt. | w ašlḥ k.ašspr k.ʿm.bʿl. | šnt.ʿm.bn il.tspr.yrḫm. | k bʿl 17[2AQHT].6.27
h. | k tǵd.arz.b ymn h. | bkm.yṯb.bʿl.l bht h. | u mlk.u bl mlk. | arṣ.drkt.yštkn. | dll.al.ilak.l bn. | ilm.mt.ʿdd.l ydd. | il 4[51].7.43
t.aṯr[t] ym.tn. | aḥd.b bn k.amlkn. | w tʿn.rbt.aṯrt ym. | bl.nmlk.ydʿ.ylḥn. | w yʿn.lṭpn.il d pi | d dq.anm.l yrẓ. | ʿm.bʿl. 6.1.48[49.1.20]
ǵr[.---]. | km.škllt.[---]. | ʿr.ym.l bl[.---]. | b[---.]ny[.--]. | l bl.sk.w [---] h. | ybm h.šbʿ[.---]. | ǵzr.ilḥu.t[---]l. | trm.tṣr.trm[16.2[125].93
.ngb. | w yṣi.ʿdn.mʿ. | ṣbu k.ul.mad. | ṯlṯ.mat.rbt. | ḫpṯ.d bl.spr. | ṯnn.d bl.hg. | hlk.l alpm.ḫdd. | w l rbt.kmyr. | [a]ṯr.ṯn. 14[KRT].2.90
pḫlt.bt.abn.bt šmm w thm. | qrit.l špš.um h.špš.um.ql.bl.ʿm. | il.mbk nhrm.b ʿdt.thmtm. | mnt.nṯk.nḥš.šmrr.nḥš. | ʿq UG5.7.2
lḥm.ʿq šr. | yʿdb.ksa.w.yṯb. | tqru.l špš.um h.špš.um.ql bl. | ʿm bʿl.mrym.ṣpn.mnt y.nṯk. | nḥš.šmrr.nḥš.ʿq šr ln h. | m UG5.7.8
m.nḥš.ʿq šr.ydb.ksa. | w yṯb. | tqru.l špš.u h.špš.um.ql.bl.ʿm. | dgn.ttl h.mnt.nṯk.nḥš.šmrr. | nḥš.ʿq šr.ln h.mlḫš.abd. UG5.7.14
.nḥš.ʿq šr.yʿdb. | ksa.w yṯb. | tqru l špš.um h.špš.um.ql bl. | ʿm ḥrn.mṣd h.mnt.nṯk nḥš. | šmrr.nḥš.ʿq šr.ln h.mlḫš. | a UG5.7.57
.nḥš ʿq. | š.yʿdb.ksa w yṯb. | tqru l špš.um h.špš.um.ql bl ʿm. | ṯṯ.w kmṯ.ḥryt h.mnt.nṯk.nḥš.šm | rr.nḥš.ʿq šr.ln h.ml UG5.7.35
dy.ḥmt.hlm.ytq. | w yṯb. | tqru.l špš.um h.špš.[um.q]l bl.ʿm. | yrḫ.lrgt h.mnt.nṯk.n[ḥš].šmrr. | nḥš.ʿq šr.ln h.mlḫš.a UG5.7.25
.nḥš. | ʿq.šr.yʿdb.ksa.w yṯb. | tqru l špš um h.špš um ql.bl.ʿm. | mlk.ʿṯtrt h.mnt.nṯk.nḥš.šmrr. | nḥš.ʿq šr.ln h.mlḫš ab UG5.7.40
. | nḥš.ʿq šr.yʿdb.ksa.w yṯb. | tqru l špš.um h.špš.um.ql.bl.ʿm. | ʿnt w ʿṯtrt inbb h.mnt.nṯk. | nḥš.šlḥm.nḥš.ʿq šr[.yʿ]db. UG5.7.19
.nḥš. | ʿq šr.yʿdb.ksa.w yṯb. | tqru.l špš.um h.špš.um.ql b.ʿm. | ršp.bbt h.mnt.nḥš.šmrr. | nḥš.ʿq šr.ln h.mlḫš.abd.ln h. UG5.7.30
.nḥš.ʿq šr.yʿdb ksa. | w yṯb. | tqru l špš.um h.špš.um.ql bl ʿm. | šḥr.w šlm šmm h mnt.nṯk.nḥš. | šmrr.nḥš ʿq šr.ln h. UG5.7.51
ḥš.yšlḥm.nḥš. | ʿq šr.yʿdb.ksa.w yṯb. | tqru.l špš.um.ql bl.ʿm | kṯr.w ḫss.kptr h.mnt.nṯk.nḥš. | šmrr.nḥš.ʿq šr.ln h.ml UG5.7.45
ẓ.ṭl.yṭll. | l ǵnbm.šbʿ.šnt. | yṣr k.bʿl.ṯmn.rkb. | ʿrpt.bl.ṭl.bl rbb. | bl.šrʿ.thmtm.bl. | ṭbn.ql.bʿl.k tmzʿ. | kst.dnil.mt.rpi. | 19[1AQHT].1.44
ʿl.l[hwt y]. | ṯn.rgm.k[ṯr.w]ḫss. | šmʿ.mʿ.l al[iy]n bʿl. | bl.ašt.ur[bt.]b bht m. | ḥln.b qr[b.hk]l m. | w ʿn.ali[yn.]bʿl. | al 4[51].6.5
n.hkl. | w yʿn.kṯr.w ḫss. | šmʿ.l aliyn bʿl. | bn.l rkb.ʿrpt. | bl.ašt.urbt.b bh[t] m. | ḥln.b qrb.hkl m. | w yʿn.aliyn bʿl. | al.t 4[51].5.123
m. | [---]t.[ ]r. | [---.--]n. | [---] h.l ʿdb. | [---]n.yd h. | [---].bl.išlḥ. | [---] h.gm. | [l --- k.]yṣḥ. | [---]d.ʿr. | [----.-]bb. | [----.]l 14[KRT].5.236
. | l ǵnbm.šbʿ.šnt. | yṣr k.bʿl.ṯmn.rkb. | ʿrpt.bl.ṭl.bl rbb. | bl.šrʿ.thmtm.bl. | ṭbn.ql.bʿl.k tmzʿ. | kst.dnil.mt.rpi. | all.ǵzr. 19[1AQHT].1.45
k.liršt. | [---.]rpi.mlk ʿlm.b ʿz. | [rpu.m]lk.ʿlm.b ḏmr h.bl. | [---].b ḥtk h.b nmrt h.l r | [--.]arṣ.ʿz k.ḏmr k.l[-] | n k.ḥtk UG5.2.2.7
.trm.tnq[--]. | km.nkyt.ṯǵr[.---]. | km.škllt.[---]. | ʿr.ym.l bl[.---]. | b[---.]ny[.--]. | l bl.sk.w [---] h. | ybm h.šbʿ[.---]. | ǵzr.i 16.2[125].91

blbl

spr.blblm. | skn uškn. | skn šbn. | skn ubrʿ. | skn ḫrṣbʿ. | rb.ntbtš. | [1033.1

bld

q'l.b q'l. | mlkm.hn.ym.yṣq.yn.ṯmk. | mrṯ.yn.srnm.yn.bld. | ǵll.yn.išryt.'nq.smd. | lbnn.ṯl mrṯ.yḫrṯ.il. | hn.ym.w ṯn.tl 22.2[124].18

bldn

'rb. | atn. | ḫryn. | bn.'nt. | llwn. | agdṯb. | aǵltn. | [-]wn. | bldn. | [-]ln. | [-]ldn. | [i]wryn. | ḫbsn. | ulmk. | 'dršp. | bn.knn. | 1061.11

blḫ

pnṯ.dq. | ṯn ḫpnm.ṯn pldm ǵlmm. | kpld.b[-.-]r[--]. | w blḫ br[-]m p[-]. | b[--.]l[-.]mat[.-]y. | ḫmšm[.--]i. | ṯlṯ m[at] ḫs 140[98].6

blẓn

.qšt.w.ql'. | ṣdqm.qšt.w.ql'. | uln.qšt.w.ql'. | uln.qšt. | bn.blẓn.qšt.w.ql'. | gb'.qšt.w.ql'. | nṣṣn.qšt. | m'r. | [']dyn.ṯt.qštm. 119[321].2.9

bly

. | bn.prsn.ṣmd.w.ḥrṣ. | bn.ilb'l. | bn.idrm. | bn.grgš. | bn.bly. | bn.apṯ. | bn.ysd. | bn.pl[-]. | bn.ṯb'nq. | brqd. | bnn. | kbln.ṣ 2113.10
.[---]. | bn.[---]. | [-----]. | bn[---]. | bn.mlkyy. | bn.atn. | bn.bly. | bn.ṯbrn. | bn.ḥgby. | bn.pity. | bn.slgyn. | 'zn.bn.mlk. | bn. 115[301].2.3
.irbn. | bn.mglb. | bn.ntp. | 'myn.bn ǵḫpn. | bn.kbln. | bn.bly. | bn.ṯ'y. | bn.nṣdn. | klby. 104[316].6
[ṯl]ṯm.ksp.'[l]. | [b]n.bly.gb'ly. | [šp]ḥ.a[n]nṯb. | w.m[--.u]škny. | [']š[r.---]t.ksp. | ['l. 2055.2
.at. | nǵṯ.w.ytn.hm.l k. | w.lḥt.alpm.ḫršm. | k.rgmt.l y.bly m. | alpm.aršt.l k.w.l y. | mn.bnš.d.l.i[--].'[m k]. | l.alpm. 2064.22
.atnb.mr[--.---]. | bn.sḫr.mr[-.---]. | bn.idrn.'š[-.---]. | bn.bly.mr[-.---]. | w.nḥl h.mr[-.---]. | ilšpš.[---]. | iḫny.[---]. | bn.[-- 88[304].10
mryn[m]. | bn.bly. | nrn. | w.nḥl h. | bn.rmyy. | bn.tlmyn. | w.nḥl h. | w.nḥl h 113[400].1.2
l h.l bn.pl. | šd.krwn.l aḫn. | šd.'yy.l aḫn. | šd.brdn.l bn.bly. | šd gzl.l.bn.ṯbr[n]. | šd.ḫzmyn.l a[--]. | ṯn šdm b uš[kn]. 2089.13
----]. | [-]mn. | b'ly. | rpan. | 'pṯrm. | bn.'bd. | šmb'l. | ykr. | bly. | ṯb'm. | ḥdṯn. | rpty. | ilym. | bn.'br. | mnip'l. | amrb'l. | dqry 1058.9
šm[n]. | alp.mitm.kbd.ṯlṯ.ḥlb. | šb'.l.'šrm.kkr.ṯlṯ. | d.ybl.blym. 1135.7

blkn

[---.]yplṭ. | [---].l.[-]npk. | [---.]l.bn.ydln. | [---].l.blkn. | [---].l.bn.k[--]. | [---].l.klṯṯb. 2136.4

bln

št aškrr w p]r ḥḏrt. | [-----]. | [---.-]n[-]. | [k yraš šśw št bln q]ṭ ydk. | [w yṣq b ap h]. | [-----]. | [-----]. | [-----]. | [---.-]rb. 160[55].14
ǵn.ḥmr[.ydk]. | aḥd h.w.yṣq.b[.ap h]. | k.yraš.šśw.[št]. | bln.qṭ.yṣq.b.a[p h]. | k yg'r[.šśw.---]. | dprn[.---]. | dr'.[---]. | tm 161[56].22

blšš

. | ilyn.'lby.ṣdkn. | gmrt.ṯlmyn. | 'bdnt. | bdy.ḥrš arkd. | blšš lmd. | ḥṯṯn.tqn. | ydd.idṯn. | šǵr.ilgdn. 1045.10

blt

.hm.brk y.tkšd. | rumm.'n.kḏd.aylt. | hm.imt.imt.npš.blt. | ḥmr.p imt.b klt. | yd y.ilḥm.hm.šb'. | ydt y.b ṣ'.hm.ks.y 5[67].1.18
'l.l y'db.mrḥ. | 'm.bn.dgn.k tms m. | w 'n.rbt.aṯrt ym. | blt.nmlk.'ṯtr.'rẓ. | ymlk.'ṯtr.'rẓ. | apnk.'ṯtr.'rẓ. | y'l.b ṣrrt.ṣpn. 6.1.54[49.1.26]
dr d.d yknn[.--]. | b'l.yṣǵd.mli[.--]. | il hd.mla.u[--.--]. | blt.p btlt.'n[t]. | w p.n'mt.aḫt[.b'l]. | y'l.b'l.b ǵ[r.---]. | w bn.dg 10[76].3.10

bm

--].ptḥ y.a[--.]dt[.---].ml[--]. | [---.-]ṯk.ytmt.dlt´tlk.[---].bm[.---]. | [---.-]qp.bn.ḥtt.bn ḥtt[.---]. | [---.--]p.km.dlt.tlk.km 1001.1.22

bmt

----]. | alp[.---.--]r. | mit.lḥ[m.---.-]dyt. | ṣl't.alp.mri. | 'šr.bmt.alp.mri. | ṯn.nšbm. | ṯmnym.tbtḫ.alp. | uz.mrat.mlḥt. | arb 1128.17
m.w dqn[.ṯṯlṯ]. | qn.ḏr' h.tḥrṯ.km.gn. | ap lb.k 'mq.ṯṯlṯ.bmt. | b'l.mt.my.lim.bn dgn. | my.hmlt.aṯr.b'l.nrd. | b arṣ.'m 6[62].1.5
i[š]. | 'l h.k irbym.kp.k.qṣm. | ǵrmn.kp.mhr.'tkt. | rišt.l bmt h.šnst. | kpt.b ḥbš h.brkm.tǵl[l]. | b dm.ḏmr.ḥlqm.b mm 3['NT].2.12
[---.šnst.kpt.b ḥb]š h.'tkt r[išt]. | [l bmt h.---.]hy bt h t'rb. | [---.tm]ṯḫṣ b 'mq. | [ṯḫtṣb.bn.qrtm.ṯṯ 7.1[131].3
ḏ.aklm.k [---]. | npl.b mšmš[.---]. | anp n m yḥr[r.---]. | bmt n m.yšḫn.[---]. | qrn h.km.ǵb[-.---]. | hw km.ḥrr[.---]. | šn 12[75].2.39
q[dš.ṯb]r.arṣ. | [---.]ǵrm[.t]ḫšn. | rḥq[.---.td']. | qdm ym.bmt.[nhr]. | ṯṯṯn.ib.b'l.tiḫd. | y'rm.šnu.hd.gpt. | ǵr.w y'n.aliyn 4[51].7.34
ḥm.w dqn. | yṯlṯ.qn.ḏr' h.yḥrṯ. | k gn.ap lb.k 'mq.yṯlṯ. | bmt.yšu.g h.w yṣḥ. | b'l.mt.my.lim.bn. | dgn.my.hmlt.aṯr. | b'l 5[67].6.22
bkm.tmdln.'r. | bkm.tṣmd.pḥl.bkm. | tšu.ab h.tštnn.l[b]mt 'r. | l ysmsm.bmt.pḥl. | y dnil.ysb.palt h. | bṣql.yph.b pal 19[1AQHT].2.59
qbnm. | 'db.gpn.atnt h. | yḥbq.qdš.w amrr. | yštn.aṯrt.l bmt.'r. | l ysmsmt.bmt.pḥl. | qdš.yuḫdm.šb'r. | amrr.k kbkb.l 4[51].4.14
m.tṣmd.pḥl.bkm. | tšu.ab h.tštnn.l[b]mt 'r. | l ysmsm.bmt.pḥl. | y dnil.ysb.palt h. | bṣql.yph.b palt.bṣ[q]l. | yph.b yǵ 19[1AQHT].2.60
nt h. | yḥbq.qdš.w amrr. | yštn.aṯrt.l bmt.'r. | l ysmsmt.bmt.pḥl. | qdš.yuḫdm.šb'r. | amrr.k kbkb.l pnm. | aṯr.btlt.'nt. 4[51].4.15

bn

y.w snry. | [b]n.sdy.bn.ṯty. | bn.ḥyn.bn.ǵlm. | bn.yyn.w.bn.au[pš]. | bn.kdrn. | 'rgzy.w.bn.'dy. | bn.gmḥn.w.ḥgbt. | bn.t 131[309].25
t.yr[ṯḫṣ.ml]k.brr. | 'lm.š.š[--].l[--.]'rb.šp | š.w ḥl[.ml]k. | bn.aup[š.--].bsbn hzpḫ ṯlṯt. | kṯr[.---.--]trt ḫmšt.bn gda[.-.]m APP.II[173].58
'nq. | brqd. | bnn. | kbln.ṣ[md]. | bn gmrt. | bn.il.ṣm[d]. | bn abbly. | yṯ'd.ṣm[d]. | bn.liy. | 'šrm.ṣ[md]. | ṯṯ kbd.b ḥ[--]. | w 2113.20
bn ils. | bn ḥšbn. | bn uryy. | bn kṯl. | bn army. | bn gln. | bn abg. | bn.nǵry. | bn.srwd. | mtnn. | bn gš[-]. | bn gbrn. | bn ul 1064.12
ln.aṯṯ. | ddy.[a]ddy. | bn.mlkr[šp]. | bn.y[k]n. | ynḥm. | bn.abd.b'[l]. | mnḥm.bn[.---]. | krmn[py]. | bn.[--]m. | bn.asr[-] 2014.48
rqd. | bn.abdg. | ilyn. | bn.tan. | bn.arm. | bn.b'l.ṣdq. | bn.army. | bn.r 1046.1.2
d'n.ilštm'y. | bn.'n.rqdy. | bn.g'yn. | bn.ǵrn. | bn.agynt. | bn.abdḥr.snry. | dqn.šlmn. | prdn.ndb[--]. | [-]rn.ḫbty. | abmn. 87[64].36
--]. | ṣbu.any[t]. | bn.kṯan. | ǵr.tš'[.'šr.b]nš. | ṣbu.any[t]. | bn abdḫ[r]. | pdym. | ḫmš.bnšm. | snrym. | tš'.bnš[m]. | gb'lym. 79[83].11
'ly. | bn.ypy.gb'ly. | bn.grgs.ilštm'y. | bn.ḫran.ilštm'y. | bn.abd'n.ilštm'y. | bn.'n.rqdy. | bn.g'yn. | bn.ǵrn. | bn.agynt. | 87[64].31
[---].rb. | [-]lpl. | bn.asrn. | bn.šḫyn. | bn.abd'n. | bn.ḫnqn. | bn.nmq. | bn.amdn. | bn.špšn. 1067.5
d.bn agmn. | bn [-]ln.bn.ṯbil. | bn is.bn tbdn. | bn uryy. | bn abd'n. | bn prkl. | bn štn. | bn annyn. | b[n] slg. | u[--] dit. | b 101[10].9

-.-]nb. | [--.--]n. | [--.--]n. | bn.[---]. | bn.ʻr[--]. | bn.nkt[-]. | bn.abd̲r. | bn.ḥrẓn. | bn.d̲qnt. | bn.gmrš. | bn.nmq. | bn.špš[yn]. 2023.3.9

---.--]ḫy. | [---.--]t. | [-----]. | [---.]l[--]. | [bn.]ubn. | kbšm. | bn.abd̲r. | bn.kpltn. | bn.prn. | ʻbdm. | bn.kd̲ǵbr. | bn.mṣrn. | bn. 114[324].2.6

.agyn. | [--]t̲n. | [--]tn.bn.ad̲mt̲n. | [-]tn bn.agyn. | ullym.bn.abynm. | antn.bn.iwr[n]r. | pwn.t̲mry. | ksyn.bn.lḥsn. | [-]k 94[313].6

miḫdym. | bn.ḥt̲b. | bn abyt. | bn ḥd̲l. | bn ṣdqn. | bn ayy. | bn dbb. | w nḥl h. | bn nʻ 2016.1.3

. | b[n.ʻr]my. | [--]t̲y. | bn.ǵdʻ. | bn.ʻyn. | bn.grb[n]. | yt̲tn. | bn.ab[l]. | kry. | psš. | ilt̲ḥm. | ḥrm. | bn.bty. | ʻby. | šm[n].bn.apn 2078.10

bn.[---]. | bn.a[--]. | w.nḥl h. | bn.alz. | w.nḥl h. | bn.sny. | bn.ablḥ. | [-----]. | w [---]. | bn.[---]. | bn.yr[--]. | bn.kt̲r[t]. | bn.š 2163.1.15

n.---]. | bn[.---.ušk]ny. | bn.kdrn.uškny. | bn.lgn.uškny. | bn.abn.uškny. | bn.arz.šʻrty. | bn.ibrd.mʻrby. | ṣdqn.gbʻly. | bn. 87[64].24

ʻ[--]. | bn.y[---]. | [-----]. | [bn.a]mdy. | bn.ḫlln. | bn.kt̲n. | bn.abn. | bn.nskn. | bn.gmrn. | bn[.-]škn. | [---.--]n. | [---.--]n. | [- 2021.2.5

]m.b km.yʻn. | [---].ydʻ.l ydʻt. | [---.]tasrn.t̲r il. | [---.]rks.bn.abnm. | [---.]upqt.ʻrb. | [---.w ẓ]r.mtn y at zd. | [---.]tʻrb.bši 1[ʻNT.X].5.23

bn iytlm. | bn ayln. | bn.kln. | bn.ʻlln. | bn.liy. | bn.nqt̲n. | bn abrḫt̲. | bn.grdy. | bn.ṣlpn. | bn ǵlmn. | bn sgld. 1064.27

[---]. | bn.plš. | bn.ubr. | bn.ʻptb. | t̲bry. | bn.ymn. | krty. | bn.abr[-]. | yrpu. | kdn. | pʻṣ. | bn.liy. | ydʻ. | šmn. | ʻdy. | ʻnbr. | aḫ 2117.1.21

. | mr[u.ibrn]. | bn.i[---]. | bn.n[---]. | bn.b[---]. | bn.iš[--]. | bn.ab[--]. | bn.al[--]. | bn.nb[dg]. | bn.ild[-]. | [-----]. | [bn.]nnr. | 113[400].5.22

rn. | bn[.-]škn. | [---.--]n. | [---.--]n. | [--.]ʻ[--]. | [bn].k[--]. | bn.ab[--]. | bn.i[--]. | bn.n[--]. | bn.ḫ[--]. | bn.[---]. | bn.k[--]. 2021.2.13

---]. | [---.]l[.---]. | [---].tbt̲t[b.---]. | [---].bn.b[--.---]. | [---].bn.ab[--.---]. | [---.]bn.a[--.---]. | [---.]bn.i[--.---]. | [---].t̲p[--.---]. 2162.A.5

pdrn.ʻšrm. | d.bn.šbʻl.uḫnpy.ḫmšm. | b.bn.t̲tm.t̲lt̲m. | b.bn.agdt̲b.ʻšrm. | b.bn.ibn.arbʻt.ʻšrt. | b.bn.mnn.t̲t̲m. | b.rpan.b 2054.1.12

ddbʻl. | [---]n.bn.agyn. | [--]t̲n. | [--]tn.bn.ad̲mt̲n. | [-]tn bn.agyn. | ullym.bn.abynm. | antn.bn.iwr[n]r. | pwn.t̲mry. | ks 94[313].5

[---]ym.mddbʻl. | [---]n.bn.agyn. | [--]t̲n. | [--]tn.bn.ad̲mt̲n. | [-]tn bn.agyn. | ullym.bn. 94[313].2

[---]. | [b]n.gʻyn.ḫr[-]. | lbnym. | grgš.[---]. | bn.ǵrn.[---]. | bn.agyn[.---]. | iyt̲[-.---]. 93[328].16

[b]n ʻntn.[---]. | bn agyn[.---]. | b[n] ʻt̲lt̲[.---]. | bn qt̲y[.---]. | bn ypʻ[.---]. | [---]bʻ 105[86].2

ʻy. | bn.abdʻn.ilštmʻy. | bn.ʻn.rqdy. | bn.gʻyn. | bn.ǵrn. | bn.agynt. | bn.abdḫr.snry. | dqn.šlmn. | prdn.ndb[--]. | [-]rn.ḫb 87[64].35

-]. | bn.al[--]. | bn.nb[dg]. | bn.ild[-]. | [-----]. | [bn.]nnr. | [bn.]aglby. | [bn.]bʻly. | [md]rǵlm. | [bn.]kdgdl. | [b]n.qt̲n. | [b]n 104[316].5

ṣ m[l]k ʻšrm. | ṣṣ abš[-] mit [ʻš]r kbd. | ṣṣ yd̲rd ʻšrm. | ṣṣ bn aglby t̲lt̲[m]. | ṣṣ bn.šršʻm.[---]. | ṣṣ mlknʻm.a[rbʻm]. | ṣṣ ml 2097.13

[s]p[r] ušknym.dt.[b d.---]. | bn.btr. | bn.ʻms. | bn.pṣn. | bn.agmz. | bn.[--]n. | bn.a[--]. | [------]. | [------]. | [------]. | [------] 2021.1.5

--]kn bn.pri. | [r]špab bn.pni. | [ab]mn bn.qṣy. | [ʻ]pt̲rm bn.agmz. | [-]n bn.iln. | [--]nn bn.ibm. | [-]n bn.ḥrn. | [š]mmn 2087.10

[-----]. | [bn.]ibln. | ysd. | bn.t̲mq. | bn.agmn. | bn.uṣb. | bn.yzg. | bn.anntn. | bn.kwn. | ǵmšd. | bn.ʻ 115[301].4.4

.nḥl h. | bn ksln.t̲lt̲ḥ. | bn yṣmḫ.bn.t̲rn w nḥl h. | bn srd.bn agmn. | bn [-]ln.bn.t̲bil. | bn is.bn tbdn. | bn uryy. | bn abdʻ 101[10].5

l.ilršp.bn[.---]. | kd.šmn.ʻl.yddn. | kd.ʻl.ššy. | kd.ʻl.nd̲bn.bn.agmn. | [k]d.ʻl.brq. | [kd]m.[ʻl].kt̲r. | [kd]m[.---].ḥ[--]. | [----- 1082.1.8

n.[---]. | bn.[---].ar. | bn.[---].b.ar. | špšyn[.---.]yt̲b.b.ar. | bn.ag[p]t̲.ḫpt.d[.yt̲b.b].šʻrt. | yly.bn.t̲rnq.[-]r.d.yt̲b.b.ilštmʻ. | i 2015.1.25

a[b]m[n]. | arbʻ.ʻl[.--]ly. | kd.[ʻl.--]ẓ. | kd.[ʻl.---]. | [--.--]ḫ.bn.ag[--]. | [---.--]m[.---]. | [kd.]šš. | [k]d.ykn.bn.ʻbdt̲rm. | kd.ʻb 1082.1.25

spr.ytnm. | bn.ḫlbym. | bn.ady. | bn.ʻt̲try. | bn.ḥrẓn. | ady. | bn.birtn. | bn.ḥrẓn. | bn.bdd 115[301].1.3

lt̲[.---].bn.t̲dnyn. | ddm.ḥ[t̲m].ʻl.šrn. | ʻšrt.ksp.ʻl.[-]lpy. | bn.ady.kkr.šʻrt. | nt̲k h. | kb[d.]mn.ʻl.abršn. | b[n.---].kršu.nt̲k 1146.9

yn. | w.nḥl h. | w.nḥl hm. | bn.ḥrm. | bn.brzn. | w.nḥl h. | bn.adld̲n. | bn.šbl. | bn.ḫnzr. | bn.arwt̲. | bn.t̲btnq. | bn.pt̲dn. | b 113[400].1.12

.bn.krwn.l bn.ʻmyn. | šd.bn.prmn.l aḫny. | šd.bn ḥnn.l bn.adld̲n. | šd.bn.nṣdn.l bn.ʻmlbi. | šd.t̲pḫln.l bn.ǵl. | w dt̲n.nḥ 2089.7

-----]. | [-----]. | [ṣṣ].b[n].ṣd[-.---]. | [ṣṣ].bn.npr.ḫmšm. | ṣṣ.bn.adld̲n.t̲lt̲m. | ṣṣ.bn.ʻglt.t̲lt̲m. | ṣṣ.bn.ʻbd.ʻšrm. | ṣṣ.bn.mṣḥ[n] 2096.16

šd.bn.adn. | [b] d.armwl. | [šd].mrnn. | b d.[-]tw[-]. | šd.bn[.---]. | 2028.1

bn.ḫran. | bn.srt. | bn.adn. | bn.ʻgw. | bn.urt. | aḫdbu. | pḥ[-]. | bn.ʻb . | bn.ud̲n[-]. | 121[307].3

[bn.]ḫdmn. | [bn.]nklb. | [---]dn. | [---]y. | [-----]. | [-----]. | bn.adn. | prtn. | bn.btry. 1073.3.3

t.w.qlʻ. | bn.znan.qšt. | bn.arz.[ar]bʻ.qšt.w.arb[ʻ.]qlʻm. | b[n.]adʻl.q[š]t.w.qlʻ. | b[n].ilyn.qšt.w.qlʻ. | šmrm.qlʻ. | ubrʻy. | a 119[321].2.46

bnšm.dt.it̲.alpm.l hm. | bn.niršn. | bn.adty. | bn.alz. | bn.birtn. | bn.mlṣ. | bn.q[--]. | bn.[---]. | bn.t̲[- 2023.1.3

| bn.ṣqn. | bn.šyn. | bn.prtn. | bn.ypr. | mrum. | bn.ʻ[--]t. | bn.adty. | bn.krwn. | bn.nǵsk. | bn.qnd̲. | bn.pity. | w.nḥl h. | bn. 113[400].3.13

| ṣṣ tmn.ḫmšm. | [ṣṣ] ʻmtd̲l t̲lt̲m. | ṣṣ ʻmlbi t̲t̲ l ʻšrm. | ṣṣ bn adty ḫmšm. | ṣṣ amtrn arbʻm. | ṣṣ iytlm mit t̲lt̲m kbd. | ṣṣ 2097.7

b t̲lt̲. | ilmlk.ʻšr.ṣin. | mlknʻm.ʻšr. | bn.adty.ʻšr. | [ṣ]dqšlm ḫmš. | krzn.ḫmš. | ubrʻym.ḫmš. | [----]. | 2039.4

[t̲]lḥn. | [---.t̲]lḥ[n]. | [---.--t̲]lḥn. | [---.]t̲lḥn. | [---.]t̲lḥn. | bn adty t̲lḥn.bn qrwl t̲lḥn. 98[11].36

[---]rn. | [--]ṣb. | [--]ps. | [--]t̲b. | [--]ln. | [---]r. | [---]y. | bn.ad̲dt. | bn.atnb. | bn.yšd. | bn.bršm. | bn.gt̲prg. | gt̲pbn. | bn. 1057.8

[---]ym.mddbʻl. | [---]n.bn.agyn. | [--]t̲n. | [--]tn.bn.ad̲mt̲n. | [-]tn bn.agyn. | ullym.bn.abynm. | antn.bn.iwr[n] 94[313].4

t. | bn.ḥdt̲.ʻšrt. | bn.ḥnyn.ʻšrt. | rpan.ḫmšt. | abǵl.ḫmšt. | bn.aḫdy.ʻšrt. | t̲t̲n.ʻṣrt. | bn.pnmn.ʻšrt. | ʻbdadt.ḫmšt. | abmn.ilš 1062.21

i[l]štmʻym. | bn.t̲k. | bn.arwdn. | tmrtn. | šdʻl.bn aḫyn. | mʻrbym. | rpan. | abršn. | atlgy. | šršn. 95[91].5

rdn. | ypq. | ʻbd. | qrḥ. | abšr. | bn.bdn. | d̲mry. | bn.pndr. | bn.aḫt. | bn.ʻdn. | bn.išbʻ[l]. 2117.4.32

n ytr. | bn ilšpš. | ubrš. | bn gmš ḫlq. | bn ʻgy. | bn zlbn. | bn.aḫ[--]. | bn[.---]. | [-----]. | bn kr[k]. | bn ḫtyn. | w nḥl h. | bn t̲ 2016.2.21

spr.ʻrbnm. | dt.ʻrb. | b.mtn.bn.ayaḫ. | b.ḥbt h.ḥwt.t̲t h. | w.mnm.šalm. | dt.tknn. | ʻl.ʻrbnm 1161.3

qrr[-]. | bn.ḥyl. | bn.gʻyn. | ḥyn. | bn.armg[-]. | bʻlmt̲pt̲. | [bn].ayḫ. | [---]rn. | ill. | ǵlmn. | bn.ytrm. | bn.ḫgbt. | mtn. | mḫtn. 1035.2.6

miḫdym. | bn.ḥt̲b. | bn abyt. | bn ḥd̲l. | bn ṣdqn. | bn ayy. | bn dbb. | w nḥl h. | bn nʻmyn. | bn at̲tyy. | bn ḫlp. | bn. 2016.1.6

.ṣmy. | bn.il[-]šy. | bn.ybšr. | bn.sly. | bn.ḫlbt. | bn.brzt. | bn.ayl. | [-----]. | ʻbd[--]. | bn.i[--]. | ʻd[--]. | ild[--]. | bn.qṣn. | ʻlpy. 2117.2.14

bn gbrn. | bn uldy. | synn.bn knʻm. | bn kbr. | bn iytlm. | bn ayln. | bn.kln. | bn.ʻlln. | bn.liy. | bn.nqt̲n. | bn abrḫt̲. | bn.gr 1064.22

. | anntn.yṣr. | annmn.w.t̲lt̲.nʻ[r] h. | rpan.w.t̲[n.]bn h. | bn.ayln.w.t̲n.bn h. | yt. 2068.27

.bt.mlk. | w.b.spr.l.št. | yrmʻl. | ṣry. | iršy. | yʻd̲rd. | ayaḫ. | bn.aylt. | ḫmš.mat.arbʻm. | kbd.ksp.anyt. | d.ʻrb.b.anyt. | l.mlk 2106.9

| b.[---.---]r. | b.ann[.---.-]ny[-]. | b.ḫqn.[---]m.ṣ[-]n. | [b].bn.ay[--.---].l.ʻšrm. | [-]gp[.---.]ʻrny.t̲t̲m. | [---.]dyn.ḫmšt.ʻšrt. | 2054.2.17

. | ʻpsn. | bn.ṣpr. | kmn. | bn.ršp. | tmn. | šmmn. | bn.rmy. | bn.aky. | ʻbdḫmn. | bn.ʻd̲t. | kt̲y. | bn.ḫny. | bn.ssm. | bn.ḫnn. | [- 1047.13

n.ʻg[w.]qšt.w qlʻ. | ḥd[t̲]n.qšt.w.qlʻ. | bn.bb.qšt.w[.ql]ʻ. | bn.aktmy.qšt. | šdyn.qšt. | bdn.qšt.w.qlʻ. | bn.šmlbi.qšt.w.qlʻ. | 119[321].4.10

t̲pn. | w qdš.u ilm.tmtn. | špḥ.ltpn.l yḥ. | w yʻny.krt.t̲ʻ. | bn.al.tbkn.al. | tdm.l y.al tkl.bn. | qr.ʻn k.mḫ.riš k. | udmʻt.ṣḥ. 16.1[125].25

t[--]. | bn.qnd̲. | ṣmq[-]. | bn.anny. | bn.ʻmtd̲l. | bn.ʻmyn. | bn.alz. | bn.birtn. | [bn.]ylkn. | [bn.]krwn. | [bn.-]ty. | [bn.]iršn. 117[325].1.12

bnšm.dt.it̲.alpm.l hm. | bn.niršn. | bn.adty. | bn.alz. | bn.birtn. | bn.mlṣ. | bn.q[--]. | bn.[---]. | bn.t̲[-]r. | bn.gr 2023.1.4

sḫrn. | mʻqb. | t̲pn. | mʻr. | lbnm. | nḫl. | yʻny. | atn. | utly. | bn.alz. | bn ḫlm. | bn.d̲mr. | bn.ʻyn. | ubnyn. | rpš d ydy. | ǵbl. | 2075.15

.bn.mlk. | bn.alṯn. | bn.ṯmyr. | ẓbr. | bn.ṯdṯb. | bn.ʻrmn. | bn.alz. | bn.mṣrn. | bn.ʻdy. | bn.ršpy. | [---.]mn. | [--.-]sn. | [bn.-] 115[301].2.14
[-----]. | b[n.---]. | b[n.---]. | bn.[---]. | bn.a[--]. | w.nḥl h. | bn.alz. | w.nḥl h. | bn.sny. | bn.ablḥ. | [-----]. | w [---]. | bn.[---]. | 2163.1.12
m.dt.l.mlk. | ʻbdyrẖ.bn.ṯyl. | ʻbdn.w.aṯt h.w.bn h. | gpn.bn[.a]ly. | bn.rqd[y].ṯbg. | iẖmlk. | ypʻn w.aṯt h. | anntn.yṣr. | a 2068.20
plšbʻl.bn.n[--]. | ḥy bn.dnn.ṯkt. | ilṯḥm.bn.dnn.ṯkt. | šbʻl.bn.aly.ṯkt. | klby.bn.iẖy.ṯkt. | psš.bn.buly.ṯkt. | ʻpṣpn.bn.ʻdy.ṯ 2085.6
mkr. | atlg. | mit.ksp.d mkr. | ilštmʻ. | ʻšrm.l mit.ksp. | ʻl.bn.alkbl.šb[ny]. | ʻšrm ksp.ʻl. | wrt.mtny.w ʻl. | prdny.aṯt h. 2107.16
nt. | bn.ṯʻl[-]. | bdl.ar.dt.inn. | mhr l ht. | artyn. | ʻdmlk. | bn.alt[-]. | iẖy[-]. | ʻbdgṯr. | ḥrr. | bn.s[-]p[-]. | bn.nrpd. | bn.ḥ[-] 1035.1.8
iyn. | bn.army. | bn.krmn. | bn.ykn. | bn.ʻṯtrab. | uṣn[-]. | bn.alṯn. | bn.aš[-]š. | bn.štn. | bn.ilš. | bn.tnabn. | bn.ḥṣn. | ṣprn. 1046.1.14
nqdm. | bn.alṯn. | bn.dly. | bn.btry. | bn.ẖdmn. | [bn].šty. | [bn].kdgdl. | [2018.2
. | bn.ṯbrn. | bn.ḥgby. | bn.pity. | bn.slgyn. | ʻzn.bn.mlk. | bn.alṯn. | bn.ṯmyr. | ẓbr. | bn.ṯdṯb. | bn.ʻrmn. | bn.alz. | bn.mṣrn. 115[301].2.9
]. | bn.i[---]. | bn.n[---]. | bn.b[---]. | bn.iš[--]. | bn.ab[--]. | bn.al[--]. | bn.nb[dg]. | bn.ild[-]. | [-----]. | [bn.]nnr. | [bn.]aglby. 113[400].5.23
t. | bn.nzʻn. | bn.slmz[-]. | bn.kʻ[--]. | bn.y[---]. | [-----]. | [bn.a]mdy. | bn.ẖlln. | bn.kṯn. | bn.abn. | bn.nskn. | bn.gmrn. | b 2021.2.2
.nq[ly]. | bn.snr[n]. | bn.pzn[y]. | bn.mg[lb]. | bn.db[--]. | bn.amd[n]. | annš[-]. 2020.13
pl. | bn.asrn. | bn.šẖyn. | bn.abdʻn. | bn.ẖnqn. | bn.nmq. | bn.amdn. | bn.špšn. 1067.8
l h. | w.nḥl hm. | bn.nqly. | bn.snrn. | bn.ṯgd. | bn.d[-]n. | bn.amdn. | bn.ṯmrn. | bn.pzny. | bn.mglb. | bn.[--]b. | bn.[---]. | 105[86].4
[w]nḥ[l h]. | [bn].amd[-]. | [bn].ṣbṭ[--]. | [bn].ẖla[n]. | [bn].ǵr[--]. | d.b[n.---]. 2164.A.2
ẖrṣ.]yd.mqm h. | [w ʻb]d.ʻlm.ṯlṯ. | [ssw]m.mrkbt b trbṣ bn.amt. | [tn.b]nm.aqny. | [tn.ṯa]rm.amid. | [w yʻn].ṯr.ab h.il. 14[KRT].2.56
rq.ẖrṣ. | yd.mqm h.w ʻbd.ʻlm. | ṯlṯ.sswm.mrkbt. | b trbṣ.bn.amt. | qḥ.krt.šlmm. | šlmm.w ng.mlk. | l bt y.rḥq.krt. | l ḥẓ 14[KRT].3.129
rṣ[.yd.mqm] h. | ʻbd[.ʻlm.ṯlṯ]. | ss[wm.mrkbt]. | b[trbṣ.bn.amt]. | [qḥ.krt.šlmm]. | [šlmm.al.tṣr]. | [udm.rbt.w udm]. | 14[KRT].5.254
.[yd.mqm h]. | w ʻbd[.ʻlm.ṯlṯ]. | sswm.m[rkbt]. | b trbṣ.[bn.amt]. | q[ḥ.kr]t[.šlmm]. | š[lmm.]al.t[ṣr]. | udm[.r]bt.w u[d 14[KRT].6.273
.ẖrṣ]. | yd.mqm h.w ʻbd. | ʻlm.ṯlṯ.sswm. | mrkbt.b trbṣ. | bn.amt.p d.[i]n. | b bt y.ttn.tn. | l y.mṯt.ḥry. | nʻmt.šbḥ.bkr k. 14[KRT].6.287
q.ẖrṣ. | yd.mqm h.w ʻbd. | ʻlm.ṯlṯ.sswm.mrkbt. | b trbṣt.bn.amt. | p d.in.b bt y.ttn. | tn.l y.mṯt.ḥry. | nʻmt.špḥ.bkr k. | d 14[KRT].3.141
---]n. | kdm.l.mḏrǵlm. | kd.l.mṣrym. | kd.mštt.mlk. | kd.bn.amht [-]t. | w.bn.mṣrym. | arbʻm.yn. | l.ẖrd. | ẖmšm.ẖmš. | 1089.9
.argb. | ydn. | ilʻnt. | bn.urt. | ydn. | qṭn. | bn.asr. | bn.ʻdy. | bn.amt[m]. | myn. | šr. | bn.zql. | bn.iẖy. | bn.iyṯr. | bn.ʻyn. | bn.ǵ 2117.3.49
.ṯlṯ. | [-]lkynt.nsk.ṯlṯ. | [-]by.nsk.ṯlṯ. | šmny. | ẖršn. | ldn. | bn.ands. | bn.ann. | bn.ʻbdpdr. | šd.iyry.l.ʻbdbʻl. | šd.šmmn.l.b 1102.14
nt.nsk.ṯlṯ. | [-]by.nsk.ṯlṯ. | šmny. | ẖršn. | ldn. | bn.ands. | bn.ann. | bn.ʻbdpdr. | šd.iyry.l.ʻbdbʻl. | šd.šmmn.l.bn.šty. | šd.b 1102.15
.kzbn.l.qr[t]. | šd.pln.bn.tiyn.b d.ilmhr nḥl h. | šd knn.bn.ann.ʻdb. | šd.iln[-].bn.irṯr.l.sẖrn.nḥl h. | šd[.ag]pṯn.b[n.]br 2029.19
.tyn.nḥl h. | šd.pǵyn[.b] d.krmn.l.ty[n.n]ḥl h. | šd.krz.[b]n.ann.ʻ[db]. | šd.ṯ[r]yn.bn.tkn.b d.qrt. | šd[.-].dyn.b d.pln.n 2029.13
n.kdgdl. | bn.smyy. | bn.lbn. | bn.šlmn. | bn.mly. | pslm. | bn.annd. | bn.glʻd. | w.nḥl h. | bn.mlkyy. | [bn].bm[--]. | [ʻš]rm. 2163.3.10
[--.lb]š.bn.sgryn.b[.ṯ]qlm. | [---.]bn.ully.b.ṯ[qlm]. | [---.]bn.annḏy.b[.---]. | [---.]bn.pd[--.---]. 135[330].6
pd[y]. | ttn. | md.ʻṯt[rt]. | kṯkt. | bn.ṯtn[--]. | [m]d.m[--]. | [b]n.annḏ[r]. | bn.ṯḏyy. | bn.grbn. | [--.]ully. | [--]ṯiy. 1054.2.2
spr.ḥrš. | qštipṯl. | bn.anny. | ilṣdq. | ypltn.bn iln. | špšm.nsl h. | [-----]. 1037.3
ḥ[l h]. | ʻbd[--]. | bn.s[---]. | bn.at[--]. | bn.qnḏ. | ṣmq[-]. | bn.anny. | bn.ʻmtḏl. | bn.ʻmyn. | bn.alz. | bn.birṯn. | [bn.]ylkn. | 117[325].1.9
n.ʻṯtry. | bn.ẖrẓn. | ady. | bn.birtn. | bn.ḥrẓn. | bn.bddn. | bn.anny. | ytršp. | bn.szn. | bn.kdgdl. | bn.glʻd. | bn.ktln. | [bn].ǵ 115[301].1.10
bn.nṣ. | [b]n.ʻṣr. | [---]m. | [bn.]ulnhr. | [bn.p]rn. | [bn.a]nny. | [---]n. | bn.kbln. | bn.pdy. | bn.ṯpdn. 1075.1.6
| bn is.bn tbdn. | bn uryy. | bn abdʻn. | bn prkl. | bn štn. | bn annyn. | b[n] slg. | u[--] dit. | bn p[-]n. | bn nẓǵil. 101[10].12
| [bn.]ibln. | ysd. | bn.ṯmq. | bn.agmn. | bn.uṣb. | bn.yzg. | bn.anntn. | bn.kwn. | ǵmšd. | bn.ʻbdḥy. | bn.ubyn. | slpd. | bn.at 115[301].4.7
[---].bn.anǵn. 2141.1
. | bn ẖnn. | b[n.-]n. | bn.ṣṣb. | bn.bʻltn ẖlq. | bn.mlkbn. | bn.asyy ẖlq. | bn.kṯly. | bn.kyn. | bn.ʻbdḥr. | [-]prm ẖlq. | [---]n 2016.2.4
gzl.bn.qldn. | gld.bt.klb. | l[---].bt.ẖzli. | bn.iẖyn. | ṣdqn.bn.ass. | bʻlyskn.bn.ss. | ṣdqn.bn.imrt. | mnḥm.bn.ẖyrn. | [-]yn 102[323].3.8
rty. | bn.ʻbṣ. | bn.argb. | ydn. | ilʻnt. | bn.urt. | ydn. | qṭn. | bn.asr. | bn.ʻdy. | bn.amt[m]. | myn. | šr. | bn.zql. | bn.iẖy. | bn.i 2117.3.47
[---].rb. | [-]lpl. | bn.asrn. | bn.šẖyn. | bn.abdʻn. | bn.ẖnqn. | bn.nmq. | bn.amdn. 1067.3
. | bn.abd.bʻ[l]. | mnḥm.bn[.---]. | krmn[py]. | bn.[--]m. | bn.asr[-]. | bn.ḏr[--]. | bn.ṣl[--]. | bn.ẖd[--]. | bn.ʻ[---]. | kbkbn b 2014.52
ṯpt.srdnnm. | rpan.uṯpt.srdnnm. | šbʻm.uṯpt.srdnnm. | bn.aǵli.uṯpt.srdnnm. | asrn.uṯpt.srdnnm. | bn.qṣn.uṯpt.srdnn 1124.8
ǵbr. | bn.mṣrn. | bn.[-]dr[-]. | [---]l[-]. | [--]ym. | [--]rm. | [bn.]aǵld. | [w.nḥ]l h. | [w.nḥ]l h[.-]. 114[324].3.4
.ṯt.qštm.w.qlʻ. | bn.ṯʻl.qšt. | bn.[ẖ]dpṯr.ṯt.qštm.[w].qlʻ. | bn.aǵlyn.ṯt.qštm[.w.ṯl]ṯ.qlʻm. | bn.ʻgw.qšt.w qlʻ. | bn.tbšn.ṯlṯ. 119[321].3.19
n. | d.lqḥt.ṯlǵḏy. | w.kd.ištir.ʻm.qrt. | ʻšt.ʻšr h.šmn. | ʻmn.bn.aǵlmn. | arbʻm.ksp.ʻl.qrt. | b.šd.bn.[u]brš. | ẖmšt.ʻšrt. | b.šd. 1083.5
l. | [b]n.qṭn. | [b]n.ǵrgn. | [b]n.tgḏn. | bn.ẖdyn. | bn.sgr. | bn.aǵltn. | bn.ktln. | bn.ʻgwn. | bn.yšmʻ. | bdl.mḏrǵlm. | bn.mm 104[316].9
bn.ab[l]. | kry. | psš. | ilṯḥm. | ḥrm. | bn.bty. | ʻby. | šm[n].bn.apn. | krty. | bn.ubr. | [bn] mdẖl. | bn.sy[n]n. | bn.šrn. 2078.17
--]. | [ʻ]bdm. | [bn].mṣrn. | [a]ršwn. | ʻb[d]. | w nḥl h. | atn.bn.ap[s]n. | nsk.ṯlṯ. | bn.[--.]m[-]ẖr. | bn.šmrm. | ṯnnm. | [ar]sw 85[80].3.7
prsn.ṣmd.w.ḥrṣ. | bn.ilbʻl. | bn.idrm. | bn.grgš. | bn.bly. | bn.apṯ. | bn.ysd. | bn.pl[-]. | bn.ṯbʻnq. | brqd. | bnn. | kbln.ṣ[md] 2113.11
yʻdd.tḥt.bn arbn. | ʻbdil.tḥt.ilmlk. | qly.tḥt bʻln.nsk. 1053.1
lmy. | ǵly. | bn.dnn. | bn.rmy. | dll. | mny. | krty. | bn.ʻbṣ. | bn.argb. | ydn. | ilʻnt. | bn.urt. | ydn. | qṭn. | bn.asr. | bn.ʻdy. | bn. 2117.3.41
].gmḥ. | [---]ty. | [b]n.ypy.gbʻly. | b[n].ḥyn. | ḏmn.šʻrty. | bn.arwdn.ilštʻy. | bn grgs. | bn.ẖran. | bn.arš[w.b]ṣry. | bn.ykn. 99[327].1.8
[---.]dd. | [---]n.dd. | [---.]dd. | bn.arwdn.dd. | mnḥm.w.kbln. | bn.ǵlm.dd. | bn.tbšn.dd. | bn.ẖ 131[309].4
i[l]štmʻym. | bn.ṯk. | bn.arwdn. | tmrtn. | šdʻl.bn aẖyn. | mʻrbym. | rpan. | abršn. | atl 95[91].3
n. | bn.ʻbdpdr. | šd.iyry.l.ʻbdbʻl. | šd.šmmn.l.bn.šty. | šd.bn.arws.l.bn.ẖlan. | šd.bn.ibryn.l.bn.ʻmnr. 1102.19
ḥrm. | bn.brzn. | w.nḥl h. | bn.adlḏn. | bn.šbl. | bn.ẖnzr. | bn.arwṯ. | bn.ṯbtnq. | bn.pṭḏn. | bn.nbdg. | bn.ḥgbn. | bn.tmr. | b 113[400].1.15
.qlʻ. | ark.qšt.w.qlʻ. | bn.ʻbdnkl.qšt.w.qlʻ. | bn.znan.qšt. | bn.arz.[ar]bʻ.qšt.w.arb[ʻ.]qlʻm. | b[n.]adʻl.q[š]t.w.qlʻ. | b[n].ily 119[321].2.45
k]ny. | bn.kdrn.uškny. | bn.lgn.uškny. | bn.abn.uškny. | bn.arz.šʻrty. | bn.ibrd.mʻrby. | ṣdqn.gbʻly. | bn.ypy.gbʻly. | bn.g 87[64].25
.d inn. | msgm.l hm. | pʻṣ.ẖbty. | artyn.ary. | brqn.ṯlḥy. | bn.aryn. | bn.lgn. | bn.bʻyn. | šdyn. | ary. | brqn. | bn.ẖlln. | bn.m 118[306].6
| bʻlyskn.bn.ss. | ṣdqn.bn.imrt. | mnḥm.bn.ẖyrn. | [-]yn.bn.arkbt. | [--]zbl.bt.mrnn. | a[--.---.-]ʻn. | ml[--.---]. | ar[--.---.-- 102[323].3.12
rn.b d.agpṯn.nḥl h. | šd.šwn.b d.ttyn.nḥl [h]. | šd.ttyn[.b]n.arkšt. | lʻq[.---]. | šd.pll.b d.qrt. | š[d].annḏr.b d.bdn.nḥ[l h 2029.4
rqd. | bn.abdg. | ilyn. | bn.tan. | bn.arm. | bn.bʻl.ṣdq. | bn.army. | bn.rpiyn. | bn.army. | bn.krm 1046.1.5

rn. | alpy. | bn.plsy. | bn.qrr[-]. | bn.ḥyl. | bn.g‘yn. | ḥyn. | bn.armg[-]. | b‘lmṯpṭ. | [bn].ayḫ. | [---]rn. | ill. | ġlmn. | bn.ytrm. 1035.2.4
l. | bn bl. | bn dkn. | bn ils. | bn ḫšbn. | bn uryy. | bn kṯl. | bn army. | bn gln. | bn abg. | bn.nġry. | bn.srwd. | mtnn. | bn gš[1064.10
n. | bn.tan. | bn.arm. | bn.b‘l.ṣdq. | bn.army. | bn.rpiyn. | bn.army. | bn.krmn. | bn.ykn. | bn.‘ṯtrab. | uṣn[-]. | bn.alṯn. | bn 1046.1.9
rqd. | bn.abdg. | ilyn. | bn.tan. | bn.arm. | bn.b‘l.ṣdq. | bn.army. | bn.rpiyn. | bn.army. | bn.krmn. | bn.ykn. | bn.‘ṯtrab. 1046.1.7
ṯ.ql‘m. | bn.‘gw.qšt.w ql‘. | bn.tbšn.ṯlṯ.qšt.w.[ṯlṯ.]ql‘m. | bn.army.ṯt.qštm.w[.]q[l‘]. | bn.rpš.qšt.w.ql‘. | bn.ġb.qšt. | bn.y 119[321].3.22
[-----]. | w [---]. | bn.[---]. | bn.yr[--]. | bn.kṯr[t]. | bn.šml. | bn.arnbt. | qdšm. | b[-.--]t. | [---.-]l[--]. | [---.]pr[--]. | [-.a]pln. | b 2163.2.7
lb. | b[n.]dtn. | w.nḥl h. | w.nḥl hm. | bn.iršyn. | bn.‘zn. | bn.aršw. | bn.ḫzrn. | bn.iġyn. | w.nḥl h. | bn.ksd. | bn.bršm. | bn 113[400].2.14
ḥyn. | ḏmn.š‘rty. | bn.arwdn.ilšt‘y. | bn grgs. | bn.ḫran. | bn.arš[w.b]ṣry. | bn.ykn. | bn.lṣn.‘rmy. | bn.b‘yn.šly. | bn.ynḫn 99[327].2.1
[-----]. | ḏ[----]. | ab[--.---]. | bn.nṣdn[.ḫm]št. | bn.arsw ‘[šr]m. | ‘šdyn.ḫmš[t]. | abršn.‘šr[t]. | b‘ln.ḫmšt. | w.n 1062.5
. | bn.irgy. | w.nḥl h. | w.nḥl hm. | [bn].pmn. | bn.gṯrn. | bn.arpḫn. | bn.ṯryn. | bn.dll. | bn.ḫswn. | mrynm. | ‘zn. | ḥyn. | ‘ 1046.3.29
bn.šyy. | bn.ḫnzr. | bn.ydb‘l. | bn.ḥyn. | [bn].ar[-]m. | [bn].ḫrp[-]. | [bn].ḫdpṯr. | [bn.-]dn. | [bn.-]lyn. | [b 124[-].2.5
. | bn.ḫrẓn. | bn.ḏqnt. | bn.gmrš. | bn.nmq. | bn.špš[yn]. | bn.ar[--]. | bn.gb[--]. | bn.ḫn[n]. | bn.gntn[-]. | [--.]nqq[-]. | b[n.- 2023.3.15
. | bn.aš[-]š. | bn.štn. | bn.ilš. | bn.tnabn. | bn.ḥṣn. | ṣprn. | bn.ašbḥ. | bn.qṭnn. | bn.ġlmn. | [bn].ṣwy. | [bn].ḫnq[n]. | [-----]. 1046.1.21
army. | bn.krmn. | bn.ykn. | bn.‘ṯtrab. | uṣn[-]. | bn.alṯn. | bn.aš[-]š. | bn.štn. | bn.ilš. | bn.tnabn. | bn.ḥṣn. | ṣprn. | bn.ašbḥ. 1046.1.15
| w.nḥl h. | w.nḥl hm. | w.[n]ḥl hm. | b[n.---]. | bn.gzry. | bn.atyn. | bn.ttn. | bn.rwy. | bn.‘myn. | bdl.mrynm. | bn.ṣqn. | b 113[400].3:2
bn.[---]. | bn.[---]. | bn.[---]. | [-----]. | bn[---]. | bn.mlkyy. | bn.atn. | bn.bly. | bn.ṭbrn. | bn.ḥgby. | bn.pity. | bn.slgyn. | ‘zn.b 115[301].2.2
. | [--]ṣb. | [--]ps. | [--]ṭb. | [--]ln. | [---]r. | [---]y. | bn.aḏdt. | bn.atnb. | bn.yšd. | bn.bršm. | bn.gṯprg. | gṯpbn. | bn.b[--]. | [b]n 1057.9
n.anntn. | bn.kwn. | ġmšd. | bn.‘bdḥy. | bn.ubyn. | slpd. | bn.atnb. | bn.ktmn. | bn.pity. | bn.iryn. | bn.‘bl. | bn.grbn. | bn.ir 115[301].4.13
n.ntp.[---]. | bn.lbnn.[----]. | ady.ḫ[--.---]. | [-]b[-]n.[---]. | bn.atnb.mr[--.---]. | bn.sḫr.mr[-.---]. | bn.idrn.‘š[-.---]. | bn.bly. 88[304].7
[spr.----]m. | bn.pi[ty]. | w.nḥ[l h]. | ‘bd[--]. | bn.s[---]. | bn.at[--]. | bn.qnḏ. | ṣmq[-]. | bn.anny. | bn.‘mtdl. | bn.‘myn. | b 117[325].1.6
ln]y[m].l mt‘t[.---]. | [-]m[.---]. | h.hn bn k.hn[.---]. | bn bn.aṯr k.hn[.---]. | yd k.ṣġr.tnšq.špt k.ṯm. | ṭkm.bm ṭkm.aḫm. 22.2[124].3
. | [ym].mġẓ.qnyt.ilm. | w tn.bt.l b‘l.km. | [i]lm.w ḥẓr.k bn. | [a]ṯrt.gm.l ġlm h. | b‘l.yṣḥ.‘n.gpn. | w ugr.bn.ġlmt. | ‘mm 8[51FRAG].4
.šbt.dqn h. | [mm‘m.-]d.l ytn.bt.l b‘l.k ilm. | [w ḥẓ]r.k bn.aṯrt.td‘ṣ.]p‘n. | [w tr.a]rṣ.id[k.l ttn.p]nm. | [‘m.i]l.mbk.nh 3[‘NT.VI].5.12
| hm.amt.aṯrt.tlbn. | lbnt.ybn.bt.l b‘l. | km ilm.w ḥẓr.k bn.aṯrt. | w t‘n.rbt.aṯrt ym. | rbt.ilm.l ḥkmt. | šbt.dqn k.l tsr k 4[51].5.63
. | [w ṣbrt.ary]h. | [wn.in.bt.l b‘l.] | [km.ilm.w ḥẓr]. | [k bn.aṯ]r[t]. | m[ṯ]b.il.mẓll. | bn h.mṯb.rbt. | aṯrt.ym.mṯb. | klt.k 4[51].1.12
w bn h.ilt.w ṣbrt.arḫ h. | wn.in.bt.l b‘l.km.ilm. | ḥẓr.k b[n.a]ṯrt.mṯb.il. | mṯll.b[n h.m]ṯb.rbt.aṯrt. | ym.mṯb.[pdr]y.bt 3[‘NT.VI].5.47
bn h.ilt.w ṣbrt. | ary h.wn.in.bt.l b‘l. | km.ilm.w ḥẓr.k bn.aṯrt. | mṯb il.mẓll.bn h. | mṯb rbt.aṯrt.ym. | mṯb.klt.knyt. | 4[51].4.51
[---.wn.in]. | [bt].l [b‘l.km.ilm.w ḥẓr]. | k bn.[aṯrt.mṯb.il.mẓll]. | bn h.m[ṯb.rbt.aṯrt.ym]. | mṯb.pdr[y.bt. 3[‘NT.VI].4.1
.l[l]im. | ṣḥ.aḫ h.b bht h.a[r]y h. | b qrb hkl h.ṣḥ. | šb‘m.bn.aṯrt. | špq.ilm.krm.y[n]. | špq.ilht.ḫprt[.yn]. | špq.ilm.alpm 4[51].6.46
yiḫd.b‘l.bn.aṯrt. | rbm.ymḫṣ.b ktp. | dk ym.ymḫṣ.b ṣmd. | ṣḥr mt.ymṣ 6[49].5.1
ḫdl. | bn ṣdqn. | bn ayy. | bn dbb. | w nḥl h. | bn n‘myn. | bn aṯyy. | bn ḫlp. | bn.ẓll. | bn ydy. | bn lzn. | bn.ṯyn. | bn g‘r. | 2016.1.10
[-]ldn. | [i]wryn. | ḫbsn. | ulmk. | ‘dršp. | bn.knn. | pdyn. | bn.aṯll.ṯn. | kdln.akdṯb. | ṯn.b gt ykn‘m. 1061.20
.mgn. | bn.‘dn. | bn.knn. | bn.py. | bn.mk[-]. | bn.by[--]. | bn.a[--]. | bn.iy[--]. | bn.ḫ[---]. | bn.plš. | bn.ubr. | bn.‘pṯb. | ṯbry. 2117.1.12
yšd. | bn.bršm. | bn.gṯprg. | gṯpbn. | bn.b[--]. | [b]n.[---]. | bn.a[--]. | bn.ml[k]. | bn.glyn. | bn.‘dr. | bn.ṯmq. | bn.ṉtp. | bn.‘g 1057.16
bn.g[--]n. | bn[.---]. | [-----]. | b[n.---]. | b[n.---]. | bn.[---]. | bn.a[--]. | w.nḥl h. | bn.alz. | w.nḥl h. | bn.sny. | bn.ablḥ. | [-----] 2163.1.10
b‘m ṯqlm.w [---] arb‘yn. | w ‘l.mnḥm.arb‘ š[mn]. | w ‘l bn a[--.-]yn ṯqlm. | [--] ksp [---] kdr [---]. | [-]ṯrn [k]sp [-]al[.-] 1103.10
--].tbtṯ[b.---]. | [---].bn.b[--.---]. | [---].bn.ab[--.---]. | [---.]bn.a[--.---]. | [---.]bn.i[--.---]. | [---].ṯp[--.---]. | [---.a]ḫt.b d[.---]. 2162.A.6
b d.---]. | bn.btr. | bn.‘ms. | bn.pṣn. | bn.agmz. | bn.[--]n. | bn.a[--]. | [------]. | [------]. | [------]. | [------]. | [------]. | [bn.]kblbn 2021.1.7
bn a[---]. | bn.byy. | bn.ily[-]. | bn.iy[--]. | bn.ṯy[--]. | bn.p[---]. | 2025.1
rwn. | [bn.-]ty. | [bn.]iršn. | bn.[---]. | bn.b[--]. | bn.š[--]. | bn.a[---]. | bn.prsn. | bn.mtyn. | bn.ḫlpn. | bn.ḥgbn. | bn.szn. | b 117[325].2.4
dnn.ṯlṯ.ṣmdm. | bn.‘mnr. | bn.kmn. | bn.ibyn. | bn.mryn.ṣmd.w.ḥrṣ. | bn.prsn.ṣmd.w.ḥrṣ. | bn.ilb‘l. 2113.4
ḫrmln. | bn.tnn. | bn.pndr. | bn.nqq. | ḥrš.bhtm. | bn.izl. | bn.ibln. | bn.ilt. | špšyn.nḥl h. | n‘mn.bn.iryn. | nrn.nḥl h. | bn. 85[80].2.4
[-----]. | [bn.]ibln. | ysd. | bn.ṯmq. | bn.agmn. | bn.uṣb. | bn.yzg. | bn.annt 115[301].4.1
[ab]mn bn.qṣy. | [‘]pṯrm bn.agmz. | [-]n bn.iln. | [--]nn bn.ibm. | [-]n bn.ḥrn. | [š]mmn bn.gmz. | [yn]ḥm bn.ilmd. 2087.12
b‘l.uḫnpy.ḫmšm. | b.bn.ṯtm.ṯlṯm. | b.bn.agdṯb.‘šrm. | b.bn.ibn.arb‘t.‘šrt. | b.bn.mnn.ṯtm. | b.rpan.bn.yyn.‘šrt. | b.yp‘r. 2054.1.13
n.uškny. | bn.lgn.uškny. | bn.abn.uškny. | bn.arz.š‘rty. | bn.ibrd.m‘rby. | ṣdqn.gb‘ly. | bn.ypy.gb‘ly. | bn.grgs.ilštm‘y. | 87[64].26
. | b‘lytn.bn.ulb. | ytr‘m.bn.swy. | ṣḥrn.bn.qrtm. | bn.špš.bn.ibrd. | ‘pṯrm.bn.‘bdy. | n[--.]bn.šnd. | [---].bn.[---]. 2024.5
.l.‘bdb‘l. | šd.šmmn.l.bn.šty. | šd.bn.arws.l.bn.ḫlan. | šd.bn.ibryn.l.bn.‘mnr. 1102.20
n.ḥgb[n]. | bn.ulbt[-]. | ḏkry[-]. | bn.tlm[yn]. | bn.y‘dd. | bn.idly[-]. | bn.‘bd[--]. | bn.ṣd[qn]. 2017.7
. | bn.mryn.ṣmd.w.ḥrṣ. | bn.prsn.ṣmd.w.ḥrṣ. | bn.ilb‘l. | bn.idrm. | bn.grgš. | bn.bly. | bn.apṯ. | bn.ysd. | bn.pl[-]. | bn.ṯb‘ 2113.8
[k]lby. | [-]ḫmn. | [š]pšyn. | [‘b]dmlk. | [---]yn. | bn.ṯ[--]. | bn.idrm. | bn.ymn. | bn.ṣry. | bn.mztn. | bn.šlgyn. | bn.[-]gštn. | 113[400].2.2
-]. | [-]b[-]n.[---]. | bn.atnb.mr[--.---]. | bn.sḫr.mr[-.---]. | bn.idrn.‘š[-.---]. | bn.bly.mr[-.---]. | w.nḥl h.mr[-.---]. | ilšpš.[-- 88[304].9
-]. | hm.[---]. | kmrṯn[.---]. | bn.ṯbln[.---]. | bn.pndr[.---]. | bn.idr[-.---]. | bn.ḥdn[-.---]. | bn.ṯbi[l.---]. 2070.2.6
bn sl[--.---]. | bn id[--.---]. 108[38].2
nn. | [bn.-]dn. | bn.ummt. | bn.ṯb[-]. | bn.[-]r[-]. | bn.tgn. | bn.iḏrn. | mnn. | b[n].skn. | bn.p‘ṣ. | bn.ḏrm. | [bn.-]ln. | [bn.-]ḏ 124[-].6.8
[s]pr.bnš.mlk.d.b.tbq. | [kr]wn. | [--]n. | [q]ṣy. | ṯn.bn.iwrḫz.[n]‘rm. | yṣr[.-]qb. | w.ṯn.bnš.iytlm. | w.‘šrm.ṣmd.al 2066.2.4
]tn.bn.aḏmṯn. | [-]tn bn.agyn. | ullym.bn.abynm. | antn.bn.iwr[n]r. | pwn.ṯmry. | ksyn.bn.lḫsn. | [-]kyn.ṯmry. 94[313].7
]. | [b]n.ḫrmln. | bn.tnn. | bn.pndr. | bn.nqq. | ḥrš.bhtm. | bn.izl. | bn.ibln. | bn.ilt. | špšyn.nḥl h. | n‘mn.bn.iryn. | nrn.nḥl 85[80].2.3
. | qtn. | bn.asr. | bn.‘dy. | bn.amt[m]. | myn. | šr. | bn.zql. | bn.iḫy. | bn.iytr. | bn.‘yn. | bn.ġzl. | bn.ṣmy. | bn.il[-]šy. | bn.ybš 2117.2.4
y bn.dnn.ṯkt. | ilthm.bn.dnn.ṯkt. | šb‘l.bn.aly.ṯkt. | klby.bn.iḫy.ṯkt. | pšš.bn.buly.ṯkt. | ‘pṣpn.bn.‘dy.ṯkt. | n‘mn.bn.‘yn.ṯ 2085.7
‘bdb‘l.bn.kdn. | gzl.bn.qldn. | gld.bt.klb. | l[---].bt.ḫzli. | bn.iḫyn. | ṣdqn.bn.ass. | b‘lyskn.bn.ss. | ṣdqn.bn.imrt. | mnḥm. 102[323].3.7
bn gš[-]. | bn gbrn. | bn uldy. | synn.bn kn‘m. | bn kbr. | bn iytlm. | bn ayln. | bn.kln. | bn.‘lln. | bn.liy. | bn.nqtn. | bn ab 1064.21
ḏm[r.---].br. | bn.i[ytlm.---]. | wr[t.---.]b d.yḥmn. | yry[.---.]br. | ydn[.---].kry 2123.2

n.asr.|bn.ʻdy.|bn.amt[m].|myn.|šr.|bn.zql.|bn.iḫy.|bn.iytr.|bn.ʻyn.|bn.ǵzl.|bn.ṣmy.|bn.il[-]šy.|bn.ybšr.|bn.sl 2117.2.5
ṯn.bn.klby.|bn.iytr.|[ʻ]bdyrḫ.|[b]n.ggʻt.|[ʻ]dy.|armwl.|uwaḫ.|ypln.w.ṯ 2086.2
.ʻdn.|bn.knn.|bn.py.|bn.mk[-].|bn.by[--].|bn.a[--].|bn.iy[--].|bn.ḫ[---].|bn.plš.|bn.ubr.|bn.ʻpṯb.|ṯbry.|bn.ymn. 2117.1.13
bn a[---].|bn.byy.|bn.ily[-].|bn.iy[--].|bn.ṯy[--].|bn.p[---].|gyn[.---].|bn.pṯ[--].|bn.db[--]. 2025.4
il b[n] il.|dr bn il.|mpḫrt bn il.|ṯrmn w šnm.|il w aṯrt.|ḫnn i 30[107].1
.|tmtn.u ḫšt k.l ntn.|ʻtq.b d.aṯt.ab.ṣrry.|ik m.yrgm.bn.il.|krt.špḥ.lṭpn.|w qdš.u ilm.tmtn.|špḥ.lṭpn.l yḥ.|w yʻn 16.1[125].20
ndbḥ.hw.ṯʻ n[ṯʻy.hw.nkt.nk]t.ytši.l ab bn il.|ytši.l d[r.bn il.l]mpḫrt.bn il.|l ṯkm[n.w šnm.]hn ʻ[r].|[---.]w npy[.--- 32[2].1.34
bḥ.hw.ṯʻ |nṯʻy.|hw.nkt.nkt.y[t]ši.l ab.bn.il.ytši.l dr.|bn il.l mpḫrt.bn.il.l ṯkmn[.w]šnm.hn.ʻr.|w.ṯb.l mspr.m[šr] 32[2].1.26
]ḥ.|[hw.ṯʻ.nṯʻy.hw.nkt.nkt.]yt[ši.l ab.bn.il].|[ytši.l dr.bn.il.l mpḫ]rt.[bn.il.l ṯkmn.w šn]m hn š.|[---.w n]py.gr[.ḥm 32[2].1.9B
[---.hw.ṯʻ.nṯʻ]y.|[hw.nkt.nkt.ytši.l ab.bn.il.ytši.l d]r.bn[.il].|[l mpḫrt.bn.il.l ṯkmn.w šnm.hn š].|[w šqrb.š.mšr m 32[2].1.2
bḥ].|hw.ṯʻ.nṯʻy.hw.nkt.n[k]t.ytši[.l ab.bn.il].|ytši.l dr.bn.il.l mpḫrt.bn.i[l.l ṯkmn.w š]nm hn š.|w šqrb.ʻr.mšr mšr 32[2].1.17
ʻy.|hw.nkt.nkt.y[t]ši.l ab.bn.il.ytši.l dr.|bn il.l mpḫrt.bn.il.l ṯkmn[.w]šnm.hn.ʻr.|w.ṯb.l mspr.m[šr] mšr.bt.ugrt.w 32[2].1.26
ʻy.hw.nkt.nk]t.ytši.l ab bn il.|ytši.l d[r.bn il.l]mpḫrt.bn il.|l ṯkm[n.w šnm.]hn ʻ[r].|[---.]w npy[.---].|[---.]w npy. 32[2].1.34
.hw.nkt.nkt.]yt[ši.l ab.bn.il].|[ytši.l dr.bn.il.l mpḫ]rt.[bn.il.l ṯkmn.w šn]m hn š.|[---.w n]py.gr[.ḥmyt.ugrt.w np]y. 32[2].1.9B
|[hw.nkt.nkt.ytši.l ab.bn.il.ytši.l d]r.bn[.il].|[l mpḫrt.bn.il.l ṯkmn.w šnm.hn š].|[w šqrb.š.mšr mšr.bn.ugrt.w npy. 32[2].1.3
y.hw.nkt.n[k]t.ytši[.l ab.bn.il].|ytši.l dr.bn.il.l mpḫrt.bn.i[l.l ṯkmn.w š]nm hn š.|w šqrb.ʻr.mšr mšr bn.ugrt.w [np 32[2].1.17
.]w l ṯʻ dbḥ n.|ndbḥ.hw.ṯʻ n[ṯʻy.hw.nkt.nk]t.ytši.l ab bn il.|ytši.l d[r.bn il.l]mpḫrt.bn il.|l ṯkm[n.w šnm.]hn ʻ[r]. 32[2].1.33
.w l.ṯʻ.dbḥ n.ndbḥ.hw.ṯʻ |nṯʻy.|hw.nkt.nkt.y[t]ši.l ab.bn.il.ytši.l dr.|bn il.l mpḫrt.bn.il.l ṯkmn[.w]šnm.hn.ʻr.|w.ṯ 32[2].1.25
.w l.ṯʻ.dbḥ n.ndb]ḥ.|[hw.ṯʻ.nṯʻy.hw.nkt.nkt.]yt[ši.l ab.bn.il].|[ytši.l dr.bn.il.l mpḫ]rt.[bn.il.l ṯkmn.w šn]m hn š.|[- 32[2].1.9A
[---.hw.ṯʻ.nṯʻ]y.|[hw.nkt.nkt.ytši.l ab.bn.il.ytši.l d]r.bn[.il].|[l mpḫrt.bn.il.l ṯkmn.w šnm.hn š].|[32[2].1.2
w l ṯʻ.d[bḥ n.ndbḥ].|hw.ṯʻ.nṯʻy.hw.nkt.n[k]t.ytši[.l ab.bn.il].|ytši.l dr.bn.il.l mpḫrt.bn.i[l.l ṯkmn.w š]nm hn š.|w š 32[2].1.16
š ḥym.w atn k.bl mt.|w ašlḥ k.ašspr k.ʻm.bʻl.|šnt.ʻm.bn il.tspr.yrḫm.|k bʻl.k yḥwy.yʻšr.ḥwy.yʻš.|r.w yšqyn h.yb 17[2AQHT].6.29
rym.ṣpn.w yʻn.|gpn.w ugr.ṯḥm.bn ilm.|mt.hwt.ydd.bn.il.|ǵzr.p np.š.npš.lbim.|thw.hm.brlt.anḫr.|b ym.hm.brk 5[67].1.13
il b[n] il.|dr bn il.|mpḫrt bn il.|ṯrmn w šnm.|il w aṯrt.|ḫnn il.|nṣbt il.| 30[107].2
n.pl[-].|bn.ṯbʻnq.|brqd.|bnn.|kbln.ṣ[md].|bn gmrt.|bn.il.ṣm[d].|bn abbly.|ytʻd.ṣm[d].|bn.liy.|ʻšrm.ṣ[md].|ṯṯ k 2113.19
].|rkby.|bn.knn.qšt.|pbyn.qšt.|yddn.qšt.w.qlʻ.|šʻrt.|bn.il.qšt.w.qlʻ.|ark.qšt.w.qlʻ.|bn.ʻbdnkl.qšt.w.qlʻ.|bn.znan. 119[321].2.41
p]n.ḥlm.|qdš.nny.ḥ[l]m.adr.|ḥl.rḥb.mk[npt].|ap.krt bn[m.il].|špḥ.lṭpn[.w qdš].|bkm.tʻrb[.ʻl.ab h].|tʻrb.ḥ[--].|b 16.2[125].110
.|ṣpn.ḥlm.qdš.|any.ḥlm.adr.ḥl.|rḥb.mknpt.ap.|[k]rt.bnm.il.špḥ.|lṭpn.w qdš.ʻl.|ab h.yʻrb.ybky.|w yšnn.ytn.g h.| 16.1[125].10
il b[n] il.|dr bn il.|mpḫrt bn il.|ṯrmn w šnm.|il w aṯrt.|ḫnn il.|nṣbt il.|šlm il.|il ḥš il 30[107].3
[---.]btlt.ʻnt.|[---.]pp.hrm.|[---].d l ydʻ bn il.|[---.]pḫr kkbm.|[---.]dr dt.šmm.|[---.al]iyn bʻl.|[---].r 10[76].1.3
[---.--]mm.hlkt.|[---.]b qrb.ʻr.|[---.m]lakm l h.|[---.]l.bn.il.|[---.--]a.ʻd h.|[---.--]rh.|[---.--]y.špš.|[---.--]h.|[---.--]t 26[135].7
qšlm ḫmš.|krzn.ḫmš.|ubrʻym.ḫmš.|[----].|[bn] itn.|[bn] il.|[---]ṯ.|klṯṯb.|gsn.|arm[w]l.|bn.ṣdqn.|ḥlbn.|tbq.alp. 2039.10
.|bn.ibyn.|bn.mryn.ṣmd.w.ḥrṣ.|bn.prsn.ṣmd.w.ḥrṣ.|bn.ilbʻl.|bn.idrm.|bn.grgš.|bn.bly.|bn.apṯ.|bn.ysd.|bn.pl[- 2113.7
tlmyn.ʻšrm.|ṣṣ.bn.krwn.ʻš[rm].|ṣṣ.bn.iršyn.[---].|[ṣṣ].bn.ilbʻl.ṯl[ṯ]m.|ṣṣ.bn.pṯdn.[--]m.|ṣṣ.[bn].gyn.[---].|[-----].|[- 2096.6
.|bn.b[---].|bn.iš[--].|bn.ab[--].|bn.al[--].|bn.nb[dg].|bn.ild[-].|[-----].|[bn.]nnr.|[bn.]aglby.|[bn.]bʻly.|[mḏ]rǵlm. 104[316].5
ḫršn.qšt.w.qlʻ.|ilrb.qšt.w.qlʻ.|psḥn.qšt.|bn.kmy.qšt.|bn.ilḫbn.qšt.w.q[lʻ].|ršpab.qšt.w.qlʻ.|pdrn.qšt.w.qlʻ.|bn.pǵ 119[321].3.44
.tknn.|ʻl.ʻrbnm.|hn hmt.|tknn.|mtn.bn.ʻbdym.|ilrb.bn.ilyn.|ʻbdadt.bn ʻbdkb.|gnʻym. 1161.11
bn.arz.[ar]bʻ.qšt.w.arb[ʻ.]qlʻm.|b[n.]adʻl.q[š]t.w.qlʻ.|b[n].ilyn.qšt.w.qlʻ.|šmrm.qlʻ.|ubrʻy.|abmn.qšt.w.ṯn.qlʻm.| 119[321].2.47
ṣṣ.bn.ilyn.ṯlṯm.|ṣṣ.bn.kzn.ṯlṯm.|ṣṣ.bn.tlmyn.ʻšrm.|ṣṣ.bn.krwn. 2096.1
.|bn.ṯbil.|bn.iryn.|ṯṯl.|bn.nṣdn.|bn.ydln.|[bn].ʻdy.|[bn].ilyn. 1071.11
bn a[---].|bn.byy.|bn.ily[-].|bn.iy[--].|bn.ṯy[--].|bn.p[---].|gyn[.---].|bn.pṯ[--]. 2025.3
bn.|bn.iršyn.|bn.nklb.|bn.mryn.|[bn.]b[--].|bn.ẓrl.|bn.illm[-].|bn.š[---].|bn.ṣ[---].|bn.š[---].|bn.[---].|bn.[---].|b 115[301].4.24
k.ksu.|ṯbt h.ḫḫ.arṣ.|nḫlt h.w ngr.|ʻnn.ilm.al.|tqrb.l bn.ilm.|mt.al.yʻdb km.|k imr.b p h.|k lli.b ṯbrn.|qn h.ṯḫta 4[51].8.16
ṣḥn.|k lsmm.mt.ql.|bʻl.ql.ʻln.špš.|tṣḥ.l mt.šmʻ.mʻ.|l bn.ilm.mt.ik.tmt[ḫ]|ṣ.ʻm.aliyn.bʻl.|ik.al.yšm[ʻ] k.ṯr.|il.ab k. 6[49].6.24
.k rs.|ipd k.ank.ispi.uṯm.|ḏrqm.amt m.l yrt.|b npš.bn ilm.mt.b mh|mrt.ydd.il.ǵzr.|tbʻ.w l.ytb ilm.idk.|l ytn.p 5[67].1.7
lb.arḫ.l ʻgl h.k lb.|ṯat.l imr h.km.lb.|ʻnt.aṯr.bʻl.tiḫd.|bn.ilm.mt.b ḥrb.|tbqʻnn.b ḫṯr.tdry|nn.b išt.tšrpnn.|b rḥm. 6[49].2.31
.|l ytn.pnm.ʻm.bʻl.|mrym.ṣpn.w yʻn.|gpn.w ugr.ṯḥm.bn ilm.|mt.hwt.ydd.bn.il.|ǵzr.p np.š.npš.lbim.|thw.hm.brl 5[67].1.12
.|mid.an[--.]ṣn[--].|nrt.ilm.špš[.ṣḥrr]t.|la.šmm.b y[d.bn.ilm.m]t.|w tʻn.btlt.ʻn[t.bnt.]bht |k.y ilm.bnt.bh[t k].a[l.t 3[ʻNT.VI].5.26
lli.b ṯbrn q y.ḫtu hw.|nrt.ilm.špš.ṣḥrrt.|la.šmm.b yd.bn ilm.mt.|ym.ymm.yʻtqn.l ymm.|l yrḫm.rḥm.ʻnt.tngṯ h.| 6[49].2.25
šsq[n h].|b qṣ.all.tšu.g h.w[tṣ]|ḥ.at.mt.tn.aḫ y.|w ʻn.bn.ilm.mt.mh.|taršn.l btlt.ʻnt.|an.itlk.w aṣd.kl.|ǵr.l kbd.ar 6[49].2.13
w yʻny.bn.|ilm.mt.npš[.-].|npš.lbun.|thw.w npš.|anḫr.b ym.|brkt. UG5.4.1
ša.|g hm.w tṣḥ.ṯḥm.aliyn.|bn.bʻl.hwt.aliy.qrdm.|bhṯ.bn.ilm.mt.ʻbd k.an.|w d ʻlm k.šmḫ.bn.ilm.mt.|[---.]g h.w a 5[67].2.19
.|ṯny.l ydd.il ǵzr.|ṯḥm.aliyn.bʻl.hwt.aliy.|qrdm.bhṯ.l bn.ilm mt.|ʻbd k.an.w d.ʻlm k.|tbʻ.w l.ytb.ilm.idk.|l ytn.pn 5[67].2.11
.l bht h.|u mlk.u bl mlk.|arṣ.drkt.yštkn.|dll.al.ilak.l bn.|ilm.mt.ʻdd.l ydd.|il.ǵzr.yqra.mt.|b npš h.ystrn ydd.|b 4[51].7.45
.|l [ym]m.l yrḫm.l yrḫm.|l šnt.[m]k.b šbʻ.|šnt.w [--].bn.ilm.mt.|ʻm.aliyn.bʻl.yšu.|g h.w yṣḥ.ʻl k.b[ʻ]l m.|pht.qltʻ 6[49].5.9
---.--]mr.limm.|[---.]bn.ilm.mt.|[--]u.šbʻt.ǵlm h.|[---].bn.ilm.mt.|p[-]n.aḫ y m.ytn.bʻl.|[s]pu y.bn m.um y.kly y.| 6[49].6.9
nhr hm.|šbʻ.ydt y.b ṣʻ.|[--.]šbʻ.rbt.|[---.]qbṯ.ṯm.|[---.]bn.ilm.|[m]t.šmḫ.p ydd.|il[.ǵ]zr.|b [-]dn.ʻ.z.w.|rgbt.zbl. UG5.4.14
.|ʻbd k.an.w d.ʻlm k.|tbʻ.w l.ytb.ilm.idk.|l ytn.pn.ʻm.bn.ilm.mt.|tk.qrt h.hmry.mk.ksu.|ṯbt.ḫḫ.arṣ.nḫlt h.tša.|g 5[67].2.14
ṣ.w pr.|ʻṣm.yraun.aliyn.bʻl.|ṯṯʻ.nn.rkb.ʻrpt.|tbʻ.rgm.l bn.ilm.mt.|ṯny.l ydd.il ǵzr.|ṯḥm.aliyn.bʻl.hwt.aliy.|qrdm.b 5[67].2.8
mn.l pʻn.mt.|hbr.w ql.|tšṯḥwy.w k|bd hwt.w rgm.|l bn.ilm.mt.|ṯny.l ydd.|il.ǵzr.ṯḥm.|aliyn.bʻl.|[hw]t.aliy.q|[r 4[51].8.30
ysʻ.alt.|ṯbt k.l yhpk.ksa.mlk k.|l ytbr.ḫṭ.mṯpṭ k.|yru.bn ilm t.ṯṯʻ.y|dd.il.ǵzr.yʻr.mt.|b ql h.y[---.---].|bʻl.yṯṯbn[.l k 6[49].6.30
h.|[---.]ru.|[----] h.|[---.--]mt.|[---.--]mr.limm.|[---.]bn.ilm.mt.|[--]u.šbʻt.ǵlm h.|[---].bn.ilm.mt.|p[-]n.aḫ y m.y 6[49].6.7
t.aliy.qrdm.|bhṯ.bn.ilm.mt.ʻbd k.an.|w d ʻlm k.šmḫ.bn.ilm.mt.|[---.]g h.w aṣḥ.ik.yṣḥn.|[bʻl.ʻm.aḫ y.ik].yqrun.h 5[67].2.20

rkb.ʻrpt. | [--].ydd.w yqlṣn. | yqm.w ywpṯn.b tk. | p[ẖ]r.bn.ilm.štt. | p[--].b ṯlḥn y.qlt. | b ks.ištyn h. | dm.ṯn.dbḥm.šna 4[51].3.14

[b]n[.---]. | bn [-]ʻy. | [b]n [i]lmd. | bn [t]bdn. | bn štn. | b[n] kdn. | bn dwn. | bn ḏrn. 2088.3

[--]nn bn.ibm. | [-]n bn.ḥrn. | [š]mmn bn.gmz. | [yn]ḥm bn.ilmd. 2087.15

spr.ḥrš. | qštipṭl. | bn.anny. | ilṣdq. | yplṭn.bn iln. | špšm.nsl h. | [-----]. 1037.5

]špab bn.pni. | [ab]mn bn.qṣy. | [ʻ]pṯrm bn.agmz. | [-]n bn.iln. | [--]nn bn.ibm. | [-]n bn.ḥrn. | [š]mmn bn.gmz. | [yn]ḥ 2087.11

--.]ubdym.b.uškn. | [---]lby. | [--]nbbl. | bn bl. | bn dkn. | bn ils. | bn ḥšbn. | bn uryy. | bn kṯl. | bn army. | bn gln. | bn abg 1064.6

r[-]m. | [bn].ḥrp[-]. | [bn].ḫdpṯr. | [bn.-]dn. | [bn.-]lyn. | [bn.i]lsk. | [bn.---]n. | bn[.---]. | bn[.---]. | bn[.---]. | bn[.---]. | bn[.- 124[-].2.10

y.ʻšrt.ṯṯt šlm.ʻšrt. | bn.ḫgby.ṯmnt.l ʻšrm.ʻšrt.ḫmš.kbd. | bn.ilṣdq.šbʻt ṯlṯt šlm. | bn.ṯmq.arbʻt ṯqlm šlmm. 1131.9

ry.w.pṯpṯ.ʻrb. | b.yrm. | [ily.w].ḏmry.ʻrb. | b.ṯbʻm. | ydn.bn.ilrpi. | w.ṯbʻm.ʻrb.b.ʻ[d]n. | ḏmry.bn.yrm. | ʻrb.b.adʻy. 2079.7

gmrš[.bn].mrnn. | ʻbdmlk.bn.ʻmyn. | agyn.rʻy. | abmlk.bn.ilrš. | iḫyn.bn.ḫryn. | [ab]ǵl.bn.gdn. | [---].bn.bqš. | [---].bn. 102[323].4.10

rišym.qnum. | bn.ilrš. | ʻ[p]ṯn. | b[n.ʻr]my. | [--]ṯy. | bn.ǵdʻ. | bn.ʻyn. | bn.grb[n] 2078.2

.bn.buly.ṯkt. | ʻpṣpn.bn.ʻdy.ṯkt. | nʻmn.bn.ʻyn.ṯkt. | ʻpṯn.bn.ilrš.ṯkt. | ilṯḥm.bn.šrn.ṯkt. | šmlbu.bn.grb.ṯkt. | šmlbu.bn.y 2085.11

n.ykn. | bn.ʻṯtrab. | uṣn[-]. | bn.alṯn. | bn.aš[-]š. | bn.štn. | bn.ilš. | bn.tnabn. | bn.ḥṣn. | ṣprn. | bn.ašbḥ. | bn.qṯnn. | bn.ǵlm 1046.1.17

-.]gt.prn. | [šd.---.]gt.prn. | [š]d.bn.š[p]šn l gt pr[n]. | šd bn.ilšḫr. | l.gt.mzln. | šd.gldy. | l.gt.mzln. | šd.glln.l.gt.mz[l]n. 1104.15

mʻnt. | bn kbdy. | bn krk. | bn srty. | bn lth ḫlq. | bn ytr. | bn ilšpš. | ubrš. | bn gmš ḫlq. | bn ʻgy. | bn zlbn. | bn.aḫ[--]. | bn 2016.2.16

n.tnn. | bn.pndr. | bn.nqq. | ḥrš.bhtm. | bn.izl. | bn.ibln. | bn.ilt. | špšyn.nḥl h. | nʻmn.bn.iryn. | nrn.nḥl h. | bn.ḫsn. | bn.ʻ 85[80].2.5

nrn. | [š]d.bn.rwy.b d.ydln. | [š].bn.trn.b d.ibrmd. | [š]d.bn.ilṯtmr.b d.tbbr. | [w.]šd.nḥl h.b d.ṯtmd. | [š]d.b d.iwrḫt. | [t 82[300].1.11

r. | bn.zql. | bn.iḫy. | bn.iyṯr. | bn.ʻyn. | bn.ǵzl. | bn.ṣmy. | bn.il[-]šy. | bn.ybšr. | bn.sly. | bn.ḫlbt. | bn.brzt. | bn.ayl. | [-----] 2117.2.9

[-----]. | bn.[---]. | bn.il[--]. | khnm[.--]. | bn.ṯ[--]. | bn.[---]. | bn.ṯʻl[-]. | bn.nq[ly]. | 2020.3

-].bt.ḫzli. | bn.iḫyn. | ṣdqn.bn.ass. | bʻlyskn.bn.ss. | ṣdqn.bn.imrt. | mnḥm.bn.ḫyrn. | [-]yn.bn.arkbt. | [--]zbl.bt.mrnn. | 102[323].3.10

bdlḥn[-]. | bn.mqwṭ. | bn.bsn. | bn.inr[-]. | bn.ṯbil. | bn.iryn. | ṯṯl. | bn.nṣdn. | bn.ydln. | [bn].ʻdy. 1071.4

. | šd.hwil.gt.prn. | šd.ḥr.gt.prn. | šd.bn.ṯbǵl.gt.prn. | šd.bn.inšr.gt.prn. | šd.[---.]gt.prn. | [šd.---.]gt.prn. | [šd.---.]gt.prn 1104.10

ḫ.bn.trn w nḥl h. | bn srd.bn agmn. | bn [-]ln.bn.ṯbil. | bn is.bn tbdn. | bn uryy. | bn abdʻn. | bn prkl. | bn štn. | bn ann 101[10].7

l h. | w.nḥl hm. | bn.iršyn. | bn.ʻzn. | bn.aršw. | bn.ḫzrn. | bn.iǵyn. | w.nḥl h. | bn.ksd. | bn.bršm. | bn.kzn. | w.nḥl h. | w.n 113[400].2.16

ʻzn.bn.irbn. | bn.mglb. | bn.ntp. | ʻmyn.bn ǵḥpn. | bn.kbln. | bn.bly. 104[316].1

[-----]. | n[----]. | bn.[---]. | bn.[---]. | bn.yk[--]. | bn.šmm. | bn.irgy. | w.nḥl h. | w.nḥl hm. | [bn].pmn. | bn.gṯrn. | bn.arpḫn 1046.2.10

n. | [--]dn. | [ṯ]bʻm. | [--]mlk. | [--]ty. | mtnbʻl. | bn.ndbn. | bn irgn. 1072.13

d.bn.bri.b d.bn.ydln. | [u]bdy.ṯǵrm. | [š]d.ṯǵr.mṯpit.b d.bn.iryn. | [u]bdy.šrm. | [š]d.bn.ḫrmln.b d.bn.tnn. | [š]d.bn.ḫr 82[300].2.8

.ʻbdḥy. | bn.ubyn. | slpd. | bn.atnb. | bn.ktmn. | bn.pity. | bn.iryn. | bn.ʻbl. | bn.grbn. | bn.iršyn. | bn.nklb. | bn.mryn. | [bn 115[301].4.16

ḥrš.bhtm. | bn.izl. | bn.ibln. | bn.ilt. | špšyn.nḥl h. | nʻmn.bn.iryn. | nrn.nḥl h. | bn.ḫsn. | bn.ʻbd. | [-----]. | [---.n]ḥ[l h]. | [-] 85[80].2.7

bdlḥn[-]. | bn.mqwṭ. | bn.bsn. | bn.inr[-]. | bn.ṯbil. | bn.iryn. | ṯṯl. | bn.nṣdn. | bn.ydln. | [bn].ʻdy. | [bn].ilyn. 1071.6

| šgn.bn b[--.---].d.yṯb.b.ilštmʻ. | abmn.bn.r[---].b.syn. | bn.irṣ[-.---.]h. | šdyn.b[n.---.--]n. 2015.2.8

.atnb. | bn.ktmn. | bn.pity. | bn.iryn. | bn.ʻbl. | bn.grbn. | bn.iršyn. | bn.nklb. | bn.mryn. | [bn.]b[--]. | bn.ẓrl. | bn.illm[-]. 115[301].4.19

bn.[-]gštn. | bn[.n]klb. | b[n.]dtn. | w.nḥl h. | w.nḥl hm. | bn.iršyn. | bn.ʻzn. | bn.aršw. | bn.ḫzrn. | bn.iǵyn. | w.nḥl h. | bn. 113[400].2.12

n.kzn.ṯlṯm. | ṣṣ.bn.tlmyn.ʻšrm. | ṣṣ.bn.krwn.ʻš[rm]. | ṣṣ.bn.iršyn.[---]. | [ṣṣ].bn.ilbʻl.ṯl[ṯ]m. | ṣṣ.bn.pṯḏn.[--]m. | ṣṣ.[bn]. 2096.5

. | bn.alz. | bn.birtn. | [bn.]ylkn. | [bn.]krwn. | [bn.-]ty. | [bn.]iršn. | bn.[---]. | bn.b[--]. | bn.š[--]. | bn.a[---]. | bn.prsn. | bn. 117[325].1.17

bn.tiyn.b d.ilmhr nḥl h. | šd knn.bn.ann.ʻdb. | šd.iln[-].bn.irṯr.l.šḫrn.nḥl h. | šd[.ag]pṯn.b[n.]brrn.l.qrt. | šd[.--]dy.bn. 2029.20

-]r. | [bn.--]tn. | [bn.-]rmn. | bn.prtn. | bn.ymn. | bn.dby. | bn.ir[--]. | bn.kr[--]. | bn.nn[-]. | [-----]. | [-----]. | [---.-]l[-]. | [bn.- 124[-].5.11

ntn bn[.---]. | bn.brzn [---]. | bnil.bn.tl[--]. | bn.brzn.ṯn. | bn.išbʻl[.---]. | bn.s[---]. | dnn.[bn.---]. | bn[.--]ʻnt. 2069.8

rḥ. | abšr. | bn.bdn. | ḏmry. | bn.pndr. | bn.aḫt. | bn.ʻdn. | bn.išbʻ[l]. 2117.4.34

]. | bn.[---]. | mr[u.ibrn]. | bn.i[---]. | bn.n[---]. | bn.b[---]. | bn.iš[--]. | bn.ab[--]. | bn.al[--]. | bn.nb[dg]. | bn.ild[-]. | [-----]. | [113[400].5.21

.ʻšr. | [ṣ]dqšlm ḫmš. | krzn.ḫmš. | ubrʻym.ḫmš. | [----]. | [bn] itn. | [bn] il. | [---]ṯ. | klṯṯb. | gsn. | arm[w]l. | bn.ṣdqn. | ḫlbn. 2039.9

kn. | [---.--]n. | [---.--]n. | [--.]ʻ[--]. | [bn].k[--]. | bn.ab[--]. | bn.i[--]. | bn.n[--]. | bn.ḫ[--]. | bn.[---]. | bn.k[--]. 2021.2.14

šr. | bn.sly. | bn.ḫlbt. | bn.brzt. | bn.ayl. | [-----]. | ʻbd[--]. | bn.i[--]. | ʻd[--]. | ild[--]. | bn.qṣn. | ʻlpy. | kṯy. | bn.ẓmn. | bn.trdn 2117.2.17

-].bn.b[--.---]. | [---].bn.ab[--.---]. | [---.]bn.a[--.---]. | [---.]bn.i[--.---]. | [---].ṯp[--.---]. | [---.a]ḥt.b d[.---]. | [---.]b d.rb.[m] 2162.A.7

t. | bn.nṯǵ[-]. | bn.gr[--]. | bn.[---]. | bn.[---]. | mr[u.ibrn]. | bn.i[---]. | bn.n[---]. | bn.b[---]. | bn.iš[--]. | bn.ab[--]. | bn.al[--]. | 113[400].5.18

bn.ʻ[---]. | w.nḥ[l h]. | w.nḥ[l h]. | bn.k[---]. | bn.y[---]. | [bn].i[---]. 116[303].14

.uṣb. | bn.yzg. | bn.anntn. | bn.kwn. | ǵmšd. | bn.ʻbdḥy. | bn.ubyn. | slpd. | bn.atnb. | bn.ktmn. | bn.pity. | bn.iryn. | bn.ʻbl 115[301].4.11

šd.snrym.dt.ʻqb. | b.ayly. | šd.abršn. | šd.kkn.[bn].ubyn. | šd.bn.li[y]. | šd.bn.š[--]y. | šd.bn.ṯ[---]. | šd.ʻdmn[.b 2026.4

[---.--]ḫy. | [---.--]t. | [-----]. | [---.]l[--]. | [bn.]ubn. | kbšm. | bn.abdr. | bn.kpltn. | bn.prn. | ʻbdm. | bn.kdǵ 114[324].2.3

[-----]. | bn.t[--.---]. | agmy[.---]. | bn.dlq[-.---]. | tǵyn.bn.ubn.ṯql[m]. | yšn.ḥrš.mrkbt.ṯq[lm]. | bn.pʻṣ.ṯqlm. | mṣrn.ḥr 122[308].1.5

psš. | ilṯḥm. | ḥrm. | bn.bty. | ʻby. | šm[n].bn.apn. | krty. | bn.ubr. | [bn] mdḫl. | bn.sy[n]n. | bn.šrn. 2078.19

k[-]. | bn.by[--]. | bn.a[--]. | bn.iy[--]. | bn.ḫ[---]. | bn.plš. | bn.ubr. | bn.ʻpṯb. | ṯbry. | bn.ymn. | krty. | bn.abr[-]. | yrpu. | kd 2117.1.16

šd.ubdy.ilštmʻ. | dt b d.skn. | šd.bn.ubrʻn b gt prn. | šd.bn.gby.gt.prn. | šd.bn.kryn.gt.prn. | šd. 1104.3

.ḥrš. | [--.]kbd. | [---]. | y[---]. | bn.ǵlyn. | bdl.ar. | bn.šyn. | bn.ubrš. | bn.d[--]b. | abrpu. | bn.k[n]y. | bn.klyn. | bn.gmḫn. | ḥ 1035.3.3

| ʻšt.ʻšr h.šmn. | ʻmn.bn.aǵlmn. | arbʻm.ksp.ʻl.qrt. | b.šd.bn.[u]brš. | ḫmšt.ʻšrt. | b.šd.bn.[-]n. | ṯl[ṯt].ʻšr[t]. | b.š[d].bn.ʻm 1083.7

.bn.gṯtn.kdm. | ynḥm.bn[.-]r[-]t.ṯlṯ. | plwn.kdm. | tmyn.bn.ubrš.kd. 136[84].12

--.-]rsd. | bn[.-]pṯ. | bn kdrn. | awldn. | arswn.yʻr[ty.--]. | bn.ugr. | gny. | ṯn.mdm. 86[305].11

n.yny.[msg]. | bn.mṣrn m[sg]. | yky msg. | ynḥm.msg. | bn.ugr.msg. | bn.ǵlṣ msg. | arbʻ l tkš[-]. | nn.arspy.ms[g]. | [---. 133[-].1.8

mpḫrt.bn.i[l.l ṯkmn.w š]nm hn š. | w šqrb.ʻr.mšr mšr bn.ugrt.w [npy.---.]ugr. | w npy.yman.w npy.ʻrmt.w npy.[--- 32[2].1.18

l mpḫrt.bn.il.l ṯkmn.w šnm.hn š]. | [w šqrb.š.mšr mšr.bn.ugrt.w npy.---.]w npy. | [---.w np]y.ugrt. | [---.u ṯḫṯu.ulp.q 32[2].1.4

---.]km. | [-----]. | [---.]ugrt. | [---].l.lim. | [---.mšr m]šr. | [bn.ugrt.---.--]y. | [---.np]y nqmd. | [---.]pḫr. | [-----]. | [-----]. | [-- APP.I[-].2.2

.srt. | bn.adn. | bn.ʻgw. | bn.urt. | aḫdbu. | pḥ[-]. | bn.ʻb . | bn.udn[-]. | bn.yṣr. 121[307].9

n.nbk[-.---]. | ršpn.bn.b'ly[.---]. | bnil.bn.yṣr[.---]. | 'dyn.bn.uḏr[-.---]. | w.'d'.nḥl h[.---]. | w.yknil.nḥl h[.---]. | w.iltm.n 90[314].1.13
. | [---.]qpḥn. | [---.a]ǵltr. | [---.]ṭml. | [---.]bn.ḥṣqt. | [---.]bn.uḏr[-]. 2132.6
b d.aḫny. | [šd.bn.--]rt.b d.ṯpṭb'l. | [ubdy.]mḫ[ṣ]m. | [šd.bn.]uzpy.b d.yšn.ḥrš. | [-----]. | [-----]. | [šd.b d.--]n. | [šd.b d.--] 82[300].2.26
--]. | nn[-.---]. | au[pš.---]. | i[---.---]. | pgl[--.---]. | šy[.---]. | bn.uḫn. | ybru.i[---]. | [p]dyn.[---]. | bnšm.d.b [d.---]. | spḫy.[--- 2161.10
n[.---]. | šd.y'ḏr[.---]. | šd.swr.[---]. | šd.bn ppn[-.---]. | šd.bn.uḫn[.---]. 83[85].7
h.ḫm[š]t. | bn.unp.arb't. | 'bdbn.ytrš ḫmšt. | krwn.'šrt. | bn.ulb ḫmšt. | bn.ḥry.ḫmšt. | swn.ḫmšt. | bn.[-]r[-.]ḫmšt. | bn. 1062.13
ilṣdq.bn.zry. | b'lytn.bn.ulb. | ytr'm.bn.swy. | šḥrn.bn.qrtm. | bn.špš.bn.ibrd. | 'pṯr 2024.2
mitm.ksp.'mn.b[n].ṣdqn. | w.kkrm.ṯlṯ. | mit.ksp.'mn. | bn.ulbtyn. | w.kkr.ṯlṯ. | ksp.d.nkly.b.šd. | mit.ḫmšt.kbd. | [l.]g 1143.4
miḫdy[m]. | bn.ḥgb[n]. | bn.ulbt[-]. | ḏkry[-]. | bn.tlm[yn]. | bn.y'dd. | bn.idly[-]. | bn.'bd 2017.3
n abg. | bn.nǵry. | bn.srwd. | mtnn. | bn gš[-]. | bn gbrn. | bn uldy. | synn.bn kn'm. | bn kbr. | bn iytlm. | bn ayln. | bn.kln 1064.18
-.l]bš.bn.grbn.b.ṯqlm. | [--.lb]š.bn.sgryn.b[.ṯ]qlm. | [---.]bn.ully.b.ṯ[qlm]. | [---.]bn.annḏy.b[.---]. | [---.]bn.pd[--.---]. 135[330].5
t. | ssw.qšt. | knn.qšt. | bn.ṯlln.qšt. | bn.šyn.qšt. | 'bd.qšt. | bn.ulmy.qšt. | ṯqbn.qšt. | bn.qnmlk.qšt. | ytḫm.qšt. | grp.qšt. | 104[316].5
bn.nṣ. | [b]n.'ṣr. | [---]m. | [bn.]ulnhr. | [bn.p]rn. | [bn.a]nny. | [---]n. | bn.kbln. | bn.pdy. | b 1075.1.4
. | [-----]. | bn.'dy. | w.nḥl h. | bn.'bl. | bn.[-]rṯn. | bn[.---]. | bn u[l]pm. | bn '[p]ty. | bn.kdgdl. | bn.smyy. | bn.lbn. | bn.šlmn 2163.3.2
r.umt. | [---.]rpat.bt. | [m]lk.itdb.d šb'. | [a]ḫm.l h.ṯmnt.bn um. | krt.ḥtk n.rš. | krt.grdš.mknt. | aṯt.ṣdq h.l ypq. | mtrḫt 14[KRT].1.9
bn[.---]. | 'bdil.bn.[---]. | 'pṯn.bn.ṯṣq[-]. | mnn.bn.krmn. | bn.umḫ. | yky.bn.slyn. | ypln.bn.ylḥn. | 'zn.bn.mll. | šrm. | [b]n 85[80].1.6
ḏdy. | agpṯr. | šb'l.mlky. | n'mn.mṣry. | y'l.kn'ny. | gdn.bn.umy. | kn'm.š'rty. | abrpu.ubr'y. | b.gt.bn.ṯlṯ. | ilḏ.b.gt.psḫn 91[311].8
--]. | [-----]. | [---.-]l[-]. | [bn.-]dt[-]. | [bn.-]nn. | [bn.-]dn. | bn.ummt. | bn.ṯb[-]. | bn.[-]r[-]. | bn.tgn. | bn.iḏrn. | mnn. | b[n]. 124[-].6.4
dyn.ḫmš[t]. | abršn.'šr[t]. | b'ln.ḫmšt. | w.nḥl h.ḫm[š]t. | bn.unp.arb't. | 'bdbn.ytrš ḫmšt. | krwn.'šrt. | bn.ulb ḫmšt. | bn 1062.10
.bn.yṣr[.---]. | sln.bn.'ṯt[-.---]. | pdy.bn.nr[-.---]. | abmlk.bn.un[-.---]. | nrn.bn.mtn[-.---]. | aḫyn.bn.nbk[-.---]. | ršpn.bn. 90[314].1.8
. | w.kkr.ṯlṯ. | ksp.d.nkly.b.šd. | mit.ḫmšt.kbd. | [l.]gmn.bn.usyy. | mit.ṯṯm.kbd. | l.bn.yšm'. | mit.arb'm.kbd. | l.liy.bn.' 1143.8
.'šrt. | b.yp'r.'šrm. | b.n'mn.bn.ply.ḫmšt.l.'šrm. | b.gdn.bn.uss.'šrm. | b.'dn.bn.ṯṯ.'šrt. | b.bn.qrdmn.ṯlṯm. | b.bṣmn[.bn 2054.1.18
[-----]. | [bn.]ibln. | ysd. | bn.ṯmq. | bn.agmn. | bn.uṣb. | bn.yzg. | bn.anntn. | bn.kwn. | ǵmšd. | bn.'bdḫy. | bn.u 115[301].4.5
l h. | bn srd.bn agmn. | bn [-]ln.bn.ṯbil. | bn is.bn tbdn. | bn uryy. | bn abd'n. | bn prkl. | bn štn. | bn annyn. | b[n] slg. | u 101[10].8
. | [---]lby. | [--]nbbl. | bn bl. | bn dkn. | bn ils. | bn ḥšbn. | bn uryy. | bn kṯl. | bn army. | bn gln. | bn abg. | bn.nǵry. | bn.sr 1064.8
.lṯḥ. | ḥgbn.lṯḥ. | spr.mkrm. | bn.sl'n.prs. | bn.ṯpdn.lṯḥ. | bn.urm.lṯḥ. 1059.9
bn.ḫran. | bn.srt. | bn.adn. | bn.'gw. | bn.urt. | aḫdbu. | pḥ[-]. | bn.'b . | bn.uḏn[-]. | bn.yṣr. 121[307].5
n.rmy. | dll. | mny. | krty. | bn.'bṣ. | bn.argb. | ydn. | il'nt. | bn.urt. | ydn. | qṭn. | bn.asr. | bn.'dy. | bn.amt[m]. | myn. | šr. | b 2117.3.44
]uḫd. | bn.n[---.]hbṭn. | bn.m[--.]skn. | bn.s[--.b]d.skn. | bn.ur[-.---]. | bn.knn[.---]y. | bn.ymlk[.b]d.skn. | bn.yḫnn.aḏd 2014.13
-]. | [------]. | [------]. | [------]. | [------]. | [bn.]kblbn[.---]. | [bn] uškny. | bn.krny[-]. | bn.mt. | bn.nz'n. | bn.slmz[-]. | bn.k'[- 2021.1.14
ṯ]mn.l.'šrm[.l.b]t.'ṯtrt. | [ṯ]lṯ.'šr h.[b]t.ršp.gn. | arb'.b d.b[n].ušryn. | kdm.l.urtn. | kdm.l.ilšpš. | kd.l.anntb. | kd.l.iwrm 1088.4
d.yšn.ḥrš. | šd.b d.aupš. | šd.b d.ršpab.aḫ.ubn. | šd.b d.bn.uṯryn. | [ubd]y.mrynm. | [š]d.bn.ṣnrn.b d.nrn. | [š]d.bn.rw 82[300].1.6
r.ytnm. | bn.ḫlbym. | bn.ady. | bn.'ṯtry. | bn.ḫrzn. | ady. | bn.birtn. | bn.ḫrzn. | bn.bddn. | bn.anny. | ytršp. | bn.szn. | bn.k 115[301].1.7
.qnḏ. | ṣmq[-]. | bn.anny. | bn.'mtḏl. | bn.'myn. | bn.alz. | bn.birtn. | [bn.]ylkn. | [bn.]krwn. | [bn.-]ty. | [bn.]iršn. | bn.[---] 117[325].1.13
bnšm.dt.iṯ.alpm.l hm. | bn.niršn. | bn.adty. | bn.alz. | bn.birtn. | bn.mlṣ. | bn.q[--]. | bn.[---]. | bn.ṯ[-]r. | bn.grdn. | [bn. 2023.1.5
tḫm.bn.dnn.ṯkt. | šb'l.bn.aly.ṯkt. | klby.bn.iḫy.ṯkt. | psš.bn.buly.ṯkt. | 'pṣpn.bn.'dy.ṯkt. | n'mn.bn.'yn.ṯkt. | 'pṯn.bn.ilrš. 2085.8
l'. | bn.šp[š.]qšt. | bn.'g[w.]qšt.w ql'. | ḥd[ṯ]n.qšt.w.ql'. | bn.bb.qšt.w[.ql]'. | bn.aktmy.qšt. | šdyn.qšt. | bdn.qšt.w.ql'. | b 119[321].4.9
bn.ady. | bn.'ṯtry. | bn.ḫrzn. | ady. | bn.birtn. | bn.ḫrzn. | bn.bddn. | bn.anny. | ytršp. | bn.szn. | bn.kdgdl. | bn.gl'd. | bn.k 115[301].1.9
---]. | bn.[---]. | bn.[---]. | w.nḥ[l h]. | bn.ẓr[-]. | mru.skn. | bn.bddn. | bn.ǵrgn. | bn.tgtn. | bn.ḫrzn. | bn.qdšt. | bn.nṯǵ[-]. | b 113[400].5.7
. | 'lpy. | kṭy. | bn.ẓmn. | bn.trdn. | ypq. | 'bd. | qrḥ. | abšr. | bn.bdn. | ḏmry. | bn.pndr. | bn.aḫt. | bn.'dn. | bn.išb'[l]. 2117.4.29
[s]ǵr.bn.bdn. | [sǵ]r.bn.psḫn. | alty. | sǵr.npr. | bn.ḫty. | ṯn.bnš ibrḏr. 2082.1
]. | bn.lky.qšt. | bn.dll.qšt.w.ql[']. | bn.pǵyn.qšt.w[.q]l'. | bn.bdn.qšt. | bn.pls.qšt. | ǵmrm. | [-]lhd.ṯt.qštm.w.ṯn.ql'm. | ul 119[321].3.30
am[-]. | ṯmn.ḥblm.šb'.šb'.ma[-]. | 'šr.kkr.rtn. | b d.šm'y.bn.bdn. 1128.33
r.irgmn. | ṯlṯ.ḫmš.alpm. | b d.brq.maḫdy. | kkr.ṯlṯ. | b d.bn.by.ar[y]. | alpm.ṯlṯ. | b d.šim.il[š]tm'y. 1134.5
bn a[---]. | bn.byy. | bn.ily[-]. | bn.iy[--]. | bn.ṯy[--]. | bn.p[---]. | gyn[.---]. | 2025.2
nn. | [--]ny. | [bn].ṯrdnt. | [bn].hyadt. | [--]lt. | šmrm. | p'ṣ.bn.byy.'šrt. 1047.25
mry[n]. | bn.mgn. | bn.'dn. | bn.knn. | bn.py. | bn.mk[-]. | bn.by[--]. | bn.a[--]. | bn.iy[--]. | bn.ḥ[---]. | bn.plš. | bn.ubr. | bn. 2117.1.11
[--.]ubdym.b.uškn. | [---]lby. | [--]nbbl. | bn bl. | bn dkn. | bn ils. | bn ḥšbn. | bn uryy. | bn kṯl. | bn army. 1064.4
m.qšt.w.ql'. | ṣdqm.qšt.w.ql'. | uln.qšt.w.ql'. | uln.qšt. | bn.blẓn.qšt.w.ql'. | gb'.qšt.w.ql'. | nṣṣn.qšt. | m'r. | [']dyn.ṯt.qšt 119[321].2.9
ḥrṣ. | bn.prsn.ṣmd.w.ḥrṣ. | bn.ilb'l. | bn.idrm. | bn.grgš. | bn.bly. | bn.apṯ. | bn.ysd. | bn.pl[-]. | bn.ṯb'nq. | brqd. | bnn. | kbl 2113.10
bn.[---]. | bn.[---]. | [-----]. | bn[---]. | bn.mlkyy. | bn.atn. | bn.bly. | bn.ṯbrn. | bn.ḥgby. | bn.pity. | bn.slgyn. | 'zn.bn.mlk. | 115[301].2.3
.bn.irbn. | bn.mglb. | bn.ntp. | 'myn.bn ǵḥpn. | bn.kbln. | bn.bly. | bn.ṯ'y. | bn.nṣdn. | klby. 104[316].6
[ṯl]ṯm.ksp.'[l]. | [b]n.bly.gb'ly. | [šp]ḥ.a[n]nṯb. | w.m[--.u]škny. | [']š[r.---]t.ksp. 2055.2
bn.atnb.mr[--.---]. | bn.šḫr.mr[-.---]. | bn.idrn.'š[-.---]. | bn.bly.mr[-.---]. | w.nḥl h.mr[-.---]. | ilšpš.[---]. | iḫny.[---]. | bn 88[304].10
mryn[m]. | bn.bly. | nrn. | w.nḥl h. | bn.rmyy. | bn.tlmyn. | w.nḥl h. | w.nḥl 113[400].1.2
.nḥl h.l bn.pl. | šd.krwn.l aḫn. | šd.'yy.l aḫn. | šd.brdn.l bn.bly. | šd gzl.l.bn.ṯbr[n]. | šd.ḫzmyn.l a[--]. | ṯn šdm b uš[kn 2089.13
.mly. | pslm. | bn.annd. | bn.gl'd. | w.nḥl h. | bn.mlkyy. | [bn].bm[--]. | ['š]rm. | [-----]. | [-----]. | bn.p[--]. | bn.'bdmlk. 2163.3.14
. | i[ln]y[m].l mṯ't[.---]. | [-]m[.---]. | h.hn bn k.hn[.---]. | bn bn.aṯr k.hn[.---]. | yd k.ṣǵr.tnšq.špt k.ṯm. | ṯkm.bm ṯkm.a 22.2[124].3
.dd.l.rpš. | [---.]šb'm.dr'.w.arb'm.drt.mit.dd. | [---].ḥpr.bn.šm. | [b.---.]knm.ṯṯm.l.mit.dr'.w.mit.drt. | w[.---.]'m.l.mit. 1098.6
'z. | [---]ḏ. | [---]. | [---]. | hm qrt tuḫd.hm mt y'l bnš. | bt bn bnš yqḥ 'z. | w yḥdy mrḥqm. RS61[24.277.30]
bdlḥn[-]. | bn.mqwṭ. | bn.bsn. | bn.inr[-]. | bn.ṯbil. | bn.iryn. | ṯṯl. | bn.nṣdn. | bn.ydln. | 1071.3
n.w[.---]. | [-]n.y'rtym. | gmm.w.bn.p[--]. | trn.w.p[-]y. | bn.b'yn.w.agytn. | [---] gnym. | [--]ry.w ary. | [---]ǵrbtym. | [--- 131[309].12
. | p'ṣ.ḫbty. | artyn.ary. | brqn.ṯlḥy. | bn.aryn. | bn.lgn. | bn.b'yn. | šdyn. | ary. | brqn. | bn.ḫlln. | bn.mṣry. | ṯmn.qšt. | w ' 118[306].8

rgs. | bn.ḫran. | bn.arš[w.b]ṣry. | bn.ykn. | bn.lṣn.ʿrmy. | bn.bʿyn.šly. | bn.ynḥn. | bn.ʿbdilm.hzpy. 99[327].2.4
spr.mdr[ǵlm]. | lt.hlk.b[.---]. | bn.bʿyn.š[--.---]. | aǵltn.mid[-.---]. | bn.lṣn.ʿrm[y]. | aršw.bṣry. 87[64].3
k.ksu. | ṯbt.ḫḫ.arṣ.nḥlt h.tša. | g hm.w tṣḥ.ṯḥm.aliyn. | bn.bʿl.hwt.aliy.qrdm. | bhṯ.bn.ilm.mt.ʿbd k.an. | w d ʿlm k.š 5[67].2.18
rqd. | bn.abdg. | ilyn. | bn.tan. | bn.arm. | bn.bʿl.ṣdq. | bn.army. | bn.rpiyn. | bn.army. | bn.krmn. | bn.yk 1046.1.6
. | bn.nb[dg]. | bn.ild[-]. | [-----]. | [bn.]nnr. | [bn.]aglby. | [bn.]bʿly. | [md]rǵlm. | [bn.]kdgdl. | [b]n.qṭn. | [b]n.ǵrgn. | [b]n.ṯ 104[316].6
.bn h. | bʿlm.w.ṯlṯ.nʿrm.w.bt.aḥt. | bn.lwn.ṯlṯtm.bʿlm. | bn.bʿly.ṯlṯtm.bʿlm. | w.aḥd.ḫbṭ. | w.arbʿ.aṯt. | bn.lg.ṯn.bn h. | bʿ 2080.7
.un[-.---]. | nrn.bn.mtn[-.---]. | aḫyn.bn.nbk[-.---]. | ršpn.bn.bʿly[.---]. | bnil.bn.yṣr[.---]. | ʿdyn.bn.udr[-.---]. | w.ʿdʿ.nḥl 90[314].1.11
bn.bʿln.biry. | ṯlṯ.bʿlm. | w.adn hm.ṯr.w.arbʿ.bnt h. | yrḫm.yd. 2080.1
n.ḥrš.mrkbt.ṯqlm. | ʿpṭn.ḥrš.qṭn.ṯqlm. | bn.pǵdn.ṯqlm. | bn.bʿln.ṯqlm. | ʿbdyrḫ.nqd.ṯqlm. | bt.sgld.ṯqlm. | bn.ʿmy.ṯqlm. 122[308].1.11
. | bn.ṯyn. | bn gʿr. | bn.prtn. | bn ḫnn. | b[n.-]n. | bn.ṣṣb. | bn.bʿltn ḫlq. | bn.mlkbn. | bn.asyy ḫlq. | bn.kṯly. | bn.kyn. | bn. 2016.2.2
lmn. | knʿm. | aḫršp. | anntn. | bʿlrm. | [-]ral. | šdn. | [-]ǵl. | bn.bʿltǵpṯ. | ḥrš.btm. | ršpab. | [r]ṣn. | [a]ǵlmn. | [a]ḫyn. | [k]rw 2060.13
[bn]šm.dt.iš[--]. | [b]n.bʿl[--]. | bn.gld. | bn.ṣmy. | bn.mry[n]. | bn.mgn. | bn.ʿdn. | b 2117.1.2
ʿy. | abmlk.bn.ilrš. | iḫyn.bn.ḫryn. | [ab]ǵl.bn.gdn. | [---].bn.bqš. | [---].bn.pdn. | [---.bn.-]ky. | [---.bn.--]r. | [-----]. | [---.--] 102[323].4.13
---.]b d.ymz. | [šd.b d].klby.psl. | [ub]dy.mri.ibrn. | [š]d.bn.bri.b d.bn.ydln. | [u]bdy.ṯǵrm. | [š]d.ṯǵr.mṯpit.b d.bn.iryn. 82[300].2.6
. | [šd.]lbny.b d.tbṯṯb. | [š]d.bn.ṯ[-]rn.b d.ʿdbmlk. | [šd.]bn.brzn.b d.nwrd. | [šd.]bn.nḥbl.b d.ʿdbym. | [šd.b]n.qṭy.b d. 82[300].1.17
ṯnnm. | bn.qqln. | w.nḥl h. | w.nḥl h. | bn.šml[-]. | bn.brzn. | bn.ḫṯr[-]. | bn.yd[--]. | bn.ʿ[---]. | w.nḥ[l h]. | w.nḥ[l h 116[303].6
. | bn.rmyy. | bn.tlmyn. | w.nḥl h. | w.nḥl hm. | bn.ḥrm. | bn.brzn. | w.nḥl h. | bn.adldn. | bn.šbl. | bn.ḫnzr. | bn.arwṭ. | bn 113[400].1.10
irṯr.l.šḫrn.nḥl h. | šd[.ag]pṯn.b[n.]brrn.l.qrt. | šd[.--]dy.bn.brzn. | l.qrt. 2029.22
šril[.---]. | anntn bn[.---]. | bn.brzn [---]. | bnil.bn.tl[--]. | bn.brzn.ṯn. | bn.išbʿl[.---]. | bn.s[---]. | dnn.[bn.---]. | bn[.--]ʿnt. 2069.7
mry[n]m. | bn rmy[y]. | yšril[.---]. | anntn bn[.---]. | bn.brzn [---]. | bnil.bn.tl[--]. | bn.brzn.ṯn. | bn.išbʿl[.---]. | bn.s[- 2069.5
y[rḫ].bn.gṯtn. | yrmn.bn.ʿn. | krwn.nḥl h. | ttn.[n]ḥl h. | bn.b[r]zn. | [---.-]ḥn. 85[80].4.12
n.ǵzl. | bn.ṣmy. | bn.il[-]šy. | bn.ybšr. | bn.sly. | bn.ḫlbt. | bn.brzt. | bn.ayl. | [-----]. | ʿbd[--]. | bn.i[--]. | ʿd[--]. | ild[--]. | bn. 2117.2.13
n.pnmn.ʿšrt. | ʿbdadt.ḫmšt. | abmn.ilštmʿy.ḫmš[t]. | ʿzn.bn.brn.ḫmšt. | mʿrt.ḫmšt. | arttb.bn.ḫmšt. | bn.ysr[.ḫmš]t. | ṣ[- 1062.26
-]tb. | [--]ln. | [---]r. | [---]y. | bn.addt. | bn.atnb. | bn.yšd. | bn.bršm. | bn.gtprg. | gtpbn. | bn.b[--]. | [b]n.[---]. | bn.a[--]. | bn 1057.11
.---]. | bn[.---]. | bn[.---]. | [bn.--]t. | [bn.---]. | [bn.--]my. | [bn.b]rq. | [bn.--]r. | [bn.--]tn. | [bn.-]rmn. | bn.prtn. | bn.ymn. | 124[-].5.4
.ṯqlm. | ʿbdyrḫ.nqd.ṯqlm. | bt.sgld.ṯqlm. | bn.ʿmy.ṯqlm. | bn.brq.ṯqlm. | bn.ḫnzr.ṯqlm. | dqn.nsk.arbʿt. | bn.ḫdyn.ṯqlm. | 122[308].1.15
b]n.[y]drn. | [---.]bn.ḫlan. | [--]r bn.mn. | [--]ry. | [--]lim bn.brq. | [--.]qtn bn.drṣy. | [--]kn bn.pri. | [r]špab bn.pni. | [ab] 2087.5
ʿmn. | bn.kbl. | knʿm. | bdlm. | bn.ṣǵr. | klb. | bn.mnḥm. | bn.brqn. | bn.ʿn. | bn.ʿbdy. | ʿbdʿṯtr. 1046.3.46
.bn.ann.ʿdb. | šd.iln[-].bn.irṯr.l.šḫrn.nḥl h. | šd[.ag]pṯn.b[n.]brrn.l.qrt. | šd[.--]dy.bn.brzn. | l.qrt. 2029.21
n.ʿzn. | bn.aršw. | bn.ḫzrn. | bn.iǵyn. | w.nḥl h. | bn.ksd. | bn.bršm. | bn.kzn. | w.nḥl h. | w.nḥl hm. | w.[n]ḥl hm. | b[n.---] 113[400].2.19
ʿbdrt[b.---]. | b ṯṯ ʿṯr ṯmn.r[qḥ.---]. | p bn btb[-.---]. | b ḫmṯ ʿṯr k[--.---]. | b ḫmṯ ʿṯr[.---]. | [-----]. | [---.- 207[57].3
n. | bn.grb[n]. | yṯtn. | bn.ab[l]. | kry. | pss. | ilṯḥm. | ḥrm. | bn.bty. | ʿby. | šm[n].bn.apn. | krty. | bn.ubr. | [bn] mdḫl. | bn.s 2078.15
[s]p[r] ušknym.dt.[b d.---]. | bn.btr. | bn.ʿms. | bn.pṣn. | bn.agmz. | bn.[--]n. | bn.a[--]. | [------ 2021.1.2
nqdm. | bn.altn. | bn.dly. | bn.btry. | bn.ḫdmn. | [bn].šty. | [bn].kdgdl. | [---.-]y[-.] 2018.4
n.]nklb. | [---]dn. | [---]y. | [-----]. | [-----]. | bn.adn. | prtn. | bn.btry. 1073.3.5
bn.hkl.w ištql šql. | tn.km.nḥšm.yḥr.tn.km. | mhr y.w bn.bṯn.itnn y. | ytt.nḥšm.mhr k.bn bṯn. | itnn k. | aṯr ršp.ʿṯtrt. UG5.7.74
.yḥr.tn.km. | mhr y.w bn.bṯn.itnn y. | ytt.nḥšm.mhr k.bn bṯn. | itnn k. | aṯr ršp.ʿṯtrt. | ʿm ʿṯtrt.mr h. | mnt.nṯk.nḥš. UG5.7.75
ryn. | bn.ʿbl. | bn.grbn. | bn.iršyn. | bn.nklb. | bn.mryn. | [bn.]b[--]. | bn.ẓrl. | bn.illm[-]. | bn.š[---]. | bn.ṣ[---]. | bn.š[---]. | b 115[301].4.22
. | [bn.]ylkn. | [bn.]krwn. | [bn.-]ty. | [bn.]iršn. | bn.[---]. | bn.b[--]. | bn.š[--]. | bn.a[---]. | bn.prsn. | bn.mtyn. | bn.ḫlpn. | b 117[325].2.2
.addt. | bn.atnb. | bn.yšd. | bn.bršm. | bn.gtprg. | gtpbn. | bn.b[--]. | [b]n.[---]. | bn.a[--]. | bn.ml[k]. | bn.glyn. | bn.ʿdr. | bn 1057.14
bt.[-]b[-.-]sy[-]h. | nn[-].b[n].py[-.d.]yṯb.b.gt.aǵld. | šgn.bn b[--.---].d.yṯb.b.ilštmʿ. | abmn.bn.r[---].b.syn. | bn.irṣ[-.---.] 2015.2.6
[---.]l[.---]. | [---.]l[.---]. | [---].tbṯṯ[b.---]. | [---].bn.b[--.---]. | [---].bn.ab[--.---]. | [---.]bn.a[--.---]. | [---.]bn.i[--.-- 2162.A.4
-]. | bn.[---]. | bn.[---]. | mr[u.ibrn]. | bn.i[---]. | bn.n[---]. | bn.b[---]. | bn.iš[--]. | bn.ab[--]. | bn.al[--]. | bn.nb[dg]. | bn.ild[-] 113[400].5.20
šd.ubdy.ilštmʿ. | dt b d.skn. | šd.bn.ubrʿn b gt prn. | šd.bn.gby.gt.prn. | šd.bn.kryn.gt.prn. | šd.bn.ky.gt.prn. | šd.hwil. 1104.4
bn gln. | bn abg. | bn.nǵry. | bn.srwd. | mtnn. | bn gš[-]. | bn gbrn. | bn uldy. | synn.bn knʿm. | bn kbr. | bn iytlm. | bn ayl 1064.17
. | bn.dqnt. | bn.gmrš. | bn.nmq. | bn.špš[yn]. | bn.ar[--]. | bn.gb[--]. | bn.ḥn[n]. | bn.gntn[-]. | [--.]nqq[-]. | b[n.---]. | bn.[--- 2023.3.16
ṯn.bn.klby. | bn.iytr. | [ʿ]bdyrḫ. | [b]n.ggʿt. | [ʿ]dy. | armwl. | uwaḫ. | ypln.w.ṯn.bn h. | ydln. | anr[2086.4
ml]k. | bn.aup[š.--].bsbn hzpḫ ṯlṯt. | kṯr[.---.--]trt ḫmšt.bn gda[.-.]mdʿ. | kl[--.---.]ṯmnt.[--.]w[.---]. | [-]m[.---.]ṣpiry[.ṯ] APP.II[173].59
l[--]. | šd.b[---]. | b d.[---]. | šd.[---]. | b d.[---]. | [-----]. | šd.bn.gdy. | b d.ddl. 2028.22
. | ildgn.qšt. | bn.yʿrn.ṯt.qštm w.qlʿ. | bn.ḥṣn.qšt.w.qlʿ. | bn.gdn.ṯt.qštm.w.qlʿ. | bn.[-]q.qšt.w.qlʿ. | gb[l]n.qšt.w.qlʿ. | bn 119[321].3.12
ʿmyn. | agyn.rʿy. | abmlk.bn.ilrš. | iḫyn.bn.ḫryn. | [ab]ǵl.bn.gdn. | [---].bn.bqš. | [---].bn.pdn. | [---.bn.-]ky. | [---.bn.--]r. | 102[323].4.12
an.mdrǵl | bn.ilh.mdrǵl | špšyn.b.ulm. | bn.qṭn.b.ulm. | bn.gdrn.b.mʿr[by]. | [w].bn.dʿm[-]. | bn.ppt.b[--]. | b[n.---]. | š 2046.1.7
. | pprn.qšt. | uln.qšt. | bn.nkl qšt. | ady.qšt. | bn.srn.qšt. | bn.gdrn.qšt. | prpr.qšt. | ugry.qšt. | bn.ṣrptn.qšt. | bn.mṣry.qšt. 119[321].1.43
.ṯn.q[l]ʿm. | kmrṯn.ṯt.qštm.ṯn.[q]lʿm. | ǵdyn.qšt.w.qlʿ. | bn.gzl.qšt.w.qlʿ. | [---]n.qšt. | ilhd.qšt. | ʿdn.qšt.w.qlʿ. | ilmhr.qš 119[321].1.5
. | bn.kzn. | w.nḥl h. | w.nḥl hm. | w.[n]ḥl hm. | b[n.---]. | bn.gzry. | bn.atyn. | bn.ttn. | bn.rwy. | bn.ʿmyn. | bdl.mrynm. | 113[400].3.1
n.iršyn.[---]. | [ṣṣ].bn.ilbʿl.ṯl[t]m. | ṣṣ.bn.pṯdn.[--]m. | ṣṣ.[bn].gyn.[---]. | [-----]. | [-----]. | [-----]. | [-----]. | [-----]. | [ṣṣ].b[n].ṣ 2096.8
[--]r.w.aṯt h. | ʿbdyrḫ.ṯn ǵlyt h. | aršmg. | ršpy.w.aṯt h. | bn.glgl.uškny. | bn.ṯny.uškny. | mnn.w.aṯt h. | slmu.ḥrš.mrkb 2068.13
[bn]šm.dt.iš[--]. | [b]n.bʿl[--]. | bn.gld. | bn.ṣmy. | bn.mry[n]. | bn.mgn. | bn.ʿdn. | bn.knn. | bn. 2117.1.3
ṯprg. | gtpbn. | bn.b[--]. | [b]n.[---]. | bn.a[--]. | bn.ml[k]. | bn.glyn. | bn.ʿdr. | bn.ṯmq. | bn.ntp. | bn.ʿgrt. 1057.18
bn dkn. | bn ils. | bn ḥšbn. | bn uryy. | bn kṯl. | bn army. | bn gln. | bn abg. | bn.nǵry. | bn.srwd. | mtnn. | bn gš[-]. | bn gbr 1064.11
.ḥrẓn. | bn.bddn. | bn.anny. | ytršp. | bn.szn. | bn.kdgdl. | bn.glʿd. | bn.ktln. | [bn].ǵrgn. | bn.pb[-]. | bn.[---]. | bn.[---]. | bn. 115[301].1.14
n.smyy. | bn.lbn. | bn.šlmn. | bn.mly. | pslm. | bn.annd. | bn.glʿd. | w.nḥl h. | bn.mlkyy. | [bn].bm[--]. | [ʿš]rm. | [-----]. | [- 2163.3.11
mz. | [-]n bn.iln. | [--]nn bn.ibm. | [-]n bn.ḥrn. | [š]mmn bn.gmz. | [yn]ḥm bn.ilmd. 2087.14

bn.ǵlmn.ary. | [bn].šdy. | [bn].gmḥ. | [---]ty. | [b]n.ypy.gb‘ly. | b[n].ḥyn. | ḏmn.š‘rty. | bn. 99[327].1.3
.ǵlm. | bn.yyn.w.bn.au[pš]. | bn.kdrn. | ‘rgzy.w.bn.‘dy. | bn.gmḥn.w.ḥgbt. | bn.tgdn. | yny. | [b]n.g‘yn dd. | [-]n.dd. | [--] 131[309].28
.šyn. | bn.ubrš. | bn.d[--]b. | abrpu. | bn.k[n]y. | bn.klyn. | bn.gmḥn. | ḥnn. | ayab. | bn.gm[--]. | bn.[---]. | g[---]. | p[---]. | b[1035.3.8
---]. | [bn.a]mdy. | bn.ḫlln. | bn.kṯn. | bn.abn. | bn.nskn. | bn.gmrn. | bn[.-]škn. | [---.--]n. | [---.--]n. | [--.]‘[--]. | [bn].k[--]. | 2021.2.7
--]. | bn.‘r[--]. | bn.nkt[-]. | bn.abḏr. | bn.ḥrẓn. | bn.ḏqnt. | bn.gmrš. | bn.nmq. | bn.špš[yn]. | bn.ar[--]. | bn.gb[--]. | bn.ḥn[2023.3.12
bn.ysd. | bn.pl[-]. | bn.ṯb‘nq. | brqd. | bnn. | kbln.ṣ[md]. | bn gmrt. | bn.il.ṣm[d]. | bn abbly. | yṯ‘d.ṣm[d]. | bn.liy. | ‘šrm.ṣ[2113.18
‘. | [---]n.qšt. | ilhd.qšt. | ‘dn.qšt.w.ql‘. | ilmhr.qšt.w.ql‘. | bn.gmrt.qšt. | ǵmrm. | bn.qṭn.qšt.w.ql‘. | mrṯd.qšt. | ssw.qšt. | k 119[321].1.10
bn krk. | bn srty. | bn lth ḫlq. | bn ytr. | bn ilšpš. | ubrš. | bn gmš ḫlq. | bn ‘gy. | bn zlbn. | bn.aḫ[--]. | bn[.---]. | [-----]. | bn 2016.2.18
. | abrpu. | bn.k[n]y. | bn.klyn. | bn.gmḥn. | ḥnn. | ayab. | bn.gm[--]. | bn.[---]. | g[---]. | p[---]. | b[---]. | [---]. | [---]. | bn[.---] 1035.3.11
bn.gnb[.msg]. | bn.twyn[.msg]. | bn.‘drš[p.msg]. | pyn.yny.[m 133[-].1.1
‘ym.---]. | qdm[n.---]. | b‘l[--.---]. | šm[---.---]. | yšr[-.---]. | bn.gnb[-.---]. | hzpym. | rišn.[---]. | bn.‘bdy.[---]. | bn.dmtn.[---] 93[328].7
bn.nmq. | bn.špš[yn]. | bn.ar[--]. | bn.gb[--]. | bn.ḥn[n]. | bn.gntn[-]. | [--.]nqq[-]. | b[n.---]. | bn.[---]. | bn.‘yn. | bn.dtn. 2023.3.18
pṯ.d[.yṯb.b].š‘rt. | yly.bn.ṯrnq.[-]r.d.yṯb.b.ilštm‘. | ilšlm.bn.gs[-.--]r.d.yṯb.b.gt.al. | ilmlk.[--]kt.[--.d.]yṯb.b.šb[n]. | bn.p 2015.1.27
m‘y. | bn.ḫran.ilštm‘y. | bn.abd‘n.ilštm‘y. | bn.‘n.rqdy. | bn.g‘yn. | bn.ǵrn. | bn.agynt. | bn.abdḫr.snry. | dqn.šlmn. | prd 87[64].33
n. | ‘rgzy.w.bn.‘dy. | bn.gmḥn.w.ḥgbt. | bn.tgdn. | yny. | [b]n.g‘yn dd. | [-]n.dd. | [--]an dd. | [-----]. | [-----]. 131[309].31
kn. | bn.‘bd. | ḫyrn. | alpy. | bn.plsy. | bn.qrr[-]. | bn.ḥyl. | bn.g‘yn. | ḥyn. | bn.armg[-]. | b‘lmṯpṯ. | [bn].ayḫ. | [---]rn. | ill. | 1035.2.2
---]. | hzpym. | rišn.[---]. | bn.‘bdy.[---]. | bn.dmtn.[---]. | [b]n.g‘yn.ḫr[-]. | lbnym. | grgš.[---]. | bn.ǵrn.[---]. | bn.agyn[.---] 93[328].12
. | bn aṯtyy. | bn ḫlp. | bn.ẓll. | bn ydy. | bn lzn. | bn.ṯyn. | bn g‘r. | bn.prtn. | bn ḫnn. | b[n.-]n. | bn.ṣṣb. | bn.b‘ltn ḫlq. | bn. 2016.1.16
. | [šd.b]n.qṭy.b d.tt. | [ubd]y.mrim. | [šd.b]n.ṯpdn.b d.bn.g‘r. | [šd.b]n.ṯqrn.b d.ḫby. | [ṯn.š]d.bn.ngzḥn.b d.gmrd. | [š 82[300].1.21
t.[---]. | krws.l.y[--.---]. | yp‘.l[.---]. | šmr[m.---]. | [-----]. | bn.g[r.---]. | ḏmry[.---]. | bn.pdr.l.[---]. 2122.6
.bn.‘yn.ṯkt. | ‘pṯn.bn.ilrš.ṯkt. | ilṯḥm.bn.šrn.ṯkt. | šmlbu.bn.grb.ṯkt. | šmlbu.bn.yp‘.ṯkt. | [---.--]m. 2085.13
[--.l]bš.mtn.b.ar‘t. | [--.l]bš.bn.ykn‘.b.ar‘t. | [--.l]bš.bn.grbn.b.ṯqlm. | [--.lb]š.bn.sgryn.b[.ṯ]qlm. | [---.]bn.ully.b.ṯ[135[330].3
. | slpd. | bn.atnb. | bn.ktmn. | bn.pity. | bn.iryn. | bn.‘bl. | bn.grbn. | bn.iršyn. | bn.nklb. | bn.mryn. | [bn.]b[--]. | bn.ẓrl. | b 115[301].4.18
. | bn.ilrš. | ‘[p]ṯn. | b[n.‘r]my. | [--]ty. | bn.ǵd‘. | bn.‘yn. | bn.grb[n]. | yṯtn. | bn.ab[l]. | kry. | psš. | ilṯḥm. | ḥrm. | bn.bty. | ‘ 2078.8
kṯkt. | bn.ṯtn[--]. | [m]d.m[--]. | [b]n.annḏ[r]. | bn.ṯdyy. | bn.grbn. | [--.]ully. | [--]ṯiy. 1054.2.4
.arz.š‘rty. | bn.ibrd.m‘rby. | ṣdqn.gb‘ly. | bn.ypy.gb‘ly. | bn.grgs.ilštm‘y. | bn.ḫran.ilštm‘y. | bn.abd‘n.ilštm‘y. | bn.‘n.r 87[64].29
]n.ypy.gb‘ly. | b[n].ḥyn. | ḏmn.š‘rty. | bn.arwdn.ilšt‘y. | bn grgs. | bn.ḫran. | bn.arš[w.b]ṣry. | bn.ykn. | bn.lṣn.‘rmy. | bn 99[327].1.9
bn.ǵlṣ msg. | arb‘ l ṯkṣ[-]. | nn.arspy.ms[g]. | [---.ms]g. | bn.[gr]gs.msg. | bn[.--]an.msg. | bn[.--].m[sg]. | b[--]n.qmy.ms 133[-].2.2
n.ṣmd.w.ḥrṣ. | bn.prsn.ṣmd.w.ḥrṣ. | bn.ilb‘l. | bn.idrm. | bn.grgš. | bn.bly. | bn.apṯ. | bn.ysd. | bn.pl[-]. | bn.ṯb‘nq. | brqd. 2113.9
k]sp [-]al[.-]r[-]. | [--]dšq krsnm. | ḫmšm [-]t ṯlṯ ty[--]. | bn.grgš. | w.npṣ bt ṯn.ṯlṯ mat. | w spl ṯlṯ.mat. | w mmskn. | w.ṯ 1103.15
bn ayln. | bn.kln. | bn.‘lln. | bn.liy. | bn.nqṭn. | bn abrḫṯ. | bn.grdy. | bn.ṣlpn. | bn ǵlmn. | bn sgld. 1064.28
n.alz. | bn.birtn. | bn.mlṣ. | bn.q[--]. | bn.[---]. | bn.ṯ[-]r. | bn.grdn. | [bn.-]ḫr. | [--.-]nb. | [--.--]n. | [--.--]n. | bn.[---]. | bn.‘r[2023.2.3
dn. | bn.ǵrgn. | bn.tgtn. | bn.ḥrẓn. | bn.qdšt. | bn.nṯǵ[-]. | bn.gr[--]. | bn.[---]. | bn.[---]. | mr[u.ibrn]. | bn.i[---]. | bn.n[---]. 113[400].5.13
n army. | bn gln. | bn abg. | bn.nǵry. | bn.srwd. | mtnn. | bn gš[-]. | bn gbrn. | bn uldy. | synn.bn kn‘m. | bn kbr. | bn iytl 1064.16
. | [---]r. | [---]y. | bn.aḏdt. | bn.atnb. | bn.yšd. | bn.bršm. | bn.gtprg. | gtpbn. | bn.b[--]. | [b]n.[---]. | bn.a[--]. | bn.ml[k]. | b 1057.12
]. | bn.šmm. | bn.irgy. | w.nḥl h. | w.nḥl hm. | [bn].pmn. | bn.gtrn. | bn.arpḫn. | bn.ṯryn. | bn.dll. | bn.ḫswn. | mrynm. | ‘zn 1046.3.28
[---.--]r. | [--.]iln. | y‘rtym. | bn.gtrn. | bq‘ty. 100[66].4
ṯn.ql‘m. | bn.ṯlṯ.ṯ[lṯ.]qšt.w.ṯn.ql‘m. | qṣn.ṯt.qštm.w.ql‘. | bn.gtrn.q[š]t. | bn.ḫdi.ṯt.qštm.w.ṯn.ql‘m. | ildgn.qšt. | bn.y‘rn. 119[321].3.7
. | liy.bn.qqln. | mnn.bn.ṣnr. | iḫy.[b]n[.--]l[-]. | ‘bdy[rḫ].bn.gttn. | yrmn.bn.‘n. | krwn.nḥl h. | ttn.[n]ḥl h. | bn.b[r]zn. | [85[80].4.8
r.ṯlṯ. | y[---.bn.]kran.ḫmš. | ‘[---].kd. | amry.kdm. | mnn.bn.gttn.kdm. | ynḫm.bn[.-]r[-]t.ṯlṯ. | plwn.kdm. | tmyn.bn.ubr 136[84].9
bn[.---]. | bn.qdšt. | bn.m‘nt. | bn.g[--]n. | bn[.---]. | [-----]. | b[n.---]. | b[n.---]. | bn.[---]. | bn.a[- 2163.1.4
iḫdym. | bn.ḥṯb. | bn abyt. | bn ḫdl. | bn ṣdqn. | bn ayy. | bn dbb. | w nḥl h. | bn n‘myn. | bn aṯtyy. | bn ḫlp. | bn.ẓll. | bn 2016.1.7
rq. | [bn.--]r. | [bn.--]tn. | [bn.-]rmn. | bn.prtn. | bn.ymn. | bn.dby. | bn.ir[--]. | bn.kr[--]. | bn.nn[-]. | [-----]. | [-----]. | [---.-]l 124[-].5.10
n.ṯ‘l[-]. | bn.nq[ly]. | bn.snr[n]. | bn.pzn[y]. | bn.mg[lb]. | bn.db[--]. | bn.amd[n]. | annš[-]. 2020.12
]. | bn.iy[--]. | bn.ṯy[--]. | bn.p[---]. | gyn[.---]. | bn.pṯ[--]. | bn.db[--]. 2025.9
| [w y‘n.]ṯr.ab h.il.‘bd k.b‘l.y ym m.‘bd k.b‘l. | [--.--]m.bn.dgn.a[s]r km.hw ybl.argmn k.k ilm. | [---.]ybl.k bn.qdš.m 2.1[137].37
.nša. | [y]d h.šmmh.dbḥ. | l ṯr.ab h.il.šrd. | [b‘l].b dbḥ h.bn dgn. | [b m]ṣd h.yrd.krt. | [l g]gt.‘db.akl.l qryt. | ḥṭt.l bt.ḫb 14[KRT].4.170
ḥm[t].ša.yd k. | šmm.dbḥ.l ṯr. | ab k.il.šrd.b‘l. | b dbḥ k.bn.dgn. | b mṣd k.w yrd. | krt.l ggt.‘db. | akl.l qryt. | ḥṭt.l bt.ḫ 14[KRT].2.78
lt.p btlt.‘n[t]. | w p.n‘mt.aḫt[.b‘l]. | y‘l.b‘l.b ǵ[r.---]. | w bn.dgn.b š[---]. | b‘l.yṯb.l ks[i.mlk h]. | bn.dgn.l kḥ[ṯ.drkt h]. | 10[76].3.13
wn.ymǵy.aklm. | w ymẓa.‘qqm. | b‘l.ḥmd m.yḥmd m. | bn.dgn.yhrr m. | b‘l.ngt hm.b p‘n h. | w il hd.b ḫrẓ‘ h. | [-----]. 12[75].1.39
.ṯpṭ.nhr.tn.il m.d tq h.d tqyn h. | [hml]t.tn.b‘l.w ‘nn h.bn.dgn.art m.pḏ h. | [w y‘n.]ṯr.ab h.il.‘bd k.b‘l.y ym m.‘bd k 2.1[137].35
[pṭ.nhr]. | tn.il m.d tq h.d tqyn.hmlt.tn.b‘l.[w ‘nn h]. | bn.dgn.art m.pḏ h.tb‘.ǵlmm.l ṯṯb.[idk.pnm]. | l ytn.tk.ǵr.ll.‘ 2.1[137].19
‘n.lṯpn.il d pi | d dq.anm.l yrẓ. | ‘m.b‘l.l y‘db.mrḥ. | ‘m.bn.dgn.k tms m. | w ‘n.rbt.aṯrt ym. | blt.nmlk.‘ṯtr.‘rẓ. | ymlk.‘ 6.1.52[49.1.24]
.b‘l.b ǵ[r.---]. | w bn.dgn.b š[---]. | b‘l.yṯb.l ks[i.mlk h]. | bn.dgn.l kḥ[ṯ.drkt h]. | l alp.ql.ẓ[--.---]. | l np ql.nd.[----]. | tlk. 10[76].3.15
r‘ h.ṯhrṯ.km.gn. | ap lb.k ‘mq.ṯṯlṯ.bmt. | b‘l.mt.my.lim.bn dgn. | my.hmlt.aṯr.b‘l.nrd. | b arṣ.‘m h.trd.nrt. | ilm.špš.‘d. 6[62].1.6
n.ap lb.k ‘mq.yṯlṯ. | bmt.yšu.g h.w yṣḥ. | b‘l.mt.my.lim.bn. | dgn.my.hmlt.aṯr. | b‘l.ard.b arṣ.ap. | ‘nt.ttlk.w tṣd.kl.ǵr. | 5[67].6.23
b‘l.[---]. | il hd.b[---]. | at.bl.at.[---]. | yisp hm.b[‘l.---]. | bn.dgn[.---]. | ‘ḏbm.[---]. | uḫry.l[---]. | mṣt.ks h.t[--.---]. | idm. 12[75].2.26
[---.]ṯlṯm.d.nlqḥt. | [bn.ḫ]tyn.yd.bt h. | [aǵ]ltn. | tdn.bn.ddy. | ‘bdil[.b]n ṣdqn. | bnšm.h[-]mt.ypḥm. | kbby.yd.bt.a 2045.4
. | bn [-]‘y̆. | [b]n [i]lmd. | bn [t]bdn. | bn štn. | b[n] kdn. | bn dwn. | bn ḏrn. 2088.7
[--.]ubdym.b.uškn. | [---]lby. | [--]nbbl. | bn bl. | bn dkn. | bn ils. | bn ḥšbn. | bn uryy. | bn kṯl. | bn army. | bn gl 1064.5
nqdm. | bn.alṯn. | bn.dly. | bn.btry. | bn.ḫdmn. | [bn].šty. | [bn].kdgdl. | [---.-]y[-.] 2018.3
dy. | [---.š]d ubdy. | [---.šd] ubdy. | [---.š]d.bn.ṣin. | [---].bn.dly. | [---.]ṯty[-.--]. 2031.12
| w.nḥl hm. | [bn].pmn. | bn.gtrn. | bn.arpḫn. | bn.ṯryn. | bn.dll. | bn.ḫswn. | mrynm. | ‘zn. | ḥyn. | ‘myn. | ilyn. | yrb‘m. | n 1046.3.31

bn.ytrm.qšt.w.ql‘. | bn.‘bdyrḫ.qšt.w.q[l‘]. | bn.lky.qšt. | bn.dll.qšt.w.ql[‘]. | bn.pǵyn.qšt.w[.q]l‘. | bn.bdn.qšt. | bn.pls.q 119[321].3.28
.]w.šǵr h. | [---.]w.šǵr h. | [---.]krwn. | [---].ḫzmyn. | [---.]bn.dll. | r[--.--]km. | w.spr h. 2072.13
[-----]. | bn.t[--.---]. | agmy[.---]. | bn.dlq[-.---]. | tǵyn.bn.ubn.ṯql[m]. | yšn.ḥrš.mrkbt.ṯq[lm]. | bn 122[308].1.4
-.---]. | bn.gnb[-.---]. | hzpym. | rišn.[---]. | bn.‘bdy.[---]. | bn.dmtn.[---]. | [b]n.g‘yn.ḫr[-]. | lbnym. | grgš.[---]. | bn.ǵrn.[-- 93[328].11
n.k nšr.b ḥbš h.km.diy. | b t‘rt h.aqht.km.ytb.l lḥ[m]. | bn.dnil.l trm.‘l h.nšr[m]. | trḫpn.ybṣr.ḥbl.diy[m.bn]. | nšrm.t 18[3AQHT].4.30
nšr.b ḥb[š y]. | km.diy.b t‘rt y.aqht.[km.ytb]. | l lḥm.w bn.dnil.l trm[.‘l h]. | nšrm.trḫpn.ybṣr.[ḥbl.d] | iym.bn.nšrm.a 18[3AQHT].4.19
bt k.dmm]. | [šbt.dq]n k.mm‘m.w[---]. | aqht.w yplṭ k.bn[.dnil.---]. | w y‘ḏr k.b yd.btlt.[‘nt]. | w y‘n.lṭpn.il d p[id]. | 18[3AQHT].1.13
‘dy. | ‘nbr. | aḫrm. | bn.qrdy. | bn.šm‘n. | bn.ǵlmy. | ǵly. | bn.dnn. | bn.rmy. | dll. | mny. | krty. | bn.‘bṣ. | bn.argb. | ydn. | il‘ 2117.3.35
šm [---]. | kn‘m.bn.[---]. | plšb‘l.bn.n[--]. | ḥy bn.dnn.ṯkt. | ilthm.bn.dnn.ṯkt. | šb‘l.bn.aly.ṯkt. | klby.bn.iḫy.ṯ 2085.4
. | kn‘m.bn.[---]. | plšb‘l.bn.n[--]. | ḥy bn.dnn.ṯkt. | ilthm.bn.dnn.ṯkt. | šb‘l.bn.aly.ṯkt. | klby.bn.iḫy.ṯkt. | psš.bn.buly.ṯkt 2085.5
bn.qrrn. | bn.dnt. | bn.ṯ‘l[-]. | bdl.ar.dt.inn. | mhr l ht. | artyn. | ‘dmlk. | bn 1035.1.2
| špšyn.b.ulm. | bn.qṯn.b.ulm. | bn.gdrn.b.m‘r[by]. | [w].bn.d‘m[-]. | bn.ppṯ.b[--]. | b[n.---]. | šm[-.---]. | tkn[.---]. | knn.b. 2046.1.8
]bn.ḫlan. | [--]r bn.mn. | [--]ry. | [--]lim bn.brq. | [--.]qtn bn.drṣy. | [--]kn bn.pri. | [r]špab bn.pni. | [ab]mn bn.qṣy. | [‘]p 2087.6
. | bn.ṣry. | bn.mztn. | bn.šlgyn. | bn.[-]gštn. | bn[.n]klb. | b[n.]dtn. | w.nḥl h. | w.nḥl hm. | bn.iršyn. | bn.‘zn. | bn.aršw. | 113[400].2.9
n]. | bn.gntn[-]. | [--.]nqq[-]. | b[n.---]. | bn.[---]. | bn.‘yn. | bn.dtn. 2023.4.4
.ṯ‘y. | w.nḥl h. | w.nḥl hm. | bn.nqly. | bn.snrn. | bn.ṯgd. | bn.d[-]n. | bn.amdn. | bn.ṯmrn. | bn.pzny. | bn.mglb. | bn.[--]b. 105[86].4
kbd. | [---]. | y[---]. | bn.ǵlyn. | bdl.ar. | bn.šyn. | bn.ubrš. | bn.d[--]b. | abrpu. | bn.k[n]y. | bn.klyn. | bn.gmḥn. | ḥnn. | ayab 1035.3.4
špy. | tmtrn.bn.pnmn. | kkr. | bn.sgttn. | kkr. | ilšpš.kkr. | bn.ḏltn. | kkr.w[.--]. | ḫ[--.---]. 1118.12
. | m‘r. | lbnm. | nḫl. | y‘ny. | atn. | utly. | bn.alz. | bn ḫlm. | bn.ḏmr. | bn.‘yn. | ubnyn. | rpš d ydy. | ǵbl. | mlk. | gwl. | rqd. | ḫ 2075.17
-]n. | bn.[---]. | bn.‘r[--]. | bn.nkt[-]. | bn.abḏr. | bn.ḫrzn. | bn.ḏqnt. | bn.gmrš. | bn.nmq. | bn.špš[yn]. | bn.ar[--]. | bn.gb[-- 2023.3.11
| bn.[-]r[-]. | bn.tgn. | bn.iḏrn. | mnn. | b[n].skn. | bn.p‘ṣ. | bn.ḏrm. | [bn.-]ln. | [bn.-]ḏprḏ. 124[-].6.12
. | [b]n [i]lmd. | bn [t]bdn. | bn štn. | b[n] kdn. | bn dwn. | bn ḏrn. 2088.8
‘[l]. | mnḥm.bn[.---]. | krmn[py]. | bn.[--]m. | bn.asr[-]. | bn.ḏr[--]. | bn.ṣl[--]. | bn.ḫd[--]. | bn.‘[---]. | kbkbn bn[.---]. | bn. 2014.53
k.m‘ṣ[d.---]. | b.ḫrbǵlm.ǵlm[n]. | w.trhy.aṯt h. | w.mlky.b[n] h. | ily.mrily.tdgr. 2048.21
s h. | any.l yṣḥ.ṯr.il.ab h.il. | mlk.d yknn h.yṣḥ.aṯrt. | w bn h.ilt.w ṣbrt.arḫ h. | wn.in.bt.l b‘l.km.ilm. | ḥẓr.k b[n.a]ṯrt. 3[‘NT.VI].5.45
. | [an]y.l yṣḥ.ṯr il.ab h. | [i]l.mlk.d yknn h.yṣḥ. | aṯrt.w bn h.ilt.w ṣbrt. | ary h.wn.in.bt.l b‘l. | km.ilm.w ḥẓr.k bn.aṯrt 4[51].4.49
ny.l yṣ]ḥ.ṯr. | [il.ab h.i]l.mlk. | [d yknn h.yṣ]ḥ.aṯ | [rt.w bn h.]ilt. | [w ṣbrt.ary]h. | [wn.in.bt.l b‘l.] | [km.ilm.w ḥẓr]. | [4[51].1.8
ql. | tštḥwy.w tkbdn h. | tšu.g h.w tṣḥ.tšmḫ ht. | aṯrt.w bn h.ilt.w ṣb | rt.ary h.k mt.aliyn. | b‘l.k ḫlq.zbl.b‘l. | arṣ.gm.y 6.1.40[49.1.12]
. | [ǵz]r.aḥd.b.bt.nwrḏ. | [at]t.adrt.b.bt.artṯb. | aṯt.w.ṯn.bn h.b.bt.iwwpzn. | aṯt.w.pǵt.b.bt.ydrm. | ṯt.aṯtm.adrtm.w.p 80[119].5
[aṯt.w].bn h.b.bt.krz. | [aṯt.]w.pǵt.b.bt.gg. | [ǵz]r.aḥd.b.bt.nwrḏ. | [at] 80[119].1
bq h.ḥmḥmt. | [---.--] n.ylt.ḥmḥmt. | [---.mt.r]pi.w ykn.bn h. | [b bt.šrš.]b qrb.hkl h. | [nṣb.skn.i]lib h.b qdš. | [ztr.‘m 17[2AQHT].1.43
.qdš. | l tbrknn l ṯr.il ab y. | tmrnn.l bny.bnwt. | w ykn.bn h b bt.šrš.b qrb. | hkl h.nṣb.skn.ilib h.b qdš. | ztr.‘m h.l ar 17[2AQHT].1.26
q.arb‘m.dr‘.w.‘šr.dd.drt. | w[.a]rb‘.l.‘šrm.dd.l.yḥšr.bl.bn h. | b.gt.m‘br.arb‘m.l.mit.dr‘.w.ṯmnym[.drt]. | w.‘šrm.l.mi 1098.11
w.aṯt h. | anntn.yṣr. | annmn.w.ṯlṯ.n‘[r] h. | rpan.w.ṯ[n.]bn h. | bn.ayln.w.ṯn.bn h. | yt. 2068.26
. | bn.b‘ly.ṯlṯtm.b‘lm. | w.aḥd.ḫbṯ. | w.arb‘.aṯt. | bn.lg.ṯn.bn h. | b‘lm.w.aḫt h. | b.šrt. | šty.w.bn h. 2080.10
iry. | ṯlṯ.b‘lm. | w.adn hm.ṯr.w.arb‘.bnt h. | yrḫm.yd.ṯn.bn h. | b‘lm.w.ṯlṯ.n‘rm.w.bt.aḫt. | bn.lwn.ṯlṯtm.b‘lm. | bn.b‘ly. 2080.4
rkbt. | bnšm.dt.l.mlk. | ‘bdyrḫ.bn.ṯyl. | ‘bdn.w.aṯt h.w.bn h. | gpn.bn[.a]ly. | bn.rqd[y].ṯbg. | iḫmlk. | yp‘n w.aṯt h. | an 2068.19
nzy.w.a[ṯt h]. | wšṯn.bn h. | ṯmgdl.ykn‘my.w.aṯt h. | w.bn h.w.alp.aḥ[d]. | aǵltn.[--]y.w.[aṯt h]. | w.bn h.w.alp.w.[---] 1080.6
h.w.ṯn.alpm. | [w.]ṯlṯm.ṣin. | anndr.ykn‘my. | w.aṯt h.w.bn h. | w.alp.w.tš[‘.]ṣin. 1080.16
w.aṯt h. | w.bn h.w.alp.aḥ[d]. | aǵltn.[--]y.w[.aṯt h]. | w.bn h.w.alp.w.[---]. | [-]ln.[---]. | w.ṯn.bn [h.---]. | [--]d m‘qby[.- 1080.8
[-]ḏmu.apsty.b[--]. | w.bn h.w aṯt h.w.alp.w ṯmn.ṣin. | [-]dln.qmnzy.w.a[ṯt h]. | wšṯn 1080.2
. | agdn.bn.nrgn. | w ynḥm.aḫ h. | w.b‘ln aḫ h. | w.ḥṯtn bn h. | w.btšy.bt h. | w.ištrmy. | bt.‘bd mlk. | w.snt. | bt.ugrt. | 1006.6
---]. | klt h.[---]. | ṯty.ary.m[--.---]. | nrn.arny[.---]. | w.ṯn.bn h.w.b[---.---]. | b tn[--.---]. | swn.qrty[.---]. | uḫ h.w.‘šr[.---]. 81[329].6
d.b.[bt.---]. | ṯt.aṯtm.w.pǵt.w.ǵzr.aḥd.b.[bt.---]. | aṯt.w.bn h.w.pǵt.aḫt.b.bt.m[--]. | aṯt.w.ṯt.bt h.b.bt.ḫdmrd. | aṯt.w.ṯ 80[119].21
.bn [h.---]. | [--]d m‘qby[.---]. | swn.qrty.w[.aṯt h]. | [w].bn h.w.ṯn.alpm. | [w.]ṯlṯm.ṣin. | anndr.ykn‘my. | w.aṯt h.w.bn 1080.13
h[.---]. | w.alp h.w.a[r]b‘.l.arb‘[m.---]. | pln.ṯmry.w.ṯn.bn h.w[.---]. | ymrn.apsny.w.aṯt h..b[n.---]. | prd.m‘qby[.w.--- 2044.8
[‘]bdyrḫ. | [b]n.gg‘t. | [‘]dy. | armwl. | uwaḫ. | ypln.w.ṯn.bn h. | ydln. | anr[my]. | mld. | krmp[y]. | bṣmn. 2086.8
annmn.w.ṯlṯ.n‘[r] h. | rpan.w.ṯ[n.]bn h. | bn.ayln.w.ṯn.bn h. | yt. 2068.27
h. | wn.in.bt.l b‘l.km.ilm. | ḥẓr.k b[n.a]ṯrt.mṯb.il. | mṯll.b[n h.m]ṯb.rbt.aṯrt. | ym.mṯb.[pdr]y.bt.ar. | [mẓll.]ṭly[.bt.]rb. 3[‘NT.VI].5.48
t.l b‘l.] | [km.ilm.w ḥẓr]. | [k bn.aṯ]r[t]. | m[ṯ]b.il.mẓll. | bn h.mṯb.rbt. | aṯrt.ym.mṯb. | klt.knyt. | mṯb.pdry.b ar. | mẓll. 4[51].1.14
h.wn.in.bt.l b‘l. | km.ilm.w ḥẓr.k bn.aṯrt. | mṯb il.mẓll.bn h. | mṯb rbt.aṯrt.ym. | mṯb.klt.knyt. | mṯb.pdry.bt.ar. | mẓll 4[51].4.52
n]. | [bt].l [b‘l.km.ilm.w ḥẓr]. | k bn.[aṯrt.mṯb.il.mẓll]. | bn h.m[ṯb.rbt.aṯrt.ym]. | mṯb.pdr[y.bt.ar.mẓll]. | ṭly.bt.r[b.mṯ 3[‘NT.VI].4.2
g.---]. | urt[n.---]. | ‘dn[.---]. | bqrt[.---]. | ṯnǵrn.[---]. | w.bn h.n[--.---]. | ḥnil.[---]. | aršmg.mru. | b‘l.šlm.‘bd. | awr.ṯǵrn.‘ 2084.7
m l.yqḥ. | bt.hnd.b d. | [‘b]dmlk. | [-]k.am‘[--]. | [w.b] d.bn h[.‘]d ‘lm. | [w.un]ṯ.in[n.]b h. | [---.]n‘m[-]. 1009.17
ḥr.‘lmt. | bnš bnšm. | l.yqḥnn.b d. | b‘ln.bn.kltn. | w.b d.bn h.‘d. | ‘lm.w unṯ. | in.b h. 1008.19
. | [ml]k.d.b riš. | [--.-]nt. | [l.‘b]dmlk. | [--.-]m[-]r. | [w.l.]bn h.‘d. | [‘l]m.mn k. | mn km l.yqḥ. | bt.hnd.b d. | [‘b]dmlk. | [1009.11
k]rm h.yd. | [k]lkl h. | [w] ytn.nn. | l.b‘ln.bn. | kltn.w l. | bn h.‘d.‘lm. | šḥr.‘lmt. | bnš bnšm. | l.yqḥnn.b d. | b‘ln.bn.kltn. 1008.14
wrnr. | alnr. | mahdt. | aby. | [-----]. | [-]nt. | ydn. | mnn.w bn h. | tkn. 107[15].12
aṯt h.w.alp.w ṯmn.ṣin. | [-]dln.qmnzy.w.a[ṯt h]. | wšṯn.bn h. | ṯmgdl.ykn‘my.w.aṯt h. | w.bn h.w.alp.aḥ[d]. | aǵltn.[--] 1080.4
yd]. | krpn.b klat yd.[---]. | km ll.kḥṣ.tusp[.---]. | tgr.il.bn h.ṯr[.---]. | w y‘n.lṭpn.il.d p[id.---]. | šm.bn y.yw.ilt.[---]. | w 1[‘NT.X].4.12
.]skn. | [---.-]im.btḏ. | [---.b]šḥr.atlgn. | [---].b šḥr. | [---.]bn h. | [-]k[--]g hn.ksp. 2167.6
n‘r h. | bn.ḫby.w.[a]ṯt h. | ynḥm.ulmy. | [--]q.w.aṯt h.w.bn h. | [--]an.w.aṯt h. | [--]y.w.aṯt h. | [--]r.w.aṯt h. | ‘bdyrḫ.ṯn 2068.6
.ṯn[.bn h.---]. | iwrm[-.]b[n.---]. | annt[n.]w[.---]. | w.ṯn.bn h.[---]. | aǵltn.ypr[y.---]. | w.šb‘.ṣin h[.---]. 2044.16

-.a]tt h[.---]. | prṯ.mgd[ly.---.]aṯ[t h]. | ʿdyn[.---]. | w.ṯn[.bn h.---]. | iwrm[-.]b[n.---]. | annt[n.]w[.---]. | w.ṯn.bn h.[---]. | 2044.13
].ʿtgrm. | [---.-]ṣbm. | [---.]nrn.mʿry. | [---.--]r. | [---.]w.ṯn.bn h. | [---.b]t h.ʿtgrm. 2043.11
h.[---]. | ḫdmtn.ṯn[.---]. | w.ṯlṯ.alp h.[---]. | swn.qrty.w.[b]n h[.---]. | w.alp h.w.a[r]bʿ.l.arbʿ[m.---]. | pln.ṯmry.w.ṯn.bn 2044.6
.[--]y.w[.aṯt h]. | w.bn h.w.alp.w.[---]. | [-]ln.[---]. | w.ṯn.bn [h.---]. | [--]d mʿqby[.---]. | swn.qrty.w[.aṯt h]. | [w].bn h.w. 1080.10
.--]a.ṯ[l]ṯ.d.a[--]. | [---].mrn. | [---.]bn pnṯbl. | [---.-]py w.bn h. 1145.2.3
w.arbʿ.aṯt. | bn.lg.ṯn.bn h. | bʿlm.w.aḫt h. | b.šrt. | šty.w.bn h. 1145.2.3
. | kṯy. | bn.ḫny. | bn.ssm. | bn.ḫnn. | [--]ny. | [bn].ṯrdnt. | [bn].hyadt. | [--]lt. | šmrm. | pʿṣ.bn.byy.ʿšrt. 2080.13
b[--.---] | b y.šnt.mlit.t[--.---]. | ymǵy k.bnm.ta[--.---]. | [b]nm.w bnt.ytn k[.---]. | [--]l.bn y.šḥt.w [---]. | [--]tt.msgr.bn 1047.22
[--.---]. | [---.]k ṯrm.l p[--.---]. | [---.]l.[--.]rlg[-.---]. | [---.]bn.w [---]. | [---.--]ṯ.kn[-.---]. | [---.--]tm.n[--.---]. | [---.-]km.tʿrb 59[100].9
--.]bn.n[--.---]. | [---.]bn.mṣ[--.---]. | [---.]bʿlš[-.---]. | [---.]bn.zzb[-.---]. | [---.]bn mt[.---]. | [---.b]n r[--.---]. 2125.11
lṯḥ ḫlq. | bn ytr. | bn ilšpš. | ubrš. | bn gmš ḫlq. | bn ʿgy. | bn zlbn. | bn.aḫ[--]. | bn[.---]. | [-----]. | bn kr[k]. | bn ḫtyn. | w n 2139.5
t. | bn.il.qšt.w.qlʿ. | ark.qšt.w.qlʿ. | bn.ʿbdnkl.qšt.w.qlʿ. | bn.znan.qšt. | bn.arz.[ar]bʿ.qšt.w.arb[ʿ.]qlʿm. | b[n.]adʿl.q[š]t. 2016.2.20
rt. | ydn. | qṭn. | bn.asr. | bn.ʿdy. | bn.amt[m]. | myn. | šr. | bn.zql. | bn.iḫy. | bn.iytr. | bn.ʿyn. | bn.ǵzl. | bn.ṣmy. | bn.il[-]šy. 119[321].2.44
ilṣdq.bn.zry. | bʿlytn.bn.ulb. | ytrʿm.bn.swy. | ṣḥrn.bn.qrtm. | bn.špš 2117.2.3
.w.qlʿ. | gln.ṯt.qštm.w.qlʿ. | gtn.qšt. | pmn.ṯt.qštm.w.qlʿ. | bn.zry.q[š]t.w.qlʿ. | bn.tlmyn.ṯt.qštm.w.qlʿ. | bn.ysd.qšt. | [ǵ] 2024.1
| [-----]. | bn[---]. | bn.mlkyy. | bn.atn. | bn.bly. | bn.ṯbrn. | bn.ḥgby. | bn.pity. | bn.slgyn. | ʿzn.bn.mlk. | bn.alṯn. | bn.ṯmyr. 104[316].9
. | ǵbl. | mlk. | gwl. | rqd. | ḫlby. | ʿn[q]pat. | m[ʿ]rb. | ʿrm. | bn.ḥgby. | mrat. 115[301].2.5
rt.šlm. | ʿbdyrḫ.šbʿt.ʿšrt ʿšrt.šlm. | yky.ʿšrt.ṯṯt šlm.ʿšrt. | bn.ḥgby.ṯmnt.l ʿšrm.ʿšrt.ḫmš.kbd. | bn.ilṣdq.šbʿt ṯlṯt šlm. | bn 2075.29
miḫdy[m]. | bn.ḥgb[n]. | bn.ulbt[-]. | ḏkry[-]. | bn.tlm[yn]. | bn.yʿdd. | bn.idl 1131.8
[--]. | bn.š[--]. | bn.a[---]. | bn.prsn. | bn.mtyn. | bn.ḫlpn. | bn.ḥgbn. | bn.szn. | bn.mglb. 2017.2
bl. | bn.ḫnzr. | bn.arwṭ. | bn.ṯbtnq. | bn.pṯdn. | bn.nbdg. | bn.ḥgbn. | bn.tmr. | bn.prsn. | bn.ršpy. | [ʿ]bdḥgb. | [k]lby. | [-]ḥ 117[325].2.8
.ḥty. | ṯn.bnš ibrdr. | bnš tlmi. | sǵr.ḫryn. | ʿdn.w sǵr h. | bn.ḥgbn. 113[400].1.19
kmrṯn[.---]. | bn.ṯbln[.---]. | bn.pndr[.---]. | bn.idr[-.---]. | bn.ḥdn[-.---]. | bn.ṯbi[l.---]. 2082.10
.ulb ḫmšt. | bn.ḥry.ḫmšt. | swn.ḫmšt. | bn.[-]r[-.]ḫmšt. | bn.ḥdṯ.ʿšrt. | bn.ḫnyn.ʿšrt. | rpan.ḫmšt. | abǵl.ḫmšt. | bn.aḫdy.ʿ 2070.2.7
miḫdym. | bn.ḥṭb. | bn abyt. | bn ḫdl. | bn ṣdqn. | bn ayy. | bn dbb. | w nḥl 1062.17
-]y. | bʿlskn. | bn.ʿbd. | ḫyrn. | alpy. | bn.plsy. | bn.qrr[-]. | bn.ḥyl. | bn.gʿyn. | ḥyn. | bn.armg[-]. | bʿlmṯpṭ. | [bn].ayḫ. | [---] 2016.1.2
bn.šyy. | bn.ḫnzr. | bn.ydbʿl. | bn.ḥyn. | [bn].ar[-]m. | [bn].ḥrp[-]. | [bn].ḫdpṯr. | [bn.-]dn. | [bn 1035.2.1
.w ykn. | [--]ndbym. | [ʿ]rmy.w snry. | [b]n.sdy.bn.ṯty. | bn.ḥyn.bn.ǵlm. | bn.yyn.w.bn.au[pš]. | bn.kdrn. | ʿrgzy.w.bn.ʿ 124[-].2.4
mn.ary. | [bn].šdy. | [bn].gmḥ. | [---]ty. | [b]n.ypy.gbʿly. | b[n].ḥyn. | ḏmn.šʿrty. | bn.arwdn.ilšʿy. | bn grgs. | bn.ḫran. | b 131[309].24
bn.ʿyn. | bn.ǵzl. | bn.ṣmy. | bn.il[-]šy. | bn.ybšr. | bn.sly. | bn.ḫlbt. | bn.brzt. | bn.ayl. | [-----]. | ʿbd[--]. | bn.i[--]. | ʿd[--]. | ild 99[327].1.6
ḫlb.rpš. | ẓẓn. | bn.ḥmny. | dqry. 2117.2.12
| bn.gmrš. | bn.nmq. | bn.špš[yn]. | bn.ar[--]. | bn.gb[--]. | bn.ḫn[n]. | bn.gntn[-]. | [--.]nqq[-]. | b[n.---]. | bn.[---]. | bn.ʿyn. 1068.3
ypḥ.ʿbdilt. | bn.m. | ypḥ.ilšlm. | bn.prqdš. | ypḥ.mnḫm. | bn.ḫnn. | brqn.spr. 2023.3.17
ʿmnr. | šd.bn.krwn.l bn.ʿmyn. | šd.bn.prmn.l aḫny. | šd.bn ḫnn.l bn.adlḏn. | šd.bn.nṣdn.l bn.ʿmlbi. | šd.ṯpḫln.l bn.ǵl. | 2116.22
. | tgyn.arty. | bn.nryn.arty. | bn.ršp.ary. | bn.ǵlmn ary. | bn.ḥsbn ary. | bn.šdy ary. | bn.ktkt.mʿqby. | bn.[---.]ṯlḥny. | b[2089.7
uṣn[-]. | bn.alṯn. | bn.aš[-]š. | bn.štn. | bn.ilš. | bn.tnabn. | bn.ḥsn. | ṣprn. | bn.ašbḥ. | bn.qṭnn. | bn.ǵlmn. | [bn].ṣwy. | [bn]. 87[64].14
i.ṯt.qštm.w.ṯn.qlʿm. | ildgn.qšt. | bn.yʿrn.ṯt.qštm w.qlʿ. | bn.ḥsn.qšt.w.qlʿ. | bn.gdn.ṯt.qštm.w.qlʿ. | bn.[-]q.qšt.w.qlʿ. | g 1046.1.19
[---.]ṯrd. | [---.]qpḫn. | [---.a]ǵlṯr. | [---.]ṭml. | [---.]bn.ḥsqt. | [---.]bn.uḏr[-]. 119[321].3.11
n.ḫlbym. | bn.ady. | bn.ʿṯtry. | bn.ḥrẓn. | ady. | bn.birtn. | bn.ḥrẓn. | bn.bddn. | bn.anny. | ytršp. | bn.szn. | bn.kdgdl. | bn. 2132.5
.--]n. | [--.--]n. | bn.[---]. | bn.ʿr[--]. | bn.nkt[-]. | bn.abḏr. | bn.ḥrẓn. | bn.ḏqnt. | bn.gmrš. | bn.nmq. | bn.špš[yn]. | bn.ar[--] 115[301].1.8
l h]. | bn.ẓr[-]. | mru.skn. | bn.bddn. | bn.ǵrgn. | bn.tgtn. | bn.ḥrẓn. | bn.qdšt. | bn.nṯǵ[-]. | bn.gr[--]. | bn.[---]. | bn.[---]. | m 2023.3.10
lʿ. | yʿrn.qšt.w.qlʿ. | klby.qšt.w.qlʿ. | bqʿt. | ily.qšt.w.qlʿ. | bn.ḥrẓn.qšt.w.qlʿ. | tgrš.qšt.w.qlʿ. | špšyn.qšt.w.qlʿ. | bn.ṯʿln.qš 113[400].5.10
unp.arbʿt. | ʿbdbn.ytrš ḫmšt. | krwn.ʿšrt. | bn.ulb ḫmšt. | bn.ḥry.ḫmšt. | swn.ḫmšt. | bn.[-]r[-.]ḫmšt. | bn.ḥdṯ.ʿšrt. | bn.ḫ 119[321].2.23
. | w.nḥl h. | bn.rmyy. | bn.tlmyn. | w.nḥl h. | w.nḥl hm. | bn.ḥrm. | bn.brzn. | w.nḥl h. | bn.adlḏn. | bn.šbl. | bn.ḫnzr. | bn. 1062.14
. | [---.-]mbʿl.[---].ʿšrt. | [---.]ḥgbn.kbs.ks[p]. | [---].ḏmrd.bn.ḥrmn. | [---.-]ǵn.ksp.ṯṯt. | [---.]ygry.ṯlṯm.ksp.b[--]. 113[400].1.9
]. | mtbʿl.bn[.---]. | ymy.bn[.---]. | ʿbdʿn.p[--.---]. | [-]d[-]l.bn.ḥrn. | aḫty.bt.abm. | [-]rbn.ʿdd.nryn. | [ab]r[p]u.bn.kbd. | [- 2153.10
ṣy. | [ʿ]pṯrm bn.agmz. | [-]n bn.iln. | [--]nn bn.ibm. | [-]n bn.ḥrn. | [š]mmn bn.gmz. | [yn]ḥm bn.ilmd. 102[322].6.1
bn.šyy. | bn.ḫnzr. | bn.ydbʿl. | bn.ḥyn. | [bn].ar[-]m. | [bn].ḥrp[-]. | [bn].ḫdpṯr. | [bn.-]dn. | [bn.-]lyn. | [bn.i]lsk. | [bn.-- 2087.13
. | ill. | ǵlmn. | bn.ytrm. | bn.ḫgbt. | mtn. | mḫtn. | [p]lsy. | bn.ḫrš. | [--.]kbd. | [---]. | y[---]. | bn.ǵlyn. | bdl.ar. | bn.šyn. | bn. 124[-].2.6
uss.ʿšrm. | b.ʿdn.bn.ṯṯ.ʿšrt. | b.bn.qrdmn.ṯlṯm. | b.bṣmn[.bn].ḥrtn.ʿ[--]. | b.t[--.---] h.[---]. | [-----]. | [--]ly.ḫmšm.b.ʿbdyr[1035.2.15
ym.b.uškn. | [---]lby. | [--]nbbl. | bn bl. | bn dkn. | bn ils. | bn ḫšbn. | bn uryy. | bn kṯl. | bn army. | bn gln. | bn abg. | bn.nǵ 2054.1.21
-].ml[--]. | [---.-]ṯk.ytmt.dlt tlk.[---].bm[.---]. | [---.-]qp.bn.ḥtt.bn ḥtt[.---]. | [---.--]p.km.dlt.tlk.km.p[---]. | [---.]bt.tḥb 1064.7
-]. | [---.-]ṯk.ytmt.dlt tlk.[---].bm[.---]. | [---.-]qp.bn.ḥtt.bn ḥtt[.---]. | [---.--]p.km.dlt.tlk.km.p[---]. | [---.]bt.tḥbṭ.km.ṣ 1001.1.23
| bn.alt[-]. | iḫy[-]. | ʿbdgṯr. | ḥrr. | bn.s[-]p[-]. | bn.nrpd. | bn.ḥ[-]y. | bʿlskn. | bn.ʿbd. | ḫyrn. | alpy. | bn.plsy. | bn.qrr[-]. | b 1001.1.23
. | bn.ṯʿ[-]. | bn.km[-]. | bn.r[--]. | [bn.]ʿ[---]. | [bn.]r[---]. | [bn.]ḥ[---]. | [bn.]šbl. | [bn.]ḫdmn. | [bn.]nklb. | [---]dn. | [---]y. | [1035.1.14
knn. | bn.py. | bn.mk[-]. | bn.by[--]. | bn.a[--]. | bn.iy[--]. | bn.ḫ[---]. | bn.plš. | bn.ubr. | bn.ʿpṭb. | ṯbry. | bn.ymn. | krty. | bn 1073.2.3
bnšm.dt.l.u[--]ṯṭb. | kṯ[r]n. | w.aṯt h.w.nʿr h. | bn.ḫby.w.[a]ṯt h. | ynḥm.ulmy. | [--]q.w.aṯt h.w.bn h. | [--]an. 2117.1.14
šd.ubdy[.---]. | šd.bn.ḫb[--.---]. | šd.srn[.---]. | šd.yʿdr[.---]. | šd.swr.[---]. | šd.bn p 2068.4
g[-]. | bʿlmṯpṭ. | [bn].ayḫ. | [---]rn. | ill. | ǵlmn. | bn.ytrm. | bn.ḫgbt. | mtn. | mḫtn. | [p]lsy. | bn.ḫrš. | [--.]kbd. | [---]. | y[---]. 83[85].2
.ṯ[lṯ].qšt.w.ṯn.qlʿm. | qṣn.ṯt.qštm.w.qlʿ. | bn.gtrn.q[š]t. | bn.ḫdi.ṯt.qštm.w.ṯn.qlʿm. | ildgn.qšt. | bn.yʿrn.ṯt.qštm w.qlʿ. | 1035.2.11
ltn.mid[-.---]. | bn.lṣn.ʿrm[y]. | aršw.bṣry. | arpṯr.yʿrty. | bn.ḫdyn.ugrty. | bn.tgdn.ugrty. | tgyn.arty. | bn.nryn.arty. | b 119[321].3.8
ḏ]rǵlm. | [bn.]kdgdl. | [b]n.qṭn. | [b]n.ǵrgn. | [b]n.tgdn. | bn.ḫdyn. | bn.sgr. | bn.aǵltn. | bn.ktln. | bn.ʿgwn. | bn.yšmʿ. | bd 87[64].8
y.ṯqlm. | bn.brq.ṯqlm. | bn.ḫnzr.ṯqlm. | dqn.nsk.arbʿt. | bn.ḫdyn.ṯqlm. | bn.ʿbd.šḫr.ṯqlm. | bn.ḫnqn.arbʿt. | [b]n.ṯrk.ṯql 104[316].9
122[308].1.18

šrm. | [š]d.bn.ḫrmln.b d.bn.tnn. | [š]d.bn.ḫrmln.tn.b d.bn.ḫdmn. | [u]bdy.nqdm. | [tlt].šdm.d.n'rb.gt.npk. | [š]d.rpan. 82[300].2.11
bn.r[--]. | [bn.]'[---]. | [bn.]r[---]. | [bn.]ḥ[---]. | [bn.]šbl. | [bn.]ḫdmn. | [bn.]nklb. | [---]dn. | [---]y. | [-----]. | [-----]. | bn.adn 1073.2.5
nqdm. | bn.altn. | bn.dly. | bn.btry. | bn.ḫdmn. | [bn].šty. | [bn].kdgdl. | [---.-]y[-.] 2018.5
t.---]. | [bn].mlṣ.qštm.w.utp[t]. | [--.q]l'.w[.---.m]rḥm. | [bn].ḫdmn.qšt.[w.u]tp[t].t[--]. | [---].arb'.[---]. | [---].kdl[.---.m 2047.9
n.ḫnzr. | bn.ydb'l. | bn.ḥyn. | [bn].ar[-]m. | [bn].ḥrp[-]. | [bn].ḫdptr. | [bn.-]dn. | [bn.-]lyn. | [bn.i]lsk. | [bn.---]n. | bn[.---]. 124[-].2.7
tt.qštm.w.tn.ql'm. | bn.[-]rkt.tt.qštm.w.ql'. | bn.t'l.qšt. | bn.[ḫ]dptr.tt.qštm.[w].ql'. | bn.aǵlyn.tt.qštm[.w.tl]t.ql'm. | b 119[321].3.18
. | krmn[py]. | bn.[--]m. | bn.asr[-]. | bn.dr[--]. | bn.ṣl[--]. | bn.ḫd[--]. | bn.'[---]. | kbkbn bn[.---]. | bn.k[--]. | bn.pdr[n.]. | b 2014.55
miḫdym. | bn.ḥṭb. | bn abyt. | bn ḫdl. | bn ṣdqn. | bn ayy. | bn dbb. | w nḥl h. | bn n'myn. | bn 2016.1.4
-]sp.mr[y-.---]. | [--]l.ttm sp[m.---]. | [p]drn.ḫm[š.---]. | l bn ḫdnr[.---]. | ttm sp.km[-.---]. | 'šrm.sp[.---]. | 'šr sp.m[ry-.-- 139[310].5
tn. | w.nḥl h. | w.nḥl hm. | bn.iršyn. | bn.'zn. | bn.aršw. | bn.ḫzrn. | bn.iǵyn. | w.nḥl h. | bn.ksd. | bn.bršm. | bn.kzn. | w.n 113[400].2.15
n. | ṣdqn.bn.ass. | b'lyskn.bn.ss. | ṣdqn.bn.imrt. | mnḫm.bn.ḥyrn. | [-]yn.bn.arkbt. | [--]zbl.bt.mrnn. | a[--.---.-]'n. | ml[-- 102[323].3.11
[w]nḥ[l h]. | [bn].amd[-]. | [bn].ṣbṭ[--]. | [bn].ḫla[n]. | [bn].ǵr[--]. | d.b[n.---]. | d.bn.[---]. | d.bn.š[--]. | d.b 2164.A.4
pdr. | šd.iyry.l.'bdb'l. | šd.šmmn.l.bn.šty. | šd.bn.arws.l.bn.ḫlan. | šd.bn.ibryn.l.bn.'mnr. 1102.19
[---.b]n.[y]drn. | [---.]bn.ḫlan. | [--]r bn.mn. | [--]ry. | [--]lim bn.brq. | [--.]qtn bn.drṣ 2087.2
spr.ytnm. | bn.ḫlbym. | bn.ady. | bn.'ttry. | bn.ḫrzn. | ady. | bn.birtn. | bn.ḫ 115[301].1.2
. | bn.slmz[-]. | bn.k'[--]. | bn.y[---]. | [-----]. | [bn.a]mdy. | bn.ḫlln. | bn.ktn. | bn.abn. | bn.nskn. | bn.gmrn. | bn[.-]škn. | [-- 2021.2.3
n.tlḥy. | bn.aryn. | bn.lgn. | bn.b'yn. | šdyn. | ary. | brqn. | bn.ḫlln. | bn.mṣry. | tmn.qšt. | w 'šr.utpt. | upšt irš[-]. 118[306].12
'qb. | tpn. | m'r. | lbnm. | nḫl. | y'ny. | atn. | utly. | bn.alz. | bn ḫlm. | bn.dmr. | bn.'yn. | ubnyn. | rpš d ydy. | ǵbl. | mlk. | gw 2075.16
qn. | bn ayy. | bn dbb. | w nḥl h. | bn n'myn. | bn attyy. | bn ḫlp. | bn.zll. | bn ydy. | bn lzn. | bn.tyn. | bn g'r. | bn.prtn. | b 2016.1.11
b.ym.ḥdt. | b.yrḫ.pgrm. | lqḥ.b'lm'dr. | w bn.ḫlp. | w[--]y.d.b'l. | miḫd.b. | arb'.mat. | ḫrṣ. 1155.4
b.ym.ḥdt. | b.yr.pgrm. | lqḥ.b'lmdr. | w.bn.ḫlp. | miḫd. | b.arb'. | mat.ḫrṣ. 1156.4
---]. | bn.b[--]. | bn.š[--]. | bn.a[---]. | bn.prsn. | bn.mtyn. | bn.ḫlpn. | bn.ḥgbn. | bn.szn. | bn.mglb. 117[325].2.7
n.ilštm'y.ḫmš[t]. | 'zn.bn.brn.ḫmšt. | m'rt.ḫmšt. | arttb.bn.ḫmšt. | bn.ysr[.ḫmš]t. | ṣ[-]r.ḫ[mšt]. | 'zn.ḫ[mšt]. 1062.28
l hm. | bn.ḥrm. | bn.brzn. | w.nḥl h. | bn.adldn. | bn.šbl. | bn.ḫnzr. | bn.arwt. | bn.tbtnq. | bn.ptdn. | bn.nbdg. | bn.ḥgbn. | 113[400].1.14
bn.šyy. | bn.ḫnzr. | bn.ydb'l. | bn.ḥyn. | [bn].ar[-]m. | [bn].ḥrp[-]. | [bn]. 124[-].2.2
.nqd.tqlm. | bt.sgld.tqlm. | bn.'my.tqlm. | bn.brq.tqlm. | bn.ḫnzr.tqlm. | dqn.nsk.arb't. | bn.ḫdyn.tqlm. | bn.'bd.šḫr.tql 122[308].1.16
mn. | šmmn. | bn.rmy. | bn.aky. | 'bdḫmn. | bn.'dt. | kty. | bn.ḫny. | bn.ssm. | bn.ḫnn. | [--]ny. | [bn].trdnt. | [bn].hyadt. | [- 1047.17
bn.ktln. | bn.'gwn. | bn.yšm'. | bdl.mdrǵlm. | bn.mmy. | bn.ḫnyn. | bn.knn. | khnm. | bn.t'y. | w.nḥl h. | w.nḥl hm. | bn.n 104[316].9
mṣrn. | bn.'dy. | bn.ršpy. | [---.]mn. | [--.-]sn. | [bn.-]ny. | [b]n.ḫnyn. | [bn].nbq. | [bn.]snrn. | [bn.-]lṣ. | bn.[---]ym. 115[301].3.2
n.ḥry.ḫmšt. | swn.ḫmšt. | bn.[-]r[-.]ḫmšt. | bn.ḥdt.'šrt. | bn.ḫnyn.'šrt. | rpan.ḫmšt. | abǵl.ḫmšt. | bn.aḫdy.'šrt. | ttn.'ṣrt. 1062.18
lp. | bn.zll. | bn ydy. | bn lzn. | bn.tyn. | bn g'r. | bn.prtn. | bn ḫnn. | b[n.-]n. | bn.ṣṣb. | bn.b'ltn ḫlq. | bn.mlkbn. | bn.asyy 2016.1.18
y. | bn.aky. | 'bdḫmn. | bn.'dt. | kty. | bn.ḫny. | bn.ssm. | bn.ḫnn. | [--]ny. | [bn].trdnt. | [bn].hyadt. | [--]lt. | šmrm. | p'ṣ.b 1047.19
[---].rb. | [-]lpl. | bn.asrn. | bn.šḫyn. | bn.abd'n. | bn.ḫnqn. | bn.nmq. | bn.amdn. | bn.špšn. 1067.6
lm. | dqn.nsk.arb't. | bn.ḫdyn.tqlm. | bn.'bd.šḫr.tqlm. | bn.ḫnqn.arb't. | [b]n.trk.tqlm. | [b]n.pdrn.tq[lm]. | pdy.[----]. | 122[308].1.20
.ḥṣn. | ṣprn. | bn.ašbḥ. | bn.qtnn. | bn.ǵlmn. | [bn].ṣwy. | [bn].ḫnq[n]. | [-----]. | [-----]. | [-----]. | [-----]. | n[----]. | bn.[---]. | b 1046.1.25
hm. | [bn].pmn. | bn.gtrn. | bn.arpḫn. | bn.tryn. | bn.dll. | bn.ḫswn. | mrynm. | 'zn. | ḥyn. | 'myn. | ilyn. | yrb'm. | n'mn. | b 1046.3.32
.ibln. | bn.ilt. | špšyn.nḥl h. | n'mn.bn.iryn. | nrn.nḥl h. | bn.ḫsn. | bn.'bd. | [-----]. | [---.n]ḥ[l h]. | [-]ntm[.---]. | [']bdm. | [85[80].2.9
tn.r'y.uzm. | sǵr.bn.ḫpsry.aḥd. | sǵr.artn.aḥd. | sǵr.'dn.aḥd. | sǵr.awldn.aḥd. | s 1140.2
spr.mḫšm. | bn.ḫpšry.b.šbn. | ilštm'ym. | y[---.]bn.'šq. | [---.]bn.tqy. | [---.]b 1041.2
d.mtkt. | tttkr.[--]dn. | 'm.krt.mswn h. | arḫ.tzǵ.l 'gl h. | bn.ḫpt.l umht hm. | k tnḥn.udmm. | w y'ny.krt.t'. 15[128].1.6
d.m'rby. | ṣdqn.gb'ly. | bn.ypy.gb'ly. | bn.grgs.ilštm'y. | bn.ḫran.ilštm'y. | bn.abd'n.ilštm'y. | bn.'n.rqdy. | bn.g'yn. | bn 87[64].30
b'ly. | b[n].ḥyn. | dmn.š'rty. | bn.arwdn.ilšt'y. | bn grgs. | bn.ḫran. | bn.arš[w.b]ṣry. | bn.ykn. | bn.lṣn.'rmy. | bn.b'yn.šly. 99[327].1.10
bn.ḫran. | bn.srt. | bn.adn. | bn.'gw. | bn.urt. | aḫdbu. | pḫ[-]. | b 121[307].1
.arwdn.dd. | mnḫm.w.kbln. | bn.ǵlm.dd. | bn.tbšn.dd. | bn.ḫran.w[.---]. | [-]n.y'rtym. | gmm.w.bn.p[--]. | trn.w.p[-]y. | 131[309].8
ḥrš.anyt. | bnš.gt.gl'd. | bnš.gt.ngr. | r'ym. | bn.ḫri[-]. | bnš.gt.'ttrt. | ad[-]l[-]m. | 'šr.ksdm.yd.lmd hm.lqḥ. 1040.5
spr.ytnm. | bn.ḫlbym. | bn.ady. | bn.'ttry. | bn.ḫrzn. | ady. | bn.birtn. | bn.ḫrzn. | bn.bddn. | bn.anny. | ytrš 115[301].1.5
rnn. | 'bdmlk.bn.'myn. | agyn.r'y. | abmlk.bn.ilrš. | iḫyn.bn.ḫryn. | [ab]ǵl.bn.gdn. | [---].bn.bqš. | [---].bn.pdn. | [---.bn.-] 102[323].4.11
y.tǵrm. | [š]d.tǵr.mtpit.b d.bn.iryn. | [u]bdy.šrm. | [š]d.bn.ḫrmln.b d.bn.tnn. | [š]d.bn.ḫrmln.tn.b d.bn.ḫdmn. | [u]bd 82[300].2.10
.slyn. | ypln.bn.ylḫn. | 'zn.bn.mll. | šrm. | [b]n.špš[yn]. | [b]n.ḫrmln. | bn.tnn. | bn.pndr. | bn.nqq. | ḥrš.bhtm. | bn.izl. | b 85[80].1.12
.bn.iryn. | [u]bdy.šrm. | [š]d.bn.ḫrmln.b d.bn.tnn. | [š]d.bn.ḫrmln.tn.b d.bn.ḫdmn. | [u]bdy.nqdm. | [tlt].šdm.d.n'rb.g 82[300].2.11
l.drdn. | b'l y.rgm. | bn.ḫrn k. | mǵy. | hbt.hw. | ḫrd.w.šl hw. | qr[-]. | akl n.b.grnt. | 2114.3
]yn.bn.tkn.b d.qrt. | šd[.-].dyn.b d.pln.nḥl h. | šd.irdyn.bn.ḫrǵš[-].l.qrt. | šd.iǵlyn.bn.kzbn.l.qr[t]. | šd.pln.bn.tiyn.b d. 2029.16
]. | ar[--.---.--]l. | aty[n.bn.]šm'nt. | ḫnn[.bn].pls. | abrš[p.bn.]ḫrpn. | gmrš[.bn].mrnn. | 'bdmlk.bn.'myn. | agyn.r'y. | ab 102[323].4.6
bn.tmy.qšt.w.ql'. | 'ky.qšt. | 'bdlbit.qšt. | kty.qšt.w.ql'. | bn.ḫršn.qšt.w.ql'. | ilrb.qšt.w.ql'. | psḫn.qšt. | bn.kmy.qšt. | bn. 119[321].3.40
šd.bn.šty.l.bn.tbrn. | šd.bn.ḫtb.l bn.y'drd. | šd.gl.b'lz.l.bn.'mnr. | šd.kn'm.l.bn.'mnr. | 2089.2
[s]ǵr.bn.bdn. | [sǵ]r.bn.psḫn. | alty. | sǵr.npr. | bn.ḫty. | tn.bnš ibrdr. | bnš tlmi. | sǵr.ḫryn. | 'dn.w sǵr h. | bn. 2082.5
n 'gy. | bn zlbn. | bn.aḫ[--]. | bn[.---]. | [-----]. | bn kr[k]. | bn ḫtyn. | w nḥl h. | bn tǵrb. | bn tdnyn. | bn pbn. 2016.3.3
[---.]tltm.d.nlqḥt. | [bn.ḫ]tyn.yd.bt h. | [aǵ]ltn. | tdn.bn.ddy. | 'bdil[.b]n ṣdqn. | bnš 2045.2
m. | bn.qqln. | w.nḥl h. | w.nḥl h. | bn.šml[-]. | bn.brzn. | bn.ḫtr[-]. | bn.yd[--]. | bn.'[---]. | w.nḥ[l h]. | w.nḥ[l h]. | bn.k[-- 116[303].7
-]n. | [--.]'[--]. | [bn].k[--]. | bn.ab[--]. | bn.i[--]. | bn.n[--]. | bn.ḫ[--]. | bn.[---]. | bn.k[--]. 2021.2.16
[---].md.'[ttr]t. | ydy. | bn.škn. | bn.mdt. | bn.ḫ[--]y. | bn.'[-]y. | kn'm. | bn.yš[-]n. | bn.pd[y]. | ttn. | md.'tt[1054.1.5
šd.bn.šty.l.bn.tbrn. | šd.bn.ḫtb.l bn.y'drd. | šd.gl.b'lz.l.bn.'mnr. | šd.kn'm 2089.1
d.krwn.l aḫn. | šd.'yy.l aḫn. | šd.brdn.l bn.bly. | šd gzl.l.bn.tbr[n]. | šd.ḫzmyn.l a[--]. | tn šdm b uš[kn]. 2089.14

.iwrḫṯ. | [ṯn].šdm.b d.gmrd. | [šd.]lbny.b d.tbṯṯb. | [š]d.bn.ṯ[-]rn.b d.ʻdbmlk. | [šd.]bn.brzn.b d.nwrḏ. | [šd.]bn.nḫbl.b 82[300].1.16
]bdḫgb. | [k]lby. | [-]ḫmn. | [š]pšyn. | [ʻb]dmlk. | [---]yn. | bn.ṯ[--]. | bn.idrm. | bn.ymn. | bn.ṣry. | bn.mztn. | bn.šlgyn. | bn 113[400].2.1
ayy. | bn dbb. | w nḥl h. | bn nʻmyn. | bn aṯtyy. | bn ḫlp. | bn.ẓll. | bn ydy. | bn lzn. | bn.ṯyn. | bn gʻr. | bn.prtn. | bn ḫnn. | b 2016.1.12
gm.l ǵlm h. | bʻl.yṣḥ.ʻn.gpn. | w ugr.bn.ǵlmt. | ʻmm ym.bn.ẓlm[t]. | rmt.prʻt.ibr[.mnt]. | ṣḥrrm.ḥbl[.--]. | ʻrpt.tḥt.[---] | 8[51FRAG].8
ǵ | [lm] h.bʻl k.yṣḥ.ʻn. | [gpn].w ugr.b ǵlmt. | [ʻmm.]ym.bn.ẓlmt.r | [mt.prʻ]t.ibr.mnt. | [ṣḥrrm.ḥbl.ʻ]rpt. | [---.---.-]ḥt. | [4[51].7.55
]. | ʻbd[--]. | bn.i[--]. | ʻd[--]. | ild[--]. | bn.qṣn. | ʻlpy. | kṭy. | bn.ẓmn. | bn.trdn. | ypq. | ʻbd. | qrḥ. | abšr. | bn.bdn. | ḏmry. | bn 2117.2.23
l. | bn.grbn. | bn.iršyn. | bn.nklb. | bn.mryn. | [bn.]b[--]. | bn.ẓrl. | bn.illm[-]. | bn.š[---]. | bn.ṣ[---]. | bn.š[---]. | bn.[---]. | bn 115[301].4.23
[-----]. | bn.[---]. | bn.[---]. | w.nḥ[l h]. | bn.ẓr[-]. | mru.skn. | bn.bddn. | bn.ǵrgn. | bn.tgtn. | bn.ḥrẓn. | b 113[400].5.4
tḥm iwrḏr. | l iwrpḫn. | bn y.aḫ y.rgm. | ilm.tǵr k. | tšlm k. | ik y.lḥt. | spr.d likt. | ʻm.ṯr 138.3
tḥm.iwrḏr. | l iwrpḫn. | bn y.aḫ y.rgm. | ilm.tǵr k. | tšlm k. | iky.lḥt. | spr.d likt. | ʻm.ṯr 138.3
mǵy.aliy[n.b]ʻl. | ik.mǵyt.b[t]lt. | ʻnt.mḫṣ y hm[.m]ḫṣ. | bn y.hm[.mkly.ṣ]brt. | ary y[.ẓl].ksp.[a]ṯrt. | k tʻn.ẓl.ksp.w n[4[51].2.25
m[.ṯṯb]. | ky.lik.bn y. | lḥt.akl.ʻm y. | mid y w ǵbn y. | w.bn y.hn kt. | yškn.anyt. | ym.yšrr. | w.ak[l.---]. | [--].š[--.--]. 2061.12
ḥ.knp.nšrm. | bʻl.yṯbr.bʻl.yṯbr.diy. | hmt.hm.tʻpn.ʻl.qbr.bn y. | tšḫṭann.b šnt h.qr.[mym]. | mlk.yṣm.y l km.qr.mym.d 19[1AQHT].3.150
[.---]. | tgr.il.bn h.tr[.---]. | w yʻn.lṭpn.il.d p[id.---]. | šm.bn y.yw.ilt.[---]. | w pʻr.šm.ym[-.---]. | tʻnyn.l zn.tn[.---]. | at.a 1[ʻNT.X].4.14
l]m. | ṯm ny.ʻ[m.]bn y. | mnm.[šl]m[.r]gm[.ṯṯb]. | ky.lik.bn y. | lḥt.akl.ʻm y. | mid y w ǵbn y. | w.bn y.hn kt. | yškn.any 2061.9
rṣ.gršm zbln. | in.b ilm.ʻny h. | w yʻn.lṭpn.il.b pid. | ṯb.bn y.lm ṯb[t] km. | l kḥṯ.zbl k[m.a]nk. | iḥtrš.w [a]škn. | aškn. 16[126].5.24
l k.[il]m. | tǵr k.tšlm k. | hn ny.ʻm n.š[l]m. | ṯm ny.ʻ[m.]bn y. | mnm.[šl]m[.r]gm[.ṯṯb]. | ky.lik.bn y. | lḥt.akl.ʻm y. | mi 2061.7
y. | bn y.yšal. | ṯryl.p rgm. | l mlk.šm y. | w l h[-] yʻl m. | bn y.yšal. | ṯryl.w rgm. | ṯṯb.l aḫ k. | l adn k. 138.16
al. | ṯryl.p rgm. | l mlk.šm y. | w l h.yʻl m. | w h[t] aḫ y. | bn y.yšal. | ṯryl.w rgm[.-]. | ṯṯb.l aḫ k. | l adn k. 138.16
| ik y.lḥt. | spr.d likt. | ʻm.ṯryl. | mh y.rgmt. | w ht.aḫ y. | bn y.yšal. | ṯryl.p rgm. | l mlk.šm y. | w l h[-] yʻl m. | bn y.yšal. 138.11
. | iky.lḥt. | spr.d likt. | ʻm.ṯryl. | mh y.rgmt. | w ht.aḫ y. | bn y.yšal. | ṯryl.p rgm. | l mlk.šm y. | w l h.yʻl m. | w h[t] aḫ y. 138.11
| ymǵy k.bnm.ta[--.---]. | [b]nm.w bnt.ytn k[.---]. | [--]l.bn y.šḥt.w [---]. | [--]tt.msgr.bn k[.---]. | [--]n.tḥm.bʻl[.---]. 59[100].10
bn.iḫy. | bn.iytr. | bn.ʻyn. | bn.ǵzl. | bn.ṣmy. | bn.il[-]šy. | bn.ybšr. | bn.sly. | bn.ḫlbt. | bn.brzt. | bn.ayl. | [-----]. | ʻbd[--]. | b 2117.2.10
bn.šyy. | bn.ḫnzr. | bn.ydbʻl. | bn.ḥyn. | [bn].ar[-]m. | [bn].ḥrp[-]. | [bn].ḫdpṯr. | [bn 124[-].2.3
.---]. | wr[t.---.]b d.yḥmn. | yry[.---.]br. | ydn[.---].kry. | bn.ydd[.---.b]r. | prkl.bʻl.any.d.b d.abr[-]. 2123.6
. | tgyn.yʻrty. | bn.krwn.b.yny.iytlm. | šgryn.ary.b.yny. | bn.yddn.b.rkby. | agyn.agny. | tqbn.mldy. 2071.7
dbb. | w nḥl h. | bn nʻmyn. | bn aṯtyy. | bn ḫlp. | bn.ẓll. | bn ydy. | bn lzn. | bn.ṯyn. | bn gʻr. | bn.prtn. | bn ḫnn. | b[n.-]n. | 2016.1.13
z. | [šd.b d].klby.psl. | [ub]dy.mri.ibrn. | [š]d.bn.bri.b d.bn.ydln. | [u]bdy.ṯǵrm. | [š]d.ṯǵr.mṯpit.b d.bn.iryn. | [u]bdy.šr 82[300].2.6
r[-]. | pqr.yḥd. | bn.ktmn.ṯǵr.hk[l]. | bn.ṯgbr.ṯǵr.hk[l]. | bn.ydln. | bn.ktmn. 1056.10
ṭ. | bn.bsn. | bn.inr[-]. | bn.ṯbil. | bn.iryn. | ṯṯl. | bn.nṣdn. | bn.ydln. | [bn].ʻdy. | [bn].ilyn. 1071.9
[---.]yplṭ. | [---].l.[-]npk. | [---.]l.bn.ydln. | [---].l.blkn. | [---].l.bn.k[--]. | [---].l.klṯṯb. 2136.3
[---.b]n.[y]drn. | [---.]bn.ḫlan. | [--]r bn.mn. | [--]ry. | [--]lim bn.brq 2087.1
ln. | w.nḥl h. | w.nḥl h. | bn.šml[-]. | bn.brzn. | bn.ḫtr[-]. | bn.yd[--]. | bn.ʻ[---]. | w.nḥ[l h]. | w.nḥ[l h]. | bn.k[---]. | bn.y[--- 116[303].8
[-----]. | [bn.]ibln. | ysd. | bn.ṯmq. | bn.agmn. | bn.uṣb. | bn.yzg. | bn.anntn. | bn.kwn. | ǵmšd. | bn.ʻbdḥy. | bn.ubyn. | slp 115[301].4.6
.skn. | bn.ur[-.---]. | bn.knn[.---]y. | bn.ymlk[.b]d.skn. | bn.yḫnn.aḏddy. | bn.pdǵy.mḫdy. | bn.yyn.mḏrǵl. | bn.ʻlr. | ḫtp 2014.16
my.qšt. | šdyn.qšt. | bdn.qšt.w.qlʻ. | bn.šmlbi.qšt.w.qlʻ. | bn.yy.qšt. | ilrb.qšt. | bn.nmš.ṯt.qšt.w.qlʻ. | bʻl.qšt.w.qlʻ. 119[321].4.14
ym. | [ʻ]rmy.w snry. | [b]n.sdy.bn.ṯty. | bn.ḥyn.bn.ǵlm. | bn.yyn.w.bn.au[pš]. | bn.kdrn. | ʻrgzy.w.bn.ʻdy. | bn.gmḥn.w. 131[309].25
bn.ymlk[.b]d.skn. | bn.yḫnn.aḏddy. | bn.pdǵy.mḫdy. | bn.yyn.mḏrǵl. | bn.ʻlr. | ḫtpy.aḏddy. | ynḥm.aḏddy. | ykny.aḏ 2014.18
gdṯb.ʻšrm. | b.bn.ibn.arbʻt.ʻšrt. | b.bn.mnn.ṯṯm. | b.rpan.bn.yyn.ʻšrt. | b.ypʻr.ʻšrm. | b.nʻmn.bn.ply.ḫmšt.l.ʻšrm. | b.gdn. 2054.1.15
| bn.arwdn.ilštʻy. | bn grgs. | bn.ḫran. | bn.arš[w.b]ṣry. | bn.ykn. | bn.lṣn.ʻrmy. | bn.bʻyn.šly. | bn.ynḥn. | bn.ʻbdilm.hzp 99[327].2.2
bn.bʻl.ṣdq. | bn.army. | bn.rpiyn. | bn.army. | bn.krmn. | bn.ykn. | bn.ʻṯtrab. | uṣn[-]. | bn.altn. | bn.aš[-]š. | bn.štn. | bn.ilš 1046.1.11
n. | ygmr.aḏddy. | gln.aṯṭ. | ddy.[a]ḏddy. | bn.mlkr[šp]. | bn.y[k]n. | ynḥm. | bn.abd.bʻ[l]. | mnḥm.bn[.---]. | krmn[py]. | 2014.46
[--.l]bš.mtn.b.arʻt. | [--.l]bš.bn.yknʻ.b.arʻt. | [--.l]bš.bn.grbn.b.ṯqlm. | [--.lb]š.bn.sgryn.b[.ṯ 135[330].2
----]. | [-----]. | [-----]. | [-----]. | n[----]. | bn.[---]. | bn.[---]. | bn.yk[--]. | bn.šmm. | bn.irgy. | w.nḥl h. | w.nḥl hm. | [bn].pmn 1046.2.8
zr.yʻdb.u ymn. | u šmal.b p hm.w l.tšbʻn y.aṯt.itrḫ. | y bn.ašld.šu.ʻdb.tk.mdbr qdš. | ṯm tgrgr.l abnm.w l.ʻṣm.šbʻ.šnt 23[52].65
n.ṯṣq[-]. | mnn.bn.krmn. | bn.umḫ. | yky.bn.slyn. | ypln.bn.ylḥn. | ʻzn.bn.mll. | šrm. | [b]n.špš[yn]. | [b]n.ḫrmln. | bn.tn 85[80].1.8
[-]. | bn.anny. | bn.ʻmtḏl. | bn.ʻmyn. | bn.alz. | bn.birtn. | [bn.]ylkn. | [bn.]krwn. | [bn.-]ty. | [bn.]iršn. | bn.[---]. | bn.b[--]. 117[325].1.14
]šr.pḫr.klat. | tqtnṣn.w tldn.tld.[ilm.]nʻmm.agzr ym. | bn.ym.ynqm.b a[p.]ḏ[d.r]gm.l il.ybl. | aṯt y.il.ylt.mh.ylt.ilmy 23[52].59
iqnu.šmt[.---]. | [b]n.šrm. | iqran.ilm.nʻmm[.agzry ym.bn]ym. | ynqm.b ap zd.aṯrt.[---]. | špš.mṣprt dlt hm[.---]. | w 23[52].23
r]gm.l il.ybl. | aṯt y.il.ylt.mh.ylt.ilmy nʻmm. | agzr ym.bn ym.ynqm.b ap.ḏd.št.špt. | l arṣ.špt l šmm.w ʻrb.b p hm.ʻṣ 23[52].61
mr[-]. | bt[.--]b bʻl.b qrb. | bt.w yʻn.aliyn. | bʻl.ašt m.kṯr bn. | ym.kṯr.bnm.ʻdt. | yptḥ.ḥln.b bht m. | urbt.b qrb.[h]kl | 4[51].7.15
. | [---d]nil. | [a]drdn. | [---]n. | pǵdn. | ṯṯpḥ. | ḥgbn. | šrm. | bn.ymil. | bn.kḏǵdl. | [-]mn. | [--]n. | [ḫr]š.qṯn. | [---]n. | [-----]. | [1039.2.3
yplṭ. | ʻbdmlk. | ynḥm. | aḏddn. | mtn. | plsy. | qṭn. | ypr. | bn.ymy. | bn.ʻrd. | [-]b.da[-]. | [--]l[--]. | [-----]. 1035.4.12
[--.]skn. | bn.s[--.b]d.skn. | bn.ur[-.---]. | bn.knn[.---]y. | bn.ymlk[.b]d.skn. | bn.yḫnn.aḏddy. | bn.pdǵy.mḫdy. | bn.yy 2014.15
y. | [bn.b]rq. | [bn.--]r. | [bn.--]tn. | [bn.-]rmn. | bn.prtn. | bn.ymn. | bn.dby. | bn.ir[--]. | bn.kr[--]. | bn.nn[-]. | [-----]. | [---- 124[-].5.9
ḫmn. | [š]pšyn. | [ʻb]dmlk. | [---]yn. | bn.ṯ[--]. | bn.idrm. | bn.ymn. | bn.ṣry. | bn.mztn. | bn.šlgyn. | bn.[-]gštn. | bn[.n]klb. 113[400].2.3
. | bn.iy[--]. | bn.ḫ[---]. | bn.plš. | bn.ubr. | bn.ʻpṯb. | ṯbry. | bn.ymn. | krty. | bn.abr[-]. | yrpu. | kdn. | pʻṣ. | bn.liy. | ydʻ. | šm 2117.1.19
. | [w a]rbʻ kkr ʻl bn[.--]. | [w] ṯlṯ šmn. | [w a]r[bʻ] ksp ʻl bn ymn. | šb šr šmn [--] ṯryn. | ḫm[š]m l ʻšr ksp ʻl bn llit. | [--]l 1103.4
byn. | šd.bn.li[y]. | šd.bn.š[--]y. | šd.bn.ṯ[---]. | šd.ʻdmn[.bn.]ynḥm. | šd.bn.ṯmr[n.m]idḫy. | šd.ṯbʻm[.--]y. 2026.8
. | bn.arš[w.b]ṣry. | bn.ykn. | bn.lṣn.ʻrmy. | bn.bʻyn.šly. | bn.ynḥn. | bn.ʻbdilm.hzpy. 99[327].2.5
[--]ps. | [--]ṯb. | [--]ln. | [---]r. | [---]y. | bn.aḏdt. | bn.atnb. | bn.yšd. | bn.bršm. | bn.gtprg. | gtpbn. | bn.b[--]. | [b]n.[---]. | bn. 1057.10
d.w.ḥrṣ. | bn.ilbʻl. | bn.idrm. | bn.grgš. | bn.bly. | bn.apṯ. | bn.ysd. | bn.pl[-]. | bn.ṯbʻnq. | brqd. | bnn. | kbln.ṣ[md]. | bn gm 2113.12
qšt.w.qlʻ. | bn.zry.q[š]t.w.qlʻ. | bn.tlmyn.ṯt.qštm.w.qlʻ. | bn.ysd.qšt. | [ǵ]mrm. | ilgn.qšt. | abršp.qšt. | ssg.qšt. | ynḥm.qšt 104[316].9

ḫmš[t]. | ʻzn.bn.brn.ḫmšt. | mʻrt.ḫmšt. | arttb.bn.ḫmšt. | bn.ysr[.ḫmš]t. | ṣ[-]r.ḫ[mšt]. | ʻzn.ḫ[mšt]. 1062.29
ḫdy[m]. | bn.ḥgb[n]. | bn.ulbt[-]. | ḏkry[-]. | bn.tlm[yn]. | bn.yʻdd. | bn.idly[-]. | bn.ʻbd[--]. | bn.ṣd[qn]. 2017.6
šd.bn.šty.l.bn.ṭbrn. | šd.bn.ḫtb.l bn.yʻḏrd. | šd.gl.bʻlz.l.bn.ʻmnr. | šd.knʻm.l.bn.ʻmnr. | šd.bn.kr 2089.2
. | bn.gṯrn.q[š]t. | bn.ḫdi.ṯt.qštm.w.ṯn.qlʻm. | ildgn.qšt. | bn.yʻrn.ṯt.qštm w.qlʻ. | bn.ḥṣn.qšt.w.qlʻ. | bn.gdn.ṯt.qštm.w.ql 119[321].3.10
abn.uškny. | bn.arz.šʻrty. | bn.ibrd.mʻrby. | ṣdqn.gbʻly. | bn.ypy.gbʻly. | bn.grgs.ilštmʻy. | bn.ḫran.ilštmʻy. | bn.abdʻn.ilš 87[64].28
bn.ǵlmn.ary. | [bn].šdy. | [bn].gmḥ. | [---]ty. | [b]n.ypy.gbʻly. | b[n].ḫyn. | ḏmn.šʻrty. | bn.arwdn.ilštʻy. | bn gr 99[327].1.5
n.ilrš.ṯkt. | ilṯḥm.bn.šrn.ṯkt. | šmlbu.bn.grb.ṯkt. | šmlbu.bn.ypʻ.ṯkt. | [---.--]m. 2085.14
n ʻntn.[---]. | bn agyn[.---]. | b[n] ʻṯlṯ[.---]. | bn qṭy[.---]. | bn ypʻ[.---]. | [---]bʻm[.---]. | [-----]. 105[86].5
y. | bn.ʻmyn. | bdl.mrynm. | bn.ṣqn. | bn.šyn. | bn.prtn. | bn.ypr. | mrum. | bn.ʻ[--]t. | bn.adty. | bn.krwn. | bn.nǵsk. | bn.q 113[400].3.10
rbn.ʻdd.nryn. | [ab]r[p]u.bn.kbd. | [-]m[-].bn.ṣmrt. | liy.bn.yṣi. | ḏmrhd.bn.srt. | [---.--]m. | ʻbdmlk.bn.šrn. | ʻbdbʻl.bn.k 102[322].6.6
[---]y. | [---.]w.nḥl h. | bn ksln.ṯlṯḥ. | bn yṣmḫ.bn.ṭrn w nḥl h. | bn srd.bn agmn. | bn [-]ln.bn.ṭbil. | 101[10].4
| w.[-----]. | w.abǵl.nḥ[l h.--]. | w.unṯ.aḫd.l h[.---]. | dnn.bn.yṣr[.---]. | sln.bn.ʻṯt[-.---]. | pdy.bn.nr[-.---]. | abmlk.bn.un[- 90[314].1.5
mtn[-.---]. | aḫyn.bn.nbk[-.---]. | ršpn.bn.bʻly[.---]. | bnil.bn.yṣr[.---]. | ʻdyn.bn.udr[-.---]. | w.ʻdʻ.nḥl h[.---]. | w.yknil.nḥ 90[314].1.12
n. | bn.ʻgw. | bn.urt. | aḫdbu. | pḫ[-]. | bn.ʻb . | bn.uḏn[-]. | bn.yṣr. 121[307].10
.ʻrb. | b.ṯbʻm. | ydn.bn.ilrpi. | w.ṯbʻm.ʻrb.b.ʻ[d]n. | ḏmry.bn.yrm. | ʻrb.b.adʻy. 2079.9
. | w.nḥl h. | bn.sny. | bn.ablḥ. | [-----]. | w [---]. | bn.[---]. | bn.yr[--]. | bn.kṯr[t]. | bn.šml. | bn.arnbt. | qdšm. | b[-.--]t. | [---.- 2163.2.4
tgḏn. | bn.ḫdyn. | bn.sgr. | bn.aǵltn. | bn.ktln. | bn.ʻgwn. | bn.yšmʻ. | bdl.mdrǵlm. | bn.mmy. | bn.ḫnyn. | bn.knn. | khnm. 104[316].9
.šd. | mit.ḫmšt.kbd. | [l.]gmn.bn.usyy. | mit.ṯṯm.kbd. | l.bn.yšmʻ. | mit.arbʻm.kbd. | l.liy.bn.ʻmyn. | mit.ḫmšm.kbd. | d. 1143.10
[---.-]bʻm. | [---.b]n.yšm[ʻ]. | [---.]mlkr[-] h.b.nṯk. | [---.]šbʻm. | [---.]ḫrg.ʻšrm. | 2153.2
]t. | ydy. | bn.škn. | bn.mdt. | bn.ḫ[--]y. | bn.ʻ[-]y. | knʻm. | bn.yš[-]n. | bn.pd[y]. | ttn. | md.ʻṯt[rt]. | kṭkt. | bn.ṯtn[--]. | [m]d. 1054.1.8
ḥnd. | ʻmṯtmr. | bn.nqmpʻ. | mlk.ugrt. | ytn.bt.anndr. | bn.ytn.bnš. | [ml]k.d.b riš. | [--.-]nt. | [l.ʻb]dmlk. | [--.-]m[-]r. | [1009.6
lq. | bn mʻnt. | bn kbdy. | bn krk. | bn srty. | bn lth ḫlq. | bn ytr. | bn ilšpš. | ubrš. | bn gmš ḫlq. | bn ʻgy. | bn zlbn. | bn.aḫ 2016.2.15
. | bn.armg[-]. | bʻlmṯpṭ. | [bn].ayḫ. | [---]rn. | ill. | ǵlmn. | bn.ytrm. | bn.ḫgbt. | mtn. | mḫtn. | [p]lsy. | bn.ḥrš. | [--.]kbd. | [- 1035.2.10
.army.ṯt.qštm.w[.]q[lʻ]. | bn.rpš.qšt.w.qlʻ. | bn.ǵb.qšt. | bn.ytrm.qšt.w.qlʻ. | bn.ʻbdyrḫ.qšt.w.q[lʻ]. | bn.lky.qšt. | bn.dll. 119[321].3.25
| bn.yd[--]. | bn.ʻ[---]. | w.nḥ[l h]. | w.nḥ[l h]. | bn.k[---]. | bn.y[---]. | [bn].i[---]. 116[303].13
. | bn.krny[-]. | bn.mt. | bn.nzʻn. | bn.slmz[-]. | bn.kʻ[--]. | bn.y[---]. | [-----]. | [bn.a]mdy. | bn.ḫlln. | bn.kṯn. | bn.abn. | bn. 2021.1.20
[.rpum.l grnt]. | i[ln]y[m].l mṯʻt[.---]. | [-]m[.---]. | h.hn bn k.hn[.---]. | bn bn.aṯr k.hn[.---]. | yd k.ṣǵr.tnšq.špt k.ṯm. | ṯ 22.2[124].2
l.ybnn. | adn y. | rgm. | ṯḥm.t[g]yn. | bn k. | l.p[ʻn.adn y]. | q[lt.---]. | l.yb[nn]. | bʻl y.r[gm]. | ṯḥm.ʻbd 2115.1.5
l.mlkt. | um y.rgm. | ṯḥm.mlk. | bn k. | l.pʻn.um y. | qlt.l.um y. | yšlm.ilm. | ṯǵr k.tšlm k. | hl ny 50[117].4
l mlkt.u[m] y. | [rg]m[.]t[ḥm]. | mlk.bn [k]. | [l].pʻn.um [y]. | qlt[.l um] y. | yšlm.il[m]. | ṯǵ[r] k.tš[l 1013.3
m.yṣḥ il. | l rbt.aṯrt ym.šmʻ. | l rbt.aṯr[t] ym.tn. | aḥd.b bn k.amlkn. | w tʻn.rbt.aṯrt ym. | bl.nmlk.ydʻ.ylḥn. | w yʻn.lṭp 6.1.46[49.1.18]
m.w bnt.ytn k[.---]. | [--]l.bn y.šḥt.w [---]. | [--]tt.msgr.bn k[.---]. | [--]n.ṯḥm.bʻl[.---]. 59[100].11
[-]l.bn.ḥrn. | aḫty.bt.abm. | [-]rbn.ʻdd.nryn. | [ab]r[p]u.bn.kbd. | [-]m[-].bn.ṣmrt. | liy.bn.yṣi. | ḏmrhd.bn.srt. | [---.--]m 102[322].6.4
| bn.kyn. | bn.ʻbdḥr. | [-]prm ḫlq. | [---]n ḫlq. | bn mʻnt. | bn kbdy. | bn krk. | bn srty. | bn lth ḫlq. | bn ytr. | bn ilšpš. | ub 2016.2.11
swn. | mrynm. | ʻzn. | ḫyn. | ʻmyn. | ilyn. | yrbʻm. | nʻmn. | bn.kbl. | knʻm. | bdlm. | bn.ṣǵr. | klb. | bn.mnḥm. | bn.brqn. | bn. 1046.3.40
n. | bn.a[--]. | [------]. | [------]. | [------]. | [------]. | [------]. | [bn.]kblbn[.---]. | [bn] uškny. | bn.krny[-]. | bn.mt. | bn.nzʻn. | b 2021.1.13
ʻzn.bn.irbn. | bn.mglb. | bn.ntp. | ʻmyn.bn ǵḫpn. | bn.kbln. | bn.bly. | bn.ṯʻy. | bn.nṣdn. | klby. 104[316].5
.ʻṣr. | [---]m. | [bn.]ulnhr. | [bn.p]rn. | [bn.a]nny. | [---]n. | bn.kbln. | bn.pdy. | bn.ṯpdn. 1075.2.1
. | mtnn. | bn gš[-]. | bn gbrn. | bn uldy. | synn.bn knʻm. | bn kbr. | bn iytlm. | bn ayln. | bn.kln. | bn.ʻlln. | bn.liy. | bn.nqṭ 1064.20
.l.iytlm. | šd.bn.nbʻm.l.ṯpṭbʻl. | šd.bn mšrn.l.ilšpš. | [šd.bn].kbr.l.snrn. | [---.--]k.l.gmrd. | [---.--]ṯ.l.yšn. | [šd.--]ln. | b d. 2030.1.6
.birtn. | bn.ḥrẓn. | bn.bddn. | bn.anny. | ytršp. | bn.szn. | bn.kdgdl. | bn.glʻd. | bn.ktln. | [bn].ǵrgn. | bn.pb[-]. | bn.[---]. | b 115[301].1.13
l h. | bn.ʻbl. | bn.[-]rṯn. | bn[.---]. | bn u[l]pm. | bn ʻ[p]ty. | bn.kdgdl. | bn.smyy. | bn.lbn. | bn.šlmn. | bn.mly. | pslm. | bn.a 2163.3.4
. | [-----]. | [bn.]nnr. | [bn.]aglby. | [bn.]bʻly. | [mḏ]rǵlm. | [bn.]kdgdl. | [b]n.qṭn. | [b]n.ǵrgn. | [b]n.tgḏn. | bn.ḫdyn. | bn.sg 104[316].9
dm. | bn.alṯn. | bn.dly. | bn.btry. | bn.ḫdmn. | [bn].šty. | [bn].kdgdl. | [---.-]y[-.] 2018.7
[b]n[.---]. | bn [-]ʻy. | [b]n [i]lmd. | bn [t]bdn. | bn štn. | b[n] kdn. | bn dwn. | bn ḏrn. 2088.6
.yṣi. | ḏmrhd.bn.srt. | [---.--]m. | ʻbdmlk.bn.šrn. | ʻbdbʻl.bn.kdn. | gzl.bn.qldn. | gld.bt.klb. | l[---].bt.ḫzli. | bn.iḫyn. | ṣd 102[323].3.3
lk. | arsw. | dqn. | ṯlṯ.klbm. | ḫmn. | [---.-]rsd. | bn[.-]pṯ. | bn kdrn. | awldn. | arswn.yʻr[ty.--]. | bn.ugr. | gny. | ṯn.mdm. 86[305].8
[n.---.ub]rʻy. | [bn.---.ubr]ʻy. | b[n.---]. | bn[.---.ušk]ny. | bn.kdrn.uškny. | bn.lgn.uškny. | bn.abn.uškny. | bn.arz.šʻrty. 87[64].22
b]n.sdy.bn.ṯty. | bn.ḥyn.bn.ǵlm. | bn.yyn.w.bn.au[pš]. | bn.kdrn. | ʻrgzy.w.bn.ʻdy. | bn.gmḥn.w.ḥgbt. | bn.tgḏn. | yny. | 131[309].26
[bn.]ubn. | kbšm. | bn.abḏr. | bn.kpltn. | bn.prn. | ʻbdm. | bn.kdǵbr. | bn.mṣrn. | bn.[-]dr[-]. | [---]l[-]. | [--]ym. | [--]rm. | [b 114[324].2.11
. | [a]drdn. | [---]n. | pǵdn. | ṯtpḫ. | ḥgbn. | šrm. | bn.ymil. | bn.kdǵdl. | [-]mn. | [--]n. | [ḥr]š.qṯn. | [---]n. | [-----]. | [--]dd. | [bʻ 1039.2.4
. | kd.ʻl.ẓrm. | kd.ʻl.šz.bn pls. | kd.ʻl.ynḥm. | tgrm.šmn.d.bn.kwy. | ʻl.šlmym.ṯmn.kbd. | ṯtm.šmn. 1082.2.8
ysd. | bn.ṯmq. | bn.agmn. | bn.uṣb. | bn.yzg. | bn.anntn. | bn.kwn. | ǵmšd. | bn.ʻbdḥy. | bn.ubyn. | slpd. | bn.atnb. | bn.kt 115[301].4.8
dyn.b d.pln.nḥl h. | šd.irdyn.bn.ḫrǵš[-].l.qrt. | šd.iǵlyn.bn.kzbn.l.qr[t]. | šd.pln.bn.tiyn.b d.ilmhr nḥl h. | šd knn.bn.a 2029.17
aršw. | bn.ḫzrn. | bn.iǵyn. | w.nḥl h. | bn.ksd. | bn.bršm. | bn.kzn. | w.nḥl h. | w.nḥl hm. | w.[n]ḥl hm. | b[n.---]. | bn.gzry. 113[400].2.20
ṣṣ.bn.ilyn.ṯlṯm. | ṣṣ.bn.kzn.ṯlṯm. | ṣṣ.bn.tlmyn.ʻšrm. | ṣṣ.bn.krwn.ʻš[rm]. | ṣṣ.bn.irš 2096.2
ʻn b gt prn. | šd.bn.gby.gt.prn. | šd.bn.kryn.gt.prn. | šd.bn.ky.gt.prn. | šd.hwil.gt.prn. | šd.ḥr.gt.prn. | šd.bn.ṯbǵl.gt.pr 1104.6
.ṣṣb. | bn.bʻltn ḫlq. | bn.mlkbn. | bn.asyy ḫlq. | bn.kṯly. | bn.kyn. | bn.ʻbdḥr. | [-]prm ḫlq. | [---]n ḫlq. | bn mʻnt. | bn kbd 2016.2.6
ṯm.w.ṯt.ṯprtm. | b.ʻšr[m.]ksp. | ḫmš.kkr.ṣml. | b.ʻšrt.b d.bn.kyn. | ʻšr.kkr.šʻrt. | b d.urtn.b.arbʻm. | arbʻt.ʻšrt.ḫrṣ. | b.ṯql 2100.13
bn.ǵs.ḥrš.šʻty. | ʻdy.bn.slʻy.gbly. | yrm.bʻl.bn.kky. 2121.3
ṯn.bn.klby. | bn.iytr. | [ʻ]bdyrḫ. | [b]n.ggʻt. | [ʻ]dy. | armwl. | uwaḫ. 2086.1
dl.ar. | bn.šyn. | bn.ubrš. | bn.d[--]b. | abrpu. | bn.k[n]y. | bn.klyn. | bn.gmḥn. | ḥnn. | ayab. | bn.gm[--]. | bn.[---]. | g[---]. | 1035.3.7
bn uldy. | synn.bn knʻm. | bn kbr. | bn iytlm. | bn ayln. | bn.kln. | bn.ʻlln. | bn.liy. | bn.nqṭn. | bn abrḫṯ. | bn.grdy. | bn.ṣl 1064.23

.|bn h.ʿd.ʿlm.|šḥr.ʿlmt.|bnš bnšm.|l.yqḥnn.b d.|bʿln.bn.kltn.|w.b d.bn h.ʿd.|ʿlm.w unṯ.|in.b h. 1008.18
.--].|[---.]yd.|[k]rm h.yd.|[k]lkl h.|[w] ytn.nn.|l.bʿln.bn.|kltn.w l.|bn h.ʿd.ʿlm.|šḥr.ʿlmt.|bnš bnšm.|l.yqḥnn.b d 1008.12
|[--]y.l arṣ[.id]y.alt.l aḫš.idy.alt.in l y.|[--]t.bʿl.ḥẓ.ršp.b[n].km.yr.klyt h.w lb h.|[ṯ]n.p k.b ǵr.ṯn.p k.b ḫlb.k tgwln. 1001.1.3
lbšt.bir.mlak.|šmm.tmr.zbl.mlk.|šmm.tlak.ṭl.amr..|bn km k bk[r.z]bl.am..|rkm.agzrt[.--].arḫ..|bʿl.azrt.ʿnt.[-]ld 13[6].28
št.w.qlʿ.|bn.ḫršn.qšt.w.qlʿ.|ilrb.qšt.w.qlʿ.|psḥn.qšt.|bn.kmy.qšt.|bn.ilḥbn.qšt.w.q[lʿ].|ršpab.qšt.w.qlʿ.|pdrn.qšt. 119[321].3.43
dnn.ṯlṯ.ṣmdm.|bn.ʿmnr.|bn.kmn.|bn.ibyn.|bn.mryn.ṣmd.w.ḥrṣ.|bn.prsn.ṣmd.w.ḥrṣ. 2113.3
n.ksln.|bn.ṣrym.|bn.ṯmq.|bn.ntp.|bn.mlk.|bn.ṯʿ[-].|bn.km[-].|bn.r[--].|[bn.]ʿ[---].|[bn.]r[---].|[bn.]ḥ[---].|[bn.]š 1073.1.12
bn.ǵlyn.|bdl.ar.|bn.šyn.|bn.ubrš.|bn.d[--]b.|abrpu.|bn.k[n]y.|bn.klyn.|bn.gmḥn.|ḥnn.|ayab.|bn.gm[--].|bn.[-- 1035.3.6
.adddy.|ildy.adddy.|grʿ.adddy.|ʿbd.ršp adddy.|ʿdn.bn.knn.|iwrḫz.b d.skn.|škny.adddy.|mšu.adddy.|plsy.add 2014.36
ʿl[--].|bn.gld.|bn.ṣmy.|bn.mry[n].|bn.mgn.|bn.ʿdn.|bn.knn.|bn.py.|bn.mk[-].|bn.by[--].|bn.a[--].|bn.iy[--].|bn. 2117.1.8
bn.ʿgwn.|bn.yšmʿ.|bdl.mdrǵlm.|bn.mmy.|bn.ḫnyn.|bn.knn.|khnm.|bn.ṯʿy.|w.nḥl h.|w.nḥl hm.|bn.nqly.|bn.s 104[316].9
n.|bldn.|[-]ln.|[-]ldn.|[i]wryn.|ḫbsn.|ulmk.|ʿdršp.|bn.knn.|pdyn.|bn.aṯtl.ṯn.|kdln.akdṯb.|ṯn.b gt yknʿm. 1061.18
.qlʿ.|ḫlb.rpš.|abmn.qšt.|ẓẓn.qšt.|dqry.qš[t].|rkby.|bn.knn.qšt.|pbyn.qšt.|yddn.qšt.w.qlʿ.|šʿrt.|bn.il.qšt.w.qlʿ.| 119[321].2.36
--.]hbṭn.|bn.m[--.]skn.|bn.s[--.b]d.skn.|bn.ur[-.---].|bn.knn[.---]y.|bn.ymlk[.b]d.skn.|bn.yḥnn.adddy.|bn.pdǵy 2014.14
.|bn.srwd.|mtnn.|bn gš[-].|bn gbrn.|bn uldy.|synn.bn knʿm.|bn kbr.|bn iytlm.|bn ayln.|bn.kln.|bn.ʿlln.|bn.li 1064.19
iršyn.|bn.ʿzn.|bn.aršw.|bn.ḫzrn.|bn.iǵyn.|w.nḥl h.|bn.ksd.|bn.bršm.|bn.kzn.|w.nḥl h.|w.nḥl hm.|w.[n]ḥl hm 113[400].2.18
ǵ]ltn.|[--]ṯm.b.gt.irbṣ.|[--]šmyn.|[w.]nḥl h.|bn.qṣn.|bn.ksln.|bn.ṣrym.|bn.ṯmq.|bn.ntp.|bn.mlk.|bn.ṯʿ[-].|bn.k 1073.1.6
[---]y.|[---.]w.nḥl h.|bn ksln.ṯlṯh.|bn yṣmḥ.bn.ṯrn w nḥl h.|bn srd.bn agmn.|bn 101[10].3
bn] uškny.|bn.krny[-].|bn.mt.|bn.nzʿn.|bn.slmz[-].|bn.kʿ[--].|bn.y[---].|[-----].|[bn.a]mdy.|bn.ḫlln.|bn.kṯn.|bn 2021.1.19
[---.--]t.|[-----].|[---.]l[--].|[bn.]ubn.|kbšm.|bn.abdr.|bn.kpltn.|bn.prn.|ʿbdm.|bn.kdǵbr.|bn.mṣrn.|bn.[-]dr[-].|[114[324].2.7
n.ṯlṯ.šmn.|a[---.]kdm.|ʿ[---]ʿm.kd.|a[----]ḥr.ṯlṯ.|y[---.bn.]kran.ḫmš.|ʿ[---].kd.|amry.kdm.|mnn.bn.gttn.kdm.|yn 136[84].6
mdrǵlm.dt.inn.|b d.tlmyn.|b d.gln.ary.|tgyn.yʿrty.|bn.krwn.b.yny.iytlm.|sgryn.ary.b.yny.|bn.yddn.b.rkby.|ag 2071.5
bn.šyn.|bn.prtn.|bn.ypr.|mrum.|bn.ʿ[--]t.|bn.adty.|bn.krwn.|bn.ngsk.|bn.qnd.|bn.pity.|w.nḥl h.|bn.rt.|bn.l[- 113[400].3.14
y.|bn.ʿmtdl.|bn.ʿmyn.|bn.alz.|bn.birtn.|[bn.]ylkn.|[bn.]krwn.|[bn.-]ty.|[bn.]iršn.|bn.[---].|bn.b[--].|bn.š[--].|b 117[325].1.15
n.yʿdrd.|šd.gl.bʿlz.l.bn.ʿmnr.|šd.knʿm.l.bn.ʿmnr.|šd.bn.krwn.l bn.ʿmyn.|šd.bn.prmn.l aḫny.|šd.bn ḥnn.l bn.adl 2089.5
ṣṣ.bn.ilyn.ṯlṯm.|ṣṣ.bn.kzn.ṯlṯm.|ṣṣ.bn.tlmyn.ʿšrm.|ṣṣ.bn.krwn.ʿš[rm].|ṣṣ.bn.iršyn.[---].|[ṣṣ].bn.ilbʿl.ṯl[ṯ]m.|ṣṣ.bn. 2096.4
t b d.skn.|šd.bn.ubrʿn b gt prn.|šd.bn.gby.gt.prn.|šd.bn.kryn.gt.prn.|šd.bn.ky.gt.prn.|šd.hwil.gt.prn.|šd.ḥr.gt.p 1104.5
mš ḫlq.|bn ʿgy.|bn zlbn.|bn.aḫ[--].|bn[.---].|[-----].|bn kr[k].|bn ḫtyn.|w nḥl h.|bn tgrb.|bn ṯdnyn.|bn pbn. 2016.3.2
bn.ʿbdḥr.|[-]prm ḫlq.|[---]n ḫlq.|bn mʿnt.|bn kbdy.|bn krk.|bn srty.|bn lth ḫlq.|bn ytr.|bn ilšpš.|ubrš.|bn gm 2016.2.12
].|[ag]dtb.bn[.---].|ʿbdil.bn.[---].|ʿpṯn.bn.ṯsq[-].|mnn.bn.krmn.|bn.umḫ.|yky.bn.slyn.|ypln.bn.ylḥn.|ʿzn.bn.mll. 85[80].1.5
.|bn.arm.|bn.bʿl.ṣdq.|bn.army.|bn.rpiyn.|bn.army.|bn.krmn.|bn.ykn.|bn.ʿṯtrab.|uṣn[-].|bn.alṯn.|bn.aš[-]š.|bn 1046.1.10
[------].|[------].|[------].|[bn.]kblbn[.---].|[bn] uškny.|bn.krny[-].|bn.mt.|bn.nzʿn.|bn.slmz[-].|bn.kʿ[--].|bn.y[---] 2021.1.15
tqrb.w ld.bn.l h.|w tqrb.w ld.bnt.l h.|mk.b šbʿ.šnt.|bn.krt.km hm.tdr.|ap.bnt.ḥry.|km hm.w ṯḫss.aṯrt.|ndr h. 15[128].3.23
]tn.|[bn.-]rmn.|bn.prtn.|bn.ymn.|bn.dby.|bn.ir[--].|bn.kr[--].|bn.nn[-].|[-----].|[-----].|[---.-]l[-].|[bn.-]dt[-].|[b 124[-].5.12
.--]ṯ.l.yšn.|[šd.--]ln.|b d.trǵds.|šd.ṯʿlb.|b d.bn.pl.|šd.bn.kt.|b d.pdy.|šd.ḫzr.|[b d].d[---]. 2030.2.5
|bn.ršp.ary.|bn.ǵlmn ary.|bn.ḥṣbn ary.|bn.šdy ary.|bn.ktkt.mʿqby.|bn.[---.]ṯlḥny.|b[n.---.ub]rʿy.|[bn.---.ubr]ʿy. 87[64].16
.|[b]n.ǵrgn.|[b]n.tgdn.|bn.ḫdyn.|bn.sgr.|bn.aǵltn.|bn.ktln.|bn.ʿgwn.|bn.yšmʿ.|bdl.mdrǵlm.|bn.mmy.|bn.ḫny 104[316].9
.bddn.|bn.anny.|ytršp.|bn.szn.|bn.kdgdl.|bn.glʿd.|bn.ktln.|[bn].ǵrgn.|bn.pb[-].|bn.[---].|bn.[---].|bn.[---].|bn. 115[301].1.15
bn.kwn.|ǵmšd.|bn.ʿbdḥy.|bn.ubyn.|slpd.|bn.atnb.|bn.ktmn.|bn.pity.|bn.iryn.|bn.ʿbl.|bn.grbn.|bn.iršyn.|bn. 115[301].4.14
[---.--]n.|[-----].|[---.-]bd.|[---]ybʿ.bʿl.ḫr[-].|pqr.yḥd.|bn.ktmn.ṯǵr.hk[l].|bn.ṯgbr.ṯǵr.hk[l].|bn.ydln.|bn.ktmn. 1056.8
.yḥd.|bn.ktmn.ṯǵr.hk[l].|bn.ṯgbr.ṯǵr.hk[l].|bn.ydln.|bn.ktmn. 1056.11
m].|mʿq[bym].|tšʿ.ʿ[šr.bnš].|ǵr.ṯ[--.---].|ṣbu.any[t].|bn.kṯan.|ǵr.tšʿ[.ʿšr.b]nš.|ṣbu.any[t].|bn abdḥ[r].|pdym.|ḫ 79[83].8
|[--]nbbl.|bn bl.|bn dkn.|bn ils.|bn ḫšbn.|bn uryy.|bn kṯl.|bn army.|bn gln.|bn abg.|bn.ngry.|bn.srwd.|mtnn 1064.9
n.-]n.|bn.ṣṣb.|bn.bʿltn ḫlq.|bn.mlkbn.|bn.asyy ḫlq.|bn.kṯly.|bn.kyn.|bn.ʿbdḥr.|[-]prm ḫlq.|[---]n ḫlq.|bn mʿnt. 2016.2.5
[-].|bn.kʿ[--].|bn.y[---].|[-----].|[bn.a]mdy.|bn.ḫlln.|bn.kṯn.|bn.abn.|bn.nskn.|bn.gmrn.|bn[.-]škn.|[---.--]n.|[-- 2021.2.4
|bn.sny.|bn.ablḥ.|[-----].|w [---].|bn.[---].|bn.yr[--].|bn.kṯr[t].|bn.šml.|bn.arnbt.|qdšm.|b[-.--]t.|[---.-]l[--].|[---. 2163.2.5
n.|bn.gmrn.|bn[.-]škn.|[---.--]n.|[---.--]n.|[--.]ʿ[--].|[bn].k[--].|bn.ab[--].|bn.i[--].|bn.n[--].|bn.ḫ[--].|bn.[---].|bn 2021.2.12
.dr[--].|bn.ṣl[--].|bn.ḫd[--].|bn.ʿ[---].|kbkbn bn[.---].|bn.k[--].|bn.pdr[n.].|bn.ʿn[--].|nḥl h[.---].|[-----]. 2014.58
---].|[---].šd ubdy.|[---.šd] u[b]dy.|[---.]šd.ubdy.|[---.]bn.k[--.]ṯ[l]ṯm ksp b[---].|[---.]šd bʿly.|[---.]šd ubdy.|[---.š]d 2031.6
]yplṭ.|[---].l.[-]npk.|[---.]l.bn.ydln.|[---].l.blkn.|[---].l.bn.k[--].|[---].l.klṯṯb. 2136.5
k[--].|bn.ab[--].|bn.i[--].|bn.n[--].|bn.ḫ[--].|bn.[---].|bn.k[--]. 2021.2.18
bn.ḫtr[-].|bn.yd[--].|bn.ʿ[---].|w.nḥ[l h].|w.nḥ[l h].|bn.k[---].|bn.y[---].|[bn].i[---]. 116[303].12
ity.|tity.ilm.l ahl hm.|dr il.l mšknt hm.|w tqrb.w ld.bn.l h.|w tqrb.w ld.bnt.l h.|mk.b šbʿ.šnt.|bn.krt.km hm.td 15[128].3.20
ḥnt h.abynt.|[d]nil.mt.rpi anḫ.ǵzr.|[mt.]hrnmy.d in.bn.l h.|km.aḫ h.w šrš.km.ary h.|bl.iṯ.bn.l h.km aḫ h.w šrš. 17[2AQHT].1.19
t.]hrnmy.d in.bn.l h.|km.aḫ h.w šrš.km.ary h.|bl.iṯ.bn.l h.km aḫ h.w šrš.|km.ary h.uzrm.ilm.ylḥm.|uzrm.yšqy 17[2AQHT].1.21
g h.w yṣḥ.aṯbn.ank.|w anḫn.w tnḫ.b irt y.|npš.k yld.bn.l y.km.|aḫ y.w šrš.km ary y.|nṣb.skn.ilib y.b qdš.|ztr.ʿ 17[2AQHT].2.14
|a[ṯt.tq]ḥ.y krt.aṯt.|tqḥ.bt k.ǵlmt.tšʿrb.|ḥqr k.tld.šbʿ.bnm.l k.|w ṯmn.tṯtmnm.|l k.tld.yṣb.ǵlm.|ynq.ḥlb.a[ṯ]rt.|m 15[128].2.23
p bl.hn.|[---].ḥ[m]t.pṯr.w.p nḥš.|[---.--]q.n[ṭ]k.l ydʿ.l bn.l pq ḥmt.|[---.--]n h.ḥmt.w tʿbtn h.abd y.|[---.ǵ]r.šrǵzz.y UG5.8.35
n knʿm.|bn kbr.|bn iytlm.|bn ayln.|bn.kln.|bn.ʿlln.|bn.liy.|bn.nqṯn.|bn abrḫṭ.|bn.grdy.|bn.ṣlpn.|bn ǵlmn.|bn 1064.25
ṯb.|ṯbry.|bn.ymn.|krty.|bn.abr[-].|yrpu.|kdn.|pʿṣ.|bn.liy.|ydʿ.|šmn.|ʿdy.|ʿnbr.|aḫrm.|bn.qrdy.|bn.šmʿn.|bn. 2117.1.25
.ṣ[md].|bn gmrt.|bn.il.ṣm[d].|bn abbly.|ytʿd.ṣm[d].|bn.liy.|ʿšrm.ṣ[md].|ṯṯ kbd.b ḥ[--].|w.arbʿ.ḥ[mrm].|b m[ʿ]rb 2113.22
nrym.dt.ʿqb.|b.ayly.|šd.abršn.|šd.kkn.[bn].ubyn.|šd.bn.li[y].|šd.bn.š[--]y.|šd.bn.ṯ[---].|šd.ʿdmn[.bn.]ynḥm.|šd.b 2026.5
|bn[.---].|bn u[l]pm.|bn ʿ[p]ty.|bn.kdgdl.|bn.smyy.|bn.lbn.|bn.šlmn.|bn.mly.|pslm.|bn.annd.|bn.glʿd.|w.nḥl 2163.3.6

[nq]dm.dt.kn.npṣ hm. | [bn].lbn.arb'.qšt.w.ar[b']. | [u]ṯpt.ql'.w.ṯt.mr[ḥ]m. | [bn].smyy 2047.2
| ṯlṯm.ar[b']. | kbd.ksp. | 'l.tgyn. | w 'l.aṯt h. | yph.m'nt. | bn.lbn. 2053.23
ḥrṯm[.---]. | bn.ṯmq[-.---]. | bn.ntp.[---]. | bn.lbnn.[----]. | ady.ḥ[--.---]. | [-]b[-]n.[---]. | bn.atnb.mr[--.---]. 88[304].4
ṯtm.b'lm. | bn.b'ly.ṯlṯtm.b'lm. | w.aḥd.ḫbṯ. | w.arb'.aṯt. | bn.lg.ṯn.bn h. | b'lm.w.aḫt h. | b.šrt. | šty.w.bn h. 2080.10
n.---.ubr]'y. | b[n.---]. | bn[.---.ušk]ny. | bn.kdrn.uškny. | bn.lgn.uškny. | bn.abn.uškny. | bn.arz.š'rty. | bn.ibrd.m'rby. | 87[64].23
sgm.l hm. | p'ṣ.ḫbty. | artyn.ary. | brqn.ṯlḥy. | bn.aryn. | bn.lgn. | bn.b'yn. | šdyn. | ary. | brqn. | bn.ḫlln. | bn.mṣry. | ṯmn. 118[306].7
'.bnt h. | yrḫm.yd.ṯn.bn h. | b'lm.w.ṯlṯ.n'rm.w.bt.aḫt. | bn.lwn.ṯlṯtm.b'lm. | bn.b'ly.ṯlṯtm.b'lm. | w.aḥd.ḫbṯ. | w.arb'.a 2080.6
nḥl h. | bn n'myn. | bn aṯtyy. | bn ḫlp. | bn.ẓll. | bn ydy. | bn lzn. | bn.ṯyn. | bn g'r. | bn.prtn. | bn ḫnn. | b[n.-]n. | bn.ṣṣb. | 2016.1.14
ullym.bn.abynm. | antn.bn.iwr[n]r. | pwn.ṯmry. | ksyn.bn.lḥsn. | [-]kyn.ṯmry. 94[313].9
| bn.ǵb.qšt. | bn.ytrm.qšt.w.ql'. | bn.'bdyrḫ.qšt.w.q[l']. | bn.lky.qšt. | bn.dll.qšt.w.ql[']. | bn.pǵyn.qšt.w[.q]l'. | bn.bdn.q 119[321].3.27
sp 'l bn ymn. | šb šr šmn [--] ṯryn. | ḫm[š]m l 'šr ksp 'l bn llit. | [--]l[-.-]p 'l [---.-]b'm arny. | w 'l [---.]rb'm ṯqlm.w [-- 1103.6
[---.]iy[ṯ]r. | [---.'bd.y]rḫ. | [---.b]n.mšrn. | [---].bn.lnn. | [-----]. | [---.-]lyr. 2135.4
lm]. | lt.hlk.b[.---]. | bn.b'yn.š[--.---]. | aǵltn.mid[-.---]. | bn.lṣn.'rm[y]. | arŝw.bṣry. | arpṯr.y'rty. | bn.ḫdyn.ugrty. | bn.t 87[64].5
n.ilšt'y. | bn grgs. | bn.ḫran. | bn.arŝ[w.b]ṣry. | bn.ykn. | bn.lṣn.'rmy. | bn.b'yn.šly. | bn.ynḥn. | bn.'bdilm.hzpy. 99[327].2.3
ḫlq. | [---]n ḫlq. | bn m'nt. | bn kbdy. | bn krk. | bn srty. | bn lṯḥ ḫlq. | bn ytr. | bn ilšpš. | ubrš. | bn gmš ḫlq. | bn 'gy. | bn 2016.2.14
n.krwn. | bn.nǵsk. | bn.qnd̠. | bn.pity. | w.nḥl h. | bn.rt. | bn.l[--]. | bn.[---]. | [---.--]y. | [--.-]d̠rm. | [--.--]y. | [--.--]y. | [-----] 113[400].3.20
-]yl.'š[rm.---]. | [---.a]rb'[.---]. | [---.ṯ]lṯm[.---]. | [---.--]m.bn l[---]. | [---].bn ṣd[-.---]. | [---.--]mn.mi[t.---]. | [---.ṯm]nym[. 149[99].7
m.b'l.ṣrrt. | ṣpn.yšu g h.w yṣḥ. | aḫ y m.ytnt.b'l. | spu y.bn m.um y.kl | y y.yt'n.k gmrm. | mt.'z.b'l.'z.ynǵḥn. | k rum 6[49].6.15
.ǵlm h. | [---].bn.ilm.mt. | p[-]n.aḫ y m.ytn.b'l. | [s]pu y.bn m.um y.kly y. | ytb.'m.b'l.ṣrrt. | ṣpn.yšu g h.w yṣḥ. | aḫ y 6[49].6.11
| tš'n. | w.hm.al[-]. | l.tš'n. | mṣrm. | tmkrn. | ypḥ.'bdilt. | bn.m. | ypḥ.ilšlm. | bn.prqdš. | ypḥ.mnḥm. | bn.ḥnn. | brqn.spr. 2116.18
. | bn.[---]. | bn.ṯ'l[-]. | bn.nq[ly]. | bn.snr[n]. | bn.pzn[y]. | bn.mg[lb]. | bn.db[--]. | bn.amd[n]. | annš[-]. 2020.11
'zn.bn.irbn. | bn.mglb. | bn.ntp. | 'myn.bn ǵḥpn. | bn.kbln. | bn.bly. | bn.ṯ'y. | 104[316].2
rn. | bn.ṯgd. | bn.d[-]n. | bn.amdn. | bn.ṯmrn. | bn.pzny. | bn.mglb. | bn.[--]b. | bn.[---]. | bn.[---]. 113[400].6.32
[---]. | bn.prsn. | bn.mtyn. | bn.ḫlpn. | bn.ḥgbn. | bn.szn. | bn.mglb. 117[325].2.10
m.dt.iš[--]. | [b]n.b'l[--]. | bn.gld. | bn.ṣmy. | bn.mry[n]. | bn.mgn. | bn.'dn. | bn.knn. | bn.py. | bn.mk[-]. | bn.by[--]. | bn.a 2117.1.6
m. | ḥrm. | bn.bty. | 'by. | šm[n].bn.apn. | krty. | bn.ubr. | [bn] mdḫl. | bn.sy[n]n. | bn.šrn. 2078.20
b'lm'd̠r. | bn.mdn. | mkrm. 1168.2
[---].md.'[ṯtr]t. | ydy. | bn.škn. | bn.mdt. | bn.ḫ[--]y. | bn.'[-]y. | kn'm. | bn.yš[-]n. | bn.pd[y]. | ṯt 1054.1.4
rnbt. | qdšm. | b[-.--]t. | [---.-]l[--]. | [---.]pr[--]. | [-.a]pln. | bn.mzt. | bn.ṯrn. | w.nḥl h. | [--.-]hs. | [--.--]nyn. | [-----]. | [-----]. 2163.2.13
b]dmlk. | [---]yn. | bn.ṯ[--]. | bn.idrm. | bn.ymn. | bn.ṣry. | bn.mztn. | bn.šlgyn. | bn.[-]gštn. | bn[.n]klb. | b[n.]dtn. | w.nḥl 113[400].2.5
.ṣmy. | bn.mry[n]. | bn.mgn. | bn.'dn. | bn.knn. | bn.py. | bn.mk[-]. | bn.by[--]. | bn.a[--]. | bn.iy[--]. | bn.ḫ[---]. | bn.plš. | b 2117.1.10
m. | bn '[p]ty. | bn.kdgdl. | bn.smyy. | bn.lbn. | bn.šlmn. | bn.mly. | pslm. | bn.annd. | bn.gl'd. | w.nḥl h. | bn.mlkyy. | [bn] 2163.3.8
n. | bn.bly. | bn.ṯbrn. | bn.ḥgby. | bn.pity. | bn.slgyn. | 'zn.bn.mlk. | bn.alṯn. | bn.ṯmyr. | ẓbr. | bn.ṯdṯb. | bn.'rmn. | bn.alz. | 115[301].2.8
rŝm. | bn.gṯprg. | gṯpbn. | bn.b[--]. | [b]n.[---]. | bn.a[--]. | bn.ml[k]. | bn.glyn. | bn.'dr. | bn.ṯmq. | bn.ntp. | bn.'grt. 1057.17
.]nḥl h. | bn.qsn. | bn.ksln. | bn.ṣrym. | bn.ṯmq. | bn.ntp. | bn.mlk. | bn.ṯ'[-]. | bn.km[-]. | bn.r[--]. | [bn.]'[---]. | [bn.]r[---]. | 1073.1.10
ṯn.ḥ[---].pgam. | ṯn[.---.b]n.mlk. | ṯ[n.---.]gpn. | [-----]. | [---.--]b. | b[--.---.b]n.'my. 1150.2
g'r. | bn.prtn. | bn ḫnn. | b[n.-]n. | bn.ṣṣb. | bn.b'ltn ḫlq. | bn.mlkbn. | bn.asyy ḫlq. | bn.kṯly. | bn.kyn. | bn.'bdḥr. | [-]prm 2016.2.3
]. | bn.[---]. | bn.[---]. | bn.[---]. | bn.[---]. | [-----]. | bn[---]. | bn.mlkyy. | bn.atn. | bn.bly. | bn.ṯbrn. | bn.ḥgby. | bn.pity. | bn. 115[301].2.1
n.šlmn. | bn.mly. | pslm. | bn.annd. | bn.gl'd. | w.nḥl h. | bn.mlkyy. | [bn].bm[--]. | ['š]rm. | [-----]. | [-----]. | bn.p[--]. | bn.' 2163.3.13
arb'.'šr h.šd. | w.kmsk.d.iwrkl. | ṯlṯ.šd.d.bn.mlkyy. | kmsk.šd.iḫmn. | širm.šd.khn. | ṯlṯ.šd.w.krm.šir.d. 1079.3
y.ad̠ddy. | aḫyn. | ygmr.ad̠ddy. | gln.aṯt. | ddy.[a]d̠ddy. | bn.mlkr[šp]. | bn.y[k]n. | ynḥm. | bn.abd.b'[l]. | mnḥm.bn[.---] 2014.45
.bn.krmn. | bn.umḫ. | yky.bn.slyn. | ypln.bn.ylḥn. | 'zn.bn.mll. | šrm. | [b]n.špš[yn]. | [b]n.ḫrmln. | bn.tnn. | bn.pndr. | 85[80].1.9
| ǵmrm. | [-]lhd.ṯt.qštm.w.ṯn.ql'm. | ulšn.ṯt.qšm.w.ql'. | bn.ml'n.qšt.w.ql'. | bn.tmy.qšt.w.ql'. | 'ky.qšt. | 'bdlbit.qšt. | kṯ 119[321].3.35
t.iṯ.alpm.l hm. | bn.niršn. | bn.adty. | bn.alz. | bn.birtn. | bn.mlṣ. | bn.q[--]. | bn.[---]. | bn.ṯ[-]r. | bn.grdn. | [bn.-]ḫr. | [--.-] 2023.1.6
.u[ṯpt]. | [w.q]l'.w.ṯt.mrḥm. | [bn].šlmn.ql'.w.ṯ[t.---]. | [bn].mlṣ.qštm.w.uṯp[t]. | [--.q]l'.w[.---.m]rḥm. | [bn].ḥdmn.qšt 2047.7
bn.aǵltn. | bn.ktln. | bn.'gwn. | bn.yšm'. | bdl.md̠rǵlm. | bn.mmy. | bn.ḫnyn. | bn.knn. | khnm. | bn.ṯ'y. | w.nḥl h. | w.nḥl 104[316].9
[---.b]n.[y]drn. | [---.]bn.ḫlan. | [--]r bn.mn. | [--]ry. | [--]lim bn.brq. | [--.]qtn bn.drṣy. | [--]kn bn.pr 2087.3
n. | yrb'm. | n'mn. | bn.kbl. | kn'm. | bdlm. | bn.ṣǵr. | klb. | bn.mnḥm. | bn.brqn. | bn.'n. | bn.'bdy. | 'bd'ṯtr. 1046.3.45
bdl.gt.bn.tbšn. | bn.mnyy.š'rty. | aryn.ad̠ddy. | agpṯr. | šb'l.mlky. | n'mn.mṣry. 91[311].2
.bn.ṯtm.ṯlṯm. | b.bn.agdṯb.'šrm. | b.bn.ibn.arb't.'šrt. | b.bn.mnn.ṯtm. | b.rpan.bn.yyn.'šrt. | b.yp'r.'šrm. | b.n'mn.bn.pl 2054.1.14
bn[.---]. | bn.qdšt. | bn.m'nt. | bn.g[--]n. | bn[.---]. | [-----]. | b[n.---]. | b[n.---]. | bn.[-- 2163.1.3
. | bn.kṯly. | bn.kyn. | bn.'bdḥr. | [-]prm ḫlq. | [---]n ḫlq. | bn m'nt. | bn kbdy. | bn krk. | bn srty. | bn lṯḥ ḫlq. | bn ytr. | bn 2016.2.10
aḥd. | sǵr.irgn.aḥd. | sǵr.ršpab.aḥd. | sǵr.arwt.aḥd. | sǵr.bn.mǵln. | aḥd. 1140.12
| ṣṣ.bn.adld̠n.ṯlṯm. | ṣṣ.bn.'glt.ṯlṯm. | ṣṣ.bn.'bd.'šrm. | ṣṣ.bn.mṣḥ[n].'šrm. | šb'.mat.ṯtm kbd. 2096.19
.qšt. | bn.gdrn.qšt. | prpr.qšt. | ugry.qšt. | bn.ṣrptn.qšt. | bn.mṣry.qšt. | arny. | abm.qšt. | ḥdṯn.ql'. | ytpṭ.qšt. | ilṯḥm.qšt. 119[321].1.47
rǵlm. | kd.l.mṣrym. | kd.mštt.mlk. | kd.bn.amht [-]t. | w.bn.mṣrym. | arb'm.yn. | l.ḥrd. | ḫmšm.ḫmš. | kbd.tgmr. | yn.d. 1089.10
n.aryn. | bn.lgn. | bn.b'yn. | šdyn. | ary. | brqn. | bn.ḫlln. | bn.mṣry. | ṯmn.qšt. | w 'šr.uṯpt. | upšt irš[-]. 118[306].13
. | bn.'bd. | [-----]. | [---.n]ḥ[l h]. | [-]ntm[.---]. | [']bdm. | [bn].mṣrn. | [a]rŝwn. | 'b[d]. | w nḥl h. | atn.bn.ap[s]n. | nsk.ṯlṯ. | 85[80].3.3
. | bn.alṯn. | bn.ṯmyr. | ẓbr. | bn.ṯdṯb. | bn.'rmn. | bn.alz. | bn.mṣrn. | bn.'dy. | bn.ršpy. | [---.]mn. | [--.-]sn. | [bn.-]ny. | [b]n 115[301].2.15
kbšm. | bn.abd̠r. | bn.kpltn. | bn.prn. | 'bdm. | bn.kd̠gbr. | bn.mṣrn. | bn.[-]dr[-]. | [---]l[-]. | [--]ym. | [--]rm. | [bn.]aǵld. | [114[324].2.12
sg]. | bn.twyn[.msg]. | bn.'drš[p.msg]. | pyn.yny.[msg]. | bn.mṣrn m[sg]. | yky msg. | ynḥm.msg. | bn.ugr.msg. | bn.ǵls 133[-].1.5
[---.]irš[-.---]. | [---.]bn.n[--.---]. | [---.]bn.mṣ[--.---]. | [---.]b'lš[-.---]. | [---.]bn.zzb[-.---]. | [---.]bn mt[.- 2139.3
bdlḥn[-]. | bn.mqwṭ. | bn.bsn. | bn.inr[-]. | bn.ṯbil. | bn.iryn. | ṯṯl. | bn.nṣdn. 1071.2

--.]bn[.---].|[---.]bn[.---].|[---.]nḫl h.|[---.b]n.špš.|[---.b]n.mradn.|[---.m]lkym.|[---.--]d. 2137.5
n.pity.|bn.iryn.|bn.ʿbl.|bn.grbn.|bn.iršyn.|bn.r.klb.|bn.mryn.|[bn.]b[--].|bn.ẓrl.|bn.illm[-].|bn.š[---].|bn.ṣ[---]. 115[301].4.21
[bn]šm.dt.iš[--].|[b]n.bʿl[--].|bn.gld.|bn.ṣmy.|bn.mry[n].|bn.mgn.|bn.ʿdn.|bn.knn.|bn.py.|bn.mk[-].|bn. 2117.1.5
ḫmš.ṯnnm.ʿšr.ḫsnm.|ṯlṯ.ʿšr.mrynm.|ḫmš.[tr]tnm.|ṯlṯ.b[n.]mrynm.|ʿšr[.m]krm.|tšʿ.hbṯnm.|ʿšr.mrum.|šbʿ.ḫsnm. 1028.4
snm.|ṯmn.ʿšr h.mrynm.|ʿšr.mkrm.|ḫmš.ṯrtnm.|ḫmš.bn.mrynm.|ʿšr.mrum.w.šbʿ.ḫsnm.|tšʿm.mḏrǵlm.|arbʿ.l ʿšr 1030.5
dnn.ṯlṯ.ṣmdm.|bn.ʿmnr.|bn.kmn.|bn.ibyn.|bn.mryn.ṣmd.w.ḥrṣ.|bn.prsn.ṣmd.w.ḥrṣ.|bn.ilbʿl.|bn.idrm. 2113.5
rum.|w.šbʿ.ḫsnm.|tšʿ.ʿšr.|mrynm.|ṯlṯ.ʿšr.mkrm.|ṯlṯ.bn.mrynm.|arbʿ.ṯrtnm.|tšʿ.ḫbṯnm.|ṯmnym.ṯlṯ.kbd.|mḏrǵl 1029.8
---].|[---]tl.|[---]ʿbl.|[---]bln.|[---]dy.|[---.n]ḫl h.|[---].bn.mryn.|[---].bn.ṯyl.|annmt.nḫl h.|abmn.bn.ʿbd.|liy.bn.rq 1036.10
y[n.bn.]šmʿnt.|ḥnn[.bn].pls.|abrš[p.bn.]ḫrpn.|gmrš[.bn].mrnn.|ʿbdmlk.bn.ʿmyn.|agyn.rʿy.|abmlk.bn.ilrš.|iḫyn. 102[323].4.7
.prsn.l.[---].|šd.bddn.l.iytlm.|šd.bn.nbʿm.l.ṯpṭbʿl.|šd.bn mšrn.l.ilšpš.|[šd.bn].kbr.l.snrn.|[---.--]k.l.gmrd.|[---.--]ṯ. 2030.1.5
[---.]iy[ṯ]r.|[---.ʿbd.y]rḫ.|[---.b]n.mšrn.|[---].bn.lnn.|[-----].|[---.-]lyr. 2135.3
[-----].|[-----].|ynḥm.|iḫy.|bn.mšt.|ʿpsn.|bn.ṣpr.|kmn.|bn.ršp.|tmn.|šmmn.|bn.rmy. 1047.5
--].|[------].|[bn.]kblbn[.---].|[bn] uškny.|bn.krny[-].|bn.mt.|bn.nzʿn.|bn.slmz[-].|bn.kʿ[--].|bn.y[---].|[-----].|[bn 2021.1.16
.]bn.mṣ[--.---].|[---.]bʿlš[-.---].|[---.]bn.zzb[-.---].|[---.]bn mt[.---].|[---.b]n r[--.---]. 2139.6
]iršn.|bn.[---].|bn.b[--].|bn.š[--].|bn.a[---].|bn.prsn.|bn.mtyn.|bn.ḫlpn.|bn.ḥgbn.|bn.szn.|bn.mglb. 117[325].2.6
bn.ʿṯt[-.---].|pdy.bn.nr[-.---].|abmlk.bn.un[-.---].|nrn.bn.mtn[-.---].|aḫyn.bn.nbk[-.---].|ršpn.bn.bʿly[.---].|bnil.bn 90[314].1.9
n.ppṭ.b[--].|b[n.---].|šm[-.---].|¡kn[.---].|knn.b.ḫ[lb].|bn mṯ.b.qmy.|nʿr.b.ulm. 2046.2.5
.|ab[---.]aḏddy.bn.skn.|bn.[---.]uḫd.|bn.n[---.]hbṯn.|bn.m[--.]skn.|bn.s[--.b]d.skn.|bn.ur[-.---].|bn.knn[.---]y.|b 2014.11
bnšm.dt.iṯ.alpm.l hm.|bn.niršn.|bn.adty.|bn.alz.|bn.birtn.|bn.mlṣ.|bn.q[--].|bn.[2023.1.2
-].|bn.n[---].|bn.b[---].|bn.iš[--].|bn.ab[--].|bn.al[--].|bn.nb[dg].|bn.ild[-].|[-----].|[bn.]nnr.|[bn.]aglby.|[bn.]bʿly 113[416].4
dlḏn.|bn.šbl.|bn.ḫnzr.|bn.arwṭ.|bn.ṯbtnq.|bn.pṯdn.|bn.nbdg.|bn.ḥgbn.|bn.tmr.|bn.prsn.|bn.ršpy.|[ʿ]bdḥgb.|[113[400].1.18
nr[-.---].|abmlk.bn.un[-.---].|nrn.bn.mtn[-.---].|aḫyn.bn.nbk[-.---].|ršpn.bn.bʿly[.---].|bnil.bn.yṣr[.---].|ʿdyn.bn.u 90[314].1.10
[-----].|šd.prsn.l.[---].|šd.bddn.l.iytlm.|šd.bn.nbʿm.l.ṯpṭbʿl.|šd.bn mšrn.l.ilšpš.|[šd.bn].kbr.l.snrn.|[---. 2030.1.4
y.|bn.ršpy.|[---.]mn.|[--.-]sn.|[bn.-]ny.|[b]n.ḫnyn.|[bn].nbq.|[bn.]snrn.|[bn.-]lṣ.|bn.[---]ym. 115[301].3.3
[šd.b]n.ṯpdn.b d.bn.gʿr.|[šd.b]n.ṯqrn.b d.ḫby.|[tn.š]d.bn.ngzḥn.b d.gmrd.|[šd.bn].pll.b d.gmrd.|[šd.bn.-]ll.b d.iw 82[300].1.23
ḥrm.b[n].ng[-]n.|atyn.š[r]šy.|ʿbdḫmn[.bn.-]bdn.|ḥṣmn.[bn.---]ln 102[322].1.1
šyn.|abmn.|[--]dn.|[ṯ]bʿm.|[--]mlk.|[--]ty.|mtnbʿl.|bn.ndbn.|bn irgn. 1072.12
-.]ṯḥr l ytn ḫs[n].|ʿbd ulm ṯn un ḫsn.|gdy lqḥ ṣṭqn gt bn ndr.|um r[-] gtn ṯṯ ḫsn l ytn.|l rḥt lqḥ ṣṭqn.|bt qbṣ urt il 1154.4
.nḫl h.|[---]n.|[--]ly.|[iw]ryn.|[--.w.n]ḫl h.|[-]ibln.|bn.nḏbn.|bn.ʿbl.|bn.tlšn.|bn.sln.|w nḫl h. 1063.11
--].|[bn.]kblbn[.---].|[bn] uškny.|bn.krny[-].|bn.mt.|bn.nzʿn.|bn.slmz[-].|bn.kʿ[--].|bn.y[---].|[-----].|[bn.a]mdy. 2021.1.17
š]d.bn.ṯ[-]rn.b d.ʿdbmlk.|[šd.]bn.brzn.b d.nwrḏ.|[šd.]bn.nḥbl.b d.ʿdbym.|[šd.b]n.qty.b d.tt.|[ubd]y.mrim.|[šd.b] 82[300].1.18
rkl.|bn štn.|bn annyn.|b[n] slg.|u[--] dit.|bn p[-]n.|bn nẓǵil. 101[10].16
št.|abršp.qšt.|ssg.qšt.|ynḥm.qšt.|pprn.qšt.|uln.qšt.|bn.nkl qšt.|ady.qšt.|bn.srn.qšt.|bn.gdrn.qšt.|prpr.qšt.|ugr 119[321].1.40
m.|bn.ymn.|bn.ṣry.|bn.mztn.|bn.šlgyn.|bn.[-]gštn.|bn[.n]klb.|b[n.]dtn.|w.nḫl h.|w.nḫl hm.|bn.iršyn.|bn.ʿzn. 113[400].2.8
.ktmn.|bn.pity.|bn.iryn.|bn.ʿbl.|bn.grbn.|bn.iršyn.|bn.nklb.|bn.mryn.|[bn.]b[--].|bn.ẓrl.|bn.illm[-].|bn.š[---].| 115[301].4.20
.]ʿ[---].|[bn.]r[---].|[bn.]ḫ[---].|[bn.]šbl.|[bn.]ḫdmn.|[bn.]nklb.|[---]dn.|[---]y.|[-----].|[-----].|bn.adn.|prtn.|bn.b 1073.2.6
bn.-]ḫr.|[--.]nb.|[--.--]n.|[--.--]n.|bn.[---].|bn.ʿr[--].|bn.nkt[-].|bn.abḏr.|bn.ḥrẓn.|bn.ḏqnt.|bn.gmrš.|bn.nmq.| 2023.3.8
--].rb.|[-]lpl.|bn.asrn.|bn.šḫyn.|bn.abdʿn.|bn.ḫnqn.|bn.nmq.|bn.amdn.|bn.špšn. 1067.7
-].|bn.nkt[-].|bn.abḏr.|bn.ḥrẓn.|bn.ḏqnt.|bn.gmrš.|bn.nmq.|bn.špš[yn].|bn.ar[--].|bn.gb[--].|bn.ḥn[n].|bn.gnt 2023.3.13
hm.rib.|w [---].|[-----].|[-]šy[.---] h.|[-]kt[.---.]nrn.|[b]n.nmq[.---].|[ḫm]št.ksp.ʿl.aṯt.|[-]ṯd[.bn.]štn. 2055.18
dn.qšt.w.qlʿ.|bn.šmlbi.qšt.w.qlʿ.|bn.yy.qšt.|ilrb.qšt.|bn.nmš.ṯṯ.qšt.w.qlʿ.|bʿl.qšt.w.qlʿ. 119[321].4.16
-].|bn.ab[--].|bn.al[--].|bn.nb[dg].|bn.ild[-].|[-----].|[bn.]nnr.|[bn.]aglby.|[bn.]bʿly.|[mḏ]rǵlm.|[bn.]kdgdl.|[b]n 104[316].5
rmn.|bn.prtn.|bn.ymn.|bn.dby.|bn.ir[--].|bn.kr[--].|bn.nn[-].|[-----].|[-----].|[---.-]l[-].|[bn.-]dt[-].|[bn.-]nn.|[bn 124[-].5.13
t.|šmmn.bn.ʿdš.ṯṯ mat.|ušknym.|ypʿ.alpm.|aḫ[m]lk.bn.nskn.alpm.|krw.šlmy.|alpm.|atn.bṣry.alpm.|lbnym.|ṯ 1060.2.3
.y[---].|[-----].|[bn.a]mdy.|bn.ḫlln.|bn.kṯn.|bn.abn.|bn.nskn.|bn.gmrn.|bn[.-]škn.|[---.--]n.|[---.--]n.|[--.]ʿ[--].|[2021.2.6
n abyt.|bn ḫdl.|bn ṣdqn.|bn ayy.|bn dbb.|w nḫl h.|bn nʿmyn.|bn aṯtyy.|bn ḫlp.|bn.ẓll.|bn ydy.|bn lzn.|bn.ṯy 2016.1.9
.prtn.|bn.ypr.|mrum.|bn.ʿ[--]t.|bn.adty.|bn.krwn.|bn.nǵsk.|bn.qnḏ.|bn.pity.|w.nḫl h.|bn.rt.|bn.l[--].|bn.[---] 113[400].3.15
n ḥšbn.|bn uryy.|bn kṯl.|bn army.|bn gln.|bn abg.|bn.nǵry.|bn.srwd.|mtnn.|bn gš[-].|bn gbrn.|bn uldy.|syn 1064.13
].|[-----].|[-----].|[-----].|[-----].|[ṣṣ].b[n].ṣd[-.---].|[ṣṣ].bn.npr.ḫmšm.|ṣṣ.bn.adlḏn.ṯlṯm.|ṣṣ.bn.ʿglt.ṯlṯm.|ṣṣ.bn.ʿbd.ʿ 2096.15
bn.nṣ.|[b]n.ʿṣr.|[---]m.|[bn.]ulnhr.|[bn.p]rn.|[bn.a]nny.|[- 1075.1.1
].|bn.mqwṭ.|bn.bsn.|bn.inr[-].|bn.ṯbil.|bn.iryn.|ṯṯl.|bn.nṣdn.|bn.ydln.|[bn].ʿdy.|[bn].ilyn. 1071.8
[-----].|ḏ[----].|ab[--.---].|bn.nṣdn[.ḫm]št.|bn.arsw ʿ[šr]m.|ʿšdyn.ḫmš[t].|abršn.ʿšr[t]. 1062.4
lb.|bn.ntp.|ʿmyn.bn ǵḥpn.|bn.kbln.|bn.bly.|bn.ṯʿy.|bn.nṣdn.|klby. 104[316].8
.ʿmyn.|šd.bn.prmn.l aḫny.|šd.bn ḥnn.l bn.adlḏn.|šd.bn.nṣdn.l bn.ʿmlbi.|šd.ṯpḫln.l bn.ǵl.|w dṯn.nḫl h.l bn.pl.|š 2089.8
|bn kbr.|bn iytlm.|bn ayln.|bn.kln.|bn.ʿlln.|bn.liy.|bn.nqṯn.|bn abrḫṭ.|bn.grdy.|bn.ṣlpn.|bn ǵlmn.|bn sgld. 1064.26
---].|bn.il[--].|khnm[.--].|bn.ṯ[--].|bn.[---].|bn.ṯʿl[-].|bn.nq[ly].|bn.snr[n].|bn.pzn[y].|bn.mg[lb].|bn.db[--].|bn. 2020.8
.ḥnyn.|bn.knn.|khnm.|bn.ṯʿy.|w.nḫl h.|w.nḫl hm.|bn.nqly.|bn.snrn.|bn.tgd.|bn.d[-]n.|bn.amdn.|bn.ṯmrn.|b 105[86].2
[šmt.n]qmpʿ.|[bn.nq]md.|[mlk.]ugrt.|bʿl ṣdq.|skn.bt.|mlk.tǵr.|[m]lk.bny 1007.2
l ym.hnd.|ʿmṯtmr.|bn.nqmpʿ.|mlk.ugrt.|ytn.bt.annḏr.|bn.ytn.bnš.|[ml]k.d.b r 1009.3
l ym hnd.|ʿmṯtmr.bn.|nqmpʿ.ml[k].|ugrt.ytn.|šd.kḏǵdl[.bn].|[-]š[-]y.d.b š[-]y 1008.2
ll.|šrm.|[b]n.špš[yn].|[b]n.ḫrmln.|bn.tnn.|bn.pndr.|bn.nqq.|ḥrš.bhtm.|bn.izl.|bn.ibln.|bn.ilt.|špšyn.nḫl h.|nʿ 85[80].2.1
l ym hnd.|iwr[k]l.pdy.|agdn.bn.nrgn.|w ynḥm.aḫ h.|w.bʿln aḫ h.|w.ḥṯtn bn h.|w.btšy.b 1006.3
pṯr.yʿrty.|bn.ḫdyn.ugrty.|bn.tgḏn.ugrty.|tgyn.arty.|bn.nryn.arty.|bn.ršp.ary.|bn.ǵlmn ary.|bn.ḥṣbn ary.|bn.šd 87[64].11

n. | ʻdmlk. | bn.alt[-]. | iẖy[-]. | ʻbdgṯr. | ḥrr. | bn.s[-]p[-]. | bn.nrpd. | bn.ḥ[-]y. | bʻlskn. | bn.ʻbd. | ẖyrn. | alpy. | bn.plsy. | b 1035.1.13
nṯ.aẖd.l h[.---]. | dnn.bn.yṣr[.---]. | sln.bn.ʻṯt[-.---]. | pdy.bn.nr[-.---]. | abmlk.bn.un[-.---]. | nrn.bn.mtn[-.---]. | aẖyn.bn. 90[314].1.7
yn. | [w.]nḥl h. | bn.qṣn. | bn.ksln. | bn.ṣrym. | bn.ṯmq. | bn.ntp. | bn.mlk. | bn.ṯʻ[-]. | bn.km[-]. | bn.r[--]. | [bn.]ʻ[---]. | [b 1073.1.9
n.[---]. | bn.a[--]. | bn.ml[k]. | bn.glyn. | bn.ʻdr. | bn.ṯmq. | bn.ntp. | bn.ʻgrt. 1057.21
ʻzn.bn.irbn. | bn.mglb. | bn.ntp. | ʻmyn.bn ǵḫpn. | bn.kbln. | bn.bly. | bn.ṯʻy. | bn.nṣdn. | 104[316].3
ḥrṯm[.---]. | bn.ṯmq[-.---]. | bn.ntp.[---]. | bn.lbnn.[----]. | ady.ḥ[--.---]. | [-]b[-]n.[---]. | bn.at 88[304].3
skn. | bn.bddn. | bn.ǵrgn. | bn.tgtn. | bn.ḥrẓn. | bn.qdšt. | bn.nṯǵ[-]. | bn.gr[--]. | bn.[---]. | bn.[---]. | mr[u.ibrn]. | bn.i[---]. 113[400].5.12
-]n. | [---.--]n. | [--.]ʻ[--]. | [bn].k[--]. | bn.ab[--]. | bn.i[--]. | bn.n[--]. | bn.ẖ[--]. | bn.[---]. | bn.k[--]. 2021.2.15
šm [---]. | knʻm.bn.[---]. | plšbʻl.bn.n[--]. | ḥy bn.dnn.ṯkt. | ilṯḥm.bn.dnn.ṯkt. | šbʻl.bn.aly.ṯkt. | 2085.3
[---.]irš[-.---]. | [---.]bn.n[--.---]. | [---.]bn.mṣ[--.---]. | [---.]bʻlš[-.---]. | [---.]bn.zzb[-. 2139.2
-]. | bn.gr[--]. | bn.[---]. | bn.[---]. | mr[u.ibrn]. | bn.i[---]. | bn.n[---]. | bn.b[---]. | bn.iš[--]. | bn.ab[--]. | bn.al[--]. | bn.nb[dg 113[400].5.19
lkt. | [---.]l.mẖṣ. | ab[---.]adddy.bn.skn. | bn.[---.]uẖd. | bn.n[---.]hbṭn. | bn.m[--.]skn. | bn.s[--.b]d.skn. | bn.ur[-.---]. | 2014.10
l. | aby. | abmn. | ynḥm. | npl. | ynḥm. | mtbʻl. | bn ǵlmn. | bn sgld. 1065.B.2
liy. | bn.nqṭn. | bn abrḫt. | bn.grdy. | bn.ṣlpn. | bn ǵlmn. | bn sgld. 1064.B.2
n.]kdgdl. | [b]n.qṭn. | [b]n.ǵrgn. | [b]n.tgdn. | bn.ẖdyn. | bn.sgr. | bn.aǵltn. | bn.ktln. | bn.ʻgwn. | bn.yšmʻ. | bdl.mdrǵlm. 104[316].9
--.l]bš.bn.yknʻ.b.arʻt. | [--.l]bš.bn.grbn.b.ṯqlm. | [--.lb]š.bn.sgryn.b[.ṯ]qlm. | [---.]bn.ully.b.ṯ[qlm]. | [---.]bn.anndy.b[.- 135[330].4
r. | ubn.ẖṣḥ.kkr. | kkr.lqḥ.ršpy. | tmtrn.bn.pnmn. | kkr. | bn.sgttn. | kkr. | ilšpš.kkr. | bn.dltn. | kkr.w[.--]. | ḥ[--.---]. 1118.9
n.nryn.arty. | bn.ršp.ary. | bn.ǵlmn ary. | bn.ḥṣbn ary. | bn.šdy ary. | bn.ktkt.mʻqby. | bn.[---.]ṯlḥny. | b[n.---.ub]rʻy. | [87[64].15
bn.ǵlmn.ary. | [bn].šdy. | [bn].gmḥ. | [---]ty. | [b]n.ypy.gbʻly. | b[n].ḥyn. | dmn. 99[327].1.2
[---.--]m. | [---]nb.w ykn. | [--]ndbym. | [ʻ]rmy.w snry. | [b]n.sdy.bn.ṯty. | bn.ḥyn.bn.ǵlm. | bn.yyn.w.bn.au[pš]. | bn.kd 131[309].23
skn.ʻšrm kk[r.---]. | mšrn.ṯlṯ.ʻš[r.kkr]. | bn.šw.šbʻ.kk[r.---]. | arbʻm.kkr.[---]. | b d.mtn.[l].šlm. 2108.3
ilṣdq.bn.zry. | bʻlytn.bn.ulb. | ytrʻm.bn.swy. | ṣḥrn.bn.qrtm. | bn.špš.bn.ibrd. | ʻpṯrm.bn.ʻbdy. | n[-- 2024.3
| ady. | bn.birtn. | bn.ḥrẓn. | bn.bddn. | bn.anny. | ytršp. | bn.szn. | bn.kdgdl. | bn.glʻd. | bn.ktln. | [bn].ǵrgn. | bn.pb[-]. | b 115[301].1.12
--]. | bn.a[---]. | bn.prsn. | bn.mtyn. | bn.ẖlpn. | bn.ḥgbn. | bn.szn. | bn.mglb. 117[325].2.9
.[----]. | ady.ḥ[--.---]. | [-]b[-]n.[---]. | bn.atnb.mr[--.---]. | bn.sẖr.mr[-.---]. | bn.idrn.ʻš[-.---]. | bn.bly.mr[-.---]. | w.nḥl h. 88[304].8
spr.rpš d l y[dy]. | atlg. | ulm. | izly. | uẖnp. | bn sẖrn. | mʻqb. | ṯpn. | mʻr. | lbnm. | nẖl. | yʻny. | atn. | utly. | bn. 2075.6
d.ʻbdym. | [ub]dy.trrm. | [šd.]bn.ṯqdy.b d.gmrd. | [š]d bn.synn.b d.gmrd. | [šd.]abyy.b d.ibrmd. | [šd.]bn.ṯṯrn.b d.bn 82[300].2.18
n.bty. | ʻby. | šm[n].bn.apn. | krty. | bn.ubr. | [bn] mdẖl. | bn.sy[n]n. | bn.šrn. 2078.21
n.ummt. | bn.ṯb[-]. | bn.[-]r[-]. | bn.tgn. | bn.idrn. | mnn. | b[n].skn. | bn.pʻṣ. | bn.drm. | [bn.-]ln. | [bn.-]dprd. 124[-].6.10
---.-]luẖ. | [---.-]tn.b d.mlkt. | [---.]l.mẖṣ. | ab[---.]adddy.bn.skn. | bn.[---.]uẖd. | bn.n[---.]hbṭn. | bn.m[--.]skn. | bn.s[--. 2014.8
dn. | bn uryy. | bn abdʻn. | bn prkl. | bn štn. | bn annyn. | b[n] slg. | u[--] dit. | bn p[-]n. | bn nẓǵil. 101[10].13
--]yn. | bn.ṯ[--]. | bn.idrm. | bn.ymn. | bn.ṣry. | bn.mztn. | bn.šlgyn. | bn.[-]gštn. | bn[.n]klb. | b[n.]dtn. | w.nḥl h. | w.nḥl 113[400].2.6
.mlkyy. | bn.atn. | bn.bly. | bn.ṯbrn. | bn.ḥgby. | bn.pity. | bn.slgyn. | ʻzn.bn.mlk. | bn.alṯn. | bn.ṯmyr. | ẓbr. | bn.ṯdṯb. | bn.ʻ 115[301].2.7
n.iyṯr. | bn.ʻyn. | bn.ǵzl. | bn.ṣmy. | bn.il[-]šy. | bn.ybšr. | bn.sly. | bn.ẖlbt. | bn.brzt. | bn.ayl. | [-----]. | ʻbd[--]. | bn.i[--]. | ʻ 2117.2.11
bn.[---]. | ʻpṯn.bn.ṯṣq[-]. | mnn.bn.krmn. | bn.umẖ. | yky.bn.slyn. | ypln.bn.ylḥn. | ʻzn.bn.mll. | šrm. | [b]n.špš[yn]. | [b]n. 85[80].1.7
blbn[.---]. | [bn] uškny. | bn.krny[-]. | bn.mt. | bn.nzʻn. | bn.slmz[-]. | bn.kʻ[--]. | bn.y[---]. | [-----]. | [bn.a]mdy. | bn.ẖlln. 2021.1.18
]ryn. | [--.w.n]ḥl h. | [-]ibln. | bn.ndbn. | bn.ʻbl. | bn.tlšn. | bn.sln. | w nḥl h. 1063.14
bn.ǵs.ḥrš.šʻty. | ʻdy.bn.slʻy.gbly. | yrm.bʻl.bn.kky. 2121.2
m. | grbn.lṯḥ. | srn.lṯḥ. | ykn.lṯḥ. | ḥgbn.lṯḥ. | spr.mkrm. | bn.slʻn.prs. | bn.ṯpdn.lṯḥ. | bn.urm.lṯḥ. 1059.7
bn sl[--.---]. | bn id[--.---]. 108[38].1
| bn.[-]rṯn. | bn[.---]. | bn u[l]pm. | bn ʻ[p]ty. | bn.kdgdl. | bn.smyy. | bn.lbn. | bn.šlmn. | bn.mly. | pslm. | bn.annd. | bn.glʻ 2163.3.5
. | [bn].lbn.arbʻ.qšt.w.ar[bʻ]. | [u]ṯpt.qlʻ.w.ṯt.mr[ḥ]m. | [bn].smyy.qšt.w.u[ṯpt]. | [w.q]lʻ.w.ṯt.mrḥm. | [bn].šlmn.qlʻ.w.ṯ 2047.4
[n.---]. | bn.[---]. | bn.a[--]. | w.nḥl h. | bn.alz. | w.nḥl h. | bn.sny. | bn.ablḥ. | [-----]. | w [---]. | bn.[---]. | bn.yr[--]. | bn.kṯr[2163.1.14
-]. | khnm[.--]. | bn.ṯ[--]. | bn.[---]. | bn.ṯʻl[-]. | bn.nq[ly]. | bn.snr[n]. | bn.pzn[y]. | bn.mg[lb]. | bn.db[--]. | bn.amd[n]. | an 2020.9
n.knn. | khnm. | bn.ṯʻy. | w.nḥl h. | w.nḥl hm. | bn.nqly. | bn.snrn. | bn.ṯgd. | bn.d[-]n. | bn.amdn. | bn.ṯmrn. | bn.pzny. | b 105[86].3
. | [---.]mn. | [--.-]sn. | [bn.-]ny. | [b]n.ẖnyn. | [bn].nbq. | [bn.]snrn. | [bn.-]lṣ. | bn.[---]ym. 115[301].3.4
.bt.klb. | l[---].bt.ẖzli. | bn.iẖyn. | ṣdqn.bn.ass. | bʻlyskn.bn.ss. | ṣdqn.bn.imrt. | mnḥm.bn.ḥyrn. | [-]yn.bn.arkbt. | [--]z 102[323].3.9
n. | bn.rmy. | bn.aky. | ʻbdḥmn. | bn.ʻdṯ. | kty. | bn.ẖny. | bn.ssm. | bn.ẖnn. | [--]ny. | [bn].trdnt. | [bn].hyadt. | [--]lt. | šmr 1047.18
[---.]w.nḥl h. | bn ksln.ṯlṯh. | bn yṣmẖ.bn.ṯrn w nḥl h. | bn srd.bn agmn. | bn [-]ln.bn.ṯbil. | bn is.bn tbdn. | bn uryy. | 101[10].5
n uryy. | bn kṯl. | bn army. | bn gln. | bn abg. | bn.nǵry. | bn.srwd. | mtnn. | bn gš[-]. | bn gbrn. | bn uldy. | synn.bn knʻm 1064.14
bn.ṣmrt. | liy.bn.yṣi. | dmrhd.bn.srt. | [---.--]m. | ʻbdmlk.bn.šrn. | ʻbdbʻl.bn.kdn. | gzl.bn.qldn. | gld.bt.klb. | l[---].bt.ẖzli 102[323].3.2
. | ynḥm.qšt. | pprn.qšt. | uln.qšt. | bn.nkl qšt. | ady.qšt. | bn.srn.qšt. | bn.gdrn.qšt. | prpr.qšt. | ugry.qšt. | bn.ṣrptn.qšt. | 119[321].1.42
n.bn.ʻdy.ṯkt. | nʻmn.bn.ʻyn.ṯkt. | ʻpṯn.bn.ilrš.ṯkt. | ilṯḥm.bn.šrn.ṯkt. | šmlbu.bn.grb.ṯkt. | šmlbu.bn.ypʻ.ṯkt. | [---.--]m. 2085.12
šm[n].bn.apn. | krty. | bn.ubr. | [bn] mdẖl. | bn.sy[n]n. | bn.šrn. 2078.22
bn.ẖran. | bn.srt. | bn.adn. | bn.ʻgw. | bn.urt. | aẖdbu. | pḥ[-]. | bn.ʻb . | bn. 121[307].2
]m[.---]. | [kd.]šš. | [k]d.ykn.bn.ʻbdṯrm. | kd.ʻbdil. | ṯlṯ.ʻl.bn.srt. | kd.ʻl.ẓrm. | kd.ʻl.šz.bn pls. | kd.ʻl.ynḥm. | tgrm.šmn.d. 1082.2.4
ab]r[p]u.bn.kbd. | [-]m[-].bn.ṣmrt. | liy.bn.yṣi. | dmrhd.bn.srt. | [---.--]m. | ʻbdmlk.bn.šrn. | ʻbdbʻl.bn.kdn. | gzl.bn.qld 102[322].6.7
. | [-]prm ẖlq. | [---]n ẖlq. | bn mʻnt. | bn kbdy. | bn krk. | bn srty. | bn lṯḥ ẖlq. | bn ytr. | bn ilšpš. | ubrš. | bn gmš ẖlq. | bn 2016.2.13
hr l ht. | artyn. | ʻdmlk. | bn.alt[-]. | iẖy[-]. | ʻbdgṯr. | ḥrr. | bn.s[-]p[-]. | bn.nrpd. | bn.ḥ[-]y. | bʻlskn. | bn.ʻbd. | ẖyrn. | alpy. 1035.1.12
y.bn.skn. | bn.[---.]uẖd. | bn.n[---.]hbṭn. | bn.m[--.]skn. | bn.s[--.b]d.skn. | bn.ur[-.---]. | bn.knn[.---]y. | bn.ymlk[.b]d.s 2014.12
[spr.----]m. | bn.pi[ty]. | w.nḥ[l h]. | ʻbd[--]. | bn.s[---]. | bn.at[--]. | bn.qnd. | ṣmq[-]. | bn.anny. | bn.ʻmtdl. | b 117[325].1.5
n.brzn [---]. | bnil.bn.tl[--]. | bn.brzn.ṯn. | bn.išbʻl[.---]. | bn.s[---]. | dnn.[bn.---]. | bn[.--]ʻnt. 2069.9
n.km[-]. | bn.r[--]. | [bn.]ʻ[---]. | [bn.]r[---]. | [bn.]ḥ[---]. | [bn.]šbl. | [bn.]ẖdmn. | [bn.]nklb. | [---]dn. | [---]y. | [-----]. | [----- 1073.2.4

h. | w.nḥl hm. | bn.ḥrm. | bn.brzn. | w.nḥl h. | bn.adlḏn. | bn.šbl. | bn.ẖnzr. | bn.arwṯ. | bn.ṯbtnq. | bn.pṯḏn. | bn.nbdg. | bn 113[400].1.13
. | ṣḥrn.bn.qrtm. | bn.špš.bn.ibrd. | ʻpṯrm.bn.ʻbdy. | n[--.]bn.šnd. | [---].bn.[---]. 2024.7
ṯ[--]. | [bn].ẖla[n]. | [bn].ǵr[--]. | d.b[n.---]. | d.bn.[---]. | d.bn.š[--]. | d.bn.ṯn[r]. | d.kmry. 2164.B.3
ran. | bn.srt. | bn.adn. | bn.ʻgw. | bn.urt. | aẖdbu. | pḥ[-]. | bn.ʻb . | bn.uḏn[-]. | bn.yṣr. 121[307].8
| ʻbdgṯr. | ḥrr. | bn.s[-]p[-]. | bn.nrpd. | bn.ḥ[-]y. | bʻlskn. | bn.ʻbd. | ẖyrn. | alpy. | bn.plsy. | bn.qrr[-]. | bn.ḥyl. | bn.gʻyn. | ḥ 1035.1.16
ḥl h. | [---].bn.mryn. | [---].bn.ṯyl. | annmt.nḥl h. | abmn.bn.ʻbd. | liy.bn.rqdy. | bn.ršp. 1036.13
bn.ṣrṯn. | bn.ʻbd. | snb.w.nḥl h. | [-]by.w.nḥl h. | [--]ilt.w.nḥl h. | [---]n. | [1063.2
].bn.npr.ẖmšm. | ṣṣ.bn.adlḏn.ṯlṯm. | ṣṣ.bn.ʻglt.ṯlṯm. | ṣṣ.bn.ʻbd.ʻšrm. | ṣṣ.bn.mṣḥ[n].ʻšrm. | šbʻ.mat.ṯṯm kbd. 2096.18
.ṯqlm. | bn.ẖnzr.ṯqlm. | dqn.nsk.arbʻt. | bn.ẖdyn.ṯqlm. | bn.ʻbd.šẖr.ṯqlm. | bn.ẖnqn.arbʻt. | [b]n.ṯrk.ṯqlm. | [b]n.pdrn.ṯ 122[308].1.19
[-----]. | [-]mn. | bʻly. | rpan. | ʻpṯrm. | bn.ʻbd. | šmbʻl. | ykr. | bly. | ṯbʻm. | ḥḏṯn. | rpty. | ilym. | bn.ʻbr. | 1058.6
.ilt. | špšyn.nḥl h. | nʻmn.bn.iryn. | nrn.nḥl h. | bn.ẖsn. | bn.ʻbd. | [-----]. | [---.n]ḥ[l h]. | [-]ntm[.---]. | [ʻ]bdm. | [bn].mṣrn 85[80].2.10
.b]ṣry. | bn.ykn. | bn.lṣn.ʻrmy. | bn.bʻyn.šly. | bn.ynḥn. | bn.ʻbdilm.hzpy. 99[327].2.6
n. | prdn.ndb[--]. | [-]rn.ẖbty. | abmn.bn.qdmn. | nʻmn.bn.ʻbdilm. 87[64].41
.agmn. | bn.uṣb. | bn.yzg. | bn.anntn. | bn.kwn. | ǵmšd. | bn.ʻbdḥy. | bn.ubyn. | slpd. | bn.atnb. | bn.ktmn. | bn.pity. | bn.i 115[301].4.10
.bʻltn ẖlq. | bn.mlkbn. | bn.asyy ẖlq. | bn.kṯly. | bn.kyn. | bn.ʻbdḥr. | [-]prm ẖlq. | [---]n ẖlq. | bn mʻnt. | bn kbdy. | bn kr 2016.2.7
| ytrʻm.bn.swy. | ṣḥrn.bn.qrtm. | bn.špš.bn.ibrd. | ʻpṯrm.bn.ʻbdy. | n[--.]bn.šnd. | [---].bn.[---]. 2024.6
ʻm. | bdlm. | bn.ṣǵr. | klb. | bn.mnḥm. | bn.brqn. | bn.ʻn. | bn.ʻbdy. | ʻbdʻṯtr. 1046.3.48
m[---.---]. | yšr[-.---]. | bn.gnb[-.---]. | hzpym. | rišn.[---]. | bn.ʻbdy.[---]. | bn.dmtn.[---]. | [b]n.gʻyn.ẖr[-]. | lbnym. | grgš.[- 93[328].10
.mnm.šalm. | dt.tknn. | ʻl.ʻrbnm. | hn hmt. | tknn. | mtn.bn.ʻbdym. | ilrb.bn.ilyn. | ʻbdadt.bn ʻbdkb. | gnʻym. 1161.10
q[lʻ]. | bn.rpš.qšt.w.qlʻ. | bn.ǵb.qšt. | bn.ytrm.qšt.w.qlʻ. | bn.ʻbdyrḫ.qšt.w.q[lʻ]. | bn.lky.qšt. | bn.dll.qšt.w.ql[ʻ]. | bn.pǵy 119[321].3.26
. | hn hmt. | tknn. | mtn.bn.ʻbdym. | ilrb.bn.ilyn. | ʻbdadt.bn ʻbdkb. | gnʻym. 1161.12
.mlkyy. | [bn].bm[--]. | [ʻš]rm. | [-----]. | [-----]. | bn.p[--]. | bn.ʻbdmlk. 2163.3.19
. | yddn.qšt.w.qlʻ. | šʻrt. | bn.il.qšt.w.qlʻ. | ark.qšt.w.qlʻ. | bn.ʻbdnkl.qšt.w.qlʻ. | bn.znan.qšt. | bn.arz.[ar]bʻ.qšt.w.arb[ʻ.] 119[321].2.43
ṯ. | [-]by.nsk.ṯlṯ. | šmny. | ḥršn. | ldn. | bn.ands. | bn.ann. | bn.ʻbdpdr. | šd.iyry.l.ʻbdbʻl. | šd.šmmn.l.bn.šty. | šd.bn.arws.l. 1102.16
-]. | [--.--]ẖ.bn.ag[--]. | [---.--]m[.---]. | [kd.]šš. | [k]d.ykn.bn.ʻbdṯrm. | kd.ʻbdil. | ṯlṯ.ʻl.bn.srt. | kd.ʻl.ẓrm. | kd.ʻl.šz.bn pls. 1082.2.2
bn.ulbt[-]. | ḏkry[-]. | bn.tlm[yn]. | bn.yʻdd. | bn.idly[-]. | bn.ʻbd[--]. | bn.ṣd[qn]. 2017.8
n.ubyn. | slpd. | bn.atnb. | bn.ktmn. | bn.pity. | bn.iryn. | bn.ʻbl. | bn.grbn. | bn.iršyn. | bn.nklb. | bn.mryn. | [bn.]b[--]. | b 115[301].4.17
---]n. | [--]ly. | [iw]ryn. | [--.w.n]ḥl h. | [-]ibln. | bn.nḏbn. | bn.ʻbl. | bn.tlšn. | bn.sln. | w nḥl h. 1063.12
. | [--.-]hs. | [--.--]nyn. | [-----]. | [-----]. | bn.ʻdy. | w.nḥl h. | bn.ʻbl. | bn.[-]rṯn. | bn[.---]. | bn u[l]pm. | bn ʻ[p]ty. | bn.kdgdl. | 2163.2.21
ʻn. | bn.ǵlmy. | ǵly. | bn.dnn. | bn.rmy. | dll. | mny. | krty. | bn.ʻbṣ. | bn.argb. | ydn. | ilʻnt. | bn.urt. | ydn. | qṯn. | bn.asr. | bn.ʻ 2117.3.40
. | bn.ʻbd. | šmbʻl. | ykr. | bly. | ṯbʻm. | ḥḏṯn. | rpty. | ilym. | bn.ʻbr. | mnipʻl. | amrbʻl. | dqry. | ṯdy. | ypʻbʻl. | bdlm. | bn.pd[-]. 1058.14
bn.ẖran. | bn.srt. | bn.adn. | bn.ʻgw. | bn.urt. | aẖdbu. | pḥ[-]. | bn.ʻb . | bn.uḏn[-]. | bn.yṣr. 121[307].4
ẖ]dpṯr.ṯt.qštm.[w].qlʻ. | bn.aǵlyn.ṯt.qštm[.w.ṯl]ṯ.qlʻm. | bn.ʻgw.qšt.w qlʻ. | bn.tbšn.ṯlṯ.qšt.w.[ṯlṯ.]qlʻm. | bn.army.ṯt.qšt 119[321].3.20
[t]. | bn.ṯǵdy[.qšt.]w.qlʻ. | ṯty.qšt[.w.]qlʻ. | bn.šp[š.]qšt. | bn.ʻg[w.]qšt.w qlʻ. | ḥd[ṯ]n.qšt.w.qlʻ. | bn.bb.qšt.w[.ql]ʻ. | bn.a 119[321].4.7
gn. | [b]n.tgḏn. | bn.ẖdyn. | bn.sgr. | bn.aǵltn. | bn.ktln. | bn.ʻgwn. | bn.yšmʻ. | bdl.mḏrǵlm. | bn.mmy. | bn.ẖnyn. | bn.kn 104[316].9
rty. | bn ltḥ ẖlq. | bn ytr. | bn ilšpš. | ubrš. | bn gmš ẖlq. | bn ʻgy. | bn zlbn. | bn.aẖ[--]. | bn[.---]. | [-----]. | bn kr[k]. | bn ẖt 2016.2.19
[n].ṣd[-.---]. | [ṣṣ].bn.npr.ẖmšm. | ṣṣ.bn.adlḏn.ṯlṯm. | ṣṣ.bn.ʻglt.ṯlṯm. | ṣṣ.bn.ʻbd.ʻšrm. | ṣṣ.bn.mṣḥ[n].ʻšrm. | šbʻ.mat.ṯṯ 2096.17
n.a[--]. | bn.ml[k]. | bn.glyn. | bn.ʻdr. | bn.ṯmq. | bn.ntp. | bn.ʻgrt. 1057.22
.ʻbṣ. | bn.argb. | ydn. | ilʻnt. | bn.urt. | ydn. | qṯn. | bn.asr. | bn.ʻdy. | bn.amt[m]. | myn. | šr. | bn.zql. | bn.iḥy. | bn.iyṯr. | bn.ʻ 2117.3.48
| bn.inr[-]. | bn.ṯbil. | bn.iryn. | ṯṯl. | bn.nṣdn. | bn.ydln. | [bn].ʻdy. | [bn].ilyn. 1071.10
.ḥyn.bn.ǵlm. | bn.yyn.w.bn.au[pš]. | bn.kdrn. | ʻrgzy.w.bn.ʻdy. | bn.gmḥn.w.ḥgbt. | bn.tgdn. | yny. | [b]n.gʻyn dd. | [-]n 131[309].27
| bn.ṯmyr. | ẓbr. | bn.ṯdṯb. | bn.ʻrmn. | bn.alz. | bn.mṣrn. | bn.ʻdy. | bn.ršpy. | [---.]mn. | [--.-]sn. | [bn.-]ny. | [b]n.ẖnyn. | [b 115[301].2.16
. | bn.ṯrn. | w.nḥl h. | [--.-]hs. | [--.--]nyn. | [-----]. | [-----]. | bn.ʻdy. | w.nḥl h. | bn.ʻbl. | bn.[-]rṯn. | bn[.---]. | bn u[l]pm. | bn 2163.2.19
ʻl.bn.aly.ṯkt. | klby.bn.iḥy.ṯkt. | psš.bn.buly.ṯkt. | ʻpṣpn.bn.ʻdy.ṯkt. | nʻmn.bn.ʻyn.ṯkt. | ʻpṯn.bn.ilrš.ṯkt. | ilṯḥm.bn.šrn.ṯ 2085.9
n.kbd. | [l.]sbrdnm. | m[i]t.l.bn.ʻẓmt.rišy. | mit.l.tlmyn.bn.ʻdy. | [---.]l.aḏddy. | [--.]l.kkln. 2095.8
. | ʻbd. | qrḥ. | abšr. | bn.bdn. | ḏmry. | bn.pndr. | bn.aẖt. | bn.ʻdn. | bn.išbʻ[l]. 2117.4.33
]. | [b]n.bʻl[--]. | bn.gld. | bn.ṣmy. | bn.mry[n]. | bn.mgn. | bn.ʻdn. | bn.knn. | bn.py. | bn.mk[-]. | bn.by[--]. | bn.a[--]. | bn.i 2117.1.7
bn. | bn.b[--]. | [b]n.[---]. | bn.a[--]. | bn.ml[k]. | bn.glyn. | bn.ʻdr. | bn.ṯmq. | bn.ntp. | bn.ʻgrt. 1057.19
ilm[.---]. | ṯšʻ.ʻš[r.---]. | bn ʻdr[.---]. | ẖmš ʻl.bn[.---]. | ẖmš ʻl rʻl[-]. | ẖmš ʻl ykn[.--]. | ẖ[2034.2.3
-.---]. | l[--.---]. | m[--.---]. | bn[.---]. | bn[.---]. | w.yn[.---]. | bn.ʻdr[.---]. | ntb[t]. | b.arb[ʻ]. | mat.ḥr[ṣ]. 2007.9
bn.gnb[.msg]. | bn.twyn[.msg]. | bn.ʻdrš[p.msg]. | pyn.yny.[msg]. | bn.mṣrn m[sg]. | yky msg. | 133[-].1.3
ṯṯ [mat]. | [-----]. | ilmlk ṯṯ mat. | ʻbdilm.ṯṯ mat. | šmmn.bn.ʻdš.ṯṯ mat. | ušknym. | ypʻ.alpm. | aẖ[m]lk.bn.nskn.alpm. | 1060.1.12
]b bʻl.b qrb. | bt.w yʻn.aliyn. | bʻl.ašt m.kṯr bn. | ym.kṯr.bnm.ʻdt. | ypṯḥ.ḥln.b bht m. | urbt.b qrb.[h]kl | m.w y[p]ṯḥ.b 4[51].7.16
n. | bn.ršp. | tmn. | šmmn. | bn.rmy. | bn.aky. | ʻbdḥmn. | bn.ʻdṯ. | kṯy. | bn.ḥny. | bn.ssm. | bn.ḥnn. | [--]ny. | [bn].ṯrdnt. | [1047.15
| bn[.n]klb. | b[n.]dtn. | w.nḥl h. | w.nḥl hm. | bn.iršyn. | bn.ʻzn. | bn.aršw. | bn.ḥzrn. | bn.iǵyn. | w.nḥl h. | bn.ksd. | bn.b 113[400].2.13
n.ʻnt. | ǵzldn. | ṯrn. | ḥdbt. | [-]ḥl.aǵltn. | [-]n. | [-]mṯ. | [--.]bn.[ʻ]zn. | [--]yn. 1043.19
ṯ ʻtr k[--.---]. | b ẖmṯ ʻtr[.---]. | [-----]. | [---.-]y[-.---]. | w bn ʻṯl.[---]. | ypẖ knʻm[.---]. | aẖmn bt[.---]. | b ẖmṯ ʻtr ṯmn[.--- 207[57].8
.mšrm. | [mi]tm.arbʻm.ṯmn.kbd. | [l.]sbrdnm. | m[i]t.l.bn.ʻẓmt.rišy. | mit.l.tlmyn.bn.ʻdy. | [---.]l.aḏddy. | [--.]l.kkln. 2095.7
nm. | nḥl. | yʻny. | atn. | utly. | bn.alz. | bn ẖlm. | bn.ḏmr. | bn.ʻyn. | ubnyn. | rpš d ydy. | ǵbl. | mlk. | gwl. | rqd. | ẖlby. | ʻn[q 2075.18
ym.qnum. | bn.ilrš. | ʻ[p]ṯn. | b[n.ʻr]my. | [--]ṯy. | bn.ǵdʻ. | bn.ʻyn. | bn.grb[n]. | yṯtn. | bn.ab[l]. | kry. | psš. | ilṯḥm. | ḥrm. | b 2078.7
. | bn.ḥn[n]. | bn.gntn[-]. | [--.]nqq[-]. | b[n.---]. | bn.[---]. | bn.ʻyn. | bn.dtn. 2023.4.3
.ʻdy. | bn.amt[m]. | myn. | šr. | bn.zql. | bn.iḥy. | bn.iyṯr. | bn.ʻyn. | bn.ǵzl. | bn.ṣmy. | bn.il[-]šy. | bn.ybšr. | bn.sly. | bn.ḥlb 2117.2.6
.bn.iḥy.ṯkt. | psš.bn.buly.ṯkt. | ʻpṣpn.bn.ʻdy.ṯkt. | nʻmn.bn.ʻyn.ṯkt. | ʻpṯn.bn.ilrš.ṯkt. | ilṯḥm.bn.šrn.ṯkt. | šmlbu.bn.grb. 2085.10

d.b d.bn.pṯd. | šd.b d.dr.khnm. | šd.b d.bn.ʻmy. | šd.b d.bn.ʻyn. | ṯn.šdm.b d.klṯṯb. | šd.b d.krz[n]. | ṯlṯ.šdm.b d.amtr[n 2090.19
| synn.bn knʻm. | bn kbr. | bn iytlm. | bn ayln. | bn.kln. | bn.ʻlln. | bn.liy. | bn.nqṭn. | bn abrḫṭ. | bn.grdy. | bn.ṣlpn. | bn ǵl 1064.24
kn. | bn.yḫnn.aḏddy. | bn.pdǵy.mḫdy. | bn.yyn.mdrǵl. | bn.ʻlr. | ḫtpy.aḏddy. | ynḥm.aḏddy. | ykny.aḏddy. | m[--].aḏdd 2014.19
šd.b d.krb[-]. | šd.b d.bn.pṯd. | šd.b d.dr.khnm. | šd.b d.bn.ʻmy. | šd.b d.bn.ʻyn. | ṯn.šdm.b d.klṯṯb. | šd.b d.krz[n]. | ṯlṯ. 2090.18
.ṯqlm. | bn.bʻln.ṯqlm. | ʻbdyrḫ.nqd.ṯqlm. | bt.sgld.ṯqlm. | bn.ʻmy.ṯqlm. | bn.brq.ṯqlm. | bn.ḫnzr.ṯqlm. | dqn.nsk.arbʻt. | b 122[308].1.14
| ṯn[.---.b]n.mlk. | ṯ[n.---.]gpn. | [-----]. | [---.--]b. | b[--.---.b]n.ʻmy. 1150.6
[.bn].pls. | abrš[p.bn.]ḫrpn. | gmrš[.bn].mrnn. | ʻbdmlk.bn.ʻmyn. | agyn.rʻy. | abmlk.bn.ilrš. | iḫyn.bn.ḫryn. | [ab]ǵl.bn. 102[323].4.8
]ḫl hm. | b[n.---]. | bn.gzry. | bn.atyn. | bn.ttn. | bn.rwy. | bn.ʻmyn. | bdl.mrynm. | bn.ṣqn. | bn.šyn. | bn.prtn. | bn.ypr. | 113[400].3.5
[---]. | bn.at[--]. | bn.qnḏ. | ṣmq[-]. | bn.anny. | bn.ʻmtḏl. | bn.ʻmyn. | bn.alz. | bn.birtn. | [bn.]ylkn. | [bn.]krwn. | [bn.-]ty. 117[325].1.11
bn.[u]brš. | ḫmšt.ʻšrt. | b.šd.bn.[-]n. | ṯl[ṯt].ʻšr[t]. | b.š[d].bn.ʻmyn. | ḫmšt. | b.[šd.--]n. | ḫ[m]št[.ʻ]šrt. | [ar]bʻm.ksp. | [---] 1083.11
.usyy. | mit.ṯṯm.kbd. | l.bn.yšmʻ. | mit.arbʻm.kbd. | l.liy.bn.ʻmyn. | mit.ḫmšm.kbd. | d.škn.l.ks.ilm. 1143.12
d.gl.bʻlz.l.bn.ʻmnr. | šd.knʻm.l.bn.ʻmnr. | šd.bn.krwn.l bn.ʻmyn. | šd.bn.prmn.l aḫny. | šd.bn ḥnn.l bn.adlḏn. | šd.bn. 2089.5
[-]k[-.---]. | ar[--.---]. | yrt.[---]. | ṯṯ.prš[.---]. | bn.ʻmyn[.---]. 2152.5
.bn.prmn.l aḫny. | šd.bn ḥnn.l bn.adlḏn. | šd.bn.nṣdn.l bn.ʻmlbi. | šd.ṯpḫln.l bn.ǵl. | w dṯn.nḫl h.l bn.pl. | šd.krwn.l a 2089.8
dnn.ṯlṯ.ṣmdm. | bn.ʻmnr. | bn.kmn. | bn.ibyn. | bn.mryn.ṣmd.w.ḥrṣ. | bn.prsn.ṣ 2113.2
| šd.bn.ḫtb.l bn.yʻḏrd. | šd.gl.bʻlz.l.bn.ʻmnr. | šd.knʻm.l.bn.ʻmnr. | šd.bn.krwn.l bn.ʻmyn. | šd.bn.prmn.l aḫny. | šd.bn 2089.4
šd.bn.šty.l.bn.ṯbrn. | šd.bn.ḫtb.l bn.yʻḏrd. | šd.gl.bʻlz.l.bn.ʻmnr. | šd.knʻm.l.bn.ʻmnr. | šd.bn.krwn.l bn.ʻmyn. | šd.bn. 2089.3
d.šmmn.l.bn.šty. | šd.bn.arws.l.bn.ḫlan. | šd.bn.ibryn.l.bn.ʻmnr. 1102.20
[s]p[r] ušknym.dt.[b d.---]. | bn.btr. | bn.ʻms. | bn.pṣn. | bn.agmz. | bn.[--]n. | bn.a[--]. | [------]. | [------ 2021.1.3
d[--]. | bn.s[---]. | bn.at[--]. | bn.qnḏ. | ṣmq[-]. | bn.anny. | bn.ʻmtḏl. | bn.ʻmyn. | bn.alz. | bn.birtn. | [bn.]ylkn. | [bn.]krwn 117[325].1.10
kbl. | knʻm. | bdlm. | bn.ṣǵr. | klb. | bn.mnḥm. | bn.brqn. | bn.ʻn. | bn.ʻbdy. | ʻbdʻṯtr. 1046.3.47
nn.bn.ṣnr. | iḫy.[b]n[.--]l[-]. | ʻbdy[rḫ].bn.gttn. | yrmn.bn.ʻn. | krwn.nḫl h. | ttn.[n]ḫl h. | bn.b[r]zn. | [---.-]ḥn. 85[80].4.9
| bn.grgs.ilštmʻy. | bn.ḫran.ilštmʻy. | bn.abdʻn.ilštmʻy. | bn.ʻn.rqdy. | bn.gʻyn. | bn.ǵrn. | bn.agynt. | bn.abdḥr.snry. | dq 87[64].32
ṯn.b gt.mzln. | ṯn.b ulm. | abmn.b gt.mʻrb. | atn. | ḫryn. | bn.ʻnt. | llwn. | agdṯb. | aǵltn. | [-]wn. | bldn. | [-]ln. | [-]ldn. | [i]w 1061.6
]ʻln. | [-]šdm. | iwryn. | nʻmn. | [-----]. | b gt.yny. | agttp. | bn.ʻnt. | ǵzldn. | trn. | ḫdbṯ. | [-]ḫl.aǵltn. | [-]n. | [-]mṯ. | [--.]bn.[ʻ 1043.12
[b]n ʻntn.[---]. | bn agyn[.---]. | b[n] ʻṯlṯ[.---]. | bn qṭy[.---]. | bn y 105[86].1
d[--]. | bn.ʻ[---]. | kbkbn bn[.---]. | bn.k[--]. | bn.pdr[n.]. | bn.ʻn[--]. | nḥl h[.---]. | [-----]. 2014.60
sp. | [--.--]n.šbʻt.l ṯlṯm. | [---].šbʻt.ʻšrt. | [---.-]kyn.ʻšrt. | b.bn.ʻsl.ʻšrm.ṯqlm kbd. | b.ṯmq.ḫmšt.l.ʻšrt. | b.[---].šbʻt.ʻšrt. | b.b 2054.1.6
.ʻdy. | w.nḥl h. | bn.ʻbl. | bn.[-]rṭn. | bn[.---]. | bn u[l]pm. | bn ʻ[p]ty. | bn.kdgdl. | bn.smyy. | bn.lbn. | bn.šlmn. | bn.mly. | p 2163.3.3
by[--]. | bn.a[--]. | bn.iy[--]. | bn.ḫ[---]. | bn.plś. | bn.ubr. | bn.ʻpṯb. | ṯbry. | bn.ymn. | krty. | bn.abr[-]. | yrpu. | kdn. | pʻṣ. | b 2117.1.17
bn.nṣ. | [b]n.ʻṣr. | [---]m. | [bn.]ulnhr. | [bn.p]rn. | [bn.a]nny. | [---]n. | bn. 1075.1.2
mlk. | ynḥm. | aḏddn. | mtn. | plsy. | qṭn. | ypr. | bn.ymy. | bn.ʻrd. | [-]b.da[-]. | [--]l[--]. | [-----]. 1035.4.13
rišym.qnum. | bn.ilrš. | ʻ[p]ṯn. | b[n.ʻr]my. | [--]ty. | bn.ǵdʻ. | bn.ʻyn. | bn.grb[n]. | yṯtn. | bn.ab[l] 2078.4
.slgyn. | ʻzn.bn.mlk. | bn.alṯn. | bn.ṯmyr. | ẓbr. | bn.ṯdṯb. | bn.ʻrmn. | bn.alz. | bn.mṣrn. | bn.ʻdy. | bn.ršpy. | [---.]mn. | [--.-] 115[301].2.13
n.grdn. | [bn.-]ḫr. | [--.-]nb. | [--.--]n. | [--.--]n. | bn.[---]. | bn.ʻr[--]. | bn.nkt[-]. | bn.abḏr. | bn.ḥrẓn. | bn.ḏqnt. | bn.gmrš. | 2023.3.7
spr.mḫṣm. | bn.ḫpśry.b.šbn. | ilštmʻym. | y[---.]bn.ʻšq. | [---.]bn.tqy. | [---.]bn.šlmy. | [-----]. | [---].ubrʻy. | [---].g 1041.4
[b]n ʻntn.[---]. | bn agyn[.---]. | b[n] ʻṯlṯ[.---]. | bn qṭy[.---]. | bn ypʻ[.---]. | [---]bʻm[.---]. | [-----]. 105[86].3
q. | bn.army. | bn.rpiyn. | bn.army. | bn.krmn. | bn.ykn. | bn.ʻṯtrab. | uṣn[-]. | bn.alṯn. | bn.aš[-]š. | bn.štn. | bn.ilš. | bn.tna 1046.1.12
spr.ytnm. | bn.ḫlbym. | bn.ady. | bn.ʻṯtry. | bn.ḥrẓn. | ady. | bn.birtn. | bn.ḥrẓn. | bn.bddn. | bn.a 115[301].1.4
l.nḥ[l h.--]. | w.unṯ.aḫd.l h[.---]. | dnn.bn.ysr[.---]. | sln.bn.ʻṯt[-.---]. | pdy.bn.nr[-.---]. | abmlk.bn.un[-.---]. | nrn.bn.mt 90[314].1.6
[---].md.ʻ[ṯtr]t. | ydy. | bn.škn. | bn.mdt. | bn.ḫ[--]y. | bn.ʻ[-]y. | knʻm. | bn.yš[-]n. | bn.pd[y]. | ttn. | md.ʻṯt[rt]. | kṯkt. | 1054.1.6
b[n.---]. | bn[.---]. | [-]d[-.---]. | bn.ʻ[--.---]. | bn.[---]. 109[-].4
l.mrynm. | bn.ṣqn. | bn.šyn. | bn.prtn. | bn.ypr. | mrum. | bn.ʻ[--]t. | bn.adty. | bn.krwn. | bn.nǵsk. | bn.qnḏ. | bn.pity. | w. 113[400].3.12
.ṯmq. | bn.ntp. | bn.mlk. | bn.ṯʻ[-]. | bn.km[-]. | bn.r[--]. | [bn.]ʻ[---]. | [bn.]r[---]. | [bn.]ḫ[---]. | [bn.]šbl. | [bn.]ḫdmn. | [bn. 1073.2.1
. | w.nḥl h. | bn.šml[-]. | bn.brzn. | bn.ḫtr[-]. | bn.yd[--]. | bn.ʻ[---]. | w.nḥ[l h]. | w.nḥ[l h]. | bn.k[---]. | bn.y[---]. | [bn].i[-- 116[303].9
. | bn.[--]m. | bn.asr[-]. | bn.ḏr[--]. | bn.ṣl[--]. | bn.ḫd[--]. | bn.ʻ[---]. | kbkbn bn[.---]. | bn.k[--]. | bn.pdr[n.]. | bn.ʻn[--]. | nḥ 2014.56
lṯ.]qlʻm. | bn.army.ṯṯ.qštm.w[.]q[lʻ]. | bn.rpš.qšt.w.qlʻ. | bn.ǵb.qšt. | bn.ytrm.qšt.w.qlʻ. | bn.ʻbdyrḫ.qšt.w.q[lʻ]. | bn.lky. 119[321].3.24
rišym.qnum. | bn.ilrš. | ʻ[p]ṯn. | b[n.ʻr]my. | [--]ty. | bn.ǵdʻ. | bn.ʻyn. | bn.grb[n]. | yṯtn. | bn.ab[l]. | kry. | psś. | ilṯḥm. 2078.6
.amt[m]. | myn. | šr. | bn.zql. | bn.iḫy. | bn.iytr. | bn.ʻyn. | bn.ǵzl. | bn.ṣmy. | bn.il[-]šy. | bn.ybšr. | bn.sly. | bn.ḫlbt. | bn.br 2117.2.7
ʻzn.bn.irbn. | bn.mglb. | bn.ntp. | ʻmyn.bn ǵḫpn. | bn.kbln. | bn.bly. | bn.ṯʻy. | bn.nṣdn. | klby. 104[316].4
.bn ḥnn.l bn.adlḏn. | šd.bn.nṣdn.l bn.ʻmlbi. | šd.ṯpḫln.l bn.ǵl. | w dṯn.nḫl h.l bn.pl. | šd.krwn.l aḫn. | šd.ʻyy.l aḫn. | šd. 2089.9
t. | mtn. | mḫtn. | [p]lsy. | bn.ḥrš. | [--.]kbd. | [---]. | y[---]. | bn.ǵlyn. | bdl.ar. | bn.šyn. | bn.ubrš. | bn.d[--]b. | abrpu. | bn.k[n 1035.2.19
. | [--]ndbym. | [ʻ]rmy.w snry. | [b]n.sdy.bn.ṯty. | bn.ḥyn.bn.ǵlm. | bn.yyn.w.bn.au[pš]. | bn.kdrn. | ʻrgzy.w.bn.ʻdy. | bn. 131[309].24
d. | [---]n.dd. | [---.]dd. | bn.arwdn.dd. | mnḥm.w.kbln. | bn.ǵlm.dd. | bn.tbšn.dd. | bn.ḫran.w[.---]. | [-]n.yʻrtym. | gmm. 131[309].6
liy. | ydʻ. | šmn. | ʻdy. | ʻnbr. | aḫrm. | bn.qrdy. | bn.šmʻn. | bn.ǵlmy. | ǵly. | bn.dnn. | bn.rmy. | dll. | mny. | krty. | bn.ʻbṣ. | b 2117.3.33
bn.tgḏn.ugrty. | tgyn.arty. | bn.nryn.arty. | bn.ršp.ary. | bn.ǵlmn ary. | bn.ḥṣbn ary. | bn.śdy ary. | bn.ktkt.mʻqby. | bn. 87[64].13
bn.ǵlmn.ary. | [bn].śdy. | [bn].gmḥ. | [---]ty. | [b]n.ypy.gbʻly. | b 99[327].1.1
n.ʻlln. | bn.liy. | bn.nqṭn. | bn abrḫṭ. | bn.grdy. | bn.ṣlpn. | bn ǵlmn. | bn sgld. 1064.B.1
| ǵldy. | iḫǵl. | aby. | abmn. | ynḥm. | npl. | ynḥm. | mtbʻl. | bn ǵlmn. | bn sgld. 1065.B.1
| bn.ilš. | bn.tnabn. | bn.ḥṣn. | ṣprn. | bn.ašbḥ. | bn.qṭnn. | bn.ǵlmn. | [bn].ṣwy. | [bn].ḫnq[n]. | [-----]. | [-----]. | [-----]. | [---- 1046.1.23
w ḥẓr.k bn. | [a]ṯrt.gm.l ǵlm h. | bʻl.yṣḥ.ʻn.gpn. | w ugr.bn.ǵlmt. | ʻmm ym.bn.ẓlm[t]. | rmt.prʻt.ibr[.mnt]. | ṣḥrrm.ḥbl 8[51FRAG].7
| [ʻ].hmlt.arṣ.gm.l ǵ[lm] h.bʻl k.yṣḥ.ʻn. | [gpn].w ugr.b ǵlmt. | [ʻmm.]ym.bn.ẓlmt.r | [mt.prʻ]t.ibr.mnt. | [ṣḥrrm.ḥbl. 4[51].7.54
| bn.mṣrn m[sg]. | yky msg. | ynḥm.msg. | bn.ugr.msg. | bn.ǵlṣ msg. | arbʻ l ṯkš[-]. | nn.arspy.ms[g]. | [---.ms]g. | bn.[gr] 133[-].1.9

bn.ǵs.ḥrš.š‘ty. | ‘dy.bn.sl‘y.gbly. | yrm.b‘l.bn.kky. 2121.1
n.anny. | ytršp. | bn.szn. | bn.kdgdl. | bn.gl‘d. | bn.ktln. | [bn].ǵrgn. | bn.pb[-]. | bn.[---]. | bn.[---]. | bn.[---]. | bn.[---]. | bn.[115[301].1.16
.]aglby. | [bn.]b‘ly. | [mḏ]rǵlm. | [bn.]kdgdl. | [b]n.qṭn. | [b]n.ǵrgn. | [b]n.tgḏn. | bn.ḫdyn. | bn.sgr. | bn.aǵltn. | bn.ktln. | 104[316].9
-]. | bn.[---]. | w.nḥ[l h]. | bn.ẓr[-]. | mru.skn. | bn.bddn. | bn.ǵrgn. | bn.tgtn. | bn.ḥrẓn. | bn.qdšt. | bn.nṯǵ[-]. | bn.gr[--]. | b 113[400].5.8
ran.ilštm‘y. | bn.abd‘n.ilštm‘y. | bn.‘n.rqdy. | bn.g‘yn. | bn.ǵrn. | bn.agynt. | bn.abdḥr.snry. | dqn.šlmn. | prdn.ndb[--]. 87[64].34
-]. | bn.dmtn.[---]. | [b]n.g‘yn.ḫr[-]. | lbnym. | grgš.[---]. | bn.ǵrn.[---]. | bn.agyn[.---]. | iyṯ[-.---]. 93[328].15
[w]nḥ[l h]. | [bn].amd[-]. | [bn].ṣbṭ[--]. | [bn].ḫla[n]. | [bn].ǵr[--]. | d.b[n.---]. | d.bn.[---]. | d.bn.s̀[--]. | d.bn.ṯn[r]. | d.k 2164.A.5
mšd. | bn.‘bdḥy. | bn.ubyn. | slpd. | bn.atnb. | bn.ktmn. | bn.pity. | bn.iryn. | bn.‘bl. | bn.grbn. | bn.iršyn. | bn.nklb. | bn. 115[301].4.15
[---]. | bn.mlkyy. | bn.atn. | bn.bly. | bn.ṯbrn. | bn.ḥgby. | bn.pity. | bn.slgyn. | ‘zn.bn.mlk. | bn.alṯn. | bn.ṯmyr. | ẓbr. | bn.ṯ 115[301].2.6
um. | bn.‘[--]t. | bn.adty. | bn.krwn. | bn.nǵsk. | bn.qnḏ. | bn.pity. | w.nḥl h. | bn.rt. | bn.l[--]. | bn.[---]. | [---.--]y. | [--.-]ḏr 113[400].3.17
[spr.----]m. | bn.pi[ty]. | w.nḥ[l h]. | ‘bd[--]. | bn.s[---]. | bn.at[--]. | bn.qnḏ. | ṣ 117[325].1.2
--]. | bn kr[k]. | bn ḫtyn. | w nḥl h. | bn ṯgrb. | bn ṯdnyn. | bn pbn. 2016.3.7
ršp. | bn.szn. | bn.kdgdl. | bn.gl‘d. | bn.ktln. | [bn].ǵrgn. | bn.pb[-]. | bn.[---]. | bn.[---]. | bn.[---]. | bn.[---]. | bn.[---]. | bn.[-- 115[301].1.17
. | [bn.]ulnhr. | [bn.p]rn. | [bn.a]nny. | [---]n. | bn.kbln. | bn.pdy. | bn.ṯpdn. 1075.2.2
.škn. | bn.mdt. | bn.ḫ[--]y. | bn.‘[-]y. | kn‘m. | bn.yš[-]n. | bn.pd[y]. | ttn. | md.‘ṯt[rt]. | kṯkt. | bn.ṯtn[--]. | [m]d.m[--]. | [b]n 1054.1.9
.ilrš. | iḫyn.bn.ḫryn. | [ab]ǵl.bn.gdn. | [---].bn.bqš. | [---].bn.pdn. | [---.bn.-]ky. | [---.bn.--]r. | [-----]. | [---.--]yn. | [---.]aṯr 102[323].4.14
. | bn.knn[.---]y. | bn.ymlk[.b]d.skn. | bn.yḥnn.aḏddy. | bn.pdǵy.mḫdy. | bn.yyn.mḏrǵl. | bn.‘lr. | ḫṯpy.aḏddy. | ynḥm. 2014.17
yp‘.l[.---]. | šmr[m.---]. | [-----]. | bn.g[r.---]. | ḏmry[.---]. | bn.pdr.l.[---]. 2122.8
.ṣl[--]. | bn.ḫd[--]. | bn.‘[---]. | kbkbn bn[.---]. | bn.k[--]. | bn.pdr[n.]. | bn.‘n[--]. | nḥl h[.---]. | [-----]. 2014.59
l.‘šrm.ṯqlm kbd. | b.ṯmq.ḫmšt.l.‘šrt. | b.[---].šb‘t.‘šrt. | b.bn.pdrn.‘šrm. | d.bn.šb‘l.uḫnpy.ḫmšm. | b.bn.ṯtm.ṯlṯm. | b.bn. 2054.1.9
lm. | bn.‘bd.šḫr.ṯqlm. | bn.ḫnqn.arb‘t. | [b]n.ṯrk.ṯqlm. | [b]n.pdrn.ṯq[lm]. | pdy.[----]. | [i]lmlk.bn.[---]. | [--]‘[-.---]. | [---. 122[308].1.22
lm. | [---.]bn.ully.b.ṯ[qlm]. | [---.]bn.annḏy.b[.---]. | [---.]bn.pd[--.---]. 135[330].7
. | bn.‘br. | mnip‘l. | amrb‘l. | dqry. | ṯdy. | yp‘b‘l. | bdlm. | bn.pḏ[-]. | bn.[---]. 1058.21
--]. | bn.ṯ[--]. | bn.[---]. | bn.ṯ‘l[-]. | bn.nq[ly]. | bn.snr[n]. | bn.pzn[y]. | bn.mg[lb]. | bn.db[--]. | bn.amd[n]. | annš[-]. 2020.10
qly. | bn.snrn. | bn.ṯgd. | bn.d[-]n. | bn.amdn. | bn.ṯmrn. | bn.pzny. | bn.mglb. | bn.[--]b. | bn.[---]. | bn.[---]. 113[400].6.31
n. | šd.b d.iwrm[--]. | šd.b d.yṯpr. | šd.b d.krb[-]. | šd.b d.bn.pṭḏ. | šd.b d.dr.khnm. | šd.b d.bn.‘my. | šd.b d.bn.‘yn. | ṯn.š 2090.16
l h. | bn.adlḏn. | bn.s̀bl. | bn.ḫnzr. | bn.arwṯ. | bn.ṯbtnq. | bn.pṭḏn. | bn.nbdg. | bn.ḥgbn. | bn.tmr. | bn.prsn. | bn.ršpy. | [‘] 113[400].1.17
.krwn.‘š[rm]. | ṣṣ.bn.iršyn.[---]. | [ṣṣ].bn.ilb‘l.ṯl[ṯ]m. | ṣṣ.bn.pṭḏn.[--]m. | ṣṣ.[bn].gyn.[---]. | [-----]. | [-----]. | [-----]. | [-----] 2096.7
.gld. | bn.ṣmy. | bn.mry[n]. | bn.mgn. | bn.‘dn. | bn.knn. | bn.py. | bn.mk[-]. | bn.by[--]. | bn.a[--]. | bn.iy[--]. | bn.ḥ[---]. | b 2117.1.9
mlk.ns[--.---]. | bn.tbd.ilšt[m‘y.---]. | mty.ilšt[m‘y.---]. | bn.pynq.‘nqp[a]t[y.---]. | ayiḫ.ilšt[m‘y.---]. | [b]dlm.dt.yṯb[.--- 90[314].2.8
. | tlš.w[.n]ḥl h[.-].ṯgd.mrum. | bt.[-]b[-.-]sy[-]h. | nn[-].b[n].py[-.d.]yṯb.b.gt.aǵld. | s̀gn.bn b[--.---].d.yṯb.b.ilštm‘. | ab 2015.2.5
gmrd. | [---.--]ṯ.l.yšn. | [šd.--]ln. | b d.trǵds. | šd.ṯ‘lb. | b d.bn.pl. | šd.bn.kt. | b d.pdy. | šd.ḫzr. | [b d].d[---]. 2030.2.4
šd.bn.nṣdn.l bn.‘mlbi. | šd.ṯpḫln.l bn.ǵl. | w dṯn.nḥl h.l bn.pl. | šd.krwn.l aḫn. | šd.‘yy.l aḫn. | šd.brdn.l bn.bly. | šd gzl 2089.10
n.mnn.ṯṯm. | b.rpan.bn.yyn.‘šrt. | b.yp‘r.‘šrm. | b.n‘mn.bn.ply.ḫmšt.l.‘šrm. | b.gdn.bn.uss.‘šrm. | b.‘dn.bn.ṯṯ.‘šrt. | b.b 2054.1.17
šd.b]n.ṯqrn.b d.ḫby. | [ṯn.š]d.bn.ngzḥn.b d.gmrd. | [šd.bn].pll.b d.gmrd. | [šd.bn.-]ll.b d.iwrḫṯ. | [šd.bn.-]nn.b d.bn.š 82[300].1.24
--.-]‘n. | ml[--.---]. | ar[--.---.--]l. | aty[n.bn.]šm‘nt. | ḥnn[.bn].pls. | abrš[p.bn.]ḫrpn. | gmrš[.bn].mrnn. | ‘bdmlk.bn.‘my 102[323].4.5
y. | bn.mk[-]. | bn.by[--]. | bn.a[--]. | bn.iy[--]. | bn.ḥ[---]. | bn.pls̀. | bn.ubr. | bn.‘pṯb. | ṯbry. | bn.ymn. | krty. | bn.abr[-]. | yr 2117.1.15
.bn.‘bdṯrm. | kd.‘bdil. | ṯlṯ.‘l.bn.srt. | kd.‘l.ẓrm. | kd.‘l.s̀z.bn pls. | kd.‘l.ynḥm. | tgrm.šmn.d.bn.kwy. | ‘l.šlmym.ṯmn.kb 1082.2.6
. | bn.dll.qšt.w.ql[‘]. | bn.pǵyn.qšt.w[.q]l‘. | bn.bdn.qšt. | bn.pls.qšt. | ǵmrm. | [-]lhd.ṯt.qštm.w.ṯn.ql‘m. | ulšn.ṯt.qšm.w. 119[321].3.31
[-]. | bn.nrpd. | bn.ḥ[-]y. | b‘lskn. | bn.‘bd. | ḫyrn. | alpy. | bn.plsy. | bn.qrr[-]. | bn.ḥyl. | bn.g‘yn. | ḥyn. | bn.armg[-]. | b‘lm 1035.1.19
bn.ilb‘l. | bn.idrm. | bn.grgš. | bn.bly. | bn.apṯ. | bn.ysd. | bn.pl[-]. | bn.ṯb‘nq. | brqd. | bnn. | kbln.ṣ[md]. | bn gmrt. | bn.il. 2113.13
. | bn.yk[--]. | bn.šmm. | bn.irgy. | w.nḥl h. | w.nḥl hm. | [bn].pmn. | bn.gṯrn. | bn.arpḫn. | bn.ṯryn. | bn.dll. | bn.ḫswn. | m 1046.3.27
--]lim bn.brq. | [--.]qtn bn.drṣy. | [--]kn bn.pri. | [r]špab bn.pni. | [ab]mn bn.qṣy. | [‘]pṯrm bn.agmz. | [-]n bn.iln. | [--]n 2087.8
mn. | bn.trdn. | ypq. | ‘bd. | qrḥ. | abšr. | bn.bdn. | ḏmry. | bn.pndr. | bn.aḫt. | bn.‘dn. | bn.išb‘[l]. 2117.4.31
‘zn.bn.mll. | šrm. | [b]n.špš[yn]. | [b]n.ḫrmln. | bn.tnn. | bn.pndr. | bn.nqq. | ḥrš.bhtm. | bn.izl. | bn.ibln. | bn.ilt. | špšyn. 85[80].1.14
l.[---]. | mr[--.---]. | hm.[---]. | kmrṯn[.---]. | bn.ṯbln[.---]. | bn.pndr[.---]. | bn.idr[-.---]. | bn.ḥdn[-.---]. | bn.ṯbi[l.---]. 2070.2.5
d.šmn. | drt.b.kkr. | ubn.ḫṣḥ.kkr. | kkr.lqḥ.ršpy. | tmtrn.bn.pnmn. | kkr. | bn.sgṯtn. | kkr. | ilšpš.kkr. | bn.ḏltn. | kkr.w[.- 1118.7
n.‘šrt. | rpan.ḫmšt. | abǵl.ḫmšt. | bn.aḫdy.‘šrt. | ṯṯn.‘ṣrt. | bn.pnmn.‘šrt. | ‘bdadt.ḫmšt. | abmn.ilštm‘y.ḫmš[t]. | ‘zn.bn.b 1062.23
. | [---.]ṯlṯ kbd.ṣin. | [---.--]a.ṯ[l]ṯ.d.a[--]. | [---].mrn. | [---.]bn pnṯbl. | [---.-]py w.bn h. 1145.2.2
[s]ǵr.bn.bdn. | [sǵ]r.bn.psḥn. | alṯy. | sǵr.npr. | bn.ḫty. | ṯn.bnš ibrḏr. | bnš tlmi. | sǵr 2082.2
bn.-]ṯtayy.b d.ṯṯmd. | [šd.bn.-]rn.b d.ṣdqšlm. | [šd.b d.]bn.p‘ṣ. | [ubdy.‘]šrm. | [šd.---]n.b d.brdd. | [---.--]m. | [šd.---.b 82[300].1.29
n.ṯb[-]. | bn.[-]r[-]. | bn.tgn. | bn.iḏrn. | mnn. | b[n].skn. | bn.p‘ṣ. | bn.ḏrm. | [bn.-]ln. | [bn.-]ḏprḏ. 124[-].6.11
lq[-.---]. | tǵyn.bn.ubn.ṯql[m]. | yšn.ḥrš.mrkbt.ṯq[lm]. | bn.p‘ṣ.ṯqlm. | mṣrn.ḥrš.mrkbt.ṯqlm. | ‘pṯn.ḥrš.qṭn.ṯqlm. | bn.p 122[308].1.7
.p‘ṣ.ṯqlm. | mṣrn.ḥrš.mrkbt.ṯqlm. | ‘pṯn.ḥrš.qṭn.ṯqlm. | bn.pǵḏn.ṯqlm. | bn.b‘ln.ṯqlm. | ‘bdyrḫ.nqd.ṯqlm. | bt.sgld.ṯql 122[308].1.10
| bn.‘bdyrḫ.qšt.w.q[l‘]. | bn.lky.qšt. | bn.dll.qšt.w.ql[‘]. | bn.pǵyn.qšt.w[.q]l‘. | bn.bdn.qšt. | bn.pls.qšt. | ǵmrm. | [-]lhd.ṯ 119[321].3.29
bn.ilḥbn.qšt.w.q[l‘]. | ršpab.qšt.w.ql‘. | pdrn.qšt.w.ql‘. | bn.pǵm[-.qšt].w.ql‘. | n‘mn.q[št.w.]ql‘. | [t]tn.qš[t]. | bn.ṯǵḏy[. 119[321].4.1
n.ḫb[--.---]. | šd.srn[.---]. | šd.y‘ḏr[.---]. | šd.swr.[---]. | šd.bn ppn[-.---]. | šd.bn.uḫn[.---]. 83[85].6
m. | bn.qṭn.b.ulm. | bn.gdrn.b.m‘r[by]. | [w].bn.d‘m[-]. | bn.ppṯ.b[--]. | b[n.---]. | šm[-.---]. | tkn[.---]. | knn.b.ḫ[lb]. | bn 2046.1.9
[s]p[r] ušknym.dt.[b d.---]. | bn.btr. | bn.‘ms. | bn.pṣn. | bn.agmz. | bn.[--]n. | bn.a[--]. | [------]. | [------]. | [------] 2021.1.4
n.mn. | [--]ry. | [--]lim bn.brq. | [--.]qtn bn.drṣy. | [--]kn bn.pri. | [r]špab bn.pni. | [ab]mn bn.qṣy. | [‘]pṯrm bn.agmz. | [- 2087.7
. | bn [-]ln.bn.ṯbil. | bn is.bn tbdn. | bn uryy. | bn abd‘n. | bn prkl. | bn štn. | bn annyn. | b[n] slg. | u[--] dit. | bn p[-]n. | bn 101[10].10
.‘mnr. | šd.kn‘m.l.bn.‘mnr. | šd.bn.krwn.l bn.‘myn. | šd.bn.prmn.l aḫny. | šd.bn ḥnn.l bn.adlḏn. | šd.bn.nṣdn.l bn.‘ml 2089.6
bn.nṣ. | [b]n.‘ṣr. | [---]m. | [bn.]ulnhr. | [bn.p]rn. | [bn.a]nny. | [---]n. | bn.kbln. | bn.pdy. | bn.ṯpdn. 1075.1.5

----]. | [---.]l[--]. | [bn.]ubn. | kbs̀m. | bn.abḏr. | bn.kpltn. | bn.prn. | ‘bdm. | bn.kḏǵbr. | bn.mṣrn. | bn.[-]dr[-]. | [---]l[-]. | [-- 114[324].2.8
r‘ym.dt.b d.iytlm. | ẖyrn.w.s̀ǵr h. | s̀ǵr.bn.prsn. | agpṯr.w.s̀ǵ[r h]. | ṯ‘ln. | mzṯn.w.s̀ǵr [h]. | s̀ǵr.plṭ. | s[d 2072.3
.-]ty. | [bn.]iršn. | bn.[---]. | bn.b[--]. | bn.š[--]. | bn.a[---]. | bn.prsn. | bn.mtyn. | bn.ẖlpn. | bn.ḥgbn. | bn.szn. | bn.mglb. 117[325].2.5
wṯ. | bn.ṯbtnq. | bn.pṯḏn. | bn.nbdg. | bn.ḥgbn. | bn.tmr. | bn.prsn. | bn.ršpy. | [‘]bdḥgb. | [k]lby. | [-]ḥmn. | [š]pšyn. | [‘b]d 113[400].1.21
. | bn.‘mnr. | bn.kmn. | bn.ibyn. | bn.mryn.ṣmd.w.ḥrṣ. | bn.prsn.ṣmd.w.ḥrṣ. | bn.ilb‘l. | bn.idrm. | bn.grgš. | bn.bly. | bn. 2113.6
| l.tš‘n. | mṣrm. | tmkrn. | ypḥ.‘bdilt. | bn.m. | ypḥ.ilšlm. | bn.prqdš. | ypḥ.mnḥm. | bn.ḥnn. | brqn.spr. 2116.20
tyy. | bn ẖlp. | bn.ẓll. | bn ydy. | bn lzn. | bn.ṯyn. | bn g‘r. | bn.prtn. | bn ẖnn. | b[n.-]n. | bn.ṣṣb. | bn.b‘ltn ẖlq. | bn.mlkbn. 2016.1.17
| [bn.--]my. | [bn.b]rq. | [bn.--]r. | [bn.--]tn. | [bn.-]rmn. | bn.prtn. | bn.ymn. | bn.dby. | bn.ir[--]. | bn.kr[--]. | bn.nn[-]. | [-- 124[-].5.8
tn. | bn.rwy. | bn.‘myn. | bdl.mrynm. | bn.ṣqn. | bn.šyn. | bn.prtn. | bn.ypr. | mrum. | bn.‘[--]t. | bn.adty. | bn.krwn. | bn.n 113[400].3.9
.gs[-.--]r.d.yṯb.b.gt.al. | ilmlk.[--]kt.[--.d.]yṯb.b.šb[n]. | bn.pr[-.]d.y[ṯb.b].šlmy. | tlš.w[.n]ḥl h[.-].ṯgd.mrum. | bt.[-]b[- 2015.2.2
y. | bn.ily[-]. | bn.iy[--]. | bn.ṯy[--]. | bn.p[---]. | gyn[.---]. | bn.pṯ[--]. | bn.db[--]. 2025.8
d‘n. | bn prkl. | bn štn. | bn annyn. | b[n] slg. | u[--] dit. | bn p[-]n. | bn nẓǵil. 101[10].15
nḥl h. | bn.mlkyy. | [bn].bm[--]. | [‘š]rm. | [-----]. | [-----]. | bn.p[--]. | bn.‘bdmlk. 2163.3.18
d. | bn.tbšn.dd. | bn.ẖran.w[.---]. | [-]n.y‘rtym. | gmm.w.bn.p[--]. | trn.w.p[-]y. | bn.b‘yn.w.agytn. | [---] gnym. | [--]ry.w 131[309].10
bn a[---]. | bn.byy. | bn.ily[-]. | bn.iy[--]. | bn.ṯy[--]. | bn.p[---]. | gyn[.---]. | bn.pṯ[--]. | bn.db[--]. 2025.6
y. | [---.]šd ubdy. | [---.š]d ubdy. | [---.šd] ubdy. | [---.š]d.bn.ṣin. | [---].bn.dly. | [---.]ṯty[-.--]. 2031.11
[w]nḥ[l h]. | [bn].amd[-]. | [bn].ṣbṭ[--]. | [bn].ẖla[n]. | [bn].ǵr[--]. | d.b[n.---]. | d.bn.[---]. | d. 2164.A.3
br‘y. | abmn.qšt.w.ṯn.ql‘m. | qdmn.ṯt.qštm.w.ṯlṯ.ql‘m. | bn.ṣdqil.ṯt.qštm.w.ṯn.ql‘m. | bn.ṯlṯ.ṯ[lṯ.]qšt.w.ṯn.ql‘m. | qṣn.ṯt. 119[321].3.4
miẖdym. | bn.ḥṭb. | bn abyt. | bn ẖdl. | bn ṣdqn. | bn ayy. | bn dbb. | w nḥl h. | bn n‘myn. | bn aṯtyy. | b 2016.1.5
nlqḥt. | [bn.ẖ]tyn.yd.bt h. | [aǵ]ltn. | tdn.bn.ddy. | ‘bdil[.b]n ṣdqn. | bnšm.h[-]mt.ypḥm. | kbby.yd.bt.amt. | ilmlk. 2045.5
mitm.ksp.‘mn.b[n].ṣdqn. | w.kkrm.ṯlṯ. | mit.ksp.‘mn. | bn.ulbtyn. | w.kkr.ṯlṯ. 1143.1
| [----]. | [bn] itn. | [bn] il. | [---]ṯ. | klṯṯb. | gsn. | arm[w]l. | bn.ṣdqn. | ẖlbn. | tbq.alp. 2039.15
ḏkry[-]. | bn.tlm[yn]. | bn.y‘dd. | bn.idly[-]. | bn.‘bd[--]. | bn.ṣd[qn]. 2017.9
n].gyn.[---]. | [-----]. | [-----]. | [-----]. | [-----]. | [-----]. | [ṣṣ].b[n].ṣd[-.---]. | [ṣṣ].bn.npr.ẖmšm. | ṣṣ.bn.adlḏn.ṯlṯm. | ṣṣ.bn.‘gl 2096.14
[---.a]rb‘[.---]. | [---.ṯ]lṯm[.---]. | [---.--]m.bn l[---]. | [---].bn ṣd[-.---]. | [---.--]mn.mi[t.---]. | [---.ṯm]nym[.---]. | [---.-]dn.ṯ 149[99].8
.tnabn. | bn.ḥṣn. | ṣprn. | bn.ašbḥ. | bn.qṭnn. | bn.ǵlmn. | [bn].ṣwy. | [bn].ẖnq[n]. | [-----]. | [-----]. | [-----]. | [-----]. | n[----]. | 1046.1.24
n.kln. | bn.‘lln. | bn.liy. | bn.nqṭn. | bn abrẖṭ. | bn.grdy. | bn.ṣlpn. | bn ǵlmn. | bn sgld. 1064.29
m.bn[.---]. | krmn[py]. | bn.[--]m. | bn.asr[-]. | bn.ḏr[--]. | bn.ṣl[--]. | bn.ẖd[--]. | bn.‘[---]. | kbkbn bn[.---]. | bn.k[--]. | bn.p 2014.54
]. | myn. | šr. | bn.zql. | bn.iẖy. | bn.iyṯr. | bn.‘yn. | bn.ǵzl. | bn.ṣmy. | bn.il[-]šy. | bn.ybšr. | bn.sly. | bn.ḥlbt. | bn.brzt. | bn.a 2117.2.8
[bn]šm.dt.iš[--]. | [b]n.b‘l[--]. | bn.gld. | bn.ṣmy. | bn.mry[n]. | bn.mgn. | bn.‘dn. | bn.knn. | bn.py. | bn. 2117.1.4
y.bt.abm. | [-]rbn.‘dd.nryn. | [ab]r[p]u.bn.kbd. | [-]m[-].bn.ṣmrt. | liy.bn.yṣi. | ḏmrhd.bn.srt. | [---.--]m. | ‘bdmlk.bn.s̀rn 102[322].6.5
n. | m[--].bn.qqln. | ‘bdil[-].bn.qqln. | liy.bn.qqln. | mnn.bn.ṣnr. | iẖy.[b]n[.--]l[-]. | ‘bdy[rẖ].bn.gṯtn. | yrmn.bn.‘n. | krw 85[80].4.6
.ršpab.aẖ.ubn. | šd.b d.bn.uṯryn. | [ubd]y.mrynm. | [š]d.bn.ṣnrn.b d.nrn. | [š]d.bn.rwy.b d.ydln. | [š].bn.trn.b d.ibrmḏ 82[300].1.8
n. | ‘myn. | ilyn. | yrb‘m. | n‘mn. | bn.kbl. | kn‘m. | bdlm. | bn.ṣǵr. | klb. | bn.mnḥm. | bn.brqn. | bn.‘n. | bn.‘bdy. | ‘bd‘ṯtr. 1046.3.43
[-----]. | [-----]. | ynḥm. | iẖy. | bn.mšt. | ‘psn. | bn.ṣpr. | kmn. | bn.ršp. | tmn. | šmmn. | bn.rmy. | bn.aky. | ‘bdẖ 1047.7
. | bn lzn. | bn.ṯyn. | bn g‘r. | bn.prtn. | bn ẖnn. | b[n.-]n. | bn.ṣṣb. | bn.b‘ltn ẖlq. | bn.mlkbn. | bn.asyy ẖlq. | bn.kṯly. | bn.k 2016.2.1
ry. | bn.atyn. | bn.ttn. | bn.rwy. | bn.‘myn. | bdl.mrynm. | bn.ṣqn. | bn.šyn. | bn.prtn. | bn.ypr. | mrum. | bn.‘[--]t. | bn.adty 113[400].3.7
.alpm.bnš.yd. | titṯm[n].w.‘l.[---]. | [-]rym.t[i]ṯtmn. | šnl.bn.ṣ[q]n.s̀[--]. | yitṯm.w.b[--]. | yšlm. | [‘]šrm̱.ks[p].yš[lm]. | [il] 2104.4
bn.ṣrṭn. | bn.‘bd. | snb.w.nḥl h. | [-]by.w.nḥl h. | [--]ilt.w.nḥl h. 1063.1
pšyn. | [‘b]dmlk. | [---]yn. | bn.ṯ[--]. | bn.idrm. | bn.ymn. | bn.ṣry. | bn.mztn. | bn.s̀lgyn. | bn.[-]gštn. | bn[.n]klb. | b[n.]dtn 113[400].2.4
]ṯm.b.gt.irbṣ. | [--]šmyn. | [w.]nḥl h. | bn.qṣn. | bn.ksln. | bn.ṣrym. | bn.ṯmq. | bn.ntp. | bn.mlk. | bn.ṯ‘[-]. | bn.km[-]. | bn.r 1073.1.7
dy.qšt. | bn.srn.qšt. | bn.gdrn.qšt. | prpr.qšt. | ugry.qšt. | bn.ṣrptn.qšt. | bn.mṣry.qšt. | arny. | abm.qšt. | ḥdṯn.ql‘. | yṯpṭ.q 119[321].1.46
b. | bn.mryn. | [bn.]b[--]. | bn.ẓrl. | bn.illm[-]. | bn.š[---]. | bn.ṣ[---]. | bn.š[---]. | bn.[---]. | bn.[---]. | b[n.---]. | b[n.---]. 115[301].4.26
ḥr.snry. | dqn.šlmn. | prdn.ndb[--]. | [-]rn.ẖbty. | abmn.bn.qdmn. | n‘mn.bn.‘bdilm. 87[64].40
]mš.ṯdṯ.ym.uzr. | [ilm].dnil.uzr.ilm.ylḥm. | [uzr.]yšqy.bn qdš.yd.ṣt h. | [dn]il.yd.ṣt h.y‘l.w yškb. | [yd.]mizrt.p yln. 17[2AQHT].1.14
rp]i.apn.ǵz[r]. | [mt.hrnmy.]uzr.ilm.ylḥm. | [uzr.yšqy.]bn.qdš.yd. | [ṣt h.y‘l.]w yškb.yd. | [mizrt.]p ynl.hn.ym. | [w ṯn 17[2AQHT].1.4
lkt.[--]pm.l mlkt.wn.in.aṯt. | [l]k.k[m.ilm]. | [w ǵlmt.k bn.qdš.]w y[--.]zbl.ym.y‘[--.]ṯpṭ.nhr. | [-------.]yšlḥn.w y‘n ‘ṯt 2.3[129].23
š ṯlṯ rb‘ ym. | [uzr.i]lm.dnil.uzr. | [ilm.y]lḥm.uzr.yšqy bn. | [qdš.ẖ]mš.ṯdṯ.ym.uzr. | [ilm].dnil.uzr.ilm.ylḥm. | [uzr.]y 17[2AQHT].1.11
[---].ybšr.qdš[.---]. | [---.--]t btm.qdš.il[.---]. | [---.b]n.qdš.k[--.---]. | [---.]‘sb.[-]ḥ[-.---]. | [---.]b[-.]mṯt k.[---]. | [--- 2125.3
m aẖ h.w šrš. | km.ary h.uzrm.ilm.ylḥm. | uzrm.yšqy.bn.qdš. | l tbrknn l ṯr.il ab y. | tmrnn.l bny.bnwt. | w ykn.bn h 17[2AQHT].1.23
k.pnm]. | l ytn.tk.ǵr.ll.‘m.phr.m‘d.ap.ilm.l lḥ[m]. | yṯb.bn qdš.l ṯrm.b‘l.qm.‘l.il.hlm. | ilm.tph hm.tphn.mlak.ym.t‘d 2.1[137].21
| [--]ḥ.b y.ṯr.il.ab y.ank.in.bt[.l] y[.km.]ilm[.w] ḥẓr[.k bn]. | [qd]š.lbum.trd.b n[p]šn y.trḥṣn.k ṯrm. | [--]b b[ht]. | [zbl 2.3[129].19
m.bn.dgn.a[s]r km.hw ybl.argmn k.k ilm. | [---.]ybl.k bn.qdš.mnḥy k.ap.anš.zbl.b‘[l]. | [-.yuẖ]d.b yd.mšẖṭ.bm.ym 2.1[137].38
.ym. | [w ṯn.uzr.]ilm.dnil. | [uzr.ilm.]ylḥm.uzr. | [yšqy.b]n.qdš ṯlṯ rb‘ ym. | [uzr.i]lm.dnil.uzr. | [ilm.y]lḥm.uzr.yšqy 17[2AQHT].1.9
bn[.---]. | bn.qdšt. | bn.m‘nt. | bn.g[--]n. | bn[.---]. | [-----]. | b[n.---]. | b[n.- 2163.1.2
[-]. | mru.skn. | bn.bddn. | bn.ǵrgn. | bn.tgtn. | bn.ḥrẓn. | bn.qdšt. | bn.nṯǵ[-]. | bn.gr[--]. | bn.[---]. | bn.[---]. | mr[u.ibrn]. 113[400].5.11
| [šd.]bn.brzn.b d.nwrḏ. | [šd.]bn.nḥbl.b d.‘dbym. | [šd.b]n.qṭy.b d.tt. | [ubd]y.mrim. | [šd.b]n.ṯpdn.b d.bn.g‘r. | [šd.b] 82[300].1.19
[b]n ‘ntn.[---]. | bn agyn[.---]. | b[n] ‘ṯlṯ[.---]. | bn qṭy[.---]. | bn yp‘[.---]. | [---]b‘m[.---]. | [-----]. 105[86].4
n.mḏrǵl. | bn.tran.mḏrǵl | bn.ilh.mḏrǵl | špšyn.b.ulm. | bn.qṭn.b.ulm. | bn.gdrn.b.m‘r[by]. | [w].bn.d‘m[-]. | bn.ppṯ.b[- 2046.1.6
.]nnr. | [bn.]aglby. | [bn.]b‘ly. | [mḏ]rǵlm. | [bn.]kdgdl. | [b]n.qṭn. | [b]n.ǵrgn. | [b]n.tgḏn. | bn.ẖdyn. | bn.sgr. | bn.aǵltn. | 104[316].9
| ‘dn.qšt.w.ql‘. | ilmhr.qšt.w.ql‘. | bn.gmrt.qšt. | ǵmrm. | bn.qṭn.qšt.w.ql‘. | mrṯd.qšt. | ssw.qšt. | knn.qšt. | bn.ṯlln.qšt. | b 119[321].1.12
š. | bn.štn. | bn.ilš. | bn.tnabn. | bn.ḥṣn. | ṣprn. | bn.ašbḥ. | bn.qṭnn. | bn.ǵlmn. | [bn].ṣwy. | [bn].ẖnq[n]. | [-----]. | [-----]. | [- 1046.1.22
.bn.srt. | [---.--]m. | ‘bdmlk.bn.s̀rn. | ‘bdb‘l.bn.kdn. | gzl.bn.qldn. | gld.bt.klb. | l[---].bt.ẖzli. | bn.iẖyn. | ṣdqn.bn.ass. | b‘ 102[323].3.4

.ypr. | mrum. | bn.'[--]t. | bn.adty. | bn.krwn. | bn.nǵsk. | bn.qnḏ. | bn.pity. | w.nḥl h. | bn.rt. | bn.l[--]. | bn.[---]. | [---.--]y. 113[400].3.16
m. | bn.pi[ty]. | w.nḥ[l h]. | 'bd[--]. | bn.s[---]. | bn.at[--]. | bn.qnḏ. | ṣmq[-]. | bn.anny. | bn.'mtḏl. | bn.'myn. | bn.alz. | bn. 117[325].1.7
h. | [w 'b]d.'lm.ṯlṯ. | [ssw]m.mrkbt b trbṣ bn.amt. | [tn.b]nm.aqny. | [tn.ṯa]rm.amid. | [w y'n].ṯr.ab h.il. | d[--].b bk.kr 14[KRT].2.57
ṯlln.qšt. | bn.šyn.qšt. | 'bd.qšt. | bn.ulmy.qšt. | ṯqbn.qšt. | bn.qnmlk.qšt. | ytḫm.qšt. | grp.qšt. | m'rby. | n'mn.ṯt.qštm.w.q 104[316].5
-.]qtn bn.drṣy. | [--]kn bn.pri. | [r]špab bn.pni. | [ab]mn bn.qṣy. | [']pṯrm bn.agmz. | [-]n bn.iln. | [--]nn bn.ibm. | [-]n b 2087.9
pt.srdnnm. | bn.aǵli.uṯpt.srdnnm. | asrn.uṯpt.srdnnm. | bn.qṣn.uṯpt.srdnnm. | yly.uṯpt.srdnnm. | arṯṯb.uṯpt.srdnnm. 1124.10
[aǵ]ltn. | [--]ṯm.b.gt.irbṣ. | [--]šmyn. | [w.]nḥl h. | bn.qṣn. | bn.ksln. | bn.ṣrym. | bn.ṯmq. | bn.ntp. | bn.mlk. | bn.ṯ'[1073.1.5
.brzt. | bn.ayl. | [-----]. | 'bd[--]. | bn.i[--]. | 'd[--]. | ild[--]. | bn.qṣn. | 'lpy. | kṯy. | bn.ẓmn. | bn.trdn. | ypq. | 'bd. | qrḥ. | abšr. 2117.2.20
ṯnnm. | bn.qqln. | w.nḥl h. | w.nḥl h. | bn.šml[-]. | bn.brzn. | bn.ḫṯr[-]. | 116[303].2
rm. | ṯnnm. | [ar]swn.bn.qqln. | m[--].bn.qqln. | 'bdil[-].bn.qqln. | liy.bn.qqln. | mnn.bn.ṣnr. | iḫy.[b]n[.--]l[-]. | 'bdy[rḫ 85[80].4.4
[ar]swn.bn.qqln. | m[--].bn.qqln. | 'bdil[-].bn.qqln. | liy.bn.qqln. | mnn.bn.ṣnr. | iḫy.[b]n[.--]l[-]. | 'bdy[rḫ].bn.gṯtn. | yr 85[80].4.5
n. | nsk.ṯlṯ. | bn.[--.]m[-]ḫr. | bn.šmrm. | ṯnnm. | [ar]swn.bn.qqln. | m[--].bn.qqln. | 'bdil[-].bn.qqln. | liy.bn.qqln. | mnn. 85[80].4.2
[--.]m[-]ḫr. | bn.šmrm. | ṯnnm. | [ar]swn.bn.qqln. | m[--].bn.qqln. | 'bdil[-].bn.qqln. | liy.bn.qqln. | mnn.bn.ṣnr. | iḫy.[b] 85[80].4.3
spr.ḥršm. | liy.bn.qqln. | [---.a]lṯy. | [-----]. | [---]tl. | [---]'bl. | [---]bln. | [---]dy. | 1036.2
.lṯpn.l yḥ. | w y'ny.krt.ṯ'. | bn.al.tbkn.al. | tdm.l y.al tkl.bn. | qr.'n k.mḫ.riš k. | udm't.ṣḥ.aḫt k. | ṯtmnt.bt.ḥmḥ h. | d[-] 16.1[125].26
yrpu. | kdn. | p'ṣ. | bn.liy. | yd'. | šmn. | 'dy. | 'nbr. | aḫrm. | bn.qrdy. | bn.šm'n. | bn.ǵlmy. | ǵly. | bn.dnn. | bn.rmy. | dll. | m 2117.3.31
ly.ḫmšt.l.'šrm. | b.gdn.bn.uss.'šrm. | b.'dn.bn.ṯṯ.'šrt. | b.bn.qrdmn.ṯlṯm. | b.bṣmn[.bn].ḥrtn.'[--]. | b.t[--.---] h.[---]. | [-- 2054.1.20
]lḥ[n]. | [---.--ṯ]lḥn. | [---.]ṯlḥn. | [---.]ṯlḥn. | bn adty ṯlḥn.bn qrwl ṯlḥn. 98[11].36
bn.qrrn. | bn.dnt. | bn.ṯ'l[-]. | bdl.ar.dt.inn. | mhr l ht. | artyn. | ' 1035.1.1
mṣry.d.'rb.b.unṯ. | bn.qrrn.mḏrǵl. | bn.tran.mḏrǵl | bn.ilh.mḏrǵl | špšyn.b.ulm. | 2046.1.2
rpd. | bn.ḥ[-]y. | b'lskn. | bn.'bd. | ḫyrn. | alpy. | bn.plsy. | bn.qrr[-]. | bn.ḥyl. | bn.g'yn. | ḥyn. | bn.armg[-]. | b'lmṯpṭ. | [bn] 1035.1.20
ilṣdq.bn.zry. | b'lytn.bn.ulb. | ytr'm.bn.swy. | ṣḥrn.bn.qrtm. | bn.špš.bn.ibrd. | 'pṯrm.bn.'bdy. | n[--.]bn.šnd. | [---]. 2024.4
.l hm. | bn.niršn. | bn.adty. | bn.alz. | bn.birtn. | bn.mlṣ. | bn.q[--]. | bn.[---]. | bn.ṯ[-]r. | bn.grdn. | [bn.-]ḫr. | [--.-]nb. | [--.- 2023.1.7
bn.uṯryn. | [ubd]y.mrynm. | [š]d.bn.ṣnrn.b d.nrn. | [š]d.bn.rwy.b d.ydln. | [š].bn.trn.b d.ibrmḏ. | [š]d.bn.ilṯtmr.b d.tb 82[300].1.9
m. | w.[n]ḥl hm. | b[n.---]. | bn.gzry. | bn.atyn. | bn.ttn. | bn.rwy. | bn.'myn. | bdl.mrynm. | bn.ṣqn. | bn.šyn. | bn.prtn. | b 113[400].3.4
. | bn.mšt. | 'psn. | bn.ṣpr. | kmn. | bn.ršp. | tmn. | šmmn. | bn.rmy. | bn.aky. | 'bdḫmn. | bn.'dṯ. | kṯy. | bn.ḫny. | bn.ssm. | b 1047.12
r. | aḫrm. | bn.qrdy. | bn.šm'n. | bn.ǵlmy. | ǵly. | bn.dnn. | bn.rmy. | dll. | mny. | krty. | bn.'bṣ. | bn.argb. | ydn. | il'nt. | bn.u 2117.3.36
mryn[m]. | bn.bly. | nrn. | w.nḥl h. | bn.rmyy. | bn.tlmyn. | w.nḥl h. | w.nḥl hm. | bn.ḥrm. | bn.brzn 113[400].1.5
mry[n]m. | bn rmy[y]. | yšril[.---]. | anntn bn[.---]. | bn.brzn [---]. | bnil.bn. 2069.2
n.abdg. | ilyn. | bn.tan. | bn.arm. | bn.b'l.ṣdq. | bn.army. | bn.rpiyn. | bn.army. | bn.krmn. | bn.ykn. | bn.'ṯtrab. | uṣn[-]. | b 1046.1.8
n.tbšn.ṯlṯ.qšt.w.[ṯlṯ.]ql'm. | bn.army.ṯt.qštm.w[.]q[l']. | bn.rpš.qšt.w.ql'. | bn.ǵb.qšt. | bn.ytrm.qšt.w.ql'. | bn.'bdyrḫ.q 119[321].3.23
n.mryn. | [---].bn.ṯyl. | annmt.nḥl h. | abmn.bn.'bd. | liy.bn.rqdy. | bn.ršp. 1036.14
k. | 'bdyrḫ.bn.ṯyl. | 'bdn.w.aṯt h.w.bn h. | gpn.bn[.a]ly. | bn.rqd[y].ṯbg. | iḫmlk. | yp'n w.aṯt h. | anntn.yṣr. | annmn.w.ṯl 1036.15
dyn.ugrty. | bn.tgḏn.ugrty. | tgyn.arty. | bn.nryn.arty. | bn.ršp.ary. | bn.ǵlmn ary. | bn.ḥṣbn ary. | bn.šdy ary. | bn.ktkt 2068.21
--]. | [-----]. | ynḫm. | iḫy. | bn.mšt. | 'psn. | bn.ṣpr. | kmn. | bn.ršp. | tmn. | šmmn. | bn.rmy. | bn.aky. | 'bdḫmn. | bn.'dṯ. | kṯ 87[64].12
---].bn.ṯyl. | annmt.nḥl h. | abmn.bn.'bd. | liy.bn.rqdy. | bn.ršp. 1047.9
tnq. | bn.pṯdn. | bn.nbdg. | bn.ḥgbn. | bn.tmr. | bn.prsn. | bn.ršpy. | [']bdḥgb. | [k]lby. | [-]ḥmn. | [š]pšyn. | ['b]dmlk. | [---] 113[400].1.22
r. | ẓbr. | bn.ṯdṯb. | bn.'rmn. | bn.alz. | bn.mṣrn. | bn.'dy. | bn.ršpy. | [---.]mn. | [--.-]sn. | [bn.-]ny. | [b]n.ḫnyn. | [bn].nbq. | 115[301].2.17
adty. | bn.krwn. | bn.nǵsk. | bn.qnḏ. | bn.pity. | w.nḥl h. | bn.rt. | bn.l[--]. | bn.[---]. | [---.--]y. | [--.-]ḏrm. | [--.--]y. | [--.--]y. 113[400].3.19
.ṣrym. | bn.ṯmq. | bn.ntp. | bn.mlk. | bn.ṯ'[-]. | bn.km[-]. | bn.r[--]. | [bn.]'[---]. | [bn.]r[---]. | [bn.]ḥ[---]. | [bn.]šbl. | [bn.]ḫ 1073.1.13
---.]b'lš[-.---]. | [---.]bn.zzb[-.---]. | [---.]bn mt[.---]. | [---.b]n r[--.---]. 2139.7
.]yṯb.b.gt.aǵld. | šgn.bn b[--.---].d.yṯb.b.ilštm'. | abmn.bn.r[---].b.syn. | bn.irṣ[-.---.]h. | šdyn.b[n.---.--]n. 2015.2.7
tp. | bn.mlk. | bn.ṯ'[-]. | bn.km[-]. | bn.r[--]. | [bn.]'[---]. | [bn.]r[---]. | [bn.]ḥ[---]. | [bn.]šbl. | [bn.]ḫdmn. | [bn.]nklb. | [---] 1073.2.2
[-]wyn.yd[-.---.]dd. | [---]n.yd.sǵ[r.---.--]k.[--]. | [---.]dd.bn.š.[---.]yd.sǵr h. | [---.--]r h.'šr[m.---.']šrm.dd. | [---.yn.d.]n 1098.42
b.ṯmq.ḫmšt.l.'šrt. | b.[---].šb't.'šrt. | b.bn.pdrn.'šrm. | d.bn.šb'l.uḫnpy.ḫmšm. | b.bn.ṯtm.ṯlṯm. | b.bn.agdṯb.'šrm. | b.bn 2054.1.10
[---].rb. | [-]lpl. | bn.asrn. | bn.šḫyn. | bn.abd'n. | bn.ḫnqn. | bn.nmq. | bn.amdn. | bn.špšn. 1067.4
bn.šyy. | bn.ḫnzr. | bn.ydb'l. | bn.ḥyn. | [bn].ar[-]m. | [bn].ḥrp[- 124[-].2.1
]lsy. | bn.ḥrš. | [--.]kbd. | [---]. | y[---]. | bn.ǵlyn. | bdl.ar. | bn.šyn. | bn.ubrš. | bn.d[--]b. | abrpu. | bn.k[n]y. | bn.klyn. | bn. 1035.3.2
tyn. | bn.ttn. | bn.rwy. | bn.'myn. | bdl.mrynm. | bn.ṣqn. | bn.šyn. | bn.prtn. | bn.ypr. | mrum. | bn.'[--]t. | bn.adty. | bn.kr 113[400].3.8
n.qšt.w.ql'. | mrṯd.qšt. | ssw.qšt. | knn.qšt. | bn.ṯlln.qšt. | bn.šyn.qšt. | 'bd.qšt. | bn.ulmy.qšt. | ṯqbn.qšt. | bn.qnmlk.qšt. | 104[316].5
---]. | mṯbt.ilm.ṯmn.ṯ[--.--]. | pamt.šb'. | iqnu.šmt[.---]. | [b]n.šrm. | iqran.ilm.n'mm[.agzry ym.bn]ym. | ynqm.b ap zd 23[52].22
[---].md.'[ṯtr]t. | ydy. | bn.škn. | bn.mdt. | bn.ḫ[--]y. | bn.'[-]y. | kn'm. | bn.yš[-]n. | bn.p 1054.1.3
pṣry.b.šbn. | ilštm'ym. | y[---.]bn.'šq. | [---.]bn.tqy. | [---.]bn.šlmy. | [-----]. | [---].ubr'y. | [---].gwl. | [---]ady. | [---]ṣry. | mi 1041.6
. | bn u[l]pm. | bn '[p]ty. | bn.kdgdl. | bn.smyy. | bn.lbn. | bn.šlmn. | bn.mly. | pslm. | bn.annd. | bn.gl'd. | w.nḥl h. | bn.ml 2163.3.7
r[ḥ]m. | [bn].smyy.qšt.w.u[ṯpt]. | [w.q]l'.w.ṯt.mrḥm. | [bn].šlmn.ql'.w.ṯ[t.---]. | [bn].mlṣ.qštm.w.uṯp[t]. | [--.q]l'.w[.--- 2047.6
n.ablḥ. | [-----]. | w [---]. | bn.[---]. | bn.yr[--]. | bn.kṯr[t]. | bn.šml. | bn.arnbt. | qdšm. | b[-.--]t. | [---.-]l[--]. | [---.]pr[--]. | [-. 2163.2.6
.qšt.w[.ql]'. | bn.aktmy.qšt. | šdyn.qšt. | bdn.qšt.w.ql'. | bn.šmlbi.qšt.w.ql'. | bn.yy.qšt. | ilrb.qšt. | bn.nmš.ṯt.qšt.w.ql'. 119[321].4.13
ṯnnm. | bn.qqln. | w.nḥl h. | w.nḥl h. | bn.šml[-]. | bn.brzn. | bn.ḫṯr[-]. | bn.yd[--]. | bn.'[---]. | w.nḥ[l h 116[303].5
]. | [-----]. | [-----]. | n[----]. | bn.[---]. | bn.[---]. | bn.yk[--]. | bn.šmm. | bn.irgy. | w.nḥl h. | w.nḥl hm. | [bn].pmn. | bn.gṯrn. 1046.2.9
]. | ṣṣ mlk mit[.---]. | ṣṣ igy.ḫmšm. | ṣṣ yrpi m[it.---]. | ṣṣ bn.š[m]mn '[šr.---]. | alp.ṯṯm. | kbd.mlḥt. 2097.19
. | p'ṣ. | bn.liy. | yd'. | šmn. | 'dy. | 'nbr. | aḫrm. | bn.qrdy. | bn.šm'n. | bn.ǵlmy. | ǵly. | bn.dnn. | bn.rmy. | dll. | mny. | krty. | 2117.3.32
l.bt.mrnn. | a[--.---.-]'n. | ml[--.---]. | ar[--.---.--]l. | aty[n.bn.]šm'nt. | ḥnn[.bn].pls. | abrš[p.bn.]ḫrpn. | gmrš[.bn].mrnn. 102[323].4.4
].pll.b d.gmrd. | [šd.bn.-]ll.b d.iwrḫṯ. | [šd.bn.-]nn.b d.bn.šmrm. | [šd.bn.-]ṯtayy.b d.ṯtmd. | [šd.bn.-]rn.b d.ṣdqšlm. | 82[300].1.26

[d]. | w nḥl h. | atn.bn.ap[s]n. | nsk.ṯlṯ. | bn.[--.]m[-]ḫr. | bn.šmrm. | ṯnnm. | [ar]swn.bn.qqln. | m[--].bn.qqln. | ʿbdil[-].b 85[80].3.10
bn.zry. | bʿlytn.bn.ulb. | ytrʿm.bn.swy. | ṣḫrn.bn.qrtm. | bn.špš.bn.ibrd. | ʿpṯrm.bn.ʿbdy. | n[--.]bn.šnd. | [---].bn.[---]. 2024.5
h. | ymn. | w.lmd h. | yʿḏrn. | w.lmd h. | ʿdn. | w.lmd h. | bn.špš. | [w.l]m[d h]. | yṣ[---]. | ʿbd[--]. | pr[--]. | ʿdr[--]. | w.lm[d 1049.1.11
.]qlʿ. | [t]tn.qš[t]. | bn.ṯǵdy[.qšt.]w.qlʿ. | ṯty.qšt[.w.]qlʿ. | bn.šp[š.]qšt. | bn.ʿg[w.]qšt.w qlʿ. | ḥd[ṯ]n.qšt.w.qlʿ. | bn.bb.qšt. 119[321].4.6
[---.]bn[.---]. | [---.]bn[.---]. | [---.]nḥl h. | [---.b]n.špš. | [---.b]n.mradn. | [---.m]lkym. | [---.--]d. 2137.4
t[-]. | bn.abḏr. | bn.ḥrẓn. | bn.ḏqnt. | bn.gmrš. | bn.nmq. | bn.špš[yn]. | bn.ar[--]. | bn.gb[--]. | bn.ḥn[n]. | bn.gntn[-]. | [--.] 2023.3.14
.umḫ. | yky.bn.slyn. | ypln.bn.ylḥn. | ʿzn.bn.mll. | šrm. | [b]n.špš[yn]. | [b]n.ḫrmln. | bn.tnn. | bn.pndr. | bn.nqq. | ḥrš.bh 85[80].1.11
n. | šd.[---.]gt.prn. | [šd.---.]gt.prn. | [šd.---.]gt.prn. | [š]d.bn.š[p]šn l gt pr[n]. | šd bn.ilšḥr. | l.gt.mzln. | šd.gldy. | l.gt.mz 1104.14
. | bn.šḫyn. | bn.abdʿn. | bn.ḫnqn. | bn.nmq. | bn.amdn. | bn.špšn. 1067.9
dbḥt.byy.bn. | šry.l ʿṯt. RS61[24.323.1]
[-] mit [ʿš]r kbd. | ṣṣ yḏrd ʿšrm. | ṣṣ bn aglby ṯlṯ[m]. | ṣṣ bn.šršʿm.[---]. | ṣṣ mlknʿm.a[rbʿm]. | ṣṣ mlk mit[.---]. | ṣṣ igy.ḫ 2097.14
nqdm. | bn.alṯn. | bn.dly. | bn.btry. | bn.ḫdmn. | [bn].šty. | [bn].kdgdl. | [---.-]y[-.] 2018.6
šd.bn.šty.l.bn.ṯbrn. | šd.bn.ḫtb.l bn.yʿḏrd. | šd.gl.bʿlz.l.bn.ʿmnr. | 2089.1
nds. | bn.ann. | bn.ʿbdpdr. | šd.iyry.l.ʿbdbʿl. | šd.šmmn.l.bn.šty. | šd.bn.arws.l.bn.ḫlan. | šd.bn.ibryn.l.bn.ʿmnr. 1102.18
[---.b]n.šty. | [---.]šlm. | [---.]šlm. | [---.]šlm. | [---.]šlm. | [---.š]lm. 2151.1
.bn.ṯbil. | bn is.bn tbdn. | bn uryy. | bn abdʿn. | bn prkl. | bn štn. | bn annyn. | b[n] slg. | u[--] dit. | bn p[-]n. | bn nẓǵil. 101[10].11
krmn. | bn.ykn. | bn.ʿṯtrab. | uṣn[-]. | bn.alṯn. | bn.aš[-]š. | bn.štn. | bn.ilš. | bn.tnabn. | bn.ḥṣn. | ṣprn. | bn.ašbḥ. | bn.qṭnn. 1046.1.16
[b]n[.---]. | bn [-]ʿy. | [b]n [i]lmd. | bn [t]bdn. | bn štn. | b[n] kdn. | bn dwn. | bn ḏrn. 2088.5
-]kt[.---.]nrn. | [b]n.nmq[.---]. | [ḫm]št.ksp.ʿl.aṯt. | [-]ṯd[.bn.]štn. 2055.20
n. | [bn.]krwn. | [bn.-]ty. | [bn.]iršn. | bn.[---]. | bn.b[--]. | bn.š[--]. | bn.a[---]. | bn.prsn. | bn.mtyn. | bn.ḫlpn. | bn.ḥgbn. | b 117[325].2.3
| b.ayly. | šd.abršn. | šd.kkn.[bn].ubyn. | šd.bn.li[y]. | šd.bn.š[--]y. | šd.bn.ṯ[---]. | šd.ʿdmn[.bn.]ynḥm. | šd.bn.ṯmr[n.m]i 2026.6
n. | bn.nklb. | bn.mryn. | [bn.]b[--]. | bn.ẓrl. | bn.illm[-]. | bn.š[---]. | bn.ṣ[---]. | bn.š[---]. | bn.[---]. | bn.[---]. | b[n.---]. | b[n 115[301].4.25
n. | [bn.]b[--]. | bn.ẓrl. | bn.illm[-]. | bn.š[---]. | bn.ṣ[---]. | bn.š[---]. | bn.[---]. | bn.[---]. | b[n.---]. | b[n.---]. 115[301].4.27
iqra.ilm.n[ʿmm.---]. | w ysmm.bn.š[---]. | ytnm.qrt.l ʿly[.---]. | b mdbr.špm.yd[.---.---]r. | l riš 23[52].2
rqd. | bn.abdg. | ilyn. | bn.tan. | bn.arm. | bn.bʿl.ṣdq. | bn.army. | bn.rpiyn. | bn.army. 1046.1.4
--]. | l šlmt.l šlm.b[--.---] | b y.šnt.mlit.t[--.---]. | ymǵy k.bnm.ta[--.---]. | [b]nm.w bnt.ytn k[.---]. | [--]l.bn y.šḥt.w [---]. 59[100].8
rdyn.bn.ḫrǵš[-].l.qrt. | šd.iǵlyn.bn.kzbn.l.qr[t]. | šd.pln.bn.tiyn.b d.ilmhr nḥl h. | šd knn.bn.ann.ʿdb. | šd.iln[-].bn.irṯr 2029.18
.d[t.---]. | ʿdn.[---]. | aḫqm bir[-.---]. | kṯrmlk.ns[--.---]. | bn.tbd.ilšt[mʿy.---]. | mty.ilšt[mʿy.---]. | bn.pynq.ʿnqp[a]t[y.--- 90[314].2.6
.ṯrn w nḥl h. | bn srd.bn agmn. | bn [-]ln.bn.ṯbil. | bn is.bn tbdn. | bn uryy. | bn abdʿn. | bn prkl. | bn štn. | bn annyn. | b 101[10].7
[b]n[.---]. | bn [-]ʿy. | [b]n [i]lmd. | bn [t]bdn. | bn štn. | b[n] kdn. | bn dwn. | bn ḏrn. 2088.4
bdl.gt.bn.tbšn. | bn.mnyy.šʿrty. | aryn.aḏddy. | agpṯr. | šbʿl.mlky. | nʿ 91[311].1
. | [---.]dd. | bn.arwdn.dd. | mnḥm.w.kbln. | bn.ǵlm.dd. | bn.tbšn.dd. | bn.ḫran.w[.---]. | [-]n.yʿrtym. | gmm.w.bn.p[--]. | 131[309].7
.qlʿ. | bn.aǵlyn.ṯt.qštm[.w.ṯl]ṯ.qlʿm. | bn.ʿgw.qšt.w qlʿ. | bn.tbšn.ṯlṯ.qšt.w.[ṯlṯ.]qlʿm. | bn.army.ṯt.qštm.w[.]q[lʿ]. | bn.rp 119[321].3.21
n.lṣn.ʿrm[y]. | aršw.bṣry. | arpṯr.yʿrty. | bn.ḫdyn.ugrty. | bn.tgḏn.ugrty. | tgyn.arty. | bn.nryn.arty. | bn.ršp.ary. | bn.ǵl 87[64].9
.]bʿly. | [md]rǵlm. | [bn.]kdgdl. | [b]n.qṭn. | [b]n.ǵrgn. | [b]n.tgḏn. | bn.ḫdyn. | bn.sgr. | bn.aǵltn. | bn.ktln. | bn.ʿgwn. | b 104[316].9
.au[pš]. | bn.kdrn. | ʿrgzy.w.bn.ʿdy. | bn.gmḥn.w.ḥgbt. | bn.tgḏn. | yny. | [b]n.gʿyn dd. | [-]n.dd. | [--]an dd. | [-----]. | [---- 131[309].29
]. | [bn.-]nn. | [bn.-]dn. | bn.ummt. | bn.ṯb[-]. | bn.[-]r[-]. | bn.tgn. | bn.iḏrn. | mnn. | b[n].skn. | bn.pʿṣ. | bn.ḏrm. | [bn.-]ln. 124[-].6.7
]. | w.nḥ[l h]. | bn.ẓr[-]. | mru.skn. | bn.bddn. | bn.ǵrgn. | bn.tgtn. | bn.ḥrẓn. | bn.qdšt. | bn.nṯǵ[-]. | bn.gr[--]. | bn.[---]. | b 113[400].5.9
bn.gnb[.msg]. | bn.twyn[.msg]. | bn.ʿdrš[p.msg]. | pyn.yny.[msg]. | bn.mṣrn m 133[-].1.2
]abyy.b d.ibrmḏ. | [šd.]bn.ṯṯrn.b d.bnš.aǵlkz. | [šd.b]d.b[n].tkwn. | [ubdy.mḏ]rǵlm. | [šd.bn.--]n.b d.aḫny. | [šd.bn.--] 82[300].2.21
d.krmn.l.ty[n.n]ḥl h. | šd.krz.[b]n.ann.ʿ[db]. | šd.ṯ[r]yn.bn.tkn.b d.qrt. | šd[.-].dyn.b d.pln.nḥl h. | šd.irdyn.bn.ḫrǵš[-] 2029.14
miḫdy[m]. | bn.ḥgb[n]. | bn.ulbt[-]. | ḏkry[-]. | bn.tlm[yn]. | bn.yʿdd. | bn.idly[-]. | bn.ʿbd[--]. | bn.ṣd[qn]. 2017.5
mryn[m]. | bn.bly. | nrn. | w.nḥl h. | bn.rmyy. | bn.tlmyn. | w.nḥl h. | w.nḥl hm. | bn.ḥrm. | bn.brzn. | w.nḥl h. 113[400].1.6
ṣṣ.bn.ilyn.ṯlṯm. | ṣṣ.bn.kzn.ṯlṯm. | ṣṣ.bn.tlmyn.ʿšrm. | ṣṣ.bn.krwn.ʿš[rm]. | ṣṣ.bn.iršyn.[---]. | [ṣṣ].bn. 2096.3
.w.qlʿ. | gtn.qšt. | pmn.ṯt.qšt.w.qlʿ. | bn.zry.q[š]t.w.qlʿ. | bn.tlmyn.ṯt.qštm.w.qlʿ. | bn.ysd.qšt. | [ǵ]mrm. | ilgn.qšt. | abrš 104[316].9
--]. | b[---]. | [---]. | [---]. | bn[.---]y. | yr[---]. | ḫdyn. | grgš. | b[n.]tlš. | ḏmr. | mkrm. | ʿzn. | yplṭ. | ʿbdmlk. | ynḥm. | aḏddn. | 1035.3.22
-]ly. | [iw]ryn. | [--.w.n]ḥl h. | [-]ibln. | bn.nḏbn. | bn.ʿbl. | bn.tlšn. | bn.sln. | w nḥl h. 1063.13
rmy[y]. | yšril[.---]. | anntn bn[.---]. | bn.brzn [---]. | bnil.bn.tl[--]. | bn.brzn.ṯn. | bn.išbʿl[.---]. | bn.s[---]. | dnn.[bn.---]. | 2069.6
štm.w.ṯn.qlʿm. | ulšn.ṯt.qšm.w.qlʿ. | bn.mlʿn.qšt.w.qlʿ. | bn.tmy.qšt.w.qlʿ. | ʿky.qšt. | ʿbdlbit.qšt. | kṯy.qšt.w.qlʿ. | bn.ḫrš 119[321].3.36
zr. | bn.arwṯ. | bn.ṯbtnq. | bn.pṯdn. | bn.nbdg. | bn.ḥgbn. | bn.tmr. | bn.prsn. | bn.ršpy. | [ʿ]bdḥgb. | [k]lby. | [-]ḥmn. | [š]pš 113[400].1.20
bn.ʿṯtrab. | uṣn[-]. | bn.alṯn. | bn.aš[-]š. | bn.štn. | bn.ilš. | bn.tnabn. | bn.ḥṣn. | ṣprn. | bn.ašbḥ. | bn.qṭnn. | bn.ǵlmn. | [bn]. 1046.1.18
n.ylḥn. | ʿzn.bn.mll. | šrm. | [b]n.špš[yn]. | [b]n.ḫrmln. | bn.tnn. | bn.pndr. | bn.nqq. | ḥrš.bhtm. | bn.izl. | bn.ibln. | bn.ilt 85[80].1.13
ǵr.mtpit.b d.bn.iryn. | [u]bdy.šrm. | [š]d.bn.ḫrmln.b d.bn.tnn. | [š]d.bn.ḫrmln.ṯn.b d.bn.ḫdmn. | [u]bdy.nqdm. | [ṯlṯ]. 82[300].2.10
. | krwn.arty. | tlmu.zlyy. | pdu.qmnzy. | bdl.qrṭy. | trgn.bn.tǵḥ. | aupš.qmnzy. | ṯrry.mṣbty. | prn.nǵty. | ṯrdn.zlyy. 89[312].7
mḫṣm. | bn.ḫpṡry.b.šbn. | ilštmʿym. | y[---.]bn.ʿšq. | [---.]bn.tqy. | [---.]bn.šlmy. | [-----]. | [---].ubrʿy. | [---].gwl. | [---]ady. 1041.5
mṣry.d.ʿrb.b.unṯ. | bn.qrrn.mḏrǵl. | bn.tran.mḏrǵl | bn.ilh.mḏrǵl | špšyn.b.ulm. | bn.qṭn.b.ulm. | b 2046.1.3
. | bn.i[--]. | ʿd[--]. | ild[--]. | bn.qṣn. | ʿlpy. | kṭy. | bn.ẓmn. | bn.trdn. | ypq. | ʿbd. | qrḥ. | abšr. | bn.bdn. | ḏmry. | bn.pndr. | bn 2117.2.24
ynm. | [š]d.bn.ṣnrn.b d.nrn. | [š]d.bn.rwy.b d.ydln. | [š].bn.trn.b d.ibrmḏ. | [š]d.bn.ilṯmr.b d.tbbr. | [w.]šd.nḥl h.b d.t 82[300].1.10
| w.nḥl hm. | w.[n]ḥl hm. | b[n.---]. | bn.gzry. | bn.atyn. | bn.ttn. | bn.rwy. | bn.ʿmyn. | bdl.mrynm. | bn.ṣqn. | bn.šyn. | bn 113[400].3.3
d. | [š]d bn.synn.b d.gmrd. | [šd.]abyy.b d.ibrmḏ. | [šd.]bn.ṯṯrn.b d.bnš.aǵlkz. | [šd.b]d.b[n].tkwn. | [ubdy.mḏ]rǵlm. | 82[300].2.20
[-----]. | bn.t[--.---]. | agmy[.---]. | bn.dlq[-.---]. | ṯǵyn.bn.ubn.ṯql[m]. | y 122[308].1.2
--.--]d.b.gnʿ. | [---].ḫbt. | [---].qmy. | [---.]qmy. | [---.--]b. | bn.t[--.---.a]ǵt. | špš[yn.---.u]brʿy. | iln.[---]. | bn.[---].ar. | bn.[-- 2015.1.19
. | bn yṣmḫ.bn.ṯrn w nḥl h. | bn srd.bn agmn. | bn [-]ln.bn.ṯbil. | bn is.bn tbdn. | bn uryy. | bn abdʿn. | bn prkl. | bn štn. 101[10].6

bdlḥn[-]. | bn.mqwṯ. | bn.bsn. | bn.inr[-]. | bn.ṯbil. | bn.iryn. | ṯṯl. | bn.nṣdn. | bn.ydln. | [bn].ʻdy. | [bn].ilyn. 1071.5
.ṯbln[.---]. | bn.pndr[.---]. | bn.idr[-.---]. | bn.ḥdn[-.---]. | bn.ṯbi[l.---]. 2070.2.8
r[ynm]. | [bʻ]l.[---]. | mr[--.---]. | hm.[---]. | kmrṯn[.---]. | bn.ṯbln[.---]. | bn.pndr[.---]. | bn.idr[-.---]. | bn.ḥdn[-.---]. | bn.ṯ 2070.2.4
bn.idrm. | bn.grgš. | bn.bly. | bn.apṯ. | bn.ysd. | bn.pl[-]. | bn.ṯbʻnq. | brqd. | bnn. | kbln.ṣ[md]. | bn gmrt. | bn.il.ṣm[d]. | b 2113.14
rn. | šd.bn.ky.gt.prn. | šd.hwil.gt.prn. | šd.ḥr.gt.prn. | šd.bn.ṯbǵl.gt.prn. | šd.bn.inšr.gt.prn. | šd.[---.]gt.prn. | [šd.---.]gt. 1104.9
mlk. | amlk.l drkt k.aṯb. | an.w yʻny.krt ṯʻ.yṯbr. | ḥrn.y bn.yṯbr.ḥrn. | riš k.ʻṯtrt.šm.bʻl. | qdqd k.tqln.b gbl. | šnt k.b ḥ 16.6[127].55
| bn.[---]. | [-----]. | bn[---]. | bn.mlkyy. | bn.atn. | bn.bly. | bn.ṯbrn. | bn.ḥgby. | bn.pity. | bn.slgyn. | ʻzn.bn.mlk. | bn.alṯn. 115[301].2.4
rzn. | w.nḥl h. | bn.adlḏn. | bn.šbl. | bn.ḫnzr. | bn.arwṯ. | bn.ṯbtnq. | bn.pṯḏn. | bn.nbdg. | bn.ḥgbn. | bn.tmr. | bn.prsn. | b 113[400].1.16
[---.-]l[-]. | [bn.-]dt[-]. | [bn.-]nn. | [bn.-]dn. | bn.ummt. | bn.ṯb[-]. | bn.[-]r[-]. | bn.tgn. | bn.iḏrn. | mnn. | b[n].skn. | bn.pʻ 124[-].6.5
-.-]bd. | [---]ybʻ.bʻl.ḫr[-]. | pqr.yḫd. | bn.ktmn.ṯǵr.hk[l]. | bn.ṯgbr.ṯǵr.hk[l]. | bn.ydln. | bn.ktmn. 1056.9
nm. | bn.ṯʻy. | w.nḥl h. | w.nḥl hm. | bn.nqly. | bn.snrn. | bn.ṯgd. | bn.d[-]n. | bn.amdn. | bn.ṯmrn. | bn.pzny. | bn.mglb. | 105[86].3
.aḫ[--]. | bn[.---]. | [-----]. | bn kr[k]. | bn ḫtyn. | w nḥl h. | bn ṯgrb. | bn ṯdnyn. | bn pbn. 2016.3.5
n[.---]. | [-----]. | bn kr[k]. | bn ḫtyn. | w nḥl h. | bn ṯgrb. | bn ṯdnyn. | bn pbn. 2016.3.6
-.]yn. | [----.-]mn. | [---.--]m.mṣl. | [---].prš.ḥtm. | ṯlṯ[.---].bn.ṯdnyn. | ddm.ḥ[ṯm].ʻl.šrn. | ʻšrt.ksp.ʻl.[-]lpy. | bn.ady.kkr.šʻ 1146.6
b.nʻmn.bn.ply.ḫmšt.l.ʻšrm. | b.gdn.bn.uss.ʻšrm. | b.ʻdn.bn.ṯṯ.ʻšrt. | b.bn.qrdmn.ṯlṯm. | b.bṣmn[.bn].ḥrtn.ʻ[--]. | b.ṯ[--.-- 2054.1.19
.pity. | bn.slgyn. | ʻzn.bn.mlk. | bn.alṯn. | bn.ṯmyr. | ẓbr. | bn.ṯdṯb. | bn.ʻrmn. | bn.alz. | bn.mṣrn. | bn.ʻdy. | bn.ršpy. | [---.] 115[301].2.12
d.ʻṯt[rt]. | kṯkt. | bn.ṯtn[--]. | [m]d.m[--]. | [b]n.annḏ[r]. | bn.ṯdyy. | bn.grbn. | [--.]ully. | [--]ṯiy. 1054.2.3
]ʻbl. | [---]bln. | [---]dy. | [---.n]ḥl h. | [---].bn.mryn. | [---].bn.ṯyl. | annmt.nḥl h. | abmn.bn.ʻbd. | liy.bn.rqdy. | bn.ršp. 1036.11
nn.w.aṯt h. | slmu.ḥrš.mrkbt. | bnšm.dt.l.mlk. | ʻbdyrḫ.bn.ṯyl. | ʻbdn.w.aṯt h.w.bn h. | gpn.bn[.a]ly. | bn.rqd[y].ṯbg. | i 2068.18
n nʻmyn. | bn aṯtyy. | bn ḫlp. | bn.ẓll. | bn ydy. | bn lzn. | bn.ṯyn. | bn gʻr. | bn.prtn. | bn ḫnn. | b[n.-]n. | bn.ṣṣb. | bn.bʻltn 2016.1.15
bn a[---]. | bn.byy. | bn.ily[-]. | bn.iy[--]. | bn.ṯy[--]. | bn.p[---]. | gyn[.---]. | bn.pṯ[--]. | bn.db[--]. 2025.5
i[l]štmʻym. | bn.ṯk. | bn.arwdn. | tmrtn. | šdʻl.bn aḫyn. | mʻrbym. | rpan. | ab 95[91].2
l.knʻny. | gdn.bn.umy. | knʻm.šʻrty. | abrpu.ubrʻy. | b.gt.bn.ṯlṯ. | ilḏ.b.gt.psḥn. 91[311].11
dmn.ṯt.qštm.w.ṯlṯ.qlʻm. | bn.ṣdqil.ṯt.qštm.w.ṯn.qlʻm. | bn.ṯlṯ.ṯ[lṯ.]qšt.w.ṯn.qlʻm. | qṣn.ṯt.qštm.w.qlʻ. | bn.gṯrn.q[š]t. | 119[321].3.5
mrm. | bn.qṯn.qšt.w.qlʻ. | mrṯd.qšt. | ssw.qšt. | knn.qšt. | bn.ṯlln.qšt. | bn.šyn.qšt. | ʻbd.qšt. | bn.ulmy.qšt. | ṯqbn.qšt. | bn. 119[316].4
. | bn.ḥgby. | bn.pity. | bn.slgyn. | ʻzn.bn.mlk. | bn.alṯn. | bn.ṯmyr. | ẓbr. | bn.ṯdṯb. | bn.ʻrmn. | bn.alz. | bn.mṣrn. | bn.ʻdy. 115[301].2.10
[-----]. | [bn.]ibln. | ysd. | bn.ṯmq. | bn.agmn. | bn.uṣb. | bn.yzg. | bn.anntn. | bn.kwn. | ǵ 115[301].4.3
bṣ. | [--]šmyn. | [w.]nḥl h. | bn.qṣn. | bn.ksln. | bn.ṣrym. | bn.ṯmq. | bn.ntp. | bn.mlk. | bn.ṯʻ[-]. | bn.km[-]. | bn.r[--]. | [bn.] 1073.1.8
b[--]. | [b]n.[---]. | bn.a[--]. | bn.ml[k]. | bn.glyn. | bn.ʻdr. | bn.ṯmq. | bn.ntp. | bn.ʻgrt. 1057.20
gby.ṯmnt.l ʻšrm.ʻšrt.ḫmš.kbd. | bn.ilṣdq.šbʻt ṯlṯt šlm. | bn.ṯmq.arbʻt ṯqlm šlmm. 1131.10
ḥrṯm[.---]. | bn.ṯmq[-.---]. | bn.ntp.[---]. | bn.lbnn.[----]. | ady.ḥ[--.---]. | [-]b[88[304].2
hm. | bn.nqly. | bn.snrn. | bn.ṯgd. | bn.d[-]n. | bn.amdn. | bn.ṯmrn. | bn.pzny. | bn.mglb. | bn.[--]b. | bn.[---]. | bn.[---]. 113[400].6.30
y]. | šd.bn.š[--]y. | šd.bn.ṯ[---]. | šd.ʻdmn[.bn.]ynḥm. | šd.bn.ṯmr[n.m]idḫy. | šd.ṯbʻm[.--]y. 2026.9
dyrḫ.ṯn ǵlyt h. | aršmg. | ršpy.w.aṯt h. | bn.glgl.uškny. | bn.ṯny.uškny. | mnn.w.aṯt h. | slmu.ḥrš.mrkbt. | bnšm.dt.l.ml 2068.14
la[n]. | [bn].ǵr[--]. | d.b[n.---]. | d.bn.[---]. | d.bn.š[--]. | d.bn.ṯn[r]. | d.kmry. 2164.в.4
| bn.mglb. | bn.ntp. | ʻmyn.bn ǵḥpn. | bn.kbln. | bn.bly. | bn.ṯʻy. | bn.nṣdn. | klby. 104[316].7
ʻ. | bdl.mdrǵlm. | bn.mmy. | bn.ḫnyn. | bn.knn. | khnm. | bn.ṯʻy. | w.nḥl h. | w.nḥl hm. | bn.nqly. | bn.snrn. | bn.ṯgd. | bn. 104[316].9
ʻ. | bn.[-]bl.ṯt.qštm.w.ṯn.qlʻm. | bn.[-]rkṯ.ṯt.qštm.w.qlʻ. | bn.ṯʻl.qšt. | bn.[ḫ]dpṯr.ṯt.qštm.[w].qlʻ. | bn.aǵlyn.ṯt.qštm[.w.ṯl 119[321].3.17
lʻ. | bn.ḥrẓn.qšt.w.qlʻ. | tgrš.qšt.w.qlʻ. | špšyn.qšt.w.qlʻ. | bn.ṯʻln.qš[t.w.q]lʻ. | ʻṯqbt.qšt. | [-]ll.qšt.w.qlʻ. | ḫlb.rpš. | abmn. 119[321].2.26
bn.qrrn. | bn.dnt. | bn.ṯʻl[-]. | bdl.ar.dt.inn. | mhr l ht. | artyn. | ʻdmlk. | bn.alt[-]. | i 1035.1.3
----]. | bn.[---]. | bn.il[--]. | khnm[.--]. | bn.ṯ[--]. | bn.[---]. | bn.ṯʻl[-]. | bn.nq[ly]. | bn.snr[n]. | bn.pzn[y]. | bn.mg[lb]. | bn.d 2020.7
n.qṣn. | bn.ksln. | bn.ṣrym. | bn.ṯmq. | bn.ntp. | bn.mlk. | bn.ṯʻ[-]. | bn.km[-]. | bn.r[--]. | [bn.]ʻ[---]. | [bn.]r[---]. | [bn.]ḥ[-- 1073.1.11
lʻ. | bn.pǵm[-.qšt].w.qlʻ. | nʻmn.q[št.w.]qlʻ. | [ṯ]tn.qš[t]. | bn.ṯǵdy[.qšt.]w.qlʻ. | ṯṯy.qšt[.w.]qlʻ. | bn.šp[š.]qšt. | bn.ʻg[w.]q 119[321].4.4
ḥbl.b d.ʻdbym. | [šd.b]n.qṯy.b d.ṯt. | [ubd]y.mrim. | [šd.b]n.ṯpdn.b d.bn.gʻr. | [šd.b]n.ṯqrn.b d.ḫby. | [ṯn.š]d.bn.ngzḥn. 82[300].1.21
| srn.lṯḥ. | ykn.lṯḥ. | ḥgbn.lṯḥ. | spr.mkrm. | bn.slʻn.prs. | bn.ṯpdn.lṯḥ. | bn.urm.lṯḥ. 1059.8
lnhr. | [bn.p]rn. | [bn.a]nny. | [---]n. | bn.kbln. | bn.pdy. | bn.ṯpdn. 1075.2.3
[---]n[.---]. | [ag]dṯb.bn[.---]. | ʻbdil.bn.[---]. | ʻpṯn.bn.ṯṣq[-]. | mnn.bn.krmn. | bn.umḫ. | yky.bn.slyn. | ypln.bn.yl 85[80].1.4
pan.b d.klṯṯb. | [š]d.ilṣy.b d.ʻbdym. | [ub]dy.trrm. | [šd.]bn.ṯqdy.b d.gmrd. | [š]d bn.synn.b d.gmrd. | [šd.]abyy.b d.ibr 82[300].2.17
ṯy.b d.ṯt. | [ubd]y.mrim. | [šd.b]n.ṯpdn.b d.bn.gʻr. | [šd.b]n.ṯqrn.b d.ḫby. | [ṯn.š]d.bn.ngzḥn.b d.gmrd. | [šd.bn].pll.b 82[300].1.22
mn. | bn.ʻdṯ. | kṯy. | bn.ḫny. | bn.ssm. | bn.ḫnn. | [--]ny. | [bn].ṯrdnt. | [bn].hyadt. | [--]lt. | šmrm. | pʻṣ.bn.byy.ʻšrt. 1047.21
| w.nḥl h. | w.nḥl hm. | [bn].pmn. | bn.gṯrn. | bn.arpḫn. | bn.ṯryn. | bn.dll. | bn.ḥswn. | mrynm. | ʻzn. | ḥyn. | ʻmyn. | ilyn. | 1046.3.30
bʻt. | bn.ḫdyn.ṯqlm. | bn.ʻbd.šḫr.ṯqlm. | bn.ḥnqn.arbʻt. | [b]n.ṯrk.ṯqlm. | [b]n.pdrn.ṯq[lm]. | pdy.[----]. | [i]lmlk.bn.[---]. | 122[308].1.21
[---]y. | [---.]w.nḥl h. | bn ksln.ṯlṯḥ. | bn yṣmḫ.bn.ṯrn w nḥl h. | bn srd.bn agmn. | bn [-]ln.bn.ṯbil. | bn is.bn t 101[10].4
šm. | b[-.--]t. | [---.-]l[--]. | [---.]pr[--]. | [-.a]pln. | bn.mzt. | bn.ṯrn. | w.nḥl h. | [--.-]hs. | [--.--]nyn. | [-----]. | [-----]. | bn.ʻdy. | 2163.2.14
| špšyn[.---.]yṯb.b.ar. | bn.ag[p]ṯ.ḫpṯ.d[.yṯb.b].šʻrt. | yly.bn.ṯrnq.[-]r.d.yṯb.b.ilštmʻ. | ilšlm.bn.gs[-.--]r.d.yṯb.b.gt.al. | il 2015.1.26
. | [---]nb.w ykn. | [--]ndbym. | [ʻ]rmy.w snry. | [b]n.sdy.bn.ṯṯy. | bn.ḥyn.bn.ǵlm. | bn.yyn.w.bn.au[pš]. | bn.kdrn. | ʻrgz 131[309].23
].šbʻt.ʻšrt. | b.bn.pdrn.ʻšrm. | d.bn.šbʻl.uḫnpy.ḫmšm. | b.bn.ṯtm.ṯlṯm. | b.bn.agdṯb.ʻšrm. | b.bn.ibn.arbʻt.ʻšrt. | b.bn.mn 2054.1.11
y. | knʻm. | bn.yš[-]n. | bn.pd[y]. | ttn. | md.ʻṯt[rt]. | kṯkt. | bn.ṯtn[--]. | [m]d.m[--]. | [b]n.annḏ[r]. | bn.ṯdyy. | bn.grbn. | [--. 1054.1.13
n.adty. | bn.alz. | bn.birtn. | bn.mlṣ. | bn.q[--]. | bn.[---]. | bn.ṯ[-]r. | bn.grdn. | [bn.-]ḫr. | [--.-]nb. | [--.--]n. | [--.--]n. | bn.[-- 2023.2.2
[-----]. | bn.[---]. | bn.il[--]. | khnm[.--]. | bn.ṯ[--]. | bn.[---]. | bn.ṯʻl[-]. | bn.nq[ly]. | bn.snr[n]. | bn.pzn[y]. 2020.5
bršn. | šd.kkn.[bn].ubyn. | šd.bn.li[y]. | šd.bn.š[--]y. | šd.bn.ṯ[---]. | šd.ʻdmn[.bn.]ynḥm. | šd.bn.ṯmr[n.m]idḫy. | šd.ṯbʻm 2026.7
ḥrm.b[n].ng[-]n. | atyn.š[r]šy. | ʻbdḫmn[.bn.-]bdn. | ḥṣmn.[bn.---]ln. | [--]dm.[bn.---]n. | bʻly.[bn.---]n. | 102[322].1.3
gdn.ṯt.qštm.w.qlʻ. | bn.[-]q.qšt.w.qlʻ. | gb[l]n.qšt.w.qlʻ. | bn.[-]bl.ṯt.qštm.w.ṯn.qlʻm. | bn.[-]rkṯ.ṯt.qštm.w.qlʻ. | bn.ṯʻl.qš 119[321].3.15

ṯ[--].|bn.idrm.|bn.ymn.|bn.ṣry.|bn.mztn.|bn.šlgyn.|bn.[-]gštn.|bn[.n]klb.|b[n.]dtn.|w.nḥl h.|w.nḥl hm.|bn.irš 113[400].2.7
ym.|ṯm[n.]alp mitm.|ilb‘l ḫmš m[at].|‘dn.ḫmš.mat.|bn.[-]d.alp.|bn.[-]pn.ṯṯ mat. 1060.2.11
n[-].|[-----].|[-----].|[---.-]l[-].|[bn.-]dt[-].|[bn.-]nn.|[bn.-]dn.|bn.ummt.|bn.ṯb[-].|bn.[-]r[-].|bn.tgn.|bn.iḏrn.|m 124[-].6.3
db‘l.|bn.ḫyn.|[bn].ar[-]m.|[bn].ḥrp[-].|[bn].ḫdpṯr.|[bn.-]dn.|[bn.-]lyn.|[bn.i]lsk.|[bn.---]n.|bn[.---].|bn[.---].|b 124[-].2.8
abḏr.|bn.kpltn.|bn.prn.|‘bdm.|bn.kdǵbr.|bn.mṣrn.|bn.[-]dr[-].|[---]l[-].|[--]ym.|[--]rm.|[bn.]aǵld.|[w.nḥ]l h.|[114[324].2.13
.ir[--].|bn.kr[--].|bn.nn[-].|[-----].|[-----].|[---.-]l[-].|[bn.-]dt[-].|[bn.-]nn.|[bn.-]dn.|bn.ummt.|bn.ṯb[-].|bn.[-]r[- 124[-].6.1
bn.iḏrn.|mnn.|b[n].skn.|bn.p‘ṣ.|bn.ḏrm.|[bn.-]ln.|[bn.-]ḏprḏ. 124[-].6.14
birtn.|bn.mlṣ.|bn.q[--].|bn.[---].|bn.ṯ[-]r.|bn.grdn.|[bn.-]ḫr.|[--.-]nb.|[--.--]n.|[--.--]n.|bn.[---].|bn.‘r[--].|bn.nkt 2023.2.4
.ḫryn.|[ab]ǵl.bn.gdn.|[---].bn.bqš.|[---].bn.pdn.|[---.bn.-]ky.|[---.bn.--]r.|[-----].|[---.--]yn.|[---.]aṯrn.|[---.--]ḫt.| 102[323].4.15
[--] yn[.--].|[---].krm.b yp‘l.y‘dd.|[---.]krm.b [-]dn.l.bn.[-]kn.|šd[.---.-]‘n.|šd[.---.-]ṣm.l.dqn.|š[d.---.--]d.pdy.|[-- 2027.1.5
yn.|[bn].ar[-]m.|[bn].ḥrp[-].|[bn].ḫdpṯr.|[bn.-]dn.|[bn.-]lyn.|[bn.i]lsk.|[bn.---]n.|bn[.---].|bn[.---].|bn[.---].|bn 124[-].2.9
[ṯn.š]d.bn.ngzḥn.b d.gmrd.|[šd.bn].pll.b d.gmrd.|[šd.bn.-]ll.b d.iwrḫṯ.|[šd.bn.-]nn.b d.bn.šmrm.|[šd.bn.-]ṯtayy.b 82[300].1.25
ksln.ṯlṯḥ.|bn yṣmḫ.bn.ṯrn w nḥl h.|bn srd.bn agmn.|bn [-]ln.bn.ṯbil.|bn is.bn tbdn.|bn uryy.|bn abd‘n.|bn prkl. 101[10].6
.|bn.tgn.|bn.iḏrn.|mnn.|b[n].skn.|bn.p‘ṣ.|bn.ḏrm.|[bn.-]ln.|[bn.-]ḏprḏ. 124[-].6.13
|[--.-]sn.|[bn.-]ny.|[b]n.ḫnyn.|[bn].nbq.|[bn.]snrn.|[bn.-]lṣ.|bn.[---]ym. 115[301].3.5
l.|bn ydy.|bn lzn.|bn.ṯyn.|bn g‘r.|bn.prtn.|bn ḫnn.|b[n.-]n.|bn.ṣṣb.|bn.b‘ltn ḫlq.|bn.mlkbn.|bn.asyy ḫlq.|bn.k 2016.1.19
mn.|arb‘m.ksp.‘l.qrt.|b.šd.bn.[u]brš.|ḫmšt.‘šrt.|b.šd.bn.[-]n.|ṯl[ṯt].‘šr[t].|b.š[d].bn.‘myn.|ḫmšt.|b.[šd.--]n.|ḫ[m] 1083.9
n.alz.|bn.mṣrn.|bn.‘dy.|bn.ršpy.|[---.]mn.|[--.-]sn.|[bn.-]ny.|[b]n.ḫnyn.|[bn].nbq.|[bn.]snrn.|[bn.-]lṣ.|bn.[---]y 115[301].3.1
mrd.|[šd.bn].pll.b d.gmrd.|[šd.bn.-]ll.b d.iwrḫṯ.|[šd.bn.-]nn.b d.bn.šmrm.|[šd.bn.-]ṯtayy.b d.ṯtmd.|[šd.bn.-]rn.b 82[300].1.26
r[--].|bn.nn[-].|[-----].|[-----].|[---.-]l[-].|[bn.-]dt[-].|[bn.-]nn.|[bn.-]dn.|bn.ummt.|bn.ṯb[-].|bn.[-]r[-].|bn.tgn.|b 124[-].6.2
[b]n[.---].|bn [-]‘y.|[b]n [i]lmd.|bn [t]bdn.|bn štn.|b[n] kdn.|bn dwn. 2088.2
lp mitm.|ilb‘l ḫmš m[at].|‘dn.ḫmš.mat.|bn.[-]d.alp.|bn.[-]pn.ṯṯ mat. 1060.2.12
.b.i[-]‘lt.mlk.|arsw.|dqn.|ṯlṯ.klbm.|ḫmn.|[---.-]rsd.|bn[.-]pt.|bn kdrn.|awldn.|arswn.y‘r[ty.--].|bn.ugr.|gny.|ṯ 86[305].7
t.qštm w.ql‘.|bn.ḥṣn.qšt.w.ql‘.|bn.gdn.ṯt.qštm.w.ql‘.|bn.[-]q.qšt.w.ql‘.|gb[l]n.qšt.w.ql‘.|bn.[-]bl.ṯt.qštm.w.ṯn.ql‘ 119[321].3.13
s.|[--.--]nyn.|[-----].|[-----].|bn.‘dy.|w.nḥl h.|bn.‘bl.|bn.[-]rṯn.|bn[.---].|bn u[l]pm.|bn ‘[p]ty.|bn.kdgdl.|bn.smy 2163.2.22
št.w.ql‘.|gb[l]n.qšt.w.ql‘.|bn.[-]bl.ṯt.qštm.w.ṯn.ql‘m.|bn.[-]rkṯ.ṯt.qštm.w.ql‘.|bn.ṯ‘l.qšt.|bn.[ḫ]dpṯr.ṯt.qštm.[w].ql‘ 119[321].3.16
]t.|[bn.---].|[bn.--]my.|[bn.b]rq.|[bn.--]r.|[bn.--]tn.|[bn.-]rmn.|bn.prtn.|bn.ymn.|bn.dby.|bn.ir[--].|bn.kr[--].|b 124[-].5.7
šd.bn.-]nn.b d.bn.šmrm.|[šd.bn.-]ṯtayy.b d.ṯtmd.|[šd.bn.-]rn.b d.ṣdqšlm.|[šd.b d.]bn.p‘ṣ.|[ubdy.‘]šrm.|[šd.---]n.b 82[300].1.28
|[bn.-]dt[-].|[bn.-]nn.|[bn.-]dn.|bn.ummt.|bn.ṯb[-].|bn.[-]r[-].|bn.tgn.|bn.iḏrn.|mnn.|b[n].skn.|bn.p‘ṣ.|bn.ḏrm 124[-].6.6
t.|krwn.‘šrt.|bn.ulb ḫmšt.|bn.ḫry.ḫmšt.|swn.ḫmšt.|bn.[-]r[-.]ḫmšt.|bn.ḥdṯ.‘šrt.|bn.ḫnyn.‘šrt.|rpan.ḫmšt.|abǵl. 1062.16
mš.|‘[---].kd.|amry.kdm.|mnn.bn.gttn.kdm.|ynḥm.bn[.-]r[-]t.ṯlṯ.|plwn.kdm.|tmyn.bn.ubrš.kd. 136[84].10
]mdy.|bn.ḫlln.|bn.kṯn.|bn.abn.|bn.nskn.|bn.gmrn.|bn[.-]škn.|[---.--]n.|[---.--]n.|[--.]‘[--].|[bn].k[--].|bn.ab[--].| 2021.2.8
hnd.|‘mṯtmr.bn.|nqmp‘.ml[k].|ugrt.ytn.|šd.kdǵdl[.bn].|[-]š[-]y.d.b š[-]y.|[---.y]d gt h[.--].|[---.]yd.|[k]rm h.yd 1008.5
.|bn.‘myn.|bn.alz.|bn.birtn.|[bn.]ylkn.|[bn.]krwn.|[bn.-]ty.|[bn.]iršn.|bn.[---].|bn.b[--].|bn.š[--].|bn.a[---].|bn. 117[325].1.16
.|[šd.bn.-]ll.b d.iwrḫṯ.|[šd.bn.-]nn.b d.bn.šmrm.|[šd.bn.-]ṯtayy.b d.ṯtmd.|[šd.bn.-]rn.b d.ṣdqšlm.|[šd.b d.]bn.p‘ṣ. 82[300].1.27
[---.]ḫ[---.]tmnym[.k]sp ḫmšt.|[w a]rb‘ kkr ‘l bn[.--].|[w] ṯlṯ šmn.|[w a]r[b‘] ksp ‘l bn ymn.|šb šr šmn [--] 1103.2
.|limm.w t‘l.‘m.il.|ab h.ḥpr.p‘l k.y[--].|šm‘ k.l arḫ.w bn.[--].|limm.ql.b udn.k w[-].|k rtqt mr[.---].|k d lbšt.bir. 13[6].22
rspy.ms[g].|[---.ms]g.|bn.[gr]gs.msg.|bn[.--]an.msg.|bn[.--].m[sg].|b[--]n.qmy.msg.|[---]n.msg.|[----].msg.|[---]. 133[-].2.4
rn.|[a]ršwn.|‘b[d].|w nḥl h.|atn.bn.ap[s]n.|nsk.ṯlṯ.|bn.[--.]m[-]ḫr.|bn.šmrm.|ṯnnm.|[ar]swn.bn.qqln.|m[--].bn 85[80].3.9
šp]ḥ.a[n]ntb.|w.m[--.u]škny.|[‘]š[r.---]t.ksp.|[‘l.---]b bn[.--].|[-]ḥ[-.---].|[-]p[-.---.-]ny.|[-]ḥ[-.---.-]dn.|arb‘[m.ksp. 2055.6
b‘ l ṯkṣ[-].|nn.arspy.ms[g].|[---.ms]g.|bn.[gr]gs.msg.|bn[.--]an.msg.|bn[.--].m[sg].|b[--]n.qmy.msg.|[---]n.msg.|[133[-].2.3
.|bn.d[-]n.|bn.amdn.|bn.ṯmrn.|bn.pzny.|bn.mglb.|bn.[--]b.|bn.[---].|bn.[---]. 113[400].6.33
qln.|‘bdil[-].bn.qqln.|liy.bn.qqln.|mnn.bn.ṣnr.|iḫy.[b]n[.--]l[-].|‘bdy[rḫ].bn.gṯtn.|yrmn.bn.‘n.|krwn.nḥl h.|ttn. 85[80].4.7
]n.|ynḥm.|bn.abd.b‘[l].|mnḥm.bn[.---].|krmn[py].|bn.[--]m.|bn.asr[-].|bn.ḏr[--].|bn.ṣl[--].|bn.ḫd[--].|bn.‘[---]. 2014.51
n[.---].|bn[.---].|bn[.---].|bn[.---].|[bn.--]t.|[bn.---].|[bn.--]my.|[bn.b]rq.|[bn.--]r.|[bn.--]tn.|[bn.-]rmn.|bn.prtn. 124[-].5.3
.bnš.aǵlkz.|[šd.b]d.b[n].tkwn.|[ubdy.mḏ]rǵlm.|[šd.bn.--]n.b d.aḫny.|[šd.bn.--]rt.b d.ṯpṭb‘l.|[ubdy.]mḫ[ṣ]m.|[š 82[300].2.23
nym.dt.[b d.---].|bn.btr.|bn.‘ms.|bn.pṣn.|bn.agmz.|bn.[--]n.|bn.a[--].|[------].|[------].|[------].|[------].|[------].|[2021.1.6
-].|tld bt.[--]t.ḫ[--.l k]|ṯrt.l bnt.hll[.snnt].|hl ǵlmt tld b[n.--]n.|‘n ha l yd h.tzd[.--].|pt l bšr h.dm a[--.--]ḥ.|w yn. 24[77].7
--].|š[d.b]d.u[--].|šd.b d.[---].|šd.b d[.---]im.|šd.b d[.bn.--]n.|šd.b d.iwrkl.|šd.b d.klb.|šd.b d.klby.|šd.b d.iytlm. 2090.7
--].|bn.brzn.ṯn.|bn.išb‘l[.---].|bn.s[---].|dnn.[bn.---].|bn[.--]‘nt. 2069.11
---].|bn[.---].|[bn.--]t.|[bn.---].|[bn.--]my.|[bn.b]rq.|[bn.--]r.|[bn.--]tn.|[bn.-]rmn.|bn.prtn.|bn.ymn.|bn.dby.|b 124[-].5.5
l.bn.gdn.|[---].bn.bqš.|[---].bn.pdn.|[---.bn.-]ky.|[---.bn.--]r.|[-----].|[---.--]yn.|[---.]aṯrn.|[---.--]ḫt.|[---.]b‘ly.|[--- 102[323].4.16
[n].tkwn.|[ubdy.mḏ]rǵlm.|[šd.bn.--]n.b d.aḫny.|[šd.bn.--]rt.b d.ṯpṭb‘l.|[ubdy.]mḫ[ṣ]m.|[šd.bn.]uzpy.b d.yšn.ḥrš 82[300].2.24
n.---]n.|bn[.---].|bn[.---].|bn[.---].|bn[.---].|bn[.---].|bn[.---].|[bn.--]t.|[bn.---].|[bn.--]my.|[bn.b]rq.|[bn.--]r.|[bn.--]tn.|[b 124[-].5.1
--].|[bn.--]t.|[bn.---].|[bn.--]my.|[bn.b]rq.|[bn.--]r.|[bn.--]tn.|[bn.-]rmn.|bn.prtn.|bn.ymn.|bn.dby.|bn.ir[--].|b 124[-].5.6
ilšt[m‘ym].|yddt[.---].|ilšn.[---].|ṣdqn.[----].|pndḏn.b[n.---].|ayaḫ.b[n.---]. 96[333].5
gd[ly.---.]aṯ[t h].|‘dyn[.---].|w.ṯn[.bn h.---].|iwrm[-.]b[n.---].|annt[n.]w[.---].|w.ṯn.bn h.[---].|aǵltn.ypr[y.---].|w 2044.14
.---].|apnm.l.‘[--].|apnm.l.[---].|apnm.l.d[--].|apnm.l.bn[.---].|apnm.l.[b]n[.---].|apnm.l.bn[.---].|ṯlṯ.ṣmdm[.---].| 145[318].6
|apnm.l.[---].|apnm.l.d[--].|apnm.l.bn[.---].|apnm.l.[b]n[.---].|apnm.l.bn[.---].|ṯlṯ.ṣmdm[.---].|mṣ[r]n[.---]. 145[318].7
.|[---.--]b.|bn.t[--.---.a]ǵt.|špš[yn.---.u]br‘y.|iln.[---].|bn.[---].ar.|bn.[---].b.ar.|špšyn[.---.]ytb.b.ar.|bn.ag[p]ṯ.ḫpṯ. 2015.1.22
b h.---].|ḥš b[ht m.tbnn.ḥš.trmmn.hkl m].|b tk.[---].|bn.[---].|a[--.---.] 1[‘NT.IX].3.29
ṣbn ary.|bn.šdy ary.|bn.ktkt.m‘qby.|bn.[---.]ṯlḥny.|b[n.---.ub]r‘y.|[bn.---.ubr]‘y.|b[n.---].|bn[.---.ušk]ny.|bn.kd 87[64].18
y ary.|bn.ktkt.m‘qby.|bn.[---.]ṯlḥny.|b[n.---.ub]r‘y.|[bn.---.ubr]‘y.|b[n.---].|bn[.---.ušk]ny.|bn.kdrn.uškny.|bn.l 87[64].19

bn[.---].|ubr[‘ym.---].|qdm[n.---].|b‘l[--.---].|šm[---.---].|yšr 93[328].1
|[---.-]tn.b d.mlkt.|[---.]l.mḫṣ.|ab[---.]aḏddy.bn.skn.|bn.[---.]uḫd.|bn.n[---.]hbṭn.|bn.m[--.]skn.|bn.s[--.b]d.skn. 2014.9
bn.[---.]ṯlḥny.|b[n.---.ub]r‘y.|[bn.---.ubr]‘y.|b[n.---].|bn[.---.ušk]ny.|bn.kdrn.uškny.|bn.lgn.uškny.|bn.abn.uškn 87[64].21
n.t[--.---.a]ǵt.|špš[yn.---.u]br‘y.|iln.[---].|bn.[---].ar.|bn.[---].b.ar.|špšyn[.---.]yṭb.b.ar.|bn.ag[p]ṯ.ḫpṯ.d[.yṭb.b].š‘r 2015.1.23
šd.bn.adn.|[b] d.armwl.|[šd].mrnn.|b d.[-]tw[-].|šd.bn[.---].|b d.dd[--].|šd.d[---].|b d.d[---].|šd.b[---].|b d.[---]. 2028.5
.atnb.|bn.yšd.|bn.bršm.|bn.gṯprg.|gṯpbn.|bn.b[--].|[b]n.[---].|bn.a[--].|bn.ml[k].|bn.glyn.|bn.‘dr.|bn.ṯmq.|bn. 1057.15
n.m‘nt.|bn.g[--]n.|bn[.---].|[-----].|b[n.---].|b[n.---].|bn.[---].|bn.a[--].|w.nḥl h.|bn.alz.|w.nḥl h.|bn.sny.|bn.abl 2163.1.9
[-----].|bn.[---].|bn.il[--].|khnm[.--].|bn.ṯ[--].|bn.[---].|bn.ṯ‘l[-].|bn 2020.2
n.|[-----].|[-----].|bn.‘dy.|w.nḥl h.|bn.‘bl.|bn.[-]rṭn.|bn[.---].|bn u[l]pm.|bn ‘[p]ty.|bn.kdgdl.|bn.smyy.|bn.lbn. 2163.3.1
mry[n]m.|bn rmy[y].|yšril[.---].|anntn bn[.---].|bn.brzn [---].|bnil.bn.tl[--].|bn.brzn.ṯn.|bn.išb‘l[.-- 2069.4
|bn.birtn.|[bn.]ylkn.|[bn.]krwn.|[bn.-]ty.|[bn.]iršn.|bn.[---].|bn.b[--].|bn.š[--].|bn.a[---].|bn.prsn.|bn.mtyn.|bn 117[325].2.1
bn.bršm.|bn.kzn.|w.nḥl h.|w.nḥl hm.|w.[n]ḥl hm.|b[n.---].|bn.gzry.|bn.atyn.|bn.ttn.|bn.rwy.|bn.‘myn.|bdl. 113[400].2.24
nq[n].|[-----].|[-----].|[-----].|[-----].|n[----].|bn.[---].|bn.[---].|bn.yk[--].|bn.šmm.|bn.irgy.|w.nḥl h.|w.nḥl hm.| 1046.2.7
h.|bn.alz.|w.nḥl h.|bn.sny.|bn.ablḥ.|[-----].|w [---].|bn.[---].|bn.yr[--].|bn.kṯr[t].|bn.šml.|bn.arnbt.|qdšm.|b[-. 2163.2.3
sr[-].|bn.ḏr[--].|bn.ṣl[--].|bn.ḫd[--].|bn.‘[---].|kbkbn bn[.---].|bn.k[--].|bn.pdr[n.].|bn.‘n[--].|nḥl h[.---].|[-----]. 2014.57
--].|[bn].k[--].|bn.ab[--].|bn.i[--].|bn.n[--].|bn.ḫ[--].|bn.[---].|bn.k[--]. 2021.2.17
bn.gb[--].|bn.ḥn[n].|bn.gntn[-].|[--.]nqq[-].|b[n.---].|bn.[---].|bn.‘yn.|bn.dtn. 2023.4.2
n.ṯ[-]r.|bn.grdn.|[bn.-]ḫr.|[--.-]nb.|[--.--]n.|[--.--]n.|bn.[---].|bn.‘r[--].|bn.nkt[-].|bn.abḏr.|bn.ḥrẓn.|bn.ḏqnt.|b 2023.3.6
bn[.---].|bn.qdšt.|bn.m‘nt.|bn.g[--]n.|bn[.---].|[-----].|b[n.- 2163.1.1
[-----].|bn.[---].|bn.il[--].|khnm[.--].|bn.ṯ[--].|bn.[---].|bn.ṯ‘l[-].|bn.nq[ly].|bn.snr[n].|bn.pzn[y].|bn.mg[l 2020.6
.niršn.|bn.adty.|bn.alz.|bn.birtn.|bn.mlṣ.|bn.q[--].|bn.[---].|bn.ṯ[-]r.|bn.grdn.|[bn.-]ḫr.|[--.-]nb.|[--.--]n.|[--.--] 2023.1.8
[b]n[.---].|bn [-]‘y.|[b]n [i]lmd.|bn [t]bdn.|bn štn.|b[n] kdn 2088.1
n[.---].|bn[.---].|bn[.---].|bn[.---].|bn[.---].|[bn.--]t.|[bn.---].|[bn.--]my.|[bn.b]rq.|[bn.--]r.|[bn.--]tn.|[bn.-]rmn. 124[-].5.2
il.bn.tl[--].|bn.brzn.ṯn.|bn.išb‘l[.---].|bn.s[---].|dnn.[bn.---].|bn[.--]‘nt. 2069.10
.i]lsk.|[bn.---]n.|bn[.---].|bn[.---].|bn[.---].|bn[.---].|bn[.---].|[bn.--]t.|[bn.---].|[bn.--]my.|[bn.b]rq.|[bn.--]r.|[b 124[-].3.5
.m‘qby.|bn.[---.]ṯlḥny.|b[n.---.ub]r‘y.|[bn.---.ubr]‘y.|b[n.---].|bn[.---.ušk]ny.|bn.kdrn.uškny.|bn.lgn.uškny.|bn. 87[64].20
n.qdšt.|bn.m‘nt.|bn.g[--]n.|bn[.---].|[-----].|b[n.---].|b[n.---].|bn.[---].|bn.a[--].|w.nḥl h.|bn.alz.|w.nḥl h.|bn.sn 2163.1.8
y.|[bn].ḫnq[n].|[-----].|[-----].|[-----].|[-----].|n[----].|bn.[---].|bn.[---].|bn.yk[--].|bn.šmm.|bn.irgy.|w.nḥl h.|w. 1046.2.6
n.ar[--].|bn.gb[--].|bn.ḥn[n].|bn.gntn[-].|[--.]nqq[-].|b[n.---].|bn.[---].|bn.‘yn.|bn.dtn. 2023.4.1
-]lyn.|[bn.i]lsk.|[bn.---]n.|bn[.---].|bn[.---].|bn[.---].|bn[.---].|bn[.---].|[bn.--]t.|[bn.---].|[bn.--]my.|[bn.b]rq.|[b 124[-].3.4
n.|bn.kdgdl.|bn.gl‘d.|bn.ktln.|[bn].ǵrgn.|bn.pb[-].|bn.[---].|bn.[---].|bn.[---].|bn.[---].|bn.[---].|bn.[---].|bn.[--- 115[301].1.18
gl‘d.|bn.ktln.|[bn].ǵrgn.|bn.pb[-].|bn.[---].|bn.[---].|bn.[---].|bn.[---].|bn.[---].|bn.[---].|bn.[---].|bn.[---].|bn.[--- 115[301].1.20
gdl.|bn.gl‘d.|bn.ktln.|[bn].ǵrgn.|bn.pb[-].|bn.[---].|bn.[---].|bn.[---].|bn.[---].|bn.[---].|bn.[---].|bn.[---].|bn.[--- 115[301].1.19
[bn].ḫdpṯr.|[bn.-]dn.|[bn.-]lyn.|[bn.i]lsk.|[bn.---]n.|bn[.---].|bn[.---].|bn[.---].|bn[.---].|bn[.---].|[bn.--]t.|[bn.--- 124[-].3.1
ktln.|[bn].ǵrgn.|bn.pb[-].|bn.[---].|bn.[---].|bn.[---].|bn.[---].|bn.[---].|bn.[---].|bn.[---].|bn.[---].|bn.[---].|bn.[--- 115[301].1.21
[--].|bn.ẓrl.|bn.illm[-].|bn.š[---].|bn.ṣ[---].|bn.š[---].|bn.[---].|bn.[---].|b[n.---].|b[n.---]. 115[301].4.28
n.pb[-].|bn.[---].|bn.[---].|bn.[---].|bn.[---].|bn.[---].|bn.[---].|bn.[---].|bn.[---].|bn.[---].|bn.[---].|bn.[---].|bn.[--- 115[301].1.23
ṯr.|[bn.-]dn.|[bn.-]lyn.|[bn.i]lsk.|[bn.---]n.|bn[.---].|bn[.---].|bn[.---].|bn[.---].|bn[.---].|[bn.--]t.|[bn.---].|[bn.--] 124[-].3.2
bn.[---].|bn.[---].|bn.[---].|bn.[---].|bn.[---].|bn.[---].|bn.[---].|bn.[---].|bn.[---].|bn.[---].|bn.[---].|bn.[---].|[-----]. 115[301].1.24
bn.[---].|bn.[---].|bn.[---].|bn.[---].|bn.[---].|bn.[---].|bn.[---].|bn.[---].|bn.[---].|bn.[---].|[-----].|bn[---].|bn.mlky 115[301].1.26
bn.[---].|bn.[---].|bn.[---].|bn.[---].|bn.[---].|bn.[---].|bn.[---].|bn.[---].|bn.[---].|bn.[---].|bn.[---].|[-----].|bn[---].| 115[301].1.25
dn.|[bn.-]lyn.|[bn.i]lsk.|[bn.---]n.|bn[.---].|bn[.---].|bn[.---].|bn[.---].|bn[.---].|[bn.--]t.|[bn.---].|[bn.--]my.|[bn. 124[-].3.3
].ǵrgn.|bn.pb[-].|bn.[---].|bn.[---].|bn.[---].|bn.[---].|bn.[---].|bn.[---].|bn.[---].|bn.[---].|bn.[---].|bn.[---].|bn.[--- 115[301].1.22
n[.---].|bn.qdšt.|bn.m‘nt.|bn.g[--]n.|bn[.---].|[-----].|b[n.---].|b[n.---].|bn.[---].|bn.a[--].|w.nḥl h.|bn.alz.|w.nḥl 2163.1.7
bn.[---].|bn.[---].|bn.[---].|bn.[---].|bn.[---].|bn.[---].|bn.[---].|bn.[---].|bn.[---].|[-----].|bn[---].|bn.mlkyy.|bn.atn 115[301].1.27
rl.|bn.illm[-].|bn.š[---].|bn.ṣ[---].|bn.š[---].|bn.[---].|bn.[---].|b[n.---].|b[n.---]. 115[301].4.29
[-----].|b[--.---].|b[--.---].|l[--.---].|m[--.---].|bn[.---].|bn[.---].|w.yn[.---].|bn.‘dr[.---].|ntb[t].|b.arb[‘].| 2007.6
[-----].|bn.[---].|bn.[---].|w.nḥ[l h].|bn.ẓr[-].|mru.skn.|bn.bddn.|b 113[400].5.1
gn.|bn.tgtn.|bn.ḥrẓn.|bn.qdšt.|bn.ntǵ[-].|bn.gr[--].|bn.[---].|bn.[---].|mr[u.ibrn].|bn.i[---].|bn.n[---].|bn.b[---]. 113[400].5.14
b[n.---].|bn[.---].|[-]d[-.---].|bn.‘[--.---].|bn.[---]. 109[-].1
bn.[---].|bn.[---].|bn.[---].|bn.[---].|bn.[---].|bn.[---].|bn.[---].|bn.[---].|[-----].|bn[---].|bn.mlkyy.|bn.atn.|bn.bly. 115[301].1.28
n.|bn.amdn.|bn.ṯmrn.|bn.pzny.|bn.mglb.|bn.[--]b.|bn.[---].|bn.[---]. 113[400].6.34
m[-].|bn.š[---].|bn.ṣ[---].|bn.š[---].|bn.[---].|bn.[---].|b[n.---].|b[n.---]. 115[301].4.30
[.---].|ḫluy.bn[.---].|ymil.bn.[---].|dly.bn[.---].|ynḥm.bn[.---].|gn.bn[.---].|klby.[bn.---].|šmmlk bn[.---].|‘myn.bn 102[322].5.6
n.k[n]y.|bn.klyn.|bn.gmḫn.|ḥnn.|ayab.|bn.gm[--].|bn.[---].|g[---].|p[---].|b[---].|[---].|[---].|bn[.---]y.|yr[---].| 1035.3.12
-].|[bn].ṣbṭ[--].|[bn].ḫla[n].|[bn].ǵr[--].|d.b[n.---].|d.bn.[---].|d.bn.š[--].|d.bn.ṯn[r].|d.kmry. 2164.в.2
|[bn].amd[-].|[bn].ṣbṭ[--].|[bn].ḫla[n].|[bn].ǵr[--].|d.b[n.---].|d.bn.[---].|d.bn.š[--].|d.bn.ṯn[r].|d.kmry. 2164.в.1
].|[---]mlk[.---].|[-----].|ilb‘l[.---].|ḫluy.bn[.---].|ymil.bn.[---].|dly.bn[.---].|ynḥm.bn[.---].|gn.bn[.---].|klby.[bn.-- 102[322].5.4
[-----].|b[--.---].|b[--.---].|l[--.---].|m[--.---].|bn[.---].|bn[.---].|w.yn[.---].|bn.‘dr[.---].|ntb[t].|b.arb[‘].|mat.ḫr[ṣ]. 2007.7
[-----].|bn.[---].|bn.[---].|w.nḥ[l h].|bn.ẓr[-].|mru.skn.|bn.bddn.|bn.ǵrgn.| 113[400].5.2
ilm[.---].|tš‘.‘š[r.---].|bn ‘dr[.---].|ḫmš ‘l.bn[.---].|ḫmš ‘l r‘l[-].|ḫmš ‘l ykn[.--].|ḫ[mš] ‘l abǵ[l].|ḫmš ‘ 2034.2.4
--].|tlby[.---].|ir[--.---].|pndyn[.---].|w.idṯ[-.---].|b.gt.b[n.---].|yḫl[.---].|b.gt.[---].|[---.]k[--]. 1078.7
[-.---].|ab[.---].|ḫyi[l.---].|iḫy[.---].|ar[.---].|‘ṯtr[.---].|bn.[---].|yly[.---].|ykn[.---].|rp[--].|ṯtw.[---].|[---.‘]šrm.ṣmd. 2131.7

. | [ʻ]bdyr[ẖ.---]. | [---]mlk[.---]. | [-----]. | ilbʻl[.---]. | ẖluy.bn[.---]. | ymil.bn.[---]. | dly.bn[.---]. | ynḥm.bn[.---]. | gn.bn[.-- 102[322].5.3
]. | klby.[bn.---]. | šmmlk bn[.---]. | ʻmyn.bn.[---]. | mtbʻl.bn[.---]. | ymy.bn[.---]. | ʻbdʻn.p[--.---]. | [-]d[-]l.bn.ḥrn. | aẖty.b 102[322].5.11
--]. | [-----]. | ilbʻl[.---]. | ẖluy.bn[.---]. | ymil.bn.[---]. | dly.bn[.---]. | ynḥm.bn[.---]. | gn.bn[.---]. | klby.[bn.---]. | šmmlk b 102[322].5.5
mn.ymtšr. | arbʻ.šmn.ʻl.ʻbdn.w.[---]. | kdm.šmn.ʻl.ilršp.bn[.---]. | kd.šmn.ʻl.yddn. | kd.ʻl.ššy. | kd.ʻl.nd̠bn.bn.agmn. | [k 1082.1.5
n[.---]. | ymil.bn.[---]. | dly.bn[.---]. | ynḥm.bn[.---]. | gn.bn[.---]. | klby.[bn.---]. | šmmlk bn[.---]. | ʻmyn.bn.[---]. | mtbʻl. 102[322].5.7
[--]ǵyn.b[n.---]. | krwn.b[n.---]. | tgyn.mʻ[---]. | w.agpṯn[.---]. | ṯynd̠r[-. 103[334].1
| bn.mlkr[šp]. | bn.y[k]n. | ynḥm. | bn.abd.bʻ[l]. | mnḥm.bn[.---]. | krmn[py]. | bn.[--]m. | bn.asr[-]. | bn.d̠r[--]. | bn.ṣl[--]. 2014.49
.ʻl.[-]lpy. | bn.ady.kkr.šʻrt. | nṯk h. | kb[d.]mn.ʻl.abršn. | b[n.---].kršu.nṯk h. | [---.--]mm.b.krsi. 1146.12
.]y[--.-]kzn. | [---.]yn.l.m[---]. | [---.]yn.l.m[--]m. | [---.]d.bn.[---.]l.dqn. | [---.--]ʻ.šdyn.l ytršn. | [---.--]ṯ.ʻbd.l.kyn. | k[rm. 2027.2.7
tn. | bn.ḥrẓn. | bn.qdšt. | bn.nṯǵ[-]. | bn.gr[--]. | bn.[---]. | bn.[---]. | mr[u.ibrn]. | bn.i[---]. | bn.n[---]. | bn.b[---]. | bn.iš[--]. 113[400].5.15
.---]. | gn.bn[.---]. | klby.[bn.---]. | šmmlk bn[.---]. | ʻmyn.bn.[---]. | mtbʻl.bn[.---]. | ymy.bn[.---]. | ʻbdʻn.p[--.---]. | [-]d[-]l. 102[322].5.10
[---]n[.---]. | [ag]dṯb.bn[.---]. | ʻbdil.bn.[---]. | ʻpṯn.bn.ṯṣq[-]. | mnn.bn.krmn. | bn.u 85[80].1.2
]. | šmmlk bn[.---]. | ʻmyn.bn.[---]. | mtbʻl.bn[.---]. | ymy.bn[.---]. | ʻbdʻn.p[--.---]. | [-]d[-]l.bn.ḥrn. | aẖty.bt.abm. | [-]rbn 102[322].5.12
---]. | ynḥm.bn[.---]. | gn.bn[.---]. | klby.[bn.---]. | šmmlk bn[.---]. | ʻmyn.bn.[---]. | mtbʻl.bn[.---]. | ymy.bn[.---]. | ʻbdʻn.p 102[322].5.9
[---]n[.---]. | [ag]dṯb.bn[.---]. | ʻbdil.bn.[---]. | ʻpṯn.bn.ṯṣq[-]. | mnn.bn.krmn. | bn.umẖ. | yky.bn.sly 85[80].1.3
šm [---]. | knʻm.bn.[---]. | plšbʻl.bn.n[--]. | ḥy bn.dnn.ṯkt. | ilṯḥm.bn.dnn.ṯkt. | š 2085.2
---]. | pln.ṯmry.w.ṯn.bn h.w[.---]. | ymrn.apsny.w.aṯt h..b[n.---]. | prd.mʻqby[.w.---.a]ṯt h[.---]. | prṯ.mgd[ly.---.]aṯ[t h]. 2044.9
rnmy.qšt.yqb.[--] | rk.ʻl.aqht.k yq[--.---]. | prʻm.ṣd k.y bn[.---]. | prʻm.ṣd k.hn pr[ʻ.--]. | ṣd.b hkl h[.---]. | [------]. | [---.l 17[2AQHT].5.37
n.[---]. | dly.bn[.---]. | ynḥm.bn[.---]. | gn.bn[.---]. | klby.[bn.---]. | šmmlk bn[.---]. | ʻmyn.bn.[---]. | mtbʻl.bn[.---]. | ymy. 102[322].5.8
lm. | bn.gdrn.b.mʻr[by]. | [w].bn.dʻm[-]. | bn.ppṯ.b[--]. | b[n.---]. | šm[-.---]. | tkn[.---]. | knn.b.ẖ[lb]. | bn mṯ.b.qmy. | nʻr. 2046.2.1
[--]ǵyn.b[n.---]. | krwn.b[n.---]. | tgyn.mʻ[---]. | w.agpṯn[.---]. | ṯynd̠r[-.---]. | gt.tg[yn.-- 103[334].2
sp.b.a[--]. | ṯqlm.ẖr[ṣ.]b.ṯmnt.ksp. | ʻšrt.ksp.b.alp.[b d].bn.[---]. | ṯšʻ.ṣin.b.ṯšʻt.ksp. | mšlt.b.ṯql.ksp. | kdwṯ.l.grgyn.b.ṯq 2101.21
.ǵlmn ary. | bn.ḥṣbn ary. | bn.šdy ary. | bn.ktkt.mʻqby. | bn.[---.]ṯlḥny. | b[n.---.ub]rʻy. | [bn.---.ubr]ʻy. | b[n.---]. | bn[.--- 87[64].17
nm.l.d[--]. | apnm.l.bn[.---]. | apnm.l.[b]n[.---]. | apnm.l.bn[.---]. | ṯlṯ.ṣmdm[.---]. | mṣ[r]n[.---]. 145[318].8
n[.---]. | [-]l[-.---]. | [-]ṯ.[---]. | mṣb[-.---]. | kṯ.aqh[r.---]. | l bn[.---]. | [ṯ]lṯ.[---]. | [---.--]yn.š.aẖ[--]. | [---.]š.nṣ[.-]al[-]. | [---.-- 143[-].2.5
b[n.---]. | bn[.---]. | [-]d[-.---]. | bn.ʻ[--.---]. | bn.[---]. 109[-].2
[šm]n.k[--.---]. | [---.ar]bʻ.dblt.d̠r[--.---]. | [--.m]itm.nṣ.l bn[.---]. | [-]l[-.---]. | [-]ṯ.[---]. | mṣb[-.---]. | kṯ.aqh[r.---]. | l bn[.- 143[-].1.10
-.]iš[--.]h[---.]išt. | [---]y.yblmm.u[---]k.yrd[.--.]i[---]n.bn. | [---.-]nn.nrt.ilm.špš.ṯšu.g h.w t[ṣḥ.šm]ʻ.mʻ. | [-.yṯ]ir ṯr.il. 2.3[129].14
š.ddm. | ṯṯ.l.ʻšrm.bn[š.mlk.---].ẖzr.lqḥ.ḥp[r]. | ʻšt.ʻšr h.bn[.---.--]ẖ.zr. | bʻl.šd. 2011.41
b.b.ilštmʻ. | abmn.bn.r[---].b.syn. | bn.irṣ[-.---.]h. | šdyn.b[n.---.--]n. 2015.2.9
. | [b]n.ṯrk.ṯqlm. | [b]n.pdrn.ṯq[lm]. | pdy.[----]. | [i]lmlk.bn.[---]. | [--]ʻ[-.---]. | [---.k]kr. | [-----]. | [---.k]kr. 122[308].1.24
[---.]bn[.---]. | [---.]bn[.---]. | [---.]nḥl h. | [---.b]n.špš. | [---.b]n.mrad 2137.1
wd.šmbnš[.---]. | [---].ksp.ʻl.k[--]. | [---.--]k. | [---.]ksp.ʻl.bn[.---]. | [---].ksp[.---]. | [---.--]ir[.---]. | [---].ʻl.ynḥ[m]. | [---.]ʻl. 1144.10
[---.]bn[.---]. | [---.]bn[.---]. | [---.]nḥl h. | [---.b]n.špš. | [---.b]n.mradn. | [---.m]lky 2137.2
[---.--]my. | [---.]bn.[---]. | [---].šd ubdy. | [---.šd] u[b]dy. | [---.]šd.ubdy. | [---.]b 2031.2
| bn.nǵsk. | bn.qnd̠. | bn.pity. | w.nḥl h. | bn.rt. | bn.l[--]. | bn.[---]. | [---.--]y. | [--.-]d̠rm. | [--.--]y. | [--.--]y. | [-----]. | [-----]. | 113[400].3.21
ilšpš. | ubrš. | bn gmš ẖlq. | bn ʻgy. | bn zlbn. | bn.aẖ[--]. | bn[.---]. | [-----]. | bn kr[k]. | bn ẖtyn. | w nḥl h. | bn ṯgrb. | bn ṯd 2016.2.22
bn[.---]. | bn.qdšt. | bn.mʻnt. | bn.g[--]n. | bn[.---]. | [-----]. | b[n.---]. | b[n.---]. | bn.[---]. | bn.a[--]. | w.nḥl h 2163.1.5
bn.[---]. | bn.[---]. | bn.[---]. | bn.[---]. | bn.[---]. | bn.[---]. | bn.[---]. | [-----]. | bn[---]. | bn.mlkyy. | bn.atn. | bn.bly. | bn.ṯbrn 115[301].1.29
[---.]m[--]. | [---].bn[.---]. | [-----]. | [---].ḥ[mr]. | [---.]w.bnš.aḥd. | [---.--]m. | [---].ʻ 2043.2
---]. | išdym.t[---]. | b k.mla[.---]. | udmʻt.d[mʻ.---]. | [---].bn.[---]. | [-----]. 27[8].12
.mẖlpt[.---.--]r. | [---.]nʻlm.[---]. | [---].hn.al[-.---]. | [---]t.bn[.---]. UG5.8.52
dn. | bn.ṯmrn. | bn.pzny. | bn.mglb. | bn.[--]b. | bn.[---]. | bn.[---]. 113[400].6.35
.š[---]. | bn.ṣ[---]. | bn.š[---]. | bn.[---]. | bn.[---]. | b[n.---]. | b[n.---]. 115[301].4.31
mnipʻl. | amrbʻl. | dqry. | ṯdy. | ypʻbʻl. | bdlm. | bn.pd̠[-]. | bn.[---]. 1058.22
bly.mr[-.---]. | w.nḥl h.mr[-.---]. | ilšpš.[---]. | iḥny.[---]. | bn.[---]. 88[304].14
---]. | ṣḥ[.---]. | ky.m[--.---]. | w pr[--.---]. | tštil[.---]. | ʻmn.bn[.---]. 1021.16
it il. | b ṣmd il. | b dṯn il. | b šrp il. | b knt il. | b ǵdyn il. | [b]n [---]. 30[107].19
b[n.---]. | bn[.---]. | [-]d[-.---]. | bn.ʻ[--.---]. | bn.[---]. 109[-].5
m. | bn.špš.bn.ibrd. | ʻpṯrm.bn.ʻbdy. | n[--.]bn.šnd. | [---].bn.[---]. 2024.8
ddt[.---]. | ilšn.[---]. | ṣdqn.[----]. | pndd̠n.b[n.---]. | ayaḥ.b[n.---]. 96[333].6
| bn.gm[--]. | bn.[---]. | g[---]. | p[---]. | b[---]. | [---]. | [---]. | bn[.---]y. | yr[---]. | ẖdyn. | grgš. | b[n.]tlš. | d̠mr. | mkrm. | ʻzn. | 1035.3.18
. | [bn.-]ny. | [b]n.ẖnyn. | [bn].nbq. | [bn.]snrn. | [bn.-]lṣ. | bn.[---]ym. 115[301].3.6
.b[n].ng[-]n. | atyn.š[r]šy. | ʻbdẖmn[.bn.-]bdn. | ḥṣmn.[bn.---]ln. | [--]dm.[bn.---]n. | bʻly.[bn.---]n. | krr[-.---]. | špš[yn. 102[322].1.4
].ḥrp[-]. | [bn].ẖdpṯr. | [bn.-]dn. | [bn.-]lyn. | [bn.i]lsk. | [bn.---]n. | bn[.---]. | bn[.---]. | bn[.---]. | bn[.---]. | bn[.---]. | [bn.-- 124[-].2.11
n.š[r]šy. | ʻbdẖmn[.bn.-]bdn. | ḥṣmn.[bn.---]ln. | [--]dm.[bn.---]n. | bʻly.[bn.---]n. | krr[-.---]. | špš[yn.---]. | [--]b[.---]. | ʻb 102[322].1.5
n[.bn.-]bdn. | ḥṣmn.[bn.---]ln. | [--]dm.[bn.---]n. | bʻly.[bn.---]n. | krr[-.---]. | špš[yn.---]. | [--]b[.---]. | ʻbdʻt[tr.---]. | bdil[102[322].1.6

bnil

.bn.mtn[-.---]. | aẖyn.bn.nbk[-.---]. | ršpn.bn.bʻly[.---]. | bnil.bn.yṣr[.---]. | ʻdyn.bn.ud̠r[-.---]. | w.ʻdʻ.nḥl h[.---]. | w.ykn 90[314].1.12
| bn rmy[y]. | yšril[.---]. | anntn bn[.---]. | bn.brzn [---]. | bnil.bn.tl[--]. | bn.brzn.ṯn. | bn.išbʻl[.---]. | bn.s[---]. | dnn.[bn.-- 2069.6
rš[bhtm.--]n.ʻbdyrẖ.ḥd̠tn.yʻr. | adbʻl[.---].ḥd̠tn.yḥmn.bnil. | ʻdn.w.ildgn.ḥṯbm. | tdǵlm.iln.bʻ[l]n.ald̠y. | tdn.ṣr[--.--]t. 2011.19
yn.unn.dqn. | ʻbdʻnt.rb ʻšrt.mnḥm.ṯbʻm.sẖr.ʻzn.ilhd. | bnil.rb ʻšrt.lkn.ypʻn.ṯ[--]. | yṣḥm.b d.ubn.krwn.ṯǵd.[m]nḥm. 2011.8

bny

ap h.---]. | ʻnt.b ṣmt.mhr h.[---]. | aqht.w tbk.y[---.---]. | abn.ank.w ʻl.[qšt k.---.ʻl]. | qṣʻt k.at.l ḥ[---.---]. | w ẖlq.ʻpmm[. 18[3AQHT].4.40
.ẖptr.l išt. | ẖbrṯ.l ẓr.pḥmm. | tʻpp.ṯr.il.d pid. | tġẓy.bny.bnwt. | b nši.ʻn h.w tphn. | hlk.bʻl.aṯtrt. | k tʻn.hlk.btlt. | ʻnt.td 4[51].2.11
. | štt.ẖptr.l išt. | ẖbrṯ.l ẓr.pḥmm. | tʻpp.ṯr.il.d pid. | tġẓy.bny.bnwt. | b nši.ʻn h.w tphn. | hlk.bʻl.aṯtrt. | k tʻn.hlk.btlt. | ʻ 4[51].2.11
ḥm. | uzrm.yšqy.bn.qdš. | l tbrknn l ṯr.il ab y. | tmrnn.l bny.bnwt. | w ykn.bn h b bt.šrš.b qrb. | hkl h.nṣb.skn.ilib h.b 17[2AQHT].1.25
ṯrt.ym.tġẓyn. | qnyt.ilm.mgntm. | ṯr.il.d pid.hm.ġẓtm. | bny.bnwt w tʻn. | btlt.ʻnt.nmgn. | [-]m.rbt.aṯrt.ym. | [nġ]ẓ.qny 4[51].3.32
y.aliyn.bʻl. | k iṯ.zbl.bʻl.arṣ. | b ḥlm.lṭpn.il d pid. | b ḏrt.bny.bnwt. | šmm.šmn.tmṭrn. | nẖlm.tlk.nbtm. | šmẖ.lṭpn.il.d 6[49].3.11
.bʻl]. | w hm.iṯ.zbl.bʻ[l.arṣ]. | b ḥlm.lṭpn.il.d pid. | b ḏrt.bny.bnwt. | šmm.šmn.tmṭrn. | nẖlm.tlk.nbtm. | w idʻ.k ḥy.ali 6[49].3.5
w yḥd. | [i]n.šmt.in.ʻẓm.yšu.g[h]. | w yṣḥ.knp.hrgb.bʻl.ybn. | [b]ʻl.ybn.diy.hwt.hrg[b]. | tpr.w du.b nši.ʻn h. | [w]yph 19[1AQHT].3.132
hm.w[yḥd]. | in.šmt.in.ʻẓm.yšu.g h. | w yṣḥ.knp.nšrm.ybn. | bʻl.ybn.diy hmt nšrm. | tpr.w du.b nši.ʻn h.w ypn. | yḥd 19[1AQHT].3.118
[.rm]m.hkl.ṯpṭ nh[r]. | [---.]hrn.w[---.]tbʻ.k[t]r w [ẖss.t]bn.bht zbl ym. | [trm]m.hk[l.ṯpṭ].nhr.bt k.[---.]šp[-.---]. | [ḥš 2.3[129].8
[.y]šṯḥw[y.]w ykb[dn h.--]r y[---]. | [---.k]ṯr.w ẖ[ss.t]bʻ.b[n.]bht.ym[.rm]m.hkl.ṯpṭ nh[r]. | [---.]hrn.w[---.]tbʻ.k[t]r w 2.3[129].7
m.b y[d.bn.ilm.m]t. | w tʻn.btlt.ʻn[t.bnt.]bht | k.y ilm.bnt.bh[t k].a[l.tš]mẖ. | al.tšmẖ.b r[m.h]kl[k]. | al.aẖd.hm.b y 3[ʻNT.VI].5.28
.špš[.ṣḥrr]t. | la.šmm.b y[d.bn.ilm.m]t. | w tʻn.btlt.ʻn[t.bnt.]bht | k.y ilm.bnt.bh[t k].a[l.tš]mẖ. | al.tšmẖ.b r[m.h]kl[3[ʻNT.VI].5.27
[---].aṯ[--.---]. | [---] h.ap.[---]. | [---].w tʻn.[btlt.ʻnt.---]. | [bnt.bht]k.y ilm[.bnt.bht k.--]. | [al.tšmẖ.]al.tš[mẖ.b rm.h] | [18[3AQHT].1.7
] h.ap.[---]. | [---].w tʻn.[btlt.ʻnt.---]. | [bnt.bht]k.y ilm[.bnt.bht k.--]. | [al.tšmẖ.]al.tš[mẖ.b rm.h] | [kl k.al.]aẖd hm.[- 18[3AQHT].1.7
.ġrm.mid.ksp. | gbʻm.mḥmd.ẖrṣ. | ybl k.udr.ilqṣm. | w bn.bht.ksp.w ẖrṣ. | bht.ṯhrm.iqnim. | šmẖ.btlt.ʻnt.tdʻṣ. | pʻnm. 4[51].5.80
qrb. | hkl k.tbl k.ġrm. | mid.ksp.gbʻm.mḥmd.. | ẖrṣ.w bn.bht.ksp. | w ẖrṣ.bht.ṯhrm. | iqnim.šmẖ.aliyn. | bʻl.ṣḥ.ẖrn.b 4[51].5.95
n.ʻnn.aṯrt. | p.ʻbd.ank.aẖd.ulṯ. | hm.amt.aṯrt.tlbn. | lbnt.ybn.bt.l bʻl. | km ilm.w ḥẓr.k bn.aṯrt. | w tʻn.rbt.aṯrt ym. | rbt. 4[51].4.62
.kmn. | ṣḥq.btlt.ʻnt.tšu. | g h.w tṣḥ.tbšr bʻl. | bšrt k.yblt.y[b]n. | bt.l k.km.aẖ k.w ḥẓr. | km.ary k.ṣḥ.ẖrn. | b bht k.ʻḏbt. 4[51].5.89
ydd. | il.ġzr.tḥm. | aliyn.bʻl. | [hw]t.aliy.q | [rdm.]bht y.bnt. | [dt.ksp.dtm]. | [ẖrṣ.hk]l y. | [---.]aẖ y. | [---.]aẖ y. | [----]y 4[51].8.35
l m. | sb.ksp.l rqm.ẖrṣ. | nṣb.l lbnt.šmẖ. | aliyn.bʻl.ht y.bnt. | dt.ksp.hkl y.dtm. | ẖrṣ.ʻdbt.bht[h.bʻ]l. | yʻdb.hd.ʻdb[.ʻd] 4[51].6.36
n.šmt.in.ʻẓm.yšu.g[h]. | w yṣḥ.knp.hrgb.bʻl.ybn. | [b]ʻl.ybn.diy.hwt.hrg[b]. | tpr.w du.b nši.ʻn h. | [w]yphn.yḥd.ṣml. 19[1AQHT].3.133
ḥd]. | in.šmt.in.ʻẓm.yšu.g h. | w yṣḥ.knp.nšrm.ybn. | bʻl.ybn.diy hmt nšrm. | tpr.w du.b nši.ʻn h.w ypn. | yḥd.hrgb.ab. 19[1AQHT].3.119
h.mlẖš. | abd.ln h.ydy.ḥmt. | b ḥrn.pnm.trġnw.w ṯtkl. | bnwt h.ykr.ʻr.d qdm. | idk.pnm.l ytn.tk aršẖ.rbt. | w aršẖ.ṯrrt UG5.7.62
r. | [---].w tpky.k[m.]nʻr.tdmʻ.km. | [ṣġ]r.bkm.yʻny[.---.bn]wt h. | [--]nn.bnt yš[--.---.-]lk. | [--]b.kmm.l k[--]. | [šp]š.b š UG5.8.41
.bʻd h.bhtm.sgrt. | bʻd h.ʻdbt.ṯlṯ.ptḥ.bt.mnt. | ptḥ.bt.w ubn.hkl.w ištql šql. | tn.km.nḥšm.yḥr.tn.km. | mhr y.w bn.bṯ UG5.7.72
uzrm.yšqy.bn.qdš. | l tbrknn l ṯr.il ab y. | tmrnn.l bny.bnwt. | w ykn.bn h b bt.šrš.b qrb. | hkl h.nṣb.skn.ilib h.b qdš. 17[2AQHT].1.25
m.tġẓyn. | qnyt.ilm.mgntm. | ṯr.il.d pid.hm.ġẓtm. | bny.bnwt w tʻn. | btlt.ʻnt.nmgn. | [-]m.rbt.aṯrt.ym. | [nġ]ẓ.qnyt.il 4[51].3.32
m. | [---.]w yʻn.kṯr. | [w ẖss.]ttb.bʻl.l hwt y. | [ḥš.]bht h.tbnn. | [ḥš.]trmm.hkl h. | y[tl]k.l lbnn.w ʻṣ h. | l[šr]yn.mḥmd. 4[51].6.16
m. | [trm]m.hk[l.ṯpṭ].nhr.bt k.[---.]šp[-.---]. | [ḥš.bh]t h.tbn[n.ḥ]š.trm[mn.hkl h.---.]bt. | [---.-]k.mnh[-.---.-]š bš[-.]t[-] 2.3[129].10
[--]b[.---]. | ḥš.bht m.k[tr]. | ḥš.rmm.hk[l m]. | ḥš.bht m.tbn[n]. | ḥš.trmmn.hk[l m]. | b tk.ṣrrt.ṣpn. | alp.šd.aẖd bt. | rbt 4[51].5.115
l]. | yšṯḥwy.[w ykbdn h.---]. | ṯr.il[.ab h.---]. | ḥš b[ht m.tbnn.ḥš.trmmn.hkl m]. | b tk.[---]. | bn.[---]. | a[--.---.] 1[ʻNT.IX].3.27
p bl.hn. | [---].ẖ[m]t.pṯr.w.p nḥš. | [---.--]q.n[t]k.l ydʻ.l bn.l pq ḥmt. | [---.--]n h.ḥmt.w tʻbtn h.abd y. | [---.ġ]r.šrġzz.y UG5.8.35
ngr.il il[š]. | ilš.ngr bt bʻl. | w aṯt k.ngrt.il[ht]. | ʻl.l ṯkm.bnw n. | l nẖnpt.mšpy. | ṯlṯ.kmm.ṯrr y. | [---.]l ġr.gm.ṣḥ. | [---.] 16[126].4.14
yn.bʻl. | k iṯ.zbl.bʻl.arṣ. | b ḥlm.lṭpn.il d pid. | b ḏrt.bny.bnwt. | šmm.šmn.tmṭrn. | nẖlm.tlk.nbtm. | šmẖ.lṭpn.il.d pid. 6[49].3.11
. | w hm.iṯ.zbl.bʻ[l.arṣ]. | b ḥlm.lṭpn.il.d pid. | b ḏrt.bny.bnwt. | šmm.šmn.tmṭrn. | nẖlm.tlk.nbtm. | w idʻ.k ḥy.aliyn.bʻ 6[49].3.5
. | limm.w tʻl.ʻm.il. | ab h.ḥpr.pʻl k.y[--]. | šmʻ k.l arẖ.w bn.[--]. | limm.ql.b udn.k w[-]. | k rtqt mr[.---]. | k d lbšt.bir. 13[6].22
.nq]md. | [mlk.]ugrt. | bʻl ṣdq. | skn.bt. | mlk.ṯġr. | [m]lk.bny. | [--].lb.mlk. | [---.]ṣmẖ. 1007.7
-.]iš[--.]h[---.]išt. | [---]y.yblmm.u[---]k.yrd[.--.]i[---]n.bn. | [---.-]nn.nrt.ilm.špš.tšu.g h.w t[ṣḥ.šm]ʻ.mʻ. | [-.yṯ]ir ṯr.il. 2.3[129].14

bnn

š. | bn.bly. | bn.apṯ. | bn.ysd. | bn.pl[-]. | bn.ṯbʻnq. | brqd. | bnn. | kbln.ṣ[md]. | bn gmrt. | bn.il.ṣm[d]. | bn abbly. | yṯʻd.ṣm[2113.16

bnny

. | bʻl y.tmġyy.hn. | alpm.ššwm.hnd. | w.mlk.bʻl y.bnš. | bnny.ʻmn. | mlakty.hnd. | ylak ʻm y. | w.tʻl.ṯh.hn. | [a]lpm.ššw 1012.34

bnš

[---.]m[--]. | [---].bn[.---]. | [-----]. | [---].ḥ[mr]. | [---.]w.bnš.aẖd. | [---.--]m. | [---].ʻtgrm. | [---.-]ṣbm. | [---.]nrn.mʻry. | [- 2043.5
ynn.b d.gmrd. | [šd.]abyy.b d.ibrmḏ. | [šd.]bn.ṯtrn.b d.bnš.aġlkz. | [šd.b]d.b[n].tkwn. | [ubdy.mḏ]rġlm. | [šd.bn.--]n. 82[300].2.20
ap. | pd. | mlk.arbʻ.ḥm[rm.w.arb]ʻ.bnšm. | ar.ḥmš.ḥmr[m.w.ḥm]š.bnšm. | atlg.ḥmr[.---.]bnšm. | 2040.3
lk.arbʻ.ḥm[rm.w.arb]ʻ.bnšm. | ar.ḥmš.ḥmr[m.w.ḥm]š.bnšm. | atlg.ḥmr[.---.]bnšm. | gbʻly.ḥmr š[--.b]nšm. | ulm.ṯn.[- 2040.4
]ġr.bn.bdn. | [sġ]r.bn.psḥn. | alṯy. | sġr.npr. | bn.ḥty. | ṯn.bnš ibrdr. | bnš tlmi. | sġr.ẖryn. | ʻdn.w sġr h. | bn.ḥgbn. 2082.6
[--]an.š[šlmt]. | bnš.iwl[--.š]šlmt. | šdyn.ššlmt. | prtwn.šʻrt. | ṯtn.šʻrt. | ʻdn.šʻrt. 97[315].2
n. | [--]n. | [q]šy. | ṯn.bn.iwrẖz.[n]ʻrm. | yṣr[.-]qb. | w.ṯn.bnš.iytlm. | w.ʻšrm.ṣmd.alpm. 2066.2.6
r.bnšm. | ʻnqpat[.---].bnš. | ubrʻy.ar[bʻ.]ḥm[r]m.w[.---.]bnšm. | ilštmʻ.arbʻ.ḥm[r]m.ḥmš.bnšm. | ġr. | ary.ḥmr w.bnš. | 2040.20
bn[š]. | gnʻy.[---.bn]š. | uškn[.---].ʻšr.bnšm. | ʻnqpat[.---].bnš. | ubrʻy.ar[bʻ.]ḥm[r]m.w[.---.]bnšm. | ilštmʻ.arbʻ.ḥm[r]m. 2040.19
m.w.ḥm]š.bnšm. | atlg.ḥmr[.---.]bnšm. | gbʻly.ḥmr š[--.b]nšm. | ulm.ṯn.[---.]bnšm. | mʻrby.[---.--]m.ṯn[.---]. | mʻr.[---]. 2040.6
.ḥmr.w.[---]. | ẖlb ʻprm.amdy.[ḥm]r.w bn[š]. | gnʻy.[---.bn]š. | uškn[.---].ʻšr.bnšm. | ʻnqpat[.---].bnš. | ubrʻy.ar[bʻ.]ḥm[2040.17
.b.š[--]. | arbʻ.bnšm.b[.---]. | ʻšrm.bnšm.[b.]ʻd[--]. | arbʻ.bnšm.b.ag[m]y. | arbʻ.bnšm.b.ḥpty. | ṯṯ.bnšm.b.bir. | ṯṯ.bnšm 2076.11
[sp]r.k[--]. | ṯ[ṯ.bn]šm[.b.a]gmy. | ṯṯ.bn[šm.---]. | ʻšr.b[nšm.---]. | arbʻ[.bnšm.-- 2076.2
.b.ġbl. | [---.b]nšm.b.mʻr.arr. | arbʻ.bnšm.b.mnt. | arbʻ.bnšm.b.irbn. | ṯn.bnšm.b.yʻrt. | ṯn.bnšm.b.ʻrmt. | arbʻ.bnšm.b. 2076.34
]šm.b.tkn. | [---.bn]šm.b.tmrm. | [---.bn]šm.b.ṯnq. | [---.b]nšm.b.ugrt. | [---.bn]šm.b.ġbl. | [---.b]nšm.b.mʻr.arr. | arbʻ.b 2076.30
.bnšm.b.ag[m]y. | arbʻ.bnšm.b.ḥpty. | ṯṯ.bnšm.b.bir. | ṯṯ.bnšm b.uẖnp. | ṯn.bnšm.b.ẖrṣbʻ. | arbʻ.bnšm.b.ḥzp. | arbʻ.bnš 2076.14

.[b.]‘d[--]. | arb‘.bnšm.b.ag[m]y. | arb‘.bnšm.b.ḫpty. | ṯṯ.bnšm.b.bir. | ṯṯ.bnšm b.uḫnp. | ṯn.bnšm.b.ḫrṣb‘. | arb‘.bnšm.b. 2076.13
n.bnšm.b.‘rmt. | arb‘.bnšm.b.šrš. | ṯṯ.bnšm.b.mlk. | arb‘.bnšm.b.bṣr. | ṯn.bnšm.[b.]rqd. | ṯn.b[nšm.b.---]y. | [---].b[nšm. 2076.39
ǵl.‘šrm.l.mit.dr‘.w.tš‘m.drt. | [w].ṯmnym.l.mit.dd.ḥpr.bnšm. | b.gt.alḫb.ṯṯm.dr‘.w.ḫmšm.drt.w.ṯṯm.dd. | ḥpr.bnšm. | 1098.15
.gt.ṯrmn.arb‘m.dr‘.w.‘šrm.drt. | w.ṯlṯm.dd.ṯṯ.kbd.ḥpr.bnšm. | b.gt.ḥdṯt.arb‘m.dr‘.w.ṯlṯm.drt. | [w].šb‘m.dd.ṯn.kbd.ḥ 1098.21
.bnšm. | b.gt.alḫb.ṯṯm.dr‘.w.ḫmšm.drt.w.ṯṯm.dd. | ḥpr.bnšm. | b.gt.knpy.mit.dr‘.ṯṯm.drt.w.šb‘m.dd.arb‘. | kbd.ḥpr.b 1098.17
rb‘m.l.mit.dr‘.w.ṯmnym[.drt]. | w.‘šrm.l.mit.dd.ḥp[r.]bnšm. | b.gt.ǵl.‘šrm.l.mit.dr‘.w.tš‘m.drt. | [w].ṯmnym.l.mit.d 1098.13
. | b.gt.knpy.mit.dr‘.ṯṯm.drt.w.šb‘m.dd.arb‘. | kbd.ḥpr.bnšm. | b.gt.ṯrmn.arb‘m.dr‘.w.‘šrm.drt. | w.ṯlṯm.dd.ṯṯ.kbd.ḥp 1098.19
ṯ.bnšm.b.bir. | ṯṯ.bnšm b.uḫnp. | ṯn.bnšm.b.ḫrṣb‘. | arb‘.bnšm.b.hzp. | arb‘.bnšm.b.šql. | arb‘.bnšm.b.nni. | ṯn.bnšm.b.s 2076.16
.---]. | ‘šrm.bnšm.[b.]‘d[--]. | arb‘.bnšm.b.ag[m]y. | arb‘.bnšm.b.ḫpty. | ṯṯ.bnšm.b.bir. | ṯṯ.bnšm b.uḫnp. | ṯn.bnšm.b.ḫr 2076.12
arb‘.bnšm.b.ḫpty. | ṯṯ.bnšm.b.bir. | ṯṯ.bnšm b.uḫnp. | ṯn.bnšm.b.ḫrṣb‘. | arb‘.bnšm.b.hzp. | arb‘.bnšm.b.šql. | arb‘.bnš 2076.15
rb‘.bnšm.b.šql. | arb‘.bnšm.b.nni. | ṯn.bnšm.b.slḫ. | [---].bnšm.b.yny. | [--.]bnšm.b.lbnm. | arb‘.bnšm.b.ypr. | [---.]bnšm 2076.20
| b.nzl.‘šrm.l.mit.dr‘.w.šb‘m.drt. | w.‘šrm.l.mit.dd.ḥpr.bnšm. | b.y‘ny.arb‘m.dr‘.w.‘šrm.drt. | w.ṯlṯm.dd.ṯṯ.kbd.ḥpr.b 1098.25
m.b.m‘r.arr. | arb‘.bnšm.b.mnt. | arb‘.bnšm.b.irbn. | ṯn.bnšm.b.y‘rt. | ṯn.bnšm.b.‘rmt. | arb‘.bnšm.b.šrš. | ṯṯ.bnšm.b.m 2076.35
nšm.b.slḫ. | [---].bnšm.b.yny. | [--.]bnšm.b.lbnm. | arb‘.bnšm.b.ypr. | [---.]bnšm.b.šbn. | [---.b]nšm.b.šmny. | [---.b]nš 2076.22
rb‘.bnšm.b.nni. | ṯn.bnšm.b.slḫ. | [---].bnšm.b.yny. | [--.]bnšm.b.lbnm. | arb‘.bnšm.b.ypr. | [---.]bnšm.b.šbn. | [---.b]nš 2076.21
| ṯn.bnšm.b.y‘rt. | ṯn.bnšm.b.‘rmt. | arb‘.bnšm.b.šrš. | ṯṯ.bnšm.b.mlk. | arb‘.bnšm.b.bṣr. | ṯn.bnšm.[b.]rqd. | ṯn.b[nšm.b 2076.38
.b.ugrt. | [---.bn]šm.b.ǵbl. | [---.b]nšm.b.m‘r.arr. | arb‘.bnšm.b.mnt. | arb‘.bnšm.b.irbn. | ṯn.bnšm.b.y‘rt. | ṯn.bnšm.b.‘ 2076.33
bn]šm.b.ṯnq. | [---.b]nšm.b.ugrt. | [---.bn]šm.b.ǵbl. | [---.b]nšm.b.m‘r.arr. | arb‘.bnšm.b.mnt. | arb‘.bnšm.b.irbn. | ṯn.b 2076.32
gt.ḥdṯt.arb‘m.dr‘.w.ṯlṯm.drt. | [w].šb‘m.dd.ṯn.kbd.ḥpr.bnšm. | b.nzl.‘šrm.l.mit.dr‘.w.šb‘m.drt. | w.‘šrm.l.mit.dd.ḥpr. 1098.23
nšm.b.ḫrṣb‘. | arb‘.bnšm.b.hzp. | arb‘.bnšm.b.šql. | arb‘.bnšm.b.nni. | ṯn.bnšm.b.slḫ. | [---].bnšm.b.yny. | [--.]bnšm.b.l 2076.18
b‘.bnšm.b.hzp. | arb‘.bnšm.b.šql. | arb‘.bnšm.b.nni. | ṯn.bnšm.b.slḫ. | [---].bnšm.b.yny. | [--.]bnšm.b.lbnm. | arb‘.bnšm 2076.19
.b.šbn. | [---.b]nšm.b.šmny. | [---.b]nšm.b.šmngy. | [---.]bnšm.b.snr.mid. | [---.bn]šm.b.tkn. | [---.bn]šm.b.tmrm. | [---. 2076.26
.bn]šm[.---]. | ṯn.bnšm.b.š[--]. | arb‘.bnšm.b[.---]. | ‘šrm.bnšm.[b.]‘d[--]. | arb‘.bnšm.b.ag[m]y. | arb‘.bnšm.b.ḫpty. | ṯṯ. 2076.10
. | b.y‘ny.arb‘m.dr‘.w.‘šrm.drt. | w.ṯlṯm.dd.ṯṯ.kbd.ḥpr.bnšm. | b.‘nmky.‘šrm.dr‘[.---.d]rt. | w.ṯn.‘šr h.dd.[---]. | iwrḏn. 1098.27
b‘.bnšm.b.mnt. | arb‘.bnšm.b.irbn. | ṯn.bnšm.b.y‘rt. | ṯn.bnšm.b.‘rmt. | arb‘.bnšm.b.šrš. | ṯṯ.bnšm.b.mlk. | arb‘.bnšm.b. 2076.36
]šm.b.tmrm. | [---.bn]šm.b.ṯnq. | [---.b]nšm.b.ugrt. | [---.bn]šm.b.ǵbl. | [---.b]nšm.b.m‘r.arr. | arb‘.bnšm.b.mnt. | arb‘.b 2076.31
arb‘.bnšm.b.šrš. | ṯṯ.bnšm.b.mlk. | arb‘.bnšm.b.bṣr. | ṯn.bnšm.[b.]rqd. | ṯn.b[nšm.b.---]y. | [---].b[nšm.b.--]nl. | [---.--]b 2076.40
nšm.b.yny. | [--.]bnšm.b.lbnm. | arb‘.bnšm.b.ypr. | [---.]bnšm.b.šbn. | [---.b]nšm.b.šmny. | [---.b]nšm.b.šmngy. | [---.]b 2076.23
nšm.b.ypr. | [---.]bnšm.b.šbn. | [---.b]nšm.b.šmny. | [---.b]nšm.b.šmngy. | [---.]bnšm.b.snr.mid. | [---.bn]šm.b.tkn. | [--- 2076.25
nšm.b.lbnm. | arb‘.bnšm.b.ypr. | [---.]bnšm.b.šbn. | [---.b]nšm.b.šmny. | [---.b]nšm.b.šmngy. | [---.]bnšm.b.snr.mid. | [2076.24
šm b.uḫnp. | ṯn.bnšm.b.ḫrṣb‘. | arb‘.bnšm.b.hzp. | arb‘.bnšm.b.šql. | arb‘.bnšm.b.nni. | ṯn.bnšm.b.slḫ. | [---].bnšm.b.y 2076.17
‘.bnšm.b.irbn. | ṯn.bnšm.b.y‘rt. | ṯn.bnšm.b.‘rmt. | arb‘.bnšm.b.šrš. | ṯṯ.bnšm.b.mlk. | arb‘.bnšm.b.bṣr. | ṯn.bnšm.[b.]r 2076.37
arb‘[.bnšm.---]. | ṯṯ.‘šr.bnš[m.---]. | ‘šr[.bn]šm[.---]. | ṯn.bnšm.b.š[--]. | arb‘.bnšm.b[.---]. | ‘šrm.bnšm.[b.]‘d[--]. | arb‘.b 2076.8
mny. | [---.b]nšm.b.šmngy. | [---.]bnšm.b.snr.mid. | [---.bn]šm.b.tkn. | [---.bn]šm.b.tmrm. | [---.bn]šm.b.ṯnq. | [---.b]nš 2076.27
b.šmngy. | [---.]bnšm.b.snr.mid. | [---.bn]šm.b.tkn. | [---.bn]šm.b.tmrm. | [---.bn]šm.b.ṯnq. | [---.b]nšm.b.ugrt. | [---.bn] 2076.28
.b.snr.mid. | [---.bn]šm.b.tkn. | [---.bn]šm.b.tmrm. | [---.bn]šm.b.ṯnq. | [---.b]nšm.b.ugrt. | [---.bn]šm.b.ǵbl. | [---.b]nšm 2076.29
.bnšm.b.bṣr. | ṯn.bnšm.[b.]rqd. | ṯn.b[nšm.b.---]y. | [---].b[nšm.b.--]nl. | [---.--]by. 2076.42
.l.rpš. | [---.]šb‘m.dr‘.w.arb‘m.drt.mit.dd. | [---].ḥpr.bn.šm. | [b.---.]knm.ṯṯm.l.mit.dr‘.w.mit.drt. | w[.---.]‘m.l.mit.dd. 1098.6
.‘šr.bnš[m.---]. | ‘šr[.bn]šm[.---]. | ṯn.bnšm.b.š[--]. | arb‘.bnšm.b[.---]. | ‘šrm.bnšm.[b.]‘d[--]. | arb‘.bnšm.b.ag[m]y. | arb 2076.9
ṯṯ.bnšm.b.mlk. | arb‘.bnšm.b.bṣr. | ṯn.bnšm.[b.]rqd. | ṯn.b[nšm.b.---]y. | [---].b[nšm.b.--]nl. | [---.--]by. 2076.41
.mlk. | b‘l y.tmǵyy.hn. | alpm.ššwm.hnd. | w.mlk.b‘l y.bnš. | bnny.‘mn. | mlakty.hnd. | ylak ‘m y. | w.t‘l.ṯh.hn. | [a]lp 1012.33
] ytn.nn. | l.b‘ln.bn. | kltn.w l. | bn h.‘d.‘lm. | šḫr.‘lmt. | bnš bnšm. | l.yqḥnn.b d. | b‘ln.bn.kltn. | w.b d.bn h.‘d. | ‘lm.w 1008.16
aṯt yqḥ ‘z. | [---]ḏ. | [---]. | [---]. | hm qrt tuḫd.hm mt y‘l bnš. | bt bn bnš yqḥ ‘z. | w yḥdy mrḥqm. RS61[24.277.29]
]‘.bnšm. | ar.ḫmš.ḥmr[m.w.ḫm]š.bnšm. | atlg.ḥmr[.---.]bnšm. | gb‘ly.ḥmr š[--.b]nšm. | ulm.ṯn.[---.]bnšm. | m‘rby.[---.- 2040.5
u.any[t]. | bn abdḫ[r]. | pdym. | ḫmš.bnšm. | snrym. | tš‘.bnš[m]. | gb‘lym. | arb‘.b[nšm]. | ṯbqym. 79[83].15
mr.w[.---]. | ṣ‘q.ḥmr.w.[---]. | ḫlb ‘prm.amdy.[ḥm]r.w bn[š]. | gn‘y.[---.bn]š. | uškn[.---].‘šr.bnšm. | ‘nqpat[.---].bnš. | 2040.16
sdm.yd.lmd hm.lqḥ. | ‘šr.mḫṣm.yd.lmd hm. | apym. | [bn]š gt.ipṯl. | [---]ym. | [----]m. | [-----]. | [bnš.g]t.ir. | bnš.gt.rb[- 1040.11
d hm. | apym. | [bn]š gt.ipṯl. | [---]ym. | [----]m. | [-----]. | [bnš.g]t.ir. | bnš.gt.rb[--]. | gpny. | bnš.mǵrt. | kbsm. | armsǵ. 1040.15
ḥrš.anyt. | bnš.gt.gl‘d. | bnš.gt.ngr. | r‘ym. | bn.ḫri[-]. | bnš.gt.‘ṯtrt. | ad[-]l[1040.2
ḥrš.anyt. | bnš.gt.gl‘d. | bnš.gt.ngr. | r‘ym. | bn.ḫri[-]. | bnš.gt.‘ṯtrt. | ad[-]l[-]m. | ‘šr.ksd 1040.3
ḥrš.anyt. | bnš.gt.gl‘d. | bnš.gt.ngr. | r‘ym. | bn.ḫri[-]. | bnš.gt.‘ṯtrt. | ad[-]l[-]m. | ‘šr.ksdm.yd.lmd hm.lqḥ. | ‘šr.mḫṣm 1040.6
m. | [bn]š gt.ipṯl. | [---]ym. | [----]m. | [-----]. | [bnš.g]t.ir. | bnš.gt.rb[--]. | gpny. | bnš.mǵrt. | kbsm. | armsǵ. 1040.16
[bn]šm.dt.iš[--]. | [b]n.b‘l[--]. | bn.gld. | bn.ṣmy. | bn.mry[n]. | b 2117.1.1
bnšm.dt.iṯ.alpm.l hm. | bn.niršn. | bn.adty. | bn.alz. | bn.birtn. 2023.1.1
[bnšm.dt.]b d.mlk. | [---.b]d.mlkt. | [---.b]d.mlk. | [---.--]ḥ.uḫ 2014.1
pgl[--.---]. | šy[.---]. | bn.uḫn. | ybru.i[---]. | [p]dyn.[---]. | bnšm.d.b [d.---]. | spḫy.[---]. | [-----]. | b[--.---]. | n‘[--.---]. | [----- 2161.13
bnšm.d.bu. | tš‘.dt.tq[ḥn]. | š‘rt. | šb‘ dt tqḥn. | ššlmt. 2099.1
lpm.ḥršm. | k.rgmt.l y.bly m. | alpm.aršt.l k.w.l y. | mn.bnš.d.l.i[--].‘[m k]. | l.alpm.w.l.y[n.--]t. | w.bl.bnš.hw[-.--]y. | 2064.24
bnšm.dt.l.u[--]ṯb. | kt[r]n. | w.aṯt h.w.n‘r h. | bn.ḫby.w.[a]ṯt h 2068.1
škny. | bn.ṯny.uškny. | mnn.w.aṯt h. | slmu.ḥrš.mrkbt. | bnšm.dt.l.mlk. | ‘bdyrḫ.bn.ṯyl. | ‘bdn.w.aṯt h.w.bn h. | gpn.bn 2068.17
bnšm.dt.[---]. | krws.l.y[--.---]. | yp‘.l[.---]. | šmr[m.---]. | [-----]. 2122.1
.l y. | mn.bnš.d.l.i[--].‘[m k]. | l.alpm.w.l.y[n.--]t. | w.bl.bnš.hw[-.--]y. | w.k.at.trg[m.--]. | w.[---]n.w.s[--]. | [--]m.m[--- 2064.26
rišym.dt.‘rb. | b bnš hm. | ḏmry.w.ptpt.‘rb. | b.yrm. | [ily.w].ḏmry.‘rb. | b.ṯb‘m. 2079.2

.ẖ]tyn.yd.bt h. | [aǵ]ltn. | tdn.bn.ddy. | ʿbdil[.b]n ṣdqn. | bnšm.h[-]mt.ypḥm. | kbby.yd.bt.amt. | ilmlk. 2045.6
khnm.tšʿ. | bnšm.w.ḥmr. | qdšm.tšʿ. | bnšm.w.ḥmr. 77[63].2
khnm.tšʿ. | bnšm.w.ḥmr. | qdšm.tšʿ. | bnšm.w.ḥmr. 77[63].4
.hwt. | [--.]iḥd.šd.gtr. | [w]ht.yšmʿ.uẖ y. | l g y.w yhbṯ.bnš. | w ytn.ilm.b d hm. | b d.iẖqm.gtr. | w b d.ytrhd. | bʿl. 55[18].18
[---.---.]l.mit.drʿ.w.šbʿm.drt. | [---.ḥpr.]bnšm.w.l.ḥrš.ʿrq.ṯn.ʿšr h. | [---.d]rʿ.w.mit.drt.w.ʿšrm.l.mit. | [1098.2
ʿrq.ṯn.ʿšr h. | [---.d]rʿ.w.mit.drt.w.ʿšrm.l.mit. | [drt.ḥpr.b]nšm.w.ṯn.ʿšr h.dd.l.rpš. | [---.]šbʿm.drʿ.w.arbʿm.drt.mit.dd. 1098.4
ǵy.bnš[.---]. | w ḥmr[.---]. | w mʿn[.---]. | w bn[š.---]. | d bnš.ḥm[r.---]. | w d.l mdl.r[--.---]. | w ṣin.ʿz.b[ʿl.---]. | llu.bn[š.- 2158.1.12
bt.alpm. | ʿšr.bnšm. | ẖmš.bnši.ṯt[---]. | ʿšr.b gt.[---]. | ṯn.ʿšr.b.gt.ir[bṣ]. | arbʿ. 2103.2
pdym. | ẖmš.bnšm. | snrym. | tšʿ.bnš[m]. | gbʿlym. | arbʿ.b[nšm]. | ṭbqym. 79[83].17
ʿl.alpm.bnš.yd. | titṯm[n].w.ʿl.[---]. | [-]rym.t[i]ṯṯmn. | šnl.bn.ṣ[q]n.š[-- 2104.1
[---.ṯ]lṯ.ʿš[r h.---]. | d bnšm.yd.grbs hm. | w.ṯn.ʿšr h.ẖpnt. | [š]šwm.amtm.ʿkyt. | yd.l 2049.2
[b.]gt.ṯpn.ʿšr.ṣmdm. | w.ṯlṯ.ʿšr.bnš. | yd.ytm.yd.rʿy.ḥmrm. | b.gt.gwl.ṯmn.ṣmdm. | w.arbʿ.ʿšr. 2038.2
d.ytm.yd.rʿy.ḥmrm. | b.gt.gwl.ṯmn.ṣmdm. | w.arbʿ.ʿšr.bnš. | yd.nǵr.mdrʿ.yd.š[--]m. | [b.]gt.ipṯl.ṯṯ.ṣmdm. | [w.ʿ]šr.bn[2038.5
. | yd.nǵr.mdrʿ.yd.š[--]m. | [b.]gt.ipṯl.ṯṯ.ṣmdm. | [w.ʿ]šr.bn[š]m.y[d].š[--]. | [-]lm.b d.r[-]m.l[-]m. | ṯṯ.ʿšr.ṣ[mdm]. | w.tšʿ 2038.8
[---.]nnd[-]. | [-]gbt. | [--]y bnš kb[š]y. | krmpy.b.bṣm. | [-]mrn.ṣd.b gl[-]. 2169.3
bnš.kld. | kbln.ʿbdyrǵ.ilgt. | ǵyrn.ybnn qrwn. | ypltn.ʿbdnt. | kl 1045.1
| ṯlṯm sp.l bnš tpnr. | arbʿ.spm.l.lbnš prwsdy. | ṯṯ spm.l bnš klnmw. | l yarš ẖswn. | ẖmš ʿšr.sp. | l bnš tpnr d yaẖd l g 137.2[93].8
.aḥd.kbd.ẖsnm. | ubnyn. | ṯṯm[.l.]mit.ṯlṯ. | kbd[.tg]mr.bnš. | l.b.bt.mlk. 1028.13
nym.ṯlṯ.kbd. | mdrǵlm. | w.šbʿ.ʿšr.ẖsnm. | ẖmšm.l.mit. | bnš.l.d. | yškb.l.b.bt.mlk. 1029.15
tn.nn. | l.bʿln.bn. | kltn.w l. | bn h.ʿd.ʿlm. | šḥr.ʿlmt. | bnš bnšm. | l.yqḥnn.b d. | bʿln.bn.kltn. | w.b d.bn h.ʿd. | ʿlm.w unṯ. 1008.16
[---]ḏ. | [---]. | [---]. | hm qrt tuḥd.hm mt yʿl bnš. | bt bn bnš yqḥ ʿz. | w yḥdy mrḥqm. RS61[24.277.30]
i[--.---]. | d.[---]. | bnš[-] mdy[-]. | w.b.glb. | phnn.w. | mndym. | bdnh. | l[q]ḥt. | [- 2129.3
spr.ḥpr.bnš mlk.b yrẖ itt[bnm]. | ršpab.rb ʿšrt.m[r]yn. | pǵdn.ilbʿl.kr 2011.1
| [---.--]n.d[--.--]i. | [--]t.mdt h[.l.]ʿṯtrt.šd. | [---.-]rt.mẖṣ.bnš.mlk.ybʿl hm. | [---.--]t.w.ẖpn.l.azzlt. | [---.]l.ʿṯtrt.šd. | [---]. 1106.53
brn. | ṯbʿm. | kyn. | bʿln. | ytršp. | ḥmšm.ṯmn.kbd. | tgmr.bnš.mlk. | d.b d.adnʿm. | [š]bʿ.b.ḥrṯm. | [ṯ]lṯ.b.ṯǵrm. | rb qrt.aẖ 1024.2.26
[sp]r.bnš.ml[k.d.b] d adn[ʿm]. | [---].riš[.---].kt. | [y]nḥm. | ilbʿl. | ʿbd 1024.1.1
spr.bnš.mlk. | d.b d.prṯ. | tšʿ.l.ʿšrm. | lqḥ.ššlmt. | ṯmn.l.arbʿm. | lqḥ. 1025.1
ʿmṯmr. | bn.nqmpʿ. | mlk.ugrt. | ytn.bt.annḏr. | bn.ytn.bnš. | [ml]k.d.b riš. | [--.-]nt. | [l.ʿb]dmlk. | [--.-]m[-]r. | [w.l.]bn 1009.6
[s]pr.bnš.mlk.d.b.tbq. | [kr]wn. | [--]n. | [q]ṣy. | ṯn.bn.iwrẖz.[n]ʿrm. | 2066.1.1
spr.bnš.mlk. | d taršn.ʿmsn. | bṣr.abn.špšyn. | dqn. | aǵlmn. | knʿm. 2067.1.1
rt.ḏkr.yṣr. | tǵǵln.ẖmš.ddm. | [---].ẖmš.ddm. | ṯṯ.l.ʿšrm.bn[š.mlk.---].ẖzr.lqḥ.ḥp[r]. | ʿšt.ʿšr h.bn[.---.--]ẖ.zr. | bʿl.šd. 2011.40
q. | [---.--]š. | [---.ṣ]dq. | tgmr. | yṣḥm. | ṯlṯm. | aḥd. | kbd. | bnš.mlk. 1055.2.6
[---.--]š. | [---.a]rbʿm. | bʿlyn.bnš. | mlkt. | ʿšrm. | [---.--]t. 138[41].3
lg.ḥmr[.---.]bnšm. | gbʿly.ḥmr š[--.b]nšm. | ulm.ṯn.[---.]bnšm. | mʿrby.[---.--]m.ṯn[.---]. | mʿr.[---]. | arny.[---]. | šʿrt.ṯn[. 2040.7
ym. | [----]m. | [-----]. | [bnš.g]t.ir. | bnš.gt.rb[--]. | gpny. | bnš.mǵrt. | kbsm. | armsǵ. 1040.18
ǵr.tšʿ[.ʿšr.b]nš. | ṣbu.any[t]. | bn abdḥ[r]. | pdym. | ẖmš.bnšm. | snrym. | tšʿ.bnš[m]. | gbʿlym. | arbʿ.b[nšm]. | ṭbqym. 79[83].13
rm.amdy.[ḥm]r.w bn[š]. | gnʿy.[---.bn]š. | uškn[.---].ʿšr.bnšm. | ʿnqpat[.---].bnš. | ubrʿy.ar[bʿ.]ḥm[r]m.w[.---.]bnšm. | i 2040.18
.ar[bʿ.]ḥm[r]m.w[.---.]bnšm. | ilštmʿ.arbʿ.ḥm[r]m.ẖmš.bnšm. | ǵr. | ary.ḥmr w.bnš. | qmy.ḥmr.w.bnš. | ṯbil. | ʿnmky.ḥ 2040.21
ṣb[u.anyt]. | ʿdn. | ṭbq[ym]. | mʿq[bym]. | tšʿ.ʿ[šr.bnš]. | ǵr.ṯ[--.---]. | ṣbu.any[t]. | bn.kṯan. | ǵr.tšʿ[.ʿšr.b]nš. | ṣbu.a 79[83].5
-.]klnmw. | [---.]w yky. | ṯlṯm sp.l bnš tpnr. | arbʿ.spm.l.lbnš prwsdy. | ṯṯ spm.l bnš klnmw. | l yarš ẖswn. | ẖmš ʿšr.sp. 137.2[93].7
.ʿ[šr.bnš]. | ǵr.ṯ[--.---]. | ṣbu.any[t]. | bn.kṯan. | ǵr.tšʿ[.ʿšr.b]nš. | ṣbu.any[t]. | bn abdḥ[r]. | pdym. | ẖmš.bnšm. | snrym. | t 79[83].9
nšm. | ilštmʿ.arbʿ.ḥm[r]m.ẖmš.bnšm. | ǵr. | ary.ḥmr w.bnš. | qmy.ḥmr.w.bnš. | ṯbil. | ʿnmky.ḥmr.w.bnš. | rqd arbʿ. | šb 2040.23
q.ṯn.qlʿm. | ẖmš.ṣmdm.w ḥrṣ. | ṯryn.sswm. | ṯryn.aḥd.d bnš. | arbʿ.ṣmdm.apnt. | w ḥrṣ. | tšʿm.mrḥ.aḥd. | kbd. 1123.6
.---]. | [-]r.l šlmt.šl[m.---.--] | r h.p šlmt.p šlm[.---]. | bt.l bnš.trg[m.---]. | l šlmt.l šlm.b[--.---] | b y.šnt.mlit.t[--.---]. | ym 59[100].5
[.-]dk[.---]. | mʿbd[.-]r[-.-]š[-.---]. | w kšt.[--]šq h[.---]. | bnš rʿym.[---]. | kbdt.bnš[.---]. | šin.[---]. | b ḥlm.[---]. | pnt[.---] 2158.2.6
ary.ḥmr w.bnš. | qmy.ḥmr.w.bnš. | ṯbil. | ʿnmky.ḥmr.w.bnš. | rqd arbʿ. | šbn aḥd. | ṭbq aḥd. | šrš aḥd. | bir aḥd. | uẖnp. | 2040.26
iwrḏn.ḥ[--.---]. | w.ṯlṯm.dd.[---.]n[--.---]. | w.a[r]bʿ[.---].bnš[.š]dyn[.---]. | agr.[---.--]n.ṯn.ʿšr h.d[--.---]. | [---.]ḥdṯn.ʿšr.d 1098.32
[l r]iš.rʿy.y[šlm.---]. | [š]lm.bnš.yš[lm.---]. | [-]r.l šlmt.šl[m.---.--] | r h.p šlmt.p šlm[.---]. | 59[100].2
p bbt. | [ʿ]ṣrm l h.ršp [-]m. | [---.]bqt[-]. | [b] ǵb.ršp mh bnš. | šrp.w ṣp ḥršḥ. | ʿlm b ǵb ḥyr. | ṯmn l ṯlṯm ṣin. | šbʿ.alpm. UG5.12.B.1
. | [sǵ]r.bn.psḥn. | alty. | sǵr.npr. | bn.ḥty. | ṯn.bnš ibrḏr. | bnš tlmi. | sǵr.ḥryn. | ʿdn.w sǵr h. | bn.ḥgbn. 2082.7
sdy. | ṯṯ spm.l bnš klnmw. | l yarš ẖswn. | ẖmš ʿšr.sp. | l bnš tpnr d yaẖd l g ynm. | ṯṯ spm l tgyn. | arbʿ spm l ll[-]. | ṯn 137.2[93].11
-]ln. | [---.]kqmṯn. | [---.]klnmw. | [---.]w yky. | ṯlṯm sp.l bnš tpnr. | arbʿ.spm.l.lbnš prwsdy. | ṯṯ spm.l bnš klnmw. | l ya 137.2[93].6
ḥm[r]m.ẖmš.bnšm. | ǵr. | ary.ḥmr w.bnš. | qmy.ḥmr.w.bnš. | ṯbil. | ʿnmky.ḥmr.w.bnš. | rqd arbʿ. | šbn aḥd. | ṭbq aḥd. | 2040.24
ṯm.l.mit.drʿ.w.mit.drt. | w[.---.]ʿm.l.mit.dd.ṯn.kbd.ḥpr.bnšm.ṯmnym.dd. | l u[-]m. | b.ṭbq.arbʿm.drʿ.w.ʿšr.dd.drt. | w[. 1098.8
bt.alpm. | ʿšr.bnšm. | ẖmš.bnši.ṯt[---]. | ʿšr.b gt.[---]. | ṯn.ʿšr.b.gt.ir[bṣ]. | arbʿ.b.gt.bʿln. | ʿšt 2103.3
bḥ k.sprt. | dt nat. | w qrwn. | l k dbḥ. | [--]r bt [--]. | [--]bnš [--]. | š š[--]. | w [--]. | d [--]. | ypḥ[--]. | w s[--]. | [---]. | qrd g RS61[24.277.14]
nš.ḥm[r.---]. | w d.l mdl.r[--.---]. | w ṣin.ʿz.b[ʿl.---]. | llu.bn[š.---]. | imr.ẖ[--.---]. | [--]n.bʿ[l.---]. | w [--]d.[---]. | idk[.-]it[. 2158.1.15
[.---]. | d ymǵy.bnš[.---]. | w ḥmr[.---]. | w mʿn[.---]. | w bn[š.---]. | d bnš.ḥm[r.---]. | w d.l mdl.r[--.---]. | w ṣin.ʿz.b[ʿl.-- 2158.1.11
rt.w ššw.ʿ[nt.---]. | w ht.[--]k.ššw[.-]rym[.---]. | d ymǵy.bnš[.---]. | w ḥmr[.---]. | w mʿn[.---]. | w bn[š.---]. | d bnš.ḥm[r. 2158.1.8
ẖmš.bnšm[.---]. | ḥdǵlm.b d.[---]. | šbʿ.lmdm.b d.s[n]rn. | lmd.aḥd. 1050.1
bn[š.---]. | ṯlṯm šurt l b[nš.---]. | arbʿ šurt [---]. | ṯṯ šurt l bnš [---]. | ẖmš kbd arbʿ[.---]. | ṯṯ šurt l tg[-.---]. | arbʿ šurt [---] 137.1[92].11
.ʿ[šr.--]m.ḥr[š]. | [---].ḥr[š.---]. | [---.ṯ]lṯ.[---.]dpm. | [---.]bnšn. | [---.ẖ]mš.ṣmd.alpm. | [---.bn]šm. | [---.]ẖmš.ṣmd.alpm. 2038.14
---.ṯ]lṯ.[---.]dpm. | [---.]bnšn. | [---.ẖ]mš.ṣmd.alpm. | [---.bn]šm. | [---.]ẖmš.ṣmd.alpm. | [---.bnš]m. | [---.]ʿšr.ṣmd.alpm. 2038.16

. | [---.]idmt.n[--.]t[--]. | [---.--]r.dlt.tḥt n. | [---.]dlt. | [---.b]nš. | [---.]yp‘. | [---.]b[--]. 2158B.5
[sp]r.k[--]. | t[t.bn]šm[.b.a]gmy. | tt.bn[šm.---]. | ‘šr.b[nšm.---]. | arb‘[.bnšm.---]. | tt.‘šr.bnš[m.---]. 2076.3
y. | tt.bn[šm.---]. | ‘šr.b[nšm.---]. | arb‘[.bnšm.---]. | tt.‘šr.bnš[m.---]. | ‘šr[.bn]šm[.---]. | tn.bnšm.b.š[--]. | arb‘.bnšm.b[.-- 2076.6
]mš.ṣmd.alpm. | [---.bn]šm. | [---.]ḫmš.ṣmd.alpm. | [---.bnš]m. | [---.]‘šr.ṣmd.alpm. | [---.bn]šm. | [---.--]m.ḫmš.ṣmdm. 2076.8
[sp]r.k[--]. | t[t.bn]šm[.b.a]gmy. | tt.bn[šm.---]. | ‘šr.b[nšm.---]. | arb‘[.bnšm.---]. | tt.‘šr.bnš[m.---]. | ‘šr[.bn]šm[.---] 2038.18
tmn ‘šr šurt l [---]. | tmn šurt l ar[--.---]. | tn šurtm l bnš [---]. | arb‘ šurt l bn[š.---]. | arb‘ šurt l q[--.---]. | tlt šurt l b 2076.4
. | tmn šurt l ar[--.---]. | tn šurtm l bnš [---]. | arb‘ šurt l bn[š.---]. | arb‘ šurt l q[--.---]. | tlt šurt l bnš [---]. | tt šurt.l bnš 137.1[92].3
--]. | tt šurt.l bnš[.---]. | tn šurtm l bn[š.---]. | tltm šurt l b[nš.---]. | arb‘ šurt [---]. | tt šurt l bnš [---]. | ḫmš kbd arb‘[.--- 137.1[92].4
]r[-.-]š[-.---]. | w kšt.[--]šq h[.---]. | bnš r‘ym.[---]. | kbdt.bnš[.---]. | šin.[---]. | b ḥlm.[---]. | pnt[.---]. 137.1[92].9
t.bn]šm[.b.a]gmy. | tt.bn[šm.---]. | ‘šr.b[nšm.---]. | arb‘[.bnšm.---]. | tt.‘šr.bnš[m.---]. | ‘šr[.bn]šm[.---]. | tn.bnšm.b.š[--]. 2158.2.7
---]. | arb‘ šurt l bn[š.---]. | arb‘ šurt l q[--.---]. | tlt šurt l bnš [---]. | tt šurt.l bnš[.---]. | tn šurtm l bn[š.---]. | tltm šurt l 2076.5
-.---]. | tlt šurt l bnš [---]. | tt šurt.l bnš[.---]. | tn šurtm l bn[š.---]. | tltm šurt l b[nš.---]. | arb‘ šurt [---]. | tt šurt l bnš [-- 137.1[92].6
| ‘šr.b[nšm.---]. | arb‘[.bnšm.---]. | tt.‘šr.bnš[m.---]. | ‘šr[.bn]šm[.---]. | tn.bnšm.b.š[--]. | arb‘.bnšm.b[.---]. | ‘šrm.bnšm.[137.1[92].8
[š.---]. | arb‘ šurt l q[--.---]. | tlt šurt l bnš [---]. | tt šurt.l bnš[.---]. | tn šurtm l bn[š.---]. | tltm šurt l b[nš.---]. | arb‘ šurt 2076.7
-.]ḫmš.ṣmd.alpm. | [---.bnš]m. | [---.]‘šr.ṣmd.alpm. | [---.bn]šm. | [---.--]m.ḫmš.ṣmdm. | [---.bnš]m. 137.1[92].7
[---.--]n.d[--.]bnš[.---]. | [---.]idmt.n[--.]t[--]. | [---.--]r.dlt.tḥt n. | [---.]dlt. | [-- 2038.20
-]. | [---.]yd‘t.k[---]. | [---].w hm. | [--]y.tb y.w [---]. | [---.]bnš.[---]. 2158B.1
.]‘šr.ṣmd.alpm. | [---.bn]šm. | [---.--]m.ḫmš.ṣmdm. | [---.bnš]m. 61[-].6
2038.22

bnt

ry b[t h]. | aqrb k ab h b‘[l]. | yǵtr.‘ttr t | rḫ l k ybrdmy.b[t.a] | b h lb[u] y‘rr.w y‘[n]. | yrḫ nyr šmm.w n‘[n]. | ‘ma nkl 24[77].29
| mrym.ṣpn.b alp.šd.rbt.kmn. | hlk.aḫt h.b‘l.y‘n.tdrq. | ybnt.ab h.šrḥq.att.l pnn h. | št.alp.qdm h.mria.w tk. | pn h.tḥ 3['NT].4.84
-]. | ymy.bn[.---]. | ‘bd‘n.p[--.---]. | [-]d[-]l.bn.ḥrn. | aḫty.bt.abm. | [-]rbn.‘dd.nryn. | [ab]r[p]u.bn.kbd. | [-]m[-].bn.ṣmrt. 102[322].6.2
um.pḫl.pḫlt.bt.abn.bt šmm w thm. | qrit.l špš.um h.špš.um.ql.bl.‘m. | il.m UG5.7.1
.tr.w.arb‘.bnt h. | yrḫm.yd.tn.bn h. | b‘lm.w.tlt.n‘rm.w.bt.aḫt. | bn.lwn.tlttm.b‘lm. | bn.b‘ly.tlttm.b‘lm. | w.aḥd.ḫbt. | 2080.5
n.ddy. | ‘bdil[.b]n ṣdqn. | bnšm.h[-]mt.ypḥm. | kbby.yd.bt.amt. | ilmlk. 2045.7
[---.t]št.rimt. | l irt h.mšr.l.dd.aliyn. | b‘l.yd.pdry.bt.ar. | ahbt.tly.bt.rb.dd.arṣy. | bt.y‘bdr.km ǵlmm. | w ‘rb n.l 3['NT].3.3
.---]. | tšt[.r]imt.[l irt h.tšr.l dd.aliyn.b‘l]. | [ahb]t pdr[y.bt.ar.ahbt.tly.bt.rb.dd]. | arṣy bt.y[‘bdr.---]. | rgm l btl[t.‘nt.t 7.2[130].11
.ǵzr.tb.ql. | ‘l.b‘l.b ṣrrt. | ṣpn.ytmr.b‘l. | bnt h.y‘n.pdry. | bt.ar.apn.tly. | [bt.r]b.pdr.yd‘. | [---]t.im[-]lt. | [-----]. | [---.--]rt. 3['NT].1.24
mẓll.bn h. | mtb rbt.atrt.ym. | mtb.klt.knyt. | mtb.pdry.bt.ar. | mẓll.tly.bt rb. | mtb.arṣ.bt y‘bdr. | w y‘n ltpn il d pid. | 4[51].4.55
a]trt.mtb.il. | mtll.b[n h.m]tb.rbt.atrt. | ym.mtb.[pdr]y.bt.ar. | [mẓll.]tly[.bt.]rb.mtb. | [arṣy.bt.y‘bdr.mtb]. | [klt.knyt] 3['NT.VI].5.49
atrt.mtb.il.mẓll]. | bn h.m[tb.rbt.atrt.ym]. | mtb.pdr[y.bt.ar.mẓll]. | tly.bt.r[b.mtb.arṣy]. | bt.y‘bdr[.mtb.klt]. | knyt.w 3['NT.VI].4.3
ẓll. | bn h.mtb.rbt. | atrt.ym.mtb. | klt.knyt. | mtb.pdry.b ar. | mẓll.tly.bt rb. | mtb.arṣy.bt.y‘bdr. | ap.mtn.rgmm. | arg 4[51].1.17
dl k. | mtrt k.‘m k.šb‘t. | ǵlm k.tmn.ḫnzr k. | ‘m k.pdry.bt.ar. | ‘m k.ttly.bt.rb.idk. | pn k.al ttn.tk.ǵr. | knkny.ša.ǵr.‘l y 5[67].5.10
al.tšt.u[rb]t.b bht m. | ḥln.b q[rb.hk]l m. | al td[.pdr]y.bt ar. | [---.tl]y.bt.rb. | [---.m]dd.il ym. | [---.-]qlṣn.wpt m. | [---. 4[51].6.10
mnnm.mt yd k.hl.‘ṣr.thrr.l išt. | w ṣḥrrt.l pḥmm.btm.bt.il.bt.il. | w ‘lm h.w hn.attm.tṣḥn y.mt mt. | nḥtm.ḫt k.mm 23[52].45
št.mdd ilm.ar[š]. | ṣmt.‘gl.il.‘tk. | mḫšt.klbt.ilm išt. | klt.bt.il.ḏbb.imtḫṣ.ksp. | itrt.ḫrṣ.trd.b‘l. | b mrym.ṣpn.mšṣṣ.[-]k‘[3['NT].3.43
m.mt yd k.hl.‘ṣr.thrr.l išt. | w ṣḥrrt.l pḥmm.btm.bt.il.bt.il. | w ‘lm h.w hn.attm.tṣḥn y.mt mt. | nḥtm.ḫt k.mmnnm. 23[52].45
ttn bn h. | w.btšy.bt h. | w.ištrmy. | bt.‘bd mlk. | w.snt. | bt.ugrt. | w.pdy h[m]. | iwrkl.mit. | ksp.b y[d]. | birtym. | [un]t 1006.11
k. | mmnnm.mt yd k.hl.‘ṣr.thrr.l išt. | w ṣḥrrt.l pḥmm.btm.bt.il.bt.il. | w ‘lm h.w hn.attm.tṣḥn y.mt mt. | nḥtm.ḫt k. 23[52].45
[---.]tltm.d.nlqḥt. | [bn.ḫ]tyn.yd.bt h. | [aǵ]ltn. | tdn.bn.ddy. | ‘bdil[.b]n ṣdqn. | bnšm.h[-]mt.yp 2045.2
.tn.ǵzrm.b.bt.ṣdqš[lm]. | [a]tt.aḥt.b.bt.rpi[--]. | [att.]w.bt h.b.bt.alḥn. | [att.w.]pǵt.aḥt.b.bt.tt. | [att.w.]bt h.b.bt.trǵd 80[119].25
d.b.[bt.---]. | att.w.bn h.w.pǵt.aḥt.b.bt.m[--]. | att.w.tt.bt h.b.bt.ḫdmrd. | att.w.tn.ǵzrm.b.bt.ṣdqš[lm]. | [a]tt.aḥt.b.bt 80[119].22
[att.]w.bt h.b.bt.alḥn. | [att.w.]pǵt.aḥt.b.bt.tt. | [att.w.]bt h.b.bt.trǵds. | [---.]att.adrt.w.pǵt.a[ḥt.b.bt.---]. | [---.‘]šrm. 80[119].27
‘l.k tmz‘. | kst.dnil.mt.rpi. | all.ǵzr.m[t.]hr[nmy]. | gm.l bt[h.dnil.k yṣḥ]. | šm‘.pǵt.tkmt[.my]. | ḥspt.l š‘r.tl.yd[‘t]. | hl 19[1AQHT].1.49
gn. | w ynḥm.aḫ h. | w.b‘ln aḫ h. | w.ḥttn bn h. | w.btšy.bt h. | w.ištrmy. | bt.‘bd mlk. | w.snt. | bt.ugrt. | w.pdy h[m]. | i 1006.7
lzn.qrty[.---]. | w.klt h.b.t[--.---]. | b‘l y.mlk[y.---]. | yd.bt h.yd[.---]. | ary.yd.t[--.---]. | ḥtn h.šb‘l[.---]. | tlḥny.yd[.---]. | 81[329].14
bn.b‘ln.biry. | tlt.b‘lm. | w.adn hm.tr.w.arb‘.bnt h. | yrḫm.yd.tn.bn h. | b‘lm.w.tlt.n‘rm.w.bt.aḫt. | bn.lwn.t 2080.3
ltm.bd.n‘m. | yšr.ǵzr.tb.ql. | ‘l.b‘l.b ṣrrt. | ṣpn.ytmr.b‘l. | bnt h.y‘n.pdry. | bt.ar.apn.tly. | [bt.r]b.pdr.yd‘. | [---]t.im[-]lt. 3['NT].1.23
y‘n ḫrḫb mlk qẓ [l]. | n‘mn.ilm l ḫt[n]. | m.b‘l trḫ pdry b[t h]. | aqrb k ab h b‘[l]. | yǵtr.‘ttr t | rḫ l k ybrdmy.b[t.a] | b 24[77].26
ašr.ar yrḫ.w y | rḫ yar k. | [ašr ilht ktrt bn] | t hll.snnt.bnt h | ll b‘l gml.yrdt. | b ‘rgzm.b bz tdm. | lla y.‘m lẓpn i | l d. 24[77].41
. | dn.il.bt h.ymǵyn. | yštql.dnil.l hkl h. | ‘rb.b bt h.ktrt.bnt. | hll.snnt.apnk.dnil. | mt.rpi.ap.hn.ǵzr.mt. | hrnmy.alp.yt 17[2AQHT].2.26
m.nkl w ib. | d ašr.ar yrḫ.w y | rḫ yar k. | [ašr ilht ktrt bn] | t hll.snnt.bnt h | ll b‘l gml.yrdt. | b ‘rgzm.b bz tdm. | lla y 24[77].40
[--.]špš. | yrḫ ytkḥ yḥ[bq] [-]. | tld bt.[--]t.ḥ[--.l k] | trt.l bnt.hll[.snnt]. | hl ǵlmt tld b[n.--]n. | ‘n ha l yd h.tzd[.--]. | pt 24[77].6
n.ǵzr.mt. | hrnmy.alp.ytbḫ.l kt | rt.yšlḥm.ktrt.w y | ššq.bnt.[hl]l.snnt. | hn.ym.w tn.yšlḥm. | ktrt.w yš[š]q.bnt.hl[l]. | s 17[2AQHT].2.31
š[š]q.bnt.hl[l]. | snnt.tlt[.r]b‘ ym.yšl | ḥm ktrt.w yššq. | bnt hll.snnt.ḫmš. | tdt.ym.yšlḥm.k[t]rt. | w y[ššq].bnt.hll.snn 17[2AQHT].2.36
ššq. | bnt hll.snnt.ḫmš. | tdt.ym.yšlḥm.k[t]rt. | w y[ššq].bnt.hll.snnt. | mk.b šb[‘.]ymm.tb‘.b bt h. | ktrt.bnt.hll.snnt. | [17[2AQHT].2.38
| ššq.bnt.[hl]l.snnt. | hn.ym.w tn.yšlḥm. | ktrt.w yš[š]q.bnt.hl[l]. | snnt.tlt[.r]b‘ ym.yšl | ḥm ktrt.w yššq. | bnt hll.snnt. 17[2AQHT].2.33
y[ššq].bnt.hll.snnt. | mk.b šb[‘.]ymm.tb‘.b bt h. | ktrt.bnt.hll.snnt. | [-]d[-]t.n‘m y.‘rš.h[--]m. | ysmsmt.‘rš.ḫlln.[-]. | 17[2AQHT].2.40
l y.al tkl.bn. | qr.‘n k.mḫ.riš k. | udm‘t.ṣḥ.aḫt k. | ttmnt.bt.ḥmḥ h. | d[-]n.tbkn.w tdm.l y.[--]. | [---].al.trgm.l aḫt k. | [- 16.1[125].29
rb.w ld.bnt.l h. | mk.b šb‘.šnt. | bn.krt.km hm.tdr. | ap.bnt.ḥry. | km hm.w thss.atrt. | ndr h.w ilt.p[--]. | w tšu.g h.w 15[128].3.24
.tštšḥ.km.ḥ[--]. | [---].‘pr.bt k.ygr[š k.---]. | [---.]y.ḥr.ḥr.bnt.ḥ[---]. | [--.]uḫd.[b‘]l m.‘[--].yd k.amṣ.yd[.--]. | [---.]ḥš[.-]n 1001.1.13
bn.šrn. | ‘bdb‘l.bn.kdn. | gzl.bn.qldn. | gld.bt.klb. | l[---].bt.ḫzli. | bn.iḫyn. | ṣdqn.bn.ass. | b‘lyskn.bn.ss. | ṣdqn.bn.imrt. 102[323].3.6

--].|[---.]nt[-.]mbk kpt.w[.--].b g[--].|[---.]ḥ[--.]bnt.ṣ‘ṣ.bnt.ḫkp[.---].|[---].aḥw.aṯm.prṯl[.---].|[---.]mnt.[l]p‘n[.-.-]b 1001.1.18
lṯpn.il d p[id].|yd‘t k.bt.k anšt.w i[n.b ilht].|qlṣ k.tb‘.bt.ḫnp.lb[k.--.ti]|ḫd.d iṯ.b kbd k.tšt.b [---].|irt k.dṯ.ydṯ.m‘q 18[3AQHT].1.17
ašr nkl w ib[.bt].|ḫrḫb.mlk qẓ ḫrḫb m|lk agzt.b sǵ[--.]špš.|yrḫ yṯkḥ yḥ[24[77].1
b.|klt.knyt.|mṯb.pdry.b ar.|mẓll.ṭly.bt rb.|mṯb.arṣy.bt.y‘bdr.|ap.mṯn.rgmm.|argm k.šskn m‘.|mgn.rbt.aṯrt ym. 4[51].1.19
ṯb.klt.knyt.|mṯb.pdry.bt.ar.|mẓll.ṭly.bt rb.|mṯb.arṣ.bt y‘bdr.|w y‘n lṭpn il d pid.|p ‘bd.an.‘nn.aṯrt.|p.‘bd.ank.a 4[51].4.57
ṯrt.ym].|mṯb.pdr[y.bt.ar.mẓll].|ṭly.bt.r[b.mṯb.arṣy].|bt.y‘bdr[.mṯb.klt].|knyt.w t‘n[.btlt.‘nt].|yṯb l y.ṯr.il[.ab y.--- 3[‘NT.VI].4.5
t.|ym.mṯb.[pdr]y.bt.ar.|[mẓll.]ṭly[.bt.]rb.mṯb.|[arṣy.bt.y‘bdr.mṯb].|[klt.knyt]. 3[‘NT.VI].5.51
.l.dd.aliyn.|b‘l.yd.pdry.bt.ar.|ahbt.ṭly.bt.rb.dd.arṣy.|bt.y‘bdr.km ǵlmm.|w ‘rb n.l p‘n.‘nt.hbr.|w ql.tšṯḥwy.kbd h 3[‘NT].3.5
.aliyn.b‘l].|[ahb]t pdr[y.bt.ar.ahbt.ṭly.bt.rb.dd].|arṣy bt.y[‘bdr.---].|rgm l btl[t.‘nt.ṯny.l ybmt.limm.tḥm.aliyn.b‘l] 7.2[130].12
[m.]n‘r.tdm‘.km.|[sǵ]r.bkm.y‘ny[.---.bn]wt h.|[--]nn.bnt yš[--.---.-]lk.|[--]b.kmm.l k[--].|[šp]š.b šmm.tq[ru.---.-]r UG5.8.42
b y.šnt.mlit.t[--.---].|ymǵy k.bnm.ta[--.---].|[b]nm.w bnt.ytn k[.---].|[--]l.bn y.šḥt.w [---].|[--]tt.msgr.bn k[.---].|[59[100].9
|w y‘ḏr k.b yd.btlt.[‘nt].|w y‘n.lṭpn.il d p[id].|yd‘t k.bt.k anšt.w i[n.b ilht].|qlṣ k.tb‘.bt.ḫnp.lb[k.--.ti]|ḫd.d iṯ.b 18[3AQHT].1.16
.mm‘m.]y‘ny.|il.b šb‘t.ḥdrm.b ṯmnt.|ap.sgrt.yd‘[t k.]bt.k an[št].|k in.b ilht.ql[ṣ] k.mh.tarš[n].|l btlt.‘nt.w t[‘]n.b 3[‘NT.VI].5.35
-]m.|‘bdmlk.bn.šrn.|‘bdb‘l.bn.kdn.|gzl.bn.qldn.|gld.bt.klb.|l[---].bt.ḫzli.|bn.iḫyn.|ṣdqn.bn.ass.|b‘lyskn.bn.ss.|ṣ 102[323].3.5
.|dr il.l mšknt hm.|w tqrb.w ld.bn.l h.|w tqrb.w ld.bnt.l h.|mk.b šb‘.šnt.|bn.krt.km hm.tdr.|ap.bnt.ḥry.|km h 15[128].3.21
.]krt.|[b tk.rpi.]arṣ.|[b pḫr].qbṣ.dtn.|[w t]qrb.w ld.|bn.tl k.|tld.pǵt.t[--]t.|tld.pǵt[.---].|tld.pǵ[t.---].|tld.pǵ[t.---] 15[128].3.6
b.dbḥ.mlk.|dbḥ ṣpn.|[-]zǵm.|[i]lib.|[i]lbldn.|[p]dry.bt.mlk.|[-]lp.izr.|[a]rz.|k.t‘rb.‘ṯtrt.šd.bt[.m]lk.|k.t‘rbn.ršp 2004.7
hn[.w.]ht.ank.|[---.--]š[-.--].w.ašt.|[---].amr k.|[---].k.ybt.mlk.|[---].w.ap.ank.|[---].l.ǵr.amn.|[---.-]ktt.hn.ib.|[---. 1012.14
‘nt.tqm.|[---.p]ḫr k.ygrš k.qr.bt k.ygrš k.|[---].bnt.ṣ‘ṣ.bnt.m‘m‘.‘bd.ḥrn.[--.]k.|[---].aǵwyn.‘n k.ẓẓ.w k mǵ.ilm.|[--. 1001.2.11
dqn.bn.imrt.|mnḥm.bn.ḫyrn.|[-]yn.bn.arkbt.|[--]zbl.bt.mrnn.|a[--.---.-]‘n.|ml[--.---].|ar[--.---.--]l.|aty[n.bn.]šm‘ 102[323].3.13
qlm.|bn.pǵdn.ṯqlm.|bn.b‘ln.ṯqlm.|‘bdyrḫ.nqd.ṯqlm.|bt.sgld.ṯqlm.|bn.‘my.ṯqlm.|bn.brq.ṯqlm.|bn.ḫnzr.ṯqlm.|dq 122[308].1.13
h.|w.b‘ln aḫ h.|w.ḥṯṯn bn h.|w.btšy.bt h.|w.ištrmy.|bt.‘bd mlk.|w.snt.|bt.ugrt.|w.pdy h[m].|iwrkl.mit.|ksp.b 1006.9
.špk[.---].|[---.]nt[-.]mbk kpt.w[.--].b g[--].|[---.]ḥ[--.]bnt.ṣ‘ṣ.bnt.ḫkp[.---].|[---].aḥw.aṯm.prṯl[.---].|[---.]mnt.[l]p‘ 1001.1.18
t tqm.‘nt.tqm.|[---.p]ḫr k.ygrš k.qr.bt k.ygrš k.|[---].bnt.ṣ‘ṣ.bnt.m‘m‘.‘bd.ḥrn.[--.]k.|[---].aǵwyn.‘n k.ẓẓ.w k mǵ.i 1001.2.11
-].|t‘ny.n[---.-]ṯq.|w š[--.---].|ḥdṯ[.---.]ḥ[--].|b bt.[-.]l bnt.q[-].|w št.b bt.ṯap[.--].|hy.yd h.w ym[ǵ].|mlak k.‘m dt[UG5.6.8
k.šb‘t.|ǵlm k.ṯmn.ḫnzr k.|‘m k.pdry.bt.ar.|‘m k.ṭṭly.bt.rb.idk.|pn k.al ttn.tk.ǵr.|knkny.ša.ǵr.‘l ydm.|ḫlb.l ẓr.rḥ 5[67].5.11
t.[l irt h.tšr.l dd.aliyn.b‘l].|[ahb]t pdr[y.bt.ar.ahbt.ṭly.bt.rb.dd].|arṣy bt.y[‘bdr.---].|rgm l btl[t.‘nt.ṯny.l ybmt.lim 7.2[130].11
mt.|l irt h.mšr.l.dd.aliyn.|b‘l.yd.pdry.bt.ar.|ahbt.ṭly.bt.rb.dd.arṣy.|bt.y‘bdr.km ǵlmm.|w ‘rb n.l p‘n.‘nt.hbr.|w 3[‘NT].3.4
.b[n h.m]ṯb.rbt.aṯrt.|ym.mṯb.[pdr]y.bt.ar.|[mẓll.]ṭly[.bt.]rb.mṯb.|[arṣy.bt.y‘bdr.mṯb].|[klt.knyt]. 3[‘NT.VI].5.50
.rbt.|aṯrt.ym.mṯb.|klt.knyt.|mṯb.pdry.b ar.|mẓll.ṭly.bt rb.|mṯb.arṣy.bt.y‘bdr.|ap.mṯn.rgmm.|argm k.šskn m‘.| 4[51].1.18
].|bn h.m[ṯb.rbt.aṯrt.ym].|mṯb.pdr[y.bt.ar.mẓll].|ṭly.bt.r[b.mṯb.arṣy].|bt.y‘bdr[.mṯb.klt].|knyt.w t‘n[.btlt.‘nt].|y 3[‘NT.VI].4.4
rbt.aṯrt.ym.|mṯb.klt.knyt.|mṯb.pdry.bt.ar.|mẓll.ṭly.bt rb.|mṯb.arṣ.bt y‘bdr.|w y‘n lṭpn il d pid.|p ‘bd.an.‘nn.aṯ 4[51].4.56
.b ṣrrt.|ṣpn.ytmr.b‘l.|bnt h.y‘n.pdry.|bt.ar.apn.ṭly.|[bt.r]b.pdr.yd‘.|[---]t.im[-]lt.|[-----].|[---.--]rt. 3[‘NT].1.25
bht m.|ḥln.b q[rb.hk]l m.|al td[.pdr]y.bt ar.|[---.ṭ]ly.bt.rb.|[---.m]dd.il ym.|[---.-]qlṣn.wpṯ m.|[---.]w y‘n.kṯr.|[w 4[51].6.11
[-]p[-]l[.---].|k lli.[---].|kpr.[šb‘.bnt.rḥ.gdm.w anhbm].|w tqr[y.ǵlmm.b št.ǵr.---].|[‘]d tš[b‘. 7.2[130].3
t m].|w ank.ib[ǵy h.---].|[-].l y‘mdn.i[---.---].|kpr.šb‘ bn[t.rḥ.gdm.w anhbm].|kla[t.ṯǵ]r[t.bht.‘nt.w tqry.ǵlmm.b š 7.2[130].23
n[--.---.-]š[--].|kpr.šb‘.bnt.rḥ.gdm.|w anhbm.klat.ṯǵrt.|bht.‘nt.w tqry.ǵlmm.|b št. 3[‘NT].2.2
].|hw km.ḥrr[.---].|šnmtm.dbṯ[.---].|tr‘.tr‘n.a[--.---].|bnt.šdm.ṣḥr[.---].|šb‘.šnt.il.mla.[-].|w ṯmn.nqpnt.‘d.|k lbš. 12[75].2.44
um.pḫl.pḫlt.bt.abn.bt šmm w thm.|qrit.l špš.um h.špš.um.ql.bl.‘m.|il.mbk nhr UG5.7.1
.|[--]dšq krsnm.|ḫmšm [-]t ṯlṯ ty[--].|bn.grgš.|w.npṣ bt tn.ṯlṯ mat.|w spl ṯlṯ.mat.|w mmskn.|w.tt.mqrtm.|w.ṯn.i 1103.16
ḫrḫb m|lk agzt.b sǵ[--.]špš.|yrḫ yṯkḥ yḥ[bq] [-].|tld bt.[--]t.ḫ[--.l k]|trt.l bnt.hll[.snnt].|hl ǵlmt tld b[n.--]n.|‘n 24[77].5
]ml.ksl h.k b[r]q.|[---.]m[-]ǵ[-].thmt.brq.|[---].tṣb.qšt.bnt.|[---.‘]n h.km.btn.yqr.|[krpn h.-.l]arṣ.ks h.tšpk m.|[l ‘ 17[2AQHT].6.13

bsbn

.brr.|‘lm.š.š[--].l[--.]‘rb.šp|š.w ḥl[.ml]k.|bn.aup[š.--].bsbn hzpḫ ṯlṯt.|kṯr[.---.--]trt ḫmšt.bn gda[.-.]mḏ‘.|kl[--.---.] APP.II[173].58

bsn

bdlḥn[-].|bn.mqwṭ.|bn.bsn.|bn.inr[-].|bn.ṯbil.|bn.iryn.|ṯṯl.|bn.nṣdn.|bn.ydln.|[bn 1071.3
mḫsrn.d.[--.]uškny m.|brq.ṯlṯ.[mat.ṯ]lṯ.|bsn.mi[t.--].|ar[--.---].|k[--.---]. 1136.3
b‘l.bt.ṯrn.|b‘l.bt.ktmn.|b‘l.bt.ndbd.|[--].ṣnr.|[b‘l].bt.bsn.|[-----].|b[--.---]. 31[14].11

b‘d

rn.l bt h.w.|yštql.l ḥṭr h.tlu ḥt.km.nḫl.|tplg.km.plg.|b‘d h.bhtm.mnt.b‘d h.bhtm.sgrt.|b‘d h.‘dbt.ṯlṯ.ptḥ.bt.mnt.| UG5.7.70
l.l ḥṭr h.tlu ḥt.km.nḫl.|tplg.km.plg.|b‘d h.bhtm.mnt.b‘d h.bhtm.sgrt.|b‘d h.‘dbt.ṯlṯ.ptḥ.bt.mnt.|ptḥ.bt.w ubn.hk UG5.7.70
.nḫl.|tplg.km.plg.|b‘d h.bhtm.mnt.b‘d h.bhtm.sgrt.|b‘d h.‘dbt.ṯlṯ.ptḥ.bt.mnt.|ptḥ.bt.w ubn.hkl.w ištql šql.|tn.k UG5.7.71
.šb‘t.|ghl.ph.ṯmnt.|nblu h.špš.ymp.|hlkt.tdr[--].|špš.b‘d h.t[--].|aṯr.aṯrm[.---].|aṯr.aṯrm[.---].|išdym.t[---].|b k.m 27[8].6
r‘.w ṣḥ hm.‘m.nǵr.mdr‘ y.nǵr.|nǵr.ptḥ.w ptḥ hw.prṣ.b‘d hm.|w ‘rb.hm.hm[.iṯ.--.l]ḥm.w t[n].|w nlḥm.hm.iṯ[.--.y 23[52].70
bu.b‘d y[.---]. 1169.1
l ṯṯpṭ.|ṯpṭ qṣr.npš.l tdy.|ṯšm.‘l.dl.l pn k.|l tšlḥm.ytm.b‘d.|ksl k.almnt.km.|aḫt.‘rš.mdw.anšt.|‘rš.zbln.rd.l mlk.|a 16.6[127].49
lt y.|b n‘m.b gb‘.tliyt.|hlm.‘nt.tph.ilm.b h.p‘nm.|ṭṭṭ.b‘d n.ksl.ṯṯbr.|‘ln.pn h.td‘.ṯǵṣ.pnt.|ksl h.anš.dt.ẓr h.tšu.|g 3[‘NT].3.30
.mǵy.hy.w kn.|[---].ḥln.d b.dmt.um.il[m.---].|[--]ḏyn.b‘d.[--]ḏyn.w l.|[--]k b‘lt bhtm[.--]tn k.|[--]y.l ihbt.yb[--].rg 1002.44
[-----].|‘r[.---].|‘r[.---].|‘r[.---].|w y[---].|b‘d[.---].|yaṯr[.---].|b d k.[---].|ṯnnt h[.---].|ṯlṯt h[.-.w y‘n].| 16[126].5.5

b‘yn

[.---].|[-]n.y‘rtym.|gmm.w.bn.p[--].|trn.w.p[-]y.|bn.b‘yn.w.agytn.|[---] gnym.|[--]ry.w ary.|[---]ǵrbtym.|[---.]w 131[309].12
p‘ṣ.ẖbty.|artyn.ary.|brqn.ṯlḥy.|bn.aryn.|bn.lgn.|bn.b‘yn.|šdyn.|ary.|brqn.|bn.ẖlln.|bn.mṣry.|ṯmn.qšt.|w ‘šr.u 118[306].8
.|bn.ẖran.|bn.arš[w.b]ṣry.|bn.ykn.|bn.lṣn.‘rmy.|bn.b‘yn.šly.|bn.ynḥn.|bn.‘bdilm.hzpy. 99[327].2.4
spr.mḏr[ǵlm].|lt.hlk.b[.---].|bn.b‘yn.š[--.---].|aǵltn.mid[-.---].|bn.lṣn.‘rm[y].|aršw.bṣry.|ar 87[64].3

b‘l

].yṯkḥ.w yiẖd.b qrb[.-].|[--.t]ṯkḥ.w tiẖd.b uš[k.--].|[-.b]‘l.yabd.l alp.|[---.bt]lt.‘nt.|[---]q.hry.w yld.|[---]m.ḥbl.kṯ[11[132].1.3
pṯt.arṣ.tspr b y|rdm.arṣ.w td‘ ilm.|k mtt.yšm‘.aliyn.b‘l.|yuhb.‘glt.b dbr.prt.|b šd.šḥlmmt.škb.|‘mn h.šb‘.l šb‘m. 5[67].5.17
.---].|[--.]yṣt ḏm[r.---].|tšt[.r]imt.[l irt h.tšr.l dd.aliyn.b‘l].|[ahb]t pdr[y.bt.ar.ahbt.ṭly.bt.rb.dd].|arṣy bt.y[‘bdr.---] 7.2[130].10
m.tiẖd.knr h.b yd[h.tšt].|rimt.l irt h.tšr.dd.al[iyn].|b‘l.ahbt. UG5.3.2.8
.ṭl.amr..|bn km k bk[r.z]bl.am..|rkm.agzrt[.--].arẖ..|b‘l.azrt.‘nt.[-]ld.|kbd h.l yd‘ hr h.[---]d[-].|tnq[.---.]in[b]b.p 13[6].30
ngṯ h.|k lb.arẖ.l ‘gl h.k lb.|ṯat.l imr h.km.lb.|‘nt.aṯr.b‘l.tiẖd.|bn.ilm.mt.b ḥrb.|tbq‘nn.b ẖṯr.tdry|nn.b išt.tšrpnn 6[49].2.30
ǵrm[.t]ẖšn.|rḥq[.---.td‘].|qdm ym.bmt.[nhr].|tṭṭn.ib.b‘l.tiẖd.|y‘rm.šnu.hd.gpt.|ǵr.w y‘n.aliyn.|b‘l.ib.hdt.lm.tḥš. 4[51].7.35
h.k lb.a[rẖ].|l ‘gl h.k lb.ṯa[t].|l imr h.km.lb.‘n[t].|aṯr.b‘l.tiẖd.m[t].|b sin.lpš.tššq[n h].|b qṣ.all.tšu.g h.w[tṣ]|ḥ.at 6[49].2.9
‘rẓ.t‘r[ẓ.---].|‘n.b‘l.a[ẖ]ḏ[.---].|ẓr h.aẖḏ.qš[t.---].|p ‘n.b‘l.aẖḏ[.---].|w ṣmt.ǵllm[.---].|aẖḏ.aklm.k [---].|npl.b mšm 12[75].2.34
|mṣt.ks h.t[--.---].|idm.adr[.---].|idm.‘rẓ.t‘r[ẓ.---].|‘n.b‘l.a[ẖ]ḏ[.---].|ẓr h.aẖḏ.qš[t.---].|p ‘n.b‘l.aẖḏ[.---].|w ṣmt.ǵl 12[75].2.32
.|bl.ašt.urbt.b bh[t] m.|ḥln.b qrb.hkl m.|w y‘n.aliyn b‘l.|al.tšt.urbt.b[bhtm].|[ḥln].b qrb.hk[l m]. 4[51].5.125
bl.ašt.ur[bt.]b bht m.|ḥln.b qr[b.hk]l m.|w ‘n.ali[yn.]b‘l.|al.tšt.u[rb]t.b bht m.|ḥln.b q[rb.hk]l m.|al td[.pdr]y.bt 4[51].6.7
yrẖ š.‘nt ṣpn.alp.|w š.pdry š.ddmš š.|w b urbt.ilib š.|b‘l alp w š.|dgn.š.il t‘ḏr.š.|b‘l š.‘nt š.ršp š.|šlmm.|w šnpt.il UG5.13.20
dbḥ.ṣp[n.---].|il.alp.w š[.---].|b‘lm.alp.w š[.---].|b‘lm.alp.w š[.---].|arṣ.w šmm.š.kṯr[t] š.yrẖ[.---].|ṣpn.š.kṯr.š. UG5.9.1.4
dbḥ.ṣp[n.---].|il.alp.w š[.---].|b‘lm.alp.w š[.---].|b‘lm.alp.w š[.---].|arṣ.w šmm.š.kṯr[t] š.yr UG5.9.1.3
|[---.]im[-.---].|[---.]š.s[--.---].|[---.-]lb[.--].š[.---].|[---.]b‘lm al[p]. UG5.9.2.21
mn.|yry[.---.]br.|ydn[.---].kry.|bn.ydd[.---.b]r.|prkl.b‘l.any.d.b d.abr[-]. 2123.7
.]dqn.b‘ln.|ǵltn.‘bd.[---].|nsk.ḥḏm.klyn[.ṣd]qn.‘bdilt.b‘l.|annmn.‘dy.klby.dqn.|ḥrṯm.ḥgbn.‘dn.ynḥm[.---].|ḥrš.m 2011.25
ilk.r[--].|aršm.b‘l [aṯt].|ttẖ.b‘l aṯt.|ayab.b‘l aṯt.|iyṯr.b‘l aṯt.|ptm.b‘l ššlmt.|‘dršp.b‘l ššl 1077.3
ilk.r[--].|aršm.b‘l [aṯt].|ttẖ.b‘l aṯt.|ayab.b‘l aṯt.|iyṯr.b‘l aṯt.|ptm.b‘l ššlmt.|‘dršp.b‘l ššlmt.|ṯtrn.b‘l š 1077.4
ilk.r[--].|aršm.b‘l [aṯt].|ttẖ.b‘l aṯt.|ayab.b‘l aṯt.|iyṯr.b‘l aṯt.|ptm.b‘l ššlmt.|‘dršp.b‘l ššlmt.|ṯtrn.b‘l ššlmt.|aršwn 1077.5
ilk.r[--].|aršm.b‘l [aṯt].|ttẖ.b‘l aṯt.|ayab.b‘l aṯt.|iyṯr.b‘l aṯt.|ptm.b‘l ššlmt. 1077.2
d.šḥlmmt.|mǵny.l b‘l.npl.l a|rṣ.mt.aliyn.b‘l.|ẖlq.zbl.b‘l.arṣ.|apnk.lṭpn.il.|d pid.yrd.l ksi.yṯb.|l hdm[.w] l.hdm.y 5[67].6.10
|k ẖlq.z[bl.b‘l.arṣ].|w hm.ḥy.a[liyn.b‘l].|w hm.iṯ.zbl.b‘[l.arṣ].|b ḥlm.lṭpn.il.d pid.|b ḏrt.bny.bnwt.|šmm.šmn.tm 6[49].3.3
.tmṭrn.|nẖlm.tlk.nbtm.|w id‘.k ḥy.aliyn.b‘l.|k iṯ.zbl.b‘l.arṣ.|b ḥlm.lṭpn.il d pid.|b ḏrt.bny.bnwt.|šmm.šmn.tmṭr 6[49].3.9
nk.w anẖn.|w tnẖ.b irt y.npš.|k ḥy.aliyn.b‘l.|k iṯ.zbl.b‘l.arṣ.|gm.yṣḥ.il.l btlt.|‘nt.šm‘.l btlt.‘n[t].|rgm.l nrt.il.šp[š 6[49].3.21
aṯrt.w bn h.ilt.w ṣb|rt.ary h.k mt.aliyn.|b‘l.k ẖlq.zbl.b‘l.|arṣ.gm.yṣḥ il.|l rbt.aṯrt ym.šm‘.|l rbt.aṯr[t] ym.tn.|aḥd 6.1.42[49.1.14]
[k mt.aliyn.b‘l].|k ẖlq.z[bl.b‘l.arṣ].|w hm.ḥy.a[liyn.b‘l].|w hm.iṯ.zbl.b‘[l.arṣ].|b ḥlm.lṭ 6[49].3.1
.‘nt.šdm.il.yš[t k].|b‘l.‘nt.mḥrṯ[-].|iy.aliyn.b‘l.|iy.zbl.b‘l.arṣ.|w t‘n.nrt.ilm.š[p]š.|šd yn.‘n.b qbt[.t]|bl lyt.‘l.umt k 6[49].4.40
gn.|b‘[l ṣ]pn.|b‘lm.|[b‘]lm.|[b‘]lm.|[b‘]lm.|[b‘]lm.|[b‘l]m.|[arṣ] w šm[m].|[-----].|[a]rṣ.|[u]šẖr[y].|[‘]ṯtrt.|i[l t]‘ 29[17].1.11
al.tǵl[.---].|prdmn.‘bd.ali[yn].|b‘l.sid.zbl.b‘l.|arṣ.qm.yṯ‘r.|w yšlḥmn h.|ybrd.ṯd.l pnw h.|b ḥrb.mlḥt. 3[‘NT].1.3
l.‘nt.šdm.il.yšt k.|[b]‘l.‘nt.mḥrṯt.|iy.aliyn.b‘l.|iy.zbl.b‘l.arṣ.|ttb‘.btlt.‘nt.|idk.l ttn.pnm.|‘m.nrt.ilm.špš.|tšu.g h. 6[49].4.29
pp.ṯr.il.d pid.|tǵẓy.bny.bnwt.|b nši.‘n h.w tphn.|hlk.b‘l.aṯtrt.|k t‘n.hlk.btlt.|‘nt.tdrq.ybmt.|[limm].b h.p‘nm.|[t 4[51].2.13
r].|tṭṭn.ib.b‘l.tiẖd.|y‘rm.šnu.hd.gpt.|ǵr.w y‘n.aliyn.|b‘l.ib.hdt.lm.tḥš.|lm.tḥš.nṯq.dmrn.|‘n.b‘l.qdm.yd h.|k tǵḏ. 4[51].7.38
.y špš.|pl.‘nt.šdm.il.yš[t k].|b‘l.‘nt.mḥrṯ[-].|iy.aliyn.b‘l.|iy.zbl.b‘l.arṣ.|w t‘n.nrt.ilm.š[p]š.|šd yn.‘n.b qbt[.t]|bl l 6[49].4.39
m.y špš.|pl.‘nt.šdm.il.yšt k.|[b]‘l.‘nt.mḥrṯt.|iy.aliyn.b‘l.|iy.zbl.b‘l.arṣ.|ttb‘.btlt.‘nt.|idk.l ttn.pnm.|‘m.nrt.ilm.šp 6[49].4.28
pš.|tṣḥ.l mt.šm‘.m‘.|l bn.ilm.mt.ik.tmt[ẖ]|ṣ.‘m.aliyn.b‘l.|ik.al.yšm[‘] k.ṯr.|il.ab k.l ys‘.alt.|ṯbt k.l yhpk.ksa.mlk 6[49].6.25
t.ks]l h.|anš.dt.ẓr.[h].|tšu.g h.w tṣḥ[.i]k.|mǵy.aliy[n.b]‘l.|ik.mǵyt.b[t]lt.|‘nt.mẖṣ y hm[.m]ẖṣ.|bn y.hm[.mkly.ṣ] 4[51].2.22
[---.b‘l.b bht h].|[il.hd.b qr]b.hkl h.|w t‘nyn.ǵlm.b‘l.|in.b‘l.b bht ht.|il hd.b qrb.hkl h.|qšt hn.aẖd.b yd h.|w 10[76].2.3
.b ǵr.|b p y.t‘lgt.b lšn[y].|ǵr[.---]b.b pš y.t[--].|hwt.b‘l.iš[--].|šm‘ l y.ypš.[---].|ḥkr[.---].|‘ṣr[.--.]tb[-].|ṯat[.---].| 2124.4
il w aṯrt.|ẖnn il.|nṣbt il.|šlm il.|il ḥš il add.|b‘l ṣpn b‘l.|ugrt.|b mrḥ il.|b nit il.|b ṣmd il.|b dṯn il.|b šrp il.|b k 30[107].10
alp.w š.l b‘l ṣpn.|dqt l ṣpn.šrp.w šlmm.|kmm.w bbt.b‘l.ugrt.|w kdm.w npš ilib.|gdlt.il š.b‘l š.‘nt.|ṣpn.alp.w š.p UG5.13.11
š.[l] b‘l.ṣpn.|[dqt.l.ṣpn.šrp].w š[l]mm.kmm.|[w bbt.b‘l.ugrt.]kdm.w npš.|[ilib.gdlt.il.š.b]‘[l.]š.‘nt ṣpn.|[---.]w [n] 36[9].1.16
lt.il š.b‘l š.‘nt.|ṣpn.alp.w š.pdry.š.|šrp.w šlmm ilib š.|b‘l ugrt š.b‘l ẖlb š.|yrẖ š.‘nt ṣpn.alp.|w š.pdry š.ddmš š.|w UG5.13.16
ṣp ẖršẖ.|‘lm b ǵb ẖyr.|ṯmn l ṯlṯm ṣin.|šb‘.alpm.|bt b‘l.ugrt.ṯn šm.|‘lm.l ršp.mlk.|alp w.š.l b‘lt.|bwrm š.iṯtqb.| UG5.12.B.6
ug[r.---].|‘nt[.---].|tmm l bt[.---].|b[‘]l.ugr[t.---].|w ‘ṣrm[.---].|ṣlyh šr[-.---].|[ṯ]lṯm.w b[--.---]. 40[134].4
.gdlt l b‘l.|ṣpn.ilbt[.---.]d[--].|l ṣpn[.---.-]lu.|ilib[.---.b]‘l.|ugrt[.---.--]n.|[w] š l [---]. UG5.13.35
.arb‘.ḥršm.|dt.tb‘ln.b.pẖn.|ṯṯtm.ẖzr.w.‘št.‘šr.ḥrš.|dt.tb‘ln.b.ugrt.|ṯṯtm.ẖzr.|dt.tb‘ln.|b.gt.ḥršm.|ṯn.ḥršm.|[-]nb 1024.3.8
[---.b‘l.b bht h].|[il.hd.b qr]b.hkl h.|w t‘nyn.ǵlm.b‘l.|in.b‘l.b b 10[76].2.1
.b‘l.b bht h].|[il.hd.b qr]b.hkl h.|w t‘nyn.ǵlm.b‘l.|in.b‘l.b bht ht.|il hd.b qrb.hkl h.|qšt hn.aẖd.b yd h.|w qṣ‘t h. 10[76].2.4
.|ṯṯtm.ẖzr.w.‘št.‘šr.ḥrš.|dt.tb‘ln.b.ugrt.|ṯṯtm.ẖzr.|dt.tb‘ln.|b.gt.ḥršm.|ṯn.ḥršm.|[-]nbkm.|ṯn.ḥršm.|b.gt.ǵl.|[-.]n 1024.3.10
|ṯkmm.ḥmt.nša.|[y]d h.šmmh.dbḥ.|l ṯr.ab h.il.šrd.|[b‘l].b dbḥ h.bn dgn.|[b m]ṣd h.yrd.krt.|[l g]gt.‘db.akl.l qryt 14[KRT].4.170
.rkb.|ṯkmm.ḥm[t].ša.yd k.|šmm.dbḥ.l ṯr.|ab k.il.šrd.b‘l.|b dbḥ k.bn.dgn.|b mṣd k.w yrd.|krt.l ggt.‘db.|akl.l qr 14[KRT].2.77
l hwt y.yptḥ.ḥ|ln.b bht m.urbt.|b qrb.hk[l m.yp]tḥ.|b‘l.b dqt[.‘rp]t.|ql h.qdš.b[‘l.y]tn.|yṯny.b‘l.ṣ[---.-]pt h.|ql h. 4[51].7.28
‘l.w yškb.|[yd.]mizrt.p yln.mk.b šb‘.ymm.|[w]yqrb.b‘l.b ḥnt h.abynt.|[d]nil.mt.rpi anẖ.ǵzr.|[mt.]hrnmy.d in.b 17[2AQHT].1.17
[-----].|[špt.l a]rṣ.špt.l šmm.|[---.l]šn.l kbkbm.y‘rb.|[b‘]l.b kbd h.b p h yrd.|k ḥrr.zt.ybl.arṣ.w pr.|‘ṣm.yraun.aliy 5[67].2.4

d.mla.u[--.--]. | blt.p btlt.‘n[t]. | w p.n‘mt.aẖt[.b‘l]. | y‘l.b‘l.b ǵ[r.---]. | w bn.dgn.b š[---]. | b‘l.yṯb.l ks[i.mlk h]. | bn.dg 10[76].3.12
. | [ṯ]lṯ.b.ṯǵrm. | rb qrt.aḥd. | ṯmn.ḫzr. | w.arb‘.ḥršm. | dt.tb‘ln.b.pḫn. | ṯṯtm.ḫzr.w.‘št.‘šr.ḥrš. | dt.tb‘ln.b.ugrt. | ṯṯtm.ḫzr 1024.3.6
sk h. | qm.ybd.w yšr. | mṣltm.bd.n‘m. | yšr.ǵzr.ṭb.ql. | ‘l.b‘l.b ṣrrt. | ṣpn.ytmr.b‘l. | bnt h.y‘n.pdry. | bt.ar.apn.ṭly. | [bt.r 3[‘NT].1.21
b‘m.šb‘.pdr. | ṯmnym.b‘l.[----]. | tš‘m.b‘l.mr[-]. | bt[.--]b b‘l.b qrb. | bt.w y‘n.aliyn. | b‘l.ašt m.kṯr bn. | ym.kṯr.bnm.‘dt. 4[51].7.13
ḫšt.klbt.ilm išt. | klt.bt.il.ḏbb.imtḫṣ.ksp. | itrṯ.ḫrṣ.ṭrd.b‘l. | b mrym.ṣpn.mšṣṣ.[-]k‘[-]. | udn h.grš h.l ksi.mlk h. | l nḫ 3[‘NT].3.44
šd.aḫd bt. | rbt.kmn.hkl. | w y‘n.kṯr.w ḫss. | šm‘.l aliyn b‘l. | bn.l rkb.‘rpt. | bl.ašt.urbt.b bh[t] m. | ḥln.b qrb.hkl m. | 4[51].5.121
ṯṭb.b‘l.l[hwt y]. | ṯn.rgm.k[ṯr.w]ḫss. | šm‘.m‘.l al[iy]n b‘l. | bl.ašt.ur[bt.]b bht m. | ḥln.b qr[b.hk]l m. | w ‘n.ali[yn.]b‘ 4[51].6.4
yiḫd.b‘l.bn.aṯrt. | rbm.ymḫṣ.b ktp. | dk ym.ymḫṣ.b ṣmd. | ṣḥr mt.y 6[49].5.1
.yd.ṯn.bn h. | b‘lm.w.ṯlṯ.n‘rm.w.bt.aḥt. | bn.lwn.ṯlṯtm.b‘lm. | bn.b‘ly.ṯlṯtm.b‘lm. | w.aḥd.ḫbṯ. | w.arb‘.aṯt. | bn.lg.ṯn.b 2080.6
bn.ǵs.ḫrš.š‘ty. | ‘dy.bn.sl‘y.gbly. | yrm.b‘l.bn.kky. 2121.3
h.w yḥd. | [i]n.šmt.in.‘ẓm.yšu.g[h]. | w yṣḥ.knp.hrgb.b‘l.ybn. | [b]‘l.ybn.diy.hwt.hrg[b]. | tpr.w du.b nši.‘n h. | [w]y 19[1AQHT].3.132
. | [i]n.šmt.in.‘ẓm.yšu.g[h]. | w yṣḥ.knp.hrgb.b‘l.ybn. | [b]‘l.ybn.diy.hwt.hrg[b]. | tpr.w du.b nši.‘n h. | [w]yphn.yḥd. 19[1AQHT].3.133
[yḥd]. | in.šmt.in.‘ẓm.yšu.g h. | w yṣḥ.knp.nšrm.ybn. | b‘l.ybn.diy hmt nšrm. | tpr.w du.b nši.‘n h.w ypn. | yḥd.hrgb 19[1AQHT].3.119
| mṣltm.bd.n‘m. | yšr.ǵzr.ṭb.ql. | ‘l.b‘l.b ṣrrt. | ṣpn.ytmr.b‘l. | bnt h.y‘n.pdry. | bt.ar.apn.ṭly. | [bt.r]b.pdr.yd‘. | [---]t.im[3[‘NT].1.22
. | i[l]. | dgn. | b‘[l ṣ]pn. | b‘lm. | [b‘]lm. | [b‘]lm. | [b‘]lm. | [b‘]lm. | [b‘]lm. | [b‘l]m. | [arṣ] w šm[m]. | [-----]. | [a]rṣ. | [u]šḫr[y]. | [‘]ṯtr 29[17].1.10
n. | il[i]b. | i[l]. | dgn. | b‘[l ṣ]pn. | b‘lm. | [b‘]lm. | [b‘]lm. | [b‘]lm. | [b‘]lm. | [b‘]lm. | [b‘l]m. | [arṣ] w šm[m]. | [-----]. | [a]rṣ. | [u]šḫr[29[17].1.9
il ṣpn. | il[i]b. | i[l]. | dgn. | b‘[l ṣ]pn. | b‘lm. | [b‘]lm. | [b‘]lm. | [b‘]lm. | [b‘]lm. | [b‘]lm. | [b‘l]m. | [arṣ] w šm[m]. | [-----]. | [a]rṣ. 29[17].1.8
il ṣpn. | il[i]b. | i[l]. | dgn. | b‘[l ṣ]pn. | b‘lm. | [b‘]lm. | [b‘]lm. | [b‘]lm. | [b‘]lm. | [b‘]lm. | [b‘l]m. | [arṣ] w šm[m]. | [----- 29[17].1.7
il ṣpn. | il[i]b. | i[l]. | dgn. | b‘[l ṣ]pn. | b‘lm. | [b‘]lm. | [b‘]lm. | [b‘]lm. | [b‘]lm. | [b‘l]m. | [arṣ] w šm[m] 29[17].1.6
. | b hm.qrnm. | km.ṯrm.w gbṯt. | km.ibrm. | w b hm.pn.b‘l. | b‘l.ytlk.w yṣd. | yḥ pat.mlbr. | wn.ymǵy.aklm. | w ymẓa.‘ 12[75].1.33
ḫrt.ilm.arṣ.b p h.rgm.l[yṣ]a. | b špt h.hwt h.knp.ṣml.b‘[l]. | b‘l.ṯbr.diy.hyt.tq[l.tḥt]. | p‘n h.ybq‘.kbd h.w yḥd. | iṯ.š 19[1AQHT].3.142
pn. | b alp.šd.rbt.kmn. | ṣḥq.btlt.‘nt.tšu. | g h.w tṣḥ.tbšr b‘l. | bšrt k.yblt.y[b]n. | bt.l k.km.aḫ k.w ḥẓr. | km.ary k.ṣḥ.ḫr 4[51].5.88
bt.il. | b‘l.bt.aḏmny. | b‘l.bt.pdy. | b‘l.bt.nqly. | b‘l.bt.‘lr. | b‘l.bt.ssl. | b 31[14].2
.bt.ssl. | b‘l.bt.ṯrn. | b‘l.bt.ktmn. | b‘l.bt.ndbd. | [--].ṣnr. | [b‘l].bt.bsn. | [-----]. | b[--.---]. 31[14].11
l]at.b hkl m. | sb.ksp.l rqm.ḫrṣ. | nṣb.l lbnt.šmḫ. | aliyn.b‘l.ht y.bnt. | dt.ksp.hkl y.dtm. | ḫrṣ.‘dbt.bht[h.b‘]l. | y‘db.hd 4[51].6.36
‘l.bt.pdy. | b‘l.bt.nqly. | b‘l.bt.‘lr. | b‘l.bt.ssl. | b‘l.bt.ṯrn. | b‘l.bt.ktmn. | b‘l.bt.ndbd. | [--].ṣnr. | [b‘l].bt.bsn. | [-----]. | b[--.- 31[14].8
.bt.nqly. | b‘l.bt.‘lr. | b‘l.bt.ssl. | b‘l.bt.ṯrn. | b‘l.bt.ktmn. | b‘l.bt.ndbd. | [--].ṣnr. | [b‘l].bt.bsn. | [-----]. | b[--.---]. 31[14].9
bt.il. | b‘l.bt.aḏmny. | b‘l.bt.pdy. | b‘l.bt.nqly. | b‘l.bt.‘lr. | b‘l.bt.ssl. | b‘l.bt.ṯrn. | b‘l.bt.ktmn. | b‘l. 31[14].4
t.il. | b‘l.bt.aḏmny. | b‘l.bt.pdy. | b‘l.bt.nqly. | b‘l.bt.‘lr. | b‘l.bt.ssl. | b‘l.bt.ṯrn. | b‘l.bt.ktmn. | b‘l.bt.ndbd. | [--].ṣnr. | [b‘l] 31[14].6
bt.il. | b‘l.bt.aḏmny. | b‘l.bt.pdy. | b‘l.bt.nqly. | b‘l.bt.‘lr. | b‘l.bt.ssl. | b‘l.bt.ṯrn. | b‘l.bt.ktmn. | b‘l.bt.ndbd. | [--] 31[14].5
bt.il. | b‘l.bt.aḏmny. | b‘l.bt.pdy. | b‘l.bt.nqly. | b‘l.bt.‘lr. | b‘l.bt.ssl. | b‘l.bt.ṯrn. | b‘l.bt 31[14].3
.aḏmny. | b‘l.bt.pdy. | b‘l.bt.nqly. | b‘l.bt.‘lr. | b‘l.bt.ssl. | b‘l.bt.ṯrn. | b‘l.bt.ktmn. | b‘l.bt.ndbd. | [--].ṣnr. | [b‘l].bt.bsn. | [- 31[14].7
‘l.w yšt.ym.ykly.ṯpṭ.nhr. | b šm.tg‘r m.‘ṯtrt.bṯ l aliyn.[b‘l.] | bṯ.l rkb.‘rpt.k šby n.zb[l.ym.k] | šby n.ṯpṭ.nhr.w yṣa b[2.4[68].28
pgr.w ṯrmnm.bt mlk. | il[bt].gdlt.ušḫry.gdlt.ym gdlt. | b‘l gdlt.yrḫ.gdlt. | gdlt.ṯrmn.gdlt.pdry.gdlt dqt. | dqt.trṯ.dqt. 34[1].14
. | [b]‘l š.aṯrt.š.ṯkmn w šnm.š. | ‘nt.š.ršp.š.dr il w p[ḫ]r b‘l. | gdlt.šlm.gdlt.w burm.[l]b. | rmṣt.ilhm.b‘lm.dṯt.w kšm.ḫ 34[1].7
b‘[l.š].aṯrt[.š.ṯkm]n w [šnm.š]. | ‘nt š ršp š[.dr.il.w pḫr.b‘l]. | gdlt.šlm[.gdlt.w burm.lb]. | rmṣt.ilh[m.b‘lm.---]. | ksm.ṯ 35[3].16
kbd.w.db[ḥ.---]. | [--].aṯrt.‘ṣr[m.l inš.ilm]. | [ṯ]ṭb.mdbḥ.b‘l.g[dlt.---]. | dqt.l.ṣpn.w.dqt[.---]. | ṯn.l.‘šrm.pamt.[---]. | š.dd 35[3].41
[l.---.kbd]. | w bdḥ.k[--.---]. | ‘ṣrm.l i[nš.ilm.ṯb.md] | bḥ.b‘l.[gdlt.---.dqt]. | l ṣpn.w [dqt.---.ṯn.l ‘š] | rm.pam[t.---]. | š dd APP.II[173].45
.b‘l.š.aṯrt.š]. | ṯkmn.w š[nm.š.‘nt.š.ršp.š.dr]. | il.w pḫr[.b‘l.gdlt.šlm.gdlt]. | w burm.l[b.rmṣt.ilhm]. | b‘lm.w mlu[.---. APP.II[173].18
rḫ.w y | rḫ yar k. | [ašr ilht kṯrt bn] | t hll.snnt.bnt h | ll b‘l gml.yrdt. | b ‘rgzm.b bz tdm. | lla y.‘m lẓpn i | l ḏ.pid.hn b 24[77].42
t]. | yrṯḥṣ.mlk.b[rr]. | b ym.mlat. | tqln.alpm. | yrḫ.‘šrt.l b‘[l]. | dqtm.w ynt.qr[t]. | w mtntm.š l rmš. | w kbd.w š.l šlm UG5.13.5
r il w p[ḫ]r b‘l. | gdlt.šlm.gdlt.w burm.[l]b. | rmṣt.ilhm.b‘lm.dṯt.w kšm.ḫmš. | ‘tr h.mlun.šnpt.ḫṣt h.b‘l.ṣpn š. | [--]ṯ š. 34[1].9
bt šbn. | iy‘dm.w b‘l h. | ddy. | ‘my. | iwrnr. | alnr. | maḫdt. | aby. | [-----]. | [-]nt. | y 107[15].2
pṭ.nhr.mlak.mṯḫr.yḥb[-.---.] | [---].mlak.bn.ktpm.rgm.b‘l h.w y[--.---]. | [---].ap.anš.zbl.b‘l.šdmt.bg[--.---]. | [---.-]dm 2.1[137].42
]at.iqnu. | argmn.nqmd.mlk. | ugrt.d ybl.l špš. | mlk.rb.b‘l h. | ks.ḫrṣ.ktn.mit.pḥm. | mit.iqni.l mlkt. | ks.ḫrṣ.ktn.mit. 64[118].26
ṯḥm.ydn.‘m.mlk. | b‘l h.nǵr.ḥwt k. | w l.a[--]t.tšknn. | ḫmšm.l mi[t].any. | tškn[n. 2062.1.2
w l n[qmd.---]. | [w]nqmd.[---]. | [-.]‘mn.šp[š.mlk.rb]. | b‘l h.šlm.[w spš]. | mlk.rb.b‘l h.[---]. | nqmd.mlk.ugr[t.--]. | ph 64[118].12
n. | [---.--]m. | [---].pi[--.-]qš. | [--]pš.šn[--]. | ṯ[-]r.b iš[-]. | b‘l h.š‘[-]rt. | ḫqr.[--.ṯq]]l rb. | ṯl[ṯ.---]. | aḥt.ḫm[-.---]. | b ym.db 39[19].9
.[---]. | [-.]‘mn.šp[š.mlk.rb]. | b‘l h.šlm.[w spš]. | mlk.rb.b‘l h.[---]. | nqmd.mlk.ugr[t.--]. | phy. | w ṯpllm.mlk.r[b.--]. | 64[118].13
ksu. | ṯbt.ḫḫ.arṣ.nḥlt h.tša. | g hm.w tṣḥ.ṯḥm.aliyn. | bn.b‘l.hwt.aliy.qrdm. | bhṯ.bn.ilm.mt.‘bd k.an. | w d ‘lm k.šmḫ. 5[67].2.18
‘rpt. | tb‘.rgm.l bn.ilm.mt. | ṯny.l ydd.il ǵzr. | ṯḥm.aliyn.b‘l.hwt.aliy. | qrdm.bhṯ.l bn.ilm mt. | ‘bd k.an.w d.‘lm k. | tb‘. 5[67].2.10
wt.w rgm. | l bn.ilm.mt. | ṯny.l ydd. | il.ǵzr.ṯḥm. | aliyn.b‘l. | [hw]t.aliy.q | [rdm.]bht y.bnt. | [dt.ksp.dtm]. | [ḫrṣ.hk]l y 4[51].8.33
y[‘bdr.---]. | rgm l btl[t.‘nt.ṯny.l ybmt.limm.ṯḥm.aliyn.b‘l]. | hw[t.aliy.qrdm.qryy.b arṣ.mlḥmt.šṯ]. | [b ‘]pr[m.ddym 7.2[130].13
d hyt. | w rgm.l btlt.‘nt. | ṯny.l ymmt.limm. | ṯḥm.aliyn.b‘l.hwt. | aliy.qrdm.qry.b arṣ. | mlḥmt šṯ.b ‘pr m.ddym. | sk.šl 3[‘NT].3.10
‘n.ǵlmm.y‘nyn.l ib.yp‘. | l b‘l.ṣrt.l rkb.‘rpt. | ṯḥm.aliyn.b‘l.hwt.aliy. | qrdm.qry.b arṣ.mlḥmt. | šṯ.b ‘p[r] m.ddym.sk.š 3[‘NT].4.51
w rgm.l kṯr. | w ḫss.ṯny.l h | yn.d ḥrš.ydm. | ṯḥm.al[iyn.b‘l]. | h[wt.aliy.qrdm]. 3[‘NT.VI].6.24
m.qrnm. | km.ṯrm.w gbṯt. | km.ibrm. | w b hm.pn.b‘l. | b‘l.ytlk.w yṣd. | yḥ pat.mlbr. | wn.ymǵy.aklm. | w ymẓa.‘qqm 12[75].1.34
.d[--.--]i. | [--]t.mdt h[.l.]‘ṯtrt.šd. | [---.-]rt.mḫṣ.bnš.mlk.yb‘l hm. | [---.--]t.w.ḫpn.l.azzlt. | [---.]l.‘ṯtrt.šd. | [---].yb‘lnn. | [1106.53
bn.b‘ln.biry. | ṯlṯ.b‘lm. | w.adn hm.ṯr.w.arb‘.bnt h. | yrḫm.yd.ṯn.bn h. | b‘lm.w. 2080.2
w.ṯlṯ.n‘rm.w.bt.aḥt. | bn.lwn.ṯlṯtm.b‘lm. | bn.b‘ly.ṯlṯtm.b‘lm. | w.aḥd.ḫbṯ. | w.arb‘.aṯt. | bn.lg.ṯn.bn h. | b‘lm.w.aḫt h. | 2080.7
‘ly.ṯlṯtm.b‘lm. | w.aḥd.ḫbṯ. | w.arb‘.aṯt. | bn.lg.ṯn.bn h. | b‘lm.w.aḫt h. | b.šrt. | šty.w.bn h. 2080.11
h.ngrt[.i]lht. | kḥṣ.k m‘r[.---]. | yṣḥ.ngr il.ilš. | ilš.ngr.bt.b‘l. | w aṯt h.ngrt.ilht. | w y‘n.lṭpn.il d pi[d]. | šm‘.l ngr.il il[š]. 16[126].4.8
ilht. | w y‘n.lṭpn.il d pi[d]. | šm‘.l ngr.il il[š]. | ilš.ngr bt b‘l. | w aṯt k.ngrt.il[ht]. | ‘l.l ṯkm.bnw n. | l nḫnpt.mšpy. | ṯlṯ.k 16[126].4.12

.[b‘]l knp. | [---.g]dlt.ṣpn.dqt.šrp.w [š]lmm. | [---.a]lp.l b‘l.w aṯrt.‘ṣr[m] l inš. | [ilm.---].lbbmm.gdlt.‘rb špš w ḥl. | [m 36[9].1.8
.w b ṣpn. | b n‘m.b ǵr.t[l]iyt. | ql.l b‘l.ttnn. | bšrt.il.bš[r.b‘]l. | w bšr.ḥtk.dgn. | k.ibr.l b‘l[.yl]d. | w rum.l rkb.‘rpt. | yšm 10[76].3.34
š.l [hrm.ǵrpl].‘l.arṣ.l an. | [ḫ]mt.i[l.w] ḥrn.yisp.ḥmt. | [b‘l.w]dgn[.yi]sp.ḥmt.‘nt.w ‘ṯtrt. | [ti]sp.ḥmt.y[r]ḫ.w.ršp.yisp UG5.8.14
[k mt.aliyn.b‘l]. | k ḫlq.z[bl.b‘l.arṣ]. | w hm.ḥy.a[liyn.b‘l]. | w hm.iṯ.zbl.b‘[l.arṣ]. | b ḥlm.lṭpn.il.d pid. | b ḏrt.bny.bn 6[49].3.2
hyt.‘n. | l arṣ.m[ṭ]r.b‘l. | w l šd.mṭr.‘ly. | n‘m.l arṣ.mṭr.b‘l. | w l šd.mṭr.‘ly. | n‘m.l ḥṭt.b gn. | bm.nrt.ksmm. | ‘l.tl[-]k.‘ṭ 16[126].3.7
.arṣ.w šmm. | sb.l qṣm.arṣ. | l ksm.mhyt.‘n. | l arṣ.m[ṭ]r.b‘l. | w l šd.mṭr.‘ly. | n‘m.l arṣ.mṭr.b‘l. | w l šd.mṭr.‘ly. | n‘m.l 16[126].3.5
.il.mt m. | y‘bš.brk n.šm.il.ǵzrm. | ṯm.ṯmq.rpu.b‘l.mhr b‘l. | w mhr.‘nt.ṯm.yḥpn.ḥyl | y.zbl.mlk.‘llm y.km.tdd. | ‘nt.ṣd 22.2[124].8
| ii.w pḫr[.b‘l.gdlt.šlm.gdlt]. | w burm.l[b.rmṣt.ilhm]. | b‘lm.w mlu[.---.ksm]. | ṯlṯm.w m‘rb[.---]. | dbḥ šmn mr[.šmn. APP.II[173].20
ṯtr.‘rẓ. | l amlk.b ṣrrt.ṣpn. | yrd.‘ṯtr.‘rẓ.yrd. | l kḥṯ.aliyn.b‘l. | w ymlk.b arṣ.il.kl h. | [---] š abn.b rḥbt. | [---] š abn.b kk 6.1.64[49.1.36]
h. | aḫd.yd h.b škrn.m‘ms h. | [k]šb‘ yn.spu.ksm h.bt.b‘l. | [w m]nt h bt.il.ṯḫ.gg h.b ym. | [ti]ṭ.rḥṣ.npṣ h.b ym.rṭ. | [- 17[2AQHT].1.32
.ln.aḫd.yd y.b š | krn m‘ms y k šb‘t yn. | spu.ksm y.bt.b‘l.[w]mn[t]. | y.bt.il.ṯḫ.gg y.b ym.ṭiṭ. | rḥṣ.npṣ y.b ym.rṭ. | d 17[2AQHT].2.21
[r.aṯr k.ṯbq]. | lḥt.niṣ k.gr[š.d ‘šy.ln k]. | spu.ksm k.bt.[b‘l.w mnt k]. | bt il.aḫd.yd k.b [škrn]. | m‘ms k.k šb‘t.yn.ṭ[ḫ]. 17[2AQHT].2.4
p.w tr.b ‘p. | tk.aḫ šmk.mlat rumm. | w yšu.‘n h.aliyn.b‘l. | w yšu.‘n h.w y‘n. | w y‘n.btlt.‘nt. | n‘mt.bn.aḫt.b‘l. | l pnn 10[76].2.13
.š[p]š. | šd yn.‘n.b qbt[.t] | bl lyt.‘l.umt k. | w abqṯ.aliyn.b‘l. | w t‘n.btlt.‘nt. | an.l an.y špš. | an.l an.il.yǵr[.-]. | ṯǵr k.š[-- 6[49].4.44
. | [adn]km.ṯpṭ.nhr.tn.il m.d tq h.d tqyn h. | [hml]t.tn.b‘l.w ‘nn h.bn.dgn.art m.pḏ h. | [w y‘n.]ṯr.ab h.il.‘bd k.b‘l.y 2.1[137].35
‘l km.adn km.ṯ[pṭ.nhr]. | tn.il m.d tq h.d tqyn.hmlt.tn.b‘l.[w ‘nn h]. | bn.dgn.art m.pḏ h.tb‘.ǵlmm.l ṯṯb.[idk.pnm]. | 2.1[137].18
ḫl]. | b n‘mm.b ys[mm.---]. | arḫ.arḫ.[---.tld]. | ibr.tld[.l b‘l]. | w rum.l[rkb.‘rpt]. | ṯḥbq.[---]. | ṯḥbq[.---]. | w tksynn.bṯn 10[76].3.21
r.yprsḥ.ym.yql. | l arṣ.tnǵṣn.pnt h.w ydlp.tmn h. | yqṯ b‘l.w yšt.ym.ykly.ṯpṭ.nhr. | b šm.tg‘r m.‘ṯtrt.bṯ l aliyn.[b‘l.] | 2.4[68].27
ṯ.b‘lm. | w.adn hm.ṯr.w.arb‘.bnt h. | yrḫm.yd.ṯn.bn h. | b‘lm.w.ṯlṯ.n‘rm.w.bt.aḥt. | bn.lwn.ṯlṯtm.b‘lm. | bn.b‘ly.ṯlṯtm. 2080.5
.zb[l.ym.k] | šby n.ṯpṭ.nhr.w yṣa b[.--]. | ybṯ.nn.aliyn.b‘l.w [---]. | ym.l mt.b‘l m.ym l[--.---]. | ḥm.l šrr.w [---]. | y‘n.y 2.4[68].31
ynsk.‘[-]. | [--]y.l arṣ[.id]y.alt.l aḫš.idy.alt.in l y. | [--]t.b‘l.ḥẓ.ršp.b[n].km.yr.klyt h.w lb h. | [ṯ]n.p k.b ǵr.ṯn.p k.b ḫl 1001.1.3
ḫss.l brlt.hyn d. | ḥrš yd.šlḥm.ššqy. | ilm sad.kbd.hmt.b‘l. | ḥkpt.il.kl h.tšm‘. | mṯt.dnty.t‘db.imr. | b pḫd.l npš.kṯr.w 17[2AQHT].5.20
| qṣ‘t.apnk.mṯt.dnty. | tšlḥm.tššqy ilm. | tsad.tkbd.hmt.b‘l. | ḥkpt il.kl h.tb‘.kṯr. | l ahl h.hyn.tb‘.l mš | knt h.apnk.dni 17[2AQHT].5.30
m]m h.nšat ẓl h kbkbm. | [---.]b km kbkbt k ṯn. | [---.]b‘l yḥmdn h.yrt y. | [---.]dmrn.l pn h yrd. | [---.]b‘l.šm[.--.]rg 2001.2.7
w yṣd. | yḥ pat.mlbr. | wn.ymǵy.aklm. | w ymẓa.‘qqm. | b‘l.ḥmd m.yḥmd m. | bn.dgn.yhrr m. | b‘l.ngṯ hm.b p‘n h. | w 12[75].1.38
-]n[-.---]. | il.ḫyr.ilib.š. | arṣ w šmm.š. | il.š.kṯrt.š. | dgn.š.b‘l.ḫlb alp w š. | b‘l ṣpn alp.w.š. | ṯrty.alp.w.š. | yrḫ.š.ṣpn.š. | kṯ UG5.9.2.4
.‘nt. | ṣpn.alp.w š.pdry.š. | šrp.w šlmm ilib š. | b‘l ugrt š.b‘l ḫlb š. | yrḫ š.‘nt ṣpn.alp. ¦ w š.pdry š.ddmš š. | w b urbt.ili UG5.13.16
br. | l ysmt.šd.šḫlmmt. | mǵny.l b‘l.npl.l a | rṣ.mt.aliyn.b‘l. | ḫlq.zbl.b‘l.arṣ. | apnk.lṭpn.il. | d pid.yrd.l ksi.yṯb. | l hdm[5[67].6.9
[-----]. | [---.--]ḫ. | [---.--]n. | [-----]. | [---.-]bd. | [---]yb‘.b‘l.ḫr[-]. | pqr.yḥd. | bn.ktmn.ṯǵr.hk[l]. | bn.ṯgbr.ṯǵr.hk[l]. | bn 1056.6
m. | [k g]mn.aliyn.b‘l. | [ṭṭ]bḫ.šb‘m.ṣin. | [k gm]n.aliyn.b‘l. | [ṭṭb]ḫ.šb‘m.aylm. | [k gmn.]aliyn.b‘l. | [ṭṭbḫ.š]b‘m.y‘lm. | 6[62].1.23
.tštnn.b ḫrt. | ilm.arṣ.ṭṭbḫ.šb‘m. | rumm.k gmn.aliyn. | [b]‘l.ṭṭbḫ.šb‘m.alpm. | [k g]mn.aliyn.b‘l. | [ṭṭ]bḫ.šb‘m.ṣin. | [k g 6[62].1.20
. | [k gmn.]aliyn.b‘l. | [ṭṭbḫ.š]b‘m.y‘lm. | [k gmn.al]iyn.b‘l. | [ṭṭbḫ.šb‘m.]ḥmrm. | [k gm]n.al[i]yn.b[‘l]. | [---]ḫ h.tšt b 6[62].1.27
. | [k gm]n.aliyn.b‘l. | [ṭṭb]ḫ.šb‘m.aylm. | [k gmn.]aliyn.b‘l. | [ṭṭbḫ.š]b‘m.y‘lm. | [k gmn.al]iyn.b‘l. | [ṭṭbḫ.šb‘m.]ḥmrm. 6[62].1.25
m.k gmn.aliyn. | [b]‘l.ṭṭbḫ.šb‘m.alpm. | [k g]mn.aliyn.b‘l. | [ṭṭ]bḫ.šb‘m.ṣin. | [k gm]n.aliyn.b‘l. | [ṭṭb]ḫ.šb‘m.aylm. | [6[62].1.21
y y. | w lḥm m ‘m aḫ y.lḥm. | w št m.‘m.a[ḫ] yn. | p nšt.b‘l.[ṭ]‘n.iṭ‘n k. | [---.]ma[---] k.k tmḫṣ. | [ltn.bṯn.br]ḥ.tkly. | [bṯ 5[67].1.26
w.k.rgm.špš. | mlk.rb.b‘l y.u. | ‘[--.]mlakt.‘bd h. | [---.]b‘l k.yḥpn. | [---.]‘m h.u ky. | [1018.2
.yrgm.mlk. | b‘l y.tmǵyy.hn. | alpm.ššwm.hnd. | w.mlk.b‘l y.bnš. | bnny.‘mn. | mlakty.hnd. | ylak ‘m y. | w.t‘l.ṯ.th.hn. | [1012.33
.---]. | mlk.r[b.b‘]l y.p.l. | ḥy.np[š.a]rš. | l.pn.b‘[l y.l].pn.b‘l y. | w.urk.ym.b‘l y. | l.pn.amn.w.l.pn. | il.mṣrm.dt.tǵrn. | n 1018.19
| l ‘bd h.alpm.š[šw]m. | rgmt.‘ly.ṯh.lm. | l.ytn.hm.mlk.[b]‘l y. | w.hn.ibm.ššq l y. | p.l.ašt.aṯt y. | n‘r y.ṯh.l pn.ib. | hn.h 1012.26
š.‘lm.l.‘ṯtrt. | l.‘nt.l.kl.il.alṯ[y]. | nmry.mlk.‘lm. | mlk n.b‘l y.ḥw[t.--]. | yšhr k.w.‘m.ṣ[--]. | ‘š[--.---]d.lik[t.---]. | w [----]. 2008.1.10
‘l.w ‘nn h.bn.dgn.art m.pḏ h. | [w y‘n.]ṯr.ab h.il.‘bd k.b‘l.y ym m.‘bd k.b‘l. | [--.--]m.bn.dgn.a[s]r km.hw ybl.argm 2.1[137].36
dt.qr[t]. | [---.]dt nzdt.m[lk]. | [---.]w.ap.bṯn[.---]. | [---.]b‘l y.y[--]. | [---.-]l[-.---]. 2127.2.7
l y.p.l. | ḥy.np[š.a]rš. | l.pn.b‘[l y.l].pn.b‘l y. | w.urk.ym.b‘l y. | l.pn.amn.w.l.pn. | il.mṣrm.dt.tǵrn. | npš.špš.mlk. | rb.b‘ 1018.20
[k.---]. | arš[.---]. | mlk.r[b.b‘]l y.p.l. | ḥy.np[š.a]rš. | l.pn.b‘[l y.l].pn.b‘l y. | w.urk.ym.b‘l y. | l.pn.amn.w.l.pn. | il.mṣrm 1018.19
l.p‘n.b‘l y[.mrḥqtm]. | šb‘ d.w.šb‘[d.qlt]. | ankn.rgmt.l.b‘l y. | l.špš.‘lm.l.‘ṯtrt. | l.‘nt.l.kl.il.alṯ[y]. | nmry.mlk.‘lm. | mlk 2008.1.6
--.]adt y.td‘. | w.ap.mlk.ud[r]. | [-]d‘.k.iḫd.[---]. | w.mlk.b‘l y. | lm.škn.hnk. | l ‘bd h.alpm.š[šw]m. | rgmt.‘ly.ṯh.lm. | l.y 1012.22
]. | klyn.apsn[y.---]. | plzn.qrty[.---]. | w.klt h.b.t[--.---]. | b‘l y.mlk[y.---]. | yd.bt h.yd[.---]. | ary.yd.t[--.---]. | ḫtn h.šb‘l[81[329].13
[--]. | ‘bd k. | l p‘n.b‘l y. | ṯn id.šb‘ d. | mrḥqtm. | qlt.‘m. | b‘l y.mnm. | šlm. | [r]gm[.ṯṯb]. | [l.]‘bd[k]. 2115.2.9
l y. | p.l.ašt.aṯt y. | n‘r y.ṯh.l pn.ib. | hn.hm.yrgm.mlk. | b‘l y.tmǵyy.hn. | alpm.ššwm.hnd. | w.mlk.b‘l y.bnš. | bnny.‘m 1012.31
[---.mlk]. | rb[.b‘l y.---]. | w.an[k.---]. | arš[.---]. | mlk.r[b.b‘]l y.p.l. | ḥy.np[š.a]rš. | l.pn.b‘[l y.l].pn.b‘l y. | w.urk.ym.b‘l 1018.17
l.ḏrdn. | b‘l y.rgm. | bn.ḫrn k. | mǵy. | hbṭ.hw. | ḫrd.w.šl hw. | qr[-]. | akl 2114.2
[l.ml]k.[b‘l y]. | rg[m]. | ṯḥm.wr[--]. | yšlm.[l] k. | ilm.t[ǵ]r k. | tšlm k. | l 2010.1
. | ṯḥm.t[g]yn. | bn k. | l.p[‘n.adn y]. | q[lt.---]. | l.yb[nn]. | b‘l y.r[gm]. | ṯḥm.‘bd[--]. | ‘bd k. | l p‘n.b‘l y. | ṯn id.šb‘ d. | mrḥ 2115.2.2
l.mlk.b[‘l y]. | r[gm]. | ṯḥm.rb.mi[--.‘]bd k. | l.p‘n.b‘l y[.mrḥqtm]. | š 2008.1.1
l.mlk.b‘[l] y. | rgm. | ṯḥm.ṯpṭb[‘l]. | [‘]bd k. | [l.p]‘n.b‘l y. | [šb‘] d.šb‘ [2063.1
l.mlk.b[‘l y]. | r[gm]. | ṯḥm.rb.mi[--.‘]bd k. | l.p‘n.b‘l y[.mrḥqtm]. | šb‘ d.w.šb‘[d.qlt]. | ankn.rgmt.l.b‘l y. | l.špš. 2008.1.4
l.mlk.b‘[l] y. | rgm. | ṯḥm.ṯpṭb[‘l]. | [‘]bd k. | [l.p]‘n.b‘l y. | [šb‘] d.šb‘ [d]. | [mr]ḥqtm. | qlt. | ‘bd k.b. | lwsnd. | [w] b 2063.5
t.---]. | l.yb[nn]. | b‘l y.r[gm]. | ṯḥm.‘bd[--]. | ‘bd k. | l p‘n.b‘l y. | ṯn id.šb‘ d. | mrḥqtm. | qlt.‘m. | b‘l y.mnm. | šlm. | [r]gm 2115.2.5
-.]mlk. | rb.b[‘l y.---]. | [-----]. | r[--.---]. | b.[---.mlk]. | rb[.b‘l y.---]. | w.an[k.---]. | arš[.---]. | mlk.r[b.b‘]l y.p.l. | ḥy.np[š.a 1018.14
---.]‘m h.u ky. | [---.--]d k.k.tmǵy. | ml[--.--]š[.ml]k.rb. | b[‘l y.---]. | yd[--.]mlk. | rb.b[‘l y.---]. | [-----]. | r[--.---]. | b.[---.m 1018.8
m.ṯn.[---]. | hn dt.[---]. | [-----]. | [-----]. | ṯḥm[.---]. | l p‘n.b‘l y[.---]. | qlt. | [--]t.mlk.d.y[mlk]. | [--.]‘bdyrḫ.l.ml[k]. | [--]t. 2064.10
.tmǵy. | ml[--.--]š[.ml]k.rb. | b[‘l y.---]. | yd[--.]mlk. | rb.b[‘l y.---]. | [-----]. | r[--.---]. | b.[---.mlk]. | rb[.b‘l y.---]. | w.an[k 1018.10
. | l.pn.amn.w.l.pn. | il.mṣrm.dt.tǵrn. | npš.špš.mlk. | rb.b‘l y. 1018.24

[---.t]št.rimt. | l irt h.mšr.l.dd.aliyn. | b‘l.yd.pdry.bt.ar. | ahbt.ṭly.bt.rb.dd.arṣy. | bt.y‘bdr.km ǵlmm 3[‘NT].3.3
t ḫbly. | špš pgr. | iltm ḫnqtm. | yrḫ kṭy. | ygb hd. | yrgb b‘l. | ydb il. | yarš il. | yrǵm il. | ‘mtr. | ydb il. | yrgb lim. | ‘mtr. | UG5.14.B.2
ydb il. | yrgb lim. | ‘mtr. | yarš il. | ydb b‘l. | yrǵm b‘l. | ‘z b‘l. | ydb hd. UG5.14.B.13
. | ql.l b‘l.ttnn. | bšrt.il.bš[r.b‘]l. | w bšr.ḥtk.dgn. | k.ibr.l b‘l[.yl]d. | w rum.l rkb.‘rpt. | yšmḫ.aliyn.b‘l. 10[76].3.36
.yšu.g h.w yṣḥ. | b‘l.mt.my.lim.bn. | dgn.my.hmlt.aṯr. | b‘l.ard.b arṣ.ap. | ‘nt.ttlk.w tṣd.kl.ǵr. | l kbd.arṣ.kl.gb‘. | l [k]b 5[67].6.25
b.k ‘mq.ttlṯ.bmt. | b‘l.mt.my.lim.bn dgn. | my.hmlt.aṯr.b‘l.nrd. | b arṣ.‘m h.trd.nrt. | ilm.špš.‘d.tšb‘.bk. | tšt.k yn.udm 6[62].1.7
ilbt. | ušḫry. | ym.b‘l. | yrḫ. | kṯr. | ṯrmn. | pdry. | dqt. | trṯ. | ršp. | ‘nt ḫbly. | špš pgr UG5.14.A.3
. | yrǵm il. | ‘mtr. | ydb il. | yrgb lim. | ‘mtr. | yarš il. | ydb b‘l. | yrǵm b‘l. | ‘z b‘l. | ydb hd. UG5.14.B.11
‘l.bkm.b arr. | bm.arr.w b ṣpn. | b n‘m.b ǵr.t[l]iyt. | ql.l b‘l.ttnn. | bšrt.il.bš[r.b‘]l. | w bšr.ḥtk.dgn. | k.ibr.l b‘l[.yl]d. | w 10[76].3.33
.urbt. | b qrb.hk[l m.yp]tḥ. | b‘l.b dqt[.‘rp]t. | ql h.qdš.b[‘l.y]tn. | ytny.b‘l.ṣ[---.-]pt h. | ql h.q[dš.ṭb]r.arṣ. | [---.]ǵrm[.t 4[51].7.29
b‘l.ytb.k ṯbt.ǵr.hd.r[‘y]. | k mdb.b tk.ǵr h.il ṣpn.b [tk]. | ǵr.tli UG5.3.1.1
p.n‘mt.aḫt[.b‘l]. | y‘l.b‘l.b ǵ[r.---]. | w bn.dgn.b š[---]. | b‘l.ytb.l ks[i.mlk h]. | bn.dgn.l kḥ[ṯ.drkt h]. | l alp.ql.ẓ[--.---]. 10[76].3.14
. | yru.bn ilm t.ṯt‘.y | dd.il.ǵzr.y‘r.mt. | b ql h.y[---.---]. | b‘l.yṯtbn[.l ksi]. | mlk h.l[nḫt.l kḥṯ]. | drkt h[.---]. | [---.]d[--.-- 6[49].6.33
ṣ. | [ašhlk].šbt h.dmm.šbt.dqn h. | [mm‘m.-]d.l ytn.bt.l b‘l.k ilm. | [w ḥẓ]r.k bn.aṯrt[.td‘ṣ.]p‘n. | [w tr.a]rṣ.id[k.l ttn.p] 3[‘NT.VI].5.11
t. | šmm.šmn.tmṭrn. | nḫlm.tlk.nbtm. | w id‘.k ḥy.aliyn.b‘l. | k iṯ.zbl.b‘l.arṣ. | b ḥlm.lṭpn.il d pid. | b ḏrt.bny.bnwt. | šm 6[49].3.8
yṣḥ. | aṯbn.ank.w anḫn. | w tnḫ.b irt y.npš. | k ḥy.aliyn.b‘l. | k iṯ.zbl.b‘l.arṣ. | gm.yṣḥ.il.l btlt. | ‘nt.šm‘.l btlt.‘n[t]. | rgm 6[49].3.20
t. | w ašlḥ k.aššpr k.‘m.b‘l. | šnt.‘m.bn il.tspr.yrḫm. | k b‘l.k yḥwy.y‘šr.ḥwy.y‘š. | r.w yšqyn h.ybd.w yšr.‘l h. | n‘m[n. 17[2AQHT].6.30
ṣḥ.tšmḫ ht. | aṯrt.w bn h.ilt.w ṣb | rt.ary h.k mt.aliyn. | b‘l.k ḫlq.zbl.b‘l. | arṣ.gm.yṣḥ il. | l rbt.aṯrt ym.šm‘. | l rbt.aṯr[t 6.1.42[49.1.14]
[k mt.aliyn.b‘l]. | k ḫlq.z[bl.b‘l.arṣ]. | w hm.ḥy.a[liyn.b‘l]. | w hm.iṯ.zbl.b‘[6[49].3.01
w.k.rgm.špš. | mlk.rb.b‘l y.u. | ‘[--.]mlakt.‘bd h. | [---.]b‘l k.yḫpn. | [---.]‘m h.u ky. | [---.--]d k.k.tmǵy. | ml[--.--]š[.ml 1018.4
]‘.l.yd‘t. | h[t.---.]l.špš.b‘l k. | ‘[--.s]glt h.at. | ht[.---.]špš.b‘l k. | yd‘m.l.yd‘t. | ‘m y.špš.b‘l k. | šnt.šntm.lm.l.tlk. | w.lḫt.a 2060.13
pš.b‘l k. | šnt.šntm.lm.l.tlk. | w.lḫt.akl.ky. | likt.‘m.špš. | b‘l k.ky.akl. | b.ḫwt k.inn. | špš n.[---]. | hm.al[k.--]. | ytnt[.---]. 2060.19
b‘l.ṯmn.rkb. | ‘rpt.bl.ṭl.bl rbb. | bl.šr‘.thmtm.bl. | ṭbn.ql.b‘l.k tmz‘. | kst.dnil.mt.rpi. | all.ǵzr.m[t.]hr[nmy]. | gm.l bt[h 19[1AQHT].1.46
.bt[.m]lk. | k.t‘rbn.ršp m.bt.mlk. | ḫlu.dg. | ḥdṯm. | dbḥ.b‘l.k.tdd.b‘lt.bhtm. | b.[-]ǵb.ršp.ṣbi. | [---.--]m. | [---.]piln. | [---] 2004.14
. | w.[---].adny.l.yḫsr. | w.[ank.yd]‘.l.yd‘t. | h[t.---.]l.špš.b‘l k. | ‘[--.s]glt h.at. | ht[.---.]špš.b‘l k. | yd‘m.l.yd‘t. | ‘m y.špš. 2060.11
.l ymru. | ilm.w nšm.d yšb | [‘].hmlt.arṣ.gm.l ǵ | [lm] h.b‘l k.yṣḥ.‘n. | [gpn].w ugr.b ǵlmt. | [‘mm.]ym.bn.ẓlmt.r | [mt. 4[51].7.53
‘[--.s]glt h.at. | ht[.---.]špš.b‘l k. | yd‘m.l.yd‘t. | ‘m y.špš.b‘l k. | šnt.šntm.lm.l.tlk. | w.lḫt.akl.ky. | likt.‘m.špš. | b‘l k.ky. 2060.15
p[-.---]. | ṣḥ.il.ytb.b[mrzḥ.---]. | bṯt.‘llm n.[---]. | ilm.bt.b‘l k.[---]. | dl.ylkn.ḥš.b a[rṣ.---]. | b ‘pr.ḫbl ṭtm.[---.] | šqy.rṭa. 1[‘NT.X].4.6
ištm.yitmr.ḥrb.lṭšt. | [--]n hm.rgm.l ṯr.ab h.il.ṯḥm.ym.b‘l km. | [adn]km.ṯpṭ.nhr.tn.il m.d tq h.d tqyn h. | [hml]t.tn. 2.1[137].33
ṯny.d‘t km.w rgm.l ṯr.a[b.-.il.ṯny.l pḫr]. | m‘d.ṯḥm.ym.b‘l km.adn km.ṯ[pṭ.nhr]. | tn.il m.d tq h.d tqyn.hmlt.tn.b‘l.[2.1[137].17
--.-]dm.mlak.ym.t‘dt.ṯpṭ.nh[r.---]. | [---].an.rgmt.l ym.b‘l km.ad[n km.ṯpṭ]. | [nhr.---.]hwt.gmr.hd.l wny[-.---]. | [---. 2.1[137].45
h.yṣ]ḥ.aṯ | [rt.w bn h.]ilt. | [w ṣbrt.ary]h. | [wn.in.bt.l b‘l.] | [km.ilm.w ḥẓr]. | [k bn.aṯ]r[t]. | m[ṯ]b.il.mẓll. | bn h.mṯb 4[51].1.10
[---.wn.in]. | [bt].l [b‘l.km.ilm.w ḥẓr]. | k bn.[aṯrt.mṯb.il.mẓll]. | bn h.m[ṯb.rbt.aṯ 3[‘NT.VI].4.01
t. | p.‘bd.ank.aḫd.ulṯ. | hm.amt.aṯrt.tlbn. | lbnt.ybn.bt.l b‘l. | km ilm.w ḥẓr.k bn.aṯrt. | w t‘n.rbt.aṯrt ym. | rbt.ilm.l ḥk 4[51].4.62
d yknn h.yṣḥ. | aṯrt.w bn h.ilt.w ṣbrt. | ary h.wn.in.bt.l b‘l. | km.ilm.w ḥẓr.k bn.aṯrt. | mṯb il.mẓll.bn h. | mṯb rbt.aṯrt. 4[51].4.50
[i]k.mgn.rbt.aṯrt. | [ym].mǵẓ.qnyt.ilm. | w tn.bt.l b‘l.km. | [i]lm.w ḥẓr.k bn. | [a]ṯrt.gm.l ǵlm h. | b‘l.yṣḥ.‘n.gpn. 8[51FRAG].3
yknn h.yṣḥ.aṯrt. | w bn h.ilt.w ṣbrt.arḫ h. | wn.in.bt.l b‘l.km.ilm. | ḥẓr.k b[n.a]ṯrt.mṯb.il. | mṯll.b[n h.m]ṯb.rbt.aṯrt. 3[‘NT.VI].5.46
mr.mr.ym.mr.ym. | l ksi h.nhr l kḥṯ.drkt h.trtqṣ. | b d b‘l.km.nšr b uṣb‘t h.hlm.qdq | d zbl ym.bn.‘nm.ṯpṭ.nhr.yprs 2.4[68].21
rš.grš ym grš ym.l ksi h. | [n]hr l kḥṯ drkt h.trtqṣ.b d b‘l km nš | r.b uṣb‘t h.hlm.ktp.zbl ym.bn ydm. | [ṯp]ṭ nhr.yrt 2.4[68].13
‘t h.hlm.ktp.zbl ym.bn ydm. | [ṯp]ṭ nhr.yrtqṣ.ṣmd.b d b‘l.km.nšr. | b[u]ṣb‘t h.ylm.ktp.zbl ym.bn ydm.ṯpṭ. | nhr.‘z.y 2.4[68].15
n.‘nm.ṯpṭ.nhr.yprsḥ ym. | w yql.l arṣ.w trtqṣ.ṣmd.b d b‘l. | [km.]nšr.b uṣb‘t h.ylm.qdqd.zbl. | [ym.]bn.‘nm.ṯpṭ.nhr. 2.4[68].23
. | w mẓa h.šr.yly h. | b skn.sknm.b ‘dn. | ‘dnm.kn.npl.b‘l. | km ṯr.w tkms.hd.p[.-]. | km.ibr.b tk.mšmš d[--]. | ittpq.l 12[75].2.54
. | [w t]‘n.mṯt.ḥry. | [l lḥ]m.l šty.ṣḥt km. | [--.dbḥ.l]krt.b‘l km. 15[128].4.28
nr.š.[--.]‘ṣrm gdlt. | b‘lm.kmm.b‘lm.kmm[.b‘lm].kmm.b‘lm.kmm. | b‘lm.kmm.b‘lm.kmm. | k t‘rb.‘ṯtrt.šd.bt.mlk[.--- UG5.9.1.11
d gbl.ṣpn.al[p]. | pḫr.ilm.š.ym.š[.k]nr.š.[--.]‘ṣrm gdlt. | b‘lm.kmm.b‘lm.kmm[.b‘lm].kmm.b‘lm.kmm. | b‘lm.kmm.b‘ UG5.9.1.11
l[p]. | pḫr.ilm.š.ym.š[.k]nr.š.[--.]‘ṣrm gdlt. | b‘lm.kmm.b‘lm.kmm[.b‘lm].kmm.b‘lm.kmm. | b‘lm.kmm.b‘lm.kmm. | UG5.9.1.11
.š.ym.š[.k]nr.š.[--.]‘ṣrm gdlt. | b‘lm.kmm.b‘lm.kmm[.b‘lm].kmm.b‘lm.kmm. | b‘lm.kmm.b‘lm.kmm. | k t‘rb.‘ṯtrt.š UG5.9.1.11
gdlt. | b‘lm.kmm.b‘lm.kmm[.b‘lm].kmm.b‘lm.kmm. | b‘lm.kmm.b‘lm.kmm. | k t‘rb.‘ṯtrt.šd.bt.mlk[.---]. | ṯn.skm.šb UG5.9.1.12
.kmm.b‘lm.kmm[.b‘lm].kmm.b‘lm.kmm. | b‘lm.kmm.b‘lm.kmm. | k t‘rb.‘ṯtrt.šd.bt.mlk[.---]. | ṯn.skm.šb‘.mšlt.arb‘. UG5.9.1.12
[---.al]p ‘nt.gdlt.b ṯlṯt mrm. | [---.i]l š.b‘l š.aṯrt.š.ym š.[b‘]l knp. | [---.g]dlt.ṣpn.dqt.šrp.w [š]lmm. | [---.a]lp.l b‘l.w aṯr 36[9].1.6
dmrn. | ‘n.b‘l.qdm.yd h. | k tǵḏ.arz.b ymn h. | bkm.ytb.b‘l.l bht h. | u mlk.u bl mlk. | arṣ.drkt.yštkn. | dll.al.ilak.l bn. 4[51].7.42
.il ym. | [---.-]qlṣn.wpṯ m. | [---.]w y‘n.kṯr. | [w ḫss.]ttb.b‘l.l hwt y. | [ḥš.]bht h.tbnn. | [ḥš.]trmm.hkl h. | y[tl]k.l lbnn. 4[51].6.15
.kṯr.w ḫss. | yšu.g h.w yṣḥ. | l rgmt.l k.l ali | yn.b‘l.ṯtbn.b‘l. | l hwt y.yptḥ.ḥ | ln.b bht m.urbt. | b qrb.hk[l m.yp]tḥ. | b‘ 4[51].7.24
w y‘n.k[ṯr.w ḫs]s. | ttb.b‘l.l[hwt y]. | ṯn.rgm.k[ṯr.w]ḫss. | šm‘.m‘.l al[iy]n b‘l. | bl.ašt. 4[51].6.2
w yṣḥ.y l k.qrt.ablm. | d ‘l k.mḫṣ.aqht.ǵzr. | ‘wrt.yšt k.b‘l.l ht. | w ‘lm h.l ‘nt.p dr.dr. | ‘db.uḫry.mṭ.yd h. | dnil.bt h.y 19[1AQHT].4.167
.b ktp. | dk ym.ymḫṣ.b ṣmd. | ṣḥr mt.ymṣḫ.l arṣ. | [ytb.]b[‘]l.l ksi.mlk h. | [---].l kḥṯ.drkt h. | l [ym]m.l yrḫm.l yrḫm. | 6[49].5.5
.špš. | ‘ms m‘.l y.aliyn.b‘l. | tšm‘.nrt.ilm.špš. | tšu.aliyn.b‘l.l ktp. | ‘nt.k tšt h.tš‘lyn h. | b ṣrrt.ṣpn.tbkyn h. | w tqbrn h. 6[62].1.14
nmlk.yd‘.ylḥn. | w y‘n.lṭpn.il d pi | d dq.anm.l yrẓ. | ‘m.b‘l.l y‘db.mrḥ. | ‘m.bn.dgn.k tms m. | w ‘n.rbt.aṯrt ym. | blt.n 6.1.51[49.1.23]
iyn.b‘l. | w yšu.‘n h.w y‘n. | w y‘n.btlt.‘nt. | n‘mt.bn.aḫt.b‘l. | l pnn h.ydd.w yqm. | l p‘n h.ykr‘.w yql. | w yšu.g h.w yṣ 10[76].2.16
‘m. | tš[‘]ly.ṯmn.l ṯmnym. | w [th]rn.w tldn mṯ. | al[iyn.b‘]l šlbšn. | i[---.---.--]l h.mǵẓ. | y[--.---.]l irt h. | n[--.---]. 5[67].5.23
. | a[lp].l btlt.‘nt. | w ypt l ybmt.li[mm]. | w y‘ny.aliyn[.b‘l]. | lm.k qnym.‘l[m.--]. | k dr d.d yknn[.--]. | b‘l.yṣǵd.mli[.-- 10[76].3.5
.hlm.rišt hm.l ẓr.brkt hm.w l kḥṯ. | zbl hm.b hm.yg‘r.b‘l.lm.ǵltm.ilm.rišt. | km l ẓr brkt km.w ln.kḥṯ.zbl km.aḥd. | 2.1[137].24
[b]n‘mm.b ysmm.ḥ[--]k.ǵrt. | [ql].l b‘l.‘nt.ttnn. | [---].b‘l m.d ip[---]. | [il.]hd.d ‘nn.n[--]. | [----.]aliyn.b[‘l]. | [---.btl]t. 10[76].2.32

.l šrr.w [---].|y‘n.ym.l mt[.---].|l šrr.w t‘[n.‘ttrt.---].|b‘l m.hmt.[---].|l šrr.št[.---].|b riš h.[---].|ib h.mš[--.---].|[b] 2.4[68].36
‘n.kṯr.w ḫss.l rgmt.|l k.l zbl.b‘l.ṯnt.l rkb.‘rpt.ht.ib k.|b‘l m.ht.ib k.tmḫṣ.ht.tṣmt.ṣrt k.|tqḥ.mlk.‘lm k.drkt.dt dr d 2.4[68].9
pṯ.nhr.w yṣa b[.--].|ybṯ.nn.aliyn.b‘l.w [---].|ym.l mt.b‘l m.ym l[--.---].|ḥm.l šrr.w [---].|y‘n.ym.l mt[.---].|l šrr.w 2.4[68].32
.‘pr.bt k.ygr[š k.---].|[---.]y.ḥr.ḥr.bnt.ḥ[---].|[--.]uḫd.[b‘]l m.‘[--].yd k.amṣ.yd[.--].|[---.]ḥš[.-]nm[.--.]k.[--].w yḫnp 1001.1.14
šnt.w [--].bn.ilm.mt.|‘m.aliyn.b‘l.yšu.|g h.w yṣḥ.‘l k.b[‘]l m.|pht.qlt.‘l k.pht.|dry.b ḥrb.‘l k.|pht.šrp.b išt.|‘l k.[6[49].5.11
[k.ym]ḫṣ.b‘l m[.--]y.tnn.w ygl.w ynsk.‘[-].|[--]y.l arṣ[.id]y.alt.l aḫš.id 1001.1.1
.ḥdṯ.|b.yrḫ.pgrm.|lqḥ.b‘lm‘ḏr.|w bn.ḫlp.|w[--]y.d.b‘l.|miḫd.b.|arb‘.mat.|ḫrṣ. 1155.5
m.ask[.šlm.]l kbd.arṣ.|ar[bdd.]l kb[d.š]dm.yšt.|[----.]b‘l.mdl h.yb‘r.|[---.]rn h.aqry.|[---.]b a[r]ṣ.mlḥmt.|ašt[.b ‘] 3[‘NT].4.70
.yṯbš.šm.il.mt m.|y‘bš.brk n.šm.il.ǵzrm.|ṯm.ṯmq.rpu.b‘l.mhr b‘l.|w mhr.‘nt.ṯm.yḥpn.ḥyl|y.zbl.mlk.‘llm y.km.td 22.2[124].8
r‘ h.yḥrṯ.|k gn.ap lb.k ‘mq.yṯlṯ.|bmt.yšu.g h.w yṣḥ.|b‘l.mt.my.lim.bn.|dgn.my.hmlt.aṯr.|b‘l.ard.b arṣ.ap.|‘nt.ttl 5[67].6.23
qn[.ṯlṯ].|qn.ḏr‘ h.tḥrṯ.km.gn.|ap lb.k ‘mq.tṯlṯ.bmt.|b‘l.mt.my.lim.bn dgn.|my.hmlt.aṯr.b‘l.nrd.|b arṣ.‘m h.trd. 6[62].1.6
ddy.[a]ḏddy.|bn.mlkr[šp].|bn.y[k]n.|ynḥm.|bn.abd.b‘[l].|mnḥm.bn[.---].|krmn[py].|bn.[--]m.|bn.asr[-].|bn.ḏr 2014.48
ht.k b h.bṯt.l tbṯ.|w b h.tdmmt.amht.|aḫr.mǵy.aliyn.b‘l.|mǵyt.btlt.‘nt.|tmgnn.rbt[.a]ṯrt ym.|tǵẓyn.qnyt.ilm.|w 4[51].3.23
|ṯṯ.l ṯtm.aḫd.‘r.|šb‘m.šb‘.pdr.|ṯmnym.b‘l.[----].|tš‘m.b‘l.mr[-].|bt[.--]b b‘l.b qrb.|bt.w y‘n.aliyn.|b‘l.ašt m.kṯr bn. 4[51].7.12
ḥ.|ḥwt.aḫt.w nar[-].|qrn.d bat k.btlt.‘nt.|qrn.d bat k b‘l.ymšḥ.|b‘l.ymšḥ.hm.b ‘p.|nṭ‘n.b arṣ.ib y.|w b ‘pr.qm.aḫ 10[76].2.22
.w nar[-].|qrn.d bat k.btlt.‘nt.|qrn.d bat k b‘l.ymšḥ.|b‘l.ymšḥ.hm.b ‘p.|nṭ‘n.b arṣ.ib y.|w b ‘pr.qm.aḫ k.|w tšu.‘ 10[76].2.23
w ymẓa.‘qqm.|b‘l.ḥmd m.yḥmd m.|bn.dgn.yhrr m.|b‘l.ngṯ hm.b p‘n h.|w il hd.b ḫrẓ‘ h.|[-----].|[--]t.[---].|[---.]‘ 12[75].1.40
--]ldm.dt ymtm.|[--.--]r.l ẓpn.|[---.]pn.ym.y[--].|[---].b‘l.tdd.|[---.]hkl.|[---.]yd h.|[---.]tmt. 25[136].7
mtm.uṣb‘[t].|[-]tr.šrk.il.|‘rb.špš.l ymǵ.|krt.ṣbia.špš.|b‘l ny.w ymlk.|[y]ṣb.‘ln.w y[-]y.|[kr]t.ṭ‘.‘ln.bḫr.|[---].aṯt k.‘ 15[128].5.20
.l hm.tḥt b‘l[.---].|h.u qšt pn hdd.b y[.----].|‘m.b ym b‘l ysy ym[.---].|rmm.ḫnpm.mḫl[.---].|mlk.nhr.ibr[.---].|zb 9[33].2.7
.tmǵ.l n‘m[y].|[arṣ.]dbr.ysmt.šd.|[šḥl]mmt.t[mǵ.]l b‘l.np[l].|[l a]rṣ[.lpš].tks.miz[rtm]. 5[67].6.30
[.m]ǵny.|l n‘m y.arṣ.dbr.|l ysmt.šd.šḥlmmt.|mǵny.l b‘l.npl.l a|rṣ.mt.aliyn.b‘l.|ḫlq.zbl.b‘l.arṣ.|apnk.lṭpn.il.|d pi 5[67].6.8
rḥm.|l šnt.[m]k.b šb‘.|šnt.w [--].bn.ilm.mt.|‘m.aliyn.b‘l.yšu.|g h.w yṣḥ.‘l k.b[‘]l m.|pht.qlt.‘l k.pht.|dry.b ḥrb.‘l 6[49].5.10
d.b ḫrẓ‘ h.|[-----].|[--]t.[---].|[---.]‘n[.---].|pnm[.---].|b‘l.n[--.---].|il.hd[.---].|at.bl[.at.---].|ḥmd m.[---].|il.hr[r.---] 12[75].2.5
al.tǵl[.---].|prdmn.‘bd.ali[yn].|b‘l.sid.zbl.b‘l.|arṣ.qm.yṯ‘r.|w yšlḥmn h.|ybrd.ṯd.l pnw h.| 3[‘NT].1.3
ly y.|yṯb.‘m.b‘l.ṣrrt.|ṣpn.yšu g h.w yṣḥ.|aḫ y m.ytnt.b‘l.|spu y.bn m.um y.kl|y y.yt‘n.k gmrm.|mt.‘z.b‘l.‘z.ynghṇ 6[49].6.14
t.|[--]u.šb‘t.ǵlm h.|[---].bn.ilm.mt.|p[-]n.aḫ y m.ytn.b‘l.|[s]pu y.bn m.um y.kly y.|yṯb.‘m.b‘l.ṣrrt.|ṣpn.yšu g h.w 6[49].6.10
]r.mrḥ h.ti[ḫd.b yd h].|š[g]r h bm ymn.t[--.---].|[--.]l b‘l.‘bd[.---].|tr ab h il.ttrm[.---].|tšlḥm yrḫ.ggn[.---].|k[.---. 2001.1.14
qdm h.mra.|w tk.pn h.t‘db.ksu.|w yṯtb.l ymn.aliyn.|b‘l.‘d.lḥm.št[y.ilm].|[w]y‘n.aliy[n.b‘l].|[--]b[.---].|ḥš.bht m 4[51].5.110
mǵt.l n‘m y.arṣ.|dbr.ysmt.šd.šḥlmmt.|ngš.ank.aliyn b‘l.|‘dbnn ank.imr.b p y.|k lli.b ṯbrn q y.ḫtu hw.|nrt.ilm.š 6[49].2.21
|aliyn.b‘l.ht y.bnt.|dt.ksp.hkl y.dtm.|ḫrṣ.‘dbt.bht[h.b‘]l.|y‘db.hd.‘db[.‘d]bt.|hkl h.ṯbḫ.alpm[.ap].|ṣin.šql.ṯrm[.w 4[51].6.38
.dr.dr.|[---.--]y k.w rḥd.|[---]y ilm.d mlk.|y[ṯ]b.aliyn.b‘l.|yt‘dd.rkb.‘rpt.|[--].ydd.w yqlṣn.|yqm.w ywpṯn.b tk.|p[4[51].3.10
šbt.dqn k.l tsr k.|rḫntt.d[-].l irt k.|wn ap.‘dn.mṭr h.|b‘l.y‘dn.‘dn.ṯkt.b glṯ.|w tn.ql h.b ‘rpt.|šrh.l arṣ.brqm.|bt.ar 4[51].5.69
‘mtr.|ydb il.|yrgb lim.|‘mtr.|yarš il.|ydb b‘l.|yrǵm b‘l.|‘z b‘l.|ydb hd. UG5.14.B.12
‘z.ynghṇ.|k rumm.mt.‘z.b‘l.|‘z.ynṯkn.k bṯnm.|mt.‘z.b‘l.‘z.ymṣḫn.|k lsmm.mt.ql.|b‘l.ql.‘ln.špš.|tṣḥ.l mt.šm‘.m‘. 6[49].6.20
ytnt.b‘l.|spu y.bn m.um y.kl|y y.yt‘n.k gmrm.|mt.‘z.b‘l.‘z.ynghṇ.|k rumm.mt.‘z.b‘l.|‘z.ynṯkn.k bṯnm.|mt.‘z.b‘l. 6[49].6.17
|y y.yt‘n.k gmrm.|mt.‘z.b‘l.‘z.ynghṇ.|k rumm.mt.‘z.b‘l.|‘z.ynṯkn.k bṯnm.|mt.‘z.b‘l.‘z.ymṣḫn.|k lsmm.mt.ql.|b‘ 6[49].6.18
[--.]ab.w il[--].|[--] šlm.šlm i[l].|[š]lm.il.šr.|dgn.w b‘l.|‘ṯ w kmṯ.|yrḫ w ksa.|yrḫ mkty.|ṯkmn w šnm.|kṯr w ḫ UG5.10.1.4
pnm.‘m.b‘l.|mrym.ṣpn.b alp.šd.rbt.kmn.|hlk.aḫt h.b‘l.y‘n.tdrq.|ybnt.ab h.šrḥq.aṯt.l pnn h.|št.alp.qdm h.mria. 3[‘NT].4.83
[.--].|il hd.mla.u[--.--].|blt.p btlt.‘n[t].|w p.n‘mt.aḫt[.b‘l].|y‘l.b‘l.b ǵ[r.---].|w bn.dgn.b š[---].|b‘l.yṯb.l ks[i.mlk h] 10[76].3.11
.|w d ‘lm k.šmḫ.bn.ilm.mt.|[---.]g h.w aṣḥ.ik.yṣḥn.|[b‘l.‘m.aḫ y.ik].yqrun.hd.|[‘m.ary y.---.--]p.mlḥm y.|[---.---]l 5[67].2.22
y.ilḥm.hm.šb‘.|ydt y.b ṣ‘.hm.ks.ymsk.|nhr.k[--].ṣḥn.b‘l.‘m.|aḫ y.qran.hd.‘m.ary y.|w lḥm m ‘m aḫ y.lḥm.|w št 5[67].1.22
wt.lṭpn.htk k.|pl.‘nt.šdm.y špš.|pl.‘nt.šdm.il.yš[t k].|b‘l.‘nt.mḥrṯ[-].|iy.aliyn.b‘l.|iy.zbl.b‘l.arṣ.|w t‘n.nrt.ilm.š[p] 6[49].4.38
.l nrt.il.šp[š].|pl.‘nt.šdm.y špš.|pl.‘nt.šdm.il.yšt k.|[b]‘l.‘nt.mḥrṯt.|iy.aliyn.b‘l.|iy.zbl.b‘l.arṣ.|ttb‘.btlt.‘nt.|idk.l 6[49].4.27
tr.b lkt.w tr.b ḫl.|[b]n‘mm.b ysmm.ḥ[--]k.ǵrt.|[ql].l b‘l.‘nt.ttnn.|[---].b‘l m.d ip[---].|[il.]hd.d ‘nn.n[--].|[----.]ali 10[76].2.31
ḥkt.ksp.w ḫrṣ ṭ‘ ṯn šm l btbt.|alp.w š šrp.alp šlmm.|l b‘l.‘ṣr l ṣpn.|npš.w.š.l ršp bbt.|[‘]ṣrm l h.ršp [-]m.|[---.]bqṯ[UG5.12.A.10
yrḫ ḥyr.b ym ḥdṯ.|alp.w š.l b‘lt bhtm.|b arb‘t ‘šrt.b‘l.|‘rkm.|b ṯmnt.‘šrt.yr|tḥṣ.mlk.brr.|‘lm.tzǵ.b ǵb.ṣpn.|nḥ UG5.12.A.3
ym[.---].|rmm.ḫnpm.mḫl[.---].|mlk.nhr.ibr[.---].|zbl b‘l.ǵlm.[---].|ṣǵr hd w r[---.---].|w l nhr nd[-.---].|[---.--]l. 9[33].2.10
l b‘l.|ǵr.b ab.td[.ps]ltm[.b y‘r].|thdy.lḥm.w dqn[.ṯlṯ].|qn.ḏr‘ 6[62].1.1
|n‘mn.ilm l ḥt[n].|m.b‘l trḫ pdry b[t h].|aqrb k ab h b‘[l].|ygtr.‘ṯtr t|rḫ l k ybrdmy.b[t.a]|b h lb[u] y‘rr.w y‘[n]. 24[77].27
.‘ṯtr.‘rẓ.|apnk.‘ṯtr.‘rẓ.|y‘l.b ṣrrt.ṣpn.|yṯb.l kḥṯ.aliyn.|b‘l.p‘n h.l tmǵyn.|hdm.riš h.l ymǵy.|aps h.w y‘n.‘ṯtr.‘rẓ.|l 6.1.59[49.1.31]
rqd.|bn.abdg.|ilyn.|bn.tan.|bn.arm.|bn.b‘l.ṣdq.|bn.army.|bn.rpiyn.|bn.army.|bn.krmn.|bn.ykn.| 1046.1.6
[šmt.n]qmp‘.|[bn.nq]md.|[mlk.]ugrt.|b‘l ṣdq.|skn.bt.|mlk.tǵr.|[m]lk.bny.|[--].lb.mlk.|[---.]ṣmḫ. 1007.4
rṣ.w bn.bht.ksp.|w ḫrṣ.bht.ṯhrm.|iqnim.šmḫ.aliyn.|b‘l.ṣḥ.ḫrn.b bht h.|‘dbt.b qrb hkl h.|yblnn ǵrm.mid.ksp.|g 4[51].5.98
bt.arzm.yklln h.|hm.bt.lbnt.y‘msn h.|l yrgm.l aliyn b‘l.|ṣḥ.ḫrn.b bhm k.|‘dbt.b qrb.hkl k.|tbl k.ǵrm.mid.ksp.| 4[51].5.74
tn.bt.l b‘l.km.|[i]lm.w ḥẓr.k bn.|[a]ṯrt.gm.l ǵlm h.|b‘l.yṣḥ.‘n.gpn.|w ugr.bn.ǵlmt.|‘mm ym.bn.ẓlm[t].|rmt.pr‘t 8[51FRAG].6
y.aliyn[.b‘l].|lm.k qnym.‘l[m.--].|k dr d.d yknn[.--].|b‘l.yṣǵd.mli[.--].|il hd.mla.u[--.--].|blt.p btlt.‘n[t].|w p.n‘mt 10[76].3.8
ilib.š.|arṣ w šmm.š.|il.š.kṯrt.š.|dgn.š.b‘l.ḫlb alp w š.|b‘l ṣpn alp.w.š.|ṯrty.alp.w.š.|yrḫ.š.ṣpn.š.|kṯr š ‘ṯtr.š.|[‘ṯt]rt. UG5.9.2.5
r‘r.|pamt ṯlṯm š l qrnt.|ṯlḥn.b‘lt.bhtm.|‘lm.‘lm.gdlt l b‘l.|ṣpn.ilbt[.---.]d[--].|l ṣpn[.---.-]lu.|ilib[.---.b]‘l.|ugrt[.---.- UG5.13.32
m.ǵṣ b šmal.|d alpm.w alp w š.|šrp.w šlmm kmm.|l b‘l.ṣpn b ‘r‘r.|pamt ṯlṯm š l qrnt.|ṯlḥn.b‘lt.bhtm.|‘lm.‘lm.g UG5.13.29
šnm.|il w aṯrt.|ḫnn il.|nṣbt il.|šlm il.|il ḥš il add.|b‘l ṣpn b‘l.|ugrt.|b mrḥ il.|b nit il.|b ṣmd il.|b dṯn il.|b šr 30[107].10
il ṣpn.|il[i]b.|i[l].|dgn.|b‘[l ṣ]pn.|b‘lm.|[b‘]lm.|[b‘]lm.|[b‘]lm.|[b‘]lm.|[b‘l]m.|[arṣ 29[17].1.5
.yrtḥṣ.mlk.brr.|[b ym.ml]at.y[ql]n.al[p]m.yrḫ.‘šrt.|[l b‘l.ṣ]pn.[dq]tm.w y[nt] qrt.|[w mtmt]m.[š.l] rm[š.]kbd.w š. 36[9].1.12

w mtmt]m.[š.l] rm[š.]kbd.w š.|[l šlm.kbd.al]p.w š.[l] b‘l.ṣpn.|[dqt.l.ṣpn.šrp].w š[l]mm.kmm.|[w bbt.b‘l.ugrt.]kd 36[9].1.14
[t].|w mtntm.š l rmš.|w kbd.w š.l šlm kbd.|alp.w š.l b‘l ṣpn.|dqt l ṣpn.šrp.w šlmm.|kmm.w bbt.b‘l.ugrt.|w kdm UG5.13.9
.|tmtn.u ḫšt k.l ntn.|‘tq.b d.att.ab ṣrry.|tbky k.ab.ġr.b‘l.|ṣpn.ḥlm.qdš.|any.ḥlm.adr.ḥl.|rḥb.mknpt.ap.|[k]rt.bn 16.1[125].6
t ab.ṣrry.|u ilm.tmtn.špḥ.|[l]tpn.l yḥ.t[b]ky k.|ab.ġr.b‘l.ṣ[p]n.ḥlm.|qdš.nny.ḥ[l]m.adr.|ḥl.rḥb.mk[npt].|ap.krt b 16.2[125].107
mṣt.ilhm.b‘lm.dṯt.w kšm.ḫmš.|‘tr h.mlun.šnpt.ḥṣt h.b‘l.ṣpn š.|[--]ṯ š.ilt.mgdl š.ilt.asrm š.|w l ll.šp. pgr.w ṯrmnm 34[1].10
dt.ẓr h.tšu.|g h.w tṣḥ.ik.mġy.gpn.w ugr.|mn.ib.yp‘.l b‘l.ṣrt.|l rkb.‘rpt.l mḫšt.mdd.|il ym.l klt.nhr.il.rbm.|l ištb 3[‘NT].3.34
.ib.yp‘.l b‘l.ṣrt.l rkb.‘rpt.|[-]‘n.ġlmm.y‘nyn.l ib.yp‘.|l b‘l.ṣrt.l rkb.‘rpt.|tḥm.aliyn.b‘l.hwt.aliy.|qrdm.qry.b arṣ.ml 3[‘NT].4.50
h.grš h.l ksi.mlk h.|l nḫt.l kḥṯ.drkt h.|mn m.ib.yp‘.l b‘l.ṣrt.l rkb.‘rpt.|[-]‘n.ġlmm.y‘nyn.l ib.yp‘.|l b‘l.ṣrt.l rkb.‘rp 3[‘NT].4.48
[-]n.aḫ y m.ytn.b‘l.|[s]pu y.bn m.um y.kly y.|yṯb.‘m.b‘l.ṣrrt.|ṣpn.yšu g h.w yṣḥ.|aḫ y m.ytnt.b‘l.|spu y.bn m.u 6[49].6.12
k[l m.yp]tḥ.|b‘l.b dqt[.‘rp]t.|ql h.qdš.b[‘l.y]tn.|ytny.b‘l.ṣ[---.-]pt h.|ql h.q[dš.ṭb]r.arṣ.|[---.]ġrm[.t]ḫšn.|rḥq[.---.t 4[51].7.30
r.w y‘n.aliyn.|b‘l.ib.hdt.lm.tḫš.|lm.tḫš.nṯq.dmrn.|‘n.b‘l.qdm.yd h.|k tġd.arz.b ymn h.|bkm.yṯb.b‘l.l bht h.|u ml 4[51].7.40
n.w y‘ny.krt ṯ‘.yṯbr.|ḥrn.y bn.yṯbr.ḥrn.|riš k.‘ṯtrt.šm.b‘l.|qdqd k.tqln.b gbl.|šnt k.b ḥpn k.w t‘n.|spr ilmlk ṯ‘y. 16.6[127].56
.---].|ṯpṭ.nhr.yṯb[r.ḥrn.y ym.yṯbr.ḥrn].|riš k.‘ṯtrt.[šm.b‘l.qdqd k.---].|[--]t.mṭ.tpln.b g[bl.šnt k.---].|[--]šnm.aṯtm.t 2.1[137].8
.tk.ġr.ll.‘m.phr.m‘d.ap.ilm.l lḥ[m].|yṯb.bn qdš.l ṯrm.b‘l.qm.‘l.il.hlm.|ilm.tph hm.tphn.mlak.ym.t‘dt.ṯpṭ[.nhr].|t[2.1[137].21
‘z.ynṯkn.k bṯnm.|mt.‘z.b‘l.‘z.ymṣḫn.|k lsmm.mt.ql.|b‘l.ql.‘ln.špš.|tṣḥ.l mt.šm‘.m‘.|l bn.ilm.mt.ik.tmt[ḫ]|ṣ.‘m.al 6[49].6.22
.yštql.|l ḥtr h.y‘msn.nn.ṯkmn.|w šnm.w ngšnn.ḥby.|b‘l.qrnm w ḏnb.ylšn.|b ḫri h.w ṯnt h.ql.il.[--].|il.k yrdm.arṣ UG5.1.1.20
bi.qšt.w.ql‘.|bn.yy.qšt.|ilrb.qšt.|bn.nmš.ṯt.qšt.w.ql‘.|b‘l.qšt.w.ql‘. 119[321].4.17
b y‘lm.mtnm.|b ‘qbt.ṯr.adr.b ġlil.qnm.|tn.l kṯr.w ḫss.yb‘l.qšt l ‘nt.|qṣ‘t.l ybmt.limm.w t‘n.btlt.|‘nt.irš ḥym.l aqht 17[2AQHT].6.24
n.mṯpdm.|tḥt.‘nt.arṣ.ṯlṯ.mtḥ.ġyrm.|idk.l ttn pnm.‘m.b‘l.|mrym.ṣpn.b alp.šd.rbt.kmn.|hlk.aḫt h.b‘l.y‘n.tdrq.|yb 3[‘NT].4.81
.|šmḫ.btlt.‘nt.td‘ṣ.|p‘nm.w tr.arṣ.|idk.l ttn.pnm.|‘m.b‘l.mrym.ṣpn.|b alp.šd.rbt.kmn.|ṣḥq.btlt.‘nt.tšu.|g h.w tṣḥ 4[51].5.85
h|mrt.ydd.il.ġzr.|tb‘.w l.yṯb ilm.idk.|l ytn.pnm.‘m.b‘l.|mrym.ṣpn.w y‘n.|gpn.w ugr.tḥm.bn ilm.|mt.hwt.ydd. 5[67].1.10
šr.|y‘db.ksa.w.yṯb.|tqru.l špš.um h.špš.um.ql bl.|‘m b‘l.mrym.ṣpn.mnt y.nṯk.|nḥš.šmrr.nḥš.‘q šr ln h.|mlḫš.abd UG5.7.9
rṣ] w šm[m].|[-----].|[a]rṣ.|[u]šḫr[y].|[‘]ṯtrt.|i[l t]‘ḏr b‘l.|ršp.|ddmš.|pḫr ilm.|ym.|uṯḫt.|knr.|mlkm.|šlm. 29[17].2.4
l.gdlt.[ṣ]pn.dqt.|[---.al]p ‘nt.gdlt.b ṯlṯt mrm.|[---.i]l š.b‘l š.aṯrt.š.ym š.[b‘]l knp.|[---.g]dlt.ṣpn.dqt.šrp.w [š]lmm.|[36[9].1.6
qt.šrp w šlmm.dqtm.|[i]lh.alp w š ilhm.gdl[t.]ilhm.|[b]‘l š.aṯrt.š.ṯkmn w šnm.š.|‘nt.š.ršp.š.dr il w p[ḫ]r b‘l.|gdlt. 34[1].6
.šrp.w š[lmm.dqtm].|ilh[.a]lp.w š[.il]hm.[gdlt.ilhm].|b‘[l.š].aṯrt[.š.ṯkm]n w [šnm.š].|‘nt š ršp š[.dr.il.w pḫr.b‘l].|g 35[3].15
ršp.šrp].|w šlmm.[dqtm.ilh.alp.w š].|ilhm.gd[lt.ilhm.b‘l.š.aṯrt.š].|ṯkmn.w š[nm.š.‘nt.š.ršp.š.dr].|il.w pḫr[.b‘l.gdlt APP.II[173].16
w[.--.k]bdm.|[---.--]mm.ṯn.šm.w alp.l[--]n.|[---.]š.il š.b‘l š.dgn š.|[---.--]r.w ṯt pl.gdlt.[ṣ]pn.dqt.|[---.al]p ‘nt.gdlt.b 36[9].1.3
m.|kmm.w bbt.b‘l.ugrt.|w kdm.w npš ilib.|gdlt.il š.b‘l š.‘nt.|ṣpn.alp.w š.pdry.š.|šrp.w šlmm ilib š.|b‘l ugrt š.b‘ UG5.13.13
mm.kmm.|[w bbt.b‘l.ugrt.]kdm.w npš.|[ilib.gdlt.il.š.b]‘[l.]š.‘nt ṣpn.|[---.]w [n]p[š.---].|[---.--]t.w[.---].|[---.--]pr.ṯ 36[9].1.17
š.ddmš š.|w b urbt.ilib š.|b‘l alp w š.|dgn.š.il t‘ḏr.š.|b‘l š.‘nt š.ršp š.|šlmm.|w šnpt.il š.|l ‘nt.ḥl š.ṯn šm.|l gṯrm. UG5.13.22
.š[.---].|aṯrt.š.‘nt.š.špš.š.arṣy.š.‘ṯtrt.š.|ušḫry.š.il.t‘ḏr.b‘l.š.ršp.š.ddmš.š.|w šlmm.ilib.š.i[l.--]m d gbl.ṣpn.al[p].|pḫ UG5.9.1.8
[ḥrš].bhtm.b‘l.šd.|[---d]nil.|[a]drdn.|[---]n.|pġdn.|ṯṯpḥ.|ḥgbn.|šrm.| 1039.1.1
m.bn[š.mlk.---].ḫzr.lqḥ.ḥp[r].|‘št.‘šr h.bn[.---.--]ḫ.zr.|b‘l.šd. 2011.42
-].mlak.bn.ktpm.rgm.b‘l h.w y[--.---].|[---].ap.anš.zbl.b‘l.šdmt.bg[--.---].|[---.-]dm.mlak.ym.t‘dt.ṯpṭ.nh[r.---].|[---]. 2.1[137].43
---].|tš‘m.b‘l.mr[-].|bt[.--]b b‘l.b qrb.|bt.w y‘n.aliyn.|b‘l.ašt m.kṯr bn.|ym.kṯr.bnm.‘dt.|yptḥ.ḥln.b bht m.|urbt.b 4[51].7.15
l aṯt.|iyṯr.b‘l aṯt.|ptm.b‘l ššlmt.|‘dršp.b‘l ššlmt.|ṯtrn.b‘l ššlmt.|aršwn.b‘l ššlmt.|ḥdṯn.b‘l ššlmt.|ssn.b‘l ššlmt. 1077.8
|ptm.b‘l ššlmt.|‘dršp.b‘l ššlmt.|ṯtrn.b‘l ššlmt.|aršwn.b‘l ššlmt.|ḥdṯn.b‘l ššlmt.|ssn.b‘l ššlmt. 1077.9
ḫ[ṣ].|aṯry.mḫṣ.|b‘ln.mḫṣ.|y[ḫ]ṣdq.mḫṣ.|ṣp[r].ks[d].|b‘l.š[lm].|ḫyrn[.---].|a[--.---].|‘[--.---].|š[--.---].|[-----].|m[--. 2084.19
‘dršp.b‘l ššlmt.|ṯtrn.b‘l ššlmt.|aršwn.b‘l ššlmt.|ḥdṯn.b‘l ššlmt.|ssn.b‘l ššlmt. 1077.10
.|ṯnġrn.[---].|w.bn h.n[--.---].|ḥnil.[---].|aršmg.mru.|b‘l.šlm.‘bd.|awr.ṯġrn.‘bd.|‘bd.ḫmn.šm‘.rgm.|šdn.[k]bš.|šd 2084.10
m.b‘l [aṯt].|ttḫ.b‘l aṯt.|ayab.b‘l aṯt.|iyṯr.b‘l aṯt.|ptm.b‘l ššlmt.|‘dršp.b‘l ššlmt.|ṯtrn.b‘l ššlmt.|aršwn.b‘l ššlmt.|ḥ 1077.6
b‘l aṯt.|ayab.b‘l aṯt.|iyṯr.b‘l aṯt.|ptm.b‘l ššlmt.|‘dršp.b‘l ššlmt.|ṯtrn.b‘l ššlmt.|aršwn.b‘l ššlmt.|ḥdṯn.b‘l ššlmt.|ss 1077.7
.|ṯtrn.b‘l ššlmt.|aršwn.b‘l ššlmt.|ḥdṯn.b‘l ššlmt.|ssn.b‘l ššlmt. 1077.11
.|[---.]b‘l yḥmdn h.yrṯ y.|[---.]dmrn.l pn h yrd.|[---.]b‘l.šm[.--.]rgbt yu.|[---]w yrmy[.q]rn h.|[---.-]ny h pdr.ttġr. 2001.2.9
tšt.k yn.udm‘t.gm.|tṣḥ.l nrt.ilm.špš.|‘ms m‘.l y.aliyn.b‘l.|tšm‘.nrt.ilm.špš.|tšu.aliyn.b‘l.l ktp.|‘nt.k tšt h.tš‘lyn h. 6[62].1.12
qht.ġzr.|irš ḥym.w atn k.bl mt.|w ašlḥ k.ašspr k.‘m.b‘l.|šnt.‘m.bn il.tspr.yrḫm.|k b‘l.k yḥwy.y‘šr.ḥwy.y‘š.|r.w 17[2AQHT].6.28
qdš.yuḫdm.šb‘r.|amrr.k kbkb.l pnm.|aṯr.btlt.‘nt.|w b‘l.tb‘.mrym.ṣpn.|idk.l ttn.pnm.|‘m.il.mbk.nhrm.|qrb.apq. 4[51].4.19
ḏġdl.|[-]mn.|[--]n.|[ḥr]š.qṯn.|[---]n.|[-----].|[--]dd.|[b‘]l.ṯġpṯm.|[k]rwn.|ḥrš.mrkbt.|mnḥm.|mṣrn.|mdrġlm.|a 1039.2.11
ḥrnqm.w |y‘n ḫrḫb mlk qẓ [l].|n‘mn.ilm l ḫt[n].|m.b‘l trḫ pdry b[t h].|aqrb k ab h b‘[l].|yġtr.‘ṯtr t|rḫ l k ybrd 24[77].26
rt.|i[lm.arṣ.b p h.rgm.l yṣa.b šp]|t h.hwt h.knp.hrgb.b‘l.ṯbr.|b‘l.ṯbr.diy.hwt.w yql.|tḥt.p‘n h.ybq‘.kbd h.w yḥd.| 19[1AQHT].3.128
ypn.|yḥd.hrgb.ab.nšrm.|yšu.g h.w yṣḥ.knp.hr[g]b.|b‘l.yṯb.b‘l.y[ṯb]r.diy[.h]wt.|w yql.tḥt.p‘n y.ibq‘.kbd[h].|w 19[1AQHT].3.123
[w]yphn.yḥd.ṣml.um.nšrm.|yšu.g h.w yṣḥ.knp.ṣml.|b‘l.yṯbr.b‘l.yṯbr.diy.|hyt.tql.tḥt.p‘n y.ibq‘.|kbd h.w aḥd.hm 19[1AQHT].3.137
t.ilm.arṣ.|b p h.rgm.l yṣa.b špt h.hwt[h].|knp.nšrm.b‘l.yṯbr.|b‘l.ṯbr.diy hmt.tqln.|tḥt.p‘n h.ybq‘.kbdt hm.w[yḥ 19[1AQHT].3.114
hn.yḥd].|b ‘rpt[.nšrm.yšu].|[g h.]w yṣḥ[.knp.nšrm].|b‘l.yṯb.b‘l.yṯb[r.diy.hmt].|tqln.tḥ p‘n y.ibq[‘.kbd hm.w] |aḥ 19[1AQHT].3.108
qbr.nn.b mdgt.b knk[-].|w yšu.g h.w yṣḥ.knp.nšrm.|b‘l.yṯbr.b‘l.yṯbr.diy.|hmt.hm.t‘pn.‘l.qbr.bn y.|tšḫṭann.b šnt 19[1AQHT].3.149
yḥd.hrgb.ab.nšrm.|yšu.g h.w yṣḥ.knp.hr[g]b.|b‘l.yṯb.b‘l.y[ṯb]r.diy[.h]wt.|w yql.tḥt.p‘n y.ibq‘.kbd[h].|w aḥd.hm 19[1AQHT].3.123
.arṣ.b p h.rgm.l yṣa.b šp]|t h.hwt h.knp.hrgb.b‘l.ṯbr.|b‘l.ṯbr.diy.hwt.w yql.|tḥt.p‘n h.ybq‘.kbd h.w yḥd.|[i]n.šmt. 19[1AQHT].3.129
m.arṣ.b p h.rgm.l[yṣ]a.|b špt h.hwt h.knp.ṣml.b‘[l].|b‘l.ṯbr.diy.hyt.tq[l.tḥt].|p‘n h.ybq‘.kbd h.w yḥd.|iṯ.šmt.iṯ.‘ẓ 19[1AQHT].3.143
n.yḥd.ṣml.um.nšrm.|yšu.g h.w yṣḥ.knp.ṣml.|b‘l.yṯbr.b‘l.yṯbr.diy.|hyt.tql.tḥt.p‘n y.ibq‘.|kbd h.w aḥd.hm.iṯ.šmt.i 19[1AQHT].3.137
mdgt.b knk[-].|w yšu.g h.w yṣḥ.knp.nšrm.|b‘l.yṯbr.b‘l.yṯbr.diy.|hmt.hm.t‘pn.‘l.qbr.bn y.|tšḫṭann.b šnt h.qr.[m 19[1AQHT].3.149
.|b p h.rgm.l yṣa.b špt h.hwt[h].|knp.nšrm.b‘l.yṯbr.|b‘l.ṯbr.diy hmt.tqln.|tḥt.p‘n h.ybq‘.kbdt hm.w[yḥd].|in.šm 19[1AQHT].3.115
].|b ‘rpt[.nšrm.yšu].|[g h.]w yṣḥ[.knp.nšrm].|b‘l.yṯb.b‘l.yṯb[r.diy.hmt].|tqln.tḥ p‘n y.ibq[‘.kbd hm.w] |aḥd.hm.i 19[1AQHT].3.108

ss.|ṣḥq.kṯr.w ḫss.|yšu.g h.w yṣḥ.|l rgmt.l k.l ali|yn.b‘l.ṯṯbn.b‘l.|l hwt y.ypth.ḥ|ln.b bht m.urbt.|b qrb.hk[l m.y 4[51].7.24
[---.‘]ṣrm.|[--]ṯpḥ b‘l.|[ṯl]ṯ.‘ṣrm.|[w]b‘lt btm.|[---.--]ṣn.l.dgn.|[---.--]m.|[---]. 39[19].2
.štt.|p[--].b ṯlḥn y.qlt.|b ks.ištyn h.|dm.ṯn.dbḥm.šna.b‘l.ṯlṯ.|rkb.‘rpt.dbḥ.|bṯt.w dbḥ.w dbḥ.|dnt.w dbḥ.tdmm.|a 4[51].3.17
m.un.yr.‘rpt.|tmṭr.b qẓ.ṭl.yṭll.|l ǵnbm.šb‘.šnt.|yṣr k.b‘l.ṯmn.rkb.|‘rpt.bl.ṭl.bl rbb.|bl.šr‘.thmtm.bl.|ṭbn.ql.b‘l.k t 19[1AQHT].1.43
l[-.---].|tḥt.ksi.zbl.ym.w ‘n.kṯr.w ḫss.l rgmt.|l k.l zbl.b‘l.ṯnt.l rkb.‘rpt.ht.ib k.|b‘l m.ht.ib k.tmḫṣ.ht.tṣmt.ṣrt k.|tq 2.4[68].8
k.il.ḥkm.ḥkm k.|‘m.‘lm.ḥyt.ḥẓt.tḥm k.|mlk n.aliyn.b‘l.ṯpṭ n.|in.d ‘ln h.klny y.qš h.|nbln.klny y.nbl.ks h.|any.l 3[‘NT.VI].5.40
k.il.ḥkm.ḥkmt.|‘m ‘lm.ḥyt.ḥẓt.|tḥm k.mlk n.aliy[n.]b‘l.|ṯpṭ n.w in.d ‘ln h.|klny n.q[š] h.n[bln].|klny n[.n]bl.ks 4[51].4.43
.rb.|khnm rb.nqdm.|ṯ‘y.nqmd.mlk ugr[t].|adn.yrgb.b‘l.ṯrmn. 6.6[62.2].57
d h.b p h yrd.|k ḥrr.zt.ybl.arṣ.w pr.|‘ṣm.yraun.aliyn.b‘l.|ṯt‘.nn.rkb.‘rpt.|tb‘.rgm.l bn.ilm.mt.|ṯny.l ydd.il ǵzr.|t 5[67].2.6
.argmn k.k ilm.|[---.]ybl.k bn.qdš.mnḥy k.ap.anš.zbl.b‘[l].|[-.yuḫ]d.b yd.mšḫṭ.bm.ymn.mḫṣ.ǵlmm.yš[--].|[ymn h 2.1[137].38
tqrm.l mt.b rn k.|[--]ḫp.an.arnn.ql.špš.ḥw.bṯnm.uḫd.b‘lm.|[--.a]ṭm.prṭl.l riš h.ḥmṯ.ṭmṯ.|[--.]ydbr.ṯrmt.al m.qḥn 1001.1.6
m]|n.w šnm.dqt[.---].|bqtm.b nbk.[---].|kmm.gdlt.l b[‘l.--.dqt].|l ṣpn.gdlt.[l.---].|ugrt.š l ili[b.---].|rt.w ‘ṣrm.l[.-- APP.II[173].36
t.aṯrt.ym.|[nǵ]ẓ.qnyt.ilm.|[---].nmgn.hwt.|[--].aliyn.b‘l.|[--.]rbt.aṯrt.ym.|[---.]btlt.‘nt.|[--.tl]ḥm.tšty.|[ilm.w tp] 4[51].3.37
.arṯ m.pḏ h.|[w y‘n.]ṯr.ab h.il.‘bd k.b‘l.y ym m.‘bd k.b‘l.|[--.--]m.bn.dgn.a[s]r km.hw ybl.argmn k.k ilm.|[---.]yb 2.1[137].36
šir.b krm.nṭṭt.dm.‘lt.b ab y.|u---].‘lt.b k.lk.l pn y.yrk.b‘l.[--].|[---.]‘nt.šzrm.tštšḥ.km.ḥ[--].|[---].‘pr.bt k.ygr[š k.--- 1001.1.10
yṯṯb.l ymn.aliyn.|b‘l.‘d.lḥm.št[y.ilm].|[w]y‘n.aliy[n.b‘l].|[--]b[.---].|ḥš.bht m.k[ṯr].|ḥš.rmm.hk[l m].|ḥš.bht m.t 4[51].5.111
ṭlb.[---].|mit.rḥ[.---].|ṭṭlb.a[--.---].|yšu.g h[.---].|i.ap.b‘[l.---].|i.hd.d[---.---].|ynp‘.b‘[l.---].|b ṯmnt.[---].|yqrb.[---] 5[67].4.6
-].|tš[.---].|t[---.---].|[-----].|[-----].|b [----].|w [----].|b‘l.[---].|il hd.b[---].|at.bl.at.[---].|yisp hm.b[‘l.---].|bn.dgn 12[75].2.22
--.---].|yšu.g h[.---].|i.ap.b‘[l.---].|i.hd.d[---.---].|ynp‘.b‘[l.---].|b ṯmnt.[---].|yqrb.[---].|lḥm.m[---.---].|[‘]d.lḥm[.št 5[67].4.8
|w [----].|b‘l.[---].|il hd.b[---].|at.bl.at.[---].|yisp hm.b[‘l.---].|bn.dgn[.---].|‘ḏbm.[---].|uḫry.l[---].|mṣt.ks h.t[--.- 12[75].2.25
w aṯb.l ntbt.k.‘ṣm l t[--].|[---.]drk.brḥ.arṣ.lk pn h.yrk.b‘[l].|[---.]bt k.ap.l pḫr k ‘nt tqm.‘nt.tqm.|[---.p]ḫr k.ygrš k 1001.2.8
n.|[---].b‘l m.d ip[---].|[il.]hd.d ‘nn.n[--].|[----.]aliyn.b[‘l].|[---.btl]t.‘n[t.-.]p h.|[---.---]n.|[-----].|[-----].|[---.]lk[.- 10[76].2.34
dd.il.y[--.---].|b ym.il.d[--.---.n]|hr.il.y[--.---].|aliyn.[b‘l.---].|btlt.[‘nt.---].|mh.k[--.---].|w at[--.---].|aṯr[t.---].|b i 4[51].2.37
[šnm.dqt.--].|[--]t.dqtm.[b nbk.---].|[--.k]mm.gdlt.l.b[‘l.---].|[dq]t.l.ṣpn.gdlt.l[.---].|u[gr]t.š.l.[il]ib.ǵ[--.--rt].|w [35[3].33
at.yp‘t.b[--.---].|aliyn.b‘l[.---].|drkt k.mšl[-.---].|b riš k.aymr[.---].|ṯpṭ.nhr.yṯb[r.ḥ 2.1[137].4
.gb‘ h d [---].|ibr.k l hm.d l h q[--.---].|l ytn.l hm.tḥt b‘l[.---].|h.u qšt pn hdd.b y[.----].|‘m.b ym b‘l ysy ym[.---]. 9[33].2.5
[---.]ḥlmt.alp.šnt.w[.---].|šntm.alp.d krr[.---].|alp.pr.b‘l.[---].|w prt.tkt.[---].|šnt.[---].|ššw.‘ṯtrt.w ššw.‘[nt.---].|w 2158.1.3
---].|w ṣin.‘z.b[‘l.---].|llu.bn[š.---].|imr.ḫ[--.---].|[--]n.b‘[l.---].|w [--]d.[---].|idk[.-]it[.---].|trgm[.-]dk[.---].|m‘bd[. 2158.1.17
rt[.---].|šm k.mdd.i[l.---].|bt ksp y.d[--.---].|b d.aliyn b[‘l.---].|kd.ynaṣn[.---].|gršnn.l k[si.mlk h.l nḫt.l kḥṯ].|drkt 1[‘NT.X].4.22
r.il.w pḫr.b‘l].|gdlt.šlm[.gdlt.w burm.lb].|rmṣt.ilh[m.b‘lm.---].|ksm.ṯlṯm.[---].|d yqḥ bt[.--]r.dbḥ[.šmn.mr].|šmn. 35[3].18
bn[š.---].|d bnš.ḥm[r.---].|w d.l mdl.r[--.---].|w ṣin.‘z.b[‘l.---].|llu.bn[š.---].|imr.ḫ[--.---].|[--]n.b‘[l.---].|w [--]d.[--- 2158.1.14
l y].|aṯr h.r[pum.l tdd.aṯr h].|l tdd.il[nym.---].|mhr.b‘l[.---.mhr].|‘nt.lk b[t y.rpim.rpim.b bt y].|aṣḥ.km.[iqra k 22.1[123].7
.hry.w yld.|[---]m.ḥbl.kṯ[r]t.|[---.bt]lt.‘nt.|[---.ali]yn.b‘l.|[---.]m‘n.|[-----].|[-----].|[---.--]r.|[---.--]qk.|[---.--]ik.|[- 11[132].1.8
spr.mr[ynm].|[b‘]l.[---].|mr[--.---].|hm.[---].|kmrṯn[.---].|bn.ṯbln[.---].|bn. 2070.1.2
n].|[---.]š[--].|[-----].|[-----].|[---.]ṯty.|[---.-]rd y.|[---.]b‘l.|[---].plz.|[---.-]tt k.|[---.]mlk. 2159.16
yd‘ bn il.|[---.]pḫr kkbm.|[---.]dr dt.šmm.|[---.al]iyn b‘l.|[---].rkb.‘rpt.|[---.]ǵš.l limm.|[---.]l yṯb.l arṣ.|[---].mtm 10[76].1.6
w yn.|[---.rk]b ‘rpt.|[---.--]n.w mnu dg.|[---.]l aliyn b‘l.|[---].rkb ‘rpt. 2001.2.17
t.ikl.b pr‘.|yṣq.b irt.lbnn.mk.b šb‘.|[ymm.---]k.aliyn.b‘l.|[---].r‘ h ab y.|[---.]‘[---]. 22.2[124].26
ytn.w [--]u.l ytn.|[aḫ]r.mǵy.‘[d]t.ilm.|[w]y‘n.aliy[n.]b‘l.|[---.]tb‘.l lṭpn.|[il.d]pid.l tbrk.|[krt.]ṯ‘.l tmr.n‘mn.|[ǵl 15[128].2.12
[---].aliyn.|[b‘l.---.-]ip.dpr k.|[---.-]mn k.ššrt.|[---.--]t.npš.‘gl.|[---.-]nk.a 5[67].5.2
].yšt.il h.|[---.]iṯm h.|[---.y]mǵy.|[---.]dr h.|[---.-]rš.l b‘l.|[---.-]ǵk.rpu mlk.|[‘lm.---.--]k.l tšt k.l iršt.|[‘lm.---.--]k. UG5.2.2.3
--.--]a h.|[---.--]d.|[---].umt n.|[---.--]yh.wn l.|[---].bt b‘l.|[---.--]y.|[---.--]nt. 28[-].12
[------.i]qnim.[--].|[---.]aliyn.b‘l.|[---.--]k.mdd il.|y[m.---.]l ṯr.qdqd h.|il[.--.]rḥq.b ǵr.|k 4[51].7.2
lk.yb‘l hm.|[---.--]t.w.ḫpn.l.azzlt.|[---.]l.‘ṯtrt.šd.|[---].yb‘lnn.|[---.--]n.b.ṯlṯ.šnt.l.nṣd.|[---.--]ršp.mlk.k.ypdd.mlbš. 1106.56
b y[--.---].|il[.---].|b‘l[.---].|[---.--]l.[---].|[---.g]dlt[.---].|[---].p[--.---].|[---.]bl[--. 46[-].1.3
[--]l.bn y.šḥt.w [---].|[--]tt.msgr.bn k[.---].|[--]n.tḥm.b‘l[.---]. 59[100].12
k gmn.al]iyn.b‘l.|[ṭṭbḫ.šb‘m.]ḥmrm.|[k gm]n.al[i]yn.b[‘l].|[---]ḥ h.tšt bm.‘[--].|[---.]zr h.ybm.l ilm.|[id]k.l ttn.pn 6.1.29[49.1.1]
.pn y[.-.]tlkn.|[---.]rḥbn.hm.[-.]aṯr[.---].|[--]šy.w ydn.b‘[l.---]n.|[--]‘.k yn.hm.l.atn.bt y.l h. 1002.61
.l pd[r.]pdrm.|ṯṯ.l ṯṯm.aḫd.‘r.|šb‘m.šb‘.pdr.|ṯmnym.b‘l.[----].|tš‘m.b‘l.mr[-].|bt[.--]b b‘l.b qrb.|bt.w y‘n.aliyn.|b 4[51].7.11
b qṣrt.npšt kn.u b qṭ]t tqṭṭ.|[ušn.yp kn.---.--]l.il.t‘ḏr b‘l.|[-----.]lšnt.|[---.--]yp.tḥt.|[-----].|[---.]w npy gr.|[ḥmyt. APP.I[-].1.8
]y.|[---.np]y nqmd.|[---.]pḫr.|[-----].|[-----].|[---.t‘ḏ]r b‘l.|[-----].|[-----].|[---.--]r.|[---.]npy.|[---.ušn.yp kn.ulp.q]ṭ APP.I[-].2.7
[-----].|[------.]ṯr.|[---.aliy]n.b‘l.|[------.]yrḫ.zbl.|[--.kṯ]r w ḫss.|[---]n.rḥm y.ršp zbl.|[w ‘ 15[128].2.3
.bnš.|w ytn.ilm.b d hm.|b d.iḫqm.gṯr.|w b d.ytrhd.|b‘l. 55[18].22
.dgn.|k.ibr.l b‘l[.yl]d.|w rum.l rkb.‘rpt.|yšmḫ.aliyn.b‘l. 10[76].3.38

b‘ldn

|ygmr.|mnṯ.|prḫ.|‘dršp.|ršpab.|ṯnw.|abmn.|abǵl.|b‘ldn.|yp‘. 1032.13

b‘ld‘

b‘ld‘.yd[.---.‘]šrt.ksp h.|lbiy.pdy.[---.k]sp h. 2112.1

b‘lz

šd.bn.šty.l.bn.ṭbrn.|šd.bn.ḫtb.l bn.y‘ḏrd.|šd.gl.b‘lz.l.bn.‘mnr.|šd.kn‘m.l.bn.‘mnr.|šd.bn.krwn.l bn.‘myn.|š 2089.3

bʻly

bdẖmn[.bn.-]bdn. | ḥṣmn.[bn.---]ln. | [--]dm.[bn.---]n. | bʻly.[bn.---]n. | krr[-.---]. | špš[yn.---]. | [--]b[.---]. | ʻbdʻṯ[tr.---]. 102[322].1.6
.nb[dg]. | bn.ild[-]. | [-----]. | [bn.]nnr. | [bn.]aglby. | [bn.]bʻly. | [mḏ]rǵlm. | [bn.]kdgdl. | [b]n.qṭn. | [b]n.ǵrgn. | [b]n.tgḏn 104[316].7
[-----]. | [-]mn. | bʻly. | rpan. | ʻpṯrm. | bn.ʻbd. | šmbʻl. | ykr. | bly. | ṯbʻm. | ḥdṯn. | r 1058.3
h. | bʻlm.w.ṯlṯ.nʻrm.w.bt.aḥt. | bn.lwn.ṯlṯtm.bʻlm. | bn.bʻly.ṯlṯtm.bʻlm. | w.aḥd.ḫbṯ. | w.arbʻ.aṯt. | bn.lg.ṯn.bn h. | bʻlm. 2080.7
[-.---]. | nrn.bn.mtn[-.---]. | aẖyn.bn.nbk[-.---]. | ršpn.bn.bʻly[.---]. | bnil.bn.yṣr[.---]. | ʻdyn.bn.uḏr[-.---]. | w.ʻdʻ.nḥl h[.-- 90[314].1.11
--.bn.--]r. | [-----]. | [---.--]yn. | [---.]aṯrn. | [---.--]ḫt. | [---.]bʻly. | [---.]nʻmy. | [---.-]ml. | [---.-]mn. | [---.-]rn. | [---.--]n. 102.5в[323.5].5
. | [---.]šd.ubdy. | [---.]bn.k[--.]ṯ[l]ṯm ksp b[---]. | [---.]šd bʻly. | [---.]šd ubdy. | [---.š]d ubdy. | [---.šd] ubdy. | [---.š]d.bn.ṣ 2031.7

bʻlyn

[---.--]š. | [---.a]rbʻm. | bʻlyn.bnš. | mlkt. | ʻšrm. | [---.--]t. 138[41].3
[-----]. | [--.-]ym[.---]. | [---.]bʻlyn[.---]. | [--.-]ṯy[.---]. 120[-].3

bʻlyskn

ldn. | gld.bt.klb. | l[---].bt.ḫzli. | bn.iẖyn. | ṣdqn.bn.ass. | bʻlyskn.bn.ss. | ṣdqn.bn.imrt. | mnḥm.bn.ḫyrn. | [-]yn.bn.arkb 102[323].3.9

bʻlytn

ilṣdq.bn.zry. | bʻlytn.bn.ulb. | ytrʻm.bn.swy. | ṣḥrn.bn.qrtm. | bn.špš.bn.ibrd. 2024.2

bʻlmḏr

b.ym.ḥdṯ. | b.yr.pgrm. | lqḥ.bʻlmḏr. | w.bn.ḫlp. | miḫd. | b.arbʻ. | mat.ḫrṣ. 1156.3

bʻlmʻḏr

bʻlmʻḏr. | bn.mdn. | mkrm. 1168.1
b.ym.ḥdṯ. | b.yrḫ.pgrm. | lqḥ.bʻlmʻḏr. | w bn.ḫlp. | w[--]y.d.bʻl. | miḫd.b. | arbʻ.mat. | ḫrṣ. 1155.3

bʻlmṯpṭ

.plsy. | bn.qrr[-]. | bn.ḥyl. | bn.gʻyn. | ḥyn. | bn.armg[-]. | bʻlmṯpṭ. | [bn].ayḫ. | [---]rn. | ill. | ǵlmn. | bn.ytrm. | bn.ḫgbt. | m 1035.2.5

bʻln

hnd. | iwr[k]l.pdy. | agdn.bn.nrgn. | w ynḥm.aḫ h. | w.bʻln aḫ h. | w.ḥṯṯn bn h. | w.btšy.bt h. | w.ištrmy. | bt.ʻbd mlk. 1006.5
ʻl[.---].ḥdṯn.yḥmn.bnil. | ʻdn.w.ildgn.ḥṭbm. | tdǵlm.iln.bʻ[l]n.alḏy. | tdn.ṣr[--.--]t.ʻzn.mtn.n[bd]g. | ḥrš qṭn[.---.]dqn.b 2011.21
bn.bʻln.biry. | ṯlṯ.bʻlm. | w.adn hm.ṯr.w.arbʻ.bnt h. | yrḫm.yd.ṯn. 2080.1
.w l. | bn h.ʻd.ʻlm. | šḫr.ʻlmt. | bnš bnšm. | l.yqḥnn.b d. | bʻln.bn.kltn. | w.b d.bn h.ʻd. | ʻlm.w unṯ. | in.b h. 1008.18
t h[.--]. | [---.]yd. | [k]rm h.yd. | [k]lkl h. | [w] ytn.nn. | l.bʻln.bn. | kltn.w l. | bn h.ʻd.ʻlm. | šḫr.ʻlmt. | bnš bnšm. | l.yqḥn 1008.12
[.ḫm]št. | bn.arsw ʻ[šr]m. | ʻšdyn.ḫmš[t]. | abršn.ʻšr[t]. | bʻln.ḫmšt. | w.nḥl h.ḫm[š]t. | bn.unp.arbʻt. | ʻbdbn.ytrš ḫmšt. 1062.8
.šmʻrgm.skn.qrt. | ḥgbn.šmʻ.skn.qrt. | ngr krm.ʻbdadt.bʻln.ypʻmlk. | ṯǵrm.mnḥm.klyn.ʻdršp.ǵlmn. | [a]bǵl.ṣṣn.ǵrn. | 2011.12
bʻln. | yrmn. | ʻnil. | pmlk. | aby. | ʻdyn. | aǵlyn. | [--]rd. | [--]qrd. | 1066.1
tsn. | rpiy. | mrṯn. | ṯnyn. | apṯ. | šbn. | gbrn. | ṯbʻm. | kyn. | bʻln. | ytršp. | ḥmšm.ṯmn.kbd. | tgmr.bnš.mlk. | d.b d.adnʻm. | 1024.2.23
[---].ḫpn. | dqn.šʻrt. | [lm]d.yrṯ. | [-.]ynḥm.ḫpn. | ṯṯ.lmd.bʻln. | l.qḥ.ḫpnt. | ṯṯ[.-]l.md.ʻṯr[t]. | l.qḥ.ḫpnt. 1117.17
bd.ḫmn.šmʻ.rgm. | šdn.[k]bš. | šdyn.mḫ[ṣ]. | aṯry.mḫṣ. | bʻln.mḫṣ. | y[ḥ]ṣdq.mḫṣ. | ṣp[r].ks[d]. | bʻl.š[lm]. | ḫyrn[.---]. | a 2084.16
yʻdd.tḥt.bn arbn. | ʻbdil.tḥt.ilmlk. | qly.tḥt bʻln.nsk. 1053.3
š.bnši.ṯt[---]. | ʻšr.b gt.[---]. | ṯn.ʻšr.b.gt.ir[bṣ]. | arbʻ.b.gt.bʻln. | ʻšt.ʻšr.b.gpn. | yd.ʻdnm. | arbʻ.ǵzlm. | ṯn.yṣrm. 2103.6
.alḏy. | tdn.ṣr[--.--]t.ʻzn.mtn.n[bd]g. | ḥrš qṭn[.---.]dqn.bʻln. | ǵltn.ʻbd.[---]. | nsk.ḥdm.klyn[.ṣd]qn.ʻbdilt.bʻl. | annmn.ʻ 2011.23
klby.dqn. | ḥrṭm.ḥgbn.ʻdn.ynḥm[.---]. | ḥrš.mrkbt.ʻzn.[b]ʻln.ṯb[--.-]nb.trtn. | [---]mm.klby.kl[--].dqn[.---]. | [-]ntn.art 2011.28
it.ḥ[p]r.ʻbdm. | mitm.drt.ṯmnym.drt. | tgmr.akl.b.gt[.b]ʻln. | ṯlṯ.mat.ṯtm.kbd. | ṯtm.ṯt.kbd.ḥpr.ʻbdm. | šbʻm.drt.arbʻ 2013.5
rš.mrkbt.ṯqlm. | ʻpṯn.ḥrš.qṭn.ṯqlm. | bn.pǵdn.ṯqlm. | bn.bʻln.ṯqlm. | ʻbdyrḫ.nqd.ṯqlm. | bt.sgld.ṯqlm. | bn.ʻmy.ṯqlm. | b 122[308].1.11
btwm. | [-]bln. | [-]bldn. | [-]bdy. | [b]ʻln. | [-]šdm. | iwryn. | nʻmn. | [-----]. | b gt.yny. | agtṯp. | bn.ʻnt 1043.5
[---]ʻ.lmdm. | [---.b]ʻln. | [---.]lmdm.b d.snrn. | [---.lm]dm.b d.nrn. | [---.ḫ]ḏǵlm. 1051.2

bʻlsip

ḥdd.ar[y.---]. | bʻlsip.a[ry.---]. | klt h.[---]. | ṯty.ary.m[--.---]. | nrn.arny[.---]. | 81[329].2

bʻlskn

. | iḫy[-]. | ʻbdgṯr. | ḥrr. | bn.s[-]p[-]. | bn.nrpd. | bn.ḥ[-]y. | bʻlskn. | bn.ʻbd. | ḫyrn. | alpy. | bn.plsy. | bn.qrr[-]. | bn.ḥyl. | bn. 1035.1.15

bʻlsr

ḥ[--]. | w.arbʻ.ḥ[mrm]. | b m[ʻ]rby. | ṯmn.ṣmd.[---]. | b d.bʻlsr. | yd.ṯdn.ʻšr. | [ḥ]mrm. | ddm.l.ybr[k]. | bdmr.prs.l.u[-]m[2102.4

bʻlṣdq

.l hm. | [---.--]ḏn. | mrkbt.mtrt. | ngršp. | ngǵln. | iltḥm. | bʻlṣdq. 1125.2.5

bʻlṣn

ṣrn. | mḏrǵlm. | agmy. | ʻdyn. | ʻbdbʻl. | ʻbdkṯr.ʻbd. | tdǵl. | bʻlṣn. | nsk.ksp. | iwrtn. | ydln. | ʻbdilm. | dqn. | nsk.ṯlṯ. | ʻbdadt. 1039.2.22

bʻlrm

. | bṣr.abn.špšyn. | dqn. | aǵlmn. | knʻm. | aḫršp. | anntn. | bʻlrm. | [-]ral. | šḏn. | [-]ǵl. | bn.bʻltǵpṯ. | ḥrš.btm. | ršpab. | [r]ṣn. 2067.1.9

b'lt

yrḫ ḫyr.b ym ḥdṯ. | alp.w š.l b'lt bhtm. | b arb't 'šrt.b'l. | 'rkm. | b ṯmnt.'šrt.yr | tḥṣ.mlk.brr UG5.12.A.2
. | k.t'rbn.ršp m.bt.mlk. | ḫlu.dg. | ḥdṯm. | dbḥ.b'l.k.tdd.b'lt.bhtm. | b.[-]ǵb.ršp.ṣbi. | [---.--]m. | [---.]piln. | [---].ṣmd[.--- 2004.14
ln.d b.dmt.um.il[m.---]. | [--]ḏyn.b'd.[--]ḏyn.w l. | [--]k b'lt bhtm[.--]tn k. | [--]y.l ihbt.yb[--].rgm y. | [---.]škb.w m[--. 1002.45
šlmm kmm. | l b'l.ṣpn b 'r'r. | pamt ṯlṯm š l qrnt. | ṯlḥn.b'lt.bhtm. | 'lm.'lm.gdlt l b'l. | ṣpn.ilbt[.---.]d[--]. | l ṣpn[.---.-]l UG5.13.31
rt.yrtḥṣ.mlk.brr]. | b arb'[t.'šrt.riš.argmn]. | w ṯn šm.l [b'lt.bhtm.'ṣrm.l inš]. | ilm.w š d[d.ilš.š.--.mlk]. | yṯb.brr[.w m 35[3].5
.yrtḥṣ.mlk. | br[r.]b a[r]b't.'šrt.riš. | arg[mn.w ṯn.]šm.l b'lt. | bhtm.'ṣ[rm.l in]š ilm.w š. | dd ilš.š[.---.]mlk.yṯb br | r.w APP.II[173].5
'ṣrm.l]. | ṣpn š.l ǵlm[t.š.w l.---]. | l yrḫ.gdlt.l [nkl.gdlt.l b'] | [lt].bht[m].[']ṣrm l [inš.ilm]. | [---.]ilh[m.dqt.š.--]. | [---.--] APP.II[173].28
[m.l ṣpn.š]. | l ǵlmt.š.w l [---.l yrḫ]. | gd[lt].l nkl[.gdlt.l b'lt.bhtm]. | 'š[rm.]l inš[.ilm.---]. | il[hm.]dqt.š[.---.rš] | [p.š]rp 35[3].26
dlt.w l ǵlmt š. | [w]pamt ṯlṯm.w yrdt.[m]dbḥt. | gdlt.l b'lt bhtm.'ṣrm. | l inš ilm. 34[1].21
| šb'.alpm. | bt b'l.ugrt.ṯn šm. | 'lm.l ršp.mlk. | alp w.š.l b'lt. | bwrm š.iṯtqb. | w š.nbk m w.š. | gt mlk š.'lm. | l kṯr.ṯn.'l UG5.12.B.8
---]. | [---.i]qni.l.ṯr[mn.art.---]. | [b.yr]ḫ.riš.yn.[---]. | [---.b']lt.bhtm.š[--.---]. | [---.-]rt.l.dml[.---]. | [b.yrḫ].nql.ṯn.ḫpn[.-- 1106.33
--]. | u[gr]t.š.l.[il]ib.ǵ[--.--rt]. | w ['ṣrm.]l.ri[--.---]. | [--]t.b'lt.bt[.---]. | [md]bḥt.b.ḫmš[.---]. | [-.]kbd.w.db[ḥ.---]. | [--].aṯ 35[3].37
]mṯbt.ilm.w.b.[---]. | [---.]tṯtbn.ilm.w.[---]. | [---.]w.ksu.b'lt.b[htm.---]. | [---.]il.bt.gdlt.[---]. | [---.]hkl[.---]. 47[33].7
-]. | [---.]qdš[.---]. | [---.k]su.p[--.---]. | [---.]agn[.---]. | [---.b'lt.b]htm[.---]. | [---.--]by.ṯ[--.---]. | [---.--]n[.---]. | [---.--]mm.g 45[45].6
[---.']ṣrm. | [--]ṯpḫ b'l. | [ṯl]ṯ.'ṣrm. | [w]b'lt btm. | [---.--]ṣn.l.dgn. | [---.--]m. | [---].pi[--.-]qš. | [--]pš.šn[39[19].4
.b m | rqdm.dšn.b.ḥbr.kṯr.ṭbm. | w tšt.'nt.gṯr.b'lt.mlk.b' | lt.drkt.b'lt.šmm.rmm. | [b'l]t.kpṯ.w 'nt.di.dit.rḫpt. | [---.-] UG5.2.1.6
y h pdr.ttǵr. | [---.n]šr k.al ttn.l n. | [---.]tn l rbd. | [---.]b'lt h w yn. | [---.rk]b 'rpt. | [---.--]n.w mnu dg. | [---.]l aliyn b' 2001.2.14
bm. | w tšt.'nt.gṯr.b'lt.mlk.b' | lt.drkt.b'lt.šmm.rmm. | [b'l]t.kpṯ.w 'nt.di.dit.rḫpt. | [---.-]rm.aklt.'gl.'l.mšt. | [---.--]r.š UG5.2.1.8
[---.--]m. | [---.]piln. | [---].ṣmd[.---.]pd[ry]. | [-----]. | [---.b]'lt. | lbnm.'šr.yn. | ḫlb.gngnt.ṯlṯ.y[n]. | bṣr.'šr.yn. | nnu arb'.y 2004.20
.w mṣltm.b m | rqdm.dšn.b.ḥbr.kṯr.ṭbm. | w tšt.'nt.gṯr.b'lt.mlk.b' | lt.drkt.b'lt.šmm.rmm. | [b'l]t.kpṯ.w 'nt.di.dit.rḫp UG5.2.1.6
m.dšn.b.ḥbr.kṯr.ṭbm. | w tšt.'nt.gṯr.b'lt.mlk.b' | lt.drkt.b'lt.šmm.rmm. | [b'l]t.kpṯ.w 'nt.di.dit.rḫpt. | [---.-]rm.aklt.'gl UG5.2.1.7
l.[----]. | l.[----]. | l.'ṯ[trt.---]. | l.mš[--.---]. | l.ilt[.---]. | l.b'lt[.---]. | l.il.bt[.---]. | l.ilt.[---]. | l.ḥtk[.---]. | l.ršp[.---]. | [l].ršp. 1004.6

b'ltdtt

. | yḥmn.aḫm[l]k.'bdrpu.adn.ṯ[--]. | bdn.qln.mtn.ydln. | b'ltdtt.tlgn.ytn. | b'ltǵpṯm.krwn.ilšn.agyn. | mnn.šr.ugrt.ḏkr. 2011.35

b'ltn

n.ṯyn. | bn g'r. | bn.prtn. | bn ḫnn. | b[n.-]n. | bn.ṣṣb. | bn.b'ltn ḫlq. | bn.mlkbn. | bn.asyy ḫlq. | bn.kṯly. | bn.kyn. | bn.'bd 2016.2.2

b'ltǵpṯ

. | kn'm. | aḫršp. | anntn. | b'lrm. | [-]ral. | šḏn. | [-]ǵl. | bn.b'ltǵpṯ. | ḥrš.btm. | ršpab. | [r]ṣn. | [a]ǵlmn. | [a]ḫyn. | [k]rwn. | [2060.13
'bdrpu.adn.ṯ[--]. | bdn.qln.mtn.ydln. | b'ltdtt.tlgn.ytn. | b'ltǵpṯm.krwn.ilšn.agyn. | mnn.šr.ugrt.ḏkr.yṣr. | tǵǵln.ḫmš.d 2011.36

b'r

rr. | yštn.aṯrt.l bmt.'r. | l ysmsmt.bmt.pḫl. | qdš.yuḫdm.šb'r. | amrr.k kbkb.l pnm. | aṯr.btlt.'nt. | w b'l.tb'.mrym.ṣpn. | 4[51].4.16
k. | mǵy. | hbṭ.hw. | ḫrd.w.šl hw. | qr[-]. | akl n.b.grnt. | l.b'r. | ap.krmm. | ḫlq. | qrt n.ḫlq. | w.d'.d'. 2114.9
l h. | [---.rg]m.ank l[.--.--]rny. | [---.]ṭm.hw.i[--]ty. | [---].ib'r.a[--.]ḏmr. | [---.]w mlk.w rg[m.---]. | [--.rg]m.ank.[b]'r.[-- 1002.52
t. | l.mlk.gbl. | w.ḫmšm.ksp. | lqḥ.mlk.gbl. | lbš.anyt h. | b'rm.ksp. | mḫr.hn. 2106.17
r. | tškr.zbl.'ršm. | yšu.'wr. | mzl.ymzl. | w ybl.trḫ.ḥdṯ. | yb'r.l ṯn.aṯt h. | w l nkr.mddt. | km irby.tškn. | šd.k ḥsn.pat. | 14[KRT].4.190
škr. | tškr.zbl.'ršm. | yšu.'wr.mzl. | ymzl.w yṣi.trḫ. | ḥdṯ.yb'r.l ṯn. | aṯt h.lm.nkr. | mddt h.k irby. | [t]škn.šd. | km.ḥsn.p 14[KRT].2.101
.ib'r.a[--.]ḏmr. | [---.]w mlk.w rg[m.---]. | [--.rg]m.ank.[b]'r.[--]ny. | [--]n.bt k.[---.]b'[r.---]. | [--]my.b d[-.--]y.[---]. | [-- 1002.54
.]l kbd.arṣ. | ar[bdd.]l kb[d.š]dm.yšt. | [----.]b'l.mdl h.yb'r. | [---.]rn h.aqry. | [---.]b a[r]ṣ.mlḥmt. | ašt[.b ']p[r] m.dd 3['NT].4.70
--]. | tr.ḥt[-.---]. | w msk.tr[.---]. | tqrb.aḫ[h.w tṣḥ]. | lm.tb'rn[.---]. | mn.yrḫ.k m[rṣ.---]. | mn.k dw.kr[t]. | w y'ny.ǵzr[. 16.2[125].80
.w rg[m.---]. | [--.rg]m.ank.[b]'r.[--]ny. | [--]n.bt k.[---.]b'[r.---]. | [--]my.b d[-.--]y.[---]. | [---.]'m.w hm[.--]yt.w.[---]. | [1002.55
ank.mnm. | [ḫ]s[r]t.w.uḫ y. | [y]'msn.ṯmn. | w.[u]ḫ y.al yb'rn. 2065.21

bǵy

mt.['mn.kbkbm.abn.brq]. | d l t[d'.šmm.at m.w ank]. | ibǵ[y h.b tk.ǵ]r y.il.ṣpn. | b q[dš.b ǵr.nḥ]lt y. | w t['n].btlt.[']n 3['NT].4.63
'.šmm. | rgm l td'.nšm.w l tbn. | hmlt.arṣ.at m.w ank. | ibǵy h.b tk.ǵr y.il.ṣpn. | b qdš.b ǵr.nḥlt y. | b n'm.b gb'.tliyt. | 3['NT].3.26
.kbkbm]. | rgm.l td'.nš[m.w l tbn.hmlt.arṣ]. | at.w ank.ib[ǵy h.---]. | w y'n.kṯr.w ḫss[.lk.lk.'nn.ilm.] | atm.bštm.w an 1['NT.IX].3.16
thmt]. | 'm kbkbm[.abn.brq.d l td'.šmm.at m]. | w ank.ib[ǵy h.---]. | [-].l y'mdn.i[---.---]. | kpr.šb' bn[t.rḥ.gdm.w anh 7.2[130].21

bǵr

n.mr]. | šmn.rqḥ[.-]bt.mtnt[.w ynt.qrt]. | w ṯn ḥṯm.w bǵr.arb['.---]. | kdm.yn.prs.qmḥ.[---]. | mdbḥt.bt.ilt.'ṣr[m.l ṣp 35[3].22
šmn mr[.šmn.rqḥ.bt]. | mtnt.w ynt.[qrt.w ṯn.ḥṯm]. | w bǵr.arb'.[---.kdm.yn]. | prs.qmḥ.m'[--.---]. | mdbḥt.bt.i[lt.'ṣr APP.II[173].24

bǵrt

wt.lṭpn[.ḥtk k.---]. | yh.kṯr.b[---]. | št.lskt.n[--.---]. | 'db.bǵrt.ṯ[--. --]. | ḥš k.'ṣ k.'[bṣ k.'m y.p'n k.tlsmn]. | 'm y twtḥ.i[1['NT.IX].3.9

bṣm

[---.]nnd[-]. | [-]gbt. | [--]y bnš kb[š]y. | krmpy.b.bṣm. | [-]mrn.ṣd.b gl[-]. 2169.4

bṣmn

dn.bn.uss.'šrm. | b.'dn.bn.ṯṯ.'šrt. | b.bn.qrdmn.ṯlṯm. | b.bṣmn[.bn].ḥrtn.'[--]. | b.t[--.---] h.[---]. | [-----]. | [--]ly.ḫmšm.b 2054.1.21
nsk.ksp. | iwrtn. | ydln. | 'bdilm. | dqn. | nsk.ṯlṯ. | 'bdadt. | bṣmn.spr. 1039.2.30

bṣmn

aẖ.|ypln.w.ṯn.bn h.|ydln.|anr[my].|mld.|krmp[y].|bṣmn. 2086.13

bṣql

y dnil.ysb.palt h.|bṣql.yph.b palt.bṣ[q]l.|yph.b yǵlm.bṣql.y[ḥb]q.|w ynšq.aḥl.an bṣ[ql].|ynp'.b palt.bṣql yp' b yǵ 19[1AQHT].2.63

yǵlm.bṣql.y[ḥb]q.|w ynšq.aḥl.an bṣ[ql].|ynp'.b palt.bṣql yp' b yǵlm.|ur.tisp k.yd.aqht.|ǵzr.tšt k.b qrb m.asm.| 19[1AQHT].2.65

b palt.bṣ[q]l.|yph.b yǵlm.bṣql.y[ḥb]q.|w ynšq.aḥl.an bṣ[ql].|ynp'.b palt.bṣql yp' b yǵlm.|ur.tisp k.yd.aqht.|ǵzr.t 19[1AQHT].2.64

--.]šš[w.---].|[---.w]yṣq b a[p h].|[k ḫr š]šw mǵmǵ w b[ṣql 'rgz].|[ydk aḥ]d h w yṣq b ap h.|[k ḫr]ššw ḫndrṯ w ṯ[160[55].4

k [ḫr ššw mǵmǵ].|w [bṣql.'rgz.ydk].|a[ḥd h.w.yṣq.b.ap h].|k.[ḫr.ššw.ḫndrṯ].|w.ṯ 161[56].3

|l ysmsm.bmt.pḥl.|y dnil.ysb.palt h.|bṣql.yph.b palt.bṣ[q]l.|yph.b yǵlm.bṣql.y[ḥb]q.|w ynšq.aḥl.an bṣ[ql].|ynp'. 19[1AQHT].2.62

tšṯnn.l[b]mt 'r.|l ysmsm.bmt.pḥl.|y dnil.ysb.palt h.|bṣql.yph.b palt.bṣ[q]l.|yph.b yǵlm.bṣql.y[ḥb]q.|w ynšq.aḥl. 19[1AQHT].2.62

bṣr

spr.bnš.mlk.|d taršn.'msn.|bṣr.abn.špšyn.|dqn.|aǵlmn.|kn'm.|aḫršp.|anntn.|b'lrm.|[2067.1.3

ht.[km.yṯb].|l lḥm.w bn.dnil.l ṯrm[.'l h].|nšrm.trḫpn.ybṣr.[ḥbl.d]|iym.bn.nšrm.arḫp.an[k.']l.|aqht.'db k.hlmn.ṯn 18[3AQHT].4.20

aqht.km.yṯb.l lḥ[m].|bn.dnil.l ṯrm.'l h.nšr[m].|trḫpn.ybṣr.ḥbl.diy[m.bn].|nšrm.trḫp.'nt.'l[.aqht].|t'dbn h.hlmn.ṯ 18[3AQHT].4.31

ḫrb[.---].|yǵly.yḫsp.ib[.---].|'l.bt.ab h.nšrm.trḫ[p]n.|ybṣr.ḥbl.diym.|tbky.pǵt.bm.lb.|tdm'.bm.kbd.|tmz'.kst.dni 19[1AQHT].1.33

t.|[--]n.|[-----].|[-----].|nnu.|šmg.|šmn.|lbnm.|ṯrm.|bṣr.|y[--].|y[--].|snr.|midḫ.|ḥ[lym].|[ḫ]lby.|'r.|'nq[pat].| 2058.2.16

d.|[---.]ḫrm.ṯn.ym.|tš[.---.]ymm.lk.|hrg.ar[b'.]ymm.bṣr.|kp.šsk k.[--].l ḥbš k.|'tk.ri[š.]l mhr k.|w 'p.l dr['].nšr k 13[6].5

l[b]nm.|nnu.|'rm.|bṣr.|m'r.|ḫlby.|mṣbt.|snr.|ṯm.|ubš.|glbt.|mi[d]ḫ.|mr[i]l. 2041.4

y].|[-----].|[---.b]'lt.|lbnm.'šr.yn.|ḫlb.gngnt.ṯlṯ.y[n].|bṣr.'šr.yn.|nnu arb'.yn.|šql ṯlṯ.yn.|šmny.kdm.yn.|šmgy.kd 2004.23

b.'rmt.|arb'.bnšm.b.šrš.|ṯṯ.bnšm.b.mlk.|arb'.bnšm.b.bṣr.|ṯn.bnšm.[b.]rqd.|ṯn.b[nšm.b.---]y.|[---].b[nšm.b.--]nl.| 2076.39

[-----].|bṣr[.---].|lbn[m].|'r[.---].|nnu[.---].|šq[--.---].|[-]r[-.---].|[--- 2145.2

bṣry

.alpm.|aḫ[m]lk.bn.nskn.alpm.|krw.šlmy.|alpm.|atn.bṣry.alpm.|lbnym.|ṯm[n.]alp mitm.|ilb'l ḫmš m[at].|'dn.ḫ 1060.2.6

n.b'yn.š[--.---].|aǵltn.mid[-.---].|bn.lṣn.'rm[y].|aršw.bṣry.|arpṯr.y'rty.|bn.ḫdyn.ugrty.|bn.tgdn.ugrty.|tgyn.arty 87[64].6

n.š'rty.|bn.arwdn.ilšt'y.|bn grgs.|bn.ḫran.|bn.arš[w.b]ṣry.|bn.ykn.|bn.lṣn.'rmy.|bn.b'yn.šly.|bn.ynḥn.|bn.'bdil 99[327].2.1

ubš.|mṣb[t].|ḥl.y[---].|'rg[z].|y'r[t].|amd[y].|atl[g].|bṣr[y].|[---].|[---]y.|ar.|agm.w.ḫpty.|ḫlb.ṣpn.|mril.|'nmky 71[113].45

bql

.w.ykhp].|mid.dblt.yṯ[nt.w].|ṣmq[m].yṯnm.w[.qmḥ.bql].|tdkn.aḥd h.w[.yṣq].|b.ap h. 161[56].34

yraš w ykhp mid.|dblt yṯnt w ṣmqm yṯn[m].|w qmḥ bql yṣq aḥd h.|b ap h. 160[55].25

bqmm

.]yd h.k šr.|knr.uṣb't h ḥrṣ.abn.|p h.tiḫd.šnt h.w akl.bqmm.|tšt ḥrṣ.k lb ilnm.|w ṯn.gprm.mn gpr h.šr.|aqht.y'n. 19[1AQHT].1.9

bq'

|arb'.uzm.mrat.bq'.|ṯlṯ.[-]ṯt.aš[']t.šmn.uz.|mi[t].ygb.bq'.|a[--].'ṭ.|a[l]pm.alpnm.|ṯlṯ.m[a]t.art.ḥkpt.|mit.dnn.|m 1128.23

|ṭat.l imr h.km.lb.|'nt.aṯr.b'l.tiḫd.|bn.ilm.mt.b ḥrb.|tbq'nn.b ḫṯr.tdry|nn.b išt.tšrpnn.|b rḥm.tṭḥnn.b šd.|tdr'nn 6[49].2.32

t h.knp.hrgb.b'l.ṯbr.|b'l.ṯbr.diy.hwt.w yql.|tḥt.p'n h.ybq'.kbd h.w yḥd.|[i]n.šmt.in.'ẓm.yšu.g[h].|w yṣḥ.knp.hrg 19[1AQHT].3.130

h.hwt h.knp.ṣml.b'[l].|b'l.ṯbr.diy.hyt.tq[l.tḥt].|p'n h.ybq'.kbd h.w yḥd.|iṯ.šmt.iṯ.'ẓm.w yqḥ b hm.|aqht.ybl.l qẓ. 19[1AQHT].3.144

yṣḥ.knp.ṣml.|b'l.yṯbr.b'l.yṯbr.diy.|hyt.tql.tḥt.p'n y.ibq'.|kbd h.w aḥd.hm.iṯ.šmt.iṯ.|'ẓm.abky w aqbrn h.aštn.| 19[1AQHT].3.138

p.hr[g]b.|b'l.yṯb.b'l.y[ṯb]r.diy[.h]wt.|w yql.tḥt.p'n y.ibq'.kbd[h].|w aḥd.hm.iṯ.šmt.hm.iṯ[.'ẓm].|abky.w aqbrn.a 19[1AQHT].3.124

].|knp.nšrm.b'l.yṯbr.|b'l.ṯbr.diy hmt.tqln.|tḥt.p'n h.ybq'.kbdt hm.w[yḥd].|in.šmt.in.'ẓm.yšu.g h.|w yṣḥ.knp.nš 19[1AQHT].3.116

[.knp.nšrm].|b'l.yṯb.b'l.yṯb[r.diy.hmt].|tqln.tḥ p'n y.ibq['.kbd hm.w] |aḥd.hm.iṯ.šmt.hm.i[ṯ].|'ẓm.abky.w aqbrn 19[1AQHT].3.109

bm.|ṯmnym.tbṯḫ.alp.|uz.mrat.mlḥt.|arb'.uzm.mrat.bq'.|ṯlṯ.[-]ṯt.aš[']t.šmn.uz.|mi[t].ygb.bq'.|a[--].'ṭ.|a[l]pm.al 1128.21

bq't

.w.ql'.|u[l]n.qšt.w.ql'.|y'rn.qšt.w.ql'.|klby.qšt.w.ql'.|bq't.|ily.qšt.w.ql'.|bn.ḥrẓn.qšt.w.ql'.|tgrš.qšt.w.ql'.|špšyn. 119[321].2.21

].b.dmt qdš.|[---].b.dmt qdš.|[---.--]n.b.anan.|[--]yl.b.bq't.b.gt.tgyn.|[--]in.b.trzy.|[--]yn.b.glltky.|ṯd[y]n.b.glltky. 2118.6

ubr'y.|arny.|m'r.|š'rt.|ḫlb rpš.|bq't.|šḥq.|y'by.|mḫr. 65[108].6

.arb' 'šr.|ṣ'.ṯmn.|šḥq.'šrm.arb'.kbd.|ḫlb rpš arb'.'šr.|bq't ṯṯ.|irab ṯn.'šr.|ḥbš.ṯmn.|amdy.arb'.'šr.|[-]n'y.ṯṯ.'šr. 67[110].8

by.[---.--]m.ṯn[.---].|m'r.[---].|arny.[---].|š'rt.ṯn[.---].|bq't.[--].ḥ[mr.---].|ḫlb krd.ḥ[mr.---].|ṣ'.ḥmr.w[.---].|ṣ'q.ḥm 2040.12

.kb]d.|š[--.---.k]bd.|ḫ[--.---.kb]d.|šr[-.---].|m'r[-.---].|bq't.[---].|šḥq[.---].|rkby ar[b'm].|bir ṯ[--].|'nqpat [---].|m[2042.13

bq'ty

[---.--]r.|[--.]iln.|y'rtym.|bn.gṯrn.|bq'ty. 100[66].5

bqr

b ṯṯ ym ḥdṯ.|ḫyr.'rbt.|špš ṯǵr h.|ršp.|w 'bdm tbqrn.|skn. 1162.5

bqrt

[-]ay[.---].|[a]rš[mg.---].|urt[n.---].|'dn[.---].|bqrt[.---].|ṯnǵrn.[---].|w.bn h.n[--.---].|ḥnil.[---].|aršmg.mr 2084.5

bqš

mt.w.anyt.hm.t'[rb].|mkr.hn d.w.rgm.ank[.--].|mlkt.ybqš.anyt.w.at[--].|w mkr n.mlk[.---]. 2008.2.13

abmlk.bn.ilrš.|iḫyn.bn.ḫryn.|[ab]ǵl.bn.gdn.|[---].bn.bqš.|[---].bn.pdn.|[---.bn.-]ky.|[---.bn.--]r.|[-----].|[---.--]yn. 102[323].4.13

bqṯ

t'n.nrt.ilm.š[p]š. | šd yn.'n.b qbt[.t] | bl lyt.'l.umt k. | w abqṯ.aliyn.b'l. | w t'n.btlt.'nt. | an.l an.y špš. | an.l an.il.yǵr[.-] 6[49].4.44
b.'ltn.a[--.--]y. | w.spr.in[.-.]'d m. | spr n.ṯhr[.--]. | aṯr.iṯ.bqṯ. | w.štn.l y. 2060.34

br

ḏm[r.---].br. | bn.i[ytlm.---]. | wr[t.---.]b d.yḫmn. | yry[.---.]br. | ydn[.---] 2123.1
anyt.miḫd[t]. | br.ṯpṭb'[l.---]. | br.dmty[.---]. | ṯkt.ydln[.---]. | ṯkt.ṯryn[.---]. | br.'bdm[lk.---]. | 84[319].1.3
[r.---].br. | bn.i[ytlm.---]. | wr[t.---.]b d.yḫmn. | yry[.---.]br. | ydn[.---].kry. | bn.ydd[.---.b]r. | prkl.b'l.any.d.b d.abr[-]. 2123.4
al[.---]. | arbḫ.'n h tšu w[.---]. | aylt tǵpy ṯr.'n[.---]. | b[b]r.mrḥ h.ti[ḫd.b yd h]. | š[g]r h bm ymn.t[--.---]. | [--.]l b'l.'b 2001.1.12
. | šmrgt.b dm.ḫrṣ. | kḥṯ.il.nḫt. | b ẓr.hdm.id. | d prša.b br. | n'l.il.d qblbl. | 'ln.ybl hm.ḫrṣ. | ṯlḥn.il.d mla. | mnm.dbb 4[51].1.36
ṯb'[l.---]. | br.dmty[.---]. | ṯkt.ydln[.---]. | ṯkt.ṯryn[.---]. | br.'bdm[lk.---]. | wry[.---]. | ṯkt[.---]. | ṯk[t.---]. | br[.---]. | br[.--- 84[319].1.6
---.]b d.yḫmn. | yry[.---.]br. | ydn[.---].kry. | bn.ydd[.---.b]r. | prkl.b'l.any.d.b d.abr[-]. 2123.6
anyt.miḫd[t]. | br.ṯpṭb'[l.---]. | br.dmty[.---]. | ṯkt.ydln[.---]. | ṯkt.ṯryn[.---]. | br 84[319].1.2
n[.---]. | br.'bdm[lk.---]. | wry[.---]. | ṯkt[.---]. | ṯk[t.---]. | br[.---]. | br[.---]. | br[.---]. | br[.---]. | br[.---]. | br[.---]. | br[.---]. | 84[319].2.1
ry[.---]. | ṯkt[.---]. | ṯk[t.---]. | br[.---]. | br[.---]. | br[.---]. | br[.---]. | br[.---]. | br[.---]. | br[.---]. | br[.---]. | br[.---]. 84[319].2.4
| ṯkt[.---]. | ṯk[t.---]. | br[.---]. | br[.---]. | br[.---]. | br[.---]. | br[.---]. | br[.---]. | br[.---]. | br[.---]. | br[.---]. 84[319].2.5
. | ṯk[t.---]. | br[.---]. | br[.---]. | br[.---]. | br[.---]. | br[.---]. | br[.---]. | br[.---]. | br[.---]. | br[.---]. 84[319].2.6
br.'bdm[lk.---]. | wry[.---]. | ṯkt[.---]. | ṯk[t.---]. | br[.---]. | br[.---]. | br[.---]. | br[.---]. | br[.---]. | br[.---]. | br[.---]. | br[.---]. | 84[319].2.2
lk.---]. | wry[.---]. | ṯkt[.---]. | ṯk[t.---]. | br[.---]. | br[.---]. | br[.---]. | br[.---]. | br[.---]. | br[.---]. | br[.---]. | br[.---]. | br[.---]. 84[319].2.3
]. | br[.---]. | br[.---]. | br[.---]. | br[.---]. | br[.---]. | br[.---]. | br[.---]. | br[.---]. | br[.---]. 84[319].2.7
]. | br[.---]. | br[.---]. | br[.---]. | br[.---]. | br[.---]. | br[.---]. | br[.---]. | br[.---]. 84[319].2.8
an[y]t.mlk[.---]. | w.[ṯ]lṯ.brm.[---]. | arb' 'tkm[.---]. 2057.2
]. | br[.---]. | br[.---]. | br[.---]. | br[.---]. | br[.---]. | br[.---]. | br[.---]. 84[319].2.9

bri

]b d.ymz. | [šd.b d].klby.psl. | [ub]dy.mri.ibrn. | [š]d.bn.bri.b d.bn.ydln. | [u]bdy.ṯǵrm. | [š]d.ṯǵr.mṯpit.b d.bn.iryn. | [u 82[300].2.6

brd

'bd.ali[yn]. | b'l.sid.zbl.b'l. | arṣ.qm.yṯ'r. | w yšlḥmn h. | ybrd.ṯd.l pnw h. | b ḥrb.mlḥt. | qṣ.mri.ndd. | y'šr.w yšqyn h. | 3['nt].1.6

brdd

d.ṣdqšlm. | [šd.b d.]bn.p'ṣ. | [ubdy.']šrm. | [šd.---]n.b d.brdd. | [---.--]m. | [šd.---.b d.]ṯpṭb'l. | [šd.---.]b d.ymz. | [šd.b d] 82[300].1.31

brdn

w dṯn.nḥl h.l bn.pl. | šd.krwn.l aḫn. | šd.'yy.l aḫn. | šd.brdn.l bn.bly. | šd gzl.l.bn.ṭbr[n]. | šd.ḫzmyn.l a[--]. | ṯn šdm 2089.13

brḏl

n. | arb'.mat. | l.alp.šmn. | nḥ.ṯṯ.mat. | šm[n].rqḥ. | kkrm.brḏl. | mit.tišrm. | ṯlṯm.almg. | ḫmšm.kkr. | qnm. | 'šrm.kk[r]. | 141[120].6

brzn

šd.]lbny.b d.tbṯṯb. | [š]d.bn.ṯ[-]rn.b d.'dbmlk. | [šd.]bn.brzn.b d.nwrḏ. | [šd.]bn.nḫbl.b d.'dbym. | [šd.b]n.qṭy.b d.tt. | 82[300].1.17
ṯnnm. | bn.qqln. | w.nḥl h. | w.nḥl h. | bn.šml[-]. | bn.brzn. | bn.ḫṯr[-]. | bn.yd[--]. | bn.'[---]. | w.nḥ[l h]. | w.nḥ[l h]. | 116[303].6
n.rmyy. | bn.tlmyn. | w.nḥl h. | w.nḥl hm. | bn.ḥrm. | bn.brzn. | w.nḥl h. | bn.adlḏn. | bn.šbl. | bn.ḫnzr. | bn.arwṯ. | bn.ṯbt 113[400].1.10
.l.sḫrn.nḥl h. | šd[.ag]pṯn.b[n.]brrn.l.qrt. | šd[.--]dy.bn.brzn. | l.qrt. 2029.22
l[.---]. | anntn bn[.---]. | bn.brzn [---]. | bnil.bn.tl[--]. | bn.brzn.ṯn. | bn.išb'l[.---]. | bn.s[---]. | dnn.[bn.---]. | bn[.--]'nt. 2069.7
mry[n]m. | bn rmy[y]. | yšril[.---]. | anntn bn[.---]. | bn.brzn [---]. | bnil.bn.tl[--]. | bn.brzn.ṯn. | bn.išb'l[.---]. | bn.s[---]. 2069.5
ḫ].bn.gṯṯn. | yrmn.bn.'n. | krwn.nḥl h. | ttn.[n]ḥl h. | bn.b[r]zn. | [---.-]ḥn. 85[80].4.12

brzt

zl. | bn.ṣmy. | bn.il[-]šy. | bn.ybšr. | bn.sly. | bn.ḫlbt. | bn.brzt. | bn.ayl. | [-----]. | 'bd[--]. | bn.i[--]. | 'd[--]. | ild[--]. | bn.qṣn. 2117.2.13

brḥ

t[.---]. | [---.]k.drḫm.w aṯb.l ntbt.k.'ṣm l t[--]. | [---.]drk.brḥ.arṣ.lk pn h.yrk.b'[l]. | [---.]bt k.ap.l pḫr k 'nt tqm.'nt.tq 1001.2.8
k tmḫṣ.ltn.bṯn.brḥ. | tkly.bṯn.'qltn. | šlyṭ.d šb'y.rašm. | ṯṯkḥ.ttrp.šmm.k rs. | i 5[67].1.1
. | p nšt.b'l.[ṭ]'n.iṭ'n k. | [---.]ma[---] k.k tmḫṣ. | [ltn.bṯn.br]ḥ.tkly. | [bṯn.'qltn.]šlyṭ. | [d šb't.rašm].ṯṯkḥ. | [ttrp.šmm.k r 5[67].1.28
l km.qr.mym.d '[l k]. | mḫṣ.aqht.ǵzr.amd.gr bt il. | 'nt.brḥ.p 'lm h.'nt.p dr[.dr]. | 'db.uḫry mṭ.yd h. | ymǵ.l mrrt.tǵll 19[1AQHT].3.154
ḫṣ.aqht. | ǵzr.šrš k.b arṣ.al. | yp'.riš.ǵly.b d.ns' k. | 'nt.brḥ.p 'lm h. | 'nt.p dr.dr.'db.uḫry mṭ yd h. | ymǵ.l qrt.ablm.a 19[1AQHT].3.161

brk

s.yiḫd. | [il.b]yd.krpn.bm. | [ymn.]brkm.ybrk. | ['bd h.]ybrk.il.krt. | [ṭ'.ymr]m.n'm[n.]ǵlm.il. | a[ṯt.tq]ḥ.y krt.aṯt. | tq 15[128].2.19
[.krt]. | b tk.rpi.ar[ṣ]. | b pḫr.qbṣ.dtn. | ṣǵrt hn.abkrn. | tbrk.ilm.tity. | tity.ilm.l ahl hm. | dr il.l mšknt hm. | w tqrb.w 15[128].3.17
mr.n'mn. | [ǵlm.]il.ks.yiḫd. | [il.b]yd.krpn.bm. | [ymn.]brkm.ybrk. | ['bd h.]ybrk.il.krt. | [ṭ'.ymr]m.n'm[n.]ǵlm.il. | a 15[128].2.18
.gg h.b ym. | [ti]ṭ.rḥṣ.npṣ h.b ym.rṭ. | [--.y]iḫd.il.'bd h.ybrk. | [dni]l mt rpi.ymr.ǵzr. | [mt.hr]nmy npš.yḥ.dnil. | [mt. 17[2AQHT].1.35
lmn.ṯnm.qdqd. | ṯlṯ id.'l.udn.špk.km.šiy. | dm.km.šḫṭ.l brk h.ṭṣi.km. | rḥ.npš h.km.iṯl.brlt h.km. | qṭr.b ap h.b ap.mh 18[3AQHT].4.24
m[.qdqd]. | ṯlṯ id.'l.udn.š[pk.km]. | šiy.dm h.km.šḫ[ṭ.l brk h]. | yṣat.km.rḥ.npš[h.km.iṯl]. | brlt h.km.qṭr.[b ap h.---] 18[3AQHT].4.35
.d ḥrš. | ydm.aḫr.ymǵy.kṯr. | w ḫss.b d.dnil.ytnn. | qšt.l brk h.y'db. | qṣ't.apnk.mṯt.dnty. | tšlḥm.tššqy ilm. | tsad.tkbd 17[2AQHT].5.27

bḥ.l ilm.|š‘ly.dǵṯ h.b šmym.|dǵṯ.hrnmy.d kbkbm.|l tbrkn.alk brkt.|tmrn.alk.nmr[rt].|imẖṣ.mẖṣ.aẖ y.akl[.m]|k 19[1AQHT].4.194

.tphn.mlak.ym.t‘dt.ṯpṭ[.nhr].|t[ǵ]ly.hlm.rišt hm.l ẓr.brkt hm.w l kḥṯ.|zbl hm.b hm.yg‘r.b‘l.lm.ǵltm.ilm.rišt.|km 2.1[137].23

.w ank.‘ny.mlak.ym.t‘dt.ṯpṭ.nhr.|tšu ilm rašt hm.l ẓr.brkt hm.ln.kḥṯ.zbl hm.|aẖr.tmǵyn.mlak ym.t‘dt.ṯpṭ.nhr.l p 2.1[137].29

il.|ǵzr.p np.š.npš.lbim.|thw.hm.brlt.anẖr.|b ym.hm.brk y.tkšd.|rumm.‘n.kḏd.aylt.|hm.imt.imt.npš.blt.|ḥmr.p i 5[67].1.16

.mlbr.|ilšiy.|kry amt.|‘pr.‘ẓm yd.|ugrm.ẖl.ld.|aklm.tbrk k.|w ld ‘qqm.|ilm.yp‘r.|šmt hm.|b hm.qrnm.|km.ṯr 12[75].1.26

l kḥṯ.|zbl hm.b hm.yg‘r.b‘l.lm.ǵltm.ilm.rišt.|km l ẓr brkt km.w ln.kḥṯ.zbl km.aḥd.|ilm.t‘ny lḥt.mlak.ym.t‘dt.ṯpṭ 2.1[137].25

ilm.t‘ny lḥt.mlak.ym.t‘dt.ṯpṭ.nhr.|šu.ilm.rašt km.l ẓr.brkt km.ln.kḥṯ.|zbl km.w ank.‘ny.mlak.ym.t‘dt.ṯpṭ.nhr.|tš 2.1[137].27

d]t.ilm.|[w]y‘n.aliy[n.]b‘l.|[---.]tb‘.l lṭpn.|[il.d]pid.l tbrk.|[krt.]ṯ‘.l tmr.n‘mn.|[ǵlm.]il.ks.yiẖd.|[il.b]yd.krpn.b 15[128].2.14

šrš.|km.ary h.uzrm.ilm.ylḥm.|uzrm.yšqy.bn.qdš.|l tbrknn l ṯr.il ab y.|tmrnn.l bny.bnwt.|w ykn.bn h b bt.šrš.b 17[2AQHT].1.24

š‘ly.dǵṯ h.b šmym.|dǵṯ.hrnmy.d kbkbm.|l tbrkn.alk brkt.|tmrn.alk.nmr[rt].|imẖṣ.mẖṣ.aẖ y.akl[.m]|kly[.‘]l.um 19[1AQHT].4.194

m ṯkm.aẖm.qym.il.|b lsmt.ṯm.yṯbš.šm.il.mt m.|y‘bš.brk n.šm.il.ǵzrm.|ṯm.ṯmq.rpu.b‘l.mhr b‘l.|w mhr.‘nt.ṯm.yḥ 22.2[124].7

n.|[ǵlm.]il.ks.yiẖd.|[il.b]yd.krpn.bm.|[ymn.]brkm.ybrk.|[‘bd h.]ybrk.il.krt.|[ṯ‘.ymr]m.n‘m[n.]ǵlm.il.|a[ṯt.tq] 15[128].2.18

m.|ǵrmn.kp.mhr.‘tkt.|rišt.l bmt h.šnst.|kpt.b ḥbš h.brkm.tǵl[l].|b dm.ḏmr.ḥlqm.b mm[‘].|mhrm.mṭm.tgrš.|šb 3[‘NT].2.13

|tǵdd.kbd h.b ṣḥq.ymlu.|lb h.b šmẖt.kbd.‘nt.|tšyt.k brkm.tǵll b dm.|ḏmr.ḥlqm.b mm‘.mhrm.|‘d.tšb‘.tmtẖṣ.b b 3[‘NT].2.27

ẖt.kbd.‘nt.tšyt.tḥt h.k]kdrt.riš.|[‘l h.k irbym.kp.---.k br]k.tǵll.b dm.|[ḏmr.---.]td[-.]rǵb.|[----]k.|[----] h. 7.1[131].9

n.|ilm.mt.npš[.-].|npš.lbun.|thw.w npš.|anẖr.b ym.|brkt.šbšt.|k rumm.hm.|‘n.kḏd.aylt.|mt hm.ks.ym|sk.nhr UG5.4.6

š[r].tštn.|[w t‘n].mṯt.ḥry.|[l lḥ]m.l šty.ṣḥt k[m].|[---.]brk.t[---].|[‘l.]krt.tbkn.|[--.]rgm.ṯrm.|[--.]mtm.tbkn.|[--]t. 15[128].5.11

brlt

ilm.|mt.hwt.ydd.bn.il.|ǵzr.p np.š.npš.lbim.|thw.hm.brlt.anẖr.|b ym.hm.brk y.tkšd.|rumm.‘n.kḏd.aylt.|hm.imt 5[67].1.15

t.rpi].|mt.aqht.ǵzr.[šṣat].|btlt.‘nt.k [rḥ.npš h].|k iṯl.brlt h.[b h.p‘nm].|ṭṭṭ.‘l[n.pn h.td‘.b ‘dn].|ksl.y[ṯbr.ygṣ.pnt. 19[1AQHT].2.93

k.km.šiy.|dm.km.šẖṭ.l brk h.tṣi.km.|rḥ.npš h.km.iṯl.brlt h.km.|qṭr.b ap h.b ap.mhr h.ank.|l aḥwy.tqḥ.yṭpn.mh 18[3AQHT].4.25

iy.dm h.km.šẖ[ṭ.l brk h].|yṣat.km.rḥ.npš[h.km.iṯl].|brlt h.km.qṭr.[b ap h.---].|‘nt.b ṣmt.mhr h.[---].|aqht.w tbk. 18[3AQHT].4.37

.|zbln.‘l.riš h.|w ṯṯb.trḥṣ.nn.b d‘t.|npš h.l lḥm.tptḥ.|brlt h.l ṯrm.|mt.dm.ẖt.š‘tqt.|dm.lan.w ypqd.|krt.ṯ‘.yšu.g h. 16.6[127].12

l h.tšm‘.|mṯt.dnty.t‘db.imr.|b pẖd.l npš.kṯr.w ẖss.|l brlt.hyn.d ḥrš.|ydm.aẖr.ymǵy.kṯr.|w ẖss.b d.dnil.ytnn.|qš 17[2AQHT].5.24

ṣḥ.|šm‘.mṯt.dnty.‘d[b].|imr.b pẖd.l npš.kṯr.|w ẖss.l brlt.hyn d.|ḥrš yd.šlḥm.ššqy.|ilm sad.kbd.hmt.b‘l.|ḥkpt.il. 17[2AQHT].5.18

.hm.brk y.tkšd.|rumm.‘n.kḏd.aylt.|hm.imt.imt.npš.blt.|ḥmr.p imt.b klt.|yd y.ilḥm.hm.šb‘.|ydt y.b ṣ‘.hm.ks.y 5[67].1.18

.|riš.r[--.--]ḥ[.---]y[.---.-]nt.[š]ṣat[k.]rḥ.npš.hm.|k.iṯl.brlt n[-.k qṭr.b ap -].|tmǵyn.tša.g h[m.w tṣḥn].|šm‘.l dnil.[19[1AQHT].2.88

i]l mt rpi.ymr.ǵzr.|[mt.hr]nmy npš.yḥ.dnil.|[mt.rp]i.brlt.ǵzr.mt hrnmy.|[---].hw.mẖ.l ‘rš h.y‘l.|[---].bm.nšq.aṯt 17[2AQHT].1.38

brn

nmn.‘šrt.|‘bdadt.ẖmšt.|abmn.ilštm‘y.ẖmš[t].|‘zn.bn.brn.ẖmšt.|m‘rt.ẖmšt.|arttb.bn.ẖmšt.|bn.ysr[.ẖmš]t.|ṣ[-]r.ẖ 1062.26

br̀šm

.|[--]ln.|[---]r.|[---]y.|bn.aḏdt.|bn.atnb.|bn.ỳsd.|bn.br̀šm.|bn.gṯprg.|gṯpbn.|bn.b[--].|[b]n.[---].|bn.a[--].|bn.ml 1057.11

brq

].|bn[.---].|bn[.---].|[bn.--]t.|[bn.---].|[bn.--]my.|[bn.b]rq.|[bn.--]r.|[bn.--]tn.|[bn.-]rmn.|bn.prtn.|bn.ymn.|bn. 124[-].5.4

ṭr h.|b‘l.y‘dn.‘dn.ṯkt.b glṯ.|w tn.ql h.b ‘rpt.|šrh.l arṣ.brqm.|bt.arzm.yklln h.|hm.bt.lbnt.y‘msn h.|l yrgm.l aliyn 4[51].5.71

[hmlt.a]rṣ.[tant.šmm.‘m.ar]ṣ.|thmt.[‘mn.kbkbm.abn.brq].|d l t[d‘.šmm.at m.w ank].|ibǵ[y h.b tk.ǵ]r y.il.ṣpn.|b 3[‘NT].4.61

|w lẖšt.abn[.tant.šmm.‘m.arṣ.thmt].|‘m kbkbm[.abn.brq.d l td‘.šmm.at m].|w ank.ib[ǵy h.---].|[-].l y‘mdn.i[---.-- 7.2[130].20

w lẖšt.abn.|tant.šmm.‘m.arṣ.|thmt.‘mn.kbkbm.|abn.brq.d l.td‘.šmm.|rgm l td‘.nšm.w l tbn.|hmlt.arṣ.at m.w an 3[‘NT].3.23

h.il ṣpn.b [tk].|ǵr.tliyt.šb‘t.brqm.[---].|ṯmnt.iṣr r‘t.‘ṣ brq y.|riš h.tply.ṭly.bn.‘n h.|uz‘rt.tmll.išd h.qrn[m].|dt.‘l h UG5.3.1.4

.šmn.‘l.yddn.|kd.‘l.ššy.|kd.‘l.nḏbn.bn.agmn.|[k]d.‘l.brq.|[kd]m.[‘l].kṯr.|[kd]m[.---].ḥ[--].|[-----].|[kd.]‘l[.---].|[k 1082.1.9

spr.irgmn.|ṯlṯ.ẖmš.alpm.|b d.brq.maẖdy.|kkr.ṯlṯ.|b d.bn.by.ar[y].|alpm.ṯlṯ.|b d.šim.il[š] 1134.3

mẖsrn.d.[--.]ušknym.|brq.ṯlṯ.[mat.ṯ]lṯ.|bsn.mi[t.--].|ar[--.---].|k[--.---]. 1136.2

m.|‘bdyrẖ.nqd.ṯqlm.|bt.sgld.ṯqlm.|bn.‘my.ṯqlm.|bn.brq.ṯqlm.|bn.ẖnzr.ṯqlm.|dqn.nsk.arb‘t.|bn.ẖdyn.ṯqlm.|bn. 122[308].1.15

.[y]drn.|[---.]bn.ẖlan.|[--]r bn.mn.|[--]ry.|[--]lim bn.brq.|[--.]qtn bn.drṣy.|[--]kn bn.pri.|[r]špab bn.pni.|[ab]mn 2087.5

qn.yṣbt.|[---.--]m.b nši.‘n h.w tphn.|[---.--]ml.ksl h.k b[r]q.|[---.]m[-]ǵ[-].thmt.brq.|[---].tṣb.qšt.bnt.|[---.‘]n h.km 17[2AQHT].6.11

h.w tphn.|[---.--]ml.ksl h.k b[r]q.|[---.]m[-]ǵ[-].thmt.brq.|[---].tṣb.qšt.bnt.|[---.‘]n h.km.bṯn.yqr.|[krpn h.-.l]arṣ. 17[2AQHT].6.12

ǵr.hd.r[‘y].|k mdb.b tk.ǵr h.il ṣpn.b [tk].|ǵr.tliyt.šb‘t.brqm.[---].|ṯmnt.iṣr r‘t.‘ṣ brq y.|riš h.tply.ṭly.bn.‘n h.|uz‘rt UG5.3.1.3

brqd

bn.grgš.|bn.bly.|bn.apṯ.|bn.ysd.|bn.pl[-].|bn.ṯb‘nq.|brqd.|bnn.|kbln.ṣ[md].|bn gmrt.|bn.il.ṣm[d].|bn abbly.|y 2113.15

brqn

[.---].kt.|[y]nḥm.|ilb‘l.|‘bdyr[ẖ].|ṯṯpḥ.|artn.|ybnil.|brqn.|adr[dn].|krwn.|arkḏn.|ilmn.|abškn.|ykn.|ršpab.|k 1024.1.9

y.|brqn.ṯlḥy.|bn.aryn.|bn.lgn.|bn.b‘yn.|šdyn.|ary.|brqn.|bn.ẖlln.|bn.mṣry.|ṯmn.qšt.|w ‘šr.uṯpt.|upšt irš[-]. 118[306].11

n.|bn.kbl.|kn‘m.|bdlm.|bn.ṣǵr.|klb.|bn.mnḥm.|bn.brqn.|bn.‘n.|bn.‘bdy.|‘bd‘ṯtr. 1046.3.46

t.|bn.m.|ypḥ.ilšlm.|bn.prqdš.|ypḥ.mnḥm.|bn.ḥnn.|brqn.spr. 2116.23

mḏrǵlm.d inn.|msgm.l hm.|p‘ṣ.ẖbty.|artyn.ary.|brqn.ṯlḥy.|bn.aryn.|bn.lgn.|bn.b‘yn.|šdyn.|ary.|brqn.|bn. 118[306].5

i]ytlm.|[-ˀ-].gmn.|[---].l.urǵṯṯb.|[---.]l.‘ṯtrum.|[---.]l.brqn.|[---].skn.|[---.‘g]ltn.|[---].‘gltn.|[---.]‘gltn.|[---.šr]t.aḥ 2162.B.7

brr

b arb‘t.‘šr[t]. | yrtḥṣ.mlk.b[rr]. | b ym.mlat. | tqln.alpm. | yrḫ.‘šrt.l b‘[l]. | dqtm.w ynt.q UG5.13.2
bmm.gdlt.‘rb špš w ḥl. | [mlk.b ar]b‘t.‘[š]rt.yrtḥṣ.mlk.brr. | [b ym.ml]at.y[ql]n.al[p]m.yrḫ.‘šrt. | [l b‘l.ṣ]pn.[dq]tm. 36[9].1.10
ym.ḥdṯ]. | šmtr.[uṯkl.l il.šlmm]. | b ṯlṯt ‘[šrt.yrtḥṣ.mlk brr]. | b arb‘[t.‘šrt.riš.argmn]. | w ṯn šm.l [b‘lt.bhtm.‘ṣrm.l inš 35[3].3
m.ḥdṯ. | [šmtr].uṯkl.l il.šlmm. | b [ṯlṯt].‘šrt.yrtḥṣ.mlk. | br[r.]b a[r]b‘t.‘šrt.riš. | arg[mn.w ṯn.]šm.l b‘lt. | bhtm.‘ṣ[rm.l APP.II[173].4
| brr.r[gm.yṯṯb.b ṯdṯ.ṯn]. | l šmn.‘[ly h.gdlt.rgm.yṯṯb]. | brr.b šb‘[.ṣbu.špš.w ḥl] | yt.‘rb špš[.w ḥl.mlk.w.b y] | m.ḥdṯ.ṯ APP.II[173].51
.brr]. | rgm.yṯṯb.b.ṯdṯ.ṯn[.--.šmn]. | ‘ly h.gdlt.rgm.yṯ[ṯb.brr]. | b.[šb]‘.ṣbu.[š]pš.w.ḥly[t].‘[r]b[.š]p[š]. | w [ḥl.]mlk.[w.]b 35[3].46
krm.alp kb[d]. | ṯlṯ.l.nskm.birtym. | b d.urtn.w.ṯṯ.mat.brr. | b.ṯmnym.ksp.ṯlṯt.kbd. | ḫmš.alp.ṯlṯ.l.ḫlby. | b d.tlmi.b.‘š 2101.4
.l [b‘lt.bhtm.‘ṣrm.l inš]. | ilm.w š d[d.ilš.š.--.mlk]. | yṯb.brr[.w mḫ-.---]. | ym.[‘]lm.y‘[--.---]. | [--.-]g[-.-]s w [---]. | w yn 35[3].7
l b‘lt. | bhtm.‘ṣ[rm.l in]š ilm.w š. | dd ilš.š[.---.]mlk.yṯb br | r.w mḫ[--.---.]w q[--]. | ym.‘lm.y[---.---]. | t.k[-]ml.[---]. | l[- APP.II[173].7
it.šmn.d.nm[-.]b d.mzy.alzy. | ḫmš.kkr.ḥlb. | ḫmš.kkr.brr. | kkr.ḫmš.mat.kbd.ṯlṯ.šm[n]. | alp.mitm.kbd.ṯlṯ.ḥlb. | šb‘.l 1135.3
it. | ḫmš.ṯnt.d ṯl | ṯ mat. | ṯṯ.ṯnt.d alp | alpm.ṯlṯ ktt. | alp.brr. | kkr.tznt. | ḫmšt.kkr tyt. 1130.15
l.yi[--.-]m[---]. | b unṯ.km.špš. | d brt.kmt. | br.ṣṯqšlm. | b unṯ.‘d ‘lm. | mišmn.nqmd. | mlk ugrt. 1001.1.19
t bhtm. | b arb‘t ‘šrt.b‘l. | ‘rkm. | b ṯmnt.‘šrt.yr | tḥṣ.mlk.brr. | ‘lm.tzǵ.b ǵb.ṣpn. | nḥkt.ksp.w ḫrṣ ṯ‘ ṯn šm l btbt. | alp.w UG5.12.A.6
dṯ.ṯn šm[.---.--]t. | b yrḫ.ši[-.b ar]b‘t.‘š | rt.yr[tḥṣ.ml]k.brr. | ‘lm.š.š[--].l[--.]‘rb.šp | š.w ḥl[.ml]k. | bn.aup[š.--].bsbn h APP.II[173].55
mit.tišrm. | ṯlṯm.almg. | ḫmšm.kkr. | qnm. | ‘šrm.kk[r]. | brr. | [‘]šrm.npš. | ‘šrm.zt.mm. | ‘rb‘m. | šmn.mr. 141[120].12
l.yi[--.-]m[---]. | b unṯ.km.špš. | d brt.kmt. | br.ṣṯqšlm. | b unṯ.‘d ‘lm. | mišmn.nqmd. | mlk ugrt. | nqmd.ml 1005.4
n.nqmd. | mlk ugrt. | nqmd.mlk.ugrt. | ktb.spr hnd. | dt brrt.ṣṯqšlm. | ‘bd h.hnd. | w mn km.l yqḥ. | spr.mlk.hnd. | b y 1005.10
ṯmn.kkr.ṯlṯ. | ṯmn.kkr.brr. | arb‘.alpm.pḥm. | ḫmš.mat.kbd. | arb‘.alpm.iqni. | ḫmš.m 1130.2
[dqt.---.ṯn.l ‘š] | rm.pam[t.---]. | š dd šmn[.gdlt.w.---]. | brr.r[gm.yṯṯb.b ṯdṯ.ṯn]. | l šmn.‘[ly h.gdlt.rgm.yṯṯb]. | brr.b šb APP.II[173].49
.w.dqt[.---]. | ṯn.l.‘šrm.pamt.[---]. | š.dd.šmn.gdlt.w.[---.brr]. | rgm.yṯṯb.b.ṯdṯ.ṯn[.--.šmn]. | ‘ly h.gdlt.rgm.yṯ[ṯb.brr]. | b 35[3].44
arb‘.ḥm[r.---]. | l ṯlṯ. | ṯn.l.brr[.---]. | arb‘.ḥmr[.---]. | l.pḫ[-.]w.[---]. | w.l.k[--]. | w.l.k[--]. 1139.3

brrn

l mt mr[b-]. | qdš mlk [---]. | kbd d ilgb[-]. | mrmnmn. | brrn aryn. | a[-]ḫn tlyn. | atdb w ‘r. | qdš w amrr. | ṯḥr w bd. | [UG5.7.71
nn.‘db. | šd.iln[-].bn.irṯr.l.sḫrn.nḥl h. | šd[.ag]pṯn.b[n.]brrn.l.qrt. | šd[.--]dy.bn.brzn. | l.qrt. 2029.21

bršm

n. | bn.aršw. | bn.ḫzrn. | bn.iǵyn. | w.nḥl h. | bn.ksd. | bn.bršm. | bn.kzn. | w.nḥl h. | w.nḥl hm. | w.[n]ḥl hm. | b[n.---]. | b 113[400].2.19

brt

.ḥbl[.--]. | ‘rpt.ṯḥt.[---] | m ‘ṣrm.ḫ[---]. | glṯ.isr[.---] | m.brt[.---]. | ymt m.[---]. | ši[.---]. | m[--.---]. 8[51FRAG].14
[--.]l tṣi.b b[--].bm.k[--]. | [--]ṯb.‘ryt k.k qlt[.---]. | [--]at.brt.lb k.‘nn.[---]. | [--.]šdq.k ttn.l y.šn[.---]. | [---.]bn.rgm.w yd 60[32].4
.l[--.---]. | [--.--]tm.w ‘[--.--]. | [---].w kl.hw[.---]. | w [--].brt.lb[--.---]. | u[-]šhr.nuš[-.---]. | b [u]grt.w ht.a[--]. | w hm.at. 54.1.5[13.1.2]

bš

kbd.š[d]m.ap.mṯn.rgmm. | argmn.lk.lk.‘nn.ilm. | atm.bštm.w an.šnt. | uǵr.l rḥq.ilm.inbb. | l rḥq.ilnym.ṯn.mṯpdm. | 3[‘NT].4.77
ank.ib[ǵy h.---]. | w y‘n.kṯr.w ḫss[.lk.lk.‘nn.ilm.] | atm.bštm.w an[.šnt.kptr]. | l rḥq.ilm.ḥkp[t.l rḥq.ilnym]. | ṯn.mṯpd 1[‘NT.IX].3.18

bši

abnm. | [---.]upqt.‘rb. | [---.w ẓ]r.mtn y at zd. | [---.]t‘rb.bši. | [---.]l tzd.l tptq. | [---].g[--.]l arṣ. 1[‘NT.X].5.26

bšr

arr. | bm.arr.w b ṣpn. | b n‘m.b ǵr.t[l]iyt. | ql.l b‘l.ttnn. | bšrt.il.bš[r.b‘]l. | w bšr.ḥtk.dgn. | k.ibr.l b‘l[.yl]d. | w rum.l rk 10[76].3.34
m.ṣpn. | b alp.šd.rbt.kmn. | ṣḥq.btlt.‘nt.tšu. | g h.w tṣḥ.tbšr b‘l. | bšrt k.yblt.y[b]n. | bt.l k.km.aḫ k.w ḥẓr. | km.ary k. 4[51].5.88
.arr.w b ṣpn. | b n‘m.b ǵr.t[l]iyt. | ql.l b‘l.ttnn. | bšrt.il.bš[r.b‘]l. | w bšr.ḥtk.dgn. | k.ibr.l b‘l[.yl]d. | w rum.l rkb.‘rpt. 10[76].3.34
.snnt]. | hl ǵlmt tld b[n.--]n. | ‘n ha l yd h.tzd[.--]. | pt l bšr h.dm a[--.--]ḥ. | w yn.k mtrḫt[.---]h. | šm‘ ilht kṯr[t.--]m 24[77].9
]. | aḫdt.plk h[.b yd h]. | plk.qlt.b ymn h. | npyn h.mks.bšr h. | tmt‘.md h.b ym.ṯn. | npyn h.b nhrm. | štt.ḫptr.l išt. | ḫ 4[51].2.5
n. | b n‘m.b ǵr.t[l]iyt. | ql.l b‘l.ttnn. | bšrt.il.bš[r.b‘]l. | w bšr.ḥtk.dgn. | k.ibr.l b‘l[.yl]d. | w rum.l rkb.‘rpt. | yšmḫ.aliyn. 10[76].3.35
---.--]‘. | [---.]idk. | [---.--]ty. | [---.--]hr. | [---.--]ḫdn. | [---.]bšr y. | [---.--]b. | [---.--]a h. | [---.--]d. | [---].umt n. | [---.--]yh.w 28[-].6
b alp.šd.rbt.kmn. | ṣḥq.btlt.‘nt.tšu. | g h.w tṣḥ.tbšr b‘l. | bšrt k.yblt.y[b]n. | bt.l k.km.aḫ k.w ḥẓr. | km.ary k.ṣḥ.ḫrn. | b 4[51].5.89
. | yd.ṣpn hm.tliy m[.--.ṣ]pn hm. | nṣḥy.šrr.m[---.--]ay. | nbšr km.dnil.[--] h[.---]. | riš.r[--.--]ḫ[.---]y[.---.-]nt.[š]ṣat[k.] 19[1AQHT].2.86
[---].ybšr.qdš[.---]. | [---.--]t btm.qdš.il[.---]. | [---.b]n.qdš.k[--.---]. | 2125.1
t[.----]. | l mṯb[.--]t[.---]. | [tqdm.]yd.b ṣ‘.t[šl]ḫ. | [ḥrb.b]bš[r].tštn. | [w t‘n].mṯt.ḥry. | [l lḥ]m.l šty.ṣḥt k[m]. | [---.]brk.t 15[128].5.8
n. | lm.mṯb[.---]. | w lḥm mr.tqdm. | yd.b ṣ‘.tšlḫ. | ḥrb.b bšr.tštn. | [w t]‘n.mṯt.ḥry. | [l lḥ]m.l šty.ṣḥt km. | [--.dbḥ.l]krt 15[128].4.25
dm‘.k]m.ṣǵr.špš.b šmm.tqru. | [---.]nplt.y[--].md‘.nplt.bšr. | [---].w tpky.k[m.]n‘r.tdm‘.km. | [ṣǵ]r.bkm.y‘ny[.---.bn] UG5.8.39

bt

aḫt.b.bt.iwrpzn. | tt.aṯtm.w.pǵt.aḫt.b bt.[-]r[-]. | [aṯ]t.b.bt.aupš. | [aṯ]t.b.bt.ṯpṯb‘l. | [---.]n[--.mḏ]rǵlm. | [---.]b.bt[.---]l. 80[119].12
h.w tphn.[---]. | b grn.yḫrb[.---]. | yǵly.yḫ-p.ib[.---]. | ‘l.bt.ab h.nšrm.trḫ[p]n. | ybṣr.ḥbl.diym. | tbky.pǵt.bm.lb. | tdm‘ 19[1AQHT].1.32
bt.il. | b‘l.bt.aḏmny. | b‘l.bt.pdy. | b‘l.bt.nqly. | b‘l.bt.‘lr. | b‘l.bt.ssl. | b‘l.b 31[14].2
m. | tštyn.ṯlṯ.rb‘.ym.ḫmš. | ṯdṯ.ym.tlḥmn.rpum. | tštyn.bt.ikl.b pr‘. | yṣq.b irt.lbnn.mk.b šb‘. | [ymm.---]k.aliyn.b‘l. | [22.2[124].24
rm.b.bt.ṣdqš[lm]. | [a]ṯt.aḫt.b.bt.rpi[--]. | [aṯt.]w.bt h.b.bt.alḫn. | [aṯt.w.]pǵt.aḫt.b.bt.tt. | [aṯt.w.]bt h.b.bt.trǵds. | [---.] 80[119].25
mrkbt.ḫmš.‘šr h.prs. | bt.mrkbt.w l šant.ṯṯ. | l bt.‘šrm. | bt alḫnm.ṯlṯm ṯṯ kbd. 2105.4
rṣ. | l špš[.w y]rḫ.l gṯr.ṯn. | [ṯql.ksp].ṯb.ap.w npš. | [---].bt.alp w š. | [---.--]m.l gṯrm. | [---.]l ‘nt m. | [---.--]rm.d krm. | [33[5].16

bt.alpm. | ‘šr.bnšm. | ḫmš.bnši.ṯt[---]. | ‘šr.b gt.[---]. | ṯn.‘šr.b.gt 2103.1
l ym.hnd. | ‘mṯtmr. | bn.nqmp‘. | mlk.ugrt. | ytn.bt.anndr. | bn.ytn.bnš. | [ml]k.d.b riš. | [--.-]nt. | [l.‘b]dmlk. | [-- 1009.5
‘l.y‘dn.‘dn.ṯkt.b glṯ. | w tn.ql h.b ‘rpt. | šrh.l arṣ.brqm. | bt.arzm.yklln h. | hm.bt.lbnt.y‘msn h. | l yrgm.l aliyn b‘l. | ṣḥ 4[51].5.72
pǵt.aḥt.b[.bt.---]. | aṯt.w ṯn.n‘rm.b.bt.ilsk. | aṯt.ad[r]t.b.bt.armwl. | aṯt.aḥt.b.bt.iwrpzn. | ṯt.aṯtm.w.pǵt.aḥt.b bt.[-]r[-] 80[119].9
[aṯt.]w.pǵt.b.bt.gg. | [ǵz]r.aḥd.b.bt.nwrḏ. | [aṯ]t.adrt.b.bt.artṯb. | aṯt.w.ṯn.bn h.b.bt.iwwpzn. | aṯt.w.pǵt.b.bt.ydrm. | ṯ 80[119].4
.aḥd.b.bt.nwrḏ. | [aṯ]t.adrt.b.bt.artṯb. | aṯt.w.ṯn.bn h.b.bt.iwwpzn. | aṯt.w.pǵt.b.bt.ydrm. | ṯt.aṯtm.adrtm.w.pǵt.aḥt.b 80[119].5
t.w ṯn.n‘rm.b.bt.ilsk. | aṯt.ad[r]t.b.bt.armwl. | aṯt.aḥt.b.bt.iwrpzn. | ṯt.aṯtm.w.pǵt.aḥt.b bt.[-]r[-]. | [aṯ]t.b.bt.aupš. | [aṯ 80[119].10
lḥt.niṣ k.gr[š.d ‘šy.ln k]. | spu.ksm k.bt.[b‘l.w mnt k]. | bt il.aḥd.yd k.b [škrn]. | m‘ms k.k šb‘t.yn.ṭ[ḫ]. | gg k.b ym.ṭiṭ 17[2AQHT].2.5
[.‘b]dym.ṯlṯ.kkr š‘rt. | iqn[i]m.ṯṯt.‘šrt.ksp h. | ḫmšt.ḫrṣ.bt.il. | b.ḫmšt.‘šrt.ksp. | ḫmš.mat.šmt. | b.‘šrt.ksp. | ‘šr.ṣin.b.ṯṯt 2100.5
bt.il. | b‘l.bt.aḏmny. | b‘l.bt.pdy. | b‘l.bt.nqly. | b‘l.bt.‘lr. | b‘l.bt. 31[14].1
q.l awl. | išttk.lm.ttkn. | štk.mlk.dn. | štk.šibt.‘n. | štk.qr.bt.il. | w mṣlt.bt.ḥr[š]. 12[75].2.61
škrn.m‘ms h. | [k]šb‘ yn.spu.ksm h.bt.b‘l. | [w m]nt h bt.il.ṯḥ.gg h.b ym. | [ṭi]ṭ.rḥṣ.npṣ h.b ym.rṭ. | [--.y]iḫd.il.‘bd h. 17[2AQHT].1.33
| krn m‘ms y k šb‘t yn. | spu.ksm y.bt.b‘l.[w]mn[t]. | y.bt.il.ṯḥ.gg y.b ym.ṭiṭ. | rḥṣ.npṣ y.b ym.rṭ. | dn.il.bt h.ymǵyn. | 17[2AQHT].2.22
.---]. | ks.ksp[.---]. | krpn.[---]. | w ṯṯtn.[---]. | t‘l.tr[-.---]. | bt.il.li[mm.---]. | ‘l.ḥbš.[---]. | mn.lik.[---]. | lik.tl[ak.---]. | t‘ddn 5[67].4.21
lk.yṣm.y l km.qr.mym.d ‘[l k]. | mḫṣ.aqht.ǵzr.amd.gr bt il. | ‘nt.brḥ.p ‘lm h.‘nt.p dr[.dr]. | ‘db.uḫry mṭ.yd h. | ymǵ.l 19[1AQHT].3.153
‘nt.ymǵy. | ‘ṯtrt.t‘db.nšb l h. | w ‘nt.ktp.b hm.yg‘r.ṯǵr. | bt.il.pn.l mgr lb.t‘dbn. | nšb.l inr.t‘dbn.ktp. | b il ab h.g‘r.yṯb. UG5.1.1.12
-]. | rt.w ‘ṣrm.l[.---]. | pamt.w bt.[---]. | rmm.w ‘l[y.---]. | bt.il.ṯq[l.---.kbd]. | w bdḥ.k[--.---]. | ‘ṣrm.l i[nš.ilm.ṯb.md] | bḥ APP.II[173].42
lk. | kdm.ǵbiš ḥry. | ḫmš yn.b d. | bḥ mlkt. | b mdr‘. | ṯlṯ bt.il | ann. | kd.bt.ilann. 1090.17
ḥry. | ḫmš yn.b d. | bḥ mlkt. | b mdr‘. | ṯlṯ bt.il | ann. | kd.bt.ilann. 1090.19
k t‘rb.‘ṯtrt.ḫr[-]. | bt mlk.‘šr.‘šr.[--].bt ilm. | kbr[-]m.[-]trmt. | lbš.w [-]tn.ušpǵt. | ḫr[-].ṯlṯt.mzn. | d 33[5].2
kd.bt ilm. | rbm. | kd l ištnm. | kd l ḫty. | maḫdh. | kd l kblbn. | kd 1090.1
. | ṯt.aṯtm.adrtm.w.pǵt.aḥt.b[.bt.---]. | aṯt.w ṯn.n‘rm.b.bt.ilsk. | aṯt.ad[r]t.b.bt.armwl. | aṯt.aḥt.b.bt.iwrpzn. | ṯt.aṯtm. 80[119].8
n ḥtm.w bǵr.arb[‘.---]. | kdm.yn.prs.qmḥ.[---]. | mdbḥt.bt.ilt.‘ṣr[m.l ṣpn.š]. | l ǵlmt.š.w l [---.l yrḫ]. | gd[lt].l nkl[.gdlt. 35[3].24
. | w bǵr.arb‘.[---.kdm.yn]. | prs.qmḥ.m‘[--.---]. | mdbḥt.bt.i[lt.‘ṣrm.l]. | ṣpn š.l ǵlm[t.š.w l.---]. | l yrḫ.gdlt.l [nkl.gdlt.l APP.II[173].26
b gt ilštm‘. | bt ubnyn š h d.ytn.ṣtqn. | tut ṭbḫ ṣtq[n]. | b bz ‘zm ṭbḫ š[h]. | 1153.2
rt.bn.il.l ṯkmn[.w]šnm.hn.‘r. | w.ṯb.l mspr.m[šr] mšr.bt.ugrt.w npy.gr. | ḥmyt.ugrt.w [np]y.nṯt.ušn.yp kn.ulp qṭy. 32[2].1.27
yrḫ ḫyr.b ym ḥdṯ. | alp.w š.l b‘lt bhtm. | b arb‘t ‘šrt.b‘l. | ‘rkm. | b ṯmnt.‘šrt.yr | ṯḥṣ.mlk.brr. | ‘l UG5.12.A.2
t‘rbn.ršp m.bt.mlk. | ḫlu.dg. | ḥdṯm. | dbḥ.b‘l.k.tdd.b‘lt.bhtm. | b.[-]ǵb.ršp.ṣbi. | [---.--]m. | [---.]piln. | [---].ṣmd[.---.]pd 2004.14
.špš[yn]. | [b]n.ḫrmln. | bn.tnn. | bn.pndr. | bn.nqq. | ḥrš.bhtm. | bn.izl. | bn.ibln. | bn.ilt. | špšyn.nḥl h. | n‘mn.bn.iryn. | 85[80].2.2
ḥ ‘z. | [---]ḏ. | [---]. | [---]. | hm qrt tuḫd.hm mt y‘l bnš. | bt bn bnš yqḥ ‘z. | w yḥdy mrḥqm. RS61[24.277.30]
sl. | b‘l.bt.ṯrn. | b‘l.bt.ktmn. | b‘l.bt.ndbd. | [--].ṣnr. | [b‘l].bt.bsn. | [-----]. | b[--.---]. 31[14].11
p.w ṣp ḫršḫ. | ‘lm b ǵb ḫyr. | ṯmn l ṯlṯm ṣin. | šb‘.alpm. | bt b‘l.ugrt.ṯn šm. | ‘lm.l ršp.mlk. | alp w.š.l b‘lt. | bwrm š.iṯtqb UG5.12.B.6
ṯt h.ngrt[.i]lht. | kḥṣ.k m‘r[.---]. | yṣḥ.ngr il.ilš. | ilš.ngr.bt.b‘l. | w aṯt h.ngrt.ilht. | w y‘n.lṭpn.il d pi[d]. | šm‘.l ngr.il il[16[126].4.8
rt.ilht. | w y‘n.lṭpn.il d pi[d]. | šm‘.l ngr.il il[š]. | ilš.ngr bt b‘l. | w aṯt k.ngrt.il[ht]. | ‘l.l ṯkm.bnw n. | l nḫnpt.mšpy. | ṯlṯ 16[126].4.12
.ln h. | aḥd.yd h.b škrn.m‘ms h. | [k]šb‘ yn.spu.ksm h.bt.b‘l. | [w m]nt h bt.il.ṯḥ.gg h.b ym. | [ṭi]ṭ.rḥṣ.npṣ h.b ym.rṭ. 17[2AQHT].1.32
‘šy.ln.aḥd.yd y.b š | krn m‘ms y k šb‘t yn. | spu.ksm y.bt.b‘l.[w]mn[t]. | y.bt.il.ṯḥ.gg y.b ym.ṭiṭ. | rḥṣ.npṣ y.b ym.rṭ. 17[2AQHT].2.21
.ḏm[r.aṯr k.ṭbq]. | lḥt.niṣ k.gr[š.d ‘šy.ln k]. | spu.ksm k.bt.[b‘l.w mnt k]. | bt il.aḥd.yd k.b [škrn]. | m‘ms k.k šb‘t.yn.ṭ 17[2AQHT].2.4
.l p[-.---]. | ṣḥ.il.yṯb.b[mrzḥ.---]. | bṯt.‘llm n.[---]. | ilm.bt.b‘l k.[---]. | dl.ylkn.ḥš.b a[rṣ.---]. | b ‘pr.ḫbl ṭtm.[---.] | šqy.r 1[‘NT.X].4.6
[ḥrš].bhtm.b‘l.šd. | [---d]nil. | [a]drdn. | [---]n. | pǵdn. | ṯṯpḥ. | ḥgbn. | 1039.1.1
| [---.--]a h. | [---.--]d. | [---].umt n. | [---.--]yh.wn l. | [---].bt b‘l. | [---.--]y. | [---.--]nt. 28[-].12
]bl[-]. | yšlm.l[k].ilm. | ṯǵr.tšl[m] k. | [-----]. | [-----]. | [--].bt.gb[-.--]. | [--]k[-].w.špš. | [---.b].ṣp[n]. | [---.]š[--]. | [-----]. | [-- 2159.8
[aṯt.w].bn h.b.bt.krz. | [aṯt.]w.pǵt.b.bt.gg. | [ǵz]r.aḥd.b.bt.nwrḏ. | [aṯ]t.adrt.b.bt.artṯb. | aṯt.w.ṯn.b 80[119].2
--.]tṯtbn.ilm.w.[---]. | [---.]w.ksu.b‘lt.b[htm.---]. | [---.]il.bt.gdlt.[---]. | [---.]hkl[.---]. 47[33].8
mṣ.w.[lt]ḥ.‘šdm. | kd yn.l.ḥḏǵb.w.kd.ḥmṣ. | prš.glbm.l.bt. | tgmǵ.kšmm.b.yrḫ.iṯtbnm. | šb‘m.dd.ṯn.kbd. | tgmr.ḥṭm.š 1099.29
‘.mhrm. | ‘d.tšb‘.tmtḫṣ.b bt. | tḫṣb.bn.ṯlḥnm.ymḫ. | [b]bt.dm.ḏmr.yṣq.šmn. | šlm.b ṣ‘.trḥṣ.yd h.bt | [l]t.‘nt.uṣb‘t h.yb 3[‘NT].2.31
ṯḥm.rgm. | mlk. | l ḥyil. | lm.tlik.‘m y. | ik y.aškn. | ‘ṣm.l bt.dml. | p ank.atn. | ‘ṣm.l k. | arb‘.‘ṣm. | ‘l.ar. | w.ṯlṯ. | ‘l.ubr‘y. | 1010.6
[.w]m | ria.il.‘glm.d[t]. | šnt.imr.qmṣ.l[l]im. | ṣḥ.aḫ h.b bht h.a[r]y h. | b qrb hkl h.ṣḥ. | šb‘m.bn.aṯrt. | špq.ilm.krm.y[4[51].6.44
[---.b‘l.b bht h]. | [il.hd.b qr]b.hkl h. | w t‘nyn.ǵlm.b‘l. | in.b‘l.b bht ht. 10[76].2.1
bht h]. | [il.hd.b qr]b.hkl h. | w t‘nyn.ǵlm.b‘l. | in.b‘l.b bht ht. | il hd.b qrb.hkl h. | qšt hn.aḥd.b yd h. | w qṣ‘t h.bm.y 10[76].2.4
d.il.k mdb.yqḥ.il.mšt‘ltm. | mšt‘ltm.l riš.agn.yqḥ.tš.b bt h. | il.ḥṭ h.nḥt.il.ymnn.mṭ.yd h.yšu. | yr.šmm h.yr.b šmm.‘ 23[52].36
n. | ‘n.b‘l.qdm.yd h. | k tǵḏ.arz.b ymn h. | bkm.yṯb.b‘l.l bht h. | u mlk.u bl mlk. | arṣ.drkt.yštkn. | dll.al.ilak.l bn. | ilm. 4[51].7.42
n.wpt m. | [---.]w y‘n.kṯr. | [w ḫss.]ṯtb.b‘l.l hwt y. | [ḥš.]bht h.tbnn. | [ḥš.]trmm.hkl h. | y[tl]k.l lbnn.w ‘ṣ h. | l[š‘r]yn. 4[51].6.16
t zbl ym. | [trm]m.hk[l.ṯpṭ].nhr.bt k.[---.]šp[-.---]. | [ḥš.bh]t h.tbn[n.h]š.trm[mn.hkl h.---.]bt. | [---.-]k.mnh[-.---.-]š b 2.3[129].10
t.šmḫ. | aliyn.b‘l.ht y.bnt. | dt.ksp.hkl y.dtm. | ḫrṣ.‘dbt.bht[h.b‘]l. | y‘db.hd.‘db[.‘d]bt. | hkl h.ṭbḫ.alpm[.ap]. | ṣin.šql. 4[51].6.38
šmm.‘m. | ḫr[ḫ]b mlk qẓ.tn nkl y | rḫ ytrḫ.ib t‘rb m b bh | t h.w atn mhr h l a | b h.alp ksp w rbt ḫ | rṣ.išlḥ ẓhrm iq | 24[77].18
. | ssnm.ysyn h.‘dtm.y‘dyn h.yb | ltm.ybln h.mǵy.ḥrn.l bt h.w. | yštql.l ḥṭr h.tlu ḥt.km.nḫl. | tplg.km.plg. | b‘d h.bht UG5.7.67
y.b ym.rṭ. | dn.il.bt h.ymǵyn. | yštql.dnil.l hkl h. | ‘rb.b bt h.kṯrt.bnt. | hll.snnt.apnk.dnil. | mt.rpi.ap.hn.ǵzr.mt. | hrn 17[2AQHT].2.26
.k[ṯ]rt. | w y[ššq].bnt.hll.snnt. | mk.b šb[‘.]ymm.tb‘.b bt h. | kṯrt.bnt.hll.snnt. | [-]d[-]t.n‘m y.‘rš.h[--]m. | ysmsmt.‘rš 17[2AQHT].2.39
. | mhrm.mṭm.tgrš. | šbm.b ksl.qšt h.mdnt. | w hln.‘nt.l bt h.tmǵyn. | tštql.ilt.l hkl h. | w l.šb‘t.tmtḫṣ h.b ‘mq. | tḫtṣb. 3[‘NT].2.17
n[t]. | y.bt.il.ṯḥ.gg y.b ym.ṭiṭ. | rḥṣ.npṣ y.b ym.rṭ. | dn.il.bt h.ymǵyn. | yštql.dnil.l hkl h. | ‘rb.b bt h.kṯrt.bnt. | hll.snnt. 17[2AQHT].2.24
b‘l.l ht. | w ‘lm h.l ‘nt.p dr.dr. | ‘db.uḫry.mṭ.yd h. | dnil.bt h.ymǵyn.yšt | ql.dnil.l hkl h.‘rb.b | kyt.b hkl h.mšspdt.b ḥ 19[1AQHT].4.170
.ḥḏḏ. | w l.rbt.kmyr. | aṯr.ṯn.ṯn.hlk. | aṯr.ṯlṯ.kl hm. | aḥd.bt h.ysgr. | almnt.škr. | tškr.zbl.‘ršm. | yšu.‘wr. | mzl.ymzl. | w 14[KRT].4.184
ḏḏ. | w l rbt.kmyr. | [a]ṯr.ṯn.ṯn.hlk. | aṯr.ṯlṯ.kl hm. | yḥd.bt h.sgr. | almnt.škr. | tškr.zbl.‘ršm. | yšu.‘wr.mzl. | ymzl.w yṣ 14[KRT].2.96

.ksp.|w ẖrṣ.bht.ṭhrm.|iqnim.šmẖ.aliyn.|b'l.ṣḥ.ẖrn.b bht h.|'ḏbt.b qrb hkl h.|yblnn ǵrm.mid.ksp.|gb'm lḥmd.ẖr 4[51].5.98
[---.šnst.kpt.b ḥb]š h.'tkt r[išt].|[l bmt h.---.]hy bt h t'rb.|[---.tm]tẖṣ b 'mq.|[tẖtṣb.bn.qrtm.tṯ'r.ṯlḥnt.]l ṣbi 7.1[131].3
--.-]ṣbm.|[---.]nrn.m'ry.|[---.--]r.|[---.]w.ṯn.bn h.|[---.b]t h.'tgrm. 2043.12
il dbḥ.b bt h.mṣd.ṣd.b qrb|hkl [h].ṣḥ.l qṣ.ilm.tlḥmn.|ilm.w tštn.tštn UG5.1.1.1
y.ršp zbl.|[w 'd]t.ilm.ṯlṯ h.|[ap]nk.krt.ṯ'.'[-]r.|[--.]b bt h.yšt.'rb.|[--] h.ytn.w [--]u.l ytn.|[aẖ]r.mǵy.'[d]t.ilm.|[w 15[128].2.9
t.]il.yṯb.b mrzḥ h.|yšt[.il.y]n.'d šb'.trṯ.'d škr.|il.hlk.l bt h.yštql.|l ḥṭr h.y'msn.nn.ṯkmn.|w šnm.w ngšnn.ḥby.|b'l UG5.1.1.17
[-----].|[---.]'l.ṯny[.---]|[---.]pẖyr.bt h.[---].|[ẖm]šm.ksp.'l.gd[--].|[---].ypḥ.'bdršp.b[--.--].|[ar 1144.3
[--.-]m[-]r.|[w.l.]bn h.'d.|['l]m.mn k.|mn km l.yqḥ.|bt.hnd.b d.|['b]dmlk.|[-]k.am'[--].|[w.b] d.bn h[.']d 'lm.|[1009.14
.mnt.b'd h.bhtm.sgrt.|b'd h.'dbt.ṯlṯ.ptḥ.bt.mnt.|ptḥ.bt.w ubn.hkl.w ištql šql.|tn.km.nḥšm.yḥr.tn.km.|mhr y.w UG5.7.72
l bbt il bt.|š l ẖlmṭ.|w tr l qlḥ.|w š ḥll ydm.|b qdš il bt.|w tlḥm aṯt.|š l ilbt.šlmm.|kll ylḥm b h.|w l bbt šqym.| UG5.7.TR3
r.|ṯmnym.b'l.[----].|tš'm.b'l.mr[-].|bt[.--]b b'l.b qrb.|bt.w y'n.aliyn.|b'l.ašt m.kṯr bn.|ym.kṯr.bnm.'dt.|yptḥ.ḥln. 4[51].7.14
r[.k bn].|[qd]š.lbum.trd.b n[p]šn y.trḥṣn.k ṯrm.|[--]b b[ht].|[zbl.]ym.b hkl.ṯpṭ.nh[r].yṯir.ṯr.il.ab h l pn[.zb]l y[m].
]m.hkl.ṯpṭ nh[r].|[---.]hrn.w[---.]tb'.k[ṯ]r w [ẖss.t]bn.bht zbl ym.|[trm]m.hk[l.ṯpṭ].nhr.bt k.[---.]šp[-.---].|[ḥš.bh]t 2.3[129].8
bn.ḥtt.bn ḥtt[.---].|[---.--]p.km.dlt.tlk.km.p[---].|[---.]bt.tḥbṭ.km.ṣq.ṣdr[.---].|[---.]kl.b kl.l pgm.pgm.l.b[---].|[---.] 1001.1.25
[t] m.|ḥln.b qrb.hkl m.|w y'n.aliyn b'l.|al.tšt.urbt.b[bhtm].|[ḥln].b qrb.hk[l m]. 4[51].5.126
lm.ttkn.|štk.mlk.dn.|štk.šibt.'n.|štk.qr.bt.il.|w mṣlt.bt.ḥr[š]. 12[75].2.62
n.dgn.|b mṣd k.w yrd.|krt.l ggt.'db.|akl.l qryt.|ḥtt.l bt.ẖbr.|yip.lḥm.d ẖmš.|mǵd.ṯdṯ.yrẖm.|'dn.ngb.w yṣi.|ṣbu. 14[KRT].2.82
n dgn.|[b m]ṣd h.yrd.krt.|[l g]gt.'db.akl.l qryt.|ḥtt.l bt.ẖbr.|yip.lḥm.d ẖmš.|[mǵ]d.ṯdṯ.yr[ẖm].|'dn.ngb.w [yṣi.ṣ 14[KRT].4.173
t.---].|aṯt.w.bn h.w.pǵt.aḥt.b.bt.m[--].|aṯt.w.ṯt.bt h.b.bt.ẖḏmrd.|aṯt.w.ṯn.ǵzrm.b.bt.ṣdqš[lm].|[a]ṯt.aḥt.b.bt.rpi[-- 80[119].22
g.|'m.tlm.ǵṣr.arṣ.|ša.ǵr.'l.ydm.|ẖlb.l ẓr.rḥtm.|w rd.bt ẖpṯt.|arṣ.tspr.b y|rdm.arṣ.|idk.al.ttn.|pnm.tk.qrt h.|h 4[51].8.7
al ttn.tk.ǵr.|knkny.ša.ǵr.'l ydm.|ẖlb.l ẓr.rḥtm w rd.|bt ẖpṯt.arṣ.tspr b y|rdm.arṣ.w td' ilm.|k mtt.yšm'.aliyn.b'l. 5[67].5.15
.tǵll b dm.|ḏmr.ḥlqm.b mm'.mhrm.|'d.tšb'.tmtẖṣ.b bt.|tẖṣb.bn.ṯlḥnm.ymḥ.|[b]bt.dm.ḏmr.yṣq.šmn.|šlm.b ṣ'.t 3['NT].2.29
rm.|mid.ksp.gb'm.mḥmd..|ẖrṣ.w bn.bht.ksp.|w ẖrṣ.bht.ṭhrm.|iqnim.šmẖ.aliyn.|b'l.ṣḥ.ẖrn.b bht h.|'ḏbt.b qrb 4[51].5.96
'm.mḥmd.ẖrṣ.|ybl k.udr.ilqṣm.|w bn.bht.ksp.w ẖrṣ.|bht.ṭhrm.iqnim.|šmẖ.btlt.'nt.td'ṣ.|p'nm.w tr.arṣ.|idk.l ttn. 4[51].5.81
.|ṯny.l ydd.|il.ǵzr.tḥm.|aliyn.b'l.|[hw]t.aliy.q|[rdm.]bht y.bnt.|[dt.ksp.dtm].|[ẖrṣ.hk]l y.|[---.]aẖ y.|[---.]aẖ y.|[4[51].8.35
.b hkl m.|sb.ksp.l rqm.ẖrṣ.|nṣb.l lbnt.šmẖ.|aliyn.b'l.ht y.bnt.|dt.ksp.hkl y.dtm.|ẖrṣ.'dbt.bht[h.b']l.|y'db.hd.'d 4[51].6.36
'bd.|'lm.ṯlṯ.sswm.|mrkbt.b trbṣ.|bn.amt.p d.[i]n.|b bt y.ttn.tn.|l y.mṯt.ḥry.|n'mt.šbḥ.bkr k.|d k n'm.'nt.|n'm 14[KRT].6.288
.w 'bd.|'lm.ṯlṯ.sswm.mrkbt.|b trbṣt.bn.amt.|p d.in.b bt y.ttn.|tn.l y.mṯt.ḥry.|n'mt.špḥ.bkr k.|d k.n'm.'nt.n'm h. 14[KRT].3.142
[-.]aṯr[.---].|[--]šy.w ydn.b'[l.---]n.|[--]'.k yn.hm.l.atn.bt y.l h. 1002.62
.ṯm.|yd[r.k]rt.ṯ'.|i.iṯt.aṯrt.ṣrm.|w ilt.ṣdynm.|hm.ḥry.bt y.|iqḥ.aš'rb.ǵlmt.|ḥẓr y.ṯn h.wspm.|atn.w ṯlṯ h.ẖrṣm.|yl 14[KRT].4.203
[dm].|[ṯ]rrt.udm.y[t]n[t].|il.ušn.ab[.ad]m.|rḥq.mlk.l bt y.|n[g.]krt.l ḥẓ[r y].|w y'n[y.k]rt[.ṯ]'.|lm.ank.ksp.|w yr[14[KRT].6.279
dm].|[ṯrrt.udm.ytnt].|[il.w ušn.ab.adm].|[rḥq.mlk.l bt y].|[ng.kr]t.l ḥ[ẓ]r y.|[-----].|[---.ttb'].|[mlakm.l yṯb].|[i 14[KRT].5.260
[nym.---].|mhr.b'l[.---.mhr].|'nt.lk b[t y.rpim.rpim.b bt y].|aṣḥ.km.[iqra km.ilnym.b] |hkl y.aṯr[h.rpum.l tdd].| 22.1[123].8
[---.m]rz'y.lk.bt y.|[rpim.rpim.b]t y.aṣḥ km.iqra.|[km.ilnym.b h]kl y.aṯr h.rpum.|[l tdd.aṯ 21[122].1.2
[--].[-]l[--.b qr]|b hkl y.[---].|lk bt y.r[pim.rpim.b bt y.aṣḥ].|km.iqr[a km.ilnym.b hkl y].|aṯr h.r[pum.l tdd.aṯ 22.1[123].3
.b qrb].hkl y.w y'n.il.|[---.mrz']y.lk.bt y.rpim.|[rpim.bt y.aṣ]ḥ km.iqra km.|[ilnym.b hkl]y.aṯr h.rpum.|[l tdd.aṯ 21[122].1.10
.ym[.---].|'l amr.yu[ẖd.ksa.mlk h].|nẖt.kḥṯ.d[rkt h.b bt y].|aṣḥ.rpi[m.iqra.ilnym].|b qrb.h[kl y.aṯr h.rpum.l] |td 22.1[123].18
kbt.|b trbṣ.bn.amt.|qḥ.krt.šlmm.|šlmm.w ng.mlk.|l bt y.rḥq.krt.|l ḥẓr y.al.tṣr.|udm.rbt.w udm ṯrrt.|udm.ytnt. 14[KRT].3.132
[--].[-]l[--.b qr]|b hkl y.[---].|lk bt y.r[pim.rpim.b bt y.aṣḥ].|km.iqr[a km.ilnym.b hkl y].|aṯ 22.1[123].3
tdd.aṯr h].|l tdd.il[nym.---].|mhr.b'l[.---.mhr].|'nt.lk b[t y.rpim.rpim.b bt y].|aṣḥ.km.[iqra km.ilnym.b] |hkl y.aṯ 22.1[123].8
[---.m]rz'y.lk.bt y.|[rpim.rpim.b]t y.aṣḥ km.iqra.|[km.ilnym.b h]kl y.aṯr 21[122].1.1
t.amǵy.l bt.|[y.---.b qrb].hkl y.w y'n.il.|[---.mrz']y.lk.bt y.rpim.|[rpim.bt y.aṣ]ḥ km.iqra km.|[ilnym.b hkl]y.aṯr 21[122].1.9
]rz'y.apnnk.yrp.|[---.]km.r'y.ht.alk.|[---.]ṯlṯt.amǵy.l bt.|[y.---.b qrb].hkl y.w y'n.il.|[---.mrz']y.lk.bt y.rpim.|[rpi 21[122].1.7
rt.b.bt.artṯb.|aṯt.w.ṯn.bn h.b.bt.iwwpzn.|aṯt.w.pǵt.b.bt.ydrm.|ṯt.aṯtm.adrtm.w.pǵt.aḥt.b[.bt.---].|aṯt.w ṯn.n'rm.b 80[119].6
ḥw[y.]w ykb[dn h.--]r y[---].|[---.k]ṯr.w ẖ[ss.t]b'.b[n.]bht.ym[.rm]m.hkl.ṯpṭ nh[r].|[---.]hrn.w[---.]tb'.k[ṯ]r w [ẖss 2.3[129].7
u[.---.ksm].|ṯlṯm.w m'rb[.---].|dbḥ šmn mr[.šmn.rqḥ.bt].|mtnt.w ynt.[qrt.w ṯn.ḥṯm].|w bǵr.arb'.[---.kdm.yn].|pr APP.II[173].22
b.dmt.um.il[m.---].|[--]ḏyn.b'd.[--]ḏyn.w l.|[--]k b'lt bhtm[.--]tn k.|[--]y.l ihbt.yb[--].rgm y.|[---.]škb.w m[--.]ml 1002.45
y[d.bn.ilm.m]t.|w t'n.btlt.'n[t.bnt.]bht |k.y ilm.bnt.bh[t k].a[l.tš]mẖ.|al.tšmẖ.b r[m.h]kl[k].|al.aẖd.hm.b y[--] 3['NT.VI].5.28
t.k.'ṣm l t[--].|[---.]drk.brḥ.arṣ.lk pn h.yrk.b'[l].|[---.]bt k.ap.l pẖr k 'nt tqm.'nt.tqm.|[---.p]ẖr k.ygrš k.qr.bt k.yg 1001.2.9
l ri[š.---].|ypt.'ṣ[--.---].|p šlm.[---].|bt k.b[--.--.m]|ǵy k[.---].|bt.[---]. 58[20].4
]bt k.ap.l pẖr k 'nt tqm.'nt.tqm.|[---.p]ẖr k.ygrš k.qr.bt k.ygrš k.|[---].bnt.ṣ'ṣ.bnt.m'm'.'bd.ḥrn.[--.]k.|[---].aǵwyn 1001.2.10
n y.yrk.b'l.[--].|[---.]'nt.šzrm.tštšḥ.km.ḥ[--].|[---].'pr.bt k.ygr[š k.---].|[---.]y.ḥr.ḥr.bnt.ḥ[---].|[--.]uẖd.[b']l m.'[--] 1001.1.12
.ṣḥrr]t.|la.šmm.b y[d.bn.ilm.m]t.|w t'n.btlt.'n[t.bnt.]bht |k.y ilm.bnt.bh[t k].a[l.tš]mẖ.|al.tšmẖ.b r[m.h]kl[k].| 3['NT.VI].5.27
aṯ[--.---].|[---] h.ap.[---].|[---].w t'n.[btlt.'nt.---].|[bnt.bht]k.y ilm[.bnt.bht k.--].|[al.tšmẖ.]al.tš[mẖ.b rm.h]|[kl k. 18[3AQHT].1.7
n h.|hm.bt.lbnt.y'msn h.|l yrgm.l aliyn b'l.|ṣḥ.ẖrn.b bhm k.|'ḏbt.b qrb.hkl k.|tbl k.ǵrm.mid.ksp.|gb'm.mḥmd. 4[51].5.75
blt.y[b]n.|bt.l k.km.aẖ k.w ḥẓr.|km.ary k.ṣḥ.ẖrn.|b bht k.'ḏbt.b qrb.|hkl k.tbl k.ǵrm.|mid.ksp.gb'm.mḥmd..|ẖ 4[51].5.92
[l]krt.|k [k]lb.b bt k.n'tq.k inr.|ap.ẖšt k.ap.ab.ik mtm.|tmtn.u ẖšt k.l ntn.|' 16.1[125].2
tn.g h.|bky.b ḥy k.ab n.ašmẖ.|b l.mt k.ngln.k klb.|b bt k.n'tq.k inr.|ap.ẖšt k.ap.ab.k mtm.|tmtn.u ẖšt k.l ntn.|' 16.1[125].16
g h.bky.b ḥ[y k.a]b n.|nšmẖ.b l.mt k.ngln.|k klb.[b]bt k.n'tq.|k inr[.ap.]ẖšt k.|ap.ab.k mtm.tmtn.|u ẖšt k.l bky 16.2[125].100
rt.|[ṯ'.ymr]m.n'm[n.]ǵlm.il.|a[ṯt.tq]ḥ.y krt.aṯt.|tqḥ.bt k.ǵlmt.tš'rb.|ḥqr k.tld.šb'.bnm.l k.|w ṯmn.tṯtmnm.|l k.t 15[128].2.22
p.[---].|[---].w t'n.[btlt.'nt.---].|[bnt.bht]k.y ilm[.bnt.bht k.--].|[al.tšmẖ.]al.tš[mẖ.b rm.h]|[kl k.al.]aẖd hm.[---].| 18[3AQHT].1.7
w [--].|d [--].|ypẖ[--].|w s[--].|[---].|qrd ga[n.--].|b bt k.[--].|w l dbḥ[--].|ṭ[--].|[--] aṯt yqḥ 'z.|[---]ḏ.|[---].|[--- RS61[24.277.22]
--.]w mlk.w rg[m.---].|[--.rg]m.ank.[b]'r.[--]ny.|[--]n.bt k.[---.]b'[r.---].|[--]my.b d[-.--]y.[---].|[---.]'m.w hm[.--]yt 1002.55

b'.k[t]r w [ẖss.t]bn.bht zbl ym.|[trm]m.hk[l.ṯpṭ].nhr.bt k.[---.]šp[-.---].|[ḥš.bh]t h.tbn[n.ḥ]š.trm[mn.hkl h.---.]bt. 2.3[129].9
[--].nk.[---].|[---.--]ḥ.an[--.---].|[---.]'ly k[.---].|[---.]at.bt k[.---].|[---.]ank[.---].|[---.-]hn.[---].|[---.--]pp h.w[.---].|[- 1002.4
b.|hkl k.tbl k.ǵrm.|mid.ksp.gb'm.mḥmd..|ẖrṣ.w bn.bht.ksp.|w ẖrṣ.bht.ṯhrm.|iqnim.šmẖ.aliyn.|b'l.šḥ.ẖrn.b bh 4[51].5.95
m.mid.ksp.|gb'm.mḥmd.ẖrṣ.|ybl k.udr.ilqṣm.|w bn.bht.ksp.w ẖrṣ.|bht.ṯhrm.iqnim.|šmẖ.btlt.'nt.td'ṣ.|p'nm.w t 4[51].5.80
lṭpn.il[.d pid.---].|'l.ydm.p'rt[.---].|šm k.mdd.i[l.---].|bt ksp y.d[--.---].|b d.aliyn b['l.---].|kd.ynaṣn[.---].|gršnn.l 1['NT.X].4.21
[aṯt.w].bn h.b.bt.krz.|[aṯt.]w.pǵt.b.bt.gg.|[ǵz]r.aḥd.b.bt.nwrd̠.|[at]t.adrt. 80[119].1
[m]t.dm.ẖt.š'tqt dm.|li.w ttb'.š'tqt.|bt.krt.bu.tbu.|bkt.tgly.w tbu.|nṣrt.tbu.pnm.|'rm.tdu.mh.| 16.6[127].3
.|'l h.ṯr h.tš'rb.|'l h.tš'rb.ẓby h.|ṯr.ẖbr.rbt.|ẖbr.ṯrrt.|bt.krt.tbun.|lm.mṯb[.---].|w lḥm mr.tqdm.|yd.b ṣ'.tšlḥ.|ḥr 15[128].4.21
dn hm.kly.|yn.b ḥmt hm.k[l]y.|šmn.b q[b't hm.---].|bt.krt.t[--]. 16[126].3.17
t.pdy.|b'l.bt.nqly.|b'l.bt.'lr.|b'l.bt.ssl.|b'l.bt.ṯrn.|b'l.bt.ktmn.|b'l.bt.ndbd.|[--].ṣnr.|[b'l].bt.bsn.|[-----].|b[--.---]. 31[14].8
spr.ḥpr.bt.k[--].|tš'.'šr h.dd.l.b[t.--].|ẖmš.ddm.l.ḥtyt.|ṯlṯm.dd.kšm 1099.1
[lm.---].|[-]r.l šlmt.šl[m.---.--]|r h.p šlmt.p šlm[.---].|bt.l bnš.trg[m.---].|l šlmt.l šlm.b[--.---]|b y.šnt.mlit.t[--.---]. 59[100].5
.l arṣ.|[ašhlk].šbt h.dmm.šbt.dqn h.|[mm'm.-]d.l ytn.bt.l b'l.k ilm.|[w ḥẓ]r.k bn.aṯrt[.td'ṣ.]p'n.|[w tr.a]rṣ.id[k.l tt 3['NT.VI].5.11
[---.wn.in].|[bt].l [b'l.km.ilm.w ḥẓr].|k bn.[aṯrt.mṯb.il.mẓll].|bn h.m[ṯb. 3['NT.VI].4.01
.aṯrt.|p.'bd.ank.aẖd.ulṯ.|hm.amt.aṯrt.tlbn.|lbnt.ybn.bt.l b'l.|km ilm.w ḥẓr.k bn.aṯrt.|w t'n.rbt.aṯrt ym.|rbt.ilm. 4[51].4.62
lk.d yknn h.yṣḥ.|aṯrt.w bn h.ilt.w ṣbrt.|ary h.wn.in.bt.l b'l.|km.ilm.w ḥẓr.k bn.aṯrt.|mṯb il.mẓll.bn h.|mṯb rbt. 4[51].4.50
yknn h.yṣ]ḥ.aṯ|[rt.w bn h.]ilt.|[w ṣbrt.ary]h.|[wn.in.bt.l b'l.]|[km.ilm.w ḥẓr].|[k bn.aṯ]r[t].|m[ṯ]b.il.mẓll.|bn h. 4[51].1.10
[i]k.mgn.rbt.aṯrt.|[ym].mǵẓ.qnyt.ilm.|w tn.bt.l b'l.km.|[i]lm.w ḥẓr.k bn.|[a]ṯrt.gm.l ǵlm h.|b'l.yṣḥ.'n. 8[51FRAG].3
lk.d yknn h.yṣḥ.aṯrt.|w bn h.ilt.w ṣbrt.arẖ h.|wn.in.bt.l b'l.km.ilm.|ḥẓr.k b[n.a]ṯrt.mṯb.il.|mṯll.b[n h.m]ṯb.rbt.a 3['NT.VI].5.46
ṯpṭ k.w y'n[.'ṯtr].dm[-]k[-].|[--]ḥ.b y.ṯr.il.ab y.ank.in.bt[.l] y[.km.]ilm[.w] ḥẓr[.k bn].|[qd]š.lbum.trd.b n[p]šn y.t 2.3[129].19
ṣḥq.btlt.'nt.tšu.|g h.w tṣḥ.tbšr b'l.|bšrt k.yblt.y[b]n.|bt.l k.km.aẖ k.w ḥẓr.|km.ary k.ṣḥ.ẖrn.|b bht k.'d̠bt.b qrb.| 4[51].5.90
tn.ql h.b 'rpt.|šrh.l arṣ.brqm.|bt.arzm.yklln h.|hm.bt.lbnt.y'msn h.|l yrgm.l aliyn b'l.|ṣḥ.ẖrn.b bhm k.|'d̠bt.b 4[51].5.73
ḥ š'rt.|ṯṯ 'šr h.lqḥ.|ẖlpnt.|ṯṯ.ḥrṯm.|lqḥ.š'rt.|'šr.ḥrš.|bhtm.lqḥ.|š'rt.|arb'.|ḥrš qṭn.|lqḥ š'rt.|ṯṯ nsk.ḥdm.|lqḥ.š'r 2052.9
.aliyn.|b'l.ašt m.kṯr bn.|ym.kṯr.bnm.'dt.|ypth.ḥln.b bht m.|urbt.b qrb.[h]kl |m.w y[p]tḥ.b dqt.'rpt.|'l h[wt].kṯr 4[51].7.17
ḥ.|l rgmt.l k.l ali|yn.b'l.ṯṯbn.b'l.|l hwt y.yptḥ.ḥ|ln.b bht m.urbt.|b qrb.hk[l m.yp]tḥ.|b'l.b dqt[.'rp]t.|ql h.qdš.b[4[51].7.26
br.w yql].|yšṯḥwy.[w ykbdn h.---].|ṯr.il[.ab h.---].|ḥš b[ht m.tbnn.ḥš.trmmn.hkl m].|b tk.[---].|bn.[---].|a[--.---.] 1['NT.IX].3.27
.b'l].|[--]b[.---].|ḥš.bht m.k[ṯr].|ḥš.rmm.hk[l m].|ḥš.bht m.tbn[n].|ḥš.trmmn.hk[l m].|b tk.ṣrrt.ṣpn.|alp.šd.aẖd 4[51].5.115
m.|ḥln.b qr[b.hk]l m.|w 'n.ali[yn.]b'l.|al.tšt.u[rb]t.b bht m.|ḥln.b q[rb.hk]l m.|al td[.pdr]y.bt ar.|[---.ṯl]y.bt.rb. 4[51].6.8
.rgm.k[ṯr.w]ẖss.|šm'.m'.l al[iy]n b'l.|bl.ašt.ur[bt.]b bht m.|ḥln.b qr[b.hk]l m.|w 'n.ali[yn.]b'l.|al.tšt.u[rb]t.b bh 4[51].6.5
kṯr.w ẖss.|šm'.l aliyn b'l.|bn.l rkb.'rpt.|bl.ašt.urbt.b bh[t] m.|ḥln.b qrb.hkl m.|w y'n.aliyn b'l.|al.tšt.urbt.b[bht 4[51].5.123
b'l.'d.lḥm.št[y.ilm].|[w]y'n.aliy[n.b'l].|[--]b[.---].|ḥš.bht m.k[ṯr].|ḥš.rmm.hk[l m].|ḥš.bht m.tbn[n].|ḥš.trmmn. 4[51].5.113
arz h.|h[n.l]bnn.w 'ṣ h.|š[r]yn.mḥmd.arz h.|tšt.išt.b bht m.|nb[l]at.b hkl m.|hn.ym.w ṯn.tikl.|išt.b bht m.nblat. 4[51].6.22
l.|išt.b bht m.nblat.|b hk[l] m.ṯlṯ.kb' ym.|tikl[.i]št.b bht m.|nbla[t.]b hkl m.|ẖmš.ṯ[d]ṯ.ym.tikl.|išt.[b]bht m.nb 4[51].6.27
t m.nblat.|b[qrb.hk]l m.mk.|b šb['.]y[mm].td.išt.|b bht m.n[bl]at.b hkl m.|sb.ksp.l rqm.ẖrṣ.|nṣb.l lbnt.šmẖ.|al 4[51].6.33
t.išt.b bht m.|nb[l]at.b hkl m.|hn.ym.w ṯn.tikl.|išt.b bht m.nblat.|b hk[l] m.ṯlṯ.kb' ym.|tikl[.i]št.b bht m.|nbla[t 4[51].6.25
t.b bht m.|nbla[t.]b hkl m.|ẖmš.ṯ[d]ṯ.ym.tikl.|išt.[b]bht m.nblat.|b[qrb.hk]l m.mk.|b šb['.]y[mm].td.išt.|b bht 4[51].6.30
[---].|[-----].|[---]m.il[.---].|[---]d nhr.umt.|[---.]rpat.bt.|[m]lk.itdb.d šb'.|[a]ẖm.l ḥ.ṯmnt.bn um.|krt.ḥtk n.rš.|k 14[KRT].1.7
š.|[--]ṯ š.ilt.mgdl š.ilt.asrm š.|w l ll.šp. pgr.w ṯrmnm.bt mlk.|il[bt].gdlt.ušẖry.gdlt.ym gdlt.|b'l gdlt.yrẖ.gdlt.|gd 34[1].12
šm.w.mšlt.|l.udmym.b.ṯmnt.'šrt.ksp.|šb'm.lbš.d.'rb.bt.mlk.|b.mit.ẖmšt.kbd.ksp.|ṯlṯ.ktnt.b d.an[r]my.|b.'šrt.ks 2101.16
ẖrṣ.b.arb'm.|mit.ẖršẖ.b.ṯqlm.|w.šb'.'šr.šmn.|d.l.yṣa.bt.mlk.|tgmr.ksp.mitm.|ẖmšm.kbd. 2100.21
spr.npš.d.|'rb.bt.mlk.|w.b.spr.l.št.|yrm'l.|ṣry.|iršy.|y'd̠rd.|ayaẖ.|bn.ayl 2106.2
[-]lp.izr.|[a]rz.|k.t'rb.'ṯtrt.šd.bt[.m]lk.|k.t'rbn.ršp m.bt.mlk.|ẖlu.dg.|ḥdṯm.|dbḥ.b'l.k.tdd.b'lt.bhtm.|b.[-]ǵb.ršp. 2004.11
ṯmn.mrkbt.dt.|'rb.bt.mlk.|yd.apnt hn.|yd.ḥẓ hn.|yd.tr hn.|w.l.ṯt.mrkbtm.|in 1121.2
i]lbldn.|[p]dry.bt.mlk.|[-]lp.izr.|[a]rz.|k.t'rb.'ṯtrt.šd.bt[.m]lk.|k.t'rbn.ršp m.bt.mlk.|ẖlu.dg.|ḥdṯm.|dbḥ.b'l.k.td 2004.10
b'l.|ṯlṯm.l.mit.š'rt.|l.šr.'ṯtrt.|mlbš.ṯrmnm.|k.yṯn.w.b.bt.|mlk.mlbš.|yṯn.l hm.|šb'.lbšm.allm.|l ušẖry.|ṯlṯ.mat.pṯt 1107.6
k t'rb.'ṯtrt.ẖr[-].|bt mlk.'šr.'šr.[--].bt ilm.|kbr[-]m.[-]trmt.|lbš.w [-]tn.ušpǵt. 33[5].2
[šmt.n]qmp'.|[bn.nq]md.|[mlk.]ugrt.|b'l ṣdq.|skn.bt.|mlk.ṯǵr.|[m]lk.bny.|[--].lb.mlk.|[---.]ṣmẖ. 1007.5
in.šlm[m.]šb' pamt.|l ilm.šb['.]l kṯr.|'lm.t'rbn.gṯrm.|bt.mlk.ṯql.ẖrṣ.|l špš.w yrẖ.l gṯr.|ṯql.ksp.ṯb.ap w np[š].|l 'nt 33[5].10
mm.b'lm.kmm.|b'lm.kmm.b'lm.kmm.|k t'rb.'ṯtrt.šd.bt.mlk[.---].|ṯn.skm.šb'.mšlt.arb'.ẖpnt.[---].|ẖmšm.ṯlṯ.rkb.n UG5.9.1.18
ntn.d.ksp.|arb'.l.ẖlby.|[---].l.bt.|arb'.l.kpslnm.|kdm.b[t.]mlk. 1087.7
rǵlm.|w.šb'.'šr.ẖsnm.|ẖmšm.l.mit.|bnš.l.d.|yškb.l.b.bt.mlk. 1029.16
d.ẖsnm.|ubnyn.|ṯṯm[.l.]mit.ṯlṯ.|kbd[.tg]mr.bnš.|l.b.bt.mlk. 1028.14
h.w.|yštql.l ḥṭr h.tlu ḥt.km.nẖl.|tplg.km.plg.|b'd h.bhtm.mnt.b'd h.bhtm.sgrt.|b'd h.'dbt.ṯlṯ.ptḥ.bt.mnt.|ptḥ.b UG5.7.70
.|b'd h.bhtm.mnt.b'd h.bhtm.sgrt.|b'd h.'dbt.ṯlṯ.ptḥ.bt.mnt.|ptḥ.bt.w ubn.hkl.w ištql šql.|tn.km.nḥšm.yḥr.tn.k UG5.7.71
l ẖmš.mrkbt.ẖmš.'šr h.prs.|bt.mrkbt.w l šant.ṯt.|l bt.'šrm.|bt alẖnm.ṯlṯm ṯt kbd. 2105.2
tm.w.pǵt.w.ǵzr.aḥd.b.[bt.---].|aṯt.w.bn h.w.pǵt.aḥt.b.bt.m[--].|aṯt.w.ṯt.bt h.b.bt.ẖdmrd.|aṯt.w.ṯn.ǵzrm.b.bt.ṣdqš[80[119].21
ym[ǵ].|mlak k.'m dt[n].|lqḥ.mṯpṭ.|w y'ny.nn.|dtn.bt n.mḫ[-].|l dg.w [-]kl.|w aṯr.hn.mr[-]. UG5.6.14
nqly.|b'l.bt.'lr.|b'l.bt.ssl.|b'l.bt.ṯrn.|b'l.bt.ktmn.|b'l.bt.ndbd.|[--].ṣnr.|[b'l].bt.bsn.|[-----].|b[--.---]. 31[14].9
[aṯt.w].bn h.b.bt.krz.|[aṯt.]w.pǵt.b.bt.gg.|[ǵz]r.aḥd.b.bt.nwrd̠.|[at]t.adrt.b.bt.arṯtb.|aṯt.w.ṯn.bn h.b.bt.iwwpzn.|a 80[119].3
bt.il.|b'l.bt.ad̠mny.|b'l.bt.pdy.|b'l.bt.nqly.|b'l.bt.'lr.|b'l.bt.ssl.|b'l.bt.ṯrn.|b'l.bt.ktmn.|b'l.bt. 31[14].4
h.tlu ḥt.km.nẖl.|tplg.km.plg.|b'd h.bhtm.mnt.b'd h.bhtm.sgrt.|b'd h.'dbt.ṯlṯ.ptḥ.bt.mnt.|ptḥ.bt.w ubn.hkl.w išt UG5.7.70
qmḥ.d.kly.b bt.skn.|l.illdrm.|lṯḥ.ẖsr.b.šb'.ddm. 2093.1
-.]b.bt[.---]l.|[t]lṯ.aṯt.adrt.w.ṯlṯ.ǵzr[m].|w.ẖmš.n'rt.b.bt.sk[n].|ṯt.aṯtm.adrtm.w.pǵt.w ǵzr[.aḥd.b.bt.---].|aṯt.w.ṯt. 80[119].17

. | b'l.bt.adṃny. | b'l.bt.pdy. | b'l.bt.nqly. | b'l.bt.'lr. | b'l.bt.ssl. | b'l.bt.ṯrn. | b'l.bt.ktmn. | b'l.bt.ndbd. | [--].ṣnr. | [b'l].bt. 31[14].6
--.--]t.b[ḥd]r.mškb. | ṯl[l.---.--]ḥ. | b lṯk.bt. | [pt]ḥ.aḥd.l.bt.'bdm. | [ṯ]n.ptḥ msb.bt.tu. | w.ptḥ[.aḥ]d.mmt. | ṯṯ.pt[ḥ.---]. 1151.9
m kmm. | l b'l.ṣpn b 'r'r. | pamt ṯlṯm š l qrnt. | ṯlḥn.b'lt.bhtm. | 'lm.'lm.gdlt l b'l. | ṣpn.ilbt[.---.]d[--]. | l ṣpn[.---.-]lu. | i UG5.13.31
bt.il. | b'l.bt.adṃny. | b'l.bt.pdy. | b'l.bt.nqly. | b'l.bt.'lr. | b'l.bt.ssl. | b'l.bt.ṯrn. | b'l.bt.ktmn. | b'l.bt.ndbd. | [--].ṣn 31[14].5
.i[---.---]. | kpr.šb' bn[t.rḥ.gdm.w anhbm]. | kla[t.ṯǵ]r[t.bht.'nt.w tqry.ǵlmm.b št.ǵr]. | ap 'nt tm[ṯḫṣ.b 'mq.ṯḫtṣb.bn. 7.2[130].24
--.---.-]š[--]. | kpr.šb'.bnt.rḥ.gdm. | w anhbm.klat.ṯǵrt. | bht.'nt.w tqry.ǵlmm. | b št.ǵr.w hln.'nt.tm | ṯḫṣ.b 'mq.ṯḫtṣb.b 3['NT].2.4
ṯḫṣ.mlk.brr]. | b arb'[t.'šrt.riš.argmn]. | w ṯn šm.l [b'lt.bhtm.'ṣrm.l inš]. | ilm.w š d[d.ilš.š.--.mlk]. | yṯb.brr[.w mḥ-.- 35[3].5
ṣ.mlk. | br[r.]b a[r]b't.'šrt.riš. | arg[mn.w ṯn.]šm.l b'lt. | bhtm.'ṣ[rm.l in]š ilm.w š. | dd ilš.š[.---.]mlk.yṯb br | r.w mḥ[- APP.II[173].6
ṣpn š.l ǵlm[t.š.w l.---]. | l yrḫ.gdlt.l [nkl.gdlt.l b'] | [lt].bht[m].[']ṣrm l [inš.ilm]. | [---.]ilh[m.dqt.š.--]. | [---.--]t.r[šp.šr APP.II[173].29
ṣpn.š]. | l ǵlmt.š.w l [---.l yrḫ]. | gd[lt].l nkl[.gdlt.l b'lt.bhtm]. | 'š[rm.]l inš[.ilm.---]. | il[hm.]dqt.š[.---.rš] | [p.š]rp.w š 35[3].26
w l ǵlmt š. | [w]pamt ṯlṯm.w yrdt.[m]dbḥt. | gdlt.l b'lt bhtm.'ṣrm. | l inš ilm. 34[1].21
l ḫmš.mrkbt.ḫmš.'šr h.prs. | bt.mrkbt.w l šant.ṯṯ. | l bt.'šrm. | bt alḫnm.ṯlṯm ṯṯ kbd. 2105.3
rim. | ṯṯ ddm l ṣin mrat. | 'šr ddm.l šm'rgm. | 'šr ddm.l bt. | 'šrm.dd.l mḫṣm. | ddm l kbs. | dd l prgṯ. | dd.l mri. | dd.l ṯ 1100.4
[--].d.ntn[.d.]ksp. | [ṯ]mn.l.'šrm[.l.b]t.'ṯtrt. | [ṯ]lṯ.'šr h.[b]t.ršp.gn. | arb'.b d.b[n].ušryn. | kdm.l.u 1088.2
bt.il. | b'l.bt.adṃny. | b'l.bt.pdy. | b'l.bt.nqly. | b'l.bt.'lr. | b'l.bt.ssl. | b'l.bt.ṯrn. | b'l.bt.kt 31[14].3
--.]l.aḥd.adr. | [---.--]t.b[ḥd]r.mškb. | ṯl[l.---.--]ḥ. | b lṯk.bt. | [pt]ḥ.aḥd.l.bt.'bdm. | [ṯ]n.ptḥ msb.bt.tu. | w.ptḥ[.aḥ]d.m 1151.8
b.bt.m[--]. | aṯt.w.ṯt.bt h.b.bt.ḫdmrd. | aṯt.w.ṯn.ǵzrm.b.bt.ṣdqš[lm]. | [a]ṯt.aḥt.b.bt.rpi[--]. | [aṯt.]w.bt h.b.bt.alḫn. | [aṯ 80[119].23
n gt bn ndr. | um r[-] gtn ṯṯ ḫsn l ytn. | l rḥt lqḥ ṣtqn. | bt qbṣ urt ilštm' dbḥ ṣtqn l. | ršp. 1154.7
[---].ybšr.qdš[.---]. | [---.--]t btm.qdš.il[.---]. | [---.b]n.qdš.k[--.---]. | [---.]'sb.[-]ḫ[-.---]. | [---. 2125.2
.tbn[n]. | ḫš.trmmn.hk[l m]. | b tk.ṣrrt.ṣpn. | alp.šd.aḫd bt. | rbt.kmn.hkl. | w y'n.kṯr.w ḫss. | šm'.l aliyn b'l. | bn.l rkb.' 4[51].5.118
b'.mat[.arb]'m.[k]bd. | d ntn.d.ksp. | arb'.l.ḫlby. | [---].l.bt. | arb'.l.kpslnm. | kdm.b[t.]mlk. 1087.5
b.bt.ḫdmrd. | aṯt.w.ṯn.ǵzrm.b.bt.ṣdqš[lm]. | [a]ṯt.aḥt.b.bt.rpi[--]. | [aṯt.]w.bt h.b.bt.alḫn. | [aṯt.w.]pǵt.aḥt.b.bt.ṯt. | [aṯt 80[119].24
[--].d.ntn[.d.]ksp. | [ṯ]mn.l.'šrm[.l.b]t.'ṯtrt. | [ṯ]lṯ.'šr h.[b]t.ršp.gn. | arb'.b d.b[n].ušryn. | kdm.l.urtn. | kdm.l.ilšpš. | k 1088.3
ršp. | anntn. | b'lrm. | [-]ral. | šdn. | [-]ǵl. | bn.b'ltǵpṯ. | ḥrš.btm. | ršpab. | [r]ṣn. | [a]ǵlmn. | [a]ḫyn. | [k]rwn. | [k]l[by]. | [--]ṯ 2060.13
lpm. | bt b'l.ugrt.ṯn šm. | 'lm.l ršp.mlk. | alp w.š.l b'lt. | bwrm š.iṯtqb. | w š.nbk m w.š. | gt mlk š.'lm. | l kṯr.ṯn.'lm. | tz UG5.12.B.9
id ydbḥ mlk. | l uš ḫ[r] ḫlmṭ. | l bbt il bt. | š l ḫlmṭ. | w tr l qlḥ. | w š ḥll ydm. | b qdš il bt. | w tlḥm aṯ UG5.7.TR3
bt šbn. | iy'dm.w b'l h. | ddy. | 'my. | iwrnr. | alnr. | maḫdt. | aby 107[15].1
db w 'r. | qdš w amrr. | ṯḫr w bd. | [k]ṯr ḫss šlm. | šlm il bt. | šlm il ḥš[t]. | ršp inšt. | [--]rm il [---]. | [---.--]m šlm [---]. UG5.7.72
[---.]šlm. | [---.--]š.lalit. | [---.]bt šp.š. | y[-]lm.w mlk. | ynṣl.l ṯ'y. 2005.2.6
spr.tbṣr. | klt.bt špš. 1175.2
mt. | [---.--] n.ylt.ḥmḥmt. | [---.mt.r]pi.w ykn.bn h. | [b bt.šrš.]b qrb.hkl h. | [nṣb.skn.i]lib h.b qdš. | [ztr.'m h.l a]rṣ.m 17[2AQHT].1.44
tbrknn l ṯr.il ab y. | tmrnn.l bny.bnwt. | w ykn.bn h b bt.šrš.b qrb. | hkl h.nṣb.skn.ilib h.b qdš. | ztr.'m h.l arṣ.mšṣu. 17[2AQHT].1.26
[---.i]qni.l.ṯr[mn.art.---]. | [b.yr]ḫ.riš.yn.[---]. | [---.b']lt.bhtm.š[--.---]. | [---.-]rt.l.dml[.---]. | [b.yrḫ].nql.ṯn.ḫpn[.---]. | [1106.33
[l.---.--]ḥ. | b lṯk.bt. | [pt]ḥ.aḥd.l.bt.'bdm. | [ṯ]n.ptḥ msb.bt.tu. | w.ptḥ[.aḥ]d.mmt. | ṯṯ.pt[ḥ.---]. | ṯn.pt[ḥ.---]. | w.pt[ḥ.--] 1151.10
.bt h.b.bt.alḫn. | [aṯt.w.]pǵt.aḥt.b.bt.ṯt. | [aṯt.w.]bt h.b.bt.trǵds. | [---.]aṯt.adrt.w.pǵt.a[ḥt.b.bt.---]. | [---.']šrm.npš.b.b 80[119].27
t.b.bt.rpi[--]. | [aṯt.]w.bt h.b.bt.alḫn. | [aṯt.w.]pǵt.aḥt.b.bt.ṯt. | [aṯt.w.]bt h.b.bt.trǵds. | [---.]aṯt.adrt.w.pǵt.a[ḥt.b.bt.-- 80[119].26
. | w š[--.---]. | ḥdṯ[.---.]ḥ[--]. | b bt.[-.]l bnt.q[-]. | w št.b bt.ṯap[.--]. | hy.yd h.w ym[ǵ]. | mlak k.'m dt[n]. | lqḥ.mṯpṭ. | w UG5.6.9
| ṯṯ.aṯtm.w.pǵt.aḥt.b bt.[-]r[-]. | [aṯ]t.b.bt.aupš. | [aṯ]t.b.bt.ṯpṭb'l. | [---.]n[--.md]rǵlm. | [---.]b.bt[.---]l. | [ṯ]lṯ.aṯt.adrt.w. 80[119].13
mny. | b'l.bt.pdy. | b'l.bt.nqly. | b'l.bt.'lr. | b'l.bt.ssl. | b'l.bt.ṯrn. | b'l.bt.ktmn. | b'l.bt.ndbd. | [--].ṣnr. | [b'l].bt.bsn. | [----- 31[14].7
-]. | [---.--]m.šr.d.yṯ[b]. | [---.--]y.d.ḫbṭ.sy[--]. | [---.--]y.b.bt.ṯr[--]. 2134.11
y.nn[.--]. | ṯ'ny.n[---.-]ṯq. | w š[--.---]. | ḥdṯ[.---.]ḥ[--]. | b bt.[-.]l bnt.q[-]. | w št.b bt.ṯap[.--]. | hy.yd h.w ym[ǵ]. | mlak k UG5.6.8
| bn.pr[-.]d.y[ṯb.b].šlmy. | tlš.w[.n]ḥl h[.-].tgd.mrum. | bt.[-]b[-.-]sy[-]h. | nn[-].b[n].py[-.d.]yṯb.b.gt.aǵld. | šgn.bn b[- 2015.2.4
.b.bt.armwl. | aṯt.aḥt.b.bt.iwrpzn. | ṯṯ.aṯtm.w.pǵt.aḥt.b bt.[-]r[-]. | [aṯ]t.b.bt.aupš. | [aṯ]t.b.bt.ṯpṭb'l. | [---.]n[--.md]rǵl 80[119].11
spr.ḥpr.bt.k[--]. | tš'.'šr h.dd.l.b[t.--]. | ḫmš.ddm.l.ḥtyt. | ṯlṯm.dd.ksmn.l.gzzm. | yyn. | ṣdqn. 1099.2
. | kl ykly. | dbḥ k.sprt. | dt nat. | w qrwn. | l k dbḥ. | [--]r bt [--]. | [--]bnš [--]. | š š[--]. | w [--]. | d [--]. | ypḫ [--]. | w s[--]. | RS61[24.277.13]
ḥd.'r. | šb'm.šb'.pdr. | ṯmnym.b'l.[----]. | tš'm.b'l.mr[-]. | bt[.--]b b'l.b qrb. | bt.w y'n.aliyn. | b'l.ašt m.kṯr bn. | ym.kṯr.b 4[51].7.13
rṯn. | ḥdǵlm.i[---]n.pbn.ndbn.sbd. | šrm.[---].ḫpn. | ḥrš[bhtm.--]n.'bdyrḫ.ḥdṯn.y'r. | adb'l[.---].ḥdṯn.yḥmn.bnil. | 'dn. 2011.18
urm.lb]. | rmṣt.ilh[m.b'lm.---]. | ksm.ṯlṯm.[---]. | d yqḥ bt[.--]r.dbḥ[.šmn.mr]. | šmn.rqḥ[.-]bt.mtnt[.w ynt.qrt]. | w ṯn 35[3].20
ǵtm.w.ǵzr.aḥd.b.[bt.---]. | ṯṯ.aṯtm.w.pǵt.w.ǵzr.aḥd.b.[bt.---]. | aṯt.w.bn h.w.pǵt.aḥt.b.bt.m[--]. | aṯt.w.ṯt.bt h.b.bt.ḫd 80[119].20
zn. | aṯt.w.pǵt.b.bt.ydrm. | ṯṯ.aṯtm.adrtm.w.pǵt.aḥt.b[.bt.---]. | aṯt.w ṯn.n'rm.b.bt.ilsk. | aṯt.ad[r]t.b.bt.armwl. | aṯt.aḥ 80[119].7
mš.n'rt.b.bt.sk[n]. | ṯṯ.aṯtm.adrtm.w.pǵt.w ǵzr[.aḥd.b.bt.---]. | aṯt.w.ṯt.pǵtm.w.ǵzr.aḥd.b.[bt.---]. | ṯṯ.aṯtm.w.pǵt.w.ǵ 80[119].18
-]. | [---.-]y[-.---]. | w bn 'ṯl.[---]. | ypḫ kn'm[.---]. | aḫmn bt[.---]. | b ḫmt 'ṯr ṯmn[.---]. 207[57].10
ug[r.---]. | 'nt[.---]. | ṯmm l bt[.---]. | b[']l.ugr[t.---]. | w 'ṣrm[.---]. | ṣlyh šr[-.---]. | [ṯ]lṯm.w 40[134].3
u[gr]t.š.l.[il]ib.ǵ[--.--rt]. | w ['ṣrm.]l.ri[--.---]. | [--]t.b'lt.bt[.---]. | [md]bḥt.b.ḫmš[.---]. | [-.]kbd.w.db[ḥ.---]. | [--].aṯrt.'ṣ 35[3].37
----]. | l.'ṯ[trt.---]. | l.mš[--.---]. | l.ilt[.---]. | l.b'lt[.---]. | l.il.bt[.---]. | l.ilt.[---]. | l.ḥtk[.---]. | l.ršp[.---]. | [l].ršp.[---.--]g.kbd. 1004.7
šmm.ttrp. | ym.ḏnbtm. | tnn.l šbm. | tšt.trks. | l mrym.l bt[.---]. | p l.tb'[.---]. | hmlt ḫt.[---]. | l.tp[-]m.[---]. | n[-]m[.---]. 1003.10
dlt.[l.---]. | ugrt.š l ili[b.---]. | rt.w 'ṣrm.l[.---]. | pamt.w bt.[---]. | rmm.w 'l[y.---]. | bt.il.ṯq[l.---.kbd]. | w bdḥ.k[--.---]. | APP.II[173].40
.pǵt.w ǵzr[.aḥd.b.bt.---]. | aṯt.w.ṯt.pǵtm.w.ǵzr.aḥd.b.[bt.---]. | ṯṯ.aṯtm.w.pǵt.w.ǵzr.aḥd.b.[bt.---]. | aṯt.w.bn h.w.pǵt. 80[119].19
.[---.]šp[-.---]. | [ḥš.bh]t h.tbn[n.h]š.trm[mn.hkl h.---.]bt. | [---.-]k.mnh[-.---.-]š bš[-.]t[-].ǵlm.l šdt[.-.]ymm. | [---.]b y 2.3[129].10
-]šn. | [---.--]m. | [---.--]l. | [---.--]m. | [---.ḫlb.]rp[š]. | [---.]bht[.---]. | [---.]amr[-]. | [---.']rg[z.-]. | [---.ḫl]b ṣpn. 72[-].2.2
bt.ilm.w.b.[---]. | [---.]ṯṯbn.ilm.w.[---]. | [---.]w.ksu.b'lt.b[htm.---]. | [---.]il.bt.gdlt.[---]. | [---.]hkl[.---]. 47[33].7
ds. | [---.]aṯt.adrt.w.pǵt.a[ḥt.b.bt.---]. | [---.']šrm.npš.b.bt.[---]. | [---.]w.pǵt.aḥt.b.bt.[---]. 80[119].29
t.ṯt. | [aṯt.w.]bt h.b.bt.trǵds. | [---.]aṯt.adrt.w.pǵt.a[ḥt.b.bt.---]. | [---.']šrm.npš.b.bt.[---]. | [---.]w.pǵt.aḥt.b.bt.[---]. 80[119].28

---.]qdš[.---]. | [---.k]su.p[--.---]. | [---.]agn[.---]. | [---.b‘lt.b]htm[.---]. | [---.--]by.ṯ[--.---]. | [---.--]n[.---]. | [---.--]mm.g[--.- 45[45].6
]. | ypt.‘ṣ[--.---]. | p šlm.[---]. | bt k.b[--.--.m] | ǵy k[.---]. | bt.[---]. 58[20].6
[ḥt.b.bt.---]. | [---.‘]šrm.npš.b.bt.[---]. | [---.]w.pǵt.aḫt.b.bt.[---]. 80[119].30
b.bt.aupš. | [aṯ]t.b.bt.ṯpṯb‘l. | [---.]n[--.md]rǵlm. | [---.]b.bt[.---]l. | [ṯ]lṯ.aṯt.adrt.w.ṯlṯ.ǵzr[m]. | w.ḫmš.n‘rt.b.bt.sk[n]. | ṯ 80[119].15
khnm. | qdšm. | mkrm. | mdm. | inšt. | ḥrš.bhtm. 75[81].6
dm. | inšt. | nsk ksp. | yṣḥm. | ḥrš mrkbt. | ḥrš qṭn. | ḥrš bhtm. 73[114].10

btbt

.mlk.brr. | ‘lm.tzǵ.b ǵb.ṣpn. | nḫkt.ksp.w ḫrṣ ṯ‘ ṯn šm l btbt. | alp.w š šrp.alp šlmm. | l b‘l.‘ṣr l ṣpn. | npš.w.š.l ršp bbt. UG5.12.A.8
]lbš.ḫmšm.iqnu. | [---].šmt.ḫmšt.ḫndlt. | [---.iqn]i.l.[-]k.btbt. | [---.l.ṯrm]nm.š[b‘].mat.š‘rt. | [---.]iqnu.[---.]lbš.ṯrmnm. 1106.18

btw

btwm. | [-]bln. | [-]bldn. | [-]bdy. | [b]‘ln. | [-]šdm. | iwryn. | n‘m 1043.1

bty

[-----]. | [---.]ršy.[---]. | [---.-]mdr. | [---.]bty. | [---.]mrṯn.[--]. | [---.]d[.---]. 2172.4
.nṯk. | [---.]šb‘m. | [---.]ḫrg.‘šrm. | [---.]abn.ksp.ṯlṯ. | [---].bty.ksp.‘šr[t]. | [---.-]mb‘l.[---].‘šrt. | [---.]ḫgbn.kbs.ks[p]. | [---] 2153.7
bn.grb[n]. | yṯtn. | bn.ab[l]. | kry. | psš. | ilthm. | ḥrm. | bn.bty. | ‘by. | šm[n].bn.apn. | krty. | bn.ubr. | [bn] mdḫl. | bn.sy[n] 2078.15

btlt

n.ap ank.aḥwy. | aqht[.ǵz]r.w y‘n.aqht.ǵzr. | al.tšrgn.y btlt m.dm.l ǵzr. | šrg k.ḫḫm.mt.uḫryt.mh.yqḥ. | mh.yqḥ.mt. 17[2AQHT].6.34
h.w[tṣ] | ḥ.at.mt.tn.aḫ y. | w ‘n.bn.ilm.mt.mh. | taršn.l btlt.‘nt. | an.itlk.w aṣd.kl. | ǵr.l kbd.arṣ.kl.gb‘. | l kbd.šdm.npš 6[49].2.14
n.‘n.b qbt[.t] | bl lyt.‘l.umt k. | w abqṯ.aliyn.b‘l. | w t‘n.btlt.‘nt. | an.l an.y špš. | an.l an.il.yǵr[.-]. | tǵr k.š[---.---]. | yštd 6[49].4.45
. | tn.l kṯr.w ḫss.yb‘l.qšt l ‘nt. | qṣ‘t.l ybmt.limm.w t‘n.btlt. | ‘nt.irš ḥym.l aqht.ǵzr. | irš ḥym.w atn k.bl mt. | w ašlḥ 17[2AQHT].6.25
mn h.b anšt[.---]. | qdqd h.w y‘n.yṭpn.[mhr.št]. | šm‘.l btlt.‘nt.at.‘[l.qšt h]. | tmḫṣ h.qṣ‘t h.hwt.l t[ḥwy]. | n‘mn.ǵzr.št 18[3AQHT].4.12
r[.---]. | [---.]uṯm.ḏr[qm.---]. | [btl]t.‘nt.l kl.[---]. | [tt]b‘.btlt.‘nt[.idk.l ttn.pnm]. | ‘m.yṭpn.mhr.š[t.tšu.g h]. | w tṣḥ.yṯb 18[3AQHT].4.5
ḫd.d iṯ.b kbd k.tšt.b [---]. | irt k.dṯ.ydṯ.m‘qb k.[ttb‘]. | [bt]lt.‘nt.idk.l ttn.[pnm]. | [‘m.a]qht.ǵzr.b alp.š[d]. | [rbt.]kmn 18[3AQHT].1.20
yšt k. | [b]‘l.‘nt.mḥrṯt. | iy.aliyn.b‘l. | iy.zbl.b‘l.arṣ. | ttb‘.btlt.‘nt. | idk.l ttn.pnm. | ‘m.nrt.ilm.špš. | tšu.g h.w tṣḥ. | ṯḥm.ṯ 6[49].4.30
nm.ymḥ. | [b]bt.dm.ḏmr.yṣq.šmn. | šlm.b ṣ‘.trḥṣ.yd h.bt | [l]t.‘nt.uṣb‘t h.ybmt.limm. | [t]rḥṣ.yd h.b dm.ḏmr. | [u]ṣb‘ 3[‘NT].2.32
]skt.n‘mn.nbl[.---]. | [--.]yṣq šmn.šlm.b ṣ[‘.trḥṣ]. | yd h.btlt.‘nt.uṣb‘t[h.ybmt]. | limm.tiḫd.knr h.b yd[h.tšt]. | rimt.l UG5.3.2.5
. | nrt.ilm.špš[.ṣḥrr]t. | la.šmm.b y[d.bn.ilm.m]t. | w t‘n.btlt.‘n[t.bnt.]bht | k.y ilm.bnt.bh[t k].a[l.tš]mḫ. | al.tšmḫ.b r[3[‘NT.VI].5.27
dr.ilqṣm. | w bn.bht.ksp.w ḫrṣ. | bht.ṯhrm.iqnim. | šmḫ.btlt.‘nt.td‘ṣ. | p‘nm.w tr.arṣ. | idk.l ttn.pnm. | ‘m.b‘l.mrym.ṣp 4[51].5.82
.bny.bnwt. | b nši.‘n h.w tphn. | hlk.b‘l.aṯtrt. | k t‘n.hlk.btlt. | ‘nt.tdrq.ybmt. | [limm].b h.p‘nm. | [ṭṭt.b ‘]dn.ksl. | [ṯṯbr.‘ 4[51].2.14
t.bmt.pḥl. | qdš.yuḫdm.šb‘r. | amrr.k kbkb.l pnm. | aṯr.btlt.‘nt. | w b‘l.tb‘.mrym.ṣpn. | idk.l ttn.pnm. | ‘m.il.mbk.nhr 4[51].4.18
[---.]arḫt.tld[n]. | a[lp].l btlt.‘nt. | w ypt l ybmt.li[mm]. | w y‘ny.aliyn[.b‘l]. | lm.k qny 10[76].3.3
hm.b ‘p. | nṭ‘n.b arṣ.ib y. | w b ‘pr.qm.aḫ k. | w tšu.‘n h.btlt.‘nt. | w tšu.‘n h.w t‘n. | w t‘n.arḫ.w tr.b lkt. | tr.b lkt.w tr. 10[76].2.26
rt.yd‘[t k.]bt.k an[št]. | k in.b ilht.ql[ṣ] k.mh.tarš[n]. | l btlt.‘nt.w t[‘]n.btlt.‘n[t]. | ṯḥm k.il.ḥkm.ḥkm k. | ‘m.‘lm.ḥyt.ḥ 3[‘NT.VI].5.37
‘m.w[---]. | aqht.w yplṭ k.bn[.dnil.---]. | w y‘dr k.b yd.btlt.[‘nt]. | w y‘n.lṭpn.il d p[id]. | yd‘t k.bt.k anšt.w i[n.b ilht]. 18[3AQHT].1.14
d yknn[.--]. | b‘l.yṣǵd.mli[.--]. | il hd.mla.u[--.--]. | blt.p btlt.‘n[t]. | w p.n‘mt.aḫt[.b‘l]. | y‘l.b‘l.b ǵ[r.---]. | w bn.dgn.b š[10[76].3.10
ṯmn.ṯṯmnm. | l k.tld.yṣb.ǵlm. | ynq.ḥlb.a[t]rt. | mṣṣ.ṯd.btlt.[‘nt]. | mšnq.[---]. 15[128].2.27
rb.mym. | tql.[---.]lb.tt[b]r. | qšt[.---]r.y[t]br. | tmn.[---.]btlt.[‘]nt. | ttb.[---.--]ša. | tlm.km[.---.]yd h.k šr. | knr.uṣb‘t h ḥ 19[1AQHT].1.5
h[m.w tṣḥn]. | šm‘.l dnil.[mt.rpi]. | mt.aqht.ǵzr.[šṣat]. | btlt.‘nt.k [rḥ.npš h]. | k iṯl.brlt h.[b h.p‘nm]. | ṭṭṭ.‘l[n.pn h.td‘ 19[1AQHT].2.92
[---.]ps[.---]. | [---].yṯbr[.---]. | [---.]uṯm.ḏr[qm.---]. | [btl]t.‘nt.l kl.[---]. | [tt]b‘.btlt.‘nt[.idk.l ttn.pnm]. | ‘m.yṭpn.mh 18[3AQHT].4.4
t.l tbṯ. | w b h.tdmmt.amht. | aḫr.mǵy.aliyn.b‘l. | mǵyt.btlt.‘nt. | tmgnn.rbt[.a]ṯrt ym. | tǵzyn.qnyt.ilm. | w t‘n.rbt.aṯr 4[51].3.24
yt.ilm.mgntm. | ṯr.il.d pid.hm.ǵẓtm. | bny.bnwt w t‘n. | btlt.‘nt.nmgn. | [-]m.rbt.aṯrt.ym. | [nǵ]ẓ.qnyt.ilm. | [---].nmgn 4[51].3.33
t.ẓr.[h]. | tšu.g h.w tṣḥ[.i]k. | mǵy.aliy[n.b]‘l. | ik.mǵyt.b[t]lt. | ‘nt.mḫṣ y hm[.m]ḫṣ. | bn y.hm[.mkly.ṣ]brt. | ary y[.ẓl] 4[51].2.23
rumm. | w yšu.‘n h.aliyn.b‘l. | w yšu.‘n h.w y‘n. | w y‘n.btlt.‘nt. | n‘mt.bn.aḫt.b‘l. | l pnn h.ydd.w yqm. | l p‘n h.ykr‘. 10[76].2.15
.l ttn.pnm. | ‘m.b‘l.mrym.ṣpn. | b alp.šd.rbt.kmn. | ṣḥq.btlt.‘nt.tšu. | g h.w tṣḥ.tbšr b‘l. | bšrt k.yblt.y[b]n. | bt.l k.km. 4[51].5.87
ttn.[pnm]. | [‘m.a]qht.ǵzr.b alp.š[d]. | [rbt.]kmn.w ṣḥq.btlt.[‘nt]. | [tšu.]g h.w tṣḥ.šm‘.m[‘.l a] | [qht.ǵ]zr.at.aḫ.w an.a 18[3AQHT].1.22
tkbd]n h.tlšn.aqht.ǵzr. | [---.kdd.dn]il.mt.rpi.w t‘n. | [btlt.‘nt.tšu.g]h.w tṣḥ.hwt. | [---.]aqht.yd[--]. | [---.--]n.ṣ[---]. | 17[2AQHT].6.53
h. | idk.l ytn pnm. | tk.aḫ.šmk.mla[t.r]umm. | tšu knp.btlt.‘n[t]. | tšu.knp.w tr.b ‘p. | tk.aḫ šmk.mlat rumm. | w yšu.‘ 10[76].2.10
--]tm.w mdbḥt. | ḫr[.---.]‘l.kbkbt. | n‘m.[--.-]llm.trṯḥṣ. | btlt.‘n[t].tptr‘ ṭd[h]. | limm.w t‘l.‘m.il. | ab h.ḥpr.p‘l k.y[--]. | 13[6].19
yql. | w yšu.g h.w yṣḥ. | ḥwt.aḫt.w nar[-]. | qrn.d bat k.btlt.‘nt. | qrn.d bat k b‘l.ymšḥ. | b‘l.ymšḥ.hm.b ‘p. | nṭ‘n.b arṣ. 10[76].2.21
y.aliyn.b‘l. | k iṯ.zbl.b‘l.arṣ. | gm.yṣḥ.il.l btlt. | ‘nt.šm‘.l btlt.‘n[t]. | rgm.l nrt.il.šp[š]. | pl.‘nt.šdm.y špš. | pl.‘nt.šdm.il. 6[49].3.23
irt y.npš. | k ḥy.aliyn.b‘l. | k iṯ.zbl.b‘l.arṣ. | gm.yṣḥ.il.l btlt. | ‘nt.šm‘.l btlt.‘n[t]. | rgm.l nrt.il.šp[š]. | pl.‘nt.šdm.y špš. 6[49].3.22
an[št]. | k in.b ilht.ql[ṣ] k.mh.tarš[n]. | l btlt.‘nt.w t[‘]n.btlt.‘n[t]. | ṯḥm k.il.ḥkm.ḥkm k. | ‘m.‘lm.ḥyt.ḥẓt.ṯḥm k. | mlk 3[‘NT.VI].5.37
| ibǵ[y h.b tk.ǵ]r y.il.ṣpn. | b q[dš.b ǵr.nḥ]lt y. | w t[‘n].btlt.[‘]nt.ṯṯb. | [ybmt.]limm.[a]n.aqry. | [b arṣ].mlḥmt.[aš]t.b 3[‘NT].4.65
‘mn.ǵzr.št.ṯrm.w[---]. | ištir.b ḏdm.w n‘rs[.---]. | w t‘n.btlt.‘nt.ṯb.ytp.w[---]. | l k.ašt k.km.nšr.b ḥb[š y]. | km.diy.b t 18[3AQHT].4.16
| ṯly.bt.r[b.mṯb.arṣy]. | bt.y‘bdr[.mṯb.klt]. | knyt.w t‘n[.btlt.‘nt]. | yṯb l y.ṯr.il[.ab y.---]. | yṯb.l y.w l h.[---]. | [--.i]mṣḫ. 3[‘NT.VI].4.6
| w ‘rb n.l p‘n.‘nt.hbr. | w ql.tšthwy.kbd hyt. | w rgm.l btlt.‘nt. | ṯny.l ymmt.limm. | ṯḥm.aliyn.b‘l.hwt. | aliy.qrdm.qr 3[‘NT].3.8
r[y.bt.ar.ahbt.ṭly.bt.rb.dd]. | arṣy bt.y[‘bdr.---]. | rgm l btl[t.‘nt.ṯny.l ybmt.limm.ṯḥm.aliyn.b‘l]. | hw[t.aliy.qrdm.qry 7.2[130].13
‘l m.d ip[---]. | [il.]hd.d ‘nn.n[--]. | [----.]aliyn.b[‘l]. | [---.btl]t.‘n[t.-.]p h. | [---.---]n. | [-----]. | [-----]. | [---.]lk[.--]t. 10[76].2.35
. | [---].nmgn.hwt. | [--].aliyn.b‘l. | [--.]rbt.aṯrt.ym. | [---.]btlt.‘nt. | [--.tl]ḥm.tšty. | [ilm.w tp]q.mrǵtm. | [ṯd.b ḥrb.m]lḥt. 4[51].3.39
[---.]btlt.‘nt. | [---.]pp.hrm. | [---].d l yd‘ bn il. | [---.]pḫr kkbm. | [-- 10[76].1.1

. | [---.bt]lt.ʻnt. | [---]q.hry.w yld. | [---]m.ḥbl.kṯ[r]t. | [---.bt]lt.ʻnt. | [---.ali]yn.bʻl. | [---.]mʻn. | [-----]. | [-----]. | [---.--]r. | [-- 11[132].1.7
[-----]. | [---].aṯ[--.---]. | [---] h.ap.[---]. | [---].w tʻn.[btlt.ʻnt.---]. | [bnt.bht]k.y ilm[.bnt.bht k.--]. | [al.tšmḫ.]al.tš[18[3AQHT].1.6
.mtm. | [---.--]d mhr.ur. | [---.]yḫnnn. | [---.--]t.ytn. | [---.btlt.]ʻnt. | [---.ybmt.]limm. | [---.---]l.limm. | [---.yt]b.l arṣ. | [--- 10[76].1.14
--.---]. | b ym.il.d[--.---.n] | hr.il.y[--.---]. | aliyn.[bʻl.---]. | btlt.[ʻnt.---]. | mh.k[--.---]. | w at[--.---]. | aṯr[t.---]. | b im[--.---]. 4[51].2.38
[.-]. | [--.t]ṯkḥ.w tiḫd.b uš[k.--]. | [-.b]ʻl.yabd.l alp. | [---.bt]lt.ʻnt. | [---]q.hry.w yld. | [---]m.ḥbl.kṯ[r]t. | [---.bt]lt.ʻnt. | [-- 11[132].1.4

btm

[---.ʻ]ṣrm. | [--]ṯpḥ bʻl. | [ṯl]ṯ.ʻṣrm. | [w]bʻlt btm. | [---.--]ṣn.l.dgn. | [---.--]m. | [---].pi[--.-]qš. | [--]pš.šn[--]. | 39[19].4

btr

[s]p[r] ušknym.dt.[b d.---]. | bn.btr. | bn.ʻms. | bn.pṣn. | bn.agmz. | bn.[--]n. | bn.a[--]. | [------]. | [2021.1.2

btry

nqdm. | bn.alṯn. | bn.dly. | bn.btry. | bn.ḫdmn. | [bn].šty. | [bn].kdgdl. | [---.-]y[-.] 2018.4
klb. | [---]dn. | [---]y. | [-----]. | [-----]. | bn.adn. | prtn. | bn.btry. 1073.3.5

btšy

n.nrgn. | w ynḥm.aḫ h. | w.bʻln aḫ h. | w.ḥttn bn h. | w.btšy.bt h. | w.ištrmy. | bt.ʻbd mlk. | w.snt. | bt.ugrt. | w.pdy h[1006.7

bṯ

. | b ks.ištyn h. | dm.ṯn.dbḥm.šna.bʻl.ṯlṯ. | rkb.ʻrpt.dbḥ. | bṯt.w dbḥ.w dbḥ. | dnt.w dbḥ.tdmm. | amht.k b h.bṯt.l tbṯ. | 4[51].3.19
n h. | yqṯ bʻl.w yšt.ym.ykly.ṯpṭ.nhr. | b šm.tgʻr m.ʻṯtrt.bṯ l aliyn.[bʻl.] | bṯ.l rkb.ʻrpt.k šby n.zb[l.ym.k] | šby n.ṯpṭ.nh 2.4[68].28
bḥ. | bṯt.w dbḥ.w dbḥ. | dnt.w dbḥ.tdmm. | amht.k b h.bṯt.l tbṯ. | w b h.tdmmt.amht. | aḫr.mǵy.aliyn.bʻl. | mǵyt.btlt.ʻ 4[51].3.21
n.pḫr.l.pḫr.ṯṯb. | ʻn.mḫr.l.mḫr.ṯṯb. | ʻn.bṯy.l.bṯy.ṯṯb. | ʻn.bṯt.l.bṯt.ṯṯb. RS225.11
yšt.ym.ykly.ṯpṭ.nhr. | b šm.tgʻr m.ʻṯtrt.bṯ l aliyn.[bʻl.] | bṯ.l rkb.ʻrpt.k šby n.zb[l.ym.k] | šby n.ṯpṭ.nhr.w yṣa b[.--]. | 2.4[68].29
b.ʻrpt.k šby n.zb[l.ym.k] | šby n.ṯpṭ.nhr.w yṣa b[.--]. | ybṯ.nn.aliyn.bʻl.w [---]. | ym.l mt.bʻl m.ym l[--.---]. | ḥm.l šrr. 2.4[68].31
m. | tspi.šir.h.l.bl.ḥrb. | tšt.dm.h.l.bl.ks. | tpnn.ʻn.bṯy.ʻn.bṯt.tpnn. | ʻn.mḫr.ʻn.pḫr.ʻn.ṯǵr. | ʻn.ṯǵr.l.ṯǵr.ṯṯb. | ʻn.pḫr.l.pḫr. RS225.5
l q[ṣ.ilm.---]. | l rḥqm.l p[-.---]. | ṣḥ.il.yṯb.b[mrzḥ.---]. | bṯt.ʻllm n.[---]. | ilm.bt.bʻl k.[---]. | dl.ylkn.ḥš.b a[rṣ.---]. | b ʻpr 1[ʻNT.X].4.5
r.l.pḫr.ṯṯb. | ʻn.mḫr.l.mḫr.ṯṯb. | ʻn.bṯy.l.bṯy.ṯṯb. | ʻn.bṯt.l.bṯt.ṯṯb. RS225.11

bṯd

[---.]l mitm.ksp. | [---.]skn. | [---.-]im.bṯd. | [---.b]šḥr.atlgn. | [---].b šḥr. | [---.]bn h. | [-]k[--]g hn.ksp 2167.3

bṯḫ

| ḥ.ḫrṣ.yṣq.ksp. | l alpm.ḫrṣ.yṣq | m.l rbbt. | yṣq-ḫym.w tbṯḫ. | kt.il.dt.rbtm. | kt.il.nbt.b ksp. | šmrgt.b dm.ḫrṣ. | kḥṯ.il. 4[51].1.30

bṯy

ʻn.ṯǵr.l.ṯǵr.ṯṯb. | ʻn.pḫr.l.pḫr.ṯṯb. | ʻn.mḫr.l.mḫr.ṯṯb. | ʻn.bṯy.l.bṯy.ṯṯb. | ʻn.bṯt.l.bṯt.ṯṯb. RS225.10
.ysmsm. | tspi.šir.h.l.bl.ḥrb. | tšt.dm.h.l.bl.ks. | tpnn.ʻn.bṯy.ʻn.bṯt.tpnn. | ʻn.mḫr.ʻn.pḫr.ʻn.ṯǵr. | ʻn.ṯǵr.l.ṯǵr.ṯṯb. | ʻn.pḫr RS225.5
.l.ṯǵr.ṯṯb. | ʻn.pḫr.l.pḫr.ṯṯb. | ʻn.mḫr.l.mḫr.ṯṯb. | ʻn.bṯy.l.bṯy.ṯṯb. | ʻn.bṯt.l.bṯt.ṯṯb. RS225.10

bṯk

ṯ]n.w nšt. | w ʻn hm.nǵr mdrʻ[.iṯ.lḥm.---]. | iṯ.yn.d ʻrb.bṯk[.---]. | mǵ hw.l hn.lg yn h[.---]. | w ḥbr h.mla yn.[---]. 23[52].74

bṯn

.l tššy.hm.tqrm.l mt.b rn k. | [--]ḫp.an.arnn.ql.špš.ḥw.bṯnm.uḫd.bʻlm. | [--.a]ṯm.prṯl.l riš h.ḥmṯ.ṯmṯ. | [--.]ydbr.ṯrmt 1001.1.6
k tmḫṣ.ltn.bṯn.brḥ. | tkly.bṯn.ʻqltn. | šlyṭ.d šbʻy.rašm. | ṯṯkḥ.ttrp.šmm.k r 5[67].1.1
] yn. | p nšt.bʻl.[ṭ]ʻn.iṭʻn k. | [---.]ma[---] k.k tmḫṣ. | [ltn.bṯn.br]ḥ.tkly. | [bṯn.ʻqltn.]šlyṭ. | [d šbʻt.rašm].ṯṯkḥ. | [ttrp.šm 5[67].1.28
.-]llm.abl.mṣrp k.[---]. | [---.]y.mṯnt.w ṯḥ.ṭbt.n[--]. | [---.b]ṯnm w ṯṯb.ʻl.bṯnt.trṯḥ[ṣ.---]. | [---.t]ṯb h.aḫt.ppšr.w ppšrt[.-- 1001.2.5
.hkl.w ištql šql. | tn.km.nḥšm.yḥr.tn.km. | mhr y.w bn.bṯn.itnn y. | ytt.nḥšm.mhr k.bn bṯn. | itnn k. | aṯr ršp.ʻṯtrt. | ʻ UG5.7.74
r.tn.km. | mhr y.w bn.bṯn.itnn y. | ytt.nḥšm.mhr k.bn bṯn. | itnn k. | aṯr ršp.ʻṯtrt. | ʻm ʻṯtrt.mr h. | mnt.nṯk.nḥš. UG5.7.75
alpm.ib.šṯ[-.]št. | ḥršm l ahlm p[---.]km. | [-]bl lb h.km.bṯn.y[--.-]ah. | ṯnm.tšqy msk.hwt.tšqy[.-.]w [---]. | w hn dt.yṯ 19[1AQHT].4.223
m. | mt.ʻz.bʻl.ʻz.ynghn. | k rumm.mt.ʻz.bʻl. | ʻz.ynṯkn.k bṯnm. | mt.ʻz.bʻl.ʻz.ymṣḫn. | k lsmm.mt.ql. | bʻl.ql.ʻln.špš. | tṣḥ 6[49].6.19
k tmḫṣ.ltn.bṯn.brḥ. | tkly.bṯn.ʻqltn. | šlyṭ.d šbʻy.rašm. | ṯṯkḥ.ttrp.šmm.k rs. | ipd k.ank.i 5[67].1.2
ṭ]ʻn.iṭʻn k. | [---.]ma[---] k.k tmḫṣ. | [ltn.bṯn.br]ḥ.tkly. | [bṯn.ʻqltn.]šlyṭ. | [d šbʻt.rašm].ṯṯkḥ. | [ttrp.šmm.k rks.ipd]k. | [5[67].1.29
dd. | il ym.l klt.nhr.il.rbm. | l ištbm.tnn.ištml h. | mḫšt.bṯn.ʻqltn. | šlyṭ.d šbʻt.rašm. | mḫšt.mdd ilm.ar[š]. | ṣmt.ʻgl.il.ʻt 3[ʻNT].3.38
[---.]m[-]ǵ[-].thmt.brq. | [---].tṣb.qšt.bnt. | [---.ʻ]n h.km.bṯn.yqr. | [krpn h.-.l]arṣ.ks h.tšpk m. | [l ʻpr.tšu.g h.]w tṣḥ.š 17[2AQHT].6.14
k.[---]. | [---.]y.mṯnt.w ṯḥ.ṭbt.n[--]. | [---.b]ṯnm w ṯṯb.ʻl.bṯnt.trṯḥ[ṣ.---]. | [---.t]ṯb h.aḫt.ppšr.w ppšrt[.---]. | [---.]k.drḫ 1001.2.5
t[.---]. | [---].nzdt.qr[t]. | [---.]dt nzdt.m[lk]. | [---.]w.ap.bṯn[.---]. | [---.]bʻl y.y[--]. | [---.-]l[-.---]. 2127.2.6

g

g

nm.il.špḥ. | lṯpn.w qdš.ʿl. | ab h.yʿrb.ybky. | w yšnn.ytn.g h. | bky.b ḥy k.ab n.ašmḫ. | b l.mt k.ngln.k klb. | b bt k.nʿtq 16.1[125].13
ǵzr.ilḥu.t[---]l. | trm.tṣr.trm[.ʿ]tqt. | tbky.w tšnn.[tt]n. | g h.bky.b ḥ[y k.a]b n. | nšmḫ.b l.mt k.ngln. | k klb.[b]bt k.nʿ 16.2[125].98
ʿl. | [s]pu y.bn m.um y.kly y. | yṯb.ʿm.bʿl.ṣrrt. | ṣpn.yšu g h.w yṣḥ. | aḫ y m.ytnt.bʿl. | spu y.bn m.um y.kl | y y.ytʿn.k 6[49].6.13
[t]. | aṯr.bʿl.tiḫd.m[t]. | b sin.lpš.tšṣq[n h]. | b qṣ.all.tšu.g h.w[tṣ] | ḥ.at.mt.tn.aḫ y. | w ʿn.bn.ilm.mt.mh. | taršn.l btlt.ʿ 6[49].2.11
ṯṯbr.ʿln.p]n h.td[ʿ]. | tǵṣ[.pnt.ks]l h. | anš.dt.ẓr.[h]. | tšu.g h.w tṣḥ[.i]k. | mǵy.aliy[n.b]ʿl. | ik.mǵyt.b[t]lt. | ʿnt.mḫṣ y h 4[51].2.21
n.ksl.ṯṯbr. | ʿln.pn h.tdʿ.tǵṣ.pnt. | ksl h.anš.dt.ẓr h.tšu. | g h.w tṣḥ.ik.mǵy.gpn.w ugr. | mn.ib.ypʿ.l bʿl.ṣrt. | l rkb.ʿrpt.l 3[ʿNT].3.33
q.lṣb.w yṣḥq. | pʿn h.l hdm.yṯpd.w ykrkr. | uṣbʿt h.yšu.g h.w y[ṣḥ]. | ik.mǵyt.rbt.aṯr[t.y]m. | ik.atwt.qnyt.i[lm]. | rǵb. 4[51].4.30
ṯ.bn.ilm.mt.ʿbd k.an. | w d ʿlm k.šmḫ.bn.ilm.mt. | [---.]g h.w aṣḥ.ik.yṣḥn. | [bʿl.ʿm.aḫ y.ik].yqrun.hd. | [ʿm.ary y.---.- 5[67].2.21
n. | yṯlṯ.qn.ḏrʿ h.yḥrṯ. | k gn.ap lb.k ʿmq.yṯlṯ. | bmt.yšu.g h.w yṣḥ. | bʿl.mt.my.lim.bn. | dgn.my.hmlt.aṯr. | bʿl.ard.b ar 5[67].6.22
ʿm.bʿl.mrym.ṣpn. | b alp.šd.rbt.kmn. | ṣḥq.btlt.ʿnt.tšu. | g h.w tṣḥ.tbšr bʿl. | bšrt k.yblt.y[b]n. | bt.l k.km.aḫ k.w ḥẓr. | 4[51].5.88
lšn.aqht.ǵzr. | [---.kdd.dn]il.mt.rpi.w tʿn. | [btlt.ʿnt.tšu.g]h.w tṣḥ.hwt. | [---.]aqht.yḏ[--]. | [---.--]n.ṣ[---]. | [spr.ilmlk.š 17[2AQHT].6.53
ḫt.bʿl. | l pnn h.ydd.w yqm. | l pʿn h.ykrʿ.w yql. | w yšu.g h.w yṣḥ. | ḥwt.aḫt.w nar[-]. | qrn.d bat k.btlt.ʿnt. | qrn.d bat 10[76].2.19
dr[.dr]. | ʿdb.uḫry mṭ.yd h. | ymǵ.l mrrt.tǵll.b nr. | yšu.g h.w yṣḥ.y l k.mrrt. | tǵll.b nr.d ʿl k.mḫṣ.aqht. | ǵzr.šrš k.b a 19[1AQHT].3.157
ḫry mṭ yd h. | ymǵ.l qrt.ablm.abl[m]. | qrt.zbl.yrḫ.yšu g h. | w yṣḥ.y l k.qrt.ablm. | d ʿl k.mḫṣ.aqht.ǵzr. | ʿwrt.yšt k.b 19[1AQHT].4.164
.il.d pid. | pʿn h.l hdm.yṯpd. | w yprq.lṣb w yṣḥq. | yšu.g h.w yṣḥ. | aṯbn.ank.w anḫn. | w tnḫ.b irt y.npš. | k ḥy.aliyn. 6[49].3.17
ʿl yṣhl pi[t]. | yprq.lṣb.w yṣḥq. | pʿn.l hdm.yṯpd.yšu. | g h.w yṣḥ.aṯbn.ank. | w anḫn.w tnḫ.b irt y. | npš.k yld.bn.l y. 17[2AQHT].2.12
-]. | [tt]bʿ.btlt.ʿnt[.idk.l ttn.pnm]. | ʿm.yṯpn.mhr.š[t.tšu.g h]. | w tṣḥ.ytb.ytp.[---]. | qrt.ablm.ablm.[qrt.zbl.yrḫ]. | ik.al. 18[3AQHT].4.6
. | tpr.w du.b nši.ʿn h.w ypn. | yḥd.hrgb.ab.nšrm. | yšu.g h.w yṣḥ.knp.hr[g]b. | bʿl.yṯb.bʿl.y[ṯb]r.diy[.h]wt. | w yql.tḥt 19[1AQHT].3.122
yql. | tḥt.pʿn h.ybqʿ.kbd h.w yḥd. | [i]n.šmt.in.ʿẓm.yšu.g[h]. | w yṣḥ.knp.hrgb.bʿl.ybn. | [b]ʿl.ybn.diy.hwt.hrg[b]. | tp 19[1AQHT].3.131
. | tḥt.pʿn h.ybqʿ.kbdt hm.w[yḥd]. | in.šmt.in.ʿẓm.yšu.g h. | w yṣḥ.knp.nšrm.ybn. | bʿl.ybn.diy hmt nšrm. | tpr.w du. 19[1AQHT].3.117
l.l qẓ.ybky.w yqbr. | yqbr.nn.b mdgt.b knk[-]. | w yšu.g h.w yṣḥ.knp.nšrm. | bʿl.yṯbr.bʿl.yṯbr.diy. | hmt.hm.tʿpn.ʿl.q 19[1AQHT].3.148
b nši[.ʿn h.w yphn.yḥd]. | b ʿrpt[.nšrm.yšu]. | [g h.]w yṣḥ[.knp.nšrm]. | bʿl.yṯb.bʿl.yṯb[r.diy.hmt]. | tqln.tḥ pʿ 19[1AQHT].3.107
tpr.w du.b nši.ʿn h. | [w]yphn.yḥd.ṣml.um.nšrm. | yšu.g h.w yṣḥ.knp.ṣml. | bʿl.yṯbr.bʿl.yṯbr.diy. | hyt.tql.tḥt.pʿn y.ib 19[1AQHT].3.136
]tḥ.b dqt.ʿrpt. | ʿl h[wt].kṯr.w ḫss. | ṣḥq.kṯr.w ḫss. | yšu.g h.w yṣḥ. | l rgmt.l k.l ali | yn.bʿl.ṯṯbn.bʿl. | l hwt y.yptḥ.ḥ | ln 4[51].7.22
nt.[m]k.b šbʿ. | šnt.w [--].bn.ilm.mt. | ʿm.aliyn.bʿl.yšu. | g h.w yṣḥ.ʿl k.b[ʿ]l m. | pht.qlt.ʿl k.pht. | dry.b ḥrb.ʿl k. | pht.š 6[49].5.11
.bnt.ḥry. | km hm.w ṯḫss.aṯrt. | ndr h.w ilt.p[--]. | w tšu.g h.w [tṣḥ]. | ph mʿ.ap.k[rt.--]. | u ṯn.ndr[.---]. | apr.[---]. | [----- 15[128].3.27
k.ab.šnm.l pʿn. | il.thbr.w tql. | tštḥwy.w tkbdn h. | tšu.g h.w tṣḥ.tšmḫ ht. | aṯrt.w bn h.ilt.w ṣb | rt.ary h.k mt.aliyn. 6.1.39[49.1.11]
t h.l trm. | mt.dm.ḫt.šʿtqt. | dm.lan.w ypqd. | krt.ṯʿ.yšu.g h. | w yṣḥ.šmʿ.l mṯt. | ḥry.ṯbḫ.imr. | w ilḥm.mgt.w iṯrm. | tš 16.6[127].15
a]qht.ǵzr.b alp.š[d]. | [rbt.]kmn.w ṣḥq.btlt.[ʿnt]. | [tšu.]g h.w tṣḥ.šmʿ.m[ʿ.l a] | [qht.ǵ]zr.at.aḫ.w an.a[ḫt k]. | [---].šbʿ. 18[3AQHT].1.23
h.km.btn.yqr. | [krpn h.-.l]arṣ.ks h.tšpk m. | [l ʿpr.tšu.g h.]w tṣḥ.šmʿ.mʿ. | [l aqht.ǵzr.i]rš.ksp.w atn k. | [ḫrṣ.w aš]lḥ 17[2AQHT].6.16
.amlk. | l drkt.k aṯb.an. | ytbʿ.yṣb ǵlm.ʿl. | ab h.yʿrb.yšu g h. | w yṣḥ.šmʿ mʿ.l krt. | ṯʿ.ištmʿ.w tqǵ udn. | k ǵz.ǵzm.tdbr. 16.6[127].40
m.u[---]k.yrd[.--.]i[---]n.bn. | [---.-]nn.nrt.ilm.špš.tšu.g h.w t[ṣḥ.šm]ʿ.mʿ. | [-.yṯ]ir ṯr.il.ab k.l pn.zbl.ym.l pn[.ṯ]pṭ[. 2.3[129].15
bʿ. | šnt.w yʿn[.dnil.mt.]rpi. | yṯb.ǵzr.m[t.hrnmy.y]šu. | g h.w yṣḥ.t[bʿ.---]. | bkyt.b hk[l]y.mšspdt. | b ḥẓr y pẓǵm.ǵr. 19[1AQHT].4.182
n.l pʿ]n.ʿnt. | [yhbr.w yql.yšt]ḥwyn.w y | [kbdn h.yšu.g h.w y]ṣḥ.tḥm. | [ṯr.il.ab k.hwt.l]ṯpn.ḥtk k. | [qryy.b arṣ.mlḥ 1[ʿNT.IX].2.17
l.arṣ. | ttbʿ.btlt.ʿnt. | idk.l ttn.pnm. | ʿm.nrt.ilm.špš. | tšu.g h.w tṣḥ. | tḥm.ṯr.il.ab k. | hwt.lṯpn.ḥtk k. | pl.ʿnt.šdm.y špš. 6[49].4.33
h.tdʿ.b ʿdn]. | ksl.y[ṯbr.yǵṣ.pnt.ksl h]. | anš.[dt.ẓr h.yšu.g h]. | w yṣ[ḥ.---]. | mḫṣ[.---]. | š[--.---]. 19[1AQHT].2.96
.šn[-.---]. | w l ṯlb.[---]. | mit.rḥ[.---]. | ṯṯlb.a[--.---]. | yšu.g h[.---]. | i.ap.bʿ[l.---]. | i.hd.d[---.---]. | ynpʿ.bʿ[l.---]. | b ṯmnt.[5[67].4.5
.thmtm]. | [tgly.ḏd.il.w]tb[a]. | [qrš.mlk.ab.]šnm. | [tša.g hm.w tṣ]ḥ.sbn. | [---]l[.---.]ʿd. | ksm.mhyt[.m]ǵny. | l nʿm y. 5[67].6.3
[k.]rḥ.npš.hm. | k.iṯl.brlt n[-.k qṯr.b ap -]. | tmǵyn.tša.g h[m.w tṣḥn]. | šmʿ.l dnil.[mt.rpi]. | mt.aqht.ǵzr.[šṣat]. | btlt. 19[1AQHT].2.89
lm.mt. | tk.qrt h.hmry.mk.ksu. | ṯbt.ḫḫ.arṣ.nḫlt h.tša. | g hm.w tṣḥ.tḥm.aliyn. | bn.bʿl.hwt.aliy.qrdm. | bhṯ.bn.ilm.mt 5[67].2.17
tbʿ.mlakm. | l yṯb.idk.pnm. | l ytn.ʿmm.pbl. | mlk.tšan. | g hm.w tṣḥn. | tḥm.krt.ṯ[ʿ]. | hwt.[n]ʿmn.[ǵlm.il]. 14[KRT].6.304
km.l yṯb]. | [idk.pnm.l ytn]. | [ʿ]m[.krt.mswn h]. | tš[an.g hm.w tṣḥn]. | tḥ[m.pbl.mlk]. | qḥ[.ksp.w yrq]. | ḫrṣ.[yd.mq 14[KRT].6.267
. | [--]ḫ[d].šd.hwt. | [--.]iḫd.šd.gtr. | [w]ht.yšmʿ.uḫ y. | l g y.w yhbṭ.bnš. | w ytn.ilm.b d hm. | b d.iḫqm.gtr. | w b d.ytr 55[18].18
klnmw. | l yarš ḫswn. | ḫmš ʿšr.sp. | l bnš tpnr d yaḫd l g ynm. | ṯṯ spm l tgyn. | arbʿ spm l ll[-]. | ṯn spm.l slyy. | ṯlṯ sp 137.2[93].11
tḥm.hl[--]. | l pḫry.a[ḫ y]. | w l g.p[-]r[--]. | yšlm[.l k]. | [i]lm[.tǵr k]. | [t]š[lm k.---]. | [-----]. | [- 56[21].3

gan

t.ǵzr.ṯb l y w l k. | [---]m.l aqry k.b ntb.pšʿ. | [---].b ntb.gan.ašql k.tḥt. | [pʿn y.a]nk.nʿmn.ʿmq.nšm. | [tdʿṣ.pʿn]m.w tr 17[2AQHT].6.44
--]. | š š[--]. | w [--]. | d [--]. | ypḫ[--]. | w s[--]. | [---]. | qrd ga[n.--]. | b bt k.[--]. | w l dbḥ[--]. | ṯ[--]. | [--] aṯt yqḥ ʿz. | [---]ḏ RS61[24.277.21]

gb

ḫmn. | ilm.w tštn.tštn y[n] ʿd šbʿ. | trṯ.ʿd.škr.yʿdb.yrḫ. | gb h.km.[---.]yqṭqt.tḥt. | ṯlḥnt.il.d ydʿnn. | yʿdb.lḥm.l h.w d l UG5.1.1.5
[---.]trks. | [---.]abnm.upqt. | [---.]l w ǵr mtn y. | [---.]rq.gb. | [---.--]kl.tǵr.mtn h. | [---.--]b.w ym ymm. | [yʿtqn.---.]ym 1[ʿNT.X].5.13

gby

.ubdy.ilštmʿ. | dt b d.skn. | šd.bn.ubrʿn b gt prn. | šd.bn.gby.gt.prn. | šd.bn.kryn.gt.prn. | šd.bn.ky.gt.prn. | šd.hwil.gt. 1104.4

gbl

. | ḫmš.mat.arbʿm. | kbd.ksp.anyt. | d.ʿrb.b.anyt. | l.mlk.gbl. | w.ḫmšm.ksp. | lqḥ.mlk.gbl. | lbš.anyt h. | bʿrm.ksp. | mḫr 2106.13
anyt. | d.ʿrb.b.anyt. | l.mlk.gbl. | w.ḫmšm.ksp. | lqḥ.mlk.gbl. | lbš.anyt h. | bʿrm.ksp. | mḫr.hn. 2106.15

.]bn ʻn km.|[---.]alp.|[---.]ym.rbt.|[---.]b nhrm.|[ʻb]r.gbl.ʻbr.|qʻl.ʻbr.iht.|np šmm.šmšr.|l dgy.aṯrt.|mǵ.l qdš.amr 3[ʻNT.VI].6.7

ry.š.il.tʻd̠r.bʻl.š.ršp.š.ddmš.š.|w šlmm.ilib.š.i[l.--]m d gbl.ṣpn.al[p].|pẖr.ilm.š.ym.š[.k]nr.š.[--.]ʻṣrm gdlt.|bʻlm.km UG5.9.1.10

.|ḥrn.y bn.yṯbr.ḥrn.|riš k.ʻṯtrt.šm.bʻl.|qdqd k.tqln.b gbl.|šnt k.b ḥpn k.w tʻn.|spr ilmlk ṯʻy. 16.6[127].57

br.ḥrn].|riš k.ʻṯtrt.[šm.bʻl.qdqd k.---].|[--]t.mṭ.tpln.b g[bl.šnt k.---].|[--]šnm.aṯtm.t[--.---].|[m]lakm.ylak.ym.[tʻdt. 2.1[137].9

gbly

bn.ǵs.ḥrš.šʻty.|ʻdy.bn.slʻy.gbly.|yrm.bʻl.bn.kky. 2121.2

gbln

ṣn.qšt.w.qlʻ.|bn.gdn.ṯt.qštm.w.qlʻ.|bn.[-]q.qšt.w.qlʻ.|gb[l]n.qšt.w.qlʻ.|bn.[-]bl.ṯt.qštm.w.ṯn.qlʻm.|bn.[-]rkṯ.ṯt.qšt 119[321].3.14

gbʻ

[-.---].|mn[-.---].|hyrm.h[--.---].|yrmm h[--.---].|mlk.gbʻ h d [---].|ibr.k l hm.d l h q[--.---].|l ytn.l hm.ṯḥt bʻl[.---] 9[33].2.3

ṣḥ.ẖrn.|b bht k.ʻd̠bt.b qrb.|hkl k.tbl k.ǵrm.|mid.ksp.gbʻm.mḥmd..|ẖrṣ.w bn.bht.ksp.|w ẖrṣ.bht.ṯhrm.|iqnim.šm 4[51].5.94

.ẖrn.b bht h.|ʻd̠bt.b qrb hkl h.|yblnn ǵrm.mid.ksp.|gbʻm lḥmd.ẖrṣ.|yblnn.udr.ilqṣm.|yak.l kṯr.w ẖss.|w ṯb l m 4[51].5.101

.ẖrn.b bhm k.|ʻd̠bt.b qrb.hkl k.|tbl k.ǵrm.mid.ksp.|gbʻm.mḥmd.ẖrṣ.|ybl k.udr.ilqṣm.|w bn.bht.ksp.w ẖrṣ.|bht 4[51].5.78

aṯr.|bʻl.ard.b arṣ.ap.|ʻnt.ttlk.w tṣd.kl.ǵr.|l kbd.arṣ.kl.gbʻ.|l [k]bd.šdm.tmǵ.l nʻm[y].|[arṣ.]dbr.ysmt.šd.|[šḥl]mm 5[67].6.27

.mh.|taršn.l btlt.ʻnt.|an.itlk.w aṣd.kl.|ǵr.l kbd.arṣ.kl.gbʻ.|l kbd.šdm.npš.ẖsrt.|bn.nšm.npš.hmlt.|arṣ.mǵt.l nʻm y 6[49].2.16

.qšt.w.qlʻ.|uln.qšt.w.qlʻ.|uln.qšt.|bn.blzn.qšt.w.qlʻ.|gbʻ.qšt.w.qlʻ.|nṣṣn.qšt.|mʻr.|[ʼ]dyn.ṯt.qštm.w.qlʻ.|[-]lrš.qšt. 119[321].2.10

k.|ibǵy h.b tk.ǵr y.il.ṣpn.|b qdš.b ǵr.nḥlt y.|b nʻm.b gbʻ.tliyt.|hlm.ʻnt.tph.ilm.b h.pʻnm.|ṯṭṭ.bʻd n.ksl.ṯṯbr.|ʻln.p 3[ʻNT].3.28

gbʻly

ap.|pd.|mlk.|ar.|atlg.|gbʻly.|ulm.|mʻrby.|mʻr.|arny.|šʻrt.|ẖlbrpš.|hry.|qmṣ.|ṣʻq 2074.6

ny.|bn.arz.šʻrty.|bn.ibrd.mʻrby.|ṣdqn.gbʻly.|bn.ypy.gbʻly.|bn.grgs.ilštmʻy.|bn.ẖran.ilštmʻy.|bn.abdʻn.ilštmʻy.| 87[64].28

bn.ǵlmn.ary.|[bn].šdy.|[bn].gmḥ.|[---]ty.|[b]n.ypy.gbʻly.|b[n].ḥyn.|d̠mn.šʻrty.|bn.arwdn.ilštʻy.|bn grgs.|bn.ẖ 99[327].1.5

y.|bn.abn.uškny.|bn.arz.šʻrty.|bn.ibrd.mʻrby.|ṣdqn.gbʻly.|bn.ypy.gbʻly.|bn.grgs.ilštmʻy.|bn.ẖran.ilštmʻy.|bn.a 87[64].27

.|ar.ẖmš.ḥmr[m.w.ẖm]š.bnšm.|atlg.ḥmr[.---.]bnšm.|gbʻly.ḥmr š[--.b]nšm.|ulm.ṯn.[---.]bnšm.|mʻrby.[---.--]m.ṯn[2040.6

šrš.|lbnm.|ẖlb.krd.|ṣʻ.|mlk.|gbʻly.|ypr.|ary.|ẓrn.|art.|ṯlḥny.|ṯlrby.|dmt.|aǵt.|w.qmnz 71[113].6

|bn abdẖ[r].|pdym.|ẖmš.bnšm.|snrym.|tšʻ.bnš[m].|gbʻlym.|arbʻ.b[nšm].|ṯbqym. 79[83].16

[ṯl]ṯm.ksp.ʻ[l].|[b]n.bly.gbʻly.|[šp]ḥ.a[n]ṯb.|w.m[--.u]škny.|[ʼ]š[r.---]t.ksp.|[ʻl.---]b 2055.2

[---].b d.š[--]mlk.|[---.b] d.gbʻly.|[---.b] d.ʻbdẖmn.|[---.b] d.ṯbq.|[---.b] d.šbn.|[---.b] d 1052.2

gbry

idṯn.d aẖd.b.ʻnqpat.|[aḥd.al]p.d aǵlmn.|[d aẖd b.g]t gbry.|[---].aḥd.aẖd.b.yʻny.|[---.-]ḥm.b.aẖd.ḥrṯ.|[---.]aẖd.b. 1129.13

gbrn

gln.|bn abg.|bn.nǵry.|bn.srwd.|mtnn.|bn gš[-].|bn gbrn.|bn uldy.|synn.bn knʻm.|bn kbr.|bn iytlm.|bn ayln.| 1064.17

|ḥṯṯn.|[--]n.|[---].|tsn.|rpiy.|mrṯn.|ṯnyn.|apṯ.|šbn.|gbrn.|ṯbʻm.|kyn.|bʻln.|ytršp.|ḥmšm.ṯmn.kbd.|tgmr.bnš. 1024.2.20

gbṯ

ld ʻqqm.|ilm.ypʻr.|šmt hm.|b hm.qrnm.|km.ṯrm.w gbṯt.|km.ibrm.|w b hm.pn.bʻl.|bʻl.ytlk.w yṣd.|yḥ pat.mlbr 12[75].1.31

gg

ʻms h.|[k]šbʻ yn.spu.ksm h.bt.bʻl.|[w m]nt h bt.il.ṯḥ.gg h.b ym.|[ṯi]ṭ.rḥṣ.npṣ h.b ym.rṭ.|[--.y]iḥd.il.ʻbd h.ybrk.|[17[2AQHT].1.33

ʻms y k šbʻt yn.|spu.ksm y.bt.bʻl.[w]mn[t].|y.bt.il.ṯḥ.gg y.b ym.ṯiṭ.|rḥṣ.npṣ y.b ym.rṭ.|dn.il.bt h.ymǵyn.|yštql.d 17[2AQHT].2.22

nt k].|bt il.aẖd.yd k.b [škrn].|mʻms k.k šbʻt.yn.ṯ[ḥ].|gg k.b ym.ṯiṭ.rḥṣ.|npṣ k.b ym rṭ.b uni[l].|pnm.tšmẖ.w ʻl yṣ 17[2AQHT].2.7

ab k.il.šrd.bʻl.|b dbḥ k.bn.dgn.|b mṣd k.w yrd.|krt.l ggt.ʻdb.|akl.l qryt.|ḥṭt.l bt.ẖbr.|yip.lḥm.d ẖmš.|mǵd.ṯdṯ.y 14[KRT].2.80

h.il.šrd.|[bʻl].b dbḥ h.bn dgn.|[b m]ṣd h.yrd.krt.|[l g]gt.ʻdb.akl.l qryt.|ḥṭt.l bt.ẖbr.|yip.lḥm.d ẖmš.|[mǵ]d.ṯdṯ. 14[KRT].4.172

[aṯt.w].bn h.b.bt.krz.|[aṯt.]w.pǵt.b.bt.gg.|[ǵz]r.aḥd.b.bt.nwrd̠.|[aṯ]t.adrt.b.bt.arṯṯb.|aṯt.w.ṯn.bn h 80[119].2

]b.ym.ḥdṯ.ṯn.šm.|l.[---]t.|i[d.yd]bḥ.mlk.l.prgl.ṣqrn.b.gg.|ar[bʻ.]arbʻ.mṯbt.azmr.b h.š.šr[-].|al[p.w].š.šlmm.pamt.š 35[3].50

ggy

[---.]d.ztm.d.si[-].|[---.]d.ztm.d ggy.[---].|[---.d].ztm.d.b[--].|[---.]ztm.[---]. 2035.2

ggn

si mlk.|l nẖt.l kḥṯ.drkt.|ap.yṣb.yṯb.b hkl.|w ywsrnn.ggn h.|lk.l ab k.yṣb.lk.|l[ab]k.w rgm.ʻny.|l k[rt.adn k.]išt 16.6[127].26

---].|[--.]l bʻl.ʻbd[.---].|ṯr ab h il.ṯtrm[.---].|tšlḥm yrẖ.ggn[.---].|k[.---.ẖ]mš.ẖssm[.---].|[---.--]m ʻṯtr[t.---].|[---.]n[-- 2001.1.16

ggʻt

by.|b d.tlmi.b.ʻšrm.ẖmšt.|kbd.ksp.|kkrm.šʻrt.štt.b d.gg[ʻt].|b.ʻšrt.ksp.|ṯlṯ.uṯbm.b d.alẖn.b.ʻšrt[.k]sp.|rṯ.l.ql.d.yb 2101.9

ṯn.bn.klby.|bn.iyṯr.|[ʼ]bdyrẖ.|[b]n.ggʻt.|[ʼ]dy.|armwl.|uwaẖ.|ypln.w.ṯn.bn h.|ydln.|anr[my]. 2086.4

gd

ʻnyn.|w šd.šd ilm.šd aṯrt.w rḥm.|ʻl.išt.šbʻ d.ǵzrm.ṭb.[g]d.b ḥlb.annẖ b ẖmat.|w ʻl.agn.šbʻ d m.dǵ[ṯ.---]t.|tlk m.rḥ 23[52].14

.ybmt.limm.|w yʻn.aqht.ǵzr.adr.ṯqbm.|[d]lbnn.adr.gdm.b rumm.|adr.qrnt.b yʻlm.mtnm.|b ʻqbt.ṯr.adr.b ǵlil.qn 17[2AQHT].6.21

[-]p[-]l[.---].|k lli.[---].|kpr.[šbʻ.bnt.rḥ.gdm.w anhbm].|w tqr[y.ǵlmm.b št.ǵr.---].|[ʼ]d tš[bʻ.tmtẖṣ.- 7.2[130].3

ank.ib[ǵy h.---].|[-].l yʻmdn.i[---.---].|kpr.šbʻ bn[t.rḥ.gdm.w anhbm].|kla[t.ṯǵ]r[t.bht.ʻnt.w tqry.ǵlmm.b št.ǵr].|a 7.2[130].23

gd

n[--.---.-]š[--].|kpr.šbʻ.bnt.rḥ.gdm.|w anhbm.klat.ṯǵrt.|bht.ʻnt.w tqry.ǵlmm.|b št.ǵr.w h 3[ʻNT].2.2

gda

]k.|bn.aup[š.--].bsbn hzpḫ ṯlṯt.|kṯr[.---.--]trt ḫmšt.bn gda[.-.]mḏʻ.|kl[--.---.]ṯmnt.[--.]w[.---].|[-]m[.---.]ṣpiry[.ṯ]lṯt[APP.II[173].59

gdy

ʻšr šṭpm.|b ḫmš.šmn.|ʻšrm.gdy.|b ḫmš.šmn.|w ḫmš ṯʻdt. 1097.3
].|šd.b[---].|b d.[---].|šd.[---].|b d.[---].|[-----].|šd.bn.gdy.|b d.ddl. 2028.22
[---.]gtn ṯṯ.|[---.]ṯḥr l ytn ḫs[n].|ʻbd ulm ṯn un ḫsn.|gdy lqḥ ṣṭqn gt bn ndr.|um r[-] gtn ṯṯ ḫsn l ytn.|l rḥt lqḥ ṣt 1154.4

gdl

.tšmḫ.]al.tš[mḫ.b rm.h]|[kl k.al.]aḫd hm.[---].|[---.b]gdlt.ar[kt y.am--].|[---.qdq]d k.ašhlk[.šbt k.dmm].|[šbt.dq] 18[3AQHT].1.10
l.tšmḫ.b r[m.h]kl[k].|al.aḫd.hm.b y[--] y.[---]b[-].|b gdlt.arkt y.am[---].|qdqd k.ašhlk.šbt[k.dmm].|[šbt.dqn k. 3[ʻNT.VI].5.31
šl]|[mm.---].dq[t.ilh.gdlt].|n.w šnm.dqt[.---].|[i]lh[m.gd]lt.i[l.dqt.ṯkm]|n.w šnm.dqt[.---].|bqtm.b nbk.[---].|km APP.II[173].33
dqt.š[.---.rš]|[p.š]rp.w šl[mm.--.dqt].|[i]lh.gdlt[.ilhm.gdlt.il].|[d]qt.ṯkmn.w [šnm.dqt.--].|[--]t.dqtm.[b nbk.---].|[35[3].30
p].w š[l]mm.kmm.|[w bbt.bʻl.ugrt.]kdm.w npš.|[ilib.gdlt.il.š.b]ʻ[l.]š.ʻnt ṣpn.|[---.]w [n]p[š.---].|[---.--]t.w[.---].|[- 36[9].1.17
rp.w šlmm.|kmm.w bbt.bʻl.ugrt.|w kdm.w npš ilib.|gdlt.il š.bʻl š.ʻnt.|ṣpn.alp.w š.pdry.š.|šrp.w šlmm ilib š.|bʻl UG5.13.13
m dqt.|ršp.dqt.šrp w šlmm.dqtm.|[i]lh.alp w š ilhm.gdl[t.]ilhm.|[b]ʻl š.aṯrt.š.ṯkmn w šnm.š.|ʻnt.š.ršp.š.dr il w p 34[1].5
m].|dqt.ršp.šrp.w š[lmm.dqtm].|ilh[.a]lp.w š[.il]hm.[gdlt.ilhm].|bʻ[l.š].aṯrt[.š.ṯkm]n w [šnm.š].|ʻnt š ršp š[.dr.il. 35[3].14
[šnm.dqt.ršp.šrp].|w šlmm.[dqtm.ilh.alp.w š].|ilhm.gd[lt.ilhm.bʻl.š.aṯrt.š].|ṯkmn.w š[nm.š.ʻnt.š.ršp.š.dr].|il.w p APP.II[173].16
--].|il[hm.]dqt.š[.---.rš]|[p.š]rp.w šl[mm.--.dqt].|[i]lh.gdlt[.ilhm.gdlt.il].|[d]qt.ṯkmn.w [šnm.dqt.--].|[--]t.dqtm.[b 35[3].30
[---].|w yn[t.q]rt.y[---].|w al[p.l]il.w bu[rm.---].|ytk.gdlt.ilhm.[ṯkmn.w šnm].|dqt.ršp.šrp.w š[lmm.dqtm].|ilh[.a 35[3].12
dqt.ṯʻ.ynt.ṯʻm.dqt.ṯʻm.|mtntm nkbd.alp.š.l il.|gdlt.ilhm.ṯkmn.w šnm dqt.|ršp.dqt.šrp w šlmm.dqtm.|[i]lh 34[1].3
.gdlt dqt.|dqt.trṯ.dqt.|[rš]p.ʻnt.ḫbly.dbḥn š[p]š pgr.|[g]dlt iltm ḫnqtm.d[q]tm.|[yr]ḫ.kṯy gdlt.w l ǵlmt š.|[w]pa 34[1].18
gdl š.ilt.asrm š.|w l ll.šp. pgr.w ṯrmnm.bt mlk.|il[bt].gdlt.ušḫry.gdlt.ym gdlt.|bʻl gdlt.yrḫ.gdlt.|gdlt.ṯrmn.gdlt.p 34[1].13
ʻl š.dgn š.|[---.--]r.w ṯt pl.gdlt.[s]pn.dqt.|[---.al]p ʻnt.gdlt.b ṯlṯt mrm.|[---.i]l š.bʻl š.aṯrt.š.ym š.[bʻ]l knp.|[---.g]dlt 36[9].1.5
ll.šp. pgr.w ṯrmnm.bt mlk.|il[bt].gdlt.ušḫry.gdlt.ym gdlt.|bʻl gdlt.yrḫ.gdlt.|gdlt.ṯrmn.gdlt.pdry.gdlt dqt.|dqt.tr 34[1].13
l.--]m d gbl.ṣpn.al[p].|pḫr.ilm.š.ym.š[.k]nr.š.[--.]ʻṣrm gdlt.|bʻlm.kmm.bʻlm.kmm[.bʻlm].kmm.bʻlm.kmm.|bʻlm.k UG5.9.1.9
m.bt mlk.|il[bt].gdlt.ušḫry.gdlt.ym gdlt.|bʻl gdlt.yrḫ.gdlt.|gdlt.ṯrmn.gdlt.pdry.gdlt dqt.|dqt.trṯ.dqt.|[rš]p.ʻnt.ḫb 34[1].14
.gdlt.ym gdlt.|bʻl gdlt.yrḫ.gdlt.|gdlt.ṯrmn.gdlt.pdry.gdlt dqt.|dqt.trṯ.dqt.|[rš]p.ʻnt.ḫbly.dbḥn š[p]š pgr.|[g]dlt il 34[1].15
m]n w [šnm.š].|ʻnt š ršp š[.dr.il.w pḫr.bʻl].|gdlt.šlm[.gdlt.w burm.lb].|rmṣt.ilh[m.bʻlm.---].|ksm.ṯlṯm.[---].|d yq 35[3].17
.ṯkmn w šnm.š.|ʻnt.š.ršp.š.dr il w p[ḫ]r bʻl.|gdlt.šlm.gdlt.w burm.[l]b.|rmṣt.ilhm.bʻlm.dṯt.w kšm.ḫmš.|ʻṯr h.mlu 34[1].8
.|ṯkmn.w š[nm.š.ʻnt.š.ršp.š.dr].|il.w pḫr[.bʻl.gdlt.šlm.gdlt].|w burm.l[b.rmṣt.ilhm].|bʻlm.w mlu[.---.ksm].|ṯlṯm. APP.II[173].18
.dbḥn š[p]š pgr.|[g]dlt iltm ḫnqtm.d[q]tm.|[yr]ḫ.kṯy gdlt.w l ǵlmt š.|[w]pamt ṯlṯm.w yrdt.[m]dbḥt.|gdlt.l bʻlt b 34[1].19
.|dqt.l.ṣpn.w.dqt[.---].|ṯn.l.ʻšrm.pamt.[---].|š.dd.šmn.gdlt.w.[---.brr].|rgm.yṯṯb.b.ṯdṯ.ṯn[.--.šmn].|ʻly h.gdlt.rgm.y 35[3].44
qt].|l ṣpn.w [dqt.---.ṯn.l ʻš]|rm.pam[t.---].|š dd šmn[.gdlt.w.---].|brr.r[gm.yṯṯb.b ṯdṯ.ṯn].|l šmn.ʻ[ly h.gdlt.rgm.yṯ APP.II[173].48
m š.|w l ll.šp. pgr.w ṯrmnm.bt mlk.|il[bt].gdlt.ušḫry.gdlt.ym gdlt.|bʻl gdlt.yrḫ.gdlt.|gdlt.ṯrmn.gdlt.pdry.gdlt dq 34[1].13
.w ṯrmnm.bt mlk.|il[bt].gdlt.ušḫry.gdlt.ym gdlt.|bʻl gdlt.yrḫ.gdlt.|gdlt.ṯrmn.gdlt.pdry.gdlt dqt.|dqt.trṯ.dqt.|[rš 34[1].14
pn b ʻrʻr.|pamt ṯlṯm š l qrnt.|ṯlḥn.bʻlt.bhtm.|ʻlm.ʻlm.gdlt l bʻl.|ṣpn.ilbt[.---.]d[--].|l ṣpn[.---.-]lu.|ilib[.---.b]ʻl.|ugr UG5.13.32
kmn.w [šnm.dqt.--].|[--]t.dqtm.[b nbk.---].|[--.k]mm.gdlt.l.b[ʻl.---].|[dq]t.l.ṣpn.gdlt.l[.---].|u[gr]t.š.l.[il]ib.ǵ[--.--rt 35[3].33
.kṯy gdlt.w l ǵlmt š.|[w]pamt ṯlṯm.w yrdt.[m]dbḥt.|gdlt.l bʻlt bhtm.ʻṣrm.|l inš ilm. 34[1].21
.ilt.ʻṣr[m.l ṣpn.š].|l ǵlmt.š.w l [---.l yrḫ].|gd[lt].l nkl[.gdlt.l bʻlt.bhtm].|ʻš[rm.]l inš[.ilm.---].|il[hm.]dqt.š[.---.rš]|[35[3].26
].|mdbḥt.bt.ilt.ʻṣr[m.l ṣpn.š].|l ǵlmt.š.w l [---.l yrḫ].|gd[lt].l nkl[.gdlt.l bʻlt.bhtm].|ʻš[rm.]l inš[.ilm.---].|il[hm.]d 35[3].26
dqtm.[b nbk.---].|[--.k]mm.gdlt.l.b[ʻl.---].|[dq]t.l.ṣpn.gdlt.l[.---].|u[gr]t.š.l.[il]ib.ǵ[--.--rt].|w [ʻṣrm.]l.ri[--.---].|[--] 35[3].34
[.---].|bqtm.b nbk.[---].|kmm.gdlt.l b[ʻl.--.dqt].|l ṣpn.gdlt.[l.---].|ugrt.š l ili[b.---].|rt.w ʻṣrm.l[.---].|pamt.w bt.[--- APP.II[173].37
h[m.dqt.š.--].|[---.--]t.r[šp.šrp.w šl]|[mm.---].dq[t.ilh.gdlt].|n.w šnm.dqt[.---].|[i]lh[m.gd]lt.i[l.dqt.ṯkm]|n.w šnm APP.II[173].32
m.|[---.a]]lp.l bʻl.w aṯrt.ʻṣr[m] l inš.|[ilm.---].lbbmm.gdlt.ʻrb špš w ḥl.|[mlk.b ar]bʻt.ʻ[š]rt.yrtḥṣ.mlk.brr.|[b ym. 36[9].1.9
.gdlt.ušḫry.gdlt.ym gdlt.|bʻl gdlt.yrḫ.gdlt.|gdlt.ṯrmn.gdlt.pdry.gdlt dqt.|dqt.trṯ.dqt.|[rš]p.ʻnt.ḫbly.dbḥn š[p]š pg 34[1].15
[---.gd]ltm.p[--.---].|[---.]arbʻt[.---].|[---.]qdš[.---].|[---.k]su.p[--. 45[45].1
lt.b ṯlṯt mrm.|[---.i]]l š.bʻl š.aṯrt.š.ym š.[bʻ]l knp.|[---.g]dlt.ṣpn.dqt.šrp.w [š]lmm.|[---.a]lp.l bʻl.w aṯrt.ʻṣr[m] l inš. 36[9].1.7
.šm.w alp.l[--]n.|[---.]š.il š.bʻl š.dgn š.|[---.--]r.w ṯt pl.gdlt.[s]pn.dqt.|[---.al]p ʻnt.gdlt.b ṯlṯt mrm.|[---.i]l š.bʻl š.aṯr 36[9].1.4
šmn[.gdlt.w.---].|brr.r[gm.yṯṯb.b ṯdṯ.ṯn].|l šmn.ʻ[ly h.gdlt.rgm.yṯṯb].|brr.b šbʻ[.ṣbu.špš.w ḥl]|yt.ʻrb špš[.w ḥl.mlk APP.II[173].50
w kšm.ḫmš.|ʻṯr h.mlun.šnpt.ḥṣt h.bʻl.ṣpn š.|[--]ṯ š.ilt.mgdl š.ilt.asrm š.|w l ll.šp. pgr.w ṯrmnm.bt mlk.|il[bt].gdlt 34[1].11
]ʻl š.aṯrt.š.ṯkmn w šnm.š.|ʻnt.š.ršp.š.dr il w p[ḫ]r bʻl.|gdlt.šlm.gdlt.w burm.[l]b.|rmṣt.ilhm.bʻlm.dṯt.w kšm.ḫmš.| 34[1].8
.aṯrt[.š.ṯkm]n w [šnm.š].|ʻnt š ršp š[.dr.il.w pḫr.bʻl].|gdlt.šlm[.gdlt.w burm.lb].|rmṣt.ilh[m.bʻlm.---].|ksm.ṯlṯm.[- 35[3].17
[---].ḫšwn.ṯṯ.mat.nṣ.|[---].ḫmšm.ḫmr.škm.|[---.ṯṯ.dd.]gdl.ṯṯ.dd.šʻrm.|[---.a]lp.arbʻ.mat.tyt.|[---.kd.]nbt.k[d.]šmn. 142[12].13
ṯ]t.mat.nṣ.ṯlṯm.ʻṣr.|[---].ḫmš[m.ḫm]r.škm.|[---.ṯṯ.dd.]gdl.ṯṯ.dd.šʻrm.|[---.hn.w.al]p.kd.nbt.kd.šmn.mr.|[---].kmn.l 142[12].7
[---.]ṯṯ.dd.gdl.ṯṯ.dd.šʻrm.|[---.-]hn.w.alp.kd.nbt.kd.šmn.mr.|[---.]arbʻ. 142[12].1
lk.|il[bt].gdlt.ušḫry.gdlt.ym gdlt.|bʻl gdlt.yrḫ.gdlt.|gdlt.ṯrmn.gdlt.pdry.gdlt dqt.|dqt.trṯ.dqt.|[rš]p.ʻnt.ḫbly.db 34[1].15
.w.db[ḥ.---].|[--].aṯrt.ʻṣr[m.l inš.ilm].|[t]ṯb.mdbḥ.bʻl.g[dlt.---].|dqt.l.ṣpn.w.dqt[.---].|ṯn.l.ʻšrm.pamt.[---].|š.dd.š 35[3].41
-.kbd].|w bdḥ.k[--.---].|ʻṣrm.l i[nš.ilm.ṯb.md]|bḥ.bʻl.[gdlt.---.dqt].|l ṣpn.w [dqt.---.ṯn.l ʻš]|rm.pam[t.---].|š dd šm APP.II[173].45
[-----].|[---.gd]lt.[---].|[---.d]dmš[.---].|[---.--]b.š.[---].|[---.yr]ḫ.š.[---].|[43[47].2
tṯtbn.ilm.w.[---].|[---.]w.ksu.bʻlt.b[htm.---].|[---.]il.bt.gdlt.[---].|[---.]hkl[.---]. 47[33].8
b y[--.---].|il[.---].|bʻl[.---].|[---.--]l.[---].|[---.g]dlt[.---].|[---].p[--.---].|[---.]bl[--.---].|[---.--]š.[---]. 46[-].2.2

[--.ʿ]ṯtrum[.---]. | [---.]ḥmr.y[--]. | [---].nʿr[.---]. | [---.]dd gdl[.---]. 2133.12

gdlt

].w y[nt.qrt.---]. | [---.--]n[.w alp.l il.w bu] | [rm.---.ytk.gdlt.ilhm]. | ṯkmn.w [šnm.dqt.ršp.šrp]. | w šlmm.[dqtm.ilh.al APP.II[173].13
.dqt.ṯkm] | n.w šnm.dqt[.---]. | bqtm.b nbk.[---]. | kmm.gdlt.l b[ʿl.--.dqt]. | l ṣpn.gdlt.[l.---]. | ugrt.š l ili[b.---]. | rt.w ʿṣr APP.II[173].36
t.i[lt.ʿṣrm.l]. | ṣpn š.l ǵlm[t.š.w l.---]. | l yrḫ.gdlt.l [nkl.gdlt.l bʿ] | [lt].bht[m].[ʿ]ṣrm l [inš.ilm]. | [---.]ilh[m.dqt.š.--]. | APP.II[173].28
]. | mdbḥt.bt.i[lt.ʿṣrm.l]. | ṣpn š.l ǵlm[t.š.w l.---]. | l yrḫ.gdlt.l [nkl.gdlt.l bʿ] | [lt].bht[m].[ʿ]ṣrm l [inš.ilm]. | [---.]ilh[m APP.II[173].28
šmn.gdlt.w.[---.brr]. | rgm.yṯtb.b.ṯdṯ.ṯn[.--.šmn]. | ʿly h.gdlt.rgm.yṯ[tb.brr]. | b.[šb]ʿ.ṣbu.[š]pš.w.ḥly[t].ʿ[r]b[.š]p[š]. | 35[3].46
.š.aṯrt.š]. | ṯkmn.w š[nm.š.ʿnt.š.ršp.š.dr]. | il.w pḫr[.bʿl.gdlt.šlm.gdlt]. | w burm.l[b.rmṣt.ilhm]. | bʿlm.w mlu[.---.ksm APP.II[173].18

gdn

yn.aḏddy. | agpṯr. | šbʿl.mlky. | nʿmn.mṣry. | yʿl.knʿny. | gdn.bn.umy. | knʿm.šʿrty. | abrpu.ubrʿy. | b.gt.bn.ṯlṯ. | ilḏ.b.gt. 91[311].8
.yyn.ʿšrt. | b.ypʿr.ʿšrm. | b.nʿmn.bn.ply.ḫmšt.l.ʿšrm. | b.gdn.bn.uss.ʿšrm. | b.ʿdn.bn.ṯṯ.ʿšrt. | b.bn.qrdmn.ṯlṯm. | b.bṣmn 2054.1.18
.aḥd.annḏr.kr[m.---]. | aǵt.mryn.ary[.]yukl.krm.[---]. | gdn.krm.aḫ[d.--]r.krm.[---]. | ary.ʿšr.arbʿ.kbd.[---]. | [--]yy.ṯṯ. 1081.17
ldgn.qšt. | bn.yʿrn.ṯt.qštm w.qlʿ. | bn.ḥṣn.qšt.w.qlʿ. | bn.gdn.ṯt.qštm.w.qlʿ. | bn.[-]q.qšt.w.qlʿ. | gb[l]n.qšt.w.qlʿ. | bn.[-] 119[321].3.12
n. | agyn.rʿy. | abmlk.bn.ilrš. | iḫyn.bn.ḫryn. | [ab]ǵl.bn.gdn. | [---].bn.bqš. | [---].bn.pdn. | [---.bn.-]ky. | [---.bn.--]r. | [--- 102[323].4.12

gdr

.gprm.mn gpr h.šr. | aqht.yʿn.kmr.kmr[.--]. | k apʿ.il.b gdrt.k lb.l | ḫṯ h.imḫṣ h.k d.ʿl.qšt h. | imḫṣ h.ʿl.qṣʿt h.hwt. | l 19[1AQHT].1.13

gdrn

.mḏrǵl | bn.ilh.mḏrǵl | špšyn.b.ulm. | bn.qṯn.b.ulm. | bn.gdrn.b.mʿr[by]. | [w].bn.dʿm[-]. | bn.ppṯ.b[--]. | b[n.---]. | šm[-.- 2046.1.7
prn.qšt. | uln.qšt. | bn.nkl qšt. | ady.qšt. | bn.srn.qšt. | bn.gdrn.qšt. | prpr.qšt. | ugry.qšt. | bn.ṣrptn.qšt. | bn.mṣry.qšt. | ar 119[321].1.43

ghl

yn.iš[ryt.-]lnr. | spr.[--]ḥ[-] k.šbʿt. | ghl.ph.ṯmnt. | nblu h.špš.ymp. | hlkt.tdr[--]. | špš.bʿd h.t[--]. | 27[8].3

gwl

ḫlm. | bn.ḏmr. | bn.ʿyn. | ubnyn. | rpš d ydy. | ǵbl. | mlk. | gwl. | rqd. | ḫlby. | ʿn[q]pat. | m[ʿ]rb. | ʿrm. | bn.ḫgby. | mrat. 2075.23
.kdm.kbd.yn.ṭb. | w.ḫmšm.k[dm.]kbd.yn.d.l.ṭb. | b.gt.gwl. | ṯlṯm.tšʿ[.kbd.yn].d.l[.ṭb].b.gt.iptl. | ṯmnym.[yn].ṭb.b.gt. 1084.18
ṣd.mqb. | b.gt.ʿmq.ḫmš.ḫrmṯt.n[it]. | krk.mʿṣd.mqb. | b.gwl.ṯmn.ḫrmṯt.[nit]. | krk.mʿṣd.mqb. | [b] gt.iptl.ṯṯ.ḫrmṯ[t.nit 2048.11
n.ʿšr.ṣmdm. | w.ṯlṯ.ʿšr.bnš. | yd.ytm.yd.rʿy.ḥmrm. | b.gt.gwl.ṯmn.ṣmdm. | w.arbʿ.ʿšr.bnš. | yd.nǵr.mdrʿ.yd.š[--]m. | [b.] 2038.4
q. | [---.]bn.tqy. | [---.]bn.šlmy. | [-----]. | [---].ubrʿy. | [---].gwl. | [---]ady. | [---]ṣry. | miḫ[-]m. | ṣdqm. | dnn. | ʿdy. 1041.9

gzz

h d.ytn.ṣtqn. | tut ṭbḫ ṣtq[n]. | b bz ʿzm ṭbḫ š[h]. | b kl ygz ḥḫ š h. 1153.5
tšʿ.ʿšr h.dd.l.b[t.--]. | ḫmš.ddm.l.ḫtyt. | ṯlṯm.dd.kšmn.l.gzzm. | yyn. | ṣdqn. | ʿbd.pdr. | myṣm. | tgt. | w.lmd h. | ytil. | w.l 1099.4
.l.ḫtn. | dd.šʿrm.l.ḥmr.ḥṭb. | dd.ḥṭm.l.ḫḏǵb. | ṯṯ.ddm.l.gzzm. | kd yn.l.ḫtn.w.kd.ḥmṣ.w.[lt]ḥ.ʿšdm. | kd yn.l.ḫḏǵb.w. 1099.26
rbʿm.kbd.yn.mṣb. | l.mḏrǵlm. | ʿšrn ʿšr.yn.mṣb.[-]ḥ[-].l.gzzm. 1084.30

gzl

rhd.bn.srt. | [---.--]m. | ʿbdmlk.bn.šrn. | ʿbdbʿl.bn.kdn. | gzl.bn.qldn. | gld.bt.klb. | l[---].bt.ḫzli. | bn.iḫyn. | ṣdqn.bn.ass. 102[323].3.4
pl. | šd.krwn.l aḫn. | šd.ʿyy.l aḫn. | šd.brdn.l bn.bly. | šd gzl.l.bn.ṭbr[n]. | šd.ḫzmyn.l a[--]. | ṯn šdm b uš[kn]. 2089.14
.q[l]ʿm. | kmrṯn.ṯt.qštm.ṯn.[q]lʿm. | ǵdyn.qšt.w.qlʿ. | bn.gzl.qšt.w.qlʿ. | [---]n.qšt. | ilhd.qšt. | ʿdn.qšt.w.qlʿ. | ilmhr.qšt.w 119[321].1.5

gzr

a[p.]ḏ[d.r]gm.l il.ybl. | aṯt y.il.ylt.mh.ylt.ilmy nʿmm. | agzr ym.bn ym.ynqm.b ap.ḏd.št.špt. | l arṣ.špt l šmm.w ʿrb. 23[52].61
mš.l ṣ[---.]šr.pḫr.klat. | tqtnṣn.w tldn.tld.[ilm.]nʿmm.agzr ym. | bn.ym.ynqm.b a[p.]ḏ[d.r]gm.l il.ybl. | aṯt y.il.ylt. 23[52].58
ṣ.špt l šmm.w ʿrb.b p hm.ʿṣr.šmm. | w dg b ym.w ndd.gzr.l zr.yʿdb.u ymn. | u šmal.b p hm.w l.tšbʿn y.aṯt.itrḫ. | y b 23[52].63
l šmm.w ʿrb.b p hm.ʿṣr.šmm. | w dg b ym.w ndd.gzr.l zr.yʿdb.u ymn. | u šmal.b p hm.w l.tšbʿn y.aṯt.itrḫ. | y bn.ašl 23[52].63

gzry

n.kzn. | w.nḥl h. | w.nḥl hm. | w.[n]ḥl hm. | b[n.---]. | bn.gzry. | bn.atyn. | bn.ttn. | bn.rwy. | bn.ʿmyn. | bdl.mrynm. | bn.ṣ 113[400].3.1

gyl

[k.ym]ḫṣ.bʿl m[.--]y.tnn.w ygl.w ynsk.ʿ[-]. | [--]y.l arṣ[.id]y.alt.l aḫš.idy.alt.in l y. | [--]t.b 1001.1.1
y.w tšnn.[tt]n. | g h.bky.b ḫ[y k.a]b n. | nšmḫ.b l.mt k.ngln. | k klb.[b]bt k.nʿtq. | k inr[.ap.]ḫšt k. | ap.ab.k mtm.tmt 16.2[125].99
ky. | w yšnn.ytn.g h. | bky.b ḫy k.ab n.ašmḫ. | b l.mt k.ngln.k klb. | b bt k.nʿtq.k inr. | ap.ḫšt k.ap.ab.k mtm. | tmtn.u 16.1[125].15
.b[n].km.yr.klyt h.w lb h. | [t]n.p k.b ǵr.ṯn.p k.b ḫlb.k tgwln.šnt k. | [--.]w špt k.l tššy.hm.tqrm.l mt.b rn k. | [--]ḫp. 1001.1.4

gyn

---]. | bn.byy. | bn.ily[-]. | bn.iy[--]. | bn.ty[--]. | bn.p[---]. | gyn[.---]. | bn.pt[--]. | bn.db[--]. 2025.7
yn.[---]. | [ṣṣ].bn.ilbʿl.ṯl[ṯ]m. | ṣṣ.bn.ptḏn.[--]m. | ṣṣ.[bn].gyn.[---]. | [-----]. | [-----]. | [-----]. | [-----]. | [-----]. | [ṣṣ].b[n].ṣd[-. 2096.8

gl

šd.bn.šty.l.bn.ṭbrn. | šd.bn.ḫtb.l bn.yʿḏrd. | šd.gl.bʿlz.l.bn.ʿmnr. | šd.knʿm.l.bn.ʿmnr. | šd.bn.krwn.l bn.ʿmyn 2089.3
a.klatnm. | klt.lḥm h.d nzl. | lqḥ.msrr.ʿṣr.db[ḥ]. | yṣq.b gl.ḥṯt.yn. | b gl.ḫrṣ.nbt.w ʿly. | l ẓr.mgdl.rkb. | ṯkmm.ḥmt.nša. 14[KRT].4.164
kl[atn]m. | klt.l[ḥm k.d]nzl. | qḥ.ms[rr.]ʿṣr. | dbḥ.ṣ[q.b g]l.ḥṯt. | yn.b gl[.ḫ]rṣ.nbt. | ʿl.l ẓr.[mg]dl. | w ʿl.l ẓr.[mg]dl.rkb 14[KRT].2.71

lt.lḥm h.d nzl. | lqḥ.msrr.ʿṣr.db[ḥ]. | yṣq.b gl.ḥtṯ.yn. | b gl.ẖrṣ.nbt.w ʿly. | l ẓr.mgdl.rkb. | ṯkmm.ḥmt.nša. | [y]d h.šm 14[KRT].4.165

.l[ḥm k.d]nzl. | qḥ.ms[rr.]ʿṣr. | dbḥ.ṣ[q.b g]l.ḥtṯ. | yn.b gl[.ẖ]rṣ.nbt. | ʿl.l ẓr.[mg]dl. | w ʿl.l ẓr.[mg]dl.rkb. | ṯkmm.ḥm[14[KRT].2.72

---.]in[b]b.pʿr. | yd h[.--.]ṣʿr.glgl. | a[---]m.rḥ.ḥḏ ʿ[r]pt. | gl[.---.]yhpk.m[---]m. | sʿ[--.]k[--]t. 13[6].35

glb

i[--.---]. | d.[---]. | bnš[-] mdy[-]. | w.b.glb. | phnn.w. | mndym. | bdnh. | l[q]ḥt. | [--]km.ʿm.mlk. | [b]ǵl 2129.4

---.]kd[r]. | [---.]ṯpr. | [---.]prš. | [---.]šdm. | [---.-]nm.prš.glbm. | [---.]ʿgd.dqr. | [---.]ṯn.alpm. | [---.ṯ]n alpm. | [---.--]r[.ʿ]š 1142.8

glbm

w.kd.ḥmṣ.w.[lt]ḥ.ʿšdm. | kd yn.l.ẖḏǵb.w.kd.ḥmṣ. | prš.glbm.l.bt. | tgmǵ.kšmm.b.yrẖ.iṯtbnm. | šbʿm.dd.ṯn.kbd. | tgm 1099.29

glbt

m. | nnu. | ʿrm. | bṣr. | mʿr. | ẖlby. | mṣbt. | snr. | ṯm. | ubš. | glbt. | mi[d]ẖ. | mr[i]l. | ẖlb. | šld. | ʿrgz. | [-----]. 2041.11

---]. | šl[-.---]. | ar[--.---]. | qrt[.---]. | ṯm[r.---]. | dm[t.---]. | gl[bt.---]. | al[-.---]. 1181.15

glbty

[---.ʿ]šrt. | ẖlb.ẖmšt.l.ʿšrm. | mril.ʿšrt. | glbty.arbʿt. | [--]ṯb.ʿšrt. 1180.4

[--]. | y[--]. | snr. | midẖ. | ḥ[lym]. | [ẖ]lby. | ʿr. | ʿnq[pat]. | glbty. | [-----]. | [-----]. | [-----]. | [-----]. | yknʿm. | šlmy. | [-----]. | [- 2058.2.25

glgl

h.l ydʿ hr h.[---]d[-]. | tnq[.---.]in[b]b.pʿr. | yd h[.--.]ṣʿr.glgl. | a[---]m.rḥ.ḥḏ ʿ[r]pt. | gl[.---.]yhpk.m[---]m. | sʿ[--.]k[--]t. 13[6].33

r.w.aṯt h. | ʿbdyrẖ.ṯn ǵlyt h. | aršmg. | ršpy.w.aṯt h. | bn.glgl.uškny. | bn.ṯny.uškny. | mnn.w.aṯt h. | slmu.ḥrš.mrkbt. | 2068.13

gld

[bn]šm.dt.iš[--]. | [b]n.bʿl[--]. | bn.gld. | bn.ṣmy. | bn.mry[n]. | bn.mgn. | bn.ʿdn. | bn.knn. | bn.py. 2117.1.3

---.--]m. | ʿbdmlk.bn.šrn. | ʿbdbʿl.bn.kdn. | gzl.bn.qldn. | gld.bt.klb. | l[---].bt.ẖzli. | bn.iẖyn. | ṣdqn.bn.ass. | bʿlyskn.bn.s 102[323].3.5

gldy

. | [š]d.bn.š[p]šn l gt pr[n]. | šd bn.ilšḥr. | l.gt.mzln. | šd.gldy. | l.gt.mzln. | šd.glln.l.gt.mz[l]n. | šd.hyabn[.l.]gt.mzln. | š 1104.17

gly

[id]k.l ttn.pnm.ʿm. | [il.]mbk nhrm.qrb. | [a]pq.thmtm.tgly.ḏd. | il.w tbu.qrš.. | mlk.ab.šnm.l pʿn. | il.thbr.w tql. | tštḥ 6.1.34[49.1.6]

k.l ttn.pnm]. | [ʿm.il.mbk.nhrm]. | [qrb.apq.thmtm]. | [tgly.ḏd.il.w]tb[a]. | [qrš.mlk.ab.]šnm. | [tša.g hm.w tṣ]ḥ.sbn. 5[67].6.1

ṣ.idk. | [l ttn.pn]m.ʿm il.mbk.nhrm. | [qrb.ap]q.thmtm tgly.ḏd il. | [w tbu.qr]š.mlk.ab.šnm. | [l pʿn.il.t]hbr.w tql.tštḥ 17[2AQHT].6.48

n. | idk.l ttn.pnm. | ʿm.il.mbk.nhrm. | qrb.apq.thmtm. | tgly.ḏd.il.w tbu. | qrš.mlk.ab.šnm. | l pʿn.il.thbr.w tql. | tštḥw 4[51].4.23

[idk.]l ytn.pnm.ʿm.[i]l.mbk.[nhrm.qrb.apq.thmtm]. | [ygly.]ḏl i[l].w ybu[.q]rš.mlk[.ab.šnm.l pʿn.il.] | [yhbr.]w yql[2.3[129].5

k.l ttn.p]nm. | [ʿm.i]l.mbk.nhr[m.qr]b.[ap]q. | [thm]tm.tgl.ḏ[d.]i[l.]w tbu. | [qr]š.m[l]k.ab[.šnm.]mṣr. | [t]bu.ḏdm.qn[3[ʿNT.VI].5.15

k.l yt[n.pnm.ʿm.lṭpn]. | il d pid.tk ẖrš[n.---.tk.ǵr.ks]. | ygly ḏd.i[l.w ybu.qrš.mlk]. | ab.šnm.l [pʿn.il.yhbr.w yql]. | yš 1[ʿNT.IX].3.23

]t.dm.ẖt.šʿtqt dm. | li.w ttbʿ.šʿtqt. | bt.krt.bu.tbu. | bkt.tgly.w tbu. | nṣrt.tbu.pnm. | ʿrm.tdu.mh. | pdrm.tdu.šrr. | ẖṭ 16.6[127].4

glyn

g. | gṯpbn. | bn.b[--]. | [b]n.[---]. | bn.a[--]. | bn.ml[k]. | bn.glyn. | bn.ʿdr. | bn.ṯmq. | bn.ntp. | bn.ʿgrt. 1057.18

gll

---]. | m[--.---]. | [-----]. | k[--.---]. | [-----]. | ẖmrn.ʿš[r.---]. | gll.tky.ṯlṯ[.---]. 2042.23

glln

pr[n]. | šd bn.ilšḥr. | l.gt.mzln. | šd.gldy. | l.gt.mzln. | šd.glln.l.gt.mz[l]n. | šd.hyabn[.l.]gt.mzln. | šd.ʿbdbʿl. | l.gt.mzln. 1104.19

glltky

bqʿt.b.gt.tgyn. | [--]in.b.trzy. | [--]yn.b.glltky. | ṯd[y]n.b.glltky. | lbw[-].uẖ.pdm.b.yʿrt. | pǵyn.b.tpḥ. | amri[l].b.šrš. | aǵl 2118.9

.b.anan. | [--]yl.b.bqʿt.b.gt.tgyn. | [--]in.b.trzy. | [--]yn.b.glltky. | ṯd[y]n.b.glltky. | lbw[-].uẖ.pdm.b.yʿrt. | pǵyn.b.tpḥ. | 2118.8

gln

ḏdy. | mšu.aḏddy. | plsy.aḏddy. | aẖyn. | ygmr.aḏddy. | gln.aṯṯ. | ddy.[a]ḏddy. | bn.mlkr[šp]. | bn.y[k]n. | ynḥm. | bn.ab 2014.43

mdrǵlm.dt.inn. | b d.tlmyn. | b d.gln.ary. | tgyn.yʿrty. | bn.krwn.b.yny.iytlm. | šgryn.ary.b.yny. 2071.3

dkn. | bn ils. | bn ḥšbn. | bn uryy. | bn kṯl. | bn army. | bn gln. | bn abg. | bn.nǵry. | bn.srwd. | mtnn. | bn gš[-]. | bn gbrn. | 1064.11

.qšt. | ytḥm.qšt. | grp.qšt. | mʿrby. | nʿmn.ṯṯ.qštm.w.qlʿ. | gln.ṯṯ.qštm.w.qlʿ. | gtn.qšt. | pmn.ṯṯ.qšt.w.qlʿ. | bn.zry.q[š]t.w. 104[316].9

glʿd

ẓn. | bn.bddn. | bn.anny. | ytršp. | bn.szn. | bn.kdgdl. | bn.glʿd. | bn.ktln. | [bn].ǵrgn. | bn.pb[-]. | bn.[---]. | bn.[---]. | bn.[--- 115[301].1.14

ḥrš.anyt. | bnš.gt.glʿd. | bnš.gt.ngr. | rʿym. | bn.ẖri[-]. | bnš.gt.ʿṯtrt. | ad[-]l[-]m. | ʿ 1040.2

myy. | bn.lbn. | bn.šlmn. | bn.mly. | pslm. | bn.annd. | bn.glʿd. | w.nḥl h. | bn.mlkyy. | [bn].bm[--]. | [ʿš]rm. | [-----]. | [-----] 2163.3.11

glṯ

r[.mnt]. | ṣḥrrm.ḥbl[.--]. | ʿrpt.tḥt.[---] | m ʿṣrm.ḥ[---]. | glṯ.isr[.---] | m.brt[.---]. | ymt m.[---]. | ši[.---]. | m[---.---]. 8[51FRAG].13

ly.ṭly.bn.ʿn h. | uzʿrt.tmll.išd h.qrn[m]. | dt.ʿl h.riš h.b glṯ.b šm[m]. | [---.i]l.ṯr.iṯ.p h.k ṯt.ǵlṯ[.--]. | [---.--] k yn.ddm.l UG5.3.1.7

rẖntt.d[-].l irt k. | wn ap.ʿdn.mṭr h. | bʿl.yʿdn.ʿdn.ṯkt.b glṯ. | w tn.ql h.b ʿrpt. | šrh.l arṣ.brqm. | bt.arzm.yklln h. | hm. 4[51].5.69

| ʿṯtrt ṣwd[t.---]. | tlk b mdb[r.---]. | tḥdṯn w hl[.---]. | w tglṯ thmt.ʿ[--.---]. | yṣi.ǵl h tḥm b[.---]. | mrḥ h l adrt[.---]. | ṯṯb 2001.1.5

gm

p[----].|gm.l[aṯt h k.yṣḥ].|šm'[.l mṯt.ḥry].|ṭbḫ.š[mn].mri k.|ptḥ.[r 15[128].4.2

[h.l g't.]alp.|ḥrṯ[.l z]ǵt.klb.|[ṣ]pr[.apn]k.|[pb]l[.mlk.g]m.l aṯt |[h.k]y[ṣḥ.]šm'.m'.|[--.]'m[.-.]aṯt y[.-].|[---.]ṯḥm.| 14[KRT].5.228

hl.yš|rb'.qṣ't.apnk.dnil.|mt.rpi.aphn.ǵzr.mt.|hrnmy.gm.l aṯt h.k yṣḥ.|šm'.mṯt.dnty.'d[b].|imr.b pḏd.l npš.kṯr.| 17[2AQHT].5.15

.ql.b'l.k tmz'.|kst.dnil.mt.rpi.|all.ǵzr.m[t.]hr[nmy].|gm.l bt[h.dnil.k yṣḥ].|šm'.pǵt.ṯkmt[.my].|ḥspt.l š'r.ṭl.yd['t 19[1AQHT].1.49

.d ym|lk.'l.ilm.l ymru.|ilm.w nšm.d yšb|['].hmlt.arṣ.gm.l ǵ|[lm] h.b'l k.yṣḥ.'n.|[gpn].w ugr.b ǵlmt.|['mm.]ym.b 4[51].7.52

ẓ.qnyt.ilm.|w tn.bt.l b'l.km.|[i]lm.w ḥẓr.k bn.|[a]ṯrt.gm.l ǵlm h.|b'l.yṣḥ.'n.gpn.|w ugr.bn.ǵlmt.|'mm ym.bn.ẓl 8[51FRAG].5

sp.[a]ṯrt.|k t'n.ẓl.ksp.w n[-]t.|ḫrṣ.šmḫ.rbt.a[ṯrt].|ym.gm.l ǵlm h.k [tṣḥ].|'n.mkṯr.ap.t[---].|dgy.rbt.aṯr[t.ym].|qḫ. 4[51].2.29

[---.--]n.|[---] h.l 'db.|[---]n.yd h.|[---].bl.išlḥ.|[---] h.gm.|[l --- k.]yṣḥ.|[---]d.'r.|[----.-]bb.|[----.]lm y.|[---.--]p.|[14[KRT].5.237

ḫn.|w tnḫ.b irt y.npš.|k ḥy.aliyn.b'l.|k iṯ.zbl.b'l.arṣ.|gm.yṣḥ.il.l btlt.|'nt.šm'.l btlt.'n[t].|rgm.l nrt.il.šp[š].|pl.'nt. 6[49].3.22

n h.ilt.w ṣb|rt.ary h.k mt.aliyn.|b'l.k ḫlq.zbl.b'l.|arṣ.gm.yṣḥ il.|l rbt.aṯrt ym.šm'.|l rbt.aṯr[t] ym.tn.|aḥd.b bn k. 6.1.43[49.1.15]

b arṣ.'m h.trd.nrt.|ilm.špš.'d.tšb'.bk.|tšt.k yn.udm't.gm.|tṣḥ.l nrt.ilm.špš.|'ms m'.l y.aliyn.b'l.|tšm'.nrt.ilm.špš. 6[62].1.10

[--]m.[---.]|gm.ṣḥ.l q[ṣ.ilm.---].|l rḥqm.l p[-.---].|ṣḥ.il.yṯb.b[mrzḥ.---].| 1['NT.X].4.2

.l ṯkm.bnw n.|l nḫnpt.mšpy.|ṯlṯ.kmm.ṯrr y.|[---.]l ǵr.gm.ṣḥ.|[---.]r[-]m. 16[126].4.17

b im[--.---].|bl.l[---.---].|mlk.[---].|dt [---].|b ṯ[--.---].|gm[.---].|y[--.---]. 4[51].2.47

gmḏ

kbd k iš.tikln.|ṯd n.km.mrm.tqrṣn.|il.yẓḥq.bm.|lb.w ygmḏ.bm kbd.|ẓi.at.l tlš.|amt.yrḫ.|l dmgy.amt.|aṯrt.qḥ.|k 12[75].1.13

gmz

.|[-]n bn.iln.|[--]nn bn.ibm.|[-]n bn.ḥrn.|[š]mmn bn.gmz.|[yn]ḥm bn.ilmd. 2087.14

gmḥ

bn.ǵlmn.ary.|[bn].šdy.|[bn].gmḥ.|[---]ty.|[b]n.ypy.gb'ly.|b[n].ḥyn.|ḏmn.š'rty.|bn.arw 99[327].1.3

gmḥn

.|bn.yyn.w.bn.au[pš].|bn.kdrn.|'rgzy.w.bn.'dy.|bn.gmḥn.w.ḥgbt.|bn.tgḏn.|yny.|[b]n.g'yn dd.|[-]n.dd.|[--]an 131[309].28

.|bn.ubrš.|bn.d[--]b.|abrpu.|bn.k[n]y.|bn.klyn.|bn.gmḥn.|ḥnn.|ayab.|bn.gm[--].|bn.[---].|g[---].|p[---].|b[---]. 1035.3.8

gml

w y|rḫ yar k.|[ašr ilht kṯrt bn]|t hll.snnt.bnt h|ll b'l gml.yrdt.|b 'rgzm.b bz tdm.|lla y.'m lẓpn i|l ḏ.pid.hn b p 24[77].42

gmm

n.ǵlm.dd.|bn.tbšn.dd.|bn.ḫran.w[.---].|[-]n.y'rtym.|gmm.w.bn.p[--].|trn.w.p[-]y.|bn.b'yn.w.agytn.|[---] gnym. 131[309].10

gmn

.|w tqbrn h.tštnn.b ḫrt.|ilm.arṣ.ṭṭbḫ.šb'm.|rumm.k gmn.aliyn.|[b]'l.ṭṭbḫ.šb'm.alpm.|[k g]mn.aliyn.b'l.|[ṭṭ]bḫ.š 6[62].1.19

bḫ.šb'm.alpm.|[k g]mn.aliyn.b'l.|[ṭṭ]bḫ.šb'm.ṣin.|[k gm]n.aliyn.b'l.|[ṭṭb]ḫ.šb'm.aylm.|[k gmn.]aliyn.b'l.|[ṭṭbḫ.š 6[62].1.23

ḫ.šb'm.aylm.|[k gmn.]aliyn.b'l.|[ṭṭbḫ.š]b'm.y'lm.|[k gmn.al]iyn.b'l.|[ṭṭbḫ.šb'm.]ḥmrm.|[k gm]n.al[i]yn.b['l].|[-- 6[62].1.27

bḫ.šb'm.ṣin.|[k gm]n.aliyn.b'l.|[ṭṭb]ḫ.šb'm.aylm.|[k gmn.]aliyn.b'l.|[ṭṭbḫ.š]b'm.y'lm.|[k gmn.al]iyn.b'l.|[ṭṭbḫ.š 6[62].1.25

ḫ.šb'm.|rumm.k gmn.aliyn.|[b]'l.ṭṭbḫ.šb'm.alpm.|[k g]mn.aliyn.b'l.|[ṭṭ]bḫ.šb'm.ṣin.|[k gm]n.aliyn.b'l.|[ṭṭb]ḫ.šb 6[62].1.21

š]b'm.y'lm.|[k gmn.al]iyn.b'l.|[ṭṭbḫ.šb'm.]ḥmrm.|[k gm]n.al[i]yn.b['l].|[---]ḥ h.tšt bm.'[--].|[---.]zr h.ybm.l ilm. 6.1.29[49.1.1]

lbtyn.|w.kkr.ṯlṯ.|ksp.d.nkly.b.šd.|mit.ḫmšt.kbd.|[l.]gmn.bn.usyy.|mit.ṯṯm.kbd.|l.bn.yšm'.|mit.arb'm.kbd.|l.liy 1143.8

-.a]ḫt.b d[.---].|[---.]b d.rb.[m]dlm.|[---.l i]ytlm.|[---].gmn.|[---].l.urǵṯb.|[---.]l.'ṯtrum.|[---.]l.brqn.|[---].skn.|[--- 2162.B.4

gmr

[sp]r.akl[.---].ṯryn.|[tg]mr.akl.b.g[t.b]ir.alp.|[']šrm.l.mit.ḫ[p]r.'bdm.|mitm.drt.ṯ 2013.2

.alp.|[']šrm.l.mit.ḫ[p]r.'bdm.|mitm.drt.ṯmnym.drt.|tgmr.akl.b.gt[.b]'ln.|ṯlṯ.mat.ṯṯm.kbd.|ṯṯm.ṯṯ.kbd.ḥpr.'bdm. 2013.5

ṯṯm.ṯṯ.kbd.ḥpr.'bdm.|šb'm.drt.arb'm.drt.|l.a[--.---].|tgm[r.ak]l.b.gt.ḥldy.|ṯlṯ.ma[t].'šr.kbd.|šb' m[at].kbd.ḥpr.'b 2013.10

šb' m[at].kbd.ḥpr.'bdm.|mit[.d]rt.arb'm.drt.|[---]m.|t[gm]r.akl.b.gt.ǵ[l].|ṯlṯ.mat.'šrm[.---].|ṯmnym.drt.a[--].|drt 2013.15

t.b.ṯql.|kkr.w.[ml]ṯḥ.tyt.[---].|[b]šb'[m.w.n]ṣp.ksp.|[tgm]r.[alp.w.]ṯlṯ.mat. 2101.28

lpm.ḫmš.mat.|šb'm[.t]š'.kbd.|tgmr.uz.ǵrn.arb'.mat.|tgmr.uz.aḫmn.arb'.mat.|arb'm.kbd.|ṯlṯ.alp.ṣpr.dt.aḥd.|ḥrṯ 1129.6

.iṯ.|[---].ṯlṯ.kbd.|[---].alpm.ḫmš.mat.|šb'm[.t]š'.kbd.|tgmr.uz.ǵrn.arb'.mat.|tgmr.uz.aḫmn.arb'.mat.|arb'm.kbd. 1129.5

.|'šrm.aḥd.kbd.ḫsnm.|ubnyn.|ṯṯm[.l.]mit.ṯlṯ.|kbd[.tg]mr.bnš.|l.b.bt.mlk. 1028.13

bn.|gbrn.|ṯb'm.|kyn.|b'ln.|ytršp.|ḫmšm.ṯmn.kbd.|tgmr.bnš.mlk.|d.b d.adn'm.|[š]b'.b.ḥrṯm.|[t]lṯ.b.ṯǵrm.|rb 1024.2.26

[---].an.rgmt.l ym.b'l km.ad[n km.ṯpṭ].|[nhr.---.]hwt.gmr.hd.l wny[-.---].|[---.]iyr h.g[-.]thbr[.---]. 2.1[137].46

bm.l.bt.|tgmǵ.kšmm.b.yrḫ.iṯtbnm.|šb'm.dd.ṯn.kbd.|tgmr.ḥṭm.šb'.ddm.|ḫmš.dd.š'rm.|kdm.yn.|kdm.ṣmṣ. 1099.32

m.|ṯlṯ.'šr.|hbṭnm.|ṯmn.|mḏrǵlm.|ṯmnym.ṯmn.kbd.|tgmr.ḫrd.|arb'm.l.mit.|ṯn.kbd. 1031.15

-]t.|w.bn.mṣrym.|arb'm.yn.|l.ḫrd.|ḫmšm.ḫmš.|kbd.tgmr.|yn.d.nkly. 1089.14

'[.---].|šrš.šb'.mṣb.|rqd.ṯlṯ.mṣb.w.[---].|uḫnp.ṯṯ.mṣb.|tgmr.[y]n.mṣb š[b'].|w ḥs[p] ṯn.k[dm]. 2004.35

[---.-]lgn.|[---.--]gbn.|[---.a]bṣdq.|[---.--]š.|[---.ṣ]dq.|tgmr.|yṣḥm.|ṯlṯm.|aḥd.|kbd.|bnš.mlk. 1055.2.1

w.[lt]ḥ.'šdm.|kd yn.l.ḥdǵb.w.kd.ḥmṣ.|prš.glbm.l.bt.|tgmǵ.kšmm.b.yrḫ.iṯtbnm.|šb'm.dd.ṯn.kbd.|tgmr.ḥṭm.šb'.d 1099.30

'm.|mit.ḫršḫ.b.ṯqlm.|w.šb'.'šr.šmn.|d.l.ysa.bt.mlk.|tgmr.ksp.mitm.|ḫmšm.kbd. 2100.22

.|[ḫ]pn.aḥd.b.ṯqlm.|lbš.aḥd.b.ṯqlm.|ḫpn.pṯtm.b 'šr.|tgmr.ksp.ṯlṯm.|ṯqlm.kbd. 1115.5

|ṯlṯ.dd.p[--].|šb't.p[--].|tš't.k[bd.---].|ḫmšt.k[bd.---].|tgmr k[--.---].|ḫmšm a[--.---].|kbd [---].|d[.a]ǵlkz[.---]. 2120.9

yṣḥ.|aḫ y m.ytnt.b'l.|spu y.bn m.um y.kl|y y.yt'n.k gmrm.|mt.'z.b'l.'z.ynghn.|k rumm.mt.'z.b'l.|'z.ynṯkn.k bṯ 6[49].6.16

. | šir.šd.krm. | d.yrmn. | šir.[š]d.mlṯḥ.šd.ʻšy. | d.ynḥm. | tgmr.šd.ṯlṯm.šd. | w.tr[--.---]. 1079.16
| ṯlṯ.ʻl.bn.srt. | kd.ʻl.ẓrm. | kd.ʻl.šz.bn pls. | kd.ʻl.ynḥm. | tgrm.šmn.d.bn.kwy. | ʻl.šlmym.ṯmn.kbd. | ṯṯm.šmn. 1082.2.8
--.---]. | [m]itm.dr[t.---]. | [ʻš]r.[k]bd[.---]. | [a]lpm[.---]. | tg[m]r.[---]. | ṯlṯ ma[t.---]. | ṯmnym[.---]. | [ṯ]mny[m.---]. | [-]r[- 2013.25
.drt.a[--]. | drt.l.alpm[.---]. | šbʻm.ṯn.kbd[.ḥpr.ʻb]dm. | tg[mr.---]. | [-]m.m[--.---]. | [m]itm.dr[t.---]. | [ʻš]r.[k]bd[.---]. | 2013.20
spr.[---]. | ṯpṭb[ʻl.---]. | mb[--.---]. | gmr[.---]. | [---]. 92[302].4
l. | [---.--]bn. | ap[n.---]. | ap[n.---]. | ap[n.---]. | ap[n.---]. | tgmr[.---]ṯm. | ṯt.ʻ[--.---]. 152[-].7
ǵlm. | arbʻ.l ʻšrm.ḫsnm. | ʻšr.hbṭnm. | ṯṯm.l.mit.ṯn.kbd. | tgmr. 1030.11

gmrd

m. | mrʻm.ʻšrm. | ʻmlbu.ʻšrm. | ʻmtdl.ʻšrm. | yʻḏrd.ʻšrm. | gmrd.ʻšrm. | ṣdqšlm.ʻšr[m]. | yknil.ḫmš. | ilmlk.ḫmš. | prṯ.ʻšr. | 1116.10
ub]dy.trrm. | [šd.]bn.ṯqdy.b d.gmrd. | [š]d bn.synn.b d.gmrd. | [šd.]abyy.b d.ibrmḏ. | [šd.]bn.ṯṯrn.b d.bnš.aǵlkz. | [šd. 82[300].2.18
. | [š]d.ilṣy.b d.ʻbdym. | [ub]dy.trrm. | [šd.]bn.ṯqdy.b d.gmrd. | [š]d bn.synn.b d.gmrd. | [šd.]abyy.b d.ibrmḏ. | [šd.]bn 82[300].2.17
d.bn.gʻr. | [šd.b]n.ṯqrn.b d.ḫby. | [ṯn.š]d.bn.ngzḥn.b d.gmrd. | [šd.bn].pll.b d.gmrd. | [šd.bn.-]ll.b d.iwrḫṭ. | [šd.bn.-] 82[300].1.23
.b d.ḫby. | [ṯn.š]d.bn.ngzḥn.b d.gmrd. | [šd.bn].pll.b d.gmrd. | [šd.bn.-]ll.b d.iwrḫṭ. | [šd.bn.-]nn.b d.bn.šmrm. | [šd.b 82[300].1.24
. | [w.]šd.nḥl h.b d.ṯṯmd. | [š]d.b d.iwrḫṭ. | [ṯn].šdm.b d.gmrd. | [šd.]lbny.b d.tbṯṯb. | [š]d.bn.ṯ[-]rn.b d.ʻdbmlk. | [šd.]b 82[300].1.14
ṭbʻl. | šd.bn mšrn.l.ilšpš. | [šd.bn].kbr.l.snrn. | [---.--]k.l.gmrd. | [---.--]ṯ.l.yšn. | [šd.--]ln. | b d.trǵds. | šd.ṯʻlb. | b d.bn.pl. 2030.1.7

gmrn

. | [bn.a]mdy. | bn.ḫlln. | bn.kṯn. | bn.abn. | bn.nskn. | bn.gmrn. | bn[.-]škn. | [---.--]n. | [---.--]n. | [--.]ʻ[--]. | [bn].k[--]. | bn. 2021.2.7

gmrš

--]l. | aty[n.bn.]šmʻnt. | ḥnn[.bn].pls. | abrš[p.bn.]ḫrpn. | gmrš[.bn].mrnn. | ʻbdmlk.bn.ʻmyn. | agyn.rʻy. | abmlk.bn.ilrš. 102[323].4.7
bn.ʻr[--]. | bn.nkt[-]. | bn.abḏr. | bn.ḥrẓn. | bn.ḏqnt. | bn.gmrš. | bn.nmq. | bn.špš[yn]. | bn.ar[--]. | bn.gb[--]. | bn.ḥn[n]. | 2023.3.12
[kd.]ʻ[l.---]. | [k]d.ʻl[.---]. | [k]d.ʻl.[---]. | kd.ʻl.[---]. | ṯlṯ.ʻl.gmrš[.---]. | kd.ʻl.ʻbd[--]. | kd.ʻl.aǵlt[n]. | ṯlṯ.ʻl.a[b]m[n]. | arbʻ.ʻl 1082.1.18

gmrt

.ysd. | bn.pl[-]. | bn.ṯbʻnq. | brqd. | bnn. | kbln.ṣ[md]. | bn gmrt. | bn.il.ṣm[d]. | bn abbly. | yṯʻd.ṣm[d]. | bn.liy. | ʻšrm.ṣ[md 2113.18
ybnn qrwn. | ypltn.ʻbdnt. | klby.aḥrṯp. | ilyn.ʻlby.ṣdkn. | gmrt.ṭlmyn. | ʻbdnt. | bdy.ḥrš arkd. | blšš lmd. | ḥṯṯn.tqn. | ydd. 1045.7
---]n.qšt. | ilhd.qšt. | ʻdn.qšt.w.qlʻ. | ilmhr.qšt.w.qlʻ. | bn.gmrt.qšt. | ǵmrm. | bn.qṯn.qšt.w.qlʻ. | mrṯd.qšt. | ssw.qšt. | knn. 119[321].1.10

gmš

krk. | bn srty. | bn lth ḫlq. | bn ytr. | bn ilšpš. | ubrš. | bn gmš ḫlq. | bn ʻgy. | bn zlbn. | bn.aḫ[--]. | bn[.---]. | [-----]. | bn kr 2016.2.18

gn

]ltm[.b yʻr]. | thdy.lḥm.w dqn[.ṯlṯ]. | qn.ḏrʻ h.tḥrṯ.km.gn. | ap lb.k ʻmq.ṯlṯ.bmt. | bʻl.mt.my.lim.bn dgn. | my.hmlt.a 6[62].1.4
.psltm.b yʻr. | yhdy.lḥm.w dqn. | yṯlṯ.qn.ḏrʻ h.yḥrṯ. | k gn.ap lb.k ʻmq.yṯlṯ. | bmt.yšu.g h.w yṣḥ. | bʻl.mt.my.lim.bn. | 5[67].6.21
mṭr.ʻly. | nʻm.l arṣ.mṭr.bʻl. | w l šd.mṭr.ʻly. | nʻm.l ḥṭt.b gn. | bm.nrt.ksmm. | ʻl.tl[-]k.ʻṭrṭrm. | nšu.[r]iš.ḥrṯm. | l ẓr.ʻdb. 16[126].3.9
y.bn[.---]. | ymil.bn.[---]. | dly.bn[.---]. | ynḥm.bn[.---]. | gn.bn[.---]. | klby.[bn.---]. | šmmlk bn[.---]. | ʻmyn.bn.[---]. | mt 102[322].5.7
ṯn[.d.]ksp. | [ṯ]mn.l.ʻšrm[.l.b]t.ʻṯtrt. | [ṯ]lṯ.ʻšr h.[b]t.ršp.gn. | arbʻ.b d.b[n].ušryn. | kdm.l.urtn. | kdm.l.ilšpš. | kd.l.annṯ 1088.3
r. | [---.]yn.l.mlkt. | [---.yrḫ.]ḫlt.šbʻ.[---].mlkt. | [---.yrḫ.]gn.šbʻ[.--]. | [---.yrḫ.]itb.šb[ʻ.---]. | [-----]. 1088.14

gnb

bn.gnb[.msg]. | bn.twyn[.msg]. | bn.ʻdrš[p.msg]. | pyn.yny.[msg]. 133[-].1.1

gngn

.mt.ʻdd.l ydd. | il.ǵzr.yqra.mt. | b npš h.ystrn ydd. | b gngn h.aḥd y.d ym | lk.ʻl.ilm.l ymru. | ilm.w nšm.d yšb | [ʻ].h 4[51].7.49
[-]y[-.---]. | iwr[--.---]. | iwr[--.---]. | tlmu[.---]. | gngn[.---]. | nwr[--.---]. | sg[---.---]. | [-]s[-.---]. 2138.5

gngnt

-].ṣmd[.---.]pd[ry]. | [-----]. | [---.b]ʻlt. | lbnm.ʻšr.yn. | ḫlb.gngnt.ṯlṯ.y[n]. | bṣr.ʻšr.yn. | nnu arbʻ.yn. | šql ṯlṯ.yn. | šmny.kd 2004.22

gny

bn[.-]pṯ. | bn kdrn. | awldn. | arswn.yʻr[ty.--]. | bn.ugr. | gny. | ṯn.mdm. 86[305].12

gnym

gmm.w.bn.p[--]. | trn.w.p[-]y. | bn.bʻyn.w.agytn. | [---] gnym. | [--]ry.w ary. | [---]ǵrbtym. | [---.]w šbʻl. | [---.-]ym. | [--- 131[309].13

gnʻ

. | tǵr k.tšlm k. | tʻzz k.alp ymm. | w rbt.šnt. | b ʻd ʻlm...gnʻ. | iršt.aršt. | l aḫ y.l rʻ y.dt. | w ytnnn. | l aḫ h.l rʻ h. | rʻ ʻlm. 1019.1.6
-----]. | [-----.-]l[-]. | [-----]. | [---.--]k. | [---.q]rt. | [---.--]d.b.gnʻ. | [---].ḫbt. | [---].qmy. | [---.]qmy. | [---.--]b. | bn.t[--.---.a]ǵt. 2015.1.14

gnʻy

gt[.-]n. | arbʻm.kbd.yn.ṭb.w.[--]. | ṯmn.kbd.yn.d.l.ṭb.b.gnʻ[y]. | mitm.yn.ḥsp.d.nkly.b.db[ḫ.--]. | mit.arbʻm.kbd.yn.ḥs 1084.23
krd. | yʻrt. | uškn. | ʻnqpat. | ilštmʻ. | šbn. | ṭbq. | rqd. | šrš. | gnʻy. | mʻqb. | agm. | bir. | ypr. | hzp. | šql. | mʻrḫ[-]. | sl[ḫ]. | snr. | 2074.26
[-----]. | [-----]. | [ḫl]bkrd. | [ḫl]bʻprm. | [q]dš. | [a]mḏy. | [gn]ʻy. | mʻqb. | agm. | ḫpty. | ypr. | ḫrṣbʻ. | uḫnp. | art. | [--]n. | [--- 2058.1.30
.w.ḫpty. | ḫlb.ṣpn. | mril. | ʻnmky. | ʻnqpat. | ṭbq. | hzp. | gnʻy. | mʻrby. | [ṣ]ʻq. | [š]ḥq. | nʻrm. | mḥrǵlm. | kzym. | mru.skn 71[113].56
.---]. | ṣʻq.ḥmr.w.[---]. | ḫlb ʻprm.amḏy.[ḥm]r.w bn[š]. | gnʻy.[---.bn]š. | uškn[.---].ʻšr.bnšm. | ʻnqpat[.---].bnš. | ubrʻy.a 2040.17
tknn. | mtn.bn.ʻbdym. | ilrb.bn.ilyn. | ʻbdadt.bn ʻbdkb. | gnʻym. 1161.13

gnryn

mlk. | šin k itn. | r‘ y šṣa idn l y. | l šmn iṯr hw. | p iḫdn gnryn. | im mlkytn yrgm. | aḫnnn. | w iḫd. 1020.7
gnryn. | l mlkytn. | ḥnn y l pn mlk. | šin k itn. | r‘ y šṣa idn l y. 1020.1

gsn

š. | ubr‘ym.ḫmš. | [----]. | [bn] itn. | [bn] il. | [---]ṯ. | klṯṯb. | gsn. | arm[w]l. | bn.ṣdqn. | ḫlbn. | tbq.alp. 2039.13

g‘yn

. | bn.ḫran.ilštm‘y. | bn.abd‘n.ilštm‘y. | bn.‘n.rqdy. | bn.g‘yn. | bn.ǵrn. | bn.agynt. | bn.abdḫr.snry. | dqn.šlmn. | prdn.n 87[64].33
gzy.w.bn.‘dy. | bn.gmḥn.w.ḥgbt. | bn.tgdn. | yny. | [b]n.g‘yn dd. | [-]n.dd. | [--]an dd. | [-----]. | [-----]. 131[309].31
. | bn.‘bd. | ḫyrn. | alpy. | bn.plsy. | bn.qrr[-]. | bn.ḥyl. | bn.g‘yn. | ḥyn. | bn.armg[-]. | b‘lmṯpṯ. | [bn].ayḫ. | [---]rn. | ill. | ǵlm 1035.2.2
| hzpym. | rišn.[---]. | bn.‘bdy.[---]. | bn.dmtn.[---]. | [b]n.g‘yn.ḫr[-]. | lbnym. | grgš.[---]. | bn.ǵrn.[---]. | bn.agyn[.---]. | iy 93[328].12

g‘r

n aṯtyy. | bn ḫlp. | bn.ẓll. | bn ydy. | bn lzn. | bn.ṯyn. | bn g‘r. | bn.prtn. | bn ḫnn. | b[n.-]n. | bn.ṣṣb. | bn.b‘ltn ḫlq. | bn.ml 2016.1.16
t[ǵ]ly.hlm.rišt hm.l ẓr.brkt hm.w l kḥṯ. | zbl hm.b hm.yg‘r.b‘l.lm.ǵltm.ilm.rišt. | km l ẓr brkt km.w ln.kḥṯ.zbl km.a 2.1[137].24
| bt.il.pn.l mgr lb.t‘dbn. | nšb.l inr.t‘dbn.ktp. | b il ab h.g‘r.yṯb.il.kb[-]. | aṯ[rt.]il.yṯb.b mrzḥ h. | yšt[.il.y]n.‘d šb‘.trṯ.‘d UG5.1.1.14
h.w ydlp.tmn h. | yqṯ b‘l.w yšt.ym.ykly.ṯpṭ.nhr. | b šm.tg‘r m.‘ṯtrt.bṯ l aliyn.[b‘l.] | bṯ.l rkb.‘rpt.k šby n.zb[l.ym.k] | 2.4[68].28
.yṣq.b[.ap h]. | k.yraš.ššw.[št]. | bln.qṭ.yṣq.b.a[p h]. | k yg‘r[.ššw.---]. | dprn[.---]. | dr‘.[---]. | tmṯl[.---]. | mǵm[ǵ.---]. | w 161[56].23
[šd.b]n.qṭy.b d.tt. | [ubd]y.mrim. | [šd.b]n.ṯpdn.b d.bn.g‘r. | [šd.b]n.ṯqrn.b d.ḫby. | [ṯn.š]d.bn.ngzḥn.b d.gmrd. | [šd.b 82[300].1.21
‘. | ‘ṯtrt.w ‘nt.ymǵy. | ‘ṯtrt.t‘db.nšb l h. | w ‘nt.ktp.b hm.yg‘r.ṯǵr. | bt.il.pn.l mgr lb.t‘dbn. | nšb.l inr.t‘dbn.ktp. | b il ab UG5.1.1.11

g‘t

b‘.w l.yšn.pbl. | mlk.l qr.ṯigt.ibr h. | l ql.nhqt.ḥmr h. | l g‘t.alp.ḥrṯ.zǵt. | klb.ṣpr.w ylak. | mlakm.l k.‘m.krt. | mswn h. 14[KRT].3.122
l.yšn.pbl. | mlk.l [qr.]ṯiqt. | ibr h[.l]ql.nhqt. | ḥmr[h.l g‘t.]alp. | ḥrṯ[.l z]ǵt.klb. | [ṣ]pr[.apn]k. | [pb]l[.mlk.g]m.l aṯt | [14[KRT].5.225

gp

.i]lm.šd.aṯrt.w rḥmy. | [---].y[ṯ]b. | [---]p.gp ym.w yṣǵd.gp..thm. | [yqḥ.]il.mšt‘ltm.mšt‘ltm.l riš.agn. | hl h.[t]špl.hl h. 23[52].30
dbḥ n‘mt. | šd[.i]lm.šd.aṯrt.w rḥmy. | [---].y[ṯ]b. | [---]p.gp ym.w yṣǵd.gp..thm. | [yqḥ.]il.mšt‘ltm.mšt‘ltm.l riš.agn. | 23[52].30
‘]. | qdm ym.bmt.[nhr]. | ṯṯṯn.ib.b‘l.tiḫd. | y‘rm.šnu.hd.gpt. | ǵr.w y‘n.aliyn. | b‘l.ib.hdt.lm.tḥš. | lm.tḥš.nṯq.dmrn. | ‘n. 4[51].7.36

gpn

mdl.‘r.ṣmd.pḥl. | št.gpnm.dt.ksp. | dt.yrq.nqbnm. | ‘db.gpn.atnt h. | yḥbq.qdš.w amrr. | yštn.aṯrt.l bmt.‘r. | l ysmsmt. 4[51].4.12
l.‘r]. | ṣmd.pḥl[.št.gpnm.dt]. | ksp.dt.yr[q.nqbnm]. | ‘db.gpn.atnt[y]. | yšm‘.qd.w amr[r]. | mdl.‘r.ṣmd.pḥl. | št.gpnm.d 4[51].4.7
| bnšm.dt.l.mlk. | ‘bdyrḫ.bn.ṯyl. | ‘bdn.w.aṯt h.w.bn h. | gpn.bn[.a]ly. | bn.rqd[y].ṯbg. | iḫmlk. | yp‘n w.aṯt h. | anntn.yṣ 2068.20
.gpn.atnt[y]. | yšm‘.qd.w amr[r]. | mdl.‘r.ṣmd.pḥl. | št.gpnm.dt.ksp. | dt.yrq.nqbnm. | ‘db.gpn.atnt h. | yḥbq.qdš.w a 4[51].4.10
š]. | w am[rr.l dgy.rbt]. | aṯrt.ym[.mdl.‘r]. | ṣmd.pḥl[.št.gpnm.dt]. | ksp.dt.yr[q.nqbnm]. | ‘db.gpn.atnt[y]. | yšm‘.qd. 4[51].4.5
rkbt. | [---.--]a.nrm. | [---.--]y.lm[.-.]b k[p]. | [---].tr[--.]gpn lk. | [---].km[-.---]. | [---.--]k yṣunn[.---]. | [---.--]dy.w.pr‘[. 1002.32
w nšm.d yšb | [‘].hmlt.arṣ.gm.l ǵ | [lm] h.b‘l k.yṣḥ.‘n. | [gpn].w ugr.b ǵlmt. | [‘mm.]ym.bn.ẓlmt.r | [mt.pr‘]t.ibr.mnt. | 4[51].7.54
‘l.km. | [i]lm.w ḥẓr.k bn. | [a]ṯrt.gm.l ǵlm h. | b‘l.yṣḥ.‘n.gpn. | w ugr.bn.ǵlmt. | ‘mm ym.bn.ẓlm[t]. | rmt.pr‘t.ibr[.mnt] 8[51FRAG].6
h.td‘.ṯǵṣ.pnt. | ksl h.anš.dt.ẓr h.tšu. | g h.w tṣḥ.ik.mǵy.gpn.w ugr. | mn.ib.yp‘.l b‘l.ṣrt. | l rkb.‘rpt.l mḫšt.mdd. | il ym 3[‘NT].3.33
.w l.yṯb ilm.idk. | l ytn.pnm.‘m.b‘l. | mrym.ṣpn.w y‘n. | gpn.w ugr.tḥm.bn ilm. | mt.hwt.ydd.bn.il. | ǵzr.p np.š.npš.lbi 5[67].1.12
[---].ṣḥt. | [---.--]t. | [---.]ilm. | [---.--]u.yd. | [---.--]k. | [---.gpn.]w ugr. | [---.---]t. 4[51].8.47
y]. | ḥspt.l š‘r.ṭl.yd[‘t]. | hlk.kbkbm.mdl.‘r. | ṣmd.pḥl.št.gpn y dt ksp. | dt.yrq.nqbn y.tš[m‘]. | pǵt.ṯkmt.my.ḥspt.l[š‘]r 19[1AQHT].2.53
‘šr.b gt.[---]. | ṯn.‘šr.b.gt.ir[bṣ]. | arb‘.b.gt.b‘ln. | ‘št.‘šr.b.gpn. | yd.‘dnm. | arb‘.ǵzlm. | ṯn.yṣrm. 2103.7
mt.w šr.yṯb.b d h.ḫṭ.ṯkl.b d h. | ḫṭ.ulmn.yzbrnn.zbrm.gpn. | yṣmdnn.ṣmdm.gpn.yšql.šdmt h. | km gpn. | šb‘ d.yrgm. 23[52].9
ṯkl.b d h. | ḫṭ.ulmn.yzbrnn.zbrm.gpn. | yṣmdnn.ṣmdm.gpn.yšql.šdmt h. | km gpn. | šb‘ d.yrgm.‘l.‘d.w ‘rbm.t‘nyn. | w 23[52].10
rnn.zbrm.gpn. | yṣmdnn.ṣmdm.gpn.yšql.šdmt h. | km gpn. | šb‘ d.yrgm.‘l.‘d.w ‘rbm.t‘nyn. | w šd.šd ilm.šd aṯrt.w r 23[52].11
ṯn.ḥ[---].pgam. | ṯn[.---.b]n.mlk. | ṯ[n.---.]gpn. | [-----]. | [---.--]b. | b[--.---.b]n.‘my. 1150.3

gpny

ṯl. | [---]ym. | [----]m. | [-----]. | [bnš.g]t.ir. | bnš.gt.rb[--]. | gpny. | bnš.mǵrt. | kbsm. | armsǵ. 1040.17

gpr

.šnt h.w akl.bqmm. | tšt ḥrṣ.k lb ilnm. | w ṯn.gprm.mn gpr h.šr. | aqht.y‘n.kmr.kmr[.--]. | k ap‘.il.b gdrt.k lb.l | ḥṯ h.i 19[1AQHT].1.11
. | p h.tiḫd.šnt h.w akl.bqmm. | tšt ḥrṣ.k lb ilnm. | w ṯn.gprm.mn gpr h.šr. | aqht.y‘n.kmr.kmr[.--]. | k ap‘.il.b gdrt.k 19[1AQHT].1.11

gr

| mlk.yṣm.y l km.qr.mym.d ‘[l k]. | mḫṣ.aqht.ǵzr.amd.gr bt il. | ‘nt.brḥ.p ‘lm h.‘nt.p dr[.dr]. | ‘db.uḫry mṭ.yd h. | ym 19[1AQHT].3.153
.t‘ḏr b‘l. | [-----.]lšnt. | [---.--]yp.tḥt. | [-----]. | [---.]w npy gr. | [ḥmyt.ugrt.w npy.yman.w npy.‘r]mt.w npy. | [---.ušn.yp APP.I[-].1.12
[.w]šnm.hn.‘r. | w.ṯb.l mspr.m[šr] mšr.bt.ugrt.w npy.gr. | ḥmyt.ugrt.w [np]y.nṯt.ušn.yp kn.ulp qṭy. | ulp.ddmy.ul[32[2].1.27
.bn.il.l mpḫ]rt.[bn.il.l ṯkmn.w šn]m hn š. | [---.w n]py.gr[.ḥmyt.ugrt.w np]y. | [---].w n[py.---].u ṯḫṭi[n.ulp.qṭy]. | ul 32[2].1.10
l.tšb‘n y.aṯt.itrḫ. | y bn.ašld.šu.‘db.tk.mdbr qdš. | ṯm tgrgr.l abnm.w l.‘ṣm.šb‘.šnt. | tmt.ṯmn.nqpt.‘d.ilm.n‘mm.ttl 23[52].66
mk.špšm. | b šb‘.w tmǵy.l udm. | rbm.w l.udm.ṯrrt. | w gr.nn.‘rm.šrn. | pdrm.s‘t.b šdm. | ḥṭb h.b grnt.ḥpšt. | s‘t.b nk. 14[KRT].3.110
ym. | aḫr.špšm.b rb‘. | ymǵy.l udm.rbt. | w udm[.ṯr]rt. | grnn.‘rm. | šrnn.pdrm. | s‘t.b šdm.ḥṭb. | w b grnt.ḥpšt. | s‘t.b n 14[KRT].4.212
--]. | krws.l.y[--.---]. | yp‘.l[.---]. | šmr[m.---]. | [-----]. | bn.g[r.---]. | ḏmry[.---]. | bn.pdr.l.[---]. 2122.6

grb

.ʻyn.ṯkt. | ʻpṯn.bn.ilrš.ṯkt. | ilṯḥm.bn.šrn.ṯkt. | šmlbu.bn.grb.ṯkt. | šmlbu.bn.ypʻ.ṯkt. | [---.--]m. 2085.13

grbn

[--.l]bš.mtn.b.arʻt. | [--.l]bš.bn.yknʻ.b.arʻt. | [--.l]bš.bn.grbn.b.ṯqlm. | [--.lb]š.bn.sgryn.b[.ṯ]qlm. | [---.]bn.ully.b.ṯ[qlm 135[330].3
lpd. | bn.atnb. | bn.ktmn. | bn.pity. | bn.iryn. | bn.ʻbl. | bn.grbn. | bn.iršyn. | bn.nklb. | bn.mryn. | [bn.]b[--]. | bn.ẓrl. | bn.il 115[301].4.18
bn.ilrš. | ʻ[p]ṯn. | b[n.ʻr]my. | [--]ṯy. | bn.ǵdʻ. | bn.ʻyn. | bn.grb[n]. | yṯtn. | bn.ab[l]. | kry. | psš. | ilṯḥm. | ḥrm. | bn.bty. | ʻby. 2078.8
maḫdym. | grbn.ltḥ. | srn.ltḥ. | ykn.ltḥ. | ḥgbn.ltḥ. | spr.mkrm. | bn.slʻn.pr 1059.2
t. | bn.ṯtn[--]. | [m]d.m[--]. | [b]n.annḏ[r]. | bn.ṯḏyy. | bn.grbn. | [--.]ully. | [--]ṯiy. 1054.2.4

grbs

[---.ṯ]lṯ.ʻš[r h.---]. | d bnšm.yd.grbs hm. | w.ṯn.ʻšr h.ḫpnt. | [š]šwm.amtm.ʻkyt. | yd.llḫ hm. | 2049.2

grgyn

b d].bn.[---]. | tšʻ.ṣin.b.tšʻt.ksp. | mšlt.b.ṯql.ksp. | kdwṯ.l.grgyn.b.ṯq[l]. | ḫmšm.šmt.b.ṯql. | kkr.w.[ml]tḥ.tyt.[---]. | [b]š 2101.24

grgs

z.šʻrty. | bn.ibrd.mʻrby. | ṣdqn.gbʻly. | bn.ypy.gbʻly. | bn.grgs.ilštmʻy. | bn.ḫran.ilštmʻy. | bn.abdʻn.ilštmʻy. | bn.ʻn.rqdy 87[64].29
ypy.gbʻly. | b[n].ḥyn. | ḏmn.šʻrty. | bn.arwdn.ilštʻy. | bn grgs. | bn.ḫran. | bn.arš[w.b]ṣry. | bn.ykn. | bn.lṣn.ʻrmy. | bn.bʻ 99[327].1.9
ǵlṣ msg. | arbʻ l ṯkṣ[-]. | nn.arspy.ms[g]. | [---.ms]g. | bn.[gr]gs.msg. | bn[.--]an.msg. | bn[.--].m[sg]. | b[--]n.qmy.msg. | [133[-].2.2

grgr

gn k.w ḫrṣ.l kl. | apnk.ǵzr.ilḥu. | [m]rḥ h.yiḫd.b yd. | [g]rgr h.bm.ymn. | [w]yqrb.trẓẓ h. | [---].mǵy h.w ǵlm. | [a]ḫt 16.1[125].48

grgš

md.w.ḫrṣ. | bn.prsn.ṣmd.w.ḫrṣ. | bn.ilbʻl. | bn.idrm. | bn.grgš. | bn.bly. | bn.apṯ. | bn.ysd. | bn.pl[-]. | bn.ṯbʻnq. | brqd. | bn 2113.9
-]. | p[---]. | b[---]. | [---]. | [---]. | bn[.---]y. | yr[---]. | ḫdyn. | grgš. | b[n.]tlš. | ḏmr. | mkrm. | ʻzn. | ypltַ. | ʻbdmlk. | ynḥm. | aḏ 1035.3.21
grgš. | w.lmd h. | aršmg. | w.lmd h. | iyṯr. | [w].lmd h. | [yn]ḥm. 1048.1
p [-]al[.-]r[-]. | [--]dšq krsnm. | ḫmšm [-]t ṯlṯ ty[--]. | bn.grgš. | w.npṣ bt ṯn.ṯlṯ mat. | w spl ṯlṯ.mat. | w mmskn. | w.ṯt.m 1103.15
[t]ḥm.uṯryn[.---]. | [g]rgš ʻbdy[--]. | [--.]l mlk [---]. | [---].aḫ y[.---]. | [--]q lpš[.---]. | 2130.1.2
mḫsm. | irpbn. | grgš. | [--]yn. | [---]n. | [--]mrt. 1042.3
bn.ʻbdy.[---]. | bn.dmtn.[---]. | [b]n.gʻyn.ḫr[-]. | lbnym. | grgš.[---]. | bn.ǵrn.[---]. | bn.agyn[.---]. | iyṯ[-.---]. 93[328].14

grdy

ayln. | bn.kln. | bn.ʻlln. | bn.liy. | bn.nqṯn. | bn abrḫṭ. | bn.grdy. | bn.ṣlpn. | bn ǵlmn. | bn sgld. 1064.28

grdn

lz. | bn.birtn. | bn.mlṣ. | bn.q[--]. | bn.[---]. | bn.ṯ[-]r. | bn.grdn. | [bn.-]ḫr. | [--.-]nb. | [--.--]n. | [--.--]n. | bn.[---]. | bn.ʻr[--]. 2023.2.3

grdš

.mšbʻt hn.b šlḥ. | ttpl.yʻn.ḥtk h. | krt yʻn.ḥtk h.rš. | mid.grdš.ṯbt h. | w b tm hn.špḥ.yitbd. | w b.pḫyr h.yrṯ. | yʻrb.b ḥd 14[KRT].1.23
.itdb.d šbʻ. | [a]ḫm.l h.ṯmnt.bn um. | krt.ḥtk n.rš. | krt.grdš.mknt. | aṯt.ṣdq h.l ypq. | mtrḫt.yšr h. | aṯt.trḫ.w tbʻt. | ṯar 14[KRT].1.11

grn

| mṯʻt.w yʻn.dnil.[mt.rpi]. | yṯb.ǵzr.mt hrnmy[.---]. | b grnt.ilm.b qrb.m[ṯʻt.ilnym]. | d tit.yspi.spu.q[--.---]. | tpḥ.ṯṣr.s 20[121].2.9
.l ʻr hm]. | tlkn.ym.w ṯa aḫr.š[pšm.b ṯlṯ]. | mǵy.rpum.l grnt.i[lnym.l] | mṯʻt.w yʻn.dnil.[mt.rpi]. | yṯb.ǵzr.mt hrnmy[20[121].2.6
l] | ʻr hm.tl[kn.ym.w ṯn.aḫr.špšm]. | b ṯlṯ.mǵy[.rpum.l grnt]. | i[ln]y[m].l mṯʻt[.---]. | [-]m[.---]. | h.hn bn k.hn[.---]. | b 22.1[123].25
| [---].aḥd.aḫd.b.yʻny. | [---.-]ḥm.b.aḫd.ḥrṯ. | [---.]aḫd.b.grn.uškn. | [---.]aḥd.ḥrṯ. 1129.16
zr. | [mt.hrn]my.ytšu. | [yṯb.b ap.ṯ]ǵr[.ṯ]ḥt. | [adrm.d b grn.y]dn. | [dn.almnt.y]ṯpṭ. | [ṯpṭ.ytm.---] h. | [---.---]n. | [-----]. 19[1AQHT].1.23
hn.ǵzr.mt.hrnm[y]. | ytšu.yṯb.b ap.ṯǵr.ṯḥt. | adrm.d b grn.ydn. | dn.almnt.yṯpṭ.ṯpṭ.ytm. | b nši ʻn h.w yphn.b alp. | š 17[2AQHT].5.7
k.aḥd h]. | w.yṣq[.b.ap h]. | k.yiḫd[.akl.ššw]. | št.mkš[r.grn]. | w.št.ašk[rr]. | w.pr.ḥḏr[t.ydk]. | aḥd h.w.yṣq[.b.ap h]. | 161[56].13
gz y]dk aḥd h w yṣq b ap h. | [k.yiḫd akl s]šw št mkšr grn. | [w št aškrr w p]r ḥḏrt. | [-----]. | [---.-]n[-]. | [k yraš ššw š 160[55].10
.udm.ṯrrt. | w gr.nn.ʻrm.šrn. | pdrm.sʻt.b šdm. | ḥṭb h.b grnt.ḥpšt. | sʻt.b nk.šibt.b bqr. | mmlat.dm.ym.w ṯn. | ṯlṯ.rbʻ.y 14[KRT].3.112
dm[.ṯr]rt. | grnn.ʻrm. | šrnn.pdrm. | sʻt.b šdm.ḥṭb. | w b grnt.ḥpšt. | sʻt.b npk.šibt.w b | mqr.mmlat. | d[m].ym.w ṯn. | ṯ 14[KRT].4.215
| [---.---]n. | [-----]. | hlk.[---.b n]ši. | ʻn h.w tphn.[---]. | b grn.yḫrb[.---]. | yǵly.yḫsp.ib[.---]. | ʻl.bt.ab h.nšrm.trḫ[p]n. | y 19[1AQHT].1.30
d h.w.yṣq[.b.ap h]. | k.yiḫd.akl.s[šw]. | št.nni.št.mk[št.grn]. | št.irǵn.ḥmr[.ydk]. | aḥd h.w.yṣq.b[.ap h]. | k.yraš.ššw.[161[56].18

grnt

bn.ḫrn k. | mǵy. | hbṭ.hw. | ḫrd.w.šl hw. | qr[-]. | akl n.b.grnt. | l.bʻr. | ap.krmm. | ḫlq. | qrt n.ḫlq. | w.dʻ.dʻ. 2114.8

grʻ

| ynḥm.aḏddy. | ǵdǵd.aḏddy. | sw.aḏddy. | ildy.aḏddy. | grʻ.aḏddy. | ʻbd.ršp aḏddy. | ʻdn.bn.knn. | iwrḫz.b d.skn. | škn 2014.34

grp

št. | bn.ulmy.qšt. | ṯqbn.qšt. | bn.qnmlk.qšt. | ytḥm.qšt. | grp.qšt. | mʻrby. | nʻmn.ṯt.qštm.w.qlʻ. | gln.ṯt.qštm.w.qlʻ. | gtn. 104[316].8

grš

.ilib y.b qdš.|ztr.ʿm y.l ʿpr.ḏmr.aṯr[y].|ṭbq lḥt.niṣ y.grš.|d ʿšy.ln.aḥd.yd y.b š|krn mʿms y k šbʿt yn.|spu.ksm y. 17[2AQHT].2.18
r.ʿm h.l arṣ.mšṣu.qṭr h.|l ʿpr.ḏmr.aṯr h.ṭbq.lḥt.|niṣ h.grš d.ʿšy.ln h.|aḥd.yd h.b škrn.mʿms h.|[k]šbʿ yn.spu.ksm 17[2AQHT].1.30
h.l a]rṣ.mšṣu.|[qṭr h.l ʿpr.ḏ]mr.a[ṯ]r h.|[ṭbq.lḥt.niṣ h.gr]š.d ʿšy.|[ln h.---].|z[tr.ʿm k.l arṣ.mšṣu.qṭr k].|l ʿpr.ḏm[r. 17[2AQHT].1.48
m k.l arṣ.mšṣu.qṭr k].|l ʿpr.ḏm[r.aṯr k.ṭbq].|lḥt.niṣ k.gr[š.d ʿšy.ln k].|spu.ksm k.bt.[bʿl.w mnt k].|bt il.aḥd.yd k. 17[2AQHT].2.3
sp.|itrṯ.ḫrṣ.ṭrd.bʿl.|b mrym.ṣpn.mšṣṣ.[-]kʿ[-].|udn h.grš h.l ksi.mlk h.|l nḫt.l kḥṯ.drkt h.|mn m.ib.ypʿ.l bʿl.ṣrt.l r 3[ʿNT].4.46
[---.yṯ]rd h.|[---.yg]rš h.|[---.]ru.|[----] h.|[---.--]mt.|[---.--]mr.limm.|[---.]b 6[49].6.2
n.b ilm].|ʿny h.y[ṯny.yṯlṯ].|rgm.my.b[ilm.ydy].|mrṣ.grš[m.zbln].|in.b ilm.ʿ[ny h.yrbʿ].|yḫmš.rgm.[my.b ilm].|y 16[126].5.15
|in.b ilm.ʿn[y h.]yṯdṯ.|yšbʿ.rgm.[my.]b ilm.|ydy.mrṣ.gršm zbln.|in.b ilm.ʿny h.|w yʿn.lṭpn.il.b pid.|ṯb.bn y.lm ṯb 16[126].5.21
|ṯlṯt h[.-.w yʿn].|lṭpn.[il.d pid.my].|b ilm.[ydy.mrṣ].|gršm.z[bln.in.b ilm].|ʿny h.y[ṯny.yṯlṯ].|rgm.my.b[ilm.ydy]. 16[126].5.12
in.b ilm.ʿ[ny h.yrbʿ].|yḫmš.rgm.[my.b ilm].|ydy.mrṣ.g[ršm.zbln].|in.b ilm.ʿn[y h.]yṯdṯ.|yšbʿ.rgm.[my.]b ilm.|yd 16[126].5.18
.|l kḥṯ.zbl k[m.a]nk.|iḥtrš.w [a]škn.|aškn.ydt.[m]rṣ gršt.|zbln.r[---].ymlu.|nʿm.[-]ṯ[-.--.]yqrṣ.|d[-] b pḫ[-.--.]mḫ 16[126].5.27
k.|kṯr ṣmdm.ynḥt.w ypʿr.šmt hm.šm k at.|ygrš.ygrš.grš ym grš ym.l ksi h.|[n]hr l kḥṯ drkt h.trtqṣ.b d bʿl km nš 2.4[68].12
mdm.ynḥt.w ypʿr.šmt hm.šm k at.|ygrš.ygrš.grš ym grš ym.l ksi h.|[n]hr l kḥṯ drkt h.trtqṣ.b d bʿl km nš|r.b uṣ 2.4[68].12
bʿ[l].|[---.]bt k.ap.l pḫr k ʿnt tqm.ʿnt.tqm.|[---.p]ḫr k.ygrš k.qr.bt k.ygrš k.|[---].bnt.ṣʿṣ.bnt.mʿmʿ.ʿbd.ḥrn.[--.]k.|[1001.2.10
.ap.l pḫr k ʿnt tqm.ʿnt.tqm.|[---.p]ḫr k.ygrš k.qr.bt k.ygrš k.|[---].bnt.ṣʿṣ.bnt.mʿmʿ.ʿbd.ḥrn.[--.]k.|[---].aǵwyn.ʿn k 1001.2.10
yrk.bʿl.[--].|[---.]ʿnt.šzrm.tštšḥ.km.ḫ[--].|[---].ʿpr.bt k.ygr[š k.---].|[---.]y.ḥr.ḥr.bnt.ḫ[---].|[--.]uḫd.[bʿ]l m.ʿ[--].yd 1001.1.12
.|bt ksp y.d[--.---].|b d.aliyn b[ʿl.---].|kd.ynaṣn[.---].|gršnn.l k[si.mlk h.l nḫt.l kḥṯ].|drkt h.š[--.--].|w hm.ap.l[--.- 1[ʿNT.X].4.24
h.brkm.tǵl[l].|b dm.ḏmr.ḥlqm.b mm[ʿ].|mhrm.mṭm.tgrš.|šbm.b ksl.qšt h.mdnt.|w hln.ʿnt.l bt h.tmǵyn.|tštql.ilt 3[ʿNT].2.15

gšm

gm.ṯṯ[b].|any kn.dt.|likt.mṣrm.|hn dt.b.ṣr.|mtt.by.|gšm.adr.|nškḥ.w.|rb.tmtt.|lqḥ.kl.ḏrʿ.|b d a[-]m.w.ank.|k[l 2059.14

gt

y.bn.ṯrnq.[-]r.d.yṯb.b.ilštmʿ.|ilšlm.bn.gs[-.--]r.d.yṯb.b.gt.al.|ilmlk.[--]kt.[--.d.]yṯb.b.šb[n].|bn.pr[-.]d.y[ṯb.b].šlmy. 2015.1.27
mit.drʿ.w.tšʿm.drt.|[w].ṯmnym.l.mit.dd.ḥpr.bnšm.|b.gt.alḥb.ṯṯm.drʿ.w.ḫmšm.drt.w.ṯṯm.dd.|ḥpr.bnšm.|b.gt.knp 1098.16
.tgd.mrum.|bt.[-]b[-.-]sy[-]h.|nn[-].b[n].py[-.d.]yṯb.b.gt.aǵld.|šgn.bn b[--.---].d.yṯb.b.ilštmʿ.|abmn.bn.r[---].b.syn. 2015.2.5
b gt ilštmʿ.|bt ubnyn š h d.ytn.ṣṭqn.|ṭut ṭbḫ ṣṭq[n].|b bz ʿzm 1153.1
ʿṣd.mqb.|b.gwl.ṯmn.ḫrmṯt.[nit].|krk.mʿṣd.mqb.|[b] gt.iptl.ṯṯ.ḫrmṯ[t.nit].|[k]rk.mʿṣd.mqb.|[b.g]t.bir.ʿš[r.---].|[-- 2048.13
n.ṣmdm.|w.arbʿ.ʿšr.bnš.|yd.nǵr.mdrʿ.yd.š[--]m.|[b.]gt.iptl.ṯṯ.ṣmdm.|[w.ʿ]šr.bn[š]m.y[d].š[--].|[-]m.b d.r[-]m.l[- 2038.7
.]kbd.yn.d.l.ṭb.|b.gt.gwl.|ṯlṯm.tšʿ[.kbd.yn].d.l[.ṭb].b.gt.iptl.|ṯmnym.[yn].ṭb.b.gt.š[---].|tšʿm.[ḫ]mš[.kbd].yn.b gt[1084.19
.yd.lmd hm.lqḥ.|ʿšr.mḫṣm.yd.lmd hm.|apym.|[bn]š gt.iptl.|[---]ym.|[----]m.|[-----].|[bnš.g]t.ir.|bnš.gt.rb[--].|g 1040.11
.|apym.|[bn]š gt.iptl.|[---]ym.|[----]m.|[-----].|[bnš.g]t.ir.|bnš.gt.rb[--].|gpny.|bnš.mǵrt.|kbsm.|armsǵ. 1040.15
pm.|ʿšr.bnšm.|ḫmš.bnši.ṯṯ[---].|ʿšr.b gt.[---].|ṯn.ʿšr.b.gt.ir[bṣ].|arbʿ.b.gt.bʿln.|ʿšt.ʿšr.b.gpn.|yd.ʿdnm.|arbʿ.ǵzlm.| 2103.5
[aǵ]ltn.|[--]ṯm.b.gt.irbṣ.|[--]šmyn.|[w.]nḥl h.|bn.qṣn.|bn.ksln.|bn.ṣrym.|bn 1073.1.2
[sp]r.akl[.---].ṯryn.|[tg]mr.akl.b.g[t.b]ir.alp.|[ʿ]šrm.l.mit.ḫ[p]r.ʿbdm.|mitm.drt.ṯmnym.drt.| 2013.2
d.mqb.|[b] gt.iptl.ṯṯ.ḫrmṯ[t.nit].|[k]rk.mʿṣd.mqb.|[b.g]t.bir.ʿš[r.---].|[---].krk.mʿ[ṣd.---].|[b.]gt.ḥrtm.ḫm[š.---].|[n 2048.15
.---.]kbd.|ṯṯ.ddm.k[--.b]rqd.|mit.tšʿm.[kb]d.ddm.|b.gt.bir. 2168.4
[---.]tḥr l ytn ḥs[n].|ʿbd ulm ṯn un ḫsn.|gdy lqḥ ṣṭqn gt bn ndr.|um r[-] gtn ṯṯ ḫsn l ytn.|l rḥt lqḥ ṣṭqn.|bt qbṣ ur 1154.4
bdl.gt.bn.ṯbšn.|bn.mnyy.šʿrty.|aryn.aḏddy.|agpṯr.|šbʿl.mlky.| 91[311].1
|yʿl.knʿny.|gdn.bn.umy.|knʿm.šʿrty.|abrpu.ubrʿy.|b.gt.bn.ṯlṯ.|ilḏ.b.gt.pshn. 91[311].11
[.---].|tlby[.---].|ir[--.---].|pndyn[.---].|w.idt[-.---].|b.gt.b[n.---].|yḫl[.---].|b.gt.[---].|[---.]k[--]. 1078.7
mš.bnši.ṯṯ[---].|ʿšr.b gt.[---].|ṯn.ʿšr.b.gt.ir[bṣ].|arbʿ.b.gt.bʿln.|ʿšt.ʿšr.b.gpn.|yd.ʿdnm.|arbʿ.ǵzlm.|ṯn.yṣrm. 2103.6
.l.mit.ḫ[p]r.ʿbdm.|mitm.drt.ṯmnym.drt.|tgmr.akl.b.gt[.b]ʿln.|ṯlṯ.mat.ṯṯm.kbd.|ṯṯm.ṯṯ.kbd.ḥpr.ʿbdm.|šbʿm.drt.a 2013.5
alp.idtn.d aḥd.b.ʿnqpat.|[aḥd.al]p.d aǵlmn.|[d aḥd b.g]t gbry.|[---].aḥd.aḥd.b.yʿny.|[---.-]ḫm.b.aḥd.ḥrt.|[---.]aḥd 1129.13
bʿm.kdm.kbd.yn.ṭb.|w.ḫmšm.k[dm.]kbd.yn.d.l.ṭb.|b.gt.gwl.|ṯlṯm.tšʿ[.kbd.yn].d.l[.ṭb].b.gt.iptl.|ṯmnym.[yn].ṭb.b. 1084.18
.ṯpn.ʿšr.ṣmdm.|w.ṯlṯ.ʿšr.bnš.|yd.ytm.yd.rʿy.ḥmrm.|b.gt.gwl.ṯmn.ṣmdm.|w.arbʿ.ʿšr.bnš.|yd.nǵr.mdrʿ.yd.š[--]m.|[2038.4
ḫrš.anyt.|bnš.gt.glʿd.|bnš.gt.ngr.|rʿym.|bn.ḫri[-].|bnš.gt.ʿttrt.|ad[-]l[-]m 1040.2
dd l ky.|dd l ʿbdkṯr.|dd[m] l rʿy.|[--] šmḫ[.---].|ddm gt dprnm.|l ḥršm.|ddm l ʿnqt.|dd l alṯt.w l lmdt h.|dd l iḫ 1101.8
].|ugrt.ytn.|šd.kḏǵdl[.bn].|[-]š[-]y.d.b š[-]y.|[---.y]d gt h[.--].|[---.]yd.|[k]rm h.yd.|[k]lkl h.|[w] ytn.nn.|l.bʿln.b 1008.7
[---.]i[y]tl[m].|[---.--]y.|[-----].|[---.k]d.|[---.]b gt.ḥgb[-].|[--.]b gt.nṯṯ[-]. 2166.5
.arbʿm.drʿ.w.ʿšrm.drt.|w.ṯlṯm.dd.ṯṯ.kbd.ḥpr.bnšm.|b.gt.ḥdṯt.arbʿm.drʿ.w.ṯlṯm.drt.|[w].šbʿm.dd.ṯn.kbd.ḥpr.bnšm. 1098.22
|yn.d.l.ṭb.b.ulm.|mit.yn.ṭb.w.ṯṯm.ṯṯ.kbd.|yn.d.l.ṭb.b.gt.ḥdṯt.|tšʿm.yn.d.l.ṭb.b.zbl.|ʿšrm.yn.ṭb.w.ṯṯm.ḫmš.k[b]d.| 1084.12
zr.w.ʿšt.ʿšr.ḥrš.|dt.tbʿln.b.ugrt.|ṯṯtm.ḥzr.|dt.tbʿln.|b.gt.ḥršm.|ṯn.ḥršm.|[-]nbkm.|ṯn.ḥršm.|b.gt.ǵl.|[-.]nǵr.mdrʿ. 1024.3.11
mʿṣd.mqb.|[b.g]t.bir.ʿš[r.---].|[---].krk.mʿ[ṣd.---].|[b.]gt.ḥrtm.ḫm[š.---].|[n]it.krk.mʿṣ[d.---].|b.ḫrbǵlm.ǵlm[n].|w. 2048.17
pr.ʿbdm.|šbʿm.drt.arbʿm.drt.|l.a[--.---].|tgm[r.ak]l.b.gt.ḥldy.|ṯlṯ.ma[t].ʿšr.kbd.|šbʿ m[at].kbd.ḥpr.ʿbdm.|mit[.d]r 2013.10
.ḫlq.b.gt.sknm.|ʿšr.yn.ṭb.w.arbʿm.ḫmš.kbd.|yn.d.l.ṭb.gt.ṭbq.|mit.ʿšr.kbd.yn.ṭb.|w.ṯṯm.arbʿ.kbd.yn.d.l.ṭb.|b.gt.mʿ 1084.5
.|ʿdršp.|bn.knn.|pdyn.|bn.aṯtl.ṯn.|kdln.akdṯb.|ṯn.b gt yknʿm. 1061.22
bldn.|[-]bdy.|[b]ʿln.|[-]šdm.|iwryn.|nʿmn.|[-----].|b gt.yny.|agṯṯp.|bn.ʿnt.|ǵzldn.|ṯrn.|ḫdbṯ.|[-]ḫl.aǵltn.|[-]n.|[1043.10
ʿm.kbd.|ṯlṯ.alp.ṣpr.dt.aḥd.|ḥrt h.aḥd.b gt.nḫl.|aḥd.b gt.knpy.w.aḥd.b gt.ṯrmn.|aḥd.alp.idtn.d aḥd.b.ʿnqpat.|[aḥ 1129.10
.gt.alḥb.ṯṯm.drʿ.w.ḫmšm.drt.w.ṯṯm.dd.|ḥpr.bnšm.|b.gt.knpy.mit.drʿ.ṯṯm.drt.w.šbʿm.dd.arbʿ.|kbd.ḥpr.bnšm.|b.g 1098.18
šd.---.]gt.prn.|[š]d.bn.š[p]šn l gt pr[n].|šd bn.ilšḥr.|l.gt.mzln.|šd.gldy.|l.gt.mzln.|šd.glln.l.gt.mz[l]n.|šd.hyabn[. 1104.16
n.š[p]šn l gt pr[n].|šd bn.ilšḥr.|l.gt.mzln.|šd.gldy.|l.gt.mzln.|šd.glln.l.gt.mz[l]n.|šd.hyabn[.l.]gt.mzln.|šd.ʿbdbʿl 1104.18

. | šd bn.ilšḥr. | l.gt.mzln. | šd.gldy. | l.gt.mzln. | šd.glln.l.gt.mz[l]n. | šd.hyabn[.l.]gt.mzln. | šd.‘bdb‘l. | l.gt.mzln. 1104.19
| šd.gldy. | l.gt.mzln. | šd.glln.l.gt.mz[l]n. | šd.hyabn[.l.]gt.mzln. | šd.‘bdb‘l. | l.gt.mzln. 1104.20
ṯn.b gt.mzln. | ṯn.b ulm. | abmn.b gt.m‘rb. | atn. | ḫryn. | bn.‘nt. | llw 1061.1
šd.glln.l.gt.mz[l]n. | šd.hyabn[.l.]gt.mzln. | šd.‘bdb‘l. | l.gt.mzln. 1104.22
šp.mlk. | alp w.š.l b‘lt. | bwrm š.iṯtqb. | w š.nbk m w.š. | gt mlk š.‘lm. | l kṯr.ṯn.‘lm. | tzǵ[.---.]nšm.pr. UG5.12.B.11
[‘]b[dm]. | ‘šrm. | inšt. | mdm. | gt.mlkym. | yqšm. | kbšm. | trrm. | khnm. | kzym. | yṣrm. | mru. 74[115].5
. | yṣḥm. | šrm. | n‘rm. | ‘bdm. | kzym. | ksdm. | [nsk].ṯlṯ. | gt.mlkym. | tmrym. | ṯnqym. | ṯǵrm. | mru.skn. | mru.ibrn. | yqš 1026.2.2
b.gt.mlkt.b.rḥbn. | ḫmšm.l.mitm.zt. | w.b d.krd. | ḫmšm.l.mit. | 1096.1
.dr‘.w.‘šr.dd.drt. | w[.a]rb‘.l.‘šrm.dd.l.yḥšr.bl.bn h. | b.gt.m‘br.arb‘m.l.mit.dr‘.w.ṯmnym[.drt]. | w.‘šrm.l.mit.dd.ḥp[1098.12
ṯn.b gt.mzln. | ṯn.b ulm. | abmn.b gt.m‘rb. | atn. | ḫryn. | bn.‘nt. | llwn. | agdṯb. | aǵltn. | [-]wn. | bld 1061.3
t.ṭbq. | mit.‘šr.kbd.yn.ṭb. | w.ṯṯm.arb‘.kbd.yn.d.l.ṭb. | b.gt.m‘rby. | ṯṯm.yn.ṭb.w.ḫmš.l.‘šrm. | yn.d.l.ṭb.b.ulm. | mit.yn. 1084.8
w.lmd h. | ‘bdrpu. | w.lmd h. | ‘dršp. | w.lmd h. | krwn b.gt.nbk. | ddm.kšmm.l.ḥṭn. | ddm.l.trbnn. | ddm.š‘rm.l.trbnn. | 1099.19
ḥrš.anyt. | bnš.gt.gl‘d. | bnš.gt.ngr. | r‘ym. | bn.ḫri[-]. | bnš.gt.‘ttrt. | ad[-]l[-]m. | ‘šr.ksdm.y 1040.3
arb‘.mat. | arb‘m.kbd. | ṯlṯ.alp.ṣpr.dt.aḥd. | ḥrṯ h.aḥd.b gt.nḫl. | aḥd.b gt.knpy.w.aḥd.b gt.ṯrmn. | aḥd.alp.idṯn.d aḥd. 1129.9
mln.ṯn.b d.bn.ḫdmn. | [u]bdy.nqdm. | [ṯlṯ].šdm.d.n‘rb.gt.npk. | [š]d.rpan.b d.klṯṭb. | [š]d.ilṣy.b d.‘bdym. | [ub]dy.trr 82[300].2.13
[m]. | [---.--]y. | [-----]. | [---.k]d. | [---.]b gt.ḥgb[-]. | [--.]b gt.nṯt[-]. 2166.6
r.yn.ṭb. | w.tš‘m.kdm.kbd.yn.d.l.ṭb. | w.arb‘m.yn.ḫlq.b.gt.sknm. | ‘šr.yn.ṭb.w.arb‘m.ḫmš.kbd. | yn.d.l.ṭb.gt.ṭbq. | mit.‘ 1084.3
.d.l.ṭb.b.zbl. | ‘šrm.yn.ṭb.w.ṯṯm.ḫmš.k[b]d. | yn.d.l.ṭb.b.gt.sǵy. | arb‘m.kdm.kbd.yn.ṭb. | w.ḫmšm.k[dm.]kbd.yn.d.l.ṭb 1084.15
m. | krk.aḥt. | b.sǵy.ḫmš.ḫrmṯt.nit. | krk.m‘ṣd.mqb. | b.gt.‘mq.ḫmš.ḫrmṯt.n[it]. | krk.m‘ṣd.mqb. | b.gwl.ṯmn.ḫrmṯt.[n 2048.9
š.anyt. | bnš.gt.gl‘d. | bnš.gt.ngr. | r‘ym. | bn.ḫri[-]. | bnš.gt.‘ttrt. | ad[-]l[-]m. | ‘šr.ksdm.yd.lmd hm.lqḥ. | ‘šr.mḫṣm.yd.l 1040.6
it.dr‘.w.ṯmnym[.drt]. | w.‘šrm.l.mit.dd.ḥp[r.]bnšm. | b.gt.ǵl.‘šrm.l.mit.dr‘.w.tš‘m.drt. | [w].ṯmnym.l.mit.dd.ḥpr.bnš 1098.14
.ḥpr.‘bdm. | mit[.d]rt.arb‘m.drt. | [---]m. | t[gm]r.akl.b.gt.ǵ[l]. | ṯlṯ.mat.‘šrm[.---]. | ṯmnym.drt.a[--]. | drt.l.alpm[.---]. 2013.15
| dt.tb‘ln. | b.gt.ḥršm. | ṯn.ḥršm. | [-]nbkm. | ṯn.ḥršm. | b.gt.ǵl. | [-.]nǵr.mdr‘. | [-].nǵr[.--]m. | [--.]psl.qšt. | [ṯl]ṯ.psl.ḥẓm. 1024.3.15
.bn.umy. | kn‘m.š‘rty. | abrpu.ubr‘y. | b.gt.bn.ṯlṯ. | ilḏ.b.gt.psḥn. 91[311].12
t.prn. | [šd.---.]gt.prn. | [šd.---.]gt.prn. | [š]d.bn.š[p]šn l gt pr[n]. | šd bn.ilšḥr. | l.gt.mzln. | šd.gldy. | l.gt.mzln. | šd.glln 1104.14
n.ky.gt.prn. | šd.hwil.gt.prn. | šd.ḥr.gt.prn. | šd.bn.ṯbǵl.gt.prn. | šd.bn.inšr.gt.prn. | šd.[---.]gt.prn. | [šd.---.]gt.prn. | [š 1104.9
šd.ubdy.ilštm‘. | dt b d.skn. | šd.bn.ubr‘n b gt prn. | šd.bn.gby.gt.prn. | šd.bn.kryn.gt.prn. | šd.bn.ky.gt.pr 1104.3
. | šd.bn.ubr‘n b gt prn. | šd.bn.gby.gt.prn. | šd.bn.kryn.gt.prn. | šd.bn.ky.gt.prn. | šd.hwil.gt.prn. | šd.ḥr.gt.prn. | šd.b 1104.5
y.ilštm‘. | dt b d.skn. | šd.bn.ubr‘n b gt prn. | šd.bn.gby.gt.prn. | šd.bn.kryn.gt.prn. | šd.bn.ky.gt.prn. | šd.hwil.gt.prn. 1104.4
bn.inšr.gt.prn. | šd.[---.]gt.prn. | [šd.---.]gt.prn. | [šd.---.]gt.prn. | [š]d.bn.š[p]šn l gt pr[n]. | šd bn.ilšḥr. | l.gt.mzln. | šd. 1104.13
.kryn.gt.prn. | šd.bn.ky.gt.prn. | šd.hwil.gt.prn. | šd.ḥr.gt.prn. | šd.bn.ṯbǵl.gt.prn. | šd.bn.inšr.gt.prn. | šd.[---.]gt.prn. 1104.8
t prn. | šd.bn.gby.gt.prn. | šd.bn.kryn.gt.prn. | šd.bn.ky.gt.prn. | šd.hwil.gt.prn. | šd.ḥr.gt.prn. | šd.bn.ṯbǵl.gt.prn. | šd. 1104.6
.gt.prn. | šd.bn.kryn.gt.prn. | šd.bn.ky.gt.prn. | šd.hwil.gt.prn. | šd.ḥr.gt.prn. | šd.bn.ṯbǵl.gt.prn. | šd.bn.inšr.gt.prn. | š 1104.7
ṯbǵl.gt.prn. | šd.bn.inšr.gt.prn. | šd.[---.]gt.prn. | [šd.---.]gt.prn. | [šd.---.]gt.prn. | [š]d.bn.š[p]šn l gt pr[n]. | šd bn.ilšḥr. 1104.12
il.gt.prn. | šd.ḥr.gt.prn. | šd.bn.ṯbǵl.gt.prn. | šd.bn.inšr.gt.prn. | šd.[---.]gt.prn. | [šd.---.]gt.prn. | [šd.---.]gt.prn. | [š]d.b 1104.10
.gt.prn. | šd.bn.ṯbǵl.gt.prn. | šd.bn.inšr.gt.prn. | šd.[---.]gt.prn. | [šd.---.]gt.prn. | [šd.---.]gt.prn. | [š]d.bn.š[p]šn l gt pr[1104.11
ṯlṯm.dd[.---]. | b.gt.ṣb[-.---]. | mit.‘šr.[---.]dd[.--]. | tš‘.dd.ḥ[ṭm.w].ḥm[šm]. | kd 2092.2
bn]š gt.iptl. | [---]ym. | [----]m. | [-----]. | [bnš.g]t.ir. | bnš.gt.rb[--]. | gpny. | bnš.mgrt. | kbsm. | armsǵ. 1040.16
spr.gt.r[---]. | ‘šrm.l.m[it.---]. | šd.dr[-.---]. 1105.1
. | ṯlṯm.tš‘[.kbd.yn].d.l[.ṭb].b.gt.iptl. | ṯmnym.[yn].ṭb.b.gt.š[---]. | tš‘m.[ḫ]mš[.kbd].yn.b gt[.-]n. | arb‘m.kbd.yn.ṭb.w.[1084.20
t qdš. | [---].b.dmt qdš. | [---.--]n.b.anan. | [--]yl.b.bq‘t.b.gt.tgyn. | [--]in.b.trzy. | [--]yn.b.glltky. | ṯd[y]n.b.glltky. | lbw[- 2118.6
wn.b[n.---]. | tgyn.m‘[---]. | w.agptn[.---]. | tyndr[-.---]. | gt.tg[yn.---]. | pwn[.---]. 103[334].6
.--]m.šb‘.[---]. | [---].‘šr.dd[.---]. | [---]mn.arb‘m.y[n]. | b.gt.trǵnds. | tš‘.‘šr.[dd].kšmm. | ṯn.‘šr[.dd.ḥ]ṭm. | w.šb[‘.---]. 2092.15
spr šd.ri[šym]. | kr[-].šdm.‘[--]. | b gt ṯm[--] yn[.--]. | [---].krm.b yp‘l.y‘dd. | [---.]krm.b [-]dn.l.bn 2027.1.3
[b.]gt.ṯpn.‘šr.ṣmdm. | w.ṯlṯ.‘šr.bnš. | yd.ytm.yd.r‘y.ḥmrm. | b.gt.g 2038.1
r.dt.aḥd. | ḥrṯ h.aḥd.b gt.nḫl. | aḥd.b gt.knpy.w.aḥd.b gt.ṯrmn. | aḥd.alp.idṯn.d aḥd.b.‘nqpat. | [aḥd.al]p.d aǵlmn. | [1129.10
aḥt.l mzy.bn[--]. | aḥt.l mkt.ǵr. | aḥt.l ‘ttrt. | arb‘.‘ṣrm. | gt.ṯrmn. | aḥt.slḫu. 39[19].18
py.mit.dr‘.ṯṯm.drt.w.šb‘m.dd.arb‘. | kbd.ḥpr.bnšm. | b.gt.ṯrmn.arb‘m.dr‘.w.‘šrm.drt. | w.ṯlṯm.dd.ṯṯ.kbd.ḥpr.bnšm. | 1098.20
pṯl. | ṯmnym.[yn].ṭb.b.gt.š[---]. | tš‘m.[ḫ]mš[.kbd].yn.b gt[.-]n. | arb‘m.kbd.yn.ṭb.w.[--]. | ṯmn.kbd.yn.d.l.ṭb.b.gn‘[y]. 1084.21
[---.--]l. | [---.--]ḏ. | [---.--]ḏ. | [---.--]aṣ. | [---.]b gt.[--]. | [---.--]n.[--]. | [--.--]ǵm.rm[-]. | [---.-]‘m. | [---.k]sp.[--]. 1148.8
r.[---.]dd[.--]. | tš‘.dd.ḥ[ṭm.w].ḥm[šm]. | kdm.kbd.yn.b.gt.[---]. | [mi]tm.ḫmšm.ḫmš.k[bd]. | [dd].kšmm.tš‘[.---]. | [š]‘r 2092.5
]. | [š]‘rm.ṯṯ.‘[šr]. | [dd].ḥṭm.w.ḥ[mšm]. | [ṯ]lṯ kbd.yn.b [gt.---]. | mit.[---].ṯlṯ.kb[d]. | [dd.--]m.šb‘.[---]. | [---].‘šr.dd[.---]. 2092.10
bt.alpm. | ‘šr.bnšm. | ḫmš.bnši.ṯt[---]. | ‘šr.b gt.[---]. | ṯn.‘šr.b.gt.ir[bṣ]. | arb‘.b.gt.b‘ln. | ‘št.‘šr.b.gpn. | yd.‘d 2103.4
-]. | pndyn[.---]. | w.idṯ[-.---]. | b.gt.b[n.---]. | yḫl[.---]. | b.gt.[---]. | [---.]k[--]. 1078.9

gtn

p.qšt. | m‘rby. | n‘mn.ṯt.qštm.w.ql‘. | gln.ṯt.qštm.w.ql‘. | gtn.qšt. | pmn.ṯt.qšt.w.ql‘. | bn.zry.q[š]t.w.ql‘. | bn.tlmyn.ṯt.qš 104[316].9
. | ‘bd ulm ṯn un ḫsn. | gdy lqḥ ṣṭqn gt bn ndr. | um r[-] gtn ṯt ḫsn l ytn. | l rḥt lqḥ ṣṭqn. | bt qbṣ urt ilštm‘ dbḥ ṣṭqn l. 1154.5
[---.]gtn ṯt. | [---.]tḥr l ytn ḫs[n]. | ‘bd ulm ṯn un ḫsn. | gdy lqḥ ṣṭq 1154.1

gṯpbn

--]y. | bn.aḏdt. | bn.atnb. | bn.yšd. | bn.bršm. | bn.gṯprg. | gṯpbn. | bn.b[--]. | [b]n.[---]. | bn.a[--]. | bn.ml[k]. | bn.glyn. | bn. 1057.13

gṯprg

---]r. | [---]y. | bn.aḏdt. | bn.atnb. | bn.yšd. | bn.bršm. | bn.gṯprg. | gṯpbn. | bn.b[--]. | [b]n.[---]. | bn.a[--]. | bn.ml[k]. | bn.gl 1057.12

gṯr

b tp.w mṣltm.b m | rqdm.dšn.b.ḥbr.kṯr.ṭbm. | w tšt.‘nt.gṯr.b‘lt.mlk.b‘ | lt.drkt.b‘lt.šmm.rmm. | [b‘l]t.kpṯ.w ‘nt.di.dit. UG5.2.1.6

ṯlṯ. | ṣin.šlm[m.]šb‘ pamt. | l ilm.šb[‘.]l kṯr. | ‘lm.t‘rbn.gṯrm. | bt.mlk.ṯql.ḫrṣ. | l špš.w yrḫ.l gṯr. | ṯql.ksp.ṭb.ap w np[š 33[5].9

.uḫ y. | l g y.w yhbṭ.bnš. | w ytn.ilm.b d hm. | b d.iḫqm.gṯr. | w b d.ytrhd. | b‘l. 55[18].20

| [---.--]m.lm. | [---.š]d.gṯr. | [--]ḥ[d].šd.hwt. | [--.]iḥd.šd.gṯr. | [w]ht.yšm‘.uḫ y. | l g y.w yhbṭ.bnš. | w ytn.ilm.b d hm. 55[18].16

[---]n.yšt.rpu.mlk.‘lm.w yšt. | [--.]gṯr.w yqr.il.yṯb.b.‘ṯtrt. | il.ṯpṭ.b hd r‘y.d yšr.w yḏmr. | b knr. UG5.2.1.2

b‘l š.‘nt š.ršp š. | šlmm. | w šnpt.il š. | l ‘nt.ḥl š.ṯn šm. | l gṯrm.ǵṣ b šmal. | d alpm.w alp w š. | šrp.w šlmm kmm. | l b‘l. UG5.13.26

. | ṯql.ksp.ṭb.ap w np[š]. | l ‘nt h.ṯql.ḫrṣ. | l špš[.w y]rḫ.l gṯr.ṯn. | [ṯql.ksp].ṭb.ap.w npš. | [---].bt.alp w š. | [---.--]m.l gṯr 33[5].14

[‘.]l kṯr. | ‘lm.t‘rbn.gṯrm. | bt.mlk.ṯql.ḫrṣ. | l špš.w yrḫ.l gṯr. | ṯql.ksp.ṭb.ap w np[š]. | l ‘nt h.ṯql.ḫrṣ. | l špš[.w y]rḫ.l gṯr 33[5].11

šil. | [-----.]šilt. | [-----]. | [-----.š]ilt. | [---.--]m.lm. | [---.š]d.gṯr. | [--]ḥ[d].šd.hwt. | [--.]iḥd.šd.gṯr. | [w]ht.yšm‘.uḫ y. | l g y. 55[18].14

.ṯn. | [ṯql.ksp].ṭb.ap.w npš. | [---].bt.alp w š. | [---.--]m.l gṯrm. | [---.]l ‘nt m. | [---.--]rm.d krm. | [---].l ‘nt m. | [---.]l šlm 33[5].17

gṯrn

n.šmm. | bn.irgy. | w.nḥl h. | w.nḥl hm. | [bn].pmn. | bn.gṯrn. | bn.arpḫn. | bn.ṯryn. | bn.dll. | bn.ḫswn. | mrynm. | ‘zn. | ḥ 1046.3.28

[---.--]r. | [--.]iln. | y‘rtym. | bn.gṯrn. | bq‘ty. 100[66].4

l‘m. | bn.ṯlṭ.ṯ[lṯ.]qšt.w.ṯn.ql‘m. | qṣn.ṯt.qštm.w.ql‘. | bn.gṯrn.q[š]t. | bn.ḫdi.ṯt.qštm.w.ṯn.ql‘m. | ildgn.qšt. | bn.y‘rn.ṯt.q 119[321].3.7

gṯtn

y.bn.qqln. | mnn.bn.ṣnr. | iḫy.[b]n[.--]l[-]. | ‘bdy[rḫ].bn.gṯtn. | yrmn.bn.‘n. | krwn.nḥl h. | ttn.[n]ḥl h. | bn.b[r]zn. | [---.- 85[80].4.8

ṯ. | y[---.bn.]kran.ḫmš. | ‘[---].kd. | amry.kdm. | mnn.bn.gṯtn.kdm. | ynḥm.bn[.-]r[-]t.ṯlṯ. | plwn.kdm. | tmyn.bn.ubrš.k 136[84].9

d

d

|širm.šd.šd.ʻšy.|w.šir.šd.krm.|d.krwn.|šir.šd.šd.ʻšy.|d.abmn.|šir.šd.krm.|d.yrmn.|šir.[š]d.mltḫ.šd.ʻšy.|d.ynḥm. 1079.11
.qpt.w.mqḥm.|w.t̲lt̲m.yn šbʻ.kbd d t̲bt̲.|w.ḫmšm.yn.d iḫ h. 1103.23
n.|aḥd.alp.idt̲n.d aḫd.b.ʻnqpat.|[aḥd.al]p.d aǵlmn.|[d aḫd b.g]t gbry.|[---].aḥd.aḫd.b.yʻny.|[---.-]ḥm.b.aḫd.ḫrt̲.| 1129.13
gt.nḫl.|aḥd.b gt.knpy.w.aḥd.b gt.t̲rmn.|aḥd.alp.idt̲n.d aḫd.b.ʻnqpat.|[aḥd.al]p.d aǵlmn.|[d aḫd b.g]t gbry.|[---]. 1129.11
mat.|tgmr.uz.aḫmn.arbʻ.mat.|arbʻm.kbd.|t̲lt̲.alp.ṣpr.dt.aḫd.|ḥrt̲ h.aḥd.b gt.nḫl.|aḥd.b gt.knpy.w.aḥd.b gt.t̲rmn. 1129.8
m.l bnš klnmw.|l yarš ḫswn.|ḫmš ʻšr.sp.|l bnš tpnr d yaḫd l g ynm.|t̲t̲ spm l tgyn.|arbʻ spm l ll[-].|t̲n spm.l sly 137.2[93].11
šlmm.|w šnpt.il š.|l ʻnt.ḥl š.t̲n šm.|l gt̲rm.ǵṣ b šmal.|d alpm.w alp w š.|šrp.w šlmm kmm.|l bʻl.ṣpn b ʻrʻr.|pamt UG5.13.27
n.arṣ.t̲l.šm[m.t]sk h.|rbb.nsk h.kbkbm.|ttpp.anhbm.d alp.šd[.ẓu h.b ym].|t̲l[.---]. 3[ʻNT].4.89
|d ttql.b ym.trtḫ[ṣ.--].|[----.a]dm.tium.b ǵlp y[m.--].|d alp šd.ẓu h.b ym.t[---].|tlbš.npṣ.ǵzr.tšt.ḫ[---.b] |nšg h.ḥrb 19[1AQHT].4.205
ttpp.anhb[m.d alp.šd].|ẓu h.b ym[.---].|[--]rn.l [---]. 3[ʻNT].3.03
ḫmšm w.|ḫmš.t̲nt.d mit.|ḫmš.t̲nt.d t̲l|t̲ mat.|t̲t.t̲nt.d alp|alpm.t̲lt̲ ktt.|alp.brr.|kkr.tznt.|ḫmšt.kkr tyt. 1130.13
šdm.ʻl k.pht.|drʻ.b ym.tn.aḥd.|b aḫ k.ispa.w ytb.|ap.d anšt.im[-].|aḥd.b aḫ k.l[--]n.|hn[-.]aḫẓ[.---]l[-].|[ʻ]nt.akl[6[49].5.21
št.k[bd.---].|tgmr k[--.---].|ḫmšm a[--.---].|kbd [---].|d[.a]ǵlkz[.---]. 2120.12
ḥd.b gt.t̲rmn.|aḥd.alp.idt̲n.d aḫd.b.ʻnqpat.|[aḥd.al]p.d aǵlmn.|[d aḫd b.g]t gbry.|[---].aḥd.aḫd.b.yʻny.|[---.-]ḥm. 1129.12
mḫ.d.kly.k ṣḥ.illd̲rm.|b d.zlb[n.--].|arbʻ.ʻš[r.]dd.nʻr.|d.apy[.--].|w.arb[ʻ.--]d.apy.ʻbd h.|w.mrbʻ[t.l ʻ]bdm. 2094.4
[---.--]m.|[-----].|[---.]d arṣ.|[---.]ln.|[---.]nb hm.|[---.-]kn.|[---.]hr n.km.šḥr.|[-- 12[75].1.3
t̲b.ǵzr.mt hrnmy[.---].|b grnt.ilm.b qrb.m[t̲ʻt.ilnym].|d tit.yspi.spu.q[--.---].|tpḫ.t̲ṣr.shr[.---].|mr[.---]. 20[121].2.10
m kbd.|[---.-]nnm t̲rm.|[---.]t̲lt̲ kbd.ṣin.|[---.--]a.t̲[l]t̲.d.a[--].|[---].mrn.|[---.]bn pnt̲bl.|[---.-]py w.bn h. 1145.1.10
arbʻ.ʻšr h.šd.|w.kmsk.d.iwrkl.|t̲lt̲.šd.d.bn.mlkyy.|kmsk.šd.iḫmn.|širm.šd.khn.|t̲l 1079.2
[---].|[--].p il[.---].|[i]l mt mr[b-].|qdš mlk [---].|kbd d ilgb[-].|mrmnmn.|brrn aryn.|a[-]ḫn tlyn.|atdb w ʻr.|qdš UG5.1.70
qm h.w ʻbd.|ʻlm.t̲lt̲.sswm.mrkbt.|b trbṣt.bn.amt.|p d.in.b bt y.ttn.|tn.l y.mt̲t.ḥry.|nʻmt.špḥ.bkr k.|d k.nʻm.ʻnt. 14[KRT].3.142
mqm h.w ʻbd.|ʻlm.t̲lt̲.sswm.|mrkbt.b trbṣ.|bn.amt.p d.[i]n.|b bt y.ttn.tn.|l y.mt̲t.ḥry.|nʻmt.šbḥ.bkr k.|d k nʻm.ʻ 14[KRT].6.287
bʻl.b ḥnt h.abynt.|[d]nil.mt.rpi anḫ.ǵzr.|[mt.]hrnmy.d in.bn.l h.|km.aḫ h.w šrš.km.ary h.|bl.it̲.bn.l h.km aḫ h.w 17[2AQHT].1.19
bn.qrrn.|bn.dnt.|bn.t̲ʻl[-].|bdl.ar.dt.inn.|mhr l ht.|artyn.|ʻdmlk.|bn.alt[-].|iḫy[-].|ʻbdgt̲r.|ḥ 1035.1.4
md̲rǵlm.dt.inn.|b d.tlmyn.|b d.gln.ary.|tgyn.yʻrty.|bn.krwn.b.yny.i 2071.1
md̲rǵlm.d inn.|msgm.l hm.|pʻṣ.ḫbty.|artyn.ary.|brqn.t̲lḫy.|bn.ary 118[306].1
mm.b ysmm.ḥ[--]k.ǵrt.|[ql].l bʻl.ʻnt.ttnn.|[---].bʻl m.d ip[---].|[il.]hd.d ʻnn.n[--].|[----.]aliyn.b[ʻl].|[---.btl]t.ʻn[t.-. 10[76].2.32
ḫpn.d.iqni.w.šmt.|l.iybʻl.|t̲lt̲m.l.mit.šʻrt.|l.šr.ʻt̲trt.|mlbš.t̲rmnm 1107.1
[bn]šm.dt.iš[--].|[b]n.bʻl[--].|bn.gld.|bn.ṣmy.|bn.mry[n].|bn.mgn. 2117.1.1
bnšm.dt.it̲.alpm.l hm.|bn.niršn.|bn.adty.|bn.alz.|bn.birtn.|bn.m 2023.1.1
.bt.k anšt.w i[n.b ilht].|qlṣ k.tbʻ.bt.ḫnp.lb[k.--.ti]|ḫd.d it̲.b kbd k.tšt.b [---].|irt k.dt̲.ydt̲.mʻqb k.[ttbʻ].|[bt]lt.ʻnt.i 18[3AQHT].1.18
[---].dt.it̲.|[---].t̲lt̲.kbd.|[---].alpm.ḫmš.mat.|šbʻm[.t]šʻ.kbd.|tgm 1129.1
|[---].t̲l[l]m.[---].|[--].r[-]y[.---].|ʻl.[--]l[-] h.|ʻdn.[---].|d.u[--.---]. 2104.13
any.al[t̲y].|d b atlg[.---].|ḫmš ʻš[r].|kkr.t̲[lt̲].|t̲t hrt[m].|t̲n mq[pm].|ul 2056.2
md̲rǵlm.d.b.i[-]ʻlt.mlk.|arsw.|dqn.|t̲lt̲.klbm.|ḫmn.|[---.-]rsd.|bn[.-] 86[305].1
]n.ǵzr.|[mt.hrn]my.ytšu.|[yt̲b.b ap.t̲]ǵr[.t]ḫt.|[adrm.d b grn.y]dn.|[dn.almnt.y]t̲pt̲.|[t̲pt̲.ytm.---] h.|[---.---]n.|[-- 19[1AQHT].1.23
pi.a hn.ǵzr.mt.hrnm[y].|ytšu.yt̲b.b ap.t̲ǵr.t̲ḫt.|adrm.d b grn.ydn.|dn.almnt.yt̲pt̲.t̲pt̲.ytm.|b nši ʻn h.w yphn.b al 17[2AQHT].5.7
-]ḫ[-]y.ilak k.|[---.--]g k.yritn.mǵy.hy.w kn.|[---].ḥln.d b.dmt.um.il[m.---].|[--]d̲yn.bʻd.[--]d̲yn.w l.|[--]k bʻlt bht 1002.43
bbm.d |msdt.arṣ.|sʻ.il.dqt.k amr.|sknt.k ḥwt.yman.|d b h.rumm.l rbbt. 4[51].1.44
iqni.ʻp[ʻp] h.|sp.trml.thgrn.[-]dm[.-].|ašlw.b ṣp.ʻn h.|d b ḥlm y.il.ytn.|b d̲rt y.ab.adm.|w ld.špḥ.l krt.|w ǵlm.l ʻb 14[KRT].3.150
h.km.tsm.|ʻt̲trt.tsm h.|d ʻq h.ib.iqni.|ʻpʻp h.sp.trml.|d b ḥlm y.il.ytn.|b d̲rt y.ab.adm.|w ld.špḥ.l krk|t.w ǵlm.l ʻ 14[KRT].6.296
y[.---.]br.|ydn[.---].kry.|bn.ydd[.---.b]r.|prkl.bʻl.any.d.b d.abr[-]. 2123.7
.|kyn.|bʻln.|ytršp.|ḥmšm.t̲mn.kbd.|tgmr.bnš.mlk.|d.b d.adnʻm.|[š]bʻ.b.ḥrt̲m.|[t̲]lt̲.b.t̲ǵrm.|rb qrt.aḥd.|t̲mn.ḥz 1024.2.27
[sp]r.bnš.ml[k.d.b] d adn[ʻm].|[---].riš[.---].kt.|[y]nḥm.|ilbʻl.|ʻbdyr[ḫ].|t̲t 1024.1.1
npṣ.ʻ[--.---].|d.b d.a[--.---].|w.b d.b[--.---].|udbr[.---].|ʻrš[.---].|t̲l[ḫn.---]. 1120.2
rʻym.dt.b d.iytlm.|ḫyrn.w.šǵr h.|šǵr.bn.prsn.|agpt̲r.w.šǵ[r h].|t̲ʻ 2072.1
[bnšm.dt.]b d.mlk.|[---.b]d.mlkt.|[---.b]d.mlk.|[---.--]ḫ.uḫd.|[---. 2014.1
spr.updt.|d b d.mlkytn.|kdrl.|slt̲mg.|adrdn.|l[l]wn.|ydln.|ldn.|tdǵl 1034.2
šd.ubdy.ilštmʻ.|dt b d.skn.|šd.bn.ubrʻn b gt prn.|šd.bn.gby.gt.prn.|šd.bn.k 1104.2
spr.bnš.mlk.|d.b d.prt̲.|tšʻ.l.ʻšrm.|lqḥ.ššlmt.|t̲mn.l.arbʻm.|lqḥ.šʻrt. 1025.2
[s]p[r] ušknym.dt.[b d.---].|bn.btr.|bn.ʻms.|bn.pṣn.|bn.agmz.|bn.[--]n.|bn 2021.1.1
.---].|šy[.---].|bn.uḫn.|ybru.i[---].|[p]dyn.[---].|bnšm.d.b [d.---].|spḫy.[---].|[-----].|b[--.---].|nʻ[--.---].|[-----].|ḫn[2161.13
.|[---.--]sʻ.hn.mlk.|[---.l]qḥ.hn.l.ḥwt h.|[---.--]p.hn.ib.d.b.mgšḫ.|[---.i]b.hn[.w.]ht.ank.|[---.--]š[-.-].w.ašt.|[---].a 1012.10
k.mnm[.š]lm.|rgm.t̲t̲[b].|any kn.dt.|likt.mṣrm.|hn dt.b.ṣr.|mtt.by.|gšm.adr.|nškḥ.w.|rb.tmtt.|lqḥ.kl.d̲rʻ.|b d 2059.12
.nqmpʻ.|mlk.ugrt.|ytn.bt.annd̲r.|bn.ytn.bnš.|[ml]k.d.b riš.|[--.-]nt.|[l.ʻb]dmlk.|[--.-]m[-]r.|[w.l.]bn h.ʻd.|[ʻl]m. 1009.7
r.bn.|nqmpʻ.ml[k].|ugrt.ytn.|šd.kd̲ǵdl[.bn].|[-]š[-]y.d.b š[-]y.|[---.y]d gt h[.--].|[---.]yd.|[k]rm h.yd.|[k]lkl h.|[1008.6
[s]pr.bnš.mlk.d.b.tbq.|[kr]wn.|[--]n.|[q]ṣy.|t̲n.bn.iwrḫz.[n]ʻrm.|yṣr[.-]qb 2066.1.1
h.w yṣḥ.|ḥwt.aḫt.w nar[-].|qrn.d bat k.btlt.ʻnt.|qrn.d bat k bʻl.ymšḥ.|bʻl.ymšḥ.hm.b ʻp.|ntʻn.b arṣ.ib y.|w b ʻpr 10[76].2.22

.ykr'.w yql. | w yšu.g h.w yṣḥ. | ḥwt.aḫt.w nar[-]. | qrn.d bat k.btlt.'nt. | qrn.d bat k b'l.ymšḥ. | b'l.ymšḥ.hm.b 'p. | nṭ 10[76].2.21
bnšm.d.bu. | tš'.dt.tq[ḥn]. | š'rt. | šb' dt tqḥn. | ššlmt. 2099.1
.'dn.m'. | ṣbu k.ul.mad. | tlṯ.mat.rbt. | ḫpṯ.d bl.spr. | ṯnn.d bl.hg. | hlk.l alpm.ḫḏḏ. | w l rbt.kmyr. | [a]ṯr.ṯn.ṯn.hlk. | aṯr. 14[KRT].2.91
bi.ngb. | w yṣi.'dn.m'. | ṣbu k.ul.mad. | ṯlṯ.mat.rbt. | ḫpṯ.d bl.spr. | ṯnn.d bl.hg. | hlk.l alpm.ḫḏḏ. | w l rbt.kmyr. | [a]ṯr.ṯ 14[KRT].2.90
rt. | kd.'l.ẓrm. | kd.'l.šz.bn pls. | kd.'l.ynḥm. | tgrm.šmn.d.bn.kwy. | 'l.šlmym.ṯmn.kbd. | ṯṯm.šmn. 1082.2.8
arb'.'šr h.šd. | w.kmsk.d.iwrkl. | ṯlṯ.šd.d.bn.mlkyy. | kmsk.šd.iḫmn. | širm.šd.khn. | ṯlṯ.šd.w.krm.šir. 1079.3
bṯ[--]. | [bn].ḫla[n]. | [bn].ǵr[--]. | d.b[n.---]. | d.bn.[---]. | d.bn.š[--]. | d.bn.ṯn[r]. | d.kmry. 2164.B.3
. | b.ṯmq.ḫmšt.l.'šrt. | b.[---].šb't.'šrt. | b.bn.pdrn.'šrm. | d.bn.šb'l.uḫnpy.ḫmšm. | b.bn.ṯtm.ṯlṯm. | b.bn.agdṯb.'šrm. | b. 2054.1.10
].ḫla[n]. | [bn].ǵr[--]. | d.b[n.---]. | d.bn.[---]. | d.bn.š[--]. | d.bn.ṯn[r]. | d.kmry. 2164.B.4
d[-]. | [bn].ṣbṭ[--]. | [bn].ḫla[n]. | [bn].ǵr[--]. | d.b[n.---]. | d.bn.[---]. | d.bn.š[--]. | d.bn.ṯn[r]. | d.kmry. 2164.B.2
]. | [bn].amd[-]. | [bn].ṣbṭ[--]. | [bn].ḫla[n]. | [bn].ǵr[--]. | d.b[n.---]. | d.bn.[---]. | d.bn.š[--]. | d.bn.ṯn[r]. | d.kmry. 2164.B.1
--.]y[--.-]kzn. | [---.]yn.l.m[---]. | [---.]yn.l.m[--]m. | [---.]d.bn.[---.]l.dqn. | [---.--]'.šdyn.l ytršn. | [---.--]t.'bd.l.kyn. | k[r 2027.2.7
mǵy.bnš[.---]. | w ḥmr[.---]. | w m'n[.---]. | w bn[š.---]. | d bnš.ḥm[r.---]. | w d.l mdl.r[--.---]. | w ṣin.'z.b['l.---]. | llu.bn[2158.1.12
[---.ṯ]lṯ.'š[r h.---]. | d bnšm.yd.grbs hm. | w.ṯn.'šr h.ḫpnt. | [š]šwm.amtm.'kyt. | y 2049.2
tq.ṯn.ql'm. | ḫmš.ṣmdm.w ḥrṣ. | tryn.ššwm. | tryn.aḥd.d bnš. | arb'.ṣmdm.apnt. | w ḥrṣ. | tš'm.mrḥ.aḥd. | kbd. 1123.6
| w.arb'.ḥršm. | dt.tb'ln.b.pḫn. | ṯṯtm.ḫzr.w.'št.'šr.ḥrš. | dt.tb'ln.b.ugrt. | ṯṯtm.ḫzr. | dt.tb'ln. | b.gt.ḥršm. | ṯn.ḥršm. | [-] 1024.3.8
ḫn. | ṯṯtm.ḫzr.w.'št.'šr.ḥrš. | dt.tb'ln.b.ugrt. | ṯṯtm.ḫzr. | dt.tb'ln. | b.gt.ḥršm. | ṯn.ḥršm. | [-]nbkm. | ṯn.ḥršm. | b.gt.ǵl. | [- 1024.3.10
ṯm. | [ṯ]lṯ.b.ṯǵrm. | rb qrt.aḥd. | ṯmn.ḫzr. | w.arb'.ḥršm. | dt.tb'ln.b.pḫn. | ṯṯtm.ḫzr.w.'št.'šr.ḥrš. | dt.tb'ln.b.ugrt. | ṯṯtm. 1024.3.6
ym.ḥdṯ. | b.yrḫ.pgrm. | lqḥ.b'lm'dr. | w bn.ḫlp. | w[--]y.d.b'l. | miḫd.b. | arb'.mat. | ḫrṣ. 1155.5
l.yi[--.-]m[---]. | b unṯ.km.špš. | d brt.kmt. | br.ṣṭqšlm. | b unṯ.'d 'lm. | mišmn.nqmd. | mlk ugr 1001.1.19
mn.nqmd. | mlk ugrt. | nqmd.mlk.ugrt. | ktb.spr hnd. | dt brrt.ṣṭqšlm. | 'bd h.hnd. | w mn km.l yqḥ. | spr.mlk.hnd. | b 1005.10
[---.]d.ztm.d.si[-]. | [---.]d.ztm.d ggy.[---]. | [---.d].ztm.d.b[--]. | [---.]ztm.[---]. 2035.3
šḫry.š.il.t'dr.b'l.š.ršp.š.ddmš.š. | w šlmm.ilib.š.i[l.--]m d gbl.ṣpn.al[p]. | pḫr.ilm.š.ym.š[.k]nr.š.[--.]'ṣrm gdlt. | b'lm.k UG5.9.1.10
[---.]d.ztm.d.si[-]. | [---.]d.ztm.d ggy.[---]. | [---.d].ztm.d.b[--]. | [---.]ztm.[---]. 2035.2
| b'l m.ht.ib k.tmḫṣ.ht.tṣmt.ṣrt k. | tqḥ.mlk.'lm k.drkt.dt dr dr k. | kṯr ṣmdm.ynḥt.w yp'r.šmt hm.šm k at. | ygrš.yg 2.4[68].10
---.-]l[-.-]hg[.---]. | [---.-]r[-.il]m.rbm.n'l[.-]gr. | [---.]'ṣ.b d h.ydrm[.]pi[-.]adm. | [---.]iṯ[-].yšql.ytk[.--]np bl.hn. | [---].ḥ UG5.8.32
spr.mḏr[ǵlm]. | lt.hlk.b[.---]. | bn.b'yn.š[--.---]. | aǵltn.mid[-.---]. | bn.lṣn.'rm[y 87[64].2
ymm. | w rbt.šnt. | b 'd 'lm...gn'. | iršt.aršt. | l aḫ y.l r' y.dt. | w ytnnn. | l aḫ h.l r' h. | r' 'lm. | ttn.w tn. | w l ttn. | w al tt 1019.1.8
w.mlk.yštal.b.hn[--]. | hmt.w.anyt.hm.t'[rb]. | mkr.hn d.w.rgm.ank[.--]. | mlkt.ybqš.anyt.w.at[--]. | w mkr n.mlk[.-- 2008.2.12
lkt. | adt y. | rgm. | tḥm.tlmyn. | 'bd k. | l.p'n. | adt y. | šb' d. | w.šb' id. | mrḥqtm. | qlt. | 'm.adt y. | mnm.šlm. | rgm.ṯṯb. | l 52[89].8
r[gm]. | tḥm.rb.mi[--.']bd k. | l.p'n.b'l y[.mrḥqtm]. | šb' d.w.šb'[d.qlt]. | ankn.rgmt.l.b'l y. | l.špš.'lm.l.'ṯtrt. | l.'nt.l.kl.i 2008.1.5
mlkt. | adt y.rgm. | tḥm.illdr. | 'bd k.. | l.p'n a[dt y]. | šb' d[.w šb' d]. | mrḥq[tm.qlt]. | mn[m.šlm]. 1014.6
[---.]d.ztm.d.si[-]. | [---.]d.ztm.d ggy.[---]. | [---.d].ztm.d.b[--]. | [---.]ztm.[---]. 2035.3
[---.]d.ztm.d.si[-]. | [---.]d.ztm.d ggy.[---]. | [---.d].ztm.d.b[--]. | [---.]ztm.[---]. 2035.2
[---.]d.ztm.d.si[-]. | [---.]d.ztm.d ggy.[---]. | [---.d].ztm.d.b[--]. | [---. 2035.1
| mṯt.dnty.t'db.imr. | b pḫd.l npš.kṯr.w ḫss. | l brlt.hyn.d ḥrš. | ydm.aḥr.ymǵy.kṯr. | w ḫss.b d.dnil.ytnn. | qšt.l brk h. 17[2AQHT].5.24
mṯt.dnty.'d[b]. | imr.b pḫd.l npš.kṯr. | w ḫss.l brlt.hyn d. | ḥrš yd.šlḥm.ššqy. | ilm sad.kbd.hmt.b'l. | ḥkpt.il.kl h.tšm' 17[2AQHT].5.18
l.tštḥ | wy.w kbd hwt. | w rgm.l kṯr. | w ḫss.ṯny.l h | yn.d ḥrš.ydm. | tḥm.al[iyn.b'l]. | h[wt.aliy.qrdm]. 3['NT.VI].6.23
l.t[štḥwy.w kbd.hwt]. | w rgm l k[ṯr.w ḫss.ṯny.l hyn]. | d ḥrš.y[dm.tḥm.ṯr.il.ab k.] | hwt.lṭpn[.ḥtk k.---]. | yh.kṯr.b[-- 1['NT.IX].3.5
abb[.---]. | [---.-]k[-.-]n[-]. | [---.--]m.šr.d.yṯ[b]. | [---.--]y.d.ḫbṯ.sy[--]. | [---.--]y.b.bt.ṯr[--]. 2134.10
lkyy. | kmsk.šd.iḫmn. | širm.šd.khn. | ṯlṯ.šd.w.krm.šir.d.ḥli. | širm.šd.šd.'šy. | w.šir.šd.krm. | d.krwn. | šir.šd.šd.'šy. | 1079.6
ḫmš.mat.kbd. | ṯlṯm.ḫmš kbd ktn. | ḫmš.rṭm. | ḫmš.ṯnt.d ḫmšm w. | ḫmš.ṯnt.d mit. | ḫmš.ṯnt.d ṯl | ṯ mat. | ṯt.ṯnt.d alp 1130.9
h.yrd.krt. | [l g]gt.'db.akl.l qryt. | ḥṯt.l bt.ḫbr. | yip.lḥm.d ḫmš. | [mǵ]d.ṯdṯ.yr[ḫm]. | 'dn.ngb.w [yṣi.ṣbu]. | ṣbi.ng[b.w 14[KRT].4.174
yrd. | krt.l ggt.'db. | akl.l qryt. | ḥṯt.l bt.ḫbr. | yip.lḥm.d ḫmš. | mǵd.ṯdṯ.yrḫm. | 'dn.ngb.w yṣi. | ṣbu.ṣbi.ngb. | w yṣi.' 14[KRT].2.83
[-]r[--.--]y. | in m.'bd k hwt. | [y]rš.'m y. | mnm.iršt k. | d ḫsrt.w.ank. | aštn..l iḫ y. | w.ap.ank.mnm. | [ḫ]s[r]t.w.uḫ y. 2065.16
ḥm. | aliyn.b'l. | [hw]t.aliy.q | [rdm.]bht y.bnt. | [dt.ksp.dtm]. | [ḫrṣ.hk]l y. | [---.]aḫ y. | [---.]aḫ y. | [----]y. | [---.]rb. | [- 4[51].8.36
.ḫrṣ. | nṣb.l lbnt.šmḫ. | aliyn.b'l.ht y.bnt. | dt.ksp.hkl y.dtm. | ḫrṣ.'dbt.bht[h.b']l. | y'db.hd.'db[.'d]bt. | hkl h.ṭbḫ.alp 4[51].6.37
. | 'šrm.ksp.d mkr. | mlk. | ṯlṯ.mat.ksp.d.šb[n]. | mit.ksp.d.ṯbq. | ṯmnym.arb't. | kbd.ksp. | d.nqdm. | ḫmšm.l mit. | ksp.d 2107.5
'nm. | ṯṯ.b'd n.ksl.ṯṯbr. | 'ln.pn h.td'.ṯǵṣ.pnt. | ksl h.anš.dt.ẓr h.tšu. | g h.w tṣḥ.ik.mǵy.gpn.w ugr. | mn.ib.yp'.l b'l.ṣrt. 3['NT].3.32
ṯṯ.b ']dn.ksl. | [ṯṯbr.'ln.p]n h.td['']. | ṯǵṣ[.pnt.ks]l h. | anš.dt.ẓr.[h]. | tšu.g h.w tṣḥ[.i]k. | mǵy.aliy[n.b]'l. | ik.mǵyt.b[t]lt. 4[51].2.20
ṯṯ.'l[n.pn h.td'.b 'dn]. | ksl.y[ṯbr.yǵṣ.pnt.ksl h]. | anš.[dt.ẓr h.yšu.g h]. | w yṣ[ḥ.---]. | mḫṣ[.---]. | š[--.---]. 19[1AQHT].2.96
d.ṯlṯ.šm[n]. | alp.mitm.kbd.ṯlṯ.ḥlb. | šb'.l.'šrm.kkr.ṯlṯ. | d.ybl.blym. 1135.7
at pḥm. | [ḫm]š[.m]at.iqnu. | argmn.nqmd.mlk. | ugrt.d ybl.l špš. | mlk.rb.b'l h. | ks.ḫrṣ.ktn.mit.pḥm. | mit.iqni.l ml 64[118].25
pllm.mlk.r[b.--]. | mṣmt.l nqmd.[---.-]št. | hl ny.argmn.d [ybl.n]qmd. | l špš.arn.ṯn[.'šr h.]mn. | 'ṣrm.ṯql.kbd[.ks].mn. 64[118].18
g['t]. | b.'šrt.ksp. | ṯlṯ.uṭbm.b d.alḫn.b.'šrt[.k]sp. | rṯ.l.ql.d.ybl.prd. | b.ṯql.w.nṣp.ksp. | ṯmn.lbšm.w.mšlt. | l.udmym.b.ṯ 2101.12
| utly. | bn.alz. | bn ḫlm. | bn.ḏmr. | bn.'yn. | ubnyn. | rpš d ydy. | ǵbl. | mlk. | gwl. | rqd. | ḫlby. | 'n[q]pat. | m[']rb. | 'rm. | b 2075.20
. | trṯ.'d.škr.y'db.yrḫ. | gb h.km.[---.]yqṭqṭ.tḥt. | ṯlḥnt.il.d yd'nn. | y'db.lḥm.l h.w d l yd'nn. | d.mṣd. | ylmn.ḫṭ.tḥt.ṯlḥn UG5.1.1.6
. | d.abmn. | šir.šd.krm. | d.yrmn. | šir.[š]d.mlth.šd.'šy. | d.ynḥm. | tgmr.šd.ṯlṯm.šd. | w.tr[--.---]. 1079.15
il.d qblbl. | 'ln.ybl hm.ḫrṣ. | ṯlḥn.il.d mla. | mnm.dbbm.d | msdt.arṣ. | s'.il.dqt.k amr. | sknt.k ḥwt.yman. | d b h.rum 4[51].1.40
ṯlṯ.d yṣa. | b d.šmmn. | l argmn. | l nskm. | ṯmn.kkrm. | alp.kbd. | [147[90].1
spr.npṣm.d yṣa.b milḫ. | 'šrm.ḫpn.ḫmš. | kbd.w lpš. | ḫmš.mispt. | mṭ. | 1109.1
tm. | inn.uṭpt. | w.ṯlṯ.ṣmdm.w.ḥrṣ. | apnt.b d.rb.ḥršm. | d.ššа.ḥwy h. 1121.10
.l ṯr.ab h.il.tḥm.ym.b'l km. | [adn]km.ṯpṭ.nhr.tn.il m.d tq h.d tqyn h. | [hml]t.tn.b'l.w 'nn h.bn.dgn.arṯ m.pḏ h. | [2.1[137].34

d

l pẖr].|m‘d.tḥm.ym.b‘l km.adn km.ṯ[pṭ.nhr].|tn.il m.d tq h.d tqyn.hmlt.tn.b‘l.[w ‘nn h].|bn.dgn.arṯ m.pḏ h.tb‘.ǵ 2.1[137].18
h.il.tḥm.ym.b‘l km.|[adn]km.ṯpṭ.nhr.tn.il m.d tq h.d tqyn h.|[hml]t.tn.b‘l.w ‘nn h.bn.dgn.arṯ m.pḏ h.|[w y‘n.] 2.1[137].34
m‘d.tḥm.ym.b‘l km.adn km.ṯ[pṭ.nhr].|tn.il m.d tq h.d tqyn.hmlt.tn.b‘l.[w ‘nn h].|bn.dgn.arṯ m.pḏ h.tb‘.ǵlmm.l 2.1[137].18
.šd.krm.|d.krwn.|šir.šd.šd.‘šy.|d.abmn.|šir.šd.krm.|d.yrmn.|šir.[š]d.mltḥ.šd.‘šy.|d.ynḥm.|tgmr.šd.ṯlṯm.šd.|w.t 1079.13
l.yd[‘t].|hlk.kbkbm.mdl.‘r.|ṣmd.pḥl.št.gpn y dt ksp.|dt.yrq.nqbn y.tš[m‘].|pǵt.ṯkmt.my.ḥspt.l[š‘]r.ṭl.|yd‘t.hlk.k 19[1AQHT].2.54
gy.rbt].|aṯrt.ym[.mdl.‘r].|ṣmd.pḥl[.št.gpnm.dt].|ksp.dt.yr[q.nqbnm].|‘db.gpn.atnt[y].|yšm‘.qd.w amr[r].|mdl.‘ 4[51].4.6
yšm‘.qd.w amr[r].|mdl.‘r.ṣmd.pḥl.|št.gpnm.dt.ksp.|dt.yrq.nqbnm.|‘db.gpn.atnt h.|yḥbq.qdš.w amrr.|yštn.aṯrt. 4[51].4.11
ṯn.‘šr.yn.[kps]lnm.|arb‘.mat[.arb]‘m.[k]bd.|d ntn.d.ksp.|arb‘.l.ẖlby.|[---].l.bt.|arb‘.l.kpslnm.|kdm.b[t.] 1087.3
[--].d.ntn[.d.]ksp.|[ṯ]mn.l.‘šrm[.l.b]t.‘ṯtrt.|[ṯ]lṯ.‘šr h.[b]t.ršp.gn. 1088.1
b gt ilštm‘.|bt ubnyn š h d.ytn.ṣṭqn.|ṭut ṭbẖ ṣṭq[n].|b bz ‘zm ṭbẖ š[h].|b kl ygz ḥẖ š 1153.2
[-]h.|nn[-].b[n].py[-.d.]yṯb.b.gt.aǵld.|šgn.bn b[--.---].d.yṯb.b.ilštm‘.|abmn.bn.r[---].b.syn.|bn.irṣ[-.---.]h.|šdyn.b[2015.2.6
yṯb.b.ar.|bn.ag[p]ṯ.ẖpṯ.d[.yṯb.b].š‘rt.|yly.bn.ṯrnq.[-]r.d.yṯb.b.ilštm‘.|ilšlm.bn.gs[-.--]r.d.yṯb.b.gt.al.|ilmlk.[--]kt.[- 2015.1.26
.š‘rt.|yly.bn.ṯrnq.[-]r.d.yṯb.b.ilštm‘.|ilšlm.bn.gs[-.--]r.d.yṯb.b.gt.al.|ilmlk.[--]kt.[--.d.]yṯb.b.šb[n].|bn.pr[-.]d.y[ṯb. 2015.1.27
]ḥl h[.-].ṯgd.mrum.|bt.[-]b[-.-]sy[-]h.|nn[-].b[n].py[-.d.]yṯb.b.gt.aǵld.|šgn.bn b[--.---].d.yṯb.b.ilštm‘.|abmn.bn.r[- 2015.2.5
.ilštm‘.|ilšlm.bn.gs[-.--]r.d.yṯb.b.gt.al.|ilmlk.[--]kt.[--.d.]yṯb.b.šb[n].|bn.pr[-.]d.y[ṯb.b].šlmy.|tlš.w[.n]ḥl h[.-].ṯgd. 2015.2.1
.d.yṯb.b.gt.al.|ilmlk.[--]kt.[--.d.]yṯb.b.šb[n].|bn.pr[-.]d.y[ṯb.b].šlmy.|tlš.w[.n]ḥl h[.-].ṯgd.mrum.|bt.[-]b[-.-]sy[-]h 2015.2.2
-].ar.|bn.[---].b.ar.|špšyn[.---.]yṯb.b.ar.|bn.ag[p]ṯ.ẖpṯ.d[.yṯb.b].š‘rt.|yly.bn.ṯrnq.[-]r.d.yṯb.b.ilštm‘.|ilšlm.bn.gs[-.-- 2015.1.25
-].|bn.pynq.‘nqp[a]t[y.---].|ayiẖ.ilšt[m‘y.---].|[b]dlm.dt.yṯb[.---].|[-]y[--].‘nqp[aty.---].|‘ṯt[r]n.[-]bṭ[-.---].|[---]n.š[- 90[314].2.10
.-]ṯby[.---].|[---].abb[.---].|[---.-]k[-.-]n[-].|[---.--]m.šr.d.yṯ[b].|[---.--]y.d.ẖbṯ.sy[--].|[---.--]y.b.bt.ṯr[--]. 2134.9
[---]m.d.yṯ[--.]l[-].|ršp.ẖmš.[m]šl[t].|[--]arš[p.-]š.l[h].|[-]ṯl[.--]š.l 2133.1
.p d.[i]n.|b bt y.ttn.tn.|l y.mṯt.ḥry.|n‘mt.šbḥ.bkr k.|d k n‘m.‘nt.|n‘m h.km.tsm.|‘ṯtrt.tsm h.|d ‘q h.ib.iqni.|‘p‘p 14[KRT].6.291
t.|p d.in.b bt y.ttn.|tn.l y.mṯt.ḥry.|n‘mt.špḥ.bkr k.|d k.n‘m.‘nt.n‘m h.|km.tsm.‘ṯtrt.ts[m h].|d ‘q h.ib.iqni.‘p[‘p 14[KRT].3.145
.|qrym.ab.dbḥ.l ilm.|š‘ly.dǵṯ h.b šmym.|dǵṯ.hrnmy.d kbkbm.|l tbrkn.alk brkt.|tmrn.alk.nmr[rt].|imẖṣ.mẖṣ.aẖ 19[1AQHT].4.193
m.ǵr.w yq.|dbḥ.ilm.yš‘ly.dǵṯ h.|b šmym.dǵṯ hrnmy[.d k]|bkbm.‘[l.---].|[-]l h.yd ‘d[.---].|ltm.mrqdm.d š[-]l[-].| 19[1AQHT].4.186
ln].|klny n[.n]bl.ks h.|[an]y.l yṣḥ.ṯr il.ab h.|[i]l.mlk.d yknn h.yṣḥ.|aṯrt.w bn h.ilt.w ṣbrt.|ary h.wn.in.bt.l b‘l.|k 4[51].4.48
š h.|nbln.klny y.nbl.ks h.|any.l yṣḥ.ṯr.il.ab h.il.|mlk.d yknn h.yṣḥ.aṯrt.|w bn h.ilt.w ṣbrt.arẖ h.|wn.in.bt.l b‘l.k 3[‘NT.VI].5.44
---].|[---.--]y.|[-----].|[any.l yṣ]ḥ.ṯr.|[il.ab h.i]l.mlk.|[d yknn h.yṣ]ḥ.aṯ|[rt.w bn h.]ilt.|[w ṣbrt.ary]h.|[wn.in.bt.l 4[51].1.7
[nq]dm.dt.kn.npṣ hm.|[bn].lbn.arb‘.qšt.w.ar[b‘].|[u]ṯpt.ql‘.w.ṯt.mr[2047.1
‘rb.|b.mtn.bn.ayaẖ.|b.ẖbṯ h.ḥwt.ṯt h.|w.mnm.šalm.|dt.tknn.|‘l.‘rbnm.|hn hmt.|tknn.|mtn.bn.‘bdym.|ilrb.bn.il 1161.6
[mm].|w y‘ny.aliyn[.b‘l].|lm.k qnym.‘l[m.--].|k dr d.d yknn[.--].|b‘l.yṣǵd.mli[.--].|il hd.mla.u[--.--].|blt.p btlt.‘n 10[76].3.7
qmḥ.d.kly.b bt.skn.|l.illḏrm.|ltḥ.ẖṣr.b.šb‘.ddm. 2093.1
yn.d.ykl.b d.[---].|b.dbḥ.mlk.|dbḥ ṣpn.|[-]zǵm.|[i]lib.|[i]lbldn 2004.1
qmḥ.d.kly.k ṣḥ.illḏrm.|b d.zlb[n.--].|arb‘.‘š[r.]dd.n‘r.|d.apy[.--]. 2094.1
].ǵr[--].|d.b[n.---].|d.bn.[---].|d.bn.š[--].|d.bn.ṯn[r].|d.kmry. 2164.B.5
il.ǵzr.tḥm.|aliyn.b‘l.|[hw]t.aliy.q|[rdm.]bht y.bnt.|[dt.ksp.dtm].|[ẖrṣ.hk]l y.|[---.]aẖ y.|[---.]aẖ y.|[----]y.|[---. 4[51].8.36
pt.l š‘r.ṭl.yd[‘t].|hlk.kbkbm.mdl.‘r.|ṣmd.pḥl.št.gpn y dt ksp.|dt.yrq.nqbn y.tš[m‘].|pǵt.ṯkmt.my.ḥspt.l[š‘]r.ṭl.|y 19[1AQHT].2.53
am[rr.l dgy.rbt].|aṯrt.ym[.mdl.‘r].|ṣmd.pḥl[.št.gpnm.dt].|ksp.dt.yr[q.nqbnm].|‘db.gpn.atnt[y].|yšm‘.qd.w amr[4[51].4.5
tnt[y].|yšm‘.qd.w amr[r].|mdl.‘r.ṣmd.pḥl.|št.gpnm.dt.ksp.|dt.yrq.nqbnm.|‘db.gpn.atnt h.|yḥbq.qdš.w amrr.| 4[51].4.10
sb.ksp.l rqm.ẖrṣ.|nṣb.l lbnt.šmẖ.|aliyn.b‘l.ht y.bnt.|dt.ksp.hkl y.dtm.|ẖrṣ.‘dbt.bht[h.b‘]l.|y‘db.hd.‘db[.‘d]bt.|h 4[51].6.37
ṯn.‘šr.yn.[kps]lnm.|arb‘.mat[.arb]‘m.[k]bd.|d ntn.d.ksp.|arb‘.l.ẖlby.|[---].l.bt.|arb‘.l.kpslnm.|kdm.b[t.]mlk. 1087.3
[--].d.ntn[.d.]ksp.|[ṯ]mn.l.‘šrm[.l.b]t.‘ṯtrt.|[ṯ]lṯ.‘šr h.[b]t.ršp.gn.|arb‘.b 1088.1
|ṯlṯ.šd.w.krm.šir.d.ẖli.|širm.šd.šd.‘šy.|w.šir.šd.krm.|d.krwn.|šir.šd.šd.‘šy.|d.abmn.|šir.šd.krm.|d.yrmn.|šir.[š] 1079.9
-].bt.alp w š.|[---.--]m.l gṯrm.|[---.]l ‘nt m.|[---.--]rm.d krm.|[---].l ‘nt m.|[---.]l šlm.|[-]l[-.-]ry.ylbš.|mlk.ylk.lqḥ. 33[5].19
[---.]ḥlmt.alp.šnt.w[.---].|šntm.alp.d krr[.---].|alp.pr.b‘l.[---].|w prt.tkt.[---].|šnt.[---].|šsw.‘ṯtrt 2158.1.2
ḥršm.|k.rgmt.l y.bly m.|alpm.aršt.l k.w.l y.|mn.bnš.d.l.i[--].‘[m k].|l.alpm.w.l.y[n.--]t.|w.bl.bnš.hw[-.--]y.|w.k. 2064.24
bnšm.dt.l.u[--]ṯṯb.|kṯ[r]n.|w.aṯt h.w.n‘r h.|bn.ẖby.w.[a]ṯt h.|ynḥ 2068.1
h[--.---].|yrmm h[--.---].|mlk.gb‘ h d [---].|ibr.k l hm.d l h q[--.---].|l ytn.l hm.tḥt b‘l[.---].|h.u qšt pn hdd.b y[.-- 9[33].2.4
bd.yn.d.l.ṭb.|b.gt.m‘rby.|ṯṯm.yn.ṭb.w.ẖmš.l.‘šrm.|yn.d.l.ṭb.b.ulm.|mit.yn.ṭb.w.ṯṯm.ṯṯ.kbd.|yn.d.l.ṭb.b.gt.ḥdṯt.|tš‘ 1084.10
bd].yn.b gt[.-]n.|arb‘m.kbd.yn.ṭb.w.[--].|ṯmn.kbd.yn.d.l.ṭb.b.gn‘[y].|mitm.yn.ḥsp.d.nkly.b.db[ḥ.--].|mit.arb‘m.k 1084.23
šm.k[dm.]kbd.yn.d.l.ṭb.|b.gt.gwl.|ṯlṯm.tš‘[.kbd.yn].d.l[.ṭb].b.gt.ipṯl.|ṯmnym.[yn].ṭb.b.gt.š[---].|tš‘m.[ẖ]mš[.kbd 1084.19
t.sǵy.|arb‘m.kdm.kbd.yn.ṭb.|w.ẖmšm.k[dm.]kbd.yn.d.l.ṭb.|b.gt.gwl.|ṯlṯm.tš‘[.kbd.yn].d.l[.ṭb].b.gt.ipṯl.|ṯmnym.[1084.17
š.l.‘šrm.|yn.d.l.ṭb.b.ulm.|mit.yn.ṭb.w.ṯṯm.ṯṯ.kbd.|yn.d.l.ṭb.b.gt.ḥdṯt.|tš‘m.yn.d.l.ṭb.b.zbl.|‘šrm.yn.ṭb.w.ṯṯm.ẖmš. 1084.12
n.d.l.ṭb.gt.ṭbq.|mit.‘šr.kbd.yn.ṭb.|w.ṯṯm.arb‘.kbd.yn.d.l.ṭb.|b.gt.m‘rby.|ṯṯm.yn.ṭb.w.ẖmš.l.‘šrm.|yn.d.l.ṭb.b.ulm. 1084.7
tš‘m.yn.d.l.ṭb.b.zbl.|‘šrm.yn.ṭb.w.ṯṯm.ẖmš.k[b]d.|yn.d.l.ṭb.b.gt.sǵy.|arb‘m.kdm.kbd.yn.ṭb.|w.ẖmšm.k[dm.]kbd. 1084.15
|mit.yn.ṭb.w.ṯṯm.ṯṯ.kbd.|yn.d.l.ṭb.b.gt.ḥdṯt.|tš‘m.yn.d.l.ṭb.b.zbl.|‘šrm.yn.ṭb.w.ṯṯm.ẖmš.k[b]d.|yn.d.l.ṭb.b.gt.sǵy. 1084.13
‘m.yn.ẖlq.b.gt.sknm.|‘šr.yn.ṭb.w.arb‘m.ẖmš.kbd.|yn.d.l.ṭb.gt.ṭbq.|mit.‘šr.kbd.yn.ṭb.|w.ṯṯm.arb‘.kbd.yn.d.l.ṭb.|b 1084.5
ẖmš.‘šr.yn.ṭb.|w.tš‘m.kdm.kbd.yn.d.l.ṭb.|w.arb‘m.yn.ẖlq.b.gt.sknm.|‘šr.yn.ṭb.w.arb‘m.ẖmš.k 1084.2
spr.rpš d l y[dy].|atlg.|ulm.|izly.|uẖnp.|bn sẖrn.|m‘qb.|ṯpn.|m‘r 2075.1
[---.]btlt.‘nt.|[---.]pp.hrm.|[---].d l yd‘ bn il.|[---.]pẖr kkbm.|[---.]dr dt.šmm.|[---.al]iyn b‘l. 10[76].1.3
h.km.[---.]yqṯqṭ.tḥt.|ṯlḥnt.il.d yd‘nn.|y‘db.lḥm.l h.w d l yd‘nn.|d.mṣd.|ylmn.ẖṭ.tḥt.ṯlḥn.|b qr‘.|‘ṯtrt.w ‘nt.ymǵy UG5.1.1.7
ẖšt.abn[.tant.šmm.‘m.arṣ.thmt].|‘m kbkbm[.abn.brq.d l td‘.šmm.at m].|w ank.ib[ǵy h.---].|[-].l y‘mdn.i[---.---].| 7.2[130].20
.a]rṣ.[tant.šmm.‘m.ar]ṣ.|thmt.[‘mn.kbkbm.abn.brq].|d l t[d‘.šmm.at m.w ank].|ibǵ[y h.b tk.ǵ]r y.il.ṣpn.|b q[dš.b 3[‘NT].4.62
št.abn.|tant.šmm.‘m.arṣ.|thmt.‘mn.kbkbm.|abn.brq.d l.td‘.šmm.|rgm l td‘.nšm.w l tbn.|hmlt.arṣ.at m.w ank.|i 3[‘NT].3.23

. | ‘šrt.ḫrṣ.b.arb‘m. | mit.ḫršḫ.b.ṯqlm. | w.šb‘.‘šr.šmn. | d.l.yṣa.bt.mlk. | tgmr.ksp.mitm. | ḫmšm.kbd. 2100.21
mr[.---]. | w m‘n[.---]. | w bn[š.---]. | d bnš.ḥm[r.---]. | w d.l mdl.r[--.---]. | w ṣin.‘z.b[‘l.---]. | llu.bn[š.---]. | imr.ḫ[--.---]. 2158.1.13
bn.ṯny.uškny. | mnn.w.aṯt h. | slmu.ḥrš.mrkbt. | bnšm.dt.l.mlk. | ‘bdyrḫ.bn.ṯyl. | ‘bdn.w.aṯt h.w.bn h. | gpn.bn[.a]ly. 2068.17
.‘m k. | [-]tn.l.stn. | [--.]d.n‘m.lbš k. | [-]dm.ṯn id. | [--]m.d.l.n‘mm. | [lm.]l.likt.‘m y. | [---.]‘bd.ank. | [---.‘b]d k. | [---.--]l 2128.1.6
m trm.d [ṣ]py. | w.trm.aḥdm. | ṣpym. | ṯlṯ mrkbt mlk. | d.l.ṣpy. | [---.t]r hm. | [---].šš̀b. | [---.]tr h. | [a]rb‘.ql‘m. | arb‘.m 1122.6
n. | šlm.ṯm ny. | ‘m k.mnm[.š]lm. | rgm.ṯṯ[b]. | any kn.dt. | likt.mṣrm. | hn dt.b.ṣr. | mtt.by. | gšm.adr. | nškḥ.w. | rb.t 2059.10
rpḫn. | bn y.aḫ y.rgm. | ilm.tǵr k. | tšlm k. | iky.lḥt. | spr.d likt. | ‘m.ṯryl. | mh y.rgmt. | w ht.aḫ y. | bn y.yšal. | ṯryl.p rg 138.7
pḫn. | bn y.aḫ y.rgm. | ilm.tǵr k. | tšlm k. | ik y.lḥt. | spr.d likt. | ‘m.ṯryl. | mh y.rgmt. | w ht.aḫ y. | bn y.yšal. | ṯryl.p rg 138.7
t.ḥš[n.---]. | y.arṣ.ḥšn[.---]. | t‘td.tkl.[---]. | tkn.lbn[.---]. | dt.lbn k[.---]. | dk k.kbkb[.---]. | dm.mt.aṣḥ[.---]. | ydd.b qr[b.- 5[67].3.7
.tq]ḥ[.q]ṣ‘t k.ybmt.limm. | w y‘n.aqht.ǵzr.adr.ṯqbm. | [d]lbnn.adr.gdm.b rumm. | adr.qrnt.b y‘lm.mtnm. | b ‘qbt.ṯr. 17[2AQHT].6.21
ḫ.w bn.[--]. | limm.ql.b udn.k w[-]. | k rtqt mr[.---]. | k d lbšt.bir.mlak. | šmm.tmr.zbl.mlk. | šmm.tlak.ṭl.amr.. | bn k 13[6].25
[---.]ṯlṯm.d.nlqḥt. | [bn.ḫ]tyn.yd.bt h. | [aǵ]ltn. | tdn.bn.ddy. | ‘bdil[.b]n 2045.1
dlt.w burm.lb]. | rmṣt.ilh[m.b‘lm.---]. | ksm.ṯlṯm.[---]. | d yqḥ bt[.--]r.dbḥ[.šmn.mr]. | šmn.rqḥ[.-]bt.mtnt[.w ynt.qrt] 35[3].20
bnšm.d.bu. | tš‘.dt.tq[ḥn]. | š‘rt. | šb‘ dt tqḥn. | ššlmt. 2099.4
bnšm.d.bu. | tš‘.dt.tq[ḥn]. | š‘rt. | šb‘ dt tqḥn. | ššlmt. 2099.2
arb‘.‘šr h.šmn. | d.lqḥt.ṯlǵdy. | w.kd.ištir.‘m.qrt. | ‘št.‘šr h.šmn. | ‘mn.bn.aǵlm 1083.2
n[--.---]. | rg[m.---]. | nǵṯ[.---]. | d.yqḥ[.---]. | hm.ṯn.[---]. | hn dt.[---]. | [-----]. | [-----]. | tḥm[.---]. 2064.4
št.šb‘ d.ǵzrm.ṭb.[g]d.b ḥlb.annḫ b ḫmat. | w ‘l.agn.šb‘ d m.dǵ[ṯ.---]t. | tlk m.rḥmy.w tṣd[.---]. | tḥgrn.ǵzr.n‘m.[---]. | 23[52].15
mš kbd ktn. | ḫmš.rṭm. | ḫmš.ṯnt.d ḫmšm w. | ḫmš.ṯnt.d mit. | ḫmš.ṯnt.d ṯl | ṯ mat. | ṯt.ṯnt.d alp | alpm.ṯlṯ ktt. | alp.brr 1130.10
.--]r.almd k.[---]. | [---.]qrt.ablm.a[blm]. | [qrt.zbl.]yrḫ.d mgdl.š[---]. | [---.]mn.‘r hm[.---]. | [---.]it[.---]. | [---.]‘p[.---]. 18[3AQHT].1.31
---]. | [---.]ilm.w ilht.dt. | [---.]šb‘.l šb‘m.aṯr. | [---.--]ldm.dt ymtm. | [--.--]r.l ẓpn. | [---.]pn.ym.y[--]. | [---].b‘l.tdd. | [---.] 25[136].4
. | ṯmnym.arb‘t. | kbd.ksp. | d.nqdm. | ḫmšm.l mit. | ksp.d.mkr.ar. | arb‘m ksp d mkr. | atlg. | mit.ksp.d mkr. | ilštm‘. | ‘ 2107.10
sp. | d.nqdm. | ḫmšm.l mit. | ksp.d.mkr.ar. | arb‘m ksp d mkr. | atlg. | mit.ksp.d mkr. | ilštm‘. | ‘šrm.l mit.ksp. | ‘l.bn.a 2107.11
mit. | ksp.d.mkr.ar. | arb‘m ksp d mkr. | atlg. | mit.ksp.d mkr. | ilštm‘. | ‘šrm.l mit.ksp. | ‘l.bn.alkbl.šb[ny]. | ‘šrm ksp.‘ 2107.13
spr.argmnm. | ‘šrm.ksp.d mkr. | mlk. | ṯlṯ.mat.ksp.d.šb[n]. | mit.ksp.d.ṭbq. | ṯmnym.ar 2107.2
id. | d pršа.b br. | n‘l.il.d qblbl. | ‘ln.ybl hm.ḫrṣ. | ṯlḥn.il.d mla. | mnm.dbbm.d | msdt.arṣ. | s‘.il.dqt.k amr. | sknt.k ḥw 4[51].1.39
-]t. | [---.]ḥw[t.---]. | [---.]š[--]. | w ym ym.yš | al. | w mlk.d mlk. | b ḥwt.špḥ. | l ydn.‘bd.mlk. | d št.‘l.ḫrd h. | špḥ.al.thbṭ. 2062.2.1
[---.]ysd k. | [---.--]r.dr.dr. | [---.--]y k.w rḥd. | [---]y ilm.d mlk. | y[ṯ]b.aliyn.b‘l. | yt‘dd.rkb.‘rpt. | [--].ydd.w yqlṣn. | yq 4[51].3.9
. | il.ǵzr.yqra.mt. | b npš h.ystrn ydd. | b gngn h.aḥd y.d ym | lk.‘l.ilm.l ymru. | ilm.w nšm.d yšb | [‘].hmlt.arṣ.gm.l ǵ 4[51].7.49
-----]. | [-----]. | tḥm[.---]. | l p‘n.b‘l y[.---]. | qlt. | [--]t.mlk.d.y[mlk]. | [--.]‘bdyrḫ.l.ml[k]. | [--]t.w.lqḥ. | yn[.--].b dn h. | w. 2064.12
. | šš̀w.‘ṯtrt.w šš̀w.‘[nt.---]. | w ht.[--]k.šš̀w[.-]rym[.---]. | d ymǵy.bnš[.---]. | w ḥmr[.---]. | w m‘n[.---]. | w bn[š.---]. | d b 2158.1.8
. | [---.]tr h. | [a]rb‘.ql‘m. | arb‘.mḏrnm. | mḏrn.w.mšḫṭ. | d.mrkbt. | mlk. | mšḫṭ.w.msg. | d.tbk. 1122.13
dbḥ klyrḫ. | ndr. | dbḥ. | dt nat. | w ytnt. | ṯrmn w. | dbḥ kl. | kl ykly. | dbḥ k.sprt. | dt na RS61[24.277.4]
t nat. | w ytnt. | ṯrmn w. | dbḥ kl. | kl ykly. | dbḥ k.sprt. | dt nat. | w qrwn. | l k dbḥ. | [--]r bt [--]. | [--]bnš [--]. | š š[--]. | RS61[24.277.10]
---.]ilṯḥm.w.[---]. | šm‘t.ḥwt[.---]. | [---].nzdt.qr[t]. | [---.]dt nzdt.m[lk]. | [---.]w.ap.bṯn[.---]. | [---.]b‘l y.y[--]. | [---.-]l[-.- 2127.2.5
.b ẓl.ḫmt.lqḥ. | imr.dbḥ.b yd h. | lla.klatnm. | klt.lḥm h.d nzl. | lqḥ.msrr.‘ṣr.db[ḥ]. | yṣq.b gl.ḥṯṯ.yn. | b gl.ḫrṣ.nbt.w ‘ly 14[KRT].3.162
b yd k]. | imr.d[bḥ.bm].ymn. | lla.kl[atn]m. | klt.l[ḥm k.d]nzl. | qḥ.ms[rr.]‘ṣr. | dbḥ.ṣ[q.b g]l.ḥṯṯ. | yn.b gl[.ḫ]rṣ.nbt. | ‘l 14[KRT].2.69
n.ṭb.w.[--]. | ṯmn.kbd.yn.d.l.ṭb.b.gn‘[y]. | mitm.yn.ḥsp.d.nkly.b.db[ḥ.--]. | mit.arb‘m.kbd.yn.ḥsp.l.m[--]. | mit.‘šrm.[1084.24
w.kkrm.ṯlṯ. | mit.ksp.‘mn. | bn.ulbtyn. | w.kkr.ṯlṯ. | ksp.d.nkly.b.šd. | mit.ḫmšt.kbd. | [l.]gmn.bn.usyy. | mit.ṯṯm.kbd. | 1143.6
[-] ym.pr‘ d nkly yn kd w kd. | w ‘l ym kdm. | w b ṯlṯ.kd yn w krsnm. | 1086.1
n.š.[---.]yd.sǵr h. | [---.--]r h.‘šr[m.---.‘]šrm.dd. | [---.yn.d.]nkly.l.r‘ym.šb‘m.l.mitm.dd. | [---.--]d.šb‘m.kbd.dr‘. | [---.] 1098.44
.lm[d h]. | ily[---]. | [-----]. | [---]lb[--]. | [---]m[.---]. | [---.]d nkly. | [---.]kbd[.---]. 1049.3.3
ṣrym. | arb‘m.yn. | l.ḫrd. | ḫmšm.ḫmš. | kbd.tgmr. | yn.d.nkly. 1089.15
mit.šmn.d.nm[-.]b d.mzy.alzy. | ḫmš.kkr.ḥlb. | ḫmš.kkr.brr. | kkr.ḫmš. 1135.1
[---.]l mdgkbr. | [---] y.‘m k. | [-]tn.l.stn. | [--.]d.n‘m.lbš k. | [-]dm.ṯn id. | [--]m.d.l.n‘mm. | [lm.]l.likt.‘m y. | [2128.1.4
].pn.b‘l y. | w.urk.ym.b‘l y. | l.pn.amn.w.l.pn. | il.mṣrm.dt.tǵrn. | npš.špš.mlk. | rb.b‘l y. 1018.22
.ksp.d.šb[n]. | mit.ksp.d.ṭbq. | ṯmnym.arb‘t. | kbd.ksp. | d.nqdm. | ḫmšm.l mit. | ksp.d.mkr.ar. | arb‘m ksp d mkr. | atl 2107.8
-]r. | [---.--]ṣ. | [-----]. | [--]lm.aḥd. | [--]l.l ḫr[-.---]. | [--]m.dt nšu. | [---.]d[--.---]. | [---.--]m aḥ[d]. | [-----]. | [---.--]m. 156[-].7
[---.nš]lm. | [---.nš]lm. | [---.nš]lm. | [---.nš]lm. | [---.pr]š̀.d.nšlm. | [---.]d.nšlm. 2036.7
[---].prš̀ qmḥ.d.nšlm. | [---].prš̀.d.nšlm. | [---.nš]lm. | [---.nš]lm. | [---.nš]lm. | [---.nš]lm. | [---.pr 2036.2
[---].prš̀ qmḥ.d.nšlm. | [---].prš̀.d.nšlm. | [---.nš]lm. | [---.nš]lm. | [---.nš]lm. | 2036.1
--.nš]lm. | [---.nš]lm. | [---.nš]lm. | [---.pr]š̀.d.nšlm. | [---.]d.nšlm. 2036.8
[---.]d.ztm.d.si[-]. | [---.]d.ztm.d ggy.[---]. | [---.d].ztm.d.b[--]. | [---.]ztm.[2035.1
ḫ. | ‘šrm.ḫpn.ḫmš. | kbd.w lpš. | ḫmš.mispt. | mṭ. | w lpš.d sgr b h. | b d.anrmy. 1109.6
[---.--]t ḥ[dr]. | [-----]. | ḫmš[.---]t.ḥdrm. | w.[---.a]ḥd.d.sgrm. | w p[tḥ.---.]l.aḥd.adr. | [---.--]t.b[ḥd]r.mškb. | ṯl[l.---. 1151.4
brq y. | riš h.tply.ṭly.bn.‘n h. | uz‘rt.tmll.išd h.qrn[m]. | dt.‘l h.riš h.b glṯ.b šm[m]. | [---.i]l.ṯr.iṯ.p h.k ṯt.ǵlt[.--]. | [---.-- UG5.3.1.7
| tšḫṭann.b šnt h.qr.[mym]. | mlk.yṣm.y l km.qr.mym.d ‘[l k]. | mḫṣ.aqht.ǵzr.amd.gr bt il. | ‘nt.brḥ.p ‘lm h.‘nt.p dr[19[1AQHT].3.152
m.abl[m]. | qrt.zbl.yrḫ.yšu g h. | w yṣḥ.y l k.qrt.ablm. | d ‘l k.mḫṣ.aqht.ǵzr. | ‘wrt.yšt k.b‘l.l ht. | w ‘lm h.l ‘nt.p dr.dr 19[1AQHT].4.166
ǵ.l mrrt.tǵll.b nr. | yšu.g h.w yṣḥ.y l k.mrrt. | tǵll.b nr.d ‘l k.mḫṣ.aqht. | ǵzr.šrš k.b arṣ.al. | yp‘.riš.ǵly.b d.ns‘ k. | ‘nt. 19[1AQHT].3.158
---.]ym.tlḥmn. | [---.rp]um.tštyn. | [---.]il.d ‘rgzm. | [---.]dt.‘l.lty. | [---.]tdbḥ.amr. | ṯmn.b qrb.hkl y.[aṯr h.rpum]. | tdd. 20[121].1.9
y‘n.kmr.kmr[.--]. | k ap‘.il.b gdrt.k lb.l | ḫṭ h.imḫṣ h.k d.‘l.qšt h. | imḫṣ h.‘l.qṣ‘t h.hwt. | l aḥw.ap.qšt h.l ttn. | l y.w b 19[1AQHT].1.14
yn. | bn.b‘l.hwt.aliy.qrdm. | bhṯ.bn.ilm.mt.‘bd k.an. | w d ‘lm k.šmḫ.bn.ilm.mt. | [---.]g h.w aṣḥ.ik.yṣḥn. | [b‘l.‘m.aḫ y 5[67].2.20
.aliyn.b‘l.hwt.aliy. | qrdm.bhṯ.l bn.ilm mt. | ‘bd k.an.w d.‘lm k. | tb‘.w l.ytb.ilm.idk. | l ytn.pn.‘m.bn.ilm.mt. | tk.qrt 5[67].2.12

d

m k.|‘m.‘lm.ḥyt.ḥẓt.tḥm k.|mlk n.aliyn.b‘l.ṯpṭ n.|in.d ‘ln h.klny y.qš h.|nbln.klny y.nbl.ks h.|any.l yṣḥ.ṯr.il.ab 3[‘NT.VI].5.41
.|‘m ‘lm.ḥyt.ḥẓt.|tḥm k.mlk n.aliy[n.]b‘l.|ṯpṭ n.w in.d ‘ln h.|klny n.q[š] h.n[bln].|klny n[.n]bl.ks h.|[an]y.l yṣḥ. 4[51].4.44
-]k.ǵrt.|[ql].l b‘l.‘nt.ttnn.|[---].b‘l m.d ip[---].|[il.]hd.d ‘nn.n[--].|[----.]aliyn.b[‘l].|[---.btl]t.‘n[t.-.]p h.|[---.---]n.|[10[76].2.33
.špḥ.bkr k.|d k.n‘m.‘nt.n‘m h.|km.tsm.‘ṯtrt.ts[m h].|d ‘q h.ib.iqni.‘p[‘p] h.|sp.ṯrml.tḥgrn.[-]dm[.-].|ašlw.b ṣp.‘n 14[KRT].3.147
t.šbḥ.bkr k.|d k n‘m.‘nt.|n‘m h.km.tsm.|‘ṯtrt.tsm h.|d ‘q h.ib.iqni.|‘p‘p h.sp.ṯrml.|d b ḥlm y.il.ytn.|b ḏrt y.ab.a 14[KRT].6.294
šd.snrym.dt.‘qb.|b.ayly.|šd.abršn.|šd.kkn.[bn].ubyn.|šd.bn.li[y].|šd. 2026.1
‘ḏrd.|ayaẖ.|bn.aylt.|ẖmš.mat.arb‘m.|kbd.ksp.anyt.|d.‘rb.b.anyt.|l.mlk.gbl.|w.ẖmšm.ksp.|lqḥ.mlk.gbl.|lbš.any 2106.12
mṣry.d.‘rb.b.unṯ.|bn.qrrn.mḏrǵl.|bn.tran.mḏrǵl|bn.ilh.mḏrǵl|šp 2046.1.1
rišym.dt.‘rb.|b bnš hm.|ḏmry.w.pṯpṯ.‘rb.|b.yrm.|[ily.w].ḏmry.‘r 2079.1
spr.‘rbnm.|dt.‘rb.|b.mtn.bn.ayaẖ.|b.ẖbṯ h.ḥwt.ṯt h.|w.mnm.šalm.|dt.t 1161.2
mn.lbšm.w.mšlt.|l.udmym.b.ṯmnt.‘šrt.ksp.|šb‘m.lbš.d.‘rb.bt.mlk.|b.mit.ẖmšt.kbd.ksp.|ṯlṯ.ktnt.b d.an[r]my.|b.‘ 2101.16
spr.npš.d.|‘rb.bt.mlk.|w.b.spr.l.št.|yrm‘l.|ṣry.|iršy.|y‘ḏrd.|ayaẖ.| 2106.1
ṯmn.mrkbt.dt.|‘rb.bt.mlk.|yd.apnt hn.|yd.ḥẓ hn.|yd.tr hn.|w.l.ṯt.mrk 1121.1
-.yn.w t]n.w nšt.|w ‘n hm.nǵr mdr‘[.iṯ.lḥm.---].|iṯ.yn.d ‘rb.bṯk[.---].|mǵ hw.l hn.lg yn h[.---].|w ḥbr h.mla yn.[--- 23[52].74
d.bn.ẖrmln.ṯn.b d.bn.ẖdmn.|[u]bdy.nqdm.|[ṯlṯ].šdm.d.n‘rb.gt.npk.|[š]d.rpan.b d.klṯṯb.|[š]d.ilṣy.b d.‘bdym.|[ub] 82[300].2.13
-]n b ym.qẓ.|[---.]ym.tlḥmn.|[---.rp]um.tštyn.|[---.]il.d ‘rgzm.|[---.]dt.‘l.lty.|[---.]tdbḥ.amr.|ṯmn.b qrb.hkl y.[aṯr 20[121].1.8
y.b qdš.|ztr.‘m y.l ‘pr.ḏmr.aṯr[y].|ṭbq lḥt.niṣ y.grš.|d ‘šy.ln.aẖd.yd y.b š|krn m‘ms y k šb‘t yn.|spu.ksm y.bt.b‘l 17[2AQHT].2.19
h.l arṣ.mšṣu.qṭr h.|l ‘pr.ḏmr.aṯr h.ṭbq.lḥt.|niṣ h.grš d.‘šy.ln h.|aẖd.yd h.b škrn.m‘ms h.|[k]šb‘ yn.spu.ksm h.bt 17[2AQHT].1.30
]rṣ.mšṣu.|[qṭr h.l ‘pr.ḏ]mr.a[ṯ]r h.|[ṭbq.lḥt.niṣ h.gr]š.d ‘šy.|[ln h.---].|z[tr.‘m k.l arṣ.mšṣu.qṭr k].|l ‘pr.ḏm[r.aṯr k 17[2AQHT].1.48
l arṣ.mšṣu.qṭr k].|l ‘pr.ḏm[r.aṯr k.ṭbq].|lḥt.niṣ k.gr[š.d ‘šy.ln k].|spu.ksm k.bt.[b‘l.w mnt k].|bt il.aẖd.yd k.b [šk 17[2AQHT].2.3
‘d.w ‘rbm.t‘nyn.|w šd.šd ilm.šd aṯrt.w rḥm.|‘l.išt.šb‘ d.ǵzrm.ṭb.[g]d.b ḥlb.annẖ b ẖmat.|w ‘l.agn.šb‘ d m.dǵ[ṯ.---] 23[52].14
m.|w id‘.k ḥy.aliyn.b‘l.|k iṯ.zbl.b‘l.arṣ.|b ḥlm.lṭpn.il d pid.|b ḏrt.bny.bnwt.|šmm.šmn.tmṭrn.|nẖlm.tlk.nbtm.|š 6[49].3.10
hm.ḥy.a[liyn.b‘l].|w hm.iṯ.zbl.b‘[l.arṣ].|b ḥlm.lṭpn.il.d pid.|b ḏrt.bny.bnwt.|šmm.šmn.tmṭrn.|nẖlm.tlk.nbtm.| 6[49].3.4
n.|w t‘n.rbt.aṯrt ym.|bl.nmlk.yd‘.ylḥn.|w y‘n.lṭpn.il d pi|d dq.anm.l yrẓ.|‘m.b‘l.l y‘db.mrḥ.|‘m.bn.dgn.k tms m 6.1.49[49.1.21]
ik.tmgnn.rbt.|aṯrt.ym.tǵẓyn.|qnyt.ilm.mgntm.|ṯr.il.d pid.hm.ǵẓtm.|bny.bnwt w t‘n.|btlt.‘nt.nmgn.|[-]m.rbt.aṯ 4[51].3.31
h|ll b‘l gml.yrdt.|b ‘rgzm.b bz tdm.|lla y.‘m lẓpn i|l ḏ.pid.hn b p y sp|r hn.b špt y mn|t hn ṯlẖ h w mlg h y|ṯtqt 24[77].45
k.bn[.dnil.---].|w y‘ḏr k.b yd.btlt.[‘nt].|w y‘n.lṭpn.il d p[id].|yd‘t k.bt.k anšt.w i[n.b ilht].|qlṣ k.tb‘.bt.ẖnp.lb[k. 18[3AQHT].1.15
.npl.l a|rṣ.mt.aliyn.b‘l.|ẖlq.zbl.b‘l.arṣ.|apnk.lṭpn.il.|d pid.yrd.l ksi.yṯb.|l hdm[.w] l.hdm.yṯb.|l arṣ.yṣq.‘mr.|un. 5[67].6.12
lm.|ydy.mrṣ.gršm zbln.|in.b ilm.‘ny h.|w y‘n.lṭpn.il.b pid.|ṭb.bn y.lm ṭb[t] km.|l kḥṯ.zbl k[m.a]nk.|iḥtrš.w [a]š 16[126].5.23
r.mǵy.‘[d]t.ilm.|[w]y‘n.aliy[n.]b‘l.|[---.]tb‘.l lṭpn.|[il.d]pid.l tbrk.|[krt.]ṯ‘.l tmr.n‘mn.|[ǵlm.]il.ks.yiẖd.|[il.b]yd. 15[128].2.14
[.---].|b d k.[---].|ṯnnt h[.---].|ṯlṯt h[.-.w y‘n].|lṭpn.[il.d pid.my].|b ilm.[ydy.mrṣ].|gršm.z[bln.in.b ilm].|‘ny h.y[ṯ 16[126].5.10
n h.b nhrm.|štt.ẖptr.l išt.|ẖbrṯ.l ẓr.pḥmm.|t‘pp.ṯr.il.d pid.|tǵẓy.bny.bnwt.|b nši.‘n h.w tphn.|hlk.b‘l.aṯtrt.|k t‘ 4[51].2.10
.bt.ar.|mẓll.ṭly.bt rb.|mṯb.arṣ.bt y‘bdr.|w y‘n lṭpn il d pid.|p ‘bd.an.‘nn.aṯrt.|p.‘bd.ank.aẖd.ulṯ.|hm.amt.aṯrt.tlb 4[51].4.58
.bnwt.|šmm.šmn.tmṭrn.|nẖlm.tlk.nbtm.|šmẖ.lṭpn.il.d pid.|p‘n h.l hdm.yṯpd.|w yprq.lṣb w yṣḥq.|yšu.g h.w yṣḥ 6[49].3.14
gr il.ilš.|ilš.ngr.bt.b‘l.|w aṯt h.ngrt.ilht.|w y‘n.lṭpn.il d pi[d].|šm‘.l ngr.il il[š].|ilš.ngr bt b‘l.|w aṯt k.ngrt.il[ht].|‘ 16[126].4.10
ḥt.[‘nt.arṣ.ṯlṯ.mtḥ].|ǵyrm.idk.l yt[n.pnm.‘m.lṭpn].|il d pid.tk ẖrš[n.---.tk.ǵr.ks].|ygly ḏd.i[l.w ybu.qrš.mlk].|ab.š 1[‘NT.IX].3.22
r.|[---].aṯt k.‘l.|[---] k.yšṣi.|[---.]ẖbr.rbt.|[ẖbr.ṯrr]t.il d.|[pid.---].b anšt.|[---.]mlu.|[---.--]tm. 15[128].5.26
-.---].|t‘nyn.l zn.tn[.---].|at.adn.tp‘r[.---].|ank.lṭpn.il[.d pid.---].|‘l.ydm.p‘rt[.---].|šm k.mdd.i[l.---].|bt ksp y.d[--.- 1[‘NT.X].4.18
|km ll.kḥṣ.tusp[.---].|tgr.il.bn h.ṯr[.---].|w y‘n.lṭpn.il.d p[id.---].|šm.bn y.yw.ilt.[---].|w p‘r.šm.ym[-.---].|t‘nyn.l 1[‘NT.X].4.13
nbt.b ksp.|šmrgt.b dm.ẖrṣ.|kḥṯ.il.nẖt.|b ẓr.hdm.id.|d prša.b br.|n‘l.il.d qblbl.|‘ln.ybl hm.ẖrṣ.|ṯlḥn.il.d mla.|m 4[51].1.36
b yrẖ.mgm[r.---].|yṣu.ẖlpn[.---].|ṯlṯ.dt.p[--.---].|dt.ṯgmi.[---].|b d [---]t.[---]. 1159.3
qṭqṭ.tḥt.|ṯlḥnt.il.d yd‘nn.|y‘db.lḥm.l h.w d l yd‘nn.|d.mṣd.|ylmn.ẖṭ.tḥt.ṯlḥn.|b qr‘.|‘ṯtrt.w ‘nt.ymǵy.|‘ṯtrt.t‘db. UG5.1.1.7B
ṯlṯ mrkb[t].|ṣpyt b ẖrṣ[.w] ṣmdm trm.d [ṣ]py.|w.trm.aḥdm.|ṣpym.|ṯlṯ mrkbt mlk.|d.l.ṣpy.|[---.t] 1122.2
t.kbd.|b d.tt.w.ṯlṯ.ktnt.b dm.tt.|w.ṯmnt.ksp.hn.|ktn.d.ṣr.pḥm.b h.w.ṯqlm.|ksp h.mitm.pḥm.b d.skn.|w.ṯt.ktnm. 1110.4
b dm.ẖrṣ.|kḥṯ.il.nẖt.|b ẓr.hdm.id.|d prša.b br.|n‘l.il.d qblbl.|‘ln.ybl hm.ẖrṣ.|ṯlḥn.il.d mla.|mnm.dbbm.d |msdt 4[51].1.37
h.ydy.ḥmt.|b ḥrn.pnm.trǵnw.w ṯtkl.|bnwt h.ykr.‘r.d qdm.|idk.pnm.l ytn.tk aršẖ.rbt.|w aršẖ.ṯrrt.ydy.b ‘ṣm.‘r‘ UG5.7.62
m.rb.mi[--.‘]bd k.|l.p‘n.b‘l y[.mrḥqtm].|šb‘ d.w.šb‘[d.qlt].|ankn.rgmt.l.b‘l y.|l.špš.‘lm.l.‘ṯtrt.|l.‘nt.l.kl.il.alṯ[y].| 2008.1.5
-]ḥ.hy.mẖ.tmẖṣ.mẖṣ[.aẖ k].|tkl.m[k]ly.‘l.umt[k.--].|d ttql.b ym.trtḥ[ṣ.--].|[----.a]dm.tium.b ǵlp y[m.--].|d alp š 19[1AQHT].4.203
b ymn h.w y‘n.yṭ[p]n[.mh]r.|št.b yn.yšt.ila.il š[--.]il.|d yqny.ḏdm.yd.mẖṣt.a[qh]t.ǵ|zr.tmẖṣ.alpm.ib.št[-.]št.|ḥrš 19[1AQHT].4.220
mṣmt.‘bs.|arr.d.qr|ht. 1173.2
.ksp.|l alpm.ẖrṣ.yṣq|m.l rbbt.|yṣq-ẖym.w tbṯẖ.|kt.il.dt.rbtm.|kt.il.nbt.b ksp.|šmrgt.b dm.ẖrṣ.|kḥṯ.il.nẖt.|b ẓr.h 4[51].1.31
k.‘m y.p‘n k.tls]|[m]n ‘m y t[wtḥ.išd k.dm.rgm.iṯ.l y.d argmn k].|[h]wt.d aṯ[ny k.---.rgm.‘ṣ].|w lẖšt.abn[.tant.š 7.2[130].17
.gpn.|yṣmdnn.ṣmdm.gpn.yšql.šdmt h.|km gpn.|šb‘ d.yrgm.‘l.‘d.w ‘rbm.t‘nyn.|w šd.šd ilm.šd aṯrt.w rḥm.|‘l.išt. 23[52].12
t y.rgm.|tḥm.illḏr.|‘bd k..|l.p‘n a[dt y].|šb‘ d[.w šb‘ d].|mrḥq[tm.qlt].|mn[m.šlm]. 1014.6
|rgm.|tḥm.ṯpṭb[‘l].|[‘]bd k.|[l.p]‘n.b‘l y.|[šb‘] d.šb‘ [d].|[mr]ḥqtm.|qlt.|‘bd k.b.|lwsnd.|[w] b ṣr.|‘m.mlk.|w.ht 2063.6
|b‘l y.r[gm].|tḥm.‘bd[--].|‘bd k.|l p‘n.b‘l y.|ṯn id.šb‘ d.|mrḥqtm.|qlt.‘m.|b‘l y.mnm.|šlm.|[r]gm[.ṯṯṯb].|[l.]‘bd[2115.2.6
spr.argmnm.|‘šrm.ksp.d mkr.|mlk.|ṯlṯ.mat.ksp.d.šb[n].|mit.ksp.d.ṭbq.|ṯmnym.arb‘t.|kbd.ksp.|d.nqdm.|ẖ 2107.4
--]m.il[.---].|[---]d nhr.umt.|[---.]rpat.bt.|[m]lk.itdb.d šb‘.|[a]ẖm.l h.ṯmnt.bn um.|krt.ḥtk n.rš.|krt.grdš.mknt.| 14[KRT].1.8
b‘[l] y.|rgm.|tḥm.ṯpṭb[‘l].|[‘]bd k.|[l.p]‘n.b‘l y.|[šb‘] d.šb‘ [d].|[mr]ḥqtm.|qlt.|‘bd k.b.|lwsnd.|[w] b ṣr.|‘m.mlk 2063.6
d.|b gngn h.aḥd y.d ym|lk.‘l.ilm.l ymru.|ilm.w nšm.d yšb|[‘].hmlt.arṣ.gm.l ǵ|[lm] h.b‘l k.yṣḥ.‘n.|[gpn].w ugr.b 4[51].7.51
.nhr.il.rbm.|l ištbm.tnn.ištml h.|mẖšt.bṯn.‘qltn.|šlyṭ.d šb‘t.rašm.|mẖšt.mdd ilm.ar[š].|ṣmt.‘gl.il.‘tk.|mẖšt.klbt.il 3[‘NT].3.39
k tmẖṣ.ltn.bṯn.brḥ.|tkly.bṯn.‘qltn.|šlyṭ.d šb‘y.rašm.|ṯṯkḥ.ttrp.šmm.k rs.|ipd k.ank.ispi.uṭm.|ḏrqm 5[67].1.3
a[---] k.k tmẖṣ.|[ltn.bṯn.br]ḥ.tkly.|[bṯn.‘qltn.]šlyṭ.|[d šb‘t.rašm].ṯṯkḥ.|[ttrp.šmm.k rks.ipd]k.|[-----]. 5[67].1.30

znm.iḫ h yṯʻr. | mšrrm.aḫt h l a | bn mznm.nkl w ib. | d ašr.ar yrḫ.w y | rḫ yar k. | [ašr ilht kṯrt bn] | t hll.snnt.bnt h 24[77].38
.ʻlm.w yšt. | [--.]gṯr.w yqr.il.yṯb.b.ʻṯtrt. | il.ṯpṭ.b hd rʻy.d yšr.w yḏmr. | b knr.w ṯlb.b tp.w mṣltm.b m | rqdm.dšn.b.ḥ UG5.2.1.3
spr ʻpsm. | dt.št. | uryn. | l mlk.ugrt. 1171.2
ym.yš | al. | w mlk.d mlk. | b ḥwt.špḥ. | l ydn.ʻbd.mlk. | d št.ʻl.ḫrd h. | špḥ.al.thbṭ. | ḫrd.ʻps.aḥd.kw | sgt. | ḫrd ksp.[--]r 2062.2.4
ṯlṯ.kbd. | mḏrġlm. | w.šbʻ.ʻšr.ḫsnm. | ḫmšm.l.mit. | bnš.l.d. | yškb.l.b.bt.mlk. 1029.15
[---].ydm. | [---].ṯdr. | [---.]mdṯn.ipd. | [---.]m[---.]d.mškbt. | [---.--]m. | [---].ṯlḥn. | [---].ṯnn. | [---.--]b.kdr. | [---.--] 1152.1.4
šmʻ. | mit.arbʻm.kbd. | l.liy.bn.ʻmyn. | mit.ḫmšm.kbd. | d.škn.l.ks.ilm. 1143.14
qrht.d.tššlmn. | ṯlrb h. | art.ṯn.yrḫm. | ṯlrby.yrḫ.w.ḫm[š.ym]m. | ṯlḥ 66[109].1
-.]pp.hrm. | [---].d l ydʻ bn il. | [---.]pḫr kkbm. | [---.]dr dt.šmm. | [---.al]iyn bʻl. | [---].rkb.ʻrpt. | [---.]ġš.l limm. | [---.]l 10[76].1.5
m.p.k mtm. | ʻz.mid. | hm.nṯkp. | mʻn k. | w.mnm. | rgm.d.tšmʻ. | ṯmt.w.št. | b.spr.ʻm y. 53[54].17
tr.ʻpt.šmm. | ṭbḫ.alpm.ap ṣin.šql.ṯrm. | w mri ilm.ʻglm.dt.šnt. | imr.qmṣ.llim.k ksp. | l ʻbrm.zt.ḫrṣ.l ʻbrm.kš. | dpr.ṯlḥ 22.2[124].13
t. | hkl h.ṭbḫ.alpm[.ap]. | ṣin.šql.ṯrm[.w]m | ria.il.ʻglm.d[t]. | šnt.imr.qmṣ.l[l]im. | ṣḥ.aḫ h.b bht h.a[r]y h. | b qrb hkl 4[51].6.42
.b[--.---]. | ṭbḫ.alp[m.ap.ṣin.šql]. | ṯrm.w [mri.ilm.ʻglm.dt.šnt]. | imr.[qmṣ.llim.---]. 1[ʻNT.X].4.31
š.]šʻrt. | [---.]tšʻ.kbd.skm. | [arb]ʻm.ḫpnt.ptt. | [-]r.pldm.dt.šʻrt. | ṯlṯm.ṯlṯ.kbd.mṣrrt. | ʻšr.ṯn.kbd.pġdrm. | ṯmn.mrbdt. 1111.8
t. | š[--].išal. | ʻm k.ybl.šd. | a[--].dʻ.k. | šld.ašld. | hn.mrṯ.d.štt. | ašld b ldt k. 2009.3.1
ṯ]trt w ʻnt[.---]. | w b hm.tṯṯb[.--]d h. | km trpa.hn nʻr. | d yšt.l.lṣb h ḫšʻr klb. | [w]riš.pqq.w šr h. | yšt.aḥd h.dm zt.ḫr UG5.1.2.4
my[.d k] | bkbm.ʻ[l.---]. | [-]l h.yd ʻd[.---]. | ltm.mrqdm.d š[-]l[-]. | w tʻn.pġt.ṯkmt.mym. | qrym.ab.dbḥ.l ilm. | šʻly.dġṯ 19[1AQHT].4.189
spr.bnš.mlk. | d taršn.ʻmsn. | bṣr.abn.špšyn. | dqn. | aġlmn. | knʻm. | aḫršp. | a 2067.1.2
ḏrnm. | mḏrn.w.mšḫṭ. | d.mrkbt. | mlk. | mšḫṭ.w.msg. | d.tbk. 1122.16
.m[--]. | mit.ʻšrm.[k]bd.yn.ḥsp.l.y[--]. | ʻšrm.yn.ḥsp.l.ql.d.tbʻ.mṣ[r]m. | mit.arbʻm.kbd.yn.mṣb. | l.mḏrġlm. | ʻšrn ʻšr.yn 1084.27
d ṯbil. | ʻṯtrt ṣwd[t.---]. | tlk b mdb[r.---]. | tḥdṯn w hl[.---]. | w 2001.1.1
.irpm.w.ṯn.trqm. | w.qpt.w.mqḥm. | w.ṯlṯm.yn šbʻ.kbd d ṭbṭ. | w.ḫmšm.yn.d iḫ h. 1103.22
b yrḫ.mgm[r.---]. | yṣu.ḫlpn[.---]. | ṯlṯ.dt.p[--.---]. | dt.ṯgmi.[---]. | b d [---]t.[---]. 1159.4
yt. | yd.llḫ hm. | w.ṯlṯ.l.ʻšrm. | ḫpnt.ššwm.ṯn. | pddm.w.d.ṯṯ. | [mr]kbt.w.ḥrṣ. 2049.8
ṯn.y[--.-]ah. | ṯnm.tšqy msk.hwt.tšqy[.-.]w [---]. | w hn dt.yṯb.l mspr. 19[1AQHT].5.1
š.rṭm. | ḫmš.ṯnt.d ḫmšm w. | ḫmš.ṯnt.d mit. | ḫmš.ṯnt.d ṯl | ṯ mat. | ṯṯ.ṯnt.d alp | alpm.ṯlṯ ktt. | alp.brr. | kkr.tznt. | ḫm 1130.11
]n ʻm y t[wtḥ.išd k.dm.rgm.iṯ.l y.d argmn k]. | [h]wt.d aṯ[ny k.---.rgm.ʻṣ]. | w lḫšt.abn[.tant.šmm.ʻm.arṣ.thmt]. | ʻ 7.2[130].18
mḫsrn.d.[--.]ušknym. | brq.ṯlṯ.[mat.ṯ]lṯ. | bsn.mi[t.--]. | ar[--.---]. | k[-- 1136.1
wn. | l k dbḥ. | [--]r bt [--]. | [--]bnš [--]. | š š[--]. | w [--]. | d [--]. | ypḫ[--]. | w s[--]. | [---]. | qrd ga[n.--]. | b bt k.[--]. | w l d RS61[24.277.17]
. | mn[-.---]. | hyrm.h[--.---]. | yrmm h[--.---]. | mlk.gbʻ h d [---]. | ibr.k l hm.d l h q[--.---]. | l ytn.l hm.tḥt bʻl[.---]. | h.u 9[33].2.3
t[--.---]. | aṯr[t.---]. | b im[--.---]. | bl.l[---.---]. | mlk.[---]. | dt [---]. | b ṯ[--.---]. | gm[.---]. | y[--.---]. 4[51].2.45
i[--.---]. | d.[---]. | bnš[-] mdy[-]. | w.b.glb. | phnn.w. | mndym. | bdnh. | l[2129.2
bnšm.dt.[---]. | krws.l.y[--.---]. | ypʻ.l[.---]. | šmr[m.---]. | [-----]. | bn.g[2122.1
]. | [---.]mnt.[l]pʻn[.-.-]bd h.aqšr[.---]. | [---].ptḥ y.a[--.]dt[.---].ml[--]. | [---.-]ṯk.ytmt.dlt tlk.[---].bm[.---]. | [---.-]qp.b 1001.1.21
[s]pr.ḫ[rš.---]. | [-]mn.n[--]. | ḫrš.d.[---]. | mrum.[---]. | yṣḥm[.---]. | mkrm[.---]. | pslm[.---]. 1038.3
--]. | w.unṯm.nḥ[l h.---]. | [---.]ʻḏr[.---]. | str[-.---]. | bdlm.d[t.---]. | ʻdn.[---]. | aḫqm bir[-.---]. | kṯrmlk.ns[--.---]. | bn.tbd.i 90[314].2.2
at.š[ʻtqt.---]. | šʻd[.---]. | rt.[---]. | ʻṯr[.---]. | b p.š[---]. | il.p.d[---]. | ʻrm.[di.mh.pdrm]. | di.š[rr.---]. | mr[ṣ.---]. | zb[ln.---]. | 16[126].5.47
[---.--]i[-.]a[--.---]. | [---.]ilm.w ilht.dt. | [---.]šbʻ.l šbʻm.aṯr. | [---.--]ldm.dt ymtm. | [--.--]r.l ẓpn. | [- 25[136].2
. | [---].adt y.yšlm. | [---.]mlk n.amṣ. | [.---].nn. | [---.]qrt.dt. | [---.--]sʻ.hn.mlk. | [---.l]qḥ.hn.l.ḥwt h. | [---.--]p.hn.ib.d.b. 1012.7
r[ṣ.---]. | [---.--]g.irb[-.---]. | [---.-]rd.pn.[---]. | [---.--]r.ṯt d.[---]. | [---.--]r.[---]. 2157.6
.---]. | rg[m.---]. | nġt[.---]. | d.yqḥ[.---]. | hm.ṯn.[---]. | hn dt.[---]. | [-----]. | [-----]. | tḥm[.---]. | l pʻn.bʻl y[.---]. | qlt. | [--]t. 2064.6
---.]ršy.[---]. | [---.-]mdr. | [---.]bty. | [---.]mrṯn.[--]. | [---.]d[.---]. 2172.6

day

ṣḥ.knp.hrgb.bʻl.ybn. | [b]ʻl.ybn.diy.hwt.hrg[b]. | tpr.w du.b nši.ʻn h. | [w]yphn.yḥd.ṣml.um.nšrm. | yšu.g h.w yṣḥ.k 19[1AQHT].3.134
. | w yṣḥ.knp.nšrm.ybn. | bʻl.ybn.diy hmt nšrm. | tpr.w du.b nši.ʻn h.w ypn. | yḥd.hrgb.ab.nšrm. | yšu.g h.w yṣḥ.knp. 19[1AQHT].3.120
.ank. | l aḥwy.tqḥ.ytpn.mhr.št. | tštn.k nšr.b ḥbš h.km.diy. | b tʻrt h.aqht.km.ytb.l lḥ[m]. | bn.dnil.l ṯrm.ʻl h.nšr[m]. 18[3AQHT].4.28
.btlt.ʻnt.ṯb.ytp.w[---]. | l k.ašt k.km.nšr.b ḥb[š y]. | km.diy.b tʻrt y.aqht.[km.ytb]. | l lḥm.w bn.dnil.l ṯrm[.ʻl h]. | nšr 18[3AQHT].4.18
]. | l lḥm.w bn.dnil.l ṯrm[.ʻl h]. | nšrm.trḫpn.ybṣr.[ḥbl.d] | iym.bn.nšrm.arḫp.an[k.ʻ]l. | aqht.ʻdb k.hlmn.ṯnm.qdqd. | 18[3AQHT].4.20
ytb.l lḥ[m]. | bn.dnil.l ṯrm.ʻl h.nšr[m]. | trḫpn.ybṣr.ḥbl.diy[m.bn]. | nšrm.trḫp.ʻnt.ʻl[.aqht]. | tʻdbn h.hlmn.ṯnm[.qdq 18[3AQHT].4.31
. | yġly.yḫsp.ib[.---]. | ʻl.bt.ab h.nšrm.trḫ[p]n. | ybṣr.ḥbl.diym. | tbky.pġt.bm.lb. | tdmʻ.bm.kbd. | tmzʻ.kst.dnil.mt. | rpi 19[1AQHT].1.33
gtr.bʻlt.mlk.bʻ | lt.drkt.bʻlt.šmm.rmm. | [bʻl]t.kpṯ.w ʻnt.di.dit.rḫpt. | [---.-]rm.aklt.ʻgl.ʻl.mšt. | [---.--]r.špr.w yšt.il. | [--- UG5.2.1.8
t.in.ʻẓm.yšu.g[h]. | w yṣḥ.knp.hrgb.bʻl.ybn. | [b]ʻl.ybn.diy.hwt.hrg[b]. | tpr.w du.b nši.ʻn h. | [w]yphn.yḥd.ṣml.um. 19[1AQHT].3.133
h.rgm.l yṣa.b š[p] | t h.hwt h.knp.hrgb.bʻl.ṯbr. | bʻl.ṯbr.diy.hwt.w yql. | tḥt.pʻn h.ybqʻ.kbd h.w yḥd. | [i]n.šmt.in.ʻẓm. 19[1AQHT].3.129
ab.nšrm. | yšu.g h.w yṣḥ.knp.hr[g]b. | bʻl.yṯb.bʻl.y[ṯb]r.diy[.h]wt. | w yql.tḥt.pʻn y.ibqʻ.kbd[h]. | w aḥd.hm.iṯ.šmt.h 19[1AQHT].3.123
b p h.rgm.l[yṣ]a. | b špt h.hwt h.knp.ṣml.bʻ[l]. | bʻl.ṯbr.diy.hyt.tq[l.tḥt]. | pʻn h.ybqʻ.kbd h.w yḥd. | iṯ.šmt.iṯ.ʻẓm.w y 19[1AQHT].3.143
l.um.nšrm. | yšu.g h.w yṣḥ.knp.ṣml. | bʻl.yṯbr.bʻl.yṯbr.diy. | hyt.tql.tḥt.pʻn y.ibqʻ. | kbd h.w aḥd.hm.iṯ.šmt.iṯ. | ʻẓm.a 19[1AQHT].3.137
knk[-]. | w yšu.g h.w yṣḥ.knp.nšrm. | bʻl.yṯbr.bʻl.yṯbr.diy. | hmt.hm.tʻpn.ʻl.qbr.bn y. | tšḫṭann.b šnt h.qr.[mym]. | m 19[1AQHT].3.149
in.šmt.in.ʻẓm.yšu.g h. | w yṣḥ.knp.nšrm.ybn. | bʻl.ybn.diy hmt nšrm. | tpr.w du.b nši.ʻn h.w ypn. | yḥd.hrgb.ab.nšr 19[1AQHT].3.119
.rgm.l yṣa.b špt h.hwt[h]. | knp.nšrm.bʻl.yṯbr. | bʻl.ṯbr.diy hmt.tqln. | tḥt.pʻn h.ybqʻ.kbdt hm.w[yḥd]. | in.šmt.in.ʻẓ 19[1AQHT].3.115
.nšrm.yšu]. | [g h.]w yṣḥ[.knp.nšrm]. | bʻl.yṯb.bʻl.yṯb[r.diy.hmt]. | tqln.tḥ pʻn y.ibq[ʻ.kbd hm.w] | aḥd.hm.iṯ.šmt.hm 19[1AQHT].3.108
qt. | bt.krt.bu.tbu. | bkt.tgly.w tbu. | nṣrt.tbu.pnm. | ʻrm.tdu.mh. | pdrm.tdu.šrr. | ḥṯ m.tʻmt.[ʻ]ṯr.[k]m. | zbln.ʻl.riš h. | 16.6[127].6
šʻd[.---]. | rt.[---]. | ʻṯr[.---]. | b p.š[---]. | il.p.d[---]. | ʻrm.[di.mh.pdrm]. | di.š[rr.---]. | mr[ṣ.---]. | zb[ln.---]. | t[--.---]. | [---- 16[126].5.48

.b'lt.mlk.b'|lt.drkt.b'lt.šmm.rmm.|[b'l]t.kpṯ.w 'nt.di.dit.rḫpt.|[---.-]rm.aklt.'gl.'l.mšt.|[---.--]r.špr.w yšt.il.|[---.-- UG5.2.1.8

u.|bkt.tgly.w tbu.|nṣrt.tbu.pnm.|'rm.tdu.mh.|pdrm.tdu.šrr.|ḥṭ m.t'mt.[']ṭr.[k]m.|zbln.'l.riš h.|w tṯb.trḥṣ.nn.b 16.6[127].7

-].|'ṭr[.---].|b p.š[---].|il.p.d[---].|'rm.[di.mh.pdrm].|di.š[rr.---].|mr[ṣ.---].|zb[ln.---].|t[--.---].|[-----]. 16[126].5.49

dit

bn abd'n.|bn prkl.|bn štn.|bn annyn.|b[n] slg.|u[--] dit.|bn p[-]n.|bn nẓġil. 101[10].14

dbb

r.|n'l.il.d qblbl.|'ln.ybl hm.ḫrṣ.|ṯlḥn.il.d mla.|mnm.dbbm.d |msdt.arṣ.|s'.il.dqt.k amr.|sknt.k ḥwt.yman.|d b h 4[51].1.40

ym.|bn.ḥṭb.|bn abyt.|bn ḫdl.|bn ṣdqn.|bn ayy.|bn dbb.|w nḥl h.|bn n'myn.|bn aṯtyy.|bn ḫlp.|bn.ẓll.|bn ydy 2016.1.7

dbḥ

.|[---.rp]um.tštyn.|[---.]il.d 'rgzm.|[---.]dt.'l.lty.|[---.]tdbḥ.amr.|ṯmn.b qrb.hkl y.[aṯr h.rpum].|tdd.aṯr h.tdd.iln[20[121].1.10

'.---].|bkyt.b hk[l]y.mšspdt.|b ḥẓr y pẓġm.ġr.w yq.|dbḥ.ilm.yš'ly.dġṯ h.|b šmym.dġṯ hrnmy[.d k]|bkbm.'[l.---]. 19[1AQHT].4.185

il dbḥ.b bt h.mṣd.ṣd.b qrb|hkl [h].ṣḥ.l qṣ.ilm.tlḥmn.|ilm.w tš UG5.1.1.1

.[il]ib.ġ[--.--rt].|w ['ṣrm.]l.ri[--.---].|[--]t.b'lt.bt[.---].|[md]bḥt.b.ḫmš[.---].|[-.]kbd.w.db[ḥ.---].|[--].aṯrt.'ṣr[m.l inš.i 35[3].38

ḥṣ.yd h.amt h.|uṣb't h.'d.ṯkm.|'rb.b ẓl.ḫmt.lqḥ.|imr.dbḥ.b yd h.|lla.klatnm.|klt.lḥm h.d nzl.|lqḥ.msrr.'ṣr.db[ḥ] 14[KRT].3.160

b['t k.]'d[.ṯ]km.|'rb[.b ẓl.ḫmt].|qḥ im[r.b yd k].|imr.d[bḥ.bm].ymn.|lla.kl[atn]m.|klt.l[ḥm k.d]nzl.|qḥ.ms[rr.]' 14[KRT].2.67

dbḥt.byy.bn.|šry.l 'ṯt. RS61[24.323.1]

-].|[-.]kbd.w.db[ḥ.---].|[--].aṯrt.'ṣr[m.l inš.ilm].|[t]ṯb.mdbḥ.b'l.g[dlt.---].|dqt.l.ṣpn.w.dqt[.---].|ṯn.l.'šrm.pamt.[--- 35[3].41

.|bt.il.ṯq[l.---.kbd].|w bdḥ.k[--.---].|'ṣrm.l i[nš.ilm.ṯb.md]|bḥ.b'l.[gdlt.---.dqt].|l ṣpn.w [dqt.---.ṯn.l 'š]|rm.pam[t. APP.II[173].44

rt.šd.bt[.m]lk.|k.t'rbn.ršp m.bt.mlk.|ḫlu.dg.|ḥdṯm.|dbḥ.b'l.k.tdd.b'lt.bhtm.|b.[-]ġb.ršp.ṣbi.|[---.--]m.|[---.]piln. 2004.14

n.ḥṭm].|w bġr.arb'.[---.kdm.yn].|prs.qmḥ.m'[--.---].|mdbḥt.bt.i[lt.'ṣrm.l].|ṣpn š.l ġlm[t.š.w l.---].|l yrḫ.gdlt.l [nk APP.II[173].26

t].|w ṯn ḥṭm.w bġr.arb['.---].|kdm.yn.prs.qmḥ.[---].|mdbḥt.bt.ilt.'ṣr[m.l ṣpn.š].|l ġlmt.š.w l [---.l yrḫ].|gd[lt].l n 35[3].24

y.qlt.|b ks.ištyn h.|dm.ṯn.dbḥm.šna.b'l.ṯlṯ.|rkb.'rpt.dbḥ.|bṯt.w dbḥ.w dbḥ.|dnt.w dbḥ.tdmm.|amht.k b h.bṯt.l 4[51].3.18

tm.|[yr]ḫ.kṯy gdlt.w l ġlmt š.|[w]pamt ṯlṯm.w yrdt.[m]dbḥt.|gdlt.l b'lt bhtm.'ṣrm.|l inš ilm. 34[1].20

dbḥ klyrḫ.|ndr.|dbḥ.|dt nat.|w ytnt.|ṯrmn w.|dbḥ kl.|kl ykly.|dbḥ k.sprt. RS61[24.277.3]

a.rbt.|špš.w tgh.nyr.|rbt.w rgm.l aḫt k.|ṯtmnt.krt n.dbḥ.|dbḥ.mlk.'šr.|'šrt.qḥ.tp k.b yd.|[-]r[-]k.bm.ymn.|tlk.š 16.1[125].39

.|[w y'ny.]ġzr.ilḥu.|[---.]mrṣ.mlk.|[--.k]rt.adn k.|[--.d]bḥ.dbḥ.|[--.']šr.'šrt.|'[---.---].|b[---.---].|t[--.---].|w[----].| 16.1[125].61

.|dm.ṯn.dbḥm.šna.b'l.ṯlṯ.|rkb.'rpt.dbḥ.|bṯt.w dbḥ.w dbḥ.|dnt.w dbḥ.tdmm.|amht.k b h.bṯt.l tbṯ.|w b h.tdmmt. 4[51].3.19

m.šna.b'l.ṯlṯ.|rkb.'rpt.dbḥ.|bṯt.w dbḥ.w dbḥ.|dnt.w dbḥ.tdmm.|amht.k b h.bṯt.l tbṯ.|w b h.tdmmt.amht.|aḫr. 4[51].3.20

.ḥmt.nša.|[y]d h.šmmh.dbḥ.|l ṯr.ab h.il.šrd.|[b'l].b dbḥ h.bn dgn.|[b m]ṣd h.yrd.krt.|[l g]gt.'db.akl.l qryt.|ḥṭt. 14[KRT].4.170

npš km.u b qṯt.tqṯṯ.|ušn yp km.l d[b]ḥm.w l.ṯ'.dbḥ n.ndbḥ.hw.ṯ' |nṯ'y.|hw.nkt.nkt.y[t]ši.l ab.bn.il.ytši.l dr.|bn il 32[2].1.24

ṣrt.npš[kn.u b qṯt].|tqṯṯn u ṯḫṭin.l bḥm.w l ṯ'.d[bḥ n.ndbḥ].|hw.ṯ'.nṯ'y.hw.nkt.n[k]t.ytši[.l ab.bn.il].|ytši.l dr.bn. 32[2].1.15

qṣrt.npš km.u b qṯt].|[tqṯṯ.u ṯḫṭu.l dbḥm.w l.ṯ'.dbḥ n.ndb]ḥ.|[hw.ṯ'.nṯ'y.hw.nkt.nkt.]yt[ši.l ab.bn.il].|[ytši.l dr.bn 32[2].1.9

pš kn.u b qṯt.|tqṯṯn.ušn y[p kn.l dbḥm.]w l ṯ' dbḥ n.|ndbḥ.hw.ṯ' n[ṯ'y.ḫw.nkt.nk]t.ytši.l ab bn il.|ytši.l d[r.bn il.l 32[2].1.33

.ištyn h.|dm.ṯn.dbḥm.šna.b'l.ṯlṯ.|rkb.'rpt.dbḥ.|bṯt.w dbḥ.w dbḥ.|dnt.w dbḥ.tdmm.|amht.k b h.bṯt.l tbṯ.|w b h.t 4[51].3.19

.b ap [kn.u b qṣ]rt.npš kn.u b qṯt.|tqṯṯn.ušn y[p kn.l dbḥm.]w l ṯ' dbḥ n.|ndbḥ.hw.ṯ' n[ṯ'y.hw.nkt.nk]t.ytši.l ab b 32[2].1.32

ṯin.b ap kn.u b [q]ṣrt.npš[kn.u b qṯt].|tqṯṯn u ṯḫṭin.l bḥm.w l ṯ'.d[bḥ n.ndbḥ].|hw.ṯ'.nṯ'y.hw.nkt.n[k]t.ytši[.l ab. 32[2].1.15

ḫṭu.u b ap km.u b qṣrt.npš km.u b qṯt].|[tqṯṯ.u ṯḫṭu.l dbḥm.w l.ṯ'.dbḥ n.ndb]ḥ.|[hw.ṯ'.nṯ'y.hw.nkt.nkt.]yt[ši.l ab. 32[2].1.9

b ap km.u b q[ṣ]rt.npš km.u b qṯt.tqṯṯ.|ušn yp km.l d[b]ḥm.w l.ṯ'.dbḥ n.ndbḥ.hw.ṯ' |nṯ'y.|hw.nkt.nkt.y[t]ši.l ab 32[2].1.24

rgm.k yrkt.'ṯqbm.|[---]m.'ẓpn.l pit.|m[--]m[.--]tm.w mdbḥt.|ḫr[.---.]'l.kbkbt.|n'm.[--.-]llm.trṯḥṣ.|btlt.'n[t].tptr' 13[6].16

.ymn.|lla.kl[atn]m.|klt.l[ḥm k.d]nzl.|qḥ.ms[rr.]'ṣr.|dbḥ.ṣ[q.b g]l.ḥṯt.|yn.b gl[.ḫ]rṣ.nbt.|'l.l ẓr.[mg]dl.|w 'l.l ẓr.[14[KRT].2.71

bḥ.b yd h.|lla.klatnm.|klt.lḥm h.d nzl.|lqḥ.msrr.'ṣr.db[ḥ].|yṣq.b gl.ḥṯt.yn.|b gl.ḫrṣ.nbt.w 'ly.|l ẓr.mgdl.rkb.|ṯk 14[KRT].3.163

ṯkmm.ḥm[t].ša.yd k.|šmm.dbḥ.l ṯr.|ab k.il.šrd.b'l.|b dbḥ k.bn.dgn.|b mṣd k.w yrd.|krt.l ggt.'db.|akl.l qryt.|ḥṭt. 14[KRT].2.78

ndr.|dbḥ.|dt nat.|w ytnt.|ṯrmn w.|dbḥ kl.|kl ykly.|dbḥ k.sprt.|dt nat.|w qrwn.|l k dbḥ.|[--]r bt [--].|[--]bnš [RS61[24.277.9]

dbḥ klyrḫ.|ndr.|dbḥ.|dt nat.|w ytnt.|ṯrmn w.|dbḥ kl.|kl ykly.|dbḥ k.sprt.|dt nat.|w qrwn.|l k dbḥ.|[--]r RS61[24.277.7]

dbḥ klyrḫ.|ndr.|dbḥ.|dt nat.|w ytnt.|ṯrmn w.|dbḥ kl.|kl RS61[24.277.1]

ltm.mrqdm.d š[-]l[-].|w t'n.pġt.ṯkmt.mym.|qrym.ab.dbḥ.l ilm.|š'ly.dġṯ h.b šmym.|dġṯ.hrnmy.d kbkbm.|l tbrkn 19[1AQHT].4.191

dm.[lḥ]m.tšty.|w t'n.mṯt ḥry.|l l[ḥ]m.l š[ty].ṣḥt km.|db[ḥ.l krt.a]dn km.|'l.krt.tbun.km.|rgm.ṯ[rm.]rgm hm.|b 15[128].6.5

.b bšr.tštn.|[w t]'n.mṯt.ḥry.|[l lḥ]m.l šty.ṣḥt km.|[--.dbḥ.l]krt.b'l km. 15[128].4.28

t.w 'ly.|l ẓr.mgdl.rkb.|ṯkmm.ḥmt.nša.|[y]d h.šmmh.dbḥ.|l ṯr.ab h.il.šrd.|[b'l].b dbḥ h.bn dgn.|[b m]ṣd h.yrd.kr 14[KRT].4.168

]dl.|w 'l.l ẓr.[mg]dl.rkb.|ṯkmm.ḥm[t].ša.yd k.|šmm.dbḥ.l ṯr.|ab k.il.šrd.b'l.|b dbḥ k.bn.dgn.|b mṣd k.w yrd.|k 14[KRT].2.76

yn.d.ykl.b d.[---].|b.dbḥ.mlk.|dbḥ ṣpn.|[-]zġm.|[i]lib.|[i]lbldn.|[p]dry.bt.mlk.| 2004.2

id ydbḥ mlk.|l ušḫ[r] ḫlmṭ.|l bbt il bt.|š l ḫlmṭ.|w tr l qlḥ.|w UG5.7.TR3

b[.š]p[š].|w [ḥl.]mlk.[w.]b.ym.ḥdṯ.ṯn.šm.|l.[---]t.|i[d.yd]bḥ.mlk.l.prgl.ṣqrn.b.gg.|ar[b'.]arb'.mṯbt.azmr.b h.š.šr[-] 35[3].50

|špš.w tgh.nyr.|rbt.w rgm.l aḫt k.|ṯtmnt.krt n.dbḥ.|dbḥ.mlk.'šr.|'šrt.qḥ.tp k.b yd.|[-]r[-]k.bm.ymn.|tlk.škn.'l. 16.1[125].40

|lwsnd.|[w] b ṣr.|'m.mlk.|w.ht.|mlk.syr.|ns.w.ṯm.|ydbḥ.|mlġ[.---].|w.m[--.--]y.|y[--.---]. 2063.16

qṣ]rt.npš kn.u b qṯt.|tqṯṯn.ušn y[p kn.l dbḥm.]w l ṯ' dbḥ n.|ndbḥ.hw.ṯ' n[ṯ'y.hw.nkt.nk]t.ytši.l ab bn il.|ytši.l d[32[2].1.32

q[ṣ]rt.npš km.u b qṯt.tqṯṯ.|ušn yp km.l d[b]ḥm.w l.ṯ'.dbḥ n.ndbḥ.hw.ṯ' |nṯ'y.|hw.nkt.nkt.y[t]ši.l ab.bn.il.ytši.l dr 32[2].1.24

.u b [q]ṣrt.npš[kn.u b qṯt].|tqṯṯn u ṯḫṭin.l bḥm.w l ṯ'.d[bḥ n.ndbḥ].|hw.ṯ'.nṯ'y.hw.nkt.n[k]t.ytši[.l ab.bn.il].|ytši.l 32[2].1.15

m.u b qṣrt.npš km.u b qṯt].|[tqṯṯ.u ṯḫṭu.l dbḥm.w l.ṯ'.dbḥ n.ndb]ḥ.|[hw.ṯ'.nṯ'y.hw.nkt.nkt.]yt[ši.l ab.bn.il].|[ytši.l 32[2].1.9

ṣprt dlt hm[.---].|w ġnbm.šlm.'rbm.ṯn[nm].|hlkm.b dbḥ n'mt.|šd[.i]lm.šd.aṯrt.w rḥmy.|[---].y[t]b.|[---]p.gp ym 23[52].27

yn.d.ykl.b d.[---].|b.dbḥ.mlk.|dbḥ ṣpn.|[-]zġm.|[i]lib.|[i]lbldn.|[p]dry.bt.mlk.|[-]lp.izr.|[2004.3

dbḥ.ṣp[n.---].|il.alp.w š[.---].|b'lm.alp.w š[.---].|b'lm.alp.w UG5.9.1.1
r[-] gtn ṯṯ ḫsn l ytn.|l rḥt lqḥ ṣtqn.|bt qbṣ urt ilštm' dbḥ ṣtqn l.|ršp. 1154.7
rmṣt.ilhm].|b'lm.w mlu[.---.ksm].|ṭlṯm.w m'rb[.---].|dbḥ šmn mr[.šmn.rqḥ.bt].|mtnt.w ynt.[qrt.w ṯn.ḥṯm].|w b APP.II[173].22
].|rmṣt.ilh[m.b'lm.---].|ksm.ṭlṯm.[---].|d yqḥ bt[.--]r.dbḥ[.šmn.mr].|šmn.rqḥ[.-]bt.mtnt[.w ynt.qrt].|w ṯn ḥṯm.w 35[3].20
ḫ]r.bn.ilm.štt.|p[--].b ṯlḥn y.qlt.|b ks.ištyn h.|dm.ṯn.dbḥm.šna.b'l.ṯlṯ.|rkb.'rpt.dbḥ.|bṯt.w dbḥ.w dbḥ.|dnt.w db 4[51].3.17
lt.ṯrmn.gdlt.pdry.gdlt dqt.|dqt.trṯ.dqt.|[rš]p.'nt.ḫbly.dbḥn š[p]š pgr.|[g]dlt iltm ḫnqtm.d[q]tm.|[yr]ḫ.kṯy gdlt.w 34[1].17
k.]yṣḥ.|[---]d.'r.|[----.-]bb.|[----.]lm y.|[---.--]p.|[---.d]bḥ.|t[---.id]k.|pn[m.al.ttn].|'m.[krt.msw]n.|w r[gm.l krt. 14[KRT].5.243
h.š'[-]rt.|ḫqr.[--.ṯq]l rb.|ṯl[ṯ.---].|aḥt.ḫm[-.---].|b ym.dbḥ.ṯp[-].|aḥt.l mzy.bn[--].|aḥt.l mkt.ǵr.|aḥt.l 'ṯtrt.|arb'.'ṣ 39[19].13
.|ypḫ[--].|w s[--].|[---].|qrd ga[n.--].|b bt k.[--].|w l dbḥ[--].|ṯ[--].|[--] aṯt yqḥ 'z.|[---]ḏ.|[---].|[---].|hm qrt tuḫ RS61[24.277.23]
-].|ṯmn.kbd.yn.d.l.ṭb.b.gn'[y].|mitm.yn.ḥsp.d.nkly.b.db[ḫ.--].|mit.arb'm.kbd.yn.ḥsp.l.m[--].|mit.'šrm.[k]bd.yn.ḥ 1084.24
y'ny.]ǵzr.ilḥu.|[---.]mrṣ.mlk.|[--.k]rt.adn k.|[--.d]bḥ.dbḥ.|[--.']šr.'šrt.|'[---.---].|b[---.---].|t[--.---].|w[----].|pǵ[t.- 16.1[125].61
w.|dbḥ kl.|kl ykly.|dbḥ k.sprt.|dt nat.|w qrwn.|l k dbḥ.|[--]r bt [--].|[--]bnš [--].|š š[--].|w [--].|d [--].|ypḫ[--] RS61[24.277.12]
]b.|[---.--]k.|[---.--]an.|[---.--]m.ank.|[---.]asrm.|[---.]dbḥm.|[---.y]rḫ.w šqr.|[---.--]b.b y[--.---].|[-----].|[-----].|[-- 1002.23
[---.]ksḫ[-.--].|[---.]mnty[.-].|[---.]rb spr ḫbb.|[---.--]n.dbḥm.|[---].'bdssm. 49[73].2.5
|drkt h.š[--.--].|w hm.ap.l[--.---].|ymḫṣ k.k[--.---].|il.dbḥ.[---].|p'r.b[--.---].|ṭbḫ.alp[m.ap.ṣin.šql].|ṯrm.w [mri.il 1['NT.X].4.28
.---].|[--]t.b'lt.bt[.---].|[md]bḥt.b.ḫmš[.---].|[-.]kbd.w.db[ḫ.---].|[--].aṯrt.'ṣr[m.l inš.ilm].|[ṯ]ṭb.mdbḥ.b'l.g[dlt.---].| 35[3].39
-].|[---.yr]ḫ.mgm[r.---].|[---.--]š.b d.h[--.---].|[---.y]rḫ.dbḥ[.---].|[---.-]pn.b d.[---].|[---.]b d.[---]. 1160.5
[---.rp]um.tdbḥn.|[----.]'d.ilnym.|[---.--]l km amt m.|[---.]b w t'rb.sd. 20[121].1.1

dbṯ

ḫn.[---].|qrn h.km.ǵb[-.---].|hw km.ḥrr[.---].|šnmtm.dbṯ[.---].|tr'.tr'n.a[--.---].|bnt.šdm.ṣḥr[.---].|šb'.šnt.il.mla.[- 12[75].2.42

dby

[bn.--]r.|[bn.--]tn.|[bn.-]rmn.|bn.prtn.|bn.ymn.|bn.dby.|bn.ir[--].|bn.kr[--].|bn.nn[-].|[-----].|[-----].|[---.-]l[-]. 124[-].5.10

dblt

rb['.d]d.š['rm.---].|[--.-]rṯm š[šm]n.k[--.---].|[---.ar]b'.dblt.ḏr[--.---].|[--.m]itm.nṣ.l bn[.---].|[-]l[-.---].|[-]ṯ.[---].|m 143[-].1.9
].|aḥd[h.w.yṣq.b.ap h].|k yr[a]š.šš[w.w.ykhp].|mid.dblt.yṯ[nt.w].|ṣmq[m].yṭnm.w[.qmḥ.bql].|tdkn.aḥd h.w[.yṣ 161[56].33
.|[---.-]rb.|[-----].|[-----].|[-----].|k yraš w ykhp mid.|dblt yṯnt w ṣmqm yṭn[m].|w qmḥ bql yṣq aḥd h.|b ap h. 160[55].24
]nbt.k[d.]šmn.mr.|[---.l]ṯḥ.sb[by]n.lṯḥ.šḥ[lt].|[---.l]ṯḥ.dblt.lṯḥ.ṣmqm.|[---.--]m.[ḫ]mšm.ḥmr.škm. 142[12].17
.|[----]d.n'r.ṯ[--]d[.---].|[---.]ṯlṯ.kṯt[.-]d.[---].|[---.a]rb'.dblt.m[--.---].|[--.mi]tm nṣ.[-]ṯ[-.]gr[-.---].|[---].arb['.d]d.š['r 143[-].1.5

dbr

.|[---.t]š'm.|[---.--]y arb'm.|[---.]l špš ṯmny[m].|[---.]dbr h l šp[š].|[---.]dbr h l šp[š].|[---.]npṯry ṯ[--].|[---.--]urm. 41[71].8
]y arb'm.|[---.]l špš ṯmny[m].|[---.]dbr h l šp[š].|[---.]dbr h l šp[š].|[---.]npṯry ṯ[--].|[---.--]urm.|[-----]. 41[71].9
--.'š]rm.kkr.ṯlṯ.|[--.]ṯlṯm.kkr.ṯlṯ.|[--.]aštn.l k.|[--]y.kl.dbrm.hm[.--].|[--]l.w.kl.mḫr k.|[--]tir.aštn.l [k].|[---].kkr.ṯl 1022.7
gm.'ny.|l k[rt.adn k.]ištm['].|w tqǵ[.udn.k ǵz.ǵzm].|tdbr.w[ǵ]rm[.ṯṯwy].|šqlt.b ǵlt.yd k.|l tdn.dn.almnt.|l ṯṯpṭ. 16.6[127].31
h.|w yṣḥ.šm' m'.l krt.|ṯ'.ištm'.w tqǵ udn.|k ǵz.ǵzm.tdbr.|w ǵrm.ṯṯwy.šqlt.|b ǵlt.yd k.l tdn.|dn.almnt.l ṯṯpṭ.|ṯp 16.6[127].43
ǵr.|l kbd.arṣ.kl.gb'.|l [k]bd.šdm.tmǵ.l n'm[y].|[arṣ.]dbr.ysmt.šd.|[šḥl]mmt.t[mǵ.]l b'l.np[l].|[l a]rṣ[.lpš].tks.miz 5[67].6.29
dm.npš.ḫsrt.|bn.nšm.npš.hmlt.|arṣ.mǵt.l n'm y.arṣ.|dbr.ysmt.šd.šḥlmmt.|ngš.ank.aliyn b'l.|'dbnn ank.imr.b p 6[49].2.20
ṣ]ḥ.sbn.|[---]l[.---.]'d.|ksm.mhyt[.m]ǵny.|l n'm y.arṣ.dbr.|l ysmt.šd.šḥlmmt.|mǵny.l b'l.npl.l a|rṣ.mt.aliyn.b'l.| 5[67].6.6
|rdm.arṣ.w td' ilm.|k mtt.yšm'.aliyn.b'l.|yuhb.'glt.b dbr.prt.|b šd.šḥlmmt.škb.|'mn h.šb'.l šb'm.|tš[']ly.ṯmn.l ṯ 5[67].5.18
ḥw.bṭnm.uḫd.b'lm.|[--.a]ṯm.prṭl.l riš h.ḥmt.ṯmṯ.|[--.]ydbr.ṯrmt.al m.qḥn y.š y.qḥn y.|[--.]šir.b krm.nṭṭt.dm.'lt.b 1001.1.8

dg

p.ḏd.št.špt.|l arṣ.špt l šmm.w 'rb.b p hm.'ṣr.šmm.|w dg b ym.w ndd.gzr.l zr.y'db.u ymn.|u šmal.b p hm.w l.tšb' 23[52].63
k k.'m dt[n].|lqḥ.mtpṭ.|w y'ny.nn.|dtn.bt n.mḫ[-].|l dg.w [-]kl.|w aṯr.hn.mr[-]. UG5.6.15
rz.|k.t'rb.'ṯtrt.šd.bt[.m]lk.|k.t'rbn.ršp m.bt.mlk.|ḫlu.dg.|ḥdṯm.|dbḥ.b'l.k.tdd.b'lt.bhtm.|b.[-]ǵb.ršp.ṣbi.|[---.--] 2004.12
l rbd.|[---.]b'lt h w yn.|[---.rk]b 'rpt.|[---.--]n.w mnu dg.|[---.]l aliyn b'l.|[---].rkb 'rpt. 2001.2.16

dgy

--.]b nhrm.|['b]r.gbl.'br.|q'l.'br.iht.|np šmm.šmšr.|l dgy.aṯrt.|mǵ.l qdš.amrr.|idk.al.tnn.|pnm.tk.ḥqkpt.|il.kl h. 3['NT.VI].6.10
.rbt.a[ṯrt].|ym.gm.l ǵlm h.k [tṣḥ].|'n.mkṯr.ap.t[---].|dgy.rbt.aṯr[t.ym].|qḥ.rṯt.b d k t[---].|rbt.'l.ydm[.---].|b md 4[51].2.31
ṯr[.il.ab -.w t'n.rbt].|aṯr[t.ym.šm'.l qdš].|w am[rr.l dgy.rbt].|aṯrt.ym[.mdl.'r].|ṣmd.pḥl[.št.gpnm.dt].|ksp.dt.yr 4[51].4.3

dgn

m.ǵrpl].'l.arṣ.l an.|[ḫ]mt.i[l.w] ḥrn.yisp.ḥmt.|[b'l.w]dgn[.yi]sp.ḥmt.'nt.w 'ṯtrt.|[ti]sp.ḥmt.y[r]ḫ.w.ršp.yisp.ḥmt. UG5.8.14
y'n.]ṯr.ab h.il.'bd k.b'l.y ym m.'bd k.b'l.|[--.--]m.bn.dgn.a[s]r km.hw ybl.argmn k.k ilm.|[---.]ybl.k bn.qdš.mnḥ 2.1[137].37
.|[y]d h.šmmh.dbḥ.|l ṯr.ab h.il.šrd.|[b'l].b dbḥ h.bn dgn.|[b m]ṣd h.yrd.krt.|[l g]gt.'db.akl.l qryt.|ḥṭt.l bt.ḫbr.| 14[KRT].4.170
[t].ša.yd k.|šmm.dbḥ.l ṯr.|ab k.il.šrd.b'l.|b dbḥ k.bn.dgn.|b mṣd k.w yrd.|krt.l ggt.'db.|akl.l qryt.|ḥṭt.l bt.ḫbr.| 14[KRT].2.78
btlt.'n[t].|w p.n'mt.aḫt[.b'l].|y'l.b'l.b ǵ[r.---].|w bn.dgn.b š[---].|b'l.yṯb.l ks[i.mlk h].|bn.dgn.l kḥ[ṯ.drkt h].|l al 10[76].3.13
il ṣpn.|il[i]b.|i[l].|dgn.|b'[l ṣ]pn.|b'lm.|[b']lm.|[b']lm.|[b']lm.|[b']lm.|[b'l]m 29[17].1.4
.ymǵy.aklm.|w ymẓa.'qqm.|b'l.ḥmd m.yḥmd m.|bn.dgn.yhrr m.|b'l.ngt hm.b p'n h.|w il hd.b ḫrẓ' h.|[-----].|[- 12[75].1.39
[--.]ab.w il[--].|[--] šlm.šlm i[l].|[š]lm.il.šr.|dgn.w b'l.|'ṯ w kmṯ.|yrḫ w ksa.|yrḫ mkṯy.|ṯkmn w šnm.| UG5.10.1.4
.nhr.tn.il m.d tq h.d tqyn h.|[hml]t.tn.b'l.w 'nn h.bn.dgn.arṯ m.pḏ h.|[w y'n.]ṯr.ab h.il.'bd k.b'l.y ym m.'bd k.b'l 2.1[137].35

.nhr].|tn.il m.d tq h.d tqyn.hmlt.tn.b‘l.[w ‘nn h].|bn.dgn.arṯ m.pḏ h.tb‘.ǵlmm.l ṯṯb.[idk.pnm].|l ytn.tk.ǵr.ll.‘m.p 2.1[137].19

.b ǵr.t[l]iyt.|ql.l b‘l.ttnn.|bšrt.il.bš[r.b‘]l.|w bšr.ḥtk.dgn.|k.ibr.l b‘l[.yl]d.|w rum.l rkb.‘rpt.|yšmẖ.aliyn.b‘l. 10[76].3.35

lṭpn.il d pi|d dq.anm.l yrẓ.|‘m.b‘l.l y‘db.mrḥ.|‘m.bn.dgn.k tms m.|w ‘n.rbt.aṯrt ym.|blt.nmlk.‘ṯtr.‘rẓ.|ymlk.‘ṯtr. 6.1.52[49.1.24]

m.nrt.ksmm.|‘l.tl[-]k.‘ṭrṭrm.|nšu.[r]iš.ḥrṯm.|l ẓr.‘db.dgn kly.|lḥm.[b]‘dn hm.kly.|yn.b ḥmt hm.k[l]y.|šmn.b q[16[126].3.13

.b ǵ[r.---].|w bn.dgn.b š[---].|b‘l.yṯb.l ks[i.mlk h].|bn.dgn.l kḥ[ṯ.drkt h].|l alp.ql.ẓ[--.---].|l np ql.nd.[----].|tlk.w t 10[76].3.15

h.tḥrṯ.km.gn.|ap lb.k ‘mq.tṯlṯ.bmt.|b‘l.mt.my.lim.bn dgn.|my.hmlt.aṯr.b‘l.nrd.|b arṣ.‘m h.trd.nrt.|ilm.špš.‘d.tšb 6[62].1.6

lb.k ‘mq.yṯlṯ.|bmt.yšu.g h.w yṣḥ.|b‘l.mt.my.lim.bn.|dgn.my.hmlt.aṯr.|b‘l.ard.b arṣ.ap.|‘nt.ttlk.w tṣd.kl.ǵr.|l kb 5[67].6.24

.alp.|w š.pdry š.ddmš š.|w b urbt.ilib š.|b‘l alp w š.|dgn.š.il t‘ḏr.š.|b‘l š.‘nt š.ršp š.|šlmm.|w šnpt.il š.|l ‘nt.ḥl š. UG5.13.21

nt.w [-]n[-.---].|il.ẖyr.ilib.š.|arṣ w šmm.š.|il.š.kṯrt.š.|dgn.š.b‘l.ẖlb alp w š.|b‘l ṣpn alp.w.š.|ṯrṯy.alp.w.š.|yrẖ.š.ṣp UG5.9.2.4

.k]bdm.|[---.--]mm.ṯn.šm.w alp.l[--]n.|[---.]š.il š.b‘l š.dgn š.|[---.--]r.w ṯt pl.gdlt.[ṣ]pn.dqt.|[---.al]p ‘nt.gdlt.b ṯlṯt 36[9].1.3

.‘q šr.ydb.ksa.|w yṯb.|tqru.l špš.u h.špš.um.ql.bl.‘m.|dgn.ttl h.mnt.nṯk.nḥš.šmrr.|nḥš.‘q šr.ln h.mlẖš.abd.ln h.|y UG5.7.15

ilht kṯr[t.--]mm.|nh l yd h tzdn[.---]n.|l ad[n h.---].|dgn tt[--.---.-]l|‘.l kṯrt hl[l.sn]nt.|ylak yrẖ ny[r] šmm.‘m.|ẖ 24[77].14

.[---].|il hd.b[---].|at.bl.at.[---].|yisp hm.b[‘l.---].|bn.dgn[.---].|‘ḏbm.[---].|uẖry.l[---].|mṣt.ks h.t[--.---].|idm.adr 12[75].2.26

‘]ṣrm.|[--]ṯpḥ b‘l.|[ṯl]ṯ.‘ṣrm.|[w]b‘lt btm.|[---.--]ṣn.l.dgn.|[---.--]m.|[---].pi[--.-]qš.|[--]pš.šn[--].|ṯ[-]r.b iš[-].|b‘l 39[19].5

dd

ṯlṯm.ktn.|ẖmšm.izml.|ẖmš.kbd.arb‘m.|dd.akl.|ṯṯ.‘šr h.yn.|kd.šmn.l.nr.ilm.|kdm.dǵm.|ṯṯ.kdm.zt 1126.4

ḥṣ.yd[h.---].|[--.]yṣt ḏm[r.---].|tšt[.r]imt.[l irt h.tšr.l dd.aliyn.b‘l].|[ahb]t pdr[y.bt.ar.ahbt.ṭly.bt.rb.dd].|arṣy bt. 7.2[130].10

.ybmt].|limm.tiẖd.knr h.b yd[h.tšt].|rimt.l irt h.tšr.dd.al[iyn].|b‘l.ahbt. UG5.3.2.7

[---.t]št.rimt.|l irt h.mšr.l.dd.aliyn.|b‘l.yd.pdry.bt.ar.|ahbt.ṭly.bt.rb.dd.arṣy.|bt.y‘bdr 3[‘NT].3.2

[d].|ḥdyn.d[d].|[-]dḏn.d[d].|qṭn.d[d].|lẖsn.d[d].|lsn.d[d].|and[--.---]. 132[331].11

irt h.mšr.l.dd.aliyn.|b‘l.yd.pdry.bt.ar.|ahbt.ṭly.bt.rb.dd.arṣy.|bt.y‘bdr.km ǵlmm.|w ‘rb n.l p‘n.‘nt.hbr.|w ql.tštḥ 3[‘NT].3.4

h.tšr.l dd.aliyn.b‘l].|[ahb]t pdr[y.bt.ar.ahbt.ṭly.bt.rb.dd].|arṣy bt.y[‘bdr.---].|rgm l btl[t.‘nt.ṯny.l ybmt.limm.tḥm 7.2[130].11

.riš.argmn].|w ṯn šm.l [b‘lt.bhtm.‘ṣrm.l inš].|ilm.w š d[d.ilš.š.--.mlk].|yṯb.brr[.w mḥ-.---].|ym.[‘]lm.y‘[--.---].|[--. 35[3].6

š.|arg[mn.w ṯn.]šm.l b‘lt.|bhtm.‘ṣ[rm.l in]š ilm.w š.|dd ilš.š[.---.]mlk.yṯb br|r.w mḥ[--.---.]w q[--].|ym.‘lm.y[---. APP.II[173].7

ṯlṯ.mat[.---.]kbd.|ṯṯ.ddm.k[--.b]rqd.|mit.tš‘m.[kb]d.ddm.|b.gt.bir. 2168.3

[---.]dd.|[---]n.dd.|[---.]dd.|bn.arwdn.dd.|mnḥm.w.kbln.|bn.ǵlm.dd.|bn.tbšn.dd.| 131[309].3

.|bn.arwdn.dd.|mnḥm.w.kbln.|bn.ǵlm.dd.|bn.tbšn.dd.|bn.ẖran.w[.---].|[-]n.y‘rtym.|gmm.w.bn.p[--].|trn.w.p[131[309].7

h.|[-]wyn.yd[-.---.]dd.|[---]n.yd.sǵ[r.---.--]k.[--].|[---.]dd.bn.š.[---.]yd.sǵr h.|[---.--]r h.‘šr[m.---.‘]šrm.dd.|[---.yn.d 1098.42

n.dd.|[---.]dd.|bn.arwdn.dd.|mnḥm.w.kbln.|bn.ǵlm.dd.|bn.tbšn.dd.|bn.ẖran.w[.---].|[-]n.y‘rtym.|gmm.w.bn.p[131[309].6

n.|[---].ẖšwn.ṯṯ.mat.nṣ.|[---].ẖmšm.ḥmr.škm.|[---.ṯṯ.dd.]gdl.ṯṯ.dd.š‘rm.|[---.a]lp.arb‘.mat.tyt.|[---.kd.]nbt.k[d.]š 142[12].13

m.[ṯ]ṯ.mat.nṣ.ṯlṯm.‘ṣr.|[---].ẖmš[m.ḥm]r.škm.|[---.ṯṯ.dd.]gdl.ṯṯ.dd.š‘rm.|[---.hn.w.al]p.kd.nbt.kd.šmn.mr.|[---].k 142[12].7

[---.]ṯṯ.dd.gdl.ṯṯ.dd.š‘rm.|[---.-]hn.w.alp.kd.nbt.kd.šmn.mr.|[---.]a 142[12].1

[--.‘]ṯtrum[.---].|[---.]ḥmr.y[--].|[---].n‘r[.---].|[---.]dd gdl[.---]. 2133.12

-]n.|dd l ky.|dd l ‘bdkṯr.|dd[m] l r‘y.|[--] šmḥ[.---].|ddm gt dprnm.|l ḥršm.|ddm l ‘nqt.|dd l alṯt.w l lmdt h.|d 1101.8

[m.---.-]rm.|‘šr[.---].alpm.|arb‘.ddm.l.k[-]ẖ.|ṯmnym.dd.dd.kbd.|[l].mḏr[ǵ]lm.|b yrẖ[ri]šyn.|šb[‘.--]n.[k]bd.|w[. 2012.19

rẖ.---].|[---.]prš.|[-----].|l.mšḥ[.---].|‘šr.d[d.---].|ṯṯm.dd.dd[.---].|l.mḏrǵlm[.---].|ṯlṯ.mat.ẖmšm.kb[d].|ẖmš.kbd.l 2012.9

.ḥpr.bnšm.ṯmnym.dd.|l u[-]m.|b.ṭbq.arb‘m.dr‘.w.‘šr.dd.drt.|w[.a]rb‘.l.‘šrm.dd.l.yḥšr.bl.bn h.|b.gt.m‘br.arb‘m.l. 1098.10

sp w rbt ẖ|rṣ.išlḥ ẓhrm iq|nim.atn šd h krm[m].|šd dd h ḥrnqm.w |y‘n ẖrẖb mlk qẓ [l].|n‘mn.ilm l ẖt[n].|m.b‘ 24[77].23

ml[--.---].|tlbr[-.---].|isg.[---].|ilwn.[---].|ṯrn.d[d].|tg d[d].|ḥdyn.d[d].|[-]dḏn.d[d].|qṭn.d[d].|lẖsn.d[d].|lsn.d[d]. 132[331].6

ṯlṯm.dd[.---].|b.gt.ṣb[-.---].|mit.‘šr.[---.]dd[.--].|tš‘.dd.ḥ[ṭm.w].ẖm[šm].|kdm.kbd.yn.b.gt.[---].|[mi]tm.ẖmšm. 2092.4

mšm.ẖmš.k[bd].|[dd].kšmm.tš‘[.---].|[š]‘rm.ṯṯ.‘[šr].|[dd].ḥṭm.w.ẖ[mšm].|[ṯ]lṯ kbd.yn.b [gt.---].|mit.[---].ṯlṯ.kb[d] 2092.9

n.arb‘m.y[n].|b.gt.trǵnds.|tš‘.‘šr.[dd].kšmm.|ṯn.‘šr[.dd.ḥ]ṭm.|w.šb[‘.---]. 2092.17

m.š‘rm.l.trbnn.|ddm.š‘rm.l.ẖtn.|dd.š‘rm.l.ḥmr.ḥṭb.|dd.ḥṭm.l.ẖḏǵb.|ṯṯ.ddm.l.gzzm.|kd yn.l.ẖtn.w.kd.ḥmṣ.w.[lt] 1099.25

-]mn.|[---.--]m.mṣl.|[---].prš.ḥṭm.|ṯlṯ[.---].bn.ṯdnyn.|ddm.ḥ[ṭm].‘l.šrn.|‘šrt.ksp.‘l.[-]lpy.|bn.ady.kkr.š‘rt.|nṯk h.| 1146.7

.|b.gt.ǵl.‘šrm.l.mit.dr‘.w.tš‘m.drt.|[w].ṯmnym.l.mit.dd.ḥpr.bnšm.|b.gt.alẖb.ṯṯm.dr‘.w.ẖmšm.drt.w.ṯṯm.dd.|ḥpr 1098.15

it.dd.ḥpr.bnšm.|b.gt.alẖb.ṯṯm.dr‘.w.ẖmšm.drt.w.ṯṯm.dd.|ḥpr.bnšm.|b.gt.knpy.mit.dr‘.ṯṯm.drt.w.šb‘m.dd.arb‘.|k 1098.16

.gt.m‘br.arb‘m.l.mit.dr‘.w.ṯmnym[.drt].|w.‘šrm.l.mit.dd.ḥp[r.]bnšm.|b.gt.ǵl.‘šrm.l.mit.dr‘.w.tš‘m.drt.|[w].ṯmny 1098.13

.bnšm.|b.nzl.‘šrm.l.mit.dr‘.w.šb‘m.drt.|w.‘šrm.l.mit.dd.ḥpr.bnšm.|b.y‘ny.arb‘m.dr‘.w.‘šrm.drt.|w.ṯlṯm.dd.ṯṯ.kb 1098.25

.kšmm.b.yrẖ.iṯtbnm.|šb‘m.dd.ṯn.kbd.|tgmr.ḥṭm.šb‘.ddm.|ẖmš.dd.š‘rm.|kdm.yn.|kdm.ṣmṣ. 1099.32

t h[.hwt h].|b nši ‘n h.w tphn.in.[---].|[-.]hlk.ǵlmm b dd y.yṣ[--].|[-.]yṣa.w l.yṣa.hlm.[ṯnm].|[q]dqd.ṯlṯ id.‘l.ud[n]. 19[1AQHT].2.77

.---.-]rm.|‘šr[.---].alpm.|arb‘.ddm.l.k[-]ẖ.|ṯmnym.dd.dd.kbd.|[l].mḏr[ǵ]lm.|b yrẖ[ri]šyn.|šb[‘.--]n.[k]bd.|w[.---. 2012.19

‘šrm ddm kbd[.-] l alpm mrim.|ṯṯ ddm l ṣin mrat.|‘šr ddm.l šm‘ 1100.1

‘ym.šb‘m.l.mitm.dd.|[---.--]d.šb‘m.kbd.dr‘.|[---.]kbd.ddm.kbd[.---].|[---.]‘m.kbd.l.r‘[ym.---].|[---].kbd.ṯmn.kb[d.- 1098.46

r.bt.k[--].|tš‘.‘šr h.dd.l.b[t.--].|ẖmš.ddm.l.ẖtyt.|ṯlṯm.dd.kšmn.l.gzzm.|yyn.|ṣdqn.|‘bd.pdr.|myṣm.|ṯgt.|w.lmd 1099.4

.|‘bdrpu.|w.lmd h.|‘dršp.|w.lmd h.|krwn b.gt.nbk.|ddm.kšmm.l.ẖtn.|ddm.l.trbnn.|ddm.š‘rm.l.trbnn.|ddm.š‘r 1099.20

].|kdm.kbd.yn.b.gt.[---].|[mi]tm.ẖmšm.ẖmš.k[bd].|[dd].kšmm.tš‘[.---].|[š]‘rm.ṯṯ.‘[šr].|[dd].ḥṭm.w.ẖ[mšm].|[ṯ]lṯ 2092.7

].‘šr.dd[.---].|[---]mn.arb‘m.y[n].|b.gt.trǵnds.|tš‘.‘šr.[dd].kšmm.|ṯn.‘šr[.dd.ḥ]ṭm.|w.šb[‘.---]. 2092.16

[---.]ksp dd qmḥ.|[---.]ṯlṯ dd ksmm.|[---.-]rbr dd š‘rm.|[---.]r[--.]ḥṭm.|kr[--.]tp[n].|k 2037.1.2

ṯlṯ.mat[.---.]kbd.|ṯṯ.ddm.k[--.b]rqd.|mit.tš‘m.[kb]d.ddm.|b.gt.bir. 2168.2

.|[--] šmḥ[.---].|ddm gt dprnm.|l ḥršm.|ddm l ‘nqt.|dd l alṯt.w l lmdt h.|dd l iẖyn.|dd l [---]. 1101.11

gt dprnm.|l ḥršm.|ddm l ‘nqt.|dd l alṯt.w l lmdt h.|dd l iẖyn.|dd l [---]. 1101.12

.mit.drt.|w[.---.]‘m.l.mit.dd.ṯn.kbd.ḥpr.bnšm.ṯmnym.dd.|l u[-]m.|b.ṭbq.arb‘m.dr‘.w.‘šr.dd.drt.|w[.a]rb‘.l.‘šrm.d 1098.8

lpm mrim. | ṯṯ ddm l ṣin mrat. | ʿšr ddm.l šmʿrgm. | ʿšr ddm.l bt. | ʿšrm.dd.l mḫṣm. | ddm l kbs. | dd l prgṯ. | dd.l mri. 1100.4
spr.ḥpr.bt.k[--]. | tšʿ.ʿšr h.dd.l.b[t.--]. | ḫmš.ddm.l.ḫtyt. | ṯlṯm.dd.kšmn.l.gzzm. | yyn. | ṣ 1099.2
glṯ.b šm[m]. | [---.i]l.ṯr.iṯ.p h.k ṯṯ.ǵlṯ[.--]. | [---.--] k yn.ddm.l b[--.---]. | [---.-]yt š[--.---]. | [---.]hl[-.---]. | [---.-]yṯr.ur[-- UG5.3.1.9
dm.šʿrm.l.ḫtn. | dd.šʿrm.l.ḥmr.ḥṭb. | dd.ḥṭm.l.ḫdǵb. | ṯṯ.ddm.l.gzzm. | kd yn.l.ḫtn.w.kd.ḥmṣ.w.[lt]ḥ.ʿšdm. | kd yn.l.ḫ 1099.26
spr.ḥpr.bt.k[--]. | tšʿ.ʿšr h.dd.l.b[t.--]. | ḫmš.ddm.l.ḫtyt. | ṯlṯm.dd.kšmn.l.gzzm. | yyn. | ṣdqn. | ʿbd.pdr. | my 1099.3
ʿ]rby. | ṯmn.ṣmd.[---]. | b d.bʿlsr. | yd.ṯdn.ʿšr. | [ḥ]mrm. | ddm.l.ybr[k]. | bdmr.prs.l.u[-]m[-]. | ṯmn.l.ʿšrm. | dmd.b d.mr 2102.6
l u[-]m. | b.ṯbq.arbʿm.drʿ.w.ʿšr.dd.drt. | w[.a]rbʿ.l.ʿšrm.dd.l.yḫšr.bl.bn h. | b.gt.mʿbr.arbʿm.l.mit.drʿ.w.ṯmnym[.drt]. 1098.11
t. | ʿšr ddm.l šmʿrgm. | ʿšr ddm.l bt. | ʿšrm.dd.l mḫṣm. | ddm l kbs. | dd l prgṯ. | dd.l mri. | dd.l ṯnǵly. | dd.l krwn. | dd.l 1100.6
[-----]. | dd l krwn. | dd l [--]n. | dd l ky. | dd l ʿbdkṯr. | dd[m] l rʿy. | [--] šmḫ[.---]. | ddm gt dpr 1101.4
l mḫṣm. | ddm l kbs. | dd l prgṯ. | dd.l mri. | dd.l ṯnǵly. | dd.l krwn. | dd.l ṯǵr. | dd.l rmt.r[---]. 1100.10
[-----]. | dd l krwn. | dd l [--]n. | dd l ky. | dd l ʿbdkṯr. | dd[m] l rʿy. | [--] 1101.2
.kbd. | w.[---.-]mʿt. | ṯlṯ[m.---.-]rm. | ʿšr[.---].alpm. | arbʿ.ddm.l.k[-]ḫ. | ṯmnym.dd.dd.kbd. | [l].mdr[ǵ]lm. | b yrḫ[ri]šy 2012.18
dm l ṣin mrat. | ʿšr ddm.l šmʿrgm. | ʿšr ddm.l bt. | ʿšrm.dd.l mḫṣm. | ddm l kbs. | dd l prgṯ. | dd.l mri. | dd.l ṯnǵly. | dd. 1100.5
ʿšr ddm.l bt. | ʿšrm.dd.l mḫṣm. | ddm l kbs. | dd l prgṯ. | dd.l mri. | dd.l ṯnǵly. | dd.l krwn. | dd.l ṯǵr. | dd.l rmt.r[---]. 1100.8
[k]bd. | w[.---.]qmʿt. | [---.]mdrǵlm. | [---.]mdm. | [w].ʿšr.dd.l np[l]. | r[p]š. 2012.26
[-----]. | dd l krwn. | dd l [--]n. | dd l ky. | dd l ʿbdkṯr. | dd[m] l rʿy. | [--] šmḫ[.---]. | ddm gt dprnm. | l ḥr 1101.5
. | dd[m] l rʿy. | [--] šmḫ[.---]. | ddm gt dprnm. | l ḥršm. | ddm l ʿnqt. | dd l alṯt.w l lmdt h. | dd l iḫyn. | dd l [---]. 1101.10
šmʿrgm. | ʿšr ddm.l bt. | ʿšrm.dd.l mḫṣm. | ddm l kbs. | dd l prgṯ. | dd.l mri. | dd.l ṯnǵly. | dd.l krwn. | dd.l ṯǵr. | dd.l r 1100.7
ʿšrm ddm kbd[.-] l alpm mrim. | ṯṯ ddm l ṣin mrat. | ʿšr ddm.l šmʿrgm. | ʿšr ddm.l bt. | ʿšrm.dd.l 1100.2
dd l prgṯ. | dd.l mri. | dd.l ṯnǵly. | dd.l krwn. | dd.l ṯǵr. | dd.l rmt.r[---]. 1100.12
[-----]. | dd l krwn. | dd l [--]n. | dd l ky. | dd l ʿbdkṯr. | dd[m] l rʿy. | [--] šmḫ[.---]. | ddm gt dprnm. | l ḥršm. | ddm l ʿ 1101.6
]rʿ.w.mit.drt.w.ʿšrm.l.mit. | [drt.ḥpr.b]nšm.w.ṯn.ʿšr h.dd.l.rpš. | [---.]šbʿm.drʿ.w.arbʿm.drt.mit.dd. | [---].ḥpr.bn.šm. 1098.4
šrm ddm kbd[.-] l alpm mrim. | ṯṯ ddm l ṣin mrat. | ʿšr ddm.l šmʿrgm. | ʿšr ddm.l bt. | ʿšrm.dd.l mḫṣm. | ddm l kbs. | 1100.3
. | ʿdršp. | w.lmd h. | krwn b.gt.nbk. | ddm.kšmm.l.ḫtn. | ddm.l.trbnn. | ddm.šʿrm.l.trbnn. | ddm.šʿrm.l.ḫtn. | dd.šʿrm.l. 1099.21
t. | ʿšrm.dd.l mḫṣm. | ddm l kbs. | dd l prgṯ. | dd.l mri. | dd.l ṯnǵly. | dd.l krwn. | dd.l ṯǵr. | dd.l rmt.r[---]. 1100.9
m l kbs. | dd l prgṯ. | dd.l mri. | dd.l ṯnǵly. | dd.l krwn. | dd.l ṯǵr. | dd.l rmt.r[---]. 1100.11
[-----]. | dd l krwn. | dd l [--]n. | dd l ky. | dd l ʿbdkṯr. | dd[m] l rʿy. | [--] šmḫ[.---]. | 1101.3
| l ḥršm. | ddm l ʿnqt. | dd l alṯt.w l lmdt h. | dd l iḫyn. | dd l [---]. 1101.13
.[---]. | ṯrn.d[d]. | tg d[d]. | ḥdyn.d[d]. | [-]dḏn.d[d]. | qṭn.d[d]. | lḫsn.d[d]. | lsn.d[d]. | and[--.---]. 132[331].9
[d]. | tg d[d]. | ḥdyn.d[d]. | [-]dḏn.d[d]. | qṭn.d[d]. | lḫsn.d[d]. | lsn.d[d]. | and[--.---]. 132[331].10
[---.]dd. | [---]n.dd. | [---.]dd. | bn.arwdn.dd. | mnḥm.w.kbln. | bn.ǵlm.dd. | bn.tbšn.dd. | bn.ḫran.w[.---] 131[309].4
qmḥ.d.kly.k ṣḥ.illdrm. | b d.zlb[n.--]. | arbʿ.ʿš[r.]dd.nʿr. | d.apy[.--]. | w.arb[ʿ.--]d.apy.ʿbd h. | w.mrbʿ[t.l ʿ]bdm. 2094.3
ḫmšm.dd. | nʿr. | ḫmšm.tišr. | ḫmš.ktnt. | ḫmš.ṯnt.alpm. | ʿšrm.hbn. | ṯl 2102.1
q[-]dr.g[--]. | q[--.---]. | kd[.--]ḥp. | dd ʿ[--]ṯr. | [-]tm[-.--]n. | mq[--.---]. 153[335].4
ṯṯm.ṯlṯ.kb[d]. | arbʿm.ṯp[rt]. | ksp h. | ṯmn.dd[.--]. | ṯlṯ.dd.p[--]. | šbʿt.p[--]. | tšʿt.k[bd.---]. | ḫmšt.k[bd.---]. | tgmr k[--. 2120.5
[---]. | ilwn.[---]. | ṯrn.d[d]. | tg d[d]. | ḥdyn.d[d]. | [-]dḏn.d[d]. | qṭn.d[d]. | lḫsn.d[d]. | lsn.d[d]. | and[--.---]. 132[331].8
[---.]ksp dd qmḥ. | [---.]ṯlṯ dd ksmm. | [---.-]rbr dd šʿrm. | [---.]r[--.]ḥṭ 2037.1.1
ṯṯm.dd. | ḥpr.bnšm. | b.gt.knpy.mit.drʿ.ṯṯm.drt.w.šbʿm.dd.arbʿ. | kbd.ḥpr.bnšm. | b.gt.ṯrmn.arbʿm.drʿ.w.ʿšrm.drt. | w. 1098.18
gdlt.---.dqt]. | l ṣpn.w [dqt.---.ṯn.l ʿš] | rm.pam[t.---]. | š dd šmn[.gdlt.w.---]. | brr.r[gm.yṯṯb.b ṯdṯ.ṯn]. | l šmn.ʿ[ly h.gd APP.II[173].48
[dlt.---]. | dqt.l.ṣpn.w.dqt[.---]. | ṯn.l.ʿšrm.pamt.[---]. | š.dd.šmn.gdlt.w.[---.brr]. | rgm.yṯṯb.b.ṯdṯ.ṯn[.--.šmn]. | ʿly h.gd 35[3].44
[ṯ]mnym.dd. | šʿrm.b.ṯydr. 1166.1
rḫ.iṯṯbnm. | šbʿm.dd.ṯn.kbd. | tgmr.ḥṭm.šbʿ.ddm. | ḫmš.dd.šʿrm. | kdm.yn. | kdm.ṣmṣ. 1099.33
n. | ddm.l.trbnn. | ddm.šʿrm.l.trbnn. | ddm.šʿrm.l.ḫtn. | dd.šʿrm.l.ḥmr.ḥṭb. | dd.ḥṭm.l.ḫdǵb. | ṯṯ.ddm.l.gzzm. | kd yn.l. 1099.24
ṯmn.ddm šʿrm.l ḥmrm. 1165.1
. | ddm.kšmm.l.ḫtn. | ddm.l.trbnn. | ddm.šʿrm.l.trbnn. | ddm.šʿrm.l.ḫtn. | dd.šʿrm.l.ḥmr.ḥṭb. | dd.ḥṭm.l.ḫdǵb. | ṯṯ.ddm 1099.23
d h. | krwn b.gt.nbk. | ddm.kšmm.l.ḫtn. | ddm.l.trbnn. | ddm.šʿrm.l.trbnn. | ddm.šʿrm.l.ḫtn. | dd.šʿrm.l.ḥmr.ḥṭb. | dd. 1099.22
šm.tišr. | ḫmš.ktnt. | ḫmš.ṯnt.alpm. | ʿšrm.hbn. | ṯlṯ.mat.dd. | šʿrm. | mit.šmn. | ʿšr.kat. | ẓrw. 2102.7
šwn.ṯṯ.mat.nṣ. | [---].ḫmšm.ḥmr.škm. | [---.ṯṯ.dd.]gdl.ṯṯ.dd.šʿrm. | [---.a]lp.arbʿ.mat.tyt. | [---.kd.]nbt.k[d.]šmn.mr. | [-- 142[12].13
t.nṣ.ṯlṯm.ʿṣr. | [---].ḫmš[m.ḥm]r.škm. | [---.ṯṯ.dd.]gdl.ṯṯ.dd.šʿrm. | [---.hn.w.al]p.kd.nbt.kd.šmn.mr. | [---].kmn.lṯḥ.sb 142[12].7
[---.]ksp dd qmḥ. | [---.]ṯlṯ dd ksmm. | [---.-]rbr dd šʿrm. | [---.]r[--.]ḥṭm. | kr[--.]tp[n]. | kkr[.---]. | kkr[.---]. | kk 2037.1.3
[---.]ṯṯ.dd.gdl.ṯṯ.dd.šʿrm. | [---.-]hn.w.alp.kd.nbt.kd.šmn.mr. | [---.]arbʿ.mat.ḫ 142[12].1
ʿ.dblt.m[--.---]. | [--.mi]tm nṣ.[-]ṯ[-.]gr[-.---]. | [---].arb[ʿ.d]d.š[ʿrm.---]. | [--.-]rṭm š[šm]n.k[--.---]. | [---.ar]bʿ.dblt.ḏr[--.- 143[-].1.7
[---]t.ddm.šʿr[m.---]. | [---].mit.ḫsw.[---]. | [----]d.nʿr.ṯ[--]d[.---]. | [--- 143[-].1.1
aḏml[--.---]. | tlbr[-.---]. | isg.[---]. | ilwn.[---]. | ṯrn.d[d]. | tg d[d]. | ḥdyn.d[d]. | [-]dḏn.d[d]. | qṭn.d[d]. | lḫsn.d[d]. 132[331].5
d.ḥpr.bnšm. | b.gt.ṯrmn.arbʿm.drʿ.w.ʿšrm.drt. | w.ṯlṯm.dd.ṯṯ.kbd.ḥpr.bnšm. | b.gt.ḥdṯt.arbʿm.drʿ.w.ṯlṯm.drt. | [w].šbʿ 1098.21
it.dd.ḥpr.bnšm. | b.yʿny.arbʿm.drʿ.w.ʿšrm.drt. | w.ṯlṯm.dd.ṯṯ.kbd.ḥpr.bnšm. | b.ʿnmky.ʿšrm.drʿ[.---.d]rt. | w.ṯn.ʿšr h.d 1098.27
gyn. | mnn.šr.ugrt.ḏkr.yṣr. | tgǵln.ḫmš.ddm. | [---].ḫmš.ddm. | ṯṯ.l.ʿšrm.bn[š.mlk.---].ḫzr.lqḥ.ḥp[r]. | ʿšt.ʿšr h.bn[.---.-- 2011.39
ḥmṣ. | prš.glbm.l.bt. | tgmǵ.kšmm.b.yrḫ.iṯṯbnm. | šbʿm.dd.ṯn.kbd. | tgmr.ḥṭm.šbʿ.ddm. | ḫmš.dd.šʿrm. | kdm.yn. | kd 1099.31
.ḥpr.bnšm. | b.gt.ḥdṯt.arbʿm.drʿ.w.ṯlṯm.drt. | [w].šbʿm.dd.ṯn.kbd.ḥpr.bnšm. | b.nzl.ʿšrm.l.mit.drʿ.w.šbʿm.drt. | w.ʿšr 1098.23
. | [b.---.]knm.ṯṯm.l.mit.drʿ.w.mit.drt. | w[.---.]ʿm.l.mit.dd.ṯn.kbd.ḥpr.bnšm.ṯmnym.dd. | l u[-]m. | b.ṯbq.arbʿm.drʿ.w 1098.8
br[-.---]. | isg.[---]. | ilwn.[---]. | ṯrn.d[d]. | tg d[d]. | ḥdyn.d[d]. | [-]dḏn.d[d]. | qṭn.d[d]. | lḫsn.d[d]. | lsn.d[d]. | and[--.---]. 132[331].7
w.bn.ʿdy. | bn.gmḥn.w.ḥgbt. | bn.tgdn. | yny. | [b]n.gʿyn dd. | [-]n.dd. | [--]an dd. | [-----]. | [-----]. 131[309].31
ṯlṯm.dd[.---]. | b.gt.ṣb[-.---]. | mit.ʿšr.[---.]dd[.--]. | tšʿ.dd.ḥ[ṭm.w].ḫm[šm]. | kdm.kbd.yn.b.gt.[---]. | [mi] 2092.3

ṯṯm.ṯlṯ.kb[d]. | arb'm.ṯp[rt]. | ksp h. | ṯmn.dd[.--]. | ṯlṯ.dd.p[--]. | šb't.p[--]. | tš't.k[bd.---]. | ḫmšt.k[bd.---]. 2120.4
. | bn.gmḥn.w.ḥgbt. | bn.tgdn. | yny. | [b]n.g'yn dd. | [-]n.dd. | [--]an dd. | [-----]. | [-----]. 131[309].32
w.ḫ[mšm]. | [t]lṯ kbd.yn.b [gt.---]. | mit.[---].ṯlṯ.kb[d]. | [dd.--]m.šb'.[---]. | [---].'šr.dd[.---]. | [---]mn.arb'm.y[n]. | b.gt.t 2092.12
.kbd.ḥpr.bnšm. | b.'nmky.'šrm.dr'[.---.d]rt. | w.ṯn.'šr h.dd.[---]. | iwrdn.ḥ[--.---]. | w.ṯlṯm.dd.[---.]n[---.---]. | w.a[r]b'[.- 1098.29
ṯlṯm.dd[.---]. | b.gt.ṣb[-.---]. | mit.'šr.[---.]dd[.--]. | tš'.dd.ḫ[ṯm.w].ḫ 2092.1
[---.]dd. | [---]n.dd. | [---.]dd. | bn.arwdn.dd. | mnḥm.w.kbln. | bn.ǵlm.dd. | bn. 131[309].2
šm.w.ṯn.'šr h.dd.l.rpš. | [---.]šb'm.dr'.w.arb'm.drt.mit.dd. | [---].ḥpr.bn.šm. | [b.---.]knm.ṯṯm.l.mit.dr'.w.mit.drt. | w[1098.5
pṯm.krwn.ilšn.agyn. | mnn.šr.ugrt.ḏkr.yṣr. | tgǵln.ḫmš.ddm. | [---].ḫmš.ddm. | ṯṯ.l.'šrm.bn[š.mlk.---].ḫzr.lqḥ.ḥp[r]. | ' 2011.38
. | [---.]dd.bn.š.[---.]yd.sǵr h. | [---.--]r h.'šr[m.---.']šrm.dd. | [---.yn.d.]nkly.l.r'ym.šb'm.l.mitm.dd. | [---.--]d.šb'm.kb 1098.43
.---]. | [---.]prš. | [-----]. | l.mšḫ[.---]. | 'šr.d[d.---]. | ṯṯm.dd.dd[.---]. | l.mdrǵlm[.---]. | ṯlṯ.mat.ḫmšm.kb[d]. | ḫmš.kbd.l.m 2012.9
'[.---.d]rt. | w.ṯn.'šr h.dd.[---]. | iwrdn.ḥ[--.---]. | w.ṯlṯm.dd.[---.]n[---.---]. | w.a[r]b'[.---].bnš[.š]dyn[.---]. | agr.[---.--]n. 1098.31
ḥdṯn.'šr.dd[.---]. | [---.]yd.sǵr[.---.--]r h. | aḥ[d.---.']šrm.d[d.---]. | 'š[r.---.--]r h. | my y[--.---.--]d. | 'šrm[.---.--]r h. | [-]w 1098.36
m[š.---]. | b[yrḫ.---]. | [---.]prš. | [-----]. | l.mšḫ[.---]. | 'šr.d[d.---]. | ṯṯm.dd.dd[.---]. | l.mdrǵlm[.---]. | ṯlṯ.mat.ḫmšm.kb[2012.8
'šr[m.---.']šrm.dd. | [---.yn.d.]nkly.l.r'ym.šb'm.l.mitm.dd. | [---.--]d.šb'm.kbd.dr'. | [---.]kbd.ddm.kbd[.---]. | [---.]'m. 1098.44
š]dyn[.---]. | agr.[---.--]n.ṯn.'šr h.d[--.---]. | [---.]ḥdṯn.'šr.dd[.---]. | [---.]yd.sǵr[.---.--]r h. | aḥ[d.---.']šrm.d[d.---]. | 'š[r.-- 1098.34
[gt.---]. | mit.[---].ṯlṯ.kb[d]. | [dd.--]m.šb'.[---]. | [---].'šr.dd[.---]. | [---]mn.arb'm.y[n]. | b.gt.trǵnds. | tš'.'šr.[dd].kšmm. 2092.13
[---.]dd. | [---]n.dd. | [---.]dd. | bn.arwdn.dd. | mnḥm.w.kbln. | bn.ǵl 131[309].1
]r h. | my y[--.---.--]d. | 'šrm[.---.--]r h. | [-]wyn.yd[-.---.]dd. | [---]n.yd.sǵ[r.---.--]k.[--]. | [---.]dd.bn.š.[---.]yd.sǵr h. | [-- 1098.40
.w.ḥgbt. | bn.tgdn. | yny. | [b]n.g'yn dd. | [-]n.dd. | [--]an dd. | [-----]. | [-----]. 131[309].33
qmḥ.d.kly.b bt.skn. | l.illdrm. | ltḥ.ḥsr.b.šb'.ddm. 2093.3

ddy

šu.adddy. | plsy.adddy. | aḫyn. | ygmr.adddy. | gln.aṭṭ. | ddy.[a]ḏddy. | bn.mlkr[šp]. | bn.y[k]n. | ynḥm. | bn.abd.b'[l]. | 2014.44
[---.]ṯlṯm.d.nlqḥt. | [bn.ḫ]tyn.yd.bt h. | [aǵ]ltn. | tdn.bn.ddy. | 'bdil[.b]n ṣdqn. | bnšm.h[-]mt.ypḥm. | kbby.yd.bt.amt. 2045.4
bt šbn. | iy'dm.w b'l h. | ddy. | 'my. | iwrnr. | alnr. | maḫdt. | aby. | [-----]. | [-]nt. | ydn. | m 107[15].3

ddym

b'l]. | hw[t.aliy.qrdm.qryy.b arṣ.mlḥmt.št]. | [b ']pr[m.ddym.sk.šlm.l kbd.arṣ.arbdd]. | l kbd.š[dm.ḥš k.'ṣ k.'bṣ k.'m 7.2[130].15
. | [---.]rn h.aqry. | [---.]b a[r]ṣ.mlḥmt. | ašt[.b ']p[r] m.ddym.ask. | šlm.l kb[d].awṣ.arbdd. | l kbd.š[d]m.ap.mṯn.rgm 3['NT].4.73
aliyn.b'l.hwt. | aliy.qrdm.qry.b arṣ. | mlḥmt št.b 'pr m.ddym. | sk.šlm.l kbd.arṣ. | arbdd.l kbd.šdm. | ḥš k.'ṣ k.'bṣ k. | ' 3['NT].3.12
[ybmt.]limm.[a]n.aqry. | [b arṣ].mlḥmt.[aš]t.b 'pr m. | ddym.ask[.šlm.]l kbd.arṣ. | ar[bdd.]l kb[d.š]dm.yšt. | [----.]b'l 3['NT].4.68
iyn.b'l.hwt.aliy. | qrdm.qry.b arṣ.mlḥmt. | št.b 'p[r] m.ddym.sk.šlm. | l kbd.arṣ.arbdd.l kbd.šdm. | [ḥ]š k.[']ṣ k.'bṣ k. 3['NT].4.53
b k.hwt.l]ṯpn.ḥtk k. | [qryy.b arṣ.mlḥ]mt.št b 'p | [r m.ddym.sk.šlm].l kbd.arṣ. | [arbdd.l kbd.š]dm.ḥš k. | ['ṣ k.'bṣ k. 1['NT.IX].2.20

ddl

-]. | b d.[---]. | šd.[---]. | b d.[---]. | [-----]. | šd.bn.gdy. | b d.ddl. 2028.23

ddmy

npy.'rmt.---.w]npy.annpdgl. | [ušn.yp kn.ulp.qṭy.ulp.]ddmy.ulp ḫry. | [ulp.ḫty.ulp.alṯy.ulp.ǵbr.ul]p.ḫbt kn. | [ulp. APP.I[-].1.4
an.w npy.'r]mt.w npy. | [---.ušn.yp km.ulp.]qṭy. | [ulp.ddmy.ulp.ḫry.ulp.ḫty.u]lp.alṯy. | [ulp.ǵbr.ulp.ḫbt km.ulp.m APP.I[-].1.15
----]. | [---.--]r. | [---.]npy. | [---.ušn.yp kn.ulp.q]ṭy. | [ulp.ddmy.ulp.ḫry.ulp.ḫty.ulp.alṯy]. | [ulp.ǵbr.ulp.ḫbt kn.ulp.md APP.I[-].2.13
py.gr. | ḥmyt.ugrt.w [np]y.nṯt.ušn.yp kn.ulp qṭy. | ulp.ddmy.ul[p.ḫ]ry.ulp.ḫty.ulp.alṯy. | ulp.ǵbr.ulp.[ḫbt] kn[.u]lp. 32[2].1.29
y.---.]w npy. | [---.w np]y.ugrt. | [---.u ṯḫṭu.ulp.qṭy.ulp.ddm]y. | [ulp.ḫry.ulp.ḫty.ulp.alṯy.ulp.ǵbr]. | [ulp.ḫbt km.ulp. 32[2].1.6
t.ugrt.w np]y. | [---].w n[py.---].u ṯḫṭi[n.ulp.qṭy]. | ulp.ddmy.ul[p.ḫry.u]lp.ḫty.ulp[.alṯy.ulp.]ǵbr. | ulp.ḫbt kn.ulp.m 32[2].1.12
mt.w npy.[---]. | w npy.nqmd.ušn.yp km.ulp.q[ṭy.ulp.ddm]y. | ulp.ḫry.ulp.ḫ[t]y.ulp.alṯy.ul[p.ǵbr.]ulp. | ḫbt km.ulp 32[2].1.20

ddmš

m]. | [-----]. | [a]rṣ. | [u]šḫr[y]. | [']ṯtrt. | i[l t]'ḏr b'l. | ršp. | ddmš. | pḫr ilm. | ym. | uṯḫt. | knr. | mlkm. | šlm. 29[17].2.6
ib š. | b'l ugrt š.b'l ḫlb š. | yrḫ š.'nt ṣpn.alp. | w š.pdry š.ddmš š. | w b urbt.ilib š. | b'l alp w š. | dgn.š.il t'ḏr.š. | b'l š.'nt UG5.13.18
ṯrt.š.'nt.š.špš.š.arṣy.š.'ṯtrt.š. | ušḫry.š.il.t'ḏr.b'l.š.ršp.š.ddmš.š. | w šlmm.ilib.š.i[l.--]m d gbl.ṣpn.al[p]. | pḫr.ilm.š.ym UG5.9.1.8
[-----]. | [---.gd]lt.[---]. | [---.d]dmš[.---]. | [---.--]b.š.[---]. | [---.yr]ḫ.š.[---]. | [---.]'[--.---]. 43[47].3

dw

t.yd k. | l tdn.dn.almnt. | l ṯpṭ.ṭpṭ.qṣr.npš. | km.aḫt.'rš.mdw. | anšt.'rš.zbln. | rd.l mlk.amlk. | l drkt.k aṯb.an. | ytb'.yṣ 16.6[127].35
'l.dl.l pn k. | l tšlḥm.ytm.b'd. | ksl k.almnt.km. | aḫt.'rš.mdw.anšt. | 'rš.zbln.rd.l mlk. | amlk.l drkt k.aṯb. | an.w y'ny. 16.6[127].51
ḫ[h.w tṣḥ]. | lm.tb'rn[.---]. | mn.yrḫ.k m[rṣ.---]. | mn.k dw.kr[t]. | w y'ny.ǵzr[.ilḥu]. | ṯlṯ.yrḫm.k m[rṣ]. | arb'.k dw.k[16.2[125].82
dw.kr[t]. | w y'ny.ǵzr[.ilḥu]. | ṯlṯ.yrḫm.k m[rṣ]. | arb'.k dw.k[rt]. | mnd'.krt.mǵ[y.---]. | w qbr.tṣr.q[br]. | tṣr.trm.tnq[- 16.2[125].85

dwn

n [-]'y. | [b]n [i]lmd. | bn [t]bdn. | bn štn. | b[n] kdn. | bn dwn. | bn ḏrn. 2088.7

dḥl

'l.w.likt. | 'm k.w.hm. | l.'l.w.lakm. | ilak.w.at. | um y.al.tdḥṣ. | w.ap.mhkm. | b.lb k.al. | tšt. 1013.21

dyy

[---.--]n. | [---.]rmṣm. | [---.]dyy. | [---.n]ḥl h. 2155.3

dyn

n. | k ǵz.ǵzm.tdbr. | w ǵrm.ṯṯwy.šqlt. | b ǵlt.yd k.l tdn. | dn.almnt.l ṯṯpṭ. | ṯpṭ qṣr.npš.l tdy. | ṯšm.ʿl.dl.l pn k. | l tšlḥm.y 16.6[127].46
ǵz.ǵzm]. | tdbr.w[ǵ]rm[.ṯṯwy]. | šqlt.b ǵlt.yd k. | l tdn.dn.almnt. | l ṯṯpṭ.ṯpṭ.qṣr.npš. | km.aḫt.ʿrš.mdw. | anšt.ʿrš.zbln. 16.6[127].33
t.hrnm[y]. | ytšu.yṯb.b ap.ṯǵr.ṯḥt. | adrm.d b grn.ydn. | dn.almnt.yṯpṭ.ṯpṭ.ytm. | b nši ʿn h.w yphn.b alp. | šd.rbt.kmn 17[2AQHT].5.8
]my.ytšu. | [yṯb.b ap.ṯ]ǵr[.t]ḥt. | [adrm.d b grn.y]dn. | [dn.almnt.y]ṯpṭ. | [ṯpṭ.ytm.---] h. | [---.---]n. | [-----]. | hlk.[---.b 19[1AQHT].1.24
šd.krz.[b]n.ann.ʿ[db]. | šd.ṯ[r]yn.bn.tkn.b d.qrt. | šd[.-].dyn.b d.pln.nḥl h. | šd.irdyn.bn.ḫrǵš[-].l.qrt. | šd.iǵlyn.bn.kz 2029.15
dn.k ǵz.ǵzm]. | tdbr.w[ǵ]rm[.ṯṯwy]. | šqlt.b ǵlt.yd k. | l tdn.dn.almnt. | l ṯṯpṭ.ṯpṭ.qṣr.npš. | km.aḫt.ʿrš.mdw. | anšt.ʿrš. 16.6[127].33
ǵ udn. | k ǵz.ǵzm.tdbr. | w ǵrm.ṯṯwy.šqlt. | b ǵlt.yd k.l tdn. | dn.almnt.l ṯṯpṭ. | ṯpṭ qṣr.npš.l tdy. | ṯšm.ʿl.dl.l pn k. | l tšl 16.6[127].45
ǵzr.mt.hrnm[y]. | ytšu.yṯb.b ap.ṯǵr.ṯḥt. | adrm.d b grn.ydn. | dn.almnt.yṯpṭ.ṯpṭ.ytm. | b nši ʿn h.w yphn.b alp. | šd.rb 17[2AQHT].5.7
[mt.hrn]my.ytšu. | [yṯb.b ap.ṯ]ǵr[.t]ḥt. | [adrm.d b grn.y]dn. | [dn.almnt.y]ṯpṭ. | [ṯpṭ.ytm.---] h. | [---.---]n. | [-----]. | hl 19[1AQHT].1.23
.ṯn.dbḥm.šna.bʿl.ṯlṯ. | rkb.ʿrpt.dbḥ. | bṯt.w dbḥ.w dbḥ. | dnt.w dbḥ.tdmm. | amht.k b h.bṯt.l tbṯ. | w b h.tdmmt.amht. 4[51].3.20
[-]n. | [b].bn.ay[--.---].l.ʿšrm. | [-]gp[.---.]ʿrny.ṯṯm. | [---.]dyn.ḫmšt.ʿšrt. | [---.-]til.ḫmšt.l ʿšrm. | [--.-]n.w.aḫt h.arbʿm. | [2054.2.19
r.b tk.mšmš d[--]. | ittpq.l awl. | išttk.lm.ttkn. | štk.mlk.dn. | štk.šibt.ʿn. | štk.qr.bt.il. | w mṣlt.bt.ḥr[š]. 12[75].2.59

dk

yṣq b ap h. | [k l yḫru w]l yṯtn mss št qlql. | [w št ʿrgz y]dk aḥd h w yṣq b ap h. | [k.yiḫd akl s]šw št mkšr grn. | [w 160[55].9
k [ḫr ššw mǵmǵ]. | w [bṣql.ʿrgz.ydk]. | a[ḥd h.w.yṣq.b.ap h]. | k.[ḫr.ššw.ḫndrṯ]. | w.ṯ[qd.mr.y 161[56].3
. | a[ḥd h.w.yṣq.b.ap h]. | k.[ḫr.ššw.ḫndrṯ]. | w.ṯ[qd.mr.ydk.aḥd h]. | w.y[ṣq.b.ap h]. | k.l.ḫ[ru.w.l.yṯtn.ššw]. | mss.[št. 161[56].6
---]. | w.š[t.nni.w.pr.ʿbk]. | w.pr[.ḥdrt.w.št]. | irǵ[n.ḥmr.ydk]. | aḥd[h.w.yṣq.b.ap h]. | k yr[a]š.šš[w.w.ykhp]. | mid.db 161[56].30
. | k.yiḫd.akl.š[šw]. | št.nni.št.mk[št.grn]. | št.irǵn.ḥmr[.ydk]. | aḥd h.w.yṣq.b[.ap h]. | k.yraš.ššw.[št]. | bln.qṭ.yṣq.b.a[161[56].19
ḥd[.akl.ššw]. | št.mkš[r.grn]. | w.št.ašk[rr]. | w.pr.ḥdr[t.ydk]. | aḥd h.w.yṣq[.b.ap h]. | k.yiḫd.akl.š[šw]. | št.nni.št.mk[161[56].15
p h]. | k.l.ḫ[ru.w.l.yṯtn.ššw]. | mss.[št.qlql.w.št]. | ʿrgz[.ydk.aḥd h]. | w.yṣq[.b.ap h]. | k.yiḫd[.akl.ššw]. | št.mkš[r.grn] 161[56].10
aḥ]d h w yṣq b ap h. | [k ḫr]ššw ḫndrṯ w ṯ[qd m]r. | [ydk aḥd h w yṣq b ap h. | [k l yḫru w]l yṯtn mss št qlql. | [w 160[55].7
[---.w]yṣq b a[p h]. | [k ḫr s]šw mǵmǵ w b[ṣql ʿrgz]. | [ydk aḥ]d h w yṣq b ap h. | [k ḫr]ššw ḫndrṯ w ṯ[qd m]r. | [yd 160[55].5
hp]. | mid.dblt.yṯ[nt.w]. | ṣmq[m].yṯnm.w[.qmḥ.bql]. | tdkn.aḥd h.w[.yṣq]. | b.ap h. 161[56].35
r w p]r ḥdrt. | [-----]. | [---.-]n[-]. | [k yraš ššw št bln q]ṭ ydk. | [w yṣq b ap h]. | [-----]. | [-----]. | [-----]. | [---.-]rb. | [-----]. 160[55].14
yiḫd.bʿl.bn.aṯrt. | rbm.ymḫṣ.b ktp. | dk ym.ymḫṣ.b ṣmd. | ṣḥr mt.ymṣḫ.l arṣ. | [yṯb.]b[ʿ]l.l ksi.mlk 6[49].5.3
rṣ.ḫšn[.---]. | tʿtd.tkl.[---]. | tkn.lbn[.---]. | dt.lbn k[.---]. | dk k.kbkb[.---]. | dm.mt.aṣḥ[.---]. | ydd.b qr[b.---]. | al.ašt.b[-- 5[67].3.8

dkn

[--.]ubdym.b.uškn. | [---]lby. | [--]nbbl. | bn bl. | bn dkn. | bn ils. | bn ḥšbn. | bn uryy. | bn kṯl. | bn army. | bn gln. | b 1064.5

dkrt

ḥtm.yn. | špq.ilht.ksat[.yn]. | špq.ilm.rḥbt yn. | špq.ilht.dkrt[.yn]. | ʿd.lḥm.šty.ilm. | w pq mrǵṯm.ṯd. | b ḥrb.mlḥt.qṣ[. 4[51].6.54

dly

nqdm. | bn.alṯn. | bn.dly. | bn.btry. | bn.ḫdmn. | [bn].šty. | [bn].kdgdl. | [---.-]y[-.] 2018.3
k[.---]. | [-----]. | ilbʿl[.---]. | ḫluy.bn[.---]. | ymil.bn.[---]. | dly.bn[.---]. | ynḥm.bn[.---]. | gn.bn[.---]. | klby.[bn.---]. | šmml 102[322].5.5
. | [---.š]d ubdy. | [---.šd] ubdy. | [---.š]d.bn.ṣin. | [---].bn.dly. | [---.]ṯty[-.--]. 2031.12

dll

bkm.yṯb.bʿl.l bht h. | u mlk.u bl mlk. | arṣ.drkt.yštkn. | dll.al.ilak.l bn. | ilm.mt.ʿdd.l ydd. | il.ǵzr.yqra.mt. | b npš h.ys 4[51].7.45
hrm.ǵ]rpl.ʿl.arṣ. | [---.]ḥmt.l p[.nṯ]k.abd.l p.ak[l]. | [ṯm.dl.]isp.ḥ[mt.---.-]hm.yasp.ḥmt. | [---.š]pš.l [hrm.ǵrpl].ʿl.arṣ.l UG5.8.11
.nḥl hm. | [bn].pmn. | bn.gṯrn. | bn.arpḫn. | bn.ṯryn. | bn.dll. | bn.ḫswn. | mrynm. | ʿzn. | ḥyn. | ʿmyn. | ilyn. | yrbʿm. | nʿm 1046.3.31
.il.yṯb.b[mrzḥ.---]. | bṯt.ʿllm n.[---]. | ilm.bt.bʿl k.[---]. | dl.ylkn.ḥš.b a[rṣ.---]. | b ʿpr.ḫbl ṯtm.[---.] | šqy.rṯa.tnm y.ytn.[1[ʿNT.X].4.7
---].bm[.---]. | [---.-]qp.bn.ḥtt.bn ḥtt[.---]. | [---.--]p.km.dlt.tlk.km.p[---]. | [---.]bt.tḥbṭ.km.ṣq.ṣdr[.---]. | [---.]kl.b kl.l 1001.1.24
qšr[.---]. | [---].ptḥ y.a[--.]dt[.---].ml[--]. | [---.-]tk.ytmt.dlt tlk.[---].bm[.---]. | [---.-]qp.bn.ḥtt.bn ḥtt[.---]. | [---.--]p.k 1001.1.22
. | [ulp.ḫry.ulp.ḫty.ulp.alṯy.ulp.ǵbr]. | [ulp.ḫbt km.ulp.mdll km.ulp.qr zbl]. | [u ṯḫṭu.u b ap km.u b qṣrt.npš km.u b 32[2].1.8
| ulp.ḫry.ulp.ḫ[t]y.ulp.alṯy.ul[p.ǵbr.]ulp. | ḫbt km.ulp.m[dl]l km.ulp.qr zbl.u[š]n yp km. | u b ap km.u b q[ṣ]rt.npš 32[2].1.22
y.ulp.ḫry.ulp.ḫty.u]lp.alṯy. | [ulp.ǵbr.ulp.ḫbt km.ulp.mdll km.ulp]. | [qr zbl.ušn.yp km.b ap km.u b qṣrt.np]št km APP.I[-].1.16
y.ul[p.ḫry.u]lp.ḫty.ulp[.alṯy.ulp.]ǵbr. | ulp.ḫbt kn.ulp.md[ll k]n.ulp.q[r zbl]. | u ṯḫṭin.b ap kn.u b [q]ṣrt.npš[kn.u 32[2].1.13
.ul[p.ḫ]ry.ulp.ḫty.ulp.alṯy. | ulp.ǵbr.ulp.[ḫbt] kn[.u]lp.mdll kn.ulp qr z[bl]. | lšn yp kn.b ap [kn.u b qṣ]rt.npš kn.u 32[2].1.30
y.ulp ḫry. | [ulp.ḫty.ulp.alṯy.ulp.ǵbr.ul]p.ḫbt kn. | [ulp.mdll kn.ulp.qr zbl.ušn.y]p kn. | [u b ap kn.u b qṣrt.npšt kn. APP.I[-].1.6
my.ulp.ḫry.ulp.ḫty.ulp.alṯy]. | [ulp.ǵbr.ulp.ḫbt kn.ulp.mdll kn.ulp.]qr zbl. | [ušn.yp kn.u b ap kn.u b qṣrt.npš kn.u APP.I[-].2.14
t.yd k.l tdn. | dn.almnt.l ṯṯpṭ. | ṯpṭ qṣr.npš.l tdy. | ṯšm.ʿl.dl.l pn k. | l tšlḥm.ytm.bʿd. | ksl k.almnt.km. | aḫt.ʿrš.mdw.an 16.6[127].48
bn.qrdy. | bn.šmʿn. | bn.ǵlmy. | ǵly. | bn.dnn. | bn.rmy. | dll. | mny. | krty. | bn.ʿbṣ. | bn.argb. | ydn. | ilʿnt. | bn.urt. | ydn. | 2117.3.37
ytrm.qšt.w.qlʿ. | bn.ʿbdyrḫ.qšt.w.q[lʿ]. | bn.lky.qšt. | bn.dll.qšt.w.ql[ʿ]. | bn.pǵyn.qšt.w[.q]lʿ. | bn.bdn.qšt. | bn.pls.qšt. | 119[321].3.28
.šǵr h. | [---.]w.šǵr h. | [---.]krwn. | [---].ḫzmyn. | [---.]bn.dll. | r[--.--]km. | w.spr h. 2072.13
š l hrm.ǵrpl.ʿl arṣ. | [l a]n ḥmt.l p[.n]ṯk.abd.l p.akl ṯm.dl. | [---.q]l.bl.tbḥ[n.l]azd.ʿr.qdm. | [---].ʿẓ q[dm.--.šp]š. | [---.š UG5.8.20

dlp

.zbl ym.bn ydm.ṯpṭ.|nhr.'z.ym.l ymk.l tnǵṣn.pnt h.l ydlp.|tmn h.kṯr.ṣmdm.ynḥt.w yp'r.šmt hm.|šm k.at.aymr. 2.4[68].17
m.]bn.'nm.ṯpṭ.nhr.yprsḥ.ym.yql.|l arṣ.tnǵṣn.pnt h.w ydlp.tmn h.|yqṯ b'l.w yšt.ym.ykly.ṯpṭ.nhr.|b šm.tg'r m.'ṯtrt 2.4[68].26

dlšpš

spm l tgyn.|arb' spm l ll[-].|ṯn spm.l slyy.|ṯlṯ spm l dlšpš amry. 137.2[93].15

dlt

agzry ym.bn]ym.|ynqm.b ap zd.aṯrt.[---].|špš.mṣprt dlt hm[.---].|w ǵnbm.šlm.'rbm.ṯn[nm].|hlkm.b dbḥ n'mt.|š 23[52].25
[---.--]n.d[--.]bnš[.---].|[---.]idmt.n[--.]t[--].|[---.--]r.dlt.tḥt n.|[---.]dlt.|[---.b]nš.|[---.]yp'.|[---.]b[--]. 2158B.3
]bnš[.---].|[---.]idmt.n[--.]t[--].|[---.--]r.dlt.tḥt n.|[---.]dlt.|[---.b]nš.|[---.]yp'.|[---.]b[--]. 2158B.4

dm

.---].|šb'.šnt.il.mla.[-].|w ṯmn.nqpnt.'d.|k lbš.km.lpš.dm a[ḫ h].|km.all.dm.ary h.|k šb't.l šb'm.aḫ h.ym[.--].|w ṯ 12[75].2.47
[-]n.tbkn.w tdm.l y.[--].|[---].al.trgm.l aḫt k.|[---.]l [ ]dm.aḫt k.|yd't.k rḥmt.|al.tšt.b šdm.mm h.|b smkt.ṣat.npš 16.1[125].32
.[-].|w ṯmn.nqpnt.'d.|k lbš.km.lpš.dm a[ḫ h].|km.all.dm.ary h.|k šb't.l šb'm.aḫ h.ym[.--].|w ṯmnt.l ṯmnym.|šr.a 12[75].2.48
.|hl ǵlmt tld b[n.--]n.|'n ha l yd h.tzd[.--].|pt l bšr h.dm a[--.--]ḥ.|w yn.k mtrḫt[.---]h.|šm' ilht kṯr[t.--]mm.|nh 24[77].9
trḥṣ.yd h.bt|[l]t.'nt.uṣb't h.ybmt.limm.|[t]rḥṣ.yd h.b dm.ḏmr.|[u]ṣb't h.b mm'.mhrm.|[ṭ]'r.ksat.l ksat.ṯlḥnt.|[l] 3['NT].2.34
hr.'tkt.|rišt.l bmt h.šnst.|kpt.b ḥbš h.brkm.tǵl[l].|b dm.ḏmr.ḥlqm.b mm['].|mhrm.mṭm.tgrš.|šbm.b ksl.qšt h. 3['NT].2.14
.b ṣḥq.ymlu.|lb h.b šmḫt.kbd.'nt.|tšyt.k brkm.tǵll b dm.|ḏmr.ḥlqm.b mm'.mhrm.|'d.tšb'.tmtḫṣ.b bt.|tḫṣb.bn.ṯl 3['NT].2.27
hrm.|'d.tšb'.tmtḫṣ.b bt.|tḫṣb.bn.ṯlḥnm.ymḥ.|[b]bt.dm.ḏmr.yṣq.šmn.|šlm.b ṣ'.trḥṣ.yd h.bt|[l]t.'nt.uṣb't h.ybmt 3['NT].2.31
šyt.tḥt h.k]kdrt.riš.|['l h.k irbym.kp.---.k br]k.tǵll.b dm.|[ḏmr.---.]td[-.]rǵb.|[----]k.|[----] h. 7.1[131].9
t'dbn h.hlmn.ṯnm[.qdqd].|ṯlṯ id.'l.udn.š[pk.km].|šiy.dm h.km.šḫ[ṭ.l brk h].|yṣat.km.rḥ.npš[h.km.iṯl].|brlt h.k 18[3AQHT].4.35
lkt.w.šnwt.|tp.aḫ.h.k.ysmsm.|tspi.šir.h.l.bl.ḥrb.|tšt.dm.h.l.bl.ks.|tpnn.'n.bṯy.'n.bṯt.tpnn.|'n.mḫr.'n.pḫr.'n.ṯǵr.| RS225.4
.|d yšt.l.lṣb h ḫš'r klb.|[w]riš.pqq.w šr h.|yšt.aḥd h.dm zt.ḫrpnt. UG5.1.2.6
ṯṯb.trḥṣ.nn.b d't.|npš h.l lḥm.tpth.|brlt h.l ṯrm.|mt.dm.ḫt.š'tqt.|dm.lan.w ypqd.|krt.ṯ'.yšu.g h.|w yṣḥ.šm'.l mṯ 16.6[127].13
[m]t.dm.ḫt.š'tqt dm.|li.w ttb'.š'tqt.|bt.krt.bu.tbu.|bkt.tgly.w tb 16.6[127].1
aqht.'db k.hlmn.ṯnm.qdqd.|ṯlṯ id.'l.udn.špk.km.šiy.|dm.km.šḫṭ.l brk h.tṣi.km.|rḥ.npš h.km.iṯl.brlt h.km.|qṭr.b 18[3AQHT].4.24
k.aḥwy.|aqht[.ǵz]r.w y'n.aqht.ǵzr.|al.tšrgn.y btlt m.dm.l ǵzr.|šrg k.ḫḫm.mt.uḫryt.mh.yqḥ.|mh.yqḥ.mt.aṯryt.sp 17[2AQHT].6.34
d't.|npš h.l lḥm.tpth.|brlt h.l ṯrm.|mt.dm.ḫt.š'tqt.|dm.lan.w ypqd.|krt.ṯ'.yšu.g h.|w yṣḥ.šm'.l mṯt.|ḥry.ṭbḫ.im 16.6[127].14
[m]t.dm.ḫt.š'tqt dm.|li.w ttb'.š'tqt.|bt.krt.bu.tbu.|bkt.tgly.w tbu.|nṣrt.tbu. 16.6[127].1
.l [---].|b mud.ṣin[.---].|mud.ṣin[.---].|iṯm.mui[-.---].|dm.mt.aṣ[ḫ.---].|ydd.b qr[b.---].|ṯmm.w lk[.---].|[--]ṯ.lk[.-- 5[67].3.25
.ilm[.---].|n'm.ilm[.---].|šgr.mu[d.---].|šgr.mud[.---].|dm.mt.aṣ[ḫ.---].|yd.b qrb[.---].|w lk.ilm.[---].|w rgm.l [---]. 5[67].3.18
tkl.[---].|tkn.lbn[.---].|dt.lbn k[.---].|dk k.kbkb[.---].|dm.mt.aṣḫ[.---].|ydd.b qr[b.---].|al.ašt.b[---].|ahpk k.l[--.-- 5[67].3.9
--.]ydbr.ṯrmt.al m.qḥn y.š y.qḥn y.|[--.]šir.b krm.nṭṭt.dm.'lt.b ab y.|u---].'lt.b k.lk.l pn y.yrk.b'l.[--].|[---.]'nt.šzr 1001.1.9
hm.štym.lḥ[m].|b ṯlḥnt.lḥm št.|b krpnm.yn.b k.ḫrṣ.|dm.'ṣm.hm.yd.il mlk.|yḫss k.ahbt.ṯr.t'rr k.|w t'n.rbt.aṯrt y 4[51].4.38
-].|b ḥrb.[mlḥt.qṣ.mri].|šty.kr[pnm.yn.---].|b ks.ḫr[ṣ.dm.'ṣm.---].|ks.ksp[.---].|krpn.[---].|w ṯṯn.[---].|t'l.tr[-.---]. 5[67].4.16
.td.|b ḥrb.mlḥt.qṣ[.m]r|i.tšty.krp[nm.y]n.|[b k]s.ḫrṣ.d[m.'ṣm].|[---.--]n.|[---.---]t.|[---.--]ṯ.|[---.--]n. 4[51].6.59
---.b ḥ]rb.mlḥ[t.qṣ].|[mri.tšty.krpnm].yn.b ks.ḫ[rṣ].|[dm.'ṣm.---]n.krpn.'l.[k]rpn.|[---.]ym.w t'l.trṯ.|[---].yn.'šy l 17[2AQHT].6.6
.|[ṯd.b ḥrb.m]lḥt.qṣ.|[mri.tšty.k]rpnm yn.|[b ks.ḫrṣ.dm].'ṣm. 4[51].3.44
.ḥš k.'ṣ k.'bṣ k.'m y.p'n k.tls]|[m]n 'm y t[wtḥ.išd k.dm.rgm.iṯ.l y.d argmn k].|[h]wt.d aṯ[ny k.---.rgm.'ṣ].|w lḥš 7.2[130].17
š k.[']ṣ k.'bṣ k.'m y.p'n k.|[tls]mn.[']m y.twtḥ.išd k.|[dm.rgm.iṯ.l y.]w argm k.hwt.|[w aṯny k.rgm.]'ṣ.w lḫšt.|[ab 3['NT].4.57
m.|ḥš k.'ṣ k.'bṣ k.|'m y.p'n k.tlsmn.'m y.|twtḥ.išd k.dm.rgm.|iṯ.l y.w argm k.|hwt.w aṯny k.rgm.|'ṣ.w lḫšt.abn. 3['NT].3.17
k.tlsmn].|'m y twtḥ.i[šd k.tk.ḫršn.-------------].|ǵr.ks.dm.r[gm.iṯ.l y.w argm k].|hwt.w aṯny k[.rgm.'ṣ.w lḫšt.abn] 1['NT.IX].3.12
.l y.w l h.[---].|[--.i]mṣḫ.nn.k imr.l arṣ.|[ašhlk].šbt h.dmm.šbt.dqn h.|[mm'm.-]d.l ytn.bt.l b'l.k ilm.|[w ḥẓ]r.k b 3['NT.VI].5.10
-].|[---.b]gdlt.ar[kt y.am--].|[---.qdq]d k.ašhlk[.šbt k.dmm].|[šbt.dq]n k.mm'm.w[---].|aqht.w ypltˍ k.bn[.dnil.--- 18[3AQHT].1.11
y.[---]b[-].|b gdlt.arkt y.am[---].|qdqd k.ašhlk.šbt[k.dmm].|[šbt.dqn k.mm'm.]y'ny.|il.b šb't.ḥdrm.b ṯmnt.|ap.s 3['NT.VI].5.32
tk.|p[ḫ]r.bn.ilm.štt.|p[--].b ṯlḥn y.qlt.|b ks.ištyn h.|dm.ṯn.dbḥm.šna.b'l.ṯlṯ.|rkb.'rpt.dbḥ.|bṯt.w dbḥ.w dbḥ.|dn 4[51].3.17
ǵlm.l šdt[.-.]ymm.|[---.]b ym.ym.y[--].yš[ ]n.ap k.'ṯtr.dm[.---.]|[---.]ḥrḥrtm.w[--.]n[--.]iš[--.]h[---.]išt.|[---]y.ybl 2.3[129].12

dmgy

.yẓḥq.bm.|lb.w ygmḏ.bm kbd.|ẓi.at.l tlš.|amt.yrḫ.|l dmgy.amt.|aṯrt.qḥ.|ksan k.ḥdg k.|ḥtl k.w ẓi.|b aln.tk m.| 12[75].1.16

dmd

rm.|ddm.l.ybr[k].|bdmr.prs.l.u[-]m[-].|ṯmn.l.'šrm.|dmd.b d.mry[n]m. 2102.11

dmy

ṯrt bn]|t hll.snnt.bnt h|ll b'l gml.yrdt.|b 'rgzm.b bz tdm.|lla y.'m lẓpn i|l ḏ.pid.hn b p y sp|r hn.b špt y mn|t h 24[77].43

dml

l.|[l.--.]mgmr.|[l.-.]qdšt.|l.'ṯtrt.ndrgd.|l.'ṯtrt.abḏr.|l.dml.|l.ilt[.-]pn.|l.uš[ḫr]y.|[---.-]mrn.|l ṯwl.|[--]ḏ[--]. 1001.1.13
.rgm.|mlk.|l ḥyil.|lm.tlik.'m y.|ik y.aškn.|'ṣm.l bt.dml.|p ank.atn.|'ṣm.l k.|arb'.'ṣm.|'l.ar.|w.ṯlṯ.|'l.ubr'y.|w. 1010.6
.|[b.yr]ḫ.riš.yn.[---].|[---.b']lt.bhtm.š[--.---].|[---.-]rt.l.dml[.---].|[b.yrḫ].nql.ṯn.ḫpn[.---].|[---].aḥd.ḫmš.am[--.---].| 1106.34

dmm

dbḥ.|dnt.w dbḥ.tdmm.|amht.k b h.bṯt.l tbṯ.|w b h.tdmmt.amht.|aḫr.mǵy.aliyn.b'l.|mǵyt.btlt.'nt.|tmgnn.rbt[. 4[51].3.22
na.b'l.ṯlṯ.|rkb.'rpt.dbḥ.|bṯt.w dbḥ.w dbḥ.|dnt.w dbḥ.tdmm.|amht.k b h.bṯt.l tbṯ.|w b h.tdmmt.amht.|aḫr.mǵy.a 4[51].3.20
b šdm.|ḥṭb h.b grnt.ḥpšt.|s't.b nk.šibt.b bqr.|mmlat.dm.ym.w ṯn.|ṯlṯ.rb'.ym.ymš.|ṯdṯ.ym.ḥẓ k.al.tš'l.|qrt h.abn. 14[KRT].3.114
.ḥṭb.|w b grnt.ḥpšt.|s't.b npk.šibt.w b |mqr.mmlat.|d[m].ym.w ṯn.|ṯlṯ.rb'.ym.|ḫmš.ṯdṯ.ym.|mk.špšm.b šb'.|w l 14[KRT].5.218
lm.tmtn.|špḥ.lṭpn.l yḥ.|w y'ny.krt.ṯ'.|bn.al.tbkn.al.|tdm.l y.al tkl.bn.|qr.'n k.mḫ.riš k.|udm't.ṣḥ.aḫt k.|ṯtmnt.b 16.1[125].26
riš k.|udm't.ṣḥ.aḫt k.|ṯtmnt.bt.ḥmḥ h.|d[-]n.tbkn.w tdm.l y.[--].|[---].al.trgm.l aḫt k.|[---.]l [ ]dm.aḫt k.|yd't.k 16.1[125].30

dm'

t.ab h.nšrm.trḫ[p]n.|ybṣr.ḥbl.diym.|tbky.pǵt.bm.lb.|tdm'.bm.kbd.|tmz'.kst.dnil.mt.|rpi.al.ǵzr.mt.hrnmy.|apnk 19[1AQHT].1.35
km.ṯqlm.arṣ h.|km ḫmšt.mṯt h.|bm.bky h.w yšn.|b dm' h.nhmmt.|šnt.tluan.|w yškb.nhmmt.|w yqmṣ.w b ḥl 14[KRT].1.32
ru.|[---.]nplt.y[--].md'.nplt.bšr.|[---].w tpky.k[m.]n'r.tdm'.km.|[ṣǵ]r.bkm.y'ny[.---.bn]wt h.|[--]nn.bnt yš[--.---.-]l UG5.8.40
.ḥmt.w t'btn h.abd y.|[---.ǵ]r.šrǵzz.ybky.km.n'r.|[w ydm'.k]m.ṣǵr.špš.b šmm.tqru.|[---.]nplt.y[--].md'.nplt.bšr.| UG5.8.38
kyt.b hkl h.mšspdt.b ḥẓr h.|pẓǵm.ǵr.ybk.l aqht.|ǵzr.ydm'.l kdd.dnil.|mt.rpi.l ymm.l yrḫm.|l yrḫm.l šnt.'d.|šb't 19[1AQHT].4.174
mm.l yrḫm.|l yrḫm.l šnt.'d.|šb't.šnt.ybk.l aq|ht.ǵzr.yd[m'.]l kdd.|dnil.mt.r[pi.mk].b šb'.|šnt.w y'n[.dnil.mt.]rp 19[1AQHT].4.178
ḏhrt h.|ab adm.w yqrb.|b šal.krt.m at.|krt.k ybky.|ydm'.n'mn.ǵlm.|il.mlk[.ṯ]r ab h.|yarš.hm.drk[t].|k ab.adm 14[KRT].1.40
.|[tn.ṯa]rm.amid.|[w y'n].ṯr.ab h.il.|d[--].b bk.krt.|b dm'.n'mn.ǵlm.|il.trḥṣ.w tadm.|rḥṣ[.y]d k.amt.|uṣb['t k.]'d 14[KRT].2.61
.|w b.pḫyr h.yrṯ.|y'rb.b ḥdr h.ybky.|b ṯn.[-]gmm.w ydm'.|tntkn.udm't h.|km.ṯqlm.arṣ h.|km ḫmšt.mṯt h.|bm. 14[KRT].1.27
---].|aṯr.aṯrm[.---].|išdym.t[---].|b k.mla[.---].|udm't.d[m'.---].|[---].bn.[---].|[-----]. 27[8].11

dm't

pdm.riš h[m.---].|'l.pd.asr.[---.]l[.---].|mḫlpt.w l.ytk.[d]m['t.]km.|rb't.ṯqlm.ṯtp[.---.]bm.|yd.ṣpn hm.tliy m[.--.ṣ]p 19[1AQHT].2.82

dmq

|t hn ṯlḫ h w mlg h y|ṯtqt 'm h b q't.|tq't 'm prbḫt.|dmqt ṣǵrt kṯrt. 24[77].50

dmrn

.|[---.]b km kbkbt k ṯn.|[---.]b'l yḥmdn h.yrṯ y.|[---.]dmrn.l pn h yrd.|[---.]b'l.šm[.--.]rgbt yu.|[---]w yrmy[.q]rn 2001.2.8
.hd.gpt.|ǵr.w y'n.aliyn.|b'l.ib.hdt.lm.tḫš.|lm.tḫš.nṯq.dmrn.|'n.b'l.qdm.yd h.|k tǵḏ.arz.b ymn h.|bkm.yṯb.b'l.l b 4[51].7.39

dmt

d.|ṣ'.|mlk.|gb'ly.|ypr.|ary.|ẓrn.|art.|ṯlḥny.|ṯlrby.|dmt.|aǵt.|w.qmnz.|slḫ.|ykn'm.|šlmy.|w.ull.|ṯmry.|qrt.|' 71[113].13
-]y.ilak k.|[---.--]g k.yritn.mǵy.hy.w kn.|[---].ḥln.d b.dmt.um.il[m.---].|[--]ḏyn.b'd.[--]ḏyn.w l.|[--]k b'lt bhtm[.-- 1002.43
bzl[.d]prn[.---].|aupṯ.krm.aḥd.nšpin.kr[m.]aḥd[.---].|dmt.lḫsn.krm.aḥd.anndr.kr[m.---].|aǵt.mryn.ary[.]yukl.kr 1081.15
[---.dmt q]dš.|[---.d]mt qdš.|[---].b.dmt qdš.|[---].b.dmt qdš.|[---.--]n.b.anan. 2118.2
[---.dmt q]dš.|[---.d]mt qdš.|[---].b.dmt qdš.|[---].b.dmt qdš.|[---.--]n.b.anan.|[--]yl.b.bq't.b.gt. 2118.3
[---.dmt q]dš.|[---.d]mt qdš.|[---].b.dmt qdš.|[---].b.dmt qdš.|[- 2118.1
[---.dmt q]dš.|[---.d]mt qdš.|[---].b.dmt qdš.|[---].b.dmt qdš.|[---.--]n.b.anan.|[--]yl.b.bq't.b.gt.tgyn.|[--]in.b.trz 2118.4
.|[-----].|[-----].|q[---].|ṯ[---].|ṯl[rby].|ṯmr[y].|aǵ[t].|dm[t].|šl[-].|[---]m.|[-]rm.|[-]dm.|[-]m.|[--]m.|[m]ru skn. 2058.2.39
dmt ṯlṯ.|qmnz tql.|zlyy ṯql.|ary ḫmšt.|ykn'm ḫmšt.|'nmk 1176.1
.w nṣp.|šlmy.ṯql.|ary ṯql.|ṯmry tql.w.nṣp.|aǵt nṣp.|dmt ṯql.|ykn'm ṯql. 69[111].6
].|qm[n]z[---].|šl[-.---].|ar[--.---].|qrt[.---].|ṯm[r.---].|dm[t.---].|gl[bt.---].|al[-.---]. 1181.14

dmty

anyt.miḫd[t].|br.ṯpṭb'[l.---].|br.dmty[.---].|ṯkt.ydln[.---].|ṯkt.ṯryn[.---].|br.'bdm[lk.---].|wr 84[319].1.3

dmtn

-].|bn.gnb[-.---].|hzpym.|rišn.[---].|bn.'bdy.[---].|bn.dmtn.[---].|[b]n.g'yn.ḫr[-].|lbnym.|grgš.[---].|bn.ǵrn.[---].| 93[328].11

dn

w]mn[t].|y.bt.il.ṯḫ.gg y.b ym.ṯiṭ.|rḥṣ.npṣ y.b ym.rṭ.|dn.il.bt h.ymǵyn.|yštql.dnil.l hkl h.|'rb.b bt h.kṯrt.bnt.|hll. 17[2AQHT].2.24
lk.d.y[mlk].|[--.]'bdyrḫ.l.ml[k].|[--]t.w.lqḥ.|yn[.--].b dn h.|w.ml[k].šświm.n'mm.|ytn.l.'bdyrḫ.|w.mlk.z[--.--]n.šś 2064.15
tpr.|šḥr w šlm.|ngh w srr.|'dw šr.|ṣdqm šr.|ḥnbn il d[n].|[-]bd w [---].|[--].p il[.---].|[i]l mt mr[b-].|qdš mlk [--- UG5.10.1.15

dnil

[ḥrš].bhtm.b'l.šd.|[---d]nil.|[a]drdn.|[---]n.|pǵdn.|ṯṯpḥ.|ḥgbn.|šrm.|bn.ymil.|b 1039.1.21
[ilm.y]lḥm.uzr.yšqy bn.|[qdš.ḫ]mš.ṯdṯ.ym.uzr.|[ilm].dnil.uzr.ilm.ylḥm.|[uzr.]yšqy.bn qdš.yd.ṣt h.|[dn]il.yd.ṣt h. 17[2AQHT].1.13
zr.ilm.]ylḥm.uzr.|[yšqy.b]n.qdš ṯlṯ rb' ym.|[uzr.i]lm.dnil.uzr.|[ilm.y]lḥm.uzr.yšqy bn.|[qdš.ḫ]mš.ṯdṯ.ym.uzr.|[il 17[2AQHT].1.10
.y'l.]w yškb.yd.|[mizrt.]p ynl.hn.ym.|[w ṯn.uzr.]ilm.dnil.|[uzr.ilm.]ylḥm.uzr.|[yšqy.b]n.qdš ṯlṯ rb' ym.|[uzr.i]l 17[2AQHT].1.7
mn[t].|y.bt.il.ṯḫ.gg y.b ym.ṯiṭ.|rḥṣ.npṣ y.b ym.rṭ.|dn.il.bt h.ymǵyn.|yštql.dnil.l hkl h.|'rb.b bt h.kṯrt.bnt.|hll.sn 17[2AQHT].2.24
št k.b'l.l ht.|w 'lm h.l 'nt.p dr.dr.|'db.uḫry.mṭ.yd h.|dnil.bt h.ymǵyn.yšt|ql.dnil.l hkl h.'rb.b|kyt.b hkl h.mšspdt 19[1AQHT].4.170
|[ilm].dnil.uzr.ilm.ylḥm.|[uzr.]yšqy.bn qdš.yd.ṣt h.|[dn]il.yd.ṣt h.y'l.w yškb.|[yd.]mizrt.p yln.mk.b šb'.ymm.|[17[2AQHT].1.15
ḫss.|l brlt.hyn.d ḥrš.|ydm.aḫr.ymǵy.kṯr.|w ḫss.b d.dnil.ytnn.|qšt.l brk h.y'db.|qs't.apnk.mṭt.dnty.|tšlḥm.tššq 17[2AQHT].5.26
z'.|kst.dnil.mt.rpi.|all.ǵzr.m[t.]hr[nmy].|gm.l bt[h.dnil.k yṣḥ].|šm'.pǵt.ṯkmt[.my].|ḥspt.l š'r.ṭl.yd['t].|hlk.kbk 19[1AQHT].1.49
.b ym.ṯiṭ.|rḥṣ.npṣ y.b ym.rṭ.|dn.il.bt h.ymǵyn.|yštql.dnil.l hkl h.|'rb.b bt h.kṯrt.bnt.|hll.snnt.apnk.dnil.|mt.rpi. 17[2AQHT].2.25
t.p dr.dr.|'db.uḫry.mṭ.yd h.|dnil.bt h.ymǵyn.yšt|ql.dnil.l hkl h.'rb.b|kyt.b hkl h.mšspdt.b ḥẓr h.|pẓǵm.ǵr.ybk. 19[1AQHT].4.171

nt.|[-]d[-]t.n'm y.'rš.h[--]m.|ysmsmt.'rš.ḫlln.[-].|yṯb.dnil.[l s]pr yrḫ h.|yrs.y[---.]y[--] h.|ṯlṯ.rb['.yrḫ.--]r[.--].|yrḫ 17[2AQHT].2.43
nšr.b ḥbš h.km.diy.|b t'rt h.aqht.km.yṯb.l lḥ[m].|bn.dnil.l ṯrm.'l h.nšr[m].|trḫpn.ybṣr.ḥbl.diy[m.bn].|nšrm.trḫp 18[3AQHT].4.30
.b ḥb[š y].|km.diy.b t'rt y.aqht.[km.yṯb].|l lḥm.w bn.dnil.l ṯrm[.'l h].|nšrm.trḫpn.ybṣr.[ḥbl.d]|iym.bn.nšrm.arḫ 18[3AQHT].4.19
pt.bl.ṭl.bl rbb.|bl.šr'.thmtm.bl.|ṭbn.ql.b'l.k tmz'.|kst.dnil.mt.rpi.|all.ģzr.m[t.]hr[nmy].|gm.l bt[h.dnil.k yṣḥ].|š 19[1AQHT].1.47
ṣr.ḥbl.diym.|tbky.pģt.bm.lb.|tdm'.bm.kbd.|tmz'.kst.dnil.mt.|rpi.al.ģzr.mt.hrnmy.|apnk.dnil.mt.|rpi.yṣly.'rpt.b 19[1AQHT].1.36
rt.p yln.mk.b šb'.ymm.|[w]yqrb.b'l.b ḥnt h.abynt.|[d]nil.mt.rpi anḫ.ģzr.|[mt.]hrnmy.d in.bn.l h.|km.aḫ h.w šr 17[2AQHT].1.18
.|yštql.dnil.l hkl h.|'rb.b bt h.kṯrt.bnt.|hll.snnt.apnk.dnil.|mt.rpi.ap.hn.ģzr.mt.|hrnmy.alp.yṭbḫ.l kṯ|rt.yšlḥm.kṯ 17[2AQHT].2.27
|[---.]abl.qšt ṯmn.|ašrb'.qṣ't.w hn šb['].|b ymm.apnk.dnil.mt.|rpi.a hn.ģzr.mt.hrnm[y].|ytšu.yṯb.b ap.ṯģr.tḥt.|ad 17[2AQHT].5.4
.|ḥkpt il.kl h.tb'.kṯr.|l ahl h.hyn.tb'.l mš|knt h.apnk.dnil.m[t].|rpi.aphn.ģzr.m[t].|hrnmy.qšt.yqb.[--]|rk.'l.aqht. 17[2AQHT].5.33
b mt[.-]ḫ.mṣṣ[-]t[.--].|pr'.qẓ.y[bl].šblt.|b ģlp h.apnk.dnil.|[m]t.rpi.ap[h]n.ģzr.|[mt.hrn]my.ytšu.|[yṯb.b ap.ṯ]ģr[. 19[1AQHT].1.19
k y'n.w y'n.tdrq.ḫss.|hlk.qšt.ybln.hl.yš|rb'.qṣ't.apnk.dnil.|mt.rpi.aphn.ģzr.mt.|hrnmy.gm.l aṯt h.k yṣḥ.|šm'.mṯt 17[2AQHT].5.13
[-----.apnk].|[dnil.mt.rp]i.apn.ģz[r].|[mt.hrnmy.]uzr.ilm.ylḥm.|[uzr.yšq 17[2AQHT].1.2
d h.ybrk.|[dni]l mt rpi.ymr.ģzr.|[mt.hr]nmy npš.yḥ.dnil.|[mt.rp]i.brlt.ģzr.mt hrnmy.|[---].hw.mḫ.l 'rš h.y'l.|[-- 17[2AQHT].1.37
hbr.w tql.tštḥ|[wy.w tkbd]n h.tlšn.aqht.ģzr.|[---.kdd.dn]il.mt.rpi.w t'n.|[btlt.'nt.tšu.g]h.w tṣḥ.hwt.|[---.]aqht.yd 17[2AQHT].6.52
mšspdt.b ḥẓr h.|pẓģm.ģr.ybk.l aqht.|ģzr.ydm'.l kdd.dnil.|mt.rpi.l ymm.l yrḫm.|l yrḫm.l šnt.'d.|šb't.šnt.ybk.l a 19[1AQHT].4.174
brlt n[-.k qṭr.b ap -].|tmģyn.tša.g h[m.w tṣḥn].|šm'.l dnil.[mt.rpi].|mt.aqht.ģzr.[šṣat].|btlt.'nt.k [rḥ.npš h].|k iṯl. 19[1AQHT].2.90
yrḫm.l šnt.'d.|šb't.šnt.ybk.l aq|ht.ģzr.yd[m'.]l kdd.|dnil.mt.r[pi.mk].b šb'.|šnt.w y'n[.dnil.mt.]rpi.|yṯb.ģzr.m[t. 19[1AQHT].4.179
ym.|[ti]ṯ.rḥṣ.npṣ h.b ym.rṯ.|[--.y]iḫd.il.'bd h.ybrk.|[dni]l mt rpi.ymr.ģzr.|[mt.hr]nmy npš.yḥ.dnil.|[mt.rp]i.brlt 17[2AQHT].1.36
mr[rt].|imḫṣ.mḫṣ.aḫ y.akl[.m]|kly[.']l.umt y.w y'n[.dn]|il.mt.rpi npš tḥ[.pģt].|t[km]t.mym.ḥspt.l š'r.|ṭl.yd't.hl 19[1AQHT].4.197
m.kbd.|tmz'.kst.dnil.mt.|rpi.al.ģzr.mt.hrnmy.|apnk.dnil.mt.|rpi.yṣly.'rpt.b |ḥm.un.yr.'rpt.|tmṭr.b qẓ.ṭl.yṭll.|l 19[1AQHT].1.38
t.ģzr.yd[m'.]l kdd.|dnil.mt.r[pi.mk].b šb'.|šnt.w y'n[.dnil.mt.]rpi.|yṯb.ģzr.m[t.hrnmy.y]šu.|g h.w yṣḥ.t[b'.---].|b 19[1AQHT].4.180
r.š[pšm.b ṯlṯ].|mģy.rpum.l grnt.i[lnym.l] |mṭ't.w y'n.dnil.[mt.rpi].|yṯb.ģzr.mt hrnmy[.---].|b grnt.ilm.b qrb.m[ṭ' 20[121].2.7
b yģlm.|ur.tisp k.yd.aqht.|ģzr.tšt k.b qrb m.asm.|y.dnh.ysb.aklt h.yph.|šblt.b akt.šblt.yp'.|b ḥmdrt.šblt.yḥ[bq] 19[1AQHT].2.68
l.bkm.|tšu.ab h.tštnn.l[b]mt 'r.|l ysmsm.bmt.pḫl.|y dnil.ysb.palt h.|bṣql.yph.b palt.bṣ[q]l.|yph.b yģlm.bṣql.y[ḥ 19[1AQHT].2.61
s k.k šb'.yn.ṭ[ḫ].|gg k.b ym.ṭiṭ.rḥṣ.|npṣ k.b ym rṯ.b uni[l].|pnm.tšmḫ.w 'l yṣhl pi[t].|yprq.lṣb.w yṣḥq.|p'n.l hd 17[2AQHT].2.8
hm.tliy m[.--.ṣ]pn hm.|nṣḥy.šrr.m[---.--]ay.|nbšr km.dnil.[--] h[.---].|riš.r[--.--]ḫ[.---]y[.---.-]nt.[š]ṣat[k.]rḥ.npš.h 19[1AQHT].2.86
.dmm].|[šbt.dq]n k.mm'm.w[---].|aqht.w yplṭ k.bn[.dnil.---].|w y'ḏr k.b yd.btlt.['nt].|w y'n.lṭpn.il d p[id].|yd't 18[3AQHT].1.13

dny

.ṯn.dbḥm.šna.b'l.ṯlṯ.|rkb.'rpt.dbḥ.|bṯt.w dbḥ.w dbḥ.|dnt.w dbḥ.tdmm.|amht.k b h.bṯt.l tbṯ.|w b h.tdmmt.amht. 4[51].3.20

dnyn

|algbṯ.arb't.|ksp h.|kkr.š'rt.|šb't.ksp h.|ḫmš.mqdm.dnyn.|b.ṯql.dprn.aḥd.|b.ṯql.|ḫmšm.'rgz.b.ḫmšt. 1127.19

dnn

----].|w.[-----].|w.abģl.nḫ[l h.--].|w.unṯ.aḫd.l h[.---].|dnn.bn.yṣr[.---].|sln.bn.'ṭt[-.---].|pdy.bn.nr[-.---].|abmlk.bn 90[314].1.5
.|'nbr.|aḫrm.|bn.qrdy.|bn.šm'n.|bn.ģlmy.|ģly.|bn.dnn.|bn.rmy.|dll.|mny.|krty.|bn.'bṣ.|bn.argb.|ydn.|il'nt. 2117.3.35
-].|bnil.bn.tl[--].|bn.brzn.ṯn.|bn.išb'l[.---].|bn.s[---].|dnn.[bn.---].|bn[.--]'nt. 2069.10
b.bq'.|a[--].'ṭ.|a[l]pm.alpnm.|ṯlṯ.m[a]t.art.ḥkpt.|mit.dnn.|mitm.iqnu.|ḫmš.'šr.qn.n'm.'n[m].|ṯn.ḥblm.alp.alp.a 1128.27
.ubr'y.|[---].gwl.|[---]ady.|[---]ṣry.|miḫ[-]m.|ṣdqm.|dnn.|'dy. 1041.14
šm [---].|kn'm.bn.[---].|plšb'l.bn.n[--].|ḥy bn.dnn.ṯkt.|ilṯḥm.bn.dnn.ṯkt.|šb'l.bn.aly.ṯkt.|klby.bn.iḫy.ṯkt. 2085.4
n'm.bn.[---].|plšb'l.bn.n[--].|ḥy bn.dnn.ṯkt.|ilṯḥm.bn.dnn.ṯkt.|šb'l.bn.aly.ṯkt.|klby.bn.iḫy.ṯkt.|psš.bn.buly.ṯkt.|' 2085.5
dnn.ṯlṯ.ṣmdm.|bn.'mnr.|bn.kmn.|bn.ibyn.|bn.mryn.ṣmd. 2113.1

dnt

bn.qrrn.|bn.dnt.|bn.ṯ'l[-].|bdl.ar.dt.inn.|mhr l ht.|artyn.|'dmlk.|bn.al 1035.1.2

dnty

|w ḫss.b d.dnil.ytnn.|qšt.l brk h.y'db.|qṣ't.apnk.mṯt.dnty.|tšlḥm.tššqy ilm.|tsad.tkbd.hmt.b'l.|ḥkpt il.kl h.tb'.k 17[2AQHT].5.28
m.ššqy.|ilm sad.kbd.hmt.b'l.|ḥkpt.il.kl h.tšm'.|mṯt.dnty.t'db.imr.|b pḫd.l npš.kṯr.w ḫss.|l brlt.hyn.d ḥrš.|ydm 17[2AQHT].5.22
t.rpi.aphn.ģzr.mt.|hrnmy.gm.l aṯt h.k yṣḥ.|šm'.mṯt.dnty.'d[b].|imr.b pḫd.l npš.kṯr.|w ḫss.l brlt.hyn d.|ḥrš yd. 17[2AQHT].5.16

d'

.|ḫlb.l ẓr.rḥtm w rd.|bt ḫpṯt.arṣ.tspr b y|rdm.arṣ.w td' ilm.|k mtt.yšm'.aliyn.b'l.|yuhb.'glt.b dbr.prt.|b šd.šḫl 5[67].5.16
.'nt.k [rḥ.npš h].|k iṯl.brlt h.[b h.p'nm].|ṭṭṭ.'l[n.pn h.td'.b 'dn].|ksl.y[ṯbr.yģṣ.pnt.ksl h].|anš.[dt.ẓr h.yšu.g h].|w 19[1AQHT].2.94
bmt.|[limm].b h.p'nm.|[ṭṭṭ.b ']dn.ksl.|[ṯṯbr.'ln.p]n h.td['].|tģṣ[.pnt.ks]l h.|anš.dt.ẓr.[h].|tšu.g h.w tṣḥ[.i]k.|mģy. 4[51].2.18
hlm.'nt.tph.ilm.b h.p'nm.|ṭṭṭ.b'd n.ksl.tṯbr.|'ln.pn h.td'.tģṣ.pnt.|ksl h.anš.dt.ẓr h.tšu.|g h.w tṣḥ.ik.mģy.gpn.w u 3['NT].3.31
r.|ḫṭ m.t'mt.[']ṭr.[k]m.|zbln.'l.riš h.|w ṯṯb.trḥṣ.nn.b d't.|npš h.l lḥm.tpth.|brlt h.l ṯrm.|mt.dm.ḫt.š'tqt.|dm.lan. 16.6[127].10
--.-]pt h.|ql h.q[dš.ṯb]r.arṣ.|[---.]ģrm[.t]ḫšn.|rḥq[.---.td'].|qdm ym.bmt.[nhr].|ṯṭtn.ib.b'l.tiḫd.|y'rm.šnu.hd.gpt.| 4[51].7.33

d'ṣ

h.|[mm'm.-]d.l ytn.bt.l b'l.k ilm.|[w ḥẓ]r.k bn.aṯrt[.td'ṣ.]p'n.|[w tr.a]rṣ.id[k.l ttn.p]nm.|['m.i]l.mbk.nhr[m.qr]b 3['NT.VI].5.12
.|w bn.bht.ksp.w ḫrṣ.|bht.ṯhrm.iqnim.|šmḫ.btlt.'nt.td'ṣ.|p'nm.w tr.arṣ.|idk.l ttn.pnm.|'m.b'l.mrym.ṣpn.|b alp 4[51].5.82
--].b ntb.gan.ašql k.tḥt.|[p'n y.a]nk.n'mn.'mq.nšm.|[td'ṣ.p'n]m.w tr.arṣ.idk.|[l ttn.pn]m.'m il.mbk.nhrm.|[qrb.a 17[2AQHT].6.46

dǵm

bd.arbʻm. | dd.akl. | t̲t̲.ʻšr h.yn. | kd.šmn.l.nr.ilm. | kdm.dǵm. | t̲t̲.kdm.ztm. 1126.7

dǵt̲

[-]l[-]. | w tʻn.pǵt.t̲kmt.mym. | qrym.ab.dbḥ.l ilm. | šʻly.dǵt̲ h.b šmym. | dǵt̲.hrnmy.d kbkbm. | l tbrkn.alk brkt. | tmr 19[1AQHT].4.192
hk[l]y.mšspdt. | b ḥz̀r y pz̀ǵm.ǵr.w yq. | dbḥ.ilm.yšʻly.dǵt̲ h. | b šmym.dǵt̲ hrnmy[.d k] | bkbm.ʻ[l.---]. | [-]l h.yd ʻd[.- 19[1AQHT].4.185
t.t̲kmt.mym. | qrym.ab.dbḥ.l ilm. | šʻly.dǵt̲ h.b šmym. | dǵt̲.hrnmy.d kbkbm. | l tbrkn.alk brkt. | tmrn.alk.nmr[rt]. | i 19[1AQHT].4.193
b ḥz̀r y pz̀ǵm.ǵr.w yq. | dbḥ.ilm.yšʻly.dǵt̲ h. | b šmym.dǵt̲ hrnmy[.d k] | bkbm.ʻ[l.---]. | [-]l h.yd ʻd[.---]. | ltm.mrqdm 19[1AQHT].4.186
ʻ d.ǵzrm.t̲b.[g]d.b ḥlb.annḫ b ḫmat. | w ʻl.agn.šbʻ d m.dǵ[t̲.---]t. | tlk m.rḥmy.w tṣd[.---]. | tḥgrn.ǵzr.nʻm.[---]. | w šm 23[52].15

dpm

dm]. | w.tšʻ.ʻ[šr.--]m.ḥr[š]. | [---].ḥr[š.---]. | [---.t̲]lt̲.[---.]dpm. | [---.]bnšn. | [---.ḫ]mš.ṣmd.alpm. | [---.bn]šm. | [---.]ḫmš. 2038.13

dpr

[---].aliyn. | [bʻl.---.-]ip.dpr k. | [---.-]mn k.ššrt. | [---.--]t.npš.ʻgl. | [---.-]nk.aštn.b ḫrt. | 5[67].5.2
.dt.šnt. | imr.qmṣ.llim.k ksp. | l ʻbrm.zt.ḫrṣ.l ʻbrm.kš. | dpr.t̲lḥn.b qʻl.b qʻl. | mlkm.hn.ym.yṣq.yn.t̲mk. | mrt̲.yn.srnm 22.2[124].16

dprn

| ksp h. | kkr.šʻrt. | šbʻt.ksp h. | ḫmš.mqdm.dnyn. | b.t̲ql.dprn.aḥd. | b.t̲ql. | ḫmšm.ʻrgz.b.ḫmšt. 1127.20
l ky. | dd l ʻbdkt̲r. | dd[m] l rʻy. | [--] šmḥ[.---]. | ddm gt dprnm. | l ḥršm. | ddm l ʻnqt. | dd l alt̲t.w l lmdt h. | dd l iḫyn. 1101.8
ʻmn.b.ḫly.ull.krm.aḥ[d.---]. | krm.uḫn.b.šdmy.t̲lt̲.bzl[.d]prn[.---]. | aupt̲.krm.aḥd.nšpin.kr[m.]aḥd[.---]. | dmt.lḫsn.k 1081.13
k.yraš.ššw.[št]. | bln.qt̲.yṣq.b.a[p h]. | k ygʻr[.ššw.---]. | dprn[.---]. | drʻ.[---]. | tmt̲l[.---]. | mǵm[ǵ.---]. | w.š[t.nni.w.pr.ʻ 161[56].24

dqn

spr.bnš.mlk. | d taršn.ʻmsn. | bṣr.abn.špšyn. | dqn. | aǵlmn. | knʻm. | aḫršp. | anntn. | bʻlrm. | [-]ral. | šd̲n. | [-]ǵl 2067.1.4
ʻ[l]n.ald̲y. | tdn.ṣr[--.--]t.ʻzn.mtn.n[bd]g. | ḥrš qt̲n[.---.]dqn.bʻln. | ǵltn.ʻbd.[---]. | nsk.ḥd̲m.klyn[.ṣd]qn.ʻbdilt.bʻl. | ann 2011.23
.[---]. | [--.i]mṣḫ.nn.k imr.l arṣ. | [ašhlk].šbt h.dmm.šbt.dqn h. | [mmʻm.-]d.l ytn.bt.l bʻl.k ilm. | [w ḥz̀]r.k bn.at̲rt[.tdʻ 3[ʻNT.VI].5.10
---]. | nsk.ḥd̲m.klyn[.ṣd]qn.ʻbdilt.bʻl. | annmn.ʻdy.klby.dqn. | ḥrtm.ḥgbn.ʻdn.ynḥm[.---]. | ḥrš.mrkbt.ʻzn.[b]ʻln.t̲b[--.- 2011.26
]k. | [-----]. | pǵd̲n. | [--]n. | [--]ntn. | ʻdn. | lkn. | ktr. | ubn. | dqn. | ḥt̲tn. | [--]n. | [---]. | tsn. | rpiy. | mrt̲n. | t̲nyn. | apt̲. | šbn. | g 1024.2.10
ḥz̀r.k bn.at̲rt. | w tʻn.rbt.at̲rt ym. | rbt.ilm.l ḥkmt. | šbt.dqn k.l tsr k. | rḫntt.d[-].l irt k. | wn ap.ʻdn.mṭr h. | bʻl.y.ʻdn.ʻ 4[51].5.66
lt.ar[kt y.am--]. | [---.qdq]d k.ašhlk[.šbt k.dmm]. | [šbt.dq]n k.mmʻm.w[---]. | aqht.w yplt̲ k.bn[.dnil.---]. | w yʻd̲r k. 18[3AQHT].1.12
gdlt.arkt y.am[---]. | qdqd k.ašhlk.šbt[k.dmm]. | [šbt.dqn k.mmʻm.]yʻny. | il.b šbʻt.ḥdrm.b t̲mnt. | ap.sgrt.ydʻ[t k.] 3[ʻNT.VI].5.33
gld.t̲qlm. | bn.ʻmy.t̲qlm. | bn.brq.t̲qlm. | bn.ḫnzr.t̲qlm. | dqn.nsk.arbʻt. | bn.ḫdyn.t̲qlm. | bn.ʻbd.šḫr.t̲qlm. | bn.ḫnqn.ar 122[308].1.17
kt̲r.ʻbd. | tdǵl. | bʻlṣn. | nsk.ksp. | iwrtn. | ydln. | ʻbdilm. | dqn. | nsk.t̲lt̲. | ʻbdadt. | bṣmn.spr. 1039.2.27
dn. | ḫyrn.mdʻ. | šmʻn.rb ʻšrt.kkln.ʻbd.absn. | šdyn.unn.dqn. | ʻbdʻnt.rb ʻšrt.mnḥm.t̲bʻm.šḫr.ʻzn.ilhd. | bnil.rb ʻšrt.lkn. 2011.6
[---.]krm.b [-]dn.l.bn.[-]kn. | šd[.---.-]ʻn. | šd[.---.-]ṣm.l.dqn. | š[d.---.--]d.pdy. | [---.dq]n. | [---.d]qn. | [---.--]b[.---]. | [--- 2027.1.7
ʻn.rqdy. | bn.gʻyn. | bn.ǵrn. | bn.agynt. | bn.abdḫr.snry. | dqn.šlmn. | prdn.ndb[--]. | [-]rn.ḫbty. | abmn.bn.qdmn. | nʻmn 87[64].37
pn. | l.ʻbdil[m].ḫpn. | tmrtn.šʻrt. | lmd.n.rn. | [---].ḫpn. | dqn.šʻrt. | [lm]d.yrt̲. | [-.]ynḥm.ḫpn. | t̲t̲.lmd.bʻln. | l.qḥ.ḫpnt. | 1117.14
mdrǵlm.d.b.i[-]ʻlt.mlk. | arsw. | dqn. | t̲lt̲.klbm. | ḫmn. | [---.-]rsd. | bn[.-]pt̲. | bn kdrn. | awldn. | 86[305].3
yks. | mizrtm.ǵr.b abn. | ydy.psltm.b yʻr. | yhdy.lḥm.w dqn. | yt̲lt̲.qn.d̲rʻ h.yḥrt̲. | k gn.ap lb.k ʻmq.yt̲lt̲. | bmt.yšu.g h. 5[67].6.19
l bʻl. | ǵr.b ab.td[.ps]ltm[.b yʻr]. | thdy.lḥm.w dqn[.t̲t̲lt̲]. | qn.d̲rʻ h.tḥrt̲.km.gn. | ap lb.k ʻmq.t̲t̲lt̲.bmt. | bʻl.mt 6[62].1.3
. | šd[.---.-]ʻn. | šd[.---.-]ṣm.l.dqn. | š[d.---.--]d.pdy. | [---.dq]n. | [---.d]qn. | [---.--]b[.---]. | [---.--]l[.--]. | [---.--]b[.---]. | [--- 2027.1.9
rš.mrkbt.ʻzn.[b]ʻln.t̲b[--.-]nb.trtn. | [---]mm.klby.kl[--].dqn[.---]. | [-]ntn.artn.b d[.--]nr[.---]. | ʻzn.w ymd.šr.b d ansn 2011.29
]ʻn. | šd[.---.-]ṣm.l.dqn. | š[d.---.--]d.pdy. | [---.dq]n. | [---.d]qn. | [---.--]b[.---]. | [---.--]l[.--]. | [---.--]b[.---]. | [---.]y[--.-]kzn 2027.1.10
n. | [---.]yn.l.m[---]. | [---.]yn.l.m[--]m. | [---.]d.bn.[---.]l.dqn. | [---.--]ʻ.šdyn.l ytršn. | [---.--]t̲.ʻbd.l.kyn. | k[rm.--.]l.i[w]r 2027.2.7

dqq

n.rbt.at̲rt ym. | bl.nmlk.ydʻ.ylḥn. | w yʻn.lt̲pn.il d pi | d dq.anm.l yrz̀. | ʻm.bʻl.l yʻdb.mrḥ. | ʻm.bn.dgn.k tms m. | w ʻn. 6.1.50[49.1.22]
.ytk.gdlt.ilhm]. | t̲kmn.w [šnm.dqt.ršp.šrp]. | w šlmm.[dqtm.ilh.alp.w š]. | ilhm.gd[lt.ilhm.bʻl.š.at̲rt.š]. | t̲kmn.w š[n APP.II[173].15
.l il. | gdlt.ilhm.t̲kmn.w šnm dqt. | ršp.dqt.šrp w šlmm.dqtm. | [i]lh.alp w š ilhm.gdl[t.]ilhm. | [b]ʻl š.at̲rt.š.t̲kmn w š 34[1].4
]. | ytk.gdlt.ilhm.[t̲kmn.w šnm]. | dqt.ršp.šrp.w š[lmm.dqtm]. | ilh[.a]lp.w š[.il]hm.[gdlt.ilhm]. | bʻ[l.š].at̲rt[.š.t̲km]n 35[3].13
l inš[.ilm.---]. | il[hm.]dqt.š[.---.rš] | [p.š]rp.w šl[mm.--.dqt]. | [i]lh.gdlt[.ilhm.gdlt.il]. | [d]qt.t̲kmn.w [šnm.dqt.--]. | [- 35[3].29
]. | [---.]ilh[m.dqt.š.--]. | [---.--]t.r[šp.šrp.w šl] | [mm.---].dq[t.ilh.gdlt]. | n.w šnm.dqt[.---]. | [i]lh[m.gd]lt.i[l.dqt.t̲km] | APP.II[173].32
qt[.---]. | [i]lh[m.gd]lt.i[l.dqt.t̲km] | n.w šnm.dqt[.---]. | bqtm.b nbk.[---]. | kmm.gdlt.l b[ʻl.--.dqt]. | l ṣpn.gdlt.[l.---]. | APP.II[173].35
h.gdlt[.ilhm.gdlt.il]. | [d]qt.t̲kmn.w [šnm.dqt.--]. | [--]t.dqtm.[b nbk.---]. | [--.k]mm.gdlt.l.b[ʻl.---]. | [dq]t.l.ṣpn.gdlt.l[35[3].32
t.ym gdlt. | bʻl gdlt.yrḫ.gdlt. | gdlt.t̲rmn.gdlt.pdry.gdlt dqt. | dqt.trt̲.dqt. | [rš]p.ʻnt.ḫbly.dbḥn š[p]š pgr. | [g]dlt iltm ḫ 34[1].15
k.brr. | [b ym.ml]at.y[ql]n.al[p]m.yrḫ.ʻšrt. | [l bʻl.ṣ]pn.[dq]tm.w y[nt] qrt. | [w mtmt]m.[š.l] rm[š.]kbd.w š. | [l šlm.k 36[9].1.12
tḥṣ.mlk.b[rr]. | b ym.mlat. | tqln.alpm. | yrḫ.ʻšrt.l bʻ[l]. | dqtm.w ynt.qr[t]. | w mtntm.š l rmš. | w kbd.w š.l šlm kbd. | UG5.13.6
dqt. | [rš]p.ʻnt.ḫbly.dbḥn š[p]š pgr. | [g]dlt iltm ḫnqtm.d[q]tm. | [yr]ḫ.kty gdlt.w l ǵlmt š. | [w]pamt t̲lt̲m.w yrdt.[m 34[1].18
hm.ḥrṣ. | t̲lḥn.il.d mla. | mnm.dbbm.d | msdt.arṣ. | sʻ.il.dqt.k amr. | sknt.k ḥwt.yman. | d b h.rumm.l rbbt. 4[51].1.42
t.--]. | [--]t.dqtm.[b nbk.---]. | [--.k]mm.gdlt.l.b[ʻl.---]. | [dq]t.l.ṣpn.gdlt.l[.---]. | u[gr]t.š.l.[il]ib.ǵ[--.--rt]. | w [ʻṣrm.]l.ri[35[3].34
.w šnm.dqt[.---]. | bqtm.b nbk.[---]. | kmm.gdlt.l b[ʻl.--.dqt]. | l ṣpn.gdlt.[l.---]. | ugrt.š l ili[b.---]. | rt.w ʻṣrm.l[.---]. | pa APP.II[173].36
w bdḥ.k[--.---]. | ʻṣrm.l i[nš.ilm.t̲b.md] | bḥ.bʻl.[gdlt.---.dqt]. | l ṣpn.w [dqt.---.t̲n.l ʻš] | rm.pam[t.---]. | š dd šmn[.gdlt. APP.II[173].45
-]. | [--].at̲rt.ʻṣr[m.l inš.ilm]. | [t̲]t̲b.mdbḥ.bʻl.g[dlt.---]. | dqt.l.ṣpn.w.dqt[.---]. | t̲n.l.ʻšrm.pamt.[---]. | š.dd.šmn.gdlt.w.[35[3].42
.[š.l] rm[š.]kbd.w š. | [l šlm.kbd.al]p.w š.[l] bʻl.ṣpn. | [dqt.l.ṣpn.šrp].w š[l]mm.kmm. | [w bbt.bʻl.ugrt.]kdm.w npš. 36[9].1.15

dqq

tntm.š l rmš. | w kbd.w š.l šlm kbd. | alp.w š.l b‘l ṣpn. | dqt l ṣpn.šrp.w šlmm. | kmm.w bbt.b‘l.ugrt. | w kdm.w npš il UG5.13.10
t.ṯ‘m. | mtntm nkbd.alp.š.l il. | gdlt.ilhm.ṯkmn.w šnm dqt. | ršp.dqt.šrp w šlmm.dqtm. | [i]lh.alp w š ilhm.gdl[t.]ilh 34[1].3
‘l gdlt.yrḫ.gdlt. | gdlt.ṯrmn.gdlt.pdry.gdlt dqt. | dqt.trṯ.dqt. | [rš]p.‘nt.ḫbly.dbḥn š[p]š pgr. | [g]dlt iltm ḫnqtm.d[q]t 34[1].16
al[p.l]il.w bu[rm.---]. | ytk.gdlt.ilhm.[ṯkmn.w šnm]. | dqt.ršp.šrp.w š[lmm.dqtm]. | ilh[.a]lp.w š[.il]hm.[gdlt.ilhm]. 35[3].13
w alp.l il.w bu] | [rm.---.ytk.gdlt.ilhm]. | ṯkmn.w [šnm.dqt.ršp.šrp]. | w šlmm.[dqtm.ilh.alp.w š]. | ilhm.gd[lt.ilhm.b‘ APP.II[173].14
nkl.gdlt.l b‘] | [lt].bht[m].[‘]ṣrm l [inš.ilm]. | [---.]ilh[m.dqt.š.--]. | [---.--]t.r[šp.šrp.w šl] | [mm.---].dq[t.ilh.gdlt]. | n.w APP.II[173].30
].l nkl[.gdlt.l b‘lt.bhtm]. | ‘š[rm.]l inš[.ilm.---]. | il[hm.]dqt.š[.---.rš] | [p.š]rp.w šl[mm.--.dqt]. | [i]lh.gdlt[.ilhm.gdlt.il 35[3].28
tntm nkbd.alp.š.l il. | gdlt.ilhm.ṯkmn.w šnm dqt. | ršp.dqt.šrp w šlmm.dqtm. | [i]lh.alp w š ilhm.gdl[t.]ilhm. | [b]‘l š 34[1].4
rm. | [---.i]l š.b‘l š.aṯrt.š.ym š.[b‘]l knp. | [---.g]dlt.ṣpn.dqt.šrp.w [š]lmm. | [---.a]lp.l b‘l.w aṯrt.‘ṣr[m] l inš. | [ilm.---]. 36[9].1.7
gdlt. | b‘l gdlt.yrḫ.gdlt. | gdlt.ṯrmn.gdlt.pdry.gdlt dqt. | dqt.trṯ.dqt. | [rš]p.‘nt.ḫbly.dbḥn š[p]š pgr. | [g]dlt iltm ḫnqt 34[1].16
ilbt. | ušḫry. | ym.b‘l. | yrḫ. | kṯr. | ṯrmn. | pdry. | dqt. | trṯ. | ršp. | ‘nt ḫbly. | špš pgr. | iltm ḫnqtm. | yrḫ kṯy. | ygb UG5.14.A.8
rš] | [p.š]rp.w šl[mm.--.dqt]. | [i]lh.gdlt[.ilhm.gdlt.il]. | [d]qt.ṯkmn.w [šnm.dqt.--]. | [--]t.dqtm.[b nbk.---]. | [--.k]mm. 35[3].31
.---].dq[t.ilh.gdlt]. | n.w šnm.dqt[.---]. | [i]lh[m.gd]lt.i[l.dqt.ṯkm] | n.w šnm.dqt[.---]. | bqtm.b nbk.[---]. | kmm.gdlt.l b APP.II[173].33
ṯn pǵn.[-]dr | m.ṯn kndwm adrm. | w knd pnṯ.dq. | ṯn ḫpnm.ṯn pldm ǵlmm. | kpld.b[-.-]r[--]. | w blḫ br[-]m 140[98].3
dqt.ṯ‘.ynt.ṯ‘m.dqt.ṯ‘m. | mtntm nkbd.alp.š.l il. | gdlt.ilhm.ṯk 34[1].1
dqt.ṯ‘.ynt.ṯ‘m.dqt.ṯ‘m. | mtntm nkbd.alp.š.l il. | gdlt.ilhm.ṯkmn.w šnm dqt. 34[1].1
.--.dqt]. | [i]lh.gdlt[.ilhm.gdlt.il]. | [d]qt.ṯkmn.w [šnm.dqt.--]. | [--]t.dqtm.[b nbk.---]. | [--.k]mm.gdlt.l.b[‘l.---]. | [dq] 35[3].31
l[--]n. | [---.]š.il š.b‘l š.dgn š. | [---.--]r.w ṯt pl.gdlt.[ṣ]pn.dqt. | [---.al]p ‘nt.gdlt.b ṯlṯt mrm. | [---.i]l š.b‘l š.aṯrt.š.ym š.[b 36[9].1.4
--.--]t.r[šp.šrp.w šl] | [mm.---].dq[t.ilh.gdlt]. | n.w šnm.dqt[.---]. | [i]lh[m.gd]lt.i[l.dqt.ṯkm] | n.w šnm.dqt[.---]. | bqtm APP.II[173].34
n.w šnm.dqt[.---]. | [i]lh[m.gd]lt.i[l.dqt.ṯkm] | n.w šnm.dqt[.---]. | bqtm.b nbk.[---]. | kmm.gdlt.l b[‘l.--.dqt]. | l ṣpn.gd APP.II[173].34
w b[--.---]. | ilib[.---]. | alp.[---]. | ili[b.---]. | t‘r[.---]. | dq[t.---]. | nb[--.---]. 44[44].6
. | ‘ṣrm.l i[nš.ilm.ṯb.md] | bḥ.b‘l.[gdlt.---.dqt]. | l ṣpn.w [dqt.---.ṯn.l ‘š] | rm.pam[t.---]. | š dd šmn[.gdlt.w.---]. | brr.r[g APP.II[173].46
‘ṣr[m.l inš.ilm]. | [ṯ]ṯb.mdbḥ.b‘l.g[dlt.---]. | dqt.l.ṣpn.w.dqt[.---]. | ṯn.l.‘šrm.pamt.[---]. | š.dd.šmn.gdlt.w.[---.brr]. | rg 35[3].42

dqr

ṯpr. | [---.]prš. | [---.]šdm. | [---.-]nm.prš.glbm. | [---.]‘gd.dqr. | [---.]ṯn.alpm. | [---.ṯ]n alpm. | [---.--]r[.‘]šr.ṣin. | [---.]klkl. 1142.8

dqry

ṯqbt.qšt. | [-]ll.qšt.w.ql‘. | ḫlb.rpš. | abmn.qšt. | ẓẓn.qšt. | dqry.qš[t]. | rkby. | bn.knn.qšt. | pbyn.qšt. | yddn.qšt.w.ql‘. | š‘r 119[321].2.33
y. | ṯb‘m. | ḥdṯn. | rpty. | ilym. | bn.‘br. | mnip‘l. | amrb‘l. | dqry. | ṯdy. | yp‘b‘l. | bdlm. | bn.pḏ[-]. | bn.[---]. 1058.17
ḫlb.rpš. | ẓẓn. | bn.ḥmny. | dqry. 1068.4

dqt

t. | yptḥ.ḥln.b bht m. | urbt.b qrb.[h]kl | m.w y[p]tḥ.b dqt.‘rpt. | ‘l h[wt].kṯr.w ḫss. | ṣḥq.kṯr.w ḫss. | yšu.g h.w yṣḥ. | l 4[51].7.19
t y.yptḥ.ḥ | ln.b bht m.urbt. | b qrb.hk[l m.yp]tḥ. | b‘l.b dqt[.‘rp]t. | ql h.qdš.b[‘l.y]tn. | yṯny.b‘l.ṣ[---.-]pt h. | ql h.q[dš. 4[51].7.28

dr

an.y špš. | an.l an.il.yǵr[.-]. | tǵr k.š[---.---]. | yštd[.---]. | dr[.---]. | r[---.---]. 6[49].4.50
dlt.ilhm]. | b‘[l.š].aṯrt[.š.ṯkm]n w [šnm.š]. | ‘nt š ršp š[.dr.il.w pḫr.b‘l]. | gdlt.šlm[.gdlt.w burm.lb]. | rmṣt.ilh[m.b‘lm 35[3].16
m.gdl[t.]ilhm. | [b]‘l š.aṯrt.š.ṯkmn w šnm.š. | ‘nt.š.ršp.š.dr il w p[ḫ]r b‘l. | gdlt.šlm.gdlt.w burm.[l]b. | rmṣt.ilhm.b‘lm 34[1].7
lhm.gd[lt.ilhm.b‘l.š.aṯrt.š]. | ṯkmn.w š[nm.š.‘nt.š.ršp.š.dr]. | il.w pḫr[.b‘l.gdlt.šlm.gdlt]. | w burm.l[b.rmṣt.ilhm]. | b‘l APP.II[173].17
.dtn. | ṣǵrt hn.abkrn. | tbrk.ilm.tity. | tity.ilm.l ahl hm. | dr il.l mšknt hm. | w tqrb.w ld.bn.l h. | w tqrb.w ld.bnt.l h. | 15[128].3.19
n. | ndbḥ.hw.ṯ‘ n[ṯ‘y.hw.nkt.nk]t.ytši.l ab bn il. | ytši.l d[r.bn il.l]mpḫrt.bn il. | l ṯkm[n.w šnm.]hn ‘[r]. | [---.]w npy[32[2].1.34
db]ḥ. | [hw.ṯ‘.nṯ‘y.hw.nkt.nkt.]yt[ši.l ab.bn.il]. | [ytši.l dr.bn.il.l mpḫ]rt.[bn.il.l ṯkmn.w šn]m hn š. | [---.w n]py.gr[. 32[2].1.9B
n.ndbḥ.hw.ṯ‘ | nṯ‘y. | hw.nkt.nkt.y[t]ši.l ab.bn.il.ytši.l dr. | bn il.l mpḫrt.bn.il.l ṯkmn[.w]šnm.hn.‘r. | w.ṯb.l mspr.m 32[2].1.25
[---.hw.ṯ‘.nṯ‘]y. | [hw.nkt.nkt.ytši.l ab.bn.il.ytši.l d]r.bn[.il]. | [l mpḫrt.bn.il.l ṯkmn.w šnm.hn š]. | [w šqrb.š.mš 32[2].1.2
ndbḥ]. | hw.ṯ‘.nṯ‘y.hw.nkt.n[k]t.ytši[.l ab.bn.il]. | ytši.l dr.bn.il.l mpḫrt.bn.i[l.l ṯkmn.w š]nm hn š. | w šqrb.‘r.mšr m 32[2].1.17
il b[n] il. | dr bn il. | mpḫrt bn il. | ṯrmn w šnm. | il w aṯrt. | ḫnn il. | nṣbt i 30[107].2
.li[mm]. | w y‘ny.aliyn[.b‘l]. | lm.k qnym.‘l[m.--]. | k dr d.d yknn[.--]. | b‘l.yṣǵd.mli[.--]. | il hd.mla.u[--.--]. | blt.p btlt.‘ 10[76].3.7
[---.]pp.hrm. | [---].d l yd‘ bn il. | [---.]pḫr kkbm. | [---.]dr dt.šmm. | [---.al]iyn b‘l. | [---].rkb.‘rpt. | [---.]ǵš.l limm. | [-- 10[76].1.5
mt.li[mm]. | w y‘ny.aliyn[.b‘l]. | lm.k qnym.‘l[m.--]. | k dr d.d yknn[.--]. | b‘l.yṣǵd.mli[.--]. | il hd.mla.u[--.--]. | blt.p b 10[76].3.7
l m.ht.ib k.tmḫṣ.ht.ṯṣmt.ṣrt k. | tqḥ.mlk.‘lm k.drkt.dt dr dr k. | kṯr ṣmdm.ynḥt.w yp‘r.šmt hm.šm k at. | ygrš.ygrš. 2.4[68].10
‘l k.mḫṣ.aqht.ǵzr. | ‘wrt.yšt k.b‘l.l ht. | w ‘lm h.l ‘nt.p dr.dr. | ‘db.uḫry.mṭ.yd h. | dnil.bt h.ymǵyn.yšt | ql.dnil.l hkl 19[1AQHT].4.168
.b arṣ.al. | yp‘.riš.ǵly.b d.ns‘ k. | ‘nt.brḥ.p ‘lm h. | ‘nt.p dr.dr.‘db.uḫry mṭ yd h. | ymǵ.l qrt.ablm.abl[m]. | qrt.zbl.yrḫ 19[1AQHT].3.162
l k]. | mḫṣ.aqht.ǵzr.amd.gr bt il. | ‘nt.brḥ.p ‘lm h.‘nt.p dr[.dr]. | ‘db.uḫry mṭ.yd h. | ymǵ.l mrrt.tǵll.b nr. | yšu.g h.w 19[1AQHT].3.154
-.--]dd. | [---.--]n.kb | [--.---.]al.yns. | [---.]ysd k. | [---.--]r.dr.dr. | [---.--]y k.w rḥd. | [---]y ilm.d mlk. | y[ṯ]b.aliyn.b‘l. | yt 4[51].3.7
d yṣd mlk. | [---].yšt.il h. | [---.]iṯm h. | [---.y]mǵy. | [---.]dr h. | [---.-]rš.l b‘l. | [---.-]ǵk.rpu mlk. | [‘lm.---.--]k.l tšt k.l irš UG5.2.2.2
.ht.ib k.tmḫṣ.ht.ṯṣmt.ṣrt k. | tqḥ.mlk.‘lm k.drkt.dt dr dr k. | kṯr ṣmdm.ynḥt.w yp‘r.šmt hm.šm k at. | ygrš.ygrš.grš 2.4[68].10
[--]. | šd.b d.yṯpr. | šd.b d.krb[-]. | šd.b d.bn.ptḏ. | šd.b d.dr.khnm. | šd.b d.bn.‘my. | šd.b d.bn.‘yn. | ṯn.šdm.b d.klṯṯb. | š 2090.17
k.mḫṣ.aqht.ǵzr. | ‘wrt.yšt k.b‘l.l ht. | w ‘lm h.l ‘nt.p dr.dr. | ‘db.uḫry.mṭ.yd h. | dnil.bt h.ymǵyn.yšt | ql.dnil.l hkl h.‘r 19[1AQHT].4.168
. | mḫṣ.aqht.ǵzr.amd.gr bt il. | ‘nt.brḥ.p ‘lm h.‘nt.p dr[.dr]. | ‘db.uḫry mṭ.yd h. | ymǵ.l mrrt.tǵll.b nr. | yšu.g h.w yṣḥ. 19[1AQHT].3.154
arṣ.al. | yp‘.riš.ǵly.b d.ns‘ k. | ‘nt.brḥ.p ‘lm h. | ‘nt.p dr.dr.‘db.uḫry mṭ yd h. | ymǵ.l qrt.ablm.abl[m]. | qrt.zbl.yrḫ.yš 19[1AQHT].3.162
]dd. | [---.--]n.kb | [--.---.]al.yns. | [---.]ysd k. | [---.--]r.dr.dr. | [---.--]y k.w rḥd. | [---]y ilm.d mlk. | y[ṯ]b.aliyn.b‘l. | yt‘dd 4[51].3.7

drb

qḥm. | w md h. | arn.w mznm. | ṯn.ḫlpnm. | ṯt.mrḥm. | drb. | mrbd. | mškbt. 2050.8

drḫm

nt.trtḥ[ṣ.---]. | [---.t]ṯb h.aḫt.ppšr.w ppšrt[.---]. | [---.]k.drḫm.w aṯb.l ntbt.k.ʿṣm l t[--]. | [---.]drk.brḥ.arṣ.lk pn h.yrk. 1001.2.7

dry

m.lb. | ʿnt.aṯr.bʿl.tiḫd. | bn.ilm.mt.b ḥrb. | tbqʿnn.b ḫṯr.tdry | nn.b išt.tšrpnn. | b rḥm.tṯḥnn.b šd. | tdrʿnn.šir h.l tikl. | 6[49].2.32
aliyn.bʿl.yšu. | g h.w yṣḥ.ʿl k.b[ʿ]l m. | pht.qlt.ʿl k.pht. | dry.b ḥrb.ʿl k. | pht.šrp.b išt. | ʿl k.[pht.ṯḥ]n.b rḥ | m.ʿ[l k.]pht 6[49].5.13
rb.ʿl k. | pht.šrp.b išt. | ʿl k.[pht.ṯḥ]n.b rḥ | m.ʿ[l k.]pht[.dr]y.b kbrt. | ʿl k.pht.[-]l[-]. | b šdm.ʿl k.pht. | drʿ.b ym.tn.aḥd 6[49].5.16

drk

pšrt[.---]. | [---.]k.drḫm.w aṯb.l ntbt.k.ʿṣm l t[--]. | [---.]drk.brḥ.arṣ.lk pn h.yrk.bʿ[l]. | [---.]bt k.ap.l pḫr k ʿnt tqm.ʿn 1001.2.8
. | kbr[-]m.[-]trmt. | lbš.w [-]tn.ušpǵt. | ḫr[-].ṯlṯt.mzn. | drk.š.alp.w ṯlṯ. | ṣin.šlm[m.]šbʿ pamt. | l ilm.šb[ʿ.]l kṯr. | ʿlm.tʿ 33[5].6

drkt

.hn.ym. | w ṯn.yṯb.krt.l ʿd h. | yṯb.l ksi mlk. | l nḫt.l kḥt.drkt. | ap.yṣb.yṯb.b hkl. | w ywsrnn.ggn h. | lk.l ab k.yṣb.lk. | l 16.6[127].24
| rqdm.dšn.b.ḥbr.kṯr.ṭbm. | w tšt.ʿnt.gṯr.bʿlt.mlk.bʿ | lt.drkt.bʿlt.šmm.rmm. | [bʿl]t.kpṯ.w ʿnt.di.dit.rḫpt. | [---.-]rm.ak UG5.2.1.7
.ib k. | bʿl m.ht.ib k.tmḫṣ.ht.tṣmt.ṣrt k. | tqḥ.mlk.ʿlm k.drkt.dt dr dr k. | kṯr ṣmdm.ynḥt.w ypʿr.šmt hm.šm k at. | yg 2.4[68].10
. | ydr.hm.ym[.---]. | ʿl amr.yu[ḫd.ksa.mlk h]. | nḫt.kḥt.d[rkt h.b bt y]. | aṣḥ.rpi[m.iqra.ilnym]. | b qrb.h[kl y.aṯr h.rp 22.1[123].18
w bn.dgn.b š[---]. | bʿl.yṯb.l ks[i.mlk h]. | bn.dgn.l kḥ[t.drkt h]. | l alp.ql.ẓ[--.---]. | l np ql.nd.[----]. | tlk.w tr.b[ḫl]. | b 10[76].3.15
| ṣḥr mt.ymṣḫ.l arṣ. | [yṯb.]b[ʿ]l.l ksi.mlk h. | [---].l kḥt.drkt h. | l [ym]m.l yrḫm.l yrḫm. | l šnt.[m]k.b šbʿ. | šnt.w [--]. 6[49].5.6
ṣpn.mšṣṣ.[-]kʿ[-]. | udn h.grš h.l ksi.mlk h. | l nḫt.l kḥt.drkt h. | mn m.ib.ypʿ.l bʿl.ṣrt.l rkb.ʿrpt. | [-]ʿn.ǵlmm.yʿnyn.l i 3[ʿNT].4.47
.šm k at. | ygrš.ygrš.grš ym grš ym.l ksi h. | [n]hr l kḥt drkt h.trtqṣ.b d bʿl km nš | r.b uṣbʿt h.hlm.ktp.zbl ym.bn yd 2.4[68].13
| šm k.at.aymr.aymr.mr.ym.mr.ym. | l ksi h.nhr l kḥt.drkt h.trtqṣ. | b d bʿl.km.nšr b uṣbʿt h.hlm.qdq | d zbl ym.bn. 2.4[68].20
ʿl.---]. | kd.ynaṣn[.---]. | gršnn.l k[si.mlk h.l nḫt.l kḥt]. | drkt h.š[--.--]. | w hm.ap.l[--.---]. | ymḫṣ k.k[--.---]. | il.dbḥ.[--- 1[ʿNT.X].4.25
b ql h.y[---.---]. | bʿl.yṯṯbn[.l ksi]. | mlk h.l[nḫt.l kḥt]. | drkt h[.---]. | [---.]d[--.---]. | [---].hn[.---]. | [---.]šn[.---]. | [---].p 6[49].6.35
rt.k ybky. | ydmʿ.nʿmn.ǵlm. | il.mlk[.ṯ]r ab h. | yarš.hm.drk[t]. | k ab.adm. | [-----]. 14[KRT].1.42
mnt.km. | aḫt.ʿrš.mdw.anšt. | ʿrš.zbln.rd.l mlk. | amlk.l drkt k.aṯb. | an.w yʿny.krt ṯʿ.yṯbr. | ḥrn.y bn.yṯbr.ḥrn. | riš k.ʿ 16.6[127].53
pš. | km.aḫt.ʿrš.mdw. | anšt.ʿrš.zbln. | rd.l mlk.amlk. | l drkt.k aṯb.an. | ytbʿ.yṣb ǵlm.ʿl. | ab h.yʿrb.yšu g h. | w yṣḥ.šmʿ 16.6[127].38
at.ypʿt.b[--.---]. | aliyn.bʿl[.---]. | drkt k.mšl[-.---]. | b riš k.aymr[.---]. | ṯpṭ.nhr.yṯb[r.ḥrn.y ym. 2.1[137].5
z.b ymn h. | bkm.yṯb.bʿl.l bht h. | u mlk.u bl mlk. | arṣ.drkt.yštkn. | dll.al.ilak.l bn. | ilm.mt.ʿdd.l ydd. | il.ǵzr.yqra.m 4[51].7.44

drm

.---]. | l y.ank.ašṣu[.---.]w[.---]. | w hm.at.tr[gm.---]. | w.drm.ʿtr[--.---]. | w ap.ht.k[--.]škn. | w.mṯnn[.---.]ʿmn k. | [-]štš. 54.1.19[13.2.4]

drʿ

t[n]. | w nlḥm.hm.iṯ[.--.yn.w t]n.w nšt. | w ʿn hm.nǵr mdrʿ[.iṯ.lḥm.---]. | iṯ.yn.d ʿrb.bṯk[.---]. | mǵ hw.l hn.lg yn h[.- 23[52].73
[l k.]pht[.dr]y.b kbrt. | ʿl k.pht.[-]l[-]. | b šdm.ʿl k.pht. | drʿ.b ym.tn.aḥd. | b aḫ k.ispa.w yṯb. | ap.d anšt.im[-]. | aḥd.b 6[49].5.19
ʿm.drt. | [w].ṯmnym.l.mit.dd.ḥpr.bnšm. | b.gt.alḫb.ṯṯm.drʿ.w.ḫmšm.drt.w.ṯṯm.dd. | ḥpr.bnšm. | b.gt.knpy.mit.drʿ.ṯṯ 1098.16
rʿ.w.šbʿm.drt. | [---.ḥpr.]bnšm.w.l.ḥrš.ʿrq.ṯn.ʿšr h. | [---.d]rʿ.w.mit.drt.w.ʿšrm.l.mit. | [drt.ḥpr.b]nšm.w.ṯn.ʿšr h.dd.l.r 1098.3
ʿm.drt.mit.dd. | [---].ḥpr.bn.šm. | [b.---.]knm.ṯṯm.l.mit.drʿ.w.mit.drt. | w[.---.]ʿm.l.mit.dd.ṯn.kbd.ḥpr.bnšm.ṯmnym. 1098.7
d.ṯn.kbd.ḥpr.bnšm.ṯmnym.dd. | l u[-]m. | b.ṯbq.arbʿm.drʿ.w.ʿšr.dd.drt. | w[.a]rbʿ.l.ʿšrm.dd.l.yḥšr.bl.bn h. | b.gt.mʿbr 1098.10
.drt.w.šbʿm.dd.arbʿ. | kbd.ḥpr.bnšm. | b.gt.ṯrmn.arbʿm.drʿ.w.ʿšrm.drt. | w.ṯlṯm.dd.ṯṯ.kbd.ḥpr.bnšm. | b.gt.ḥdṯt.arbʿm 1098.20
w.šbʿm.drt. | w.ʿšrm.l.mit.dd.ḥpr.bnšm. | b.yʿny.arbʿm.drʿ.w.ʿšrm.drt. | w.ṯlṯm.dd.ṯṯ.kbd.ḥpr.bnšm. | b.ʿnmky.ʿšrm.d 1098.26
.ʿd.ilm.nʿmm.ttlkn. | šd.tṣdn.pat.mdbr.w ngš.hm.nǵr. | mdrʿ.w ṣḥ hm.ʿm.nǵr.mdrʿ y.nǵr. | nǵr.ptḥ.w ptḥ hw.prṣ.bʿd 23[52].69
.l.mit. | [drt.ḥpr.b]nšm.w.ṯn.ʿšr h.dd.l.rpš. | [---.]šbʿm.drʿ.w.arbʿm.drt.mit.dd. | [---].ḥpr.bn.šm. | [b.---.]knm.ṯṯm.l. 1098.5
.drt. | [w].šbʿm.dd.ṯn.kbd.ḥpr.bnšm. | b.nzl.ʿšrm.l.mit.drʿ.w.šbʿm.drt. | w.ʿšrm.l.mit.dd.ḥpr.bnšm. | b.yʿny.arbʿm.dr 1098.24
[---.---.]l.mit.drʿ.w.šbʿm.drt. | [---.ḥpr.]bnšm.w.l.ḥrš.ʿrq.ṯn.ʿšr h. | [---.d]rʿ. 1098.1
[.drt]. | w.ʿšrm.l.mit.dd.ḥp[r.]bnšm. | b.gt.ǵl.ʿšrm.l.mit.drʿ.w.tšʿm.drt. | [w].ṯmnym.l.mit.dd.ḥpr.bnšm. | b.gt.alḫb.ṯṯ 1098.14
rm.drt. | w.ṯlṯm.dd.ṯṯ.kbd.ḥpr.bnšm. | b.gt.ḥdṯt.arbʿm.drʿ.w.ṯlṯm.drt. | [w].šbʿm.dd.ṯn.kbd.ḥpr.bnšm. | b.nzl.ʿšrm.l. 1098.22
[.a]rbʿ.l.ʿšrm.dd.l.yḥšr.bl.bn h. | b.gt.mʿbr.arbʿm.l.mit.drʿ.w.ṯmnym[.drt]. | w.ʿšrm.l.mit.dd.ḥp[r.]bnšm. | b.gt.ǵl.ʿšr 1098.12
.tṣdn.pat.mdbr.w ngš.hm.nǵr. | mdrʿ.w ṣḥ hm.ʿm.nǵr.mdrʿ y.nǵr. | nǵr.ptḥ.w ptḥ hw.prṣ.bʿd hm. | w ʿrb.hm.hm[.iṯ 23[52].69
m.bṣr. | kp.šsk k.[--].l ḥbš k. | ʿtk.ri[š.]l mhr k. | w ʿp.l drʿ[ʿ].nšr k. | w rbṣ.l ǵr k.inbb. | kt ǵr k.ank.ydʿt. | [-]n.atn.at. 13[6].8
tbqʿnn.b ḫṯr.tdry | nn.b išt.tšrpnn. | b rḥm.tṯḥnn.b šd. | tdrʿnn.šir h.l tikl. | ʿṣrm.mnt h.l tkly. | npr[m.]šir.l šir.yṣḥ. 6[49].2.35
drʿ.w.ḫmšm.drt.w.ṯṯm.dd. | ḥpr.bnšm. | b.gt.knpy.mit.drʿ.ṯṯm.drt.w.šbʿm.dd.arbʿ. | kbd.ḥpr.bnšm. | b.gt.ṯrmn.arbʿ 1098.18
.ʿšrm.drt. | w.ṯlṯm.dd.ṯṯ.kbd.ḥpr.bnšm. | b.ʿnmky.ʿšrm.drʿ[.---.d]rt. | w.ṯn.ʿšr h.dd.[---]. | iwrdn.ḥ[--.---]. | w.ṯlṯm.dd.[- 1098.28
.yn.d.]nkly.l.rʿym.šbʿm.l.mitm.dd. | [---.--]d.šbʿm.kbd.drʿ. | [---.]kbd.ddm.kbd[.---]. | [---.]ʿm.kbd.l.rʿ[ym.---]. | [---].k 1098.45
.[št]. | bln.qṯ.yṣq.b.a[p h]. | k ygʿr[.ššw.---]. | dprn[.---]. | drʿ.[---]. | tmṯl[.---]. | mǵm[ǵ.---]. | w.š[t.nni.w.pr.ʿbk]. | w.pr[. 161[56].25

drṣy

.ḫlan. | [--]r bn.mn. | [--]ry. | [--]lim bn.brq. | [--.]qtn bn.drṣy. | [--]kn bn.pri. | [r]špab bn.pni. | [ab]mn bn.qṣy. | [ʿ]pṯrm 2087.6

drq

ʿm.bʿl. | mrym.ṣpn.b alp.šd.rbt.kmn. | hlk.aḫt h.bʿl.yʿn.tdrq. | ybnt.ab h.šrḥq.aṯt.l pnn h. | št.alp.qdm h.mria.w tk. | p 3[ʿNT].4.83
i ʿn h.w yphn.b alp. | šd.rbt.kmn.hlk.kṯr. | k yʿn.w yʿn.tdrq.ḫss. | hlk.qšt.ybln.hl.yš | rbʿ.qṣʿt.apnk.dnil. | mt.rpi.aphn 17[2AQHT].5.11

drq

t.|b nši.ʻn h.w tphn.|hlk.bʻl.aṯtrt.|k tʻn.hlk.btlt.|ʻnt.tdrq.ybmt.|[limm].b h.pʻnm.|[tṭṭ.b ʻ]dn.ksl.|[ṯṯbr.ʻln.p]n h. 4[51].2.15

drt

---]m.|t[gm]r.akl.b.gt.ǵ[l].|ṯlṯ.mat.ʻšrm[.---].|ṯmnym.drt.a[--].|drt.l.alpm[.---].|šbʻm.ṯn.kbd[.ḥpr.ʻb]dm.|tg[mr.-- 2013.17
lqḥ.šʻrt.|urẖ.ln.kkrm.|w.rḥd.kd.šmn.|drt.b.kkr.|ubn.ẖṣḥ.kkr.|kkr.lqḥ.ršpy.|tmtrn.bn.pnmn.|kk 1118.4
[t.b]ir.alp.|[ʻ]šrm.l.mit.ḥ[p]r.ʻbdm.|mitm.drt.ṯmnym.drt.|tgmr.akl.b.gt[.b]ʻln.|ṯlṯ.mat.ṯṯm.kbd.|ṯṯm.ṯṯ.kbd.ḥpr.ʻ 2013.4
d.l.yḥšr.bl.bn h.|b.gt.mʻbr.arbʻm.l.mit.drʻ.w.ṯmnym[.drt].|w.ʻšrm.l.mit.dd.ḥp[r.]bnšm.|b.gt.ǵl.ʻšrm.l.mit.drʻ.w.tš 1098.12
bʻm.dd.ṯn.kbd.ḥpr.bnšm.|b.nzl.ʻšrm.l.mit.drʻ.w.šbʻm.drt.|w.ʻšrm.l.mit.dd.ḥpr.bnšm.|b.yʻny.arbʻm.drʻ.w.ʻšrm.drt 1098.24
rt.|[---.ḥpr.]bnšm.w.l.ḥrš.ʻrq.ṯn.ʻšr h.|[---.d]rʻ.w.mit.drt.w.ʻšrm.l.mit.|[drt.ḥpr.b]nšm.w.ṯn.ʻšr h.dd.l.rpš.|[---.]šb 1098.3
r.bnšm.ṯmnym.dd.|l u[-]m.|b.ṭbq.arbʻm.drʻ.w.ʻšr.dd.drt.|w[.a]rbʻ.l.ʻšrm.dd.l.yḥšr.bl.bn h.|b.gt.mʻbr.arbʻm.l.mit 1098.10
mšm.drt.w.ṯṯm.dd.|ḥpr.bnšm.|b.gt.knpy.mit.drʻ.ṯṯm.drt.w.šbʻm.dd.arbʻ.|kbd.ḥpr.bnšm.|b.gt.ṯrmn.arbʻm.drʻ.w.ʻ 1098.18
.ṯlṯm.dd.ṯṯ.kbd.ḥpr.bnšm.|b.gt.ḥdṯt.arbʻm.drʻ.w.ṯlṯm.drt.|[w].šbʻm.dd.ṯn.kbd.ḥpr.bnšm.|b.nzl.ʻšrm.l.mit.drʻ.w.š 1098.22
mnym.l.mit.dd.ḥpr.bnšm.|b.gt.alẖb.ṯṯm.drʻ.w.ẖmšm.drt.w.ṯṯm.dd.|ḥpr.bnšm.|b.gt.knpy.mit.drʻ.ṯṯm.drt.w.šbʻm. 1098.16
|w.ʻšrm.l.mit.dd.ḥpr.bnšm.|b.yʻny.arbʻm.drʻ.w.ʻšrm.drt.|w.ṯlṯm.dd.ṯṯ.kbd.ḥpr.bnšm.|b.ʻnmky.ʻšrm.drʻ[.---.d]rt. 1098.26
.dd.arbʻ.|kbd.ḥpr.bnšm.|b.gt.ṯrmn.arbʻm.drʻ.w.ʻšrm.drt.|w.ṯlṯm.dd.ṯṯ.kbd.ḥpr.bnšm.|b.gt.ḥdṯt.arbʻm.drʻ.w.ṯlṯm 1098.20
rm.l.mit.dd.ḥp[r.]bnšm.|b.gt.ǵl.ʻšrm.l.mit.drʻ.w.tšʻm.drt.|[w].ṯmnym.l.mit.dd.ḥpr.bnšm.|b.gt.alẖb.ṯṯm.drʻ.w.ẖm 1098.14
rt.|w.ṯlṯm.dd.ṯṯ.kbd.ḥpr.bnšm.|b.ʻnmky.ʻšrm.drʻ[.---.d]rt.|w.ṯn.ʻšr h.dd.[---].|iwrḏn.ḥ[--.---].|w.ṯlṯm.dd.[---.]n[-- 1098.28
t.dd.|[---].ḥpr.bn.šm.|[b.---.]knm.ṯṯm.l.mit.drʻ.w.mit.drt.|w[.---.]ʻm.l.mit.dd.ṯn.kbd.ḥpr.bnšm.ṯmnym.dd.|l u[-] 1098.7
.w.l.ḥrš.ʻrq.ṯn.ʻšr h.|[---.d]rʻ.w.mit.drt.w.ʻšrm.l.mit.|[drt.ḥpr.b]nšm.w.ṯn.ʻšr h.dd.l.rpš.|[---.]šbʻm.drʻ.w.arbʻm.drt 1098.4
m]r.akl.b.gt.ǵ[l].|ṯlṯ.mat.ʻšrm[.---].|ṯmnym.drt.a[--].|drt.l.alpm[.---].|šbʻm.ṯn.kbd[.ḥpr.ʻb]dm.|tg[mr.---].|[-]m.m 2013.18
ṯ.mat.ṯṯm.kbd.|ṯṯm.ṯṯ.kbd.ḥpr.ʻbdm.|šbʻm.drt.arbʻm.drt.|l.a[--.---].|tgm[r.ak]l.b.gt.ẖldy.|ṯlṯ.ma[t].ʻšr.kbd.|šbʻ 2013.8
.ḥpr.b]nšm.w.ṯn.ʻšr h.dd.l.rpš.|[---.]šbʻm.drʻ.w.arbʻm.drt.mit.dd.|[---].ḥpr.bn.šm.|[b.---.]knm.ṯṯm.l.mit.drʻ.w.mit. 1098.5
t[.b]ʻln.|ṯlṯ.mat.ṯṯm.kbd.|ṯṯm.ṯṯ.kbd.ḥpr.ʻbdm.|šbʻm.drt.arbʻm.drt.|l.a[--.---].|tgm[r.ak]l.b.gt.ẖldy.|ṯlṯ.ma[t].ʻšr. 2013.8
ldy.|ṯlṯ.ma[t].ʻšr.kbd.|šbʻ m[at].kbd.ḥpr.ʻbdm.|mit[.d]rt.arbʻm.drt.|[---]m.|t[gm]r.akl.b.gt.ǵ[l].|ṯlṯ.mat.ʻšrm[.--- 2013.13
]mr.akl.b.g[t.b]ir.alp.|[ʻ]šrm.l.mit.ḥ[p]r.ʻbdm.|mitm.drt.ṯmnym.drt.|tgmr.akl.b.gt[.b]ʻln.|ṯlṯ.mat.ṯṯm.kbd.|ṯṯm.ṯ 2013.4
[---.---.]l.mit.drʻ.w.šbʻm.drt.|[---.ḥpr.]bnšm.w.l.ḥrš.ʻrq.ṯn.ʻšr h.|[---.d]rʻ.w.mit.drt.w 1098.1
ṯn.kbd[.ḥpr.ʻb]dm.|tg[mr.---].|[-]m.m[--.---].|[m]itm.dr[t.---].|[ʻš]r.[k]bd[.---].|[a]lpm[.---].|tg[m]r.[---].|ṯlṯ ma[t. 2013.22
[ṯ]mny[m.---].|[-]r[-.---].|[--]m.l.[---].|a[---.---].|ʻšrm.drt[.---]. 2013.32
[t].ʻšr.kbd.|šbʻ m[at].kbd.ḥpr.ʻbdm.|mit[.d]rt.arbʻm.drt.|[---]m.|t[gm]r.akl.b.gt.ǵ[l].|ṯlṯ.mat.ʻšrm[.---].|ṯmnym. 2013.13

dšn

.d yšr.w yḏmr.|b knr.w ṯlb.b tp.w mṣltm.b m|rqdm.dšn.b.ḥbr.kṯr.ṭbm.|w tšt.ʻnt.gṯr.bʻlt.mlk.bʻ|lt.drkt.bʻlt.šmm UG5.2.1.5

dtn

h.w ym[ǵ].|mlak k.ʻm dt[n].|lqḥ.mṯpṭ.|w yʻny.nn.|dtn.bt n.mḥ[-].|l dg.w [-]kl.|w aṯr.hn.mr[-]. UG5.6.14
.ṣry.|bn.mztn.|bn.šlgyn.|bn.[-]gštn.|bn[.n]klb.|b[n.]dtn.|w.nḥl h.|w.nḥl hm.|bn.iršyn.|bn.ʻzn.|bn.aršw.|bn.ẖz 113[400].2.9
[-----].|[---.mid.rm.]krt.|[b tk.rpi.]arṣ.|[b pẖr].qbṣ.dtn.|[w t]qrb.w ld.|bn.tl k.|tld.pǵt.t[--]t.|tld.pǵt[.---].|tld. 15[128].3.4
k ymǵy.adn.|ilm.rbm ʻm dtn.|w yšal.mṯpṭ.yld.|w yʻny.nn[.--].|tʻny.n[---.-]ṯq.|w š[--. UG5.6.2
.q[-].|w št.b bt.ṭap[.--].|hy.yd h.w ym[ǵ].|mlak k.ʻm dt[n].|lqḥ.mṯpṭ.|w yʻny.nn.|dtn.bt n.mḥ[-].|l dg.w [-]kl.| UG5.6.11
|tld.p[ǵt.---].|mid.rm[.krt].|b tk.rpi.ar[ṣ].|b pẖr.qbṣ.dtn.|ṣǵrt hn.abkrn.|tbrk.ilm.tity.|tity.ilm.l ahl hm.|dr il.l 15[128].3.15
bn.gntn[-].|[--.]nqq[-].|b[n.---].|bn.[---].|bn.ʻyn.|bn.dtn. 2023.4.4

dṯ

.tbʻ.bt.ẖnp.lb[k.--.ti]|ẖd.d iṯ.b kbd k.tšt.b [---].|irt k.dṯ.ydṯ.mʻqb k.[ttbʻ].|[bt]lt.ʻnt.idk.l ttn.[pnm].|[ʻm.a]qht.ǵz 18[3AQHT].1.19
ʻ.bt.ẖnp.lb[k.--.ti]|ẖd.d iṯ.b kbd k.tšt.b [---].|irt k.dṯ.ydṯ.mʻqb k.[ttbʻ].|[bt]lt.ʻnt.idk.l ttn.[pnm].|[ʻm.a]qht.ǵzr.b 18[3AQHT].1.19

dṯn

add.|bʻl ṣpn bʻl.|ugrt.|b mrḥ il.|b nit il.|b ṣmd il.|b dṯn il.|b šrp il.|b knt il.|b ǵdyn il.|[b]n [---]. 30[107].15
bn.adlḏn.|šd.bn.nṣdn.l bn.ʻmlbi.|šd.ṯpẖln.l bn.ǵl.|w dṯn.nḥl h.l bn.pl.|šd.krwn.l aẖn.|šd.ʻyy.l aẖn.|šd.brdn.l bn 2089.10

dṯt

p[ẖ]r bʻl.|gdlt.šlm.gdlt.w burm.[l]b.|rmṣt.ilhm.bʻlm.dṯt.w kšm.ẖmš.|ʻṯr h.mlun.šnpt.ẖṣt h.bʻl.ṣpn š.|[--]ṯ š.ilt.m 34[1].9

ḏ

ḏ

h | ll bʿl gml.yrdt. | b ʿrgzm.b bz tdm. | lla y.ʿm lẓpn i | l ḏ.pid.hn b p y sp | r hn.b špt y mn | t hn ṯlḥ h w mlg h y | ṯtqt 24[77].45

ḏbb

d ilm.ar[š]. | ṣmt.ʿgl.il.ʿtk. | mḫšt.klbt.ilm išt. | klt.bt.il.ḏbb.imtḫṣ.ksp. | itrṯ.ḫrṣ.ṭrd.bʿl. | b mrym.ṣpn.mšṣṣ.[-]kʿ[-]. | u 3[ʿNT].3.43

ḏd

.l ttn.pnm.ʿm. | [il.]mbk nhrm.qrb. | [a]pq.thmtm.tgly.ḏd. | il.w tbu.qrš.. | mlk.ab.šnm.l pʿn. | il.thbr.w tql. | tšthwy. 6.1.34[49.1.6]
tn.p]nm. | [ʿm.i]l.mbk.nhr[m.qr]b.[ap]q. | [thm]tm.tgl.ḏ[d.]i[l.]w tbu. | [qr]š.m[l]k.ab[.šnm.]mṣr. | [t]bu.ḏdm.qn[-.-] 3[ʿNT.VI].5.15
tn.pnm]. | [ʿm.il.mbk.nhrm]. | [qrb.apq.thmtm]. | [tgly.ḏd.il.w]tb[a]. | [qrš.mlk.ab.]šnm. | [tša.g hm.w tṣ]ḥ.sbn. | [---] 5[67].6.1
k.l ttn.pnm. | ʿm.il.mbk.nhrm. | qrb.apq.thmtm. | tgly.ḏd.il.w tbu. | qrš.mlk.ab.šnm. | l pʿn.il.thbr.w tql. | tšthwy.w t 4[51].4.23
l ytn.pnm.ʿm.[i]l.mbk.[nhrm.qrb.apq.thmtm]. | [ygly.]ḏl i[l].w ybu[.q]rš.mlk[.ab.šnm.l pʿn.il.] | [yhbr.]w yql[.y]šthʷ 2.3[129].5
t[n.pnm.ʿm.lṭpn]. | il d pid.tk ḫrš[n.---.tk.ǵr.ks]. | ygly ḏd.i[l.w ybu.qrš.mlk]. | ab.šnm.l [pʿn.il.yhbr.w yql]. | yšthwy 1[ʿNT.IX].3.23
. | [l ttn.pn]m.ʿm il.mbk.nhrm. | [qrb.ap]q.thmtm tgly.ḏd il. | [w tbu.qr]š.mlk.ab.šnm. | [l pʿn.il.t]hbr.w tql.tšth | [wy 17[2AQHT].6.48
h.qṣʿt h.hwt.l t[ḥwy]. | nʿmn.ǵzr.št.ṭrm.w[---]. | ištir.b ḏdm.w nʿrs[.---]. | w tʿn.btlt.ʿnt.ṯb.ytp.w[---]. | l k.ašt k.km.n 18[3AQHT].4.15
.w yʿn.yṭ[p]n[.mh]r. | št.b yn.yšt.ila.il š[--.]il. | d yqny.ḏdm.yd.mḫṣt.a[qh]t.ǵ | zr.tmḫṣ.alpm.ib.št[-.]št. | ḥršm l ahl 19[1AQHT].4.220
.špš.mǵy[t]. | pǵt.l ahlm.rgm.l yṭ[pn.y] | bl.agrtn.bat.b ḏd k.[pǵt]. | bat.b hlm w yʿn.yṭpn[.mhr]. | št.qḥn.w tšqyn.yn. 19[1AQHT].4.213
m.tgl.ḏ[d.]i[l.]w tbu. | [qr]š.m[l]k.ab[.šnm.]mṣr. | [t]bu.ḏdm.qn[-.-]n[-.-]lt. | ql h.yš[mʿ].ṭr.[il].ab h.[---]l. | b šbʿt.ḥdr 3[ʿNT.VI].5.17
.w tldn.tld.[ilm.]nʿmm.agzr ym. | bn.ym.ynqm.b a[p.]ḏ[d.r]gm.l il.ybl. | aṯt y.il.ylt.mh.ylt.ilmy nʿmm. | agzr ym.bn 23[52].59
.il.ylt.mh.ylt.ilmy nʿmm. | agzr ym.bn ym.ynqm.b ap.ḏd.št.špt. | l arṣ.špt l šmm.w ʿrb.b p hm.ʿṣr.šmm. | w dg b ym 23[52].61

ḏkr

ltdtt.tlgn.ytn. | bʿltǵpṭm.krwn.ilšn.agyn. | mnn.šr.ugrt.ḏkr.yṣr. | tgǵln.ḫmš.ddm. | [---].ḫmš.ddm. | ṯṯ.l.ʿšrm.bn[š.mlk 2011.37

ḏkry

spr.argmn.nskm. | rqdym. | šṭšm.ṯṯ mat. | ṣprn.ṯṯ mat. | ḏkry.ṯṯ mat. | [p]lsy.ṯṯ mat. | ʿdn.ḫmš [m]at. | [--]kbʿl ṯṯ [mat]. 1060.1.5

ḏltn

. | tmtrn.bn.pnmn. | kkr. | bn.sgṯtn. | kkr. | ilšpš.kkr. | bn.ḏltn. | kkr.w[.--]. | ḫ[--.---]. 1118.12

ḏmn

l ttn. | w al ttn. | tn ks yn. | w ištn. | ʿbd.prṭ.ṯḥm. | qrq.pṭ.ḏmn. | l iṯtl. 1019.2.2
n].šdy. | [bn].gmḥ. | [---]ty. | [b]n.ypy.gbʿly. | b[n].ḥyn. | ḏmn.šʿrty. | bn.arwdn.ilštʿy. | bn grgs. | bn.ḫran. | bn.arš[w.b]ṣ 99[327].1.7

ḏmr

b.skn.i]lib h.b qdš. | [ztr.ʿm h.l a]rṣ.mšṣu. | [qṭr h.l ʿpr.ḏ]mr.a[ṯ]r h. | [ṭbq.lḥt.niṣ h.gr]š.d ʿšy. | [ln h.---]. | z[tr.ʿm k.l 17[2AQHT].1.47
.nṣb.skn.ilib h.b qdš. | ztr.ʿm h.l arṣ.mšṣu.qṭr h. | l ʿpr.ḏmr.aṯr h.ṭbq.lḥt. | niṣ h.grš d.ʿšy.ln h. | aḫd.yd h.b škrn.mʿ 17[2AQHT].1.29
y.w šrš.km ary y. | nṣb.skn.ilib y.b qdš. | ztr.ʿm y.l ʿpr.ḏmr.aṯr[y]. | ṭbq lḥt.niṣ y.grš. | d ʿšy.ln.aḫd.yd y.b š | krn mʿ 17[2AQHT].2.17
gr]š.d ʿšy. | [ln h.---]. | z[tr.ʿm k.l arṣ.mšṣu.qṭr k]. | l ʿpr.ḏm[r.aṯr k.ṭbq]. | lḥt.niṣ k.gr[š.d ʿšy.ln k]. | spu.ksm k.bt.[bʿl. 17[2AQHT].2.2
.yd h.bt | [l]t.ʿnt.uṣbʿt h.ybmt.limm. | [t]rḥṣ.yd h.b dm.ḏmr. | [u]ṣbʿt h.b mmʿ.mhrm. | [ṯ]ʿr.ksat.l ksat.ṯlḥnt. | [l]ṯlḥn 3[ʿNT].2.34
št. | [--.]gṯr.w yqr.il.ytb.b.ʿṯtrt. | il.ṯpṭ.b hd rʿy.d yšr.w yḏmr. | b knr.w ṯlb.b tp.w mṣltm.b m | rqdm.dšn.b.ḥbr.kṯr.ṭ UG5.2.1.3
ʿr. | lbnm. | nḫl. | yʿny. | atn. | utly. | bn.alz. | bn ḫlm. | bn.ḏmr. | bn.ʿyn. | ubnyn. | rpš d ydy. | ǵbl. | mlk. | gwl. | rqd. | ḫlby 2075.17
-]k.l tšt k.liršt. | [---.]rpi.mlk ʿlm.b ʿz. | [rpu.m]lk.ʿlm.b ḏmr h.bl. | [---].b ḥtk h.b nmrt h.l r | [--.]arṣ.ʿz k.ḏmr k.l[-] | n UG5.2.2.7
ʿtkt. | rišt.l bmt h.šnst. | kpt.b ḥbš h.brkm.tǵl[l]. | b dm.ḏmr.ḥlqm.b mm[ʿ]. | mhrm.mṭm.tgrš. | šbm.b ksl.qšt h.mdnt 3[ʿNT].2.14
q.ymlu. | lb h.b šmḫt.kbd.ʿnt. | tšyt.k brkm.tǵll b dm. | ḏmr.ḥlqm.b mmʿ.mhrm. | ʿd.tšbʿ.tmtḫṣ.b bt. | tḫṣb.bn.ṯlḥnm. 3[ʿNT].2.28
. | ʿd.tšbʿ.tmtḫṣ.b bt. | tḫṣb.bn.ṯlḥnm.ymḫ. | [b]bt.dm.ḏmr.yṣq.šmn. | šlm.b ṣʿ.trḥṣ.yd h.bt | [l]t.ʿnt.uṣbʿt h.ybmt.lim 3[ʿNT].2.31
ʿlm.b ḏmr h.bl. | [---].b ḥtk h.b nmrt h.l r | [--.]arṣ.ʿz k.ḏmr k.l[-] | n k.ḥtk k.nmrt k.b tk. | ugrt.l ymt.špš.w yrḫ. | w UG5.2.2.9
. | [---]. | [---]. | bn[.---]y. | yr[---]. | ḫdyn. | grgš. | b[n.]tlš. | ḏmr. | mkrm. | ʿzn. | yplṭ. | ʿbdmlk. | ynḥm. | aḏddn. | mtn. | plsy 1035.4.1
ḏm[r.---].br. | bn.i[ytlm.---]. | wr[t.---.]b d.yḥmn. | yry[.---.]br. 2123.1
g]m.ank l[.--.--]rny. | [---.]tm.hw.i[--]ty. | [---].ibʿr.a[--.]ḏmr. | [---.]w mlk.w rg[m.---]. | [--.rg]m.ank.[b]ʿr.[--]ny. | [--] 1002.52
tḫṣ.---]. | klyn[.---]. | špk.l[---]. | trḥṣ.yd[h.---]. | [--.]yṣt ḏm[r.---]. | tšt[.r]imt.[l irt h.tšr.l dd.aliyn.bʿl]. | [ahb]t pdr[y. 7.2[130].9
t h.k]kdrt.riš. | [ʿl h.k irbym.kp.---.k br]k.tǵll.b dm. | [ḏmr.---.]td[-.]rǵb. | [----]k. | [----] h. 7.1[131].10

ḏmrbʿl

]. | [--]b[.---]. | ʿbdʿṯ[tr.---]. | bdil[.---]. | abǵl.[---]. | [.---]. | ḏmrbʿ[l.---]. | iḫyn.[---]. | ʿbdbʿ[l.---]. | uwil[.---]. | ušry[n.---]. | 102[322].2.5

ḏmrd

.ʿšr[t]. | [---.-]mbʿl.[---].ʿšrt. | [---.]ḥgbn.kbs.ks[p]. | [---].ḏmrd.bn.ḫrmn. | [---.-]ǵn.ksp.ṯṯt. | [---.]ygry.ṯlṯm.ksp.b[--]. 2153.10

ḏmrhd

.nryn. | [ab]r[p]u.bn.kbd. | [-]m[-].bn.ṣmrt. | liy.bn.yṣi. | ḏmrhd.bn.srt. | [---.--]m. | ʿbdmlk.bn.šrn. | ʿbdbʿl.bn.kdn. | gzl. 102[322].6.7

ḏmry

].ḏmry.ʻrb.|b.ṯbʻm.|ydn.bn.ilrpi.|w.ṯbʻm.ʻrb.b.ʻ[d]n.|ḏmry.bn.yrm.|ʻrb.b.adʻy. 2079.9
ty.|bn.ẓmn.|bn.trdn.|ypq.|ʻbd.|qrḥ.|abšr.|bn.bdn.|ḏmry.|bn.pndr.|bn.aẖt.|bn.ʻdn.|bn.išbʻ[l]. 2117.4.30
rišym.dt.ʻrb.|b bnš hm.|ḏmry.w.pṯpṯ.ʻrb.|b.yrm.|[ily.w].ḏmry.ʻrb.|b.ṯbʻm.|ydn.bn. 2079.3
.dt.ʻrb.|b bnš hm.|ḏmry.w.pṯpṯ.ʻrb.|b.yrm.|[ily.w].ḏmry.ʻrb.|b.ṯbʻm.|ydn.bn.ilrpi.|w.ṯbʻm.ʻrb.b.ʻ[d]n.|ḏmry.b 2079.5
.l.y[--.---].|ypʻ.l[.---].|šmr[m.---].|[-----].|bn.g[r.---].|ḏmry[.---].|bn.pdr.l.[---]. 2122.7

ḏn

[---].|lg.šmn.rqḥ.šrʻm.ušpǵtm.p[--.---].|kṯ.ẓrw.kṯ.nbt.ḏnt.w [-]n[-.---].|il.ẖyr.ilib.š.|arṣ w šmm.š.|il.š.kṯrt.š.|dgn. UG5.9.1.22

ḏnb

h.yʻmsn.nn.ṯkmn.|w šnm.w ngšnn.ḥby.|bʻl.qrnm w ḏnb.ylšn.|b ẖri h.w ṯnt h.ql.il.[--].|il.k yrdm.arṣ.ʻnt.|w ʻṯtrt UG5.1.1.20
]un.b arṣ.|mẖnm.ṯrp ym.|lšnm.tlḥk.|šmm.tṯrp.|ym.ḏnbtm.|tnn.l šbm.|tšt.trks.|l mrym.l bt[.---].|p l.tbʻ[.---].| 1003.7

ḏqnt

.|bn.[---].|bn.ʻr[--].|bn.nkt[-].|bn.abḏr.|bn.ḥrẓn.|bn.ḏqnt.|bn.gmrš.|bn.nmq.|bn.špš[yn].|bn.ar[--].|bn.gb[--].| 2023.3.11

ḏrdn

l.ḏrdn.|bʻl y.rgm.|bn.ẖrn k.|mǵy.|hbṭ.hw.|ẖrd.w.šl hw.|qr 2114.1

ḏrm

.[-]r[-].|bn.tgn.|bn.iḏrn.|mnn.|b[n].skn.|bn.pʻṣ.|bn.ḏrm.|[bn.-]ln.|[bn.-]ḏprḏ. 124[-].6.12

ḏrn

]n [i]lmd.|bn [t]bdn.|bn štn.|b[n] kdn.|bn dwn.|bn ḏrn. 2088.8

ḏrʻ

n dt.b.ṣr.|mtt.by.|gšm.adr.|nškḥ.w.|rb.tmtt.|lqḥ.kl.ḏrʻ.|b d a[-]m.w.ank.|k[l.]ḏrʻ hm.|[--.n]pš[.-].|w [k]l hm.b 2059.17
.ǵr.b abn.|ydy.psltm.b yʻr.|yhdy.lḥm.w dqn.|yṯlṯ.qn.ḏrʻ h.yḥrṯ.|k gn.ap lb.k ʻmq.yṯlṯ.|bmt.yšu.g h.w yṣḥ.|bʻl.m 5[67].6.20
ǵr.b ab.td[.ps]ltm[.b yʻr].|thdy.lḥm.w dqn[.ṯṯlṯ].|qn.ḏrʻ h.tḥrṯ.km.gn.|ap lb.k ʻmq.ṯṯlṯ.bmt.|bʻl.mt.my.lim.bn dg 6[62].1.4
.|nškḥ.w.|rb.tmtt.|lqḥ.kl.ḏrʻ.|b d a[-]m.w.ank.|k[l.]ḏrʻ hm.|[--.n]pš[.-].|w [k]l hm.b d.|rb.tmtt.lqḥt.|w.ṯṯb.ank 2059.19

ḏrq

šbʻy.rašm.|ṯṯkḥ.ttrp.šmm.k rs.|ipd k.ank.ispi.uṭm.|ḏrqm.amt m.l yrt.|b npš.bn ilm.mt.b mh|mrt.ydd.il.ǵzr.|t 5[67].1.6
[---.]ps[.---].|[---].yṯbr[.---].|[---.]uṭm.ḏr[qm.---].|[btl]t.ʻnt.l kl.[---].|[tt]bʻ.btlt.ʻnt[.idk.l ttn.pnm]. 18[3AQHT].4.3

ḏrt

.k ḥy.aliyn.bʻl.|k iṯ.zbl.bʻl.arṣ.|b ḥlm.lṭpn.il d pid.|b ḏrt.bny.bnwt.|šmm.šmn.tmṭrn.|nẖlm.tlk.nbtm.|šmẖ.lṭpn.i 6[49].3.11
liyn.bʻl].|w hm.iṯ.zbl.bʻ[l.arṣ].|b ḥlm.lṭpn.il.d pid.|b ḏrt.bny.bnwt.|šmm.šmn.tmṭrn.|nẖlm.tlk.nbtm.|w idʻ.k ḥy 6[49].3.5
t.tluan.|w yškb.nhmmt.|w yqmṣ.w b ḥlm h.|il.yrd.b ḏhrt h.|ab adm.w yqrb.|b šal.krt.m at.|krt.k ybky.|ydmʻ.n 14[KRT].1.36
h.|d ʻq h.ib.iqni.|ʻpʻp h.sp.ṯrml.|d b ḥlm y.il.ytn.|b ḏrt y.ab.adm.|w ld.špḥ.l krk|t.w ǵlm.l ʻbd.|il.ttbʻ.mlakm.| 14[KRT].6.297
l.tḥgrn.[-]dm[.-].|ašlw.b ṣp.ʻn h.|d b ḥlm y.il.ytn.|b ḏrt y.ab.adm.|w ld.špḥ.l krt.|w ǵlm.l ʻbd.il.|krt.yẖṭ.w ḥlm. 14[KRT].3.151
l krt.a]dn km.|ʻl.krt.tbun.km.|rgm.ṯ[rm.]rgm hm.|b ḏrt[.---.]krt.|[----]. 15[128].6.8

h

h

m.---].|pln.ṯmry.w.ṯn.bn h.w[.---].|ymrn.apsny.w.aṯt h..b[n.---].|prd.m'qby[.w.---.a]ṯt h[.---].|prṯ.mgd[ly.---.]aṯ[t 2044.9
n.|w yškb.nhmmt.|w yqmṣ.w b ḥlm h.|il.yrd.b ḏhrt h.|ab adm.w yqrb.|b šal.krt.m at.|krt.k ybky.|ydm'.n'mn. 14[KRT].1.36
yṣq.b irt.lbnn.mk.b šb'.|[ymm.---]k.aliyn.b'l.|[---].r' h ab y.|[---.]'[---]. 22.2[124].27
-.--]q.n[ṯ]k.l yd'.l bn.l pq ḥmt.|[---.--]n h.ḥmt.w t'btn h.abd y.|[---.ǵ]r.šrǵzz.ybky.km.n'r.|[w ydm'.k]m.ṣǵr.špš.b UG5.8.36
.|[yd.]mizrt.p yln.mk.b šb'.ymm.|[w]yqrb.b'l.b ḥnt h.abynt.|[d]nil.mt.rpi anẖ.ǵzr.|[mt.]hrnmy.d in.bn.l h.|km 17[2AQHT].1.17
y.|[---.n]ḥl h.|[---].bn.mryn.|[---].bn.ṯyl.|annmt.nḥl h.|abmn.bn.'bd.|liy.bn.rqdy.|bn.ršp. 1036.12
dm.ym.w ṯn.|ṯlṯ.rb'.ym.ymš.|ṯdṯ.ym.ḥẓ k.al.tš'l.|qrt h.abn.yd k.|mšdpt.w hn.špšm.|b šb'.w l.yšn.pbl.|mlk.l qr.ṯ 14[KRT].3.117
z.aẖmn.arb'.mat.|arb'm.kbd.|ṯlṯ.alp.ṣpr.dt.aẖd.|ḥrṯ h.aḥd.b gt.nẖl.|aḥd.b gt.knpy.w.aḥd.b gt.ṯrmn.|aḥd.alp.idṯ 1129.9
'dd.l ydd.|il.ǵzr.yqra.mt.|b npš h.ystrn ydd.|b gngn h.aḥd y.d ym|lk.'l.ilm.l ymru.|ilm.w nšm.d yšb|['].hmlt.ar 4[51].7.49
r h.d[--.---].|[---.]ḥdṯn.'šr.dd[.---].|[---.]yd.sǵr[.---.--]r h.|aḥ[d.---.']šrm.d[d.---].|'š[r.---.--]r h.|my y[--.---.--]d.|'šr 1098.35
.šqrb.[---].|b mgn k.w ẖrṣ.l kl.|apnk.ǵzr.ilḥu.|[m]rḥ h.yiḥd.b yd.|[g]rgr h.bm.ymn.|[w]yqrb.trẓẓ h.|[---].mǵy h 16.1[125].47
arbẖ.'n h tšu w[.---].|aylt tǵpy ṯr.'n[.---].|b[b]r.mrḥ h.ti[ẖd.b yd h].|š[g]r h bm ymn.t[--.---].|[--.]l b'l.'bd[.---].|ṯ 2001.1.12
mšṣu.qṭr h.|l 'pr.ḏmr.aṯr h.ṭbq.lḥt.|niṣ h.grš d.'šy.ln h.|aẖd.yd h.b škrn.m'ms h.|[k]šb' yn.spu.ksm h.bt.b'l.|[w 17[2AQHT].1.30
šẖṭ.bm.ymn.mẖṣ.ǵlmm.yš[--].|[ymn h.'n]t.tuẖd.šmal h.tuẖd.'ṯtrt.ik.m[ẖṣt.ml]|[ak.ym.t']dt.ṯpṭ.nhr.mlak.mṯẖr.yḥ 2.1[137].40
|idm.adr[.---].|idm.'rẓ.t'r[ẓ.---].|'n.b'l.a[ẖ]ḏ[.---].|ẓr h.aẖḏ.qš[t.---].|p 'n.b'l.aẖḏ[.---].|w ṣmt.ǵllm[.---].|aẖḏ.akl 12[75].2.33
-.--]ša.|tlm.km[.---.]yd h.k šr.|knr.uṣb't h ḥrṣ.abn.|p h.tiẖd.šnt h.w akl.bqmm.|tšt ḥrṣ.k lb ilnm.|w ṯn.gprm.mn 19[1AQHT].1.9
[---.]ydm ym.|[---.]ydm nhr.|[---.]trǵt.|[---.]h aẖd[.--].|[---.]iln[-.---].|[---.--]ẖ[.---].|[---.]dt[-.---].|[---.]ks 49[73].1.4
ḥ.ṭbt.n[--].|[---.b]ṯnm w ṯṯb.'l.bṯnt.trtḥ[ṣ.---].|[---.t]ṯb h.aẖt.ppšr.w ppšrt[.---].|[---.]k.drẖm.w aṯb.l ntbt.k.'ṣm l t[- 1001.2.6
ank.l hm.|w.any k.ṯt.|by.'ky.'ryt.|w.aẖ y.mhk.|b lb h.al.yšt. 2059.27
.|tšu.knp.w tr.b 'p.|tk.aẖ šmk.mlat rumm.|w yšu.'n h.aliyn.b'l.|w yšu.'n h.w y'n.|w y'n.btlt.'nt.|n'mt.bn.aẖt.b' 10[76].2.13
n nkl y|rẖ ytrẖ.ib t'rb m b bh|t h.w atn mhr h l a|b h.alp ksp w rbt ẖ|rṣ.išlḥ ẓhrm iq|nim.atn šd h krm[m].|šd 24[77].20
ḏ[r].|[-]d'.k.iẖd.[---].|w.mlk.b'l y.|lm.škn.hnk.|l 'bd h.alpm.ṡ[ṡw]m.|rgmt.'ly.ṯh.lm.|l.ytn.hm.mlk.[b]'l y.|w.hn. 1012.24
rt.yẖṭ.w ḥlm.|'bd.il.w hdrt.|yrtḥṣ.w yadm.|yrḥṣ.yd h.amt h.|uṣb't h.'d.ṯkm.|'rb.b ẓl.ẖmt.lqḥ.|imr.dbḥ.b yd h. 14[KRT].3.157
ṭ n.w in.d 'ln h.|klny n.q[š] h.n[bln].|klny n[.n]bl.ks h.|[an]y.l yṣḥ.ṯr il.ab h.|[i]l.mlk.d yknn h.yṣḥ.|aṯrt.w bn h. 4[51].4.46
n.b'l.ṯpṭ n.|in.d 'ln h.klny y.qš h.|nbln.klny y.nbl.ks h.|any.l yṣḥ.ṯr.il.ab h.il.|mlk.d yknn h.yṣḥ.aṯrt.|w bn h.ilt. 3['NT.VI].5.42
i.km.|rḥ.npš h.km.iṯl.brlt h.km.|qṭr.b ap h.b ap.mhr h.ank.|l aḥwy.tqḥ.yṭpn.mhr.št.|tštn.k nšr.b ḥbš h.km.diy.| 18[3AQHT].4.26
n h.|gpn.bn[.a]ly.|bn.rqd[y].ṯbg.|iẖmlk.|yp'n w.aṯt h.|anntn.yṣr.|annmn.w.ṯlṯ.n'[r] h.|rpan.w.ṯ[n.]bn h.|bn.ay 2068.23
h.p'nm].|ṭṭṭ.'l[n.pn h.td'.b 'dn].|ksl.y[ṯbr.yǵṣ.pnt.ksl h].|anš.[dt.ẓr h.yšu.g h].|w yṣ[ḥ.---].|mẖṣ[.---].|š[--.---]. 19[1AQHT].2.95
nm.|[ṭṭṭ.b ']dn.ksl.|[ṯṯbr.'ln.p]n h.td['].|tǵṣ[.pnt.ks]l h.|anš.dt.ẓr.[h].|tšu.g h.w tṣḥ[.i]k.|mǵy.aliy[n.b]'l.|ik.mǵy 4[51].2.19
.b h.p'nm.|ṭṭṭ.b'd n.ksl.ṯṯbr.|'ln.pn h.td'.tǵṣ.pnt.|ksl h.anš.dt.ẓr h.tšu.|g h.w tṣḥ.ik.mǵy.gpn.w ugr.|mn.ib.yp'.l 3['NT].3.32
.b klat.yd h.|b krb.'ẓm.ridn.|mt.šmm.ks.qdš.|l tphn h.aṯt.krpn.|l t'n.aṯrt.alp.|kd.yqḥ.b ẖmr.|rbt.ymsk.b msk h. 3['NT].1.14
t.ḥtk n.rš.|krt.grdš.mknt.|aṯt.ṣdq h.l ypq.|mtrẖt.yšr h.|aṯt.trẖ.w tb't.|ṯar um.tkn l h.|mṯlṯt.kṯrm.tmt.|mrb't.zbl 14[KRT].1.13
[---.]ṯlṯm.d.nlqḥt.|[bn.ẖ]tyn.yd.bt h.|[aǵ]ltn.|tdn.bn.ddy.|'bdil[.b]n ṣdqn.|bnšm.h[-]mt.ypḥ 2045.2
[-----].|[---].aṯ[--.---].|[---] h.ap.[---].|[---].w t'n.[btlt.'nt.---].|[bnt.bht]k.y ilm[.bnt.bht 18[3AQHT].1.5
n.|l y.w b mt[.-]ḥ.mṣṣ[-]t[.--].|pr'.qẓ.y[bl].šblt.|b ǵlp h.apnk.dnil.|[m]t.rpi.ap[h]n.ǵzr.|[mt.hrn]my.ytšu.|[yṯb.b 19[1AQHT].1.19
hmt.b'l.|ḥkpt il.kl h.tb'.kṯr.|l ahl h.hyn.tb'.l mš|knt h.apnk.dnil.m[t].|rpi.aphn.ǵzr.m[t].|hrnmy.qšt.yqb.[--]|rk 17[2AQHT].5.33
l.|[--.kṯ]r w ẖss.|[---]n.rḥm y.ršp zbl.|[w 'd]t.ilm.ṯlṯ h.|[ap]nk.krt.ṯ'.'[-]r.|[--.]b bt h.yšt.'rb.|[--] h.ytn.w [--]u.l y 15[128].2.7
y.tqḥ.yṭpn.mhr.št.|tštn.k nšr.b ḥbš h.km.diy.|b t'rt h.aqht.km.ytb.l lḥ[m].|bn.dnil.l ṯrm.'l h.nšr[m].|trẖpn.ybṣ 18[3AQHT].4.29
d.m[ṯkt].|mẓma.yd.mṯkt.|ṯṯkr.[--]dn.|'m.krt.mswn h.|arẖ.tzǵ.l 'gl h.|bn.ẖpṯ.l umht hm.|k tnḥn.udmm.|w y'n 15[128].1.4
]m|ria.il.'glm.d[t].|šnt.imr.qmṣ.l[l]im.|ṣḥ.aẖ h.b bht h.a[r]y h.|b qrb hkl h.ṣḥ.|šb'm.bn.aṯrt.|špq.ilm.krm.y[n].| 4[51].6.44
r.npṣ.krw.|ṯt.ẖṯrm.ṯn.kst.|spl.mšlt.w.mqḥm.|w md h.|arn.w mznm.|ṯn.ẖlpnm.|ṯt.mrḥm.|drb.|mrbd.|mškbt. 2050.4
.krt.m at.|krt.k ybky.|ydm'.n'mn.ǵlm.|il.mlk[.ṯ]r ab h.|yarš.hm.drk[t].|k ab.adm.|[-----]. 14[KRT].1.41
grgš.|w.lmd h.|aršmg.|w.lmd h.|iyṯr.|[w].lmd h.|[yn]ḥm.|[w.]lmd h.| 1048.2
n.w.aṯt h.|[--]y.w.aṯt h.|[--]r.w.aṯt h.|'bdyrẖ.ṯn ǵlyt h.|aršmg.|ršpy.w.aṯt h.|bn.glgl.uškny.|bn.ṯny.uškny.|mn 2068.10
qrht.d.tššlmn.|ṯlrb h.|art.ṯn.yrẖm.|ṯlrby.yrẖ.w.ẖm[š.ym]m.|ṯlḥny.yrẖ.w.ẖm[š 66[109].2
.yẖsr.|w.[ank.yd]'.l.yd't.|h[t.---.]l.špš.b'l k.|'[--.s]glt h.at.|ht[.---.]špš.b'l k.|yd'm.l.yd't.|'m y.špš.b'l k.|šnt.šntm 2060.12
]ntm[.---].|[']bdm.|[bn].mṣrn.|[a]rṡwn.|'b[d].|w nḥl h.|atn.bn.ap[s]n.|nsk.ṯlṯ.|bn.[--.]m[-]ẖr.|bn.šmrm.|ṯnnm.| 85[80].3.6
.bkr k.|d k.n'm.'nt.n'm h.|km.tsm.'ṯtrt.ts[m h].|d 'q h.ib.iqni.'p['p] h.|sp.ṯrml.ṯhgrn.[-]dm[.-].|ašlw.b ṣp.'n h.|d 14[KRT].3.147
.bkr k.|d k n'm.'nt.|n'm h.km.tsm.|'ṯtrt.tsm h.|d 'q h.ib.iqni.|'p'p h.sp.ṯrml.|d b ḥlm y.il.ytn.|b ḏrt y.ab.adm.| 14[KRT].6.294
hd.b qrb.hkl h.|qšt hn.aẖd.b yd h.|w qṣ't h.bm.ymn h.|idk.l ytn pnm.|tk.aẖ.šmk.mla[t.r]umm.|tšu knp.btlt.'n[10[76].2.7
aršmg.|w.lmd h.|iyṯr.|[w].lmd h.|[yn]ḥm.|[w.]lmd h.|[i]wrmẖ.|[w.]lmd h. 1048.8
grgš.|w.lmd h.|aršmg.|w.lmd h.|iyṯr.|[w].lmd h.|[yn]ḥm.|[w.]lmd h.|[i]wrmẖ.|[w.]lmd 1048.4
n.amt.|[tn.b]nm.aqny.|[tn.ṯa]rm.amid.|[w y'n].ṯr.ab h.il.|d[--].b bk.krt.|b dm'.n'mn.ǵlm.|il.trḥṣ.w tadm.|rḥṣ[.y 14[KRT].2.59
[---.b'l.b bht h].|[il.hd.b qr]b.hkl h.|w t'nyn.ǵlm.b'l.|in.b'l.b bht ht.|il h 10[76].2.1
h].|[il.hd.b qr]b.hkl h.|w t'nyn.ǵlm.b'l.|in.b'l.b bht ht.|il hd.b qrb.hkl h.|qšt hn.aẖd.b yd h.|w qṣ't h.bm.ymn 10[76].2.4
il.k mdb.yqḥ.il.mšt'ltm.|mšt'ltm.l riš.agn.yqḥ.tš.b bt h.|il.ẖṭ h.nḥt.il.ymnn.mṭ.yd h.yšu.|yr.šmm h.yr.b šmm.'ṣr. 23[52].36
hmmt.|šnt.tluan.|w yškb.nhmmt.|w yqmṣ.w b ḥlm h.|il.yrd.b ḏhrt h.|ab adm.w yqrb.|b šal.krt.m at.|krt.k yb 14[KRT].1.35
mgdl.rkb.|ṯkmm.ḥmt.nša.|[y]d h.šmmh.dbḥ.|l ṯr.ab h.il.šrd.|[b'l].b dbḥ h.bn dgn.|[b m]ṣd h.yrd.krt.|[l g]gt.'db 14[KRT].4.169

n.q[š] h.n[bln].|klny n[.n]bl.ks h.|[an]y.l yṣḥ.ṯr il.ab h.|[i]l.mlk.d yknn h.yṣḥ.|aṯrt.w bn h.ilt.w ṣbrt.|ary h.wn.i 4[51].4.47

.klny y.qš h.|nbln.klny y.nbl.ks h.|any.l yṣḥ.ṯr.il.ab h.il.|mlk.d yknn h.yṣḥ.aṯrt.|w bn h.ilt.w ṣbrt.arḫ h.|wn.in. 3[‘NT.VI].5.43

[-----].|[---.--]y.|[-----].|[any.l yṣ]ḥ.ṯr.|[il.ab h.i]l.mlk.|[d yknn h.yṣ]ḥ.aṯ|[rt.w bn h.]ilt.|[w ṣbrt.ary]h.| 4[51].1.5

hml]t.tn.b‘l.w ‘nn h.bn.dgn.arṯ m.pḏ h.|[w y‘n.]ṯr.ab h.il.‘bd k.b‘l.y ym m.‘bd k.b‘l.|[--.--]m.bn.dgn.a[s]r km.hw 2.1[137].36

b‘l.yṯb.k ṯbt.ǵr.hd.r[‘y].|k mdb.b tk.ǵr h.il ṣpn.b [tk].|ǵr.tliyt.šb‘t.brqm.[---].|ṯmnt.iṣr r‘t.‘ṣ brq y.| UG5.3.1.2

]y.d‘t hm.išt.ištm.yitmr.ḥrb.ltšt.|[--]n hm.rgm.l ṯr.ab h.il.tḥm.ym.b‘l km.|[adn]km.ṯpṭ.nhr.tn.il m.d tq h.d tqyn 2.1[137].33

h].|š[g]r h bm ymn.t[--.---].|[--.]l b‘l.‘bd[.---].|ṯr ab h il.tṯrm[.---].|tšlḥm yrḫ.ggn[.---].|k[.---.ḫ]mš.ḫssm[.---].|[- 2001.1.15

[--].|[---.]aliyn.b‘l.|[---.--]k.mdd il.|y[m.---.]l ṯr.qdqd h.|il[.--.]rḥq.b ǵr.|km.y[--.]ilm.b ṣpn.|‘dr.l[‘r].‘rm.|ṯb.l pd 4[51].7.4

ṣ[d.---].|b.ḫrbǵlm.ǵlm[n].|w.trhy.aṯt h.|w.mlky.b[n] h.|ily.mrily.tdgr. 2048.21

.|[w.l]m[d h].|yṣ[---].|‘bd[--].|pr[--].|‘dr[--].|w.lm[d h].|ily[---].|[-----].|[---]lb[--].|[---]m[.---].|[---.]d nkly.|[---.] 1049.2.10

.w.r‘ h.|ṯrm[-].w[.r‘ h].|[‘]ṯtr[-].w.[r‘ h].|ḫlly[-].w.r‘[h].|ilmškl.w.r‘[h].|šŝw[.--].w.r[‘ h].|kr[mn.--.]w.r[‘ h].|šd. 2083.2.1

n]y.l yṣḥ.ṯr il.ab h.|[i]l.mlk.d yknn h.yṣḥ.|aṯrt.w bn h.ilt.w ṣbrt.|ary h.wn.in.bt.l b‘l.|km.ilm.w ḥẓr.k bn.aṯrt.| 4[51].4.49

.|any.l yṣḥ.ṯr.il.ab h.il.|mlk.d yknn h.yṣḥ.aṯrt.|w bn h.ilt.w ṣbrt.arḫ h.|wn.in.bt.l b‘l.km.ilm.|ḥẓr.k b[n.a]ṯrt.mṯ 3[‘NT.VI].5.45

.l yṣ]ḥ.ṯr.|[il.ab h.i]l.mlk.|[d yknn h.yṣ]ḥ.aṯ|[rt.w bn h.]ilt.|[w ṣbrt.ary]h.|[wn.in.bt.l b‘l.]|[km.ilm.w ḥẓr].|[k b 4[51].1.8

|tšṯḥwy.w tkbdn h.|tšu.g h.w tṣḥ.tšmḫ ht.|aṯrt.w bn h.ilt.w ṣb|rt.ary h.k mt.aliyn.|b‘l.k ḫlq.zbl.b‘l.|arṣ.gm.yṣḥ 6.1.40[49.1.12]

.rb.b‘l y.u.|‘[--.]mlakt.‘bd h.|[---.]b‘l k.yḫpn.|[---.]‘m h.u ky.|[---.--]d k.k.tmǵy.|ml[--.--]š[.ml]k.rb.|b[‘l y.---].|yd 1018.5

.b‘l.qdm.yd h.|k tǵḏ.arz.b ymn h.|bkm.yṯb.b‘l.l bht h.|u mlk.u bl mlk.|arṣ.drkt.yštkn.|dll.al.ilak.l bn.|ilm.mt.‘ 4[51].7.42

[---].|ibr.k l hm.d l h q[--.---].|l ytn.l hm.tḥt b‘l[.---].|h.u qšt pn hdd.b y[.----].|‘m.b ym b‘l ysy ym[.---].|rmm.ḫn 9[33].2.6

‘t.brqm.[---].|ṯmnt.iṣr r‘t.‘ṣ brq y.|riš h.tply.ṭly.bn.‘n h.|uz‘rt.tmll.išd h.qrn[m].|dt.‘l h.riš h.b glṯ.b šm[m].|[---.i] UG5.3.1.5

h.w šrš.km.ary h.|bl.iṯ.bn.l h.km aḫ h.w šrš.|km.ary h.uzrm.ilm.ylḥm.|uzrm.yšqy.bn.qdš.|l tbrknn l ṯr.il ab y.|t 17[2AQHT].1.22

rpi.rgm.|‘m špš.kll.mid m.|šlm.|l.[--]n.špš.|ad[.‘]bd h.uk.škn.|k.[---.]sglt h.hw.|w.b[.---.]uk.nǵr.|w.[---].adny.l. 2060.6

].|‘dn.ngb.w [yṣi.ṣbu].|ṣbi.ng[b.w yṣi.‘dn].|m‘[.ṣ]bu h.u[l.mad].|ṯlṯ.mat.rbt.|hlk.l alpm.ḫḏḏ.|w l.rbt.kmyr.|aṯr. 14[KRT].4.178

‘y.ṯlṯ.|ar.ṯmn ‘šr h.|mlk.arb‘.|ǵbl.ḫmš.|atlg.ḫmš ‘šr[h].|ulm ṯ[ṯ].|m‘rby.ḫmš.|ṭbq.arb‘.|tkm[.---].|uḫnp[.---].|u 68[65].1.8

.w ḥlm.|‘bd.il.w hdrt.|yrtḥṣ.w yadm.|yrḥṣ.yd h.amt h.|uṣb‘t h.‘d.ṯkm.|‘rb.b ẓl.ḫmt.lqḥ.|imr.dbḥ.b yd h.|lla.kla 14[KRT].3.157

ǵr krm.|[---].ab h.krm ar.|[---.]h.mḥtrt.pṭtm.|[---.-]t h.ušpǵt tišr.|[---.šm]m h.nšat ẓl h kbkbm.|[---.]b km kbkb 2001.2.4

pnm.tk.ḥqkpt.|il.kl h.kptr.|ksu.ṯbt h.ḥkpt.|arṣ.nḥlt h.|b alp.šd.rbt.|kmn.l p‘n.kṯ.|hbr.w ql.tšṯḥ|wy.w kbd hwt. 3[‘NT.VI].6.16

.pnm.tk.ḥkpt.il.kl h].|[kptr.]ks[u.ṯbt h.ḥkpt.arṣ.nḥlt h].|b alp.šd.r[bt.kmn.l p‘n.kṯr].|hbr.w ql.t[šṯḥwy.w kbd.hw 1[‘NT.IX].3.1

.ablm.[qrt.zbl.yrḫ].|ik.al.yḥdṯ.yrḫ.b[---].|b qrn.ymn h.b anšt[.---].|qdqd h.w y‘n.yṭpn.[mhr.št].|šm‘.l btlt.‘nt.at.‘ 18[3AQHT].4.10

mid.|dblt yṯnt w ṣmqm yṯn[m].|w qmḥ bql ysq aḥd h.|b ap h. 160[55].25

ḫṭ.l brk h.tṣi.km.|rḥ.npš h.km.iṯl.brlt h.km.|qṭr.b ap h.b ap.mhr h.ank.|l aḥwy.tqḥ.yṭpn.mhr.št.|tštn.k nšr.b ḥbš 18[3AQHT].4.26

ydm‘.|tntkn.udm‘t h.|km.ṯqlm.arṣ h.|km ḫmšt.mṭt h.|bm.bky h.w yšn.|b dm‘ h.nhmmt.|šnt.tluan.|w yškb.nh 14[KRT].1.30

.ǵzrm.b.bt.ṣdqš[lm].|[a]ṯt.aḥt.b.bt.rpi[--].|[aṯt.]w.bt h.b.bt.alḫn.|[aṯt.w.]pǵt.aḥt.b.bt.tt.|[aṯt.w.]bt h.b.bt.trǵds.| 80[119].25

ǵz]r.aḥd.b.bt.nwrḏ.|[aṯ]t.adrt.b.bt.artṯb.|aṯt.w.ṯn.bn h.b.bt.iwwpzn.|aṯt.w.pǵt.b.bt.ydrm.|ṯt.aṯtm.adrtm.w.pǵt.a 80[119].5

ṯrm[.w]m|ria.il.‘glm.d[t].|šnt.imr.qmṣ.l[l]im.|ṣḥ.aḫ h.b bht h.a[r]y h.|b qrb hkl h.ṣḥ.|šb‘m.bn.aṯrt.|špq.ilm.kr 4[51].6.44

b.[bt.---].|aṯt.w.bn h.w.pǵt.aḥt.b.bt.m[--].|aṯt.w.ṯt.bt h.b.bt.ḫḏmrd.|aṯt.w.ṯn.ǵzrm.b.bt.ṣdqš[lm].|[a]ṯt.aḥt.b.bt.r 80[119].22

.hm.ym[.---].|‘l amr.yu[ḫd.ksa.mlk h].|nḫt.kḥṯ.d[rkt h.b bt y].|aṣḥ.rpi[m.iqra.ilnym].|b qrb.h[kl y.aṯr h.rpum.l] 22.1[123].18

[aṯt.w].bn h.b.bt.krz.|[aṯt.]w.pǵt.b.bt.gg.|[ǵz]r.aḥd.b.bt.nwrḏ.|[aṯ]t.a 80[119].1

.ḥmḥmt.|[---.--] n.ylt.ḥmḥmt.|[---.mt.r]pi.w ykn.bn h.|[b bt.šrš.]b qrb.hkl h.|[nṣb.skn.i]lib h.b qdš.|[ztr.‘m h.l 17[2AQHT].1.43

š.|l tbrknn l ṯr.il ab y.|tmrnn.l bny.bnwt.|w ykn.bn h b bt.šrš.b qrb.|hkl h.nṣb.skn.ilib h.b qdš.|ztr.‘m h.l arṣ.m 17[2AQHT].1.26

t.]w.bt h.b.bt.alḫn.|[aṯt.w.]pǵt.aḥt.b.bt.tt.|[aṯt.w.]bt h.b.bt.trǵds.|[---.]aṯt.adrt.w.pǵt.a[ḥt.b.bt.---].|[---.‘]šrm.npš 80[119].27

h.tply.ṭly.bn.‘n h.|uz‘rt.tmll.išd h.qrn[m].|dt.‘l h.riš h.b glṯ.b šm[m].|[---.i]l.ṯr.iṯ.p h.k ṯt.ǵlt[.--].|[---.--] k yn.dd UG5.3.1.7

.w l.udm.ṯrrt.|w gr.nn.‘rm.šrn.|pdrm.s‘t.b šdm.|ḥṭb h.b grnt.ḥpšt.|s‘t.b nk.šibt.b bqr.|mmlat.dm.ym.w ṯn.|ṯlṯ.r 14[KRT].3.112

rb‘m.dr‘.w.‘šr.dd.drt.|w[.a]rb‘.l.‘šrm.dd.l.yḥšr.bl.bn h.|b.gt.m‘br.arb‘m.l.mit.dr‘.w.ṯmnym[.drt].|w.‘šrm.l.mit.d 1098.11

ṣ‘.trḥṣ.yd h.bt|[l]t.‘nt.uṣb‘t h.ybmt.limm.|[t]rḥṣ.yd h.b dm.ḏmr.|[u]ṣb‘t h.b mm‘.mhrm.|[ṯ]‘r.ksat.l ksat.ṯlḥnt. 3[‘NT].2.34

i].|mt.aqht.ǵzr.[šṣat].|btlt.‘nt.k [rḥ.npš h].|k iṯl.brlt h.[b h.p‘nm].|ṭṭṭ.‘l[n.pn h.td‘.b ‘dn].|ksl.y[ṯbr.yǵṣ.pnt.ksl h 19[1AQHT].2.93

l.sid.zbl.b‘l.|arṣ.qm.yṯ‘r.|w yšlḥmn h.|ybrd.ṯd.l pnw h.|b ḥrb.mlḥt.|qṣ.mri.ndd.|y‘šr.w yšqyn h.|ytn.ks.b d h.| 3[‘NT].1.6

.ḫpn.ḫmš.|kbd.w lpš.|ḫmš.mispt.|mṭ.|w lpš.d sgr b h.|b d.anrmy. 1109.6

[-----].|l abn[.---].|aḫdt.plk h[.b yd h].|plk.qlt.b ymn h.|npyn h.mks.bšr h.|tmt‘.md h. 4[51].2.3

ṣ[‘.trḥṣ].|yd h.btlt.‘nt.uṣb‘t[h.ybmt].|limm.tiḫd.knr h.b yd[h.tšt].|rimt.l irt h.tšr.dd.al[iyn].|b‘l.ahbt. UG5.3.2.6

bn.trn.b d.ibrmḏ.|[š]d.bn.ilṯtmr.b d.tbbr.|[w.]šd.nḥl h.b d.ṯtmd.|[š]d.b d.iwrḫṭ.|[ṯn].šdm.b d.gmrd.|[šd.]lbny.b 82[300].1.12

.t]sk h.|rbb.nsk h.kbkbm.|ttpp.anhbm.d alp.šd[.ẓu h.b ym].|ṭl[.---]. 3[‘NT].4.89

h.bt.b‘l.|[w m]nt h bt.il.ṯḫ.gg h.b ym.|[ṯi]ṭ.rḥṣ.npṣ h.b ym.rṯ.|[--.y]iḫd.il.‘bd h.ybrk.|[dni]l mt rpi.ymr.ǵzr.|[17[2AQHT].1.34

.trtḥ[ṣ.--].|[----.a]dm.tium.b ǵlp y[m.--].|d alp šd.ẓu h.b ym.t[---].|tlbš.npṣ.ǵzr.tšt.ḫ[---.b] |nšg h.ḥrb.tšt.b t‘r[t h 19[1AQHT].4.205

s h.|[k]šb‘ yn.spu.ksm h.bt.b‘l.|[w m]nt h bt.il.ṯḫ.gg h.b ym.|[ṯi]ṭ.rḥṣ.npṣ h.b ym.rṯ.|[--.y]iḫd.il.‘bd h.ybrk.|[dni 17[2AQHT].1.33

yd h].|plk.qlt.b ymn h.|npyn h.mks.bšr h.|tmt‘.md h.b ym.ṯn.|npyn h.b nhrm.|štt.ḫptr.l išt.|ḫbrṯ.l ẓr.pḥmm.| 4[51].2.6

ttpp.anhb[m.d alp.šd].|ẓu h.b ym[.---].|[--]rn.l [---]. 3[‘NT].3.02

bht ht.|il hd.b qrb.hkl h.|qšt hn.aḫd.b yd h.|w qṣ‘t h.bm.ymn h.|idk.l ytn pnm.|tk.aḫ.šmk.mla[t.r]umm.|tšu 10[76].2.7

.w ḫrṣ.l kl.|apnk.ǵzr.ilḥu.|[m]rḥ h.yiḫd.b yd.|[g]rgr h.bm.ymn.|[w]yqrb.trẓẓ h.|[---].mǵy h.w ǵlm.|[a]ḫt h.šib. 16.1[125].48

aylt tǵpy ṯr.‘n[.---].|b[b]r.mrḥ h.ti[ḫd.b yd h].|š[g]r h bm ymn.t[--.---].|[--.]l b‘l.‘bd[.---].|ṯr ab h il.tṯrm[.---].|tšl 2001.1.13

ubnyn š h d.ytn.ṣṭqn.|ṯut ṭbḫ ṣtq[n].|b bz ‘zm ṭbḫ š[h].|b kl ygz ḥḫ š h. 1153.4

ri.ndd.|y‘šr.w yšqyn h.|ytn.ks.b d h.|krpn.b klat.yd h.|b krb.‘ẓm.ridn.|mt.šmm.ks.qdš.|l tphn h.aṯt.krpn.|l t‘n. 3[‘NT].1.11

nt.uṣb‘t h.ybmt.limm.|[t]rḥṣ.yd h.b dm.ḏmr.|[u]ṣb‘t h.b mm‘.mhrm.|[ṯ]‘r.ksat.l ksat.ṯlḥnt.|[l]ṯlḥn.hdmm.tṯ‘r.l 3[‘NT].2.35

pi.mlk ‘lm.b ‘z.|[rpu.m]lk.‘lm.b ḏmr h.bl.|[---].b ḥtk h.b nmrt h.l r|[--.]arṣ.‘z k.ḏmr k.l[-]|n k.ḥtk k.nmrt k.b tk. UG5.2.2.8

mn h. | npyn h.mks.bšr h. | tmt'.md h.b ym.ṯn. | npyn h.b nhrm. | štt.ḫptr.l išt. | ḫbrṯ.l ẓr.pḥmm. | t'pp.ṯr.il.d pid. | t 4[51].2.7
r]. | tšt k.bm.qrb m.asm. | b p h.rgm.l yṣa.b špt h[.hwt h]. | b nši 'n h.w tphn.in.[---]. | [-.]hlk.ǵlmm b dd y.yṣ[--]. | [-. 19[1AQHT].2.75
[---.-]b'm. | [---.b]n.yšm[']. | [---.]mlkr[-] h.b.nṯk. | [---.]šb'm. | [---.]ḫrg.'šrm. | [---.]abn.ksp.ṯlṯ. | [---].bty 2153.3
]. | w ṯmnt.l ṯmnym. | šr.aḫy h.mẓa h. | w mẓa h.šr.yly h. | b skn.sknm.b 'dn. | 'dnm.kn.npl.b'l. | km ṯr.w tkms.hd.p[. 12[75].2.52
t k. | [---.]l [ ]dm.aḫt k. | yd't.k rḥmt. | al.tšt.b šdm.mm h. | b smkt.ṣat.npš h. | [-]mt[-].ṣba.rbt. | špš.w tgh.nyr. | rbt.w 16.1[125].34
hln.'nt.l bt h.tmǵyn. | tštql.ilt.l hkl h. | w l.šb't.tmtḫṣ h.b 'mq. | tḫtṣb.bn.qrtm.tṯ'r. | ksat.l mhr.ṯ'r.ṯlḥnt. | l ṣbim.hd 3['NT].2.19
rt k. | wn ap.'dn.mṭr h. | b'l.y'dn.'dn.ṯkt.b glṯ. | w tn.ql h.b 'rpt. | šrh.l arṣ.brqm. | bt.arzm.yklln h. | hm.bt.lbnt.y'ms 4[51].5.70
t.l a]rṣ.špt.l šmm. | [---.l]šn.l kbkbm.y'rb. | [b']l.b kbd h.b p h yrd. | k ḫrr.zt.ybl.arṣ.w pr. | 'ṣm.yraun.aliyn.b'l. | ṯt'. 5[67].2.4
zrm. | mid.tmtḫṣn.w t'n. | tḫtṣb.w tḥdy.'nt. | tǵdd.kbd h.b ṣḥq.ymlu. | lb h.b šmḫt.kbd.'nt. | tšyt.k brkm.tǵll b dm. | 3['NT].2.25
ǵzrm.mid.tmtḫṣn.w t]'n.tḫtṣb. | [w tḥdy.'nt.tǵdd.kbd h.b ṣḥ]q.ymlu.lb h. | [b šmḫt.kbd.'nt.tšyt.tḥt h.k]kdrt.riš. | [' 7.1[131].7
tšm'.nrt.ilm.špš. | tšu.aliyn.b'l.l ktp. | 'nt.k tšt h.tš'lyn h. | b ṣrrt.ṣpn.tbkyn h. | w tqbrn h.tštnn.b ḫrt. | ilm.arṣ.ṯṭbḫ.š 6[62].1.15
y.bnwt. | w ykn.bn h b bt.šrš.b qrb. | hkl h.nṣb.skn.ilib h.b qdš. | ztr.'m h.l arṣ.mšṣu.qṭr h. | l 'pr.ḏmr.aṯr h.ṭbq.lḥt. | 17[2AQHT].1.27
r]pi.w ykn.bn h. | [b bt.šrš.]b qrb.hkl h. | [nṣb.skn.i]lib h.b qdš. | [ztr.'m h.l a]rṣ.mšṣu. | [qṭr h.l 'pr.ḏ]mr.a[ṯ]r h. | [ṭb 17[2AQHT].1.45
p y sp | r hn.b špt y mn | t hn ṯlḥ h w mlg h y | ṯtqt 'm h b q't. | tq't 'm prbḫṯ. | dmqt ṣǵrt kṯrt. 24[77].48
l imr h.km.lb.'n[t]. | aṯr.b'l.tiḫd.m[t]. | b sin.lpš.tšṣq[n h]. | b qṣ.all.tšu.g h.w[tṣ] | ḥ.at.mt.tn.aḫ y. | w 'n.bn.ilm.mt. 6[49].2.10
l.'glm.d[t]. | šnt.imr.qmṣ.l[l]im. | ṣḥ.aḫ h.b bht h.a[r]y h. | b qrb hkl h.ṣḥ. | šb'm.bn.aṯrt. | špq.ilm.krm.y[n]. | špq.ilht 4[51].6.44
šš[r]t.ḫrṣ.ṯqlm.kbd.'šrt.mzn h. | b [ar]b'm.ksp. | b d[.'b]dym.ṯlṯ.kkr š'rt. | iqn[i]m.ṯṯt.'šrt.k 2100.1
. | l 'pr.ḏmr.aṯr h.ṭbq.lḥt. | niṣ h.grš d.'šy.ln h. | aḫd.yd h.b škrn.m'ms h. | [k]šb' yn.spu.ksm h.bt.b'l. | [w m]nt h bt. 17[2AQHT].1.31
.w t'n. | tḫtṣb.w tḥdy.'nt. | tǵdd.kbd h.b ṣḥq.ymlu. | lb h.b šmḫt.kbd.'nt. | tšyt.k brkm.tǵll b dm. | ḏmr.ḥlqm.b mm'. 3['NT].2.26
.w t]'n.tḫtṣb. | [w tḥdy.'nt.tǵdd.kbd h.b ṣḥ]q.ymlu.lb h. | [b šmḫt.kbd.'nt.tšyt.tḥt h.k]kdrt.riš. | ['l h.k irbym.kp.--- 7.1[131].7
-]. | w t'n.pǵt.ṯkmt.mym. | qrym.ab.dbḥ.l ilm. | š'ly.dǵṯ h.b šmym. | dǵṯ.hrnmy.d kbkbm. | l tbrkn.alk brkt. | tmrn.al 19[1AQHT].4.192
]y.mšspdt. | b ḥẓr y pẓǵm.ǵr.w yq. | dbḥ.ilm.yš'ly.dǵṯ h. | b šmym.dǵṯ hrnmy[.d k] | bkbm.'[l.---]. | [-]l h.yd 'd[.---]. 19[1AQHT].4.185
m. | w.aḥd.ḫbṯ. | w.arb'.aṯt. | bn.lg.ṯn.bn h. | b'lm.w.aḫt h. | b.šrt. | šty.w.bn h. 2080.11
. | rgm l td'.nšm.w l tbn. | hmlt.arṣ.at m.w ank. | ibǵy h.b tk.ǵr y.il.ṣpn. | b qdš.b ǵr.nḥlt y. | b n'm.b gb'.tliyt. | hlm. 3['NT].3.26
n.kbkbm.abn.brq]. | d l t[d'.šmm.at m.w ank]. | ibǵ[y h.b tk.ǵ]r y.il.ṣpn. | b q[dš.b ǵr.nḥ]lt y. | w t['n].btlt.[']nt.ṯṭb. 3['NT].4.63
ḫ h.w.'šr[.---]. | klyn.apsn[y.---]. | plzn.qrty[.---]. | w.klt h.b.t[--.---]. | b'l y.mlk[y.---]. | yd.bt h.yd[.---]. | ary.yd.t[--.--- 81[329].12
n il.tspr.yrḫm. | k b'l.k yḥwy.y'šr.ḥwy.y'š. | r.w yšqyn h.ybd.w yšr.'l h. | n'm[n.w t]'nynn.ap ank.aḥwy. | aqht[.ǵz]r. 17[2AQHT].6.31
.il.špḥ. | lṭpn.w qdš.'l. | ab h.y'rb.ybky. | w yšnn.ytn.g h. | bky.b ḥy k.ab n.ašmḫ. | b l.mt k.ngln.k klb. | b bt k.n'tq.k 16.1[125].13
r.ilḥu.t[---]l. | trm.tṣr.trm[.']tqt. | tbky.w tšnn.[tt]n. | g h.bky.b ḥ[y k.a]b n. | nšmḫ.b l.mt k.ngln. | k klb.[b]bt k.n'tq 16.2[125].98
h. | w b tm hn.špḥ.yitbd. | w b.pḫyr h.yrṯ. | y'rb.b ḥdr h.ybky. | b ṯn.[-]gmm.w ydm'. | tntkn.udm't h. | km.ṯqlm.arṣ 14[KRT].1.26
| lm.tḫš.nṯq.dmrn. | 'n.b'l.qdm.yd h. | k tǵd.arz.b ymn h. | bkm.ytb.b'l.l bht h. | u mlk.u bl mlk. | arṣ.drkt.yštkn. | dll. 4[51].7.41
n h.tǵr. | yṣu.hlm.aḫ h.tph. | [ksl]h.l arṣ.ṯtbr. | [---.]aḫ h.tbky. | [--.m]rṣ.mlk. | [---.]krt.adn k. | [w y'ny.]ǵzr.ilḥu. | [--- 16.1[125].55
.ǵzr. | [mt.]hrnmy.d in.bn.l h. | km.aḫ h.w šrš.km.ary h. | bl.iṯ.bn.l h.km aḫ h.w šrš. | km.ary h.uzrm.ilm.ylḥm. | uz 17[2AQHT].1.20
tšt k.liršt. | [---.]rpi.mlk 'lm.b 'z. | [rpu.m]lk.'lm.b ḏmr h.bl. | [---].b ḥtk h.b nmrt h.l r | [--.]arṣ.'z k.ḏmr k.l[-] | n k.ḥt UG5.2.2.7
lmyn. | w.nḥl h. | w.nḥl hm. | bn.ḥrm. | bn.brzn. | w.nḥl h. | bn.adlḏn. | bn.šbl. | bn.ḫnzr. | bn.arwṯ. | bn.ṯbtnq. | bn.pṭḏn 113[400].1.11
ṯt h. | anntn.yṣr. | annmn.w.ṯlṯ.n'[r] h. | rpan.w.ṯ[n.]bn h. | bn.ayln.w.ṯn.bn h. | yt. 2068.26
--]. | [-----]. | b[n.---]. | b[n.---]. | bn.[---]. | bn.a[--]. | w.nḥl h. | bn.alz. | w.nḥl h. | bn.sny. | bn.ablḥ. | [-----]. | w [---]. | bn.[-- 2163.1.11
[w]nḥ[l h]. | [bn].amd[-]. | [bn].ṣbṭ[--]. | [bn].ḫla[n]. | [bn].ǵr[--]. | d.b[n 2164.A.1
'bdy[rḫ].bn.gṯtn. | yrmn.bn.'n. | krwn.nḥl h. | ttn.[n]ḥl h. | bn.b[r]zn. | [---.-]ḫn. 85[80].4.11
h. | [--]r.w.aṯt h. | 'bdyrḫ.ṯn ǵlyt h. | aršmg. | ršpy.w.aṯt h. | bn.glgl.uškny. | bn.ṯny.uškny. | mnn.w.aṯt h. | slmu.ḥrš.mr 2068.12
t.nša. | [y]d h.šmmh.dbḥ. | l ṯr.ab h.il.šrd. | [b'l].b dbḥ h.bn dgn. | [b m]ṣd h.yrd.krt. | [l g]gt.'db.akl.l qryt. | ḥṭt.l bt. 14[KRT].4.170
m.ṯpṭ.nhr.tn.il m.d tq h.d tqyn h. | [hml]t.tn.b'l.w 'nn h.bn.dgn.art m.pḏ h. | [w y'n.]ṯr.ab h.il.'bd k.b'l.y ym m.'bd 2.1[137].35
km.ṯ[pṭ.nhr]. | tn.il m.d tq h.d tqyn.hmlt.tn.b'l.[w 'nn h]. | bn.dgn.art m.pḏ h.tb'.ǵlmm.l ṯṯb.[idk.pnm]. | l ytn.tk.ǵr. 2.1[137].18
| y'l.b'l.b ǵ[r.---]. | w bn.dgn.b š[---]. | b'l.ytb.l ks[i.mlk h]. | bn.dgn.l kḥ[ṯ.drkt h]. | l alp.ql.ẓ[--.---]. | l np ql.nd.[----]. 10[76].3.14
| bn.ḫty. | ṯn.bnš ibrḏr. | bnš tlmi. | sǵr.ḫryn. | 'dn.w sǵr h. | bn.ḫgbn. 2082.9
bnšm.dt.l.u[--]ṯtb. | kṯ[r]n. | w.aṯt h.w.n'r h. | bn.ḫby.w.[a]ṯt h. | ynḥm.ulmy. | [--]q.w.aṯt h.w.bn h. | [--] 2068.3
| bn.ibln. | bn.ilt. | špšyn.nḥl h. | n'mn.bn.iryn. | nrn.nḥl h. | bn.ḫsn. | bn.'bd. | [-----]. | [---.n]ḥ[l h]. | [-]ntm[.---]. | [']bdm 85[80].2.8
a.yd.mṯkt. | ṯṯkr.[--]dn. | 'm.krt.mswn h. | arḫ.tzǵ.l 'gl h. | bn.ḫpṯ.l umht hm. | k tnḥn.udmm. | w y'ny.krt.ṯ'. 15[128].1.5
[-----]. | bn.[---]. | bn.[---]. | w.nḥ[l h]. | bn.ẓr[-]. | mru.skn. | bn.bddn. | bn.ǵrgn. | bn.tgtn. | bn.ḥrẓ 113[400].5.3
bn.iršyn. | bn.'zn. | bn.aršw. | bn.ḫzrn. | bn.iǵyn. | w.nḥl h. | bn.ksd. | bn.bršm. | bn.kzn. | w.nḥl h. | w.nḥl hm. | w.[n]ḥl 113[400].2.17
[---]y. | [---.]w.nḥl h. | bn ksln.ṯlṯḥ. | bn yṣmḫ.bn.ṯrn w nḥl h. | bn srd.bn agmn. | 101[10].2
zn. | bn.ḫṭr[-]. | bn.yd[--]. | bn.'[---]. | w.nḥ[l h]. | w.nḥ[l h]. | bn.k[---]. | bn.y[---]. | [bn].i[---]. 116[303].11
. | bn.šlmn. | bn.mly. | pslm. | bn.annd. | bn.gl'd. | w.nḥl h. | bn.mlkyy. | [bn].bm[--]. | ['š]rm. | [-----]. | [-----]. | bn.p[--]. | 2163.3.12
. | bn abyt. | bn ḫdl. | bn ṣdqn. | bn ayy. | bn dbb. | w nḥl h. | bn n'myn. | bn aṯtyy. | bn ḫlp. | bn.ẓll. | bn ydy. | bn lzn. | bn 2016.1.8
]. | b[n.---]. | bn.[---]. | bn.a[--]. | w.nḥl h. | bn.alz. | w.nḥl h. | bn.sny. | bn.ablḥ. | [-----]. | w [---]. | bn.[---]. | bn.yr[--]. | bn.k 2163.1.13
]y. | [---.]w.nḥl h. | bn ksln.ṯlṯḥ. | bn yṣmḫ.bn.ṯrn w nḥl h. | bn srd.bn agmn. | bn [-]ln.bn.ṯbil. | bn is.bn tbdn. | bn ury 101[10].4
l h. | [--.-]hs. | [--.--]nyn. | [-----]. | [-----]. | bn.'dy. | w.nḥl h. | bn.'bl. | bn.[-]rṯn. | bn[.---]. | bn u[l]pm. | bn '[p]ty. | bn.kdg 2163.2.20
[aǵ]ltn. | [--]ṯm.b.gt.irbṣ. | [--]šmyn. | [w.]nḥl h. | bn.qṣn. | bn.ksln. | bn.ṣrym. | bn.ṯmq. | bn.ntp. | bn.mlk. | bn 1073.1.4
mryn[m]. | bn.bly. | nrn. | w.nḥl h. | bn.rmyy. | bn.tlmyn. | w.nḥl h. | w.nḥl hm. | bn.ḥrm. | bn.b 113[400].1.4
bn.adty. | bn.krwn. | bn.ngśk. | bn.qnḏ. | bn.pity. | w.nḥl h. | bn.rt. | bn.l[--]. | bn.[---]. | [---.--]y. | [--.-]ḏrm. | [--.--]y. | [--.- 113[400].3.18
ṯnnm. | bn.qqln. | w.nḥl h. | w.nḥl h. | bn.šml[-]. | bn.brzn. | bn.ḫṭr[-]. | bn.yd[--]. | bn.'[---]. | w.nḥ 116[303].4
lmd h. | ymn. | w.lmd h. | y'drn. | w.lmd h. | 'dn. | w.lmd h. | bn.špš. | [w.l]m[d h]. | yṣ[---]. | 'bd[--]. | pr[--]. | 'dr[--]. | w.l 1049.1.10
bn.aḫ[--]. | bn[.---]. | [-----]. | bn kr[k]. | bn ḫtyn. | w nḥl h. | bn tgrb. | bn ṯdnyn. | bn pbn. 2016.3.4

mš.ddm. | ṯṯ.l.ʿšrm.bn[š.mlk.---].ẖzr.lqḥ.ḥp[r]. | ʿšt.ʿšr h.bn[.---.--]ẖ.zr. | bʿl.šd. 2011.41
pṯ m. | [---.]w yʿn.kṯr. | [w ẖss.]tṯb.bʿl.l hwt y. | [ḥš.]bht h.tbnn. | [ḥš.]trmm.hkl h. | y[tl]k.l lbnn.w ʿṣ h. | l[šr]yn.mḥm 4[51].6.16
ym. | [trm]m.hk[l.ṯpṯ].nhr.bt k.[---.]šp[-.---]. | [ḥš.bh]t h.tbn[n.ḥ]š.trm[mn.hkl h.---.]bt. | [---.-]k.mnh[-.---.-]š bš[-.]t 2.3[129].10
n.bʿly.ṯlṯtm.bʿlm. | w.aḥd.ẖbṯ. | w.arbʿ.aṯt. | bn.lg.ṯn.bn h. | bʿlm.w.aẖt h. | b.šrt. | šty.w.bn h. 2080.10
. | ṯlṯ.bʿlm. | w.adn hm.ṯr.w.arbʿ.bnt h. | yrẖm.yd.ṯn.bn h. | bʿlm.w.ṯlṯ.nʿrm.w.bt.aẖt. | bn.lwn.ṯlṯtm.bʿlm. | bn.bʿly.ṯlṯt 2080.4
lm.l ymru. | ilm.w nšm.d yšb | [ʿ].hmlt.arṣ.gm.l ǵ | [lm] h.bʿl k.yṣḥ.ʿn. | [gpn].w ugr.b ǵlmt. | [ʿmm.]ym.bn.ẓlmt.r | [m 4[51].7.53
ẖ. | aliyn.bʿl.ht y.bnt. | dt.ksp.hkl y.dtm. | ḫrṣ.ʿdbt.bht[h.bʿ]l. | yʿdb.hd.ʿdb[.ʿd]bt. | hkl h.ṭbḫ.alpm[.ap]. | ṣin.šql.ṯrm[4[51].6.38
t. | šbt.dqn k.l tsr k. | rḫntt.d[-].l irt k. | wn ap.ʿdn.mṭr h. | bʿl.yʿdn.ʿdn.ṯkt.b glṯ. | w tn.ql h.b ʿrpt. | šrh.l arṣ.brqm. | b 4[51].5.68
ttn pnm.ʿm.bʿl. | mrym.ṣpn.b alp.šd.rbt.kmn. | hlk.aẖt h.bʿl.yʿn.tdrq. | ybnt.ab h.šrḥq.aṯt.l pnn h. | št.alp.qdm h.mri 3[ʿNT].4.83
l]. | nʿmn.ilm l ẖt[n]. | m.bʿl trẖ pdry b[t h]. | aqrb k ab h bʿ[l]. | yǵtr.ʿṯtr t | rẖ l k ybrdmy.b[t.a] | b h lb[u] yʿrr.w yʿ[n 24[77].27
. | w tn.bt.l bʿl.km. | [i]lm.w ḥẓr.k bn. | [a]ṯrt.gm.l ǵlm h. | bʿl.yṣḥ.ʿn.gpn. | w ugr.bn.ǵlmt. | ʿmm ym.bn.ẓlm[t]. | rmt. 8[51FRAG].5
| rmṣt.ilhm.bʿlm.dṯt.w kšm.ḥmš. | ʿtr h.mlun.šnpt.ḥṣt h.bʿl.ṣpn š. | [--]t š.ilt.mgdl š.ilt.asrm š. | w l ll.šp. pgr.w ṯrmn 34[1].10
anyt. | l.mlk.gbl. | w.ḫmšm.ksp. | lqḥ.mlk.gbl. | lbš.anyt h. | bʿrm.ksp. | mḫr.hn. 2106.16
šlm.]l kbd.arṣ. | ar[bdd.]l kb[d.š]dm.yšt. | [----.]bʿl.mdl h.ybʿr. | [---.]rn h.aqry. | [---.]b a[r]ṣ.mlḥmt. | ašt[.b ʿ]p[r] m. 3[ʿNT].4.70
h.tštnn.l[b]mt ʿr. | l ysmsm.bmt.pḥl. | y dnil.ysb.palt h. | bṣql.yph.b palt.bṣ[q]l. | yph.b yǵlm.bṣql.y[ḥb]q. | w ynšq. 19[1AQHT].2.61
wt h.knp.hrgb.bʿl.ṯbr. | bʿl.ṯbr.diy.hwt.w yql. | tḥt.pʿn h.ybqʿ.kbd h.w yḥd. | [i]n.šmt.in.ʿẓm.yšu.g[h]. | w yṣḥ.knp.h 19[1AQHT].3.130
t h.hwt h.knp.ṣml.bʿ[l]. | bʿl.ṯbr.diy.hyt.tq[l.tḥt]. | pʿn h.ybqʿ.kbd h.w yḥd. | iṯ.šmt.iṯ.ʿẓm.w yqḥ b hm. | aqht.ybl.l q 19[1AQHT].3.144
[h]. | knp.nšrm.bʿl.yṯbr. | bʿl.ṯbr.diy hmt.tqln. | tḥt.pʿn h.ybqʿ.kbdt hm.w[yḥd]. | in.šmt.in.ʿẓm.yšu.g h. | w yṣḥ.knp. 19[1AQHT].3.116
n.ʿbd.ali[yn]. | bʿl.sid.zbl.bʿl. | arṣ.qm.yṯʿr. | w yšlḥmn h. | ybrd.ṯd.l pnw h. | b ḥrb.mlḥt. | qṣ.mri.ndd. | yʿšr.w yšqyn 3[ʿNT].1.5
l.ks.yiẖd. | [il.b]yd.krpn.bm. | [ymn.]brkm.ybrk. | [ʿbd h.]ybrk.il.krt. | [ṯʿ.ymr]m.nʿm[n.]ǵlm.il. | a[ṯt.tq]ḥ.y krt.aṯt. | 15[128].2.19
.ṯḥ.gg h.b ym. | [ti]ṯ.rḥṣ.npṣ h.b ym.rṯ. | [--.y]iẖd.il.ʿbd h.ybrk. | [dni]l mt rpi.ymr.ǵzr. | [mt.hr]nmy npš.yḥ.dnil. | [m 17[2AQHT].1.35
.qṣm. | ǵrmn.kp.mhr.ʿtkt. | rišt.l bmt h.šnst. | kpt.b ḥbš h.brkm.tǵl[l]. | b dm.ḏmr.ḥlqm.b mm[ʿ]. | mhrm.mṭm.tgrš. | 3[ʿNT].2.13
.b škrn.mʿms h. | [k]šbʿ yn.spu.ksm h.bt.bʿl. | [w m]nt h bt.il.ṯḥ.gg h.b ym. | [ti]ṯ.rḥṣ.npṣ h.b ym.rṯ. | [--.y]iẖd.il.ʿbd 17[2AQHT].1.33
šy.ln h. | aẖd.yd h.b škrn.mʿms h. | [k]šbʿ yn.spu.ksm h.bt.bʿl. | [w m]nt h bt.il.ṯḥ.gg h.b ym. | [ti]ṯ.rḥṣ.npṣ h.b ym.r 17[2AQHT].1.32
bt h.w. | yštql.l ḥṭr h.tlu ḥt.km.nḫl. | tplg.km.plg. | bʿd h.bhtm.mnt.bʿd h.bhtm.sgrt. | bʿd h.ʿdbt.ṯlṯ.ptḥ.bt.mnt. | ptḥ UG5.7.70
ṭr h.tlu ḥt.km.nḫl. | tplg.km.plg. | bʿd h.bhtm.mnt.bʿd h.bhtm.sgrt. | bʿd h.ʿdbt.ṯlṯ.ptḥ.bt.mnt. | ptḥ.bt.w ubn.hkl.w UG5.7.70
[--].d.ntn[.d.]ksp. | [ṯ]mn.l.ʿšrm[.l.b]t.ʿṯtrt. | [ṯ]lṯ.ʿšr h.[b]t.ršp.gn. | arbʿ.b d.b[n].ušryn. | kdm.l.urtn. | kdm.l.ilšpš. 1088.3
.n]skt.nʿmn.nbl[.---]. | [--.]yṣq šmn.šlm.b ṣ[ʿ.trḥṣ]. | yd h.btlt.ʿnt.uṣbʿt[h.ybmt]. | limm.tiẖd.knr h.b yd[h.tšt]. | rimt UG5.3.2.5
lḥnm.ymḥ. | [b]bt.dm.ḏmr.yṣq.šmn. | šlm.b ṣʿ.trḥṣ.yd h.bt | [l]t.ʿnt.uṣbʿt h.ybmt.limm. | [t]rḥṣ.yd h.b dm.ḏmr. | [u]ṣ 3[ʿNT].2.32
ḥ.hm.b ʿp. | nṭʿn.b arṣ.ib y. | w b ʿpr.qm.aẖ k. | w tšu.ʿn h.btlt.ʿnt. | w tšu.ʿn h.w tʿn. | w tʿn.arẖ.w tr.b lkt. | tr.b lkt.w t 10[76].2.26
.dbḥ. | bṯt.w dbḥ.w dbḥ. | dnt.w dbḥ.tdmm. | amht.k b h.bṯt.l tbṯ. | w b h.tdmmt.amht. | aḫr.mǵy.aliyn.bʿl. | mǵyt.btl 4[51].3.21
d šmn[.gdlt.w.---]. | brr.r[gm.yṯṯb.b ṯdt.ṯn]. | l šmn.ʿ[ly h.gdlt.rgm.yṯṯb]. | brr.b šbʿ[.ṣbu.špš.w ḥl]. | yt.ʿrb špš[.w ḥl.m APP.II[173].50
d.šmn.gdlt.w.[---.brr]. | rgm.yṯṯb.b.ṯdṯ.ṯn[.--.šmn]. | ʿly h.gdlt.rgm.yṯ[ṯb.brr]. | b.[šb]ʿ.ṣbu.[š]pš.w.ḥly[t].ʿ[r]b[.š]p[š]. 35[3].46
. | [---.--]n. | [---] h.l ʿdb. | [---]n.yd h. | [---].bl.išlḥ. | [---] h.gm. | [l --- k.]yṣḥ. | [---]d.ʿr. | [----.-]bb. | [----.]lm y. | [---.--]p. 14[KRT].5.237
r. | bt.il.pn.l mgr lb.tʿdbn. | nšb.l inr.tʿdbn.ktp. | b il ab h.gʿr.ytb.il.kb[-]. | aṯ[rt.]il.ytb.b mrzḥ h. | yšt[.il.y]n.ʿd šbʿ.trṯ. UG5.1.1.14
bt. | bnšm.dt.l.mlk. | ʿbdyrẖ.bn.ṯyl. | ʿbdn.w.aṯt h.w.bn h. | gpn.bn[.a]ly. | bn.rqd[y].ṯbg. | iḫmlk. | ypʿn w.aṯt h. | anntn 2068.19
ztr.ʿm h.l arṣ.mšṣu.qṭr h. | l ʿpr.ḏmr.aṯr h.ṭbq.lḥt. | niṣ h.grš d.ʿšy.ln h. | aẖd.yd h.b škrn.mʿms h. | [k]šbʿ yn.spu.ks 17[2AQHT].1.30
h.l a]rṣ.mšṣu. | [qṭr h.l ʿpr.ḏ]mr.a[ṯ]r h. | [ṭbq.lḥt.niṣ h.gr]š.d ʿšy. | [ln h.---]. | z[tr.ʿm k.l arṣ.mšṣu.qṭr k]. | l ʿpr.ḏm[17[2AQHT].1.48
ṣ.ksp. | itrṯ.ḫrṣ.ṯrd.bʿl. | b mrym.ṣpn.mšṣṣ.[-]kʿ[-]. | udn h.grš h.l ksi.mlk h. | l nḫt.l kḥṯ.drkt h. | mn m.ib.ypʿ.l bʿl.ṣrt. 3[ʿNT].4.46
n km.ṯpṭ]. | [nhr.---.]hwt.gmr.hd.l wny[-.---]. | [---.]iyr h.g[-.]thbr[.---]. 2.1[137].47
.ib.iqni.ʿp[ʿp] h. | sp.ṯrml.tḥgrn.[-]dm[.-]. | ašlw.b ṣp.ʿn h. | d b ḥlm y.il.ytn. | b ḏrt y.ab.adm. | w ld.špḥ.l krt. | w ǵlm. 14[KRT].3.149
ab h.il.tḥm.ym.bʿl km. | [adn]km.ṯpṭ.nhr.tn.il m.d tq h.d tqyn h. | [hml]t.tn.bʿl.w ʿnn h.bn.dgn.arṯ m.pḏ h. | [w yʿn 2.1[137].34
]. | mʿd.tḥm.ym.bʿl km.adn km.ṯ[pṭ.nhr]. | tn.il m.d tq h.d tqyn.hmlt.tn.bʿl.[w ʿnn h]. | bn.dgn.arṯ m.pḏ h.tbʿ.ǵlmm 2.1[137].18
b gt ilštmʿ. | bt ubnyn š h d.ytn.ṣtqn. | ṭut ṭbḫ ṣtq[n]. | b bz ʿzm ṭbḫ š[h]. | b kl ygz ḥḫ 1153.2
b.b ẓl.ḫmt.lqḥ. | imr.dbḥ.b yd h. | lla.klatnm. | klt.lḥm h.d nzl. | lqḥ.msrr.ʿṣr.db[ḥ]. | yṣq.b gl.ḥtṯ.yn. | b gl.ḫrṣ.nbt.w 14[KRT].3.162
ʿmt.špḥ.bkr k. | d k.nʿm.ʿnt.nʿm h. | km.tsm.ʿṯtrt.ts[m h]. | d ʿq h.ib.iqni.ʿp[ʿp] h. | sp.ṯrml.tḥgrn.[-]dm[.-]. | ašlw.b ṣ 14[KRT].3.146
ʿmt.šbḥ.bkr k. | d k nʿm.ʿnt. | nʿm h.km.tsm. | ʿṯtrt.tsm h. | d ʿq h.ib.iqni. | ʿpʿp h.sp.ṯrml. | d b ḥlm y.il.ytn. | b ḏrt y.a 14[KRT].6.293
-]. | mn[-.---]. | hyrm.h[--.---]. | yrmm h[--.---]. | mlk.gbʿ h d [---]. | ibr.k l hm.d l h q[--.---]. | l ytn.l hm.tḥt bʿl[.---]. | h. 9[33].2.3
dm gt dprnm. | l ḥršm. | ddm l ʿnqt. | dd l alṯt.w l lmdt h. | dd l iḫyn. | dd l [---]. 1101.11
spr.ḥpr.bt.k[--]. | tšʿ.ʿšr h.dd.l.b[t.--]. | ḫmš.ddm.l.ḫtyt. | ṯlṯm.dd.kšmn.l.gzzm. | yyn. | 1099.2
-.d]rʿ.w.mit.drt.w.ʿšrm.l.mit. | [drt.ḥpr.b]nšm.w.ṯn.ʿšr h.dd.l.rpš. | [---.]šbʿm.drʿ.w.arbʿm.drt.mit.dd. | [---].ḥpr.bn.š 1098.4
ṯṯ.kbd.ḥpr.bnšm. | b.ʿnmky.ʿšrm.drʿ[.---.d]rt. | w.ṯn.ʿšr h.dd.[---]. | iwrdn.ḥ[--.---]. | w.ṯlṯm.dd.[---.]n[---.---]. | w.a[r]bʿ 1098.29
bt šbn. | iyʿdm.w bʿl h. | ddy. | ʿmy. | iwrnr. | alnr. | maḫdt. | aby. | [-----]. | [-]nt. | ydn. 107[15].2
t]. | hl ǵlmt tld b[n.--]n. | ʿn ha l yd h.tzd[.--]. | pt l bšr h.dm a[--.--]ḥ. | w yn.k mtrḫt[.---]h. | šmʿ ilht kṯr[t.--]mm. | 24[77].9
ʿr. | d yšt.l.lṣb h ḫšʿr klb. | [w]riš.pqq.w šr h. | yšt.aḥd h.dm zt.ḫrpnt. UG5.1.2.6
ṭb.l y.w l h.[---]. | [--.i]mṣḫ.nn.k imr.l arṣ. | [ašhlk].šbt h.dmm.šbt.dqn h. | [mmʿm.-]d.l ytn.bt.l bʿl.k ilm. | [w ḥẓ]r.k 3[ʿNT.VI].5.10
n.b tk. | p[ḫ]r.bn.ilm.štt. | p[--].b ṯlḥn y.qlt. | b ks.ištyn h. | dm.ṯn.dbḥm.šna.bʿl.ṯlṯ. | rkb.ʿrpt.dbḥ. | bṯt.w dbḥ.w dbḥ. 4[51].3.16
.w dbḥ. | dnt.w dbḥ.tdmm. | amht.k b h.bṯt.l tbṯ. | w b h.tdmmt.amht. | aḫr.mǵy.aliyn.bʿl. | mǵyt.btlt.ʿnt. | tmgnn.rb 4[51].3.22
t.yšt k.bʿl.l ht. | w ʿlm h.l ʿnt.p dr.dr. | ʿdb.uḫry.mṭ.yd h. | dnil.bt h.ymǵyn.yšt | ql.dnil.l hkl h.ʿrb.b | kyt.b hkl h.mšs 19[1AQHT].4.169
zr. | [ilm].dnil.uzr.ilm.ylḥm. | [uzr.]yšqy.bn qdš.yd.ṣt h. | [dn]il.yd.ṣt h.yʿl.w yškb. | [yd.]mizrt.p yln.mk.b šbʿ.ymm 17[2AQHT].1.14
tmzʿ. | kst.dnil.mt.rpi. | all.ǵzr.m[t.]hr[nmy]. | gm.l bt[h.dnil.k yṣḥ]. | šmʿ.pǵt.ṯkmt[.my]. | ḥspt.l šʿr.ṭl.yd[ʿt]. | hlk.kb 19[1AQHT].1.49
tlt.ʿnt.k [rḥ.npš h]. | k iṯl.brlt h.[b h.pʿnm]. | ṭṭṭ.ʿl[n.pn h.tdʿ.b ʿdn]. | ksl.y[ṯbr.yǵṣ.pnt.ksl h]. | anš.[dt.ẓr h.yšu.g h]. | 19[1AQHT].2.94
. | hlm.ʿnt.tph.ilm.b h.pʿnm. | ṭṭṭ.bʿd n.ksl.ṯṯbr. | ʿln.pn h.tdʿ.tǵṣ.pnt. | ksl h.anš.dt.ẓr h.tšu. | g h.w tṣḥ.ik.mǵy.gpn.w 3[ʿNT].3.31

.ybmt. | [limm].b h.p'nm. | [tṯṯ.b ']dn.ksl. | [ṯṯbr.'ln.p]n h.td[']. | tǵṣ[.pnt.ks]l h. | anš.dt.ẓr.[h]. | tšu.g h.w tṣḥ[.i]k. | m 4[51].2.18
.bn. | qr.'n k.mḫ.riš k. | udm't.ṣḥ.aḫt k. | ṯtmnt.bt.ḥmḥ h. | d[-]n.tbkn.w tdm.l y.[--]. | [---].al.trgm.l aḫt k. | [---.]l [ ]d 16.1[125].29
.---]. | w.a[r]b'[.---].bnš[.š]dyn[.---]. | agr.[---.--]n.ṯn.'šr h.d[--.---]. | [---.]ḥdṯn.'šr.dd[.---]. | [---.]yd.sǵr[.---.--]r h. | aḥ[d 1098.33
ṣr. | ṯḥrr.l išt.w ṣḥrt.l pḥmm.aṯtm.a[ṯt.il]. | aṯt.il.w 'lm h.yhbr.špt hm.yš[q]. | hn.špt hm.mtqtm.mtqtm.k lrmn[.--]. | 23[52].49
id m. | šlm. | l.[--]n.špš. | ad[.']bd h.uk.škn. | k.[---.]sglt h.hw. | w.b[.---.]uk.nǵr. | w.[---].adny.l.yḫsr. | w.[ank.yd]'.l.y 2060.7
qht.ǵz[r]. | tšt k.bm.qrb m.asm. | b p h.rgm.l yṣa.b špt h[.hwt h]. | b nši 'n h.w tphn.in.[---]. | [-.]hlk.ǵlmm b dd y.yṣ 19[1AQHT].2.75
ky.w aqbrn.ašt.b ḫrt. | i[lm.arṣ.b p h.rgm.l yṣa.b šp] | t h.hwt h.knp.hrgb.b'l.ṯbr. | b'l.ṯbr.diy.hwt.w yql. | tḥt.p'n h.y 19[1AQHT].3.128
y.w aqbrn h. | ašt.b ḫrt.ilm.arṣ. | b p h.rgm.l yṣa.b špt h.hwt[h]. | knp.nšrm.b'l.yṯbr. | b'l.ṯbr.diy hmt.tqln. | tḥt.p'n 19[1AQHT].3.113
aqbrn h.aštn. | b ḫrt.ilm.arṣ.b p h.rgm.l[yṣ]a. | b špt h.hwt h.knp.ṣml.b'[l]. | b'l.ṯbr.diy.hyt.tq[l.tḥt]. | p'n h.ybq'.k 19[1AQHT].3.142
l.b gdrt.k lb.l | ḥṯ h.imḫṣ h.k d.'l.qšt h. | imḫṣ h.'l.qṣ't h.hwt. | l aḥw.ap.qšt h.l ttn. | l y.w b mt[.-]ḥ.mṣṣ[-]t[.--]. | pr'. 19[1AQHT].1.15
.ytpn.[mhr.št]. | šm'.l btlt.'nt.at.'[l.qšt h]. | tmḫṣ h.qṣ't h.hwt.l t[ḥwy]. | n'mn.ǵzr.št.ṯrm.w[---]. | ištir.b ḏdm.w n'rs[18[3AQHT].4.13
šqy ilm. | tsad.tkbd.hmt.b'l. | ḥkpt il.kl h.tb'.kṯr. | l ahl h.hyn.tb'.l mš | knt h.apnk.dnil.m[t]. | rpi.aphn.ǵzr.m[t]. | hr 17[2AQHT].5.32
lk. | l nḫt.l kḥṯ.drkt. | ap.yṣb.ytb.b hkl. | w ywsrnn.ggn h. | lk.l ab k.yṣb.lk. | l[ab]k.w rgm.'ny. | l k[rt.adn k.]ištm['']. 16.6[127].26
ḫss.]ṯtb.b'l.l hwt y. | [ḥš.]bht h.tbnn. | [ḥš.]trmm.hkl h. | y[tl]k.l lbnn.w 'ṣ h. | l[šr]yn.mḥmd.arz h. | h[n.l]bnn.w 'ṣ 4[51].6.17
. | qrš.mlk.ab.šnm. | l p'n.il.thbr.w tql. | tštḥwy.w tkbd h. | hlm.il.k yphn h. | yprq.lṣb.w yṣḥq. | p'n h.l hdm.ytpd.w y 4[51].4.26
ksi h. | [n]hr l kḥṯ drkt h.trtqṣ.b d b'l km nš | r.b uṣb't h.hlm.ktp.zbl ym.bn ydm. | [tp]ṭ nhr.yrtqṣ.ṣmd.b d b'l.km.n 2.4[68].14
n ydm. | [tp]ṭ nhr.yrtqṣ.ṣmd.b d b'l.km.nšr. | b[u]ṣb't h.ylm.ktp.zbl ym.bn ydm.ṯpṭ. | nhr.'z.ym.l ymk.l tngṣn.pnt 2.4[68].16
. | l ksi h.nhr l kḥṯ.drkt h.trtqṣ. | b d b'l.km.nšr b uṣb't h.hlm.qdq | d zbl ym.bn.'nm.ṯpṭ.nhr.yprsḥ ym. | w yql.l arṣ. 2.4[68].21
ym. | w yql.l arṣ.w trtqṣ.ṣmd.b d b'l. | [km.]nšr.b uṣb't h.ylm.qdqd.zbl. | [ym.]bn.'nm.ṯpṭ.nhr.yprsḥ.ym.yql. | l arṣ.t 2.4[68].24
pn.ybṣr.ḥbl.diy[m.bn]. | nšrm.trḫp.'nt.'l[.aqht]. | t'dbn h.hlmn.ṯnm[.qdqd]. | ṯlṯ id.'l.udn.š[pk.km]. | šiy.dm h.km.šḫ 18[3AQHT].4.33
b glṯ. | w tn.ql h.b 'rpt. | šrh.l arṣ.brqm. | bt.arzm.yklln h. | hm.bt.lbnt.y'msn h. | l yrgm.l aliyn b'l. | ṣḥ.ḫrn.b bhm k. 4[51].5.72
m.ym.b'l km. | [adn]km.ṯpṭ.nhr.tn.il m.d tq h.d tqyn h. | [hml]t.tn.b'l.w 'nn h.bn.dgn.art m.pḏ h. | [w y'n.]ṯr.ab h. 2.1[137].34
bt ḫpṯt. | arṣ.tspr.b y | rdm.arṣ. | idk.al.ttn. | pnm.tk.qrt h. | hmry.mk.ksu. | ṯbt h.ḫḫ.arṣ. | nḫlt h.w nǵr. | 'nn.ilm.al. | tq 4[51].8.11
k. | tb'.w l.ytb.ilm.idk. | l ytn.pn.'m.bn.ilm.mt. | tk.qrt h.hmry.mk.ksu. | ṯbt.ḫḫ.arṣ.nḫlt h.tša. | g hm.w tṣḥ.ṯḥm.aliy 5[67].2.15
ṯ.mǵy[.rpum.l grnt]. | i[ln]y[m].l mṭ'ṭ[.---]. | [-]m[.---]. | h.hn bn k.hn[.---]. | bn bn.aṯr k.hn[.---]. | yd k.ṣǵr.tnšq.špt k. 22.2[124].2
]trmm.hkl h. | y[tl]k.l lbnn.w 'ṣ h. | l[šr]yn.mḥmd.arz h. | h[n.l]bnn.w 'ṣ h. | š[r]yn.mḥmd.arz h. | tšt.išt.b bht m. | n 4[51].6.19
rt. | nqmd.mlk.ugrt. | ktb.spr hnd. | dt brrt.ṣṯqšlm. | 'bd h.hnd. | w mn km.l yqḥ. | spr.mlk.hnd. | b yd.ṣṯqšlm. | 'd 'lm. 1005.11
.km[.---.]yd h.k šr. | knr.uṣb't h ḫrṣ.abn. | p h.tiḥd.šnt h.w akl.bqmm. | tšt ḫrṣ.k lb ilnm. | w tn.gprm.mn gpr h.šr. | 19[1AQHT].1.9
y.w.a[ṯt h]. | wšṯn.bn h. | ṯmgdl.ykn'my.w.aṯt h. | w.bn h.w.alp.aḥ[d]. | aǵltn.[--]y.w[.aṯt h]. | w.bn h.w.alp.w.[---]. | [- 1080.6
.ṯn.alpm. | [w.]ṯlṯm.ṣin. | anndr.ykn'my. | w.aṯt h.w.bn h. | w.alp.w.ṯš['.]ṣin. 1080.16
[-]ḏmu.apsty.b[--]. | w.bn h.w aṯt h.w.alp.w ṯmn.ṣin. | [-]dln.qmnzy.w.a[ṯt h]. | wšṯn.bn h. | ṯmg 1080.2
ṯt h. | w.bn h.w.alp.aḥ[d]. | aǵltn.[--]y.w[.aṯt h]. | w.bn h.w.alp.w.[---]. | [-]ln.[---]. | w.ṯn.bn [h.---]. | [--]d m'qby[.---]. 1080.8
[-]ḏmu.apsty.b[--]. | w.bn h.w aṯt h.w.alp.w ṯmn.ṣin. | [-]dln.qmnzy.w.a[ṯt h]. | wšṯn.bn 1080.2
'l.ḥmd m.yḥmd m. | bn.dgn.yhrr m. | b'l.ngṯ hm.b p'n h. | w il hd.b ḫrẓ' h. | [-----]. | [--]t.[---]. | [---.]'n[.---]. | pnm[.---] 12[75].1.40
krt.km hm.tdr. | ap.bnt.ḥry. | km hm.w ṯḫss.aṯrt. | ndr h.w ilt.p[--]. | w tšu.g h.w [tṣḥ]. | ph m'.ap.k[rt.--]. | u ṯn.ndr[. 15[128].3.26
. | w ynḥm.aḫ h. | w.b'ln aḫ h. | w.ḥṯtn bn h. | w.btšy.bt h. | w.ištrmy. | bt.'bd mlk. | w.snt. | bt.ugrt. | w.pdy h[m]. | iwr 1006.7
'm ml[kt]. | tǵsdb.šmlšn. | w tb' ank. | 'm mlakt h šm' h. | w b.'ly skn.yd' rgm h. | w ht ab y ǵm[--]. | t[--.---]. | ls[--.-- 1021.7
.b šlḥ. | ttpl.y'n.ḥtk h. | krt y'n.ḥtk h.rš. | mid.grdš.ṯbt h. | w b tm hn.špḥ.yitbd. | w b.pḫyr h.yrṯ. | y'rb.b ḥdr h.ybky. 14[KRT].1.23
ḫrš.mrkbt. | bnšm.dt.l.mlk. | 'bdyrḫ.bn.ṯyl. | 'bdn.w.aṯt h.w.bn h. | gpn.bn[.a]ly. | bn.rqd[y].ṯbg. | iḫmlk. | yp'n w.aṯt h 2068.19
ln.qmnzy.w.a[ṯt h]. | wšṯn.bn h. | ṯmgdl.ykn'my.w.aṯt h. | w.bn h.w.alp.aḥ[d]. | aǵltn.[--]y.w[.aṯt h]. | w.bn h.w.alp. 1080.5
.bn h.w.ṯn.alpm. | [w.]ṯlṯm.ṣin. | anndr.ykn'my. | w.aṯt h.w.bn h. | w.alp.w.ṯš['.]ṣin. 1080.16
n'my.w.aṯt h. | w.bn h.w.alp.aḥ[d]. | aǵltn.[--]y.w[.aṯt h]. | w.bn h.w.alp.w.[---]. | [-]ln.[---]. | w.ṯn.bn [h.---]. | [--]d m' 1080.7
--]. | w.ṯn.bn [h.---]. | [--]d m'qby[.---]. | swn.qrty.w[.aṯt h]. | [w].bn h.w.ṯn.alpm. | [w.]ṯlṯm.ṣin. | anndr.ykn'my. | w.aṯt 1080.12
h.w.n'r h. | bn.ḫby.w.[a]ṯt h. | ynḥm.ulmy. | [--]q.w.aṯt h.w.bn h. | [--]an.w.aṯt h. | [--]y.w.aṯt h. | [--]r.w.aṯt h. | 'bdyrḫ 2068.6
l ym hnd. | iwr[k]l.pdy. | agdn.bn.nrgn. | w ynḥm.aḫ h. | w.b'ln aḫ h. | w.ḥṯtn bn h. | w.btšy.bt h. | w.ištrmy. | bt.'bd 1006.4
gdn.bn.nrgn. | w ynḥm.aḫ h. | w.b'ln aḫ h. | w.ḥṯtn bn h. | w.btšy.bt h. | w.ištrmy. | bt.'bd mlk. | w.snt. | bt.ugrt. | w.p 1006.6
. | klt h.[---]. | ṯty.ary.m[--.---]. | nrn.arny[.---]. | w.ṯn.bn h.w.b[---.---]. | b tn[--.---]. | swn.qrty[.---]. | uḫ h.w.'šr[.---]. | kl 81[329].6
| gb h.km.[---.]yqṯqṭ.tḥt. | ṯlḥnt.il.d yd'nn. | y'db.lḥm.l h.w d l yd'nn. | d.mṣd. | ylmn.ḥṭ.tḥt.ṯlḥn. | b qr'. | 'ṯtrt.w 'nt.y UG5.1.1.7
l. | [ym.]bn.'nm.ṯpṭ.nhr.yprsḥ.ym.yql. | l arṣ.tngṣn.pnt h.w ydlp.tmn h. | yqṭ b'l.w yšt.ym.ykly.ṯpṭ.nhr. | b šm.tg'r m 2.4[68].26
l.]'ṣr.ṯḥrr.l išt.ṣḥrrt.l pḥmm. | a[ṯ]tm.aṯt.il.aṯt.il.w 'lm h.w hm. | aṯtm.tṣḥn y.ad ad.nḥtm.ḥṭ k. | mmnnm.mṭ yd k.hl 23[52].42
ṯb.l] y. | hl ny.'mn. | mlk.b.ṯy ndr. | iṯt.w.ht. | [-]sny.uḏr h. | w.hm.ḫt. | 'l.w.likt. | 'm k.w.hm. | l.'l.w.lakm. | ilak.w.at. | 1013.15
hl.'ṣr.ṯḥrr.l išt. | w ṣḥrrt.l pḥmm.btm.bt.il.bt.il. | w 'lm h.w hn.aṯtm.tṣḥn y.mt mt. | nḥtm.ḥṭ k.mmnnm.mṭ yd k.hl.' 23[52].46
n. | w tb' ank. | 'm mlakt h šm' h. | w b.'ly skn.yd' rgm h. | w ht ab y ǵm[--]. | t[--.---]. | ls[--.---]. | ṣḥ[.---]. | ky.m[--.---]. 1021.8
rgb.b'l.ṯbr. | b'l.ṯbr.diy.hwt.w yql. | tḥt.p'n h.ybq'.kbd h.w yḥd. | [i]n.šmt.in.'ẓm.yšu.g[h]. | w yṣḥ.knp.hrgb.b'l.ybn. 19[1AQHT].3.130
np.ṣml.b'[l]. | b'l.ṯbr.diy.hyt.tq[l.tḥt]. | p'n h.ybq'.kbd h.w yḥd. | iṯ.šmt.iṯ.'ẓm.w yqḥ b hm. | aqht.ybl.l qz.ybky.w y 19[1AQHT].3.144
.ṣml. | b'l.yṯbr.b'l.yṯbr.diy. | hyt.tql.tḥt.p'n y.ibq'. | kbd h.w aḥd.hm.iṯ.šmt.iṯ. | 'ẓm.abky w aqbrn h.aštn. | b ḫrt.ilm.a 19[1AQHT].3.139
b'l.yṯb.b'l.y[ṯb]r.diy[.h]wt. | w yql.tḥt.p'n y.ibq'.kbd[h]. | w aḥd.hm.iṯ.šmt.hm.iṯ[.'ẓm]. | abky.w aqbrn.ašt.b ḫrt. | i 19[1AQHT].3.124
iwr[k]l.pdy. | agdn.bn.nrgn. | w ynḥm.aḫ h. | w.b'ln aḫ h. | w.ḥṯtn bn h. | w.btšy.bt h. | w.ištrmy. | bt.'bd mlk. | w.snt. | 1006.5
pdr.ttgr. | [---.n]šr k.al ttn.l n. | [---.]tn l rbd. | [---.]b'lt h w yn. | [---.rk]b 'rpt. | [---.--]n.w mnu dg. | [---.]l aliyn b'l. | [2001.2.14
.ḫ[ru.w.l.yṯtn.ššw]. | mss.[št.qlql.w.št]. | 'rgz.[ydk.aḥd h]. | w.yṣq[.b.ap h]. | k.yiḫd[.akl.ššw]. | št.mkš[r.grn]. | w.št.aš 161[56].10
]. | št.mkš[r.grn]. | w.št.ašk[rr]. | w.pr.ḥdr[t.ydk]. | aḥd h.w.yṣq[.b.ap h]. | k.yiḫd.akl.š[šw]. | št.nni.št.mk[št.grn]. | št.i 161[56].16
. | [k l yḫru w]l yṯtn mss št qlql. | [w št 'rgz y]dk aḥd h w yṣq b ap h. | [k.yiḫd akl š]šw št mkšr grn. | [w št aškrr w 160[55].9
k [ḫr ššw mǵmǵ]. | w [bṣql.'rgz.ydk]. | a[ḥd h.w.yṣq.b.ap h]. | k.[ḫr.ššw.ḫndrṯ]. | w.ṯ[qd.mr.ydk.aḥd h]. | 161[56].4

b a[p h]. | [k ẖr š]šw mǵmǵ w b[ṣql ʻrgz]. | [ydk aḥ]d h w yṣq b ap h. | [k ẖr]ššw ẖndrṯ w ṯ[qd m]r. | [ydk aḥd h w 160[55].5
w yṣq b ap h. | [k ẖr]ššw ẖndrṯ w ṯ[qd m]r. | [ydk aḥd h w yṣq b ap h. | [k l yẖru w]l yttn mss št qlql. | [w št ʻrgz y] 160[55].7
.w.yṣq.b.ap h]. | k.[ẖr.ššw.ẖndrṯ]. | w.ṯ[qd.mr.ydk.aḥd h]. | w.y[ṣq.b.ap h]. | k.l.ẖ[ru.w.l.yttn.ššw]. | mss.[št.qlql.w.št] 161[56].6
ni.w.pr.ʻbk]. | w.pr[.ḥdrt.w.št]. | irǵ[n.ḥmr.ydk]. | aḥd[h.w.yṣq.b.ap h]. | k yr[a]š.šš[w.w.ykhp]. | mid.dblt.yṯ[nt.w]. | 161[56].31
l.š[šw]. | št.nni.št.mk[št.grn]. | št.irǵn.ḥmr[.ydk]. | aḥd h.w.yṣq.b[.ap h]. | k.yraš.ššw.[št]. | bln.qṭ.yṣq.b.a[p h]. | k ygʻ 161[56].20
.dblt.yṯ[nt.w]. | ṣmq[m].yṯnm.w[.qmḥ.bql]. | tdkn.aḥd h.w[.yṣq]. | b.ap h. 161[56].35
n.udmʻt h. | km.ṯqlm.arṣ h. | km ẖmšt.mṯt h. | bm.bky h.w yšn. | b dmʻ h.nhmmt. | šnt.tluan. | w yškb.nhmmt. | w yq 14[KRT].1.31
.ʻm. | ẖr[ẖ]b mlk qẓ.tn nkl y | rẖ ytrẖ.ib tʻrb m b bh | t h.w atn mhr h l a | b h.alp ksp w rbt ẖ | rṣ.išlḥ ẓhrm iq | nim. 24[77].19
.b š[-]y. | [---.y]d gt h[.--]. | [---].yd. | [k]rm h.yd. | [k]lkl h. | [w] ytn.nn. | l.bʻln.bn. | kltn.w l. | bn h.ʻd.ʻlm. | šḫr.ʻlmt. | b 1008.10
nhr.mlak.mṯẖr.yḥb[-.---.] | [---].mlak.bn.ktpm.rgm.bʻl h.w y[--.---]. | [---].ap.anš.zbl.bʻl.šdmt.bg[--.---]. | [---.-]dm.ml 2.1[137].42
m. | b qdš il bt. | w tlḥm aṯt. | š l ilbt.šlmm. | kll ylḥm b h. | w l bbt šqym. | š l uẖr ẖlmṭ. | w tr l qlḥ. | ym aḥd. UG5.11.10
ršm. | yšu.ʻwr. | mzl.ymzl. | w ybl.trẖ.ḥdṯ. | ybʻr.l ṯn.aṯt h. | w l nkr.mddt. | km irby.tškn. | šd.k ḥsn.pat. | mdbr.tlkn. | 14[KRT].4.190
ksl.qšt h.mdnt. | w hln.ʻnt.l bt h.tmǵyn. | tštql.ilt.l hkl h. | w l.šbʻt.tmtḫṣ h.b ʻmq. | tḫtṣb.bn.qrtm.ṯṯʻr. | ksat.l mhr.ṯʻr 3[ʻNT].2.18
.alt.l aḥš.idy.alt.in l y. | [--]t.bʻl.ḥẓ.ršp.b[n].km.yr.klyt h.w lb h. | [ṯ]n.p k.b ǵr.ṯn.p k.b ẖlb.k tgwln.šnt k. | [--.]w špt 1001.1.3
m lẓpn i | l ḏ.pid.hn b p y sp | r hn.b špt y mn | t hn ṯlẖ h w mlg h y | ṯtqt ʻm h b qʻt. | tqʻt ʻm prbẖṯ. | dmqt ṣǵrt kṯrt. 24[77].47
.y[mlk]. | [--.]ʻbdyrẖ.l.ml[k]. | [--]t.w.lqḥ. | yn[.--].b dn h. | w.ml[k].ššwm.nʻmm. | ytn.l.ʻbdyrẖ. | w.mlk.z[--.--]n.ššw 2064.15
--]. | [n]it.krk.mʻṣ[d.---]. | b.ẖrbǵlm.ǵlm[n]. | w.trhy.aṯt h. | w.mlky.b[n] h. | ily.mrily.tdgr. 2048.20
spr.ʻrbnm. | dt.ʻrb. | b.mtn.bn.ayaẖ. | b.ẖbṯ h.ḥwt.ṯt h. | w.mnm.šalm. | dt.tknn. | ʻl.ʻrbnm. | hn hmt. | tknn. | mtn.b 1161.4
.---.]ḥ[--]. | b bt.[-.]l bnt.q[-]. | w št.b bt.ṯap[.--]. | hy.yd h.w ym[ǵ]. | mlak k.ʻm dt[n]. | lqḥ.mṭpṭ. | w yʻny.nn. | dtn.bt UG5.6.10
.l šbʻm.aẖ h.ym[.--]. | w ṯmnt.l ṯmnym. | šr.aẖy h.mẓa h. | w mẓa h.šr.yly h. | b skn.sknm.b ʻdn. | ʻdnm.kn.npl.bʻl. | k 12[75].2.51
l[-]. | bn.brzn. | bn.ẖṯr[-]. | bn.yd[--]. | bn.ʻ[---]. | w.nḥ[l h]. | w.nḥ[l h]. | bn.k[---]. | bn.y[---]. | [bn].i[---]. 116[303].10
ṯnnm. | bn.qqln. | w.nḥl h. | w.nḥl h. | bn.šml[-]. | bn.brzn. | bn.ẖṯr[-]. | bn.yd[--]. | bn.ʻ[- 116[303].3
.[-]dr[-]. | [---]l[-]. | [--]ym. | [--]rm. | [bn.]aǵld. | [w.nḥ]l h. | [w.nḥ]l h[.-]. 114[324].3.5
tn. | bn.šlgyn. | bn.[-]gštn. | bn[.n]klb. | b[n.]dtn. | w.nḥl h. | w.nḥl hm. | bn.iršyn. | bn.ʻzn. | bn.aršw. | bn.ẖzrn. | bn.iǵyn 113[400].2.10
]. | bn.bly. | nrn. | w.nḥl h. | bn.rmyy. | bn.tlmyn. | w.nḥl h. | w.nḥl hm. | bn.ḥrm. | bn.brzn. | w.nḥl h. | bn.adlḏn. | bn.šbl 113[400].1.7
. | bn.mmy. | bn.ẖnyn. | bn.knn. | khnm. | bn.ṯʻy. | w.nḥl h. | w.nḥl hm. | bn.nqly. | bn.snrn. | bn.ṯgd. | bn.d[-]n. | bn.amd 105[86].1
bn.[---]. | bn.[---]. | bn.yk[--]. | bn.šmm. | bn.irgy. | w.nḥl h. | w.nḥl hm. | [bn].pmn. | bn.gṯrn. | bn.arpẖn. | bn.ṯryn. | bn.d 1046.2.11
| bn.iǵyn. | w.nḥl h. | bn.ksd. | bn.bršm. | bn.kzn. | w.nḥl h. | w.nḥl hm. | w.[n]ḥl hm. | b[n.---]. | bn.gzry. | bn.atyn. | bn.t 113[400].2.21
bnšm.dt.l.u[--]ṯṯb. | kṯ[r]n. | w.aṯt h.w.nʻr h. | bn.ẖby.w.[a]ṯt h. | ynḥm.ulmy. | [--]q.w.aṯt h.w.b 2068.3
.ttn. | pnm.tk.qrt h. | hmry.mk.ksu. | ṯbt h.ẖẖ.arṣ. | nḫlt h.w nǵr. | ʻnn.ilm.al. | tqrb.l bn.ilm. | mt.al.yʻdb km. | k imr.b 4[51].8.14
.w ṯtb. | mlakm.l h.lm.ank. | ksp.w yrq.ẖrṣ. | yd.mqm h.w ʻbd. | ʻlm.ṯlṯ.sswm.mrkbt. | b trbṣt.bn.amt. | p d.in.b bt y. 14[KRT].3.139
| w yʻn[y.k]rt[.ṯ]ʻ. | lm.ank.ksp. | w yr[q.ẖrṣ]. | yd.mqm h.w ʻbd. | ʻlm.ṯlṯ.sswm. | mrkbt.b trbṣ. | bn.amt.p d.[i]n. | b bt 14[KRT].6.284
t. | mswn h.tḥm.pbl.mlk. | qḥ.ksp.w yrq.ẖrṣ. | yd.mqm h.w ʻbd.ʻlm. | ṯlṯ.sswm.mrkbt. | b trbṣ.bn.amt. | qḥ.krt.šlmm. 14[KRT].3.127
tṣḥn]. | tḥ[m.pbl.mlk]. | qḥ[.ksp.w yrq]. | ẖrṣ.[yd.mqm h]. | w ʻbd[.ʻlm.ṯlṯ]. | sswm.m[rkbt]. | b trbṣ.[bn.amt]. | q[ḥ.kr] 14[KRT].6.270
-]. | [-----]. | [-----.lm]. | [ank.ksp.w yrq]. | [ẖrṣ.]yd.mqm h. | [w ʻb]d.ʻlm.ṯlṯ. | [ssw]m.mrkbt b trbṣ bn.amt. | [tn.b]nm.a 14[KRT].2.54
rṣ.ib y. | w b ʻpr.qm.aẖ k. | w tšu.ʻn h.btlt.ʻnt. | w tšu.ʻn h.w tʻn. | w tʻn.arẖ.w tr.b lkt. | tr.b lkt.w tr.b ẖl. | [b]nʻmm.b 10[76].2.27
k.aẖ šmk.mlat rumm. | w yšu.ʻn h.aliyn.bʻl. | w yšu.ʻn h.w yʻn. | w yʻn.btlt.ʻnt. | nʻmt.bn.aẖt.bʻl. | l pnn h.ydd.w yq 10[76].2.14
m.t[---]. | tlbš.npṣ.ǵzr.tšt.ẖ[---.b] | nšg h.ḥrb.tšt.b tʻr[t h]. | w ʻl.tlbš.npṣ.aṯt.[--]. | ṣbi nrt.ilm.špš.[-]r[--]. | pǵt.minš.šd 19[1AQHT].4.207
n y[.t]q | ḥ.pǵt.w tšqyn h.tq[ḥ.ks.]b d h. | qbʻt.b ymn h.w yʻn.yṭ[p]n[.mh]r. | št.b yn.yšt.ila.il š[--.]il. | d yqny.ḏdm. 19[1AQHT].4.218
| ik.al.yḥdṯ.yrẖ.b[---]. | b qrn.ymn h.b anšt[.---]. | qdqd h.w yʻn.yṭpn.[mhr.št]. | šmʻ.l btlt.ʻnt.at.ʻ[l.qšt h]. | tmḫṣ h.qṣʻ 18[3AQHT].4.11
šbʻ.rgm.[my.]b ilm. | ydy.mrṣ.gršm zbln. | in.b ilm.ʻny h. | w yʻn.lṭpn.il.b pid. | ṯb.bn y.lm ṯb[t] km. | l kḥṯ.zbl k[m.a] 16[126].5.22
kḥṯ.aliyn. | bʻl.pʻn h.l tmǵyn. | hdm.riš h.l ymǵy. | aps h.w yʻn.ʻṯtr.ʻrẓ. | l amlk.b ṣrrt.ṣpn. | yrd.ʻṯtr.ʻrẓ.yrd. | l kḥṯ.ali 6.1.61[49.1.33]
[---.bʻl.b bht h]. | [il.hd.b qr]b.hkl h. | w tʻnyn.ǵlm.bʻl. | in.bʻl.b bht ht. | il hd.b qrb.hkl h. | qšt h 10[76].2.2
tq h.d tqyn h. | [hml]t.tn.bʻl.w ʻnn h.bn.dgn.art m.pḏ h. | [w yʻn.]ṯr.ab h.il.ʻbd k.bʻl.y ym m.ʻbd k.bʻl. | [--.--]m.bn.d 2.1[137].35
n.ẖṯ.tḥt.ṯlḥn. | b qrʻ. | ʻṯtrt.w ʻnt.ymǵy. | ʻṯtrt.tʻdb.nšb l h. | w ʻnt.ktp.b hm.ygʻr.ṯǵr. | bt.il.pn.l mgr lb.tʻdbn. | nšb.l inr UG5.1.1.10
w.ṯn.bn h.w.b[---.---]. | b tn[--.---]. | swn.qrty[.---]. | uẖ h.w.ʻšr[.---]. | klyn.apsn[y.---]. | plzn.qrty[.---]. | w.klt h.b.t[--. 81[329].9
d.b yd. | [g]rgr h.bm.ymn. | [w]yqrb.trẓẓ h. | [---].mǵy h.w ǵlm. | [a]ẖt h.šib.yṣat.mrḥ h. | l tl.yṣb.pn h.ṯǵr. | yṣu.hlm. 16.1[125].50
.qrb m.asm. | b p h.rgm.l yṣa.b špt h[.hwt h]. | b nši ʻn h.w tphn.in.[---]. | [-.]hlk.ǵlmm b dd y.yṣ[--]. | [-.]yṣa.w l.yṣa. 19[1AQHT].2.76
. | adrm.d b grn.ydn. | dn.almnt.yṯpṭ.ṯpṭ.ytm. | b nši ʻn h.w yphn.b alp. | šd.rbt.kmn.hlk.kṯr. | k yʻn.w yʻn.tdrq.ẖss. | 17[2AQHT].5.9
.l ẓr.pḥmm. | tʻpp.ṯr.il.d pid. | tǵẓy.bny.bnwt. | b nši.ʻn h.w tphn. | hlk.bʻl.aṯtrt. | k tʻn.hlk.btlt. | ʻnt.tdrq.ybmt. | [lim 4[51].2.12
b nši[.ʻn h.w yphn.yḥd]. | b ʻrpt[.nšrm.yšu]. | [g h.]w yṣḥ[.knp.nšrm]. 19[1AQHT].2.105
p.nšrm.ybn. | bʻl.ybn.diy hmt nšrm. | tpr.w du.b nši.ʻn h.w ypn. | yḥd.hrgb.ab.nšrm. | yšu.g h.w yṣḥ.knp.hr[g]b. | bʻl. 19[1AQHT].3.120
b.bʻl.ybn. | [b]ʻl.ybn.diy.hwt.hrg[b]. | tpr.w du.b nši.ʻn h. | [w]yphn.yḥd.ṣml.um.nšrm. | yšu.g h.w yṣḥ.knp.ṣml. | bʻl. 19[1AQHT].3.134
ṭ. | [ṭpṭ.ytm.---] h. | [---.---]n. | [-----]. | hlk.[---.b n]ši. | ʻn h.w tphn.[---]. | b grn.yḥrb[.---]. | yǵly.yḥsp.ib[.---]. | ʻl.bt.ab h 19[1AQHT].1.29
| [---].yn.ʻšy l ḥbš. | [---.]ḥtn.qn.yṣbt. | [---.--]m.b nši.ʻn h.w tphn. | [---.--]ml.ksl h.k b[r]q. | [---.]m[-]ǵ[-].thmt.brq. | [- 17[2AQHT].6.10
.[bt.---]. | ṯt.aṯtm.w.pǵt.w.ǵzr.aḥd.b.[bt.---]. | aṯt.w.bn h.w.pǵt.aḫt.b.bt.m[--]. | aṯt.w.ṯt.bt h.b.bt.ẖḏmrd. | aṯt.w.ṯn.ǵ 80[119].21
. | [s]pu y.bn m.um y.kly y. | ytb.ʻm.bʻl.ṣrrt. | ṣpn.yšu g h.w yṣḥ. | aẖ y m.ytnt.bʻl. | spu y.bn m.um y.kl | y y.ytʻn.k g 6[49].6.13
t]. | aṯr.bʻl.tiẖd.m[t]. | b sin.lpš.tšṣq[n h]. | b qṣ.all.tšu.g h.w[tṣ] | ḥ.at.mt.tn.aẖ y. | w ʻn.bn.ilm.mt.mh. | taršn.l btlt.ʻn 6[49].2.11
br.ʻln.p]n h.td[ʻ]. | tǵṣ[.pnt.ks]l h. | anš.dt.ẓr.[h]. | tšu.g h.w tṣḥ[.i]k. | mǵy.aliy[n.b]ʻl. | ik.mǵyt.b[t]lt. | ʻnt.mḫṣ y hm[. 4[51].2.21
ksl.ṯṯbr. | ʻln.pn h.tdʻ.tǵṣ.pnt. | ksl h.anš.dt.ẓr h.tšu. | g h.w tṣḥ.ik.mǵy.gpn.w ugr. | mn.ib.ypʻ.l bʻl.ṣrt. | l rkb.ʻrpt.l m 3[ʻNT].3.33
lṣb.w yṣḥq. | pʻn h.l hdm.ytpd.w ykrkr. | uṣbʻt h.yšu.g h.w y[ṣḥ]. | ik.mǵyt.rbt.aṯr[t.y]m. | ik.atwt.qnyt.i[lm]. | rǵb.rǵ 4[51].4.30
bn.ilm.mt.ʻbd k.an. | w d ʻlm k.šmẖ.bn.ilm.mt. | [---.]g h.w aṣḥ.ik.yṣḥn. | [bʻl.ʻm.aẖ y.ik].yqrun.hd. | [ʻm.ary y.---.--] 5[67].2.21
. | yṯlṯ.qn.ḏrʻ h.yḥrṯ. | k gn.ap lb.k ʻmq.yṯlṯ. | bmt.yšu.g h.w yṣḥ. | bʻl.mt.my.lim.bn. | dgn.my.hmlt.aṯr. | bʻl.ard.b arṣ. 5[67].6.22

.b‘l.mrym.ṣpn. | b alp.šd.rbt.kmn. | ṣḥq.btlt.‘nt.tšu. | g h.w tṣḥ.tbšr b‘l. | bšrt k.yblt.y[b]n. | bt.l k.km.aḫ k.w ḥẓr. | k 4[51].5.88

.aqht.ǵzr. | [---.kdd.dn]il.mt.rpi.w t‘n. | [btlt.‘nt.tšu.g]h.w tṣḥ.hwt. | [---.]aqht.yd̲[--]. | [---.--]n.ṣ[---]. | [spr.ilmlk.šbn 17[2AQHT].6.53

.b‘l. | l pnn h.ydd.w yqm. | l p‘n h.ykr‘.w yql. | w yšu.g h.w yṣḥ. | ḥwt.aḫt.w nar[-]. | qrn.d bat k.btlt.‘nt. | qrn.d bat k 10[76].2.19

r[.dr]. | ‘db.uḫry mṭ.yd h. | ymǵ.l mrrt.tǵll.b nr. | yšu.g h.w yṣḥ.y l k.mrrt. | tǵll.b nr.d ‘l k.mḫṣ.aqht. | ǵzr.šrš k.b arṣ 19[1AQHT].3.157

y mṭ yd h. | ymǵ.l qrt.ablm.abl[m]. | qrt.zbl.yrḫ.yšu g h. | w yṣḥ.y l k.qrt.ablm. | d ‘l k.mḫṣ.aqht.ǵzr. | ‘wrt.yšt k.b‘l. 19[1AQHT].4.164

‘l yṣhl pi[t]. | yprq.lṣb.w yṣḥq. | p‘n.l hdm.yṯpd.yšu. | g h.w yṣḥ.aṯbn.ank. | w anḫn.w tnḫ.b irt y. | npš.k yld.bn.l y.k 17[2AQHT].2.12

il.d pid. | p‘n h.l hdm.yṯpd. | w yprq.lṣb w yṣḥq. | yšu.g h.w yṣḥ. | aṯbn.ank.w anḫn. | w tnḫ.b irt y.npš. | k ḥy.aliyn.b‘ 6[49].3.17

. | [tt]b‘.btlt.‘nt[.idk.l ttn.pnm]. | ‘m.yṯpn.mhr.š[t.tšu.g h]. | w tṣḥ.ytb.ytp.[---]. | qrt.ablm.ablm.[qrt.zbl.yrḫ]. | ik.al.y 18[3AQHT].4.6

l. | tḥt.p‘n h.ybq‘.kbd h.w yḥd. | [i]n.šmt.in.‘ẓm.yšu.g[h]. | w yṣḥ.knp.hrgb.b‘l.ybn. | [b]‘l.ybn.diy.hwt.hrg[b]. | tpr.w 19[1AQHT].3.131

tpr.w du.b nši.‘n h.w ypn. | yḥd.hrgb.ab.nšrm. | yšu.g h.w yṣḥ.knp.hr[g]b. | b‘l.yṯb.b‘l.y[ṯb]r.diy[.h]wt. | w yql.tḥt.p 19[1AQHT].3.122

tḥt.p‘n h.ybq‘.kbdt hm.w[yḥd]. | in.šmt.in.‘ẓm.yšu.g h. | w yṣḥ.knp.nšrm.ybn. | b‘l.ybn.diy hmt nšrm. | tpr.w du.b 19[1AQHT].3.117

l qẓ.ybky.w yqbr. | yqbr.nn.b mdgt.b knk[-]. | w yšu.g h.w yṣḥ.knp.nšrm. | b‘l.yṯbr.b‘l.yṯbr.diy. | hmt.hm.t‘pn.‘l.qbr 19[1AQHT].3.148

b nši[.‘n h.w yphn.yḥd]. | b ‘rpt[.nšrm.yšu]. | [g h.]w yṣḥ[.knp.nšrm]. | b‘l.yṯb.b‘l.yṯb[r.diy.hmt]. | tqln.tḥ p‘n 19[1AQHT].3.107

r.w du.b nši.‘n h. | [w]yphn.yḥd.ṣml.um.nšrm. | yšu.g h.w yṣḥ.knp.ṣml. | b‘l.yṯbr.b‘l.yṯbr.diy. | hyt.tql.tḥt.p‘n y.ibq‘ 19[1AQHT].3.136

ḫ.b dqt.‘rpt. | ‘l h[wt].kṯr.w ḫss. | ṣḥq.kṯr.w ḫss. | yšu.g h.w yṣḥ. | l rgmt.l k.l ali | yn.b‘l.ṯtbn.b‘l. | l hwt y.ypṯḥ.ḥ | ln.b 4[51].7.22

[.---]. | tšqy[.---]. | tr.ḥt[-.---]. | w msk.tr[.---]. | tqrb.aḫ[h.w tṣḥ]. | lm.tb‘rn[.---]. | mn.yrḫ.k m[rṣ.---]. | mn.k dw.kr[t]. 16.2[125].79

.[m]k.b šb‘. | šnt.w [--].bn.ilm.mt. | ‘m.aliyn.b‘l.yšu. | g h.w yṣḥ.‘l k.b[‘]l m. | pht.qlt.‘l k.pht. | dry.b ḥrb.‘l k. | pht.šrp 6[49].5.11

nt.ḥry. | km hm.w tḫss.aṯrt. | ndr h.w ilt.p[--]. | w tšu.g h.w [tṣḥ]. | ph m‘.ap.k[rt.--]. | u ṯn.ndr[.---]. | apr.[---]. | [-----]. 15[128].3.27

.ab.šnm.l p‘n. | il.thbr.w tql. | tštḥwy.w tkbdn h. | tšu.g h.w tṣḥ.tšmḫ ht. | aṯrt.w bn h.ilt.w ṣb | rt.ary h.k mt.aliyn. | b 6.1.39[49.1.11]

h.l trm. | mt.dm.ḫt.š‘tqt. | dm.lan.w ypqd. | krt.ṯ‘.yšu.g h. | w yṣḥ.šm‘.l mṯt. | ḥry.ṭbḫ.imr. | w ilḥm.mgṯ.w iṯrm. | tšm‘. 16.6[127].15

qht.ǵzr.b alp.š[d]. | [rbt.]kmn.w ṣḥq.btlt.[‘nt]. | [tšu.]g h.w tṣḥ.šm‘.m[‘.l a] | [qht.ǵ]zr.at.aḫ.w an.a[ḫt k]. | [---].šb‘.ṯi 18[3AQHT].1.23

.km.btn.yqr. | [krpn h.-.l]arṣ.ks h.tšpk m. | [l ‘pr.tšu.g h.]w tṣḥ.šm‘.m‘. | [l aqht.ǵzr.i]rš.ksp.w atn k. | [ḫrṣ.w aš]lḥ k 17[2AQHT].6.16

mlk. | l drkt.k aṯb.an. | ytb‘.yṣb ǵlm.‘l. | ab h.y‘rb.yšu g h. | w yṣḥ.šm‘ m‘.l krt. | ṯ‘.ištm‘.w tqǵ udn. | k ǵz.ǵzm.tdbr. | 16.6[127].40

.u[---]k.yrd[.--.]i[---]n.bn. | [---.-]nn.nrt.ilm.špš.tšu.g h.w t[ṣḥ.šm]‘.m‘. | [-.yṯ]ir tr.il.ab k.l pn.zbl.ym.l pn[.ṯ]pṭ[.n] 2.3[129].15

‘. | šnt.w y‘n[.dnil.mt.]rpi. | ytb.ǵzr.m[t.hrnmy.y]šu. | g h.w yṣḥ.t[b‘.---]. | bkyt.b hk[l]y.mšspdt. | b ḥẓr y pẓǵm.ǵr.w 19[1AQHT].4.182

.l p‘]n.‘nt. | [yhbr.w yql.yšt]ḥwyn.w y | [kbdn h.yšu.g h.w y]ṣḥ.tḥm. | [tr.il.ab k.hwt.l]ṭpn.ḥtk k. | [qryy.b arṣ.mlḥ] 1[‘NT.IX].2.17

rṣ. | ttb‘.btlt.‘nt. | idk.l ttn.pnm. | ‘m.nrt.ilm.špš. | tšu.g h.w tṣḥ. | tḥm.ṯr.il.ab k. | hwt.lṭpn.ḥtk k. | pl.‘nt.šdm.y špš. | p 6[49].4.33

td‘.b ‘dn]. | ksl.y[ṯbr.yǵṣ.pnt.ksl h]. | anš.[dt.ẓr h.yšu.g h]. | w yṣ[ḥ.---]. | mḫṣ[.---]. | š[--.---]. 19[1AQHT].2.96

u.aliyn.b‘l.l ktp. | ‘nt.k tšt h.tš‘lyn h. | b ṣrrt.ṣpn.tbkyn h. | w tqbrn h.tštnn.b ḫrt. | ilm.arṣ.tṭbḫ.šb‘m. | rumm.k gmn. 6[62].1.16

‘l. | in.b‘l.b bht ht. | il hd.b qrb.hkl h. | qšt hn.aḫd.b yd h. | w qṣ‘t h.bm.ymn h. | idk.l ytn pnm. | tk.aḫ.šmk.mla[t.r]u 10[76].2.6

tity.ilm.l ahl hm. | dr il.l mšknt hm. | w tqrb.w ld.bn.l h. | w tqrb.w ld.bnt.l h. | mk.b šb‘.šnt. | bn.krt.km hm.tdr. | ap 15[128].3.20

.--]. | arb‘.‘š[r.]dd.n‘r. | d.apy[.--]. | w.arb[‘.--]d.apy.‘bd h. | w.mrb‘[t.l ‘]bdm. 2094.5

[.---]. | w.ṯlṯ.alp h.[---]. | swn.qrty.w.[b]n h[.---]. | w.alp h.w.a[r]b‘.l.arb‘[m.---]. | pln.tmry.w.ṯn.bn h.w[.---]. | ymrn.a 2044.7

q.aṯt.l pnn h. | št.alp.qdm h.mria.w tk. | pn h.tḥspn.m h.w trḥṣ. | ṭl.šmm.šmn.arṣ.ṭl.šm[m.t]sk h. | rbb.nsk h.kbkbm 3[‘NT].4.86

t.l ksat.ṯlḥnt. | [l]ṯlḥn.hdmm.tt‘r.l hdmm. | [t]ḥspn.m h.w trḥṣ. | [ṭ]l.šmm.šmn.arṣ.rbb. | [r]kb ‘rpt.ṭl.šmm.tsk h. | [r 3[‘NT].2.38

.‘rpt]. | ṯḥbq.[---]. | ṯḥbq[.---]. | w tksynn.btn[-.] | y[--.]šr h.w šḫp h. | [--.]šḫp.ṣǵrt h. | yrk.t‘l.b ǵr. | mslmt.b ǵr.tliyt. | w 10[76].3.26

snm.ysyn h.‘dtm.y‘dyn h.yb | ltm.ybln h.mǵy.ḥrn.l bt h.w. | yštql.l ḥṭr h.tlu ḥt.km.nḫl. | tplg.km.plg. | b‘d h.bhtm. UG5.7.67

n.bn.l h. | km.aḫ h.w šrš.km.ary h. | bl.iṯ.bn.l h.km aḫ h.w šrš. | km.ary h.uzrm.ilm.ylḥm. | uzrm.yšqy.bn.qdš. | l tbr 17[2AQHT].1.21

d]nil.mt.rpi anḫ.ǵzr. | [mt.]hrnmy.d in.bn.l h. | km.aḫ h.w šrš.km.ary h. | bl.iṯ.bn.l h.km aḫ h.w šrš. | km.ary h.uzr 17[2AQHT].1.20

u.mh. | pdrm.tdu.šrr. | ḥṭ m.t‘mt.[‘]ṭr.[k]m. | zbln.‘l.riš h. | w ttb.trḥṣ.nn.b d‘t. | npš h.l lḥm.tptḥ. | brlt h.l trm. | mt.d 16.6[127].9

n. | w šnm.w ngšnn.ḥby. | b‘l.qrnm w d̲nb.ylšn. | b ḫri h.w ṯnt h.ql.il.[--]. | il.k yrdm.arṣ.‘nt. | w ‘ṯtrt.tṣdn.[---]. | [---.- UG5.1.1.21

[h.---]. | [--]d m‘qby[.---]. | swn.qrty.w[.aṯt h]. | [w].bn h.w.ṯn.alpm. | [w.]ṯlṯm.ṣin. | anndr.ykn‘my. | w.aṯt h.w.bn h. 1080.13

tt.w.ṯlṯ.ktnt.b dm.tt. | w.ṯmnt.ksp.hn. | ktn.d.ṣr.pḥm.b h.w.ṯqlm. | ksp h.mitm.pḥm.b d.skn. | w.tt.ktnm.ḫmšt.w.nṣp 1110.4

.---]. | w.alp h.w.a[r]b‘.l.arb‘[m.---]. | pln.tmry.w.ṯn.bn h.w[.---]. | ymrn.apsny.w.aṯt h..b[n.---]. | prd.m‘qby[.w.---.a]ṯ 2044.8

-.]at.bt k[.---]. | [---.]ank[.---]. | [---.-]hn.[---]. | [---.--]pp h.w[.---]. | [---.]l k[.---]. | [-----]. | [-----]. | [-----]. | [---].al.tš[--.--- 1002.7

.ab h.il. | mlk.d yknn h.yṣḥ.aṯrt. | w bn h.ilt.w ṣbrt.arḫ h. | wn.in.bt.l b‘l.km.ilm. | ḥẓr.k b[n.a]ṯrt.mṯb.il. | mṯll.b[n h. 3[‘NT.VI].5.45

l.mlk. | [d yknn h.yṣ]ḥ.aṯ | [rt.w bn h.]ilt. | [w ṣbrt.ary]h. | [wn.in.bt.l b‘l.] | [km.ilm.w ḥẓr]. | [k bn.aṯ]r[t]. | m[ṯ]b.il. 4[51].1.9

h. | [i]l.mlk.d yknn h.yṣḥ. | aṯrt.w bn h.ilt.w ṣbrt. | ary h.wn.in.bt.l b‘l. | km.ilm.w ḥẓr.k bn.aṯrt. | mṯb il.mẓll.bn h. | 4[51].4.50

k] | ṯrt.l bnt.hll[.snnt]. | hl ǵlmt tld b[n.--]n. | ‘n ha l yd h.tzd[.--]. | pt l bšr h.dm a[--.--]ḥ. | w yn.k mtrḫt[.---]h. | šm‘ 24[77].8

. | w yn.k mtrḫt[.---]h. | šm‘ ilht kṯr[t.--]mm. | nh l yd h tzdn[.---]n. | l ad[n h.---]. | dgn tt[--.---.-]l | ‘.l kṯrt hl[l.sn]nt. 24[77].12

d.pḫl. | št.gpnm.dt.ksp. | dt.yrq.nqbnm. | ‘db.gpn.atnt h. | yḥbq.qdš.w amrr. | yštn.aṯrt.l bmt.‘r. | l ysmsmt.bmt.pḫl. 4[51].4.12

spr.‘rbnm. | dt.‘rb. | b.mtn.bn.ayaḫ. | b.ḫbṭ h.ḥwt.tt h. | w.mnm.šalm. | dt.tknn. | ‘l.‘rbnm. | hn hmt. | tknn 1161.4

kli. | plǵn. | apšny. | ‘rb[.---]. | w.b.p[.--]. | apš[ny]. | b.yṣi h. | ḥwt.[---]. | alp.k[sp]. | tš‘n. | w.hm.al[-]. | l.tš‘n. | mṣrm. | tm 2116.9

mrr. | idk.al.tnn. | pnm.tk.ḥqkpt. | il.kl h.kptr. | ksu.ṯbt h.ḥkpt. | arṣ.nḥlt h. | b alp.šd.rbt. | kmn.l p‘n.kṯ. | hbr.w ql.tšt 3[‘NT.VI].6.15

[idk.al.ttn.pnm.tk.ḥkpt.il.kl h]. | [kptr.]ks[u.ṯbt h.ḥkpt.arṣ.nḥlt h]. | b alp.šd.r[bt.kmn.l p‘n.kṯr]. | hbr.w ql.t[1[‘NT.IX].3.1

[---].hw.mḫ.l ‘rš h.y‘l. | [---].bm.nšq.aṯt h. | [---.]b ḥbq h.ḥmḥmt. | [---.--] n.ylt.ḥmḥmt. | [---.mt.r]pi.w ykn.bn h. | [b 17[2AQHT].1.41

ṯr.w.p nḥš. | [---.--]q.n[ṯ]k.l yd‘.l bn.l pq ḥmt. | [---.--]n h.ḥmt.w t‘btn h.abd y. | [---.ǵ]r.šrǵzz.ybky.km.n‘r. | [w ydm‘ UG5.8.36

.an.arnn.ql.špš.ḥw.btnm.uḫd.b‘lm. | [--.a]ṯm.prṯl.l riš h.ḥmṯ.ṯmṯ. | [--.]ydbr.ṯrmt.al m.qḥn y.š y.qḥn y. | [--.]šir.b kr 1001.1.7

nt.ab h.šrḥq.aṯt.l pnn h. | št.alp.qdm h.mria.w tk. | pn h.tḥspn.m h.w trḥṣ. | ṭl.šmm.šmn.arṣ.ṭl.šm[m.t]sk h. | rbb.ns 3[‘NT].4.86

]llm.trtḥṣ. | btlt.‘n[t].tptr‘ ṭd[h]. | limm.w t‘l.‘m.il. | ab h.ḥpr.p‘l k.y[--]. | šm‘ k.l arḫ.w bn.[--]. | limm.ql.b udn.k w[- 13[6].21

alp šd.ẓu h.b ym.t[---]. | tlbš.npṣ.ǵzr.tšt.ḫ[---.b] | nšg h.ḥrb.tšt.b t‘r[t h]. | w ‘l.tlbš.npṣ.aṯt.[--]. | ṣbi nrt.ilm.špš.[-]r[19[1AQHT].4.207

w rbt ḫ | rṣ.išlḥ ẓhrm iq | nim.atn šd h krm[m]. | šd dd h ḥrnqm.w | y‘n ḫrḫb mlk qẓ [l]. | n‘mn.ilm l ḥt[n]. | m.b‘l tr 24[77].23

.[‘]nt. | ṯṭb.[---.--]ša. | tlm.km[.---.]yd h.k šr. | knr.uṣb‘t h ḫrṣ.abn. | p h.tiḥd.šnt h.w akl.bqmm. | tšt ḫrṣ.k lb ilnm. | w 19[1AQHT].1.8

b abn.|ydy.psltm.b y‘r.|yhdy.lḥm.w dqn.|yṯlṯ.qn.ḏr‘ h.yḥrṯ.|k gn.ap lb.k ‘mq.yṯlṯ.|bmt.yšu.g h.w yṣḥ.|b‘l.mt.m 5[67].6.20
b ab.td[.ps]ltm[.b y‘r].|thdy.lḥm.w dqn[.tṯlṯ].|qn.ḏr‘ h.tḥrṯ.km.gn.|ap lb.k ‘mq.tṯlṯ.bmt.|b‘l.mt.my.lim.bn dgn.| 6[62].1.4
[---.]ktb nǵr krm.|[---].ab h.krm ar.|[---.]h.mḥtrt.pṯtm.|[---.-]t h.ušpǵt tišr.|[---.šm]m h.nšat ẓl h kb 2001.2.3
dm.arṣ.|idk.al.ttn.|pnm.tk.qrt h.|hmry.mk.ksu.|ṯbt h.ẖẖ.arṣ.|nḥlt h.w nǵr.|‘nn.ilm.al.|tqrb.l bn.ilm.|mt.al.y‘d 4[51].8.13
.šlm.mlkt.‘rbm m.ṯnnm.|mt.w šr.yṯb.b d h.ẖṭ.ṯkl.b d h.|ẖṭ.ulmn.yzbrnn.zbrm.gpn.|yṣmdnn.ṣmdm.gpn.yšql.šdm 23[52].8
ay.|šlm.mlk.šlm.mlkt.‘rbm m.ṯnnm.|mt.w šr.yṯb.b d h.ẖṭ.ṯkl.b d h.|ẖṭ.ulmn.yzbrnn.zbrm.gpn.|yṣmdnn.ṣmdm.g 23[52].8
[h].|s̀sw[.--].w.r[‘ h].|kr[mn.--.]w.r[‘ h].|šd.[--.w.]r[‘ h].|ẖla[n.---].|w lšṯr[.---]. 2083.2.5
lwš.w.r‘ h.|kdrš.w.r‘ h.|ṯrm[-].w[.r‘ h].|[‘]ṯtr[-].w.[r‘ h].|ẖlly[-].w.r‘[h].|ilmškl.w.r‘[h].|s̀sw[.--].w.r[‘ h].|kr[mn 2083.1.7
.khn[m.---.]k p‘n.|[---.--]y.yd.nšy.[---.--]š.l mdb.|[---] h.mẖlpt[.---.--]r.|[---.]n‘lm.[---].|[---].hn.al[-.---].|[---]t.bn[.- UG5.8.49
‘[šr]m.|‘šdyn.ẖmš[t].|abršn.‘šr[t].|b‘ln.ẖmšt.|w.nḥl h.ẖm[š]t.|bn.unp.arb‘t.|‘bdbn.ytrš ẖmšt.|krwn.‘šrt.|bn.ulb 1062.9
b‘m.ksp.|b d[.‘b]dym.ṯlṯ.kkr š‘rt.|iqn[i]m.ṯṯt.‘šrt.ksp h.|ẖmšt.ẖrṣ.bt.il.|b.ẖmšt.‘šrt.ksp.|ẖmš.mat.šmt.|b.‘šrt.ksp 2100.4
it.adrm.b.‘šrt.|‘šr.ydt.b.‘šrt.|ẖmš.kkrm.ṣml.|‘šrt.ksp h.|ẖmš.kkr.qnm.|ṯlṯt.w.ṯlṯt.ksp h.|arb‘.kkr.|algbṯ.arb‘t.|k 1127.11
sp h.|arb‘.kkr.|algbṯ.arb‘t.|ksp h.|kkr.š‘rt.|šb‘t.ksp h.|ẖmš.mqdm.dnyn.|b.ṯql.dprn.aḥd.|b.ṯql.|ẖmšm.‘rgz.b.ẖ 1127.18
[---.ṯ]lṯ.‘š[r h.---].|d bnšm.yd.grbs hm.|w.ṯn.‘šr h.ẖpnt.|[s̀]s̀wm.amtm.‘kyt.|yd.llẖ hm.|w.ṯlṯ.l.‘šrm.|ẖpnt.s̀ 2049.3
it.mit.krk.mit.|m‘ṣd.ẖmšm.mqb.[‘]šrm.|b.ulm.ṯṯ.‘šr h.ẖrmṯt.|ṯt.nitm.ṯn.m‘ṣdm.ṯn.mqbm.|krk.aḥt.|b.sǵy.ẖmš.ẖ 2048.4
.ḥry.bt y.|iqḥ.aš‘rb.ǵlmt.|ḥẓr y.ṯn h.wspm.|atn.w ṯlṯ h.ẖrṣm.|ylk ym.w ṯn.|ṯlṯ.rb‘.ym.|aẖr.špšm.b rb‘.|ymǵy.l u 14[KRT].4.206
.---].|w b hm.tṯṯb[.--]d h.|km trpa.hn n‘r.|d yšt.l.lṣb h ẖš‘r klb.|[w]riš.pqq.w šr h.|yšt.aḥd h.dm zt.ẖrpnt. UG5.1.2.4
bn.ilm.|mt.al.y‘db km.|k imr.b p h.|k lli.b ṯbrn.|qn h.ṯẖtan.|nrt.ilm.špš.|ṣḥrrt.la.|šmm.b yd.md|d.ilm.mt.b a| 4[51].8.20
---.ḥ]rn.|[-]rk.ḥ[--.---.-]lk.|[-]sr.n[--.---.]ḥrn.|[--]p.ẖp h.ẖ[--.---.šp]š.l hrm.|[ǵrpl.]‘l.ar[ṣ.---.ḥ]mt.|[---.šp]š.l [hrm.ǵ UG5.8.7
l y.dtm.|ẖrṣ.‘dbt.bht[h.b‘]l.|y‘db.hd.‘db[.‘d]bt.|hkl h.ṭbẖ.alpm[.ap].|ṣin.šql.ṯrm[.w]m|ria.il.‘glm.d[t].|šnt.imr. 4[51].6.40
.ilib h.b qdš.|ztr.‘m h.l arṣ.mšṣu.qṭr h.|l ‘pr.ḏmr.aṯr h.ṭbq.lḥt.|niṣ h.grš d.‘šy.ln h.|aẖd.yd h.b škrn.m‘ms h.|[k 17[2AQHT].1.29
h.b qdš.|[ztr.‘m h.l a]rṣ.mšṣu.|[qṭr h.l ‘pr.ḏ]mr.a[ṯ]r h.|[ṭbq.lḥt.niṣ h.gr]š.d ‘šy.|[ln h.---].|z[tr.‘m k.l arṣ.mšṣu.q 17[2AQHT].1.47
w b šḥt.‘s.mt.‘r‘rm.yn‘rn h.|ssnm.ysyn h.‘dtm.y‘dyn h.yb|ltm.ybln h.mǵy.ḥrn.l bt h.w.|yštql.l ḥṭr h.tlu ḥt.km.n UG5.7.66
.|iqnim.šmẖ.aliyn.|b‘l.ṣḥ.ẖrn.b bht h.|‘ḏbt.b qrb hkl h.|yblnn ǵrm.mid.ksp.|gb‘m lḥmd.ẖrṣ.|yblnn.udr.ilqṣm.|y 4[51].5.99
škllt.[---].|‘r.ym.l bl[.---].|b[---.]ny[.--].|l bl.sk.w [---] h.|ybm h.šb‘[.---].|ǵzr.ilḥu.t[---]l.|trm.tṣr.trm[.‘]tqt.|tbky. 16.2[125].93
m.|[k gm]n.al[i]yn.b[‘l].|[---]ḥ h.tšt bm.‘[--].|[---.]zr h.ybm.l ilm.|[id]k.l ttn.pnm.‘m.|[il.]mbk nhrm.qrb.|[a]pq. 6.1.31[49.1.3]
[.---].|[--.]yṣq šmn.šlm.b ṣ[‘.trḥṣ].|yd h.btlt.‘nt.uṣb‘t[h.ybmt].|limm.tiẖd.knr h.b yd[h.tšt].|rimt.l irt h.tšr.dd.al[UG5.3.2.5
.dm.ḏmr.yṣq.šmn.|šlm.b ṣ‘.trḥṣ.yd h.bt|[l]t.‘nt.uṣb‘t h.ybmt.limm.|[t]rḥṣ.yd h.b dm.ḏmr.|[u]ṣb‘t h.b mm‘.mhr 3[‘NT].2.33
[---.]h.yb[--].|[---.--]n.irš[.---].|[---.--]mr.ph.|[---.--]mm.hlkt.|[--- 26[135].1
].|[-]š[-]y.d.b š[-]y.|[---.y]d gt h[.--].|[---.]yd.|[k]rm h.yd.|[k]lkl h.|[w] ytn.nn.|l.b‘ln.bn.|kltn.w l.|bn h.‘d.‘lm. 1008.9
‘ly.dǵṯ h.|b šmym.dǵṯ hrnmy[.d k]|bkbm.‘[l.---].|[-]l h.yd ‘d[.---].|ltm.mrqdm.d š[-]l[-].|w t‘n.pǵt.ṯkmt.mym.|qr 19[1AQHT].4.188
n.qrty[.---].|w.klt h.b.t[--.---].|b‘l y.mlk[y.---].|yd.bt h.yd[.---].|ary.yd.t[--.---].|ẖtn h.šb‘l[.---].|ṯlḥny.yd[.---].|yd 81[329].14
yšu.‘n h.w y‘n.|w y‘n.btlt.‘nt.|n‘mt.bn.aẖt.b‘l.|l pnn h.ydd.w yqm.|l p‘n h.ykr‘.w yql.|w yšu.g h.w yṣḥ.|ḥwt.aẖt 10[76].2.17
ṣd h.mnt.nṯk nḥš.|šmrr.nḥš.‘q šr.ln h.mlẖš.|abd.ln h.ydy.ḥmt.|b ḥrn.pnm.trǵnw.w tṯkl.|bnwt h.ykr.‘r.d qdm. UG5.7.60
q šr[.y‘]db.ksa.|nḥš.šmrr.nḥš.‘q šr.ln h.ml|ẖš.abd.ln h.ydy.ḥmt.hlm.yṯq.|w yṯb.|tqru.l špš.um h.špš.[um.q]l bl.‘ UG5.7.22
hmtm.|mnt.nṯk.nḥš.šmrr.nḥš.|‘q šr.ln h.mlẖš abd.ln h.ydy.|ḥmt.hlm.yṯq yṯqšqy.nḥš.yšlḥm.‘q šr.|y‘db.ksa.w.yṯ UG5.7.5
.ḥryt h.mnt.nṯk.nḥš.šm|rr.nḥš.‘q šr.ln h.mlẖš abd.ln h.|ydy.ḥmt.hlm.yṯq nḥš yšlḥm.nḥš.|‘q.šr.y‘db.ksa.w yṯb.|t UG5.7.37
gn.ttl h.mnt.nṯk.nḥš.šmrr.|nḥš.‘q šr.ln h.mlẖš.abd.ln h.|ydy.ḥmt.hlm.yṯq.nḥš.yšlḥm.|nḥš.‘q šr.y‘db.ksa.w yṯb.|t UG5.7.16
.|ršp.bbt h.mnt.nḥš.šmrr.|nḥš.‘q šr.ln h.mlẖš.abd.ln h.ydy.|ḥmt.hlm.yṯq.nḥš.yšlḥm.nḥš ‘q.|š.y‘db.ksa w yṯb.|tq UG5.7.32
.ṣpn.mnt y.nṯk.|nḥš.šmrr.nḥš.‘q šr ln h.|mlẖš.abd.ln h.ydy.ḥmt.hlm.yṯq.|nḥš.yšlḥm.nḥš.‘q šr.ydb.ksa.|w yṯb.|t UG5.7.11
.‘ṯtrt h.mnt.nṯk.nḥš.šmrr.|nḥš.‘q šr.ln h.mlẖš abd.ln h.ydy.|ḥmt.hlm.yṯq.nḥš.yšlḥm.nḥš.|‘q šr.y‘db.ksa.w yṯb.|t UG5.7.42
ptr h.mnt.nṯk.nḥš.|šmrr.nḥš.‘q šr.ln h.mlẖš.abd.|ln h.ydy.ḥmt.hlm yṯq.nḥš.|yšlḥm.nḥš.‘q šr.y‘db ksa.|w yṯb.|t UG5.7.48
lrgt h.mnt.nṯk.n[ḥš].šmrr.|nḥš.‘q šr.ln h.mlẖš.abd.ln h.ydy.|ḥmt.hlm.yṯq.nḥš.yšlḥm.nḥš.|‘q šr.y‘db.ksa.w yṯb.|t UG5.7.27
mm h mnt.nṯk.nḥš.|šmrr.nḥš ‘q šr.ln h.mlẖš.|abd.ln h.ydy ḥmt.hlm.yṯq šqy.|nḥš.yšlḥm.nḥš.‘q šr.y‘db.|ksa.w yṯ UG5.7.54
dyrẖ.|[b]n.gg‘t.|[‘]dy.|armwl.|uwaẖ.|ypln.w.ṯn.bn h.|ydln.|anr[my].|mld.|krmp[y].|bṣmn. 2086.8
.-]l[-.-]hg[.---].|[---.-]r[-.il]m.rbm.n‘l[.-]gr.|[---.]‘ṣ.b d h.ydrm[.]pi[-.]adm.|[---.]iṯ[-].yšql.yṯk[.--]np bl.hn.|[---].ḥ[UG5.8.32
.km.lpš.dm a[ẖ h].|km.all.dm.ary h.|k šb‘t.l šb‘m.aẖ h.ym[.--].|w ṯmnt.l ṯmnym.|šr.aẖy h.mẓa h.|w mẓa h.šr.yl 12[75].2.49
[-----].|w.lmd h.|mtn.|w.lmd h.|ymn.|w.lmd h.|y‘ḏrn.|w.lmd h.|‘dn.|w.lmd h.|bn.špš. 1049.1.4
lṯm.ktn.|ẖmšm.izml.|ẖmš.kbd.arb‘m.|dd.akl.|ṯṯ.‘šr h.yn.|kd.šmn.l.nr.ilm.|kdm.dǵm.|ṯṯ.kdm.ztm. 1126.5
.dt.l.u[--]tṯb.|kṯ[r]n.|w.aṯt h.w.n‘r h.|bn.ẖby.w.[a]ṯt h.|ynḥm.ulmy.|[--]q.w.aṯt h.w.bn h.|[--]an.w.aṯt h.|[--]y.w 2068.4
grgš.|w.lmd h.|aršmg.|w.lmd h.|iyṯr.|[w].lmd h.|[yn]ḥm.|[w.]lmd h.|[i]wrmẖ.|[w.]lmd h. 1048.6
[-----].|w.lmd h.|mtn.|w.lmd h.|ymn.|w.lmd h.|y‘ḏrn.|w.lmd h.|‘dn.|w.lmd h.|bn.špš.|[w.l]m[d h].|yṣ 1049.1.6
‘ṣd].|w ẖrmṯt.|ṯlṯm.ar[b‘].|kbd.ksp.|‘l.tgyn.|w ‘l.aṯt h.|ypḥ.m‘nt.|bn.lbn. 2053.21
qdqd].|ṯlṯ id.‘l.udn.š[pk.km].|šiy.dm h.km.šẖ[ṭ.l brk h].|yṣat.km.rḥ.npš[h.km.iṯl].|brlt h.km.qṭr.[b ap h.---].|‘n 18[3AQHT].4.35
ṯnm.qdqd.|ṯlṯ id.‘l.udn.špk.km.šiy.|dm.km.šẖṭ.l brk h.tṣi.km.|rḥ.npš h.km.iṯl.brlt h.km.|qṭr.b ap h.b ap.mhr h. 18[3AQHT].4.24
h.|y‘ḏrn.|w.lmd h.|‘dn.|w.lmd h.|bn.špš.|[w.l]m[d h].|yṣ[---].|‘bd[--].|pr[--].|‘dr[--].|w.lm[d h].|ily[---].|[----- 1049.1.12
rṣ.špt.l šmm.|[---.l]šn.l kbkbm.y‘rb.|[b‘]l.b kbd h.b p h yrd.|k ḥrr.zt.ybl.arṣ.w pr.|‘ṣm.yraun.aliyn.b‘l.|ṯt‘.nn.rkb 5[67].2.4
h.dbḥ.|l ṯr.ab h.il.šrd.|[b‘l].b dbḥ h.bn dgn.|[b m]ṣd h.yrd.krt.|[l g]gt.‘db.akl.l qryt.|ḥṭt.l bt.ẖbr.|yip.lḥm.d ẖmš 14[KRT].4.171
b‘l.mt.my.lim.bn dgn.|my.hmlt.aṯr.b‘l.nrd.|b arṣ.‘m h.trd.nrt.|ilm.špš.‘d.tšb‘.bk.|tšt.k yn.udm‘t.gm.|tṣḥ.l nrt.il 6[62].1.8
kbkbt k ṯn.|[---.]b‘l yḥmdn h.yrṯ y.|[---.]dmrn.l pn h yrd.|[---.]b‘l.šm[.--.]rgbt yu.|[---]w yrmy[.q]rn h.|[---.-]n 2001.2.8
bn.b‘ln.biry.|ṯlṯ.b‘lm.|w.adn hm.ṯr.w.arb‘.bnt h.|yrẖm.yd.ṯn.bn h.|b‘lm.w.ṯlṯ.n‘rm.w.bt.aḥt.|bn.lwn.ṯlṯt 2080.3
ḥ.tš.b bt h.|il.ẖṭ h.nḥt.il.ymnn.mṭ.yd h.yšu.|yr.šmm h.yr.b šmm.‘ṣr.yẖrṭ yšt.|l pḥm.il.aṯtm.k ypt.hm.aṯtm.tṣḥn. 23[52].38
rẖm.w aṯb.l ntbt.k.‘ṣm l t[--].|[---.]drk.brḥ.arṣ.lk pn h.yrk.b‘[l].|[---.]bt k.ap.l pẖr k ‘nt tqm.‘nt.tqm.|[---.p]ẖr k. 1001.2.8

---].|w tksynn.bṯn[-.]|y[--.]šr h.w šḫp h.|[--.]šḫp.ṣǵrt h.|yrk.tʻl.b ǵr.|mslmt.b ǵr.tliyt.|w tʻl.bkm.b arr.|bm.arr.w 10[76].3.27

y.ʻrš.h[--]m.|ysmsmt.ʻrš.ḫlln.[-].|yṯb.dnil.[l s]pr yrḫ h.|yrs.y[---.]y[--] h.|ṯlṯ.rb[ʻ.yrḫ.--]r[.--].|yrḫm.ymǵy[.---].| 17[2AQHT].2.43

t ẓl h kbkbm.|[---.]b km kbkbt k ṯn.|[---.]bʻl yḥmdn h.yrṯ y.|[---.]dmrn.l pn h yrd.|[---.]bʻl.šm[.--.]rgbt yu.|[---] 2001.2.7

h.rš.|mid.grdš.ṯbt h.|w b tm hn.špḥ.yitbd.|w b.pḫyr h.yrṯ.|yʻrb.b ḥdr h.ybky.|b ṯn.[-]gmm.w ydmʻ.|tntkn.udmʻ 14[KRT].1.25

bʻ.mṯbt.azmr.b h.š.šr[-].|al[p.w].š.šlmm.pamt.šbʻ.klb h.|yr[--.]mlk.ṣbu.špš.w.ḥl.mlk.|w.[---].ypm.w.mḫ[--].t[ṯ]tb 35[3].52

nmn.w.ṯlṯ.nʻ[r] h.|rpan.w.ṯ[n.]bn h.|bn.ayln.w.ṯn.bn h.|yt. 2068.27

]t.ilm.ṯlṯ h.|[ap]nk.krt.ṯʻ.ʻ[-]r.|[--.]b bt h.yšt.ʻrb.|[--] h.ytn.w [--]u.l ytn.|[aḫ]r.mǵy.ʻ[d]t.ilm.|[w]yʻn.aliy[n.]bʻl.| 15[128].2.10

rd.ṯd.l pnw h.|b ḥrb.mlḥt.|qṣ.mri.ndd.|yʻšr.w yšqyn h.|ytn.ks.b d h.|krpn.b klat.yd h.|b krb.ʻẓm.ridn.|mt.šmm 3[ʻNT].1.9

mš.[m]šl[t].|[--]arš[p.-]š.l[h].|[-]ṯl[.--]š.l h.|[---]l[.--] h.|mtn[.---.]l h.|[---.]l h.|[---.--]š.l h.|[---].l h.|[--.]spr[.---]. 2133.5

mn.l.gzzm.|yyn.|ṣdqn.|ʻbd.pdr.|myṣm.|ṯgt.|w.lmd h.|yṯil.|w.lmd h.|rpan.|w.lmd h.|ʻbdrpu.|w.lmd h.|ʻdršp. 1099.10

ṯbḫ.imr.w lḥm.|mgṯ.w yṯrm.hn.ym.|w ṯn.yṯb.krt.l ʻd h.|yṯb.l ksi mlk.|l nḫt.l kḥṯ.drkt.|ap.yṣb.yṯb.b hkl.|w ywsr 16.6[127].22

bʻl.]|[km.ilm.w ḥẓr].|[k bn.aṯ]r[t].|m[ṯ]b.il.mẓll.|bn h.mṯb.rbt.|aṯrt.ym.mṯb.|klt.knyt.|mṯb.pdry.b ar.|mẓll.ṭly. 4[51].1.14

n.in.bt.l bʻl.|km.ilm.w ḥẓr.k bn.aṯrt.|mṯb il.mẓll.bn h.|mṯb rbt.aṯrt.ym.|mṯb.klt.knyt.|mṯb.pdry.bt.ar.|mẓll.ṭly 4[51].4.52

n.in.bt.l bʻl.km.ilm.|ḥẓr.k b[n.a]ṯrt.mṯb.il.|mṯll.b[n h.m]ṯb.rbt.aṯrt.|ym.mṯb.[pdr]y.bt.ar.|[mẓll.]ṭly[.bt.]rb.mṯb 3[ʻNT.VI].5.48

[bt].l [bʻl.km.ilm.w ḥẓr].|k bn.[aṯrt.mṯb.il.mẓll].|bn h.m[ṯb.rbt.aṯrt.ym].|mṯb.pdr[y.bt.ar.mẓll].|ṭly.bt.r[b.mṯb.a 3[ʻNT.VI].4.2

br.ḥṯ.mṭpṭ k.|yru.bn ilm t.ṯṯʻ.y|dd.il.ǵẓr.yʻr.mt.|b ql h.y[---.---].|bʻl.yṯṯbn[.l ksi].|mlk h.l[nḫt.l kḥṯ].|drkt h[.---] 6[49].6.32

w].|mss.[št.qlql.w.št].|ʻrgz[.ydk.aḥd h].|w.yṣq[.b.ap h].|k.yiḫd[.akl.ššw].|št.mkš[r.grn].|w.št.ašk[rr].|w.pr.ḥdr[161[56].11

]l yṯtn mss št qlql.|[w št ʻrgz y]dk aḥd h w yṣq b ap h.|[k.yiḫd akl s]šw št mkšr grn.|[w št aškrr w p]r ḥdrt.|[--- 160[55].9

n].|w.št.ašk[rr].|w.pr.ḥdr[t.ydk].|aḥd h.w.yṣq[.b.ap h].|k.yiḫd.akl.š[šw].|št.nni.št.mk[št.grn].|št.irǵn.ḥmr[.ydk 161[56].16

im.ḫp y[m].|ṭṣmt.adm.ṣat.š[p]š.|tḥt h.k kdrt.ri[š].|ʻl h.k irbym.kp.k.qṣm.|ǵrmn.kp.mhr.ʻtkt.|rišt.l bmt h.šnst.| 3[ʻNT].2.10

.ymlu.lb h.|[b šmḫt.kbd.ʻnt.tšyt.tḥt h.k]kdrt.riš.|[ʻl h.k irbym.kp.---.k br]k.tǵll.b dm.|[ḏmr.---.]td[-.]rǵb.|[----] 7.1[131].9

l.|ymzl.w yṣi.trḫ.|ḥdṯ.ybʻr.l ṯn.|aṯt h.lm.nkr.|mddt h.k irby.|[t]škn.šd.|km.ḥsn.pat.mdbr.|lk.ym.w ṯn.ṯlṯ.rbʻ y 14[KRT].2.103

ʻ.l dnil.[mt.rpi].|mt.aqht.ǵzr.[šṣat].|btlt.ʻnt.k [rḥ.npš h].|k iṯl.brlt h.[b h.pʻnm].|ṭṭ.ʻl[n.pn h.td]ʻ.b ʻdn].|ksl.y[ṯbr. 19[1AQHT].2.92

ḥtn.qn.yṣbt.|[---.--]m.b nši.ʻn h.w tphn.|[---.--]ml.ksl h.k b[r]q.|[---.]m[-]ǵ[-].thmt.brq.|[---].tṣb.qšt.bnt.|[---.ʻ]n h 17[2AQHT].6.11

ḥd h.w.yṣq.b[.ap h].|k.yraš.ššw.[št].|bln.qt.yṣq.b.a[p h].|k ygʻr[.ššw.---].|dprn[.---].|drʻ.[---].|tmṯl[.---].|mǵm[ǵ.- 161[56].22

ht.yʻn.kmr.kmr[.--].|k apʻ.il.b gdrt.k lb.l |ḥt h.imḫṣ h.k d.ʻl.qšt h.|imḫṣ h.ʻl.qṣʻt h.hwt.|l aḥw.ap.qšt h.l ttn.|l y. 19[1AQHT].1.14

ḫr ššw mǵmǵ].|w [bṣql.ʻrgz.ydk].|a[ḥd h.w.yṣq.b.ap h].|k.[ḫr.ššw.ḫndrṯ].|w.ṯ[qd.mr.ydk.aḥd h].|w.y[ṣq.b.ap h] 161[56].4

ḫr s]šw mǵmǵ w b[ṣql ʻrgz].|[ydk aḥ]d h w yṣq b ap h.|[k ḫr]ššw ḫndrṯ w ṯ[qd m]r.|[ydk aḥd h w yṣq b ap h.|[160[55].5

[k.---.]šš[w.---].|[---.w]yṣq b a[p h].|[k ḫr s]šw mǵmǵ w b[ṣql ʻrgz].|[ydk aḥ]d h w yṣq b ap 160[55].3

ʻnt.hlkt.w.šnwt.|tp.aḫ.h.k.ysmsm.|tspi.šir.h.l.bl.ḥrb.|tšt.dm.h.l.bl.ks.|tpnn.ʻn.bty RS225.2

ǵdd.kbd h.b ṣḥ]q.ymlu.lb h.|[b šmḫt.kbd.ʻnt.tšyt.tḥt h.k]kdrt.riš.|[ʻl h.k irbym.kp.---.k br]k.tǵll.b dm.|[ḏmr.---. 7.1[131].8

n.|qrytm tmḫṣ.lim.ḫp y[m].|ṭṣmt.adm.ṣat.š[p]š.|tḥt h.k kdrt.ri[š].|ʻl h.k irbym.kp.k.qṣm.|ǵrmn.kp.mhr.ʻtkt.|ri 3[ʻNT].2.9

|[k ḫr]ššw ḫndrṯ w ṯ[qd m]r.|[ydk aḥd h w yṣq b ap h.|[k l yḫru w]l yṯtn mss št qlql.|[w št ʻrgz y]dk aḥd h w y 160[55].7

k.[ḫr.ššw.ḫndrṯ].|w.ṯ[qd.mr.ydk.aḥd h].|w.y[ṣq.b.ap h].|k.l.ḫ[ru.w.l.yṯtn.ššw].|mss.[št.qlql.w.št].|ʻrgz[.ydk.aḥd 161[56].7

ilm.mt.|ym.ymm.yʻtqn.l ymm.|l yrḫm.rḥm.ʻnt.tngṯ h.|k lb.arḫ.l ʻgl h.k lb.|ṯat.l imr h.km.lb.|ʻnt.aṯr.bʻl.tiḫd.|b 6[49].2.27

|kd.[---].|kd.t[---.ym.ymm].|yʻtqn.w[rḥm.ʻnt].|tngṯ h.k lb.a[rḫ].|l ʻgl h.k lb.ṯa[t].|l imr h.km.lb.ʻn[t].|aṯr.bʻl.tiḫ 6[49].2.6

ym.ymm].|yʻtqn.w[rḥm.ʻnt].|tngṯ h.k lb.a[rḫ].|l ʻgl h.k lb.ṯa[t].|l imr h.km.lb.ʻn[t].|aṯr.bʻl.tiḫd.m[t].|b sin.lpš.t 6[49].2.7

m.yʻtqn.l ymm.|l yrḫm.rḥm.ʻnt.tngṯ h.|k lb.arḫ.l ʻgl h.k lb.|ṯat.l imr h.km.lb.|ʻnt.aṯr.bʻl.tiḫd.|bn.ilm.mt.b ḥrb.| 6[49].2.28

.|ʻnn.ilm.al.|tqrb.l bn.ilm.|mt.al.yʻdb km.|k imr.b p h.|k lli.b ṯbrn.|qn h.tḫtan.|nrt.ilm.špš.|ṣḥrrt.la.|šmm.b yd 4[51].8.18

h.|tšu.g h.w tṣḥ.tšmḫ ht.|aṯrt.w bn h.ilt.w ṣb|rt.ary h.k mt.aliyn.|bʻl.k ḫlq.zbl.bʻl.|arṣ.gm.yṣḥ il.|l rbt.aṯrt ym.š 6.1.41[49.1.13]

k tʻn.ẓl.ksp.w n[-]t.|ḫrṣ.šmḫ.rbt.a[ṯrt].|ym.gm.l ǵlm h.k [tṣḥ].|ʻn.mkṯr.ap.t[---].|dgy.rbt.aṯr[t.ym].|qḫ.rṯt.b d k t 4[51].2.29

p[----].|gm.l[aṯt h k.yṣḥ].|šmʻ[.l mṯt.ḥry].|ṭbḫ.š[mn].mri k.|ptḥ.[rḥ]bt.yn.| 15[128].4.2

.|ḥrṯ[.l z]ǵt.klb.|[ṣ]pr[.apn]k.|[pb]l[.mlk.g]m.l aṯt |[h.k]y[ṣḥ.]šmʻ.mʻ.|[--.]ʻm[.-.]aṯt y[.-].|[---.]ṯḥm.|[---]t.[ ]r.|[14[KRT].5.229

.qṣʻt.apnk.dnil.|mt.rpi.aphn.ǵzr.mt.|hrnmy.gm.l aṯt h.k yṣḥ.|šmʻ.mṯt.dnty.ʻd[b].|imr.b pḫd.l npš.kṯr.|w ḫss.l br 17[2AQHT].5.15

w.pr[.ḥdrt.w.št].|irǵ[n.ḥmr.ydk].|aḥd[h.w.yṣq.b.ap h].|k yr[a]š.šš[w.w.ykhp].|mid.dblt.yṯ[nt.w].|ṣmq[m].ytn 161[56].31

i.št.mk[št.grn].|št.irǵn.ḥmr[.ydk].|aḥd h.w.yṣq.b[.ap h].|k.yraš.ššw.[št].|bln.qt.yṣq.b.a[p h].|k ygʻr[.ššw.---].|dp 161[56].20

h.ṯbq.lḥt.|niṣ h.grš d.ʻšy.ln h.|aḥd.yd h.b škrn.mʻms h.|[k]šbʻ yn.spu.ksm h.bt.bʻl.|[w m]nt h bt.il.ṯḥ.gg h.b ym. 17[2AQHT].1.31

mn.nqpnt.ʻd.|k lbš.km.lpš.dm a[ḫ] h].|km.all.dm.ary h.|k šbʻt.l šbʻm.aḫ h.ym[.--].|w ṯmnt.l ṯmnym.|šr.aḫy h.m 12[75].2.48

]br.|ṯmn.[---.]btlt.[ʻ]nt.|ṯṯb.[---.--]ša.|tlm.km[.---.]yd h.k šr.|knr.uṣbʻt h ḫrṣ.abn.|p h.tiḫd.šnt h.w akl.bqmm.|tšt 19[1AQHT].1.7

n.|bʻl.ib.hdt.lm.ṯḫš.|lm.ṯḫš.ntq.dmrn.|ʻn.bʻl.qdm.yd h.|k tǵḏ.arz.b ymn h.|bkm.yṯb.bʻl.l bht h.|u mlk.u bl mlk. 4[51].7.40

šd h.qrn[m].|dt.ʻl h.riš h.b glṯ.b šm[m].|[---.i]l.tr.iṯ.p h.k ṯt.ǵlt[.--].|[---.--] k yn.ddm.l b[--.---].|[---.-]yt š[--.---].|[UG5.3.1.8

.ḥ[tm].ʻl.šrn.|ʻšrt.ksp.ʻl.[-]lpy.|bn.ady.kkr.šʻrt.|nṯk h.|kb[d.]mn.ʻl.abršn.|b[n.---].kršu.nṯk h.|[---.--]mm.b.krsi. 1146.10

.m h.w trḥṣ.|ṭl.šmm.šmn.arṣ.ṭl.šm[m.t]sk h.|rbb.nsk h.kbkbm.|ttpp.anhbm.d alp.šd[.ẓu h.b ym].|ṭl[.---]. 3[ʻNT].4.88

.mḫtrt.pṯtm.|[---.-]t h.ušpǵt tišr.|[---.šm]m h.nšat ẓl h kbkbm.|[---.]b km kbkbt k ṯn.|[---.]bʻl yḥmdn h.yrṯ y.|[- 2001.2.5

šmm.šmn.arṣ.rbb.|[r]kb ʻrpt.ṭl.šmm.tsk h.|[rb]b.nsk h.kbkbm. 3[ʻNT].2.41

arbʻ.yn.l.mrynm.ḥ[--].kl h.|kdm.l.zn[-.---].|kd.l.aṯr[y]m.|kdm.ʻm.[--]n.|kd.mštt.[--- 1089.1

ḫrny.w.rʻ h.|klbr.w.rʻ h.|tškrǵ.w.rʻ h.|ǵlwš.w.rʻ h.|kdrš.w.rʻ h.|trm[-].w[.rʻ h].|[ʻ]ṯtr[-].w.[rʻ h].|ḫlly[-].w.rʻ 2083.1.4

kr.qnm.|ṯlṯt.w.ṯlṯt.ksp h.|arbʻ.kkr.|algbṯ.arbʻt.|ksp h.|kkr.šʻrt.|šbʻt.ksp h.|ḫmš.mqdm.dnyn.|b.ṯql.dprn.aḥd.| 1127.16

ḫrny.w.rʻ h.|klbr.w.rʻ h.|tškrǵ.w.rʻ h.|ǵlwš.w.rʻ h.|kdrš.w.rʻ h.|trm[2083.1.1

ʻm.ʻlm.ḥyt.ḥẓt.ṯḥm k.|mlk n.aliyn.bʻl.ṯpṭ n.|in.d ʻln h.klny y.qš h.|nbln.klny y.nbl.ks h.|any.l yṣḥ.ṯr.il.ab h.il.| 3[ʻNT.VI].5.41

ʻlm.ḥyt.ḥẓt.|ṯḥm k.mlk n.aliy[n.]bʻl.|ṯpṭ n.w in.d ʻln h.|klny n.q[š] h.n[bln].|klny n[.n]bl.ks h.|[an]y.l yṣḥ.ṯr il.a 4[51].4.44

rnmy.d in.bn.l h.|km.aḫ h.w šrš.km.ary h.|bl.iṯ.bn.l h.km aḫ h.w šrš.|km.ary h.uzrm.ilm.ylḥm.|uzrm.yšqy.bn. 17[2AQHT].1.21

h.abynt.|[d]nil.mt.rpi anḫ.ǵzr.|[mt.]hrnmy.d in.bn.l h.|km.aḫ h.w šrš.km.ary h.|bl.iṯ.bn.l h.km aḫ h.w šrš.|km. 17[2AQHT].1.19

'.šnt.il.mla.[-].|w ṯmn.nqpnt.'d.|k lbš.km.lpš.dm a[ḫ h].|km.all.dm.ary h.|k šb't.l šb'm.aḫ h.ym[.--].|w ṯmnt.l ṯ 12[75].2.47
[pk.km].|šiy.dm h.km.šḫ[ṭ.l brk h].|yṣat.km.rḥ.npš[h.km.iṯl].|brlt h.km.qṭr.[b ap h.---].|'nt.b ṣmt.mhr h.[---].| 18[3AQHT].4.36
.'l.udn.špk.km.šiy.|dm.km.šḫṭ.l brk h.tṣi.km.|rḥ.npš h.km.iṯl.brlt h.km.|qṭr.b ap h.b ap.mhr h.ank.|l aḥwy.tqḥ. 18[3AQHT].4.25
tmḫṣ.alpm.ib.št[-.]št.|ḥršm l ahlm p[---.]km.|[-]bl lb h.km.bṯn.y[--.-]ah.|ṯnm.tšqy msk.hwt.tšqy[.-.]w [---].|w hn 19[1AQHT].4.223
[r]q.|[---.]m[-]ǵ[-].thmt.brq.|[---].tṣb.qšt.bnt.|[---.']n h.km.bṯn.yqr.|[krpn h.-.l]arṣ.ks h.tšpk m.|[l 'pr.tšu.g h.]w 17[2AQHT].6.14
mn.yzbrnn.zbrm.gpn.|yṣmdnn.ṣmdm.gpn.yšql.šdmt h.|km gpn.|šb' d.yrgm.'l.'d.w 'rbm.t'nyn.|w šd.šd ilm.šd a 23[52].10
mhr h.ank.|l aḥwy.tqḥ.ytpn.mhr.št.|tštn.k nšr.b ḥbš h.km.diy.|b t'rt h.aqht.km.ytb.l lḥ[m].|bn.dnil.l ṯrm.'l h.nš 18[3AQHT].4.28
.|b ṯn.[-]gmm.w ydm'.|tntkn.udm't h.|km.ṯqlm.arṣ h.|km ḫmšt.mṭt h.|bm.bky h.w yšn.|b dm' h.nhmmt.|šnt. 14[KRT].1.29
ttn.|tn.l y.mṯt.ḥry.|n'mt.špḥ.bkr k.|d k.n'm.'nt.n'm h.|km.tsm.'ṯtrt.ts[m h].|d 'q h.ib.iqni.'p['p] h.|sp.ṯrml.tḥgr 14[KRT].3.145
tn.tn.|l y.mṯt.ḥry.|n'mt.šbḥ.bkr k.|d k n'm.'nt.|n'm h.km.tsm.|'ṯtrt.tsm h.|d 'q h.ib.iqni.|'p'p h.sp.ṯrml.|d b ḥl 14[KRT].6.292
l yrḫm.rḥm.'nt.tngṯ h.|k lb.arḫ.l 'gl h.k lb.|ṯat.l imr h.km.lb.|'nt.aṯr.b'l.tiḫd.|bn.ilm.mt.b ḥrb.|tbq'nn.b ḫṯr.tdr 6[49].2.29
[rḥm.'nt].|tngṯ h.k lb.a[rḫ].|l 'gl h.k lb.ṯa[t].|l imr h.km.lb.'n[t].|aṯr.b'l.tiḫd.m[t].|b sin.lpš.tššq[n h].|b qṣ.all. 6[49].2.8
mš[.---].|anp n m yḥr[r.---].|bmt n m.yšḫn.[---].|qrn h.km.ǵb[-.---].|hw km.ḥrr[.---].|šnmtm.dbṭ[.---].|tr'.tr'n.a[- 12[75].2.40
.šiy.|dm.km.šḫṭ.l brk h.tṣi.km.|rḥ.npš h.km.iṯl.brlt h.km.|qṭr.b ap h.b ap.mhr h.ank.|l aḥwy.tqḥ.ytpn.mhr.št.| 18[3AQHT].4.25
m h.km.šḫ[ṭ.l brk h].|yṣat.km.rḥ.npš[h.km.iṯl].|brlt h.km.qṭr.[b ap h.---].|'nt.b ṣmt.mhr h.[---].|aqht.w tbk.y[-- 18[3AQHT].4.37
---].|[---.-]b[-.---].|['ṯ]trt w 'nt[.---].|w b hm.ṯṯtb[.--]d h.|km trpa.hn n'r.|d yšt.l.lṣb h ḫš'r klb.|[w]riš.pqq.w šr h. UG5.1.2.2
n h.hlmn.ṯnm[.qdqd].|ṯlṯ id.'l.udn.š[pk.km].|šiy.dm h.km.šḫ[ṭ.l brk h].|yṣat.km.rḥ.npš[h.km.iṯl].|brlt h.km.qṭr 18[3AQHT].4.35
'rb.b ḥdr h.ybky.|b ṯn.[-]gmm.w ydm'.|tntkn.udm't h.|km.ṯqlm.arṣ h.|km ḫmšt.mṭt h.|bm.bky h.w yšn.|b dm' 14[KRT].1.28
n.|ilm.w tštn.tštn y[n] 'd šb'.|trṯ.'d.škr.y'db.yrḫ.|gb h.km.[---.]yqṭqṭ.tḥt.|ṯlḥnt.il.d yd'nn.|y'db.lḥm.l h.w d l yd' UG5.1.1.5
qbrn.ašt.b ḫrt.|i[lm.arṣ.b p h.rgm.l yṣa.b šp]|t h.hwt h.knp.hrgb.b'l.ṯbr.|b'l.ṯbr.diy.hwt.w yql.|tḥt.p'n h.ybq'.kb 19[1AQHT].3.128
brn h.|ašt.b ḫrt.ilm.arṣ.|b p h.rgm.l yṣa.b špt h.hwt[h].|knp.nšrm.b'l.yṯbr.|b'l.ṯbr.diy hmt.tqln.|tḥt.p'n h.ybq'. 19[1AQHT].3.113
n h.aštn.|b ḫrt.ilm.arṣ.b p h.rgm.l[yṣ]a.|b špt h.hwt h.knp.ṣml.b'[l].|b'l.ṯbr.diy.hyt.tq[l.tḥt].|p'n h.ybq'.kbd h.w 19[1AQHT].3.142
iqnu.|argmn.nqmd.mlk.|ugrt.d ybl.l špš.|mlk.rb.b'l h.|ks.ḫrṣ.ktn.mit.pḥm.|mit.iqni.l mlkt.|ks.ḫrṣ.ktn.mit.pḥ 64[118].26
bn[.---].|aḫdt.plk h[.b yd h].|plk.qlt.b ymn h.|npyn h.mks.bšr h.|tmt'.md h.b ym.ṯn.|npyn h.b nhrm.|štt.ḫptr.l 4[51].2.5
.|w ilt.ṣdynm.|hm.ḥry.bt y.|iqḥ.aš'rb.ǵlmt.|ḥẓr y.ṯn h.wspm.|atn.w ṯlṯ h.ḫrṣm.|ylk ym.w ṯn.|ṯlṯ.rb'.ym.|aḫr.šp 14[KRT].4.205
l ḫtn y.a[ḫ]r.|nkl yrḫ ytrḫ.adn h.|yšt mṣb.mznm.um h.|kp mznm.iḫ h yṯ'r.|mšrrm.aḫt h l a|bn mznm.nkl w ib. 24[77].34
aṯrt.|mǵ.l qdš.amrr.|idk.al.tnn.|pnm.tk.ḥqkpt.|il.kl h.kptr.|ksu.ṯbt h.ḥkpt.|arṣ.nḥlt h.|b alp.šd.rbt.|kmn.l p'n. 3['NT.VI].6.14
[idk.al.ttn.pnm.tk.ḥkpt.il.kl h].|[kptr.]ks[u.ṯbt h.ḥkpt.arṣ.nḥlt h].|b alp.šd.r[bt.kmn.l p' 1['NT.IX].3.01
h.|rpan.|w.lmd h.|'bdrpu.|w.lmd h.|'dršp.|w.lmd h.|krwn b.gt.nbk.|ddm.kšmm.l.ḥtn.|ddm.l.trbnn.|ddm.š'r 1099.18
[---.]ktb nǵr krm.|[---].ab h.krm ar.|[---.]h.mḥtrt.pṯtm.|[---.-]t h.ušpǵt tišr.|[---.šm]m 2001.2.2
h l a|b h.alp ksp w rbt ḫ|rṣ.išlḥ ẓhrm iq|nim.atn šd h krm[m].|šd dd h ḥrnqm.w |y'n ḫrḫb mlk qẓ [l].|n'mn.il 24[77].22
.[r' h].|ḫlly[-].w.r'[h].|ilmškl.w.r'[h].|ššw[.--].w.r[' h].|kr[mn.--.]w.r[' h].|šd.[--.w.]r[' h].|ḫla[n.---].|w lšṯr[.--- 2083.2.3
n.btlt.'nt.|n'mt.bn.aḫt.b'l.|l pnn h.ydd.w yqm.|l p'n h.ykr'.w yql.|w yšu.g h.w yṣḥ.|ḥwt.aḫt.w nar[-].|qrn.d bat 10[76].2.18
|b ḥrb.mlḥt.|qṣ.mri.ndd.|y'šr.w yšqyn h.|ytn.ks.b d h.|krpn.b klat.yd h.|b krb.'ẓm.ridn.|mt.šmm.ks.qdš.|l tph 3['NT].1.10
yitsp.|ršp.nṯdṯt.ǵlm.|ym.mšb't hn.b šlḥ.|ttpl.y'n.ḥtk h.|krt y'n.ḥtk h.rš.|mid.grdš.ṯbt h.|w b tm hn.špḥ.yitbd.| 14[KRT].1.21
ydm.ṯpṭ.|nhr.'z.ym.l ymk.l tnǵṣn.pnt h.l ydlp.|tmn h.kṯr.ṣmdm.ynḥt.w yp'r.šmt hm.|šm k.at.aymr.aymr.mr.y 2.4[68].18
ym.rṯ.|dn.il.bt h.ymǵyn.|yštql.dnil.l hkl h.|'rb.b bt h.kṯrt.bnt.|hll.snnt.apnk.dnil.|mt.rpi.ap.hn.ǵzr.mt.|hrnmy 17[2AQHT].2.26
[ṯ]rt.|w y[ššq].bnt.hll.snnt.|mk.b šb['.]ymm.tb'.b bt h.kṯrt.bnt.hll.snnt.|[-]d[-]t.n'm y.'rš.h[--]m.|ysmsmt.'rš.ḫl 17[2AQHT].2.39
lk qẓ.tn nkl y|rḫ ytrḫ.ib t'rb m b bh|t h.w atn mhr h l a|b h.alp ksp w rbt ḫ|rṣ.išlḥ ẓhrm iq|nim.atn šd h krm[24[77].19
št mṣb.mznm.um h.|kp mznm.iḫ h yṯ'r.|mšrrm.aḫt h l a|bn mznm.nkl w ib.|d ašr.ar yrḫ.w y|rḫ yar k.|[ašr il 24[77].36
l[.---].|w tglṯ thmt.'[--.---].|yṣi.ǵl h tḥm b[.---].|mrḥ h l adrt[.---].|ṯtb 'ṯtrt b ǵl[.---].|qrẓ tšt.l šmal[.---].|arbḫ.'n 2001.1.7
ṯr.tdry|nn.b išt.tšrpnn.|b rḥm.tṭḥnn.b šd.|tdr'nn.šir h.l tikl.|'ṣrm.mnt h.l tkly.|npr[m.]šir.l šir.yṣḥ. 6[49].2.35
.dgn.b š[---].|b'l.ytb.l ks[i.mlk h].|bn.dgn.l kḥ[ṯ.drkt h].|l alp.ql.ẓ[--.---].|l np ql.nd.[----].|tlk.w tr.b[ḫl].|b n'm 10[76].3.15
n h b bt.šrš.b qrb.|hkl h.nṣb.skn.ilib h.b qdš.|ẓtr.'m h.l arṣ.mššu.qṭr h.|l 'pr.ḏmr.aṯr h.ṭbq.lḥt.|niṣ h.grš d.'šy.ln 17[2AQHT].1.28
[b bt.šrš.]b qrb.hkl h.|[nṣb.skn.i]lib h.b qdš.|[ẓtr.'m h.l a]rṣ.mššu.|[qṭr h.l 'pr.ḏ]mr.a[ṯ]r h.|[ṭbq.lḥt.niṣ h.gr]š.d 17[2AQHT].1.46
ṣat.mrḥ h.|l tl.yṣb.pn h.ṯǵr.|yṣu.hlm.aḫ h.tph.|[ksl]h.l arṣ.ṯṯbr.|[---.]aḫ h.tbky.|[--.m]rṣ.mlk.|[---.]krt.adn k.|[16.1[125].54
bq.l.iytlm.|[---].l.iytlm.|[---.]'bdilm.l.iytlm.|[---.n]ḫl h.lm.iytlm. 1076.6
'nt.hlkt.w.šnwt.|tp.aḫ.h.k.ysmsm.|tspi.šir.h.l.bl.ḥrb.|tšt.dm.h.l.bl.ks.|tpnn.'n.bty.'n.btt.tpnn.|'n.mḫr. RS225.3
w.šnwt.|tp.aḫ.h.k.ysmsm.|tspi.šir.h.l.bl.ḥrb.|tšt.dm.h.l.bl.ks.|tpnn.'n.bty.'n.btt.tpnn.|'n.mḫr.'n.pḫr.'n.ṯǵr.|'n.ṯ RS225.4
n.|šd.bn.nṣdn.l bn.'mlbi.|šd.ṯpḫln.l bn.ǵl.|w dṯn.nḫl h.l bn.pl.|šd.krwn.l aḫn.|šd.'yy.l aḫn.|šd.brdn.l bn.bly.|šd 2089.10
.|b šb'.w l.yšn.pbl.|mlk.l qr.ṯigt.ibr h.|l ql.nhqt.ḥmr h.|l g't.alp.ḥrṯ.zǵt.|klb.ṣpr.w ylak.|mlakm.l k.'m.krt.|msw 14[KRT].3.121
.|w l.yšn.pbl.|mlk.l [qr.]ṯiqt.|ibr h[.l]ql.nhqt.|ḥmr[h.l g't.]alp.|ḥrṯ[.l z]ǵt.klb.|[ṣ]pr[.apn]k.|[pb]l[.mlk.g]m.l aṯ 14[KRT].5.225
.ktp.zbl ym.bn ydm.ṯpṭ.|nhr.'z.ym.l ymk.l tnǵṣn.pnt h.l ydlp.|tmn h.kṯr.ṣmdm.ynḥt.w yp'r.šmt hm.|šm k.at.ay 2.4[68].17
wy.w tkbd h.|hlm.il.k yphn h.|yprq.lṣb.w yṣḥq.|p'n h.l hdm.ytpd.w ykrkr.|uṣb't h.yšu.g h.w y[ṣḥ].|ik.mǵyt.rbt 4[51].4.29
.šmn.tmtrn.|nḫlm.tlk.nbtm.|šmḫ.lṭpn.il.d pid.|p'n h.l hdm.ytpd.|w yprq.lṣb w yṣḥq.|yšu.g h.w yṣḥ.|aṯbn.ank 6[49].3.15
r.z]bl.am..|rkm.agzrt[.--].arḫ..|b'l.azrt.'nt.[-]ld.|kbd h.l yd' hr h.[---]d[-].|tnq[.---.]in[b]b.p'r.|yd h[.--.]ṣ'r.glgl.|a 13[6].31
mt.ymṣḫ.l arṣ.|[ytb.]b[']l.l ksi.mlk h.|[---].l kḥṯ.drkt h.|l [ym]m.l yrḫm.l yrḫm.|l šnt.[m]k.b šb'.|šnt.w [--].bn.il 6[49].5.6
mḫṣ h.k d.'l.qšt h.|imḫṣ h.'l.qṣ't h.hwt.|l aḥw.ap.qšt h.l ttn.|l y.w b mt[.-]ḥ.mṣṣ[-]t[.--].|pr'.qẓ.y[bl].šblt.|b ǵlp h 19[1AQHT].1.16
pnn.|b rḥm.tṭḥnn.b šd.|tdr'nn.šir h.l tikl.|'ṣrm.mnt h.l tkly.|npr[m.]šir.l šir.yṣḥ. 6[49].2.36
|itrṯ.ḫrṣ.ṭrd.b'l.|b mrym.ṣpn.mšṣṣ.[-]k'[-].|udn h.grš h.l ksi.mlk h.|l nḫt.l kḥṯ.drkt h.|mn m.ib.yp'.l b'l.ṣrt.l rkb.' 3['NT].4.46
t'mt.[']ṯr.[k]m.|zbln.'l.riš h.|w ṯtb.trḥṣ.nn.b d't.|npš h.l lḥm.tpth.|brlt h.l ṯrm.|mt.dm.ḫt.š'tqt.|dm.lan.w ypqd. 16.6[127].11
ṣrrt.ṣpn.|ytb.l kḥṯ.aliyn.|b'l.p'n h.l tmǵyn.|hdm.riš h.l ymǵy.|aps h.w y'n.'ṯtr.'rẓ.|l amlk.b ṣrrt.ṣpn.|yrd.'ṯtr.'r 6.1.60[49.1.32]
.|apnk.'ṯtr.'rẓ.|y'l.b ṣrrt.ṣpn.|ytb.l kḥṯ.aliyn.|b'l.p'n h.l tmǵyn.|hdm.riš h.l ymǵy.|aps h.w y'n.'ṯtr.'rẓ.|l amlk.b 6.1.59[49.1.31]

i[m.iqra.ilnym].|b qrb.h[kl y.atr h.rpum.l] |tdd.atr[h.l tdd.ilnym].|asr.mr[kbt.---].|t'ln.l mr[kbt hm.tity.l] |'r h 22.1[123].21
.km.[iqra km.ilnym.b] |hkl y.atr[h.rpum.l tdd].|atr h.l t[dd.ilnym].|yḥpn.ḥy[ly.zbl.mlk.'llm y].|šm'.atm[.-- 22.1[123].11
].|km.iqr[a km.ilnym.b hkl y].|atr h.r[pum.l tdd.atr h].|l tdd.il[nym.---].|mhr.b'l[.---.mhr].|'nt.lk b[t y.rpim.rpi 22.1[123].5
ḥ km.iqra.|[km.ilnym.b h]kl y.atr h.rpum.|[l tdd.atr h].l tdd.ilnym.|[---.m]rz'y.apnnk.yrp.|[---.]km.r'y.ht.alk.|[21[122].1.4
km.iqra km.|[ilnym.b hkl]y.atr h.rpum.|[l tdd.atr]h.l tdd.i[lnym].|[---.]r[--.---].|[---.yt]b.l arṣ. 21[122].1.12
.b'l.|b mrym.ṣpn.mšṣṣ.[-]k'[-].|udn h.grš h.l ksi.mlk h.|l nḥt.l kḥt.drkt h.|mn m.ib.yp'.l b'l.ṣrt.l rkb.'rpt.|[-]'n.ǵ 3['NT].4.46
-].|b d.aliyn b['l.---].|kd.ynaṣn[.---].|gršnn.l k[si.mlk h.l nḥt.l kḥt].|drkt h.š[--.--].|w hm.ap.l[--.---].|ymḫṣ k.k[--. 1['NT.X].4.24
d.il.ǵzr.y'r.mt.|b ql h.y[---.---].|b'l.yṯṯbn[.l ksi].|mlk h.l[nḥt.l kḥt].|drkt h[.---].|[---.]d[--.---].|[---].hn[.---].|[---. 6[49].6.34
[--.]'m[.-.]att y[.-].|[---.]tḥm.|[---]t.[ ]r.|[---.--]n.|[---] h.l 'db.|[---]n.yd h.|[---].bl.išlḥ.|[---] h.gm.|[l --- k.]ysḥ.|[-- 14[KRT].5.234
.ablm.|d 'l k.mḫṣ.aqht.ǵzr.|'wrt.yšt k.b'l.l ht.|w 'lm h.l 'nt.p dr.dr.|'db.uḫry.mṭ.yd h.|dnil.bt h.ymǵyn.yšt|ql.d 19[1AQHT].4.168
h.|[nṣb.skn.i]lib h.b qdš.|[ztr.'m h.l a]rṣ.mšṣu.|[qṭr h.l 'pr.ḏ]mr.a[t]r h.|[ṭbq.lḥt.niṣ h.gr]š.d 'šy.|[ln h.---].|z[tr. 17[2AQHT].1.47
b.|hkl h.nṣb.skn.ilib h.b qdš.|ztr.'m h.l arṣ.mšṣu.qṭr h.|l 'pr.ḏmr.atr h.ṭbq.lḥt.|niṣ h.grš d.'šy.ln h.|aḫd.yd h.b š 17[2AQHT].1.28
.|[---.š]mt.|[---].y[--.--]m.|[---.--]n.d[--.--]i.|[--]t.mdt h[.l.]'ṯtrt.šd.|[---.-]rt.mḫṣ.bnš.mlk.yb'l hm.|[---.--]t.w.ḫpn.l. 1106.52
ṯrm.|[--]b b[ht].|[zbl.]ym.b hkl.ṯpṭ.nh[r].ytir.ṯr.il.ab h l pn[.zb]l y[m].|[l pn.ṯp]ṭ[.nhr.]mlkt.[--]pm.l mlkt.wn.in. 2.3[129].21
l h.ṯmnt.bn um.|krt.ḥtk n.rš.|krt.grdš.mknt.|att.ṣdq h.l ypq.|mtrḫt.yšr h.|att.trḫ.w tb't.|ṯar um.tkn l h.|mtltt.k 14[KRT].1.12
šdpt.w hn.špšm.|b šb'.w l.yšn.pbl.|mlk.l qr.ṯigt.ibr h.|l ql.nhqt.ḥmr h.|l g't.alp.ḥrṯ.zǵt.|klb.ṣpr.w ylak.|mlak 14[KRT].3.120
.ym.|mk.špšm.b šb'.|w l.yšn.pbl.|mlk.l [qr.]ṯiqt.|ibr h[.l]ql.nhqt.|ḥmr[h.l g't.]alp.|ḥrṯ[.l z]ǵt.klb.|[ṣ]pr[.apn]k. 14[KRT].5.224
.|šrh.l arṣ.brqm.|bt.arzm.yklln h.|hm.bt.lbnt.y'msn h.|l yrgm.l aliyn b'l.|ṣḥ.ḫrn.b bhm k.|'dbt.b qrb.hkl k.|tbl 4[51].5.73
'd 'lm...gn'.|iršt.aršt.|l aḫ y.l r' y.dt.|w ytnnn.|l aḫ h.l r' h.|r' 'lm.|ttn.w tn.|w l ttn.|w al ttn.|tn ks yn.|w ištn 1019.1.10
.b 'z.|[rpu.m]lk.'lm.b ḏmr h.bl.|[---].b ḥtk h.b nmrt h.l r|[--.]arṣ.'z k.ḏmr k.l[-]|n k.ḥtk k.nmrt k.b tk.|ugrt.l y UG5.2.2.8
--.t]š'm.|[---.--]y arb'm.|[---.]l špš ṯmny[m].|[---.]dbr h l šp[š].|[---.]dbr h l šp[š].|[---.]nptry ṯ[--].|[---.--]urm.|[--- 41[71].8
b'm.|[---.]l špš ṯmny[m].|[---.]dbr h l šp[š].|[---.]dbr h l šp[š].|[---.]nptry ṯ[--].|[---.--]urm.|[-----]. 41[71].9
.|[ḥš.]bht h.tbnn.|[ḥš.]trmm.hkl h.|y[tl]k.l lbnn.w 'ṣ h.|l[šr]yn.mḥmd.arz h.|h[n.l]bnn.w 'ṣ h.|š[r]yn.mḥmd.arz 4[51].6.18
]yqrb.trẓẓ h.|[---].mǵy h.w ǵlm.|[a]ḫt h.šib.yṣat.mrḥ h.|l tl.yṣb.pn h.tǵr.|yṣu.hlm.aḫ h.tph.|[ksl]h.l arṣ.ṯṯbr.|[-- 16.1[125].51
ln.'l.riš h.|w ṯṯb.trḥṣ.nn.b d't.|npš h.l lḥm.tpth.|brlt h.l ṯrm.|mt.dm.ḫt.š'tqt.|dm.lan.w ypqd.|krt.ṯ'.yšu.g h.|w 16.6[127].12
.y'dyn h.yb|ltm.ybln h.mǵy.ḥrn.l bt h.w.|yštql.l ḥṭr h.tlu ḫt.km.nḫl.|tplg.km.plg.|b'd h.bhtm.mnt.b'd h.bhtm.s UG5.7.68
r[.---.]'l.kbkbt.|n'm.[--.-]llm.trtḥṣ.|btlt.'n[t].tptr' ṭd[h].|limm.w t'l.'m.il.|ab h.ḥpr.p'l k.y[--].|šm' k.l arḫ.w bn.[13[6].19
.|aqrb k ab h b'[l].|yǵtr.'ṯtr t|rḫ l k ybrdmy.b[t.a]|b h lb[u] y'rr.w y'[n].|yrḫ nyr šmm.w n'[n].|'ma nkl ḫtn y.a[24[77].30
b'ld'.yd[.---.']šrt.ksp h.|lbiy.pdy.[---.k]sp h. 2112.1
.ql bl.|'m ḥrn.mṣd h.mnt.nṯk nḥš.|šmrr.nḥš.'q šr.ln h.mlḫš.|abd.ln h.ydy.ḥmt.|b ḥrn.pnm.trǵnw.w ṯtkl.|bnwt UG5.7.59
'm.|šḥr.w šlm šmm h mnt.nṯk.nḥš.|šmrr.nḥš 'q šr.ln h.mlḫš.|abd.ln h.ydy ḥmt.hlm.ytq šqy.|nḥš.yšlḥm.nḥš.'q šr UG5.7.53
|nḥš.šlḥm.nḥš.'q šr[.y']db.ksa.|nḥš.šmrr.nḥš.'q šr.ln h.ml|ḫš.abd.ln h.ydy.ḥmt.hlm.ytq.|w ytb.|tqru.l špš.um h. UG5.7.21
k nhrm.b 'dt.thmtm.|mnt.nṯk.nḥš.šmrr.nḥš.|'q šr.ln h.mlḫš abd.ln h.ydy.|ḥmt.hlm.ytq ytqšqy.nḥš.yšlḥm.'q šr.| UG5.7.5
m.ql.bl.'m.|dgn.ttl h.mnt.nṯk.nḥš.šmrr.|nḥš.'q šr.ln h.mlḫš.abd.ln h.|ydy.ḥmt.hlm.ytq.nḥš.yšlḥm.|nḥš.'q šr.y'd UG5.7.16
l.|'m b'l.mrym.ṣpn.mnt y.nṯk.|nḥš.šmrr.nḥš.'q šr ln h.|mlḫš.abd.ln h.ydy.ḥmt.hlm.ytq.|nḥš.yšlḥm.nḥš.'q šr.yd UG5.7.10
l 'm.|ṯt.w kmṯ.ḥryt h.mnt.nṯk.nḥš.šm|rr.nḥš.'q šr.ln h.mlḫš abd.ln h.|ydy.ḥmt.hlm.ytq nḥš yšlḥm.nḥš.|'q.šr.y'd UG5.7.37
ql.bl.'m.|mlk.'ṯtrt h.mnt.nṯk.nḥš.šmrr.|nḥš.'q šr.ln h.mlḫš abd.ln h.ydy.|ḥmt.hlm.ytq.nḥš.yšlḥm.nḥš.|'q šr.y'd UG5.7.42
špš.um.ql b.'m.|ršp.bbt h.mnt.nḥš.šmrr.|nḥš.'q šr.ln h.mlḫš.abd.ln h.ydy.|ḥmt.hlm.ytq.nḥš.yšlḥm.nḥš 'q.|š.y'd UG5.7.32
l.'m|kṯr.w ḫss.kptr h.mnt.nṯk.nḥš.|šmrr.nḥš.'q šr.ln h.mlḫš.abd.|ln h.ydy.ḥmt.hlm ytq.nḥš.|yšlḥm.nḥš.'q šr.y'd UG5.7.47
q]l bl.'m.|yrḫ.lrgt h.mnt.nṯk.n[ḥš].šmrr.|nḥš.'q šr.ln h.mlḫš.abd.ln h.ydy.|ḥmt.hlm.ytq.nḥš.yšlḥm.nḥš.|'q šr.y'd UG5.7.27
t h.|uṣb't h.'d.ṯkm.|'rb.b ẓl.ḥmt.lqḥ.|imr.dbḥ.b yd h.|lla.klatnm.|klt.lḥm h.d nzl.|lqḥ.msrr.'ṣr.db[ḥ].|yṣq.b gl 14[KRT].3.160
dm ṯrrt.|udm.ytnt.il w ušn.|ab.adm.w ṯṯb.|mlakm.l h.lm.ank.|ksp.w yrq.ḫrṣ.|yd.mqm h.w 'bd.|'lm.ṯlṯ.sswm.m 14[KRT].3.137
'ršm.|yšu.'wr.mzl.|ymzl.w yṣi.trḫ.|ḥdṯ.yb'r.l ṯn.|att h.lm.nkr.|mddt h.k irby.|[t]škn.šd.|km.ḥsn.pat.mdbr.|lk. 14[KRT].2.102
] l.hdm.ytb.|l arṣ.yṣq.'mr.|un.l riš h.'pr.plṯt.|l qdqd h.lpš.yks.|mizrtm.ǵr.b abn.|ydy.psltm.b y'r.|yhdy.lḥm.w 5[67].6.16
aḥd.kbd.|arb'm.b ḫzr.|lqḥ š'rt.|ṯt 'šr h.lqḥ.|ḫlpnt.|ṯt.ḥrtm.|lqḥ.š'rt.|'šr.ḥrš.|bhtm.lqḥ.|š'rt.|ar 2052.4
qyn.yn.qḥ.|ks.b d y.qb't.b ymn y[.t]q|ḥ.pǵt.w tšqyn h.tq[ḥ.ks.]b d h.|qb't.b ymn h.w y'n.yṯ[p]n[.mh]r.|št.b yn. 19[1AQHT].4.217
š.mlk.ab.šnm.|[l p'n.il.t]hbr.w tql.tštḥ|[wy.w tkbd]n h.tlšn.aqht.ǵzr.|[---.kdd.dn]il.mt.rpi.w t'n.|[btlt.'nt.tšu.g]h 17[2AQHT].6.51
m.tt.|w.ṯmnt.ksp.hn.|ktn.d.ṣr.pḥm.b h.w.ṯqlm.|ksp h.mitm.pḥm.b d.skn.|w.ṯt.ktnm.ḥmšt.w.nṣp.ksp.hn. 1110.5
.ḏmr.ḫlqm.b mm['].|mhrm.mṭm.tgrš.|šbm.b ksl.qšt h.mdnt.|w hln.'nt.l bt h.tmǵyn.|tštql.ilt.l hkl h.|w l.šb't.t 3['NT].2.16
h.šr.|aqht.y'n.kmr.kmr[.--].|k ap'.il.b gdrt.k lb.l |ḥt h.imḫṣ h.k d.'l.qšt h.|imḫṣ h.'l.qṣ't h.hwt.|l aḥw.ap.qšt h.l 19[1AQHT].1.14
.kmr[.--].|k ap'.il.b gdrt.k lb.l |ḥt h.imḫṣ h.k d.'l.qšt h.|imḫṣ h.'l.qṣ't h.hwt.|l aḥw.ap.qšt h.l ttn.|l y.w b mt[.-]ḥ 19[1AQHT].1.14
].|qdqd h.w y'n.ytpn.[mhr.št].|šm'.l btlt.'nt.at.'[l.qšt h].|tmḫṣ h.qṣ't h.hwt.l t[ḥwy].|n'mn.ǵzr.št.ṯrm.w[---].|išti 18[3AQHT].4.12
l mḫšt.mdd.|il ym.l klt.nhr.il.rbm.|l ištbm.tnn.ištml h.|mḫšt.bṯn.'qltn.|šlyṭ.d šb't.rašm.|mḫšt.mdd ilm.ar[š].|ṣ 3['NT].3.37
-.]yd.sǵr[.---.--]r h.|aḥ[d.---.']šrm.d[d.---].|'š[r.---.--]r h.|my y[--.---.--]d.|'šrm[.---.--]r h.|[-]wyn.yd[-.---.]dd.|[---] 1098.37
il.l mšknt hm.|w tqrb.w ld.bn.l h.|w tqrb.w ld.bnt.l h.|mk.b šb'.šnt.|bn.krt.km hm.tdr.|ap.bnt.ḥry.|km hm.w 15[128].3.21
|iṯ.yn.d 'rb.bṯk[.---].|mǵ hw.l hn.lg yn h[.---].|w ḥbr h.mla yn.[---]. 23[52].76
dlt.w burm.[l]b.|rmṣt.ilhm.b'lm.dṯt.w kšm.ḫmš.|'ṯr h.mlun.šnpt.ḫṣt h.b'l.ṣpn š.|[--]ṯ š.ilt.mgdl š.ilt.asrm š.|w l 34[1].10
-.]wmrkm.|bir.ḫmš.|uškn.arb'.|ubr'y.ṯlṯ.|ar.ṯmn 'šr h.|mlk.arb'.|ǵbl.ḫmš.|atlg.ḫmš 'šr[h].|ulm ṯ[ṯ].|m'rby.ḫ 68[65].1.5
.|[--.i]mṣḫ.nn.k imr.l arṣ.|[ašhlk].šbt h.dmm.šbt.dqn h.|[mm'm.-]d.l ytn.bt.l b'l.k ilm.|[w ḥẓ]r.k bn.atrt[.td'ṣ.]p' 3['NT.VI].5.10
šṣṣ.[-]k'[-].|udn h.grš h.l ksi.mlk h.|l nḥt.l kḥt.drkt h.|mn m.ib.yp'.l b'l.ṣrt.l rkb.'rpt.|[-]'n.ǵlmm.y'nyn.l ib.yp'. 3['NT].4.47
.[---.-]št.|hl ny.argmn.d [ybl.n]qmd.|l špš.arn.ṯn[.'šr h.]mn.|'ṣrm.ṯql.kbd[.ks].mn.ḫrṣ.|w arb'.ktnt.w [---]b.|[ḫm 64[118].19
b.ksa.w ytb.|tqru.l špš.um h.špš.um.ql b.'m.|ršp.bbt h.mnt.nḥš.šmrr.|nḥš.'q šr.ln h.mlḫš.abd.ln h.ydy.|ḥmt.hl UG5.7.31
ytb.|tqru l špš.um h.špš.um.ql.bl.'m.|'nt w 'ṯtrt inbb h.mnt.nṯk.|nḥš.šlḥm.nḥš.'q šr[.y']db.ksa.|nḥš.šmrr.nḥš.'q UG5.7.20

ṯb.|tqru l špš.um h.špš.um.ql bl ʻm.|šḥr.w šlm šmm h mnt.nṯk.nḥš.|šmrr.nḥš ʻq šr.ln h.mlḫš.|abd.ln h.ydy ḥmt UG5.7.52
ʻdb.ksa.w yṯb.|tqru.l špš.um.ql bl.ʻm|kṯr.w ḫss.kptr h.mnt.nṯk.nḥš.|šmrr.nḥš.ʻq šr.ln h.mlḫš.abd.|ln h.ydy.ḥmt UG5.7.46
ksa.w yṯb.|tqru l špš um h.špš um ql.bl.ʻm.|mlk.ʻṯtrt h.mnt.nṯk.nḥš.šmrr.|nḥš.ʻq šr.ln h.mlḫš abd.ln h.ydy.|ḥmt UG5.7.41
b.ksa.|w yṯb.|tqru.l špš.u h.špš.um.ql.bl.ʻm.|dgn.ttl h.mnt.nṯk.nḥš.šmrr.|nḥš.ʻq šr.ln h.mlḫš.abd.ln h.|ydy.ḥmt UG5.7.15
ksa.w yṯb.|tqru l špš.um h.špš.um.ql bl.|ʻm ḥrn.mṣd h.mnt.nṯk nḥš.|šmrr.nḥš.ʻq šr.ln h.mlḫš.|abd.ln h.ydy.ḥmt UG5.7.58
q.|w yṯb.|tqru.l špš.um h.špš.[um.q]l bl.ʻm.|yrḫ.lrgt h.mnt.nṯk.n[ḥš].šmrr.|nḥš.ʻq šr.ln h.mlḫš.abd.ln h.ydy.|ḥ UG5.7.26
yṯb.|tqru l špš.um h.špš.um.ql bl ʻm.|ṯṯ.w kmṯ.ḥryt h.mnt.nṯk.nḥš.šm|rr.nḥš.ʻq šr.ln h.mlḫš abd.ln h.|ydy.ḥmt UG5.7.36
nḥšm.mhr k.bn bṯn.|itnn k.|aṯr ršp.ʻṯtrt.|ʻm ʻṯtrt.mr h.|mnt.nṯk.nḥš. UG5.7.TR2
rʻrm.ynʻrn h.|ssnm.ysyn h.ʻdtm.yʻdyn h.yb|ltm.ybln h.mǵy.ḥrn.l bt h.w.|yštql.l ḥṭr h.tlu ḥt.km.nḥl.|tplg.km.pl UG5.7.67
gr bt il.|ʻnt.brḫ.p ʻlm h.ʻnt.p dr[.dr].|ʻdb.uḫry mṭ.yd h.|ymǵ.l mrrt.tǵll.b nr.|yšu.g h.w yṣḥ.y l k.mrrt.|tǵll.b nr. 19[1AQHT].3.155
b d.nsʻ k.|ʻnt.brḫ.p ʻlm h.|ʻnt.p dr.dr.ʻdb.uḫry mṭ yd h.|ymǵ.l qrt.ablm.abl[m].|qrt.zbl.yrḫ.yšu g h.|w yṣḥ.y l k. 19[1AQHT].3.162
hrm.mṭm.tgrš.|šbm.b ksl.qšt h.mdnt.|w hln.ʻnt.l bt h.tmǵyn.|tštql.ilt.l hkl h.|w l.šbʻt.tmtḫṣ h.b ʻmq.|tḫtṣb.bn. 3[ʻNT].2.17
l ht.|w ʻlm h.l ʻnt.p dr.dr.|ʻdb.uḫry.mṭ.yd h.|dnil.bt h.ymǵyn.yšt|ql.dnil.l hkl h.ʻrb.b|kyt.b hkl h.mšspdt.b ḥẓr 19[1AQHT].4.170
].|y.bt.il.ṯḥ.gg y.b ym.ṭiṭ.|rḥṣ.npṣ y.b ym.rṭ.|dn.il.bt h.ymǵyn.|yštql.dnil.l hkl h.|ʻrb.b bt h.kṯrt.bnt.|hll.snnt.ap 17[2AQHT].2.24
.|k šbʻt.l šbʻm.aḫ h.ym[.--].|w ṯmnt.l ṯmnym.|šr.aḫy h.mẓa h.|w mẓa h.šr.yly h.|b skn.sknm.b ʻdn.|ʻdnm.kn.np 12[75].2.51
.bʻl.yʻn.tdrq.|ybnt.ab h.šrḥq.aṯt.l pnn h.|št.alp.qdm h.mria.w tk.|pn h.tḥspn.m h.w trḥṣ.|ṭl.šmm.šmn.arṣ.ṭl.šm[3[ʻNT].4.85
spr..k tlakn.|ǵlmm.|aḫr.mǵy.kṯr.w ḫss.|št.alp.qdm h.mra.|w tk.pn h.tʻdb.ksu.|w yṯtb.l ymn.aliyn.|bʻl.ʻd.lḥm.š 4[51].5.107
šbʻ.ṯnnm.w.šbʻ.ḫsnm.|ṯmn.ʻšr h.mrynm.|ʻšr.mkrm.|ḫmš.ṯrtnm.|ḫmš.bn.mrynm.|ʻšr.mru 1030.2
ḫr.mr[-.---].|bn.idrn.ʻš[-.---].|bn.bly.mr[-.---].|w.nḥl h.mr[-.---].|ilšpš.[---].|iḫny.[---].|bn.[---]. 88[304].11
ʻṯtrt.---].|bʻl m.hmt.[---].|l šrr.šṯ[.---].|b riš h.[---].|ib h.mš[--.---].|[b]n.ʻn h[.---]. 2.4[68].39
[-----].|w.lmd h.|mtn.|w.lmd h.|ymn.|w.lmd h.|yʻḏrn.|w.lmd h.|ʻdn.|w 1049.1.2
ḫdt.plk h[.b yd h].|plk.qlt.b ymn h.|npyn h.mks.bšr h.|tmtʻ.md h.b ym.ṯn.|npyn h.b nhrm.|štt.ḫptr.l išt.|ḫbrṯ.l 4[51].2.5
ḥẓt.tḥm k.|mlk n.aliyn.bʻl.ṯpṭ n.|in.d ʻln h.klny y.qš h.|nbln.klny y.nbl.ks h.|any.l yṣḥ.ṯr.il.ab h.il.|mlk.d yknn 3[ʻNT.VI].5.41
m k.mlk n.aliy[n.]bʻl.|ṯpṭ n.w in.d ʻln h.|klny n.q[š] h.n[bln].|klny n[.n]bl.ks h.|[an]y.l yṣḥ.ṯr il.ab h.|[i]l.mlk.d 4[51].4.45
t.|kḥṣ.k mʻr[.---].|yṣḥ.ngr il.ilš.|ilš.ngr.bt.bʻl.|w aṯt h.ngrt.ilht.|w yʻn.lṭpn.il d pi[d].|šmʻ.l ngr.il il[š].|ilš.ngr bt 16[126].4.9
k.ph[.-].|k il.ḥkmt.k ṯr.lṭpn.|ṣḥ.ngr.il.ilš.il[š].|w aṯt h.ngrt[.i]lht.|kḥṣ.k mʻr[.---].|yṣḥ.ngr il.ilš.|ilš.ngr.bt.bʻl.|w 16[126].4.5
---.]tdbḥ.amr.|ṯmn.b qrb.hkl y.[aṯr h.rpum].|tdd.aṯr h.tdd.iln[ym.---].|asr.sswm.tṣmd.dg[-.---].|tʻln.l mrkbt hm. 20[121].2.2
pʻr.šmt hm.|šm k.at.aymr.aymr.mr.ym.mr.ym.|l ksi h.nhr l kḥṯ.drkt h.trtqṣ.|b d bʻl.km.nšr b uṣbʻt h.hlm.qdq| 2.4[68].20
ypʻr.šmt hm.šm k at.|ygrš.ygrš.grš ym grš ym.l ksi h.|[n]hr l kḥṯ drkt h.trtqṣ.b d bʻl km nš|r.b uṣbʻt h.hlm.ktp 2.4[68].12
mn.prst[.---].|ydr.hm.ym[.---].|ʻl amr.yu[ḫd.ksa.mlk h].|nḥṯ.kḥṯ.d[rkt h.b bt y].|aṣḥ.rpi[m.iqra.ilnym].|b qrb.h[22.1[123].17
ṯqlm.arṣ h.|km ḫmšt.mṯt h.|bm.bky h.w yšn.|b dmʻ h.nhmmt.|šnt.tluan.|w yškb.nhmmt.|w yqmṣ.w b ḥlm h.|i 14[KRT].1.32
.yqḥ.il.mštʻltm.|mštʻltm.l riš.agn.yqḥ.tš.b bt h.|il.ḥṭ h.nḥt.il.ymnn.mṭ.yd h.yšu.|yr.šmm h.yr.b šmm.ʻṣr.yḫrṭ yšt 23[52].37
š.|abd.ln h.ydy.ḥmt.|b ḥrn.pnm.trǵnw.w ttkl.|bnwt h.ykr.ʻr.d qdm.|idk.pnm.l ytn.tk aršḫ.rbt.|w aršḫ.ṯrrt.ydy. UG5.7.62
bn.nqq.|ḥrš.bhtm.|bn.izl.|bn.ibln.|bn.ilt.|špšyn.nḥl h.|nʻmn.bn.iryn.|nrn.nḥl h.|bn.ḫsn.|bn.ʻbd.|[-----].|[---.n] 85[80].2.6
.|k bʻl.k yḥwy.yʻšr.ḥwy.yʻš.|r.w yšqyn h.ybd.w yšr.ʻl h.|nʻm[n.w t]ʻnynn.ap ank.aḥwy.|aqht[.ǵz]r.w yʻn.aqht.ǵzr 17[2AQHT].6.31
tḥm.ydn.ʻm.mlk.|bʻl h.ngr.ḥwt k.|w l.a[--]t.tšknn.|ḫmšm.l mi[t].any.|tškn[n.--] 2062.1.2
[-----].|l abn[.---].|aḫdt.plk h[.b yd h].|plk.qlt.b ymn h.|npyn h.mks.bšr h.|tmtʻ.md h.b ym.ṯn.|npyn h.b nhrm.| 4[51].2.4
y.|tmrnn.l bny.bnwt.|w ykn.bn h b bt.šrš.b qrb.|hkl h.nṣb.skn.ilib h.b qdš.|ztr.ʻm h.l arṣ.mšṣu.qṭr h.|l ʻpr.ḏmr. 17[2AQHT].1.27
ḥmḥmt.|[---.mt.r]pi.w ykn.bn h.|[b bt.šrš.]b qrb.hkl h.|[nṣb.skn.i]lib h.b qdš.|[ztr.ʻm h.l a]rṣ.mšṣu.|[qṭr h.l ʻpr. 17[2AQHT].1.44
ṯṯ.bʻd n.ksl.ttbr.|ʻln.pn h.tdʻ.tǵṣ.pnt.|ksl h.anš.dt.ẓr h.tšu.|g h.w tṣḥ.ik.mǵy.gpn.w ugr.|mn.ib.ypʻ.l bʻl.ṣrt.|l rk 3[ʻNT].3.32
n.ksl.|[ttbr.ʻln.p]n h.td[ʻ].|tǵṣ[.pnt.ks]l h.|anš.dt.ẓr.[h].|tšu.g h.w tṣḥ[.i]k.|mǵy.aliy[n.b]ʻl.|ik.mǵyt.b[t]lt.|ʻnt.m 4[51].2.20
.|yprq.lṣb.w yṣḥq.|pʻn h.l hdm.ytpd.w ykrkr.|uṣbʻt h.yšu.g h.w y[ṣḥ].|ik.mǵyt.rbt.aṯr[t.y]m.|ik.atwt.qnyt.i[lm] 4[51].4.30
rš..|mlk.ab.šnm.l pʻn.|il.thbr.w tql.|tštḥwy.w tkbdn h.|tšu.g h.w tṣḥ.tšmḫ ht.|aṯrt.w bn h.ilt.w ṣb|rt.ary h.k mt 6.1.38[49.1.10]
[rbt.kmn.l pʻ]n.ʻnt.|[yhbr.w yql.yšt]ḥwyn.w y|[kbdn h.yšu.g h.w y]ṣḥ.tḥm.|[ṯr.il.ab k.hwt.l]ṭpn.ḥtk k.|[qryy.b a 1[ʻNT.IX].2.17
[n.pn h.tdʻ.b ʻdn].|ksl.y[ṯbr.yǵṣ.pnt.ksl h].|anš.[dt.ẓr h.yšu.g h].|w yṣ[ḥ.---].|mḫṣ[.---].|š[--.---]. 19[1AQHT].2.96
ʻm.bn.ilm.mt.|tk.qrt h.hmry.mk.ksu.|ṯbt.ḫḫ.arṣ.nḥlt h.tša.|g hm.w tṣḥ.tḥm.aliyn.|bn.bʻl.hwt.aliy.qrdm.|bhṯ.bn. 5[67].2.16
bʻ].|[mlakm.l yṯb].|[idk.pnm.l ytn].|[ʻ]m[.krt.mswn h].|tš[an.g hm.w tṣḥn].|tḥ[m.pbl.mlk].|qḥ[.ksp.w yrq].|ḫr 14[KRT].6.266
rt[.---].|ṯṯb ʻṯtrt b ǵl[.---].|qrẓ tšt.l šmal[.---].|arbḫ.ʻn h tšu w[.---].|aylt tǵpy ṯr.ʻn[.---].|b[b]r.mrḫ h.ti[ḫd.b yd h] 2001.1.10
ar.|[---.]h.mḥtrt.pṯtm.|[---.-]t h.ušpǵt tišr.|[---.šm]m h.nšat ẓl h kbkbm.|[---.]b km kbkbt k ṯn.|[---.]bʻl yḥmdn 2001.2.5
ʻltm.l riš.agn.yqḥ.tš.b bt h.|il.ḥṭ h.nḥt.il.ymnn.mṭ.yd h.yšu.|yr.šmm h.yr.b šmm.ʻṣr.yḫrṭ yšt.|l pḥm.il.aṯtm.k ypt 23[52].37
.diy.b tʻrt y.aqht.[km.yṯb].|l lḥm.w bn.dnil.l ṯrm[.ʻl h].|nšrm.trḫpn.ybṣr.[ḥbl.d]|iym.bn.nšrm.arḫp.an[k.ʻ]l.|aq 18[3AQHT].4.19
km.diy.|b tʻrt h.aqht.km.yṯb.l lḥ[m].|bn.dnil.l ṯrm.ʻl h.nšr[m].|trḫpn.ybṣr.ḥbl.diy[m.bn].|nšrm.trḫp.ʻnt.ʻl[.aqht] 18[3AQHT].4.30
phn.[---].|b grn.yḫrb[.---].|yǵly.yḫsp.ib[.---].|ʻl.bt.ab h.nšrm.trḫ[p]n.|ybṣr.ḥbl.diym.|tbky.pǵt.bm.lb.|tdmʻ.bm.k 19[1AQHT].1.32
---].|urt[n.---].|ʻdn[.---].|bqrt[.---].|ṯnǵrn.[---].|w.bn h.n[--.---].|ḥnil.[---].|aršmg.mru.|bʻl.šlm.ʻbd.|awr.ṯǵrn.ʻbd. 2084.7
mṭ.|al[iyn.bʻ]l šlbšn.|i[---.---.--]l h.mǵẓ.|y[--.---.]l irt h.|n[--.---]. 5[67].5.25
ḏ.|w l.rbt.kmyr.|aṯr.ṯn.ṯn.hlk.|aṯr.ṯlṯ.kl hm.|aḥd.bt h.ysgr.|almnt.škr.|tškr.zbl.ʻršm.|yšu.ʻwr.|mzl.ymzl.|w yb 14[KRT].4.184
.|w l rbt.kmyr.|[a]ṯr.ṯn.ṯn.hlk.|aṯr.ṯlṯ.kl hm.|yḥd.bt h.sgr.|almnt.škr.|tškr.zbl.ʻršm.|yšu.ʻwr.mzl.|ymzl.w yṣi.tr 14[KRT].2.96
py.w.aṯt h.|bn.glgl.uškny.|bn.ṯny.uškny.|mnn.w.aṯt h.|slmu.ḥrš.mrkbt.|bnšm.dt.l.mlk.|ʻbdyrḫ.bn.ṯyl.|ʻbdn.w. 2068.15
[.rʻ h].|[ʻ]ṯtr[-].w.[rʻ h].|ḫlly[-].w.rʻ[h].|ilmškl.w.rʻ[h].|ššw[.--].w.r[ʻ h].|kr[mn.--.]w.r[ʻ h].|šd.[--.w.]r[ʻ h].|ḫla 2083.2.2
|w aršḫ.ṯrrt.ydy.b ʻṣm.ʻrʻr.|w b šḥt.ʻs.mt.ʻrʻrm.ynʻrn h.|ssnm.ysyn h.ʻdtm.yʻdyn h.yb|ltm.ybln h.mǵy.ḥrn.l bt h. UG5.7.65
rʻym.dt.b d.iytlm.|ḫyrn.w.šǵr h.|šǵr.bn.prsn.|agpṯr.w.šǵ[r h].|ṭʻln.|mztn.w.šǵr [h].|šǵr.p 2072.2
ǵr h.|šǵr.bn.prsn.|agpṯr.w.šǵ[r h].|ṭʻln.|mztn.w.šǵr [h].|šǵr.plṭ.|s[d]rn [w].ṯn.šǵr h.|[---.]w.šǵr h.|[---.]w.šǵr h.| 2072.6
.ʻnt.|nʻm h.km.tsm.|ʻṯtrt.tsm h.|d ʻq h.ib.iqni.|ʻpʻp h.sp.ṯrml.|d b ḥlm y.il.ytn.|b ḏrt y.ab.adm.|w ld.špḥ.l krk 14[KRT].6.295

.ʻnt.nʻm h.|km.tsm.ʻṯtrt.ts[m h].|d ʻq h.ib.iqni.ʻp[ʻp] h.|sp.ṯrml.tḥgrn.[-]dm[.-].|ašlw.b ṣp.ʻn h.|d b ḥlm y.il.ytn. 14[KRT].3.147
.|dnil.bt h.ymǵyn.yšt|ql.dnil.l hkl h.ʻrb.b|kyt.b hkl h.mšspdt.b ḥẓr h.|pẓǵm.ǵr.ybk.l aqht.|ǵzr.ydmʻ.l kdd.dnil. 19[1AQHT].4.172
l.al.ilak.l bn.|ilm.mt.ʻdd.l ydd.|il.ǵzr.yqra.mt.|b npš h.ystrn ydd.|b gngn h.aḥd y.d ym|lk.ʻl.ilm.l ymru.|ilm.w 4[51].7.48
rt.]ṯʻ.|tḥm[.pbl.mlk].|qḥ.[ksp.w yr]q.|ḫrṣ[.yd.mqm] h.|ʻbd[.ʻlm.ṯlṯ].|ss[wm.mrkbt].|b[trbṣ.bn.amt].|[qḥ.krt.šl 14[KRT].5.251
aṯt h.w.bn h.|[--]an.w.aṯt h.|[--]y.w.aṯt h.|[--]r.w.aṯt h.|ʻbdyrḫ.ṯn ǵlyt h.|aršmg.|ršpy.w.aṯt h.|bn.glgl.uškny.|b 2068.9
.|myṣm.|ṯgt.|w.lmd h.|ytil.|w.lmd h.|rpan.|w.lmd h.|ʻbdrpu.|w.lmd h.|ʻdršp.|w.lmd h.|krwn b.gt.nbk.|ddm 1099.14
[spr.----]m.|bn.pi[ty].|w.nḫ[l h].|ʻbd[--].|bn.s[---].|bn.at[--].|bn.qnd̲.|ṣmq[-].|bn.anny.| 117[325].1.3
l.yqḥ.|bt.hnd.b d.|[ʻb]dmlk.|[-]k.amʻ[--].|[w.b] d.bn h[.ʻ]d ʻlm.|[w.un]ṯ.in[n.]b h.|[---.]nʻm[-]. 1009.17
ʻlmt.|bnš bnšm.|l.yqḥnn.b d.|bʻln.bn.kltn.|w.b d.bn h.ʻd.|ʻlm.w unṯ.|in.b h. 1008.19
ml]k.d.b riš.|[--.-]nt.|[l.ʻb]dmlk.|[--.-]m[-]r.|[w.l.]bn h.ʻd.|[ʻl]m.mn k.|mn km l.yqḥ.|bt.hnd.b d.|[ʻb]dmlk.|[-]k 1009.11
m h.yd.|[k]lkl h.|[w] ytn.nn.|l.bʻln.bn.|kltn.w l.|bn h.ʻd.ʻlm.|šḫr.ʻlmt.|bnš bnšm.|l.yqḥnn.b d.|bʻln.bn.kltn.|w 1008.14
ʻbd.il.w hdrt.|yrtḥṣ.w yadm.|yrḥṣ.yd h.amt h.|uṣbʻt h.ʻd.ṯkm.|ʻrb.b ẓl.ḫmt.lqḥ.|imr.dbḥ.b yd h.|lla.klatnm.|klt 14[KRT].3.158
mm.|aḫr.mǵy.kṯr.w ḫss.|št.alp.qdm h.mra.|w tk.pn h.tʻdb.ksu.|w yṯṯb.l ymn.aliyn.|bʻl.ʻd.lḥm.št[y.ilm].|[w]yʻn 4[51].5.108
š.|ydm.aḫr.ymǵy.kṯr.|w ḫss.b d.dnil.ytnn.|qšt.l brk h.yʻdb.|qṣʻt.apnk.mṯt.dnty.|tšlḥm.tššqy ilm.|tsad.tkbd.hm 17[2AQHT].5.27
l.|tplg.km.plg.|bʻd h.bhtm.mnt.bʻd h.bhtm.sgrt.|bʻd h.ʻdbt.ṯlṯ.ptḥ.bt.mnt.|ptḥ.bt.w ubn.hkl.w ištql šql.|tn.km.n UG5.7.71
dy.b ʻṣm.ʻrʻr.|w b šḫt.ʻs.mt.ʻrʻrm.ynʻrn h.|ssnm.ysyn h.ʻdtm.yʻdyn h.yb|ltm.ybln h.mǵy.ḥrn.l bt h.w.|yštql.l ḥṭr UG5.7.66
---].|prd.mʻqby[.w.---.a]ṯt h[.---].|prṯ.mgd[ly.---.]aṯ[t h].|ʻdyn[.---].|w.ṯn[.bn h.---].|iwrm[-.]b[n.---].|annt[n.]w[.- 2044.11
d h.|mtn.|w.lmd h.|ymn.|w.lmd h.|yʻd̲rn.|w.lmd h.|ʻdn.|w.lmd h.|bn.špš.|[w.l]m[d h].|yṣ[---].|ʻbd[--].|pr[- 1049.1.8
ḫm.b d[.---].|[---].ṯl[l]m.[---].|[--].r[-]y[.---].|ʻl.[--]l[-] h.|ʻdn.[---].|d.u[--.---]. 2104.11
d h.|ytil.|w.lmd h.|rpan.|w.lmd h.|ʻbdrpu.|w.lmd h.|ʻdršp.|w.lmd h.|krwn b.gt.nbk.|ddm.kšmm.l.ḫtn.|ddm 1099.16
.|w ḫrṣ.bht.ṯhrm.|iqnim.šmḫ.aliyn.|bʻl.ṣḥ.ḫrn.b bht h.|ʻd̲bt.b qrb hkl h.|yblnn ǵrm.mid.ksp.|gbʻm lḥmd.ḫrṣ.|y 4[51].5.98
bd.nʻm.|yšr.ǵzr.ṭb.ql.|ʻl.bʻl.b ṣrrt.|ṣpn.ytmr.bʻl.|bnt h.yʻn.pdry.|bt.ar.apn.ṭly.|[bt.r]b.pdr.ydʻ.|[---]t.im[-]lt.|[--- 3[ʻNT].1.23
.|k apʻ.il.b gdrt.k lb.l|ḥt h.imḫṣ h.k d.ʻl.qšt h.|imḫṣ h.ʻl.qṣʻt h.hwt.|l aḥw.ap.qšt h.l ttn.|l y.w b mt[.-]ḫ.mṣṣ[-]t[19[1AQHT].1.15
liyn.bʻl.|tšmʻ.nrt.ilm.špš.|tšu.aliyn.bʻl.l ktp.|ʻnt.k tšt h.tšʻlyn h.|b ṣrrt.ṣpn.tbkyn h.|w tqbrn h.tštnn.b ḫrt.|ilm.a 6[62].1.15
uzr.ilm.ylḥm.|[uzr.]yšqy.bn qdš.yd.ṣt h.|[dn]il.yd.ṣt h.yʻl.w yškb.|[yd.]mizrt.p yln.mk.b šbʻ.ymm.|[w]yqrb.bʻl. 17[2AQHT].1.15
[mt.hrnmy.]uzr.ilm.ylḥm.|[uzr.yšqy.]bn.qdš.yd.|[ṣt h.yʻl.]w yškb.yd.|[mizrt.]p ynl.hn.ym.|[w ṯn.uzr.]ilm.dnil. 17[2AQHT].1.5
t.|w ht.aḫ y.|bn y.yšal.|tryl.p rgm.|l mlk.šm y.|w l h.yʻl m.|w h[t] aḫ y.|bn y.yšal.|tryl.w rgm[.-].|ṯṯb.l aḫ k.|l 138.14
ḥ.dnil.|[mt.rp]i.brlt.ǵzr.mt hrnmy.|[---].hw.mḫ.l ʻrš h.yʻl.|[---].bm.nšq.aṯt h.|[---.]b ḥbq h.ḥmḥmt.|[---.--] n.ylt. 17[2AQHT].1.39
h.|yšt[.il.y]n.ʻd šbʻ.trṯ.ʻd škr.|il.hlk.l bt h.yštql.|l ḥṭr h.yʻmsn.nn.ṯkmn.|w šnm.w ngšnn.ḥby.|bʻl.qrnm w d̲nb.ylš UG5.1.1.18
[-.yuḫ]d.b yd.mšḫṭ.bm.ymn.mḫṣ.ǵlmm.yš[--].|[ymn h.ʻn]t.tuḫd.šmal h.tuḫd.ʻṯtrt.ik.m[ḫṣt.ml]|[ak.ym.tʻ]dt.ṯpṭ.n 2.1[137].40
ǵzr.šrš k.b arṣ.al.|ypʻ.riš.ǵly.b d.nsʻ k.|ʻnt.brḥ.p ʻlm h.|ʻnt.p dr.dr.ʻdb.uḫry mṭ yd h.|ymǵ.l qrt.ablm.abl[m].|qr 19[1AQHT].3.161
ym.d ʻ[l k].|mḫṣ.aqht.ǵzr.amd.gr bt il.|ʻnt.brḥ.p ʻlm h.ʻnt.p dr[.dr].|ʻdb.uḫry mṭ.yd h.|ymǵ.l mrrt.tǵll.b nr.|yšu 19[1AQHT].3.154
ksi.ytb.|l hdm[.w] l.hdm.ytb.|l arṣ.yṣq.ʻmr.|un.l riš h.ʻpr.plṯt.|l qdqd h.lpš.yks.|mizrtm.ǵr.b abn.|ydy.psltm.b 5[67].6.15
rḥṣ.npṣ y.b ym.rṭ.|dn.il.bt h.ymǵyn.|yštql.dnil.l hkl h.|ʻrb.b bt h.kṯrt.bnt.|hll.snnt.apnk.dnil.|mt.rpi.ap.hn.ǵzr. 17[2AQHT].2.25
|ʻdb.uḫry.mṭ.yd h.|dnil.bt h.ymǵyn.yšt|ql.dnil.l hkl h.ʻrb.b|kyt.b hkl h.mšspdt.b ḥẓr h.|pẓǵm.ǵr.ybk.l aqht.|ǵz 19[1AQHT].4.171
l.|rḥb.mknpt.ap.|[k]rt.bnm.il.špḥ.|lṭpn.w qdš.ʻl.|ab h.yʻrb.ybky.|w yšnn.ytn.g h.|bky.b ḥy k.ab n.ašmḫ.|b l.mt 16.1[125].12
t].|ap.krt bn[m.il].|špḥ.lṭpn[.w qdš].|bkm.tʻr[b.ʻl.ab h].|tʻrb.ḥ[--].|b ṯtm.t[---].|šknt.[---].|bkym[.---].|ǵr.y[----]. 16.2[125].112
.|ṯṭbḫ.šmn.[m]ri h.|t[p]tḥ.rḥbt.yn.|ʻl h.ṯr h.tšʻrb.|ʻl h.tšʻrb.ẓby h.|ṯr.ḥbr.rbt.|ḥbr.ṯrrt.|bt.krt.tbun.|lm.mṯb[.---] 15[128].4.18
.|rd.l mlk.amlk.|l drkt.k aṯb.an.|ytbʻ.yṣb ǵlm.ʻl.|ab h.yʻrb.yšu g h.|w yṣḥ.šmʻ mʻ.l krt.|ṯʻ.ištmʻ.w tqǵ udn.|k ǵz 16.6[127].40
ʻ.mtt.[ḥ]ry.|ṯṭbḫ.šmn.[m]ri h.|t[p]tḥ.rḥbt.yn.|ʻl h.ṯr h.tšʻrb.|ʻl h.tšʻrb.ẓby h.|ṯr.ḥbr.rbt.|ḥbr.ṯrrt.|bt.krt.tbun.|l 15[128].4.17
[---.šnst.kpt.b ḥb]š h.ʻtkt r[išt].|[l bmt h.---.]hy bt h tʻrb.|[---.tm]tḫṣ b ʻmq.|[tḫtṣb.bn.qrtm.ttʻr.ṯlḥnt.]l ṣbim.| 7.1[131].3
d.sǵ[r.---.--]k.[--].|[---.]dd.bn.š.[---.]yd.sǵr h.|[---.--]r h.ʻšr[m.---.ʻ]šrm.dd.|[---.yn.d.]nkly.l.rʻym.šbʻm.l.mitm.dd.| 1098.43
ṣbm.|[---.]nrn.mʻry.|[---.--]r.|[---.]w.ṯn.bn h.|[---.b]t h.ʻtgrm. 2043.12
[---.šnst.kpt.b ḥb]š h.ʻtkt r[išt].|[l bmt h.---.]hy bt h tʻrb.|[---.tm]tḫṣ b ʻmq.|[t 7.1[131].2
.|tškrǵ.w.rʻ h.|ǵlwš.w.rʻ h.|kdrš.w.rʻ h.|ṯrm[-].w[.rʻ h].|[ʻ]ṯtr[-].w.[rʻ h].|ḫlly[-].w.rʻ[h].|ilmškl.w.rʻ[h].|ššw[.-- 2083.1.6
m.|w [th]rn.w tldn mṯ.|al[iyn.bʻ]l šlbšn.|i[---.---.--]l h.mǵẓ.|y[--.---.]l irt h.|n[--.---]. 5[67].5.24
ḫrny.w.rʻ h.|klbr.w.rʻ h.|tškrǵ.w.rʻ h.|ǵlwš.w.rʻ h.|kdrš.w.rʻ h.|ṯrm[-].w[.rʻ h].|[ʻ]ṯtr[-].w.[rʻ h 2083.1.3
šlm.---].|[š]lm.bnš.yš[lm.---].|[-]r.l šlmt.šl[m.---.--]|r h.p šlmt.p šlm[.---].|bt.l bnš.trg[m.---].|l šlmt.l šlm.b[--.---] 59[100].4
[---.]bʻl.šm[.--.]rgbt yu.|[---]w yrmy[.q]rn h.|[---.-]ny h pdr.ttǵr.|[---.n]šr k.al ttn.l n.|[---.]tn l rbd.|[---.]bʻlt h w 2001.2.11
[a]ḫt h.šib.yṣat.mrḥ h.|l tl.yṣb.pn h.tǵr.|yṣu.hlm.aḫ h.tph.|[ksl]h.l arṣ.ttbr.|[---.]aḫ h.tbky.|[--.m]rṣ.mlk.|[---.] 16.1[125].53
isp k.yd.aqht.|ǵzr.tšt k.b qrb m.asm.|y.dnh.ysb.aklt h.yph.|šblt.b akt.šblt.ypʻ.|b ḥmdrt.šblt.yḫ[bq].|w ynšq.aḫl. 19[1AQHT].2.68
yn.yšt|ql.dnil.l hkl h.ʻrb.b|kyt.b hkl h.mšspdt.b ḥẓr h.|pẓǵm.ǵr.ybk.l aqht.|ǵzr.ydmʻ.l kdd.dnil.|mt.rpi.l ymm. 19[1AQHT].4.172
[tk].|ǵr.tliyt.šbʻt.brqm.[---].|ṯmnt.iṣr rʻt.ʻṣ brq y.|riš h.tply.ṭly.bn.ʻn h.|uzʻrt.tmll.išd h.qrn[m].|dt.ʻl h.riš.h.b glṯ UG5.3.1.5
[-----].|l abn[.---].|aḫdt.plk h[.b yd h].|plk.qlt.b ymn h.|npyn h.mks.bšr h.|tmtʻ.md h.b ym.ṯn. 4[51].2.3
hlk.bʻl.aṯtrt.|k tʻn.hlk.btlt.|ʻnt.tdrq.ybmt.|[limm].b h.pʻnm.|[ṭṭ.b ʻ]dn.ksl.|[ṯtbr.ʻln.p]n h.td[ʻ].|tǵṣ[.pnt.ks]l h. 4[51].2.16
qdš.b ǵr.nḥlt y.|b nʻm.b gbʻ.tliyt.|hlm.ʻnt.tph.ilm.b h.pʻnm.|ṭṭ.bʻd n.ksl.ṯtbr.|ʻln.pn h.tdʻ.tǵṣ.pnt.|ksl h.anš.dt. 3[ʻNT].3.29
t.aqht.ǵzr.[šṣat].|btlt.ʻnt.k [rḥ.npš h].|k iṯl.brlt h.[b h.pʻnm].|ṭṭ.ʻl[n.pn h.tdʻ.b ʻdn].|ksl.y[ṯbr.yǵṣ.pnt.ksl h].|a 19[1AQHT].2.93
l ḥmš.mrkbt.ḥmš.ʻšr h.prs.|bt.mrkbt.w l šant.ṯṯ.|l bt.ʻšrm.|bt alḥnm.ṯlṯm ṯṯ kbd 2105.1
.|l pʻn.il.thbr.w tql.|tštḥwy.w tkbd h.|hlm.il.k yphn h.|yprq.lṣb.w yṣḥq.|pʻn h.l hdm.ytpd.w ykrkr.|uṣbʻt h.yšu. 4[51].4.27
.|lḥn š[-]ʻ[--.]aḥd[.-].|tšmʻ.mtt.[ḥ]ry.|ṯṭbḫ.šmn.[m]ri h.|t[p]tḥ.rḥbt.yn.|ʻl h.ṯr h.tšʻrb.|ʻl h.tšʻrb.ẓby h.|ṯr.ḥbr.rbt 15[128].4.15
[-----].|[ṯṭbḫ.šm]n.[mri h].|[tptḥ.rḥ]bt.[yn].|[---.]rp[.---].|[---.ḥ]br[.---].|bḥr[.--]t[.- 15[128].5.1
il dbḥ.b bt h.mṣd.ṣd.b qrb|hkl [h].ṣḥ.l qṣ.ilm.tlḥmn.|ilm.w tštn.tštn y[UG5.1.1.1
ḥ.]il.mštʻltm.mštʻltm.l riš.agn.|hl h.[t]špl.hl h.trm.hl h.tṣḥ.ad ad.|w hl h.tṣḥ.um.um.tirk m.yd.il.k ym.|w yd il.k 23[52].32

h

y n[.n]bl.ks h.|[an]y.l yṣḥ.ṯr il.ab h.|[i]l.mlk.d yknn h.yṣḥ.|aṯrt.w bn h.ilt.w ṣbrt.|ary h.wn.in.bt.l b'l.|km.ilm. 4[51].4.48
n.klny y.nbl.ks h.|any.l yṣḥ.ṯr.il.ab h.il.|mlk.d yknn h.yṣḥ.aṯrt.|w bn h.ilt.w ṣbrt.arḫ h.|wn.in.bt.l b'l.km.ilm.|ḥ 3['NT.VI].5.44
-.--]y.|[-----].|[any.l yṣ]ḥ.ṯr.|[il.ab h.i]l.mlk.|[d yknn h.yṣ]ḥ.aṯ|[rt.w bn h.]ilt.|[w ṣbrt.ary]h.|[wn.in.bt.l b'l.]|[k 4[51].1.7
tm.l riš.agn.|hl h.[t]špl.hl h.trm.hl h.tṣḥ.ad ad.|w hl h.tṣḥ.um.um.tirk m.yd.il.k ym.|w yd il.k mdb.ark.yd.il.k y 23[52].33
il dbḥ.b bt h.mṣd.ṣd.b qrb|hkl [h].ṣḥ.l qṣ.ilm.tlḥmn.|ilm.w tštn.tštn y[n] 'd šb'.|trṯ.'d.škr.y UG5.1.1.2
nt.imr.qmṣ.l[l]im.|ṣḥ.aḫ h.b bht h.a[r]y h.|b qrb hkl h.ṣḥ.|šb'm.bn.aṯrt.|špq.ilm.krm.y[n].|špq.ilht.ḫprt[.yn].|š 4[51].6.45
ṣṣ mr'm ḫmšm ḫmš kbd.|ṣṣ ubn ḫmš 'šr h.|ṣṣ 'myd ḫmšm.|ṣṣ tmn.ḫmšm.|[ṣṣ] 'mtḏl ṯlṯm.|ṣṣ 'mlbi ṯ 2097.2
.b d y.qb't.b ymn y[.t]q|ḥ.pǵt.w tšqyn h.tq[ḥ.ks.]b d h.|qb't.b ymn h.w y'n.yṯ[p]n[.mh]r.|št.b yn.yšt.ila.il š[--.]il. 19[1AQHT].4.217
b bht m.urbt.|b qrb.hk[l m.yp]tḥ.|b'l.b dqt[.'rp]t.|ql h.qdš.b['l.y]tn.|yṯny.b'l.ṣ[---.-]pt h.|ql h.q[dš.ṯb]r.arṣ.|[---.] 4[51].7.29
dqt[.'rp]t.|ql h.qdš.b['l.y]tn.|yṯny.b'l.ṣ[---.-]pt h.|ql h.q[dš.ṯb]r.arṣ.|[---.]ǵrm[.t]ḫšn.|rḥq[.---.td'].|qdm ym.bmt. 4[51].7.31
.krpn.|l t'n.aṯrt.alp.|kd.yqḥ.b ḫmr.|rbt.ymsk.b msk h.|qm.ybd.w yšr.|mṣltm.bd.n'm.|yšr.ǵzr.ṭb.ql.|'l.b'l.b ṣrrt. 3['NT].1.17
m.w ngšnn.ḥby.|b'l.qrnm w ḏnb.ylšn.|b ḫri h.w ṭnt h.ql.il.[--].|il.k yrdm.arṣ.'nt.|w 'ṯtrt.tṣdn.[---].|[---.-]b[-.---]. UG5.1.1.21
.|b'l.b dqt[.'rp]t.|ql h.qdš.b['l.y]tn.|yṯny.b'l.ṣ[---.-]pt h.|ql h.q[dš.ṯb]r.arṣ.|[---.]ǵrm[.t]ḫšn.|rḥq[.---.td'].|qdm y 4[51].7.30
.w y'n.yṯpn.[mhr.št].|šm'.l btlt.'nt.at.'[l.qšt h].|tmḫṣ h.qṣ't h.hwt.l t[ḥwy].|n'mn.ǵzr.št.ṯrm.w[---].|ištir.b ḏdm. 18[3AQHT].4.13
.b'l.yṯbr.diy.|hmt.hm.t'pn.'l.qbr.bn y.|tšḫṭann.b šnt h.qr.[mym].|mlk.yṣm.y l km.qr.mym.d '[l k].|mḫṣ.aqht.ǵz 19[1AQHT].3.151
ḫrḫb mlk qẓ [l].|n'mn.ilm l ḫt[n].|m.b'l trḫ pdry b[t h].|aqrb k ab h b'[l].|yǵtr.'ṯtr t|rḫ l k ybrdmy.b[t.a]|b h lb 24[77].26
r[bdd.]l kb[d.š]dm.yšt.|[----.]b'l.mdl h.yb'r.|[---.]rn h.aqry.|[---.]b a[r]ṣ.mlḥmt.|ašt[.b ']p[r] m.ddym.ask.|šlm.l 3['NT].4.71
t.iṣr r't.'ṣ brq y.|riš h.tply.ṭly.bn.'n h.|uz'rt.tmll.išd h.qrn[m].|dt.'l h.riš h.b glṯ.b šm[m].|[---.i]l.ṯr.iṯ.p h.k ṯt.ǵlt UG5.3.1.6
[.---].|[---].aḥw.aṭm.prṭl[.---].|[---.]mnt.[l]p'n[.-.-]bd h.aqšr[.---].|[---].ptḥ y.a[--.]dt[.---].ml[--].|[---.-]ṯk.ytmt.dlt 1001.1.20
kl h.|w t'nyn.ǵlm.b'l.|in.b'l.b bht ht.|il hd.b qrb.hkl h.|qšt hn.aḫd.b yd h.|w qṣ't h.bm.ymn h.|idk.l ytn pnm.|t 10[76].2.5
.ṭpṭ.nhr.yprsḥ.ym.yql.|l arṣ.tnǵṣn.pnt h.w ydlp.tmn h.|yqṯ b'l.w yšt.ym.ykly.ṯpṭ.nhr.|b šm.tg'r m.'ṯtrt.bṯ l aliyn 2.4[68].26
.---].|yrmm h[--.---].|mlk.gb' h d [---].|ibr.k l hm.d l h q[--.---].|l ytn.l hm.tḥt b'l[.---].|h.u qšt pn hdd.b y[.----]. 9[33].2.4
.|riš h.tply.ṭly.bn.'n h.|uz'rt.tmll.išd h.qrn[m].|dt.'l h.riš h.b glṯ.b šm[m].|[---.i]l.ṯr.iṯ.p h.k ṯt.ǵlt[.--].|[---.--] k y UG5.3.1.7
.d |msdt.arṣ.|s'.il.dqt.k amr.|sknt.k ḥwt.yman.|d b h.rumm.l rbbt. 4[51].1.44
pn h.tḥspn.m h.w trḥṣ.|ṭl.šmm.šmn.arṣ.ṭl.šm[m.t]sk h.|rbb.nsk h.kbkbm.|ttpp.anhbm.d alp.šd[.ẓu h.b ym].|ṭl[. 3['NT].4.87
.w trḥṣ.|[ṭ]l.šmm.šmn.arṣ.rbb.|[r]kb 'rpt.ṭl.šmm.tsk h.|[rb]b.nsk h.kbkbm. 3['NT].2.40
|rgm.my.b[ilm.ydy].|mrṣ.grš[m.zbln].|in.b ilm.'[ny h.yrb'].|yḫmš.rgm.[my.b ilm].|ydy.mrṣ.g[ršm.zbln].|in.b il 16[126].5.16
š.kkrm.ṣml.|'šrt.ksp h.|ḫmš.kkr.qnm.|ṯlṯ.w.ṯlṯ.ksp h.|arb'.kkr.|algbṯ.arb't.|ksp h.|kkr.š'rt.|šb't.ksp h.|ḫmš. 1127.13
|ṯlṯ mrkbt mlk.|d.l.ṣpy.|[---.t]r hm.|[---].ššb.|[---.]tr h.|[a]rb'.ql'm.|arb'.mdrnm.|mdrn.w.mšḫṭ.|d.mrkbt.|mlk. 1122.9
[---.]dyn.ḫmšt.'šrt.|[---.-]til.ḫmšt.l 'šrm.|[--.-]n.w.aḫt h.arb'm.|[--.-]dn.'šrm.|[--.-]dwn.ṯlṯm.w.šb'.alpm.|[kt]rmlk 2054.2.21
iṯ.šmt.iṯ.|'ẓm.abky w aqbrn h.aštn.|b ḫrt.ilm.arṣ.b p h.rgm.l[yṣ]a.|b špt h.hwt h.knp.ṣml.b'[l].|b'l.ṯbr.diy.hyt.tq 19[1AQHT].3.141
mt.hm.iṯ[.'ẓm].|abky.w aqbrn.aštn.b ḫrt.|i[lm.arṣ.b p h.rgm.l yṣa.b šp]|t h.hwt h.knp.hrgb.b'l.ṯbr.|b'l.ṯbr.diy.hw 19[1AQHT].3.127
t.hm.i[ṯ].|'ẓm.abky.w aqbrn h.|ašt.b ḫrt.ilm.arṣ.|b p h.rgm.l yṣa.b špt h.hwt[h].|knp.nšrm.b'l.yṯbr.|b'l.ṯbr.diy 19[1AQHT].3.113
rt.|ur.tisp k.yd.aqht.ǵz[r].|tšt k.bm.qrb m.asm.|b p h.rgm.l yṣa.b špt h[.hwt h].|b nši 'n h.w tphn.in.[---].|[-.]hl 19[1AQHT].2.75
thm.|[yqḥ.]il.mšt'ltm.mšt'ltm.l riš.agn.|hl h.[t]špl.hl h.trm.hl h.tṣḥ.ad ad.|w hl h.tṣḥ.um.um.tirk m.yd.il.k ym.| 23[52].32
ṣpn.b alp.šd.rbt.kmn.|hlk.aḫt h.b'l.y'n.tdrq.|ybnt.ab h.šrḥq.aṯt.l pnn h.|št.alp.qdm h.mria.w tk.|pn h.tḥspn.m h 3['NT].4.84
...gn'.|iršt.aršt.|l aḫ y.l r' y.dt.|w ytnnn.|l aḫ h.l r' h.|r' 'lm.|ttn.w tn.|w l ttn.|w al ttn.|tn ks yn.|w ištn.|'bd. 1019.1.10
im.|[rpim.bt y.aṣ]ḥ km.iqra km.|[ilnym.b hkl]y.aṯr h.rpum.|[l tdd.aṯr]h.l tdd.i[lnym].|[---.]r[--.---].|[---.yṯ]b.l 21[122].1.11
rpim.rpim.b]t y.aṣḥ km.iqra.|[km.ilnym.b h]kl y.aṯr h.rpum.|[l tdd.aṯr h].l tdd.ilnym.|[---.m]rz'y.apnnk.yrp.|[- 21[122].1.3
m.rpim.b bt y.aṣḥ].|km.iqr[a km.ilnym.b hkl y].|aṯr h.r[pum.l tdd.aṯr h].|l tdd.il[nym.---].|mhr.b'l[.---.mhr].|'n 22.1[123].5
rkt h.b bt y].|aṣḥ.rpi[m.iqra.ilnym].|b qrb.h[kl y.aṯr h.rpum.l] |tdd.aṯr[h.l tdd.ilnym].|asr.mr[kbt.---].|t'ln.l m 22.1[123].20
.rpim.b bt y].|aṣḥ.km.[iqra km.ilnym.b] |hkl y.aṯr[h.rpum.l tdd].|aṯr h.l t[dd.ilnym.ṯm].|yḥpn.ḥy[ly.zbl.mlk.' 22.1[123].10
.|[---.]dt.'l.lty.|[---.]tdbḥ.amr.|ṯmn.b qrb.hkl y.[aṯr h.rpum].|tdd.aṯr h.tdd.iln[ym.---].|asr.sswm.tṣmd.dg[-.---]. 20[121].2.1
.|ṣdqn.|'bd.pdr.|myṣm.|ṯgt.|w.lmd h.|yṯil.|w.lmd h.|rpan.|w.lmd h.|'bdrpu.|w.lmd h.|'dršp.|w.lmd h.|krw 1099.12
.|iḫmlk.|yp'n w.aṯt h.|anntn.yṣr.|annmn.w.ṯlṯ.n'[r] h.|rpan.w.ṯ[n.]bn h.|bn.ayln.w.ṯn.bn h.|yt. 2068.25
k.at.aymr.aymr.mr.ym.mr.ym.|l ksi h.nhr l kḥṯ.drkt h.trtqṣ.|b d b'l.km.nšr b uṣb't h.hlm.qdq|d zbl ym.bn.'nm. 2.4[68].20
at.|ygrš.ygrš.grš ym grš ym.l ksi h.|[n]hr l kḥṯ drkt h.trtqṣ.b d b'l km nš|r.b uṣb't h.hlm.ktp.zbl ym.bn ydm.|[ṯ 2.4[68].13
t.ǵlm.|ym.mšb't hn.b šlḥ.|ttpl.y'n.ḥtk h.|krt y'n.ḥtk h.rš.|mid.grdš.ṯbt h.|w b tm hn.šph.yitbd.|w b.pḫyr h.yrṯ. 14[KRT].1.22
b ṯṯ ym ḥdṯ.|ḥyr.'rbt.|špš tǵr h.|ršp.|w 'bdm tbqrn.|skn. 1162.3
p.alp šlmm.|l b'l.'ṣr l ṣpn.|npš.w.š.l ršp bbt.|[']ṣrm l h.ršp [-]m.|[---.]bqt[-].|[b] ǵb.ršp mh bnš.|šrp.w ṣp ḫrš̱ḫ.|' UG5.12.A.12
.yd]bḥ.mlk.l.prgl.ṣqrn.b.gg.|ar[b'.]arb'.mṯbt.azmr.b h.š.šr[-].|al[p.w].š.šlmm.pamt.šb'.klb h.|yr[--.]mlk.ṣbu.špš. 35[3].51
.bm.ymn.|[w]yqrb.trẓẓ h.|[---].mǵy h.w ǵlm.|[a]ḫt h.šib.yṣat.mrḥ h.|l tl.yṣb.pn h.tǵr.|yṣu.hlm.aḫ h.tph.|[ksl] 16.1[125].51
aliyn.b'l.|yuhb.'glt.b dbr.prt.|b šd.šḥlmmt.škb.|'mn h.šb'.l šb'm.|tš[']ly.ṯmn.l ṯmnym.|w [th]rn.w tldn mṯ.|al[iy 5[67].5.20
.|'r.ym.l bl[.---].|b[---.]ny[.--].|l bl.sk.w [---] h.|ybm h.šb'[.---].|ǵzr.ilḥu.t[---]l.|trm.tṣr.trm[.']tqt.|tbky.w tšnn.[t 16.2[125].94
b'l y.mlk[y.---].|yd.bt h.yd[.---].|ary.yd.t[--.---].|ḫtn h.šb'l[.---].|ṯlḥny.yd[.---].|yd.ṯlṯ.kl[t h.---].|w.ṯṯm.ṣi[n.---].| 81[329].16
w[.---].|aylt tǵpy ṯr.'n[.---].|b[b]r.mrḥ h.ti[ḫd.b yd h].|š[g]r h bm ymn.t[--.---].|[--.]l b'l.'bd[.---].|ṯr ab h il.ṯṯr 2001.1.12
rkšt.|l'q[.---].|šd.pll.b d.qrt.|š[d].anndr.b d.bdn.nḥ[l h].|[šd.]agyn.b d.kmrn.n[ḥl] h.|[š]d.nbzn.[-]l.qrt.|[š]d.agpṯ 2029.7
nḥl h.|šd knn.bn.ann.'db.|šd.iln[-].bn.irṯr.l.šḫrn.nḥl h.|šd[.ag]pṯn.b[n.]brrn.l.qrt.|šd[.--]dy.bn.brzn.|l.qrt. 2029.20
rn.n[ḥl] h.|[š]d.nbzn.[-]l.qrt.|[š]d.agpṯr.b d.šḫrn.nḥl h.|šd.annmn.b d.tyn.nḥl h.|šd.pǵyn[.b] d.krmn.l.ty[n.n]ḥl 2029.10
'[db].|šd.ṯ[r]yn.bn.tkn.b d.qrt.|šd[.-].dyn.b d.pln.nḥl h.|šd.irdyn.bn.ḫrǵš[-].l.qrt.|šd.iǵlyn.bn.kzbn.l.qr[t].|šd.pln 2029.15
arb'.'šr h.šd.|w.kmsk.d.iwrkl.|ṯlṯ.šd.d.bn.mlkyy.|kmsk.šd.iḫmn.|š 1079.1
šd.iǵlyn.bn.kzbn.l.qr[t].|šd.pln.bn.tiyn.b d.ilmhr nḥl h.|šd knn.bn.ann.'db.|šd.iln[-].bn.irṯr.l.šḫrn.nḥl h.|šd[.ag] 2029.18
annmn.b d.tyn.nḥl h.|šd.pǵyn[.b] d.krmn.l.ty[n.n]ḥl h.|šd.krz.[b]n.ann.'[db].|šd.ṯ[r]yn.bn.tkn.b d.qrt.|šd[.-].dy 2029.12

š[d].annḏr.b d.bdn.nḥ[l h]. | [šd.]agyn.b d.kmrn.n[ḥl] h. | [š]d.nbzn.[-]l.qrt. | [š]d.agpṯr.b d.šḫrn.nḥl h. | šd.annmn.b 2029.8
spr.ubdy.art. | šd.prn.b d.agpṯn.nḥl h. | šd.s̀wn.b d.ttyn.nḥl [h]. | šd.tṯyn[.b]n.arkšt. | l‘q[.---]. | šd. 2029.2
qrt. | [š]d.agpṯr.b d.sḫrn.nḥl h. | šd.annmn.b d.tyn.nḥl h. | šd.pǵyn[.b] d.krmn.l.ty[n.n]ḥl h. | šd.krz.[b]n.ann.‘[db]. | 2029.11
dy.art. | šd.prn.b d.agpṯn.nḥl h. | šd.s̀wn.b d.ttyn.nḥl [h]. | šd.tṯyn[.b]n.arkšt. | l‘q[.---]. | šd.pll.b d.qrt. | š[d].annḏr.b 2029.3
h]. | ilmškl.w.r‘[h]. | s̀šw[.--].w.r[‘ h]. | kr[mn.--.]w.r[‘ h]. | šd.[--.w.]r[‘ h]. | ḫla[n.---]. | w lštr[.---]. 2083.2.4
.---].d.yṯb.b.ilštm‘. | abmn.bn.r[---].b.syn. | bn.irṣ[-.---.]h. | šdyn.b[n.---.--]n. 2015.2.8
ṣb‘t[h.ybmt]. | limm.tiḫd.knr h.b yd[h.tšt]. | rimt.l irt h.tšr.dd.al[iyn]. | b‘l.ahbt. UG5.3.2.7
---]. | trḥṣ.yd[h.---]. | [--.]yṣt ḏm[r.---]. | tšt[.r]imt.[l irt h.tšr.l dd.aliyn.b‘l]. | [ahb]t pdr[y.bt.ar.ahbt.ṭly.bt.rb.dd]. | a 7.2[130].10
[---.t]št.rimt. | l irt h.mšr.l.dd.aliyn. | b‘l.yd.pdry.bt.ar. | ahbt.ṭly.bt.rb.dd.arṣy. | 3[‘NT].3.2
]rš.mr[k]bt. | [--].‘šr h[.---]. | [ḫm]š.‘šr h[.---]. | ḫmš.‘šr h. | šrm. 1024.4.1
kmn. | hlk.aḫt h.b‘l.y‘n.tdrq. | ybnt.ab h.šrḫq.aṯt.l pnn h. | št.alp.qdm h.mria.w tk. | pn h.tḥspn.m h.w trḥṣ. | ṭl.šmm. 3[‘NT].4.84
]yn.mḥmd.arz h. | h[n.l]bnn.w ‘ṣ h. | š[r]yn.mḥmd.arz h. | tšt.išt.b bht m. | nb[l]at.b hkl m. | hn.ym.w ṯn.tikl. | išt.b b 4[51].6.21
y.ibq‘. | kbd h.w aḥd.hm.iṯ.šmt.iṯ. | ‘ẓm.abky w aqbrn h.aštn. | b ḫrt.ilm.arṣ.b p h.rgm.l[yṣ]a. | b špt h.hwt h.knp.ṣ 19[1AQHT].3.140
bd hm.w] | aḥd.hm.iṯ.šmt.hm.i[ṯ]. | ‘ẓm.abky.w aqbrn h. | ašt.b ḫrt.ilm.arṣ. | b p h.rgm.l yṣa.b špt h.hwt[h]. | knp.n 19[1AQHT].3.111
ktp. | ‘nt.k tšt h.tš‘lyn h. | b ṣrrt.ṣpn.tbkyn h. | w tqbrn h.tštnn.b ḫrt. | ilm.arṣ.ṭṭbḫ.šb‘m. | rumm.k gmn.aliyn. | [b]‘l.t 6[62].1.17
n.b‘l. | [ṭṭbḫ.šb‘m.]ḥmrm. | [k gm]n.al[i]yn.b[‘l]. | [---]ḥ h.tšt bm.‘[--]. | [---.]zr h.ybm.l ilm. | [id]k.l ttn.pnm.‘m. | [il.] 6.1.30[49.1.2]
k.kbkbm. | bkm.tmdln.‘r. | bkm.tṣmd.pḥl.bkm. | tšu.ab h.tštnn.l[b]mt ‘r. | l ysmsm.bmt.pḥl. | y dnil.ysb.palt h. | bṣql 19[1AQHT].2.59
šmm.w n‘[n]. | ‘ma nkl ḫtn y.a[ḫ]r. | nkl yrḫ ytrḫ.adn h. | yšt mṣb.mznm.um h. | kp mznm.iḫ h yṯ‘r. | mšrrm.aḫt h l 24[77].33
.ršp zbl. | [w ‘d]t.ilm.ṯlṯ h. | [ap]nk.krt.ṯ‘.‘[-]r. | [--.]b bt h.yšt.‘rb. | [--] h.ytn.w [--]u.l ytn. | [aḫ]r.mǵy.‘[d]t.ilm. | [w]y 15[128].2.9
. | yd h.btlt.‘nt.uṣb‘t[h.ybmt]. | limm.tiḫd.knr h.b yd[h.tšt]. | rimt.l irt h.tšr.dd.al[iyn]. | b‘l.ahbt. UG5.3.2.6
n[qmd.---]. | [w]nqmd.[---]. | [-.]‘mn.šp[š.mlk.rb]. | b‘l h.šlm.[w spš]. | mlk.rb.b‘l h.[---]. | nqmd.mlk.ugr[t.--]. | phy. | 64[118].12
gl.ḫrṣ.nbt.w ‘ly. | l ẓr.mgdl.rkb. | ṯkmm.ḥmt.nša. | [y]d h.šmmh.dbḥ. | l ṯr.ab h.il.šrd. | [b‘l].b dbḥ h.bn dgn. | [b m]ṣd 14[KRT].4.168
arb‘.‘šr h.šmn. | d.lqḥt.ṯlǵdy. | w.kd.ištir.‘m.qrt. | ‘št.‘šr h.šmn. | ‘mn.b 1083.1
arb‘.‘šr h.šmn. | d.lqḥt.ṯlǵdy. | w.kd.ištir.‘m.qrt. | ‘št.‘šr h.šmn. | ‘mn.bn.aǵlmn. | arb‘m.ksp.‘l.qrt. | b.šd.bn.[u]brš. | ḫ 1083.4
h.tzd[.--]. | pt l bšr h.dm a[--.--]ḥ. | w yn.k mtrḫt[.---]h. | šm‘ ilht kṯr[t.--]mm. | nh l yd h tzdn[.---]n. | l ad[n h.---]. 24[77].10
ht.luk ‘m ml[kt]. | tǵsdb.šmlšn. | w tb‘ ank. | ‘m mlakt h šm‘ h. | w b.‘ly skn.yd‘ rgm h. | w ht ab y ǵm[--]. | t[--.---]. | l 1021.7
d. | ḥrš yd.šlḥm.ššqy. | ilm sad.kbd.hmt.b‘l. | ḥkpt.il.kl h.tšm‘. | mṯt.dnty.t‘db.imr. | b pḫd.l npš.kṯr.w ḫss. | l brlt.hyn 17[2AQHT].5.21
qr]š.m[l]k.ab[.šnm.]mṣr. | [t]bu.ḏdm.qn[-.-]n[-.-]lt. | ql h.yš[m‘].ṯr.[il].ab h.[---]l. | b šb‘t.ḥdrm.[b ṯ]mn[t.ap]. | sgrt.g[3[‘NT.VI].5.18
‘l h.k irbym.kp.k.qṣm. | ǵrmn.kp.mhr.‘tkt. | rišt.l bmt h.šnst. | kpt.b ḥbš h.brkm.ṯǵl[l]. | b dm.ḏmr.ḥlqm.b mm[‘]. | 3[‘NT].2.12
[---.--]m. | [---].pi[--.-]qš. | [--]pš.šn[--]. | ṯ[-]r.b iš[-]. | b‘l h.š‘[-]rt. | ḫqr.[--.ṭq]l rb. | ṯl[ṯ.---]. | aḥt.ḫm[-.---]. | b ym.dbḥ.ṯp 39[19].9
| w mlk.d mlk. | b ḫwt.šph. | l ydn.‘bd.mlk. | d št.‘l.ḥrd h. | šph.al.thbṭ. | ḥrd.‘ps.aḥd.kw | sgt. | ḥrd ksp.[--]r. | ymm.w[2062.2.4
.tṣb.qšt.bnt. | [---.‘]n h.km.bṯn.yqr. | [krpn h.-.l]arṣ.ks h.tšpk m. | [l ‘pr.tšu.g h.]w tṣḥ.šm‘.m‘. | [l aqht.ǵzr.i]rš.ksp. 17[2AQHT].6.15
yṣǵd.gp..thm. | [yqḥ.]il.mšt‘ltm.mšt‘ltm.l riš.agn. | hl h.[t]špl.hl h.trm.hl h.tṣḥ.ad ad. | w hl h.tṣḥ.um.um.tirk m.y 23[52].32
um.pḥl.pḥlt.bt.abn.bt šmm w thm. | qrit.l špš.um h.špš.um.ql.bl.‘m. | il.mbk nhrm.b ‘dt.thmtm. | mnt.nṯk.nḥš. UG5.7.2
ṯqšqy.nḥš.yšlḥm.‘q šr. | y‘db.ksa.w.yṯb. | tqru.l špš.um h.špš.um.ql bl. | ‘m b‘l.mrym.ṣpn.mnt y.nṯk. | nḥš.šmrr.nḥš.‘ UG5.7.8
ṯq. | nḥš.yšlḥm.nḥš.‘q šr.ydb.ksa. | w yṯb. | tqru.l špš.u h.špš.um.ql.bl.‘m. | dgn.ttl h.mnt.nṯk.nḥš.šmrr. | nḥš.‘q šr.ln UG5.7.14
. | nḥš.yšlḥm.nḥš.‘q šr.y‘db. | ksa.w yṯb. | tqru l špš.um h.špš.um.ql bl. | ‘m ḥrn.mṣd h.mnt.nṯk nḥš. | šmrr.nḥš.‘q šr.l UG5.7.57
ṯq.nḥš.yšlḥm.nḥš ‘q. | š.y‘db.ksa w yṯb. | tqru l špš.um h.špš.um.ql bl ‘m. | ṯṯ.w kmṯ.ḥryt h.mnt.nṯk.nḥš.šm | rr.nḥš.‘ UG5.7.35
| ḥš.abd.ln h.ydy.ḥmt.hlm.yṯq. | w yṯb. | tqru.l špš.um h.špš.[um.q]l bl.‘m. | yrḫ.lrgt h.mnt.nṯk.n[ḥš].šmrr. | nḥš.‘q š UG5.7.25
q nḥš yšlḥm.nḥš. | ‘q.šr.y‘db.ksa.w yṯb. | tqru l špš um h.špš um ql.bl.‘m. | mlk.‘ṯtrt h.mnt.nṯk.nḥš.šmrr. | nḥš.‘q šr.l UG5.7.40
q.nḥš.yšlḥm. | nḥš.‘q šr.y‘db.ksa.w yṯb. | tqru l špš.um h.špš.um.ql.bl.‘m. | ‘nt w ‘ṯtrt inbb h.mnt.nṯk. | nḥš.šlḥm.nḥš UG5.7.19
q.nḥš.yšlḥm.nḥš. | ‘q šr.y‘db.ksa.w yṯb. | tqru.l špš.um h.špš.um.ql b.‘m. | ršp.bbt h.mnt.nḥš.šmrr. | nḥš.‘q šr.ln h.m UG5.7.30
.nḥš. | yšlḥm.nḥš.‘q šr.y‘db ksa. | w yṯb. | tqru l špš.um h.špš.um.ql bl ‘m. | šḥr.w šlm šmm h mnt.nṯk.nḥš. | šmrr.nḥ UG5.7.51
yn.iš[ryt.-]lnr. | spr.[--]ḥ[-] k.šb‘t. | ghl.ph.ṯmnt. | nblu h.špš.ymp. | hlkt.tdr[--]. | špš.b‘d h.t[--]. | aṯr.aṯrm[.---]. | aṯr.a 27[8].4
il.yṯb.b mrzḥ h. | yšt[.il.y]n.‘d šb‘.trṯ.‘d škr. | il.hlk.l bt h.yštql. | l ḥṭr h.y‘msn.nn.ṯkmn. | w šnm.w ngšnn.ḥby. | b‘l.q UG5.1.1.17
h.w akl.bqmm. | tšt ḥrṣ.k lb ilnm. | w ṯn.gprm.mn gpr h.šr. | aqht.y‘n.kmr.kmr[.--]. | k ap‘.il.b gdrt.k lb.l | ḥt h.imḫ 19[1AQHT].1.11
h.ym[.--]. | w ṯmnt.l ṯmnym. | šr.aḫy h.mẓa h. | w mẓa h.šr.yly h. | b skn.sknm.b ‘dn. | ‘dnm.kn.npl.b‘l. | km ṯr.w tk 12[75].2.52
]k.l lbnn.w ‘ṣ h. | l[šr]yn.mḥmd.arz h. | h[n.l]bnn.w ‘ṣ h. | š[r]yn.mḥmd.arz h. | tšt.išt.b bht m. | nb[l]at.b hkl m. | hn 4[51].6.20
m trpa.hn n‘r. | d yšt.l.lṣb h ḫš‘r klb. | [w]riš.pqq.w šr h. | yšt.aḥd h.dm zt.ḫrpnt. UG5.1.2.5
bn.ktp. | b il ab h.g‘r.yṯb.il.kb[-]. | aṯ[rt.]il.yṯb.b mrzḥ h. | yšt[.il.y]n.‘d šb‘.trṯ.‘d škr. | il.hlk.l bt h.yštql. | l ḥṭr h.y‘m UG5.1.1.15
. | kd.ynaṣn[.---]. | gršnn.l k[si.mlk h.l nḫt.l kḥṯ]. | drkt h.š[--.--]. | w hm.ap.l[--.---]. | ymḫṣ k.k[--.---]. | il.dbḥ.[---]. | p‘ 1[‘NT.X].4.25
.dnty. | tšlḥm.tššqy ilm. | tsad.tkbd.hmt.b‘l. | ḥkpt il.kl h.tb‘.kṯr. | l ahl h.hyn.tb‘.l mš | knt h.apnk.dnil.m[t]. | rpi.ap 17[2AQHT].5.31
.d tq h.d tqyn.hmlt.tn.b‘l.[w ‘nn h]. | bn.dgn.arṯ m.pḏ h.tb‘.ǵlmm.l ṯṯb.[idk.pnm]. | l ytn.tk.ǵr.ll.‘m.phr.m‘d.ap.ilm 2.1[137].19
db[r.---]. | ṯḥdṯn w hl[.---]. | w tglṯ thmt.‘[--.---]. | yṣi.ǵl h tḥm b[.---]. | mrḥ h l adrt[.---]. | ṯṭb ‘ṯtrt b ǵl[.---]. | qrẓ tšt.l 2001.1.6
lp.ḫrṭ.zǵt. | klb.ṣpr.w ylak. | mlakm.l k.‘m.krt. | mswn h.ṯḥm.pbl.mlk. | qḥ.ksp.w yrq.ḫrṣ. | yd.mqm h.w ‘bd.‘lm. | ṯlṯ 14[KRT].3.125
ḫrny.w.r‘ h. | klbr.w.r‘ h. | tškrǵ.w.r‘ h. | ǵlwš.w.r‘ h. | kdrš.w.r‘ h. | ṯrm[-].w[.r‘ h]. | [‘ 2083.1.2
[b]n[.--]l[-]. | ‘bdy[rḫ].bn.gttn. | yrmn.bn.‘n. | krwn.nḥl h. | ttn.[n]ḥl h. | bn.b[r]zn. | [---.-]ḥn. 85[80].4.10
. | ghl.ph.ṯmnt. | nblu h.špš.ymp. | hlkt.tdr[--]. | špš.b‘d h.t[--]. | aṯr.aṯrm[.---]. | aṯr.aṯrm[.---]. | išdym.t[---]. | b k.mla[. 27[8].6
b[‘l.---]. | bn.dgn[.---]. | ‘dbm.[---]. | uḫry.l[---]. | mṣt.ks h.t[--.---]. | idm.adr[.---]. | idm.‘rẓ.t‘r[ẓ.---]. | ‘n.b‘l.a[ḫ]d[.---]. 12[75].2.29
.rgm.[my.b ilm]. | ydy.mrṣ.g[ršm.zbln]. | in.b ilm.‘n[y h.]yṯdṯ. | yšb‘.rgm.[my.]b ilm. | ydy.mrṣ.gršm zbln. | in.b ilm. 16[126].5.19
nr. | alnr. | maḫdt. | aby. | [-----]. | [-]nt. | ydn. | mnn.w bn h. | ṯkn. 107[15].12
dq h.l ypq. | mtrḫt.yšr h. | aṯt.trḫ.w tb‘t. | ṯar um.tkn l h. | mṯlṯt.kṯrm.tmt. | mrb‘t.zblnm. | mḫmšt.yitsp. | ršp.nṯdṯt.ǵl 14[KRT].1.15
smt.‘rš.ḫlln.[-]. | yṯb.dnil.[l s]pr yrḫ h. | yrs.y[---.]y[--] h. | ṯlṯ.rb[‘.yrḫ.--]r[.--]. | yrḫm.ymǵy[.---]. | ḫ[--.]r[---]. 17[2AQHT].2.44

h.w.alp.w ṯmn.ṣin. | [-]dln.qmnzy.w.a[ṯt h]. | wšṯn.bn h. | ṯmgdl.ykn‘my.w.aṯt h. | w.bn h.w.alp.aḫ[d]. | aǵltn.[--]y. 1080.4
---]d nhr.umt. | [---.]rpat.bt. | [m]lk.itdb.d šb‘. | [a]ḫm.l h.ṯmnt.bn um. | krt.ḥtk n.rš. | krt.grdš.mknt. | aṯt.ṣdq h.l ypq 14[KRT].1.9
ṯṯm.ṯlṯ.kb[d]. | arb‘m.ṯp[rt]. | ksp h. | ṯmn.dd[.--]. | ṯlṯ.dd.p[--]. | šb‘t.p[--]. | tš‘t.k[bd.---]. | ḫmšt.k 2120.3
w.bn h.w aṯt h.w.alp.w ṯmn.ṣin. | [-]dln.qmnzy.w.a[ṯt h]. | wšṯn.bn h. | ṯmgdl.ykn‘my.w.aṯt h. | w.bn h.w.alp.aḫ[d]. 1080.3
š.idy.alt.in l y. | [--]t.b‘l.ḥẓ.ršp.b[n].km.yr.klyt h.w lb h. | [ṯ]n.p k.b ǵr.ṯn.p k.b ḫlb.k tgwln.šnt k. | [--.]w špt k.l tšš 1001.1.3
pid.my]. | b ilm.[ydy.mrṣ]. | gršm.z[bln.in.b ilm]. | ‘ny h.y[ṯny.yṯlṯ]. | rgm.my.b[ilm.ydy]. | mrṣ.grš[m.zbln]. | in.b il 16[126].5.13
t.b d.iytlm. | ḫyrn.w.šǵr h. | šǵr.bn.prsn. | agpṯr.w.šǵ[r h]. | ṯ‘ln. | mztn.w.šǵr [h]. | šǵr.plṭ. | s[d]rn [w].ṯn.šǵr h. | [---.] 2072.4
l yrḫ ytrḫ.adn h. | yšt mṣb.mznm.um h. | kp mznm.iḫ h yṯ‘r. | mšrrm.aḫt h l a | bn mznm.nkl w ib. | d ašr.ar yrḫ.w 24[77].35
[---].mǵy h.w ǵlm. | [a]ḫt h.šib.yṣat.mrḥ h. | l tl.yṣb.pn h.ṯǵr. | yṣu.hlm.aḫ h.tph. | [ksl]h.l arṣ.ṯṯbr. | [---.]aḫ h.tbky. | 16.1[125].52
.ṯql.ḫrṣ. | l špš.w yrḫ.l gṯr. | ṯql.ksp.ṯb.ap w np[š]. | l ‘nt h.ṯql.ḫrṣ. | l špš[.w y]rḫ.l gṯr.ṯn. | [ṯql.ksp].ṯb.ap.w npš. | [---]. 33[5].13
| tšm‘.mṯt.[ḥ]ry. | ṯṯbḫ.šmn.[m]ri h. | t[p]tḥ.rḥbt.yn. | ‘l h.ṯr h.tš‘rb. | ‘l h.tš‘rb.ẓby h. | ṯr.ḫbr.rbt. | ḫbr.ṯrrt. | bt.krt.tbu 15[128].4.17
.[m]ri h. | t[p]tḥ.rḥbt.yn. | ‘l h.ṯr h.tš‘rb. | ‘l h.tš‘rb.ẓby h. | ṯr.ḫbr.rbt. | ḫbr.ṯrrt. | bt.krt.tbun. | lm.mṯb[.---]. | w lḥm m 15[128].4.18
]. | krpn.b klat yd.[---]. | km ll.kḥṣ.tusp[.---]. | tgr.il.bn h.ṯr[.---]. | w y‘n.lṭpn.il.d p[id.---]. | šm.bn y.yw.ilt.[---]. | w p‘ 1['NT.X].4.12
‘ h. | klbr.w.r‘ h. | tškrǵ.w.r‘ h. | ǵlwš.w.r‘ h. | kdrš.w.r‘ h. | ṯrm[-].w[.r‘ h]. | [‘]ṯtr[-].w.[r‘ h]. | ḫlly[-].w.r‘[h]. | ilmškl. 2083.1.5
l ḏ.pid.hn b p y sp | r hn.b špt y mn | t hn ṯlḥ h w mlg h y | ṯtqt ‘m h b q‘t. | tq‘t ‘m prbḫt. | dmqt ṣǵrt kṯrt. 24[77].47
[---]. | b‘d[.---]. | yatr[.---]. | b d k.[---]. | ṯnnt h[.---]. | ṯlṯt h[.-.w y‘n]. | lṭpn.[il.d pid.my]. | b ilm.[ydy.mrṣ]. | gršm.z[bln 16[126].5.9
t.brq. | [---].ṯṣb.qšt.bnt. | [---.‘]n h.km.bṯn.yqr. | [krpn h.-.l]arṣ.ks h.tšpk m. | [l ‘pr.tšu.g h.]w tṣḥ.šm‘.m‘. | [l aqht.ǵ 17[2AQHT].6.15
[--.d.]yṯb.b.šb[n]. | bn.pr[-.]d.y[ṯb.b].šlmy. | tlš.w[.n]ḥl h[.-].ṯgd.mrum. | bt.[-]b[-.-]sy[-]h. | nn[-].b[n].py[-.d.]yṯb.b.gt 2015.2.3
---]l[-]. | [--]ym. | [--]rm. | [bn.]aǵld. | [w.nḥ]l h. | [w.nḥ]l h[.-]. 114[324].3.6
l h. | [--]ilt.w.nḥl h. | [---]n. | [--]ly. | [iw]ryn. | [--.w.n]ḥl h. | [-]ibln. | bn.nḏbn. | bn.‘bl. | bn.tlšn. | bn.sln. | w nḥl h. 1063.9
bn.ṣrṯn. | bn.‘bd. | snb.w.nḥl h. | [-]by.w.nḥl h. | [--]ilt.w.nḥl h. | [---]n. | [--]ly. | [iw]ryn. | [--. 1063.3
.d[d.---]. | ‘š[r.---.--]r h. | my y[--.---.--]d. | ‘šrm[.---.--]r h. | [-]wyn.yd[-.---.]dd. | [---]n.yd.sǵ[r.---.--]k.[--]. | [---.]dd.bn. 1098.39
kny[.w]mit. | zt.b d hm.rib. | w [---]. | [-----]. | [-]šy[.---] h. | [-]kt[.---.]nrn. | [b]n.nmq[.---]. | [ḫm]št.ksp.‘l.aṯt. | [-]td[.bn 2055.16
n. | [---.-]im.bṯd. | [---.b]šḥr.atlgn. | [---].b šḥr. | [---.]bn h. | [-]k[--]g hn.ksp. 2167.6
t k. | yd‘t.k rḥmt. | al.tšt.b šdm.mm h. | b smkt.ṣat.npš h. | [-]mt[-].ṣba.rbt. | špš.w tgh.nyr. | rbt.w rgm.l aḫt k. | ttmn 16.1[125].35
bn.iryn. | nrn.nḥl h. | bn.ḫsn. | bn.‘bd. | [-----]. | [---.n]ḥ[l h]. | [-]ntm[.---]. | [‘]bdm. | [bn].mṣrn. | [a]ršwn. | ‘b[d]. | w nḥl 85[80].2.12
[---]m.d.yṯ[--.]l[-]. | ršp.ḫmš.[m]šl[t]. | [--]arš[p.-]š.l[h]. | [-]ṯl[.--]š.l h. | [---]l[.--] h. | mtn[.---.]l h. | [---.]l h. | [---.--]š. 2133.3
[-----]. | w.[-----]. | w.abǵl.nḥ[l h.--]. | w.unṯ.aḥd.l h[.---]. | dnn.bn.yṣr[.---]. | sln.bn.‘tt[-.---]. | 90[314].1.3
[---]l[.--] h. | mtn[.---.]l h. | [---.]l h. | [---.--]š.l h. | [---].l h. | [--.]spr[.---]. | [--.]ḫrd[.---]. | [---.]l h. 2133.9
]ld. | kbd h.l yd‘ hr h.[---]d[-]. | tnq[.---.]in[b]b.p‘r. | yd h[.--.]ṣ‘r.glgl. | a[---]m.rḥ.ḥḏ ‘[r]pt. | gl[.---.]yhpk.m[---]m. | s‘[13[6].33
bq.[---]. | tḥbq[.---]. | w tksynn.bṯn[-.] | y[--.]šr h.w šḫp h. | [--.]šḫp.ṣǵrt h. | yrk.t‘l.b ǵr. | mslmt.b ǵr.tliyt. | w t‘l.bkm. 10[76].3.26
--.-]l[--]. | [---.]pr[--]. | [-.a]pln. | bn.mzt. | bn.ṯrn. | w.nḥl h. | [--.-]hs. | [--.--]nyn. | [-----]. | [-----]. | bn.‘dy. | w.nḥl h. | bn.‘b 2163.2.15
ugrt.ytn. | šd.kdǵdl[.bn]. | [-]š[-]y.d.b š[-]y. | [---.y]d gt h[.--]. | [---.]yd. | [k]rm h.yd. | [k]lkl h. | [w] ytn.nn. | l.b‘ln.bn. 1008.7
----]. | [-----]. | [-----]. | [-----]. | [-----]. | [---.--]yn. | [w.nḥ]l h. | [--.---]n. | [-----]. | [-----]. | [-----]. | [-----]. | [--.-]gn. | [--.--]n. | [113[400].4.18
h. | bn.ḫby.w.[a]ṯt h. | ynḥm.ulmy. | [--]q.w.aṯt h.w.bn h. | [--]an.w.aṯt h. | [--]y.w.aṯt h. | [--]r.w.aṯt h. | ‘bdyrḫ.ṯn ǵlyt 2068.6
bn.ṣrṯn. | bn.‘bd. | snb.w.nḥl h. | [-]by.w.nḥl h. | [--]ilt.w.nḥl h. | [---]n. | [--]ly. | [iw]ryn. | [--.w.n]ḥl h. | [-]ibl 1063.4
]ṯt h. | ynḥm.ulmy. | [--]q.w.aṯt h.w.bn h. | [--]an.w.aṯt h. | [--]y.w.aṯt h. | [--]r.w.aṯt h. | ‘bdyrḫ.ṯn ǵlyt h. | aršmg. | ršp 2068.7
.w tpky.k[m.]n‘r.tdm‘.km. | [ṣǵ]r.bkm.y‘ny[.---.bn]wt h. | [--]nn.bnt yš[--.---.-]lk. | [--]b.kmm.l k[--]. | [šp]š.b šmm.t UG5.8.41
lmy. | [--]q.w.aṯt h.w.bn h. | [--]an.w.aṯt h. | [--]y.w.aṯt h. | [--]r.w.aṯt h. | ‘bdyrḫ.ṯn ǵlyt h. | aršmg. | ršpy.w.aṯt h. | bn. 2068.8
k[.ab.šnm.l p‘n.il.] | [yhbr.]w yql[.y]šṯḥw[y.]w ykb[dn h.--]r y[---]. | [---.k]ṯr.w ḫ[ss.t]b‘.b[n.]bht.ym[.rm]m.hkl.ṯpṭ 2.3[129].6
[---.šnst.kpt.b ḥb]š h.‘tkt r[išt]. | [l bmt h.---.]hy bt h t‘rb. | [---.tm]ṯḫṣ b ‘mq. | [ṯḥtṣb.bn.qrtm.ṯṭ‘r.ṯl 7.1[131].3
[---.yṯ]rd h. | [---.yg]rš h. | [---.]ru. | [----] h. | [---.--]mt. | [---.--]mr.limm. | [---.]bn.ilm. 6[49].6.2
[.bn h.---]. | iwrm[-.]b[n.---]. | annt[n.]w[.---]. | w.ṯn.bn h.[---]. | aǵltn.ypr[y.---]. | w.šb‘.ṣin h[.---]. 2044.16
š[h.km.iṯl]. | brlt h.km.qṭr.[b ap h.---]. | ‘nt.b ṣmt.mhr h.[---]. | aqht.w tbk.y[---.---]. | abn.ank.w ‘l.[qšt k.---.‘l]. | qṣ‘t 18[3AQHT].4.38
[---.--]n.il ǵnṯ.‘gl il. | [---.--]d.il.šd yṣd mlk. | [---].yšt.il h. | [---.]iṯm h. | [---.y]mǵy. | [---.]dr h. | [---.-]rš.l b‘l. | [---.-]ǵk. UG5.2.1.13
n[-.---]. | w l ṯlb.[---]. | mit.rḥ[.---]. | ṯṯlb.a[--.---]. | yšu.g h[.---]. | i.ap.b‘[l.---]. | i.hd.d[---.---]. | ynp‘.b‘[l.---]. | b ṯmnt.[--- 5[67].4.5
šrr.w t‘[n.‘ṯtrt.---]. | b‘l m.hmt.[---]. | l šrr.št[.---]. | b riš h.[---]. | ib h.mš[--.---]. | [b]n.‘n h[.---]. 2.4[68].38
]ṯt h[.---]. | prṯ.mgd[ly.---.]aṯ[t h]. | ‘dyn[.---]. | w.ṯn[.bn h.---]. | iwrm[-.]b[n.---]. | annt[n.]w[.---]. | w.ṯn.bn h.[---]. | aǵlt 2044.13
nm. | [---].ṯlṯm.iqnu. | [---.l.]ṯrmn.mlk. | [---.]š‘rt.šb‘.‘šr h. | [---.iqn]i.l.ṯrmn.qrt. | [---.]lbš.ḫmšm.iqnu. | [---].šmt.ḫmšt. 1106.14
zr.mt hrnmy. | [---].hw.mḫ.l ‘rš h.y‘l. | [---].bm.nšq.aṯt h. | [---.]b ḥbq h.ḥmḥmt. | [---.--] n.ylt.ḥmḥmt. | [---.mt.r]pi.w 17[2AQHT].1.40
[---.w ym.ym]m. | [y‘tqn.---.ymǵy.]npš. | [---.h]d.tngṯn h. | [---].b ṣpn. | [---].nšb.b ‘n. | [---.]b km.y‘n. | [---.yd‘.l] yd‘t. | 1['NT.X].5.4
. | [---.]tḥm. | [---]t.[ ]r. | [---.--]n. | [---] h.l ‘db. | [---]n.yd h. | [---].bl.išlḫ. | [---] h.gm. | [l --- k.]yṣḥ. | [---]d.‘r. | [----.-]bb. | 14[KRT].5.235
--]mt. | [---.--]mr.limm. | [---.]bn.ilm.mt. | [--]u.šb‘t.ǵlm h. | [---].bn.ilm.mt. | p[-]n.aḫ y m.ytn.b‘l. | [s]pu y.bn m.um y. 6[49].6.8
]lṯy. | [-----]. | [---]tl. | [---]‘bl. | [---]bln. | [---]dy. | [---.n]ḥl h. | [---].bn.mryn. | [---].bn.ṯyl. | annmt.nḥl h. | abmn.bn.‘bd. | l 1036.9
[---.]bn[.---]. | [---.]bn[.---]. | [---.]nḥl h. | [---.b]n.špš. | [---.b]n.mradn. | [---.m]lkym. | [---.--]d. 2137.3
--]. | trgm[.-]dk[.---]. | m‘bd[.-]r[-.-]š[-.---]. | w kšt.[--]šq h[.---]. | bnš r‘ym.[---]. | kbdt.bnš[.---]. | šin.[---]. | b ḥlm.[---]. | 2158.2.5
w.k.rgm.špš. | mlk.rb.b‘l y.u. | ‘[--.]mlakt.‘bd h. | [---.]b‘l k.yḫpn. | [---.]‘m h.u ky. | [---.--]d k.k.tmǵy. | ml[-- 1018.3
rm. | [---.-]ṣbm. | [---.]nrn.m‘ry. | [---.--]r. | [---.]w.ṯn.bn h. | [---.b]t h.‘tgrm. 2043.11
hr.bt k.[---.]šp[-.---]. | [ḫš.bh]t h.tbn[n.ḫ]š.trm[mn.hkl h.---.]bt. | [---.-]k.mnh[-.---.-]š bš[-.]t[-].ǵlm.l šdt[.-.]ymm. | [- 2.3[129].10
[---.yṯ]rd h. | [---.yg]rš h. | [---.]ru. | [----] h. | [---.--]mt. | [---.--]mr.limm. 6[49].6.1
[---.ṯ]lt.‘š[r h.---]. | d bnšm.yd.grbs hm. | w.ṯn.‘šr h.ḫpnt. | [š]šwm.amtm.‘ 2049.1
h. | šm‘ ilht kṯr[t.--]mm. | nh l yd h tzdn[.---]n. | l ad[n h.---]. | dgn tt[--.---.-]l | ‘.l kṯrt hl[l.sn]nt. | ylak yrḫ ny[r] šmm 24[77].13
[-----]. | w.[-----]. | w.abǵl.nḥ[l h.--]. | w.unṯ.aḥd.l h[.---]. | dnn.bn.yṣr[.---]. | sln.bn.‘tt[-.---]. | pdy.bn.nr[-.---]. | a 90[314].1.4

l.mit.dr'.w.šb'm.drt.|[---.ḫpr.]bnšm.w.l.ḥrš.'rq.tn.'šr h.|[---.d]r'.w.mit.drt.w.'šrm.l.mit.|[drt.ḫpr.b]nšm.w.tn.'šr 1098.2
--].|ḫdmtn.ṯn[.---].|w.ṯlṯ.alp h.[---].|swn.qrty.w.[b]n h[.---].|w.alp h.w.a[r]b'.l.arb'[m.---].|pln.ṯmry.w.ṯn.bn h.w 2044.6
.---].|'dyn.bn.udr[-.---].|w.'d'.nḥl h[.---].|w.yknil.nḥl h[.---].|w.iltm.nḥl h[.---].|w.unṯm.nḥ[l h.---].|[---.]'dr[.---]. 90[314].1.15
.---].|w.'d'.nḥl h[.---].|w.yknil.nḥl h[.---].|w.iltm.nḥl h[.---].|w.unṯm.nḥ[l h.---].|[---.]'dr[.---].|str[-.---].|bdlm.d[t 90[314].1.16
r'[.iṯ.lḥm.---].|iṯ.yn.d 'rb.bṯk[.---].|mǵ hw.l hn.lg yn h[.---].|w ḥbr h.mla yn.[---]. 23[52].75
ly[.---].|bnil.bn.yṣr[.---].|'dyn.bn.udr[-.---].|w.'d'.nḥl h[.---].|w.yknil.nḥl h[.---].|w.iltm.nḥl h[.---].|w.unṯm.nḥ[l 90[314].1.14
[r h].|ṯ'ln.|mztn.w.šǵr [h].|šǵr.plṭ.|s[d]rn [w].ṯn.šǵr h.|[---.]w.šǵr h.|[---.]w.šǵr h.|[---.]krwn.|[---].ḫzmyn.|[---. 2072.8
ztn.w.šǵr [h].|šǵr.plṭ.|s[d]rn [w].ṯn.šǵr h.|[---.]w.šǵr h.|[---.]w.šǵr h.|[---.]krwn.|[---].ḫzmyn.|[---.]bn.dll.|r[--.-- 2072.9
m].|rgm.l td'.nš[m.w l tbn.hmlt.arṣ].|at.w ank.ib[ǵy h.---].|w y'n.kṯr.w ḫss[.lk.lk.'nn.ilm.]|atm.bštm.w an[.šnt.k 1['NT.IX].3.16
.yd.ṭ[--.---].|ḫtn h.šb'l[.---].|ṯlḥny.yd[.---].|yd.ṯlṯ.kl[ṭ h.---].|w.ṯṯm.ṣi[n.---].|tn[--].|agyn.[---].|[w].ṯn.[---]. 81[329].18
[qṭr h.l 'pr.d]mr.a[t]r h.|[ṭbq.lḥt.niṣ h.gr]š.d 'šy.|[ln h.---].|z[tr.'m k.l arṣ.mšṣu.qṭr k].|l 'pr.ḏm[r.aṯr k.ṭbq].|lḥt. 17[2AQHT].1.49
[p'n.il.yhbr.w yql].|yštḥwy.[w ykbdn h.---].|ṯr.il[.ab h.---].|ḥš b[ht m.tbnn.ḥš.trmmn.hkl m].|b tk.[---].|bn.[---]. 1['NT.IX].3.26
yd.[---].|am[-]n.[---].|w.a[ṯt] h.[---].|ḫdmtn.ṯn[.---].|w.ṯlṯ.alp h.[---].|swn.qrty.w.[b]n h[. 2044.3
[-----].|[---.]'l.ṯny[.---]|[---.]pḫyr.bt h.[---].|[ḫm]šm.ksp.'l.gd[--].|[---].yph.'bdršp.b[--.--].|[ar]b' 1144.3
ṯ.psl.ḥzm.|[---.ḥ]rš.mr[k]bt.|[--].'šr h[.---].|[ḫm]š.'šr h[.---].|ḫmš.'šr h.|šrm. 1024.3.22
.|[--.]psl.qšt.|[ṯl]ṯ.psl.ḥzm.|[---.ḥ]rš.mr[k]bt.|[--].'šr h[.---].|[ḫm]š.'šr h[.---].|ḫmš.'šr h.|šrm. 1024.3.21
[---.]yd.npṣ h.|[---.]yd.npṣ h.|[---.]yd.npṣ h.|[---.yd].npṣ h.|[---.yd.np]ṣ h.|[---.yd.np]ṣ 1119.2
.]yd.npṣ h.|[---.]yd.npṣ h.|[---.yd].npṣ h.|[---.yd.np]ṣ h.|[---.yd.np]ṣ h.|[---.yd.npṣ] h.|[---.-]nm.|[---.--]ṯ. 1119.5
[---.]yd.npṣ h.|[---.]yd.npṣ h.|[---.]yd.npṣ h.|[---.yd].npṣ h.|[---.yd.np]ṣ h.|[---.yd.np]ṣ h.|[---.yd.npṣ] 1119.3
[---.]yd.npṣ h.|[---.]yd.npṣ h.|[---.]yd.npṣ h.|[---.yd].npṣ h.|[---.yd.np]ṣ 1119.1
.]yd.npṣ h.|[---.]yd.npṣ h.|[---.]yd.npṣ h.|[---.yd].npṣ h.|[---.yd.np]ṣ h.|[---.yd.np]ṣ h.|[---.yd.npṣ] h.|[---.-]nm.|[1119.4
.]yd.npṣ h.|[---.yd].npṣ h.|[---.yd.np]ṣ h.|[---.yd.np]ṣ h.|[---.yd.npṣ] h.|[---.-]nm.|[---.--]ṯ. 1119.6
šǵr.plṭ.|s[d]rn [w].ṯn.šǵr h.|[---.]w.šǵr h.|[---.]w.šǵr h.|[---.]krwn.|[---].ḫzmyn.|[---.]bn.dll.|r[--.--]km.|w.spr h. 2072.10
-]mr.ph.|[---.--]mm.hlkt.|[---.]b qrb.'r.|[---.m]lakm l h.|[---.]l.bn.il.|[---.--]a.'d h.|[---.--]rh.|[---.--]y.špš.|[---.--]h. 26[135].6
[.--]š.l h.|[---]l[.--] h.|mtn[.---.]l h.|[---.]l h.|[---.--]š.l h.|[---].l h.|[--.]spr[.---].|[--.]ḫrd[.---].|[---.]l h. 2133.8
--]arš[p.-]š.l[h].|[-]ṯl[.--]š.l h.|[---]l[.--] h.|mtn[.---.]l h.|[---.]l h.|[---.--]š.l h.|[---].l h.|[--.]spr[.---].|[--.]ḫrd[.---]. 2133.6
.ymḫṣ.b smd.|ṣḥr mt.ymṣḫ.l arṣ.|[yṯb.]b['].l.l ksi.mlk h.|[---].l kḥṯ.drkt h.|l [ym]m.l yrḫm.l yrḫm.|l šnt.[m]k.b š 6[49].5.5
-]t.š l i[l.---].|[--.aṯ]rt.š[.---].|[---.]l pdr[-.---].|ṣin aḥd h[.---].|l 'ṯrt[.---].|'lm.kmm[.---].|w b ṯlṯ.ṣ[in.---].|l ll.pr[-.- 37[22].5
ẓpn.|[---.]pn.ym.y[--].|[---].b'l.tdd.|[---.]hkl.|[---.]yd h.|[---.]tmt. 25[136].9
pdd.mlbš.|u---].mlk.ytn.mlbš.|[---.-]rn.k.ypdd.mlbš h.|[---.]mlk.ytn.lbš.l h. 1106.60
|[m]rḫ h.yiḫd.b yd.|[g]rgr h.bm.ymn.|[w]yqrb.trẓẓ h.|[---].mǵy h.w ǵlm.|[a]ḫt h.šib.yṣat.mrḫ h.|l tl.yṣb.pn h.ṯ 16.1[125].49
nṯ.'gl il.|[---.--]d.il.šd yṣd mlk.|[---].yšt.il h.|[---.]iṯm h.|[---.y]mǵy.|[---.]dr h.|[---.-]rš.l b'l.|[---.-]ǵk.rpu mlk.|['l UG5.2.1.14
[--.-]ln.|[---.n]ḫl h.|[---.n]ḫl h.|[---.n]ḫl h. 126[-].2
[--.-]ln.|[---.n]ḫl h.|[---.n]ḫl h.|[---.n]ḫl h. 126[-].3
k.|[-]k.am'[--].|[w.b] d.bn h[.']d 'lm.|[w.un]ṯ.in[n.]b h.|[---.]n'm[-]. 1009.18
-].|[-.]'mn.šp[š.mlk.rb].|b'l h.šlm.[w spš].|mlk.rb.b'l h.[---].|nqmd.mlk.ugr[t.--].|phy.|w ṯpllm.mlk.r[b.--].|mṣm 64[118].13
am[-]n.[---].|w.a[ṯt] h.[---].|ḫdmtn.ṯn[.---].|w.ṯlṯ.alp h.[---].|swn.qrty.w.[b]n h[.---].|w.alp h.w.a[r]b'.l.arb'[m.--- 2044.5
l[q]ḥt.|[--]km.'m.mlk.|[b]ǵl hm.w.iblbl hm.|w.b.ṯb h.[---].|spr ḥ[--.---].|w.'m[.---].|yqḥ[.---].|w.n[--.---]. 2129.11
h.[---]l.|b šb't.ḥdrm.[b ṯ]mn[t.ap].|sgrt.g[-].[-]ẓ[.---] h[.---].|'n.ṯk[.---].|'ln.ṯ[--.---].|l p'n.ǵl[m]m[.---].|mid.an[-- 3['NT.VI].5.20
rk h].|yṣat.km.rḥ.npš[h.km.iṯl].|brlt h.km.qṭr.[b ap h.---].|'nt.b ṣmt.mhr h.[---].|aqht.w tbk.y[---.---].|abn.ank. 18[3AQHT].4.37
].|ymrn.apsny.w.aṯt h..b[n.---].|prd.m'qby[.w.---.a]ṯt h[.---].|prṯ.mgd[ly.---.]aṯ[t h].|'dyn[.---].|w.ṯn[.bn h.---].|i 2044.10
[.--.ṣ]pn hm.|nṣḥy.šrr.m[---.--]ay.|nbšr km.dnil.[--] h[.---].|riš.r[--.--]ḥ[.---]y[.---.-]nt.[š]ṣat[k.]rḥ.npš.hm.|k.iṯl. 19[1AQHT].2.86
|[---.]'l.w tš'[d]n.npṣ h.|[---.]rgm.hn.[--]n.w aspt.[q]l h.|[---.rg]m.ank l[.--.--]rny.|[---.]ṯm.hw.i[--]ty.|[---].ib'r.a[-- 1002.49
].rgm y.|[---.]škb.w m[--.]mlakt.|[---.]'l.w tš'[d]n.npṣ h.|[---.]rgm.hn.[--]n.w aspt.[q]l h.|[---.rg]m.ank l[.--.--]rny. 1002.48
n.|yrd.'ṯtr.'rẓ.yrd.|l kḥṯ.aliyn.b'l.|w ymlk.b arṣ.il.kl h.|[---] š abn.b rḥbt.|[---] š abn.b kknt. 6.1.65[49.1.37]
'r[.---].|w y[---].|b'd[.---].|yaṯr[.---].|b d k.[---].|ṯnnt h[.---].|ṯlṯt h[.-.w y'n].|lṭpn.[il.d pid.my].|b ilm.[ydy.mrṣ]. 16[126].5.8
mlk].|ab.šnm.l [p'n.il.yhbr.w yql].|yštḥwy.[w ykbdn h.---].|ṯr.il[.ab h.---].|ḥš b[ht m.tbnn.ḥš.trmmn.hkl m].|b t 1['NT.IX].3.25
ḥdd.ar[y.---].|b'lsip.a[ry.---].|klt h.[---].|ṯty.ary.m[--.---].|nrn.arny[.---].|w.ṯn.bn h.w.b[---.--- 81[329].3
.|'m kbkbm[.abn.brq.d l td'.šmm.at m].|w ank.ib[ǵy h.---].|[-].l y'mdn.i[---.---].|kpr.šb' bn[t.rḥ.gdm.w anhbm].| 7.2[130].21
[---.]w rm ṯlbm ṯlb.|[---.-]pr l n'm.|[---.-]mt w rm tp h.|[---.-]ḫb l n'm.|[---.]ymǵy.|[---.]rm ṯlbm.|[---.--]m.|[---.- UG5.5.5
.w ym ymm.|[y'tqn.---].ymǵy.npš.|[---.--]t.hd.tngṯm h.|[---.-]ḫm k b ṣpn.|[---.]išqb.aylt.|[---.--]m.b km.y'n.|[---] 1['NT.X].5.17
[---.]w rm tp h.|[---.-]lu mm l n'm.|[---.]w rm ṯlbm ṯlb.|[---.-]pr l n'm.|[- UG5.5.1
l pn h yrd.|[---.]b'l.šm[.--.]rgbt yu.|[---]w yrmy[.q]rn h.|[---.-]ny h pdr.ttǵr.|[---.n]šr k.al ttn.l n.|[---.]tn l rbd.|[- 2001.2.10
.yd].npṣ h.|[---.yd.np]ṣ h.|[---.yd.np]ṣ h.|[---.yd.npṣ] h.|[---.-]nm.|[---.--]ṯ. 1119.7
ṣd mlk.|[---].yšt.il h.|[---.]iṯm h.|[---.y]mǵy.|[---.]dr h.|[---.-]rš.l b'l.|[---.-]ǵk.rpu mlk.|['lm.---.--]k.l tšt k.l iršt.| UG5.2.2.2
].|[']d tš[b'.tmtḫṣ.---].|klyn[.---].|špk.l[---].|trḥṣ.yd[h.---].|[--.]yṣt ḏm[r.---].|tšt[.r]imt.[l irt h.tšr.l dd.aliyn.b'l]. 7.2[130].8
nyt.w t'n[.btlt.'nt].|yṯb l y.ṯr.il[.ab y.---].|yṯb.l y.w l h.[---].|[--.i]mṣḫ.nn.k imr.l arṣ.|[ašhlk].šbt h.dmm.šbt.dqn 3['NT.VI].4.8
upqt.|[---.]l w ǵr mtn y.|[---.]rq.gb.|[---.--]kl.tǵr.mtn h.|[---.--]b.w ym ymm.|[y'tqn.---].ymǵy.npš.|[---.--]t.hd.tn 1['NT.X].5.14
y.w[.aṯt h].|w.bn h.w.alp.w.[---].|[-]ln.[---].|w.ṯn.bn [h.---].|[--]d m'qby[.---].|swn.qrty.w[.aṯt h].|[w].bn h.w.ṯn.a 1080.10
y.|[---.--]hr.|[---.--]ḫdn.|[---.]bšr y.|[---.--]b.|[---.--]a h.|[---.--]d.|[---].umt n.|[---.--]yh.wn l.|[---].bt b'l.|[---.--]y. 28[-].8
[---.--]y.npš[.---].|[---.k]si h.|[---.--]y.rb.šm[.---]. 2160.2
m y.|[-]wd.r[-.]pǵt.|[---.--]t.yd't.|[----.r]gm.|[---].kll h.|[---.--]l y.|[---.--]r.|[--.]wk[--.---].|[--]lm.l[--.---].|[-]m.in 54.1.[7]
.kkr.š'rt.|nṯk h.|kb[d.]mn.'l.abršn.|b[n.---].kršu.nṯk h.|[---.--]mm.b.krsi. 1146.12

[---.yṭ]rd h.|[---.yg]rš h.|[---.]ru.|[----] h.|[---.--]mt.|[---.--]mr.limm.|[---.]bn.ilm.mt.|[--]u.šb‘t.ǵlm 6[49].6.4

-].nn.|[---.]qrt.dt.|[---.--]s‘.hn.mlk.|[---.l]qḥ.hn.l.ḥwt h.|[---.--]p.hn.ib.d.b.mgšẖ.|[---.i]b.hn[.w.]ht.ank.|[---.--]š[-. 1012.9

dd.|[---]n.yd.sǵ[r.---.--]k.[--].|[---.]dd.bn.š.[---.]yd.sǵr h.|[---.--]r h.‘šr[m.---.‘]šrm.dd.|[---.yn.d.]nkly.l.r‘ym.šb‘m.l 1098.42

[---.]b qrb.‘r.|[---.m]lakm l h.|[---.]l.bn.il.|[---.--]a.‘d h.|[---.--]rh.|[---.--]y.špš.|[---.--]h.|[---.--]th. 26[135].8

]š.l[h].|[-]ṯl[.--]š.l h.|[---]l[.--] h.|mtn[.---.]l h.|[---.]l h.|[---.--]š.l h.|[---].l h.|[--.]spr[.---].|[--.]ẖrd[.---].|[---.]l h. 2133.7

h.y[---.---].|b‘l.yṯṯbn[.l ksi].|mlk h.l[nẖt.l kḥṯ].|drkt h[.---].|[---.]d[--.---].|[---].hn[.---].|[---.]šn[.---].|[---].pit.|[- 6[49].6.35

.|w.yknil.nḥl h[.---].|w.iltm.nḥl h[.---].|w.unṯm.nḥ[l h.---].|[---.]‘d̠r[.---].|str[-.---].|bdlm.d[t.---].|‘dn.[---].|aẖq 90[314].1.17

t.|[adrm.d b grn.y]dn.|[dn.almnt.y]ṯpṭ.|[ṯpṭ.ytm.---] h.|[---.---]n.|[-----].|hlk.[---.b n]ši.|‘n h.w tphn.[---].|b grn. 19[1AQHT].1.25

|[il.]hd.d ‘nn.n[--].|[----.]aliyn.b[‘l].|[---.btl]t.‘n[t.-.]p h.|[---.---]n.|[-----].|[-----].|[---.]lk[.--]t. 10[76].2.35

t.|b.bn.qrdmn.ṯlṯm.|b.bṣmn[.bn].ḥrtn.‘[--].|b.t[--.---] h.[---].|[-----].|[--]ly.ẖmšm.b.‘bdyr[ẖ].|[---].‘šrm.|[-----].|[-- 2054.1.22

.|kbkbn bn[.---].|bn.k[--].|bn.pdr[n.].|bn.‘n[--].|nḥl h[.---].|[-----]. 2014.61

.|pr‘m.ṣd k.y bn[.---].|pr‘m.ṣd k.hn pr[‘.--].|ṣd.b hkl h[.---].|[------].|[---.l]ḥm[.---].|[---].ay š[---].|[---.b ḥ]rb.mlḥ[17[2AQHT].5.39

[n.]w[.---].|w.ṯn.bn h.[---].|aǵltn.ypr[y.---].|w.šb‘.ṣin h[.---]. 2044.18

[---].|l šrr.št[.---].|b riš h.[---].|ib h.mš[--.---].|[b]n.‘n h[.---]. 2.4[68].40

|rkm.agzrt[.--].arẖ..|b‘l.azrt.‘nt.[-]ld.|kbd h.l yd‘ hr h.[---]d[-].|tnq[.---.]in[b]b.p‘r.|yd h[.--.]ṣ‘r.glgl.|a[---]m.rḥ. 13[6].31

.]mṣr.|[t]bu.d̠dm.qn[-.-]n[-.-]lt.|ql h.yš[m‘].ṯr.[il].ab h.[---]l.|b šb‘t.ḥdrm.[b ṯ]mn[t.ap].|sgrt.g[-].[-]ẓ[.---] h[.---]. 3[‘NT.VI].5.18

-.]l[-].|ršp.ẖmš.[m]šl[t].|[--]arš[p.-]š.l[h].|[-]ṯl[.--]š.l h.|[---]l[.--] h.|mtn[.---.]l h.|[---.]l h.|[---.--]š.l h.|[---].l h.|[2133.4

rṭn.|bn.‘bd.|snb.w.nḥl h.|[-]by.w.nḥl h.|[--]ilt.w.nḥl h.|[---]n.|[--]ly.|[iw]ryn.|[--.w.n]ḥl h.|[-]ibln.|bn.nd̠bn.|b 1063.5

[---.a]rgmn.špš.|[-----].|[-----].|[-----].|[----] h.|[-----].|[-]b‘l.|[--]m.|[m‘]rby.|m‘r.|arny.|‘nqpat.|š‘rt.| 2058.1.5

.|bn.dgn.yhrr m.|b‘l.ngṯ hm.b p‘n h.|w il hd.b ẖrẓ‘ h.|[-----].|[--]t.[---].|[---.]‘n[.---].|pnm[.---].|b‘l.n[--.---].|il. 12[75].1.41

-].|[---.-]n[-].|[k yraš ššw št bln q]ṭ ydk.|[w yṣq b ap h].|[-----].|[-----].|[-----].|[---.-]rb.|[-----].|[-----].|[-----].|k y 160[55].15

.ḥrš.|qštipṭl.|bn.anny.|ilṣdq.|ypltn.bn iln.|špšm.nsl h.|[-----]. 1037.6

.|mrḥqtm.|qlt.|‘m.adt y.|mnm.šlm.|rgm.tṯṯb.|l.‘bd h. 52[89].15

---.]krwn.|[---].ẖzmyn.|[---.]bn.dll.|r[--.--]km.|w.spr h. 2072.15

.w.mqḥm.|w.ṯlṯm.yn šb‘.kbd d ṭbṭ.|w.ẖmšm.yn.d iẖ h. 1103.23

l h.|[-]ibln.|bn.nd̠bn.|bn.‘bl.|bn.tlšn.|bn.sln.|w nḥl h. 1063.15

]s[-]n.|[--.-]nyn.|[---].[-]ǵtyn.|[---].[-]tyn.|[---.w.]nḥl h. 123[326].2.6

a.ṯ[l]ṯ.d.a[--].|[---].mrn.|[---.]bn pnṯbl.|[---.-]py w.bn h. 1145.2.3

rb‘.aṯt.|bn.lg.ṯn.bn h.|b‘lm.w.aẖt h.|b.šrt.|šty.w.bn h. 2080.13

nn.b d.|b‘ln.bn.kltn.|w.b d.bn h.‘d.|‘lm.w unṯ.|in.b h. 1008.21

n.alkbl.šb[ny].|‘šrm ksp.‘l.|wrt.mtny.w ‘l.|prdny.aṯt h. 2107.19

lt yṯnt w ṣmqm yṯn[m].|w qmḥ bql yṣq aḥd h.|b ap h. 160[55].26

mq[m].yṯnm.w[.qmḥ.bql].|tdkn.aḥd h.w[.yṣq].|b.ap h. 161[56].36

ṭpt.|w.ṯlṯ.ṣmdm.w.ḥrṣ.|apnt.b d.rb.ḥršm.|d.šṣa.ḥwy h. 1121.10

.|[w].lmd h.|[yn]ḥm.|[w.]lmd h.|[i]wrmẖ.|[w.]lmd h. 1048.10

b‘ld‘.yd[.---.‘]šrt.ksp h.|lbiy.pdy.[---.k]sp h. 2112.2

tqn.|tut ṭbẖ ṣtq[n].|b bz ‘zm ṭbẖ š[h].|b kl ygz ẖẖ š h. 1153.5

r.mnt.|[ṣḥrrm.ḥbl.‘]rpt.|[---.---.-]ḥt.|[---.---]m.|[----] h. 4[51].7.60

[---.--]n.|[---.]rmṣm.|[---.]dyy.|[---.n]ḥl h. 2155.4

.ytn.mlbš.|[---.-]rn.k.ypdd.mlbš h.|[---.]mlk.ytn.lbš.l h. 1106.61

[.---].|[--]šy.w ydn.b‘[l.---]n.|[--]‘.k yn.hm.l.atn.bt y.l h. 1002.62

[---.--]š.l h.|[---].l h.|[--.]spr[.---].|[--.]ẖrd[.---].|[---.]l h. 2133.12

[--.-]ln.|[---.n]ḥl h.|[---.n]ḥl h.|[---.n]ḥl h. 126[-].4

--.k br]k.tǵll.b dm.|[d̠mr.---.]td[-.]rǵb.|[----]k.|[----] h. 7.1[131].12

hbṭ

[d].šd.hwt.|[--.]iḥd.šd.gṯr.|[w]ht.yšm‘.uẖ y.|l g y.w yhbṭ.bnš.|w ytn.ilm.b d hm.|b d.iẖqm.gṯr.|w b d.ytrhd.|b‘ 55[18].18

l.d̠rdn.|b‘l y.rgm.|bn.ẖrn k.|mǵy.|hbṭ.hw.|ẖrd.w.šl hw.|qr[-].|akl n.b.grnt.|l.b‘r.|ap.krmm.| 2114.5

mlk.|b ḥwt.špḥ.|l ydn.‘bd.mlk.|d št.‘l.ẖrd h.|špḥ.al.thbṭ.|ẖrd.‘ps.aḥd.kw|sgt.|ẖrd ksp.[--]r.|ymm.w[.---].|[----- 2062.2.5

hbṯn

.]l.mẖṣ.|ab[---.]ad̠ddy.bn.skn.|bn.[---.]uẖd.|bn.n[---.]hbṯn.|bn.m[--.]skn.|bn.s[--.b]d.skn.|bn.ur[-.---].|bn.knn[.- 2014.10

ynm.|ẖmš.[ṯr]tnm.|ṯlṯ.b[n.]mrynm.|‘šr[.m]krm.|tš‘.hbṯnm.|‘šr.mrum.|šb‘.ẖsnm.|tš‘m.ṯṯ.kbd.md̠rǵlm.|‘šrm.aḥ 1028.6

um.w.šb‘.ẖsnm.|tš‘m.md̠rǵlm.|arb‘.l ‘šrm.ẖsnm.|‘šr.hbṯnm.|ṯṯm.l.mit.ṯn.kbd.|tgmr. 1030.9

.ẖmš.|mrum.‘šr.|šb‘.ẖsnm.|mkrm.|mrynm.|ṯlṯ.‘šr.|hbṯnm.|ṯmn.|md̠rǵlm.|ṯmnym.ṯmn.kbd.|tgmr.ẖrd.|arb‘m 1031.11

rynm.|ṯlṯ.‘šr.mkrm.|ṯlṯ.bn.mrynm.|arb‘.ṯrtnm.|tš‘.hbṯnm.|ṯmnym.ṯlṯ.kbd.|md̠rǵlm.|w.šb‘.‘šr.ẖsnm.|ẖmšm.l. 1029.10

hbm

kd.šmn.‘l.hbm.šlmy.|kd.šmn.ṯbil.|kd.šmn.ymtšr.|arb‘.šmn.‘l.‘bdn.w. 1082.1.1

hbn

.dd.|n‘r.|ẖmšm.tišr.|ẖmš.ktnt.|ẖmš.ṯnt.alpm.|‘šrm.hbn.|ṯlṯ.mat.dd.|š‘rm.|mit.šmn.|‘šr.kat.|ẓrw. 2102.6

hbr

pq.thmtm. | tgly.ḏd.il.w tbu. | qrš.mlk.ab.šnm. | l p‘n.il.thbr.w tql. | tštḥwy.w tkbd h. | hlm.il.k yphn h. | yprq.lṣb.w y 4[51].4.25
| [l ytn.pnm.tk.]in.bb.b alp ḫẓr. | [rbt.kmn.l p‘]n.‘nt. | [yhbr.w yql.yšt]ḥwyn.w y | [kbdn h.yšu.g h.w y]ṣḥ.tḥm. | [ṯr.i 1[‘NT.IX].2.16
q.thmtm.tgly.ḏd. | il.w tbu.qrš.. | mlk.ab.šnm.l p‘n. | il.thbr.w tql. | tštḥwy.w tkbdn h. | tšu.g h.w tṣḥ.tšmḫ ht. | aṯrt. 6.1.37[49.1.9]
q.thmtm tgly.ḏd il. | [w tbu.qr]š.mlk.ab.šnm. | [l p‘n.il.t]hbr.w tql.tštḥ | [wy.w tkbd]n h.tlšn.aqht.ġzr. | [---.kdd.dn]i 17[2AQHT].6.50
k.ġr.ks]. | ygly ḏd.i[l.w ybu.qrš.mlk]. | ab.šnm.l [p‘n.il.yhbr.w yql]. | yštḥwy.[w ykbdn h.---]. | ṯr.il[.ab h.---]. | ḥš b[h 1[‘NT.IX].3.24
.ṯbt h.ḥkpt.arṣ.nḫlt h]. | b alp.šd.r[bt.kmn.l p‘n.kṯr]. | hbr.w ql.t[štḥwy.w kbd.hwt]. | w rgm l k[ṯr.w ḫss.ṯny.l hyn] 1[‘NT.IX].3.3
šmm.b yd.md | d.ilm.mt.b a | lp.šd.rbt.k | mn.l p‘n.mt. | hbr.w ql. | tštḥwy.w k | bd hwt.w rgm. | l bn.ilm.mt. | ṯny.l yd 4[51].8.27
u.ṯbt h.ḥkpt. | arṣ.nḫlt h. | b alp.šd.rbt. | kmn.l p‘n.kṯ. | hbr.w ql.tštḥ | wy.w kbd hwt. | w rgm.l kṯr. | w ḫss.ṯny.l h | y 3[‘NT.VI].6.19
ly.bt.rb.dd.arṣy. | bt.y‘bdr.km ġlmm. | w ‘rb n.l p‘n.‘nt.hbr. | w ql.tštḥwy.kbd hyt. | w rgm.l btlt.‘nt. | ṯny.l ymmt.lim 3[‘NT].3.6
. | ṯḥrr.l išt.w ṣḥrt.l pḥmm.aṯtm.a[ṯt.il]. | aṯt.il.w ‘lm h.yhbr.špt hm.yš[q]. | hn.špt hm.mtqtm.mtqtm.k lrmn[.--]. | b 23[52].49
t.yld y.šḥr.w šl[m]. | šu.‘db.l špš.rbt.w l kbkbm.kn[-]. | yhbr.špt hm.yšq.hn.[š]pt hm.mtqtm. | bm.nšq.w hr.[b]ḥbq. 23[52].55
ṯpṯ]. | [nhr.---.]hwt.gmr.hd.l wny[-.---]. | [---.]iyr h.g[-.]thbr[.---]. 2.1[137].47

hgg

n.‘n k.ẓẓ.w k mġ.ilm. | [--.]k ‘ṣm.k ‘šm.l ttn.k abnm.l thggn. 1001.2.13

hgy

m‘. | ṣbu k.ul.mad. | ṯlṯ.mat.rbt. | ḫpṯ.d bl.spr. | ṯnn.d bl.hg. | hlk.l alpm.ḫḏḏ. | w l rbt.kmyr. | [a]ṯr.ṯn.ṯn.hlk. | aṯr.ṯlṯ.kl 14[KRT].2.91

hd

m.yḥmd m. | bn.dgn.yhrr m. | b‘l.ngṯ hm.b p‘n h. | w il hd.b ḫrẓ‘ h. | [-----]. | [--]t.[---]. | [---.]‘n[.---]. | pnm[.---]. | b‘l.n[12[75].1.41
l hm.d l h q[--.---]. | l ytn.l hm.tḥt b‘l[.---]. | h.u qšt pn hdd.b y[.----]. | ‘m.b ym b‘l ysy ym[.---]. | rmm.ḫnpm.mḫl[.- 9[33].2.6
[---.b‘l.b bht h]. | [il.hd.b qr]b.hkl h. | w t‘nyn.ġlm.b‘l. | in.b‘l.b bht ht. | il hd.b qr 10[76].2.2
il.hd.b qr]b.hkl h. | w t‘nyn.ġlm.b‘l. | in.b‘l.b bht ht. | il hd.b qrb.hkl h. | qšt hn.aḫd.b yd h. | w qṣ‘t h.bm.ymn h. | idk 10[76].2.5
| t[---.---]. | [-----]. | [-----]. | b [----]. | w [----]. | b‘l.[---]. | il hd.b[---]. | at.bl.at.[---]. | yisp hm.b[‘l.---]. | bn.dgn[.---]. | ‘ḏb 12[75].2.23
--.td‘]. | qdm ym.bmt.[nhr]. | ṯṯn.ib.b‘l.tiḫd. | y‘rm.šnu.hd.gpt. | ġr.w y‘n.aliyn. | b‘l.ib.hdt.lm.tḫš. | lm.tḫš.nṯq.dmrn. 4[51].7.36
.ḥ[--]k.ġrt. | [ql].l b‘l.‘nt.ttnn. | [---].b‘l m.d ip[---]. | [il.]hd.d ‘nn.n[--]. | [----.]aliyn.b[‘l]. | [---.btl]t.‘n[t.-.]p h. | [---.---] 10[76].2.33
it.rḥ[.---]. | ṯṯlb.a[--.---]. | yšu.g h[.---]. | i.ap.b‘[l.---]. | i.hd.d[---.---]. | ynp‘.b‘[l.---]. | b ṯmnt.[---]. | yqrb.[---]. | lḥm.m[- 5[67].4.7
pm.mḫl[.---]. | mlk.nhr.ibr[.---]. | zbl b‘l.ġlm.[---]. | ṣġr hd w r[---.---]. | w l nhr nd[-.---]. | [---.--]l. 9[33].2.11
ṯ. | ršp. | ‘nt ḫbly. | špš pgr. | iltm ḫnqtm. | yrḫ kty. | ygb hd. | yrgb b‘l. | ydb il. | yarš il. | yrġm il. | ‘mtr. | ydb il. | yrgb li UG5.14.B.1
an.rgmt.l ym.b‘l km.ad[n km.ṯpṯ]. | [nhr.---.]hwt.gmr.hd.l wny[-.---]. | [---.]iyr h.g[-.]thbr[.---]. 2.1[137].46
ṯn.ib.b‘l.tiḫd. | y‘rm.šnu.hd.gpt. | ġr.w y‘n.aliyn. | b‘l.ib.hdt.lm.tḫš. | lm.tḫš.nṯq.dmrn. | ‘n.b‘l.qdm.yd h. | k tġḏ.arz.b 4[51].7.38
nym.‘l[m.--]. | k dr d.d yknn[.--]. | b‘l.yṣġd.mli[.--]. | il hd.mla.u[--.--]. | blt.p btlt.‘n[t]. | w p.n‘mt.aḫt[.b‘l]. | y‘l.b‘l.b 10[76].3.9
[---.--]b. | [---.w ym.ym]m. | [y‘tqn.---.ymġy.]npš. | [---.h]d.tngtn h. | [---].b ṣpn. | [---].nšb.b ‘n. | [---.]b km.y‘n. | [---.y 1[‘NT.X].5.4
h. | [---.--]b.w ym ymm. | [y‘tqn.---].ymġy.npš. | [---.-]t.hd.tngṯm h. | [---.-]ḥm k b ṣpn. | [---.]išqb.aylt. | [---.--]m.b k 1[‘NT.X].5.17
ht y.bnt. | dt.ksp.hkl y.dtm. | ḫrṣ.‘dbt.bht[h.b‘]l. | y‘db.hd.‘db[.‘d]bt. | hkl h.ṯbḫ.alpm[.ap]. | ṣin.šql.ṯrm[.w]m | ria.il. 4[51].6.39
t y.b ṣ‘.hm.ks.ymsk. | nhr.k[--].ṣḥn.b‘l.‘m. | aḫ y.qran.hd.‘m.ary y. | w lḥm m ‘m aḫ y.lḥm. | w št m.‘m.a[ḫ] yn. | p n 5[67].1.23
m.mt. | [---.]g h.w aṣḥ.ik.yṣḥn. | [b‘l.‘m.aḫ y.ik].yqrun.hd. | [‘m.ary y.---.--]p.mlḥm y. | [---.---]lt.qẓb. | [---.]šmḫ y. | [- 5[67].2.22
. | b skn.sknm.b ‘dn. | ‘dnm.kn.npl.b‘l. | km ṯr.w tkms.hd.p[.-]. | km.ibr.b tk.mšmš d[--]. | ittpq.l awl. | išttk.lm.ttkn. 12[75].2.55
pu.mlk.‘lm.w yšt. | [--.]gṯr.w yqr.il.yṯb.b.‘ṯtrt. | il.ṯpṭ.b hd r‘y.d yšr.w yḏmr. | b knr.w ṯlb.b tp.w mṣltm.b m | rqdm. UG5.2.1.3
b‘l.yṯb.k ṯbt.ġr.hd.r[‘y]. | k mdb.b tk.ġr h.il ṣpn.b [tk]. | ġr.tliyt.šb‘t.brqm.[-- UG5.3.1.1
.--]slm.w.yṯb. | [----.--]t.hw[-]y.h[--]r.w rgm.ank. | [---.]hdd tr[--.--]l.aṯrt y. | [--]ptm.šḥq. | [---.]rgm.hy.[-]ḫ[-]y.ilak k. 1002.39
---]. | [--]t.[---]. | [---.]‘n[.---]. | pnm[.---]. | b‘l.n[--.---]. | il.hd[.---]. | at.bl[.at.---]. | ḥmd m.[---]. | il.hr[r.---]. | kb[-.---]. | y 12[75].2.6
rgb lim. | ‘mtr. | yarš il. | ydb b‘l. | yrġm b‘l. | ‘z b‘l. | ydb hd. UG5.14.B.14

hdy

zr.ilm.ylḥm. | [uzr.yšqy.]bn.qdš.yd. | [ṣt h.y‘l.]w yškb.yd. | [mizrt.]p ynl.hn.ym. | [w ṯn.uzr.]ilm.dnil. | [uzr.ilm.]ylḥ 17[2AQHT].1.5
[uzr.]yšqy.bn qdš.yd.ṣt h. | [dn]il.yd.ṣt h.y‘l.w yškb. | [yd.]mizrt.p yln.mk.b šb‘.ymm. | [w]yqrb.b‘l.b ḥnt h.abynt. | 17[2AQHT].1.16
l qdqd h.lpš.yks. | mizrtm.ġr.b abn. | ydy.psltm.b y‘r. | yhdy.lḥm.w dqn. | yṯlṯ.qn.ḏr‘ h.yḥrṯ. | k gn.ap lb.k ‘mq.yṯlṯ. | 5[67].6.19
l b‘l. | ġr.b ab.td[.ps]ltm[.b y‘r]. | thdy.lḥm.w dqn[.ṯṯlṯ]. | qn.ḏr‘ h.tḥrṯ.km.gn. | ap lb.k ‘mq.ṯṯlṯ 6[62].1.3
n.l riš h.‘pr.plṯt. | l qdqd h.lpš.yks. | mizrtm.ġr.b abn. | ydy.psltm.b y‘r. | yhdy.lḥm.w dqn. | yṯlṯ.qn.ḏr‘ h.yḥrṯ. | k gn. 5[67].6.18
l b‘l. | ġr.b ab.td[.ps]ltm[.b y‘r]. | thdy.lḥm.w dqn[.ṯṯlṯ]. | qn.ḏr‘ h.tḥrṯ.km. 6[62].1.2
ṯ.ym.uzr. | [ilm].dnil.uzr.ilm.ylḥm. | [uzr.]yšqy.bn qdš.yd.ṣt h. | [dn]il.yd.ṣt h.y‘l.w yškb. | [yd.]mizrt.p yln.mk.b šb‘ 17[2AQHT].1.14
.ġz[r]. | [mt.hrnmy.]uzr.ilm.ylḥm. | [uzr.yšqy.]bn.qdš.yd. | [ṣt h.y‘l.]w yškb.yd. | [mizrt.]p ynl.hn.ym. | [w ṯn.uzr.]il 17[2AQHT].1.4
.dnil.uzr.ilm.ylḥm. | [uzr.]yšqy.bn qdš.yd.ṣt h. | [dn]il.yd.ṣt h.y‘l.w yškb. | [yd.]mizrt.p yln.mk.b šb‘.ymm. | [w]yqr 17[2AQHT].1.15

hdm

tm. | kt.il.nbt.b ksp. | šmrgt.b dm.ḫrṣ. | kḥṯ.il.nḫt. | b zr.hdm.id. | d prša.b br. | n‘l.il.d qblbl. | ‘ln.ybl hm.ḫrṣ. | ṯlḥn.il.d 4[51].1.35
‘l. | ḫlq.zbl.b‘l.arṣ. | apnk.lṭpn.il. | d pid.yrd.l ksi.yṯb. | l hdm[.w] l.hdm.yṯb. | l arṣ.yṣq.‘mr. | un.l riš h.‘pr.plṯt. | l qdq 5[67].6.13
m‘.mhrm. | [ṯ]‘r.ksat.l ksat.ṯlḥnt. | [l]ṯlḥn.hdmm.ṯṯ‘r.l hdmm. | [t]ḥspn.m h.w trḥṣ. | [ṯ]l.šmm.šmn.arṣ.rbb. | [r]kb ‘r 3[‘NT].2.37
.b‘l.arṣ. | apnk.lṭpn.il. | d pid.yrd.l ksi.yṯb. | l hdm[.w] l.hdm.yṯb. | l arṣ.yṣq.‘mr. | un.l riš h.‘pr.plṯt. | l qdqd h.lpš.yks. 5[67].6.13
‘mq. | tḫtṣb.bn.qrtm.ṯṯ‘r. | ksat.l mhr.ṯ‘r.ṯlḥnt. | l ṣbim.hdmm.l ġzrm. | mid.tmtḫṣn.w t‘n. | tḫtṣb.w tḥdy.‘nt. | tġdd.k 3[‘NT].2.22
[---.tm]tḫṣ b ‘mq. | [tḫtṣb.bn.qrtm.ṯṯ‘r.ṯlḥnt.]l ṣbim. | [hdmm.l ġzrm.mid.tmtḫṣn.w t]‘n.tḫtṣb. | [w tḥdy.‘nt.tġdd.kb 7.1[131].6

ʻrẓ. | yʻl.b ṣrrt.ṣpn. | yṯb.l kḥṯ.aliyn. | bʻl.pʻn h.l tmǵyn. | hdm.riš h.l ymǵy. | aps h.w yʻn.ʻṯtr.ʻrẓ. | l amlk.b ṣrrt.ṣpn. | y 6.1.60[49.1.32]

u]ṣbʻt h.b mmʻ.mhrm. | [ṯ]ʻr.ksat.l ksat.ṯlḥnt. | [l]ṯlḥn.hdmm.ṯṯʻr.l hdmm. | [t]ḫspn.m h.w trḥṣ. | [ṭ]l.šmm.šmn.arṣ. 3[ʻNT].2.37

.w tkbd h. | hlm.il.k yphn h. | yprq.lṣb.w yṣḥq. | pʻn h.l hdm.yṯpd.w ykrkr. | uṣbʻt h.yšu.g h.w y[ṣḥ]. | ik.mǵyt.rbt.aṯr 4[51].4.29

mn.tmṯrn. | nḫlm.tlk.nbtm. | šmḫ.lṭpn.il.d pid. | pʻn h.l hdm.yṯpd. | w yprq.lṣb w yṣḥq. | yšu.g h.w yṣḥ. | aṯbn.ank.w 6[49].3.15

i[l]. | pnm.tšmḫ.w ʻl yṣhl pi[t]. | yprq.lṣb.w yṣḥq. | pʻn.l hdm.yṯpd.yšu. | g h.w yṣḥ.aṯbn.ank. | w anḫn.w tnḫ.b irt y. | 17[2AQHT].2.11

hdrt

ld.špḥ.l krt. | w ǵlm.l ʻbd.il. | krt.yḫṭ.w ḥlm. | ʻbd.il.w hdrt. | yrtḥṣ.w yadm. | yrḥṣ.yd h.amt h. | uṣbʻt h.ʻd.ṯkm. | ʻrb. 14[KRT].3.155

hw

t.tbʻ[.---]. | qrt.mlk[.---]. | w.ʻl.ap.s[--.---]. | b hm.w.rgm.hw.al[--]. | atn.ksp.l hm.ʻd. | ilak.ʻm.mlk. | ht.lik[t.--.]mlk[.--]. 2008.2.6

.[--]n.w aspt.[q]l h. | [---.rg]m.ank l[.--.--]rny. | [---.]ṯm.hw.i[--]ty. | [---].ibʻr.a[--.]ḏmr. | [---.]w mlk.w rg[m.---]. | [--.r 1002.51

]. | w ank.u šbt[--.---]. | ank.n[--]n[.---]. | kst.l[--.---]. | w.hw.uy.ʻn[--.---]. | l ytn.w rgm[.---]. | w yrdnn.an[--.---]. | [---].a 54.1.13[13.1.10]

m. | šlm. | l.[--]n.špš. | ad[.ʻ]bd h.uk.škn. | k.[---.]sglt h.hw. | w.b[.---.]uk.nǵr. | w.[---].adny.l.yḫsr. | w.[ank.yd]ʻ.l.ydʻt 2060.7

l.ḏrdn. | bʻl y.rgm. | bn.ḫrn k. | mǵy. | hbṭ.hw. | ḫrd.w.šl hw. | qr[-]. | akl n.b.grnt. | l.bʻr. | ap.krmm. | ḫlq. 2114.5

il.ʻbd k.bʻl.y ym m.ʻbd k.bʻl. | [--.--]m.bn.dgn.a[s]r km.hw ybl.argmn k.k ilm. | [---.]ybl.k bn.qdš.mnḥy k.ap.anš.zbl 2.1[137].37

m yḥr[r.---]. | bmt n m.yšḫn.[---]. | qrn h.km.ǵb[-.---]. | hw km.ḥrr[.---]. | šnmtm.dbṭ[.---]. | trʻ.trʻn.a[--.---]. | bnt.šdm. 12[75].2.41

ʻn hm.nǵr mdrʻ[.iṯ.lḥm.---]. | iṯ.yn.d ʻrb.bṯk[.---]. | mǵ hw.l hn.lg yn h[.---]. | w hbr h.mla yn.[---]. 23[52].75

r]nmy npš.yḥ.dnil. | [mt.rp]i.brlt.ǵzr.mt hrnmy. | [---].hw.mḫ.l ʻrš h.yʻl. | [---].bm.nšq.aṯt h. | [---.]b ḥbq h.ḥmḥmt. | 17[2AQHT].1.39

[---.hw.ṯʻ.nṯʻ]y. | [hw.nkt.nkt.ytši.l ab.bn.il.ytši.l d]r.bn[.il]. | [l mpḫrt.bn.il.l ṯ 32[2].1.2

. | ušn yp km.l d[b]ḥm.w l.ṯʻ.dbḥ n.ndbḥ.hw.ṯʻ |nṯʻy. | hw.nkt.nkt.y[t]ši.l ab.bn.il.ytši.l dr. | bn il.l mpḫrt.bn.il.l ṯk 32[2].1.25

]. | tqṯṯn u ṯḫṭin.l bḥm.w l ṯʻ.d[bḥ n.ndbḥ]. | hw.ṯʻ.nṯʻy.hw.nkt.n[k]t.ytši[.l ab.bn.il]. | ytši.l dr.bn.il.l mpḫrt.bn.i[l.l ṯ 32[2].1.16

ṯṭn.ušn y[p kn.l dbḥm.]w l ṯʻ dbḥ n. | ndbḥ.hw.ṯʻ n[ṯʻy.hw.nkt.nk]t.ytši.l ab bn il. | ytši.l d[r.bn il.l]mpḫrt.bn il. | l ṯ 32[2].1.33

]. | [tqṯṯ.u ṯḫṭu.l dbḥm.w l.ṯʻ.dbḥ n.ndb]ḥ. | [hw.ṯʻ.nṯʻy.hw.nkt.nkt.]yt[ši.l ab.bn.il]. | [ytši.l dr.bn.il.l mpḫ]rt.[bn.il.l 32[2].1.9A

k.aliyn bʻl. | ʻdbnn ank.imr.b p y. | k lli.b ṯbrn q y.ḫṭu hw. | nrt.ilm.špš.ṣḥrrt. | la.šmm.b yd.bn ilm.mt. | ym.ymm.yʻ 6[49].2.23

. | ḥnn y l pn mlk. | šin k itn. | rʻ y šṣa idn l y. | l šmn iṯr hw. | p iḫdn gnryn. | im mlkytn yrgm. | aḫnnn. | w iḫd. 1020.6

ǵr. | mdrʻ.w ṣḥ hm.ʻm.nǵr.mdrʻ y.nǵr. | nǵr.ptḥ.w ptḥ hw.prṣ.bʻd hm. | w ʻrb.hm.hm[.iṯ.--.l]ḥm.w t[n]. | w nlḥm.h 23[52].70

l.ḏrdn. | bʻl y.rgm. | bn.ḫrn k. | mǵy. | hbṭ.hw. | ḫrd.w.šl hw. | qr[-]. | akl n.b.grnt. | l.bʻr. | ap.krmm. | ḫlq. | qrt n.ḫlq. | w 2114.6

[---.hw.ṯʻ.nṯʻ]y. | [hw.nkt.nkt.ytši.l ab.bn.il.ytši.l d]r.bn[.il]. | [l m 32[2].1.1

.u b qṯṯ.tqṯṯ. | ušn yp km.l d[b]ḥm.w l.ṯʻ.dbḥ n.ndbḥ.hw.ṯʻ |nṯʻy. | hw.nkt.nkt.y[t]ši.l ab.bn.il.ytši.l dr. | bn il.l mp 32[2].1.24

kn.u b qṯt]. | tqṯṯn u ṯḫṭin.l bḥm.w l ṯʻ.d[bḥ n.ndbḥ]. | hw.ṯʻ.nṯʻy.hw.nkt.n[k]t.ytši[.l ab.bn.il]. | ytši.l dr.bn.il.l mpḫ 32[2].1.16

.u b qṯt. | tqṯṯn.ušn y[p kn.l dbḥm.]w l ṯʻ dbḥ n. | ndbḥ.hw.ṯʻ n[ṯʻy.hw.nkt.nk]t.ytši.l ab bn il. | ytši.l d[r.bn il.l]mpḫ 32[2].1.33

km.u b qṯt]. | [tqṯṯ.u ṯḫṭu.l dbḥm.w l.ṯʻ.dbḥ n.ndb]ḥ. | [hw.ṯʻ.nṯʻy.hw.nkt.nkt.]yt[ši.l ab.bn.il]. | [ytši.l dr.bn.il.l mpḫ 32[2].1.9A

-.---]. | b [u]grt.w ht.a[--]. | w hm.at.trg[m.---]. | w sip.u hw[.---]. | w ank.u šbt[--.---]. | ank.n[--]n[.---]. | kst.l[--.---]. | w. 54.1.9[13.1.6]

[-----]. | [---.--]ty.l[--.---]. | [--.--]tm.w ʻ[--.--]. | [---].w kl.hw[.---]. | w [--].brt.lb[--.---]. | u[-]šhr.nuš[-.---]. | b [u]grt.w ht 54.1.4[13.1.1]

hwil

n.gby.gt.prn. | šd.bn.kryn.gt.prn. | šd.bn.ky.gt.prn. | šd.hwil.gt.prn. | šd.ḥr.gt.prn. | šd.bn.ṯbǵl.gt.prn. | šd.bn.inšr.gt.p 1104.7

hwy

.ṯḥm.bn ilm. | mt.hwt.ydd.bn.il. | ǵzr.p np.š.npš.lbim. | thw.hm.brlt.anḫr. | b ym.hm.brk y.tkšd. | rumm.ʻn.kḏd.aylt. 5[67].1.15

w yʻny.bn. | ilm.mt.npš[.-]. | npš.lbun. | thw.w npš. | anḫr.b ym. | brkt.šbšt. | k rumm.hm. | ʻn.kḏd.aylt UG5.4.4

hwt

. | ṯbt.ḫḫ.arṣ.nḫlt h.tša. | g hm.w tṣḥ.ṯḥm.aliyn. | bn.bʻl.hwt.aliy.qrdm. | bhṯ.bn.ilm.mt.ʻbd k.an. | w d ʻlm k.šmḫ.bn.i 5[67].2.18

. | tbʻ.rgm.l bn.ilm.mt. | ṯny.l ydd.il ǵzr. | ṯḥm.aliyn.bʻl.hwt.aliy. | qrdm.bhṯ.l bn.ilm mt. | ʻbd k.an.w d.ʻlm k. | tbʻ.w l 5[67].2.10

rgm. | l bn.ilm.mt. | ṯny.l ydd. | il.ǵzr.ṯḥm. | aliyn.bʻl. | [hw]t.aliy.q | [rdm.]bht y.bnt. | [dt.ksp.dtm]. | [ḫrṣ.hk]l y. | [---. 4[51].8.34

r.---]. | rgm l btl[t.ʻnt.ṯny.l ybmt.limm.ṯḥm.aliyn.bʻl]. | hw[t.aliy.qrdm.qryy.b arṣ.mlḥmt.št]. | [b ʻ]pr[m.ddym.sk.šl 7.2[130].14

ǵlmm.yʻnyn.l ib.ypʻ. | l bʻl.ṣrt.l rkb.ʻrpt. | ṯḥm.aliyn.bʻl.hwt.aliy. | qrdm.qry.b arṣ.mlḥmt. | št.b ʻp[r] m.ddym.sk.šlm. 3[ʻNT].4.51

yt. | w rgm.l btlt.ʻnt. | ṯny.l ymmt.limm. | ṯḥm.aliyn.bʻl.hwt. | aliy.qrdm.qry.b arṣ. | mlḥmt št.b ʻpr m.ddym. | sk.šlm. 3[ʻNT].3.10

.l kṯr. | w ḫss.ṯny.l h | yn.d ḥrš.ydm. | ṯḥm.al[iyn.bʻl]. | h[wt.aliy.qrdm]. 3[ʻNT.VI].6.25

d.rgm.b ǵr. | b p y.tʻlgt.b lšn[y]. | ǵr[.---]b.b pš y.t[--]. | hwt.bʻl.iš[--]. | šmʻ l y.ypš.[---]. | ḥkr[.---]. | ʻṣr[--.]tb[-]. | ṯat[.-- 2124.4

---]. | [---].an.rgmt.l ym.bʻl km.ad[n km.ṯpṭ]. | [nhr.---.]hwt.gmr.hd.l wny[-.---]. | [---.]iyr h.g[-.]thbr[.---]. 2.1[137].46

ls] | [m]n ʻm y t[wtḥ.išd k.dm.rgm.iṯ.l y.d argmn k]. | [h]wt.d aṯ[ny k.---.rgm.ʻṣ]. | w lḫšt.abn[.tant.šmm.ʻm.arṣ.thm 7.2[130].18

t.ǵz[r]. | tšt k.bm.qrb m.asm. | b p h.rgm.l yṣa.b špt h[.hwt h]. | b nši ʻn h.w tphn.in.[---]. | [-.]hlk.ǵlmm b dd y.yṣ[--] 19[1AQHT].2.75

.w aqbrn.ašt.b ḫrt. | i[lm.arṣ.b p h.rgm.l yṣa.b šp] | t h.hwt h.knp.hrgb.bʻl.ṯbr. | bʻl.ṯbr.diy.hwt.w yql. | tḥt.pʻn h.ybq 19[1AQHT].3.128

.w aqbrn h. | ašt.b ḫrt.ilm.arṣ. | b p h.rgm.l yṣa.b špt h.hwt[h]. | knp.nšrm.bʻl.yṯbr. | bʻl.ṯbr.diy hmt.tqln. | tḥt.pʻn h. 19[1AQHT].3.113

aqbrn h.aštn. | b ḫrt.ilm.arṣ.b p h.rgm.l[yṣ]a. | b špt h.hwt h.knp.ṣml.bʻ[l]. | bʻl.ṯbr.diy.hyt.tq[l.tḥt]. | pʻn h.ybqʻ.kbd 19[1AQHT].3.142

.ʻẓm.yšu.g[h]. | w yṣḥ.knp.hrgb.bʻl.ybn. | [b]ʻl.ybn.diy.hwt.hrg[b]. | tpr.w du.b nši.ʻn h. | [w]yphn.yḥd.ṣml.um.nšr 19[1AQHT].3.133

gm.l yṣa.b šp] | t h.hwt h.knp.hrgb.bʻl.ṯbr. | bʻl.ṯbr.diy.hwt.w yql. | tḥt.pʻn h.ybqʻ.kbd h.w yḥd. | [i]n.šmt.in.ʻẓm.yšu 19[1AQHT].3.129

šrm. | yšu.g h.w yṣḥ.knp.hr[g]b. | bʻl.yṯb.bʻl.y[ṯb]r.diy[.h]wt. | w yql.tḥt.pʻn y.ibqʻ.kbd[h]. | w aḥd.hm.iṯ.šmt.hm.iṯ[. 19[1AQHT].3.123

a | lp.šd.rbt.k | mn.l pʻn.mt. | hbr.w ql. | tšthwy.w k | bd hwt.w rgm. | l bn.ilm.mt. | ṯny.l ydd. | il.ǵzr.ṯḥm. | aliyn.bʻl. | [4[51].8.29

b alp.šd.r[bt.kmn.l pʻn.kṯr]. | hbr.w ql.t[šthwy.w kbd.hwt]. | w rgm l k[ṯr.w ḫss.ṯny.l hyn]. | d ḥrš.y[dm.ṯḥm.ṯr.il.a 1[ʻNT.IX].3.3

| b alp.šd.rbt. | kmn.l pʻn.kṯ. | hbr.w ql.tšth | wy.w kbd hwt. | w rgm.l kṯr. | w ḫss.ṯny.l h | yn.d ḥrš.ydm. | ṯḥm.al[iyn. 3[ʻNT.VI].6.20

| [tls]mn.[ʻ]m y.twtḥ.išd k. | [dm.rgm.iṯ.l y.]w argm k.hwt. | [w aṯny k.rgm.]ʻṣ.w lḫšt. | [abn.rgm.l td]ʻ.nš[m.w l t]b 3[ʻNT].4.57

n k.tlsmn.ʿm y.|twtḥ.išd k.dm.rgm.|iṯ.l y.w argm k.|hwt.w aṯny k.rgm.|ʿṣ.w lḫšt.abn.|tant.šmm.ʿm.arṣ.|thmt.ʿ 3[ʿNT].3.19
.tk.ḫršn.-------------].|ǵr.ks.dm.r[gm.iṯ.l y.w argm k].|hwt.w aṯny k[.rgm.ʿṣ.w lḫšt.abn].|tunt.šmm.ʿm[.arṣ.thmt.ʿ 1[ʿNT.IX].3.13
m.|[---.-]qlṣn.wpṯ m.|[---.]w yʿn.kṯr.|[w ḫss.]ṯtb.bʿl.l hwt y.|[ḥš.]bht h.tbnn.|[ḥš.]trmm.hkl h.|y[tl]k.l lbnn.w ʿṣ 4[51].6.15
ḫss.|yšu.g h.w yṣḥ.|l rgmt.l k.l ali|yn.bʿl.ṯtbn.bʿl.|l hwt y.yptḥ.ḥ|ln.b bht m.urbt.|b qrb.hk[l m.yp]tḥ.|bʿl.b dq 4[51].7.25
w yʿn.k[ṯr.w ḫs]s.|ṯtb.bʿl.l[hwt y].|ṯn.rgm.k[ṯr.w]ḫss.|šmʿ.mʿ.l al[iy]n bʿl.|bl.ašt.ur[bt 4[51].6.2
ʿm.bʿl.|mrym.ṣpn.w yʿn.|gpn.w ugr.tḥm.bn ilm.|mt.hwt.ydd.bn.il.|ǵzr.p np.š.npš.lbim.|thw.hm.brlt.anḫr.|b y 5[67].1.13
.|[---.--]m.|[-----].|[-]š[--.---].|[-]r[--.--]y.|in m.ʿbd k hwt.|[y]rš.ʿm y.|mnm.iršt k.|d ḫsrt.w.ank.|aštn..l.iḫ y.|w. 2065.13
.b bht m.|urbt.b qrb.[h]kl |m.w y[p]tḥ.b dqt.ʿrpt.|ʿl h[wt].kṯr.w ḫss.|ṣḥq.kṯr.w ḫss.|yšu.g h.w yṣḥ.|l rgmt.l k.l 4[51].7.20
gdrt.k lb.l |ḥt h.imḫṣ h.k d.ʿl.qšt h.|imḫṣ h.ʿl.qṣʿt h.hwt.|l aḫw.ap.qšt h.l ttn.|l y.w b mt[.-]ḫ.mṣṣ[-]t[.--].|prʿ.q 19[1AQHT].1.15
ṭpn.[mhr.št].|šmʿ.l btlt.ʿnt.at.ʿ[l.qšt h].|tmḫṣ h.qṣʿt h.hwt.l t[ḥwy].|nʿmn.ǵzr.št.trm.w[---].|ištir.b ḏdm.w nʿrs[.-- 18[3AQHT].4.13
.pnm.|ʿm.nrt.ilm.špš.|tšu.g h.w tṣḥ.|tḥm.ṯr.il.ab k.|hwt.lṭpn.ḥtk k.|pl.ʿnt.šdm.y špš.|pl.ʿnt.šdm.il.yš[t k].|bʿl.ʿ 6[49].4.35
št]ḥwyn.w y|[kbdn h.yšu.g h.w y]ṣḥ.tḥm.|[ṯr.il.ab k.hwt.l]ṭpn.ḥtk k.|[qryy.b arṣ.mlḥ]mt.št b ʿp|[r m.ddym.sk.š 1[ʿNT.IX].2.18
l k[ṯr.w ḫss.ṯny.l hyn].|d ḥrš.y[dm.tḥm.ṯr.il.ab k.]|hwt.lṭpn[.ḥtk k.---].|yh.kṯr.b[---].|št.lskt.n[--.---].|ʿdb.bǵrt. 1[ʿNT.IX].3.6
l ytn.ʿmm.pbl.|mlk.tšan.|g hm.w tṣḥn.|tḥm.krt.ṯ[ʿ].|hwt.[n]ʿmn.[ǵlm.il]. 14[KRT].6.306
p[---.]km.|[-]bl lb h.km.btn.y[--.-]ah.|tnm.tšqy msk.hwt.tšqy[.-.]w [---].|w hn dt.ytb.l mspr. 19[1AQHT].4.224
.nmgn.|[-]m.rbt.aṯrt.ym.|[nǵ]ẓ.qnyt.ilm.|[---].nmgn.hwt.|[--].aliyn.bʿl.|[--.]rbt.aṯrt.ym.|[---.]btlt.ʿnt.|[--.tl]ḥm.t 4[51].3.36
-----].|[-----.š]ilt.|[---.--]m.lm.|[---.š]d.gṯr.|[--]ḥ[d].šd.hwt.|[--.]iḥd.šd.gṯr.|[w]ht.yšmʿ.uḫ y.|l g y.w yhbṭ.bnš.|w 55[18].15
r.|[---.kdd.dn]il.mt.rpi.w tʿn.|[btlt.ʿnt.tšu.g]h.w tṣḥ.hwt.|[---.]aqht.yd[--].|[---.--]n.ṣ[---].|[spr.ilmlk.šbny.lmd.at 17[2AQHT].6.53
rt.|[---.]mn mn[-.---.--]n.nmr.|[--.]l ytk.bl[-.---.]m[--.]hwt.|[---].ṯllt.khn[m.---.]k pʿn.|[---.--]y.yd.nšy.[---.--]š.l md UG5.8.46

hzp

r.|agm.w.ḫpty.|ḫlb.ṣpn.|mril.|ʿnmky.|ʿnqpat.|ṭbq.|hzp.|gnʿy.|mʿrby.|[ṣ]ʿq.|[š]ḥq.|nʿrm.|mḫrǵlm.|kzym.|mr 71[113].55
.bir.|ṯṯ.bnšm b.uḫnp.|ṯn.bnšm.b.ḫrṣbʿ.|arbʿ.bnšm.b.hzp.|arbʿ.bnšm.b.šql.|arbʿ.bnšm.b.nni.|ṯn.bnšm.b.slḫ.|[---] 2076.16
ʿ.|šbn.|ṭbq.|rqd.|šrš.|gnʿy.|mʿqb.|agm.|bir.|ypr.|hzp.|šql.|mʿrḫ[-].|sl[ḫ].|snr.|ʿrgz.|yknʿm.|ʿnmky.|ǵr. 2074.31
nnu arbʿ.yn.|šql ṯlṯ.yn.|šmny.kdm.yn.|šmgy.kd.yn.|hzp.tšʿ.yn.|[b]ir.ʿšr[.---]m ḥsp.|ḫpty.kdm[.---].|[a]gm.arbʿ[. 2004.28
-].ʿšr.|[---].ṯlṯ.|[---].ṯmn.|[---].ṯlṯ.|[---].aḥd.|u[--].ṯn.|hz[p].ṯṯ.|ḫrṣbʿ.aḥd.|ypr.arb.|m[-]qb.ʿšr.|ṯnʿy.ṯlṯ.|ḫlb ʿprm. 70[112].7
qd arbʿ.|šbn aḥd.|ṭbq aḥd.|šrš aḥd.|bir aḥd.|uḫnp.|hzp ṯn.|mʿqb arbʿ. 2040.33

hzpḫ

ʿlm.š.š[--].l[--.]ʿrb.špš|š.w ḥl[.ml]k.|bn.aup[š.--].bsbn hzpḫ ṯlṯt.|kṯr[.---.--]trt ḫmšt.bn gda[.-.]mdʿ.|kl[--.---.]ṯmnt. APP.II[173].58

hzpy

n.---].|bʿl[--.---].|šm[---.---].|yšr[-.---].|bn.gnb[-.---].|hzpym.|rišn.[---].|bn.ʿbdy.[---].|bn.dmtn.[---].|[b]n.gʿyn.ḫr 93[328].8
.ykn.|bn.lṣn.ʿrmy.|bn.bʿyn.šly.|bn.ynḫn.|bn.ʿbdilm.hzpy. 99[327].2.6

hy

[---.šnst.kpt.b ḥb]š h.ʿtkt r[išt].|[l bmt h.---.]hy bt h tʿrb.|[---.tm]tḫṣ b ʿmq.|[tḫtṣb.bn.qrtm.ṯṯʿr.ṯlḥnt.]l ṣ 7.1[131].3
ṣḥq.|[---.]rgm.hy.[-]ḫ[-]y.ilak k.|[---.--]g k.yritn.mǵy.hy.w kn.|[---].ḥln.d b.dmt.um.il[m.---].|[--]ḏyn.bʿd.[--]ḏyn. 1002.42
].|ḥdṯ[.---.]ḥ[--].|b bt.[-.]l bnt.q[-].|w št.b bt.ṯap[.--].|hy.yd h.w ym[ǵ].|mlak k.ʿm dt[n].|lqḥ.mṭpṭ.|w yʿny.nn.|d UG5.6.10
rdr.|l iwrpḫn.|bn y.aḫ y.rgm.|ilm.tǵr k.|tšlm k.|ik y.lḥt.|spr.d likt.|ʿm.ṯryl.|mh y.rgmt.|w ht.aḫ y.|bn y.yšal. 138.6
ǵt].|ṯ[km]t.mym.ḥspt.l šʿr.|ṭl.ydʿt.hlk.kbkbm.|a[-]ḫ.hy.mḫ.tmḫṣ.mḫṣ[.aḫ k].|tkl.m[k]ly.ʿl.umt[k.--].|d ttql.b y 19[1AQHT].4.201
.|ilm.tǵr k.|tšlm k.|iky.lḥt.|spr.d likt.|ʿm.ṯryl.|mh y.rgmt.|w ht.aḫ y.|bn y.yšal.|ṯryl.p rgm.|l mlk.šm y.|w l 138.9
.|ilm.tǵr k.|tšlm k.|ik y.lḥt.|spr.d likt.|ʿm.ṯryl.|mh y.rgmt.|w ht.aḫ y.|bn y.yšal.|ṯryl.p rgm.|l mlk.šm y.|w l 138.9
tḥm.rgm.|mlk.|l ḥyil.|lm.tlik.ʿm y.|ik y.aškn.|ʿṣm.l bt.dml.|p ank.atn.|ʿṣm.l k.|arbʿ.ʿṣm.|ʿl.ar.|w 1010.5
.ank.|[---.]hdd tr[--.--]l.aṯrt y.|[--]ptm.ṣḥq.|[---.]rgm.hy.[-]ḫ[-]y.ilak k.|[---.--]g k.yritn.mǵy.hy.w kn.|[---].ḥln.d 1002.41
.---].|ql.[---].|w mlk[.nhš.w mlk.mg]šḫ.|ʿmn.[---].|ik y.[---].|w l n[qmd.---].|[w]nqmd.[---].|[-.]ʿmn.šp[š.mlk.rb]. 64[118].8

hyabn

l.gt.mzln.|šd.gldy.|l.gt.mzln.|šd.glln.l.gt.mz[l]n.|šd.hyabn[.l.]gt.mzln.|šd.ʿbdbʿl.|l.gt.mzln. 1104.20

hyadt

y.|bn.ḫny.|bn.ssm.|bn.ḫnn.|[--]ny.|[bn].ṯrdnt.|[bn].hyadt.|[--]lt.|šmrm.|pʿṣ.bn.byy.ʿšrt. 1047.22

hyn

šmʿ.|mṯt.dnty.tʿdb.imr.|b pḫd.l npš.kṯr.w ḫss.|l brlt.hyn.d ḥrš.|ydm.aḫr.ymǵy.kṯr.|w ḫss.b d.dnil.ytnn.|qšt.l br 17[2AQHT].5.24
šmʿ.mṯt.dnty.ʿd[b].|imr.b pḫd.l npš.kṯr.|w ḫss.l brlt.hyn d.|ḥrš yd.šlḥm.ššqy.|ilm sad.kbd.hmt.bʿl.|ḥkpt.il.kl h. 17[2AQHT].5.18
br.w ql.tštḥ|wy.w kbd hwt.|w rgm.l kṯr.|w ḫss.ṯny.l h|yn.d ḥrš.ydm.|tḥm.al[iyn.bʿl].|h[wt.aliy.qrdm]. 3[ʿNT.VI].6.22
br.w ql.t[štḥwy.w kbd.hwt].|w rgm l k[ṯr.w ḫss.ṯny.l hyn].|d ḥrš.y[dm.tḥm.ṯr.il.ab k.]|hwt.lṭpn[.ḥtk k.---].|yh.k 1[ʿNT.IX].3.4
.|argm k.šskn mʿ.|mgn.rbt.aṯrt ym.|mǵẓ.qnyt.ilm.|hyn.ʿly.l mpḫm.|b d.ḫss.mṣbṭm.|yṣq.ksp.yšl|ḥ.ḫrṣ.yṣq.ksp. 4[51].1.24
y ilm.|tsad.tkbd.hmt.bʿl.|ḥkpt il.kl h.tbʿ.kṯr.|l ahl h.hyn.tbʿ.l mš|knt h.apnk.dnil.m[t].|rpi.aphn.ǵzr.m[t].|hrn 17[2AQHT].5.32

hyrm

-].|rb[-.---].|šr[-.---].|[-.]ʿl[.---].|rʿm[-.---].|mn[-.---].|hyrm.h[--.---].|yrmm h[--.---].|mlk.gbʿ h d [---].|ibr.k l hm. 9[33].2.1

hyt

dr.km ǵlmm.|w ‘rb n.l p‘n.‘nt.hbr.|w ql.tštḥwy.kbd hyt.|w rgm.l btlt.‘nt.|ṯny.l ymmt.limm.|tḥm.aliyn.b‘l.hwt. 3[‘NT].3.7
.rgm.l[yṣ]a.|b špt h.hwt h.knp.ṣml.b‘[l].|b‘l.ṯbr.diy.hyt.tq[l.tḥt].|p‘n h.ybq‘.kbd h.w yḥd.|iṯ.šmt.iṯ.‘ẓm.w yqḥ b 19[1AQHT].3.143
.nšrm.|yšu.g h.w yṣḥ.knp.ṣml.|b‘l.yṯbr.b‘l.yṯbr.diy.|hyt.tql.tḥt.p‘n y.ibq‘.|kbd h.w aḥd.hm.iṯ.šmt.iṯ.|‘ẓm.abky 19[1AQHT].3.138

hkl

b‘.b‘l.ḫr[-].|pqr.yḥd.|bn.ktmn.ṯǵr.hk[l].|bn.ṯgbr.ṯǵr.hk[l].|bn.ydln.|bn.ktmn. 1056.9
--].|[---.-]bd.|[---]yb‘.b‘l.ḫr[-].|pqr.yḥd.|bn.ktmn.ṯǵr.hk[l].|bn.ṯgbr.ṯǵr.hk[l].|bn.ydln.|bn.ktmn. 1056.8
r.|[w ḫss.]ṯṯb.b‘l.l hwt y.|[ḥš.]bht h.tbnn.|[ḥš.]trmm.hkl h.|y[tl]k.l lbnn.w ‘ṣ h.|l[šr]yn.mḥmd.arz h.|h[n.l]bnn. 4[51].6.17
.b ksl.qšt h.mdnt.|w hln.‘nt.l bt h.tmǵyn.|tštql.ilt.l hkl h.|w l.šb‘t.tmtḫṣ h.b ‘mq.|tḫtṣb.bn.qrtm.tṯ‘r.|ksat.l mh 3[‘NT].2.18
[---.b‘l.b bht h].|[il.hd.b qr]b.hkl h.|w t‘nyn.ǵlm.b‘l.|in.b‘l.b bht ht.|il hd.b qrb.hkl h.|q 10[76].2.2
p.hkl y.dtm.|ḫrṣ.‘dbt.bht[h.b‘]l.|y‘db.hd.‘db[.‘d]bt.|hkl h.ṭbḫ.alpm[.ap].|ṣin.šql.ṯrm[.w]m|ria.il.‘glm.d[t].|šnt. 4[51].6.40
rm.|iqnim.šmḫ.aliyn.|b‘l.ṣḥ.ḫrn.b bht h.|‘ḏbt.b qrb hkl h.|yblnn ǵrm.mid.ksp.|gb‘m lḥmd.ḫrṣ.|yblnn.udr.ilqṣ 4[51].5.99
.ylt.ḥmḥmt.|[---.mt.r]pi.w ykn.bn h.|[b bt.šrš.]b qrb.hkl h.|[nṣb.skn.i]lib h.b qdš.|[ztr.‘m h.l a]rṣ.mšṣu.|[qṭr h.l 17[2AQHT].1.44
ab y.|tmrnn.l bny.bnwt.|w ykn.bn h b bt.šrš.b qrb.|hkl h.nṣb.skn.ilib h.b qdš.|ztr.‘m h.l arṣ.mšṣu.qṭr h.|l ‘pr.ḏ 17[2AQHT].1.27
yd h.|dnil.bt h.ymǵyn.yšt|ql.dnil.l hkl h.‘rb.b|kyt.b hkl h.mšspdt.b ḥẓr h.|pẓǵm.ǵr.ybk.l aqht.|ǵzr.ydm‘.l kdd. 19[1AQHT].4.172
.ṯiṯ.|rḥṣ.npṣ y.b ym.rṯ.|dn.il.bt h.ymǵyn.|yštql.dnil.l hkl h.|‘rb.b bt h.kṯrt.bnt.|hll.snnt.apnk.dnil.|mt.rpi.ap.hn. 17[2AQHT].2.25
.dr.|‘db.uḫry.mṭ.yd h.|dnil.bt h.ymǵyn.yšt|ql.dnil.l hkl h.‘rb.b|kyt.b hkl h.mšspdt.b ḥẓr h.|pẓǵm.ǵr.ybk.l aqht 19[1AQHT].4.171
t].|šnt.imr.qmṣ.l[l]im.|ṣḥ.aḫ h.b bht h.a[r]y h.|b qrb hkl h.ṣḥ.|šb‘m.bn.aṯrt.|špq.ilm.krm.y[n].|špq.ilht.ḫprt[.yn 4[51].6.45
]b.hkl h.|w t‘nyn.ǵlm.b‘l.|in.b‘l.b bht ht.|il hd.b qrb.hkl h.|qšt hn.aḫd.b yd h.|w qṣ‘t h.bm.ymn h.|idk.l ytn pn 10[76].2.5
ṭ].nhr.bt k.[---.]šp[-.---].|[ḥš.bh]t h.tbn[n.ḥ]š.trm[mn.hkl h.---.]bt.|[---.-]k.mnh[-.---.-]š bš[-.]t[-].ǵlm.l šdt[.-.]ymm 2.3[129].10
.---].|pr‘m.ṣd k.y bn[.---].|pr‘m.ṣd k.hn pr[‘.--].|ṣd.b hkl h[.---].|[------].|[---.l]ḥm[.---].|[---].ay š[---].|[---.b ḥ]rb. 17[2AQHT].5.39
h.bhtm.sgrt.|b‘d h.‘dbt.ṯlṯ.ptḥ.bt.mnt.|ptḥ.bt.w ubn.hkl.w ištql šql.|tn.km.nḥšm.yḥr.tn.km.|mhr y.w bn.bṯn.itn UG5.7.72
rt.l ‘d h.|yṯb.l ksi mlk.|l nḫt.l kḥṯ.drkt.|ap.yṣb.yṯb.b hkl.|w ywsrnn.ggn h.|lk.l ab k.yṣb.lk.|l[ab]k.w rgm.‘ny.| 16.6[127].25
mmn.hk[l m].|b tk.ṣrrt.ṣpn.|alp.šd.aḫd bt.|rbt.kmn.hkl.|w y‘n.kṯr.w ḫss.|šm‘.l aliyn b‘l.|bn.l rkb.‘rpt.|bl.ašt.u 4[51].5.119
.lk.bt y.rpim.|[rpim.bt y.aṣ]ḥ km.iqra km.|[ilnym.b hkl]y.aṯr h.rpum.|[l tdd.aṯr]h.l tdd.i[lnym].|[---.]r[--.---].| 21[122].1.11
nḫt.kḥṯ.d[rkt h.b bt y].|aṣḥ.rpi[m.iqra.ilnym].|b qrb.h[kl y.aṯr h.rpum.l] |tdd.aṯr[h.l tdd.ilnym].|asr.mr[kbt.---] 22.1[123].20
.lk.bt y.|[rpim.rpim.b]t y.aṣḥ km.iqra.|[km.ilnym.b h]kl y.aṯr h.rpum.|[l tdd.aṯr h].l tdd.ilnym.|[---.m]rz‘y.apn 21[122].1.3
lk bt y.r[pim.rpim.b bt y.aṣḥ].|km.iqr[a km.ilnym.b hkl y].|aṯr h.r[pum.l tdd.aṯr h].|l tdd.il[nym.---].|mhr.b‘l[. 22.1[123].4
b[t y.rpim.rpim.b bt y].|aṣḥ.km.[iqra km.ilnym.b] |hkl y.aṯr[h.rpum.l tdd].|aṯr h.l t[dd.ilnym.ṯm].|yḥpn.ḥy[ly 22.1[123].10
.]il.d ‘rgzm.|[---.]dt.‘l.lty.|[---.]tdbḥ.amr.|ṯmn.b qrb.hkl y.[aṯr h.rpum].|tdd.aṯr h.tdd.iln[ym.---].|asr.sswm.tṣm 20[121].2.1
.l rqm.ḫrṣ.|nṣb.l lbnt.šmḫ.|aliyn.b‘l.ht y.bnt.|dt.ksp.hkl y.dtm.|ḫrṣ.‘dbt.bht[h.b‘]l.|y‘db.hd.‘db[.‘d]bt.|hkl h.ṭb 4[51].6.37
.|[---.]km.r‘y.ht.alk.|[---.]ṯlṯt.amǵy.l bt.|[y.---.b qrb].hkl y.w y‘n.il.|[---.mrz‘]y.lk.bt y.rpim.|[rpim.bt y.aṣ]ḥ km. 21[122].1.8
.|yṯb.ǵzr.m[t.hrnmy.y]šu.|g h.w yṣḥ.t[b‘.---].|bkyt.b hk[l]y.mšspdt.|b ḥẓr y pẓǵm.ǵr.w yq.|dbḥ.ilm.yš‘ly.dǵṯ h. 19[1AQHT].4.183
b‘l.|[hw]t.aliy.q|[rdm.]bht y.bnt.|[dt.ksp.dtm].|[ḫrṣ.hk]l y.|[---.]aḫ y.|[---.]aḫ y.|[----]y.|[---.]rb.|[---].ṣḥt.|[---. 4[51].8.37
[--].[-]l[--.b qr]|b hkl y.[---].|lk bt y.r[pim.rpim.b bt y.aṣḥ].|km.iqr[a km.ilny 22.1[123].2
nt.]bht |k.y ilm.bnt.bh[t k].a[l.tš]mḫ.|al.tšmḫ.b r[m.h]kl[k].|al.aḫd.hm.b y[--] y.[---]b[-].|b gdlt.arkt y.am[---]. 3[‘NT.VI].5.29
t.bht]k.y ilm[.bnt.bht k.--].|[al.tšmḫ.]al.tš[mḫ.b rm.h]|[kl k.al.]aḫd hm.[---].|[---.b]gdlt.ar[kt y.am--].|[---.qdq] 18[3AQHT].1.8
m.aḫ k.w ḥẓr.|km.ary k.ṣḥ.ḫrn.|b bht k.‘ḏbt.b qrb.|hkl k.tbl k.ǵrm.|mid.ksp.gb‘m.mḥmd..|ḫrṣ.w bn.bht.ksp.| 4[51].5.93
sn h.|l yrgm.l aliyn b‘l.|ṣḥ.ḫrn.b bhm k.|‘ḏbt.b qrb.hkl k.|tbl k.ǵrm.mid.ksp.|gb‘m.mḥmd.ḫrṣ.|ybl k.udr.ilqṣ 4[51].5.76
m.|w ‘n.ali[yn.]b‘l.|al.tšt.u[rb]t.b bht m.|ḥln.b q[rb.hk]l m.|al td[.pdr]y.bt ar.|[---.ṭl]y.bt.rb.|[---.m]dd.il ym.|[4[51].6.9
.k[ṯr].|ḥš.rmm.hk[l m].|ḥš.bht m.tbn[n].|ḥš.trmmn.hk[l m].|b tk.ṣrrt.ṣpn.|alp.šd.aḫd bt.|rbt.kmn.hkl.|w y‘n.k 4[51].5.116
kbdn h.---].|ṯr.il[.ab h.---].|ḥš b[ht m.tbnn.ḥš.trmmn.hkl m].|b tk.[---].|bn.[---].|a[--.---.] 1[‘NT.IX].3.27
w ‘ṣ h.|š[r]yn.mḥmd.arz h.|tšt.išt.b bht m.|nb[l]at.b hkl m.|hn.ym.w ṯn.tikl.|išt.b bht m.nblat.|b hk[l] m.ṯlṯ.kb‘ 4[51].6.23
šm‘.m‘.l al[iy]n b‘l.|bl.ašt.ur[bt.]b bht m.|ḥln.b qr[b.hk]l m.|w ‘n.ali[yn.]b‘l.|al.tšt.u[rb]t.b bht m.|ḥln.b q[rb.h 4[51].6.6
yn b‘l.|bn.l rkb.‘rpt.|bl.ašt.urbt.b bh[t] m.|ḥln.b qrb.hkl m.|w y‘n.aliyn b‘l.|al.tšt.urbt.b[bhtm].|[ḥln].b qrb.hk[4[51].5.124
r bn.|ym.kṯr.bnm.‘dt.|yptḥ.ḥln.b bht m.|urbt.b qrb.[h]kl |m.w y[p]tḥ.b dqt.‘rpt.|‘l h[wt].kṯr.w ḫss.|ṣḥq.kṯr.w ḫ 4[51].7.18
w]y‘n.aliy[n.b‘l].|[--]b[.---].|ḥš.bht m.k[ṯr].|ḥš.rmm.hk[l m].|ḥš.bht m.tbn[n].|ḥš.trmmn.hk[l m].|b tk.ṣrrt.ṣpn. 4[51].5.114
lat.|b hk[l] m.ṯlṯ.kb‘ ym.|tikl[.i]št.b bht m.|nbla[t.]b hkl m.|ḫmš.ṯ[d]ṯ.ym.tikl.|išt.[b]bht m.nblat.|b[qrb.hk]l 4[51].6.28
hkl m.|ḫmš.ṯ[d]ṯ.ym.tikl.|išt.[b]bht m.nblat.|b[qrb.hk]l m.mk.|b šb[‘.]y[mm].td.išt.|b bht m.n[bl]at.b hkl m.|s 4[51].6.31
b.hk]l m.mk.|b šb[‘.]y[mm].td.išt.|b bht m.n[bl]at.b hkl m.|sb.ksp.l rqm.ḫrṣ.|nṣb.l lbnt.šmḫ.|aliyn.b‘l.ht y.bnt. 4[51].6.33
n.b‘l.ṯṯbn.b‘l.|l hwt y.yptḥ.ḥ|ln.b bht m.urbt.|b qrb.hk[l m.yp]tḥ.|b‘l.b dqt[.‘rp]t.|ql h.qdš.b[‘l.y]tn.|yṯny.b‘l.ṣ[- 4[51].7.27
b[l]at.b hkl m.|hn.ym.w ṯn.tikl.|išt.b bht m.nblat.|b hk[l] m.ṯlṯ.kb‘ ym.|tikl[.i]št.b bht m.|nbla[t.]b hkl m.|ḫmš. 4[51].6.26
m.|w y‘n.aliyn b‘l.|al.tšt.urbt.b[bhtm].|[ḥln].b qrb.hk[l m]. 4[51].5.127
.]hrn.w[---.]tb‘.k[ṯ]r w [ḫss.t]bn.bht zbl ym.|[trm]m.hk[l.ṯpṭ].nhr.bt k.[---.]šp[-.---].|[ḥš.bh]t h.tbn[n.ḥ]š.trm[mn 2.3[129].9
m.trd.b n[p]šn y.trḥṣn.k ṯrm.|[--]b b[ht].|[zbl.]ym.b hkl.ṯpṭ.nh[r].yṯir.ṯr.il.ab h l pn[.zb]l y[m].|[l pn.ṯp]ṭ[.nhr.] 2.3[129].21
n h.--]r y[---].|[---.k]ṯr.w ḫ[ss.t]b‘.b[n.]bht.ym[.rm]m.hkl.ṯpṭ nh[r].|[---.]hrn.w[---.]tb‘.k[ṯ]r w [ḫss.t]bn.bht zbl y 2.3[129].7
tm.|[--.--]r.l ẓpn.|[---.]pn.ym.y[--].|[---].b‘l.tdd.|[---.]hkl.|[---.]yd h.|[---.]tmt. 25[136].8
].|[---.]w.ksu.b‘lt.b[htm.---].|[---.]il.bt.gdlt.[---].|[---.]hkl[.---]. 47[33].9

hl

yqḥ.]il.mšt‘ltm.mšt‘ltm.l riš.agn.|hl h.[t]špl.hl h.trm.hl h.tṣḥ.ad ad.|w hl h.tṣḥ.um.um.tirk m.yd.il.k ym.|w yd il 23[52].32
št‘ltm.l riš.agn.|hl h.[t]špl.hl h.trm.hl h.tṣḥ.ad ad.|w hl h.tṣḥ.um.um.tirk m.yd.il.k ym.|w yd il.k mdb.ark.yd.il. 23[52].33

p..thm. | [yqḥ.]il.mšt‘ltm.mšt‘ltm.l riš.agn. | hl h.[t]špl.hl h.trm.hl h.tṣḥ.ad ad. | w hl h.tṣḥ.um.um.tirk m.yd.il.k y 23[52].32
.w yṣǵd.gp..thm. | [yqḥ.]il.mšt‘ltm.mšt‘ltm.l riš.agn. | hl h.[t]špl.hl h.trm.hl h.tṣḥ.ad ad. | w hl h.tṣḥ.um.um.tirk m 23[52].32
--]. | phy. | w ṯpllm.mlk.r[b.--]. | mṣmt.l nqmd.[---.-]št. | hl ny.argmn.d [ybl.n]qmd. | l špš.arn.ṯn[.‘šr h.]mn. | ‘ṣrm.ṯql. 64[118].18
n.um [y]. | qlt[.l um] y. | yšlm.il[m]. | tǵ[r] k.tš[lm] k. | [h]l ny.‘m n[.š]lm. | w.ṯm [ny.‘m.mlkt.u]m y. | mnm[.šlm]. | w 1013.8
n k. | l.p‘n.um y. | qlt.l.um y. | yšlm.ilm. | tǵr k.tšlm k. | hl ny.‘m n[y]. | kll.šlm. | ṯm ny.‘m.um y. | mnm.šlm. | w.rgm.ṯ 50[117].9
.ṯm [ny.‘m.mlkt.u]m y. | mnm[.šlm]. | w.rgm[.ṯṯb.l] y. | hl ny.‘mn. | mlk.b.ṯy ndr. | iṯt.w.ht. | [-]sny.uḏr h. | w.hm.ḫt. | ‘ 1013.12
[yš]lm[.ilm]. | tǵr k[.tšlm k]. | hl ny.[---]. | w.pdr[--.---]. | tmǵyn[.---]. | w.mli[.---]. | [-]kl.w [-- 57[101].3
hn.aṯtm.tṣḥn y.mt mt. | nḥtm.ḫṭ k.mmnnm.mṭ yd k.hl.‘ṣr. | tḥrr.l išt.w ṣḥrt.l pḥmm.aṯtm.a[ṯt.il]. | aṯt.il.w ‘lm h.y 23[52].47
hm. | aṯtm.tṣḥn y.ad ad.nḥtm.ḫṭ k. | mmnnm.mṭ yd k.hl.‘ṣr.tḥrr.l išt. | w ṣḥrrt.l pḥmm.btm.bt.il.bt.il. | w ‘lm h.w h 23[52].44
hm.aṯtm.tṣḥn. | y mt.mt.nḥtm.ḫṭ k.mmnnm.mṭ.yd k. | h[l.]‘ṣr.tḥrr.l išt.ṣḥrrt.l pḥmm. | a[ṯ]tm.aṯt.il.aṯt.il.w ‘lm h.w 23[52].41
kḥ yḫ[bq] [-]. | tld bt.[--]t.ḫ[--.l k] | ṯrt.l bnt.hll[.snnt]. | hl ǵlmt tld b[n.--]n. | ‘n ha l yd h.tzd[.--]. | pt l bšr h.dm a[--. 24[77].7
.rbt.kmn.hlk.kṯr. | k y‘n.w y‘n.tdrq.ḫss. | hlk.qšt.ybln.hl.yš | rb‘.qṣ‘t.apnk.dnil. | mt.rpi.aphn.ǵzr.mt. | hrnmy.gm.l a 17[2AQHT].5.12
d ṯbil. | ‘ṯtrt ṣwd[t.---]. | tlk b mdb[r.---]. | tḥdṯn w hl[.---]. | w tglṯ thmt.‘[--.---]. | yṣi.ǵl h tḥm b[.---]. | mrḥ h l ad 2001.1.4

hlk

. | idk.l ttn pnm.‘m.b‘l. | mrym.ṣpn.b alp.šd.rbt.kmn. | hlk.aḫt h.b‘l.y‘n.tdrq. | ybnt.ab h.šrḥq.aṯt.l pnn h. | št.alp.qd 3['NT].4.83
| ṯlṯ.mat.rbt. | hlk.l alpm.ḫḏḏ. | w l.rbt.kmyr. | aṯr.ṯn.ṯn.hlk. | aṯr.ṯlṯ.kl hm. | aḥd.bt h.ysgr. | almnt.škr. | tškr.zbl.‘ršm. 14[KRT].4.182
n.d bl.hg. | hlk.l alpm.ḫḏḏ. | w l rbt.kmyr. | [a]ṯr.ṯn.ṯn.hlk. | aṯr.ṯlṯ.kl hm. | yḥd.bt h.sgr. | almnt.škr. | tškr.zbl.‘ršm. | 14[KRT].2.94
---]. | šgr.mud[.---]. | dm.mt.aṣ[ḥ.---]. | yd.b qrb[.---]. | w lk.ilm.[---]. | w rgm.l [---]. | b mud.ṣin[.---]. | mud.ṣin[.---]. | iṯ 5[67].3.20
.---]. | al.ašt.b[---]. | ahpk k.l[--.---]. | ṯmm.w lk[.---]. | w lk.ilm[.---]. | n‘m.ilm[.---]. | šgr.mu[d.---]. | šgr.mud[.---]. | dm. 5[67].3.14
]. | špš.mṣprt dlt hm[.---]. | w ǵnbm.šlm.‘rbm.ṯn[nm]. | hlkm.b dbḥ n‘mt. | šd[.i]lm.šd.aṯrt.w rḥmy. | [---].y[ṯ]b. | [---] 23[52].27
d ṯbil. | ‘ṯtrt ṣwd[t.---]. | tlk b mdb[r.---]. | tḥdṯn w hl[.---]. | w tglṯ thmt.‘[--.---]. | yṣi.ǵl 2001.1.3
---].šb‘.ṯir k.[---]. | [---.]ab y.ndt.ank[.---]. | [---.--]l.mlk.tlk.b ṣd[.---]. | [---.]mt.išryt[.---]. | [---.--]r.almd k.[---]. | [---.]q 18[3AQHT].1.27
spr.mḏr[ǵlm]. | lt.hlk.b[.---]. | bn.b‘yn.š[--.---]. | aǵltn.mid[-.---]. | bn.lṣn.‘rm[y]. 87[64].2
. | t‘pp.ṯr.il.d pid. | tǵẓy.bny.bnwt. | b nši.‘n h.w tphn. | hlk.b‘l.aṯtrt. | k t‘n.hlk.btlt. | ‘nt.tdrq.ybmt. | [limm].b h.p‘nm 4[51].2.13
m. | š‘ly.dǵṯ h.b šmym. | dǵṯ.hrnmy.d kbkbm. | l tbrkn.alk brkt. | tmrn.alk.nmr[rt]. | imḫṣ.mḫṣ.aḫ y.akl[.m] | kly[.‘]l. 19[1AQHT].4.194
[--].[-]l[--.b qr] | b hkl y.[---]. | lk bt y.r[pim.rpim.b bt y.aṣḥ]. | km.iqr[a km.ilnym.b hkl y]. 22.1[123].3
.l tdd.aṯr h]. | l tdd.il[nym.---]. | mhr.b‘l[.---.mhr]. | ‘nt.lk b[t y.rpim.rpim.b bt y]. | aṣḥ.km.[iqra km.ilnym.b] | hkl y 22.1[123].8
[---.m]rz‘y.lk.bt y. | [rpim.rpim.b]t y.aṣḥ km.iqra. | [km.ilnym.b h]kl y.a 21[122].1.1
ṯlṯt.amǵy.l bt. | [y.---.b qrb].hkl y.w y‘n.il. | [---.mrz‘]y.lk.bt y.rpim. | [rpim.bt y.aṣ]ḥ km.iqra km. | [ilnym.b hkl]y.a 21[122].1.9
tǵẓy.bny.bnwt. | b nši.‘n h.w tphn. | hlk.b‘l.aṯtrt. | k t‘n.hlk.btlt. | ‘nt.tdrq.ybmt. | [limm].b h.p‘nm. | [ṭṭṭ.b ‘]dn.ksl. | [t 4[51].2.14
kb[d].awṣ.arbdd. | l kbd.š[d]m.ap.mṯn.rgmm. | argmn.lk.lk.‘nn.ilm. | atm.bštm.w an.šnt. | uǵr.l rḥq.ilm.inbb. | l rḥq. 3['NT].4.76
tbn.hmlt.arṣ]. | at.w ank.ib[ǵy h.---]. | w y‘n.kṯr.w ḫss[.lk.lk.‘nn.ilm.] | atm.bštm.w an[.šnt.kptr]. | l rḥq.ilm.ḥkp[t.l r 1['NT.IX].3.17
[-----]. | [---.r]ḥm.tld. | [---.]ḫrm.ṯn.ym. | tš[.---.]ymm.lk. | hrg.ar[b‘.]ymm.bṣr. | kp.šsk k.[--].l ḥbš k. | ‘tk.ri[š.]l mhr 13[6].4
h.btlt.‘nt. | w tšu.‘n h.w t‘n. | w t‘n.arḫ.w tr.b lkt. | tr.b lkt.w tr.b ḫl. | [b]n‘mm.b ysmm.ḥ[--]k.ǵrt. | [ql].l b‘l.‘nt.ttn 10[76].2.29
.dgn.l kḥ[ṯ.drkt h]. | l alp.ql.ẓ[--.---]. | l np ql.nd.[----]. | tlk.w tr.b[ḫl]. | b n‘mm.b ys[mm.---]. | arḫ.arḫ.[---.tld]. | ibr.t 10[76].3.18
.]špš.b‘l k. | yd‘m.l.yd‘t. | ‘m y.špš.b‘l k. | šnt.šntm.lm.l.tlk. | w.lḥt.akl.ky. | likt.‘m.špš. | b‘l k.ky.akl. | b.ḥwt k.inn. | šp 2060.16
t.mt.tn.aḫ y. | w ‘n.bn.ilm.mt.mh. | taršn.l btlt.‘nt. | an.itlk.w aṣd.kl. | ǵr.l kbd.arṣ.kl.gb‘. | l kbd.šdm.npš.ḫsrt. | bn.nš 6[49].2.15
t.my.lim.bn. | dgn.my.hmlt.aṯr. | b‘l.ard.b arṣ.ap. | ‘nt.ttlk.w tṣd.kl.ǵr. | l kbd.arṣ.kl.gb‘. | l [k]bd.šdm.tmǵ.l n‘m[y]. 5[67].6.26
qrnm. | km.ṯrm.w gbṯt. | km.ibrm. | w b hm.pn.b‘l. | b‘l.ytlk.w yṣd. | yḥ pat.mlbr. | wn.ymǵy.aklm. | w ymẓa.‘qqm. | b 12[75].1.34
‘nt.hlkt.w.šnwt. | tp.aḫ.h.k.ysmsm. | tspi.šir.h.l.bl.ḥrb. | tšt.dm.h. RS225.1
yṯb.b[mrzḥ.---]. | bṯt.‘llm n.[---]. | ilm.bt.b‘l k.[---]. | dl.ylkn.ḥš.b a[rṣ.---]. | b ‘pr.ḫbl ṭtm.[---.] | šqy.rṭa.tnm y.ytn.[ks 1['NT.X].4.7
r.sswm.tṣmd.dg[-.---]. | t‘ln.l mrkbt hm.ti[ty.l ‘r hm]. | tlkn.ym.w ṯa aḫr.š[pšm.b ṯlṯ]. | mǵy.rpum.l grnt.i[lnym.l] | 20[121].2.5
ym]. | asr.mr[kbt.---]. | t‘ln.l mr[kbt hm.tity.l] | ‘r hm.tl[kn.ym.w ṯn.aḫr.špšm]. | b ṯlṯ.mǵy[.rpum.l grnt]. | i[ln]y[m] 22.1[123].24
h. | w l nkr.mddt. | km irby.tškn. | šd.k ḥsn.pat. | mdbr.tlkn. | ym.w ṯn.aḫr. | šp[š]m.b [ṯ]lṯ. | ym[ǵy.]l qdš. | a[ṯrt.]ṣrm. 14[KRT].4.194
| iqḥ.aš‘rb.ǵlmt. | ḥẓr y.ṯn h.wspm. | atn.w ṯlṯ h.ḫrṣm. | ylk ym.w ṯn. | ṯlṯ.rb‘.ym. | aḫr.špšm.b rb‘. | ymǵy.l udm.rbt. | 14[KRT].4.207
m.nkr. | mddt h.k irby. | [t]škn.šd. | km.ḥsn.pat.mdbr. | lk.ym.w ṯn.ṯlṯ.rb‘ ym. | ḫmš.ṯdṯ.ym.mk.špšm. | b šb‘.w tmǵy. 14[KRT].3.106
w tšu.‘n h.btlt.‘nt. | w tšu.‘n h.w t‘n. | w t‘n.arḫ.w tr.b lkt. | tr.b lkt.w tr.b ḫl. | [b]n‘mm.b ysmm.ḥ[--]k.ǵrt. | [ql].l b 10[76].2.28
| il.mt.rpi npš tḥ[.pǵt]. | ṯ[km]t.mym.ḥspt.l š‘r. | ṭl.yd‘t.hlk.kbkbm. | a[-]ḥ.hy.mḫ.tmḫṣ.mḫṣ[.aḫ k]. | tkl.m[k]ly.‘l.um 19[1AQHT].4.200
t.yrq.nqbn y.tš[m‘]. | pǵt.ṯkmt.my.ḥspt.l[š‘]r.ṭl. | yd‘t.hlk.kbkbm. | bkm.tmdln.‘r. | bkm.tṣmd.pḥl.bkm. | tšu.ab h.tš 19[1AQHT].2.56
h.dnil.k yṣḥ]. | šm‘.pǵt.ṯkmt[.my]. | ḥspt.l š‘r.ṭl.yd[‘t]. | hlk.kbkbm.mdl.‘r. | ṣmd.pḥl.št.gpn y dt ksp. | dt.yrq.nqbn y. 19[1AQHT].2.52
.bm[.---]. | [---.-]qp.bn.ḥtt.bn ḥtt[.---]. | [---.--]p.km.dlt.tlk.km.p[---]. | [---.]bt.tḥbṭ.km.ṣq.ṣdr[.---]. | [---.]kl.b kl.l pgm 1001.1.24
nt.yṯpṭ.ṯpṭ.ytm. | b nši ‘n h.w yphn.b alp. | šd.rbt.kmn.hlk.kṯr. | k y‘n.w y‘n.tdrq.ḫss. | hlk.qšt.ybln.hl.yš | rb‘.qṣ‘t.ap 17[2AQHT].5.10
rkt. | ap.yṣb.yṯb.b hkl. | w ywsrnn.ggn h. | lk.l ab k.yṣb.lk. | l[ab]k.w rgm.‘ny. | l k[rt.adn k.]ištm[‘]. | w tqǵ[.udn.k ǵ 16.6[127].27
l nḫt.l kḥṯ.drkt. | ap.yṣb.yṯb.b hkl. | w ywsrnn.ggn h. | lk.l ab k.yṣb.lk. | l[ab]k.w rgm.‘ny. | l k[rt.adn k.]ištm[‘]. | w 16.6[127].27
ṣbi.ng[b.w yṣi.‘dn]. | m‘[.ṣ]bu h.u[l.mad]. | ṯlṯ.mat.rbt. | hlk.l alpm.ḫḏḏ. | w l.rbt.kmyr. | aṯr.ṯn.ṯn.hlk. | aṯr.ṯlṯ.kl hm. | 14[KRT].4.180
ṣbu k.ul.mad. | ṯlṯ.mat.rbt. | ḫpṯ.d bl.spr. | ṯnn.d bl.hg. | hlk.l alpm.ḫḏḏ. | w l rbt.kmyr. | [a]ṯr.ṯn.ṯn.hlk. | aṯr.ṯlṯ.kl hm. 14[KRT].2.92
. | aṯ[rt.]il.yṯb.b mrzḥ h. | yšt[.il.y]n.‘d šb‘.trṯ.‘d škr. | il.hlk.l bt h.yštql. | l ḥṭr h.y‘msn.nn.ṯkmn. | w šnm.w ngšnn.ḥb UG5.1.1.17
ss.]ṯtb.b‘l.l hwt y. | [ḥš.]bht h.tbnn. | [ḥš.]trmm.hkl h. | y[tl]k.l lbnn.w ‘ṣ h. | l[šr]yn.mḥmd.arz h. | h[n.l]bnn.w ‘ṣ h. 4[51].6.18
y.qḥn y. | [--.]šir.b krm.nṭṭt.dm.‘lt.b ab y. | u---].‘lt.b k.lk.l pn y.yrk.b‘l.[--]. | [---.]‘nt.šzrm.tštšḥ.km.ḥ[--]. | [---].‘pr.b 1001.1.10
.d krm. | [---].l ‘nt m. | [---.]l šlm. | [-]l[-.-]ry.ylbš. | mlk.ylk.lqḥ.ilm. | aṯr.ilm.ylk.p‘nm. | mlk.p‘nm.yl[k]. | šb‘.pamt.l k 33[5].23
.[g]d.b ḥlb.annḫ b ḫmat. | w ‘l.agn.šb‘ d m.dǵ[ṯ.---]t. | tlk m.rḥmy.w tṣd[.---]. | tḥgrn.ǵzr.n‘m.[---]. | w šm.‘rbm.yr[. 23[52].16
šmym. | dǵṯ.hrnmy.d kbkbm. | l tbrkn.alk brkt. | tmrn.alk.nmr[rt]. | imḫṣ.mḫṣ.aḫ y.akl[.m] | kly[.‘]l.umt y.w y‘n[.d 19[1AQHT].4.195

pn.il.d pid. | b d̲rt.bny.bnwt. | šmm.šmn.tmṭrn. | nh̲lm.tlk.nbtm. | w id‘.k ḥy.aliyn.b‘l. | k iṯ.zbl.b‘l.arṣ. | b ḥlm.lṭpn.il 6[49].3.7
pn.il d pid. | b d̲rt.bny.bnwt. | šmm.šmn.tmṭrn. | nh̲lm.tlk.nbtm. | šmh̲.lṭpn.il.d pid. | p‘n h.l hdm.yṯpd. | w yprq.lṣb 6[49].3.13
.hmlt.arṣ]. | at.w ank.ib[ǵy h.---]. | w y‘n.kṯr.w h̲ss[.lk.lk.‘nn.ilm.] | atm.bštm.w an[.šnt.kptr]. | l rḥq.ilm.ḥkp[t.l rḥq 1['NT.IX].3.17
[d].awṣ.arbdd. | l kbd.š[d]m.ap.mṯn.rgmm. | argmn.lk.lk.‘nn.ilm. | atm.bštm.w an.šnt. | uǵr.l rḥq.ilm.inbb. | l rḥq.iln 3['NT].4.76
m.l yṣa.b špt h[.hwt h]. | b nši ‘n h.w tphn.in.[---]. | [-.]hlk.ǵlmm b dd y.yṣ[--]. | [-.]yṣa.w l.yṣa.hlm.[ṯnm]. | [q]dqd.ṯl 19[1AQHT].2.77
---.]k.drh̲m.w aṯb.l ntbt.k.‘ṣm l t[--]. | [---.]drk.brḥ.arṣ.lk pn h.yrk.b‘[l]. | [---.]bt k.ap.l ph̲r k ‘nt tqm.‘nt.tqm. | [---.p 1001.2.8
. | [---.]l šlm. | [-]l[-.-]ry.ylbš. | mlk.ylk.lqḥ.ilm. | aṯr.ilm.ylk.p‘nm. | mlk.p‘nm.yl[k]. | šb‘.pamt.l kl hm. 33[5].24
. | kt ǵr k.ank.yd‘t. | [-]n.atn.at.mṯb k[.---]. | [š]mm.rm.lk.prẓ kt. | [k]bkbm.ṯm.tpl k.lbnt. | [-.]rgm.k yrkt.‘ṯqbm. | [--- 13[6].12
phn.b alp. | šd.rbt.kmn.hlk.kṯr. | k y‘n.w y‘n.tdrq.h̲ss. | hlk.qšt.ybln.hl.yš | rb‘.qṣ‘t.apnk.dnil. | mt.rpi.aphn.ǵzr.mt. | 17[2AQHT].5.12
.ylbš. | mlk.ylk.lqḥ.ilm. | aṯr.ilm.ylk.p‘nm. | mlk.p‘nm.yl[k]. | šb‘.pamt.l kl hm. 33[5].25
gr.l abnm.w l.‘ṣm.šb‘.šnt. | tmt.ṯmn.nqpt.‘d.ilm.n‘mm.ttlkn. | šd.tṣdn.pat.mdbr.w ngš.hm.nǵr. | mdr‘.w ṣḥ hm.‘m.n 23[52].67
ab y.---]. | yṯb.l y.w l h.[---]. | [--.i]mṣh̲.nn.k imr.l arṣ. | [ašhlk].šbt h.dmm.šbt.dqn h. | [mm‘m.-]d.l ytn.bt.l b‘l.k ilm. 3['NT.VI].5.10
d.hm.b y[--] y.[---]b[-]. | b gdlt.arkt y.am[---]. | qdqd k.ašhlk.šbt[k.dmm]. | [šbt.dqn k.mm‘m.]y‘ny. | il.b šb‘t.h̲drm. 3['NT.VI].5.32
.]ah̲d hm.[---]. | [---.b]gdlt.ar[kt y.am--]. | [---.qdq]d k.ašhlk[.šbt k.dmm]. | [šbt.dq]n k.mm‘m.w[---]. | aqht.w yplṭ 18[3AQHT].1.11
ḥ. | dbḥ.mlk.‘šr. | ‘šrt.qḥ.tp k.b yd. | [-]r[-]k.bm.ymn. | tlk.škn.‘l.ṣrrt. | adn k.šqrb.[---]. | b mgn k.w h̲rṣ.l kl. | apnk.ǵ 16.1[125].43
nr. | spr.[--]ḥ[-] k.šb‘t. | ghl.ph.ṯmnt. | nblu h.špš.ymp. | hlkt.tdr[--]. | špš.b‘d h.t[--]. | aṯr.aṯrm[.---]. | aṯr.aṯrm[.---]. | iš 27[8].5
ikt.‘m.špš. | b‘l k.ky.akl. | b.ḥwt k.inn. | špš n.[---]. | hm.al[k.--]. | ytnt[.---]. | ṯn[.---]. | w[.-----]. | l[.-----]. | h[--.---]. | šp[š. 2060.22
n. | [dn.almnt.y]ṯpṭ. | [ṯpṭ.ytm.---] h. | [---.---]n. | [-----]. | hlk.[---.b n]ši. | ‘n h.w tphn.[---]. | b grn.yh̲rb[.---]. | yǵly.yh̲sp 19[1AQHT].1.28
-.]h.yb[--]. | [---.--]n.irš[.---]. | [---.--]mr.ph. | [---.--]mm.hlkt. | [---.]b qrb.‘r. | [---.m]lakm l h. | [---.]l.bn.il. | [---.--]a.‘d 26[135].4
[.---]. | [---].ptḥ y.a[--.]dt[.---].ml[--]. | [---.-]ṯk.ytmt.dlt tlk.[---].bm[.---]. | [---.-]qp.bn.ḥtt.bn ḥtt[.---]. | [---.--]p.km.dl 1001.1.22
ydd.b qr[b.---]. | al.ašt.b[---]. | ahpk k.l[--.---]. | ṯmm.w lk[.---]. | w lk.ilm[.---]. | n‘m.ilm[.---]. | šgr.mu[d.---]. | šgr.mu 5[67].3.13
t. | [---.--]a.nrm. | [---.--]y.lm[.-.]b k[p]. | [---].tr[--.]gpn lk. | [---].km[-.---]. | [---.--]k yṣunn[.---]. | [---.--]dy.w.pr‘[.---]. | 1002.32
w.[---]. | [---.ṯ]y.al.an[k.--.]il[m.--]y. | [--.m]ṣlm.pn y[.-.]tlkn. | [---.]rḥbn.hm.[-.]aṯr[.---]. | [--]šy.w ydn.b‘[l.---]n. | [--]‘. 1002.59
h].l tdd.ilnym. | [---.m]rz‘y.apnnk.yrp. | [---.]km.r‘y.ht.alk. | [---.]ṯlṯt.amǵy.l bt. | [y.---.b qrb].hkl y.w y‘n.il. | [---.mrz 21[122].1.6
.mui[-.---]. | dm.mt.aṣ[ḥ.---]. | ydd.b qr[b.---]. | ṯmm.w lk[.---]. | [--]ṯ.lk[.---]. | [--]kṯ.i[---.---]. | p.šn[-.---]. | w l ṯlb.[---]. 5[67].3.27

hll

.ar yrh̲.w y | rh̲ yar k. | [ašr ilht kṯrt bn] | t hll.snnt.bnt h | ll b‘l gml.yrdt. | b ‘rgzm.b bz tdm. | lla y.‘m lẓpn i | l d̲.pid. 24[77].41
il.bt h.ymǵyn. | yštql.dnil.l hkl h. | ‘rb.b bt h.kṯrt.bnt. | hll.snnt.apnk.dnil. | mt.rpi.ap.hn.ǵzr.mt. | hrnmy.alp.yṭbh̲.l 17[2AQHT].2.27
l w ib. | d ašr.ar yrh̲.w y | rh̲ yar k. | [ašr ilht kṯrt bn] | t hll.snnt.bnt h | ll b‘l gml.yrdt. | b ‘rgzm.b bz tdm. | lla y.‘m lẓ 24[77].41
špš. | yrh̲ ytkḥ yḥ[bq] [-]. | tld bt.[--]t.h̲[--.l k] | ṯrt.l bnt.hll[.snnt]. | hl ǵlmt tld b[n.--]n. | ‘n ha l yd h.tzd[.--]. | pt l bšr 24[77].6
.mt. | hrnmy.alp.yṭbh̲.l kṯ | rt.yšlḥm.kṯrt.w y | ššq.bnt.[hl]l.snnt. | hn.ym.w ṯn.yšlḥm. | kṯrt.w yš[š]q.bnt.hl[l]. | snnt.ṯ 17[2AQHT].2.31
q.bnt.hl[l]. | snnt.ṯlṯ[.r]b‘ ym.yšl | ḥm kṯrt.w yššq. | bnt hll.snnt.h̲mš. | ṯdṯ.ym.yšlḥm.k[ṯ]rt. | w y[ššq].bnt.hll.snnt. | 17[2AQHT].2.36
yd h tzdn[.---]n. | l ad[n h.---]. | dgn tt[--.---.-]l | ‘.l kṯrt hl[l.sn]nt. | ylak yrh̲ ny[r] šmm.‘m. | h̲r[h̲]b mlk qẓ.tn nkl y | 24[77].15
| bnt hll.snnt.h̲mš. | ṯdṯ.ym.yšlḥm.k[ṯ]rt. | w y[ššq].bnt.hll.snnt. | mk.b šb[‘.]ymm.tb‘.b bt h. | kṯrt.bnt.hll.snnt. | [-]d[17[2AQHT].2.38
.bnt.[hl]l.snnt. | hn.ym.w ṯn.yšlḥm. | kṯrt.w yš[š]q.bnt.hl[l]. | snnt.ṯlṯ[.r]b‘ ym.yšl | ḥm kṯrt.w yššq. | bnt hll.snnt.h̲m 17[2AQHT].2.33
šq].bnt.hll.snnt. | mk.b šb[‘.]ymm.tb‘.b bt h. | kṯrt.bnt.hll.snnt. | [-]d[-]t.n‘m y.‘rš.h[--]m. | ysmsmt.‘rš.h̲lln.[-]. | yṯb. 17[2AQHT].2.40

hlm

.w ǵlm. | [a]h̲t h.šib.yṣat.mrḥ h. | l tl.yṣb.pn h.ṯǵr. | yṣu.hlm.ah̲ h.tph. | [ksl]h.l arṣ.ṯṯbr. | [---.]ah̲ h.tbky. | [--.m]rṣ.ml 16.1[125].53
rš.mlk.ab.šnm. | l p‘n.il.thbr.w tql. | tštḥwy.w tkbd h. | hlm.il.k yphn h. | yprq.lṣb.w yṣḥq. | p‘n h.l hdm.yṯpd.w ykrk 4[51].4.27
.phr.m‘d.ap.ilm.l lḥ[m]. | yṯb.bn qdš.l ṯrm.b‘l.qm.‘l.il.hlm. | ilm.tph hm.tphn.mlak.ym.t‘dt.ṯpṭ[.nhr]. | t[ǵ]ly.hlm.ri 2.1[137].21
mṣ.yd[.--]. | [---.]hš[.-]nm[.--.]k.[--].w yh̲np[.---]. | [---.]ylm.b[n.‘]n k.ṣmdm.špk[.---]. | [---.]nt[-.]mbk kpt.w[.--].b g[- 1001.1.16
ksa. | nḥš.šmrr.nḥš.‘q šr.ln h.ml | h̲š.abd.ln h.ydy.ḥmt.hlm.ytq. | w yṯb. | tqru.l špš.um h.špš.[um.q]l bl.‘m. | yrh̲.lrgt UG5.7.22
nṯk.nḥš.šmrr.nḥš. | ‘q šr.ln h.mlh̲š abd.ln h.ydy. | ḥmt.hlm.ytq ytqšqy.nḥš.yšlḥm.‘q šr. | y‘db.ksa.w.yṯb. | tqru.l špš. UG5.7.6
nṯk.nḥš.šmrr. | nḥš.‘q šr.ln h.mlh̲š.abd.ln h. | ydy.ḥmt.hlm.ytq.nḥš.yšlḥm. | nḥš.‘q šr.y‘db.ksa.w yṯb. | tqru l špš.um UG5.7.17
nṯk.nḥš.šm | rr.nḥš.‘q šr.ln h.mlh̲š abd.ln h. | ydy.ḥmt.hlm.ytq nḥš yšlḥm.nḥš. | ‘q.šr.y‘db.ksa.w yṯb. | tqru l špš um UG5.7.38
nṯk.nḥš. | šmrr.nḥš.‘q šr.ln h.mlh̲š.abd. | ln h.ydy.ḥmt.hlm ytq.nḥš. | yšlḥm.nḥš.‘q šr.y‘db ksa. | w yṯb. | tqru l špš.u UG5.7.48
ṯk.n[ḥš].šmrr. | nḥš.‘q šr.ln h.mlh̲š.abd.ln h.ydy. | ḥmt.hlm.ytq.nḥš.yšlḥm.nḥš. | ‘q šr.y‘db.ksa.w yṯb. | tqru.l špš.um UG5.7.28
nt.nḥš.šmrr. | nḥš.‘q šr.ln h.mlh̲š.abd.ln h.ydy. | ḥmt.hlm.ytq.nḥš.yšlḥm.nḥš ‘q. | š.y‘db.ksa w yṯb. | tqru l špš.um UG5.7.33
nṯk.nḥš.šmrr. | nḥš.‘q šr.ln h.mlh̲š abd.ln h.ydy. | ḥmt.hlm.ytq.nḥš.yšlḥm.nḥš. | ‘q šr.y‘db.ksa.w yṯb. | tqru.l špš.um UG5.7.43
nṯk. | nḥš.šmrr.nḥš.‘q šr ln h. | mlh̲š.abd.ln h.ydy.ḥmt.hlm.ytq. | nḥš.yšlḥm.nḥš.‘q šr.ydb.ksa. | w yṯb. | tqru.l špš.u UG5.7.11
nṯk.nḥš. | šmrr.nḥš ‘q šr.ln h.mlh̲š. | abd.ln h.ydy ḥmt.hlm.ytq šqy. | nḥš.yšlḥm.nḥš.‘q šr.y‘db. | ksa.w yṯb. | tqru l š UG5.7.54
]r. | qšt[.---]r.y[ṯ]br. | ṯmn.[---.]btlt.[‘]nt. | ṯṯb.[---.--]ša. | tlm.km[.---.]yd h.k šr. | knr.uṣb‘t h ḥrṣ.abn. | p h.tiḥd.šnt h. 19[1AQHT].1.7
i h. | [n]hr l kḥṯ drkt h.trtqṣ.b d b‘l km nš | r.b uṣb‘t h.hlm.ktp.zbl ym.bn ydm. | [ṯp]ṭ nhr.yrtqṣ.ṣmd.b d b‘l.km.nšr 2.4[68].14
ydm. | [ṯp]ṭ nhr.yrtqṣ.ṣmd.b d b‘l.km.nšr. | b[u]ṣb‘t h.ylm.ktp.zbl ym.bn ydm.ṯpṭ. | nhr.‘z.ym.l ymk.l tnǵṣn.pnt h.l 2.4[68].16
.b tk.ǵr y.il.ṣpn. | b qdš.b ǵr.nḥlt y. | b n‘m.b gb‘.tliyt. | hlm.‘nt.tph.ilm.b h.p‘nm. | ṭṭt.b‘d n.ksl.ṯṯbr. | ‘ln.pn h.td‘.tǵṣ 3['NT].3.29
. | w yql.l arṣ.w trtqṣ.ṣmd.b d b‘l. | [km.]nšr.b uṣb‘t h.ylm.qdqd.zbl. | [ym.]bn.‘nm.ṯpṭ.nhr.yprsḥ.ym.yql. | l arṣ.tnǵ 2.4[68].24
ksi h.nhr l kḥṯ.drkt h.trtqṣ. | b d b‘l.km.nšr b uṣb‘t h.hlm.qdq | d zbl ym.bn.‘nm.ṯpṭ.nhr.yprsḥ ym. | w yql.l arṣ.w 2.4[68].21
n.ybṣr.[ḥbl.d] | iym.bn.nšrm.arḥp.an[k.‘]l. | aqht.‘db k.hlmn.ṯnm.qdqd. | ṯlṯ id.‘l.udn.špk.km.šiy. | dm.km.šḥṭ.l brk 18[3AQHT].4.22
hn.in.[---]. | [-.]hlk.ǵlmm b dd y.yṣ[--]. | [-.]yṣa.w l.yṣa.hlm.[ṯnm]. | [q]dqd.ṯlṯ id.‘l.ud[n]. | [---.-]sr.pdm.riš h[m.---]. | 19[1AQHT].2.78
.ybṣr.ḥbl.diy[m.bn]. | nšrm.trḥp.‘nt.‘l[.aqht]. | t‘dbn h.hlmn.ṯnm[.qdqd]. | ṯlṯ id.‘l.udn.š[pk.km]. | šiy.dm h.km.šh̲[ṭ. 18[3AQHT].4.33

hln

.b mm[ʿ]. | mhrm.mṭm.tgrš. | šbm.b ksl.qšt h.mdnt. | w hln.ʿnt.l bt h.tmǵyn. | tštql.ilt.l hkl h. | w l.šbʿt.tmtḫṣ h.b ʿmq 3[ʿNT].2.17
. | w anhbm.klat.ṯǵrt. | bht.ʿnt.w tqry.ǵlmm. | b št.ǵr.w hln.ʿnt.tm | tḫṣ.b ʿmq.tḫtṣb.bn. | qrytm tmḫṣ.lim.ḫp y[m]. | tṣ 3[ʿNT].2.5

hm

lk.l alpm.ḫḏḏ. | w l.rbt.kmyr. | aṯr.ṯn.ṯn.hlk. | aṯr.ṯlṯ.kl hm. | aḥd.bt h.ysgr. | almnt.škr. | tškr.zbl.ʿršm. | yšu.ʿwr. | mzl 14[KRT].4.183
.tʿdt.ṯpṭ.nhr. | tšu ilm rašt hm.l ẓr.brkt hm.ln.kḥṯ.zbl hm. | aḫr.tmǵyn.mlak ym.tʿdt.ṯpṭ.nhr.l pʿn.il. | [l t]pl.l tštḥw 2.1[137].29
p[.--]. | apš[ny]. | b.yṣi h. | ḥwt.[---]. | alp.k[sp]. | tšʿn. | w.hm.al[-]. | l.tšʿn. | mṣrm. | tmkrn. | ypḥ.ʿbdilt. | bn.m. | ypḥ.ilšl 2116.13
ʿn lṭpn il d pid. | p ʿbd.an.ʿnn.aṯrt. | p.ʿbd.ank.aḫd.ulṯ. | hm.amt.aṯrt.tlbn. | lbnt.ybn.bt.l bʿl. | km ilm.w ḥẓr.k bn.aṯrt. 4[51].4.61
.ṯḥrr.l išt.ṣḥrrt.l pḥmm. | a[ṯ]tm.aṯt.il.aṯt.il.w ʿlm h.w hm. | aṯtm.tṣḥn y.ad ad.nḥtm.ḫṭ k. | mmnnm.mṭ yd k.hl.ʿṣr.t 23[52].42
yr.šmm h.yr.b šmm.ʿṣr.yḫrṭ yšt. | l pḥm.il.aṯtm.k ypt.hm.aṯtm.tṣḥn. | y mt.mt.nḥtm.ḫṭ k.mmnnm.mṭ.yd k. | h[l.]ʿṣ 23[52].39
---]. | gršnn.l k[si.mlk h.l nḫt.l kḥṯ]. | drkt h.š[--.--]. | w hm.ap.l[--.---]. | ymḫṣ k.k[--.---]. | il.dbḥ.[---]. | pʿr.b[--.---]. | ṯb 1[ʿNT.X].4.26
[---.]y[--].ḫtt.mtt[--]. | [--.]ḥy[--.--.]l ašṣi.hm.ap.amr[--]. | [---].w b ym.mnḫ l abd.b ym.irtm.m[--]. | [ṯp 2.4[68].2
[-]l[-]m. | ʿšr.ksdm.yd.lmd hm.lqḥ. | ʿšr.mḫṣm.yd.lmd hm. | apym. | [bn]š gt.ipṯl. | [---]ym. | [----]m. | [-----]. | [bnš.g]t.i 1040.9
l.tḥt]. | pʿn h.ybqʿ.kbd h.w yḥd. | iṯ.šmt.iṯ.ʿẓm.w yqḥ b hm. | aqht.ybl.l qẓ.ybky.w yqbr. | yqbr.nn.b mdgt.b knk[-]. | 19[1AQHT].3.145
-.---]. | [---].ank.l km[.---]. | l y.ank.ašṣu[.---.]w[.---]. | w hm.at.tr[gm.---]. | w.drm.ʿtr[--.---]. | w ap.ht.k[--.]škn. | w.mṯ 54.1.18[13.2.3]
brt.lb[--.---]. | u[-]šhr.nuš[-.---]. | b [u]grt.w ht.a[--]. | w hm.at.trg[m.---]. | w sip.u hw[.---]. | w ank.u šbt[--.---]. | ank. 54.1.8[13.1.5]
tdd.iln[ym.---]. | asr.sswm.tṣmd.dg[-.---]. | tʿln.l mrkbt hm.ti[ty.l ʿr hm]. | tlkn.ym.w ṯa aḫr.š[pšm.b ṯlṯ]. | mǵy.rpum 20[121].2.4
tdd.aṯr[h.l tdd.ilnym]. | asr.mr[kbt.---]. | tʿln.l mr[kbt hm.tity.l] | ʿr hm.tl[kn.ym.w ṯn.aḫr.špšm]. | b ṯlṯ.mǵy[.rpum 22.1[123].23
y.bt h. | w.ištrmy. | bt.ʿbd mlk. | w.snt. | bt.ugrt. | w.pdy h[m]. | iwrkl.mit. | ksp.b y[d]. | birtym. | [un]ṯ inn. | l [h]m ʿd t 1006.12
.brlt.anḫr. | b ym.hm.brk y.tkšd. | rumm.ʿn.kdd.aylt. | hm.imt.imt.npš.blt. | ḥmr.p imt.b klt. | yd y.ilḥm.hm.šbʿ. | yd 5[67].1.18
rgm. | yšlm.l k. | l.trǵds. | w.l.klby. | šmʿt.ḫti. | nḫtu.ht. | hm.in mm. | nḫtu.w.lak. | ʿm y.w.yd. | ilm.p.k mtm. | ʿz.mid. | 53[54].9
.il. | [l t]pl.l tštḥwy.pḥr.mʿd.qmm.a[--].amr. | [ṯn]y.dʿt hm.išt.ištm.yitmr.ḥrb.lṭšt. | [--]n hm.rgm.l ṯr.ab h.il.tḥm.ym 2.1[137].32
aliyn.bʿl]. | k ḫlq.z[bl.bʿl.arṣ]. | w hm.ḥy.a[liyn.bʿl]. | w hm.iṯ.zbl.bʿ[l.arṣ]. | b ḥlm.lṭpn.il.d pid. | b ḏrt.bny.bnwt. | šm 6[49].3.3
.hmt]. | tqln.tḥ pʿn y.ibq[ʿ.kbd hm.w] | aḥd.hm.iṯ.šmt.hm.i[ṯ]. | ʿẓm.abky.w aqbrn h. | ašt.b ḫrt.ilm.arṣ. | b p h.rgm.l 19[1AQHT].3.110
.h]wt. | w yql.tḥt.pʿn y.ibqʿ.kbd[h]. | w aḥd.hm.iṯ.šmt.hm.iṯ[.ʿẓm]. | abky.w aqbrn.ašt.b ḫrt. | i[lm.arṣ.b p h.rgm.l y 19[1AQHT].3.125
yṯbr.bʿl.yṯbr.diy. | hyt.tql.tḥt.pʿn y.ibqʿ. | kbd h.w aḥd.hm.iṯ.šmt.iṯ. | ʿẓm.abky w aqbrn h.aštn. | b ḫrt.ilm.arṣ.b p h. 19[1AQHT].3.139
y[ṯb]r.diy[.h]wt. | w yql.tḥt.pʿn y.ibqʿ.kbd[h]. | w aḥd.hm.iṯ.šmt.hm.iṯ[.ʿẓm]. | abky.w aqbrn.ašt.b ḫrt. | i[lm.arṣ.b p 19[1AQHT].3.125
ʿl.yṯb[r.diy.hmt]. | tqln.tḥ pʿn y.ibq[ʿ.kbd hm.w] | aḥd.hm.iṯ.šmt.hm.i[ṯ]. | ʿẓm.abky.w aqbrn h. | ašt.b ḫrt.ilm.arṣ. | 19[1AQHT].3.110
.prṣ.bʿd hm. | w ʿrb.hm.hm[.iṯ.--.l]ḥm.w t[n]. | w nlḥm.hm.iṯ[.--.yn.w t]n.w nšt. | w ʿn hm.nǵr mdrʿ[.iṯ.lḥm.---]. | iṯ.y 23[52].72
mdrʿ y.nǵr. | nǵr.ptḥ.w ptḥ hw.prṣ.bʿd hm. | w ʿrb.hm.hm[.iṯ.--.l]ḥm.w t[n]. | w nlḥm.hm.iṯ[.--.yn.w t]n.w nšt. | w ʿ 23[52].71
. | db[ḥ.l krt.a]dn km. | ʿl.krt.tbun.km. | rgm.ṯ[rm.]rgm hm. | b ḏrt[.---.]krt. | [----]. 15[128].6.7
pṯ[.nhr]. | t[ǵ]ly.hlm.rišt hm.l ẓr.brkt hm.w l kḥṯ. | zbl hm.b hm.ygʿr.bʿl.lm.ǵltm.ilm.rišt. | km l ẓr brkt km.w ln.kḥ 2.1[137].24
| ugrm.ḫl.ld. | aklm.tbrk k. | w ld ʿqqm. | ilm.ypʿr. | šmt hm. | b hm.qrnm. | km.ṯrm.w gbṯt. | km.ibrm. | w b hm.pn.bʿl. 12[75].1.29
r. | [w]ht.yšmʿ.uḫ y. | l g y.w yhbṭ.bnš. | w ytn.ilm.b d hm. | b d.iḫqm.gṯr. | w b d.ytrhd. | bʿl. 55[18].19
rʿ. | b d a[-]m.w.ank. | k[l.]ḏrʿ hm. | [--.n]pš[.-]. | w [k]l hm.b d. | rb.tmtt.lqḥt. | w.ṯṯb.ank.l hm. | w.any k.ṯt. | by.ʿky.ʿr 2059.21
.bnt.bh[t k].a[l.tš]mḫ. | al.tšmḫ.b r[m.h]kl[k]. | al.aḫd.hm.b y[--] y.[---]b[-]. | b gdlt.arkt y.am[---]. | qdqd k.ašhlk.šb 3[ʿNT.VI].5.30
| qrn.d bat k.btlt.ʿnt. | qrn.d bat k bʿl.ymšḥ. | bʿl.ymšḥ.hm.b ʿp. | nṭʿn.b arṣ.ib y. | w b ʿpr.qm.aḫ k. | w tšu.ʿn h.btlt.ʿn 10[76].2.23
a.ʿqqm. | bʿl.hmd m.yḥmd m. | bn.dgn.yhrr m. | bʿl.ngṯ hm.b pʿn h. | w il hd.b ḫrẓʿ h. | [-----]. | [--]t.[---]. | [---.]ʿn[.---]. 12[75].1.40
yn. | bn.[-]gštn. | bn[.n]klb. | b[n.]dtn. | w.nḥl h. | w.nḥl hm. | bn.iršyn. | bn.ʿzn. | bn.aršw. | bn.ḫzrn. | bn.iǵyn. | w.nḥl h 113[400].2.11
| nrn. | w.nḥl h. | bn.rmyy. | bn.tlmyn. | w.nḥl h. | w.nḥl hm. | bn.ḥrm. | bn.brzn. | w.nḥl h. | bn.adldn. | bn.šbl. | bn.ḫnz 113[400].1.8
[nq]dm.dt.kn.npṣ hm. | [bn].lbn.arbʿ.qšt.w.ar[bʿ]. | [u]ṯpt.qlʿ.w.ṯṯ.mr[ḥ]m. | [bn] 2047.1
bnšm.dt.iṯ.alpm.l hm. | bn.niršn. | bn.adty. | bn.alz. | bn.birtn. | bn.mlṣ. | bn.q[--]. 2023.1.1
y. | bn.ḫnyn. | bn.knn. | khnm. | bn.ṯʿy. | w.nḥl h. | w.nḥl hm. | bn.nqly. | bn.snrn. | bn.ṯgd. | bn.d[-]n. | bn.amdn. | bn.ṯm 105[86].2
n.[---]. | bn.yk[--]. | bn.šmm. | bn.irgy. | w.nḥl h. | w.nḥl hm. | [bn].pmn. | bn.gtrn. | bn.arpḫn. | bn.ṯryn. | bn.dll. | bn.ḫs 1046.2.12
.ksd. | bn.bršm. | bn.kzn. | w.nḥl h. | w.nḥl hm. | w.[n]ḥl hm. | b[n.---]. | bn.gzry. | bn.atyn. | bn.ttn. | bn.rwy. | bn.ʿmyn. | 113[400].2.23
---]. | w [----]. | bʿl.[---]. | il hd.b[---]. | at.bl.at.[---]. | yisp hm.b[ʿl.---]. | bn.dgn[.---]. | ʿḏbm.[---]. | uḫry.l[---]. | mṣt.ks h. 12[75].2.25
.bn.il. | ǵzr.p np.š.npš.lbim. | thw.hm.brlt.anḫr. | b ym.hm.brk y.tkšd. | rumm.ʿn.kdd.aylt. | hm.imt.imt.npš.blt. | ḥm 5[67].1.16
.bn ilm. | mt.hwt.ydd.bn.il. | ǵzr.p np.š.npš.lbim. | thw.hm.brlt.anḫr. | b ym.hm.brk y.tkšd. | rumm.ʿn.kdd.aylt. | hm 5[67].1.15
lṯ. | w tn.ql h.b ʿrpt. | šrh.l arṣ.brqm. | bt.arzm.yklln h. | hm.bt.lbnt.yʿmsn h. | l yrgm.l aliyn bʿl. | ṣḥ.ḫrn.b bhm k. | ʿḏ 4[51].5.73
r]. | t[ǵ]ly.hlm.rišt hm.l ẓr.brkt hm.w l kḥṯ. | zbl hm.b hm.ygʿr.bʿl.lm.ǵltm.ilm.rišt. | km l ẓr brkt km.w ln.kḥṯ.zbl 2.1[137].24
b qrʿ. | ʿṯtrt.w ʿnt.ymǵy. | ʿṯtrt.tʿdb.nšb l h. | w ʿnt.ktp.b hm.ygʿr.ṯǵr. | bt.il.pn.l mgr lb.tʿdbn. | nšb.l inr.tʿdbn.ktp. | b i UG5.1.1.11
rm.h[--.---]. | yrmm h[--.---]. | mlk.gbʿ h d [---]. | ibr.k l hm.d l h q[--.---]. | l ytn.l hm.tḥt bʿl[.---]. | h.u qšt pn hdd.b y 9[33].2.4
r.qbṣ.dtn. | ṣǵrt hn.abkrn. | tbrk.ilm.tity. | tity.ilm.l ahl hm. | dr il.l mšknt hm. | w tqrb.w ld.bn.l h. | w tqrb.w ld.bnt. 15[128].3.18
t. | krt.k ybky. | ydmʿ.nʿmn.ǵlm. | il.mlk[.ṯ]r ab h. | yarš.hm.drk[t]. | k ab.adm. | [-----]. 14[KRT].1.42
rišym.dt.ʿrb. | b bnš hm. | ḏmry.w.ptpt.ʿrb. | b.yrm. | [ily.w].ḏmry.ʿrb. | b.ṯbʿm. | yd 2079.2
d.ilnym]. | asr.mr[kbt.---]. | tʿln.l mr[kbt hm.tity.l] | ʿr hm.tl[kn.ym.w ṯn.aḫr.špšm]. | b ṯlṯ.mǵy[.rpum.l grnt]. | i[ln] 22.1[123].24
--]. | asr.sswm.tṣmd.dg[-.---]. | tʿln.l mrkbt hm.ti[ty.l ʿr hm]. | tlkn.ym.w ṯa aḫr.š[pšm.b ṯlṯ]. | mǵy.rpum.l grnt.i[lny 20[121].2.4
y. | likt.ʿm.špš. | bʿl k.ky.akl. | b.ḥwt k.inn. | špš n.[---]. | hm.al[k.--]. | ytnt[.---]. | ṯn[.---]. | w[.-----]. | l[.-----]. | h[--.---]. | š 2060.22
nǵr.mdrʿ y.nǵr. | nǵr.ptḥ.w ptḥ hw.prṣ.bʿd hm. | w ʿrb.hm.hm[.iṯ.--.l]ḥm.w t[n]. | w nlḥm.hm.iṯ[.--.yn.w t]n.w nšt. | 23[52].71
[--.n]pš[.-]. | w [k]l hm.b d. | rb.tmtt.lqḥt. | w.ṯṯb.ank.l hm. | w.any k.ṯt. | by.ʿky.ʿryt. | w.aḫ y.mhk. | b lb h.al.yšt. 2059.23
nn.w. | mndym. | bdnh. | l[q]ḥt. | [--]km.ʿm.mlk. | [b]ǵl hm.w.iblbl hm. | w.b.ṯb h.[---]. | spr ḥ[--.---]. | w.ʿm[.---]. | yqḥ 2129.10
ym. | bdnh. | l[q]ḥt. | [--]km.ʿm.mlk. | [b]ǵl hm.w.iblbl hm. | w.b.ṯb h.[---]. | spr ḥ[--.---]. | w.ʿm[.---]. | yqḥ[.---]. | w.n[- 2129.10

rm.bʿl.yṯbr.|bʿl.ṯbr.diy hmt.tqln.|tḥt.pʿn h.ybqʿ.kbdt hm.w[yḥd].|in.šmt.in.ʿẓm.yšu.g h.|w yṣḥ.knp.nšrm.ybn.| 19[1AQHT].3.116
m].|bʿl.yṯb.bʿl.yṯb[r.diy.hmt].|tqln.tḥ pʿn y.ibq[ʿ.kbd hm.w] |aḥd.hm.iṯ.šmt.hm.i[ṯ].|ʿẓm.abky.w aqbrn h.|ašt.b 19[1AQHT].3.109
.]rkb[.---].|[---].d[--.---].|b ql[.-----].|w tštqdn[.-----].|hm.|w yḥ.mlk.|w ik m.kn.w [---].|tšknnnn[.---]. 62[26].8
h.|mk.b šbʿ.šnt.|bn.krt.km hm.tdr.|ap.bnt.ḥry.|km hm.w tḥss.aṯrt.|ndr h.w ilt.p[--].|w tšu.g h.w [tṣḥ].|ph mʿ. 15[128].3.25
-].|ytnm.qrt.l ʿly[.---].|b mdbr.špm.yd[.---.---]r.|l riš hm.w yš[--.--]m.|lḥm.b lḥm ay.w šty.b ḫmr yn ay.|šlm.mlk 23[52].5
k.tšlm k].|ʿbd[.---]y.|ʿm[.---]y.|šk[--.--.]kll.|šk[--.--.]hm.|w.k[b--.---].|ʿm[.---]m ib.|[---.--]m.|[-----].|[-]š[--.---].| 2065.6
n.mlak.ym.tʿdt.ṯpṭ[.nhr].|t[ǵ]ly.hlm.rišt hm.l ẓr.brkt hm.w l kḥṯ.|zbl hm.b hm.ygʿr.bʿl.lm.ǵltm.ilm.rišt.|km l ẓr 2.1[137].23
.|w dg b ym.w ndd.gzr.l zr.yʿdb.u ymn.|u šmal.b p hm.w l.tšbʿn y.aṯt.itrḫ.|y bn.ašld.šu.ʿdb.tk.mdbr qdš.|ṯm tg 23[52].64
w.nḫl h.|bn.ksd.|bn.bršm.|bn.kzn.|w.nḫl h.|w.nḫl hm.|w.[n]ḫl hm.|b[n.---].|bn.gzry.|bn.atyn.|bn.ttn.|bn.rw 113[400].2.22
ṣḥ hm.ʿm.nǵr.mdrʿ y.nǵr.|nǵr.ptḥ.w ptḥ hw.prṣ.bʿd hm.|w ʿrb.hm.hm[.iṯ.--.l]ḥm.w t[n].|w nlḥm.hm.iṯ[.--.yn.w 23[52].70
mtm].|[tgly.ḏd.il.w]tb[a].|[qrš.mlk.ab.]šnm.|[tša.g hm.w tṣ]ḥ.sbn.|[---]l[.---.]ʿd.|ksm.mhyt[.m]ǵny.|l nʿm y.ar 5[67].6.3
k.]rḥ.npš.hm.|k.iṯl.brlt n[-.k qṭr.b ap -].|tmǵyn.tša.g h[m.w tṣḥn].|šmʿ.l dnil.[mt.rpi].|mt.aqht.ǵzr.[šṣat].|btlt.ʿn 19[1AQHT].2.89
.mt.|tk.qrt h.hmry.mk.ksu.|ṯbt.ḫḫ.arṣ.nḫlt h.tša.|g hm.w tṣḥ.tḥm.aliyn.|bn.bʿl.hwt.aliy.qrdm.|bhṯ.bn.ilm.mt.ʿ 5[67].2.17
ʿ.mlakm.|l yṯb.idk.pnm.|l ytn.ʿmm.pbl.|mlk.tšan.|g hm.w tṣḥn.|tḥm.krt.ṯ[ʿ].|hwt.[n]ʿmn.[ǵlm.il]. 14[KRT].6.304
.l yṯb].|[idk.pnm.l ytn].|[ʿ]m[.krt.mswn h].|tš[an.g hm.w tṣḥn].|tḥ[m.pbl.mlk].|qḥ[.ksp.w yrq].|ḫrṣ.[yd.mqm 14[KRT].6.267
abkrn.|tbrk.ilm.tity.|tity.ilm.l ahl hm.|dr il.l mšknt hm.|w tqrb.w ld.bn.l h.|w tqrb.w ld.bnt.l h.|mk.b šbʿ.šnt.| 15[128].3.19
rm[.---].|tšt.tbʿ[.---].|qrt.mlk[.---].|w.ʿl.ap.s[--.---].|b hm.w.rgm.hw.al[--].|atn.ksp.l hm.ʿd.|ilak.ʿm.mlk.|ht.lik[t. 2008.2.6
grbs hm.|w.ṯn.ʿšr h.ḫpnt.|[š]šwm.amtm.ʿkyt.|yd.llḫ hm.|w.ṯlṯ.l.ʿšrm.|ḫpnt.ššwm.ṯn.|pddm.w.d.ṯṯ.|[mr]kbt.w.ḥ 2049.5
[---.ṯ]lṯ.ʿš[r h.---].|d bnšm.yd.grbs hm.|w.ṯn.ʿšr h.ḫpnt.|[š]šwm.amtm.ʿkyt.|yd.llḫ hm.|w.ṯlṯ.l 2049.2
[k mt.aliyn.bʿl].|k ḫlq.z[bl.bʿl.arṣ].|w hm.ḥy.a[liyn.bʿl].|w hm.iṯ.zbl.bʿ[l.arṣ].|b ḥlm.lṭpn.il.d pid. 6[49].3.2
d[yn]m.ṯm.|yd[r.k]rt.ṯʿ.|i.iṯt.aṯrt.ṣrm.|w ilt.ṣdynm.|hm.ḥry.bt y.|iqḥ.ašʿrb.ǵlmt.|ḥẓr y.ṯn h.wspm.|atn.w ṯlṯ h. 14[KRT].4.203
.nḫt.|b ẓr.hdm.id.|d pršа.b br.|nʿl.il.d qblbl.|ʿln.ybl hm.ḫrṣ.|ṯlḥn.il.d mla.|mnm.dbbm.d |msdt.arṣ.|sʿ.il.dqt.k 4[51].1.38
.|hl ny.ʿmn.|mlk.b.ṯy ndr.|iṯt.w.ht.|[-]sny.uḏr h.|w.hm.ḫt.|ʿl.w.likt.|ʿm k.w.hm.|l.ʿl.w.lakm.|ilak.w.at.|um y. 1013.16
.lḥ[m].|b ṯlḥnt.lḥm št.|b krpnm.yn.b k.ḫrṣ.|dm.ʿṣm.hm.yd.il mlk.|yḫss k.ahbt.ṯr.tʿrr k.|w tʿn.rbt.aṯrt ym.|tḥm 4[51].4.38
.l alpm.ḫḏḏ.|w l rbt.kmyr.|[a]ṯr.ṯn.ṯn.hlk.|aṯr.ṯlṯ.kl hm.|yḥd.bt h.sgr.|almnt.škr.|tškr.zbl.ʿršm.|yšu.ʿwr.mzl.| 14[KRT].2.95
].|šmʿ.atm[.---].|ym.lm.qd[.---].|šmn.prst[.---].|ydr.hm.ym[.---].|ʿl amr.yu[ḫd.ksa.mlk h].|nḫt.kḥṯ.d[rkt h.b bt 22.1[123].16
.[--] h[.---].|riš.r[--.--]ḥ[.---]y[.---.-]nt.[š]šat[k.]rḥ.npš.hm.|k.iṯl.brlt n[-.k qṭr.b ap -].|tmǵyn.tša.g h[m.w tṣḥn].|š 19[1AQHT].2.87
--]dn.|ʿm.krt.mswn h.|arḫ.tzǵ.l ʿgl h.|bn.ḫpṯ.l umht hm.|k tnḥn.udmm.|w yʿny.krt.ṯʿ. 15[128].1.6
.ʿṯrṯrm.|nšu.[r]iš.ḥrṯm.|l ẓr.ʿdb.dgn kly.|lḥm.[b]ʿdn hm.kly.|yn.b ḥmt hm.k[l]y.|šmn.b q[bʿt hm.---].|bt.krt.t[-- 16[126].3.14
aliy[n.b]ʿl.|ik.mǵyt.b[t]lt.|ʿnt.mḫṣ y hm[.m]ḫṣ.|bn y.hm[.mkly.ṣ]brt.|ary y[.ẓl].ksp.[a]ṯrt.|k tʿn.ẓl.ksp.w n[-]t.|ḫ 4[51].2.25
rṯm.|l ẓr.ʿdb.dgn kly.|lḥm.[b]ʿdn hm.kly.|yn.b ḥmt hm.k[l]y.|šmn.b q[bʿt hm.---].|bt.krt.t[--]. 16[126].3.15
anḫr.b ym.|brkt.šbšt.|k rumm.hm.|ʿn.kdd.aylt.|mt hm.ks.ym|sk.nhr hm.|šbʿ.ydt y.b ṣʿ.|[--.]šbʿ.rbt.|[---.]qbṭ.ṯ UG5.4.9
pš.blt.|ḥmr.p imt.b klt.|yd y.ilḥm.hm.šbʿ.|ydt y.b ṣʿ.hm.ks.ymsk.|nhr.k[--].ṣḥn.bʿl.ʿm.|aḫ y.qran.hd.ʿm.ary y.| 5[67].1.21
.tph hm.tphn.mlak.ym.tʿdt.ṯpṭ[.nhr].|t[ǵ]ly.hlm.rišt hm.l ẓr.brkt hm.w l kḥṯ.|zbl hm.b hm.ygʿr.bʿl.lm.ǵltm.ilm. 2.1[137].23
zbl km.w ank.ʿny.mlak.ym.tʿdt.ṯpṭ.nhr.|tšu ilm rašt hm.l ẓr.brkt hm.ln.kḥṯ.zbl hm.|aḫr.tmǵyn.mlak ym.tʿdt.ṯp 2.1[137].29
l yblt.ḫbṭm.|ap ksp hm.|l yblt.|w ht.luk ʿm ml[kt].|tǵsdb.šmlšn.|w tbʿ ank.|ʿ 1021.2
ḥbn.hm.[-.]aṯr[.---].|[--]šy.w ydn.bʿ[l.---]n.|[--]ʿ.k yn.hm.l.atn.bt y.l h. 1002.62
[---.-]lk[.---].|[---.ʿ]šr.ym[.---].|[---].hm.l y[--.---].|[---].mṣrm[.---].|[---.--]n mkr[.---].|[---].ank.[2126.3
w.mlk.z[--.--]n.ššwm.|nʿmm.[--].ṯṯm.w.at.|nǵṯ.w.ytn.hm.l k.|w.lḥt.alpm.ḥršm.|k.rgmt.l y.bly m.|alpm.aršt.l k. 2064.20
k.ʿny.mlak.ym.tʿdt.ṯpṭ.nhr.|tšu ilm rašt hm.l ẓr.brkt hm.ln.kḥṯ.zbl hm.|aḫr.tmǵyn.mlak ym.tʿdt.ṯpṭ.nhr.l pʿn.il. 2.1[137].29
r.|iṯt.w.ht.|[-]sny.uḏr h.|w.hm.ḫt.|ʿl.w.likt.|ʿm k.w.hm.|l.ʿl.w.lakm.|ilak.w.at.|um y.al.tdḥṣ.|w.ap.mhkm.|b.l 1013.18
t.w l.ytk.[d]m[ʿt.]km.|rbʿt.ṯqlm.ṯṯp[.---.]bm.|yd.ṣpn hm.tliy m[.--.ṣ]pn hm.|nṣḥy.šrr.m[---.--]ay.|nbšr km.dnil.[- 19[1AQHT].2.84
.|bn.ḫri[-].|bnš.gt.ʿṯtrt.|ad[-]l[-]m.|ʿšr.ksdm.yd.lmd hm.lqḥ.|ʿšr.mḫṣm.yd.lmd hm.|apym.|[bn]š gt.ipṯl.|[---]ym 1040.8
w tṣḥ[.i]k.|mǵy.aliy[n.b]ʿl.|ik.mǵyt.b[t]lt.|ʿnt.mḫṣ y hm[.m]ḫṣ.|bn y.hm[.mkly.ṣ]brt.|ary y[.ẓl].ksp.[a]ṯrt.|k tʿn. 4[51].2.24
.škn.hnk.|l ʿbd h.alpm.š[šw]m.|rgmt.ʿly.ṯh.lm.|l.ytn.hm.mlk.[b]ʿl y.|w.hn.ibm.ššq l y.|p.l.ašt.aṯt y.|nʿr y.ṯh.l pn 1012.26
|ṯ[--].|[--] aṯt yqḥ ʿz.|[---]ḏ.|[---].|[---].|hm qrt tuḫd.hm mt yʿl bnš.|bt bn bnš yqḥ ʿz.|w yḥdy mrḥqm. RS61[24.277.29]
.l špš.rbt.w l kbkbm.kn[-].|yhbr.špt hm.yšq.hn.[š]pt hm.mtqtm.|bm.nšq.w hr.[b]ḥbq.w ḥ[m]ḥmt.ytb[n].|yspr.l 23[52].55
aṯtm.a[ṯt.il].|aṯt.il.w ʿlm h.yhbr.špt hm.yš[q].|hn.špt hm.mtqtm.mtqtm.k lrmn[.--].|bm.nšq.w hr.b ḥbq.ḥmḥmt.t 23[52].50
.bn.l h.|w tqrb.w ld.bnt.l h.|mk.b šbʿ.šnt.|bn.krt.km hm.tdr.|ap.bnt.ḥry.|km hm.w tḥss.aṯrt.|ndr h.w ilt.p[--].| 15[128].3.23
-.l]ḥm.w t[n].|w nlḥm.hm.iṯ[.--.yn.w t]n.w nšt.|w ʿn hm.nǵr mdrʿ[.iṯ.lḥm.---].|iṯ.yn.d ʿrb.bṯk[.---].|mǵ hw.l hn.l 23[52].73
mn.nqpt.ʿd.ilm.nʿmm.ttlkn.|šd.tṣdn.pat.mdbr.w ngš.hm.nǵr.|mdrʿ.w ṣḥ hm.ʿm.nǵr.mdrʿ y.nǵr.|nǵr.ptḥ.w ptḥ h 23[52].68
r.w šl[m].|šu.ʿdb.l špš.rbt.w l kbkbm.kn[-].|yhbr.špt hm.yšq.hn.[š]pt hm.mtqtm.|bm.nšq.w hr.[b]ḥbq.w ḥ[m]ḥ 23[52].55
t.w šḥrt.l pḥmm.aṯtm.a[ṯt.il].|aṯt.il.w ʿlm h.yhbr.špt hm.yš[q].|hn.špt hm.mtqtm.mtqtm.k lrmn[.--].|bm.nšq.w 23[52].49
.mit.šmn.|arbʿm.l.mit.tišr.|ṯṯ.ṯṯ.b [ṯ]ql.ṯlṯt.l.ʿšrm.ksp hm.|šstm.b.šbʿm.|ṯlṯ.mat.trm.b.ʿšrt.|mit.adrm.b.ʿšrt.|ʿšr.y 1127.5
---].|w.ʿl.ap.s[--.---].|b hm.w.rgm.hw.al[--].|atn.ksp.l hm.ʿd.|ilak.ʿm.mlk.|ht.lik[t.--.]mlk[.--].|w.mlk.yštal.b.hn[- 2008.2.7
y h[m].|iwrkl.mit.|ksp.b y[d].|birtym.|[un]ṯ inn.|l [h]m ʿd ṯṯtbn.|ksp.iwrkl.|w ṯb.l unṯ hm. 1006.17
m.ttlkn.|šd.tṣdn.pat.mdbr.w ngš.hm.nǵr.|mdrʿ.w ṣḥ hm.ʿm.nǵr.mdrʿ y.nǵr.|nǵr.ptḥ.w ptḥ hw.prṣ.bʿd hm.|w ʿr 23[52].69
pš.lbun.|thw.w npš.|anḫr.b ym.|brkt.šbšt.|k rumm.hm.|ʿn.kdd.aylt.|mt hm.ks.ym|sk.nhr hm.|šbʿ.ydt y.b ṣʿ.|[UG5.4.7
yšu.g h.w yṣḥ.knp.nšrm.|bʿl.yṯbr.bʿl.yṯbr.diy.|hmt.hm.tʿpn.ʿl.qbr.bn y.|tšḫṭann.b šnt h.qr.[mym].|mlk.yṣm.y l 19[1AQHT].3.150
bn ym.ynqm.b ap.ḏd.št.špt.|l arṣ.špt l šmm.w ʿrb.b p hm.ʿṣr.šmm.|w dg b ym.w ndd.gzr.l zr.yʿdb.u ymn.|u šmal 23[52].62
t.lik[t.--.]mlk[.--].|w.mlk.yštal.b.hn[--].|hmt.w.anyt.hm.tʿ[rb].|mkr.hn d.w.rgm.ank[.--].|mlkt.ybqš.anyt.w.at[-- 2008.2.11
gnn.rbt.|aṯrt.ym.tǵẓyn.|qnyt.ilm.mgntm.|ṯr.il.d pid.hm.ǵẓtm.|bny.bnwt w tʿn.|btlt.ʿnt.nmgn.|[-]m.rbt.aṯrt.ym. 4[51].3.31
.rbt.aṯr[t.y]m.|ik.atwt.qnyt.i[lm].|rǵb.rǵbt.w tǵt[--].|hm.ǵmu.ǵmit.w ʿs[--].|lḥm.hm.štym.lḥ[m].|b ṯlḥnt.lḥm št. 4[51].4.34

lm.l lḫ[m]. | yṯb.bn qdš.l ṯrm.b'l.qm.'l.il.hlm. | ilm.tph hm.tphn.mlak.ym.t'dt.ṯpṭ[.nhr]. | t[ǵ]ly.hlm.rišt hm.l ẓr.brk 2.1[137].22
mt hm. | b hm.qrnm. | km.ṯrm.w gbṯt. | km.ibrm. | w b hm.pn.b'l. | b'l.ytlk.w yṣd. | yḫ pat.mlbr. | wn.ymǵy.aklm. | w 12[75].1.33
mḏrǵlm.d inn. | msgm.l hm. | p'ṣ.ḫbty. | artyn.ary. | brqn.ṯlḥy. | bn.aryn. | bn.lgn. | bn.b 118[306].2
km. | rb't.ṯqlm.ṯtp[.---.]bm. | yd.ṣpn hm.tliy m[.--.ṣ]pn hm. | nṣḥy.šrr.m[---.--]ay. | nbšr km.dnil.[--] h[.---]. | riš.r[--.-- 19[1AQHT].2.84
p k.b ǵr.ṯn.p k.b ḫlb.k tgwln.šnt k. | [--.]w špt k.l tššy.hm.tqrm.l mt.b rn k. | [--]ḫp.an.arnn.ql.špš.ḥw.bṯnm.uḫd.b' 1001.1.5
ḫl.ld. | aklm.tbrk k. | w ld 'qqm. | ilm.yp'r. | šmt hm. | b hm.qrnm. | km.ṯrm.w gbṯt. | km.ibrm. | w b hm.pn.b'l. | b'l.ytl 12[75].1.30
| w l dbḥ[--]. | ṯ[--]. | [--] aṯt yqḥ 'z. | [---]ḏ. | [---]. | [---]. | hm qrt tuḫd.hm mt y'l bnš. | bt bn bnš yqḥ 'z. | w yḥdy mrḥ RS61[24.277.29]
rb'[m.ksp.]'l. | il[m]l[k.a]rgnd. | uškny[.w]mit. | zt.b d hm.rib. | w [---]. | [-----]. | [-]šy[.---] h. | [-]kt[.---.]nrn. | [b]n.nm 2055.13
.a[--].amr. | [ṯn]y.d't hm.išt.ištm.yitmr.ḥrb.ltšt. | [--]n hm.rgm.l ṯr.ab h.il.ṯḥm.ym.b'l km. | [adn]km.ṯpṭ.nhr.tn.il 2.1[137].33
. | w.hn.ibm.šṣq l y. | p.l.ašt.aṯt y. | n'r y.ṯh.l pn.ib. | hn.hm.yrgm.mlk. | b'l y.tmǵyy.hn. | alpm.ššwm.hnd. | w.mlk.b'l 1012.30
ylt. | hm.imt.imt.npš.blt. | ḥmr.p imt.b klt. | yd y.ilḥm.hm.šb'. | ydt y.b ṣ'.hm.ks.ymsk. | nhr.k[--].ṣḥn.b'l.'m. | aḫ y.q 5[67].1.20
bšt. | k rumm.hm. | 'n.kḏd.aylt. | mt hm.ks.ym | sk.nhr hm. | šb'.ydt y.b ṣ'. | [--.]šb'.rbt. | [---.]qbṭ.ṯm. | [---.]bn.ilm. | [UG5.4.10
.šr.'ṯtrt. | mlbš.ṯrmnm. | k.ytn.w.b.bt. | mlk.mlbš. | ytn.l hm. | šb'.lbšm.allm. | l ušḫry. | ṯlṯ.mat.pṯtm. | l.mgmr.b.ṯlṯ. | šn 1107.8
tnǵṣn.pnt h.l ydlp. | tmn h.kṯr.ṣmdm.ynḥt.w yp'r.šmt hm. | šm k.at.aymr.aymr.mr.ym.mr.ym. | l ksi h.nhr l kḥṯ.dr 2.4[68].18
lk.'lm k.drkt.dt dr dr k. | kṯr ṣmdm.ynḥt.w yp'r.šmt hm.šm k at. | ygrš.ygrš.grš ym grš ym.l ksi h. | [n]hr l kḥṯ dr 2.4[68].11
i[lm]. | rǵb.rǵbt.w tǵt[--]. | hm.ǵmu.ǵmit.w 's[--]. | lḥm.hm.štym.lḥ[m]. | b ṯlḥnt.lḥm št. | b krpnm.yn.b k.ḫrṣ. | dm.'ṣ 4[51].4.35
ak.ym.[t'dt.ṯpṭ.nhr]. | b 'lṣ.'lṣm.npr.š[--.---]. | uṯ.ṯbr.ap hm.tb'.ǵlm[m.al.ṯṯb.idk.pnm]. | al.ttn.'m.pḫr.m'd.t[k.ǵr.ll.l 2.1[137].13
--]. | mlk.gb' h d [---]. | ibr.k l hm.d l h q[--.---]. | l ytn.l hm.ṯḥt b'l[.---]. | h.u qšt pn hdd.b y[.----]. | 'm.b ym b'l ysy y 9[33].2.5
lk. | w.aḥd. | 'l atlg. | w l.'ṣm. | tspr. | nrn.al.tud | ad.at.l hm. | ṯṯm.ksp. 1010.20
w 'ṯtrt.tṣdn.[---]. | [---.-]b[-.---]. | ['ṯ]trt w 'nt[.---]. | w b hm.tṯṯb[.--]d h. | km trpa.hn n'r. | d yšt.l.lṣb h ḫš'r klb. | [w]r UG5.1.2.2
mm. | nḫtu.w.lak. | 'm y.w.yd. | ilm.p.k mtm. | 'z.mid. | hm.nṯkp. | m'n k. | w.mnm. | rgm.d.tšm'. | ṯmt.w.št. | b.spr.'m 53[54].14
n[--.---]. | rg[m.---]. | nǵṯ[.---]. | d.yqḥ[.---]. | hm.ṯn.[---]. | hn dt.[---]. | [-----]. | [-----]. | ṯḥm[.---]. | l p'n.b'l y[2064.5
bn.b'ln.biry. | ṯlṯ.b'lm. | w.adn hm.ṯr.w.arb'.bnt h. | yrḫm.yd.ṯn.bn h. | b'lm.w.ṯlṯ.n'rm.w.bt. 2080.3
l.an[k.--.]il[m.--]y. | [--.m]ṣlm.pn y[.-.]tlkn. | [---.]rḫbn.hm.[-.]aṯr[.---]. | [--]šy.w ydn.b'[l.---]n. | [--]'.k yn.hm.l.atn.bt 1002.60
škḥ.w. | rb.tmtt. | lqḥ.kl.ḏr'. | b d a[-]m.w.ank. | k[l.]ḏr' hm. | [--.n]pš[.-]. | w [k]l hm.b d. | rb.tmtt.lqḥt. | w.ṯṯb.ank.l h 2059.19
[---.--]d.'m y. | [--.]spr.lm.likt. | [--]y.k išal hm. | [--.'š]rm.kkr.ṯlṯ. | [--.]ṯlṯm.kkr.ṯlṯ. | [--.]aštn.l k. | [--]y.kl. 1022.3
.kkr.ṯlṯ. | [--.]ṯlṯm.kkr.ṯlṯ. | [--.]aštn.l k. | [--]y.kl.dbrm.hm[.--]. | [--]l.w.kl.mḫr k. | [--]tir.aštn.l [k]. | [---].kkr.ṯl[ṯ]. 1022.7
]km.t[--.---]. | [--.n]pš.ttn[.---]. | [---.]yd't.k[---]. | [---].w hm. | [--]y.ṯb y.w [---]. | [---.]bnš.[---]. 61[-].4
]n.bt k.[---.]b'[r.---]. | [--]my.b d[-.--]y.[---]. | [---.]'m.w hm[.--]yt.w.[---]. | [---.ṯ]y.al.an[k.--.]il[m.--]y. | [--.m]ṣlm.pn y 1002.57
lḥm.[b]'dn hm.kly. | yn.b ḥmt hm.k[l]y. | šmn.b q[b't hm.---]. | bt.krt.t[--]. 16[126].3.16
ry ym.bn]ym. | ynqm.b ap zd.aṯrt.[---]. | špš.mṣprt dlt hm[.---]. | w ǵnbm.šlm.'rbm.ṯn[nm]. | hlkm.b dbḥ n'mt. | šd[.i 23[52].25
spr.mr[ynm]. | [b']l.[---]. | mr[--.---]. | hm.[---]. | kmrṯn[.---]. | bn.ṯbln[.---]. | bn.pndr[.---]. | bn.idr[-.- 2070.2.2
| w.trm.aḥdm. | ṣpym. | ṯlṯ mrkbt mlk. | d.l.ṣpy. | [---.t]r hm. | [---].ššb. | [---.]tr h. | [a]rb'.ql'm. | arb'.mḏrnm. | mḏrn.w. 1122.7
ṣa.hlm.[ṯnm]. | [q]dqd.ṯlṯ id.'l.ud[n]. | [---.-]sr.pdm.riš h[m.---]. | 'l.pd.asr.[---.]l[.---]. | mḫlpt.w l.ytk.[d]m['t.]km. | r 19[1AQHT].2.80
[---.--]m. | [-----]. | [---.]d arṣ. | [---.]ln. | [---.]nb hm. | [---.-]kn. | [---.]hr n.km.šḥr. | [---.y]lt n.km.qdm. | [-.k]bd 12[75].1.5
[---].in ḥẓm.l hm. | [---.--]ḏn. | mrkbt.mtrt. | ngršp. | ngǵln. | ilṯḥm. | b'lṣdq. 1125.1.1
.--]i. | [--]t.mdt h[.l.]'ṯtrt.šd. | [---.-]rt.mḫṣ.bnš.mlk.yb'l hm. | [---.--]t.w.ḫpn.l.azzlt. | [---.]l.'ṯtrt.šd. | [---].yb'lnn. | [---.- 1106.53
.pgm.l.b[---]. | [---.]mdbm.l ḥrn.ḥr[n.---]. | [---.--]m.ql.hm[.---]. | [---].aṯt n.r[---]. | [---.]ḫr[-.--]. | [---.]plnt.[---]. | [---.]' 1001.1.28
t.ablm.a[blm]. | [qrt.zbl.]yrḫ.d mgdl.š[---]. | [---.]mn.'r hm[.---]. | [---.]it[.---]. | [---.]'p[.---]. 18[3AQHT].1.32
nt.bht k.--]. | [al.tšmḫ.]al.tš[mḫ.b rm.h]| [kl k.al.]aḫd hm.[---]. | [---.b]gdlt.ar[kt y.am--]. | [---.qdq]d k.ašhlk[.šbt k. 18[3AQHT].1.9
ilm. | aṯr.ilm.ylk.p'nm. | mlk.p'nm.yl[k]. | šb'.pamt.l kl hm. 33[5].26
tš'.ṣmdm. | ṯlṯm.b d. | ibrtlm. | w.pat.aḥt. | in.b hm. 1141.5
ym. | [un]ṯ inn. | l [h]m 'd ṯṯbn. | ksp.iwrkl. | w ṯb.l unṯ hm. 1006.19

hmlt

kbkbm. | abn.brq.d l.td'.šmm. | rgm l td'.nšm.w l tbn. | hmlt.arṣ.at m.w ank. | ibǵy h.b tk.ǵr y.il.ṣpn. | b qdš.b ǵr.nḥl 3['NT].3.25
m.'m[.arṣ.thmt.'mn.kbkbm]. | rgm.l td'.nš[m.w l tbn.hmlt.arṣ]. | at.w ank.ib[ǵy h.---]. | w y'n.kṯr.w ḫss[.lk.lk.'nn.i 1['NT.IX].3.15
h.aḥd y.d ym | lk.'l.ilm.l ymru. | ilm.w nšm.d yšb | [']hmlt.arṣ.gm.l ǵ | [lm] h.b'l k.yṣḥ.'n. | [gpn].w ugr.b ǵlmt. | [' 4[51].7.52
aḫ k.l[--]n. | hn[-.]aḥẓ[.---]l[-]. | [']nt.akl[y.nšm]. | akly.hml[t.arṣ]. | w y[-]l.a[---]. | š[--.---]. | bl[.---]. 6[49].5.25
| ǵr.l kbd.arṣ.kl.gb'. | l kbd.šdm.npš.ḫsrt. | bn.nšm.npš.hmlt. | arṣ.mǵt.l n'm y.arṣ. | dbr.ysmt.šd.šḥlmmt. | ngš.ank.al 6[49].2.18
ṯny k.rgm.]'ṣ.w lḫšt. | [abn.rgm.l td]'.nš[m.w l t]bn. | [hmlt.a]rṣ.[tant.šmm.'m.ar]ṣ. | thmt.['mn.kbkbm.abn.brq]. | d 3['NT].4.60
.gn. | ap lb.k 'mq.tṯlṯ.bmt. | b'l.mt.my.lim.bn dgn. | my.hmlt.aṯr.b'l.nrd. | b arṣ.'m h.trd.nrt. | ilm.špš.'d.tšb'.bk. | tšt. 6[62].1.7
.ytlṯ. | bmt.yšu.g h.w yṣḥ. | b'l.mt.my.lim.bn. | dgn.my.hmlt.aṯr. | b'l.ard.b arṣ.ap. | 'nt.ttlk.w tṣd.kl.ǵr. | l kbd.arṣ.kl. 5[67].6.24
. | tnn.l šbm. | tšt.trks. | l mrym.l bt[.---]. | p l.tb'[.---]. | hmlt ḫt.[---]. | l.tp[-]m.[---]. | n[-]m[.---]. 1003.12
m.ym.b'l km.adn km.ṯ[pṭ.nhr]. | tn.il m.d tq h.d tqyn.hmlt.tn.b'l.[w 'nn h]. | bn.dgn.arṯ m.pḏ h.tb'.ǵlmm.l ṯṯb.[idk 2.1[137].18
m.b'l km. | [adn]km.ṯpṭ.nhr.tn.il m.d tq h.d tqyn h. | [hml]t.tn.b'l.w 'nn h.bn.dgn.arṯ m.pḏ h. | [w y'n.]ṯr.ab h.il.'b 2.1[137].35

hmr

.ank.ispi.uṭm. | ḏrqm.amt m.l yrt. | b npš.bn ilm.mt.b mh | mrt.ydd.il.ǵzr. | tb'.w l.ytb ilm.idk. | l ytn.pnm.'m.b'l. | 5[67].1.7

hmry

pṯt. | arṣ.tspr.b y | rdm.arṣ. | idk.al.ttn. | pnm.tk.qrt h. | hmry.mk.ksu. | tbt h.ḫḫ.arṣ. | nḫlt h.w nǵr. | 'nn.ilm.al. | tqrb. 4[51].8.12
. | tb'.w l.yṯb.ilm.idk. | l ytn.pn.'m.bn.ilm.mt. | tk.qrt h.hmry.mk.ksu. | tbt.ḫḫ.arṣ.nḫlt h.tša. | g hm.w tṣḥ.tḥm.aliyn. 5[67].2.15

hmt

‘db.|qṣ‘t.apnk.mṯt.dnty.|tšlḥm.tššqy ilm.|tsad.tkbd.hmt.b‘l.|ḥkpt il.kl h.tb‘.kṯr.|l ahl h.hyn.tb‘.l mš|knt h.apn 17[2AQHT].5.30
r.|w ḫss.l brlt.hyn d.|ḥrš yd.šlḥm.ššqy.|ilm sad.kbd.hmt.b‘l.|ḥkpt.il.kl h.tšm‘.|mṯt.dnty.t‘db.imr.|b pḫd.l npš.k 17[2AQHT].5.20
[-].|w yšu.g h.w yṣḥ.knp.nšrm.|b‘l.yṯbr.b‘l.yṯbr.diy.|hmt.hm.t‘pn.‘l.qbr.bn y.|tšḫṭann.b šnt h.qr.[mym].|mlk.yṣ 19[1AQHT].3.150
k.‘m.mlk.|ht.lik[t.--.]mlk[.--].|w.mlk.yštal.b.hn[--].|hmt.w.anyt.hm.t‘[rb].|mkr.hn d.w.rgm.ank[.--].|mlkt.ybqš 2008.2.11
.ḫbṯ h.ḥwt.ṯt h.|w.mnm.šalm.|dt.tknn.|‘l.‘rbnm.|hn hmt.|tknn.|mtn.bn.‘bdym.|ilrb.bn.ilyn.|‘bdadt.bn ‘bdkb.| 1161.8
mt.in.‘ẓm.yšu.g h.|w yṣḥ.knp.nšrm.ybn.|b‘l.ybn.diy hmt nšrm.|tpr.w du.b nši.‘n h.w ypn.|yḥd.hrgb.ab.nšrm.|y 19[1AQHT].3.119
.l yṣa.b špt h.hwt[h].|knp.nšrm.b‘l.yṯbr.|b‘l.ṯbr.diy hmt.tqln.|tḥt.p‘n h.ybq‘.kbdt hm.w[yḥd].|in.šmt.in.‘ẓm.yš 19[1AQHT].3.115
m.yšu].|[g h.]w yṣḥ[.knp.nšrm].|b‘l.yṯb.b‘l.yṯb[r.diy.hmt].|tqln.tḥ p‘n y.ibq[‘.kbd hm.w] |aḥd.hm.iṯ.šmt.hm.i[ṯ] 19[1AQHT].3.108
.w [---].|y‘n.ym.l mt[.---].|l šrr.w t‘[n.‘ṯtrt.---].|b‘l m.hmt.[---].|l šrr.št[.---].|b riš h.[---].|ib h.mš[--.---].|[b]n.‘n h 2.4[68].36

hn

].|mlk h.l[nḫt.l kḥṯ].|drkt h[.---].|[---.]d[--.---].|[---].hn[.---].|[---.]šn[.---].|[---].pit.|[---.]qbat.|[---.]inšt.|[--]u.l 6[49].6.37
t‘nyn.ǵlm.b‘l.|in.b‘l.b bht ht.|il hd.b qrb.hkl h.|qšt hn.aḫd.b yd h.|w qṣ‘t h.bm.ymn h.|idk.l ytn pnm.|tk.aḫ.š 10[76].2.6
aṯt y.|n‘r y.ṯh.l pn.ib.|hn.hm.yrgm.mlk.|b‘l y.tmǵyy.hn.|alpm.ššwm.hnd.|w.mlk.b‘l y.bnš.|bnny.‘mn.|mlakty.h 1012.31
‘l y.bnš.|bnny.‘mn.|mlakty.hnd.|ylak ‘m y.|w.t‘l.ṯh.hn.|[a]lpm.ššwm.|[---].w.ṯb. 1012.37
--]š.l mdb.|[---] h.mḫlpt[.---.--]r.|[---.]n‘lm.[---].|[---].hn.al[-.---].|[---]t.bn[.---]. UG5.8.51
[---].|lb.ab[d k].al[.---].|[-]tm.iph.adt y.w.[---].|tšṣḥq.hn.aṯt.l.‘bd.|šb‘t.w.nṣp.ksp.|[-]tm.rb[.--.a]ḫd.|[---.--]t.b[-].| 1017.4
.ṯhrr.l išt.|w ṣḥrrt.l pḥmm.btm.bt.il.bt.il.|w ‘lm h.w hn.aṯtm.tṣḥn y.mt mt.|nḥtm.ḫṭ k.mmnnm.mṭ yd k.hl.‘ṣr.|t 23[52].46
qrt.dt.|[---.--]s‘.hn.mlk.|[---.l]qḥ.hn.l.ḥwt h.|[---.--]p.hn.ib.d.b.mgšḫ.|[---.i]b.hn[.w.]ht.ank.|[---.--]š[-.--].w.ašt.|[1012.10
lpm.š[šw]m.|rgmt.‘ly.ṯh.lm.|l.ytn.hm.mlk.[b]‘l y.|w.hn.ibm.ššq l y.|p.l.ašt.aṯt y.|n‘r y.ṯh.l pn.ib.|hn.hm.yrgm. 1012.27
--].k.ybt.mlk.|[---].w.ap.ank.|[---].l.ǵr.amn.|[---.-]ktt.hn.ib.|[---.]mlk.|[---.]adt y.td‘.|w.ap.mlk.uḏ[r].|[-]d‘.k.iḫd. 1012.17
tḥm.ml[k.---].|l.mlk.[---].|rg[m].|hn.i[---].|ds[-.---].|t[--.---].|a[--.---].|[---].ksp.‘m[.---].|[---.]i 2127.1.4
l gml.yrdt.|b ‘rgzm.b bz tdm.|lla y.‘m lẓpn i|l ḏ.pid.hn b p y sp|r hn.b špt y mn|t hn ṯlḫ h w mlg h y|ṯtqt ‘m h 24[77].45
rb‘t.zblnm.|mḫmšt.yitsp.|ršp.nṯdṯt.ǵlm.|ym.mšb‘t hn.b šlḥ.|ttpl.y‘n.ḥtk h.|krt y‘n.ḥtk h.rš.|mid.grdš.ṯbt h.| 14[KRT].1.20
‘rgzm.b bz tdm.|lla y.‘m lẓpn i|l ḏ.pid.hn b p y sp|r hn.b špt y mn|t hn ṯlḫ h w mlg h y|ṯtqt ‘m h b q‘t.|tq‘t ‘m 24[77].46
---].|mid.rm[.krt].|b tk.rpi.ar[ṣ].|b pḫr.qbṣ.dtn.|ṣǵrt hn.abkrn.|tbrk.ilm.tity.|tity.ilm.l ahl hm.|dr il.l mšknt hm 15[128].3.16
ǵy[.rpum.l grnt].|i[ln]y[m].l mṯ‘t[.---].|[-]m[.---].|h.hn bn k.hn[.---].|bn bn.aṯr k.hn[.---].|yd k.ṣǵr.tnšq.špt k.ṯ 22.2[124].2
|‘m k.mnm[.š]lm.|rgm.ṯṯ[b].|any kn.dt.|likt.mṣrm.|hn dt.b.ṣr.|mtt.by.|gšm.adr.|nškḥ.w.|rb.tmtt.|lqḥ.kl.ḏr‘.| 2059.12
-].|w.mlk.yštal.b.hn[--].|hmt.w.anyt.hm.t‘[rb].|mkr.hn d.w.rgm.ank[.--].|mlkt.ybqš.anyt.w.at[--].|w mkr n.mlk 2008.2.12
m.bṯn.y[--.-]ah.|ṯnm.tšqy msk.hwt.tšqy[.-.]w [---].|w hn dt.yṯb.l mspr. 19[1AQHT].5.1
n[--.---].|rg[m.---].|nǵṯ[.---].|d.yqḥ[.---].|hm.ṯn.[---].|hn dt.[---].|[-----].|[-----].|tḥm[.---].|l p‘n.b‘l y[.---].|qlt.|[-- 2064.6
]‘l y.|w.hn.ibm.ššq l y.|p.l.ašt.aṯt y.|n‘r y.ṯh.l pn.ib.|hn.hm.yrgm.mlk.|b‘l y.tmǵyy.hn.|alpm.ššwm.hnd.|w.mlk 1012.30
.|b.ḫbṯ h.ḥwt.ṯt h.|w.mnm.šalm.|dt.tknn.|‘l.‘rbnm.|hn hmt.|tknn.|mtn.bn.‘bdym.|ilrb.bn.ilyn.|‘bdadt.bn ‘bdk 1161.8
[---].ḫmš[m.ḥm]r.škm.|[---.ṯṯ.dd.]gdl.ṯṯ.dd.š‘rm.|[---.hn.w.al]p.kd.nbt.kd.šmn.mr.|[---].kmn.lṯḥ.sbbyn.|[---.-]‘t.lt 142[12].8
|[---.l]qḥ.hn.l.ḥwt h.|[---.--]p.hn.ib.d.b.mgšḫ.|[---.i]b.hn[.w.]ht.ank.|[---.--]š[-.--].w.ašt.|[---].amr k.|[---].k.ybt.ml 1012.11
n.mrkbt.dt.|‘rb.bt.mlk.|yd.apnt hn.|yd.ḥẓ hn.|yd.tr hn.|w.l.ṯt.mrkbtm.|inn.uṯpt.|w.ṯlṯ.ṣmdm.w.ḥrṣ.|apnt.b d.r 1121.5
ṯmn.mrkbt.dt.|‘rb.bt.mlk.|yd.apnt hn.|yd.ḥẓ hn.|yd.tr hn.|w.l.ṯt.mrkbtm.|inn.uṯpt.|w.ṯlṯ.ṣm 1121.3
ṯmn.mrkbt.dt.|‘rb.bt.mlk.|yd.apnt hn.|yd.ḥẓ hn.|yd.tr hn.|w.l.ṯt.mrkbtm.|inn.uṯpt.|w.ṯlṯ.ṣmdm.w.ḥrṣ.| 1121.4
š[r]yn.mḥmd.arz h.|tšt.išt.b bht m.|nb[l]at.b hkl m.|hn.ym.w ṯn.tikl.|išt.b bht m.nblat.|b hk[l] m.ṯlṯ.kb‘ ym.|ti 4[51].6.24
r.yšqy.]bn.qdš.yd.|[ṣt h.y‘l.]w yškb.yd.|[mizrt.]p ynl.hn.ym.|[w ṯn.uzr.]ilm.dnil.|[uzr.ilm.]ylḥm.uzr.|[yšqy.b]n. 17[2AQHT].1.6
.w iṯrm.|tšm‘.mṯt.ḥry.|tṭbḫ.imr.w lḥm.|mgṯ.w yṯrm.hn.ym.|w ṯn.yṯb.krt.l ‘d h.|yṯb.l ksi mlk.|l nḫt.l kḥṯ.drkt.| 16.6[127].21
y.alp.yṭbḫ.l kṯ|rt.yšlḥm.kṯrt.w y|ššq.bnt.[hl]l.snnt.|hn.ym.w ṯn.yšlḥm.|kṯrt.w yš[š]q.bnt.hl[l].|snnt.ṯlṯ[.r]b‘ ym 17[2AQHT].2.32
nm.yn.bld.|ǵll.yn.išryt.‘nq.smd.|lbnn.ṯl mrṯ.yḥrṯ.il.|hn.ym.w ṯn.tlḥmn.rpum.|tštyn.ṯlṯ.rb‘.ym.ḫmš.|ṯdṯ.ym.tlḥ 22.2[124].21
p.|l ‘brm.zt.ḫrṣ.l ‘brm.kš.|dpr.ṯlḥn.b q‘l.b q‘l.|mlkm.hn.ym.yṣq.yn.ṯmk.|mrṯ.yn.srnm.yn.bld.|ǵll.yn.išryt.‘nq.sm 22.2[124].17
.bṯd.|[---.b]šḥr.atlgn.|[---].b šḥr.|[---.]bn h.|[-]k[--]g hn.ksp. 2167.7
b].|ky.lik.bn y.|lḥt.akl.‘m y.|mid y w ǵbn y.|w.bn y.hn kt.|yškn.anyt.|ym.yšrr.|w.ak[l.---].|[--].š[--.--]. 2061.12
m[š].mat.kbd.|b d.tt.w.ṯlṯ.ktnt.b dm.tt.|w.ṯmnt.ksp.hn.|ktn.d.ṣr.pḥm.b h.w.ṯqlm.|ksp h.mitm.pḥm.b d.skn.|w. 1110.3
amṣ.|[---].nn.|[---.]qrt.dt.|[---.--]s‘.hn.mlk.|[---.l]qḥ.hn.l.ḥwt h.|[---.--]p.hn.ib.d.b.mgšḫ.|[---.i]b.hn[.w.]ht.ank.| 1012.9
t.ḫ[--.l k]|ṯrt.l bnt.hll[.snnt].|hl ǵlmt tld b[n.--]n.|‘n ha l yd h.tzd[.--].|pt l bšr h.dm a[--.--]ḥ.|w yn.k mtrḫt[.---] 24[77].8
m.hkl h.|y[tl]k.l lbnn.w ‘ṣ h.|l[šr]yn.mḥmd.arz h.|h[n.l]bnn.w ‘ṣ h.|š[r]yn.mḥmd.arz h.|tšt.išt.b bht m.|nb[l] 4[51].6.20
m.nǵr mdr‘[.iṯ.lḥm.---].|iṯ.yn.d ‘rb.bṯk[.---].|mǵ hw.l hn.lg yn h[.---].|w ḥbr h.mla yn.[---]. 23[52].75
št.|yn.tǵẓyt.špš.|rpim.tḥtk.|špš.tḥtk.ilnym.|‘d k.ilm.hn.mtm.|‘d k.kṯr m.ḥbr k.|w ḫss.d‘t k.|b ym.arš.w tnn.|kṯ 6.6[62.2].47
yšlm.|[---.]mlk n.amṣ.|[---].nn.|[---.]qrt.dt.|[---.--]s‘.hn.mlk.|[---.l]qḥ.hn.l.ḥwt h.|[---.--]p.hn.ib.d.b.mgšḫ.|[---.i] 1012.8
[---.]mat.|š[--].išal.|‘m k.ybl.šd.|a[--].d‘.k.|šld.ašld.|hn.mrṯ.d.štt.|ašld b ldt k. 2009.3.1
mṭpṭ.|w y‘ny.nn.|dtn.bt n.mḥ[-].|l dg.w [-]kl.|w aṯr.hn.mr[-]. UG5.6.16
.rgm.|tḥm.mlk.ṣr.aḫ k.|y[š]lm.l k.ilm.|tǵr k.tšlm k.|hn ny.‘m n.|šlm.ṯm ny.|‘m k.mnm[.š]lm.|rgm.ṯṯ[b].|any k 2059.6
.pgn.|l.mlk.ugrt.|rgm.|yšlm.l k.[il]m.|tǵr k.tšlm k.|hn ny.‘m n.š[l]m.|ṯm ny.‘[m.]bn y.|mnm.[šl]m[.r]gm[.ṯṯ]b]. 2061.6
d k.|l.p‘n.adt ny.|mrḥqtm.|qlny.ilm.|tǵr k.|tšlm k.|hn ny.‘m ny.|kll.mid.|šlm.|w.ap.ank.|nḫt.ṯm ny.|‘m.adt n 51[95].10
-.---].|[‘ṯ]trt w ‘nt[.---].|w b hm.tṯtb[.--]d h.|km trpa.hn n‘r.|d yšt.l.lṣb h ḫš‘r klb.|[w]riš.pqq.w šr h.|yšt.aḥd h. UG5.1.2.3
l ab.bn.il.ytši.l dr.|bn il.l mpḫrt.bn.il.l ṯkmn[.w]šnm.hn.‘r.|w.ṯb.l mspr.m[šr] mšr.bt.ugrt.w npy.gr.|ḥmyt.ugrt. 32[2].1.26
bn il.|ytši.l d[r.bn il.l]mpḫrt.bn il.|l ṯkm[n.w šnm.]hn ‘[r].|[---.]w npy[.---].|[---.]w npy.u[grt.---].|[---.--]y.ulp.[32[2].1.35
l h.|‘rb.b bt h.kṯrt.bnt.|hll.snnt.apnk.dnil.|mt.rpi.ap.hn.ǵzr.mt.|hrnmy.alp.yṭbḫ.l kṯ|rt.yšlḥm.kṯrt.w y|ššq.bnt.[17[2AQHT].2.28

n. | ašrb'.qṣ't.w hn šb['] . | b ymm.apnk.dnil.mt. | rpi.a hn.ǵzr.mt.hrnm[y]. | ytšu.yṯb.b ap.ṯǵr.tḥt. | adrm.d b grn.yd 17[2AQHT].5.5
rk.'l.aqht.k yq[--.---]. | pr'm.ṣd k.y bn[.---]. | pr'm.ṣd k.hn pr['.--]. | ṣd.b hkl h[.---]. | [------]. | [---.l]ḥm[.---]. | [---].ay š 17[2AQHT].5.38
ab.bn.il]. | ytši.l dr.bn.il.l mpḫrt.bn.i[l.l ṯkmn.w š]nm hn š. | w šqrb.'r.mšr mšr bn.ugrt.w [npy.---.]ugr. | w npy.ym 32[2].1.17
b.bn.il.ytši.l d]r.bn[.il]. | [l mpḫrt.bn.il.l ṯkmn.w šnm.hn š]. | [w šqrb.š.mšr mšr.bn.ugrt.w npy.---.]w npy. | [---.w n 32[2].1.3
b.bn.il]. | [ytši.l dr.bn.il.l mpḫ]rt.[bn.il.l ṯkmn.w šn]m hn š. | [---.w n]py.gr[.ḥmyt.ugrt.w np]y. | [---].w n[py.---].u t 32[2].1.9B
[-----]. | [---.]abl.qšt ṯmn. | ašrb'.qṣ't.w hn šb['] . | b ymm.apnk.dnil.mt. | rpi.a hn.ǵzr.mt.hrnm[y]. | yt 17[2AQHT].5.3
l.y'n.ḥtk h. | krt y'n.ḥtk h.rš. | mid.grdš.ṯbt h. | w b tm hn.šph.yitbd. | w b.pḫyr h.yrṯ. | y'rb.b ḥdr h.ybky. | b ṯn.[-]g 14[KRT].1.24
m.ymš. | ṯdṯ.ym.ḥẓ k.al.tš'l. | qrt h.abn.yd k. | mšdpt.w hn.špšm. | b šb'.w l.yšn.pbl. | mlk.l qr.ṯigt.ibr h. | l ql.nhqt.ḥ 14[KRT].3.118
]. | šu.'db.l špš.rbt.w l kbkbm.kn[-]. | yhbr.špt hm.yšq.hn.[š]pt hm.mtqtm. | bm.nšq.w hr.[b]ḥbq.w ḥ[m]ḥmt.yṯb[n 23[52].55
ḥmm.aṯtm.a[ṯt.il]. | aṯt.il.w 'lm h.yhbr.špt hm.yš[q]. | hn.špt hm.mtqtm.mtqtm.k lrmn[.--]. | bm.nšq.w hr.b ḥbq.ḥ 23[52].50
lla y.'m lẓpn i | l ḏ.pid.hn b p y sp | r hn.b špt y mn | t hn ṯlḫ h w mlg h y | ṯtqt 'm h b q't. | tq't 'm prbḫt. | dmqt ṣǵr 24[77].47
.]škb.w m[--.]mlakt. | [---.]'l.w tš'[d]n.npṣ h. | [---.]rgm.hn.[--]n.w aspt.[q]l h. | [---.rg]m.ank l[.--.--]rny. | [---.]ṯm.hw. 1002.49
m.l grnt]. | i[ln]y[m].l mṯ't[.---]. | [-]m[.---]. | h.hn bn k.hn[.---]. | bn bn.aṯr k.hn[.---]. | yd k.ṣǵr.tnšq.špt k.ṯm. | ṯkm.b 22.2[124].2
'ṣ.b d h.ydrm[.]pi[-.]adm. | [---.]iṯ[-].yšql.yṯk[.--]np bl.hn. | [---].ḥ[m]t.pṯr.w.p nḥš. | [---.--]q.n[ṯ]k.l yd'.l bn.l pq ḥm UG5.8.33
l mṯ't[.---]. | [-]m[.---]. | h.hn bn k.hn[.---]. | bn bn.aṯr k.hn[.---]. | yd k.ṣǵr.tnšq.špt k.ṯm. | ṯkm.bm ṯkm.aḫm.qym.il. | 22.2[124].3
.ḫmšm.ksp. | lqḥ.mlk.gbl. | lbš.anyt h. | b'rm.ksp. | mḫr.hn. 2106.18
ksp h.mitm.pḥm.b d.skn. | w.ṯt.ktnm.ḫmšt.w.nṣp.ksp.hn. 1110.6

hnd

l ym hnd. | iwr[k]l.pdy. | agdn.bn.nrgn. | w ynḥm.aḫ h. | w.b'ln aḫ 1006.1
.-]m[-]r. | [w.l.]bn h.'d. | ['l]m.mn k. | mn km l.yqḥ. | bt.hnd.b d. | ['b]dmlk. | [-]k.am'[--]. | [w.b] d.bn h[.']d 'lm. | [w.u 1009.14
dt brrt.ṣṯqšlm. | 'bd h.hnd. | w mn km.l yqḥ. | spr.mlk.hnd. | b yd.ṣṯqšlm. | 'd 'lm. 1005.13
. | mišmn.nqmd. | mlk ugrt. | nqmd.mlk.ugrt. | ktb.spr hnd. | dt brrt.ṣṯqšlm. | 'bd h.hnd. | w mn km.l yqḥ. | spr.mlk.h 1005.9
n.ib. | hn.hm.yrgm.mlk. | b'l y.tmǵyy.hn. | alpm.ššwm.hnd. | w.mlk.b'l y.bnš. | bnny.'mn. | mlakty.hnd. | ylak 'm y. | 1012.32
| nqmd.mlk.ugrt. | ktb.spr hnd. | dt brrt.ṣṯqšlm. | 'bd h.hnd. | w mn km.l yqḥ. | spr.mlk.hnd. | b yd.ṣṯqšlm. | 'd 'lm. 1005.11
lpm.ššwm.hnd. | w.mlk.b'l y.bnš. | bnny.'mn. | mlakty.hnd. | ylak 'm y. | w.t'l.ṯh.hn. | [a]lpm.ššwm. | [---].w.ṯb. 1012.35
l ym hnd. | 'mṯtmr.bn. | nqmp'.ml[k]. | ugrt.ytn. | šd.kḏǵdl[.bn]. | [-] 1008.1
l ym.hnd. | 'mṯtmr. | bn.nqmp'. | mlk.ugrt. | ytn.bt.annḏr. | bn.ytn.b 1009.1

hnk

.ap.mlk.uḏ[r]. | [-]d'.k.iḫd.[---]. | w.mlk.b'l y. | lm.škn.hnk. | l 'bd h.alpm.š[šw]m. | rgmt.'ly.ṯh.lm. | l.ytn.hm.mlk.[b 1012.23

hnn

[---.--]y.hnn. | [---.kll].šlm. | [---.ṯ]mn.'m k. | [m]nm.šlm. | [---.w.r]gm.ṯ 2171.1

hpk

[.---]. | dm.mt.aṣḥ[.---]. | ydd.b qr[b.---]. | al.ašt.b[---]. | ahpk k.l[--.---]. | ṯmm.w lk[.---]. | w lk.ilm[.---]. | n'm.ilm[.---]. 5[67].3.12
'm.aliyn.b'l. | ik.al.yšm['] k.ṯr. | il.ab k.l ys'.alt. | ṯbt k.l yhpk.ksa.mlk k. | l yṯbr.ḫṭ.mṯpṭ k. | yru.bn ilm t.ṯt'.y | dd.il.ǵ 6[49].6.28
]pṯ[.n]hr. | [ik.a]l.yšm' k.ṯr.[i]l.ab k.l ys'.[alt.]ṯ[bt | k.l y]hpk. | [ksa.]mlk k.l yṯbr.ḫṭ.mṯpṭ k.w y'n[.'ṯtr].dm[-]k[-]. | [
]b.p'r. | yd h[.--.]ṣ'r.glgl. | a[---]m.rḥ.ḫd '[r]pt. | gl[.---.]yhpk.m[---]m. | s'[--.]k[--]t. 13[6].35

hrg

---]. | [---.r]ḫm.tld. | [---.]ḫrm.ṯn.ym. | tš[.---.]ymm.lk. | hrg.ar[b'.]ymm.bṣr. | kp.ššk k.[--].l ḥbš k. | 'tk.ri[š.]l mhr k. | 13[6].5

hrgb

'l.ybn.diy hmt nšrm. | tpr.w du.b nši.'n h.w ypn. | yḥd.hrgb.ab.nšrm. | yšu.g h.w yṣḥ.knp.hr[g]b. | b'l.yṯb.b'l.y[ṯb]r. 19[1AQHT].3.121
'.kbd h.w yḥd. | [i]n.šmt.in.'ẓm.yšu.g[h]. | w yṣḥ.knp.hrgb.b'l.ybn. | [b]'l.ybn.diy.hwt.hrg[b]. | tpr.w du.b nši.'n h. | 19[1AQHT].3.132
št.b ḫrt. | i[lm.arṣ.b p h.rgm.l yṣa.b šp]|t h.hwt h.knp.hrgb.b'l.ṯbr. | b'l.ṯbr.diy.hwt.w yql. | tḥt.p'n h.ybq'.kbd h.w 19[1AQHT].3.128
ši.'n h.w ypn. | yḥd.hrgb.ab.nšrm. | yšu.g h.w yṣḥ.knp.hr[g]b. | b'l.yṯb.b'l.y[ṯb]r.diy[.h]wt. | w yql.tḥt.p'n y.ibq'.kbd 19[1AQHT].3.122
.yšu.g[h]. | w yṣḥ.knp.hrgb.b'l.ybn. | [b]'l.ybn.diy.hwt.hrg[b]. | tpr.w du.b nši.'n h. | [w]yphn.yḥd.ṣml.um.nšrm. | yš 19[1AQHT].3.133

hry

[-]. | yhbr.špt hm.yšq.hn.[š]pt hm.mtqtm. | bm.nšq.w hr.[b]ḥbq.w ḥ[m]ḥmt.yṯb[n]. | yspr.l ḫmš.l ṣ[---.]šr.pḫr.klat 23[52].56
[q]. | hn.špt hm.mtqtm.mtqtm.k lrmn[.--]. | bm.nšq.w hr.b ḥbq.ḥmḥmt.tqt[nṣn]. | tldn.šḥr.w šlm.rgm.l il.ybl.a[ṯt y 23[52].51
m.. | rkm.agzrt[.--].arḫ.. | b'l.azrt.'nt.[-]ld. | kbd h.l yd' hr h.[---]d[-]. | tnq[.---.]in[b]b.p'r. | yd h[.--.]ṣ'r.glgl. | a[---]m. 13[6].31
mmt.škb. | 'mn h.šb'.l šb'm. | tš[']ly.ṯmn.l ṯmnym. | w [th]rn.w tldn mṯ. | al[iyn.b']l šlbšn. | i[---.---.--]l h.mǵẓ. | y[--.-- 5[67].5.22
tiḫd.b uš[k.--]. | [-.b]'l.yabd.l alp. | [---.bt]lt.'nt. | [---]q.hry.w yld. | [---]m.ḥbl.kt[r]t. | [---.bt]lt.'nt. | [---.ali]yn.b'l. | [--- 11[132].1.5
----]. | [---.]d arṣ. | [---.]ln. | [---.]nb hm. | [---.-]kn. | [---.]hr n.km.šḥr. | [---.y]lt n.km.qdm. | [-.k]bd n.il.ab n. | kbd k iš. 12[75].1.7
. | atlg. | gb'ly. | ulm. | m'rby. | m'r. | arny. | š'rt. | ḫlbrpš. | hry. | qmṣ. | ṣ'q. | qmy. | ḫlbkrd. | y'rt. | uškn. | 'nqpat. | ilštm'. | š 2074.13

hrm

ṯ]r w ḫss.y[i]sp.ḥmt.šḥr.w šlm. | [yis]p.ḥmt.isp.[šp]š l hrm.ǵrpl.'l arṣ. | [l a]n ḥmt.l p[.n]ṯk.abd.l p.akl ṯm.dl. | [---.q UG5.8.19
.ak[l]. | [ṯm.dl.]isp.ḥ[mt.---.-]hm.yasp.ḥmt. | [---.š]pš.l [hrm.ǵrpl].'l.arṣ.l an. | [ḥ]mt.i[l.w] ḥrn.yisp.ḥmt. | [b'l.w]dgn UG5.8.12
h.ḫ[--.---.šp]š.l hrm. | [ǵrpl.]'l.ar[ṣ.---.ḥ]mt. | [---.šp]š.l [hrm.ǵ]rpl.'l.arṣ. | [---.]ḥmt.l p[.nṯ]k.abd.l p.ak[l]. | [ṯm.dl.]isp UG5.8.9
[--.---.-]lk. | [-]sr.n[--.---.]ḥrn. | [--]p.ḫp h.ḫ[--.---.šp]š.l hrm. | [ǵrpl.]'l.ar[ṣ.---.ḥ]mt. | [---.šp]š.l [hrm.ǵ]rpl.'l.arṣ. | [---. UG5.8.7
[---.]btlt.'nt. | [---.]pp.hrm. | [---].d l yd' bn il. | [---.]pḫr kkbm. | [---.]dr dt.šmm. | [-- 10[76].1.2

hrn

]ṯr.w ẖ[ss.t]b'.b[n.]bht.ym[.rm]m.hkl.ṯpṭ nh[r]. | [---.]hrn.w[---.]tb'.k[ṯ]r w [ẖss.t]bn.bht zbl ym. | [trm]m.hk[l.ṯpṭ 2.3[129].8

hrnmy

h.kṯrt.bnt. | hll.snnt.apnk.dnil. | mt.rpi.ap.hn.ǵzr.mt. | hrnmy.alp.yṯbḫ.l kṯ | rt.yšlḥm.kṯrt.w y | ššq.bnt.[hl]l.snnt. | h 17[2AQHT].2.29
bm.lb. | tdm'.bm.kbd. | tmz'.kst.dnil.mt. | rpi.al.ǵzr.mt.hrnmy. | apnk.dnil.mt. | rpi.yṣly.'rpt.b | ḥm.un.yr.'rpt. | tmṭr. 19[1AQHT].1.37
[-----.apnk]. | [dnil.mt.rp]i.apn.ǵz[r]. | [mt.hrnmy.]uzr.ilm.ylḥm. | [uzr.yšqy.]bn.qdš.yd. | [ṣt h.y'l.]w yš 17[2AQHT].1.3
št.ybln.hl.yš | rb'.qṣ't.apnk.dnil. | mt.rpi.aphn.ǵzr.mt. | hrnmy.gm.l aṯt h.k yṣḥ. | šm'.mṯt.dnty.'d[b]. | imr.b pḫd.l np 17[2AQHT].5.15
tm.bl. | ṯbn.ql.b'l.k tmz'. | kst.dnil.mt.rpi. | all.ǵzr.m[t.]hr[nmy]. | gm.l bt[h.dnil.k yṣḥ]. | šm'.pǵt.ṯkmt[.my]. | ḥspt.l 19[1AQHT].1.48
]yqrb.b'l.b ḥnt h.abynt. | [d]nil.mt.rpi anḫ.ǵzr. | [mt.]hrnmy.d in.bn.l h. | km.aḫ h.w šrš.km.ary h. | bl.iṯ.bn.l h.km 17[2AQHT].1.19
t.mym. | qrym.ab.dbḥ.l ilm. | š'ly.dǵṯ h.b šmym. | dǵṯ.hrnmy.d kbkbm. | l tbrkn.alk brkt. | tmrn.alk.nmr[rt]. | imḫṣ. 19[1AQHT].4.193
ẓr y pẓǵm.ǵr.w yq. | dbḥ.ilm.yš'ly.dǵṯ h. | b šmym.dǵṯ hrnmy[.d k] | bkbm.'[l.---]. | [-]l h.yd 'd[.---]. | ltm.mrqdm.d š 19[1AQHT].4.186
rṯ. | [--.y]iḫd.il.'bd h.ybrk. | [dni]l mt rpi.ymr.ǵzr. | [mt.hr]nmy npš.yḥ.dnil. | [mt.rp]i.brlt.ǵzr.mt hrnmy. | [---].hw. 17[2AQHT].1.37
t.r[pi.mk].b šb'. | šnt.w y'n[.dnil.mt.]rpi. | yṯb.ǵzr.m[t.hrnmy.y]šu. | g h.w yṣḥ.t[b'.---]. | bkyt.b hk[l]y.mšspdt. | b ḥ 19[1AQHT].4.181
ṣ't.w hn šb['']. | b ymm.apnk.dnil.mt. | rpi.a hn.ǵzr.mt.hrnm[y]. | ytšu.yṯb.b ap.ṯǵr.ṯḥt. | adrm.d b grn.ydn. | dn.alm 17[2AQHT].5.5
[bl].šblt. | b ǵlp h.apnk.dnil. | [m]t.rpi.ap[h]n.ǵzr. | [mt.hrn]my.ytšu. | [yṯb.b ap.ṯ]ǵr[.t]ḥt. | [adrm.d b grn.y]dn. | [dn. 19[1AQHT].1.21
yn.tb'.l mš | knt h.apnk.dnil.m[t]. | rpi.aphn.ǵzr.m[t]. | hrnmy.qšt.yqb.[--] | rk.'l.aqht.k yq[--.---]. | pr'm.ṣd k.y bn[.-- 17[2AQHT].5.35
.l grnt.i[lnym.l] | mṭ't.w y'n.dnil.[mt.rpi]. | yṯb.ǵzr.mt hrnmy[.---]. | b grnt.ilm.b qrb.m[ṭ't.ilnym]. | d tit.yspi.spu.q[20[121].2.8
r.ǵzr. | [mt.hr]nmy npš.yḥ.dnil. | [mt.rp]i.brlt.ǵzr.mt hrnmy. | [---].hw.mḫ.l 'rš h.y'l. | [---].bm.nšq.aṯt h. | [---.]b ḥb 17[2AQHT].1.38

hrr

y.aklm. | w ymẓa.'qqm. | b'l.ḥmd m.yḥmd m. | bn.dgn.yhrr m. | b'l.ngṯ hm.b p'n h. | w il hd.b ẖrẓ' h. | [-----]. | [--]t.[- 12[75].1.39
| b'l.n[--.---]. | il.hd[.---]. | at.bl[.at.---]. | ḥmd m.[---]. | il.hr[r.---]. | kb[-.---]. | ym.[---]. | yšḥr[.---]. | yikl[.---]. | km.s[--.--- 12[75].2.10

hrt

any.al[ṯy]. | d b atlg[.---]. | ẖmš 'š[r]. | kkr.ṯ[lt]. | ṯt hrt[m]. | ṯn mq[pm]. | ulṯ.ṯl[t]. | krk.kly[.--]. | ẖmš.mr[kbt]. | ṯṯ 2056.5

ht

tb' ank. | 'm mlakt h šm' h. | w b.'ly skn.yd' rgm h. | w ht ab y ǵm[--]. | t[--.---]. | ls[--.---]. | ṣḥ[.---]. | ky.m[--.---]. | w p 1021.9
y. | bn y.yšal. | ṯryl.p rgm. | l mlk.šm y. | w l h.y'l m. | w h[t] aḫ y. | bn y.yšal. | ṯryl.w rgm[.-]. | ṯṯb.l aḫ k. | l adn k. 138.15
. | tšlm k. | ik y.lḥt. | spr.d likt. | 'm.ṯryl. | mh y.rgmt. | w ht.aḫ y. | bn y.yšal. | ṯryl.p rgm. | l mlk.šm y. | w l h[-] y'l m. | 138.10
. | tšlm k. | iky.lḥt. | spr.d likt. | 'm.ṯryl. | mh y.rgmt. | w ht.aḫ y. | bn y.yšal. | ṯryl.p rgm. | l mlk.šm y. | w l h.y'l m. | w 138.10
ḥ.hn.l.ḥwt h. | [---.--]p.hn.ib.d.b.mgšḫ. | [---.i]b.hn[.w.]ht.ank. | [---.--]š[-.--].w.ašt. | [---].amr k. | [---].k.ybt.mlk. | [---] 1012.11
.--]y.ns[--.---]. | [---.]trgm[.-----]. | [---.]alp.p[--.---]. | [--.]ht.ap[.---]. | [---.]iln[--.---]. 63[26].2.4
bn.qrrn. | bn.dnt. | bn.ṯ'l[-]. | bdl.ar.dt.inn. | mhr l ht. | artyn. | 'dmlk. | bn.alt[-]. | iḫy[-]. | 'bdgṯr. | ḥrr. | bn.s[-]p[-]. 1035.1.5
| il.thbr.w tql. | tštḥwy.w tkbdn h. | tšu.g h.w tṣḥ.tšmḫ ht. | aṯrt.w bn h.ilt.w ṣb | rt.ary h.k mt.aliyn. | b'l.k ḫlq.zbl.b'l 6.1.39[49.1.11]
---]. | w [--].brt.lb[--.---]. | u[-]šhr.nuš[-.---]. | b [u]grt.w ht.a[--]. | w hm.at.trg[m.---]. | w sip.u hw[.---]. | w ank.u šbt[- 54.1.7[13.1.4]
bl.ym.w 'n.kṯr.w ẖss.l rgmt. | l k.l zbl.b'l.ṯnt.l rkb.'rpt.ht.ib k. | b'l m.ht.ib k.tmḫṣ.ht.tṣmt.ṣrt k. | tqḥ.mlk.'lm k.drk 2.4[68].8
.w ẖss.l rgmt. | l k.l zbl.b'l.ṯnt.l rkb.'rpt.ht.ib k. | b'l m.ht.ib k.tmḫṣ.ht.tṣmt.ṣrt k. | tqḥ.mlk.'lm k.drkt.dt dr dr k. | k 2.4[68].9
ṯr h].l tdd.ilnym. | [---.m]rz'y.apnnk.yrp. | [---.]km.r'y.ht.alk. | [---.]ṯlṯt.amǵy.l bt. | [y.---.b qrb].hkl y.w y'n.il. | [---. 21[122].1.6
lsy. | rgm. | yšlm.l k. | l.trǵds. | w.l.klby. | šm't.ẖti. | nḫtu.ht. | hm.in mm. | nḫtu.w.lak. | 'm y.w.yd. | ilm.p.k mtm. | 'z.m 53[54].8
ḥ.y l k.qrt.ablm. | d 'l k.mḫṣ.aqht.ǵzr. | 'wrt.yšt k.b'l.l ht. | w 'lm h.l 'nt.p dr.dr. | 'db.uḫry.mṭ.yd h. | dnil.bt h.ymǵy 19[1AQHT].4.167
-.]w[.---]. | w hm.at.tr[gm.---]. | w.drm.'tr[--.---]. | w ap.ht.k[--.]škn. | w.mṯnn[.---.]'mn k. | [-]štš.[---.]rgm y. | [-]wd.r[54.1.20[13.2.5]
l yblt.ẖbṯm. | ap ksp hm. | l yblt. | w ht.luk 'm ml[kt]. | tǵsdb.šmlšn. | w tb' ank. | 'm mlakt h šm' 1021.4
hm.w.rgm.hw.al[--]. | atn.ksp.l hm.'d. | ilak.'m.mlk. | ht.lik[t.--.]mlk[.--]. | w.mlk.yštal.b.hn[--]. | hmt.w.anyt.hm.t' 2008.2.9
[mr]ḥqtm. | qlt. | 'bd k.b. | lwsnd. | [w] b ṣr. | 'm.mlk. | w.ht. | mlk.syr. | ns.w.ṯm. | ydbḥ. | mlǵ[.---]. | w.m[--.--]y. | y[--.--- 2063.13
šlm.l k.ilm. | ṯǵr k.tšlm k. | lḥt.šlm.k.lik[t]. | um y.'m y.ht.'m[ny]. | kll.šlm.ṯm ny. | 'm.um y.mnm.šlm. | w.rgm.ṯṯb.l 2009.1.6
.mtm.amt. | [ap.m]ṯn.rgmm.argm.qštm. | [----.]mhrm.ht.tṣdn.tinṯt. | [---]m.tṣḥq.'nt.w b lb.tqny. | [---.]ṯb l y.l aqht.ǵ 17[2AQHT].6.40
. | l k.l zbl.b'l.ṯnt.l rkb.'rpt.ht.ib k. | b'l m.ht.ib k.tmḫṣ.ht.tṣmt.ṣrt k. | tqḥ.mlk.'lm k.drkt.dt dr dr k. | kṯr ṣmdm.ynḥ 2.4[68].9
.lm. | [---.š]d.gṯr. | [--]ḥ[d].šd.hwt. | [--.]iḫd.šd.gṯr. | [w]ht.yšm'.uḫ y. | l g y.w yhbṭ.bnš. | w ytn.ilm.b d hm. | b d.iḫq 55[18].17
lm]. | w.rgm[.ṯṯb.l] y. | hl ny.'mn. | mlk.b.ṯy ndr. | iṯt.w.ht. | [-]sny.udr h. | w.hm.ḫt. | 'l.w.likt. | 'm k.w.hm. | l.'l.w.lak 1013.14
. | w prt.tkt.[---]. | šnt.[---]. | ššw.'ṯtrt.w ššw.'[nt.---]. | w ht.[--]k.ššw[.-]rym[.---]. | d ymǵy.bnš[.---]. | w ḥmr[.---]. | w 2158.1.7
[.---.]uk.ngr. | w.[---].adny.l.yḫsr. | w.[ank.yd]'.l.yd't. | h[t.---.]l.špš.b'l k. | '[--.s]glt h.at. | ht[.---.]špš.b'l k. | yd'm.l.yd 2060.11
| w.[ank.yd]'.l.yd't. | h[t.---.]l.špš.b'l k. | '[--.s]glt h.at. | ht[.---.]špš.b'l k. | yd'm.l.yd't. | 'm y.špš.b'l k. | šnt.šntm.lm.l. 2060.13

W

w

[-----].|w.[-----].|w.abǵl.nḫ[l h.--].|w.unṯ.aḫd.l h[.---].|dnn.bn.yṣr[.---].|sln.b 90[314].1.3
.|[-]n.y'rtym.|gmm.w.bn.p[--].|trn.w.p[-]y.|bn.b'yn.w.agytn.|[---] gnym.|[--]ry.w ary.|[---]ǵrbtym.|[---.]w šb'l. 131[309].12
[--]ǵyn.b[n.---].|krwn.b[n.---].|tgyn.m'[---].|w.agpṯn[.---].|ṯyndr[-.---].|gt.tg[yn.---].|pwn[.---]. 103[334].4
t.|w ǵlm.l 'bd.il.|krt.yḫt.w ḥlm.|'bd.il.w hdrt.|yrtḥṣ.w yadm.|yrḥṣ.yd h.amt h.|uṣb't h.'d.ṯkm.|'rb.b ẓl.ḫmt.lqḥ 14[KRT].3.156
'n].ṯr.ab h.il.|d[--].b bk.krt.|b dm'.n'mn.ǵlm.|il.trḥṣ.w tadm.|rḥṣ[.y]d k.amt.|uṣb['t k.]'d[.ṯ]km.|'rb[.b ẓl.ḫmt].| 14[KRT].2.62
bn.b'ln.biry.|ṯlṯ.b'lm.|w.adn hm.ṯr.w.arb'.bnt h.|yrḫm.yd.ṯn.bn h.|b'lm.w.ṯlṯ.n'r 2080.3
ṯlṯ.alp.ṣpr.dt.aḥd.|ḥrṯ h.aḥd.b gt.nḫl.|aḥd.b gt.knpy.w.aḥd.b gt.ṯrmn.|aḥd.alp.idṯn.d aḥd.b.'nqpat.|[aḥd.al]p.d 1129.10
'rm.w.bt.aḥt.|bn.lwn.ṯlṯtm.b'lm.|bn.b'ly.ṯlṯtm.b'lm.|w.aḥd.ḫbṯ.|w.arb'.aṯt.|bn.lg.ṯn.bn h.|b'lm.w.aḫt h.|b.šrt.| 2080.8
ṣm.l k.|arb'.'ṣm.|'l.ar.|w.ṯlṯ.|'l.ubr'y.|w.ṯn.'l.|mlk.|w.aḥd.|'l atlg.|w l.'ṣm.|tspr.|nrn.al.tud|ad.at.l hm.|ṯṯm.k 1010.15
.iḫ y.|w.ap.ank.mnm.|[ḫ]s[r]t.w.uḫ y.|[y]'msn.ṯmn.|w.[u]ḫ y.al yb'rn. 2065.21
b.tmtt.lqḥt.|w.ṯṯb.ank.l hm.|w.any k.ṯt.|by.'ky.'ryt.|w.aḫ y.mhk.|b lb h.al.yšt. 2059.26
.|d ḫsrt.w.ank.|aštn..l.iḫ y.|w.ap.ank.mnm.|[ḫ]s[r]t.w.uḫ y.|[y]'msn.ṯmn.|w.[u]ḫ y.al yb'rn. 2065.19
[--].yṯkḥ.w yiḫd.b qrb[.-].|[--.t]ṯkḥ.w tiḫd.b uš[k.--].|[-.b]'l.yabd.l alp.|[---.bt]lt.'nt.|[---]q.hry. 11[132].1.2
[--].yṯkḥ.w yiḫd.b qrb[.-].|[--.t]ṯkḥ.w tiḫd.b uš[k.--].|[-.b]'l.yabd.l al 11[132].1.1
mn iṯr hw.|p iḫdn gnryn.|im mlkytn yrgm.|aḫnnn.|w iḫd. 1020.10
tm.b'lm.|w.aḥd.ḫbṯ.|w.arb'.aṯt.|bn.lg.ṯn.bn h.|b'lm.w.aḫt h.|b.šrt.|šty.w.bn h. 2080.11
.ṯṯm.|[---.]dyn.ḫmšt.'šrt.|[---.-]til.ḫmšt.l 'šrm.|[--.-]n.w.aḫt h.arb'm.|[--.-]dn.'šrm.|[--.-]dwn.ṯlṯm.w.šb'.alpm.|[k 2054.2.21
l um y.adt ny.|rgm.|ṯhm.tlmyn.|w.aḫtmlk 'bd k.|l.p'n.adt ny.|mrḥqtm.|qlny.ilm.|tǵr k.|tš 51[95].4
m[.---.]yd h.k šr.|knr.uṣb't h ḫrṣ.abn.|p h.tiḫd.šnt h.w akl.bqmm.|tšt ḫrṣ.k lb ilnm.|w ṯn.gprm.mn gpr h.šr.|aq 19[1AQHT].1.9
|mid y w ǵbn y.|w.bn y.hn kt.|yškn.anyt.|ym.yšrr.|w.ak[l.---].|[--].š[--.--]. 2061.15
.dt.|w ytnnn.|l aḫ h.l r' h.|r' 'lm.|ttn.w tn.|w l ttn.|w al ttn.|tn ks yn.|w ištn.|'bd.prt.ṯhm.|qrq.pt.ḏmn.|l ittl. 1019.1.14
.|l pn.špš.|w pn.špš.nr.|b y.mid.w um.|tšmḫ.m ab.|w al.trḫln.|'tn.ḫrd.ank.|'m ny.šlm.|kll.|w mnm.|šlm 'm.| 1015.12
w.a[ṯt h].|wšṯn.bn h.|ṯmgdl.ykn'my.w.aṯt h.|w.bn h.w.alp.aḥ[d].|aǵltn.[--]y.w[.aṯt h].|w.bn h.w.alp.w.[---].|[-]l 1080.6
tn.ṯn[.---].|w.ṯlṯ.alp h.[---].|swn.qrty.w.[b]n h[.---].|w.alp h.w.a[r]b'.l.arb'[m.---].|pln.ṯmry.w.ṯn.bn h.w[.---].|y 2044.7
šnpt.il š.|l 'nt.ḥl š.ṯn šm.|l gṯrm.ǵṣ b šmal.|d alpm.w alp w š.|šrp.w šlmm kmm.|l b'l.ṣpn b 'r'r.|pamt ṯlṯm š l UG5.13.27
.alpm.|[w.]ṯlṯm.ṣin.|anndr.ykn'my.|w.aṯt h.w.bn h.|w.alp.w.tš['.]ṣin. 1080.17
[-]ḏmu.apsty.b[--].|w.bn h.w aṯt h.w.alp.w ṯmn.ṣin.|[-]dln.qmnzy.w.a[ṯt h].|wšṯn.bn h.|ṯmgdl 1080.2
h.|w.bn h.w.alp.aḥ[d].|aǵltn.[--]y.w[.aṯt h].|w.bn h.w.alp.w.[---].|[-]ln.[---].|w.ṯn.bn [h.---].|[--]d m'qby[.---].|s 1080.8
].ḫmš[m.ḥm]r.škm.|[---.ṯṯ.dd.]gdl.ṯṯ.dd.š'rm.|[---.hn.w.al]p.kd.nbt.kd.šmn.mr.|[---].kmn.lṯḥ.sbbyn.|[---.-]'t.lṯḥ.š 142[12].8
[---.]ṯṯ.dd.gdl.ṯṯ.dd.š'rm.|[---.-]hn.w.alp.kd.nbt.kd.šmn.mr.|[---.]arb'.mat.ḫswn.lṯḥ.aqhr.|[---. 142[12].2
y[---.---].|t.k[-]ml.[---].|l[---].w y[nt.qrt.---].|[---.--]n[.w alp.l il.w bu]|[rm.---.ytk.gdlt.ilhm].|tkmn.w [šnm.dqt.rš APP.II[173].12
.[']lm.y'[--.---].|[--.-]g[-.-]s w [---].|w yn[t.q]rt.y[---].|w al[p.l]il.w bu[rm.---].|ytk.gdlt.ilhm.[tkmn.w šnm].|dqt.r 35[3].11
[---.--]ṯ.slḫ.npš.ṯ' w[.--.k]bdm.|[---.--]mm.ṯn.šm.w alp.l[--]n.|[---.]š.il š.b'l š.dgn š.|[---.--]r.w tt pl.gdlt.[ṣ]pn. 36[9].1.2
arb'm.qšt.|alp ḥẓm.w alp.|nṯq.ṯn.ql'm.|ḫmš.ṣmdm.w ḫrṣ.|tryn.ššwm.|tryn.aḥ 1123.2
ṯr[.il.ab -.w t'n.rbt].|aṯr[t.ym.šm'.l qdš].|w am[rr.l dgy.rbt].|aṯrt.ym[.mdl.'r].|ṣmd.pḥl[.št.gpnm.dt]. 4[51].4.3
.dt].|ksp.dt.yr[q.nqbnm].|'db.gpn.atnt[y].|yšm'.qd.w amr[r].|mdl.'r.ṣmd.pḥl.|št.gpnm.dt.ksp.|dt.yrq.nqbnm. 4[51].4.8
nm.dt.ksp.|dt.yrq.nqbnm.|'db.gpn.atnt h.|yḥbq.qdš.w amrr.|yštn.aṯrt.l bmt.'r.|l ysmsmt.bmt.pḥl.|qdš.yuḫdm. 4[51].4.13
].|mrmnmn.|brrn aryn.|a[-]ḫn tlyn.|atdb w 'r.|qdš w amrr.|ṯḥr w bd.|[k]ṯr ḫss šlm.|šlm il bt.|šlm il ḫš[t].|ršp UG5.7.71
.btlt.['nt].|[tšu.]g h.w tṣḥ.šm'.m['.l a]|[qht.ǵ]zr.at.aḫ.w an.a[ḫt k].|[---].šb'.ṯir k.[---].|[---.]ab y.ndt.ank[.---].|[---. 18[3AQHT].1.24
.aṯryt.spsg.ysk.|[l]riš.ḫrṣ.l ẓr.qdqd y.|[--.]mt.kl.amt.w an.mtm.amt.|[ap.m]ṯn.rgmm.argm.qštm.|[----.]mhrm.ht 17[2AQHT].6.38
š[d]m.ap.mṯn.rgmm.|argmn.lk.lk.'nn.ilm.|atm.bštm.w an.šnt.|uǵr.l rḥq.ilm.inbb.|l rḥq.ilnym.ṯn.mṯpdm.|ṯḥt.'n 3['NT].4.77
b[ǵy h.---].|w y'n.kṯr.w ḫss[.lk.lk.'nn.ilm.]|atm.bštm.w an[.šnt.kpṯr].|l rḥq.ilm.ḥkp[t.l rḥq.ilnym].|ṯn.mṯpdm.ṯḥt 1['NT.IX].3.18
[-]p[-]l[.---].|k lli.[---].|kpr.[šb'.bnt.rḥ.gdm.w anhbm].|w tqr[y.ǵlmm.b št.ǵr.---].|[']d tš[b'.tmtḫṣ.---].| 7.2[130].3
ib[ǵy h.---].|[-].l y'mdn.i[---.---].|kpr.šb' bn[t.rḥ.gdm.w anhbm].|kla[t.ṯǵ]r[t.bht.'nt.w tqry.ǵlmm.b št.ǵr].|ap 'nt 7.2[130].23
n[--.---.-]š[--].|kpr.šb'.bnt.rḥ.gdm.|w anhbm.klat.ṯǵrt.|bht.'nt.w tqry.ǵlmm.|b št.ǵr.w hln.'nt.t 3['NT].2.3
.mlk.|ht.lik[t.--.]mlk[.--].|w.mlk.yštal.b.hn[--].|hmt.w.anyt.hm.t'[rb].|mkr.hn d.w.rgm.ank[.--].|mlkt.ybqš.anyt 2008.2.11
]pš[.-].|w [k]l hm.b d.|rb.tmtt.lqḥt.|w.ṯṯb.ank.l hm.|w.any k.ṯt.|by.'ky.'ryt.|w.aḫ y.mhk.|b lb h.al.yšt. 2059.24
]grt.w ht.a[--].|w hm.at.trg[m.---].|w sip.u hw[.---].|w ank.u šbt[--.---].|ank.n[--]n[.---].|kst.l[--.---].|w.hw.uy.'n 54.1.10[13.1.7]
rq.d l.td'.šmm.|rgm l td'.nšm.w l tbn.|hmlt.arṣ.at m.w ank.|ibǵy h.b tk.ǵr y.il.ṣpn.|b qdš.b ǵr.nḥlt y.|b n'm.b g 3['NT].3.25
.ar]ṣ.|thmt.['mn.kbkbm.abn.brq].|d l t[d'.šmm.at m.w ank].|ibǵ[y h.b tk.ǵ]r y.il.ṣpn.|b q[dš.b ǵr.nḥ]lt y.|w t['n 3['NT].4.62
t.'mn.kbkbm].|rgm.l td'.nš[m.w l tbn.hmlt.arṣ].|at.w ank.ib[ǵy h.---].|w y'n.kṯr.w ḫss[.lk.lk.'nn.ilm.]|atm.bšt 1['NT.IX].3.16
'm.arṣ.thmt].|'m kbkbm[.abn.brq.d l td'.šmm.at m].|w ank.ib[ǵy h.---].|[-].l y'mdn.i[---.---].|kpr.šb' bn[t.rḥ.gdm 7.2[130].21
.[---.]sglt h.hw.|w.b[.---.]uk.nǵr.|w.[---].adny.l.yḫsr.|w.[ank.yd]'.l.yd't.|h[t.---.]l.špš.b'l k.|'[--.s]glt h.at.|ht[.---.] 2060.10
by.|gšm.adr.|nškḥ.w.|rb.tmtt.|lqḥ.kl.ḏr'.|b d a[-]m.w.ank.|k[l.]ḏr' hm.|[--.n]pš[.-].|w [k]l hm.b d.|rb.tmtt.lqḥ 2059.18
t.ṭpṭ.nhr.|šu.ilm.rašt km.l ẓr.brkt km.ln.kḥṯ.|zbl km.w ank.'ny.mlak.ym.t'dt.ṭpṭ.nhr.|tšu ilm rašt hm.l ẓr.brkt h 2.1[137].28
.--]y.|in m.'bd k hwt.|[y]rš.'m y.|mnm.iršt k.|d ḫsrt.w.ank.|aštn..l.iḫ y.|w.ap.ank.mnm.|[ḫ]s[r]t.w.uḫ y.|[y]'ms 2065.16
.b['l y.---].|[-----].|r[--.---].|b.[---.mlk].|rb[.b'l y.---].|w.an[k.---].|arš[.---].|mlk.r[b.b']l y.p.l.|ḥy.np[š.a]rš.|l.pn.b 1018.15
.arb'[m.---].|pln.ṯmry.w.ṯn.bn h.w[.---].|ymrn.apsny.w.aṯt h..b[n.---].|prd.m'qby[.w.---.a]ṯt h[.---].|prṭ.mgd[ly.-- 2044.9

h.w.bn h. | gpn.bn[.a]ly. | bn.rqd[y].ṯbg. | iḫmlk. | yp‘n w.aṯt h. | anntn.yṣr. | annmn.w.ṯlṯ.n‘[r] h. | rpan.w.ṯ[n.]bn h. | 2068.23
w.aṯt h. | [--]r.w.aṯt h. | ‘bdyrḫ.ṯn ǵlyt h. | aršmg. | ršpy.w.aṯt h. | bn.glgl.uškny. | bn.ṯny.uškny. | mnn.w.aṯt h. | slmu. 2068.12
[-]ḏmu.apsty.b[--]. | w.bn h.w aṯt h.w.alp.w ṯmn.ṣin. | [-]dln.qmnzy.w.a[ṯt h]. | wšṯn.bn h 1080.2
slmu.ḥrš.mrkbt. | bnšm.dt.l.mlk. | ‘bdyrḫ.bn.ṯyl. | ‘bdn.w.aṯt h.w.bn h. | gpn.bn[.a]ly. | bn.rqd[y].ṯbg. | iḫmlk. | yp‘n 2068.19
. | [-]dln.qmnzy.w.a[ṯt h]. | wšṯn.bn h. | ṯmgdl.ykn‘my.w.aṯt h. | w.bn h.w.alp.aḫ[d]. | aǵltn.[--]y.w[.aṯt h]. | w.bn h. 1080.5
]. | [w].bn h.w.ṯn.alpm. | [w.]ṯlṯm.ṣin. | annḏr.ykn‘my. | w.aṯt h.w.bn h. | w.alp.w.tš[‘.]ṣin. 1080.16
gdl.ykn‘my.w.aṯt h. | w.bn h.w.alp.aḫ[d]. | aǵltn.[--]y.w[.aṯt h]. | w.bn h.w.alp.w.[---]. | [-]ln.[---]. | w.ṯn.bn [h.---]. | [1080.7
[-]ln.[---]. | w.ṯn.bn [h.---]. | [--]d m‘qby[.---]. | swn.qrty.w[.aṯt h]. | [w].bn h.w.ṯn.alpm. | [w.]ṯlṯm.ṣin. | annḏr.ykn‘my. 1080.12
w.aṯt h.w.n‘r h. | bn.ḫby.w.[a]ṯt h. | ynḥm.ulmy. | [--]q.w.aṯt h.w.bn h. | [--]an.w.aṯt h. | [--]y.w.aṯt h. | [--]r.w.aṯt h. | ‘ 2068.6
bnšm.dt.l.u[--]ṯtb. | kṯ[r]n. | w.aṯt h.w.n‘r h. | bn.ḫby.w.[a]ṯt h. | ynḥm.ulmy. | [--]q.w.aṯt 2068.3
bnšm.dt.l.u[--]ṯtb. | kṯ[r]n. | w.aṯt h.w.n‘r h. | bn.ḫby.w.[a]ṯt h. | ynḥm.ulmy. | [--]q.w.aṯt h.w.bn h. | [--]an.w.aṯt h. 2068.4
rt[.i]lht. | kḥṣ.k m‘r[.---]. | yṣḥ.ngr il.ilš. | ilš.ngr.bt.b‘l. | w aṯt h.ngrt.ilht. | w y‘n.lṭpn.il d pi[d]. | šm‘.l ngr.il il[š]. | ilš. 16[126].4.9
‘.amr k.ph[.-]. | k il.ḥkmt.k ṯr.lṭpn. | ṣḥ.ngr.il.ilš.il[š]. | w aṯt h.ngrt[.i]lht. | kḥṣ.k m‘r[.---]. | yṣḥ.ngr il.ilš. | ilš.ngr.bt. 16[126].4.5
g. | ršpy.w.aṯt h. | bn.glgl.uškny. | bn.ṯny.uškny. | mnn.w.aṯt h. | slmu.ḥrš.mrkbt. | bnšm.dt.l.mlk. | ‘bdyrḫ.bn.ṯyl. | ‘b 2068.15
-]q.w.aṯt h.w.bn h. | [--]an.w.aṯt h. | [--]y.w.aṯt h. | [--]r.w.aṯt h. | ‘bdyrḫ.ṯn ǵlyt h. | aršmg. | ršpy.w.aṯt h. | bn.glgl.ušk 2068.9
.b[--]. | w.bn h.w aṯt h.w.alp.w ṯmn.ṣin. | [-]dln.qmnzy.w.a[ṯt h]. | wšṯn.bn h. | ṯmgdl.ykn‘my.w.aṯt h. | w.bn h.w.alp. 1080.3
y.w.[a]ṯt h. | ynḥm.ulmy. | [--]q.w.aṯt h.w.bn h. | [--]an.w.aṯt h. | [--]y.w.aṯt h. | [--]r.w.aṯt h. | ‘bdyrḫ.ṯn ǵlyt h. | aršm 2068.7
nḥm.ulmy. | [--]q.w.aṯt h.w.bn h. | [--]an.w.aṯt h. | [--]y.w.aṯt h. | [--]r.w.aṯt h. | ‘bdyrḫ.ṯn ǵlyt h. | aršmg. | ršpy.w.aṯt 2068.8
yd.[---]. | am[-]n.[---]. | w.a[ṯt] h.[---]. | ḫḏmtn.ṯn[.---]. | w.ṯlṯ.alp h.[---]. | swn.qrty.w. 2044.3
| w y‘n.lṭpn.il d pi[d]. | šm‘.l ngr.il il[š]. | ilš.ngr bt b‘l. | w aṯt k.ngrt.il[ht]. | ‘l.l ṯkm.bnw n. | l nḫnpt.mšpy. | ṯlṯ.kmm. 16[126].4.13
[--.]mlakt. | [---.]‘l.w tš‘[d]n.npṣ h. | [---.]rgm.hn.[--]n.w aspt.[q]l h. | [---.rg]m.ank l[.--.--]rny. | [---.]ṯm.hw.i[--]ty. | [1002.49
. | [y]rš.‘m y. | mnm.iršt k. | d ḫsrt.w.ank. | aštn..l.iḫ y. | w.ap.ank.mnm. | [ḫ]s[r]t.w.uḫ y. | [y]‘msn.ṯmn. | w.[u]ḫ y.al 2065.18
qlny.ilm. | ṯǵr k. | tšlm k. | hn ny.‘m ny. | kll.mid. | šlm. | w.ap.ank. | nḫṯ.ṯm ny. | ‘m.adt ny. | mnm.šlm. | rgm.ṯṯb. | l.‘bd 51[95].13
| [---.--]š[-.--].w.ašt. | [---].amr k. | [---].k.ybt.mlk. | [---].w.ap.ank. | [---].l.ǵr.amn. | [---.-]ktt.hn.ib. | [---.]mlk. | [---.]adt 1012.15
‘t.ḫwt[.---]. | [---].nzdt.qr[t]. | [---.]dt nzdt.m[lk]. | [---.]w.ap.bṯn[.---]. | [---.]b‘l y.y[--]. | [---.-]l[-.---]. 2127.2.6
ṣu[.---.]w[.---]. | w hm.at.tr[gm.---]. | w.drm.‘tr[--.---]. | w ap.ht.k[--.]škn. | w.mṯnn[.---.]‘mn k. | [-]štš.[---.]rgm y. | [-] 54.1.20[13.2.5]
t. | ‘m k.w.hm. | l.‘l.w.lakm. | ilak.w.at. | um y.al.tdḥṣ. | w.ap.mhkm. | b.lb k.al. | tšt. 1013.22
-].l.ǵr.amn. | [---.-]ktt.hn.ib. | [---.]mlk. | [---.]adt y.td‘. | w.ap.mlk.uḏ[r]. | [-]d‘.k.iḫd.[---]. | w.mlk.b‘l y. | lm.škn.hnk. | 1012.20
[--]. | trn.w.p[-]y. | bn.b‘yn.w.agytn. | [---] gnym. | [--]ry.w ary. | [---]ǵrbtym. | [---.]w šb‘l. | [---.-]ym. | [---.--]ḫm. | [---.-- 131[309].14
lk.r[b.b‘]l y.p.l. | ḥy.np[š.a]rš. | l.pn.b‘[l y.l].pn.b‘l y. | w.urk.ym.b‘l y. | l.pn.amn.w.l.pn. | il.mṣrm.dt.tǵrn. | npš.špš. 1018.20
ṯkl. | bnwt h.ykr.‘r.d qdm. | idk.pnm.l ytn.tk aršḫ.rbt. | w aršḫ.ṯrrt.ydy.b ‘ṣm.‘r‘r. | w b šḫt.‘s.mt.‘r‘rm.yn‘rn h. | ssn UG5.7.64
h. | w.hm.ḫt. | ‘l.w.likt. | ‘m k.w.hm. | l.‘l.w.lakm. | ilak.w.at. | um y.al.tdḥṣ. | w.ap.mhkm. | b.lb k.al. | tšt. 1013.20
n k.šsrt. | [---.--]t.npš.‘gl. | [---.-]nk.aštn.b ḫrt. | ilm.arṣ.w at.qḥ. | ‘rpt k.rḥ k.mdl k. | mṭrt k.‘m k.šb‘t. | ǵlm k.ṯmn.ḫn 5[67].5.6
. | ytn.l.‘bdyrḫ. | w.mlk.z[--.--]n.ššwm. | n‘mm.[--].ṯtm.w.at. | nǵt.w.ytn.hm.l k. | w.lḥt.alpm.ḫršm. | k.rgmt.l y.bly m 2064.19
.hm.t‘[rb]. | mkr.hn d.w.rgm.ank[.--]. | mlkt.ybqš.anyt.w.at[--]. | w mkr n.mlk[.---]. 2008.2.13
r.il.y[--.---]. | aliyn.[b‘l.---]. | btlt.[‘nt.---]. | mh.k[--.---]. | w at[--.---]. | aṯr[t.---]. | b im[--.---]. | bl.l[---.---]. | mlk.[---]. | dt 4[51].2.40
. | lqḥ.mṭpṭ. | w y‘ny.nn. | dtn.bt n.mḫ[-]. | l dg.w [-]kl. | w aṯr.hn.mr[-]. UG5.6.16
il b[n] il. | dr bn il. | mpḫrt bn il. | ṯrmn w šnm. | il w aṯrt. | ḫnn il. | nṣbt il. | šlm il. | il ḥš il add. | b‘l ṣpn b‘l. | ugrt 30[107].5
‘]l knp. | [---.g]dlt.ṣpn.dqt.šrp.w [š]lmm. | [---.a]lp.l b‘l.w aṯrt.‘ṣr[m] l inš. | [ilm.---].lbbmm.gdlt.‘rb špš w ḥl. | [mlk. 36[9].1.8
ašr nkl w ib[.bt]. | ḫrḫb.mlk qẓ ḫrḫb m | lk aǵzt.b sǵ[--.]špš. | yrḫ ytk 24[77].1
. | kp mznm.iḫ h yṯ‘r. | mšrrm.aḫt h l a | bn mznm.nkl w ib. | d ašr.ar yrḫ.w y | rḫ yar k. | [ašr ilht kṯrt bn] | t hll.snnt 24[77].37
w. | mndym. | bdnh. | l[q]ḥt. | [--]km.‘m.mlk. | [b]ǵl hm.w.iblbl hm. | w.b.ṯb h.[---]. | spr ḥ[--.---]. | w.‘m[.---]. | yqḥ[.---] 2129.10
w.[---]. | ity[.---]. | tlby[.---]. | ir[--.---]. | pndyn[.---]. | w.idt[-.---]. | b.gt.b[n.---]. | yḫl[.---]. | b.gt.[---]. | [---.]k[--]. 1078.6
]r. | ḥmr.ḥmr. | ḥmr.ḥmr. | ḥmr.ḥmr. | ḥmr.ḥmr. | ḥmr.w izml.aḥt. 146[87].7
[--.---]. | b ql[.-----]. | w tštqdn[.-----]. | hm. | w yḫ.mlk. | w ik m.kn.w [---]. | tšknnnn[.---]. 62[26].10
md m.yḥmd m. | bn.dgn.yhrr m. | b‘l.ngṯ hm.b p‘n h. | w il hd.b ḫrẓ‘ h. | [-----]. | [--]t.[---]. | [---.]‘n[.---]. | pnm[.---]. | b 12[75].1.41
.--]n.‘bdyrḫ.ḥdṯn.y‘r. | adb‘l[.---].ḥdṯn.yḥmn.bnil. | ‘dn.w.ildgn.ḥṯbm. | tdǵlm.iln.b‘[l]n.alḏy. | tdn.ṣr[--.--]t.‘zn.mtn.n 2011.20
[---.--]i[-.]a[--.---]. | [---.]ilm.w ilht.dt. | [---.]šb‘.l šb‘m.aṯr. | [---.--]ldm.dt ymtm. | [--.--]r.l 25[136].2
t.km hm.tdr. | ap.bnt.ḥry. | km hm.w ṯḫss.aṯrt. | ndr h.w ilt.p[--]. | w tšu.g h.w [tṣḥ]. | ph m‘.ap.k[rt.--]. | u ṯn.ndr[.-- 15[128].3.26
.]ṣrm.w l ilt. | ṣd[yn]m.ṯm. | yd[r.k]rt.ṯ‘. | i.ṯt.aṯrt.ṣrm. | w ilt.ṣdynm. | hm.ḥry.bt y. | iqḥ.aš‘rb.ǵlmt. | ḥẓr y.ṯn h.wspm 14[KRT].4.202
n.bn.uḏr[-.---]. | w.‘d‘.nḥl h[.---]. | w.yknil.nḥl h[.---]. | w.iltm.nḥl h[.---]. | w.unṭm.nḥ[l h.---]. | [---.]‘ḏr[.---]. | str[-.--- 90[314].1.16
[--.]ab.w il[--]. | [--] šlm.šlm i[l]. | [š]lm.il.šr. | dgn.w b‘l. | ‘ṯ w kmṯ. | y UG5.10.1.1
.b yd.btlt.[‘nt]. | w y‘n.lṭpn.il d p[id]. | yd‘t k.bt.k anšt.w i[n.b ilht]. | qlṣ k.tb‘.bt.ḫnp.lb[k.--.ti] | ḫd.d iṯ.b kbd k.tšt. 18[3AQHT].1.16
ḥkmt. | ‘m ‘lm.ḥyt.ḥẓt. | ṯḥm k.mlk n.aliy[n.]b‘l. | ṯpṭ n.w in.d ‘ln h. | klny n.q[š] h.n[bln]. | klny n[.n]bl.ks h. | [an]y.l 4[51].4.44
n.---]. | tšnpn.‘lm.km[m.---]. | w.l ll.‘ṣrm.w [---]. | kmm.w.in.‘ṣr[.---]. | w mit.š‘rt.[-]y[-.---]. | w.kdr.w.npt t[--.---]. | w. 38[23].8
ṯm.sgrt. | b‘d h.‘dbt.ṯlṯ.ptḥ.bt.mnt. | ptḥ.bt.w ubn.hkl.w ištql šql. | tn.km.nḥšm.yḥr.tn.km. | mhr y.w bn.bṯn.itnn y. UG5.7.72
ynḥm.aḫ h. | w.b‘ln aḫ h. | w.ḥṯtn bn h. | w.btšy.bt h. | w.ištrmy. | bt.‘bd mlk. | w.snt. | bt.ugrt. | w.pdy h[m]. | iwrkl. 1006.8
.š. | trṯy.alp.w.š. | yrḫ.š.ṣpn.š. | kṯr š ‘ṯtr.š. | [‘ṯ]rt.š.šgr w iṯm š. | [---.]š.ršp.idrp.š. | [---.il.t‘]ḏr.š. | [---.-]mt.š. | [-----]. | [UG5.9.2.9
| w.rgm.ṯṯb.l y. | w.mnd‘.k.ank. | aḥš.mǵy.mnd‘. | k.igr.w.u.[--]. | ‘m.špš.[---]. | nšlḥ[.---]. | [---.m]at. | [---.]mat. | š[--].iš 2009.1.12
nt.b‘d h.bhtm.sgrt. | b‘d h.‘dbt.ṯlṯ.ptḥ.bt.mnt. | ptḥ.bt.w ubn.hkl.w ištql šql. | tn.km.nḥšm.yḥr.tn.km. | mhr y.w bn. UG5.7.72
| [i]lm.w ḥẓr.k bn. | [a]ṯrt.gm.l ǵlm h. | b‘l.yṣḥ.‘n.gpn. | w ugr.bn.ǵlmt. | ‘mm ym.bn.ẓlm[t]. | rmt.pr‘t.ibr[.mnt]. | ṣḥr 8[51FRAG].7
.d yšb | [‘].hmlt.arṣ.gm.l ǵ | [lm] h.b‘l k.yṣḥ.‘n. | [gpn].w ugr.b ǵlmt. | [‘mm.]ym.bn.ẓlmt.r | [mt.pr‘]t.ibr.mnt. | [ṣḥrr 4[51].7.54
‘.tǵṣ.pnt. | ksl h.anš.dt.ẓr h.tšu. | g h.w tṣḥ.ik.mǵy.gpn.w ugr. | mn.ib.yp‘.l b‘l.ṣrt. | l rkb.‘rpt.l mḫšt.mdd. | il ym.l klt 3[‘NT].3.33

ytb ilm.idk. | l ytn.pnm.ʿm.bʿl. | mrym.ṣpn.w yʿn. | gpn.w ugr.tḥm.bn ilm. | mt.hwt.ydd.bn.il. | ǵzr.p np.š.npš.lbim. | 5[67].1.12
ṣḥt. | [---.--]t. | [---.]ilm. | [---.--]u.yd. | [---.--]k. | [---.gpn.]w ugr. | [---.---]t. 4[51].8.47
bn.amt]. | q[ḥ.kr]t[.šlmm]. | š[lmm.]al.t[ṣr]. | udm[.r]bt.w u[dm]. | [t]rrt.udm.y[t]n[t]. | il.ušn.ab[.ad]m. | rḥq.mlk.l bt 14[KRT].6.276
mm.w ng.mlk. | l bt y.rḥq.krt. | l ḥẓr y.al.tṣr. | udm.rbt.w udm ṯrrt. | udm.ytnt.il w ušn. | ab.adm.w ṯṯb. | mlakm.l h.l 14[KRT].3.134
rbṣ.bn.amt]. | [qḥ.krt.šlmm]. | [šlmm.al.tṣr]. | [udm.rbt.w udm]. | [ṯrrt.udm.ytnt]. | [il.w ušn.ab.adm]. | [rḥq.mlk.l bt 14[KRT].5.257
.w ṯn. | ṯlṯ.rbʿ.ym. | aḫr.špšm.b rbʿ. | ymǵy.l udm.rbt. | w udm[.ṯr]rt. | grnn.ʿrm. | šrnn.pdrm. | sʿt.b šdm.ḥṭb. | w b gr 14[KRT].4.211
lḥny. | ṯlrby. | dmt. | aǵt. | w.qmnz. | slḫ. | ykn'm. | šlmy. | w.ull. | ṯmry. | qrt. | ʿrm. | nnu. | [--]. | [---]. | mʿr. | arny. | ubrʿy. | i 71[113].19
k.um y. | tdʿ.ky.ʿrbt. | l pn.špš. | w pn.špš.nr. | b y.mid.w um. | tšmḫ.m ab. | w al.trḫln. | ʿtn.ḫrd.ank. | ʿm ny.šlm. | kll. 1015.10
[-----]. | w.[-----]. | w.abǵl.nḫ[l h.--]. | w.unṯ.aḫd.l h[.---]. | dnn.bn.yṣr[.---]. | sln.bn.ʿṯt[-.---]. | pdy.bn 90[314].1.4
d.b d. | [ʿb]dmlk. | [-]k.amʿ[--]. | [w.b] d.bn h[.ʿ]d ʿlm. | [w.un]ṯ.in[n.]b h. | [---.]nʿm[-]. 1009.18
bnšm. | l.yqḥnn.b d. | bʿln.bn.kltn. | w.b d.bn h.ʿd. | ʿlm.w unṯ. | in.b h. 1008.20
ʿdʿ.nḫl h[.---]. | w.yknil.nḫl h[.---]. | w.iltm.nḫl h[.---]. | w.unṯm.nḫ[l h.---]. | [---.]ʿdr[.---]. | str[-.---]. | bdlm.d[t.---]. | ʿd 90[314].1.17
.krt. | l ḥẓr y.al.tṣr. | udm.rbt.w udm ṯrrt. | udm.ytnt.il w ušn. | ab.adm.w ṯṯb. | mlakm.l h.lm.ank. | ksp.w yrq.ḫrṣ. | y 14[KRT].3.135
[šlmm.al.tṣr]. | [udm.rbt.w udm]. | [ṯrrt.udm.ytnt]. | [il.w ušn.ab.adm]. | [rḥq.mlk.l bt y]. | [ng.kr]t.l ḥ[ẓ]r y. | [-----]. | 14[KRT].5.259
ʿ.qšt.w.ar[bʿ]. | [u]ṯpt.qlʿ.w.ṯt.mr[ḫ]m. | [bn].smyy.qšt.w.u[ṯpt]. | [w.q]lʿ.w.ṯt.mrḫm. | [bn].šlmn.qlʿ.w.ṯ[t.---]. | [bn]. 2047.4
iḫyn.uṯpt.ḥẓm. | anšrm.uṯpt.ḥẓm. | w uṯpt.srdnnm. | awpn.uṯpt.ḥẓm. | w uṯpt.srdnnm. | rpan.uṯp 1124.3
| anšrm.uṯpt.ḥẓm. | w uṯpt.srdnnm. | awpn.uṯpt.ḥẓm. | w uṯpt.srdnnm. | rpan.uṯpt.srdnnm. | šbʿm.uṯpt.srdnnm. | bn. 1124.5
.qštm.w.uṯp[t]. | [--.q]lʿ.w[.---.m]rḫm. | [bn].ḫdmn.qšt.[w.u]ṯp[t].ṯ[--]. | [---].arbʿ.[---]. | [---].kdl[.---.mr]ḫm.w.ṯ[t.---]. 2047.9
]lʿ.w.ṯt.mrḫm. | [bn].šlmn.qlʿ.w.ṯ[t.---]. | [bn].mlṣ.qštm.w.uṯp[t]. | [--.q]lʿ.w[.---.m]rḫm. | [bn].ḫdmn.qšt.[w.u]ṯp[t].ṯ[- 2047.7
grt š.bʿl ḫlb š. | yrḫ š.ʿnt ṣpn.alp. | w š.pdry š.ddmš š. | w b urbt.ilib š. | bʿl alp w š. | dgn.š.il tʿdr.š. | bʿl š.ʿnt š.ršp š. | š UG5.13.19
l.iybʿl. | ṯlṯm.l.mit.šʿrt. | l.šr.ʿṯtrt. | mlbš.ṯrmnm. | k.ytn.w.b.bt. | mlk.mlbš. | ytn.l hm. | šbʿ.lbšm.allm. | l ušḫry. | ṯlṯ.ma 1107.6
i[--.---]. | d.[---]. | bnš[-] mdy[-]. | w.b.glb. | phnn.w. | mndym. | bdnh. | l[q]ḥt. | [--]km.ʿm.mlk. | [2129.4
w udm[.ṯr]rt. | grnn.ʿrm. | šrnn.pdrm. | sʿt.b šdm.ḥṭb. | w b grnt.ḥpšt. | sʿt.b npk.šibt.w b | mqr.mmlat. | d[m].ym.w 14[KRT].4.215
dbḫ.w dbḫ. | dnt.w dbḫ.tdmm. | amht.k b h.bṯt.l tbṯ. | w b h.tdmmt.amht. | aḫr.mǵy.aliyn.bʿl. | mǵyt.btlt.ʿnt. | tmgn 4[51].3.22
ʿr. | šmt hm. | b hm.qrnm. | km.ṯrm.w gbṯt. | km.ibrm. | w b hm.pn.bʿl. | bʿl.ytlk.w yṣd. | yḥ pat.mlbr. | wn.ymǵy.aklm 12[75].1.33
ʿnt. | w ʿṯtrt.tṣdn.[---]. | [---.-]b[-.---]. | [ʿ]ṯrt w ʿnt[.---]. | w b hm.tṯṯb[.--]d h. | km trpa.hn nʿr. | d yšt.l.lṣb h ḫšʿr klb. | [UG5.1.2.2
b dmʿ h.nhmmt. | šnt.tluan. | w yškb.nhmmt. | w yqmṣ.w b ḥlm h. | il.yrd.b ḏhrt h. | ab adm.w yqrb. | b šal.krt.m at. 14[KRT].1.35
ʿl ym kdm. | w b ṯlṯ.kd yn w krsnm. | w b rbʿ kdm yn. | w b ḫmš kd yn. 1086.5
. | mn km l.yqḥ. | bt.hnd.b d. | [ʿb]dmlk. | [-]k.amʿ[--]. | [w.b] d.bn h[.ʿ]d ʿlm. | [w.un]ṯ.in[n.]b h. | [---.]nʿm[-]. 1009.17
ʿlm. | šḥr.ʿlmt. | bnš bnšm. | l.yqḥnn.b d. | bʿln.bn.kltn. | w.b d.bn h.ʿd. | ʿlm.w unṯ. | in.b h. 1008.19
npṣ.ʿ[--.---]. | d.b d.a[--.---]. | w.b d.b[--.---]. | udbr[.---]. | ʿrš[.---]. | tl[ḥn.---]. | a[--.---]. | ṯn[.-- 1120.3
. | l g y.w yhbt.bnš. | w ytn.ilm.b d hm. | b d.iḫqm.gṯr. | w b d.ytrhd. | bʿl. 55[18].21
b.gt.mlkt.b.rḥbn. | ḫmšm.l.mitm.zt. | w.b d.krd. | ḫmšm.l.mit. | arbʿ.kbd. 1096.3
r]. | b.[šb]ʿ.ṣbu.[š]pš.w.ḥly[t].ʿ[r]b[.š]p[š]. | w [ḥl.]mlk.[w.]b.ym.ḥdṯ.ṯn.šm. | l.[---]t. | i[d.yd]bḥ.mlk.l.prgl.ṣqrn.b.gg. | 35[3].48
m.yṯb]. | brr.b šbʿ[.ṣbu.špš.w ḥl] | yt.ʿrb špš[.w ḥl.mlk.w.b y] | m.ḥdṯ.ṯn šm[.---.--]t. | b yrḫ.ši[-.b ar]bʿt.ʿš | rt.yr[ṯḥṣ. APP.II[173].52
--].ḫtt.mtt[--]. | [--.]ḫy[--.--.]l ašṣi.hm.ap.amr[--]. | [---].w b ym.mnḫ l abd.b ym.irtm.m[--]. | [ṯpṭ].nhr.tlʿm.ṯm.ḥrbm 2.4[68].3
argm.qštm. | [----.]mhrm.ht.tṣdn.tinṯt. | [---]m.tṣḥq.ʿnt.w b lb.tqny. | [---.]tb l y.l aqht.ǵzr.ṯb l y w l k. | [---]m.l aqry 17[2AQHT].6.41
[---]. | [ʿl.]krt.tbkn. | [--.]rgm.ṯrm. | [--.]mtm.tbkn. | [--]t.w b lb.tqb[-]. | [--]m[-].mtm.uṣbʿ[t]. | [-]tr.šrk.il. | ʿrb.špš.l ym 15[128].5.15
l.qšt h. | imḫṣ h.ʿl.qṣʿt h.hwt. | l aḥw.ap.qšt h.l ttn. | l y.w b mt[.-]ḫ.mṣṣ[-]t[.--]. | prʿ.qẓ.y[bl].šblt. | b ǵlp h.apnk.dnil. 19[1AQHT].1.17
n.pdrm. | sʿt.b šdm.ḥṭb. | w b grnt.ḥpšt. | sʿt.b npk.šibt.w b | mqr.mmlat. | d[m].ym.w ṯn. | ṯlṯ.rbʿ.ym. | ḫmš.ṯdṯ.ym. | 14[KRT].5.216
spr.npš.d. | ʿrb.bt.mlk. | w.b.spr.l.št. | yrmʿl. | ṣry. | iršy. | yʿdrd. | ayaḫ. | bn.aylt. | ḫmš. 2106.3
ml[kt]. | tǵsdb.šmlšn. | w tbʿ ank. | ʿm mlakt h šmʿ h. | w b.ʿly skn.ydʿ rgm h. | w ht ab y ǵm[--]. | t[--.---]. | ls[--.---]. | 1021.8
.d bat k bʿl.ymšḫ. | bʿl.ymšḫ.hm.b ʿp. | ntʿn.b arṣ.ib y. | w b ʿpr.qm.aḫ k. | w tšu.ʿn h.btlt.ʿnt. | w tšu.ʿn h.w tʿn. | w tʿn 10[76].2.25
tldn. | trkn. | kli. | plǵn. | apšny. | ʿrb[.---]. | w.b.p[.--]. | apš[ny]. | b.yṣi h. | ḥwt.[---]. | alp.k[sp]. | tšʿn. | w.h 2116.7
t yʿn.ḥtk h.rš. | mid.grdš.ṯbt h. | w b tm hn.špḥ.yitbd. | w b.pḫyr h.yrṯ. | yʿrb.b ḥdr h.ybky. | b ṯn.[-]gmm.w ydmʿ. | t 14[KRT].1.25
rk.tʿl.b ǵr. | mslmt.b ǵr.tliyt. | w tʿl.bkm.b arr. | bm.arr.w b ṣpn. | b nʿm.b ǵr.t[l]iyt. | ql.l bʿl.ttnn. | bšrt.il.bš[r.bʿ]l. | w 10[76].3.31
ʿl y. | [šb'] d.šbʿ [d]. | [mr]ḫqtm. | qlt. | ʿbd k.b. | lwsnd. | [w] b ṣr. | ʿm.mlk. | w.ht. | mlk.syr. | ns.w.ṯm. | ydbḥ. | mlǵ[.---]. 2063.11
y yn kd w kd. | w ʿl ym kdm. | w b ṯlṯ.kd yn w krsnm. | w b rbʿ kdm yn. | w b ḫmš kd yn. 1086.4
idk.pnm.l ytn.tk aršḫ.rbt. | w aršḫ.ṯrrt.ydy.b ʿṣm.ʿrʿr. | w b šḫṭ.ʿs.mt.ʿrʿrm.ynʿrn h. | ssnm.ysyn h.ʿdtm.yʿdyn h.yb | l UG5.7.65
šlḥ. | ttpl.yʿn.ḥtk h. | krt yʿn.ḥtk h.rš. | mid.grdš.ṯbt h. | w b tm hn.špḥ.yitbd. | w b.pḫyr h.yrṯ. | yʿrb.b ḥdr h.ybky. | b 14[KRT].1.24
bdnh. | l[q]ḥt. | [--]km.ʿm.mlk. | [b]ǵl hm.w.iblbl hm. | w.b.ṯb h.[---]. | spr ḥ[--.---]. | w.ʿm[.---]. | yqḥ[.---]. | w.n[--.---]. 2129.11
[-] ym.prʿ d nkly yn kd w kd. | w ʿl ym kdm. | w b ṯlṯ.kd yn w krsnm. | w b rbʿ kdm yn. | w b ḫmš kd yn. 1086.3
pdr[-.---]. | ṣin aḥd h[.---]. | l ʿṯtrt[.---]. | ʿlm.kmm[.---]. | w b ṯlṯ.ṣ[in.---]. | l ll.pr[-.---]. | mit šʿ[rt.---]. | ptr.k[--.---]. | [-]y 37[22].8
šlm. | l.[--]n.špš. | ad[.ʿ]bd h.uk.škn. | k.[---.]sglt h.hw. | w.b[.---.]uk.nǵr. | w.[---].adny.l.yḫsr. | w.[ank.yd]ʿ.l.ydʿt. | h[t. 2060.8
. | [---].mr[--.---]. | [---].mr[--.]ydm[.---]. | [---.]mṯbt.ilm.w.b.[---]. | [---.]ṯṯbn.ilm.w.[---]. | [---.]w.ksu.bʿlt.b[htm.---]. | [47[33].5
w [šnm.š]. | ʿnt š ršp š[.dr.il.w pḫr.bʿl]. | gdlt.šlm[.gdlt.w burm.lb]. | rmṣt.ilh[m.bʿlm.---]. | ksm.ṯlṯm.[---]. | d yqḥ bt[. 35[3].17
n w šnm.š. | ʿnt.š.ršp.š.dr il w p[ḫ]r bʿl. | gdlt.šlm.gdlt.w burm.[l]b. | rmṣt.ilhm.bʿlm.dṯt.w kšm.ḫmš. | ʿtr h.mlun.šn 34[1].8
.w š[nm.š.ʿnt.š.ršp.š.dr]. | il.w pḫr[.bʿl.gdlt.šlm.gdlt]. | w burm.l[b.rmṣt.ilhm]. | bʿlm.w mlu[.---.ksm]. | ṯlṯm.w mʿrb[APP.II[173].19
---]. | [--.-]g[-.-]s w [---]. | w yn[t.q]rt.y[---]. | w al[p.l]il.w bu[rm.---]. | ytk.gdlt.ilhm.[ṯkmn.w šnm]. | dqt.ršp.šrp.w š[35[3].11
t.k[-]ml.[---]. | l[---].w y[nt.qrt.---]. | [---.--]n[.w alp.l il.w bu] | [rm.---.ytk.gdlt.ilhm]. | ṯkmn.w [šnm.dqt.ršp.šrp]. | w APP.II[173].12
kbd. | alp.w š.l bʿl ṣpn. | dqt l ṣpn.šrp.w šlmm. | kmm.w bbt.bʿl.ugrt. | w kdm.w npš ilib. | gdlt.il š.bʿl š.ʿnt. | ṣpn.alp. UG5.13.11
.al]p.w š.[l] bʿl.ṣpn. | [dqt.l.ṣpn.šrp].w š[l]mm.kmm. | [w bbt.bʿl.ugrt.]kdm.w npš. | [ilib.gdlt.il.š.b]ʿ[l.]š.ʿnt ṣpn. | [--- 36[9].1.16
| brrn aryn. | a[-]ḥn tlyn. | atdb w ʿr. | qdš w amrr. | ṯḫr w bd. | [k]ṯr ḫss šlm. | šlm il bt. | šlm il ḫš[t]. | ršp inšt. | [--]rm UG5.7.71

. | pamt.w bt.[---]. | rmm.w ʻl[y.---]. | bt.il.ṯq[l.---.kbd]. | w bdḥ.k[--.---]. | ʻṣrm.l i[nš.ilm.ṯb.md] | bḥ.bʻl.[gdlt.---.dqt]. | APP.II[173].43
m.ḫt.šʻtqt dm. | li.w ttbʻ.šʻtqt. | bt.krt.bu.tbu. | bkt.tgly.w tbu. | nṣrt.tbu.pnm. | ʻrm.tdu.mh. | pdrm.tdu.šrr. | ḫṭ m.tʻm 16.6[127].4
nm.ʻm. | [il.]mbk nhrm.qrb. | [a]pq.thmtm.tgly.ḏd. | il.w tbu.qrš.. | mlk.ab.šnm.l pʻn. | il.thbr.w tql. | tštḥwy.w tkbd 6.1.35[49.1.7]
nm.ʻm.[i]l.mbk.[nhrm.qrb.apq.thmtm]. | [ygly.]ḏl i[l].w ybu[.q]rš.mlk[.ab.šnm.l pʻn.il.] | [yhbr.]w yql[.y]štḥw[y.] 2.3[129].5
m.ʻm.lṭpn]. | il d pid.tk ḫrš[n.---.tk.ǵr.ks]. | ygly ḏd.i[l.w ybu.qrš.mlk]. | ab.šnm.l [pʻn.il.yhbr.w yql]. | yštḥwy.[w yk 1[ʻNT.IX].3.23
tn.pnm. | ʻm.il.mbk.nhrm. | qrb.apq.thmtm. | tgly.ḏd.il.w tbu. | qrš.mlk.ab.šnm. | l pʻn.il.thbr.w tql. | tštḥwy.w tkbd 4[51].4.23
.pn]m.ʻm il.mbk.nhrm. | [qrb.ap]q.thmtm tgly.ḏd il. | [w tbu.qr]š.mlk.ab.šnm. | [l pʻn.il.t]hbr.w tql.tšth | [wy.w tkb 17[2AQHT].6.49
. | [ʻm.i]l.mbk.nhr[m.qr]b.[ap]q. | [thm]tm.tgl.ḏ[d.]i[l.]w tbu. | [qr]š.m[l]k.ab[.šnm.]mṣr. | [t]bu.ḏdm.qn[-.-]n[-.-]lt. | 3[ʻNT.VI].5.15
m]. | [ʻm.il.mbk.nhrm]. | [qrb.apq.thmtm]. | [tgly.ḏd.il.w]tb[a]. | [qrš.mlk.ab.]šnm. | [tša.g hm.w tṣ]ḥ.sbn. | [---]l[.---. 5[67].6.1
brlt h.km.qṭr.[b ap h.---]. | ʻnt.b ṣmt.mhr h.[---]. | aqht.w tbk.y[---.---]. | abn.ank.w ʻl.[qšt k.---.ʻl]. | qṣʻt k.at.l ḥ[---.--- 18[3AQHT].4.39
ṣǵr.špš.b šmm.tqru. | [---.]nplt.y[--].mdʻ.nplt.bšr. | [---].w tpky.k[m.]nʻr.tdmʻ.km. | [ṣǵ]r.bkm.yʻny[.---.bn]wt h. | [--] UG5.8.40
.l k.w.l y. | mn.bnš.d.l.i[--].ʻ[m k]. | l.alpm.w.l.y[n.--]t. | w.bl.bnš.hw[-.--]y. | w.k.at.trg[m.--]. | w.[---]n.w.s[--]. | [--]m. 2064.26
nd pnṯ.dq. | ṯn ḫpnm.ṯn pldm ǵlmm. | kpld.b[-.-]r[--]. | w blḫ br[-]m p[-]. | b[--.]l[-.]mat[.-]y. | ḫmšm[.--]i. | ṯlṯ m[at] 140[98].6
my.w snry. | [b]n.sdy.bn.ṯty. | bn.ḥyn.bn.ǵlm. | bn.yyn.w.bn.au[pš]. | bn.kdrn. | ʻrgzy.w.bn.ʻdy. | bn.gmḥn.w.ḥgbt. | b 131[309].25
ubn.hkl.w ištql šql. | tn.km.nḥšm.yḥr.tn.km. | mhr y.w bn.bṯn.itnn y. | ytt.nḥšm.mhr k.bn bṯn. | itnn k. | aṯr ršp.ʻṯt UG5.7.74
. | blt.p btlt.ʻn[t]. | w p.nʻmt.aḫt[.bʻl]. | yʻl.bʻl.b ǵ[r.---]. | w bn.dgn.b š[---]. | bʻl.yṯb.l ks[i.mlk h]. | bn.dgn.l kḥ[ṯ.drkt h 10[76].3.13
.nšr.b ḥb[š y]. | km.diy.b tʻrt y.aqht.[km.yṯb]. | l lḥm.w bn.dnil.l ṯrm[.ʻl h]. | nšrm.trḫpn.ybṣr.[ḥbl.d] | iym.bn.nšr 18[3AQHT].4.19
rǵl | špšyn.b.ulm. | bn.qṯn.b.ulm. | bn.gdrn.b.mʻr[by]. | [w].bn.dʻm[-]. | bn.ppṯ.b[--]. | b[n.---]. | šm[-.---]. | tkn[.---]. | kn 2046.1.8
tql. | tštḥwy.w tkbdn h. | tšu.g h.w tṣḥ.tšmḫ ht. | aṯrt.w bn h.ilt.w ṣb | rt.ary h.k mt.aliyn. | bʻl.k ḫlq.zbl.bʻl. | arṣ.g 6.1.40[49.1.12]
l.ks h. | any.l yṣḥ.ṯr.il.ab h.il. | mlk.d yknn h.yṣḥ.aṯrt. | w bn h.ilt.w ṣbrt.arḫ h. | wn.in.bt.l bʻl.km.ilm. | ḥẓr.k b[n.a]ṯ 3[ʻNT.VI].5.45
[any.l yṣ]ḥ.ṯr. | [il.ab h.i]l.mlk. | [d yknn h.yṣ]ḥ.aṯ | [rt.w bn h.]ilt. | [w ṣbrt.ary]h. | [wn.in.bt.l bʻl.] | [km.ilm.w ḥẓr]. 4[51].1.8
s h. | [an]y.l yṣḥ.ṯr il.ab h. | [i]l.mlk.d yknn h.yṣḥ. | aṯrt.w bn h.ilt.w ṣbrt. | ary h.wn.in.bt.l bʻl. | km.ilm.w ḥẓr.k bn.a 4[51].4.49
[aṯt.w].bn h.b.bt.krz. | [aṯt.]w.pǵt.b.bt.gg. | [ǵz]r.aḥd.b.bt.nwrḏ. | 80[119].1
š.mrkbt. | bnšm.dt.l.mlk. | ʻbdyrḫ.bn.ṯyl. | ʻbdn.w.aṯt h.w.bn h. | gpn.bn[.a]ly. | bn.rqd[y].ṯbg. | iḫmlk. | ypʻn w.aṯt h. | 2068.19
qmnzy.w.a[ṯt h]. | wštn.bn h. | ṯmgdl.yknʻmy.w.aṯt h. | w.bn h.w.alp.aḥ[d]. | aǵltn.[--]y.w[.aṯt h]. | w.bn h.w.alp.w.[- 1080.6
n h.w.ṯn.alpm. | [w.]ṯlṯm.ṣin. | anndr.yknʻmy. | w.aṯt h.w.bn h. | w.alp.w.tš[ʻ.]ṣin. 1080.16
y.w.aṯt h. | w.bn h.w.alp.aḥ[d]. | aǵltn.[--]y.w[.aṯt h]. | w.bn h.w.alp.w.[---]. | [-]ln.[---]. | w.ṯn.bn [h.---]. | [--]d mʻqby 1080.8
[-]ḏmu.apsty.b[--]. | w.bn h.w aṯt h.w.alp.w ṯmn.ṣin. | [-]dln.qmnzy.w.a[ṯt h]. | w 1080.2
.aḥd.b.[bt.---]. | ṯt.aṯtm.w.pǵt.w.ǵzr.aḥd.b.[bt.---]. | aṯt.w.bn h.w.pǵt.aḫt.b.bt.m[--]. | aṯt.w.ṯt.bt h.b.bt.ḫḏmrd. | aṯt. 80[119].21
.ṯn.bn [h.---]. | [--]d mʻqby[.---]. | swn.qrty.w[.aṯt h]. | [w].bn h.w.ṯn.alpm. | [w.]ṯlṯm.ṣin. | anndr.yknʻmy. | w.aṯt h.w 1080.13
š[mg.---]. | urt[n.---]. | ʻdn[.---]. | bqrt[.---]. | ṯnǵrn.[---]. | w.bn h.n[--.---]. | ḥnil.[---]. | aršmg.mru. | bʻl.šlm.ʻbd. | awr.ṯǵr 2084.7
. | iwrnr. | alnr. | maḫdt. | aby. | [-----]. | [-]nt. | ydn. | mnn.w bn h. | ṯkn. 107[15].12
w.nʻr h. | bn.ḫby.w.[a]ṯt h. | ynḥm.ulmy. | [--]q.w.aṯt h.w.bn h. | [--]an.w.aṯt h. | [--]y.w.aṯt h. | [--]r.w.aṯt h. | ʻbdyrḫ.ṯ 2068.6
[ṯt] h.[---]. | ḫḏmtn.ṯn[.---]. | w.ṯlṯ.alp h.[---]. | swn.qrty.w.[b]n h[.---]. | w.alp h.w.a[r]bʻ.l.arbʻ[m.---]. | pln.ṯmry.w.ṯn. 2044.6
---.--]a.ṯ[l]ṯ.d.a[--]. | [---].mrn. | [---.]bn pnṯbl. | [---.-]py w.bn h. 1145.2.3
ṯ. | w.arbʻ.aṯt. | bn.lg.ṯn.bn h. | bʻlm.w.aḫt h. | b.šrt. | šty.w.bn h. 2080.13
b.ym.ḥdṯ. | b.yrḫ.pgrm. | lqḥ.bʻlmʻḏr. | w bn.ḫlp. | w[--]y.d.bʻl. | miḫd.b. | arbʻ.mat. | ḫrṣ. 1155.4
b.ym.ḥdṯ. | b.yr.pgrm. | lqḥ.bʻlmḏr. | w.bn.ḫlp. | miḫd. | b.arbʻ. | mat.ḫrṣ. 1156.4
]gm[.ṯṯb]. | ky.lik.bn y. | lḥt.akl.ʻm y. | mid y w ǵbn y. | w.bn y.hn kt. | yškn.anyt. | ym.yšrr. | w.ak[l.---]. | [--].š[--.--]. 2061.12
ḏrǵlm. | kd.l.mṣrym. | kd.mštt.mlk. | kd.bn.amht [-]t. | w.bn.mṣrym. | arbʻm.yn. | l.ḫrd. | ḫmšm.ḫmš. | kbd.tgmr. | yn. 1089.10
bn.ḥyn.bn.ǵlm. | bn.yyn.w.bn.au[pš]. | bn.kdrn. | ʻrgzy.w.bn.ʻdy. | bn.gmḥn.w.ḥgbt. | bn.tgḏn. | yny. | [b]n.gʻyn dd. | [- 131[309].27
ḫmṯ ʻṯr k[--.---]. | b ḫmṯ ʻṯr[.---]. | [-----]. | [---.-]y[-.---]. | w bn ʻṯl.[---]. | ypḫ knʻm[.---]. | aḫmn bt[.---]. | b ḫmṯ ʻṯr ṯmn[. 207[57].8
.dd. | bn.tbšn.dd. | bn.ḫran.w[.---]. | [-]n.yʻrtym. | gmm.w.bn.p[--]. | trn.w.p[-]y. | bn.bʻyn.w.agytn. | [---] gnym. | [--]ry 131[309].10
t.b qrb. | hkl k.tbl k.ǵrm. | mid.ksp.gbʻm.mḥmd.. | ḫrṣ.w bn.bht.ksp. | w ḫrṣ.bht.ṯhrm. | iqnim.šmḫ.aliyn. | bʻl.ṣḥ.ḫrn 4[51].5.95
l k.ǵrm.mid.ksp. | gbʻm.mḥmd.ḫrṣ. | ybl k.udr.ilqṣm. | w bn.bht.ksp.w ḫrṣ. | bht.ṯhrm.iqnim. | šmḫ.btlt.ʻnt.tdʻṣ. | pʻn 4[51].5.80
h]. | limm.w tʻl.ʻm.il. | ab h.ḥpr.pʻl k.y[--]. | šmʻ k.l arḫ.w bn.[--]. | limm.ql.b udn.k w[-]. | k rtqt mr[.---]. | k d lbšt.bi 13[6].22
[---.]m[--]. | [---].bn[.---]. | [-----]. | [---].ḥ[mr]. | [---.]w.bnš.aḥd. | [---.--]m. | [---].ʻtgrm. | [---.-]ṣbm. | [---.]nrn.mʻry. 2043.5
ṣʻ.ḥmr.w[.---]. | ṣʻq.ḥmr.w.[---]. | ḫlb ʻprm.amḏy.[ḥm]r.w bn[š]. | gnʻy.[---.bn]š. | uškn[.---].ʻšr.bnšm. | ʻnqpat[.---].bnš 2040.16
-.]bnšm. | ilštmʻ.arbʻ.ḥm[r]m.ḫmš.bnšm. | ǵr. | ary.ḥmr w.bnš. | qmy.ḥmr.w.bnš. | ṯbil. | ʻnmky.ḥmr.w.bnš. | rqd arbʻ. 2040.23
. | ary.ḥmr w.bnš. | qmy.ḥmr.w.bnš. | ṯbil. | ʻnmky.ḥmr.w.bnš. | rqd arbʻ. | šbn aḥd. | ṯbq aḥd. | šrš aḥd. | bir aḥd. | uḫn 2040.26
bʻ.ḥm[r]m.ḫmš.bnšm. | ǵr. | ary.ḥmr w.bnš. | qmy.ḥmr.w.bnš. | ṯbil. | ʻnmky.ḥmr.w.bnš. | rqd arbʻ. | šbn aḥd. | ṯbq aḥd 2040.24
ym[.---]. | d ymǵy.bnš[.---]. | w ḥmr[.---]. | w mʻn[.---]. | w bn[š.---]. | d bnš.ḥm[r.---]. | w d.l mdl.r[--.---]. | w ṣin.ʻz.b[ʻl 2158.1.11
m.ṯr.w.arbʻ.bnt h. | yrḫm.yd.ṯn.bn h. | bʻlm.w.ṯlṯ.nʻrm.w.bt.aḫt. | bn.lwn.ṯlṯtm.bʻlm. | bn.bʻly.ṯlṯtm.bʻlm. | w.aḥd.ḫbṯ 2080.5
t.w.ṯn.ǵzrm.b.bt.ṣdqš[lm]. | [a]ṯt.aḫt.b.bt.rpi[--]. | [aṯt.]w.bt h.b.bt.alḫn. | [aṯt.w.]pǵt.aḫt.b.bt.tt. | [aṯt.w.]bt h.b.bt.tr 80[119].25
-]. | [aṯt.]w.bt h.b.bt.alḫn. | [aṯt.w.]pǵt.aḫt.b.bt.tt. | [aṯt.w.]bt h.b.bt.trǵds. | [---.]aṯt.adrt.w.pǵt.a[ḫt.b.bt.---]. | [---.ʻ]šr 80[119].27
-] | b y.šnt.mlit.t[--.---]. | ymǵy k.bnm.ta[--.---]. | [b]nm.w bnt.ytn k[.---]. | [--]l.bn y.šḫt.w [---]. | [--]tt.msgr.bn k[.---]. 59[100].9
bt šbn. | iyʻdm.w bʻl h. | ddy. | ʻmy. | iwrnr. | alnr. | maḫdt. | aby. | [-----]. | [-]nt. 107[15].2
[--.]ab.w il[--]. | [--] šlm.šlm i[l]. | [š]lm.il.šr. | dgn.w bʻl. | ʻṯ w kmṯ. | yrḫ w ksa. | yrḫ mkṯy. | ṯkmn w šnm. | kṯr w UG5.10.1.4
l. | qdš.yuḫdm.šbʻr. | amrr.k kbkb.l pnm. | aṯr.btlt.ʻnt. | w bʻl.tbʻ.mrym.ṣpn. | idk.l ttn.pnm. | ʻm.il.mbk.nhrm. | qrb.a 4[51].4.19
ym hnd. | iwr[k]l.pdy. | agdn.bn.nrgn. | w ynḥm.aḫ h. | w.bʻln aḫ h. | w.ḥṯtn bn h. | w.btšy.bt h. | w.ištrmy. | bt.ʻbd ml 1006.5
[---.ʻ]ṣrm. | [--]ṯpḫ bʻl. | [ṯl]ṯ.ʻṣrm. | [w]bʻlt btm. | [---.--]ṣn.l.dgn. | [---.--]m. | [---].pi[--.-]qš. | [--]pš. 39[19].4
.šmn.mr]. | šmn.rqḥ[.-]bt.mtnt[.w ynt.qrt]. | w ṯn ḥṯm.w bǵr.arb[ʻ.---]. | kdm.yn.prs.qmḥ.[---]. | mdbḥt.bt.ilt.ʻṣr[m.l 35[3].22
ḥ šmn mr[.šmn.rqḥ.bt]. | mtnt.w ynt.[qrt.w ṯn.ḥṯm]. | w bǵr.arbʻ.[---.kdm.yn]. | prs.qmḥ.mʻ[--.---]. | mdbḥt.bt.i[lt.ʻṣ APP.II[173].24

k.---.]šš[w.---]. | [---.w]yṣq b a[p h]. | [k ḫr š]šw mǵmǵ w b[ṣql ʻrgz]. | [ydk aḫ]d h w yṣq b ap h. | [k ḫr]ššw ḫndrṯ w 160[55].4
k [ḫr ššw mǵnǵ]. | w [bṣql.ʻrgz.ydk]. | a[ḥd h.w.yṣq.b.ap h]. | k.[ḫr.ššw.ḫndrṯ]. | 161[56].3
w tʻn.nrt.ilm.š[p]š. | šd yn.ʻn.b qbt[.t] | bl lyt.ʻl.umt k. | w abqṯ.aliyn.bʻl. | w tʻn.btlt.ʻnt. | an.l an.y špš. | an.l an.il.yǵr[6[49].4.44
ṣpn. | b nʻm.b ǵr.t[l]iyt. | ql.l bʻl.ttnn. | bšrt.il.bš[r.bʻ]l. | w bšr.ḥtk.dgn. | k.ibr.l bʻl[.yl]d. | w rum.l rkb.ʻrpt. | yšmḫ.ali 10[76].3.35
n.gdlt.[l.---]. | ugrt.š l ili[b.---]. | rt.w ʻṣrm.l[.---]. | pamt.w bt.[---]. | rmm.w ʻl[y.---]. | bt.il.ṯq[l.---.kbd]. | w bdḥ.k[--.---] APP.II[173].40
n.bn.nrgn. | w ynḥm.aḫ h. | w.bʻln aḫ h. | w.ḥṯṯn bn h. | w.btšy.bt h. | w.ištrmy. | bt.ʻbd mlk. | w.snt. | bt.ugrt. | w.pdy 1006.7
šl | ḥ.ḫrṣ.yṣq.ksp. | l alpm.ḫrṣ.yṣq | m.l rbbt. | yṣq-ḫym.w tbṯḫ. | kt.il.dt.rbtm. | kt.il.nbt.b ksp. | šmrgt.b dm.ḫrṣ. | kḥṯ. 4[51].1.30
].w.ʻl.[---]. | [-]rym.t[i]ṯtmn. | šnl.bn.ṣ[q]n.š[--]. | yitṯm.w.b[--]. | yšlm. | [ʻ]šrm.ks[p].yš[lm]. | [il]ṯhm.b d[.---]. | [---].ṯl[2104.5
w b[--.---]. | ilib[.---]. | alp.[---]. | ili[b.---]. | tʻr[.---]. | dq[t.---]. | n 44[44].1
---]. | b[ʻ]l.ugr[t.---]. | w ʻṣrm[.---]. | ṣlyh šr[-.---]. | [t]ltm.w b[--.---]. | l il limm[.---]. | w ṯt.npš[.---]. | kbd.w [---]. | l ṣp[n. 40[134].7
klt h.[---]. | ṯty.ary.m[--.---]. | nrn.arny[.---]. | w.ṯn.bn h.w.b[---.---]. | b tn[--.---]. | swn.qrty[.---]. | uḫ h.w.ʻšr[.---]. | kly 81[329].6
w ld ʻqqm. | ilm.ypʻr. | šmt hm. | b hm.qrnm. | km.ṯrm.w gbṯt. | km.ibrm. | w b hm.pn.bʻl. | bʻl.ytlk.w yṣd. | yḥ pat.ml 12[75].1.31
[k.ym]ḫṣ.bʻl m[.--]y.tnn.w ygl.w ynsk.ʻ[-]. | [--]y.l arṣ[.id]y.alt.l aḫš.idy.alt.in l y. | [--] 1001.1.1
il. | ʻṯtrt ṣwd[t.---]. | tlk b mdb[r.---]. | ṯḥdtn w hl[.---]. | w tglṯ thmt.ʻ[--.---]. | yṣi.ǵl h ṯḥm b[.---]. | mrḥ h l adrt[.---]. | 2001.1.5
. | kbd k iš.tikln. | ṯd n.km.mrm.tqrṣn. | il.yẓḥq.bm. | lb.w ygmḏ.bm kbd. | ẓi.at.l tlš. | amt.yrḫ. | l dmgy.amt. | aṯrt.qḥ. 12[75].1.13
m.mk.špšm. | b šbʻ.w tmǵy.l udm. | rbm.w l.udm.ṯrrt. | w gr.nn.ʻrm.šrn. | pdrm.sʻt.b šdm. | ḥṭb h.b grnt.ḥpšt. | sʻt.b n 14[KRT].3.110
b h.km.[---.]yqṯqṭ.ṯḥt. | ṯlḥnt.il.d ydʻnn. | yʻdb.lḥm.l h.w d l ydʻnn. | d.mṣd. | ylmn.ḥṭ.ṯḥt.ṯlḥn. | b qrʻ. | ʻṯtrt.w ʻnt.ym UG5.1.1.7
ḥmr[.---]. | w mʻn[.---]. | w bn[š.---]. | d bnš.ḥm[r.---]. | w d.l mdl.r[--.---]. | w ṣin.ʻz.b[ʻl.---]. | llu.bn[š.---]. | imr.ḫ[--.-- 2158.1.13
liyn. | bn.bʻl.hwt.aliy.qrdm. | bhṯ.bn.ilm.mt.ʻbd k.an. | w d ʻlm k.šmḫ.bn.ilm.mt. | [---.]g h.w aṣḥ.ik.yṣḥn. | [bʻl.ʻm.a 5[67].2.20
m.aliyn.bʻl.hwt.aliy. | qrdm.bhṯ.l bn.ilm mt. | ʻbd k.an.w d.ʻlm k. | tbʻ.w l.ytb.ilm.idk. | l ytn.pn.ʻm.bn.ilm.mt. | tk.qr 5[67].2.12
.ʻkyt. | yd.llḫ hm. | w.ṯlṯ.l.ʻšrm. | ḫpnt.sšwm.ṯn. | pddm.w.d.ṯṯ. | [mr]kbt.w.ḥrṣ. 2049.8
yṣḥ.knp.hrgb.bʻl.ybn. | [b]ʻl.ybn.diy.hwt.hrg[b]. | tpr.w du.b nši.ʻn h. | [w]yphn.yḥd.ṣml.um.nšrm. | yšu.g h.w yṣḥ 19[1AQHT].3.134
h. | w yṣḥ.knp.nšrm.ybn. | bʻl.ybn.diy hmt nšrm. | tpr.w du.b nši.ʻn h.w ypn. | yḥd.hrgb.ab.nšrm. | yšu.g h.w yṣḥ.k 19[1AQHT].3.120
h. | dm.ṯn.dbḥm.šna.bʻl.ṯlṯ. | rkb.ʻrpt.dbḥ. | bṯt.w dbḥ.w dbḥ. | dnt.w dbḥ.tdmm. | amht.k b h.bṯt.l tbṯ. | w b h.tdm 4[51].3.19
bḥm.šna.bʻl.ṯlṯ. | rkb.ʻrpt.dbḥ. | bṯt.w dbḥ.w dbḥ. | dnt.w dbḥ.tdmm. | amht.k b h.bṯt.l tbṯ. | w b h.tdmmt.amht. | aḫ 4[51].3.20
ks.ištyn h. | dm.ṯn.dbḥm.šna.bʻl.ṯlṯ. | rkb.ʻrpt.dbḥ. | bṯt.w dbḥ.w dbḥ. | dnt.w dbḥ.tdmm. | amht.k b h.bṯt.l tbṯ. | w b 4[51].3.19
[-.]rgm.k yrkt.ʻṯqbm. | [---]m.ʻẓpn.l pit. | m[--]m[.---]tm.w mdbḥt. | ḫr[.---.]ʻl.kbkbt. | nʻm.[--.-]llm.trṯḥṣ. | btlt.ʻn[t].tpt 13[6].16
dbḥ klyrḫ. | ndr. | dbḥ. | dt nat. | w ytnt. | ṯrmn w. | dbḥ kl. | kl ykly. | dbḥ k.sprt. | dt nat. | w qrwn. | l k dbḥ. | [RS61[24.277.6]
[--.---]. | [--]t.bʻlt.bt[.---]. | [md]bḥt.b.ḫmš[.---]. | [-.]kbd.w.db[ḥ.---]. | [--].aṯrt.ʻṣr[m.l inš.ilm]. | [t]ṯb.mdbḥ.bʻl.g[dlt.--- 35[3].39
ap.ḏd.št.špt. | l arṣ.špt l šmm.w ʻrb.b p hm.ʻṣr.šmm. | w dg b ym.w ndd.gzr.l zr.yʻdb.u ymn. | u šmal.b p hm.w l.tš 23[52].63
[hrm.ǵrpl].ʻl.arṣ.l an. | [ḫ]mt.i[l.w] ḥrn.yisp.ḥmt. | [bʻl.w]dgn[.yi]sp.ḥmt.ʻnt.w ʻṯtrt. | [ti]sp.ḥmt.y[r]ḫ.w.ršp.yisp.ḥ UG5.8.14
[ym.]bn.ʻnm.ṯpṭ.nhr.yprsḥ.ym.yql. | l arṣ.tngṣn.pnt h.w ydlp.tmn h. | yqṭ bʻl.w yšt.ym.ykly.ṯpṭ.nhr. | b šm.tgʻr m.ʻṯ 2.4[68].26
ḫ.riš k. | udmʻt.ṣḥ.aḫt k. | ṯtmnt.bt.ḥmḥ h. | d[-]n.tbkn.w tdm.l y.[--]. | [---].al.trgm.l aḫt k. | [---.]l [ ]dm.aḫt k. | ydʻt. 16.1[125].30
h.ḥmt.w tʻbtn h.abd y. | [---.ǵ]r.šrǵzz.ybky.km.nʻr. | [w ydmʻ.k]m.ṣǵr.špš.b šmm.tqru. | [---.]nplt.y[--].mdʻ.nplt.bš UG5.8.38
tbd. | w b.pḫyr h.yrṯ. | yʻrb.b ḥdr h.ybky. | b ṯn.[-]gmm.w ydmʻ. | tntkn.udmʻt h. | km.ṯqlm.arṣ h. | km ḫmšt.mṭt h. | b 14[KRT].1.27
dm. | ḫlb.l ẓr.rḥtm w rd. | bt ḫpṯt.arṣ.tspr b y | rdm.arṣ.w tdʻ ilm. | k mtt.yšmʻ.aliyn.bʻl. | yuhb.ʻglt.b dbr.prt. | b šd.šḥ 5[67].5.16
pš.yks. | mizrtm.ǵr.b abn. | ydy.psltm.b yʻr. | yhdy.lḥm.w dqn. | yṯlṯ.qn.ḏrʻ h.yḥrṯ. | k gn.ap lb.k ʻmq.yṯlṯ. | bmt.yšu.g 5[67].6.19
l bʻl. | ǵr.b ab.td[.ps]ltm[.b yʻr]. | thdy.lḥm.w dqn[.ṯṯlṯ]. | qn.ḏrʻ h.tḥrṯ.km.gn. | ap lb.k ʻmq.ṯṯlṯ.bmt. | bʻl. 6[62].1.3
rt.ʻṣr[m.l inš.ilm]. | [t]ṯb.mdbḥ.bʻl.g[dlt.---]. | dqt.l.ṣpn.w.dqt[.---]. | ṯn.l.ʻšrm.pamt.[---]. | š.dd.šmn.gdlt.w.[---.brr]. | r 35[3].42
---]. | ʻṣrm.l i[nš.ilm.ṯb.md] | bḥ.bʻl.[gdlt.---.dqt]. | l ṣpn.w [dqt.---.ṯn.l ʻš] | rm.pam[t.---]. | š dd šmn[.gdlt.w.---]. | brr.r APP.II[173].46
m[.---]. | l y.ank.aššu[.---.]w[.---]. | w hm.at.tr[gm.---]. | w.drm.ʻtr[--.---]. | w ap.ht.k[--.]škn. | w.mṯnn[.---.]ʻmn k. | [-]š 54.1.19[13.2.4]
.l bn.adlḏn. | šd.bn.nṣdn.l bn.ʻmlbi. | šd.ṯpḫln.l bn.ǵl. | w dṯn.nḥl h.l bn.pl. | šd.krwn.l aḫn. | šd.ʻyy.l aḫn. | šd.brdn.l 2089.10
yšt. | [--.]gṯr.w yqr.il.ytb.b.ʻṯtrt. | il.ṯpṭ.b hd rʻy.d yšr.w yḏmr. | b knr.w ṯlb.b tp.w mṣltm.b m | rqdm.dšn.b.ḥbr.kṯr UG5.2.1.3
išym.dt.ʻrb. | b bnš hm. | ḏmry.w.pṯpṭ.ʻrb. | b.yrm. | [ily.w].ḏmry.ʻrb. | b.ṯbʻm. | ydn.bn.ilrpi. | w.ṯbʻm.ʻrb.b.ʻ[d]n. | ḏmr 2079.5
ṯr h.yʻmsn.nn.ṯkmn. | w šnm.w ngšnn.ḥby. | bʻl.qrnm w ḏnb.ylšn. | b ḫri h.w ṯnt h.ql.il.[--]. | il.k yrdm.arṣ.ʻnt. | w ʻṯ UG5.1.1.20
-]ḥ[d].šd.hwt. | [--.]iḥd.šd.gṯr. | [w]ht.yšmʻ.uḫ y. | l g y.w yhbṭ.bnš. | w ytn.ilm.b d hm. | b d.iḫqm.gṯr. | w b d.ytrhd. 55[18].18
| w ld.špḥ.l krt. | w ǵlm.l ʻbd.il. | krt.yḫṭ.w ḥlm. | ʻbd.il.w hdrt. | yrtḥṣ.w yadm. | yrḥṣ.yd h.amt h. | uṣbʻt h.ʻd.ṯkm. | ʻr 14[KRT].3.155
.---]. | w ank.u šbt[--.---]. | ank.n[--]n[.---]. | kst.l[--.---]. | w.hw.uy.ʻn[--.---]. | l ytn.w rgm[.---]. | w yrdnn.an[--.---]. | [--- 54.1.13[13.1.10]
mštʻltm.l riš.agn. | hl h.[t]špl.hl h.trm.hl h.tṣḥ.ad ad. | w hl h.tṣḥ.um.um.tirk m.yd.il.k ym. | w yd il.k mdb.ark.yd.i 23[52].33
d ṯbil. | ʻṯtrt ṣwd[t.---]. | tlk b mdb[r.---]. | ṯḥdṯn w hl[.---]. | w tglṯ thmt.ʻ[--.---]. | yṣi.ǵl h ṯḥm b[.---]. | mrḥ h l 2001.1.4
d.---]. | šgr.mud[.---]. | dm.mt.aṣ[ḥ.---]. | yd.b qrb[.---]. | w lk.ilm.[---]. | w rgm.l [---]. | b mud.ṣin[.---]. | mud.ṣin[.---]. | 5[67].3.20
[b.---]. | al.ašt.b[---]. | ahpk k.l[--.---]. | ṯmm.w lk[.---]. | w lk.ilm[.---]. | nʻm.ilm[.---]. | šgr.mu[d.---]. | šgr.mud[.---]. | d 5[67].3.14
]. | ydd.b qr[b.---]. | al.ašt.b[---]. | ahpk k.l[--.---]. | ṯmm.w lk[.---]. | w lk.ilm[.---]. | nʻm.ilm[.---]. | šgr.mu[d.---]. | šgr.m 5[67].3.13
iṯm.mui[-.---]. | dm.mt.aṣ[ḥ.---]. | ydd.b qr[b.---]. | ṯmm.w lk[.---]. | [--]ṯ.lk[.---]. | [--]kṯ.i[---.---]. | p.šn[-.---]. | w l ṯlb.[-- 5[67].3.27
m.b mm[ʻ]. | mhrm.mṭm.tgrš. | šbm.b ksl.qšt h.mdnt. | w hln.ʻnt.l bt h.tmǵyn. | tštql.ilt.l hkl h. | w l.šbʻt.tmtḫṣ h.b ʻ 3[ʻNT].2.17
m. | w anhbm.klat.ṯǵrt. | bht.ʻnt.w tqry.ǵlmm. | b št.ǵr.w hln.ʻnt.tm | ṯḫṣ.b ʻmq.tḫtṣb.bn. | qrytm tmḫṣ.lim.ḫp y[m]. 3[ʻNT].2.5
.b.p[.--]. | apš[ny]. | b.yṣi h. | ḥwt.[---]. | alp.k[sp]. | tšʻn. | w.hm.al[-]. | l.tšʻn. | mṣrm. | tmkrn. | ypḥ.ʻbdilt. | bn.m. | ypḥ.il 2116.13
ʻṣr.tḥrr.l išt.ṣḥrrt.l pḥmm. | a[t]tm.aṯt.il.aṯt.il.w ʻlm h.w hm. | aṯtm.tṣḥn y.ad ad.nḥtm.ḫṭ k. | mmnnm.mṭ yd k.hl.ʻṣ 23[52].42
n[.---]. | gršnn.l k[si.mlk h.l nḫt.l kḥṯ]. | drkt h.š[--.--]. | w hm.ap.l[--.---]. | ymḫṣ k.k[--.---]. | il.dbḥ.[---]. | pʻr.b[--.---]. | 1[ʻNT.X].4.26
[--.---]. | [---].ank.l km[.---]. | l y.ank.aššu[.---.]w[.---]. | w hm.at.tr[gm.---]. | w.drm.ʻtr[--.---]. | w ap.ht.k[--.]škn. | w. 54.1.18[13.2.3]
-].brt.lb[--.---]. | u[-]šhr.nuš[-.---]. | b [u]grt.w ht.a[--]. | w hm.at.trg[m.---]. | w sip.u hw[.---]. | w ank.u šbt[--.---]. | an 54.1.8[13.1.5]
t.aliyn.bʻl]. | k ḫlq.z[bl.bʻl.arṣ]. | w hm.ḥy.a[liyn.bʻl]. | w hm.iṯ.zbl.bʻ[l.arṣ]. | b ḫlm.lṭpn.il.d pid. | b ḏrt.bny.bnwt. | š 6[49].3.3
[k mt.aliyn.bʻl]. | k ḫlq.z[bl.bʻl.arṣ]. | w hm.ḥy.a[liyn.bʻl]. | w hm.iṯ.zbl.bʻ[l.arṣ]. | b ḫlm.lṭpn.il.d pi 6[49].3.2

] y. | hl ny.‘mn. | mlk.b.ṯy ndr. | iṯt.w.ht. | [-]sny.udr h. | w.hm.ḫt. | ‘l.w.likt. | ‘m k.w.hm. | l.‘l.w.lakm. | ilak.w.at. | um 1013.16
ndr. | iṯt.w.ht. | [-]sny.udr h. | w.hm.ḫt. | ‘l.w.likt. | ‘m k.w.hm. | l.‘l.w.lakm. | ilak.w.at. | um y.al.tdḥṣ. | w.ap.mhkm. | 1013.18
--.]km.t[--.---]. | [--.n]pš.ttn[.---]. | [---.]yd‘t.k[---]. | [---].w hm. | [--]y.ṯb y.w [---]. | [---.]bnš.[---]. 61[-].4
[--]n.bt k.[---.]b‘[r.---]. | [--]my.b d[-.--]y.[---]. | [---.]‘m.w hm[.--]yt.w.[---]. | [---.ṯ]y.al.an[k.--.]il[m.--]y. | [--.m]ṣlm.p 1002.57
.‘ṣr.tḥrr.l išt. | w ṣḥrrt.l pḥmm.btm.bt.il.bt.il. | w ‘lm h.w hn.aṯtm.tṣḥn y.mt mt. | nḥtm.ḫṭ k.mmnnm.mṭ yd k.hl.‘ṣr 23[52].46
.alpm.š[šw]m. | rgmt.‘ly.ṯh.lm. | l.ytn.hm.mlk.[b]‘l y. | w.hn.ibm.šṣq l y. | p.l.ašt.aṯt y. | n‘r y.ṯh.l pn.ib. | hn.hm.yrg 1012.27
.km.bṯn.y[--.-]ah. | ṯnm.tšqy msk.hwt.tšqy[.-.]w [---]. | w hn dt.yṯb.l mspr. 19[1AQHT].5.1
[-----]. | [---.]abl.qšt ṯmn. | ašrb‘.qṣ‘t.w hn šb[‘]. | b ymm.apnk.dnil.mt. | rpi.a hn.ǵzr.mt.hrnm[y]. 17[2AQHT].5.3
‘.ym.ymš. | ṯdṯ.ym.ḥẓ k.al.tš‘l. | qrt h.abn.yd k. | mšdpt.w hn.špšm. | b šb‘.w l.yšn.pbl. | mlk.l qr.ṯigt.ibr h. | l ql.nhqt. 14[KRT].3.118
.kn[-]. | yhbr.špt hm.yšq.hn.[š]pt hm.mtqtm. | bm.nšq.w hr.[b]ḥbq.w ḥ[m]ḥmt.yṯb[n]. | yspr.l ḫmš.l ṣ[---.]šr.pḫr.k 23[52].56
.yš[q]. | hn.špt hm.mtqtm.mtqtm.k lrmn[.--]. | bm.nšq.w hr.b ḥbq.ḥmḥmt.tqt[nṣn]. | tldn.šḥr.w šlm.rgm.l il.ybl.a[ṯt 23[52].51
.šḥlmmt.škb. | ‘mn h.šb‘.l šb‘m. | tš[‘]ly.ṯmn.l ṯmnym. | w [th]rn.w tldn mṯ. | al[iyn.b‘]l šlbšn. | i[---.---.--]l h.mǵẓ. | y[- 5[67].5.22
w tb‘ ank. | ‘m mlakt h šm‘ h. | w b.‘ly skn.yd‘ rgm h. | w ht ab y ǵm[--]. | t[--.---]. | ls[--.---]. | ṣḥ[.---]. | ky.m[--.---]. | w 1021.9
ḫ y. | bn y.yšal. | ṯryl.p rgm. | l mlk.šm y. | w l h.y‘l m. | w h[t] aḫ y. | bn y.yšal. | ṯryl.w rgm[.-]. | ṯṯb.l aḫ k. | l adn k. 138.15
r k. | tšlm k. | iky.lḥt. | spr.d likt. | ‘m.ṯryl. | mh y.rgmt. | w ht.aḫ y. | bn y.yšal. | ṯryl.p rgm. | l mlk.šm y. | w l h.y‘l m. | 138.10
k. | tšlm k. | ik y.lḥt. | spr.d likt. | ‘m.ṯryl. | mh y.rgmt. | w ht.aḫ y. | bn y.yšal. | ṯryl.p rgm. | l mlk.šm y. | w l h[-] y‘l m 138.10
.l]qḥ.hn.l.ḥwt h. | [---.--]p.hn.ib.d.b.mgšḫ. | [---.i]b.hn[.w.]ht.ank. | [---.--]š[-.--].w.ašt. | [---].amr k. | [---].k.ybt.mlk. | [1012.11
[.---]. | w [--].brt.lb[--.---]. | u[-]šhr.nuš[-.---]. | b [u]grt.w ht.a[--]. | w hm.at.trg[m.---]. | w sip.u hw[.---]. | w ank.u šb 54.1.7[13.1.4]
l yblt.ḫbṯm. | ap ksp hm. | l yblt. | w ht.luk ‘m ml[kt]. | tǵsdb.šmlšn. | w tb‘ ank. | ‘m mlakt h š 1021.4
. | [mr]ḥqtm. | qlt. | ‘bd k.b. | lwsnd. | [w] b ṣr. | ‘m.mlk. | w.ht. | mlk.syr. | ns.w.ṯm. | ydbḥ. | mlǵ[.---]. | w.m[--.--]y. | y[--. 2063.13
-]m.lm. | [---.š]d.gṯr. | [--]ḥ[d].šd.hwt. | [--.]iḥd.šd.gṯr. | [w]ht.yšm‘.uḫ y. | l g y.w yhbṭ.bnš. | w ytn.ilm.b d hm. | b d.i 55[18].17
[.šlm]. | w.rgm[.ṯṯb.l] y. | hl ny.‘mn. | mlk.b.ṯy ndr. | iṯt.w.ht. | [-]sny.udr h. | w.hm.ḫt. | ‘l.w.likt. | ‘m k.w.hm. | l.‘l.w.l 1013.14
--]. | w prt.tkt.[---]. | šnt.[---]. | ššw.‘ṯtrt.w ššw.‘[nt.---]. | w ht.[--]k.ššw[.-]rym[.---]. | d ymǵy.bnš[.---]. | w ḥmr[.---]. | w 2158.1.7
m.---]. | iṯ.yn.d ‘rb.bṯk[.---]. | mǵ hw.l hn.lg yn h[.---]. | w ḥbr h.mla yn.[---]. 23[52].76
yyn.w.bn.au[pš]. | bn.kdrn. | ‘rgzy.w.bn.‘dy. | bn.gmḥn.w.ḥgbt. | bn.tgdn. | yny. | [b]n.g‘yn dd. | [-]n.dd. | [--]an dd. | [-- 131[309].28
b.b‘l.ṯbr. | b‘l.ṯbr.diy.hwt.w yql. | tḥt.p‘n h.ybq‘.kbd h.w yḥd. | [i]n.šmt.in.‘ẓm.yšu.g[h]. | w yṣḥ.knp.hrgb.b‘l.ybn. | [19[1AQHT].3.130
‘l.yṯbr. | b‘l.ṯbr.diy hmt.tqln. | tḥt.p‘n h.ybq‘.kbdt hm.w[yḥd]. | in.šmt.in.‘ẓm.yšu.g h. | w yṣḥ.knp.nšrm.ybn. | b‘l.y 19[1AQHT].3.116
p.ṣml.b‘[l]. | b‘l.ṯbr.diy.hyt.tq[l.tḥt]. | p‘n h.ybq‘.kbd h.w yḥd. | iṯ.šmt.iṯ.‘ẓm.w yqḥ b hm. | aqht.ybl.l qẓ.ybky.w yqb 19[1AQHT].3.144
l. | b‘l.yṯbr.b‘l.yṯbr.diy. | hyt.tql.tḥt.p‘n y.ibq‘. | kbd h.w aḥd.hm.iṯ.šmt.iṯ. | ‘ẓm.abky w aqbrn h.aštn. | b ḫrt.ilm.arṣ 19[1AQHT].3.139
yṯb.b‘l.y[ṯb]r.diy[.h]wt. | w yql.tḥt.p‘n y.ibq‘.kbd[h]. | w aḥd.hm.iṯ.šmt.hm.iṯ[.‘ẓm]. | abky.w aqbrn.ašt.b ḫrt. | i[lm. 19[1AQHT].3.125
b‘l.yṯb.b‘l.yṯb[r.diy.hmt]. | tqln.tḥ p‘n y.ibq[‘.kbd hm.w] | aḥd.hm.iṯ.šmt.hm.i[ṯ]. | ‘ẓm.abky.w aqbrn h. | ašt.b ḫrt.i 19[1AQHT].3.109
nt.]l ṣbim. | [hdmm.l ǵzrm.mid.tmtḫṣn.w t]‘n.tḫtṣb. | [w tḥdy.‘nt.tǵdd.kbd h.b ṣḥ]q.ymlu.lb h. | [b šmḫt.kbd.‘nt.tš 7.1[131].7
lḥnt. | l ṣbim.hdmm.l ǵzrm. | mid.tmtḫṣn.w t‘n. | tḫtṣb.w tḥdy.‘nt. | tǵdd.kbd h.b ṣḥq.ymlu. | lb h.b šmḫt.kbd.‘nt. | tš 3[‘NT].2.24
| [---]. | hm qrt tuḫd.hm mt y‘l bnš. | bt bn bnš yqḥ ‘z. | w yḥdy mrḥqm. RS61[24.277.31]
.rbt.aṯrt. | [ym].mǵẓ.qnyt.ilm. | w tn.bt.l b‘l.km. | [i]lm.w ḥẓr.k bn. | [a]ṯrt.gm.l ǵlm h. | b‘l.yṣḥ.‘n.gpn. | w ugr.bn.ǵl 8[51FRAG].4
bt h.dmm.šbt.dqn h. | [mm‘m.-]d.l ytn.bt.l b‘l.k ilm. | [w ḥẓ]r.k bn.aṯrt[.td‘ṣ.]p‘n. | [w tr.a]rṣ.id[k.l ttn.p]nm. | [‘m.i] 3[‘NT.VI].5.12
.aḫd.ulṯ. | hm.amt.aṯrt.tlbn. | lbnt.ybn.bt.l b‘l. | km ilm.w ḥẓr.k bn.aṯrt. | w t‘n.rbt.aṯrt ym. | rbt.ilm.l ḥkmt. | šbt.dqn 4[51].5.63
.w bn h.]ilt. | [w ṣbrt.ary]h. | [wn.in.bt.l b‘l.] | [km.ilm.w ḥẓr]. | [k bn.aṯ]r[t]. | m[ṯ]b.il.mẓll. | bn h.mṯb.rbt. | aṯrt.ym. 4[51].1.11
. | aṯrt.w bn h.ilt.w ṣbrt. | ary h.wn.in.bt.l b‘l. | km.ilm.w ḥẓr.k bn.aṯrt. | mṯb il.mẓll.bn h. | mṯb rbt.aṯrt.ym. | mṯb.kl 4[51].4.51
[---.wn.in]. | [bt].l [b‘l.km.ilm.w ḥẓr]. | k bn.[aṯrt.mṯb.il.mẓll]. | bn h.m[ṯb.rbt.aṯrt.ym]. | mṯ 3[‘NT.VI].4.01
dm[-]k[-]. | [--]ḥ.b y.ṯr.il.ab y.ank.in.bt[.l] y[.km.]ilm[.w] ḥẓr[.k bn]. | [qd]š.lbum.trd.b n[p]šn y.trḥṣn.k ṯrm. | [--]b 2.3[129].19
. | g h.w tṣḥ.tbšr b‘l. | bšrt k.yblt.y[b]n. | bt.l k.km.aḫ k.w ḥẓr. | km.ary k.ṣḥ.ḫrn. | b bht k.‘ḏbt.b qrb. | hkl k.tbl k.ǵr 4[51].5.90
t.l ql.rpi[.---]. | [---.-]llm.abl.mṣrp k.[---]. | [---.]y.mṭnt.w th.ṭbt.n[--]. | [---.b]ṯnm w ṯṯb.‘l.bṯnt.trtḥ[ṣ.---]. | [---.t]ṯb h. 1001.2.4
[.---]. | [---].d[--.---]. | b ql[.-----]. | w tštqdn[.-----]. | hm. | w yḥ.mlk. | w ik m.kn.w [---]. | tšknnnn[.---]. 62[26].9
p.l b‘l.w aṯrt.‘ṣr[m] l inš. | [ilm.---].lbbmm.gdlt.‘rb špš w ḥl. | [mlk.b ar]b‘t.‘[š]rt.yrtḥṣ.mlk.brr. | [b ym.ml]at.y[ql]n. 36[9].1.9
.b ar]b‘t.‘š | rt.yr[tḥṣ.ml]k.brr. | ‘lm.š.š[--].l[--.]‘rb.šp | š.w ḥl[.ml]k. | bn.aup[š.--].bsbn hzpḫ ṯlṯt. | kṯr[.---.--]trt ḫmšt. APP.II[173].57
h.gdlt.rgm.yṯṯb]. | brr.b šb‘[.ṣbu.špš.w ḥl] | yt.‘rb špš[.w ḥl.mlk.w.b y] | m.ḥdṯ.ṯn šm[.---.--]t. | b yrḫ.ši[-.b ar]b‘t.‘š | APP.II[173].52
rgm.yṯ[ṯb.brr]. | b.[šb]‘.ṣbu.[š]pš.w.ḥly[t].‘[r]b[.š]p[š]. | w [ḥl.]mlk.[w.]b.ym.ḥdṯ.ṯn.šm. | l.[---]t. | i[d.yd]bḥ.mlk.l.prgl 35[3].48
-]. | al[p.w].š.šlmm.pamt.šb‘.klb h. | yr[--.]mlk.ṣbu.špš.w.ḥl.mlk. | w.[---].ypm.w.mḥ[--].t[ṯ]ṯbn.[-]. | b.[--].w.km.iṯ.y[35[3].53
n[.--.šmn]. | ‘ly h.gdlt.rgm.yṯ[ṯb.brr]. | b.[šb]‘.ṣbu.[š]pš.w.ḥly[t].‘[r]b[.š]p[š]. | w [ḥl.]mlk.[w.]b.ym.ḥdṯ.ṯn.šm. | l.[---]t 35[3].47
dṯ.ṯn]. | l šmn.‘[ly h.gdlt.rgm.yṯṯb]. | brr.b šb‘[.ṣbu.špš.w ḥl] | yt.‘rb špš[.w ḥl.mlk.w.b y] | m.ḥdṯ.ṯn šm[.---.--]t. | b yr APP.II[173].51
ḏrt y.ab.adm. | w ld.špḥ.l krt. | w ǵlm.l ‘bd.il. | krt.yḫṭ.w ḥlm. | ‘bd.il.w hdrt. | yrtḥṣ.w yadm. | yrḥṣ.yd h.amt h. | uṣb 14[KRT].3.154
špt hm.yšq.hn.[š]pt hm.mtqtm. | bm.nšq.w hr.[b]ḥbq.w ḥ[m]ḥmt.yṯb[n]. | yspr.l ḫmš.l ṣ[---.]šr.pḫr.klat. | tqtnṣn.w 23[52].56
khnm.tš‘. | bnšm.w.ḥmr. | qdšm.tš‘. | bnšm.w.ḥmr. 77[63].2
[nt.---]. | w ht.[--]k.ššw[.-]rym[.---]. | d ymǵy.bnš[.---]. | w ḥmr[.---]. | w m‘n[.---]. | w bn[š.---]. | d bnš.ḥm[r.---]. | w d.l 2158.1.9
khnm.tš‘. | bnšm.w.ḥmr. | qdšm.tš‘. | bnšm.w.ḥmr. 77[63].4
d.ṯlṯ.mṣb.w.[---]. | uḫnp.ṯṯ.mṣb. | tgmr.[y]n.mṣb š[b‘]. | w ḥs[p] ṯn.k[dm]. 2004.36
.yasp.ḥmt. | [---.š]pš.l [hrm.ǵrpl].‘l.arṣ.l an. | [ḥ]mt.i[l.w] ḥrn.yisp.ḥmt. | [b‘l.w]dgn[.yi]sp.ḥmt.‘nt.w ‘ṯtrt. | [ti]sp.ḥ UG5.8.13
hn. | yd.tr hn. | w.l.ṯt.mrkbtm. | inn.uṯpt. | w.ṯlṯ.ṣmdm.w.ḥrṣ. | apnt.b d.rb.ḥršm. | d.šṣa.ḥwy h. 1121.8
bn.kmn. | bn.ibyn. | bn.mryn.ṣmd.w.ḥrṣ. | bn.prsn.ṣmd.w.ḥrṣ. | bn.ilb‘l. | bn.idrm. | bn.grgš. | bn.bly. | bn.apṯ. | bn.ysd. 2113.6
lṯ.ṣmdm. | bn.‘mnr. | bn.kmn. | bn.ibyn. | bn.mryn.ṣmd.w.ḥrṣ. | bn.prsn.ṣmd.w.ḥrṣ. | bn.ilb‘l. | bn.idrm. | bn.grgš. | bn. 2113.5
ḥrṣ. | ṯryn.sšwm. | ṯryn.aḥd.d bnš. | arb‘.ṣmdm.apnt. | w ḥrṣ. | tš‘m.mrḥ.aḥd. | kbd. 1123.8
arb‘m.qšt. | alp ḥẓm.w alp. | nṯq.ṯn.ql‘m. | ḫmš.ṣmdm.w ḥrṣ. | ṯryn.sšwm. | ṯryn.aḥd.d bnš. | arb‘.ṣmdm.apnt. | w ḥrṣ 1123.4

--].tlmdm.|[y]bnn.ṣmdm.|ṯp[ṯ]b'l.ṣmdm.|[---.ṣ]mdm.w.ḥrṣ.|[---].aḥdm.|[iwr]pzn.aḥdm.|[i]lšpš.aḥd. 2033.2.5
.|w.ṯlṯ.l.'šrm.|ḫpnt.ššwm.ṯn.|pddm.w.d.ṯṯ.|[mr]kbt.w.ḥrṣ. 2049.9
[k]l.pdy.|agdn.bn.nrgn.|w ynḥm.aḫ h.|w.b'ln aḫ h.|w.ḥṯṯn bn h.|w.btšy.bt h.|w.ištrmy.|bt.'bd mlk.|w.snt.|bt. 1006.6
d.yph.mlk.|r[š]p.ḥgb.ap.|w[.n]pš.ksp.|w ḫrṣ.km[-].|w.ḥ[--.-]lp.|w.š.l[--]p.|w[.--.-]nš.|i[--.---].|w[.---].|k[--.---].| 2005.1.5
--.---].|abn.ank.w 'l.[qšt k.---.'l].|qṣ't k.at.l ḥ[---.---].|w ḫlq.'pmm[.---]. 18[3AQHT].4.42
.|pd.|mlk.arb'.ḥm[rm.w.arb]'.bnšm.|ar.ḥmš.ḥmr[m.w.ḥm]š.bnšm.|atlg.ḥmr[.---.]bnšm.|gb'ly.ḥmr š[--.b]nšm.| 2040.4
rt.|[w].ṯmnym.l.mit.dd.ḥpr.bnšm.|b.gt.alḫb.ṯṯm.dr'.w.ḥmšm.drt.w.ṯṯm.dd.|ḥpr.bnšm.|b.gt.knpy.mit.dr'.ṯṯm.dr 1098.16
h.|art.ṯn.yrḫm.|ṯlrby.yrḫ.w.ḥm[š.ym]m.|ṯlḥny.yrḫ.w.ḥm[š.ymm].|ẓrn.yrḫ.w.ḥmš.y[m]m.|mrat.ḥmš.'šr.ymm. 66[109].5
rḫ.w.ḥm[š.ym]m.|ṯlḥny.yrḫ.w.ḥm[š.ymm].|ẓrn.yrḫ.w.ḥmš.y[m]m.|mrat.ḥmš.'šr.ymm.|qmnz.yrḫ.w.ḥmš.ymm. 66[109].6
rn.yrḫ.w.ḥmš.y[m]m.|mrat.ḥmš.'šr.ymm.|qmnz.yrḫ.w.ḥmš.ymm.|'nmk.yrḫ.|ypr.yrḫ.w.ḥmš.ymm. 66[109].8
qrht.d.ṯššlmn.|ṯlrb h.|art.ṯn.yrḫm.|ṯlrby.yrḫ.w.ḥm[š.ym]m.|ṯlḥny.yrḫ.w.ḥm[š.ymm].|ẓrn.yrḫ.w.ḥmš.y[66[109].4
šr.ymm.|qmnz.yrḫ.w.ḥmš.ymm.|'nmk.yrḫ.|ypr.yrḫ.w.ḥmš.ymm. 66[109].10
.ṯn.trqm.|w.qpt.w.mqḥm.|w.ṯlṯm.yn šb'.kbd d ṭbṭ.|w.ḥmšm.yn.d iḫ h. 1103.23
d[.---].|b.gt.ṣb[-.---].|mit.'šr.[---.]dd[.--].|tš'.dd.ḥ[ṭm.w].ḥm[šm].|kdm.kbd.yn.b.gt.[---].|[mi]tm.ḥmšm.ḥmš.k[bd 2092.4
mš.k[b]d.|yn.d.l.ṭb.b.gt.sǵy.|arb'm.kdm.kbd.yn.ṭb.|w.ḥmšm.k[dm.]kbd.yn.d.l.ṭb.|b.gt.gwl.|ṯlṯm.tš'[.kbd.yn].d. 1084.17
š.mat.arb'm.|kbd.ksp.anyt.|d.'rb.b.anyt.|l.mlk.gbl.|w.ḥmšm.ksp.|lqḥ.mlk.gbl.|lbš.anyt h.|b'rm.ksp.|mḫr.hn. 2106.14
.ṭb.|w.ṯṯm.arb'.kbd.yn.d.l.ṭb.|b.gt.m'rby.|ṯṯm.yn.ṭb.w.ḥmš.l.'šrm.|yn.d.l.ṭb.b.ulm.|mit.yn.ṭb.w.ṯṯm.ṯṯ.kbd.|yn. 1084.9
.mḏ]rǵlm.|[---.]b.bt[.---]l.|[ṯ]lṯ.aṯt.adrt.w.ṯlṯ.ǵzr[m].|w.ḥmš.n'rt.b.bt.sk[n].|ṯt.aṯtm.adrtm.w.pǵt.w ǵzr[.aḥd.b.bt. 80[119].17
š.k[bd].|[dd].kšmm.tš'[.---].|[š]'rm.ṯṯ.'[šr].|[dd].ḥṭm.w.ḥ[mšm].|[ṯ]lṯ kbd.yn.b [gt.---].|mit.[---].ṯlṯ.kb[d].|[dd.--] 2092.9
.kbd.|ṯlṯm.ḥmš kbd ktn.|ḥmš.rṭm.|ḥmš.ṯnt.d ḥmšm w.|ḥmš.ṯnt.d mit.|ḥmš.ṯnt.d ṯl|ṯ mat.|ṯt.ṯnt.d alp|alpm.ṯlṯ 1130.9
'šr šṭpm.|b ḥmš.šmn.|'šrm.gdy.|b ḥmš.šmn.|w ḥmš ṯ'dt. 1097.5
.[b']l m.'[--].yd k.amṣ.yd[.--].|[---.]ḥš[.-]nm[.--.]k.[--].w yḫnp[.---].|[---.]ylm.b[n.']n k.ṣmdm.špk[.---].|[---.]nt[-.] 1001.1.15
.ḥmt.ṯṯ.w ktṯ.|[yus]p.ḥmt.mlk.b 'ṯtrt.yisp.ḥmt.|[kṯ]r w ḫss.y[i]sp.ḥmt.šḥr.w šlm.|[yis]p.ḥmt.isp.[šp]š l hrm.ǵrpl. UG5.8.18
mk.b šb'.šnt.|bn.krt.km hm.tdr.|ap.bnt.ḥry.|km hm.w ṯḫss.aṯrt.|ndr h.w ilt.p[--].|w tšu.g h.w [tṣḥ].|ph m'.ap.k 15[128].3.25
l npš.kṯr.w ḫss.|l brlt.hyn.d ḥrš.|ydm.aḫr.ymǵy.kṯr.|w ḫss.b d.dnil.ytnn.|qšt.l brk h.y'db.|qṣ't.apnk.mṯt.dnty.|t 17[2AQHT].5.26
bht.ym[.rm]m.hkl.ṯpṭ nh[r].|[---.]hrn.w[---.]tb'.k[ṯ]r w [ḫss.t]bn.bht zbl ym.|[trm]m.hk[l.ṯpṭ].nhr.bt k.[---.]šp[-.- 2.3[129].8
.qrnt.b y'lm.mtnm.|b 'qbt.ṯr.adr.b ǵlil.qnm.|tn.l kṯr.w ḫss.yb'l.qšt l 'nt.|qṣ't.l ybmt.limm.w t'n.btlt.|'nt.irš ḥym 17[2AQHT].6.24
[m.w l tbn.hmlt.arṣ].|at.w ank.ib[ǵy h.---].|w y'n.kṯr.w ḫss[.lk.lk.'nn.ilm.]|atm.bštm.w an[.šnt.kptr].|l rḥq.ilm.ḥ 1['NT.IX].3.17
mid.ksp.|gb'm lḥmd.ḫrṣ.|yblnn.udr.ilqṣm.|yak.l kṯr.w ḫss.|w ṯb l mspr..k tlakn.|ǵlmm.|aḫr.mǵy.kṯr.w ḫss.|št. 4[51].5.103
.|'d k.kṯr m.ḥbr k.|w ḫss.d't k.|b ym.arš.w tnn.|kṯr.w ḫss.yd.|ytr.kṯr.w ḫss.|spr.ilmlk šbny.|lmd.atn.prln.rb.|k 6.6[62.2].51
|špš.ṯḥtk.ilnym.|'d k.ilm.hn.mtm.|'d k.kṯr m.ḥbr k.|w ḫss.d't k.|b ym.arš.w tnn.|kṯr.w ḫss.yd.|ytr.kṯr.w ḫss.|s 6.6[62.2].49
nḥš.|'q šr.y'db.ksa.w yṯb.|tqru.l špš.um.ql bl.'m|kṯr.w ḫss.kptr h.mnt.nṯk.nḥš.|šmrr.nḥš.'q šr.ln h.mlḫš.abd.|ln UG5.7.46
ḥkpt.il.kl h.tšm'.|mṯt.dnty.t'db.imr.|b pḫd.l npš.kṯr.w ḫss.|l brlt.hyn.d ḥrš.|ydm.aḫr.ymǵy.kṯr.|w ḫss.b d.dnil. 17[2AQHT].5.23
aṯt h.k yṣḥ.|šm'.mṯt.dnty.'d[b].|imr.b pḫd.l npš.kṯr.|w ḫss.l brlt.hyn d.|ḥrš yd.šlḥm.ššqy.|ilm sad.kbd.hmt.b'l.| 17[2AQHT].5.18
ny.w l.'pr.'ẓm ny.|l b'l[-.---].|tḥt.ksi.zbl.ym.w 'n.kṯr.w ḫss.l rgmt.|l k.l zbl.b'l.ṯnt.l rkb.'rpt.ht.ib k.|b'l m.ht.ib k 2.4[68].7
kl |m.w y[p]tḥ.b dqt.'rpt.|'l h[wt].kṯr.w ḫss.|ṣḥq.kṯr.w ḫss.|yšu.g h.w yṣḥ.|l rgmt.l k.l ali|yn.b'l.ṯṯbn.b'l.|l hwt 4[51].7.21
.|w ḫss.d't k.|b ym.arš.w tnn.|kṯr.w ḫss.yd.|ytr.kṯr.w ḫss.|spr.ilmlk šbny.|lmd.atn.prln.rb.|khnm rb.nqdm.|ṯ' 6.6[62.2].52
.|'ṭ w kmṯ.|yrḫ w ksa.|yrḫ mkṯy.|ṯkmn w šnm.|kṯr w ḫss.|'ṯtr 'ṯtpr.|šḥr w šlm.|ngh w srr.|'dw šr.|ṣdqm šr.|ḥ UG5.10.1.9
|urbt.b qrb.[h]kl |m.w y[p]tḥ.b dqt.'rpt.|'l h[wt].kṯr.w ḫss.|ṣḥq.kṯr.w ḫss.|yšu.g h.w yṣḥ.|l rgmt.l k.l ali|yn.b'l. 4[51].7.20
kṯr.w ḫss.|w ṯb l mspr..k tlakn.|ǵlmm.|aḫr.mǵy.kṯr.w ḫss.|št.alp.qdm h.mra.|w tk.pn h.t'db.ksu.|w yṯṯb.l ymn 4[51].5.106
b tk.ṣrrt.ṣpn.|alp.šd.aḥd bt.|rbt.kmn.hkl.|w y'n.kṯr.w ḫss.|šm'.l aliyn b'l.|bn.l rkb.'rpt.|bl.ašt.urbt.b bh[t] m.| 4[51].5.120
w y'n.k[ṯr.w ḫs]s.|ṯtb.b'l.l[hwt y].|tn.rgm.k[ṯr.w]ḫss.|šm'.m'.l al[iy]n b'l.|bl.ašt.ur[bt.]b bht m.|ḥln.b qr[4[51].6.3
hbr.]w yql[.y]šṯḥw[y.]w ykb[dn h.--]r y[---].|[---.k]ṯr.w ḫ[ss.t]b'.b[n.]bht.ym[.rm]m.hkl.ṯpṭ nh[r].|[---.]hrn.w[---. 2.3[129].7
.|[---.m]dd.il ym.|[---.-]qlṣn.wpṯ m.|[---.]w y'n.kṯr.|[w ḫss.]ṯtb.b'l.l hwt y.|[ḥš.]bht h.tbnn.|[ḥš.]trmm.hkl h.|y[t 4[51].6.15
w y'n.k[ṯr.w ḫs]s.|ṯtb.b'l.l[hwt y].|tn.rgm.k[ṯr.w]ḫss.|šm'.m'.l al[iy] 4[51].6.1
p'n.kṯr].|hbr.w ql.t[šṯḥwy.w kbd.hwt].|w rgm l k[ṯr.w ḫss.tny.l hyn].|d ḥrš.y[dm.tḥm.ṯr.il.ab k.]|hwt.lṭpn[.ḥtk 1['NT.IX].3.4
.l p'n.kṯ.|hbr.w ql.tšṯḥ|wy.w kbd hwt.|w rgm.l kṯr.|w ḫss.tny.l h|yn.d ḥrš.ydm.|tḥm.al[iyn.b'l].|h[wt.aliy.qrd 3['NT.VI].6.22
---].|[------.]ṯr.|[---.aliy]n.b'l.|[------.]yrḫ.zbl.|[--.kṯ]r w ḫss.|[---]n.rḥm y.ršp zbl.|[w 'd]t.ilm.ṯlṯ h.|[ap]nk.krt.ṯ'.' 15[128].2.5
t h[.l.]'ṯtrt.šd.|[---.-]rt.mḫṣ.bnš.mlk.yb'l hm.|[---.--]t.w.ḫpn.l.azzlt.|[---.]l.'ṯtrt.šd.|[---].yb'lnn.|[---.--]n.b.ṯlṯ.šnt.l. 1106.54
|y'r[t].|amd[y].|atl[g].|bṣr[y].|[---].|[---]y.|ar.|agm.w.ḫpty.|ḫlb.ṣpn.|mril.|'nmky.|'nqpat.|ṭbq.|hzp.|gn'y.|m 71[113].49
ḫmšt.'š[rt].|ksp.'l.agd[ṯb].|w nit w m'ṣd.|w ḫrmṯt.|'šrt.ksp.|'l.ḫ[z]rn.|w.nit.w[.m'ṣd].|w.ḫ[rmṯt].|'š[2053.4
].|w.ḫ[rmṯt].|'š[r.---].|'l[.---].|w.ni[t.---].|w[.m'ṣd].|w ḫr[mṯt].|[']šr[.---].|[']l [-]g[-.---].|w ni[t.w.m'ṣd].|w ḫrmṯ 2053.13
m'ṣd.|w ḫrmṯt.|'šrt.ksp.|'l.ḫ[z]rn.|w.nit.w[.m'ṣd].|w.ḫ[rmṯt].|'š[r.---].|'l[.---].|w.ni[t.---].|w[.m'ṣd].|w ḫr[mṯt] 2053.8
|w ḫr[mṯt].|[']šr[.---].|[']l [-]g[-.---].|w ni[t.w.m'ṣd].|w ḫrmṯt.|ṯlṯm.ar[b'].|kbd.ksp.|'l.tgyn.|w 'l.aṯt h.|yph.m'n 2053.17
tbl k.ǵrm.|mid.ksp.gb'm.mḥmd..|ḫrṣ.w bn.bht.ksp.|w ḫrṣ.bht.ṯhrm.|iqnim.šmḫ.aliyn.|b'l.ṣḥ.ḥrn.b bht h.|'ḏbt. 4[51].5.96
sp.|gb'm.mḥmd.ḫrṣ.|ybl k.udr.ilqṣm.|w bn.bht.ksp.w ḫrṣ.|bht.ṯhrm.iqnim.|šmḫ.btlt.'nt.td'ṣ.|p'nm.w tr.arṣ.|i 4[51].5.80
id.yph.mlk.|r[š]p.ḥgb.ap.|w[.n]pš.ksp.|w ḫrṣ.km[-].|w.ḥ[--.-]lp.|w.š.l[--]p.|w[.--.-]nš.|i[--.---].|w[.- 2005.1.4
]k.bm.ymn.|tlk.škn.'l.ṣrrt.|adn k.šqrb.[---].|b mgn k.w ḫrṣ.l kl.|apnk.ǵzr.ilḥu.|[m]rḥ h.yiḫd.b yd.|[g]rgr h.bm.y 16.1[125].45
ṯmnt.'šrt.yr|tḥṣ.mlk.brr.|'lm.tzǵ.b ǵb.ṣpn.|nḥkt.ksp.w ḫrṣ ṯ' ṯn šm l btbt.|alp.w š šrp.alp šlmm.|l b'l.'ṣr l ṣpn.|n UG5.12.A.8
--.---].|t[--.---].|w[----].|pǵ[t.---].|lk[.---].|ki[--.---].|w ḫ[--.---].|my[.---].|at[t.---].|aḫ k[.---].|tr.ḥ[---].|w tṣḥ[.--- 16.2[125].70
[---.]tasrn.ṯr il.|[---.]rks.bn.abnm.|[---.]upqt.'rb.|[---.w ẓ]r.mtn y at zd.|[---.]t'rb.bši.|[---.]l tzd.l tptq.|[---].g[--.]l 1['NT.X].5.25
.ysgr.|almnt.škr.|tškr.zbl.'ršm.|yšu.'wr.|mzl.ymzl.|w ybl.trḫ.ḥdṯ.|yb'r.l ṯn.aṯt h.|w l nkr.mddt.|km irby.tškn. 14[KRT].4.189
.hl h.tṣḥ.ad ad.|w hl h.tṣḥ.um.um.tirk m.yd.il.k ym.|w yd il.k mdb.ark.yd.il.k ym.|w yd.il.k mdb.yqḥ.il.mšt'ltm. 23[52].34

um.tirk m.yd.il.k ym.|w yd il.k mdb.ark.yd.il.k ym.|w yd.il.k mdb.yqḥ.il.mšt'ltm.|mšt'ltm.l riš.agn.yqḥ.tš.b bt 23[52].35
by.|šm't.ḫti.|nḫtu.ht.|hm.in mm.|nḫtu.w.lak.|'m y.w.yd.|ilm.p.k mtm.|'z.mid.|hm.nṯkp.|m'n k.|w.mnm.|rg 53[54].11
.m]ṣlm.pn y[.-.]tlkn.|[---.]rḥbn.hm.[-.]aṯr[.---].|[--]šy.w ydn.b'[l.---]n.|[--]'.k yn.hm.l.atn.bt y.l h. 1002.61
qr[-].|akl n.b.grnt.|l.b'r.|ap.krmm.|ḫlq.|qrt n.ḫlq.|w.d'.d'. 2114.13
].|kll.šlm.ṯm ny.|'m.um y.mnm.šlm.|w.rgm.ṯṯb.l y.|w.mnd'.k.ank.|aḥš.mǵy.mnd'.|k.igr.w.u.[--].|'m.špš.[---].| 2009.1.10
.|b ḏrt.bny.bnwt.|šmm.šmn.tmṭrn.|nḫlm.tlk.nbtm.|w id'.k ḥy.aliyn.b'l.|k iṯ.zbl.b'l.arṣ.|b ḥlm.lṭpn.il d pid.|b ḏ 6[49].3.8
t.lb k.'nn.[---].|[--.]šdq.k ttn.l y.šn[.---].|[---.]bn.rgm.w yd'[.---]. 60[32].6
[-----.]a[---].|[---.--]ln.|[---.]kqmṯn.|[---.]klnmw.|[---.]w yky.|ṯlṯm sp.l bnš tpnr.|arb'.spm.l.lbnš prwsdy.|ṯṯ spm.l 137.2[93].5
.|[---.]w šb'l.|[---.-]ym.|[---.--]ḫm.|[---.--]m.|[---]nb.w ykn.|[--]ndbym.|[']rmy.w snry.|[b]n.sdy.bn.ṯty.|bn.ḥyn. 131[309].20
bnil.bn.yṣr[.---].|'dyn.bn.uḏr[-.---].|w.'d'.nḥl h[.---].|w.yknil.nḥl h[.---].|w.iltm.nḥl h[.---].|w.unṯm.nḥ[l h.---].|[90[314].1.15
.ilm.tity.|tity.ilm.l ahl hm.|dr il.l mšknt hm.|w tqrb.w ld.bn.l h.|w tqrb.w ld.bnt.l h.|mk.b šb'.šnt.|bn.krt.km h 15[128].3.20
hl hm.|dr il.l mšknt hm.|w tqrb.w ld.bn.l h.|w tqrb.w ld.bnt.l h.|mk.b šb'.šnt.|bn.krt.km hm.tdr.|ap.bnt.ḫry.| 15[128].3.21
id.rm.]krt.|[b tk.rpi.]arṣ.|[b pḫr].qbṣ.dtn.|[w t]qrb.w ld.|bn.tl k.|tld.pǵt.t[--]t.|tld.pǵt[.---].|tld.pǵ[t.---].|tld.p 15[128].3.5
m]ḫmt.yṯb[n].|yspr.l ḫmš.l ṣ[---.]šr.pḫr.klat.|tqtnṣn.w tldn.tld.[ilm.]n'mm.agzr ym.|bn.ym.ynqm.b a[p.]ḏ[d.r]g 23[52].58
škb.|'mn h.šb'.l šb'm.|tš[']ly.ṯmn.l ṯmnym.|w [th]rn.w tldn mṯ.|al[iyn.b']l šlbšn.|i[---.---.--]l h.mǵẓ.|y[--.---.]l irt 5[67].5.22
lšiy.|kry amt.|'pr.'ẓm yd.|ugrm.ḫl.ld.|aklm.tbrk k.|w ld 'qqm.|ilm.yp'r.|šmt hm.|b hm.qrnm.|km.ṯrm.w gbṯt. 12[75].1.27
ni.|'p'p h.sp.ṯrml.|d b ḥlm y.il.ytn.|b ḏrt y.ab.adm.|w ld.špḥ.l krk|t.w ǵlm.l 'bd.|il.ttb'.mlakm.|l yṯb.idk.pnm. 14[KRT].6.298
.-].|ašlw.b ṣp.'n h.|d b ḥlm y.il.ytn.|b ḏrt y.ab.adm.|w ld.špḥ.l krt.|w ǵlm.l 'bd.il.|krt.yḫṭ.w ḥlm.|'bd.il.w hdrt. 14[KRT].3.152
.b uš[k.--].|[-.b]'l.yabd.l alp.|[---.bt]lt.'nt.|[---]q.hry.w yld.|[---]m.ḫbl.kṯ[r]t.|[---.bt]lt.'nt.|[---.ali]yn.b'l.|[---.]m' 11[132].1.5
w ǵr mtn y.|[---.]rq.gb.|[---.--]kl.tǵr.mtn h.|[---.--]b.w ym ymm.|[y'tqn.---].ymǵy.npš.|[---.--]t.hd.tngṯm h.|[---. 1['NT.X].5.15
[---.--]b.|[---.w ym.ym]m.|[y'tqn.---.ymǵy.]npš.|[---.h]d.tngṯn h.|[---].b 1['NT.X].5.2
m.a[--.--]n.|[--.]ḥ[--.]d[--]t.|[---.]ḫw[t.---].|[---.]š[--].|w ym ym.yš|al.|w mlk.d mlk.|b ḥwt.špḥ.|l ydn.'bd.mlk.| 2062.2.02
.klby.kl[--].dqn[.---].|[-]ntn.artn.b d[.--]nr[.---].|'zn.w ymd.šr.b d ansny.|nsk.ks[p.--]mrtn.kṯrmlk.|yḥmn.aḫm[l 2011.31
b[n.--]n.|'n ha l yd h.tzd[.--].|pt l bšr h.dm a[--.--]ḥ.|w yn.k mtrḫt[.---]h.|šm' ilht kṯr[t.--]mm.|nh l yd h tzdn[.- 24[77].10
[--.---].|b[--.---].|l[--.---].|m[--.---].|bn[.---].|bn[.---].|w.yn[.---].|bn.'dr[.---].|ntb[t].|b.arb['].|mat.ḫr[ṣ]. 2007.8
dr.ttǵr.|[---.n]šr k.al ttn.l n.|[---.]tn l rbd.|[---.]b'lt h w yn.|[---.rk]b 'rpt.|[---.--]n.w mnu dg.|[---.]l aliyn b'l.|[--- 2001.2.14
l ym hnd.|iwr[k]l.pdy.|agdn.bn.nrgn.|w ynḥm.aḫ h.|w.b'ln aḫ h.|w.ḥṯṯn bn h.|w.btšy.bt h.|w.išt 1006.4
[b ym.ml]at.y[ql]n.al[p]m.yrḫ.'šrt.|[l b'l.ṣ]pn.[dq]tm.w y[nt] qrt.|[w mtmt]m.[š.l] rm[š.]kbd.w š.|[l šlm.kbd.al]p 36[9].1.12
k.b[rr].|b ym.mlat.|tqln.alpm.|yrḫ.'šrt.l b'[l].|dqtm.w ynt.qr[t].|w mtntm.š l rmš.|w kbd.w š.l šlm kbd.|alp.w UG5.13.6
-].|d yqḥ bt[.--]r.dbḥ[.šmn.mr].|šmn.rqḥ[.-]bt.mtnt[.w ynt.qrt].|w ṯn ḥṯm.w bǵr.arb['.---].|kdm.yn.prs.qmḥ.[---] 35[3].21
.|ṯlṯm.w m'rb[.---].|dbḥ šmn mr[.šmn.rqḥ.bt].|mtnt.w ynt.[qrt.w ṯn.ḥṯm].|w bǵr.arb'.[---.kdm.yn].|prs.qmḥ.m'[APP.II[173].23
rr[.w mḫ-.---].|ym.[']lm.y'[--.---].|[--.-]g[-.-]s w [---].|w yn[t.q]rt.y[---].|w al[p.l]il.w bu[rm.---].|ytk.gdlt.ilhm.[ṯ 35[3].10
ḥ[--.---.]w q[--].|ym.'lm.y[---.---].|t.k[-]ml.[---].|l[---].w y[nt.qrt.---].|[---.--]n[.w alp.l il.w bu]|[rm.---.ytk.gdlt.ilh APP.II[173].11
iqra.ilm.n['mm.---].|w ysmm.bn.š[---].|ytnm.qrt.l 'ly[.---].|b mdbr.špm.yd[.---.-- 23[52].2
h.|ytb.l ksi mlk.|l nḥt.l kḥṯ.drkt.|ap.yṣb.yṯb.b hkl.|w ywsrnn.ggn h.|lk.l ab k.yṣb.lk.|l[ab]k.w rgm.'ny.|l k[rt 16.6[127].26
[---.]arḫt.tld[n].|a[lp].l btlt.'nt.|w ypt l ybmt.li[mm].|w y'ny.aliyn[.b'l].|lm.k qnym.'l[m.--] 10[76].3.4
y[ṯ]b.aliyn.b'l.|yt'dd.rkb.'rpt.|[--].ydd.w yqlṣn.|yqm.w ywpṯn.b tk.|p[ḫ]r.bn.ilm.štt.|p[--].b ṯlḥn y.qlt.|b ks.ištyn 4[51].3.13
.[b'l.]|bṯ.l rkb.'rpt.k šby n.zb[l.ym.k] |šby n.ṭpṭ.nhr.w yṣa b[.--].|ybṯ.nn.aliyn.b'l.w [---].|ym.l mt.b'l m.ym l[--. 2.4[68].30
|amt.yrḫ.|l dmgy.amt.|aṯrt.qḥ.|ksan k.ḥdg k.|ḥtl k.w ẓi.|b aln.tk m.|b tk.mlbr.|ilšiy.|kry amt.|'pr.'ẓm yd.|ug 12[75].1.19
mš.|[mǵ]d.ṯdṯ.yr[ḫm].|'dn.ngb.w [yṣi.ṣbu].|ṣbi.ng[b.w yṣi.'dn].|m'[.ṣ]bu h.u[l.mad].|ṯlṯ.mat.rbt.|hlk.l alpm.ḫḏ 14[KRT].4.177
.d ḫmš.|mǵd.ṯdṯ.yrḫm.|'dn.ngb.w yṣi.|ṣbu.ṣbi.ngb.|w yṣi.'dn.m'.|ṣbu k.ul.mad.|ṯlṯ.mat.rbt.|ḫpṯ.d bl.spr.|ṯnn. 14[KRT].2.87
ḥṯt.l bt.ḫbr.|yip.lḥm.d ḫmš.|mǵd.ṯdṯ.yrḫm.|'dn.ngb.w yṣi.|ṣbu.ṣbi.ngb.|w yṣi.'dn.m'.|ṣbu k.ul.mad.|ṯlṯ.mat.rbt 14[KRT].2.85
.l bt.ḫbr.|yip.lḥm.d ḫmš.|[mǵ]d.ṯdṯ.yr[ḫm].|'dn.ngb.w [yṣi.ṣbu].|ṣbi.ng[b.w yṣi.'dn].|m'[.ṣ]bu h.u[l.mad].|ṯlṯ.m 14[KRT].4.176
t h.sgr.|almnt.škr.|tškr.zbl.'ršm.|yšu.'wr.mzl.|ymzl.w yṣi.trḫ.|ḥdṯ.yb'r.l ṯn.|aṯt h.lm.nkr.|mddt h.k irby.|[t]šk 14[KRT].2.100
[k l yḫru w]l yṯtn mss št qlql.|[w št 'rgz y]dk aḥd h w yṣq b ap h.|[k.yiḫd akl s]šw št mkšr grn.|[w št aškrr w p 160[55].9
u.w.l.yṯtn.ššw].|mss.[št.qlql.w.št].|'rgz[.ydk.aḥd h].|w.yṣq[.b.ap h].|k.yiḫd[.akl.ššw].|št.mkš[r.grn].|w.št.ašk[rr 161[56].11
|št.mkš[r.grn].|w.št.ašk[rr].|w.pr.ḥdr[t.ydk].|aḥd h.w.yṣq[.b.ap h].|k.yiḫd.akl.š[šw].|št.nni.št.mk[št.grn].|št.irǵ 161[56].16
k [ḫr ššw mǵmǵ].|w [bṣql.'rgz.ydk].|a[ḥd h.w.yṣq.b.ap h].|k.[ḫr.ššw.ḥndrt].|w.ṯ[qd.mr.ydk.aḥd h].|w. 161[56].4
a[p h].|[k ḫr s]šw mǵmǵ w b[ṣql 'rgz].|[ydk aḥ]d h w yṣq b ap h.|[k ḫr]ššw ḥndrt w ṯ[qd m]r.|[ydk aḥd h w y 160[55].5
[k.---.]šs[w.---].|[---.w]yṣq b a[p h].|[k ḫr s]šw mǵmǵ w b[ṣql 'rgz].|[ydk aḥ]d 160[55].3
ṣq.b.ap h].|k.[ḫr.ššw.ḥndrt].|w.ṯ[qd.mr.ydk.aḥd h].|w.y[ṣq.b.ap h].|k.l.ḫ[ru.w.l.yṯtn.ššw].|mss.[št.qlql.w.št].|'r 161[56].7
yṣq b ap h.|[k ḫr]ššw ḥndrt w ṯ[qd m]r.|[ydk aḥd h w yṣq b ap h.|[k l yḫru w]l yṯtn mss št qlql.|[w št 'rgz y]d 160[55].7
š[šw].|št.nni.št.mk[št.grn].|št.irǵn.ḥmr[.ydk].|aḥd h.w.yṣq.b[.ap h].|k.yraš.ššw.[št].|bln.qṭ.yṣq.b.a[p h].|k yǵ'r[. 161[56].20
.w.pr.'bk].|w.pr[.ḥdrt.w.št].|irǵ[n.ḥmr.ydk].|aḥd[h.w.yṣq.b.ap h].|k yr[a]š.šš[w.w.ykhp].|mid.dblt.yṯ[nt.w].|ṣ 161[56].31
r ḥdrt.|[-----].|[---.-]n[-].|[k yraš ššw št bln q]ṭ ydk.|[w yṣq b ap h].|[-----].|[-----].|[-----].|[---.-]rb.|[-----].|[-----]. 160[55].15
blt.yṯ[nt.w].|ṣmq[m].yṯnm.w[.qmḥ.bql].|tdkn.aḥd h.w[.yṣq].|b.ap h. 161[56].35
ab k.yṣb.lk.|l[ab]k.w rgm.'ny.|l k[rt.adn k.]ištm['].|w tqǵ[.udn.k ǵz.ǵzm].|tdbr.w[ǵ]rm[.ṯṯwy].|šqlt.b ǵlt.yd k. 16.6[127].30
lm.'l.|ab h.y'rb.yšu g h.|w yṣḥ.šm' m'.l krt.|ṯ'.ištm'.w tqǵ udn.|k ǵz.ǵzm.tdbr.|w ǵrm.ṯṯwy.šqlt.|b ǵlt.yd k.l td 16.6[127].42
[---]n.yšt.rpu.mlk.'lm.w yšt.|[--.]gṯr.w yqr.il.yṯb.b.'ṯtrt.|il.ṯpṭ.b hd r'y.d yšr.w yḏmr.|b knr.w ṯl UG5.2.1.2
--].|kst.l[--.---].|w.hw.uy.'n[--.---].|l ytn.w rgm[.---].|w yrdnn.an[--.---].|[---].ank.l km[.---].|l y.ank.ašṣu[.---.]w[. 54.1.15[13.1.12]
r.ṯrmg.|'m.tlm.ǵṣr.arṣ.|ša.ǵr.'l.ydm.|ḫlb.l ẓr.rḥtm.|w rd.bt ḫpṯt.|arṣ.tspr.b y|rdm.arṣ.|idk.al.ttn.|pnm.tk.qrt 4[51].8.7
|pn k.al ttn.tk.ǵr.|knkny.ša.ǵr.'l ydm.|ḫlb.l ẓr.rḥtm w rd.|bt ḫpṯt.arṣ.tspr b y|rdm.arṣ.w td' ilm.|k mtt.yšm'.ali 5[67].5.14
tm.d[q]tm.|[yr]ḫ.kty gdlt.w l ǵlmt š.|[w]pamt ṯlṯm.w yrdt.[m]dbḥt.|gdlt.l b'lt bhtm.'ṣrm.|l inš ilm. 34[1].20

m.dbḥ.l ṯr.|ab k.il.šrd.b‘l.|b dbḥ k.bn.dgn.|b mṣd k.w yrd.|krt.l ggt.‘db.|akl.l qryt.|ḥṭt.l bt.ḫbr.|yip.lḥm.d ḫm 14[KRT].2.79
ṯ‘r.|mšrrm.aḫt h l a|bn mznm.nkl w ib.|d ašr.ar yrḫ.w y|rḫ yar k.|[ašr ilht kṯrt bn]|t hll.snnt.bnt h|ll b‘l gml.y 24[77].38
.‘z k.ḏmr k.l[-]|n k.ḥtk k.nmrt k.b tk.|ugrt.l ymt.špš.w yrḫ.|w n‘mt.šnt.il. UG5.2.2.11
yrḫ.l gṯr.|ṯql.ksp.ṭb.ap w np[š].|l ‘nt h.ṯql.ḫrṣ.|l špš[.w y]rḫ.l gṯr.ṯn.|[ṯql.ksp].ṭb.ap.w npš.|[---].bt.alp w š.|[---.-- 33[5].14
l ilm.šb[‘.]l kṯr.|‘lm.t‘rbn.gṯrm.|bt.mlk.ṯql.ḫrṣ.|l špš.w yrḫ.l gṯr.|ṯql.ksp.ṭb.ap w np[š].|l ‘nt h.ṯql.ḫrṣ.|l špš[.w y 33[5].11
n.ašql k.tḥt.|[p‘n y.a]nk.n‘mn.‘mq.nšm.|[td‘ṣ.p‘n]m.w tr.arṣ.idk.|[l ttn.pn]m.‘m il.mbk.nhrm.|[qrb.ap]q.thmtm 17[2AQHT].6.46
.ksp.w ḫrṣ.|bht.ṭhrm.iqnim.|šmḫ.btlt.‘nt.td‘ṣ.|p‘nm.w tr.arṣ.|idk.l ttn.pnm.|‘m.b‘l.mrym.ṣpn.|b alp.šd.rbt.kmn 4[51].5.83
.-]d.l ytn.bt.l b‘l.k ilm.|[w ḥẓ]r.k bn.aṯrt[.td‘ṣ.]p‘n.|[w tr.a]rṣ.id[k.l ttn.p]nm.|[‘m.i]l.mbk.nhr[m.qr]b.[ap]q.|[th 3[‘NT.VI].5.13
.aḫ k.|w tšu.‘n h.btlt.‘nt.|w tšu.‘n h.w t‘n.|w t‘n.arḫ.w tr.b lkt.|tr.b lkt.w tr.b ḫl.|[b]n‘mm.b ysmm.ḥ[--]k.ǵrt.| 10[76].2.28
tlt.‘nt.|w tšu.‘n h.w t‘n.|w t‘n.arḫ.w tr.b lkt.|tr.b lkt.w tr.b ḫl.|[b]n‘mm.b ysmm.ḥ[--]k.ǵrt.|[ql].l b‘l.‘nt.ttnn.|[10[76].2.29
n.l kḥ[ṯ.drkt h].|l alp.ql.ẓ[--.---].|l np ql.nd.[----].|tlk.w tr.b[ḫl].|b n‘mm.b ys[mm.---].|arḫ.arḫ.[---.tld].|ibr.tld[. 10[76].3.18
|tk.aḫ.šmk.mla[t.r]umm.|tšu knp.btlt.‘n[t].|tšu.knp.w tr.b ‘p.|tk.aḫ šmk.mlat rumm.|w yšu.‘n h.aliyn.b‘l.|w yš 10[76].2.11
ak.|mlakm.l k.‘m.krt.|mswn h.tḥm.pbl.mlk.|qḥ.ksp.w yrq.ḫrṣ.|yd.mqm h.w ‘bd.‘lm.|ṯlṯ.sswm.mrkbt.|b trbṣ.bn 14[KRT].3.126
ytnt.il w ušn.|ab.adm.w ṯṯb.|mlakm.l h.lm.ank.|ksp.w yrq.ḫrṣ.|yd.mqm h.w ‘bd.|‘lm.ṯlṯ.sswm.mrkbt.|b trbṣt.b 14[KRT].3.138
[-----].|[-----].|[-----.lm].|[ank.ksp.w yrq].|[ḫrṣ.]yd.mqm h.|[w ‘b]d.‘lm.ṯlṯ.|[ssw]m.mrkbt b tr 14[KRT].1.53
t y.|n[g.]krt.l ḥẓ[r y].|w y‘n[y.k]rt[.ṯ]‘.|lm.ank.ksp.|w yr[q.ḫrṣ].|yd.mqm h.w ‘bd.|‘lm.ṯlṯ.sswm.|mrkbt.b trbṣ. 14[KRT].6.283
swn h].|tš[an.g hm.w tṣḥn].|tḥ[m.pbl.mlk].|qḥ[.ksp.w yrq].|ḫrṣ.[yd.mqm h].|w ‘bd[.‘lm.ṯlṯ].|sswm.m[rkbt].|b 14[KRT].6.269
krt.msw]n.|w r[gm.l krt.]ṯ‘.|tḥm[.pbl.mlk].|qḥ.[ksp.w yr]q.|ḫrṣ[.yd.mqm] h.|‘bd[.‘lm.ṯlṯ].|ss[wm.mrkbt].|b[tr 14[KRT].5.250
.udm‘t h.|km.ṯqlm.arṣ h.|km ḫmšt.mṭt h.|bm.bky h.w yšn.|b dm‘ h.nhmmt.|šnt.tluan.|w yškb.nhmmt.|w yqm 14[KRT].1.31
ytnm.qrt.l ‘ly[.---].|b mdbr.špm.yd[.---.---]r.|l riš hm.w yš[--.--]m.|lḥm.b lḥm ay.w šty.b ḫmr yn ay.|šlm.mlk.šl 23[52].5
.|[--.]iḥd.šd.gṯr.|[w]ht.yšm‘.uḫ y.|l g y.w yhbṭ.bnš.|w ytn.ilm.b d hm.|b d.iḫqm.gṯr.|w b d.ytrhd.|b‘l. 55[18].19
[i]k.mgn.rbt.aṯrt.|[ym].mǵẓ.qnyt.ilm.|w tn.bt.l b‘l.km.|[i]lm.w ḥẓr.k bn.|[a]ṯrt.gm.l ǵlm h.|b‘l.yṣ 8[51FRAG].3
yrḫ.|w.mlk.z[--.--]n.ššwm.|n‘mm.[--].ṯṯm.w.at.|nǵṯ.w.ytn.hm.l k.|w.lḥt.alpm.ḥršm.|k.rgmt.l y.bly m.|alpm.ar 2064.20
št.|l aḫ y.l r‘ y.dt.|w ytnnn.|l aḫ h.l r‘ h.|r‘ ‘lm.|ttn.w tn.|w l ttn.|w al ttn.|tn ks yn.|w ištn.|‘bd.prṯ.tḥm.|qrq. 1019.1.12
ǵr.ptḥ.w ptḥ hw.prṣ.b‘d hm.|w ‘rb.hm.hm[.iṯ.--.l]ḥm.w t[n].|w nlḥm.hm.iṯ[.--.yn.w t]n.w nšt.|w ‘n hm.nǵr mdr‘ 23[52].71
|w ‘rb.hm.hm[.iṯ.--.l]ḥm.w t[n].|w nlḥm.hm.iṯ[.--.yn.w t]n.w nšt.|w ‘n hm.nǵr mdr‘[.iṯ.lḥm.---].|iṯ.yn.d ‘rb.bṯk[. 23[52].72
k m.|[l ‘pr.tšu.g h.]w tṣḥ.šm‘.m‘.|[l aqht.ǵzr.i]rš.ksp.w atn k.|[ḫrṣ.w aš]lḥ k.w tn.qšt k.[l].|[‘nt.tq]ḥ[.q]ṣ‘t k.ybm 17[2AQHT].6.17
.|w rbt.šnt.|b ‘d ‘lm...gn‘.|iršt.aršt.|l aḫ y.l r‘ y.dt.|w ytnnn.|l aḫ h.l r‘ h.|r‘ ‘lm.|ttn.w tn.|w l ttn.|w al ttn.|t 1019.1.9
m.|ḫr[ḫ]b mlk qẓ.tn nkl y|rḫ ytrḫ.ib t‘rb m b bh|t h.w atn mhr h l a|b h.alp ksp w rbt ḫ|rṣ.išlḥ ẓhrm iq|nim.at 24[77].19
-]y.|[---.y]d gt h[.--].|[---.]yd.|[k]rm h.yd.|[k]lkl h.|[w] ytn.nn.|l.b‘ln.bn.|kltn.w l.|bn h.‘d.‘lm.|šḥr.‘lmt.|bnš b 1008.11
t.d[-].l irt k.|wn ap.‘dn.mṭr h.|b‘l.y‘dn.‘dn.ṯkt.b glṯ.|w tn.ql h.b ‘rpt.|šrh.l arṣ.brqm.|bt.arzm.yklln h.|hm.bt.lb 4[51].5.70
ḥ.šm‘.m‘.|[l aqht.ǵzr.i]rš.ksp.w atn k.|[ḫrṣ.w aš]lḥ k.w tn.qšt k.[l].|[‘nt.tq]ḥ[.q]ṣ‘t k.ybmt.limm.|w y‘n.aqht.ǵzr. 17[2AQHT].6.18
.mlat.|tqln.alpm.|yrḫ.‘šrt.l b‘[l].|dqtm.w ynt.qr[t].|w mtntm.š l rmš.|w kbd.w š.l šlm kbd.|alp.w š.l b‘l ṣpn.|d UG5.13.7
[ql]n.al[p]m.yrḫ.‘šrt.|[l b‘l.ṣ]pn.[dq]tm.w y[nt] qrt.|[w mtmt]m.[š.l] rm[š.]kbd.w š.|[l šlm.kbd.al]p.w š.[l] b‘l.ṣp 36[9].1.13
dbḥ klyrḫ.|ndr.|dbḥ.|dt nat.|w ytnt.|ṯrmn w.|dbḥ kl.|kl ykly.|dbḥ k.sprt.|dt nat.|w qr RS61[24.277.5]
t.[-]l[-].|b šdm.‘l k.pht.|dr‘.b ym.tn.aḥd.|b aḫ k.ispa.w yṯb.|ap.d anšt.im[-].|aḥd.b aḫ k.l[--]n.|hn[-.]aḥẓ[.---]l[-]. 6[49].5.20
ǵy.kṯr.w ḫss.|št.alp.qdm h.mra.|w tk.pn h.t‘db.ksu.|w yṯṯb.l ymn.aliyn.|b‘l.‘d.lḥm.št[y.ilm].|[w]y‘n.aliy[n.b‘l]. 4[51].5.109
[ṣ.---].|[---.t]ṯb h.aḫt.ppšr.w ppšrt[.---].|[---.]k.drḫm.w aṯb.l ntbt.k.‘ṣm l t[--].|[---.]drk.brḥ.arṣ.lk pn h.yrk.b‘[l].| 1001.2.7
bl.mṣrp k.[---].|[---.]y.mṭnt.w tḥ.ṭbt.n[--].|[---.b]tnm w ṯṯb.‘l.bṯnt.trtḥ[ṣ.---].|[---.t]ṯb h.aḫt.ppšr.w ppšrt[.---].|[--- 1001.2.5
ydy ḥmt.hlm.yṯq šqy.|nḥš.yšlḥm.nḥš.‘q šr.y‘db.|ksa.w yṯb.|tqru l špš.um h.špš.um.ql bl.|‘m ḥrn.mṣd h.mnt.nṯk UG5.7.56
.ln h.ydy.|ḥmt.hlm.yṯq.nḥš.yšlḥm.nḥš ‘q.|š.y‘db.ksa w yṯb.|tqru l špš.um h.špš.um.ql bl ‘m.|ṯṯ.w kmṯ.ḥryt h.m UG5.7.34
ln h.ydy.|ḥmt.hlm.yṯq.nḥš.yšlḥm.nḥš.|‘q šr.y‘db.ksa.w yṯb.|tqru.l špš.um h.špš.um.ql b.‘m.|ršp.bbt h.mnt.nḥš.š UG5.7.29
ln h.ydy.ḥmt.hlm yṯq.nḥš.|yšlḥm.nḥš.‘q šr.y‘db ksa.|w yṯb.|tqru l špš.um h.špš.um.ql bl ‘m.|šḥr.w šlm šmm h UG5.7.50
ln h.|ydy.ḥmt.hlm.yṯq nḥš yšlḥm.nḥš.|‘q.šr.y‘db.ksa.w yṯb.|tqru l špš um h.špš um ql.bl.‘m.|mlk.‘ṯtrt h.mnt.nṯk UG5.7.39
.ln h.ydy.ḥmt.hlm.yṯq.|nḥš.yšlḥm.nḥš.‘q šr.ydb.ksa.|w yṯb.|tqru.l špš.u h.špš.um.ql.bl.‘m.|dgn.ttl h.mnt.nṯk.nḥ UG5.7.13
.ydy.|ḥmt.hlm.yṯq yṯqšqy.nḥš.yšlḥm.‘q šr.|y‘db.ksa.w.yṯb.|tqru.l špš.um h.špš.um.ql bl.|‘m b‘l.mrym.ṣpn.mnt UG5.7.7
šmrr.nḥš.‘q šr.ln h.ml|ḫš.abd.ln h.ydy.ḥmt.hlm.yṯq.|w yṯb.|tqru.l špš.um h.špš.[um.q]l bl.‘m.|yrḫ.lrgt h.mnt.nṯ UG5.7.24
ln h.|ydy.ḥmt.hlm.yṯq.nḥš.yšlḥm.|nḥš.‘q šr.y‘db.ksa.w yṯb.|tqru l špš.um h.špš.um.ql.bl.‘m.|‘nt w ‘ṯtrt inbb h.m UG5.7.18
ln h.ydy.|ḥmt.hlm.yṯq.nḥš.yšlḥm.nḥš.|‘q šr.y‘db.ksa.w yṯb.|tqru.l špš.um.ql bl.‘m|kṯr.w ḫss.kptr h.mnt.nṯk.nḥš. UG5.7.44
r‘[.---].|[---.]ytn.ml[--].ank.iphn.|[---.a]nk.i[--.--]slm.w.yṯb.|[----.--]t.hw[-]y.h[--]r.w rgm.ank.|[---.]hdd tr[--.--]l. 1002.37
|‘rb.špš.l ymǵ.|krt.ṣbia.špš.|b‘l ny.w ymlk.|[y]ṣb.‘ln.w y[-]y.|[kr]t.ṯ‘.‘ln.bḫr.|[---].aṯt k.‘l.|[---] k.yšṣi.|[---.]ḫbr.r 15[128].5.21
hn[-.]aḥẓ[.---]l[-].|[‘]nt.akl[y.nšm].|akly.hml[t.arṣ].|w y[-]l.a[---].|š[--.---].|bl[.---]. 6[49].5.26
.l mlkt.wn.in.aṯt.|[l]k.k[m.ilm].|[w ǵlmt.k bn.qdš.]w y[--.]zbl.ym.y‘[--.]ṯpṭ.nhr.|[-------.]yšlḥn.w y‘n ‘ṯtr[.-]. 2.3[129].23
r.mlak.mṭḫr.yḥb[-.---.]|[---].mlak.bn.ktpm.rgm.b‘l h.w y[--.---].|[---].ap.anš.zbl.b‘l.šdmt.bg[--.---].|[---.-]dm.mla 2.1[137].42
[-----].|‘r[.---].|‘r[.---].|‘r[.---].|w y[---].|b‘d[.---].|yaṯr[.---].|b d k.[---].|ṯnnt h[.---].|ṯlṯt h[. 16[126].5.4
.l.i[--].‘[m k].|l.alpm.w.l.y[n.--]t.|w.bl.bnš.hw[-.--]y.|w.k.at.trg[m.--].|w.[---]n.w.s[--].|[--]m.m[---].|[---.m]nd‘[.-- 2064.27
--].bnt.ṣ‘ṣ.bnt.m‘m‘.‘bd.ḥrn.[--.]k.|[---].aǵwyn.‘n k.ẓẓ.w k mǵ.ilm.|[--.]k ‘ṣm.k ‘šm.l ttn.k abnm.l thggn. 1001.2.12
w.k.rgm.špš.|mlk.rb.b‘l y.u.|‘[--.]mlakt.‘bd h.|[---.]b‘l k.yḫ 1018.1
il.w tbu.|qrš.mlk.ab.šnm.|l p‘n.il.thbr.w tql.|tšthwy.w tkbd h.|hlm.il.k yphn h.|yprq.lṣb.w yṣḥq.|p‘n h.l hdm.y 4[51].4.26
w tbu.qr]š.mlk.ab.šnm.|[l p‘n.il.t]hbr.w tql.tštḥ|[wy.w tkbd]n h.tlšn.aqht.ǵzr.|[---.kdd.dn]il.mt.rpi.w t‘n.|[btlt.‘ 17[2AQHT].6.51
.b alp ḥẓr.|[rbt.kmn.l p‘]n.‘nt.|[yhbr.w yql.yšt]ḥwyn.w y|[kbdn h.yšu.g h.w y]ṣḥ.tḥm.|[ṯr.il.ab k.hwt.l]ṭpn.ḥtk k 1[‘NT.IX].2.16
l.w tbu.qrš..|mlk.ab.šnm.l p‘n.|il.thbr.w tql.|tšthwy.w tkbdn h.|tšu.g h.w tṣḥ.tšmḫ ht.|aṯrt.w bn h.ilt.w ṣb|rt.a 6.1.38[49.1.10]
u[.q]rš.mlk[.ab.šnm.l p‘n.il.]|[yhbr.]w yql[.y]šthw[y.]w ykb[dn h.--]r y[---].|[---.k]ṯr.w ḫ[ss.t]b‘.b[n.]bht.ym[.rm] 2.3[129].6

ybu.qrš.mlk].|ab.šnm.l [p'n.il.yhbr.w yql].|yštḥwy.[w ykbdn h.---].|ṯr.il[.ab h.---].|ḥš b[ht m.tbnn.ḥš.trmmn.hk 1['NT.IX].3.25

m.mt.b a|lp.šd.rbt.k|mn.l p'n.mt.|hbr.w ql.|tštḥwy.w k|bd hwt.w rgm.|l bn.ilm.mt.|ṯny.l ydd.|il.ǵzr.tḥm.|ali 4[51].8.28

ḥlt h].|b alp.šd.r[bt.kmn.l p'n.kṯr].|hbr.w ql.t[štḥwy.w kbd.hwt].|w rgm l k[ṯr.w ḫss.ṯny.l hyn].|d ḥrš.y[dm.tḥm 1['NT.IX].3.3

nḥlt h.|b alp.šd.rbt.|kmn.l p'n.kṯ.|hbr.w ql.tštḥ|wy.w kbd hwt.|w rgm.l kṯr.|w ḫss.ṯny.l h|yn.d ḥrš.ydm.|tḥm. 3['NT.VI].6.20

|yrḫ.'šrt.l b'[l].|dqtm.w ynt.qr[t].|w mtntm.š l rmš.|w kbd.w š.l šlm kbd.|alp.w š.l b'l ṣpn.|dqt l ṣpn.šrp.w šlm UG5.13.8

[---.]dd.|[---]n.dd.|[---.]dd.|bn.arwdn.dd.|mnḥm.w.kbln.|bn.ǵlm.dd.|bn.tbšn.dd.|bn.ḫran.w[.---].|[-]n.y'rty 131[309].5

m k].|'bd[.---]y.|'m[.---]y.|šk[--.--.]kll.|šk[--.--.]hm.|w.k[b--.---].|'m[.---]m ib.|[---.--]m.|[-----].|[-]š[--.---].|[-]r[- 2065.7

arb'.'šr h.šmn.|d.lqḥt.ṯlǵdy.|w.kd.ištir.'m.qrt.|'št.'šr h.šmn.|'mn.bn.aǵlmn.|arb'm.ksp.' 1083.3

b'l ṣpn.|dqt l ṣpn.šrp.w šlmm.|kmm.w bbt.b'l.ugrt.|w kdm.w npš ilib.|gdlt.il š.b'l š.'nt.|ṣpn.alp.w š.pdry.š.|šrp UG5.13.12

[-] ym.pr' d nkly yn kd w kd.|w 'l ym kdm.|w b ṯlṯ.kd yn w krsnm.|w b rb' kdm y 1086.1

mr.ḥṭb.|dd.ḥṭm.l.ḫdǵb.|ṯṯ.ddm.l.gzzm.|kd yn.l.ḫtn.w.kd.ḥmṣ.w.[lt]ḥ.'šdm.|kd yn.l.ḫdǵb.w.kd.ḥmṣ.|prš.glbm.l 1099.27

m.|kd yn.l.ḫtn.w.kd.ḥmṣ.w.[lt]ḥ.'šdm.|kd yn.l.ḫdǵb.w.kd.ḥmṣ.|prš.glbm.l.bt.|tgmǵ.kšmm.b.yrḫ.iṯtbnm.|šb'm. 1099.28

ṣrm.w [---].|kmm.w.in.'ṣr[.---].|w mit.š'rt.[-]y[-.---].|w.kdr.w.npt t[--.---].|w.ksp.y'db.[---]. 38[23].10

|irǵ[n.ḥmr.ydk].|aḥd[h.w.yṣq.b.ap h].|k yr[a]š.šš[w.w.ykhp].|mid.dblt.yṯ[nt.w].|ṣmq[m].yṯnm.w[.qmḥ.bql].|td 161[56].32

|[-----].|[-----].|[---.-]rb.|[-----].|[-----].|[-----].|k yraš w ykhp mid.|dblt yṯnt w ṣmqm yṯn[m].|w qmḥ bql yṣq aḥ 160[55].23

šqy.bn.qdš.|l tbrknn l ṯr.il ab y.|tmrnn.l bny.bnwt.|w ykn.bn h b bt.šrš.b qrb.|hkl h.nṣb.skn.ilib h.b qdš.|ztr.' 17[2AQHT].1.26

--.]b ḥbq h.ḥmḥmt.|[---.--] n.ylt.ḥmḥmt.|[---.mt.r]pi.w ykn.bn h.|[b bt.šrš.]b qrb.hkl h.|[nṣb.skn.i]lib h.b qdš.|[17[2AQHT].1.43

mn.b[n].ṣdqn.|w.kkrm.ṯlṯ.|mit.ksp.'mn.|bn.ulbtyn.|w.kkr.ṯlṯ.|ksp.d.nkly.b.šd.|mit.ḫmšt.kbd.|[l.]gmn.bn.usyy. 1143.5

mitm.ksp.'mn.b[n].ṣdqn.|w.kkrm.ṯlṯ.|mit.ksp.'mn.|bn.ulbtyn.|w.kkr.ṯlṯ.|ksp.d.nkly. 1143.2

[-----].|[---.--]ty.l[--.---].|[--.--]tm.w '[--.--].|[---].w kl.hw[.---].|w [--].brt.lb[--.---].|u[-]šhr.nuš[-.---].|b [u]grt 54.1.4[13.1.1]

qḥ.kl.ḏr'.|b d a[-]m.w.ank.|k[l.]ḏr' hm.|[--.n]pš[.-].|w [k]l hm.b d.|rb.tmtt.lqḥt.|w.ṯṯb.ank.l hm.|w.any k.ṯt.|b 2059.21

]ṯlṯm.kkr.ṯlṯ.|[--.]aštn.l k.|[--]y.kl.dbrm.hm[.--].|[--]l.w.kl.mḫr k.|[--]tir.aštn.l [k].|[---].kkr.ṯl[ṯ]. 1022.8

--].|uḫ h.w.'šr[.---].|klyn.apsn[y.---].|plzn.qrty[.---].|w.klt h.b.t[--.---].|b'l y.mlk[y.---].|yd.bt h.yd[.---].|ary.yd.t 81[329].12

.špš.w.ḥl.mlk.|w.[---].ypm.w.mḫ[--].t[t]ṯbn.[-].|b.[--].w.km.iṯ.y[--.]šqm.yd[-]. 35[3].55

.šr.yly h.|b skn.sknm.b 'dn.|'dnm.kn.npl.b'l.|km ṯr.w tkms.hd.p[.-].|km.ibr.b tk.mšmš d[--].|ittpq.l awl.|išttk.l 12[75].2.55

arb'.'šr h.šd.|w.kmsk.d.iwrkl.|ṯlṯ.šd.d.bn.mlkyy.|kmsk.šd.iḫmn.|širm.š 1079.2

.ḫmšt.'šrt.ksp.|ḫmš.mat.šmt.|b.'šrt.ksp.|'šr.ṣin.b.ṯṯt.w.kmsk.|arb'[.k]dwṯm.w.ṯt.ṯprtm.|b.'šr[m.]ksp.|ḫmš.kkr.ṣ 2100.9

p.ḥmt.y[r]ḫ.w.ršp.yisp.ḥmt.|['ṯt]r.w 'ṯtpr.yisp.ḥmt.ṯṯ.w kṯṯ.|[yus]p.ḥmt.mlk.b 'ṯtrt.yisp.ḥmt.|[kṯ]r w ḫss.y[i]sp.ḥ UG5.8.16

š.y'db.ksa w yṯb.|tqru l špš.um h.špš.um.ql bl 'm.|ṯṯ.w kmṯ.ḥryt h.mnt.nṯk.nḥš.šm|rr.nḥš.'q šr.ln h.mlḫš abd.ln UG5.7.36

ab.w il[--].|[--] šlm.šlm i[l].|[š]lm.il.šr.|dgn.w b'l.|'ṯ w kmṯ.|yrḫ w ksa.|yrḫ mkty.|ṯkmn w šnm.|kṯr w ḫss.|'ṯtr UG5.10.1.5

.|[---.]rgm.hy.[-]ḫ[-]y.ilak k.|[---.--]g k.yritn.mǵy.hy.w kn.|[---].ḥln.d b.dmt.um.il[m.---].|[--]ḏyn.b'd.[--]ḏyn.w l. 1002.42

ṯn pǵn.[-]dr|m.ṯn kndwm adrm.|w knd pnṯ.dq.|ṯn ḫpnm.ṯn pldm ǵlmm.|kpld.b[-.-]r[--].|w 140[98].3

]r b'l.|gdlt.šlm.gdlt.w burm.[l]b.|rmṣt.ilhm.b'lm.dṯt.w kšm.ḫmš.|'ṯr h.mlun.šnpt.ḥṣt h.b'l.ṣpn š.|[--]ṯ š.ilt.mgdl 34[1].9

].|[---.]mṯbt.ilm.w.b.[---].|[---.]ṯṯtbn.ilm.w.[---].|[---.]w.ksu.b'lt.b[htm.---].|[---.]il.bt.gdlt.[---].|[---.]hkl[.---]. 47[33].7

--] šlm.šlm i[l].|[š]lm.il.šr.|dgn.w b'l.|'ṯ w kmṯ.|yrḫ w ksa.|yrḫ mkty.|ṯkmn w šnm.|kṯr w ḫss.|'ṯtr 'ṯtpr.|šḥr w UG5.10.1.6

.tld[.l b'l].|w rum.l[rkb.'rpt].|tḥbq.[---].|tḥbq[.---].|w tksynn.bṯn[-.]|y[--.]šr h.w šḫp h.|[--.]šḫp.ṣǵrt h.|yrk.t'l. 10[76].3.25

n.'ṣr[.---].|w mit.š'rt.[-]y[-.---].|w.kdr.w.npt t[--.---].|w.ksp.y'db.[---]. 38[23].11

.|idk[.-]it[.---].|trgm[.-]dk[.---].|m'bd[.-]r[-.-]š[-.---].|w kšt.[--]šq h[.---].|bnš r'ym.[---].|kbdt.bnš[.---].|šin.[---].| 2158.2.5

hlm.il.k yphn h.|yprq.lṣb.w yṣḥq.|p'n h.l hdm.yṯpd.w ykrkr.|uṣb't h.yšu.g h.w y[ṣḥ].|ik.mǵyt.rbt.aṯr[t.y]m.|ik. 4[51].4.29

ṯ.šd.d.bn.mlkyy.|kmsk.šd.iḫmn.|širm.šd.khn.|ṯlṯ.šd.w.krm.šir.d.ḫli.|širm.šd.šd.'šy.|w.šir.šd.krm.|d.krwn.|šir.š 1079.6

.pr' d nkly yn kd w kd.|w 'l ym kdm.|w b ṯlṯ.kd yn w krsnm.|w b rb' kdm yn.|w b ḫmš kd yn. 1086.3

[--].w rbb.|š[---]npš išt.|w.l.tikl w l tš[t]. 2003.3

tḥm.ydn.'m.mlk.|b'l h.ngr.ḥwt k.|w l.a[--]t.tšknn.|ḫmšm.l mi[t].any.|tškn[n.--]h.k[--].|w šn 2062.1.3

ym.w ṯn.aḫr.|šp[š]m.b [ṯ]lṯ.|ym[ǵy.]l qdš.|a[ṯrt.]ṣrm.w l ilt.|ṣd[yn]m.ṯm.|yd[r.k]rt.ṯ'.|i.iṯ.aṯrt.ṣrm.|w ilt.ṣdynm 14[KRT].4.198

m.|ḫmš.ṯdṯ.ym.mk.špšm.|b šb'.w tmǵy.l udm.|rbm.w l.udm.ṯrrt.|w gr.nn.'rm.šrn.|pdrm.s't.b šdm.|ḥṭb h.b gr 14[KRT].3.109

|b qdš il bt.|w tlḥm aṯt.|š l ilbt.šlmm.|kll ylḥm b h.|w l bbt šqym.|š l uḫr ḫlmt.|w tr l qlḥ.|ym aḥd. UG5.11.11

mt.'mn.kbkbm.|abn.brq.d l.td'.šmm.|rgm l td'.nšm.w l tbn.|hmlt.arṣ.at m.w ank.|ibǵy h.b tk.ǵr y.il.ṣpn.|b qdš 3['NT].3.24

tunt.šmm.'m[.arṣ.thmt.'mn.kbkbm].|rgm.l td'.nš[m.w l tbn.hmlt.arṣ].|at.w ank.ib[ǵy h.---].|w y'n.kṯr.w ḫss[.lk. 1['NT.IX].3.15

.hwt.|[w aṯny k.rgm.]'ṣ.w lḫšt.|[abn.rgm.l td]'.nš[m.w l t]bn.|[hmlt.a]rṣ.[tant.šmm.'m.ar]ṣ.|thmt.['mn.kbkbm.a 3['NT].4.59

.bnš.|[ml]k.d.b riš.|[--.-]nt.|[l.'b]dmlk.|[--.-]m[-]r.|[w.l.]bn h.'d.|['l]m.mn k.|mn km l.yqḥ.|bt.hnd.b d.|['b]dm 1009.11

yd.|[k]rm h.yd.|[k]lkl h.|[w] ytn.nn.|l.b'ln.bn.|kltn.w l.|bn h.'d.'lm.|šḥr.'lmt.|bnš bnšm.|l.yqḥnn.b d.|b'ln.bn. 1008.13

tḥm.hl[--].|l pḫry.a[ḫ y].|w l g.p[-]r[--].|yšlm[.l k].|[i]lm[.tǵr k].|[t]š[lm k.---].|[-----] 56[21].3

[--].|ypḫ[--].|w s[--].|[---].|qrd ga[n.--].|b bt k.[--].|w l dbḥ[--].|t[--].|[--] aṯt yqḥ 'z.|[---]ḏ.|[---].|[---].|hm qrt RS61[24.277.23]

rgmt.|w ht.aḫ y.|bn y.yšal.|ṯryl.p rgm.|l mlk.šm y.|w l h.y'l m.|w h[t] aḫ y.|bn y.yšal.|ṯryl.w rgm[.-].|ṯṯb.l aḫ 138.14

t].|knyt.w t'n[.btlt.'nt].|yṯb l y.ṯr.il[.ab y.---].|yṯb.l y.w l h.[---].|[--.i]mṣḫ.nn.k imr.l arṣ.|[ašhlk].šbt h.dmm.šbt. 3['NT.VI].4.8

.zbl.b'l.arṣ.|apnk.lṭpn.il.|d pid.yrd.l ksi.yṯb.|l hdm[.w] l.hdm.yṯb.|l arṣ.yṣq.'mr.|un.l riš h.'pr.plṯt.|l qdqd h.lpš 5[67].6.13

rgmt.|w ht.aḫ y.|bn y.yšal.|ṯryl.p rgm.|l mlk.šm y.|w l h[-] y'l m.|bn y.yšal.|ṯryl.w rgm.|ṯṯb.l aḫ k.|l adn k. 138.15

[---.---.]l.mit.dr'.w.šb'm.drt.|[---.ḥpr.]bnšm.w.l.ḥrš.'rq.ṯn.'šr h.|[---.d]r'.w.mit.drt.w.'šrm.l.mit.|[drt.ḥp 1098.2

m.w lk[.---].|[--]ṯ.lk[.---].|[--]kṯ.i[---.---].|p.šn[-.---].|w l ṭlb.[---].|mit.rḥ[.---].|ṭṭlb.a[--.---].|yšu.g h[.---].|i.ap.b'[5[67].4.2

k.|w.lḥt.alpm.ḫršm.|k.rgmt.l y.bly m.|alpm.arštl k.w.l y.|mn.bnš.d.l.i[--].'[m k].|l.alpm.w.l.y[n.--]t.|w.bl.bnš. 2064.23

.|alpm.ar.št.l k.w.l y.|mn.bnš.d.l.i[--].'[m k].|l.alpm.w.l.y[n.--]t.|w.bl.bnš.hw[-.--]y.|w.k.at.trg[m.--].|w.[---]n.w 2064.25

h.w tphn.in.[---].|[-.]hlk.ǵlmm b dd y.yṣ[--].|[-.]yṣa.w l.yṣa.hlm.[ṯnm].|[q]dqd.ṯlṯ id.'l.ud[n].|[---.-]sr.pdm.riš h[19[1AQHT].2.78

].ym.w ṯn.|ṯlṯ.rb'.ym.|ḫmš.ṯdṯ.ym.|mk.špšm.b šb'.|w l.yšn.pbl.|mlk.l [qr.]ṯiqt.|ibr h[.l]ql.nhqt.|ḥmr[h.l g't.]a 14[KRT].5.222

ḥẓ k.al.tšʻl. | qrt h.abn.yd k. | mšdpt.w hn.špšm. | b šbʻ.w l.yšn.pbl. | mlk.l qr.ṯigt.ibr h. | l ql.nhqt.ḥmr h. | l gʻt.alp.ḥ 14[KRT].3.119

ḫ y.l rʻ y.dt. | w ytnnn. | l aḫ h.l rʻ h. | rʻ ʻlm. | ttn.w tn. | w l ttn. | w al ttn. | tn ks yn. | w ištn. | ʻbd.prṯ.ṯḥm. | qrq.pt.ḏm 1019.1.13

t.aliy. | qrdm.bhṯ.l bn.ilm mt. | ʻbd k.an.w d.ʻlm k. | tbʻ.w l.yṯb.ilm.idk. | l ytn.pn.ʻm.bn.ilm.mt. | tk.qrt h.hmry.mk.k 5[67].2.13

t m.l yrt. | b npš.bn ilm.mt.b mh | mrt.ydd.il.ǵzr. | tbʻ.w l.yṯb ilm.idk. | l ytn.pnm.ʻm.bʻl. | mrym.ṣpn.w yʻn. | gpn.w 5[67].1.9

---]m.tṣḥq.ʻnt.w b lb.tqny. | [---.]ṯb l y.l aqht.ǵzr.ṯb l y w l k. | [---]m.l aqry k.b ntb.pšʻ. | [---].b ntb.gan.ašql k.tḥt. | [17[2AQHT].6.42

[ṯt y]. | il.ylt.mh.ylt.yld y.šḫr.w šl[m]. | šu.ʻdb.l špš.rbt.w l kbkbm.kn[-]. | yhbr.špt hm.yšq.hn.[š]pt hm.mtqtm. | bm. 23[52].54

lak.ym.tʻdt.ṯpṭ[.nhr]. | t[ǵ]ly.hlm.rišt hm.l ẓr.brkt hm.w l kḥṯ. | zbl hm.b hm.ygʻr.bʻl.lm.ǵltm.ilm.rišt. | km l ẓr brkt 2.1[137].23

l hm.b hm.ygʻr.bʻl.lm.ǵltm.ilm.rišt. | km l ẓr brkt km.w ln.kḥṯ.zbl km.aḥd. | ilm.tʻny lḥt.mlak.ym.tʻdt.ṯpṭ.nhr. | šu. 2.1[137].25

ṯḥm.iwrḏr. | l.plsy. | rgm. | yšlm.l k. | l.trǵds. | w.l.klby. | šmʻt.ḫti. | nḫtu.ht. | hm.in mm. | nḫtu.w.lak. | ʻm y. 53[54].6

--]. | l ṯlṯ. | ṯn.l.brr[.---]. | arbʻ.ḥmr[.---]. | l.pḫ[-.]w.[---]. | w.l.k[--]. | w.l.k[--]. 1139.6

ṯn.l.brr[.---]. | arbʻ.ḥmr[.---]. | l.pḫ[-.]w.[---]. | w.l.k[--]. | w.l.k[--]. 1139.7

ʻṯt[rt.---]. | [ʻ]ṣr.l pdr ṯṯ.ṣ[in.---]. | tšnpn.ʻlm.km[m.---]. | w.l ll.ʻṣrm.w [---]. | kmm.w.in.ʻṣr[.---]. | w mit.šʻrt.[-]y[-.---]. | 38[23].7

lun.šnpt.ḫṣt h.bʻl.ṣpn š. | [--]ṯ š.ilt.mgdl š.ilt.asrm š. | w l ll.šp. pgr.w ṯrmnm.bt mlk. | il[bt].gdlt.ušḫry.gdlt.ym gdl 34[1].12

ḫ[.---]. | ddm gt dprnm. | l ḥršm. | ddm l ʻnqt. | dd l altt.w l lmdt h. | dd l iḫyn. | dd l [---]. 1101.11

lk.nhr.ibr[.---]. | zbl bʻl.ǵlm.[---]. | ṣǵr hd w r[---.---]. | w l nhr nd[-.---]. | [---.--]l. 9[33].2.12

. | yšu.ʻwr. | mzl.ymzl. | w ybl.trḫ.ḥdṯ. | ybʻr.l ṯn.aṯt h. | w l nkr.mddt. | km irby.tškn. | šd.k ḥsn.pat. | mdbr.tlkn. | ym. 14[KRT].4.191

.[---]. | w mlk[.nhš.w mlk.mg]šḫ. | ʻmn.[---]. | ik y.[---]. | w l n[qmd.---]. | [w]nqmd.[---]. | [-.]ʻmn.šp[š.mlk.rb]. | bʻl h.š 64[118].9

[---.-]sr.pdm.riš h[m.---]. | ʻl.pd.asr.[---.]l[.---]. | mḫlpt.w l.ytk.[d]m[ʻt.]km. | rbʻt.ṯqlm.ṯtp[.---.]bm. | yd.ṣpn hm.tliy 19[1AQHT].2.82

ṯpṭ].nhr.tlʻm.ṯm.ḥrbm.its.anšq. | [-]htm.l arṣ.ypl.ul ny.w l.ʻpr.ʻẓm ny. | l bʻl[-.---]. | tḥt.ksi.zbl.ym.w ʻn.kṯr.w ḫss.l rg 2.4[68].5

. | ʻl.ar. | w.ṯlṯ. | ʻl.ubrʻy. | w.ṯn.ʻl. | mlk. | w.aḥd. | ʻl atlg. | w l.ʻṣm. | tspr. | nrn.al.tud | ad.at.l hm. | ṯṯm.ksp. 1010.17

.itrḫ. | y bn.ašld.šu.ʻdb.tk.mdbr qdš. | ṯm tgrgr.l abnm.w l.ʻṣm.šbʻ.šnt. | tmt.ṯmn.nqpt.ʻd.ilm.nʻmm.ttlkn. | šd.tṣdn.p 23[52].66

n š[p]š pgr. | [g]dlt iltm ḫnqtm.d[q]tm. | [yr]ḫ.kty gdlt.w l ǵlmt š. | [w]pamt ṯlṯm.w yrdt.[m]dbḥt. | gdlt.l bʻlt bhtm. 34[1].19

a]rš. | l.pn.bʻ[l y.l].pn.bʻl y. | w.urk.ym.bʻl y. | l.pn.amn.w.l.pn. | il.mṣrm.dt.tǵrn. | npš.špš.mlk. | rb.bʻl y. 1018.21

]. | mʻ[.ṣ]bu h.u[l.mad]. | ṯlṯ.mat.rbt. | hlk.l alpm.ḫḏḏ. | w l.rbt.kmyr. | aṯr.ṯn.ṯn.hlk. | aṯr.ṯlṯ.kl hm. | aḥd.bt h.ysgr. | al 14[KRT].4.181

.mat.rbt. | ḫpṯ.d bl.spr. | ṯnn.d bl.hg. | hlk.l alpm.ḫḏḏ. | w l rbt.kmyr. | [a]ṯr.ṯn.ṯn.hlk. | aṯr.ṯlṯ.kl hm. | yḥd.bt h.sgr. | a 14[KRT].2.93

l ḫmš.mrkbt.ḫmš.ʻšr h.prs. | bt.mrkbt.w l šant.ṯṯ. | l bt.ʻšrm. | bt alḫnm.ṯlṯm ṯt kbd. 2105.2

dg b ym.w ndd.gzr.l zr.yʻdb.u ymn. | u šmal.b p hm.w l.tšbʻn y.aṯt.itrḫ. | y bn.ašld.šu.ʻdb.tk.mdbr qdš. | ṯm tgrgr. 23[52].64

.qšt h.mdnt. | w hln.ʻnt.l bt h.tmǵyn. | tštql.ilt.l hkl h. | w l.šbʻt.tmtḫṣ h.b ʻmq. | tḥtṣb.bn.qrtm.ttʻr. | ksat.l mhr.ṯʻr.ṯl 3[ʻNT].2.19

šmm. | sb.l qṣm.arṣ. | l ksm.mhyt.ʻn. | l arṣ.m[ṭ]r.bʻl. | w l šd.mṭr.ʻly. | nʻm.l arṣ.mṭr.bʻl. | w l šd.mṭr.ʻly. | nʻm.l ḥṭt.b 16[126].3.6

.ʻn. | l arṣ.m[ṭ]r.bʻl. | w l šd.mṭr.ʻly. | nʻm.l arṣ.mṭr.bʻl. | w l šd.mṭr.ʻly. | nʻm.l ḥṭt.b gn. | bm.nrt.ksmm. | ʻl.tl[-]k.ʻṭrṭr 16[126].3.8

[--].w rbb. | š[---]npš išt. | w.l.tikl w l tš[t]. 2003.3

ndrṯ w ṯ[qd m]r. | [ydk aḥd h w yṣq b ap h. | [k l yḫru w]l yttn mss št qlql. | [w št ʻrgz y]dk aḥd h w yṣq b ap h. | [k 160[55].8

drṯ]. | w.ṯ[qd.mr.ydk.aḥd h]. | w.y[ṣq.b.ap h]. | k.l.ḫ[ru.w.l.yttn.ššw]. | mss.[št.qlql.w.št]. | ʻrgz[.ydk.aḥd h]. | w.yṣq[.b 161[56].8

kbt.dt. | ʻrb.bt.mlk. | yd.apnt hn. | yd.ḥẓ hn. | yd.tr hn. | w.l.ṯt.mrkbtm. | inn.uṯpt. | w.ṯlṯ.ṣmdm.w.ḥrṣ. | apnt.b d.rb.ḥr 1121.6

kn.u b qṣ]rt.npš kn.u b qṭt. | tqṭṭn.ušn y[p kn.l dbḥm.]w l ṯʻ dbḥ n. | ndbḥ.hw.ṯʻ n[ṯʻy.hw.nkt.nk]t.ytši.l ab bn il. | yt 32[2].1.32

ap km.u b qṣrt.npš km.u b qṭt]. | [tqṭṭ.u ṯḫṭu.l dbḥm.w l.ṯʻ.dbḥ n.ndb]ḥ. | [hw.ṯʻ.nṯʻy.hw.nkt.nkt.]yt[ši.l ab.bn.il]. 32[2].1.9

.u b q[ṣ]rt.npš km.u b qṭt.tqṭṭ. | ušn yp km.l d[b]ḥm.w l.ṯʻ.dbḥ n.ndbḥ.hw.ṯʻ | nṯʻy. | hw.nkt.nkt.y[t]ši.l ab.bn.il.yt 32[2].1.24

ap kn.u b [q]ṣrt.npš[kn.u b qṭt]. | tqṭṭn u ṯḫṭin.l bḥm.w l ṯʻ.d[bḥ n.ndbḥ]. | hw.ṯʻ.nṯʻy.hw.nkt.n[k]t.ytši[.l ab.bn.il]. 32[2].1.15

n. | [---].ḥln.d b.dmt.um.il[m.---]. | [--]ḏyn.bʻd.[--]ḏyn.w l. | [--]k bʻlt bhtm[.--]tn k. | [--]y.l ihbt.yb[--].rgm y. | [---.]š 1002.44

l [----]. | w l [---]. | kd.[---]. | kd.t[---.ym.ymm]. | yʻtqn.w[rḥm.ʻnt]. | tn 6[49].2.2

yn.prs.qmḥ.[---]. | mdbḥt.bt.ilt.ʻṣr[m.l ṣpn.š]. | l ǵlmt.š.w l [---.l yrḫ]. | gd[lt].l nkl[.gdlt.l bʻlt.bhtm]. | ʻš[rm.]l inš[.il 35[3].25

s.qmḥ.m[--.---]. | mdbḥt.bt.i[lt.ʻṣrm.l]. | ṣpn š.l ǵlm[t.š.w l.---]. | l yrḫ.gdlt.l [nkl.gdlt.l bʻ] | [lt].bht[m].[ʻ]ṣrm l [inš.il APP.II[173].27

.ṯigt.ibr h. | l ql.nhqt.ḥmr h. | l gʻt.alp.ḥrṯ.zǵt. | klb.ṣpr.w ylak. | mlakm.l k.ʻm.krt. | mswn h.ṯḥm.pbl.mlk. | qḥ.ksp.w 14[KRT].3.123

trǵds. | w.l.klby. | šmʻt.ḫti. | nḫtu.ht. | hm.in mm. | nḫtu.w.lak. | ʻm y.w.yd. | ilm.p.k mtm. | ʻz.mid. | hm.nṯkp. | mʻn k. | 53[54].10

n. | mlk.b.ṯy ndr. | iṯt.w.ht. | [-]sny.udr h. | w.hm.ḫt. | ʻl.w.likt. | ʻm k.w.hm. | l.ʻl.w.lakm. | ilak.w.at. | um y.al.tdḥṣ. | w 1013.17

t.l aḥš.idy.alt.in l y. | [--]t.bʻl.ḥẓ.ršp.b[n].km.yr.klyt h.w lb h. | [ṯ]n.p k.b ǵr.ṯn.p k.b ḫlb.k tgwln.šnt k. | [--.]w špt k. 1001.1.3

t il bt. | š l ḫlmt. | w tr l qlḥ. | w š ḥll ydm. | b qdš il bt. | w tlḥm aṯt. | š l ilbt.šlmm. | kll ylḥm b h. | w l bbt šqym. | š l u UG5.7.TR3

[.---]. | prdmn.ʻbd.ali[yn]. | bʻl.sid.zbl.bʻl. | arṣ.qm.yṯʻr. | w yšlḥmn h. | ybrd.ṯd.l pnw h. | b ḥrb.mlḥt. | qṣ.mri.ndd. | yʻš 3[ʻNT].1.5

ptḥ hw.prṣ.bʻd hm. | w ʻrb.hm.hm[.iṯ.--.l]ḥm.w t[n]. | w nlḥm.hm.iṯ[.--.yn.w t]n.w nšt. | w ʻn hm.nǵr mdrʻ[.iṯ.lḥm. 23[52].72

s.ymsk. | nhr.k[--].ṣḥn.bʻl.ʻm. | aḫ y.qran.hd.ʻm.ary y. | w lḥm m ʻm aḫ y.lḥm. | w št m.ʻm.a[ḫ] yn. | p nšt.bʻl.[ṭ]ʻn.iṭʻ 5[67].1.24

ṭbḫ.imr. | w ilḥm.mgṯ.w iṯrm. | tšmʻ.mtt.ḥry. | ṭṭbḫ.imr.w lḥm. | mgṯ.w yṯrm.hn.ym. | w ṯn.yṯb.krt.l ʻd h. | yṯb.l ksi m 16.6[127].20

ypqd. | krt.ṯʻ.yšu.g h. | w yṣḥ.šmʻ.l mtt. | ḥry.ṭbḫ.imr. | w ilḥm.mgṯ.w iṯrm. | tšmʻ.mtt.ḥry. | ṭṭbḫ.imr.w lḥm. | mgṯ.w 16.6[127].18

.bʻl k. | ydʻm.l.ydʻt. | ʻm y.špš.bʻl k. | šnt.šntm.lm.l.tlk. | w.lḥt.akl.ky. | likt.ʻm.špš. | bʻl k.ky.akl. | b.hwt k.inn. | špš n.[-- 2060.17

--.--]n.ššwm. | nʻmm.[--].ṯṯm.w.at. | nǵṯ.w.ytn.hm.l k. | w.lḥt.alpm.ḫršm. | k.rgmt.l y.bly m. | alpm.aršt.l k.w.l y. | m 2064.21

by h. | ṯr.ḫbr.rbt. | ḫbr.ṯrrt. | bt.krt.tbun. | lm.mṯb[.---]. | w lḥm mr.tqdm. | yd.b ṣʻ.tšlḥ. | ḥrb.b bšr.tštn. | [w t]ʻn.mtt.ḥr 15[128].4.23

k. | [dm.rgm.iṯ.l y.]w argm k.hwt. | [w aṯny k.rgm.]ʻṣ.w lḫšt. | [abn.rgm.l td]ʻ.nš[m.w l t]bn. | [hmlt.a]rṣ.[tant.šmm 3[ʻNT].4.58

šd k.dm.rgm. | iṯ.l y.w argm k. | hwt.w aṯny k.rgm. | ʻṣ.w lḫšt.abn. | tant.šmm.ʻm.arṣ. | thmt.ʻmn.kbkbm. | abn.brq.d 3[ʻNT].3.20

m.rgm.iṯ.l y.d argmn k]. | [h]wt.d aṯ[ny k.---.rgm.ʻṣ]. | w lḫšt.abn[.tant.šmm.ʻm.arṣ.thmt]. | ʻm kbkbm[.abn.brq.d l 7.2[130].19

r.ks.dm.r[gm.iṯ.l y.w argm k]. | hwt.w atny k[.rgm.ʻṣ.w lḫšt.abn]. | tunt.šmm.ʻm[.arṣ.thmt.ʻmn.kbkbm]. | rgm.l tdʻ 1[ʻNT.IX].3.13

-.]ʻbd.ank. | [---.ʻb]d k. | [---.--]l y.ʻm. | [---.]ʻm. | [---.--]y.w.lm. | [---.]il.šlm. | [---.]ank. | [---]t.mly. 2128.2.4

mlkt.ugrt. | [--]kt.rgmt. | [--]y.l.ilak. | [---].ʻm y. | [---]m.w.lm. | [---.]w.ʻm k. | [---]m.ksp. | [---].ʻm. | [---.-]n[-]. | [---.]l k 1016.13

grgš. | w.lmd h. | aršmg. | w.lmd h. | iyṯr. | [w].lmd h. | [yn]ḥm. | [w.]l 1048.2

.lmd h. | aršmg. | w.lmd h. | iyṯr. | [w].lmd h. | [yn]ḥm. | [w.]lmd h. | [i]wrmḫ. | [w.]lmd h. 1048.8

grgš. | w.lmd h. | aršmg. | w.lmd h. | iyṯr. | [w].lmd h. | [yn]ḥm. | [w.]lmd h. | [i]wrmẖ. | [1048.4
| bn.špš. | [w.l]m[d h]. | yṣ[---]. | ʿbd[--]. | pr[--]. | ʿdr[--]. | w.lm[d h]. | ily[---]. | [-----]. | [---]lb[--]. | [---]m[.---]. | [---.]d nkl 1049.2.10
tn. | w.lmd h. | ymn. | w.lmd h. | yʿḏrn. | w.lmd h. | ʿdn. | w.lmd h. | bn.špš. | [w.l]m[d h]. | yṣ[---]. | ʿbd[--]. | pr[--]. | ʿdr[-- 1049.1.10
[-----]. | w.lmd h. | mtn. | w.lmd h. | ymn. | w.lmd h. | yʿḏrn. | w.lmd h. | ʿdn. | w.lmd h. | 1049.1.4
grgš. | w.lmd h. | aršmg. | w.lmd h. | iyṯr. | [w].lmd h. | [yn]ḥm. | [w.]lmd h. | [i]wrmẖ. | [w.]lmd h. 1048.6
[-----]. | w.lmd h. | mtn. | w.lmd h. | ymn. | w.lmd h. | yʿḏrn. | w.lmd h. | ʿdn. | w.lmd h. | bn.špš. | [w.l]m[d 1049.1.6
. | w.lmd h. | yʿḏrn. | w.lmd h. | ʿdn. | w.lmd h. | bn.špš. | [w.l]m[d h]. | yṣ[---]. | ʿbd[--]. | pr[--]. | ʿdr[--]. | w.lm[d h]. | ily[-- 1049.1.12
.dd.kšmn.l.gzzm. | yyn. | ṣdqn. | ʿbd.pdr. | myṣm. | ṯgt. | w.lmd h. | yṯil. | w.lmd h. | rpan. | w.lmd h. | ʿbdrpu. | w.lmd h. 1099.10
| w.lmd h. | rpan. | w.lmd h. | ʿbdrpu. | w.lmd h. | ʿdršp. | w.lmd h. | krwn b.gt.nbk. | ddm.kšmm.l.ẖtn. | ddm.l.trbnn. | 1099.18
[-----]. | w.lmd h. | mtn. | w.lmd h. | ymn. | w.lmd h. | yʿḏrn. | w.lmd h. 1049.1.2
ʿbd.pdr. | myṣm. | ṯgt. | w.lmd h. | yṯil. | w.lmd h. | rpan. | w.lmd h. | ʿbdrpu. | w.lmd h. | ʿdršp. | w.lmd h. | krwn b.gt.nb 1099.14
-]. | w.lmd h. | mtn. | w.lmd h. | ymn. | w.lmd h. | yʿḏrn. | w.lmd h. | ʿdn. | w.lmd h. | bn.špš. | [w.l]m[d h]. | yṣ[---]. | ʿbd[- 1049.1.8
t. | w.lmd h. | yṯil. | w.lmd h. | rpan. | w.lmd h. | ʿbdrpu. | w.lmd h. | ʿdršp. | w.lmd h. | krwn b.gt.nbk. | ddm.kšmm.l.ẖt 1099.16
m. | yyn. | ṣdqn. | ʿbd.pdr. | myṣm. | ṯgt. | w.lmd h. | yṯil. | w.lmd h. | rpan. | w.lmd h. | ʿbdrpu. | w.lmd h. | ʿdršp. | w.lmd 1099.12
h. | iyṯr. | [w].lmd h. | [yn]ḥm. | [w.]lmd h. | [i]wrmẖ. | [w.]lmd h. 1048.10
.b milẖ. | ʿšrm.ẖpn.ẖmš. | kbd.w lpš. | ẖmš.mispt. | mṭ. | w lpš.d sgr b h. | b d.anrmy. 1109.6
spr.npṣm.d yṣa.b milẖ. | ʿšrm.ẖpn.ẖmš. | kbd.w lpš. | ẖmš.mispt. | mṭ. | w lpš.d sgr b h. | b d.anrmy. 1109.3
y.hyt.tq[l.tḥt]. | pʿn h.ybqʿ.kbd h.w yḥd. | iṯ.šmt.iṯ.ʿẓm.w yqḥ b hm. | aqht.ybl.l qẓ.ybky.w yqbr. | yqbr.nn.b mdgt.b 19[1AQHT].3.145
spr.npṣ.krw. | ṯt.ẖṭrm.ṯn.kst. | spl.mšlt.w.mqḥm. | w md h. | arn.w mznm. | ṯn.ẖlpnm. | ṯt.mrḥm. | drb 2050.3
---]. | qlt. | [--]t.mlk.d.y[mlk]. | [--.]ʿbdyrẖ.l.ml[k]. | [--]t.w.lqḥ. | yn[.--].b dn h. | w.ml[k].ššwm.nʿmm. | ytn.l.ʿbdyrẖ. | 2064.14
.r[ʿ h]. | kr[mn.--.]w.r[ʿ h]. | šd.[--.w.]r[ʿ h]. | ẖla[n.---]. | w lšṭr[.---]. 2083.2.7
d.ḥṭm.l.ḥḏǵb. | ṯṯ.ddm.l.gzzm. | kd yn.l.ẖtn.w.kd.ḥmṣ.w.[lt]ḥ.ʿšdm. | kd yn.l.ḥḏǵb.w.kd.ḥmṣ. | prš.glbm.l.bt. | tgmǵ. 1099.27
.šbʿm.drt. | [---.ḥpr.]bnšm.w.l.ḥrš.ʿrq.ṯn.ʿšr h. | [---.d]rʿ.w.mit.drt.w.ʿšrm.l.mit. | [drt.ḥpr.b]nšm.w.ṯn.ʿšr h.dd.l.rpš. | 1098.3
drt.mit.dd. | [---].ḥpr.bn.šm. | [b.---.]knm.ṯṯm.l.mit.drʿ.w.mit.drt. | w[.---.]ʿm.l.mit.dd.ṯn.kbd.ḥpr.bnšm.ṯmnym.dd. | 1098.7
-]ḥ[-.---.-]dn. | arbʿ[m.ksp.]ʿl. | il[m]l[k.a]rgnd. | uškny[.w]mit. | zt.b d hm.rib. | w [---]. | [-----]. | [-]šy[.---] h. | [-]kt[.--- 2055.12
lm.km[m.---]. | w.l ll.ʿṣrm.w [---]. | kmm.w.in.ʿṣr[.---]. | w mit.šʿrt.[-]y[-.---]. | w.kdr.w.npt t[--.---]. | w.ksp.yʿdb.[---]. 38[23].9
spr.npṣ.krw. | ṯt.ẖṭrm.ṯn.kst. | spl.mšlt.w.mqḥm. | w md h. | arn.w mznm. | ṯn.ẖlpnm. | ṯt.mrḥm. | drb. | mrbd. | 2050.4
t m. | yʿbš.brk n.šm.il.ǵzrm. | ṭm.ṭmq.rpu.bʿl.mhr bʿl. | w mhr.ʿnt.ṭm.yḥpn.ḥyl | y.zbl.mlk.ʿllm y.km.tdd. | ʿnt.ṣd.tštr 22.2[124].9
[--.---]. | [---.]ʿsb.[-]ẖ[-.---]. | [---.]b[-.]mṭt k.[---]. | [---.]k.w tmt[.---]. | [---.]k.w ṯṯ[--.---]. | [---.]k.w ṯ[--.---]. | [---.]k ṯrm.l 2125.6
rw. | ṯt.ẖṭrm.ṯn.kst. | spl.mšlt.w.mqḥm. | w md h. | arn.w mznm. | ṯn.ẖlpnm. | ṯt.mrḥm. | drb. | mrbd. | mškbt. 2050.5
lt.bhtm.ʿṣrm.l inš]. | ilm.w š d[d.ilš.š.--.mlk]. | ytb.brr[.w mḥ-.---]. | ym.[ʿ]lm.yʿ[--.---]. | [--.-]g[-.-]s w [---]. | w yn[t.q] 35[3].7
t.šbʿ.klb h. | yr[--.]mlk.ṣbu.špš.w.ḥl.mlk. | w.[---].ypm.w.mḥ[--].t[ṯ]tbn.[-]. | b.[--].w.km.iṯ.y[--.]šqm.yd[-]. 35[3].54
| bhtm.ʿṣ[rm.l in]š ilm.w š. | dd ilš.š[.---.]mlk.ytb br | r.w mḥ[--.---.]w q[--]. | ym.ʿlm.y[---.---]. | t.k[-]ml.[---]. | l[---].w APP.II[173].8
. | mkr.hn d.w.rgm.ank[.--]. | mlkt.ybqš.anyt.w.at[--]. | w mkr n.mlk[.---]. 2008.2.14
pẖr[.bʿl.gdlt.šlm.gdlt]. | w burm.l[b.rmṣt.ilhm]. | bʿlm.w mlu[.---.ksm]. | ṯlṯm.w mʿrb[.---]. | dbḥ šmn mr[.šmn.rqḥ.b APP.II[173].20
ṯǵr k[.tšlm k]. | hl ny.[---]. | w.pdr[--.---]. | tmǵyn[.---]. | w.mli[.---]. | [-]kl.w [---]. | ʿd.mǵt[.---]. 57[101].6
ht. | [-]sny.uḏr h. | w.hm.ẖt. | ʿl.w.likt. | ʿm k.w.hm. | l.ʿl.w.lakm. | ilak.w.at. | um y.al.tdḥṣ. | w.ap.mhkm. | b.lb k.al. | tš 1013.19
lẓpn i | l ḏ.pid.hn b p y sp | r hn.b špt y mn | t hn ṯlẖ h w mlg h y | ṯtqt ʿm h b qʿt. | tqʿt ʿm prbẖṭ. | dmqt ṣǵrt kṯrt. 24[77].47
ẓ. | l amlk.b ṣrrt.ṣpn. | yrd.ʿṯtr.ʿrẓ.yrd. | l kḥṯ.aliyn.bʿl. | w ymlk.b arṣ.il.kl h. | [---] š abn.b rḥbt. | [---] š abn.b kknt. 6.1.65[49.1.37]
hn.hm.yrgm.mlk. | bʿl y.tmǵyy.hn. | alpm.ššwm.hnd. | w.mlk.bʿl y.bnš. | bnny.ʿmn. | mlakty.hnd. | ylak ʿm y. | w.tʿl.ṯ 1012.33
lk. | [---.]adt y.tdʿ. | w.ap.mlk.uḏ[r]. | [-]dʿ.k.iḥd.[---]. | w.mlk.bʿl y. | lm.škn.hnk. | l ʿbd h.alpm.š[šw]m. | rgmt.ʿly.ṯh. 1012.22
[--.]d[--]t. | [---.]ḥw[t.---]. | [---.]š[--]. | w ym ym.yš | al. | w mlk.d mlk. | b ḥwt.špḥ. | l ydn.ʿbd.mlk. | d št.ʿl.ḥrd h. | špḥ. 2062.2.1
.--.--]rny. | [---.]tm.hw.i[--]ty. | [---].ibʿr.a[--.]dmr. | [---.]w mlk.w rg[m.---]. | [--.rg]m.ank.[b]ʿr.[--]ny. | [--]n.bt k.[---.] 1002.53
. | yn[.--].b dn h. | w.ml[k].ššwm.nʿmm. | ytn.l.ʿbdyrẖ. | w.mlk.z[--.--]n.ššwm. | nʿmm.[--].ṯṯm.w.at. | nǵṯ.w.ytn.hm.l 2064.18
ṣbʿ[t]. | [-]tr.šrk.il. | ʿrb.špš.l ymǵ. | krt.ṣbia.špš. | bʿl ny.w ymlk. | [y]ṣb.ʿln.w y[-]y. | [kr]t.ṯʿ.ʿln.bẖr. | [---].aṯt k.ʿl. | [---] 15[128].5.20
-]. | ʿm[-.---]. | mǵ[-.---]. | šp[š.---]. | ql.[---]. | w mlk[.nhš.w mlk.mg]šẖ. | ʿmn.[---]. | ik y.[---]. | w l n[qmd.---]. | [w]nqm 64[118].6
[-----]. | ʿm[-.---]. | mǵ[-.---]. | šp[š.---]. | ql.[---]. | w mlk[.nhš.w mlk.mg]šẖ. | ʿmn.[---]. | ik y.[---]. | w l n[qmd.-- 64[118].6
[---.]šlm. | [---.--]š.lalit. | [---.]bt šp.š. | y[-]lm.w mlk. | ynṣl.l ṯʿy. 2005.2.7
mlk]. | [--.]ʿbdyrẖ.l.ml[k]. | [--]t.w.lqḥ. | yn[.--].b dn h. | w.ml[k].ššwm.nʿmm. | ytn.l.ʿbdyrẖ. | w.mlk.z[--.--]n.ššwm. | 2064.16
]. | atn.ksp.l hm.ʿd. | ilak.ʿm.mlk. | ht.lik[t.--.]mlk[.--]. | w.mlk.yštal.b.hn[--]. | hmt.w.anyt.hm.tʿ[rb]. | mkr.hn d.w.rg 2008.2.10
| [n]it.krk.mʿṣ[d.---]. | b.ḥrbǵlm.ǵlm[n]. | w.trhy.aṯt h. | w.mlky.b[n] h. | ily.mrily.tdgr. 2048.21
.ṭql.ksp. | kdwṯ.l.grgyn.b.ṭq[l]. | ḥmšm.šmt.b.ṭql. | kkr.w.[ml]tḥ.tyt.[---]. | [b]šbʿ[m.w.n]ṣp.ksp. | [tgm]r.[alp.w.]ṯlṯ. 2101.26
lṯ ty[--]. | bn.grgš. | w.npṣ bt ṯn.ṯlṯ mat. | w spl ṯlṯ.mat. | w mmskn. | w.ṯt.mqrtm. | w.ṯn.irpm.w.ṯn.trqm. | w.qpt.w.mq 1103.18
d.mlk.ugrt. | ktb.spr hnd. | dt brrt.ṣṭqšlm. | ʿbd h.hnd. | w mn km.l yqḥ. | spr.mlk.hnd. | b yd.ṣṭqšlm. | ʿd ʿlm. 1005.12
[---.]tn l rbd. | [---.]bʿlt h w yn. | [---.rk]b ʿrpt. | [---.--]n.w mnu dg. | [---.]l aliyn bʿl. | [---].rkb ʿrpt. 2001.2.16
| ʿm y.w.yd. | ilm.p.k mtm. | ʿz.mid. | hm.nṯkp. | mʿn k. | w.mnm. | rgm.d.tšmʿ. | ṯmt.w.št. | b.spr.ʿm y. 53[54].16
spr.ʿrbnm. | dt.ʿrb. | b.mtn.bn.ayaẖ. | b.ḥbṭ h.ḥwt.ṯt h. | w.mnm.šalm. | dt.tknn. | ʿl.ʿrbnm. | hn hmt. | tknn. | mtn.bn.ʿb 1161.5
tšmẖ.m ab. | w al.trḥln. | ʿtn.ḥrd.ank. | ʿm ny.šlm. | kll. | w mnm. | šlm ʿm. | um y. | ʿm y.tṯṯb. | rgm. 1015.16
ẖd.yd h.b škrn.mʿms h. | [k]šbʿ yn.spu.ksm h.bt.bʿl. | [w m]nt h bt.il.ṯḥ.gg h.b ym. | [ṭi]ṭ.rḥṣ.npṣ h.b ym.rṭ. | [--.y]iẖ 17[2AQHT].1.33
aẖd.yd y.b š | krn mʿms y k šbʿt yn. | spu.ksm y.bt.bʿl.[w]mn[t]. | y.bt.il.ṯḥ.gg y.b ym.ṭiṭ. | rḥṣ.npṣ y.b ym.rṭ. | dn.il. 17[2AQHT].2.21
ṭr k.ṭbq]. | lḥt.niṣ k.gr[š.d ʿšy.ln k]. | spu.ksm k.bt.[bʿl.w mnt k]. | bt il.aẖd.yd k.b [škrn]. | mʿms k.k šbʿt.yn.ṭ[ẖ]. | g 17[2AQHT].2.4
. | arbʿ.mḏrnm. | mḏrn.w.mšẖṭ. | d.mrkbt. | mlk. | mšẖṭ.w.msg. | d.tbk. 1122.15
ẖ k[.---]. | tr.ḥ[---]. | w tṣḥ[.---]. | tšqy[.---]. | tr.ḥt[-.---]. | w msk.tr[.---]. | tqrb.aẖ[h.w tṣḥ]. | lm.tbʿrn[.---]. | mn.yrẖ.k 16.2[125].78

.[--]k.šśw[.-]rym[.---].|d ymǵy.bnš[.---].|w ḫmr[.---].|w mʿn[.---].|w bn[š.---].|d bnš.ḥm[r.---].|w d.l mdl.r[--.---]. 2158.1.10
ḫmšt.ʿš[rt].|ksp.ʿl.agd[ṯb].|w nit w mʿṣd.|w ḫrmṯt.|ʿšrt.ksp.|ʿl.ḫ[z]rn.|w.nit.w[.mʿṣd].|w.ḫ[2053.3
b].|w nit w mʿṣd.|w ḫrmṯt.|ʿšrt.ksp.|ʿl.ḫ[z]rn.|w.nit.w[.mʿṣd].|w.ḫ[rmṯt].|ʿš[r.---].|ʿl[.---].|w.ni[t.---].|w[.mʿṣd]. 2053.7
nit.w[.mʿṣd].|w.ḫ[rmṯt].|ʿš[r.---].|ʿl[.---].|w.ni[t.---].|w[.mʿṣd].|w ḫr[mṯt].|[ʿ]šr[.---].|[ʿ]l [-]g[-.---].|w ni[t.w.mʿṣ 2053.12
w[.mʿṣd].|w ḫr[mṯt].|[ʿ]šr[.---].|[ʿ]l [-]g[-.---].|w ni[t.w.mʿṣd].|w ḫrmṯt.|ṯlṯm.ar[bʿ].|kbd.ksp.|ʿl.tgyn.|w ʿl.aṯt h. 2053.16
.|lk.ym.w ṯn.ṯlṯ.rbʿ ym.|ḫmš.ṯdṯ.ym.mk.špšm.|b šbʿ.w tmǵy.l udm.|rbm.w l.udm.ṯrrt.|w gr.nn.ʿrm.šrn.|pdrm.s 14[KRT].3.108
--.]ḫ[--].|b bt.[-.]l bnt.q[-].|w št.b bt.ṯap[.--].|hy.yd h.w ym[ǵ].|mlak k.ʿm dt[n].|lqḥ.mṯpṭ.|w yʿny.nn.|dtn.bt n. UG5.6.10
bʿm.aḫ h.ym[.--].|w ṯmnt.l ṯmnym.|šr.aḫy h.mẓa h.|w mẓa h.šr.yly h.|b skn.sknm.b ʿdn.|ʿdnm.kn.npl.bʿl.|km ṯ 12[75].2.52
pn.bʿl.|bʿl.ytlk.w yṣd.|yḥ pat.mlbr.|wn.ymǵy.aklm.|w ymẓa.ʿqqm.|bʿl.ḥmd m.yḥmd m.|bn.dgn.yhrr m.|bʿl.ngṯ 12[75].1.37
mmskn.|w.ṯt.mqrtm.|w.ṯn.irpm.w.ṯn.trqm.|w.qpt.w.mqḥm.|w.ṯlṯm.yn šbʿ.kbd d ṭbṭ.|w.ḫmšm.yn.d iḫ h. 1103.21
yʿdb.hd.ʿdb[.ʿd]bt.|hkl h.ṭbḫ.alpm[.ap].|ṣin.šql.ṯrm[.w]m|ria.il.ʿglm.d[t].|šnt.imr.qmṣ.l[l]im.|ṣḥ.aḫ h.b bht h.a 4[51].6.41
.|il.dbḥ.[---].|pʿr.b[--.---].|ṭbḫ.alp[m.ap.ṣin.šql].|ṯrm.w [mri.ilm.ʿglm.dt.šnt].|imr.[qmṣ.llim.---]. 1[ʿNT.X].4.31
m.tdd.|ʿnt.ṣd.tštr.ʿpt.šmm.|ṭbḫ.alpm.ap ṣin.šql.ṯrm.|w mri ilm.ʿglm.dt.šnt.|imr.qmṣ.llim.k ksp.|l ʿbrm.zt.ḫrṣ.l ʿ 22.2[124].13
ṯn.pld.ptt[.-]r.|lpš.sgr.rq.|ṯt.prqt.|w.mrdt.prqt.ptt.|lbš.psm.rq.|ṯn.mrdt.az.|ṯlṯ.pld.šʿrt.|ṯ[---]. 1112.4
|[---].šśb.|[---.]tr h.|[a]rbʿ.qlʿm.|arbʿ.mdrnm.|mdrn.w.mšḫṭ.|d.mrkbt.|mlk.|mšḫṭ.w.msg.|d.tbk. 1122.12
rt[.k]sp.|rṭ.l.ql.d.ybl.prd.|b.ṯql.w.nṣp.ksp.|ṯmn.lbšm.w.mšlt.|l.udmym.b.ṯmnt.ʿšrt.ksp.|šbʿm.lbš.d.ʿrb.bt.mlk.|b. 2101.14
m.at.tr[gm.---].|w.drm.ʿtr[--.---].|w ap.ht.k[--.]škn.|w.mṯnn[.---.]ʿmn k.|[-]štš.[---.]rgm y.|[-]wd.r[-.]pǵt.|[---.--] 54.1.21[13.2.6]
[ṯl]ṯm.ksp.ʿ[l].|[b]n.bly.gbʿly.|[šp]ḥ.a[n]ntb.|w.m[--.u]škny.|[ʿ]š[r.---]t.ksp.|[ʿl.---]b bn[.--].|[-]ḥ[-.---].|[- 2055.4
bʿlt bhtm[.--]tn k.|[--]y.l ihbt.yb[--].rgm y.|[---.]škb.w m[--.]mlakt.|[---.]ʿl.w tšʿ[d]n.npṣ h.|[---.]rgm.hn.[--]n.w 1002.47
.|ʿm.mlk.|w.ht.|mlk.syr.|ns.w.ṯm.|ydbḥ.|mlǵ[.---].|w.m[--.--]y.|y[--.---]. 2063.18
yqm.|l pʿn h.ykrʿ.w yql.|w yšu.g h.w yṣḥ.|hwt.aḫt.w nar[-].|qrn.d bat k.btlt.ʿnt.|qrn.d bat k bʿl.ymšḥ.|bʿl.ymš 10[76].2.20
ḫmšt.ʿš[rt].|ksp.ʿl.agd[ṯb].|w nit w mʿṣd.|w ḫrmṯt.|ʿšrt.ksp.|ʿl.ḫ[z]rn.|w.nit.w[.mʿṣd]. 2053.3
agd[ṯb].|w nit w mʿṣd.|w ḫrmṯt.|ʿšrt.ksp.|ʿl.ḫ[z]rn.|w.nit.w[.mʿṣd].|w.ḫ[rmṯt].|ʿš[r.---].|ʿl[.---].|w.ni[t.---].|w[. 2053.7
t.---].|w[.mʿṣd].|w ḫr[mṯt].|[ʿ]šr[.---].|[ʿ]l [-]g[-.---].|w ni[t.w.mʿṣd].|w ḫrmṯt.|ṯlṯm.ar[bʿ].|kbd.ksp.|ʿl.tgyn.|w ʿ 2053.16
.ḫ[z]rn.|w.nit.w[.mʿṣd].|w.ḫ[rmṯt].|ʿš[r.---].|ʿl[.---].|w.ni[t.---].|w[.mʿṣd].|w ḫr[mṯt].|[ʿ]šr[.---].|[ʿ]l [-]g[-.---].|w 2053.11
b šdm.mm h.|b smkt.ṣat.npš h.|[-]mt[-].ṣba.rbt.|špš.w tgh.nyr.|rbt.w rgm.l aḫt k.|ṯtmnt.krt n.dbḥ.|dbḥ.mlk.ʿšr 16.1[125].37
ṯlṯ.sswm.mrkbt.|b trbṣ.bn.amt.|qḥ.krt.šlmm.|šlmm.w ng.mlk.|l bt y.rḥq.krt.|l ḥẓr y.al.tṣr.|udm.rbt.w udm ṯrr 14[KRT].3.131
.|tmt.ṯmn.nqpt.ʿd.ilm.nʿmm.ttlkn.|šd.tṣdn.pat.mdbr.w ngš.hm.nǵr.|mdrʿ.w ṣḥ hm.ʿm.nǵr.mdrʿ y.nǵr.|nǵr.ptḥ. 23[52].68
r.|il.hlk.l bt h.yštql.|l ḥṭr h.yʿmsn.nn.ṯkmn.|w šnm.w ngšnn.ḥby.|bʿl.qrnm w ḏnb.ylšn.|b ḫri h.w ṯnt h.ql.il.[--] UG5.1.1.19
t.|l arṣ.špt l šmm.w ʿrb.b p hm.ʿṣr.šmm.|w dg b ym.w ndd.gzr.l zr.yʿdb.u ymn.|u šmal.b p hm.w l.tšbʿn y.aṯt.itr 23[52].63
i[--.---].|d.[---].|bnš[-] mdy[-].|w.b.glb.|phnn.w.|mndym.|bdnh.|l[q]ḥt.|[--]km.ʿm.mlk.|[b]ǵl hm.w.iblb 2129.5
yprq.lṣb w yṣḥq.|yšu.g h.w yṣḥ.|aṯbn.ank.w anḫn.|w tnḫ.b irt y.npš.|k ḥy.aliyn.bʿl.|k iṯ.zbl.bʿl.arṣ.|gm.yṣḥ.il.l 6[49].3.19
q.|pʿn.l hdm.ytpd.yšu.|g h.w yṣḥ.aṯbn.ank.|w anḫn.w tnḫ.b irt y.|npš.k yld.bn.l y.km.|aḫ y.w šrš.km ary y.|nṣ 17[2AQHT].2.13
ṣb.w yṣḥq.|pʿn.l hdm.ytpd.yšu.|g h.w yṣḥ.aṯbn.ank.|w anḫn.w tnḫ.b irt y.|npš.k yld.bn.l y.km.|aḫ y.w šrš.km a 17[2AQHT].2.13
.ytpd.|w yprq.lṣb w yṣḥq.|yšu.g h.w yṣḥ.|aṯbn.ank.w anḫn.|w tnḫ.b irt y.npš.|k ḥy.aliyn.bʿl.|k iṯ.zbl.bʿl.arṣ.|g 6[49].3.18
h].|[-]ntm[.---].|[ʿ]bdm.|[bn].mṣrn.|[a]ršwn.|ʿb[d].|w nḥl h.|atn.bn.ap[s]n.|nsk.ṯlṯ.|bn.[--.]m[-]ḫr.|bn.šmrm.|ṯ 85[80].3.6
.|bn.tlmyn.|w.nḥl h.|w.nḥl hm.|bn.ḥrm.|bn.brzn.|w.nḥl h.|bn.adlḏn.|bn.šbl.|bn.ḫnzr.|bn.arwt.|bn.ṯbtnq.|b 113[400].1.11
|bn[.---].|[-----].|b[n.---].|b[n.---].|bn.[---].|bn.a[--].|w.nḥl h.|bn.alz.|w.nḥl h.|bn.sny.|bn.ablḥ.|[-----].|w [---]. 2163.1.11
[w]nḥ[l h].|[bn].amd[-].|[bn].ṣbṭ[--].|[bn].ḫla[n].|[bn].ǵr[-- 2164.A.1
[-----].|bn.[---].|bn.[---].|w.nḥ[l h].|bn.ẓr[-].|mru.skn.|bn.bddn.|bn.ǵrgn.|bn.tgtn.| 113[400].5.3
l hm.|bn.iršyn.|bn.ʿzn.|bn.aršw.|bn.ḫzrn.|bn.iǵyn.|w.nḥl h.|bn.ksd.|bn.bršm.|bn.kzn.|w.nḥl h.|w.nḥl hm.|w 113[400].2.17
[---]y.|[---.]w.nḥl h.|bn ksln.ṯlṯḫ.|bn yṣmḫ.bn.ṯrn w nḥl h.|bn srd.bn a 101[10].2
.|bn.brzn.|bn.ḫtr[-].|bn.yd[--].|bn.ʿ[---].|w.nḥ[l h].|w.nḥ[l h].|bn.k[---].|bn.y[---].|[bn].i[---]. 116[303].11
bn.lbn.|bn.šlmn.|bn.mly.|pslm.|bn.annd.|bn.glʿd.|w.nḥl h.|bn.mlkyy.|[bn].bm[--].|[ʿš]rm.|[-----].|[-----].|bn. 2163.3.12
bn.ḥṭb.|bn abyt.|bn ḥdl.|bn ṣdqn.|bn ayy.|bn dbb.|w nḥl h.|bn nʿmyn.|bn aṯtyy.|bn ḫlp.|bn.ẓll.|bn ydy.|bn l 2016.1.8
b[n.---].|b[n.---].|bn.[---].|bn.a[--].|w.nḥl h.|bn.alz.|w.nḥl h.|bn.sny.|bn.ablḥ.|[-----].|w [---].|bn.[---].|bn.yr[-- 2163.1.13
[---]y.|[---.]w.nḥl h.|bn ksln.ṯlṯḫ.|bn yṣmḫ.bn.ṯrn w nḥl h.|bn srd.bn agmn.|bn [-]ln.bn.ṯbil.|bn is.bn tbdn.|b 101[10].4
.|w.nḥl h.|[--.-]hs.|[--.--]nyn.|[-----].|[-----].|bn.ʿdy.|w.nḥl h.|bn.ʿbl.|bn.[-]rṯn.|bn[.---].|bn u[l]pm.|bn ʿ[p]ty.|b 2163.2.20
[aǵ]ltn.|[--]tm.b.gt.irbṣ.|[--]šmyn.|[w.]nḥl h.|bn.qṣn.|bn.ksln.|bn.ṣrym.|bn.ṯmq.|bn.ntp.|bn. 1073.1.4
mryn[m].|bn.bly.|nrn.|w.nḥl h.|bn.rmyy.|bn.tlmyn.|w.nḥl h.|w.nḥl hm.|bn.ḥrm. 113[400].1.4
ʿ[--]t.|bn.adty.|bn.krwn.|bn.ngśk.|bn.qnd.|bn.pity.|w.nḥl h.|bn.rt.|bn.l[--].|bn.[---].|[---.--]y.|[--.-]drm.|[--.--] 113[400].3.18
tnnm.|bn.qqln.|w.nḥl h.|w.nḥl h.|bn.šml[-].|bn.brzn.|bn.ḫtr[-].|bn.yd[--].|bn.ʿ[---]. 116[303].4
zlbn.|bn.aḫ[--].|bn[.---].|[-----].|bn kr[k].|bn ḫtyn.|w nḥl h.|bn tgrb.|bn tdnyn.|bn pbn. 2016.3.4
.|bn.šml[-].|bn.brzn.|bn.ḫtr[-].|bn.yd[--].|bn.ʿ[---].|w.nḥ[l h].|w.nḥ[l h].|bn.k[---].|bn.y[---].|[bn].i[---]. 116[303].10
tnnm.|bn.qqln.|w.nḥl h.|w.nḥl h.|bn.šml[-].|bn.brzn.|bn.ḫtr[-].|bn.yd[--]. 116[303].3
ṣrn.|bn.[-]dr[-].|[---]l[-].|[--]ym.|[--]rm.|[bn.]aǵld.|[w.nḥ]l h.|[w.nḥ]l h[.-]. 114[324].3.5
bn.mztn.|bn.šlgyn.|bn.[-]gštn.|bn[.n]klb.|b[n.]dtn.|w.nḥl h.|w.nḥl hm.|bn.iršyn.|bn.ʿzn.|bn.aršw.|bn.ḫzrn.|b 113[400].2.10
ryn[m].|bn.bly.|nrn.|w.nḥl h.|bn.rmyy.|bn.tlmyn.|w.nḥl h.|w.nḥl hm.|bn.ḥrm.|bn.brzn.|w.nḥl h.|bn.adlḏn. 113[400].1.7
ḏrǵlm.|bn.mmy.|bn.ḫnyn.|bn.knn.|khnm.|bn.ṯʿy.|w.nḥl h.|w.nḥl hm.|bn.nqly.|bn.snrn.|bn.tgd.|bn.d[-]n.|b 105[86].1
[----].|bn.[---].|bn.[---].|bn.yk[--].|bn.šmm.|bn.irgy.|w.nḥl h.|w.nḥl hm.|[bn].pmn.|bn.gtrn.|bn.arpḫn.|bn.tryn 1046.2.11
.ḫzrn.|bn.iǵyn.|w.nḥl h.|bn.ksd.|bn.bršm.|bn.kzn.|w.nḥl h.|w.nḥl hm.|w.[n]ḥl hm.|b[n.---].|bn.gzry.|bn.atyn 113[400].2.21
.arsw ʿ[šr]m.|ʿšdyn.ḫmš[t].|abršn.ʿšr[t].|bʿln.ḫmšt.|w.nḥl h.ḫm[š]t.|bn.unp.arbʿt.|ʿbdbn.ytrš ḫmšt.|krwn.ʿšrt.| 1062.9
].|bn.sḫr.mr[-.---].|bn.idrn.ʿš[-.---].|bn.bly.mr[-.---].|w.nḥl h.mr[-.---].|ilšpš.[---].|iḫny.[---].|bn.[---]. 88[304].11

w

[spr.----]m.|bn.pi[ty].|w.nḥ[l h].|‘bd[--].|bn.s[---].|bn.at[--].|bn.qnd̠.|ṣmq[-].|bn. 117[325].1.3
k.[--]kt.[--.d.]yṯb.b.šb[n].|bn.pr[-.]d.y[ṯb.b].šlmy.|tlš.w[.n]ḥl h[.-].ṯgd.mrum.|bt.[-]b[-.-]sy[-]h.|nn[-].b[n].py[-.d. 2015.2.3
r[-].|[---]l[-].|[--]ym.|[--]rm.|[bn.]aǵld.|[w.nḥ]l h.|[w.nḥ]l h[.-]. 114[324].3.6
y.w.nḥl h.|[--]ilt.w.nḥl h.|[---]n.|[--]ly.|[iw]ryn.|[--.w.n]ḥl h.|[-]ibln.|bn.nd̠bn.|bn.‘bl.|bn.tlšn.|bn.sln.|w nḥl 1063.9
bn.ṣrṯn.|bn.‘bd.|snb.w.nḥl h.|[-]by.w.nḥl h.|[--]ilt.w.nḥl h.|[---]n.|[--]ly.|[iw]ry 1063.3
--]t.|[---.-]l[--].|[---.]pr[--].|[-.a]pln.|bn.mzt.|bn.ṯrn.|w.nḥl h.|[--.-]hs.|[--.--]nyn.|[-----].|[-----].|bn.‘dy.|w.nḥl h 2163.2.15
----].|[-----].|[-----].|[-----].|[-----].|[-----].|[---.--]yn.|[w.nḥ]l h.|[--.---]n.|[-----].|[-----].|[-----].|[-----].|[--.-]gn.|[-- 113[400].4.18
bn.ṣrṯn.|bn.‘bd.|snb.w.nḥl h.|[-]by.w.nḥl h.|[--]ilt.w.nḥl h.|[---]n.|[--]ly.|[iw]ryn.|[--.w.n]ḥl h. 1063.4
bn.ṣrṯn.|bn.‘bd.|snb.w.nḥl h.|[-]by.w.nḥl h.|[--]ilt.w.nḥl h.|[---]n.|[--]ly.|[iw]ryn.|[--.w.n]ḥl h.|[-]ibln.|bn.nd̠ 1063.5
.w.n]ḥl h.|[-]ibln.|bn.nd̠bn.|bn.‘bl.|bn.tlšn.|bn.sln.|w nḥl h. 1063.15
-].|[--.-]s[-]n.|[--.-]nyn.|[---].[-]ǵtyn.|[---].[-]tyn.|[---.w.]nḥl h. 123[326].2.6
|bn.šlgyn.|bn.[-]gštn.|bn[.n]klb.|b[n.]dtn.|w.nḥl h.|w.nḥl hm.|bn.iršyn.|bn.‘zn.|bn.aršw.|bn.ḫzrn.|bn.iǵyn.| 113[400].2.11
n.bly.|nrn.|w.nḥl h.|bn.rmyy.|bn.tlmyn.|w.nḥl h.|w.nḥl hm.|bn.ḥrm.|bn.brzn.|w.nḥl h.|bn.adld̠n.|bn.šbl.|b 113[400].1.8
n.mmy.|bn.ḫnyn.|bn.knn.|khnm.|bn.ṯ‘y.|w.nḥl h.|w.nḥl hm.|bn.nqly.|bn.snrn.|bn.ṯgd.|bn.d[-]n.|bn.amdn.| 105[86].1
[---].|bn.[---].|bn.yk[--].|bn.šmm.|bn.irgy.|w.nḥl h.|w.nḥl hm.|[bn].pmn.|bn.gṯrn.|bn.arpḫn.|bn.ṯryn.|bn.dll.| 1046.2.12
l h.|bn.ksd.|bn.bršm.|bn.kzn.|w.nḥl h.|w.nḥl hm.|w.[n]ḥl hm.|b[n.---].|bn.gzry.|bn.atyn.|bn.ttn.|bn.rwy.|b 113[400].2.23
.iǵyn.|w.nḥl h.|bn.ksd.|bn.bršm.|bn.kzn.|w.nḥl h.|w.nḥl hm.|w.[n]ḥl hm.|b[n.---].|bn.gzry.|bn.atyn.|bn.ttn. 113[400].2.22
[k.ym]ḫṣ.b‘l m[.--]y.tnn.w ygl.w ynsk.‘[-].|[--]y.l arṣ[.id]y.alt.l aḫš.idy.alt.in l y.|[--]t.b‘l.ḫ 1001.1.1
r k.l[-]|n k.ḥtk k.nmrt k.b tk.|ugrt.l ymt.špš.w yrḫ.|w n‘mt.šnt.il. UG5.2.2.12
bnšm.dt.l.u[--]ṯṯb.|kṯ[r]n.|w.aṯt h.w.n‘r h.|bn.ḫby.w.[a]ṯt h.|ynḥm.ulmy.|[--]q.w.aṯt h.w.bn 2068.3
n.|pnm.tk.qrt h.|hmry.mk.ksu.|ṯbt h.ḫḫ.arṣ.|nḫlt h.w nǵr.|‘nn.ilm.al.|tqrb.l bn.ilm.|mt.al.y‘db km.|k imr.b p 4[51].8.14
[---.--]t ugrt.|[---.w n]py.yman.|[w npy.‘rmt.---.w]npy.annpdgl.|[ušn.yp kn.ulp.qṭy.ulp.]ddmy.ulp ḫry.|[ul APP.I[-].1.3
š].|[w šqrb.š.mšr mšr.bn.ugrt.w npy.---.]w npy.|[---.w np]y.ugrt.|[---.u ṯḫṭu.ulp.qṭy.ulp.ddm]y.|[ulp.ḫry.ulp.ḫt 32[2].1.5
t.bn il.|l ṯkm[n.w šnm.]hn ‘[r].|[---.]w npy[.---].|[---.]w npy.u[grt.---].|[---.--]y.ulp.[---].|[---.]ǵbr.u[lp.---].|[---.--] 32[2].2.2
.l ṯkmn[.w]šnm.hn.‘r.|w.ṯb.l mspr.m[šr] mšr.bt.ugrt.w npy.gr.|ḥmyt.ugrt.w [np]y.nṯt.ušn.yp kn.ulp qṭy.|ulp.dd 32[2].1.27
ytši.l dr.bn.il.l mpḫ]rt.[bn.il.l ṯkmn.w šn]m hn š.|[---.w n]py.gr[.ḥmyt.ugrt.w np]y.|[---].w n[py.---].u ṯḫṭi[n.ulp.q 32[2].1.10
--.--]l.il.t‘d̠r b‘l.|[-----.]lšnt.|[---.--]yp.tḥt.|[-----].|[---.]w npy gr.|[ḥmyt.ugrt.w npy.yman.w npy.‘r]mt.w npy.|[---. APP.I[-].1.12
lšnt.|[---.--]yp.tḥt.|[-----].|[---.]w npy gr.|[ḥmyt.ugrt.w npy.yman.w npy.‘r]mt.w npy.|[---.ušn.yp km.ulp.]qṭy.|[APP.I[-].1.13
nm hn š.|w šqrb.‘r.mšr mšr bn.ugrt.w [npy.---.]ugr.|w npy.yman.w npy.‘rmt.w npy.[---].|w npy.nqmd.ušn.yp k 32[2].1.19
[---.--]t ugrt.|[---.w n]py.yman.|[w npy.‘rmt.---.w]npy.annpdgl.|[ušn.yp kn. APP.I[-].1.2
[npy.---.]ugr.|w npy.yman.w npy.‘rmt.w npy.[---].|w npy.nqmd.ušn.yp km.ulp.q[ṭy.ulp.ddm]y.|ulp.ḫry.ulp.ḫ[32[2].1.20
.|w.ṯb.l mspr.m[šr] mšr.bt.ugrt.w npy.gr.|ḥmyt.ugrt.w [np]y.nṯt.ušn.yp kn.ulp qṭy.|ulp.ddmy.ul[p.ḫ]ry.ulp.ḫty. 32[2].1.28
.tḥt.|[-----].|[---.]w npy gr.|[ḥmyt.ugrt.w npy.yman.w npy.‘r]mt.w npy.|[---.ušn.yp km.ulp.]qṭy.|[ulp.ddmy.ulp APP.I[-].1.13
qrb.‘r.mšr mšr bn.ugrt.w [npy.---.]ugr.|w npy.yman.w npy.‘rmt.w npy.[---].|w npy.nqmd.ušn.yp km.ulp.q[ṭy.ul 32[2].1.19
[---.--]t ugrt.|[---.w n]py.yman.|[w npy.‘rmt.---.w]npy.annpdgl.|[ušn.yp kn.ulp.qṭy.ulp.]dd APP.I[-].1.3
.w šn]m hn š.|[---.w n]py.gr[.ḥmyt.ugrt.w np]y.|[---].w n[py.---].u ṯḫṭi[n.ulp.qṭy].|ulp.ddmy.ul[p.ḫry.u]lp.ḫty.ul 32[2].1.11
bn.i[l.l ṯkmn.w š]nm hn š.|w šqrb.‘r.mšr mšr bn.ugrt.w [npy.---.]ugr.|w npy.yman.w npy.‘rmt.w npy.[---].|w np 32[2].1.18
|[---.]w npy gr.|[ḥmyt.ugrt.w npy.yman.w npy.‘r]mt.w npy.|[---.ušn.yp km.ulp.]qṭy.|[ulp.ddmy.ulp.ḫry.ulp.ḫty. APP.I[-].1.13
n.w šnm.hn š].|[w šqrb.š.mšr mšr.bn.ugrt.w npy.---.]w npy.|[---.w np]y.ugrt.|[---.u ṯḫṭu.ulp.qṭy.ulp.ddm]y.|[ul 32[2].1.4
šr bn.ugrt.w [npy.---.]ugr.|w npy.yman.w npy.‘rmt.w npy.[---].|w npy.nqmd.ušn.yp km.ulp.q[ṭy.ulp.ddm]y.|ul 32[2].1.19
.[bn.il.l ṯkmn.w šn]m hn š.|[---.w n]py.gr[.ḥmyt.ugrt.w np]y.|[---].w n[py.---].u ṯḫṭi[n.ulp.qṭy].|ulp.ddmy.ul[p.ḫr 32[2].1.10
.bn.il.l ṯkmn.w šnm.hn š].|[w šqrb.š.mšr mšr.bn.ugrt.w npy.---.]w npy.|[---.w np]y.ugrt.|[---.u ṯḫṭu.ulp.qṭy.ulp.d 32[2].1.4
d[r.bn il.l]mpḫrt.bn il.|l ṯkm[n.w šnm.]hn ‘[r].|[---.]w npy[.---].|[---.]w npy.u[grt.---].|[---.--]y.ulp.[---].|[---.]ǵbr 32[2].2.1
[.-]r[-].|[--]dšq krsnm.|ḫmšm [-]t ṯlṯ ty[--].|bn.grgš.|w.npṣ bt ṯn.ṯlṯ mat.|w spl ṯlṯ.mat.|w mmskn.|w.ṯt.mqrtm. 1103.16
w y‘ny.bn.|ilm.mt.npš[.-].|npš.lbun.|thw.w npš.|anḫr.b ym.|brkt.šbšt.|k rumm.hm.|‘n.kd̠d.aylt.|m UG5.4.4
|dqt l ṣpn.šrp.w šlmm.|kmm.w bbt.b‘l.ugrt.|w kdm.w npš ilib.|gdlt.il š.b‘l š.‘nt.|ṣpn.alp.w š.pdry.š.|šrp.w šlm UG5.13.12
[dqt.l.ṣpn.šrp].w š[l]mm.kmm.|[w bbt.b‘l.ugrt.]kdm.w npš.|[ilib.gdlt.il.š.b]‘[l.]š.‘nt ṣpn.|[---.]w [n]p[š.---].|[---.-- 36[9].1.16
id.yph.mlk.|r[š]p.ḫgb.ap.|w[.n]pš.ksp.|w ḫrṣ.km[-].|w.ḥ[--.-]lp.|w.š.l[--]p.|w[.--.-]nš. 2005.1.3
gṯrm.|bt.mlk.ṯql.ḫrṣ.|l špš.w yrḫ.l gṯr.|ṯql.ksp.ṯb.ap w np[š].|l ‘nt h.ṯql.ḫrṣ.|l špš[.w y]rḫ.l gṯr.ṯn.|[ṯql.ksp].ṯb.a 33[5].12
.|l ‘nt h.ṯql.ḫrṣ.|l špš[.w y]rḫ.l gṯr.ṯn.|[ṯql.ksp].ṯb.ap.w npš.|[---].bt.alp w š.|[---.--]m.l gṯrm.|[---.]l ‘nt m.|[---.--] 33[5].15
‘l.ugrt.]kdm.w npš.|[ilib.gdlt.il.š.b]‘[l.]š.‘nt ṣpn.|[---.]w [n]p[š.---].|[---.--]t.w[.---].|[---.--]pr.ṯ[--.---].|[-----].|[---.-- 36[9].1.18
[---].|kmm.w.in.‘ṣr[.---].|w mit.š‘rt.[-]y[-.---].|w.kdr.w.npt t[--.---].|w.ksp.y‘db.[---]. 38[23].10
qrt ṯqlm.w nṣp.|šlmy.ṯql.|ary ṯql.|ṯmry ṯql.w.nṣp.|aǵt nṣp.|dmt ṯql.|ykn‘m ṯql. 69[111].4
[-]b[-.---.--]|r ṯṯm lḥm.|l[.-]ry ṯlṯ spm w ‘šr lḥm.|[--.]w nṣp w ṯlṯ spm w ‘šrm lḥ[m].|l[.-]dt ḫnd[r]ṯ ar‘ s[p]m w ‘š 134[-].4
l].|ḫmšm.šmt.b.ṯql.|kkr.w.[ml]tḫ.tyt.[---].|[b]šb‘[m.w.n]ṣp.ksp.|[tgm]r.[alp.w.]ṯlṯ.mat. 2101.27
h.w.ṯqlm.|ksp h.mitm.pḥm.b d.skn.|w.ṯt.ktnm.ḫmšt.w.nṣp.ksp.hn. 1110.6
ṯlṯ.uṭbm.b d.alḫn.b.‘šrt[.k]sp.|rṯ.l.ql.d.ybl.prd.|b.ṯql.w.nṣp.ksp.|ṯmn.lbšm.w.mšlt.|l.udmym.b.ṯmnt.‘šrt.ksp.|šb‘ 2101.13
l[.---].|[-]tm.iph.adt y.w.[---].|tšṣḥq.hn.aṯt.l.‘bd.|šb‘t.w.nṣp.ksp.|[-]tm.rb[.--.a]ḫd.|[---.--]t.b[-].|[---.-]y[-]. 1017.5
qrt ṯqlm.w nṣp.|šlmy.ṯql.|ary ṯql.|ṯmry ṯql.w.nṣp.|aǵt nṣp.|dmt ṯql 69[111].1
nsk k[sp].|‘šrt.|w nṣ[p]. 1164.3
].yq[--.--].|w [---.]rkb[.---].|[---].d[--.---].|b ql[.-----].|w tštqdn[.-----].|hm.|w yḥ.mlk.|w ik m.kn.w [---].|tšknnn 62[26].7
š.w mlk.mg]šḫ.|‘mn.[---].|ik y.[---].|w l n[qmd.---].|[w]nqmd.[---].|[-.]‘mn.šp[š.mlk.rb].|b‘l h.šlm.[w spš].|mlk. 64[118].10
t.bn.aḫt.b‘l.|l pnn h.ydd.w yqm.|l p‘n h.ykr‘.w yql.|w yšu.g h.w yṣḥ.|ḥwt.aḫt.w nar[-].|qrn.d bat k.btlt.‘nt.|qr 10[76].2.19

qht.ybl.l qẓ.ybky.w yqbr. | yqbr.nn.b mdgt.b knk[-]. | w yšu.g h.w yṣḥ.knp.nšrm. | b'l.yṯbr.b'l.yṯbr.diy. | hmt.hm.t' 19[1AQHT].3.148
r. | ap.bnt.ḥry. | km hm.w tẖss.aṯrt. | ndr h.w ilt.p[--]. | w tšu.g h.w [tṣḥ]. | ph m'.ap.k[rt.--]. | u ṯn.ndr[.---]. | apr.[---]. 15[128].3.27
.btlt.'n[t]. | tšu.knp.w tr.b 'p. | tk.aẖ šmk.mlat rumm. | w yšu.'n h.aliyn.b'l. | w yšu.'n h.w y'n. | w y'n.btlt.'nt. | n'mt. 10[76].2.13
| b'l.ymšḫ.hm.b 'p. | nṭ'n.b arṣ.ib y. | w b 'pr.qm.aẖ k. | w tšu.'n h.btlt.'nt. | w tšu.'n h.w t'n. | w t'n.arẖ.w tr.b lkt. | tr 10[76].2.26
tr.b 'p. | tk.aẖ šmk.mlat rumm. | w yšu.'n h.aliyn.b'l. | w yšu.'n h.w y'n. | w y'n.btlt.'nt. | n'mt.bn.aẖt.b'l. | l pnn h.y 10[76].2.14
nṭ'n.b arṣ.ib y. | w b 'pr.qm.aẖ k. | w tšu.'n h.btlt.'nt. | w tšu.'n h.w t'n. | w t'n.arẖ.w tr.b lkt. | tr.b lkt.w tr.b ẖl. | [b 10[76].2.27
strn ydd. | b gngn h.aḥd y.d ym | lk.'l.ilm.l ymru. | ilm.w nšm.d yšb | ['].hmlt.arṣ.gm.l ǵ | [lm] h.b'l k.yṣḥ.'n. | [gpn]. 4[51].7.51
ǵ[ṯ.---]t. | tlk m.rḥmy.w tṣd[.---]. | tḥgrn.ǵzr.n'm.[.--]. | w šm.'rbm.yr[.---]. | mṯbt.ilm.ṯmn.ṯ[--.--]. | pamt.šb'. | iqnu.š 23[52].18
lt h. | bṣql.yph.b palt.bṣ[q]l. | yph.b yǵlm.bṣql.y[ḥb]q. | w ynšq.aḥl.an bṣ[ql]. | ynp'.b palt.bṣql yp' b yǵlm. | ur.tisp k. 19[1AQHT].2.64
.aklt h.yph. | šblt.b akt.šblt.yp'. | b ḥmdrt.šblt.yḥ[bq]. | w ynšq.aḥl.an.šblt. | tp'.b aklt.šblt.tp'[.b ḥm]drt. | ur.tisp k.y 19[1AQHT].2.71
bmt.limm.w t'n.btlt. | 'nt.irš ḥym.l aqht.ǵzr. | irš ḥym.w atn k.bl mt. | w ašlḥ k.ašspr k.'m.b'l. | šnt.'m.bn il.tspr.yrẖ 17[2AQHT].6.27
n y.hm[.mkly.ṣ]brt. | ary y[.ẓl].ksp.[a]ṯrt. | k t'n.ẓl.ksp.w n[-]t. | ẖrṣ.šmẖ.rbt.a[ṯrt]. | ym.gm.l ǵlm h.k [tṣḥ]. | 'n.mkṯr. 4[51].2.27
m. | w.b.ṯb h.[---]. | spr ḥ[--.---]. | w.'m[.---]. | yqḥ[.---]. | w.n[--.---]. 2129.15
hr.nuš[-.---]. | b [u]grt.w ht.a[--]. | w hm.at.trg[m.---]. | w sip.u hw[.---]. | w ank.u šbt[--.---]. | ank.n[--]n[.---]. | kst.l[-- 54.1.9[13.1.6]
m. | p[---]r.aḥd. | [-----]. | [-----]. | [---.--]y. | [---.-]ṯt. | [---.]w.sbsg. | [-----]. | [-----]. | [---.--]ṯ. | [---.-]b.m.lk. | kdwṯ.ḥdṯ. | b d 1112.14
--.--]ẖm. | [---.--]m. | [---]nb.w ykn. | [--]ndbym. | [']rmy.w snry. | [b]n.sdy.bn.ṯty. | bn.ḥyn.bn.ǵlm. | bn.yyn.w.bn.au[p 131[309].22
h. | w.ḥṯṯn bn h. | w.btšy.bt h. | w.ištrmy. | bt.'bd mlk. | w.snt. | bt.ugrt. | w.pdy h[m]. | iwrkl.mit. | ksp.b y[d]. | birtym 1006.10
--]. | alp.pr.b'l.[---]. | w prt.tkt.[---]. | šnt.[---]. | s̀sw.'ṯtrt.w s̀sw.'[nt.---]. | w ht.[--]k.s̀sw[.-]rym[.---]. | d ymǵy.bnš[.---]. 2158.1.6
r.npr. | bn.ẖty. | ṯn.bnš ıbrḏr. | bnš tlmi. | sǵr.ẖryn. | 'dn.w sǵr h. | bn.ḥgbn. 2082.9
r'ym.dt.b d.iytlm. | ẖyrn.w.s̀ǵr h. | s̀ǵr.bn.prsn. | agpṯr.w.s̀ǵ[r h]. | ṯ'ln. | mztn.w.s̀ǵr [h]. 2072.2
rn.w.s̀ǵr h. | s̀ǵr.bn.prsn. | agpṯr.w.s̀ǵ[r h]. | ṯ'ln. | mztn.w.s̀ǵr [h]. | s̀ǵr.plṭ. | s[d]rn [w].ṯn.s̀ǵr h. | [---.]w.s̀ǵr h. | [---.]w. 2072.6
r'ym.dt.b d.iytlm. | ẖyrn.w.s̀ǵr h. | s̀ǵr.bn.prsn. | agpṯr.w.s̀ǵ[r h]. | ṯ'ln. | mztn.w.s̀ǵr [h]. | s̀ǵr.plṭ. | s[d]rn [w].ṯn.s̀ǵr h. 2072.4
ln. | mztn.w.s̀ǵr [h]. | s̀ǵr.plṭ. | s[d]rn [w].ṯn.s̀ǵr h. | [---.]w.s̀ǵr h. | [---.]w.s̀ǵr h. | [---.]krwn. | [---].ẖzmyn. | [---.]bn.dll. 2072.9
r [h]. | s̀ǵr.plṭ. | s[d]rn [w].ṯn.s̀ǵr h. | [---.]w.s̀ǵr h. | [---.]w.s̀ǵr h. | [---.]krwn. | [---].ẖzmyn. | [---.]bn.dll. | r[--.--]km. | w 2072.10
. | ẖmšm [-]t ṯlṯ ty[--]. | bn.grgš. | w.npṣ bt ṯn.ṯlṯ mat. | w spl ṯlṯ.mat. | w mmskn. | w.ṯt.mqrtm. | w.ṯn.irpm.w.ṯn.trq 1103.17
p[š.---]. | 'm.k[--.lḥt]. | akl.yṯ[ṯb.--]pt. | ib.'ltn.a[--.--]y. | w.spr.in[.-.]'d m. | spr n.ṯhr[.--]. | aṯr.iṯ.bqṯ. | w.štn.l y. 2060.32
r h. | [---.]krwn. | [---].ẖzmyn. | [---.]bn.dll. | r[--.--]km. | w.spr h. 2072.15
.---]. | [w]nqmd.[---]. | [-.]'mn.šp[š.mlk.rb]. | b'l h.šlm.[w spš]. | mlk.rb.b'l h.[---]. | nqmd.mlk.ugr[t.--]. | phy. | w ṯpll 64[118].12
. | ṯkmn w šnm. | kṯr w ẖss. | 'ṯtr 'ṯtpr. | šḥr w šlm. | ngh w srr. | 'dw šr. | ṣdqm šr. | ḥnbn il d[n]. | [-]bd w [---]. | [--].p il[UG5.10.1.12
[n.--]t. | w.bl.bnš.hw[-.--]y. | w.k.at.trg[m.--]. | w.[---]n.w.s[--]. | [--]m.m[---]. | [---.m]nd'[.--]. 2064.28
]r bt [--]. | [--]bnš [--]. | š š[--]. | w [--]. | d [--]. | ypẖ[--]. | w s[--]. | [---]. | qrd ga[n.--]. | b bt k.[--]. | w l dbḥ[--]. | ṭ[--]. | [-- RS61[24.277.19]
b ṯṯ ym ḥdṯ. | ẖyr.'rbt. | špš ṯǵr h. | ršp. | w 'bdm tbqrn. | skn. 1162.5
w ṯṯb. | mlakm.l h.lm.ank. | ksp.w yrq.ẖrṣ. | yd.mqm h.w 'bd. | 'lm.ṯlṯ.sswm.mrkbt. | b trbṣt.bn.amt. | p d.in.b bt y.tt 14[KRT].3.139
[-----]. | [-----.lm]. | [ank.ksp.w yrq]. | [ẖrṣ.]yd.mqm h. | [w 'b]d.'lm.ṯlṯ. | [ssw]m.mrkbt b trbṣ bn.amt. | [ṯn.b]nm.aqny. 14[KRT].2.55
mswn h.tḥm.pbl.mlk. | qḥ.ksp.w yrq.ẖrṣ. | yd.mqm h.w 'bd.'lm. | ṯlṯ.sswm.mrkbt. | b trbṣ.bn.amt. | qḥ.krt.šlmm. | šl 14[KRT].3.127
]. | tḥ[m.pbl.mlk]. | qḥ[.ksp.w yrq]. | ẖrṣ.[yd.mqm h]. | w 'bd[.'lm.ṯlṯ]. | sswm.m[rkbt]. | b trbṣ.[bn.amt]. | q[ḥ.kr]t[.šl 14[KRT].6.271
y'n[y.k]rt[.ṯ]'. | lm.ank.ksp. | w yr[q.ẖrṣ]. | yd.mqm h.w 'bd. | 'lm.ṯlṯ.sswm. | mrkbt.b trbṣ. | bn.amt.p d.[i]n. | b bt y. 14[KRT].6.284
nḥš. | [---.--]q.n[ṯ]k.l yd'.l bn.l pq ḥmt. | [---.--]n h.ḥmt.w t'btn h.abd y. | [---.ǵ]r.šrǵzz.ybky.km.n'r. | [w ydm'.k]m.ṣ UG5.8.36
špn.bn.b'ly[.---]. | bnil.bn.yṣr[.---]. | 'dyn.bn.udr[-.---]. | w.'d'.nḥl h[.---]. | w.yknil.nḥl h[.---]. | w.iltm.nḥl h[.---]. | w.u 90[314].1.14
| [------.]yrẖ.zbl. | [--.kṯ]r w ẖss. | [---]n.rḥm y.ršp zbl. | [w 'd]t.ilm.ṯlṯ h. | [ap]nk.krt.ṯ'.'[-]r. | [--.]b bt h.yšt.'rb. | [--] h. 15[128].2.7
šbt.dq]n k.mm'm.w[---]. | aqht.w ypltṭ k.bn[.dnil.---]. | w y'ḏr k.b yd.btlt.['nt]. | w y'n.lṭpn.il d p[id]. | yd't k.bt.k an 18[3AQHT].1.14
]y.l ihbt.yb[--].rgm y. | [---.]škb.w m[--.]mlakt. | [---.]'l.w tš'[d]n.npṣ h. | [---.]rgm.hn.[--]n.w aspt.[q]l h. | [---.rg]m.a 1002.48
b 'pr.qm.aẖ k. | w tšu.'n h.btlt.'nt. | w tšu.'n h.w t'n. | w t'n.arẖ.w tr.b lkt. | tr.b lkt.w tr.b ẖl. | [b]n'mm.b ysmm.ḥ[10[76].2.28
.mlat rumm. | w yšu.'n h.aliyn.b'l. | w yšu.'n h.w y'n. | w y'n.btlt.'nt. | n'mt.bn.aẖt.b'l. | l pnn h.ydd.w yqm. | l p'n h. 10[76].2.15
. | b nši 'n h.w yphn.b alp. | šd.rbt.kmn.hlk.kṯr. | k y'n.w y'n.tdrq.ẖss. | hlk.qšt.ybln.hl.yš | rb'.qṣ't.apnk.dnil. | mt.rp 17[2AQHT].5.11
ib y. | w b 'pr.qm.aẖ k. | w tšu.'n h.btlt.'nt. | w tšu.'n h.w t'n. | w t'n.arẖ.w tr.b lkt. | tr.b lkt.w tr.b ẖl. | [b]n'mm.b ys 10[76].2.27
.aẖ šmk.mlat rumm. | w yšu.'n h.aliyn.b'l. | w yšu.'n h.w y'n. | w y'n.btlt.'nt. | n'mt.bn.aẖt.b'l. | l pnn h.ydd.w yqm. | 10[76].2.14
n.qrtm.tṯ'r.ṯlḥnt.]l ṣbim. | [hdmm.l ǵzrm.mid.tmtẖṣn.w t]'n.tẖtṣb. | [w tḥdy.'nt.tǵdd.kbd h.b ṣḥ]q.ymlu.lb h. | [b š 7.1[131].6
at.l mhr.ṯ'r.ṯlḥnt. | l ṣbim.hdmm.l ǵzrm. | mid.tmtẖṣn.w t'n. | tẖtṣb.w tḥdy.'nt. | tǵdd.kbd h.b ṣḥq.ymlu. | lb h.b šm 3['NT].2.23
t.w rḥm. | 'l.išt.šb' d.ǵzrm.ṭb.[g]d.b ḥlb.annẖ b ẖmat. | w 'l.agn.šb' d m.dǵ[ṯ.---]t. | tlk m.rḥmy.w tṣd[.---]. | tḥgrn.ǵz 23[52].15
i[t.w.m'ṣd]. | w ẖrmṯt. | ṯlṯm.ar[b']. | kbd.ksp. | 'l.tgyn. | w 'l.aṯt h. | ypḥ.m'nt. | bn.lbn. 2053.21
[----]. | k[--.---]. | 'šrm[.---]. | tšt.tb'[.---]. | qrt.mlk[.---]. | w.'l.ap.s[--.---]. | b hm.w.rgm.hw.al[--]. | atn.ksp.l hm.'d. | ila 2008.2.5
---.]rb'm ṯqlm.w [---] arb'yn. | w 'l.mnḥm.arb' š[mn]. | w 'l bn a[--.-]yn ṯqlm. | [--] ksp [---] kdr [---]. | [-]ṯrn [k]sp [-] 1103.10
[-] ym.pr' d nkly yn kd w kd. | w 'l ym kdm. | w b ṯlṯ.kd yn w krsnm. | w b rb' kdm yn. | w b 1086.2
[---]. | tlbš.npṣ.ǵzr.tšt.ẖ[---.b] | nšg h.ḥrb.tšt.b t'r[t h]. | w 'l.tlbš.npṣ.aṯt.[--]. | ṣbi nrt.ilm.špš.[-]r[--]. | pǵt.minš.šdm l 19[1AQHT].4.208
'l [---.-]b'm arny. | w 'l [---.]rb'm ṯqlm.w [---] arb'yn. | w 'l.mnḥm.arb' š[mn]. | w 'l bn a[--.-]yn ṯqlm. | [--] ksp [---] 1103.9
.l mit.ksp. | 'l.bn.alkbl.šb[ny]. | 'šrm ksp.'l. | wrt.mtny.w 'l. | prdny.aṯt h. 2107.18
gg k.b ym.ṯiṭ.rḥṣ. | npṣ k.b ym rṯ.b uni[l]. | pnm.tšmẖ.w 'l yṣhl pi[t]. | yprq.lṣb.w yṣḥq. | p'n.l hdm.yṯpd.yšu. | g h.w 17[2AQHT].2.9
| 'nt.b ṣmt.mhr h.[---]. | aqht.w tbk.y[---.---]. | abn.ank.w 'l.[qšt k.---.'l]. | qṣ't k.at.l ḥ[---.---]. | w ẖlq.'pmm[.---]. 18[3AQHT].4.40
m[š]m l 'šr ksp 'l bn llit. | [--]l[-.-]p 'l [---.-]b'm arny. | w 'l [---.]rb'm ṯqlm.w [---] arb'yn. | w 'l.mnḥm.arb' š[mn]. | 1103.8
'l.alpm.bnš.yd. | titṯm[n].w.'l.[---]. | [-]rym.t[i]ṯtmn. | šnl.bn.ṣ[q]n.s̀[--]. | yitṯm.w.b[--]. | 2104.2
šẖp h. | [--.]šẖp.ṣǵrt h. | yrk.t'l.b ǵr. | mslmt.b ǵr.tliyt. | w t'l.bkm.b arr. | bm.arr.w b ṣpn. | b n'm.b ǵr.t[l]iyt. | ql.l b'l. 10[76].3.30
r. | dbḥ.ṣ[q.b g]l.ḥtṯ. | yn.b gl[.ẖ]rṣ.nbt. | 'l.l ẓr.[mg]dl. | w 'l.l ẓr.[mg]dl.rkb. | ṯkmm.ḥm[t].ša.yd k. | šmm.dbḥ.l ṯr. | a 14[KRT].2.74

nzl. | lqḥ.msrr.ʿṣr.db[ḥ]. | yṣq.b gl.ḥtṯ.yn. | b gl.ẖrṣ.nbt.w ʿly. | l ẓr.mgdl.rkb. | ṯkmm.ḥmt.nša. | [y]d h.šmmh.dbḥ. | l ṯ 14[KRT].4.165

bkbt. | nʿm.[--.-]llm.trtḥṣ. | btlt.ʿn[t].tptrʿ ṯd[h]. | limm.w tʿl.ʿm.il. | ab h.ḥpr.pʿl k.y[--]. | šmʿ k.l arẖ.w bn.[--]. | limm. 13[6].20

].yn.b ks.ẖ[rṣ]. | [dm.ʿṣm.---]n.krpn.ʿl.[k]rpn. | [---.]ym.w tʿl.trṯ. | [---].yn.ʿšy l ḥbš. | [---.]ḥtn.qn.yṣbt. | [---.--]m.b nši.ʿ 17[2AQHT].6.7

w.mlk.bʿl y.bnš. | bnny.ʿmn. | mlakty.hnd. | ylak ʿm y. | w.tʿl.ṯh.hn. | [a]lpm.šŝwm. | [---].w.ṯb. 1012.37

rt.š l ili[b.---]. | rt.w ʿṣrm.l[.---]. | pamt.w bt.[---]. | rmm.w ʿl[y.---]. | bt.il.ṯq[l.---.kbd]. | w bdḥ.k[--.---]. | ʿṣrm.l i[nš.ilm APP.II[173].41

k.hl.ʿṣr. | tḥrr.l išt.w ṣḥrt.l pḥmm.aṯtm.a[ṯt.il]. | aṯt.il.w ʿlm h.yhbr.špt hm.yš[q]. | hn.špt hm.mtqtm.mtqtm.k lrm 23[52].49

k. | h[l.]ʿṣr.tḥrr.l išt.ṣḥrrt.l pḥmm. | a[ṯ]tm.aṯt.il.aṯt.il.w ʿlm h.w hm. | aṯtm.tṣḥn y.ad ad.nḥtm.ẖṭ k. | mmnnm.mṭ y 23[52].42

yd k.hl.ʿṣr.tḥrr.l išt. | w ṣḥrrt.l pḥmm.btm.bt.il.bt.il. | w ʿlm h.w hn.aṯtm.tṣḥn y.mt mt. | nḥtm.ẖṭ k.mmnnm.mṭ yd 23[52].46

l k.qrt.ablm. | d ʿl k.mẖṣ.aqht.ǵzr. | ʿwrt.yšt k.bʿl.l ht. | w ʿlm h.l ʿnt.p dr.dr. | ʿdb.uẖry.mṭ.yd h. | dnil.bt h.ymǵyn.yš 19[1AQHT].4.168

[--]kt.rgmt. | [--]y.l.ilak. | [---].ʿm y. | [---]m.w.lm. | [---.]w.ʿm k. | [---]m.ksp. | [---].ʿm. | [---.-]n[-]. | [---.]l km. | [---.-]lk. 1016.14

.il.alṯ[y]. | nmry.mlk.ʿlm. | mlk n.bʿl y.ḥw[t.--]. | yšhr k.w.ʿm.ṣ[--]. | ʿš[--.---]d.lik[t.---]. | w [----]. | k[--.---]. | ʿšrm[.---]. | 2008.1.11

k. | [b]ǵl hm.w.iblbl hm. | w.b.ṯb h.[---]. | spr ḥ[--.---]. | w.ʿm[.---]. | yqḥ[.---]. | w.n[--.---]. 2129.13

al[iy]n bʿl. | bl.ašt.ur[bt.]b bht m. | ḥln.b qr[b.hk]l m. | w ʿn.ali[yn.]bʿl. | al.tšt.u[rb]t.b bht m. | ḥln.b q[rb.hk]l m. | al 4[51].6.7

n.l rkb.ʿrpt. | bl.ašt.urbt.b bh[t] m. | ḥln.b qrb.hkl m. | w yʿn.aliyn bʿl. | al.tšt.urbt.b[bhtm]. | [ḥln].b qrb.hk[l m]. 4[51].5.125

ym.bmt.[nhr]. | tṯṭn.ib.bʿl.tiẖd. | yʿrm.šnu.hd.gpt. | ǵr.w yʿn.aliyn. | bʿl.ib.hdt.lm.tḥš. | lm.tḥš.nṯq.dmrn. | ʿn.bʿl.qdm 4[51].7.37

---.]arẖt.tld[n]. | a[lp].l btlt.ʿnt. | w ypt l ybmt.li[mm]. | w yʿny.aliyn[.bʿl]. | lm.k qnym.ʿl[m.--]. | k dr d.d yknn[.--]. | b 10[76].3.5

ṯmnym.bʿl.[----]. | tšʿm.bʿl.mr[-]. | bt[.--]b bʿl.b qrb. | bt.w yʿn.aliyn. | bʿl.ašt m.kṯr bn. | ym.kṯr.bnm.ʿdt. | ypth.ḥln.b b 4[51].7.14

h.tʿdb.ksu. | w yṯṯb.l ymn.aliyn. | bʿl.ʿd.lḥm.št[y.ilm]. | [w]yʿn.aliy[n.bʿl]. | [--]b[.---]. | ḥš.bht m.k[ṯr]. | ḥš.rmm.hk[l 4[51].5.111

.yšt.ʿrb. | [--] h.ytn.w [--]u.l ytn. | [aẖ]r.mǵy.ʿ[d]t.ilm. | [w]yʿn.aliy[n.]bʿl. | [---.]tbʿ.l lṭpn. | [il.d]pid.l tbrk. | [krt.]ṯʿ.l t 15[128].2.12

ḥwy.yʿšr.ḥwy.yʿš. | r.w yšqyn h.ybd.w yšr.ʿl h. | nʿm[n.w t]ʿnynn.ap ank.aḥwy. | aqht[.ǵz]r.w yʿn.aqht.ǵzr. | al.tšrgn 17[2AQHT].6.32

aš]lḥ k.w tn.qšt k.[l]. | [ʿnt.tq]ḥ[.q]ṣʿt k.ybmt.limm. | w yʿn.aqht.ǵzr.adr.ṯqbm. | [d]lbnn.adr.gdm.b rumm. | adr.q 17[2AQHT].6.20

w yšr.ʿl h. | nʿm[n.w t]ʿnynn.ap ank.aḥwy. | aqht[.ǵz]r.w yʿn.aqht.ǵzr. | al.tšrgn.y btlt m.dm.l ǵzr. | šrg k.ẖẖm.mt.u 17[2AQHT].6.33

]km.rʿy.ht.alk. | [---.]ṯlṯt.amǵy.l bt. | [y.---.b qrb].hkl y.w yʿn.il. | [---.mrzʿ]y.lk.bt y.rpim. | [rpim.bt y.aṣ]ḥ km.iqra k 21[122].1.8

.lpš.tšṣq[n h]. | b qṣ.all.tšu.g h.w[tṣ] | ḥ.at.mt.tn.aẖ y. | w ʿn.bn.ilm.mt.mh. | taršn.l btlt.ʿnt. | an.itlk.w aṣd.kl. | ǵr.l k 6[49].2.13

w yʿny.bn. | ilm.mt.npš[.-]. | npš.lbun. | thw.w npš. | anẖr.b y UG5.4.1

š. | šd yn.ʿn.b qbt[.t] | bl lyt.ʿl.umt k. | w abqṯ.aliyn.bʿl. | w tʿn.btlt.ʿnt. | an.l an.y špš. | an.l an.il.yǵr[.-]. | tǵr k.š[---.---] 6[49].4.45

il.qnm. | tn.l kṯr.w ẖss.ybʿl.qšt l ʿnt. | qṣʿt.l ybmt.limm.w tʿn.btlt. | ʿnt.irš ḥym.l aqht.ǵzr. | irš ḥym.w atn k.bl mt. | w 17[2AQHT].6.25

ṣn[--]. | nrt.ilm.špš[.ṣḥrr]t. | la.šmm.b y[d.bn.ilm.m]t. | w tʿn.btlt.ʿn[t.bnt.]bht | k.y ilm.bnt.bh[t k].a[l.tš]mẖ. | al.tš 3[ʿNT.VI].5.27

yn. | qnyt.ilm.mgntm. | ṯr.il.d pid.hm.ǵẓtm. | bny.bnwt w tʿn. | btlt.ʿnt.nmgn. | [-]m.rbt.aṯrt.ym. | [nǵ]ẓ.qnyt.ilm. | [--- 4[51].3.32

ḥ | [wy.w tkbd]n h.tlšn.aqht.ǵzr. | [---.kdd.dn]il.mt.rpi.w tʿn. | [btlt.ʿnt.tšu.g]h.w tṣḥ.hwt. | [---.]aqht.yḏ[--]. | [---.--]n 17[2AQHT].6.52

k.]bt.k an[št]. | k in.b ilht.ql[ṣ] k.mh.tarš[n]. | l btlt.ʿnt.w t[ʿ]n.btlt.ʿn[t]. | tḥm k.il.ḥkm.ḥkm k. | ʿm.ʿlm.ḥyt.ḥẓt.tḥm 3[ʿNT.VI].5.37

w ank]. | ibǵ[y h.b tk.ǵ]r y.il.ṣpn. | b q[dš.b ǵr.nḥ]lt y. | w t[ʿn].btlt.[ʿ]nt.ṯṯb. | [ybmt.]limm.[a]n.aqry. | [b arṣ].mlḥmt. 3[ʿNT].4.65

y]. | nʿmn.ǵzr.št.ṯrm.w[---]. | ištir.b ḏdm.w nʿrs[.---]. | w tʿn.btlt.ʿnt.ṯb.ytp.w[---]. | l k.ašt k.km.nšr.b ḥb[š y]. | km. 18[3AQHT].4.16

.mẓll]. | ṭly.bt.r[b.mṯb.arṣy]. | bt.yʿbdr[.mṯb.klt]. | knyt.w tʿn[.btlt.ʿnt]. | yṯb l y.ṯr.il[.ab y.---]. | yṯb.l y.w l h.[---]. | [--.i 3[ʿNT.VI].4.6

[-----]. | [---].aṯ[--.---]. | [---] h.ap.[---]. | [---].w tʿn.[btlt.ʿnt.---]. | [bnt.bht]k.y ilm[.bnt.bht k.--]. | [al.tšmẖ. 18[3AQHT].1.6

zr. | tbʿ.w l.yṯb ilm.idk. | l ytn.pnm.ʿm.bʿl. | mrym.ṣpn.w yʿn. | gpn.w ugr.tḥm.bn ilm. | mt.hwt.ydd.bn.il. | ǵzr.p np.š 5[67].1.11

rn.alk.nmr[rt]. | imẖṣ.mẖṣ.aẖ y.akl[.m] | kly[.ʿ]l.umt y.w yʿn[.dn] | il.mt.rpi npš tḥ[.pǵt]. | ṯ[km]t.mym.ḥspt.l šʿr. | ṭl. 19[1AQHT].4.197

ṯa aẖr.š[pšm.b ṯlṯ]. | mǵy.rpum.l grnt.i[lnym.l] | mṭʿt.w yʿn.dnil.[mt.rpi]. | yṯb.ǵzr.mt hrnmy[.---]. | b grnt.ilm.b qr 20[121].2.7

.l aq | ht.ǵzr.yd[mʿ.]l kdd. | dnil.mt.r[pi.mk].b šbʿ. | šnt.w yʿn[.dnil.mt.]rpi. | yṯb.ǵzr.m[t.hrnmy.y]šu. | g h.w yṣḥ.t[bʿ 19[1AQHT].4.180

[.iṯ.--.l]ḥm.w t[n]. | w nlḥm.hm.iṯ[.--.yn.w t]n.w nšt. | w ʿn hm.nǵr mdrʿ[.iṯ.lḥm.---]. | iṯ.yn.d ʿrb.bṯk[.---]. | mǵ hw.l 23[52].73

ṣ.išlḥ ẓhrm iq | nim.atn šd h krm[m]. | šd dd h ḥrnqm.w | yʿn ẖrẖb mlk qẓ [l]. | nʿmn.ilm l ẖt[n]. | m.bʿl trẖ pdry b[24[77].23

n y[.t]q | ḥ.pǵt.w tšqyn h.tq[ḥ.ks.]b d h. | qbʿt.b ymn h.w yʿn.yṭ[p]n[.mh]r. | št.b yn.yšt.ila.il š[--.]il. | d yqny.ḏdm.yd 19[1AQHT].4.218

.rgm.l yṭ[pn.y] | bl.agrtn.bat.b ḏd k.[pǵt]. | bat.b hlm w yʿn.yṭpn[.mhr]. | št.qḥn.w tšqyn.yn.qḥ. | ks.b d y.qbʿt.b y 19[1AQHT].4.214

.al.yḥdṯ.yrẖ.b[---]. | b qrn.ymn h.b anšt[.---]. | qdqd h.w yʿn.yṭpn.[mhr.št]. | šmʿ.l btlt.ʿnt.at.ʿ[l.qšt h]. | tmẖṣ h.qṣʿt 18[3AQHT].4.11

h bʿ[l]. | yǵtr.ʿṯtr t | rẖ l k ybrdmy.b[t.a] | b h lb[u] yʿrr.w yʿ[n]. | yrẖ nyr šmm.w nʿ[n]. | ʿma nkl ẖtn y.a[ẖ]r. | nkl yr 24[77].30

bn.il. | krt.špḥ.lṭpn. | w qdš.u ilm.tmtn. | špḥ.lṭpn.l yḥ. | w yʿny.krt.ṯʿ. | bn.al.tbkn.al. | tdm.l y.al tkl.bn. | qr.ʿn k.mẖ.ri 16.1[125].24

]. | il.ušn.ab[.ad]m. | rḥq.mlk.l bt y. | n[g.]krt.l ḥẓ[r y]. | w yʿn[y.k]rt[.ṯ]ʿ. | lm.ank.ksp. | w yr[q.ẖrṣ]. | yd.mqm h.w ʿbd 14[KRT].6.281

š.mdw.anšt. | ʿrš.zbln.rd.l mlk. | amlk.l drkt k.aṯb. | an.w yʿny.krt ṯʿ.yṯbr. | ḥrn.y bn.yṯbr.ḥrn. | riš k.ʿṯtrt.šm.bʿl. | qdq 16.6[127].54

. | arẖ.tzǵ.l ʿgl h. | bn.ẖpṯ.l umht hm. | k tnḥn.udmm. | w yʿny.krt.ṯʿ. 15[128].1.8

m.l tdʿ.nš[m.w l tbn.hmlt.arṣ]. | at.w ank.ib[ǵy h.---]. | w yʿn.kṯr.w ẖss[.lk.lk.ʿnn.ilm.] | atm.bštm.w an[.šnt.kptr]. | l 1[ʿNT.IX].3.17

rṣ.ypl.ul ny.w l.ʿpr.ʿẓm ny. | l bʿl[-.---]. | tḥt.ksi.zbl.ym.w ʿn.kṯr.w ẖss.l rgmt. | l k.l zbl.bʿl.ṯnt.l rkb.ʿrpt.ht.ib k. | bʿl 2.4[68].7

.hk[l m]. | b tk.ṣrrt.ṣpn. | alp.šd.aẖd bt. | rbt.kmn.hkl. | w yʿn.kṯr.w ẖss. | šmʿ.l aliyn bʿl. | bn.l rkb.ʿrpt. | bl.ašt.urbt.b 4[51].5.120

w yʿn.k[ṯr.w ẖs]s. | ṯṯb.bʿl.l[hwt y]. | ṯn.rgm.k[ṯr.w]ẖss. | šmʿ 4[51].6.1

---.ṭl]y.bt.rb. | [---.m]dd.il ym. | [---.-]qlṣn.wpṯ m. | [---.]w yʿn.kṯr. | [w ẖss.]ṯṯb.bʿl.l hwt y. | [ḥš.]bht h.tbnn. | [ḥš.]trm 4[51].6.14

.b bn k.amlkn. | w tʿn.rbt.aṯrt ym. | bl.nmlk.ydʿ.ylḥn. | w yʿn.lṭpn.il d pi | d dq.anm.l yrẓ. | ʿm.bʿl.l yʿdb.mrḥ. | ʿm.bn. 6.1.49[49.1.21]

. | aqht.w ypltૃ k.bn[.dnil.---]. | w yʿḏr k.b yd.btlt.[ʿnt]. | w yʿn.lṭpn.il d p[id]. | ydʿt k.bt.k anšt.w i[n.b ilht]. | qlṣ k.tbʿ. 18[3AQHT].1.15

.rgm.[my.]b ilm. | ydy.mrṣ.gršm zbln. | in.b ilm.ʿny h. | w yʿn.lṭpn.il.b pid. | ṯb.bn y.lm ṯb[t] km. | l kḥṯ.zbl k[m.a]nk. 16[126].5.23

. | bʿd[.---]. | yaṯr[.---]. | b d k.[---]. | ṯnnt h[.---]. | ṯlṯt h[.-.w yʿn]. | lṭpn.[il.d pid.my]. | b ilm.[ydy.mrṣ]. | gršm.z[bln.in.b 16[126].5.9

yt. | mṯb.pdry.bt.ar. | mẓll.ṭly.bt rb. | mṯb.arṣ.bt yʿbdr. | w yʿn lṭpn il d pid. | p ʿbd.an.ʿnn.aṯrt. | p.ʿbd.ank.aẖd.ulṯ. | h 4[51].4.58

r[.---]. | yṣḥ.ngr il.ilš. | ilš.ngr.bt.bʿl. | w aṯt h.ngrt.ilht. | w yʿn.lṭpn.il d pi[d]. | šmʿ.l ngr.il il[š]. | ilš.ngr bt bʿl. | w aṯt k 16[126].4.10

klat yd.[---]. | km ll.kḥṣ.tusp[.---]. | tgr.il.bn h.ṯr[.---]. | w yʿn.lṭpn.il.d p[id.---]. | šm.bn y.yw.ilt.[---]. | w pʿr.šm.ym[-. 1[ʿNT.X].4.13

[-----]. | šmʿ.l [-]mt[.-]m.l[-]ṯnm. | ʿdm.[lḥ]m.tšty. | w tʿn.mṯt ḥry. | l l[ḥ]m.l š[ty].ṣḥt km. | db[ḥ.l krt.a]dn km. | ʿl 15[128].6.3

[.---]. | w lẖm mr.tqdm. | yd.b ṣʿ.tšlḥ. | ḥrb.b bšr.tštn. | [w t]ʿn.mṯt.ḥry. | [l lḥ]m.l šty.ṣḥt km. | [--.dbḥ.l]krt.bʿl km. 15[128].4.26

b[.--]t[.---].|[tqdm.]yd.b ṣ'.t[šl]ḥ.|[ḥrb.b]bš[r].tštn.|[w t'n].mṯt.ḥry.|[l lḥ]m.l šty.ṣḥt k[m].|[---.]brk.t[---].|['l.]kr 15[128].5.9
p[.--].|hy.yd h.w ym[ǵ].|mlak k.'m dt[n].|lqḥ.mṯpṭ.|w y'ny.nn.|dtn.bt n.mḫ[-].|l dg.w [-]kl.|w aṯr.hn.mr[-]. UG5.6.13
k ymǵy.adn.|ilm.rbm 'm dtn.|w yšal.mṯpṭ.yld.|w y'ny.nn[.--].|t'ny.n[---.-]ṯq.|w š[--.---].|ḥdṯ[.---.]ḥ[--].|b b UG5.6.4
.il.yš[t k].|b'l.'nt.mḫrṯ[-].|iy.aliyn.b'l.|iy.zbl.b'l.arṣ.|w t'n.nrt.ilm.š[p]š.|šd yn.'n.b qbt[.t]|bl lyt.'l.umt k.|w abq 6[49].4.41
n.|riš k.'ṯtrt.šm.b'l.|qdqd k.tqln.b gbl.|šnt k.b ḥpn k.w t'n.|spr ilmlk ṯ'y. 16.6[127].58
k ybrdmy.b[t.a]|b h lb[u] y'rr.w y'[n].|yrḫ nyr šmm.w n'[n].|'ma nkl ḫtn y.a[ḫ]r.|nkl yrḫ ytrḫ.adn h.|yšt mṣb. 24[77].31
ys'.[alt.]ṯ[bt |k.l y]hpk.|[ksa.]mlk k.l yṯbr.ḫṭ.mṯpṭ k.w y'n[.'ṯtr].dm[-]k[-].|[--]ḥ.b y.ṯr.il.ab y.ank.in.bt[.l] y[.km. 2.3[129].18
ḫṭ.aliyn.|b'l.p'n h.l tmǵyn.|hdm.riš h.l ymǵy.|aps h.w y'n.'ṯtr.'rẓ.|l amlk.b ṣrrt.ṣpn.|yrd.'ṯtr.'rẓ.yrd.|l kḥṯ.aliyn 6.1.61[49.1.33]
.k bn.qdš.]w y[--.]zbl.ym.y'[--.]ṯpṭ.nhr.|[-------.]yšlḥn.w y'n 'ṯtr[.-]. 2.3[129].24
.ym l[--.---].|ḥm.l šrr.w [---].|y'n.ym.l mt[.---].|l šrr.w t'[n.'ṯtrt.---].|b'l m.hmt.[---].|l šrr.št[.---].|b riš h.[---].|ib 2.4[68].35
].|lm.tb'rn[.---].|mn.yrḫ.k m[rṣ.---].|mn.k dw.kr[t].|w y'ny.ǵzr[.ilḥu].|ṯlṯ.yrḫm.k m[rṣ].|arb'.k dw.k[rt].|mnd'. 16.2[125].83
ṣ.ṯṯbr.|[---.]aḫ h.tbky.|[--.m]rṣ.mlk.|[---.]krt.adn k.|[w y'ny.]ǵzr.ilḥu.|[---.]mrṣ.mlk.|[--.k]rt.adn k.|[--.d]bḥ.dbḥ 16.1[125].58
[---.b'l.b bht h].|[il.hd.b qr]b.hkl h.|w t'nyn.ǵlm.b'l.|in.b'l.b bht ht.|il hd.b qrb.hkl h.|qšt hn.a 10[76].2.3
bkbm.'[l.---].|[-]l h.yd 'd[.---].|ltm.mrqdm.d š[-]l[-].|w t'n.pǵt.ṯkmt.mym.|qrym.ab.dbḥ.l ilm.|š'ly.dǵt h.b šmy 19[1AQHT].4.190
mǵyt.btlt.'nt.|tmgnn.rbt[.a]ṯrt ym.|tǵẓyn.qnyt.ilm.|w t'n.rbt.aṯrt ym.|ik.tmgnn.rbt.|aṯrt.ym.tǵẓyn.|qnyt.ilm. 4[51].3.27
t.aṯrt ym.šm'.|l rbt.aṯr[t] ym.tn.|aḥd.b bn k.amlkn.|w t'n.rbt.aṯrt ym.|bl.nmlk.yd'.ylḥn.|w y'n.lṭpn.il d pi|d dq 6.1.47[49.1.19]
q.anm.l yrẓ.|'m.b'l.l y'db.mrḥ.|'m.bn.dgn.k tms m.|w 'n.rbt.aṯrt ym.|blt.nmlk.'ṯtr.'rẓ.|ymlk.'ṯtr.'rẓ.|apnk.'ṯtr.' 6.1.53[49.1.25]
.aṯrt.tlbn.|lbnt.ybn.bt.l b'l.|km ilm.w ḥẓr.k bn.aṯrt.|w t'n.rbt.aṯrt ym.|rbt.ilm.l ḥkmt.|šbt.dqn k.l tsr k.|rḫntt.d 4[51].5.64
ṯr[.il.ab -.w t'n.rbt].|aṯr[t.ym.šm'.l qdš].|w am[rr.l dgy.rbt].|aṯrt.ym 4[51].4.1
b k.ḫrṣ.|dm.'ṣm.hm.yd.il mlk.|yḫss k.ahbt.ṯr.t'rr k.|w t'n.rbt.aṯrt ym.|ṯḥm k.il.ḥkm.ḥkmt.|'m 'lm.ḥyt.ḥẓt.|ṯḥ 4[51].4.40
kbt b trbṣ bn.amt.|[tn.b]nm.aqny.|[tn.ṯa]rm.amid.|[w y'n].ṯr.ab h.il.|d[--].b bk.krt.|b dm'.n'mn.ǵlm.|il.trḥṣ.w 14[KRT].2.59
.d tqyn h.|[hml]t.tn.b'l.w 'nn h.bn.dgn.arṯ m.pd h.|[w y'n.]ṯr.ab h.il.'bd k.b'l.y ym m.'bd k.b'l.|[--.--]m.bn.dgn. 2.1[137].36
dn]km.ṯpṭ.nhr.tn.il m.d tq h.d tqyn h.|[hml]t.tn.b'l.w 'nn h.bn.dgn.arṯ m.pd h.|[w y'n.]ṯr.ab h.il.'bd k.b'l.y ym 2.1[137].35
.adn km.ṯ[pṭ.nhr].|tn.il m.d tq h.d tqyn.hmlt.tn.b'l.[w 'nn h].|bn.dgn.arṯ m.pd h.tb'.ǵlmm.l ṯṯb.[idk.pnm].|l yt 2.1[137].18
št.'nt.gṯr.b'lt.mlk.b'|lt.drkt.b'lt.šmm.rmm.|[b'l]t.kpṯ.w 'nt.di.dit.rḫpt.|[---.-]rm.aklt.'gl.'l.mšt.|[---.--]r.špr.w yšt.i UG5.2.1.8
ṯ.ṯḥt.ṯlḥn.|b qr'.|'ṯtrt.w 'nt.ymǵy.|'ṯtrt.t'db.nšb l h.|w 'nt.ktp.b hm.yg'r.ṯǵr.|bt.il.pn.l mgr lb.t'dbn.|nšb.l inr.t' UG5.1.1.11
l h.w d l yd'nn.|d.mṣd.|ylmn.ḫṭ.ṯḥt.ṯlḥn.|b qr'.|'ṯtrt.w 'nt.ymǵy.|'ṯtrt.t'db.nšb l h.|w 'nt.ktp.b hm.yg'r.ṯǵr.|bt.il UG5.1.1.9
k yrdm.arṣ.'nt.|w 'ṯtrt.tṣdn.[---].|[---.-]b[-.---].|['ṯ]trt w 'nt[.---].|w b hm.tṯṯb[.--]d h.|km trpa.hn n'r.|d yšt.l.lṣb UG5.1.2.1
ik.atwt.qnyt.i[lm].|rǵb.rǵbt.w tǵt[--].|hm.ǵmu.ǵmit.w 's[--].|lḥm.hm.štym.lḥ[m].|b ṯlḥnt.lḥm št.|b krpnm.yn.b 4[51].4.34
[b'.]ymm.bṣr.|kp.šsk k.[--].l ḥbš k.|'tk.ri[š.]l mhr k.|w 'p.l dr['].nšr k.|w rbṣ.l ǵr k.inbb.|kt ǵr k.ank.yd't.|[-]n.a 13[6].8
mšm.l mi[t].any.|tškn[n.--]h.k[--].|w šnm[.--.]w[.--].|w 'prm.a[--.--]n.|[--.]ḥ[--.]d[--]t.|[---.]ḥw[t.---].|[---.]š[--].| 2062.1.7
wt y.|[ḥš.]bht h.tbnn.|[ḥš.]trmm.hkl h.|y[tl]k.l lbnn.w 'ṣ h.|l[šr]yn.mḥmd.arz h.|h[n.l]bnn.w 'ṣ h.|š[r]yn.mḥm 4[51].6.18
|y[tl]k.l lbnn.w 'ṣ h.|l[šr]yn.mḥmd.arz h.|h[n.l]bnn.w 'ṣ h.|š[r]yn.mḥmd.arz h.|tšt.išt.b bht m.|nb[l]at.b hkl m 4[51].6.20
l.---].|[dq]t.l.ṣpn.gdlt.l[.---].|u[gr]t.š.l.[il]ib.g[--.--rt].|w ['ṣrm.]l.ri[--.---].|[--]t.b'lt.bt[.---].|[md]bḥt.b.ḫmš[.---].|[- 35[3].36
dlt.l b['l.--.dqt].|l ṣpn.gdlt.[l.---].|ugrt.š l ili[b.---].|rt.w 'ṣrm.l[.---].|pamt.w bt.[---].|rmm.w 'l[y.---].|bt.il.ṯq[l.---. APP.II[173].39
ug[r.---].|'nt[.---].|tmm l bt[.---].|b['l].ugr[t.---].|w 'ṣrm[.---].|ṣlyh šr[-.---].|[ṯ]lṯm.w b[--.---].|l il limm[.---].| 40[134].5
bd d ilgb[-].|mrmnmn.|brrn aryn.|a[-]ḥn tlyn.|atdb w 'r.|qdš w amrr.|ṯḥr w bd.|[k]ṯr ḫss šlm.|šlm il bt.|šlm il UG5.7.71
agzr ym.bn ym.ynqm.b ap.ḏd.št.špt.|l arṣ.špt l šmm.w 'rb.b p hm.'ṣr.šmm.|w dg b ym.w ndd.gzr.l zr.y'db.u ym 23[52].62
m.'m.nǵr.mdr' y.nǵr.|nǵr.ptḥ.w ptḥ hw.prṣ.b'd hm.|w 'rb.hm.hm[.iṯ.--.l]ḥm.w t[n].|w nlḥm.hm.iṯ[.--.yn.w t]n. 23[52].71
ry.bt.ar.|ahbt.ṭly.bt.rb.dd.arṣy.|bt.y'bdr.km ǵlmm.|w 'rb n.l p'n.'nt.hbr.|w ql.tšthwy.kbd hyt.|w rgm.l btlt.'nt. 3['NT].3.6
um.tdbḥn.|[----.]'d.ilnym.|[---.--]l km amt m.|[---.]b w t'rb.sd.|[---.--]n b ym.qẓ.|[---.]ym.tlḥmn.|[---.rp]um.tšty 20[121].1.4
nn.ṣmdm.gpn.yšql.šdmt h.|km gpn.|šb' d.yrgm.'l.'d.w 'rbm.t'nyn.|w šd.šd ilm.šd aṯrt.w rḥm.|'l.išt.šb' d.ǵzrm.ṭ 23[52].12
.|w burm.l[b.rmṣt.ilhm].|b'lm.w mlu[.---.ksm].|ṯlṯm.w m'rb[.---].|dbḥ šmn mr[.šmn.rqḥ.bt].|mtnt.w ynt.[qrt.w APP.II[173].21
h.hwt.l t[ḥwy].|n'mn.ǵzr.št.ṯrm.w[---].|ištir.b ḏdm.w n'rs[.---].|w t'n.btlt.'nt.ṯb.ytp.w[---].|l k.ašt k.km.nšr.b ḥ 18[3AQHT].4.15
.b'yn.|šdyn.|ary.|brqn.|bn.ḫlln.|bn.mṣry.|ṯmn.qšt.|w 'šr.uṯpt.|upšt irš[-]. 118[306].15
'šr.bnš.|yd.nǵr.mdr'.yd.š[--]m.|[b.]gt.iptl.ṯṯ.ṣmdm.|[w.']šr.bn[š]m.y[d].š[--].|[-]lm.b d.r[-]m.l[-]m.|ṯṯ.'šr.ṣ[mdm] 2038.8
n.kbd.ḥpr.bnšm.ṯmnym.dd.|l u[-]m.|b.ṯbq.arb'm.dr'.w.'šr.dd.drt.|w[.a]rb'.l.'šrm.dd.l.yḥšr.bl.bn h.|b.gt.m'br.ar 1098.10
['.--]n.[k]bd.|w[.---.]qm't.|[---.]mdrǵlm.|[---.]mdm.|[w].'šr.dd.l np[l].|r[p]š. 2012.26
'm.drt.|w.'šrm.l.mit.dd.ḥpr.bnšm.|b.y'ny.arb'm.dr'.w.'šrm.drt.|w.ṯlṯm.dd.ṯṯ.kbd.ḥpr.bnšm.|b.'nmky.'šrm.dr'[. 1098.26
.w.šb'm.dd.arb'.|kbd.ḥpr.bnšm.|b.gt.ṯrmn.arb'm.dr'.w.'šrm.drt.|w.ṯlṯm.dd.ṯṯ.kbd.ḥpr.bnšm.|b.gt.ḥdṯt.arb'm.dr' 1098.20
šr.bl.bn h.|b.gt.m'br.arb'm.l.mit.dr'.w.ṯmnym[.drt].|w.'šrm.l.mit.dd.ḥp[r.]bnšm.|b.gt.ǵl.'šrm.l.mit.dr'.w.tš'm.dr 1098.13
d.ṯn.kbd.ḥpr.bnšm.|b.nzl.'šrm.l.mit.dr'.w.šb'm.drt.|w.'šrm.l.mit.dd.ḥpr.bnšm.|b.y'ny.arb'm.dr'.w.'šrm.drt.|w. 1098.25
[---.ḥpr.]bnšm.w.l.ḥrš.'rq.ṯn.'šr h.|[---.d]r'.w.mit.drt.w.'šrm.l.mit.|[drt.ḥpr.b]nšm.w.ṯn.'šr h.dd.l.rpš.|[---.]šb'm. 1098.3
lḥm.|l[.-]ry ṯlṯ spm w 'šr lḥm.|[--.]w nsp w ṯlṯ spm w 'šrm lḥ[m].|l[.-]dt ḫnd[r]ṯ ar' s[p]m w 'š[r].|[---.]ḫndrṯm 134[-].4
[-]b[-.---.--]|r ṯṯm lḥm.|l[.-]ry ṯlṯ spm w 'šr lḥm.|[--.]w nsp w ṯlṯ spm w 'šrm lḥ[m].|l[.-]dt ḫnd[r] 134[-].3
q]ṣy.|ṯn.bn.iwrḫz.[n]'rm.|ysr[.-]qb.|w.ṯn.bnš.iytlm.|w.'šrm.ṣmd.alpm. 2066.2.7
nsp w ṯlṯ spm w 'šrm lḥ[m].|l[.-]dt ḫnd[r]ṯ ar' s[p]m w 'š[r].|[---.]ḫndrṯm ṯṯ spm [w] ṯlṯm l[ḥm].|[---.]ar' spm w 134[-].5
.ṯn.bn h.w.b[---.---].|b ṯn[--.---].|swn.qrty[.---].|uḫ h.w.'šr[.---].|klyn.apsn[y.---].|plzn.qrty[.---].|w.klt h.b.t[--.--- 81[329].9
ḫd.|ṯmn.ḫzr.|w.arb'.ḥršm.|dt.tb'ln.b.pḫn.|ṯṯṯm.ḫzr.w.'št.'šr.ḥrš.|dt.tb'ln.b.ugrt.|ṯṯṯm.ḫzr.|dt.tb'ln.|b.gt.ḥršm. 1024.3.7
mt.'nt.w 'ṯtrt.|[ti]sp.ḥmt.y[r]ḫ.w.ršp.yisp.ḥmt.|['ṯ]r.w 'ṯpr.yisp.ḥmt.ṯṯ.w ktṯ.|[yus]p.ḥmt.mlk.b 'ṯtrt.yisp.ḥmt.| UG5.8.16
[ḥ]mt.i[l.w] ḥrn.yisp.ḥmt.|[b'l.w]dgn[.yi]sp.ḥmt.'nt.w 'ṯtrt.|[ti]sp.ḥmt.y[r]ḫ.w.ršp.yisp.ḥmt.|['ṯ]r.w 'ṯpr.yisp. UG5.8.14
.y'db.ksa.w yṯb.|tqru l špš.um h.špš.um.ql.bl.'m.|'nt w 'ṯtrt inbb h.mnt.nṯk.|nḥš.šlḥm.nḥš.'q šr[.y']db.ksa.|nḥš.š UG5.7.20
ḏnb.ylšn.|b ḫri h.w tnt h.ql.il.[--].|il.k yrdm.arṣ.'nt.|w 'ṯtrt.tṣdn.[---].|[---.-]b[-.---].|['ṯ]trt w 'nt[.---].|w b hm.tṯṯ UG5.1.1.23

[-----].|[---.--]ty.l[--.---].|[--.--]tm.w ʿ[--.--].|[---].w kl.hw[.---].|w [--].brt.lb[--.---].|u[-]šhr.nuš 54[-].1.3
m.[šl]m[.r]gm[.ṯṯb].|ky.lik.bn y.|lḥt.akl.ʿm y.|mid y w ǵbn y.|w.bn y.hn kt.|yškn.anyt.|ym.yšrr.|w.ak[l.---].|[-- 2061.11
---].|aṯt.w.ṯt.pǵtm.w.ǵzr.aḥd.b.[bt.---].|ṯt.aṯtm.w.pǵt.w.ǵzr.aḥd.b.[bt.---].|aṯt.w.bn h.w.pǵt.aḥt.b.bt.m[--].|aṯt.w.ṯ 80[119].20
ṯ.ǵzr[m].|w.ḫmš.nʿrt.b.bt.sk[n].|ṯt.aṯtm.adrtm.w.pǵt.w ǵzr[.aḥd.b.bt.---].|aṯt.w.ṯt.pǵtm.w.ǵzr.aḥd.b.[bt.---].|ṯt.aṯ 80[119].18
.aṯtm.adrtm.w.pǵt.w ǵzr[.aḥd.b.bt.---].|aṯt.w.ṯt.pǵtm.w.ǵzr.aḥd.b.[bt.---].|ṯt.aṯtm.w.pǵt.w.ǵzr.aḥd.b.[bt.---].|aṯt. 80[119].19
b yd.|[g]rgr h.bm.ymn.|[w]yqrb.trẓẓ h.|[---].mǵy h.w ǵlm.|[a]ḫt h.šib.yṣat.mrḥ h.|l tl.yṣb.pn h.ṯǵr.|yṣu.hlm.a 16.1[125].50
h.|d b ḥlm y.il.ytn.|b ḏrt y.ab.adm.|w ld.špḥ.l krt.|w ǵlm.l ʿbd.il.|krt.yḫṯ.w ḥlm.|ʿbd.il.w hdrt.|yrtḥṣ.w yadm. 14[KRT].3.153
l.|d b ḥlm y.il.ytn.|b ḏrt y.ab.adm.|w ld.špḥ.l krk|t.w ǵlm.l ʿbd.|il.ttbʿ.mlakm.|l yṯb.idk.pnm.|l ytn.ʿmm.pbl.| 14[KRT].6.299
ṯ[.nhr.]mlkt.[--]pm.l mlkt.wn.in.aṯt.|[l]k.k[m.ilm].|[w ǵlmt.k bn.qdš.]w y[--.]zbl.ym.yʿ[--.]ṯpṭ.nhr.|[-------.]yšlḥn 2.3[129].23
]ym.|ynqm.b ap zd.aṯrt.[---].|špš.mṣprt dlt hm[.---].|w ǵnbm.šlm.ʿrbm.ṯn[nm].|hlkm.b dbḥ nʿmt.|šd[.i]lm.šd.aṯ 23[52].26
.l] ydʿt.|[---.t]asrn.|[---.]trks.|[---.]abnm.upqt.|[---.]l w ǵr mtn y.|[---.]rq.gb.|[---.--]kl.ṯǵr.mtn h.|[---.--]b.w ym y 1[ʿNT.X].5.12
ny.|l k[rt.adn k.]ištm[ʿ].|w tqǵ[.udn.k ǵz.ǵzm].|tdbr.w[ǵ]rm[.ṯṯwy].|šqlt.b ǵlt.yd k.|l tdn.dn.almnt.|l ṯpṭ.ṯpṭ.qṣ 16.6[127].31
yṣḥ.šmʿ mʿ.l krt.|ṯʿ.ištmʿ.w tqǵ udn.|k ǵz.ǵzm.tdbr.|w ǵrm.ṯṯwy.šqlt.|b ǵlt.yd k.l tdn.|dn.almnt.l ṯpṭ.|ṯpṭ qṣr.n 16.6[127].44
-.]adm.|[---.]iṯ[-].yšql.ytk[.--]np bl.hn.|[---].ḫ[m]t.pṭr.w.p nḥš.|[---.--]q.n[t]k.l ydʿ.l bn.l pq ḥmt.|[---.--]n h.ḥmt.w UG5.8.34
].|bʿl.yṣǵd.mli[.--].|il hd.mla.u[--.--].|blt.p btlt.ʿn[t].|w p.nʿmt.aḫt[.bʿl].|yʿl.bʿl.b ǵ[r.---].|w bn.dgn.b š[---].|bʿl.yṯ 10[76].3.11
[g]dlt iltm ḫnqtm.d[q]tm.|[yr]ḫ.kty gdlt.w l ǵlmt š.|[w]pamt ṯlṯm.w yrdt.[m]dbḥt.|gdlt.l bʿlt bhtm.ʿṣrm.|l inš il 34[1].20
tšʿ.ṣmdm.|ṯlṯm.b d.|ibrtlm.|w.pat.aḫt.|in.b hm. 1141.4
.|w.btšy.bt h.|w.ištrmy.|bt.ʿbd mlk.|w.snt.|bt.ugrt.|w.pdy h[m].|iwrkl.mit.|ksp.b y[d].|birtym.|[un]ṯ inn.|l [h 1006.12
[yš]lm[.ilm].|ṯǵr k[.tšlm k].|hl ny.[---].|w.pdr[--.---].|tmǵyn[.---].|w.mli[.---].|[-]kl.w [---].|ʿd.mǵt[. 57[101].4
rb m.asm.|b p h.rgm.l yṣa.b špt h[.hwt h].|b nši ʿn h.w tphn.in.[---].|[-.]hlk.ǵlmm b dd y.yṣ[--].|[-.]yṣa.w l.yṣa.hl 19[1AQHT].2.76
adrm.d b grn.ydn.|dn.almnt.yṯpṭ.ṯpṭ.ytm.|b nši ʿn h.w yphn.b alp.|šd.rbt.kmn.hlk.kṯr.|k yʿn.w yʿn.tdrq.ḫss.|hl 17[2AQHT].5.9
ẓr.pḥmm.|tʿpp.ṯr.il.d pid.|tǵẓy.bny.bnwt.|b nši.ʿn h.w tphn.|hlk.bʿl.aṯtrt.|k tʿn.hlk.btlt.|ʿnt.tdrq.ybmt.|[limm]. 4[51].2.12
b nši[.ʿn h.w yphn.yḥd].|b ʿrpt[.nšrm.yšu].|[g h.]w yṣḥ[.knp.nšrm].|b 19[1AQHT].2.105
nšrm.ybn.|bʿl.ybn.diy hmt nšrm.|tpr.w du.b nši.ʿn h.w ypn.|yḥd.hrgb.ab.nšrm.|yšu.g h.w yṣḥ.knp.hr[g]b.|bʿl.yṯ 19[1AQHT].3.120
l.ybn.|[b]ʿl.ybn.diy.hwt.hrg[b].|tpr.w du.b nši.ʿn h.|[w]yphn.yḥd.ṣml.um.nšrm.|yšu.g h.w yṣḥ.knp.ṣml.|bʿl.yṯb 19[1AQHT].3.135
|[ṯpṭ.ytm.---] h.|[---.---]n.|[-----].|hlk.[---.b n]ši.|ʿn h.w tphn.[---].|b grn.yḥrb[.---].|yǵly.yḥsp.ib[.---].|ʿl.bt.ab h.n 19[1AQHT].1.29
---].yn.ʿšy l ḥbš.|[---.]ḥtn.qn.yṣbt.|[---.--]m.b nši.ʿn h.w tphn.|[---.--]ml.ksl h.k b[r]q.|[---.]m[-]ǵ[-].thmt.brq.|[--- 17[2AQHT].6.10
l[t.]ilhm.|[b]ʿl š.aṯrt.š.ṯkmn w šnm.š.|ʿnt.š.ršp.š.dr il w p[ḫ]r bʿl.|gdlt.šlm.gdlt.w burm.[l]b.|rmṣt.ilhm.bʿlm.dṯt. 34[1].7
lhm].|bʿ[l.š].aṯrt[.š.ṯkm]n w [šnm.š].|ʿnt š ršp š[.dr.il.w pḫr.bʿl].|gdlt.šlm[.gdlt.w burm.lb].|rmṣt.ilh[m.bʿlm.---]. 35[3].16
[lt.ilhm.bʿl.š.aṯrt.š].|ṯkmn.w š[nm.š.ʿnt.š.ršp.š.dr].|il.w pḫr[.bʿl.gdlt.šlm.gdlt].|w burm.l[b.rmṣt.ilhm].|bʿlm.w m APP.II[173].18
.ašhlk[.šbt k.dmm].|[šbt.dq]n k.mmʿm.w[---].|aqht.w yplṭ k.bn[.dnil.---].|w yʿḏr k.b yd.btlt.[ʿnt].|w yʿn.lṭpn.il 18[3AQHT].1.13
.ṯṯb.l y.|bm.ṭy.ndr.|iṯt.ʿmn.mlkt.|w.rgm y.l[--].|lqt.w.pn.|mlk.nr b n. 50[117].17
ṯǵr k.|ugrt.ṯǵr k.|tšlm k.um y.|tdʿ.ky.ʿrbt.|l pn.špš.|w pn.špš.nr.|b y.mid.w um.|tšmḫ.m ab.|w al.trḥln.|ʿtn.ḥr 1015.9
ym.l ymk.l tnǵṣn.pnt h.l ydlp.|tmn h.kṯr.ṣmdm.ynḥt.w ypʿr.šmt hm.|šm k.at.aymr.aymr.mr.ym.mr.ym.|l ksi h. 2.4[68].18
ṣrt k.|tqḥ.mlk.ʿlm k.drkt.dt dr dr k.|kṯr ṣmdm.ynḥt.w ypʿr.šmt hm.šm k at.|ygrš.ygrš.grš ym grš ym.l ksi h.|[n 2.4[68].11
.ṯr[.---].|w yʿn.lṭpn.il.d p[id.---].|šm.bn y.yw.ilt.[---].|w pʿr.šm.ym[-.---].|tʿnyn.l zn.tn[.---].|at.adn.tpʿr[.---].|ank. 1[ʿNT.X].4.15
arbʿ.ʿšr.ǵzrm.|arbʿ.aṯt.|pǵt.aḥt.|w.pǵy.aḥ. 2081.4
bt.---].|ṯt.aṯtm.w.pǵt.w.ǵzr.aḥd.b.[bt.---].|aṯt.w.bn h.w.pǵt.aḥt.b.bt.m[--].|aṯt.w.ṯt.bt h.b.bt.ḫdmrd.|aṯt.w.ṯn.ǵzr 80[119].21
lm].|[a]ṯt.aḥt.b.bt.rpi[--].|[aṯt.]w.bt h.b.bt.alḥn.|[aṯt.w.]pǵt.aḥt.b.bt.tt.|[aṯt.w.]bt h.b.bt.trǵds.|[---.]aṯt.adrt.w.pǵ 80[119].26
.|aṯt.ad[r]t.b.bt.armwl.|aṯt.aḥt.b.bt.iwrpzn.|ṯt.aṯtm.w.pǵt.aḥt.b bt.[-]r[-].|[aṯ]t.b.bt.aupš.|[aṯ]t.b.bt.ṯpṭbʿl.|[---.] 80[119].11
h.b.bt.iwwpzn.|aṯt.w.pǵt.b.bt.ydrm.|ṯt.aṯtm.adrtm.w.pǵt.aḥt.b[.bt.---].|aṯt.w ṯn.nʿrm.b.bt.ilsk.|aṯt.ad[r]t.b.bt.a 80[119].7
.]pǵt.aḥt.b.bt.tt.|[aṯt.w.]bt h.b.bt.trǵds.|[---.]aṯt.adrt.w.pǵt.a[ḥt.b.bt.---].|[---.ʿ]šrm.npš.b.bt.[---].|[---.]w.pǵt.aḥt. 80[119].28
adrt.w.pǵt.a[ḥt.b.bt.---].|[---.ʿ]šrm.npš.b.bt.[---].|[---.]w.pǵt.aḥt.b.bt.[---]. 80[119].30
[aṯt.w].bn h.b.bt.krz.|[aṯt.]w.pǵt.b.bt.gg.|[ǵz]r.aḥd.b.bt.nwrḏ.|[aṯ]t.adrt.b.bt.arṯṯb.|aṯ 80[119].2
|[aṯ]t.adrt.b.bt.arṯṯb.|aṯt.w.ṯn.bn h.b.bt.iwwpzn.|aṯt.w.pǵt.b.bt.ydrm.|ṯt.aṯtm.adrtm.w.pǵt.aḥt.b[.bt.---].|aṯt.w ṯ 80[119].6
rt.w.ṯlṯ.ǵzr[m].|w.ḫmš.nʿrt.b.bt.sk[n].|ṯt.aṯtm.adrtm.w.pǵt.w ǵzr[.aḥd.b.bt.---].|aṯt.w.ṯt.pǵtm.w.ǵzr.aḥd.b.[bt.--- 80[119].18
d.b.bt.---].|aṯt.w.ṯt.pǵtm.w.ǵzr.aḥd.b.[bt.---].|ṯt.aṯtm.w.pǵt.w.ǵzr.aḥd.b.[bt.---].|aṯt.w.bn h.w.pǵt.aḥt.b.bt.m[--].| 80[119].20
[---.b]ṯnm w ttb.ʿl.bṯnt.trtḥ[ṣ.---].|[---.t]ṯb h.aḥt.ppšr.w ppšrt[.---].|[---.]k.drḥm.w aṯb.l ntbt.k.ʿṣm l t[--].|[---.]drk 1001.2.6
bʿl.|[--.]rbt.aṯrt.ym.|[---.]btlt.ʿnt.|[--.tl]ḥm.tšty.|[ilm.w tp]q.mrǵtm.|[td.b ḥrb.m]lḥt.qṣ.|[mri.tšty.k]rpnm yn.|[b 4[51].3.41
|špq.ilm.rḥbt yn.|špq.ilht.dkrt[.yn].|ʿd.lḥm.šty.ilm.|w pq mrǵtm.td.|b ḥrb.mlḥt.qṣ[.m]r|i.tšty.krp[nm.y]n.|[b k 4[51].6.56
nt.[---].|yqrb.[---].|lḥm.m[---.---].|[ʿ]d.lḥm[.šty.ilm].|w pq.mr[ǵtm.td.---].|b ḥrb.[mlḥt.qṣ.mri].|šty.kr[pnm.yn.--- 5[67].4.13
š h.l lḥm.tpth.|brlt h.l trm.|mt.dm.ḫt.šʿtqt.|dm.lan.w ypqd.|krt.ṯʿ.yšu.g h.|w yṣḥ.šmʿ.l mṯt.|ḥry.ṭbḫ.imr.|w ilḥ 16.6[127].14
.ap h].|k.yiḫd[.akl.ššw].|št.mkš[r.grn].|w.št.ašk[rr].|w.pr.ḥḏr[t.ydk].|aḥd h.w.yṣq[.b.ap h].|k.yiḫd.akl.š[šw].|št. 161[56].15
drʿ.[---].|tmṯl[.---].|mǵm[ǵ.---].|w.š[t.nni.w.pr.ʿbk].|w.pr[.ḥḏrt.w.št].|irǵ[n.ḥmr.ydk].|aḥd[h.w.yṣq.b.ap h].|k 161[56].29
yṣq b ap h.|[k.yiḫd akl š]šw št mkšr grn.|[w št aškrr w p]r ḥḏrt.|[-----].|[---.-]n[-].|[k yraš ššw št bln q]ṭ ydk.|[w 160[55].11
dprn[.---].|drʿ.[---].|tmṯl[.---].|mǵm[ǵ.---].|w.š[t.nni.w.pr.ʿbk].|w.pr[.ḥḏrt.w.št].|irǵ[n.ḥmr.ydk].|aḥd[h.w.yṣq. 161[56].28
kbkbm.yʿrb.|[bʿ]l.b kbd h.b p h yrd.|k ḥrr.zt.ybl.arṣ.w pr.|ʿṣm.yraun.aliyn.bʿl.|ṯtʿ.nn.rkb.ʿrpt.|tbʿ.rgm.l bn.ilm. 5[67].2.5
--].|[-----].|[-----].|[---].al.tš[--.---].|[---.]l ksi y.w pr[ʿ].|[---].prʿ.ank.[---].|[---.]ank.nši[.---].|[---.ṯ]br.ḫss.[--- 1002.13
]gpn lk.|[---].km[-.---].|[---.--]k yṣunn[.---].|[---.--]dy.w.prʿ[.---].|[---.]ytn.ml[--].ank.iphn.|[---.a]nk.i[--.--]slm.w.y 1002.35
ḫlm.tlk.nbtm.|šmḫ.lṭpn.il.d pid.|pʿn h.l hdm.yṯpd.|w yprq.lṣb w yṣḥq.|yšu.g h.w yṣḥ.|aṯbn.ank.w anḫn.|w tn 6[49].3.16
t.alp.šnt.w[.---].|šntm.alp.d krr[.---].|alp.pr.bʿl.[---].|w prt.tkt.[---].|šnt.[---].|ššw.ʿṯrt.w ššw.ʿ[nt.---].|w ht.[--]k. 2158.1.4
ab y ǵm[--].|t[--.---].|ls[--.---].|ṣḥ[.---].|ky.m[--.---].|w pr[--.---].|tštil[.---].|ʿmn.bn[.---]. 1021.14
]ḥ.|b lṯk.bt.|[pt]ḥ.aḥd.l.bt.ʿbdm.|[t]n.ptḥ msb.bt.tu.|w.ptḥ[.aḥ]d.mmt.|ṯt.pt[ḥ.---].|ṯn.pt[ḥ.---].|w.pt[ḥ.--]r.ṯǵr.| 1151.11

.kṯr.bnm.ʻdt.|ypth̩.h̩ln.b bht m.|urbt.b qrb.[h]kl |m.w y[p]th̩.b dqt.ʻrpt.|ʻl h[wt].kṯr.w ẖss.|ṣh̩q.kṯr.w ẖss.|yšu. 4[51].7.19
š.hm.nǵr.|mdrʻ.w ṣh̩ hm.ʻm.nǵr.mdrʻ y.nǵr.|nǵr.pth̩.w pth̩ hw.prṣ.bʻd hm.|w ʻrb.hm.hm[.iṯ.--.l]h̩m.w t[n].|w nl 23[52].70
sb.bt.tu.|w.pth̩[.ah̩]d.mmt.|ṯṯ.pt[h̩.---].|ṯn.pt[h̩.---].|w.pt[h̩.--]r.ṯǵr.|ṯmn.h̩lnm.|ṯt.tẖ[--].l.mtm. 1151.14
t h̩[dr].|[-----].|ẖmš[.---]t.h̩drm.|w.[---.a]h̩d.d.sgrm.|w p[th̩.---.]l.ah̩d.adr.|[---.--]t.b[h̩d]r.mškb.|ṯl[l.---.--]h̩.|b lṯ 1151.5
rišym.dt.ʻrb.|b bnš hm.|ḏmry.w.pṯpṯ.ʻrb.|b.yrm.|[ily.w].ḏmry.ʻrb.|b.ṯbʻm.|ydn.bn.ilrpi.| 2079.3
.|bn.ẖran.w[.---].|[-]n.yʻrtym.|gmm.w.bn.p[--].|trn.w.p[-]y.|bn.bʻyn.w.agytn.|[---] gnym.|[--]ry.w ary.|[---]ǵrb 131[309].11
.---].|w bn[š.---].|d bnš.h̩m[r.---].|w d.l mdl.r[--.---].|w ṣin.ʻz.b[ʻl.---].|llu.bn[š.---].|imr.ẖ[--.---].|[--]n.bʻ[l.---].|w 2158.1.14
y.l yṣh̩.ṯr.il.ab h.il.|mlk.d yknn h.yṣh̩.aṯrt.|w bn h.ilt.w ṣbrt.arẖ h.|wn.in.bt.l bʻl.km.ilm.|h̩ẓr.k b[n.a]ṯrt.mṯb.il.| 3[ʻNT.VI].5.45
l yṣh̩.ṯr il.ab h.|[i]l.mlk.d yknn h.yṣh̩.|aṯrt.w bn h.ilt.w ṣbrt.|ary h.wn.in.bt.l bʻl.|km.ilm.w h̩ẓr.k bn.aṯrt.|mṯb il 4[51].4.49
r.|[il.ab h.i]l.mlk.|[d yknn h.yṣ]h̩.aṯ|[rt.w bn h.]ilt.|[w ṣbrt.ary]h.|[wn.in.bt.l bʻl.]|[km.ilm.w h̩ẓr].|[k bn.aṯ]r[t] 4[51].1.9
wy.w tkbdn h.|tšu.g h.w tṣh̩.tšmẖ ht.|aṯrt.w bn h.ilt.w ṣb|rt.ary h.k mt.aliyn.|bʻl.k ẖlq.zbl.bʻl.|arṣ.gm.yṣh̩ il.|l 6.1.40[49.1.12]
.tn.aẖ y.|w ʻn.bn.ilm.mt.mh.|taršn.l btlt.ʻnt.|an.itlk.w aṣd.kl.|ǵr.l kbd.arṣ.kl.gbʻ.|l kbd.šdm.npš.ẖsrt.|bn.nšm.n 6[49].2.15
y.lim.bn.|dgn.my.hmlt.aṯr.|bʻl.ard.b arṣ.ap.|ʻnt.ttlk.w tṣd.kl.ǵr.|l kbd.arṣ.kl.gbʻ.|l [k]bd.šdm.tmǵ.l nʻm[y].|[ar 5[67].6.26
.|km.ṯrm.w gbṯt.|km.ibrm.|w b hm.pn.bʻl.|bʻl.ytlk.w yṣd.|yh̩ pat.mlbr.|wn.ymǵy.aklm.|w ymẓa.ʻqqm.|bʻl.h̩ 12[75].1.34
annẖ b ẖmat.|w ʻl.agn.šbʻ d m.dǵ[ṯ.---]t.|tlk m.rh̩my.w tṣd[.---].|th̩grn.ǵzr.nʻm.[---].|w šm.ʻrbm.yr[.---].|mṯbt.il 23[52].16
t.idk.l ttn.[pnm].|[ʻm.a]qht.ǵzr.b alp.š[d].|[rbt.]kmn.w ṣh̩q.btlt.[ʻnt].|[tšu.]g h.w tṣh̩.šmʻ.m[ʻ.l a]|[qht.ǵ]zr.at.aẖ. 18[3AQHT].1.22
tm.|šmẖ.lṭpn.il.d pid.|pʻn h.l hdm.yṯpd.|w yprq.lṣb w yṣh̩q.|yšu.g h.w yṣh̩.|aṯbn.ank.w anẖn.|w tnẖ.b irt y.npš 6[49].3.16
r.w tql.|tštẖwy.w tkbd h.|hlm.il.k yphn h.|yprq.lṣb.w yṣh̩q.|pʻn h.l hdm.yṯpd.w ykrkr.|uṣbʻt h.yšu.g h.w y[ṣh̩]. 4[51].4.28
.b ym rṯ.b uni[l].|pnm.tšmẖ.w ʻl yṣhl pi[t].|yprq.lṣb.w yṣh̩q.|pʻn.l hdm.yṯpd.yšu.|g h.w yṣh̩.aṯbn.ank.|w anẖn. 17[2AQHT].2.10
.mt mt.|nh̩tm.ẖṭ k.mmnnm.mṭ yd k.hl.ʻṣr.|th̩rr.l išt.w ṣh̩rt.l ph̩mm.aṯtm.a[ṯt.il].|aṯt.il.w ʻlm h.yhbr.špt hm.yš[q 23[52].48
y.ad ad.nh̩tm.ẖṭ k.|mmnnm.mṭ yd k.hl.ʻṣr.th̩rr.l išt.|w ṣh̩rrt.l ph̩mm.btm.bt.il.bt.il.|w ʻlm h.w hn.aṯtm.tṣh̩n y.m 23[52].45
[s]pu y.bn m.um y.kly y.|yṯb.ʻm.bʻl.ṣrrt.|ṣpn.yšu g h.w yṣh̩.|aẖ y m.ytnt.bʻl.|spu y.bn m.um y.kl|y y.ytʻn.k gmr 6[49].6.13
|aṯr.bʻl.tiẖd.m[t].|b sin.lpš.tšṣq[n h].|b qṣ.all.tšu.g h.w[tṣ]|h̩.at.mt.tn.aẖ y.|w ʻn.bn.ilm.mt.mh.|taršn.l btlt.ʻnt. 6[49].2.11
.ʻln.p]n h.td[ʻ].|tǵṣ[.pnt.ks]l h.|anš.dt.ẓr.[h].|tšu.g h.w tṣh̩[.i]k.|mǵy.aliy[n.b]ʻl.|ik.mǵyt.b[t]lt.|ʻnt.mẖṣ y hm[. 4[51].2.21
l.ṯṯbr.|ʻln.pn h.tdʻ.tǵṣ.pnt.|ksl h.anš.dt.ẓr h.tšu.|g h.w tṣh̩.ik.mǵy.gpn.w ugr.|mn.ib.ypʻ.l bʻl.ṣrt.|l rkb.ʻrpt.l mẖ 3[ʻNT].3.33
b.w yṣh̩q.|pʻn h.l hdm.yṯpd.w ykrkr.|uṣbʻt h.yšu.g h.w y[ṣh̩].|ik.mǵyt.rbt.aṯr[t.y]m.|ik.atwt.qnyt.i[lm].|rǵb.rǵbt 4[51].4.30
.ilm.mt.ʻbd k.an.|w d ʻlm k.šmẖ.bn.ilm.mt.|[---.]g h.w aṣh̩.ik.yṣh̩n.|[bʻl.ʻm.aẖ y.ik].yqrun.hd.|[ʻm.ary y.---.--]p. 5[67].2.21
yṯlṯ.qn.ḏrʻ h.yh̩rṯ.|k gn.ap lb.k ʻmq.yṯlṯ.|bmt.yšu.g h.w yṣh̩.|bʻl.mt.my.lim.bn.|dgn.my.hmlt.aṯr.|bʻl.ard.b arṣ.ap 5[67].6.22
ʻl.mrym.ṣpn.|b alp.šd.rbt.kmn.|ṣh̩q.btlt.ʻnt.tšu.|g h.w tṣh̩.tbšr bʻl.|bšrt k.yblt.y[b]n.|bt.l k.km.aẖ k.w h̩ẓr.|km. 4[51].5.88
qht.ǵzr.|[---.kdd.dn]il.mt.rpi.w tʻn.|[btlt.ʻnt.tšu.g]h.w tṣh̩.hwt.|[---.]aqht.yḏ[--].|[---.--]n.ṣ[---].|[spr.ilmlk.šbny.l 17[2AQHT].6.53
.nʻmm.ttlkn.|šd.tṣdn.pat.mdbr.w ngš.hm.nǵr.|mdrʻ.w ṣh̩ hm.ʻm.nǵr.mdrʻ y.nǵr.|nǵr.pth̩.w pth̩ hw.prṣ.bʻd hm. 23[52].69
ʻl.|l pnn h.ydd.w yqm.|l pʻn h.ykrʻ.w yql.|w yšu.g h.w yṣh̩.|h̩wt.aẖt.w nar[-].|qrn.d bat k.btlt.ʻnt.|qrn.d bat k b 10[76].2.19
dr].|ʻdb.uẖry mṭ.yd h.|ymǵ.l mrrt.tǵll.b nr.|yšu.g h.w yṣh̩.y l k.mrrt.|tǵll.b nr.d ʻl k.mẖṣ.aqht.|ǵzr.šrš k.b arṣ.a 19[1AQHT].3.157
ṭ yd h.|ymǵ.l qrt.ablm.abl[m].|qrt.zbl.yrẖ.yšu g h.|w yṣh̩.y l k.qrt.ablm.|d ʻl k.mẖṣ.aqht.ǵzr.|ʻwrt.yšt k.bʻl.l ht 19[1AQHT].4.165
yṣhl pi[t].|yprq.lṣb.w yṣh̩q.|pʻn.l hdm.yṯpd.yšu.|g h.w yṣh̩.aṯbn.ank.|w anẖn.w tnẖ.b irt y.|npš.k yld.bn.l y.km. 17[2AQHT].2.12
d pid.|pʻn h.l hdm.yṯpd.|w yprq.lṣb w yṣh̩q.|yšu.g h.w yṣh̩.|aṯbn.ank.w anẖn.|w tnẖ.b irt y.npš.|k h̩y.aliyn.bʻl. 6[49].3.17
]bʻ.btlt.ʻnt[.idk.l ttn.pnm].|ʻm.yṭpn.mhr.š[t.tšu.g h].|w tṣh̩.yṯb.ytp.[---].|qrt.ablm.ablm.[qrt.zbl.yrẖ].|ik.al.yh̩dṯ. 18[3AQHT].4.7
t.pʻn h.ybqʻ.kbd h.w yh̩d.|[i]n.šmt.in.ʻẓm.yšu.g[h].|w yṣh̩.knp.hrgb.bʻl.ybn.|[b]ʻl.ybn.diy.hwt.hrg[b].|tpr.w du. 19[1AQHT].3.132
r.w du.b nši.ʻn h.w ypn.|yh̩d.hrgb.ab.nšrm.|yšu.g h.w yṣh̩.knp.hr[g]b.|bʻl.yṯb.bʻl.y[ṯb]r.diy[.h]wt.|w yql.th̩t.pʻn 19[1AQHT].3.122
.pʻn h.ybqʻ.kbdt hm.w[yh̩d].|in.šmt.in.ʻẓm.yšu.g h.|w yṣh̩.knp.nšrm.ybn.|bʻl.ybn.diy hmt nšrm.|tpr.w du.b nši 19[1AQHT].3.118
b nši[.ʻn h.w yphn.yh̩d].|b ʻrpt[.nšrm.yšu].|[g h.]w yṣh̩[.knp.nšrm].|bʻl.yṯb.bʻl.yṯb[r.diy.hmt].|tqln.th̩ pʻn y.i 19[1AQHT].3.107
ẓ.ybky.w yqbr.|yqbr.nn.b mdgt.b knk[-].|w yšu.g h.w yṣh̩.knp.nšrm.|bʻl.yṯbr.bʻl.yṯbr.diy.|hmt.hm.tʻpn.ʻl.qbr.b 19[1AQHT].3.148
du.b nši.ʻn h.|[w]yphn.yh̩d.ṣml.um.nšrm.|yšu.g h.w yṣh̩.knp.ṣml.|bʻl.yṯbr.bʻl.yṯbr.diy.|hyt.tql.th̩t.pʻn y.ibqʻ.| 19[1AQHT].3.136
b dqt.ʻrpt.|ʻl h[wt].kṯr.w ẖss.|ṣh̩q.kṯr.w ẖss.|yšu.g h.w yṣh̩.|l rgmt.l k.l ali|yn.bʻl.ṯṯbn.bʻl.|l hwt y.ypth̩.h̩|ln.b b 4[51].7.22
.---].|tšqy[.---].|tr.h̩t[-.---].|w msk.tr[.---].|tqrb.aẖ[h.w tṣh̩].|lm.tbʻrn[.---].|mn.yrẖ.k m[rṣ.---].|mn.k dw.kr[t].| 16.2[125].79
m].|[tgly.ḏd.il.w]tb[a].|[qrš.mlk.ab.]šnm.|[tša.g hm.w tṣ]h̩.sbn.|[---]l[.---.]ʻd.|ksm.mhyt[.m]ǵny.|l nʻm y.arṣ.db 5[67].6.3
m]k.b šbʻ.|šnt.w [--].bn.ilm.mt.|ʻm.aliyn.bʻl.yšu.|g h.w yṣh̩.ʻl k.b[ʻ]l m.|pht.qlt.ʻl k.pht.|dry.b h̩rb.ʻl k.|pht.šrp.b 6[49].5.11
.h̩ry.|km hm.w tẖss.aṯrt.|ndr h.w ilt.p[--].|w tšu.g h.w [tṣh̩].|ph mʻ.ap.k[rt.--].|u ṯn.ndr[.---].|apr.[---].|[-----]. 15[128].3.27
.šnm.l pʻn.|il.thbr.w tql.|tštẖwy.w tkbdn h.|tšu.g h.w tṣh̩.tšmẖ ht.|aṯrt.w bn h.ilt.w ṣb|rt.ary h.k mt.aliyn.|bʻl. 6.1.39[49.1.11]
.npš.hm.|k.iṯl.brlt n[-.k qṭr.b ap -].|tmǵyn.tša.g h[m.w tṣh̩n].|šmʻ.l dnil.[mt.rpi].|mt.aqht.ǵzr.[šṣat].|btlt.ʻnt.k [r 19[1AQHT].2.89
ṯrm.|mt.dm.ẖt.šʻtqt.|dm.lan.w ypqd.|krt.ṯʻ.yšu.g h.|w yṣh̩.šmʻ.l mṯt.|h̩ry.ṭbẖ.imr.|w ilh̩m.mgṯ.w iṯrm.|tšmʻ.mṯ 16.6[127].16
t.ǵzr.b alp.š[d].|[rbt.]kmn.w ṣh̩q.btlt.[ʻnt].|[tšu.]g h.w tṣh̩.šmʻ.m[ʻ.l a]|[qht.ǵ]zr.at.aẖ.w an.a[ẖt k].|[---].šbʻ.ṯir 18[3AQHT].1.23
.bṯn.yqr.|[krpn h.-.l]arṣ.ks h.tšpk m.|[l ʻpr.tšu.g h.]w tṣh̩.šmʻ.mʻ.|[l aqht.ǵzr.i]rš.ksp.w atn k.|[ẖrṣ.w aš]lh̩ k.w 17[2AQHT].6.16
.|l drkt.k aṯb.an.|ytbʻ.yṣb ǵlm.ʻl.|ab h.yʻrb.yšu g h.|w yṣh̩.šmʻ mʻ.l krt.|ṯʻ.ištmʻ.w tqǵ udn.|k ǵz.ǵzm.tdbr.|w ǵ 16.6[127].41
u[---]k.yrd[.--.]i[---]n.bn.|[---.-]nn.nrt.ilm.špš.tšu.g h.w t[ṣh̩.šm]ʻ.mʻ.|[-.yṯ]ir ṯr.il.ab k.l pn.zbl.ym.l pn[.ṯ]pṭ[.n]hr 2.3[129].15
šnt.w yʻn[.dnil.mt.]rpi.|yṯb.ǵzr.m[t.hrnmy.y]šu.|g h.w yṣh̩.t[bʻ.---].|bkyt.b hk[l]y.mšspdt.|b h̩ẓr y pẓǵm.ǵr.w y 19[1AQHT].4.182
.|tk.qrt h.hmry.mk.ksu.|ṯbt.ẖẖ.arṣ.nh̩lt h.tša.|g hm.w tṣh̩.th̩m.aliyn.|bn.bʻl.hwt.aliy.qrdm.|bhṯ.bn.ilm.mt.ʻbd k 5[67].2.17
akm.|l yṯb.idk.pnm.|l ytn.ʻmm.pbl.|mlk.tšan.|g hm.w tṣh̩n.|th̩m.krt.ṯ[ʻ].|hwt.[n]ʻmn.[ǵlm.il]. 14[KRT].6.304
ṯb].|[idk.pnm.l ytn].|[ʻ]m[.krt.mswn h].|tš[an.g hm.w tṣh̩n].|th̩[m.pbl.mlk].|qh̩[.ksp.w yrq].|ẖrṣ.[yd.mqm h].| 14[KRT].6.267
.|ttbʻ.btlt.ʻnt.|idk.l ttn.pnm.|ʻm.nrt.ilm.špš.|tšu.g h.w tṣh̩.|th̩m.ṯr.il.ab k.|hwt.lṭpn.h̩tk k.|pl.ʻnt.šdm.y špš.|pl.ʻ 6[49].4.33
pʻ]n.ʻnt.|[yhbr.w yql.yšt]h̩wyn.w y|[kbdn h.yšu.g h.w y]ṣh̩.th̩m.|[ṯr.il.ab k.hwt.l]ṭpn.h̩tk k.|[qryy.b arṣ.mlh̩]mt 1[ʻNT.IX].2.17
ʻdn].|ksl.y[ṯbr.yǵṣ.pnt.ksl h].|anš.[dt.ẓr h.yšu.g h].|w yṣ[h̩.---].|mẖṣ[.---].|š[--.---]. 19[1AQHT].2.97
-].|w ẖ[--.---].|my[.---].|aṯ[t.---].|aẖ k[.---].|tr.h̩[---].|w tṣh̩[.---].|tšqy[.---].|tr.h̩t[-.---].|w msk.tr[.---].|tqrb.aẖ[h. 16.2[125].75

b.‘ṯtrt.|il.ṯpṭ.b hd r‘y.d yšr.w yḏmr.|b knr.w ṯlb.b tp.w mṣltm.b m|rqdm.dšn.b.ḥbr.kṯr.ṭbm.|w tšt.‘nt.gṯr.b‘lt.ml UG5.2.1.4
l.|išttk.lm.ttkn.|štk.mlk.dn.|štk.šibt.‘n.|štk.qr.bt.il.|w mṣlt.bt.ḥr[š]. 12[75].2.62
ṯlṯ mrkb[t].|ṣpyt b ẖrṣ[.w] ṣmdm trm.d [ṣ]py.|w.trm.aḥdm.|ṣpym.|ṯlṯ mrkbt mlk. 1122.2
.|[-----].|[-----].|[-----].|k yraš w ykhp mid.|dblt yṯnt w ṣmqm yṯn[m].|w qmḥ bql yṣq aḥd h.|b ap h. 160[55].24
w.yṣq.b.ap h].|k yr[a]š.šš[w.w.ykhp].|mid.dblt.yṯ[nt.w].|ṣmq[m].yṯnm.w[.qmḥ.bql].|tdkn.aḥd h.w[.yṣq].|b.ap h 161[56].33
‘n.b‘l.a[ẖ]ḏ[.---].|ẓr h.aẖḏ.qš[t.---].|p ‘n.b‘l.aẖḏ[.---].|w ṣmt.ǵllm[.---].|aẖḏ.aklm.k [---].|npl.b mšmš[.---].|anp n 12[75].2.35
mt.|šd[.i]lm.šd.aṯrt.w rḥmy.|[---].y[ṯ]b.|[---]p.gp ym.w yṣǵd.gp..thm.|[yqḥ.]il.mšt‘ltm.mšt‘ltm.l riš.agn.|hl h.[t]š 23[52].30
]ṣrm l h.ršp [-]m.|[---.]bqt[-].|[b] ǵb.ršp mh bnš.|šrp.w ṣp ẖršẖ.|‘lm b ǵb ẖyr.|ṯmn l ṯlṯm ṣin.|šb‘.alpm.|bt b‘l.u UG5.12.B.2
y.ibq[‘.kbd hm.w] |aḥd.hm.iṯ.šmt.hm.i[ṯ].|‘ẓm.abky.w aqbrn h.|ašt.b ẖrt.ilm.arṣ.|b p h.rgm.l yṣa.b špt h.hwt[h 19[1AQHT].3.111
l.tḥt.p‘n y.ibq‘.|kbd h.w aḥd.hm.iṯ.šmt.iṯ.|‘ẓm.abky w aqbrn h.aštn.|b ẖrt.ilm.arṣ.b p h.rgm.l[yṣ]a.|b špt h.hwt 19[1AQHT].3.140
liyn.b‘l.l ktp.|‘nt.k tšt h.tš‘lyn h.|b ṣrrt.ṣpn.tbkyn h.|w tqbrn h.tštnn.b ẖrt.|ilm.arṣ.tṭbẖ.šb‘m.|rumm.k gmn.aliy 6[62].1.17
ṯ.yrẖm.k m[rṣ].|arb‘.k dw.k[rt].|mnd‘.krt.mǵ[y.---].|w qbr.tṣr.q[br].|tṣr.trm.tnq[--].|km.nkyt.ṯǵr[.---].|km.škllt. 16.2[125].87
w yḥd.|iṯ.šmt.iṯ.‘ẓm.w yqḥ b hm.|aqht.ybl.l qẓ.ybky.w yqbr.|yqbr.nn.b mdgt.b knk[-].|w yšu.g h.w yṣḥ.knp.nšr 19[1AQHT].3.146
‘n y.ibq‘.kbd[h].|w aḥd.hm.iṯ.šmt.hm.iṯ[.‘ẓm].|abky.w aqbrn.ašt.b ẖrt.|i[lm.arṣ.b p h.rgm.l yṣa.b šp]|t h.hwt h. 19[1AQHT].3.126
n.|‘tq.b d.aṯt.ab.ṣrry.|ik m.yrgm.bn.il.|krt.špḥ.lṭpn.|w qdš.u ilm.tmtn.|špḥ.lṭpn.l yḥ.|w y‘ny.krt.ṯ‘.|bn.al.tbkn.a 16.1[125].22
[l]m.adr.|ḥl.rḥb.mk[npt].|ap.krt bn[m.il].|špḥ.lṭpn[.w qdš].|bkm.t‘r[b.‘l.ab h].|t‘rb.ḥ[--].|b ṯtm.t[---].|šknt.[---] 16.2[125].111
ny.ḥlm.adr.ḥl.|rḥb.mknpt.ap.|[k]rt.bnm.il.špḥ.|lṭpn.w qdš.‘l.|ab h.y‘rb.ybky.|w yšnn.ytn.g h.|bky.b ḥy k.ab n. 16.1[125].11
h.w y‘n.|w y‘n.btlt.‘nt.|n‘mt.bn.aẖt.b‘l.|l pnn h.ydd.w yqm.|l p‘n h.ykr‘.w yql.|w yšu.g h.w yṣḥ.|ḥwt.aẖt.w nar 10[76].2.17
nt.|n‘mt.bn.aẖt.b‘l.|l pnn h.ydd.w yqm.|l p‘n h.ykr‘.w yql.|w yšu.g h.w yṣḥ.|ḥwt.aẖt.w nar[-].|qrn.d bat k.btlt. 10[76].2.18
mtm.|tgly.ḏd.il.w tbu.|qrš.mlk.ab.šnm.|l p‘n.il.thbr.w tql.|tštḥwy.w tkbd h.|hlm.il.k yphn h.|yprq.lṣb.w yṣḥq. 4[51].4.25
tm tgly.ḏd il.|[w tbu.qr]š.mlk.ab.šnm.|[l p‘n.il.t]hbr.w tql.tštḥ|[wy.w tkbd]n h.tlšn.aqht.ǵzr.|[---.kdd.dn]il.mt.r 17[2AQHT].6.50
tm.tgly.ḏd.|il.w tbu.qrš..|mlk.ab.šnm.l p‘n.|il.thbr.w tql.|tštḥwy.w tkbdn h.|tšu.g h.w tṣḥ.tšmẖ ht.|aṯrt.w bn 6.1.37[49.1.9]
n.pnm.tk.]in.bb.b alp ḥẓr.|[rbt.kmn.l p‘]n.‘nt.|[yhbr.w yql.yšt]ḥwyn.w y|[kbdn h.yšu.g h.w y]ṣḥ.tḥm.|[ṯr.il.ab k 1[‘NT.IX].2.16
ygly.]ḏl i[l].w ybu[.q]rš.mlk[.ab.šnm.l p‘n.il.]|[yhbr.]w yql[.y]štḥw[y.]w ykb[dn h.--]r y[---].|[---.k]ṯr.w ẖ[ss.t]b‘. 2.3[129].6
s].|ygly ḏd.i[l.w ybu.qrš.mlk].|ab.šnm.l [p‘n.il.yhbr.w yql].|yštḥwy.[w ykbdn h.---].|ṯr.il[.ab h.---].|ḥš b[ht m.t 1[‘NT.IX].3.24
h.ḥkpt.arṣ.nḥlt h].|b alp.šd.r[bt.kmn.l p‘n.kṯr].|hbr.w ql.t[štḥwy.w kbd.hwt].|w rgm l k[ṯr.w ẖss.ṯny.l hyn].|d 1[‘NT.IX].3.3
.b yd.md|d.ilm.mt.b a|lp.šd.rbt.k|mn.l p‘n.mt.|hbr.w ql.|tštḥwy.w k|bd hwt.w rgm.|l bn.ilm.mt.|ṯny.l ydd.|il 4[51].8.27
t h.ḥkpt.|arṣ.nḥlt h.|b alp.šd.rbt.|kmn.l p‘n.kṯ.|hbr.w ql.tštḥ|wy.w kbd hwt.|w rgm.l kṯr.|w ẖss.ṯny.l h|yn.d ḥ 3[‘NT.VI].6.19
b.dd.arṣy.|bt.y‘bdr.km ǵlmm.|w ‘rb n.l p‘n.‘nt.hbr.|w ql.tštḥwy.kbd hyt.|w rgm.l btlt.‘nt.|ṯny.l ymmt.limm.|t 3[‘NT].3.7
uṣb‘t h.hlm.qdq|d zbl ym.bn.‘nm.ṯpṭ.nhr.yprsḥ ym.|w yql.l arṣ.w trtqṣ.ṣmd.b d b‘l.|[km.]nšr.b uṣb‘t h.ylm.qdq 2.4[68].23
yṣa.b šp]|t h.hwt h.knp.hrgb.b‘l.ṯbr.|b‘l.ṯbr.diy.hwt.w yql.|tḥt.p‘n h.ybq‘.kbd h.w yḥd.|[i]n.šmt.in.‘ẓm.yšu.g[h 19[1AQHT].3.129
šu.g h.w yṣḥ.knp.hr[g]b.|b‘l.yṯb.b‘l.y[ṯb]r.diy[.h]wt.|w yql.tḥt.p‘n y.ibq‘.kbd[h].|w aḥd.hm.iṯ.šmt.hm.iṯ[.‘ẓm].| 19[1AQHT].3.124
bn.knn.qšt.|pbyn.qšt.|yddn.qšt.w.ql‘.|š‘rt.|bn.il.qšt.w.ql‘.|ark.qšt.w.ql‘.|bn.‘bdnkl.qšt.w.ql‘.|bn.znan.qšt.|bn.a 119[321].2.41
t.w.ql‘.|bn.gzl.qšt.w.ql‘.|[---]n.qšt.|ilhd.qšt.|‘dn.qšt.w.ql‘.|ilmhr.qšt.w.ql‘.|bn.gmrt.qšt.|ǵmrm.|bn.qṭn.qšt.w.ql 119[321].1.8
w.ql‘.|‘ky.qšt.|‘bdlbit.qšt.|kṯy.qšt.w.ql‘.|bn.ẖršn.qšt.w.ql‘.|ilrb.qšt.w.ql‘.|psḥn.qšt.|bn.kmy.qšt.|bn.ilḥbn.qšt.w. 119[321].3.40
l‘.|yṯpṭ.qšt.|ilṯḥm.qšt.w.ql‘.|ṣdqm.qšt.w.ql‘.|uln.qšt.w.ql‘.|uln.qšt.|bn.blẓn.qšt.w.ql‘.|gb‘.qšt.w.ql‘.|nṣṣn.qšt.| 119[321].2.7
m.qšt.|ḥdṯn.ql‘.|yṯpṭ.qšt.|ilṯḥm.qšt.w.ql‘.|ṣdqm.qšt.w.ql‘.|uln.qšt.w.ql‘.|uln.qšt.|bn.blẓn.qšt.w.ql‘.|gb‘.qšt.w.ql 119[321].2.6
.|m‘r.|[‘]dyn.ṯt.qštm.w.ql‘.|[-]lrš.qšt.w.ql‘.|t[t]n.qšt.w.ql‘.|u[l]n.qšt.w.ql‘.|y‘rn.qšt.w.ql‘.|klby.qšt.w.ql‘.|bq‘t.|i 119[321].2.16
š.]qšt.|bn.‘g[w.]qšt.w ql‘.|ḥd[ṯ]n.qšt.w.ql‘.|bn.bb.qšt.w[.ql]‘.|bn.aktmy.qšt.|šdyn.qšt.|bdn.qšt.w.ql‘.|bn.šmlbi.qš 119[321].4.9
n.[-]rkṯ.ṯt.qštm.w.ql‘.|bn.ṯ‘l.qšt.|bn.[ẖ]dpṯr.ṯt.qštm.[w].ql‘.|bn.aǵlyn.ṯt.qštm[.w.ṯl]ṯ.ql‘m.|bn.‘gw.qšt.w ql‘.|bn.t 119[321].3.18
an.qšt.|bn.arz.[ar]b‘.qšt.w.arb[‘.]ql‘m.|b[n.]ad‘l.q[š]t.w.ql‘.|b[n].ilyn.qšt.w.ql‘.|šmrm.ql‘.|ubr‘y.|abmn.qšt.w.ṯn. 119[321].2.46
št[.w.]ql‘.|bn.šp[š.]qšt.|bn.‘g[w.]qšt.w ql‘.|ḥd[ṯ]n.qšt.w.ql‘.|bn.bb.qšt.w[.ql]‘.|bn.aktmy.qšt.|šdyn.qšt.|bdn.qšt. 119[321].4.8
št.w.q[l‘].|bn.lky.qšt.|bn.dll.qšt.w.ql[‘].|bn.pǵyn.qšt.w[.q]l‘.|bn.bdn.qšt.|bn.pls.qšt.|ǵmrm.|[-]lhd.ṯt.qštm.w.ṯn. 119[321].3.29
.ṯn.ql‘m.|ildgn.qšt.|bn.y‘rn.ṯt.qštm w.ql‘.|bn.ḥṣn.qšt.w.ql‘.|bn.gdn.ṯt.qštm.w.ql‘.|bn.[-]q.qšt.w.ql‘.|gb[l]n.qšt.w. 119[321].3.11
qštm.w.ṯn.q[l]‘m.|kmrṯn.ṯt.qštm.ṯn.[q]l‘m.|ǵdyn.qšt.w.ql‘.|bn.gzl.qšt.w.ql‘.|[---]n.qšt.|ilhd.qšt.|‘dn.qšt.w.ql‘.|il 119[321].1.4
št.w.ql‘.|[---]n.qšt.|ilhd.qšt.|‘dn.qšt.w.ql‘.|ilmhr.qšt.w.ql‘.|bn.gmrt.qšt.|ǵmrm.|bn.qṭn.qšt.w.ql‘.|mrṯd.qšt.|ssw 119[321].1.9
štm.w.ṯn.ql‘m.|bn.ṯlṯ.ṯ[lṯ.]qšt.w.ṯn.ql‘m.|qṣn.ṯt.qštm.w.ql‘.|bn.gṯrn.q[š]t.|bn.ẖdi.ṯt.qštm.w.ṯn.ql‘m.|ildgn.qšt.|b 119[321].3.6
ql‘.|š‘rt.|bn.il.qšt.w.ql‘.|ark.qšt.w.ql‘.|bn.‘bdnkl.qšt.w.ql‘.|bn.znan.qšt.|bn.arz.[ar]b‘.qšt.w.arb[‘.]ql‘m.|b[n.]ad‘ 119[321].2.43
.ṯt.qštm.w.ql‘.|gln.ṯt.qštm.w.ql‘.|gtn.qšt.|pmn.ṯt.qšt.w.ql‘.|bn.zry.q[š]t.w.ql‘.|bn.tlmyn.ṯt.qštm.w.ql‘.|bn.ysd.qš 104[316].9
bn.ẖdi.ṯt.qštm.w.ṯn.ql‘m.|ildgn.qšt.|bn.y‘rn.ṯt.qštm w.ql‘.|bn.ḥṣn.qšt.w.ql‘.|bn.gdn.ṯt.qštm.w.ql‘.|bn.[-]q.qšt.w 119[321].3.10
qšt.w.ql‘.|y‘rn.qšt.w.ql‘.|klby.qšt.w.ql‘.|bq‘t.|ily.qšt.w.ql‘.|bn.ḥrẓn.qšt.w.ql‘.|tgrš.qšt.w.ql‘.|špšyn.qšt.w.ql‘.|bn 119[321].2.22
.w.ql‘.|bn.tmy.qšt.w.ql‘.|‘ky.qšt.|‘bdlbit.qšt.|kṯy.qšt.w.ql‘.|bn.ẖršn.qšt.w.ql‘.|ilrb.qšt.w.ql‘.|psḥn.qšt.|bn.kmy.q 119[321].3.39
bn.aktmy.qšt.|šdyn.qšt.|bdn.qšt.w.ql‘.|bn.šmlbi.qšt.w.ql‘.|bn.yy.qšt.|ilrb.qšt.|bn.nmš.ṯt.qšt.w.ql‘.|b‘l.qšt.w.ql‘. 119[321].4.13
mn.ṯt.qšt.w.ql‘.|bn.zry.q[š]t.w.ql‘.|bn.tlmyn.ṯt.qštm.w.ql‘.|bn.ysd.qšt.|[ǵ]mrm.|ilgn.qšt.|abršp.qšt.|ssg.qšt.|yn 104[316].9
št.w.ql‘.|bn.ǵb.qšt.|bn.ytrm.qšt.w.ql‘.|bn.‘bdyrẖ.qšt.w.q[l‘].|bn.lky.qšt.|bn.dll.qšt.w.ql[‘].|bn.pǵyn.qšt.w[.q]l‘.| 119[321].3.26
pls.qšt.|ǵmrm.|[-]lhd.ṯt.qštm.w.ṯn.ql‘m.|ulšn.ṯt.qšm.w.ql‘.|bn.ml‘n.qšt.w.ql‘.|bn.tmy.qšt.w.ql‘.|‘ky.qšt.|‘bdlbit. 119[321].3.34
m.w[.]q[l‘].|bn.rpš.qšt.w.ql‘.|bn.ǵb.qšt.|bn.ytrm.qšt.w.ql‘.|bn.‘bdyrẖ.qšt.w.q[l‘].|bn.lky.qšt.|bn.dll.qšt.w.ql[‘].| 119[321].3.25
byn.qšt.|yddn.qšt.w.ql‘.|š‘rt.|bn.il.qšt.w.ql‘.|ark.qšt.w.ql‘.|bn.‘bdnkl.qšt.w.ql‘.|bn.znan.qšt.|bn.arz.[ar]b‘.qšt.w 119[321].2.42
št.w.[ṯlṯ.]ql‘m.|bn.army.ṯt.qštm.w[.]q[l‘].|bn.rpš.qšt.w.ql‘.|bn.ǵb.qšt.|bn.ytrm.qšt.w.ql‘.|bn.‘bdyrẖ.qšt.w.q[l‘].| 119[321].3.23
št.w.ql‘.|bn.‘bdyrẖ.qšt.w.q[l‘].|bn.lky.qšt.|bn.dll.qšt.w.ql[‘].|bn.pǵyn.qšt.w[.q]l‘.|bn.bdn.qšt.|bn.pls.qšt.|ǵmrm. 119[321].3.28
y.qšt.|bn.ilḥbn.qšt.w.q[l‘].|ršpab.qšt.w.ql‘.|pdrn.qšt.w.ql‘.|bn.pǵm[-.qšt].w.ql‘.|n‘mn.q[št.w.]ql‘.|[t]tn.qš[t].|bn 119[321].3.46
t.w ql‘.|bn.tbšn.ṯlṯ.qšt.w.[ṯlṯ.]ql‘m.|bn.army.ṯt.qštm.w[.]q[l‘].|bn.rpš.qšt.w.ql‘.|bn.ǵb.qšt.|bn.ytrm.qšt.w.ql‘.|bn 119[321].3.22
.|bn.bb.qšt.w[.ql]‘.|bn.aktmy.qšt.|šdyn.qšt.|bdn.qšt.w.ql‘.|bn.šmlbi.qšt.w.ql‘.|bn.yy.qšt.|ilrb.qšt.|bn.nmš.ṯt.qšt 119[321].4.12

n.q[št.w.]ql'. | [t]tn.qš[t]. | bn.tǵdy[.qšt.]w.ql'. | tty.qšt[.w.]ql'. | bn.šp[š.]qšt. | bn.'g[w.]qšt.w ql'. | ḥd[t]n.qšt.w.ql'. | b 119[321].4.5
tm.[w].ql'. | bn.aǵlyn.tt.qštm[.w.tl]t.ql'm. | bn.'gw.qšt.w ql'. | bn.tbšn.tlt.qšt.w.[tlt.]ql'm. | bn.army.tt.qštm.w[.]q[l'] 119[321].3.20
tt.qštm.w.ql'. | gtn.qšt. | pmn.tt.qšt.w.ql'. | bn.zry.q[š]t.w.ql'. | bn.tlmyn.tt.qštm.w.ql'. | bn.ysd.qšt. | [ǵ]mrm. | ilgn.qš 104[316].9
hd.tt.qštm.w.tn.ql'm. | ulšn.tt.qšm.w.ql'. | bn.ml'n.qšt.w.ql'. | bn.tmy.qšt.w.ql'. | 'ky.qšt. | 'bdlbit.qšt. | kty.qšt.w.ql'. | 119[321].3.35
št.w.ql'. | bn.[-]bl.tt.qštm.w.tn.ql'm. | bn.[-]rkt.tt.qštm.w.ql'. | bn.t'l.qšt. | bn.[h]dptr.tt.qštm.[w].ql'. | bn.aǵlyn.tt.qšt 119[321].3.16
št.w.ql'. | bn.ḥrzn.qšt.w.ql'. | tgrš.qšt.w.ql'. | špšyn.qšt.w.ql'. | bn.t'ln.qš[t.w.q]l'. | 'tqbt.qšt. | [-]ll.qšt.w.ql'. | hlb.rpš. | 119[321].2.25
l'. | bn.gdn.tt.qštm.w.ql'. | bn.[-]q.qšt.w.ql'. | gb[l]n.qšt.w.ql'. | bn.[-]bl.tt.qštm.w.tn.ql'm. | bn.[-]rkt.tt.qštm.w.ql'. | b 119[321].3.14
.y'rn.tt.qštm w.ql'. | bn.ḥsn.qšt.w.ql'. | bn.gdn.tt.qštm.w.ql'. | bn.[-]q.qšt.w.ql'. | gb[l]n.qšt.w.ql'. | bn.[-]bl.tt.qštm.w. 119[321].3.12
bn.šmlbi.qšt.w.ql'. | bn.yy.qšt. | ilrb.qšt. | bn.nmš.tt.qšt.w.ql'. | b'l.qšt.w.ql'. 119[321].4.16
t]n.qšt.w.ql'. | u[l]n.qšt.w.ql'. | y'rn.qšt.w.ql'. | klby.qšt.w.ql'. | bq't. | ily.qšt.w.ql'. | bn.ḥrzn.qšt.w.ql'. | tgrš.qšt.w.ql'. | 119[321].2.19
'. | bn.ḥsn.qšt.w.ql'. | bn.gdn.tt.qštm.w.ql'. | bn.[-]q.qšt.w.ql'. | gb[l]n.qšt.w.ql'. | bn.[-]bl.tt.qštm.w.tn.ql'm. | bn.[-]rkt 119[321].3.13
'. | ṣdqm.qšt.w.ql'. | uln.qšt.w.ql'. | uln.qšt. | bn.blzn.qšt.w.ql'. | gb'.qšt.w.ql'. | nṣṣn.qšt. | m'r. | [']dyn.tt.qštm.w.ql'. | [-] 119[321].2.9
.qnmlk.qšt. | ytḥm.qšt. | grp.qšt. | m'rby. | n'mn.tt.qštm.w.ql'. | gln.tt.qštm.w.ql'. | gtn.qšt. | pmn.tt.qšt.w.ql'. | bn.zry. 104[316].9
qšt. | grp.qšt. | m'rby. | n'mn.tt.qštm.w.ql'. | gln.tt.qštm.w.ql'. | gtn.qšt. | pmn.tt.qšt.w.ql'. | bn.zry.q[š]t.w.ql'. | bn.tlm 104[316].9
b']. | [u]tpt.ql'.w.tt.mr[h]m. | [bn].smyy.qšt.w.u[tpt]. | [w.q]l'.w.tt.mrḥm. | [bn].šlmn.ql'.w.t[t.---]. | [bn].mlṣ.qštm.w. 2047.5
[.qšt.]w.ql'. | tty.qšt[.w.]ql'. | bn.šp[š.]qšt. | bn.'g[w.]qšt.w ql'. | ḥd[t]n.qšt.w.ql'. | bn.bb.qšt.w[.ql]'. | bn.aktmy.qšt. | šd 119[321].4.7
pšyn.qšt.w.ql'. | bn.t'ln.qš[t.w.q]l'. | 'tqbt.qšt. | [-]ll.qšt.w.ql'. | hlb.rpš. | abmn.qšt. | zzn.qšt. | dqry.qš[t]. | rkby. | bn.kn 119[321].2.28
.qštm.w.ql'. | [-]lrš.qšt.w.ql'. | t[t]n.qšt.w.ql'. | u[l]n.qšt.w.ql'. | y'rn.qšt.w.ql'. | klby.qšt.w.ql'. | bq't. | ily.qšt.w.ql'. | bn. 119[321].2.17
lrš.qšt.w.ql'. | t[t]n.qšt.w.ql'. | u[l]n.qšt.w.ql'. | y'rn.qšt.w.ql'. | klby.qšt.w.ql'. | bq't. | ily.qšt.w.ql'. | bn.ḥrzn.qšt.w.ql'. 119[321].2.18
ql'. | ilmhr.qšt.w.ql'. | bn.gmrt.qšt. | ǵmrm. | bn.qtn.qšt.w.ql'. | mrtd.qšt. | ssw.qšt. | knn.qšt. | bn.tlln.qšt. | bn.šyn.qšt. | 119[321].1.12
.q[l']. | ršpab.qšt.w.ql'. | pdrn.qšt.w.ql'. | bn.pǵm[-.qšt].w.ql'. | n'mn.q[št.w.]ql'. | [t]tn.qš[t]. | bn.tǵdy[.qšt.]w.ql'. | tty. 119[321].4.1
ql'. | uln.qšt.w.ql'. | uln.qšt. | bn.blzn.qšt.w.ql'. | gb'.qšt.w.ql'. | nṣṣn.qšt. | m'r. | [']dyn.tt.qštm.w.ql'. | [-]lrš.qšt.w.ql'. | 119[321].2.10
'm. | ulšn.tt.qšm.w.ql'. | bn.ml'n.qšt.w.ql'. | bn.tmy.qšt.w.ql'. | 'ky.qšt. | 'bdlbit.qšt. | kty.qšt.w.ql'. | bn.hršn.qšt.w.ql'. 119[321].3.36
qšt.w.ql'. | tgrš.qšt.w.ql'. | špšyn.qšt.w.ql'. | bn.t'ln.qš[t.w.q]l'. | 'tqbt.qšt. | [-]ll.qšt.w.ql'. | hlb.rpš. | abmn.qšt. | zzn.qšt 119[321].2.26
sḥn.qšt. | bn.kmy.qšt. | bn.ilḥbn.qšt.w.q[l']. | ršpab.qšt.w.ql'. | pdrn.qšt.w.ql'. | bn.pǵm[-.qšt].w.ql'. | n'mn.q[št.w.]ql' 119[321].3.45
'bdlbit.qšt. | kty.qšt.w.ql'. | bn.hršn.qšt.w.ql'. | ilrb.qšt.w.ql'. | psḥn.qšt. | bn.kmy.qšt. | bn.ilḥbn.qšt.w.q[l']. | ršpab.qš 119[321].3.41
ṣry.qšt. | arny. | abm.qšt. | ḥdtn.ql'. | ytpt.qšt. | iltḥm.qšt.w.ql'. | ṣdqm.qšt.w.ql'. | uln.qšt.w.ql'. | uln.qšt. | bn.blzn.qšt.w 119[321].2.5
l'. | ilrb.qšt.w.ql'. | psḥn.qšt. | bn.kmy.qšt. | bn.ilḥbn.qšt.w.q[l']. | ršpab.qšt.w.ql'. | pdrn.qšt.w.ql'. | bn.pǵm[-.qšt].w.ql' 119[321].3.44
'.qšt.w.arb['.]ql'm. | b[n.]ad'l.q[š]t.w.ql'. | b[n].ilyn.qšt.w.ql'. | šmrm.ql'. | ubr'y. | abmn.qšt.w.tn.ql'm. | qdmn.tt.qštm 119[321].2.47
t. | dqry.qš[t]. | rkby. | bn.knn.qšt. | pbyn.qšt. | yddn.qšt.w.ql'. | š'rt. | bn.il.qšt.w.ql'. | ark.qšt.w.ql'. | bn.'bdnkl.qšt.w.ql 119[321].2.38
.w.ql'. | bq't. | ily.qšt.w.ql'. | bn.ḥrzn.qšt.w.ql'. | tgrš.qšt.w.ql'. | špšyn.qšt.w.ql'. | bn.t'ln.qš[t.w.q]l'. | 'tqbt.qšt. | [-]ll.qš 119[321].2.24
w.ql'. | klby.qšt.w.ql'. | bq't. | ily.qšt.w.ql'. | bn.ḥrzn.qšt.w.ql'. | tgrš.qšt.w.ql'. | špšyn.qšt.w.ql'. | bn.t'ln.qš[t.w.q]l'. | 't 119[321].2.23
.ql'. | pdrn.qšt.w.ql'. | bn.pǵm[-.qšt].w.ql'. | n'mn.q[št.w.]ql'. | [t]tn.qš[t]. | bn.tǵdy[.qšt.]w.ql'. | tty.qšt[.w.]ql'. | bn.š 119[321].4.2
.w.ql'. | nṣṣn.qšt. | m'r. | [']dyn.tt.qštm.w.ql'. | [-]lrš.qšt.w.ql'. | t[t]n.qšt.w.ql'. | u[l]n.qšt.w.ql'. | y'rn.qšt.w.ql'. | klby.q 119[321].2.15
št].w.ql'. | n'mn.q[št.w.]ql'. | [t]tn.qš[t]. | bn.tǵdy[.qšt.]w.ql'. | tty.qšt[.w.]ql'. | bn.šp[š.]qšt. | bn.'g[w.]qšt.w ql'. | ḥd[t] 119[321].4.4
št.w.ql'. | gb'.qšt.w.ql'. | nṣṣn.qšt. | m'r. | [']dyn.tt.qštm.w.ql'. | [-]lrš.qšt.w.ql'. | t[t]n.qšt.w.ql'. | u[l]n.qšt.w.ql'. | y'rn.q 119[321].2.14
. | kmrtn.tt.qštm.tn.[q]l'm. | ǵdyn.qšt.w.ql'. | bn.gzl.qšt.w.ql'. | [---]n.qšt. | ilhd.qšt. | 'dn.qšt.w.ql'. | ilmhr.qšt.w.ql'. | b 119[321].1.5
.ql'. | bn.yy.qšt. | ilrb.qšt. | bn.nmš.tt.qšt.w.ql'. | b'l.qšt.w.ql'. 119[321].4.17
]y ilm.d mlk. | y[t]b.aliyn.b'l. | yt'dd.rkb.'rpt. | [--].ydd.w yqlṣn. | yqm.w ywptn.b tk. | p[h]r.bn.ilm.štt. | p[--].b tlḥn y 4[51].3.12
r[a]š.šš[w.w.ykhp]. | mid.dblt.yt[nt.w]. | ṣmq[m].ytnm.w[.qmḥ.bql]. | tdkn.aḥd h.w[.yṣq]. | b.ap h. 161[56].34
----]. | k yraš w ykhp mid. | dblt ytnt w ṣmqm ytn[m]. | w qmḥ bql yṣq aḥd h. | b ap h. 160[55].25
. | gb'ly. | ypr. | ary. | zrn. | art. | tlḥny. | tlrby. | dmt. | aǵt. | w.qmnz. | slh. | ykn'm. | šlmy. | w.ull. | tmry. | qrt. | 'rm. | nnu. | [71[113].15
.w yšn. | b dm' h.nhmmt. | šnt.tluan. | w yškb.nhmmt. | w yqmṣ.w b ḥlm h. | il.yrd.b dhrt h. | ab adm.w yqrb. | b šal.k 14[KRT].1.35
mat. | w mmskn. | w.tt.mqrtm. | w.tn.irpm.w.tn.trqm. | w.qpt.w.mqḥm. | w.tltm.yn šb'.kbd d tbt. | w.hmšm.yn.d ih 1103.21
in.b'l.b bht ht. | il hd.b qrb.hkl h. | qšt hn.aḥd.b yd h. | w qṣ't h.bm.ymn h. | idk.l ytn pnm. | tk.aḥ.šmk.mla[t.r]umm 10[76].2.7
hmmt. | w yqmṣ.w b ḥlm h. | il.yrd.b dhrt h. | ab adm.w yqrb. | b šal.krt.m at. | krt.k ybky. | ydm'.n'mn.ǵlm. | il.mlk 14[KRT].1.37
.yd.ṣt h.y'l.w yškb. | [yd.]mizrt.p yln.mk.b šb'.ymm. | [w]yqrb.b'l.b ḥnt h.abynt. | [d]nil.mt.rpi anḫ.ǵzr. | [mt.]hrn 17[2AQHT].1.17
n. | tbrk.ilm.tity. | tity.ilm.l ahl hm. | dr il.l mšknt hm. | w tqrb.w ld.bn.l h. | w tqrb.w ld.bnt.l h. | mk.b šb'.šnt. | bn.k 15[128].3.20
.ilm.l ahl hm. | dr il.l mšknt hm. | w tqrb.w ld.bn.l h. | w tqrb.w ld.bnt.l h. | mk.b šb'.šnt. | bn.krt.km hm.tdr. | ap.bn 15[128].3.21
-]. | [---.mid.rm.]krt. | [b tk.rpi.]arṣ. | [b pḫr].qbṣ.dtn. | [w t]qrb.w ld. | bn.tl k. | tld.pǵt.t[--]t. | tld.pǵt[.---]. | tld.pǵ[t.--- 15[128].3.5
.il]. | ytši.l dr.bn.il.l mpḫrt.bn.i[l.l tkmn.w š]nm hn š. | w šqrb.'r.mšr mšr bn.ugrt.w [npy.---.]ugr. | w npy.yman.w n 32[2].1.18
pnk.ǵzr.ilḥu. | [m]rḥ h.yiḫd.b yd. | [g]rgr h.bm.ymn. | [w]yqrb.trzz h. | [---].mǵy h.w ǵlm. | [a]ḫt h.šib.yṣat.mrḥ h. | 16.1[125].49
ytši.l d]r.bn[.il]. | [l mpḫrt.bn.il.l tkmn.w šnm.hn š]. | [w šqrb.š.mšr mšr.bn.ugrt.w npy.---.]w npy. | [---.w np]y.ugr 32[2].1.4
ytnt. | trmn w. | dbḥ kl. | kl ykly. | dbḥ k.sprt. | dt nat. | w qrwn. | l k dbḥ. | [--]r bt [--]. | [--]bnš [--]. | š š[--]. | w [--]. | d RS61[24.277.11]
yṣḥ.t[b'.---]. | bkyt.b hk[l]y.mšspdt. | b ḥzr y pzǵm.ǵr.w yq. | dbḥ.ilm.yš'ly.dǵt h. | b šmym.dǵt hrnmy[.d k] | bkbm. 19[1AQHT].4.184
]. | kpr.šb' bn[t.rḥ.gdm.w anhbm]. | kla[t.tǵ]r[t.bht.'nt.w tqry.ǵlmm.b št.ǵr]. | ap 'nt tm[tḫṣ.b 'mq.tḫtṣb.bn.qrytm.t 7.2[130].24
[--]. | kpr.šb'.bnt.rḥ.gdm. | w anhbm.klat.tǵrt. | bht.'nt.w tqry.ǵlmm. | b št.ǵr.w hln.'nt.tm | tḫṣ.b 'mq.tḫtṣb.bn. | qryt 3['NT].2.4
p[-]l[.---]. | k lli.[---]. | kpr.[šb'.bnt.rḥ.gdm.w anhbm]. | w tqr[y.ǵlmm.b št.ǵr.---]. | [']d tš[b'.tmtḫṣ.---]. | klyn[.---]. | šp 7.2[130].4
.l in]š ilm.w š. | dd ilš.š[.---.]mlk.ytb br | r.w mḫ[--.---.]w q[--]. | ym.'lm.y[---.---]. | t.k[-]ml.[---]. | l[---].w y[nt.qrt.---]. APP.II[173].8
.tttb[.--]d h. | km trpa.hn n'r. | d yšt.l.lṣb h ḫš'r klb. | [w]riš.pqq.w šr h. | yšt.aḥd h.dm zt.hrpnt. UG5.1.2.5
n'mm.b ys[mm.---]. | arḫ.arḫ.[---.tld]. | ibr.tld[.l b'l]. | w rum.l[rkb.'rpt]. | tḥbq.[---]. | tḥbq[.---]. | w tksynn.btn[-.] | 10[76].3.22
tnn. | bšrt.il.bš[r.b']l. | w bšr.ḥtk.dgn. | k.ibr.l b'l[.yl]d. | w rum.l rkb.'rpt. | yšmḫ.aliyn.b'l. 10[76].3.37
n.dt. | likt.mṣrm. | hn dt.b.ṣr. | mtt.by. | gšm.adr. | nškḥ.w. | rb.tmtt. | lqḥ.kl.dr'. | b d a[-]m.w.ank. | k[l.]dr' hm. | [--.n] 2059.15

ẖ ytrẖ.ib t‘rb m b bh|t h.w atn mhr h l a|b h.alp ksp w rbt ẖ|rṣ.išlḥ ẓhrm iq|nim.atn šd h krm[m].|šd dd h ḥrn 24[77].20
[t]ḥm.iṯtl.|l mnn.ilm.|tǵr k.tšlm k.|t‘zz k.alp ymm.|w rbt.šnt.|b ‘d ‘lm...gn‘.|iršt.aršt.|l aẖ y.l r‘ y.dt.|w ytnnn. 1019.1.5
[--].w rbb.|š[---]npš išt.|w.l.tikl w l tš[t]. 2003.1
.|bn.lwn.ṯlṯtm.b‘lm.|bn.b‘ly.ṯlṯtm.b‘lm.|w.aḥd.ẖbṯ.|w.arb‘.aṯt.|bn.lg.ṯn.bn h.|b‘lm.w.aẖt h.|b.šrt.|šty.w.bn h. 2080.9
[nq]dm.dt.kn.npṣ hm.|[bn].lbn.arb‘.qšt.w.ar[b‘].|[u]ṯpt.ql‘.w.ṯt.mr[ḥ]m.|[bn].smyy.qšt.w.u[ṯpt].|[2047.2
ap.|pd.|mlk.arb‘.ḥm[rm.w.arb]‘.bnšm.|ar.ẖmš.ḥmr[m.w.ẖm]š.bnšm.|atlg.ḥmr[.---.] 2040.3
bn.b‘ln.biry.|ṯlṯ.b‘lm.|w.adn hm.ṯr.w.arb‘.bnt h.|yrẖm.yd.ṯn.bn h.|b‘lm.w.ṯlṯ.n‘rm.w.bt.aḥt.|b 2080.3
it.|[drt.ḥpr.b]nšm.w.ṯn.‘šr h.dd.l.rpš.|[---.]šb‘m.dr‘.w.arb‘m.drt.mit.dd.|[---].ḥpr.bn.šm.|[b.---.]knm.ṯṯm.l.mit. 1098.5
bbly.|yṯ‘d.ṣm[d].|bn.liy.|‘šrm.ṣ[md].|ṯṯ kbd.b ḥ[--].|w.arb‘.ḥ[mrm].|b m[‘]rby.|ṯmn.ṣmd.[---].|b d.b‘lsr.|yd.ṯdn 2102.1
‘m.|[š]b‘.b.ḥrṯm.|[ṯ]lṯ.b.ṯǵrm.|rb qrt.aẖd.|ṯmn.ẖzr.|w.arb‘.ḥršm.|dt.tb‘ln.b.pẖn.|ṯṯtm.ẖzr.w.‘št.‘šr.ḥrš.|dt.tb‘ln 1024.3.5
.kbd.yn.d.l.ṭb.|w.arb‘m.yn.ẖlq.b.gt.sknm.|‘šr.yn.ṭb.w.arb‘m.ẖmš.kbd.|yn.d.l.ṭb.gt.ṭbq.|mit.‘šr.kbd.yn.ṭb.|w.ṯṯ 1084.4
tš‘.ṯnnm.|w.arb‘.ẖsnm.|‘šr.mrum.|w.šb‘.ẖsnm.|tš‘.‘šr.|mrynm.|ṯlṯ.‘š 1029.2
ẖmš.‘šr.yn.ṭb.|w.tš‘m.kdm.kbd.yn.d.l.ṭb.|w.arb‘m.yn.ẖlq.b.gt.sknm.|‘šr.yn.ṭb.w.arb‘m.ẖmš.kbd.|yn. 1084.3
[---.]ẖ[---.]ṯmnym[.k]sp ẖmšt.|[w a]rb‘ kkr ‘l bn[.--].|[w] ṯlṯ šmn.|[w a]r[b‘] ksp ‘l bn ymn. 1103.2
ym[.k]sp ẖmšt.|[w a]rb‘ kkr ‘l bn[.--].|[w] ṯlṯ šmn.|[w a]r[b‘] ksp ‘l bn ymn.|šb šr šmn [--] ṯryn.|ẖm[š]m l ‘šr ks 1103.4
d.|l špš.arn.ṯn[.‘šr h.]mn.|‘ṣrm.ṯql.kbd[.ks].mn.ẖrṣ.|w arb‘.ktnt.w [---]b.|[ẖm]š.mat pḥm.|[ẖm]š[.m]at.iqnu.|ar 64[118].21
.|arb‘.‘š[r.]dd.n‘r.|d.apy[.--].|w.arb[‘.--]d.apy.‘bd h.|w.mrb‘[t.l ‘]bdm. 2094.6
m.ṯmnym.dd.|l u[-]m.|b.ṭbq.arb‘m.dr‘.w.‘šr.dd.drt.|w[.a]rb‘.l.‘šrm.dd.l.yḥšr.bl.bn h.|b.gt.m‘br.arb‘m.l.mit.dr‘. 1098.11
--].|w.ṯlṯ.alp h.[---].|swn.qrty.w.[b]n h[.---].|w.alp h.w.a[r]b‘.l.arb‘[m.---].|pln.ṯmry.w.ṯn.bn h.w[.---].|ymrn.aps 2044.7
[---.--]ǵz.|[---.]qrt.|[---].aṯt.|[---.]w arb‘.n‘r[m].|[---.a]ḥd.|[---.]ṯlṯ.aṯt. 2142.4
ṯ.‘šr.bnš.|yd.ytm.yd.r‘y.ḥmrm.|b.gt.gwl.ṯmn.ṣmdm.|w.arb‘.‘šr.bnš.|yd.nǵr.mdr‘.yd.š[--]m.|[b.]gt.ipṯl.ṯṯ.ṣmdm.| 2038.5
‘.|bn.‘bdnkl.qšt.w.ql‘.|bn.znan.qšt.|bn.arz.[ar]b‘.qšt.w.arb[‘.]ql‘m.|b[n.]ad‘l.q[š]t.w.ql‘.|b[n].ilyn.qšt.w.ql‘.|šmr 119[321].2.45
ṣḥ.illḏrm.|b d.zlb[n.--].|arb‘.‘š[r.]dd.n‘r.|d.apy[.--].|w.arb[‘.--]d.apy.‘bd h.|w.mrb‘[t.l ‘]bdm. 2094.5
r h.dd.[---].|iwrḏn.ḥ[--.---].|w.ṯlṯm.dd.[---.]n[---.---].|w.a[r]b‘[.---].bnš[.š]dyn[.---].|agr.[---.--]n.ṯn.‘šr h.d[--.---].|[1098.32
šsk k.[--].l ḥbš k.|‘tk.ri[š.]l mhr k.|w ‘p.l dr[‘].nšr k.|w rbṣ.l ǵr k.inbb.|kt ǵr k.ank.yd‘t.|[-]n.atn.at.mṯb k[.---].|[13[6].9
m.|[---.]bn.ilm.|[m]t.šmḥ.p ydd.|il[.ǵ]zr.|b [-]dn.‘.z.w.|rgbt.zbl. UG5.4.17
.mlk.yštal.b.hn[--].|hmt.w.anyt.hm.t‘[rb].|mkr.hn d.w.rgm.ank[.--].|mlkt.ybqš.anyt.w.at[--].|w mkr n.mlk[.---]. 2008.2.12
phn.|[---.a]nk.i[--.--]slm.w.yṯb.|[----.--]t.hw[-]y.h[--]r.w rgm.ank.|[---.]hdd tr[--.--]l.aṯrt y.|[--]ptm.ṣḥq.|[---.]rgm. 1002.38
.---].|tšt.tb‘[.---].|qrt.mlk[.---].|w.‘l.ap.s[--.---].|b hm.w.rgm.hw.al[--].|atn.ksp.l hm.‘d.|ilak.‘m.mlk.|ht.lik[t.--.] 2008.2.6
|mnm.šlm.|w.rgm.ṯṯb.l y.|bm.ṯy.ndr.|iṯt.‘mn.mlkt.|w.rgm y.l[--].|lqt.w.pn.|mlk.nr b n. 50[117].16
m y.p‘n k.|[tls]mn.[‘]m y.twtḥ.išd k.|[dm.rgm.iṯ.l y.]w argm k.hwt.|[w aṯny k.rgm.]‘ṣ.w lẖšt.|[abn.rgm.l td]‘.nš[3[‘NT].4.57
k.|‘m y.p‘n k.tlsmn.‘m y.|twtḥ.išd k.dm.rgm.|iṯ.l y.w argm k.|hwt.w aṯny k.rgm.|‘ṣ.w lẖšt.abn.|tant.šmm.‘m. 3[‘NT].3.18
twtḥ.i[šd k.tk.ẖršn.-------------].|ǵr.ks.dm.r[gm.iṯ.l y.w argm k].|hwt.w aṯny k[.rgm.‘ṣ.w lẖšt.abn].|tunt.šmm.‘m 1[‘NT.IX].3.12
smkt.ṣat.npš h.|[-]mt[-].ṣba.rbt.|špš.w tgh.nyr.|rbt.w rgm.l aẖt k.|ṯtmnt.krt n.dbḥ.|dbḥ.mlk.‘šr.|‘šrt.qḥ.tp k.b 16.1[125].38
.šd.rbt.k|mn.l p‘n.mt.|hbr.w ql.|tštḥwy.w k|bd hwt.w rgm.|l bn.ilm.mt.|ṯny.l ydd.|il.ǵzr.tḥm.|aliyn.b‘l.|[hw]t 4[51].8.29
ǵlmm.|w ‘rb n.l p‘n.‘nt.hbr.|w ql.tštḥwy.kbd hyt.|w rgm.l btlt.‘nt.|ṯny.l ymmt.limm.|tḥm.aliyn.b‘l.hwt.|aliy. 3[‘NT].3.8
.|[---.d]bḥ.|t[---.id]k.|pn[m.al.ttn].|‘m.[krt.msw]n.|w r[gm.l krt.]ṯ‘.|tḥm[.pbl.mlk].|qḥ.[ksp.w yr]q.|ẖrṣ[.yd.m 14[KRT].5.248
.šd.rbt.|kmn.l p‘n.kṯ.|hbr.w ql.tštḥ|wy.w kbd hwt.|w rgm.l kṯr.|w ẖss.ṯny.l h|yn.d ḥrš.ydm.|tḥm.al[iyn.b‘l].| 3[‘NT.VI].6.21
d.r[bt.kmn.l p‘n.kṯr].|hbr.w ql.t[štḥwy.w kbd.hwt].|w rgm l k[ṯr.w ẖss.ṯny.l hyn].|d ḥrš.y[dm.tḥm.ṯr.il.ab k.]|h 1[‘NT.IX].3.4
|al.tpl.al.tštḥwy.pẖr [m‘d.qmm.a--.am]|r ṯny.d‘t km.w rgm.l ṯr.a[b.-.il.ṯny.l pẖr].|m‘d.tḥm.ym.b‘l km.adn km.ṯ[2.1[137].16
[.---].|dm.mt.aṣ[ḥ.---].|yd.b qrb[.---].|w lk.ilm.[---].|w rgm.l [---].|b mud.ṣin[.---].|mud.ṣin[.---].|iṯm.mui[-.---]. 5[67].3.21
.yṯb.b hkl.|w ywsrnn.ggn h.|lk.l ab k.yṣb.lk.|l[ab]k.w rgm.‘ny.|l k[rt.adn k.]ištm[‘].|w tqǵ[.udn.k ǵz.ǵzm].|tdb 16.6[127].28
ryl.p rgm.|l mlk.šm y.|w l h[-] y‘l m.|bn y.yšal.|ṯryl.w rgm.|ṯṯb.l aẖ k.|l adn k. 138.17
.|hl ny.‘m n[y].|kll.šlm.|ṯm ny.‘m.um y.|mnm.šlm.|w.rgm.ṯṯb.l y.|bm.ṯy.ndr.|iṯt.‘mn.mlkt.|w.rgm y.l[--].|lqt. 50[117].13
y.‘m n[.š]lm.|w.ṯm [ny.‘m.mlkt.u]m y.|mnm[.šlm].|w.rgm[.ṯṯb.l] y.|hl ny.‘mn.|mlk.b.ṯy ndr.|iṯt.w.ht.|[-]sny.u 1013.11
.‘m y.ht.‘m[ny].|kll.šlm.ṯm ny.|‘m.um y.mnm.šlm.|w.rgm.ṯṯb.l y.|w.mnd‘.k.ank.|aḥš.mǵy.mnd‘.|k.igr.w.u.[--] 2009.1.9
]y.hnn.|[---.kll].šlm.|[---.ṯ]mn.‘m k.|[m]nm.šlm.|[---.w.r]gm.ṯṯb. 2171.5
l mlk.šm y.|w l h.y‘l m.|w h[t] aẖ y.|bn y.yšal.|ṯryl.w rgm[.-].|ṯṯb.l aẖ k.|l adn k. 138.17
ank.n[--]n[.---].|kst.l[--.---].|w.hw.uy.‘n[--.---].|l ytn.w rgm[.---].|w yrdnn.an[--.---].|[---].ank.l km[.---].|l y.ank. 54.1.14[13.1.11]
y.|[---.]ṯm.hw.i[--]ty.|[---].ib‘r.a[--.]ḏmr.|[---.]w mlk.w rg[m.---].|[--.rg]m.ank.[b]‘r.[--]ny.|[--]n.bt k.[---.]b‘[r.---] 1002.53
l n‘m.|[---.]w rm ṯlbm ṯlb.|[---.-]pr l n‘m.|[---.-]mt w rm tp h.|[---.-]ḥb l n‘m.|[---.]ymǵy.|[---.]rm ṯlbm.|[---.--] UG5.5.5
[---.]w rm tp h.|[---.-]lu mm l n‘m.|[---.]w rm ṯlbm ṯlb.|[---.-]pr UG5.5.1
[---.]w rm tp h.|[---.-]lu mm l n‘m.|[---.]w rm ṯlbm ṯlb.|[---.-]pr l n‘m.|[---.-]mt w rm tp h.|[---.-]ḥb UG5.5.3
lqḥ.š‘rt.|urẖ.ln.kkrm.|w.rḥd.kd.šmn.|drt.b.kkr.|ubn.ẖṣḥ.kkr.|kkr.lqḥ.ršpy.|tmtr 1118.3
b|[--.---.]al.yns.|[---.]ysd k.|[---.--]r.dr.dr.|[---.--]y k.w rḥd.|[---]y ilm.d mlk.|y[ṯ]b.aliyn.b‘l.|yt‘dd.rkb.‘rpt.|[--]. 4[51].3.8
l [----].|w l [---].|kd.[---].|kd.t[---.ym.ymm].|y‘tqn.w[rḥm.‘nt].|tngṯ h.k lb.a[rẖ].|l ‘gl h.k lb.ṯa[t].|l imr h.km. 6[49].2.5
n.|šb‘ d.yrgm.‘l.‘d.w ‘rbm.t‘nyn.|w šd.šd ilm.šd aṯrt.w rḥm.|‘l.išt.šb‘ d.ǵzrm.ṭb.[g]d.b ḥlb.annẖ b ẖmat.|w ‘l.ag 23[52].13
.šlm.‘rbm.ṯn[nm].|hlkm.b dbḥ n‘mt.|šd[.i]lm.šd.aṯrt.w rḥmy.|[---].y[ṯ]b.|[---]p.gp ym.w yṣǵd.gp..thm.|[yqḥ.]il. 23[52].28
aṯt.l pnn h.|št.alp.qdm h.mria.w tk.|pn h.tḥspn.m h.w trḥṣ.|ṭl.šmm.šmn.arṣ.ṭl.šm[m.t]sk h.|rbb.nsk h.kbkbm.| 3[‘NT].4.86
l ksat.ṯlḥnt.|[l.]ṯlḥn.hdmm.ṯṯ‘r.l hdmm.|[t]ḥspn.m h.w trḥṣ.|[ṭ]l.šmm.šmn.arṣ.rbb.|[r]kb ‘rpt.ṭl.šmm.tsk h.|[rb] 3[‘NT].2.38
kdrš.w.r‘ h.|ṯrm[-].w[.r‘ h].|[‘]ṯtr[-].w.[r‘ h].|ẖlly[-].w.r‘[h].|ilmškl.w.r‘[h].|ššw[.--].w.r[‘ h].|kr[mn.--.]w.r[‘ h 2083.2.1
l.w.r‘[h].|ššw[.--].w.r[‘ h].|kr[mn.--.]w.r[‘ h].|šd.[--.w.]r[‘ h].|ẖla[n.---].|w lšṭr[.---]. 2083.2.5
h.|ǵlwš.w.r‘ h.|kdrš.w.r‘ h.|ṯrm[-].w[.r‘ h].|[‘]ṯtr[-].w.[r‘ h].|ẖlly[-].w.r‘[h].|ilmškl.w.r‘[h].|ššw[.--].w.r[‘ h].| 2083.1.7

ẖrny.w.r‘ h. | klbr.w.r‘ h. | tškrǵ.w.r‘ h. | ǵlwš.w.r‘ h. | kdrš.w.r‘ h. | ṯrm[-].w[.r‘ h]. | [‘]ṯtr[-].w.[r‘ h]. | ẖlly[-] 2083.1.4
ẖrny.w.r‘ h. | klbr.w.r‘ h. | tškrǵ.w.r‘ h. | ǵlwš.w.r‘ h. | kdrš.w.r‘ h. | 2083.1.1
r[-].w.[r‘ h]. | ẖlly[-].w.r‘[h]. | ilmškl.w.r‘[h]. | ššw[.--].w.r[‘ h]. | kr[mn.--.]w.r[‘ h]. | šd.[--.w.]r[‘ h]. | ẖla[n.---]. | w lšṯ 2083.2.3
[-].w[.r‘ h]. | [‘]ṯtr[-].w.[r‘ h]. | ẖlly[-].w.r‘[h]. | ilmškl.w.r‘[h]. | ššw[.--].w.r[‘ h]. | kr[mn.--.]w.r[‘ h]. | šd.[--.w.]r[‘ h] 2083.2.2
w.r‘ h. | tškrǵ.w.r‘ h. | ǵlwš.w.r‘ h. | kdrš.w.r‘ h. | ṯrm[-].w[.r‘ h]. | [‘]ṯtr[-].w.[r‘ h]. | ẖlly[-].w.r‘[h]. | ilmškl.w.r‘[h]. | š 2083.1.6
ẖrny.w.r‘ h. | klbr.w.r‘ h. | tškrǵ.w.r‘ h. | ǵlwš.w.r‘ h. | kdrš.w.r‘ h. | ṯrm[-].w[.r‘ h]. | [‘]ṯtr[-].w. 2083.1.3
.w.r‘[h]. | ilmškl.w.r‘[h]. | ššw[.--].w.r[‘ h]. | kr[mn.--.]w.r[‘ h]. | šd.[--.w.]r[‘ h]. | ẖla[n.---]. | w lšṯr[.---]. 2083.2.4
ẖrny.w.r‘ h. | klbr.w.r‘ h. | tškrǵ.w.r‘ h. | ǵlwš.w.r‘ h. | kdrš.w.r‘ h. | ṯrm[-].w[.r‘ 2083.1.2
y.w.r‘ h. | klbr.w.r‘ h. | tškrǵ.w.r‘ h. | ǵlwš.w.r‘ h. | kdrš.w.r‘ h. | ṯrm[-].w[.r‘ h]. | [‘]ṯtr[-].w.[r‘ h]. | ẖlly[-].w.r‘[h]. | il 2083.1.5
.qdq | d zbl ym.bn.‘nm.ṯpṭ.nhr.yprsḥ ym. | w yql.l arṣ.w trtqṣ.ṣmd.b d b‘l. | [km.]nšr.b uṣb‘t h.ylm.qdqd.zbl. | [ym.] 2.4[68].23
t. | [b‘l.w]dgn[.yi]sp.ḥmt.‘nt.w ‘ṯtrt. | [ti]sp.ḥmt.y[r]ẖ.w.ršp.yisp.ḥmt. | [‘ṯ]r.w ‘ṯpr.yisp.ḥmt.ṯṯ.w kṯṯ. | [yus]p.ḥmt UG5.8.15
.mẖl[.---]. | mlk.nhr.ibr[.---]. | zbl b‘l.ǵlm.[---]. | ṣǵr hd w r[---.---]. | w l nhr nd[-.---]. | [---.--]l. 9[33].2.11
kmn.w šnm dqt. | ršp.dqt.šrp w šlmm.dqtm. | [i]lh.alp w š ilhm.gdl[t.]ilhm. | [b]‘l š.aṯrt.š.ṯkmn w šnm.š. | ‘nt.š.ršp.š 34[1].5
[ṯkmn.w šnm]. | dqt.ršp.šrp.w š[lmm.dqtm]. | ilh[.a]lp.w š[.il]hm.[gdlt.ilhm]. | b‘[l.š].aṯrt[.š.ṯkm]n w [šnm.š]. | ‘nt š 35[3].14
]. | ṯkmn.w [šnm.dqt.ršp.šrp]. | w šlmm.[dqtm.ilh.alp.w š]. | ilhm.gd[lt.ilhm.b‘l.š.aṯrt.š]. | ṯkmn.w š[nm.š.‘nt.š.ršp.š APP.II[173].15
l.ḥyr.ilib.š. | arṣ w šmm.š. | il.š.kṯrt.š. | dgn.š.b‘l.ẖlb alp w š. | b‘l ṣpn alp.w.š. | ṯrṯy.alp.w.š. | yrẖ.š.ṣpn.š. | kṯr š ‘ṯtr.š. | [UG5.9.2.4
m.l ršp.mlk. | alp w.š.l b‘lt. | bwrm š.iṯtqb. | w š.nbk m w.š. | gt mlk š.‘lm. | l kṯr.ṯn.‘lm. | tzǵ[.---.]nšm.pr. UG5.12.B.10
t ṣpn.alp. | w š.pdry š.ddmš š. | w b urbt.ilib š. | b‘l alp w š. | dgn.š.il t‘ḏr.š. | b‘l š.‘nt š.ršp š. | šlmm. | w šnpt.il š. | l ‘nt UG5.13.20
.‘šrt.riš.argmn]. | w ṯn šm.l [b‘lt.bhtm.‘ṣrm.l inš]. | ilm.w š d[d.ilš.š.--.mlk]. | yṯb.brr[.w mḥ-.---]. | ym.[‘]lm.y‘[--.---]. 35[3].6
‘šrt.riš. | arg[mn.w ṯn.]šm.l b‘lt. | bhtm.‘ṣ[rm.l in]š ilm.w š. | dd ilš.š[.---.]mlk.yṯb br | r.w mḥ[--.---.]w q[--]. | ym.‘lm. APP.II[173].6
mlk. | l ušẖ[r] ẖlmṭ. | l bbt il bt. | š l ẖlmṭ. | w tr l qlḥ. | w š ḥll ydm. | b qdš il bt. | w tlḥm aṯt. | š l ilbt.šlmm. | kll ylḥ UG5.7.TR3
kṯrt.š. | dgn.š.b‘l.ẖlb alp w š. | b‘l ṣpn alp.w.š. | ṯrṯy.alp.w.š. | yrẖ.š.ṣpn.š. | kṯr š ‘ṯtr.š. | [‘ṯ]rt.š.šgr w iṯm š. | [---.]š.ršp. UG5.9.2.6
nt.qr[t]. | w mtntm.š l rmš. | w kbd.w š.l šlm kbd. | alp.w š.l b‘l ṣpn. | dqt l ṣpn.šrp.w šlmm. | kmm.w bbt.b‘l.ugrt. | w UG5.13.9
] qrt. | [w mtmt]m.[š.l] rm[š.]kbd.w š. | [l šlm.kbd.al]p.w š.[l] b‘l.ṣpn. | [dqt.l.ṣpn.šrp].w š[l]mm.kmm. | [w bbt.b‘l.u 36[9].1.14
yrẖ ẖyr.b ym ḥdt. | alp.w š.l b‘lt bhtm. | b arb‘t ‘šrt.b‘l. | ‘rkm. | b ṯmnt.‘šrt.yr | tḥṣ.ml UG5.12.A.2
ṣin. | šb‘.alpm. | bt b‘l.ugrt.ṯn šm. | ‘lm.l ršp.mlk. | alp w.š.l b‘lt. | bwrm š.iṯtqb. | w š.nbk m w.š. | gt mlk š.‘lm. | l kṯr UG5.12.B.8
n šm l btbt. | alp.w š šrp.alp šlmm. | l b‘l.‘ṣr l ṣpn. | npš.w.š.l ršp bbt. | [‘]ṣrm l h.ršp [-]m. | [---.]bqt[-]. | [b] ǵb.ršp mh UG5.12.A.11
rt.l b‘[l]. | dqtm.w ynt.qr[t]. | w mtntm.š l rmš. | w kbd.w š.l šlm kbd. | alp.w š.l b‘l ṣpn. | dqt l ṣpn.šrp.w šlmm. | km UG5.13.8
l.ṣ]pn.[dq]tm.w y[nt] qrt. | [w mtmt]m.[š.l] rm[š.]kbd.w š. | [l šlm.kbd.al]p.w š.[l] b‘l.ṣpn. | [dqt.l.ṣpn.šrp].w š[l]mm 36[9].1.13
[.---.]d[--]. | l ṣpn[.---.-]lu. | ilib[.---.b]‘l. | ugrt[.---.--]n. | [w] š l [---]. UG5.13.37
r[š]p.ḥgb.ap. | w[.n]pš.ksp. | w ẖrṣ.km[-]. | w.ḥ[--.-]lp. | w.š.l[--]p. | w[.--.-]nš. | i[--.---]. | w[.---]. | k[--.---]. | tql[.---]. 2005.1.6
rt.ṯn šm. | ‘lm.l ršp.mlk. | alp w.š.l b‘lt. | bwrm š.iṯtqb. | w š.nbk m w.š. | gt mlk š.‘lm. | l kṯr.ṯn.‘lm. | tzǵ[.---.]nšm.pr. UG5.12.B.10
spr[.---]. | ybnil[.---.]kd yn.w š. | spr.m[--]. | spr d[---]b.w š. | tt.ẖmš.[---]. | skn.ul[m.---]. | [1093.2
.w šlmm ilib š. | b‘l ugrt š.b‘l ẖlb š. | yrẖ š.‘nt ṣpn.alp. | w š.pdry š.ddmš š. | w b urbt.ilib š. | b‘l alp w š. | dgn.š.il t‘ḏr. UG5.13.18
b‘l.ugrt. | w kdm.w npš ilib. | gdlt.il š.b‘l š.‘nt. | ṣpn.alp.w š.pdry.š. | šrp.w šlmm ilib š. | b‘l ugrt š.b‘l ẖlb š. | yrẖ š.‘nt UG5.13.14
prgl.ṣqrn.b.gg. | ar[b‘.]arb‘.mṯbt.azmr.b h.š.šr[-]. | al[p.w].š.šlmm.pamt.šb‘.klb h. | yr[--.]mlk.ṣbu.špš.w.ḥl.mlk. | w.[35[3].52
‘lm.tzǵ.b ǵb.ṣpn. | nḥkt.ksp.w ẖrṣ ṭ‘ ṯn šm l btbt. | alp.w š šrp.alp šlmm. | l b‘l.‘ṣr l ṣpn. | npš.w.š.l ršp bbt. | [‘]ṣrm l UG5.12.A.9
.il š. | l ‘nt.ḥl š.ṯn šm. | l gṯrm.ǵṣ b šmal. | d alpm.w alp w š. | šrp.w šlmm kmm. | l b‘l.ṣpn b ‘r‘r. | pamt ṯlṯm š l qrnt. | UG5.13.27
spr[.---]. | ybnil[.---.]kd yn.w š. | spr.m[--]. | spr d[---]b.w š. | tt.ẖmš.[---]. | skn.ul[m.---]. | [---]š.[---]. | [---]y[.---]. | sk[n. 1093.4
šmm.š. | il.š.kṯrt.š. | dgn.š.b‘l.ẖlb alp w š. | b‘l ṣpn alp.w.š. | ṯrṯy.alp.w.š. | yrẖ.š.ṣpn.š. | kṯr š ‘ṯtr.š. | [‘ṯ]rt.š.šgr w iṯm UG5.9.2.5
.---]. | [---]š.[---]. | [---]y[.---]. | sk[n.---]. | u[---.]w š. | [---].w š. | [--]b.šd.[---]. | [--]kz[--]. 1093.11
.ṣp[n.---]. | il.alp.w š[.---]. | b‘lm.alp.w š[.---]. | b‘lm.alp.w š[.---]. | arṣ.w šmm.š.kṯr[t] š.yrẖ[.---]. | ṣpn.š.kṯr.š.pdry.š.ǵ UG5.9.1.4
dbḥ.ṣp[n.---]. | il.alp.w š[.---]. | b‘lm.alp.w š[.---]. | b‘lm.alp.w š[.---]. | arṣ.w šmm.š. UG5.9.1.2
dbḥ.ṣp[n.---]. | il.alp.w š[.---]. | b‘lm.alp.w š[.---]. | b‘lm.alp.w š[.---]. | arṣ.w šmm.š.kṯr[t] š.yrẖ[.---]. | ṣ UG5.9.1.3
skn.ul[m.---]. | [---]š.[---]. | [---]y[.---]. | sk[n.---]. | u[---.]w š. | [---].w š. | [--]b.šd.[---]. | [--]kz[--]. 1093.10
pš[.w y]rẖ.l gṯr.ṯn. | [tql.ksp].ṯb.ap.w npš. | [---].bt.alp w š. | [---.--]m.l gṯrm. | [---.]l ‘nt m. | [---.--]rm.d krm. | [---].l ‘ 33[5].16
k ymǵy.adn. | ilm.rbm ‘m dtn. | w yšal.mṯpṭ.yld. | w y‘ny.nn[.--]. | t‘ny.n[---.-]ṯq. | w š[--.---]. | UG5.6.3
--].šḥr.[---]. | [---].al yṯb‘[.--]. | [---.]l adn.ḥwt[.--]. | [--]h.w yššil[.--]. | [---.]lp[--]. 1023.5
. | širm.šd.khn. | ṯlṯ.šd.w.krm.šir.d.ḥli. | širm.šd.šd.‘šy. | w.šir.šd.krm. | d.krwn. | šir.šd.šd.‘šy. | d.abmn. | šir.šd.krm. | d 1079.8
. | [--.-]n.w.aẖt h.arb‘m. | [--.-]dn.‘šrm. | [--.-]dwn.ṯlṯm.w.šb‘.alpm. | [kṯ]rmlk.‘šrm. | [--]ny.‘šrt.trbyt. | [--.]‘bd.ṯlṯm. | [2054.2.23
| adt y. | rgm. | ṯḥm.tlmyn. | ‘bd k. | l.p‘n. | adt y. | šb‘ d. | w.šb‘ id. | mrḥqtm. | qlt. | ‘m.adt y. | mnm.šlm. | rgm.ṯṯb. | l.‘b 52[89].9
m]. | ṯḥm.rb.mi[--.‘]bd k. | l.p‘n.b‘l y[.mrḥqtm]. | šb‘ d.w.šb‘[d.qlt]. | ankn.rgmt.l.b‘l y. | l.špš.‘lm.l.‘ṯtrt. | l.‘nt.l.kl.il. 2008.1.5
kt. | adt y.rgm. | ṯḥm.illḏr. | ‘bd k.. | l.p‘n a[dt y]. | šb‘ d[.w šb‘ d]. | mrḥq[tm.qlt]. | mn[m.šlm]. 1014.6
.drt.w.ṯṯm.dd. | ḥpr.bnšm. | b.gt.knpy.mit.dr‘.ṯṯm.drt.w.šb‘m.dd.arb‘. | kbd.ḥpr.bnšm. | b.gt.ṯrmn.arb‘m.dr‘.w.‘šrm 1098.18
dd.ṯṯ.kbd.ḥpr.bnšm. | b.gt.ḥdṯt.arb‘m.dr‘.w.ṯlṯm.drt. | [w].šb‘m.dd.ṯn.kbd.ḥpr.bnšm. | b.nzl.‘šrm.l.mit.dr‘.w.šb‘m.d 1098.23
t. | [w].šb‘m.dd.ṯn.kbd.ḥpr.bnšm. | b.nzl.‘šrm.l.mit.dr‘.w.šb‘m.drt. | w.‘šrm.l.mit.dd.ḥpr.bnšm. | b.y‘ny.arb‘m.dr‘.w. 1098.24
[---.---.]l.mit.dr‘.w.šb‘m.drt. | [---.ḥpr.]bnšm.w.l.ḥrš.‘rq.ṯn.‘šr h. | [---.d]r‘.w.m 1098.1
. | ‘šr.mkrm. | ẖmš.ṯrtnm. | ẖmš.bn.mrynm. | ‘šr.mrum.w.šb‘.ẖsnm. | tš‘m.mdrǵlm. | arb‘.l ‘šrm.ẖsnm. | ‘šr.hbṭnm. | ṯṯ 1030.6
tš‘.ṯnnm. | w.arb‘.ẖsnm. | ‘šr.mrum. | w.šb‘.ẖsnm. | tš‘.‘šr. | mrynm. | ṯlṯ.‘šr.mkrm. | ṯlṯ.bn.mrynm. | 1029.4
šb‘.ṯnnm.w.šb‘.ẖsnm. | ṯmn.‘šr h.mrynm. | ‘šr.mkrm. | ẖmš.ṯrtnm. | ẖm 1030.1
. | arb‘.ṯrtnm. | tš‘.ẖbṭnm. | ṯmnym.ṯlṯ.kbd. | mdrǵlm. | w.šb‘.‘šr.ẖsnm. | ẖmšm.l.mit. | bnš.l.d. | yškb.l.b.bt.mlk. 1029.13
.tqlm.kbd.arb‘m. | ‘šrt.ẖrṣ.b.arb‘m. | mit.ẖršḫ.b.tqlm. | w.šb‘.‘šr.šmn. | d.l.yṣa.bt.mlk. | tgmr.ksp.mitm. | ẖmšm.kbd. 2100.20
---]. | annt[n.]w[.---]. | w.ṯn.bn h.[---]. | aǵltn.ypr[y.---]. | w.šb‘.ṣin h[.---]. 2044.18

[n].|b.gt.trǵnds.|tš'.'šr.[dd].kšmm.|tn.'šr[.dd.ḥ]tm.|w.šb['.---]. 2092.18
.w.agytn.|[---] gnym.|[--]ry.w ary.|[---]ǵrbtym.|[---.]w šb'l.|[---.-]ym.|[---.--]ḫm.|[---.--]m.|[---]nb.w ykn.|[--]nd 131[309].16
.ydln.|[š].bn.trn.b d.ibrmd̠.|[š]d.bn.iltmr.b d.tbbr.|[w.]šd.nḥl h.b d.ttmd.|[š]d.b d.iwrḫt.|[tn].šdm.b d.gmrd.|[š 82[300].1.12
yšql.šdmt h.|km gpn.|šb' d.yrgm.'l.'d.w 'rbm.t'nyn.|w šd.šd ilm.šd atrt.w rḥm.|'l.išt.šb' d.ǵzrm.tb.[g]d.b ḥlb.an 23[52].13
pt].|tḥbq.[---].|tḥbq[.---].|w tksynn.btn[-.]|y[--.]šr h.w šḫp h.|[--.]šḫp.ṣǵrt h.|yrk.t'l.b ǵr.|mslmt.b ǵr.tliyt.|w t'l 10[76].3.26
h.|km trpa.hn n'r.|d yšt.l.lṣb h ḫš'r klb.|[w]riš.pqq.w šr h.|yšt.aḥd h.dm zt.ḫrpnt. UG5.1.2.5
r.yrḫm.|k b'l.k yḥwy.y'šr.ḥwy.y'š.|r.w yšqyn h.ybd.w yšr.'l h.|n'm[n.w t]'nynn.ap ank.aḥwy.|aqht[.ǵz]r.w y'n. 17[2AQHT].6.31
.atrt.alp.|kd.yqḥ.b ḫmr.|rbt.ymsk.b msk h.|qm.ybd.w yšr.|mṣltm.bd.n'm.|yšr.ǵzr.tb.ql.|'l.b'l.b ṣrrt.|ṣpn.ytmr. 3['NT].1.18
h].|w.yṣq[.b.ap h].|k.yiḫd[.akl.ššw].|št.mkš[r.grn].|w.št.ašk[rr].|w.pr.ḥd̠r[t.ydk].|aḥd h.w.yṣq[.b.ap h].|k.yiḫd 161[56].14
k aḥd h w yṣq b ap h.|[k.yiḫd akl s]šw št mkšr grn.|[w št aškrr w p]r ḥd̠rt.|[-----].|[---.-]n[-].|[k yraš ššw št bln 160[55].11
tl[.---].|mǵm[ǵ.---].|w.š[t.nni.w.pr.'bk].|w.pr[.ḥd̠rt.w.št].|irǵ[n.ḥmr.ydk].|aḥd[h.w.yṣq.b.ap h].|k yr[a]š.ššw. 161[56].29
[---.-]tq.|w š[--.---].|ḥdt[.---.]ḥ[--].|b bt.[-.]l bnt.q[-].|w št.b bt.tap[.--].|hy.yd h.w ym[ǵ].|mlak k.'m dt[n].|lqḥ. UG5.6.9
'z.mid.|hm.ntkp.|m'n k.|w.mnm.|rgm.d.tšm'.|tmt.w.št.|b.spr.'m y. 53[54].18
.a[--.--]y.|w.spr.in[.-.]'d m.|spr n.tḥr[.--].|atr.it.bqt.|w.štn.l y. 2060.35
.ššw.---].|dprn[.---].|dr'.[---].|tmtl[.---].|mǵm[ǵ.---].|w.š[t.nni.w.pr.'bk].|w.pr[.ḥd̠rt.w.št].|irǵ[n.ḥmr.ydk].|aḥd[161[56].28
].|w.y[ṣq.b.ap h].|k.l.ḫ[ru.w.l.yttn.ššw].|mss.[št.qlql.w.št].|'rgz[.ydk.aḥd h].|w.yṣq[.b.ap h].|k.yiḫd[.akl.ššw].|š 161[56].9
aḥd h w yṣq b ap h.|[k l yḫru w]l yttn mss št qlql.|[w št 'rgz y]dk aḥd h w yṣq b ap h.|[k.yiḫd akl s]šw št mkšr 160[55].9
p.hn.ib.d.b.mgšḫ.|[---.i]b.hn[.w.]ht.ank.|[---.--]š[-.--].w.ašt.|[---].amr k.|[---].k.ybt.mlk.|[---].w.ap.ank.|[---].l.ǵr. 1012.12
rnmy.]uzr.ilm.ylḥm.|[uzr.yšqy.]bn.qdš.yd.|[ṣt h.y'l.]w yškb.yd.|[mizrt.]p ynl.hn.ym.|[w tn.uzr.]ilm.dnil.|[uzr.i 17[2AQHT].1.5
lm.ylḥm.|[uzr.]yšqy.bn qdš.yd.ṣt h.|[dn]il.yd.ṣt h.y'l.w yškb.|[yd.]mizrt.p yln.mk.b šb'.ymm.|[w]yqrb.b'l.b ḥnt 17[2AQHT].1.15
mtt h.|bm.bky h.w yšn.|b dm' h.nhmmt.|šnt.tluan.|w yškb.nhmmt.|w yqmṣ.w b ḥlm h.|il.yrd.b d̠hrt h.|ab ad 14[KRT].1.34
b pid.|tb.bn y.lm tb[t] km.|l kht.zbl k[m.a]nk.|iḥtrš.w [a]škn.|aškn.ydt.[m]rṣ gršt.|zbln.r[---].ymlu.|n'm.[-]t[-.- 16[126].5.26
l.d̠rdn.|b'l y.rgm.|bn.ḫrn k.|mǵy.|hbt.hw.|ḫrd.w.šl hw.|qr[-].|akl n.b.grnt.|l.b'r.|ap.krmm.|ḫlq.|qrt n.ḫl 2114.6
.g h.]w tṣḥ.šm'.m'.|[l aqht.ǵzr.i]rš.ksp.w atn k.|[ḫrṣ.w aš]lḥ k.w tn.qšt k.[l].|['nt.tq]ḥ[.q]ṣ't k.ybmt.limm.|w y'n 17[2AQHT].6.18
.btlt.|'nt.irš ḥym.l aqht.ǵzr.|irš ḥym.w atn k.bl mt.|w ašlḥ k.ašspr k.'m.b'l.|šnt.'m.bn il.tspr.yrḫm.|k b'l.k yḥw 17[2AQHT].6.28
.ḥmt.mlk.b 'ttrt.yisp.ḥmt.|[kt]r w ḫss.y[i]sp.ḥmt.šḥr.w šlm.|[yis]p.ḥmt.isp.[šp]š l hrm.ǵrpl.'l arṣ.|[l a]n ḥmt.l p[. UG5.8.18
š.špš.š.arṣy.š.'ttrt.š.|ušḫry.š.il.t'd̠r.b'l.š.ršp.š.ddmš.š.|w šlmm.ilib.š.i[l.--]m d gbl.ṣpn.al[p].|pḫr.ilm.š.ym.š[.k]nr.š UG5.9.1.10
.w npš ilib.|gdlt.il š.b'l š.'nt.|ṣpn.alp.w š.pdry.š.|šrp.w šlmm ilib š.|b'l ugrt š.b'l ḫlb š.|yrḫ š.'nt ṣpn.alp.|w š.pd UG5.13.15
bd.alp.š.l il.|gdlt.ilhm.tkmn.w šnm dqt.|ršp.dqt.šrp w šlmm.dqtm.|[i]lh.alp w š ilhm.gdl[t.]ilhm.|[b]'l š.atrt.š.t 34[1].4
]|[rm.---.ytk.gdlt.ilhm].|tkmn.w [šnm.dqt.ršp.šrp].|w šlmm.[dqtm.ilh.alp.w š].|ilhm.gd[lt.ilhm.b'l.š.atrt.š].|tk APP.II[173].15
bu[rm.---].|ytk.gdlt.ilhm.[tkmn.w šnm].|dqt.ršp.šrp.w š[lmm.dqtm].|ilh[.a]lp.w š[.il]hm.[gdlt.ilhm].|b'[l.š].atrt 35[3].13
bd.w š.|[l šlm.kbd.al]p.w š.[l] b'l.ṣpn.|[dqt.l.ṣpn.šrp].w š[l]mm.kmm.|[w bbt.b'l.ugrt.]kdm.w npš.|[ilib.gdlt.il.š.b 36[9].1.15
w kbd.w š.l šlm kbd.|alp.w š.l b'l ṣpn.|dqt l ṣpn.šrp.w šlmm.|kmm.w bbt.b'l.ugrt.|w kdm.w npš ilib.|gdlt.il š.b UG5.13.10
t.ḥl š.tn šm.|l gtrm.ǵṣ b šmal.|d alpm.w alp w š.|šrp.w šlmm kmm.|l b'l.ṣpn b 'r'r.|pamt tltm š l qrnt.|tlḥn.b'lt. UG5.13.28
a.|yrḫ mkty.|tkmn w šnm.|ktr w ḫss.|'ttr 'ttpr.|šḥr w šlm.|ngh w srr.|'dw šr.|ṣdqm šr.|ḥnbn il d[n].|[-]bd w [UG5.10.1.11
.šḥr.w šlm.rgm.l il.ybl.a[tt y].|il.ylt.mh.ylt.yld y.šḥr.w šl[m].|šu.'db.l špš.rbt.w l kbkbm.kn[-].|yhbr.špt hm.yšq. 23[52].53
n[.--].|bm.nšq.w hr.b ḥbq.ḥmḥmt.tqt[nṣn].|tldn.šḥr.w šlm.rgm.l il.ybl.a[tt y].|il.ylt.mh.ylt.yld y.šḥr.w šl[m].|šu 23[52].52
'db ksa.|w ytb.|tqru l špš.um h.špš.um.ql bl 'm.|šḥr.w šlm šmm h mnt.ntk.nḥš.|šmrr.nḥš 'q šr.ln h.mlḫš.|abd.l UG5.7.52
tm].|'š[rm.]l inš[.ilm.---].|il[hm.]dqt.š[.---.rš]|[p.š]rp.w šl[mm.--.dqt].|[i]lh.gdlt[.ilhm.gdlt.il].|[d]qt.tkmn.w [šn 35[3].29
-.i]l š.b'l š.atrt.š.ym š.[b']l knp.|[---.g]dlt.ṣpn.dqt.šrp.w [š]lmm.|[---.a]lp.l b'l.w atrt.'ṣr[m] l inš.|[ilm.---].lbbmm. 36[9].1.7
']ṣrm l [inš.ilm].|[---.]ilh[m.dqt.š.--].|[---.--]t.r[šp.šrp.w šl]|[mm.---].dq[t.ilh.gdlt].|n.w šnm.dqt[.---].|[i]lh[m.gd] APP.II[173].31
[-----].|yṣq.šm[n.---].|'n.tr.arṣ.w šmm.|sb.l qṣm.arṣ.|l ksm.mhyt.'n.|l arṣ.m[t]r.b'l.|w l šd 16[126].3.2
-.---].|kt.zrw.kt.nbt.d̠nt.w [-]n[-.---].|il.ḫyr.ilib.š.|arṣ w šmm.š.|il.š.ktrt.š.|dgn.š.b'l.ḫlb alp w š.|b'l ṣpn alp.w.š.| UG5.9.2.2
lp.w š[.---].|b'lm.alp.w š[.---].|b'lm.alp.w š[.---].|arṣ.w šmm.š.ktr[t] š.yrḫ[.---].|ṣpn.š.ktr.š.pdry.š.ǵrm.š[.---].|atr UG5.9.1.5
.|b'lm.|[b']lm.|[b']lm.|[b']lm.|[b']lm.|[b'l]m.|[arṣ] w šm[m].|[-----].|[a]rṣ.|[u]šḫr[y].|[']ttrt.|i[l t]'d̠r b'l.|ršp.| 29[17].1.12
ḫpn.d.iqni.w.šmt.|l.iyb'l.|tltm.l.mit.š'rt.|l.šr.'ttrt.|mlbš.trmnm.|k.yt 1107.1
w l.a[--]t.tšknn.|ḫmšm.l mi[t].any.|tškn[n.--]h.k[--].|w šnm[.--.]w[.--].|w 'prm.a[--.--]n.|[--.]ḥ[--.]d[--]t.|[---.]ḥw[2062.1.6
'nt.hlkt.w.šnwt.|tp.aḫ.h.k.ysmsm.|tspi.šir.h.l.bl.ḥrb.|tšt.dm.h.l.bl. RS225.1
il b[n] il.|dr bn il.|mpḫrt bn il.|trmn w šnm.|il w atrt.|ḫnn il.|nṣbt il.|šlm il.|il ḥš il add.|b'l ṣp 30[107].4
t.t'm.dqt.t'm.|mtntm nkbd.alp.š.l il.|gdlt.ilhm.tkmn.w šnm dqt.|ršp.dqt.šrp w šlmm.dqtm.|[i]lh.alp w š ilhm.g 34[1].3
---.--]n[.w alp.l il.w bu]|[rm.---.ytk.gdlt.ilhm].|tkmn.w [šnm.dqt.ršp.šrp].|w šlmm.[dqtm.ilh.alp.w š].|ilhm.gd[lt APP.II[173].14
.y[---].|w al[p.l]il.w bu[rm.---].|ytk.gdlt.ilhm.[tkmn.w šnm].|dqt.ršp.šrp.w š[lmm.dqtm].|ilh[.a]lp.w š[.il]hm.[g 35[3].12
.w šl[mm.--.dqt].|[i]lh.gdlt[.ilhm.gdlt.il].|[d]qt.tkmn.w [šnm.dqt.--].|[--]t.dqtm.[b nbk.---].|[--.k]mm.gdlt.l.b['l.-- 35[3].31
.š.--].|[---.--]t.r[šp.šrp.w šl]|[mm.---].dq[t.ilh.gdlt].|n.w šnm.dqt[.---].|[i]lh[m.gd]lt.i[l.dqt.tkm]|n.w šnm.dqt[.---] APP.II[173].34
.gdlt].|n.w šnm.dqt[.---].|[i]lh[m.gd]lt.i[l.dqt.tkm]|n.w šnm.dqt[.---].|bqtm.b nbk.[---].|kmm.gdlt.l b['l.--.dqt].|l APP.II[173].34
t.y[t]ši.l ab.bn.il.ytši.l dr.|bn il.l mpḫrt.bn.il.l tkmn[.w]šnm.hn.'r.|w.tb.l mspr.m[šr] mšr.bt.ugrt.w npy.gr.|ḥm 32[2].1.26
.ytši.l ab bn il.|ytši.l d[r.bn il.l]mpḫrt.bn il.|l tkm[n.w šnm.]hn '[r].|[---.]w npy[.---].|[---.]w npy.u[grt.---].|[---.- 32[2].1.35
]t.ytši[.l ab.bn.il].|ytši.l dr.bn.il.l mpḫrt.bn.i[l.l tkmn.w š]nm hn š.|w šqrb.'r.mšr mšr bn.ugrt.w [npy.---.]ugr.|w 32[2].1.17
t.ytši.l ab.bn.il.ytši.l d]r.bn[.il].|[l mpḫrt.bn.il.l tkmn.w šnm.hn š].|[w šqrb.š.mšr mšr.bn.ugrt.w npy.---.]w npy.| 32[2].1.3
]yt[ši.l ab.bn.il].|[ytši.l dr.bn.il.l mpḫ]rt.[bn.il.l tkmn.w šn]m hn š.|[---.w n]py.gr[.ḥmyt.ugrt.w np]y.|[---].w n[py 32[2].1.9B
trt.'d škr.|il.hlk.l bt h.yštql.|l ḥtr h.y'msn.nn.tkmn.|w šnm.w ngšnn.ḥby.|b'l.qrnm w d̠nb.ylšn.|b ḫri h.w tnt h. UG5.1.1.19
r.|dgn.w b'l.|'t w kmt.|yrḫ w ksa.|yrḫ mkty.|tkmn w šnm.|ktr w ḫss.|'ttr 'ttpr.|šḥr w šlm.|ngh w srr.|'dw šr. UG5.10.1.8
tm.|[i]lh.alp w š ilhm.gdl[t.]ilhm.|[b]'l š.atrt.š.tkmn w šnm.š.|'nt.š.ršp.š.dr il w p[ḫ]r b'l.|gdlt.šlm.gdlt.w burm. 34[1].6

dqtm.ilh.alp.w š]. | ilhm.gd[lt.ilhm.b'l.š.atrt.š]. | ṯkmn.w š[nm.š.'nt.š.ršp.š.dr]. | il.w pẖr[.b'l.gdlt.šlm.gdlt]. | w bur APP.II[173].17
. | ilh[.a]lp.w š[.il]hm.[gdlt.ilhm]. | b'[l.š].aṯrt[.š.ṯkm]n w [šnm.š]. | 'nt š ršp š[.dr.il.w pẖr.b'l]. | gdlt.šlm[.gdlt.w bur 35[3].15
.ap. | [k]rt.bnm.il.špḥ. | lṯpn.w qdš.'l. | ab h.y'rb.ybky. | w yšnn.ytn.g h. | bky.b ḥy k.ab n.ašmẖ. | b l.mt k.ngln.k klb. 16.1[125].13
m h.šb'[.---]. | ġzr.ilḥu.t[---]l. | trm.ṯṣr.trm[.']tqt. | tbky.w tšnn.[tt]n. | g h.bky.b ḥ[y k.a]b n. | nšmẖ.b l.mt k.ngln. | k 16.2[125].97
š. | b'l alp w š. | dgn.š.il t'ḏr.š. | b'l š.'nt š.ršp š. | šlmm. | w šnpt.il š. | l 'nt.ḥl š.ṯn šm. | l gṯrm.ġṣ b šmal. | d alpm.w alp UG5.13.24
. | tġr.tšl[m] k. | [-----]. | [-----]. | [--].bt.gb[-.--]. | [--]k[-].w.špš. | [---.b].ṣp[n]. | [---.]š[--]. | [-----]. | [-----]. | [---.]tty. | [---.-] 2159.9
.w lb h. | [ṯ]n.p k.b ġr.ṯn.p k.b ẖlb.k tgwln.šnt k. | [--.]w špt k.l tššy.hm.tqrm.l mt.b rn k. | [--]ẖp.an.arnn.ql.špš.ḥ 1001.1.5
.rpi.ap.hn.ġzr.mt. | hrnmy.alp.yṯbẖ.l kṯ | rt.yšlḥm.kṯrt.w y | ššq.bnt.[hl]l.snnt. | hn.ym.w ṯn.yšlḥm. | kṯrt.w yš[š]q.bn 17[2AQHT].2.30
| kṯrt.w yš[š]q.bnt.hl[l]. | snnt.ṯlṯ[.r]b' ym.yšl | ḥm kṯrt.w yššq. | bnt hll.snnt.ḫmš. | ṯdṯ.ym.yšlḥm.k[ṯ]rt. | w y[ššq].bn 17[2AQHT].2.35
kṯrt.w yššq. | bnt hll.snnt.ḫmš. | ṯdṯ.ym.yšlḥm.k[ṯ]rt. | w y[ššq].bnt.hll.snnt. | mk.b šb['.]ymm.tb'.b bt h. | kṯrt.bnt.h 17[2AQHT].2.38
.kṯrt.w y | ššq.bnt.[hl]l.snnt. | hn.ym.w ṯn.yšlḥm. | kṯrt.w yš[š]q.bnt.hl[l]. | snnt.ṯlṯ[.r]b' ym.yšl | ḥm kṯrt.w yššq. | bnt 17[2AQHT].2.33
| šnt.'m.bn il.tspr.yrḫm. | k b'l.k yḥwy.y'šr.ḥwy.y'š. | r.w yšqyn h.ybd.w yšr.'l h. | n'm[n.w ṯ]'nynn.ap ank.aḥwy. | a 17[2AQHT].6.31
n h. | ybrd.ṯd.l pnw h. | b ḥrb.mlḥt. | qṣ.mri.ndd. | y'šr.w yšqyn h. | ytn.ks.b d h. | krpn.b klat.yd h. | b krb.'ẓm.ridn. 3['NT].1.9
.qḥn.w tšqyn.yn.qḥ. | ks.b d y.qb't.b ymn y[.t]q | ḥ.pġt.w tšqyn h.tq[ḥ.ks.]b d h. | qb't.b ymn h.w y'n.yṯ[p]n[.mh]r. | 19[1AQHT].4.217
bat.b ḏd k.[pġt]. | bat.b hlm w y'n.yṯpn[.mhr]. | šṯ.qḥn.w tšqyn.yn.qḥ. | ks.b d y.qb't.b ymn y[.t]q | ḥ.pġt.w tšqyn h.t 19[1AQHT].4.215
m.ysyn h.'dtm.y'dyn h.yb | ltm.ybln h.mġy.ḥrn.l bt h.w. | yštql.l ḥṭr h.tlu ḥt.km.nḫl. | tplg.km.plg. | b'd h.bhtm.mn UG5.7.67
.--]an. | [---.--]m.ank. | [---.]asrm. | [---.]dbḥm. | [---.y]rḫ.w šqr. | [---.--]b.b y[--.---]. | [-----]. | [-----]. | [-----]. | [---.]mrkbt. 1002.24
ty.b ẖmr yn ay. | šlm.mlk.šlm.mlkt.'rbm m.ṯnnm. | mt.w šr.yṯb.b d h.ḥṭ.ṯkl.b d h. | ḥṭ.ulmn.yzbrnn.zbrm.gpn. | yṣm 23[52].8
bn.l h. | km.aḫ h.w šrš.km.ary h. | bl.iṯ.bn.l h.km aḫ h.w šrš. | km.ary h.uzrm.ilm.ylḥm. | uzrm.yšqy.bn.qdš. | l tbrk 17[2AQHT].1.21
nil.mt.rpi anḫ.ġzr. | [mt.]hrnmy.d in.bn.l h. | km.aḫ h.w šrš.km.ary h. | bl.iṯ.bn.l h.km aḫ h.w šrš. | km.ary h.uzrm. 17[2AQHT].1.20
nk. | w anḫn.w tnḫ.b irt y. | npš.k yld.bn.l y.km. | aḫ y.w šrš.km ary y. | nṣb.skn.ilib y.b qdš. | ztr.'m y.l 'pr.ḏmr.aṯr[17[2AQHT].2.15
['[n k. | [tlsmn.'m y.twt]ḥ.išd k. | [tk.ḫršn.---]r.[-]ḥm k.w št. | [---.]ẓ[--.-]rdy k. | [---.i]qnim. | [---.-]šu.b qrb. | [---].asr. 1['NT.IX].2.3
w 'nt.di.dit.rḫpt. | [---.-]rm.aklt.'gl.'l.mšt. | [---.--]r.špr.w yšt.il. | [---.--]n.il ġnṯ.'gl il. | [---.--]d.il.šd yṣd mlk. | [---].yšt UG5.2.1.10
špm.yd[.---.---]r. | l riš hm.w yš[--.--]m. | lḥm.b lḥm ay.w šty.b ẖmr yn ay. | šlm.mlk.šlm.mlkt.'rbm m.ṯnnm. | mt.w 23[52].6
.hm.hm[.iṯ.--.l]ḥm.w t[n]. | w nlḥm.hm.iṯ[.--.yn.w t]n.w nšt. | w 'n hm.nġr mdr'[.iṯ.lḥm.---]. | iṯ.yn.d 'rb.bṯk[.---]. | 23[52].72
prsḥ.ym.yql. | l arṣ.tngṣn.pnt h.w ydlp.tmn h. | yqṯ b'l.w yšt.ym.ykly.ṯpṭ.nhr. | b šm.tg'r m.'ṯtrt.bṯ l aliyn.[b'l.] | bṯ.l 2.4[68].27
'l.'m. | aḫ y.qran.hd.'m.ary y. | w lḥm m 'm aḫ y.lḥm. | w št m.'m.a[ḫ] yn. | p nšt.b'l.[ṭ]'n.iṭ'n k. | [---.]ma[---] k.k tm 5[67].1.25
h.l r' h. | r' 'lm. | ttn.w tn. | w l ttn. | w al ttn. | tn ks yn. | w ištn. | 'bd.prṭ.ṯḥm. | qrq.pṭ.ḏmn. | l iṯtl. 1019.1.16
nr.w ṯlb.b tp.w mṣltm.b m | rqdm.dšn.b.ḥbr.kṯr.ṭbm. | w tšt.'nt.gṯr.b'lt.mlk.b' | lt.drkt.b'lt.šmm.rmm. | [b'l]t.kpṯ.w ' UG5.2.1.6
ḥ.b bt h.mṣd.ṣd.b qrb | hkl [h].ṣḥ.l qṣ.ilm.tlḥmn. | ilm.w tštn.tštn y[n] 'd šb'. | trṯ.'d.škr.y'db.yrḫ. | gb h.km.[---.]yqṯ UG5.1.1.3
[---]n.yšt.rpu.mlk.'lm.w yšt. | [--.]gṯr.w yqr.il.yṯb.b.'ṯtrt. | il.ṯpṭ.b hd r'y.d yšr.w yḏ UG5.2.1.1
dtn. | w yšal.mṯpṭ.yld. | w y'ny.nn[.--]. | t'ny.n[---.-]tq. | w š[--.---]. | ḥdṯ[.---.]ḥ[--]. | b bt.[-.]l bnt.q[-]. | w št.b bt.ṯap[.-- UG5.6.6
ap ksp hm. | l yblt. | w ht.luk 'm ml[kt]. | tġsdb.šmlšn. | w tb' ank. | 'm mlakt h šm' h. | w b.'ly skn.yd' rgm h. | w ht a 1021.6
[m]t.dm.ḥt.š'tqt dm. | li.w ttb'.š'tqt. | bt.krt.bu.tbu. | bkt.tgly.w tbu. | nṣrt.tbu.pnm. | 'r 16.6[127].2
krt.grdš.mknt. | aṯt.ṣdq h.l ypq. | mtrḫt.yšr h. | aṯt.trḫ.w tb't. | ṯar um.tkn l h. | mṯlṯt.kṯrm.tmt. | mrb't.zblnm. | mḫ 14[KRT].1.14
um.pḫl.pḫlt.bt.abn.bt šmm w thm. | qrit.l špš.um h.špš.um.ql.bl.'m. | il.mbk nhrm.b 'dt. UG5.7.1
.tdrq. | ybnt.ab h.šrḥq.aṯt.l pnn h. | št.alp.qdm h.mria.w tk. | pn h.tḥspn.m h.w trḥṣ. | ṭl.šmm.šmn.arṣ.ṭl.šm[m.t]sk 3['NT].4.85
lakn. | ġlmm. | aḫr.mġy.kṯr.w ḫss. | št.alp.qdm h.mra. | w tk.pn h.t'db.ksu. | w yṯṯb.l ymn.aliyn. | b'l.'d.lḥm.šṯ[y.ilm]. 4[51].5.108
lm.hn.mtm. | 'd k.kṯr m.ḥbr k. | w ḫss.d't k. | b ym.arš.w tnn. | kṯr.w ḫss.yd. | ytr.kṯr.w ḫss. | spr.ilmlk šbny. | lmd.at 6.6[62.2].50
. | ik.mġyt.rbt.aṯr[t.y]m. | ik.atwt.qnyt.i[lm]. | rġb.rġbt.w tġt[--]. | hm.ġmu.ġmit.w 's[--]. | lḥm.hm.štym.lḥ[m]. | b ṯlḥ 4[51].4.33
ṯlṯ mrkb[t]. | ṣpyt b ḥrṣ[.w] ṣmdm trm.d [ṣ]py. | w.trm.aḥdm. | ṣpym. | ṯlṯ mrkbt mlk. | d.l.ṣpy. | [---.t]r hm. | [- 1122.3
id ydbḥ mlk. | l ušḫ[r] ḫlmṭ. | l bbt il bt. | š l ḫlmṭ. | w tr l qlḥ. | w š ḥll ydm. | b qdš il bt. | w tlḥm aṯt. | š l ilbt.šlm UG5.7.TR3
lbt.šlmm. | kll ylḥm b h. | w l bbt šqym. | š l uḫr ḫlmṭ. | w tr l qlḥ. | ym aḥd. UG5.11.13
rṯm.ḫm[š.---]. | [n]it.krk.m'ṣ[d.---]. | b.ḫrbġlm.ġlm[n]. | w.trhy.aṯt h. | w.mlky.b[n] h. | ily.mrily.tdgr. 2048.20
rmn. | šir.[š]d.mlṯḥ.šd.'šy. | d.ynḥm. | tgmr.šd.ṯlṯm.šd. | w.tr[--.---]. 1079.17
t]. | w.'šrm.l.mit.dd.ḥp[r.]bnšm. | b.gt.ġl.'šrm.l.mit.dr'.w.tš'm.drt. | [w].ṯmnym.l.mit.dd.ḥpr.bnšm. | b.gt.alḫb.ṯṯm.d 1098.14
ḫmš.'šr.yn.ṭb. | w.tš'm.kdm.kbd.yn.d.l.ṭb. | w.arb'm.yn.ḫlq.b.gt.sknm. | 'šr.y 1084.2
[š]m.y[d].š[--]. | [-]lm.b d.r[-]m.l[-]m. | ṯṯ.'šr.ṣ[mdm]. | w.tš'.'[šr.--]m.ḥr[š]. | [---].ḥr[š.---]. | [---.ṯ]lṯ.[---.]dpm. | [---.]b 2038.11
| [w.]ṯlṯm.ṣin. | anndr.ykn'my. | w.aṯt h.w.bn h. | w.alp.w.tš['.]ṣin. 1080.17
[-.---]. | [---.]b[-.]mṯt k.[---]. | [---.]k.w tmt[.---]. | [---.]k.w tṯ[--.---]. | [---.]k.w ṯ[--.---]. | [---.]k ṯrm.l p[--.---]. | [---.]l.[--. 2125.7
.[---]. | yšlm[.l k.ilm]. | tšlm[k.tġr] k. | t'zz[k.---.]lm. | w ṯ[--.--]ṣm k. | [-----]. | [-----.]šil. | [-----.]šilt. | [-----]. | [-----.š]ilt 55[18].7
ṯ.'rb. | b.yrm. | [ily.w].ḏmry.'rb. | b.ṯb'm. | ydn.bn.ilrpi. | w.ṯb'm.'rb.b.'[d]n. | ḏmry.bn.yrm. | 'rb.b.ad'y. 2079.8
m.l.mit.dd.ḥpr.bnšm. | b.gt.alḫb.ṯṯm.dr'.w.ḫmšm.drt.w.ṯṯm.dd. | ḥpr.bnšm. | b.gt.knpy.mit.dr'.ṯṯm.drt.w.šb'm.dd. 1098.16
. | yn.d.l.ṭb.b.gt.ḥḏṯt. | tš'm.yn.d.l.ṭb.b.zbl. | 'šrm.yn.ṭb.w.ṯṯm.ḫmš.k[b]d. | yn.d.l.ṭb.b.gt.sġy. | arb'm.kdm.kbd.yn.ṭb. 1084.14
m. | ḫmš.kkrm.alp kb[d]. | ṯlṯ.l.nskm.birtym. | b d.urtn.w.ṯṯ.mat.brr. | b.ṯmnym.ksp.ṯlṯt.kbd. | ḫmš.alp.ṯlṯ.l.ḫlby. | b d 2101.4
.---]. | ḫtn h.šb'l[.---]. | ṯlḥny.yd[.---]. | yd.ṯlṯ.kl[t h.---]. | w.ṯṯm.ṣi[n.---]. | tn[--]. | agyn.[---]. | [w].tn.[---]. 81[329].19
.arb'm.ḫmš.kbd. | yn.d.l.ṭb.gt.ṭbq. | mit.'šr.kbd.yn.ṭb. | w.ṯṯm.arb'.kbd.yn.d.l.ṭb. | b.gt.m'rby. | ṯṯm.yn.ṭb.w.ḫmš.l.'šr 1084.7
. | ṯṯm.yn.ṭb.w.ḫmš.l.'šrm. | yn.d.l.ṭb.b.ulm. | mit.yn.ṭb.w.ṯṯm.ṯṯ.kbd. | yn.d.l.ṭb.b.gt.ḥḏṯt. | tš'm.yn.d.l.ṭb.b.zbl. | 'šrm. 1084.11
-]. | ksp[.---]. | k[--.---]. | ar[b'.---]. | ṯmn[.---]. | [-]r[-.---]. | w ṯṯ.[---]. | ṯlṯm[.---]. | mil[-.---]. 148[96].12
[l.]ḏr' hm. | [--.n]pš[.-]. | w [k]l hm.b d. | rb.tmtt.lqḥt. | w.ṯṯb.ank.l hm. | w.any k.ṯṯ. | by.'ky.'ryt. | w.aḫ y.mhk. | b lb 2059.23
y[d]. | birtym. | [un]ṯ inn. | l [h]m 'd ṯṯtbn. | ksp.iwrkl. | w ṯb.l unṯ hm. 1006.19
. | gb'm lḥmd.ḫrṣ. | yblnn.udr.ilqṣm. | yak.l kṯr.w ḫss. | w ṯb l mspr..k tlakn. | ġlmm. | aḫr.mġy.kṯr.w ḫss. | št.alp.qd 4[51].5.104
.il.ytši.l dr. | bn il.l mpḫrt.bn.il.l ṯkmn[.w]šnm.hn.'r. | w.ṯb.l mspr.m[šr] mšr.bt.ugrt.w npy.gr. | ḥmyt.ugrt.w [np]y 32[2].1.27

ṣr.|udm.rbt.w udm ṯrrt.|udm.ytnt.il w ušn.|ab.adm.w ṯṯb.|mlakm.l h.lm.ank.|ksp.w yrq.ḫrṣ.|yd.mqm h.w ‘bd. 14[KRT].3.136
h.|pdrm.tdu.šrr.|ḫṭ m.t‘mt.[‘]ṭr.[k]m.|zbln.‘l.riš h.|w tṯb.trḥṣ.nn.b d‘t.|npš h.l lḥm.tpṯḥ.|brlt h.l ṯrm.|mt.dm. 16.6[127].10
akty.hnd.|ylak ‘m y.|w.t‘l.ṯh.hn.|[a]lpm.ššwm.|[---].w.ṯb. 1012.39
.|w šnm.w ngšnn.ḥby.|b‘l.qrnm w ḏnb.ylšn.|b ḫri h.w ṯnt h.ql.il.[--].|il.k yrdm.arṣ.‘nt.|w ‘ṯtrt.tṣdn.[---].|[---.-]b UG5.1.1.21
‘q šr.ln h.mlḫš.|abd.ln h.ydy.ḥmt.|b ḥrn.pnm.trǵnw.w ṯṯkl.|bnwt h.ykr.‘r.d qdm.|idk.pnm.l ytn.tk aršḫ.rbt.|w UG5.7.61
yqr.il.yṯb.b.‘ṯtrt.|il.ṯpṭ.b hd r‘y.d yšr.w yḏmr.|b knr.w ṯlb.b tp.w mṣltm.b m|rqdm.dšn.b.ḥbr.kṯr.ṭbm.|w tšt.‘nt. UG5.2.1.4
yd.[---].|am[-]n.[---].|w.a[ṯt] h.[---].|ḫḏmtn.ṯn[.---].|w.ṯlṯ.alp h.[---].|swn.qrty.w.[b]n h[.---].|w.alp h.w.a[r]b‘.l.a 2044.5
m.ubdym.l mlkt.b.‘nmky[.---].|mgdly.ǵlpṯr.ṯn.krmm.w.ṯlṯ.ub[dym.---].|qmnz.ṯṯ.krm.ykn‘m.ṯmn.krm[.---].|krm. 1081.10
an[y]t.mlk[.---].|w.[ṯ]lṯ.brm.[---].|arb‘ ‘tkm[.---]. 2057.2
rm.l.mit.dd.ḥpr.bnšm.|b.y‘ny.arb‘m.dr‘.w.‘šrm.drt.|w.ṯlṯm.dd.ṯṯ.kbd.ḥpr.bnšm.|b.‘nmky.‘šrm.dr‘[.---.d]rt.|w.ṯ 1098.27
rb‘.|kbd.ḥpr.bnšm.|b.gt.ṯrmn.arb‘m.dr‘.w.‘šrm.drt.|w.ṯlṯm.dd.ṯṯ.kbd.ḥpr.bnšm.|b.gt.ḥdṯt.arb‘m.dr‘.w.ṯlṯm.drt. 1098.21
.‘šrm.dr‘[.---.d]rt.|w.ṯn.‘šr h.dd.[---].|iwrḏn.ḥ[--.---].|w.ṯlṯm.dd.[---.]n[---.---].|w.a[r]b‘[.---].bnš[.š]dyn[.---].|agr.[1098.31
.drt.|w.ṯlṯm.dd.ṯṯ.kbd.ḥpr.bnšm.|b.gt.ḥdṯt.arb‘m.dr‘.w.ṯlṯm.drt.|[w].šb‘m.dd.ṯn.kbd.ḥpr.bnšm.|b.nzl.‘šrm.l.mit. 1098.22
.|hm.ḥry.bt y.|iqḥ.aš‘rb.ǵlmt.|ḥzr y.ṯn h.wspm.|atn.w ṯlṯ h.ḫrṣm.|ylk ym.w ṯn.|ṯlṯ.rb‘.ym.|aḫr.špšm.b rb‘.|ym 14[KRT].4.206
w.ṯt.mqrtm.|w.ṯn.irpm.w.ṯn.trqm.|w.qpt.w.mqḥm.|w.ṯlṯm.yn šb‘.kbd d ṯbṭ.|w.ḫmšm.yn.d iḫ h. 1103.22
b.‘šrt.|ḫmš.kkrm.ṣml.|‘šrt.ksp h.|ḫmš.kkr.qnm.|ṯlṯt.w.ṯlṯt.ksp h.|arb‘.kkr.|algbṯ.arb‘t.|ksp h.|kkr.š‘rt.|šb‘t.ksp 1127.13
alpm.pḥm.ḫm[š].mat.kbd.|b d.tt.w.ṯlṯ.ktnt.b dm.tt.|w.ṯmnt.ksp.hn.|ktn.d.ṣr.pḥm.b h.w.ṯql 1110.2
hm.|w.ṯn.‘šr h.ḫpnt.|[š]šwm.amtm.‘kyt.|yd.llḫ hm.|w.ṯlṯ.l.‘šrm.|ḫpnt.ššwm.ṯn.|pddm.w.d.ṯṯ.|[mr]kbt.w.ḥrṣ. 2049.6
l[.-]dt ḫnd[r]ṯ ar‘ s[p]m w ‘š[r].|[---.]ḫndrṯm ṯṯ spm [w] ṯlṯm l[ḥm].|[---.]ar‘ spm w [---].|[---]š[.---.--]b[.---].|[--.]s 134[-].6
.w.[ml]tḥ.tyt.[---].|[b]šb‘[m.w.n]ṣp.ksp.|[tgm]r.[alp.w.]ṯlṯ.mat. 2101.28
.rqd[y].ṯbg.|iḫmlk.|yp‘n w.aṯt h.|anntn.yṣr.|annmn.w.ṯlṯ.n‘[r] h.|rpan.w.ṯ[n.]bn h.|bn.ayln.w.ṯn.bn h.|yt. 2068.25
.|w.adn hm.ṯr.w.arb‘.bnt h.|yrḫm.yd.ṯn.bn h.|b‘lm.w.ṯlṯ.n‘rm.w.bt.aḥt.|bn.lwn.ṯlṯtm.b‘lm.|bn.b‘ly.ṯlṯtm.b‘lm. 2080.5
--.--]|r ṯṯm lḥm.|l[.-]ry ṯlṯ spm w ‘šr lḥm.|[--.]w nṣp w ṯlṯ spm w ‘šrm lḥ[m].|l[.-]dt ḫnd[r]ṯ ar‘ s[p]m w ‘š[r].|[-- 134[-].4
n.|‘ṣm.l bt.dml.|p ank.atn.|‘ṣm.l k.|arb‘.‘ṣm.|‘l.ar.|w.ṯlṯ.|‘l.ubr‘y.|w.ṯn.‘l.|mlk.|w.aḥd.|‘l atlg.|w l.‘ṣm.|tspr. 1010.11
[b.]gt.ṯpn.‘šr.ṣmdm.|w.ṯlṯ.‘šr.bnš.|yd.ytm.yd.r‘y.ḥmrm.|b.gt.gwl.ṯmn.ṣmdm.|w. 2038.2
ṭb‘l.|[---.]n[--.mḏ]rǵlm.|[---.]b.bt[.---]l.|[ṯ]lṯ.aṯt.adrt.w.ṯlṯ.ǵzr[m].|w.ḫmš.n‘rt.b.bt.sk[n].|ṯt.aṯtm.adrtm.w.pǵt.w 80[119].16
‘qby[.---].|swn.qrty.w[.aṯt h].|[w].bn h.w.ṯn.alpm.|[w.]ṯlṯm.ṣin.|annḏr.ykn‘my.|w.aṯt h.w.bn h.|w.alp.w.tš[‘.]ṣi 1080.14
.[-]trmt.|lbš.w [-]tn.ušpǵt.|ḫr[-].ṯlṯt.mzn.|drk.š.alp.w ṯlṯ.|ṣin.šlm[m.]šb‘ pamt.|l ilm.šb[‘.]l kṯr.|‘lm.t‘rbn.gṯrm. 33[5].6
t hn.|yd.ḥẓ hn.|yd.tr hn.|w.l.ṯt.mrkbtm.|inn.uṯpt.|w.ṯlṯ.ṣmdm.w.ḥrṣ.|apnt.b d.rb.ḥršm.|d.šṣa.ḥwy h. 1121.8
ṯt.qštm[.w.ṯl]ṯ.ql‘m.|bn.‘gw.qšt.w ql‘.|bn.tbšn.ṯlṯ.qšt.w.[ṯlṯ.]ql‘m.|bn.army.ṯt.qštm.w[.]q[l‘].|bn.rpš.qšt.w.ql‘.|bn 119[321].3.21
.ṯ‘l.qšt.|bn.[ḫ]dpṯr.ṯt.qštm.[w].ql‘.|bn.aǵlyn.ṯt.qštm[.w.ṯl]ṯ.ql‘m.|bn.‘gw.qšt.w ql‘.|bn.tbšn.ṯlṯ.qšt.w.[ṯlṯ.]ql‘m.|b 119[321].3.19
šmrm.ql‘.|ubr‘y.|abmn.qšt.w.ṯn.ql‘m.|qdmn.ṯt.qštm.w.ṯlṯ.ql‘m.|bn.ṣdqil.ṯt.qštm.w.ṯn.ql‘m.|bn.ṯlṭ.ṯ[lṯ.]qšt.w.ṯn. 119[321].3.3
---.]ḫ[---.]ṯmnym[.k]sp ḫmšt.|[w a]rb‘ kkr ‘l bn[.--].|[w] ṯlṯ šmn.|[w a]r[b‘] ksp ‘l bn ymn.|šb šr šmn [--] ṯryn.|ḫ 1103.3
‘bd k.b.|lwsnd.|[w] b ṣr.|‘m.mlk.|w.ht.|mlk.syr.|ns.w.ṭm.|ydbḥ.|mlǵ[.---].|w.m[--.--]y.|y[--.---]. 2063.15
] y.|yšlm.il[m].|tǵ[r] k.tš[lm] k.|[h]l ny.‘m n[.š]lm.|w.ṯm [ny.‘m.mlkt.u]m y.|mnm[.šlm].|w.rgm[.ṯṯb.l] y.|hl n 1013.9
rb‘.l.‘šrm.dd.l.yḥšr.bl.bn h.|b.gt.m‘br.arb‘m.l.mit.dr‘.w.ṯmnym[.drt].|w.‘šrm.l.mit.dd.ḥp[r.]bnšm.|b.gt.ǵl.‘šrm.l. 1098.12
alpm.pḥm.ḫm[š].mat.kbd.|b d.tt.w.ṯlṯ.ktnt.b dm.tt.|w.ṯmnt.ksp.hn.|ktn.d.ṣr.pḥm.b h.w.ṯqlm.|ksp h.mitm.pḥm 1110.3
it.dd.ḥp[r.]bnšm.|b.gt.ǵl.‘šrm.l.mit.dr‘.w.tš‘m.drt.|[w].ṯmnym.l.mit.dd.ḥpr.bnšm.|b.gt.alḫb.ṯṯm.dr‘.w.ḫmšm.dr 1098.15
a[ḫ h].|km.all.dm.ary h.|k šb‘t.l šb‘m.aḫ h.ym[.--].|w ṯmnt.l ṯmnym.|šr.aḫy h.mẓa h.|w mẓa h.šr.yly h.|b skn. 12[75].2.50
|tr‘.tr‘n.a[--.---].|bnt.šdm.ṣḥr[.---].|šb‘.šnt.il.mla.[-].|w ṯmn.nqpnt.‘d.|k lbš.km.lpš.dm a[ḫ h].|km.all.dm.ary h. 12[75].2.46
[-]ḏmu.apsty.b[--].|w.bn h.w aṯt h.w.alp.w ṯmn.ṣin.|[-]dln.qmnzy.w.a[ṯt h].|wšṯn.bn h.|ṯmgdl.ykn‘ 1080.2
.y krt.aṯt.|tqḥ.bt k.ǵlmt.tš‘rb.|ḥqr k.tld.šb‘.bnm.l k.|w ṯmn.ṯṯmnm.|l k.tld.yṣb.ǵlm.|ynq.ḥlb.a[ṯ]rt.|mṣṣ.ṯd.btlt. 15[128].2.24
r.mddt.|km irby.tškn.|šd.k ḥsn.pat.|mdbr.tlkn.|ym.w ṯn.aḫr.|šp[š]m.b [ṯ]lṯ.|ym[ǵy.]l qdš.|a[ṯrt.]ṣrm.w l ilt.|ṣd 14[KRT].4.195
ṣmd.dg[-.---].|t‘ln.l mrkbt hm.ti[ty.l ‘r hm].|tlkn.ym.w ṯa aḫr.š[pšm.b ṯlṯ].|mǵy.rpum.l grnt.i[lnym.l] |mṯ‘t.w y‘ 20[121].2.5
.mr[kbt.---].|t‘ln.l mr[kbt hm.tity.l] |‘r hm.tl[kn.ym.w ṯn.aḫr.špšm].|b ṯlṯ.mǵy[.rpum.l grnt].|i[ln]y[m].l mṯ‘t[.-- 22.1[123].24
ḥmd.arz h.|tšt.išt.b bht m.|nb[l]at.b hkl m.|hn.ym.w ṯn.tikl.|išt.b bht m.nblat.|b hk[l] m.ṯlṯ.kb‘ ym.|tikl[.i]št. 4[51].6.24
h.---].|[--]d m‘qby[.---].|swn.qrty.w[.aṯt h].|[w].bn h.w.ṯn.alpm.|[w.]ṯlṯm.ṣin.|annḏr.ykn‘my.|w.aṯt h.w.bn h.|w 1080.13
bt ṯn.ṯlṯ mat.|w spl ṯlṯ.mat.|w mmskn.|w.ṯt.mqrtm.|w.ṯn.irpm.w.ṯn.trqm.|w.qpt.w.mqḥm.|w.ṯlṯm.yn šb‘.kbd d 1103.20
.qdš.yd.|[ṣt h.y‘l.]w yškb.yd.|[mizrt.]p ynl.hn.ym.|[w ṯn.uzr.]ilm.dnil.|[uzr.ilm.]ylḥm.uzr.|[yšqy.b]n.qdš ṯlṯ rb‘ 17[2AQHT].1.7
lbš.aḥd.|b.‘šrt.|w.ṯn.b.ḫmšt.|ṯprt.b.ṯlṯt.|mṯyn.b.ṯṯt.|ṯn.lbšm.b.‘šrt.|pld.b.a 1108.3
.bt.gg.|[ǵz]r.aḥd.b.bt.nwrḏ.|[aṯ]t.adrt.b.bt.arṯṯb.|aṯt.w.ṯn.bn h.b.bt.iwwpzn.|aṯt.w.pǵt.b.bt.ydrm.|ṯt.aṯtm.adrtm 80[119].5
.|yp‘n w.aṯt h.|anntn.yṣr.|annmn.w.ṯlṯ.n‘[r] h.|rpan.w.ṯ[n.]bn h.|bn.ayln.w.ṯn.bn h.|yt. 2068.26
.a[ry.---].|klt h.[---].|ṯty.ary.m[--.---].|nrn.arny[.---].|w.ṯn.bn h.w.b[---.---].|b tn[--.---].|swn.qrty[.---].|uḫ h.w.‘šr 81[329].6
.[b]n h[.---].|w.alp h.w.a[r]b‘.l.arb‘[m.---].|pln.ṯmry.w.ṯn.bn h.w[.---].|ymrn.apsny.w.aṯt h..b[n.---].|prd.m‘qby[2044.8
iyṯr.|[‘]bdyrḫ.|[b]n.gg‘t.|[‘]dy.|armwl.|uwaḫ.|ypln.w.ṯn.bn h.|ydln.|anr[my].|mld.|krmp[y].|bṣmn. 2086.8
.yṣr.|annmn.w.ṯlṯ.n‘[r] h.|rpan.w.ṯ[n.]bn h.|bn.ayln.w.ṯn.bn h.|yt. 2068.27
--].|w.ṯn[.bn h.---].|iwrm[-.]b[n.---].|annt[n.]w[.---].|w.ṯn.bn h.[---].|aǵltn.ypr[y.---].|w.šb‘.ṣin h[.---]. 2044.16
y[.w.---.a]ṯt h[.---].|prṯ.mgd[ly.---.]aṯ[t h].|‘dyn[.---].|w.ṯn[.bn h.---].|iwrm[-.]b[n.---].|annt[n.]w[.---].|w.ṯn.bn h. 2044.13
.|[---].‘tgrm.|[---.-]ṣbm.|[---.]nrn.m‘ry.|[---.--]r.|[---.]w.ṯn.bn h.|[---.b]t h.‘tgrm. 2043.11
aǵltn.[--]y.w[.aṯt h].|w.bn h.w.alp.w.[---].|[-]ln.[---].|w.ṯn.bn [h.---].|[--]d m‘qby[.---].|swn.qrty.w[.aṯt h].|[w].b 1080.10
[kr]wn.|[--]n.|[q]ṣy.|ṯn.bn.iwrḫz.[n]‘rm.|yṣr[.-]qb.|w.ṯn.bnš.iytlm.|w.‘šrm.ṣmd.alpm. 2066.2.6
zr.aḥd.b.[bt.---].|aṯt.w.bn h.w.pǵt.aḥt.b.bt.m[--].|aṯt.w.ṯt.bt h.b.bt.ḫḏmrd.|aṯt.w.ṯn.ǵzrm.b.bt.ṣdqš[lm].|[a]ṯt.aḥt 80[119].22
ṣ.abn.|p h.tiḫd.šnt h.w akl.bqmm.|tšt ḥrṣ.k lb ilnm.|w ṯn.gprm.mn gpr h.šr.|aqht.y‘n.kmr.kmr[.--].|k ap‘.il.b g 19[1AQHT].1.11

[.--]r.dbḥ[.šmn.mr].|šmn.rqḥ[.-]bt.mtnt[.w ynt.qrt].|w tn ḥtm.w bǵr.arb['.---].|kdm.yn.prs.qmḥ.[---].|mdbḥt.bt. 35[3].22
'rb[.---].|dbḥ šmn mr[.šmn.rqḥ.bt].|mtnt.w ynt.[qrt.w tn.ḥtm].|w bǵr.arb'.[---.kdm.yn].|prs.qmḥ.m'[--.---].|md APP.II[173].23
|tšm'.mṯt.ḥry.|ṯṭbḫ.imr.w lḥm.|mgṯ.w yṯrm.hn.ym.|w ṯn.yṯb.krt.l 'd h.|yṯb.l ksi mlk.|l nḫt.l kḥṯ.drkt.|ap.yṣb.y 16.6[127].22
lsmn.'m y.|twtḥ.išd k.dm.rgm.|iṯ.l y.w argm k.|hwt.w aṯny k.rgm.|'ṣ.w lḫšt.abn.|tant.šmm.'m.arṣ.|thmt.'mn.k 3['NT].3.19
n.[']m y.twtḥ.išd k.|[dm.rgm.iṯ.l y.]w argm k.hwt.|[w aṯny k.rgm.]'ṣ.w lḫšt.|[abn.rgm.l td]'.nš[m.w l t]bn.|[hm 3['NT].4.58
ršn.-------------].|ǵr.ks.dm.r[gm.iṯ.l y.w argm k].|hwt.w aṯny k[.rgm.'ṣ.w lḫšt.abn].|tunt.šmm.'m[.arṣ.thmt.'mn.k 1['NT.IX].3.13
ktn.d.ṣr.pḥm.b h.w.ṯqlm.|ksp h.mitm.pḥm.b d.skn.|w.ṯṯ.ktnm.ḫmšt.w.nṣp.ksp.hn. 1110.6
ṭbḫ.l kṯ|rt.yšlḥm.kṯrt.w y|ššq.bnt.[hl]l.snnt.|hn.ym.w ṯn.yšlḥm.|kṯrt.w yš[š]q.bnt.hl[l].|snnt.ṯlṯ[.r]b' ym.yšl|ḥ 17[2AQHT].2.32
bld.|ǵll.yn.išryt.'nq.smd.|lbnn.ṯl mrṯ.yḥrṯ.il.|hn.ym.w ṯn.tlḥmn.rpum.|tštyn.ṯlṯ.rb'.ym.ḫmš.|ṯdṯ.ym.tlḥmn.rpu 22.2[124].21
.grgš.|w.npṣ bt ṯn.ṯlṯ mat.|w spl ṯlṯ.mat.|w mmskn.|w.ṯṯ.mqrtm.|w.ṯn.irpm.w.ṯn.trqm.|w.qpt.w.mqḥm.|w.ṯlṯm 1103.19
.dt.kn.npṣ hm.|[bn].lbn.arb'.qšt.w.ar[b'].|[u]ṯpt.ql'.w.ṯṯ.mr[ḥ]m.|[bn].smyy.qšt.w.u[ṯpt].|[w.q]l'.w.ṯṯ.mrḥm.|[2047.3
]ṯpt.ql'.w.ṯṯ.mr[ḥ]m.|[bn].smyy.qšt.w.u[ṯpt].|[w.q]l'.w.ṯṯ.mrḥm.|[bn].šlmn.ql'.w.ṯ[t.---].|[bn].mlṣ.qštm.w.uṯp[t]. 2047.5
ǵt.b.bt.ydrm.|ṯṯ.aṯṯm.adrtm.w.pǵt.aḥt.b[.bt.---].|aṯt.w ṯn.n'rm.b.bt.ilsk.|aṯt.ad[r]t.b.bt.armwl.|aṯt.aḥt.b.bt.iwrp 80[119].8
[.---].|ṣlyh šr[-.---].|[ṯ]lṯm.w b[--.---].|l il limm[.---].|w ṯt.npš[.---].|kbd.w [---].|l ṣp[n.---].|š.[---].|w [----].|k[--.- 40[134].9
gptr.w.šǵ[r h].|ṯ'ln.|mztn.w.šǵr [h].|šǵr.plṭ.|s[d]rn [w].ṯn.šǵr h.|[---.]w.šǵr h.|[---.]w.šǵr h.|[---.]krwn.|[---].ḫz 2072.8
.|p ank.atn.|'ṣm.l k.|arb'.'ṣm.|'l.ar.|w.ṯlṯ.|'l.ubr'y.|w.ṯn.'l.|mlk.|w.aḥd.|'l atlg.|w l.'ṣm.|tspr.|nrn.al.tud|ad.a 1010.13
šr h.|[---.d]r'.w.mit.drt.w.'šrm.l.mit.|[drt.ḥpr.b]nšm.w.ṯn.'šr h.dd.l.rpš.|[---.]šb'm.dr'.w.arb'm.drt.mit.dd.|[---]. 1098.4
ṯlṯm.dd.ṯṯ.kbd.ḥpr.bnšm.|b.'nmky.'šrm.dr'[.---.d]rt.|w.ṯn.'šr h.dd.[---].|iwrḏn.ḥ[--.---].|w.ṯlṯm.dd.[---.]n[---.---].| 1098.29
[---.ṯ]lṯ.'š[r h.---].|d bnšm.yd.grbs hm.|w.ṯn.'šr h.ḫpnt.|[š]šwm.amtm.'kyt.|yd.llḫ hm.|w.ṯlṯ.l.'šrm 2049.3
h.w.pǵt.aḥt.b.bt.m[--].|aṯt.w.ṯṯ.bt h.b.bt.ḫdmrd.|aṯt.w.ṯn.ǵzrm.b.bt.ṣdqš[lm].|[a]ṯt.aḥt.b.bt.rpi[--].|[aṯt.]w.bt h. 80[119].23
]mm.ṯn.šm.w alp.l[--]n.|[---.]š.il š.b'l š.dgn š.|[---.--]r.w ṯt pl.gdlt.[s]pn.dqt.|[---.al]p 'nt.gdlt.b ṯlṯt mrm.|[---.i]l š. 36[9].1.4
t.sk[n].|ṯṯ.aṯṯm.adrtm.w.pǵt.w ǵzr[.aḥd.b.bt.---].|aṯt.w.ṯt.pǵtm.w.ǵzr.aḥd.b.[bt.---].|ṯṯ.aṯṯm.w.pǵt.w.ǵzr.aḥd.b.[b 80[119].19
l'm.|qṣn.ṯt.qštm.w.ql'.|bn.gṯrn.q[š]t.|bn.ḫdi.ṯt.qštm.w.ṯn.ql'm.|ildgn.qšt.|bn.y'rn.ṯt.qštm w.ql'.|bn.ḥṣn.qšt.w.ql 119[321].3.8
[.q]l'.|bn.bdn.qšt.|bn.pls.qšt.|ǵmrm.|[-]lhd.ṯt.qštm.w.ṯn.ql'm.|ulšn.ṯt.qšm.w.ql'.|bn.ml'n.qšt.w.ql'.|bn.tmy.qšt 119[321].3.33
.ṯn.ql'm.|qdmn.ṯt.qštm.w.ṯlṯ.ql'm.|bn.ṣdqil.ṯt.qštm.w.ṯn.ql'm.|bn.ṯlṯ.ṯ[lṯ.]qšt.w.ṯn.ql'm.|qṣn.ṯt.qštm.w.ql'.|bn. 119[321].3.4
l'.|bn.[-]q.qšt.w.ql'.|gb[l]n.qšt.w.ql'.|bn.[-]bl.ṯt.qštm.w.ṯn.ql'm.|bn.[-]rkṯ.ṯt.qštm.w.ql'.|bn.ṯ'l.qšt.|bn.[ḫ]dpṯr.ṯt. 119[321].3.15
[u]lm.|mṯpṯ.ṯt.qštm.w.ṯn.q[l]'m.|kmrṯn.ṯt.qštm.ṯn.[q]l'm.|ǵdyn.qšt.w.ql'.|bn.g 119[321].1.2
.ql'.|b[n].ilyn.qšt.w.ql'.|šmrm.ql'.|ubr'y.|abmn.qšt.w.ṯn.ql'm.|qdmn.ṯt.qštm.w.ṯlṯ.ql'm.|bn.ṣdqil.ṯt.qštm.w.ṯn. 119[321].3.2
w.ṯlṯ.ql'm.|bn.ṣdqil.ṯt.qštm.w.ṯn.ql'm.|bn.ṯlṯ.ṯ[lṯ.]qšt.w.ṯn.ql'm.|qṣn.ṯt.qštm.w.ql'.|bn.gṯrn.q[š]t.|bn.ḫdi.ṯt.qštm. 119[321].3.5
b [ṯlṯt].'šrt.yrṯḥṣ.mlk.|br[r.]b a[r]b't.'šrt.riš.|arg[mn.w ṯn.]šm.l b'lt.|bhtm.'ṣ[rm.l in]š ilm.w š.|dd ilš.š[.---.]mlk. APP.II[173].5
].|b ṯlṯt '[šrt.yrṯḥṣ.mlk.brr].|b arb'[t.'šrt.riš.argmn].|w ṯn šm.l [b'lt.bhtm.'ṣrm.l inš].|ilm.w š d[d.ilš.š.--.mlk].|yṯ 35[3].5
t.|w spl ṯlṯ.mat.|w mmskn.|w.ṯṯ.mqrtm.|w.ṯn.irpm.w.ṯn.trqm.|w.qpt.w.mqḥm.|w.ṯlṯm.yn šb'.kbd d ṭbṭ.|w.ḫm 1103.20
rb.ǵlmt.|ḥẓr y.ṯn h.wspm.|atn.w ṯlṯ h.ḫrṣm.|ylk ym.w ṯn.|ṯlṯ.rb'.ym.|aḫr.špšm.b rb'.|ymǵy.l udm.rbt.|w udm[. 14[KRT].4.207
grnt.ḥpšt.|s't.b npk.šibt.w b |mqr.mmlat.|d[m].ym.w ṯn.|ṯlṯ.rb'.ym.|ḫmš.ṯdṯ.ym.|mk.špšm.b šb'.|w l.yšn.pbl. 14[KRT].5.218
|mddt h.k irby.|[t]škn.šd.|km.ḥsn.pat.mdbr.|lk.ym.w ṯn.ṯlṯ.rb' ym.|ḫmš.ṯdṯ.ym.mk.špšm.|b šb'.w tmǵy.l udm. 14[KRT].3.106
ḥṭb h.b grnt.ḥpšt.|s't.b nk.šibt.b bqr.|mmlat.dm.ym.w ṯn.|ṯlṯ.rb'.ym.ymš.|ṯdṯ.ym.ḥẓ k.al.tš'l.|qrt h.abn.yd k.| 14[KRT].3.114
t.šmt.|b.'šrt.ksp.|'šr.ṣin.b.ṯṯt.w.kmsk.|arb'[.k]dwṯm.w.ṯt.ṯprtm.|b.'šr[m.]ksp.|ḫmš.kkr.ṣml.|b.'šrt.b d.bn.kyn.|' 2100.10
.smyy.qšt.w.u[ṯpt].|[w.q]l'.w.ṯṯ.mrḥm.|[bn].šlmn.ql'.w.ṯ[t.---].|[bn].mlṣ.qštm.w.uṯp[t].|[--.q]l'.w[.---.m]rḥm.|[b 2047.6
n.---].|b ks.ḫr[ṣ.dm.'ṣm.---].|ks.ksp[.---].|krpn.[---].|w ṯṯn.[---].|t'l.tr[-.---].|bt.il.li[mm.---].|'l.ḥbš.[---].|mn.lik. 5[67].4.19
št.[w.u]ṯp[t].ṯ[--].|[---].arb'.[---].|[---].kdl[.---.mr]ḥm.w.ṯ[t.---].|[---.mr]ḥm.w.ṯ[t.---].|[---].ql'[.---].|[---.a]rb'[.---]. 2047.11
].arb'.[---].|[---].kdl[.---.mr]ḥm.w.ṯ[t.---].|[---.mr]ḥm.w.ṯ[t.---].|[---].ql'[.---].|[---.a]rb'[.---]. 2047.12
.|yd.ṯlṯ.kl[t h.---].|w.ṯṯm.ṣi[n.---].|tn[--].|agyn.[---].|[w].ṯn.[---]. 81[329].22
[w spš].|mlk.rb.b'l h.[---].|nqmd.mlk.ugr[t.--].|phy.|w ṯpllm.mlk.r[b.--].|mṣmt.l nqmd.[---.-]št.|hl ny.argmn.d [64[118].16
l.'rgz.ydk].|a[ḥd h.w.yṣq.b.ap h].|k.[ḫr.ššw.ḫndrṯ].|w.ṯ[qd.mr.ydk.aḥd h].|w.y[ṣq.b.ap h].|k.l.ḫ[ru.w.l.yṯtn.ššw 161[56].6
ṣql 'rgz].|[ydk aḥ]d h w yṣq b ap h.|[k ḫr]ššw ḫndrṯ w ṯ[qd m]r.|[ydk aḥd h w yṣq b ap h.|[k l yḫru w]l yṯtn m 160[55].6
w.ṯlṯ.ktnt.b dm.tt.|w.ṯmnt.ksp.hn.|ktn.d.ṣr.pḥm.b h.w.ṯqlm.|ksp h.mitm.pḥm.b d.skn.|w.ṯt.ktnm.ḫmšt.w.nṣp.k 1110.4
ḥm.mgṯ.w iṯrm.|tšm'.mṯt.ḥry.|ṯṭbḫ.imr.w lḥm.|mgṯ.w yṯrm.hn.ym.|w ṯn.yṯb.krt.l 'd h.|yṯb.l ksi mlk.|l nḫt.l kḥ 16.6[127].21
'.yšu.g h.|w yṣḥ.šm'.l mṯt.|ḥry.ṭbḫ.imr.|w ilḥm.mgṯ.w iṯrm.|tšm'.mṯt.ḥry.|ṯṭbḫ.imr.w lḥm.|mgṯ.w yṯrm.hn.ym. 16.6[127].18
h.b'l.ṣpn š.|[--]ṯ š.ilt.mgdl š.ilt.asrm š.|w l ll.šp. pgr.w ṯrmnm.bt mlk.|il[bt].gdlt.ušḫry.gdlt.ym gdlt.|b'l gdlt.yr 34[1].12
ṯt k.[---].|[---.]k.w tmt[.---].|[---.]k.w ṯt[--.---].|[---.]k.w ṯ[--.---].|[---.]k trm.l p[--.---].|[---.]l.[--.]rlg[-.---].|[---.]bn. 2125.8
.'m dt[n].|lqḥ.mṯpṭ.|w y'ny.nn.|dtn.bt n.mḫ[-].|l dg.w [-]kl.|w aṯr.hn.mr[-]. UG5.6.15
.|lg.šmn.rqḥ.šr'm.ušpǵtm.p[--.---].|kṯ.ẓrw.kṯ.nbt.ḏnt.w [-]n[-.---].|il.ḥyr.ilib.š.|arṣ w šmm.š.|il.š.kṯrt.š.|dgn.š.b'l. UG5.9.1.22
t.ḫr[-].|bt mlk.'šr.'šr.[--].bt ilm.|kbr[-]m.[-]trmt.|lbš.w [-]tn.ušpǵt.|ḫr[-].ṯlṯt.mzn.|drk.š.alp.w ṯlṯ.|ṣin.šlm[m.]šb' 33[5].4
[---.]ylm.b[n.']n k.ṣmdm.špk[.---].|[---.]nt[-.]mbk kpt.w[.--].b g[--].|[---.]ḫ[--.]bnt.ṣ'ṣ.bnt.ḫkp[.---].|[---].aḥw.aṭm. 1001.1.17
drkt h.|l [ym]m.l yrḫm.l yrḫm.|l šnt.[m]k.b šb'.|šnt.w [--].bn.ilm.mt.|'m.aliyn.b'l.yšu.|g h.w yṣḥ.'l k.b[']l m.|p 6[49].5.9
--.--]ty.l[--.---].|[--.--]tm.w '[--.--].|[---].w kl.hw[.---].|w [--].brt.lb[--.---].|u[-]šhr.nuš[-.---].|b [u]grt.w ht.a[--].|w 54.1.5[13.1.2]
t.|w qrwn.|l k dbḥ.|[--]r bt [--].|[--]bnš [--].|š š[--].|w [--].|d [--].|ypḫ[--].|w s[--].|[---].|qrd ga[n.--].|b bt k.[-- RS61[24.277.16]
knn.|ḫmšm.l mi[t].any.|tškn[n.--]h.k[--].|w šnm[.--.]w[.--].|w 'prm.a[--.--]n.|[--.]ḥ[--.]d[--]t.|[---.]hw[t.---].|[---.] 2062.1.6
.pnmn.|kkr.|bn.sgttn.|kkr.|ilšpš.kkr.|bn.ḏltn.|kkr.w[.--].|ḫ[--.---]. 1118.13
[---.--]ṯ.slḫ.npš.ṭ' w[.--.k]bdm.|[---.--]mm.ṯn.šm.w alp.l[--]n.|[---.]š.il š.b'l š.d 36[9].1.1
-.]b ym.ym.y[--].yš[ ]n.ap k.'ṯtr.dm[.---.]|[---.]ḥrḥrtm.w[--.]n[--.]iš[--.]h[---.]išt.|[---]y.yblmm.u[---]k.yrd[.--.]i[--- 2.3[129].13
yrḫ.[---].|šb'.yn[.---].|mlkt[.---].|kd.yn.l.[---].|armwl w [--].|arb'.yn.[--].|l adrm.b[--].|šqym. 1092.5
[---].|tš'm.[ḫ]mš[.kbd].yn.b gt[.-]n.|arb'm.kbd.yn.ṭb.w.[--].|ṯmn.kbd.yn.d.l.ṭb.b.gn'[y].|mitm.yn.ḥsp.d.nkly.b.db 1084.22

p. | w[.n]pš.ksp. | w ḫrṣ.km[-]. | w.ḫ[--.-]lp. | w.š.l[--]p. | w[.--.-]nš. | i[--.---]. | w[.---]. | k[--.---]. | ṯql[.---]. 2005.1.7
.ṯlṯ h. | [ap]nk.krt.ṯ‘.‘[-]r. | [--.]b bt h.yšt.‘rb. | [--] h.ytn.w [--]u.l ytn. | [aḫ]r.mǵy.‘[d]t.ilm. | [w]y‘n.aliy[n.]b‘l. | [---.]t 15[128].2.10
n.‘z.b[‘l.---]. | llu.bn[š.---]. | imr.ḫ[--.---]. | [--]n.b‘[l.---]. | w [--]d.[---]. | idk[.-]it[.---]. | trgm[.-]dk[.---]. | m‘bd[.-]r[-.-]š[-. 2158.2.1
b.ym.ḥdṯ. | b.yrḫ.pgrm. | lqḥ.b‘lm‘ḏr. | w bn.ḫlp. | w[--]y.d.b‘l. | miḫd.b. | arb‘.mat. | ḫrṣ. 1155.5
ad[.‘]bd h.uk.škn. | k.[---.]sglt h.hw. | w.b[.---.]uk.nǵr. | w.[---].adny.l.yḫsr. | w.[ank.yd]‘.l.yd‘t. | h[t.---.]l.špš.b‘l k. | ‘[- 2060.9
[---.--]t ḥ[dr]. | [-----]. | ḫmš[.---]t.ḥdrm. | w.[---.a]ḥd.d.sgrm. | w p[tḥ.---.]l.aḥd.adr. | [---.--]t.b[ḥd]r.mš 1151.4
]. | ṯṯb ‘ṯtrt b ǵl[.---]. | qrẓ tšt.l šmal[.---]. | arbḫ.‘n h tšu w[.---]. | aylt tǵpy tr.‘n[.---]. | b[b]r.mrḫ h.ti[ḫd.b yd h]. | š[g] 2001.1.10
n h.w[.---]. | ymrn.apsny.w.aṯt h..b[n.---]. | prd.m‘qby[.w.---.a]ṯt h[.---]. | prṯ.mgd[ly.---.]aṯ[t h]. | ‘dyn[.---]. | w.ṯn[.bn 2044.10
]. | [---.qdq]d k.ašhlk[.šbt k.dmm]. | [šbt.dq]n k.mm‘m.w[---]. | aqht.w yplṭ k.bn[.dnil.---]. | w y‘ḏr k.b yd.btlt.[‘nt]. | 18[3AQHT].1.12
n llit. | [--]l[-.-]p ‘l [---.-]b‘m arny. | w ‘l [---.]rb‘m ṯqlm.w [---] arb‘yn. | w ‘l.mnḥm.arb‘ š[mn]. | w ‘l bn a[--.-]yn ṯqlm 1103.8
l.qšt h]. | tmḫṣ h.qṣ‘t h.hwt.l t[ḥwy]. | n‘mn.ǵzr.št.ṯrm.w[---]. | ištir.b ḏdm.w n‘rs[.---]. | w t‘n.btlt.‘nt.ṯb.yṯp.w[---]. 18[3AQHT].4.14
w.[---]. | ity[.---]. | tlby[.---]. | ir[--.---]. | pndyn[.---]. | w.idṯ[-.--- 1078.1
.kdm[.---]. | [a]gm.arb‘[.---]. | šrš.šb‘.mṣb. | rqd.ṯlṯ.mṣb.w.[---]. | uḫnp.ṯṯ.mṣb. | tgmr.[y]n.mṣb š[b‘]. | w ḥs[p] ṯn.k[dm 2004.33
| w.nḥl h. | bn.alz. | w.nḥl h. | bn.sny. | bn.ablḥ. | [-----]. | w [---]. | bn.[---]. | bn.yr[--]. | bn.kṯr[t]. | bn.šml. | bn.arnbt. | qd 2163.2.2
[.---].‘šr.bnšm. | ‘nqpat[.---].bnš. | ubr‘y.ar[b‘.]ḥm[r]m.w[.---.]bnšm. | ilštm‘.arb‘.ḥm[r]m.ḫmš.bnšm. | ǵr. | ary.ḥmr 2040.20
.l.ṣpn.w.dqt[.---]. | ṯn.l.‘šrm.pamt.[---]. | š.dd.šmn.gdlt.w.[---.brr]. | rgm.yṯṯb.b.ṯdṯ.ṯn[.--.šmn]. | ‘ly h.gdlt.rgm.yṯ[ṯb. 35[3].44
l ṣpn.w [dqt.---.ṯn.l ‘š] | rm.pam[t.---]. | š dd šmn[.gdlt.w.---]. | brr.r[gm.yṯṯb.b ṯdṯ.ṯn]. | l šmn.‘[ly h.gdlt.rgm.yṯṯb]. | APP.II[173].48
]. | km.škllt.[---]. | ‘r.ym.l bl[.---]. | b[---.]ny[.--]. | l bl.sk.w [---] h. | ybm h.šb‘[.---]. | ǵzr.ilḥu.t[---]l. | trm.tṣr.trm[.‘]tqt. 16.2[125].93
yrdnn.an[--.---]. | [---].ank.l km[.---]. | l y.ank.ašṣu[.---.]w[.---]. | w hm.at.tr[gm.---]. | w.drm.‘tr[--.---]. | w ap.ht.k[--.]š 54.1.17[13.2.2]
-]bl lb h.km.bṯn.y[--.-]ah. | ṯnm.tšqy msk.hwt.tšqy[.-.]w [---]. | w hn dt.yṯb.l mspr. 19[1AQHT].4.224
]. | yṯb.brr[.w mḫ-.---]. | ym.[‘]lm.y‘[--.---]. | [--.-]g[-.-]s w [---]. | w yn[t.q]rt.y[---]. | w al[p.l]il.w bu[rm.---]. | ytk.gdlt 35[3].9
‘.ḥm[r.---]. | l ṯlṯ. | ṯn.l.brr[.---]. | arb‘.ḥmr[.---]. | l.pḫ[-.]w.[---]. | w.l.k[--]. | w.l.k[--]. 1139.5
. | ‘dyn[.---]. | w.ṯn[.bn h.---]. | iwrm[-.]b[n.---]. | annt[n.]w[.---]. | w.ṯn.bn h.[---]. | aǵltn.ypr[y.---]. | w.šb‘.ṣin h[.---]. 2044.15
.ḥ[mr.---]. | ḫlb krd.ḥ[mr.---]. | ṣ‘.ḥmr.w[.---]. | ṣ‘q.ḥmr.w.[---]. | ḫlb ‘prm.amḏy.[ḥm]r.w bn[š]. | gn‘y.[---.bn]š. | uškn[2040.15
[l.ym.k] | šby n.ṯpṭ.nhr.w yṣa b[.--]. | ybṯ.nn.aliyn.b‘l.w [---]. | ym.l mt.b‘l m.ym l[--.---]. | ḥm.l šrr.w [---]. | y‘n.ym.l 2.4[68].31
-]. | w.alp h.w.a[r]b‘.l.arb‘[m.---]. | pln.ṯmry.w.ṯn.bn h.w[.---]. | ymrn.apsny.w.aṯt h..b[n.---]. | prd.m‘qby[.w.---.a]ṯt 2044.8
.š.šlmm.pamt.šb‘.klb h. | yr[--.]mlk.ṣbu.špš.w.ḥl.mlk. | w.[---].ypm.w.mḫ[--].t[ṯ]tbn.[-]. | b.[--].w.km.iṯ.y[--.]šqm.yd[35[3].54
.šlmy. | kd.šmn.ṯbil. | kd.šmn.ymtšr. | arb‘.šmn.‘l.‘bdn.w.[---]. | kdm.šmn.‘l.ilršp.bn[.---]. | kd.šmn.‘l.yddn. | kd.‘l.ššy. 1082.1.4
‘]ṣr.l pdr ṯṯ.ṣ[in.---]. | tšnpn.‘lm.km[m.---]. | w.l ll.‘ṣrm.w [---]. | kmm.w.in.‘ṣr[.---]. | w mit.š‘rt.[-]y[-.---]. | w.kdr.w.n 38[23].7
ḫrṣ.km[-]. | w.ḫ[--.-]lp. | w.š.l[--]p. | w[.--.-]nš. | i[--.---]. | w[.---]. | k[--.---]. | ṯql[.---]. 2005.1.9
.w[---]. | ištir.b ḏdm.w n‘rs[.---]. | w t‘n.btlt.‘nt.ṯb.yṯp.w[---]. | l k.ašt k.km.nšr.b ḥb[š y]. | km.diy.b t‘rt y.aqht.[km 18[3AQHT].4.16
. | [ṯ]lṯm.w b[--.---]. | l il limm[.---]. | w ṯt.npš[.---]. | kbd.w [---]. | l ṣp[n.---]. | š.[---]. | w [----]. | k[--.---]. | ‘n[t.---]. 40[134].10
m]. | [---.]ar‘ spm w [---]. | [---]š[.---.--]b[.---]. | [--.]sp[m.w ---.l]ḥm. 134[-].9
[---.ṣ]mdm[.---]. | [ul]l.aḥdm.w[.---]. | [m‘q]b.aḥdm.w[.---]. | [‘r]gz.ṯlṯ.ṣmd[m.---]. | [m]ṣbt.ṣ 1179.2
n].šlmn.ql‘.w.ṯ[t.---]. | [bn].mlṣ.qštm.w.uṯp[t]. | [--.q]l‘.w[.---.m]rḥm. | [bn].ḫdmn.qšt.[w.u]ṯp[t].ṯ[--]. | [---].arb‘.[---]. 2047.8
l ny.[---]. | w.pdr[--.---]. | tmǵyn[.---]. | w.mli[.---]. | [-]kl.w [---]. | ‘d.mǵt[.---]. 57[101].7
.aliyn.b‘l.w [---]. | ym.l mt.b‘l m.ym l[--.---]. | ḥm.l šrr.w [---]. | y‘n.ym.l mt[.---]. | l šrr.w t‘[n.‘ṯtrt.---]. | b‘l m.hmt.[-- 2.4[68].33
[---].ḥpr.bn.šm. | [b.---.]knm.ṯṯm.l.mit.dr‘.w.mit.drt. | w[.---.]‘m.l.mit.dd.ṯn.kbd.ḥpr.bnšm.ṯmnym.dd. | l u[-]m. | b. 1098.8
[---.ṣ]mdm[.---]. | [ul]l.aḥdm.w[.---]. | [m‘q]b.aḥdm.w[.---]. | [‘r]gz.ṯlṯ.ṣmd[m.---]. | [m]ṣbt.ṣmdm.[---]. | [--]nr.arb‘. 1179.3
adt y.[---]. | lb.ab[d k].al[.---]. | [-]tm.iph.adt y.w.[---]. | tšṣḥq.hn.aṯt.l.‘bd. | šb‘t.w.nṣp.ksp. | [-]tm.rb[.--.a]ḥd. 1017.3
.ṯn[.---]. | bq‘t.[--].ḥ[mr.---]. | ḫlb krd.ḥ[mr.---]. | ṣ‘.ḥmr.w[.---]. | ṣ‘q.ḥmr.w.[---]. | ḫlb ‘prm.amḏy.[ḥm]r.w bn[š]. | gn‘ 2040.14
dd.kbd. | [l].mḏr[ǵ]lm. | b yrḫ[ri]šyn. | šb[‘.--]n.[k]bd. | w[.---.]qm‘t. | [---.]mḏrǵlm. | [---.]mdm. | [w].‘šr.dd.l np[l]. | r[2012.23
[---.--]ṯ[.---]. | [---.]mt[--.---]. | bk[--.--].yq[--.--]. | w [---.]rkb[.---]. | [---].d[--.---]. | b ql[.-----]. | w tštqdn[.-----]. | 62[26].4
ql[.-----]. | w tštqdn[.-----]. | hm. | w yḫ.mlk. | w ik m.kn.w [---]. | tšknnnn[.---]. 62[26].10
[-.---]. | t[--.---]. | a[--.---]. | [---].ksp.‘m[.---]. | [---.]ilthm.w.[---]. | šm‘t.ḫwt[.---]. | [---].nzdt.qr[t]. | [---.]dt nzdt.m[lk]. | [2127.2.2
[---.]ḫlmt.alp.šnt.w[.---]. | šntm.alp.d krr[.---]. | alp.pr.b‘l.[---]. | w prt.tkt.[---]. | 2158.1.1
w ḫ[ss.t]b‘.b[n.]bht.ym[.rm]m.hkl.ṯpṭ nh[r]. | [---.]hrn.w[---.]tb‘.k[ṯ]r w [ḫss.t]bn.bht zbl ym. | [trm]m.hk[l.ṯpṭ].nh 2.3[129].8
.bn h.w.alp.aḫ[d]. | aǵltn.[--]y.w[.aṯt h]. | w.bn h.w.alp.w.[---]. | [-]ln.[---]. | w.ṯn.bn [h.---]. | [--]d m‘qby[.---]. | swn.qr 1080.8
| kṯr[.---.--]trt ḫmšt.bn gda[.-]mḏ‘. | kl[--.---.]ṯmnt[.--.]w[.---]. | [-]m[.---.]ṣpiry[.ṯ]lṯt[.---]. APP.II[173].60
. | ḫmš.kbd.l.md‘. | b yr[ḫ.iṯtb]nm. | ṯlṯ[.mat.a]rb‘.kbd. | w.[---.-]m‘t. | ṯlṯ[m.---.-]rm. | ‘šr[.---].alpm. | arb‘.ddm.l.k[-]ḫ. 2012.15
dd. | mnḥm.w.kbln. | bn.ǵlm.dd. | bn.tbšn.dd. | bn.ḫran.w[.---]. | [-]n.y‘rtym. | gmm.w.bn.p[--]. | trn.w.p[-]y. | bn.b‘yn. 131[309].8
lm. | ngh w srr. | ‘dw šr. | ṣdqm šr. | ḥnbn il d[n]. | [-]bd w [---]. | [--].p il[.---]. | [i]l mt mr[b-]. | qdš mlk [---]. | kbd d ilg UG5.10.1.16
y[--.---]. | [--.]dn[--.---]. | [--.]lq[--.---]. | [--.]g[--.---]. | [--.]w[.---]. | [--]rṣ.[---]. | [--.]nk[--]. 45[45].8
.bnm.ta[--.---]. | [b]nm.w bnt.ytn k[.---]. | [--]l.bn y.šḥt.w [---]. | [--]tt.msgr.bn k[.---]. | [--]n.tḥm.b‘l[.---]. 59[100].10
-.n]pš.ttn[.---]. | [---.]yd‘t.k[---]. | [---].w hm. | [--]y.ṯb y.w [---]. | [---.]bnš.[---]. 61[-].5
r[--.]ydm[.---]. | [---.]mṯbt.ilm.w.b.[---]. | [---.]ṯṯtbn.ilm.w.[---]. | [---.]w.ksu.b‘lt.b[htm.---]. | [---.]il.bt.gdlt.[---]. | [---.] 47[33].6
]at.bt k[.---]. | [---.]ank[.---]. | [---.-]hn.[---]. | [---.--]pp h.w[.---]. | [---.]l k[.---]. | [-----]. | [-----]. | [-----]. | [---].al.tš[--.---]. | 1002.7
[-----.]w[.---]. | [---.]l špš[.---]. 42[-].1
[-----]. | [---].w [---]. | [---].mr[--.---]. | [---].mr[--.]ydm[.---]. | [---.]mṯbt.ilm. 47[33].2
-.]b‘[r.---]. | [--]my.b d[-.--]y.[---]. | [---.]‘m.w hm[.--]yt.w.[---]. | [---.ṯ]y.al.an[k.--.]il[m.--]y. | [--.m]ṣlm.pn y[.-.]tlkn. | 1002.57
ilib.gdlt.il.š.b]‘[l].š.‘nt ṣpn. | [---.]w [n]p[š.---]. | [---.--]t.w[.---]. | [---.--]pr.ṭ[--.---]. | [-----]. | [---.--]lk[.---]. | [---.--]g.tuṣl[36[9].2.1
---]. | [---.]k ṯrm.l p[--.---]. | [---.]l.[--.]rlg[-.---]. | [---.]bn.w [---]. | [---.--]t.kn[-.---]. | [---.--]tm.n[--.---]. | [---.-]km.t‘rb[.-- 2125.11
[r]. | [---.]ḫndrṯm ṯṯ spm [w] ṯlṯm l[ḥm]. | [---.]ar‘ spm w [---]. | [---]š[.---.--]b[.---]. | [--.]sp[m.w ---.l]ḥm. 134[-].7

špḥ.al.thbṭ.|ḫrd.ʻps.aḫd.kw|sgt.|ḫrd ksp.[--]r.|ymm.w[.---].|[-----].|w[.-----].|[-----]. 2062.2.9
p.]ʻl.|il[m]l[k.a]rgnd.|uškny[.w]mit.|zt.b d hm.rib.|w [---].|[-----].|[-]šy[.---] h.|[-]kt[.---.]nrn.|[b]n.nmq[.---].|[2055.14
.ṯn[.ʻšr h.]mn.|ʻṣrm.ṯql.kbd[.ks].mn.ḫrṣ.|w arbʻ.ktnt.w [---]b.|[ḫm]š.mat pḥm.|[ḫm]š[.m]at.iqnu.|argmn.nqmd. 64[118].21
pm.w.l.y[n.--]t.|w.bl.bnš.hw[-.--]y.|w.k.at.trg[m.--].|w.[---]n.w.s[--].|[--]m.m[---].|[---.m]ndʻ[.--]. 2064.28
km.s[--.---].|tš[.---].|t[---.---].|[-----].|[-----].|b [----].|w [----].|bʻl.[---].|il hd.b[---].|at.bl.at.[---].|yisp hm.b[ʻl.---] 12[75].2.21
.tǵr k].|[t]š[lm k.---].|[-----].|[-----].|h[--.---].|[-----].|w [----].|w [----].|w [----].|t[--.---]. 56[21].11
t]š[lm k.---].|[-----].|[-----].|h[--.---].|[-----].|w [----].|w [----].|w [----].|t[--.---]. 56[21].12
m[.---].|w ṯt.npš[.---].|kbd.w [---].|l ṣp[n.---].|š.[---].|w [----].|k[--.---].|ʻn[t.---]. 40[134].13
.bʻl y.ḥw[t.--].|yšhr k.w.ʻm.ṣ[--].|ʻš[--.---]d.lik[t.---].|w [----].|k[--.---].|ʻšrm[.---].|tšt.tbʻ[.---].|qrt.mlk[.---].|w.ʻl. 2008.1.13
--.d]bḥ.dbḥ.|[--.ʻ]šr.ʻšrt.|ʻ[---.---].|b[---.---].|t[--.---].|w[----].|pǵ[t.---].|lk[.---].|ki[--.---].|w ḫ[--.---].|my[.---].|a 16.2[125].66
---].|[-----].|[-----].|h[--.---].|[-----].|w [----].|w [----].|w [----].|t[--.---]. 56[21].13
[-----].|w.[-----].|w.abǵl.nḥ[l h.--].|w.unṯ.aḫd.l h[.---].|dnn.bn.yṣr[. 90[314].1.2
wt k.inn.|špš n.[---].|hm.al[k.--].|ytnt[.---].|ṯn[.---].|w[.-----].|l[.-----].|h[--.---].|šp[š.---].|ʻm.k[--.lḥt].|akl.yṯ[ṯb.- 2060.25
.ʻps.aḫd.kw|sgt.|ḫrd ksp.[--]r.|ymm.w[.---].|[-----].|w[.-----].|[-----]. 2062.2.11

wṭm

|šlyṭ.d šbʻy.rašm.|ṯṯkḥ.ttrp.šmm.k rs.|ipd k.ank.ispi.uṭm.|ḏrqm.amt m.l yrt.|b npš.bn ilm.mt.b mh|mrt.ydd.il. 5[67].1.5

wmrkm

[--.]wmrkm.|bir.ḫmš.|uškn.arbʻ.|ubrʻy.ṯlṯ.|ar.ṯmn ʻšr h.|mlk. 68[65].1.1

wn

.|rbt.ilm.l ḥkmt.|šbt.dqn k.l tsr k.|rḫntt.d[-].l irt k.|wn ap.ʻdn.mṭr h.|bʻl.yʻdn.ʻdn.ṯkt.b glṯ.|w tn.ql h.b ʻrpt.|šr 4[51].5.68
h l pn[.zb]l y[m].|[l pn.ṯp]ṭ[.nhr.]mlkt.[--]pm.l mlkt.wn.in.aṯt.|[l]k.k[m.ilm].|[w ǵlmt.k bn.qdš.]w y[--.]zbl.ym. 2.3[129].22
k.|[d yknn h.yṣ]ḥ.aṯ|[rt.w bn h.]ilt.|[w ṣbrt.ary]h.|[wn.in.bt.l bʻl.]|[km.ilm.w ḥẓr].|[k bn.aṯ]r[t].|m[ṯ]b.il.mẓll. 4[51].1.10
.|[i]l.mlk.d yknn h.yṣḥ.|aṯrt.w bn h.ilt.w ṣbrt.|ary h.wn.in.bt.l bʻl.|km.ilm.w ḥẓr.k bn.aṯrt.|mṯb il.mẓll.bn h.|m 4[51].4.50
[---.wn.in].|[bt].l [bʻl.km.ilm.w ḥẓr].|k bn.[aṯrt.mṯb.il.mẓll].|b 3[ʻNT.VI].4.02
h.il.|mlk.d yknn h.yṣḥ.aṯrt.|w bn h.ilt.w ṣbrt.arḫ h.|wn.in.bt.l bʻl.km.ilm.|ḥẓr.k b[n.a]ṯrt.mṯb.il.|mṯll.b[n h.m]ṯ 3[ʻNT.VI].5.46
.|[---.--]b.|[---.--]a h.|[---.--]d.|[---].umt n.|[---.--]yh.wn l.|[---].bt bʻl.|[---.--]y.|[---.--]nt. 28[-].11
.ibrm.|w b hm.pn.bʻl.|bʻl.ytlk.w yṣd.|yḥ pat.mlbr.|wn.ymǵy.aklm.|w ymẓa.ʻqqm.|bʻl.ḥmd m.yḥmd m.|bn.dg 12[75].1.36

wql

ʻd[rš]p.|pqr.|ṯǵr.|ttǵl.|ṯn.yṣḥm.|slṯmg.|kdrl.|wql.|adrdn.|prn.|ʻbdil.|ušy.šbn[-].|aḫt.ab.|krwn.|nnḏ.|m 1069.8

wry

ty[.---].|ṯkt.ydln[.---].|ṯkt.ṯryn[.---].|br.ʻbdm[lk.---].|wry[.---].|ṯkt[.---].|ṯk[t.---].|br[.---].|br[.---].|br[.---].|br[.-- 84[319].1.7

wrt

štmʻ.|ʻšrm.l mit.ksp.|ʻl.bn.alkbl.šb[ny].|ʻšrm ksp.ʻl.|wrt.mtny.w ʻl.|prdny.aṯt h. 2107.18
ḏm[r.---].br.|bn.i[ytlm.---].|wr[t.---.]b d.yḥmn.|yry[.---.]br.|ydn[.---].kry.|bn.ydd[.---.b 2123.3

wšy

[ṯ]n.p k.b ǵr.ṯn.p k.b ḫlb.k tgwln.šnt k.|[--.]w špt k.l tššy.hm.tqrm.l mt.b rn k.|[--]ḫp.an.arnn.ql.špš.ḥw.bṯnm.u 1001.1.5
dy.ʻnt.|tǵdd.kbd h.b ṣḥq.ymlu.|lb h.b šmḫt.kbd.ʻnt.|tšyt.k brkm.tǵll b dm.|ḏmr.ḥlqm.b mmʻ.mhrm.|ʻd.tšbʻ.tmt 3[ʻNT].2.27

wtḥ

bd.šdm.|[ḥ]š k.[ʻ]ṣ k.ʻbṣ k.ʻm y.pʻn k.|[tls]mn.[ʻ]m y.twtḥ.išd k.|[dm.rgm.iṯ.l y.]w argm k.hwt.|[w aṯny k.rgm.]ʻ 3[ʻNT].4.56
d.l kbd.šdm.|ḥš k.ʻṣ k.ʻbṣ k.|ʻm y.pʻn k.tlsmn.ʻm y.|twtḥ.išd k.dm.rgm.|iṯ.l y.w argm k.|hwt.w aṯny k.rgm.|ʻṣ. 3[ʻNT].3.17
.|l kbd.š[dm.ḥš k.ʻṣ k.ʻbṣ k.ʻm y.pʻn k.tls]|[m]n ʻm y t[wtḥ.išd k.dm.rgm.iṯ.l y.d argmn k].|[h]wt.d aṯ[ny k.---.rg 7.2[130].17
.l kbd.š]dm.ḥš k.|[ʻṣ k.ʻbṣ k.ʻm y.pʻ]n k.tlsmn.|[ʻm y.twtḥ.išd] k.tk.ḫršn.|[---.-]bd k.spr.|[---.-]nk. 1[ʻNT.IX].2.23
[ḥš k.ʻṣ k.ʻbṣ k.ʻ]m y.p[ʻ]n k.|[tlsmn.ʻm y.twt]ḥ.išd k.|[tk.ḫršn.---]r.[-]ḥm k.w št.|[---.]ẓ[--.-]rdy k.|[-- 1[ʻNT.IX].2.2
.bǵrt.ṯ[--. --].|ḥš k.ʻṣ k.ʻ[bṣ k.ʻm y.pʻn k.tlsmn].|ʻm y twtḥ.i[šd k.tk.ḫršn.-------------].|ǵr.ks.dm.r[gm.iṯ.l y.w argm 1[ʻNT.IX].3.11

Z

z

ṭ.ṯm.|[---.]bn.ilm.|[m]t.šmḫ.p ydd.|il[.ǵ]zr.|b [-]dn.ʻ.z.w.|rgbt.zbl.	UG5.4.17

zbl

.|šmm.tmr.zbl.mlk.|šmm.tlak.ṭl.amr..|bn km k bk[r.z]bl.am..|rkm.agzrt[.--].arḫ..|bʻl.azrt.ʻnt.[-]ld.|kbd h.l ydʻ	13[6].28
ty.ulp.alṯy.ulp.ǵbr].|[ulp.ḫbt km.ulp.mdll km.ulp.qr zbl].|[u ṯḫṭu.u b ap km.u b qṣrt.npš km.u b qṭt].|[tqṭṭ.u ṯḫṭ	32[2].1.8
y.ulp[.alṯy.ulp.]ǵbr.|ulp.ḫbt kn.uìp.md[ll k]n.ulp.q[r zbl].|u ṯḫṭin.b ap kn.u b [q]ṣrt.npš[kn.u b qṭt].|tqṭṭn u ṯḫṭi	32[2].1.13
.ulp.alṯy.ul[p.ǵbr.]ulp.|ḫbt km.ulp.m[dl]l km.ulp.qr zbl.u[š]n yp km.|u b ap km.u b q[ṣ]rt.npš km.u b qṭt.tqṭṭ.|	32[2].1.22
u]lp.alṯy.|[ulp.ǵbr.ulp.ḫbt km.ulp.mdll km.ulp].|[qr zbl.ušn.yp km.b ap km.u b qṣrt.np]št km.|[u b qṭt.tqṭṭ.ušn.	APP.I[-].1.17
ty.ulp.alṯy].|[ulp.ǵbr.ulp.ḫbt kn.ulp.mdll kn.ulp.]qr zbl.|[ušn.yp kn.u b ap kn.u b qṣrt.npš kn.u b]qṭt.|[tqṭṭn.uš	APP.I[-].2.14
ḫty.ulp.alṯy.ulp.ǵbr.ul]p.ḫbt kn.|[ulp.mdll kn.ulp.qr zbl.ušn.y]p kn.|[u b ap kn.u b qṣrt.npšt kn.u b qṭ]t tqṭṭ.|[u	APP.I[-].1.6
ty.ulp.alṯy.|ulp.ǵbr.ulp.[ḫbt] kn[.u]lp.mdll kn.ulp qr z[bl].|lšn yp kn.b ap [kn.u b qṣ]rt.npš kn.u b qṭt.|tqṭṭn.ušn	32[2].1.30
t.šd.šḫlmmt.|mǵny.l bʻl.npl.l a|rṣ.mt.aliyn.bʻl.|ḫlq.zbl.bʻl.arṣ.|apnk.lṭpn.il.|d pid.yrd.l ksi.yṯb.|l hdm[.w] l.hd	5[67].6.10
bʻl].|k ḫlq.z[bl.bʻl.arṣ].|w hm.ḥy.a[liyn.bʻl].|w hm.iṯ.zbl.bʻ[l.arṣ].|b ḥlm.lṭpn.il.d pid.|b ḏrt.bny.bnwt.|šmm.šmn	6[49].3.3
šmn.tmṭrn.|nḫlm.tlk.nbtm.|w idʻ.k ḥy.aliyn.bʻl.|k iṯ.zbl.bʻl.arṣ.|b ḥlm.lṭpn.il d pid.|b ḏrt.bny.bnwt.|šmm.šmn.t	6[49].3.9
ht.|aṯrt.w bn h.ilt.w ṣb|rt.ary h.k mt.aliyn.|bʻl.k ḫlq.zbl.bʻl.|arṣ.gm.yṣḥ il.|l rbt.aṯrt ym.šmʻ.|l rbt.aṯr[t] ym.tn.|	6.1.42[49.1.14]
n.ank.w anḫn.|w tnḫ.b irt y.npš.|k ḥy.aliyn.bʻl.|k iṯ.zbl.bʻl.arṣ.|gm.yṣḥ.il.l btlt.|ʻnt.šmʻ.l btlt.ʻn[t].|rgm.l nrt.il.š	6[49].3.21
[k mt.aliyn.bʻl].|k ḫlq.z[bl.bʻl.arṣ].|w hm.ḥy.a[liyn.bʻl].|w hm.iṯ.zbl.bʻ[l.arṣ].|b ḥl	6[49].3.1
.|pl.ʻnt.šdm.il.yš[t k].|bʻl.ʻnt.mḥrṯ[-].|iy.aliyn.bʻl.|iy.zbl.bʻl.arṣ.|w tʻn.nrt.ilm.š[p]š.|šd yn.ʻn.b qbt[.t]|bl lyt.ʻl.u	6[49].4.40
al.tǵl[.---].|prdmn.ʻbd.ali[yn].|bʻl.sid.zbl.bʻl.|arṣ.qm.yṯʻr.|w yšlḥmn h.|ybrd.ṯd.l pnw h.|b ḥrb.	3[ʻNT].1.3
š.|pl.ʻnt.šdm.il.yšt k.|[b]ʻl.ʻnt.mḥrṯt.|iy.aliyn.bʻl.|iy.zbl.bʻl.arṣ.|ttbʻ.btlt.ʻnt.|idk.l ttn.pnm.|ʻm.nrt.ilm.špš.|tšu.	6[49].4.29
sy ym[.---].|rmm.ḫnpm.mḫl[.---].|mlk.nhr.ibr[.---].|zbl bʻl.ǵlm.[---].|ṣǵr hd w r[---.---].|w l nhr nd[-.---].|[---.--]	9[33].2.10
|[---].mlak.bn.ktpm.rgm.bʻl h.w y[--.---].|[---].ap.anš.zbl.bʻl.šdmt.bg[--.---].|[---.-]dm.mlak.ym.tʻdt.ṯpṭ.nh[r.---].|[	2.1[137].43
l bʻl[-.---].|ṯḥt.ksi.zbl.ym.w ʻn.kṯr.w ḫss.l rgmt.|l k.l zbl.bʻl.ṯnt.l rkb.ʻrpt.ht.ib k.|bʻl m.ht.ib k.tmḫṣ.ht.tṣmt.ṣrt k	2.4[68].8
ybl.argmn k.k ilm.|[---.]ybl.k bn.qdš.mnḥy k.ap.anš.zbl.bʻ[l].|[-.yuḫ]d.b yd.mšḫṭ.bm.ymn.mḫṣ.ǵlmm.yš[--].|[y	2.1[137].38
.ym.tʻdt.ṯpṭ.nhr.|tšu ilm rašt hm.l ẓr.brkt hm.ln.kḥṯ.zbl hm.|aḫr.tmǵyn.mlak ym.tʻdt.ṯpṭ.nhr.l pʻn.il.|[l t]pl.l tšt	2.1[137].29
dt.ṯpṭ[.nhr].|t[ǵ]ly.hlm.rišt hm.l ẓr.brkt hm.w l kḥṯ.|zbl hm.b hm.ygʻr.bʻl.lm.ǵltm.ilm.rišt.|km l ẓr brkt km.w ln	2.1[137].24
n.bʻl.|[------.]yrḫ.zbl.|[--.kṯ]r w ḫss.|[---]n.rḥm y.ršp zbl.|[w ʻd]t.ilm.ṯlṯ h.|[ap]nk.krt.ṯʻ.ʻ[-]r.|[--.]b bt h.yšt.ʻrb.|	15[128].2.6
.|[qd]š.lbum.trd.b n[p]šn y.trḥṣn.k ṯrm.|[--]b b[ht].|[zbl.]ym.b hkl.ṯpṭ.nh[r].yṯir.ṯr.il.ab h l pn[.zb]l y[m].|[l pn.ṯ	2.3[129].21
r l kḥṯ drkt h.trtqṣ.b d bʻl km nš|r.b uṣbʻt h.hlm.ktp.zbl ym.bn ydm.|[ṯp]ṭ nhr.yrtqṣ.ṣmd.b d bʻl.km.nšr.|b[u]ṣb	2.4[68].14
p]ṭ nhr.yrtqṣ.ṣmd.b d bʻl.km.nšr.|b[u]ṣbʻt h.ylm.ktp.zbl ym.bn ydm.ṯpṭ.|nhr.ʻz.ym.l ymk.l tngṣn.pnt h.l ydlp.|t	2.4[68].16
kḥṯ.drkt h.trtqṣ.|b d bʻl.km.nšr b uṣbʻt h.hlm.qdq|d zbl ym.bn.ʻnm.ṯpṭ.nhr.yprsḥ ym.|w yql.l arṣ.w trtqṣ.ṣmd.b	2.4[68].22
arṣ.w trtqṣ.ṣmd.b d bʻl.|[km.]nšr.b uṣbʻt h.ylm.qdqd.zbl.|[ym.]bn.ʻnm.ṯpṭ.nhr.yprsḥ.ym.yql.|l arṣ.tngṣn.pnt h.w	2.4[68].24
htm.l arṣ.ypl.ul ny.w l.ʻpr.ʻẓm ny.|l bʻl[-.---].|ṯḥt.ksi.zbl.ym.w ʻn.kṯr.w ḫss.l rgmt.|l k.l zbl.bʻl.ṯnt.l rkb.ʻrpt.ht.ib	2.4[68].7
t.wn.in.aṯt.|[l]k.k[m.ilm].|[w ǵlmt.k bn.qdš.]w y[--.]zbl.ym.yʻ[--.]ṯpṭ.nhr.|[-------.]yšlḥn.w yʻn ʻṯtr[.-].	2.3[129].23
|b šm.tgʻr m.ʻṯtrt.bṯ l aliyn.[bʻl.]|bṯ.l rkb.ʻrpt.k šby n.zb[l.ym.k]|šby n.ṯpṭ.nhr.w yṣa b[.--].|ybṯ.nn.aliyn.bʻl.w [-	2.4[68].29
t.ilm.špš.tšu.g h.w t[ṣḥ.šm]ʻ.mʻ.|[-.yṯ]ir ṯr.il.ab k.l pn.zbl.ym.l pn[.ṯ]pṭ[.n]hr.|[ik.a]l.yšmʻ k.ṯr.[i]l.ab k.l ysʻ.[alt.]ṯ[	2.3[129].16
-]b b[ht].|[zbl.]ym.b hkl.ṯpṭ.nh[r].yṯir.ṯr.il.ab h l pn[.zb]l y[m].|[l pn.ṯp]ṭ[.nhr.]mlkt.[--]pm.l mlkt.wn.in.aṯt.|[l]	2.3[129].21
kl.ṯpṭ nh[r].|[---.]hrn.w[---.]tbʻ.k[ṯ]r w [ḫss.t]bn.bht zbl ym.|[trm]m.hk[l.ṯpṭ].nhr.bt k.[---.]šp[-.---].|[ḫš.bh]t h.t	2.3[129].8
r.š[t.tšu.g h].|w tṣḥ.ytb.ytp.[---].|qrt.ablm.ablm.[qrt.zbl.yrḫ].|ik.al.yḥdṯ.yrḫ.b[---].|b qrn.ymn h.b anšt[.---].|qd	18[3AQHT].4.8
.---].|[---.--]r.almd k.[---].|[---.]qrt.ablm.a[blm].|[qrt.zbl.]yrḫ.d mgdl.š[---].|[---.]mn.ʻr hm[.---].|[---.]it[.---].|[---.	18[3AQHT].1.31
dr.dr.ʻdb.uḫry mṯ yd h.|ymǵ.l qrt.ablm.abl[m].|qrt.zbl.yrḫ.yšu g h.|w yṣḥ.y l k.qrt.ablm.|d ʻl k.mḫṣ.aqht.ǵzr.|	19[1AQHT].4.164
.ʻny h.|w yʻn.lṭpn.il.b pid.|ṭb.bn y.lm ṭb[t] km.|l kḥṯ.zbl k[m.a]nk.|iḥtrš.w [a]škn.|aškn.ydt.[m]rṣ gršt.|zbln.r[--	16[126].5.25
.ym.tʻdt.ṯpṭ.nhr.|šu.ilm.rašt km.l ẓr.brkt km.ln.kḥṯ.|zbl km.w ank.ʻny.mlak.ym.tʻdt.ṯpṭ.nhr.|tšu ilm rašt hm.l ẓ	2.1[137].28
m.ygʻr.bʻl.lm.ǵltm.ilm.rišt.|km l ẓr brkt km.w ln.kḥṯ.zbl km.aḥd.|ilm.tʻny lḥt.mlak.ym.tʻdt.ṯpṭ.nhr.|šu.ilm.rašt	2.1[137].25
.|ṯm.ṯmq.rpu.bʻl.mhr bʻl.|w mhr.ʻnt.ṯm.yḥpn.ḥyl|y.zbl.mlk.ʻllm y.km.tdd.|ʻnt.ṣd.tštr.ʻpt.šmm.|ṭbḫ.alpm.ap ṣin	22.2[124].10
ṯr[h.rpum.l tdd].|aṯr h.l t[dd.ilnym.ṯm].|yḥpn.ḥy[ly.zbl.mlk.ʻllm y].|šmʻ.atm[.---].|ym.lm.qd[.---].|šmn.prst[.--	22.1[123].12
.k w[-].|k rtqt mr[.---].|k d lbšt.bir.mlak.|šmm.tmr.zbl.mlk.|šmm.tlak.ṭl.amr..|bn km k bk[r.z]bl.am..|rkm.ag	13[6].26
.ṯn.hlk.|aṯr.ṯlṯ.kl hm.|yḥd.bt h.sgr.|almnt.škr.|tškr.zbl.ʻršm.|yšu.ʻwr.mzl.|ymzl.w yṣi.trḫ.|ḥdṯ.ybʻr.l ṯn.|aṯt h.l	14[KRT].2.98
ṯn.hlk.|aṯr.ṯlṯ.kl hm.|aḥd.bt h.ysgr.|almnt.škr.|tškr.zbl.ʻršm.|yšu.ʻwr.|mzl.ymzl.|w ybl.trḫ.ḥdṯ.|ybʻr.l ṯn.aṯt h.	14[KRT].4.186
.ṭb.w.ṯṯm.ṯṯ.kbd.|yn.d.l.ṭb.b.gt.ḥdṯt.|tšʻm.yn.d.l.ṭb.b.zbl.|ʻšrm.yn.ṭb.w.ṯtm.ḫmš.k[b]d.|yn.d.l.ṭb.b.gt.sǵy.|arbʻm.	1084.13
[-----].|[------.]ṯr.|[---.aliy]n.bʻl.|[------.]yrḫ.zbl.|[--.kṯ]r w ḫss.|[---]n.rḥm y.ršp zbl.|[w ʻd]t.ilm.ṯlṯ h.|[	15[128].2.4
bn.ilm.|[m]t.šmḫ.p ydd.|il[.ǵ]zr.|b [-]dn.ʻ.z.w.|rgbt.zbl.	UG5.4.18

zbln

ilm.ʻn[y h.]ytdṯ.|yšbʻ.rgm.[my.]b ilm.|ydy.mrṣ.gršm zbln.|in.b ilm.ʻny h.|w yʻn.lṭpn.il.b pid.|ṭb.bn y.lm ṭb[t] k	16[126].5.21
].|ʻny h.y[ṯny.yṯlṯ].|rgm.my.b[ilm.ydy].|mrṣ.grš[m.zbln].|in.b ilm.ʻ[ny h.yrb].|yḫmš.rgm.[my.b ilm].|ydy.mrṣ	16[126].5.15
.ʻ[ny h.yrbʻ].|yḫmš.rgm.[my.b ilm].|ydy.mrṣ.g[ršm.zbln].|in.b ilm.ʻn[y h.]ytdṯ.|yšbʻ.rgm.[my.]b ilm.|ydy.mrṣ.	16[126].5.18
[.-.w yʻn].|lṭpn.[il.d pid.my].|b ilm.[ydy.mrṣ].|gršm.z[bln.in.b ilm].|ʻny h.y[ṯny.yṯlṯ].|rgm.my.b[ilm.ydy].|mrṣ.	16[126].5.12
aṯt.trḫ.w tbʻt.|ṯar um.tkn l h.|mṯlṯt.kṯrm.tmt.|mrbʻt.zblnm.|mḫmšt.yitsp.|ršp.nṯdṯt.ǵlm.|ym.mšbʻt hn.b šlḥ.|tt	14[KRT].1.17

n.almnt. | l ṯṯpṯ.ṯpṯ.qṣr.npš. | km.aẖt.ʿrš.mdw. | anšt.ʿrš.zbln. | rd.l mlk.amlk. | l drkt.k aṯb.an. | ytbʿ.yṣb ǵlm.ʿl. | ab h. 16.6[127].36
lḥm.ytm.bʿd. | ksl k.almnt.km. | aẖt.ʿrš.mdw.anšt. | ʿrš.zbln.rd.l mlk. | amlk.l drkt k.aṯb. | an.w yʿny.krt ṯʿ.yṯbr. | ḥrn 16.6[127].52
m. | ʿrm.tdu.mh. | pdrm.tdu.šrr. | ẖṯ m.tʿmt.[ʾ]ṯr.[k]m. | zbln.ʿl.riš h. | w ṯṯb.trḥṣ.nn.b dʿt. | npš h.l lḥm.tptḥ. | brlt h.l ṯ 16.6[127].9
ṯ.zbl k[m.a]nk. | iḥtrš.w [a]škn. | aškn.ydt.[m]rṣ gršt. | zbln.r[---].ymlu. | nʿm.[-]ṯ[-.--.]yqrṣ. | d[-] b pẖ[-.--.]mẖt. | [---. 16[126].5.28
il.p.d[---]. | ʿrm.[di.mh.pdrm]. | di.š[rr.---]. | mr[ṣ.---]. | zb[ln.---]. | t[--.---]. | [-----]. 16[126].5.51

zbr

nm. | mt.w šr.yṯb.b d h.ẖṭ.ṯkl.b d h. | ẖṭ.ulmn.yzbrnn.zbrm.gpn. | yṣmdnn.ṣmdm.gpn.yšql.šdmt h. | km gpn. | šbʿ d. 23[52].9
bm m.ṯnnm. | mt.w šr.yṯb.b d h.ẖṭ.ṯkl.b d h. | ẖṭ.ulmn.yzbrnn.zbrm.gpn. | yṣmdnn.ṣmdm.gpn.yšql.šdmt h. | km gp 23[52].9

zd

šrm. | iqran.ilm.nʿmm[.agzry ym.bn]ym. | ynqm.b ap zd.aṯrt.[---]. | špš.mṣprt dlt hm[.---]. | w ǵnbm.šlm.ʿrbm.ṯn[n 23[52].24
.]upqt.ʿrb. | [---.w ẓ]r.mtn y at zd. | [---.]tʿrb.bši. | [---.]l tzd.l tptq. | [---].g[--.]l arṣ. 1[ʿNT.X].5.27
| ṯrt.l bnt.hll[.snnt]. | hl ǵlmt tld b[n.--]n. | ʿn ha l yd h.tzd[.--]. | pt l bšr h.dm a[--.--]ḥ. | w yn.k mtrẖt[.---]h. | šmʿ il 24[77].8
| [---.]rks.bn.abnm. | [---.]upqt.ʿrb. | [---.w ẓ]r.mtn y at zd. | [---.]tʿrb.bši. | [---.]l tzd.l tptq. | [---].g[--.]l arṣ. 1[ʿNT.X].5.25
w yn.k mtrẖt[.---]h. | šmʿ ilht kṯr[t.--]mm. | nh l yd h tzdn[.---]n. | l ad[n h.---]. | dgn tt[--.---.-]l | ʿ.l kṯrt hl[l.sn]nt. | 24[77].12

zlbn

ẖlq. | bn ytr. | bn ilšpš. | ubrš. | bn gmš ẖlq. | bn ʿgy. | bn zlbn. | bn.aẖ[--]. | bn[.---]. | [-----]. | bn kr[k]. | bn ẖtyn. | w nḥl 2016.2.20
qmḥ.d.kly.k ṣḥ.illdrm. | b d.zlb[n.--]. | arbʿ.ʿš[r.]dd.nʿr. | d.apy[.--]. | w.arb[ʿ.--]d.apy.ʿbd h 2094.2

zlyy

qrṭym.mddbʿl. | kdn.zlyy. | krwn.arty. | tlmu.zlyy. | pdu.qmnzy. | bdl.qrṭy. | trgn.bn 89[312].2
qrṭym.mddbʿl. | kdn.zlyy. | krwn.arty. | tlmu.zlyy. | pdu.qmnzy. | bdl.qrṭy. | trgn.bn.tǵh. | aupš.qmnzy. | ṯrr 89[312].4
dmt ṯlṯ. | qmnz ṯql. | zlyy ṯql. | ary ẖmšt. | yknʿm ẖmšt. | ʿnmky ṯqlm. | [-]kt ʿšrt. | q 1176.3
gn.bn.tǵh. | aupš.qmnzy. | ṯrry.mṣbty. | prn.nǵty. | ṯrdn.zlyy. 89[312].11

zmr

---]t. | i[d.yd]bḥ.mlk.l.prgl.ṣqrn.b.gg. | ar[bʿ.]arbʿ.mṯbt.azmr.b h.š.šr[-]. | al[p.w].š.šlmm.pamt.šbʿ.klb h. | yr[--.]mlk. 35[3].51

zn

.---]. | šm.bn y.yw.ilt.[---]. | w pʿr.šm.ym[-.---]. | tʿnyn.l zn.tn[.---]. | at.adn.tpʿr[.---]. | ank.lṭpn.il[.d pid.---]. | ʿl.ydm.pʿ 1[ʿNT.X].4.16

znan

bn.il.qšt.w.qlʿ. | ark.qšt.w.qlʿ. | bn.ʿbdnkl.qšt.w.qlʿ. | bn.znan.qšt. | bn.arz.[ar]bʿ.qšt.w.arb[ʿ.]qlʿm. | b[n.]adʿl.q[š]t.w.q 119[321].2.44

zǵ

arbʿt ʿšrt.bʿl. | ʿrkm. | b ṯmnt.ʿšrt.yr | ṯḥṣ.mlk.brr. | ʿlm.tzǵ.b ǵb.ṣpn. | nḥkt.ksp.w ẖrṣ ṯʿ ṯn šm l btbt. | alp.w š šrp.alp UG5.12.A.7
t]. | mẓma.yd.mṯkt. | ṯṯkr.[--]dn. | ʿm.krt.mswn h. | arẖ.tzǵ.l ʿgl h. | bn.ẖpṯ.l umht hm. | k tnḥn.udmm. | w yʿny.krt.ṯʿ. 15[128].1.5
m š.iṯtqb. | w š.nbk m w.š. | gt mlk š.ʿlm. | l kṯr.ṯn.ʿlm. | tzǵ[.---.]nšm.pr. UG5.12.B.13

zǵt

.l [qr.]ṯiqt. | ibr h[.l]ql.nhqt. | ḥmr[h.l gʿt.]alp. | ḥrṯ[.l z]ǵt.klb. | [ṣ]pr[.apn]k. | [pb]l[.mlk.g]m.l aṯt | [h.k]y[ṣḥ.]šmʿ. 14[KRT].5.226
pbl. | mlk.l qr.ṯigt.ibr h. | l ql.nhqt.ḥmr h. | l gʿt.alp.ḥrṯ.zǵt. | klb.ṣpr.w ylak. | mlakm.l k.ʿm.krt. | mswn h.ṯḥm.pbl.ml 14[KRT].3.122

zql

ydn. | qṭn. | bn.asr. | bn.ʿdy. | bn.amt[m]. | myn. | šr. | bn.zql. | bn.iẖy. | bn.iyṯr. | bn.ʿyn. | bn.ǵzl. | bn.ṣmy. | bn.il[-]šy. | b 2117.2.3

zr

l.ʿšrm.bn[š.mlk.---].ẖzr.lqḥ.ḥp[r]. | ʿšt.ʿšr h.bn[.---.--]ẖ.zr. | bʿl.šd. 2011.41
mrm. | [k gm]n.al[i]yn.b[ʿl]. | [---]ḥ h.tšt bm.ʿ[--]. | [---.]zr h.ybm.l ilm. | [id]k.l ttn.pnm.ʿn.. | [il.]mbk nhrm.qrb. | [a] 6.1.31[49.1.3]

zry

ilṣdq.bn.zry. | bʿlytn.bn.ulb. | ytrʿm.bn.swy. | ṣḥrn.bn.qrtm. | bn.špš.bn 2024.1
.qlʿ. | gln.ṯt.qštm.w.qlʿ. | gtn.qšt. | pmn.ṯt.qšt.w.qlʿ. | bn.zry.q[š]t.w.qlʿ. | bn.tlmyn.ṯt.qštm.w.qlʿ. | bn.ysd.qšt. | [ǵ]mrm 104[316].9

zrm

.ʿlt.b ab y. | u---].ʿlt.b k.lk.l pn y.yrk.bʿl.[--]. | [---.]ʿnt.šzrm.tštšḥ.km.ḥ[--]. | [---].ʿpr.bt k.ygr[š k.---]. | [---.]y.ḥr.ḥr.b 1001.1.11

zt

ṯlṯ.mat. | šbʿm kbd. | zt.ubdym. | b mlk. 1095.3
]dn. | arbʿ[m.ksp.]ʿl. | il[m]l[k.a]rgnd. | uškny[.w]mit. | zt.b d hm.rib. | w [---]. | [-----]. | [-]šy[.---] h. | [-]kt[.---.]nrn. | [2055.13
[---.]d.ztm.d.si[-]. | [---.]d.ztm.d ggy.[---]. | [---.d].ztm.d.b[--]. | [---.]ztm.[---]. 2035.3
[---.]d.ztm.d.si[-]. | [---.]d.ztm.d ggy.[---]. | [---.d].ztm.d.b[--]. | [---.]ztm.[---]. 2035.2
[---.]d.ztm.d.si[-]. | [---.]d.ztm.d ggy.[---]. | [---.d].ztm.d.b[--]. | [---.]z 2035.1
b.gt.mlkt.b.rḥbn. | ẖmšm.l.mitm.zt. | w.b d.krd. | ẖmšm.l.mit. | arbʿ.kbd. 1096.2
yšt.l.lṣb h ẖšʿr klb. | [w]riš.pqq.w šr h. | yšt.aḥd h.dm zt.ẖrpnt. UG5.1.2.6
. | w mri ilm.ʿglm.dt.šnt. | imr.qmṣ.llim.k ksp. | l ʿbrm.zt.ẖrṣ.l ʿbrm.kš. | dpr.ṯlḥn.b qʿl.b qʿl. | mlkm.hn.ym.yṣq.yn.ṯ 22.2[124].15

zt

[---.l]šn.l kbkbm.y'rb. | [b']l.b kbd h.b p h yrd. | k ḫrr.zt.ybl.arṣ.w pr. | 'ṣm.yraun.aliyn.b'l. | ṯṯ'.nn.rkb.'rpt. | tb'.rg	5[67].2.5
ḫmšm.kkr. | qnm. | 'šrm.kk[r]. | brr. | [']šrm.npš. | 'šrm.zt.mm. | 'rb'm. | šmn.mr.	141[120].14
.si[-]. | [---.]d.ztm.d ggy.[---]. | [---.d].ztm.d.b[--]. | [---.]ztm.[---].	2035.4
.akl. | ṯṯ.'šr h.yn. | kd.šmn.l.nr.ilm. | kdm.dǵm. | ṯṯ.kdm.ztm.	1126.8

ztr

ykn.bn h b bt.šrš.b qrb. | hkl h.nṣb.skn.ilib h.b qdš. | ztr.'m h.l arṣ.mšṣu.qṭr h. | l 'pr.ḏmr.aṯr h.ṭbq.lḥt. | niṣ h.grš	17[2AQHT].1.28
.bn h. | [b bt.šrš.]b qrb.hkl h. | [nṣb.skn.i]lib h.b qdš. | [ztr.'m h.l a]rṣ.mšṣu. | [qṭr h.l 'pr.ḏ]mr.a[ṯ]r h. | [ṭbq.lḥt.niṣ h	17[2AQHT].1.46
n.l y.km. | aḫ y.w šrš.km ary y. | nṣb.skn.ilib y.b qdš. | ztr.'m y.l 'pr.ḏmr.aṯr[y]. | ṭbq lḥt.niṣ y.grš. | d 'šy.ln.aḫd.yd	17[2AQHT].2.17
l 'pr.ḏ]mr.a[ṯ]r h. | [ṭbq.lḥt.niṣ h.gr]š.d 'šy. | [ln h.---]. | z[tr.'m k.l arṣ.mšṣu.qṭr k]. | l 'pr.ḏm[r.aṯr k.ṭbq]. | lḥt.niṣ k.g	17[2AQHT].2.1

ḥ

ḥbṭ

.ḥtt.bn ḥtt[.---].|[---.--]p.km.dlt.tlk.km.p[---].|[---.]bt.tḥbṭ.km.ṣq.ṣdr[.---].|[---.]kl.b kl.l pgm.pgm.l.b[---].|[---.]m 1001.1.25

ḥby

.l bt h.yštql.|l ḥṭr h.y'msn.nn.ṯkmn.|w šnm.w ngšnn.ḥby.|b'l.qrnm w ḏnb.ylšn.|b ḫri h.w ṯnt h.ql.il.[--].|il.k yrd UG5.1.1.19

ḥbl

.ǵlmt.|'mm ym.bn.ẓlm[t].|rmt.pr't.ibr[.mnt].|ṣḥrrm.ḥbl[.--].|'rpt.tḥt.[---]|m 'ṣrm.ḥ[---].|glṯ.isr[.---]|m.brt[.--- 8[51FRAG].10
kpt.|mit.dnn.|mitm.iqnu.|ḫmš.'šr.qn.n'm.'n[m].|ṯn.ḥblm.alp.alp.am[-].|ṯmn.ḥblm.šb'.šb'.ma[-].|'šr.kkr.rtn.|b 1128.30
.yṯb].|l lḥm.w bn.dnil.l ṯrm[.'l h].|nšrm.trḫpn.ybṣr.[ḥbl.d]|iym.bn.nšrm.arḫp.an[k.']l.|aqht.'db k.hlmn.ṯnm.qd 18[3AQHT].4.20
km.yṯb.l lḥ[m].|bn.dnil.l ṯrm.'l h.nšr[m].|trḫpn.ybṣr.ḥbl.diy[m.bn].|nšrm.trḫp.'nt.'l[.aqht].|t'dbn h.hlmn.ṯnm[. 18[3AQHT].4.31
.---].|yǵly.yḫsp.ib[.---].|'l.bt.ab h.nšrm.trḫ[p]n.|ybṣr.ḥbl.diym.|tbky.pǵt.bm.lb.|tdm'.bm.kbd.|tmz'.kst.dnil.mt. 19[1AQHT].1.33
.b]'l.yabd.l alp.|[---.bt]lt.'nt.|[---]q.hry.w yld.|[---]m.ḥbl.kṯ[r]t.|[---.bt]lt.'nt.|[---.ali]yn.b'l.|[---.]m'n.|[-----].|[--- 11[132].1.6
ǵlmt.|['mm.]ym.bn.ẓlmt.r|[mt.pr']t.ibr.mnt.|[ṣḥrrm.ḥbl.']rpt.|[---.---.-]ḥt.|[---.---]m.|[----] h. 4[51].7.57
.|ḫmš.'šr.qn.n'm.'n[m].|ṯn.ḥblm.alp.alp.am[-].|ṯmn.ḥblm.šb'.šb'.ma[-].|'šr.kkr.rtn.|b d.šm'y.bn.bdn. 1128.31

ḥbq

my.|[---].hw.mḫ.l 'rš h.y'l.|[---].bm.nšq.aṯt h.|[---.]b ḥbq h.ḥmḥmt.|[---.--] n.ylt.ḥmḥmt.|[---.mt.r]pi.w ykn.bn h 17[2AQHT].1.41
hbr.špt hm.yšq.hn.[š]pt hm.mtqtm.|bm.nšq.w hr.[b]ḥbq.w ḥ[m]ḥmt.ytb[n].|yspr.l ḫmš.l ṣ[---.]šr.pḫr.klat.|tqtn 23[52].56
il.ysb.palt h.|bṣql.yph.b palt.bṣ[q]l.|yph.b yǵlm.bṣql.y[ḥb]q.|w ynšq.aḥl.an bṣ[ql].|ynp'.b palt.bṣql yp' b yǵlm.| 19[1AQHT].2.63
.dnh.ysb.aklt h.yph.|šblt.b akt.šblt.yp'.|b ḥmdrt.šblt.yḥ[bq].|w ynšq.aḥl.an.šblt.|tp'.b aklt.šblt.tp'[.b ḥm]drt.|ur 19[1AQHT].2.70
hn.špt hm.mtqtm.mtqtm.k lrmn[.--].|bm.nšq.w hr.b ḥbq.ḥmḥmt.tqt[nṣn].|tldn.šḥr.w šlm.rgm.l il.ybl.a[ṯt y].|il. 23[52].51
pḥl.|št.gpnm.dt.ksp.|dt.yrq.nqbnm.|'db.gpn.atnt h.|yḥbq.qdš.w amrr.|yštn.aṯrt.l bmt.'r.|l ysmsmt.bmt.pḥl.|qd 4[51].4.13
.|ḫrḫb.mlk qẓ ḫrḫb m|lk aǵzt.b sǵ[--.]špš.|yrḫ yṯkḥ yḥ[bq] [-].|tld bt.[--]t.ḫ[--.l k]|ṯrt.l bnt.hll[.snnt].|hl ǵlmt tl 24[77].4
---.tld].|ibr.tld[.l b'l].|w rum.l[rkb.'rpt].|tḥbq.[---].|tḥbq[.---].|w tksynn.bṯn[-.]|y[--.]šr h.w šḫp h.|[--.]šḫp.ṣǵrt 10[76].3.24
].|arḫ.arḫ.[---.tld].|ibr.tld[.l b'l].|w rum.l[rkb.'rpt].|tḥbq.[---].|tḥbq[.---].|w tksynn.bṯn[-.]|y[--.]šr h.w šḫp h.|[- 10[76].3.23

ḥbr

.---].|iṯ.yn.d 'rb.bṯk[.---].|mǵ hw.l hn.lg yn h[.---].|w ḥbr h.mla yn.[---]. 23[52].76
.tḥtk.|špš.tḥtk.ilnym.|'d k.ilm.hn.mtm.|'d k.kṯr m.ḥbr k.|w ḫss.d't k.|b ym.arš.w tnn.|kṯr.w ḫss.yd.|ytr.kṯr. 6.6[62.2].48
.w yḏmr.|b knr.w ṯlb.b tp.w mṣltm.b m|rqdm.dšn.b.ḥbr.kṯr.ṭbm.|w tšt.'nt.gṯr.b'lt.mlk.b'|lt.drkt.b'lt.šmm.rmm. UG5.2.1.5

ḥbš

p.k.qṣm.|ǵrmn.kp.mhr.'tkt.|rišt.l bmt h.šnst.|kpt.b ḥbš h.brkm.tǵl[l].|b dm.ḏmr.ḥlqm.b mm['].|mhrm.mṭm.tg 3['NT].2.13
ap.mhr h.ank.|l aḥwy.tqḥ.yṭpn.mhr.št.|tštn.k nšr.b ḥbš h.km.diy.|b t'rt h.aqht.km.ytb.l lḥ[m].|bn.dnil.l ṯrm.'l 18[3AQHT].4.28
[---.šnst.kpt.b ḥb]š h.'tkt r[išt].|[l bmt h.---.]hy bt h t'rb.|[---.tm]ṯḥṣ b 'm 7.1[131].2
s[.---].|w t'n.btlt.'nt.ṯb.ytp.w[---].|l k.ašt k.km.nšr.b ḥb[š y].|km.diy.b t'rt y.aqht.[km.ytb].|l lḥm.w bn.dnil.l ṯr 18[3AQHT].4.17
.|tš[.---.]ymm.lk.|hrg.ar[b'.]ymm.bṣr.|kp.šsk k.[--].l ḥbš k.|'tk.ri[š.]l mhr k.|w 'p.l dr['].nšr k.|w rbṣ.l ǵr k.inbb. 13[6].6
q.'šrm.arb'.kbd.|ḫlb rpš arb'.'šr.|bq't ṯṯ.|irab ṯn.'šr.|ḥbš.ṯmn.|amḏy.arb'.'šr.|[-]n'y.ṯṯ.'šr. 67[110].10
m.---]n.krpn.'l.[k]rpn.|[---.]ym.w t'l.trṯ.|[---].yn.'šy l ḥbš.|[---.]ḥtn.qn.yṣbt.|[---.--]m.b nši.'n h.w tphn.|[---.--]ml. 17[2AQHT].6.8
krpn.[---].|w tṯtn.[---].|t'l.tr[-.---].|bt.il.li[mm.---].|'l.ḥbš.[---].|mn.lik.[---].|lik.tl[ak.---].|t'ddn[.---].|niṣ.p[---.---] 5[67].4.22

ḥgb

id.yph.mlk.|r[š]p.ḥgb.ap.|w[.n]pš.ksp.|w ḫrṣ.km[-].|w.ḥ[--.-]lp.|w.š.l[--]p.| 2005.1.2

ḥgby

---].|bn[---].|bn.mlkyy.|bn.atn.|bn.bly.|bn.ṯbrn.|bn.ḥgby.|bn.pity.|bn.slgyn.|'zn.bn.mlk.|bn.alṯn.|bn.ṯmyr.|ẓb 115[301].2.5
bl.|mlk.|gwl.|rqd.|ḫlby.|'n[q]pat.|m[']rb.|'rm.|bn.ḥgby.|mrat. 2075.29
lm.|'bdyrḫ.šb't.'šrt 'šrt.šlm.|yky.'šrt.ṯṯt šlm.'šrt.|bn.ḥgby.ṯmnt.l 'šrm.'šrt.ḫmš.kbd.|bn.ilṣdq.šb't ṯlṯt šlm.|bn.ṯm 1131.8

ḥgbn

miḫdy[m].|bn.ḥgb[n].|bn.ulbt[-].|ḏkry[-].|bn.tlm[yn].|bn.y'dd.|bn.idly[- 2017.2
.|bn.š[--].|bn.a[---].|bn.prsn.|bn.mtyn.|bn.ḫlpn.|bn.ḥgbn.|bn.szn.|bn.mglb. 117[325].2.8
bn.ḫnzr.|bn.arwṯ.|bn.ṯbtnq.|bn.pṭḏn.|bn.nbdg.|bn.ḥgbn.|bn.tmr.|bn.prsn.|bn.ršpy.|[']bdḥgb.|[k]lby.|[-]ḥmn 113[400].1.19
dn].|krwn.|arkḏn.|ilmn.|abškn.|ykn.|ršpab.|klyn.|ḥgbn.|ḥṯn.|'bdmlk.|y[--]k.|[-----].|pǵḏn.|[--]n.|[--]ntn.|' 1024.1.18
.ksp.ṯlṯ.|[---].bty.ksp.'šr[t].|[---.-]mb'l.[---].'šrt.|[---.]ḥgbn.kbs.ks[p].|[---].ḏmrd.bn.ḫrmn.|[---.-]ǵn.ksp.ṯṯt.|[---.] 2153.9
maḫdym.|grbn.ltḥ.|srn.ltḥ.|ykn.ltḥ.|ḥgbn.ltḥ.|spr.mkrm.|bn.sl'n.prs.|bn.ṯpdn.ltḥ.|bn.urm.ltḥ. 1059.5
m.klyn[.ṣd]qn.'bdilt.b'l.|annmn.'dy.klby.dqn.|ḥrṯm.ḥgbn.'dn.ynḥm[.---].|ḥrš.mrkbt.'zn.[b]'ln.ṯb[--.-]nb.trtn.|[-- 2011.27
].bhtm.b'l.šd.|[---d]nil.|[a]drdn.|[---]n.|pǵḏn.|ṯṯpḥ.|ḥgbn.|šrm.|bn.ymil.|bn.kḏgdl.|[-]mn.|[--]n.|[ḫr]š.qṯn.|[-- 1039.1.26
.b d.ubn.krwn.tǵd.[m]nḥm.|'pṯrm.šm'rgm.skn.qrt.|ḥgbn.šm'.skn.qrt.|nǵr krm.'bdadt.b'ln.yp'mlk.|ṯǵrm.mnḥ 2011.11
y.|ṯn.bnš ibrḏr.|bnš tlmi.|sǵr.ḫryn.|'dn.w sǵr h.|bn.ḥgbn. 2082.10

ḥgbt

n.w.bn.au[pš].|bn.kdrn.|‘rgzy.w.bn.‘dy.|bn.gmḫn.w.ḥgbt.|bn.tgdn.|yny.|[b]n.g‘yn dd.|[-]n.dd.|[--]an dd.|[----- 131[309].28

ḥgr

t.|w ‘l.agn.šb‘ d m.dǵ[ṯ.---]t.|tlk m.rḥmy.w tṣd[.---].|tḥgrn.ǵzr.n‘m.[---].|w šm.‘rbm.yr[.---].|mṯbt.ilm.ṯmn.ṯ[--.- 23[52].17
|km.tsm.‘ṯtrt.ts[m h].|d ‘q h.ib.iqni.‘p[‘p] h.|sp.ṯrml.tḥgrn.[-]dm[.-].|ašlw.b ṣp.‘n h.|d b ḥlm y.il.ytn.|b ḏrt y.ab. 14[KRT].3.148

ḥdg

d.|ẓi.at.l tlš.|amt.yrḫ.|l dmgy.amt.|aṯrt.qḥ.|ksan k.ḥdg k.|ḥtl k.w ẓi.|b aln.tk m.|b tk.mlbr.|ilšiy.|kry amt.|‘ 12[75].1.18

ḥdd

ḥdd.ar[y.---].|b‘lsip.a[ry.---].|klt h.[---].|ṯty.ary.m[--.---].|n 81[329].1

ḥdy

‘l.lm.ǵltm.ilm.rišt.|km l ẓr brkt km.w ln.kḥṯ.zbl km.aḥd.|ilm.t‘ny lḥt.mlak.ym.t‘dt.ṯpṭ.nhr.|šu.ilm.rašt km.l ẓr. 2.1[137].25
ṯbr.|b‘l.ṯbr.diy hmt.tqln.|tḥt.p‘n h.ybq‘.kbdt hm.w[yḥd].|in.šmt.in.‘ẓm.yšu.g h.|w yṣḥ.knp.nšrm.ybn.|b‘l.ybn. 19[1AQHT].3.116
b‘l.ṯbr.|b‘l.ṯbr.diy.hwt.w yql.|tḥt.p‘n h.ybq‘.kbd h.w yḥd.|[i]n.šmt.in.‘ẓm.yšu.g[h].|w yṣḥ.knp.hrgb.b‘l.ybn.|[b] 19[1AQHT].3.130
ml.b‘[l].|b‘l.ṯbr.diy.hyt.tq[l.tḥt].|p‘n h.ybq‘.kbd h.w yḥd.|iṯ.šmt.iṯ.‘ẓm.w yqḥ b hm.|aqht.ybl.l qẓ.ybky.w yqbr. 19[1AQHT].3.144
b nši[.‘n h.w yphn.yḥd].|b ‘rpt[.nšrm.yšu].|[g h.]w yṣḥ[.knp.nšrm].|b‘l.yṯb.b‘l 19[1AQHT].2.105
|b‘l.yṯbr.b‘l.yṯbr.diy.|hyt.tql.tḥt.p‘n y.ibq‘.|kbd h.w aḥd.hm.iṯ.šmt.iṯ.|‘ẓm.abky w aqbrn h.aštn.|b ḫrt.ilm.arṣ.b 19[1AQHT].3.139
ṯb.b‘l.yṯb[r.diy.hmt].|tqln.tḥ p‘n y.ibq[‘.kbd hm.w] |aḥd.hm.iṯ.šmt.hm.i[ṯ].|‘ẓm.abky.w aqbrn h.|ašt.b ḫrt.ilm.a 19[1AQHT].3.110
.b‘l.y[ṯb]r.diy[.h]wt.|w yql.tḥt.p‘n y.ibq‘.kbd[h].|w aḥd.hm.iṯ.šmt.hm.iṯ[.‘ẓm].|abky.w aqbrn.ašt.b ḫrt.|i[lm.ar 19[1AQHT].3.125
n.|b‘l.ybn.diy hmt nšrm.|tpr.w du.b nši.‘n h.w ypn.|yḥd.hrgb.ab.nšrm.|yšu.g h.w yṣḥ.knp.hr[g]b.|b‘l.yṯb.b‘l.y[ṯ 19[1AQHT].3.121
.]l ṣbim.|[hdmm.l ǵzrm.mid.tmtḫṣn.w t]‘n.tḫtṣb.|[w tḥdy.‘nt.tǵdd.kbd h.b ṣḥ]q.ymlu.lb h.|[b šmḫt.kbd.‘nt.tšyt.t 7.1[131].7
nt.|l ṣbim.hdmm.l ǵzrm.|mid.tmtḫṣn.w t‘n.|tḫtṣb.w tḥdy.‘nt.|tǵdd.kbd h.b ṣḥq.ymlu.|lb h.b šmḫt.kbd.‘nt.|tšyt. 3[‘NT].2.24
]‘l.ybn.diy.hwt.hrg[b].|tpr.w du.b nši.‘n h.|[w]yphn.yḥd.ṣml.um.nšrm.|yšu.g h.w yṣḥ.knp.ṣml.|b‘l.yṯbr.b‘l.yṯbr. 19[1AQHT].3.135
--].|hm qrt tuḫd.hm mt y‘l bnš.|bt bn bnš yqḥ ‘z.|w yḥdy mrḥqm. RS61[24.277.31]

ḥdyn

--].|tlbr[-.---].|isg.[---].|ilwn.[---].|ṯrn.d[d].|tg d[d].|ḥdyn.d[d].|[-]dḏn.d[d].|qṭn.d[d].|lḫsn.d[d].|lsn.d[d].|and[132[331].7

ḥdr

dm.qn[-.-]n[-.-]lt.|ql h.yš[m‘].ṯr.[il].ab h.[---]l.|b šb‘t.ḥdrm.[b ṯ]mn[t.ap].|sgrt.g[-].[-]ẓ[.---] h[.---].|‘n.ṯk[.---].|‘l 3[‘NT.VI].5.19
.ašhlk.šbt[k.dmm].|[šbt.dqn k.mm‘m.]y‘ny.|il.b šb‘t.ḥdrm.b ṯmnt.|ap.sgrt.yd‘[t k.]bt.k an[št].|k in.b ilht.ql[ṣ] k. 3[‘NT.VI].5.34
š.ṯbt h.|w b tm hn.špḥ.yitbd.|w b.pḫyr h.yrṯ.|y‘rb.b ḥdr h.ybky.|b ṯn.[-]gmm.w ydm‘.|tntkn.udm‘t h.|km.ṯqlm 14[KRT].1.26
[---.--]t ḥ[dr].|[-----].|ḫmš[.---]t.ḥdrm.|w.[---.a]ḥd.d.sgrm.|w p[tḥ.---.]l.aḥd.adr.|[---.--]t.b[1151.3
|w.[---.a]ḥd.d.sgrm.|w p[tḥ.---.]l.aḥd.adr.|[---.--]t.b[ḥd]r.mškb.|ṯl[l.---.--]ḥ.|b lṯk.bt.|[pt]ḥ.aḥd.l.bt.‘bdm.|[ṯ]n.p 1151.6
[---.--]t ḥ[dr].|[-----].|ḫmš[.---]t.ḥdrm.|w.[---.a]ḥd.d.sgrm.|w p[tḥ.- 1151.1

ḥdṯ

yrḫ ḫyr.b ym ḥdṯ.|alp.w š.l b‘lt bhtm.|b arb‘t ‘šrt.b‘l.|‘rkm.|b ṯmnt.‘šrt. UG5.12.A.1
-.]w.sbsg.|[-----].|[-----].|[---.--]ṯ.|[---.-]b.m.lk.|kdwṯ.ḥdṯ.|b d ‘lpy. 1112.19
b ym ḥdṯ.|b.yrḫ.pgrm.|lqḥ.iwrpzn.|argḏḏ.|tṯkn.|ybrk.|ntbt.|b. 2006.1
b.ym.ḥdṯ.|b.yrḫ.pgrm.|lqḥ.b‘lm‘ḏr.|w bn.ḫlp.|w[--]y.d.b‘l.|miḫ 1155.1
b.ym.ḥdṯ.|b.yr.pgrm.|lqḥ.b‘lmḏr.|w.bn.ḫlp.|miḫd.|b.arb‘.|mat. 1156.1
nt.škr.|tškr.zbl.‘ršm.|yšu.‘wr.|mzl.ymzl.|w ybl.trḫ.ḥdṯ.|yb‘r.l ṯn.aṯt h.|w l nkr.mddt.|km irby.tškn.|šd.k ḥsn. 14[KRT].4.189
nt.škr.|tškr.zbl.‘ršm.|yšu.‘wr.mzl.|ymzl.w yṣi.trḫ.|ḥdṯ.yb‘r.l ṯn.|aṯt h.lm.nkr.|mddt h.k irby.|[t]škn.šd.|km.ḥ 14[KRT].2.101
.t‘rb.‘ṯtrt.šd.bt[.m]lk.|k.t‘rbn.ršp m.bt.mlk.|ḫlu.dg.|ḥdṯm.|dbḥ.b‘l.k.tdd.b‘lt.bhtm.|b.[-]ǵb.ršp.ṣbi.|[---.--]m.|[-- 2004.13
d ṯbil.|‘ṯtrt ṣwd[t.---].|tlk b mdb[r.---].|tḥdṯn w hl[.---].|w tglṯ thmt.‘[--.---].|yṣi.ǵl h tḥm b[.---].|m 2001.1.4
b ṯṯ ym ḥdṯ.|ḫyr.‘rbt.|špš ṯǵr h.|ršp.|w ‘bdm tbqrn.|skn. 1162.1
w tṣḥ.yṯb.yṭp.[---].|qrt.ablm.ablm.[qrt.zbl.yrḫ].|ik.al.yḥdṯ.yrḫ.b[---].|b qrn.ymn h.b anšt[.---].|qdqd h.w y‘n.yṭp 18[3AQHT].4.9
ḫmšt.|bn.ḥry.ḫmšt.|swn.ḫmšt.|bn.[-]r[-.]ḫmšt.|bn.ḥdṯ.‘šrt.|bn.ḫnyn.‘šrt.|rpan.ḫmšt.|abǵl.ḫmšt.|bn.aḫdy.‘šrt. 1062.17
[b yr]ḫ[.r]išyn.b ym.ḥdṯ.|[šmtr].uṯkl.l il.šlmm.|b [ṯlṯt].‘šrt.yrtḥṣ.mlk.|br[r.]b a[APP.II[173].1
b yrḫ.[rišyn.b ym.ḥdṯ].|šmtr.[uṯkl.l il.šlmm].|b ṯlṯt ‘[šrt.yrtḥṣ.mlk.brr].|b arb 35[3].1
]‘.ṣbu.[š]pš.w.ḥly[t].‘[r]b[.š]p[š].|w [ḥl.]mlk.[w.]b.ym.ḥdṯ.ṯn.šm.|l.[---]t.|i[d.yd]bḥ.mlk.l.prgl.ṣqrn.b.gg.|ar[b‘.]ar 35[3].48
rr.b šb‘[.ṣbu.špš.w ḥl]|yt.‘rb špš[.w ḥl.mlk.w.b y]|m.ḥdṯ.ṯn šm[.---.--]t.|b yrḫ.ši[-.b ar]b‘t.‘š|rt.yr[tḥṣ.ml]k.brr.|‘ APP.II[173].53
l.mṯpṭ.yld.|w y‘ny.nn[.--].|t‘ny.n[---.-]ṯq.|w š[--.---].|ḥdṯ[.---.]ḥ[--].|b bt.[-.]l bnt.q[-].|w št.b bt.ṯap[.--].|hy.yd h. UG5.6.7
[---.--]mn.|[---].ḥdṯ.|[---.š]mt.|[---].y[--.--]m.|[---.--]n.d[--.--]i.|[--]t.mdt h[.l 1106.48

ḥdṯn

lmt.|‘dršp.b‘l ššlmt.|ṯtrn.b‘l ššlmt.|ar̀šwn.b‘l ššlmt.|ḥdṯn.b‘l ššlmt.|ssn.b‘l ššlmt. 1077.10
.[---].ḫpn.|ḥrš[bhtm.--]n.‘bdyrḫ.ḥdṯn.y‘r.|adb‘l[.---].ḥdṯn.yḥmn.bnil.|‘dn.w.ildgn.ḥṭbm.|tdǵlm.iln.b‘[l]n.alḏy.|t 2011.19
.pbn.nḏbn.sbd.|šrm.[---].ḫpn.|ḥrš[bhtm.--]n.‘bdyrḫ.ḥdṯn.y‘r.|adb‘l[.---].ḥdṯn.yḥmn.bnil.|‘dn.w.ildgn.ḥṭbm.|td 2011.18
--].bnš[.š]dyn[.---].|agr.[---.--]n.ṯn.‘šr h.d[--.---].|[---.]ḥdṯn.‘šr.dd[.---].|[---.]yd.sǵr[.---.--]r h.|aḥ[d.---.‘]šrm.d[d.--- 1098.34
gry.qšt.|bn.ṣrptn.qšt.|bn.mṣry.qšt.|arny.|abm.qšt.|ḥdṯn.ql‘.|yṭpṭ.qšt.|ilthm.qšt.w.ql‘.|ṣdqm.qšt.w.ql‘.|uln.qšt. 119[321].2.3
.ql‘.|ṯty.qšt[.w.]ql‘.|bn.šp[š.]qšt.|bn.‘g[w.]qšt.w ql‘.|ḥd[ṯ]n.qšt.w.ql‘.|bn.bb.qšt.w[.ql]‘.|bn.aktmy.qšt.|šdyn.qšt. 119[321].4.8

.| b'ly.| rpan.| 'pṯrm.| bn.'bd.| šmb'l.| ykr.| bly.| ṯb'm.| ḥdṯn.| rpty.| ilym.| bn.'br.| mnip'l.| amrb'l.| dqry.| ṯdy.| yp'b 1058.11

ḥdṯt

b'm.dr'.w.'šrm.drt.| w.ṯlṯm.dd.ṯṯ.kbd.ḥpr.bnšm.| b.gt.ḥdṯt.arb'm.dr'.w.ṯlṯm.drt.| [w].šb'm.dd.ṯn.kbd.ḥpr.bnšm.| b 1098.22
n.d.l.ṭb.b.ulm.| mit.yn.ṭb.w.ṯṯm.ṯṯ.kbd.| yn.d.l.ṭb.b.gt.ḥdṯt.| tš'm.yn.d.l.ṭb.b.zbl.| 'šrm.yn.ṭb.w.ṯṯm.ḫmš.k[b]d.| yn. 1084.12

ḥḏm

tn.n[bd]g.| ḥrš qṭn[.---.]dqn.b'ln.| ǵltn.'bd.[---].| nsk.ḥḏm.klyn[.ṣd]qn.'bdilt.b'l.| annmn.'dy.klby.dqn.| ḥrṯm.ḥgb 2011.25
r.ḥrš.| bhtm.lqḥ.| š'rt.| arb'.| ḥrš qṭn.| lqḥ š'rt.| ṯṯ nsk.ḥḏm.| lqḥ.š'rt. 2052.14

ḥḏrt

.| k.yiḫd[.akl.ššw].| št.mkš[r.grn].| w.št.ašk[rr].| w.pr.ḥḏr[t.ydk].| aḥd h.w.yṣq[.b.ap h].| k.yiḫd.akl.š[šw].| št.nni.š 161[56].15
-].| tmṯl[.---].| mǵm[ǵ.---].| w.š[t.nni.w.pr.'bk].| w.pr[.ḥḏrt.w.št].| irǵ[n.ḥmr.ydk].| aḥd[h.w.yṣq.b.ap h].| k yr[a]š. 161[56].29
ap h.| [k.yiḫd akl š]šw št mkšr grn.| [w št aškrr w p]r ḥḏrt.| [-----].| [---.-]n[-].| [k yraš ššw št bln q]ṭ ydk.| [w yṣq b 160[55].11

ḥw

kpt.w[.--].b g[--].| [---.]ḫ[--.]bnt.ṣ'ṣ.bnt.ḫkp[.---].| [---].aḥw.aṭm.prṯl[.---].| [---.]mnt.[l]p'n[.-.-]bd h.aqšr[.---].| [---]. 1001.1.19

ḥwy

tgly.ḏd.il.w tbu.| qrš.mlk.ab.šnm.| l p'n.il.thbr.w tql.| tšṯḥwy.w tkbd h.| hlm.il.k yphn h.| yprq.lṣb.w yṣḥq.| p'n h.l 4[51].4.26
ly.ḏd il.| [w tbu.qr]š.mlk.ab.šnm.| [l p'n.il.t]hbr.w tql.tšṯḥ| [wy.w tkbd]n h.tlšn.aqht.ǵzr.| [---.kdd.dn]il.mt.rpi.w t 17[2AQHT].6.50
.tk.]in.bb.b alp ḥẓr.| [rbt.kmn.l p']n.'nt.| [yhbr.w yql.yšt]ḥwyn.w y| [kbdn h.yšu.g h.w y]ṣḥ.ṯḥm.| [ṯr.il.ab k.hwt.l 1['NT.IX].2.16
ly.ḏd.| il.w tbu.qrš..| mlk.ab.šnm.l p'n.| il.thbr.w tql.| tšṯḥwy.w tkbdn h.| tšu.g h.w tṣḥ.tšmḫ ht.| aṯrt.w bn h.ilt.w 6.1.38[49.1.10]
l i[l].w ybu[.q]rš.mlk[.ab.šnm.l p'n.il.]| [yhbr.]w yql[.y]šṯḥw[y.]w ykb[dn h.--]r y[---].| [---.k]ṯr.w ḫ[ss.t]b'.b[n.]bh 2.3[129].6
ḏd.i[l.w ybu.qrš.mlk].| ab.šnm.l [p'n.il.yhbr.w yql].| yšṯḥwy.[w ykbdn h.---].| ṯr.il[.ab h.---].| ḥš b[ht m.tbnn.ḥš.t 1['NT.IX].3.25
md| d.ilm.mt.b a| lp.šd.rbt.k| mn.l p'n.mt.| hbr.w ql.| tšṯḥwy.w k| bd hwt.w rgm.| l bn.ilm.mt.| ṯny.l ydd.| il.ǵzr.t 4[51].8.28
pt.arṣ.nḥlt h].| b alp.šd.r[bt.kmn.l p'n.kṯr].| hbr.w ql.t[šṯḥwy.w kbd.hwt].| w rgm l k[ṯr.w ḫss.ṯny.l hyn].| d ḥrš.y 1['NT.IX].3.3
kpt.| arṣ.nḥlt h.| b alp.šd.rbt.| kmn.l p'n.kṯ.| hbr.w ql.tšṯḥ| wy.w kbd hwt.| w rgm.l kṯr.| w ḫss.ṯny.l h| yn.d ḥrš.yd 3['NT.VI].6.19
.arṣy.| bt.y'bdr.km ǵlmm.| w 'rb n.l p'n.'nt.hbr.| w ql.tšṯḥwy.kbd hyt.| w rgm.l btlt.'nt.| ṯny.l ymmt.limm.| ṯḥm.al 3['NT].3.7
hm.| aḫr.tmǵyn.mlak ym.t'dt.ṯpṭ.nhr.l p'n.il.| [l t]pl.l tšṯḥwy.pḫr.m'd.qmm.a[--].amr.| [ṯn]y.d't hm.išt.ištm.yitmr. 2.1[137].31
k.pnm].| al.ttn.'m.pḫr.m'd.t[k.ǵr.ll.l p'n.il].| al.tpl.al.tšṯḥwy.pḫr [m'd.qmm.a--.am]| r ṯny.d't km.w rgm.l ṯr.a[b.- 2.1[137].15

ḥwt

la.| mnm.dbbm.d | msdt.arṣ.| s'.il.dqt.k amr.| sknt.k ḥwt.yman.| d b h.rumm.l rbbt. 4[51].1.43

ḥḫ

ytn.ṣṭqn.| tut ṭbḫ ṣtq[n].| b bz 'zm ṭbḫ š[h].| b kl ygz ḥḫ š h. 1153.5

ḥṭ

ṯlṯm.dd[.---].| b.gt.ṣb[-.---].| mit.'šr.[---.]dd[.--].| tš'.dd.ḥ[ṭm.w].ḫm[šm].| kdm.kbd.yn.b.gt.[---].| [mi]tm.ḫmšm.ḫmš 2092.4
.ḫmš.k[bd].| [dd].kšmm.tš'[.---].| [š]'rm.ṯṯ.'[šr].| [dd].ḥṭm.w.ḫ[mšm].| [ṯ]lṯ kbd.yn.b [gt.---].| mit.[---].ṯlṯ.kb[d].| [d 2092.9
rb'm.y[n].| b.gt.trǵnds.| tš'.'šr.[dd].kšmm.| ṯn.'šr[.dd.ḥ]ṭm.| w.šb['.---]. 2092.17
qmḥ.| [---.]ṯlṯ dd ksmm.| [---.-]rbr dd š'rm.| [---.]r[--.]ḥṭm.| kr[--.]tp[n].| kkr[.---].| kkr[.---].| kkr[.---].| kkr[.---].| k 2037.1.4
š'rm.l.trbnn.| ddm.š'rm.l.ḥtn.| dd.š'rm.l.ḥmr.ḥṭb.| dd.ḥṭm.l.ḫḏǵb.| ṯṯ.ddm.l.gzzm.| kd yn.l.ḥtn.w.kd.ḥmṣ.w.[lt]ḥ.' 1099.25
.| [---.--]m.mṣl.| [---].prš.ḥṭm.| ṯlṯ[.---].bn.ṯdnyn.| ddm.ḥ[ṭm].'l.šrn.| 'šrt.ksp.'l.[-]lpy.| bn.ady.kkr.š'rt.| nṯk h.| kb[d. 1146.7
bt.| tgmǵ.kšmm.b.yrḫ.ittbnm.| šb'm.dd.ṯn.kbd.| tgmr.ḥṭm.šb'.ddm.| ḫmš.dd.š'rm.| kdm.yn.| kdm.ṣmṣ. 1099.32
m.b.mṣbt.| mit.'šrm.ṯn kbd.| [kš]mm.| [']š[r]m.ṯn.kbd.ḥṭm.| [-]m[-.-]'[-.-]ag š'rm.| [---.--]mi.| [--.]ṯṯ[m] šb'.k[bd].| [- 2091.5

ḥṭb

miḫdym.| bn.ḥṭb.| bn abyt.| bn ḫdl.| bn ṣdqn.| bn ayy.| bn dbb.| w nḥl h.| 2016.1.2
n.| ddm.š'rm.l.trbnn.| ddm.š'rm.l.ḥtn.| dd.š'rm.l.ḥmr.ḥṭb.| dd.ḥṭm.l.ḫḏǵb.| ṯṯ.ddm.l.gzzm.| kd yn.l.ḥtn.w.kd.ḥmṣ. 1099.24
rbm.w l.udm.ṯrrt.| w gr.nn.'rm.šrn.| pdrm.s't.b šdm.| ḥṭb h.b grnt.ḥpšt.| s't.b nk.šibt.b bqr.| mmlat.dm.ym.w ṯn.| 14[KRT].3.112
.rbt.| w udm[.ṯr]rt.| grnn.'rm.| šrnn.pdrm.| s't.b šdm.ḥṭb.| w b grnt.ḥpšt.| s't.b npk.šibt.w b | mqr.mmlat.| d[m].y 14[KRT].4.214
yrḫ.ḥdṯn.y'r.| adb'l[.---].ḥdṯn.yḥmn.bnil.| 'dn.w.ildgn.ḥṭbm.| tdǵlm.iln.b'[l]n.aldy.| tdn.ṣr[--.--]t.'zn.mtn.n[bd]g.| 2011.20

ḥṭr

dtm.y'dyn h.yb| ltm.ybln h.mǵy.ḥrn.l bt h.w.| yštql.l ḥṭr h.tlu ht.km.nḫl.| tplg.km.plg.| b'd h.bhtm.mnt.b'd h.bht UG5.7.68
zḥ h.| yšt[.il.y]n.'d šb'.trṯ.'d škr.| il.hlk.l bt h.yštql.| l ḥṭr h.y'msn.nn.ṯkmn.| w šnm.w ngšnn.ḥby.| b'l.qrnm w ḏn UG5.1.1.18

ḥẓ

iḫyn.utpt.ḥẓm.| anšrm.utpt.ḥẓm.| w utpt.srdnnm.| awpn.utpt.ḥẓm.| 1124.1
ṯmn.mrkbt.dt.| 'rb.bt.mlk.| yd.apnt hn.| yd.ḥẓ hn.| yd.tr hn.| w.l.ṯt.mrkbtm.| inn.utpt.| w.ṯlṯ.ṣmdm.w.ḥ 1121.4
arb'm.qšt.| alp ḥẓm.w alp.| ntq.ṯn.ql'm.| ḫmš.ṣmdm.w ḥrṣ.| tryn.ššwm.| try 1123.2
iḫyn.utpt.ḥẓm.| anšrm.utpt.ḥẓm.| w utpt.srdnnm.| awpn.utpt.ḥẓm.| w utpt.srdnnm.| rp 1124.2
t.ḥẓm.| anšrm.utpt.ḥẓm.| w utpt.srdnnm.| awpn.utpt.ḥẓm.| w utpt.srdnnm.| rpan.utpt.srdnnm.| šb'm.utpt.srdnn 1124.4
t.b bqr.| mmlat.dm.ym.w ṯn.| ṯlṯ.rb'.ym.ymš.| ṯdṯ.ym.ḥẓ k.al.tš'l.| qrt h.abn.yd k.| mšdpt.w hn.špšm.| b šb'.w l.yš 14[KRT].3.116
[---].in ḥẓm.l hm.| [---.--]ḏn.| mrkbt.mtrt.| ngršp.| ngǵln.| ilṯḥm.| b' 1125.1.1

ḥẓ

sk.'[-].|[--]y.l arṣ[.id]y.alt.l aḥš.idy.alt.in l y.|[--]t.b'l.ḥẓ.ršp.b[n].km.yr.klyt h.w lb h.|[ṯ]n.p k.b ǵr.ṯn.p k.b ḫlb.k 1001.1.3
nt.w t[']n.btlt.'n[t].|tḥm k.il.ḥkm.ḥkm k.|'m.'lm.ḥyt.ḥẓt.tḥm k.|mlk n.aliyn.b'l.ṯpṭ n.|in.d 'ln h.klny y.qš h.|nbl 3['NT.VI].5.39
.|w t'n.rbt.aṯrt ym.|tḥm k.il.ḥkm.ḥkmt.|'m 'lm.ḥyt.ḥẓt.|tḥm k.mlk n.aliy[n.]b'l.|ṯpṭ n.w in.d 'ln h.|klny n.q[š] 4[51].4.42
t.ǵl.|[-.]nǵr.mdr'.|[-].nǵr[.--]m.|[--.]psl.qšt.|[ṯl]ṯ.psl.ḥẓm.|[---.ḫ]rš.mr[k]bt.|[--].'šr h[.---].|[ḫm]š.'šr h[.---].|ḫm 1024.3.19

ḥẓr

dtm.y'dyn h.yb|ltm.ybln h.mǵy.ḥrn.l bt h.w.|yštql.l ḥṭr h.tlu ḥt.km.nḫl.|tplg.km.plg.|b'd h.bhtm.mnt.b'd h.bht UG5.7.68
ymǵyn.yšt|ql.dnil.l hkl h.'rb.b|kyt.b hkl h.mšspdt.b ḥẓr h.|pẓǵm.ǵr.ybk.l aqht.|ǵzr.ydm'.l kdd.dnil.|mt.rpi.l y 19[1AQHT].4.172
amt.|qḥ.krt.šlmm.|šlmm.w ng.mlk.|l bt y.rḥq.krt.|l ḥẓr y.al.tṣr.|udm.rbt.w udm ṯrrt.|udm.ytnt.il w ušn.|ab.ad 14[KRT].3.133
.y[t]n[t].|il.ušn.ab[.ad]m.|rḥq.mlk.l bt y.|n[g.]krt.l ḥẓ[r y].|w y'n[y.k]rt[.ṯ]'.|lm.ank.ksp.|w yr[q.ḫrṣ].|yd.mq 14[KRT].6.280
y.y]šu.|g h.w yṣḥ.t[b'.---].|bkyt.b hk[l]y.mšspdt.|b ḥẓr y pẓǵm.ǵr.w yq.|dbḥ.ilm.yš'ly.dǵṯ h.|b šmym.dǵṯ hrn 19[1AQHT].4.184
aṯrt.ṣrm.|w ilt.ṣdynm.|hm.ḥry.bt y.|iqḥ.aš'rb.ǵlmt.|ḥẓr y.ṯn h.wspm.|atn.w ṯlṯ h.ḫrṣm.|ylk ym.w ṯn.|ṯlṯ.rb'.ym 14[KRT].4.205
.ytnt].|[il.w ušn.ab.adm].|[rḥq.mlk.l bt y].|[ng.kr]t.l ḥ[ẓ]r y.|[-----].|[---.ttb'].|[mlakm.l yṯb].|[idk.pnm.l ytn].|[' 14[KRT].5.261
t.aṯrt.|[ym].mǵẓ.qnyt.ilm.|w tn.bt.l b'l.km.|[i]lm.w ḥẓr.k bn.|[a]ṯrt.gm.l ǵlm h.|b'l.yṣḥ.'n.gpn.|w ugr.bn.ǵlmt. 8[51FRAG].4
h.dmm.šbt.dqn h.|[mm'm.-]d.l ytn.bt.l b'l.k ilm.|[w ḥẓ]r.k bn.aṯrt[.td'ṣ.]p'n.|[w tr.a]rṣ.id[k.l ttn.p]nm.|['m.i]l. 3['NT.VI].5.12
d.ulṯ.|hm.amt.aṯrt.tlbn.|lbnt.ybn.bt.l b'l.|km ilm.w ḥẓr.k bn.aṯrt.|w t'n.rbt.aṯrt ym.|rbt.ilm.l ḥkmt.|šbt.dqn k. 4[51].5.63
bn h.]ilt.|[w ṣbrt.ary]h.|[wn.in.bt.l b'l.]|[km.ilm.w ḥẓr].|[k bn.aṯ]r[t].|m[ṯ]b.il.mẓll.|bn h.mṯb.rbt.|aṯrt.ym.mṯ 4[51].1.11
aṯrt.w bn h.ilt.w ṣbrt.|ary h.wn.in.bt.l b'l.|km.ilm.w ḥẓr.k bn.aṯrt.|mṯb il.mẓll.bn h.|mṯb rbt.aṯrt.ym.|mṯb.klt.k 4[51].4.51
[---.wn.in].|[bt].l [b'l.km.ilm.w ḥẓr].|k bn.[aṯrt.mṯb.il.mẓll].|bn h.m[ṯb.rbt.aṯrt.ym].|mṯb. 3['NT.VI].4.01
.aṯrt.|w bn h.ilt.w ṣbrt.arḫ h.|wn.in.bt.l b'l.km.ilm.|ḥẓr.k b[n.a]ṯrt.mṯb.il.|mṯll.b[n h.m]ṯb.rbt.aṯrt.|ym.mṯb.[pd 3['NT.VI].5.47
[-]k[-].|[--]ḥ.b y.ṯr.il.ab y.ank.in.bt[.l] y[.km.]ilm[.w] ḥẓr[.k bn].|[qd]š.lbum.trd.b n[p]šn y.trḥṣn.k ṯrm.|[--]b b[h 2.3[129].19
'm[n.]ǵlm.il.|a[ṯt.tq]ḥ.y krt.aṯt.|tqḥ.bt k.ǵlmt.tš'rb.|ḥqr k.tld.šb'.bnm.l k.|w ṯmn.ṯṯmnm.|l k.tld.yṣb.ǵlm.|ynq. 15[128].2.23
h.w tṣḥ.tbšr b'l.|bšrt k.yblt.y[b]n.|bt.l k.km.aḫ k.w ḥẓr.|km.ary k.ṣḥ.ḫrn.|b bht k.'ḏbt.b qrb.|hkl k.tbl k.ǵrm.| 4[51].5.90
b.|[---].t'tqn.|[---.-]'b.idk.|[l ytn.pnm.tk.]in.bb.b alp ḥẓr.|[rbt.kmn.l p']n.'nt.|[yhbr.w yql.yšt]ḥwyn.w y|[kbdn 1['NT.IX].2.14

ḥy

šm [---].|kn'm.bn.[---].|plšb'l.bn.n[--].|ḥy bn.dnn.ṯkt.|ilṯḥm.bn.dnn.ṯkt.|šb'l.bn.aly.ṯkt.|klby.bn.iḫ 2085.4

ḥyil

tḥm.rgm.|mlk.|l ḥyil.|lm.tlik.'m y.|ik y.aškn.|'ṣm.l bt.dml.|p ank.atn.|'ṣm. 1010.3
ṯb[-.---].|ab[.---].|ḥyi[l.---].|iḫy[.---].|ar[.---].|'ṯtr[.---].|bn.[---].|yly[.---].|ykn 2131.3

ḥyy

h.ydd.w yqm.|l p'n h.ykr'.w yql.|w yšu.g h.w yṣḥ.|ḥwt.aḫt.w nar[-].|qrn.d bat k.btlt.'nt.|qrn.d bat k b'l.ymšḥ.
[k mt.aliyn.b'l].|k ḫlq.z[bl.b'l.arṣ].|w hm.ḥy.a[liyn.b'l].|w hm.iṯ.zbl.b'[l.arṣ].|b ḥlm.lṭpn.il.d pid.|b ḏ 10[76].2.20
šu.g h.w yṣḥ.|aṯbn.ank.w anḫn.|w tnḫ.b irt y.npš.|k ḥy.aliyn.b'l.|k iṯ.zbl.b'l.arṣ.|gm.yṣḥ.il.l btlt.|'nt.šm'.l btlt.' 6[49].3.2
bny.bnwt.|šmm.šmn.tmṭrn.|nḫlm.tlk.nbtm.|w id'.k ḥy.aliyn.b'l.|k iṯ.zbl.b'l.arṣ.|b ḥlm.lṭpn.il d pid.|b ḏrt.bny. 6[49].3.20
lb.l |ḫṭ h.imḫṣ h.k d.'l.qšt h.|imḫṣ h.'l.qṣ't h.hwt.|l aḥw.ap.qšt h.l ttn.|l y.w b mt[.-]ḥ.mṣṣ[-]t[.--].|pr'.qẓ.y[bl].š 6[49].3.8
|r.w yšqyn h.ybd.w yšr.'l h.|n'm[n.w t]'nynn.ap ank.aḥwy.|aqht[.ǵz]r.w y'n.aqht.ǵzr.|al.tšrgn.y btlt m.dm.l ǵzr 19[1AQHT].1.16
k.l bky.'tq.|b d.aṯt ab.ṣrry.|u ilm.tmtn.špḥ.|[l]ṭpn.l yḥ.t[b]ky k.|ab.ǵr.b'l.ṣ[p]n.ḥlm.|qdš.nny.ḥ[l]m.adr.|ḥl.rḥb 17[2AQHT].6.32
pt k.l tššy.hm.tqrm.l mt.b rn k.|[--]ḫp.an.arnn.ql.špš.ḥw.bṯnm.uḫd.b'lm.|[--.a]ṭm.prṭl.l riš h.ḥmṯ.ṭmṯ.|[--.]ydbr.ṯ 16.2[125].106
il.'bd h.ybrk.|[dni]l mt rpi.ymr.ǵzr.|[mt.hr]nmy npš.yḥ.dnil.|[mt.rp]i.brlt.ǵzr.mt hrnmy.|[---].hw.mḫ.l 'rš h.y'l. 1001.1.6
.|[.---].nn.|[---.]qrt.dt.|[---.--]s'.hn.mlk.|[---.l]qḥ.hn.l.ḥwt h.|[---.--]p.hn.ib.d.b.mgšḫ.|[---.i]b.hn[.w.]ht.ank.|[---.- 17[2AQHT].1.37
inn.uṯpt.|w.ṯlṯ.ṣmdm.w.ḥrṣ.|apnt.b d.rb.ḥršm.|d.šṣa.ḥwy h. 1012.9
ṣ't.l ybmt.limm.w t'n.btlt.|'nt.irš ḥym.l aqht.ǵzr.|irš ḥym.w atn k.bl mt.|w ašlḥ k.ašspr k.'m.b'l.|šnt.'m.bn il.tsp 1121.10
gm.bn.il.|krt.špḥ.lṭpn.|w qdš.u ilm.tmtn.|špḥ.lṭpn.l yḥ.|w y'ny.krt.ṯ'.|bn.al.tbkn.al.|tdm.l y.al tkl.bn.|qr.'n k. 17[2AQHT].6.27
tlt.'nt.w t[']n.btlt.'n[t].|tḥm k.il.ḥkm.ḥkm k.|'m.'lm.ḥyt.ḥẓt.tḥm k.|mlk n.aliyn.b'l.ṯpṭ n.|in.d 'ln h.klny y.qš h. 16.1[125].23
'rr k.|w t'n.rbt.aṯrt ym.|tḥm k.il.ḥkm.ḥkmt.|'m 'lm.ḥyt.ḥẓt.|tḥm k.mlk n.aliy[n.]b'l.|ṯpṭ n.w in.d 'ln h.|klny n. 3['NT.VI].5.39
l ql.rpi[.---].|[---.-]llm.abl.mṣrp k.[---].|[---.]y.mṭnt.w tḥ.ṭbt.n[--].|[---.b]ṯnm w ṯṯb.'l.bṯnt.trtḥ[ṣ.---].|[---.t]ṯb h.aḫt 4[51].4.42
pr k.'m.b'l.|šnt.'m.bn il.tspr.yrḫm.|k b'l.k yḥwy.y'šr.ḥwy.y'š.|r.w yšqyn h.ybd.w yšr.'l h.|n'm[n.w t]'nynn.ap a 1001.2.4
---]l.|trm.tṣr.trm[.']tqt.|tbky.w tšnn.[tt]n.|g h.bky.b ḥ[y k.a]b n.|nšmḫ.b l.mt k.ngln.|k klb.[b]bt k.n'tq.|k inr[. 17[2AQHT].6.30
lṭpn.w qdš.'l.|ab h.y'rb.ybky.|w yšnn.ytn.g h.|bky.b ḥy k.ab n.ašmḫ.|b l.mt k.ngln.k klb.|b bt k.n'tq.k inr.|ap.ḫ 16.2[125].98
tm.lm.l.tlk.|w.lḥt.akl.ky.|likt.'m.špš.|b'l k.ky.akl.|b.ḥwt k.inn.|špš n.[---].|hm.al[k.--].|ytnt[.---].|ṯn[.---].|w[.--- 16.1[125].14
tḥm.ydn.'m.mlk.|b'l h.nǵr.ḥwt k.|w l.a[--]t.tšknn.|ḫmšm.l mi[t].any.|tškn[n.--]h.k[--] 2060.20
n h.yb|ltm.ybln h.mǵy.ḥrn.l bt h.w.|yštql.l ḥṭr h.tlu ḥt.km.nḫl.|tplg.km.plg.|b'd h.bhtm.mnt.b'd h.bhtm.sgrt.| 2062.1.2
ḫss.yb'l.qšt l 'nt.|qṣ't.l ybmt.limm.w t'n.btlt.|'nt.irš ḥym.l aqht.ǵzr.|irš ḥym.w atn k.bl mt.|w ašlḥ k.ašspr k.'m UG5.7.68
npš h.km.iṯl.brlt h.km.|qṭr.b ap h.b ap.mhr h.ank.|l aḥwy.tqḥ.yṭpn.mhr.št.|tštn.k nšr.b ḥbš h.km.diy.|b t'rt h.a 17[2AQHT].6.26
--].|[---].d[--.---].|b ql[.-----].|w tštqdn[.-----].|hm.|w yḥ.mlk.|w ik m.kn.w [---].|tšknnnn[.---]. 18[3AQHT].4.27
hr.št].|šm'.l btlt.'nt.at.'[l.qšt h].|tmḫṣ h.qṣ't h.hwt.l t[ḥwy].|n'mn.ǵzr.št.ṯrm.w[---].|ištir.b ḏdm.w n'rs[.---].|w 62[26].9
rb[.b'l y.---].|w.an[k.---].|arš[.---].|mlk.r[b.b']l y.p.l.|ḥy.np[š.a]rš.|l.pn.b'[l y.l].pn.b'l y.|w.urk.ym.b'l y.|l.pn.am 18[3AQHT].4.13
ašlḥ k.ašspr k.'m.b'l.|šnt.'m.bn il.tspr.yrḫm.|k b'l.k yḥwy.y'šr.ḥwy.y'š.|r.w yšqyn h.ybd.w yšr.'l h.|n'm[n.w t]' 1018.18
ṣ.aḫ y.akl[.m]|kly[.']l.umt y.w y'n[.dn]|il.mt.rpi npš tḥ[.pǵt].|ṯ[km]t.mym.ḥspt.l š'r.|ṭl.yd't.hlk.kbkbm.|a[-]ḥ.h 17[2AQHT].6.30
w[t.---].|[---.]š[--].|w ym ym.yš|al.|w mlk.d mlk.|b ḥwt.špḥ.|l ydn.'bd.mlk.|d št.'l.ḫrd h.|špḥ.al.thbṭ.|ḫrd.'ps. 19[1AQHT].4.198
spr.'rbnm.|dt.'rb.|b.mtn.bn.ayaḫ.|b.ḫbṯ h.ḥwt.ṯt h.|w.mnm.šalm.|dt.tknn.|'l.'rbnm.|hn hmt.|tknn.| 2062.2.2
1161.4

.l.ʻṯtrt. | l.ʻnt.l.kl.il.alṯ[y]. | nmry.mlk.ʻlm. | mlk n.bʻl y.ḥw[t.--]. | yšhr k.w.ʻm.ṣ[--]. | ʻš[--.---]d.lik[t.---]. | w [----]. | k[-- 2008.1.10

[---.]b[--]. | [---].šḫr.[---]. | [---].al ytbʻ[.--]. | [---.]l adn.ḥwt[.--]. | [--]h.w yššil[.--]. | [---.]lp[--]. 1023.4

. | plǵn. | apšny. | ʻrb[.---]. | w.b.p[.--]. | apš[ny]. | b.yṣi h. | ḥwt.[---]. | alp.k[sp]. | tšʻn. | w.hm.al[-]. | l.tšʻn. | mṣrm. | tmkrn 2116.10

-]. | a[--.---]. | [---].ksp.ʻm[.---]. | [---.]ilṯḥm.w.[---]. | šmʻt.ḥwt[.---]. | [---].nzdt.qr[t]. | [---.]dt nzdt.m[lk]. | [---.]w.ap.bṯn 2127.2.3

šnm[.--.]w[.--]. | w ʻprm.a[--.--]n. | [--.]ḥ[--.]d[--]t. | [---.]ḥw[t.---]. | [---.]š[--]. | w ym ym.yš | al. | w mlk.d mlk. | b ḥwt.š 2062.1.9

sb[--]. | yqḥ.mi[t]. | b.ḥwt. 1174.3

ḥyl

. | bʻlskn. | bn.ʻbd. | ḫyrn. | alpy. | bn.plsy. | bn.qrr[-]. | bn.ḥyl. | bn.gʻyn. | ḥyn. | bn.armg[-]. | bʻlmṯpṭ. | [bn].ayḫ. | [---]rn. 1035.2.1

ḥyly

il.ǵzrm. | ṯm.ṯmq.rpu.bʻl.mhr bʻl. | w mhr.ʻnt.ṯm.yḥpn.ḥyl | y.zbl.mlk.ʻllm y.km.tdd. | ʻnt.ṣd.tštr.ʻpt.šmm. | ṭbḫ.alpm 22.2[124].9

kl y.aṯr[h.rpum.l tdd]. | aṯr h.l t[dd.ilnym.ṯm]. | yḥpn.ḥy[ly.zbl.mlk.ʻllm y]. | šmʻ.atm[.---]. | ym.lm.qd[.---]. | šmn.p 22.1[123].12

ḥyn

d. | ḫyrn. | alpy. | bn.plsy. | bn.qrr[-]. | bn.ḥyl. | bn.gʻyn. | ḥyn. | bn.armg[-]. | bʻlmṯpṭ. | [bn].ayḫ. | [---]rn. | ill. | ǵlmn. | bn. 1035.2.3

bn.šyy. | bn.ḫnzr. | bn.ydbʻl. | bn.ḥyn. | [bn].ar[-]m. | [bn].ḥrp[-]. | [bn].ḫdpṯr. | [bn.-]dn. | [bn.-]l 124[-].2.4

ykn. | [--]ndbym. | [ʻ]rmy.w snry. | [b]n.sdy.bn.ṯty. | bn.ḥyn.bn.ǵlm. | bn.yyn.w.bn.au[pš]. | bn.kdrn. | ʻrgzy.w.bn.ʻdy. 131[309].24

ry. | [bn].šdy. | [bn].gmḥ. | [---]ty. | [b]n.ypy.gbʻly. | b[n].ḥyn. | ḏmn.šʻrty. | bn.arwdn.ilštʻy. | bn grgs. | bn.ḫran. | bn.arš 99[327].1.6

| bn.arpḫn. | bn.ṯryn. | bn.dll. | bn.ḫswn. | mrynm. | ʻzn. | ḥyn. | ʻmyn. | ilyn. | yrbʻm. | nʻmn. | bn.kbl. | knʻm. | bdlm. | bn.ṣ 1046.3.35

ḥkm

l[ṣ] k.mh.tarš[n]. | l btlt.ʻnt.w t[ʻ]n.btlt.ʻn[t]. | tḥm k.il.ḥkm.ḥkm k. | ʻm.ʻlm.ḥyt.ḥẓt.tḥm k. | mlk n.aliyn.bʻl.ṯpṭ n. | i 3[ʻNT.VI].5.38

lk. | yḫss k.ahbt.ṯr.tʻrr k. | w tʻn.rbt.aṯrt ym. | tḥm k.il.ḥkm.ḥkmt. | ʻm ʻlm.ḥyt.ḥẓt. | tḥm k.mlk n.aliy[n.]bʻl. | ṯpṭ n. 4[51].4.41

.mh.tarš[n]. | l btlt.ʻnt.w t[ʻ]n.btlt.ʻn[t]. | tḥm k.il.ḥkm.ḥkm k. | ʻm.ʻlm.ḥyt.ḥẓt.tḥm k. | mlk n.aliyn.bʻl.ṯpṭ n. | in.d ʻl 3[ʻNT.VI].5.38

[-----]. | [-----]. | il.šmʻ.amr k.ph[.-]. | k il.ḥkmt.k ṯr.lṭpn. | ṣḥ.ngr.il.ilš.il[š]. | w aṯt h.ngrt[.i]lht. | kḥṣ.k 16[126].4.3

ḫss k.ahbt.ṯr.tʻrr k. | w tʻn.rbt.aṯrt ym. | tḥm k.il.ḥkm.ḥkmt. | ʻm ʻlm.ḥyt.ḥẓt. | tḥm k.mlk n.aliy[n.]bʻl. | ṯpṭ n.w in.d 4[51].4.41

| km ilm.w ḥẓr.k bn.aṯrt. | w tʻn.rbt.aṯrt ym. | rbt.ilm.l ḥkmt. | šbt.dqn k.l tsr k. | rḫntt.d[-].l irt k. | wn ap.ʻdn.mṭr h. 4[51].5.65

ḥkpt

rr. | idk.al.tnn. | pnm.tk.ḥqkpt. | il.kl h.kptr. | ksu.ṯbt h.ḥkpt. | arṣ.nḥlt h. | b alp.šd.rbt. | kmn.l pʻn.kṯ. | hbr.w ql.tštḥ | 3[ʻNT.VI].6.15

[idk.al.ttn.pnm.tk.ḥkpt.il.kl h]. | [kptr.]ks[u.ṯbt h.ḥkpt.arṣ.nḥlt h]. | b alp.šd.r[bt.kmn.l pʻn.kṯr]. | hbr.w ql.t[št 1[ʻNT.IX].3.1

[idk.al.ttn.pnm.tk.ḥkpt.il.kl h]. | [kptr.]ks[u.ṯbt h.ḥkpt.arṣ.nḥlt h]. | b alp.šd.r[b 1[ʻNT.IX].3.01

šmšr. | l dgy.aṯrt. | mǵ.l qdš.amrr. | idk.al.tnn. | pnm.tk.ḥqkpt. | il.kl h.kptr. | ksu.ṯbt h.ḥkpt. | arṣ.nḥlt h. | b alp.šd.rbt 3[ʻNT.VI].6.13

l brlt.hyn d. | ḥrš yd.šlḥm.ššqy. | ilm sad.kbd.hmt.bʻl. | ḥkpt.il.kl h.tšmʻ. | mṯt.dnty.tʻdb.imr. | b pḫd.l npš.kṯr.w ḫss. 17[2AQHT].5.21

.apnk.mṯt.dnty. | tšlḥm.tššqy ilm. | tsad.tkbd.hmt.bʻl. | ḥkpt il.kl h.tbʻ.kṯr. | l ahl h.hyn.tbʻ.l mš | knt h.apnk.dnil.m[17[2AQHT].5.31

[---.]n[--.---]. | [---.kpt]r.l r[ḥq.ilm.ḥkpt.l rḥq]. | [ilnym.ṯn.mṯpd]m.t[ḥt.ʻnt.arṣ.ṯlṯ.mtḥ.ǵyrm]. | [i 2.3[129].2

s[.lk.lk.ʻnn.ilm.] | atm.bštm.w an[.šnt.kptr]. | l rḥq.ilm.ḥkp[t.l rḥq.ilnym]. | ṯn.mṯpdm.tḥt.[ʻnt.arṣ.ṯlṯ.mtḥ]. | ǵyrm.id 1[ʻNT.IX].3.19

. | mi[t].ygb.bqʻ. | a[--].ʻṭ. | a[l]pm.alpnm. | ṯlṯ.m[a]t.art.ḥkpt. | mit.dnn. | mitm.iqnu. | ḫmš.ʻšr.qn.nʻm.ʻn[m]. | ṯn.ḥblm 1128.26

ḥkr

| ǵr[.---]b.b pš y.t[--]. | hwt.bʻl.iš[--]. | šmʻ l y.ypš.[---]. | ḥkr[.---]. | ʻṣr[.--.]tb[-]. | ṯat[.---]. | yn[-.---]. | i[--.---]. 2124.6

ḥl

]ʻ.šdyn.l ytršn. | [---.--]ṯ.ʻbd.l.kyn. | k[rm.--.]l.i[w]rtḏl. | ḥl.d[--.ʻbd]yrḫ.b d.apn. | krm.i[--].l.[---.]a[-]bn. 2027.2.11

. | uškn. | snr. | rq[d]. | [---]. | [---]. | mid[-]. | ubš. | mṣb[t]. | ḥl.y[---]. | ʻrg[z]. | yʻr[t]. | amḏ[y]. | atl[g]. | bṣr[y]. | [---]. | [---]y. 71[113].40

bʻl.w aṯrt.ʻṣr[m] l inš. | [ilm.---].lbbmm.gdlt.ʻrb špš w ḥl. | [mlk.b ar]bʻt.ʻ[š]rt.yrtḥṣ.mlk.brr. | [b ym.ml]at.y[ql]n.al[36[9].1.9

ar]bʻt.ʻš | rt.yr[tḥṣ.ml]k.brr. | ʻlm.š.š[--].l[--.]ʻrb.šp | š.w ḥl[.ml]k. | bn.aup[š.--].bsbn hzpḫ ṯlṯt. | kṯr[.---.--]trt ḫmšt.bn APP.II[173].57

.gdlt.rgm.yṯṯb]. | brr.b šbʻ[.ṣbu.špš.w ḥl] | yt.ʻrb špš[.w ḥl.mlk.w.b y] | m.ḥdṯ.ṯn šm[.---.--]t. | b yrḫ.ši[-.b ar]bʻt.ʻš | rt. APP.II[173].52

.yṯ[ṯb.brr]. | b.[šb]ʻ.ṣbu.[š]pš.w.ḥly[t].ʻ[r]b[.š]p[š]. | w [ḥl.]mlk.[w.]b.ym.ḥdṯ.ṯn.šm. | l.[---]t. | i[d.yd]bḥ.mlk.l.prgl.ṣq 35[3].48

| al[p.w].š.šlmm.pamt.šbʻ.klb h. | yr[--.]mlk.ṣbu.špš.w.ḥl.mlk. | w.[---].ypm.w.mḥ[--].t[ṯ]ṯbn.[-]. | b.[--].w.km.iṯ.y[--. 35[3].53

.ab ṣrry. | tbky k.ab.ǵr.bʻl. | ṣpn.ḥlm.qdš. | any.ḥlm.adr.ḥl. | rḥb.mknpt.ap. | [k]rt.bnm.il.špḥ. | lṭpn.w qdš.ʻl. | ab h.yʻr 16.1[125].8

yḥ.t[b]ky k. | ab.ǵr.bʻl.ṣ[p]n.ḥlm. | qdš.nny.ḥ[l]m.adr. | ḥl.rḥb.mk[npt]. | ap.krt bn[m.il]. | špḥ.lṭpn[.w qdš]. | bkm.tʻr[16.2[125].109

n.š.il tʻḏr.š. | bʻl š.ʻnt š.ršp š. | šlmm. | w šnpt.il š. | l ʻnt.ḥl š.ṯn šm. | l gṯrm.ǵṣ b šmal. | d alpm.w alp w š. | šrp.w šlm UG5.13.25

ḥlb

w šd.šd ilm.šd aṯrt.w rḥm. | ʻl.išt.šbʻ d.ǵzrm.ṭb.[g]d.b ḥlb.annḫ b ḫmat. | w ʻl.agn.šbʻ d m.dǵ[ṯ.---]t. | tlk m.rḥmy.w 23[52].14

tld.šbʻ.bnm.l k. | w ṯmn.tṯtmnm. | l k.tld.yṣb.ǵlm. | ynq.ḥlb.a[ṯ]rt. | mṣṣ.ṯd.btlt.[ʻnt]. | mšnq.[---]. 15[128].2.26

mit.šmn.d.nm[-.]b d.mzy.alzy. | ḫmš.kkr.ḥlb. | ḫmš.kkr.brr. | kkr.ḫmš.mat.kbd.ṯlṯ.šm[n]. | alp.mitm.kb 1135.2

kr.brr. | kkr.ḫmš.mat.kbd.ṯlṯ.šm[n]. | alp.mitm.kbd.ṯlṯ.ḥlb. | šbʻ.l.ʻšrm.kkr.ṯlṯ. | d.ybl.blym. 1135.5

ḥlbt

ʻyn. | bn.ǵzl. | bn.ṣmy. | bn.il[-]šy. | bn.ybšr. | bn.sly. | bn.ḥlbt. | bn.brzt. | bn.ayl. | [-----]. | ʻbd[--]. | bn.i[--]. | ʻd[--]. | ild[--] 2117.2.12

ḥlym

mg. | šmn. | lbnm. | ṯrm. | bṣr. | y[--]. | y[--]. | snr. | midḫ. | ḥ[lym]. | [ḫ]lby. | ʻr. | ʻnq[pat]. | glbty. | [-----]. | [-----]. | [-----]. | [- 2058.2.21

ḫlyt

--.šmn]. | ‘ly h.gdlt.rgm.yṯ[ṯb.brr]. | b.[šb]‘.ṣbu.[š]pš.w.ḫly[t].‘[r]b[.š]p[š]. | w [ḥl.]mlk.[w.]b.ym.ḥdṯ.ṯn.šm. | l.[---]t. | 35[3].47
.ṯn]. | l šmn.‘[ly h.gdlt.rgm.yṯṯb]. | brr.b šb‘[.ṣbu.špš.w ḫl] | yt.‘rb špš[.w ḥl.mlk.w.b y] | m.ḥdṯ.ṯn šm[.---.--]t. | b yrḫ. APP.II[173].51

ḫll

k. | l ušḫ[r] ḫlmṭ. | l bbt il bt. | š l ḫlmṭ. | w tr l qlḥ. | w š ḫll ydm. | b qdš il bt. | w tlḥm aṯt. | š l ilbt.šlmm. | kll ylḥm b UG5.7.TR3

ḫlm

ḥ. | [l]ṭpn.l yḥ.t[b]ky k. | ab.ǵr.b‘l.ṣ[p]n.ḫlm. | qdš.nny.ḫ[l]m.adr. | ḥl.rḥb.mk[npt]. | ap.krt bn[m.il]. | špḥ.lṭpn[.w qd 16.2[125].108
q.b d.aṯt.ab ṣrry. | tbky k.ab.ǵr.b‘l. | ṣpn.ḫlm.qdš. | any.ḫlm.adr.ḥl. | rḥb.mknpt.ap. | [k]rt.bnm.il.špḥ. | lṭpn.w qdš.‘l. 16.1[125].8
[---.]ḫlmt.alp.šnt.w[.---]. | šntm.alp.d krr[.---]. | alp.pr.b‘l.[---]. | w 2158.1.1
‘ h.nhmmt. | šnt.tluan. | w yškb.nhmmt. | w yqmṣ.w b ḫlm h. | il.yrd.b ḏhrt h. | ab adm.w yqrb. | b šal.krt.m at. | krt. 14[KRT].1.35
.‘p[‘p] h. | sp.ṯrml.ṯhgrn.[-]dm[.-]. | ašlw.b ṣp.‘n h. | d b ḫlm y.il.ytn. | b ḏrt y.ab.adm. | w ld.špḥ.l krt. | w ǵlm.l ‘bd.il. 14[KRT].3.150
.tsm. | ‘ṯtrt.tsm h. | d ‘q h.ib.iqni. | ‘p‘p h.sp.ṯrml. | d b ḫlm y.il.ytn. | b ḏrt y.ab.adm. | w ld.špḥ.l krk | t.w ǵlm.l ‘bd. 14[KRT].6.296
b‘l.arṣ]. | w hm.ḥy.a[liyn.b‘l]. | w hm.iṯ.zbl.b‘[l.arṣ]. | b ḫlm.lṭpn.il.d pid. | b ḏrt.bny.bnwt. | šmm.šmn.tmṭrn. | nḫlm.t 6[49].3.4
ḫlm.tlk.nbtm. | w id‘.k ḥy.aliyn.b‘l. | k iṯ.zbl.b‘l.arṣ. | b ḫlm.lṭpn.il d pid. | b ḏrt.bny.bnwt. | šmm.šmn.tmṭrn. | nḫlm.t 6[49].3.10
t y.ab.adm. | w ld.špḥ.l krt. | w ǵlm.l ‘bd.il. | krt.yḫṯ.w ḫlm. | ‘bd.il.w hdrt. | yrtḥṣ.w yadm. | yrḥṣ.yd h.amt h. | uṣb‘t 14[KRT].3.154
. | u ilm.tmtn.špḥ. | [l]ṭpn.l yḥ.t[b]ky k. | ab.ǵr.b‘l.ṣ[p]n.ḫlm. | qdš.nny.ḫ[l]m.adr. | ḥl.rḥb.mk[npt]. | ap.krt bn[m.il]. | 16.2[125].107
ḫšt k.l ntn. | ‘tq.b d.aṯt.ab ṣrry. | tbky k.ab.ǵr.b‘l. | ṣpn.ḫlm.qdš. | any.ḫlm.adr.ḥl. | rḥb.mknpt.ap. | [k]rt.bnm.il.špḥ. 16.1[125].7
-]šq h[.---]. | bnš r‘ym.[---]. | kbdt.bnš[.---]. | šin.[---]. | b ḫlm.[---]. | pnt[.---]. 2158.2.9

ḫln

.w y‘n.aliyn. | b‘l.ašt m.kṯr bn. | ym.kṯr.bnm.‘dt. | ypth.ḫln.b bht m. | urbt.b qrb.[h]kl | m.w y[p]tḥ.b dqt.‘rpt. | ‘l h[4[51].7.17
h.w yṣḥ. | l rgmt.l k.l ali | yn.b‘l.ṯṯbn.b‘l. | l hwt y.yptḥ.ḫ | ln.b bht m.urbt. | b qrb.hk[l m.yp]tḥ. | b‘l.b dqt[.‘rp]t. | ql 4[51].7.25
b qr[b.hk]l m. | w ‘n.ali[yn.]b‘l. | al.tšt.u[rb]t.b bht m. | ḫln.b q[rb.hk]l m. | al td[.pdr]y.bt ar. | [---.ṯl]y.bt.rb. | [---.m] 4[51].6.9
. | šm‘.l aliyn b‘l. | bn.l rkb.‘rpt. | bl.ašt.urbt.b bh[t] m. | ḫln.b qrb.hkl m. | w y‘n.aliyn b‘l. | al.tšt.urbt.b[bhtm]. | [ḫln] 4[51].5.124
[ṯr.w]ḫss. | šm‘.m‘.l al[iy]n b‘l. | bl.ašt.ur[bt.]b bht m. | ḫln.b qr[b.hk]l m. | w ‘n.ali[yn.]b‘l. | al.tšt.u[rb]t.b bht m. | ḫl 4[51].6.6
n.b qrb.hkl m. | w y‘n.aliyn b‘l. | al.tšt.urbt.b[bhtm]. | [ḫln].b qrb.hk[l m]. 4[51].5.127
hy.[-]ḫ[-]y.ilak k. | [---.--]g k.yritn.mǵy.hy.w kn. | [---].ḫln.d b.dmt.um.il[m.---]. | [--]ḏyn.b‘d.[--]ḏyn.w l. | [--]k b‘lt 1002.43
d.mmt. | ṯṯ.pt[ḫ.---]. | ṯn.pt[ḫ.---]. | w.pt[ḫ.--]r.ṭǵr. | ṯmn.ḫlnm. | ṯṯ.ṯḫ[--].l.mtm. 1151.15

ḫlq

rišt.l bmt h.šnst. | kpt.b ḫbš h.brkm.tǵl[l]. | b dm.ḏmr.ḫlqm.b mm[‘]. | mhrm.mṭm.tgrš. | šbm.b ksl.qšt h.mdnt. | w 3[‘NT].2.14
lu. | lb h.b šmḫt.kbd.‘nt. | tšyt.k brkm.tǵll b dm. | ḏmr.ḫlqm.b mm‘.mhrm. | ‘d.tšb‘.tmtḫṣ.b bt. | tḫṣb.bn.ṯlḥnm.ymḫ 3[‘NT].2.28

ḫlt

mḏ. | kd.l.ydn. | [---.y]rḫ.ḫyr. | [---.]yn.l.mlkt. | [---.yrḫ.]ḫlt.šb‘.[---].mlkt. | [---.yrḫ.]gn.šb‘[.--]. | [---.yrḫ.]iṯb.šb[‘.---]. | [1088.13
[---.-]bd[.---]. | [---.]yrḫ.ḫyr[.---]. | [---].yrḫ.ḫl[t.---]. | [---].yrḫ.gn[-.---]. | [---.]yrḫ.iṯ[b.---]. 1088.A.3

ḫm

| rpi.al.ǵzr.mt.hrnmy. | apnk.dnil.mt. | rpi.yṣly.‘rpt.b | ḫm.un.yr.‘rpt. | tmṭr.b qẓ.ṭl.yṭll. | l ǵnbm.šb‘.šnt. | yṣr k.b‘l.ṯ 19[1AQHT].1.40
]. | ybṯ.nn.aliyn.b‘l.w [---]. | ym.l mt.b‘l m.ym l[--.---]. | ḫm.l šrr.w [---]. | y‘n.ym.l mt[.---]. | l šrr.w t‘[n.‘ṯtrt.---]. | b‘l 2.4[68].33

ḫmd

. | b bht k.‘ḏbt.b qrb. | hkl k.tbl k.ǵrm. | mid.ksp.gb‘m.mḫmd.. | ḫrṣ.w bn.bht.ksp. | w ḫrṣ.bht.ṯhrm. | iqnim.šmḫ.aliy 4[51].5.94
.tbnn. | [ḫš.]trmm.hkl h. | y[tl]k.l lbnn.w ‘ṣ h. | l[šr]yn.mḫmd.arz h. | h[n.l]bnn.w ‘ṣ h. | š[r]yn.mḫmd.arz h. | tšt.išt. 4[51].6.19
‘ṣ h. | l[šr]yn.mḫmd.arz h. | h[n.l]bnn.w ‘ṣ h. | š[r]yn.mḫmd.arz h. | tšt.išt.b bht m. | nb[l]at.b hkl m. | hn.ym.w ṯn. 4[51].6.21
m h.nšat ẓl h kbkbm. | [---.]b km kbkbt k ṯn. | [---.]b‘l yḫmdn h.yrṯ y. | [---.]dmrn.l pn h yrd. | [---.]b‘l.šm[--.]rgbt y 2001.2.7
b bht h. | ‘ḏbt.b qrb hkl h. | yblnn ǵrm.mid.ksp. | gb‘m lḥmd.ḫrṣ. | yblnn.udr.ilqṣm. | yak.l kṯr.w ḫss. | w ṯb l mspr..k 4[51].5.101
b bhm k. | ‘ḏbt.b qrb.hkl k. | tbl k.ǵrm.mid.ksp. | gb‘m.mḫmd.ḫrṣ. | ybl k.udr.ilqṣm. | w bn.bht.ksp.w ḫrṣ. | bht.ṯhrm 4[51].5.78
at.mlbr. | wn.ymǵy.aklm. | w ymẓa.‘qqm. | b‘l.ḫmd m.yḫmd m. | bn.dgn.yhrr m. | b‘l.ngṯ hm.b p‘n h. | w il hd.b ḫrẓ 12[75].1.38
ṣd. | yḥ pat.mlbr. | wn.ymǵy.aklm. | w ymẓa.‘qqm. | b‘l.ḫmd m.yḫmd m. | bn.dgn.yhrr m. | b‘l.ngṯ hm.b p‘n h. | w il 12[75].1.38
.---]. | pnm[.---]. | b‘l.n[--.---]. | il.hd[.---]. | at.bl[.at.---]. | ḫmd m.[---]. | il.hr[r.---]. | kb[-.---]. | ym.[---]. | yšḫr[.---]. | yikl[12[75].2.9

ḫmdrt

.šblt.yḫ[bq]. | w ynšq.aḫl.an.šblt. | tp‘.b aklt.šblt.tp‘[.b ḫm]drt. | ur.tisp k.yd.aqht.ǵz[r]. | tšt k.bm.qrb m.asm. | b p h 19[1AQHT].2.72
m.asm. | y.dnh.ysb.aklt h.yph. | šblt.b akt.šblt.yp‘. | b ḫmdrt.šblt.yḫ[bq]. | w ynšq.aḫl.an.šblt. | tp‘.b aklt.šblt.tp‘[.b 19[1AQHT].2.70

ḫmḫ

al tkl.bn. | qr.‘n k.mḫ.riš k. | udm‘t.ṣḥ.aḫt k. | ṯtmnt.bt.ḫmḫ h. | d[-]n.tbkn.w tdm.l y.[--]. | [---].al.trgm.l aḫt k. | [---.] 16.1[125].29

ḫmḫmt

pt hm.mtqtm.mtqtm.k lrmn[.--]. | bm.nšq.w hr.b ḫbq.ḫmḫmt.tqt[nṣn]. | tldn.šḫr.w šlm.rgm.l il.ybl.a[ṯt y]. | il.ylt.m 23[52].51
hm.yšq.hn.[š]pt hm.mtqtm. | bm.nšq.w hr.[b]ḫbq.w ḫ[m]ḫmt.ytb[n]. | yspr.l ḫmš.l ṣ[---.]šr.pḫr.klat. | tqtnṣn.w tl 23[52].56
[---].bm.nšq.aṯt h. | [---.]b ḫbq h.ḫmḫmt. | [---.--] n.ylt.ḫmḫmt. | [---.mt.r]pi.w ykn.bn h. | [b bt.šrš.]b qrb.hkl h. | [nṣ 17[2AQHT].1.42
--].hw.mḫ.l ‘rš h.y‘l. | [---].bm.nšq.aṯt h. | [---.]b ḫbq h.ḫmḫmt. | [---.--] n.ylt.ḫmḫmt. | [---.mt.r]pi.w ykn.bn h. | [b bt 17[2AQHT].1.41

ḥmyt

b‘l. | [-----.]lšnt. | [---.--]yp.tḥt. | [-----]. | [---.]w npy gr. | [ḥmyt.ugrt.w npy.yman.w npy.‘r]mt.w npy. | [---.ušn.yp km. APP.I[-].1.13
]šnm.hn.‘r. | w.tb.l mspr.m[šr] mšr.bt.ugrt.w npy.gr. | ḥmyt.ugrt.w [np]y.nṯt.ušn.yp kn.ulp qṭy. | ulp.ddmy.ul[p.ḫ] 32[2].1.28
.il.l mpḫ]rt.[bn.il.l ṯkmn.w šn]m hn š. | [---.w n]py.gr[.ḥmyt.ugrt.w np]y. | [---].w n[py.---].u tḫṭi[n.ulp.qṭy]. | ulp.dd 32[2].1.10

ḥmny

ḫlb.rpš. | ẓẓn. | bn.ḥmny. | dqry. 1068.3

ḥmṣ

ṭb. | dd.ḥṭm.l.ḫdǵb. | ṯṯ.ddm.l.gzzm. | kd yn.l.ḫtn.w.kd.ḥmṣ.w.[lt]ḥ.‘šdm. | kd yn.l.ḫdǵb.w.kd.ḥmṣ. | prš.glbm.l.bt. | t 1099.27
yn.l.ḫtn.w.kd.ḥmṣ.w.[lt]ḥ.‘šdm. | kd yn.l.ḫdǵb.w.kd.ḥmṣ. | prš.glbm.l.bt. | tgmǵ.kšmm.b.yrḫ.iṯtbnm. | šb‘m.dd.ṯn. 1099.28

ḥmr

[b.]gt.ṯpn.‘šr.ṣmdm. | w.ṯlṯ.‘šr.bnš. | yd.ytm.yd.r‘y.ḥmrm. | b.gt.gwl.ṯmn.ṣmdm. | w.arb‘.‘šr.bnš. | yd.nǵr.mdr‘.y 2038.3
ṯ‘d.ṣm[d]. | bn.liy. | ‘šrm.ṣ[md]. | ṯṯ kbd.b ḥ[--]. | w.arb‘.ḥ[mrm]. | b m[‘]rby. | ṯmn.ṣmd.[---]. | b d.b‘lsr. | yd.ṯdn.‘šr. | [ḥ 2102.1
m]. | b m[‘]rby. | ṯmn.ṣmd.[---]. | b d.b‘lsr. | yd.ṯdn.‘šr. | [ḥ]mrm. | ddm.l.ybr[k]. | bdmr.prs.l.u[-]m[-]. | ṯmn.l.‘šrm. | d 2102.5
.ap h]. | k.yiḫd.akl.š[šw]. | št.nni.št.mk[št.grn]. | št.irǵn.ḥmr[.ydk]. | aḥd h.w.yṣq.b[.ap h]. | k.yraš.ššw.[št]. | bln.qṭ.yṣ 161[56].19
m[ǵ.---]. | w.š[t.nni.w.pr.‘bk]. | w.pr[.ḫdrt.w.št]. | irǵ[n.ḥmr.ydk]. | aḥd[h.w.yṣq.b.ap h]. | k yr[a]š.šš[w.w.ykhp]. | mi 161[56].30
špšm. | b šb‘.w l.yšn.pbl. | mlk.l qr.ṯigt.ibr h. | l ql.nhqt.ḥmr h. | l g‘t.alp.ḥrṯ.zǵt. | klb.ṣpr.w ylak. | mlakm.l k.‘m.krt. 14[KRT].3.121
.b šb‘. | w l.yšn.pbl. | mlk.l [qr.]ṯiqt. | ibr h[.l]ql.nhqt. | ḥmr[h.l g‘t.]alp. | ḥrṯ[.l z]ǵt.klb. | [ṣ]pr[.apn]k. | [pb]l[.mlk.g] 14[KRT].5.225
r.ḥ[m]r. | ḥmr.ḥmr. | ḥmr.ḥmr. | ḥmr.ḥmr. | ḥmr.ḥmr. | ḥmr.w izml.aḥt. 146[87].7
.---]. | ṣ‘.ḥmr.w[.---]. | ṣ‘q.ḥmr.w.[---]. | ḫlb ‘prm.amdy.[ḥm]r.w bn[š]. | gn‘y.[---.bn]š. | uškn[.---].‘šr.bnšm. | ‘nqpat[.-- 2040.16
w[.---.]bnšm. | ilštm‘.arb‘.ḥm[r]m.ḫmš.bnšm. | ǵr. | ary.ḥmr w.bnš. | qmy.ḥmr.w.bnš. | ṯbil. | ‘nmky.ḥmr.w.bnš. | rqd 2040.23
. | ǵr. | ary.ḥmr w.bnš. | qmy.ḥmr.w.bnš. | ṯbil. | ‘nmky.ḥmr.w.bnš. | rqd arb‘. | šbn aḥd. | ṯbq aḥd. | šrš aḥd. | bir aḥd. | 2040.26
‘.arb‘.ḥm[r]m.ḫmš.bnšm. | ǵr. | ary.ḥmr w.bnš. | qmy.ḥmr.w.bnš. | ṯbil. | ‘nmky.ḥmr.w.bnš. | rqd arb‘. | šbn aḥd. | ṯb 2040.24
ap. | pd. | mlk.arb‘.ḥm[rm.w.arb]‘.bnšm. | ar.ḫmš.ḥmr[m.w.ḫm]š.bnšm. | atlg.ḥmr[.---.]bnšm. | gb‘ly.ḥmr š[--.b 2040.4
ap. | pd. | mlk.arb‘.ḥm[rm.w.arb]‘.bnšm. | ar.ḫmš.ḥmr[m.w.ḫm]š.bnšm. | atlg.ḥ 2040.3
]š. | uškn[.---].‘šr.bnšm. | ‘nqpat[.---].bnš. | ubr‘y.ar[b‘.]ḥm[r]m.w[.---.]bnšm. | ilštm‘.arb‘.ḥm[r]m.ḫmš.bnšm. | ǵr. | a 2040.20
‘t.[--].ḥ[mr.---]. | ḫlb krd.ḥ[mr.---]. | ṣ‘.ḥmr.w[.---]. | ṣ‘q.ḥmr.w.[---]. | ḫlb ‘prm.amdy.[ḥm]r.w bn[š]. | gn‘y.[---.bn]š. | 2040.15
| š‘rt.ṯn[.---]. | bq‘t.[--].ḥ[mr.---]. | ḫlb krd.ḥ[mr.---]. | ṣ‘.ḥmr.w[.---]. | ṣ‘q.ḥmr.w.[---]. | ḫlb ‘prm.amdy.[ḥm]r.w bn[š]. 2040.14
.trbnn. | ddm.š‘rm.l.trbnn. | ddm.š‘rm.l.ḫtn. | dd.š‘rm.l.ḥmr.ḥṭb. | dd.ḥṭm.l.ḫdǵb. | ṯṯ.ddm.l.gzzm. | kd yn.l.ḫtn.w.kd. 1099.24
r. | ḥmr.ḥ[m]r. | ḥmr.ḥmr. | ḥmr.ḥmr. | ḥmr.ḥmr. | ḥmr.ḥmr. | ḥmr.w izml.aḥt. 146[87].6
.ḥm]r. | ḥmr.ḥ[m]r. | ḥmr.ḥmr. | ḥmr.ḥmr. | ḥmr.ḥmr. | ḥmr.ḥmr. | ḥmr.w izml.aḥt. 146[87].6
ḥm[r.ḥm]r. | ḥmr.ḥ[m]r. | ḥmr.ḥmr. | ḥmr.ḥmr. | ḥmr.ḥmr. | ḥmr.ḥmr. | ḥmr.w izml.aḥt. 146[87].5
ḥm[r.ḥm]r. | ḥmr.ḥ[m]r. | ḥmr.ḥmr. | ḥmr.ḥmr. | ḥmr.ḥmr. | ḥmr.ḥmr. | ḥmr.w izml.aḥt. 146[87].5
ḥm[r.ḥm]r. | ḥmr.ḥ[m]r. | ḥmr.ḥmr. | ḥmr.ḥmr. | ḥmr.ḥmr. | ḥmr.ḥmr. | ḥmr.w i 146[87].2
ḥm[r.ḥm]r. | ḥmr.ḥ[m]r. | ḥmr.ḥmr. | ḥmr.ḥmr. | ḥmr.ḥmr. | ḥmr.ḥmr. | ḥmr.w izml.aḥt 146[87].3
ḥm[r.ḥm]r. | ḥmr.ḥ[m]r. | ḥmr.ḥmr. | ḥmr.ḥmr. | ḥmr.ḥmr. | ḥmr.ḥmr. | ḥm 146[87].2
ḥm[r.ḥm]r. | ḥmr.ḥ[m]r. | ḥmr.ḥmr. | ḥmr.ḥmr. | ḥmr.ḥmr. | ḥmr.ḥmr. | ḥmr.w izml.aḥt. 146[87].3
ḥm[r.ḥm]r. | ḥmr.ḥ[m]r. | ḥmr.ḥmr. | ḥmr.ḥmr. | ḥmr.ḥmr. | ḥmr.ḥmr. | ḥmr.w izml.aḥt. 146[87].4
ḥm[r.ḥm]r. | ḥmr.ḥ[m]r. | ḥmr.ḥmr. | ḥmr.ḥmr. | ḥmr.ḥmr. | ḥ 146[87].1
ḥm[r.ḥm]r. | ḥmr.ḥ[m]r. | ḥmr.ḥmr. | ḥmr.ḥmr. | ḥmr.ḥmr. | ḥmr.ḥmr. | ḥmr.w izml.aḥt. 146[87].4
ḥm[r.ḥm]r. | ḥmr.ḥ[m]r. | ḥmr.ḥmr. | ḥmr.ḥmr. | ḥmr.ḥmr. | ḥmr.ḥ 146[87].1
--].bnš. | ubr‘y.ar[b‘.]ḥm[r]m.w[.---.]bnšm. | ilštm‘.arb‘.ḥm[r]m.ḫmš.bnšm. | ǵr. | ary.ḥmr w.bnš. | qmy.ḥmr.w.bnš. | ṯ 2040.21
[--.‘]ttrum[.---]. | [---.]ḥmr.y[--]. | [---].n‘r[.---]. | [---.]dd gdl[.---]. 2133.12
.b‘l. | [ṯṭbḫ.š]b‘m.y‘lm. | [k gmn.al]iyn.b‘l. | [ṯṭbḫ.šb‘m.]ḥmrm. | [k gm]n.al[i]yn.b[‘l]. | [---]ḥ h.tšt bm.‘[--]. | [---.]zr h. 6[62].1.28
.brk y.tkšd. | rumm.‘n.kdd.aylt. | hm.imt.imt.npš.blt. | ḥmr.p imt.b klt. | yd y.ilḫm.hm.šb‘. | ydt y.b ṣ‘.hm.ks.ymsk. 5[67].1.19
khnm.tš‘. | bnšm.w.ḥmr. | qdšm.tš‘. | bnšm.w.ḥmr. 77[63].2
n. | [---.-]‘t.lth.ššmn. | [---].ḫswn.ṯṯ.mat.nṣ. | [---].ḫmšm.ḥmr.škm. | [---.ṯṯ.dd.]gdl.ṯṯ.dd.š‘rm. | [---.a]lp.arb‘.mat.tyt. | [142[12].12
.šḥlt. | [---.lth.]ṣmqm.[t]t.mat.nṣ.ṯlṯm.‘ṣr. | [---].ḫmš[m.ḥm]r.škm. | [---.ṯṯ.dd.]gdl.ṯṯ.dd.š‘rm. | [---.hn.w.al]p.kd.nbt.k 142[12].6
n.lth.šḥ[lt]. | [---.l]th.dblt.lth.ṣmqm. | [---.--]m.[ḫ]mšm.ḥmr.škm. 142[12].18
mš.ḥmr[m.w.ḫm]š.bnšm. | atlg.ḥmr[.---.]bnšm. | gb‘ly.ḥmr š[--.b]nšm. | ulm.ṯn.[---.]bnšm. | m‘rby.[---.--]m.ṯn[.---]. | 2040.6
rm.w.arb]‘.bnšm. | ar.ḫmš.ḥmr[m.w.ḫm]š.bnšm. | atlg.ḥmr[.---.]bnšm. | gb‘ly.ḥmr š[--.b]nšm. | ulm.ṯn.[---.]bnšm. | 2040.5
[---.]m[--]. | [---].bn[.---]. | [-----]. | [---].ḥ[mr]. | [---.]w.bnš.aḥd. | [---.--]m. | [---].‘tgrm. | [---.-]ṣbm. | [-- 2043.4
bnš[.---]. | w ḥmr[.---]. | w m‘n[.---]. | w bn[š.---]. | d bnš.ḥm[r.---]. | w d.l mdl.r[--.---]. | w ṣin.‘z.b[‘l.---]. | llu.bn[š.---]. | 2158.1.12
.---]. | w ht.[--]k.ššw[.-]rym[.---]. | d ymǵy.bnš[.---]. | w ḥmr[.---]. | w m‘n[.---]. | w bn[š.---]. | d bnš.ḥm[r.---]. | w d.l m 2158.1.9
]m.ṯn[.---]. | m‘r.[---]. | arny.[---]. | š‘rt.ṯn[.---]. | bq‘t.[--].ḥ[mr.---]. | ḫlb krd.ḥ[mr.---]. | ṣ‘.ḥmr.w[.---]. | ṣ‘q.ḥmr.w.[---]. 2040.12
arb‘.ḥm[r.---]. | l ṯlṯ. | ṯn.l.brr[.---]. | arb‘.ḥmr[.---]. | l.pḫ[-.]w.[---]. | w.l.k[--]. | w.l.k[--]. 1139.4
arb‘.ḥm[r.---]. | l ṯlṯ. | ṯn.l.brr[.---]. | arb‘.ḥmr[.---]. | l.pḫ[-.]w.[---]. | 1139.1
-]. | arny.[---]. | š‘rt.ṯn[.---]. | bq‘t.[--].ḥ[mr.---]. | ḫlb krd.ḥ[mr.---]. | ṣ‘.ḥmr.w[.---]. | ṣ‘q.ḥmr.w.[---]. | ḫlb ‘prm.amdy.[ḥ 2040.13
ṯmn.ddm š‘rm.l ḥmrm. 1165.1
khnm.tš‘. | bnšm.w.ḥmr. | qdšm.tš‘. | bnšm.w.ḥmr. 77[63].4

ḥmt

rt.yisp.ḥmt.|[kt̠]r w ḫss.y[i]sp.ḥmt.šḥr.w šlm.|[yis]p.ḥmt.isp.[šp]š l hrm.ǵrpl.ʻl arṣ.|[l a]n ḥmt.l p[.n]t̠k.abd.l p.a UG5.8.19
t.---.-]hm.yasp.ḥmt.|[---.š]pš.l [hrm.ǵrpl].ʻl.arṣ.l an.|[ḥ]mt.i[l.w] ḥrn.yisp.ḥmt.|[bʻl.w]dgn[.yi]sp.ḥmt.ʻnt.w ʻt̠trt. UG5.8.13
mnt.nt̠k nḥš.|šmrr.nḥš.ʻq šr.ln h.mlḫš.|abd.ln h.ydy.ḥmt.|b ḥrn.pnm.trǵnw.w t̠tkl.|bnwt h.ykr.ʻr.d qdm.|idk.p UG5.7.60
[---.š]pš.l [hrm.ǵrpl].ʻl.arṣ.l an.|[ḥ]mt.i[l.w] ḥrn.yisp.ḥmt.|[bʻl.w]dgn[.yi]sp.ḥmt.ʻnt.w ʻt̠trt.|[ti]sp.ḥmt.y[r]ḫ.w.r UG5.8.13
ʻ]db.ksa.|nḥš.šmrr.nḥš.ʻq šr.ln h.ml|ḫš.abd.ln h.ydy.ḥmt.hlm.yt̠q.|w yt̠b.|tqru.l špš.um h.špš.[um.q]l bl.ʻm.|yr UG5.7.22
mnt.nt̠k.nḥš.šmrr.nḥš.|ʻq šr.ln h.mlḫš abd.ln h.ydy.|ḥmt.hlm.yt̠q yt̠qšqy.nḥš.yšlḥm.ʻq šr.|yʻdb.ksa.w.yt̠b.|tqru.l UG5.7.6
mnt.nt̠k.nḥš.šmrr.|nḥš.ʻq šr.ln h.mlḫš abd.ln h.ydy.|ḥmt.hlm.yt̠q.nḥš.yšlḥm.nḥš.|ʻq šr.yʻdb.ksa.w yt̠b.|tqru.l šp UG5.7.43
nt y.nt̠k.|nḥš.šmrr.nḥš.ʻq šr ln h.|mlḫš.abd.ln h.ydy.ḥmt.hlm.yt̠q.|nḥš.yšlḥm.nḥš.ʻq šr.ydb.ksa.|w yt̠b.|tqru.l š UG5.7.11
t h.mnt.nḥš.šmrr.|nḥš.ʻq šr.ln h.mlḫš.abd.ln h.ydy.|ḥmt.hlm.yt̠q.nḥš.yšlḥm.nḥš ʻq.|š.yʻdb.ksa w yt̠b.|tqru l špš UG5.7.33
nt.nt̠k.n[ḥš].šmrr.|nḥš.ʻq šr.ln h.mlḫš.abd.ln h.ydy.|ḥmt.hlm.yt̠q.nḥš.yšlḥm.nḥš.|ʻq šr.yʻdb.ksa.w yt̠b.|tqru.l šp UG5.7.28
mnt.nt̠k.nḥš.šm|rr.nḥš.ʻq šr.ln h.mlḫš abd.ln h.|ydy.ḥmt.hlm.yt̠q nḥš yšlḥm.nḥš.|ʻq.šr.yʻdb.ksa.w yt̠b.|tqru l šp UG5.7.38
mnt.nt̠k.nḥš.šmrr.|nḥš.ʻq šr.ln h.mlḫš.abd.ln h.|ydy.ḥmt.hlm.yt̠q.nḥš.yšlḥm.|nḥš.ʻq šr.yʻdb.ksa.w yt̠b.|tqru l šp UG5.7.17
mnt.nt̠k.nḥš.|šmrr.nḥš.ʻq šr.ln h.mlḫš.abd.|ln h.ydy.ḥmt.hlm yt̠q.nḥš.|yšlḥm.nḥš.ʻq šr.yʻdb ksa.|w yt̠b.|tqru l š UG5.7.48
mnt.nt̠k.nḥš.|šmrr.nḥš ʻq šr.ln h.mlḫš.|abd.ln h.ydy ḥmt.hlm.yt̠q šqy.|nḥš.yšlḥm.nḥš.ʻq šr.yʻdb.|ksa.w yt̠b.|tqr UG5.7.54
]iš.ḥrt̠m.|l ẓr.ʻdb.dgn kly.|lḥm.[b]ʻdn hm.kly.|yn.b ḥmt hm.k[l]y.|šmn.b q[bʻt hm.---].|bt.krt.t[--]. 16[126].3.15
.w.p nḥš.|[---.--]q.n[t̠]k.l ydʻ.l bn.l pq ḥmt.|[---.--]n h.ḥmt.w tʻbtn h.abd y.|[---.ǵ]r.šrǵzz.ybky.km.nʻr.|[w ydmʻ.k UG5.8.36
t.|[ti]sp.ḥmt.y[r]ḫ.w.ršp.yisp.ḥmt.|[ʻt̠]r.w ʻt̠pr.yisp.ḥmt.t̠t̠.w ktt̠.|[yus]p.ḥmt.mlk.b ʻt̠trt.yisp.ḥmt.|[kt̠]r w ḫss. UG5.8.16
rn.yisp.ḥmt.|[bʻl.w]dgn[.yi]sp.ḥmt.ʻnt.w ʻt̠trt.|[ti]sp.ḥmt.y[r]ḫ.w.ršp.yisp.ḥmt.|[ʻt̠]r.w ʻt̠pr.yisp.ḥmt.t̠t̠.w ktt̠.|[UG5.8.15
w ʻt̠pr.yisp.ḥmt.t̠t̠.w ktt̠.|[yus]p.ḥmt.mlk.b ʻt̠trt.yisp.ḥmt.|[kt̠]r w ḫss.y[i]sp.ḥmt.šḥr.w šlm.|[yis]p.ḥmt.isp.[šp]š UG5.8.17
ǵrpl.]ʻl.ar[ṣ.---.ḥ]mt.|[---.šp]š.l [hrm.ǵ]rpl.ʻl.arṣ.|[---.]ḥmt.l p[.nt̠]k.abd.l p.ak[l].|[t̠m.dl.]isp.ḥ[mt.---.-]hm.yasp.ḥ UG5.8.10
r.w šlm.|[yis]p.ḥmt.isp.[šp]š l hrm.ǵrpl.ʻl arṣ.|[l a]n ḥmt.l p[.n]t̠k.abd.l p.akl t̠m.dl.|[---.q]l.bl.tbḥ[n.l]azd.ʻr.qd UG5.8.20
.ršp.yisp.ḥmt.|[ʻt̠]r.w ʻt̠pr.yisp.ḥmt.t̠t̠.w ktt̠.|[yus]p.ḥmt.mlk.b ʻt̠trt.yisp.ḥmt.|[kt̠]r w ḫss.y[i]sp.ḥmt.šḥr.w šlm. UG5.8.17
.b gl.ḥt̠t̠.yn.|b gl.ḫrṣ.nbt.w ʻly.|l ẓr.mgdl.rkb.|t̠kmm.ḥmt.nša.|[y]d h.šmmh.dbḥ.|l t̠r.ab h.il.šrd.|[bʻl].b dbḥ h.b 14[KRT].4.167
[.ḫ]rṣ.nbt.|ʻl.l ẓr.[mg]dl.|w ʻl.l ẓr.[mg]dl.rkb.|t̠kmm.ḥm[t].ša.yd k.|šmm.dbḥ.l t̠r.|ab k.il.šrd.bʻl.|b dbḥ k.bn.dg 14[KRT].2.75
rṣ.l an.|[ḥ]mt.i[l.w] ḥrn.yisp.ḥmt.|[bʻl.w]dgn[.yi]sp.ḥmt.ʻnt.w ʻt̠trt.|[ti]sp.ḥmt.y[r]ḫ.w.ršp.yisp.ḥmt.|[ʻt̠]r.w ʻt̠ UG5.8.14
gn[.yi]sp.ḥmt.ʻnt.w ʻt̠trt.|[ti]sp.ḥmt.y[r]ḫ.w.ršp.yisp.ḥmt.|[ʻt̠]r.w ʻt̠pr.yisp.ḥmt.t̠t̠.w ktt̠.|[yus]p.ḥmt.mlk.b ʻt̠trt UG5.8.15
drm[.]pi[-.]adm.|[---.]it̠[-].yšql.ytk[.--]np bl.hn.|[---].ḥ[m]t.pt̠r.w.p nḥš.|[---.--]q.n[t̠]k.l ydʻ.l bn.l pq ḥmt.|[---.--] UG5.8.34
t̠.|[yus]p.ḥmt.mlk.b ʻt̠trt.yisp.ḥmt.|[kt̠]r w ḫss.y[i]sp.ḥmt.šḥr.w šlm.|[yis]p.ḥmt.isp.[šp]š l hrm.ǵrpl.ʻl arṣ.|[l a]n UG5.8.18
.l p[.nt̠]k.abd.l p.ak[l].|[t̠m.dl.]isp.ḥ[mt.---.-]hm.yasp.ḥmt.|[---.š]pš.l [hrm.ǵrpl].ʻl.arṣ.l an.|[ḥ]mt.i[l.w] ḥrn.yisp. UG5.8.11
--.]ḥrn.|[--]p.ḫp h.ḫ[--.---.šp]š.l hrm.|[ǵrpl.]ʻl.ar[ṣ.---.ḥ]mt.|[---.šp]š.l [hrm.ǵ]rpl.ʻl.arṣ.|[---.]ḥmt.l p[.nt̠]k.abd.l p. UG5.8.8
rpl.ʻl.arṣ.|[---.]ḥmt.l p[.nt̠]k.abd.l p.ak[l].|[t̠m.dl.]isp.ḥ[mt.---.-]hm.yasp.ḥmt.|[---.š]pš.l [hrm.ǵrpl].ʻl.arṣ.l an.|[ḥ] UG5.8.11
.|[---].ḥ[m]t.pt̠r.w.p nḥš.|[---.--]q.n[t̠]k.l ydʻ.l bn.l pq ḥmt.|[---.--]n h.ḥmt.w tʻbtn h.abd y.|[---.ǵ]r.šrǵzz.ybky.km UG5.8.35

ḥmt̠

n.arnn.ql.špš.ḥw.bt̠nm.uḫd.bʻlm.|[--.a]t̠m.prt̠l.l riš h.ḥmt̠.t̠mt̠.|[--.]ydbr.t̠rmt.al m.qḥn y.š y.qḥn y.|[--.]šir.b krm 1001.1.7

ḫnil

---].|ʻdn[.---].|bqrt[.---].|t̠nǵrn.[---].|w.bn h.n[--.---].|ḫnil.[---].|aršmg.mru.|bʻl.šlm.ʻbd.|awr.t̠ǵrn.ʻbd.|ʻbd.ḫmn.š 2084.8

ḫnbn

s.|ʻt̠r ʻt̠pr.|šḥr w šlm.|ngh w srr.|ʻdw šr.|ṣdqm šr.|ḫnbn il d[n].|[-]bd w [---].|[--].p il[.---].|[i]l mt mr[b-].|qdš UG5.10.1.15

ḥnt̠

l šd.mt̠r.ʻly.|nʻm.l arṣ.mt̠r.bʻl.|w l šd.mt̠r.ʻly.|nʻm.l ḥt̠t.b gn.|bm.nrt.ksmm.|ʻl.tl[-]k.ʻt̠rt̠rm.|nšu.[r]iš.ḥrt̠m.|l ẓ 16[126].3.9
k.bn.dgn.|b mṣd k.w yrd.|krt.l ggt.ʻdb.|akl.l qryt.|ḥt̠t.l bt.ḫbr.|yip.lḥm.d ḫmš.|mǵd.t̠dt̠.yrḫm.|ʻdn.ngb.w yṣi. 14[KRT].2.82
ḥ h.bn dgn.|[b m]ṣd h.yrd.krt.|[l g]gt.ʻdb.akl.l qryt.|ḥt̠t.l bt.ḫbr.|yip.lḥm.d ḫmš.|[mǵ]d.t̠dt̠.yr[ḫm].|ʻdn.ngb.w [14[KRT].4.173

ḥnn

rš.|bn.d[--]b.|abrpu.|bn.k[n]y.|bn.klyn.|bn.gmḥn.|ḥnn.|ayab.|bn.gm[--].|bn.[---].|g[---].|p[---].|b[---].|[---].|[1035.3.9
.gmrš.|bn.nmq.|bn.špš[yn].|bn.ar[--].|bn.gb[--].|bn.ḥn[n].|bn.gntn[-].|[--.]nqq[-].|b[n.---].|bn.[---].|bn.ʻyn.|bn 2023.3.17
a[--.---.-]ʻn.|ml[--.---].|ar[--.---.--]l.|aty[n.bn.]šmʻnt.|ḥnn[.bn].pls.|abrš[p.bn.]ḫrpn.|gmrš[.bn].mrnn.|ʻbdmlk.bn 102[323].4.5
.ʻbdilt.|bn.m.|ypḥ.ilšlm.|bn.prqdš.|ypḥ.mnḥm.|bn.ḥnn.|brqn.spr. 2116.22
yškb.|[yd.]mizrt.p yln.mk.b šbʻ.ymm.|[w]yqrb.bʻl.b ḥnt h.abynt.|[d]nil.mt.rpi anḫ.ǵzr.|[mt.]hrnmy.d in.bn.l h. 17[2AQHT].1.17
gnryn.|l mlkytn.|ḥnn y l pn mlk.|šin k itn.|rʻ y šṣa idn l y.|l šmn it̠r hw.|p i 1020.3
r.|šd.bn.krwn.l bn.ʻmyn.|šd.bn.prmn.l aḫny.|šd.bn ḥnn.l bn.adldn.|šd.bn.nṣdn.l bn.ʻmlbi.|šd.t̠pḫln.l bn.ǵl.|w 2089.7
m.|[---.]l yt̠b.l arṣ.|[---].mtm.|[---.--]d mhr.ur.|[---.]yḥnnn.|[---.--]t.ytn.|[---.btlt.]ʻnt.|[---.ybmt.]limm.|[---.---]l. 10[76].1.12

ḥsn

dt̠.|ybʻr.l t̠n.at̠t h.|w l nkr.mddt.|km irby.tškn.|šd.k ḥsn.pat.|mdbr.tlkn.|ym.w t̠n.aḫr.|šp[š]m.b [t̠]lt̠.|ym[ǵy.]l 14[KRT].4.193
bʻr.l t̠n.|at̠t h.lm.nkr.|mddt h.k irby.|[t]škn.šd.|km.ḥsn.pat.mdbr.|lk.ym.w t̠n.t̠lt̠.rbʻ ym.|ḫmš.t̠dt̠.ym.mk.špšm 14[KRT].2.105

ḥsp

bd.yn.t̠b.w.[--].|t̠mn.kbd.yn.d.l.t̠b.b.gnʻ[y].|mitm.yn.ḥsp.d.nkly.b.db[ḥ.--].|mit.arbʻm.kbd.yn.ḥsp.l.m[--].|mit.ʻšr 1084.24
ny.kdm.yn.|šmgy.kd.yn.|hzp.tšʻ.yn.|[b]ir.ʻšr[.---]m ḥsp.|ḫpty.kdm[.---].|[a]gm.arbʻ[.---].|šrš.šbʻ.mṣb.|rqd.t̠lt̠. 2004.29

.--]. | mit.arb'm.kbd.yn.ḥsp.l.m[--]. | mit.'šrm.[k]bd.yn.ḥsp.l.y[--]. | 'šrm.yn.ḥsp.l.ql.d.tb'.mṣ[r]m. | mit.arb'm.kbd.yn 1084.26
y]. | mitm.yn.ḥsp.d.nkly.b.db[ḥ.--]. | mit.arb'm.kbd.yn.ḥsp.l.m[--]. | mit.'šrm.[k]bd.yn.ḥsp.l.y[--]. | 'šrm.yn.ḥsp.l.ql.d 1084.25
yn.ḥsp.l.m[--]. | mit.'šrm.[k]bd.yn.ḥsp.l.y[--]. | 'šrm.yn.ḥsp.l.ql.d.tb'.mṣ[r]m. | mit.arb'm.kbd.yn.mṣb. | l.mdrǵlm. | 'š 1084.27
hr[nmy]. | gm.l bt[h.dnil.k yṣḥ]. | šm'.pǵt.ṯkmt[.my]. | ḥspt.l š'r.ṭl.yd['t]. | hlk.kbkbm.mdl.'r. | ṣmd.pḥl.št.gpn y dt k 19[1AQHT].2.51
l.št.gpn y dt ksp. | dt.yrq.nqbn y.tš[m']. | pǵt.ṯkmt.my.ḥspt.l[š']r.ṭl. | yd't.hlk.kbkbm. | bkm.tmdln.'r. | bkm.tṣmd.p 19[1AQHT].2.55
umt y.w y'n[.dn] | il.mt.rpi npš ṯḥ[.pǵt]. | ṯ[km]t.mym.ḥspt.l š'r. | ṭl.yd't.hlk.kbkbm. | a[-]ḥ.hy.mḫ.tmḫṣ.mḫṣ[.aḫ k]. 19[1AQHT].4.199
.ab h.šrḥq.aṯt.l pnn h. | št.alp.qdm h.mria.w tk. | pn h.tḥspn.m h.w trḥṣ. | ṭl.šmm.šmn.arṣ.ṭl.šm[m.t]sk h. | rbb.nsk 3['NT].4.86
. | [ṭ]'r.ksat.l ksat.ṯlḥnt. | [l]ṯlḥn.hdmm.ṯṭ'r.l hdmm. | [t]ḥspn.m h.w trḥṣ. | [ṭ]l.šmm.šmn.arṣ.rbb. | [r]kb 'rpt.ṭl.šmm 3['NT].2.38
ṯlṯ.mṣb.w.[---]. | uḫnp.ṯṯ.mṣb. | tgmr.[y]n.mṣb š[b']. | w ḥs[p] ṯn.k[dm]. 2004.36

ḥpn

n.šm.il.ǵzrm. | ṯm.ṯmq.rpu.b'l.mhr b'l. | w mhr.'nt.ṯm.yḥpn.ḥyl | y.zbl.mlk.'llm y.km.tdd. | 'nt.ṣd.tštr.'pt.šmm. | ṭbḫ 22.2[124].9
.b] | hkl y.aṯr[h.rpum.l tdd]. | aṯr h.l t[dd.ilnym.ṯm]. | yḥpn.ḥy[ly.zbl.mlk.'llm y]. | šm'.atm[.---]. | ym.lm.qd[.---]. | 22.1[123].12
ṯbr.ḥrn. | riš k.'ṯtrt.šm.b'l. | qdqd k.tqln.b gbl. | šnt k.b ḥpn k.w t'n. | spr ilmlk ṯ'y. 16.6[127].58

ḥpr

'šr h.dd.l.rpš. | [---.]šb'm.dr'.w.arb'm.drt.mit.dd. | [---].ḥpr.bn.šm. | [b.---.]knm.ṯṯm.l.mit.dr'.w.mit.drt. | w[.---.]'m.l. 1098.6
b.gt.ǵl.'šrm.l.mit.dr'.w.tš'm.drt. | [w].ṯmnym.l.mit.dd.ḥpr.bnšm. | b.gt.alḫb.ṯṯm.dr'.w.ḫmšm.drt.w.ṯṯm.dd. | ḥpr.bn 1098.15
m. | b.gt.ṯrmn.arb'm.dr'.w.'šrm.drt. | w.ṯlṯm.dd.ṯṯ.kbd.ḥpr.bnšm. | b.gt.ḥdṯt.arb'm.dr'.w.ṯlṯm.drt. | [w].šb'm.dd.ṯn.k 1098.21
.ḥpr.bnšm. | b.gt.alḫb.ṯṯm.dr'.w.ḫmšm.drt.w.ṯṯm.dd. | ḥpr.bnšm. | b.gt.knpy.mit.dr'.ṯṯm.drt.w.šb'm.dd.arb'. | kbd.ḥ 1098.17
m'br.arb'm.l.mit.dr'.w.ṯmnym[.drt]. | w.'šrm.l.mit.dd.ḥp[r.]bnšm. | b.gt.ǵl.'šrm.l.mit.dr'.w.tš'm.drt. | [w].ṯmnym.l. 1098.13
nšm. | b.gt.knpy.mit.dr'.ṯṯm.drt.w.šb'm.dd.arb'. | kbd.ḥpr.bnšm. | b.gt.ṯrmn.arb'm.dr'.w.'šrm.drt. | w.ṯlṯm.dd.ṯṯ.kb 1098.19
šm. | b.nzl.'šrm.l.mit.dr'.w.šb'm.drt. | w.'šrm.l.mit.dd.ḥpr.bnšm. | b.y'ny.arb'm.dr'.w.'šrm.drt. | w.ṯlṯm.dd.ṯṯ.kbd.ḥ 1098.25
. | b.gt.ḥdṯt.arb'm.dr'.w.ṯlṯm.drt. | [w].šb'm.dd.ṯn.kbd.ḥpr.bnšm. | b.nzl.'šrm.l.mit.dr'.w.šb'm.drt. | w.'šrm.l.mit.dd. 1098.23
bnšm. | b.y'ny.arb'm.dr'.w.'šrm.drt. | w.ṯlṯm.dd.ṯṯ.kbd.ḥpr.bnšm. | b.'nmky.'šrm.dr'[.---.d]rt. | w.ṯn.'šr h.dd.[---]. | iw 1098.27
[---.---.]l.mit.dr'.w.šb'm.drt. | [---.ḥpr.]bnšm.w.l.ḥrš.'rq.ṯn.'šr h. | [---.d]r'.w.mit.drt.w.'šrm.l.m 1098.2
.ḥrš.'rq.ṯn.'šr h. | [---.d]r'.w.mit.drt.w.'šrm.l.mit. | [drt.ḥpr.b]nšm.w.ṯn.'šr h.dd.l.rpš. | [---.]šb'm.dr'.w.arb'm.drt.mi 1098.4
spr.ḥpr.bnš mlk.b yrḫ iṯt[bnm]. | ršpab.rb 'šrt.m[r]yn. | pǵdn.ilb' 2011.1
m.ṯṯm.l.mit.dr'.w.mit.drt. | w[.---.]'m.l.mit.dd.ṯn.kbd.ḥpr.bnšm.ṯmnym.dd. | l u[-]m. | b.ṭbq.arb'm.dr'.w.'šr.dd.drt. 1098.8
spr.ḥpr.bt.k[--]. | tš'.'šr h.dd.l.b[t.--]. | ḫmš.ddm.l.ḫtyt. | ṯlṯm.dd. 1099.1
[.---]. | ṯmnym.drt.a[--]. | drt.l.alpm[.---]. | šb'm.ṯn.kbd[.ḥpr.'b]dm. | tg[mr.---]. | [-]m.m[--.---]. | [m]itm.dr[t.---]. | ['š]r. 2013.19
tgm[r.ak]l.b.gt.ḫldy. | ṯlṯ.ma[t].'šr.kbd. | šb' m[at].kbd.ḥpr.'bdm. | mit[.d]rt.arb'm.drt. | [---]m. | t[gm]r.akl.b.gt.ǵ[l]. 2013.12
r.akl[.---].ṯryn. | [tǵ]mr.akl.b.g[t.b]ir.alp. | [']šrm.l.mit.ḥ[p]r.'bdm. | mitm.drt.ṯmnym.drt. | tgmr.akl.b.gt[.b]'ln. | ṯlṯ. 2013.3
rt. | tgmr.akl.b.gt[.b]'ln. | ṯlṯ.mat.ṯṯm.kbd. | ṯṯm.ṯṯ.kbd.ḥpr.'bdm. | šb'm.drt.arb'm.drt. | l.a[--.---]. | tgm[r.ak]l.b.gt.ḫl 2013.7
š.ddm. | [---].ḫmš.ddm. | ṯṯ.l.'šrm.bn[š.mlk.---].ḫzr.lqḥ.ḥp[r]. | 'št.'šr h.bn[.---.--]ḫ.zr. | b'l.šd. 2011.40
m.trtḥṣ. | btlt.'n[t].tptr' ṭd[h]. | limm.w t'l.'m.il. | ab h.ḥpr.p'l k.y[--]. | šm' k.l arḫ.w bn.[--]. | limm.ql.b udn.k w[-]. 13[6].21

ḥpš

.ṯrrt. | w gr.nn.'rm.šrn. | pdrm.s't.b šdm. | ḥṭb h.b grnt.ḥpšt. | s't.b nk.šibt.b bqr. | mmlat.dm.ym.w ṯn. | ṯlṯ.rb'.ym.y 14[KRT].3.112
ṯr]rt. | grnn.'rm. | šrnn.pdrm. | s't.b šdm.ḥṭb. | w b grnt.ḥpšt. | s't.b npk.šibt.w b | mqr.mmlat. | d[m].ym.w ṯn. | ṯlṯ.rb' 14[KRT].4.215

ḥṣbn

yn.arty. | bn.nryn.arty. | bn.ršp.ary. | bn.ǵlmn ary. | bn.ḥṣbn ary. | bn.šdy ary. | bn.ktkt.m'qby. | bn.[---.]ṯlḥny. | b[n.-- 87[64].14

ḥṣmn

ḥrm.b[n].ng[-]n. | atyn.š[r]šy. | 'bdḫmn[.bn.-]bdn. | ḥṣmn.[bn.---]ln. | [--]dm.[bn.---]n. | b'ly.[bn.---]n. | krr[-.---]. | 102[322].1.4

ḥṣn

[-]. | bn.alṯn. | bn.aš[-]š. | bn.štn. | bn.ilš. | bn.tnabn. | bn.ḥṣn. | ṣprn. | bn.ašbḥ. | bn.qṭnn. | bn.ǵlmn. | [bn].ṣwy. | [bn].ḫn 1046.1.19
qštm.w.ṯn.ql'm. | ildgn.qšt. | bn.y'rn.ṯṯ.qštm w.ql'. | bn.ḥṣn.qšt.w.ql'. | bn.gdn.ṯṯ.qštm.w.ql'. | bn.[-]q.qšt.w.ql'. | gb[l] 119[321].3.11

ḥṣqt

[---.]ṯrd. | [---.]qpḥn. | [---.a]ǵlṯr. | [---.]ṭml. | [---.]bn.ḥṣqt. | [---.]bn.udr[-]. 2132.5

ḥr

rm.tštšḥ.km.ḥ[--]. | [---].'pr.bt k.ygr[š k.---]. | [---.]y.ḥr.ḥr.bnt.ḥ[---]. | [--.]uḫd.[b']l m.'[--].yd k.amṣ.yd[.--]. | [---.]ḥš[. 1001.1.13
pt k.l tššy.hm.tqrm.l mt.b rn k. | [--]ḫp.an.arnn.ql.špš.ḥw.btnm.uḫd.b'lm. | [--.a]ṯm.prṯl.l riš h.ḥmṭ.ṯmt. | [--.]ydbr.ṯ 1001.1.6
.bn.kryn.gt.prn. | šd.bn.ky.gt.prn. | šd.hwil.gt.prn. | šd.ḥr.gt.prn. | šd.bn.ṯbǵl.gt.prn. | šd.bn.inšr.gt.prn. | šd.[---.]gt.p 1104.8
.šzrm.tštšḥ.km.ḥ[--]. | [---].'pr.bt k.ygr[š k.---]. | [---.]y.ḥr.ḥr.bnt.ḥ[---]. | [--.]uḫd.[b']l m.'[--].yd k.amṣ.yd[.--]. | [---.] 1001.1.13
n.š'rt. | 'bd.yrḫ š'rt. | ḫbd.ṯr yṣr š'r. | pdy.yṣr š'rt. | atnb.ḥr. | š'rt.š'rt. 97[315].13

ḥrb

ḫr[.--]t[.----]. | l mṯb[.--]t[.---]. | [tqdm.]yd.b ṣ'.t[šl]ḥ. | [ḥrb.b]bš[r].tštn. | [w t'n].mṯt.ḥry. | [l lḥ]m.l šty.ṣḥt k[m]. | [-- 15[128].5.8
rt.tbun. | lm.mṯb[.---]. | w lḥm mr.tqdm. | yd.b ṣ'.tšlḥ. | ḥrb.b bšr.tštn. | [w t]'n.mṯt.ḥry. | [l lḥ]m.l šty.ṣḥt km. | [--.db 15[128].4.25
.k lb. | ṯat.l imr h.km.lb. | 'nt.aṯr.b'l.tiḫd. | bn.ilm.mt.b ḥrb. | tbq'nn.b ḫṯr.tdry | nn.b išt.tšrpnn. | b rḥm.tṭḥnn.b šd. | t 6[49].2.31
.pḫr.m'd.qmm.a[--].amr. | [ṯn]y.d't hm.išt.ištm.yitmr.ḥrb.lṭšt. | [--]n hm.rgm.l ṯr.ab h.il.ṯḥm.ym.b'l km. | [adn]km 2.1[137].32

bl.b'l.|arṣ.qm.yṯ'r.|w yšlḥmn h.|ybrd.ṯd.l pnw h.|b ḥrb.mlḥt.|qṣ.mri.ndd.|y'šr.w yšqyn h.|ytn.ks.b d h.|krpn. 3['NT].1.7
pq.ilht.dkrt[.yn].|'d.lḥm.šty.ilm.|w pq mrǵtm.ṯd.|b ḥrb.mlḥt.qṣ[.m]r|i.tšty.krp[nm.y]n.|[b k]s.ḫrṣ.d[m.'ṣm].|[- 4[51].6.57
.m[---.---].|[']d.lḥm[.šty.ilm].|w pq.mr[ǵtm.ṯd.---].|b ḥrb.[mlḥt.qṣ.mri].|šty.kr[pnm.yn.---].|b ks.ḫr[ṣ.dm.'ṣm.---] 5[67].4.14
kl h[.---].|[------].|[---.l]ḥm[.---].|[---].ay š[---].|[---.b ḥ]rb.mlḥ[t.qṣ].|[mri.tšty.krpnm].yn.b ks.ḫ[rṣ].|[dm.'ṣm.---] 17[2AQHT].6.4
---.]btlt.'nt.|[--.tl]ḥm.tšty.|[ilm.w tp]q.mrǵtm.|[ṯd.b ḥrb.m]lḥt.qṣ.|[mri.tšty.k]rpnm yn.|[b ks.ḫrṣ.dm].'ṣm. 4[51].3.42
b ym.mnḫ l abd.b ym.irtm.m[--].|[ṯpṭ].nhr.tl'm.tm.ḥrbm.its.anšq.|[-]htm.l arṣ.ypl.ul ny.w l.'pr.'ẓm ny.|l b'l[-.- 2.4[68].4
b'l.yšu.|g h.w yṣḥ.'l k.b[']l m.|pht.qlt.'l k.pht.|dry.b ḥrb.'l k.|pht.šrp.b išt.|'l k.[pht.ṭḥ]n.b rḥ|m.'[l k.]pht[.dr]y. 6[49].5.13
lp šd.ẓu h.b ym.t[---].|tlbš.npṣ.ǵzr.tšt.ḫ[---.b] |nšg h.ḥrb.tšt.b t'r[t h].|w 'l.tlbš.npṣ.aṯt.[--].|ṣbi nrt.ilm.špš.[-]r[--] 19[1AQHT].4.207
'nt.hlkt.w.šnwt.|tp.aḫ.h.k.ysmsm.|tspi.šir.h.l.bl.ḥrb.|tšt.dm.h.l.bl.ks.|tpnn.'n.bṯy.'n.bṯt.tpnn.|'n.mḫr.'n.pḫ RS225.3

ḥrḥrtm

m.|[---.]b ym.ym.y[--].yš[ ]n.ap k.'ṯtr.dm[.---.]|[---.]ḥrḥrtm.w[--.]n[--.]iš[--.]h[---.]išt.|[---]y.yblmm.u[---]k.yrd 2.3[129].13

ḫrẓn

lbym.|bn.ady.|bn.'ṯtry.|bn.ḫrẓn.|ady.|bn.birtn.|bn.ḫrẓn.|bn.bddn.|bn.anny.|ytršp.|bn.szn.|bn.kdgdl.|bn.gl'd 115[301].1.8
n.|[--.--]n.|bn.[---].|bn.'r[--].|bn.nkt[-].|bn.abḏr.|bn.ḫrẓn.|bn.ḏqnt.|bn.gmrš.|bn.nmq.|bn.špš[yn].|bn.ar[--].|b 2023.3.10
.|bn.ẓr[-].|mru.skn.|bn.bddn.|bn.ǵrgn.|bn.tgtn.|bn.ḫrẓn.|bn.qdšt.|bn.nṯǵ[-].|bn.gr[--].|bn.[---].|bn.[---].|mr[u 113[400].5.10
y'rn.qšt.w.ql'.|klby.qšt.w.ql'.|bq't.|ily.qšt.w.ql'.|bn.ḫrẓn.qšt.w.ql'.|tgrš.qšt.w.ql'.|špšyn.qšt.w.ql'.|bn.ṯ'ln.qš[t. 119[321].2.23

ḥry

n]m.tm.|yd[r.k]rt.ṯ'.|i.iṯt.aṯrt.ṣrm.|w ilt.ṣdynm.|hm.ḥry.bt y.|iqḥ.aš'rb.ǵlmt.|ḥẓr y.ṯn h.wspm.|atn.w ṯlṯ h.ḫrṣ 14[KRT].4.203
.arb't.|'bdbn.ytrš ḫmšt.|krwn.'šrt.|bn.ulb ḫmšt.|bn.ḥry.ḫmšt.|swn.ḫmšt.|bn.[-]r[-.]ḫmšt.|bn.ḥdṯ.'šrt.|bn.ḫnyn 1062.14
m'.l mṯt.|ḥry.ṭbḫ.imr.|w ilḥm.mgṯ.w iṯrm.|tšm'.mṯt.ḥry.|tṭbḫ.imr.w lḥm.|mgṯ.w yṯrm.hn.ym.|w ṯn.yṯb.krt.l 'd 16.6[127].19
tqt.|dm.lan.w ypqd.|krt.ṯ'.yšu.g h.|w yṣḥ.šm'.l mṯt.|ḥry.ṭbḫ.imr.|w ilḥm.mgṯ.w iṯrm.|tšm'.mṯt.ḥry.|tṭbḫ.imr.w 16.6[127].17
--]š[.--]qm.|id.u [---]t.|lḥn š[-]'[--.]aḫd[.-].|tšm'.mṯt.[ḥ]ry.|tṭbḫ.šmn.[m]ri h.|t[p]tḥ.rḥbt.yn.|'l h.ṯr h.tš'rb.|'l h.t 15[128].4.14
p[----].|gm.l[aṯt h k.yṣḥ].|šm'[.l mṯt.ḥry].|ṭbḫ.š[mn].mri k.|ptḥ.[rḥ]bt.yn.|ṣḥ.šb'm.ṯr y.|ṯmnym 15[128].4.3
ld.bnt.l h.|mk.b šb'.šnt.|bn.krt.km hm.tdr.|ap.bnt.ḥry.|km hm.w ṯbss.aṯrt.|ndr h.w ilt.p[--].|w tšu.g h.w [tṣḥ] 15[128].3.24
.|[tqdm.]yd.b ṣ'.t[šl]ḥ.|[ḥrb.b]bš[r].tštn.|[w t'n].mṯt.ḥry.|[l lḥ]m.l šty.ṣḥt k[m].|[---.]brk.t[---].|['l.]krt.tbkn.|[--. 15[128].5.9
.|šm'.l [-]mt[.-]m.l[-]ṯnm.|'dm.[lḥ]m.tšty.|w t'n.mṯt ḥry.|l l[ḥ]m.l š[ty].ṣḥt km.|db[ḥ.l krt.a]dn km.|'l.krt.tbun. 15[128].6.3
m mr.tqdm.|yd.b ṣ'.tšlḥ.|ḥrb.b bšr.tštn.|[w t]'n.mṯt.ḥry.|[l lḥ]m.l šty.ṣḥt km.|[--.dbḥ.l]krt.b'l km. 15[128].4.26
mrkbt.b trbṣ.|bn.amt.p d.[i]n.|b bt y.ttn.tn.|l y.mṯt.ḥry.|n'mt.šbḥ.bkr k.|d k n'm.'nt.|n'm h.km.tsm.|'ṯtrt.tsm 14[KRT].6.289
.mrkbt.|b trbṣt.bn.amt.|p d.in.b bt y.ttn.|tn.l y.mṯt.ḥry.|n'mt.špḥ.bkr k.|d k.n'm.'nt.n'm h.|km.tsm.'ṯtrt.ts[m 14[KRT].3.143

ḥryt

sa w yṯb.|tqru l špš.um h.špš.um.ql bl 'm.|ṯṯ.w kmṯ.ḥryt h.mnt.nṯk.nḥš.šm|rr.nḥš.'q šr.ln h.mlḫš abd.ln h.|ydy UG5.7.36

ḥrm

.nḥl h.|bn.rmyy.|bn.tlmyn.|w.nḥl h.|w.nḥl hm.|bn.ḥrm.|bn.brzn.|w.nḥl h.|bn.adldn.|bn.šbl.|bn.ḫnzr.|bn.ar 113[400].1.9
|bn.'yn.|bn.grb[n].|yṯtn.|bn.ab[l].|kry.|psš.|ilthm.|ḥrm.|bn.bty.|'by.|šm[n].bn.apn.|krty.|bn.ubr.|[bn] mdḫl. 2078.14
ḥrm.b[n].ng[-]n.|atyn.š[r]šy.|'bdḫmn[.bn.-]bdn.|ḥṣmn.[bn. 102[322].1.1

ḥrmn

--.-]mb'l.[---].'šrt.|[---.]ḥgbn.kbs.ks[p].|[---].ḏmrd.bn.ḥrmn.|[---.-]ǵn.ksp.ṯṯt.|[---.]ygry.ṯlṯm.ksp.b[--]. 2153.10

ḥrn

tb'l.bn[.---].|ymy.bn[.---].|'bd'n.p[--.---].|[-]d[-]l.bn.ḥrn.|aḫty.bt.abm.|[-]rbn.'dd.nryn.|[ab]r[p]u.bn.kbd.|[-]m[102[322].6.1
sp.ḥmt.|[---.š]pš.l [hrm.ǵrpl].'l.arṣ.l an.|[ḥ]mt.i[l.w] ḥrn.yisp.ḥmt.|[b'l.w]dgn[.yi]sp.ḥmt.'nt.w 'ṯtrt.|[ti]sp.ḥmt. UG5.8.13
ṣdr[.---].|[---.]kl.b kl.l pgm.pgm.l.b[---].|[---.]mdbm.l ḥrn.ḥr[n.---].|[---.--]m.ql.hm[.---].|[---].aṯt n.r[---].|[---.]ḥr[- 1001.1.27
ln.rd.l mlk.|amlk.l drkt k.aṯb.|an.w y'ny.krt ṯ'.ytbr.|ḥrn.y bn.ytbr.ḥrn.|riš k.'ṯtrt.šm.b'l.|qdqd k.tqln.b gbl.|šnt 16.6[127].55
--].|drkt k.mšl[-.---].|b riš k.aymr[.---].|ṯpṭ.nhr.ytb[r.ḥrn.y ym.ytbr.ḥrn].|riš k.'ṯtrt.[šm.b'l.qdqd k.---].|[--]t.mṯ.t 2.1[137].7
'rn h.|ssnm.ysyn h.'dtm.y'dyn h.yb|ltm.ybln h.mǵy.ḥrn.l bt h.w.|yštql.l ḥṭr h.tlu ḥt.km.nḫl.|tplg.km.plg.|b'd UG5.7.67
nḥš.|šmrr.nḥš.'q šr.ln h.mlḫš.|abd.ln h.ydy.ḥmt.|b ḥrn.pnm.trǵnw.w ṯṯkl.|bnwt h.ykr.'r.d qdm.|idk.pnm.l ytn UG5.7.61
šr.y'db.|ksa.w yṯb.|tqru l špš.um h.špš.um.ql bl.|'m ḥrn.mṣd h.mnt.nṯk nḥš.|šmrr.nḥš.'q šr.ln h.mlḫš.|abd.ln h UG5.7.58
[-.---].|b riš k.aymr[.---].|ṯpṭ.nhr.ytb[r.ḥrn.y ym.ytbr.ḥrn].|riš k.'ṯtrt.[šm.b'l.qdqd k.---].|[--]t.mṯ.tpln.b g[bl.šnt k 2.1[137].7
lk.l drkt k.aṯb.|an.w y'ny.krt ṯ'.ytbr.|ḥrn.y bn.ytbr.ḥrn.|riš k.'ṯtrt.šm.b'l.|qdqd k.tqln.b gbl.|šnt k.b ḥpn k.w t' 16.6[127].55
[']pṯrm bn.agmz.|[-]n bn.iln.|[--]nn bn.ibm.|[-]n bn.ḥrn.|[š]mmn bn.gmz.|[yn]ḥm bn.ilmd. 2087.13
--.-]bt.np[-.---].|[-] l šd.ql.[---.---].aṯr.|[--.]ǵrm.y[--.---.ḥ]rn.|[-]rk.ḥ[--.---.-]lk.|[-]sr.n[--.---.]ḥrn.|[--]p.ḫp h.ḫ[--.---. UG5.8.4
]ḥr k.ygrš k.qr.bt k.ygrš k.|[---].bnt.ṣ'ṣ.bnt.m'm'.'bd.ḥrn.[--.]k.|[---].aǵwyn.'n k.ẓẓ.w k mǵ.ilm.|[--.]k 'ṣm.k 'šm.l 1001.2.11
|[--.]ǵrm.y[--.---.ḥ]rn.|[-]rk.ḥ[--.---.-]lk.|[-]sr.n[--.---.]ḥrn.|[--]p.ḫp h.ḫ[--.---.šp]š.l hrm.|[ǵrpl.]'l.ar[ṣ.---.ḥ]mt.|[-- UG5.8.6
---].|[---.]kl.b kl.l pgm.pgm.l.b[---].|[---.]mdbm.l ḥrn.ḥr[n.---].|[---.--]m.ql.hm[.---].|[---].aṯt n.r[---].|[---.]ḥr[-.--]. 1001.1.27

ḫrnq

rbt ḫ|rṣ.išlḥ ẓhrm iq|nim.atn šd h krm[m].|šd dd h ḫrnqm.w |y'n ḫrḫb mlk qẓ [l].|n'mn.ilm l ḫt[n].|m.b'l trḫ 24[77].23

ḥrṣ

ʿ]nt. | ṯṯb.[---.--]ša. | tlm.km[.---.]yd h.k šr. | knr.uṣbʿt h ḥrṣ.abn. | p h.tiḫd.šnt h.w akl.bqmm. | tšt ḥrṣ.k lb ilnm. | w ṯ 19[1AQHT].1.8
n. | yd.tr hn. | w.l.ṯt.mrkbtm. | inn.uṯpt. | w.ṯlṯ.ṣmdm.w.ḥrṣ. | apnt.b d.rb.ḥršm. | d.šṣa.ḥwy h. 1121.8
.kmn. | bn.ibyn. | bn.mryn.ṣmd.w.ḥrṣ. | bn.prsn.ṣmd.w.ḥrṣ. | bn.ilbʿl. | bn.idrm. | bn.grgš. | bn.bly. | bn.apṯ. | bn.ysd. | b 2113.6
ṣmdm. | bn.ʿmnr. | bn.kmn. | bn.ibyn. | bn.mryn.ṣmd.w.ḥrṣ. | bn.prsn.ṣmd.w.ḥrṣ. | bn.ilbʿl. | bn.idrm. | bn.grgš. | bn.bly 2113.5
knr.uṣbʿt h ḥrṣ.abn. | p h.tiḫd.šnt h.w akl.bqmm. | tšt ḥrṣ.k lb ilnm. | w ṯn.gprm.mn gpr h.šr. | aqht.yʿn.kmr.kmr[.- 19[1AQHT].1.10
.mt.uḫryt.mh.yqḥ. | mh.yqḥ.mt.aṯryt.spsg.ysk. | [l]riš.ḥrṣ.l ẓr.qdqd y. | [--.]mt.kl.amt.w an.mtm.amt. | [ap.m]ṯn.rg 17[2AQHT].6.37
rṣ. | ṯryn.ššwm. | ṯryn.aḥd.d bnš. | arbʿ.ṣmdm.apnt. | w ḥrṣ. | tšʿm.mrḥ.aḥd. | kbd. 1123.8
rbʿm.qšt. | alp ḥẓm.w alp. | nṯq.ṯn.qlʿm. | ḫmš.ṣmdm.w ḥrṣ. | ṯryn.ššwm. | ṯryn.aḥd.d bnš. | arbʿ.ṣmdm.apnt. | w ḥrṣ. | t 1123.4
tlmdm. | [y]bnn.ṣmdm. | ṯp[ṯ]bʿl.ṣmdm. | [---.ṣ]mdm.w.ḥrṣ. | [---].aḥdm. | [iwr]pzn.aḥdm. | [i]lšpš.aḥd. 2033.2.5
w.ṯlṯ.l.ʿšrm. | ḫpnt.ššwm.ṯn. | pddm.w.d.ṯṯ. | [mr]kbt.w.ḥrṣ. 2049.9

ḫrr

n. | mhr l ht. | artyn. | ʿdmlk. | bn.alt[-]. | iḫy[-]. | ʿbdgtr. | ḫrr. | bn.s[-]p[-]. | bn.nrpd. | bn.ḥ[-]y. | bʿlskn. | bn.ʿbd. | ḫyrn. | 1035.1.11
m. | [---.l]šn.l kbkbm.yʿrb. | [bʿ]l.b kbd h.b p h yrd. | k ḫrr.zt.ybl.arṣ.w pr. | ʿṣm.yraun.aliyn.bʿl. | ṯtʿ.nn.rkb.ʿrpt. | tbʿ. 5[67].2.5
tm.tṣḥn y.mt mt. | nḥtm.ḫṭ k.mmnnm.mṭ yd k.hl.ʿṣr. | tḥrr.l išt.w ṣḥrt.l pḥmm.aṯtm.a[ṯt.il]. | aṯt.il.w ʿlm h.yhbr.špt 23[52].48
aṯtm.tṣḥn y.ad ad.nḥtm.ḫṭ k. | mmnnm.mṭ yd k.hl.ʿṣr.tḥrr.l išt. | w ṣḥrrt.l pḥmm.btm.bt.il.bt.il. | w ʿlm h.w hn.aṯt 23[52].44
.tṣḥn. | y mt.mt.nḥtm.ḫṭ k.mmnnm.mṭ.yd k. | h[l.]ʿṣr.tḥrr.l išt.ṣḥrrt.l pḥmm. | a[ṯ]tm.aṯt.il.aṯt.il.w ʿlm h.w hm. | aṯ 23[52].41
lm[.---]. | aḫd.aklm.k [---]. | npl.b mšmš[.---]. | anp n m yḥr[r.---]. | bmt n m.yšḫn.[---]. | qrn h.km.ǵb[-.---]. | hw km.ḫ 12[75].2.38
.---]. | bmt n m.yšḫn.[---]. | qrn h.km.ǵb[-.---]. | hw km.ḫrr[.---]. | šnmtm.dbṭ[.---]. | trʿ.trʿn.a[--.---]. | bnt.šdm.ṣḥr[.---] 12[75].2.41

ḫrš

ḫrš.anyt. | bnš.gt.glʿd. | bnš.gt.ngr. | rʿym. | bn.ḫri[-]. | bnš.gt.ʿṯ 1040.1
klby.aḫrtp. | ilyn.ʿlby.ṣdkn. | gmrt.ṯlmyn. | ʿbdnt. | bdy.ḫrš arkd. | blšš lmd. | ḥṯṯn.tqn. | ydd.idṯn. | šǵr.ilgdn. 1045.9
ṯṯtm.ḫzr. | dt.tbʿln. | b.gt.ḫršm. | ṯn.ḫršm. | [-]nbkm. | ṯn.ḫršm. | b.gt.ǵl. | [-.]nǵr.mdrʿ. | [-].nǵr[.--]m. | [--.]psl.qšt. | [ṯl]ṯ. 1024.3.14
[b]n.špš[yn]. | [b]n.ḫrmln. | bn.tnn. | bn.pndr. | bn.nqq. | ḫrš.bhtm. | bn.izl. | bn.ibln. | bn.ilt. | špšyn.nḫl h. | nʿmn.bn.iry 85[80].2.2
[ḫrš].bhtm.bʿl.šd. | [---d]nil. | [a]drdn. | [---]n. | pǵdn. | ṯṯpḥ. | ḥg 1039.1.1
r. | lqḥ šʿrt. | ṯṯ ʿšr h.lqḥ. | ḫlpnt. | ṯṯ.ḫrṯm. | lqḥ.šʿrt. | ʿšr.ḫrš. | bhtm.lqḥ. | šʿrt. | arbʿ. | ḫrš qṭn. | lqḥ šʿrt. | ṯṯ nsk.ḥdm. | lq 2052.8
| aḫršp. | anntn. | bʿlrm. | [-]ral. | šdn. | [-]ǵl. | bn.bʿltǵpṯ. | ḫrš.btm. | ršpab. | [r]ṣn. | [a]ǵlmn. | [a]ḫyn. | [k]rwn. | [k]l[by]. | 2060.13
ḥ.mrṯn. | ḫdǵlm.i[---]n.pbn.ndbn.sbd. | šrm.[---]. ḫpn. | ḫrš[bhtm.--]n.ʿbdyrḫ.ḥdṯn.yʿr. | adbʿl[.---].ḥdṯn.yḥmn.bnil. | 2011.18
]. | mdm. | inšt. | nsk ksp. | yṣḥm. | ḫrš mrkbt. | ḫrš qṭn. | ḫrš bhtm. 73[114].10
khnm. | qdšm. | mkrm. | mdm. | inšt. | ḫrš.bhtm. 75[81].6
.ḫzr. | w.arbʿ.ḫršm. | dt.tbʿln.b.pḫn. | ṯṯtm.ḫzr.w.ʿšt.ʿšr.ḫrš. | dt.tbʿln.b.ugrt. | ṯṯtm.ḫzr. | dt.tbʿln. | b.gt.ḫršm. | ṯn.ḫršm 1024.3.7
bʿ.b.ḫrṯm. | [ṯ]lṯ.b.ṯǵrm. | rb qrt.aḥd. | ṯmn.ḫzr. | w.arbʿ.ḫršm. | dt.tbʿln.b.pḫn. | ṯṯtm.ḫzr.w.ʿšt.ʿšr.ḫrš. | dt.tbʿln.b.ugrt. 1024.3.5
ṯt.mrkbtm. | inn.uṯpt. | w.ṯlṯ.ṣmdm.w.ḥrṣ. | apnt.b d.rb.ḫršm. | d.šṣa.ḥwy h. 1121.9
[s]pr.ḥ[rš.---]. | [-]mn.n[--]. | ḫrš.d.[---]. | mrum.[---]. | yṣḥm[.---]. | mkrm[.---]. | pslm[.---]. 1038.3
ʿbdkṯr. | dd[m] l rʿy. | [--] šmḫ[.---]. | ddm gt dprnm. | l ḫršm. | ddm l ʿnqt. | dd l alṯt.w l lmdt h. | dd l iḫyn. | dd l [---] 1101.9
pn.il.b pid. | tb.bn y.lm ṯb[t] km. | l kḥṯ.zbl k[m.a]nk. | iḥtrš.w [a]škn. | aškn.ydt.[m]rṣ gršt. | zbln.r[---].ymlu. | nʿm.[16[126].5.26
ṯt.dnty.tʿdb.imr. | b pḫd.l npš.kṯr.w ḫss. | l brlt.hyn.d ḫrš. | ydm.aḫr.ymǵy.kṯr. | w ḫss.b d.dnil.ytnn. | qšt.l brk h.yʿ 17[2AQHT].5.24
t.dnty.ʿd[b]. | imr.b pḫd.l npš.kṯr. | w ḫss.l brlt.hyn d. | ḫrš yd.šlḥm.ššqy. | ilm sad.kbd.hmt.bʿl. | ḥkpt.il.kl h.tšmʿ. | 17[2AQHT].5.19
tšṯḥ | wy.w kbd hwt. | w rgm.l kṯr. | w ḫss.ṯny.l h | yn.d ḫrš.ydm. | ṯḥm.al[iyn.bʿl]. | h[wt.aliy.qrdm]. 3[ʿNT.VI].6.23
[šṯḥwy.w kbd.hwt]. | w rgm l k[ṯr.w ḫss.ṯny.l hyn]. | d ḫrš.y[dm.ṯḥm.ṯr.il.ab k.] | hwt.lṭpn[.ḥtk k.---]. | yh.kṯr.b[---]. 1[ʿNT.IX].3.5
. | nʿmm.[--].ṯṯm.w.at. | nǵṯ.w.ytn.hm.l k. | w.lḥt.alpm.ḫršm. | k.rgmt.l y.bly m. | alpm.aršt.l k.w.l y. | mn.bnš.d.l.i[-- 2064.21
yqny.ḏdm.yd.mḫṣt.a[qh]t.ǵ | zr.tmḫṣ.alpm.ib.št[-.]št. | ḫršm l ahlm p[---.]km. | [-]bl lb h.km.bṯn.y[--.-]ah. | ṯnm.tšqy 19[1AQHT].4.222
spr.ḫršm. | liy.bn.qqln. | [---.a]lṯy. | [-----]. | [---]tl. | [---]ʿbl. | [---]bln 1036.1
h. | bn.glgl.uškny. | bn.ṯny.uškny. | mnn.w.aṯt h. | slmu.ḫrš.mrkbt. | bnšm.dt.l.mlk. | ʿbdyrḫ.bn.ṯyl. | ʿbdn.w.aṯt h.w.b 2068.16
mru s[kn]. | mru ib[rn]. | mdm. | inšt. | nsk ksp. | yṣḥm. | ḫrš mrkbt. | ḫrš qṭn. | ḫrš bhtm. 73[114].8
[ḫr]š.qṭn. | [---]n. | [-----]. | [--]dd. | [bʿ]l.ṯǵpṯm. | [k]rwn. | ḫrš.mrkbt. | mnḥm. | mṣrn. | mdrǵlm. | agmy. | ʿdyn. | ʿbdbʿl. | ʿ 1039.2.13
ʿl. | annmn.ʿdy.klby.dqn. | ḫrṯm.ḥgbn.ʿdn.ynḥm[.---]. | ḫrš.mrkbt.ʿzn.[b]ʿln.ṯb[--.-]nb.trtn. | [---]mm.klby.kl[--].dqn[2011.28
-]. | agmy[.---]. | bn.dlq[-.---]. | ṯǵyn.bn.ubn.ṯql[m]. | yšn.ḫrš.mrkbt.ṯq[lm]. | bn.pʿṣ.ṯqlm. | mṣrn.ḫrš.mrkbt.ṯqlm. | ʿpṯn. 122[308].1.6
bn.ṯql[m]. | yšn.ḫrš.mrkbt.ṯq[lm]. | bn.pʿṣ.ṯqlm. | mṣrn.ḫrš.mrkbt.ṯqlm. | ʿpṯn.ḫrš.qṭn.ṯqlm. | bn.pǵdn.ṯqlm. | bn.bʿln. 122[308].1.8
ǵr.mdrʿ. | [-].nǵr[.--]m. | [--.]psl.qšt. | [ṯl]ṯ.psl.ḥẓm. | [---.ḫ]rš.mr[k]bt. | [--].ʿšr h[.---]. | [ḫm]š.ʿšr h[.---]. | ḫmš.ʿšr h. | šr 1024.3.20
[---.---.]l.mit.drʿ.w.šbʿm.drt. | [---.ḥpr.]bnšm.w.l.ḫrš.ʿrq.ṯn.ʿšr h. | [---.d]rʿ.w.mit.drt.w.ʿšrm.l.mit. | [drt.ḥpr.b] 1098.2
mru ib[rn]. | mdm. | inšt. | nsk ksp. | yṣḥm. | ḫrš mrkbt. | ḫrš qṭn. | ḫrš bhtm. 73[114].9
pnt. | ṯṯ.ḫrṯm. | lqḥ.šʿrt. | ʿšr.ḫrš. | bhtm.lqḥ. | šʿrt. | arbʿ. | ḫrš qṭn. | lqḥ šʿrt. | ṯṯ nsk.ḥdm. | lqḥ.šʿrt. 2052.12
kbt.ṯq[lm]. | bn.pʿṣ.ṯqlm. | mṣrn.ḫrš.mrkbt.ṯqlm. | ʿpṯn.ḫrš.qṭn.ṯqlm. | bn.pǵdn.ṯqlm. | bn.bʿln.ṯqlm. | ʿbdyrḫ.nqd.ṯql 122[308].1.9
. | ṯdǵlm.iln.bʿ[l]n.aldy. | ṯdn.ṣr[--.--]t.ʿzn.mtn.n[bd]g. | ḫrš qṭn[.---.]dqn.bʿln. | ǵltn.ʿbd.[---]. | nsk.ḥdm.klyn[.ṣd]qn.ʿb 2011.23
ṯṯpḥ. | ḥgbn. | šrm. | bn.ymil. | bn.kdǵdl. | [-]mn. | [--]n. | [ḫr]š.qṭn. | [---]n. | [-----]. | [--]dd. | [bʿ]l.ṯǵpṯm. | [k]rwn. | ḫrš.mr 1039.2.7
spr.ḫrš. | qštipṭl. | bn.anny. | ilṣdq. | ypltn.bn iln. | špšm.nsl h. | [---- 1037.1
ubdy.mdm. | šd.b d.ʿbdmlk. | šd.b d.yšn.ḫrš. | šd.b d.aupš. | šd.b d.ršpab.aḫ.ubn. | šd.b d.bn.uṯryn. | [u 82[300].1.3
bn.ǵs.ḫrš.šʿty. | ʿdy.bn.slʿy.gbly. | yrm.bʿl.bn.kky. 2121.1
w.ʿšt.ʿšr.ḫrš. | dt.tbʿln.b.ugrt. | ṯṯtm.ḫzr. | dt.tbʿln. | b.gt.ḫršm. | ṯn.ḫršm. | [-]nbkm. | ṯn.ḫršm. | b.gt.ǵl. | [-.]nǵr.mdrʿ. | [- 1024.3.11
rš. | dt.tbʿln.b.ugrt. | ṯṯtm.ḫzr. | dt.tbʿln. | b.gt.ḫršm. | ṯn.ḫršm. | [-]nbkm. | ṯn.ḫršm. | b.gt.ǵl. | [-.]nǵr.mdrʿ. | [-].nǵr[.--] 1024.3.12

ll. | ǵlmn. | bn.ytrm. | bn.ḫgbt. | mtn. | mḫtn. | [p]lsy. | bn.ḥrš. | [--.]kbd. | [---]. | y[---]. | bn.ǵlyn. | bdl.ar. | bn.šyn. | bn.ubr 1035.2.15
. | [-]lm.b d.r[-]m.l[-]m. | ṯṯ.'šr.ṣ[mdm]. | w.tš'.'[šr.--]m.ḥr[š]. | [---].ḥr[š.---]. | [---.ṯ]lṯ.[---.]dpm. | [---.]bnšn. | [---.ḫ]mš. 2038.11
šb'.yn.l [---]. | ṯlṯ.l ḥr[š.---]. | ṯṯ[.l.]mštt[.---]. | ṯlṯ.l.mḏr[ǵlm]. | kd[.--].lm[d.---]. | k 1091.2
[s]pr.ḥ[rš.---]. | [-]mn.n[--]. | ḥrš.d.[---]. | mrum.[---]. | yṣḥm[.---]. | m 1038.1
.r[-]m.l[-]m. | ṯṯ.'šr.ṣ[mdm]. | w.tš'.'[šr.--]m.ḥr[š]. | [---].ḥr[š.---]. | [---.ṯ]lṯ.[---.]dpm. | [---.]bnšn. | [---.ḫ]mš.ṣmd.alpm. 2038.12
--]rt.b d.ṯpṭb'l. | [ubdy.]mḫ[s]m. | [šd.bn.]uzpy.b d.yšn.ḥrš. | [-----]. | [-----]. | [šd.b d.--]n. | [šd.b d.--]n. | [šd.b d.--]ǵl. | [82[300].2.26
.ttkn. | štk.mlk.dn. | štk.šibt.'n. | štk.qr.bt.il. | w mṣlt.bt.ḥr[š]. 12[75].2.62

ḥrtn

šrm. | b.'dn.bn.ṯṯ.'šrt. | b.bn.qrdmn.ṯlṯm. | b.bṣmn[.bn].ḥrtn.'[--]. | b.t[--.---] h.[---]. | [-----]. | [--]ly.ḫmšm.b.'bdyr[ḫ]. | 2054.1.21

ḥrṯ

.ḥtk k. | pl.'nt.šdm.y špš. | pl.'nt.šdm.il.yš[t k]. | b'l.'nt.mḥrṯ[-]. | iy.aliyn.b'l. | iy.zbl.b'l.arṣ. | w t'n.nrt.ilm.š[p]š. | šd y 6[49].4.38
il.šp[š]. | pl.'nt.šdm.y špš. | pl.'nt.šdm.il.yšt k. | [b]'l.'nt.mḥrṯt. | iy.aliyn.b'l. | iy.zbl.b'l.arṣ. | ttb'.btlt.'nt. | idk.l ttn.pn 6[49].4.27
rṯ.yn.srnm.yn.bld. | ǵll.yn.išryt.'nq.smd. | lbnn.ṭl mrṯ.yḥrṯ.il. | hn.ym.w ṯn.tlḥmn.rpum. | tštyn.ṯlṯ.rb'.ym.ḫmš. | ṯdṯ. 22.2[124].20
r.uz.aḫmn.arb'.mat. | arb'm.kbd. | ṯlṯ.alp.ṣpr.dt.aḥd. | ḥrṯ h.aḥd.b gt.nḫl. | aḥd.b gt.knpy.w.aḥd.b gt.ṯrmn. | aḥd.alp 1129.9
šn.pbl. | mlk.l qr.ṯigt.ibr h. | l ql.nhqt.ḥmr h. | l g't.alp.ḥrṯ.zǵt. | klb.ṣpr.w ylak. | mlakm.l k.'m.krt. | mswn h.tḥm.pb 14[KRT].3.122
sk.ḥḏm.klyn[.ṣd]qn.'bdilt.b'l. | annmn.'dy.klby.dqn. | ḥrṯm.ḥgbn.'dn.ynḥm[.---]. | ḥrš.mrkbt.'zn.[b]'ln.ṯb[--.-]nb.tr 2011.27
ṣd.mqb. | [b.g]t.bir.'š[r.---]. | [---].krk.m'[ṣd.---]. | [b.]gt.ḥrṯm.ḫm[š.---]. | [n]it.krk.m'ṣ[d.---]. | b.ḫrbǵlm.ǵlm[n]. | w.tr 2048.17
bn. | ydy.psltm.b y'r. | yhdy.lḥm.w dqn. | ytlṯ.qn.ḏr' h.yḥrṯ. | k gn.ap lb.k 'mq.ytlṯ. | bmt.yšu.g h.w yṣḥ. | b'l.mt.my.l 5[67].6.20
ab.td[.ps]ltm[.b y'r]. | thdy.lḥm.w dqn[.ṯlṯ]. | qn.ḏr' h.tḥrṯ.km.gn. | ap lb.k 'mq.ṯlṯ.bmt. | b'l.mt.my.lim.bn dgn. | m 6[62].1.4
l. | mlk.l [qr.]ṯiqt. | ibr h[.l]ql.nhqt. | ḥmr[h.l g't.]alp. | ḥrṯ[.l z]ǵt.klb. | [ṣ]pr[.apn]k. | [pb]l[.mlk.g]m.l aṯt | [h.k]y[ṣḥ 14[KRT].5.226
m.l ḥṯt.b gn. | bm.nrt.ksmm. | 'l.tl[-]k.'ṭrṭrm. | nšu.[r]iš.ḥrṯm. | l ẓr.'db.dgn kly. | lḥm.[b]'dn hm.kly. | yn.b ḥmt hm. 16[126].3.12
ḥd.kbd. | arb'm.b ḫzr. | lqḥ š'rt. | ṯṯ 'šr h.lqḥ. | ḫlpnt. | ṯṯ.ḥrṯm. | lqḥ.š'rt. | 'šr.ḥrš. | bhtm.lqḥ. | š'rt. | arb'. | ḥrš qṭn. | lqḥ š 2052.6
ḥmšm.ṯmn.kbd. | tgmr.bnš.mlk. | d.b d.adn'm. | [š]b'.b.ḥrṯm. | [ṯ]lṯ.b.ṯǵrm. | rb qrt.aḥd. | ṯmn.ḫzr. | w.arb'.ḥršm. | dt.t 1024.3.1
aḫd b.g]t gbry. | [---].aḥd.aḫd.b.y'ny. | [---.-]ḥm.b.aḫd.ḥrṯ. | [---.]aḫd.b.grn.uškn. | [---.]aḫd.ḥrṯ. 1129.15
ḥrṯm[.---]. | bn.ṯmq[-.---]. | bn.ntp.[---]. | bn.lbnn.[----]. | ady.ḥ[88[304].1
. | [---.-]ḥm.b.aḫd.ḥrṯ. | [---.]aḫd.b.grn.uškn. | [---.]aḫd.ḥrṯ. 1129.17

ḥš

.b'l m[.--]y.tnn.w ygl.w ynsk.'[-]. | [--]y.l arṣ[.id]y.alt.l aḥš.idy.alt.in l y. | [--]t.b'l.ḥẓ.ršp.b[n].km.yr.klyt h.w lb h. | [1001.1.2
il. | ṯrmn w šnm. | il w aṯrt. | ḫnn il. | nṣbt il. | šlm il. | il ḥš il add. | b'l ṣpn b'l. | ugrt. | b mrḥ il. | b nit il. | b ṣmd il. | b d 30[107].9
[mrzḥ.---]. | bṯt.'llm n.[---]. | ilm.bt.b'l k.[---]. | dl.ylkn.ḥš.b a[rṣ.---]. | b 'pr.ḫbl ṭtm.[---.] | šqy.rṯa.tnm y.ytn.[ks.b yd 1['NT.X].4.7
.bht zbl ym. | [trm]m.hk[l.ṯpṭ].nhr.bt k.[---.]šp[-.---]. | [ḥš.bh]t h.tbn[n.ḥ]š.trm[mn.hkl h.---.]bt. | [---.-]k.mnh[-.---.-] 2.3[129].10
]qlṣn.wpṯ m. | [---.]w y'n.kṯr. | [w ḫss.]ṯṯb.b'l.l hwt y. | [ḥš.]bht h.tbnn. | [ḥš.]trmm.hkl h. | y[tl]k.l lbnn.w 'ṣ h. | l[šr] 4[51].6.16
y[n.b'l]. | [--]b[.---]. | ḥš.bht m.k[ṯr]. | ḥš.rmm.hk[l m]. | ḥš.bht m.tbn[n]. | ḥš.trmmn.hk[l m]. | b tk.ṣrrt.ṣpn. | alp.šd.a 4[51].5.115
yhbr.w yql]. | yšṯḥwy.[w ykbdn h.---]. | ṯr.il[.ab h.---]. | ḥš b[ht m.tbnn.ḥš.trmmn.hkl m]. | b tk.[---]. | bn.[---]. | a[--.-- 1['NT.IX].3.27
n. | b'l.'d.lḥm.šṯ[y.ilm]. | [w]y'n.aliy[n.b'l]. | [--]b[.---]. | ḥš.bht m.k[ṯr]. | ḥš.rmm.hk[l m]. | ḥš.bht m.tbn[n]. | ḥš.trmm 4[51].5.113
[ḥš k.'ṣ k.'bṣ k.']m y.p['n k. | [tlsmn.'m y.twt]ḥ.išd k. | [tk.ḫr 1['NT.IX].2.1
b 'p | [r m.ddym.sk.šlm].l kbd.arṣ. | [arbdd.l kbd.š]dm.ḥš k. | ['ṣ k.'bṣ k.'m y.p']n k.tlsmn. | ['m y.twtḥ.išd] k.tk.ḫršn 1['NT.IX].2.21
.---]. | yh.kṯr.b[---]. | št.lskt.n[--.---]. | 'db.bǵrt.ṯ[--. --]. | ḥš k.'ṣ k.'[bṣ k.'m y.p'n k.tlsmn]. | 'm y twtḥ.i[šd k.tk.ḫršn.- 1['NT.IX].3.10
[b ']pr[m.ddym.sk.šlm.l kbd.arṣ.arbdd]. | l kbd.š[dm.ḥš k.'ṣ k.'bṣ k.'m y.p'n k.tls] | [m]n 'm y t[wtḥ.išd k.dm.rgm 7.2[130].16
.b 'p[r] m.ddym.sk.šlm. | l kbd.arṣ.arbdd.l kbd.šdm. | [ḥ]š k.[']ṣ k.'bṣ k.'m y.p'n k. | [tls]mn.[']m y.twtḥ.išd k. | [dm. 3['NT].4.55
t.b 'pr m.ddym. | sk.šlm.l kbd.arṣ. | arbdd.l kbd.šdm. | ḥš k.'ṣ k.'bṣ k. | 'm y.p'n k.tlsmn.'m y. | twtḥ.išd k.dm.rgm. | 3['NT].3.15
.tiḫd. | y'rm.šnu.hd.gpt. | ǵr.w y'n.aliyn. | b'l.ib.hdt.lm.tḥš. | lm.tḥš.ntq.dmrn. | 'n.b'l.qdm.yd h. | k tǵd.arz.b ymn h. 4[51].7.38
. | 'm.um y.mnm.šlm. | w.rgm.ṯṯb.l y. | w.mnd'.k.ank. | aḥš.mǵy.mnd'. | k.igr.w.u.[--]. | 'm.špš.[---]. | nšlḥ[.---]. | [---.m 2009.1.11
'rm.šnu.hd.gpt. | ǵr.w y'n.aliyn. | b'l.ib.hdt.lm.tḥš. | lm.tḥš.ntq.dmrn. | 'n.b'l.qdm.yd h. | k tǵd.arz.b ymn h. | bkm.yṯ 4[51].7.39
.]w y'n.kṯr. | [w ḫss.]ṯṯb.b'l.l hwt y. | [ḥš.]bht h.tbnn. | [ḥš.]trmm.hkl h. | y[tl]k.l lbnn.w 'ṣ h. | l[šr]yn.mḥmd.arz h. | 4[51].6.17
m]m.hk[l.ṯpṭ].nhr.bt k.[---.]šp[-.---]. | [ḥš.bh]t h.tbn[n.h]š.trm[mn.hkl h.---.]bt. | [---.-]k.mnh[-.---.-]š bš[-.]t[-].ǵlm.l 2.3[129].10
]. | ḥš.bht m.k[ṯr]. | ḥš.rmm.hk[l m]. | ḥš.bht m.tbn[n]. | ḥš.trmmn.hk[l m]. | b tk.ṣrrt.ṣpn. | alp.šd.aḫd bt. | rbt.kmn.h 4[51].5.116
tḥwy.[w ykbdn h.---]. | ṯr.il[.ab h.---]. | ḥš b[ht m.tbnn.ḥš.trmmn.hkl m]. | b tk.[---]. | bn.[---]. | a[--.---.] 1['NT.IX].3.27
y.ilm]. | [w]y'n.aliy[n.b'l]. | [--]b[.---]. | ḥš.bht m.k[ṯr]. | ḥš.rmm.hk[l m]. | ḥš.bht m.tbn[n]. | ḥš.trmmn.hk[l m]. | b tk. 4[51].5.114
bnt.ḥ[---]. | [--.]uḫd.[b']l m.'[--].yd k.amṣ.yd[.--]. | [---.]ḥš[.-]nm[.--.]k.[--].w yḫnp[.---]. | [---.]ylm.b[n.']n k.ṣmdm.šp 1001.1.15

ḥšbn

.b.uškn. | [---]lby. | [--]nbbl. | bn bl. | bn dkn. | bn ils. | bn ḥšbn. | bn uryy. | bn kṯl. | bn army. | bn gln. | bn abg. | bn.ngry. 1064.7

ḥšn

[---.--]m[.---]. | [-.]rbt.ṯbt.[---]. | rbt.ṯbt.ḥš[n.---]. | y.arṣ.ḥšn[.---]. | t'td.tkl.[---]. | tkn.lbn[.---]. | dt.lbn 5[67].3.3
[---.--]m[.---]. | [-.]rbt.ṯbt.[---]. | rbt.ṯbt.ḥš[n.---]. | y.arṣ.ḥšn[.---]. | t'td.tkl.[---]. | tkn.lbn[.---]. | dt.lbn k[.---]. | dk k.kbk 5[67].3.4

ḥt

--.']ṯtry. | [-----.]yn. | [----.-]mn. | [---.--]m.mṣl. | [---].prš.ḥtm. | ṯlṯ[.---].bn.ṯdnyn. | ddm.ḥ[ṯm].'l.šrn. | 'šrt.ksp.'l.[-]lpy. 1146.5

ḥtk

ḥm. | [l]ḥm.trmmt.l tšt. | yn.tǵẓyt.špš. | rpim.tḥtk. | špš.tḥtk.ilnym. | ʻd k.ilm.hn.mtm. | ʻd k.kṯr m.ḥbr k. | w ḫss.dʻt k 6.6[62.2].46
nʻm.b ǵr.t[l]iyt. | ql.l bʻl.ttnn. | bšrt.il.bš[r.bʻ]l. | w bšr.ḥtk.dgn. | k.ibr.l bʻl[.yl]d. | w rum.l rkb.ʻrpt. | yšmḫ.aliyn.bʻl. 10[76].3.35
--.]rpi.mlk ʻlm.b ʻz. | [rpu.m]lk.ʻlm.b ḏmr h.bl. | [---].b ḥtk h.b nmrt h.l r | [--.]arṣ.ʻz k.ḏmr k.l[-] | n k.ḥtk k.nmrt k. UG5.2.2.8
št.yitsp. | ršp.nṯdṯt.ǵlm. | ym.mšbʻt hn.b šlḥ. | ttpl.yʻn.ḥtk h. | krt yʻn.ḥtk h.rš. | mid.grdš.ṯbt h. | w b tm hn.špḥ.yitb 14[KRT].1.21
ṯdṯt.ǵlm. | ym.mšbʻt hn.b šlḥ. | ttpl.yʻn.ḥtk h. | krt yʻn.ḥtk h.rš. | mid.grdš.ṯbt h. | w b tm hn.špḥ.yitbd. | w b.pḫyr h. 14[KRT].1.22
. | [---].b ḥtk h.b nmrt h.l r | [--.]arṣ.ʻz k.ḏmr k.l[-] | n k.ḥtk k.nmrt k.b tk. | ugrt.l ymt.špš.w yrḫ. | w nʻmt.šnt.il. UG5.2.2.10
.nrt.ilm.špš. | tšu.g h.w tṣḥ. | tḥm.ṯr.il.ab k. | hwt.lṭpn.ḥtk k. | pl.ʻnt.šdm.y špš. | pl.ʻnt.šdm.il.yš[t k]. | bʻl.ʻnt.mḥrṯ[-] 6[49].4.35
y | [kbdn h.yšu.g h.w y]ṣḥ.tḥm. | [ṯr.il.ab k.hwt.l]ṭpn.ḥtk k. | [qryy.b arṣ.mlḥ]mt.št b ʻp | [r m.ddym.sk.šlm].l kbd. 1[ʻNT.IX].2.18
ḫss.ṯny.l hyn]. | d ḥrš.y[dm.tḥm.ṯr.il.ab k.] | hwt.lṭpn[.ḥtk k.---]. | yh.kṯr.b[---]. | št.lskt.n[--.---]. | ʻdb.bǵrt.ṯ[--. --]. | ḥ 1[ʻNT.IX].3.6
rpat.bt. | [m]lk.itdb.d šbʻ. | [a]ḫm.l h.ṯmnt.bn um. | krt.ḥtk n.rš. | krt.grdš.mknt. | aṯt.ṣdq h.l ypq. | mtrḫt.yšr h. | aṯt.t 14[KRT].1.10
.ṭry.ap.l tlḥm. | [l]ḥm.trmmt.l tšt. | yn.tǵẓyt.špš. | rpim.tḥtk. | špš.tḥtk.ilnym. | ʻd k.ilm.hn.mtm. | ʻd k.kṯr m.ḥbr k. | 6.6[62.2].45
š[--.---]. | l.ilt[.---]. | l.bʻlt[.---]. | l.il.bt[.---]. | l.ilt.[---]. | l.ḥtk[.---]. | l.ršp[.---]. | [l].ršp.[---.--]g.kbd. | [l.i]lt.qb[-.---]. | [l.a] 1004.9

ḥtl

t.l tlš. | amt.yrḫ. | l dmgy.amt. | aṯrt.qḥ. | ksan k.ḥdg k. | ḥtl k.w ẓi. | b aln.tk m. | b tk.mlbr. | ilšiy. | kry amt. | ʻpr.ʻẓm y 12[75].1.19

ḥtn

pn.ʻl.[k]rpn. | [---.]ym.w tʻl.trṯ. | [---].yn.ʻšy l ḥbš. | [---.]ḥtn.qn.yṣbt. | [---.--]m.b nši.ʻn h.w tphn. | [---.--]ml.ksl h.k b[17[2AQHT].6.9

ḥtr

[---.]ktb nǵr krm. | [---].ab h.krm ar. | [---.]h.mḥtrt.pṯtm. | [---.-]t h.ušpǵt tišr. | [---.šm]m h.nšat ẓl h kbkb 2001.2.3

ḥtt

l[--]. | [---.-]ṯk.ytmt.dlt tlk.[---].bm[.---]. | [---.-]qp.bn.ḥtt.bn ḥtt[.---]. | [---.--]p.km.dlt.tlk.km.p[---]. | [---.]bt.tḥbṭ.k 1001.1.23
[---.-]ṯk.ytmt.dlt tlk.[---].bm[.---]. | [---.-]qp.bn.ḥtt.bn ḥtt[.---]. | [---.--]p.km.dlt.tlk.km.p[---]. | [---.]bt.tḥbṭ.km.ṣq.ṣd 1001.1.23

ḥtṯ

latnm. | klt.lḥm h.d nzl. | lqḥ.msrr.ʻṣr.db[ḥ]. | yṣq.b gl.ḥtṯ.yn. | b gl.ḫrṣ.nbt.w ʻly. | l ẓr.mgdl.rkb. | ṯkmm.ḥmt.nša. | [14[KRT].4.164
tn]m. | klt.l[ḥm k.d]nzl. | qḥ.ms[rr.]ʻṣr. | dbḥ.ṣ[q.b g]l.ḥtṯ. | yn.b gl[.ḫ]rṣ.nbt. | ʻl.l ẓr.[mg]dl. | w ʻl.l ẓr.[mg]dl.rkb. | ṯ 14[KRT].2.71

ḥtṯn

]l.pdy. | agdn.bn.nrgn. | w ynḥm.aḫ h. | w.bʻln aḫ h. | w.ḥtṯn bn h. | w.btšy.bt h. | w.ištrmy. | bt.ʻbd mlk. | w.snt. | bt.ug 1006.6
wn. | arkḏn. | ilmn. | abškn. | ykn. | ršpab. | klyn. | ḥgbn. | ḥtṯn. | ʻbdmlk. | y[--]k. | [-----]. | pǵḏn. | [--]n. | [--]ntn. | ʻdn. | lkn 1024.1.19
.ṣdkn. | gmrt.ṭlmyn. | ʻbdnt. | bdy.ḥrš arkd. | blšš lmd. | ḥtṯn.tqn. | ydd.idṯn. | šǵr.ilgdn. 1045.11
----]. | pǵḏn. | [--]n. | [--]ntn. | ʻdn. | lkn. | ktr. | ubn. | dqn. | ḥtṯn. | [--]n. | [---]. | tsn. | rpiy. | mrṭn. | ṯnyn. | apṯ. | šbn. | gbrn. | ṯ 1024.2.11

ḥṯbn

ṯṯ.mat.ksp. | ḥṯbn.ybnn. | arbʻm.l.mit.šmn. | arbʻm.l.mit.tišr. | ṯṯ.ṯṯ.b [ṯ]ql.ṯ 1127.2
spr.ḥṯbn.sbrdnm. | ḫmš.kkrm.alp kb[d]. | ṯlṯ.l.nskm.birtym. | b d. 2101.1

ḥṯm

---]. | dbḥ šmn mr[.šmn.rqḥ.bt]. | mtnt.w ynt.[qrt.w ṯn.ḥṯm]. | w bǵr.arbʻ.[---.kdm.yn]. | prs.qmḥ.mʻ[--.---]. | mdbḥt.b APP.II[173].23
.dbḥ[.šmn.mr]. | šmn.rqḥ[.-]bt.mtnt[.w ynt.qrt]. | w ṯn ḥṯm.w bǵr.arb[ʻ.---]. | kdm.yn.prs.qmḥ.[---]. | mdbḥt.bt.ilt.ʻṣr 35[3].22

ḫ

ḫbb

[---.]dt[-.---].|[---.]ksḥ[-.--].|[---.]mnty[.-].|[---.]rb spr ḫbb.|[---.--]n.dbḥm.|[---].ʻbdssm. 49[73].2.4

ḫbd

.|ʻdn.šʻrt.|mnn.šʻrt.|bdn.šʻrt.|ʻpṯn.šʻrt.|ʻbd.yrḫ šʻrt.|ḫbd.ṯr yṣr šʻr.|pdy.yṣr šʻrt.|atnb.ḥr.|šʻrt.šʻrt. 97[315].11

ḫby

bnšm.dt.l.u[--]ṯṯb.|kṯ[r]n.|w.aṯt h.w.nʻr h.|bn.ḫby.w.[a]ṯt h.|ynḫm.ulmy.|[--]q.w.aṯt h.w.bn h.|[--]an.w.a 2068.4
bd]y.mrim.|[šd.b]n.ṯpdn.b d.bn.gʻr.|[šd.b]n.ṯqrn.b d.ḫby.|[ṯn.š]d.bn.ngzḥn.b d.gmrd.|[šd.bn].pll.b d.gmrd.|[šd. 82[300].1.22

ḫbl

n.[---].|ilm.bt.bʻl k.[---].|dl.ylkn.ḥš.b a[rṣ.---].|b ʻpr.ḫbl ṭtm.[---.]|šqy.rṯa.tnm y.ytn.[ks.b yd].|krpn.b klat yd.[-- 1[ʻNT.X].4.8

ḫbly

t.|gdlt.ṯrmn.gdlt.pdry.gdlt dqt.|dqt.ṯrṯ.dqt.|[rš]p.ʻnt.ḫbly.dbḥn š[p]š pgr.|[g]dlt iltm ḫnqtm.d[q]tm.|[yr]ḫ.kṯy g 34[1].17
ry.|ym.bʻl.|yrḫ.|kṯr.|ṯrmn.|pdry.|dqt.|ṯrṯ.|ršp.|ʻnt ḫbly.|špš pgr.|iltm ḫnqtm.|yrḫ kṯy.|ygb hd.|yrgb bʻl.|ydb UG5.14.A.11

ḫbsn

.|agdṯb.|aǵltn.|[-]wn.|bldn.|[-]ln.|[-]ldn.|[i]wryn.|ḫbsn.|ulmk.|ʻdršp.|bn.knn.|pdyn.|bn.aṯtl.ṯn.|kdln.akdṯb. 1061.15

ḫbr

gn.|[b m]ṣd h.yrd.krt.|[l g]gt.ʻdb.akl.l qryt.|ḥṭt.l bt.ḫbr.|yip.lḥm.d ḫmš.|[mǵ]d.ṯdṯ.yr[ḫm].|ʻdn.ngb.w [yṣi.ṣbu] 14[KRT].4.173
gn.|b mṣd k.w yrd.|krt.l ggt.ʻdb.|akl.l qryt.|ḥṭt.l bt.ḫbr.|yip.lḥm.d ḫmš.|mǵd.ṯdṯ.yrḫm.|ʻdn.ngb.w yṣi.|ṣbu.ṣbi 14[KRT].2.82
y[-]y.|[kr]t.ṯʻ.ʻln.bḫr.|[---].aṯt k.ʻl.|[---] k.yššṣi.|[---.]ḫbr.rbt.|[ḫbr.ṯrr]t.il d.|[pid.---].b anšt.|[---.]mlu.|[---.--]tm. 15[128].5.25
i h.|t[p]ṯḥ.rḥbt.yn.|ʻl h.ṯr h.tšʻrb.|ʻl h.tšʻrb.ẓby h.|ṯr.ḫbr.rbt.|ḫbr.ṯrrt.|bt.krt.tbun.|lm.mṯb[.---].|w lḥm mr.tqd 15[128].4.19
ri k.|ptḥ.[rḥ]bt.yn.|ṣḥ.šbʻm.ṯr y.|ṯmnym.[ẓ]by y.|ṯr.ḫbr[.rb]t.|ḫbr[.ṯrrt].|[-]ʻb[-].š[--]m.|[----]r[.---]š[.--]qm.|id. 15[128].4.8
r]t.ṯʻ.ʻln.bḫr.|[---].aṯt k.ʻl.|[---] k.yššṣi.|[---.]ḫbr.rbt.|[ḫbr.ṯrr]t.il d.|[pid.---].b anšt.|[---.]mlu.|[---.--]tm. 15[128].5.26
ḥ.rḥbt.yn.|ʻl h.ṯr h.tšʻrb.|ʻl h.tšʻrb.ẓby h.|ṯr.ḫbr.rbt.|ḫbr.ṯrrt.|bt.krt.tbun.|lm.mṯb[.---].|w lḥm mr.tqdm.|yd.b ṣ 15[128].4.20
rḥ]bt.yn.|ṣḥ.šbʻm.ṯr y.|ṯmnym.[ẓ]by y.|ṯr.ḫbr[.rb]t.|ḫbr[.ṯrrt].|[-]ʻb[-].š[--]m.|[----]r[.---]š[.--]qm.|id.u [---]t.|lḥ 15[128].4.9
ṭbḫ.šm]n.[mri h].|[tpṯḥ.rḥ]bt.[yn].|[---.]rp[.---].|[---.ḫ]br[.---].|bḫr[.--]t[.----].|l mṯb[.--]t[.---].|[tqdm.]yd.b ṣʻ.t[šl 15[128].5.4

ḫbrtnr

|mit.iqni.l tpnr.|[ks.ksp.kt]n.mit.pḫ[m].|[mit.iqni.l]ḫbrtn[r].|[ks.ksp.ktn.mit.pḫ]m.|[mit.iqni.l ḫbrtn]r ṯn.|[ks. 64[118].34
it.iqni.l]ḫbrtn[r].|[ks.ksp.ktn.mit.pḫ]m.|[mit.iqni.l ḫbrtn]r ṯn.|[ks.ksp.ktn.mit.pḫm].|[mit.iqn]i.l skl.[--].|[---. 64[118].36

ḫbrṯ

.|tmtʻ.md h.b ym.ṯn.|npyn h.b nhrm.|štt.ḫptr.l išt.|ḫbrṯ.l ẓr.pḫmm.|tʻpp.ṯr.il.d pid.|tǵẓy.bny.bnwt.|b nši.ʻn h. 4[51].2.9

ḫbt

il[štmʻ].|šbn.|ṭbq.|rqd.|uškn.|ḫbt.|[ḫlb].kr[d]. 1177.6
y.ulp.ddm]y.|[ulp.ḫry.ulp.ḫty.ulp.alṯy.ulp.ǵbr].|[ulp.ḫbt km.ulp.mdll km.ulp.qr zbl].|[u ṯḫṭu.u b ap km.u b qṣrt 32[2].1.8
.ulp.ddm]y.|ulp.ḫry.ulp.ḫ[t]y.ulp.alṯy.ul[p.ǵbr.]ulp.|ḫbt km.ulp.m[dl]l km.ulp.qr zbl.u[š]n yp km.|u b ap km.u 32[2].1.22
ṯy.|[ulp.ddmy.ulp.ḫry.ulp.ḫty.u]lp.alṯy.|[ulp.ǵbr.ulp.ḫbt km.ulp.mdll km.ulp].|[qr zbl.ušn.yp km.b ap km.u b q APP.I[-].1.16
ṯy.|[ulp.ddmy.ulp.ḫry.ulp.ḫty.ulp.alṯy].|[ulp.ǵbr.ulp.ḫbt kn.ulp.mdll kn.ulp.]qr zbl.|[ušn.yp kn.u b ap kn.u b qṣ APP.I[-].2.14
qṯy.ulp.]ddmy.ulp ḫry.|[ulp.ḫty.ulp.alṯy.ulp.ǵbr.ul]p.ḫbt kn.|[ulp.mdll kn.ulp.qr zbl.ušn.y]p kn.|[u b ap kn.u b APP.I[-].1.5
].|ulp.ddmy.ul[p.ḫry.u]lp.ḫty.ulp[.alṯy.ulp.]ǵbr.|ulp.ḫbt kn.ulp.md[ll k]n.ulp.q[r zbl].|u ṯḫṭin.b ap kn.u b [q]ṣrt. 32[2].1.13
ṯy.|ulp.ddmy.ul[p.ḫ]ry.ulp.ḫty.ulp.alṯy.|ulp.ǵbr.ulp.[ḫbt] kn[.u]lp.mdll kn.ulp qr z[bl].|lšn yp kn.b ap [kn.u b qṣ 32[2].1.30
--.-]l[-].|[-----].|[---.--]k.|[---.q]rt.|[---.--]d.b.gnʻ.|[---].ḫbt.|[---].qmy.|[---.]qmy.|[---.--]b.|bn.t[--.---.a]ǵt.|špš[yn.- 2015.1.15

ḫbty

gynt.|bn.abdḫr.snry.|dqn.šlmn.|prdn.ndb[--].|[-]rn.ḫbty.|abmn.bn.qdmn.|nʻmn.bn.ʻbdilm. 87[64].39
mḏrǵlm.d inn.|msgm.l hm.|pʻṣ.ḫbty.|artyn.ary.|brqn.ṯlḥy.|bn.aryn.|bn.lgn.|bn.bʻyn.|šdy 118[306].3

ḫbṯ

l yblt.ḫbṯm.|ap ksp hm.|l yblt.|w ht.luk ʻm ml[kt].|tǵsdb.šmlšn. 1021.1
spr.ʻrbnm.|dt.ʻrb.|b.mtn.bn.ayaḫ.|b.ḫbṯ h.ḥwt.ṯt h.|w.mnm.šalm.|dt.tknn.|ʻl.ʻrbnm.|hn hmt.|t 1161.4
bt.aḫt.|bn.lwn.ṯlṯtm.bʻlm.|bn.bʻly.ṯlṯtm.bʻlm.|w.aḥd.ḫbṯ.|w.arbʻ.aṯt.|bn.lg.ṯn.bn h.|bʻlm.w.aḫt h.|b.šrt.|šty.w.b 2080.8
b[.---].|[---.-]k[-.-]n[-].|[---.--]m.šr.d.yṯ[b].|[---.--]y.d.ḫbṯ.sy[--].|[---.--]y.b.bt.ṯr[--]. 2134.10

ḫgbt

.|bʻlmṯpṭ.|[bn].ayḫ.|[---]rn.|ill.|ǵlmn.|bn.ytrm.|bn.ḫgbt.|mtn.|mḫtn.|[p]lsy.|bn.ḫrš.|[--.]kbd.|[---].|y[---].|bn 1035.2.11

ḫdi

ṯ.]qšt.w.ṯn.ql'm. | qṣn.ṯt.qštm.w.ql'. | bn.gṯrn.q[š]t. | bn.ḫdi.ṯt.qštm.w.ṯn.ql'm. | ildgn.qšt. | bn.y'rn.ṯt.qštm w.ql'. | bn. 119[321].3.8

ḫdbṯ

. | n'mn. | [-----]. | b gt.yny. | agtṯp. | bn.'nt. | ǵzldn. | ṯrn. | ḫdbṯ. | [-]ḥl.aǵltn. | [-]n. | [-]mṯ. | [--.]bn.[']zn. | [--]yn. 1043.15

ḫdyn

.mid[-.---]. | bn.lṣn.'rm[y]. | aršw.bṣry. | arpṯr.y'rty. | bn.ḫdyn.ugrty. | bn.tgdn.ugrty. | tgyn.arty. | bn.nryn.arty. | bn.rš 87[64].8
ǵlm. | [bn.]kdgdl. | [b]n.qṯn. | [b]n.ǵrgn. | [b]n.tgdn. | bn.ḫdyn. | bn.sgr. | bn.aǵltn. | bn.ktln. | bn.'gwn. | bn.yšm'. | bdl.m 104[316].9
-]. | g[---]. | p[---]. | b[---]. | [---]. | [---]. | bn[.---]y. | yr[---]. | ḫdyn. | grgš. | b[n.]tlš. | ḏmr. | mkrm. | 'zn. | yplṭ. | 'bdmlk. | ynḥ 1035.3.20
qlm. | bn.brq.ṯqlm. | bn.ḫnzr.ṯqlm. | dqn.nsk.arb't. | bn.ḫdyn.ṯqlm. | bn.'bd.šḫr.ṯqlm. | bn.ḫnqn.arb't. | [b]n.ṯrk.ṯqlm. 122[308].1.18

ḫdmn

. | [š]d.bn.ḫrmln.b d.bn.tnn. | [š]d.bn.ḫrmln.ṯn.b d.bn.ḫdmn. | [u]bdy.nqdm. | [ṯlṯ].šdm.d.n'rb.gt.npk. | [š]d.rpan.b d 82[300].2.11
[--]. | [bn.]'[---]. | [bn.]r[---]. | [bn.]ḫ[---]. | [bn.]šbl. | [bn.]ḫdmn. | [bn.]nklb. | [---]dn. | [---]y. | [-----]. | [-----]. | bn.adn. | pr 1073.2.5
nqdm. | bn.alṯn. | bn.dly. | bn.btry. | bn.ḫdmn. | [bn].šty. | [bn].kdgdl. | [---.-]y[-.] 2018.5
]. | [bn].mlṣ.qštm.w.uṯp[t]. | [--.q]l'.w[.---.m]rḥm. | [bn].ḫdmn.qšt.[w.u]ṯp[t].ṯ[--]. | [---].arb'.[---]. | [---].kdl[.---.mr]ḥ 2047.9

ḫdpṯr

zr. | bn.ydb'l. | bn.ḥyn. | [bn].ar[-]m. | [bn].ḥrp[-]. | [bn].ḫdpṯr. | [bn.-]dn. | [bn.-]lyn. | [bn.i]lsk. | [bn.---]n. | bn[.---]. | bn 124[-].2.7
tm.w.ṯn.ql'm. | bn.[-]rkṯ.ṯt.qštm.w.ql'. | bn.ṯ'l.qšt. | bn.[ḫ]dpṯr.ṯt.qštm.[w].ql'. | bn.aǵlyn.ṯt.qštm[.w.ṯl]ṯ.ql'm. | bn.'g 119[321].3.18

ḫḏ

d[-]. | tnq[.---.]in[b]b.p'r. | yd h[.--.]ṣ'r.glgl. | a[---]m.rḥ.ḫḏ '[r]pt. | gl[.---.]yhpk.m[---]m. | s'[--.]k[--]t. 13[6].34

ḫḏḏ

yṣi.'dn]. | m'[.ṣ]bu h.u[l.mad]. | ṯlṯ.mat.rbt. | hlk.l alpm.ḫḏḏ. | w l.rbt.kmyr. | aṯr.ṯn.ṯn.hlk. | aṯr.ṯlṯ.kl hm. | aḥd.bt h.ys 14[KRT].4.180
d. | ṯlṯ.mat.rbt. | ḫpṯ.d bl.spr. | ṯnn.d bl.hg. | hlk.l alpm.ḫḏḏ. | w l rbt.kmyr. | [a]ṯr.ṯn.ṯn.hlk. | aṯr.ṯlṯ.kl hm. | yḥd.bt h. 14[KRT].2.92

ḫḏl

miḫdym. | bn.ḥṭb. | bn abyt. | bn ḫḏl. | bn ṣdqn. | bn ayy. | bn dbb. | w nḥl h. | bn n'myn. | bn aṯt 2016.1.4

ḫḏmḏr

š. | [---.--]ty. | [---.-]i[-.--]. | [-----]. | [---.--]y. | [---.--]lm. | ḫḏmḏr.b.kṯ[t]ǵlm. | mḏl.b.kṯtǵlm. 2118.23

ḫḏmrd

--]. | aṯt.w.bn h.w.pǵt.aḥt.b.bt.m[--]. | aṯt.w.ṯt.bt h.b.bt.ḫḏmrd. | aṯt.w.ṯn.ǵzrm.b.bt.ṣdqš[lm]. | [a]ṯt.aḥt.b.bt.rpi[--]. | [80[119].22

ḫḏmtn

yd.[---]. | am[-]n.[---]. | w.a[ṯt] h.[---]. | ḫḏmtn.ṯn[.---]. | w.ṯlṯ.alp h.[---]. | swn.qrty.w.[b]n h[.---]. | w. 2044.4

ḫḏnr

.mr[y-.---]. | [--]l.ṯṯm sp[m.---]. | [p]drn.ḫm[š.---]. | l bn ḫḏnr[.---]. | ṯṯm sp.km[-.---]. | 'šrm.sp[.---]. | 'šr sp.m[ry-.---]. | 139[310].5

ḫḏǵb

.l.gzzm. | kd yn.l.ḫtn.w.kd.ḥmṣ.w.[lt]ḥ.'šdm. | kd yn.l.ḫḏǵb.w.kd.ḥmṣ. | prš.glbm.l.bt. | tgmǵ.kšmm.b.yrḫ.iṯtbnm. | 1099.28
trbnn. | ddm.š'rm.l.ḫtn. | dd.š'rm.l.ḥmr.ḥṭb. | dd.ḥṭm.l.ḫḏǵb. | ṯt.ddm.l.gzzm. | kd yn.l.ḫtn.w.kd.ḥmṣ.w.[lt]ḥ.'šdm. | 1099.25

ḫḏǵl

lmn. | [a]bǵl.ṣṣn.ǵrn. | šib.mqdšt.'b[dml]k.ṯtpḥ.mrṯn. | ḫḏǵlm.i[---]n.pbn.nḏbn.sbd. | šrm.[---].ḫpn. | ḥrš[bhtm.--]n.' 2011.16
ḫmš.bnšm[.---]. | ḫḏǵlm.b d.[---]. | šb'.lmdm.b d.s[n]rn. | lmd.aḥd.b d.yr[š]. | l 1050.2
šb'.ḫḏǵlm. | l.[---]mn ḫpn. | l[.--.]škn.ḫpn. | l.k[-]w.ḫpn. | l.ṣ[--].š'[1117.1
-.b]'ln. | [---.]lmdm.b d.snrn. | [---.lm]dm.b d.nrn. | [---.ḫ]ḏǵlm. | [lmd.]aḥd.b d.yrš. 1051.5

ḫzli

.šrn. | 'bdb'l.bn.kdn. | gzl.bn.qldn. | gld.bt.klb. | l[---].bt.ḫzli. | bn.iḫyn. | ṣdqn.bn.ass. | b'lyskn.bn.ss. | ṣdqn.bn.imrt. | 102[323].3.6

ḫzmyn

šd.'yy.l aḫn. | šd.brdn.l bn.bly. | šd gzl.l.bn.ṭbr[n]. | šd.ḫzmyn.l a[--]. | ṯn šdm b uš[kn]. 2089.15
.ṯn.šǵr h. | [---.]w.šǵr h. | [---.]w.šǵr h. | [---.]krwn. | [---].ḫzmyn. | [---.]bn.dll. | r[--.--]km. | w.spr h. 2072.12

ḫzr

. | b d.trǵds. | šd.ṯ'lb. | b d.bn.pl. | šd.bn.kt. | b d.pdy. | šd.ḫzr. | [b d].d[---]. 2030.2.7
l.'šrm.bn[š.mlk.---].ḫzr.lqḥ.ḥp[r]. | 'št.'šr h.bn[.---.--]ḫ.zr. | b'l.šd. 2011.41
ln.b.pḫn. | ṯṯm.ḫzr.w.'št.'šr.ḥrš. | dt.tb'ln.b.ugrt. | ṯṯm.ḫzr. | dt.tb'ln. | b.gt.ḥršm. | ṯn.ḥršm. | [-]nbkm. | ṯn.ḥršm. | b.gt. 1024.3.9
rt.aḫd. | ṯmn.ḫzr. | w.arb'.ḥršm. | dt.tb'ln.b.pḫn. | ṯṯm.ḫzr.w.'št.'šr.ḥrš. | dt.tb'ln.b.ugrt. | ṯṯm.ḫzr. | dt.tb'ln. | b.gt.ḥr 1024.3.7
d.adn'm. | [š]b'.b.ḥrṯm. | [ṯ]lṯ.b.ṯǵrm. | rb qrt.aḫd. | ṯmn.ḫzr. | w.arb'.ḥršm. | dt.tb'ln.b.pḫn. | ṯṯm.ḫzr.w.'št.'šr.ḥrš. | dt 1024.3.4
ǵln.ḫmš.ddm. | [---].ḫmš.ddm. | ṯt.l.'šrm.bn[š.mlk.---].ḫzr.lqḥ.ḥp[r]. | 'št.'šr h.bn[.---.--]ḫ.zr. | b'l.šd. 2011.40
aḥd.kbd. | arb'm.b ḫzr. | lqḥ š'rt. | ṯt 'šr h.lqḥ. | ḫlpnt. | ṯt.ḥrṯm. | lqḥ.š'rt. | 'šr.ḥrš. 2052.2

ẖzr

[.l.]mštt[.---].|ṯlṯ.l.md̮r[ǵlm].|kd[.--].lm[d.---].|kd[.l.]ẖzr[m.---].|kd[.l.]ṯrtn[m].|arbʻ l.mry[nm].|kdm l.ẖty.[---].| 1091.6

ẖzrn

|w.nḥl h.|w.nḥl hm.|bn.iršyn.|bn.ʻzn.|bn.arŝw.|bn.ẖzrn.|bn.iǵyn.|w.nḥl h.|bn.ksd.|bn.bršm.|bn.kzn.|w.nḥl 113[400].2.15
].|ksp.ʻl.agd[ṯb].|w nit w mʻṣd.|w ẖrmṯt.|ʻšrt.ksp.|ʻl.ẖ[z]rn.|w.nit.w[.mʻṣd].|w.ẖ[rmṯt].|ʻš[r.---].|ʻl[.---].|w.ni[t.- 2053.6

ẖẖ

.arṣ.|idk.al.ttn.|pnm.tk.qrt h.|hmry.mk.ksu.|ṯbt h.ẖẖ.arṣ.|nḥlt h.w nǵr.|ʻnn.ilm.al.|tqrb.l bn.ilm.|mt.al.yʻdb 4[51].8.13
k.|l ytn.pn.ʻm.bn.ilm.mt.|tk.qrt h.hmry.mk.ksu.|ṯbt.ẖẖ.arṣ.nḥlt h.tša.|g hm.w tṣḥ.tḥm.aliyn.|bn.bʻl.hwt.aliy.qr 5[67].2.16

ẖẖm

ǵz]r.w yʻn.aqht.ǵzr.|al.tšrgn.y btlt m.dm.l ǵzr.|šrg k.ẖẖm.mt.uẖryt.mh.yqḥ.|mh.yqḥ.mt.aṯryt.spsg.ysk.|[l]riš.ḥ 17[2AQHT].6.35

ẖṭ

.mlkt.ʻrbm m.ṯnnm.|mt.w šr.yṯb.b d h.ẖṭ.ṯkl.b d h.|ẖṭ.ulmn.yzbrnn.zbrm.gpn.|yṣmdnn.ṣmdm.gpn.yšql.šdmt h 23[52].9
nšrm.|bʻl.yṯbr.bʻl.yṯbr.diy.|hmt.hm.tʻpn.ʻl.qbr.bn y.|tšẖṭann.b šnt h.qr.[mym].|mlk.yṣm.y l km.qr.mym.d ʻ[l k]. 19[1AQHT].3.151
pr h.šr.|aqht.yʻn.kmr.kmr[.--].|k apʻ.il.b gdrt.k lb.l |ẖṭ h.imẖṣ h.k d.ʻl.qšt h.|imẖṣ h.ʻl.qṣʻt h.hwt.|l aḥw.ap.qšt 19[1AQHT].1.14
db.yqḥ.il.mštʻltm.|mštʻltm.l riš.agn.yqḥ.tš.b bt h.|il.ẖṭ h.nḥt.il.ymnn.mṭ.yd h.yšu.|yr.šmm h.yr.b šmm.ʻṣr.yẖrṭ 23[52].37
.|b d̮rt y.ab.adm.|w ld.špḥ.l krt.|w ǵlm.l ʻbd.il.|krt.yẖṭ.w ḥlm.|ʻbd.il.w hdrt.|yrtḥṣ.w yadm.|yrḥṣ.yd h.amt h. 14[KRT].3.154
m.aṯt.il.aṯt.il.w ʻlm h.w hm.|aṯtm.tṣḥn y.ad ad.nḥtm.ẖṭ k.|mmnnm.mṭ yd k.hl.ʻṣr.tḥrr.l išt.|w ṣḥrrt.l pḥmm.btm 23[52].43
m.bt.il.bt.il.|w ʻlm h.w hn.aṯtm.tṣḥn y.mt mt.|nḥtm.ẖṭ k.mmnnm.mṭ yd k.hl.ʻṣr.|tḥrr.l išt.w ṣḥrt.l pḥmm.aṯtm. 23[52].47
št.|l pḥm.il.aṯtm.k ypt.hm.aṯtm.tṣḥn.|y mt.mt.nḥtm.ẖṭ k.mmnnm.mṭ.yd k.|h[l.]ʻṣr.tḥrr.l išt.ṣḥrrt.l pḥmm.|a[t]t 23[52].40
ly.w tbu.|nṣrt.tbu.pnm.|ʻrm.tdu.mh.|pdrm.tdu.šrr.|ẖṭ m.tʻmt.[ʻ]ṯr.[k]m.|zbln.ʻl.riš h.|w ṯṯb.trḥṣ.nn.b dʻt.|npš 16.6[127].8
t.il.d ydʻnn.|yʻdb.lḥm.l h.w d l ydʻnn.|d.mṣd.|ylmn.ẖṭ.ṯḥt.ṯlḥn.|b qrʻ.|ʻṯtrt.w ʻnt.ymǵy.|ʻṯtrt.tʻdb.nšb l h.|w ʻnt UG5.1.1.8
.|šlm.mlk.šlm.mlkt.ʻrbm m.ṯnnm.|mt.w šr.yṯb.b d h.ẖṭ.ṯkl.b d h.|ẖṭ.ulmn.yzbrnn.zbrm.gpn.|yṣmdnn.ṣmdm.gp 23[52].8
km.r[--].|amr.[---].|ẖṭ.ṯk[l.---].|[-]l[--.---]. 2002.3
.[i]l.ab k.l ysʻ.[alt.]ṯ[bt |k.l y]hpk.|[ksa.]mlk k.l yṯbr.ẖṭ.mṯpṭ k.w yʻn[.ʻṯtr].dm[-]k[-].|[--]ḥ.b y.ṯr.il.ab y.ank.in.bt 2.3[129].18
ʻ] k.ṯr.|il.ab k.l ysʻ.alt.|ṯbt k.l yhpk.ksa.mlk k.|l yṯbr.ẖṭ.mṯpṭ k.|yru.bn ilm t.ṯtʻ.y|dd.il.ǵzr.yʻr.mt.|b ql h.y[---.-- 6[49].6.29

ẖṭa

ṯy.ulp.ǵbr].|[ulp.ẖbt km.ulp.mdll km.ulp.qr zbl].|[u ṯḥṭu.u b ap km.u b qṣrt.npš km.u b qṭt].|[tqṭṭ.u ṯḥṭu.l dbḥ 32[2].1.8A
|[---.w n]py.gr[.ḥmyt.ugrt.w np]y.|[---].w n[py.---].u ṯḥṭi[n.ulp.qṭy].|ulp.ddmy.ul[p.ẖry.u]lp.ẖty.ulp[.alṯy.ulp.]ǵ 32[2].1.11
šr.bn.ugrt.w npy.---.]w npy.|[---.w np]y.ugrt.|[---.u ṯḥṭu.ulp.qṭy.ulp.ddm]y.|[ulp.ẖry.ulp.ẖty.ulp.alṯy.ulp.ǵbr].| 32[2].1.6
lṯy.ulp.]ǵbr.|ulp.ẖbt kn.ulp.md[ll k]n.ulp.q[r zbl].|u ṯḥṭin.b ap kn.u b [q]ṣrt.npš[kn.u b qṭt].|tqṭṭn u ṯḥṭin.l bḥm 32[2].1.14
].|[u ṯḥṭu.u b ap km.u b qṣrt.npš km.u b qṭt].|[tqṭṭ.u ṯḥṭu.l dbḥm.w l.ṯʻ.dbḥ n.ndb]ḥ.|[hw.ṯʻ.nṯʻy.hw.nkt.nkt.]yt[š 32[2].1.9
l].|u ṯḥṭin.b ap kn.u b [q]ṣrt.npš[kn.u b qṭt].|tqṭṭn u ṯḥṭin.l bḥm.w l ṯʻ.d[bḥ n.ndbḥ].|hw.ṯʻ.nṯʻy.hw.nkt.n[k]t.ytši 32[2].1.15

ẖyl

n.tk m.|b tk.mlbr.|ilšiy.|kry amt.|ʻpr.ʻẓm yd.|ugrm.ẖl.ld.|aklm.tbrk k.|w ld ʻqqm.|ilm.ypʻr.|šmt hm.|b hm.qr 12[75].1.25

ẖym

.ksp.yšl|ḥ.ẖrṣ.yṣq.ksp.|l alpm.ẖrṣ.yṣq|m.l rbbt.|yṣq-ẖym.w tbṯẖ.|kt.il.dt.rbtm.|kt.il.nbt.b ksp.|šmrgt.b dm.ẖrṣ. 4[51].1.30

ẖyml

skn.ṯlṯm.|iytlm.ṯlṯm.|ẖyml.ṯlṯm.|ǵlkz.ṯlṯm.|mlknʻm.ʻšrm.|mrʻm.ʻšrm.|ʻmlbu.ʻšr 1116.3

ẖyr

ʻm.ušpǵtm.p[--.---].|kṯ.ẓrw.kṯ.nbt.d̮nt.w [-]n[-.---].|il.ẖyr.ilib.š.|arṣ w šmm.š.|il.š.kṯrt.š.|dgn.š.bʻl.ẖlb alp w š.|bʻ UG5.9.2.1
yrẖ ẖyr.b ym ḥdṯ.|alp.w š.l bʻlt bhtm.|b arbʻt ʻšrt.bʻl.|ʻrkm.|b UG5.12.A.1
b ṯṯ ym ḥdṯ.|ẖyr.ʻrbt.|špš ṯǵr h.|ršp.|w ʻbdm tbqrn.|skn. 1162.2
-.]bqt[-].|[b] ǵb.ršp mh bnš.|šrp.w ṣp ẖršẖ.|ʻlm b ǵb ẖyr.|ṯmn l ṯlṯm ṣin.|šbʻ.alpm.|bt bʻl.ugrt.ṯn šm.|ʻlm.l ršp. UG5.12.B.3
.l.ilšpš.|kd.l.annṯb.|kd.l.iwrmd̮.|kd.l.ydn.|[---.y]rẖ.ẖyr.|[---.]yn.l.mlkt.|[---.yrẖ.]ẖlt.šbʻ.[---].mlkt.|[---.yrẖ.]gn. 1088.11
[---.-]bd[.---].|[---.]yrẖ.ẖyr[.---].|[---].yrẖ.ḥl[t.---].|[---].yrẖ.gn[-.---].|[---.]yrẖ.iṯ[b.- 1088.A.2

ẖyrn

ḥrr.|bn.s[-]p[-].|bn.nrpd.|bn.ḥ[-]y.|bʻlskn.|bn.ʻbd.|ẖyrn.|alpy.|bn.plsy.|bn.qrr[-].|bn.ḥyl.|bn.gʻyn.|ḥyn.|bn.a 1035.1.17
rʻym.dt.b d.iytlm.|ẖyrn.w.ŝǵr h.|ŝǵr.bn.prsn.|agpṯr.w.šǵ[r h].|ṯʻln.|mztn.w.ŝ 2072.2
ʻbdyrẖ.|ubn.ẖyrn.|ybnil.adrdn.|klyn.kkln.|ʻdmlk.tdn.|ʻzn.pǵd̮n.|[a]nn 1070.2
nm].|ršpab.rb ʻšrt.m[r]yn.|pǵd̮n.ilbʻl.krwn.lbn.ʻdn.|ẖyrn.mdʻ.|šmʻn.rb ʻšrt.kkln.ʻbd.abṣn.|šdyn.unn.dqn.|ʻbdʻn 2011.4
spr.rʻym.|lqḥ.šʻrt.|anntn.|ʻdn.|sdwn.|mztn.|ẖyrn.|šdn.|[ʻš]rm.ṯn kbd.|šǵrm.|lqḥ.ššlmt. 2098.7
ṣdqn.bn.ass.|bʻlyskn.bn.ss.|ṣdqn.bn.imrt.|mnḥm.bn.ẖyrn.|[-]yn.bn.arkbt.|[--]zbl.bt.mrnn.|a[--.---.-]ʻn.|ml[--.--- 102[323].3.11
mẖṣ.|bʻln.mẖṣ.|y[ḥ]ṣdq.mẖṣ.|ṣp[r].ks[d].|bʻl.š[lm].|ẖyrn[.---].|a[--.---].|ʻ[--.---].|š[--.---].|[-----].|m[--.---]. 2084.20

ẖkp

[---.]nt[-.]mbk kpt.w[.--].b g[--].|[---.]ḥ[--.]bnt.ṣʻṣ.bnt.ẖkp[.---].|[---].aḥw.aṭm.prṭl[.---].|[---.]mnt.[l]pʻn[.-.-]bd h. 1001.1.18

ẖlan

[w]nḥ[l h]. | [bn].amd[-]. | [bn].ṣbṯ[--]. | [bn].ẖla[n]. | [bn].ǵr[--]. | d.b[n.---]. | d.bn.[---]. | d.bn.š[--]. | d.bn.ṯn 2164.A.4
. | šd.iyry.l.ʿbdbʿl. | šd.šmmn.l.bn.šty. | šd.bn.arws.l.bn.ẖlan. | šd.bn.ibryn.l.bn.ʿmnr. 1102.19
[---.b]n.[y]drn. | [---.]bn.ẖlan. | [--]r bn.mn. | [--]ry. | [--]lim bn.brq. | [--.]qtn bn.drṣy. | [2087.2
| ššw[.--].w.r[ʿ h]. | kr[mn.--.]w.r[ʿ h]. | šd.[--.w.]r[ʿ h]. | ẖla[n.---]. | w lšṯr[.---]. 2083.2.6

ẖli

kyy. | kmsk.šd.iẖmn. | širm.šd.khn. | ṯlṯ.šd.w.krm.šir.d.ẖli. | širm.šd.šd.ʿšy. | w.šir.šd.krm. | d.krwn. | šir.šd.šd.ʿšy. | d.a 1079.6

ẖlu

| [a]rz. | k.tʿrb.ʿṯtrt.šd.bt[.m]lk. | k.tʿrbn.ršp m.bt.mlk. | ẖlu.dg. | ḥdṯm. | dbḥ.bʿl.k.tdd.bʿlt.bhtm. | b.[-]ǵb.ršp.ṣbi. | [---. 2004.12

ẖluy

[.---]. | [ʿ]bdyr[ẖ.---]. | [---]mlk[.---]. | [-----]. | ilbʿl[.---]. | ẖluy.bn[.---]. | ymil.bn.[---]. | dly.bn[.---]. | ynḥm.bn[.---]. | gn. 102[322].5.3

ẖlb

-.---]. | il.ẖyr.ilib.š. | arṣ w šmm.š. | il.š.kṯrt.š. | dgn.š.bʿl.ẖlb alp w š. | bʿl ṣpn alp.w.š. | ṯrṯy.alp.w.š. | yrẖ.š.ṣpn.š. | kṯr š UG5.9.2.4
[-]. | bn.ppṯ.b[--]. | b[n.---]. | šm[-.---]. | tkn[.---]. | knn.b.ẖ[lb]. | bn mṯ.b.qmy. | nʿr.b.ulm. 2046.2.4
| [---].ṣmd[.---.]pd[ry]. | [-----]. | [---.b]ʿlt. | lbnm.ʿšr.yn. | ẖlb.gngnt.ṯlṯ.y[n]. | bṣr.ʿšr.yn. | nnu arbʿ.yn. | šql ṯlṯ.yn. | šmny 2004.22
[---.ʿ]šrt. | ẖlb.ẖmšt.l.ʿšrm. | mril.ʿšrt. | glbty.arbʿt. | [--]ṯb.ʿšrt. 1180.2
ẓ.ršp.b[n].km.yr.klyt h.w lb h. | [t]n.p k.b ǵr.ṯn.p k.b ẖlb.k tgwln.šnt k. | [--.]w špt k.l tššy.hm.tqrm.l mt.b rn k. | [1001.1.4
š[--.---]. | ṣʿ[-.---]. | ṣʿq[.---]. | ẖlb.k[rd]. | uškn. | ʿnqp[at]. | ubrʿ[y]. | ilšt[mʿ]. | šbn. | ṭbq. 2146.4
| mʿr.[---]. | arny.[---]. | šʿrt.ṯn[.---]. | bqʿt.[--].ḥ[mr.---]. | ẖlb krd.ḥ[mr.---]. | ṣʿ.ḥmr.w[.---]. | ṣʿq.ḥmr.w.[---]. | ẖlb ʿprm. 2040.13
šrš. | lbnm. | ẖlb.krd. | ṣʿ. | mlk. | gbʿly. | ypr. | ary. | ẓrn. | art. | ṯlḥny. | ṯlrby. | 71[113].3
ẖlb k[rd]. | ṣʿq. | š[---]. 1178.1
ẖlb ʿprm.ṯṯ. | ẖlb krd.ṯn ʿšr. | qmy.arbʿ.ʿšr. | ṣʿq.arbʿ ʿšr. | ṣʿ.ṯmn. | šḥq.ʿšrm.a 67[110].2
il[štmʿ]. | šbn. | ṭbq. | rqd. | uškn. | ẖbt. | [ẖlb].kr[d]. 1177.7
ṯṯly.bt.rb.idk. | pn k.al ttn.tk.ǵr. | knkny.ša.ǵr.ʿl ydm. | ẖlb.l ẓr.rḥtm w rd. | bt ẖpṯt.arṣ.tspr b y | rdm.arṣ.w tdʿ ilm. | 5[67].5.14
.ǵr.trǵzz. | ʿm.ǵr.ṯrmg. | ʿm.tlm.ǵṣr.arṣ. | ša.ǵr.ʿl.ydm. | ẖlb.l ẓr.rḥtm. | w rd.bt ẖpṯt. | arṣ.tspr.b y | rdm.arṣ. | idk.al.tt 4[51].8.6
ʿr. | ẖlby. | mṣbt. | snr. | ṯm. | ubš. | glbt. | mi[d]ẖ. | mr[i]l. | ẖlb. | šld. | ʿrgz. | [-----]. 2041.14
-]. | ẖlb krd.ḥ[mr.---]. | ṣʿ.ḥmr.w[.---]. | ṣʿq.ḥmr.w.[---]. | ẖlb ʿprm.amḏy.[ḥm]r.w bn[š]. | gnʿy.[---.bn]š. | uškn[.---].ʿšr. 2040.16
ẖlb ʿprm.ṯṯ. | ẖlb krd.ṯn ʿšr. | qmy.arbʿ.ʿšr. | ṣʿq.arbʿ ʿšr. | ṣʿ.ṯm 67[110].1
n. | hz[p].ṯṯ. | ẖrṣbʿ.aḥd. | ypr.arb. | m[-]qb.ʿšr. | ṯnʿy.ṯlṯ. | ẖlb ʿprm.ṯn. | tmḏy.ṯlṯ. | [--]rt.arbʿ. | [---].ʿšr. 70[112].12
mḏ[y]. | atl[g]. | bṣr[y]. | [---]. | [---]y. | ar. | agm.w.ẖpty. | ẖlb.ṣpn. | mril. | ʿnmky. | ʿnqpat. | ṭbq. | hzp. | gnʿy. | mʿrby. | [ṣ]ʿ 71[113].50
lb.]rp[š]. | [---.]bht[.---]. | [---.]amr[-]. | [---.ʿ]rg[z.-]. | [---.ẖl]b ṣpn. 72[-].2.5
št.w.qlʿ. | bn.ṯʿln.qš[t.w.q]lʿ. | ʿṯqbt.qšt. | [-]ll.qšt.w.qlʿ. | ẖlb.rpš. | abmn.qšt. | ẓẓn.qšt. | dqry.qš[t]. | rkby. | bn.knn.qšt. | 119[321].2.30
ubrʿy. | arny. | mʿr. | šʿrt. | ẖlb rpš. | bqʿt. | šḥq. | yʿby. | mẖr. 65[108].5
ẖlb.rpš. | ẓẓn. | bn.ḥmny. | dqry. 1068.1
my.arbʿ.ʿšr. | ṣʿq.arbʿ ʿšr. | ṣʿ.ṯmn. | šḥq.ʿšrm.arbʿ.kbd. | ẖlb rpš arbʿ.ʿšr. | bqʿt ṯṯ. | irab ṯn.ʿšr. | ḥbš.ṯmn. | amḏy.arbʿ.ʿšr 67[110].7
| [---.--]dm. | [--.--]šn. | [---.--]m. | [---.--]l. | [---.--]m. | [---.ẖlb.]rp[š]. | [---.]bht[.---]. | [---.]amr[-]. | [---.ʿ]rg[z.-]. | [---.ẖl]b 72[-].2.1
. | ṣpn.alp.w š.pdry.š. | šrp.w šlmm ilib š. | bʿl ugrt š.bʿl ẖlb š. | yrẖ š.ʿnt ṣpn.alp. | w š.pdry š.ddmš š. | w b urbt.ilib š. UG5.13.16

ẖlby

tn.w.ṯṯ.mat.brr. | b.ṯmnym.ksp.ṯlṯt.kbd. | ẖmš.alp.ṯlṯ.l.ẖlby. | b d.tlmi.b.ʿšrm.ẖmšt. | kbd.ksp. | kkrm.šʿrt.štt.b d.gg[ʿ 2101.6
spr.ytnm. | bn.ẖlbym. | bn.ady. | bn.ʿṯtry. | bn.ẖrẓn. | ady. | bn.birtn. | bn.ḥrẓn 115[301].1.2
l[b]nm. | nnu. | ʿrm. | bṣr. | mʿr. | ẖlby. | mṣbt. | snr. | ṯm. | ubš. | glbt. | mi[d]ẖ. | mr[i]l. | ẖlb. | šld. | 2041.6
r. | bn.ʿyn. | ubnyn. | rpš d ydy. | ǵbl. | mlk. | gwl. | rqd. | ẖlby. | ʿn[q]pat. | m[ʿ]rb. | ʿrm. | bn.ẖgby. | mrat. 2075.25
. | lbnm. | ṯrm. | bṣr. | y[--]. | y[--]. | snr. | midẖ. | ḥ[lym]. | [ẖ]lby. | ʿr. | ʿnq[pat]. | glbty. | [-----]. | [-----]. | [-----]. | [-----]. | yk 2058.2.22
kps]lnm. | arbʿ.mat[.arb]ʿm.[k]bd. | d ntn.d.ksp. | arbʿ.l.ẖlby. | [---].l.bt. | arbʿ.l.kpslnm. | kdm.b[t.]mlk. 1087.4

ẖlbkrd

d. | [š]rš. | [-----]. | [-----]. | [-----]. | [-----]. | [-----]. | [-----]. | [ẖl]bkrd. | [ẖl]bʿprm. | [q]dš. | [a]mḏy. | [gn]ʿy. | mʿqb. | agm. | ẖ 2058.1.26
ʿrby. | mʿr. | arny. | šʿrt. | ẖlbrpš. | hry. | qmṣ. | ṣʿq. | qmy. | ẖlbkrd. | yʿrt. | uškn. | ʿnqpat. | ilštmʿ. | šbn. | ṭbq. | rqd. | šrš. | gn 2074.17

ẖlbn

n] itn. | [bn] il. | [---]ṯ. | klṯṯb. | gsn. | arm[w]l. | bn.ṣdqn. | ẖlbn. | tbq.alp. 2039.16

ẖlbʿprm

rkby. | šḥq. | ǵn. | ṣʿ. | mld. | amḏy. | ẖlbʿprm. | ẖpty. | [ẖr]ṣbʿ. | [mʿ]rb. 2077.7
-----]. | [-----]. | [-----]. | [-----]. | [-----]. | [-----]. | [ẖl]bkrd. | [ẖl]bʿprm. | [q]dš. | [a]mḏy. | [gn]ʿy. | mʿqb. | agm. | ẖpty. | ypr. | 2058.1.27

ẖlbrpš

mlk. | ar. | atlg. | gbʿly. | ulm. | mʿrby. | mʿr. | arny. | šʿrt. | ẖlbrpš. | hry. | qmṣ. | ṣʿq. | qmy. | ẖlbkrd. | yʿrt. | uškn. | ʿnqpat. | 2074.12

ḫldy

.ʻbdm.|šbʻm.drt.arbʻm.drt.|l.a[--.---].|tgm[r.ak]l.b.gt.ḫldy.|ṯlṯ.ma[t].ʻšr.kbd.|šbʻ m[at].kbd.ḫpr.ʻbdm.|mit[.d]rt.a 2013.10

ḫly

---].|qmnz.ṯṯ.krm.yknʻm.ṯmn.krm[.---].|krm.nʻmn.b.ḫly.ull.krm.aḫ[d.---].|krm.uḫn.b.šdmy.ṯlṯ.bzl[.d]prn[.---].|a 1081.12

ḫll

w tšu.ʻn h.w tʻn.|w tʻn.arḫ.w tr.b lkt.|tr.b lkt.w tr.b ḫl.|[b]nʻmm.b ysmm.ḥ[--]k.ǵrt.|[ql].l bʻl.ʻnt.ttnn.|[---].bʻl 10[76].2.29

.drkt h].|l alp.ql.ẓ[--.---].|l np ql.nd.[----].|tlk.w tr.b[ḫl].|b nʻmm.b ys[mm.---].|arḫ.arḫ.[---.tld].|ibr.tld[.l bʻl].| 10[76].3.18

ṯrt.bnt.hll.snnt.|[-]d[-]t.nʻm y.ʻrš.h[--]m.|ysmsmt.ʻrš.ḫlln.[-].|yṯb.dnil.[l s]pr yrḫ h.|yrs.y[---.]y[--] h.|ṯlṯ.rb[ʻ.yrḫ. 17[2AQHT].2.42

ḫlln

n.slmz[-].|bn.kʻ[--].|bn.y[---].|[-----].|[bn.a]mdy.|bn.ḫlln.|bn.kṯn.|bn.abn.|bn.nskn.|bn.gmrn.|bn[.-]škn.|[---.-- 2021.2.3

lḥy.|bn.aryn.|bn.lgn.|bn.bʻyn.|šdyn.|ary.|brqn.|bn.ḫlln.|bn.mṣry.|ṯmn.qšt.|w ʻšr.uṯpt.|upšt irš[-]. 118[306].12

ḫlm

.|ṯpn.|mʻr.|lbnm.|nḫl.|yʻny.|atn.|utly.|bn.alz.|bn ḫlm.|bn.ḏmr.|bn.ʻyn.|ubnyn.|rpš d ydy.|ǵbl.|mlk.|gwl.|r 2075.16

ḫlmṭ

id ydbḥ mlk.|l ušḫ[r] ḫlmṭ.|l bbt il bt.|š l ḫlmṭ.|w tr l qlḥ.|w š ḥll ydm.|b qdš il bt.|w tlḥm aṯt.|š l il UG5.7.TR3

ṯt.|š l ilbt.šlmm.|kll ylḥm b h.|w l bbt šqym.|š l uḫr ḫlmṭ.|w tr l qlḥ.|ym aḥd. UG5.11.12

id ydbḥ mlk.|l ušḫ[r] ḫlmṭ.|l bbt il bt.|š l ḫlmṭ.|w tr l qlḥ.|w š ḥll ydm.|b qdš il UG5.7.TR3

ḫlp

.|bn ayy.|bn dbb.|w nḥl h.|bn nʻmyn.|bn aṯtyy.|bn ḫlp.|bn.ẓll.|bn ydy.|bn lzn.|bn.ṯyn.|bn gʻr.|bn.prtn.|bn ḫ 2016.1.11

ud[n].|[---.-]sr.pdm.riš h[m.---].|ʻl.pd.asr.[---.]l[.---].|mḫlpt.w l.ytk.[d]m[ʻt.]km.|rbʻt.ṯqlm.ṯtp[.---.]bm.|yd.ṣpn h 19[1AQHT].2.82

b.ym.ḥdṯ.|b.yrḫ.pgrm.|lqḥ.bʻlmʻḏr.|w bn.ḫlp.|w[--]y.d.bʻl.|miḥd.b.|arbʻ.mat.|ḫrṣ. 1155.4

b.ym.ḥdṯ.|b.yr.pgrm.|lqḥ.bʻlmḏr.|w.bn.ḫlp.|miḫd.|b.arbʻ.|mat.ḫrṣ. 1156.4

hn[m.---.]k pʻn.|[---.--]y.yd.nšy.[---.--]š.l mdb.|[---] h.mḫlpt[.---.--]r.|[---.]nʻlm.[---].|[---].hn.al[-.---].|[---]t.bn[.--- UG5.8.49

ḫlpn

.|bn.b[--].|bn.š[--].|bn.a[---].|bn.prsn.|bn.mtyn.|bn.ḫlpn.|bn.ḥgbn.|bn.szn.|bn.mglb. 117[325].2.7

aḥd.kbd.|arbʻm.b ḫzr.|lqḥ šʻrt.|ṯṯ ʻšr h.lqḥ.|ḫlpnt.|ṯṯ.ḥrṭm.|lqḥ.šʻrt.|ʻšr.ḥrš.|bhtm.lqḥ.|šʻrt.|arbʻ.|ḥrš 2052.5

ṯn.kst.|spl.mšlt.w.mqḥm.|w md h.|arn.w mznm.|ṯn.ḫlpnm.|ṯṯ.mrḥm.|drb.|mrbd.|mškbt. 2050.6

b yrḫ.mgm[r.---].|yṣu.ḫlpn[.---].|ṯlṯ.dt.p[--.---].|dt.ṯgmi.[---].|b d [---]t.[---]. 1159.2

ḫlq

mš.ʻšr.yn.ṭb.|w.tšʻm.kdm.kbd.yn.d.l.ṭb.|w.arbʻm.yn.ḫlq.b.gt.sknm.|ʻšr.yn.ṭb.w.arbʻm.ḫmš.kbd.|yn.d.l.ṭb.gt.ṭbq. 1084.3

--]n ḫlq.|bn mʻnt.|bn kbdy.|bn krk.|bn srty.|bn ltḥ ḫlq.|bn ytr.|bn ilšpš.|ubrš.|bn gmš ḫlq.|bn ʻgy.|bn zlbn.| 2016.2.14

n.|b[n.-]n.|bn.ṣṣb.|bn.bʻltn ḫlq.|bn.mlkbn.|bn.asyy ḫlq.|bn.kṯly.|bn.kyn.|bn.ʻbdḥr.|[-]prm ḫlq.|[---]n ḫlq.|bn 2016.2.4

.|bn gʻr.|bn.prtn.|bn ḫnn.|b[n.-]n.|bn.ṣṣb.|bn.bʻltn ḫlq.|bn.mlkbn.|bn.asyy ḫlq.|bn.kṯly.|bn.kyn.|bn.ʻbdḥr.|[- 2016.2.2

y ḫlq.|bn.kṯly.|bn.kyn.|bn.ʻbdḥr.|[-]prm ḫlq.|[---]n ḫlq.|bn mʻnt.|bn kbdy.|bn krk.|bn srty.|bn ltḥ ḫlq.|bn yt 2016.2.9

|bn srty.|bn ltḥ ḫlq.|bn ytr.|bn ilšpš.|ubrš.|bn gmš ḫlq.|bn ʻgy.|bn zlbn.|bn.aḫ[--].|bn[.---].|[-----].|bn kr[k].| 2016.2.18

hw.|qr[-].|akl n.b.grnt.|l.bʻr.|ap.krmm.|ḫlq.|qrt n.ḫlq.|w.dʻ.dʻ. 2114.12

l ysmt.šd.šḥlmmt.|mǵny.l bʻl.npl.l a|rṣ.mt.aliyn.bʻl.|ḫlq.zbl.bʻl.arṣ.|apnk.lṭpn.il.|d pid.yrd.l ksi.yṯb.|l hdm[.w] 5[67].6.10

mḫ ht.|aṯrt.w bn h.ilt.w ṣb|rt.ary h.k mt.aliyn.|bʻl.k ḫlq.zbl.bʻl.|arṣ.gm.yṣḥ il.|l rbt.aṯrt ym.šmʻ.|l rbt.aṯr[t] ym. 6.1.42[49.1.14]

[k mt.aliyn.bʻl].|k ḫlq.z[bl.bʻl.arṣ].|w hm.ḥy.a[liyn.bʻl].|w hm.iṯ.zbl.bʻ[l.arṣ].| 6[49].3.1

---].|abn.ank.w ʻl.[qšt k.---.ʻl].|qṣʻt k.at.l ḥ[---.---].|w ḫlq.ʻpmm[.---]. 18[3AQHT].4.42

.|ḥrd.w.šl hw.|qr[-].|akl n.b.grnt.|l.bʻr.|ap.krmm.|ḫlq.|qrt n.ḫlq.|w.dʻ.dʻ. 2114.11

bn.|bn.asyy ḫlq.|bn.kṯly.|bn.kyn.|bn.ʻbdḥr.|[-]prm ḫlq.|[---]n ḫlq.|bn mʻnt.|bn kbdy.|bn krk.|bn srty.|bn ltḥ 2016.2.8

ḫmat

.šd aṯrt.w rḥm.|ʻl.išt.šbʻ d.ǵzrm.ṭb.[g]d.b ḥlb.annḫ b ḫmat.|w ʻl.agn.šbʻ d m.dǵ[ṯ.---]t.|tlk m.rḥmy.w tṣd[.---].|t 23[52].14

ḫmn

ḥnil.[---].|aršmg.mru.|bʻl.šlm.ʻbd.|awr.ṯǵrn.ʻbd.|ʻbd.ḫmn.šmʻ.rgm.|šdn.[k]bš.|šdyn.mḫ[ṣ].|aṯry.mḫṣ.|bʻln.mḫṣ. 2084.12

mḏrǵlm.d.b.i[-]ʻlt.mlk.|arsw.|dqn.|ṯlṯ.klbm.|ḫmn.|[---.-]rsd.|bn[.-]pṯ.|bn kdrn.|awldn.|arswn.yʻr[ty.--]. 86[305].5

ḫmr

.---.---]r.|l riš hm.w yš[--.--]m.|lḥm.b lḥm ay.w šty.b ḫmr yn ay.|šlm.mlk.šlm.mlkt.ʻrbm m.ṯnnm.|mt.w šr.yṯb.b 23[52].6

m.ks.qdš.|l tphn h.aṯt.krpn.|l tʻn.aṯrt.alp.|kd.yqḥ.b ḫmr.|rbt.ymsk.b msk h.|qm.ybd.w yšr.|mṣltm.bd.nʻm.|yš 3[ʻNT].1.16

.šl[-.---].|[---.]ʻšrm.krm.[---].|[ṯ]lrby.ʻšr.ṯn.kb[d.---].|ḫmrm.ṯṯ.krm[m.---].|krm.ǵlkz.b.p[--.---].|krm.ilyy.b.m[--.- 1081.22

ḫmrn

r ṯ[--].|ʻnqpat [---].|m[--.---].|[-----].|k[--.---].|[-----].|ḫmrn.ʻš[r.---].|gll.tky.ṯlṯ[.---]. 2042.22

l.ḫmšt.|bn.aḫdy.‘šrt.|ṯṯn.‘ṣrt.|bn.pnmn.‘šrt.|‘bdadt.ḫmšt.|abmn.ilštm‘y.ḫmš[t].|‘zn.bn.brn.ḫmšt.|m‘rt.ḫmšt.|a 1062.24
mšt.|bn.[-]r[-.]ḫmšt.|bn.ḥdṯ.‘šrt.|bn.ḫnyn.‘šrt.|rpan.ḫmšt.|abġl.ḫmšt.|bn.aḫdy.‘šrt.|ṯṯn.‘ṣrt.|bn.pnmn.‘šrt.|‘bd 1062.19
-].|ab[--.---].|bn.nṣdn[.ḫm]št.|bn.arsw ‘[šr]m.|‘šdyn.ḫmš[t].|abršn.‘šr[t].|b‘ln.ḫmšt.|w.nḥl h.ḫm[š]t.|bn.unp.ar 1062.6
spr.irgmn.|ṯlṯ.ḫmš.alpm.|b d.brq.maḫdy.|kkr.ṯlṯ.|b d.bn.by.ar[y].|alpm.ṯ 1134.2
irtym.|b d.urtn.w.ṯṯ.mat.brr.|b.ṯmnym.ksp.ṯlṯt.kbd.|ḫmš.alp.ṯlṯ.l.ḫlby.|b d.tlmi.b.‘šrm.ḫmšt.|kbd.ksp.|kkrm.š‘r 2101.6
|[---.-]rt.l.dml[.---].|[b.yrḫ].nql.ṯn.ḫpn[.---].|[---].aḥd.ḫmš.am[--.---].|[---.--]m.qmṣ.ṯlṯm.i[qnu.---].|[b.yr]ḫ.mgmr. 1106.36
tb‘t.|ṯar um.tkn l h.|mṯlṯt.kṯrm.tmt.|mrb‘t.zblnm.|mḫmšt.yitsp.|ršp.nṯdṯt.ġlm.|ym.mšb‘t hn.b šlḥ.|ṯṯpl.y‘n.ḥt 14[KRT].1.18
t.ḫmšt.|abmn.ilštm‘y.ḫmš[t].|‘zn.bn.brn.ḫmšt.|m‘rt.ḫmšt.|arṯṯb.bn.ḫmšt.|bn.ysr[.ḫmš]t.|ṣ[-]r.ḫ[mšt].|‘zn.ḫ[mš 1062.27
š.|uškn.arb‘.|ubr‘y.ṯlṯ.|ar.ṯmn ‘šr h.|mlk.arb‘.|ġbl.ḫmš.|atlg.ḫmš ‘šr[h].|ulm ṯ[ṯ].|m‘rby.ḫmš.|ṭbq.arb‘.|tkm 68[65].1.7
‘t.p[--].|tš‘t.k[bd.---].|ḫmšt.k[bd.---].|tgmr k[--.---].|ḫmšm a[--.---].|kbd [---].|d[.a]ġlkz[.---]. 2120.10
ṯlṯm.ktn.|ḫmšm.izml.|ḫmš.kbd.arb‘m.|dd.akl.|ṯṯ.‘šr h.yn.|kd.šmn.l. 1126.2
l.‘šrm.|y‘ḏrd.‘šrm.|gmrd.‘šrm.|ṣdqšlm.‘šr[m].|yknil.ḫmš.|ilmlk.ḫmš.|prṯ.‘šr.|ubn.‘šr. 1116.12
.mlk.|[---.]š‘rt.šb‘.‘šr h.|[---.iqn]i.l.ṯrmn.qrt.|[---.]lbš.ḫmšm.iqnu.|[---].šmt.ḫmšt.ḫndlt.|[---.iqn]i.l.[-]k.btbt.|[---.l 1106.16
šr.ṣin.|mlkn‘m.‘šr.|bn.adty.‘šr.|[ṣ]dqšlm ḫmš.|krzn.ḫmš.|ubr‘ym.ḫmš.|[----].|[bn] itn.|[bn] il.|[---]ṯ.|klṯṯb.|gs 2039.6
[--.]wmrkm.|bir.ḫmš.|uškn.arb‘.|ubr‘y.ṯlṯ.|ar.ṯmn ‘šr h.|mlk.arb‘.|ġbl.ḫmš 68[65].1.2
šrt.|b.[---].šb‘t.‘šrt.|b.bn.pdrn.‘šrm.|d.bn.šb‘l.uḫnpy.ḫmšm.|b.bn.ṯtm.ṯlṯm.|b.bn.agdṯb.‘šrm.|b.bn.ibn.arb‘t.‘šrt. 2054.1.10
b.bṣmn[.bn].ḥrtn.‘[--].|b.ṯ[--.---] h.[---].|[-----].|[--]ly.ḫmšm.b.‘bdyr[ḫ].|[---].‘šrm.|[-----].|[---.‘]šr[.---].|[---.-]‘rm. 2054.1.24
|ḫmšt.‘šrt.|b.šd.bn.[-]n.|ṯl[ṯt].‘šr[t].|b.š[d].bn.‘myn.|ḫmšt.|b.[šd.--]n.|ḫ[m]št[.‘]šrt.|[ar]b‘m.ksp.|[---]yn.|[---.]k 1083.12
[-.]ḫmšt.|bn.ḥdṯ.‘šrt.|bn.ḫnyn.‘šrt.|rpan.ḫmšt.|abġl.ḫmšt.|bn.aḫdy.‘šrt.|ṯṯn.‘ṣrt.|bn.pnmn.‘šrt.|‘bdadt.ḫmšt.|a 1062.20
[-----].|ḏ[----].|ab[--.---].|bn.nṣdn[.ḫm]št.|bn.arsw ‘[šr]m.|‘šdyn.ḫmš[t].|abršn.‘šr[t].|b‘ln.ḫm 1062.4
šr]m.|‘šdyn.ḫmš[t].|abršn.‘šr[t].|b‘ln.ḫmšt.|w.nḥl h.ḫm[š]t.|bn.unp.arb‘t.|‘bdbn.ytrš ḫmšt.|krwn.‘šrt.|bn.ulb ḫ 1062.9
w ḥl[.ml]k.|bn.aup[š.--].bsbn hzpḫ ṯlṯt.|kṯr[.---.--]trt ḫmšt.bn gda[.-.]mḏ‘.|kl[--.---.]ṯmnt.[--.]w[.---].|[-]m[.---.]ṣp APP.II[173].59
šrt.|bn.ulb ḫmšt.|bn.ḫry.ḫmšt.|swn.ḫmšt.|bn.[-]r[-.]ḫmšt.|bn.ḥdṯ.‘šrt.|bn.ḫnyn.‘šrt.|rpan.ḫmšt.|abġl.ḫmšt.|bn 1062.16
]t.|bn.unp.arb‘t.|‘bdbn.ytrš ḫmšt.|krwn.‘šrt.|bn.ulb ḫmšt.|bn.ḫry.ḫmšt.|swn.ḫmšt.|bn.[-]r[-.]ḫmšt.|bn.ḥdṯ.‘šrt. 1062.13
lštm‘y.ḫmš[t].|‘zn.bn.brn.ḫmšt.|m‘rt.ḫmšt.|arṯṯb.bn.ḫmšt.|bn.ysr[.ḫmš]t.|ṣ[-]r.ḫ[mšt].|‘zn.ḫ[mšt]. 1062.28
šb‘.ḫsnm.|ṯmn.‘šr h.mrynm.|‘šr.mkrm.|ḫmš.ṯrtnm.|ḫmš.bn.mrynm.|‘šr.mrum.w.šb‘.ḫsnm.|tš‘m.mḏrġlm.|arb‘. 1030.5
rš ḫmšt.|krwn.‘šrt.|bn.ulb ḫmšt.|bn.ḫry.ḫmšt.|swn.ḫmšt.|bn.[-]r[-.]ḫmšt.|bn.ḥdṯ.‘šrt.|bn.ḫnyn.‘šrt.|rpan.ḫmšt 1062.15
d.|mlk.arb‘.ḥm[rm.w.arb]‘.bnšm.|ar.ḫmš.ḥmr[m.w.ḫm]š.bnšm.|atlg.ḥmr[.---.]bnšm.|gb‘ly.ḥmr š[--.b]nšm.|ul 2040.4
ṯan.|ġr.tš‘[.‘šr.b]nš.|ṣbu.any[t].|bn abdḫ[r].|pdym.|ḫmš.bnšm.|snrym.|tš‘.bnš[m].|gb‘lym.|arb‘.b[nšm].|ṭbqy 79[83].13
br‘y.ar[b‘.]ḥm[r]m.w[.---.]bnšm.|ilštm‘.arb‘.ḥm[r]m.ḫmš.bnšm.|ġr.|ary.ḥmr w.bnš.|qmy.ḥmr.w.bnš.|ṭbil.|‘nm 2040.21
bt.alpm.|‘šr.bnšm.|ḫmš.bnši.ṯt[---].|‘šr.b gt.[---].|ṯn.‘šr.b.gt.ir[bṣ].|arb‘.b.gt.b‘l 2103.3
ḫmš.bnšm[.---].|ḥḏġlm.b d.[---].|šb‘.lmdm.b d.s[n]rn.|lmd. 1050.1
spr.ḫpr.bt.k[--].|tš‘.‘šr h.dd.l.b[t.--].|ḫmš.ddm.l.ḥtyt.|ṯlṯm.dd.kšmn.l.gzzm.|yyn.|ṣdqn.|‘bd.pdr 1099.3
ḫmšm.dd.|n‘r.|ḫmšm.tišr.|ḫmš.ktnt.|ḫmš.ṯnt.alpm.|‘šrm. 2102.1
.b.yrḫ.ittbnm.|šb‘m.dd.ṯn.kbd.|tgmr.ḥṭm.šb‘.ddm.|ḫmš.dd.š‘rm.|kdm.yn.|kdm.ṣmṣ. 1099.33
lšn.agyn.|mnn.šr.ugrt.ḏkr.yṣr.|tġġln.ḫmš.ddm.|[---].ḫmš.ddm.|ṯṯ.l.‘šrm.bn[š.mlk.---].ḫzr.lqḥ.ḥp[r].|‘šṯ.‘šr h.bn[2011.39
b‘ltġptm.krwn.ilšn.agyn.|mnn.šr.ugrt.ḏkr.yṣr.|tġġln.ḫmš.ddm.|[---].ḫmš.ddm.|ṯṯ.l.‘šrm.bn[š.mlk.---].ḫzr.lqḥ.ḥp 2011.38
.|[w].ṯmnym.l.mit.dd.ḥpr.bnšm.|b.gt.alḫb.ṯṯm.dr‘.w.ḫmšm.drt.w.ṯṯm.dd.|ḥpr.bnšm.|b.gt.knpy.mit.dr‘.ṯṯm.drt. 1098.16
š.mat.kbd.|ṯlṯm.ḫmš kbd ktn.|ḫmš.rṭm.|ḫmš.ṯnt.d ḫmšm w.|ḫmš.ṯnt.d mit.|ḫmš.ṯnt.d ṯl|ṯ mat.|ṯṯ.ṯnt.d alp|a 1130.9
]št.|bn.arsw ‘[šr]m.|‘šdyn.ḫmš[t].|abršn.‘šr[t].|b‘ln.ḫmšt.|w.nḥl h.ḫm[š]t.|bn.unp.arb‘t.|‘bdbn.ytrš ḫmšt.|krw 1062.8
m.b h.w.ṯqlm.|ksp h.mitm.pḥm.b d.skn.|w.ṯṯ.ktnm.ḫmšt.w.nṣp.ksp.hn. 1110.6
[---.]ḫ[---.]ṯmnym[.k]sp ḫmšt.|[w a]rb‘ kkr ‘l bn[.--].|[w] ṯlṯ šmn.|[w a]r[b‘] ksp ‘l b 1103.1
ap.|pd.|mlk.arb‘.ḥm[rm.w.arb]‘.bnšm.|ar.ḫmš.ḥmr[m.w.ḫm]š.bnšm.|atlg.ḥmr[.---.]bnšm.|gb‘ly.ḥmr 2040.4
šmn.ltḥ.šḥlt.|[---.ltḥ.]ṣmqm.[t]ṯ.mat.nṣ.ṯlṯm.‘ṣr.|[---].ḫmš[m.ḥm]r.škm.|[---.ṯṯ.dd.]gdl.ṯṯ.dd.š‘rm.|[---.hn.w.al]p. 142[12].6
ḥ.sbbyn.|[---.-]‘t.ltḥ.ššmn.|[---].ḫšwn.ṯṯ.mat.nṣ.|[---].ḫmšm.ḥmr.škm.|[---.ṯṯ.dd.]gdl.ṯṯ.dd.š‘rm.|[---.a]lp.arb‘.ma 142[12].12
.sb[by]n.ltḥ.šḥ[lt].|[---.l]tḥ.dblt.ltḥ.ṣmqm.|[---.--]m.[ḫ]mšm.ḥmr.škm. 142[12].18
lk.|kd.bn.amht [-]t.|w.bn.mṣrym.|arb‘m.yn.|l.ḫrd.|ḫmšm.ḫmš.|kbd.tgmr.|yn.d.nkly. 1089.13
‘.dd.ḥ[ṭm.w].ḫm[šm].|kdm.kbd.yn.b.gt.[---].|[mi]tm.ḫmšm.ḫmš.k[bd].|[dd].kšmm.tš‘[.---].|[š]‘rm.ṯṯ.‘[šr].|[dd]. 2092.6
ṣṣ mr‘m ḫmšm ḫmš kbd.|ṣṣ ubn ḫmš ‘šr h.|ṣṣ ‘myd ḫmšm.|ṣṣ tmn. 2097.1
.|[---.iqn]i.l.ṯrmn.qrt.|[---.]lbš.ḫmšm.iqnu.|[---].šmt.ḫmšt.ḫndlt.|[---.iqn]i.l.[-]k.btbt.|[---.l.ṯrm]nm.š[b‘].mat.š‘rt 1106.17
[.---].|ṯr ab h il.ttrm[.---].|tšlḥm yrḫ.ggn[.---].|k[.---.ḫ]mš.ḫssm[.---].|[---.--]m ‘ttr[t.---].|[---.]n[--.---]. 2001.1.17
kdwṯm.[---].|ḫmš.pld š‘rt.|ṯṯ pld pṯt.|arb‘ ḥpnt pṯt.|ḫmš ḥpnt.š‘rt.|ṯlṯ.‘šr kdwṯm. 1113.10
k.aḥt.|b.sġy.ḫmš.ḫrmṯt.nit.|krk.m‘ṣd.mqb.|b.gt.‘mq.ḫmš.ḫrmṯt.n[it].|krk.m‘ṣd.mqb.|b.gwl.ṯmn.ḫrmṯt.[nit].|kr 2048.9
h.ḫrmṯt.|ṯṯ.nitm.ṯn.m‘ṣdm.ṯn.mqbm.|krk.aḥt.|b.sġy.ḫmš.ḫrmṯt.nit.|krk.m‘ṣd.mqb.|b.gt.‘mq.ḫmš.ḫrmṯt.n[it].|k 2048.7
.ksp.|b d[.‘b]dym.ṯlṯ.kkr š‘rt.|iqn[i]m.ṯṯṯ.‘šrt.ksp h.|ḫmšt.ḥrṣ.bt.il.|b.ḫmšt.‘šrt.ksp.|ḫmš.mat.šmt.|b.‘šrt.ksp.|‘š 2100.5
mlk.arb‘.|ġbl.ḫmš.|atlg.ḫmš ‘šr[h].|ulm ṯ[ṯ].|m‘rby.ḫmš.|ṭbq.arb‘.|tkm[.---].|uḫnp[.---].|ušk[n.---].|ubr[‘y.---]. 68[65].1.10
dmt ṯlṯ.|qmnz ṯql.|zlyy ṯql.|ary ḫmšt.|ykn‘m ḫmšt.|‘nmky ṯqlm.|[-]kt ‘šrt.|qrn šb‘t. 1176.4
.|art.ṯn.yrḫm.|ṯlrby.yrḫ.w.ḫm[š.ym]m.|ṯlḥny.yrḫ.w.ḫm[š.ymm].|ẓrn.yrḫ.w.ḫmš.y[m]m.|mrat.ḫmš.‘šr.ymm.|q 66[109].5
.w.ḫm[š.ym]m.|ṯlḥny.yrḫ.w.ḫm[š.ymm].|ẓrn.yrḫ.w.ḫmš.y[m]m.|mrat.ḫmš.‘šr.ymm.|qmnz.yrḫ.w.ḫmš.ymm.|‘ 66[109].6
yrḫ.w.ḫmš.y[m]m.|mrat.ḫmš.‘šr.ymm.|qmnz.yrḫ.w.ḫmš.ymm.|‘nmk.yrḫ.|ypr.yrḫ.w.ḫmš.ymm. 66[109].8
qrht.d.tššlmn.|ṯlrb h.|art.ṯn.yrḫm.|ṯlrby.yrḫ.w.ḫm[š.ym]m.|ṯlḥny.yrḫ.w.ḫm[š.ymm].|ẓrn.yrḫ.w.ḫmš.y[m] 66[109].4

ymm. | qmnz.yrḫ.w.ḫmš.ymm. | ʿnmk.yrḫ. | ypr.yrḫ.w.ḫmš.ymm. 66[109].10

mrynm. | šbʿ yn. | l mrynm. | b yṯbmlk. | kdm.ǵbiš ḫry. | ḫmš yn.b d. | bḫ mlkt. | b mdrʿ. | ṯlṯ bt.il | ann. | kd.bt.ilann. 1090.14

n.trqm. | w.qpt.w.mqḥm. | w.ṯlṯm.yn šbʿ.kbd d ṭbṭ. | w.ḫmšm.yn.d iḫ h. 1103.23

.yn. | ʿbdiltp.ṯm[n].y[n]. | qṣn.ḫ[---]. | arny.[---]. | aǵltn.ḫmš[.yn]. 1085.12

rt.šlm. | yky.ʿšrt.ṯṯt šlm.ʿšrt. | bn.ḥgby.ṯmnt.l ʿšrm.ʿšrt.ḫmš.kbd. | bn.ilṣdq.šbʿt ṯlṯt šlm. | bn.ṯmq.arbʿt ṯqlm šlmm. 1131.8

.bn.amht [-]t. | w.bn.mṣrym. | arbʿm.yn. | l.ḫrd. | ḫmšm.ḫmš. | kbd.tgmr. | yn.d.nkly. 1089.13

.kbd. | l.bn.yšmʿ. | mit.arbʿm.kbd. | l.liy.bn.ʿmyn. | mit.ḫmšm.kbd. | d.škn.l.ks.ilm. 1143.13

ṭm.w].ḫm[šm]. | kdm.kbd.yn.b.gt.[---]. | [mi]tm.ḫmšm.ḫmš.k[bd]. | [dd].kšmm.tšʿ[.---]. | [š]ʿrm.ṯṯ.ʿ[šr]. | [dd].ḥṭm.w. 2092.6

spr.npṣm.d yṣa.b milḫ. | ʿšrm.ḫpn.ḫmš. | kbd.w lpš. | ḫmš.mispt. | mṭ. | w lpš.d sgr b h. | b d.anr 1109.2

. | ʿšr.d[d.---]. | ṯṯm.dd.dd[.---]. | l.mdrǵlm[.---]. | ṯlṯ.mat.ḫmšm.kb[d]. | ḫmš.kbd.l.mdʿ. | b yr[ḫ.iṯtb]nm. | ṯlṯ[.mat.a]rbʿ 2012.11

yn].d.l[.ṭb].b.gt.ipṯl. | ṯmnym.[yn].ṭb.b.gt.š[---]. | tšʿm.[ḫ]mš[.kbd].yn.b gt[.-]n. | arbʿm.kbd.yn.ṭb.w.[--]. | ṯmn.kbd.y 1084.21

.l.ṭb.b.gt.ḥdṯt. | tšʿm.yn.d.l.ṭb.b.zbl. | ʿšrm.yn.ṭb.w.ṯṯm.ḫmš.k[b]d. | yn.d.l.ṭb.b.gt.sǵy. | arbʿm.kdm.kbd.yn.ṭb. | w.ḫm 1084.14

.d.l.ṭb. | w.arbʿm.yn.ḫlq.b.gt.sknm. | ʿšr.yn.ṭb.w.arbʿm.ḫmš.kbd. | yn.d.l.ṭb.gt.ṭbq. | mit.ʿšr.kbd.yn.ṭb. | w.ṯṯm.arbʿ.kb 1084.4

nym.ksp.ṯlṯt.kbd. | ḫmš.alp.ṯlṯ.l.ḫlby. | b d.tlmi.b.ʿšrm.ḫmšt. | kbd.ksp. | kkrm.šʿrt.štt.b d.gg[ʿt]. | b.ʿšrt.ksp. | ṯlṯ.uṭb 2101.7

udmym.b.ṯmnt.ʿšrt.ksp. | šbʿm.lbš.d.ʿrb.bt.mlk. | b.mit.ḫmšt.kbd.ksp. | ṯlṯ.ktnt.b d.an[r]my. | b.ʿšrt.ksp.b.a[--]. | ṯqlm 2101.17

. | ḫmš.mat.kbd. | arbʿ.alpm.iqni. | ḫmš.mat.kbd. | ṯlṯm.ḫmš kbd ktn. | ḫmš.rṭm. | ḫmš.ṯnt.d ḫmšm w. | ḫmš.ṯnt.d mit 1130.7

ksp.ʿmn. | bn.ulbtyn. | w.kkr.ṯlṯ. | ksp.d.nkly.b.šd. | mit.ḫmšt.kbd. | [l.]gmn.bn.usyy. | mit.ṯṯm.kbd. | l.bn.yšmʿ. | mit.a 1143.7

ṯṯm.dd.dd[.---]. | l.mdrǵlm[.---]. | ṯlṯ.mat.ḫmšm.kb[d]. | ḫmš.kbd.l.mdʿ. | b yr[ḫ.iṯtb]nm. | ṯlṯ[.mat.a]rbʿ.kbd. | w.[---.-] 2012.12

spr.ḫrd.arr. | ap arbʿm[.--]. | pd[.---.ḫm]šm.kb[d]. | ǵb[-.---.]kbd. | m[--.---.k]bd. | a[--.---.]kbd. | m[2042.3

ṣṣ mrʿm ḫmšm ḫmš kbd. | ṣṣ ubn ḫmš ʿšr h. | ṣṣ ʿmyd ḫmšm. | ṣṣ tmn.ḫmšm. 2097.1

ṯlṯm.ktn. | ḫmšm.izml. | ḫmš.kbd.arbʿm. | dd.akl. | ṯṯ.ʿšr h.yn. | kd.šmn.l.nr.ilm. | kdm. 1126.3

ṯlṯm šurt l b[nš.---]. | arbʿ šurt [---]. | ṯṯ šurt l bnš [---]. | ḫmš kbd arbʿ[.---]. | ṯṯ šurt l tg[-.---]. | arbʿ šurt [---]. | [ḫm]šm 137.1[92].12

h. | ṯmn.dd[.--]. | ṯlṯ.dd.p[--]. | šbʿt.p[--]. | tšʿt.k[bd.---]. | ḫmšt.k[bd.---]. | tgmr k[--.---]. | ḫmšm a[--.---]. | kbd [---]. | d[. 2120.8

[--]t.ilhnm.b šnt. | [---.]šbʿ.mat.šʿrt.ḫmšm.kbd. | [---.-]nd.l.mlbš.ṯrmnm. | [---]h.lbš.allm.lbnm. | [- 1106.2

qlm. | w.šbʿ.ʿšr.šmn. | d.l.yṣa.bt.mlk. | tgmr.ksp.mitm. | ḫmšm.kbd. 2100.23

npṣm. | b d.mri. | skn. | ʿšrm. | ḫmš. | kbd. 157[116].5

kdm. | w b ṯlṯ.kd yn w krsnm. | w b rbʿ kdm yn. | w b ḫmš kd yn. 1086.5

---]. | b.gt.ṣb[-.---]. | mit.ʿšr.[---.]dd[.--]. | tšʿ.dd.ḥ[ṭm.w].ḫm[šm]. | kdm.kbd.yn.b.gt.[---]. | [mi]tm.ḫmšm.ḫmš.k[bd]. | [2092.4

š.k[b]d. | yn.d.l.ṭb.b.gt.sǵy. | arbʿm.kdm.kbd.yn.ṭb. | w.ḫmšm.k[dm.]kbd.yn.d.l.ṭb. | b.gt.gwl. | ṯlṯm.tšʿ[.kbd.yn].d.l[. 1084.17

spr.ḥtbn.sbrdnm. | ḫmš.kkrm.alp kb[d]. | ṯlṯ.l.nskm.birtym. | b d.urtn.w.ṯṯ.mat. 2101.2

mit.šmn.d.nm[-.]b d.mzy.alzy. | ḫmš.kkr.ḥlb. | ḫmš.kkr.brr. | kkr.ḫmš.mat.kbd.ṯlṯ.šm[n]. | alp.mitm.kbd.ṯlṯ. 1135.3

mit.šmn.d.nm[-.]b d.mzy.alzy. | ḫmš.kkr.ḥlb. | ḫmš.kkr.brr. | kkr.ḫmš.mat.kbd.ṯlṯ.šm[n]. | alp 1135.2

.ṯṯt.w.kmsk. | arbʿ[.k]dwṯm.w.ṯt.ṯprtm. | b.ʿšr[m.]ksp. | ḫmš.kkr.ṣml. | b.ʿšrt.b d.bn.kyn. | ʿšr.kkr.šʿrt. | b d.urtn.b.arbʿ 2100.12

m. | ṯlṯ.mat.trm.b.ʿšrt. | mit.adrm.b.ʿšrt. | ʿšr.ydt.b.ʿšrt. | ḫmš.kkrm.ṣml. | ʿšrt.ksp h. | ḫmš.kkr.qnm. | ṯlṯt.w.ṯlṯt.ksp h. 1127.10

.mat. | šm[n].rqḥ. | kkrm.brdl. | mit.tišrm. | ṯlṯm.almg. | ḫmšm.kkr. | qnm. | ʿšrm.kk[r]. | brr. | [ʿ]šrm.npš. | ʿšrm.zt.mm. 141[120].9

drm.b.ʿšrt. | ʿšr.ydt.b.ʿšrt. | ḫmš.kkrm.ṣml. | ʿšrt.ksp h. | ḫmš.kkr.qnm. | ṯlṯt.w.ṯlṯt.ksp h. | arbʿ.kkr. | algbṯ.arbʿt. | ksp 1127.12

l | ṯ mat. | ṯt.ṯnt.d alp | alpm.ṯlṯ ktt. | alp.brr. | kkr.tznt. | ḫmšt.kkr tyt. 1130.17

at.arbʿm. | kbd.ksp.anyt. | d.ʿrb.b.anyt. | l.mlk.gbl. | w.ḫmšm.ksp. | lqḥ.mlk.gbl. | lbš.anyt h. | bʿrm.ksp. | mḫr.hn. 2106.14

. | [-----]. | [-]šy[.---] h. | [-]kt[.---.]nrn. | [b]n.nmq[.---]. | [ḫm]št.ksp.ʿl.aṯt. | [-]ṯd[.bn.]štn. 2055.19

[-----]. | [---.]ʿl.ṯny[.---] | [---.]pḫyr.bt h.[---]. | [ḫm]šm.ksp.ʿl.gd[--]. | [---].ypḫ.ʿbdršp.b[--.--]. | [ar]bʿt.ʿšrt.kb 1144.4

anntb.ḫmšm.ksp ṯlṯm.šl[m.---]. | iwrpzn.ʿšrm ʿšrm š[lm.---]. | ilabn.ʿ 1131.1

bʿln.ḫmšt. | w.nḥl h.ḫm[š]t. | bn.unp.arbʿt. | ʿbdbn.ytrš ḫmšt. | krwn.ʿšrt. | bn.ulb ḫmšt. | bn.ḫry.ḫmšt. | swn.ḫmšt. | b 1062.11

ṯlṯ. | ilmlk.ʿšr.ṣin. | mlknʿm.ʿšr. | bn.adty.ʿšr. | [ṣ]dqšlm ḫmš. | krzn.ḫmš. | ubrʿym.ḫmš. | [----]. | [bn] itn. | [bn] il. | [---]t 2039.5

ḫmšm.dd. | nʿr. | ḫmšm.tišr. | ḫmš.ktnt. | ḫmš.ṯnt.alpm. | ʿšrm.hbn. | ṯlṯ.mat.dd. | šʿrm. | mit. 2102.4

spr[.---]. | ḫmš.k[--.---]. | ḫmš[.---]. | ʿš[r.---]. | [-----]. | [-----]. | [-----]. | [----- 1128.2

tḥm.ydn.ʿm.mlk. | bʿl h.ngr.ḥwt k. | w l.a[--]t.tšknn. | ḫmšm.l mi[t].any. | tškn[n.--]h.k[--]. | w šnm[.--.]w[.--]. | w ʿp 2062.1.4

šʿ.ḫbṯnm. | ṯmnym.ṯlṯ.kbd. | mdrǵlm. | w.šbʿ.ʿšr.ḫsnm. | ḫmšm.l.mit. | bnš.l.d. | yškb.l.b.bt.mlk. 1029.14

b.gt.mlkt.b.rḫbn. | ḫmšm.l.mitm.zt. | w.b d.krd. | ḫmšm.l.mit. | arbʿ.kbd. 1096.2

n]. | mit.ksp.d.ṯbq. | ṯmnym.arbʿt. | kbd.ksp. | d.nqdm. | ḫmšm.l mit. | ksp.d.mkr.ar. | arbʿm ksp d mkr. | atlg. | mit.ks 2107.9

b.gt.mlkt.b.rḫbn. | ḫmšm.l.mitm.zt. | w.b d.krd. | ḫmšm.l.mit. | arbʿ.kbd. 1096.4

.ṯṯm. | b.rpan.bn.yyn.ʿšrt. | b.ypʿr.ʿšrm. | b.nʿmn.bn.ply.ḫmšt.l.ʿšrm. | b.gdn.bn.uss.ʿšrm. | b.ʿdn.bn.ṯṯ.ʿšrt. | b.bn.qrdm 2054.1.17

ʿt.ʿšrt. | [---.-]kyn.ʿšrt. | b.bn.ʿsl.ʿšrm.ṯqlm kbd. | b.ṯmq.ḫmšt.l.ʿšrt. | b.[---].šbʿt.ʿšrt. | b.bn.pdrn.ʿšrm. | d.bn.šbʿl.uḫnp 2054.1.7

b. | w.ṯṯm.arbʿ.kbd.yn.d.l.ṭb. | b.gt.mʿrby. | ṯṯm.yn.ṭb.w.ḫmš.l.ʿšrm. | yn.d.l.ṭb.b.ulm. | mit.yn.ṭb.w.ṯṯm.ṯṯ.kbd. | yn.d.l. 1084.9

lṯ šmn. | [w a]r[bʿ] ksp ʿl bn ymn. | šb šr šmn [--] tryn. | ḫm[š]m l ʿšr ksp ʿl bn llit. | [--]l[-.-]p ʿl [---.-]bʿm arny. | w ʿl [1103.6

[---.ʿ]šrt. | ḫlb.ḫmšt.l.ʿšrm. | mril.ʿšrt. | glbty.arbʿt. | [--]tb.ʿšrt. 1180.2

[ḫm]š l ʿšrm. | [-]dmm. | b.ubn. 1167.1

šrm. | [-]gp[.---.]ʿrny.ṯṯm. | [---.]dyn.ḫmšt.ʿšrt. | [---.-]til.ḫmšt.l ʿšrm. | [--.-]n.w.aḫt h.arbʿm. | [--.-]dn.ʿšrm. | [--.-]dwn. 2054.2.20

qtm. | bm.nšq.w hr.[b]ḥbq.w ḥ[m]ḥmt.ytb[n]. | yspr.l ḫmš.l ṣ[---.]šr.pḫr.klat. | tqtnṣn.w tldn.tld.[ilm.]nʿmm.agzr 23[52].57

[.ks].mn.ḫrṣ. | w arbʿ.ktnt.w [---]b. | [ḫm]š.mat pḥm. | [ḫm]š[.m]at.iqnu. | argmn.nqmd.mlk. | ugrt.d ybl.l špš. | mlk.r 64[118].23

.alpm. | lbnym. | ṯm[n.]alp mitm. | ilbʿl ḫmš m[at]. | ʿdn.ḫmš.mat. | bn.[-]d.alp. | bn.[-]pn.ṯṯ mat. 1060.2.10

m. | ṯmn.mat.kbd. | pwt. | ṯmn.mat.pṯtm. | kkrm.alpm. | ḫmš.mat.kbd. | abn.ṣrp. 2051.9

alpm.pḥm.ḫm[š].mat.kbd. | b d.tt.w.ṯlṯ.ktnt.b dm.tt. | w.ṯmnt.ksp.hn. | k 1110.1

alpm.arbʿ.mat.k[bd]. | mit.b d.yd[r]m. | alp ḫmš mat.kbd.d[--]. 2109.3

tmn.kkr.tlt. | tmn.kkr.brr. | arbʻ.alpm.pḥm. | ḫmš.mat.kbd. | arbʻ.alpm.iqni. | ḫmš.mat.kbd. | tltm.ḫmš kbd 1130.4
.brr. | arbʻ.alpm.pḥm. | ḫmš.mat.kbd. | arbʻ.alpm.iqni. | ḫmš.mat.kbd. | tltm.ḫmš kbd ktn. | ḫmš.rṭm. | ḫmš.tnt.d ḫmš 1130.6
.nm[-.]b d.mzy.alzy. | ḫmš.kkr.ḥlb. | ḫmš.kkr.brr. | kkr.ḫmš.mat.kbd.tlt.šm[n]. | alp.mitm.kbd.tlt.ḥlb. | šbʻ.l.ʻšrm.kkr 1135.4
alpm. | atn.bṣry.alpm. | lbnym. | tm[n.]alp mitm. | ilbʻl ḫmš m[at]. | ʻdn.ḫmš.mat. | bn.[-]d.alp. | bn.[-]pn.tt mat. 1060.2.9
mn. | ʻṣrm.tql.kbd[.ks].mn.ḫrṣ. | w arbʻ.ktnt.w [---]b. | [ḫm]š.mat pḥm. | [ḫm]š[.m]at.iqnu. | argmn.nqmd.mlk. | ugrt. 64[118].22
w.b.spr.l.št. | yrmʻl. | ṣry. | iršy. | yʻdrd. | ayaḫ. | bn.aylt. | ḫmš.mat.arbʻm. | kbd.ksp.anyt. | d.ʻrb.b.anyt. | l.mlk.gbl. | w. 2106.10
[---].dt.it. | [---].tlt.kbd. | [---].alpm.ḫmš.mat. | šbʻm[.t]šʻ.kbd. | tgmr.uz.ǵrn.arbʻ.mat. | tgmr.uz.a 1129.3
qn[i]m.ttt.ʻšrt.ksp h. | ḫmšt.ḫrṣ.bt.il. | b.ḫmšt.ʻšrt.ksp. | ḫmš.mat.šmt. | b.ʻšrt.ksp. | ʻšr.ṣin.b.ttt.w.kmsk. | arbʻ[.k]dwt 2100.7
| mtbʻl.rišy. | tltm.tlt.ʻl.nsk. | arym. | alp.tlt.ʻl. | nsk.art. | ḫmš.mat.tlt. | ʻl.mtn.rišy. 1137.9
.tt mat. | ṣprn.tt mat. | dkry.tt mat. | [p]lsy.tt mat. | ʻdn.ḫmš [m]at. | [--]kbʻl tt [mat]. | [-----]. | ilmlk tt mat. | ʻbdilm.tt 1060.1.7
spr.npṣm.d yṣa.b milḫ. | ʻšrm.ḫpn.ḫmš. | kbd.w lpš. | ḫmš.mispt. | mṭ. | w lpš.d sgr b h. | b d.anrmy. 1109.4
[-]gmm.w ydmʻ. | tntkn.udmʻt h. | km.tqlm.arṣ h. | km ḫmšt.mṭt h. | bm.bky h.w yšn. | b dmʻ h.nhmmt. | šnt.tluan. | 14[KRT].1.30
.ʻšrt. | ʻbdadt.ḫmšt. | abmn.ilštmʻy.ḫmš[t]. | ʻzn.bn.brn.ḫmšt. | mʻrt.ḫmšt. | arttb.bn.ḫmšt. | bn.ysr[.ḫmš]t. | ṣ[-]r.ḫ[mš 1062.26
yrd. | krt.l ggt.ʻdb. | akl.l qryt. | ḥtt.l bt.ḫbr. | yip.lḥm.d ḫmš. | mǵd.tdt.yrḫm. | ʻdn.ngb.w yṣi. | ṣbu.ṣbi.ngb. | w yṣi.ʻdn 14[KRT].2.83
yrd.krt. | [l g]gt.ʻdb.akl.l qryt. | ḥtt.l bt.ḫbr. | yip.lḥm.d ḫmš. | [mǵ]d.tdt.yr[ḫm]. | ʻdn.ngb.w [yṣi.ṣbu]. | ṣbi.ng[b.w yṣi 14[KRT].4.174
b.atlg.tlt.ḫrmtt.ttm. | mḫrhn.nit.mit.krk.mit. | mʻṣd.ḫmšm.mqb.[ʻ]šrm. | b.ulm.tt.ʻšr h.ḫrmtt. | tt.nitm.tn.mʻṣdm.t 2048.3
h. | arbʻ.kkr. | algbt.arbʻt. | ksp h. | kkr.šʻrt. | šbʻt.ksp h. | ḫmš.mqdm.dnyn. | b.tql.dprn.aḥd. | b.tql. | ḫmšm.ʻrgz.b.ḫmš 1127.19
tnnm.tt. | ʻšr.ḫsnm. | nʻr.mrynm. | ḫmš. | trtnm.ḫmš. | mrum.ʻšr. | šbʻ.ḫsnm. | mkrm. | mrynm. | tlt.ʻšr. | hbṭnm. 1031.5
l ḫmš.mrkbt.ḫmš.ʻšr h.prs. | bt.mrkbt.w l šant.tt. | l bt.ʻšrm. | b 2105.1
kr.t[lt]. | tt hrt[m]. | tn mq[pm]. | ult.tl[t]. | krk.kly[.--]. | ḫmš.mr[kbt]. | tt [-]az[-]. | ʻšt[--.---]. | irg[mn.---]. | krk[.---]. 2056.9
[---]m.d.yt[--.]l[-]. | ršp.ḫmš.[m]šl[t]. | [--]arš[p.-]š.l[h]. | [-]tl[.--]š.l h. | [---]l[.--] h. | m 2133.2
d]rǵlm. | [---.]b.bt[.---]l. | [t]lt.att.adrt.w.tlt.ǵzr[m]. | w.ḫmš.nʻrt.b.bt.sk[n]. | tt.attm.adrtm.w.pǵt.w ǵzr[.aḥd.b.bt.--- 80[119].17
[---.n]pš. | [---.--]ʻ.npš. | [---.-]bʻ.npš. | [---].npš. | [---.ḫm]š.npš. | [---].npš. | [---].npš. | [---.a]ḥd. 1142.5
ʻt. | ʻbdbn.ytrš ḫmšt. | krwn.ʻšrt. | bn.ulb ḫmšt. | bn.ḫry.ḫmšt. | swn.ḫmšt. | bn.[-]r[-.]ḫmšt. | bn.ḥdt.ʻšrt. | bn.ḫnyn.ʻšrt. 1062.14
. | ttn.ʻṣrt. | bn.pnmn.ʻšrt. | ʻbdadt.ḫmšt. | abmn.ilštmʻy.ḫmš[t]. | ʻzn.bn.brn.ḫmšt. | mʻrt.ḫmšt. | arttb.bn.ḫmšt. | bn.ysr 1062.25
mšt. | mʻrt.ḫmšt. | arttb.bn.ḫmšt. | bn.ysr[.ḫmš]t. | ṣ[-]r.ḫ[mšt]. | ʻzn.ḫ[mšt]. 1062.30
dr[.---]. | ḫmš ʻl.bn[.---]. | ḫmš ʻl rʻl[-]. | ḫmš ʻl ykn[.--]. | ḫ[mš] ʻl abǵ[l]. | ḫmš ʻl ilb[ʻl]. | ʻšr ʻl [---]. 2034.2.7
n[.---]. | ḫmš ʻl rʻl[-]. | ḫmš ʻl ykn[.--]. | ḫ[mš] ʻl abǵ[l]. | ḫmš ʻl ilb[ʻl]. | ʻšr ʻl [---]. 2034.2.8
ilm[.---]. | tšʻ.ʻš[r.---]. | bn ʻdr[.---]. | ḫmš ʻl.bn[.---]. | ḫmš ʻl rʻl[-]. | ḫmš ʻl ykn[.--]. | ḫ[mš] ʻl abǵ[l]. 2034.2.4
tšʻ.ʻš[r.---]. | bn ʻdr[.---]. | ḫmš ʻl.bn[.---]. | ḫmš ʻl rʻl[-]. | ḫmš ʻl ykn[.--]. | ḫ[mš] ʻl abǵ[l]. | ḫmš ʻl ilb[ʻl]. | ʻšr ʻl [---]. 2034.2.6
ilm[.---]. | tšʻ.ʻš[r.---]. | bn ʻdr[.---]. | ḫmš ʻl.bn[.---]. | ḫmš ʻl rʻl[-]. | ḫmš ʻl ykn[.--]. | ḫ[mš] ʻl abǵ[l]. | ḫmš ʻl ilb[ʻl]. | 2034.2.5
dmt tlt. | qmnz tql. | zlyy tql. | ary ḫmšt. | yknʻm ḫmšt. | ʻnmky tqlm. | [-]kt ʻšrt. | qrn šbʻt. 1176.5
šbʻt.ksp h. | ḫmš.mqdm.dnyn. | b.tql.dprn.aḥd. | b.tql. | ḫmšm.ʻrgz.b.ḫmšt. 1127.22
n. | ʻmn.bn.aǵlmn. | arbʻm.ksp.ʻl.qrt. | b.šd.bn.[u]brš. | ḫmšt.ʻšrt. | b.šd.bn.[-]n. | tl[tt].ʻšr[t]. | b.š[d].bn.ʻmyn. | ḫmšt. | 1083.8
rbʻ. | ubrʻy.tlt. | ar.tmn ʻšr h. | mlk.arbʻ. | ǵbl.ḫmš. | atlg.ḫmš ʻšr[h]. | ulm t[t]. | mʻrby.ḫmš. | tbq.arbʻ. | tkm[.---]. | uḫn 68[65].1.8
l ḫmš.mrkbt.ḫmš.ʻšr h.prs. | bt.mrkbt.w l šant.tt. | l bt.ʻšrm. | bt alḫnm.tlt 2105.1
ṣṣ mrʻm ḫmšm ḫmš kbd. | ṣṣ ubn ḫmš ʻšr h. | ṣṣ ʻmyd ḫmšm. | ṣṣ tmn.ḫmšm. | [ṣṣ] ʻmtdl tltm. | ṣ 2097.2
m. | [---.ḫ]rš.mr[k]bt. | [--].ʻšr h[.---]. | [ḫm]š.ʻšr h[.---]. | ḫmš.ʻšr h. | šrm. 1024.4.1
l.qšt. | [tl]t.psl.ḥzm. | [---.ḫ]rš.mr[k]bt. | [--].ʻšr h[.---]. | [ḫm]š.ʻšr h[.---]. | ḫmš.ʻšr h. | šrm. 1024.3.22
ny.yrḫ.w.ḫm[š.ymm]. | ẓrn.yrḫ.w.ḫmš.y[m]m. | mrat.ḫmš.ʻšr.ymm. | qmnz.yrḫ.w.ḫmš.ymm. | ʻnmk.yrḫ. | ypr.yrḫ. 66[109].7
ḫmš.ʻšr.yn.ṭb. | w.tšʻm.kdm.kbd.yn.d.l.ṭb. | w.arbʻm.yn.ḫlq.b 1084.1
any.al[ty]. | d b atlg[.---]. | ḫmš ʻš[r]. | kkr.t[lt]. | tt hrt[m]. | tn mq[pm]. | ult.tl[t]. | krk.kl 2056.3
.tlt.kkr šʻrt. | iqn[i]m.ttt.ʻšrt.ksp h. | ḫmšt.ḫrṣ.bt.il. | b.ḫmšt.ʻšrt.ksp. | ḫmš.mat.šmt. | b.ʻšrt.ksp. | ʻšr.ṣin.b.ttt.w.kms 2100.6
ḫmšt.ʻš[rt]. | ksp.ʻl.agd[tb]. | w nit w mʻṣd. | w ḫrmtt. | ʻšrt.ksp 2053.1
ʻbdrt[b.---]. | b tt ʻtr tmn.r[qḥ.---]. | p bn btb[-.---]. | b ḫmt ʻtr k[--.---]. | b ḫmt ʻtr[.---]. | [-----]. | [---.-]y[-.---]. | w bn ʻ 207[57].4
pm.l.lbnš prwsdy. | tt spm.l bnš klnmw. | l yarš ḫswn. | ḫmš ʻšr.sp. | l bnš tpnr d yaḫd l g ynm. | tt spm l tgyn. | arbʻ s 137.2[93].10
pm.alpnm. | tlt.m[a]t.art.ḥkpt. | mit.dnn. | mitm.iqnu. | ḫmš.ʻšr.qn.nʻm.ʻn[m]. | tn.ḥblm.alp.alp.am[-]. | tmn.ḥblm.šbʻ 1128.29
n.[-]n. | tl[tt].ʻšr[t]. | b.š[d].bn.ʻmyn. | ḫmšt. | b.[šd.--]n. | ḫ[m]št[.ʻ]šrt. | [ar]bʻm.ksp. | [---]yn. | [---.]ksp. | [---.]mit. | [----- 1083.14
[-.---]. | w bn ʻtl.[---]. | ypḫ knʻm[.---]. | aḫmn bt[.---]. | b ḫmt ʻtr tmn[.---]. 207[57].11
-.-]ʻrm. | [---.--]n.ʻšrm. | [---.-]rn.mit.[---]. | [---.--]t. | [---.]ḫmšt.ʻšrt. | [---.]ʻšrm. | [---.--]št.ʻšrt. | [---.--]m. | [---.--]tm. | [---. 2054.2.7
| [b].bn.ay[--.---].l.ʻšrm. | [-]gp[.---.]ʻrny.ttm. | [---.]dyn.ḫmšt.ʻšrt. | [---.-]til.ḫmšt.l ʻšrm. | [--.-]n.w.aḫt h.arbʻm. | [--.-] 2054.2.19
ʻtr tmn.r[qḥ.---]. | p bn btb[-.---]. | b ḫmt ʻtr k[--.---]. | b ḫmt ʻtr[.---]. | [-----]. | [---.-]y[-.---]. | w bn ʻtl.[---]. | ypḫ knʻm[. 207[57].5
gdlt.šlm.gdlt.w burm.[l]b. | rmṣt.ilhm.bʻlm.dtt.w kšm.ḫmš. | ʻtr h.mlun.šnpt.ḥṣt h.bʻl.ṣpn š. | [--]t š.ilt.mgdl š.ilt.asr 34[1].9
. | a[---.]kdm. | ʻ[---]ʻm.kd. | a[----]ḫr.tlt. | y[---.bn.]kran.ḫmš. | ʻ[---].kd. | amry.kdm. | mnn.bn.gttn.kdm. | ynḥm.bn[.-] 136[84].6
-.---]. | tn pld mḫ[--.---]. | t[--] ḫpnt. | [---] kdwtm.[---]. | ḫmš.pld šʻrt. | tt pld ptt. | arbʻ ḫpnt ptt. | ḫmš ḫpnt.šʻrt. | tlt.ʻš 1113.7
.ʻšrm. | gmrd.ʻšrm. | ṣdqšlm.ʻšr[m]. | yknil.ḫmš. | ilmlk.ḫmš. | prt.ʻšr. | ubn.ʻšr. 1116.13
ḫr[š]. | [---].ḫr[š.---]. | [---.t]lt.[---.]dpm. | [---.]bnšn. | [---.ḫ]mš.ṣmd.alpm. | [---.bn]šm. | [---.]ḫmš.ṣmd.alpm. | [---.bnš] 2038.15
pm. | [---.]bnšn. | [---.ḫ]mš.ṣmd.alpm. | [---.bn]šm. | [---.]ḫmš.ṣmd.alpm. | [---.bnš]m. | [---.]ʻšr.ṣmd.alpm. | [---.bn]šm. | 2038.17
arbʻm.qšt. | alp ḥẓm.w alp. | ntq.tn.qlʻm. | ḫmš.ṣmdm.w ḥrṣ. | tryn.ššwm. | tryn.aḥd.d bnš. | arbʻ.ṣmdm. 1123.4
. | [---.bnš]m. | [---.]ʻšr.ṣmd.alpm. | [---.bn]šm. | [---.--]m.ḫmš.ṣmdm. | [---.bnš]m. 2038.21
.ḫmšm. | [ṣṣ] ʻmtdl tltm. | ṣṣ ʻmlbi tt l ʻšrm. | ṣṣ bn adty ḫmšm. | ṣṣ amtrn arbʻm. | ṣṣ iytlm mit tltm kbd. | ṣṣ m[l]k ʻšr 2097.7
. | [-----]. | [-----]. | [-----]. | [ṣṣ].b[n].ṣd[-.---]. | [ṣṣ].bn.npr.ḫmšm. | ṣṣ.bn.adldn.tltm. | ṣṣ.bn.ʻglt.tltm. | ṣṣ.bn.ʻbd.ʻšrm. | ṣṣ 2096.15
šʻm.[---]. | ṣṣ mlknʻm.a[rbʻm]. | ṣṣ mlk mit[.---]. | ṣṣ igy.ḫmšm. | ṣṣ yrpi m[it.---]. | ṣṣ bn.š[m]mn ʻ[šr.---]. | alp.ttm. | kb 2097.17

ḫmš kbd. | ṣṣ ubn ḫmš ʿšr h. | ṣṣ ʿmyd ḫmšm. | ṣṣ tmn.ḫmšm. | [ṣṣ] ʿmtdl tlṯm. | ṣṣ ʿmlbi ṯṯ l ʿšrm. | ṣṣ bn adty ḫmšm. 2097.4
ṣṣ mrʿm ḫmšm ḫmš kbd. | ṣṣ ubn ḫmš ʿšr h. | ṣṣ ʿmyd ḫmšm. | ṣṣ tmn.ḫmšm. | [ṣṣ] ʿmtdl tlṯm. | ṣṣ ʿmlbi ṯṯ l ʿšrm. | ṣṣ 2097.3
ʿzn.bn.brn.ḫmšt. | mʿrt.ḫmšt. | arttb.bn.ḫmšt. | bn.ysr[.ḫmš]t. | ṣ[-]r.ḫ[mšt]. | ʿzn.ḫ[mšt]. 1062.29
.b[ilm.ydy]. | mrṣ.grš[m.zbln]. | in.b ilm.ʿ[ny h.yrbʿ]. | yḫmš.rgm.[my.b ilm]. | ydy.mrṣ.g[ršm.zbln]. | in.b ilm.ʿn[y h 16[126].5.17
d. | arbʿ.alpm.iqni. | ḫmš.mat.kbd. | tlṯm.ḫmš kbd ktn. | ḫmš.rṯm. | ḫmš.ṯnt.d ḫmšm w. | ḫmš.ṯnt.d mit. | ḫmš.ṯnt.d ṯl | 1130.8
| ḫmš kbd arbʿ[.---]. | ṯṯ šurt l tg[-.---]. | arbʿ šurt [---]. | [ḫm]šm šurt [---]. | ṯlṯ šurt l [---]. | ṯn šurtm l [---]. | [-----.]a[---] 137.1[92].15
.---]. | iwrpzn.ʿšrm ʿšrm š[lm.---]. | ilabn.ʿšrt ṯqlm kbd.ḫmš.šl[m.---]. | tlmyn.šbʿt.ʿšrt ʿšrt[.šlm.---]. | ybn.ṯmnt.ʿšrt ʿšr 1131.3
ʿšr šṭpm. | b ḫmš.šmn. | ʿšrm.gdy. | b ḫmš.šmn. | w ḫmš ṯʿdt. 1097.4
ʿšr šṭpm. | b ḫmš.šmn. | ʿšrm.gdy. | b ḫmš.šmn. | w ḫmš ṯʿdt. 1097.2
šʿ.ṣin.b.tšʿt.ksp. | mšlt.b.ṯql.ksp. | kdwṯ.l.grgyn.b.ṯq[l]. | ḫmšm.šmt.b.ṯql. | kkr.w.[ml]tḥ.tyt.[---]. | [b]šbʿ[m.w.n]ṣp.ks 2101.25
[---.-]kn. | [---.]tlṯm. | kuwṯ.ṯlṯ.kbd. | m[i]t.arbʿt.kbd. | ḫ[mš.]šʿrt. | [---.]tšʿ.kbd.skm. | [arb]ʿm.ḫpnt.pṯt. | [-]r.pldm.dt 1111.5
ḫmšm.dd. | nʿr. | ḫmšm.tišr. | ḫmš.ktnt. | ḫmš.ṯnt.alpm. | ʿšrm.hbn. | ṯlṯ.mat.dd. 2102.3
k[l] m.ṯlṯ.kbʿ ym. | tikl[.i]št.b bht m. | nbla[t.]b hkl m. | ḫmš.ṯ[d]ṯ.ym.tikl. | išt.[b]bht m.nblat. | b[qrb.hk]l m.mk. | b 4[51].6.29
m. | [uzr.i]lm.dnil.uzr. | [ilm.y]lḥm.uzr.yšqy bn. | [qdš.ḫ]mš.ṯdṯ.ym.uzr. | [ilm].dnil.uzr.ilm.ylḥm. | [uzr.]yšqy.bn qd 17[2AQHT].1.12
t. | sʿt.b nk.šibt.b bqr. | mmlat.dm.ym.w ṯn. | ṯlṯ.rbʿ.ym.ymš. | ṯdṯ.ym.ḥẓ k.al.tšʿl. | qrt h.abn.yd k. | mšdpt.w hn.špšm 14[KRT].3.115
l]. | snnt.ṯlṯ[.r]bʿ ym.yšl | ḥm kṯrt.w yššq. | bnt hll.snnt.ḫmš. | ṯdṯ.ym.yšlḥm.k[ṯ]rt. | w y[ššq].bnt.hll.snnt. | mk.b šb[ʿ. 17[2AQHT].2.36
rṯ.yḥrṯ.il. | hn.ym.w ṯn.tlḥmn.rpum. | tštyn.ṯlṯ.rbʿ.ym.ḫmš. | ṯdṯ.ym.tlḥmn.rpum. | tštyn.bt.ikl.b prʿ. | yṣq.b irt.lbnn. 22.2[124].22
[t]škn.šd. | km.ḥsn.pat.mdbr. | lk.ym.w ṯn.ṯlṯ.rbʿ ym. | ḫmš.ṯdṯ.ym.mk.špšm. | b šbʿ.w tmǵy.l udm. | rbm.w l.udm.ṯr 14[KRT].3.107
pk.šibt.w b | mqr.mmlat. | d[m].ym.w ṯn. | ṯlṯ.rbʿ.ym. | ḫmš.ṯdṯ.ym. | mk.špšm.b šbʿ. | w l.yšn.pbl. | mlk.l [qr.]ṯiqt. | ib 14[KRT].5.220
[bd]. | [dd].kšmm.tšʿ[.---]. | [š]ʿrm.ṯṯ.ʿ[šr]. | [dd].ḥṯm.w.ḫ[mšm]. | [ṯ]lṯ kbd.yn.b [gt.---]. | mit.[---].ṯlṯ.kb[d]. | [dd.--]m. 2092.9
.ʿṯrt.šd.bt.mlk[.---]. | ṯn.skm.šbʿ.mšlt.arbʿ.ḫpnt.[---]. | ḫmšm.ṯlṯ.rkb.ntn.ṯlṯ.mat.[---]. | lg.šmn.rqḥ.šrʿm.ušpǵtm.p[-- UG5.9.1.20
rṭn. | ṯnyn. | apṯ. | šbn. | gbrn. | ṭbʿm. | kyn. | bʿln. | ytršp. | ḫmšm.ṯmn.kbd. | tgmr.bnš.mlk. | d.b d.adnʿm. | [š]bʿ.b.ḥrṯm. 1024.2.25
ḫmšm.dd. | nʿr. | ḫmšm.tišr. | ḫmš.ktnt. | ḫmš.ṯnt.alpm. | ʿšrm.hbn. | ṯlṯ.mat.dd. | šʿrm. | mit.šmn. | ʿšr.k 2102.5
ḫmš.ṯnnm.ʿšr.ḫsnm. | ṯlṯ.ʿšr.mrynm. | ḫmš.[tr]tnm. | ṯlṯ.b[n.] 1028.1
m.iqni. | ḫmš.mat.kbd. | tlṯm.ḫmš kbd ktn. | ḫmš.rṯm. | ḫmš.ṯnt.d ḫmšm w. | ḫmš.ṯnt.d mit. | ḫmš.ṯnt.d ṯl | ṯ mat. | ṯṯ.ṯ 1130.9
d. | tlṯm.ḫmš kbd ktn. | ḫmš.rṯm. | ḫmš.ṯnt.d ḫmšm w. | ḫmš.ṯnt.d mit. | ḫmš.ṯnt.d ṯl | ṯ mat. | ṯṯ.ṯnt.d alp | alpm.ṯlṯ ktt. 1130.10
ktn. | ḫmš.rṯm. | ḫmš.ṯnt.d ḫmšm w. | ḫmš.ṯnt.d mit. | ḫmš.ṯnt.d ṯl | ṯ mat. | ṯṯ.ṯnt.d alp | alpm.ṯlṯ ktt. | alp.brr. | kkr.t 1130.11
ʿšr šṭpm. | b ḫmš.šmn. | ʿšrm.gdy. | b ḫmš.šmn. | w ḫmš ṯʿdt. 1097.5
lbš.aḥd. | b.ʿšrt. | w.ṯn.b.ḫmšt. | tprt.b.ṯlṯt. | mṯyn.b.ṯṯt. | ṯn.lbšm.b.ʿšrt. | pld.b.arbʿt. | lb 1108.3
šbʿ.ṯnnm.w.šbʿ.ḫsnm. | ṯmn.ʿšr h.mrynm. | ʿšr.mkrm. | ḫmš.ṯrtnm. | ḫmš.bn.mrynm. | ʿšr.mrum.w.šbʿ.ḫsnm. | tšʿm.m 1030.4
ṯnnm.ṯṯ. | ʿšr.ḫsnm. | nʿr.mrynm. | ḫmš. | ṯrtnm.ḫmš. | mrum.ʿšr. | šbʿ.ḫsnm. | mkrm. | mrynm. | ṯl 1031.4
ḫmš.ṯnnm.ʿšr.ḫsnm. | ṯlṯ.ʿšr.mrynm. | ḫmš.[tr]tnm. | ṯlṯ.b[n.]mrynm. | ʿšr[.m]krm. | tšʿ.hbṯnm. | ʿšr. 1028.3
[---] kdr [---]. | [-]trn [k]sp [-]al[.-]r[-]. | [--]dšq krsnm. | ḫmšm [-]t ṯlṯ ty[--]. | bn.grgš. | w.npṣ bt ṯn.ṯlṯ mat. | w spl ṯlṯ. 1103.14
kpld.b[-.-]r[--]. | w blḫ br[-]m p[-]. | b[--.]l[-.]mat[.-]y. | ḫmšm[.--]i. | ṯlṯ m[at] ḫswn. | ṯlṯ ṯ[-].ṯṯ ḥ[--]. 140[98].8
ṣ.ṯlṯm.i[qnu.---]. | [b.yr]ḫ.mgmr.mš[--.---]. | [---].iqnu.ḫmš[.---]. | [b.yr]ḫ.pgrm[.---]. 1106.39
b y[rḫ.---]. | ʿš[r.---]. | ḫm[š.---]. | b[yrḫ.---]. | [---.]prš. | [-----]. | l.mšḫ[.---]. | ʿšr.d[d.-- 2012.3
alp[.---]. | mat[.---]. | ḫrṣ[.---]. | ṯlṯ.k[---]. | ṯlṯ.a[--.---]. | ḫmš[.---]. | ksp[.---]. | k[--.---]. | ar[bʿ.---]. | ṯmn[.---]. | [-]r[-.---]. 148[96].6
r[y-.---]. | [--]sp.mr[y-.---]. | [--]l.ṯṯm sp[m.---]. | [p]drn.ḫm[š.---]. | l bn ḥdnr[.---]. | ṯṯm sp.km[-.---]. | ʿšrm.sp[.---]. | ʿšr 139[310].4
b. | [b.g]t.bir.ʿš[r.---]. | [---].krk.mʿ[ṣd.---]. | [b.]gt.ḥrṯm.ḫm[š.---]. | [n]it.krk.mʿṣ[d.---]. | b.ḫrbǵlm.ǵlm[n]. | w.trhy.aṯt 2048.17
]. | ybnil[.---.]kd yn.w š. | spr.m[--]. | spr d[---]b.w š. | ṯṯ.ḫmš.[---]. | skn.ul[m.---]. | [---]š.[---]. | [---]y[.---]. | sk[n.---]. | u[1093.5
spr[.---]. | ḫmš.k[--.---]. | ḫmš[.---]. | ʿš[r.---]. | [-----]. | [-----]. | [-----]. | [-----]. | [-----]. | [---- 1128.3
[-]š[-.---]. | [-]š[-.---]. | arb[ʿ.---]. | ḫmš.[---]. | ǵ[--.---]. 150[36].4
--rt]. | w [ʿṣrm.]l.ri[--.---]. | [--]t.bʿlt.bt[.---]. | [md]bḥt.b.ḫmš[.---]. | [-.]kbd.w.db[ḥ.---]. | [--].aṯrt.ʿṣr[m.l inš.ilm]. | [ṯ]tb 35[3].38
[---]t ṯm[n.---]. | [--]l ḫmš[.---]. | [----.]ḫmš[.---]. | [--.-]rn.ʿrbt[.---]. | [---].ṯmnym[.---]. | [---.--]p.mit[.- 151[25].3
]ʿd.admn[.---]. | [---.--]d.ytr.mṯ[--]. | [-----]. | [-----]. | [---].ḫmš[.---]. | [---.]urš[-.---]. | [---.]yd.kl.[---]. 2156.8
[---]t ṯm[n.---]. | [--]l ḫmš[.---]. | [----.]ḫmš[.---]. | [--.-]rn.ʿrbt[.---]. | [---].ṯmnym[.--- 151[25].2
[---.--]t ḥ[dr]. | [-----]. | ḫmš[.---]t.ḥdrm. | w.[---.a]ḥd.d.sgrm. | w p[tḥ.---.]l.aḥd.adr. | 1151.3
.ʿšr. | bn.adty.ʿšr. | [ṣ]dqšlm ḫmš. | krzn.ḫmš. | ubrʿym.ḫmš. | [----]. | [bn] itn. | [bn] il. | [---]ṯ. | klṯtb. | gsn. | arm[w]l. | b 2039.7
mšt. | arttb.bn.ḫmšt. | bn.ysr[.ḫmš]t. | ṣ[-]r.ḫ[mšt]. | ʿzn.ḫ[mšt]. 1062.31
mš.mqdm.dnyn. | b.ṯql.dprn.aḥd. | b.ṯql. | ḫmšm.ʿrgz.b.ḫmšt. 1127.22

ḫmt

.w tadm. | rḥṣ[.y]d k.amt. | uṣb[ʿt k.]ʿd[.ṯ]km. | ʿrb[.b ẓl.ḫmt]. | qḥ im[r.b yd k]. | imr.d[bḥ.bm].ymn. | lla.kl[atn]m. | kl 14[KRT].2.65
ṣ.w yadm. | yrḥṣ.yd h.amt h. | uṣbʿt h.ʿd.ṯkm. | ʿrb.b ẓl.ḫmt.lqḥ. | imr.dbḥ.b yd h. | lla.klatnm. | klt.lḥm h.d nzl. | lqḥ. 14[KRT].3.159

ḫndlt

.iqn]i.l.ṯrmn.qrt. | [---.]lbš.ḫmšm.iqnu. | [---].šmt.ḫmšt.ḫndlt. | [---.iqn]i.l.[-]k.btbt. | [---.l.ṯrm]nm.š[bʿ].mat.šʿrt. | [---. 1106.17

ḫndrṯ

]. | w [bṣql.ʿrgz.ydk]. | a[ḥd h.w.yṣq.b.ap h]. | k.[ḫr.ššw.ḫndrṯ]. | w.ṯ[qd.mr.ydk.aḥd h]. | w.y[ṣq.b.ap h]. | k.l.ḫ[ru.w.l. 161[56].5
ǵ w b[ṣql ʿrgz]. | [ydk aḥ]d h w yṣq b ap h. | [k ḫr]ššw ḫndrṯ w ṯ[qd m]r. | [ydk aḥd h w yṣq b ap h. | [k l yḫru w]l 160[55].6
w ʿšr lḥm. | [--.]w nṣp w ṯlṯ spm w ʿšrm lḥ[m]. | l[.-]dt ḫnd[r]ṯ arʿ s[p]m w ʿš[r]. | [---.]ḫndrṯm ṯṯ spm [w] ṯlṯm l[ḥm 134[-].5
w ʿšrm lḥ[m]. | l[.-]dt ḫnd[r]ṯ arʿ s[p]m w ʿš[r]. | [---.]ḫndrṯm ṯṯ spm [w] ṯlṯm l[ḥm]. | [---.]arʿ spm w [---]. | [---]š[.- 134[-].6

ḫnzr

. | bn.ḥrm. | bn.brzn. | w.nḥl h. | bn.adlḏn. | bn.šbl. | bn.ḫnzr. | bn.arwṯ. | bn.ṯbtnq. | bn.ptḏn. | bn.nbdg. | bn.ḥgbn. | bn. 113[400].1.14
bn.šyy. | bn.ḫnzr. | bn.ydbʻl. | bn.ḥyn. | [bn].ar[-]m. | [bn].ḥrp[-]. | [bn].ḫdp 124[-].2.2
t.qḥ. | ʻrpt k.rḥ k.mdl k. | mṭrt k.ʻm k.šbʻt. | ǵlm k.ṯmn.ḫnzr k. | ʻm k.pdry.bt.ar. | ʻm k.ṭṭly.bt.rb.idk. | pn k.al ttn.tk. 5[67].5.9
d.ṯqlm. | bt.sgld.ṯqlm. | bn.ʻmy.ṯqlm. | bn.brq.ṯqlm. | bn.ḫnzr.ṯqlm. | dqn.nsk.arbʻt. | bn.ḫdyn.ṯqlm. | bn.ʻbd.šḫr.ṯqlm. 122[308].1.16

ḫny

. | šmmn. | bn.rmy. | bn.aky. | ʻbdḫmn. | bn.ʻdṯ. | kṯy. | bn.ḫny. | bn.ssm. | bn.ḫnn. | [--]ny. | [bn].ṯrdnt. | [bn].hyadt. | [--]lt 1047.17

ḫnyn

.ktln. | bn.ʻgwn. | bn.yšmʻ. | bdl.mdrǵlm. | bn.mmy. | bn.ḫnyn. | bn.knn. | khnm. | bn.ṯʻy. | w.nḥl h. | w.nḥl hm. | bn.nqly 104[316].9
n. | bn.ʻdy. | bn.ršpy. | [---.]mn. | [--.-]sn. | [bn.-]ny. | [b]n.ḫnyn. | [bn].nbq. | [bn.]snrn. | [bn.-]lṣ. | bn.[---]ym. 115[301].3.2
ry.ḫmšt. | swn.ḫmšt. | bn.[-]r[-.]ḫmšt. | bn.ḥdṯ.ʻšrt. | bn.ḫnyn.ʻšrt. | rpan.ḫmšt. | abǵl.ḫmšt. | bn.aḫdy.ʻšrt. | ṯṯn.ʻṣrt. | bn 1062.18

ḫnn

[n] il. | dr bn il. | mpḫrt bn il. | ṯrmn w šnm. | il w aṯrt. | ḫnn il. | nṣbt il. | šlm il. | il ḥš il add. | bʻl ṣpn bʻl. | ugrt. | b mrḥ 30[107].6
bn.ẓll. | bn ydy. | bn lzn. | bn.ṯyn. | bn gʻr. | bn.prtn. | bn ḫnn. | b[n.-]n. | bn.ṣṣb. | bn.bʻltn ḫlq. | bn.mlkbn. | bn.asyy ḫlq. 2016.1.18
n l y. | l šmn iṯr hw. | p iḫdn gnryn. | im mlkytn yrgm. | aḫnnn. | w iḫd. 1020.9
| bn.aky. | ʻbdḫmn. | bn.ʻdṯ. | kṯy. | bn.ḫny. | bn.ssm. | bn.ḫnn. | [--]ny. | [bn].ṯrdnt. | [bn].hyadt. | [--]lt. | šmrm. | pʻṣ.bn.b 1047.19

ḫnp

n.il d p[id]. | ydʻt k.bt.k anšt.w i[n.b ilht]. | qlṣ k.tbʻ.bt.ḫnp.lb[k.--.ti] | ḫd.d iṯ.b kbd k.tšt.b [---]. | irt k.dṯ.ydṯ.mʻqb 18[3AQHT].1.17
qšt pn hdd.b y[.----]. | ʻm.b ym bʻl ysy ym[.---]. | rmm.ḫnpm.mḫl[.---]. | mlk.nhr.ibr[.---]. | zbl bʻl.ǵlm.[---]. | ṣǵr hd 9[33].2.8
]. | ilš.ngr bt bʻl. | w aṯt k.ngrt.il[ht]. | ʻl.l ṯkm.bnw n. | l nḫnpt.mšpy. | ṯlṯ.kmm.ṯrr y. | [---.]l ǵr.gm.ṣḥ. | [---.]r[-]m. 16[126].4.15
ʻ]l m.ʻ[--].yd k.amṣ.yd[.--]. | [---.]ḥš[.-]nm[.--.]k.[--].w yḫnp[.---]. | [---.]ylm.b[n.ʻ]n k.ṣmdm.špk[.---]. | [---.]nt[-.]mb 1001.1.15

ḫnq

dqt.trṯ.dqt. | [rš]p.ʻnt.ḫbly.dbḥn š[p]š pgr. | [g]dlt iltm ḫnqtm.d[q]tm. | [yr]ḫ.kṯy gdlt.w l ǵlmt š. | [w]pamt ṯlṯm.w 34[1].18
. | ṯrmn. | pdry. | dqt. | trṯ. | ršp. | ʻnt ḫbly. | špš pgr. | iltm ḫnqtm. | yrḫ kṯy. | ygb hd. | yrgb bʻl. | ydb il. | yarš il. | yrǵm il. UG5.14.A.13

ḫnqn

[---].rb. | [-]lpl. | bn.asrn. | bn.šḫyn. | bn.abdʻn. | bn.ḫnqn. | bn.nmq. | bn.amdn. | bn.špšn. 1067.6
. | dqn.nsk.arbʻt. | bn.ḫdyn.ṯqlm. | bn.ʻbd.šḫr.ṯqlm. | bn.ḫnqn.arbʻt. | [b]n.ṯrk.ṯqlm. | [b]n.pdrn.ṯq[lm]. | pdy.[----]. | [i]l 122[308].1.20
. | ṣprn. | bn.ašbḥ. | bn.qṯnn. | bn.ǵlmn. | [bn].ṣwy. | [bn].ḫnq[n]. | [-----]. | [-----]. | [-----]. | [-----]. | n[----]. | bn.[---]. | bn.[-- 1046.1.25

ḫsw

[---]t.ddm.šʻr[m.---]. | [---].mit.ḫsw.[---]. | [----]d.nʻr.ṯ[--]d[.---]. | [---.]ṯlṯ.kṯt[.-]d.[---]. | [---.a]r 143[-].1.2

ḫswn

| arbʻ.spm.l.lbnš prwsdy. | ṯṯ spm.l bnš klnmw. | l yarš ḫswn. | ḫmš ʻšr.sp. | l bnš tpnr d yaḫd l g ynm. | ṯṯ spm l tgyn 137.2[93].9
ʻrm. | [---.-]hn.w.alp.kd.nbt.kd.šmn.mr. | [---.]arbʻ.mat.ḫswn.lṯḥ.aqhr. | [---.lṯḥ.]sbbyn.lṯḥ.ššmn.lṯḥ.šḫlt. | [---.lṯḥ.]sm 142[12].3
. | [bn].pmn. | bn.gṯrn. | bn.arpḫn. | bn.ṯryn. | bn.dll. | bn.ḫswn. | mrynm. | ʻzn. | ḥyn. | ʻmyn. | ilyn. | yrbʻm. | nʻmn. | bn.k 1046.3.32
.šmn.mr. | [---].kmn.lṯḥ.sbbyn. | [---.-]ʻt.lṯḥ.ššmn. | [---].ḫswn.ṯṯ.mat.nṣ. | [---].ḫmšm.ḥmr.škm. | [---.ṯṯ.dd.]gdl.ṯṯ.dd.šʻ 142[12].11
br[-]m p[-]. | b[--.]l[-.]mat[.-]y. | ḫmšm[.--]i. | ṯlṯ m[at] ḫswn. | ṯlṯ ṯ[-].ṯṯ ḥ[--]. 140[98].9

ḫsyn

[---.--]n.aḥd. | [p]dr.ḫsyn.aḥd. | pdr.mlk.aḥd. 130[29].2

ḫsn

rum. | šbʻ.ḫsnm. | tšʻm.ṯṯ.kbd.mdrǵlm. | ʻšrm.aḥd.kbd.ḫsnm. | ubnyn. | ṯtm[.l.]mit.ṯlṯ. | kbd[.tg]mr.bnš. | l.b.bt.mlk. 1028.10
n. | bn.ilt. | špšyn.nḥl h. | nʻmn.bn.iryn. | nrn.nḥl h. | bn.ḫsn. | bn.ʻbd. | [-----]. | [---.n]ḥ[l h]. | [-]ntm[.---]. | [ʻ]bdm. | [bn] 85[80].2.9
[---.]gtn ṯṯ. | [---.]tḥr l ytn ḫs[n]. | ʻbd ulm ṯn un ḫsn. | gdy lqḥ ṣṭqn gt bn ndr. | um r[-] gtn ṯṯ ḫsn l ytn. | l rḥt 1154.3
rtnm. | tšʻ.ḫbṭnm. | ṯmnym.ṯlṯ.kbd. | mdrǵlm. | w.šbʻ.ʻšr.ḫsnm. | ḫmšm.l.mit. | bnš.l.d. | yškb.l.b.bt.mlk. 1029.13
lm ṯn un ḫsn. | gdy lqḥ ṣṭqn gt bn ndr. | um r[-] gtn ṯṯ ḫsn l ytn. | l rḥt lqḥ ṣṭqn. | bt qbṣ urt ilštmʻ dbḥ ṣṭqn l. | ršp. 1154.5
ḫsnm. | nʻr.mrynm. | ḫmš. | ṯrtnm.ḫmš. | mrum.ʻšr. | šbʻ.ḫsnm. | mkrm. | mrynm. | ṯlṯ.ʻšr. | hbṭnm. | ṯmn. | mdrǵlm. | ṯm 1031.7
ṯnnm.ṯṯ. | ʻšr.ḫsnm. | nʻr.mrynm. | ḫmš. | ṯrtnm.ḫmš. | mrum.ʻšr. | šbʻ.ḫsnm. 1031.2
[---.]gtn ṯṯ. | [---.]tḥr l ytn ḫs[n]. | ʻbd ulm ṯn un ḫsn. | gdy lqḥ ṣṭqn gt bn ndr. | um r[-] 1154.2
m. | ʻšr.mrum.w.šbʻ.ḫsnm. | tšʻm.mdrǵlm. | arbʻ.l ʻšrm.ḫsnm. | ʻšr.hbṭnm. | ṯtm.l.mit.ṯn.kbd. | tgmr. 1030.8
tšʻ.ṯnnm. | w.arbʻ.ḫsnm. | ʻšr.mrum. | w.šbʻ.ḫsnm. | tšʻ.ʻšr. | mrynm. | ṯlṯ.ʻšr.mkr 1029.2
mkrm. | ḫmš.ṯrtnm. | ḫmš.bn.mrynm. | ʻšr.mrum.w.šbʻ.ḫsnm. | tšʻm.mdrǵlm. | arbʻ.l ʻšrm.ḫsnm. | ʻšr.hbṭnm. | ṯtm.l.m 1030.6
tšʻ.ṯnnm. | w.arbʻ.ḫsnm. | ʻšr.mrum. | w.šbʻ.ḫsnm. | tšʻ.ʻšr. | mrynm. | ṯlṯ.ʻšr.mkrm. | ṯlṯ.bn.mrynm. | arbʻ.ṯr 1029.4
.b[n.]mrynm. | ʻšr[.m]krm. | tšʻ.hbṭnm. | ʻšr.mrum. | šbʻ.ḫsnm. | tšʻm.ṯṯ.kbd.mdrǵlm. | ʻšrm.aḥd.kbd.ḫsnm. | ubnyn. | ṯ 1028.8
ḫmš.ṯnnm.ʻšr.ḫsnm. | ṯlṯ.ʻšr.mrynm. | ḫmš.[tr]ṯnm. | ṯlṯ.b[n.]mrynm. | ʻšr[.m 1028.1
šbʻ.ṯnnm.w.šbʻ.ḫsnm. | ṯmn.ʻšr h.mrynm. | ʻšr.mkrm. | ḫmš.ṯrtnm. | ḫmš.bn. 1030.1

ḫss

mt.ṯṯ.w kṯṯ. | [yus]p.ḥmt.mlk.b ‘ṯtrt.yisp.ḥmt. | [kṯ]r w ḫss.y[i]sp.ḥmt.šḥr.w šlm. | [yis]p.ḥmt.isp.[šp]š l hrm.ǵrpl.‘l UG5.8.18
.b šb‘.šnt. | bn.krt.km hm.tdr. | ap.bnt.ḥry. | km hm.w ṯhss.aṯrt. | ndr h.w ilt.p[--]. | w tšu.g h.w [tṣḥ]. | ph m‘.ap.k[rt 15[128].3.25
pš.kṯr.w ḫss. | l brlt.hyn.d ḥrš. | ydm.aḫr.ymǵy.kṯr. | w ḫss.b d.dnil.ytnn. | qšt.l brk h.y‘db. | qṣ‘t.apnk.mṯt.dnty. | tšl 17[2AQHT].5.26
.ym[.rm]m.hkl.ṯpṯ nh[r]. | [---.]hrn.w[---.]tb‘.k[ṯ]r w [ḫss.t]bn.bht zbl ym. | [trm]m.hk[l.ṯpṯ].nhr.bt k.[---.]šp[-.---]. 2.3[129].8
rnt.b y‘lm.mtnm. | b ‘qbt.ṯr.adr.b ǵlil.qnm. | tn.l kṯr.w ḫss.yb‘l.qšt l ‘nt. | qṣ‘t.l ybmt.limm.w t‘n.btlt. | ‘nt.irš ḥym.l 17[2AQHT].6.24
.w l tbn.hmlt.arṣ. | at.w ank.ib[ǵy h.---]. | w y‘n.kṯr.w ḫss[.lk.lk.‘nn.ilm.] | atm.bštm.w an[.šnt.kptr]. | l rḥq.ilm.ḥkp 1['NT.IX].3.17
.w yphn.b alp. | šd.rbt.kmn.hlk.kṯr. | k y‘n.w y‘n.tdrq.ḫss. | hlk.qšt.ybln.hl.yš | rb‘.qṣ‘t.apnk.dnil. | mt.rpi.aphn.ǵzr. 17[2AQHT].5.11
d.ksp. | gb‘m lḥmd.ḫrṣ. | yblnn.udr.ilqṣm. | yak.l kṯr.w ḫss. | w ṯb l mspr..k tlakn. | ǵlmm. | aḫr.mǵy.kṯr.w ḫss. | št.alp 4[51].5.103
‘d k.kṯr m.ḥbr k. | w ḫss.d‘t k. | b ym.arš.w tnn. | kṯr.w ḫss.yd. | ytr.kṯr.w ḫss. | spr.ilmlk šbny. | lmd.atn.prln.rb. | kh 6.6[62.2].51
š.ṯḥtk.ilnym. | ‘d k.ilm.hn.mtm. | ‘d k.kṯr m.ḥbr k. | w ḫss.d‘t k. | b ym.arš.w tnn. | kṯr.w ḫss.yd. | ytr.kṯr.w ḫss. | spr. 6.6[62.2].49
t.lḥm št. | b krpnm.yn.b k.ḫrṣ. | dm.‘ṣm.hm.yd.il mlk. | yḫss k.ahbt.ṯr.t‘rr k. | w t‘n.rbt.aṯrt ym. | ṯḥm k.il.ḥkm.ḥkmt 4[51].4.39
š. | ‘q šr.y‘db.ksa.w yṯb. | tqru.l špš.um.ql bl.‘m | kṯr.w ḫss.kptr h.mnt.nṯk.nḥš. | šmrr.nḥš.‘q šr.ln h.mlḫš.abd. | ln h. UG5.7.46
h.k yṣḥ. | šm‘.mṯt.dnty.‘d[b]. | imr.b pḥd.l npš.kṯr. | w ḫss.l brlt.hyn d. | ḥrš yd.šlḥm.ššqy. | ilm sad.kbd.hmt.b‘l. | ḥk 17[2AQHT].5.18
pt.il.kl h.tšm‘. | mṯt.dnty.t‘db.imr. | b pḥd.l npš.kṯr.w ḫss. | l brlt.hyn.d ḥrš. | ydm.aḫr.ymǵy.kṯr. | w ḫss.b d.dnil.yt 17[2AQHT].5.23
.w l.‘pr.‘ẓm ny. | l b‘l[-.---]. | ṯḥt.ksi.zbl.ym.w ‘n.kṯr.w ḫss.l rgmt. | l k.l zbl.b‘l.ṯnt.l rkb.‘rpt.ht.ib k. | b‘l m.ht.ib k.t 2.4[68].7
| m.w y[p]ṯḥ.b dqt.‘rpt. | ‘l h[wt].kṯr.w ḫss. | ṣḥq.kṯr.w ḫss. | yšu.g h.w yṣḥ. | l rgmt.l k.l ali | yn.b‘l.ṯtbn.b‘l. | l hwt y.y 4[51].7.21
w ḫss.d‘t k. | b ym.arš.w tnn. | kṯr.w ḫss.yd. | ytr.kṯr.w ḫss. | spr.ilmlk šbny. | lmd.atn.prln.rb. | khnm rb.nqdm. | ṯ‘y. 6.6[62.2].52
‘ṯ w kmṯ. | yrḫ w ksa. | yrḫ mkṯy. | ṯkmn w šnm. | kṯr w ḫss. | ‘ṯtr ‘ṯtpr. | šḥr w šlm. | ngh w srr. | ‘dw šr. | ṣdqm šr. | ḥnb UG5.10.1.9
gn.rbt.aṯrt ym. | mǵẓ.qnyt.ilm. | hyn.‘ly.l mpḫm. | b d.ḫss.mṣbṭm. | yṣq.ksp.yšl | ḥ.ḫrṣ.yṣq.ksp. | l alpm.ḫrṣ.yṣq | m.l 4[51].1.25
rbt.b qrb.[h]kl | m.w y[p]ṯḥ.b dqt.‘rpt. | ‘l h[wt].kṯr.w ḫss. | ṣḥq.kṯr.w ḫss. | yšu.g h.w yṣḥ. | l rgmt.l k.l ali | yn.b‘l.ṯtb 4[51].7.20
r.w ḫss. | w ṯb l mspr..k tlakn. | ǵlmm. | aḫr.mǵy.kṯr.w ḫss. | št.alp.qdm h.mra. | w tk.pn h.t‘db.ksu. | w yṯtb.l ymn.al 4[51].5.106
| a[-]ḫn tlyn. | atdb w ‘r. | qdš w amrr. | ṯḥr w bd. | [k]ṯr ḫss šlm. | šlm il bt. | šlm il ḫš[t]. | ršp inšt. | [--]rm il [---]. | [---. UG5.7.71
tk.ṣrrt.ṣpn. | alp.šd.aḫd bt. | rbt.kmn.hkl. | w y‘n.kṯr.w ḫss. | šm‘.l aliyn b‘l. | bn.l rkb.‘rpt. | bl.ašt.urbt.b bh[t] m. | ḥl 4[51].5.120
w y‘n.k[ṯr.w ḫs]s. | ṯtb.b‘l.l[hwt y]. | ṯn.rgm.k[ṯr.w]ḫss. | šm‘.m‘.l al[iy]n b‘l. | bl.ašt.ur[bt.]b bht m. | ḥln.b qr[b.h 4[51].6.3
r.]w yql[.y]šṯḥw[y.]w ykb[dn h.--]r y[---]. | [---.k]ṯr.w ḫ[ss.t]b‘.b[n.]bht.ym[.rm]m.hkl.ṯpṯ nh[r]. | [---.]hrn.w[---.]t 2.3[129].7
[---.m]dd.il ym. | [---.-]qlṣn.wpṯ m. | [---.]w y‘n.kṯr. | [w ḫss.]ṯtb.b‘l.l hwt y. | [ḥš.]bht h.tbnn. | [ḥš.]trmm.hkl h. | y[tl] 4[51].6.15
w y‘n.k[ṯr.w ḫs]s. | ṯtb.b‘l.l[hwt y]. | ṯn.rgm.k[ṯr.w]ḫss. | šm‘.m‘.l al[iy]n 4[51].6.1
n.kṯr]. | hbr.w ql.t[šṯḥwy.w kbd.hwt]. | w rgm l k[ṯr.w ḫss.ṯny.l hyn]. | d ḥrš.y[dm.ṯḥm.ṯr.il.ab k.] | hwt.lṭpn[.ḥtk k.- 1['NT.IX].3.4
p‘n.kṯ. | hbr.w ql.tšṯḥ | wy.w kbd hwt. | w rgm.l kṯr. | w ḫss.ṯny.l h | yn.d ḥrš.ydm. | ṯḥm.al[iyn.b‘l]. | h[wt.aliy.qrdm]. 3['NT.VI].6.22
. | ṯr ab h il.ṯtrm[.---]. | tšlḥm yrḫ.ggn[.---]. | k[.---.ḫ]mš.ḫssm[.---]. | [---.--]m ‘ṯtr[t.---]. | [---.]n[--.---]. 2001.1.17
.w pr[‘]. | [---].pr‘.ank.[---]. | [---.]ank.nši[.---]. | [---.ṯ]br.ḫss.[---]. | [---.--]št.b [---]. | [---.--]b. | [---.--]k. | [---.--]an. | [---.-- 1002.16
]. | [------.]ṯr. | [---.aliy]n.b‘l. | [------.]yrḫ.zbl. | [--.kṯ]r w ḫss. | [---]n.rḥm y.ršp zbl. | [w ‘d]t.ilm.ṯlṯ h. | [ap]nk.krt.ṯ‘.‘[-] 15[128].2.5

ḫsp

lk.[---.b n]ši. | ‘n h.w tphn.[---]. | b grn.yḫrb[.---]. | yǵly.yḫsp.ib[.---]. | ‘l.bt.ab h.nšrm.trḫ[p]n. | ybṣr.ḥbl.diym. | tbky. 19[1AQHT].1.31

ḫsr

. | an.itlk.w aṣd.kl. | ǵr.l kbd.arṣ.kl.gb‘. | l kbd.šdm.npš.ḫsrt. | bn.nšm.npš.hmlt. | arṣ.mǵt.l n‘m y.arṣ. | dbr.ysmt.šd.š 6[49].2.17
.iršt k. | d ḫsrt.w.ank. | aštn..l.iḫ y. | w.ap.ank.mnm. | [ḫ]s[r]t.w.uḫ y. | [y]‘msn.ṯmn. | w.[u]ḫ y.al yb‘rn. 2065.19
kn. | k.[---.]sglt h.hw. | w.b[.---.]uk.nǵr. | w.[---].adny.l.yḫsr. | w.[ank.yd]‘.l.yd‘t. | h[t.---.]l.špš.b‘l k. | ‘[--.s]glt h.at. | h 2060.9
]r[--.--]y. | in m.‘bd k hwt. | [y]rš.‘m y. | mnm.iršt k. | d ḫsrt.w.ank. | aštn..l.iḫ y. | w.ap.ank.mnm. | [ḫ]s[r]t.w.uḫ y. | [2065.16

ḫšwn

.šmn.mr. | [---].kmn.lṯḥ.sbbyn. | [---.-]‘t.lṯḥ.ššmn. | [---].ḫšwn.ṯṯ.mat.nṣ. | [---].ḫmšm.ḥmr.škm. | [---.ṯṯ.dd.]gdl.ṯṯ.dd.š‘ 142[12].11

ḫp

[--.---.ḥ]rn. | [-]rk.ḫ[--.---.-]lk. | [-]sr.n[--.---.]ḥrn. | [--]p.ḫp h.ḫ[--.---.šp]š.l hrm. | [ǵrpl.]‘l.ar[ṣ.---.ḥ]mt. | [---.šp]š.l [hr UG5.8.7
dbḥ n‘mt. | šd[.i]lm.šd.aṯrt.w rḥmy. | [---].y[ṯ]b. | [---]p.gp ym.w yṣǵd.gp..thm. | [yqḥ.]il.mšt‘ltm.mšt‘ltm.l riš.agn. | 23[52].30
.ǵr.w hln.‘nt.tm | ṯḥṣ.b ‘mq.ṯḥtṣb.bn. | qrytm tmḫṣ.lim.ḫp y[m]. | tṣmt.adm.ṣat.š[p]š. | ṯḥt h.k kdrt.ri[š]. | ‘l h.k irby 3['NT].2.7
t.ǵr]. | ap ‘nt tm[ṯḫṣ.b ‘mq.ṯḥtṣb.bn.qrytm.tmḫṣ]. | lim ḫ[p.ym.---]. | [--]m.t[-]t[.---]. | m[-]mt[.---]. | [-----]. | t[---.---]. | t 7.2[130].26

ḫpn

[-----]. | [ḫ]pn.aḥd.b.ṯqlm. | lbš.aḥd.b.ṯqlm. | ḫpn.pṯtm.b ‘šr. | tgmr.ksp 1115.2
ḫpn.d.iqni.w.šmt. | l.iyb‘l. | ṯlṯm.l.mit.š‘rt. | l.šr.‘ṯtrt. | mlbš.ṯr 1107.1
rmlk.ḫpn. | l.‘bdil[m].ḫpn. | tmrtn.š‘rt. | lmd.n.rn. | [---].ḫpn. | dqn.š‘rt. | [lm]d.yrṯ. | [-.]ynḥm.ḫpn. | ṯṯ.lmd.b‘ln. | l.qḥ.ḫ 1117.13
l]k.ṯṯpḥ.mrṯn. | ḫdǵlm.i[---]n.pbn.ndbn.sbd. | šrm.[---].ḫpn. | ḥrš[bhtm.--]n.‘bdyrḫ.ḫdṯn.y‘r. | adb‘l[.---].ḫdṯn.yḥmn. 2011.17
spr.npṣm.d yṣa.b milḫ. | ‘šrm.ḫpn.ḫmš. | kbd.w lpš. | ḫmš.mispt. | mṯ. | w lpš.d sgr b h. | b d. 1109.2
[.l.]‘ṯtrt.šd. | [---.-]rt.mḫṣ.bnš.mlk.yb‘l hm. | [---.--]t.w.ḫpn.l.azzlt. | [---.]l.‘ṯtrt.šd. | [---].yb‘lnn. | [---.--]n.b.ṯlṯ.šnt.l.nṣ 1106.54
šb‘.ḫdǵlm. | l.[---]mn ḫpn. | l[.--.]škn.ḫpn. | l.k[-]w.ḫpn. | l.ṣ[--].š‘[rt]. | l.‘dy.š[‘]r[t]. | ṯlṯ.l.‘d.ab[ǵ]l. | l 1117.3
[rt]. | l.‘dy.š[‘]r[t]. | ṯlṯ.l.‘d.ab[ǵ]l. | l.ydln.š‘rt. | l.kṯrmlk.ḫpn. | l.‘bdil[m].ḫpn. | tmrtn.š‘rt. | lmd.n.rn. | [---].ḫpn. | dqn.š 1117.9
šb‘.ḫdǵlm. | l.[---]mn ḫpn. | l[.--.]škn.ḫpn. | l.k[-]w.ḫpn. | l.ṣ[--].š‘[rt]. | l.‘dy.š[‘]r[t]. | ṯlṯ.l.‘d.ab[ǵ]l. | l.ydln.š‘rt. | l. 1117.4
šb‘.ḫdǵlm. | l.[---]mn ḫpn. | l[.--.]škn.ḫpn. | l.k[-]w.ḫpn. | l.ṣ[--].š‘[rt]. | l.‘dy.š[‘]r[t]. | 1117.2
[---.ṯ]lṯ.‘š[r h.---]. | d bnšm.yd.grbs hm. | w.ṯn.‘šr h.ḫpnt. | [š]šwm.amtm.‘kyt. | yd.llḫ hm. | w.ṯlṯ.l.‘šrm. | ḫpnt.šš 2049.3

h.ẖpnt. | [š]šwm.amtm.ʿkyt. | yd.llẖ hm. | w.ṯlṯ.l.ʿšrm. | ẖpnt.ššwm.ṯn. | pddm.w.d.ṯṯ. | [mr]kbt.w.ḥrṣ. 2049.7
[-----]. | [ẖ]pn.aḥd.b.ṯqlm. | lbš.aḥd.b.ṯqlm. | ẖpn.pṯtm.b ʿšr. | tgmr.ksp.ṯlṯm. | ṯqlm.kbd. 1115.4
pnt. | [---] kdwṯm.[---]. | ẖmš.pld šʿrt. | ṯṯ pld pṯt. | arbʿ ẖpnt pṯt. | ẖmš ẖpnt.šʿrt. | ṯlṯ.ʿšr kdwṯm. 1113.9
[i]t.arbʿt.kbd. | ẖ[mš.]šʿrt. | [---.]tšʿ.kbd.skm. | [arb]ʿm.ẖpnt.pṯt. | [-]r.pldm.dt.šʿrt. | ṯlṯm.ṯlṯ.kbd.mṣrrt. | ʿšr.ṯn.kbd.p 1111.7
ṯm.[---]. | ẖmš.pld šʿrt. | ṯṯ pld pṯt. | arbʿ ẖpnt pṯt. | ẖmš ẖpnt.šʿrt. | ṯlṯ.ʿšr kdwṯm. 1113.10
]. | ṯlṯ.l.ʿd.ab[ǵ]l. | l.ydln.šʿrt. | l.kṯrmlk.ẖpn. | l.ʿbdil[m].ẖpn. | tmrtn.šʿrt. | lmd.n.rn. | [---].ẖpn. | dqn.šʿrt. | [lm]d.yrṯ. | [1117.10
t. | lmd.n.rn. | [---].ẖpn. | dqn.šʿrt. | [lm]d.yrṯ. | [-.]ynḥm.ẖpn. | ṯṯ.lmd.bʿln. | l.qḥ.ẖpnt. | ṯṯ[.-]l.md.ʿṯtr[t]. | l.qḥ.ẖpnt. 1117.16
dqn.šʿrt. | [lm]d.yrṯ. | [-.]ynḥm.ẖpn. | ṯṯ.lmd.bʿln. | l.qḥ.ẖpnt. | ṯṯ[.-]l.md.ʿṯtr[t]. | l.qḥ.ẖpnt. 1117.18
ṯn pǵn.[-]dr | m.ṯn kndwm adrm. | w knd pnṯ.dq. | ṯn ẖpnm.ṯn pldm ǵlmm. | kpld.b[-.-]r[--]. | w blẖ br[-]m p[-]. | b[140[98].4
mm. | k tʿrb.ʿṯtrt.šd.bt.mlk[.---]. | ṯn.skm.šbʿ.mšlt.arbʿ.ẖpnt.[---]. | ẖmšm.ṯlṯ.rkb.ntn.ṯlṯ.mat.[---]. | lg.šmn.rqḥ.šrʿm. UG5.9.1.19
[-----]. | ʿšr[.---]. | ud[-.---]. | ṯn pld mẖ[--.---]. | ṯ[--] ẖpnt. | [---] kdwṯm.[---]. | ẖmš.pld šʿrt. | ṯṯ pld pṯt. | arbʿ ẖpnt 1113.5
.rgm.špš. | mlk.rb.bʿl y.u. | ʿ[--.]mlakt.ʿbd h. | [---.]bʿl k.yẖpn. | [---.]ʿm h.u ky. | [---.--]d k.k.tmǵy. | ml[--.--]š[.ml]k.rb 1018.4
.bʿ]lt.bhtm.š[--.---]. | [---.-]rt.l.dml[.---]. | [b.yrẖ].nql.ṯn.ẖpn[.---]. | [---].aḥd.ẖmš.am[--.---]. | [---.--]m.qmṣ.ṯlṯm.i[qnu. 1106.35
m.ẖpn. | ṯṯ.lmd.bʿln. | l.qḥ.ẖpnt. | ṯṯ[.-]l.md.ʿṯtr[t]. | l.qḥ.ẖpnt. 1117.20

ẖpsry

ṯn.rʿy.uzm. | sǵr.bn.ẖpsry.aḥd. | sǵr.artn.aḥd. | sǵr.ʿdn.aḥd. | sǵr.awldn.aḥd. | sǵr.i 1140.2
spr.mẖṣm. | bn.ẖpšry.b.šbn. | ilštmʿym. | y[---.]bn.ʿšq. | [---.]bn.tqy. | [---.]bn.šl 1041.2

ẖpšry

spr.mẖṣm. | bn.ẖpšry.b.šbn. | ilštmʿym. | y[---.]bn.ʿšq. | [---.]bn.tqy. | [---.]bn.šl 1041.2

ẖpr

b hkl h.ṣḥ. | šbʿm.bn.aṯrt. | špq.ilm.krm.y[n]. | špq.ilht.ẖprt[.yn]. | špq.ilm.alpm.y[n]. | špq.ilht.arẖt[.yn]. | špq.ilm.k 4[51].6.48

ẖpty

ʿr[t]. | amd[y]. | atl[g]. | bṣr[y]. | [---]. | [---]y. | ar. | agm.w.ẖpty. | ẖlb.ṣpn. | mril. | ʿnmky. | ʿnqpat. | ṭbq. | hzp. | gnʿy. | mʿrb 71[113].49
rkby. | šḥq. | ǵn. | ṣʿ. | mld. | amdy. | ẖlbʿprm. | ẖpty. | [ẖr]ṣbʿ. | [mʿ]rb. 2077.8
krd. | [ẖl]bʿprm. | [q]dš. | [a]mdy. | [gn]ʿy. | mʿqb. | agm. | ẖpty. | ypr. | ẖrṣbʿ. | uẖnp. | art. | [--]n. | [-----]. | [-----]. | nnu. | šm 2058.2.3
dm.yn. | šmgy.kd.yn. | hzp.tšʿ.yn. | [b]ir.ʿšr[.---]m hsp. | ẖpty.kdm[.---]. | [a]gm.arbʿ[.---]. | šrš.šbʿ.mṣb. | rqd.ṯlṯ.mṣb.w. 2004.30
m.bnšm.[b.]ʿd[--]. | arbʿ.bnšm.b.ag[m]y. | arbʿ.bnšm.b.ẖpty. | ṯṯ.bnšm.b.bir. | ṯṯ.bnšm b.uẖnp. | ṯn.bnšm.b.ẖrṣbʿ. | arb 2076.12
]. | art.[---]. | [-----]. | [-----]. | l [----]. | b[--.---]. | ẖl[--.---]. | ẖp[ty.---]. 1147.9

ẖptr

.mks.bšr h. | tmtʿ.md h.b ym.ṯn. | npyn h.b nhrm. | štt.ẖptr.l išt. | ẖbrṯ.l ẓr.pḥmm. | tʿpp.ṯr.il.d pid. | tǵẓy.bny.bnwt. 4[51].2.8

ẖpṯ

bu.ṣbi.ngb. | w yṣi.ʿdn.mʿ. | ṣbu k.ul.mad. | ṯlṯ.mat.rbt. | ẖpṯ.d bl.spr. | ṯnn.d bl.hg. | hlk.l alpm.ẖdd. | w l rbt.kmyr. | [a 14[KRT].2.90
.[---].ar. | bn.[---].b.ar. | špšyn[.---.]yṯb.b.ar. | bn.ag[p]ṯ.ẖpṯ.d[.yṯb.b].šʿrt. | yly.bn.ṯrnq.[-]r.d.yṯb.b.ilštmʿ. | ilšlm.bn.g 2015.1.25
ṯkt. | ṯṯkr.[--]dn. | ʿm.krt.mswn h. | arẖ.tzǵ.l ʿgl h. | bn.ẖpṯ.l umht hm. | k tnḥn.udmm. | w yʿny.krt.ṯʿ. 15[128].1.6

ẖpṯt

ttn.tk.ǵr. | knkny.ša.ǵr.ʿl ydm. | ẖlb.l ẓr.rḥtm w rd. | bt ẖpṯt.arṣ.tspr b y | rdm.arṣ.w tdʿ ilm. | k mtt.yšmʿ.aliyn.bʿl. | y 5[67].5.15
| ʿm.tlm.ǵṣr.arṣ. | ša.ǵr.ʿl.ydm. | ẖlb.l ẓr.rḥtm. | w rd.bt ẖpṯt. | arṣ.tspr.b y | rdm.arṣ. | idk.al.ttn. | pnm.tk.qrt h. | hmry 4[51].8.7

ẖṣb

r[t.bht.ʿnt.w tqry.ǵlmm.b št.ǵr]. | ap ʿnt tm[tẖṣ.b ʿmq.tẖtṣb.bn.qrytm.tmẖṣ]. | lim ẖ[p.ym.---]. | [--]m.t[-]t[.---]. | m[- 7.2[130].25
bht.ʿnt.w tqry.ǵlmm. | b št.ǵr.w hln.ʿnt.tm | tẖṣ.b ʿmq.tẖtṣb.bn. | qrytm tmẖṣ.lim.ẖp y[m]. | tṣmt.adm.ṣat.š[p]š. | tḥt 3[ʿNT].2.6
bt h.tmǵyn. | tštql.ilt.l hkl h. | w l.šbʿt.tmtẖṣ h.b ʿmq. | tẖtṣb.bn.qrtm.ttʿr. | ksat.l mhr.ṯʿr.ṯlḥnt. | l ṣbim.hdmm.l ǵzr 3[ʿNT].2.20
t r[išt]. | [l bmt h.---.]hy bt h tʿrb. | [---.tm]tẖṣ b ʿmq. | [tẖtṣb.bn.qrtm.ttʿr.ṯlḥnt.]l ṣbim. | [hdmm.l ǵzrm.mid.tmtẖṣn 7.1[131].5
l b dm. | ḏmr.ḥlqm.b mmʿ.mhrm. | ʿd.tšbʿ.tmtẖṣ.b bt. | tẖṣb.bn.ṯlḥnm.ymḥ. | [b]bt.dm.ḏmr.yṣq.šmn. | šlm.b ṣʿ.trḥṣ. 3[ʿNT].2.30
r.ṯʿr.ṯlḥnt. | l ṣbim.hdmm.l ǵzrm. | mid.tmtẖṣn.w tʿn. | tẖtṣb.w tḥdy.ʿnt. | tǵdd.kbd h.b ṣḥq.ymlu. | lb h.b šmẖt.kbd.ʿ 3[ʿNT].2.24
.ttʿr.ṯlḥnt.]l ṣbim. | [hdmm.l ǵzrm.mid.tmtẖṣn.w t]ʿn.tẖtṣb. | [w tḥdy.ʿnt.tǵdd.kbd h.b ṣḥ]q.ymlu.lb h. | [b šmẖt.kb 7.1[131].6

ẖṣḥ

qḥ.šʿrt. | urẖ.ln.kkrm. | w.rḥd.kd.šmn. | drt.b.kkr. | ubn.ẖṣḥ.kkr. | kkr.lqḥ.ršpy. | tmtrn.bn.pnmn. | kkr. | bn.sgṯtn. | kk 1118.5

ẖṣr

qmḥ.d.kly.b bt.skn. | l.illḏrm. | ltḥ.ẖṣr.b.šbʿ.ddm. 2093.3

ẖṣt

[l]b. | rmṣt.ilhm.bʿlm.dṯt.w kšm.ẖmš. | ʿṯr h.mlun.šnpt.ẖṣt h.bʿl.ṣpn š. | [--]ṯ š.ilt.mgdl š.ilt.asrm š. | w l ll.šp. pgr.w ṯ 34[1].10

ẖqn

ṯm. | [---.]ʿšrt. | [-----]. | b.[---.---]r. | b.ann[.---.-]ny[-]. | b.ẖqn.[---]m.ṣ[-]n. | [b].bn.ay[--.---].l.ʿšrm. | [-]gp[.---.]ʿrny.ṯṯm. 2054.2.16

ẖqr

[---].pi[--.-]qš. | [--]pš.šn[--]. | t̠[-]r.b iš[-]. | bʿl h.šʿ[-]rt. | ẖqr.[--.t̠q]l rb. | t̠l[t̠.---]. | aḥt.ẖm[-.---]. | b ym.dbḥ.t̠p[-]. | aḥt.l 39[19].10

ẖr

w mǵmǵ w b[ṣql ʿrgz]. | [ydk aḥ]d h w yṣq b ap h. | [k ẖr]ššw ẖndrt̠ w t̠[qd m]r. | [ydk aḥd h w yṣq b ap h. | [k l yẖ 160[55].6
mǵmǵ]. | w [bṣql.ʿrgz.ydk]. | a[ḥd h.w.yṣq.b.ap h]. | k.[ẖr.ššw.ẖndrt̠]. | w.t̠[qd.mr.ydk.aḥd h]. | w.y[ṣq.b.ap h]. | k.l.ẖ 161[56].5
k [ẖr ššw mǵmǵ]. | w [bṣql.ʿrgz.ydk]. | a[ḥd h.w.yṣq.b.ap h]. | k.[161[56].2
[k.---.]šš[w.---]. | [---.w]yṣq b a[p h]. | [k ẖr š]šw mǵmǵ w b[ṣql ʿrgz]. | [ydk aḥ]d h w yṣq b ap h. | [k 160[55].4
[-----]. | [---.r]ḥm.tld. | [---.]ẖrm.t̠n.ym. | tš[.---.]ymm.lk. | hrg.ar[bʿ.]ymm.bṣr. | kp.šsk k. 13[6].3
kt.ʿt̠qbm. | [---]m.ʿẓpn.l pit. | m[--]m[.--]tm.w mdbḥt. | ẖr[.---.]ʿl.kbkbt. | nʿm.[--.-]llm.trtḥṣ. | btlt.ʿn[t].tptrʿ t̠d[h]. | li 13[6].17

ẖra

.t̠kmn. | w šnm.w ngšnn.ḥby. | bʿl.qrnm w d̠nb.ylšn. | b ẖri h.w t̠nt h.ql.il.[--]. | il.k yrdm.arṣ.ʿnt. | w ʿt̠trt.tṣdn.[---]. | [UG5.1.1.21
ššw ẖndrt̠ w t̠[qd m]r. | [ydk aḥd h w yṣq b ap h. | [k l yẖru w]l yt̠tn mss št qlql. | [w št ʿrgz y]dk aḥd h w yṣq b ap 160[55].8
w.ẖndrt̠]. | w.t̠[qd.mr.ydk.aḥd h]. | w.y[ṣq.b.ap h]. | k.l.ẖ[ru.w.l.yt̠tn.ššw]. | mss.[št.qlql.w.št]. | ʿrgz[.ydk.aḥd h]. | w. 161[56].8

ẖran

ʿrby. | ṣdqn.gbʿly. | bn.ypy.gbʿly. | bn.grgs.ilštmʿy. | bn.ẖran.ilštmʿy. | bn.abdʿn.ilštmʿy. | bn.ʿn.rqdy. | bn.gʿyn. | bn.ǵr 87[64].30
. | b[n].ḥyn. | d̠mn.šʿrty. | bn.arwdn.ilštʿy. | bn grgs. | bn.ẖran. | bn.arš[w.b]ṣry. | bn.ykn. | bn.lṣn.ʿrmy. | bn.bʿyn.šly. | b 99[327].1.10
bn.ẖran. | bn.srt. | bn.adn. | bn.ʿgw. | bn.urt. | aẖdbu. | pḥ[-]. | bn.ʿb 121[307].1
wdn.dd. | mnḥm.w.kbln. | bn.ǵlm.dd. | bn.tbšn.dd. | bn.ẖran.w[.---]. | [-]n.yʿrtym. | gmm.w.bn.p[--]. | trn.w.p[-]y. | bn. 131[309].8

ẖrb

.---]n. | [-----]. | hlk.[---.b n]ši. | ʿn h.w tphn.[---]. | b grn.yẖrb[.---]. | yǵly.yẖsp.ib[.---]. | ʿl.bt.ab h.nšrm.trẖ[p]n. | ybṣr. 19[1AQHT].1.30

ẖrbǵlm

ʿ[ṣd.---]. | [b.]gt.ḥrt̠m.ẖm[š.---]. | [n]it.krk.mʿṣ[d.---]. | b.ẖrbǵlm.ǵlm[n]. | w.trhy.at̠t h. | w.mlky.b[n] h. | ily.mrily.tdgr 2048.19

ẖrg

[---.b]n.yšm[ʿ]. | [---.]mlkr[-] h.b.nt̠k. | [---.]šbʿm. | [---.]ẖrg.ʿšrm. | [---.]abn.ksp.t̠lt̠. | [---].bty.ksp.ʿšr[t]. | [---.-]mbʿl.[-- 2153.5

ẖrd

n.špš.nr. | b y.mid.w um. | tšmẖ.m ab. | w al.trẖln. | ʿtn.ẖrd.ank. | ʿm ny.šlm. | kll. | w mnm. | šlm ʿm. | um y. | ʿm y.tt̠tb 1015.13
spr.ẖrd.arr. | ap arbʿm[.--]. | pd[.---.ẖm]šm.kb[d]. | ǵb[-.---.]kbd. | 2042.1
š | al. | w mlk.d mlk. | b ḥwt.špḥ. | l ydn.ʿbd.mlk. | d št.ʿl.ẖrd h. | špḥ.al.thbṭ. | ẖrd.ʿps.aẖd.kw | sgt. | ẖrd ksp.[--]r. | ym 2062.2.4
l.d̠rdn. | bʿl y.rgm. | bn.ẖrn k. | mǵy. | hbṭ.hw. | ẖrd.w.šl hw. | qr[-]. | akl n.b.grnt. | l.bʿr. | ap.krmm. | ẖlq. | qrt 2114.6
štt.mlk. | kd.bn.amht [-]t. | w.bn.mṣrym. | arbʿm.yn. | l.ẖrd. | ẖmšm.ẖmš. | kbd.tgmr. | yn.d.nkly. 1089.12
.mlk. | d št.ʿl.ẖrd h. | špḥ.al.thbṭ. | ẖrd.ʿps.aẖd.kw | sgt. | ẖrd ksp.[--]r. | ymm.w[.---]. | [-----]. | w[.-----]. | [-----]. 2062.2.8
b ḥwt.špḥ. | l ydn.ʿbd.mlk. | d št.ʿl.ẖrd h. | špḥ.al.thbṭ. | ẖrd.ʿps.aẖd.kw | sgt. | ẖrd ksp.[--]r. | ymm.w[.---]. | [-----]. | w[. 2062.2.6
.ʿšr. | hbt̠nm. | t̠mn. | md̠rǵlm. | t̠mnym.t̠mn.kbd. | tgmr.ẖrd. | arbʿm.l.mit. | t̠n.kbd. 1031.15
-.]l h. | [---.]l h. | [---.--]š.l h. | [---].l h. | [--.]spr[.---]. | [--.]ẖrd[.---]. | [---.]l h. 2133.11

ẖrẖb

ašr nkl w ib[.bt]. | ẖrẖb.mlk qẓ ẖrẖb m | lk aǵzt.b sǵ[--.]špš. | yrẖ yt̠kḥ yẖ[bq] [-]. | tld bt.[--]t 24[77].2
ašr nkl w ib[.bt]. | ẖrẖb.mlk qẓ ẖrẖb m | lk aǵzt.b sǵ[--.]špš. | yrẖ yt̠kḥ yẖ[bq] [- 24[77].2
tt[--.---.-]l | ʿ.l kt̠rt hl[l.sn]nt. | ylak yrẖ ny[r] šmm.ʿm. | ẖr[ẖ]b mlk qẓ.tn nkl y | rẖ ytrẖ.ib tʿrb m b bh | t h.w atn mh 24[77].17
hrm iq | nim.atn šd h krm[m]. | šd dd h ḥrnqm.w | yʿn ẖrẖb mlk qẓ [l]. | nʿmn.ilm l ẖt[n]. | m.bʿl trẖ pdry b[t h]. | aq 24[77].24

ẖrṭ

ṭ h.nẖt.il.ymnn.mṭ.yd h.yšu. | yr.šmm h.yr.b šmm.ʿṣr.yẖrṭ yšt. | l pḥm.il.at̠tm.k ypt.hm.at̠tm.tṣḥn. | y mt.mt.nḥtm. 23[52].38

ẖrẓn

spr.ytnm. | bn.ẖlbym. | bn.ady. | bn.ʿt̠try. | bn.ẖrẓn. | ady. | bn.birtn. | bn.ḥrẓn. | bn.bddn. | bn.anny. | ytršp. | 115[301].1.5

ẖrẓʿ

md m. | bn.dgn.yhrr m. | bʿl.ngt̠ hm.b pʿn h. | w il hd.b ẖrẓʿ h. | [-----]. | [--]t.[---]. | [---.]ʿn[.---]. | pnm[.---]. | bʿl.n[--.---] 12[75].1.41

ẖry

t.ugrt.w [np]y.nt̠t.ušn.yp kn.ulp qty. | ulp.ddmy.ul[p.ẖ]ry.ulp.ẖty.ulp.alt̠y. | ulp.ǵbr.ulp.[ẖbt] kn[.u]lp.mdll kn.ul 32[2].1.29
]y. | [---].w n[py.---].u t̠ẖt̠i[n.ulp.qty]. | ulp.ddmy.ul[p.ẖry.u]lp.ẖty.ulp[.alt̠y.ulp.]ǵbr. | ulp.ẖbt kn.ulp.md[ll k]n.ul 32[2].1.12
--]. | w npy.nqmd.ušn.yp km.ulp.q[ty.ulp.ddm]y. | ulp.ẖry.ulp.ẖ[t]y.ulp.alt̠y.ul[p.ǵbr.]ulp. | ẖbt km.ulp.m[dl]l km. 32[2].1.21
[---.w np]y.ugrt. | [---.u t̠ẖt̠u.ulp.qty.ulp.ddm]y. | [ulp.ẖry.ulp.ẖty.ulp.alt̠y.ulp.ǵbr]. | [ulp.ẖbt km.ulp.mdll km.ulp. 32[2].1.7
-]r. | [---.]npy. | [---.ušn.yp kn.ulp.q]ty. | [ulp.ddmy.ulp.ẖry.ulp.ẖty.ulp.alt̠y]. | [ulp.ǵbr.ulp.ẖbt kn.ulp.mdll kn.ulp.] APP.I[-].2.13
-.w]npy.annpdgl. | [ušn.yp kn.ulp.qty.ulp.]ddmy.ulp ẖry. | [ulp.ẖty.ulp.alt̠y.ulp.ǵbr.ul]p.ẖbt kn. | [ulp.mdll kn.ulp APP.I[-].1.4
ʿr]mt.w npy. | [---.ušn.yp km.ulp.]qty. | [ulp.ddmy.ulp.ẖry.ulp.ẖty.u]lp.alt̠y. | [ulp.ǵbr.ulp.ẖbt km.ulp.mdll km.ulp] APP.I[-].1.15
kd.l mrynm. | šbʿ yn. | l mrynm. | b yt̠bmlk. | kdm.ǵbiš ẖry. | ẖmš yn.b d. | bḥ mlkt. | b mdrʿ. | t̠lt̠ bt.il | ann. | kd.bt.ila 1090.13

ḫryn

.|ʿbdmlk.bn.ʿmyn.|agyn.rʿy.|abmlk.bn.ilrš.|iḫyn.bn.ḫryn.|[ab]ǵl.bn.gdn.|[---].bn.bqš.|[---].bn.pdn.|[---.bn.-]ky. 102[323].4.11
ṯn.b gt.mzln.|ṯn.b ulm.|abmn.b gt.mʿrb.|atn.|ḫryn.|bn.ʿnt.|llwn.|agdṯb.|aǵltn.|[-]wn.|bldn.|[-]ln.|[-]ld 1061.5
n.|alṯy.|sǵr.npr.|bn.ḫty.|ṯn.bnš ibrdr.|bnš tlmi.|sǵr.ḫryn.|ʿdn.w sǵr h.|bn.ḥgbn. 2082.8

ḫrmln

ǵrm.|[š]d.ṯǵr.mṯpit.b d.bn.iryn.|[u]bdy.šrm.|[š]d.bn.ḫrmln.b d.bn.tnn.|[š]d.bn.ḫrmln.ṯn.b d.bn.ḫdmn.|[u]bdy.n 82[300].2.10
.|ypln.bn.ylḥn.|ʿzn.bn.mll.|šrm.|[b]n.špš[yn].|[b]n.ḫrmln.|bn.tnn.|bn.pndr.|bn.nqq.|ḥrš.bhtm.|bn.izl.|bn.ibl 85[80].1.12
.iryn.|[u]bdy.šrm.|[š]d.bn.ḫrmln.b d.bn.tnn.|[š]d.bn.ḫrmln.ṯn.b d.bn.ḫdmn.|[u]bdy.nqdm.|[ṯlṯ].šdm.d.nʿrb.gt.n 82[300].2.11

ḫrmṯt

.|b.gwl.ṯmn.ḫrmṯt.[nit].|krk.mʿṣd.mqb.|[b] gt.ipṯl.ṯṯ.ḫrmṯ[t.nit].|[k]rk.mʿṣd.mqb.|[b.g]t.bir.ʿš[r.---].|[---].krk.mʿ 2048.13
b.gt.ʿmq.ḫmš.ḫrmṯt.n[it].|krk.mʿṣd.mqb.|b.gwl.ṯmn.ḫrmṯt.[nit].|krk.mʿṣd.mqb.|[b] gt.ipṯl.ṯṯ.ḫrmṯ[t.nit].|[k]rk. 2048.11
ṯt.|ṯt.nitm.ṯn.mʿṣdm.ṯn.mqbm.|krk.aḥt.|b.sǵy.ḫmš.ḫrmṯt.nit.|krk.mʿṣd.mqb.|b.gt.ʿmq.ḫmš.ḫrmṯt.n[it].|krk.m 2048.7
.|b.sǵy.ḫmš.ḫrmṯt.nit.|krk.mʿṣd.mqb.|b.gt.ʿmq.ḫmš.ḫrmṯt.n[it].|krk.mʿṣd.mqb.|b.gwl.ṯmn.ḫrmṯt.[nit].|krk.mʿṣ 2048.9
ḫmšt.ʿš[rt].|ksp.ʿl.agd[ṯb].|w nit w mʿṣd.|w ḫrmṯt.|ʿšrt.ksp.|ʿl.ḫ[z]rn.|w.nit.w[.mʿṣd].|w.ḫ[rmṯt].|ʿš[r.- 2053.4
|w.ḫ[rmṯt].|ʿš[r.---].|ʿl[.---].|w.ni[t.---].|w[.mʿṣd].|w ḫr[mṯt].|[ʿ]šr[.---].|[ʿ]l [-]g[-.---].|w ni[t.w.mʿṣd].|w ḫrmṯt. 2053.13
ʿṣd.|w ḫrmṯt.|ʿšrt.ksp.|ʿl.ḫ[z]rn.|w.nit.w[.mʿṣd].|w.ḫ[rmṯt].|ʿš[r.---].|ʿl[.---].|w.ni[t.---].|w[.mʿṣd].|w ḫr[mṯt].| 2053.8
b.atlg.ṯlṯ.ḫrmṯt.ṯṯm.|mḫrhn.nit.mit.krk.mit.|mʿṣd.ḫmšm.mqb.[ʿ]šrm 2048.1
ḫr[mṯt].|[ʿ]šr[.---].|[ʿ]l [-]g[-.---].|w ni[t.w.mʿṣd].|w ḫrmṯt.|ṯlṯm.ar[bʿ].|kbd.ksp.|ʿl.tgyn.|w ʿl.aṯt h.|yph.mʿnt.| 2053.17
.mit.krk.mit.|mʿṣd.ḫmšm.mqb.[ʿ]šrm.|b.ulm.ṯṯ.ʿšr h.ḫrmṯt.|ṯt.nitm.ṯn.mʿṣdm.ṯn.mqbm.|krk.aḥt.|b.sǵy.ḫmš.ḫr 2048.4

ḫrn

n.bht.ksp.|w ḫrṣ.bht.ṯhrm.|iqnim.šmḫ.aliyn.|bʿl.ṣḥ.ḫrn.b bht h.|ʿḏbt.b qrb hkl h.|yblnn ǵrm.mid.ksp.|gbʿm lḥ 4[51].5.98
bšrt k.yblt.y[b]n.|bt.l k.km.aḫ k.w ḥẓr.|km.ary k.ṣḥ.ḫrn.|b bht k.ʿḏbt.b qrb.|hkl k.tbl k.ǵrm.|mid.ksp.gbʿm.mḥ 4[51].5.91
.yklln h.|hm.bt.lbnt.yʿmsn h.|l yrgm.l aliyn bʿl.|ṣḥ.ḫrn.b bhm k.|ʿḏbt.b qrb.hkl k.|tbl k.ǵrm.mid.ksp.|gbʿm.m 4[51].5.75
l.ḏrdn.|bʿl y.rgm.|bn.ḫrn k.|mǵy.|hbṭ.hw.|ḫrd.w.šl hw.|qr[-].|akl n.b.grnt.|l.bʿ 2114.3

ḫrny

ḫrny.w.rʿ h.|klbr.w.rʿ h.|tškrǵ.w.rʿ h.|ǵlwš.w.rʿ h.|kdrš.w. 2083.1.1

ḫrpn

[--.---.--]l.|aty[n.bn.]šmʿnt.|ḥnn[.bn].pls.|abrš[p.bn.]ḫrpn.|gmrš[.bn].mrnn.|ʿbdmlk.bn.ʿmyn.|agyn.rʿy.|abmlk. 102[323].4.6

ḫrpnt

t.l.lṣb h ḫšʿr klb.|[w]riš.pqq.w šr h.|yšt.aḥd h.dm zt.ḫrpnt. UG5.1.2.6

ḫrṣ

.urtn.b.arbʿm.|arbʿt.ʿšrt.ḫrṣ.|b.ṯqlm.kbd.arbʿm.|ʿšrt.ḫrṣ.b.arbʿm.|mit.ḫršḫ.b.ṯqlm.|w.šbʿ.ʿšr.šmn.|d.l.yṣa.bt.mlk 2100.18
bd.ksp.|ṯlṯ.ktnt.b d.an[r]my.|b.ʿšrt.ksp.b.a[--].|ṯqlm.ḫr[ṣ.]b.ṯmnt.ksp.|ʿšrt.ksp.b.alp.[b d].bn.[---].|tšʿ.ṣin.b.tšʿt.k 2101.20
.b d.bn.kyn.|ʿšr.kkr.šʿrt.|b d.urtn.b.arbʿm.|arbʿt.ʿšrt.ḫrṣ.|b.ṯqlm.kbd.arbʿm.|ʿšrt.ḫrṣ.b.arbʿm.|mit.ḫršḫ.b.ṯqlm.| 2100.16
|b d[.ʿb]dym.ṯlṯ.kkr šʿrt.|iqn[i]m.ṯṯt.ʿšrt.ksp h.|ḫmšt.ḫrṣ.bt.il.|b.ḫmšt.ʿšrt.ksp.|ḫmš.mat.šmt.|b.ʿšrt.ksp.|ʿšr.ṣin. 2100.5
l k.ǵrm.|mid.ksp.gbʿm.mḥmd..|ḫrṣ.w bn.bht.ksp.|w ḫrṣ.bht.ṯhrm.|iqnim.šmḫ.aliyn.|bʿl.ṣḥ.ḫrn.b bht h.|ʿḏbt.b q 4[51].5.96
.|gbʿm.mḥmd.ḫrṣ.|ybl k.udr.ilqṣm.|w bn.bht.ksp.w ḫrṣ.|bht.ṯhrm.iqnim.|šmḫ.btlt.ʿnt.tdʿṣ.|pʿnm.w tr.arṣ.|idk. 4[51].5.80
lḥm.hm.štym.lḥ[m].|b ṯlḥnt.lḥm št.|b krpnm.yn.b k.ḫrṣ.|dm.ʿṣm.hm.yd.il mlk.|yḫss k.ahbt.ṯr.tʿrr k.|w tʿn.rbt.a 4[51].4.37
ṯd.---].|b ḥrb.[mlḥt.qṣ.mri].|šty.kr[pnm.yn.---].|b ks.ḫr[ṣ.dm.ʿṣm.---].|ks.ksp[.---].|krpn.[---].|w ṯṯn.[---].|tʿl.tr[- 5[67].4.16
ǵtm.ṯd.|b ḥrb.mlḥt.qṣ[.m]r|i.tšty.krp[nm.y]n.|[b k]s.ḫrṣ.d[m.ʿṣm].|[---.--]n.|[---.---]t.|[---.--]ṯ.|[---.--]n. 4[51].6.59
š[---].|[---.b ḥ]rb.mlḥ[t.qṣ].|[mri.tšty.krpnm].yn.b ks.ḫ[rṣ].|[dm.ʿṣm.---]n.krpn.ʿl.[k]rpn.|[---.]ym.w tʿl.trṯ.|[---].y 17[2AQHT].6.5
ǵtm.|[ṯd.b ḥrb.m]lḥt.qṣ.|[mri.tšty.k]rpnm yn.|[b ks.ḫrṣ.dm].ʿṣm. 4[51].3.44
iyn.bʿl.|[hw]t.aliy.q|[rdm.]bht y.bnt.|[dt.ksp.dtm].|[ḫrṣ.hk]l y.|[---.]aḫ y.|[---.]aḫ y.|[----]y.|[---.]rb.|[---].ṣḥt.| 4[51].8.37
ry.bt y.|iqḥ.ašʿrb.ǵlmt.|ḥẓr y.ṯn h.wspm.|atn.w ṯlṯ h.ḫrṣm.|ylk ym.w ṯn.|ṯlṯ.rbʿ.ym.|aḫr.špšm.b rbʿ.|ymǵy.l ud 14[KRT].4.206
.ʿḏbt.b qrb.|hkl k.tbl k.ǵrm.|mid.ksp.gbʿm.mḥmd..|ḫrṣ.w bn.bht.ksp.|w ḫrṣ.bht.ṯhrm.|iqnim.šmḫ.aliyn.|bʿl.ṣḥ 4[51].5.95
ṯlṯ mrkb[t].|ṣpyt b ḫrṣ[.w] ṣmdm trm.d [ṣ]py.|w.trm.aḥdm.|ṣpym.|ṯlṯ mrkbt 1122.2
n]qmd.|l špš.arn.ṯn[.ʿšr h.]mn.|ʿṣrm.ṯql.kbd[.ks].mn.ḫrṣ.|w arbʿ.ktnt.w [---]b.|[ḫm]š.mat pḥm.|[ḫm]š[.m]at.iqn 64[118].20
r.tšu.g h.]w tṣḥ.šmʿ.mʿ.|[l aqht.ǵzr.i]rš.ksp.w atn k.|[ḫrṣ.w aš]lḥ k.w tn.qšt k.[l].|[ʿnt.tq]ḥ[.q]ṣʿt k.ybmt.limm.|w 17[2AQHT].6.18
.il.ʿtk.|mḫšt.klbt.ilm išt.|klt.bt.il.ḏbb.imtḫṣ.ksp.|itrṯ.ḫrṣ.ṭrd.bʿl.|b mrym.ṣpn.mšṣṣ.[-]kʿ[-].|udn h.grš h.l ksi.mlk 3[ʿNT].3.44
h.|ʿḏbt.b qrb hkl h.|yblnn ǵrm.mid.ksp.|gbʿm lḥmd.ḫrṣ.|yblnn.udr.ilqṣm.|yak.l kṯr.w ḫss.|w ṯb l mspr..k tlakn 4[51].5.101
k.|ʿḏbt.b qrb.hkl k.|tbl k.ǵrm.mid.ksp.|gbʿm.mḥmd.ḫrṣ.|ybl k.udr.ilqṣm.|w bn.bht.ksp.w ḫrṣ.|bht.ṯhrm.iqnim. 4[51].5.78
w ušn.|ab.adm.w ṯṯb.|mlakm.l h.lm.ank.|ksp.w yrq.ḫrṣ.|yd.mqm h.w ʿbd.|ʿlm.ṯlṯ.sswm.mrkbt.|b trbṣt.bn.amt. 14[KRT].3.138
lakm.l k.ʿm.krt.|mswn h.ṯḥm.pbl.mlk.|qḥ.ksp.w yrq.ḫrṣ.|yd.mqm h.w ʿbd.ʿlm.|ṯlṯ.sswm.mrkbt.|b trbṣ.bn.amt.| 14[KRT].3.126
[-----].|[-----].|[-----.lm].|[ank.ksp.w yrq].|[ḫrṣ.]yd.mqm h.|[w ʿb]d.ʿlm.ṯlṯ.|[ssw]m.mrkbt b trbṣ bn.am 14[KRT].2.54
tš[an.g hm.w tṣḥn].|ṯḥ[m.pbl.mlk].|qḥ[.ksp.w yrq].|ḫrṣ.[yd.mqm h].|w ʿbd[.ʿlm.ṯlṯ].|sswm.m[rkbt].|b trbṣ.[bn. 14[KRT].6.270
g.]krt.l ḥẓ[r y].|w yʿn[y.k]rt[.ṯ]ʿ.|lm.ank.ksp.|w yr[q.ḫrṣ].|yd.mqm h.w ʿbd.|ʿlm.ṯlṯ.sswm.|mrkbt.b trbṣ.|bn.amt 14[KRT].6.283
]n.|w r[gm.l krt.]ṯʿ.|ṯḥm[.pbl.mlk].|qḥ.[ksp.w yr]q.|ḫrṣ[.yd.mqm] h.|ʿbd[.ʿlm.ṯlṯ].|ss[wm.mrkbt].|b[trbṣ.bn.a 14[KRT].5.251
.ilm.|hyn.ʿly.l mpḫm.|b d.ḫss.mṣbṭm.|yṣq.ksp.yšl|ḥ.ḫrṣ.yṣq.ksp.|l alpm.ḫrṣ.yṣq|m.l rbbt.|yṣq-ḫym.w tbṯḫ.|kt.i 4[51].1.27

ḫrṣ

. | b d.ḫss.mṣbṭm. | yṣq.ksp.yšl | ḥ.ḫrṣ.yṣq.ksp. | l alpm.ḫrṣ.yṣq | m.l rbbt. | yṣq-ḫym.w tbṯḫ. | kt.il.dt.rbtm. | kt.il.nbt. 4[51].1.28
m.w tbṯḫ. | kt.il.dt.rbtm. | kt.il.nbt.b ksp. | šmrgt.b dm.ḫrṣ. | kḥt.il.nḥt. | b ẓr.hdm.id. | d prša.b br. | n'l.il.d qblbl. | 'ln. 4[51].1.33
id.yph.mlk. | r[š]p.ḫgb.ap. | w[.n]pš.ksp. | w ḫrṣ.km[-]. | w.ḫ[--.-]lp. | w.š.l[--]p. | w[.--.-]nš. | i[--.---]. | w[.---] 2005.1.4
lk.rb.b'l h. | ks.ḫrṣ.ktn.mit.pḥm. | mit.iqni.l mlkt. | ks.ḫrṣ.ktn.mit.pḥm. | mit.iqni.l uṯryn. | ks.ksp.ktn.mit.pḥm. | mi 64[118].29
argmn.nqmd.mlk. | ugrt.d ybl.l špš. | mlk.rb.b'l h. | ks.ḫrṣ.ktn.mit.pḥm. | mit.iqni.l mlkt. | ks.ḫrṣ.ktn.mit.pḥm. | mit 64[118].27
bm.ymn. | tlk.škn.'l.ṣrrt. | adn k.šqrb.[---]. | b mgn k.w ḫrṣ.l kl. | apnk.ģzr.ilḥu. | [m]rḥ h.yiḫd.b yd. | [g]rgr h.bm.ym 16.1[125].45
w mri ilm.'glm.dt.šnt. | imr.qmṣ.llim.k ksp. | l 'brm.zt.ḫrṣ.l 'brm.kš. | dpr.ṯlḥn.b q'l.b q'l. | mlkm.hn.ym.yṣq.yn.ṯmk 22.2[124].15
šb' pamt. | l ilm.šb['.]l kṯr. | 'lm.t'rbn.gṯrm. | bt.mlk.ṯql.ḫrṣ. | l špš.w yrḫ.l gṯr. | ṯql.ksp.ṭb.ap w np[š]. | l 'nt h.ṯql.ḫrṣ. 33[5].10
rṣ. | l špš.w yrḫ.l gṯr. | ṯql.ksp.ṭb.ap w np[š]. | l 'nt h.ṯql.ḫrṣ. | l špš[.w y]rḫ.l gṯr.ṯn. | [ṯql.ksp].ṭb.ap.w npš. | [---].bt.alp 33[5].13
ḥm h.d nzl. | lqḥ.msrr.'ṣr.db[ḥ]. | yṣq.b gl.ḥṯt.yn. | b gl.ḫrṣ.nbt.w 'ly. | l ẓr.mgdl.rkb. | ṯkmm.ḥmt.nša. | [y]d h.šmmh. 14[KRT].4.165
m k.d]nzl. | qḥ.ms[rr.]'ṣr. | dbḥ.ṣ[q.b g]l.ḥṯt. | yn.b gl[.ḫ]rṣ.nbt. | 'l.l ẓr.[mg]dl. | w 'l.l ẓr.[mg]dl.rkb. | ṯkmm.ḥm[t].š 14[KRT].2.72
]y[mm].td.išt. | b bht m.n[bl]at.b hkl m. | sb.ksp.l rqm.ḫrṣ. | nṣb.l lbnt.šmḫ. | aliyn.b'l.ht y.bnt. | dt.ksp.hkl y.dtm. | ḫ 4[51].6.34
nṣb.l lbnt.šmḫ. | aliyn.b'l.ht y.bnt. | dt.ksp.hkl y.dtm. | ḫrṣ.'dbt.bht[h.b']l. | y'db.hd.'db[.'d]bt. | hkl h.ṭbḫ.alpm[.ap]. 4[51].6.38
.ib t'rb m b bh | t h.w atn mhr h l a | b h.alp ksp w rbt ḫ | rṣ.išlḥ ẓhrm iq | nim.atn šd h krm[m]. | šd dd h ḫrnqm.w 24[77].20
mkly.ṣ]brt. | ary y[.ẓl].ksp.[a]ṯrt. | k t'n.ẓl.ksp.w n[-]t. | ḫrṣ.šmḫ.rbt.a[ṯrt]. | ym.gm.l ģlm h.k [tṣḥ]. | 'n.mkṯr.ap.t[---]. 4[51].2.28
. | b ẓr.hdm.id. | d prša.b br. | n'l.il.d qblbl. | 'ln.ybl hm.ḫrṣ. | ṯlḥn.il.d mla. | mnm.dbbm.d | msdt.arṣ. | s'.il.dqt.k amr 4[51].1.38
nt.'šrt.yr | tḥṣ.mlk.brr. | 'lm.tzģ.b ģb.ṣpn. | nḥkt.ksp.w ḫrṣ ṯ' ṯn šm l btbt. | alp.w š šrp.alp šlmm. | l b'l.'ṣr l ṣpn. | npš UG5.12.A.8
šš[r]t.ḫrṣ.ṯqlm.kbd.'šrt.mzn h. | b [ar]b'm.ksp. | b d[.'b]dym.ṯlṯ.kkr 2100.1
alp[.---]. | mat[.---]. | ḫrṣ[.---]. | ṯlṯ.k[---]. | ṯlṯ.a[--.---]. | ḫmš[.---]. | ksp[.---]. | k[--.---]. 148[96].3
rpzn. | argdd. | ṯṯkn. | ybrk. | ntbt. | b.mitm. | 'šrm. | kbd.ḫrṣ. 2006.10
bn[.---]. | w.yn[.---]. | bn.'dr[.---]. | ntb[t]. | b.arb['']. | mat.ḫr[ṣ]. 2007.12
.b'lm'dr. | w bn.ḫlp. | w[--]y.d.b'l. | miḫd.b. | arb'.mat. | ḫrṣ. 1155.8
.yr.pgrm. | lqḥ.b'lmdr. | w.bn.ḫlp. | miḫd. | b.arb'. | mat.ḫrṣ. 1156.7
mšq.mlkt. | mitm.ṯṯm. | kbd.ks[p]. | ksp. | ṯmnym. | ḫrṣ. 1157.6

ḫrṣb'

-].ṯlṯ. | [---].ṯmn. | [---].ṯlṯ. | [---].aḥd. | u[--].ṯn. | hz[p].ṯṯ. | ḫrṣb'.aḥd. | ypr.arb. | m[-]qb.'šr. | ṯn'y.ṯlṯ. | ḫlb 'prm.ṯn. | tmdy 70[112].8
rm. | [q]dš. | [a]mdy. | [gn]'y. | m'qb. | agm. | ḫpty. | ypr. | ḫrṣb'. | uḫnp. | art. | [--]n. | [-----]. | [-----]. | nnu. | šmg. | šmn. | lb 2058.2.5
rkby. | šḥq. | ģn. | ṣ'. | mld. | amdy. | ḫlb'prm. | ḫpty. | [ḫr]ṣb'. | [m']rb. 2077.9
spr.blblm. | skn uškn. | skn šbn. | skn ubr'. | skn ḫrṣb'. | rb.ntbtš. | [---].'bd.r[--]. | arb'.k[--]. | ṯlṯ.ktt. 1033.5
m.b.ḫpty. | ṯṯ.bnšm.b.bir. | ṯṯ.bnšm b.uḫnp. | ṯn.bnšm.b.ḫrṣb'. | arb'.bnšm.b.hzp. | arb'.bnšm.b.šql. | arb'.bnšm.b.nni. | 2076.15

ḫrṣn

ḫrṣn rb khnm. A.1

ḫršḫ

b't.'šrt.ḫrṣ. | b.ṯqlm.kbd.arb'm. | 'šrt.ḫrṣ.b.arb'm. | mit.ḫršḫ.b.ṯqlm. | w.šb'.'šr.šmn. | d.l.yṣa.bt.mlk. | tgmr.ksp.mitm. 2100.19
l h.ršp [-]m. | [---.]bqt[-]. | [b] ģb.ršp mh bnš. | šrp.w ṣp ḫršḫ. | 'lm b ģb ḫyr. | ṯmn l ṯlṯm ṣin. | šb'.alpm. | bt b'l.ugrt.ṯn UG5.12.B.2

ḫršn

'b]dršp.nsk.ṯlṯ. | [-]lkynt.nsk.ṯlṯ. | [-]by.nsk.ṯlṯ. | šmny. | ḫršn. | ldn. | bn.ands. | bn.ann. | bn.'bdpdr. | šd.iyry.l.'bdb'l. | š 1102.12
.tmy.qšt.w.ql'. | 'ky.qšt. | 'bdlbit.qšt. | kṯy.qšt.w.ql'. | bn.ḫršn.qšt.w.ql'. | ilrb.qšt.w.ql'. | pšḫn.qšt. | bn.kmy.qšt. | bn.ilḥ 119[321].3.40
rṣ.ṯlṯ.mṯḥ]. | ģyrm.idk.l yt[n.pnm.'m.lṯpn]. | il d pid.tk ḫrš[n.---.tk.ģr.ks]. | ygly ḏd.i[l.w ybu.qrš.mlk]. | ab.šnm.l [p' 1['NT.IX].3.22
k. | ['ṣ k.'bṣ k.'m y.p']n k.tlsmn. | ['m y.twtḥ.išd] k.tk.ḫršn. | [---.-]bd k.spr. | [---.-]nk. 1['NT.IX].2.23
.'ṣ k.'bṣ k.']m y.p[']n k. | [tlsmn.'m y.twt]ḥ.išd k. | [tk.ḫršn.---]r.[-]ḫm k.w št. | [---.]ẓ[--.-]rdy k. | [---.i]qnim. | [---.-]š 1['NT.IX].2.3
ḥš k.'ṣ k.'[bṣ k.'m y.p'n k.tlsmn]. | 'm y twtḥ.i[šd k.tk.ḫršn.-------------]. | ģr.ks.dm.r[gm.iṯ.l y.w argm k]. | hwt.w aṯ 1['NT.IX].3.11

ḫrt

]. | w aḥd.hm.iṯ.šmt.hm.iṯ[.'ẓm]. | abky.w aqbrn.ašt.b ḫrt. | i[lm.arṣ.b p h.rgm.l yṣa.b šp] | t h.hwt h.knp.hrgb.b'l.ṯb 19[1AQHT].3.126
] | aḥd.hm.iṯ.šmt.hm.i[ṯ]. | 'ẓm.abky.w aqbrn h. | ašt.b ḫrt.ilm.arṣ. | b p h.rgm.l yṣa.b špt h.hwt[h]. | knp.nšrm.b'l.y 19[1AQHT].3.112
d h.w aḥd.hm.iṯ.šmt.iṯ. | 'ẓm.abky w aqbrn h.aštn. | b ḫrt.ilm.arṣ.b p h.rgm.l[yṣ]a. | b špt h.hwt h.knp.ṣml.b'[l]. | b 19[1AQHT].3.141
pr k. | [---.-]mn k.ššrt. | [---.--]t.npš.'gl. | [---.-]nk.aštn.b ḫrt. | ilm.arṣ.w at.qḥ. | 'rpt k.rḥ k.mdl k. | mṭrt k.'m k.šb't. | ģ 5[67].5.5
tšt h.tš'lyn h. | b ṣrrt.ṣpn.tbkyn h. | w tqbrn h.tštnn.b ḫrt. | ilm.arṣ.ṭṭbḫ.šb'm. | rumm.k gmn.aliyn. | [b]'l.ṭṭbḫ.šb'm. 6[62].1.17

ḫš

]tn. | yṯny.b'l.ṣ[---.-]pt h. | ql h.q[dš.ṭb]r.arṣ. | [---.]ģrm[.t]ḫšn. | rḥq[.---.td']. | qdm ym.bmt.[nhr]. | ṭṭṭn.ib.b'l.tiḫd. | y'r 4[51].7.32

ḫš'r

--]. | w b hm.ṭṭṭb[.--]d h. | km trpa.hn n'r. | d yšt.l.lṣb h ḫš'r klb. | [w]riš.pqq.w šr h. | yšt.aḥd h.dm zt.ḫrpnt. UG5.1.2.4

ḫšt

[l]krt. | k [k]lb.b bt k.n'tq.k inr. | ap.ḫšt k.ap.ab.ik mtm. | tmtn.u ḫšt k.l ntn. | 'tq.b d.aṯt.ab ṣrry. | 16.1[125].3
n. | nšmḫ.b l.mt k.ngln. | k klb.[b]bt k.n'tq. | k inr[.ap.]ḫšt k. | ap.ab.k mtm.tmtn. | u ḫšt k.l bky.'tq. | b d.aṯt ab.ṣrry. 16.2[125].101
ab n.ašmḫ. | b l.mt k.ngln.k klb. | b bt k.n'tq.k inr. | ap.ḫšt k.ap.ab.k mtm. | tmtn.u ḫšt k.l ntn. | 'tq.b d.aṯt.ab.ṣrry. | i 16.1[125].17
.[b]bt k.n'tq. | k inr[.ap.]ḫšt k. | ap.ab.k mtm.tmtn. | u ḫšt k.l bky.'tq. | b d.aṯt ab.ṣrry. | u ilm.tmtn.špḥ. | [l]ṭpn.l yḥ. 16.2[125].103
klb. | b bt k.n'tq.k inr. | ap.ḫšt k.ap.ab.k mtm. | tmtn.u ḫšt k.l ntn. | 'tq.b d.aṯt.ab.ṣrry. | ik m.yrgm.bn.il. | krt.špḥ.lṭp 16.1[125].18

k]lb.b bt k.nʿtq.k inr. | ap.ḫšt k.ap.ab.ik mtm. | tmtn.u ḫšt k.l ntn. | ʿtq.b d.aṯt.ab ṣrry. | tbky k.ab.ġr.bʿl. | ṣpn.ḥlm.q 16.1[125].4
dš w amrr. | ṯḫr w bd. | [k]ṯr ḫss šlm. | šlm il bt. | šlm il ḫš[t]. | ršp inšt. | [--]rm il [---]. | [---.--]m šlm [---]. UG5.7.72

ḫt

ʿšr.ktnt. | ʿšr.rṭm. | kkr[.-].ḫt. | mitm[.p]ttm. | ṯlṯm[.---].kst. | alp.a[bn.ṣ]rp. 1114.3
ny.ʿmn. | mlk.b.ṯy ndr. | iṯt.w.ht. | [-]sny.uḏr h. | w.hm.ḫt. | ʿl.w.likt. | ʿm k.w.hm. | l.ʿl.w.lakm. | ilak.w.at. | um y.al.td 1013.16
n.l šbm. | tšt.trks. | l mrym.l bt[.---]. | p l.tbʿ[.---]. | hmlt ḫt.[---]. | l.tp[-]m.[---]. | n[-]m[.---]. 1003.12

ḫta

š.ank.aliyn bʿl. | ʿdbnn ank.imr.b p y. | k lli.b ṯbrn q y.ḫtu hw. | nrt.ilm.špš.ṣḥrrt. | la.šmm.b yd.bn ilm.mt. | ym.ym 6[49].2.23
r. | l.plsy. | rgm. | yšlm.l k. | l.trġds. | w.l.klby. | šmʿt.ḫti. | nḫtu.ht. | hm.in mm. | nḫtu.w.lak. | ʿm y.w.yd. | ilm.p.k mtm. 53[54].8
k. | l.trġds. | w.l.klby. | šmʿt.ḫti. | nḫtu.ht. | hm.in mm. | nḫtu.w.lak. | ʿm y.w.yd. | ilm.p.k mtm. | ʿz.mid. | hm.nṯkp. | m 53[54].10
iwrḏr. | l.plsy. | rgm. | yšlm.l k. | l.trġds. | w.l.klby. | šmʿt.ḫti. | nḫtu.ht. | hm.in mm. | nḫtu.w.lak. | ʿm y.w.yd. | ilm.p.k 53[54].7
.ilm. | mt.al.yʿdb km. | k imr.b p h. | k lli.b ṯbrn. | qn h.tḫtan. | nrt.ilm.špš. | ṣḥrrt.la. | šmm.b yd.md | d.ilm.mt.b a | lp 4[51].8.20

ḫtb

šd.bn.šty.l.bn.ṭbrn. | šd.bn.ḫtb.l bn.yʿḏrd. | šd.gl.bʿlz.l.bn.ʿmnr. | šd.knʿm.l.bn.ʿmnr. | šd. 2089.2

ḫty

npy. | [---.ušn.yp km.ulp.]qṯy. | [ulp.ddmy.ulp.ḫry.ulp.ḫty.u]lp.alṯy. | [ulp.ġbr.ulp.ḫbt km.ulp.mdll km.ulp]. | [qr zb APP.I[-].1.15
]npy. | [---.ušn.yp kn.ulp.q]ṯy. | [ulp.ddmy.ulp.ḫry.ulp.ḫty.ulp.alṯy]. | [ulp.ġbr.ulp.ḫbt kn.ulp.mdll kn.ulp.]qr zbl. | [APP.I[-].2.13
nnpdgl. | [ušn.yp kn.ulp.qṯy.ulp.]ddmy.ulp ḫry. | [ulp.ḫty.ulp.alṯy.ulp.ġbr.ul]p.ḫbt kn. | [ulp.mdll kn.ulp.qr zbl.uš APP.I[-].1.5
p]y.ugrt. | [---.u ṯḫṭu.ulp.qṯy.ulp.ddm]y. | [ulp.ḫry.ulp.ḫty.ulp.alṯy.ulp.ġbr]. | [ulp.ḫbt km.ulp.mdll km.ulp.qr zbl]. 32[2].1.7
py.nqmd.ušn.yp km.ulp.q[ṯy.ulp.ddm]y. | ulp.ḫry.ulp.ḫ[t]y.ulp.alṯy.ul[p.ġbr.]ulp. | ḫbt km.ulp.m[dl]l km.ulp.qr z 32[2].1.21
[np]y.nṯt.ušn.yp kn.ulp qṯy. | ulp.ddmy.ul[p.ḫ]ry.ulp.ḫty.ulp.alṯy. | ulp.ġbr.ulp.[ḫbt] kn[.u]lp.mdll kn.ulp qr z[bl]. 32[2].1.29
.w n[py.---].u ṯḫṭi[n.ulp.qṯy]. | ulp.ddmy.ul[p.ḫry.u]lp.ḫty.ulp[.alṯy.ulp.]ġbr. | ulp.ḫbt kn.ulp.md[ll k]n.ulp.q[r zbl]. 32[2].1.12
kd.bt ilm. | rbm. | kd l ištnm. | kd l ḫty. | maḫdh. | kd l kblbn. | kdm.mṭḫ. | l.alṯy. | kd.l mrynm. | š 1090.4
[s]ġr.bn.bdn. | [sġ]r.bn.psḫn. | alṯy. | sġr.npr. | bn.ḫty. | ṯn.bnš ibrḏr. | bnš tlmi. | sġr.ḥryn. | ʿdn.w sġr h. | bn.ḥgb 2082.5
[.l.]ḫzr[m.---]. | kd[.l.]ṯrtn[m]. | arbʿ l.mry[nm]. | kdm l.ḫty.[---]. | kdm l.ʿṯtr[t]. | kd l.m[ḏ]rġl[m]. | kd l.mryn[m]. 1091.9

ḫtyn

gy. | bn zlbn. | bn.aḫ[--]. | bn[.---]. | [-----]. | bn kr[k]. | bn ḫtyn. | w nḥl h. | bn ṯgrb. | bn ṯdnyn. | bn pbn. 2016.3.3
[---.]ṯlṯm.d.nlqḥt. | [bn.ḫ]tyn.yd.bt h. | [aġ]ltn. | tdn.bn.ddy. | ʿbdil[.b]n ṣdqn. | bnšm. 2045.2

ḫtyt

spr.ḥpr.bt.k[--]. | tšʿ.ʿšr h.dd.l.b[t.--]. | ḫmš.ddm.l.ḫtyt. | ṯlṯm.dd.ksmn.l.gzzm. | yyn. | ṣdqn. | ʿbd.pdr. | myṣm. | ṯ 1099.3

ḫtn

md h. | ʿdršp. | w.lmd h. | krwn b.gt.nbk. | ddm.ksmm.l.ḫtn. | ddm.l.trbnn. | ddm.šʿrm.l.trbnn. | ddm.šʿrm.l.ḫtn. | dd.š 1099.20
.l.ḫtn. | ddm.l.trbnn. | ddm.šʿrm.l.trbnn. | ddm.šʿrm.l.ḫtn. | dd.šʿrm.l.ḥmr.ḥṭb. | dd.ḥṭm.l.ḫdġb. | ṯṯ.ddm.l.gzzm. | kd 1099.23
--]. | bʿl y.mlk[y.---]. | yd.bt h.yd[.---]. | ary.yd.t[--.---]. | ḫtn h.šbʿl[.---]. | ṯlḥny.yd[.---]. | yd.ṯlṯ.kl[t h.---]. | w.ṯṯm.ṣi[n.- 81[329].16
.l.ḥmr.ḥṭb. | dd.ḥṭm.l.ḫdġb. | ṯṯ.ddm.l.gzzm. | kd yn.l.ḫtn.w.kd.ḥmṣ.w.[lt]ḥ.ʿšdm. | kd yn.l.ḫdġb.w.kd.ḥmṣ. | prš.gl 1099.27
b h lb[u] yʿrr.w yʿ[n]. | yrḫ nyr šmm.w nʿ[n]. | ʿma nkl ḫtn y.a[ḫ]r. | nkl yrḫ ytrḫ.adn h. | yšt mṣb.mznm.um h. | kp 24[77].32
]. | šd dd h ḥrnqm.w | yʿn ḫrḫb mlk qẓ [l]. | nʿmn.ilm l ḫt[n]. | m.bʿl trḫ pdry b[t h]. | aqrb k ab h bʿ[l]. | yġtr.ʿṯtr t | rḫ 24[77].25

ḫtt

[---.]y[--].ḫtt.mtt[--]. | [--.]ḥy[--.--.]l ašši.hm.ap.amr[--]. | [---].w b ym. 2.4[68].1
.trḥṣ.nn.b dʿt. | npš h.l lḥm.tptḥ. | brlt h.l ṯrm. | mt.dm.ḫt.šʿtqt. | dm.lan.w ypqd. | krt.ṯʿ.yšu.g h. | w yṣḥ.šmʿ.l mṯt. | ḥ 16.6[127].13
[m]t.dm.ḫt.šʿtqt dm. | li.w ttbʿ.šʿtqt. | bt.krt.bu.tbu. | bkt.tgly.w tbu. | n 16.6[127].1

ḫtpy

.yḥnn.aḏddy. | bn.pdġy.mḫdy. | bn.yyn.mdrġl. | bn.ʿlr. | ḫtpy.aḏddy. | ynḥm.aḏddy. | ykny.aḏddy. | m[--].aḏddy. | ypʿ. 2014.20
mšu. | ḫtpy. | ġldy. | iḫġl. | aby. | abmn. | ynḥm. | npl. | ynḥm. | mtbʿl. | 1065.2

ḫṯr

h.km.lb. | ʿnt.aṯr.bʿl.tiḫd. | bn.ilm.mt.b ḥrb. | tbqʿnn.b ḫṯr.tdry | nn.b išt.tšrpnn. | b rḥm.tṭḥnn.b šd. | tdrʿnn.šir h.l ti 6[49].2.32
spr.npṣ.krw. | ṯt.ḫṯrm.ṯn.kst. | spl.mšlt.w.mqḥm. | w md h. | arn.w mznm. | ṯn. 2050.2

ṭ

ṭb

.tʿrbn.gṯrm. | bt.mlk.ṯql.ḫrṣ. | l špš.w yrḫ.l gṯr. | ṯql.ksp.ṭb.ap w np[š]. | l ʿnt h.ṯql.ḫrṣ. | l špš[.w y]rḫ.l gṯr.ṯn. | [ṯql.ksp 33[5].12
np[š]. | l ʿnt h.ṯql.ḫrṣ. | l špš[.w y]rḫ.l gṯr.ṯn. | [ṯql.ksp].ṭb.ap.w npš. | [---].bt.alp w š. | [---.--]m.l gṯrm. | [---.]l ʿnt m. | [33[5].15
n.d.l.ṭb. | b.gt.mʿrby. | ṯṯm.yn.ṭb.w.ḫmš.l.ʿšrm. | yn.d.l.ṭb.b.ulm. | mit.yn.ṭb.w.ṯṯm.ṯṯ.kbd. | yn.d.l.ṭb.b.gt.ḥdṯt. | tšʿm. 1084.10
.yn.b gt[.-]n. | arbʿm.kbd.yn.ṭb.w.[--]. | ṯmn.kbd.yn.d.l.ṭb.b.gnʿ[y]. | mitm.yn.ḥsp.d.nkly.b.db[ḫ.--]. | mit.arbʿm.kbd. 1084.23
.k[dm.]kbd.yn.d.l.ṭb. | b.gt.gwl. | ṯlṯm.tšʿ[.kbd.yn].d.l[.ṭb].b.gt.ipṯl. | ṯmnym.[yn].ṭb.b.gt.š[---]. | tšʿm.[ḫ]mš[.kbd].yn 1084.19
y. | arbʿm.kdm.kbd.yn.ṭb. | w.ḫmšm.k[dm.]kbd.yn.d.l.ṭb. | b.gt.gwl. | ṯlṯm.tšʿ[.kbd.yn].d.l[.ṭb].b.gt.ipṯl. | ṯmnym.[yn 1084.17
ʿšrm. | yn.d.l.ṭb.b.ulm. | mit.yn.ṭb.w.ṯṯm.ṯṯ.kbd. | yn.d.l.ṭb.b.gt.ḥdṯt. | tšʿm.yn.d.l.ṭb.b.zbl. | ʿšrm.yn.ṭb.w.ṯṯm.ḫmš.k[b 1084.12
.l.ṭb.gt.ṭbq. | mit.ʿšr.kbd.yn.ṭb. | w.ṯṯm.arbʿ.kbd.yn.d.l.ṭb. | b.gt.mʿrby. | ṯṯm.yn.ṭb.w.ḫmš.l.ʿšrm. | yn.d.l.ṭb.b.ulm. | m 1084.7
.yn.d.l.ṭb.b.zbl. | ʿšrm.yn.ṭb.w.ṯṯm.ḫmš.k[b]d. | yn.d.l.ṭb.b.gt.sġy. | arbʿm.kdm.kbd.yn.ṭb. | w.ḫmšm.k[dm.]kbd.yn. 1084.15
t.gwl. | ṯlṯm.tšʿ[.kbd.yn].d.l[.ṭb].b.gt.ipṯl. | ṯmnym.[yn].ṭb.b.gt.š[---]. | tšʿm.[ḫ]mš[.kbd].yn.b gt[.-]n. | arbʿm.kbd.yn.ṭ 1084.20
it.yn.ṭb.w.ṯṯm.ṯṯ.kbd. | yn.d.l.ṭb.b.gt.ḥdṯt. | tšʿm.yn.d.l.ṭb.b.zbl. | ʿšrm.yn.ṭb.w.ṯṯm.ḫmš.k[b]d. | yn.d.l.ṭb.b.gt.sġy. | ar 1084.13
m.tʿnyn. | w šd.šd ilm.šd aṯrt.w rḥm. | ʿl.išt.šbʿ d.ġzrm.ṭb.[g]d.b ḥlb.annḫ b ḫmat. | w ʿl.agn.šbʿ d m.dġ[ṯ.---]t. | tlk 23[52].14
yn.ḫlq.b.gt.sknm. | ʿšr.yn.ṭb.w.arbʿm.ḫmš.kbd. | yn.d.l.ṭb.gt.ṭbq. | mit.ʿšr.kbd.yn.ṭb. | w.ṯṯm.arbʿ.kbd.yn.d.l.ṭb. | b.gt. 1084.5
ṯm.ḫmš.k[b]d. | yn.d.l.ṭb.b.gt.sġy. | arbʿm.kdm.kbd.yn.ṭb. | w.ḫmšm.k[dm.]kbd.yn.d.l.ṭb. | b.gt.gwl. | ṯlṯm.tšʿ[.kbd.y 1084.16
.yn.ṭb. | w.ṯṯm.arbʿ.kbd.yn.d.l.ṭb. | b.gt.mʿrby. | ṯṯm.yn.ṭb.w.ḫmš.l.ʿšrm. | yn.d.l.ṭb.b.ulm. | mit.yn.ṭb.w.ṯṯm.ṯṯ.kbd. | y 1084.9
dm.kbd.yn.d.l.ṭb. | w.arbʿm.yn.ḫlq.b.gt.sknm. | ʿšr.yn.ṭb.w.arbʿm.ḫmš.kbd. | yn.d.l.ṭb.gt.ṭbq. | mit.ʿšr.kbd.yn.ṭb. | w. 1084.4
ḫmš.ʿšr.yn.ṭb. | w.tšʿm.kdm.kbd.yn.d.l.ṭb. | w.arbʿm.yn.ḫlq.b.gt.sknm. | ʿšr.yn.ṭb.w.arbʿm.ḫmš.kbd. 1084.2
r. | b knr.w ṯlb.b tp.w mṣltm.b m | rqdm.dšn.b.ḥbr.kṯr.ṭbm. | w tšt.ʿnt.gṯr.bʿlt.mlk.bʿ | lt.drkt.bʿlt.šmm.rmm. | [bʿl]t. UG5.2.1.5
ḫmš.ʿšr.yn.ṭb. | w.tšʿm.kdm.kbd.yn.d.l.ṭb. | w.arbʿm.yn.ḫlq.b.gt.sknm. | ʿ 1084.1
bd. | yn.d.l.ṭb.b.gt.ḥdṯt. | tšʿm.yn.d.l.ṭb.b.zbl. | ʿšrm.yn.ṭb.w.ṯṯm.ḫmš.k[b]d. | yn.d.l.ṭb.b.gt.sġy. | arbʿm.kdm.kbd.yn. 1084.14
ṭb.w.arbʿm.ḫmš.kbd. | yn.d.l.ṭb.gt.ṭbq. | mit.ʿšr.kbd.yn.ṭb. | w.ṯṯm.arbʿ.kbd.yn.d.l.ṭb. | b.gt.mʿrby. | ṯṯm.yn.ṭb.w.ḫmš. 1084.6
by. | ṯṯm.yn.ṭb.w.ḫmš.l.ʿšrm. | yn.d.l.ṭb.b.ulm. | mit.yn.ṭb.w.ṯṯm.ṯṯ.kbd. | yn.d.l.ṭb.b.gt.ḥdṯt. | tšʿm.yn.d.l.ṭb.b.zbl. | ʿš 1084.11
t.š[---]. | tšʿm.[ḫ]mš[.kbd].yn.b gt[.-]n. | arbʿm.kbd.yn.ṭb.w.[--]. | ṯmn.kbd.yn.d.l.ṭb.b.gnʿ[y]. | mitm.yn.ḥsp.d.nkly.b 1084.22
.rpi[.---]. | [---.-]llm.abl.mṣrp k.[---]. | [---.]y.mṯnt.w th.ṭbt.n[--]. | [---.b]ṯnm w ṭṭb.ʿl.bṯnt.trth[ṣ.---]. | [---.t]ṭb h.aḫt.p 1001.2.4
msk.b msk h. | qm.ybd.w yšr. | mṣltm.bd.nʿm. | yšr.ġzr.ṭb.ql. | ʿl.bʿl.b ṣrrt. | ṣpn.ytmr.bʿl. | bnt h.yʿn.pdry. | bt.ar.apn.ṭ 3[ʿNT].1.20

ṭbḫ

y.dtm. | ḫrṣ.ʿdbt.bht[h.bʿ]l. | yʿdb.hd.ʿdb[.ʿd]bt. | hkl h.ṭbḫ.alpm[.ap]. | ṣin.šql.ṯrm[.w]m | ria.il.ʿglm.d[t]. | šnt.imr.q 4[51].6.40
ap.l[--.---]. | ymḫṣ k.k[--.---]. | il.dbḥ.[---]. | pʿr.b[--.---]. | ṭbḫ.alp[m.ap.ṣin.šql]. | ṯrm.w [mri.ilm.ʿglm.dt.šnt]. | imr.[qm 1[ʿNT.X].4.30
pn.ḥyl | y.zbl.mlk.ʿllm y.km.tdd. | ʿnt.ṣd.tštr.ʿpt.šmm. | ṭbḫ.alpm.ap ṣin.šql.ṯrm. | w mri ilm.ʿglm.dt.šnt. | imr.qmṣ.lli 22.2[124].12
dm.lan.w ypqd. | krt.ṯʿ.yšu.g h. | w yṣḥ.šmʿ.l mtt. | ḥry.ṭbḫ.imr. | w ilḥm.mgt.w iṯrm. | tšmʿ.mtt.ḥry. | tṭbḫ.imr.w lḥ 16.6[127].17
ṯt. | ḥry.ṭbḫ.imr. | w ilḥm.mgt.w iṯrm. | tšmʿ.mtt.ḥry. | tṭbḫ.imr.w lḥm. | mgt.w ytrm.hn.ym. | w ṯn.ytb.krt.l ʿd h. | yt 16.6[127].20
| hll.snnt.apnk.dnil. | mt.rpi.ap.hn.ġzr.mt. | hrnmy.alp.yṭbḫ.l kṯ | rt.yšlḥm.kṯrt.w y | ššq.bnt.[hl]l.snnt. | hn.ym.w ṯn. 17[2AQHT].2.29
b gt ilštmʿ. | bt ubnyn š h d.ytn.ṣtqn. | tut ṭbḫ ṣtq[n]. | b bz ʿzm ṭbḫ š[h]. | b kl ygz ḥḥ š h. 1153.3
ʿ. | bt ubnyn š h d.ytn.ṣtqn. | tut ṭbḫ ṣtq[n]. | b bz ʿzm ṭbḫ š[h]. | b kl ygz ḥḥ š h. 1153.4
ytn.ṣtqn. | tut ṭbḫ ṣtq[n]. | b bz ʿzm ṭbḫ š[h]. | b kl ygz ḥḥ š h. 1153.5
k g]mn.aliyn.bʿl. | [tṭ]bḫ.šbʿm.ṣin. | [k gm]n.aliyn.bʿl. | [tṭb]ḫ.šbʿm.aylm. | [k gmn.]aliyn.bʿl. | [tṭbḫ.š]bʿm.yʿlm. | [k g 6[62].1.24
n.b ḫrt. | ilm.arṣ.tṭbḫ.šbʿm. | rumm.k gmn.aliyn. | [b]ʿl.tṭbḫ.šbʿm.alpm. | [k g]mn.aliyn.bʿl. | [tṭ]bḫ.šbʿm.ṣin. | [k gm] 6[62].1.20
gmn.]aliyn.bʿl. | [tṭbḫ.š]bʿm.yʿlm. | [k gmn.al]iyn.bʿl. | [tṭbḫ.šbʿm.]ḥmrm. | [k gm]n.al[i]yn.b[ʿl]. | [---]ḫ h.tšt bm.ʿ[--]. 6[62].1.28
m]n.aliyn.bʿl. | [tṭb]ḫ.šbʿm.aylm. | [k gmn.]aliyn.bʿl. | [tṭbḫ.š]bʿm.yʿlm. | [k gmn.al]iyn.bʿl. | [tṭbḫ.šbʿm.]ḥmrm. | [k g 6[62].1.26
gmn.aliyn. | [b]ʿl.tṭbḫ.šbʿm.alpm. | [k g]mn.aliyn.bʿl. | [tṭ]bḫ.šbʿm.ṣin. | [k gm]n.aliyn.bʿl. | [tṭb]ḫ.šbʿm.aylm. | [k gm 6[62].1.22
h. | b ṣrrt.ṣpn.tbkyn h. | w tqbrn h.tštnn.b ḫrt. | ilm.arṣ.tṭbḫ.šbʿm. | rumm.k gmn.aliyn. | [b]ʿl.tṭbḫ.šbʿm.alpm. | [k g] 6[62].1.18
]qm. | id.u [---]t. | lḥn š[-]ʿ[--.]aḫd[.-]. | tšmʿ.mtt.[ḥ]ry. | tṭbḫ.šmn.[m]ri h. | t[p]tḥ.rḥbt.yn. | ʿl h.ṯr h.tšʿrb. | ʿl h.tšʿrb.ẓ 15[128].4.15
[-----]. | [tṭbḫ.šm]n.[mri h]. | [tpth.rḥ]bt.[yn]. | [---.]rp[.---]. | [---.ḫ]br[. 15[128].5.1
p[----]. | gm.l[aṯt h k.yṣḥ]. | šmʿ[.l mtt.ḥry]. | ṭbḫ.š[mn].mri k. | ptḥ.[rḥ]bt.yn. | ṣḥ.šbʿm.ṯr y. | ṯmnym.[ẓ]by 15[128].4.4

ṭbn

| yṣr k.bʿl.ṯmn.rkb. | ʿrpt.bl.ṭl.bl rbb. | bl.šrʿ.thmtm.bl. | ṭbn.ql.bʿl.k tmzʿ. | kst.dnil.mt.rpi. | all.ġzr.m[t.]hr[nmy]. | gm 19[1AQHT].1.46

ṭbq

r.w.bnš. | ṯbil. | ʿnmky.ḥmr.w.bnš. | rqd arbʿ. | šbn aḥd. | ṭbq aḥd. | šrš aḥd. | bir aḥd. | uḫnp. | hzp ṯn. | mʿqb arbʿ. 2040.29
]y. | ar. | agm.w.ḫpty. | ḫlb.ṣpn. | mril. | ʿnmky. | ʿnqpat. | ṭbq. | hzp. | gnʿy. | mʿrby. | [ṣ]ʿq. | [š]ḥq. | nʿrm. | mḥrġlm. | kzy 71[113].54
[--]n.bu[-]bd.ubln. | [---].l.ubl[n]. | [--.]ṭbq.l.iytlm. | [---].l.iytlm. | [---.]ʿbdilm.l.iytlm. | [---.n]ḥl h.lm.i 1076.3
lib h.b qdš. | ẓtr.ʿm h.l arṣ.mšṣu.qṭr h. | l ʿpr.ḏmr.aṯr h.ṭbq.lḥt. | niṣ h.grš d.ʿšy.ln h. | aḥd.yd h.b škrn.mʿms h. | [k]š 17[2AQHT].1.29
qdš. | [ẓtr.ʿm h.l a]rṣ.mšṣu. | [qṭr h.l ʿpr.ḏ]mr.a[ṯ]r h. | [ṭbq.lḥt.niṣ h.gr]š.d ʿšy. | [ln h.---]. | z[tr.ʿm k.l arṣ.mšṣu.qṭr k] 17[2AQHT].1.48
ry y. | nṣb.skn.ilib y.b qdš. | ẓtr.ʿm y.l ʿpr.ḏmr.aṯr[y]. | ṭbq lḥt.niṣ y.grš. | d ʿšy.ln.aḥd.yd y.b š | krn mʿms y k šbʿt yn 17[2AQHT].2.18
[ln h.---]. | z[tr.ʿm k.l arṣ.mšṣu.qṭr k]. | l ʿpr.ḏm[r.aṯr k.ṭbq]. | lḥt.niṣ k.gr[š.d ʿšy.ln k]. | spu.ksm k.bt.[bʿl.w mnt k]. | 17[2AQHT].2.2
q.b.gt.sknm. | ʿšr.yn.ṭb.w.arbʿm.ḫmš.kbd. | yn.d.l.ṭb.gt.ṭbq. | mit.ʿšr.kbd.yn.ṭb. | w.ṯṯm.arbʿ.kbd.yn.d.l.ṭb. | b.gt.mʿrb 1084.5
.]ʿm.l.mit.dd.ṯn.kbd.ḥpr.bnšm.ṯmnym.dd. | l u[-]m. | b.ṭbq.arbʿm.drʿ.w.ʿšr.dd.drt. | w[.a]rbʿ.l.ʿšrm.dd.l.yḥšr.bl.bn h. 1098.10

b‘. | ǵbl.ḫmš. | atlg.ḫmš ‘šr[h]. | ulm ṯ[ṯ]. | m‘rby.ḫmš. | ṭbq.arb‘. | tkm[.---]. | uḫnp[.---]. | ušk[n.---]. | ubr[‘y.---]. | ar[.-- 68[65].1.11
il[štm‘]. | šbn. | ṭbq. | rqd. | uškn. | ḫbt. | [ḫlb].kr[d]. 1177.3
ṣ‘q. | qmy. | ḫlbkrd. | y‘rt. | uškn. | ‘nqpat. | ilštm‘. | šbn. | ṭbq. | rqd. | šrš. | gn‘y. | m‘qb. | agm. | bir. | ypr. | hzp. | šql. | m‘rḥ 2074.23
‘šrm.ksp.d mkr. | mlk. | ṯlṯ.mat.ksp.d.šb[n]. | mit.ksp.d.ṭbq. | ṯmnym.arb‘t. | kbd.ksp. | d.nqdm. | ḫmšm.l mit. | ksp.d. 2107.5
| mlk[.---]. | ǵbl[.---]. | atl[g.---]. | u[lm.---]. | m[‘rby.---]. | ṭ[bq.---]. 68[65].2.11
-]. | ḫlb.k[rd]. | uškn. | ‘nqp[at]. | ubr‘[y]. | ilšt[m‘]. | šbn. | ṭbq. 2146.10

ṭbqy

ṣb[u.anyt]. | ‘dn. | ṭbq[ym]. | m‘q[bym]. | tš‘.‘[šr.bnš]. | ǵr.ṯ[--.---]. | ṣbu.any[t]. | b 79[83].3
mš.bnšm. | snrym. | tš‘.bnš[m]. | gb‘lym. | arb‘.b[nšm]. | ṭbqym. 79[83].18

ṭbrn

šd.bn.šty.l.bn.ṭbrn. | šd.bn.ḥtb.l bn.y‘ḏrd. | šd.gl.b‘lz.l.bn.‘mnr. | šd.kn‘m.l.b 2089.1
rwn.l aḫn. | šd.‘yy.l aḫn. | šd.brdn.l bn.bly. | šd gzl.l.bn.ṭbr[n]. | šd.ḫzmyn.l a[--]. | ṯn šdm b uš[kn]. 2089.14

ṭhr

b bh | t h.w atn mhr h l a | b h.alp ksp w rbt ḫ | rṣ.išlḥ ẓhrm iq | nim.atn šd h krm[m]. | šd dd h ḥrnqm.w | y‘n ḫrḫb 24[77].21
| mid.ksp.gb‘m.mḥmd.. | ḫrṣ.w bn.bht.ksp. | w ḫrṣ.bht.ṭhrm. | iqnim.šmḫ.aliyn. | b‘l.ṣḥ.ḥrn.b bht h. | ‘ḏbt.b qrb hkl 4[51].5.96
ḥmd.ḫrṣ. | ybl k.udr.ilqṣm. | w bn.bht.ksp.w ḫrṣ. | bht.ṭhrm.iqnim. | šmḫ.btlt.‘nt.td‘ṣ. | p‘nm.w tr.arṣ. | idk.l ttn.pnm 4[51].5.81
l.yṯ[ṯb.--]pt. | ib.‘ltn.a[--.--]y. | w.spr.in[.-.]‘d m. | spr n.ṭhr[.--]. | aṯr.iṯ.bqṯ. | w.štn.l y. 2060.33

ṭḥn

ht.qlt.‘l k.pht. | dry.b ḥrb.‘l k. | pht.šrp.b išt. | ‘l k.[pht.ṭḥ]n.b rḥ | m.‘[l k.]pht[.dr]y.b kbrt. | ‘l k.pht.[-]l[-]. | b šdm.‘l 6[49].5.15
.mt.b ḥrb. | tbq‘nn.b ḫṯr.tdry | nn.b išt.tšrpnn. | b rḥm.tṭḥnn.b šd. | tdr‘nn.šir h.l tikl. | ‘ṣrm.mnt h.l tkly. | npr[m.]šir 6[49].2.34

ṭḫ

.m‘ms h. | [k]šb‘ yn.spu.ksm h.bt.b‘l. | [w m]nt h bt.il.ṭḫ.gg h.b ym. | [ṭi]ṭ.rḥṣ.npṣ h.b ym.rṯ. | [--.y]iḫd.il.‘bd h.ybrk 17[2AQHT].1.33
m‘ms y k šb‘t yn. | spu.ksm y.bt.b‘l.[w]mn[t]. | y.bt.il.ṭḫ.gg y.b ym.ṭiṭ. | rḥṣ.npṣ y.b ym.rṯ. | dn.il.bt h.ymǵyn. | yštql 17[2AQHT].2.22
l.w mnt k]. | bt il.aḫd.yd k.b [škrn]. | m‘ms k.k šb‘t.yn.ṭ[ḫ]. | gg k.b ym.ṭiṭ.rḥṣ. | npṣ k.b ym rṯ.b uni[l]. | pnm.tšmḫ.w 17[2AQHT].2.6

ṭḫr

l h.tuḫd.‘ṯtrt.ik.m[ḫṣt.ml] | [ak.ym.t‘]dt.ṯpṭ.nhr.mlak.mṭḫr.yḥb[-.---.] | [---].mlak.bn.ktpm.rgm.b‘l h.w y[--.---]. | [-- 2.1[137].41

ṭṭ

i]sp.ḥmt.y[r]ḫ.w.ršp.yisp.ḥmt. | [‘ṯ]r.w ‘ṯtpr.yisp.ḥmt.ṭṭ.w kṯṯ. | [yus]p.ḥmt.mlk.b ‘ṯtrt.yisp.ḥmt. | [kṯ]r w ḫss.y[i]sp UG5.8.16
. | š.y‘db.ksa w yṯb. | tqru l špš.um h.špš.um.ql bl ‘m. | ṭṭ.w kmṯ.ḥryt h.mnt.nṯk.nḥš.šm | rr.nḥš.‘q šr.ln h.mlḫš abd. UG5.7.36

ṭl

.---]. | k d lbšt.bir.mlak. | šmm.tmr.zbl.mlk. | šmm.tlak.ṭl.amr.. | bn km k bk[r.z]bl.am.. | rkm.agzrt[.--].arḫ.. | b‘l.azrt 13[6].27
b qẓ.ṭl.yṭll. | l ǵnbm.šb‘.šnt. | yṣr k.b‘l.ṯmn.rkb. | ‘rpt.bl.ṭl.bl rbb. | bl.šr‘.thmtm.bl. | ṭbn.ql.b‘l.k tmz‘. | kst.dnil.mt.rpi. 19[1AQHT].1.44
nk.dnil.mt. | rpi.yṣly.‘rpt.b | ḥm.un.yr.‘rpt. | tmṭr.b qẓ.ṭl.yṭll. | l ǵnbm.šb‘.šnt. | yṣr k.b‘l.ṯmn.rkb. | ‘rpt.bl.ṭl.bl rbb. | 19[1AQHT].1.41
n[.dn] | il.mt.rpi npš ṭḥ[.pǵt]. | ṭ[km]t.mym.ḥspt.l š‘r. | ṭl.yd‘t.hlk.kbkbm. | a[-]ḥ.hy.mḫ.tmḫṣ.mḫṣ[.aḫ k]. | tkl.m[k]l 19[1AQHT].4.200
t ksp. | dt.yrq.nqbn y.tš[m‘]. | pǵt.ṭkmt.my.ḥspt.l[š‘]r.ṭl. | yd‘t.hlk.kbkbm. | bkm.tmdln.‘r. | bkm.tṣmd.pḥl.bkm. | tš 19[1AQHT].2.55
gm.l bt[h.dnil.k yṣḥ]. | šm‘.pǵt.ṭkmt[.my]. | ḥspt.l š‘r.ṭl.yd[‘t]. | hlk.kbkbm.mdl.‘r. | ṣmd.pḥl.št.gpn y dt ksp. | dt.yr 19[1AQHT].2.51
mk. | mrṯ.yn.srnm.yn.bld. | ǵll.yn.išryt.‘nq.smd. | lbnn.ṭl mrṯ.yḥrṯ.il. | hn.ym.w ṯn.tlḥmn.rpum. | tštyn.ṯlṯ.rb‘.ym.ḫ 22.2[124].20
[t]ḥspn.m h.w trḥṣ. | [ṭ]l.šmm.šmn.arṣ.rbb. | [r]kb ‘rpt.ṭl.šmm.tsk h. | [rb]b.nsk h.kbkbm. 3[‘NT].2.40
.mria.w tk. | pn h.tḥspn.m h.w trḥṣ. | ṭl.šmm.šmn.arṣ.ṭl.šm[m.t]sk h. | rbb.nsk h.kbkbm. | ttpp.anhbm.d alp.šd[.ẓu 3[‘NT].4.87
h. | št.alp.qdm h.mria.w tk. | pn h.tḥspn.m h.w trḥṣ. | ṭl.šmm.šmn.arṣ.ṭl.šm[m.t]sk h. | rbb.nsk h.kbkbm. | ttpp.anh 3[‘NT].4.87
nt. | [l]ṭlḥn.hdmm.ṭṭ‘r.l hdmm. | [t]ḥspn.m h.w trḥṣ. | [ṭ]l.šmm.šmn.arṣ.rbb. | [r]kb ‘rpt.ṭl.šmm.tsk h. | [rb]b.nsk h.k 3[‘NT].2.39
rbb.nsk h.kbkbm. | ttpp.anhbm.d alp.šd[.ẓu h.b ym]. | ṭl[.---]. 3[‘NT].4.90

ṭlb

| [--]kṭ.i[---.---]. | p.šn[-.---]. | w l ṭlb.[---]. | mit.rḥ[.---]. | ṭṭlb.a[--.---]. | yšu.g h[.---]. | i.ap.b‘[l.---]. | i.hd.d[---.---]. | ynp‘. 5[67].4.4
lk[.---]. | [--]ṭ.lk[.---]. | [--]kṭ.i[---.---]. | p.šn[-.---]. | w l ṭlb.[---]. | mit.rḥ[.---]. | ṭṭlb.a[--.---]. | yšu.g h[.---]. | i.ap.b‘[l.--- 5[67].4.2

ṭly

r.tliyt.šb‘t.brqm.[---]. | ṯmnt.iṣr r‘t.‘ṣ brq y. | riš h.tply.ṭly.bn.‘n h. | uz‘rt.tmll.išd h.qrn[m]. | dt.‘l h.riš h.b glṯ.b šm[UG5.3.1.5
.‘m k.šb‘t. | ǵlm k.ṯmn.ḫnzr k. | ‘m k.pdry.bt.ar. | ‘m k.ṭṭly.bt.rb.idk. | pn k.al ttn.tk.ǵr. | knkny.ša.ǵr.‘l ydm. | ḫlb.l ẓ 5[67].5.11
t.rimt. | l irt h.mšr.l.dd.aliyn. | b‘l.yd.pdry.bt.ar. | ahbt.ṭly.bt.rb.dd.arṣy. | bt.y‘bdr.km ǵlmm. | w ‘rb n.l p‘n.‘nt.hbr. | 3[‘NT].3.4
imt.[l irt h.tšr.l dd.aliyn.b‘l]. | [ahb]t pdr[y.bt.ar.ahbt.ṭly.bt.rb.dd]. | arṣy bt.y[‘bdr.---]. | rgm l btl[t.‘nt.ṯny.l ybmt.li 7.2[130].11
ṯb.rbt. | aṯrt.ym.mṯb. | klt.knyt. | mṯb.pdry.b ar. | mẓll.ṭly.bt rb. | mṯb.arṣy.bt.y‘bdr. | ap.mṯn.rgmm. | argm k.šskn m 4[51].1.18
ṭll.b[n h.m]ṯb.rbt.aṯrt. | ym.mṯb.[pdr]y.bt.ar. | [mẓll.]ṭly[.bt.]rb.mṯb. | [arṣy.bt.y‘bdr.mṯb]. | [klt.knyt]. 3[‘NT.VI].5.50
ẓll]. | bn h.m[ṯb.rbt.aṯrt.ym]. | mṯb.pdr[y.bt.ar.mẓll]. | ṭly.bt.r[b.mṯb.arṣy]. | bt.y‘bdr[.mṯb.klt]. | knyt.w t‘n[.btlt.‘nt] 3[‘NT.VI].4.4
mṯb rbt.aṯrt.ym. | mṯb.klt.knyt. | mṯb.pdry.bt.ar. | mẓll.ṭly.bt rb. | mṯb.arṣ.bt y‘bdr. | w y‘n lṭpn il d pid. | p ‘bd.an.‘nn 4[51].4.56
| ‘l.b‘l.b ṣrrt. | ṣpn.ytmr.b‘l. | bnt h.y‘n.pdry. | bt.ar.apn.ṭly. | [bt.r]b.pdr.yd‘. | [---]t.im[-]lt. | [-----]. | [---.--]rt. 3[‘NT].1.24
]t.b bht m. | ḥln.b q[rb.hk]l m. | al td[.pdr]y.bt ar. | [---.ṭl]y.bt.rb. | [---.m]dd.il ym. | [---.-]qlṣn.wpṯ m. | [---.]w y‘n.kṯr 4[51].6.11

ṯll

.dnil.mt.|rpi.yṣly.ʻrpt.b |ḥm.un.yr.ʻrpt.|tmṭr.b qẓ.ṭl.yṭll.|l ǵnbm.šbʻ.šnt.|yṣr k.bʻl.ṯmn.rkb.|ʻrpt.bl.ṭl.bl rbb.|bl. 19[1AQHT].1.41

ṯlmyn

qrwn.|ypltn.ʻbdnt.|klby.aḥrṯp.|ilyn.ʻlby.ṣdkn.|gmrt.ṯlmyn.|ʻbdnt.|bdy.ḥrš arkd.|blšš lmd.|ḥtṯn.tqn.|ydd.idṯn. 1045.7

ṯml

[---.]ṯrd.|[---.]qpḥn.|[---.a]ǵlṯr.|[---.]ṯml.|[---.]bn.ḥṣqt.|[---.]bn.uḏr[-]. 2132.4

ṯmṯ

n.ql.špš.ḥw.bṯnm.uḫd.bʻlm.|[--.a]ṯm.prṭl.l riš h.ḥmṯ.ṯmṯ.|[--.]ydbr.ṯrmt.al m.qḥn y.š y.qḥn y.|[--.]šir.b krm.nṭṭt. 1001.1.7

ṯʻn

w lḥm m ʻm aḫ y.lḥm.|w št m.ʻm.a[ḫ] yn.|p nšt.bʻl.[ṯ]ʻn.iṯʻn k.|[---.]ma[---] k.k tmḫṣ.|[ltn.bṯn.br]ḥ.tkly.|[bṯn.ʻq 5[67].1.26
m m ʻm aḫ y.lḥm.|w št m.ʻm.a[ḫ] yn.|p nšt.bʻl.[ṯ]ʻn.iṯʻn k.|[---.]ma[---] k.k tmḫṣ.|[ltn.bṯn.br]ḥ.tkly.|[bṯn.ʻqltn.] 5[67].1.26

ṯrd

k.|mḫšt.klbt.ilm išt.|klt.bt.il.ḏbb.imtḫṣ.ksp.|itrṯ.ḫrṣ.ṯrd.bʻl.|b mrym.ṣpn.mšṣṣ.[-]kʻ[-].|udn h.grš h.l ksi.mlk h.|l 3[ʻNT].3.44
[---.yṯ]rd h.|[---.yg]rš h.|[---.]ru.|[----] h.|[---.--]mt.|[---.--]mr. 6[49].6.1
[---.]ṯrd.|[---.]qpḥn.|[---.a]ǵlṯr.|[---.]ṯml.|[---.]bn.ḥṣqt.|[---.]bn. 2132.1

ṯry

.---].|[---].pit.|[---.]qbat.|[---.]inšt.|[--]u.l tštql.|[---].ṯry.ap.l tlḥm.|[l]ḥm.trmmt.l tšt.|yn.tǵẓyt.špš.|rpim.tḥtk.|š 6.6[62.2].42

ṯtm

---].|ilm.bt.bʻl k.[---].|dl.ylkn.ḥš.b a[rṣ.---].|b ʻpr.ḫbl ṯtm.[---.]|šqy.rṯa.tnm y.ytn.[ks.b yd].|krpn.b klat yd.[---].| 1[ʻNT.X].4.8

Ẓ

ẓu

m[m.t]sk h. | rbb.nsk h.kbkbm. | ttpp.anhbm.d alp.šd[.ẓu h.b ym]. | ṯl[.---]. 3['NT].4.89
ym.trtḥ[ṣ.--]. | [----.a]dm.tium.b ǵlp y[m.--]. | d alp šd.ẓu h.b ym.t[---]. | tlbš.npṣ.ǵzr.tšt.ẖ[---.b] | nšg h.ḥrb.tšt.b t'r[19[1AQHT].4.205
ttpp.anhb[m.d alp.šd]. | ẓu h.b ym[.---]. | [--]rn.l [---]. 3['NT].3.02

ẓby

.šmn.[m]ri h. | t[p]ṯḥ.rḥbt.yn. | 'l h.ṯr h.tš'rb. | 'l h.tš'rb.ẓby h. | ṯr.ẖbr.rbt. | ẖbr.ṯrrt. | bt.krt.tbun. | lm.mṯb[.---]. | w lḥ 15[128].4.18
ẖ.š[mn].mri k. | pṯḥ.[rḥ]bt.yn. | ṣḥ.šb'm.ṯr y. | ṯmnym.[ẓ]by y. | ṯr.ẖbr[.rb]t. | ẖbr[.ṯrrt]. | [-]'b[-].š[--]m. | [----]r[.---]š[. 15[128].4.7

ẓbr

. | bn.pity. | bn.slgyn. | 'zn.bn.mlk. | bn.alṯn. | bn.ṯmyr. | ẓbr. | bn.ṯdṯb. | bn.'rmn. | bn.alz. | bn.mṣrn. | bn.'dy. | bn.ršpy. | 115[301].2.11

ẓhr

b bh | t h.w atn mhr h l a | b h.alp ksp w rbt ẖ | rṣ.išlḥ ẓhrm iq | nim.atn šd h krm[m]. | šd dd h ḥrnqm.w | y'n ḥrẖb 24[77].21

ẓẓ

| [---].bnt.ṣ'ṣ.bnt.m'm'.'bd.ḥrn.[--.]k. | [---].aǵwyn.'n k.ẓẓ.w k mǵ.ilm. | [--.]k 'ṣm.k 'šm.l ttn.k abnm.l thggn. 1001.2.12

ẓẓn

ẖlb.rpš. | ẓẓn. | bn.ḥmny. | dqry. 1068.2
.w.q]l'. | 'ṯqbt.qšt. | [-]ll.qšt.w.ql'. | ẖlb.rpš. | abmn.qšt. | ẓẓn.qšt. | dqry.qš[t]. | rkby. | bn.knn.qšt. | pbyn.qšt. | yddn.qšt. 119[321].2.32

ẓl

.]h.mḥtrt.pṯtm. | [---.-]t h.ušpǵt tišr. | [---.šm]m h.nšat ẓl h kbkbm. | [---.]b km kbkbt k ṯn. | [---.]b'l yḥmdn h.yrṯ y. 2001.2.5
lt. | 'nt.mḥṣ y hm[.m]ẖṣ. | bn y.hm[.mkly.ṣ]brt. | ary y[.ẓl].ksp.[a]ṯrt. | k t'n.ẓl.ksp.w n[-]t. | ẖrṣ.šmẖ.rbt.a[ṯrt]. | ym.g 4[51].2.26
]ẖṣ. | bn y.hm[.mkly.ṣ]brt. | ary y[.ẓl].ksp.[a]ṯrt. | k t'n.ẓl.ksp.w n[-]t. | ẖrṣ.šmẖ.rbt.a[ṯrt]. | ym.gm.l ǵlm h.k [ṯṣḥ]. | ' 4[51].2.27

ẓll

n.in.bt.l b'l.] | [km.ilm.w ḥẓr]. | [k bn.aṯ]r[t]. | m[ṯ]b.il.mẓll. | bn h.mṯb.rbt. | aṯrt.ym.mṯb. | klt.knyt. | mṯb.pdry.b ar. 4[51].1.13
.arẖ h. | wn.in.bt.l b'l.km.ilm. | ḥẓr.k b[n.a]ṯrt.mṯb.il. | mṯll.b[n h.m]ṯb.rbt.aṯrt. | ym.mṯb.[pdr]y.bt.ar. | [mẓll.]ṯly[.bt 3['NT.VI].5.48
. | ary h.wn.in.bt.l b'l. | km.ilm.w ḥẓr.k bn.aṯrt. | mṯb il.mẓll.bn h. | mṯb rbt.aṯrt.ym. | mṯb.klt.knyt. | mṯb.pdry.bt.ar. 4[51].4.52
---.wn.in]. | [bt].l [b'l.km.ilm.w ḥẓr]. | k bn.[aṯrt.mṯb.il.mẓll]. | bn h.m[ṯb.rbt.aṯrt.ym]. | mṯb.pdr[y.bt.ar.mẓll]. | ṯly.bt 3['NT.VI].4.1
. | bn dbb. | w nḥl h. | bn n'myn. | bn aṯtyy. | bn ẖlp. | bn.ẓll. | bn ydy. | bn lzn. | bn.ṯyn. | bn g'r. | bn.prtn. | bn ẖnn. | b[n. 2016.1.12
ḥṣ.w tadm. | rḥṣ[.y]d k.amt. | uṣb['t k.]'d[.ṯ]km. | 'rb[.b ẓl.ẖmt]. | qḥ im[r.b yd k]. | imr.d[bḥ.bm].ymn. | lla.kl[atn]m. 14[KRT].2.65
rtḥṣ.w yadm. | yrḥṣ.yd h.amt h. | uṣb't h.'d.ṯkm. | 'rb.b ẓl.ẖmt.lqḥ. | imr.dbḥ.b yd h. | lla.klatnm. | klt.lḥm h.d nzl. | l 14[KRT].3.159
ṯb.il.mẓll]. | bn h.m[ṯb.rbt.aṯrt.ym]. | mṯb.pdr[y.bt.ar.mẓll]. | ṯly.bt.r[b.mṯb.arṣy]. | bt.y'bdr[.mṯb.klt]. | knyt.w t'n[. 3['NT.VI].4.3
n h. | mṯb rbt.aṯrt.ym. | mṯb.klt.knyt. | mṯb.pdry.bt.ar. | mẓll.ṯly.bt rb. | mṯb.arṣ.bt y'bdr. | w y'n lṯpn il d pid. | p 'bd.a 4[51].4.56
b.il. | mṯll.b[n h.m]ṯb.rbt.aṯrt. | ym.mṯb.[pdr]y.bt.ar. | [mẓll.]ṯly[.bt.]rb.mṯb. | [arṣy.bt.y'bdr.mṯb]. | [klt.knyt]. 3['NT.VI].5.50
n h.mṯb.rbt. | aṯrt.ym.mṯb. | klt.knyt. | mṯb.pdry.b ar. | mẓll.ṯly.bt rb. | mṯb.arṣy.bt.y'bdr. | ap.mṯn.rgmm. | argm k.šs 4[51].1.18

ẓlmt

.l ǵlm h. | b'l.yṣḥ.'n.gpn. | w ugr.bn.ǵlmt. | 'mm ym.bn.ẓlm[t]. | rmt.pr't.ibr[.mnt]. | ṣḥrrm.ḥbl[.--]. | 'rpt.ṯḥt.[---] | m ' 8[51FRAG].8
lm] h.b'l k.yṣḥ.'n. | [gpn].w ugr.b ǵlmt. | ['mm.]ym.bn.ẓlmt.r | [mt.pr']t.ibr.mnt. | [ṣḥrrm.ḥbl.']rpt. | [---.---.-]ḥt. | [---. 4[51].7.55

ẓma

[mrǵ]b.yd.m[ṯkt]. | mẓma.yd.mṯkt. | ṯṯkr.[--]dn. | 'm.krt.mswn h. | arẖ.tzǵ.l 'gl h 15[128].1.2

ẓmn

'bd[--]. | bn.i[--]. | 'd[--]. | ild[--]. | bn.qṣn. | 'lpy. | kṯy. | bn.ẓmn. | bn.trdn. | ypq. | 'bd. | qrḥ. | abšr. | bn.bdn. | ḏmry. | bn.pn 2117.2.23

ẓpn

.dt. | [---.]šb'.l šb'm.aṯr. | [---.--]ldm.dt ymtm. | [--.--]r.l ẓpn. | [---.]pn.ym.y[--]. | [---].b'l.tdd. | [---.]hkl. | [---.]yd h. | [--- 25[136].5

ẓr

hm.tphn.mlak.ym.t'dt.ṯpṭ[.nhr]. | t[ǵ]ly.hlm.rišt hm.l ẓr.brkt hm.w l kḥṯ. | zbl hm.b hm.yg'r.b'l.lm.ǵltm.ilm.rišt. | 2.1[137].23
m.w ank.'ny.mlak.ym.t'dt.ṯpṭ.nhr. | tšu ilm rašt hm.l ẓr.brkt hm.ln.kḥṯ.zbl hm. | aẖr.tmǵyn.mlak ym.t'dt.ṯpṭ.nhr. 2.1[137].29
.w l kḥṯ. | zbl hm.b hm.yg'r.b'l.lm.ǵltm.ilm.rišt. | km l ẓr brkt km.w ln.kḥṯ.zbl km.aḥd. | ilm.t'ny lḥt.mlak.ym.t'dt. 2.1[137].25
. | ilm.t'ny lḥt.mlak.ym.t'dt.ṯpṭ.nhr. | šu.ilm.rašt km.l ẓr.brkt km.ln.kḥṯ. | zbl km.w ank.'ny.mlak.ym.t'dt.ṯpṭ.nhr. 2.1[137].27
--]. | idm.adr[.---]. | idm.'rẓ.t'r[ẓ.---]. | 'n.b'l.a[ẖ]d[.---]. | ẓr h.aḥd.qš[t.---]. | p 'n.b'l.aḥd[.---]. | w ṣmt.ǵllm[.---]. | aḥd.a 12[75].2.33
']dn.ksl. | [ṯṯbr.'ln.p]n h.td[']. | ṯǵṣ[.pnt.ks]l h. | anš.dt.ẓr.[h]. | tšu.g h.w tṣḥ[.i]k. | mǵy.aliy[n.b]'l. | ik.mǵyt.b[t]lt. | ' 4[51].2.20
. | ṯṯt.b'd n.ksl.ṯṯbr. | 'ln.pn h.td'.ṯǵṣ.pnt. | ksl h.anš.dt.ẓr h.tšu. | g h.w tṣḥ.ik.mǵy.gpn.w ugr. | mn.ib.yp'.l b'l.ṣrt. | l 3['NT].3.32
ṯ.'l[n.pn h.td'.b 'dn]. | ksl.y[ṯbr.yǵṣ.pnt.ksl h]. | anš.[dt.ẓr h.yšu.g h]. | w yṣ[ḥ.---]. | mḥṣ[.---]. | š[--.---]. 19[1AQHT].2.96
.rbtm. | kt.il.nbt.b ksp. | šmrgt.b dm.ḥrṣ. | kḥṯ.il.nḥt. | b ẓr.hdm.id. | d prša.b br. | n'l.il.d qblbl. | 'ln.ybl hm.ḥrṣ. | ṯlḥn.i 4[51].1.35
ḥ.ms[rr.]'ṣr. | dbḥ.ṣ[q.b g]l.ḥṯṯ. | yn.b gl[.ẖ]rṣ.nbt. | 'l.l ẓr.[mg]dl. | w 'l.l ẓr.[mg]dl.rkb. | ṯkmm.ḥm[t].ša.yd k. | šmm. 14[KRT].2.73

ẓr

.msrr.'ṣr.db[ḥ]. | yṣq.b gl.ḥtṯ.yn. | b gl.ḫrṣ.nbt.w 'ly. | l ẓr.mgdl.rkb. | ṯkmm.ḥmt.nša. | [y]d h.šmmh.dbḥ. | l ṯr.ab h.il 14[KRT].4.166
ḥ.ṣ[q.b g]l.ḥtṯ. | yn.b gl[.ḫ]rṣ.nbt. | 'l.l ẓr.[mg]dl. | w 'l.l ẓr.[mg]dl.rkb. | ṯkmm.ḥm[t].ša.yd k. | šmm.dbḥ.l ṯr. | ab k.il.š 14[KRT].2.74
--.]tasrn.ṯr il. | [---.]rks.bn.abnm. | [---.]upqt.'rb. | [---.w ẓ]r.mtn y at zd. | [---.]t'rb.bši. | [---.]l tzd.l tptq. | [---].g[--.]l a 1['NT.X].5.25
gn. | bm.nrt.ksmm. | 'l.tl[-]k.'ṭrṭrm. | nšu.[r]iš.ḥrṯm. | l ẓr.'db.dgn kly. | lḥm.[b]'dn hm.kly. | yn.b ḥmt hm.k[l]y. | šm 16[126].3.13
'.md h.b ym.ṯn. | npyn h.b nhrm. | štt.ḫptr.l išt. | ḫbrṯ.l ẓr.pḥmm. | t'pp.ṯr.il.d pid. | tǵẓy.bny.bnwt. | b nši.'n h.w tph 4[51].2.9
ḫryt.mh.yqḥ. | mh.yqḥ.mt.aṯryt.spsg.ysk. | [l]riš.ḥrṣ.l ẓr.qdqd y. | [--.]mt.kl.amt.w an.mtm.amt. | [ap.m]ṯn.rgmm.a 17[2AQHT].6.37
rǵzz. | 'm.ǵr.ṯrmg. | 'm.tlm.ǵṣr.arṣ. | ša.ǵr.'l.ydm. | ḫlb.l ẓr.rḥtm. | w rd.bt ḫpṯt. | arṣ.tspr.b y | rdm.arṣ. | idk.al.ttn. | pn 4[51].8.6
t.rb.idk. | pn k.al ttn.tk.ǵr. | knkny.ša.ǵr.'l ydm. | ḫlb.l ẓr.rḥtm w rd. | bt ḫpṯt.arṣ.tspr b y | rdm.arṣ.w td' ilm. | k mtt 5[67].5.14

ẓrw

tn.ṯlṯ.mat.[---]. | lg.šmn.rqḥ.šr'm.ušpǵtm.p[--.---]. | kṯ.ẓrw.kṯ.nbt.ḏnt.w [-]n[-.---]. | il.ḫyr.ilib.š. | arṣ w šmm.š. | il.š. UG5.9.1.22
lpm. | 'šrm.hbn. | ṯlṯ.mat.dd. | š'rm. | mit.šmn. | 'šr.kat. | ẓrw. 2102.11

ẓrl

bn.grbn. | bn.iršyn. | bn.nklb. | bn.mryn. | [bn.]b[--]. | bn.ẓrl. | bn.illm[-]. | bn.š[---]. | bn.ṣ[---]. | bn.š[---]. | bn.[---]. | bn.[-- 115[301].4.23

ẓrm

.]šš. | [k]d.ykn.bn.'bdṯrm. | kd.'bdil. | ṯlṯ.'l.bn.srt. | kd.'l.ẓrm. | kd.'l.šz.bn pls. | kd.'l.ynḥm. | tgrm.šmn.d.bn.kwy. | 'l.šl 1082.2.5

ẓrn

šrš. | lbnm. | ḫlb.krd. | ṣ'. | mlk. | gb'ly. | ypr. | ary. | ẓrn. | art. | ṯlḥny. | ṯlrby. | dmt. | aǵt. | w.qmnz. | slḫ. | ykn'm. | šl 71[113].9
. | ṯlrby.yrḫ.w.ḫm[š.ym]m. | ṯlḥny.yrḫ.w.ḫm[š.ymm]. | ẓrn.yrḫ.w.ḫmš.y[m]m. | mrat.ḫmš.'šr.ymm. | qmnz.yrḫ.w.ḫ 66[109].6
ag[--]. | ḫp[--]. | m'q[b]. | ar[--]. | ẓr[n]. | ṯlḥ[n]. | ṯlr[by]. | qm[--]. | šl[--]. | a[---]. | d[---]. | q[---]. | ' 2147.5

y

y

l h q[--.---]. | l ytn.l hm.tḥt bʿl[.---]. | h.u qšt pn hdd.b y[.----]. | ʿm.b ym bʿl ysy ym[.---]. | rmm.ḫnpm.mḫl[.---]. | ml 9[33].2.6
grn.[-]dm[.-]. | ašlw.b ṣp.ʿn h. | d b ḫlm y.il.ytn. | b ḏrt y.ab.adm. | w ld.špḥ.l krt. | w ǵlm.l ʿbd.il. | krt.yḫṯ.w ḫlm. | ʿb 14[KRT].3.151
d ʿq h.ib.iqni. | ʿpʿp h.sp.ṯrml. | d b ḫlm y.il.ytn. | b ḏrt y.ab.adm. | w ld.špḥ.l krk | t.w ǵlm.l ʿbd. | il.ttbʿ.mlakm. | l yṯ 14[KRT].6.297
l pḥmm. | a[ṯ]tm.aṯt.il.aṯt.il.w ʿlm h.w hm. | aṯtm.tṣḥn y.ad ad.nḥtm.ḫṭ k. | mmnnm.mṭ yd k.hl.ʿṣr.tḥrr.l išt. | w ṣḥr 23[52].43
l um y.adt ny. | rgm. | tḥm.tlmyn. | w.aḫtmlk ʿbd k. | l.pʿn.adt ny. | 51[95].1
tḥm iwrḏr. | l iwrpḫn. | bn y.aḫ y.rgm. | ilm.tǵr k. | tšlm k. | ik y.lḥt. | spr.d likt. | ʿm.ṯryl. 138.3
tḥm.iwrḏr. | l iwrpḫn. | bn y.aḫ y.rgm. | ilm.tǵr k. | tšlm k. | iky.lḥt. | spr.d likt. | ʿm.ṯryl. | 138.3
lb[u] yʿrr.w yʿ[n]. | yrḫ nyr šmm.w nʿ[n]. | ʿma nkl ḫtn y.a[ḫ]r. | nkl yrḫ ytrḫ.adn h. | yšt mṣb.mznm.um h. | kp mzn 24[77].32
.ap.ank.mnm. | [ḫ]s[r]t.w.uḫ y. | [y]ʿmsn.ṯmn. | w.[u]ḫ y.al ybʿrn. 2065.21
ḫt. | ʿl.w.likt. | ʿm k.w.hm. | l.ʿl.w.lakm. | ilak.w.at. | um y.al.tdḥṣ. | w.ap.mhkm. | b.lb k.al. | tšt. 1013.21
tn. | špḥ.lṯpn.l yḥ. | w yʿny.krt.ṯʿ. | bn.al.tbkn.al. | tdm.l y.al tkl.bn. | qr.ʿn k.mḫ.riš k. | udmʿt.ṣḥ.aḫt k. | ṯtmnt.bt.ḥmḥ 16.1[125].26
. | qḥ.krt.šlmm. | šlmm.w ng.mlk. | l bt y.rḥq.krt. | l ḥẓr y.al.tṣr. | udm.rbt.w udm ṯrrt. | udm.ytnt.il w ušn. | ab.adm. 14[KRT].3.133
bʿ.bk. | tšt.k yn.udmʿt.gm. | tṣḥ.l nrt.ilm.špš. | ʿms mʿ.l y.aliyn.bʿl. | tšmʿ.nrt.ilm.špš. | tšu.aliyn.bʿl.l ktp. | ʿnt.k tšt h.t 6[62].1.12
š[mḫ.b rm.h] | [kl k.al.]aḫd hm.[---]. | [---.b]gdlt.ar[kt y.am--]. | [---.qdq]d k.ašhlk[.šbt k.dmm]. | [šbt.dq]n k.mmʿm 18[3AQHT].1.10
r[m.h]kl[k]. | al.aḫd.hm.b y[--] y.[---]b[-]. | b gdlt.arkt y.am[---]. | qdqd k.ašhlk.šbt[k.dmm]. | [šbt.dqn k.mmʿm.]yʿ 3[ʿNT.VI].5.31
yṯbr.ḫṭ.mṯpṭ k.w yʿn[.ʿṯtr].dm[-]k[-]. | [--]h.b y.ṯr.il.ab y.ank.in.bt[.l] y[.km.]ilm[.w] ḥẓr[.k bn]. | [qd]š.lbum.trd.b n 2.3[129].19
w rgm[.---]. | w yrdnn.an[--.---]. | [---].ank.l km[.---]. | l y.ank.ašṣu[.---.]w[.---]. | w hm.at.tr[gm.---]. | w.drm.ʿtr[--.---] 54.1.17[13.2.2]
-]m.l aqry k.b ntb.pšʿ. | [---].b ntb.gan.ašql k.tḥt. | [pʿn y.a]nk.nʿmn.ʿmq.nšm. | [tdʿṣ.pʿn]m.w tr.arṣ.idk. | [l ttn.pn]m 17[2AQHT].6.45
.w ndd.gzr.l zr.yʿdb.u ymn. | u šmal.b p hm.w l.tšbʿn y.aṯt.itrḫ. | y bn.ašld.šu.ʿdb.tk.mdbr qdš. | ṯm tgrgr.l abnm.w 23[52].64
.yṯp.w[---]. | l k.ašt k.km.nšr.b ḥb[š y]. | km.diy.b tʿrt y.aqht.[km.yṯb]. | l lḥm.w bn.dnil.l ṯrm[.ʿl h]. | nšrm.trḫpn.y 18[3AQHT].4.18
.w tṣd.kl.ǵr. | l kbd.arṣ.kl.gbʿ. | l [k]bd.šdm.tmǵ.l nʿm[y]. | [arṣ.]dbr.ysmt.šd. | [šḥl]mmt.t[mǵ.]l bʿl.np[l]. | [l a]rṣ[.lp 5[67].6.28
l kbd.šdm.npš.ḫsrt. | bn.nšm.npš.hmlt. | arṣ.mǵt.l nʿm y.arṣ. | dbr.ysmt.šd.šḥlmmt. | ngš.ank.aliyn bʿl. | ʿdbnn ank.i 6[49].2.19
.w tṣ]ḥ.sbn. | [---]l[.---.]ʿd. | ksm.mhyt[.m]ǵny. | l nʿm y.arṣ.dbr. | l ysmt.šd.šḥlmmt. | mǵny.l bʿl.npl.l a | rṣ.mt.aliyn. 5[67].6.6
[---.--]m[.---]. | [-.]rbt.ṯbt.[---]. | rbt.ṯbt.ḫš[n.---]. | y.arṣ.ḫšn[.---]. | tʿtd.tkl.[---]. | tkn.lbn[.---]. | dt.lbn k[.---]. | dk 5[67].3.4
ṯr il. | [---.]rks.bn.abnm. | [---.]upqt.ʿrb. | [---.w ẓ]r.mtn y at zd. | [---.]tʿrb.bši. | [---.]l tzd.l tptq. | [---].g[--.]l arṣ. 1[ʿNT.X].5.25
y.rpim.rpim.b bt y]. | aṣḥ.km.[iqra km.ilnym.b] | hkl y.aṯr[h.rpum.l tdd]. | aṯr h.l t[dd.ilnym.ṯm]. | yḥpn.ḥy[ly.zbl 22.1[123].10
t y.rpim. | [rpim.bt y.aṣ]ḥ km.iqra km. | [ilnym.b hkl]y.aṯr h.rpum. | [l tdd.aṯr]h.l tdd.i[lnym]. | [---.]r[--.---]. | [---.y 21[122].1.11
ḥṯ.d[rkt h.b bt y]. | aṣḥ.rpi[m.iqra.ilnym]. | b qrb.h[kl y.aṯr h.rpum.l] | tdd.aṯr[h.l tdd.ilnym]. | asr.mr[kbt.---]. | tʿl 22.1[123].20
t y.r[pim.rpim.b bt y.aṣḥ]. | km.iqr[a km.ilnym.b hkl y]. | aṯr h.r[pum.l tdd.aṯr h]. | l tdd.il[nym.---]. | mhr.bʿl[.---. 22.1[123].4
t y. | [rpim.rpim.b]t y.aṣḥ km.iqra. | [km.ilnym.b h]kl y.aṯr h.rpum. | [l tdd.aṯr h].l tdd.ilnym. | [---.m]rzʿy.apnnk.y 21[122].1.3
d ʿrgzm. | [---.]dt.ʿl.lty. | [---.]tdbḥ.amr. | ṯmn.b qrb.hkl y.[aṯr h.rpum]. | tdd.aṯr h.tdd.iln[ym.---]. | asr.sswm.tṣmd.dg 20[121].2.1
rṯl[.---]. | [---.]mnt.[l]pʿn[.-.-]bd h.aqšr[.---]. | [---].ptḥ y.a[--.]dt[.---].ml[--]. | [---.-]ṯk.ytmt.dlt tlk.[---].bm[.---]. | [--- 1001.1.21
tḥm.rgm. | mlk. | l ḥyil. | lm.tlik.ʿm y. | ik y.aškn. | ʿṣm.l bt.dml. | p ank.atn. | ʿṣm.l k. | arbʿ.ʿṣm. | ʿl. 1010.4
k.šmḫ.bn.ilm.mt. | [---.]g h.w aṣḥ.ik.yṣḥn. | [bʿl.ʿm.aḫ y.ik].yqrun.hd. | [ʿm.ary y.---.--]p.mlḥm y. | [---.---]lt.qẓb. | [-- 5[67].2.22
m.agzr ym. | bn.ym.ynqm.b a[p.]ḏ[d.r]gm.l il.ybl. | aṯt y.il.ylt.mh.ylt.ilmy nʿmm. | agzr ym.bn ym.ynqm.b ap.ḏd.št 23[52].60
ḥbq.ḥmḥmt.tqt[nṣn]. | tldn.šḥr.w šlm.rgm.l il.ybl.a[ṯt y]. | il.ylt.mh.ylt.yld y.šḥr.w šl[m]. | šu.ʿdb.l špš.rbt.w l kbkb 23[52].52
] h. | sp.ṯrml.tḥgrn.[-]dm[.-]. | ašlw.b ṣp.ʿn h. | d b ḫlm y.il.ytn. | b ḏrt y.ab.adm. | w ld.špḥ.l krt. | w ǵlm.l ʿbd.il. | krt. 14[KRT].3.150
. | ʿṯtrt.tsm h. | d ʿq h.ib.iqni. | ʿpʿp h.sp.ṯrml. | d b ḫlm y.il.ytn. | b ḏrt y.ab.adm. | w ld.špḥ.l krk | t.w ǵlm.l ʿbd. | il.tt 14[KRT].6.296
.abn.brq]. | d l t[dʿ.šmm.at m.w ank]. | ibǵ[y h.b tk.ǵ]r y.il.ṣpn. | b q[dš.b ǵr.nḥ]lt y. | w t[ʿn].btlt.[ʿ]nt.ṯṯb. | [ybmt.]li 3[ʿNT].4.63
tdʿ.nšm.w l tbn. | hmlt.arṣ.at m.w ank. | ibǵy h.b tk.ǵr y.il.ṣpn. | b qdš.b ǵr.nḥlt y. | b nʿm.b gbʿ.tliyt. | hlm.ʿnt.tph.il 3[ʿNT].3.26
| la.šmm.b y[d.bn.ilm.m]t. | w tʿn.btlt.ʿn[t.bnt.]bht | k.y ilm.bnt.bh[t k].a[l.tš]mḫ. | al.tšmḫ.b r[m.h]kl[k]. | al.aḫd.h 3[ʿNT.VI].5.28
-]. | [---] h.ap.[---]. | [---].w tʿn.[btlt.ʿnt.---]. | [bnt.bht]k.y ilm[.bnt.bht k.--]. | [al.tšmḫ.]al.tš[mḫ.b rm.h] | [kl k.al.]aḫ 18[3AQHT].1.7
w.k.rgm.špš. | mlk.rb.bʿl y.u. | ʿ[--.]mlakt.ʿbd h. | [---.]bʿl k.yḫpn. | [---.]ʿm h.u ky. | [---.- 1018.2
t.al m.qḥn y.š y.qḥn y. | [--.]šir.b krm.nṭṭt.dm.ʿlt.b ab y. | u---].ʿlt.b k.lk.l pn y.yrk.bʿl.[--]. | [---.]ʿnt.šzrm.tštšḥ.km.ḥ 1001.1.9
m y.bt.bʿl.[w]mn[t]. | y.bt.il.ṯḥ.gg y.b ym.ṭiṭ. | rḥṣ.npṣ y.b ym.rṭ. | dn.il.bt h.ymǵyn. | yštql.dnil.l hkl h. | ʿrb.b bt h.k 17[2AQHT].2.23
y k šbʿt yn. | spu.ksm y.bt.bʿl.[w]mn[t]. | y.bt.il.ṯḥ.gg y.b ym.ṭiṭ. | rḥṣ.npṣ y.b ym.rṭ. | dn.il.bt h.ymǵyn. | yštql.dnil. 17[2AQHT].2.22
ṣ.at m.w ank. | ibǵy h.b tk.ǵr y.il.ṣpn. | b qdš.b ǵr.nḥlt y. | b nʿm.b gbʿ.tliyt. | hlm.ʿnt.tph.ilm.b h.pʿnm. | ṭṭṭ.bʿd n.ksl 3[ʿNT].3.27
.imt.npš.blt. | ḥmr.p imt.b klt. | yd y.ilḥm.hm.šbʿ. | ydt y.b ṣʿ.hm.ks.ymsk. | nhr.k[--].ṣḥn.bʿl.ʿm. | aḫ y.qran.hd.ʿm.ar 5[67].1.21
.hm. | ʿn.kdd.aylt. | mt hm.ks.ym | sk.nhr hm. | šbʿ.ydt y.b ṣʿ. | [--.]šbʿ.rbt. | [---.]qbṭ.ṯm. | [---.]bn.ilm. | [m]t.šmḫ.p yd UG5.4.11
pš.k yld.bn.l y.km. | aḫ y.w šrš.km ary y. | nṣb.skn.ilib y.b qdš. | ztr.ʿm y.l ʿpr.ḏmr.aṯr[y]. | ṭbq lḥt.niṣ y.grš. | d ʿšy.l 17[2AQHT].2.16
y.l ʿpr.ḏmr.aṯr[y]. | ṭbq lḥt.niṣ y.grš. | d ʿšy.ln.aḫd.yd y.b š | krn mʿms y k šbʿt yn. | spu.ksm y.bt.bʿl.[w]mn[t]. | y.b 17[2AQHT].2.19
[y]. | kll.šlm. | ṯm ny.ʿm.um y. | mnm.šlm. | w.rgm.ṯṯb.l y. | bm.ṯy.ndr. | iṯt.ʿmn.mlkt. | w.rgm y.l[--]. | lqt.w.pn. | mlk.n 50[117].13
.w.at. | nǵṯ.w.ytn.hm.l k. | w.lḥt.alpm.ḫršm. | k.rgmt.l y.bly m. | alpm.aršt.l k.w.l y. | mn.bnš.d.l.i[--].ʿ[m k]. | l.alpm 2064.22
.yšal. | ṯryl.p rgm. | l mlk.šm y. | w l h.yʿl m. | w h[t] aḫ y. | bn y.yšal. | ṯryl.w rgm[.-]. | ṯṯb.l aḫ k. | l adn k. 138.15
k. | iky.lḥt. | spr.d likt. | ʿm.ṯryl. | mh y.rgmt. | w ht.aḫ y. | bn y.yšal. | ṯryl.p rgm. | l mlk.šm y. | w l h.yʿl m. | w h[t] a 138.10
k. | ik y.lḥt. | spr.d likt. | ʿm.ṯryl. | mh y.rgmt. | w ht.aḫ y. | bn y.yšal. | ṯryl.p rgm. | l mlk.šm y. | w l h[-] yʿl m. | bn y.y 138.10
.l zr.yʿdb.u ymn. | u šmal.b p hm.w l.tšbʿn y.aṯt.itrḫ. | y bn.ašld.šu.ʿdb.tk.mdbr qdš. | ṯm tgrgr.l abnm.w l.ʿṣm.šbʿ.š 23[52].65
.ʿm.bʿl.ṣrrt. | ṣpn.yšu g h.w yṣḥ. | aḫ y m.ytnt.bʿl. | spu y.bn m.um y.kl | y y.ytʿn.k gmrm. | mt.ʿz.bʿl.ʿz.ynghn. | k ru 6[49].6.15

y

‘t.ǵlm h. | [---].bn.ilm.mt. | p[-]n.aḫ y m.ytn.b‘l. | [s]pu y.bn m.um y.kly y. | yṯb.‘m.b‘l.ṣrrt. | ṣpn.yšu g h.w yṣḥ. | aḫ y 6[49].6.11
.l mlk. | amlk.l drkt k.aṯb. | an.w y‘ny.krt ṯ‘.yṯbr. | ḥrn.y bn.yṯbr.ḥrn. | riš k.‘ṯtrt.šm.b‘l. | qdqd k.tqln.b gbl. | šnt k.b 16.6[127].55
| hrnmy.qšt.yqb.[--] | rk.‘l.aqht.k yq[--.---]. | pr‘m.ṣd k.y bn[.---]. | pr‘m.ṣd k.hn pr[‘.--]. | ṣd.b hkl h[.---]. | [------]. | [-- 17[2AQHT].5.37
.l ydd. | il.ǵzr.tḥm. | aliyn.b‘l. | [hw]t.aliy.q | [rdm.]bht y.bnt. | [dt.ksp.dtm]. | [ḫrṣ.hk]l y. | [---.]aḫ y. | [---.]aḫ y. | [---- 4[51].8.35
hkl m. | sb.ksp.l rqm.ḫrṣ. | nṣb.l lbnt.šmḫ. | aliyn.b‘l.ht y.bnt. | dt.ksp.hkl y.dtm. | ḫrṣ.‘dbt.bht[h.b‘]l. | y‘db.hd.‘db[.‘ 4[51].6.36
m.mlk. | b‘l y.tmǵyy.hn. | alpm.s̀s̀wm.hnd. | w.mlk.b‘l y.bnš. | bnny.‘mn. | mlakty.hnd. | ylak ‘m y. | w.t‘l.ṯh.hn. | [a]l 1012.33
knp.hr[g]b. | b‘l.yṯb.b‘l.y[ṯb]r.diy[.h]wt. | w yql.tḥt.p‘n y.ibq‘.kbd[h]. | w aḥd.hm.iṯ.šmt.hm.iṯ[.‘ẓm]. | abky.w aqbrn 19[1AQHT].3.124
.w yṣḥ.knp.ṣml. | b‘l.yṯbr.b‘l.yṯbr.diy. | hyt.tql.tḥt.p‘n y.ibq‘. | kbd h.w aḥd.hm.iṯ.šmt.iṯ. | ‘ẓm.abky w aqbrn h.aštn. 19[1AQHT].3.138
ṣḥ[.knp.nšrm]. | b‘l.yṯb.b‘l.yṯb[r.diy.hmt]. | tqln.tḥ p‘n y.ibq[‘.kbd hm.w] | aḥd.hm.iṯ.šmt.hm.i[ṯ]. | ‘ẓm.abky.w aqb 19[1AQHT].3.109
š | krn m‘ms y k šb‘t yn. | spu.ksm y.bt.b‘l.[w]mn[t]. | y.bt.il.ṭḫ.gg y.b ym.ṭiṭ. | rḥṣ.npṣ y.b ym.rṯ. | dn.il.bt h.ymǵyn 17[2AQHT].2.22
d ‘šy.ln.aḫd.yd y.b š | krn m‘ms y k šb‘t yn. | spu.ksm y.bt.b‘l.[w]mn[t]. | y.bt.il.ṭḫ.gg y.b ym.ṭiṭ. | rḥṣ.npṣ y.b ym.r 17[2AQHT].2.21
nn.ap ank.aḥwy. | aqht[.ǵz]r.w y‘n.aqht.ǵzr. | al.tšrgn.y btlt m.dm.l ǵzr. | šrg k.ḫḫm.mt.uḫryt.mh.yqḥ. | mh.yqḥ.m 17[2AQHT].6.34
kn.ilib y.b qdš. | ztr.‘m y.l ‘pr.ḏmr.aṯr[y]. | ṭbq lḥt.niṣ y.grš. | d ‘šy.ln.aḫd.yd y.b š | krn m‘ms y k šb‘t yn. | spu.ksm 17[2AQHT].2.18
p ymm. | w rbt.šnt. | b ‘d ‘lm...gn‘. | iršt.aršt. | l aḫ y.l r‘ y.dt. | w ytnnn. | l aḫ h.l r‘ h. | r‘ ‘lm. | ttn.w tn. | w l ttn. | w al 1019.1.8
m.ḫrṣ. | nṣb.l lbnt.šmḫ. | aliyn.b‘l.ht y.bnt. | dt.ksp.hkl y.dtm. | ḫrṣ.‘dbt.bht[h.b‘]l. | y‘db.hd.‘db[.‘d]bt. | hkl h.ṭbḫ.al 4[51].6.37
spt.l š‘r.ṭl.yd[‘t]. | hlk.kbkbm.mdl.‘r. | ṣmd.pḥl.št.gpn y dt ksp. | dt.yrq.nqbn y.tš[m‘]. | pǵt.ṯkmt.my.ḥspt.l[š‘]r.ṭl. | 19[1AQHT].2.53
dd. | il.ǵzr.yqra.mt. | b npš h.ystrn ydd. | b gngn h.aḥd y.d ym | lk.‘l.ilm.l ymru. | ilm.w nšm.d yšb | [‘].hmlt.arṣ.gm.l 4[51].7.49
ṣ k.‘m y.p‘n k.tls] | [m]n ‘m y t[wtḥ.išd k.dm.rgm.iṯ.l y.d argmn k]. | [h]wt.d aṯ[ny k.---.rgm.‘ṣ]. | w lḫšt.abn[.tant.š 7.2[130].17
p‘ b yǵlm. | ur.tisp k.yd.aqht. | ǵzr.tšt k.b qrb m.asm. | y.dnh.ysb.aklt h.yph. | šblt.b akt.šblt.yp‘. | b ḥmdrt.šblt.yḥ[b 19[1AQHT].2.68
ḥl.bkm. | tšu.ab h.tštnn.l[b]mt ‘r. | l ysmsm.bmt.pḥl. | y dnil.ysb.palt h. | bṣql.yph.b palt.bṣ[q]l. | yph.b yǵlm.bṣql.y[19[1AQHT].2.61
.d pid.---]. | ‘l.ydm.p‘rt[.---]. | šm k.mdd.i[l.---]. | bt ksp y.d[--.---]. | b d.aliyn b[‘l.---]. | kd.ynaṣn[.---]. | gršnn.l k[si.ml 1[‘NT.X].4.21
| w.ṯm [ny.‘m.mlkt.u]m y. | mnm[.šlm]. | w.rgm[.ṯṯb.l] y. | hl ny.‘mn. | mlk.b.ṯy ndr. | iṯt.w.ht. | [-]sny.uḏr h. | w.hm.ḫ 1013.11
y.aliy[n.b]‘l. | ik.mǵyt.b[t]lt. | ‘nt.mḫṣ y hm[.m]ḫṣ. | bn y.hm[.mkly.ṣ]brt. | ary y[.ẓl].ksp.[a]ṯrt. | k t‘n.ẓl.ksp.w n[-]t. 4[51].2.25
h.w tṣḥ[.i]k. | mǵy.aliy[n.b]‘l. | ik.mǵyt.b[t]lt. | ‘nt.mḫṣ y hm[.m]ḫṣ. | bn y.hm[.mkly.ṣ]brt. | ary y[.ẓl].ksp.[a]ṯrt. | k t‘ 4[51].2.24
ṯṯb]. | ky.lik.bn y. | lḥt.akl.‘m y. | mid y w ǵbn y. | w.bn y.hn kt. | yškn.anyt. | ym.yšrr. | w.ak[l.---]. | [--].š[--.--]. 2061.12
yšlm.l k.ilm. | tǵr k.tšlm k. | lḥt.šlm.k.lik[t]. | um y.‘m y.ht.‘m[ny]. | kll.šlm.ṯm ny. | ‘m.um y.mnm.šlm. | w.rgm.ṯṯb. 2009.1.6
wt. | [y]rš.‘m y. | mnm.iršt k. | d ḫsrt.w.ank. | aštn..l.iḫ y. | w.ap.ank.mnm. | [ḫ]s[r]t.w.uḫ y. | [y]‘msn.ṯmn. | w.[u]ḫ y. 2065.17
]. | mlk.r[b.b‘]l y.p.l. | ḥy.np[š.a]rš. | l.pn.b‘[l y.l].pn.b‘l y. | w.urk.ym.b‘l y. | l.pn.amn.w.l.pn. | il.mṣrm.dt.tǵrn. | npš.š 1018.19
.‘l.qšt h. | imḫṣ h.‘l.qṣ‘t h.hwt. | l aḥw.ap.qšt h.l ttn. | l y.w b mt[.-]ḥ.mṣṣ[-]t[.--]. | pr‘.qẓ.y[bl].šblt. | b ǵlp h.apnk.dn 19[1AQHT].1.17
qrn.d bat k b‘l.ymšḥ. | b‘l.ymšḥ.hm.b ‘p. | nṭ‘n.b arṣ.ib y. | w b ‘pr.qm.aḫ k. | w tšu.‘n h.btlt.‘nt. | w tšu.‘n h.w t‘n. | w 10[76].2.24
.w ubn.hkl.w ištql šql. | tn.km.nḥšm.yḥr.tn.km. | mhr y.w bn.bṯn.itnn y. | ytt.nḥšm.mhr k.bn bṯn. | itnn k. | aṯr ršp.‘ UG5.7.74
[.r]gm[.ṯṯb]. | ky.lik.bn y. | lḥt.akl.‘m y. | mid y w ǵbn y. | w.bn y.hn kt. | yškn.anyt. | ym.yšrr. | w.ak[l.---]. | [--].š[--.-- 2061.11
[--]ḥ[d].šd.hwt. | [--.]iḥd.šd.gṯr. | [w]ht.yšm‘.uḫ y. | l g y.w yhbṭ.bnš. | w ytn.ilm.b d hm. | b d.iḫqm.gṯr. | w b d.ytrh 55[18].18
d h.alpm.s̀[s̀w]m. | rgmt.‘ly.ṯh.lm. | l.ytn.hm.mlk.[b]‘l y. | w.hn.ibm.šṣq l y. | p.l.ašt.aṯt y. | n‘r y.ṯh.l pn.ib. | hn.hm.y 1012.26
klby. | šm‘t.ḫti. | nḫtu.ht. | hm.in mm. | nḫtu.w.lak. | ‘m y.w.yd. | ilm.p.k mtm. | ‘z.mid. | hm.nṯkp. | m‘n k. | w.mnm. | r 53[54].11
ny]. | kll.šlm.ṯm ny. | ‘m.um y.mnm.šlm. | w.rgm.ṯṯb.l y. | w.mnd‘.k.ank. | aḥš.mǵy.mnd‘. | k.igr.w.u.[--]. | ‘m.špš.[--- 2009.1.9
tḥm.hl[--]. | l pḫry.a[ḫ y]. | w l g.p[-]r[--]. | yšlm[.l k]. | [i]lm[.tǵr k]. | [t]š[lm k.---]. | [- 56[21].2
y.rgmt. | w ht.aḫ y. | bn y.yšal. | ṯryl.p rgm. | l mlk.šm y. | w l h.y‘l m. | w h[t] aḫ y. | bn y.yšal. | ṯryl.w rgm[.-]. | ṯṯb.l 138.13
klt]. | knyt.w t‘n[.btlt.‘nt]. | yṯb l y.ṯr.il[.ab y.---]. | yṯb.l y.w l h.[---]. | [--.i]mṣḫ.nn.k imr.l arṣ. | [ašhlk].šbt h.dmm.šbt 3[‘NT.VI].4.8
y.rgmt. | w ht.aḫ y. | bn y.yšal. | ṯryl.p rgm. | l mlk.šm y. | w l h[-] y‘l m. | bn y.yšal. | ṯryl.w rgm. | ṯṯb.l aḫ k. | l adn k. 138.13
[---]m.tṣḥq.‘nt.w b lb.tqny. | [---.]ṯb l y.l aqht.ǵzr.ṯb l y w l k. | [---]m.l aqry k.b ntb.pš‘. | [---].b ntb.gan.ašql k.tḥt. | 17[2AQHT].6.42
.ks.ymsk. | nhr.k[--].ṣḥn.b‘l.‘m. | aḫ y.qran.hd.‘m.ary y. | w lḥm m ‘m aḫ y.lḥm. | w št m.‘m.a[ḫ] yn. | p nšt.b‘l.[ṭ]‘n. 5[67].1.23
d. | w.mlk.b‘l y.bnš. | bnny.‘mn. | mlakty.hnd. | ylak ‘m y. | w.t‘l.ṯh.hn. | [a]lpm.s̀s̀wm. | [---].w.ṯb. 1012.36
--.]km.r‘y.ht.alk. | [---.]ṯlṯt.amǵy.l bt. | [y.---.b qrb].hkl y.w y‘n.il. | [---.mrz‘]y.lk.bt y.rpim. | [rpim.bt y.aṣ]ḥ km.iqra 21[122].1.8
sin.lpš.tššq[n h]. | b qṣ.all.tšu.g h.w[tṣ] | ḥ.at.mt.tn.aḫ y. | w ‘n.bn.ilm.mt.mh. | taršn.l btlt.‘nt. | an.itlk.w aṣd.kl. | ǵr. 6[49].2.12
m.w ank]. | ibǵ[y h.b tk.ǵ]r y.il.ṣpn. | b q[dš.b ǵr.nḥ]lt y. | w t[‘n].btlt.[‘]nt.ṯṯb. | [ybmt.]limm.[a]n.aqry. | [b arṣ].mlḥ 3[‘NT].4.64
mrn.alk.nmr[rt]. | imḫṣ.mḫṣ.aḫ y.akl[.m] | kly[.‘]l.umt y.w y‘n[.dn] | il.mt.rpi npš tḥ[.pǵt]. | ṯ[km]t.mym.ḥspt.l š‘r. | 19[1AQHT].4.197
]n[t]. | il.ušn.ab[.ad]m. | rḥq.mlk.l bt y. | n[g.]krt.l ḥẓ[r y]. | w y‘n[y.k]rt[.ṯ]‘. | lm.ank.ksp. | w yr[q.ḫrṣ]. | yd.mqm h.w 14[KRT].6.280
nm.[šl]m[.r]gm[.ṯṯb]. | ky.lik.bn y. | lḥt.akl.‘m y. | mid y w ǵbn y. | w.bn y.hn kt. | yškn.anyt. | ym.yšrr. | w.ak[l.---]. | 2061.11
.---]. | [-----]. | [-----]. | [-----]. | [---].al.tš[--.---]. | [---.]l ksi y.w pr[‘]. | [---].pr‘.ank.[---]. | [---.]ank.nši[.---]. | [---.ṯ]br.ḫss.[1002.13
bṣ k. | ‘m y.p‘n k.tlsmn.‘m y. | twtḥ.išd k.dm.rgm. | iṯ.l y.w argm k. | hwt.w aṯny k.rgm. | ‘ṣ.w lḫšt.abn. | tant.šmm.‘ 3[‘NT].3.18
k.‘m y.p‘n k. | [tls]mn.[‘]m y.twtḥ.išd k. | [dm.rgm.iṯ.l y.]w argm k.hwt. | [w aṯny k.rgm.]‘ṣ.w lḫšt. | [abn.rgm.l td]‘. 3[‘NT].4.57
y twtḥ.i[šd k.tk.ḫršn.------------]. | ǵr.ks.dm.r[gm.iṯ.l y.w argm k]. | hwt.w aṯny k[.rgm.‘ṣ.w lḫšt.abn]. | tunt.šmm.‘ 1[‘NT.IX].3.12
.ank. | w anḫn.w tnḫ.b irt y. | npš.k yld.bn.l y.km. | aḫ y.w šrš.km ary y. | nṣb.skn.ilib y.b qdš. | ztr.‘m y.l ‘pr.ḏmr.aṯ 17[2AQHT].2.15
adt y.[---]. | lb.ab[d k].al[.---]. | [-]tm.iph.adt y.w.[---]. | tšṣḥq.hn.aṯt.l.‘bd. | šb‘t.w.nṣp.ksp. | [-]tm.rb[.--.a]ḥ 1017.3
[--.n]pš.ttn[.---]. | [---.]yd‘t.k[---]. | [---].w hm. | [--]y.ṯb y.w [---]. | [---.]bnš.[---]. 61[-].5
rbdd.l kbd.šdm. | ḥš k.‘ṣ k.‘bṣ k. | ‘m y.p‘n k.tlsmn.‘m y. | twtḥ.išd k.dm.rgm. | iṯ.l y.w argm k. | hwt.w aṯny k.rgm. 3[‘NT].3.16
kbd.šdm. | [ḥ]š k.[‘]ṣ k.‘bṣ k.‘m y.p‘n k. | [tls]mn.[‘]m y.twtḥ.išd k. | [dm.rgm.iṯ.l y.]w argm k.hwt. | [w aṯny k.rgm 3[‘NT].4.56
d]. | l kbd.š[dm.ḥš k.‘ṣ k.‘bṣ k.‘m y.p‘n k.tls] | [m]n ‘m y t[wtḥ.išd k.dm.rgm.iṯ.l y.d argmn k]. | [h]wt.d aṯ[ny k.---.r 7.2[130].17
b.bǵrt.ṯ[--. --]. | ḥš k.‘ṣ k.‘[bṣ k.‘m y.p‘n k.tlsmn]. | ‘m y twtḥ.i[šd k.tk.ḫršn.------------]. | ǵr.ks.dm.r[gm.iṯ.l y.w arg 1[‘NT.IX].3.11
[ḥš k.‘ṣ k.‘bṣ k.‘]m y.p[‘]n k. | [tlsmn.‘m y.twt]ḥ.išd k. | [tk.ḫršn.---]r.[-]ḥm k.w št. | [---.]ẓ[--.-]rdy k. | 1[‘NT.IX].2.2
d.l kbd.š]dm.ḥš k. | [‘ṣ k.‘bṣ k.‘m y.p‘]n k.tlsmn. | [‘m y.twtḥ.išd] k.tk.ḫršn. | [---.-]bd k.spr. | [---.-]nk. 1[‘NT.IX].2.23
lm.l.‘ṯtrt. | l.‘nt.l.kl.il.alṯ[y]. | nmry.mlk.‘lm. | mlk n.b‘l y.ḥw[t.--]. | yšhr k.w.‘m.ṣ[--]. | ‘š[--.---]d.lik[t.---]. | w [----]. | k[2008.1.10

nt.šzrm.tštšḥ.km.ḥ[--].|[---].ʿpr.bt k.ygr[š k.---].|[---.]y.ḥr.ḥr.bnt.ḥ[---].|[--.]uḫd.[bʿ]l m.ʿ[--].yd k.amṣ.yd[.--].|[--- 1001.1.13
---.-]qlṣn.wpṯ m.|[---.]w yʿn.kṯr.|[w ḫss.]ṯṯb.bʿl.l hwt y.|[ḥš.]bht h.tbnn.|[ḥš.]trmm.hkl h.|y[tl]k.l lbnn.w ʿṣ h.|l[4[51].6.15
np.nšrm.|bʿl.yṯbr.bʿl.yṯbr.diy.|hmt.hm.tʿpn.ʿl.qbr.bn y.|tšḫṭann.b šnt h.qr.[mym].|mlk.yṣm.y l km.qr.mym.d ʿ[l 19[1AQHT].3.150
ngš.ank.aliyn bʿl.|ʿdbnn ank.imr.b p y.|k lli.b ṯbrn q y.ḫtu hw.|nrt.ilm.špš.ṣḥrrt.|la.šmm.b yd.bn ilm.mt.|ym.y 6[49].2.23
m ary y.|nṣb.skn.ilib y.b qdš.|ztr.ʿm y.l ʿpr.ḏmr.aṯr[y].|ṭbq lḥt.niṣ y.grš.|d ʿšy.ln.aḫd.yd y.b š|krn mʿms y k šbʿ 17[2AQHT].2.17
[t]lt.|ʿnt.mḫṣ y hm[.m]ḫṣ.|bn y.hm[.mkly.ṣ]brt.|ary y[.ẓl].ksp.[a]ṯrt.|k tʿn.ẓl.ksp.w n[-]t.|ḫrṣ.šmḫ.rbt.a[ṯrt].|y 4[51].2.26
.dm[.---.]|[---.]ḥrḥrtm.w[--.]n[--.]iš[--.]h[---.]išt.|[---]y.yblmm.u[---]k.yrd[.--.]i[---]n.bn.|[---.-]nn.nrt.ilm.špš.tšu. 2.3[129].14
nk.|[---].l.ǵr.amn.|[---.-]ktt.hn.ib.|[---.]mlk.|[---.]adt y.tdʿ.|w.ap.mlk.uḏ[r].|[-]dʿ.k.iḫd.[---].|w.mlk.bʿl y.|lm.škn 1012.19
|l ṯryl.um y.|rgm.|ugrt.tǵr k.|ugrt.tǵr k.|tšlm k.um y.|tdʿ.ky.ʿrbt.|l pn.špš.|w pn.špš.nr.|b y.mid.w um.|tšmḫ. 1015.6
-].|tgr.il.bn h.ṯr[.---].|w yʿn.lṭpn.il.d p[id.---].|šm.bn y.yw.ilt.[---].|w pʿr.šm.ym[-.---].|tʿnyn.l zn.tn[.---].|at.adn. 1[ʿNT.X].4.14
ʿnn h.bn.dgn.arṯ m.pḏ h.|[w yʿn.]ṯr.ab h.il.ʿbd k.bʿl.y ym m.ʿbd k.bʿl.|[--.--]m.bn.dgn.a[s]r km.hw ybl.argmn k. 2.1[137].36
drkt k.mšl[-.---].|b riš k.aymr[.---].|ṯpṭ.nhr.yṯb[r.ḥrn.y ym.yṯbr.ḥrn].|riš k.ʿṯtrt.[šm.bʿl.qdqd k.---].|[--]t.mṭ.tpln. 2.1[137].7
lgt.b lšn[y].|ǵr[.---]b.b pš y.t[--].|hwt.bʿl.iš[--].|šmʿ l y.ypš.[---].|ḥkr[.---].|ʿṣr[.--.]tb[-].|ṯat[.---].|yn[-.---].|i[--.---] 2124.5
gnryn.|l mlkytn.|ḥnn y l pn mlk.|šin k itn.|rʿ y šṣa idn l y.|l šmn iṯr hw.|p iḫdn gnryn.|im mlkytn yrgm. 1020.5
.hwt h].|b nši ʿn h.w tphn.in.[---].|[-.]hlk.ǵlmm b dd y.yṣ[--].|[-.]yṣa.w l.yṣa.hlm.[ṯnm].|[q]dqd.ṯlṯ id.ʿl.ud[n].|[-- 19[1AQHT].2.77
.|[--.]šir.b krm.nṭṭt.dm.ʿlt.b ab y.|u---].ʿlt.b k.lk.l pn y.yrk.bʿl.[--].|[---.]ʿnt.šzrm.tštšḥ.km.ḥ[--].|[---].ʿpr.bt k.ygr[1001.1.10
d.|ʿlm.ṯlṯ.sswm.|mrkbt.b trbṣ.|bn.amt.p d.[i]n.|b bt y.ttn.tn.|l y.mṯt.ḥry.|nʿmt.šbḥ.bkr k.|d k nʿm.ʿnt.|nʿm h.k 14[KRT].6.288
ʿbd.|ʿlm.ṯlṯ.sswm.mrkbt.|b trbṣt.bn.amt.|p d.in.b bt y.ttn.|tn.l y.mṯt.ḥry.|nʿmt.špḥ.bkr k.|d k.nʿm.ʿnt.nʿm h.|k 14[KRT].3.142
dl.ylkn.ḥš.b a[rṣ.---].|b ʿpr.ḫbl ṭtm.[---.]|šqy.rṯa.tnm y.ytn.[ks.b yd].|krpn.b klat yd.[---].|km ll.kḥṣ.tusp[.---].|tg 1[ʿNT.X].4.9
tql šql.|tn.km.nḥšm.yḥr.tn.km.|mhr y.w bn.bṯn.itnn y.|ytt.nḥšm.mhr k.bn bṯn.|itnn k.|aṯr ršp.ʿṯtrt.|ʿm ʿṯtrt.mr UG5.7.74
qr[t].|[---.]dt nzdt.m[lk].|[---.]w.ap.bṯn[.---].|[---.]bʿl y.y[--].|[---.-]l[-.---]. 2127.2.7
mt.šd.šḥlmmt.|ngš.ank.aliyn bʿl.|ʿdbnn ank.imr.b p y.|k lli.b ṯbrn q y.ḫtu hw.|nrt.ilm.špš.ṣḥrrt.|la.šmm.b yd.b 6[49].2.22
y].|ṭbq lḥt.niṣ y.grš.|d ʿšy.ln.aḫd.yd y.b š|krn mʿms y k šbʿt yn.|spu.ksm y.bt.bʿl.[w]mn[t].|y.bt.il.ṯḥ.gg y.b ym 17[2AQHT].2.20
|ṣpn.yšu g h.w yṣḥ.|aḫ y m.ytnt.bʿl.|spu y.bn m.um y.kl|y y.ytʿn.k gmrm.|mt.ʿz.bʿl.ʿz.ynghn.|k rumm.mt.ʿz.bʿl 6[49].6.15
--].bn.ilm.mt.|p[-]n.aḫ y m.ytn.bʿl.|[s]pu y.bn m.um y.kly y.|yṯb.ʿm.bʿl.ṣrrt.|ṣpn.yšu g h.w yṣḥ.|aḫ y m.ytnt.bʿl. 6[49].6.11
m.|l tbrkn.alk brkt.|tmrn.alk.nmr[rt].|imḫṣ.mḫṣ.aḫ y.akl[.m]|kly[.ʿ]l.umt y.w yʿn[.dn]|il.mt.rpi npš tḥ[.pǵt].|ṯ[19[1AQHT].4.196
yṣḥ.aṯbn.ank.|w anḫn.w tnḫ.b irt y.|npš.k yld.bn.l y.km.|aḫ y.w šrš.km ary y.|nṣb.skn.ilib y.b qdš.|ztr.ʿm y.l 17[2AQHT].2.14
.w yʿn[.ʿṯtr].dm[-]k[-].|[--]ḥ.b y.ṯr.il.ab y.ank.in.bt[.l] y[.km.]ilm[.w] ḥẓr[.k bn].|[qd]š.lbum.trd.b n[p]šn y.trḥṣn. 2.3[129].19
].|w tʿn.btlt.ʿnt.ṯb.yṭp.w[---].|l k.ašt k.km.nšr.b ḥb[š y].|km.diy.b tʿrt y.aqht.[km.yṯb].|l lḥm.w bn.dnil.l ṯrm[.ʿl 18[3AQHT].4.17
u.bʿl.mhr bʿl.|w mhr.ʿnt.ṯm.yḥpn.ḥyl|y.zbl.mlk.ʿllm y.km.tdd.|ʿnt.ṣd.tštr.ʿpt.šmm.|ṭbḫ.alpm.ap ṣin.šql.ṯrm.|w 22.2[124].10
ʿbd h.]ybrk.il.krt.|[ṯʿ.ymr]m.nʿm[n.]ǵlm.il.|a[ṯt.tq]ḥ.y krt.aṯt.|tqḥ.bt k.ǵlmt.tšʿrb.|ḥqr k.tld.šbʿ.bnm.l k.|w ṯmn. 15[128].2.21
zr.p np.š.npš.lbim.|thw.hm.brlt.anḫr.|b ym.hm.brk y.tkšd.|rumm.ʿn.kḏd.aylt.|hm.imt.imt.npš.blt.|ḥmr.p imt. 5[67].1.16
m.ht.tṣdn.tinṯt.|[---]m.tṣḥq.ʿnt.w b lb.tqny.|[---.]ṯb l y.l aqht.ǵzr.ṯb l y w l k.|[---]m.l aqry k.b ntb.pšʿ.|[---].b ntb 17[2AQHT].6.42
d.gṯr.|[--]ḥ[d].šd.hwt.|[--.]iḥd.šd.gṯr.|[w]ht.yšmʿ.uḫ y.|l g y.w yhbṭ.bnš.|w ytn.ilm.b d hm.|b d.iḫqm.gṯr.|w b 55[18].17
aṯr[.---].|[--]šy.w ydn.bʿ[l.---]n.|[--]ʿ.k yn.hm.l.atn.bt y.l h. 1002.62
b.uḫry mṭ.yd h.|ymǵ.l mrrt.tǵll.b nr.|yšu.g h.w yṣḥ.y l k.mrrt.|tǵll.b nr.d ʿl k.mḫṣ.aqht.|ǵzr.šrš k.b arṣ.al.|ypʿ. 19[1AQHT].3.157
.|ymǵ.l qrt.ablm.abl[m].|qrt.zbl.yrḫ.yšu g h.|w yṣḥ.y l k.qrt.ablm.|d ʿl k.mḫṣ.aqht.ǵzr.|ʿwrt.yšt k.bʿl.l ht.|w ʿl 19[1AQHT].4.165
tʿpn.ʿl.qbr.bn y.|tšḫṭann.b šnt h.qr.[mym].|mlk.yṣm.y l km.qr.mym.d ʿ[l k].|mḫṣ.aqht.ǵzr.amd.gr bt il.|ʿnt.brḥ. 19[1AQHT].3.152
m.|aḫ y.w šrš.km ary y.|nṣb.skn.ilib y.b qdš.|ztr.ʿm y.l ʿpr.ḏmr.aṯr[y].|ṭbq lḥt.niṣ y.grš.|d ʿšy.ln.aḫd.yd y.b š|k 17[2AQHT].2.17
p.l.|ḥy.np[š.a]rš.|l.pn.bʿ[l y.l].pn.bʿl y.|w.urk.ym.bʿl y.|l.pn.amn.w.l.pn.|il.mṣrm.dt.tǵrn.|npš.špš.mlk.|rb.bʿl y. 1018.20
-].|arš[.---].|mlk.r[b.bʿ]l y.p.l.|ḥy.np[š.a]rš.|l.pn.bʿ[l y.l].pn.bʿl y.|w.urk.ym.bʿl y.|l.pn.amn.w.l.pn.|il.mṣrm.dt.t 1018.19
gnryn.|l mlkytn.|ḥnn y l pn mlk.|šin k itn.|rʿ y šṣa idn l y.|l šmn iṯr hw.|p iḫdn 1020.3
k.alp ymm.|w rbt.šnt.|b ʿd ʿlm...gnʿ.|iršt.aršt.|l aḫ y.l rʿ y.dt.|w ytnnn.|l aḫ h.l rʿ h.|rʿ ʿlm.|ttn.w tn.|w l ttn.| 1019.1.8
n.|l mlkytn.|ḥnn y l pn mlk.|šin k itn.|rʿ y šṣa idn l y.|l šmn iṯr hw.|p iḫdn gnryn.|im mlkytn yrgm.|aḫnnn.| 1020.5
n.bʿl y[.mrḥqtm].|šbʿ d.w.šbʿ[d.qlt].|ankn.rgmt.l.bʿl y.|l.špš.ʿlm.l.ʿṯtrt.|l.ʿnt.l.kl.il.alṯ[y].|nmry.mlk.ʿlm.|mlk n. 2008.1.6
[---].ap[.---].|[---].l y.l [---].|[---] ny.ṯp[--.---].|[---.--]zn.a[--.---].|[---.--]y.ns[--.-- 63[26].1.2
n.kḏd.aylt.|hm.imt.imt.npš.blt.|ḥmr.p imt.b klt.|yd y.ilḥm.hm.šbʿ.|ydt y.b ṣʿ.hm.ks.ymsk.|nhr.k[--].ṣḥn.bʿl.ʿm. 5[67].1.20
-].ṣḥn.bʿl.ʿm.|aḫ y.qran.hd.ʿm.ary y.|w lḥm m ʿm aḫ y.lḥm.|w št m.ʿm.a[ḫ] yn.|p nšt.bʿl.[ṭ]ʿn.iṭʿn k.|[---.]ma[---] 5[67].1.24
.|ṯm ny.ʿ[m.]bn y.|mnm.[šl]m[.r]gm[.ṯṯb].|ky.lik.bn y.|lḥt.akl.ʿm y.|mid y w ǵbn y.|w.bn y.hn kt.|yškn.anyt.| 2061.9
.gršm zbln.|in.b ilm.ʿny h.|w yʿn.lṭpn.il.b pid.|ṯb.bn y.lm ṯb[t] km.|l kḥṯ.zbl k[m.a]nk.|iḥtrš.w [a]škn.|aškn.ydt 16[126].5.24
ši[l.š]lm y.|[ʿ]d.r[-]š.|[-]ly.l.likt.|[a]nk.[---].|šil.[šlm y].|[l]m.li[kt].|[-]t.ʿ[--]. 2010.12
adt y.tdʿ.|w.ap.mlk.uḏ[r].|[-]dʿ.k.iḫd.[---].|w.mlk.bʿl y.|lm.škn.hnk.|l ʿbd h.alpm.ś[św]m.|rgmt.ʿly.ṯh.lm.|l.ytn. 1012.22
a]ṭm.prṭl.l riš h.ḥmṯ.ṭmṯ.|[--.]ydbr.ṯrmt.al m.qḥn y.š y.qḥn y.|[--.]šir.b krm.nṭṭt.dm.ʿlt.b ab y.|u---].ʿlt.b k.lk.l pn 1001.1.8
.|yd[r.k]rt.ṯʿ.|i.iṯt.aṯrt.ṣrm.|w ilt.ṣdynm.|hm.ḥry.bt y.|iqḥ.ašʿrb.ǵlmt.|ḥẓr y.ṯn h.wspm.|atn.w ṯlṯ h.ḫrṣm.|ylk 14[KRT].4.203
n[.mhr].|št.qḥn.w tšqyn.yn.qḥ.|ks.b d y.qbʿt.b ymn y[.t]q|ḥ.pǵt.w tšqyn h.tq[ḥ.ks.]b d h.|qbʿt.b ymn h.w yʿn.y 19[1AQHT].4.216
šlm.|w.rgm.ṯṯb.l y.|bm.ṯy.ndr.|iṯt.ʿmn.mlkt.|w.rgm y.l[--].|lqt.w.pn.|mlk.nr b n. 50[117].16
m.um y.kly y.|yṯb.ʿm.bʿl.ṣrrt.|ṣpn.yšu g h.w yṣḥ.|aḫ y m.ytnt.bʿl.|spu y.bn m.um y.kl|y y.ytʿn.k gmrm.|mt.ʿz.b 6[49].6.14
bn.ilm.mt.|[--]u.šbʿt.ǵlm h.|[---].bn.ilm.mt.|p[-]n.aḫ y m.ytn.bʿl.|[s]pu y.bn m.um y.kly y.|yṯb.ʿm.bʿl.ṣrrt.|ṣpn.y 6[49].6.10
k.|tšlm k.um y.|tdʿ.ky.ʿrbt.|l pn.špš.|w pn.špš.nr.|b y.mid.w um.|tšmḫ.m ab.|w al.trḥln.|ʿtn.ḫrd.ank.|ʿm ny.šl 1015.10
bn y.|mnm.[šl]m[.r]gm[.ṯṯb].|ky.lik.bn y.|lḥt.akl.ʿm y.|mid y w ǵbn y.|w.bn y.hn kt.|yškn.anyt.|ym.yšrr.|w.ak 2061.10
t.lqḥt.|w.ṯṯb.ank.l hm.|w.any k.ṯt.|by.ʿky.ʿryt.|w.aḫ y.mhk.|b lb h.al.yšt. 2059.26
|[---.]ʿmt.l ql.rpi[.---].|[---.-]llm.abl.mṣrp k.[---].|[---.]y.mṭnt.w tḥ.ṭbt.n[--].|[---.b]ṯnm w ṯṯb.ʿl.bṯnt.trtḥ[ṣ.---].|[--- 1001.2.4
lyn.apsn[y.---].|plzn.qrty[.---].|w.klt h.b.t[--.---].|bʿl y.mlk[y.---].|yd.bt h.yd[.---].|ary.yd.t[--.---].|ḫtn h.šbʿl[.--- 81[329].13

y

w.lḥt.alpm.ḫršm.|k.rgmt.l y.bly m.|alpm.aršt.l k.w.l y.|mn.bnš.d.l.i[--].'[m k].|l.alpm.w.l.y[n.--]t.|w.bl.bnš.hw[- 2064.23

----].|[-]š[--.---].|[-]r[--.--]y.|in m.'bd k hwt.|[y]rš.'m y.|mnm.iršt k.|d ḫsrt.w.ank.|aštn..l.iḫ y.|w.ap.ank.mnm.| 2065.14

.|tģr k.tšlm k.|hl ny.'m n[y].|kll.šlm.|ṯm ny.'m.um y.|mnm.šlm.|w.rgm.ṯṯb.l y.|bm.ṯy.ndr.|iṯt.'mn.mlkt.|w.rg 50[117].11

.tš[lm] k.|[h]l ny.'m n[.š]lm.|w.ṯm [ny.'m.mlkt.u]m y.|mnm[.šlm].|w.rgm[.ṯṯb.l] y.|hl ny.'mn.|mlk.b.ṯy ndr.|iṯ 1013.9

.lik[t].|um y.'m y.ht.'m[ny].|kll.šlm.ṯm ny.|'m.um y.mnm.šlm.|w.rgm.ṯṯb.l y.|w.mnd'.k.ank.|aḫš.mģy.mnd'.| 2009.1.8

[il]m.|tģr k.tšlm k.|hn ny.'m n.š[l]m.|ṯm ny.'[m.]bn y.|mnm.[šl]m[.r]gm[.ṯṯb].|ky.lik.bn y.|lḥt.akl.'m y.|mid y 2061.7

.|'bd k.|l p'n.b'l y.|ṯn id.šb' d.|mrḫqtm.|qlt.'m.|b'l y.mnm.|šlm.|[r]gm[.ṯṯb].|[l.]'bd[k]. 2115.2.9

.|l.p'n.|adt y.|šb' d.|w.šb' id.|mrḫqtm.|qlt.|'m.adt y.|mnm.šlm.|rgm.ṯṯb.|l.'bd h. 52[89].12

bz tdm.|lla y.'m lẓpn i|l ḏ.pid.hn b p y sp|r hn.b špt y mn|t hn ṯlḫ h w mlg h y|ṯtqt 'm h b q't.|tq't 'm prbḫṯ.|d 24[77].46

.|p.l.ašt.aṯt y.|n'r y.ṯh.l pn.ib.|hn.hm.yrgm.mlk.|b'l y.tmģyy.hn.|alpm.ššwm.hnd.|w.mlk.b'l y.bnš.|bnny.'mn.| 1012.31

zrm.ilm.ylḥm.|uzrm.yšqy.bn.qdš.|l tbrknn l ṯr.il ab y.|tmrnn.l bny.bnwt.|w ykn.bn h b bt.šrš.b qrb.|hkl h.nṣb. 17[2AQHT].1.24

šmm.'ṣr.yḫrṭ yšt.|l pḥm.il.aṯtm.k ypt.hm.aṯtm.tṣḥn.|y mt.mt.nḥtm.ḫṭ k.mmnnm.mṭ.yd k.|h[l.]'ṣr.tḥrr.l išt.ṣḥrrt 23[52].40

ṣḥrrt.l pḥmm.btm.bt.il.bt.il.|w 'lm h.w hn.aṯtm.tṣḥn y.mt mt.|nḥtm.ḫṭ k.mmnnm.mṭ yd k.hl.'ṣr.|tḥrr.l išt.w ṣḥr 23[52].46

swm.|mrkbt.b trbṣ.|bn.amt.p d.[i]n.|b bt y.ttn.tn.|l y.mṯt.ḥry.|n'mt.šbḥ.bkr k.|d k n'm.'nt.|n'm h.km.tsm.|'ṯt 14[KRT].6.289

ṯ.sswm.mrkbt.|b trbṣt.bn.amt.|p d.in.b bt y.ttn.|tn.l y.mṯt.ḥry.|n'mt.špḥ.bkr k.|d k.n'm.'nt.n'm h.|km.tsm.'ṯtrt 14[KRT].3.143

lk n.aliyn.b'l.ṯpṭ n.|in.d 'ln h.klny y.qš h.|nbln.klny y.nbl.ks h.|any.l yṣḥ.ṯr.il.ab h.il.|mlk.d yknn h.yṣḥ.aṯrt.|w 3['NT.VI].5.42

].|[ṯ]rrt.udm.y[t]n[t].|il.ušn.ab[.ad]m.|rḥq.mlk.l bt y.|n[g.]krt.l ḥẓ[r y].|w y'n[y.k]rt[.ṯ]'.|lm.ank.ksp.|w yr[q. 14[KRT].6.279

].|[ṯrrt.udm.ytnt].|[il.w ušn.ab.adm].|[rḥq.mlk.l bt y].|[ng.kr]t.l ḥ[ẓ]r y.|[-----].|[---.ttb'].|[mlakm.l yṯb].|[idk. 14[KRT].5.260

ht.ģ]zr.at.aḫ.w an.a[ḫt k].|[---].šb'.ṯir k.[---].|[---.]ab y.ndt.ank[.---].|[---.--]l.mlk.tlk.b ṣd[.---].|[---.]mt.išryt[.---]. 18[3AQHT].1.26

m.|l.ytn.hm.mlk.[b]'l y.|w.hn.ibm.šṣq l y.|p.l.ašt.aṯt y.|n'r y.ṯh.l pn.ib.|hn.hm.yrgm.mlk.|b'l y.tmģyy.hn.|alpm 1012.28

.pat.mdbr.w ngš.hm.nģr.|mdr'.w ṣḥ hm.'m.nģr.mdr' y.nģr.|nģr.ptḥ.w ptḥ hw.prṣ.b'd hm.|w 'rb.hm.hm[.iṯ.--.l]ḥ 23[52].69

yṣḥq.|yšu.g h.w yṣḥ.|aṯbn.ank.w anḫn.|w tnḫ.b irt y.npš.|k ḥy.aliyn.b'l.|k iṯ.zbl.b'l.arṣ.|gm.yṣḥ.il.l btlt.|'nt.š 6[49].3.19

m.yṯpd.yšu.|g h.w yṣḥ.aṯbn.ank.|w anḫn.w tnḫ.b irt y.|npš.k yld.bn.l y.km.|aḫ y.w šrš.km ary y.|nṣb.skn.ilib y. 17[2AQHT].2.13

tnḫ.b irt y.|npš.k yld.bn.l y.km.|aḫ y.w šrš.km ary y.|nṣb.skn.ilib y.b qdš.|ztr.'m y.l 'pr.ḏmr.aṯr[y].|ṯbq lḥt.ni 17[2AQHT].2.15

.|tqru.l špš.um h.špš.um.ql bl.|'m b'l.mrym.ṣpn.mnt y.nṯk.|nḥš.šmrr.nḥš.'q šr ln h.|mlḫš.abd.ln h.ydy.ḥmt.hlm. UG5.7.9

ģzr.m[t.hrnmy.y]šu.|g h.w yṣḥ.t[b'.---].|bkyt.b hk[l]y.mšspdt.|b ḥẓr y pẓģm.ģr.w yq.|dbḥ.ilm.yš'ly.dģṯ h.|b šm 19[1AQHT].4.183

rdt.|b 'rgzm.b bz tdm.|lla y.'m lẓpn i|l ḏ.pid.hn b p y sp|r hn.b špt y mn|t hn ṯlḫ h w mlg h y|ṯtqt 'm h b q't.|t 24[77].45

.|yšlm.[l] k.|ilm.t[ģ]r k.|tšlm k.|lm[.l.]likt.|ši[l.š]lm y.|[']d.r[-]š.|[-]ly.l.likt.|[a]nk.[---].|šil.[šlm y].|[l]m.li[kt].| 2010.8

rgm.|yšlm.l k.ilm.|tģr k.tšlm k.|lḥt.šlm.k.lik[t].|um y.'m y.ht.'m[ny].|kll.šlm.ṯm ny.|'m.um y.mnm.šlm.|w.rg 2009.1.6

.|'tn.ḫrd.ank.|'m ny.šlm.|kll.|w mnm.|šlm 'm.|um y.|'m y.ṯṯb.|rgm. 1015.18

[---.]l mdgkbr.|[---] y.'m k.|[-]tn.l.stn.|[--.]d.n'm.lbš k.|[-]dm.ṯn id.|[--]m.d.l.n' 2128.1.2

hll.snnt.bnt h|ll b'l gml.yrdt.|b 'rgzm.b bz tdm.|lla y.'m lẓpn i|l ḏ.pid.hn b p y sp|r hn.b špt y mn|t hn ṯlḫ h w 24[77].44

m.|[lm.]l.likt.'m y.|[---.]'bd.ank.|[---.'b]d k.|[---.--]l y.'m.|[---.]'m.|[---.--]y.w.lm.|[---.]il.šlm.|[---.]ank.|[---].ml 2128.2.2

rt.w.ank.|aštn..l.iḫ y.|w.ap.ank.mnm.|[ḫ]s[r]t.w.uḫ y.|[y]'msn.ṯmn.|w.[u]ḫ y.al yb'rn. 2065.19

šu g h.w yṣḥ.|aḫ y m.ytnt.b'l.|spu y.bn m.um y.kl|y y.yt'n.k gmrm.|mt.'z.b'l.'z.ynghn.|k rumm.mt.'z.b'l.|'z.yn 6[49].6.16

b šb['.]ymm.tb'.b bt h.|kṯrt.bnt.hll.snnt.|[-]d[-]t.n'm y.'rš.h[--]m.|ysmsmt.'rš.ḫlln.[-].|yṯb.dnil.[l s]pr yrḫ h.|yrs. 17[2AQHT].2.41

k.|'m mlakt h šm' h.|w b.'ly skn.yd' rgm h.|w ht ab y ģm[--].|t[--.---].|ls[--.---].|ṣḥ[.---].|ky.m[--.---].|w pr[--.--- 1021.9

arḫ.td.rgm.b ģr.|b p y.t'lgt.b lšn[y].|ģr[.---]b.b pš y.t[--].|hwt.b'l.iš[--].|šm' l y.ypš.[---].|ḥkr 2124.2

lk].|rb[.b'l y.---].|w.an[k.---].|arš[.---].|mlk.r[b.b']l y.p.l.|ḥy.np[š.a]rš.|l.pn.b'[l y.l].pn.b'l y.|w.urk.ym.b'l y.|l. 1018.17

rgmt.'ly.ṯh.lm.|l.ytn.hm.mlk.[b]'l y.|w.hn.ibm.šṣq l y.|p.l.ašt.aṯt y.|n'r y.ṯh.l pn.ib.|hn.hm.yrgm.mlk.|b'l y.tm 1012.27

]šu.|g h.w yṣḥ.t[b'.---].|bkyt.b hk[l]y.mšspdt.|b ḥẓr y pẓģm.ģr.w yq.|dbḥ.ilm.yš'ly.dģṯ h.|b šmym.dģṯ hrnmy[. 19[1AQHT].4.184

šlm.|l kbd.arṣ.arbdd.l kbd.šdm.|[ḥ]š k.[']ṣ k.'bṣ k.'m y.p'n k.|[tls]mn.[']m y.twtḥ.išd k.|[dm.rgm.iṯ.l y.]w argm 3['NT].4.55

k.šlm.l kbd.arṣ.|arbdd.l kbd.šdm.|ḥš k.'ṣ k.'bṣ k.|'m y.p'n k.tlsmn.'m y.|twtḥ.išd k.dm.rgm.|iṯ.l y.w argm k.|h 3['NT].3.16

k.šlm.l kbd.arṣ.arbdd].|l kbd.š[dm.ḥš k.'ṣ k.'bṣ k.'m y.p'n k.tls]|[m]n 'm y t[wtḥ.išd k.dm.rgm.iṯ.l y.d argmn k]. 7.2[130].16

[ḥš k.'ṣ k.'bṣ k.']m y.p[']n k.|[tlsmn.'m y.twt]ḥ.išd k.|[tk.ḫršn.---]r.[-]ḥm k.w 1['NT.IX].2.1

šlm].l kbd.arṣ.|[arbdd.l kbd.š]dm.ḥš k.|['ṣ k.'bṣ k.'m y.p']n k.tlsmn.|['m y.twtḥ.išd] k.tk.ḫršn.|[---.-]bd k.spr.|[- 1['NT.IX].2.22

.|št.lskt.n[--.---].|'db.bģrt.ṯ[--. --].|ḥš k.'ṣ k.'[bṣ k.'m y.p'n k.tlsmn].|'m y twtḥ.i[šd k.tk.ḫršn.-------------].|ģr.ks.d 1['NT.IX].3.10

.|yšu.g h.w yṣḥ.|l rgmt.l k.l ali|yn.b'l.ṯṯbn.b'l.|l hwt y.yptḥ.ḥ|ln.b bht m.urbt.|b qrb.hk[l m.yp]tḥ.|b'l.b dqt[.'r 4[51].7.25

m.---].|mhr.b'l[.---.mhr].|'nt.lk b[t y.rpim.rpim.b bt y].|aṣḥ.km.[iqra km.ilnym.b] |hkl y.aṯr[h.rpum.l tdd].|aṯr 22.1[123].8

[---.m]rz'y.lk.bt y.|[rpim.rpim.b]t y.aṣḥ km.iqra.|[km.ilnym.b h]kl y.aṯr h.rpum.|[l tdd.aṯr h] 21[122].1.2

[--].[-]l[--.b qr]|b hkl y.[---].|lk bt y.r[pim.rpim.b bt y.aṣḥ].|km.iqr[a km.ilnym.b hkl y].|aṯr h.r[pum.l tdd.aṯr h 22.1[123].3

qrb].hkl y.w y'n.il.|[---.mrz']y.lk.bt y.rpim.|[rpim.bt y.aṣ]ḥ km.iqra km.|[ilnym.b hkl]y.aṯr h.rpum.|[l tdd.aṯr] 21[122].1.10

[.---].|'l amr.yu[ḫd.ksa.mlk h].|nḫt.kḥṯ.d[rkt h.b bt y].|aṣḥ.rpi[m.iqra.ilnym].|b qrb.h[kl y.aṯr h.rpum.l] |tdd.a 22.1[123].18

hlm w y'n.ytpn[.mhr].|št.qḥn.w tšqyn.yn.qḥ.|ks.b d y.qb't.b ymn y[.t]q|ḥ.pģt.w tšqyn h.tq[ḥ.ks.]b d h.|qb't.b y 19[1AQHT].4.216

lṣn.|yqm.w ywpṯn.b tk.|p[ḫ]r.bn.ilm.štt.|p[--].b ṯlḥn y.qlt.|b ks.ištyn h.|dm.ṯn.dbḥm.šna.b'l.ṯlṯ.|rkb.'rpt.dbḥ.|b 4[51].3.15

mlkt.u[m] y.|[rg]m[.]t[ḥm].|mlk.bn [k].|[l].p'n.um [y].|qlt[.l um] y.|yšlm.il[m].|tģ[r] k.tš[lm] k.|[h]l ny.'m n[. 1013.4

l.mlkt.|um y.rgm.|tḥm.mlk.|bn k.|l.p'n.um y.|qlt.l.um y.|yšlm.ilm.|tģr k.tšlm k.|hl ny.'m n[y].|kll.šl 50[117].5

l.ybnn.|adn y.|rgm.|tḥm.t[g]yn.|bn k.|l.p['n.adn y].|q[lt.---].|l.yb[nn].|b'l y.r[gm].|tḥm.'bd[--].|'bd k.|l p'n 2115.1.6

.šb'.|ydt y.b ṣ'.hm.ks.ymsk.|nhr.k[--].ṣḥn.b'l.'m.|aḫ y.qran.hd.'m.ary y.|w lḥm m 'm aḫ y.lḥm.|w št m.'m.a[ḫ] 5[67].1.23

.ḥyt.ḥẓt.tḥm k.|mlk n.aliyn.b'l.ṯpṭ n.|in.d 'ln h.klny y.qš h.|nbln.klny y.nbl.ks h.|any.l yṣḥ.ṯr.il.ab h.il.|mlk.d y 3['NT.VI].5.41

ṣpn.b [tk].|ģr.tliyt.šb't.brqm.[---].|ṯmnt.iṣr r't.'ṣ brq y.|riš h.tply.ṭly.bn.'n h.|uz'rt.tmll.išd h.qrn[m].|dt.'l h.riš UG5.3.1.4

tḥm iwrḏr.|l iwrpḫn.|bn y.aḫ y.rgm.|ilm.tģr k.|tšlm k.|ik y.lḥt.|spr.d likt.|'m.ṯryl.|mh 138.3

tḥm.iwrḏr.|l iwrpḫn.|bn y.aḫ y.rgm.|ilm.tģr k.|tšlm k.|iky.lḥt.|spr.d likt.|'m.ṯryl.|mh y 138.3

tḥm[.t]lm[yn].|l ṯryl.um y.|rgm.|ugrt.tǵr k.|ugrt.tǵr k.|tšlm k.um y.|td‘.ky.‘rbt.|l 1015.2
l.ḏrdn.|b‘l y.rgm.|bn.ḫrn k.|mǵy.|hbṭ.hw.|ḫrd.w.šl hw.|qr[-].|akl n. 2114.2
tḥm.mlk.|l.ṯryl.um y.rgm.|yšlm.l k.ilm.|tǵr k.tšlm k.|lḥt.šlm.k.lik[t].|um y.‘m 2009.1.2
[tḥm.---].|[l.---].|[a]ḫt y.rgm.|[y]šlm.l k.|[il]m.tšlm k.|[tǵ]r k.|[--]y.ibr[-].|[--]wy. 1016.3
l.mlkt.|adt y.rgm.|tḥm.illḏr.|‘bd k..|l.p‘n a[dt y].|šb‘ d[.w šb‘ d].|mrḫ 1014.2
[l.ml]k.[b‘l y].|rg[m].|tḥm.wr[--].|yšlm.[l] k.|ilm.t[ǵ]r k.|tšlm k.|lm[. 2010.1
l mlkt.u[m] y.|[rg]m[.]t[ḥm].|mlk.bn [k].|[l].p‘n.um [y].|qlt[.l um] y.| 1013.1
l.mlkt.|um y.rgm.|tḥm.mlk.|bn k.|l.p‘n.um y.|qlt.l.um y.|yšlm.ilm.|t 50[117].2
l.mlk.ugrt.|aḫ y.rgm.|tḥm.mlk.ṣr.aḫ k.|y[š]lm.l k.ilm.|tǵr k.tšlm k.|hn n 2059.2
l.mlk[.u]grt.|iḫ y.rgm.|[tḥ]m.m[lk.-]bl[-].|yšlm.l[k].ilm.|tǵr.tšl[m] k.|[---- 2159.2
m.t[g]yn.|bn k.|l.p[‘n.adn y].|q[lt.---].|l.yb[nn].|b‘l y.r[gm].|tḥm.‘bd[--].|‘bd k.|l p‘n.b‘l y.|ṯn id.šb‘ d.|mrḥqt 2115.2.2
l.mlk.b[‘l y].|r[gm].|tḥm.rb.mi[--.‘]bd k.|l.p‘n.b‘l y[.mrḥqtm].|šb‘ d. 2008.1.1
l.ybnn.|adn y.|rgm.|tḥm.t[g]yn.|bn k.|l.p[‘n.adn y].|q[lt.---].|l.yb[nn]. 2115.1.2
l.mlkt.|adt y.|rgm.|tḥm.tlmyn.|‘bd k.|l.p‘n.|adt y.|šb‘ d.|w.šb‘ id.|m 52[89].2
l.mlk.b‘[l] y.|rgm.|tḥm.ṯpṭb[‘l].|[‘]bd k.|[l.p]‘n.b‘l y.|[šb‘] d.šb‘ [d].|[2063.1
.l] y[.km.]ilm[.w] ḥẓr[.k bn].|[qd]š.lbum.trd.b n[p]šn y.trḥṣn.k ṯrm.|[--]b b[ht].|[zbl.]ym.b hkl.ṯpṭ.nh[r].ytir.ṯr.il. 2.3[129].20
t.|b trbṣ.bn.amt.|qḥ.krt.šlmm.|šlmm.w ng.mlk.|l bt y.rḥq.krt.|l ḥẓr y.al.tṣr.|udm.rbt.w udm ṯrrt.|udm.ytnt.il 14[KRT].3.132
l.mlk.b[‘l y].|r[gm].|tḥm.rb.mi[--.‘]bd k.|l.p‘n.b‘l y[.mrḥqtm].|šb‘ d.w.šb‘[d.qlt].|ankn.rgmt.l.b‘l y.|l.špš.‘lm 2008.1.4
[---.a]dt y.|[---].irrṯwm.‘bd k.|[---.a]dt y.mrḥqm.|[---].adt y.yšlm.|[---.]mlk n.amṣ.|[.---].nn.|[---.] 1012.3
.aṯr h].|l tdd.il[nym.---].|mhr.b‘l[.---.mhr].|‘nt.lk b[t y.rpim.rpim.b bt y].|aṣḥ.km.[iqra km.ilnym.b] |hkl y.aṯr[22.1[123].8
[--].[-]l[--.b qr]|b hkl y.[---].|lk bt y.r[pim.rpim.b bt y.aṣḥ].|km.iqr[a km.ilnym.b hkl y].|aṯr 22.1[123].3
ǵy.l bt.|[y.---.b qrb].hkl y.w y‘n.il.|[---.mrz‘]y.lk.bt y.rpim.|[rpim.bt y.aṣ]ḥ km.iqra km.|[ilnym.b hkl]y.aṯr h.r 21[122].1.9
[---.m]rz‘y.lk.bt y.|[rpim.rpim.b]t y.aṣḥ km.iqra.|[km.ilnym.b h]kl y.aṯr h.r 21[122].1.1
-.aliy]n.b‘l.|[------.]yrḫ.zbl.|[--.kṯ]r w ḫss.|[---]n.rḥm y.ršp zbl.|[w ‘d]t.ilm.ṯlṯ h.|[ap]nk.krt.ṯ‘.‘[-]r.|[--.]b bt h.yšt 15[128].2.6
[--.a]ṯm.prṯl.l riš h.ḥmṯ.ṯmṯ.|[--.]ydbr.ṯrmt.al m.qḥn y.š y.qḥn y.|[--.]šir.b krm.nṯṯt.dm.‘lt.b ab y.|u---].‘lt.b k.lk. 1001.1.8
bn y.yšal.|ṯryl.p rgm.|l mlk.šm y.|w l h[-] y‘l m.|bn y.yšal.|ṯryl.w rgm.|ṯṯb.l aḫ k.|l adn k. 138.16
ṯryl.p rgm.|l mlk.šm y.|w l h.y‘l m.|w h[t] aḫ y.|bn y.yšal.|ṯryl.w rgm[.-].|ṯṯb.l aḫ k.|l adn k. 138.16
y.lḥt.|spr.d likt.|‘m.ṯryl.|mh y.rgmt.|w ht.aḫ y.|bn y.yšal.|ṯryl.p rgm.|l mlk.šm y.|w l h[-] y‘l m.|bn y.yšal.|ṯr 138.11
y.lḥt.|spr.d likt.|‘m.ṯryl.|mh y.rgmt.|w ht.aḫ y.|bn y.yšal.|ṯryl.p rgm.|l mlk.šm y.|w l h.y‘l m.|w h[t] aḫ y.|b 138.11
l.mlkt.|adt y.|rgm.|tḥm.tlmyn.|‘bd k.|l.p‘n.|adt y.|šb‘ d.|w.šb‘ id.|mrḥqtm.|qlt.|‘m.adt y.|mnm.šlm.|rgm 52[89].7
l.mlkt.|adt y.rgm.|tḥm.illḏr.|‘bd k..|l.p‘n a[dt y].|šb‘ d[.w šb‘ d].|mrḥq[tm.qlt].|mn[m.šlm]. 1014.5
l.mlk.b‘[l] y.|rgm.|tḥm.ṯpṭb[‘l].|[‘]bd k.|[l.p]‘n.b‘l y.|[šb‘] d.šb‘ [d].|[mr]ḥqtm.|qlt.|‘bd k.b.|lwsnd.|[w] b ṣr. 2063.5
.|tldn.šḥr.w šlm.rgm.l il.ybl.a[tt y].|il.ylt.mh.ylt.yld y.šḥr.w šl[m].|šu.‘db.l špš.rbt.w l kbkbm.kn[-].|yhbr.špt h 23[52].53
ǵy k.bnm.ta[--.---].|[b]nm.w bnt.ytn k[.---].|[--]l.bn y.šḥt.w [---].|[--]tt.msgr.bn k[.---].|[--]n.tḥm.b‘l[.---]. 59[100].10
--].|[--.]l mlk [---].|[---].aḫ y[.---].|[--]q lpš[.---].|[---] y št k[.---].|[---.]l m[lk]. 2130.2.2
kt.|um y.rgm.|tḥm.mlk.|bn k.|l.p‘n.um y.|qlt.l.um y.|yšlm.ilm.|tǵr k.tšlm k.|hl ny.‘m n[y].|kll.šlm.|ṯm ny.‘ 50[117].6
[rg]m[.]t[ḥm].|mlk.bn [k].|[l].p‘n.um [y].|qlt[.l um] y.|yšlm.il[m].|tǵ[r] k.tš[lm] k.|[h]l ny.‘m n[.š]lm.|w.ṯm [n 1013.5
]dt y.|[---].irrṯwm.‘bd k.|[---.a]dt y.mrḥqm.|[---].adt y.yšlm.|[---.]mlk n.amṣ.|[.---].nn.|[---.]qrt.dt.|[---.--]s‘.hn. 1012.4
dd].|aṯr h.l t[dd.ilnym.ṯm].|yḥpn.ḥy[ly.zbl.mlk.‘llm y].|šm‘.atm[.---].|ym.lm.qd[.---].|šmn.prst[.---].|ydr.hm.y 22.1[123].12
kbkbm.mdl.‘r.|ṣmd.pḥl.št.gpn y dt ksp.|dt.yrq.nqbn y.tš[m‘].|pǵt.ṯkmt.my.ḥspt.l[š‘]r.ṭl.|yd‘t.hlk.kbkbm.|bkm. 19[1AQHT].2.54
pḥl[.št.gpnm.dt].|ksp.dt.yr[q.nqbnm].|‘db.gpn.atnt[y].|yšm‘.qd.w amr[r].|mdl.‘r.ṣmd.pḥl.|št.gpnm.dt.ksp.|dt. 4[51].4.7
p šlm[.---].|bt.l bnš.trg[m.---].|l šlmt.l šlm.b[--.---]|b y.šnt.mlit.t[--.---].|ymǵy k.bnm.ta[--.---].|[b]nm.w bnt.ytn 59[100].7
yt k.k qlt[.---].|[--]at.brt.lb k.‘nn.[---].|[--.]šdq.k ttn.l y.šn[.---].|[---.]bn.rgm.w yd‘[.---]. 60[32].5
l lyt.‘l.umt k.|w abqṯ.aliyn.b‘l.|w t‘n.btlt.‘nt.|an.l an.y špš.|an.l an.il.yǵr[.-].|tǵr k.š[---.---].|yštd[.---].|dr[.---].| 6[49].4.46
‘l k.|‘[--.s]glt h.at.|ht[.---.]špš.b‘l k.|yd‘m.l.yd‘t.|‘m y.špš.b‘l k.|šnt.šntm.lm.l.tlk.|w.lḥt.akl.ky.|likt.‘m.špš.|b‘l 2060.15
btlt.|‘nt.šm‘.l btlt.‘n[t].|rgm.l nrt.il.šp[š].|pl.‘nt.šdm.y špš.|pl.‘nt.šdm.il.yšt k.|[b]‘l.‘nt.mḥrṯt.|iy.aliyn.b‘l.|iy.zb 6[49].4.25
g h.w tṣḥ.|tḥm.ṯr.il.ab k.|hwt.lṭpn.ḥtk k.|pl.‘nt.šdm.y špš.|pl.‘nt.šdm.il.yš[t k].|b‘l.‘nt.mḥrṯ[-].|iy.aliyn.b‘l.|iy.z 6[49].4.36
arḫ.td.rgm.b ǵr.|b p y.t‘lgt.b lšn[y].|ǵr[.---]b.b pš y.t[--].|hwt.b‘l.iš[--].|šm‘ l y. 2124.2
arḫ.td.rgm.b ǵr.|b p y.t‘lgt.b lšn[y].|ǵr[.---]b.b pš y.t[--].|hwt.b‘l.iš[--].|šm‘ l y.ypš.[---].|ḥkr[.---].|‘šr[.--.]tb[-] 2124.3
n.hm.mlk.[b]‘l y.|w.hn.ibm.šṣq l y.|p.l.ašt.aṯt y.|n‘r y.ṯh.l pn.ib.|hn.hm.yrgm.mlk.|b‘l y.tmǵyy.hn.|alpm.ššwm 1012.29
.ilm.mt.|p[-]n.aḫ y m.ytn.b‘l.|[s]pu y.bn m.um y.kly y.|yṯb.‘m.b‘l.ṣrrt.|ṣpn.yšu g h.w yṣḥ.|aḫ y m.ytnt.b‘l.|spu 6[49].6.11
rd.ank.|‘m ny.šlm.|kll.|w mnm.|šlm ‘m.|um y.|‘m y.ṯṯṯb.|rgm. 1015.19
mṯt.ḥry].|ṭbḫ.š[mn].mri k.|ptḥ.[rḥ]bt.yn.|ṣḥ.šb‘m.ṯr y.|ṯmnym.[ẓ]by y.|ṯr.ḫbr[.rb]t.|ḫbr[.ṯrrt].|[-]‘b[-].š[--]m.|[15[128].4.6
-].|l.yb[nn].|b‘l y.r[gm].|tḥm.‘bd[--].|‘bd k.|l p‘n.b‘l y.|ṯn id.šb‘ d.|mrḥqtm.|qlt.‘m.|b‘l y.mnm.|šlm.|[r]gm[.ṯṯṯ 2115.2.5
.ṣrm.|w ilt.ṣdynm.|hm.ḥry.bt y.|iqḥ.aš‘rb.ǵlmt.|ḥẓr y.ṯn h.wspm.|atn.w tlṯ h.ḫrṣm.|ylk ym.w ṯn.|ṯlṯ.rb‘.ym.|a 14[KRT].4.205
w y‘n.k[ṯr.w ḫs]s.|ṯṯb.b‘l.l[hwt y].|ṯn.rgm.k[ṯr.w]ḫss.|šm‘.m‘.l al[iy]n b‘l.|bl.ašt.ur[bt.]b b 4[51].6.2
.]mlk k.l ytbr.ḫṭ.mṯpṭ k.w y‘n[.‘ṯtr].dm[-]k[-].|[--]ḫ.b y.ṯr.il.ab y.ank.in.bt[.l] y[.km.]ilm[.w] ḥẓr[.k bn].|[qd]š.lbu 2.3[129].19
.arṣy].|bt.y‘bdr[.mṯb.klt].|knyt.w t‘n[.btlt.‘nt].|ytb l y.ṯr.il[.ab y.---].|ytb.l y.w l h.[---].|[--.i]mṣḫ.nn.k imr.l arṣ.| 3[‘NT.VI].4.7
n].mri k.|ptḥ.[rḥ]bt.yn.|ṣḥ.šb‘m.ṯr y.|ṯmnym.[ẓ]by y.|ṯr.ḫbr[.rb]t.|ḫbr[.ṯrrt].|[-]‘b[-].š[--]m.|[----]r[.---]š[.--]qm 15[128].4.7
-]yt.w.[---].|[---.ṯ]y.al.an[k.--.]il[m.--]y.|[--.m]šlm.pn y[.-.]tlkn.|[---.]rḫbn.hm.[-.]aṯr[.---].|[--]šy.w ydn.b‘[l.---]n.| 1002.59
pb]l[.mlk.g]m.l aṯt |[h.k]y[ṣḥ.]šm‘.m‘.|[--.]‘m[.-.]aṯt y[.-].|[---].tḥm.|[---]t.[ ]r.|[---.--]n.|[---] h.l ‘db.|[---]n.yd h. 14[KRT].5.230
ap.ht.k[--.]škn.|w.mṯnn[.---.]‘mn k.|[-]štš.[---.]rgm y.|[-]wd.r[-.]pǵt.|[---.--]t.yd‘t.|[----.r]gm.|[---].kll h.|[---.--] 54.1.22[13.2.7]
.yqḥ.|mh.yqḥ.mt.aṯryt.spsg.ysk.|[l]riš.ḥrṣ.l ẓr.qdqd y.|[--.]mt.kl.amt.w an.mtm.amt.|[ap.m]ṯn.rgmm.argm.qšt 17[2AQHT].6.37

y

[---.--]d.‘m y. | [--.]spr.lm.likt. | [--]y.k išal hm. | [--.‘š]rm.kkr.ṯlṯ. | [--.]ṯlṯ 1022.1
rṯl.l riš h.ḥmṯ.ṯmṯ. | [--.]ydbr.ṯrmt.al m.qḥn y.š y.qḥn y. | [--.]šir.b krm.nṭṭt.dm.‘lt.b ab y. | u---].‘lt.b k.lk.l pn y.yrk 1001.1.8
udm‘t.ṣḥ.aḫt k. | ṯtmnt.bt.ḥmḥ h. | d[-]n.tbkn.w tdm.l y.[--]. | [---].al.trgm.l aḫt k. | [---.]l [ ]dm.aḫt k. | yd‘t.k rḥmt. | 16.1[125].30
--.--]t.hw[-]y.h[--]r.w rgm.ank. | [---.]hdd tr[--.--]l.aṯrt y. | [--]ptm.ṣḥq. | [---.]rgm.hy.[-]ḫ[-]y.ilak k. | [---.--]g k.yritn. 1002.39
w ygl.w ynsk.‘[-]. | [--]y.l arṣ[.id]y.alt.l aḥš.idy.alt.in l y. | [--]t.b‘l.ḥẓ.ršp.b[n].km.yr.klyt h.w lb h. | [ṯ]n.p k.b ǵr.ṯn. 1001.1.2
[dt.ksp.dtm]. | [ḫrṣ.hk]l y. | [---.]aḫ y. | [---.]aḫ y. | [----]y. | [---.]rb. | [---].ṣḥt. | [---.--]t. | [---.]ilm. | [---.--]u.yd. | [---.--]k 4[51].8.40
hw]t.aliy.q | [rdm.]bht y.bnt. | [dt.ksp.dtm]. | [ḫrṣ.hk]l y. | [---.]aḫ y. | [---.]aḫ y. | [----]y. | [---.]rb. | [---].ṣḥt. | [---.--]t. | 4[51].8.37
| [rdm.]bht y.bnt. | [dt.ksp.dtm]. | [ḫrṣ.hk]l y. | [---.]aḫ y. | [---.]aḫ y. | [----]y. | [---.]rb. | [---].ṣḥt. | [---.--]t. | [---.]ilm. | [4[51].8.38
[---.a]dt y. | [---].irrṯwm.‘bd k. | [---.a]dt y.mrḥqm. | [---].adt y.yšlm. | [1012.1
.apnnk.yrp. | [---.]km.r‘y.ht.alk. | [---.]ṯlṯt.amǵy.l bt. | [y.---.b qrb].hkl y.w y‘n.il. | [---.mrz‘]y.lk.bt y.rpim. | [rpim.bt 21[122].1.8
-.b].ṣp[n]. | [---.]š[--]. | [-----]. | [-----]. | [---.]ṯty. | [---.-]rd y. | [---.]b‘l. | [---].plz. | [---.-]tt k. | [---.]mlk. 2159.15
kbkbm. | [---.]b km kbkbt k ṯn. | [---.]b‘l yḥmdn h.yrṯ y. | [---.]dmrn.l pn h yrd. | [---.]b‘l.šm[.--.]rgbt yu. | [---]w yr 2001.2.7
[--].[-]l[--.b qr]| b hkl y.[---]. | lk bt y.r[pim.rpim.b bt y.aṣḥ]. | km.iqr[a km.ilnym.b 22.1[123].2
lk. | rb.b[‘l y.---]. | [-----]. | r[--.---]. | b.[---.mlk]. | rb[.b‘l y.---]. | w.an[k.---]. | arš[.---]. | mlk.r[b.b‘]l y.p.l. | ḥy.np[š.a]rš. 1018.14
n[y.---]. | plzn.qrty[.---]. | w.klt h.b.t[--.---]. | b‘l y.mlk[y.---]. | yd.bt h.yd[.---]. | ary.yd.t[--.---]. | ḫtn h.šb‘l[.---]. | ṯlḫn 81[329].13
m h.u ky. | [---.--]d k.k.tmǵy. | ml[--.--]š[.ml]k.rb. | b[‘l y.---]. | yd[--.]mlk. | rb.b[‘l y.---]. | [-----]. | r[--.---]. | b.[---.mlk]. 1018.8
grt.il[ht]. | ‘l.l ṯkm.bnw n. | l nḫnpt.mšpy. | ṯlṯ.kmm.ṯrr y. | [---.]l ǵr.gm.ṣḥ. | [---.]r[-]m. 16[126].4.16
adt y.[---]. | lb.ab[d k].al[.---]. | [-]tm.iph.adt y.w.[---]. | tšṣḥq.hn.a 1017.1
‘m.lbš k. | [-]dm.ṯn id. | [--]m.d.l.n‘mm. | [lm.]l.likt.‘m y. | [---.]‘bd.ank. | [---.‘b]d k. | [---.--]l y.‘m. | [---.]‘m. | [---.--]y. 2128.1.7
irt.lbnn.mk.b šb‘. | [ymm.---]k.aliyn.b‘l. | [---].r‘ h ab y. | [---.]‘[---]. 22.2[124].27
[ṯ]k.l yd‘.l bn.l pq ḥmt. | [---.--]n h.ḥmt.w t‘btn h.abd y. | [---.ǵ]r.šrǵzz.ybky.km.n‘r. | [w ydm‘.k]m.ṣǵr.špš.b šmm.t UG5.8.36
ṯn.[---]. | hn dt.[---]. | [-----]. | [-----]. | tḥm[.---]. | l p‘n.b‘l y[.---]. | qlt. | [--]t.mlk.d.y[mlk]. | [--.]‘bdyrḫ.l.ml[k]. | [--]t.w.l 2064.10
--.t]asrn. | [---.]trks. | [---.]abnm.upqt. | [---.]l w ǵr mtn y. | [---.]rq.gb. | [---.--]kl.tǵr.mtn h. | [---.--]b.w ym ymm. | [y‘t 1[‘NT.X].5.12
yn.w l. | [--]k b‘lt bhtm[.--]tn k. | [--]y.l ihbt.yb[--].rgm y. | [---.]škb.w m[--.]mlakt. | [---.]‘l.w tš‘[d]n.npṣ h. | [---.]rgm. 1002.46
d. | [‘m.ary y.---.--]p.mlḥm y. | [---.---]lt.qẓb. | [---.]šmḫ y. | [---.]tb‘. | [---.-]nnm. 5[67].2.25
.y‘bdr[.mṯb.klt]. | knyt.w t‘n[.btlt.‘nt]. | yṯb l y.ṯr.il[.ab y.---]. | yṯb.l y.w l h.[---]. | [--.i]mṣḫ.nn.k imr.l arṣ. | [ašhlk].šb 3[‘NT.VI].4.7
| [---.yṯ]b.l arṣ. | [---.--]l.šir. | [---.-]tm. | [---.]yd y. | [----]y. | [---.-]lm. | [---.r]umm. 10[76].1.21
-]‘. | [---.]idk. | [---.--]ty. | [---.--]hr. | [---.--]ḫdn. | [---.]bšr y. | [---.--]b. | [---.--]a h. | [---.--]d. | [---].umt n. | [---.--]yh.wn l. 28[-].6
h.w aṣḥ.ik.yṣḥn. | [b‘l.‘m.aḫ y.ik].yqrun.hd. | [‘m.ary y.---.--]p.mlḥm y. | [---.---]lt.qẓb. | [---.]šmḫ y. | [---.]tb‘. | [---.-] 5[67].2.23
[---] h.gm. | [l --- k.]yṣḥ. | [---]d.‘r. | [----.-]bb. | [----.]lm y. | [---.--]p. | [---.d]bḥ. | t[---.id]k. | pn[m.al.ttn]. | ‘m.[krt.msw] 14[KRT].5.241
m.uṯryn[.---]. | [g]rgš ‘bdy[--]. | [--.]l mlk [---]. | [---].aḫ y[.---]. | [--]q lpš[.---]. | [---] y št k[.---]. | [---.]l m[lk]. 2130.1.4
d.r[-.]pǵt. | [---.--]t.yd‘t. | [----.r]gm. | [---].kll h. | [---.--]l y. | [---.--]r. | [--.]wk[--.---]. | [--].lm.l[--.---]. | [-]m.in[.---]. | [--.] 45[45].1
n. | [b‘l.‘m.aḫ y.ik].yqrun.hd. | [‘m.ary y.---.--]p.mlḥm y. | [---.---]lt.qẓb. | [---.]šmḫ y. | [---.]tb‘. | [---.-]nnm. 5[67].2.23
ǵy. | ml[--.--]š[.ml]k.rb. | b[‘l y.---]. | yd[--.]mlk. | rb.b[‘l y.---]. | [-----]. | r[--.---]. | b.[---.mlk]. | rb[.b‘l y.---]. | w.an[k.---]. 1018.10
bu.b‘d y[.---]. 1169.1
].a[l.tš]mḫ. | al.tšmḫ.b r[m.h]kl[k]. | al.aḫd.hm.b y[--] y.[---]b[-]. | b gdlt.arkt y.am[---]. | qdqd k.ašhlk.šbt[k.dmm]. 3[‘NT.VI].5.30
y.rgm l. | mlkt.ugrt. | [--]kt.rgmt. | [--]y.l.ilak. | [---].‘m y. | [---]m.w.lm. | [---.]w.‘m k. | [---]m.ksp. | [---].‘m. | [---.-]n[-]. 1016.12
t y.bnt. | [dt.ksp.dtm]. | [ḫrṣ.hk]l y. | [---.]aḫ y. | [---.]aḫ y. | [----]y. | [---.]rb. | [---].ṣḥt. | [---.--]t. | [---.]ilm. | [---.--]u.yd. 4[51].8.39
-]l.limm. | [---.yṯ]b.l arṣ. | [---.--]l.šir. | [---.-]tm. | [---.]yd y. | [----]y. | [---.-]lm. | [---.r]umm. 10[76].1.20
. | [il.w ušn.ab.adm]. | [rḥq.mlk.l bt y]. | [ng.kr]t.l ḥ[ẓ]r y. | [-----]. | [---.ttb‘]. | [mlakm.l yṯb]. | [idk.pnm.l ytn]. | [‘]m[.k 14[KRT].5.261
kp. | m‘n k. | w.mnm. | rgm.d.tšm‘. | ṯmt.w.št. | b.spr.‘m y. 53[54].19
pn.amn.w.l.pn. | il.mṣrm.dt.tǵrn. | npš.špš.mlk. | rb.b‘l y. 1018.24
y. | w.spr.in[.-.]‘d m. | spr n.ṯhr[.--]. | aṯr.iṯ.bqṯ. | w.štn.l y. 2060.35

yarš

db il. | yarš il. | yrǵm il. | ‘mtr. | ydb il. | yrgb lim. | ‘mtr. | yarš il. | ydb b‘l. | yrǵm b‘l. | ‘z b‘l. | ydb hd. UG5.14.B.10
pgr. | iltm ḫnqtm. | yrḫ kty. | ygb hd. | yrgb b‘l. | ydb il. | yarš il. | yrǵm il. | ‘mtr. | ydb il. | yrgb lim. | ‘mtr. | yarš il. | ydb UG5.14.B.4
tpnr. | arb‘.spm.l.lbnš prwsdy. | ṯṯ spm.l bnš klnmw. | l yarš ḫswn. | ḫmš ‘šr.sp. | l bnš tpnr d yaḫd l g ynm. | ṯṯ spm l 137.2[93].9

yu

n h.yrṯ y. | [---.]dmrn.l pn h yrd. | [---.]b‘l.šm[.--.]rgbt yu. | [---]w yrmy[.q]rn h. | [---.-]ny h pdr.ttǵr. | [---.n]šr k.al tt 2001.2.9

yukl

. | dmt.lḫsn.krm.aḥd.anndr.kr[m.---]. | aǵt.mryn.ary[.]yukl.krm.[---]. | gdn.krm.aḫ[d.--]r.krm.[---]. | ary.‘šr.arb‘.kb 1081.16

ybl

l m‘[rb]. | nrt.ilm.špš.mǵy[t]. | pǵt.l ahlm.rgm.l yṯ[pn.y] | bl.agrtn.bat.b ḏd k.[pǵt]. | bat.b hlm w y‘n.yṯpn[.mhr]. | š 19[1AQHT].4.212
lm.]n‘mm.agzr ym. | bn.ym.ynqm.b a[p.]ḏ[d.r]gm.l il.ybl. | aṯt y.il.ylt.mh.ylt.ilmy n‘mm. | agzr ym.bn ym.ynqm.b 23[52].59
.w hr.b hbq.ḥmḥmt.tqt[nṣn]. | tldn.šḥr.w šlm.rgm.l il.ybl.a[ṯt y]. | il.ylt.mh.ylt.yld y.šḥr.w šl[m]. | šu.‘db.l špš.rbt. 23[52].52
d k.b‘l.y ym m.‘bd k.b‘l. | [--.--]m.bn.dgn.a[s]r km.hw ybl.argmn k.k ilm. | [---.]ybl.k bn.qdš.mnḥy k.ap.anš.zbl.b‘[l 2.1[137].37
--.l]šn.l kbkbm.y‘rb. | [b‘]l.b kbd h.b p h yrd. | k ḫrr.zt.ybl.arṣ.w pr. | ‘ṣm.yraun.aliyn.b‘l. | ṯt‘.nn.rkb.‘rpt. | tb‘.rgm.l 5[67].2.5
bt.b qrb hkl h. | yblnn ǵrm.mid.ksp. | gb‘m lḥmd.ḫrṣ. | yblnn.udr.ilqṣm. | yak.l ktr.w ḫss. | w ṯb l mspr..k tlakn. | ǵl 4[51].5.102
m[.---.]| [---.]ḥrḥrtm.w[--.]n[--.]iš[--.]h[---.]išt. | [---]y.yblmm.u[---]k.yrd[.--.]i[---]n.bn. | [---.-]nn.nrt.ilm.špš.tšu.g 2.3[129].14
.ṯlṯ.šm[n]. | alp.mitm.kbd.ṯlṯ.ḥlb. | šb‘.l.‘šrm.kkr.ṯlṯ. | d.ybl.blym. 1135.7

d.rbt.kmn. | ṣḥq.btlt.ʿnt.tšu. | g h.w tṣḥ.tbšr bʿl. | bšrt k.yblt.y[b]n. | bt.l k.km.aḫ k.w ḥẓr. | km.ary k.ṣḥ.ḫrn. | b bht k. 4[51].5.89
.mt.ʿrʿrm.ynʿrn h. | ssnm.ysyn h.ʿdtm.yʿdyn h.yb | ltm.ybln h.mǵy.ḥrn.l bt h.w. | yštql.l ḥṭr h.tlu ḥt.km.nḫl. | tplg.k UG5.7.67
lp. | šd.rbt.kmn.hlk.kṯr. | k yʿn.w yʿn.tdrq.ḫss. | hlk.qšt.ybln.hl.yš | rbʿ.qṣʿt.apnk.dnil. | mt.rpi.aphn.ǵzr.mt. | hrnmy.g 17[2AQHT].5.12
ḥṯ.il.nḫt. | b ẓr.hdm.id. | d pršа.b br. | nʿl.il.d qblbl. | ʿln.ybl hm.ḫrṣ. | ṯlḥn.il.d mla. | mnm.dbbm.d | msdt.arṣ. | sʿ.il.dq 4[51].1.38
l yblt.ḫbṯm. | ap ksp hm. | l yblt. | w ht.luk ʿm ml[kt]. | tǵsdb.šmlšn. | w tbʿ ank. | ʿm mlak 1021.3
l yblt.ḫbṯm. | ap ksp hm. | l yblt. | w ht.luk ʿm ml[kt]. | tǵsdb.š 1021.1
b šḥt.ʿs.mt.ʿrʿrm.ynʿrn h. | ssnm.ysyn h.ʿdtm.yʿdyn h.yb | ltm.ybln h.mǵy.ḥrn.l bt h.w. | yštql.l ḥṭr h.tlu ḥt.km.nḫl UG5.7.66
bt.b qrb.hkl k. | tbl k.ǵrm.mid.ksp. | gbʿm.mḥmd.ḫrṣ. | ybl k.udr.ilqṣm. | w bn.bht.ksp.w ḫrṣ. | bht.ṭhrm.iqnim. | šmḫ 4[51].5.79
[--.--]m.bn.dgn.a[s]r km.hw ybl.argmn k.k ilm. | [---.]ybl.k bn.qdš.mnḥy k.ap.anš.zbl.bʿ[l]. | [-.yuḫ]d.b yd.mšḫṭ.b 2.1[137].38
l yrgm.l aliyn bʿl. | ṣḥ.ḫrn.b bhm k. | ʿḏbt.b qrb.hkl k. | tbl k.ǵrm.mid.ksp. | gbʿm.mḥmd.ḫrṣ. | ybl k.udr.ilqṣm. | w bn 4[51].5.77
k.w ḥẓr. | km.ary k.ṣḥ.ḫrn. | b bht k.ʿḏbt.b qrb. | hkl k.tbl k.ǵrm. | mid.ksp.gbʿm.mḥmd.. | ḫrṣ.w bn.bht.ksp. | w ḫrṣ. 4[51].5.93
h.ybqʿ.kbd h.w yḥd. | iṯ.šmt.iṯ.ʿẓm.w yqḥ b hm. | aqht.ybl.l qẓ.ybky.w yqbr. | yqbr.nn.b mdgt.b knk[-]. | w yšu.g h. 19[1AQHT].3.146
t pḥm. | [ḫm]š[.m]at.iqnu. | argmn.nqmd.mlk. | ugrt.d ybl.l špš. | mlk.rb.bʿl h. | ks.ḫrṣ.ktn.mit.pḥm. | mit.iqni.l mlkt 64[118].25
bʿl. | iy.zbl.bʿl.arṣ. | w tʿn.nrt.ilm.š[p]š. | šd yn.ʿn.b qbt[.t] | bl lyt.ʿl.umt k. | w abqṯ.aliyn.bʿl. | w tʿn.btlt.ʿnt. | an.l an.y 6[49].4.42
m.mlk.r[b.--]. | mṣmt.l nqmd.[---.-]št. | hl ny.argmn.d [ybl.n]qmd. | l špš.arn.ṯn[.ʿšr h.]mn. | ʿṣrm.ṯql.kbd[.ks].mn.ḫr 64[118].18
nim.šmḫ.aliyn. | bʿl.ṣḥ.ḫrn.b bht h. | ʿḏbt.b qrb hkl h. | yblnn ǵrm.mid.ksp. | gbʿm lḥmd.ḫrṣ. | yblnn.udr.ilqṣm. | yak. 4[51].5.100
ʿt]. | b.ʿšrt.ksp. | ṯlṯ.uṭbm.b d.alḫn.b.ʿšrt[.k]sp. | rṭ.l.ql.d.ybl.prd. | b.ṯql.w.nṣp.ksp. | ṯmn.lbšm.w.mšlt. | l.udmym.b.ṯm 2101.12
r[-.--]. | [---.]plnt.[---]. | [---.]ʿmt.l ql.rpi[.---]. | [---.-]llm.abl.mṣrp k.[---]. | [---.]y.mṭnt.w tḥ.ṭbt.n[--]. | [---.b]ṯnm w ṯṯb 1001.2.3
[-----]. | [---.]abl.qšt ṯmn. | ašrbʿ.qṣʿt.w hn šb[ʿ]. | b ymm.apnk.dnil.mt. | rp 17[2AQHT].5.2
aḥw.ap.qšt h.l ttn. | l y.w b mt[.-]ḥ.mṣṣ[-]t[.--]. | prʿ.qẓ.y[bl].šblt. | b ǵlp h.apnk.dnil. | [m]t.rpi.ap[h]n.ǵzr. | [mt.hrn] 19[1AQHT].1.18
š.[---]. | nšlḥ[.---]. | [---.m]at. | [---.]mat. | š[--].išal. | ʿm k.ybl.šd. | a[--].dʿ.k. | šld.ašld. | hn.mrṯ.d.štt. | ašld b ldt k. 2009.2.4
sgr. | almnt.škr. | tškr.zbl.ʿršm. | yšu.ʿwr. | mzl.ymzl. | w ybl.trḫ.ḥdṯ. | ybʿr.l ṯn.aṯt h. | w l nkr.mddt. | km irby.tškn. | š 14[KRT].4.189

ybm

t.[---]. | ʿr.ym.l bl[.---]. | b[---.]ny[.--]. | l bl.sk.w [---] h. | ybm h.šbʿ[.---]. | ǵzr.ilḥu.t[---]l. | trm.tṣr.trm[.ʿ]tqt. | tbky.w tš 16.2[125].94
. | [k gm]n.al[i]yn.b[ʿl]. | [---]ḥ h.tšt bm.ʿ[--]. | [---.]zr h.ybm.l ilm. | [id]k.l ttn.pnm.ʿm. | [il.]mbk nhrm.qrb. | [a]pq.th 6.1.31[49.1.3]

ybmt

--]. | [--.]yṣq šmn.šlm.b ṣ[ʿ.trḥṣ]. | yd h.btlt.ʿnt.uṣbʿt[h.ybmt]. | limm.tiḫd.knr h.b yd[h.tšt]. | rimt.l irt h.tšr.dd.al[iy UG5.3.2.5
]r y.il.ṣpn. | b q[dš.b ǵr.nḥ]lt y. | w t[ʿn].btlt.[ʿ]nt.ṯṯb. | [ybmt.]limm.[a]n.aqry. | [b arṣ].mlḥmt.[aš]t.b ʿpr m. | ddym.a 3[ʿNT].4.66
nši.ʿn h.w tphn. | hlk.bʿl.aṯtrt. | k tʿn.hlk.btlt. | ʿnt.tdrq.ybmt. | [limm].b h.pʿnm. | [tṭṭ.b ʿ]dn.ksl. | [ṯṯbr.ʿln.p]n h.td[ʿ]. 4[51].2.15
[---.]arḫt.tld[n]. | a[lp].l btlt.ʿnt. | w ypt l ybmt.li[mm]. | w yʿny.aliyn[.bʿl]. | lm.k qnym.ʿl[m.--]. | k dr 10[76].3.4
atn k. | [ḫrṣ.w aš]lḥ k.w tn.qšt k.[l]. | [ʿnt.tq]ḥ[.q]ṣʿt k.ybmt.limm. | w yʿn.aqht.ǵzr.adr.ṯqbm. | [d]lbnn.adr.gdm.b r 17[2AQHT].6.19
t.ṯr.adr.b ǵlil.qnm. | tn.l kṯr.w ḫss.ybʿl.qšt l ʿnt. | qṣʿt.l ybmt.limm.w tʿn.btlt. | ʿnt.irš ḥym.l aqht.ǵzr. | irš ḥym.w at 17[2AQHT].6.25
m.ḏmr.yṣq.šmn. | šlm.b ṣʿ.trḥṣ.yd h.bt | [l]t.ʿnt.uṣbʿt h.ybmt.limm. | [t]rḥṣ.yd h.b dm.ḏmr. | [u]ṣbʿt h.b mmʿ.mhrm. 3[ʿNT].2.33
.ʿnt.hbr. | w ql.tštḥwy.kbd hyt. | w rgm.l btlt.ʿnt. | ṯny.l ymmt.limm. | tḥm.aliyn.bʿl.hwt. | aliy.qrdm.qry.b arṣ. | mlḥ 3[ʿNT].3.9
:ṭly.bt.rb.dd]. | arṣy bt.y[ʿbdr.---]. | rgm l btl[t.ʿnt.ṯny.l ybmt.limm.tḥm.aliyn.bʿl]. | hw[t.aliy.qrdm.qryy.b arṣ.mlḥm 7.2[130].13
d mhr.ur. | [---.]yḥnnn. | [---.--]t.ytn. | [---.btlt.]ʿnt. | [---.ybmt.]limm. | [---.---]l.limm. | [---.yṯ]b.l arṣ. | [---.--]l.šir. | [---.- 10[76].1.15

ybn

ṯqlm kbd.ḫmš.šl[m.---]. | tlmyn.šbʿt.ʿšrt ʿšrt[.šlm.---]. | ybn.ṯmnt.ʿšrt ʿšrt.šlm. | ʿbdyrḫ.šbʿt.ʿšrt ʿšrt.šlm. | yky.ʿšrt.ṯṯt 1131.5

ybnil

ʿbdyrḫ. | ubn.ḫyrn. | ybnil.adrdn. | klyn.kkln. | ʿdmlk.tdn. | ʿzn.pǵḏn. | [a]nndn. | [r] 1070.3
[---].riš[.---].kt. | [y]nḥm. | ilbʿl. | ʿbdyr[ḫ]. | ṯṯpḥ. | artn. | ybnil. | brqn. | adr[dn]. | krwn. | arkḏn. | ilmn. | abškn. | ykn. | rš 1024.1.8
[-----]. | ubyn[.---]. | annt[n.---]. | ipṯn[.---]. | ybni[l.---]. | ikrn[.---]. | tlmyn[.---]. | tldn[.---]. | annḏr[.---]. | [-] 106[332].5
spr[.---]. | ybnil[.---.]kd yn.w š. | spr.m[--]. | spr d[---]b.w š. | tt.ḫmš.[---]. 1093.2

ybnn

l.ybnn. | adn y. | rgm. | tḥm.t[g]yn. | bn k. | l.p[ʿn.adn y]. | q[lt.--- 2115.1.1
y. | rgm. | tḥm.t[g]yn. | bn k. | l.p[ʿn.adn y]. | q[lt.---]. | l.yb[nn]. | bʿl y.r[gm]. | tḥm.ʿbd[--]. | ʿbd k. | l pʿn.bʿl y. | ṯn id.šb 2115.2.1
dm.b.mʿrby. | [--.šd]m.b.uškn. | [---.--]n. | [---].tlmdm. | [y]bnn.ṣmdm. | ṯp[ṭ]bʿl.ṣmdm. | [---.ṣ]mdm.w.ḥrṣ. | [---].aḥdm. 2033.2.3
bnš.kld. | kbln.ʿbdyrǵ.ilgt. | ǵyrn.ybnn qrwn. | ypltn.ʿbdnt. | klby.aḥrṯp. | ilyn.ʿlby.ṣdkn. | gmrt. 1045.3
ṯṯ.mat.ksp. | ḥṯbn.ybnn. | arbʿm.l.mit.šmn. | arbʿm.l.mit.tišr. | ṯṯ.ṯṯ.b [ṯ]ql.ṯlṯt.l.ʿš 1127.2
mnḥ.b d.ybnn. | arbʿ.mat. | l.alp.šmn. | nḥ.ṯṯ.mat. | šm[n].rqḥ. | kkrm.br 141[120].1
spr.[---]. | iytlm[.---]. | ybnn[.---]. | ilšp[š.---]. 2140.3
[---.]ybnn. | [---.]mlknʿm. | [---.]tǵpṯn. | [--.]ubln. | [--.-]ḥ[-]. | [--.-]s[- 123[326].1.1

ybru

---]. | au[pš.---]. | i[---.---]. | pgl[--.---]. | šy[.---]. | bn.uḫn. | ybru.i[---]. | [p]dyn.[---]. | bnšm.d.b [d.---]. | spḫy.[---]. | [-----]. 2161.11

ybrdmy

ʿl trḫ pdry b[t h]. | aqrb k ab h bʿ[l]. | yǵtr.ʿṯtr t | rḫ l k ybrdmy.b[t.a] | b h lb[u] yʿrr.w yʿ[n]. | yrḫ nyr šmm.w nʿ[n]. 24[77].29

ybrk

ṯmn.ṣmd.[---].|b d.b‘lsr.|yd.ṯdn.‘šr.|[ḫ]mrm.|ddm.l.ybr[k].|bdmr.prs.l.u[-]m[-].|ṯmn.l.‘šrm.|dmd.b d.mry[n]m 2102.6

b ym ḥdṯ.|b.yrḫ.pgrm.|lqḥ.iwrpzn.|argdd.|ttkn.|ybrk.|ntbt.|b.mitm.|‘šrm.|kbd.ḫrṣ. 2006.6

ybšr

.iḫy.|bn.iyṯr.|bn.‘yn.|bn.ǵzl.|bn.ṣmy.|bn.il[-]šy.|bn.ybšr.|bn.sly.|bn.ḥlbt.|bn.brzt.|bn.ayl.|[-----].|‘bd[--].|bn.i 2117.2.10

ygb

lḥt.|arb‘.uzm.mrat.bq‘.|ṯlṯ.[-]ṯt.aš[‘]t.šmn.uz.|mi[t].ygb.bq‘.|a[--].‘ṭ.|a[l]pm.alpnm.|ṯlṯ.m[a]t.art.ḥkpt.|mit.dnn 1128.23

t.|trṯ.|ršp.|‘nt ḫbly.|špš pgr.|iltm ḫnqtm.|yrḫ kṯy.|ygb hd.|yrgb b‘l.|ydb il.|yarš il.|yrǵm il.|‘mtr.|ydb il.|yr UG5.14.B.1

ygmr

d.skn.|škny.adddy.|mšu.adddy.|plsy.adddy.|aḫyn.|ygmr.adddy.|gln.aṯṯ.|ddy.[a]dddy.|bn.mlkr[šp].|bn.y[k]n. 2014.42

spr.bdlm.|n‘mn.|rbil.|plsy.|ygmr.|mnṯ.|prḫ.|‘dršp.|ršpab.|ṯnw.|abmn.|abǵl.|b‘ldn.| 1032.5

ygry

kbs.ks[p].|[---].ḏmrd.bn.ḥrmn.|[---.-]ǵn.ksp.ṯṯ.|[---.]ygry.ṯlṯm.ksp.b[--]. 2153.12

ygrš

r dr k.|kṯr ṣmdm.ynḥt.w yp‘r.šmt hm.šm k at.|ygrš.ygrš.grš ym grš ym.l ksi h.|[n]hr l kḥṯ drkt h.trtqṣ.b d b‘l k 2.4[68].12

t.dt dr dr k.|kṯr ṣmdm.ynḥt.w yp‘r.šmt hm.šm k at.|ygrš.ygrš.grš ym grš ym.l ksi h.|[n]hr l kḥṯ drkt h.trtqṣ.b d 2.4[68].12

yd

ubdy.mdm.|šd.b d.‘bdmlk.|šd.b d.yšn.ḥrš.|šd.b d.aupš.|šd.b d.ršpab.aḫ.ubn.|šd.b d.bn.uṯryn.|[ubd]y.mryn 82[300].1.4

--.]br.|ydn[.---].kry.|bn.ydd[.---.b]r.|prkl.b‘l.any.d.b d.abr[-]. 2123.7

spr.ubdy.art.|šd.prn.b d.agpṯn.nḥl h.|šd.śwn.b d.ttyn.nḥl [h].|šd.ṯtyn[.b]n.arkšt.| 2029.2

ṯlṯ.mat.ṯlṯm.|kbd.šmn.|l kny.|ṯmnym.šmn.|b d.adnn‘m. 1094.5

yn.|b‘ln.|ytršp.|ḫmšm.ṯmn.kbd.|tgmr.bnš.mlk.|d.b d.adn‘m.|[š]b‘.b.ḥrṯm.|[ṯ]lṯ.b.ṯǵrm.|rb qrt.aḥd.|ṯmn.ḫzr.| 1024.2.27

[sp]r.bnš.ml[k.d.b] d adn[‘m].|[---].riš[.---].kt.|[y]nḥm.|ilb‘l.|‘bdyr[ḫ].|ṯtpḥ.|a 1024.1.1

z.|[šd.b]d.b[n].tkwn.|[ubdy.mḏ]rǵlm.|[šd.bn.--]n.b d.aḫny.|[šd.bn.--]rt.b d.ṯpṯb‘l.|[ubdy.]mḫ[ṣ]m.|[šd.bn.]uzp 82[300].2.23

ty.t‘db.imr.|b pḫd.l npš.kṯr.w ḫss.|l brlt.hyn.d ḥrš.|ydm.aḫr.ymǵy.kṯr.|w ḫss.b d.dnil.ytnn.|qšt.l brk h.y‘db.|q 17[2AQHT].5.25

.ydm.p‘rt[.---].|šm k.mdd.i[l.---].|bt ksp y.d[--.---].|b d.aliyn b[‘l.---].|kd.ynaṣn[.---].|gršnn.l k[si.mlk h.l nḫt.l kḥ 1[‘NT.X].4.22

d.ksp.|kkrm.š‘rt.štt.b d.gg[‘t].|b.‘šrt.ksp.|ṯlṯ.uṯbm.b d.alḫn.b.‘šrt[.k]sp.|rṯ.l.ql.d.ybl.prd.|b.ṯql.w.nṣp.ksp.|ṯmn.l 2101.11

rkl.|šd.b d.klb.|šd.b d.klby.|šd.b d.iytlm.|ṯn.šdm.b d.amtrn.|šd.b d.iwrm[--].|šd.b d.yṯpr.|šd.b d.krb[-].|šd.b d 2090.12

d.bn.‘yn.|ṯn.šdm.b d.klṯṯb.|šd.b d.krz[n].|ṯlṯ.šdm.b d.amtr[n].|ṯn.šdm.b d.skn.|šd.b d[.‘b]dyrḫ.|šd.b [d.--]ṯtb. 2090.22

.dqn[.---].|[-]ntn.artn.b d[.--]nr[.---].|‘zn.w ymd.šr.b d ansny.|nsk.ks[p.--]mrtn.kṯrmlk.|yḥmn.aḫm[l]k.‘bdrpu.a 2011.31

šb‘m.lbš.d.‘rb.bt.mlk.|b.mit.ḫmšt.kbd.ksp.|ṯlṯ.ktnt.b d.an[r]my.|b.‘šrt.ksp.b.a[--].|ṯqlm.ḫr[ṣ.]b.ṯmnt.ksp.|‘šrt.ks 2101.18

.ḫmš.|kbd.w lpš.|ḫmš.mispt.|mṯ.|w lpš.d sgr b h.|b d.anrmy. 1109.7

inr.|ap.ḫšt k.ap.ab.k mtm.|tmtn.u ḫšt k.l ntn.|‘tq.b d.aṯt.ab.ṣrry.|ik m.yrgm.bn.il.|krt.špḥ.lṭpn.|w qdš.u ilm.t 16.1[125].19

r[.ap.]ḫšt k.|ap.ab.k mtm.tmtn.|u ḫšt k.l bky.‘tq.|b d.aṯt ab.ṣrry.|u ilm.tmtn.špḥ.|[l]ṭpn.l yḥ.t[b]ky k.|ab.ǵr.b‘l 16.2[125].104

inr.|ap.ḫšt k.ap.ab.ik mtm.|tmtn.u ḫšt k.l ntn.|‘tq.b d.aṯt.ab ṣrry.|tbky k.ab.ǵr.b‘l.|ṣpn.ḥlm.qdš.|any.ḥlm.adr.ḥ 16.1[125].5

ṯmn.mrkbt.dt.|‘rb.bt.mlk.|yd.apnt hn.|yd.ḥẓ hn.|yd.tr hn.|w.l.ṯt.mrkbtm.|inn.uṯpt.| 1121.3

---.--]ṯ.‘bd.l.kyn.|k[rm.--.]l.i[w]rtdl.|ḥl.d[--.‘bd]yrḫ.b d.apn.|krm.i[--].l.[---.]a[-]bn. 2027.2.11

šq.aḥl.an.šblt.|tp‘.b aklt.šblt.tp‘[.b ḥm]drt.|ur.tisp k.yd.aqht.ǵz[r].|tšt k.bm.qrb m.asm.|b p h.rgm.l yṣa.b špt h[19[1AQHT].2.73

.aḥl.an bṣ[ql].|ynp‘.b palt.bṣql yp‘ b yǵlm.|ur.tisp k.yd.aqht.|ǵzr.tšt k.b qrb m.asm.|y.dnh.ysb.aklt h.yph.|šblt. 19[1AQHT].2.66

šd.bn.adn.|[b] d.armwl.|[šd].mrnn.|b d.[-]tw[-].|šd.bn[.---].|b d.dd[--].|š 2028.2

|lmd.aḥd.b d.yḫ[--].|ṯlṯ.lmdm.b d.nḫ[--].|lmd.aḥd.b d.ar[--].|ṯlṯ.lmdm.b d.[---].|ṯlṯ.lmdm.b d.[---]. 1050.7

‘l.alpm.bnš.yd.|titṯm[n].w.‘l.[---].|[-]rym.t[i]ṯmn.|šnl.bn.ṣ[q]n.š[--].|yi 2104.1

ṣr.|mtt.by.|gšm.adr.|nškḥ.w.|rb.tmtt.|lqḥ.kl.ḏr‘.|b d a[-]m.w.ank.|k[l.]ḏr‘ hm.|[--.n]pš[.-].|w [k]l hm.b d.|rb.t 2059.18

npṣ.‘[--.---].|d.b d.a[--.---].|w.b d.b[--.---].|udbr[.---].|‘rš[.---].|ṯl[ḥn.---].|a[- 1120.2

d.bn.ṣnrn.b d.nrn.|[š]d.bn.rwy.b d.ydln.|[š].bn.trn.b d.ibrmḏ.|[š]d.bn.ilṯtmr.b d.tbbr.|[w.]šd.nḥl h.b d.ṯtmd.|[š] 82[300].1.10

.ṯqdy.b d.gmrd.|[š]d bn.synn.b d.gmrd.|[šd.]abyy.b d.ibrmḏ.|[šd.]bn.ṯṯrn.b d.bnš.aǵlkz.|[šd.b]d.b[n].tkwn.|[u 82[300].2.19

tš‘.ṣmdm.|ṯlṯm.b d.|ibrtlm.|w.pat.aḥt.|in.b hm. 1141.2

.ngzḥn.b d.gmrd.|[šd.bn].pll.b d.gmrd.|[šd.bn.-]ll.b d.iwrḫṭ.|[šd.bn.-]nn.b d.bn.šmrm.|[šd.bn.-]ṯtayy.b d.ṯtmd. 82[300].1.25

[š]d.bn.ilṯtmr.b d.tbbr.|[w.]šd.nḥl h.b d.ṯtmd.|[š]d.b d.iwrḫṭ.|[ṯn].šdm.b d.gmrd.|[šd.]lbny.b d.tbṯṯb.|[š]d.bn.ṯ[- 82[300].1.13

[--].|šd.b d.[---].|šd.b d[.---]im.|šd.b d[.bn.--]n.|šd.b d.iwrkl.|šd.b d.klb.|šd.b d.klby.|šd.b d.iytlm.|ṯn.šdm.b d. 2090.8

.|šd.b d.klby.|šd.b d.iytlm.|ṯn.šdm.b d.amtrn.|šd.b d.iwrm[--].|šd.b d.yṯpr.|šd.b d.krb[-].|šd.b d.bn.pṯḏ.|šd.b 2090.13

ht.yšm‘.uḫ y.|l g y.w yhbṭ.bnš.|w ytn.ilm.b d hm.|b d.iḫqm.gṯr.|w b d.ytrhd.|b‘l. 55[18].20

r‘ym.dt.b d.iytlm.|ḫyrn.w.śǵr h.|śǵr.bn.prsn.|agpṯr.w.śǵ[r h].|ṯ‘ln.| 2072.1

[--.-]d[-.---].|[--.šd]m.b d.iyt[lm].|[šd.b]d.s[--].|š[d.b]d.u[--].|šd.b d.[---].|šd.b d[.- 2090.2

[.bn.--]n.|šd.b d.iwrkl.|šd.b d.klb.|šd.b d.klby.|šd.b d.iytlm.|ṯn.šdm.b d.amtrn.|šd.b d.iwrm[--].|šd.b d.yṯpr.|š 2090.11

špl.hl h.trm.hl h.tṣḥ.ad ad.|w hl h.tṣḥ.um.um.tirk m.yd.il.k ym.|w yd il.k mdb.ark.yd.il.k ym.|w yd.il.k mdb.yq 23[52].33

hl h.tṣḥ.um.um.tirk m.yd.il.k ym.|w yd il.k mdb.ark.yd.il.k ym.|w yd.il.k mdb.yqḥ.il.mšt‘ltm.|mšt‘ltm.l riš.agn. 23[52].34

h.tṣḥ.ad ad.|w hl h.tṣḥ.um.um.tirk m.yd.il.k ym.|w yd il.k mdb.ark.yd.il.k ym.|w yd.il.k mdb.yqḥ.il.mšt‘ltm.| 23[52].34

.tirk m.yd.il.k ym.|w yd il.k mdb.ark.yd.il.k ym.|w yd.il.k mdb.yqḥ.il.mšt‘ltm.|mšt‘ltm.l riš.agn.yqḥ.tš.b bt h.| 23[52].35

m].|b tlhnt.lhm št.|b krpnm.yn.b k.hrṣ.|dm.ʿṣm.hm.yd.il mlk.|yhss k.ahbt.ṯr.tʿrr k.|w tʿn.rbt.aṯrt ym.|thm k.il. 4[51].4.38
.|šmʿt.hti.|nhtu.ht.|hm.in mm.|nhtu.w.lak.|ʿm y.w.yd.|ilm.p.k mtm.|ʿz.mid.|hm.nṯkp.|mʿn k.|w.mnm.|rgm. 53[54].11
rǵš[-].l.qrt.|šd.iǵlyn.bn.kzbn.l.qr[t].|šd.pln.bn.tiyn.b d.ilmhr nhl h.|šd knn.bn.ann.ʿdb.|šd.iln[-].bn.irṯr.l.shrn.nh 2029.18
.ṯbʿm.shr.ʿzn.ilhd.|bnil.rb ʿšrt.lkn.ypʿn.ṯ[--].|yṣhm.b d.ubn.krwn.ṯǵd.[m]nhm.|ʿpṯrm.šmʿrgm.skn.qrt.|hgbn.šmʿ. 2011.9
.w ẓi.|b aln.tk m.|b tk.mlbr.|ilšiy.|kry amt.|ʿpr.ʿẓm yd.|ugrm.hl.ld.|aklm.tbrk k.|w ld ʿqqm.|ilm.ypʿr.|šmt h 12[75].1.24
.|[---.b] d.ʿbdhmn.|[---.b] d.ṯbq.|[---.b] d.šbn.|[---.b] d.ulm.|[---.b] d.ǵbl.|[---.b] d.ʿbdkṯr.|[---.b] d.urǵnr. 1052.6
n.|[---.b] d.ulm.|[---.b] d.ǵbl.|[---.b] d.ʿbdkṯr.|[---.b] d.urǵnr. 1052.9
]ksp.|hmš.kkr.ṣml.|b.ʿšrt.b d.bn.kyn.|ʿšr.kkr.šʿrt.|b d.urtn.b.arbʿm.|arbʿt.ʿšrt.hrṣ.|b.ṯqlm.kbd.arbʿm.|ʿšrt.hrṣ.b. 2100.15
.sbrdnm.|hmš.kkrm.alp kb[d].|ṯlṯ.l.nskm.birtym.|b d.urtn.w.ṯṯ.mat.brr.|b.ṯmnym.ksp.ṯlṯt.kbd.|hmš.alp.ṯlṯ.l.hl 2101.4
--.-]d[-.---].|[--.šd]m.b d.iyt[lm].|[šd.b]d.s[--].|š[d.b]d.u[--].|šd.b d.[---].|šd.b d[.---]im.|šd.b d[.bn.--]n.|šd.b d.i 2090.4
šstm.b.šbʿm.|ṯlṯ.mat.trm.b.ʿšrt.|mit.adrm.b.ʿšrt.|ʿšr.ydt.b.ʿšrt.|hmš.kkrm.ṣml.|ʿšrt.ksp h.|hmš.kkr.qnm.|ṯlṯt.w 1127.9
hbr.trrt.|bt.krt.tbun.|lm.mṯb[.---].|w lhm mr.tqdm.|yd.b ṣʿ.tšlh.|hrb.b bšr.tštn.|[w t]ʿn.mṯt.hry.|[l lh]m.l šty.ṣh 15[128].4.24
[---.h]br[.---].|bhr[.--]t[.----].|l mṯb[.--]t[.---].|[tqdm.]yd.b ṣʿ.t[šl]h.|[hrb.b]bš[r].tštn.|[w tʿn].mṯt.hry.|[l lh]m.l š 15[128].5.7
mlk.|w.snt.|bt.ugrt.|w.pdy h[m].|iwrkl.mit.|ksp.b y[d].|birtym.|[un]ṯ inn.|l [h]m ʿd ṯṯbn.|ksp.iwrkl.|w ṯb.l 1006.14
.ṯṯyn[.b]n.arkšt.|lʿq[.---].|šd.pll.b d.qrt.|š[d].anndr.b d.bdn.nh[l h].|[šd.]agyn.b d.kmrn.n[hl] h.|[š]d.nbzn.[-]l.qr 2029.7
bʿ yn.|l mrynm.|b yṯbmlk.|kdm.ǵbiš hry.|hmš yn.b d.|bh mlkt.|b mdrʿ.|ṯlṯ bt.il|ann.|kd.bt.ilann. 1090.14
[.---].|mid.an[--.]ṣn[--].|nrt.ilm.špš[.ṣhrr]t.|la.šmm.b y[d.bn.ilm.m]t.|w tʿn.btlt.ʿn[t.bnt.]bht |k.y ilm.bnt.bh[t k]. 3[ʿNT.VI].5.26
|k lli.b ṯbrn q y.htu hw.|nrt.ilm.špš.ṣhrrt.|la.šmm.b yd.bn ilm.mt.|ym.ymm.yʿtqn.l ymm.|l yrhm.rhm.ʿnt.tngṯ 6[49].2.25
š]d.bn.bri.b d.bn.ydln.|[u]bdy.ṯǵrm.|[š]d.ṯǵr.mṯpit.b d.bn.iryn.|[u]bdy.šrm.|[š]d.bn.hrmln.b d.bn.tnn.|[š]d.bn.h 82[300].2.8
|[ṯ]mn.l.ʿšrm[.l.b]t.ʿṯtrt.|[ṯ]lṯ.ʿšr h.[b]t.ršp.gn.|arbʿ.b d.b[n].ušryn.|kdm.l.urtn.|kdm.l.ilšpš.|kd.l.anntb.|kd.l.iwr 1088.4
.b d.yšn.hrš.|šd.b d.aupš.|šd.b d.ršpab.ah.ubn.|šd.b d.bn.uṯryn.|[ubd]y.mrynm.|[š]d.bn.ṣnrn.b d.nrn.|[š]d.bn.r 82[300].1.6
spr.irgmn.|ṯlṯ.hmš.alpm.|b d.brq.mahdy.|kkr.ṯlṯ.|b d.bn.by.ar[y].|alpm.ṯlṯ.|b d.šim.il[š]tmʿy. 1134.5
ym.|[šd.b]n.qṭy.b d.tt.|[ubd]y.mrim.|[šd.b]n.ṯpdn.b d.bn.gʿr.|[šd.b]n.ṯqrn.b d.hby.|[tn.š]d.bn.ngzhn.b d.gmrd.| 82[300].1.21
km l.yqh.|bt.hnd.b d.|[ʿb]dmlk.|[-]k.amʿ[--].|[w.b] d.bn h[.ʿ]d ʿlm.|[w.un]ṯ.in[n.]b h.|[---.]nʿm[-]. 1009.17
|šhr.ʿlmt.|bnš bnšm.|l.yqhnn.b d.|bʿln.bn.kltn.|w.b d.bn h.ʿd.|ʿlm.w unṯ.|in.b h. 1008.19
y.šrm.|[š]d.bn.hrmln.b d.bn.tnn.|[š]d.bn.hrmln.ṯn.b d.bn.hdmn.|[u]bdy.nqdm.|[ṯlṯ].šdm.d.nʿrb.gt.npk.|[š]d.rpa 82[300].2.11
mz.|[šd.b d].klby.psl.|[ub]dy.mri.ibrn.|[š]d.bn.bri.b d.bn.ydln.|[u]bdy.ṯǵrm.|[š]d.ṯǵr.mṯpit.b d.bn.iryn.|[u]bdy. 82[300].2.6
wṯm.w.ṯṯ.ṯprtm.|b.ʿšr[m.]ksp.|hmš.kkr.ṣml.|b.ʿšrt.b d.bn.kyn.|ʿšr.kkr.šʿrt.|b d.urtn.b.arbʿm.|arbʿt.ʿšrt.hrṣ.|b.ṯq 2100.13
|šd.b d.bn.pṯd.|šd.b d.dr.khnm.|šd.b d.bn.ʿmy.|šd.b d.bn.ʿyn.|ṯn.šdm.b d.klṯṯb.|šd.b d.krz[n].|ṯlṯ.šdm.b d.amtr 2090.19
.|šd.b d.krb[-].|šd.b d.bn.pṯd.|šd.b d.dr.khnm.|šd.b d.bn.ʿmy.|šd.b d.bn.ʿyn.|ṯn.šdm.b d.klṯṯb.|šd.b d.krz[n].|ṯl 2090.18
trn.|šd.b d.iwrm[--].|šd.b d.ytpr.|šd.b d.krb[-].|šd.b d.bn.pṯd.|šd.b d.dr.khnm.|šd.b d.bn.ʿmy.|šd.b d.bn.ʿyn.|ṯ 2090.16
.l.gmrd.|[---.--]t.l.yšn.|[šd.--]ln.|b d.trǵds.|šd.ṯʿlb.|b d.bn.pl.|šd.bn.kt.|b d.pdy.|šd.hzr.|[b d].d[---]. 2030.2.4
šd.bn.-]ṯtayy.b d.ṯṯmd.|[šd.bn.-]rn.b d.ṣdqšlm.|[šd.b d.]bn.pʿṣ.|[ubdy.ʿ]šrm.|[šd.---]n.b d.brdd.|[---.--]m.|[šd.---. 82[300].1.29
bn].pll.b d.gmrd.|[šd.bn.-]ll.b d.iwrht.|[šd.bn.-]nn.b d.bn.šmrm.|[šd.bn.-]ṯtayy.b d.ṯṯmd.|[šd.bn.-]rn.b d.ṣdqšlm 82[300].1.26
d.]abyy.b d.ibrmd.|[šd.]bn.ṯṯrn.b d.bnš.aǵlkz.|[šd.b]d.b[n].tkwn.|[ubdy.md]rǵlm.|[šd.bn.--]n.b d.ahny.|[šd.bn. 82[300].2.21
.ṯǵr.mṯpit.b d.bn.iryn.|[u]bdy.šrm.|[š]d.bn.hrmln.b d.bn.tnn.|[š]d.bn.hrmln.ṯn.b d.bn.hdmn.|[u]bdy.nqdm.|[ṯl 82[300].2.10
.s[--].|š[d.b]d.u[--].|šd.b d.[---].|šd.b d[.---]im.|šd.b d[.bn.--]n.|šd.b d.iwrkl.|šd.b d.klb.|šd.b d.klby.|šd.b d.iytl 2090.7
t.ksp.b.a[--].|ṯqlm.hr[ṣ.]b.ṯmnt.ksp.|ʿšrt.ksp.b.alp.[b d].bn.[---].|tšʿ.ṣin.b.tšʿt.ksp.|mšlt.b.ṯql.ksp.|kdwṯ.l.grgyn.b 2101.21
.synn.b d.gmrd.|[šd.]abyy.b d.ibrmd.|[šd.]bn.ṯṯrn.b d.bnš.aǵlkz.|[šd.b]d.b[n].tkwn.|[ubdy.md]rǵlm.|[šd.bn.--] 82[300].2.20
n.bn.ddy.|ʿbdil[.b]n ṣdqn.|bnšm.h[-]mt.yphm.|kbby.yd.bt.amt.|ilmlk. 2045.7
[---.]ṯlṯm.d.nlqht.|[bn.h]tyn.yd.bt h.|[aǵ]ltn.|tdn.bn.ddy.|ʿbdil[.b]n ṣdqn.|bnšm.h[-]mt 2045.2
].|plzn.qrty[.---].|w.klt h.b.t[--.---].|bʿl y.mlk[y.---].|yd.bt h.yd[.---].|ary.yd.t[--.---].|htn h.šbʿl[.---].|ṯlhny.yd[.-- 81[329].14
aymr.mr.ym.mr.ym.|l ksi h.nhr l kht.drkt h.trtqṣ.|b d bʿl.km.nšr b uṣbʿt h.hlm.qdq|d zbl ym.bn.ʿnm.ṯpṭ.nhr.yp 2.4[68].21
.bn.ʿnm.ṯpṭ.nhr.yprsh ym.|w yql.l arṣ.w trtqṣ.ṣmd.b d bʿl.|[km.]nšr.b uṣbʿt h.ylm.qdqd.zbl.|[ym.]bn.ʿnm.ṯpṭ.nh 2.4[68].23
.ygrš.grš ym grš ym.l ksi h.|[n]hr l kht drkt h.trtqṣ.b d bʿl km nš|r.b uṣbʿt h.hlm.ktp.zbl ym.bn ydm.|[ṯp]ṭ nhr.y 2.4[68].13
ṣbʿt h.hlm.ktp.zbl ym.bn ydm.|[ṯp]ṭ nhr.yrtqṣ.ṣmd.b d bʿl.km.nšr.|b[u]ṣbʿt h.ylm.ktp.zbl ym.bn ydm.ṯpṭ.|nhr.ʿz 2.4[68].15
kltn.w l.|bn h.ʿd.ʿlm.|šhr.ʿlmt.|bnš bnšm.|l.yqhnn.b d.|bʿln.bn.kltn.|w.b d.bn h.ʿd.|ʿlm.w unṯ.|in.b h. 1008.17
.b h[--].|w.arbʿ.h[mrm].|b m[ʿ]rby.|ṯmn.ṣmd.[---].|b d.bʿlsr.|yd.ṯdn.ʿšr.|[h]mrm.|ddm.l.ybr[k].|bdmr.prs.l.u[-] 2102.4
.b d.ṣdqšlm.|[šd.b d.]bn.pʿṣ.|[ubdy.ʿ]šrm.|[šd.---]n.b d.brdd.|[---.--]m.|[šd.---.b d.]ṯpṭbʿl.|[šd.---.]b d.ymz.|[šd.b 82[300].1.31
spr.irgmn.|ṯlṯ.hmš.alpm.|b d.brq.mahdy.|kkr.ṯlṯ.|b d.bn.by.ar[y].|alpm.ṯlṯ.|b d.šim.il[1134.3
mmʿm.w[---].|aqht.w yplṭ k.bn[.dnil.---].|w yʿdr k.b yd.btlt.[ʿnt].|w yʿn.lṭpn.il d p[id].|ydʿt k.bt.k anšt.w i[n.b il 18[3AQHT].1.14
npṣ.ʿ[--.---].|d.b d.a[--.---].|w.b d.b[--.---].|udbr[.---].|ʿrš[.---].|ṯl[hn.---].|a[--.---].|ṯn[.---].| 1120.3
[---].b d.š[--]mlk.|[---.b] d.gbʿly.|[---.b] d.ʿbdhmn.|[---.b] d.ṯbq.|[---.b] d.šbn.|[---.b] 1052.2
hlby.|b d.tlmi.b.ʿšrm.hmšt.|kbd.ksp.|kkrm.šʿrt.šṯt.b d.gg[ʿt].|b.ʿšrt.ksp.|ṯlṯ.uṯbm.b d.alhn.b.ʿšrt[.k]sp.|rṯ.l.ql.d. 2101.9
mdrǵlm.dt.inn.|b d.tlmyn.|b d.gln.ary.|tgyn.yʿrty.|bn.krwn.b.yny.iytlm.|sgryn.ary.b.yn 2071.3
|[ub]dy.trrm.|[šd.]bn.ṯqdy.b d.gmrd.|[š]d bn.synn.b d.gmrd.|[šd.]abyy.b d.ibrmd.|[šd.]bn.ṯṯrn.b d.bnš.aǵlkz.|[š 82[300].2.18
ṯtb.|[š]d.ilṣy.b d.ʿbdym.|[ub]dy.trrm.|[šd.]bn.ṯqdy.b d.gmrd.|[š]d bn.synn.b d.gmrd.|[šd.]abyy.b d.ibrmd.|[šd.] 82[300].2.17
.b d.bn.gʿr.|[šd.b]n.ṯqrn.b d.hby.|[ṯn.š]d.bn.ngzhn.b d.gmrd.|[šd.bn].pll.b d.gmrd.|[šd.bn.-]ll.b d.iwrht.|[šd.bn. 82[300].1.23
rn.b d.hby.|[ṯn.š]d.bn.ngzhn.b d.gmrd.|[šd.bn].pll.b d.gmrd.|[šd.bn.-]ll.b d.iwrht.|[šd.bn.-]nn.b d.bn.šmrm.|[šd 82[300].1.24
br.|[w.]šd.nhl h.b d.ṯṯmd.|[š]d.b d.iwrht.|[ṯn].šdm.b d.gmrd.|[šd.]lbny.b d.tbṯtb.|[š]d.bn.ṯ[-]rn.b d.ʿdbmlk.|[šd.] 82[300].1.14
[---.ṯ]lṯ.ʿš[r h.---].|d bnšm.yd.grbs hm.|w.ṯn.ʿšr h.hpnt.|[š]šwm.amtm.ʿkyt.|yd.llh hm 2049.2
].|b mgn k.w hrṣ.l kl.|apnk.ǵzr.ilhu.|[m]rh h.yihd.b yd.|[g]rgr h.bm.ymn.|[w]yqrb.trẓẓ h.|[---].mǵy h.w ǵlm.| 16.1[125].47
ml[k].|ugrt.ytn.|šd.kdǵdl[.bn].|[-]š[-]y.d.b š[-]y.|[---.y]d gt h[.--].|[---.]yd.|[k]rm h.yd.|[k]lkl h.|[w] ytn.nn.|l.bʿ 1008.7

---]. | b d.[---]. | šd.[---]. | b d.[---]. | [-----]. | šd.bn.gdy. | b d.ddl. 2028.23
. | [b] d.armwl. | [šd].mrnn. | b d.[-]tw[-]. | šd.bn[.---]. | b d.dd[--]. | šd.d[---]. | b d.d[---]. | šd.b[---]. | b d.[---]. | šd[.---]. | b 2028.6
.w ḫss. | l brlt.hyn.d ḥrš. | ydm.aḥr.ymǵy.kṯr. | w ḫss.b d.dnil.ytnn. | qšt.l brk h.y'db. | qṣ't.apnk.mṯt.dnty. | tšlḥm.tšš 17[2AQHT].5.26
m[--]. | šd.b d.yṯpr. | šd.b d.krb[-]. | šd.b d.bn.pṯd. | šd.b d.dr.khnm. | šd.b d.bn.'my. | šd.b d.bn.'yn. | ṯn.šdm.b d.klṯṯb. 2090.17
rnn. | b d.[-]tw[-]. | šd.bn[.---]. | b d.dd[--]. | šd.d[---]. | b d.d[---]. | šd.b[---]. | b d.[---]. | šd[.---]. | b d[.---]. | š[d.---]. | b d[. 2028.8
ds. | šd.ṯ'lb. | b d.bn.pl. | šd.bn.kt. | b d.pdy. | šd.ḫzr. | [b d].d[---]. 2030.2.8
l. | krt.yḫṭ.w ḥlm. | 'bd.il.w hdrt. | yrtḥṣ.w yadm. | yrḥṣ.yd h.amt h. | uṣb't h.'d.ṯkm. | 'rb.b ẓl.ḫmt.lqḥ. | imr.dbḥ.b yd 14[KRT].3.157
m.b ṣ'.trḥṣ.yd h.bt | [l]t.'nt.uṣb't h.ybmt.limm. | [t]rḥṣ.yd h.b dm.ḏmr. | [u]ṣb't h.b mm'.mhrm. | [ṯ]'r.ksat.l ksat.ṯlḥ 3['NT].2.34
ṣ.mri.ndd. | y'šr.w yšqyn h. | ytn.ks.b d h. | krpn.b klat.yd h. | b krb.'ẓm.ridn. | mt.šmm.ks.qdš. | l tphn h.aṯt.krpn. | l 3['NT].1.11
r h. | l 'pr.ḏmr.aṯr h.ṭbq.lḥt. | niṣ h.grš d.'šy.ln h. | aḫd.yd h.b škrn.m'ms h. | [k]šb' yn.spu.ksm h.bt.b'l. | [w m]nt h 17[2AQHT].1.31
n.ṯlḥnm.ymḫ. | [b]bt.dm.ḏmr.yṣq.šmn. | šlm.b ṣ'.trḥṣ.yd h.bt | [l]t.'nt.uṣb't h.ybmt.limm. | [t]rḥṣ.yd h.b dm.ḏmr. | [3['NT].2.32
[---.n]skt.n'mn.nbl[.---]. | [--.]yṣq šmn.šlm.b ṣ['.trḥṣ]. | yd h.btlt.'nt.uṣb't[h.ybmt]. | limm.tiḫd.knr h.b yd[h.tšt]. | ri UG5.3.2.5
'wrt.yšt k.b'l.l ht. | w 'lm h.l 'nt.p dr.dr. | 'db.uḫry.mṭ.yd h. | dnil.bt h.ymǵyn.yšt | ql.dnil.l hkl h.'rb.b | kyt.b hkl h. 19[1AQHT].4.169
dṯ[.---.]ḥ[--]. | b bt.[-.]l bnt.q[-]. | w št.b bt.ṯap[.--]. | hy.yd h.w ym[ǵ]. | mlak k.'m dt[n]. | lqḥ.mṯpṭ. | w y'ny.nn. | dtn. UG5.6.10
.b'l. | in.b'l.b bht ht. | il hd.b qrb.hkl h. | qšt hn.aḫd.b yd h. | w qṣ't h.bm.ymn h. | idk.l ytn pnm. | tk.aḫ.šmk.mla[t. 10[76].2.6
-.l k] | ṯrt.l bnt.hll[.snnt]. | hl ǵlmt tld b[n.--]n. | 'n ha l yd h.tzd[.--]. | pt l bšr h.dm a[--.--]ḥ. | w yn.k mtrḫt[.---]h. | š 24[77].8
--]ḥ. | w yn.k mtrḫt[.---]h. | šm' ilht kṯr[t.--]mm. | nh l yd h tzdn[.---]n. | l ad[n h.---]. | dgn tt[--.---.-]l | '.l kṯrt hl[l.sn 24[77].12
lk.šlm.mlkt.'rbm m.ṯnnm. | mt.w šr.yṯb.b d h.ḫṭ.ṯkl.b d h. | ḫṭ.ulmn.yzbrnn.zbrm.gpn. | yṣmdnn.ṣmdm.gpn.yšql.šd 23[52].8
n ay. | šlm.mlk.šlm.mlkt.'rbm m.ṯnnm. | mt.w šr.yṯb.b d h.ḫṭ.ṯkl.b d h. | ḫṭ.ulmn.yzbrnn.zbrm.gpn. | yṣmdnn.ṣmdm 23[52].8
.y[ṯ]br. | ṯmn.[---.]btlt.[']nt. | ṯṯb.[---.--]ša. | tlm.km[.---.]yd h.k šr. | knr.uṣb't h ḫrṣ.abn. | p h.tiḫd.šnt h.w akl.bqmm. 19[1AQHT].1.7
liyn. | b'l.ib.hdt.lm.ṯḥš. | lm.ṯḥš.nṯq.dmrn. | 'n.b'l.qdm.yd h. | k tǵḏ.arz.b ymn h. | bkm.yṯb.b'l.l bht h. | u mlk.u bl m 4[51].7.40
h. | b ḥrb.mlḥt. | qṣ.mri.ndd. | y'šr.w yšqyn h. | ytn.ks.b d h. | krpn.b klat.yd h. | b krb.'ẓm.ridn. | mt.šmm.ks.qdš. | l t 3['NT].1.10
h.amt h. | uṣb't h.'d.ṯkm. | 'rb.b ẓl.ḫmt.lqḥ. | imr.dbḥ.b yd h. | lla.klatnm. | klt.lḥm h.d nzl. | lqḥ.msrr.'ṣr.db[ḥ]. | yṣq. 14[KRT].3.160
d.gr bt il. | 'nt.brḥ.p 'lm h.'nt.p dr[.dr]. | 'db.uḫry mṭ.yd h. | ymǵ.l mrrt.tǵll.b nr. | yšu.g h.w yṣḥ.y l k.mrrt. | tǵll.b 19[1AQHT].3.155
ly.b d.ns' k. | 'nt.brḥ.p 'lm h. | 'nt.p dr.dr.'db.uḫry mṭ yd h. | ymǵ.l qrt.ablm.abl[m]. | qrt.zbl.yrḫ.yšu g h. | w yṣḥ.y l 19[1AQHT].3.162
št'ltm.l riš.agn.yqḥ.tš.b bt h. | il.ḫṭ h.nḥt.il.ymnn.mṭ.yd h.yšu. | yr.šmm h.yr.b šmm.'ṣr.yḫrṯ yšt. | l pḥm.il.aṯtm.k 23[52].37
[-----]. | l abn[.---]. | aḫdt.plk h[.b yd h]. | plk.qlt.b ymn h. | npyn h.mks.bšr h. | tmt'.md h.b ym 4[51].2.3
ks.b d y.qb't.b ymn y[.t]q | ḥ.pǵt.w tšqyn h.tq[ḥ.ks.]b d h. | qb't.b ymn h.w y'n.yṯ[p]n[.mh]r. | št.b yn.yšt.ila.il š[--.] 19[1AQHT].4.217
tšu w[.---]. | aylt tǵpy ṯr.'n[.---]. | b[b]r.mrḥ h.ti[ḫd.b yd h]. | š[g]r h bm ymn.t[--.---]. | [--.]l b'l.'bd[.---]. | ṯr ab h il.t 2001.1.12
rḥṣ]. | yd h.btlt.'nt.uṣb't[h.ybmt]. | limm.tiḫd.knr h.b yd[h.tšt]. | rimt.l irt h.tšr.dd.al[iyn]. | b'l.ahbt. UG5.3.2.6
. | b gl.ḫrṣ.nbt.w 'ly. | l ẓr.mgdl.rkb. | ṯkmm.ḥmt.nša. | [y]d h.šmmh.dbḥ. | l ṯr.ab h.il.šrd. | [b'l].b dbḥ h.bn dgn. | [b 14[KRT].4.168
t.[-]ld. | kbd h.l yd' hr h.[---]d[-]. | tnq[.---.]in[b]b.p'r. | yd h[.--.]ṣ'r.glgl. | a[---]m.rḥ.ḥd '[r]pt. | gl[.---.]yhpk.m[---]m. 13[6].33
[.-]. | [---.]ṯḥm. | [---]t.[ ]r. | [---.--]n. | [---] h.l 'db. | [---]n.yd h. | [---].bl.išlḥ. | [---] h.gm. | [l --- k.]yṣḥ. | [---]d.'r. | [----.-]b 14[KRT].5.235
r.l ẓpn. | [---.]pn.ym.y[--]. | [---].b'l.tdd. | [---.]hkl. | [---.]yd h. | [---.]tmt. 25[136].9
r.---]. | [']d tš[b'.tmtḫṣ.---]. | klyn[.---]. | špk.l[---]. | trḥṣ.yd[h.---]. | [--.]yṣt ḏm[r.---]. | tšt[.r]imt.[l irt h.tšr.l dd.aliyn. 7.2[130].8
.gṯr. | [w]ht.yšm'.uḫ y. | l g y.w yhbṭ.bnš. | w ytn.ilm.b d hm. | b d.iḫqm.gṯr. | w b d.ytrhd. | b'l. 55[18].19
| arb'[m.ksp.]'l. | il[m]l[k.a]rgnd. | uškny[.w]mit. | zt.b d hm.rib. | w [---]. | [-----]. | [-]šy[.---] h. | [-]kt[.---.]nrn. | [b]n.n 2055.13
.n[ql.---]. | [---.]m[---]. | [---.yr]ḫ.mgm[r.---]. | [---.--]š.b d.h[--.---]. | [---.y]rḫ.dbḥ[.---]. | [---.-]pn.b d.[---]. | [---.]b d.[--- 1160.4
qmḥ.d.kly.k ṣḥ.illḏrm. | b d.zlb[n.--]. | arb'.'š[r.]dd.n'r. | d.apy[.--]. | w.arb['.--]d.apy.'bd 2094.2
ṯmn.mrkbt.dt. | 'rb.bt.mlk. | yd.apnt hn. | yd.ḥẓ hn. | yd.tr hn. | w.l.ṯt.mrkbtm. | inn.uṯpt. | w.ṯlṯ.ṣmdm. 1121.4
[ubd]y.mrim. | [šd.b]n.ṯpdn.b d.bn.g'r. | [šd.b]n.ṯqrn.b d.ḫby. | [ṯn.š]d.bn.ngẓhn.b d.gmrd. | [šd.bn].pll.b d.gmrd. | [š 82[300].1.22
m. | 'm.ǵr.trǵzz. | 'm.ǵr.trmg. | 'm.tlm.ǵṣr.arṣ. | ša.ǵr.'l.ydm. | ḫlb.l ẓr.rḥtm. | w rd.bt ḫpṯt. | arṣ.tspr.b y | rdm.arṣ. | id 4[51].8.5
| 'm k.ṯṯly.bt.rb.idk. | pn k.al ttn.tk.ǵr. | knkny.ša.ǵr.'l ydm. | ḫlb.l ẓr.rḥtm w rd. | bt ḫpṯt.arṣ.tspr b y | rdm.arṣ.w td' 5[67].5.13
| mgn.rbt.aṯrt ym. | mǵẓ.qnyt.ilm. | hyn.'ly.l mpḫm. | b d.ḫss.mṣbṭm. | yṣq.ksp.yšl | ḥ.ḫrṣ.yṣq.ksp. | l alpm.ḫrṣ.yṣq | m. 4[51].1.25
-ḫym.w tbṯḫ. | kt.il.dt.rbtm. | kt.il.nbt.b ksp. | šmrgt.b dm.ḫrṣ. | kḥṯ.il.nḥt. | b ẓr.hdm.id. | d pršа.b br. | n'l.il.d qblbl. 4[51].1.33
.'m y.l 'pr.ḏmr.aṯr[y]. | ṭbq lḥt.niṣ y.grš. | d 'šy.ln.aḫd.yd y.b š | krn m'ms y k šb't yn. | spu.ksm y.bt.b'l.[w]mn[t]. | 17[2AQHT].2.19
m.'n.kḏd.aylt. | hm.imt.imt.npš.blt. | ḥmr.p imt.b klt. | yd y.ilḥm.hm.šb'. | ydt y.b ṣ'.hm.ks.ymsk. | nhr.k[--].ṣḥn.b'l.' 5[67].1.20
.b hlm w y'n.yṯpn[.mhr]. | št.qḥn.w tšqyn.yn.qḥ. | ks.b d y.qb't.b ymn y[.t]q | ḥ.pǵt.w tšqyn h.tq[ḥ.ks.]b d h. | qb't.b 19[1AQHT].4.216
-.---]l.limm. | [---.yṯ]b.l arṣ. | [---.--]l.šir. | [---.-]tm. | [---.]yd y. | [----]y. | [---.-]lm. | [---.r]umm. 10[76].1.20
mnḥ.b d.ybnn. | arb'.mat. | l.alp.šmn. | nḥ.ṭt.mat. | šm[n].rqḥ. | kkrm. 141[120].1
lli.b ṯbrn. | qn h.ṯḥtan. | nrt.ilm.špš. | ṣḥrrt.la. | šmm.b yd.md | d.ilm.mt.b a | lp.šd.rbt.k | mn.l p'n.mt. | hbr.w ql. | tšt 4[51].8.23
| [ubd]y.mrynm. | [š]d.bn.ṣnrn.b d.nrn. | [š]d.bn.rwy.b d.ydln. | [š].bn.trn.b d.ibrmd. | [š]d.bn.ilṯtmr.b d.tbbr. | [w.]š 82[300].1.9
alpm.arb'.mat.k[bd]. | mit.b d.yd[r]m. | alp ḫmš mat.kbd.d[--]. 2109.2
ḏm[r.---].br. | bn.i[ytlm.---]. | wr[t.---.]b d.yḫmn. | yry[.---.]br. | ydn[.---].kry. | bn.ydd[.---.b]r. | prkl.b'l 2123.3
. | šb'.lmdm.b d.s[n]rn. | lmd.aḥd.b d.yr[š]. | lmd.aḥd.b d.yḥ[--]. | ṯlṯ.lmdm.b d.nḥ[--]. | lmd.aḥd.b d.ar[--]. | ṯlṯ.lmdm. 1050.5
[---.]ydm ym. | [---.]ydm nhr. | [---.]trǵt. | [---.]h aḫd[.--]. | [---.]iln[- 49[73].1.1
.---]n.b d.brdd. | [---.--]m. | [šd.---.b d.]ṯpṯb'l. | [šd.---.]b d.ymz. | [šd.b d].klby.psl. | [ub]dy.mri.ibrn. | [š]d.bn.bri.b d.b 82[300].2.3
--]. | ḫdǵlm.b d.[---]. | šb'.lmdm.b d.s[n]rn. | lmd.aḥd.b d.yr[š]. | lmd.aḥd.b d.yḥ[--]. | ṯlṯ.lmdm.b d.nḥ[--]. | lmd.aḥd.b 1050.4
d.snrn. | [---.lm]dm.b d.nrn. | [---.ḫ]dǵlm. | [lmd.]aḥd.b d.yrš. 1051.6
ubdy.mdm. | šd.b d.'bdmlk. | šd.b d.yšn.ḥrš. | šd.b d.aupš. | šd.b d.ršpab.aḫ.ubn. | šd.b d.bn.uṯry 82[300].1.3
šd.bn.--]rt.b d.ṯpṯb'l. | [ubdy.]mḫ[ṣ]m. | [šd.bn.]uzpy.b d.yšn.ḥrš. | [-----]. | [šd.b d.--]n. | [šd.b d.--]n. | [šd.b d.- 82[300].2.26
[b.]gt.ṯpn.'šr.ṣmdm. | w.ṯlṯ.'šr.bnš. | yd.ytm.yd.r'y.ḥmrm. | b.gt.gwl.ṯmn.ṣmdm. | w.arb'.'šr.bnš. | 2038.3
.kṯr m.ḥbr k. | w ḫss.d't k. | b ym.arš.w tnn. | kṯr.w ḫss.yd. | ytr.kṯr.w ḫss. | spr.ilmlk šbny. | lmd.atn.prln.rb. | khnm 6.6[62.2].51

y.w yhbṭ.bnš. | w ytn.ilm.b d hm. | b d.iḫqm.gṯr. | w b d.ytrhd. | b'l. 55[18].21
.b d.iytlm. | ṯn.šdm.b d.amtrn. | šd.b d.iwrm[--]. | šd.b d.yṯpr. | šd.b d.krb[-]. | šd.b d.bn.pṯḏ. | šd.b d.dr.khnm. | šd.b 2090.14
r[š k.---]. | [---.]y.ḥr.ḥr.bnt.ḥ[---]. | [--.]uḫd.[b'l] m.'[--].yd k.amṣ.yd[.--]. | [---.]ḥš[.-]nm[.--.]k.[--].w yḫnp[.---]. | [---.] 1001.1.14
d[--].b bk.krt. | b dm'.n'mn.ǵlm. | il.trḥṣ.w tadm. | rḥṣ[.y]d k.amt. | uṣb['t k.]'d[.ṯ]km. | 'rb[.b ẓl.ḫmt]. | qḥ im[r.b yd 14[KRT].2.63
k.amt. | uṣb['t k.]'d[.ṯ]km. | 'rb[.b ẓl.ḫmt]. | qḥ im[r.b yd k]. | imr.d[bḥ.bm].ymn. | lla.kl[atn]m. | klt.l[ḥm k.d]nzl. | 14[KRT].2.66
gr[š.d 'šy.ln k]. | spu.ksm k.bt.[b'l.w mnt k]. | bt il.aḥd.yd k.b [škrn]. | m'ms k.k šb't.yn.ṭ[ḥ]. | gg k.b ym.ṭiṭ.rḥṣ. | npṣ 17[2AQHT].2.5
h.w hm. | aṯtm.tṣḥn y.ad ad.nḥtm.ḫṭ k. | mmnnm.mṭ yd k.hl.'ṣr.tḥrr.l išt. | w ṣḥrrt.l pḥmm.btm.bt.il.bt.il. | w 'lm 23[52].44
m h.w hn.aṯtm.tṣḥn y.mt mt. | nḥtm.ḫṭ k.mmnnm.mṭ yd k.hl.'ṣr. | tḥrr.l išt.w ṣḥrt.l pḥmm.aṯtm.a[ṯt.il]. | aṯt.il.w 'l 23[52].47
k ypt.hm.aṯtm.tṣḥn. | y mt.mt.nḥtm.ḫṭ k.mmnnm.mṭ.yd k. | h[l.]'ṣr.tḥrr.l išt.ṣḥrrt.l pḥmm. | a[ṯ]tm.aṯt.il.aṯt.il.w 'l 23[52].40
tqǵ[.udn.k ǵz.ǵzm]. | tdbr.w[ǵ]rm[.ṯṯwy]. | šqlt.b ǵlt.yd k. | l tdn.dn.almnt. | l ṯṯpṭ.ṯpṭ.qṣr.npš. | km.aḫt.'rš.mdw. | a 16.6[127].32
'.w tqǵ udn. | k ǵz.ǵzm.tdbr. | w ǵrm.ṯṯwy.šqlt. | b ǵlt.yd k.l tdn. | dn.almnt.l ṯṯpṭ. | ṯpṭ qṣr.npš.l tdy. | ṯšm.'l.dl.l pn 16.6[127].45
.w ṯn. | ṯlṯ.rb'.ym.ymš. | ṯdṯ.ym.ḥẓ k.al.tš'l. | qrt h.abn.yd k. | mšdpt.w hn.špšm. | b šb'.w l.yšn.pbl. | mlk.l qr.ṯigt.ibr 14[KRT].3.117
]. | [-]m[.---]. | h.hn bn k.hn[.---]. | bn bn.aṯr k.hn[.---]. | yd k.ṣǵr.tnšq.špt k.ṯm. | ṯkm.bm ṯkm.aḫm.qym.il. | b lsmt.ṯ 22.2[124].4
t. | 'l.l ẓr.[mg]dl. | w 'l.l ẓr.[mg]dl.rkb. | ṯkmm.ḥm[t].ša.yd k. | šmm.dbḥ.l ṯr. | ab k.il.šrd.b'l. | b dbḥ k.bn.dgn. | b mṣd 14[KRT].2.75
k [ṯṣḥ]. | 'n.mkṯr.ap.t[---]. | dgy.rbt.aṯr[t.ym]. | qḥ.rṯt.b d k t[---]. | rbt.'l.ydm[.---]. | b mdd.il.y[--.---]. | b ym.il.d[--.---. 4[51].2.32
[.---]. | 'r[.---]. | 'r[.---]. | w y[---]. | b'd[.---]. | yaṯr[.---]. | b d k.[---]. | ṯnnt h[.---]. | ṯlṯt h[.-.w y'n]. | lṯpn.[il.d pid.my]. | b i 16[126].5.7
--]. | šd.b d[.---]im. | šd.b d[.bn.--]n. | šd.b d.iwrkl. | šd.b d.klb. | šd.b d.klby. | šd.b d.iytlm. | ṯn.šdm.b d.amtrn. | šd.b d. 2090.9
. | [---.--]m. | [šd.---.b d.]ṯpṭb'l. | [šd.---.]b d.ymz. | [šd.b d].klby.psl. | [ub]dy.mri.ibrn. | [š]d.bn.bri.b d.bn.ydln. | [u]bd 82[300].2.4
--]im. | šd.b d[.bn.--]n. | šd.b d.iwrkl. | šd.b d.klb. | šd.b d.klby. | šd.b d.iytlm. | ṯn.šdm.b d.amtrn. | šd.b d.iwrm[--]. | š 2090.10
. | [-]š[-]y.d.b š[-]y. | [---.y]d gt h[.--]. | [---.]yd. | [k]rm h.yd. | [k]lkl h. | [w] ytn.nn. | l.b'ln.bn. | kltn.w l. | bn h.'d.'lm. | š 1008.9
--]. | [-----]. | [-----]. | [---].ḫmš[.---]. | [---.]urš[-.---]. | [---.]yd.kl.[---]. 2156.10
. | [u]bdy.nqdm. | [ṯlṯ].šdm.d.n'rb.gt.npk. | [š]d.rpan.b d.klṯṯb. | [š]d.ilṣy.b d.'bdym. | [ub]dy.trrm. | [šd.]bn.ṯqdy.b d. 82[300].2.14
d.dr.khnm. | šd.b d.bn.'my. | šd.b d.bn.'yn. | ṯn.šdm.b d.klṯṯb. | šd.b d.krz[n]. | ṯlṯ.šdm.b d.amtr[n]. | ṯn.šdm.b d.skn. 2090.20
d.pll.b d.qrt. | š[d].anndr.b d.bdn.nḥ[l h]. | [šd.]agyn.b d.kmrn.n[ḥl] h. | [š]d.nbzn.[-]l.qrt. | [š]d.agpṯr.b d.šḫrn.nḥl h 2029.8
ṯn.šdm.b d.amtrn. | šd.b d.iwrm[--]. | šd.b d.yṯpr. | šd.b d.krb[-]. | šd.b d.bn.pṯḏ. | šd.b d.dr.khnm. | šd.b d.bn.'my. | šd 2090.15
b.gt.mlkt.b.rḥbn. | ḫmšm.l.mitm.zt. | w.b d.krd. | ḫmšm.l.mit. | arb'.kbd. 1096.3
šd.b d.bn.'my. | šd.b d.bn.'yn. | ṯn.šdm.b d.klṯṯb. | šd.b d.krz[n]. | ṯlṯ.šdm.b d.amtr[n]. | ṯn.šdm.b d.skn. | šd.b d[.'b]d 2090.21
d.kḏǵdl[.bn]. | [-]š[-]y.d.b š[-]y. | [---.y]d gt h[.--]. | [---.]yd. | [k]rm h.yd. | [k]lkl h. | [w] ytn.nn. | l.b'ln.bn. | kltn.w l. | b 1008.8
b d.šḫrn.nḥl h. | šd.annmn.b d.tyn.nḥl h. | šd.pǵyn[.b] d.krmn.l.ty[n.n]ḥl h. | šd.krz.[b]n.ann.'[db]. | šd.ṯ[r]yn.bn.tk 2029.12
id.l tbrk. | [krt.]ṯ'.l tmr.n'mn. | [ǵlm.]il.ks.yiḫd. | [il.b]yd.krpn.bm. | [ymn.]brkm.ybrk. | ['bd h.]ybrk.il.krt. | [ṯ'.ymr 15[128].2.17
a[rṣ.---]. | b 'pr.ḫbl ṯtm.[---.] | šqy.rṯa.tnm y.ytn.[ks.b yd]. | krpn.b klat yd.[---]. | km ll.ḫṣ.tusp[.---]. | tgr.il.bn h.tr[1['NT.X].4.9
ty.'d[b]. | imr.b pḥd.l npš.kṯr. | w ḫss.l brlt.hyn d. | ḥrš yd.šlḥm.ššqy. | ilm sad.kbd.hmt.b'l. | ḥkpt.il.kl h.tšm'. | mṯt.d 17[2AQHT].5.19
šm.yd.grbs hm. | w.ṯn.'šr h.ḫpnt. | [š]šwm.amtm.'kyt. | yd.llḫ hm. | w.ṯlṯ.l.'šrm. | ḫpnt.ššwm.ṯn. | pddm.w.d.ṯṯ. | [mr] 2049.5
'ṯtrt. | ad[-]l[-]m. | 'šr.ksdm.yd.lmd hm.lqḥ. | 'šr.mḫṣm.yd.lmd hm. | apym. | [bn]š gt.ipṯl. | [---]ym. | [----]m. | [-----]. | [1040.9
r. | r'ym. | bn.ḫri[-]. | bnš.gt.'ṯtrt. | ad[-]l[-]m. | 'šr.ksdm.yd.lmd hm.lqḥ. | 'šr.mḫṣm.yd.lmd hm. | apym. | [bn]š gt.ipṯl. 1040.8
mit.šmn.d.nm[-.]b d.mzy.alzy. | ḫmš.kkr.hlb. | ḫmš.kkr.brr. | kkr.ḫmš.mat.kbd.ṯ 1135.1
'n.yṯ[p]n[.mh]r. | št.b yn.yšt.ila.il š[--.]il. | d yqny.ḏdm.yd.mḫṣt.a[qh]t.ǵ | zr.tmḫṣ.alpm.ib.št[-.]št. | ḥršm l ahlm p[-- 19[1AQHT].4.220
[bnšm.dt.]b d.mlk. | [---.b]d.mlkt. | [---.b]d.mlk. | [---.--]ḥ.uḫd. | [---.-]luḫ. 2014.1
[bnšm.dt.]b d.mlk. | [---.b]d.mlkt. | [---.b]d.mlk. | [---.--]ḥ.uḫd. | [---.-]luḫ. | [---.-]tn.b d.mlkt. | [---.]l.mḫ 2014.3
spr.updt. | d b d.mlkytn. | kdrl. | slṯmg. | adrdn. | l[l]wn. | ydln. | ldn. | tdǵl. | ib 1034.2
[bnšm.dt.]b d.mlk. | [---.b]d.mlkt. | [---.b]d.mlk. | [---.--]ḥ.uḫd. | [---.-]luḫ. | [---.-]tn.b d. 2014.2
[---.--]y.bṭr.b d.mlkt. | [---.]bṭr.b d.mlkt. | [---].b d.mršp. | [---.m]rbṣ. | [---.r]b.ṯnnm. | [---.]asrm. 2015.1.2
[---.--]y.bṭr.b d.mlkt. | [---.]bṭr.b d.mlkt. | [---].b d.mršp. | [---.m]rbṣ. | [---.r] 2015.1.1
lkt. | [---.b]d.mlk. | [---.--]ḥ.uḫd. | [---.-]luḫ. | [---.-]tn.b d.mlkt. | [---.]l.mḫṣ. | ab[---.]adddy.bn.skn. | bn.[---.]uḫd. | bn. 2014.6
.[---]. | šd[.---]. | b d[.---]. | š[d.---]. | b d[.---]. | šd[.---]. | b d.ml[--]. | šd.b[---]. | b d.[---]. | šd.[---]. | b d.[---]. | [-----]. | šd.bn 2028.16
npṣm. | b d.mri. | skn. | 'šrm. | ḫmš. | kbd. 157[116].2
dm.l.ybr[k]. | bdmr.prs.l.u[-]m[-]. | ṯmn.l.'šrm. | dmd.b d.mry[n]m. 2102.11
[---.--]y.bṭr.b d.mlkt. | [---.]bṭr.b d.mlkt. | [---].b d.mršp. | [---.m]rbṣ. | [---.r]b.ṯnnm. | [---.]asrm. | [---.--]kn. | [--- 2015.1.3
[---.]ybl.k bn.qdš.mnḥy k.ap.anš.zbl.b'[l]. | [-.yuḫ]d.b yd.mšḫṭ.bm.ymn.mḫṣ.ǵlmm.yš[--]. | [ymn h.'n]t.tuḫd.šmal 2.1[137].39
n.ṯlṯ.'š[r.kkr]. | bn.šw.šb'.kk[r.---]. | arb'm.kkr.[---]. | b d.mtn.[l].šlm. 2108.5
[mrǵ]b.yd.m[ṯkt]. | mẓma.yd.mṯkt. | ṯṯkr.[--]dn. | 'm.krt.mswn h. | ar 15[128].1.1
[mrǵ]b.yd.m[ṯkt]. | mẓma.yd.mṯkt. | ṯṯkr.[--]dn. | 'm.krt.mswn h. | arḫ.tzǵ.l 'gl h. | bn.ḫ 15[128].1.2
[---.]ydm ym. | [---.]ydm nhr. | [---.]trǵt. | [---.]h aḥd[.--]. | [---.]iln[-.---]. | [---.--]ḫ[. 49[73].1.2
y.b d.tbṯṯb. | [š]d.bn.ṯ[-]rn.b d.'dbmlk. | [šd.]bn.brzn.b d.nwrḏ. | [šd.]bn.nḥbl.b d.'dbym. | [šd.b]n.qty.b d.tt. | [ubd]y. 82[300].1.17
. | lmd.aḥd.b d.yr[š]. | lmd.aḥd.b d.yḫ[--]. | ṯlṯ.lmdm.b d.nḫ[--]. | lmd.aḥd.b d.ar[--]. | ṯlṯ.lmdm.b d.[---]. | ṯlṯ.lmdm.b 1050.6
.b nr.d 'l k.mḫṣ.aqht. | ǵzr.šrš k.b arṣ.al. | yp'.riš.ǵly.b d.ns' k. | 'nt.brḥ.p 'lm h. | 'nt.p dr.dr.'db.uḫry mṭ yd h. | ymǵ 19[1AQHT].3.160
.yd.r'y.ḥmrm. | b.gt.gwl.ṯmn.ṣmdm. | w.arb'.'šr.bnš. | yd.nǵr.mdr'.yd.š[--]m. | [b.]gt.ipṯl.ṯṯ.ṣmdm. | [w.']šr.bn[š]m.y 2038.6
[---.]yd.npṣ h. | [---.]yd.npṣ h. | [---.]yd.npṣ h. | [---.yd].npṣ h. | [---.yd.np]ṣ h. | [---.yd.np]ṣ h. | [---. 1119.3
ṣ h. | [---.]yd.npṣ h. | [---.yd].npṣ h. | [---.yd.np]ṣ h. | [---.yd.np]ṣ h. | [---.yd.npṣ] h. | [---.-]nm. | [---.--]ṯ. 1119.6
ṣ h. | [---.]yd.npṣ h. | [---.]yd.npṣ h. | [---.yd].npṣ h. | [---.yd.np]ṣ h. | [---.yd.np]ṣ h. | [---.yd.npṣ] h. | [---.-]nm. | [---.--]ṯ. 1119.5
[---.]yd.npṣ h. | [---.]yd.npṣ h. | [---.]yd.npṣ h. | [---.yd].npṣ h. | [---.yd.np]ṣ h. | [---. 1119.2
[---.]yd.npṣ h. | [---.]yd.npṣ h. | [---.]yd.npṣ h. | [---.yd].npṣ h. | [---. 1119.1
[---.]yd.npṣ h. | [---.]yd.npṣ h. | [---.]yd.npṣ h. | [---.yd].npṣ h. | [---.yd.np]ṣ h. | [---.yd.np]ṣ h. | [---.yd.npṣ] h. | [---. 1119.4

ṣ h.|[---.yd].npṣ h.|[---.yd.np]ṣ h.|[---.yd.np]ṣ h.|[---.yd.npṣ] h.|[---.-]nm.|[---.--]ṯ. 1119.7
bn.|šd.b d.bn.uṯryn.|[ubd]y.mrynm.|[š]d.bn.ṣnrn.b d.nrn.|[š]d.bn.rwy.b d.ydln.|[š].bn.trn.b d.ibrmḏ.|[š]d.bn.i 82[300].1.8
ʿ.lmdm.|[---.b]ʿln.|[---.]lmdm.b d.snrn.|[---.lm]dm.b d.nrn.|[---.ẖ]dǵlm.|[lmd.]aḥd.b d.yrš. 1051.4
bl[-.---.]m[--.]hwt.|[---].ṯllt.khn[m.---.]k pʿn.|[---.--]y.yd.nšy.[---.--]š.l mdb.|[---] h.mẖlpt[.---.--]r.|[---.]nʿlm.[---].| UG5.8.48
gyn.b d.kmrn.n[ḥl] h.|[š]d.nbzn.[-]l.qrt.|[š]d.agpṯr.b d.sẖrn.nḥl h.|šd.annmn.b d.tyn.nḥl h.|šd.pǵyn[.b] d.krmn. 2029.10
bn.[---.]uẖd.|bn.n[---.]hbṯn.|bn.m[--.]skn.|bn.s[--.b]d.skn.|bn.ur[-.---].|bn.knn[.---]y.|bn.ymlk[.b]d.skn.|bn.yḥ 2014.12
s[--.b]d.skn.|bn.ur[-.---].|bn.knn[.---]y.|bn.ymlk[.b]d.skn.|bn.yḥnn.aḏddy.|bn.pdǵy.mẖdy.|bn.yyn.mḏrǵl.|bn. 2014.15
sp.hn.|ktn.d.ṣr.pḥm.b h.w.ṯqlm.|ksp h.mitm.pḥm.b d.skn.|w.ṯt.ktnm.ẖmšt.w.nṣp.ksp.hn. 1110.5
.klṯṯb.|šd.b d.krz[n].|ṯlṯ.šdm.b d.amtr[n].|ṯn.šdm.b d.skn.|šd.b d[.ʿb]dyrẖ.|šd.b [d.--]ṯṯb. 2090.23
šd.ubdy.ilštmʿ.|dt b d.skn.|šd.bn.ubrʿn b gt prn.|šd.bn.gby.gt.prn.|šd.bn.kryn. 1104.2
dy.|grʿ.aḏddy.|ʿbd.ršp aḏddy.|ʿdn.bn.knn.|iwrẖz.b d.skn.|škny.aḏddy.|mšu.aḏddy.|plsy.aḏddy.|aẖyn.|ygmr. 2014.37
ẖmš.bnšm[.---].|ẖdǵlm.b d.[---].|šbʿ.lmdm.b d.s[n]rn.|lmd.aḥd.b d.yr[š].|lmd.aḥd.b d.yḥ[--].|ṯlṯ.lmdm. 1050.3
[---]ʿ.lmdm.|[---.b]ʿln.|[---.]lmdm.b d.snrn.|[---.lm]dm.b d.nrn.|[---.ẖ]dǵlm.|[lmd.]aḥd.b d.yrš. 1051.3
[-.---.]dd.|[---]n.yd.sǵ[r.---.--]k.[--].|[---.]dd.bn.š.[---.]yd.sǵr h.|[---.--]r h.ʿšr[m.---.ʿ]šrm.dd.|[---.yn.d.]nkly.l.rʿym 1098.42
[--.---.--]d.|ʿšrm[.---.--]r h.|[-]wyn.yd[-.---.]dd.|[---]n.yd.sǵ[r.---.--]k.[--].|[---.]dd.bn.š.[---.]yd.sǵr h.|[---.--]r h.ʿšr[1098.41
r.[---.--]n.ṯn.ʿšr h.d[--.---].|[---.]ḥdṯn.ʿšr.dd[.---].|[---.]yd.sǵr[.---.--]r h.|aḥ[d.---.ʿ]šrm.d[d.---].|ʿš[r.---.--]r h.|my y 1098.35
[--.-]d[-.---].|[--.šd]m.b d.iyt[lm].|[šd.b]d.s[--].|š[d.b]d.u[--].|šd.b d.[---].|šd.b d[.---]im.|šd.b d[.bn 2090.3
[---].b d.š[--]mlk.|[---.b] d.gbʿly.|[---.b] d.ʿbdẖmn.|[---.b] d.ṯbq.|[---.b] d.šbn.|[---.b] d.ulm.|[---.b] 1052.3
lṯ].šdm.d.nʿrb.gt.npk.|[š]d.rpan.b d.klṯṯb.|[š]d.ilṣy.b d.ʿbdym.|[ub]dy.trrm.|[šd.]bn.ṯqdy.b d.gmrd.|[š]d bn.syn 82[300].2.15
šš[r]t.ẖrṣ.ṯqlm.kbd.ʿšrt.mzn h.|b [ar]bʿm.ksp.|b d[.ʿb]dym.ṯlṯ.kkr šʿrt.|iqn[i]m.ṯṯt.ʿšrt.ksp h.|ẖmšt.ẖrṣ.bt.il. 2100.3
d.krz[n].|ṯlṯ.šdm.b d.amtr[n].|ṯn.šdm.b d.skn.|šd.b d[.ʿb]dyrẖ.|šd.b [d.--]ṯṯb. 2090.24
.ṯbq.|[---.b] d.šbn.|[---.b] d.ulm.|[---.b] d.ǵbl.|[---.b] d.ʿbdkṯr.|[---.b] d.urǵnr. 1052.8
ubdy.mdm.|šd.b d.ʿbdmlk.|šd.b d.yšn.ḥrš.|šd.b d.aupš.|šd.b d.ršpab.aẖ.ubn 82[300].1.2
r.|[w.l.]bn h.ʿd.|[ʿl]m.mn k.|mn km l.yqẖ.|bt.hnd.b d.|[ʿb]dmlk.|[-]k.amʿ[--].|[w.b] d.bn h[.ʿ]d ʿlm.|[w.un]ṯ.in[1009.14
.dǵt h.|b šmym.dǵt hrnmy[.d k]|bkbm.ʿ[l.---].|[-]l h.yd ʿd[.---].|ltm.mrqdm.d š[-]l[-].|w tʿn.pǵt.ṯkmt.mym.|qry 19[1AQHT].4.188
n.b d.ʿdbmlk.|[šd.]bn.brzn.b d.nwrḏ.|[šd.]bn.nḥbl.b d.ʿdbym.|[šd.b]n.qty.b d.tt.|[ubd]y.mrim.|[šd.b]n.ṯpdn.b d 82[300].1.18
].šdm.b d.gmrd.|[šd.]lbny.b d.tbṯṯb.|[š]d.bn.ṯ[-]rn.b d.ʿdbmlk.|[šd.]bn.brzn.b d.nwrḏ.|[šd.]bn.nḥbl.b d.ʿdbym.| 82[300].1.16
t.[---].|ṯn.ʿšr.b.gt.ir[bṣ].|arbʿ.b.gt.bʿln.|ʿšt.ʿšr.b.gpn.|yd.ʿdnm.|arbʿ.ǵzlm.|ṯn.yṣrm. 2103.8
sg.|[-----].|[-----].|[---.--]ṯ.|[---.-]b.m.lk.|kdwṯ.ḥdṯ.|b d ʿlpy. 1112.20
mn.|[---.b] d.ṯbq.|[---.b] d.šbn.|[---.b] d.ulm.|[---.b] d.ǵbl.|[---.b] d.ʿbdkṯr.|[---.b] d.urǵnr. 1052.7
liy.krm.aḥd[.---].|ʿbdmlk.krm.aḥ[d.---].|krm.ubdy.b d.ǵ[--.---].|krm.pyn.arty[.---].|ṯlṯ.krm.ubdym.l mlkt.b.ʿnmk 1081.7
.|[šd.--]ln.|b d.trǵds.|šd.ṯʿlb.|b d.bn.pl.|šd.bn.kt.|b d.pdy.|šd.ẖzr.|[b d].d[---]. 2030.2.6
[---.t]št.rimt.|l irt h.mšr.l.dd.aliyn.|bʿl.yd.pdry.bt.ar.|ahbt.ṭly.bt.rb.dd.arṣy.|bt.yʿbdr.km ǵlmm.| 3[ʿNT].3.3
.[b]n.ann.ʿ[db].|šd.ṯ[r]yn.bn.tkn.b d.qrt.|šd[.-].dyn.b d.pln.nḥl h.|šd.irdyn.bn.ẖrǵš[-].l.qrt.|šd.iǵlyn.bn.kzbn.l.qr 2029.15
zn.tn[.---].|at.adn.tpʿr[.---].|ank.ltpn.il[.d pid.---].|ʿl.ydm.pʿrt[.---].|šm k.mdd.i[l.---].|bt ksp y.d[--.---].|b d.aliy 1[ʿNT.X].4.19
ṣmdm.a[--.---].|b d.prẖ[-.---].|apnm.l.ʿ[--].|apnm.l.[---].|apnm.l.d[--].|apnm. 145[318].2
spr.bnš.mlk.|d.b d.prṯ.|ṯšʿ.l.ʿšrm.|lqḥ.šślmt.|ṯmn.l.arbʿm.|lqḥ.šʿrt. 1025.2
.b d.bn.šmrm.|[šd.bn.-]ṯtayy.b d.ṯṯmd.|[šd.bn.-]rn.b d.šdqšlm.|[šd.b d.]bn.pʿṣ.|[ubdy.ʿ]šrm.|[šd.---]n.b d.brdd.| 82[300].1.28
.ṣṭqšlm.|ʿbd h.hnd.|w mn km.l yqẖ.|spr.mlk.hnd.|b yd.ṣṭqšlm.|ʿd ʿlm. 1005.14
].|mẖlpt.w l.ytk.[d]m[ʿt.]km.|rbʿt.ṯqlm.ṯtp[.---.]bm.|yd.ṣpn hm.tliy m[.--.ṣ]pn hm.|nṣḥy.šrr.m[---.--]ay.|nbšr k 19[1AQHT].2.84
l ẖz[r y].|w yʿn[y.k]rt[.ṯ]ʿ.|lm.ank.ksp.|w yr[q.ẖrṣ].|yd.mqm h.w ʿbd.|ʿlm.ṯlṯ.sswm.|mrkbt.b trbṣ.|bn.amt.p d.[14[KRT].6.284
n.|ab.adm.w ṯtb.|mlakm.l h.lm.ank.|ksp.w yrq.ẖrṣ.|yd.mqm h.w ʿbd.|ʿlm.ṯlṯ.sswm.mrkbt.|b trbṣt.bn.amt.|p d. 14[KRT].3.139
.g hm.w tṣḥn].|ṯḥ[m.pbl.mlk].|qḥ[.ksp.w yrq].|ẖrṣ.[yd.mqm h].|w ʿbd[.ʿlm.ṯlṯ].|sswm.m[rkbt].|b trbṣ.[bn.amt] 14[KRT].6.270
.l k.ʿm.krt.|mswn h.ṯḥm.pbl.mlk.|qḥ.ksp.w yrq.ẖrṣ.|yd.mqm h.w ʿbd.ʿlm.|ṯlṯ.sswm.mrkbt.|b trbṣ.bn.amt.|qḥ.k 14[KRT].3.127
[-----].|[-----].|[-----.lm].|[ank.ksp.w yrq].|[ẖrṣ.]yd.mqm h.|[w ʿb]d.ʿlm.ṯlṯ.|[ssw]m.mrkbt b trbṣ bn.amt.|[t 14[KRT].2.54
r[gm.l krt.]ṯʿ.|ṯḥm[.pbl.mlk].|qḥ.[ksp.w yr]q.|ẖrṣ[.yd.mqm] h.|ʿbd[.ʿlm.ṯlṯ].|ss[wm.mrkbt].|b[trbṣ.bn.amt].|[14[KRT].5.251
b d.ttyn.nḥl [h].|šd.ṯṯyn[.b]n.arkšt.|lʿq[.---].|šd.pll.b d.qrt.|š[d].anndr.b d.bdn.nḥ[l h].|[šd.]agyn.b d.kmrn.n[ḥl] 2029.6
ty[n.n]ḥl h.|šd.krz.[b]n.ann.ʿ[db].|šd.ṯ[r]yn.bn.tkn.b d.qrt.|šd[.-].dyn.b d.pln.nḥl h.|šd.irdyn.bn.ẖrǵš[-].l.qrt.|šd 2029.14
|w.l.ṯt.mrkbtm.|inn.uṯpt.|w.ṯlṯ.ṣmdm.w.ḥrṣ.|apnt.b d.rb.ḥršm.|d.šṣa.ḥwy h. 1121.9
--.]bn.i[--.---].|[---].ṯp[--.---].|[---.a]ḥt.b d[.---].|[---.]b d.rb.[m]dlm.|[---.l i]ytlm.|[---].gmn.|[---].l.urǵṯb.|[---.]l.ʿṯt 2162.B.2
d a[-]m.w.ank.|k[l.]drʿ hm.|[--.n]pš[-.].|w [k]l hm.b d.|rb.tmtt.lqḥt.|w.ṯṯb.ank.l hm.|w.any k.ṯt.|by.ʿky.ʿryt.|w 2059.21
[b.]gt.ṯpn.ʿšr.ṣmdm.|w.ṯlṯ.ʿšr.bnš.|yd.ytm.yd.rʿy.ḥmrm.|b.gt.gwl.ṯmn.ṣmdm.|w.arbʿ.ʿšr.bnš.|yd.nǵr. 2038.3
m.|šd.b d.ʿbdmlk.|šd.b d.yšn.ḥrš.|šd.b d.aupš.|šd.b d.ršpab.aẖ.ubn.|šd.b d.bn.uṯryn.|[ubd]y.mrynm.|[š]d.bn.ṣ 82[300].1.5
[b.]gt.iptl.ṯt.ṣmdm.|[w.ʿ]šr.bn[š]m.y[d].š[--].|[-]lm.b d.r[-]m.l[-]m.|ṯt.ʿšr.ṣ[mdm].|w.ṯšʿ.ʿ[šr.--]m.ḥr[š].|[---].ḥr[š. 2038.9
b d.brq.maẖdy.|kkr.ṯlṯ.|b d.bn.by.ar[y].|alpm.ṯlṯ.|b d.šim.il[š]tmʿy. 1134.7
[---.b] d.gbʿly.|[---.b] d.ʿbdẖmn.|[---.b] d.ṯbq.|[---.b] d.šbn.|[---.b] d.ulm.|[---.b] d.ǵbl.|[---.b] d.ʿbdkṯr.|[---.b] d. 1052.5
ṯlṯ.d yṣa.|b d.šmmn.|l argmn.|l nskm.|ṯmn.kkrm.|alp.kbd.|[m]itm.kb 147[90].2
alp.alp.am[-].|ṯmn.ḥblm.šbʿ.šbʿ.ma[-].|ʿšr.kkr.rtn.|b d.šmʿy.bn.bdn. 1128.33
r.mdrʿ.yd.š[--]m.|[b.]gt.iptl.ṯt.ṣmdm.|[w.ʿ]šr.bn[š]m.y[d].š[--].|[-]lm.b d.r[-]m.l[-]m.|ṯt.ʿšr.ṣ[mdm].|w.ṯšʿ.ʿ[šr.--] 2038.8
m.|b.gt.gwl.ṯmn.ṣmdm.|w.arbʿ.ʿšr.bnš.|yd.nǵr.mdrʿ.yd.š[--]m.|[b.]gt.iptl.ṯt.ṣmdm.|[w.ʿ]šr.bn[š]m.y[d].š[--].|[-]l 2038.6
[---].b d.š[--]mlk.|[---.b] d.gbʿly.|[---.b] d.ʿbdẖmn.|[---.b] d.ṯbq.|[- 1052.1
.rwy.b d.ydln.|[š].bn.trn.b d.ibrmḏ.|[š]d.bn.ilṯtmr.b d.tbbr.|[w.]šd.nḥl h.b d.ṯtmd.|[š]d.b d.iwrẖṭ.|[ṯn].šdm.b d. 82[300].1.11
ṯṯmd.|[š]d.b d.iwrẖṭ.|[ṯn].šdm.b d.gmrd.|[šd.]lbny.b d.tbṯṯb.|[š]d.bn.ṯ[-]rn.b d.ʿdbmlk.|[šd.]bn.brzn.b d.nwrḏ.|[82[300].1.15

|wy.w kbd hwt.|w rgm.l kṯr.|w ẖss.ṯny.l h|yn.d ḥrš.ydm.|tḥm.al[iyn.b'l].|h[wt.aliy.qrdm]. 3['NT.VI].6.23
wy.w kbd.hwt].|w rgm l k[ṯr.w ẖss.ṯny.l hyn].|d ḥrš.y[dm.tḥm.ṯr.il.ab k.]|hwt.lṭpn[.ḥtk k.---].|yh.kṯr.b[---].|št. 1['NT.IX].3.5
.nbzn.[-]l.qrt.|[š]d.agpṯr.b d.sẖrn.nḥl h.|šd.annmn.b d.tyn.nḥl h.|šd.pǵyn[.b] d.krmn.l.ty[n.n]ḥl h.|šd.krz.[b]n.a 2029.11
mat.brr.|b.ṯmnym.ksp.ṯlṯt.kbd.|ẖmš.alp.ṯlṯ.l.ẖlby.|b d.tlmi.b.'šrm.ẖmšt.|kbd.ksp.|kkrm.š'rt.štt.b d.gg['t].|b.'šrt 2101.7
mḏrǵlm.dt.inn.|b d.tlmyn.|b d.gln.ary.|tgyn.y'rty.|bn.krwn.b.yny.iytlm.|šgr 2071.2
ṯmn.mrkbt.dt.|'rb.bt.mlk.|yd.apnt hn.|yd.ḥẓ hn.|yd.tr hn.|w.l.ṯt.mrkbtm.|inn.uṯpt.|w.ṯlṯ.ṣmdm.w.ḥrṣ.|apnt 1121.5
br.l.snrn.|[---.--]k.l.gmrd.|[---.--]ṯ.l.yšn.|[šd.--]ln.|b d.trǵds.|šd.ṯ'lb.|b d.bn.pl.|šd.bn.kt.|b d.pdy.|šd.ẖzr.|[b d] 2030.2.2
rzn.b d.nwrḏ.|[šd.]bn.nḥbl.b d.'dbym.|[šd.b]n.qṭy.b d.tt.|[ubd]y.mrim.|[šd.b]n.ṯpdn.b d.bn.g'r.|[šd.b]n.ṯqrn.b 82[300].1.19
alpm.pḥm.ẖm[š].mat.kbd.|b d.tt.w.ṯlṯ.ktnt.b dm.tt.|w.ṯmnt.ksp.hn.|ktn.d.ṣr.pḥm.b h.w. 1110.2
alpm.pḥm.ẖm[š].mat.kbd.|b d.tt.w.ṯlṯ.ktnt.b dm.tt.|w.ṯmnt.ksp.hn.|ktn.d.ṣr.pḥm.b h.w.ṯqlm.|ksp h.mit 1110.2
spr.ubdy.art.|šd.prn.b d.agpṯn.nḥl h.|šd.šwn.b d.ttyn.nḥl [h].|šd.tṯyn[.b]n.arkšt.|l'q[.---].|šd.pll.b d.qrt.|š[2029.3
rn.b d.ibrmḏ.|[š]d.bn.ilṯtmr.b d.tbbr.|[w.]šd.nḥl h.b d.ṯtmd.|[š]d.b d.iwrẖṭ.|[ṯn].šdm.b d.gmrd.|[šd.]lbny.b d.tb 82[300].1.12
b d.iwrẖṭ.|[šd.bn.-]nn.b d.bn.šmrm.|[šd.bn.-]ṯtayy.b d.ṯtmd.|[šd.bn.-]rn.b d.ṣdqšlm.|[šd.b d.]bn.p'ṣ.|[ubdy.']šr 82[300].1.27
klt h.b.t[--.---].|b'l y.mlk[y.---].|yd.bt h.yd[.---].|ary.yd.t[--.---].|ẖtn h.šb'l[.---].|ṯlḥny.yd[.---].|yd.ṯlṯ.kl[t h.---].| 81[329].15
.b d.š[--]mlk.|[---.b] d.gb'ly.|[---.b] d.'bdẖmn.|[---.b] d.ṯbq.|[---.b] d.šbn.|[---.b] d.ulm.|[---.b] d.ǵbl.|[---.b] d.'bd 1052.4
w.arb'.ḥ[mrm].|b m[']rby.|ṯmn.ṣmd.[---].|b d.b'lsr.|yd.ṯdn.'šr.|[ḥ]mrm.|ddm.l.ybr[k].|bdmr.prs.l.u[-]m[-].|ṯm 2102.4
[.---].|ary.yd.t[--.---].|ẖtn h.šb'l[.---].|ṯlḥny.yd[.---].|yd.ṯlṯ.kl[t h.---].|w.ṯṯm.ṣi[n.---].|tn[--].|agyn.[---].|[w].ṯn.[- 81[329].18
.b'ln.biry.|ṯlṯ.b'lm.|w.adn hm.ṯr.w.arb'.bnt h.|yrẖm.yd.ṯn.bn h.|b'lm.w.ṯlṯ.n'rm.w.bt.aḥt.|bn.lwn.ṯlṯtm.b'lm.|b 2080.4
qṣ.ṣmd.b d b'l.km.nšr.|b[u]ṣb't h.ylm.ktp.zbl ym.bn ydm.ṯpṭ.|nhr.'z.ym.l ymk.l tnǵṣn.pnt h.l ydlp.|tmn h.kṯr.ṣ 2.4[68].16
t h.trtqṣ.b d b'l km nš|r.b uṣb't h.hlm.ktp.zbl ym.bn ydm.|[ṯp]ṭ nhr.yrtqṣ.ṣmd.b d b'l.km.nšr.|b[u]ṣb't h.ylm.kt 2.4[68].14
|[ubdy.mḏ]rǵlm.|[šd.bn.--]n.b d.aẖny.|[šd.bn.--]rt.b d.ṯpṭb'l.|[ubdy.]mẖ[ṣ]m.|[šd.bn.]uzpy.b d.yšn.ḥrš.|[-----].| 82[300].2.24
ṣ.|[ubdy.']šrm.|[šd.---]n.b d.brdd.|[---.--]m.|[šd.---.b d.]ṯpṭb'l.|[šd.---.]b d.ymz.|[šd.b d].klby.psl.|[ub]dy.mri.ibr 82[300].2.2
.l aẖt k.|ṯtmnt.krt n.dbḥ.|dbḥ.mlk.'šr.|'šrt.qḥ.tp k.b yd.|[-]r[-]k.bm.ymn.|tlk.škn.'l.ṣrrt.|adn k.šqrb.[---].|b mg 16.1[125].41
šd.bn.adn.|[b] d.armwl.|[šd].mrnn.|b d.[-]tw[-].|šd.bn[.---].|b d.dd[--].|šd.d[---].|b d.d[---].|šd.b[2028.4
[---.]y.ḥr.ḥr.bnt.ḥ[---].|[--.]uẖd.[b']l m.'[--].yd k.amṣ.yd[.--].|[---.]ḥš[.-]nm[.--.]k.[--].w yẖnp[.---].|[---.]ylm.b[n.'] 1001.1.14
ẖ[ṣ]m.|[šd.bn.]uzpy.b d.yšn.ḥrš.|[-----].|[-----].|[šd.b d.--]n.|[šd.b d.--]n.|[šd.b d.--]ǵl.|[šd.b d.--]pšm.šyr. 82[300].2.29
.]uzpy.b d.yšn.ḥrš.|[-----].|[-----].|[šd.b d.--]n.|[šd.b d.--]n.|[šd.b d.--]ǵl.|[šd.b d.--]pšm.šyr. 82[300].2.30
.-]nb.trtn.|[---]mm.klby.kl[--].dqn[.---].|[-]ntn.artn.b d[.--]nr[.---].|'zn.w ymd.šr.b d ansny.|nsk.ks[p.--]mrtn.kṯr 2011.30
šn.ḥrš.|[-----].|[-----].|[šd.b d.--]n.|[šd.b d.--]n.|[šd.b d.--]ǵl.|[šd.b d.--]pšm.šyr. 82[300].2.31
|[-----].|[šd.b d.--]n.|[šd.b d.--]n.|[šd.b d.--]ǵl.|[šd.b d.--]pšm.šyr. 82[300].2.32
.b d.amtr[n].|ṯn.šdm.b d.skn.|šd.b d[.'b]dyrẖ.|šd.b [d.--]tṯb. 2090.25
yd.[---].|am[-]n.[---].|w.a[ṯt] h.[---].|ẖḏmtn.ṯn[.---].|w.ṯlṯ.al 2044.1
.ḥ[--].|b ṯtm.t[---].|šknt.[---].|bkym[.---].|ǵr.y[----].|ydm.[---].|apn.[---].|[--.]b[.---]. 16.2[125].118
qrty[.---].|w.klt h.b.t[--.---].|b'l y.mlk[y.---].|yd.bt h.yd[.---].|ary.yd.t[--.---].|ẖtn h.šb'l[.---].|ṯlḥny.yd[.---].|yd.ṯl 81[329].14
yn.d.ykl.b d.[---].|b.dbḥ.mlk.|dbḥ ṣpn.|[-]zǵm.|[i]lib.|[i]lbldn.|[p]dr 2004.1
.ap.t[---].|dgy.rbt.aṯr[t.ym].|qḥ.rṯt.b d k t[---].|rbt.'l.ydm[.---].|b mdd.il.y[--.---].|b ym.il.d[--.---.n]|hr.il.y[--.---]. 4[51].2.33
[s]p[r] ušknym.dt.[b d.---].|bn.btr.|bn.'ms.|bn.pṣn.|bn.agmz.|bn.[--]n.|bn.a[--]. 2021.1.1
d.bt h.yd[.---].|ary.yd.t[--.---].|ẖtn h.šb'l[.---].|ṯlḥny.yd[.---].|yd.ṯlṯ.kl[t h.---].|w.ṯṯm.ṣi[n.---].|tn[--].|agyn.[---]. 81[329].17
bl ṭtm.[---.]|šqy.rṯa.tnm y.ytn.[ks.b yd].|krpn.b klat yd.[---].|km ll.kḥṣ.tusp[.---].|tgr.il.bn h.ṯr[.---].|w y'n.lṭpn.i 1['NT.X].4.10
šy[.---].|bn.uẖn.|ybru.i[---].|[p]dyn.[---].|bnšm.d.b [d.---].|spẖy.[---].|[-----].|b[--.---].|n'[--.---].|[-----].|ẖn[--.--- 2161.13
b'ld'.yd[.---.']šrt.ksp h.|lbiy.pdy.[---.k]sp h. 2112.1
ẖmš.bnšm[.---].|ẖḏǵlm.b d.[---].|šb'.lmdm.b d.s[n]rn.|lmd.aḥd.b d.yr[š].|lmd.aḥd.b 1050.2
--.šd]m.b d.iyt[lm].|[šd.b]d.s[--].|š[d.b]d.u[--].|šd.b d.[---].|šd.b d[.---]im.|šd.b d[.bn.--]n.|šd.b d.iwrkl.|šd.b d. 2090.5
[---].|šd.b[---].|b d.[---].|šd[.---].|b d[.---].|š[d.---].|b d[.---].|šd[.---].|b d.ml[--].|šd.b[---].|b d.[---].|šd.[---].|b d. 2028.14
.bn[.---].|b d.dd[--].|šd.d[---].|b d.d[---].|šd.b[---].|b d.[---].|šd[.---].|b d[.---].|š[d.---].|b d[.---].|šd[.---].|b d.ml[2028.10
].|šd.d[---].|b d.d[---].|šd.b[---].|b d.[---].|šd[.---].|b d[.---].|š[d.---].|b d[.---].|šd[.---].|b d.ml[--].|šd.b[---].|b d. 2028.12
-].|š[d.---].|b d[.---].|šd[.---].|b d.ml[--].|šd.b[---].|b d.[---].|šd.[---].|b d.[---].|[-----].|šd.bn.gdy.|b d.ddl. 2028.18
[---].ydm.|[---].ṯdr.|[---.]mdṯn.ipd.|[---.]m[---.]d.mškbt.|[---.--] 1152.1.1
|ṯlṯ.lmdm.b d.nḥ[--].|lmd.aḥd.b d.ar[--].|ṯlṯ.lmdm.b d.[---].|ṯlṯ.lmdm.b d.[---]. 1050.8
[----]y.|[---.]rb.|[---].ṣḥt.|[---.--]t.|[---.]ilm.|[---.--]u.yd.|[---.--]k.|[---.gpn.]w ugr.|[---.---]t. 4[51].8.45
bn.a[--.---].|[---.]bn.i[--.---].|[---].ṯp[--.---].|[---.a]ḥt.b d[.---].|[---.]b d.rb.[m]dlm.|[---.l i]ytlm.|[---].gmn.|[---].l.ur 2162.B.1
-].|[---.--]š.b d.h[--.---].|[---.y]rẖ.dbḥ[.---].|[---.-]pn.b d.[---].|[---.]b d.[---]. 1160.6
[-----].|[---].w [---].|[---].mr[--.---].|[---].mr[--.]ydm[.---].|[---.]mṯbt.ilm.w.b.[---].|[---.]tṯṯbn.ilm.w.[---].|[--- 47[33].4
.|yitṯm.w.b[--].|yšlm.|[']šrm.ks[p].yš[lm].|[il]tḥm.b d[.---].|[---].ṯl[l]m.[---].|[--].r[-]y[.---].|'l.[--]l[-] h.|'dn.[---]. 2104.8
.|w ysmm.bn.š[---].|ytnm.qrt.l 'ly[.---].|b mdbr.špm.yd[.---.---]r.|l riš hm.w yš[--.--]m.|lḥm.b lḥm ay.w šty.b ẖm 23[52].4
-].|šd[.---].|b d.ml[--].|šd.b[---].|b d.[---].|šd.[---].|b d.[---].|[-----].|šd.bn.gdy.|b d.ddl. 2028.20
[-].|[-]b.m[--].|b y[rẖ].|pgr[m].|yṣa[.---].|lb[-.---].|b d[.---]. 1158.2.5
-].|lmd.aḥd.b d.ar[--].|ṯlṯ.lmdm.b d.[---].|ṯlṯ.lmdm.b d.[---]. 1050.9
.h[--.---].|[---.y]rẖ.dbḥ[.---].|[---.-]pn.b d.[---].|[---.]b d.[---]. 1160.7
yt[lm].|[šd.b]d.s[--].|š[d.b]d.u[--].|šd.b d.[---].|šd.b d[.---]im.|šd.b d[.bn.--]n.|šd.b d.iwrkl.|šd.b d.klb.|šd.b d.k 2090.6
[r.---].|yṣu.ẖlpn[.---].|ṯlṯ.dt.p[--.---].|dt.ṯgmi.[---].|b d [---]t.[---]. 1159.5

ydb

ly. | špš pgr. | iltm ẖnqtm. | yrẖ kṯy. | ygb hd. | yrgb bʿl. | ydb il. | yarš il. | yrǵm il. | ʿmtr. | ydb il. | yrgb lim. | ʿmtr. | yarš UG5.14.B.3
ṯy. | ygb hd. | yrgb bʿl. | ydb il. | yarš il. | yrǵm il. | ʿmtr. | ydb il. | yrgb lim. | ʿmtr. | yarš il. | ydb bʿl. | yrǵm bʿl. | ʿz bʿl. | y UG5.14.B.7
rš il. | yrǵm il. | ʿmtr. | ydb il. | yrgb lim. | ʿmtr. | yarš il. | ydb bʿl. | yrǵm bʿl. | ʿz bʿl. | ydb hd. UG5.14.B.11
il. | yrgb lim. | ʿmtr. | yarš il. | ydb bʿl. | yrǵm bʿl. | ʿz bʿl. | ydb hd. UG5.14.B.14

ydbʿl

bn.šyy. | bn.ẖnzr. | bn.ydbʿl. | bn.ḥyn. | [bn].ar[-]m. | [bn].ḥrp[-]. | [bn].ẖdpṯr. | [bn.-] 124[-].2.3

ydd

rt.ṯlmyn. | ʿbdnt. | bdy.ḥrš arkd. | blšš lmd. | ḥṯṯn.tqn. | ydd.idṯn. | šǵr.ilgdn. 1045.12
.mǵy.gpn.w ugr. | mn.ib.ypʿ.l bʿl.ṣrt. | l rkb.ʿrpt.l mẖšt.mdd. | il ym.l klt.nhr.il.rbm. | l ištbm.tnn.ištml h. | mẖšt.bṯn.ʿ 3[ʿNT].3.35
[------.i]qnim.[--]. | [---.]aliyn.bʿl. | [---.--]k.mdd il. | y[m.---.]l ṯr.qdqd h. | il[.--.]rḥq.b ǵr. | km.y[--.]ilm.b 4[51].7.3
.b q[rb.hk]l m. | al td[.pdr]y.bt ar. | [---.ṯl]y.bt.rb. | [---.m]dd.il ym. | [---.-]qlṣn.wpṯ m. | [---.]w yʿn.kṯr. | [w ẖss.]ṯṯb.bʿ 4[51].6.12
y.rbt.aṯr[t.ym]. | qḥ.rṯt.b d k t[---]. | rbt.ʿl.ydm[.---]. | b mdd.il.y[--.---]. | b ym.il.d[--.---.n] | hr.il.y[--.---]. | aliyn.[bʿl.-- 4[51].2.34
ṣʿ. | [--.]šbʿ.rbt. | [---.]qbṯ.ṯm. | [---.]bn.ilm. | [m]t.šmḥ.p ydd. | il[.ǵ]zr. | b [-]dn.ʿ.z.w. | rgbt.zbl. UG5.4.15
k.l yhpk.ksa.mlk k. | l yṯbr.ẖṭ.mṯpṭ k. | yru.bn ilm t.ṯṯʿ.y | dd.il.ǵzr.yʿr.mt. | b ql h.y[---.---]. | bʿl.yṯṯbn[.l ksi]. | mlk h.l 6[49].6.30
bl mlk. | arṣ.drkt.yštkn. | dll.al.ilak.l bn. | ilm.mt.ʿdd.l ydd. | il.ǵzr.yqra.mt. | b npš h.ystrn ydd. | b gngn h.aḥd y.d y 4[51].7.46
.uṯm. | ḏrqm.amt m.l yrt. | b npš.bn ilm.mt.b mh | mrt.ydd.il.ǵzr. | tbʿ.w l.yṯb ilm.idk. | l ytn.pnm.ʿm.bʿl. | mrym.ṣpn 5[67].1.8
.w ql. | tštḥwy.w k | bd hwt.w rgm. | l bn.ilm.mt. | ṯny.l ydd. | il.ǵzr.tḥm. | aliyn.bʿl. | [hw]t.aliy.q | [rdm.]bht y.bnt. | [d 4[51].8.31
.aliyn.bʿl. | ṯṯʿ.nn.rkb.ʿrpt. | tbʿ.rgm.l bn.ilm.mt. | ṯny.l ydd.il ǵzr. | tḥm.aliyn.bʿl.hwt.aliy. | qrdm.bhṯ.l bn.ilm mt. | ʿ 5[67].2.9
ʿr[.---]. | ank.lṯpn.il[.d pid.---]. | ʿl.ydm.pʿrt[.---]. | šm k.mdd.i[l.---]. | bt ksp y.d[--.---]. | b d.aliyn b[ʿl.---]. | kd.ynaṣn[. 1[ʿNT.X].4.20
.tnn.ištml h. | mẖšt.bṯn.ʿqltn. | šlyṭ.d šbʿt.rašm. | mẖšt.mdd ilm.ar[š]. | ṣmt.ʿgl.il.ʿtk. | mẖšt.klbt.ilm išt. | klt.bt.il.ḏbb 3[ʿNT].3.40
.b ṯbrn. | qn h.ṯẖtan. | nrt.ilm.špš. | ṣḥrrt.la. | šmm.b yd.md | d.ilm.mt.b a | lp.šd.rbt.k | mn.l pʿn.mt. | hbr.w ql. | tštḥw 4[51].8.23
l bn. | ilm.mt.ʿdd.l ydd. | il.ǵzr.yqra.mt. | b npš h.ystrn ydd. | b gngn h.aḥd y.d ym | lk.ʿl.ilm.l ymru. | ilm.w nšm.d y 4[51].7.48
.---]. | dt.lbn k[.---]. | dk k.kbkb[.---]. | dm.mt.aṣḥ[.---]. | ydd.b qr[b.---]. | al.ašt.b[---]. | ahpk k.l[--.---]. | ṯmm.w lk[.--- 5[67].3.10
[.---]. | šgr.mu[d.---]. | šgr.mud[.---]. | dm.mt.aṣ[ḥ.---]. | yd.b qrb[.---]. | w lk.ilm.[---]. | w rgm.l [---]. | b mud.ṣin[.---]. | 5[67].3.19
[.---]. | mud.ṣin[.---]. | iṯm.mui[-.---]. | dm.mt.aṣ[ḥ.---]. | ydd.b qr[b.---]. | ṯmm.w lk[.---]. | [--]ṯ.lk[.---]. | [--]kṯ.i[---.---]. 5[67].3.26
ʿl. | mrym.ṣpn.w yʿn. | gpn.w ugr.tḥm.bn ilm. | mt.hwt.ydd.bn.il. | ǵzr.p np.š.npš.lbim. | thw.hm.brlt.anẖr. | b ym.h 5[67].1.13
wr.mzl. | ymzl.w yṣi.trḥ. | ḥdṯ.ybʿr.l ṯn. | aṯt h.lm.nkr. | mddt h.k irby. | [t]škn.šd. | km.ḥsn.pat.mdbr. | lk.ym.w ṯn.ṯlṯ 14[KRT].2.103
u.ʿn h.w yʿn. | w yʿn.btlt.ʿnt. | nʿmt.bn.aẖt.bʿl. | l pnn h.ydd.w yqm. | l pʿn h.ykrʿ.w yql. | w yšu.g h.w yṣḥ. | ḥwt.aẖt. 10[76].2.17
| [---]y ilm.d mlk. | y[ṯ]b.aliyn.bʿl. | ytʿdd.rkb.ʿrpt. | [--].ydd.w yqlṣn. | yqm.w ywpṯn.b tk. | p[ẖ]r.bn.ilm.štt. | p[--].b ṯl 4[51].3.12
r. | mzl.ymzl. | w ybl.trḥ.ḥdṯ. | ybʿr.l ṯn.aṯt h. | w l nkr.mddt. | km irby.tškn. | šd.k ḥsn.pat. | mdbr.tlkn. | ym.w ṯn.aẖ 14[KRT].4.191
-]. | wr[t.---.]b d.yḥmn. | yry[.---.]br. | ydn[.---].kry. | bn.ydd[.---.b]r. | prkl.bʿl.any.d.b d.abr[-]. 2123.6

yddn

yn.yʿrty. | bn.krwn.b.yny.iytlm. | šgryn.ary.b.yny. | bn.yddn.b.rkby. | agyn.agny. | ṯqbn.mldy. 2071.7
n.ʿl.ʿbdn.w.[---]. | kdm.šmn.ʿl.ilršp.bn[.---]. | kd.šmn.ʿl.yddn. | kd.ʿl.ššy. | kd.ʿl.nḏbn.bn.agmn. | [k]d.ʿl.brq. | [kd]m.[ʿl 1082.1.6
št. | ẓẓn.qšt. | dqry.qš[t]. | rkby. | bn.knn.qšt. | pbyn.qšt. | yddn.qšt.w.qlʿ. | šʿrt. | bn.il.qšt.w.qlʿ. | ark.qšt.w.qlʿ. | bn.ʿbdn 119[321].2.38

yddt

ilšt[mʿym]. | yddt[.---]. | ilšn.[---]. | ṣdqn.[----]. | pndḏn.b[n.---]. | ayaẖ.b[n.-- 96[333].2

ydy

spr.rpš d l y[dy]. | atlg. | ulm. | izly. | uẖnp. | bn sẖrn. | mʿqb. | ṯpn. | mʿr. | l 2075.1
.ykr.ʿr.d qdm. | idk.pnm.l ytn.tk aršẖ.rbt. | w aršẖ.ṯrrt.ydy.b ʿṣm.ʿrʿr. | w b šḥt.ʿs.mt.ʿrʿrm.ynʿrn h. | ssnm.ysyn h.ʿdt UG5.7.64
b. | w nḥl h. | bn nʿmyn. | bn aṯtyy. | bn ẖlp. | bn.ẓll. | bn ydy. | bn lzn. | bn.ṯyn. | bn gʿr. | bn.prtn. | bn ẖnn. | b[n.-]n. | bn. 2016.1.13
[---].md.ʿ[ṯr]t. | ydy. | bn.škn. | bn.mdt. | bn.ẖ[--]y. | bn.ʿ[-]y. | knʿm. | bn.yš[-]n. 1054.1.2
ṣd h.mnt.nṯk nḥš. | šmrr.nḥš.ʿq šr.ln h.mlẖš. | abd.ln h.ydy.ḥmt. | b ḥrn.pnm.trǵnw.w ṯṯkl. | bnwt h.ykr.ʿr.d qdm. | i UG5.7.60
šr[.yʿ]db.ksa. | nḥš.šmrr.nḥš.ʿq šr.ln h.ml | ẖš.abd.ln h.ydy.ḥmt.hlm.ytq. | w yṯb. | tqru.l špš.um h.špš.[um.q]l bl.ʿm. UG5.7.22
tm. | mnt.nṯk.nḥš.šmrr.nḥš. | ʿq šr.ln h.mlẖš abd.ln h.ydy. | ḥmt.hlm.ytq ytqšqy.nḥš.yšlḥm.ʿq šr. | yʿdb.ksa.w.yṯb. | UG5.7.5
yt h.mnt.nṯk.nḥš.šm | rr.nḥš.ʿq šr.ln h.mlẖš abd.ln h. | ydy.ḥmt.hlm.ytq nḥš yšlḥm.nḥš. | ʿq.šr.yʿdb.ksa.w yṯb. | tqru UG5.7.38
t h.mnt.nṯk.n[ḥš].šmrr. | nḥš.ʿq šr.ln h.mlẖš.abd.ln h.ydy. | ḥmt.hlm.ytq.nḥš.yšlḥm.nḥš. | ʿq šr.yʿdb.ksa.w yṯb. | tqr UG5.7.27
ršp.bbt h.mnt.nḥš.šmrr. | nḥš.ʿq šr.ln h.mlẖš.abd.ln h.ydy. | ḥmt.hlm.ytq.nḥš.yšlḥm.nḥš ʿq. | š.yʿdb.ksa w yṯb. | tqr UG5.7.32
tl h.mnt.nṯk.nḥš.šmrr. | nḥš.ʿq šr.ln h.mlẖš.abd.ln h. | ydy.ḥmt.hlm.ytq.nḥš.yšlḥm. | nḥš.ʿq šr.yʿdb.ksa.w yṯb. | tqru UG5.7.17
n.mnt y.nṯk. | nḥš.šmrr.nḥš.ʿq šr ln h. | mlẖš.abd.ln h.ydy.ḥmt.hlm.ytq. | nḥš.yšlḥm.nḥš.ʿq šr.ydb.ksa. | w yṯb. | tqr UG5.7.11
tr h.mnt.nṯk.nḥš. | šmrr.nḥš.ʿq šr.ln h.mlẖš.abd. | ln h.ydy.ḥmt.hlm ytq.nḥš. | yšlḥm.nḥš.ʿq šr.yʿdb ksa. | w yṯb. | tqr UG5.7.48
ṯṯrt h.mnt.nṯk.nḥš.šmrr. | nḥš.ʿq šr.ln h.mlẖš abd.ln h.ydy. | ḥmt.hlm.ytq.nḥš.yšlḥm.nḥš. | ʿq šr.yʿdb.ksa.w yṯb. | tqr UG5.7.42
m h mnt.nṯk.nḥš. | šmrr.nḥš ʿq šr.ln h.mlẖš. | abd.ln h.ydy ḥmt.hlm.ytq šqy. | nḥš.yšlḥm.nḥš.ʿq šr.yʿdb. | ksa.w yṯb. UG5.7.54
[y-]n. | yny. | ydn. | ytršp. | ydrm. | ydy. | ydlm. | yʿḏrd. | yrmt. | yyn. | yn. | ydln. | ymn. | yṯky. | [y]r 112[16].6
m.zbln]. | in.b ilm.ʿn[y h.]yṯdṯ. | yšbʿ.rgm.[my.]b ilm. | ydy.mrṣ.gršm zbln. | in.b ilm.ʿny h. | w yʿn.lṯpn.il.b pid. | ṯb.b 16[126].5.21
.zbln]. | in.b ilm.ʿ[ny h.yrbʿ]. | yẖmš.rgm.[my.b ilm]. | ydy.mrṣ.g[ršm.zbln]. | in.b ilm.ʿn[y h.]yṯdṯ. | yšbʿ.rgm.[my.]b 16[126].5.18
ršm.z[bln.in.b ilm]. | ʿny h.y[ṯny.yṯlṯ]. | rgm.my.b[ilm.ydy]. | mrṣ.grš[m.zbln]. | in.b ilm.ʿ[ny h.yrbʿ]. | yẖmš.rgm.[m 16[126].5.14
nnt h[.---]. | ṯlṯt h[.-.w yʿn]. | lṯpn.[il.d pid.my]. | b ilm.[ydy.mrṣ]. | gršm.z[bln.in.b ilm]. | ʿny h.y[ṯny.yṯlṯ]. | rgm.my. 16[126].5.11

m ṯb[t] km. | l kẖṯ.zbl k[m.a]nk. | iḥtrš.w [a]škn. | aškn.ydt.[m]rṣ gršt. | zbln.r[---].ymlu. | n‘m.[-]ṯ[-.--.]yqrṣ. | d[-] b p 16[126].5.27
tly. | bn.alz. | bn ẖlm. | bn.ḏmr. | bn.‘yn. | ubnyn. | rpš d ydy. | ǵbl. | mlk. | gwl. | rqd. | ẖlby. | ‘n[q]pat. | m[‘]rb. | ‘rm. | bn. 2075.20
y.šqlt. | b ǵlt.yd k.l tdn. | dn.almnt.l ṯpṭ. | ṯpṭ qṣr.npš.l tdy. | ṯšm.‘l.dl.l pn k. | l tšlḥm.ytm.b‘d. | ksl k.almnt.km. | aẖt. 16.6[127].47

ydlm

[y-]n. | yny. | ydn. | ytršp. | ydrm. | ydy. | ydlm. | y‘ḏrd. | yrmt. | yyn. | yn. | ydln. | ymn. | yṯky. | [y]rm. 112[16].7

ydln

rẖ. | [b]n.gg‘t. | [‘]dy. | armwl. | uwaẖ. | ypln.w.ṯn.bn h. | ydln. | anr[my]. | mld. | krmp[y]. | bṣmn. 2086.9
[šd.b d].klby.psl. | [ub]dy.mri.ibrn. | [š]d.bn.bri.b d.bn.ydln. | [u]bdy.ṯǵrm. | [š]d.ṯǵr.mṯpit.b d.bn.iryn. | [u]bdy.šrm. 82[300].2.6
]. | pqr.yẖd. | bn.ktmn.ṯǵr.hk[l]. | bn.ṯgbr.ṯǵr.hk[l]. | bn.ydln. | bn.ktmn. 1056.10
bn.bsn. | bn.inr[-]. | bn.ṯbil. | bn.iryn. | ṯtl. | bn.nṣdn. | bn.ydln. | [bn].‘dy. | [bn].ilyn. 1071.9
ṯrmlk. | yḥmn.aẖm[l]k.‘bdrpu.adn.ṯ[--]. | bdn.qln.mtn.ydln. | b‘ltdtt.tlgn.ytn. | b‘ltǵpṯm.krwn.ilšn.agyn. | mnn.šr.ug 2011.34
. | ytršp. | ydrm. | ydy. | ydlm. | y‘ḏrd. | yrmt. | yyn. | yn. | ydln. | ymn. | yṯky. | [y]rm. 112[16].12
pr.updt. | d b d.mlkytn. | kdrl. | slṯmg. | adrdn. | l[l]wn. | ydln. | ldn. | tdǵl. | ibrkyṯ. 1034.7
yn. | ‘bdb‘l. | ‘bdkṯr.‘bd. | tdǵl. | b‘lṣn. | nsk.ksp. | iwrtn. | ydln. | ‘bdilm. | dqn. | nsk.ṯlṯ. | ‘bdadt. | bṣmn.spr. 1039.2.25
ubd]y.mrynm. | [š]d.bn.ṣnrn.b d.nrn. | [š]d.bn.rwy.b d.ydln. | [š].bn.trn.b d.ibrmḏ. | [š]d.bn.ilṯtmr.b d.tbbr. | [w.]šd. 82[300].1.9
k[-]w.ẖpn. | l.ṣ[--].š‘[rt]. | l.‘dy.š[‘]r[t]. | ṯlṯ.l.‘d.ab[ǵ]l. | l.ydln.š‘rt. | l.kṯrmlk.ẖpn. | l.‘bdil[m].ẖpn. | tmrtn.š‘rt. | lmd.n.r 1117.8
[---.]yplṭ. | [---].l.[-]npk. | [---.]l.bn.ydln. | [---].l.blkn. | [---].l.bn.k[--]. | [---].l.klṯtb. 2136.3
anyt.miẖd[t]. | br.ṯpṭb‘[l.---]. | br.dmty[.---]. | ṯkt.ydln[.---]. | ṯkt.ṯryn[.---]. | br.‘bdm[lk.---]. | wry[.---]. | ṯkt[.---]. 84[319].1.4

ydm

l ušẖ[r] ẖlmṭ. | l bbt il bt. | š l ẖlmṭ. | w tr l qlḥ. | w š ḥll ydm. | b qdš il bt. | w tlḥm aṯt. | š l ilbt.šlmm. | kll ylḥm b h. | UG5.7.TR3

ydn

| bn.dnn. | bn.rmy. | dll. | mny. | krty. | bn.‘bṣ. | bn.argb. | ydn. | il‘nt. | bn.urt. | ydn. | qṯn. | bn.asr. | bn.‘dy. | bn.amt[m]. | 2117.3.42
. | ḏmry.w.pṯpṭ.‘rb. | b.yrm. | [ily.w].ḏmry.‘rb. | b.ṯb‘m. | ydn.bn.ilrpi. | w.ṯb‘m.‘rb.b.‘[d]n. | ḏmry.bn.yrm. | ‘rb.b.ad‘y. 2079.7
]ṣlm.pn y[.-.]tlkn. | [---.]rḥbn.hm.[-.]aṯr[.---]. | [--]šy.w ydn.b‘[l.---]n. | [--]‘.k yn.hm.l.atn.bt y.l h. 1002.61
[y-]n. | yny. | ydn. | ytršp. | ydrm. | ydy. | ydlm. | y‘ḏrd. | yrmt. | yyn. | yn. | ydl 112[16].3
| ddy. | ‘my. | iwrnr. | alnr. | maẖdt. | aby. | [-----]. | [-]nt. | ydn. | mnn.w bn h. | ṯkn. 107[15].11
--.]š[--]. | w ym ym.yš | al. | w mlk.d mlk. | b ḥwt.špḥ. | l ydn.‘bd.mlk. | d št.‘l.ẖrd h. | špḥ.al.thbṭ. | ẖrd.‘ps.aẖd.kw | sgt 2062.2.3
ṯḥm.ydn.‘m.mlk. | b‘l h.nǵr.ḥwt k. | w l.a[--]t.tšknn. | ẖmšm.l mi[t 2062.1.1
ll. | mny. | krty. | bn.‘bṣ. | bn.argb. | ydn. | il‘nt. | bn.urt. | ydn. | qṯn. | bn.asr. | bn.‘dy. | bn.amt[m]. | myn. | šr. | bn.zql. | b 2117.3.45
m.l.urtn. | kdm.l.ilšpš. | kd.l.anntb. | kd.l.iwrmḏ. | kd.l.ydn. | [---.y]rẖ.ẖyr. | [---.]yn.l.mlkt. | [---.yrẖ.]ẖlt.šb‘.[---].mlkt 1088.9
-].br. | bn.i[ytlm.---]. | wr[t.---.]b d.yḥmn. | yry[.---.]br. | ydn[.---].kry. | bn.ydd[.---.b]r. | prkl.b‘l.any.d.b d.abr[-]. 2123.5

yd‘

[---.]btlt.‘nt. | [---.]pp.hrm. | [---].d l yd‘ bn il. | [---.]pẖr kkbm. | [---.]dr dt.šmm. | [---.al]iyn b‘l. | [- 10[76].1.3
m.[---.]yqṯqṭ.ṯḥt. | ṯlḥnt.il.d yd‘nn. | y‘db.lḥm.l h.w d l yd‘nn. | d.mṣd. | ylmn.ẖṭ.ṯḥt.ṯlḥn. | b qr‘. | ‘ṯtrt.w ‘nt.ymǵy. | ‘ṯ UG5.1.1.7
.dn] | il.mt.rpi npš ṯḥ[.pǵt]. | ṯ[km]t.mym.ḥspt.l š‘r. | ṯl.yd‘t.hlk.kbkbm. | a[-]ḥ.hy.mẖ.tmẖṣ.mẖṣ[.aẖ k]. | tkl.m[k]ly.‘ 19[1AQHT].4.200
sp. | dt.yrq.nqbn y.tš[m‘]. | pǵt.ṯkmt.my.ḥspt.l[š‘]r.ṯl. | yd‘t.hlk.kbkbm. | bkm.tmdln.‘r. | bkm.tṣmd.pḥl.bkm. | tšu.ab 19[1AQHT].2.56
m.l bt[h.dnil.k yṣḥ]. | šm‘.pǵt.ṯkmt[.my]. | ḥspt.l š‘r.ṯl.yd[‘t]. | hlk.kbkbm.mdl.‘r. | ṣmd.pḥl.št.gpn y dt ksp. | dt.yrq. 19[1AQHT].2.51
p‘n.il. | [l t]pl.l tštḥwy.pẖr.m‘d.qmm.a[--].amr. | [ṯn]y.d‘t hm.išt.ištm.yitmr.ḥrb.ltšt. | [--]n hm.rgm.l ṯr.ab h.il.ṯḥm. 2.1[137].32
bl.am.. | rkm.agzrt[.--].arẖ.. | b‘l.azrt.‘nt.[-]ld. | kbd h.l yd‘ hr h.[---]d[-]. | tnq[.---.]in[b]b.p‘r. | yd h[.--.]ṣ‘r.glgl. | a[--- 13[6].31
. | w.b[.---.]uk.nǵr. | w.[---].adny.l.yẖsr. | w.[ank.yd]‘.l.yd‘t. | h[t.---.]l.špš.b‘l k. | ‘[--.s]glt h.at. | ht[.---.]špš.b‘l k. | yd‘ 2060.10
. | [---].l.ǵr.amn. | [---.-]ktt.hn.ib. | [---.]mlk. | [---.]adt y.td‘. | w.ap.mlk.uḏ[r]. | [-]d‘.k.iẖd.[---]. | w.mlk.b‘l y. | lm.škn.h 1012.19
[-]. | akl n.b.grnt. | l.b‘r. | ap.krmm. | ẖlq. | qrt n.ẖlq. | w.d‘.d‘. 2114.13
y.mnm.šlm. | w.rgm.ṯṯb.l y. | w.mnd‘.k.ank. | aḥš.mǵy.mnd‘. | k.igr.w.u.[--]. | ‘m.špš.[---]. | nšlḥ[.---]. | [---.m]at. | [---.] 2009.1.11
kll.šlm.ṯm ny. | ‘m.um y.mnm.šlm. | w.rgm.ṯṯb.l y. | w.mnd‘.k.ank. | aḥš.mǵy.mnd‘. | k.igr.w.u.[--]. | ‘m.špš.[---]. | nšl 2009.1.10
tk.ilnym. | ‘d k.ilm.hn.mtm. | ‘d k.kṯr m.ḥbr k. | w ẖss.d‘t k. | b ym.arš.w tnn. | kṯr.w ẖss.yd. | ytr.kṯr.w ẖss. | spr.ilm 6.6[62.2].49
il.---]. | w y‘ḏr k.b yd.btlt.[‘nt]. | w y‘n.lṭpn.il d p[id]. | yd‘t k.bt.k anšt.w i[n.b ilht]. | qlṣ k.tb‘.bt.ẖnp.lb[k.--.ti] | ẖd. 18[3AQHT].1.16
bt.dqn k.mm‘m.]y‘ny. | il.b šb‘t.ḥdrm.b ṯmnt. | ap.sgrt.yd‘[t k.]bt.k an[št]. | k in.b ilht.ql[ṣ] k.mh.tarš[n]. | l btlt.‘nt. 3[‘NT.VI].5.35
b ḏrt.bny.bnwt. | šmm.šmn.tmṭrn. | nẖlm.tlk.nbtm. | w id‘.k ḥy.aliyn.b‘l. | k iṯ.zbl.b‘l.arṣ. | b ẖlm.lṭpn.il d pid. | b ḏrt. 6[49].3.8
---]. | [---.m]at. | [---.]mat. | š[--].išal. | ‘m k.ybl.šd. | a[--].d‘.k. | šld.ašld. | hn.mrṯ.d.štt. | ašld b ldt k. 2009.2.5
tdm.l y.[--]. | [---].al.trgm.l aẖt k. | [---.]l [ ]dm.aẖt k. | yd‘t.k rḥmt. | al.tšt.b šdm.mm h. | b smkt.ṣat.npš h. | [-]mt[-]. 16.1[125].33
ryl.um y. | rgm. | ugrt.ṯǵr k. | ugrt.ṯǵr k. | tšlm k.um y. | td‘.ky.‘rbt. | l pn.špš. | w pn.špš.nr. | b y.mid.w um. | tšmẖ.m 1015.7
p‘n.il]. | al.tpl.al.tštḥwy.pẖr [m‘d.qmm.a--.am] | r ṯny.d‘t km.w rgm.l ṯr.a[b.-.il.ṯny.l pẖr]. | m‘d.ṯḥm.ym.b‘l km.ad 2.1[137].16
[---.]km.t[--.---]. | [--.n]pš.ttn[.---]. | [---.]yd‘t.k[---]. | [---].w hm. | [--]y.ṯb y.w [---]. | [---.]bnš.[---]. 61[-].3
[.--]np bl.hn. | [---].ẖ[m]t.pṭr.w.p nḥš. | [---.--]q.n[ṯ]k.l yd‘.l bn.l pq ḥmt. | [---.--]n h.ḥmt.w t‘btn h.abd y. | [---.ǵ]r.šr UG5.8.35
lt h.hw. | w.b[.---.]uk.nǵr. | w.[---].adny.l.yẖsr. | w.[ank.yd]‘.l.yd‘t. | h[t.---.]l.špš.b‘l k. | ‘[--.s]glt h.at. | ht[.---.]špš.b‘l 2060.10
‘t. | h[t.---.]l.špš.b‘l k. | ‘[--.s]glt h.at. | ht[.---.]špš.b‘l k. | yd‘m.l.yd‘t. | ‘m y.špš.b‘l k. | šnt.šntm.lm.l.tlk. | w.lḥt.akl.ky. 2060.14
-]ḥm k b ṣpn. | [---.]išqb.aylt. | [---.--]m.b km.y‘n. | [---].yd‘.l yd‘t. | [---.]tasrn.ṯr il. | [---.]rks.bn.abnm. | [---.]upqt.‘rb. 1[‘NT.X].5.21
ngṯn h. | [---].b ṣpn. | [---].nšb.b ‘n. | [---.]b km.y‘n. | [---.yd‘.l] yd‘t. | [---.t]asrn. | [---.]trks. | [---.]abnm.upqt. | [---.]l w 1[‘NT.X].5.8
m.tn. | aḥd.b bn k.amlkn. | w t‘n.rbt.aṯrt ym. | bl.nmlk.yd‘.ylḥn. | w y‘n.lṭpn.il d pi | d dq.anm.l yrẓ. | ‘m.b‘l.l y‘db.m 6.1.48[49.1.20]
n‘r. | [w ydm‘.k]m.ṣǵr.špš.b šmm.tqru. | [---.]nplt.y[--].md‘.nplt.bšr. | [---].w tpky.k[m.]n‘r.tdm‘.km. | [ṣǵ]r.bkm.y‘n UG5.8.39

yd‘

ḫšt.abn]. | tunt.šmm.‘m[.arṣ.thmt.‘mn.kbkbm]. | rgm.l td‘.nš[m.w l tbn.hmlt.arṣ]. | at.w ank.ib[ǵy h.---]. | w y‘n.kṯr. 1[‘NT.IX].3.15
]w argm k.hwt. | [w aṯny k.rgm.]‘ṣ.w lḫšt. | [abn.rgm.l td]‘.nš[m.w l t]bn. | [hmlt.a]rṣ.[tant.šmm.‘m.ar]ṣ. | thmt.[‘m 3[‘NT].4.59
.arṣ. | thmt.‘mn.kbkbm. | abn.brq.d l.td‘.šmm. | rgm l td‘.nšm.w l tbn. | hmlt.arṣ.at m.w ank. | ibǵy h.b tk.ǵr y.il.ṣp 3[‘NT].3.24
trṯ.‘d.škr.y‘db.yrḫ. | gb h.km.[---.]yqṯqṭ.tḥt. | ṯlḥnt.il.d yd‘nn. | y‘db.lḥm.l h.w d l yd‘nn. | d.mṣd. | ylmn.ḫṭ.tḥt.ṯlḥn. | UG5.1.1.6
---.]l.špš.b‘l k. | ‘[--.s]glt h.at. | ht[.---.]špš.b‘l k. | yd‘m.l.yd‘t. | ‘m y.špš.b‘l k. | šnt.šntm.lm.l.tlk. | w.lḥt.akl.ky. | likt.‘m 2060.14
sdb.šmlšn. | w tb‘ ank. | ‘m mlakt h šm‘ h. | w b.‘ly skn.yd‘ rgm h. | w ht ab y ǵm[--]. | t[--.---]. | ls[--.---]. | ṣḫ[.---]. | ky. 1021.8
ṣ.[tant.šmm.‘m.ar]ṣ. | thmt.[‘mn.kbkbm.abn.brq]. | d l t[d‘.šmm.at m.w ank]. | ibǵ[y h.b tk.ǵ]r y.il.ṣpn. | b q[dš.b ǵr. 3[‘NT].4.62
.abn[.tant.šmm.‘m.arṣ.thmt]. | ‘m kbkbm[.abn.brq.d l td‘.šmm.at m]. | w ank.ib[ǵy h.---]. | [-].l y‘mdn.i[---.---]. | kpr 7.2[130].20
bn. | tant.šmm.‘m.arṣ. | thmt.‘mn.kbkbm. | abn.brq.d l.td‘.šmm. | rgm l td‘.nšm.w l tbn. | hmlt.arṣ.at m.w ank. | ibǵy 3[‘NT].3.23
. | bn.ymn. | krty. | bn.abr[-]. | yrpu. | kdn. | p‘ṣ. | bn.liy. | yd‘. | šmn. | ‘dy. | ‘nbr. | aḫrm. | bn.qrdy. | bn.šm‘n. | bn.ǵlmy. | 2117.1.26
r k. | w ‘p.l dr[‘].nšr k. | w rbṣ.l ǵr k.inbb. | kt ǵr k.ank.yd‘t. | [-]n.atn.at.mṯb k[.---]. | [š]mm.rm.lk.prẓ kt. | [k]bkbm.ṯ 13[6].10
. | w.k.at.trg[m.--]. | w.[---]n.w.s[--]. | [--]m.m[---]. | [---.m]nd‘[.--]. 2064.30
k b ṣpn. | [---.]išqb.aylt. | [---.--]m.b km.y‘n. | [---].yd‘.l yd‘t. | [---.]tasrn.ṯr il. | [---.]rks.bn.abnm. | [---.]upqt.‘rb. | [---. 1[‘NT.X].5.21
. | [---].b ṣpn. | [---].nšb.b ‘n. | [---.]b km.y‘n. | [---.yd‘.l] yd‘t. | [---.t]asrn. | [---.]trks. | [---.]abnm.upqt. | [---.]l w ǵr mtn 1[‘NT.X].5.8
b k.‘nn.[---]. | [--.]šdq.k ttn.l y.šn[.---]. | [---.]bn.rgm.w yd‘[.---]. 60[32].6
n.ytmr.b‘l. | bnt h.y‘n.pdry. | bt.ar.apn.ṯly. | [bt.r]b.pdr.yd‘. | [---]t.im[-]lt. | [-----]. | [---.--]rt. 3[‘NT].1.25
[.---.]‘mn k. | [-]štš.[---.]rgm y. | [-]wd.r[-.]pǵt. | [---.--]t.yd‘t. | [----.r]gm. | [---].kll h. | [---.--]l y. | [---.--]r. | [--.]wk[--.--- 54.1.24[43.7]
. | akl n.b.grnt. | l.b‘r. | ap.krmm. | ḫlq. | qrt n.ḫlq. | w.d‘.d‘. 2114.13

ydrm

alpm.arb‘.mat.k[bd]. | mit.b d.yd[r]m. | alp ḫmš mat.kbd.d[--]. 2109.2
[y-]n. | yny. | ydn. | ytršp. | ydrm. | ydy. | ydlm. | y‘ḏrd. | yrmt. | yyn. | yn. | ydln. | ymn. | yṯk 112[16].5
l[-.-]hg[.---]. | [---.-]r[-.il]m.rbm.n‘l[.-]gr. | [---.]‘ṣ.b d h.ydrm[.]pi[-.]adm. | [---.]it[-].yšql.yṯk[.--]np bl.hn. | [---].ḥ[m]t UG5.8.32
b.bt.arttb. | aṯt.w.ṯn.bn h.b.bt.iwwpzn. | aṯt.w.pǵt.b.bt.ydrm. | ṯt.aṯtm.adrtm.w.pǵt.aḥt.b[.bt.---]. | aṯt.w ṯn.n‘rm.b.bt 80[119].6

ydrn

[---.b]n.[y]drn. | [---.]bn.ḫlan. | [--]r bn.mn. | [--]ry. | [--]lim bn.brq. | [--. 2087.1

ydt

.imt.imt.npš.blt. | ḥmr.p imt.b klt. | yd y.ilḥm.hm.šb‘. | ydt y.b ṣ‘.hm.ks.ymsk. | nhr.k[--].ṣḥn.b‘l.‘m. | aḫ y.qran.hd.‘ 5[67].1.21
mm.hm. | ‘n.kḏd.aylt. | mt hm.ks.ym | sk.nhr hm. | šb‘.ydt y.b ṣ‘. | [--.]šb‘.rbt. | [---.]qbṭ.ṯm. | [---.]bn.ilm. | [m]t.šmḥ. UG5.4.11

yḏrd

it ṯlṯm kbd. | ṣṣ m[l]k ‘šrm. | ṣṣ abš[-] mit [‘š]r kbd. | ṣṣ yḏrd ‘šrm. | ṣṣ bn aglby ṯlṯ[m]. | ṣṣ bn.šrš‘m.[---]. | ṣṣ mlkn‘m. 2097.12

yh

yn]. | d ḥrš.y[dm.tḥm.ṯr.il.ab k.] | hwt.lṭpn[.ḥtk k.---]. | yh.kṯr.b[---]. | št.lskt.n[--.---]. | ‘db.bǵrt.ṯ[--. --]. | ḥš k.‘ṣ k.‘[bṣ 1[‘NT.IX].3.7

yw

. | tgr.il.bn h.ṯr[.---]. | w y‘n.lṭpn.il.d p[id.---]. | šm.bn y.yw.ilt.[---]. | w p‘r.šm.ym[-.---]. | t‘nyn.l zn.tn[.---]. | at.adn.tp 1[‘NT.X].4.14

yzg

-----]. | [bn.]ibln. | ysd. | bn.ṯmq. | bn.agmn. | bn.uṣb. | bn.yzg. | bn.anntn. | bn.kwn. | ǵmšd. | bn.‘bdḥy. | bn.ubyn. | slpd. | 115[301].4.6

yḥd

.--]ḫ. | [---.--]n. | [-----]. | [---.-]bd. | [---]yb‘.b‘l.ḫr[-]. | pqr.yḥd. | bn.ktmn.ṯǵr.hk[l]. | bn.ṯgbr.ṯǵr.hk[l]. | bn.ydln. | bn.kt 1056.7
m.ḫḏḏ. | w l rbt.kmyr. | [a]ṯr.ṯn.ṯn.hlk. | aṯr.ṯlṯ.kl hm. | yḥd.bt h.sgr. | almnt.škr. | tškr.zbl.‘ršm. | yšu.‘wr.mzl. | ymzl. 14[KRT].2.96

yḥmn

]. | ‘zn.w ymd.šr.b d ansny. | nsk.ks[p.--]mrtn.kṯrmlk. | yḥmn.aḫm[l]k.‘bdrpu.adn.ṯ[--]. | bdn.qln.mtn.ydln. | b‘ltdtt.t 2011.33
ḫpn. | ḥrš[bhtm.--]n.‘bdyrḫ.ḥdṯn.y‘r. | adb‘l[.---].ḥdṯn.yḥmn.bnil. | ‘dn.w.ildgn.ḥṭbm. | tdǵlm.iln.b‘[l]n.alḏy. | tdn.ṣr 2011.19
ḏm[r.---].br. | bn.i[ytlm.---]. | wr[t.---.]b d.yḥmn. | yry[.---.]br. | ydn[.---].kry. | bn.ydd[.---.b]r. | prkl.b‘l.a 2123.3
šlmym.lqḥ.akl. | yḥmn.ṯlṯ.šmn. | a[---.]kdm. | ‘[---]‘m.kd. | a[----]ḥr.ṯlṯ. | y[---.bn 136[84].2

yḥnn

n. | bn.ur[-.---]. | bn.knn[.---]y. | bn.ymlk[.b]d.skn. | bn.yḥnn.aḏddy. | bn.pdǵy.mḫdy. | bn.yyn.mḏrǵl. | bn.‘lr. | ḥṯpy.a 2014.16

yḥṣdq

‘.rgm. | šdn.[k]bš. | šdyn.mḫ[ṣ]. | aṯry.mḫṣ. | b‘ln.mḫṣ. | y[ḥ]ṣdq.mḫṣ. | ṣp[r].ks[d]. | b‘l.š[lm]. | ḫyrn[.---]. | a[--.---]. | ‘[-- 2084.17

yḥr

tḥ.bt.mnt. | ptḥ.bt.w ubn.hkl.w ištql šql. | tn.km.nḥšm.yḥr.tn.km. | mhr y.w bn.bṯn.itnn y. | ytt.nḥšm.mhr k.bn bṯn. UG5.7.73

yḥšr

]m. | b.ṯbq.arb‘m.dr‘.w.‘šr.dd.drt. | w[.a]rb‘.l.‘šrm.dd.l.yḥšr.bl.bn h. | b.gt.m‘br.arb‘m.l.mit.dr‘.w.ṯmnym[.drt]. | w.‘š 1098.11

yẖl

.---]. | ir[--.---]. | pndyn[.---]. | w.idṯ[-.---]. | b.gt.b[n.---]. | yẖl[.---]. | b.gt.[---]. | [---.]k[--]. 1078.8

yṭp

.ṭrm.w[---]. | ištir.b ḏdm.w n'rs[.---]. | w t'n.btlt.'nt.ṯb.yṭp.w[---]. | l k.ašt k.km.nšr.b ḥb[š y]. | km.diy.b t'rt y.aqht. 18[3AQHT].4.16
[.idk.l ttn.pnm]. | 'm.yṭpn.mhr.š[t.tšu.g h]. | w tṣḥ.yṯb.yṭp.[---]. | qrt.ablm.ablm.[qrt.zbl.yrẖ]. | ik.al.yḥdṯ.yrẖ.b[---]. 18[3AQHT].4.7

yṭpn

š.šdm l m'[rb]. | nrt.ilm.špš.mǵy[t]. | pǵt.l ahlm.rgm.l yṭ[pn.y] | bl.agrtn.bat.b ḏd k.[pǵt]. | bat.b hlm w y'n.yṭpn[.m 19[1AQHT].4.212
| ḥ.pǵt.w tšqyn h.tq[ḥ.ks.]b d h. | qb't.b ymn h.w y'n.yṭ[p]n[.mh]r. | št.b yn.yšt.ila.il š[--.]il. | d yqny.ḏdm.yd.mḫṣt. 19[1AQHT].4.218
.l yṭ[pn.y] | bl.agrtn.bat.b ḏd k.[pǵt]. | bat.b hlm w y'n.yṭpn[.mhr]. | št.qḥn.w tšqyn.yn.qḥ. | ks.b d y.qb't.b ymn y[.t 19[1AQHT].4.214
. | [btl]t.'nt.l kl.[---]. | [tt]b'.btlt.'nt[.idk.l ttn.pnm]. | 'm.yṭpn.mhr.š[t.tšu.g h]. | w tṣḥ.yṯb.yṭp.[---]. | qrt.ablm.ablm.[q 18[3AQHT].4.6
iṯl.brlt h.km. | qṭr.b ap h.b ap.mhr h.ank. | l aḥwy.tqḥ.yṭpn.mhr.št. | tštn.k nšr.b ḥbš h.km.diy. | b t'rt h.aqht.km.yṯ 18[3AQHT].4.27
dṯ.yrẖ.b[---]. | b qrn.ymn h.b anšt[.---]. | qdqd h.w y'n.yṭpn.[mhr.št]. | šm'.l btlt.'nt.at.'[l.qšt h]. | tmẖṣ h.qṣ't h.hwt. 18[3AQHT].4.11

yy

.qšt. | šdyn.qšt. | bdn.qšt.w.ql'. | bn.šmlbi.qšt.w.ql'. | bn.yy.qšt. | ilrb.qšt. | bn.nmš.ṯt.qšt.w.ql'. | b'l.qšt.w.ql'. 119[321].4.14

yyn

. | [']rmy.w snry. | [b]n.sdy.bn.ṯty. | bn.ḥyn.bn.ǵlm. | bn.yyn.w.bn.au[pš]. | bn.kdrn. | 'rgzy.w.bn.'dy. | bn.gmḥn.w.ḥgb 131[309].25
| yny. | ydn. | ytršp. | ydrm. | ydy. | ydlm. | y'ḏrd. | yrmt. | yyn. | yn. | ydln. | ymn. | yṯky. | [y]rm. 112[16].10
ymlk[.b]d.skn. | bn.yḥnn.aḏddy. | bn.pdǵy.mḥdy. | bn.yyn.mḏrǵl. | bn.'lr. | ḥtpy.aḏddy. | ynḥm.aḏddy. | ykny.aḏddy 2014.18
b.'šrm. | b.bn.ibn.arb't.'šrt. | b.bn.mnn.ṯṯm. | b.rpan.bn.yyn.'šrt. | b.yp'r.'šrm. | b.n'mn.bn.ply.ẖmšt.l.'šrm. | b.gdn.bn. 2054.1.15
.dd.l.b[t.--]. | ẖmš.ddm.l.ḥtyt. | ṯlṯm.dd.kšmn.l.gzzm. | yyn. | ṣdqn. | 'bd.pdr. | myṣm. | ṯgt. | w.lmd h. | yṯil. | w.lmd h. | 1099.5

yky

bdil.bn.[---]. | 'pṯn.bn.ṯṣq[-]. | mnn.bn.krmn. | bn.umẖ. | yky.bn.slyn. | ypln.bn.ylḥn. | 'zn.bn.mll. | šrm. | [b]n.špš[yn]. | 85[80].1.7
---.]a[---]. | [---.--]ln. | [---.]kqmṯn. | [---.]klnmw. | [---.]w yky. | ṯlṯm sp.l bnš tpnr. | arb'.spm.l.lbnš prwsdy. | ṯṯ spm.l b 137.2[93].5
sg]. | bn.'drš[p.msg]. | pyn.yny.[msg]. | bn.mṣrn m[sg]. | yky msg. | ynḥm.msg. | bn.ugr.msg. | bn.ǵlṣ msg. | arb' l ṯkṣ[-] 133[-].1.6
.---]. | ybn.ṯmnt.'šrt 'šrt.šlm. | 'bdyrẖ.šb't.'šrt 'šrt.šlm. | yky.'šrt.ṯṯt šlm.'šrt. | bn.ḥgby.ṯmnt.l 'šrm.'šrt.ẖmš.kbd. | bn.i 1131.7

ykn

.arwdn.ilšt'y. | bn grgs. | bn.ḥran. | bn.arš[w.b]ṣry. | bn.ykn. | bn.lṣn.'rmy. | bn.b'yn.šly. | bn.ynḥn. | bn.'bdilm.hzpy. 99[327].2.2
.['l.---]. | [--.--]ẖ.bn.ag[--]. | [---.--]m[.---]. | [kd.]šš. | [k]d.ykn.bn.'bdṯrm. | kd.'bdil. | ṯlṯ.'l.bn.srt. | kd.'l.ẓrm. | kd.'l.šz.bn 1082.2.2
b'l.ṣdq. | bn.army. | bn.rpiyn. | bn.army. | bn.krmn. | bn.ykn. | bn.'ṯtrab. | uṣn[-]. | bn.alṯn. | bn.aš[-]š. | bn.štn. | bn.ilš. | b 1046.1.11
ygmr.aḏddy. | gln.aṯṯ. | ddy.[a]ḏddy. | bn.mlkr[šp]. | bn.y[k]n. | ynḥm. | bn.abd.b'[l]. | mnḥm.bn[.---]. | krmn[py]. | bn.[2014.46
mahdym. | grbn.ltḥ. | srn.ltḥ. | ykn.ltḥ. | ḥgbn.ltḥ. | spr.mkrm. | bn.sl'n.prs. | bn.ṯpdn.ltḥ. | bn. 1059.4
| ybnil. | brqn. | adr[dn]. | krwn. | arkdn. | ilmn. | abškn. | ykn. | ršpab. | klyn. | ḥgbn. | ḥṯṯn. | 'bdmlk. | y[--]k. | [-----]. | pǵḏ 1024.1.15
.---]. | bn 'dr[.---]. | ẖmš 'l.bn[.---]. | ẖmš 'l r'l[-]. | ẖmš 'l ykn[.--]. | ẖ[mš] 'l abǵ[l]. | ẖmš 'l ilb['l]. | 'šr 'l [---]. 2034.2.6
[---.]w šb'l. | [---.-]ym. | [---.--]ẖm. | [---.--]m. | [---]nb.w ykn. | [--]ndbym. | [']rmy.w snry. | [b]n.sdy.bn.ṯty. | bn.ḥyn.bn 131[309].20
i[l.---]. | iẖy[.---]. | ar[.---]. | 'ṯtr[.---]. | bn.[---]. | yly[.---]. | ykn[.---]. | rp[--]. | ṯṯw.[---]. | [---.']šrm.ṣmd.ššw. 2131.9

yknil

'mtḏl.'šrm. | y'ḏrd.'šrm. | gmrd.'šrm. | ṣdqšlm.'šr[m]. | yknil.ẖmš. | ilmlk.ẖmš. | prṯ.'šr. | ubn.'šr. 1116.12
il.bn.yṣr[.---]. | 'dyn.bn.uḏr[-.---]. | w.'d'.nḥl h[.---]. | w.yknil.nḥl h[.---]. | w.iltm.nḥl h[.---]. | w.unṯm.nḥ[l h.---]. | [---. 90[314].1.15

ykny

y. | bn.yyn.mḏrǵl. | bn.'lr. | ḥtpy.aḏddy. | ynḥm.aḏddy. | ykny.aḏddy. | m[--].aḏddy. | yp'.aḏddy. | abǵl.aḏ[ddy]. | abǵl.a 2014.22

ykn'

[--.l]bš.mtn.b.ar't. | [--.l]bš.bn.ykn'.b.ar't. | [--.l]bš.bn.grbn.b.ṯqlm. | [--.lb]š.bn.sgryn.b[.ṯ]ql 135[330].2

ykn'm

dmt ṯlṯ. | qmnz ṯql. | zlyy ṯql. | ary ẖmšt. | ykn'm ẖmšt. | 'nmky ṯqlm. | [-]kt 'šrt. | qrn šb't. 1176.5
| agm. | bir. | ypr. | hzp. | šql. | m'rḥ[-]. | sl[ẖ]. | snr. | 'rgz. | ykn'm. | 'nmky. | ǵr. 2074.37
]. | qm[--]. | šl[--]. | a[---]. | d[---]. | q[---]. | 'm[--]. | ar[--]. | ykn['m]. | ṣlyy. | 'nm[ky]. | l[bnm]. | 'r[--]. 2133.8
ry. | ẓrn. | art. | ṯlḥny. | ṯlrby. | dmt. | aǵt. | w.qmnz. | slẖ. | ykn'm. | šlmy. | w.ull. | ṯmry. | qrt. | 'rm. | nnu. | [--]. | [---]. | m'r. 71[113].17
by. | 'r. | 'nq[pat]. | glbty. | [-----]. | [-----]. | [-----]. | [-----]. | ykn'm. | šlmy. | [-----]. | [-----]. | q[---]. | ṯ[---]. | ṯl[rby]. | ṯmr[y]. | 2058.2.30
gdly.ǵlpṯr.ṯn.krmm.w.ṯlṯ.ub[dym.---]. | qmnz.ṯṯ.krm.ykn'm.ṯmn.krm[.---]. | krm.n'mn.b.ẖly.ull.krm.aḥ[d.---]. | kr 1081.11
šlmy.ṯql. | ary ṯql. | ṯmry ṯql.w.nṣp. | aǵt nṣp. | dmt ṯql. | ykn'm ṯql. 69[111].7
n[.---]. | [-----]. | yṯ[--.---]. | ṯl[ṯ.---]. | ṯl[ṯ.---]. | 'nmk[.---]. | ykn'm[.---]. | qm[n]z[---]. | šl[-.---]. | ar[--.---]. | qrt[.---]. | ṯm[r.- 1181.8
dršp. | bn.knn. | pdyn. | bn.aṯtl.ṯn. | kdln.akdṯb. | ṯn.b gt ykn'm. 1061.22

ykn'my

y.w[.aṯt h]. | [w].bn h.w.ṯn.alpm. | [w.]ṯlṯm.ṣin. | anndr.ykn'my. | w.aṯt h.w.bn h. | w.alp.w.tš['.]ṣin. 1080.15
ṯmn.ṣin. | [-]dln.qmnzy.w.a[ṯt h]. | wšṯn.bn h. | ṯmgdl.ykn'my.w.aṯt h. | w.bn h.w.alp.aḥ[d]. | aǵltn.[--]y.w[.aṯt h]. | 1080.5

ykr

[-----].|[-]mn.|b'ly.|rpan.|'pṯrm.|bn.'bd.|šmb'l.|ykr.|bly.|ṯb'm.|ḥdṯn.|rpty.|ilym.|bn.'br.|mnip'l.|amrb'l. 1058.8

yld

k m.|b tk.mlbr.|ilšiy.|kry amt.|'pr.'ẓm yd.|ugrm.ḫl.ld.|aklm.tbrk k.|w ld 'qqm.|ilm.yp'r.|šmt hm.|b hm.qrn 12[75].1.25
[---.]arḫt.tld[n].|a[lp].l btlt.'nt.|w ypt l ybmt.li[mm].|w y'ny.aliyn[.b 10[76].3.2
-].|tlk.w tr.b[ḫl].|b n'mm.b ys[mm.---].|arḫ.arḫ.[---.tld].|ibr.tld[.l b'l].|w rum.l[rkb.'rpt].|tḥbq.[---].|tḥbq[.---]. 10[76].3.20
|bn.ym.ynqm.b a[p.]ḏ[d.r]gm.l il.ybl.|aṯt y.il.ylt.mh.ylt.ilmy n'mm.|agzr ym.bn ym.ynqm.b ap.ḏd.št.špt.|l arṣ.š 23[52].60
.yṯb[n].|yspr.l ḫmš.l ṣ[---.]šr.pḫr.klat.|tqtnṣn.w tldn.tld.[ilm.]n'mm.agzr ym.|bn.ym.ynqm.b a[p.]ḏ[d.r]gm.l il.y 23[52].58
].išal.|'m k.ybl.šd.|a[--].d'.k.|šld.ašld.|hn.mrṯ.d.štt.|ašld b ldt k. 2009.3.2
.tity.|tity.ilm.l ahl hm.|dr il.l mšknt hm.|w tqrb.w ld.bn.l h.|w tqrb.w ld.bnt.l h.|mk.b šb'.šnt.|bn.krt.km hm. 15[128].3.20
šu.|g h.w yṣḥ.aṯbn.ank.|w anḫn.w tnḫ.b irt y.|npš.k yld.bn.l y.km.|aḫ y.w šrš.km ary y.|nṣb.skn.ilib y.b qdš.|zt 17[2AQHT].2.14
q] [-].|tld bt.[--]t.ḫ[--.l k]|ṯrt.l bnt.hll[.snnt].|hl ǵlmt tld b[n.--]n.|'n ha l yd h.tzd[.--].|pt l bšr h.dm a[--.--]ḫ.|w 24[77].7
hm.|dr il.l mšknt hm.|w tqrb.w ld.bn.l h.|w tqrb.w ld.bnt.l h.|mk.b šb'.šnt.|bn.krt.km hm.tdr.|ap.bnt.ḫry.|k 15[128].3.21
d.rm.]krt.|[b tk.rpi.]arṣ.|[b pḫr].qbṣ.dtn.|[w t]qrb.w ld.|bn.tl k.|tld.pǵt.t[--]t.|tld.pǵt[.---].|tld.pǵ[t.---].|tld.pǵ[t 15[128].3.5
qẓ ḫrḫb m|lk aǵzt.b sǵ[--.]špš.|yrḫ yṯkḥ yḫ[bq] [-].|tld bt.[--]t.ḫ[--.l k]|ṯrt.l bnt.hll[.snnt].|hl ǵlmt tld b[n.--]n.| 24[77].5
m]at.|[---.]mat.|š[--].išal.|'m k.ybl.šd.|a[--].d'.k.|šld.ašld.|hn.mrṯ.d.štt.|ašld b ldt k. 2009.2.6
k ymǵy.adn.|ilm.rbm 'm dtn.|w yšal.mṯpṭ.yld.|w y'ny.nn[.--].|t'ny.n[---.-]ṯq.|w š[--.---].|ḥdṯ[.---.]ḫ[--] UG5.6.3
.l b'l.ttnn.|bšrt.il.bš[r.b']l.|w bšr.ḥtk.dgn.|k.ibr.l b'l[.yl]d.|w rum.l rkb.'rpt.|yšmḫ.aliyn.b'l. 10[76].3.36
'l.|[---].bm.nšq.aṯt h.|[---.]b ḥbq h.ḥmḥmt.|[---.--] n.ylt.ḥmḥmt.|[---.mt.r]pi.w ykn.bn h.|[b bt.šrš.]b qrb.hkl h.| 17[2AQHT].1.42
nṣn].|tldn.šḥr.w šlm.rgm.l il.ybl.a[ṯt y].|il.ylt.mh.ylt.yld y.šḥr.w šl[m].|šu.'db.l špš.rbt.w l kbkbm.kn[-].|yhbr.šp 23[52].53
]ḥmt.yṯb[n].|yspr.l ḫmš.l ṣ[---.]šr.pḫr.klat.|tqtnṣn.w tldn.tld.[ilm.]n'mm.agzr ym.|bn.ym.ynqm.b a[p.]ḏ[d.r]gm. 23[52].58
---.m]at.|[---.]mat.|š[--].išal.|'m k.ybl.šd.|a[--].d'.k.|šld.ašld.|hn.mrṯ.d.štt.|ašld b ldt k. 2009.2.6
qt[nṣn].|tldn.šḥr.w šlm.rgm.l il.ybl.a[ṯt y].|il.ylt.mh.ylt.yld y.šḥr.w šl[m].|šu.'db.l špš.rbt.w l kbkbm.kn[-].|yhb 23[52].53
lmt.tš'rb.|ḥqr k.tld.šb'.bnm.l k.|w ṯmn.tṯtmnm.|l k.tld.yṣb.ǵlm.|ynq.ḥlb.a[ṯ]rt.|mṣṣ.ṯd.btlt.['nt].|mšnq.[---]. 15[128].2.25
'm k.ybl.šd.|a[--].d'.k.|šld.ašld.|hn.mrṯ.d.štt.|ašld b ldt k. 2009.3.2
tr.b[ḫl].|b n'mm.b ys[mm.---].|arḫ.arḫ.[---.tld].|ibr.tld[.l b'l].|w rum.l[rkb.'rpt].|tḥbq.[---].|tḥbq[.---].|w tksy 10[76].3.21
gzr ym.|bn.ym.ynqm.b a[p.]ḏ[d.r]gm.l il.ybl.|aṯt y.il.ylt.mh.ylt.ilmy n'mm.|agzr ym.bn ym.ynqm.b ap.ḏd.št.špt. 23[52].60
mḥmt.tqt[nṣn].|tldn.šḥr.w šlm.rgm.l il.ybl.a[ṯt y].|il.ylt.mh.ylt.yld y.šḥr.w šl[m].|šu.'db.l špš.rbt.w l kbkbm.kn[23[52].53
b.|'mn h.šb'.l šb'm.|tš['l]y.ṯmn.l ṯmnym.|w [th]rn.w tldn mṯ.|al[iyn.b']l šlbšn.|i[---.---.--]l h.mǵẓ.|y[--.---.]l irt h. 5[67].5.22
---.]ln.|[---.]nb hm.|[---.-]kn.|[---.]hr n.km.šḥr.|[---.y]lt n.km.qdm.|[-.k]bd n.il.ab n.|kbd k iš.tikln.|ṯd n.km.m 12[75].1.8
y'db.u ymn.|u šmal.b p hm.w l.tšb'n y.aṯt.itrḫ.|y bn.ašld.šu.'db.tk.mdbr qdš.|ṯm tgrgr.l abnm.w l.'ṣm.šb'.šnt.|t 23[52].65
y.|kry amt.|'pr.'ẓm yd.|ugrm.ḫl.ld.|aklm.tbrk k.|w ld 'qqm.|ilm.yp'r.|šmt hm.|b hm.qrnm.|km.ṯrm.w gbṯt.|k 12[75].1.27
tk.rpi.]arṣ.|[b pḫr].qbṣ.dtn.|[w t]qrb.w ld.|bn.tl k.|tld.pǵt.t[--]t.|tld.pǵt[.---].|tld.pǵ[t.---].|tld.pǵ[t.---].|tld.pǵ[15[128].3.7
ld.|bn.tl k.|tld.pǵt.t[--]t.|tld.pǵt[.---].|tld.pǵ[t.---].|tld.pǵ[t.---].|tld.pǵ[t.---].|tld.p[ǵt.---].|mid.rm[.krt].|b tk.r 15[128].3.10
tld.pǵt.t[--]t.|tld.pǵt[.---].|tld.pǵ[t.---].|tld.pǵ[t.---].|tld.pǵ[t.---].|tld.p[ǵt.---].|mid.rm[.krt].|b tk.rpi.ar[ṣ].|b pḫ 15[128].3.11
b pḫr].qbṣ.dtn.|[w t]qrb.w ld.|bn.tl k.|tld.pǵt.t[--]t.|tld.pǵt[.---].|tld.pǵ[t.---].|tld.pǵ[t.---].|tld.pǵ[t.---].|tld.p[ǵt 15[128].3.8
n.|[w t]qrb.w ld.|bn.tl k.|tld.pǵt.t[--]t.|tld.pǵt[.---].|tld.pǵ[t.---].|tld.pǵ[t.---].|tld.pǵ[t.---].|tld.p[ǵt.---].|mid.rm 15[128].3.9
|tld.pǵt[.---].|tld.pǵ[t.---].|tld.pǵ[t.---].|tld.pǵ[t.---].|tld.p[ǵt.---].|mid.rm[.krt].|b tk.rpi.ar[ṣ].|b pḫr.qbṣ.dtn.|ṣǵ 15[128].3.12
]ǵlm.il.|a[ṯt.tq]ḥ.y krt.aṯt.|tqḥ.bt k.ǵlmt.tš'rb.|ḥqr k.tld.šb'.bnm.l k.|w ṯmn.tṯtmnm.|l k.tld.yṣb.ǵlm.|ynq.ḥlb.a[15[128].2.23
tm.k lrmn[.--].|bm.nšq.w hr.b ḥbq.ḥmḥmt.tqt[nṣn].|tldn.šḥr.w šlm.rgm.l il.ybl.a[ṯt y].|il.ylt.mh.ylt.yld y.šḥr.w 23[52].52
.|'p'p h.sp.ṯrml.|d b ḥlm y.il.ytn.|b ḏrt y.ab.adm.|w ld.špḥ.l krk|t.w ǵlm.l 'bd.|il.ttb'.mlakm.|l yṭb.idk.pnm.|l 14[KRT].6.298
.|ašlw.b ṣp.'n h.|d b ḥlm y.il.ytn.|b ḏrt y.ab.adm.|w ld.špḥ.l krt.|w ǵlm.l 'bd.il.|krt.yḫṭ.w ḥlm.|'bd.il.w hdrt.|y 14[KRT].3.152
[-----].|[---.r]ḥm.tld.|[---.]ḫrm.ṯn.ym.|tš[.---.]ymm.lk.|hrg.ar[b'.]ymm.bṣr.| 13[6].2
uš[k.--].|[-.b]'l.yabd.l alp.|[---.bt]lt.'nt.|[---]q.hry.w yld.|[---]m.ḥbl.kṯ[r]t.|[---.bt]lt.'nt.|[---.ali]yn.b'l.|[---.]m'n. 11[132].1.5

ylḥn

ṣq[-].|mnn.bn.krmn.|bn.umḫ.|yky.bn.slyn.|ypln.bn.ylḥn.|'zn.bn.mll.|šrm.|[b]n.špš[yn].|[b]n.ḫrmln.|bn.tnn.| 85[80].1.8

yly

pt.srdnnm.|asrn.uṯpt.srdnnm.|bn.qṣn.uṯpt.srdnnm.|yly.uṯpt.srdnnm.|arṯtb.uṯpt.srdnnm. 1124.11
.ar.|špšyn[.---.]yṯb.b.ar.|bn.ag[p]ṯ.ḫpt.d[.yṯb.b].š'rt.|yly.bn.ṯrnq.[-]r.d.yṯb.b.ilštm'.|ilšlm.bn.gs[-.--]r.d.yṯb.b.gt.al 2015.1.26
[.--].|w ṯmnt.l ṯmnym.|šr.aḫy h.mẓa h.|w mẓa h.šr.yly h.|b skn.sknm.b 'dn.|'dnm.kn.npl.b'l.|km ṯr.w tkms.h 12[75].2.52
[.---].|ḥyi[l.---].|iḫy[.---].|ar[.---].|'ttr[.---].|bn.[---].|yly[.---].|ykn[.---].|rp[--].|ṯtw.[---].|[---.']šrm.ṣmd.ššw. 2131.8

ylkn

bn.anny.|bn.'mtḏl.|bn.'myn.|bn.alz.|bn.birtn.|[bn.]ylkn.|[bn.]krwn.|[bn.-]ty.|[bn.]iršn.|bn.[---].|bn.b[--].|bn. 117[325].1.14

yln

[uzr.yšqy.]bn.qdš.yd.|[ṣt h.y'l.]w yškb.yd.|[mizrt.]p ynl.hn.ym.|[w ṯn.uzr.]ilm.dnil.|[uzr.ilm.]ylḥm.uzr.|[yšqy. 17[2AQHT].1.6
n qdš.yd.ṣt h.|[dn]il.yd.ṣt h.y'l.w yškb.|[yd.]mizrt.p yln.mk.b šb'.ymm.|[w]yqrb.b'l.b ḥnt h.abynt.|[d]nil.mt.rp 17[2AQHT].1.16

ym

kll ylḥm b h.|w l bbt šqym.|š l uḫr ḫlmṭ.|w tr l qlḥ.|ym aḥd. UG5.11.14
y.ṯn h.wspm.|atn.w ṯlṯ h.ḫrṣm.|ylk ym.w ṯn.|ṯlṯ.rb'.ym.|aḫr.špšm.b rb'.|ymǵy.l udm.rbt.|w udm[.ṯr]rt.|grnn.' 14[KRT].4.208

| hn.ym.w ṯn.tikl. | išt.b bht m.nblat. | b hk[l] m.ṯlṯ.kbʻ ym. | tikl[.i]št.b bht m. | nbla[t.]b hkl m. | ḫmš.ṯ[d]ṯ.ym.tikl. | i 4[51].6.26

bʻ ym. | tikl[.i]št.b bht m. | nbla[t.]b hkl m. | ḫmš.ṯ[d]ṯ.ym.tikl. | išt.[b]bht m.nblat. | b[qrb.hk]l m.mk. | b šb[ʻ.]y[m 4[51].6.29

[-----]. | [---.]abl.qšt ṯmn. | ašrbʻ.qṣʻt.w hn šb[ʻ]. | b ymm.apnk.dnil.mt. | rpi.a hn.ġzr.mt.hrnm[y]. | ytšu.yṯb.b ap 17[2AQHT].5.4

. | ʻd k.ilm.hn.mtm. | ʻd k.kṯr m.ḥbr k. | w ḫss.dʻt k. | b ym.arš.w tnn. | kṯr.w ḫss.yd. | ytr.kṯr.w ḫss. | spr.ilmlk šbny. 6.6[62.2].50

d.w ykrkr. | uṣbʻt h.yšu.g h.w y[ṣḥ]. | ik.mġyt.rbt.aṯr[t.y]m. | ik.atwt.qnyt.i[lm]. | rġb.rġbt.w tġt[--]. | hm.ġmu.ġmit. 4[51].4.31

| tmgnn.rbt[.a]ṯrt ym. | tġẓyn.qnyt.ilm. | w tʻn.rbt.aṯrt ym. | ik.tmgnn.rbt. | aṯrt.ym.tġẓyn. | qnyt.ilm.mgntm. | ṯr.il.d 4[51].3.27

ḥ.rṯt.b d k t[---]. | rbt.ʻl.ydm[.---]. | b mdd.il.y[--.---]. | b ym.il.d[--.---.n] | hr.il.y[--.---]. | aliyn.[bʻl.---]. | btlt.[ʻnt.---]. | m 4[51].2.35

[--.--.]l ašṣi.hm.ap.amr[--]. | [---].w b ym.mnḫ l abd.b ym.irtm.m[--]. | [ṯpṭ].nhr.tlʻm.ṯm.ḥrbm.its.anšq. | [-]htm.l ar 2.4[68].3

r.]ilm.dnil. | [uzr.ilm.]ylḥm.uzr. | [yšqy.b]n.qdš ṯlṯ rbʻ ym. | [uzr.i]lm.dnil.uzr. | [ilm.y]lḥm.uzr.yšqy bn. | [qdš.ḫ]mš. 17[2AQHT].1.9

i]lm.dnil.uzr. | [ilm.y]lḥm.uzr.yšqy bn. | [qdš.ḫ]mš.ṯdṯ.ym.uzr. | [ilm].dnil.uzr.ilm.ylḥm. | [uzr.]yšqy.bn qdš.yd.ṣt h. 17[2AQHT].1.12

. | [u]šḫr[y]. | [ʻ]ṯtrt. | i[l t]ʻḏr bʻl. | ršp. | ddmš. | pḫr ilm. | ym. | uṯḫt. | knr. | mlkm. | šlm. 29[17].2.8

]š.lbum.trd.b n[p]šn y.trḥṣn.k trm. | [--]b b[ht]. | [zbl.]ym.b hkl.ṯpṭ.nh[r].ytir.ṯr.il.ab h l pn[.zb]l y[m]. | [l pn.ṯp]ṭ[. 2.3[129].21

nhr.yrtqṣ.ṣmd.b d bʻl.km.nšr. | b[u]ṣbʻt h.ylm.ktp.zbl ym.bn ydm.ṯpṭ. | nhr.ʻz.ym.l ymk.l tngṣn.pnt h.l ydlp. | tmn 2.4[68].16

ḥṯ drkt h.trtqṣ.b d bʻl km nš | r.b uṣbʻt h.hlm.ktp.zbl ym.bn ydm. | [ṯp]ṭ nhr.yrtqṣ.ṣmd.b d bʻl.km.nšr. | b[u]ṣbʻt h 2.4[68].14

.drkt h.trtqṣ. | b d bʻl.km.nšr b uṣbʻt h.hlm.qdq | d zbl ym.bn.ʻnm.ṯpṭ.nhr.yprsḥ ym. | w yql.l arṣ.w trtqṣ.ṣmd.b d bʻ 2.4[68].22

trtqṣ.ṣmd.b d bʻl. | [km.]nšr.b uṣbʻt h.ylm.qdqd.zbl. | [ym.]bn.ʻnm.ṯpṭ.nhr.yprsḥ.ym.yql. | l arṣ.tngṣn.pnt h.w ydlp. 2.4[68].25

. | l rbt.aṯr[t] ym.tn. | aḥd.b bn k.amlkn. | w tʻn.rbt.aṯrt ym. | bl.nmlk.ydʻ.ylḥn. | w yʻn.lṭpn.il d pi | d dq.anm.l yrẓ. | ʻ 6.1.47[49.1.19]

ʻm.bʻl.l yʻdb.mrḥ. | ʻm.bn.dgn.k tms m. | w ʻn.rbt.aṯrt ym. | blt.nmlk.ʻṯtr.ʻrẓ. | ymlk.ʻṯtr.ʻrẓ. | apnk.ʻṯtr.ʻrẓ. | yʻl.b ṣrrt. 6.1.53[49.1.25]

l h.q[dš.ṯb]r.arṣ. | [---.]ġrm[.t]ḫšn. | rḥq[.---.td‘]. | qdm ym.bmt.[nhr]. | ṯṯn.ib.bʻl.tiḫd. | yʻrm.šnu.hd.gpt. | ġr.w yʻn.a 4[51].7.34

m.l ġ | [lm] h.bʻl k.yṣḥ.ʻn. | [gpn].w ugr.b ġlmt. | [ʻmm.]ym.bn.ẓlmt.r | [mt.prʻ]t.ibr.mnt. | [ṣḥrrm.ḥbl.ʻ]rpt. | [---.---.-] 4[51].7.55

]ṯrt.gm.l ġlm h. | bʻl.yṣḥ.ʻn.gpn. | w ugr.bn.ġlmt. | ʻmm ym.bn.ẓlm[t]. | rmt.prʻt.ibr[.mnt]. | ṣḥrrm.ḥbl[.--]. | ʻrpt.ṯḥt.[8[51FRAG].8

ṣ[---.]šr.pḫr.klat. | tqtnṣn.w tldn.tld.[ilm.]nʻmm.agzr ym. | bn.ym.ynqm.b a[p.]ḏ[d.r]gm.l il.ybl. | aṯt y.il.ylt.mh.ylt 23[52].58

šbʻ. | iqnu.šmt[.---]. | [b]n.šrm. | iqran.ilm.nʻmm[.agzry ym.bn]ym. | ynqm.b ap zd.aṯrt.[---]. | špš.mṣprt dlt hm[.---]. 23[52].23

ḏ[d.r]gm.l il.ybl. | aṯt y.il.ylt.mh.ylt.ilmy nʻmm. | agzr ym.bn ym.ynqm.b ap.ḏd.št.špt. | l arṣ.špt l šmm.w ʻrb.b p h 23[52].61

.bʻ]l y.p.l. | ḥy.np[š.a]rš. | l.pn.bʻ[l y.l].pn.bʻl y. | w.urk.ym.bʻl y. | l.pn.amn.w.l.pn. | il.mṣrm.dt.tġrn. | npš.špš.mlk. | r 1018.20

ilbt. | ušḫry. | ym.bʻl. | yrḫ. | kṯr. | ṯrmn. | pdry. | dqt. | trṯ. | ršp. | ʻnt ḫbly. | špš UG5.14.A.3

]. | [---.-]dm.mlak.ym.tʻdt.ṯpṭ.nh[r.---]. | [---].an.rgmt.l ym.bʻl km.ad[n km.ṯpṭ]. | [nhr.---.]hwt.gmr.hd.l wny[-.---]. | 2.1[137].45

.išt.ištm.yitmr.ḥrb.lṭšt. | [--]n hm.rgm.l ṯr.ab h.il.ṯḥm.ym.bʻl km. | [adn]km.ṯpṭ.nhr.tn.il m.d tq h.d tqyn h. | [hml] 2.1[137].33

] | r ṯny.dʻt km.w rgm.l ṯr.a[b.-.il.ṯny.l pḫr]. | mʻd.ṯḥm.ym.bʻl km.adn km.ṯ[pṭ.nhr]. | tn.il m.d tq h.d tqyn.hmlt.tn. 2.1[137].17

ytn.l hm.ṯḥt bʻl[.---]. | h.u qšt pn hdd.b y[.----]. | ʻm.b ym bʻl ysy ym[.---]. | rmm.ḫnpm.mḫl[.---]. | mlk.nhr.ibr[.---]. 9[33].2.7

ḥm.tld. | [---.]ḫrm.ṯn.ym. | tš[.---.]ymm.lk. | hrg.ar[bʻ.]ymm.bṣr. | kp.šsk k.[--].l ḥbš k. | ʻtk.ri[š.]l mhr k. | w ʻp.l dr[ʻ] 13[6].5

ʻny.bn. | ilm.mt.npš[.-]. | npš.lbun. | thw.w npš. | anḫr.b ym. | brkt.šbšt. | k rumm.hm. | ʻn.kdd.aylt. | mt hm.ks.ym | sk. UG5.4.5

w l ll.šp. pgr.w ṯrmnm.bt mlk. | il[bt].gdlt.ušḫry.gdlt.ym gdlt. | bʻl gdlt.yrḫ.gdlt. | gdlt.ṯrmn.gdlt.pdry.gdlt dqt. | dq 34[1].13

l].ksp.[a]ṯrt. | k tʻn.ẓl.ksp.w n[-]t. | ḫrṣ.šmḫ.rbt.a[ṯrt]. | ym.gm.l ġlm h.k [ṯṣḥ]. | ʻn.mkṯr.ap.t[---]. | dgy.rbt.aṯr[t.ym]. 4[51].2.29

kṯr ṣmdm.ynḥt.w ypʻr.šmt hm.šm k at. | ygrš.ygrš.grš ym grš ym.l ksi h. | [n]hr l kḥṯ drkt h.trtqṣ.b d bʻl km nš | r.b 2.4[68].12

bʻl h.šʻ[-]rt. | ḫqr.[--.tq]l rb. | tl[t.---]. | aḥt.ḫm[-.---]. | b ym.dbḥ.ṯp[-]. | aḥt.l mzy.bn[--]. | aḥt.l mkt.ġr. | aḥt.l ʻṯtrt. | ar 39[19].13

. | [ṯṣ]un.b arṣ. | mḫnm.ṯrp ym. | lšnm.tlḥk. | šmm.ṯṯrp. | ym.ḏnbtm. | tnn.l šbm. | tšt.trks. | l mrym.l bt[.---]. | p l.tbʻ[.--- 1003.7

[-----]. | [---.r]ḫm.tld. | [---.]ḫrm.ṯn.ym. | tš[.---.]ymm.lk. | hrg.ar[bʻ.]ymm.bṣr. | kp.šsk k.[--].l ḥbš k. | ʻtk.ri[š.] 13[6].4

.ydd.bn.il. | ġzr.p np.š.npš.lbim. | thw.hm.brlt.anḫr. | b ym.hm.brk y.tkšd. | rumm.ʻn.kdd.aylt. | hm.imt.imt.npš.blt. 5[67].1.16

l ym hnd. | iwr[k]l.pdy. | agdn.bn.nrgn. | w ynḥm.aḫ h. | w.bʻln 1006.1

l ym hnd. | ʻmṯtmr.bn. | nqmpʻ.ml[k]. | ugrt.ytn. | šd.kdġdl[.bn] 1008.1

l ym.hnd. | ʻmṯtmr. | bn.nqmpʻ. | mlk.ugrt. | ytn.bt.anndr. | bn.y 1009.1

.trm.hl h.tṣḥ.ad ad. | w hl h.tṣḥ.um.um.tirk m.yd.il.k ym. | w yd il.k mdb.ark.yd.il.k ym. | w yd.il.k mdb.yqḥ.il.mš 23[52].33

.um.um.tirk m.yd.il.k ym. | w yd il.k mdb.ark.yd.il.k ym. | w yd.il.k mdb.yqḥ.il.mštʻltm. | mštʻltm.l riš.agn.yqḥ.tš. 23[52].34

št.špt. | l arṣ.špt l šmm.w ʻrb.b p hm.ʻṣr.šmm. | w dg b ym.w ndd.gzr.l zr.yʻdb.u ymn. | u šmal.b p hm.w l.tšbʻn y.aṯ 23[52].63

nm].yn.b ks.ḫ[rṣ]. | [dm.ʻṣm.---]n.krpn.ʻl.[k]rpn. | [---.]ym.w tʻl.trṯ. | [---].yn.ʻšy l ḥbš. | [---.]ḥtn.qn.yṣbt. | [---.--]m.b 17[2AQHT].6.7

.l arṣ.ypl.ul ny.w l.ʻpr.ʻẓm ny. | l bʻl[-.---]. | ṯḥt.ksi.zbl.ym.w ʻn.kṯr.w ḫss.l rgmt. | l k.l zbl.bʻl.ṯnt.l rkb.ʻrpt.ht.ib k. | 2.4[68].7

ḫ nʻmt. | šd[.i]lm.šd.aṯrt.w rḥmy. | [---].y[t]b. | [---]p.gp ym.w yṣġd.gp..thm. | [yqḥ.]il.mštʻltm.mštʻltm.l riš.agn. | hl h 23[52].30

šr b uṣbʻt h.hlm.qdq | d zbl ym.bn.ʻnm.ṯpṭ.nhr.yprsḥ ym. | w yql.l arṣ.w trtqṣ.ṣmd.b d bʻl. | [km.]nšr.b uṣbʻt h.ylm. 2.4[68].22

. | [dn]il.yd.ṣt h.yʻl.w yškb. | [yd.]mizrt.p yln.mk.b šbʻ.ymm. | [w]yqrb.bʻl.b ḥnt h.abynt. | [d]nil.mt.rpi anḫ.ġzr. | [17[2AQHT].1.16

[t]ḥm.iṯtl. | l mnn.ilm. | tġr k.tšlm k. | tʻzz k.alp ymm. | w rbt.šnt. | b ʻd ʻlm...gnʻ. | iršt.aršt. | l aḫ y.l rʻ y.dt. | w 1019.1.4

| asr.mr[kbt.---]. | tʻln.l mr[kbt hm.tity.l] | ʻr hm.tl[kn.ym.w ṯn.aḫr.špšm]. | b ṯlṯ.mġy[.rpum.l grnt]. | i[ln]y[m].l mṭʻ 22.1[123].24

m.tṣmd.dg[-.---]. | tʻln.l mrkbt hm.ti[ty.l ʻr hm]. | tlkn.ym.w ṯa aḫr.š[pšm.b ṯlṯ]. | mġy.rpum.l grnt.i[lnym.l] | mṭʻt. 20[121].2.5

l nkr.mddt. | km irby.tškn. | šd.k ḥsn.pat. | mdbr.tlkn. | ym.w ṯn.aḫr. | šp[š]m.b [ṯ]lṯ. | ym[ġy.]l qdš. | a[ṯrt.]ṣrm.w l ilt 14[KRT].4.195

yn.mḫmd.arz h. | tšt.išt.b bht m. | nb[l]at.b hkl m. | hn.ym.w ṯn.tikl. | išt.b bht m.nblat. | b hk[l] m.ṯlṯ.kbʻ ym. | tikl[.i 4[51].6.24

qy.]bn.qdš.yd. | [ṣt h.yʻl.]w yškb.yd. | [mizrt.]p ynl.hn.ym. | [w ṯn.uzr.]ilm.dnil. | [uzr.ilm.]ylḥm.uzr. | [yšqy.b]n.qdš 17[2AQHT].1.6

iṯrm. | tšmʻ.mtt.ḥry. | ṯṭbḫ.imr.w lḥm. | mgṯ.w ytrm.hn.ym. | w ṯn.ytb.krt.l ʻd h. | yṯb.l ksi mlk. | l nḫt.l kḥṯ.drkt. | ap. 16.6[127].21

lp.yṭbḫ.l kṯ | rt.yšlḥm.kṯrt.w y | ššq.bnt.[hl]l.snnt. | hn.ym.w ṯn.yšlḥm. | kṯrt.w yš[š]q.bnt.hl[l]. | snnt.ṯlṯ[.r]bʻ ym.yšl 17[2AQHT].2.32

.yn.bld. | ġll.yn.išryt.ʻnq.smd. | lbnn.ṯl mrt.yḥrt.il. | hn.ym.w ṯn.tlḥmn.rpum. | tštyn.ṯlṯ.rbʻ.ym.ḫmš. | ṯdṯ.ym.tlḥmn.r 22.2[124].21

.ašʻrb.ġlmt. | ḥẓr y.ṯn h.wspm. | atn.w ṯlṯ h.ḫrṣm. | ylk ym.w ṯn. | ṯlṯ.rbʻ.ym. | aḫr.špšm.b rbʻ. | ymġy.l udm.rbt. | w u 14[KRT].4.207

w b grnt.ḥpšt. | sʻt.b npk.šibt.w b | mqr.mmlat. | d[m].ym.w ṯn. | ṯlṯ.rbʻ.ym. | ḫmš.ṯdṯ.ym. | mk.špšm.b šbʻ. | w l.yšn. 14[KRT].5.218

nkr. | mddt h.k irby. | [t]škn.šd. | km.ḥsn.pat.mdbr. | lk.ym.w ṯn.ṯlṯ.rbʻ ym. | ḫmš.ṯdṯ.ym.mk.špšm. | b šbʻ.w tmġy.l u 14[KRT].3.106

m. | ḥṭb h.b grnt.ḥpšt. | sʻt.b nk.šibt.b bqr. | mmlat.dm.ym.w ṯn. | ṯlṯ.rbʻ.ym.ymš. | ṯdṯ.ym.ḥẓ k.al.tšʻl. | qrt h.abn.yd 14[KRT].3.114

d h.|šp̣ḥ.al.thbṭ.|ḫrd.ʻps.aḫd.kw|sgt.|ḫrd ksp.[--]r.|ymm.w[.---].|[-----].|w[.-----].|[-----]. 2062.2.9
yrḫ ḫyr.b ym ḥdṯ.|alp.w š.l bʻlt bhtm.|b arbʻt ʻšrt.bʻl.|ʻrkm.|b ṯmnt.ʻ UG5.12.A.1
b ym ḥdṯ.|b.yrḫ.pgrm.|lqḥ.iwrpzn.|argdd.|ttkn.|ybrk.|ntbt 2006.1
b.ym.ḥdṯ.|b.yr.pgrm.|lqḥ.bʻlmdr.|w.bn.ḫlp.|miḫd.|b.arbʻ.| 1156.1
b.ym.ḥdṯ.|b.yrḫ.pgrm.|lqḥ.bʻlmʻdr.|w bn.ḫlp.|w[--]y.d.bʻl.| 1155.1
b ṯṯ ym ḥdṯ.|ḫyr.ʻrbt.|špš ṯǵr h.|ršp.|w ʻbdm tbqrn.|skn. 1162.1
b yrḫ.[rišyn.b ym.ḥdṯ].|šmtr.[uṯkl.l il.šlmm].|b ṯlṯt ʻ[šrt.yrtḥṣ.mlk.brr].|b 35[3].1
[b yr]ḫ[.r]išyn.b ym.ḥdṯ.|[šmtr].uṯkl.l il.šlmm.|b [ṯlṯt].ʻšrt.yrtḥṣ.mlk.|br[r.] APP.II[173].1
.[šb]ʻ.ṣbu.[š]pš.w.ḥly[t].ʻ[r]b[.š]p[š].|w [ḥl.]mlk.[w.]b.ym.ḥdṯ.ṯn.šm.|l.[---]t.|i[d.yd]bḥ.mlk.l.prgl.ṣqrn.b.gg.|ar[bʻ 35[3].48
ṯb].|brr.b šbʻ[.ṣbu.špš.w ḥl]|yt.ʻrb špš[.w ḥl.mlk.w.b y]|m.ḥdṯ.ṯn šm[.---.--]t.|b yrḫ.ši[-.b ar]bʻt.ʻš|rt.yr[tḥṣ.ml]k. APP.II[173].52
.šibt.b bqr.|mmlat.dm.ym.w ṯn.|ṯlṯ.rbʻ.ym.ymš.|ṯdṯ.ym.ḥẓ k.al.tšʻl.|qrt h.abn.yd k.|mšdpt.w hn.špšm.|b šbʻ.w 14[KRT].3.116
ḥpšt.|sʻt.b nk.šibt.b bqr.|mmlat.dm.ym.w ṯn.|ṯlṯ.rbʻ.ym.ymš.|ṯdṯ.ym.ḥẓ k.al.tšʻl.|qrt h.abn.yd k.|mšdpt.w hn.š 14[KRT].3.115
.ṯl mrṯ.yḥrṯ.il.|hn.ym.w ṯn.tlḥmn.rpum.|tštyn.ṯlṯ.rbʻ.ym.ḫmš.|ṯdṯ.ym.tlḥmn.rpum.|tštyn.bt.ikl.b prʻ.|yṣq.b irt.l 22.2[124].22
irby.|[t]škn.šd.|km.ḥsn.pat.mdbr.|lk.ym.w ṯn.ṯlṯ.rbʻ ym.|ḫmš.ṯdṯ.ym.mk.špšm.|b šbʻ.w tmǵy.l udm.|rbm.w l.u 14[KRT].3.106
ʻt.b npk.šibt.w b |mqr.mmlat.|d[m].ym.w ṯn.|ṯlṯ.rbʻ.ym.|ḫmš.ṯdṯ.ym.|mk.špšm.b šbʻ.|w l.yšn.pbl.|mlk.l [qr.]ṯi 14[KRT].5.219
sk h.|rbb.nsk h.kbkbm.|ttpp.anhbm.d alp.šd[.ẓu h.b ym].|ṯl[.---]. 3[ʻNT].4.89
ṯn.yrḫm.|ṯlrby.yrḫ.w.ḫm[š.ym]m.|tlḥny.yrḫ.w.ḫm[š.ymm].|ẓrn.yrḫ.w.ḫmš.y[m]m.|mrat.ḫmš.ʻšr.ymm.|qmnz.y 66[109].5
q[dm.--.šp]š.|[---.šm]n.mšḫt.kṯpm.a[-]ṯ[-].|[---.--]ḥ b ym.tld[---.]b[-.]y[--.---].|[---.il]m.rb[m.--]š[-].|[---].nš.b [---]. UG5.8.24
--.-]k.mnh[-.---.-]š bš[-.]t[-].ǵlm.l šdt[.-.]ymm.|[---.]b ym.ym.y[--].yš[ ]n.ap k.ʻṯtr.dm[.---.]|[---.]ḥrḥrtm.w[--.]n[-- 2.3[129].12
l [----].|w l [---].|kd.[---].|kd.t[---.ym.ymm].|yʻtqn.w[rḥm.ʻnt].|tngṯ h.k lb.a[rḫ].|l ʻgl h.k lb. 6[49].2.4
y.ḫtu hw.|nrt.ilm.špš.ṣḥrrt.|la.šmm.b yd.bn ilm.mt.|ym.ymm.yʻtqn.l ymm.|l yrḫm.rḥm.ʻnt.tngṯ h.|k lb.arḫ.l ʻgl 6[49].2.26
[---.--]b.|[---.w ym.ym]m.|[yʻtqn.---.ymǵy.]npš.|[---.h]d.tngṯn h.|[---].b ṣp 1[ʻNT.X].5.2
ǵr mtn y.|[---.]rq.gb.|[---.--]kl.ṭǵr.mtn h.|[---.--]b.w ym ymm.|[yʻtqn.---].ymǵy.npš.|[---.--]t.hd.tngṯm h.|[---.-] 1[ʻNT.X].5.15
.a[--.--]n.|[--.]ḥ[--.]d[--]t.|[---.]ḥw[t.---].|[---.]š[--].|w ym ym.yš|al.|w mlk.d mlk.|b ḥwt.šp̣ḥ.|l ydn.ʻbd.mlk.|d š 2062.2.02
.pḫr.klat.|tqtnṣn.w tldn.tld.[ilm.]nʻmm.agzr ym.|bn.ym.ynqm.b a[p.]ḏ[d.r]gm.l il.ybl.|aṯt y.il.ylt.mh.ylt.ilmy nʻ 23[52].59
u.šmt[.---].|[b]n.šrm.|iqran.ilm.nʻmm[.agzry ym.bn]ym.|ynqm.b ap zd.aṯrt.[---].|špš.mṣprt dlt hm[.---].|w ǵnb 23[52].23
m.l il.ybl.|aṯt y.il.ylt.mh.ylt.ilmy nʻmm.|agzr ym.bn ym.ynqm.b ap.ḏd.št.špt.|l arṣ.špt l šmm.w ʻrb.b p hm.ʻṣr.š 23[52].61
.in.aṯt.|[l]k.k[m.ilm].|[w ǵlmt.k bn.qdš.]w y[--.]zbl.ym.yʻ[--.]ṯpṭ.nhr.|[-------.]yšlḥn.w yʻn ʻṯtr[.-]. 2.3[129].23
ʻbrm.zt.ḫrṣ.l ʻbrm.kš.|dpr.ṯlḥn.b qʻl.b qʻl.|mlkm.hn.ym.yṣq.yn.ṯmk.|mrṯ.yn.srnm.yn.bld.|ǵll.yn.išryt.ʻnq.smd.| 22.2[124].17
ht[.dr]y.b kbrt.|ʻl k.pht.[-]l[-].|b šdm.ʻl k.pht.|drʻ.b ym.tn.aḥd.|b aḫ k.ispa.w yṯb.|ap.d anšt.im[-].|aḥd.b aḫ k.l 6[49].5.19
.zbl.bʻl.|arṣ.gm.yṣḥ il.|l rbt.aṯrt ym.šmʻ.|l rbt.aṯr[t] ym.tn.|aḥd.b bn k.amlkn.|w tʻn.rbt.aṯrt ym.|bl.nmlk.ydʻ.y 6.1.45[49.1.17]
.ilm.w ḥẓr.k bn.aṯrt.|mṯb il.mẓll.bn h.|mṯb rbt.aṯrt.ym.|mṯb.klt.knyt.|mṯb.pdry.bt.ar.|mẓll.ṭly.bt rb.|mṯb.arṣ. 4[51].4.53
ḥẓr].|[k bn.aṯ]r[t].|m[ṯ]b.il.mẓll.|bn h.mṯb.rbt.|aṯrt.ym.mṯb.|klt.knyt.|mṯb.pdry.b ar.|mẓll.ṭly.bt rb.|mṯb.arṣy. 4[51].1.15
.ilm.|ḥẓr.k b[n.a]ṯrt.mṯb.il.|mṯll.b[n h.m]ṯb.rbt.aṯrt.|ym.mṯb.[pdr]y.bt.ar.|[mẓll.]ṭly[.bt.]rb.mṯb.|[arṣy.bt.yʻbdr. 3[ʻNT.VI].5.49
m.w ḥẓr].|k bn.[aṯrt.mṯb.il.mẓll].|bn h.m[ṯb.rbt.aṯrt.ym].|mṯb.pdr[y.bt.ar.mẓll].|ṭly.bt.r[b.mṯb.arṣy].|bt.yʻbdr[. 3[ʻNT.VI].4.2
k.mnh[-.---.-]š bš[-.]t[-].ǵlm.l šdt[.-.]ymm.|[---.]b ym.ym.y[--].yš[ ]n.ap k.ʻṯtr.dm[.---.]|[---.]ḥrḥrtm.w[--.]n[--.]iš[2.3[129].12
šbʻm.aṯr.|[---.--]ldm.dt ymtm.|[--.--]r.l ẓpn.|[---.]pn.ym.y[--].|[---].bʻl.tdd.|[---.]hkl.|[---.]yd h.|[---.]tmt. 25[136].6
.tǵʻr m.ʻṯtrt.bṯ l aliyn.[bʻl.]|bṯ.l rkb.ʻrpt.k šby n.zb[l.ym.k] |šby n.ṯpṭ.nhr.w yṣa b[.--].|ybṯ.nn.aliyn.bʻl.w [---].| 2.4[68].29
[-] ym.prʻ d nkly yn kd w kd.|w ʻl ym kdm.|w b ṯlṯ.kd yn w krsnm.|w b rbʻ kdm yn.|w b ḫm 1086.2
m.yql.|l arṣ.tngṣn.pnt h.w ydlp.tmn h.|yqṭ bʻl.w yšt.ym.ykly.ṯpṭ.nhr.|b šm.tgʻr m.ʻṯtrt.bṯ l aliyn.[bʻl.]|bṯ.l rkb.ʻr 2.4[68].27
].|bt[.--]b bʻl.b qrb.|bt.w yʻn.aliyn.|bʻl.ašt m.kṯr bn.|ym.kṯr.bnm.ʻdt.|ypth.ḥln.b bht m.|urbt.b qrb.[h]kl |m.w y 4[51].7.16
].|tṣr.trm.tnq[--].|km.nkyt.ṯǵr[.---].|km.škllt.[---].|ʻr.ym.l bl[.---].|b[---.]ny[.--].|l bl.sk.w [---] h.|ybm h.šbʻ[.---]. 16.2[125].91
mṣḫ.l arṣ.|[yṯb.]b[ʻ]l.l ksi.mlk h.|[---].l kḥṯ.drkt h.|l [ym]m.l yrḫm.l yrḫm.|l šnt.[m]k.b šbʻ.|šnt.w [--].bn.ilm.mt. 6[49].5.7
h.|pǵm.ǵr.ybk.l aqht.|ǵzr.ydmʻ.l kdd.dnil.|mt.rpi.l ymm.l yrḫm.|l yrḫm.l šnt.ʻd.|šbʻt.šnt.ybk.l aq|ht.ǵzr.yd[m 19[1AQHT].4.175
.špš.ṣḥrrt.|la.šmm.b yd.bn ilm.mt.|ym.ymm.yʻtqn.l ymm.|l yrḫm.rḥm.ʻnt.tngṯ h.|k lb.arḫ.l ʻgl h.k lb.|ṯat.l imr 6[49].2.26
.w ugr.|mn.ib.ypʻ.l bʻl.ṣrt.|l rkb.ʻrpt.l mḫšt.mdd.|il ym.l klt.nhr.il.rbm.|l ištbm.tnn.ištml h.|mḫšt.bṯn.ʻqltn.|šl 3[ʻNT].3.36
.ynḫt.w ypʻr.šmt hm.|šm k.at.aymr.aymr.mr.ym.mr.ym.|l ksi h.nhr l kḥṯ.drkt h.trtqṣ.|b d bʻl.km.nšr b uṣbʻt h. 2.4[68].19
m.ynḫt.w ypʻr.šmt hm.šm k at.|ygrš.ygrš.grš ym grš ym.l ksi h.|[n]hr l kḥṯ drkt h.trtqṣ.b d bʻl km nš|r.b uṣbʻt h 2.4[68].12
|šby n.ṯpṭ.nhr.w yṣa b[.--].|ybṯ.nn.aliyn.bʻl.w [---].|ym.l mt.bʻl m.ym l[--.---].|ḥm.l šrr.w [---].|yʻn.ym.l mt[.---] 2.4[68].32
[---].|ym.l mt.bʻl m.ym l[--.---].|ḥm.l šrr.w [---].|yʻn.ym.l mt[.---].|l šrr.w t[n.ʻṯtrt.---].|bʻl m.hmt.[---].|l šrr.št[.- 2.4[68].34
.nšr.|b[u]ṣbʻt h.ylm.ktp.zbl ym.bn ydm.ṯpṭ.|nhr.ʻz.ym.l ymk.l tngṣn.pnt h.l ydlp.|tmn h.kṯr.ṣmdm.ynḫt.w ypʻ 2.4[68].17
.špš.tšu.g h.w t[ṣḥ.šm]ʻ.mʻ.|[-.yṯ]ir ṯr.il.ab k.l pn.zbl.ym.l pn[.ṯ]pṭ[.n]hr.|[ik.a]l.yšmʻ k.ṯr.[i]l.ab k.l ysʻ.[alt.]ṯ[bt | 2.3[129].16
[ht].|[zbl.]ym.b hkl.ṯpṭ.nh[r].yṯir.ṯr.il.ab h l pn[.zb]l y[m].|[l pn.ṯp]ṭ[.nhr.]mlkt.[--]pm.l mlkt.wn.in.aṯt.|[l]k.k[2.3[129].21
nym.ṯm].|yḥpn.ḥy[ly.zbl.mlk.ʻllm y].|šmʻ.atm[.---].|ym.lm.qd[.---].|šmn.prst[.---].|ydr.hm.ym[.---].|ʻl amr.yu[22.1[123].14
lṯ[.r]bʻ ym.yšl|ḥm kṯrt.w yššq.|bnt hll.snnt.ḫmš.|ṯdṯ.ym.yšlḥm.k[ṯ]rt.|w y[šš]q].bnt.hll.snnt.|mk.b šb[ʻ.]ymm.tbʻ. 17[2AQHT].2.37
.ym.w ṯn.yšlḥm.|kṯrt.w yš[š]q.bnt.hl[l].|snnt.ṯlṯ[.r]bʻ ym.yšl|ḥm kṯrt.w yššq.|bnt hll.snnt.ḫmš.|ṯdṯ.ym.yšlḥm.k[17[2AQHT].2.34
.|hn.ym.w ṯn.tlḥmn.rpum.|tštyn.ṯlṯ.rbʻ.ym.ḫmš.|ṯdṯ.ym.tlḥmn.rpum.|tštyn.bt.ikl.b prʻ.|yṣq.b irt.lbnn.mk.b šbʻ. 22.2[124].23
]l km amt m.|[---.]b w tʻrb.sd.|[---.--]n b ym.qẓ.|[---.]ym.tlḥmn.|[---.rp]um.tštyn.|[---.]il.d ʻrgzm.|[---.]dt.ʻl.lty.|[20[121].1.6
m.gm.l ǵlm h.k [tṣḥ].|ʻn.mkṯr.ap.t[---].|dgy.rbt.aṯr[t.ym].|qḥ.rṭt.b d k t[---].|rbt.ʻl.ydm[.---].|b mdd.il.y[--.---].| 4[51].2.31
[--]r.[---].|[---.]il.[---].|[tṣ]un.b arṣ.|mḫnm.ṭrp ym.|lšnm.tlḥk.|šmm.ṭṭrp.|ym.dnbtm.|tnn.l šbm.|tšt.trks. 1003.4
r.w yṣa b[.--].|ybṯ.nn.aliyn.bʻl.w [---].|ym.l mt.bʻl m.ym l[--.---].|ḥm.l šrr.w [---].|yʻn.ym.l mt[.---].|l šrr.w t[n.ʻṯ 2.4[68].32
ʻnn h.bn.dgn.arṯ m.pḏ h.|[w yʻn.]ṯr.ab h.il.ʻbd k.bʻl.y ym m.ʻbd k.bʻl.|[--.--]m.bn.dgn.a[s]r km.hw ybl.argmn k.k 2.1[137].36
tʻn.rbt].|aṯr[t.ym.šmʻ.l qdš].|w am[rr.l dgy.rbt].|aṯrt.ym[.mdl.ʻr].|ṣmd.pḥl[.št.gpnm.dt].|ksp.dt.yr[q.nqbnm].|ʻd 4[51].4.4

yiḫd.b'l.bn.aṯrt.|rbm.ymḫṣ.b ktp.|dk ym.ymḫṣ.b ṣmd.|ṣḥr mt.ymṣḫ.l arṣ.|[yṯb.]b['l].l ksi.mlk h.| 6[49].5.3
b |mqr.mmlat.|d[m].ym.w ṯn.|ṯlṯ.rb'.ym.|ḫmš.ṯdṯ.ym.|mk.špšm.b šb'.|w l.yšn.pbl.|mlk.l [qr.]ṯiqt.|ibr h[.l]ql 14[KRT].5.220
d.|km.ḥsn.pat.mdbr.|lk.ym.w ṯn.ṯlṯ.rb' ym.|ḫmš.ṯdṯ.ym.mk.špšm.|b šb'.w tmģy.l udm.|rbm.w l.udm.ṯrrt.|w gr 14[KRT].3.107
dlt.'rb špš w ḥl.|[mlk.b ar]b't.'[š]rt.yrtḥṣ.mlk.brr.|[b ym.ml]at.y[ql]n.al[p]m.yrḫ.'šrt.|[l b'l.ṣ]pn.[dq]tm.w y[nt] q 36[9].1.11
b arb't.'šr[t].|yrtḥṣ.mlk.b[rr].|b ym.mlat.|tqln.alpm.|yrḫ.'šrt.l b'[l].|dqtm.w ynt.qr[t].|w UG5.13.3
tt.mtt[--].|[--.]ḥy[--.--.]l aššj.hm.ap.amr[--].|[---].w b ym.mnḫ l abd.b ym.irtm.m[--].|[ṯpṭ].nhr.tl'm.ṯm.ḥrbm.its. 2.4[68].3
r.ṣmdm.ynḥt.w yp'r.šmt hm.|šm k.at.aymr.aymr.mr.ym.mr.ym.|l ksi h.nhr l kḥṯ.drkt h.trtqṣ.|b d b'l.km.nšr b 2.4[68].19
m[š.ym]m.|ṯlḥny.yrḫ.w.ḫm[š.ymm].|ẓrn.yrḫ.w.ḫmš.y[m]m.|mrat.ḫmš.'šr.ymm.|qmnz.yrḫ.w.ḫmš.ymm.|'nmk. 66[109].6
.tikl.|išt.[b]bht m.nblat.|b[qrb.hk]l m.mk.|b šb['.]y[mm].td.išt.|b bht m.n[bl]at.b hkl m.|sb.ksp.l rqm.ḫrṣ.|n 4[51].6.32
.l inš].|ilm.w š d[d.ilš.š.--.mlk].|yṯb.brr[.w mḫ-.---].|ym.[']lm.y'[--.---].|[--.-]g[-.-]s w [---].|w yn[t.q]rt.y[---].|w 35[3].8
.w š.|dd ilš.š[.---.]mlk.yṯb br|r.w mḫ[--.---.]w q[--].|ym.'lm.y[---.---].|t.k[-]ml.[---].|l[---].w y[nt.qrt.---].|[---.--]n APP.II[173].9
.ḫmš.y[m]m.|mrat.ḫmš.'šr.ymm.|qmnz.yrḫ.w.ḫmš.ymm.|'nmk.yrḫ.|ypr.yrḫ.w.ḫmš.ymm. 66[109].8
l [----].|w l [---].|kd.[---].|kd.t[---.ym.ymm].|y'tqn.w[rḥm.'nt].|tngṯ h.k lb.a[rḫ].|l 'gl h.k lb.ṯa[t 6[49].2.4
u hw.|nrt.ilm.špš.ṣḥrrt.|la.šmm.b yd.bn ilm.mt.|ym.ymm.y'tqn.l ymm.|l yrḫm.rḥm.'nt.tngṯ h.|k lb.arḫ.l 'gl h.k 6[49].2.26
mtn y.|[---.]rq.gb.|[---.--]kl.tģr.mtn h.|[---.--]b.w ym ymm.|[y'tqn.---].ymģy.npš.|[---.--]t.hd.tngṯm h.|[---.-]ḥm 1['NT.X].5.15
[---.--]b.|[---.w ym.ym]m.|[y'tqn.---.ymģy.]npš.|[---.h]d.tngṯn h.|[---].b ṣpn.|[- 1['NT.X].5.2
y'bdr.|ap.mṯn.rgmm.|argm k.šskn m'.|mgn.rbt.aṯrt ym.|mģẓ.qnyt.ilm.|hyn.'ly.l mpḫm.|b d.ḥss.mṣbṭm.|yṣq.k 4[51].1.22
[i]k.mgn.rbt.aṯrt.|[ym].mģẓ.qnyt.ilm.|w tn.bt.l b'l.km.|[i]lm.w ḥẓr.k bn.|[a]ṯr 8[51FRAG].2
t.|aḫr.mģy.aliyn.b'l.|mģyt.btlt.'nt.|tmgnn.rbt[.a]ṯrt ym.|tģẓyn.qnyt.ilm.|w t'n.rbt.aṯrt ym.|ik.tmgnn.rbt.|aṯrt. 4[51].3.25
ģẓyn.qnyt.ilm.|w t'n.rbt.aṯrt ym.|ik.tmgnn.rbt.|aṯrt.ym.tģẓyn.|qnyt.ilm.mgntm.|ṯr.il.d pid.hm.ģẓtm.|bny.bnw 4[51].3.29
.ģẓtm.|bny.bnwt w t'n.|btlt.'nt.nmgn.|[-]m.rbt.aṯrt.ym.|[nģ]ẓ.qnyt.ilm.|[---].nmgn.hwt.|[--].aliyn.b'l.|[--.]rbt. 4[51].3.34
[-] ym.pr' d nkly yn kd w kd.|w 'l ym kdm.|w b ṯlṯ.kd yn w k 1086.1
w hln.'nt.tm|tḥṣ.b 'mq.tḥtṣb.bn.|qrytm tmḫṣ.lim.ḫp y[m].|tṣmt.adm.ṣat.š[p]š.|tḥt h.k kdrt.ri[š].|'l h.k irbym.k 3['NT].2.7
lnym.|[---.--]l km amt m.|[---.]b w t'rb.sd.|[---.--]n b ym.qẓ.|[---.]ym.tlḥmn.|[---.rp]um.tštyn.|[---.]il.d 'rgzm.|[- 20[121].1.5
r.b uṣb't h.ylm.qdqd.zbl.|[ym.]bn.'nm.ṯpṭ.nhr.yprsḥ.ym.yql.|l arṣ.tngṣn.pnt h.w ydlp.tmn h.|yqṯ b'l.w yšt.ym.y 2.4[68].25
w.ḫm[š.ymm].|ẓrn.yrḫ.w.ḫmš.y[m]m.|mrat.ḫmš.'šr.ymm.|qmnz.yrḫ.w.ḫmš.ymm.|'nmk.yrḫ.|ypr.yrḫ.w.ḫmš.y 66[109].7
t.ybn.bt.l b'l.|km ilm.w ḥẓr.k bn.aṯrt.|w t'n.rbt.aṯrt ym.|rbt.ilm.l ḥkmt.|šbt.dqn k.l tsr k.|rḫntt.d[-].l irt k.|wn 4[51].5.64
[---.--]b.|[---.r]iš k.|[---.]bn 'n km.|[---.]alp.|[---.]ym.rbt.|[---.]b nhrm.|['b]r.gbl.'br.|q'l.'br.iht.|np šmm.šmš 3['NT.VI].6.5
pṯ nh[r].|[---.]ḥrn.w[---.]tb'.k[ṯ]r w [ḫss.t]bn.bht zbl ym.|[trm]m.hk[l.ṯpṭ].nhr.bt k.[---.]šp[-.---].|[ḥš.bh]t h.tbn[2.3[129].8
y.]w ykb[dn h.--]r y[---].|[---.k]ṯr.w ḫ[ss.t]b'.b[n.]bht.ym[.rm]m.hkl.ṯpṭ nh[r].|[---.]ḥrn.w[---.]tb'.k[ṯ]r w [ḫss.t]b 2.3[129].7
ḫ.tmḫṣ.mḫṣ[.aḫ k].|tkl.m[k]ly.'l.umt[k.--].|d ttql.b ym.trtḥ[ṣ.--].|[----.a]dm.tium.b ģlp y[m.--].|d alp šd.ẓu h.b 19[1AQHT].4.203
n].|m'ms k.k šb't.yn.t[ḫ].|gg k.b ym.ṭiṭ.rḥṣ.|npṣ k.b ym rṭ.b uni[l].|pnm.tšmḫ.w 'l yṣhl pi[t].|yprq.lṣb.w yṣḥq.| 17[2AQHT].2.8
.bt.b'l.[w]mn[t].|y.bt.il.ṯḥ.gg y.b ym.ṭiṭ.|rḥṣ.npṣ y.b ym.rṭ.|dn.il.bt h.ymģyn.|yštql.dnil.l hkl h.|'rb.b bt h.kṯrt. 17[2AQHT].2.23
.bt.b'l.|[w m]nt h bt.il.ṯḥ.gg h.b ym.|[ṭi]ṭ.rḥṣ.npṣ h.b ym.rṭ.|[--.y]iḫd.il.'bd h.ybrk.|[dni]l mt rpi.ymr.ģzr.|[mt.hr 17[2AQHT].1.34
.dqt.|[---.al]p 'nt.gdlt.b ṯlṯt mrm.|[---.i]l š.b'l š.aṯrt.š.ym š.[b']l knp.|[---.g]dlt.ṣpn.dqt.šrp.w [š]lmm.|[---.a]lp.l b' 36[9].1.6
š.š.|w šlmm.ilib.š.i[l.--]m d gbl.ṣpn.al[p].|pḫr.ilm.š.ym.š[.k]nr.š.[--.]'ṣrm gdlt.|b'lm.kmm.b'lm.kmm[.b'lm].km UG5.9.1.9
.--]n.|[--.]ḥ[--.]d[--]t.|[---.]ḥw[t.---].|[---.]š[--].|w ym ym.yš|al.|w mlk.d mlk.|b ḥwt.špḥ.|l ydn.'bd.mlk.|d št.'l. 2062.2.02
ṯrm.tmt.|mrb't.zblnm.|mḫmšt.yitsp.|ršp.nṯdṯt.ģlm.|ym.mšb't hn.b šlḥ.|ttpl.y'n.ḥtk h.|krt y'n.ḥtk h.rš.|mid.gr 14[KRT].1.20
ṯr[.il.ab -.w t'n.rbt].|aṯr[t.ym.šm'.l qdš].|w am[rr.l dgy.rbt].|aṯrt.ym[.mdl.'r].|ṣmd.p 4[51].4.2
.k mt.aliyn.|b'l.k ḫlq.zbl.b'l.|arṣ.gm.yṣḥ il.|l rbt.aṯrt ym.šm'.|l rbt.aṯr[t] ym.tn.|aḥd.b bn k.amlkn.|w t'n.rbt.aṯr 6.1.44[49.1.16]
.akl.'m y.|mid y w ģbn y.|w.bn y.hn kt.|yškn.anyt.|ym.yšrr.|w.ak[l.---].|[--].š[--.--]. 2061.14
dṯ.ym.yšlḥm.k[ṯ]rt.|w y[ššq].bnt.hll.snnt.|mk.b šb['.]ymm.tb'.b bt h.|kṯrt.bnt.hll.snnt.|[-]d[-]t.n'm y.'rš.h[--]m.| 17[2AQHT].2.39
ṣm.hm.yd.il mlk.|yḫss k.ahbt.ṯr.t'rr k.|w t'n.rbt.aṯrt ym.|tḥm k.il.ḥkm.ḥkmt.|'m 'lm.ḥyt.ḥẓt.|tḥm k.mlk n.aliy[4[51].4.40
.b g[bl.šnt k.---].|[--]šnm.aṯtm.t[--.---].|[m]lakm.ylak.ym.[t'dt.ṯpṭ.nhr].|b 'lṣ.'lṣm.npr.š[--.---].|uṯ.ṭbr.ap hm.tb'.ģl 2.1[137].11
rašt hm.l ẓr.brkt hm.ln.kḥṯ.zbl hm.|aḫr.tmģyn.mlak ym.t'dt.ṯpṭ.nhr.l p'n.il.|[l t]pl.l tštḥwy.pḫr.m'd.qmm.a[--].a 2.1[137].30
|[ymn h.'n]t.tuḥd.šmal h.tuḥd.'ṯtrt.ik.m[ḫṣt.ml]|[ak.ym.t']dt.ṯpṭ.nhr.mlak.mṯhr.yḥb[-.---.]|[---].mlak.bn.ktpm.r 2.1[137].41
.rašt km.l ẓr.brkt km.ln.kḥṯ.|zbl km.w ank.'ny.mlak.ym.t'dt.ṯpṭ.nhr.|tšu ilm rašt hm.l ẓr.brkt hm.ln.kḥṯ.zbl hm 2.1[137].28
l ẓr brkt km.w ln.kḥṯ.zbl km.aḥd.|ilm.t'ny lḥt.mlak.ym.t'dt.ṯpṭ.nhr.|šu.ilm.rašt km.l ẓr.brkt km.ln.kḥṯ.|zbl km 2.1[137].26
.bn qdš.l ṯrm.b'l.qm.'l.il.hlm.|ilm.tph hm.tphn.mlak.ym.t'dt.ṯpṭ[.nhr].|t[ģ]ly.hlm.rišt hm.l ẓr.brkt hm.w l kḥṯ.|z 2.1[137].22
--].|[---].ap.anš.zbl.b'l.šdmt.bg[--.---].|[---.-]dm.mlak.ym.t'dt.ṯpṭ.nh[r.---].|[---].an.rgmt.l ym.b'l km.ad[n km.ṯpṭ] 2.1[137].44
[-----].|[---.r]ḥm.tld.|[---.]ḫrm.ṯn.ym.|tš[.---.]ymm.lk.|hrg.ar[b'.]ymm.bṣr.|kp.šsk k.[--].l ḥb 13[6].3
ḫ[ṣ.--].|[----.a]dm.tium.b ģlp y[m.--].|d alp šd.ẓu h.b ym.t[---].|tlbš.npṣ.ģzr.tšt.ḫ[---.b] |nšg h.ḥrb.tšt.b t'r[t h].| 19[1AQHT].4.205
[k]šb' yn.spu.ksm h.bt.b'l.|[w m]nt h bt.il.ṯḥ.gg h.b ym.|[ṭi]ṭ.rḥṣ.npṣ h.b ym.rṭ.|[--.y]iḫd.il.'bd h.ybrk.|[dni]l m 17[2AQHT].1.33
šb't yn.|spu.ksm y.bt.b'l.[w]mn[t].|y.bt.il.ṯḥ.gg y.b ym.ṭiṭ.|rḥṣ.npṣ y.b ym.rṭ.|dn.il.bt h.ymģyn.|yštql.dnil.l hk 17[2AQHT].2.22
bt il.aḥd.yd k.b [škrn].|m'ms k.k šb't.yn.t[ḫ].|gg k.b ym.ṭiṭ.rḥṣ.|npṣ k.b ym rṭ.b uni[l].|pnm.tšmḫ.w 'l yṣhl pi[t]. 17[2AQHT].2.7
kt k.mšl[-.---].|b riš k.aymr[.---].|ṯpṭ.nhr.yṯb[r.ḥrn.y ym.yṯbr.ḥrn].|riš k.'ṯtrt.[šm.b'l.qdqd k.---].|[--]t.mt.tpln.b 2.1[137].7
rht.d.tššlmn.|ṯlrb h.|art.ṯn.yrḫm.|ṯlrby.yrḫ.w.ḫm[š.ym]m.|ṯlḥny.yrḫ.w.ḫm[š.ymm].|ẓrn.yrḫ.w.ḫmš.y[m]m.|m 66[109].4
h].|plk.qlt.b ymn h.|npyn h.mks.bšr h.|tmt'.md h.b ym.ṯn.|npyn h.b nhrm.|štt.ḫptr.l išt.|ḫbrt.l ẓr.pḥmm.|t'pp 4[51].2.6
mt[k.--].|d ttql.b ym.trtḥ[ṣ.--].|[----.a]dm.tium.b ģlp y[m.--].|d alp šd.ẓu h.b ym.t[---].|tlbš.npṣ.ģzr.tšt.ḫ[---.b] | 19[1AQHT].4.204
m.lpš.dm a[ḫ h].|km.all.dm.ary h.|k šb't.l šb'm.aḫ h.ym[.--].|w ṯmnt.l ṯmnym.|šr.aḫy h.mẓa h.|w mẓa h.šr.yly 12[75].2.49
kl h.---.]bt.|[---.-]k.mnh[-.---.-]š bš[-.]t[-].ģlm.l šdt[.-.]ymm.|[---.]b ym.ym.y[--].yš[ ]n.ap k.'ṯtr.dm[.---.]|[---.]ḥrḥr 2.3[129].11
.qnyt.ilm.|[---].nmgn.hwt.|[--].aliyn.b'l.|[--.]rbt.aṯrt.ym.|[---.]btlt.'nt.|[--.tl]ḥm.tšty.|[ilm.w tp]q.mrġtm.|[ṭd.b 4[51].3.38
[---.]ydm ym.|[---.]ydm nhr.|[---.]trģt.|[---.]h aḥd[.--].|[---.]iln[-.---]. 49[73].1.1

n.rpum.|tštyn.bt.ikl.b pr'.|yṣq.b irt.lbnn.mk.b šb'.|[ymm.---]k.aliyn.b'l.|[---].r' h ab y.|[---.]'[---]. 22.2[124].26
[------.i]qnim.[--].|[---.]aliyn.b'l.|[---.--]k.mdd il.|y[m.---.]l ṯr.qdqd h.|il[.--.]rḥq.b ǵr.|km.y[--.]ilm.b ṣpn.|'dr 4[51].7.4
m'.atm[.---].|ym.lm.qd[.---].|šmn.prst[.---].|ydr.hm.ym[.---].|'l amr.yu[ḫd.ksa.mlk h].|nḫt.kḥṯ.d[rkt h.b bt y].| 22.1[123].16
hk]l m.|al td[.pdr]y.bt ar.|[---.ṯl]y.bt.rb.|[---.m]dd.il ym.|[---.-]qlṣn.wpṯ m.|[---.]w y'n.kṯr.|[w ḫss.]tṯb.b'l.l hwt 4[51].6.12
t b'l[.---].|h.u qšt pn hdd.b y[.----].|'m.b ym b'l ysy ym[.---].|rmm.ḫnpm.mḫl[.---].|mlk.nhr.ibr[.---].|zbl b'l.ǵl 9[33].2.7
.---].|at.bl[.at.---].|ḥmd m.[---].|il.hr[r.---].|kb[-.---].|ym.[---].|yšḥr[.---].|yikl[.---].|km.s[--.---].|tš[.---].|t[---.---] 12[75].2.12
.|ap 'nt tm[ṯḫṣ.b 'mq.tḫtṣb.bn.qrytm.tmḫṣ].|lim ḫ[p.ym.---].|[--]m.t[-]t[.---].|m[-]mt[.---].|[-----].|t[---.---].|t[---. 7.2[130].26
ttpp.anhb[m.d alp.šd].|ẓu h.b ym[.---].|[--]rn.l [---]. 3['NT].3.02
[---.-]lk[.---].|[---.']šr.ym[.---].|[---].hm.l y[--.---].|[---].mṣrm[.---].|[---.--]n mkr[.- 2126.2
.|qmnz.yrḫ.w.ḫmš.ymm.|'nmk.yrḫ.|ypr.yrḫ.w.ḫmš.ymm. 66[109].10

yman

mnm.dbbm.d |msdt.arṣ.|s'.il.dqt.k amr.|sknt.k ḥwt.yman.|d b h.rumm.l rbbt. 4[51].1.43
š.|w šqrb.'r.mšr mšr bn.ugrt.w [npy.---.]ugr.|w npy.yman.w npy.'rmt.w npy.[---].|w npy.nqmd.ušn.yp km.ulp. 32[2].1.19
--.--]yp.tḥt.|[-----].|[---.]w npy gr.|[ḥmyt.ugrt.w npy.yman.w npy.'r]mt.w npy.|[---.ušn.yp km.ulp.]qṭy.|[ulp.dd APP.I[-].1.13
[---.--]t ugrt.|[---.w n]py.yman.|[w npy.'rmt.---.w]npy.annpdgl.|[ušn.yp kn.ulp.qṭy. APP.I[-].1.2

ymil

--d]nil.|[a]drdn.|[---]n.|pǵdn.|ṯṯpḥ.|ḥgbn.|šrm.|bn.ymil.|bn.kḏǵdl.|[-]mn.|[--]n.|[ḫr]š.qṭn.|[---]n.|[-----].|[--] 1039.2.3
[ḫ.---].|[---]mlk[.---].|[-----].|ilb'l[.---].|ḫluy.bn[.---].|ymil.bn.[---].|dly.bn[.---].|ynḥm.bn[.---].|gn.bn[.---].|klby.[102[322].5.4

ymd

klby.kl[--].dqn[.---].|[-]ntn.artn.b d[.--]nr[.---].|'zn.w ymd.šr.b d ansny.|nsk.ks[p.--]mrtn.kṯrmlk.|yḥmn.aḫm[l]k 2011.31

ymz

-]n.b d.brdd.|[---.--]m.|[šd.---.b d.]ṯpṭb'l.|[šd.---.]b d.ymz.|[šd.b d].klby.psl.|[ub]dy.mri.ibrn.|[š]d.bn.bri.b d.bn. 82[300].2.3

ymḥ

lqm.b mm'.mhrm.|'d.tšb'.tmtḫṣ.b bt.|tḫṣb.bn.ṯlḥnm.ymḥ.|[b]bt.dm.ḏmr.yṣq.šmn.|šlm.b ṣ'.trḥṣ.yd h.bt|[l]t.'nt. 3['NT].2.30

ymy

lṭ.|'bdmlk.|ynḥm.|aḏddn.|mtn.|plsy.|qṭn.|ypr.|bn.ymy.|bn.'rd.|[-]b.da[-].|[--]l[--].|[-----]. 1035.4.12
n.---].|šmmlk bn[.---].|'myn.bn.[---].|mtb'l.bn[.---].|ymy.bn[.---].|'bd'n.p[--.---].|[-]d[-]l.bn.ḥrn.|aḫty.bt.abm.|[102[322].5.12

ymlk

]skn.|bn.s[--.b]d.skn.|bn.ur[-.---].|bn.knn[.---]y.|bn.ymlk[.b]d.skn.|bn.yḥnn.aḏddy.|bn.pdǵy.mḫdy.|bn.yyn.m 2014.15

ymn

ḫss.|št.alp.qdm h.mra.|w tk.pn h.t'db.ksu.|w yṯṯb.l ymn.aliyn.|b'l.'d.lḥm.št[y.ilm].|[w]y'n.aliy[n.b'l].|[--]b[.--- 4[51].5.109
rb.b p hm.'ṣr.šmm.|w dg b ym.w ndd.gzr.l zr.y'db.u ymn.|u šmal.b p hm.w l.tšb'n y.aṯt.itrḫ.|y bn.ašld.šu.'db.tk 23[52].63
[bn.b]rq.|[bn.--]r.|[bn.--]tn.|[bn.-]rmn.|bn.prtn.|bn.ymn.|bn.dby.|bn.ir[--].|bn.kr[--].|bn.nn[-].|[-----].|[-----].| 124[-].5.9
n.|[š]pšyn.|['b]dmlk.|[---]yn.|bn.ṯ[--].|bn.idrm.|bn.ymn.|bn.ṣry.|bn.mztn.|bn.šlgyn.|bn.[-]gštn.|bn[.n]klb.|b[113[400].2.3
.]ṯ'.l tmr.n'mn.|[ǵlm.]il.ks.yiḫd.|[il.b]yd.krpn.bm.|[ymn.]brkm.ybrk.|['bd h.]ybrk.il.krt.|[ṯ'.ymr]m.n'm[n.]ǵl 15[128].2.18
t.|il hd.b qrb.hkl h.|qšt hn.aḫd.b yd h.|w qṣ't h.bm.ymn h.|idk.l ytn pnm.|tk.aḫ.šmk.mla[t.r]umm.|tšu knp.bt 10[76].2.7
.ablm.ablm.[qrt.zbl.yrḫ].|ik.al.yḥdṯ.yrḫ.b[---].|b qrn.ymn h.b anšt[.---].|qdqd h.w y'n.yṭpn.[mhr.št].|šm'.l btlt.' 18[3AQHT].4.10
.tḫš.|lm.tḫš.nṯq.dmrn.|'n.b'l.qdm.yd h.|k tǵd.arz.b ymn h.|bkm.yṯb.b'l.l bht h.|u mlk.u bl mlk.|arṣ.drkt.yštkn 4[51].7.41
t.b ymn y[.t]q|ḥ.pǵt.w tšqyn h.tq[ḥ.ks.]b d h.|qb't.b ymn h.w y'n.yṭ[p]n[.mh]r.|št.b yn.yšt.ila.il š[--.]il.|d yqny. 19[1AQHT].4.218
[-----].|l abn[.---].|aḫdt.plk h[.b yd h].|plk.qlt.b ymn h.|npyn h.mks.bšr h.|tmt'.md h.b ym.ṯn.|npyn h.b n 4[51].2.4
b'[l].|[-.yuḫ]d.b yd.mšḫṭ.bm.ymn.mḫṣ.ǵlmm.yš[--].|[ymn h.'n]t.tuḫd.šmal h.tuḫd.'ttrt.ik.m[ḫṣt.ml]|[ak.ym.t']dt 2.1[137].40
rt n.dbḥ.|dbḥ.mlk.'šr.|'šrt.qḥ.tp k.b yd.|[-]r[-]k.bm.ymn.|tlk.škn.'l.ṣrrt.|adn k.šqrb.[---].|b mgn k.w ḫrṣ.l kl.|a 16.1[125].42
[-----].|w.lmd h.|mtn.|w.lmd h.|ymn.|w.lmd h.|y'ḏrn.|w.lmd h.|'dn.|w.lmd h.|bn.špš.|[w 1049.1.5
.l kl.|apnk.ǵzr.ilḥu.|[m]rḥ h.yiḫd.b yd.|[g]rgr h.bm.ymn.|[w]yqrb.trẓẓ h.|[---].mǵy h.w ǵlm.|[a]ḫt h.šib.yṣat. 16.1[125].48
'n.yṭpn[.mhr].|št.qḥn.w tšqyn.yn.qḥ.|ks.b d y.qb't.b ymn y[.t]q|ḥ.pǵt.w tšqyn h.tq[ḥ.ks.]b d h.|qb't.b ymn h.w 19[1AQHT].4.216
p.|ydrm.|ydy.|ydlm.|y'ḏrd.|yrmt.|yyn.|yn.|ydln.|ymn.|yṯky.|[y]rm. 112[16].13
m.|iǵlkḏ.|[i]ly[-]n.|[-----].|m[--.---].|[-]n.qrqr.|[--]n.ymn.y[--].|ilḫr.ṣdqn[.--]. 2022.25
n.iy[--].|bn.ḥ[---].|bn.plš.|bn.ubr.|bn.'pṯb.|ṯbry.|bn.ymn.|krty.|bn.abr[-].|yrpu.|kdn.|p'ṣ.|bn.liy.|yd'.|šmn.|' 2117.1.19
.ṯ]km.|'rb[.b ẓl.ḫmt].|qḥ im[r.b yd k].|imr.d[bḥ.bm].ymn.|lla.kl[atn]m.|klt.l[ḥm k.d]nzl.|qḥ.ms[rr.]'ṣr.|dbḥ.ṣ[14[KRT].2.67
.qdš.mnḥy k.ap.anš.zbl.b'[l].|[-.yuḫ]d.b yd.mšḫṭ.bm.ymn.mḫṣ.ǵlmm.yš[--].|[ymn h.'n]t.tuḫd.šmal h.tuḫd.'ttrt.i 2.1[137].39
a]rb' kkr 'l bn[.--].|[w] ṯlṯ šmn.|[w a]r[b'] ksp 'l bn ymn.|šb šr šmn [--] ṯryn.|ḫm[š]m l 'šr ksp 'l bn llit.|[--]l[-.- 1103.4
ǵpy ṯr.'n[.---].|b[b]r.mrḥ h.ti[ḫd.b yd h].|š[g]r h bm ymn.t[--.---].|[--.]l b'l.'bd[.---].|ṯr ab h il.ṯṯrm[.---].|tšlḥm y 2001.1.13

ymp

ryt.-]lnr.|spr.[--]ḥ[-] k.šb't.|ghl.ph.ṯmnt.|nblu h.špš.ymp.|hlkt.tdr[--].|špš.b'd h.t[--].|aṯr.aṯrm[.---].|aṯr.aṯrm[.- 27[8].4

ymrn

p h.w.a[r]b'.l.arb'[m.---].|pln.ṯmry.w.ṯn.bn h.w[.---].|ymrn.apsny.w.aṯt h..b[n.---].|prd.m'qby[.w.---.a]ṯt h[.---].| 2044.9

ymtšr

kd.šmn.ʿl.hbm.šlmy. | kd.šmn.ṯbil. | kd.šmn.ymtšr. | arbʿ.šmn.ʿl.ʿbdn.w.[---]. | kdm.šmn.ʿl.ilršp.bn[.---]. | k 1082.1.3

yn

-.arb]ʿ.yn. | [---].ṯmn.yn. | [---.-]ṯr.kdm.yn. | [-]dyn.arbʿ.yn. | abškn.kdm.yn. | šbn.kdm.yn. | ʿbdiltp.ṯm[n].y[n]. | qṣn.ḫ[1085.6
-]r. | l riš hm.w yš[--.--]m. | lḥm.b lḥm ay.w šty.b ḫmr yn ay. | šlm.mlk.šlm.mlkt.ʿrbm m.ṯnnm. | mt.w šr.yṯb.b d h. 23[52].6
. | mlkm.hn.ym.yṣq.yn.ṯmk. | mrṯ.yn.srnm.yn.bld. | ǵll.yn.išryt.ʿnq.smd. | lbnn.ṯl mrṯ.yḥrṯ.il. | hn.ym.w ṯn.tlḥmn.rp 22.2[124].19
yn.iš[ryt.-]lnr. | spr.[--]ḥ[-] k.šbʿt. | ghl.ph.ṯmnt. | nblu h.špš.y 27[8].1
r.bʿl.nrd. | b arṣ.ʿm h.trd.nrt. | ilm.špš.ʿd.tšbʿ.bk. | tšt.k yn.udmʿt.gm. | tṣḥ.l nrt.ilm.špš. | ʿms mʿ.l y.aliyn.bʿl. | tšmʿ.n 6[62].1.10
nm. | klt.lḥm h.d nzl. | lqḥ.msrr.ʿṣr.db[ḥ]. | yṣq.b gl.ḥṯt.yn. | b gl.ḫrṣ.nbt.w ʿly. | l ẓr.mgdl.rkb. | ṯkmm.ḥmt.nša. | [y]d 14[KRT].4.164
. | klt.l[ḥm k.d]nzl. | qḥ.ms[rr.]ʿṣr. | dbḥ.ṣ[q.b g]l.ḥṯt. | yn.b gl[.ḫ]rṣ.nbt. | ʿl.l ẓr.[mg]dl. | w ʿl.l ẓr.[mg]dl.rkb. | ṯkmm 14[KRT].2.72
[d]. | [dd.--]m.šbʿ.[---]. | [---].ʿšr.dd[.---]. | [---]mn.arbʿm.y[n]. | b.gt.trǵnds. | tšʿ.ʿšr.[dd].kšmm. | ṯn.ʿšr[.dd.ḥ]ṭm. | w.šb[2092.14
b.gt.ipṯl. | ṯmnym.[yn].ṭb.b.gt.š[---]. | tšʿm.[ḫ]mš[.kbd].yn.b gt[.-]n. | arbʿm.kbd.yn.ṭb.w.[--]. | ṯmn.kbd.yn.d.l.ṭb.b.gn 1084.21
it.ʿšr.[---.]dd[.--]. | tšʿ.dd.ḥ[ṭm.w].ḫm[šm]. | kdm.kbd.yn.b.gt.[---]. | [mi]tm.ḫmšm.ḫmš.k[bd]. | [dd].kšmm.tšʿ[.---]. 2092.5
šʿ[.---]. | [š]ʿrm.ṯṯ.ʿ[šr]. | [dd].ḥṭm.w.ḫ[mšm]. | [ṯ]lṯ kbd.yn.b [gt.---]. | mit.[---].ṯlṯ.kb[d]. | [dd.--]m.šbʿ.[---]. | [---].ʿšr.d 2092.10
šu.[r]iš.ḥrṭm. | l ẓr.ʿdb.dgn kly. | lḥm.[b]ʿdn hm.kly. | yn.b ḥmt hm.k[l]y. | šmn.b q[bʿt hm.---]. | bt.krt.t[--]. 16[126].3.15
m. | šbʿ yn. | l mrynm. | b yṯbmlk. | kdm.ǵbiš ḫry. | ḫmš yn.b d. | bḥ mlkt. | b mdrʿ. | ṯlṯ bt.il | ann. | kd.bt.ilann. 1090.14
ʿs[--]. | lḥm.hm.štym.lḥ[m]. | b ṯlḥnt.lḥm št. | b krpnm.yn.b k.ḫrṣ. | dm.ʿṣm.hm.yd.il mlk. | yḫss k.ahbt.ṯr.tʿrr k. | w t 4[51].4.37
. | w pq mrǵṯm.ṯd. | b ḥrb.mlḥt.qṣ[.m]r | i.tšty.krp[nm.y]n. | [b k]s.ḫrṣ.d[m.ʿṣm]. | [---.--]n. | [---.---]t. | [---.--]ṯ. | [---.--] 4[51].6.58
[---].ay š[---]. | [---.b ḥ]rb.mlḥ[t.qṣ]. | [mri.tšty.krpnm].yn.b ks.ḫ[rṣ]. | [dm.ʿṣm.---]n.krpn.ʿl.[k]rpn. | [---.]ym.w tʿl.trṯ 17[2AQHT].6.5
.w tp]q.mrǵṯm. | [ṯd.b ḥrb.m]lḥt.qṣ. | [mri.tšty.k]rpnm yn. | [b ks.ḫrṣ.dm].ʿṣm. 4[51].3.43
ʿ.yn. | šql ṯlṯ.yn. | šmny.kdm.yn. | šmgy.kd.yn. | hzp.tšʿ.yn. | [b]ir.ʿšr[.---]m ḥsp. | ḫpty.kdm[.---]. | [a]gm.arbʿ[.---]. | šr 2004.28
n.b qʿl.b qʿl. | mlkm.hn.ym.yṣq.yn.ṯmk. | mrṯ.yn.srnm.yn.bld. | ǵll.yn.išryt.ʿnq.smd. | lbnn.ṯl mrṯ.yḥrṯ.il. | hn.ym.w ṯ 22.2[124].18
-.]pd[ry]. | [-----]. | [---.b]ʿlt. | lbnm.ʿšr.yn. | ḫlb.gngnt.ṯlṯ.y[n]. | bṣr.ʿšr.yn. | nnu arbʿ.yn. | šql ṯlṯ.yn. | šmny.kdm.yn. | šm 2004.22
. | w.qpt.w.mqḥm. | w.ṯlṯm.yn šbʿ.kbd d ṭbt. | w.ḫmšm.yn.d iḫ h. 1103.23
yn.d.ykl.b d.[---]. | b.dbḥ.mlk. | dbḥ ṣpn. | [-]zǵm. | [i]lib. | [i]lb 2004.1
ʿ.kbd.yn.d.l.ṭb. | b.gt.mʿrby. | ṯṯm.yn.ṭb.w.ḫmš.l.ʿšrm. | yn.d.l.ṭb.b.ulm. | mit.yn.ṭb.w.ṯṯm.ṯṯ.kbd. | yn.d.l.ṭb.b.gt.ḥdṯt. 1084.10
[.kbd].yn.b gt[.-]n. | arbʿm.kbd.yn.ṭb.w.[--]. | ṯmn.kbd.yn.d.l.ṭb.b.gnʿ[y]. | mitm.yn.ḥsp.d.nkly.b.db[ḥ.--]. | mit.arbʿ 1084.23
w.ḫmšm.k[dm.]kbd.yn.d.l.ṭb. | b.gt.gwl. | ṯlṯm.tšʿ[.kbd.yn].d.l[.ṭb].b.gt.ipṯl. | ṯmnym.[yn].ṭb.b.gt.š[---]. | tšʿm.[ḫ]mš[. 1084.19
b.gt.sǵy. | arbʿm.kdm.kbd.yn.ṭb. | w.ḫmšm.k[dm.]kbd.yn.d.l.ṭb. | b.gt.gwl. | ṯlṯm.tšʿ[.kbd.yn].d.l[.ṭb].b.gt.ipṯl. | ṯmny 1084.17
ḫmš.l.ʿšrm. | yn.d.l.ṭb.b.ulm. | mit.yn.ṭb.w.ṯṯm.ṯṯ.kbd. | yn.d.l.ṭb.b.gt.ḥdṯt. | tšʿm.yn.d.l.ṭb.b.zbl. | ʿšrm.yn.ṭb.w.ṯṯm.ḫ 1084.12
. | yn.d.l.ṭb.gt.ṭbq. | mit.ʿšr.kbd.yn.ṭb. | w.ṯṯm.arbʿ.kbd.yn.d.l.ṭb. | b.gt.mʿrby. | ṯṯm.yn.ṭb.w.ḫmš.l.ʿšrm. | yn.d.l.ṭb.b.u 1084.7
tt. | tšʿm.yn.d.l.ṭb.b.zbl. | ʿšrm.yn.ṭb.w.ṯṯm.ḫmš.k[b]d. | yn.d.l.ṭb.b.gt.sǵy. | arbʿm.kdm.kbd.yn.ṭb. | w.ḫmšm.k[dm.]k 1084.15
lm. | mit.yn.ṭb.w.ṯṯm.ṯṯ.kbd. | yn.d.l.ṭb.b.gt.ḥdṯt. | tšʿm.yn.d.l.ṭb.b.zbl. | ʿšrm.yn.ṭb.w.ṯṯm.ḫmš.k[b]d. | yn.d.l.ṭb.b.gt.s 1084.13
rbʿm.yn.ḫlq.b.gt.sknm. | ʿšr.yn.ṭb.w.arbʿm.ḫmš.kbd. | yn.d.l.ṭb.gt.ṭbq. | mit.ʿšr.kbd.yn.ṭb. | w.ṯṯm.arbʿ.kbd.yn.d.l.ṭb 1084.5
ḫmš.ʿšr.yn.ṭb. | w.tšʿm.kdm.kbd.yn.d.l.ṭb. | w.arbʿm.yn.ḫlq.b.gt.sknm. | ʿšr.yn.ṭb.w.arbʿm.ḫm 1084.2
d.bn.š.[---.]yd.sǵr h. | [---.--]r h.ʿšr[m.---.ʿ]šrm.dd. | [---.yn.d.]nkly.l.rʿym.šbʿm.l.mitm.dd. | [---.--]d.šbʿm.kbd.drʿ. | [-- 1098.44
n.mṣrym. | arbʿm.yn. | l.ḫrd. | ḫmšm.ḫmš. | kbd.tgmr. | yn.d.nkly. 1089.15
ṯ[.--.yn.w ṯ]n.w nšt. | w ʿn hm.ngr mdrʿ[.iṯ.lḥm.---]. | iṯ.yn.d ʿrb.bṯk[.---]. | mǵ hw.l hn.lg yn h[.---]. | w ḥbr h.mla yn. 23[52].74
h.b glṯ.b šm[m]. | [---.i]l.ṯr.iṯ.p h.k ṯt.ǵlṯ[.--]. | [---.--] k yn.ddm.l b[--.---]. | [---.-]yṯ š[--.---]. | [---.]hl[-.---]. | [---.-]yṯr.u UG5.3.1.9
mdrʿ[.iṯ.lḥm.---]. | iṯ.yn.d ʿrb.bṯk[.---]. | mǵ hw.l hn.lg yn h[.---]. | w ḥbr h.mla yn.[---]. 23[52].75
yn. | nnu arbʿ.yn. | šql ṯlṯ.yn. | šmny.kdm.yn. | šmgy.kd.yn. | hzp.tšʿ.yn. | [b]ir.ʿšr[.---]m ḥsp. | ḫpty.kdm[.---]. | [a]gm.a 2004.27
--.]rḥbn.hm.[-.]aṯr[.---]. | [--]šy.w ydn.bʿ[l.---]n. | [--]ʿ.k yn.hm.l.atn.bt y.l h. 1002.62
. | w ʿl ym kdm. | w b ṯlṯ.kd yn w krsnm. | w b rbʿ kdm yn. | w b ḫmš kd yn. 1086.4
m. | w ʿrb.hm.hm[.iṯ.--.l]ḥm.w t[n]. | w nlḥm.hm.iṯ[.--.yn.w ṯ]n.w nšt. | w ʿn hm.ngr mdrʿ[.iṯ.lḥm.---]. | iṯ.yn.d ʿrb.bṯ 23[52].72
ym.prʿ d nkly yn kd w kd. | w ʿl ym kdm. | w b ṯlṯ.kd yn w krsnm. | w b rbʿ kdm yn. | w b ḫmš kd yn. 1086.3
spr[.---]. | ybnil[.---.]kd yn.w š. | spr.m[--]. | spr d[---]b.w š. | tt.ḫmš.[---]. | skn.ul[m.--- 1093.2
l aḫ h.l rʿ h. | rʿ ʿlm. | ttn.w tn. | w l ttn. | w al ttn. | tn ks yn. | w ištn. | ʿbd.prṯ.ṯḥm. | qrq.pt.ḏmn. | l iṯtl. 1019.1.15
.kbd.yn.ṭb.w.[--]. | ṯmn.kbd.yn.d.l.ṭb.b.gnʿ[y]. | mitm.yn.ḥsp.d.nkly.b.db[ḥ.--]. | mit.arbʿm.kbd.yn.ḥsp.l.m[--]. | mit 1084.24
[ḥ.--]. | mit.arbʿm.kbd.yn.ḥsp.l.m[--]. | mit.ʿšrm.[k]bd.yn.ḥsp.l.y[--]. | ʿšrm.yn.ḥsp.l.ql.d.tbʿ.mṣ[r]m. | mit.arbʿm.kbd 1084.26
nʿ[y]. | mitm.yn.ḥsp.d.nkly.b.db[ḥ.--]. | mit.arbʿm.kbd.yn.ḥsp.l.m[--]. | mit.ʿšrm.[k]bd.yn.ḥsp.l.y[--]. | ʿšrm.yn.ḥsp.l. 1084.25
bd.yn.ḥsp.l.m[--]. | mit.ʿšrm.[k]bd.yn.ḥsp.l.y[--]. | ʿšrm.yn.ḥsp.l.ql.d.tbʿ.mṣ[r]m. | mit.arbʿm.kbd.yn.mṣb. | l.mdrǵlm. 1084.27
piln. | [---].ṣmd[.---.]pd[ry]. | [-----]. | [---.b]ʿlt. | lbnm.ʿšr.yn. | ḫlb.gngnt.ṯlṯ.y[n]. | bṣr.ʿšr.yn. | nnu arbʿ.yn. | šql ṯlṯ.yn. | š 2004.21
ḫmš.ʿšr.yn.ṭb. | w.tšʿm.kdm.kbd.yn.d.l.ṭb. | w.arbʿm.yn.ḫlq.b.gt.sknm. | ʿšr.yn.ṭb.w.arbʿm.ḫmš.kbd. | yn.d.l.ṭb.gt.ṭ 1084.3
b.gt.gwl. | ṯlṯm.tšʿ[.kbd.yn].d.l[.ṭb].b.gt.ipṯl. | ṯmnym.[yn].ṭb.b.gt.š[---]. | tšʿm.[ḫ]mš[.kbd].yn.b gt[.-]n. | arbʿm.kbd. 1084.20
w.ṯṯm.ḫmš.k[b]d. | yn.d.l.ṭb.b.gt.sǵy. | arbʿm.kdm.kbd.yn.ṭb. | w.ḫmšm.k[dm.]kbd.yn.d.l.ṭb. | b.gt.gwl. | ṯlṯm.tšʿ[.kb 1084.16
bd.yn.ṭb. | w.ṯṯm.arbʿ.kbd.yn.d.l.ṭb. | b.gt.mʿrby. | ṯṯm.yn.ṭb.w.ḫmš.l.ʿšrm. | yn.d.l.ṭb.b.ulm. | mit.yn.ṭb.w.ṯṯm.ṯṯ.kbd 1084.9
m.kdm.kbd.yn.d.l.ṭb. | w.arbʿm.yn.ḫlq.b.gt.sknm. | ʿšr.yn.ṭb.w.arbʿm.ḫmš.kbd. | yn.d.l.ṭb.gt.ṭbq. | mit.ʿšr.kbd.yn.ṭb. 1084.4
ḫmš.ʿšr.yn.ṭb. | w.tšʿm.kdm.kbd.yn.d.l.ṭb. | w.arbʿm.yn.ḫlq.b.gt.skn 1084.1
ṯt.kbd. | yn.d.l.ṭb.b.gt.ḥdṯt. | tšʿm.yn.d.l.ṭb.b.zbl. | ʿšrm.yn.ṭb.w.ṯṯm.ḫmš.k[b]d. | yn.d.l.ṭb.b.gt.sǵy. | arbʿm.kdm.kbd. 1084.14
yn.ṭb.w.arbʿm.ḫmš.kbd. | yn.d.l.ṭb.gt.ṭbq. | mit.ʿšr.kbd.yn.ṭb. | w.ṯṯm.arbʿ.kbd.yn.d.l.ṭb. | b.gt.mʿrby. | ṯṯm.yn.ṭb.w.ḫ 1084.6
mʿrby. | ṯṯm.yn.ṭb.w.ḫmš.l.ʿšrm. | yn.d.l.ṭb.b.ulm. | mit.yn.ṭb.w.ṯṯm.ṯṯ.kbd. | yn.d.l.ṭb.b.gt.ḥdṯt. | tšʿm.yn.d.l.ṭb.b.zbl. 1084.11
.b.gt.š[---]. | tšʿm.[ḫ]mš[.kbd].yn.b gt[.-]n. | arbʿm.kbd.yn.ṭb.w.[--]. | ṯmn.kbd.yn.d.l.ṭb.b.gnʿ[y]. | mitm.yn.ḥsp.d.nkl 1084.22

.[b'l.w mnt k].|bt il.aḫd.yd k.b [škrn].|m'ms k.k šb't.yn.ṭ[ḥ].|gg k.b ym.ṭiṭ.rḥṣ.|npṣ k.b ym rṯ.b uni[l].|pnm.tšm 17[2AQHT].2.6
|ydn.|ytršp.|ydrm.|ydy.|ydlm.|y'ḏrd.|yrmt.|yyn.|yn.|ydln.|ymn.|yṯky.|[y]rm. 112[16].11
.--]n.|'n ha l yd h.tzd[.--].|pt l bšr h.dm a[--.--]ḥ.|w yn.k mtrḫt[.---]h.|šm' ilht kṯr[t.--]mm.|nh l yd h tzdn[.---] 24[77].10
[-] ym.pr' d nkly yn kd w kd.|w 'l ym kdm.|w b ṯlṯ.kd yn w krsnm.|w b rb' 1086.1
.dd.ṯn.kbd.|tgmr.ḥṭm.šb'.ddm.|ḫmš.dd.š'rm.|kdm.yn.|kdm.ṣmṣ. 1099.34
m.ktn.|ḫmšm.izml.|ḫmš.kbd.arb'm.|dd.akl.|ṯṯ.'šr h.yn.|kd.šmn.l.nr.ilm.|kdm.dǵm.|ṯṯ.kdm.ztm. 1126.5
ṯn.'šr.yn.[kps]lnm.|arb'.mat[.arb]'m.[k]bd.|d ntn.d.ksp.|arb'.l.ḫl 1087.1
ddm.l.gzzm.|kd yn.l.ḫtn.w.kd.ḥmṣ.w.[lt]ḥ.'šdm.|kd yn.l.ḫdǵb.w.kd.ḥmṣ.|prš.glbm.l.bt.|tgmǵ.kšmm.b.yrḫ.iṯtbn 1099.28
|kd.mštt.mlk.|kd.bn.amht [-]t.|w.bn.mṣrym.|arb'm.yn.|l.ḫrd.|ḫmšm.ḫmš.|kbd.tgmr.|yn.d.nkly. 1089.11
.š'rm.l.ḥmr.ḥṭb.|dd.ḥṭm.l.ḫdǵb.|ṯṯ.ddm.l.gzzm.|kd yn.l.ḫtn.w.kd.ḥmṣ.w.[lt]ḥ.'šdm.|kd yn.l.ḫdǵb.w.kd.ḥmṣ.|p 1099.27
kd.l.annṯb.|kd.l.iwrmḏ.|kd.l.ydn.|[---.y]rḫ.ḫyr.|[---.]yn.l.mlkt.|[---.yrḫ.]ḫlt.šb'.[---].mlkt.|[---.yrḫ.]gn.šb'[.--].|[- 1088.12
ḫdh.|kd l kblbn.|kdm.mṯḫ.|l.alṯy.|kd.l mrynm.|šb' yn.|l mrynm.|b yṯbmlk.|kdm.ǵbiš ḫry.|ḫmš yn.b d.|bḥ ml 1090.10
arb'.yn.l.mrynm.ḫ[--].kl h.|kdm.l.zn[-.---].|kd.l.aṯr[y]m.|kdm.' 1089.1
].|[---.--]b[.---].|[---.]y[--.-]kzn.|[---.]yn.l.m[---].|[---.]yn.l.m[--]m.|[---.]d.bn.[---.]l.dqn.|[---.--]'.šdyn.l ytršn.|[---. 2027.2.6
b[.---].|[---.--]l[.--].|[---.--]b[.---].|[---.]y[--.-]kzn.|[---.]yn.l.m[---].|[---.]yn.l.m[--]m.|[---.]d.bn.[---.]l.dqn.|[---.--]'.š 2027.2.5
kd.yn.|l prṯ. 159[59].1
b yrḫ.[---].|šb'.yn[.---].|mlkt[.---].|kd.yn.l.[---].|armwl w [--].|arb'.yn.[--].|l adrm.b[--].|šqym. 1092.4
šb'.yn.l [---].|ṯlṯ.l ḥr[š.---].|ṯṯ[.l.]mštt[.---].|ṯlṯ.l.mḏr[ǵlm].|kd[. 1091.1
k.[pǵt].|bat.b hlm w y'n.yṯpn[.mhr].|šṯ.qḥn.w tšqyn.yn.qḥ.|ks.b d y.qb't.b ymn y[.t]q|ḥ.pǵt.w tšqyn h.tq[ḥ.ks.] 19[1AQHT].4.215
l.y[--].|'šrm.yn.ḥsp.l.ql.d.tb'.mṣ[r]m.|mit.arb'm.kbd.yn.mṣb.|l.mḏrǵlm.|'šrn 'šr.yn.mṣb.[-]ḥ[-].l.gzzm. 1084.28
'.mṣ[r]m.|mit.arb'm.kbd.yn.mṣb.|l.mḏrǵlm.|'šrn 'šr.yn.mṣb.[-]ḥ[-].l.gzzm. 1084.30
--].|[---.b]'lt.|lbnm.'šr.yn.|ḫlb.gngnt.ṯlṯ.y[n].|bṣr.'šr.yn.|nnu arb'.yn.|šql ṯlṯ.yn.|šmny.kdm.yn.|šmgy.kd.yn.|h 2004.23
šrš.šb'.mṣb.|rqd.ṯlṯ.mṣb.w.[---].|uḫnp.ṯṯ.mṣb.|tgmr.[y]n.mṣb š[b'].|w ḥs[p] ṯn.k[dm]. 2004.35
niṣ h.grš d.'šy.ln h.|aḫd.yd h.b škrn.m'ms h.|[k]šb' yn.spu.ksm h.bt.b'l.|[w m]nt h bt.il.ṯḥ.gg h.b ym.|[ti]ṭ.rḥṣ. 17[2AQHT].1.32
lḥt.niṣ y.grš.|d 'šy.ln.aḫd.yd y.b š|krn m'ms y k šb't yn.|spu.ksm y.bt.b'l.[w]mn[t].|y.bt.il.ṯḥ.gg y.b ym.ṭiṭ.|rḥṣ 17[2AQHT].2.20
.|dpr.ṯlḥn.b q'l.b q'l.|mlkm.hn.ym.yṣq.yn.ṯmk.|mrṯ.yn.srnm.yn.bld.|ǵll.yn.išryt.'nq.smd.|lbnn.ṯl mrṯ.yḥrṯ.il.|h 22.2[124].18
]ṯr.kdm.yn.|[-]dyn.arb'.yn.|abškn.kdm.yn.|šbn.kdm.yn.|'bdiltp.ṯm[n].y[n].|qṣn.ḫ[---].|arny.[---].|aǵltn.ḫmš[.yn 1085.8
n.|špq.ilht.ksat[.yn].|špq.ilm.rḥbt yn.|špq.ilht.dkrt[.yn].|'d.lḥm.šty.ilm.|w pq mrǵtm.ṯd.|b ḥrb.mlḥt.qṣ[.m]r|i. 4[51].6.54
b il ab h.g'r.yṯb.il.kb[-].|aṯ[rt.]il.yṯb.b mrzḥ h.|yšt[.il.y]n.'d šb'.trṯ.'d škr.|il.hlk.l bt h.yštql.|l ḥṭr h.y'msn.nn.ṯk UG5.1.1.16
ṣd.ṣd.b qrb|hkl [h].ṣḥ.l qṣ.ilm.tlḥmn.|ilm.w tštn.tštn y[n] 'd šb'.|trṯ.'d.škr.y'db.yrḫ.|gb h.km.[---.]yqṯqṭ.ṯḥt.|ṯlḥ UG5.1.1.3
ḫd[.-].|tšm'.mṯt.[ḥ]ry.|ṭṭbḫ.šmn.[m]ri h.|t[p]ṯḥ.rḥbt.yn.|'l h.ṯr h.tš'rb.|'l h.tš'rb.ẓby h.|ṯr.ḫbr.rbt.|ḫbr.ṯrrt.|bt. 15[128].4.16
[-].|iy.aliyn.b'l.|iy.zbl.b'l.arṣ.|w t'n.nrt.ilm.š[p]š.|šd yn.'n.b qbt[.t]|bl lyt.'l.umt k.|w abqt.aliyn.b'l.|w t'n.btlt.'n 6[49].4.42
.|[dm.'ṣm.---]n.krpn.'l.[k]rpn.|[---.]ym.w t'l.trṯ.|[---].yn.'šy l ḥbš.|[---.]ḫtn.qn.yṣbt.|[---.--]m.b nši.'n h.w tphn.|[17[2AQHT].6.8
t.|[--]u.l tštql.|[---].ṭry.ap.l tlḥm.|[l]ḥm.trmmt.l tšt.|yn.tǵẓyt.špš.|rpim.ṯḥtk.|špš.ṯḥtk.ilnym.|'d k.ilm.hn.mtm.| 6.6[62.2].44
.hd.'m.ary y.|w lḥm m 'm aḫ y.lḥm.|w št m.'m.a[ḫ] yn.|p nšt.b'l.[t]'n.iṭ'n k.|[---.]ma[---] k.k tmḫṣ.|[ltn.bṯn.br] 5[67].1.25
.|špq.ilm.krm.y[n].|špq.ilht.ḫprt[.yn].|špq.ilm.alpm.y[n].|špq.ilht.arḫt[.yn].|špq.ilm.kḥṯm.yn.|špq.ilht.ksat[.yn 4[51].6.49
].|špq.ilm.kḥṯm.yn.|špq.ilht.ksat[.yn].|špq.ilm.rḥbt yn.|špq.ilht.dkrt[.yn].|'d.lḥm.šty.ilm.|w pq mrǵtm.ṯd.|b ḥ 4[51].6.53
h.a[r]y h.|b qrb hkl h.ṣḥ.|šb'm.bn.aṯrt.|špq.ilm.krm.y[n].|špq.ilht.ḫprt[.yn].|špq.ilm.alpm.y[n].|špq.ilht.arḫt[.y 4[51].6.47
špq.ilm.alpm.y[n].|špq.ilht.arḫt[.yn].|špq.ilm.kḥṯm.yn.|špq.ilht.ksat[.yn].|špq.ilm.rḥbt yn.|špq.ilht.dkrt[.yn].| 4[51].6.51
h.ṣḥ.|šb'm.bn.aṯrt.|špq.ilm.krm.y[n].|špq.ilht.ḫprt[.yn].|špq.ilm.alpm.y[n].|špq.ilht.arḫt[.yn].|špq.ilm.kḥṯm.y 4[51].6.48
|špq.ilht.ḫprt[.yn].|špq.ilm.alpm.y[n].|špq.ilht.arḫt[.yn].|špq.ilm.kḥṯm.yn.|špq.ilht.ksat[.yn].|špq.ilm.rḥbt yn.| 4[51].6.50
].|špq.ilht.arḫt[.yn].|špq.ilm.kḥṯm.yn.|špq.ilht.ksat[.yn].|špq.ilm.rḥbt yn.|špq.ilht.dkrt[.yn].|'d.lḥm.šty.ilm.|w 4[51].6.52
.bt].|mtnt.w ynt.[qrt.w ṯn.ḥṭm].|w bǵr.arb'.[---.kdm.yn].|prs.qmḥ.m'[--.---].|mdbḥt.bt.i[lt.'ṣrm.l].|ṣpn š.l ǵlm[t. APP.II[173].24
]bt.mtnt[.w ynt.qrt].|w ṯn ḥṭm.w bǵr.arb['.---].|kdm.yn.prs.qmḥ.[---].|mdbḥt.bt.ilt.'ṣr[m.l ṣpn.š].|l ǵlmt.š.w l [-- 35[3].23
k.yṣḥ].|šm'[.l mṯt.ḥry].|ṭbḫ.š[mn].mri k.|ptḥ.[rḥ]bt.yn.|ṣḥ.šb'm.ṯr y.|ṯmnym.[ẓ]by y.|ṯr.ḫbr[.rb]t.|ḫbr[.ṯrrt].|[15[128].4.5
.arb'.yn.|abškn.kdm.yn.|šbn.kdm.yn.|'bdiltp.ṯm[n].y[n].|qṣn.ḫ[---].|arny.[---].|aǵltn.ḫmš[.yn]. 1085.9
ṯmn.yn.|[---.-]ṯr.kdm.yn.|[-]dyn.arb'.yn.|abškn.kdm.yn.|šbn.kdm.yn.|'bdiltp.ṯm[n].y[n].|qṣn.ḫ[---].|arny.[---].| 1085.7
qrtm.|w.ṯn.irpm.w.ṯn.trqm.|w.qpt.w.mqḥm.|w.ṯlṯm.yn šb'.kbd d ṭbt.|w.ḫmšm.yn.d iḫ h. 1103.22
.y[n].|bṣr.'šr.yn.|nnu arb'.yn.|šql ṯlṯ.yn.|šmny.kdm.yn.|šmgy.kd.yn.|hzp.tš'.yn.|[b]ir.'šr[.---]m ḥsp.|ḫpty.kdm 2004.26
n.|ḫlb.gngnt.ṯlṯ.y[n].|bṣr.'šr.yn.|nnu arb'.yn.|šql ṯlṯ.yn.|šmny.kdm.yn.|šmgy.kd.yn.|hzp.tš'.yn.|[b]ir.'šr[.---]m 2004.25
lbnm.'šr.yn.|ḫlb.gngnt.ṯlṯ.y[n].|bṣr.'šr.yn.|nnu arb'.yn.|šql ṯlṯ.yn.|šmny.kdm.yn.|šmgy.kd.yn.|hzp.tš'.yn.|[b]i 2004.24
tq[ḥ.ks.]b d h.|qb't.b ymn h.w y'n.yṯ[p]n[.mh]r.|šṯ.b yn.yšt.ila.il š[--.]il.|d yqny.ḏdm.yd.mḫṣt.a[qh]t.ǵ|zr.tmḫṣ.a 19[1AQHT].4.219
.ḫrṣ.l 'brm.kš.|dpr.ṯlḥn.b q'l.b q'l.|mlkm.hn.ym.yṣq.yn.ṯmk.|mrṯ.yn.srnm.yn.bld.|ǵll.yn.išryt.'nq.smd.|lbnn.ṯl 22.2[124].17
[---.a]rb'.yn.|[---.arb]'.yn.|[---].ṯmn.yn.|[---.-]ṯr.kdm.yn.|[-]dyn.arb'.yn.|abškn.kdm.yn.|šbn.kdm.yn.|'bdiltp.ṯm 1085.5
.|[--]t.mlk.d.y[mlk].|[--.]'bdyrḫ.l.ml[k].|[--]t.w.lqḥ.|yn[.--].b dn h.|w.ml[k].ššwm.n'mm.|ytn.l.'bdyrḫ.|w.mlk.z 2064.15
'.yn[.---].|mlkt[.---].|kd.yn.l.[---].|armwl w [--].|arb'.yn.[--].|l adrm.b[--].|šqym. 1092.6
spr šd.ri[šym].|kr[-].šdm.'[--].|b gt ṯm[--] yn[.--].|[---].krm.b yp'l.y'dd.|[---.]krm.b [-]dn.l.bn.[-]kn.|š 2027.1.3
lpm.aršt.l k.w.l y.|mn.bnš.d.l.i[--].'[m k].|l.alpm.w.l.y[n.--]t.|w.bl.bnš.hw[-.--]y.|w.k.at.trg[m.--].|w.[---]n.w.s[-- 2064.25
[-----].|[ṭṭbḫ.šm]n.[mri h].|[tpṯḥ.rḥ]bt.[yn].|[---.]rp[.---].|[---.ḫ]br[.---].|bḫr[.--]t[.----].|l mṯb[.--]t[. 15[128].5.2
pq.mr[ǵtm.ṯd.---].|b ḥrb.[mlḥt.qṣ.mri].|šty.kr[pnm.yn.---].|b ks.ḫr[ṣ.dm.'ṣm.---].|ks.ksp[.---].|krpn.[---].|w ṯṯt 5[67].4.15
.---].|b[--.---].|l[--.---].|m[--.---].|bn[.---].|bn[.---].|w.yn[.---].|bn.'dr[.---].|ntb[t].|b.arb['].|mat.ḫr[ṣ]. 2007.8
b yrḫ.[---].|šb'.yn[.---].|mlkt[.---].|kd.yn.l.[---].|armwl w [--].|arb'.yn.[--]. 1092.2
[---.ṯl]š.yn.|[---.a]rb'.yn.|[---.arb]'.yn.|[---].ṯmn.yn.|[---.-]ṯr.kdm.y 1085.1

[---.ṯl]š.yn. | [---.a]rb'.yn. | [---.arb]'.yn. | [---].ṯmn.yn. | [---.-]ṯr.kdm.yn. | [-]dyn.arb'. 1085.2
.ttǵr. | [---.n]šr k.al ttn.l n. | [---.]tn l rbd. | [---.]b'lt h w yn. | [---.rk]b 'rpt. | [---.--]n.w mnu dg. | [---.]l aliyn b'l. | [---].r 2001.2.14
[---.ṯl]š.yn. | [---.a]rb'.yn. | [---.arb]'.yn. | [---].ṯmn.yn. | [---.-]ṯr.kdm.yn. | [-]dyn.arb'.yn. | abškn.kd 1085.3
[---.ṯl]š.yn. | [---.a]rb'.yn. | [---.arb]'.yn. | [---].ṯmn.yn. | [---.-]ṯr.kdm.yn. | [-]dyn.arb'.yn. | abškn.kdm.yn. | šbn.k 1085.4
---.--]rt.š'rt[.---]. | [---.i]qni.l.ṯr[mn.art.---]. | [b.yr]ẖ.riš.yn.[---]. | [---.b']lt.bhtm.š[--.---]. | [---.-]rt.l.dml[.---]. | [b.yrẖ]. 1106.32
. | [---].yrẖ.[---]. | [---].yrẖ.[---]. | [---].yrẖ.[---]. | [---.-]pd.yn.[---]. | [---.]yn[.---]. 1088.B.5
]. | [---].yrẖ.[---]. | [---].yrẖ.[---]. | [---.-]pd.yn.[---]. | [---.]yn[.---]. 1088.B.6
d 'rb.bṯk[.---]. | mǵ hw.l hn.lg yn h[.---]. | w ḥbr h.mla yn.[---]. 23[52].76
[---.']ṯtry. | [-----.]yn. | [----.-]mn. | [---.--]m.mṣl. | [---].prš.ḥtm. | ṯlṯ[.---].bn.ṯdny 1146.2
w b ṯlṯ.kd yn w krsnm. | w b rb' kdm yn. | w b ḫmš kd yn. 1086.5
'bdiltp.ṯm[n].y[n]. | qṣn.ẖ[---]. | arny.[---]. | aǵltn.ḫmš[.yn]. 1085.12

ynḥm

| bn.pdǵy.mḫdy. | bn.yyn.mdrǵl. | bn.'lr. | ḫtpy.adddy. | ynḥm.adddy. | ykny.adddy. | m[--].adddy. | yp'.adddy. | abǵl. 2014.21
a[---]. | rbil.[---]. | kdyn.[---.-]gṯ. | šmrm.a[ddd]y.tb[--]. | ynḥm.adddy. | ǵdǵd.adddy. | sw.adddy. | ildy.adddy. | gr'.add 2014.30
yn. | grgš. | b[n.]tlš. | dmr. | mkrm. | 'zn. | yplṭ. | 'bdmlk. | ynḥm. | adddn. | mtn. | plsy. | qṭn. | ypr. | bn.ymy. | bn.'rd. | [-]b. 1035.4.6
l ym hnd. | iwr[k]l.pdy. | agdn.bn.nrgn. | w ynḥm.aẖ h. | w.b'ln aẖ h. | w.ḥṯtn bn h. | w.btšy.bt h. | w.ištr 1006.4
[-----]. | [-----]. | ynḥm. | iḫy. | bn.mšt. | 'psn. | bn.ṣpr. | kmn. | bn.ršp. | tmn. | šm 1047.3
[sp]r.bnš.ml[k.d.b] d adn['m]. | [---].riš[.---].kt. | [y]nḥm. | ilb'l. | 'bdyr[ẖ]. | ṯtpḥ. | artn. | ybnil. | brqn. | adr[dn]. | 1024.1.3
.l.u[--]ṯtb. | kṯ[r]n. | w.aṯt h.w.n'r h. | bn.ḫby.w.[a]ṯt h. | ynḥm.ulmy. | [--]q.w.aṯt h.w.bn h. | [--]an.w.aṯt h. | [--]y.w.aṯ 2068.5
ddy. | gln.aṯṯ. | ddy.[a]dddy. | bn.mlkr[šp]. | bn.y[k]n. | ynḥm. | bn.abd.b'[l]. | mnḥm.bn[.---]. | krmn[py]. | bn.[--]m. | b 2014.47
n.iln. | [--]nn bn.ibm. | [-]n bn.ḥrn. | [š]mmn bn.gmz. | [yn]ḥm bn.ilmd. 2087.15
]kran.ḫmš. | '[---].kd. | amry.kdm. | mnn.bn.gṯtn.kdm. | ynḥm.bn[.-]r[-]t.ṯlṯ. | plwn.kdm. | tmyn.bn.ubrš.kd. 136[84].10
]. | ilb'l[.---]. | ḫluy.bn[.---]. | ymil.bn.[---]. | dly.bn[.---]. | ynḥm.bn[.---]. | gn.bn[.---]. | klby.[bn.---]. | šmmlk bn[.---]. | ' 102[322].5.6
d.abmn. | šir.šd.krm. | d.yrmn. | šir.[š]d.mlṯḥ.šd.'šy. | d.ynḥm. | tgmr.šd.ṯlṯm.šd. | w.tr[--.---]. 1079.15
d.'bdil. | ṯlṯ.'l.bn.srt. | kd.'l.ẓrm. | kd.'l.šz.bn pls. | kd.'l.ynḥm. | tgrm.šmn.d.bn.kwy. | 'l.šlmym.ṯmn.kbd. | ṯtm.šmn. 1082.2.7
grgš. | w.lmd h. | aršmg. | w.lmd h. | iyṯr. | [w].lmd h. | [yn]ḥm. | [w.]lmd h. | [i]wrmẖ. | [w.]lmd h. 1048.7
rtn.š'rt. | lmd.n.rn. | [---].ḫpn. | dqn.š'rt. | [lm]d.yrṯ. | [-.]ynḥm.ḫpn. | ṯt.lmd.b'ln. | l.qḥ.ḫpnt. | ṯt[.-]l.md.'ṯtr[t]. | l.qḥ.ẖ 1117.16
š[p.msg]. | pyn.yny.[msg]. | bn.mṣrn m[sg]. | yky msg. | ynḥm.msg. | bn.ugr.msg. | bn.ǵlṣ msg. | arb' l ṯkṣ[-]. | nn.arspy 133[-].1.7
mšu. | ḫtpy. | ǵldy. | iḫǵl. | aby. | abmn. | ynḥm. | npl. | ynḥm. | mtb'l. | bn ǵlmn. | bn sgld. 1065.9
mšu. | ḫtpy. | ǵldy. | iḫǵl. | aby. | abmn. | ynḥm. | npl. | ynḥm. | mtb'l. | bn ǵlmn. | bn sgld. 1065.7
l'. | bn.ysd.qšt. | [ǵ]mrm. | ilgn.qšt. | abršp.qšt. | ssg.qšt. | ynḥm.qšt. | pprn.qšt. | uln.qšt. | bn.nkl qšt. | ady.qšt. | bn.srn.q 105[86].3
. | šd.bn.li[y]. | šd.bn.š[--]y. | šd.bn.ṯ[---]. | šd.'dmn[.bn.]ynḥm. | šd.bn.ṯmr[n.m]idḫy. | šd.ṯb'm[.--]y. 2026.8
d]qn.'bdilt.b'l. | annmn.'dy.klby.dqn. | ḥrṯm.ḥgbn.'dn.ynḥm[.---]. | ḥrš.mrkbt.'zn.[b]'ln.ṯb[--.-]nb.trtn. | [---]mm.klb 2011.27
---.]ksp.'l.bn[.---]. | [---].ksp[.---]. | [---.--]ir[.---]. | [---].'l.ynḥ[m]. | [---.]'l.ab.b[---]. | [---.]'l.'[--]. | [---.']'.'[--]. 1144.13

ynḥn

n.arš[w.b]ṣry. | bn.ykn. | bn.lṣn.'rmy. | bn.b'yn.šly. | bn.ynḥn. | bn.'bdilm.hzpy. 99[327].2.5

yny

n. | [-]bdy. | [b]'ln. | [-]šdm. | iwryn. | n'mn. | [-----]. | b gt.yny. | agtṯp. | bn.'nt. | ǵzldn. | ṯrn. | ḫdbṭ. | [-]ḫl.aǵltn. | [-]n. | [-] 1043.10
t.inn. | b d.tlmyn. | b d.gln.ary. | tgyn.y'rty. | bn.krwn.b.yny.iytlm. | šgryn.ary.b.yny. | bn.yddn.b.rkby. | agyn.agny. | ṯ 2071.5
n.kdrn. | 'rgzy.w.bn.'dy. | bn.gmḥn.w.ḥgbt. | bn.tgdn. | yny. | [b]n.g'yn dd. | [-]n.dd. | [--]an dd. | [-----]. | [-----]. 131[309].30
n.ary. | tgyn.y'rty. | bn.krwn.b.yny.iytlm. | šgryn.ary.b.yny. | bn.yddn.b.rkby. | agyn.agny. | ṯqbn.mldy. 2071.6
[y-]n. | yny. | ydn. | ytršp. | ydrm. | ydy. | ydlm. | y'drd. | yrmt. | yyn. | y 112[16].2
bn.gnb[.msg]. | bn.twyn[.msg]. | bn.'drš[p.msg]. | pyn.yny.[msg]. | bn.mṣrn m[sg]. | yky msg. | ynḥm.msg. | bn.ugr. 133[-].1.4
.b.šql. | arb'.bnšm.b.nni. | ṯn.bnšm.b.slẖ. | [---].bnšm.b.yny. | [--.]bnšm.b.lbnm. | arb'.bnšm.b.ypr. | [---.]bnšm.b.šbn. | 2076.20

ynm

nmw. | l yarš ḫswn. | ḫmš 'šr.sp. | l bnš tpnr d yaḫd l g ynm. | ṯt spm l tgyn. | arb' spm l ll[-]. | ṯn spm.l slyy. | ṯlṯ spm 137.2[93].11

ynq

.klat. | tqtnṣn.w tldn.tld.[ilm.]n'mm.agzr ym. | bn.ym.ynqm.b a[p.]d[d.r]gm.l il.ybl. | aṯt y.il.ylt.mh.ylt.ilmy n'mm 23[52].59
t[.---]. | [b]n.šrm. | iqran.ilm.n'mm[.agzry ym.bn]ym. | ynqm.b ap zd.aṯrt.[---]. | špš.mṣprt dlt hm[.---]. | w ǵnbm.šl 23[52].24
il.ybl. | aṯt y.il.ylt.mh.ylt.ilmy n'mm. | agzr ym.bn ym.ynqm.b ap.dd.št.špt. | l arṣ.špt l šmm.w 'rb.b p hm.'ṣr.šmm. 23[52].61
r k.tld.šb'.bnm.l k. | w ṯmn.ṯtmnm. | l k.tld.yṣb.ǵlm. | ynq.ḥlb.a[ṯ]rt. | mṣṣ.ṯd.btlt.['nt]. | mšnq.[---]. 15[128].2.26
[.--].arḫ.. | b'l.azrt.'nt.[-]ld. | kbd h.l yd' hr h.[---]d[-]. | tnq[.---.]in[b]b.p'r. | yd h[.--.]ṣ'r.glgl. | a[---]m.rḥ.ḥd '[r]pt. | g 13[6].32
m. | l k.tld.yṣb.ǵlm. | ynq.ḥlb.a[ṯ]rt. | mṣṣ.ṯd.btlt.['nt]. | mšnq.[---]. 15[128].2.28

ynt

[rr]. | b ym.mlat. | tqln.alpm. | yrẖ.'šrt.l b'[l]. | dqtm.w ynt.qr[t]. | w mtntm.š l rmš. | w kbd.w š.l šlm kbd. | alp.w š.l UG5.13.6
ym.ml]at.y[ql]n.al[p]m.yrẖ.'šrt. | [l b'l.ṣ]pn.[dq]tm.w y[nt] qrt. | [w mtmt]m.[š.l] rm[š.]kbd.w š. | [l šlm.kbd.al]p.w 36[9].1.12
| d yqḥ bt[.--]r.dbḥ[.šmn.mr]. | šmn.rqḥ[.-]bt.mtnt[.w ynt.qrt]. | w ṯn ḥtm.w bǵr.arb['.---]. | kdm.yn.prs.qmḥ.[---]. | 35[3].21
ṯlṯm.w m'rb[.---]. | dbḥ šmn mr[.šmn.rqḥ.bt]. | mtnt.w ynt.[qrt.w ṯn.ḥtm]. | w bǵr.arb'.[---.kdm.yn]. | prs.qmḥ.m'[--. APP.II[173].23
'.w mḥ-.---]. | ym.[']lm.y'[--.---]. | [--.-]g[-.-]s w [---]. | w yn[t.q]rt.y[---]. | w al[p.l]il.w bu[rm.---]. | ytk.gdlt.ilhm.[ṯkm 35[3].10

--.---.]w q[--].|ym.ʿlm.y[---.---].|t.k[-]ml.[---].|l[---].w y[nt.qrt.---].|[---.--]n[.w alp.l il.w bu]|[rm.---.ytk.gdlt.ilhm] APP.II[173].11
dqt.ṯʿ.ynt.ṯʿm.dqt.ṯʿm.|mtntm nkbd.alp.š.l il.|gdlt.ilhm.ṯkmn.w š 34[1].1

ysd

qblbl.|ʿln.ybl hm.ḫrṣ.|ṯlḥn.il.d mla.|mnm.dbbm.d |msdt.arṣ.|sʿ.il.dqt.k amr.|sknt.k ḥwt.yman.|d b h.rumm.l 4[51].1.41
ps.|[--]ṯb.|[--]ln.|[---]r.|[---]y.|bn.adḏt.|bn.atnb.|bn.yšd.|bn.bršm.|bn.gṯprg.|gṯpbn.|bn.b[--].|[b]n.[---].|bn.a[-- 1057.10
.ḫrṣ.|bn.ilbʿl.|bn.idrm.|bn.grgš.|bn.bly.|bn.apṯ.|bn.ysd.|bn.pl[-].|bn.ṯbʿnq.|brqd.|bnn.|kbln.ṣ[md].|bn gmrt.| 2113.12
[-----].|[bn.]ibln.|ysd.|bn.ṯmq.|bn.agmn.|bn.uṣb.|bn.yzg.|bn.anntn.|bn.kw 115[301].4.2
.|[---.--]dn.|[---.--]dd.|[---.--]n.kb|[--.---.]al.yns.|[---.]ysd k.|[---.--]r.dr.dr.|[---.--]y k.w rḥd.|[---]y ilm.d mlk.|y[ṯ 4[51].3.6
w.qlʿ.|bn.zry.q[š]t.w.qlʿ.|bn.tlmyn.ṯt.qštm.w.qlʿ.|bn.ysd.qšt.|[ǵ]mrm.|ilgn.qšt.|abršp.qšt.|ssg.qšt.|ynḥm.qšt.|p 104[316].9

ysm

ln.ʿr.|bkm.tṣmd.pḥl.bkm.|tšu.ab h.tštnn.l[b]mt ʿr.|l ysmsm.bmt.pḥl.|y dnil.ysb.palt h.|bṣql.yph.b palt.bṣ[q]l.|y 19[1AQHT].2.60
b.gpn.atnt h.|yḥbq.qdš.w amrr.|yštn.aṯrt.l bmt.ʿr.|l ysmsmt.bmt.pḥl.|qdš.yuḫdm.šbʿr.|amrr.k kbkb.l pnm.|aṯr 4[51].4.15
iqra.ilm.n[ʿmm.---].|w ysmm.bn.š[---].|ytnm.qrt.l ʿly[.---].|b mdbr.špm.yd[.---.---]r 23[52].2
ry.|nʿmt.špḥ.bkr k.|d k.nʿm.ʿnt.nʿm h.|km.tsm.ʿṯtrt.ts[m h].|d ʿq h.ib.iqni.ʿp[ʿp] h.|sp.ṯrml.ṯḥgrn.[-]dm[.-].|ašl 14[KRT].3.146
y.|nʿmt.šbḥ.bkr k.|d k nʿm.ʿnt.|nʿm h.km.tsm.|ʿṯtrt.tsm h.|d ʿq h.ib.iqni.|ʿpʿp h.sp.ṯrml.|d b ḥlm y.il.ytn.|b ḏrt 14[KRT].6.293
.|w tʿn.arḫ.w tr.b lkt.|tr.b lkt.w tr.b ḫl.|[b]nʿmm.b ysmm.ḥ[--]k.ǵrt.|[ql].l bʿl.ʿnt.ttnn.|[---].bʿl m.d ip[---].|[il.] 10[76].2.30
ʿnt.hlkt.w.šnwt.|tp.aḫ.h.k.ysmsm.|tspi.šir.h.l.bl.ḥrb.|tšt.dm.h.l.bl.ks.|tpnn.ʿn.bṯy.ʿn.b RS225.2
bʿ.b bt h.|kṯrt.bnt.hll.snnt.|[-]d[-]t.nʿm y.ʿrš.h[--]m.|ysmsmt.ʿrš.ḫlln.[-].|yṯb.dnil.[l s]pr yrḫ h.|yrs.y[---.]y[--] h. 17[2AQHT].2.42
.l y.mṯt.ḥry.|nʿmt.špḥ.bkr k.|d k.nʿm.ʿnt.nʿm h.|km.tsm.ʿṯtrt.ts[m h].|d ʿq h.ib.iqni.ʿp[ʿp] h.|sp.ṯrml.ṯḥgrn.[-]d 14[KRT].3.146
l y.mṯt.ḥry.|nʿmt.šbḥ.bkr k.|d k nʿm.ʿnt.|nʿm h.km.tsm.|ʿṯtrt.tsm h.|d ʿq h.ib.iqni.|ʿpʿp h.sp.ṯrml.|d b ḥlm y.il 14[KRT].6.292
.|[---]l[.---.]ʿd.|ksm.mhyt[.m]ǵny.|l nʿm y.arṣ.dbr.|l ysmt.šd.šḥlmmt.|mǵny.l bʿl.npl.l a|rṣ.mt.aliyn.bʿl.|ḫlq.zbl. 5[67].6.7
l kbd.arṣ.kl.gbʿ.|l [k]bd.šdm.tmǵ.l nʿm[y].|[arṣ.]dbr.ysmt.šd.|[šḥ]lmmt.t[mǵ.]l bʿl.np[l].|[l a]rṣ[.lpš].tks.miz[rt 5[67].6.29
npš.ḫsrt.|bn.nšm.npš.hmlt.|arṣ.mǵt.l nʿm y.arṣ.|dbr.ysmt.šd.šḥlmmt.|ngš.ank.aliyn bʿl.|ʿdbnn ank.imr.b p y.|k 6[49].2.20
l.ẓ[--.---].|l np ql.nd.[----].|tlk.w tr.b[ḫl].|b nʿmm.b ys[mm.---].|arḫ.arḫ.[---.tld].|ibr.tld[.l bʿl].|w rum.l[rkb.ʿr 10[76].3.19

ysr

.|yṯb.l ksi mlk.|l nḫt.l kḥṯ.drkt.|ap.yṣb.yṯb.b hkl.|w ywsrnn.ggn h.|lk.l ab k.yṣb.lk.|l[ab]k.w rgm.ʿny.|l k[rt.a 16.6[127].26
š[t].|ʿzn.bn.brn.ḫmšt.|mʿrt.ḫmšt.|arttb.bn.ḫmšt.|bn.ysr[.ḫmš]t.|ṣ[-]r.ḫ[mšt].|ʿzn.ḫ[mšt]. 1062.29
n.aṯrt.|w tʿn.rbt.aṯrt ym.|rbt.ilm.l ḥkmt.|šbt.dqn k.l tsr k.|rḫntt.d[-].l irt k.|wn ap.ʿdn.mṭr h.|bʿl.yʿdn.ʿdn.ṯkt.b 4[51].5.66

yšd

ps.|[--]ṯb.|[--]ln.|[---]r.|[---]y.|bn.adḏt.|bn.atnb.|bn.yšd.|bn.bršm.|bn.gṯprg.|gṯpbn.|bn.b[--].|[b]n.[---].|bn.a[-- 1057.10

yʿbdr

klt.knyt.|mṯb.pdry.b ar.|mẓll.ṭly.bt rb.|mṯb.arṣy.bt.yʿbdr.|ap.mṯn.rgmm.|argm k.šskn mʿ.|mgn.rbt.aṯrt ym.| 4[51].1.19
.klt.knyt.|mṯb.pdry.bt.ar.|mẓll.ṭly.bt rb.|mṯb.arṣ.bt yʿbdr.|w yʿn lṭpn il d pid.|p ʿbd.an.ʿnn.aṯrt.|p.ʿbd.ank.aḫd. 4[51].4.57
.ym].|mṯb.pdr[y.bt.ar.mẓll].|ṭly.bt.r[b.mṯb.arṣy].|bt.yʿbdr[.mṯb.klt].|knyt.w tʿn[.btlt.ʿnt].|yṯb l y.ṯr.il[.ab y.---].| 3[ʿNT.VI].4.5
ym.mṯb.[pdr]y.bt.ar.|[mẓll.]ṭly[.bt.]rb.mṯb.|[arṣy.bt.yʿbdr.mṯb].|[klt.knyt]. 3[ʿNT.VI].5.51
d.aliyn.|bʿl.yd.pdry.bt.ar.|ahbt.ṭly.bt.rb.dd.arṣy.|bt.yʿbdr.km ǵlmm.|w ʿrb n.l pʿn.ʿnt.hbr.|w ql.tštḥwy.kbd hyt. 3[ʿNT].3.5
yn.bʿl].|[ahb]t pdr[y.bt.ar.ahbt.ṭly.bt.rb.dd].|arṣy bt.y[ʿbdr.---].|rgm l btl[t.ʿnt.ṯny.l ybmt.limm.tḥm.aliyn.bʿl].|h 7.2[130].12

yʿby

ubrʿy.|arny.|mʿr.|šʿrt.|ḫlb rpš.|bqʿt.|šḥq.|yʿby.|mḫr. 65[108].8

yʿdd

[m].|bn.ḥgb[n].|bn.ulbt[-].|ḏkry[-].|bn.tlm[yn].|bn.yʿdd.|bn.idly[-].|bn.ʿbd[--].|bn.ṣd[qn]. 2017.6
yʿdd.tḥt.bn arbn.|ʿbdil.tḥt.ilmlk.|qly.tḥt bʿln.nsk. 1053.1
].|kr[-].šdm.ʿ[--].|b gt ṯm[--] yn[.--].|[---].krm.b ypʿl.yʿdd.|[---.]krm.b [-]dn.l.bn.[-]kn.|šd[.---.-]ʿn.|šd[.---.-]ṣm.l. 2027.1.4

yʿḏr

šd.ubdy[.---].|šd.bn.ḫb[--.---].|šd.srn[.---].|šd.yʿḏr[.---].|šd.swr.[---].|šd.bn ppn[-.---].|šd.bn.uḫn[.---]. 83[85].4

yʿḏrd

spr.npš.d.|ʿrb.bt.mlk.|w.b.spr.l.št.|yrmʿl.|ṣry.|iršy.|yʿḏrd.|ayaḫ.|bn.aylt.|ḫmš.mat.arbʿm.|kbd.ksp.anyt.|d.ʿrb 2106.7
[y-]n.|yny.|ydn.|ytršp.|ydrm.|ydy.|ydlm.|yʿḏrd.|yrmt.|yyn.|yn.|ydln.|ymn.|yṯky.|[y]rm. 112[16].8
|mlknʿm.ʿšrm.|mrʿm.ʿšrm.|ʿmlbu.ʿšrm.|ʿmtḏl.ʿšrm.|yʿḏrd.ʿšrm.|gmrd.ʿšrm.|ṣdqšlm.ʿšr[m].|yknil.ḫmš.|ilmlk.ḫ 1116.9
šd.bn.šty.l.bn.ṭbrn.|šd.bn.ḫtb.l bn.yʿḏrd.|šd.gl.bʿlz.l.bn.ʿmnr.|šd.knʿm.l.bn.ʿmnr.|šd.bn.krwn. 2089.2

yʿḏrn

[-----].|w.lmd h.|mtn.|w.lmd h.|ymn.|w.lmd h.|yʿḏrn.|w.lmd h.|ʿdn.|w.lmd h.|bn.špš.|[w.l]m[d h].|yṣ[--- 1049.1.7
ʿ[l.---].|iḫyn.[---].|ʿbdbʿ[l.---].|uwil[.---].|ušry[n.---].|yʿḏrn[.---].|[ʿ]bdyr[ḫ.---].|[---]mlk[.---].|[-----].|ilbʿl[.---].|ḫl 102[322].2.10

yʿl

bʿl.|[ṯṭb]ḫ.šbʿm.aylm.|[k gmn.]aliyn.bʿl.|[ṯṭbḫ.š]bʿm.yʿlm.|[k gmn.al]iyn.bʿl.|[ṯṭbḫ.šbʿm.]ḥmrm.|[k gm]n.al[i]yn 6[62].1.26
yy.šʿrty.|aryn.adḏdy.|agpṯr.|šbʿl.mlky.|nʿmn.mṣry.|yʿl.knʿny.|gdn.bn.umy.|knʿm.šʿrty.|abrpu.ubrʿy.|b.gt.bn.ṯl 91[311].7

ǵzr.adr.ṯqbm. | [d]lbnn.adr.gdm.b rumm. | adr.qrnt.b y'lm.mtnm. | b 'qbt.ṯr.adr.b ǵlil.qnm. | tn.l kṯr.w ẖss.yb'l.qšt 17[2AQHT].6.22

y'ny

. | izly. | uẖnp. | bn sẖrn. | m'qb. | ṯpn. | m'r. | lbnm. | nẖl. | y'ny. | atn. | utly. | bn.alz. | bn ẖlm. | bn.ḏmr. | bn.'yn. | ubnyn. | 2075.12
m.l.mit.dr'.w.šb'm.drt. | w.'šrm.l.mit.dd.ḥpr.bnšm. | b.y'ny.arb'm.dr'.w.'šrm.drt. | w.ṯlṯm.dd.ṯṯ.kbd.ḥpr.bnšm. | b.'n 1098.26
[aḥd.al]p.d aǵlmn. | [d aẖd b.g]t gbry. | [---].aḥd.aẖd.b.y'ny. | [---.-]ḥm.b.aẖd.ḥrṯ. | [---.]aẖd.b.grn.uškn. | [---.]aẖd.ḥr 1129.14

y'r

nḏbn.sbd. | šrm.[---].ẖpn. | ḥrš[bhtm.--]n.'bdyrẖ.ḥdṯn.y'r. | adb'l[.---].ḥdṯn.yḥmn.bnil. | 'dn.w.ildgn.ḥṭbm. | tdǵlm.il 2011.18
l b'l. | ǵr.b ab.td[.ps]ltm[.b y'r]. | thdy.lḥm.w dqn[.ṯṯlṯ]. | qn.ḏr' h.ṯḥrṯ.km.gn. | ap lb.k ' 6[62].1.2
lṯt. | l qdqd h.lpš.yks. | mizrtm.ǵr.b abn. | ydy.psltm.b y'r. | yhdy.lḥm.w dqn. | yṯlṯ.qn.ḏr' h.yḥrṯ. | k gn.ap lb.k 'mq. 5[67].6.18
n. | rḥq[.---.td']. | qdm ym.bmt.[nhr]. | ṯṭṯn.ib.b'l.tiẖd. | y'rm.šnu.hd.gpt. | ǵr.w y'n.aliyn. | b'l.ib.hdt.lm.ṯḥš. | lm.ṯḥš.n 4[51].7.36

y'rn

.ql'. | [-]lrš.qšt.w.ql'. | t[t]n.qšt.w.ql'. | u[l]n.qšt.w.ql'. | y'rn.qšt.w.ql'. | klby.qšt.w.ql'. | bq't. | ily.qšt.w.ql'. | bn.ḥrẓn.q 119[321].2.18
n.gṯrn.q[š]t. | bn.ẖdi.ṯt.qštm.w.ṯn.ql'm. | ildgn.qšt. | bn.y'rn.ṯt.qštm w.ql'. | bn.ḥṣn.qšt.w.ql'. | bn.gdn.ṯt.qštm.w.ql'. | 119[321].3.10

y'rt

]. | [---]. | [---]. | mid[-]. | ubš. | mṣb[t]. | ẖl.y[---]. | 'rg[z]. | y'r[t]. | amḏ[y]. | atl[g]. | bṣr[y]. | [---]. | [---]y. | ar. | agm.w.ẖpty 71[113].42
r. | arny. | š'rt. | ẖlbrpš. | hry. | qmṣ. | ṣ'q. | qmy. | ẖlbkrd. | y'rt. | uškn. | 'nqpat. | ilštm'. | šbn. | ṭbq. | rqd. | šrš. | gn'y. | m'qb 2074.18
zy. | [--]yn.b.glltky. | td[y]n.b.glltky. | lbw[-].uẖ.pdm.b.y'rt. | pǵyn.b.ṭpẖ. | amri[l].b.šrš. | aǵltn.b.midẖ. | [--]n.b.ayly. | 2118.10
.arr. | arb'.bnšm.b.mnt. | arb'.bnšm.b.irbn. | ṯn.bnšm.b.y'rt. | ṯn.bnšm.b.'rmt. | arb'.bnšm.b.šrš. | ṯṯ.bnšm.b.mlk. | arb'. 2076.35

y'rty

[---.--]r. | [--.]iln. | y'rtym. | bn.gṯrn. | bq'ty. 100[66].3
--]. | aǵltn.mid[-.---]. | bn.lṣn.'rm[y]. | aršw.bṣry. | arpṯr.y'rty. | bn.ẖdyn.ugrty. | bn.tgḏn.ugrty. | tgyn.arty. | bn.nryn.a 87[64].7
mḏrǵlm.dt.inn. | b d.tlmyn. | b d.gln.ary. | tgyn.y'rty. | bn.krwn.b.yny.iytlm. | šgryn.ary.b.yny. | bn.yddn.b.rk 2071.4
.kbln. | bn.ǵlm.dd. | bn.tbšn.dd. | bn.ẖran.w[.---]. | [-]n.y'rtym. | gmm.w.bn.p[--]. | trn.w.p[-]y. | bn.b'yn.w.agytn. | [-- 131[309].9
. | ẖmn. | [---.-]rsd. | bn[.-]pṯ. | bn kdrn. | awldn. | arswn.y'r[ty.--]. | bn.ugr. | gny. | ṯn.mdm. 86[305].10

y'š

m.b'l. | šnt.'m.bn il.tspr.yrẖm. | k b'l.k yḥwy.y'šr.ḥwy.y'š. | r.w yšqyn h.ybd.w yšr.'l h. | n'm[n.w t]'nynn.ap ank.aḥ 17[2AQHT].6.30

yǵl

l.y[ḥb]q. | w ynšq.aḥl.an bṣ[ql]. | ynp'.b palt.bṣql yp' b yǵlm. | ur.tisp k.yd.aqht. | ǵzr.tšt k.b qrb m.asm. | y.dnh.ysb. 19[1AQHT].2.65
.pḥl. | y dnil.ysb.palt h. | bṣql.yph.b palt.bṣ[q]l. | yph.b yǵlm.bṣql.y[ḥb]q. | w ynšq.aḥl.an bṣ[ql]. | ynp'.b palt.bṣql yp 19[1AQHT].2.63

yp

.pamt.šb'.klb h. | yr[--.]mlk.ṣbu.špš.w.ḥl.mlk. | w.[---].ypm.w.mḥ[--].t[ṯ]ṯbn.[-]. | b.[--].w.km.iṯ.y[--.]šqm.yd[-]. 35[3].54
.ul[p.ǵbr.]ulp. | ẖbt km.ulp.m[dl]l km.ulp.qr zbl.u[š]n yp km. | u b ap km.u b q[ṣ]rt.npš km.u b qṭt.tqṭṭ. | ušn yp k 32[2].1.22
npy.yman.w npy.'rmt.w npy.[---]. | w npy.nqmd.ušn.yp km.ulp.q[ṭy.ulp.ddm]y. | ulp.ẖry.ulp.ẖ[t]y.ulp.alṭy.ul[p.ǵ 32[2].1.20
[ḥmyt.ugrt.w npy.yman.w npy.'r]mt.w npy. | [---.ušn.yp km.ulp.]qṭy. | [ulp.ddmy.ulp.ẖry.ulp.ẖty.u]lp.alṭy. | [ulp. APP.I[-].1.14
. | [ulp.ǵbr.ulp.ẖbt km.ulp.mdll km.ulp]. | [qr zbl.ušn.yp km.b ap km.u b qṣrt.np]št km. | [u b qṭt.tqṭṭ.ušn.yp km.- APP.I[-].1.17
p km. | u b ap km.u b q[ṣ]rt.npš km.u b qṭt.tqṭṭ. | ušn yp km.l d[b]ḥm.w l.ṯ'.dbḥ n.ndbḥ.hw.ṯ' | nṯ'y. | hw.nkt.nkt. 32[2].1.24
n.yp km.b ap km.u b qṣrt.np]št km. | [u b qṭt.tqṭṭ.ušn.yp km.---.-]yt km. | [---.]km. | [-----]. | [---.]ugrt. | [---].l.lim. | [- APP.I[-].1.18
.alṭy.ulp.ǵbr.ul]p.ẖbt kn. | [ulp.mdll kn.ulp.qr zbl.ušn.y]p kn. | [u b ap kn.u b qṣrt.npšt kn.u b qṭ]t tqṭṭ. | [ušn.yp kn APP.I[-].1.6
y]. | [ulp.ǵbr.ulp.ẖbt kn.ulp.mdll kn.ulp.]qr zbl. | [ušn.yp kn.u b ap kn.u b qṣrt.npš kn.u b]qṭt. | [tqṭṭn.ušn.yp kn.-- APP.I[-].2.15
.w n]py.yman. | [w npy.'rmt.---.w]npy.annpdgl. | [ušn.yp kn.ulp.qṭy.ulp.]ddmy.ulp ẖry. | [ulp.ẖty.ulp.alṭy.ulp.ǵbr. APP.I[-].1.4
--.t'ḏ]r b'l. | [-----]. | [-----]. | [---.--]r. | [---.]npy. | [---.ušn.yp kn.ulp.q]ṭy. | [ulp.ddmy.ulp.ẖry.ulp.ẖty.ulp.alṭy]. | [ulp.ǵ APP.I[-].2.12
[šr] mšr.bt.ugrt.w npy.gr. | ḥmyt.ugrt.w [np]y.nṯt.ušn.yp kn.ulp qṭy. | ulp.ddmy.ul[p.ẖ]ry.ulp.ẖty.ulp.alṭy. | ulp.ǵbr 32[2].1.28
. | ulp.ǵbr.ulp.[ẖbt] kn[.u]lp.mdll kn.ulp qr z[bl]. | lšn yp kn.b ap [kn.u b qṣ]rt.npš kn.u b qṭt. | tqṭṭn.ušn y[p kn.l d 32[2].1.31
lšn yp kn.b ap [kn.u b qṣ]rt.npš kn.u b qṭt. | tqṭṭn.ušn y[p kn.l dbḥm.]w l ṯ' dbḥ n. | ndbḥ.hw.ṯ' n[ṯ'y.hw.nkt.nk]t.y 32[2].1.32
.yp kn.u b ap kn.u b qṣrt.npš kn.u b]qṭt. | [tqṭṭn.ušn.yp kn.---.-]gym. | [---.]l kbkb. | [-----]. APP.I[-].2.16
]p kn. | [u b ap kn.u b qṣrt.npšt kn.u b qṭ]t tqṭṭ. | [ušn.yp kn.---.--]l.il.t'ḏr b'l. | [-----.]lšnt. | [---.--]yp.tḥt. | [-----]. | [--- APP.I[-].1.8

ypḥ

w.hm.al[-]. | l.tš'n. | mṣrm. | tmkrn. | ypḥ.'bdilt. | bn.m. | ypḥ.ilšlm. | bn.prqdš. | ypḥ.mnḥm. | bn.ḥnn. | brqn.spr. 2116.19
. | [aǵ]ltn. | tdn.bn.ddy. | 'bdil[.b]n ṣdqn. | bnšm.h[-]mt.ypḥm. | kbby.yd.bt.amt. | ilmlk. 2045.6
-]. | b ḥmṯ 'tr[.---]. | [-----]. | [---.-]y[-.---]. | w bn 'ṭl.[---]. | ypḥ kn'm[.---]. | aḥmn bt[.---]. | b ḥmṯ 'tr ṯmn[.---]. 207[57].9
rm. | tmkrn. | ypḥ.'bdilt. | bn.m. | ypḥ.ilšlm. | bn.prqdš. | ypḥ.mnḥm. | bn.ḥnn. | brqn.spr. 2116.21
. | w ẖrmṯt. | ṯlṯm.ar[b']. | kbd.ksp. | 'l.tgyn. | w 'l.aṯt h. | ypḥ.m'nt. | bn.lbn. 2053.22
]. | alp.k[sp]. | tš'n. | w.hm.al[-]. | l.tš'n. | mṣrm. | tmkrn. | ypḥ.'bdilt. | bn.m. | ypḥ.ilšlm. | bn.prqdš. | ypḥ.mnḥm. | bn.ḥn 2116.17
y[.---] | [---.]pẖyr.bt h.[---]. | [ẖm]šm.ksp.'l.gd[--]. | [---].ypḥ.'bdršp.b[--.--]. | [ar]b't.'šrt.kbd[.---]. | [---.-]rwd.šmbnš[.- 1144.5

ypẖ

dbḥ. | [--]r bt [--]. | [--]bnš [--]. | š š[--]. | w [--]. | d [--]. | ypẖ[--]. | w s[--]. | [---]. | qrd ga[n.--]. | b bt k.[--]. | w l dbḥ[--]. RS61[24.277.18]

ypy

.uškny. | bn.arz.š'rty. | bn.ibrd.m'rby. | ṣdqn.gb'ly. | bn.ypy.gb'ly. | bn.grgs.ilštm'y. | bn.ḫran.ilštm'y. | bn.abd'n.ilštm 87[64].28
bn.ǵlmn.ary. | [bn].šdy. | [bn].gmḫ. | [---]ty. | [b]n.ypy.gb'ly. | b[n].ḥyn. | ḏmn.š'rty. | bn.arwdn.ilšt'y. | bn grgs. | 99[327].1.5

ypl̇ṭ

-]y. | yr[---]. | ḫdyn. | grgš. | b[n.]tlš. | ḏmr. | mkrm. | 'zn. | yplṭ. | 'bdmlk. | ynḥm. | aḏddn. | mtn. | plsy. | qṭn. | ypr. | bn.ym 1035.4.4
[---.]yplṭ. | [---].l.[-]npk. | [---.]l.bn.ydln. | [---].l.blkn. | [---].l.bn.k[-- 2136.1
[---.--]l[-.---]. | [---.]yplṭ[.---]. | [---.--]l.rb.kzym. | [---]y. | [-----]. | [-----]. | [--]dt.nsk. 1102.2

ypltn

spr.ḥrš. | qštiptl. | bn.anny. | ilṣdq. | ypltn.bn iln. | špšm.nsl h. | [-----]. 1037.5

ypln

pṯn.bn.ṯsq[-]. | mnn.bn.krmn. | bn.umḫ. | yky.bn.slyn. | ypln.bn.ylḥn. | 'zn.bn.mll. | šrm. | [b]n.špš[yn]. | [b]n.ḫrmln. | 85[80].1.8
. | bn.iyṯr. | [']bdyrḫ. | [b]n.gg't. | [']dy. | armwl. | uwaḫ. | ypln.w.ṯn.bn h. | ydln. | anr[my]. | mld. | krmp[y]. | bṣmn. 2086.8

ypltn

bnš.kld. | kbln.'bdyrǵ.ilgt. | ǵyrn.ybnn qrwn. | ypltn.'bdnt. | klby.aḥrṯp. | ilyn.'lby.ṣdkn. | gmrt.ṯlmyn. | 'bdnt 1045.4

yp'

py.aḏddy. | ynḥm.aḏddy. | ykny.aḏddy. | m[--].aḏddy. | yp'.aḏddy. | abǵl.aḏ[ddy]. | abǵl.a[---]. | rbil.[---]. | kḏyn.[---.-] 2014.24
ṯ mat. | 'bdilm.ṯṯ mat. | šmmn.bn.'dš.ṯṯ mat. | ušknym. | yp'.alpm. | aḫ[m]lk.bn.nskn.alpm. | krw.šlmy. | alpm. | atn.bṣr 1060.2.2
at.yp't.b[--.---]. | aliyn.b'l[.---]. | drkt k.mšl[-.---]. | b riš k.aymr[. 2.1[137].3
udn h.grš h.l ksi.mlk h. | l nḫt.l kḥṯ.drkt h. | mn m.ib.yp'.l b'l.ṣrt.l rkb.'rpt. | [-]'n.ǵlmm.y'nyn.l ib.yp'. | l b'l.ṣrt.l r 3['NT].4.48
.anš.dt.ẓr h.tšu. | g h.w tṣḥ.ik.mǵy.gpn.w ugr. | mn.ib.yp'.l b'l.ṣrt. | l rkb.'rpt.l mḫšt.mdd. | il ym.l klt.nhr.il.rbm. | l 3['NT].3.34
mn m.ib.yp'.l b'l.ṣrt.l rkb.'rpt. | [-]'n.ǵlmm.y'nyn.l ib.yp'. | l b'l.ṣrt.l rkb.'rpt. | ṯḥm.aliyn.b'l.hwt.aliy. | qrdm.qry.b 3['NT].4.49
bnšm.dt.[---]. | krws.l.y[--.---]. | yp'.l[.---]. | šmr[m.---]. | [-----]. | bn.g[r.---]. | ḏmry[.---]. | bn.pd 2122.3
rš.ṯkt. | ilṯḥm.bn.šrn.ṯkt. | šmlbu.bn.grb.ṯkt. | šmlbu.bn.yp'.ṯkt. | [---.--]m. 2085.14
t.n[--.]t[--]. | [---.--]r.dlt.tḥt n. | [---.]dlt. | [---.b]nš. | [---.]yp'. | [---.]b[--]. 2158B.6
tn.[---]. | bn agyn[.---]. | b[n] 'tlt[.---]. | bn qṭy[.---]. | bn yp'[.---]. | [---]b'm[.---]. | [-----]. 105[86].5
. | mnṯ. | prḫ. | 'dršp. | ršpab. | ṯnw. | abmn. | abǵl. | b'ldn. | yp'. 1032.14

yp'b'l

ṯn. | rpty. | ilym. | bn.'br. | mnip'l. | amrb'l. | dqry. | ṯdy. | yp'b'l. | bdlm. | bn.pḏ[-]. | bn.[---]. 1058.19

yp'l

[šym]. | kr[-].šdm.'[--]. | b gt ṯm[--] yn[.--]. | [---].krm.b yp'l.y'dd. | [---.]krm.b [-]dn.l.bn.[-]kn. | šd[.---.-]'n. | šd[.---.-]ṣ 2027.1.4

yp'mlk

'rgm.skn.qrt. | ḥgbn.šm'.skn.qrt. | nǵr krm.'bdadt.b'ln.yp'mlk. | ṯǵrm.mnḥm.klyn.'dršp.ǵlmn. | [a]bǵl.ṣṣn.ǵrn. | šib. 2011.12

yp'n

w.aṯt h.w.bn h. | gpn.bn[.a]ly. | bn.rqd[y].ṯbg. | iḫmlk. | yp'n w.aṯt h. | anntn.yṣr. | annmn.w.ṯlṯ.n'[r] h. | rpan.w.ṯ[n.]b 2068.23
bd'nt.rb 'šrt.mnḥm.ṯb'm.sḫr.'zn.ilhd. | bnil.rb 'šrt.lkn.yp'n.ṯ[--]. | yṣḥm.b d.ubn.krwn.ṯǵd.[m]nḥm. | 'pṯrm.šm'rgm. 2011.8

yp'r

n.ibn.arb't.'šrt. | b.bn.mnn.ṯṯm. | b.rpan.bn.yyn.'šrt. | b.yp'r.'šrm. | b.n'mn.bn.ply.ḫmšt.l.'šrm. | b.gdn.bn.uss.'šrm. | b 2054.1.16

ypq

| 'd[--]. | ild[--]. | bn.qṣn. | 'lpy. | kṭy. | bn.ẓmn. | bn.trdn. | ypq. | 'bd. | qrḥ. | abšr. | bn.bdn. | ḏmry. | bn.pndr. | bn.aḫt. | bn. 2117.2.25

ypr

šrš. | lbnm. | ḫlb.krd. | ṣ'. | mlk. | gb'ly. | ypr. | ary. | ẓrn. | art. | ṯlḥny. | ṯlrby. | dmt. | aǵt. | w.qmnz. | slḫ. | 71[113].7
'zn. | yplṭ. | 'bdmlk. | ynḥm. | aḏddn. | mtn. | plsy. | qṭn. | ypr. | bn.ymy. | bn.'rd. | [-]b.da[-]. | [--]l[--]. | [-----]. 1035.4.11
. | ilštm'. | šbn. | ṯbq. | rqd. | šrš. | gn'y. | m'qb. | agm. | bir. | ypr. | hzp. | šql. | m'rḫ[-]. | sl[ḫ]. | snr. | 'rgz. | ykn'm. | 'nmky. | ǵ 2074.30
l]b'prm. | [q]dš. | [a]mḏy. | [gn]'y. | m'qb. | agm. | ḫpty. | ypr. | ḫrsb'. | uḫnp. | art. | [--]n. | [-----]. | [-----]. | nnu. | šmg. | šm 2058.2.4
at.ḫmš.'šr.ymm. | qmnz.yrḫ.w.ḫmš.ymm. | 'nmk.yrḫ. | ypr.yrḫ.w.ḫmš.ymm. 66[109].10
bn.'myn. | bdl.mrynm. | bn.ṣqn. | bn.šyn. | bn.prtn. | bn.ypr. | mrum. | bn.'[--]t. | bn.adty. | bn.krwn. | bn.nǵsk. | bn.qnḏ 113[400].3.10
mn. | [---].ṯlṯ. | [---].aḥd. | u[--].ṯn. | hz[p].ṯṯ. | ḫrṣb'.aḥd. | ypr.arb. | m[-]qb.'šr. | ṯn'y.ṯlṯ. | ḫlb 'prm.ṯn. | tmdy.ṯlṯ. | [--]rt.a 70[112].9
lḫ. | [---].bnšm.b.yny. | [--.]bnšm.b.lbnm. | arb'.bnšm.b.ypr. | [---.]bnšm.b.šbn. | [---.b]nšm.b.šmny. | [---.b]nšm.b.šmn 2076.22

ypry

rm[-.]b[n.---]. | annt[n.]w[.---]. | w.ṯn.bn h.[---]. | aǵltn.ypr[y.---]. | w.šb'.ṣin h[.---]. 2044.17

ypš

t.b lšn[y]. | ǵr[.---]b.b pš y.t[--]. | hwt.b'l.iš[--]. | šm' l y.ypš.[---]. | ḥkr[.---]. | 'ṣr[.--.]tb[-]. | ṯat[.---]. | yn[-.---]. | i[--.---]. 2124.5

ypt

[---.]arẖt.tld[n]. | a[lp].l btlt.ʻnt. | w ypt l ybmt.li[mm]. | w yʻny.aliyn[.bʻl]. | lm.k qnym.ʻl[m.--]. | 10[76].3.4
l ri[š.---]. | ypt.ʻṣ[--.---]. | p šlm.[---]. | bt k.b[--.--.m] | ǵy k[.---]. | bt.[---]. 58[20].2

ypṯ

]b.aliyn.bʻl. | ytʻdd.rkb.ʻrpt. | [--].ydd.w yqlṣn. | yqm.w ywpṯn.b tk. | p[ẖ]r.bn.ilm.štt. | p[--].b ṯlḥn y.qlt. | b ks.ištyn h 4[51].3.13
dr]y.bt ar. | [---.ṯl]y.bt.rb. | [---.m]dd.il ym. | [---.-]qlṣn.wpṯ m. | [---.]w yʻn.kṯr. | [w ẖss.]ṯṯb.bʻl.l hwt y. | [ḥš.]bht h.tb 4[51].6.13

yṣa

d n.km.mrm.tqrṣn. | il.yẓḥq.bm. | lb.w ygmḏ.bm kbd. | ẓi.at.l tlš. | amt.yrẖ. | l dmgy.amt. | aṯrt.qḥ. | ksan k.ḥdg k. | ḥt 12[75].1.14
gnryn. | l mlkytn. | ḥnn y l pn mlk. | šin k itn. | rʻ y šṣa idn l y. | l šmn iṯr hw. | p iḫdn gnryn. | im mlkytn yrgm. | 1020.5
bʻl.] | bṯ.l rkb.ʻrpt.k šby n.zb[l.ym.k] | šby n.ṯpṭ.nhr.w yṣa b[.--]. | ybṯ.nn.aliyn.bʻl.w [---]. | ym.l mt.bʻl m.ym l[--.--- 2.4[68].30
mt.yrẖ. | l dmgy.amt. | aṯrt.qḥ. | ksan k.ḥdg k. | ḥtl k.w ẓi. | b aln.tk m. | b tk.mlbr. | ilšiy. | kry amt. | ʻpr.ʻẓm yd. | ugr 12[75].1.19
[--]r.[---]. | [---.]il.[---]. | [ṯṣ]un.b arṣ. | mḫnm.ṯrp ym. | lšnm.tlḥk. | šmm.ṯṯrp. | ym.ḏnbt 1003.3
[-----]. | [--.]l ṯṣi.b b[--].bm.k[--]. | [--]ṯb.ʻryt k.k qlt[.---]. | [--]at.brt.lb k.ʻnn 60[32].2
ṯlṯ.d yṣa. | b d.šmmn. | l argmn. | l nskm. | ṯmn.kkrm. | alp.kbd. | [m 147[90].1
spr.npṣm.d yṣa.b milḫ. | ʻšrm.ḫpn.ḫmš. | kbd.w lpš. | ḫmš.mispt. | mṭ. | w l 1109.1
isp k.yd.aqht.ǵz[r]. | tšt k.bm.qrb m.asm. | b p h.rgm.l yṣa.b špt h[.hwt h]. | b nši ʻn h.w tphn.in.[---]. | [-.]hlk.ǵlmm 19[1AQHT].2.75
ṯ[.ʻẓm]. | abky.w aqbrn.ašt.b ḫrt. | i[lm.arṣ.b p h.rgm.l yṣa.b šp] | t h.hwt h.knp.hrgb.bʻl.ṯbr. | bʻl.ṯbr.diy.hwt.w yql. 19[1AQHT].3.127
. | ʻẓm.abky.w aqbrn h. | ašt.b ḫrt.ilm.arṣ. | b p h.rgm.l yṣa.b špt h.hwt[h]. | knp.nšrm.bʻl.yṯbr. | bʻl.ṯbr.diy hmt.tqln 19[1AQHT].3.113
| ʻẓm.abky w aqbrn h.aštn. | b ḫrt.ilm.arṣ.b p h.rgm.l[yṣ]a. | b špt h.hwt h.knp.ṣml.bʻ[l]. | bʻl.ṯbr.diy.hyt.tq[l.tḥt]. | p 19[1AQHT].3.141
ʻšrt.ḫrṣ.b.arbʻm. | mit.ḫršḫ.b.ṯqlm. | w.šbʻ.ʻšr.šmn. | d.l.yṣa.bt.mlk. | tgmr.ksp.mitm. | ḫmšm.kbd. 2100.21
.tša.g h[m.w tṣḥn]. | šmʻ.l dnil.[mt.rpi]. | mt.aqht.ǵzr.[šṣat]. | btlt.ʻnt.k [rḥ.npš h]. | k iṯl.brlt h.[b h.pʻnm]. | ṯṭṭ.ʻl[n.p 19[1AQHT].2.91
n. | kli. | plǵn. | apšny. | ʻrb[.---]. | w.b.p[.--]. | apš[ny]. | b.yṣi h. | ḥwt.[---]. | alp.k[sp]. | tšʻn. | w.hm.al[-]. | l.tšʻn. | mṣrm. | 2116.9
y h.w ǵlm. | [a]ḫt h.šib.yṣat.mrḥ h. | l tl.yṣb.pn h.tǵr. | yṣu.hlm.aḫ h.tph. | [ksl]h.l arṣ.ṯṯbr. | [---.]aḫ h.tbky. | [--.m]r 16.1[125].53
tphn.in.[---]. | [-.]hlk.ǵlmm b dd y.yṣ[--]. | [-.]yṣa.w l.yṣa.hlm.[ṯnm]. | [q]dqd.ṯlṯ id.ʻl.ud[n]. | [---.-]sr.pdm.riš h[m.- 19[1AQHT].2.78
[---.]y[--].ḫtt.mtt[--]. | [--.]ḥy[--.--.]l ašṣi.hm.ap.amr[--]. | [---].w b ym.mnḫ l abd.b ym.irtm.m[--] 2.4[68].2
ši ʻn h.w tphn.in.[---]. | [-.]hlk.ǵlmm b dd y.yṣ[--]. | [-.]yṣa.w l.yṣa.hlm.[ṯnm]. | [q]dqd.ṯlṯ id.ʻl.ud[n]. | [---.-]sr.pdm.r 19[1AQHT].2.78
. | inn.uṯpt. | w.ṯlṯ.ṣmdm.w.ḥrṣ. | apnt.b d.rb.ḥršm. | d.šṣa.ḥwy h. 1121.10
b yrḫ.mgm[r.---]. | yṣu.ḫlpn[.---]. | ṯlṯ.dt.p[--.---]. | dt.ṯgmi.[---]. | b d [---]t.[---]. 1159.2
y. | nbšr km.dnil.[--] h[.---]. | riš.r[--.--]ḥ[.---]y[.---.-]nt.[š]ṣat[k.]rḥ.npš.hm. | k.iṯl.brlt n[-.k qṭr.b ap -]. | tmǵyn.tša.g 19[1AQHT].2.87
m.qdqd. | ṯlṯ id.ʻl.udn.špk.km.šiy. | dm.km.šḫṭ.l brk h.ṯṣi.km. | rḥ.npš h.km.iṯl.brlt h.km. | qṭr.b ap h.b ap.mhr h.an 18[3AQHT].4.24
d]. | ṯlṯ id.ʻl.udn.š[pk.km]. | šiy.dm h.km.šḫ[ṭ.l brk h]. | yṣat.km.rḥ.npš[h.km.iṯl]. | brlt h.km.qṭr.[b ap h.---]. | ʻnt.b ṣ 18[3AQHT].4.36
ymn. | [w]yqrb.trẓẓ h. | [---].mǵy h.w ǵlm. | [a]ḫt h.šib.yṣat.mrḥ h. | l tl.yṣb.pn h.tǵr. | yṣu.hlm.aḫ h.tph. | [ksl]h.l ar 16.1[125].51
]dm.aḫt k. | ydʻt.k rḥmt. | al.tšt.b šdm.mm h. | b smkt.ṣat.npš h. | [-]mt[-].ṣba.rbt. | špš.w tgh.nyr. | rbt.w rgm.l aḫt 16.1[125].35
š. | [mǵ]d.ṯdt.yr[ḫm]. | ʻdn.ngb.w [yṣi.ṣbu]. | ṣbi.ng[b.w yṣi.ʻdn]. | mʻ[.ṣ]bu h.u[l.mad]. | ṯlṯ.mat.rbt. | hlk.l alpm.ḫḏd. | 14[KRT].4.177
ḫmš. | mǵd.ṯdt.yrḫm. | ʻdn.ngb.w yṣi. | ṣbu.ṣbi.ngb. | w yṣi.ʻdn.mʻ. | ṣbu k.ul.mad. | ṯlṯ.mat.rbt. | ḫpṯ.d bl.spr. | ṯnn.d b 14[KRT].2.87
lk b mdb[r.---]. | ṯḥdṯn w hl[.---]. | w tglṯ thmt.ʻ[--.---]. | yṣi.ǵl h tḥm b[.---]. | mrḥ h l adrt[.---]. | ṯṯb ʻṯrt b ǵl[.---]. | qr 2001.1.6
t.ḫbr. | yip.lḥm.d ḫmš. | [mǵ]d.ṯdt.yr[ḫm]. | ʻdn.ngb.w [yṣi.ṣbu]. | ṣbi.ng[b.w yṣi.ʻdn]. | mʻ[.ṣ]bu h.u[l.mad]. | ṯlṯ.mat.r 14[KRT].4.176
t.l bt.ḫbr. | yip.lḥm.d ḫmš. | mǵd.ṯdt.yrḫm. | ʻdn.ngb.w yṣi. | ṣbu.ṣbi.ngb. | w yṣi.ʻdn.mʻ. | ṣbu k.ul.mad. | ṯlṯ.mat.rbt. | 14[KRT].2.85
t.šrš.b qrb. | hkl h.nṣb.skn.ilib h.b qdš. | ztr.ʻm h.l arṣ.mšṣu.qṭr h. | l ʻpr.ḏmr.aṯr h.ṭbq.lḥt. | niṣ h.grš d.ʻšy.ln h. | aḫ 17[2AQHT].1.28
š.]b qrb.hkl h. | [nṣb.skn.i]lib h.b qdš. | [ztr.ʻm h.l a]rṣ.mšṣu. | [qṭr h.l ʻpr.ḏ]mr.a[ṯ]r h. | [ṭbq.lḥt.niṣ h.gr]š.d ʻšy. | [ln 17[2AQHT].1.46
h. | [ṭbq.lḥt.niṣ h.gr]š.d ʻšy. | [ln h.---]. | z[tr.ʻm k.l arṣ.mšṣu.qṭr k]. | l ʻpr.ḏm[r.aṯr k.ṭbq]. | lḥt.niṣ k.gr[š.d ʻšy.ln k]. 17[2AQHT].2.1
.b ʻmq.ṯḥtṣb.bn. | qrytm tmḫṣ.lim.ḫp y[m]. | tṣmt.adm.ṣat.š[p]š. | tḥt h.k kdrt.ri[š]. | ʻl h.k irbym.kp.k.qṣm. | ǵrmn.k 3[ʻNT].2.8
.sgr. | almnt.škr. | tškr.zbl.ʻršm. | yšu.ʻwr.mzl. | ymzl.w yṣi.trḫ. | ḥdṯ.ybʻr.l ṯn. | aṯt h.lm.nkr. | mddt h.k irby. | [t]škn.š 14[KRT].2.100
[.---]. | w yrdnn.an[--.---]. | [---].ank.l km[.---]. | l y.ank.ašṣu[.---.]w[.---]. | w hm.at.tr[gm.---]. | w.drm.ʻtr[--.---]. | w ap 54.1.17[13.2.2]
[y]ṣb.ʻln.w y[-]y. | [kr]t.ṯʻ.ʻln.bḫr. | [---].aṯt k.ʻl. | [---] k.yšṣi. | [---.]ḫbr.rbt. | [ḫbr.ṯrr]t.il d. | [pid.---].b anšt. | [---.]mlu. 15[128].5.24
gr[m]. | yṣa[.---]. | mšr[-]. | [-]b.m[--]. | b y[rḫ]. | pgr[m]. | yṣa[.---]. | lb[-.---]. | b d[.---]. 1158.2.3
b yr[ḫ]. | pgr[m]. | yṣa[.---]. | mšr[-]. | [-]b.m[--]. | b y[rḫ]. | pgr[m]. | yṣa[.---]. | lb[-. 1158.1.3
[.-.]b k[p]. | [---].tr[--.]gpn lk. | [---].km[-.---]. | [---.--]k yṣunn[.---]. | [---.--]dy.w.prʻ[.---]. | [---.]ytn.ml[--].ank.iphn. | [1002.34

yṣi

.ʻdd.nryn. | [ab]r[p]u.bn.kbd. | [-]m[-].bn.ṣmrt. | liy.bn.yṣi. | ḏmrhd.bn.srt. | [---.--]m. | ʻbdmlk.bn.šrn. | ʻbdbʻl.bn.kdn. 102[322].6.6

yṣb

ḥṯ.drkt. | ap.yṣb.yṯb.b hkl. | w ywsrnn.ggn h. | lk.l ab k.yṣb.lk. | l[ab]k.w rgm.ʻny. | l k[rt.adn k.]ištm[ʻ]. | w tqǵ[.udn 16.6[127].27
ṯn.yṯb.krt.l ʻd h. | yṯb.l ksi mlk. | l nḥt.l kḥṯ.drkt. | ap.yṣb.yṯb.b hkl. | w ywsrnn.ggn h. | lk.l ab k.yṣb.lk. | l[ab]k.w 16.6[127].25
tr.šrk.il. | ʻrb.špš.l ymǵ. | krt.ṣbia.špš. | bʻl ny.w ymlk. | [y]ṣb.ʻln.w y[-]y. | [kr]t.ṯʻ.ʻln.bḫr. | [---].aṯt k.ʻl. | [---] k.yšṣi. | [- 15[128].5.21
t.tšʻrb. | ḥqr k.tld.šbʻ.bnm.l k. | w ṯmn.ṯṯmnm. | l k.tld.yṣb.ǵlm. | ynq.ḥlb.a[ṯ]rt. | mṣṣ.ṯd.btlt.[ʻnt]. | mšnq.[---]. 15[128].2.25
. | anšt.ʻrš.zbln. | rd.l mlk.amlk. | l drkt.k aṯb.an. | ytbʻ.yṣb ǵlm.ʻl. | ab h.yʻrb.yšu g h. | w yṣḥ.šmʻ mʻ.l krt. | ṯʻ.ištmʻ.w 16.6[127].39

yṣbt

]rpn. | [---.]ym.w tʻl.trṯ. | [---].yn.ʻšy l ḥbš. | [---.]ḥtn.qn.yṣbt. | [---.--]m.b nši.ʻn h.w tphn. | [---.--]ml.ksl h.k b[r]q. | [-- 17[2AQHT].6.9

yṣḥ

t.mnḥm.ṯb'm.sẖr.'zn.ilhd. | bnil.rb 'šrt.lkn.yp'n.ṯ[--]. | yṣḥm.b d.ubn.krwn.tǵd.[m]nḥm. | 'pṯrm.šm'rgm.skn.qrt. | ḥ 2011.9
[šm]. | mru s[kn]. | mru ib[rn]. | mdm. | inšt. | nsk ksp. | yṣḥm. | ḥrš mrkbt. | ḥrš qṭn. | ḥrš bhtm. 73[114].7
'd[rš]p. | pqr. | ṯǵr. | ttǵl. | ṯn.yṣḥm. | slṯmg. | kdrl. | wql. | adrdn. | prn. | 'bdil. | ušy.šbn[-]. | a 1069.5
. | mẖrǵlm. | kzym. | mru.skn. | mru.ibrn. | pslm. | šrm. | yṣḥm. | 'šrm. | mrum. | ṯnnm. | mqdm. | khnm. | qdšm. | nsk.ksp 71[113].67
iršt.yṣḥm. | arb'.alpm. | mitm.kbd.ṯlṯ. | arb'.kkrm. | ṯmn.mat.kbd. 2051.1
. | 'šrm. | ṯnnm. | nqdm. | khnm. | qdšm. | pslm. | mkrm. | yṣḥm. | šrm. | n'rm. | 'bdm. | kzym. | ksdm. | [nsk].ṯlṯ. | gt.mlky 1026.1.10
gn. | [---.--]gbn. | [---.a]bṣdq. | [---.--]š. | [---.ṣ]dq. | tgmr. | yṣḥm. | ṯlṯm. | aḥd. | kbd. | bnš.mlk. 1055.2.2
[s]pr.ḥ[rš.---]. | [-]mn.n[--]. | ḥrš.d.[---]. | mrum.[---]. | yṣḥm[.---]. | mkrm[.---]. | pslm[.---]. 1038.5
[---.]mru ib[rn.---]. | [---.]yṣḥm[.---]. | [---.]'bd[m.---]. | [---.-]ẖy[-.---]. | [---.-]ml[-.---]. | [- 1027.2
. | mru.skn. | nsk.ksp | mẖṣm. | ksdm. | mḏrǵlm. | pslm. | yṣḥm. 74[115].19

yṣmẖ

[---]y. | [---.]w.nḥl h. | bn ksln.ṯlṯh. | bn yṣmẖ.bn.ṯrn w nḥl h. | bn srd.bn agmn. | bn [-]ln.bn.ṯbil. | bn 101[10].4

yṣq

w ykhp mid. | dblt yṯnt w ṣmqm yṯn[m]. | w qmḥ bql yṣq aḥd h. | b ap h. 160[55].25
l yẖru w]l yṯtn mss št qlql. | [w št 'rgz y]dk aḥd h w yṣq b ap h. | [k.yiḫd akl š]šw št mkšr grn. | [w št aškrr w p]r 160[55].9
t.mkš[r.grn]. | w.št.ašk[rr]. | w.pr.ḥḏr[t.ydk]. | aḥd h.w.yṣq[.b.ap h]. | k.yiḫd.akl.š[šw]. | št.nni.št.mk[št.grn]. | št.irǵn. 161[56].16
.l.yṯtn.ššw]. | mss.[št.qlql.w.št]. | 'rgz[.ydk.aḥd h]. | w.yṣq[.b.ap h]. | k.yiḫd[.akl.ššw]. | št.mkš[r.grn]. | w.št.ašk[rr]. | 161[56].11
r[.ydk]. | aḥd h.w.yṣq.b[.ap h]. | k.yraš.ššw.[št]. | bln.qṭ.yṣq.b.a[p h]. | k yg'r[.ššw.---]. | dprn[.---]. | dr'.[---]. | tmṯl[.---]. 161[56].22
k [ẖr ššw mǵmǵ]. | w [bṣql.'rgz.ydk]. | a[ḥd h.w.yṣq.b.ap h]. | k.[ẖr.ššw.ẖndrṯ]. | w.ṯ[qd.mr.ydk.aḥd h]. | w.y[ṣ 161[56].4
[p h]. | [k ẖr š]šw mǵmǵ w b[ṣql 'rgz]. | [ydk aḥ]d h w yṣq b ap h. | [k ẖr]ššw ẖndrṯ w ṯ[qd m]r. | [ydk aḥd h w yṣq 160[55].5
[k.---.]šš[w.---]. | [---.w]yṣq b a[p h]. | [k ẖr š]šw mǵmǵ w b[ṣql 'rgz]. | [ydk aḥ]d h w 160[55].3
.b.ap h]. | k.[ẖr.ššw.ẖndrṯ]. | w.ṯ[qd.mr.ydk.aḥd h]. | w.y[ṣq.b.ap h]. | k.l.ẖ[ru.w.l.yṯtn.ššw]. | mss.[št.qlql.w.št]. | 'rgz[161[56].7
q b ap h. | [k ẖr]ššw ẖndrṯ w ṯ[qd m]r. | [ydk aḥd h w yṣq b ap h. | [k l yẖru w]l yṯtn mss št qlql. | [w št 'rgz y]dk a 160[55].7
.pr.'bk]. | w.pr[.ḥḏrt.w.št]. | irǵ[n.ḥmr.ydk]. | aḥd[h.w.yṣq.b.ap h]. | k yr[a]š.šš[w.w.ykhp]. | mid.dblt.yṯ[nt.w]. | ṣmq 161[56].31
w]. | št.nni.št.mk[št.grn]. | št.irǵn.ḥmr[.ydk]. | aḥd h.w.yṣq.b[.ap h]. | k.yraš.ššw.[št]. | bln.qṭ.yṣq.b.a[p h]. | k yg'r[.šš 161[56].20
ḏrt. | [-----]. | [---.-]n[-]. | [k yraš ššw št bln q]ṭ ydk. | [w yṣq b ap h]. | [-----]. | [-----]. | [-----]. | [---.-]rb. | [-----]. | [-----]. | [160[55].15
.yṯ[nt.w]. | ṣmq[m].yṯnm.w[.qmḥ.bql]. | tdkn.aḥd h.w[.yṣq]. | b.ap h. 161[56].35
.rb'.ym.ẖmš. | ṯdṯ.ym.tlḥmn.rpum. | tštyn.bt.ikl.b pr'. | yṣq.b irt.lbnn.mk.b šb'. | [ymm.---]k.aliyn.b'l. | [---].r' h ab y 22.2[124].25
. | lla.kl[atn]m. | klt.l[ḥm k.d]nzl. | qḥ.ms[rr.]'ṣr. | dbḥ.ṣ[q.b g]l.ḥtṯ. | yn.b gl[.ẖ]rṣ.nbt. | 'l.l ẓr.[mg]dl. | w 'l.l ẓr.[mg] 14[KRT].2.71
h. | lla.klatnm. | klt.lḥm h.d nzl. | lqḥ.msrr.'ṣr.db[ḥ]. | yṣq.b gl.ḥtṯ.yn. | b gl.ẖrṣ.nbt.w 'ly. | l ẓr.mgdl.rkb. | ṯkmm.ḥ 14[KRT].4.164
m.zt.ẖrṣ.l 'brm.kš. | dpr.ṯlḥn.b q'l.b q'l. | mlkm.hn.ym.yṣq.yn.ṯmk. | mrṯ.yn.srnm.yn.bld. | ǵll.yn.išryt.'nq.smd. | lbn 22.2[124].17
. | hyn.'ly.l mpḥm. | b d.ẖss.mṣbṭm. | yṣq.ksp.yšl | ḥ.ẖrṣ.yṣq.ksp. | l alpm.ẖrṣ.yṣq | m.l rbbt. | yṣq-ẖym.w tbṯẖ. | kt.il.dt. 4[51].1.27
m. | mǵẓ.qnyt.ilm. | hyn.'ly.l mpḥm. | b d.ẖss.mṣbṭm. | yṣq.ksp.yšl | ḥ.ẖrṣ.yṣq.ksp. | l alpm.ẖrṣ.yṣq | m.l rbbt. | yṣq-ẖy 4[51].1.26
d.ẖss.mṣbṭm. | yṣq.ksp.yšl | ḥ.ẖrṣ.yṣq.ksp. | l alpm.ẖrṣ.yṣq | m.l rbbt. | yṣq-ẖym.w tbṯẖ. | kt.il.dt.rbtm. | kt.il.nbt.b ks 4[51].1.28
pn.il. | d pid.yrd.l ksi.yṯb. | l hdm[.w] l.hdm.yṯb. | l arṣ.yṣq.'mr. | un.l riš h.'pr.plṯt. | l qdqd h.lpš.yks. | mizrtm.ǵr.b a 5[67].6.14
.tšb'.tmtẖṣ.b bt. | ṯẖṣb.bn.ṯlḥnm.ymḥ. | [b]bt.dm.ḏmr.yṣq.šmn. | šlm.b ṣ'.trḥṣ.yd h.bt | [l]t.'nt.uṣb't h.ybmt.limm. | [3['NT].2.31
.---]. | [---.-]yṯr.ur[--.---]. | [---.n]skt.n'mn.nbl[.---]. | [--.]yṣq šmn.šlm.b ṣ['.trḥṣ]. | yd h.btlt.'nt.uṣb't[h.ybmt]. | limm.t UG5.3.2.4
[-----]. | yṣq.šm[n.---]. | 'n.tr.arṣ.w šmm. | sb.l qṣm.arṣ. | l ksm.mhyt.' 16[126].3.1

yṣr

.bn[.a]ly. | bn.rqd[y].ṯbg. | iẖmlk. | yp'n w.aṯt h. | anntn.yṣr. | annmn.w.ṯlṯ.n'[r] h. | rpan.w.ṯ[n.]bn h. | bn.ayln.w.ṯn.b 2068.24
. | ṯǵrm. | mru.skn. | mru.ibrn. | yqšm. | trrm. | kkrdnm. | yṣrm. | ktrm. | mṣlm. | tkn[m]. | ǵ[---]. | ǵm[--]. 1026.2.11
dm. | gt.mlkym. | yqšm. | kbšm. | trrm. | khnm. | kzym. | yṣrm. | mru.ibrn. | mru.skn. | nsk.ksp | mẖṣm. | ksdm. | mḏrǵl 74[115].11
. | bdn.š'rt. | 'pṯn.š'rt. | 'bd.yrẖ š'rt. | ẖbd.ṯr yṣr š'r. | pdy.yṣr š'rt. | atnb.ẖr. | š'rt.š'rt. 97[315].12
rt. | mnn.š'rt. | bdn.š'rt. | 'pṯn.š'rt. | 'bd.yrẖ š'rt. | ẖbd.ṯr yṣr š'r. | pdy.yṣr š'rt. | atnb.ẖr. | š'rt.š'rt. 97[315].11
.tlgn.ytn. | b'ltǵpṯm.krwn.ilšn.agyn. | mnn.šr.ugrt.ḏkr.yṣr. | tǵǵln.ẖmš.ddm. | [---].ẖmš.ddm. | ṯṯ.l.'šrm.bn[š.mlk.---]. 2011.37
lk.d.b.tbq. | [kr]wn. | [--]n. | [q]ṣy. | ṯn.bn.iwrẖz.[n]'rm. | yṣr[.-]qb. | w.ṯn.bnš.iytlm. | w.'šrm.ṣmd.alpm. 2066.2.5
[-]rm. | ['b]dm. | [yṣ]rm. | [-]qy[m]. 78[-].3
.[-----]. | w.abǵl.nẖ[l h.--]. | w.unṯ.aẖd.l h[.---]. | dnn.bn.yṣr[.---]. | sln.bn.'ṯt[-.---]. | pdy.bn.nr[-.---]. | abmlk.bn.un[-.--- 90[314].1.5
[-.---]. | aẖyn.bn.nbk[-.---]. | ršpn.bn.b'ly[.---]. | bnil.bn.yṣr[.---]. | 'dyn.bn.udr[-.---]. | w.'d'.nḥl h[.---]. | w.yknil.nḥl h[90[314].1.12
bn.'gw. | bn.urt. | aẖdbu. | pḥ[-]. | bn.'b . | bn.uḏn[-]. | bn.yṣr. 121[307].10
arb'.b.gt.b'ln. | 'št.'šr.b.gpn. | yd.'dnm. | arb'.ǵzlm. | ṯn.yṣrm. 2103.10

yṣt

'.tmtẖṣ.---]. | klyn[.---]. | špk.l[---]. | trḥṣ.yd[h.---]. | [--.]yṣt ḏm[r.---]. | tšt[.r]imt.[l irt h.tšr.l dd.aliyn.b'l]. | [ahb]t pdr 7.2[130].9

yqb

knt h.apnk.dnil.m[t]. | rpi.aphn.ǵzr.m[t]. | hrnmy.qšt.yqb.[--] | rk.'l.aqht.k yq[--.---]. | pr'm.ṣd k.y bn[.---]. | pr'm.ṣd 17[2AQHT].5.35

yqy

ṯr.ab h.il.ṯḥm.ym.b'l km. | [adn]km.ṯpṭ.nhr.tn.il m.d tq h.d tqyn h. | [hml]t.tn.b'l.w 'nn h.bn.dgn.arṯ m.pḏ h. | [w 2.1[137].34
ẖr]. | m'd.ṯḥm.ym.b'l km.adn km.ṯ[pṭ.nhr]. | tn.il m.d tq h.d tqyn.hmlt.tn.b'l.[w 'nn h]. | bn.dgn.arṯ m.pḏ h.tb'.ǵl 2.1[137].18

.il.ṯḥm.ym.bʻl km.|[adn]km.ṭpṭ.nhr.tn.il m.d tq h.d tqyn h.|[hml]t.tn.bʻl.w ʻnn h.bn.dgn.arṯ m.pḏ h.|[w yʻn.]ṯr. 2.1[137].34

ʻd.ṯḥm.ym.bʻl km.adn km.ṯ[pṭ.nhr].|tn.il m.d tq h.d tqyn.hmlt.tn.bʻl.[w ʻnn h].|bn.dgn.arṯ m.pḏ h.tbʻ.ǵlmm.l ṯṯ 2.1[137].18

yqǵ

k.yṣb.lk.|l[ab]k.w rgm.ʻny.|l k[rt.adn k.]ištm[ʻ].|w tqǵ[.udn.k ǵz.ǵzm].|tdbr.w[ǵ]rm[.ṯṯwy].|šqlt.b ǵlt.yd k.|l 16.6[127].30

.ʻl.|ab h.yʻrb.yšu g h.|w yṣḥ.šmʻ mʻ.l krt.|ṯʻ.ištmʻ.w tqǵ udn.|k ǵz.ǵzm.tdbr.|w ǵrm.ṯṯwy.šqlt.|b ǵlt.yd k.l tdn. 16.6[127].42

yqr

[---]n.yšt.rpu.mlk.ʻlm.w yšt.|[--.]gṯr.w yqr.il.yṯb.b.ʻṯtrt.|il.ṯpṭ.b hd rʻy.d yšr.w yḏmr.|b knr.w ṯlb.b UG5.2.1.2

yqš

[ʻ]b[dm].|ʻšrm.|inšt.|mdm.|gt.mlkym.|yqšm.|kbšm.|trrm.|khnm.|kzym.|yṣrm.|mru.ibrn.|mru.s 74[115].6

lkym.|tmrym.|ṯnqym.|ṯǵrm.|mru.skn.|mru.ibrn.|yqšm.|trrm.|kkrdnm.|yṣrm.|ktrm.|mṣlm.|tkn[m].|ǵ[---]. 1026.2.8

[---].|mtn[.---].|ṯdpṯn[.--].|tny[.--].|sll[.--].|mld[.--].|yqš[.--].|[-----].|inš[r.---].|ršp[.---].|iḫy[-.--].|iwr[--.--].|ʻd[- 1074.8

yr

m.rḥmy.w tṣd[.---].|ṯḥgrn.ǵzr.nʻm.[---].|w šm.ʻrbm.yr[.---].|mṯbt.ilm.ṯmn.ṯ[--.--].|pamt.šbʻ.|iqnu.šmt[.---].|[b] 23[52].18

yra

b.|[bʻ]l.b kbd h.b p h yrd.|k ḫrr.zt.ybl.arṣ.w pr.|ʻṣm.yraun.aliyn.bʻl.|ṯṯʻ.nn.rkb.ʻrpt.|tbʻ.rgm.l bn.ilm.mt.|ṯny.l y 5[67].2.6

k.l ysʻ.alt.|ṯbt k.l yhpk.ksa.mlk k.|l yṯbr.ḫṭ.mṯpṭ k.|yru.bn ilm t.ṯṯʻ.y|dd.il.ǵzr.yʻr.mt.|b ql h.y[---.---].|bʻl.yṯṯbn 6[49].6.30

y.|[--]ptm.ṣḥq.|[---.]rgm.hy.[-]ḫ[-]y.ilak k.|[---.--]g k.yritn.mǵy.hy.w kn.|[---].ḥln.d b.dmt.um.il[m.---].|[--]ḏyn.b 1002.42

yrbʻm

n.|bn.dll.|bn.ḫswn.|mrynm.|ʻzn.|ḥyn.|ʻmyn.|ilyn.|yrbʻm.|nʻmn.|bn.kbl.|knʻm.|bdlm.|bn.ṣǵr.|klb.|bn.mnḥ 1046.3.38

yrgb

p.|ʻnt ḫbly.|špš pgr.|iltm ḫnqtm.|yrḫ kṯy.|ygb hd.|yrgb bʻl.|ydb il.|yarš il.|yrǵm il.|ʻmtr.|ydb il.|yrgb lim.|ʻ UG5.14.B.2

.prln.rb.|khnm rb.nqdm.|ṯʻy.nqmd.mlk ugr[t].|adn.yrgb.bʻl.ṯrmn. 6.6[62.2].57

hd.|yrgb bʻl.|ydb il.|yarš il.|yrǵm il.|ʻmtr.|ydb il.|yrgb lim.|ʻmtr.|yarš il.|ydb bʻl.|yrǵm bʻl.|ʻz bʻl.|ydb hd. UG5.14.B.8

yrd

.|kst.l[--.---].|w.hw.uy.ʻn[--.---].|l ytn.w rgm[.---].|w yrdnn.an[--.---].|[---].ank.l km[.---].|l y.ank.ašṣu[.---.]w[.--- 54.1.15[13.1.12]

|ša.ǵr.ʻl.ydm.|ḫlb.l ẓr.rḥtm.|w rd.bt ḫpṯt.|arṣ.tspr.b y|rdm.arṣ.|idk.al.ttn.|pnm.tk.qrt h.|hmry.mk.ksu.|ṯbt h. 4[51].8.8

y.ša.ǵr.ʻl ydm.|ḫlb.l ẓr.rḥtm w rd.|bt ḫpṯt.arṣ.tspr b y|rdm.arṣ.w tdʻ ilm.|k mtt.yšmʻ.aliyn.bʻl.|yuhb.ʻglt.b dbr. 5[67].5.15

y.|bʻl.qrnm w ḏnb.ylšn.|b ḫri h.w ṯnt h.ql.il.[--].|il.k yrdm.arṣ.ʻnt.|w ʻṯtrt.tṣdn.[---].|[---.-]b[-.---].|[ʻt]trt w ʻnt[.-- UG5.1.1.22

u.g h.w yṣḥ.|bʻl.mt.my.lim.bn.|dgn.my.hmlt.aṯr.|bʻl.ard.b arṣ.ap.|ʻnt.ttlk.w tṣd.kl.ǵr.|l kbd.arṣ.kl.gbʻ.|l [k]bd.š 5[67].6.25

ʻmq.ṯṯlṯ.bmt.|bʻl.mt.my.lim.bn dgn.|my.hmlt.aṯr.bʻl.nrd.|b arṣ.ʻm h.trd.nrt.|ilm.špš.ʻd.tšbʻ.bk.|tšt.k yn.udmʻt.g 6[62].1.7

t.|šnt.tluan.|w yškb.nhmmt.|w yqmṣ.w b ḥlm h.|il.yrd.b ḏhrt h.|ab adm.w yqrb.|b šal.krt.m at.|krt.k ybky.|y 14[KRT].1.36

kḥ.ttrp.šmm.k rs.|ipd k.ank.ispi.uṯm.|ḏrqm.amt m.l yrt.|b npš.bn ilm.mt.b mh|mrt.ydd.il.ǵzr.|tbʻ.w l.yṯb ilm.i 5[67].1.6

y.ank.in.bt[.l] y[.km.]ilm[.w] ḥẓr[.k bn].|[qd]š.lbum.trd.b n[p]šn y.trḥṣn.k ṯrm.|[--]b b[ht].|[zbl.]ym.b hkl.ṯpṭ.n 2.3[129].20

rḫ yar k.|[ašr ilht kṯrt bn]|t hll.snnt.bnt h|ll bʻl gml.yrdt.|b ʻrgzm.b bz tdm.|lla y.ʻm lẓpn i|l ḏ.pid.hn b p y sp| 24[77].42

l.rkb.|ṯkmm.ḥmt.nša.|[y]d h.šmmh.dbḥ.|l ṯr.ab h.il.šrd.|[bʻl].b dbḥ h.bn dgn.|[b m]ṣd h.yrd.krt.|[l g]gt.ʻdb.akl 14[KRT].4.169

g]dl.rkb.|ṯkmm.ḥm[t].ša.yd k.|šmm.dbḥ.l ṯr.|ab k.il.šrd.bʻl.|b dbḥ k.bn.dgn.|b mṣd k.w yrd.|krt.l ggt.ʻdb.|akl.l 14[KRT].2.77

n k.al ttn.tk.ǵr.|knkny.ša.ǵr.ʻl ydm.|ḫlb.l ẓr.rḥtm w rd.|bt ḫpṯt.arṣ.tspr b y|rdm.arṣ.w tdʻ ilm.|k mtt.yšmʻ.aliyn 5[67].5.14

ṯrmg.|ʻm.tlm.ǵṣr.arṣ.|ša.ǵr.ʻl.ydm.|ḫlb.l ẓr.rḥtm.|w rd.bt ḫpṯt.|arṣ.tspr.b y|rdm.arṣ.|idk.al.ttn.|pnm.tk.qrt h.| 4[51].8.7

.d[q]tm.|[yr]ḫ.kṯy gdlt.w l ǵlmt š.|[w]pamt ṯlṯm.w yrdt.[m]dbḥt.|gdlt.l bʻlt bhtm.ʻṣrm.|l inš ilm. 34[1].20

špt.l šmm.|[---.l]šn.l kbkbm.yʻrb.|[bʻ]l.b kbd h.b p h yrd.|k ḫrr.zt.ybl.arṣ.w pr.|ʻṣm.yraun.aliyn.bʻl.|ṯṯʻ.nn.rkb.ʻr 5[67].2.4

dbḥ.|l ṯr.ab h.il.šrd.|[bʻl].b dbḥ h.bn dgn.|[b m]ṣd h.yrd.krt.|[l g]gt.ʻdb.akl.l qryt.|ḥṭt.l bt.ḫbr.|yip.lḥm.d ḫmš.| 14[KRT].4.171

.dbḥ.l ṯr.|ab k.il.šrd.bʻl.|b dbḥ k.bn.dgn.|b mṣd k.w yrd.|krt.l ggt.ʻdb.|akl.l qryt.|ḥṭt.l bt.ḫbr.|yip.lḥm.d ḫmš.| 14[KRT].2.79

y.|aps h.w yʻn.ʻṯtr.ʻrẓ.|l amlk.b ṣrrt.ṣpn.|yrd.ʻṯtr.ʻrẓ.yrd.|l kḥṯ.aliyn.bʻl.|w ymlk.b arṣ.il.kl h.|[---] š abn.b rḥbt. 6.1.63[49.1.35]

a|rṣ.mt.aliyn.bʻl.|ḫlq.zbl.bʻl.arṣ.|apnk.lṭpn.il.|d pid.yrd.l ksi.yṯb.|l hdm[.w] l.hdm.yṯb.|l arṣ.yṣq.ʻmr.|un.l riš h 5[67].6.12

t.|l ṯṯpṭ.ṯpṭ.qṣr.npš.|km.aḫt.ʻrš.mdw.|anšt.ʻrš.zbln.|rd.l mlk.amlk.|l drkt.k aṯb.an.|ytbʻ.yṣb ǵlm.ʻl.|ab h.yʻrb.yš 16.6[127].37

ytm.bʻd.|ksl k.almnt.km.|aḫt.ʻrš.mdw.anšt.|ʻrš.zbln.rd.l mlk.|amlk.l drkt k.aṯb.|an.w yʻny.krt ṯʻ.yṯbr.|ḥrn.y bn 16.6[127].52

l.mt.my.lim.bn dgn.|my.hmlt.aṯr.bʻl.nrd.|b arṣ.ʻm h.trd.nrt.|ilm.špš.ʻd.tšbʻ.bk.|tšt.k yn.udmʻt.gm.|tṣḥ.l nrt.ilm. 6[62].1.8

.riš h.l ymǵy.|aps h.w yʻn.ʻṯtr.ʻrẓ.|l amlk.b ṣrrt.ṣpn.|yrd.ʻṯtr.ʻrẓ.yrd.|l kḥṯ.aliyn.bʻl.|w ymlk.b arṣ.il.kl h.|[---] š 6.1.63[49.1.35]

rtm.w[--.]n[--.]iš[--.]h[---.]išt.|[---]y.yblmm.u[---]k.yrd[.--.]i[---]n.bn.|[---.-]nn.nrt.ilm.špš.tšu.g h.w t[ṣḥ.šm]ʻ.m 2.3[129].14

kbkbt k ṯn.|[---.]bʻl yḥmdn h.yrṯ y.|[---.]dmrn.l pn h yrd.|[---.]bʻl.šm[.--.]rgbt yu.|[---]w yrmy[.q]rn h.|[---.-]ny 2001.2.8

[---.]spr[.---].|[---.]yrd[.---]. 2154.2

yrḫ

.|mšrrm.aḫt h l a|bn mznm.nkl w ib.|d ašr.ar yrḫ.w y|rḫ yar k.|[ašr ilht kṯrt bn]|t hll.snnt.bnt h|ll bʻl gml.yrdt 24[77].38

t.tšu.g h].|w tṣḥ.yṯb.ytp.[---].|qrt.ablm.ablm.[qrt.zbl.yrḫ].|ik.al.yḥdṯ.yrḫ.b[---].|b qrn.ymn h.b anšt[.---].|qdqd 18[3AQHT].4.8

t.|[---.yrḫ.]ḫlt.šbʻ.[---].mlkt.|[---.yrḫ.]gn.šbʻ[.--].|[---.yrḫ.]iṯb.šb[ʻ.---].|[-----]. 1088.15

rḫ.ḫyr[.---].|[---].yrḫ.ḥl[t.---].|[---].yrḫ.gn[-.---].|[---.]yrḫ.iṯ[b.---]. 1088.A.5

spr.ḥpr.bnš mlk.b yrḫ iṯt[bnm].|ršpab.rb ʻšrt.m[r]yn.|pǵḏn.ilbʻl.krwn.lbn.ʻdn. 2011.1

yrẖ

d yn.l.ẖḏǵb.w.kd.ḥmṣ.|prš̀.glbm.l.bt.|tgmǵ.ks̀mm.b.yrẖ.iṯtbnm.|šb‘m.dd.ṯn.kbd.|tgmr.ḥṭm.šb‘.ddm.|ẖmš.dd.š‘ 1099.30
ḏrǵlm[.---].|ṯlṯ.mat.ẖmšm.kb[d].|ẖmš.kbd.l.md‘.|b yr[ẖ.iṯtb]nm.|ṯlṯ[.mat.a]rb‘.kbd.|w.[---.-]m‘t.|ṯlṯ[m.---.-]rm 2012.13
.yṯb.ytp.[---].|qrt.ablm.ablm.[qrt.zbl.yrẖ].|ik.al.yḥdṯ.yrẖ.b[---].|b qrn.ymn h.b anšt[.---].|qdqd h.w y‘n.yṭpn.[mh 18[3AQHT].4.9
ilm.tlḥmn.|ilm.w tštn.tštn y[n] ‘d šb‘.|trṯ.‘d.škr.y‘db.yrẖ.|gb h.km.[---.]yqṯqṭ.tḥt.|ṯlḥnt.il.d yd‘nn.|y‘db.lḥm.l h. UG5.1.1.4
.t[--.---].|[--.]l b‘l.‘bd[.---].|ṯr ab h il.tṯrm[.---].|tšlḥm yrẖ.ggn[.---].|k[.---.ẖ]mš.ẖssm[.---].|[---.--]m ‘ṯtr[t.---].|[---. 2001.1.16
rmnm.bt mlk.|il[bt].gdlt.ušẖry.gdlt.ym gdlt.|b‘l gdlt.yrẖ.gdlt.|gdlt.ṯrmn.gdlt.pdry.gdlt dqt.|dqt.trṯ.dqt.|[rš]p.‘n 34[1].14
ḥ.[---].|mdbḥt.bt.ilt.‘ṣr[m.l ṣpn.š].|l ǵlmt.š.w l [---.l yrẖ].|gd[lt].l nkl[.gdlt.l b‘lt.bhtm].|‘š[rm.]l inš[.ilm.---].|il[35[3].25
--.---].|mdbḥt.bt.i[lt.‘ṣrm.l].|ṣpn š.l ǵlm[t.š.w l.---].|l yrẖ.gdlt.l [nkl.gdlt.l b‘]|[lt].bht[m].[‘]ṣrm l [inš.ilm].|[---.]il APP.II[173].28
ẖ.ẖyr.|[---.]yn.l.mlkt.|[---.yrẖ.]ḥlt.šb‘.[---].mlkt.|[---.yrẖ.]gn.šb‘[.--].|[---.yrẖ.]iṯb.šb[‘.---].|[-----]. 1088.14
--.-]bd[.---].|[---.]yrẖ.ẖyr[.---].|[---].yrẖ.ḥl[t.---].|[---].yrẖ.gn[-.---].|[---.]yrẖ.iṯ[b.---]. 1088.A.4
|[---.--]r.almd k.[---].|[---.]qrt.ablm.a[blm].|[qrt.zbl.]yrẖ.d mgdl.š[---].|[---.]mn.‘r hm[.---].|[---.]it[.---].|[---.]‘p[18[3AQHT].1.31
m[---].|[---.yr]ẖ.mgm[r.---].|[---.--]š.b d.h[--.---].|[---.y]rẖ.dbḥ[.---].|[---.-]pn.b d.[---].|[---.]b d.[---]. 1160.5
n‘m y.‘rš.h[--]m.|ysmsmt.‘rš.ẖlln.[-].|yṯb.dnil.[l s]pr yrẖ h.|yrs.y[---.]y[--] h.|ṯlṯ.rb[‘.yrẖ.--]r[.--].|yrẖm.ymǵy[.-- 17[2AQHT].2.43
|ṯlrb h.|art.ṯn.yrẖm.|ṯlrby.yrẖ.w.ẖm[š.ym]m.|ṯlḥny.yrẖ.w.ẖm[š.ymm].|ẓrn.yrẖ.w.ẖmš.y[m]m.|mrat.ẖmš.‘šr.y 66[109].5
by.yrẖ.w.ẖm[š.ym]m.|ṯlḥny.yrẖ.w.ẖm[š.ymm].|ẓrn.yrẖ.w.ẖmš.y[m]m.|mrat.ẖmš.‘šr.ymm.|qmnz.yrẖ.w.ẖmš.y 66[109].6
].|ẓrn.yrẖ.w.ẖmš.y[m]m.|mrat.ẖmš.‘šr.ymm.|qmnz.yrẖ.w.ẖmš.ymm.|‘nmk.yrẖ.|ypr.yrẖ.w.ẖmš.ymm. 66[109].8
qrht.d.tššlmn.|ṯlrb h.|art.ṯn.yrẖm.|ṯlrby.yrẖ.w.ẖm[š.ym]m.|ṯlḥny.yrẖ.w.ẖm[š.ymm].|ẓrn.yrẖ.w.ẖm 66[109].4
mš.‘šr.ymm.|qmnz.yrẖ.w.ẖmš.ymm.|‘nmk.yrẖ.|ypr.yrẖ.w.ẖmš.ymm. 66[109].10
h yṯ‘r.|mšrrm.aẖt h l a|bn mznm.nkl w ib.|d ašr.ar yrẖ.w y|rẖ yar k.|[ašr ilht kṯrt bn]|t hll.snnt.bnt h|ll b‘l g 24[77].38
-].|[--] šlm.šlm i[l].|[š]lm.il.šr.|dgn.w b‘l.|‘ṯ w kmṯ.|yrẖ w ksa.|yrẖ mkṯy.|ṯkmn w šnm.|kṯr w ẖss.|‘ṯtr ‘ṯtpr.|š UG5.10.1.6
k.ḏmr k.l[-]|n k.ḥtk k.nmrt k.b tk.|ugrt.l ymt.špš.w yrẖ.|w n‘mt.šnt.il. UG5.2.2.11
sp.ḥmt.|[b‘l.w]dgn[.yi]sp.ḥmt.‘nt.w ‘ṯtrt.|[ti]sp.ḥmt.y[r]ẖ.w.ršp.yisp.ḥmt.|[‘ṯt]r.w ‘ṯtpr.yisp.ḥmt.ṯṯ.w kṯṯ.|[yus] UG5.8.15
.|[---.--]an.|[---.--]m.ank.|[---.]asrm.|[---.]dbḥm.|[---.y]rẖ.w šqr.|[---.--]b.b y[--.---].|[-----].|[-----].|[-----].|[---.]m 1002.24
[-----].|[------.]ṯr.|[---.aliy]n.b‘l.|[------.]yrẖ.zbl.|[--.kṯ]r w ẖss.|[---]n.rḥm y.ršp zbl.|[w ‘d]t.ilm.ṯlṯ 15[128].2.4
l.iwrmḏ.|kd.l.ydn.|[---.y]rẖ.ẖyr.|[---.]yn.l.mlkt.|[---.yrẖ.]ḥlt.šb‘.[---].mlkt.|[---.yrẖ.]gn.šb‘[.--].|[---.yrẖ.]iṯb.šb[‘.- 1088.13
[---.-]bd[.---].|[---.]yrẖ.ẖyr[.---].|[---].yrẖ.ḥl[t.---].|[---].yrẖ.gn[-.---].|[---.]yrẖ.iṯ[b.---]. 1088.A.3
yrẖ ẖyr.b ym ḥdṯ.|alp.w š.l b‘lt bhtm.|b arb‘t ‘šrt.b‘l.|‘rkm UG5.12.A.1
.|kdm.l.ilšpš.|kd.l.annṯb.|kd.l.iwrmḏ.|kd.l.ydn.|[---.y]rẖ.ẖyr.|[---.]yn.l.mlkt.|[---.yrẖ.]ḥlt.šb‘.[---].mlkt.|[---.yrẖ 1088.11
[---.-]bd[.---].|[---.]yrẖ.ẖyr[.---].|[---].yrẖ.ḥl[t.---].|[---].yrẖ.gn[-.---].|[---.]yrẖ.i 1088.A.2
.|mrat.ẖmš.‘šr.ymm.|qmnz.yrẖ.w.ẖmš.ymm.|‘nmk.yrẖ.|ypr.yrẖ.w.ẖmš.ymm. 66[109].9
tn k.bl mt.|w ašlḥ k.ašspr k.‘m.b‘l.|šnt.‘m.bn il.tspr.yrẖm.|k b‘l.k yḥwy.y‘šr.ḥwy.y‘š.|r.w yšqyn h.ybd.w yšr.‘l 17[2AQHT].6.29
yrẖ.k m[rṣ.---].|mn.k dw.kr[t].|w y‘ny.ǵzr[.ilḥu].|ṯlṯ.yrẖm.k m[rṣ].|arb‘.k dw.k[rt].|mnd‘.krt.mǵ[y.---].|w qbr.t 16.2[125].84
|w msk.tr[.---].|tqrb.aẖ[h.w tṣḥ].|lm.tb‘rn[.---].|mn.yrẖ.k m[rṣ.---].|mn.k dw.kr[t].|w y‘ny.ǵzr[.ilḥu].|ṯlṯ.yrẖm. 16.2[125].81
.‘nt.ẖbly.dbḥn š[p]š pgr.|[g]dlt iltm ẖnqtm.d[q]tm.|[yr]ẖ.kṯy gdlt.w l ǵlmt š.|[w]pamt ṯlṯm.w yrdt.[m]dbḥt.|gd 34[1].19
pdry.|dqt.|trṯ.|ršp.|‘nt ẖbly.|špš pgr.|iltm ẖnqtm.|yrẖ kṯy.|ygb hd.|yrgb b‘l.|ydb il.|yarš il.|yrǵm il.|‘mtr.|y UG5.14.A.14
ilbt.|ušẖry.|ym.b‘l.|yrẖ.|kṯr.|ṯrmn.|pdry.|dqt.|trṯ.|ršp.|‘nt ẖbly.|špš pgr.|ilt UG5.14.A.4
ẖ.l gṯr.|ṯql.ksp.ṭb.ap w np[š].|l ‘nt h.ṯql.ẖrṣ.|l špš[.w y]rẖ.l gṯr.ṯn.|[ṯql.ksp].ṭb.ap.w npš.|[---].bt.alp w š.|[---.--] 33[5].14
lm.šb[‘.]l kṯr.|‘lm.t‘rbn.gṯrm.|bt.mlk.ṯql.ẖrṣ.|l špš.w yrẖ.l gṯr.|ṯql.ksp.ṭb.ap w np[š].|l ‘nt h.ṯql.ẖrṣ.|l špš[.w y]r 33[5].11
rṣn.|il.yẓḥq.bm.|lb.w ygmḏ.bm kbd.|ẓi.at.l tlš.|amt.yrẖ.|l dmgy.amt.|aṯrt.qḥ.|ksan k.ḥdg k.|ḥtl k.w ẓi.|b aln.t 12[75].1.15
ṣ.|[yṯb.]b[‘]l.l ksi.mlk h.|[---].l kḥṯ.drkt h.|l [ym]m.l yrẖm.l yrẖm.|l šnt.[m]k.b šb‘.|šnt.w [--].bn.ilm.mt.|‘m.ali 6[49].5.7
.ǵr.ybk.l aqht.|ǵzr.ydm‘.l kdd.dnil.|mt.rpi.l ymm.l yrẖm.|l yrẖm.l šnt.‘d.|šb‘t.šnt.ybk.l aq|ht.ǵzr.yd[m‘.]l kdd 19[1AQHT].4.175
]b[‘]l.l ksi.mlk h.|[---].l kḥṯ.drkt h.|l [ym]m.l yrẖm.l yrẖm.|l šnt.[m]k.b šb‘.|šnt.w [--].bn.ilm.mt.|‘m.aliyn.b‘l.yš 6[49].5.7
.l aqht.|ǵzr.ydm‘.l kdd.dnil.|mt.rpi.l ymm.l yrẖm.|l yrẖm.l šnt.‘d.|šb‘t.šnt.ybk.l aq|ht.ǵzr.yd[m‘.]l kdd.|dnil.m 19[1AQHT].4.176
t.hlm.yṯq.|w yṯb.|tqru.l špš.um h.špš.[um.q]l bl.‘m.|yrẖ.lrgt h.mnt.nṯk.n[ḥš].šmrr.|nḥš.‘q šr.ln h.mlẖš.abd.ln h. UG5.7.26
].aḥd.ẖmš.am[--.---].|[---.--]m.qmṣ.ṯlṯm.i[qnu.---].|[b.yr]ẖ.mgmr.mš[--.---].|[---].iqnu.ẖmš[.---].|[b.yr]ẖ.pgrm[.--- 1106.38
b yrẖ.mgm[r.---].|yṣu.ẖlpn[.---].|ṯlṯ.dt.p[--.---].|dt.ṯgmi.[---]. 1159.1
[---.y]rẖ.n[ql.---].|[---.]m[---].|[---.yr]ẖ.mgm[r.---].|[---.--]š.b d.h[--.---].|[---.y]rẖ.dbḥ[.---].|[--- 1160.3
šlm i[l].|[š]lm.il.šr.|dgn.w b‘l.|‘ṯ w kmṯ.|yrẖ w ksa.|yrẖ mkṯy.|ṯkmn w šnm.|kṯr w ẖss.|‘ṯtr ‘ṯtpr.|šḥr w šlm.|n UG5.10.1.7
il.[l s]pr yrẖ h.|yrs.y[---.]y[--] h.|ṯlṯ.rb[‘.yrẖ.--]r[.--].|yrẖm.ymǵy[.---].|ẖ[--.]r[---]. 17[2AQHT].2.46
ǵtr.‘ṯtr t|rẖ l k ybrdmy.b[t.a]|b h lb[u] y‘rr.w y‘[n].|yrẖ nyr šmm.w n‘[n].|‘ma nkl ẖtn y.a[ẖ]r.|nkl yrẖ ytrẖ.ad 24[77].31
.|l ad[n h.---].|dgn tt[--.---.-]l|‘.l kṯrt hl[l.sn]nt.|ylak yrẖ ny[r] šmm.‘m.|ẖr[ẖ]b mlk qẓ.tn nkl y|rẖ ytrẖ.ib t‘rb m 24[77].16
n.[---].|[---.b‘]lt.bhtm.š[--.---].|[---.-]rt.l.dml[.---].|[b.yrẖ].nql.ṯn.ẖpn[.---].|[---].aḥd.ẖmš.am[--.---].|[---.--]m.qmṣ 1106.35
[---.y]rẖ.n[ql.---].|[---.]m[---].|[---.yr]ẖ.mgm[r.---].|[---.--]š.b d. 1160.1
.dr.‘db.uẖry mṭ yd h.|ymǵ.l qrt.ablm.abl[m].|qrt.zbl.yrẖ.yšu g h.|w yṣḥ.y l k.qrt.ablm.|d ‘l k.mẖṣ.aqht.ǵzr.|‘wr 19[1AQHT].4.164
db.akl.l qryt.|ḥṭt.l bt.ẖbr.|yip.lḥm.d ẖmš.|[mǵ]d.ṯdṯ.yr[ẖm].|‘dn.ngb.w [yṣi.ṣbu].|ṣbi.ng[b.w yṣi.‘dn].|m‘[.ṣ]bu 14[KRT].4.175
db.|akl.l qryt.|ḥṭt.l bt.ẖbr.|yip.lḥm.d ẖmš.|mǵd.ṯdṯ.yrẖm.|‘dn.ngb.w yṣi.|ṣbu.ṣbi.ngb.|w yṣi.‘dn.m‘.|ṣbu k.ul. 14[KRT].2.84
arb‘t.‘šr[t].|yrtḥṣ.mlk.b[rr].|b ym.mlat.|tqln.alpm.|yrẖ.‘šrt.l b‘[l].|dqtm.w ynt.qr[t].|w mtntm.š l rmš.|w kbd. UG5.13.5
ar]b‘t.‘[š]rt.yrtḥṣ.mlk.brr.|[b ym.ml]at.y[ql]n.al[p]m.yrẖ.‘šrt.|[l b‘l.ṣ]pn.[dq]tm.w y[nt] qrt.|[w mtmt]m.[š.l] rm[36[9].1.11
b yr[ẖ].|pgr[m].|yṣa[.---].|mšr[-].|[-]b.m[--].|b y[rẖ].|pgr[m].|yṣa[.---].|lb[-.---].|b d[.---]. 1158.2.1
b yr[ẖ].|pgr[m].|yṣa[.---].|mšr[-].|[-]b.m[--].|b y[rẖ].|pgr[m 1158.1.1
b ym ḥdṯ.|b.yrẖ.pgrm.|lqḥ.iwrpzn.|argḏḏ.|ṯṯkn.|ybrk.|ntbt.|b.mitm.| 2006.2
b.ym.ḥdṯ.|b.yr.pgrm.|lqḥ.b‘lmḏr.|w.bn.ẖlp.|miẖd.|b.arb‘.|mat.ẖrṣ. 1156.2
b.ym.ḥdṯ.|b.yrẖ.pgrm.|lqḥ.b‘lm‘ḏr.|w bn.ẖlp.|w[--]y.d.b‘l.|miẖd.b.|ar 1155.2

.---].|[b.yr]ḫ.mgmr.mš[--.---].|[---].iqnu.ḫmš[.---].|[b.yr]ḫ.pgrm[.---]. 1106.40
lk.---].|[---.--]rt.š'rt[.---].|[---.i]qni.l.ṯr[mn.art.---].|[b.yr]ḫ.riš.yn.[---].|[---.b']lt.bhtm.š[--.---].|[---.-]rt.l.dml[.---].| 1106.32
rb'.ddm.l.k[-]ḫ.|ṯmnym.dd.dd.kbd.|[l].md̲r[ǵ]lm.|b yrḫ[ri]šyn.|šb['.--]n.[k]bd.|w[.---.]qm't.|[---.]md̲rǵlm.|[---. 2012.21
b yrḫ.[rišyn.b ym.ḥdṯ].|šmtr.[uṯkl.l il.šlmm].|b ṯlṯt '[šrt.yrtḥṣ 35[3].1
[b yr]ḫ[.r]išyn.b ym.ḥdṯ.|[šmtr].uṯkl.l il.šlmm.|b [ṯlṯt].'šrt.yrt APP.II[173].1
rt.|la.šmm.b yd.bn ilm.mt.|ym.ymm.y'tqn.l ymm.|l yrḫm.rḥm.'nt.tngṯ h.|k lb.arḫ.l 'gl h.k lb.|ṯat.l imr h.km.lb 6[49].2.27
lp.w š.pdry.š.|šrp.w šlmm ilib š.|b'l ugrt š.b'l ḫlb š.|yrḫ š.'nt ṣpn.alp.|w š.pdry š.ddmš š.|w b urbt.ilib š.|b'l alp UG5.13.17
.|dgn.š.b'l.ḫlb alp w š.|b'l ṣpn alp.w.š.|ṯrṯy.alp.w.š.|yrḫ.š.ṣpn.š.|kṯr š 'ṯtr.š.|['ṯt]rt.š.šgr w iṯm š.|[---.]š.ršp.idrp. UG5.9.2.7
-].|[---.gd]lt.[---].|[---.d]dmš[.---].|[---.--]b.š.[---].|[---.yr]ḫ.š.[---].|[---.]'[--.---]. 43[47].5
l]|yt.'rb špš[.w ḫl.mlk.w.b y]|m.ḥdṯ.ṯn šm[.---.--]t.|b yrḫ.ši[-.b ar]b't.'š|rt.yr[tḥṣ.ml]k.brr.|'lm.š.š[--].l[--.]'rb.šp| APP.II[173].54
.|ṯṯn.š'rt.|'dn.š'rt.|mnn.š'rt.|bdn.š'rt.|'pṯn.š'rt.|'bd.yrḫ š'rt.|ḫbd.ṯr yṣr š'r.|pdy.yṣr š'rt.|atnb.ḫr.|š'rt.š'rt. 97[315].10
'[n].|yrḫ nyr šmm.w n'[n].|'ma nkl ḫtn y.a[ḫ]r.|nkl yrḫ ytrḫ.adn h.|yšt mṣb.mznm.um h.|kp mznm.iḫ h yṯ'r.| 24[77].33
.sn]nt.|ylak yrḫ ny[r] šmm.'m.|ḫr[ḫ]b mlk qẓ.tn nkl y|rḫ ytrḫ.ib t'rb m b bh|t h.w atn mhr h l a|b h.alp ksp w 24[77].17
l w ib[.bt].|ḫrḫb.mlk qẓ ḫrḫb m|lk aǵzt.b sǵ[--.]špš.|yrḫ ytkḥ yḫ[bq] [-].|tld bt.[--]t.ḫ[--.l k]|ṯrt.l bnt.hll[.snnt].| 24[77].4
qrht.d.tššlmn.|tlrb h.|art.ṯn.yrḫm.|ṯlrby.yrḫ.w.ḫm[š.ym]m.|ṯlḥny.yrḫ.w.ḫm[š.ymm].|ẓ 66[109].3
ln.[-].|yṯb.dnil.[l s]pr yrḫ h.|yrs.y[---.]y[--] h.|ṯlṯ.rb['.yrḫ.--]r[.--].|yrḫm.ymǵy[.---].|ḫ[--.]r[---]. 17[2AQHT].2.45
[---.]iy[ṯ]r.|[---.'bd.y]rḫ.|[---.b]n.mšrn.|[---].bn.lnn.|[-----].|[---.-]lyr. 2135.2
b y[rḫ.---].|'š[r.---].|ḫm[š.---].|b[yrḫ.---].|[---.]prš.|[-----].|l. 2012.1
.alp.w š[.---].|b'lm.alp.w š[.---].|arṣ.w šmm.š.kṯr[t] š.yrḫ[.---].|ṣpn.š.kṯr.š.pdry.š.ǵrm.š[.---].|aṯrt.š.'nt.š.špš.š.arṣy UG5.9.1.5
b yrḫ.[---].|šb'.yn[.---].|mlkt[.---].|kd.yn.l.[---].|armwl w [--]. 1092.1
[-----].|[---].yrḫ.[---].|[---].yrḫ.[---].|[---].yrḫ.[---].|[---.-]pd.yn.[---].|[---. 1088.B.2
[-----].|[---].yrḫ.[---].|[---].yrḫ.[---].|[---].yrḫ.[---].|[---.-]pd.yn.[---].|[---.]yn[.---]. 1088.B.3
b y[rḫ.---].|'š[r.---].|ḫm[š.---].|b[yrḫ.---].|[---.]prš.|[-----].|l.mšḫ[.---].|'šr.d[d.---].|ṯṯm.dd.dd 2012.4
[-----].|[---].yrḫ.[---].|[---].yrḫ.[---].|[---].yrḫ.[---].|[---.-]pd.yn.[---].|[---.]yn[.---]. 1088.B.4

yrḫm

bn.b'ln.biry.|ṯlṯ.b'lm.|w.adn hm.ṯr.w.arb'.bnt h.|yrḫm.yd.ṯn.bn h.|b'lm.w.ṯlṯ.n'rm.w.bt.aḥt.|bn.lwn.ṯlṯtm.b' 2080.4

yry

ašql k.ṯḥt.|[p'n y.a]nk.n'mn.'mq.nšm.|[td'ṣ.p'n]m.w tr.arṣ.idk.|[l ttn.pn]m.'m il.mbk.nhrm.|[qrb.ap]q.thmtm tg 17[2AQHT].6.46
sp.w ḫrṣ.|bht.thrm.iqnim.|šmḫ.btlt.'nt.td'ṣ.|p'nm.w tr.arṣ.|idk.l ttn.pnm.|'m.b'l.mrym.ṣpn.|b alp.šd.rbt.kmn.| 4[51].5.83
]d.l ytn.bt.l b'l.k ilm.|[w ḥẓ]r.k bn.aṯrt[.td'ṣ.]p'n.|[w tr.a]rṣ.id[k.l ttn.p]nm.|['m.i]l.mbk.nhr[m.qr]b.[ap]q.|[thm] 3['NT.VI].5.13
u.'n h.btlt.'nt.|w tšu.'n h.w t'n.|w t'n.arḫ.w tr.b lkt.|tr.b lkt.w tr.b ḫl.|[b]n'mm.b ysmm.ḥ[--]k.ǵrt.|[ql].l b'l.'nt 10[76].2.29
k.|w tšu.'n h.btlt.'nt.|w tšu.'n h.w t'n.|w t'n.arḫ.w tr.b lkt.|tr.b lkt.w tr.b ḫl.|[b]n'mm.b ysmm.ḥ[--]k.ǵrt.|[ql 10[76].2.28
.'nt.|w tšu.'n h.w t'n.|w t'n.arḫ.w tr.b lkt.|tr.b lkt.w tr.b ḫl.|[b]n'mm.b ysmm.ḥ[--]k.ǵrt.|[ql].l b'l.'nt.ttnn.|[--- 10[76].2.29
kḫ[ṯ.drkt h].|l alp.ql.ẓ[--.---].|l np ql.nd.[----].|tlk.w tr.b[ḫl].|b n'mm.b ys[mm.---].|arḫ.arḫ.[---.tld].|ibr.tld[.l b 10[76].3.18
k.aḫ.šmk.mla[t.r]umm.|tšu knp.btlt.'n[t].|tšu.knp.w tr.b 'p.|tk.aḫ šmk.mlat rumm.|w yšu.'n h.aliyn.b'l.|w yšu.' 10[76].2.11
tš.b bt h.|il.ḥṯ h.nḥt.il.ymnn.mṯ.yd h.yšu.|yr.šmm h.yr.b šmm.'ṣr.yḫrṯ yšt.|l pḥm.il.aṯtm.k ypt.hm.aṯtm.tṣḥn.|y 23[52].38
rṣ[.id]y.alt.l aḫš.idy.alt.in l y.|[--]t.b'l.ḥẓ.ršp.b[n].km.yr.klyt h.w lb h.|[ṯ]n.p k.b ǵr.ṯn.p k.b ḫlb.k tgwln.šnt k.|[-- 1001.1.3
mhr.'nt.ṯm.yḥpn.ḥyl|y.zbl.mlk.'llm y.km.tdd.|'nt.ṣd.tštr.'pt.šmm.|ṭbḫ.alpm.ap ṣin.šql.ṯrm.|w mri ilm.'glm.dt.š 22.2[124].11
ǵzr.mt.hrnmy.|apnk.dnil.mt.|rpi.yṣly.'rpt.b |ḥm.un.yr.'rpt.|tmṭr.b qẓ.ṭl.yṭll.|l ǵnbm.šb'.šnt.|yṣr k.b'l.ṯmn.rkb. 19[1AQHT].1.40
š.agn.yqḥ.tš.b bt h.|il.ḥṯ h.nḥt.il.ymnn.mṯ.yd h.yšu.|yr.šmm h.yr.b šmm.'ṣr.yḫrṯ yšt.|l pḥm.il.aṯtm.k ypt.hm.aṯt 23[52].38
d̲m[r.---].br.|bn.i[ytlm.---].|wr[t.---.]b d.yḥmn.|yry[.---.]br.|ydn[.---].kry.|bn.ydd[.---.b]r.|prkl.b'l.any.d.b 2123.4

yryt

[---].yryt.|[---.a]drt.|[--.ṯṯ]m.ṯmn.k[bd].|[---.yr]yt.dq[-].|[--.ṯ]lṯm.l.mi[t].|[---.]arb'.kbd. 2170.4
[---].yryt.|[---.a]drt.|[--.ṯṯ]m.ṯmn.k[bd].|[---.yr]yt.dq[-].|[--.ṯ]lṯ 2170.1

yrk

[--.]šir.b krm.nṭṭt.dm.'lt.b ab y.|u---].'lt.b k.lk.l pn y.yrk.b'l.[--].|[---.]'nt.šzrm.tštšḥ.km.ḥ[--].|[---].'pr.bt k.ygr[š 1001.1.10
ḫm.w aṯb.l ntbt.k.'šm l t[--].|[---.]drk.brḥ.arṣ.lk pn h.yrk.b'[l].|[---.]bt k.ap.l pḫr k 'nt tqm.'nt.tqm.|[---.p]ḫr k.yg 1001.2.8
|w tksynn.btn[-.]|y[--.]šr h.w šḫp h.|[--.]šḫp.ṣǵrt h.|yrk.t'l.b ǵr.|mslmt.b ǵr.tliyt.|w t'l.bkm.b arr.|bm.arr.w b ṣ 10[76].3.28
š]mm.rm.lk.prẓ kt.|[k]bkbm.ṯm.tpl k.lbnt.|[-.]rgm.k yrkt.'tqbm.|[---]m.'ẓpn.l pit.|m[--]m[.--]tm.w mdbḥt.|ḫr[.- 13[6].14

yrm

rišym.dt.'rb.|b bnš hm.|d̲mry.w.pṯpṯ.'rb.|b.yrm.|[ily.w].d̲mry.'rb.|b.ṯb'm.|ydn.bn.ilrpi.|w.ṯb'm.'rb.b.' 2079.4
bn.ǵs.ḥrš.š'ty.|'dy.bn.sl'y.gbly.|yrm.b'l.bn.kky. 2121.3
.|b.ṯb'm.|ydn.bn.ilrpi.|w.ṯb'm.'rb.b.'[d]n.|d̲mry.bn.yrm.|'rb.b.ad'y. 2079.9
.|ydlm.|y'd̲rd.|yrmt.|yyn.|yn.|ydln.|ymn.|yṯky.|[y]rm. 112[16].15

yrml

.|[---.]b.yrml.|[---.]b.yrml.|[---.--]n.b.yrml.|[---.--]ny.yrml.|šwn.qrty.|b.šlmy. 2119.24
|[---].b.ndb.|[---].b.kmkty.|[---.]yrmly.qrtym.|[---].b.yrml.|[---.]b.yrml.|[---.]b.yrml.|[---.]b.yrml.|[---.]b.yrml.|[2119.18
[---].b.kmkty.|[---.]yrmly.qrtym.|[---].b.yrml.|[---.]b.yrml.|[---.]b.yrml.|[---.]b.yrml.|[---.]b.yrml.|[---.--]n.b.yrm 2119.19
.|[---.]yrmly.qrtym.|[---].b.yrml.|[---.]b.yrml.|[---.]b.yrml.|[---.]b.yrml.|[---.]b.yrml.|[---.--]n.b.yrml.|[---.--]ny.y 2119.20

qrtym.|[---].b.yrml.|[---.]b.yrml.|[---.]b.yrml.|[---.]b.yrml.|[---.]b.yrml.|[---.--]n.b.yrml.|[---.--]ny.yrml.|s̀wn.qrt 2119.21
--].|[-----].|[---.--]y.|[---.--]y.|[---.yr]ml.|[---.--]y.|[---.yr]ml.|[---.y]rml.|[---.]kmkty.|[---].b.kmkty.|[---].b.ndb.|[- 2119.9
[---.--]y.|[---.--]y.|[---.yr]ml.|[---.--]y.|[---.yr]ml.|[---.y]rml.|[---.]kmkty.|[---].b.kmkty.|[---].b.ndb.|[---].b.ndb.| 2119.10
[---.-]yn.|[-----].|[-----].|[-----].|[---.--]y.|[---.--]y.|[---.yr]ml.|[---.--]y.|[---.yr]ml.|[---.y]rml.|[---.]kmkty.|[---].b.k 2119.7
.yrml.|[---.]b.yrml.|[---.]b.yrml.|[---.]b.yrml.|[---.]b.yrml.|[---.--]n.b.yrml.|[---.--]ny.yrml.|s̀wn.qrty.|b.šlmy. 2119.22
ml.|[---.]b.yrml.|[---.]b.yrml.|[---.]b.yrml.|[---.--]n.b.yrml.|[---.--]ny.yrml.|s̀wn.qrty.|b.šlmy. 2119.23

yrmly

-].b.ndb.|[---].b.ndb.|[---].b.ndb.|[---].b.kmkty.|[---.]yrmly.qrtym.|[---].b.yrml.|[---.]b.yrml.|[---.]b.yrml.|[---.]b 2119.17

yrmn

qln.|mnn.bn.ṣnr.|iẖy.[b]n[.--]l[-].|‘bdy[rẖ].bn.gṯtn.|yrmn.bn.‘n.|krwn.nḥl h.|ttn.[n]ḥl h.|bn.b[r]zn.|[---.-]ḥn. 85[80].4.9
b‘ln.|yrmn.|‘nil.|pmlk.|aby.|‘dyn.|aǵlyn.|[--]rd.|[--]qrd.|[--]r. 1066.2
.krm.|d.krwn.|šir.šd.šd.‘šy.|d.abmn.|šir.šd.krm.|d.yrmn.|šir.[š]d.mltḥ.šd.‘šy.|d.ynḥm.|tgmr.šd.ṯlṯm.šd.|w.tr[1079.13

yrm‘l

spr.npš.d.|‘rb.bt.mlk.|w.b.spr.l.št.|yrm‘l.|ṣry.|iršy.|y‘ḏrd.|ayaẖ.|bn.aylt.|ẖmš.mat.arb‘m.|k 2106.4

yrmt

[y-]n.|yny.|ydn.|ytršp.|ydrm.|ydy.|ydlm.|y‘ḏrd.|yrmt.|yyn.|yn.|ydln.|ymn.|yṯky.|[y]rm. 112[16].9

yrs

rš.h[--]m.|ysmsmt.‘rš.ẖlln.[-].|yṯb.dnil.[l s]pr yrẖ h.|yrs.y[---.]y[--] h.|ṯlṯ.rb[‘.yrẖ.--]r[.--].|yrẖm.ymǵy[.---].|ẖ[--. 17[2AQHT].2.44

yrǵm

ẖnqtm.|yrẖ kṯy.|ygb hd.|yrgb b‘l.|ydb il.|yarš il.|yrǵm il.|‘mtr.|ydb il.|yrgb lim.|‘mtr.|yarš il.|ydb b‘l.|yrǵ UG5.14.B.5
m il.|‘mtr.|ydb il.|yrgb lim.|‘mtr.|yarš il.|ydb b‘l.|yrǵm b‘l.|‘z b‘l.|ydb hd. UG5.14.B.12

yrp

h.rpum.|[l tdd.aṯr h].l tdd.ilnym.|[---.m]rz‘y.apnnk.yrp.|[---.]km.r‘y.ht.alk.|[---.]ṯlṯt.amǵy.l bt.|[y.---.b qrb].hkl 21[122].1.5.

yrpi

ṣṣ mlkn‘m.a[rb‘m].|ṣṣ mlk mit[.---].|ṣṣ igy.ẖmšm.|ṣṣ yrpi m[it.---].|ṣṣ bn.š[m]mn ‘[šr.---].|alp.ṯṯm.|kbd.mlḥt. 2097.18

yrpu

ls̀.|bn.ubr.|bn.‘pṯb.|ṯbry.|bn.ymn.|krty.|bn.abr[-].|yrpu.|kdn.|p‘ṣ.|bn.liy.|yd‘.|šmn.|‘dy.|‘nbr.|aẖrm.|bn.qr 2117.1.22

yrq

.|n[g.]krt.l ḥẓ[r y].|w y‘n[y.k]rt[.ṯ]‘.|lm.ank.ksp.|w yr[q.ẖrṣ].|yd.mqm h.w ‘bd.|‘lm.ṯlṯ.sswm.|mrkbt.b trbṣ.|b 14[KRT].6.283
[-----].|[-----].|[-----.lm].|[ank.ksp.w yrq].|[ẖrṣ.]yd.mqm h.|[w ‘b]d.‘lm.ṯlṯ.|[ssw]m.mrkbt b trbṣ 14[KRT].1.53
.|mlakm.l k.‘m.krt.|mswn h.tḥm.pbl.mlk.|qḥ.ksp.w yrq.ẖrṣ.|yd.mqm h.w ‘bd.‘lm.|ṯlṯ.sswm.mrkbt.|b trbṣ.bn.a 14[KRT].3.126
n h].|tš[an.g hm.w tṣḥn].|tḥ[m.pbl.mlk].|qḥ[.ksp.w yrq].|ẖrṣ.[yd.mqm h].|w ‘bd[.‘lm.ṯlṯ].|sswm.m[rkbt].|b tr 14[KRT].6.269
t.il w ušn.|ab.adm.w ṯṯb.|mlakm.l h.lm.ank.|ksp.w yrq.ẖrṣ.|yd.mqm h.w ‘bd.|‘lm.ṯlṯ.sswm.mrkbt.|b trbṣt.bn. 14[KRT].3.138
t.msw]n.|w r[gm.l krt.]ṯ‘.|tḥm[.pbl.mlk].|qḥ.[ksp.w yr]q.|ẖrṣ[.yd.mqm] h.|‘bd[.‘lm.ṯlṯ].|ss[wm.mrkbt].|b[trbṣ. 14[KRT].5.250
[‘t].|hlk.kbkbm.mdl.‘r.|ṣmd.pḥl.št.gpn y dt ksp.|dt.yrq.nqbn y.tš[m‘].|pǵt.ṯkmt.my.ḥspt.l[š‘]r.ṭl.|yd‘t.hlk.kbk 19[1AQHT].2.54
m‘.qd.w amr[r].|mdl.‘r.ṣmd.pḥl.|št.gpnm.dt.ksp.|dt.yrq.nqbnm.|‘db.gpn.atnt h.|yḥbq.qdš.w amrr.|yštn.aṯrt.l b 4[51].4.11
.rbt].|aṯrt.ym[.mdl.‘r].|ṣmd.pḥl[.št.gpnm.dt].|ksp.dt.yr[q.nqbnm].|‘db.gpn.atnt[y].|yšm‘.qd.w amr[r].|mdl.‘r.ṣ 4[51].4.6

yrš

].|ẖḏǵlm.b d.[---].|šb‘.lmdm.b d.s[n]rn.|lmd.aḥd.b d.yr[š].|lmd.aḥd.b d.yḥ[--].|ṯlṯ.lmdm.b d.nḥ[--].|lmd.aḥd.b d 1050.4
--]m.|[-----].|[-]š[--.---].|[-]r[--.--]y.|in m.‘bd k hwt.|[y]rš.‘m y.|mnm.iršt k.|d ẖsrt.w.ank.|aštn..l.iẖ y.|w.ap.ank 2065.14
snrn.|[---.lm]dm.b d.nrn.|[---.ẖ]ḏǵlm.|[lmd.]aḥd.b d.yrš. 1051.6

yrt

[-]k[-.---].|ar[--.---].|yrt.[---].|ṯṯ.prs̀[.---].|bn.‘myn[.---]. 2152.3

yrṯ

t.‘gl.il.‘tk.|mẖšt.klbt.ilm išt.|klt.bt.il.ḏbb.imtẖṣ.ksp.|itrṯ.ẖrṣ.ṭrd.b‘l.|b mrym.ṣpn.mšṣṣ.[-]k‘[-].|udn h.grš h.l ksi. 3[‘NT].3.44
l h kbkbm.|[---.]b km kbkbt k ṯn.|[---.]b‘l yḥmdn h.yrṯ y.|[---.]dmrn.l pn h yrd.|[---.]b‘l.šm[.--.]rgbt yu.|[---]w 2001.2.7
.tn.il m.d tq h.d tqyn h.|[hml]t.tn.b‘l.w ‘nn h.bn.dgn.arṯ m.pḏ h.|[w y‘n.]ṯr.ab h.il.‘bd k.b‘l.y ym m.‘bd k.b‘l.|[--. 2.1[137].35
].|tn.il m.d tq h.d tqyn.hmlt.tn.b‘l.[w ‘nn h].|bn.dgn.arṯ m.pḏ h.tb‘.ǵlmm.l ṯṯb.[idk.pnm].|l ytn.tk.ǵr.ll.‘m.phr.m 2.1[137].19
rš.|mid.grdš.ṯbt h.|w b tm hn.špḥ.yitbd.|w b.pẖyr h.yrṯ.|y‘rb.b ḥdr h.ybky.|b ṯn.[-]gmm.w ydm‘.|tntkn.udm‘t 14[KRT].1.25
pn.|tmrtn.š‘rt.|lmd.n.rn.|[---].ẖpn.|dqn.š‘rt.|[lm]d.yrṯ.|[-.]ynḥm.ẖpn.|ṯṯ.lmd.b‘ln.|l.qḥ.ẖpnt.|ṯṯ[.-]l.md.‘ṯtr[t]. 1117.15

yš

---.-]š bš[-.]t[-].ǵlm.l šdt[.-.]ymm.|[---.]b ym.ym.y[--].yš[ ]n.ap k.‘ṯtr.dm[.---.]|[---.]ḥrḥrtm.w[--.]n[--.]iš[--.]h[---.] 2.3[129].12

yšmʻ

n. | bn.ḫdyn. | bn.sgr. | bn.aǵltn. | bn.ktln. | bn.ʻgwn. | bn.yšmʻ. | bdl.mdrǵlm. | bn.mmy. | bn.ḫnyn. | bn.knn. | khnm. | bn 104[316].9
. | mit.ḫmšt.kbd. | [l.]gmn.bn.usyy. | mit.ṯṯm.kbd. | l.bn.yšmʻ. | mit.arbʻm.kbd. | l.liy.bn.ʻmyn. | mit.ḫmšm.kbd. | d.škn 1143.10
[---.-]bʻm. | [---.b]n.yšm[ʻ]. | [---.]mlkr[-] h.b.nṯk. | [---.]šbʻm. | [---.]ḫrg.ʻšrm. | [---. 2153.2

yšn

mʻt h. | km.ṯqlm.arṣ h. | km ḫmšt.mṯt h. | bm.bky h.w yšn. | b dmʻ h.nhmmt. | šnt.tluan. | w yškb.nhmmt. | w yqmṣ. 14[KRT].1.31
--.---]. | agmy[.---]. | bn.dlq[-.---]. | tǵyn.bn.ubn.ṯql[m]. | yšn.ḥrš.mrkbt.ṯq[lm]. | bn.pʻṣ.ṯqlm. | mṣrn.ḥrš.mrkbt.ṯqlm. | ʻ 122[308].1.6
ubdy.mdm. | šd.b d.ʻbdmlk. | šd.b d.yšn.ḥrš. | šd.b d.aupš. | šd.b d.ršpab.aḫ.ubn. | šd.b d.bn.uṯryn. 82[300].1.3
.bn.--]rt.b d.ṯpṭbʻl. | [ubdy.]mḫ[ṣ]m. | [šd.bn.]uzpy.b d.yšn.ḥrš. | [-----]. | [-----]. | [šd.b d.--]n. | [šd.b d.--]n. | [šd.b d.--] 82[300].2.26
| km ḫmšt.mṯt h. | bm.bky h.w yšn. | b dmʻ h.nhmmt. | šnt.tluan. | w yškb.nhmmt. | w yqmṣ.w b ḥlm h. | il.yrd.b ḏhr 14[KRT].1.33
m.w ṯn. | ṯlṯ.rbʻ.ym. | ḫmš.ṯdṯ.ym. | mk.špšm.b šbʻ. | w l.yšn.pbl. | mlk.l [qr.]ṯiqt. | ibr h[.l]ql.nhqt. | ḥmr[h.l gʻt.]alp. 14[KRT].5.222
.al.tšʻl. | qrt h.abn.yd k. | mšdpt.w hn.špšm. | b šbʻ.w l.yšn.pbl. | mlk.l qr.ṯigt.ibr h. | l ql.nhqt.ḥmr h. | l gʻt.alp.ḥrṯ.z 14[KRT].3.119
.l.ilšpš. | [šd.bn].kbr.l.snrn. | [---.--]k.l.gmrd. | [---.--]ṯ.l.yšn. | [šd.--]ln. | b d.trǵds. | šd.ṯʻlb. | b d.bn.pl. | šd.bn.kt. | b d.p 2030.1.8

yšr

| krt.ḥtk n.rš. | krt.grdš.mknt. | aṯt.ṣdq h.l ypq. | mtrḫt.yšr h. | aṯt.trḫ.w tbʻt. | ṯar um.tkn l h. | mṯlṯt.kṯrm.tmt. | mrbʻt 14[KRT].1.13

yšril

mry[n]m. | bn rmy[y]. | yšril[.---]. | anntn bn[.---]. | bn.brzn [---]. | bnil.bn.tl[--]. | bn.br 2069.3

yštd

lt.ʻnt. | an.l an.y špš. | an.l an.il.yǵr[.-]. | tǵr k.š[---.---]. | yštd[.---]. | dr[.---]. | r[---.---]. 6[49].4.49

yt

n.w.ṯlṯ.nʻ[r] h. | rpan.w.ṯ[n.]bn h. | bn.ayln.w.ṯn.bn h. | yt. 2068.28

ytḥm

.qšt. | ʻbd.qšt. | bn.ulmy.qšt. | ṯqbn.qšt. | bn.qnmlk.qšt. | ytḥm.qšt. | grp.qšt. | mʻrby. | nʻmn.ṯt.qštm.w.qlʻ. | gln.ṯt.qštm. 104[316].7

ytm

ṯb.b ap.ṯǵr.tḥt. | adrm.d b grn.ydn. | dn.almnt.yṯpṭ.ṯpṭ.ytm. | b nši ʻn h.w yphn.b alp. | šd.rbt.kmn.hlk.kṯr. | k yʻn.w 17[2AQHT].5.8
mnt.l ṯṯpṭ. | ṯpṭ qṣr.npš.l tdy. | ṯšm.ʻl.dl.l pn k. | l tšlḥm.ytm.bʻd. | ksl k.almnt.km. | aḫt.ʻrš.mdw.anšt. | ʻrš.zbln.rd.l m 16.6[127].49
d h.aqšr[.---]. | [---].pṯh y.a[--.]dt[.---].ml[--]. | [---.-]ṯk.ytmt.dlt tlk.[---].bm[.---]. | [---.-]qp.bn.ḥtt.bn ḥtt[.---]. | [---.-- 1001.1.22
[b.]gt.ṯpn.ʻšr.ṣmdm. | w.ṯlṯ.ʻšr.bnš. | yd.ytm.yd.rʻy.ḥmrm. | b.gt.gwl.ṯmn.ṣmdm. | w.arbʻ.ʻšr.bnš. | yd. 2038.3
ṯ]ǵr[.t]ḥt. | [adrm.d b grn.y]dn. | [dn.almnt.y]ṯpṭ. | [ṯpṭ.ytm.---] h. | [---.---]n. | [-----]. | hlk.[---.b n]ši. | ʻn h.w tphn.[---] 19[1AQHT].1.25

ytn

.dr]y.b kbrt. | ʻl k.pht.[-]l[-]. | b šdm.ʻl k.pht. | drʻ.b ym.tn.aḥd. | b aḫ k.ispa.w ytb. | ap.d anšt.im[-]. | aḥd.b aḫ k.l[--] 6[49].5.19
l.bʻl. | arṣ.gm.yṣḥ il. | l rbt.aṯrt ym.šmʻ. | l rbt.aṯr[t] ym.tn. | aḥd.b bn k.amlkn. | w tʻn.rbt.aṯrt ym. | bl.nmlk.ydʻ.ylḥn. 6.1.45[49.1.17]
[t]. | b sin.lpš.tšṣq[n h]. | b qṣ.all.tšu.g h.w[tṣ] | ḥ.at.mt.tn.aḫ y. | w ʻn.bn.ilm.mt.mh. | taršn.l btlt.ʻnt. | an.itlk.w aṣd. 6[49].2.12
p]nk.krt.ṯʻ.ʻ[-]r. | [--.]b bt h.yšt.ʻrb. | [--] h.ytn.w [--]u.l ytn. | [aḫ]r.mǵy.ʻ[d]t.ilm. | [w]yʻn.aliy[n.]bʻl. | [---.]tbʻ.l ltpn. 15[128].2.10
l dr[ʻ].nšr k. | w rbṣ.l ǵr k.inbb. | kt ǵr k.ank.ydʻt. | [-]n.atn.at.mtb k[.---]. | [š]mm.rm.lk.prẓ kt. | [k]bkbm.ṯm.tpl k.lb 13[6].11
m]. | š[lmm.]al.t[ṣr]. | udm[.r]bt.w u[dm]. | [ṯ]rrt.udm.y[t]n[t]. | il.ušn.ab[.ad]m. | rḥq.mlk.l bt y. | n[g.]krt.l ḥẓ[r y]. 14[KRT].6.277
t y.rḥq.krt. | l ḥẓr y.al.tṣr. | udm.rbt.w udm ṯrrt. | udm.ytnt.il w ušn. | ab.adm.w ṯtb. | mlakm.l h.lm.ank. | ksp.w yrq. 14[KRT].3.135
t.šlmm]. | [šlmm.al.tṣr]. | [udm.rbt.w udm]. | [ṯrrt.udm.ytnt]. | [il.w ušn.ab.adm]. | [rḥq.mlk.l bt y]. | [ng.kr]t.l ḥ[ẓ]r y 14[KRT].5.258
-.il.ṯny.l pḫr]. | mʻd.tḥm.ym.bʻl km.adn km.ṯ[pṭ.nhr]. | tn.il m.d tq h.d tqyn.hmlt.tn.bʻl.[w ʻnn h]. | bn.dgn.arṯ m.pḏ 2.1[137].18
hm.rgm.l ṯr.ab h.il.tḥm.ym.bʻl km. | [adn]km.ṯpṭ.nhr.tn.il m.d tq h.d tqyn h. | [hml]t.tn.bʻl.w ʻnn h.bn.dgn.arṯ m. 2.1[137].34
--.]iḥd.šd.gṯr. | [w]ht.yšmʻ.uḫ y. | l g y.w yhbṭ.bnš. | w ytn.ilm.b d hm. | b d.iḥqm.gṯr. | w b d.ytrhd. | bʻl. 55[18].19
| sp.ṯrml.ṯḫgrn.[-]dm[.-]. | ašlw.b ṣp.ʻn h. | d b ḥlm y.il.ytn. | b ḏrt y.ab.adm. | w ld.špḥ.l krt. | w ǵlm.l ʻbd.il. | krt.yḫṭ. 14[KRT].3.150
trt.tsm h. | d ʻq h.ib.iqni. | ʻpʻp h.sp.ṯrml. | d b ḥlm y.il.ytn. | b ḏrt y.ab.adm. | w ld.špḥ.l krk | t.w ǵlm.l ʻbd. | il.ttbʻ.m 14[KRT].6.296
spr.ytnm. | bn.ḫlbym. | bn.ady. | bn.ʻṯtry. | bn.ḫrzn. | ady. | bn.birtn 115[301].1.1
qm h. | [w ʻb]d.ʻlm.ṯlṯ. | [ssw]m.mrkbt b trbṣ bn.amt. | [tn.b]nm.aqny. | [tn.ṯa]rm.amid. | [w yʻn].ṯr.ab h.il. | d[--].b bk 14[KRT].2.57
nd. | ʻmṯtmr. | bn.nqmpʻ. | mlk.ugrt. | ytn.bt.annḏr. | bn.ytn.bnš. | [ml]k.d.b riš. | [--.-]nt. | [l.ʻb]dmlk. | [--.-]m[-]r. | [w.l. 1009.6
m. | [adn]km.ṯpṭ.nhr.tn.il m.d tq h.d tqyn h. | [hml]t.tn.bʻl.w ʻnn h.bn.dgn.arṯ m.pḏ h. | [w yʻn.]ṯr.ab h.il.ʻbd k.bʻl 2.1[137].35
.bʻl km.adn km.ṯ[pṭ.nhr]. | tn.il m.d tq h.d tqyn.hmlt.tn.bʻl.[w ʻnn h]. | bn.dgn.arṯ m.pḏ h.tbʻ.ǵlmm.l ṯṯb.[idk.pnm 2.1[137].18
m.mt. | [--]u.šbʻt.ǵlm h. | [---].bn.ilm.mt. | p[-]n.aḫ y m.ytn.bʻl. | [s]pu y.bn m.um y.kly y. | yṯb.ʻm.bʻl.ṣrrt. | ṣpn.yšu g 6[49].6.10
y.kly y. | yṯb.ʻm.bʻl.ṣrrt. | ṣpn.yšu g h.w yṣḥ. | aḫ y m.ytnt.bʻl. | spu y.bn m.um y.kl | y y.ytʻn.k gmrm. | mt.ʻz.bʻl.ʻz. 6[49].6.14
[l]k.ʻbdrpu.adn.ṯ[--]. | bdn.qln.mtn.ydln. | bʻltdtt.tlgn.ytn. | bʻltǵptm.krwn.ilšn.agyn. | mnn.šr.ugrt.ḏkr.yṣr. | tgǵln.ḫ 2011.35
km.b arr. | bm.arr.w b ṣpn. | b nʻm.b ǵr.t[l]iyt. | ql.l bʻl.ttnn. | bšrt.il.bš[r.bʻ]l. | w bšr.ḥtk.dgn. | k.ibr.l bʻl[.yl]d. | w ru 10[76].3.33
l ym.hnd. | ʻmṯtmr. | bn.nqmpʻ. | mlk.ugrt. | ytn.bt.annḏr. | bn.ytn.bnš. | [ml]k.d.b riš. | [--.-]nt. | [l.ʻb]dmlk 1009.5
hm.[-.]aṯr[.---]. | [--]šy.w ydn.bʻ[l.---]n. | [--]ʻ.k yn.hm.l.atn.bt y.l h. 1002.62
imr.l arṣ. | [ašhlk].šbt h.dmm.šbt.dqn h. | [mmʻm.-]d.l ytn.bt.l bʻl.k ilm. | [w ḥẓ]r.k bn.aṯrt[.tdʻṣ.]pʻn. | [w tr.a]rṣ.id[3[ʻNT.VI].5.11
[i]k.mgn.rbt.aṯrt. | [ym].mǵẓ.qnyt.ilm. | w tn.bt.l bʻl.km. | [i]lm.w ḥẓr.k bn. | [a]ṯrt.gm.l ǵlm h. | bʻl.yṣḥ.ʻ 8[51FRAG].3
.---]. | ǵzr.ilḥu.t[---]l. | trm.tṣr.trm[.ʻ]tqt. | tbky.w tšnn.[tt]n. | g h.bky.b ḥ[y k.a]b n. | nšmḫ.b l.mt k.ngln. | k klb.[b]b 16.2[125].97
rt.bnm.il.špḥ. | lṭpn.w qdš.ʻl. | ab h.yʻrb.ybky. | w yšnn.ytn.g h. | bky.b ḥy k.ab n.ašmḫ. | b l.mt k.ngln.k klb. | b bt k. 16.1[125].13

ṯn.ʿšr.yn.[kps]lnm.|arbʿ.mat[.arb]ʿm.[k]bd.|d ntn.d.ksp.|arbʿ.l.ḫlby.|[---].l.bt.|arbʿ.l.kpslnm.|kdm.b[t.]m 1087.3
[--].d.ntn[.d.]ksp.|[t]mn.l.ʿšrm[.l.b]t.ʿṯtrt.|[ṯ]lṯ.ʿšr h.[b]t.ršp.gn.|a 1088.1
rḫ.|w.mlk.z[--.--]n.šswm.|nʿmm.[--].ṯtm.w.at.|nǵṯ.w.ytn.hm.l k.|w.lḥt.alpm.ḫršm.|k.rgmt.l y.bly m.|alpm.aršt.l 2064.20
|lm.škn.hnk.|l ʿbd h.alpm.š[šw]m.|rgmt.ʿly.ṯh.lm.|l.ytn.hm.mlk.[b]ʿl y.|w.hn.ibm.šṣq l y.|p.l.ašt.atṯ y.|nʿr y.ṯh. 1012.26
l rʿ y.dt.|w ytnnn.|l aḫ h.l rʿ h.|rʿ ʿlm.|ttn.w tn.|w l ttn.|w al ttn.|tn ks yn.|w ištn.|ʿbd.prṯ.ṯhm.|qrq.pṯ.ḏmn.|l 1019.1.13
.ksm].|ṯlṯm.w mʿrb[.---].|dbḥ šmn mr[.šmn.rqḥ.bt].|mtnt.w ynt.[qrt.w ṯn.ḥṯm].|w bǵr.arbʿ.[---.kdm.yn].|prs.q APP.II[173].23
lṯm.[---].|d yqḥ bt[.--]r.dbḥ[.šmn.mr].|šmn.rqḥ[.-]bt.mtnt[.w ynt.qrt].|w ṯn ḥṯm.w bǵr.arb[ʿ.---].|kdm.yn.prs.q 35[3].21
t.aršt.|l aḫ y.l rʿ y.dt.|w ytnnn.|l aḫ h.l rʿ h.|rʿ ʿlm.|ttn.w tn.|w l ttn.|w al ttn.|tn ks yn.|w ištn.|ʿbd.prṯ.ṯhm.| 1019.1.12
|l aḫ y.l rʿ y.dt.|w ytnnn.|l aḫ h.l rʿ h.|rʿ ʿlm.|ttn.w tn.|w l ttn.|w al ttn.|tn ks yn.|w ištn.|ʿbd.prṯ.ṯhm.|qrq.pṯ. 1019.1.12
ptḥ.w ptḥ hw.prṣ.bʿd hm.|w ʿrb.hm.hm[.iṯ.--.l]ḥm.w t[n].|w nlḥm.hm.iṯ[.--.yn.w t]n.w nšt.|w ʿn hm.nǵr mdrʿ[.iṯ 23[52].71
--].|ank.n[--]n[.---].|kst.l[--.---].|w.hw.uy.ʿn[--.---].|l ytn.w rgm[.---].|w yrdnn.an[--.---].|[---].ank.l km[.---].|l y. 54.1.14[13.1.11]
ʿrb.hm.hm[.iṯ.--.l]ḥm.w t[n].|w nlḥm.hm.iṯ[.--.yn.w t]n.w nšt.|w ʿn hm.nǵr mdrʿ[.iṯ.lḥm.---].|iṯ.yn.d ʿrb.bṯk[.--- 23[52].72
nm.|hm.ḥry.bt y.|iqḥ.ašʿrb.ǵlmt.|ḥẓr y.ṯn h.wspm.|atn.w ṯlṯ h.ḫrṣm.|ylk ym.w ṯn.|ṯlṯ.rbʿ.ym.|aḫr.špšm.b rbʿ.| 14[KRT].4.206
.ilm.ṯlṯ h.|[ap]nk.krt.ṯʿ.ʿ[-]r.|[--.]b bt h.yšt.ʿrb.|[--] h.ytn.w [--]u.l ytn.|[aḫ]r.mǵy.ʿ[d]t.ilm.|[w]yʿn.aliy[n.]bʿl.|[- 15[128].2.10
[---.]gtn ṯṯ.|[---.]ṯḥr l ytn ḫs[n].|ʿbd ulm ṯn un ḫsn.|gdy lqḥ ṣtqn gt bn ndr.|um r 1154.2
.w ištql šql.|tn.km.nḥšm.yḥr.tn.km.|mhr y.w bn.bṯn.itnn y.|ytt.nḥšm.mhr k.bn bṯn.|itnn k.|aṯr ršp.ʿṯtrt.|ʿm ʿṯtr UG5.7.74
w ytnnn.|l aḫ h.l rʿ h.|rʿ ʿlm.|ttn.w tn.|w l ttn.|w al ttn.|tn ks yn.|w ištn.|ʿbd.prṯ.ṯhm.|qrq.pṯ.ḏmn.|l iṯtl. 1019.1.14
d.|ʿlm.ṯlṯ.sswm.mrkbt.|b trbṣt.bn.amt.|p d.in.b bt y.ttn.|tn.l y.mṯt.ḥry.|nʿmt.špḥ.bkr k.|d k.nʿm.ʿnt.nʿm h.|km 14[KRT].3.142
|ʿlm.ṯlṯ.sswm.|mrkbt.b trbṣ.|bn.amt.p d.[i]n.|b bt y.ttn.tn.|l y.mṯt.ḥry.|nʿmt.šbḥ.bkr k.|d k nʿm.ʿnt.|nʿm h.km 14[KRT].6.288
]k.|[---].aǵwyn.ʿn k.ẓẓ.w k mǵ.ilm.|[--.]k ʿṣm.k ʿšm.l ttn.k abnm.l thggn. 1001.2.13
m.|mhr y.w bn.bṯn.itnn y.|ytt.nḥšm.mhr k.bn bṯn.|itnn k.|aṯr ršp.ʿṯtrt.|ʿm ʿṯtrt.mr h.|mnt.nṯk.nḥš. UG5.7.76
t.limm.w tʿn.btlt.|ʿnt.irš ḥym.l aqht.ǵzr.|irš ḥym.w atn k.bl mt.|w ašlḥ k.ašspr k.ʿm.bʿl.|šnt.ʿm.bn il.tspr.yrḫm 17[2AQHT].6.27
m.|[l ʿpr.tšu.g h.]w tṣḥ.šmʿ.mʿ.|[l aqht.ǵzr.i]rš.ksp.w atn k.|[ḫrṣ.w aš]lḥ k.w tn.qšt k.[l].|[ʿnt.tq]ḥ[.q]ṣʿt k.ybmt.li 17[2AQHT].6.17
šnt.mlit.t[--.---].|ymǵy k.bnm.ta[--.---].|[b]nm.w bnt.ytn k[.---].|[--]l.bn y.šḥt.w [---].|[--]tt.msgr.bn k[.---].|[--]n. 59[100].9
dqt.ṯʿ.ynt.ṯʿm.dqt.ṯʿm.|mtntm nkbd.alp.š.l il.|gdlt.ilhm.ṯkmn.w šnm dqt.|ršp.dqt. 34[1].2
t.mnt.|ptḥ.bt.w ubn.hkl.w ištql šql.|tn.km.nḥšm.yḥr.tn.km.|mhr y.w bn.bṯn.itnn y.|ytt.nḥšm.mhr k.bn bṯn.|itn UG5.7.73
d h.ʿdbt.ṯlṯ.ptḥ.bt.mnt.|ptḥ.bt.w ubn.hkl.w ištql šql.|tn.km.nḥšm.yḥr.tn.km.|mhr y.w bn.bṯn.itnn y.|ytt.nḥšm. UG5.7.73
d.l pnw h.|b ḥrb.mlḥt.|qṣ.mri.ndd.|yʿšr.w yšqyn h.|ytn.ks.b d h.|krpn.b klat.yd h.|b krb.ʿẓm.ridn.|mt.šmm.ks 3[ʿNT].1.10
l.ylkn.ḫš.b a[rṣ.---].|b ʿpr.ḫbl ṯtm.[---.]|šqy.rṯa.tnm y.ytn.[ks.b yd].|krpn.b klat yd.[---].|ḳm ll.kḥṣ.tusp[.---].|tgr. 1[ʿNT.X].4.9
nn.|l aḫ h.l rʿ h.|rʿ ʿlm.|ttn.w tn.|w l ttn.|w al ttn.|tn ks yn.|w ištn.|ʿbd.prṯ.ṯhm.|qrq.pṯ.ḏmn.|l iṯtl. 1019.1.15
qrt.mlk[.---].|w.ʿl.ap.s[--.---].|b hm.w.rgm.hw.al[--].|atn.ksp.l hm.ʿd.|ilak.ʿm.mlk.|ht.lik[t.--.]mlk[.--].|w.mlk.yš 2008.2.7
w rbt.šnt.|b ʿd ʿlm...gnʿ.|iršt.aršt.|l aḫ y.l rʿ y.dt.|w ytnnn.|l aḫ h.l rʿ h.|rʿ ʿlm.|ttn.w tn.|w l ttn.|w al ttn.|tn 1019.1.9
ʿrt.|l.šr.ʿṯtrt.|mlbš.ṯrmnm.|k.ytn.w.b.bt.|mlk.mlbš.|ytn.l hm.|šbʿ.lbšm.allm.|l ušḫry.|ṯlṯ.mat.pṯtm.|l.mgmr.b.ṯ 1107.8
h[--.---].|mlk.gbʿ h d [---].|ibr.k l hm.d l h q[--.---].|l ytn.l hm.ṯḥt bʿl[.---].|h.u qšt pn hdd.b y[.---].|ʿm.b ym bʿl 9[33].2.5
ṣ h.k d.ʿl.qšt h.|imḫṣ h.ʿl.qṣʿt h.hwt.|l aḥw.ap.qšt h.l ttn.|l y.w b mt[.-]ḫ.mṣṣ[-]t[.--].|prʿ.qẓ.y[bl].šblt.|b ǵlp h.ap 19[1AQHT].1.16
.ṯlṯ.sswm.|mrkbt.b trbṣ.|bn.amt.p d.[i]n.|b bt y.ttn.tn.|l y.mṯt.ḥry.|nʿmt.šbḥ.bkr k.|d k nʿm.ʿnt.|nʿm h.km.ts 14[KRT].6.288
m.ṯlṯ.sswm.mrkbt.|b trbṣt.bn.amt.|p d.in.b bt y.ttn.|tn.l y.mṯt.ḥry.|nʿmt.špḥ.bkr k.|d k.nʿm.ʿnt.nʿm h.|km.tsm. 14[KRT].3.143
]tb.ʿryt k.k qlt[.---].|[--]at.brt.lb k.ʿnn.[---].|[--.]šdq.k ttn.l y.šn[.---].|[---.]bn.rgm.w ydʿ[.---]. 60[32].5
m.|adr.qrnt.b yʿlm.mtnm.|b ʿqbt.ṯr.adr.b ǵlil.qnm.|tn.l kṯr.w ḫss.ybʿl.qšt l ʿnt.|qṣʿt.l ybmt.limm.w tʿn.btlt.|ʿnt. 17[2AQHT].6.24
---]w yrmy[.q]rn h.|[---.-]ny h pdr.ttǵr.|[---.n]šr k.al ttn.l n.|[---.]tn l rbd.|[---.]bʿlt h w yn.|[---.rk]b ʿrpt.|[---.--] 2001.2.12
k].|[--]t.w.lqḥ.|yn[.--].b dn h.|w.ml[k].šswm.nʿmm.|ytn.l.ʿbdyrḫ.|w.mlk.z[--.--]n.šswm.|nʿmm.[--].ṯtm.w.at.|nǵ 2064.17
q]rn h.|[---.-]ny h pdr.ttǵr.|[---.n]šr k.al ttn.l n.|[---.]tn l rbd.|[---.]bʿlt h w yn.|[---.rk]b ʿrpt.|[---.--]n.w mnu dg. 2001.2.13
un ḫsn.|gdy lqḥ ṣtqn gt bn ndr.|um r[-] gtn ṯṯ ḫsn l ytn.|l rḥt lqḥ ṣtqn.|bt qbṣ urt ilštmʿ dbḥ ṣtqn l.|ršp. 1154.5
u---].mlk.ytn.mlbš.|[---.-]rn.k.ypdd.mlbš h.|[---.]mlk.ytn.lbš.l h. 1106.61
b.ṯlṯ.šnt.l.nṣd.|[---.--]ršp.mlk.k.ypdd.mlbš.|u---].mlk.ytn.mlbš.|[---.-]rn.k.ypdd.mlbš h.|[---.]mlk.ytn.lbš.l h. 1106.59
|ḫr[ḫ]b mlk qẓ.tn nkl y|rḫ ytrḫ.ib tʿrb m b bh|t h.w atn mhr h l a|b h.alp ksp w rbt ḫ|rṣ.išlḥ ẓhrm iq|nim.atn š 24[77].19
[-.---].|[---.--]k yṣunn[.---].|[---.--]dy.w.prʿ[.---].|[---.]ytn.ml[--].ank.iphn.|[---.a]nk.i[--.--]slm.w.yṯb.|[----.--]t.hw[1002.36
šql.|tn.km.nḥšm.yḥr.tn.km.|mhr y.w bn.bṯn.itnn y.|ytt.nḥšm.mhr k.bn bṯn.|itnn k.|aṯr ršp.ʿṯtrt.|ʿm ʿṯtrt.mr h. UG5.7.75
ṯrt hl[l.sn]nt.|ylak yrḫ ny[r] šmm.ʿm.|ḫr[ḫ]b mlk qẓ.tn nkl y|rḫ ytrḫ.ib tʿrb m b bh|t h.w atn mhr h l a|b h.alp 24[77].17
.|[---.y]d gt h[.--].|[---.]yd.|[k]rm h.yd.|[k]lkl h.|[w] ytn.nn.|l.bʿln.bn.|kltn.w l.|bn h.ʿd.ʿlm.|šḥr.ʿlmt.|bnš bnš 1008.11
l ḥ[ẓ]r y.|[-----].|[---.ttbʿ].|[mlakm.l yṯb].|[idk.pnm.l ytn].|[ʿ]m[.krt.mswn h].|tš[an.g hm.w tṣḥn].|tḥ[m.pbl.mlk 14[KRT].6.265
b.|[----.]lm y.|[---.--]p.|[---.d]bḥ.|t[---.id]k.|pn[m.al.ttn].|ʿm.[krt.msw]n.|w r[gm.l krt.]ṯʿ.|tḥm[.pbl.mlk].|qḥ.[k 14[KRT].5.246
.l krk|t.w ǵlm.l ʿbd.|il.ttbʿ.mlakm.|l yṯb.idk.pnm.|l ytn.ʿmm.pbl.|mlk.tšan.|g hm.w tṣḥn.|tḥm.krt.ṯ[ʿ].|hwt.[n] 14[KRT].6.302
r.š[--.---].|uṯ.ṯbr.ap hm.tbʿ.ǵlm[m.al.ṯṯb.idk.pnm].|al.ttn.ʿm.pḫr.mʿd.t[k.ǵr.ll.l pʿn.il].|al.tpl.al.tšthwy.pḫr [mʿd.q 2.1[137].14
.|l ḥyil.|lm.tlik.ʿm y.|ik y.aškn.|ʿṣm.l bt.dml.|p ank.atn.|ʿṣm.l k.|arbʿ.ʿṣm.|ʿl.ar.|w.ṯlṯ.|ʿl.ubrʿy.|w.ṯn.ʿl.|mlk.| 1010.7
k.tšt.b [---].|irt k.dṯ.ydṯ.mʿqb k.[ttbʿ].|[bt]lt.ʿnt.idk.l ttn.[pnm].|[ʿm.a]qht.ǵzr.b alp.š[d].|[rbt.]kmn.w ṣḥq.btlt.[ʿ 18[3AQHT].1.20
ʿn y.a]nk.nʿmn.ʿmq.nšm.|[tdʿṣ.pʿn]m.w tr.arṣ.idk.|[l ttn.pn]m.ʿm il.mbk.nhrm.|[qrb.ap]q.thmtm tgly.ḏd il.|[w t 17[2AQHT].6.47
|[ilnym.ṯn.mṯpd]m.ṯ[ḥt.ʿnt.arṣ.ṯlṯ.mtḥ.ǵyrm].|[idk.]l ytn.pnm.ʿm.[i]l.mbk.[nhrm.qrb.apq.thmtm].|[ygly.]ḏl i[l]. 2.3[129].4
k kbkb.l pnm.|aṯr.btlt.ʿnt.|w bʿl.tbʿ.mrym.ṣpn.|idk.l ttn.pnm.|ʿm.il.mbk.nhrm.|qrb.apq.thmtm.|tgly.ḏd.il.w tb 4[51].4.20
ʿl.k ilm.|[w ḥẓ]r.k bn.aṯrt[.tdʿṣ.]pʿn.|[w tr.a]rṣ.id[k.l ttn.p]nm.|[ʿm.i]l.mbk.nhr[m.qr]b.[ap]q.|[thm]tm.tgl.ḏ[d.]i 3[ʿNT.VI].5.13
[idk.l ttn.pnm].|[ʿm.il.mbk.nhrm].|[qrb.apq.thmtm].|[tgly.ḏd.il. 5[67].6.03
b[ʿl].|[---]ḫ h.tšt bm.ʿ[--].|[---.]zr h.ybm.l ilm.|[id]k.l ttn.pnm.ʿm.|[il.]mbk nhrm.qrb.|[a]pq.thmtm.tgly.ḏd.|il.w 6.1.32[49.1.4]
bn.ilm mt.|ʿbd k.an.w d.ʿlm k.|tbʿ.w l.yṯb.ilm.idk.|l ytn.pn.ʿm.bn.ilm.mt.|tk.qrt h.hmry.mk.ksu.|ṯbt.ḫḫ.arṣ.nḥl 5[67].2.14
t.ṯhrm.iqnim.|šmḫ.btlt.ʿnt.tdʿṣ.|pʿnm.w tr.arṣ.|idk.l ttn.pnm.|ʿm.bʿl.mrym.ṣpn.|b alp.šd.rbt.kmn.|ṣḥq.btlt.ʿnt.t 4[51].5.84

rḥq.ilnym.ṯn.mṯpdm.|ṯḥt.ʻnt.arṣ.ṯlṯ.mtḥ.ǵyrm.|idk.l ttn pnm.ʻm.bʻl.|mrym.ṣpn.b alp.šd.rbt.kmn.|hlk.aḫt h.bʻl.y 3[ʻNT].4.81
n ilm.mt.b mh|mrt.ydd.il.ǵzr.|tbʻ.w l.yṯb ilm.idk.|l ytn.pnm.ʻm.bʻl.|mrym.ṣpn.w yʻn.|gpn.w ugr.ṯḥm.bn ilm.| 5[67].1.10
ṯm.ḏr[qm.---].|[btl]t.ʻnt.l kl.[---].|[tt]bʻ.btlt.ʻnt[.idk.l ttn.pnm].|ʻm.yṭpn.mhr.š[t.tšu.g h].|w tṣḥ.yṯb.yṯp.[---].|qrt. 18[3AQHT].4.5
q.ilnym].|ṯn.mṯpdm.ṯḥt.[ʻnt.arṣ.ṯlṯ.mtḥ].|ǵyrm.idk.l yt[n.pnm.ʻm.lṭpn].|il d pid.tk ḫrš[n.---.tk.ǵr.ks].|ygly ḏd.i[l 1[ʻNT.IX].3.21
t.mḫrtt.|iy.aliyn.bʻl.|iy.zbl.bʻl.arṣ.|ttbʻ.btlt.ʻnt.|idk.l ttn.pnm.|ʻm.nrt.ilm.špš.|tšu.g h.w tṣḥ.|ṯḥm.ṯr.il.ab k.|hwt 6[49].4.31
idk.al.ttn.pnm.|ʻm.ǵr.trǵzz.|ʻm.ǵr.ṯrmg.|ʻm.tlm.ǵṣr.arṣ.|ša.ǵr.ʻl. 4[51].8.1
.hkl h.|qšt hn.aḫd.b yd h.|w qṣʻt h.bm.ymn h.|idk.l ytn pnm.|tk.aḫ.šmk.mla[t.r]umm.|tšu knp.btlt.ʻn[t].|tšu.k 10[76].2.8
]m.ʻdb.l arṣ.|[---.]špm.ʻdb.|[---].tʻtqn.|[---.-]ʻb.idk.|[l ytn.pnm.tk.]in.bb.b alp ḥẓr.|[rbt.kmn.l pʻ]n.ʻnt.|[yhbr.w y 1[ʻNT.IX].2.14
[idk.al.ttn.pnm.tk.ḫkpt.il.kl h].|[kptr.]ks[u.ṯbt h.ḫkpt.arṣ.nḫlt h].| 1[ʻNT.IX].3.01
iht.|np šmm.šmšr.|l dgy.aṯrt.|mǵ.l qdš.amrr.|idk.al.tnn.|pnm.tk.ḫqkpt.|il.kl h.kptr.|ksu.ṯbt h.ḫkpt.|arṣ.nḫlt h 3[ʻNT.VI].6.12
l ẓr.rḥtm.|w rd.bt ḫptt.|arṣ.tspr.b y|rdm.arṣ.|idk.al.ttn.|pnm.tk.qrt h.|hmry.mk.ksu.|ṯbt h.ḫḫ.arṣ.|nḫlt h.w nǵ 4[51].8.10
b gt ilštmʻ.|bt ubnyn š h d.ytn.ṣtqn.|ṯut ṯbḫ ṣtq[n].|b bz ʻzm ṯbḫ š[h].|b kl ygz ḫḫ š h 1153.2
[-].l irt k.|wn ap.ʻdn.mṭr h.|bʻl.yʻdn.ʻdn.ṯkt.b glṯ.|w tn.ql h.b ʻrpt.|šrh.l arṣ.brqm.|bt.arzm.yklln h.|hm.bt.lbnt. 4[51].5.70
iqra.ilm.n[ʻmm.---].|w ysmm.bn.š[---].|ytnm.qrt.l ʻly[.---].|b mdbr.špm.yd[.---.---]r.|l riš hm.w yš[- 23[52].3
mʻ.mʻ.|[l aqht.ǵzr.i]rš.ksp.w atn k.|[ḫrṣ.w aš]lḥ k.w tn.qšt k.[l].|[ʻnt.tq]ḥ[.q]ṣʻt k.ybmt.limm.|w yʻn.aqht.ǵzr.ad 17[2AQHT].6.18
.|l brlt.hyn.d ḥrš.|ydm.aḫr.ymǵy.kṯr.|w ḫss.b d.dnil.ytnn.|qšt.l brk h.yʻdb.|qṣʻt.apnk.mṯt.dnty.|tšlḥm.tššqy ilm 17[2AQHT].5.26
gnryn.|l mlkytn.|ḥnn y l pn mlk.|šin k itn.|rʻ y šša idn l y.|l šmn iṯr hw.|p iḫdn gnryn.|im mlkyt 1020.4
lat.|tqln.alpm.|yrḫ.ʻšrt.l bʻ[l].|dqtm.w ynt.qr[t].|w mtntm.š l rmš.|w kbd.w š.l šlm kbd.|alp.w š.l bʻl ṣpn.|dqt UG5.13.7
l]n.al[p]m.yrḫ.ʻšrt.|[l bʻl.ṣ]pn.[dq]tm.w y[nt] qrt.|[w mtmt]m.[š.l] rm[š.]kbd.w š.|[l šlm.kbd.al]p.w š.[l] bʻl.ṣpn.| 36[9].1.13
n mhr h l a|b h.alp ksp w rbt ḫ|rṣ.išlḥ ẓhrm iq|nim.atn šd h krm[m].|šd dd h ḥrnqm.w |yʻn ḫrḫb mlk qẓ [l].|n 24[77].22
l ym hnd.|ʻmṯtmr.bn.|nqmpʻ.ml[k].|ugrt.ytn.|šd.kdǵdl[.bn].|[-]š[-]y.d.b š[-]y.|[---.y]d gt h[.--].|[---.] 1008.4
.pnm.trǵnw.w ttkl.|bnwt h.ykr.ʻr.d qdm.|idk.pnm.l ytn.tk aršḫ.rbt.|w aršḫ.ṯrrt.ydy.b ʻṣm.ʻrʻr.|w b šḫt.ʻs.mt.ʻrʻr UG5.7.63
.ḫnzr k.|ʻm k.pdry.bt.ar.|ʻm k.ṭṭly.bt.rb.idk.|pn k.al ttn.tk.ǵr.|knkny.ša.ǵr.ʻl ydm.|ḫlb.l ẓr.rḥtm w rd.|bt ḫptt.a 5[67].5.12
nn h].|bn.dgn.arṯ m.pḏ h.tbʻ.ǵlmm.l ttb.[idk.pnm].|l ytn.tk.ǵr.ll.ʻm.phr.mʻd.ap.ilm.l lḥ[m].|yṯb.bn qdš.l ṯrm.bʻl. 2.1[137].20
m.ṯlṯ.|[ssw]m.mrkbt b trbṣ bn.amt.|[tn.b]nm.aqny.|[tn.ṯa]rm.amid.|[w yʻn].ṯr.ab h.il.|d[--].b bk.krt.|b dmʻ.nʻm 14[KRT].2.58
bt.|b qrb.hk[l m.yp]tḥ.|bʻl.b dqt[.ʻrp]t.|ql h.qdš.b[ʻl.y]tn.|yṯny.bʻl.ṣ[---.-]pt h.|ql h.q[dš.ṯb]r.arṣ.|[---.]ǵrm[.t]ḫš 4[51].7.29
].|šm.bn y.yw.ilt.[---].|w pʻr.šm.ym[-.---].|tʻnyn.l zn.tn[.---].|at.adn.tpʻr[.---].|ank.lṭpn.il[.d pid.---].|ʻl.ydm.pʻrt[1[ʻNT.X].4.16
.w tr.b ḫl.|[b]nʻmm.b ysmm.ḥ[--]k.ǵrt.|[ql].l bʻl.ʻnt.ttnn.|[---].bʻl m.d ip[---].|[il.]hd.d ʻnn.n[--].|[----.]aliyn.b[ʻl] 10[76].2.31
arṣ.|[---].mtm.|[---.--]d mhr.ur.|[---.]yḥnnn.|[---.--]t.ytn.|[---.btlt.]ʻnt.|[---.ybmt.]limm.|[---.---]l.limm.|[---.yṯ]b. 10[76].1.13
.[m]šl[t].|[--]arš[p.-]š.l[h].|[-]ṯl[.--]š.l h.|[---]l[.--] h.|mtn[.---.]l h.|[---.]l h.|[---.--]š.l h.|[---].l h.|[--.]spr[.---].|[--. 2133.6
š.|bʻl k.ky.akl.|b.ḥwt k.inn.|špš n.[---].|hm.al[k.--].|ytnt[.---].|ṯn[.---].|w[.-----].|l[.-----].|h[--.---].|šp[š.---].|ʻm. 2060.23
[---.]km.t[--.---].|[--.n]pš.ttn[.---].|[---.]ydʻt.k[---].|[---].w hm.|[--]y.ṯb y.w [---].|[---.] 61[-].2
mašmn.|ytn. 1182.2

ytnt

dbḥ klyrḫ.|ndr.|dbḥ.|dt nat.|w ytnt.|ṯrmn w.|dbḥ kl.|kl ykly.|dbḥ k.sprt.|dt nat.|w qrwn RS61[24.277.5]

ytr

|bn mʻnt.|bn kbdy.|bn krk.|bn srty.|bn lth ḫlq.|bn ytr.|bn ilšpš.|ubrš.|bn gmš ḫlq.|bn ʻgy.|bn zlbn.|bn.aḫ[--] 2016.2.15
m.ḥbr k.|w ḫss.dʻt k.|b ym.arš.w tnn.|kṯr.w ḫss.yd.|ytr.kṯr.w ḫss.|spr.ilmlk šbny.|lmd.atn.prln.rb.|khnm rb.n 6.6[62.2].52
rq[-.---].|[---.]ʻd ʻlm[.---].|[---.]ʻd.admn[.---].|[---.--]d.ytr.mṯ[--].|[-----].|[-----].|[---].ḫmš[.---].|[---.]urš[-.---].|[---. 2156.5

ytrhd

.w yhbṯ.bnš.|w ytn.ilm.b d hm.|b d.iḫqm.gṯr.|w b d.ytrhd.|bʻl. 55[18].21

ytrm

n.armg[-].|bʻlmṯpṯ.|[bn].ayḫ.|[---]rn.|ill.|ǵlmn.|bn.ytrm.|bn.ḫgbt.|mtn.|mḫtn.|[p]lsy.|bn.ḥrš.|[--.]kbd.|[---]. 1035.2.10
my.ṯt.qštm.w[.]q[lʻ].|bn.rpš.qšt.w.qlʻ.|bn.ǵb.qšt.|bn.ytrm.qšt.w.qlʻ.|bn.ʻbdyrḫ.qšt.w.q[lʻ].|bn.lky.qšt.|bn.dll.qšt 119[321].3.25

ytrʻm

ilṣdq.bn.zry.|bʻlytn.bn.ulb.|ytrʻm.bn.swy.|ṣḥrn.bn.qrtm.|bn.špš.bn.ibrd.|ʻpṯrm.bn.ʻbd 2024.3

ytrš

[t].|bʻln.ḫmšt.|w.nḥl h.ḫm[š]t.|bn.unp.arbʻt.|ʻbdbn.ytrš ḫmšt.|krwn.ʻšrt.|bn.ulb ḫmšt.|bn.ḥry.ḫmšt.|swn.ḫmš 1062.11

ytršn

[---.]yn.l.m[--]m.|[---.]d.bn.[---.]l.dqn.|[---.--]ʻ.šdyn.l ytršn.|[---.--]ṯ.ʻbd.l.kyn.|k[rm.--.]l.i[w]rtḏl.|ḥl.d[--.ʻbd]yrḫ. 2027.2.8

ytršp

n.ḫrzn.|ady.|bn.birtn.|bn.ḥrẓn.|bn.bddn.|bn.anny.|ytršp.|bn.szn.|bn.kdǵdl.|bn.glʻd.|bn.ktln.|[bn].ǵrgn.|bn.p 115[301].1.11
piy.|mrṭn.|ṯnyn.|apṯ.|šbn.|gbrn.|ṯbʻm.|kyn.|bʻln.|ytršp.|ḫmšm.ṯmn.kbd.|tgmr.bnš.mlk.|d.b d.adnʻm.|[š]bʻ.b 1024.2.24
[y-]n.|yny.|ydn.|ytršp.|ydrm.|ydy.|ydlm.|yʻḏrd.|yrmt.|yyn.|yn.|ydln.|y 112[16].4

yṯil

.l.gzzm.|yyn.|ṣdqn.|ʻbd.pdr.|myṣm.|ṯgt.|w.lmd h.|yṯil.|w.lmd h.|rpan.|w.lmd h.|ʻbdrpu.|w.lmd h.|ʻdršp.|w. 1099.11

yṯb

k.|[---.--]r.dr.dr.|[---.--]y k.w rḥd.|[---]y ilm.d mlk.|y[ṯ]b.aliyn.b‘l.|yt‘dd.rkb.‘rpt.|[--].ydd.w yqlṣn.|yqm.w yw 4[51].3.10

.|aḫt.‘rš.mdw.anšt.|‘rš.zbln.rd.l mlk.|amlk.l drkt k.aṯb.|an.w y‘ny.krt ṯ‘.yṯbr.|ḥrn.y bn.yṯbr.ḥrn.|riš k.‘ṯtrt.šm. 16.6[127].53

.aḫt.‘rš.mdw.|anšt.‘rš.zbln.|rd.l mlk.amlk.|l drkt.k aṯb.an.|ytb‘.yṣb ǵlm.‘l.|ab h.y‘rb.yšu g h.|w yṣḥ.šm‘ m‘.l k 16.6[127].38

i[t].|yprq.lṣb.w yṣḥq.|p‘n.l hdm.yṯpd.yšu.|g h.w yṣḥ.aṯbn.ank.|w anḫn.w tnḫ.b irt y.|npš.k yld.bn.l y.km.|aḫ y. 17[2AQHT].2.12

‘n h.l hdm.yṯpd.|w yprq.lṣb w yṣḥq.|yšu.g h.w yṣḥ.|aṯbn.ank.w anḫn.|w tnḫ.b irt y.npš.|k ḥy.aliyn.b‘l.|k iṯ.zbl 6[49].3.18

-]l[-].|b šdm.‘l k.pht.|dr‘.b ym.tn.aḥd.|b aḫ k.ispa.w yṯb.|ap.d anšt.im[-].|aḥd.b aḫ k.l[--]n.|hn[-.]aḥẓ[.---]l[-].|[‘ 6[49].5.20

ṯrt.ym.mṯb.|klt.knyt.|mṯb.pdry.b ar.|mẓll.ṭly.bt rb.|mṯb.arṣy.bt.y‘bdr.|ap.mṯn.rgmm.|argm k.šskn m‘.|mgn.rb 4[51].1.19

rt.ym.|mṯb.klt.knyt.|mṯb.pdry.bt.ar.|mẓll.ṭly.bt rb.|mṯb.arṣ.bt y‘bdr.|w y‘n lṭpn il d pid.|p ‘bd.an.‘nn.aṯrt.|p.‘b 4[51].4.57

m]ṯb.rbt.aṯrt.|ym.mṯb.[pdr]y.bt.ar.|[mẓll.]ṭly[.bt.]rb.mṯb.|[arṣy.bt.y‘bdr.mṯb].|[klt.knyt]. 3[‘NT.VI].5.50

.m[ṯb.rbt.aṯrt.ym].|mṯb.pdr[y.bt.ar.mẓll].|ṭly.bt.r[b.mṯb.arṣy].|bt.y‘bdr[.mṯb.klt].|knyt.w t‘n[.btlt.‘nt].|yṯb l y.ṯ 3[‘NT.VI].4.4

hr].|b ‘lṣ.‘lṣm.npr.š[--.---].|uṭ.ṯbr.ap hm.tb‘.ǵlm[m.al.ṯṯb.idk.pnm].|al.ttn.‘m.pḫr.m‘d.t[k.ǵr.ll.l p‘n.il].|al.tpl.al.tš 2.1[137].13

.l bt y].|[ng.kr]t.l ḥ[ẓ]r y.|[-----].|[---.ttb‘].|[mlakm.l yṯb].|[idk.pnm.l ytn].|[‘]m[.krt.mswn h].|tš[an.g hm.w tṣḥ 14[KRT].6.264

.adm.|w ld.špḥ.l krk|t.w ǵlm.l ‘bd.|il.ttb‘.mlakm.|l yṯb.idk.pnm.|l ytn.‘mm.pbl.|mlk.tšan.|g hm.w tṣḥn.|tḥm. 14[KRT].6.301

ry]h.|[wn.in.bt.l b‘l.]|[km.ilm.w ḥẓr].|[k bn.aṯ]r[t].|m[ṯ]b.il.mẓll.|bn h.mṯb.rbt.|aṯrt.ym.mṯb.|klt.knyt.|mṯb.p 4[51].1.13

lt.w ṣbrt.arḫ h.|wn.in.bt.l b‘l.km.ilm.|ḥẓr.k b[n.a]ṯrt.mṯb.il.|mṯll.b[n h.m]ṯb.rbt.aṯrt.|ym.mṯb.[pdr]y.bt.ar.|[mẓl 3[‘NT.VI].5.47

[---.wn.in].|[bt].l [b‘l.km.ilm.w ḥẓr].|k bn.[aṯrt.mṯb.il.mẓll].|bn h.m[ṯb.rbt.aṯrt.ym].|mṯb.pdr[y.bt.ar.mẓll] 3[‘NT.VI].4.1

w ṣbrt.|ary h.wn.in.bt.l b‘l.|km.ilm.w ḥẓr.k bn.aṯrt.|mṯb il.mẓll.bn h.|mṯb rbt.aṯrt.ym.|mṯb.klt.knyt.|mṯb.pdry 4[51].4.52

.il.pn.l mgr lb.t‘dbn.|nšb.l inr.t‘dbn.ktp.|b il ab h.g‘r.yṯb.il.kb[-].|aṯ[rt.]il.yṯb.b mrzḥ h.|yšt[.il.y]n.‘d šb‘.trṯ.‘d šk UG5.1.1.14

y.|qrdm.bhṯ.l bn.ilm mt.|‘bd k.an.w d.‘lm k.|tb‘.w l.yṯb.ilm.idk.|l ytn.pn.‘m.bn.ilm.mt.|tk.qrt h.hmry.mk.ksu. 5[67].2.13

.l yrt.|b npš.bn ilm.mt.b mh|mrt.ydd.il.ǵzr.|tb‘.w l.yṯb ilm.idk.|l ytn.pnm.‘m.b‘l.|mrym.ṣpn.w y‘n.|gpn.w ugr 5[67].1.9

---].w [---].|[---].mr[--.---].|[---].mr[--.]ydm[.---].|[---.]mṯbt.ilm.w.b.[---].|[---.]tṯṯbn.ilm.w.[---].|[---.]w.ksu.b‘lt.b[h 47[33].5

.w tṣd[.---].|tḥgrn.ǵzr.n‘m.[---].|w šm.‘rbm.yr[.---].|mṯbt.ilm.ṯmn.ṯ[--.--].|pamt.šb‘.|iqnu.šmt[.---].|[b]n.šrm.|i 23[52].19

b ymm.apnk.dnil.mt.|rpi.a hn.ǵzr.mt.hrnm[y].|ytšu.yṯb.b ap.ṯǵr.tḥt.|adrm.d b grn.ydn.|dn.almnt.yṯpṭ.ṯpṭ.ytm. 17[2AQHT].5.6

h.apnk.dnil.|[m]t.rpi.ap[h]n.ǵzr.|[mt.hrn]my.ytšu.|[yṯb.b ap.ṯ]ǵr[.t]ḥt.|[adrm.d b grn.y]dn.|[dn.almnt.y]ṯpṭ.|[ṯ 19[1AQHT].1.22

.u]br‘y.|iln.[---].|bn.[---].ar.|bn.[---].b.ar.|špšyn[.---.]yṯb.b.ar.|bn.ag[p]ṯ.ḫpṯ.d[.yṯb.b].š‘rt.|yly.bn.ṯrnq.[-]r.d.yṯb. 2015.1.24

]h.|nn[-].b[n].py[-.d.]yṯb.b.gt.aǵld.|sgn.bn b[--.---].d.yṯb.b.ilštm‘.|abmn.bn.r[---].b.syn.|bn.irṣ[-.---.]h.|šdyn.b[n. 2015.2.6

b.b.ar.|bn.ag[p]ṯ.ḫpṯ.d[.yṯb.b].š‘rt.|yly.bn.ṯrnq.[-]r.d.yṯb.b.ilštm‘.|ilšlm.bn.gs[-.--]r.d.yṯb.b.gt.al.|ilmlk.[--]kt.[--. 2015.1.26

rt.|yly.bn.ṯrnq.[-]r.d.yṯb.b.ilštm‘.|ilšlm.bn.gs[-.--]r.d.yṯb.b.gt.al.|ilmlk.[--]kt.[--.d.]yṯb.b.šb[n].|bn.pr[-.]d.y[ṯb.b]. 2015.1.27

l h[.-].ṯgd.mrum.|bt.[-]b[-.-]sy[-]h.|nn[-].b[n].py[-.d.]yṯb.b.gt.aǵld.|sgn.bn b[--.---].d.yṯb.b.ilštm‘.|abmn.bn.r[---]. 2015.2.5

.yṯb.krt.l ‘d h.|yṯb.l ksi mlk.|l nḫt.l kḥṯ.drkt.|ap.yṣb.yṯb.b hkl.|w ywsrnn.ggn h.|lk.l ab k.yṣb.lk.|l[ab]k.w rgm 16.6[127].25

mr yn ay.|šlm.mlk.šlm.mlkt.‘rbm m.ṯnnm.|mt.w šr.yṯb.b d h.ḫṭ.ṯkl.b d h.|ḫṭ.ulmn.yzbrnn.zbrm.gpn.|yṣmdnn. 23[52].8

|nšb.l inr.t‘dbn.ktp.|b il ab h.g‘r.yṯb.il.kb[-].|aṯ[rt.]il.yṯb.b mrzḥ h.|yšt[.il.y]n.‘d šb‘.trṯ.‘d škr.|il.hlk.l bt h.yštql. UG5.1.1.15

--]m.[---.]|gm.ṣḥ.l q[ṣ.ilm.---].|l rḥqm.l p[-.---].|ṣḥ.il.yṯb.b[mrzḥ.---].|bṯt.‘llm n.[---].|ilm.bt.b‘l k.[---].|dl.ylkn.ḥ 1[‘NT.X].4.4

[---]n.yšt.rpu.mlk.‘lm.w yšt.|[--.]gṯr.w yqr.il.yṯb.b.‘ṯtrt.|il.ṯpṭ.b hd r‘y.d yšr.w yḏmr.|b knr.w ṯlb.b tp.w UG5.2.1.2

tm‘.|ilšlm.bn.gs[-.--]r.d.yṯb.b.gt.al.|ilmlk.[--]kt.[--.d.]yṯb.b.šb[n].|bn.pr[-.]d.y[ṯb.b].šlmy.|tlš.w[.n]ḥl h[.-].ṯgd.mr 2015.2.1

.yṯb.b.gt.al.|ilmlk.[--]kt.[--.d.]yṯb.b.šb[n].|bn.pr[-.]d.y[ṯb.b].šlmy.|tlš.w[.n]ḥl h[.-].ṯgd.mrum.|bt.[-]b[-.-]sy[-]h.| 2015.2.2

r.|bn.[---].b.ar.|špšyn[.---.]yṯb.b.ar.|bn.ag[p]ṯ.ḫpṯ.d[.yṯb.b].š‘rt.|yly.bn.ṯrnq.[-]r.d.yṯb.b.ilštm‘.|ilšlm.bn.gs[-.--]r. 2015.1.25

y.mrṣ.gršm zbln.|in.b ilm.‘ny h.|w y‘n.lṭpn.il.b pid.|ṯb.bn y.lm ṯb[t] km.|l kḥṯ.zbl k[m.a]nk.|iḥtrš.w [a]škn.|aš 16[126].5.24

.[idk.pnm].|l ytn.tk.ǵr.ll.‘m.phr.m‘d.ap.ilm.l lḥ[m].|yṯb.bn qdš.l ṯrm.b‘l.qm.‘l.il.hlm.|ilm.tph hm.tphn.mlak.ym 2.1[137].21

mḫṣ.b ktp.|dk ym.ymḫṣ.b ṣmd.|ṣḥr mt.ymṣḫ.l arṣ.|[yṯb.]b[‘]l.l ksi.mlk h.|[---].l kḥṯ.drkt h.|l [ym]m.l yrḫm.l yr 6[49].5.5

šm.l [b‘lt.bhtm.‘ṣrm.l inš].|ilm.w š d[d.ilš.š.--.mlk].|yṯb.brr[.w mḥ-.---].|ym.[‘]lm.y‘[--.---].|[--.-]g[-.-]s w [---].| 35[3].7

.w tḥ.ṭbt.n[--].|[---.b]ṯnm w ṯṯb.‘l.bṯnt.trtḥ[ṣ.---].|[---.t]ṯb h.aḫt.ppšr.w ppšrt[.---].|[---.]k.drḫm.w aṯb.l ntbt.k.‘ṣm 1001.2.6

t hn.b šlḥ.|ttpl.y‘n.ḥtk h.|krt y‘n.ḥtk h.rš.|mid.grdš.ṯbt h.|w b tm hn.špḥ.yitbd.|w b.pḫyr h.yrṯ.|y‘rb.b ḥdr h.y 14[KRT].1.23

[idk.al.ttn.pnm.tk.ḥkpt.il.kl h].|[kptr.]ks[u.ṯbt h.ḥkpt.arṣ.nḥlt h].|b alp.šd.r[bt.kmn.l p‘n.kṯr].|hbr.w q 1[‘NT.IX].3.1

dš.amrr.|idk.al.tnn.|pnm.tk.ḥqkpt.|il.kl h.kptr.|ksu.ṯbt h.ḥkpt.|arṣ.nḥlt h.|b alp.šd.rbt.|kmn.l p‘n.kṯ.|hbr.w ql 3[‘NT.VI].6.15

y|rdm.arṣ.|idk.al.ttn.|pnm.tk.qrt h.|hmry.mk.ksu.|ṯbt h.ḫḫ.arṣ.|nḥlt h.w nǵr.|‘nn.ilm.al.|tqrb.l bn.ilm.|mt.al. 4[51].8.13

.|l.[---]t.|i[d.yd]bḥ.mlk.l.prgl.ṣqrn.b.gg.|ar[b‘.]arb‘.mṯbt.azmr.b h.š.šr[-].|al[p.w].š.šlmm.pamt.šb‘.klb h.|yr[--. 35[3].51

[---.--]m[.---].|[-.]rbt.ṯbt.[---].|rbt.ṯbt.ḥš[n.---].|y.arṣ.ḥšn[.---].|t‘td.tkl.[---].|tkn.lbn[.---].|dt.l 5[67].3.3

.idk.|l ytn.pn.‘m.bn.ilm.mt.|tk.qrt h.hmry.mk.ksu.|ṯbt.ḫḫ.arṣ.nḥlt h.tša.|g hm.w tṣḥ.tḥm.aliyn.|bn.b‘l.hwt.aliy 5[67].2.16

t.‘nt[.idk.l ttn.pnm].|‘m.yṭpn.mhr.š[t.tšu.g h].|w tṣḥ.yṯb.ytp.[---].|qrt.ablm.ablm.[qrt.zbl.yrḫ].|ik.al.yḥdṯ.yrḫ.b[- 18[3AQHT].4.7

b‘l.yṯb.k ṯbt.ǵr.hd.r[‘y].|k mdb.b tk.ǵr h.il ṣpn.b [tk].|ǵr.tliyt.š UG5.3.1.1

t[ḫ]|ṣ.‘m.aliyn.b‘l.|ik.al.yšm[‘] k.ṯr.|il.ab k.l ys‘.alt.|ṯbt k.l yhpk.ksa.mlk k.|l yṯbr.ḫṭ.mṯpṭ k.|yru.bn ilm t.ṯt‘.y| 6[49].6.28

m.l pn[.ṯ]pṭ[.n]hr.|[ik.a]l.yšm‘ k.ṯr.[i]l.ab k.l ys‘.[alt.]ṯ[bt |k.l y]hpk.|[ksa.]mlk k.l yṯbr.ḫṭ.mṯpṭ k.w y‘n[.‘ṯtr].dm 2.3[129].17

nšr k.|w rbṣ.l ǵr k.inbb.|kt ǵr k.ank.yd‘t.|[-]n.atn.at.mṯb k[.---].|[š]mm.rm.lk.prẓ kt.|[k]bkbm.ṯm.tpl k.lbnt.|[-. 13[6].11

mṯb.pdr[y.bt.ar.mẓll].|ṭly.bt.r[b.mṯb.arṣy].|bt.y‘bdr[.mṯb.klt].|knyt.w t‘n[.btlt.‘nt].|yṯb l y.ṯr.il[.ab y.---].|yṯb.l y 3[‘NT.VI].4.5

.w ḥẓr.k bn.aṯrt.|mṯb il.mẓll.bn h.|mṯb rbt.aṯrt.ym.|mṯb.klt.knyt.|mṯb.pdry.bt.ar.|mẓll.ṭly.bt rb.|mṯb.arṣ.bt y‘ 4[51].4.54

].|[k bn.aṯ]r[t].|m[ṯ]b.il.mẓll.|bn h.mṯb.rbt.|aṯrt.ym.mṯb.|klt.knyt.|mṯb.pdry.b ar.|mẓll.ṭly.bt rb.|mṯb.arṣy.bt.y 4[51].1.15

ṯb.[pdr]y.bt.ar.|[mẓll.]ṭly[.bt.]rb.mṯb.|[arṣy.bt.y‘bdr.mṯb].|[klt.knyt]. 3[‘NT.VI].5.51

zbln.|in.b ilm.‘ny h.|w y‘n.lṭpn.il.b pid.|ṯb.bn y.lm ṯb[t] km.|l kḥṯ.zbl k[m.a]nk.|iḥtrš.w [a]škn.|aškn.ydt.[m]r 16[126].5.24

.mṯt.ḥry.|ṭṭbḫ.imr.w lḥm.|mgṯ.w yṯrm.hn.ym.|w ṯn.yṯb.krt.l ‘d h.|yṯb.l ksi mlk.|l nḫt.l kḥṯ.drkt.|ap.yṣb.yṯb.b 16.6[127].22

ṣ.|apnk.lṭpn.il.|d pid.yrd.l ksi.yṯb.|l hdm[.w] l.hdm.yṯb.|l arṣ.yṣq.‘mr.|un.l riš h.‘pr.plṯt.|l qdqd h.lpš.yks.|miz 5[67].6.13

h.rpum. | [l tdd.aṯr]h.l tdd.i[lnym]. | [---.]r[--.---]. | [---.yṯ]b.l arṣ. 21[122].2.1
aliyn.b'l. | ḫlq.zbl.b'l.arṣ. | apnk.lṭpn.il. | d pid.yrd.l ksi.yṯb. | l hdm[.w] l.hdm.yṯb. | l arṣ.yṣq.'mr. | un.l riš h.'pr.plṯt. 5[67].6.12
.kṯr.w ḫss. | št.alp.qdm h.mra. | w tk.pn h.t'db.ksu. | w yṯṯb.l ymn.aliyn. | b'l.'d.lḥm.št[y.ilm]. | [w]y'n.aliy[n.b'l]. | [- 4[51].5.109
lk.'ṯtr.'rẓ. | ymlk.'ṯtr.'rẓ. | apnk.'ṯtr.'rẓ. | y'l.b ṣrrt.ṣpn. | yṯb.l kḥṯ.aliyn. | b'l.p'n h.l tmǵyn. | hdm.riš h.l ymǵy. | aps h. 6.1.58[49.1.30]
n'mt.aḫt[.b'l]. | y'l.b'l.b ǵ[r.---]. | w bn.dgn.b š[---]. | b'l.yṯb.l ks[i.mlk h]. | bn.dgn.l kḥ[ṯ.drkt h]. | l alp.ql.ẓ[--.---]. | l n 10[76].3.14
ru.bn ilm t.ṯt'.y | dd.il.ǵzr.y'r.mt. | b ql h.y[---.---]. | b'l.yṯṯbn[.l ksi]. | mlk h.l[nḥt.l kḥṯ]. | drkt h[.---]. | [---.]d[--.---]. | 6[49].6.33
.imr.w lḥm. | mgṯ.w yṯrm.hn.ym. | w ṯn.yṯb.krt.l 'd h. | yṯb.l ksi mlk. | l nḥt.l kḥṯ.drkt. | ap.yṣb.yṯb.b hkl. | w ywsrnn. 16.6[127].23
.mhr.št. | tštn.k nšr.b ḥbš h.km.diy. | b t'rt h.aqht.km.yṯb.l lḥ[m]. | bn.dnil.l ṯrm.'l h.nšr[m]. | trḫpn.ybṣr.ḥbl.diy[m 18[3AQHT].4.29
. | l k.ašt k.km.nšr.b ḥb[š y]. | km.diy.b t'rt y.aqht.[km.yṯb]. | l lḥm.w bn.dnil.l ṯrm[.'l h]. | nšrm.trḫpn.ybṣr.[ḥbl.d] | i 18[3AQHT].4.18
.---]. | [---.t]ṯb h.aḫt.ppšr.w ppšrt[.---]. | [---.]k.drḫm.w aṯb.l ntbt.k.'ṣm l t[--]. | [---.]drk.brḥ.arṣ.lk pn h.yrk.b'[l]. | [-- 1001.2.7
.mṣrp k.[---]. | [---.]y.mṭnt.w tḥ.ṭbt.n[--]. | [---.b]ṯnm w ṯṯb.'l.bṯnt.trṯḥ[ṣ.---]. | [---.t]ṯb h.aḫt.ppšr.w ppšrt[.---]. | [---.]k 1001.2.5
b'l.yṯb.k ṯbt.ǵr.hd.r['y]. | k mdb.b tk.ǵr h.il ṣpn.b [tk]. | ǵr.tliyt.šb't.br UG5.3.1.1
ẓr]. | k bn.[aṯrt.mṯb.il.mẓll]. | bn h.m[ṯb.rbt.aṯrt.ym]. | mṯb.pdr[y.bt.ar.mẓll]. | ṭly.bt.r[b.mṯb.arṣy]. | bt.y'bdr[.mṯb.k 3['NT.VI].4.3
. | ḥẓr.k b[n.a]ṯrt.mṯb.il. | mṯll.b[n h.m]ṯb.rbt.aṯrt. | ym.mṯb.[pdr]y.bt.ar. | [mẓll.]ṭly[.bt.]rb.mṯb. | [arṣy.bt.y'bdr.mṯb 3['NT.VI].5.49
m[ṯ]b.il.mẓll. | bn h.mṯb.rbt. | aṯrt.ym.mṯb. | klt.knyt. | mṯb.pdry.b ar. | mẓll.ṭly.bt rb. | mṯb.arṣy.bt.y'bdr. | ap.mṯn.r 4[51].1.17
rt. | mṯb il.mẓll.bn h. | mṯb rbt.aṯrt.ym. | mṯb.klt.knyt. | mṯb.pdry.bt.ar. | mẓll.ṭly.bt rb. | mṯb.arṣ.bt y'bdr. | w y'n lṭp 4[51].4.55
dy. | ḥmt.hlm.yṯq yṯqšqy.nḥš.yšlḥm.'q šr. | y'db.ksa.w.yṯb. | tqru.l špš.um h.špš.um.ql bl. | 'm b'l.mrym.ṣpn.mnt y. UG5.7.7
h.ydy. | ḥmt.hlm.yṯq.nḥš.yšlḥm.nḥš. | 'q šr.y'db.ksa.w yṯb. | tqru.l špš.um h.špš.um.ql b.'m. | ršp.bbt h.mnt.nḥš.šmr UG5.7.29
h.ydy. | ḥmt.hlm.yṯq.nḥš.yšlḥm.nḥš 'q. | š.y'db.ksa w yṯb. | tqru l špš.um h.špš.um.ql bl 'm. | ṯṯ.w kmṯ.ḥryt h.mnt. UG5.7.34
h. | ydy.ḥmt.hlm.yṯq nḥš yšlḥm.nḥš. | 'q.šr.y'db.ksa.w yṯb. | tqru l špš um h.špš um ql.bl.'m. | mlk.'ṯtrt h.mnt.nṯk.n UG5.7.39
h.ydy.ḥmt.hlm.yṯq. | nḥš.yšlḥm.nḥš.'q šr.ydb.ksa. | w yṯb. | tqru.l špš.u h.špš.um.ql.bl.'m. | dgn.ttl h.mnt.nṯk.nḥš.š UG5.7.13
h. | ydy.ḥmt.hlm.yṯq.nḥš.yšlḥm. | nḥš.'q šr.y'db.ksa.w yṯb. | tqru l špš.um h.špš.um.ql.bl.'m. | 'nt w 'ṯtrt inbb h.mnt UG5.7.18
y ḥmt.hlm.yṯq šqy. | nḥš.yšlḥm.nḥš.'q šr.y'db. | ksa.w yṯb. | tqru l špš.um h.špš.um.ql bl. | 'm ḥrn.mṣd h.mnt.nṯk n UG5.7.56
rr.nḥš.'q šr.ln h.ml | ḫš.abd.ln h.ydy.ḥmt.hlm.yṯq. | w yṯb. | tqru.l špš.um h.špš.[um.q]l bl.'m. | yrḫ.lrgt h.mnt.nṯk. UG5.7.24
h.ydy.ḥmt.hlm yṯq.nḥš. | yšlḥm.nḥš.'q šr.y'db ksa. | w yṯb. | tqru l špš.um h.špš.um.ql bl 'm. | šḥr.w šlm šmm h mn UG5.7.50
h.ydy. | ḥmt.hlm.yṯq.nḥš.yšlḥm.nḥš. | 'q šr.y'db.ksa.w yṯb. | tqru.l špš.um.ql bl.'m | kṯr.w ḫss.kptr h.mnt.nṯk.nḥš. | š UG5.7.44
n.bt.l b'l. | km.ilm.w ḥẓr.k bn.aṯrt. | mṯb il.mẓll.bn h. | mṯb rbt.aṯrt.ym. | mṯb.klt.knyt. | mṯb.pdry.bt.ar. | mẓll.ṭly.bt 4[51].4.53
l.] | [km.ilm.w ḥẓr]. | [k bn.aṯ]r[t]. | m[ṯ]b.il.mẓll. | bn h.mṯb.rbt. | aṯrt.ym.mṯb. | klt.knyt. | mṯb.pdry.b ar. | mẓll.ṭly.bt 4[51].1.14
t].l [b'l.km.ilm.w ḥẓr]. | k bn.[aṯrt.mṯb.il.mẓll]. | bn h.m[ṯb.rbt.aṯrt.ym]. | mṯb.pdr[y.bt.ar.mẓll]. | ṭly.bt.r[b.mṯb.arṣ 3['NT.VI].4.2
.in.bt.l b'l.km.ilm. | ḥẓr.k b[n.a]ṯrt.mṯb.il. | mṯll.b[n h.m]ṯb.rbt.aṯrt. | ym.mṯb.[pdr]y.bt.ar. | [mẓll.]ṭly[.bt.]rb.mṯb. | 3['NT.VI].5.48
bt.[yn]. | [---.]rp[.---]. | [---.ḫ]br[.---]. | bḫr[.--]t[.----]. | l mṯb[.--]t[.---]. | [tqdm.]yd.b ṣ'.t[šl]ḥ. | [ḥrb.b]bš[r].tštn. | [w t' 15[128].5.6
'l h.tš'rb.ẓby h. | ṯr.ḫbr.rbt. | ḫbr.ṯrrt. | bt.krt.tbun. | lm.mṯb[.---]. | w lḥm mr.tqdm. | yd.b ṣ'.tšlḥ. | ḥrb.b bšr.tštn. | [w 15[128].4.22
[---.--]m[.---]. | [-.]rbt.ṯbt.[---]. | rbt.ṯbt.ḫš[n.---]. | y.arṣ.ḫšn[.---]. | t'td.tkl.[---]. | tkn.l 5[67].3.2
bn.pynq.'nqp[a]t[y.---]. | ayiḫ.ilšt[m'y.---]. | [b]dlm.dt.yṯb[.---]. | [-]y[--].'nqp[aty.---]. | 'ṯt[r]n.[-]bṯ[-.---]. | [---]n.š[--.- 90[314].2.10
]ṯby[.---]. | [---].abb[.---]. | [---.-]k[-.-]n[-]. | [---.--]m.šr.d.yṯ[b]. | [---.--]y.d.ḫbṯ.sy[--]. | [---.--]y.b.bt.ṯr[--]. 2134.9
tql.[---.]lb.ṯṯ[b]r. | qšt[.---]r.y[ṯ]br. | tmn.[---.]btlt.[']nt. | ṯṯb.[---.--]ša. | tlm.km[.---.]yd h.k šr. | knr.uṣb't h ḥrṣ.abn. | p 19[1AQHT].1.6
m]. | hlkm.b dbḥ n'mt. | šd[.i]lm.šd.aṯrt.w rḥmy. | [---].y[ṯ]b. | [---]p.gp ym.w yṣǵd.gp..thm. | [yqḥ.]il.mšt'ltm.mšt'lt 23[52].29
[.---]. | [---.]ytn.ml[--].ank.iphn. | [---.a]nk.i[--.--]slm.w.yṯb. | [----.--]t.hw[-]y.h[--]r.w rgm.ank. | [---.]hdd tr[--.--]l.aṯr 1002.37

yṯbmlk

| kdm.mṯḫ. | l.alty. | kd.l mrynm. | šb' yn. | l mrynm. | b yṯbmlk. | kdm.ǵbiš ḫry. | ḫmš yn.b d. | bḥ mlkt. | b mdr'. | ṯlṯ b 1090.12

yṯky

m. | ydy. | ydlm. | y'ḏrd. | yrmt. | yyn. | yn. | ydln. | ymn. | yṯky. | [y]rm. 112[16].14

yṯn

mt. | l.iyb'l. | ṯlṯm.l.mit.š'rt. | l.šr.'ṯtrt. | mlbš.ṯrmnm. | k.yṯn.w.b.bt. | mlk.mlbš. | yṯn.l hm. | šb'.lbšm.allm. | l ušḫry. | ṯl 1107.6
.-]rb. | [-----]. | [-----]. | [-----]. | k yraš w ykhp mid. | dblt yṯnt w ṣmqm yṯn[m]. | w qmḥ bql yṣq aḥd h. | b ap h. 160[55].24
d[h.w.yṣq.b.ap h]. | k yr[a]š.šš[w.w.ykhp]. | mid.dblt.yṯ[nt.w]. | ṣmq[m].yṯnm.w[.qmḥ.bql]. | tdkn.aḥd h.w[.yṣq]. | 161[56].33
]. | k yr[a]š.šš[w.w.ykhp]. | mid.dblt.yṯ[nt.w]. | ṣmq[m].yṯnm.w[.qmḥ.bql]. | tdkn.aḥd h.w[.yṣq]. | b.ap h. 161[56].34
[-----]. | [-----]. | k yraš w ykhp mid. | dblt yṯnt w ṣmqm yṯn[m]. | w qmḥ bql yṣq aḥd h. | b ap h. 160[55].24

yṯ'd

. | bnn. | kbln.ṣ[md]. | bn gmrt. | bn.il.ṣm[d]. | bn abbly. | yṯ'd.ṣm[d]. | bn.liy. | 'šrm.ṣ[md]. | ṯṯ kbd.b ḥ[--]. | w.arb'.ḥ[mr 2113.21

yṯpṭ

bn.ṣrptn.qšt. | bn.mṣry.qšt. | arny. | abm.qšt. | ḥdṯn.ql'. | yṯpṭ.qšt. | ilṯḥm.qšt.w.ql'. | ṣdqm.qšt.w.ql'. | uln.qšt.w.ql'. | ul 119[321].2.4

yṯpr

d.iytlm. | ṯn.šdm.b d.amtrn. | šd.b d.iwrm[--]. | šd.b d.yṯpr. | šd.b d.krb[-]. | šd.b d.bn.pṯḏ. | šd.b d.dr.khnm. | šd.b d. 2090.14

yṯq

nḥš.šmrr.nḥš.'q šr.ln h.ml | ḫš.abd.ln h.ydy.ḥmt.hlm.yṯq. | w yṯb. | tqru.l špš.um h.špš.[um.q]l bl.'m. | yrḫ.lrgt h.m UG5.7.22
ḥš.šmrr.nḥš. | 'q šr.ln h.mlḫš abd.ln h.ydy. | ḥmt.hlm.yṯq yṯqšqy.nḥš.yšlḥm.'q šr. | y'db.ksa.w.yṯb. | tqru.l špš.um UG5.7.6
ḥš.šmrr. | nḥš.'q šr.ln h.mlḫš.abd.ln h.ydy. | ḥmt.hlm.yṯq.nḥš.yšlḥm.nḥš 'q. | š.y'db.ksa w yṯb. | tqru l špš.um h.špš UG5.7.33

yṯq

ḥš.šmrr.|nḥš.ʿq šr.ln h.mlḫš.abd.ln h.|ydy.ḥmt.hlm.yṯq.nḥš.yšlḥm.|nḥš.ʿq šr.yʿdb.ksa.w yṯb.|tqru l špš.um h.šp UG5.7.17
ḥš.|šmrr.nḥš.ʿq šr.ln h.mlḫš.abd.|ln h.ydy.ḥmt.hlm yṯq.nḥš.|yšlḥm.nḥš.ʿq šr.yʿdb ksa.|w yṯb.|tqru l špš.um h.š UG5.7.48
ḥš.šmrr.|nḥš.ʿq šr.ln h.mlḫš abd.ln h.ydy.|ḥmt.hlm.yṯq.nḥš.yšlḥm.nḥš.|ʿq šr.yʿdb.ksa.w yṯb.|tqru.l špš.um.ql b UG5.7.43
ḥš.šm|rr.nḥš.ʿq šr.ln h.mlḫš abd.ln h.|ydy.ḥmt.hlm.yṯq nḥš yšlḥm.nḥš.|ʿq.šr.yʿdb.ksa.w yṯb.|tqru l špš um h.šp UG5.7.38
ḥš].šmrr.|nḥš.ʿq šr.ln h.mlḫš.abd.ln h.ydy.|ḥmt.hlm.yṯq.nḥš.yšlḥm.nḥš.|ʿq šr.yʿdb.ksa.w yṯb.|tqru.l špš.um h.šp UG5.7.28
nḥš.šmrr.nḥš.ʿq šr ln h.|mlḫš.abd.ln h.ydy.ḥmt.hlm.yṯq.|nḥš.yšlḥm.nḥš.ʿq šr.ydb.ksa.|w yṯb.|tqru.l špš.u h.špš. UG5.7.11
ḥš.|šmrr.nḥš ʿq šr.ln h.mlḫš.|abd.ln h.ydy ḥmt.hlm.yṯq šqy.|nḥš.yšlḥm.nḥš.ʿq šr.yʿdb.|ksa.w yṯb.|tqru l špš.u UG5.7.54

yṯtn

ʿ[p]ṯn.|b[n.ʿr]my.|[--]ty.|bn.ǵdʿ.|bn.ʿyn.|bn.grb[n].|yṯtn.|bn.ab[l].|kry.|psś.|ilṯḥm.|ḥrm.|bn.bty.|ʿby.|šm[n]. 2078.9

k

k

l.mlkt.|adt y.rgm.|tḥm.illdr.|ʿbd k..|l.pʿn a[dt y].|šbʿ d[.w šbʿ d].|mrḥq[tm.qlt].|mn[m.šlm]. 1014.4
y.|ydmʿ.nʿmn.ǵlm.|il.mlk[.t̲]r ab h.|yarš.hm.drk[t].|k ab.adm.|[-----]. 14[KRT].1.43
qẓ [l].|nʿmn.ilm l ḫt[n].|m.bʿl trḫ pdry b[t h].|aqrb k ab h bʿ[l].|yǵtr.ʿt̲tr t|rḫ l k ybrdmy.b[t.a]|b h lb[u] yʿrr.w 24[77].27
.w qdš.ʿl.|ab h.yʿrb.ybky.|w yšnn.ytn.g h.|bky.b ḥy k.ab n.ašmḫ.|b l.mt k.ngln.k klb.|b bt k.nʿtq.k inr.|ap.ḫšt 16.1[125].14
.|trm.tṣr.trm[.ʿ]tqt.|tbky.w tšnn.[tt]n.|g h.bky.b ḥ[y k.a]b n.|nšmḫ.b l.mt k.ngln.|k klb.[b]bt k.nʿtq.|k inr[.ap.] 16.2[125].98
q.|b d.at̲t ab.ṣrry.|u ilm.tmtn.špḥ.|[l]tpn.l yḫ.t[b]ky k.|ab.ǵr.bʿl.ṣ[p]n.ḥlm.|qdš.nny.ḥ[l]m.adr.|ḥl.rḥb.mk[npt]. 16.2[125].106
ik mtm.|tmtn.u ḫšt k.l ntn.|ʿtq.b d.at̲t.ab ṣrry.|tbky k.ab.ǵr.bʿl.|ṣpn.ḥlm.qdš.|any.ḥlm.adr.ḥl.|rḥb.mknpt.ap.|[16.1[125].6
[---].aǵwyn.ʿn k.ẓẓ.w k mǵ.ilm.|[--.]k ʿṣm.k ʿšm.l ttn.k abnm.l thggn. 1001.2.13
.šlm.|w.rgm.t̲t̲b.l y.|w.mndʿ.k.ank.|aḥš.mǵy.mndʿ.|k.igr.w.u.[--].|ʿm.špš.[---].|nšlḥ[.---].|[---.m]at.|[---.]mat.|š 2009.1.12
št.|b krpnm.yn.b k.ḫrṣ.|dm.ʿṣm.hm.yd.il mlk.|yḫss k.ahbt.t̲r.tʿrr k.|w tʿn.rbt.at̲rt ym.|tḥm k.il.ḥkm.ḥkmt.|ʿm 4[51].4.39
mss.[št.qlql.w.št].|ʿrgz[.ydk.aḥd h].|w.yṣq[.b.ap h].|k.yiḫd[.akl.s̀sw].|št.mkš[r.grn].|w.št.ašk[rr].|w.pr.ḥdr[t.yd 161[56].12
t̲tn mss št qlql.|[w št ʿrgz y]dk aḥd h w yṣq b ap h.|[k.yiḫd akl s̀]šw št mkšr grn.|[w št aškrr w p]r ḥdrt.|[-----]. 160[55].10
w.št.ašk[rr].|w.pr.ḥdr[t.ydk].|aḥd h.w.yṣq[.b.ap h].|k.yiḫd.akl.s̀[šw].|št.nni.št.mk[št.grn].|št.irǵn.ḥmr[.ydk].|a 161[56].17
n.ib.|[---.]mlk.|[---.]adt y.tdʿ.|w.ap.mlk.ud[r].|[-]dʿ.k.iḫd.[---].|w.mlk.bʿl y.|lm.škn.hnk.|l ʿbd h.alpm.s̀[šw]m.| 1012.21
at.ypʿt.b[--.---].|aliyn.bʿl[.---].|drkt k.mšl[-.---].|b riš k.aymr[.---].|t̲pṭ.nhr.ytb[r.ḥrn.y ym.ytbr.ḥrn].|riš k.ʿt̲trt.[š 2.1[137].6
ht |k.y ilm.bnt.bh[t k].a[l.tš]mḫ.|al.tšmḫ.b r[m.h]kl[k].|al.aḫd.hm.b y[--] y.[---]b[-].|b gdlt.arkt y.am[---].|qdqd 3[ʿNT.VI].5.29
k.y ilm[.bnt.bht k.--].|[al.tšmḫ.]al.tš[mḫ.b rm.h]|[kl k.al.]aḫd hm.[---].|[---.b]gdlt.ar[kt y.am--].|[---.qdq]d k.aš 18[3AQHT].1.9
u.|[---]w yrmy[.q]rn h.|[---.-]ny h pdr.ttǵr.|[---.n]šr k.al ttn.l n.|[---.]tn l rbd.|[---.]bʿlt h w yn.|[---.rk]b ʿrpt.|[-- 2001.2.12
t̲mn.ḫnzr k.|ʿm k.pdry.bt.ar.|ʿm k.t̲ṭly.bt.rb.idk.|pn k.al ttn.tk.ǵr.|knkny.ša.ǵr.ʿl ydm.|ḫlb.l ẓr.rḥtm w rd.|bt ḫ 5[67].5.12
bqr.|mmlat.dm.ym.w t̲n.|t̲lt̲.rbʿ.ym.ymš.|t̲dt̲.ym.ḥẓ k.al.tšʿl.|qrt h.abn.yd k.|mšdpt.w hn.špšm.|b šbʿ.w l.yšn.p 14[KRT].3.116
l.w.lakm.|ilak.w.at.|um y.al.tdḥṣ.|w.ap.mhkm.|b.lb k.al.|tšt. 1013.23
.bn.ilm.m]t.|w tʿn.btlt.ʿn[t.bnt.]bht |k.y ilm.bnt.bh[t k].a[l.tš]mḫ.|al.tšmḫ.b r[m.h]kl[k].|al.aḫd.hm.b y[--] y.[--- 3[ʿNT.VI].5.28
adt y.[---].|lb.ab[d k].al[.---].|[-]tm.iph.adt y.w.[---].|tšṣḥq.hn.at̲t.l.ʿbd.|šbʿt.w. 1017.2
tštyn.bt.ikl.b prʿ.|yṣq.b irt.lbnn.mk.b šbʿ.|[ymm.---]k.aliyn.bʿl.|[---].rʿ h ab y.|[---.]ʿ[---]. 22.2[124].26
t̲ qṣr.npš.l tdy.|t̲šm.ʿl.dl.l pn k.|l tšlḥm.ytm.bʿd.|ksl k.almnt.km.|aḫt.ʿrš.mdw.anšt.|ʿrš.zbln.rd.l mlk.|amlk.l dr 16.6[127].50
[t]ḥm.ittl.|l mnn.ilm.|tǵr k.tšlm k.|tʿzz k.alp ymm.|w rbt.šnt.|b ʿd ʿlm...gnʿ.|iršt.aršt.|l aḫ y.l rʿ y. 1019.1.4
k.---].|[---.]y.ḫr.ḫr.bnt.ḫ[---].|[--.]uḫd.[bʿ]l m.ʿ[--].yd k.amṣ.yd[.--].|[---.]ḥš[.-]nm[.--.]k.[--].w yḫnp[.---].|[---.]ylm 1001.1.14
ḫrṣ.|t̲lḥn.il.d mla.|mnm.dbbm.d |msdt.arṣ.|sʿ.il.dqt.k amr.|sknt.k ḥwt.yman.|d b h.rumm.l rbbt. 4[51].1.42
].b bk.krt.|b dmʿ.nʿmn.ǵlm.|il.trḥṣ.w tadm.|rḥṣ[.y]d k.amt.|uṣb[ʿt k.]ʿd[.t̲]km.|ʿrb[.b ẓl.ḫmt].|qḥ im[r.b yd k].|i 14[KRT].2.63
.tḥm.aliyn.|bn.bʿl.hwt.aliy.qrdm.|bht̲.bn.ilm.mt.ʿbd k.an.|w d ʿlm k.šmḫ.bn.ilm.mt.|[---.]g h.w aṣḥ.ik.yṣḥn.|[bʿ 5[67].2.19
r.|tḥm.aliyn.bʿl.hwt.aliy.|qrdm.bht̲.l bn.ilm mt.|ʿbd k.an.w d.ʿlm k.|tbʿ.w l.ytb.ilm.idk.|l ytn.pn.ʿm.bn.ilm.mt.| 5[67].2.12
.t̲m ny.|ʿm.um y.mnm.šlm.|w.rgm.t̲t̲b.l y.|w.mndʿ.k.ank.|aḥš.mǵy.mndʿ.|k.igr.w.u.[--].|ʿm.špš.[---].|nšlḥ[.---] 2009.1.10
š.]l mhr k.|w ʿp.l dr[ʿ].nšr k.|w rbṣ.l ǵr k.inbb.|kt ǵr k.ank.ydʿt.|[-]n.atn.at.mtb k[.---].|[š]mm.rm.lk.prẓ kt.|[k] 13[6].10
.btn.ʿqltn.|šlyṭ.d šbʿy.rašm.|t̲t̲kḥ.ttrp.šmm.k rs.|ipd k.ank.ispi.ut̲m.|drqm.amt m.l yrt.|b npš.bn ilm.mt.b mh| 5[67].1.5
yʿdr k.b yd.btlt.[ʿnt].|w yʿn.ltpn.il d p[id].|ydʿt k.bt.k anšt.w i[n.b ilht].|qlṣ k.tbʿ.bt.ḫnp.lb[k.--.ti]|ḫd.d it̲.b kb 18[3AQHT].1.16
mʿm.]yʿny.|il.b šbʿt.ḥdrm.b t̲mnt.|ap.sgrt.ydʿ[t k.]bt.k an[št].|k in.b ilht.ql[ṣ] k.mh.tarš[n].|l btlt.ʿnt.w t[ʿ]n.btlt. 3[ʿNT.VI].5.35
[l]krt.|k [k]lb.b bt k.nʿtq.k inr.|ap.ḫšt k.ap.ab.ik mtm.|tmtn.u ḫšt k.l ntn.|ʿtq.b d.at̲t.ab ṣrry.|tbk 16.1[125].3
.ašmḫ.|b l.mt k.ngln.k klb.|b bt k.nʿtq.k inr.|ap.ḫšt k.ap.ab.k mtm.|tmtn.u ḫšt k.l ntn.|ʿtq.b d.at̲t.ab.ṣrry.|ik 16.1[125].17
šmḫ.b l.mt k.ngln.|k klb.[b]bt k.nʿtq.|k inr[.ap.]ḫšt k.|ap.ab.k mtm.tmtn.|u ḫšt k.l bky.ʿtq.|b d.at̲t ab.ṣrry.|u i 16.2[125].101
]r km.hw ybl.argmn k.k ilm.|[---.]ybl.k bn.qdš.mnḥy k.ap.anš.zbl.bʿ[l].|[-.yuḫ]d.b yd.mšḫt.bm.ymn.mḫṣ.ǵlmm.y 2.1[137].38
.ʿṣm l t[--].|[---.]drk.brḥ.arṣ.lk pn h.yrk.bʿ[l].|[---.]bt k.ap.l pḫr k ʿnt tqm.ʿnt.tqm.|[---.p]ḫr k.ygrš k.qr.bt k.ygrš 1001.2.9
k.rpu mlk.|[ʿlm.---.--]k.l tšt k.l iršt.|[ʿlm.---.--]k.l tšt k.liršt.|[---.]rpi.mlk ʿlm.b ʿz.|[rpu.m]lk.ʿlm.b d̲mr h.bl.|[--- UG5.2.2.5
t h.l ydlp.|tmn h.kt̲r.ṣmdm.ynḥt.w ypʿr.šmt hm.|šm k.at.aymr.aymr.mr.ym.mr.ym.|l ksi h.nhr l kḥt̲.drkt h.trtq 2.4[68].19
k.drkt.dt dr dr k.|kt̲r ṣmdm.ynḥt.w ypʿr.šmt hm.šm k at.|ygrš.ygrš.grš ym grš ym.l ksi h.|[n]hr l kḥt̲ drkt h.trt 2.4[68].11
.|aqht.w tbk.y[---.---].|abn.ank.w ʿl.[qšt k.---.ʿl].|qṣʿt k.at.l ḥ[---.---].|w ḫlq.ʿpmm[.---]. 18[3AQHT].4.41
[--].ʿ[m k].|l.alpm.w.l.y[n.--]t.|w.bl.bnš.hw[-.--]y.|w.k.at.trg[m.--].|w.[---]n.w.s[--].|[--]m.m[---].|[---.m]ndʿ[.--]. 2064.27
mhr y.w bn.bt̲n.itnn y.|ytt.nḫšm.mhr k.bn bt̲n.|itnn k.|at̲r ršp.ʿt̲trt.|ʿm ʿt̲trt.mr h.|mnt.nt̲k.nḫš. UG5.7.76
.t[l]iyt.|ql.l bʿl.ttnn.|bšrt.il.bš[r.bʿ]l.|w bšr.ḥtk.dgn.|k.ibr.l bʿl[.yl]d.|w rum.l rkb.ʿrpt.|yšmḫ.aliyn.bʿl. 10[76].3.36
ḥm iwrdr.|l iwrpḫn.|bn y.aḫ y.rgm.|ilm.tǵr k.|tšlm k.|ik y.lḥt.|spr.d likt.|ʿm.t̲ryl.|mh y.rgmt.|w ht.aḫ y.|bn 138.5
ḥm.iwrdr.|l iwrpḫn.|bn y.aḫ y.rgm.|ilm.tǵr k.|tšlm k.|iky.lḥt.|spr.d likt.|ʿm.t̲ryl.|mh y.rgmt.|w ht.aḫ y.|bn y 138.5
ht.ql[ṣ] k.mh.tarš[n].|l btlt.ʿnt.w t[ʿ]n.btlt.ʿn[t].|tḥm k.il.ḥkm.ḥkm k.|ʿm.ʿlm.ḥyt.ḥẓt.tḥm k.|mlk n.aliyn.bʿl.t̲pṭ 3[ʿNT.VI].5.38
.il mlk.|yḫss k.ahbt.t̲r.tʿrr k.|w tʿn.rbt.at̲rt ym.|tḥm k.il.ḥkm.ḥkmt.|ʿm ʿlm.ḥyt.ḥẓt.|tḥm k.mlk n.aliy[n.]bʿl.|tp 4[51].4.41
[-----].|[-----].|il.šmʿ.amr k.ph[.-].|k il.ḥkmt.k t̲r.ltpn.|ṣḥ.ngr.il.ilš.il[š].|w at̲t h.ngrt[.i]lht.|kḫ 16[126].4.3
.[mg]dl.rkb.|t̲kmm.ḥm[t].ša.yd k.|šmm.dbḥ.l t̲r.|ab k.il.šrd.bʿl.|b dbḥ k.bn.dgn.|b mṣd k.w yrd.|krt.l ggt.ʿdb.| 14[KRT].2.77
mt.l tšt.|yn.tǵzyt.špš.|rpim.tḥtk.|špš.tḥtk.ilnym.|ʿd k.ilm.hn.mtm.|ʿd k.kt̲r m.ḫbr k.|w ḫss.dʿt k.|b ym.arš.w t 6.6[62.2].47
ašhlk].šbt h.dmm.šbt.dqn h.|[mmʿm.-]d.l ytn.bt.l bʿl.k ilm.|[w ḥẓ]r.k bn.at̲rt[.tdʿṣ.]pʿn.|[w tr.a]rṣ.id[k.l ttn.p]n 3[ʿNT.VI].5.11
tḥm.pgn.|l.mlk.ugrt.|rgm.|yšlm.l k.[il]m.|tǵr k.tšlm k.|hn ny.ʿm n.š[l]m.|t̲m ny.ʿ[m.]bn y.| 2061.4
l.mlk.ugrt.|aḫ y.rgm.|tḥm.mlk.ṣr.aḫ k.|y[š]lm.l k.ilm.|tǵr k.tšlm k.|hn ny.ʿm n.|šlm.t̲m ny.|ʿm k.mnm[.š]l 2059.4

tḥm.mlk.|l.ṯryl.um y.rgm.|yšlm.l k.ilm.|tġr k.tšlm k.|lḥt.šlm.k.lik[t].|um y.ʿm y.ht.ʿm[ny].| 2009.1.3
[l.ml]k.[bʿl y].|rg[m].|tḥm.wr[--].|yšlm.[l] k.|ilm.t[ġ]r k.|tšlm k.|lm[.l.]likt.|ši[l.š]lm y.|[ʿ]d.r[-]š.|[-]l 2010.4
y[šlm.l k.ilm].|tġ[r k.tšlm k].|ʿbd[.---]y.|ʿm[.---]y.|šk[--.--.]kll.|šk[2065.1
tḥm.hl[--].|l pḫry.a[ḫ y].|w l g.p[-]r[--].|yšlm[.l k].|[i]lm[.tġr k].|[t]š[lm k.---].|[-----].|[-----].|h[--.---].|[---- 56[21].4
l.mlk[.u]grt.|iḫ y.rgm.|[tḥ]m.m[lk.-]bl[-].|yšlm.l[k].ilm.|tġr.tšl[m] k.|[-----].|[-----].|[--].bt.gb[-.--].|[--]k[-].w 2159.4
l.rb.khnm.|rgm.|tḥm.[---].|yšlm[.l k.ilm].|tšlm[k.tġr] k.|tʿzz[k.---.]lm.|w t[--.--]ṣm k.|[-----]. 55[18].4
[tḥm.---].|[l.---].|[a]ḫt y.rgm.|[y]šlm.l k.|[il]m.tšlm k.|[tġ]r k.|[--]y.ibr[-].|[--]wy.rgm l.|mlkt.ugr 1016.4
.ʿbd k.bʿl.|[--.--]m.bn.dgn.a[s]r km.hw ybl.argmn k.k ilm.|[---.]ybl.k bn.qdš.mnḥy k.ap.anš.zbl.bʿ[l].|[-.yuḫ]d.b 2.1[137].37
lt h.w nġr.|ʿnn.ilm.al.|tqrb.l bn.ilm.|mt.al.yʿdb km.|k imr.b p h.|k lli.b ṯbrn.|qn h.tḫtan.|nrt.ilm.špš.|ṣḥrrt.la.| 4[51].8.18
amt.|uṣb[ʿt k.]ʿd[.ṯ]km.|ʿrb[.b ẓl.ḫmt].|qḥ im[r.b yd k].|imr.d[bḥ.bm].ymn.|lla.kl[atn]m.|klt.l[ḥm k.d]nzl.|qḥ. 14[KRT].2.66
yṯb l y.ṯr.il[.ab y.---].|yṯb.l y.w l h.[---].|[--.i]mṣḫ.nn.k imr.l arṣ.|[ašhlk].šbt h.dmm.šbt.dqn h.|[mmʿm.-]d.l ytn. 3[ʿNT.VI].5.9
y.|il.b šbʿt.ḥdrm.b ṯmnt.|ap.sgrt.ydʿ[t k.]bt.k an[št].|k in.b ilht.ql[ṣ] k.mh.tarš[n].|l btlt.ʿnt.w t[ʿ]n.btlt.ʿn[t].|tḥ 3[ʿNT.VI].5.36
.l.tlk.|w.lḥt.akl.ky.|likt.ʿm.špš.|bʿl k.ky.akl.|b.ḫwt k.inn.|špš n.[---].|hm.al[k.--].|ytnt[.---].|ṯn[.---].|w[.-----].| 2060.20
ḥbš k.|ʿtk.ri[š.]l mhr k.|w ʿp.l dr[ʿ].nšr k.|w rbṣ.l ġr k.inbb.|kt ġr k.ank.ydʿt.|[-]n.atn.at.mṯb k[.---].|[š]mm.rm. 13[6].9
[l]krt.|k [k]lb.b bt k.nʿtq.k inr.|ap.ḫšt k.ap.ab.ik mtm.|tmtn.u ḫšt k.l ntn.|ʿtq.b d.aṯ 16.1[125].2
y.b ḥy k.ab n.ašmḫ.|b l.mt k.ngln.k klb.|b bt k.nʿtq.k inr.|ap.ḫšt k.ap.ab.k mtm.|tmtn.u ḫšt k.l ntn.|ʿtq.b d.aṯt. 16.1[125].16
ḥ[y k.a]b n.|nšmḫ.b l.mt k.ngln.|k klb.[b]bt k.nʿtq.|k inr[.ap.]ḫšt k.|ap.ab.k mtm.tmtn.|u ḫšt k.l bky.ʿtq.|b d.a 16.2[125].101
.ḥp y[m].|tṣmt.adm.ṣat.š[p]š.|tḥt h.k kdrt.ri[š].|ʿl h.k irbym.kp.k.qṣm.|ġrmn.kp.mhr.ʿtkt.|rišt.l bmt h.šnst.|kp 3[ʿNT].2.10
mlu.lb h.|[b šmḫt.kbd.ʿnt.tšyt.tḥt h.k]kdrt.riš.|[ʿl h.k irbym.kp.---.k br]k.tġll.b dm.|[ḏmr.---.]td[-.]rġb.|[----]k. 7.1[131].9
|ymzl.w yṣi.trḫ.|ḥdṯ.ybʿr.l ṯn.|aṯt h.lm.nkr.|mddt h.k irby.|[t]škn.šd.|km.ḥsn.pat.mdbr.|lk.ym.w ṯn.ṯlṯ.rbʿ ym. 14[KRT].2.103
n.km.šḥr.|[---.y]lt n.km.qdm.|[-.k]bd n.il.ab n.|kbd k iš.tikln.|td n.km.mrm.tqrṣn.|il.yẓḥq.bm.|lb.w ygmd.bm 12[75].1.10
m.šmn.tmṭrn.|nḫlm.tlk.nbtm.|w idʿ.k ḥy.aliyn.bʿl.|k iṯ.zbl.bʿl.arṣ.|b ḥlm.lṭpn.il d pid.|b ḏrt.bny.bnwt.|šmm.š 6[49].3.9
|aṯbn.ank.w anḫn.|w tnḫ.b irt y.npš.|k ḥy.aliyn.bʿl.|k iṯ.zbl.bʿl.arṣ.|gm.yṣḥ.il.l btlt.|ʿnt.šmʿ.l btlt.ʿn[t].|rgm.l nr 6[49].3.21
nil.[mt.rpi].|mt.aqht.ġzr.[šṣat].|btlt.ʿnt.k [rḥ.npš h].|k iṯl.brlt h.[b h.p ʿnm].|ṭṭ.ʿl[n.pn h.td]ʿ.b ʿdn].|ksl.y[ṯbr.ygṣ. 19[1AQHT].2.93
[.---].|riš.r[--.--]ḫ[.---]y[.---.-]nt.[š]ṣat[k.]rḥ.npš.hm.|k.iṯl.brlt n[-.k qṭr.b ap -].|tmġyn.tša.g h[m.w tṣḥn].|šmʿ.l d 19[1AQHT].2.88
qnim.|[---.-]šu.b qrb.|[---].asr.|[---.--]m.ymt m.|[---].k iṯl.|[---.--]m.ʿdb.l arṣ.|[---.]špm.ʿdb.|[---].tʿtqn.|[---.-]ʿb.id 1[ʿNT.IX].2.9
tḥm[.t]lm[yn].|l ṯryl.um y.|rgm.|ugrt.tġr k.|ugrt.tġr k.|tšlm k.um y.|tdʿ.ky.ʿrbt.|l pn.špš.|w pn.špš. 1015.5
rt.ṯʿ.|bn.al.tbkn.al.|tdm.l y.al tkl.bn.|qr.ʿn k.mḫ.riš k.|udmʿt.ṣḥ.aḫt k.|ṯtmnt.bt.ḥmḥ h.|d[-]n.tbkn.w tdm.l y.[- 16.1[125].27
qrb.hkl k.|tbl k.ġrm.mid.ksp.|gbʿm.mḥmd.ḫrṣ.|ybl k.udr.ilqṣm.|w bn.bht.ksp.w ḫrṣ.|bht.ṭhrm.iqnim.|šmḫ.btl 4[51].5.79
rḥm.|ʿdn.ngb.w yṣi.|ṣbu.ṣbi.ngb.|w yṣi.ʿdn.mʿ.|ṣbu k.ul.mad.|ṯlṯ.mat.rbt.|ḫpṯ.d bl.spr.|ṯnn.d bl.hg.|hlk.l alpm 14[KRT].2.88
[yn].|l ṯryl.um y.|rgm.|ugrt.tġr k.|ugrt.tġr k.|tšlm k.um y.|tdʿ.ky.ʿrbt.|l pn.špš.|w pn.špš.nr.|b y.mid.w um.| 1015.6
h.w yṣḥ.y l k.mrrt.|tġll.b nr.d ʿl k.mḥṣ.aqht.|ġzr.šrš k.b arṣ.al.|ypʿ.riš.ġly.b d.nsʿ k.|ʿnt.brḥ.p ʿlm h.|ʿnt.p dr.dr. 19[1AQHT].3.159
.ʿrpt.dbḥ.|bṯt.w dbḥ.w dbḥ.|dnt.w dbḥ.tdmm.|amht.k b h.bṯt.l tbṯ.|w b h.tdmmt.amht.|aḫr.mġy.aliyn.bʿl.|mġy 4[51].3.21
bn.yṯbr.ḥrn.|riš k.ʿṯtrt.šm.bʿl.|qdqd k.tqln.b gbl.|šnt k.b ḥpn k.w tʿn.|spr ilmlk ṯʿy. 16.6[127].58
bʿl.ḥẓ.ršp.b[n].km.yr.klyt h.w lb h.|[ṯ]n.p k.b ġr.ṯn.p k.b ḫlb.k tgwln.šnt k.|[--.]w špt k.l tššy.hm.tqrm.l mt.b rn 1001.1.4
n k.mmʿm.w[---].|aqht.w yplṭ k.bn[.dnil.---].|w yʿḏr k.b yd.btlt.[ʿnt].|w yʿn.lṭpn.il d p[id].|ydʿt k.bt.k anšt.w i[n 18[3AQHT].1.14
gm.l aḫt k.|ttmnt.krt n.dbḥ.|dbḥ.mlk.ʿšr.|ʿšrt.qḥ.tp k.b yd.|[-]r[-]k.bm.ymn.|tlk.škn.ʿl.ṣrrt.|adn k.šqrb.[---].|b 16.1[125].41
ilnym.|ʿd k.ilm.hn.mtm.|ʿd k.kṯr m.ḥbr k.|w ḫss.dʿt k.|b ym.arš.w tnn.|kṯr.w ḫss.yd.|ytr.kṯr.w ḫss.|spr.ilmlk š 6.6[62.2].49
[škrn].|mʿms k.k šbʿt.yn.ṭ[ḫ].|gg k.b ym.ṭiṭ.rḥṣ.|npṣ k.b ym rṭ.b uni[l].|pnm.tšmḫ.w ʿl yṣhl pi[t].|yprq.lṣb.w yṣḥ 17[2AQHT].2.8
k].|bt il.aḫd.yd k.b [škrn].|mʿms k.k šbʿt.yn.ṭ[ḫ].|gg k.b ym.ṭiṭ.rḥṣ.|npṣ k.b ym rṭ.b uni[l].|pnm.tšmḫ.w ʿl yṣhl 17[2AQHT].2.7
mnt.krt n.dbḥ.|dbḥ.mlk.ʿšr.|ʿšrt.qḥ.tp k.b yd.|[-]r[-]k.bm.ymn.|tlk.škn.ʿl.ṣrrt.|adn k.šqrb.[---].|b mgn k.w ḫrṣ.l 16.1[125].42
d k.|[l.p]ʿn.bʿl y.|[šbʿ] d.šbʿ [d].|[mr]ḥqtm.|qlt.|ʿbd k.b.|lwsnd.|[w] b ṣr.|ʿm.mlk.|w.ht.|mlk.syr.|ns.w.ṯm.|yd 2063.9
.tqny.|[---.]ṯb l y.l aqht.ġzr.ṯb l y w l k.|[---]m.l aqry k.b ntb.pšʿ.|[---].b ntb.gan.ašql k.tḥt.|[pʿn y.a]nk.nʿmn.ʿmq 17[2AQHT].6.43
in l y.|[--]t.bʿl.ḥẓ.ršp.b[n].km.yr.klyt h.w lb h.|[ṯ]n.p k.b ġr.ṯn.p k.b ḫlb.k tgwln.šnt k.|[--.]w špt k.l tššy.hm.tqr 1001.1.4
.|[yʿtqn.---].ymġy.npš.|[---.--]t.hd.tngṯm h.|[---.-]ḥm k b ṣpn.|[---.]išqb.aylt.|[---.--]m.b km.yʿn.|[---].ydʿ.l ydʿt.|[1[ʿNT.X].5.18
.b aklt.šblt.tpʿ[.b ḥm]drt.|ur.tisp k.yd.aqht.ġz[r].|tšt k.bm.qrb m.asm.|b p h.rgm.l yṣa.b špt h[.hwt h].|b nši ʿn h 19[1AQHT].2.74
npʿ.b palt.bṣql ypʿ b yġlm.|ur.tisp k.yd.aqht.|ġzr.tšt k.b qrb m.asm.|y.dnh.ysb.aklt h.yph.|šblt.b akt.šblt.ypʿ.|b 19[1AQHT].2.67
.d ʿšy.ln k].|spu.ksm k.bt.[bʿl.w mnt k].|bt il.aḫd.yd k.b [škrn].|mʿms k.k šbʿt.yn.ṭ[ḫ].|gg k.b ym.ṭiṭ.rḥṣ.|npṣ k. 17[2AQHT].2.5
h.b nmrt h.l r|[--.]arṣ.ʿz k.ḏmr k.l[-]|n k.ḥtk k.nmrt k.b tk.|ugrt.l ymt.špš.w yrḫ.|w nʿmt.šnt.il. UG5.2.2.10
.|il.yrd.b ḏhrt h.|ab adm.w yqrb.|b šal.krt.m at.|krt.k ybky.|ydmʿ.nʿmn.ġlm.|il.mlk[.ṯ]r ab h.|yarš.hm.drk[t].| 14[KRT].1.39
r.mlak.|šmm.tmr.zbl.mlk.|šmm.tlak.ṭl.amr..|bn km k bk[r.z]bl.am..|rkm.agzrt[.--].arḫ..|bʿl.azrt.ʿnt.[-]ld.|kbd 13[6].28
mm.w tʿn.btlt.|ʿnt.irš ḥym.l aqht.ġzr.|irš ḥym.w atn k.bl mt.|w ašlḥ k.ašspr k.ʿm.bʿl.|šnt.ʿm.bn il.tspr.yrḫm.|k 17[2AQHT].6.27
rt.|[ym].mġẓ.qnyt.ilm.|w tn.bt.l bʿl.km.|[i]lm.w ḥẓr.k bn.|[a]ṯrt.gm.l ġlm h.|bʿl.yṣḥ.ʿn.gpn.|w ugr.bn.ġlmt.|ʿm 8[51FRAG].4
m.šbt.dqn h.|[mmʿm.-]d.l ytn.bt.l bʿl.k ilm.|[w ḥẓ]r.k bn.aṯrt[.tdʿṣ.]pʿn.|[w tr.a]rṣ.id[k.l ttn.p]nm.|[ʿm.i]l.mbk. 3[ʿNT.VI].5.12
lṯ.|hm.amt.aṯrt.tlbn.|lbnt.ybn.bt.l bʿl.|km ilm.w ḥẓr.k bn.aṯrt.|w tʿn.rbt.aṯrt ym.|rbt.ilm.l ḥkmt.|šbt.dqn k.l tsr 4[51].5.63
t.|w bn h.ilt.w ṣbrt.arḫ h.|wn.in.bt.l bʿl.km.ilm.|ḥẓr.k b[n.a]ṯrt.mṯb.il.|mṯll.b[n h.m]ṯb.rbt.aṯrt.|ym.mṯb.[pdr]y. 3[ʿNT.VI].5.47
[---.wn.in].|[bt].l [bʿl.km.ilm.w ḥẓr].|k bn.[aṯrt.mṯb.il.mẓll].|bn h.m[ṯb.rbt.aṯrt.ym].|mṯb.pdr[y. 3[ʿNT.VI].4.1
.w bn h.ilt.w ṣbrt.|ary h.wn.in.bt.l bʿl.|km.ilm.w ḥẓr.k bn.aṯrt.|mṯb il.mẓll.bn h.|mṯb rbt.aṯrt.ym.|mṯb.klt.knyt. 4[51].4.51
ilt.|[w ṣbrt.ary]h.|[wn.in.bt.l bʿl.]|[km.ilm.w ḥẓr].|[k bn.aṯ]r[t].|m[ṯ]b.il.mẓll.|bn h.mṯb.rbt.|aṯrt.ym.mṯb.|klt. 4[51].1.12
m.yḥr.tn.km.|mhr y.w bn.bṯn.itnn y.|ytt.nḫšm.mhr k.bn bṯn.|itnn k.|aṯr ršp.ʿṯtrt.|ʿm ʿṯtrt.mr h.|mnt.nṯk.nḫš. UG5.7.75
.ḥm[t].ša.yd k.|šmm.dbḥ.l ṯr.|ab k.il.šrd.bʿl.|b dbḥ k.bn.dgn.|b mṣd k.w yrd.|krt.l ggt.ʿdb.|akl.l qryt.|ḥṭt.l bt. 14[KRT].2.78
[.šbt k.dmm].|[šbt.dq]n k.mmʿm.w[---].|aqht.w yplṭ k.bn[.dnil.---].|w yʿḏr k.b yd.btlt.[ʿnt].|w yʿn.lṭpn.il d p[id]. 18[3AQHT].1.13
mlkt.[--]pm.l mlkt.wn.in.aṯt.|[l]k.k[m.ilm].|[w ġlmt.k bn.qdš.]w y[--.]zbl.ym.yʿ[--.]ṯpṭ.nhr.|[-------.]yšlḥn.w yʿn ʿ 2.3[129].23

-].|[--]ḫ.b y.ṯr.il.ab y.ank.in.bt[.l] y[.km.]ilm[.w] ḥẓr[.k bn].|[qd]š.lbum.trd.b n[p]šn y.trḥṣn.k ṯrm.|[--]b b[ht].|[z 2.3[129].19
--]m.bn.dgn.a[s]r km.hw ybl.argmn k.k ilm.|[---.]ybl.k bn.qdš.mnḥy k.ap.anš.zbl.b'[l].|[-.yuḫ]d.b yd.mšḫṭ.bm.y 2.1[137].38
.---].|l šlmt.l šlm.b[--.---]|b y.šnt.mlit.t[--.---].|ymǵy k.bnm.ta[--.---].|[b]nm.w bnt.ytn k[.---].|[--]l.bn y.šḥt.w [-- 59[100].8
-].|w y'dr k.b yd.btlt.['nt].|w y'n.lṭpn.il d p[id].|yd't k.bt.k anšt.w i[n.b ilht].|qlṣ k.tb'.bt.ḫnp.lb[k.--.ti]|ḫd.d iṯ. 18[3AQHT].1.16
n k.mm'm.]y'ny.|il.b šb't.ḥdrm.b ṯmnt.|ap.sgrt.yd'[t k.]bt.k an[št].|k in.b ilht.ql[ṣ] k.mh.tarš[n].|l btlt.'nt.w t['] 3['NT.VI].5.35
b.hn[.w.]ht.ank.|[---.--]š[-.--].w.ašt.|[---].amr k.|[---].k.ybt.mlk.|[---].w.ap.ank.|[---].l.ǵr.amn.|[---.-]ktt.hn.ib.|[- 1012.14
.b'l.w 'nn h.bn.dgn.art m.pḏ h.|[w y'n.]ṯr.ab h.il.'bd k.b'l.y ym m.'bd k.b'l.|[--.--]m.bn.dgn.a[s]r km.hw ybl.arg 2.1[137].36
mt.|w ašlḥ k.ašspr k.'m.b'l.|šnt.'m.bn il.tspr.yrḫm.|k b'l.k yḥwy.y'šr.ḥwy.y'š.|r.w yšqyn h.ybd.w yšr.'l h.|n'm[17[2AQHT].6.30
.|w yšḥ.y l k.qrt.ablm.|d 'l k.mḫṣ.aqht.ǵzr.|'wrt.yšt k.b'l.l ht.|w 'lm h.l 'nt.p dr.dr.|'db.uḫry.mṭ.yd h.|dnil.bt h 19[1AQHT].4.167
.w 'n.kṯr.w ḫss.l rgmt.|l k.l zbl.b'l.ṯnt.l rkb.'rpt.ht.ib k.|b'l m.ht.ib k.tmḫṣ.ht.tṣmt.ṣrt k.|tqḥ.mlk.'lm k.drkt.dt d 2.4[68].8
'.|šnt.w [--].bn.ilm.mt.|'m.aliyn.b'l.yšu.|g h.w yṣḥ.'l k.b[']l m.|pht.qlt.'l k.pht.|dry.b ḥrb.'l k.|pht.šrp.b išt.|'l k. 6[49].5.11
ṣḥ.|ḥwt.aḫt.w nar[-].|qrn.d bat k.btlt.'nt.|qrn.d bat k b'l.ymšḥ.|b'l.ymšḥ.hm.b 'p.|nṭ'n.b arṣ.ib y.|w b 'pr.qm.a 10[76].2.22
.|hwt.lṭpn.ḥtk k.|pl.'nt.šdm.y špš.|pl.'nt.šdm.il.yš[t k].|b'l.'nt.mḥrṯ[-].|iy.aliyn.b'l.|iy.zbl.b'l.arṣ.|w t'n.nrt.ilm. 6[49].4.37
|rgm.l nrt.il.šp[š].|pl.'nt.šdm.y špš.|pl.'nt.šdm.il.yšt k.|[b]'l.'nt.mḥrṯt.|iy.aliyn.b'l.|iy.zbl.b'l.arṣ.|ttb'.btlt.'nt.|i 6[49].4.26
|ḥm.un.yr.'rpt.|tmṭr.b qẓ.ṭl.yṭll.|l ǵnbm.šb'.šnt.|yṣr k.b'l.ṯmn.rkb.|'rpt.bl.ṭl.bl rbb.|bl.šr'.thmtm.bl.|ṭbn.ql.b'l.k 19[1AQHT].1.43
gn.art m.pḏ h.|[w y'n.]ṯr.ab h.il.'bd k.b'l.y ym m.'bd k.b'l.|[--.--]m.bn.dgn.a[s]r km.hw ybl.argmn k.k ilm.|[---.] 2.1[137].36
t.|tǵdd.kbd h.b ṣḥq.ymlu.|lb h.b šmḫt.kbd.'nt.|tšyt.k brkm.tǵll b dm.|ḏmr.ḥlqm.b mm'.mhrm.|'d.tšb'.tmtḫṣ.b 3['NT].2.27
ḫt.kbd.'nt.tšyt.tḥt h.k]kdrt.riš.|['l h.k irbym.kp.---.k br]k.tǵll.b dm.|[ḏmr.---.]td[-.]rǵb.|[----]k.|[----] h. 7.1[131].9
n.qn.yṣbt.|[---.--]m.b nši.'n h.w tphn.|[---.--]ml.ksl h.k b[r]q.|[---.]m[-]ǵ[-].thmt.brq.|[---].tṣb.qšt.bnt.|[---.']n h.k 17[2AQHT].6.11
q].|lḥt.niṣ k.gr[š.d 'šy.ln k].|spu.ksm k.bt.[b'l.w mnt k].|bt il.aḥd.yd k.b [škrn].|m'ms k.k šb't.yn.ṭ[ḫ].|gg k.b y 17[2AQHT].2.4
r.ḏm[r.aṯr k.ṭbq].|lḥt.niṣ k.gr[š.d 'šy.ln k].|spu.ksm k.bt.[b'l.w mnt k].|bt il.aḥd.yd k.b [škrn].|m'ms k.k šb't.y 17[2AQHT].2.4
w yql.|w yšu.g h.w yṣḥ.|ḥwt.aḫt.w nar[-].|qrn.d bat k.btlt.'nt.|qrn.d bat k b'l.ymšḥ.|b'l.ymšḥ.hm.b 'p.|nṭ'n.b a 10[76].2.21
rm.|mt.'z.b'l.'z.ynghn.|k rumm.mt.'z.b'l.|'z.ynṯkn.k bṯnm.|mt.'z.b'l.'z.ymṣḫn.|k lsmm.mt.ql.|b'l.ql.'ln.špš.|tṣ 6[49].6.19
l ri[š.---].|ypt.'ṣ[--.---].|p šlm.[---].|bt k.b[--.--.m]|ǵy k[.---].|bt.[---]. 58[20].4
ybky.|w yšnn.ytn.g h.|bky.b ḥy k.ab n.ašmḫ.|b l.mt k.ngln.k klb.|b bt k.n'tq.k inr.|ap.ḫšt k.ap.ab.k mtm.|tmtn 16.1[125].15
bky.w tšnn.[tt]n.|g h.bky.b ḥ[y k.a]b n.|nšmḫ.b l.mt k.ngln.|k klb.[b]bt k.n'tq.|k inr[.ap.]ḫšt k.|ap.ab.k mtm.t 16.2[125].99
p.b[n].km.yr.klyt h.w lb h.|[t]n.p k.b ǵr.ṯn.p k.b ḫlb.k tgwln.šnt k.|[--.]w špt k.l tššy.hm.tqrm.l mt.b rn k.|[--]ḫ 1001.1.4
bḫ.šb'm.|rumm.k gmn.aliyn.|[b]'l.ṭṭbḫ.šb'm.alpm.|[k g]mn.aliyn.b'l.|[ṭṭ]bḫ.šb'm.ṣin.|[k gm]n.aliyn.b'l.|[ṭṭb]ḫ. 6[62].1.21
ṭṭ]bḫ.šb'm.ṣin.|[k gm]n.aliyn.b'l.|[ṭṭb]ḫ.šb'm.aylm.|[k gmn.]aliyn.b'l.|[ṭṭbḫ.š]b'm.y'lm.|[k gmn.al]iyn.b'l.|[ṭṭbḫ 6[62].1.25
.ṭṭbḫ.šb'm.alpm.|[k g]mn.aliyn.b'l.|[ṭṭ]bḫ.šb'm.ṣin.|[k gm]n.aliyn.b'l.|[ṭṭb]ḫ.šb'm.aylm.|[k gmn.]aliyn.b'l.|[ṭṭbḫ 6[62].1.23
h.|w tqbrn h.tštnn.b ḫrt.|ilm.arṣ.ṭṭbḫ.šb'm.|rumm.k gmn.aliyn.|[b]'l.ṭṭbḫ.šb'm.alpm.|[k g]mn.aliyn.b'l.|[ṭṭ]bḫ 6[62].1.19
b]ḫ.šb'm.aylm.|[k gmn.]aliyn.b'l.|[ṭṭbḫ.š]b'm.y'lm.|[k gmn.al]iyn.b'l.|[ṭṭbḫ.šb'm.]ḥmrm.|[k gm]n.al[i]yn.b['l].| 6[62].1.27
ḫ.š]b'm.y'lm.|[k gmn.al]iyn.b'l.|[ṭṭbḫ.šb'm.]ḥmrm.|[k gm]n.al[i]yn.b['l].|[---]ḥ h.tšt bm.'[--].|[---.]zr h.ybm.l il 6.1.29[49.1.1]
w yṣḥ.|aḫ y m.ytnt.b'l.|spu y.bn m.um y.kl|y y.yt'n.k gmrm.|mt.'z.b'l.'z.ynghn.|k rumm.mt.'z.b'l.|'z.ynṯkn.k 6[49].6.16
dy.psltm.b y'r.|yhdy.lḥm.w dqn.|yṯlṯ.qn.ḏr' h.yḥrṯ.|k gn.ap lb.k 'mq.yṯlṯ.|bmt.yšu.g h.w yṣḥ.|b'l.mt.my.lim.bn 5[67].6.21
.w.yṣq.b[.ap h].|k.yraš.ššw.[št].|bln.qt.yṣq.b.a[p h].|k yǵ'r[.ššw.---].|dprn[.---].|dr'.[---].|tmṯl[.---].|mǵm[ǵ.---]. 161[56].23
r.'m k.l arṣ.mšṣu.qṭr k].|l 'pr.ḏm[r.aṯr k.ṭbq].|lḥt.niṣ k.gr[š.d 'šy.ln k].|spu.ksm k.bt.[b'l.w mnt k].|bt il.aḥd.yd 17[2AQHT].2.3
k.b'[l].|[---.]bt k.ap.l pḫr k 'nt tqm.'nt.tqm.|[---.p]ḫr k.ygrš k.qr.bt k.ygrš k.|[---].bnt.ṣ'ṣ.bnt.m'm'.'bd.ḥrn.[--.]k. 1001.2.10
k.ap.l pḫr k 'nt tqm.'nt.tqm.|[---.p]ḫr k.ygrš k.qr.bt k.ygrš k.|[---].bnt.ṣ'ṣ.bnt.m'm'.'bd.ḥrn.[--.]k.|[---].aǵwyn.'n 1001.2.10
y.yrk.b'l.[--].|[---.]'nt.šzrm.tštšḥ.km.ḥ[--].|[---].'pr.bt k.ygr[š k.---].|[---.]y.ḥr.ḥr.bnt.ḥ[---].|[--.]uḫd.[b']l m.'[--].y 1001.1.12
--].|[-]r[--.--]y.|in m.'bd k hwt.|[y]rš.'m y.|mnm.iršt k.|d ḫsrt.w.ank.|aštn..l.iḫ y.|w.ap.ank.mnm.|[ḫ]s[r]t.w.uḫ 2065.15
.amt.|p d.in.b bt y.ttn.|tn.l y.mṯt.ḥry.|n'mt.šbḥ.bkr k.|d k.n'm.'nt.n'm h.|km.tsm.'ṯtrt.ts[m h].|d 'q h.ib.iqni.'p 14[KRT].3.144
mt.p d.[i]n.|b bt y.ttn.tn.|l y.mṯt.ḥry.|n'mt.šbḥ.bkr k.|d k n'm.'nt.|n'm h.km.tsm.|'ṯtrt.tsm h.|d 'q h.ib.iqni.|' 14[KRT].6.290
arḫ.w bn.[--].|limm.ql.b udn.k w[-].|k rtqt mr[.---].|k d lbšt.bir.mlak.|šmm.tmr.zbl.mlk.|šmm.tlak.ṭl.amr..|bn 13[6].25
r.b yd k].|imr.d[bḥ.bm].ymn.|lla.kl[atn]m.|klt.l[ḥm k.d]nzl.|qḥ.ms[rr.]'ṣr.|dbḥ.ṣ[q.b g]l.ḥtt.|yn.b gl[.ḫ]rṣ.nbt. 14[KRT].2.69
t.y'n.kmr.kmr[.--].|k ap'.il.b gdrt.k lb.l |ḥt h.imḫṣ h.k d.'l.qšt h.|imḫṣ h.'l.qṣ't h.hwt.|l aḥw.ap.qšt h.l ttn.|l y.w 19[1AQHT].1.14
n w.|dbḥ kl.|kl ykly.|dbḥ k.sprt.|dt nat.|w qrwn.|l k dbḥ.|[--]r bt [--].|[--]bnš [--].|š š[--].|w [--].|d [--].|ypḥ[RS61[24.277.12]
.aḫ[h.w tṣḥ].|lm.tb'rn[.---].|mn.yrḫ.k m[rṣ.---].|mn.k dw.kr[t].|w y'ny.ǵzr[.ilḥu].|ṯlṯ.yrḫm.k m[rṣ].|arb'.k dw. 16.2[125].82
k dw.kr[t].|w y'ny.ǵzr[.ilḥu].|ṯlṯ.yrḫm.k m[rṣ].|arb'.k dw.k[rt].|mnd'.krt.mǵ[y.---].|w qbr.tṣr.q[br].|tṣr.trm.tnq 16.2[125].85
dm.ḥš k.'ṣ k.'bṣ k.'m y.p'n k.tls]|[m]n 'm y t[wtḥ.išd k.dm.rgm.iṯ.l y.d argmn k].|[h]wt.d aṯ[ny k.---.rgm.'ṣ].|w l 7.2[130].17
šdm.|ḥš k.'ṣ k.'bṣ k.|'m y.p'n k.tlsmn.'m y.|twtḥ.išd k.dm.rgm.|iṯ.l y.w argm k.|hwt.w aṯny k.rgm.|'ṣ.w lḫšt.ab 3['NT].3.17
[h]š k.[']ṣ k.'bṣ k.'m y.p'n k.|[tls]mn.[']m y.twtḥ.išd k.|[dm.rgm.iṯ.l y.]w argm k.hwt.|[w aṯny k.rgm.]'ṣ.w lḫšt. 3['NT].4.56
---].|[---.b]gdlt.ar[kt y.am--].|[---.qdq]d k.ašhlk[.šbt k.dmm].|[šbt.dq]n k.mm'm.w[---].|aqht.w yplṭ k.bn[.dnil. 18[3AQHT].1.11
-] y.[---]b[-].|b gdlt.arkt y.am[---].|qdqd k.ašhlk.šbt[k.dmm].|[šbt.dqn k.mm'm.]y'ny.|il.b šb't.ḥdrm.b ṯmnt.|a 3['NT.VI].5.32
bmt.li[mm].|w y'ny.aliyn[.b'l].|lm.k qnym.'l[m.--].|k dr d.d yknn[.--].|b'l.yṣǵd.mli[.--].|il hd.mla.u[--.--].|blt.p 10[76].3.7
bṯnt.trtḥ[ṣ.---].|[---.t]tb h.aḫt.ppšr.w ppšrt[.---].|[---.]k.drḫm.w aṯb.l ntbt.k.'šm l t[--].|[---.]drk.brḥ.arṣ.lk pn h.yr 1001.2.7
t.ib k.|b'l m.ht.ib k.tmḫṣ.ht.tṣmt.ṣrt k.|tqḥ.mlk.'lm k.drkt.dt dr dr k.|kṯr ṣmdm.ynḥt.w yp'r.šmt hm.šm k at.| 2.4[68].10
k.tb'.bt.ḫnp.lb[k.--.ti]|ḫd.d iṯ.b kbd k.tšt.b [---].|irt k.dṯ.ydṯ.m'qb k.[ttb'].|[bt]lt.'nt.idk.l ttn.[pnm].|['m.a]qht.ǵ 18[3AQHT].1.19
k.'lm.b ḏmr h.bl.|[---].b ḥtk h.b nmrt h.l r|[--.]arṣ.'z k.ḏmr k.l[-]|n k.ḥtk k.nmrt k.b tk.|ugrt.l ymt.špš.w yrḫ.| UG5.2.2.9
n k.tls]|[m]n 'm y t[wtḥ.išd k.dm.rgm.iṯ.l y.d argmn k].|[h]wt.d aṯ[ny k.---.rgm.'ṣ].|w lḫšt.abn[.tant.šmm.'m.arṣ 7.2[130].17
d k.tk.ḫršn.-------------].|ǵr.ks.dm.r[gm.iṯ.l y.w argm k].|hwt.w aṯny k[.rgm.'ṣ.w lḫšt.abn].|tunt.šmm.'m[.arṣ.th 1['NT.IX].3.12
k.|[tls]mn.[']m y.twtḥ.išd k.|[dm.rgm.iṯ.l y.]w argm k.hwt.|[w aṯny k.rgm.]'ṣ.w lḫšt.|[abn.rgm.l td]'.nš[m.w l t] 3['NT].4.57
.p'n k.tlsmn.'m y.|twtḥ.išd k.dm.rgm.|iṯ.l y.w argm k.|hwt.w aṯny k.rgm.|'ṣ.w lḫšt.abn.|tant.šmm.'m.arṣ.|thm 3['NT].3.18

ib.|[---.--]m.|[-----].|[-]š[--.---].|[-]r[--.--]y.|in m.‘bd k hwt.|[y]rš.‘m y.|mnm.iršt k.|d ḫsrt.w.ank.|aštn..l.iḫ y.| 2065.13
ttn.pnm.|‘m.nrt.ilm.špš.|tšu.g h.w tṣḥ.|tḥm.ṯr.il.ab k.|hwt.lṭpn.ḥtk k.|pl.‘nt.šdm.y špš.|pl.‘nt.šdm.il.yš[t k].|b‘ 6[49].4.34
l.yšt]ḫwyn.w y|[kbdn h.yšu.g h.w y]ṣḥ.tḥm.|[ṯr.il.ab k.hwt.l]ṭpn.ḥtk k.|[qryy.b arṣ.mlḥ]mt.št b ‘p|[r m.ddym.sk 1[‘NT.IX].2.18
rgm l k[ṯr.w ḫss.ṯny.l hyn].|d ḥrš.y[dm.tḥm.ṯr.il.ab k.]|hwt.lṭpn[.ḥtk k.---].|yh.kṯr.b[---].|št.lskt.n[--.---].|‘db. 1[‘NT.IX].3.5
l].p‘n.um [y].|qlt[.l um] y.|yšlm.il[m].|tǵ[r] k.tš[lm] k.|[h]l ny.‘m n[.š]lm.|w.ṯm [ny.‘m.mlkt.u]m y.|mnm[.šlm] 1013.7
.|bn k.|l.p‘n.um y.|qlt.l.um y.|yšlm.ilm.|tǵr k.tšlm k.|hl ny.‘m n[y].|kll.šlm.|ṯm ny.‘m.um y.|mnm.šlm.|w.rg 50[117].8
[yš]lm[.ilm].|tǵr k[.tšlm k].|hl ny.[---].|w.pdr[--.---].|tmǵyn[.---].|w.mli[.---].|[-]kl. 57[101].2
w hm.|aṯtm.tṣḥn y.ad ad.nḥtm.ḫṭ k.|mmnnm.mṭ yd k.hl.‘ṣr.tḥrr.l išt.|w ṣḥrrt.l pḥmm.btm.bt.il.bt.il.|w ‘lm h.w 23[52].44
.w hn.aṯtm.tṣḥn y.mt mt.|nḥtm.ḫṭ k.mmnnm.mṭ yd k.hl.‘ṣr.|tḥrr.l išt.w ṣḥrt.l pḥmm.aṯtm.a[ṯt.il].|aṯt.il.w ‘lm h 23[52].47
pt.hm.aṯtm.tṣḥn.|y mt.mt.nḥtm.ḫṭ k.mmnnm.mṭ.yd k.|h[l.]‘ṣr.tḥrr.l išt.ṣḥrrt.l pḥmm.|a[ṯ]tm.aṯt.il.aṯt.il.w ‘lm h 23[52].40
.š y.qḥn y.|[--.]šir.b krm.nṭṭt.dm.‘lt.b ab y.|u---].‘lt.b k.lk.l pn y.yrk.b‘l.[--].|[---.]‘nt.šzrm.tštšḥ.km.ḥ[--].|[---].‘pr 1001.1.10
ḫd.hm.b y[--] y.[---]b[-].|b gdlt.arkt y.am[---].|qdqd k.ašhlk.šbt[k.dmm].|[šbt.dqn k.mm‘m.]y‘ny.|il.b šb‘t.ḥdr 3[‘NT.VI].5.32
al.]aḫd hm.[---].|[---.b]gdlt.ar[kt y.am--].|[---.qdq]d k.ašhlk[.šbt k.dmm].|[šbt.dq]n k.mm‘m.w[---].|aqht.w ypl 18[3AQHT].1.11
pn.ybṣr.[ḥbl.d]|iym.bn.nšrm.arḫp.an[k.‘]l.|aqht.‘db k.hlmn.ṯnm.qdqd.|ṯlṯ id.‘l.udn.špk.km.šiy.|dm.km.šḫṭ.l br 18[3AQHT].4.22
ḥm.pgn.|l.mlk.ugrt.|rgm.|yšlm.l k.[il]m.|tǵr k.tšlm k.|hn ny.‘m n.š[l]m.|ṯm ny.‘[m.]bn y.|mnm.[šl]m[.r]gm[.ṯṯ 2061.5
ḫ y.rgm.|tḥm.mlk.ṣr.aḫ k.|y[š]lm.l k.ilm.|tǵr k.tšlm k.|hn ny.‘m n.|šlm.ṯm ny.|‘m k.mnm[.š]lm.|rgm.ṯṯ[b].|an 2059.5
‘bd k.|l.p‘n.adt ny.|mrḥqtm.|qlny.ilm.|tǵr k.|tšlm k.|hn ny.‘m ny.|kll.mid.|šlm.|w.ap.ank.|nḫt.ṯm ny.|‘m.a 51[95].9
]|rk.‘l.aqht.k yq[--.---].|pr‘m.ṣd k.y bn[.---].|pr‘m.ṣd k.hn pr[‘.--].|ṣd.b hkl h[.---].|[------].|[---.l]ḫm[.---].|[---].ay 17[2AQHT].5.38
um.l grnt].|i[ln]y[m].l mṭ‘t[.---].|[-]m[.---].|h.hn bn k.hn[.---].|bn bn.aṯr k.hn[.---].|yd k.ṣǵr.tnšq.špt k.ṭm.|ṭkm 22.2[124].2
].l mṭ‘t[.---].|[-]m[.---].|h.hn bn k.hn[.---].|bn bn.aṯr k.hn[.---].|yd k.ṣǵr.tnšq.špt k.ṭm.|ṭkm.bm ṭkm.aḫm.qym.il 22.2[124].3
ṣ.|w t‘n.nrt.ilm.š[p]š.|šd yn.‘n.b qbt[.t]|bl lyt.‘l.umt k.|w abqṯ.aliyn.b‘l.|w t‘n.btlt.‘nt.|an.l an.y špš.|an.l an.il.y 6[49].4.43
y ndr.|iṯt.w.ht.|[-]sny.udr h.|w.hm.ḫt.|‘l.w.likt.|‘m k.w.hm.|l.‘l.w.lakm.|ilak.w.at.|um y.al.tdḥṣ.|w.ap.mhkm. 1013.18
u.|g h.w tṣḥ.tbšr b‘l.|bšrt k.yblt.y[b]n.|bt.l k.km.aḫ k.w ḥẓr.|km.ary k.ṣḥ.ḫrn.|b bht k.‘ḏbt.b qrb.|hkl k.tbl k.ǵ 4[51].5.90
tk.|špš.tḥtk.ilnym.|‘d k.ilm.hn.mtm.|‘d k.kṯr m.ḥbr k.|w ḫss.d‘t k.|b ym.arš.w tnn.|kṯr.w ḫss.yd.|ytr.kṯr.w ḫss 6.6[62.2].48
-]k.bm.ymn.|tlk.škn.‘l.ṣrrt.|adn k.šqrb.[---].|b mgn k.w ḫrṣ.l kl.|apnk.ǵzr.ilḥu.|[m]rḥ h.yiḫd.b yd.|[g]rgr h.bm 16.1[125].45
.|ilšiy.|kry amt.|‘pr.‘ẓm yd.|ugrm.ḫl.ld.|aklm.tbrk k.|w ld ‘qqm.|ilm.yp‘r.|šmt hm.|b hm.qrnm.|km.ṭrm.w g 12[75].1.26
lš.|amt.yrḫ.|l dmgy.amt.|aṯrt.qḥ.|ksan k.ḥdg k.|ḥtl k.w ẓi.|b aln.tk m.|b tk.mlbr.|ilšiy.|kry amt.|‘pr.‘ẓm yd.| 12[75].1.19
šmm.dbḥ.l ṯr.|ab k.il.šrd.b‘l.|b dbḥ k.bn.dgn.|b mṣd k.w yrd.|krt.l ggt.‘db.|akl.l qryt.|ḥṭt.l bt.ḫbr.|yip.lḥm.d ḫ 14[KRT].2.79
tṣḥ.šm‘.m‘.|[l aqht.ǵzr.i]rš.ksp.w atn k.|[ḫrṣ.w aš]lḥ k.w tn.qšt k.[l].|[‘nt.tq]ḥ[.q]ṣ‘t k.ybmt.limm.|w y‘n.aqht.ǵz 17[2AQHT].6.18
tḥm.ydn.‘m.mlk.|b‘l h.ngr.ḥwt k.|w l.a[--]t.tšknn.|ḫmšm.l mi[t].any.|tškn[n.--]h.k[--].|w 2062.1.2
.l k.|w.lḥt.alpm.ḫršm.|k.rgmt.l y.bly m.|alpm.aršt.l k.w.l y.|mn.bnš.d.l.i[--].‘[m k].|l.alpm.w.l.y[n.--]t.|w.bl.bn 2064.23
k.z[--.--]n.ššwm.|n‘mm.[--].ṯtm.w.at.|nǵṯ.w.ytn.hm.l k.|w.lḥt.alpm.ḫršm.|k.rgmt.l y.bly m.|alpm.aršt.l k.w.l y.| 2064.20
.k[--.---].|[---.]‘sb.[-]ḥ[-.---].|[---.]b[-.]mṭt k.[---].|[---.]k.w tmt[.---].|[---.]k.w tṯ[--.---].|[---.]k.w ṯ[--.---].|[---.]k ṯr 2125.6
ak.|‘m y.w.yd.|ilm.p.k mtm.|‘z.mid.|hm.nṯkp.|m‘n k.|w.mnm.|rgm.d.tšm‘.|ṯmt.w.št.|b.spr.‘m y. 53[54].15
šḥ.|b‘l.ymšḫ.hm.b ‘p.|nṭ‘n.b arṣ.ib y.|w b ‘pr.qm.aḫ k.|w tšu.‘n h.btlt.‘nt.|w tšu.‘n h.w t‘n.|w t‘n.arḫ.w tr.b lkt. 10[76].2.25
kl.il.alṯ[y].|nmry.mlk.‘lm.|mlk n.b‘l y.ḥw[t.--].|yšhr k.w.‘m.ṣ[--].|‘š[--.---]d.lik[t.---].|w [----].|k[--.---].|‘šrm[.---] 2008.1.11
rn.|riš k.‘ṯtrt.šm.b‘l.|qdqd k.tqln.b gbl.|šnt k.b ḥpn k.w t‘n.|spr ilmlk ṯ‘y. 16.6[127].58
.l ys‘.[alt.]ṯ[bt |k.l y]hpk.|[ksa.]mlk k.l ytbr.ḫṭ.mṭpṭ k.w y‘n[.‘ṯtr].dm[-]k[-].|[--]ḥ.b y.ṯr.il.ab y.ank.in.bt[.l] y[.k 2.3[129].18
.l arṣ.ṯtbr.|[---.]aḫ h.tbky.|[--.m]rṣ.mlk.|[---.]krt.adn k.|[w y‘ny.]ǵzr.ilḥu.|[---.]mrṣ.mlk.|[--.k]rt.adn k.|[--.d]bḥ. 16.1[125].57
yn.b k.ḫrṣ.|dm.‘ṣm.hm.yd.il mlk.|yḫss k.ahbt.ṯr.t‘rr k.|w t‘n.rbt.aṯrt ym.|tḥm k.il.ḥkm.ḥkmt.|‘m ‘lm.ḥyt.ḥẓt.|t 4[51].4.39
.ar[b‘.]ymm.bṣr.|kp.šsk k.[--].l ḥbš k.|‘tk.ri[š.]l mhr k.|w ‘p.l dr[‘].nšr k.|w rbṣ.l ǵr k.inbb.|kt ǵr k.ank.yd‘t.|[-] 13[6].7
kp.šsk k.[--].l ḥbš k.|‘tk.ri[š.]l mhr k.|w ‘p.l dr[‘].nšr k.|w rbṣ.l ǵr k.inbb.|kt ǵr k.ank.yd‘t.|[-]n.atn.at.mṯb k[.--- 13[6].8
b.yṯb.b hkl.|w ywsrnn.ggn h.|lk.l ab k.yṣb.lk.|l[ab]k.w rgm.‘ny.|l k[rt.adn k.]ištm[‘].|w tqǵ[.udn.k ǵz.ǵzm].|t 16.6[127].28
.kb|[--.---.]al.yns.|[---.]ysd k.|[---.--]r.dr.dr.|[---.--]y k.w rḥd.|[---]y ilm.d mlk.|y[ṯ]b.aliyn.b‘l.|yt‘dd.rkb.‘rpt.|[- 4[51].3.8
.p[‘]n k.|[tlsmn.‘m y.twt]ḥ.išd k.|[tk.ḫršn.---]r.[-]ḥm k.w št.|[---.]ẓ[--.-]rdy k.|[---.i]qnim.|[---.-]šu.b qrb.|[---].as 1[‘NT.IX].2.3
-]ḥ[-.---].|[---.]b[-.]mṭt k.[---].|[---.]k.w tmt[.---].|[---.]k.w tṯ[--.---].|[---.]k.w ṯ[--.---].|[---.]k ṯrm.l p[--.---].|[---.]l.[- 2125.7
q]ḥ.y krt.aṯt.|tqḥ.bt k.ǵlmt.tš‘rb.|ḥqr k.tld.šb‘.bnm.l k.|w ṯmn.tṯtmnm.|l k.tld.yṣb.ǵlm.|ynq.ḥlb.a[ṯ]rt.|mṣṣ.ṯd.b 15[128].2.23
mṭt k.[---].|[---.]k.w tmt[.---].|[---.]k.w tṯ[--.---].|[---.]k.w ṯ[--.---].|[---.]k ṯrm.l p[--.---].|[---.]l.[--.]rlg[-.---].|[---.]b 2125.8
ym.|rbt.ilm.l ḥkmt.|šbt.dqn k.l tsr k.|rḥntt.d[-].l irt k.|wn ap.‘dn.mṭr h.|b‘l.y‘dn.‘dn.ṯkt.b glṯ.|w tn.ql h.b ‘rpt. 4[51].5.67
.ḥpr.p‘l k.y[--].|šm‘ k.l arḫ.w bn.[--].|limm.ql.b udn.k w[-].|k rtqt mr[.---].|k d lbšt.bir.mlak.|šmm.tmr.zbl.ml 13[6].23
kbd.|ẓi.at.l tlš.|amt.yrḫ.|l dmgy.amt.|aṯrt.qḥ.|ksan k.ḥdg k.|ḥtl k.w ẓi.|b aln.tk m.|b tk.mlbr.|ilšiy.|kry amt. 12[75].1.18
mla.|mnm.dbbm.d |msdt.arṣ.|s‘.il.dqt.k amr.|sknt.k ḥwt.yman.|d b h.rumm.l rbbt. 4[51].1.43
yšu.g h.w yṣḥ.|aṯbn.ank.w anḫn.|w tnḫ.b irt y.npš.|k ḥy.aliyn.b‘l.|k iṯ.zbl.b‘l.arṣ.|gm.yṣḥ.il.l btlt.|‘nt.šm‘.l btlt 6[49].3.20
rt.bny.bnwt.|šmm.šmn.tmṭrn.|nḫlm.tlk.nbtm.|w id‘.k ḥy.aliyn.b‘l.|k iṯ.zbl.b‘l.arṣ.|b ḥlm.lṭpn.il d pid.|b ḏrt.bn 6[49].3.8
w ašlḥ k.ašspr k.‘m.b‘l.|šnt.‘m.bn il.tspr.yrḫm.|k b‘l.k yḥwy.y‘šr.ḥwy.y‘š.|r.w yšqyn h.ybd.w yšr.‘l h.|n‘m[n.w t 17[2AQHT].6.30
.ḥdṯ.|yb‘r.l ṯn.aṯt h.|w l nkr.mddt.|km irby.tškn.|šd.k ḥsn.pat.|mdbr.tlkn.|ym.w ṯn.aḫr.|šp[š]m.b [ṯ]lṯ.|ym[ǵy.] 14[KRT].4.193
šmm.|[---.l]šn.l kbkbm.y‘rb.|[b‘]l.b kbd h.b p h yrd.|k ḫrr.zt.ybl.arṣ.w pr.|‘ṣm.yraun.aliyn.b‘l.|ṯt‘.nn.rkb.‘rpt.|t 5[67].2.5
bl.|[---].b ḥtk h.b nmrt h.l r|[--.]arṣ.‘z k.ḏmr k.l[-]|n k.ḥtk k.nmrt k.b tk.|ugrt.l ymt.špš.w yrḫ.|w n‘mt.šnt.il. UG5.2.2.10
i.at.l tlš.|amt.yrḫ.|l dmgy.amt.|aṯrt.qḥ.|ksan k.ḥdg k.|ḥtl k.w ẓi.|b aln.tk m.|b tk.mlbr.|ilšiy.|kry amt.|‘pr.‘ẓ 12[75].1.18
[.ǵz]r.w y‘n.aqht.ǵzr.|al.tšrgn.y btlt m.dm.l ǵzr.|šrg k.ḫḫm.mt.uḫryt.mh.yqḥ.|mh.yqḥ.mt.aṯryt.spsg.ysk.|[l]riš. 17[2AQHT].6.35
tšmḫ ht.|aṯrt.w bn h.ilt.w ṣb|rt.ary h.k mt.aliyn.|b‘l.k ḫlq.zbl.b‘l.|arṣ.gm.yṣḥ il.|l rbt.aṯrt ym.šm‘.|l rbt.aṯr[t] y 6.1.42[49.1.14]
[k mt.aliyn.b‘l].|k ḫlq.z[bl.b‘l.arṣ].|w hm.ḥy.a[liyn.b‘l].|w hm.iṯ.zbl.b‘[l.arṣ] 6[49].3.1
.k.rgm.špš.|mlk.rb.b‘l y.u.|‘[--.]mlakt.‘bd h.|[---.]b‘l k.yḥpn.|[---.]‘m h.u ky.|[---.--]d k.k.tmǵy.|ml[--.--]š[.ml]k. 1018.4

šw mǵmǵ].|w [bṣql.ʻrgz.ydk].|a[ḥd h.w.yṣq.b.ap h].|k.[ḫr.ššw.ḫndrṯ].|w.ṯ[qd.mr.ydk.aḥd h].|w.y[ṣq.b.ap h].|k. 161[56].5
]šw mǵmǵ w b[ṣql ʻrgz].|[ydk aḥ]d h w yṣq b ap h.|[k ḫr]ššw ḫndrṯ w ṯ[qd m]r.|[ydk aḥd h w yṣq b ap h.|[k l 160[55].6
k [ḫr ššw mǵmǵ].|w [bṣql.ʻrgz.ydk].|a[ḥd h.w.yṣq.b.ap h].| 161[56].2
[k.---.]šš[w.---].|[---.w]yṣq b a[p h].|[k ḫr š]šw mǵmǵ w b[ṣql ʻrgz].|[ydk aḥ]d h w yṣq b ap h.|[160[55].4
l ʻpr.tšu.g h.]w tṣḥ.šmʻ.mʻ.|[l aqht.ǵzr.i]rš.ksp.w atn k.|[ḫrṣ.w aš]lḥ k.w tn.qšt k.[l].|[ʻnt.tq]ḥ[.q]ṣʻt k.ybmt.limm 17[2AQHT].6.17
.|[ln h.---].|z[tr.ʻm k.l arṣ.mšṣu.qṭr k].|l ʻpr.ḏm[r.aṯr k.ṭbq].|lḥt.niṣ k.gr[š.d ʻšy.ln k].|spu.ksm k.bt.[bʻl.w mnt k] 17[2AQHT].2.2
k.ʻm k.šbʻt.|ǵlm k.ṯmn.ḫnzr k.|ʻm k.pdry.bt.ar.|ʻm k.ṭṭly.bt.rb.idk.|pn k.al ttn.tk.ǵr.|knkny.ša.ǵr.ʻl ydm.|ḫlb.l 5[67].5.11
k.|[---].bnt.ṣʻṣ.bnt.mʻmʻ.ʻbd.ḥrn.[--.]k.|[---].aǵwyn.ʻn k.ẓẓ.w k mǵ.ilm.|[--.]k ʻṣm.k ʻšm.l ttn.k abnm.l thggn. 1001.2.12
]t.|la.šmm.b y[d.bn.ilm.m]t.|w tʻn.btlt.ʻn[t.bnt.]bht |k.y ilm.bnt.bh[t k].a[l.tš]mḫ.|al.tšmḫ.b r[m.h]kl[k].|al.aḫd 3[ʻNT.VI].5.28
.---].|[---] h.ap.[---].|[---].w tʻn.[btlt.ʻnt.---].|[bnt.bht]k.y ilm[.bnt.bht k.--].|[al.tšmḫ.]al.tš[mḫ.b rm.h]|[kl k.al.]a 18[3AQHT].1.7
t].|hrnmy.qšt.yqb.[--]|rk.ʻl.aqht.k yq[--.---].|prʻm.ṣd k.y bn[.---].|prʻm.ṣd k.hn pr[ʻ.--].|ṣd.b hkl h[.---].|[------].|[17[2AQHT].5.37
.šd.rbt.kmn.|ṣḥq.btlt.ʻnt.tšu.|g h.w tṣḥ.tbšr bʻl.|bšrt k.yblt.y[b]n.|bt.l k.km.aḫ k.w ḥẓr.|km.ary k.ṣḥ.ḥrn.|b bht 4[51].5.89
h.|l yrgm.l aliyn bʻl.|ṣḥ.ḥrn.b bhm k.|ʻḏbt.b qrb.hkl k.|tbl k.ǵrm.mid.ksp.|gbʻm.mḥmd.ḫrṣ.|ybl k.udr.ilqṣm.|w 4[51].5.76
ḫ k.w ḥẓr.|km.ary k.ṣḥ.ḥrn.|b bht k.ʻḏbt.b qrb.|hkl k.tbl k.ǵrm.|mid.ksp.gbʻm.mḥmd..|ḫrṣ.w bn.bht.ksp.|w ḫr 4[51].5.93
špš.[---].|nšlḥ[.---].|[---.m]at.|[---.]mat.|š[--].išal.|ʻm k.ybl.šd.|a[--].dʻ.k.|šld.ašld.|hn.mrṯ.d.štt.|ašld b ldt k. 2009.2.4
.w atn k.|[ḫrṣ.w aš]lḥ k.w tn.qšt k.[l].|[ʻnt.tq]ḥ[.q]ṣʻt k.ybmt.limm.|w yʻn.aqht.ǵzr.adr.ṯqbm.|[d]lbnn.adr.gdm. 17[2AQHT].6.19
.bʻl trḫ pdry b[t h].|aqrb k ab h bʻ[l].|yǵtr.ʻṯtr t|rḫ l k ybrdmy.b[t.a]|b h lb[u] yʻrr.w yʻ[n].|yrḫ nyr šmm.w nʻ[n 24[77].29
šq.aḫl.an bṣ[ql].|ynpʻ.b palt.bṣql ypʻ b yǵlm.|ur.tisp k.yd.aqht.|ǵzr.tšt k.b qrb m.asm.|y.dnh.ysb.aklt h.yph.|šb 19[1AQHT].2.66
ynšq.aḫl.an.šblt.|tpʻ.b aklt.šblt.tpʻ[.b ḥm]drt.|ur.tisp k.yd.aqht.ǵz[r].|tšt k.bm.qrb m.asm.|b p h.rgm.l yṣa.b špt 19[1AQHT].2.73
.tpʻr[.---].|ank.lṭpn.il[.d pid.---].|ʻl.ydm.pʻrt[.---].|šm k.mdd.i[l.---].|bt ksp y.d[--.---].|b d.aliyn b[ʻl.---].|kd.ynaṣ 1[ʻNT.X].4.20
n.w tdm.l y.[--].|[---].al.trgm.l aḫt k.|[---.]l [ ]dm.aḫt k.|ydʻt.k rḥmt.|al.tšt.b šdm.mm h.|b smkt.ṣat.npš h.|[-]mt 16.1[125].32
.ydʻt.|h[t.---.]l.špš.bʻl k.|ʻ[--.s]glt h.at.|ht[.---.]špš.bʻl k.|ydʻm.l.ydʻt.|ʻm y.špš.bʻl k.|šnt.šntm.lm.l.tlk.|w.lḥt.akl. 2060.13
.yšu.|g h.w yṣḥ.aṯbn.ank.|w anḫn.w tnḫ.b irt y.|npš.k yld.bn.l y.km.|aḫ y.w šrš.km ary y.|nṣb.skn.ilib y.b qdš.| 17[2AQHT].2.14
].|[---.m]at.|[---.]mat.|š[--].išal.|ʻm k.ybl.šd.|a[--].dʻ.k.|šld.ašld.|hn.mrṯ.d.štt.|ašld b ldt k. 2009.2.5
.ǵlmt.tšʻrb.|ḥqr k.tld.šbʻ.bnm.l k.|w ṯmn.ṯṯmnm.|l k.tld.yṣb.ǵlm.|ynq.ḥlb.a[ṯ]rt.|mṣṣ.ṯd.btlt.[ʻnt].|mšnq.[---]. 15[128].2.25
.|[b tk.rpi.]arṣ.|[b pḫr].qbṣ.dtn.|[w t]qrb.w ld.|bn.tl k.|tld.pǵt.t[--]t.|tld.pǵt[.---].|tld.pǵ[t.---].|tld.pǵ[t.---].|tld. 15[128].3.6
n.]ǵlm.il.|a[ṯt.tq]ḥ.y krt.aṯt.|tqḥ.bt k.ǵlmt.tšʻrb.|ḥqr k.tld.šbʻ.bnm.l k.|w ṯmn.ṯṯmnm.|l k.tld.yṣb.ǵlm.|ynq.ḥlb. 15[128].2.23
l h.trm.hl h.tṣḥ.ad ad.|w hl h.tṣḥ.um.um.tirk m.yd.il.k ym.|w yd il.k mdb.ark.yd.il.k ym.|w yd.il.k mdb.yqḥ.il. 23[52].33
ṣḥ.um.um.tirk m.yd.il.k ym.|w yd il.k mdb.ark.yd.il.k ym.|w yd.il.k mdb.yqḥ.il.mštʻltm.|mštʻltm.l riš.agn.yqḥ.t 23[52].34
aṯr.bʻl.nrd.|b arṣ.ʻm h.trd.nrt.|ilm.špš.ʻd.tšbʻ.bk.|tšt.k yn.udmʻt.gm.|tṣḥ.l nrt.ilm.špš.|ʻms mʻ.l y.aliyn.bʻl.|tšmʻ. 6[62].1.10
iš h.b glṯ.b šm[m].|[---.i]l.ṯr.iṯ.p h.k ṯt.ǵlt[.--].|[---.--] k yn.ddm.l b[--.---].|[---.]yt š[--.---].|[---.]hl[-.---].|[---.-]yṯr. UG5.3.1.9
[---.]rḫbn.hm.[-.]aṯr[.---].|[--]šy.w ydn.b[ʻl.---]n.|[--]ʻ.k yn.hm.l.atn.bt y.l h. 1002.62
ʻnt.hlkt.w.šnwt.|tp.aḫ.h.k.ysmsm.|tspi.šir.h.l.bl.ḥrb.|tšt.dm.h.l.bl.ks.|tpnn.ʻn.bty.ʻ RS225.2
.|[y]ṣb.ʻln.w y[-]y.|[kr]t.ṯʻ.ʻln.bḫr.|[---].aṯt k.ʻl.|[---] k.yšṣi.|[---.]ḫbr.rbt.|[ḫbr.ṯrr]t.il d.|[pid.---].b anšt.|[---.]ml 15[128].5.24
kḥṯ.drkt.|ap.yṣb.ytb.b hkl.|w ywsrnn.ggn h.|lk.l ab k.yṣb.lk.|l[ab]k.w rgm.ʻny.|l k[rt.adn k.]ištm[ʻ].|w tqǵ[.u 16.6[127].27
[t].|rpi.aphn.ǵzr.m[t].|hrnmy.qšt.yqb.[--]|rk.ʻl.aqht.k yq[--.---].|prʻm.ṣd k.y bn[.---].|prʻm.ṣd k.hn pr[ʻ.--].|ṣd.b 17[2AQHT].5.36
.ab k.l ysʻ.alt.|ṯbt k.l yhpk.ksa.mlk k.|l ytbr.ḫṭ.mṯpṭ k.|yru.bn ilm t.ṯtʻ.y|dd.il.ǵzr.yʻr.mt.|b ql h.y[---.---].|bʻl.yṯ 6[49].6.29
t y.|[--]ptm.ṣḥq.|[---.]rgm.hy.[-]ḫ[-]y.ilak k.|[---.--]g k.yritn.mǵy.hy.w kn.|[---].ḥln.d b.dmt.um.il[m.---].|[--]ḏyn 1002.42
by.|bʻl.qrnm w ḏnb.ylšn.|b ḫri h.w ṯnt h.ql.il.[--].|il.k yrdm.arṣ.ʻnt.|w ʻṯtrt.tṣdn.[---].|[---.-]b[-.---].|[ʻṯ]trt w ʻnt[UG5.1.1.22
rḥrtm.w[--.]n[--.]iš[--.]h[---.]išt.|[---]y.yblmm.u[---]k.yrd[.--.]i[---]n.bn.|[---.-]nn.nrt.ilm.špš.tšu.g h.w t[ṣḥ.šm]ʻ. 2.3[129].14
|[š]mm.rm.lk.prẓ kt.|[k]bkbm.ṯm.tpl k.lbnt.|[-.]rgm.k yrkt.ʻṯqbm.|[---]m.ʻzpn.l pit.|m[--]m[.--]tm.w mdbḥt.|ḫr 13[6].14
--]ṯb.ʻryt k.k qlt[.---].|[--]at.brt.lb k.ʻnn.[---].|[--.]šdq.k ttn.l y.šn[.---].|[---.]bn.rgm.w ydʻ[.---]. 60[32].5
gnryn.|l mlkytn.|ḥnn y l pn mlk.|šin k itn.|rʻ y šṣa idn l y.|l šmn iṯr hw.|p iḫdn gnryn.|im mlky 1020.4
m.|aḫt.ʻrš.mdw.anšt.|ʻrš.zbln.rd.l mlk.|amlk.l drkt k.aṯb.|an.w yʻny.krt ṯʻ.ytbr.|ḥrn.y bn.ytbr.ḥrn.|riš k.ʻṯtrt.š 16.6[127].53
m.aḫt.ʻrš.mdw.|anšt.ʻrš.zbln.|rd.l mlk.amlk.|l drkt.k aṯb.an.|ytbʻ.yṣb ǵlm.ʻl.|ab h.yʻrb.yšu g h.|w yṣḥ.šmʻ mʻ.l 16.6[127].38
bʻl.ytb.k ṯbt.ǵr.hd.r[ʻy].|k mdb.b tk.ǵr h.il ṣpn.b [tk].|ǵr.tliyt.šbʻt. UG5.3.1.1
.šmt.|l.iybʻl.|ṯlṯm.l.mit.šʻrt.|l.šr.ʻṯtrt.|mlbš.ṯrmnm.|k.ytn.w.b.bt.|mlk.mlbš.|ytn.l hm.|šbʻ.lbšm.allm.|l ušḫry.| 1107.6
.|btlt.ʻn[t].tptrʻ ṯd[h].|limm.w tʻl.ʻm.il.|ab h.ḥpr.pʻl k.y[--].|šmʻ k.l arḫ.w bn.[--].|limm.ql.b udn.k w[-].|k rtqt 13[6].21
m.ʻbd k.bʻl.|[--.--]m.bn.dgn.a[s]r km.hw ybl.argmn k.k ilm.|[---.]ybl.k bn.qdš.mnḥy k.ap.anš.zbl.bʻ[l].|[-.yuḫ]d 2.1[137].37
|w št m.ʻm.a[ḫ] yn.|p nšt.bʻl.[ṭ]ʻn.iṭʻn k.|[---.]ma[---] k.k tmḫṣ.|[ltn.bṯn.br]ḥ.tkly.|[bṯn.ʻqltn.]šlyṭ.|[d šbʻt.rašm].t 5[67].1.27
lakt.ʻbd h.|[---.]bʻl k.yḫpn.|[---.]ʻm h.u ky.|[---.--]d k.k.tmǵy.|ml[--.--]š[.ml]k.rb.|b[ʻl y.---].|yd[--.]mlk.|rb.b[ʻl 1018.6
[-----].|[--.]l tṣi.b b[--].bm.k[--].|[--]ṯb.ʻryt k.k qlt[.---].|[--]at.brt.lb k.ʻnn.[---].|[--.]šdq.k ttn.l y.šn[.---] 60[32].3
sm k.bt.[bʻl.w mnt k].|bt il.aḥd.yd k.b [škrn].|mʻms k.k šbʻt.yn.ṯ[ḫ].|gg k.b ym.ṭiṭ.rḥṣ.|npṣ k.b ym rṯ.b uni[l].|p 17[2AQHT].2.6
t.l bmt.ʻr.|l ysmsmt.bmt.pḥl.|qdš.yuḫdm.šbʻr.|amrr.k kbkb.l pnm.|aṯr.btlt.ʻnt.|w bʻl.tbʻ.mrym.ṣpn.|idk.l ttn.pn 4[51].4.17
šn[.---].|tʻtd.tkl.[---].|tkn.lbn[.---].|dt.lbn k[.---].|dk k.kbkb[.---].|dm.mt.aṣḥ[.---].|ydd.b qr[b.---].|al.ašt.b[---].| 5[67].3.8
d.kbd h.b ṣḥ]q.ymlu.lb h.|[b šmḫt.kbd.ʻnt.tšyt.tḥt h.k]kdrt.riš.|[ʻl h.k irbym.kp.---.k br]k.tǵll.b dm.|[ḏmr.---.]t 7.1[131].8
|qrytm tmḫṣ.lim.ḫp y[m].|tṣmt.adm.ṣat.š[p]š.|tḥt h.k kdrt.ri[š].|ʻl h.k irbym.kp.k.qṣm.|ǵrmn.kp.mhr.ʻtkt.|rišt. 3[ʻNT].2.9
ʻl k.|šnt.šntm.lm.l.tlk.|w.lḥt.akl.ky.|likt.ʻm.špš.|bʻl k.ky.akl.|b.ḫwt k.inn.|špš n.[---].|hm.al[k.--].|ytnt[.---].|tn 2060.19
[l]krt.|k [k]lb.b bt k.nʻtq.k inr.|ap.ḫšt k.ap.ab.ik mtm.|tmtn.u ḫšt 16.1[125].2
nn.[tt]n.|g h.bky.b ḥ[y k.a]b n.|nšmḫ.b l.mt k.ngln.|k klb.[b]bt k.nʻtq.|k inr[.ap.]ḫšt k.|ap.ab.k mtm.tmtn.|u ḫ 16.2[125].100
w yšnn.ytn.g h.|bky.b ḥy k.ab n.ašmḫ.|b l.mt k.ngln.k klb.|b bt k.nʻtq.k inr.|ap.ḫšt k.ap.ab.k mtm.|tmtn.u ḫšt 16.1[125].15
t.l šʻr.|ṯl.ydʻt.hlk.kbkbm.|a[-]ḥ.hy.mḫ.tmḫṣ.mḫṣ[.aḫ k].|tkl.m[k]ly.ʻl.umt[k.--].|d ttql.b ym.trth[ṣ.--].|[----.a]d 19[1AQHT].4.201
btlt.ʻnt.tšu.|g h.w tṣḥ.tbšr bʻl.|bšrt k.yblt.y[b]n.|bt.l k.km.aḫ k.w ḥẓr.|km.ary k.ṣḥ.ḥrn.|b bht k.ʻḏbt.b qrb.|hkl 4[51].5.90

[m].|[l pn.tp]t[.nhr.]mlkt.[--]pm.l mlkt.wn.in.att.|[l]k.k[m.ilm].|[w ǵlmt.k bn.qdš.]w y[--.]zbl.ym.y'[--.]tpt.nhr.
ddm.w n'rs[.---].|w t'n.btlt.'nt.tb.ytp.w[---].|l k.ašt k.km.nšr.b ḥb[š y].|km.diy.b t'rt y.aqht.[km.ytb].|l lḥm.w 18[3AQHT].4.17
.ap ṣin.šql.trm.|w mri ilm.'glm.dt.šnt.|imr.qmṣ.llim.k ksp.|l 'brm.zt.ḫrṣ.l 'brm.kš.|dpr.tlḥn.b q'l.b q'l.|mlkm.h 22.2[124].14
špš.|rpim.tḥtk.|špš.tḥtk.ilnym.|'d k.ilm.hn.mtm.|'d k.ktr m.ḥbr k.|w ḫss.d't k.|b ym.arš.w tnn.|ktr.w ḫss.yd.| 6.6[62.2].48
t.ib k.tmḫṣ.ht.tṣmt.ṣrt k.|tqḥ.mlk.'lm k.drkt.dt dr dr k.|ktr ṣmdm.ynḥt.w yp'r.šmt hm.šm k at.|ygrš.ygrš.grš y 2.4[68].10
h.l nḫt.l kḥt].|drkt h.š[--.--].|w hm.ap.l[--.---].|ymḫṣ k.k[--.---].|il.dbḥ.[---].|p'r.b[--.---].|tbḫ.alp[m.ap.ṣin.šql].|t 1['NT.X].4.27
.šm y.|w l h[-] y'l m.|bn y.yšal.|tryl.w rgm.|ttb.l aḫ k.|l adn k. 138.18
'l m.|w h[t] aḫ y.|bn y.yšal.|tryl.w rgm[.-].|ttb.l aḫ k.|l adn k. 138.18
t].ktr.w ḫss.|ṣḥq.ktr.w ḫss.|yšu.g h.w yṣḥ.|l rgmt.l k.l ali|yn.b'l.ttbn.b'l.|l hwt y.yptḥ.ḥ|ln.b bht m.urbt.|b qr 4[51].7.23
t.l y.bly m.|alpm.aršt.l k.w.l y.|mn.bnš.d.l.i[--].'[m k].|l.alpm.w.l.y[n.--]t.|w.bl.bnš.hw[-.--]y.|w.k.at.trg[m.--]. 2064.24
ptr' td[h].|limm.w t'l.'m.il.|ab h.ḥpr.p'l k.y[--].|šm' k.l arḫ.w bn.[--].|limm.ql.b udn.k w[-].|k rtqt mr[.---].|k d 13[6].22
r.a[t]r h.|[tbq.lḥt.niṣ h.gr]š.d 'šy.|[ln h.---].|z[tr.'m k.l arṣ.mšṣu.qtr k].|l 'pr.dm[r.atr k.tbq].|lḥt.niṣ k.gr[š.d 'šy 17[2AQHT].2.1
r h.|[---.-]rš.l b'l.|[---.-]ǵk.rpu mlk.|['lm.---.--]k.l tšt k.l iršt.|['lm.---.--]k.l tšt k.liršt.|[---.]rpi.mlk 'lm.b 'z.|[rpu. UG5.2.2.5
]bt k.n'tq.|k inr[.ap.]ḫšt k.|ap.ab.k mtm.tmtn.|u ḫšt k.l bky.'tq.|b d.att ab.ṣrry.|u ilm.tmtn.špḥ.|[l]tpn.l yḥ.t[b] 16.2[125].103
tqǵ udn.|k ǵz.ǵzm.tdbr.|w ǵrm.ttwy.šqlt.|b ǵlt.yd k.l tdn.|dn.almnt.l ttpt.|tpt qṣr.npš.l tdy.|tšm.'l.dl.l pn k.| 16.6[127].45
ǵ[.udn.k ǵz.ǵzm].|tdbr.w[ǵ]rm[.ttwy].|šqlt.b ǵlt.yd k.|l tdn.dn.almnt.|l ttpt.tpt.qṣr.npš.|km.aḫt.'rš.mdw.|anšt 16.6[127].32
hyrm.h[--.---].|yrmm h[--.---].|mlk.gb' h d [---].|ibr.k l hm.d l h q[--.---].|l ytn.l hm.tḥt b'l[.---].|h.u qšt pn hdd. 9[33].2.4
]|ṣ.'m.aliyn.b'l.|ik.al.yšm['] k.tr.|il.ab k.l ys'.alt.|tbt k.l yhpk.ksa.mlk k.|l ytbr.ḫt.mtpt k.|yru.bn ilm t.tt'.y|dd.i 6[49].6.28
n[.t]pt[.n]hr.|[ik.a]l.yšm' k.tr.[i]l.ab k.l ys'.[alt.]t[bt |k.l y]hpk.|[ksa.]mlk k.l ytbr.ḫt.mtpt k.w y'n[.'ttr].dm[-]k[-]
h.|[t]n.p k.b ǵr.tn.p k.b ḫlb.k tgwln.šnt k.|[--.]w špt k.l tššy.hm.tqrm.l mt.b rn k.|[--]ḫp.an.arnn.ql.špš.ḥw.btnm 1001.1.5
y.|l b'l[-.---].|tḥt.ksi.zbl.ym.w 'n.ktr.w ḫss.l rgmt.|l k.l zbl.b'l.tnt.l rkb.'rpt.ht.ib k.|b'l m.ht.ib k.tmḫṣ.ht.tṣmt.ṣ 2.4[68].8
ḫr]ššw ḫndrt w t[qd m]r.|[ydk aḥd h w yṣq b ap h.|[k l yḫru w]l yttn mss št qlql.|[w št 'rgz y]dk aḥd h w yṣq b 160[55].8
r.ššw.ḫndrt].|w.t[qd.mr.ydk.aḥd h].|w.y[ṣq.b.ap h].|k.l.ḫ[ru.w.l.yttn.ššw].|mss.[št.qlql.w.št].|'rgz[.ydk.aḥd h].| 161[56].8
k bn.atrt.|w t'n.rbt.atrt ym.|rbt.ilm.l ḥkmt.|šbt.dqn k.l tsr k.|rḫntt.d[-].l irt k.|wn ap.'dn.mtr h.|b'l.y'dn.'dn.tk 4[51].5.66
tdn.|dn.almnt.l ttpt.|tpt qṣr.npš.l tdy.|tšm.'l.dl.l pn k.|l tšlḥm.ytm.b'd.|ksl k.almnt.km.|aḫt.'rš.mdw.anšt.|'rš. 16.6[127].48
k.l pn.zbl.ym.l pn[.t]pt[.n]hr.|[ik.a]l.yšm' k.tr.[i]l.ab k.l ys'.[alt.]t[bt |k.l y]hpk.|[ksa.]mlk k.l ytbr.ḫt.mtpt k.w y 2.3[129].17
m.mt.ik.tmt[ḫ]|ṣ.'m.aliyn.b'l.|ik.al.yšm['] k.tr.|il.ab k.l ys'.alt.|tbt k.l yhpk.ksa.mlk k.|l ytbr.ḫt.mtpt k.|yru.bn 6[49].6.27
|b bt k.n'tq.k inr.|ap.ḫšt k.ap.ab.k mtm.|tmtn.u ḫšt k.l ntn.|'tq.b d.att.ab.ṣrry.|ik m.yrgm.bn.il.|krt.špḥ.ltpn.| 16.1[125].18
.b bt k.n'tq.k inr.|ap.ḫšt k.ap.ab.ik mtm.|tmtn.u ḫšt k.l ntn.|'tq.b d.att.ab ṣrry.|tbky k.ab.ǵr.b'l.|ṣpn.ḥlm.qdš.| 16.1[125].4
.|[l aqht.ǵzr.i]rš.ksp.w atn k.|[ḫrṣ.w aš]lḥ k.w tn.qšt k.[l].|['nt.tq]ḥ[.q]ṣ't k.ybmt.limm.|w y'n.aqht.ǵzr.adr.tqb 17[2AQHT].6.18
ḥt.niṣ h.gr]š.d 'šy.|[ln h.---].|z[tr.'m k.l arṣ.mšṣu.qtr k].|l 'pr.dm[r.atr k.tbq].|lḥt.niṣ k.gr[š.d 'šy.ln k].|spu.ksm 17[2AQHT].2.1
]nn.nrt.ilm.špš.tšu.g h.w t[ṣḥ.šm]'.m'.|[-.yt]ir tr.il.ab k.l pn.zbl.ym.l pn[.t]pt[.n]hr.|[ik.a]l.yšm' k.tr.[i]l.ab k.l ys'. 2.3[129].16
l.ybnn.|adn y.|rgm.|tḥm.t[g]yn.|bn k.|l.p['n.adn y].|q[lt.---].|l.yb[nn].|b'l y.r[gm].|tḥm.'bd[--] 2115.1.5
l.mlkt.|adt y.|rgm.|tḥm.tlmyn.|'bd k.|l.p'n.|adt y.|šb' d.|w.šb' id.|mrḥqtm.|qlt.|'m.adt y.|m 52[89].5
l um y.adt ny.|rgm.|tḥm.tlmyn.|w.aḫtmlk 'bd k.|l.p'n.adt ny.|mrḥqtm.|qlny.ilm.|tǵr k.|tšlm k.|hn ny.' 51[95].4
l.mlkt.|um y.rgm.|tḥm.mlk.|bn k.|l.p'n.um y.|qlt.l.um y.|yšlm.ilm.|tǵr k.tšlm k.|hl ny.'m 50[117].4
l mlkt.u[m] y.|[rg]m[.]t[ḥm].|mlk.bn [k].|[l].p'n.um [y].|qlt[.l um] y.|yšlm.il[m].|tǵ[r] k.tš[lm] k. 1013.3
l.mlk.b['l y].|r[gm].|tḥm.rb.mi[--.']bd k.|l.p'n.b'l y[.mrḥqtm].|šb' d.w.šb'[d.qlt].|ankn.rgmt.l.b'l 2008.1.3
l.mlk.b'[l] y.|rgm.|tḥm.tptb['l].|[']bd k.|[l.p]'n.b'l y.|[šb'] d.šb' [d].|[mr]ḥqtm.|qlt.|'bd k.b.|lws 2063.4
n y].|q[lt.---].|l.yb[nn].|b'l y.r[gm].|tḥm.'bd[--].|'bd k.|l p'n.b'l y.|tn id.šb' d.|mrḥqtm.|qlt.'m.|b'l y.mnm.|šl 2115.2.4
tḥm.iwrdr.|l.plsy.|rgm.|yšlm.l k.|l.trǵds.|w.l.klby.|šm't.ḫti.|nḫtu.ht.|hm.in mm.|nḫtu.w 53[54].4
šm' k.tr.[i]l.ab k.l ys'.[alt.]t[bt |k.l y]hpk.|[ksa.]mlk k.l ytbr.ḫt.mtpt k.w y'n[.'ttr].dm[-]k[-].|[--]ḥ.b y.tr.il.ab y.a 2.3[129].18
k.al.yšm['] k.tr.|il.ab k.l ys'.alt.|tbt k.l yhpk.ksa.mlk k.|l ytbr.ḫt.mtpt k.|yru.bn ilm t.tt'.y|dd.il.ǵzr.y'r.mt.|b ql 6[49].6.28
|l.tryl.um y.rgm.|yšlm.l k.ilm.|tǵr k.tšlm k.|lḥt.šlm.k.lik[t].|um y.'m y.ht.'m[ny].|kll.šlm.tm ny.|'m.um y.mn 2009.1.5
.ḫrṣ.|yblnn.udr.ilqṣm.|yak.l ktr.w ḫss.|w tb l mspr..k tlakn.|ǵlmm.|aḫr.mǵy.ktr.w ḫss.|št.alp.qdm h.mra.|w t 4[51].5.104
d.[---].|kd.t[---.ym.ymm].|y'tqn.w[rḥm.'nt].|tngt h.k lb.a[rḫ].|l 'gl h.k lb.ta[t].|l imr h.km.lb.'n[t].|atr.b'l.tiḥd. 6[49].2.6
.mt.|ym.ymm.y'tqn.l ymm.|l yrḫm.rḥm.'nt.tngt h.|k lb.arḫ.l 'gl h.k lb.|tat.l imr h.km.lb.|'nt.atr.b'l.tiḫd.|bn.il 6[49].2.28
.uṣb't h ḫrṣ.abn.|p h.tiḫd.šnt h.w akl.bqmm.|tšt ḫrṣ.k lb ilnm.|w tn.gprm.mn gpr h.šr.|aqht.y'n.kmr.kmr[.--].| 19[1AQHT].1.10
.mn gpr h.šr.|aqht.y'n.kmr.kmr[.--].|k ap'.il.b gdrt.k lb.l |ḫt h.imḫṣ h.k d.'l.qšt h.|imḫṣ h.'l.qṣ't h.hwt.|l aḥw. 19[1AQHT].1.13
.ymm].|y'tqn.w[rḥm.'nt].|tngt h.k lb.a[rḫ].|l 'gl h.k lb.ta[t].|l imr h.km.lb.'n[t].|atr.b'l.tiḫd.m[t].|b sin.lpš.tšṣ 6[49].2.7
.y'tqn.l ymm.|l yrḫm.rḥm.'nt.tngt h.|k lb.arḫ.l 'gl h.k lb.|tat.l imr h.km.lb.|'nt.atr.b'l.tiḫd.|bn.ilm.mt.b ḥrb.|tb 6[49].2.28
.at.mtb k[.---].|[š]mm.rm.lk.prz kt.|[k]bkbm.tm.tpl k.lbnt.|[-.]rgm.k yrkt.'tqbm.|[---]m.'ẓpn.l pit.|m[--]m[.--]t 13[6].13
bnt.šdm.ṣḥr[.---].|šb'.šnt.il.mla.[-].|w tmn.nqpnt.'d.|k lbš.km.lpš.dm a[ḫ h].|km.all.dm.ary h.|k šb't.l šb'm.aḫ h 12[75].2.47
tḥm.mlk.|l.tryl.um y.rgm.|yšlm.l k.ilm.|tǵr k.tšlm k.|lḥt.šlm.k.lik[t].|um y.'m y.ht.'m[ny].|kll.šlm.tm ny.|' 2009.1.4
n.ilm.al.|tqrb.l bn.ilm.|mt.al.y'db km.|k imr.b p h.|k lli.b tbrn.|qn h.tḫtan.|nrt.ilm.špš.|ṣḥrrt.la.|šmm.b yd.m 4[51].8.19
.šd.šḥlmmt.|ngš.ank.aliyn b'l.|'dbnn ank.imr.b p y.|k lli.b tbrn q y.ḫtu hw.|nrt.ilm.špš.ṣḥrrt.|la.šmm.b yd.bn il 6[49].2.23
[-]p[-]l[.---].|k lli.[---].|kpr.[šb'.bnt.rḥ.gdm.w anhbm].|w tqr[y.ǵlmm.b š 7.2[130].2
l y].|rg[m].|tḥm.wr[--].|yšlm.[l] k.|ilm.t[ǵ]r k.|tšlm k.|lm[.l.]likt.|ši[l.š]lm y.|[']d.r[-]š.|[-]ly.l.likt.|[a]nk.[---].| 2010.6
mm.mt.'z.b'l.|'z.yntkn.k btnm.|mt.'z.b'l.'z.ymšḫn.|k lsmm.mt.ql.|b'l.ql.'ln.špš.|tṣḥ.l mt.šm'.m'.|l bn.ilm.mt.i 6[49].6.21
.l kbd.arṣ.arbdd].|l kbd.š[dm.ḥš k.'ṣ k.'bṣ k.'m y.p'n k.tls]|[m]n 'm y t[wtḥ.išd k.dm.rgm.it.l y.d argmn k].|[h]w 7.2[130].16
kbd.arṣ.arbdd.l kbd.šdm.|[ḥ]š k.[']ṣ k.'bṣ k.'m y.p'n k.|[tls]mn.[']m y.twtḥ.išd k.|[dm.rgm.it.l y.]w argm k.hwt. 3['NT].4.55
l kbd.arṣ.|arbdd.l kbd.šdm.|ḥš k.'ṣ k.'bṣ k.|'m y.p'n k.tlsmn.'m y.|twtḥ.išd k.dm.rgm.|it.l y.w argm k.|hwt.w a 3['NT].3.16
[ḥš k.'ṣ k.'bṣ k.']m y.p[']n k.|[tlsmn.'m y.twt]ḥ.išd k.|[tk.ḫršn.---]r.[-]ḥm k.w št.|[---.] 1['NT.IX].2.1

bd.arṣ.|[arbdd.l kbd.š]dm.ḥš k.|[ʿṣ k.ʿbṣ k.ʿm y.pʿ]n k.tlsmn.|[ʿm y.twtḥ.išd] k.tk.ḫršn.|[---.-]bd k.spr.|[---.-]nk. 1[ʿNT.IX].2.22
kt.n[--.---].|ʿdb.ǵrt.ṯ[--. --].|ḥš k.ʿṣ k.ʿ[bṣ k.ʿm y.pʿn k.tlsmn].|ʿm y twtḥ.i[šd k.tk.ḫršn.-------------].|ǵr.ks.dm.r[g 1[ʿNT.IX].3.10
ʿl.ṯnt.l rkb.ʿrpt.ht.ib k.|bʿl m.ht.ib k.tmḫṣ.ht.tṣmt.ṣrt k.|tqḥ.mlk.ʿlm k.drkt.dt dr dr k.|kṯr ṣmdm.ynḥt.w ypʿr.šm 2.4[68].9
w ʿlm h.yhbr.špt hm.yš[q].|hn.špt hm.mtqtm.mtqtm.k lrmn[.--].|bm.nšq.w hr.b ḥbq.ḥmḥmt.tqt[nṣn].|tldn.šḥr. 23[52].50
ḏmr h.bl.|[---].b ḥtk h.b nmrt h.l r|[--.]arṣ.ʿz k.ḏmr k.l[-]|n k.ḥtk k.nmrt k.b tk.|ugrt.l ymt.špš.w yrḫ.|w nʿmt. UG5.2.2.9
|dm.mt.aṣḥ[.---].|ydd.b qr[b.---].|al.ašt.b[---].|ahpk k.l[--.---].|ṯmm.w lk[.---].|w lk.ilm[.---].|nʿm.ilm[.---].|šgr. 5[67].3.12
tn.aḥd.|b aḫ k.ispa.w yṯb.|ap.d anšt.im[-].|aḥd.b aḫ k.l[--]n.|hn[-.]aḥẓ[.---]l[-].|[ʿ]nt.akl[y.nšm].|akly.hml[t.arṣ] 6[49].5.22
.ad ad.|w hl h.tṣḥ.um.um.tirk m.yd.il.k ym.|w yd il.k mdb.ark.yd.il.k ym.|w yd.il.k mdb.yqḥ.il.mštʿltm.|mštʿlt 23[52].34
bʿl.yṯb.k ṯbt.ǵr.hd.r[ʿy].|k mdb.b tk.ǵr h.il ṣpn.b [tk].|ǵr.tliyt.šbʿt.brqm.[---].|ṯmnt.i UG5.3.1.2
m.yd.il.k ym.|w yd il.k mdb.ark.yd.il.k ym.|w yd.il.k mdb.yqḥ.il.mštʿltm.|mštʿltm.l riš.agn.yqḥ.tš.b bt h.|il.ḥṭ 23[52].35
pš.ʿgl.|[---.-]nk.aštn.b ḫrt.|ilm.arṣ.w at.qḥ.|ʿrpt k.rḥ k.mdl k.|mṭrt k.ʿm k.šbʿt.|ǵlm k.ṯmn.ḫnzr k.|ʿm k.pdry.bt 5[67].5.7
.b ṯmnt.|ap.sgrt.ydʿ[t k.]bt.k an[št].|k in.b ilht.ql[ṣ] k.mh.tarš[n].|l btlt.ʿnt.w t[ʿ]n.btlt.ʿn[t].|tḥm k.il.ḥkm.ḥkm 3[ʿNT.VI].5.36
.|tšu.g h.w tṣḥ.tšmḫ ht.|aṯrt.w bn h.ilt.w ṣb|rt.ary h.k mt.aliyn.|bʿl.k ḫlq.zbl.bʿl.|arṣ.gm.yṣḥ il.|l rbt.aṯrt ym.šm 6.1.41[49.1.13]
[k mt.aliyn.bʿl].|k ḫlq.z[bl.bʿl.arṣ].|w hm.ḥy.a[liyn.bʿl].|w h 6[49].3.01
t k.ngln.|k klb.[b]bt k.nʿtq.|k inr[.ap.]ḫšt k.|ap.ab.k mtm.tmtn.|u ḫšt k.l bky.ʿtq.|b d.aṯt ab.ṣrry.|u ilm.tmtn. 16.2[125].102
b l.mt k.ngln.k klb.|b bt k.nʿtq.k inr.|ap.ḫšt k.ap.ab.k mtm.|tmtn.u ḫšt k.l ntn.|ʿtq.b d.aṯt.ab.ṣrry.|ik m.yrgm.b 16.1[125].17
[l]krt.|k [k]lb.b bt k.nʿtq.k inr.|ap.ḫšt k.ap.ab.ik mtm.|tmtn.u ḫšt k.l ntn.|ʿtq.b d.aṯt.ab ṣrry.|tbky k.ab.ǵ 16.1[125].3
|nḫtu.ht.|hm.in mm.|nḫtu.w.lak.|ʿm y.w.yd.|ilm.p.k mtm.|ʿz.mid.|hm.nṯkp.|mʿn k.|w.mnm.|rgm.d.tšmʿ.|ṯm 53[54].12
r.rḥtm w rd.|bt ḫpṯt.arṣ.tspr b y|rdm.arṣ.w tdʿ ilm.|k mtt.yšmʿ.aliyn.bʿl.|yuhb.ʿglt.b dbr.prt.|b šd.šḥlmmt.škb. 5[67].5.17
ṯmn.rkb.|ʿrpt.bl.ṯl.bl rbb.|bl.šrʿ.thmtm.bl.|ṭbn.ql.bʿl.k tmzʿ.|kst.dnil.mt.rpi.|all.ǵzr.m[t.]hr[nmy].|gm.l bt[h.dn 19[1AQHT].1.46
|w yʿny.krt.ṯʿ.|bn.al.tbkn.al.|tdm.l y.al tkl.bn.|qr.ʿn k.mḫ.riš k.|udmʿt.ṣḥ.aḫt k.|ṯtmnt.bt.ḥmḥ h.|d[-]n.tbkn.w 16.1[125].27
ṭann.b šnt h.qr.[mym].|mlk.yṣm.y l km.qr.mym.d ʿ[l k].|mḫṣ.aqht.ǵzr.amd.gr bt il.|ʿnt.brḥ.p ʿlm h.ʿnt.p dr[.dr]. 19[1AQHT].3.152
bl[m].|qrt.zbl.yrḫ.yšu g h.|w yṣḥ.y l k.qrt.ablm.|d ʿl k.mḫṣ.aqht.ǵzr.|ʿwrt.yšt k.bʿl.l ht.|w ʿlm h.l ʿnt.p dr.dr.|ʿd 19[1AQHT].4.166
mrrt.tǵll.b nr.|yšu.g h.w yṣḥ.y l k.mrrt.|tǵll.b nr.d ʿl k.mḫṣ.aqht.|ǵzr.šrš k.b arṣ.al.|ypʿ.riš.ǵly.b d.nsʿ k.|ʿnt.brḥ 19[1AQHT].3.158
[k.ym]ḫṣ.bʿl m[.--]y.tnn.w ygl.w ynsk.ʿ[-].|[--]y.l arṣ[.id]y.alt 1001.1.1
s.l rgmt.|l k.l zbl.bʿl.ṯnt.l rkb.ʿrpt.ht.ib k.|bʿl m.ht.ib k.tmḫṣ.ht.tṣmt.ṣrt k.|tqḥ.mlk.ʿlm k.drkt.dt dr dr k.|kṯr ṣm 2.4[68].9
št m.ʿm.a[ḫ] yn.|p nšt.bʿl.[ṭ]ʿn.iṭʿn k.|[---.]ma[---] k.k tmḫṣ.|[ltn.btn.br]ḥ.tkly.|[btn.ʿqltn.]šlyṭ.|[d šbʿt.rašm].ṯṯ 5[67].1.27
k tmḫṣ.ltn.btn.brḥ.|tkly.btn.ʿqltn.|šlyṭ.d šbʿy.rašm.|ṯṯkḥ.ṯt 5[67].1.1
[---.-]nk.aštn.b ḫrt.|ilm.arṣ.w at.qḥ.|ʿrpt k.rḥ k.mdl k.|mṭrt k.ʿm k.šbʿt.|ǵlm k.ṯmn.ḫnzr k.|ʿm k.pdry.bt.ar.|ʿ 5[67].5.7
h.t[--].|aṯr.aṯrm[.---].|aṯr.aṯrm[.---].|išdym.t[---].|b k.mla[.---].|udmʿt.d[mʿ.---].|[---].bn.[---].|[-----]. 27[8].10
yṣḥ il.|l rbt.aṯrt ym.šmʿ.|l rbt.aṯr[t] ym.tn.|aḥd.b bn k.amlkn.|w tʿn.rbt.aṯrt ym.|bl.nmlk.ydʿ.ylḥn.|w yʿn.lṭpn.il 6.1.46[49.1.18]
.btlt.ʿn[t].|tḥm k.il.ḥkm.ḥkm k.|ʿm.ʿlm.ḥyt.ḥẓt.tḥm k.|mlk n.aliyn.bʿl.ṯpṭ n.|in.d ʿln h.klny y.qš h.|nbln.klny y. 3[ʿNT.VI].5.39
t.aṯrt ym.|tḥm k.il.ḥkm.ḥkmt.|ʿm ʿlm.ḥyt.ḥẓt.|tḥm k.mlk n.aliy[n.]bʿl.|ṯpṭ n.w in.d ʿln h.|klny n.q[š] h.n[bln]. 4[51].4.43
kt y.am--].|[---.qdq]d k.ašhlk[.šbt k.dmm].|[šbt.dq]n k.mmʿm.w[---].|aqht.w yplṭ k.bn[.dnil.---].|w yʿdr k.b yd.b 18[3AQHT].1.12
t.arkt y.am[---].|qdqd k.ašhlk.šbt[k.dmm].|[šbt.dqn k.mmʿm.]yʿny.|il.b šbʿt.ḥdrm.b ṯmnt.|ap.sgrt.ydʿ[t k.]bt.k 3[ʿNT.VI].5.33
.-]nt.|[l.ʿb]dmlk.|[--.-]m[-]r.|[w.l.]bn h.ʿd.|[ʿl]m.mn k.|mn km l.yqḥ.|bt.hnd.b d.|[ʿb]dmlk.|[-]k.amʿ[--].|[w.b] 1009.12
lm.l k.ilm.|tǵr k.tšlm k.|hn ny.ʿm n.|šlm.ṯm ny.|ʿm k.mnm[.š]lm.|rgm.ṯṯ[b].|any kn.dt.|likt.mṣrm.|hn dt.b.ṣr. 2059.8
[---.--]y.hnn.|[---.kll].šlm.|[---.ṯ]mn.ʿm k.|[m]nm.šlm.|[---.w.r]gm.ṯṯb. 2171.3
l pḥm.il.aṯtm.k ypt.hm.aṯtm.tṣḥn.|y mt.mt.nḥtm.ḫṭ k.mmnnm.mṭ.yd k.|h[l.]ʿṣr.thrr.l išt.ṣḥrrt.l pḥmm.|a[ṯ]tm. 23[52].40
bt.il.bt.il.|w ʿlm h.w hn.aṯtm.tṣḥn y.mt mt.|nḥtm.ḫṭ k.mmnnm.mṭ yd k.hl.ʿṣr.|thrr.l išt.w ṣḥrt.l pḥmm.aṯtm.a[ṯt 23[52].47
aṯt.il.aṯt.il.w ʿlm h.w hm.|aṯtm.tṣḥn y.ad ad.nḥtm.ḫṭ k.|mmnnm.mṭ yd k.hl.ʿṣr.thrr.l išt.|w ṣḥrrt.l pḥmm.btm.bt 23[52].43
il d pi|d dq.anm.l yrẓ.|ʿm.bʿl.l yʿdb.mrḥ.|ʿm.bn.dgn.k tms m.|w ʿn.rbt.aṯrt ym.|blt.nmlk.ʿṯtr.ʿrẓ.|ymlk.ʿṯtr.ʿrẓ.| 6.1.52[49.1.24]
t.k ṯr.lṭpn.|ṣḥ.ngr.il.ilš.il[š].|w aṯt h.ngrt[.i]lht.|kḥṣ.k mʿr[.---].|yṣḥ.ngr il.ilš.|ilš.ngr.bt.bʿl.|w aṯt h.ngrt.ilht.|w 16[126].4.6
k ymǵy.adn.|ilm.rbm ʿm dtn.|w yšal.mṯpṭ.yld.|w yʿny.nn[. UG5.6.1
bnt.ṣʿṣ.bnt.mʿmʿ.ʿbd.ḥrn.[--.]k.|[---].aǵwyn.ʿn k.ẓẓ.w k mǵ.ilm.|[--.]k ʿṣm.k ʿšm.l ttn.k abnm.l thggn. 1001.2.12
l.ḏrdn.|bʿl y.rgm.|bn.ḫrn k.|mǵy.|hbt.hw.|ḫrd.w.šl hw.|qr[-].|akl n.b.grnt.|l.bʿr.|a 2114.3
akt.ʿbd h.|[---.]bʿl k.yḫpn.|[---.]ʿm h.u ky.|[---.--]d k.k.tmǵy.|ml[--.--]š[.ml]k.rb.|b[ʿl y.---].|yd[--.]mlk.|rb.b[ʿl y. 1018.6
m[rṣ.---].|mn.k dw.kr[t].|w yʿny.ǵzr[.ilḥu].|ṯlṯ.yrḫm.k m[rṣ].|arbʿ.k dw.k[rt].|mndʿ.krt.mǵ[y.---].|w qbr.tṣr.q[br 16.2[125].84
sk.tr[.---].|tqrb.aḫ[h.w tṣḥ].|lm.tbʿrn[.---].|mn.yrḫ.k m[rṣ.---].|mn.k dw.kr[t].|w yʿny.ǵzr[.ilḥu].|ṯlṯ.yrḫm.k m 16.2[125].81
-].b ḥtk h.b nmrt h.l r|[--.]arṣ.ʿz k.ḏmr k.l[-]|n k.ḥtk k.nmrt k.b tk.|ugrt.l ymt.špš.w yrḫ.|w nʿmt.šnt.il. UG5.2.2.10
ḫry mṭ.yd h.|ymǵ.l mrrt.tǵll.b nr.|yšu.g h.w yṣḥ.y l k.mrrt.|tǵll.b nr.d ʿl k.mḫṣ.aqht.|ǵzr.šrš k.b arṣ.al.|ypʿ.riš. 19[1AQHT].3.157
ṯn.|ṯlṯ.rbʿ.ym.ymš.|ṯdṯ.ym.ḥẓ k.al.tšʿl.|qrt h.abn.yd k.|mšdpt.w hn.špšm.|b šbʿ.w l.yšn.pbl.|mlk.l qr.ṯigt.ibr h. 14[KRT].3.117
at.ypʿt.b[--.---].|aliyn.bʿl[.---].|drkt k.mšl[-.---].|b riš k.aymr[.---].|ṯpṭ.nhr.yṯb[r.ḥrn.y ym.yṯbr. 2.1[137].5
.lṭpn.il d pi[d].|šmʿ.l ngr.il il[š].|ilš.ngr bt bʿl.|w aṯt k.ngrt.il[ht].|ʿl.l ṯkm.bnw n.|l nḫnpt.mšpy.|ṯlṯ.kmm.ṯrr y. 16[126].4.13
[.m]lk.|k.tʿrbn.ršp m.bt.mlk.|ḫlu.dg.|ḥdṯm.|dbḥ.bʿl.k.tdd.bʿlt.bhtm.|b.[-]ǵb.ršp.ṣbi.|[---.--]m.|[---.]piln.|[---].ṣ 2004.14
.|ʿm.krt.mswn h.|arḫ.tẓǵ.l ʿgl h.|bn.ḫpṯ.l umht hm.|k tnḥn.udmm.|w yʿny.krt.ṯʿ. 15[128].1.7
.|p d.in.b bt y.ttn.|tn.l y.mṯt.ḥry.|nʿmt.šph.bkr k.|d k.nʿm.ʿnt.nʿm h.|km.tsm.ʿṯtrt.ts[m h].|d ʿq h.ib.iqni.ʿp[ʿp] 14[KRT].3.145
d.[i]n.|b bt y.ttn.tn.|l y.mṯt.ḥry.|nʿmt.šbḥ.bkr k.|d k nʿm.ʿnt.|nʿm h.km.tsm.|ʿṯtrt.tsm h.|d ʿq h.ib.iqni.|ʿpʿp h 14[KRT].6.291
l.rb.khnm.|rgm.|tḥm.[---].|yšlm[.l k.ilm].|tšlm[k.tǵr] k.|tʿzz[k.---.]lm.|w t[--.--]ṣm k.|[-----].|[-----.]šil.|[-- 55[18].5
[tḥm.---].|[l.---].|[a]ḫt y.rgm.|[y]šlm.l k.|[il]m.tšlm k.|[tǵ]r k.|[--]y.ibr[-].|[--]wy.rgm l.|mlkt.ugrt.|[--]kt.rgmt 1016.5
nm.|w ṯn.gprm.mn gpr h.šr.|aqht.yʿn.kmr.kmr[.--].|k apʿ.il.b gdrt.k lb.l|ḫt h.imḫṣ h.k d.ʿl.qšt h.|imḫṣ h.ʿl.qṣʿt 19[1AQHT].1.13
b ap h.b ap.mhr h.ank.|l aḥwy.tqḥ.yṭpn.mhr.št.|tštn.k nšr.b ḥbš h.km.diy.|b tʿrt h.aqht.km.yṯb.l lḥ[m].|bn.dnil. 18[3AQHT].4.28
ll.ṯly.bt rb.|mṯb.arṣy.bt.yʿbdr.|ap.mṯn.rgmm.|argm k.šskn mʿ.|mgn.rbt.aṯrt ym.|mǵẓ.qnyt.ilm.|hyn.ʿly.l mpḫ 4[51].1.21

ʿl k.pht.[-]l[-].|b šdm.ʿl k.pht.|drʿ.b ym.tn.aḥd.|b aḫ k.ispa.w yṯb.|ap.d anšt.im[-].|aḥd.b aḫ k.l[--]n.|hn[-.]aḫẓ[. 6[49].5.20
ṣu.qṯr k].|l ʿpr.ḏm[r.aṯr k.ṭbq].|lḥt.niṣ k.gr[š.d ʿšy.ln k].|spu.ksm k.bt.[bʿl.w mnt k].|bt il.aḥd.yd k.b [škrn].|mʿ 17[2AQHT].2.3
dbḥ.|dt nat.|w ytnt.|ṯrmn w.|dbḥ kl.|kl ykly.|dbḥ k.sprt.|dt nat.|w qrwn.|l k dbḥ.|[--]r bt [--].|[--]bnš [--].|š RS61[24.277.9]
nt.irš ḥym.l aqht.ǵzr.|irš ḥym.w atn k.bl mt.|w ašlḥ k.ašspr k.ʿm.bʿl.|šnt.ʿm.bn il.tspr.yrḫm.|k bʿl.k yḥwy.yʿšr. 17[2AQHT].6.28
m y.pʿ]n k.tlsmn.|[ʿm y.twtḥ.išd] k.tk.ḫršn.|[---.-]bd k.spr.|[---.-]nk. 1[ʿNT.IX].2.24
y[šlm.l k.ilm].|tǵ[r k.tšlm k].|ʿbd[.---]y.|ʿm[.---]y.|šk[--.--.]kll.|šk[--.--.]hm.|w.k[b--.- 2065.2
.ddym.sk.šlm].l kbd.arṣ.|[arbdd.l kbd.š]dm.ḥš k.|[ʿṣ k.ʿbṣ k.ʿm y.pʿ]n k.tlsmn.|[ʿm y.twtḥ.išd] k.tk.ḫršn.|[---.-]b 1[ʿNT.IX].2.22
[ḥš k.ʿṣ k.ʿbṣ k.ʿ]m y.p[ʿ]n k.|[tlsmn.ʿm y.twt]ḥ.išd k.|[tk.ḫršn.---]r. 1[ʿNT.IX].2.1
m.ddym.|sk.šlm.l kbd.arṣ.|arbdd.l kbd.šdm.|ḥš k.ʿṣ k.ʿbṣ k.|ʿm y.pʿn k.tlsmn.ʿm y.|twtḥ.išd k.dm.rgm.|iṯ.l y.w 3[ʿNT].3.15
h.kṯr.b[---].|št.lskt.n[--.---].|ʿdb.bǵrt.ṯ[--. --].|ḥš k.ʿṣ k.ʿ[bṣ k.ʿm y.pʿn k.tlsmn].|ʿm y twtḥ.i[šd k.tk.ḫršn.---------- 1[ʿNT.IX].3.10
[m.ddym.sk.šlm.l kbd.arṣ.arbdd].|l kbd.š[dm.ḥš k.ʿṣ k.ʿbṣ k.ʿm y.pʿn k.tls]|[m]n ʿm y t[wtḥ.išd k.dm.rgm.iṯ.l y.d 7.2[130].16
.ddym.sk.šlm.|l kbd.arṣ.arbdd.l kbd.šdm.|[ḥ]š k.[ʿ]ṣ k.ʿbṣ k.ʿm y.pʿn k.|[tls]mn.[ʿ]m y.twtḥ.išd k.|[dm.rgm.iṯ.l y 3[ʿNT].4.55
mʿ.nʿmn.ǵlm.|il.trḥṣ.w tadm.|rḥṣ[.y]d k.amt.|uṣb[ʿt k.]ʿd[.ṯ]km.|ʿrb[.b ẓl.ḫmt].|qḥ im[r.b yd k].|imr.d[bḥ.bm]. 14[KRT].2.64
m.bt.lbnt.yʿmsn h.|l yrgm.l aliyn bʿl.|ṣḥ.ḫrn.b bhm k.|ʿḏbt.b qrb.hkl k.|tbl k.ǵrm.mid.ksp.|gbʿm.mḥmd.ḫrṣ.|y 4[51].5.75
y[b]n.|bt.l k.km.aḫ k.w ḥẓr.|km.ary k.ṣḥ.ḫrn.|b bht k.ʿḏbt.b qrb.|hkl k.tbl k.ǵrm.|mid.ksp.gbʿm.mḥmd..|ḫrṣ.w 4[51].5.92
[t]ḥm.iṯtl.|l mnn.ilm.|tǵr k.tšlm k.|tʿzz k.alp ymm.|w rbt.šnt.|b ʿd ʿlm...gnʿ.|iršt.aršt.|l aḫ 1019.1.3
b.khnm.|rgm.|tḥm.[---].|yšlm[.l k.ilm].|tšlm[k.tǵr] k.|tʿzz[k.---.]lm.|w t[--.--]ṣm k.|[-----].|[-----.]šil.|[-----.]šilt 55[18].5
pid.|tǵẓy.bny.bnwt.|b nši.ʿn h.w tphn.|hlk.bʿl.aṯtrt.|k tʿn.hlk.btlt.|ʿnt.tdrq.ybmt.|[limm].b h.pʿnm.|[ṭṭt.b ʿ]dn.k 4[51].2.14
ṭ.ytm.|b nši ʿn h.w yphn.b alp.|šd.rbt.kmn.hlk.kṯr.|k yʿn.w yʿn.tdrq.ḫss.|hlk.qšt.ybln.hl.yš|rbʿ.qṣʿt.apnk.dnil.| 17[2AQHT].5.11
m[.m]ḫṣ.|bn y.hm[.mkly.ṣ]brt.|ary y[.ẓl].ksp.[a]ṯrt.|k tʿn.ẓl.ksp.w n[-]t.|ḫrṣ.šmḫ.rbt.a[ṯrt].|ym.gm.l ǵlm h.k [tṣ 4[51].2.27
y.w ymlk.|[y]ṣb.ʿln.w y[-]y.|[kr]t.ṯʿ.ʿln.bḫr.|[---].aṯt k.ʿl.|[---] k.yšṣi.|[---.]ḫbr.rbt.|[ḫbr.ṯrr]t.il d.|[pid.---].b anšt 15[128].5.23
m.l aqht.ǵzr.|irš ḥym.w atn k.bl mt.|w ašlḥ k.ašspr k.ʿm.bʿl.|šnt.ʿm.bn il.tspr.yrḫm.|k bʿl.k yḥwy.yʿšr.ḥwy.yʿš. 17[2AQHT].6.28
]l bnt.q[-].|w št.b bt.ṯap[.--].|hy.yd h.w ym[ǵ].|mlak k.ʿm dt[n].|lqḥ.mṯpṭ.|w yʿny.nn.|dtn.bt n.mḥ[-].|l dg.w [-] UG5.6.11
.sk.šlm.|l kbd.arṣ.arbdd.l kbd.šdm.|[ḥ]š k.[ʿ]ṣ k.ʿbṣ k.ʿm y.pʿn k.|[tls]mn.[ʿ]m y.twtḥ.išd k.|[dm.rgm.iṯ.l y.]w a 3[ʿNT].4.55
dym.sk.šlm.l kbd.arṣ.arbdd].|l kbd.š[dm.ḥš k.ʿṣ k.ʿbṣ k.ʿm y.pʿn k.tls]|[m]n ʿm y t[wtḥ.išd k.dm.rgm.iṯ.l y.d arg 7.2[130].16
b[---].|št.lskt.n[--.---].|ʿdb.bǵrt.ṯ[--. --].|ḥš k.ʿṣ k.ʿ[bṣ k.ʿm y.pʿn k.tlsmn].|ʿm y twtḥ.i[šd k.tk.ḫršn.-------------].|ǵ 1[ʿNT.IX].3.10
[ḥš k.ʿṣ k.ʿbṣ k.ʿ]m y.p[ʿ]n k.|[tlsmn.ʿm y.twt]ḥ.išd k.|[tk.ḫršn.---]r.[-]ḥ 1[ʿNT.IX].2.1
.sk.šlm].l kbd.arṣ.|[arbdd.l kbd.š]dm.ḥš k.|[ʿṣ k.ʿbṣ k.ʿm y.pʿ]n k.tlsmn.|[ʿm y.twtḥ.išd] k.tk.ḫršn.|[---.-]bd k.s 1[ʿNT.IX].2.22
ym.|sk.šlm.l kbd.arṣ.|arbdd.l kbd.šdm.|ḥš k.ʿṣ k.ʿbṣ k.|ʿm y.pʿn k.tlsmn.ʿm y.|twtḥ.išd k.dm.rgm.|iṯ.l y.w arg 3[ʿNT].3.15
ʿrpt k.rḥ k.mdl k.|mṭrt k.ʿm k.šbʿt.|ǵlm k.ṯmn.ḫnzr k.|ʿm k.pdry.bt.ar.|ʿm k.ṭṭly.bt.rb.idk.|pn k.al ttn.tk.ǵr.|k 5[67].5.9
.aštn.b ḫrt.|ilm.arṣ.w at.qḥ.|ʿrpt k.rḥ k.mdl k.|mṭrt k.ʿm k.šbʿt.|ǵlm k.ṯmn.ḫnzr k.|ʿm k.pdry.bt.ar.|ʿm k.ṭṭly.b 5[67].5.8
qt.ḥmr h.|l gʿt.alp.ḥrṯ.zǵt.|klb.ṣpr.w ylak.|mlakm.l k.ʿm.krt.|mswn h.tḥm.pbl.mlk.|qḥ.ksp.w yrq.ḫrṣ.|yd.mq 14[KRT].3.124
arš[n].|l btlt.ʿnt.w t[ʿ]n.btlt.ʿn[t].|tḥm k.il.ḥkm.ḥkm k.|ʿm.ʿlm.ḥyt.ḥẓt.tḥm k.|mlk n.aliyn.bʿl.ṯpṭ n.|in.d ʿln h.kl 3[ʿNT.VI].5.38
r].|thdy.lḥm.w dqn[.ṯṯlt].|qn.ḏrʿ h.tḥrṯ.km.gn.|ap lb.k ʿmq.ṯṯlṯ.bmt.|bʿl.mt.my.lim.bn dgn.|my.hmlt.aṯr.bʿl.nrd. 6[62].1.5
yʿr.|yhdy.lḥm.w dqn.|yṯlṯ.qn.ḏrʿ h.yḥrṯ.|k gn.ap lb.k ʿmq.yṯlṯ.|bmt.yšu.g h.w yṣḥ.|bʿl.mt.my.lim.bn.|dgn.my. 5[67].6.21
ṣi.b b[--].bm.k[--].|[--]ṯb.ʿryt k.k qlt[.---].|[--]at.brt.lb k.ʿnn.[---].|[--.]šdq.k ttn.l y.šn[.---].|[---.]bn.rgm.w ydʿ[.---]. 60[32].4
d ʿl k.mḫṣ.aqht.|ǵzr.šrš k.b arṣ.al.|ypʿ.riš.ǵly.b d.nsʿ k.|ʿnt.brḥ.p ʿlm h.|ʿnt.p dr.dr.ʿdb.uḫry mṭ yd h.|ymǵ.l qrt. 19[1AQHT].3.160
.|[---.]drk.brḥ.arṣ.lk pn h.yrk.bʿ[l].|[---.]bt k.ap.l pḫr k ʿnt tqm.ʿnt.tqm.|[---.p]ḫr k.ygrš k.qr.bt k.ygrš k.|[---.]bnt 1001.2.9
ʿ]pr[m.ddym.sk.šlm.l kbd.arṣ.arbdd].|l kbd.š[dm.ḥš k.ʿṣ k.ʿbṣ k.ʿm y.pʿn k.tls]|[m]n ʿm y t[wtḥ.išd k.dm.rgm.iṯ. 7.2[130].16
[r] m.ddym.sk.šlm.|l kbd.arṣ.arbdd.l kbd.šdm.|[ḥ]š k.[ʿ]ṣ k.ʿbṣ k.ʿm y.pʿn k.|[tls]mn.[ʿ]m y.twtḥ.išd k.|[dm.rg 3[ʿNT].4.55
|[r m.ddym.sk.šlm].l kbd.arṣ.|[arbdd.l kbd.š]dm.ḥš k.|[ʿṣ k.ʿbṣ k.ʿm y.pʿ]n k.tlsmn.|[ʿm y.twtḥ.išd] k.tk.ḫršn.|[1[ʿNT.IX].2.21
[ḥš k.ʿṣ k.ʿbṣ k.ʿ]m y.p[ʿ]n k.|[tlsmn.ʿm y.twt]ḥ.išd k.|[tk.ḫršn. 1[ʿNT.IX].2.1
-].|yh.kṯr.b[---].|št.lskt.n[--.---].|ʿdb.bǵrt.ṯ[--. --].|ḥš k.ʿṣ k.ʿ[bṣ k.ʿm y.pʿn k.tlsmn].|ʿm y twtḥ.i[šd k.tk.ḫršn.----- 1[ʿNT.IX].3.10
ʿpr m.ddym.|sk.šlm.l kbd.arṣ.|arbdd.l kbd.šdm.|ḥš k.ʿṣ k.ʿbṣ k.|ʿm y.pʿn k.tlsmn.ʿm y.|twtḥ.išd k.dm.rgm.|iṯ.l 3[ʿNT].3.15
]ṯb h.aḫt.ppšr.w ppšrt[.---].|[---.]k.drḫm.w aṯb.l ntbt.k.ʿṣm l t[--].|[---.]drk.brḥ.arṣ.lk pn h.yrk.bʿ[l].|[---.]bt k.ap. 1001.2.7
ʿ.ʿbd.ḥrn.[--.]k.|[---].aǵwyn.ʿn k.ẓẓ.w k mǵ.ilm.|[--.]k ʿṣm.k ʿšm.l ttn.k abnm.l thggn. 1001.2.13
k tʿrb.ʿṯtrt.ḫr[-].|bt mlk.ʿšr.ʿšr.[--].bt ilm.|kbr[-]m.[-]trmt.| 33[5].1
zǵm.|[i]lib.|[i]lbldn.|[p]dry.bt.mlk.|[-]lp.izr.|[a]rz.|k.tʿrb.ʿṯtrt.šd.bt[.m]lk.|k.tʿrbn.ršp m.bt.mlk.|ḫlu.dg.|ḥdṯm 2004.10
mm[.bʿlm].kmm.bʿlm.kmm.|bʿlm.kmm.bʿlm.kmm.|k tʿrb.ʿṯtrt.šd.bt.mlk[.---].|ṯn.skm.šbʿ.mšlt.arbʿ.ḫpnt.[---].|ḫ UG5.9.1.18
]dry.bt.mlk.|[-]lp.izr.|[a]rz.|k.tʿrb.ʿṯtrt.šd.bt[.m]lk.|k.tʿrbn.ršp m.bt.mlk.|ḫlu.dg.|ḥdṯm.|dbḥ.bʿl.k.tdd.bʿlt.bht 2004.11
.ḥrn.[--.]k.|[---].aǵwyn.ʿn k.ẓẓ.w k mǵ.ilm.|[--.]k ʿṣm.k ʿšm.l ttn.k abnm.l thggn. 1001.2.13
.---.]ymm.lk.|hrg.ar[bʿ.]ymm.bṣr.|kp.šsk k.[--].l ḥbš k.|ʿtk.ri[š.]l mhr k.|w ʿp.l dr[ʿ].nšr k.|w rbṣ.l ǵr k.inbb.|kt 13[6].6
[l]krt.|k [k]lb.b bt k.nʿtq.k inr.|ap.ḫšt k.ap.ab.ik mtm.|tmtn.u ḫšt k.l ntn.|ʿtq 16.1[125].2
g h.|bky.b ḥy k.ab n.ašmḫ.|b l.mt k.ngln.k klb.|b bt k.nʿtq.k inr.|ap.ḫšt k.ap.ab.k mtm.|tmtn.u ḫšt k.l ntn.|ʿtq. 16.1[125].16
h.bky.b ḥ[y k.a]b n.|nšmḫ.b l.mt k.ngln.|k klb.[b]bt k.nʿtq.|k inr[.ap.]ḫšt k.|ap.ab.k mtm.tmtn.|u ḫšt k.l bky.ʿt 16.2[125].100
-.]t[-].ǵlm.l šdt[.-.]ymm.|[---.]b ym.ym.y[--].yš[ ]n.ap k.ʿṯtr.dm[.---.]|[---.]ḥrḥrtm.w[--.]n[--.]iš[--.]h[---.]išt.|[---] 2.3[129].12
t k.aṯb.|an.w yʿny.krt ṯʿ.yṯbr.|ḥrn.y bn.yṯbr.ḥrn.|riš k.ʿṯtrt.šm.bʿl.|qdqd k.tqln.b gbl.|šnt k.b ḥpn k.w tʿn.|spr il 16.6[127].56
iš k.aymr[.---].|ṯpṭ.nhr.yṯb[r.ḥrn.y ym.yṯbr.ḥrn].|riš k.ʿṯtrt.[šm.bʿl.qdqd k.---].|[--]t.mṯ.tpln.b g[bl.šnt k.---].|[--] 2.1[137].8
.[---].adny.l.yḫsr.|w.[ank.yd]ʿ.l.ydʿt.|h[t.---.]l.špš.bʿl k.|ʿ[--.s]glt h.at.|ht[.---.]špš.bʿl k.|ydʿm.l.ydʿt.|ʿm y.špš.bʿl 2060.11
yʿrb.yšu g h.|w yṣḥ.šmʿ mʿ.l krt.|ṯʿ.ištmʿ.w tqǵ udn.|k ǵz.ǵzm.tdbr.|w ǵrm.ṯṯwy.šqlt.|b ǵlt.yd k.l tdn.|dn.almnt 16.6[127].43
l[ab]k.w rgm.ʿny.|l k[rt.adn k.]ištm[ʿ].|w tqǵ[.udn.k ǵz.ǵzm].|tdbr.w[ǵ]rm[.ṯṯwy].|šqlt.b ǵlt.yd k.|l tdn.dn.al 16.6[127].30
.|[ṯʿ.ymr]m.n.ʿm[n.]ǵlm.il.|a[ṯt.tq]ḥ.y krt.aṯt.|tqḥ.bt k.ǵlmt.tšʿrb.|ḥqr k.tld.šbʿ.bnm.l k.|w ṯmn.ṯṯmnm.|l k.tld. 15[128].2.22
ḥẓr.|km.ary k.ṣḥ.ḫrn.|b bht k.ʿḏbt.b qrb.|hkl k.tbl k.ǵrm.|mid.ksp.gbʿm.mḥmd..|ḫrṣ.w bn.bht.ksp.|w ḫrṣ.bht 4[51].5.93

gm.l aliyn b'l. | ṣḥ.ḫrn.b bhm k. | 'd̠bt.b qrb.hkl k. | tbl k.ǵrm.mid.ksp. | gb'm.mḥmd.ḫrṣ. | ybl k.udr.ilqṣm. | w bn.bh 4[51].5.77
.w tr.b lkt. | tr.b lkt.w tr.b ḫl. | [b]n'mm.b ysmm.ḥ[--]k.ǵrt. | [ql].l b'l.'nt.ttnn. | [---].b'l m.d ip[---]. | [il.]hd.d 'nn.n[10[76].2.30
d. | [---].yb'lnn. | [---.--]n.b.t̠lt̠.šnt.l.nṣd. | [---.--]ršp.mlk.k.ypdd.mlbš. | u---].mlk.ytn.mlbš. | [---.-]rn.k.ypdd.mlbš h. | [1106.58
--]ršp.mlk.k.ypdd.mlbš. | u---].mlk.ytn.mlbš. | [---.-]rn.k.ypdd.mlbš h. | [---.]mlk.ytn.lbš.l h. 1106.60
.rḥ k.mdl k. | mṭrt k.'m k.šb't. | ǵlm k.t̠mn.ḫnzr k. | 'm k.pdry.bt.ar. | 'm k.ṭṭly.bt.rb.idk. | pn k.al ttn.tk.ǵr. | knkny.š 5[67].5.10
t. | 'm.aliyn.b'l.yšu. | g h.w yṣḥ.'l k.b[']l m. | pht.qlt.'l k.pht. | dry.b ḥrb.'l k. | pht.šrp.b išt. | 'l k.[pht.ṭḥ]n.b rḥ | m.'[l 6[49].5.12
dry.b ḥrb.'l k. | pht.šrp.b išt. | 'l k.[pht.ṭḥ]n.b rḥ | m.'[l k.]pht[.dr]y.b kbrt. | 'l k.pht.[-]l[-]. | b šdm.'l k.pht. | dr'.b ym 6[49].5.16
rḥ | m.'[l k.]pht[.dr]y.b kbrt. | 'l k.pht.[-]l[-]. | b šdm.'l k.pht. | dr'.b ym.tn.aḥd. | b aḫ k.ispa.w ytb. | ap.d anšt.im[-]. 6[49].5.18
.ab.šnm. | l p'n.il.thbr.w tql. | tšt̠ḥwy.w tkbd h. | hlm.il.k yphn h. | yprq.lṣb.w yṣḥq. | p'n h.l hdm.yt̠pd.w ykrkr. | uṣb 4[51].4.27
]l m. | pht.qlt.'l k.pht. | dry.b ḥrb.'l k. | pht.šrp.b išt. | 'l k.[pht.ṭḥ]n.b rḥ | m.'[l k.]pht[.dr]y.b kbrt. | 'l k.pht.[-]l[-]. | b 6[49].5.15
. | g h.w yṣḥ.'l k.b[']l m. | pht.qlt.'l k.pht. | dry.b ḥrb.'l k. | pht.šrp.b išt. | 'l k.[pht.ṭḥ]n.b rḥ | m.'[l k.]pht[.dr]y.b kbrt 6[49].5.13
[-----]. | [-----]. | il.šm'.amr k.ph[.-]. | k il.ḥkmt.k tr.lṭpn. | ṣḥ.ngr.il.ilš.il[š]. | w att h.ngrt[16[126].4.2
.b išt. | 'l k.[pht.ṭḥ]n.b rḥ | m.'[l k.]pht[.dr]y.b kbrt. | 'l k.pht.[-]l[-]. | b šdm.'l k.pht. | dr'.b ym.tn.aḥd. | b aḫ k.ispa.w 6[49].5.17
t.ilm.špš. | tšu.g h.w tṣḥ. | t̠ḥm.t̠r.il.ab k. | hwt.lṭpn.ḥtk k. | pl.'nt.šdm.y špš. | pl.'nt.šdm.il.yš[t k]. | b'l.'nt.mḥrt[-]. | iy. 6[49].4.35
nmr. | [--.]l ytk.bl[-.---.]m[--.]hwt. | [---].t̠llt.khn[m.---.]k p'n. | [---.--]y.yd.nšy.[---.--]š.l mdb. | [---] h.mḫlpt[.---.--]r. | UG5.8.47
š.mǵy[t]. | pǵt.l ahlm.rgm.l yt̠[pn.y] | bl.agrtn.bat.b d̠d k.[pǵt]. | bat.b hlm w y'n.yt̠pn[.mhr]. | št.qḥn.w tšqyn.yn.qḥ. 19[1AQHT].4.213
-]. | gm.l[at̠t̠ h k.yṣḥ]. | šm'[.l mt̠t.ḥry]. | t̠bḫ.š[mn].mri k. | ptḥ.[rḥ]bt.yn. | ṣḥ.šb'm.t̠r y. | t̠mnym.[ẓ]by y. | t̠r.ḫbr[.rb]t 15[128].4.4
.yšu. | yr.šmm h.yr.b šmm.'ṣr.yḫrt̠ yšt. | l pḥm.il.at̠tm.k ypt.hm.at̠tm.tṣḥn. | y mt.mt.nḥtm.ḫt̠ k.mmnnm.mt̠.yd k. | 23[52].39
qmḥ.d.kly.k ṣḥ.illdrm. | b d.zlb[n.--]. | arb'.'š[r.]dd.n'r. | d.apy[.--]. | w.ar 2094.1
b'l. | bšrt k.yblt.y[b]n. | bt.l k.km.aḫ k.w ḥẓr. | km.ary k.ṣḥ.ḫrn. | b bht k.'d̠bt.b qrb. | hkl k.tbl k.ǵrm. | mid.ksp.gb' 4[51].5.91
mru. | ilm.w nšm.d yšb | ['].hmlt.arṣ.gm.l ǵ | [lm] h.b'l k.yṣḥ.'n. | [gpn].w ugr.b ǵlmt. | ['mm.]ym.bn.ẓlmt.r | [mt.pr'] 4[51].7.53
t'n.ẓl.ksp.w n[-]t. | ḫrṣ.šmḫ.rbt.a[trt]. | ym.gm.l ǵlm h.k [tṣḥ]. | 'n.mktr.ap.t[---]. | dgy.rbt.at̠r[t.ym]. | qḥ.rt̠t.b d k t[- 4[51].2.29
p[----]. | gm.l[at̠t̠ h k.yṣḥ]. | šm'[.l mt̠t.ḥry]. | t̠bḫ.š[mn].mri k. | ptḥ.[rḥ]bt.yn. | ṣḥ 15[128].4.2
ḥrt̠[.l z]ǵt.klb. | [ṣ]pr[.apn]k. | [pb]l[.mlk.g]m.l at̠t̠ | [h.k]y[ṣ.ḥ.]šm'.m'. | [--.]'m[.-.]at̠t̠ y[.-]. | [---.]t̠ḥm. | [---]t.[ ]r. | [-- 14[KRT].5.229
ṣ't.apnk.dnil. | mt.rpi.aphn.ǵzr.mt. | hrnmy.gm.l at̠t̠ h.k yṣḥ. | šm'.mt̠t.dnty.'d[b]. | imr.b pḫd.l npš.kt̠r. | w ḫss.l brlt 17[2AQHT].5.15
kst.dnil.mt.rpi. | all.ǵzr.m[t.]hr[nmy]. | gm.l bt[h.dnil.k yṣḥ]. | šm'.pǵt.t̠kmt[.my]. | ḥspt.l š'r.t̠l.yd['t]. | hlk.kbkbm. 19[1AQHT].1.49
---] h.l 'db. | [---]n.yd h. | [---].bl.išlḥ. | [---] h.gm. | [l --- k.]yṣḥ. | [---]d.'r. | [----.-]bb. | [----.]lm y. | [---.--]p. | [---.d]bḥ. | 14[KRT].5.238
[---.]ḥš[.-]nm[.--.]k.[--].w yḫnp[.---]. | [---.]ylm.b[n.']n k.ṣmdm.špk[.---]. | [---.]nt[-.]mbk kpt.w[.--].b g[--]. | [---.]ḫ[-- 1001.1.16
-]m[.---]. | h.hn bn k.hn[.---]. | bn bn.at̠r k.hn[.---]. | yd k.ṣǵr.tnšq.špt k.t̠m. | t̠km.bm t̠km.aḫm.qym.il. | b lsmt.t̠m.yt̠ 22.2[124].4
-.--]ḫ[.---]y[.---.-]nt.[š]ṣat[k.]rḥ.npš.hm. | k.it̠l.brlt n[-.k qtr.b ap -]. | tmǵyn.tša.g h[m.w tṣḥn]. | šm'.l dnil.[mt.rpi]. 19[1AQHT].2.88
rt t̠'.ytbr. | ḥrn.y bn.ytbr.ḥrn. | riš k.'t̠trt.šm.b'l. | qdqd k.tqln.b gbl. | šnt k.b ḥpn k.w t'n. | spr ilmlk t̠'y. 16.6[127].57
[-----]. | [--.]l tṣi.b b[--].bm.k[--]. | [--]tb.'ryt k.k qlt[.---]. | [--]at.brt.lb k.'nn.[---]. | [--.]šdq.k ttn.l y.šn[.---]. | 60[32].3
btlt.'nt. | w ypt l ybmt.li[mm]. | w y'ny.aliyn[.b'l]. | lm.k qnym.'l[m.--]. | k dr d.d yknn[.--]. | b'l.yṣǵd.mli[.--]. | il hd. 10[76].3.6
ṣmt.adm.ṣat.š[p]š. | t̠ḥt h.k kdrt.ri[š]. | 'l h.k irbym.kp.k.qṣm. | ǵrmn.kp.mhr.'tkt. | rišt.l bmt h.šnst. | kpt.b ḥbš h.br 3['NT].2.10
| [---.]bt k.ap.l pḫr k 'nt tqm.'nt.tqm. | [---.p]ḫr k.ygrš k.qr.bt k.ygrš k. | [---].bnt.ṣ'ṣ.bnt.m'm'.'bd.ḥrn.[--.]k. | [---].a 1001.2.10
t.qḥ.tp k.b yd. | [-]r[-]k.bm.ymn. | tlk.škn.'l.ṣrrt. | adn k.šqrb.[---]. | b mgn k.w ḫrṣ.l kl. | apnk.ǵzr.ilḥu. | [m]rḥ h.yiḫ 16.1[125].44
[kbdn h.yšu.g h.w y]ṣḥ.t̠ḥm. | [t̠r.il.ab k.hwt.l]t̠pn.ḥtk k. | [qryy.b arṣ.mlḥ]mt.št b 'p | [r m.ddym.sk.šlm].l kbd.arṣ. 1['NT.IX].2.18
mǵ.l qrt.ablm.abl[m]. | qrt.zbl.yrḫ.yšu g h. | w yṣḥ.y l k.qrt.ablm. | d 'l k.mḫṣ.aqht.ǵzr. | 'wrt.yšt k.b'l.l ht. | w 'lm h 19[1AQHT].4.165
[-----]. | [-----]. | [-----]. | [---.-]rb. | [-----]. | [-----]. | [-----]. | k yraš w ykhp mid. | dblt ytnt w ṣmqm ytn[m]. | w qmḥ bql 160[55].23
r[.ḥdrt.w.št]. | irǵ[n.ḥmr.ydk]. | aḥd[h.w.yṣq.b.ap h]. | k yr[a]š.šš[w.w.ykhp]. | mid.dblt.yt̠[nt.w]. | ṣmq[m].ytnm.w[. 161[56].32
mkšr grn. | [w št aškrr w p]r ḥdrt. | [-----]. | [---.-]n[-]. | [k yraš ššw št bln q]t ydk. | [w yṣq b ap h]. | [-----]. | [-----]. | [--- 160[55].14
k[št.grn]. | št.irǵn.ḥmr[.ydk]. | aḥd h.w.yṣq.b[.ap h]. | k.yraš.ššw.[št]. | bln.qt.yṣq.b.a[p h]. | k yǵ'r[.ššw.---]. | dprn[.- 161[56].21
pš[.-]. | npš.lbun. | thw.w npš. | anḫr.b ym. | brkt.šbšt. | k rumm.hm. | 'n.kd̠d.aylt. | mt hm.ks.ym | sk.nhr hm. | šb'.yd UG5.4.7
.bn m.um y.kl | y y.yt'n.k gmrm. | mt.'z.b'l.'z.ynghn. | k rumm.mt.'z.b'l. | 'z.ynt̠kn.k bt̠nm. | mt.'z.b'l.'z.ymṣḫn. | k l 6[49].6.18
.tlik.'m y. | ik y.aškn. | 'ṣm.l bt.dml. | p ank.atn. | 'ṣm.l k. | arb'.'ṣm. | 'l.ar. | w.t̠lt̠. | 'l.ubr'y. | w.tn.'l. | mlk. | w.aḥd. | 'l a 1010.8
.[--.]t̠m.w.at. | ngt̠.w.ytn.hm.l k. | w.lḥt.alpm.ḫršm. | k.rgmt.l y.bly m. | alpm.aršt.l k.w.l y. | mn.bnš.d.l.i[--].'[m k 2064.22
y.twtḥ.išd k. | [dm.rgm.it̠.l y.]w argm k.hwt. | [w at̠ny k.rgm.]'ṣ.w lḫšt. | [abn.rgm.l td]'.nš[m.w l t]bn. | [hmlt.a]rṣ.[3['NT].4.58
y. | twtḥ.išd k.dm.rgm. | it̠.l y.w argm k. | hwt.w at̠ny k.rgm. | 'ṣ.w lḫšt.abn. | tant.šmm.'m.arṣ. | thmt.'mn.kbkbm. | 3['NT].3.19
--------]. | ǵr.ks.dm.r[gm.it̠.l y.w argm k]. | hwt.w at̠ny k[.rgm.'ṣ.w lḫšt.abn]. | tunt.šmm.'m[.arṣ.thmt.'mn.kbkbm]. 1['NT.IX].3.13
w.k.rgm.špš. | mlk.rb.b'l y.u. | '[--.]mlakt.'bd h. | [---.]b'l k.yḫpn 1018.1
--]t.npš.'gl. | [---.-]nk.aštn.b ḫrt. | ilm.arṣ.w at.qḥ. | 'rpt k.rḥ k.mdl k. | mṭrt k.'m k.šb't. | ǵlm k.t̠mn.ḫnzr k. | 'm k.pd 5[67].5.7
ṣḥn]. | šm'.l dnil.[mt.rpi]. | mt.aqht.ǵzr.[šṣat]. | btlt.'nt.k [rḥ.npš h]. | k it̠l.brlt h.[b h.p'nm]. | tt̠t.'l[n.pn h.td'.b 'dn]. 19[1AQHT].2.92
r km.dnil.[--] h[.---]. | riš.r[--.--]ḫ[.---]y[.---.-]nt.[š]ṣat[k.]rḥ.npš.hm. | k.it̠l.brlt n[-.k qtr.b ap -]. | tmǵyn.tša.g h[m. 19[1AQHT].2.87
.l y.[--]. | [---].al.trgm.l aḫt k. | [---.]l [ ]dm.aḫt k. | yd't.k rḥmt. | al.tšt.b šdm.mm h. | b smkt.ṣat.npš h. | [-]mt[-].ṣba. 16.1[125].33
trt. | w t'n.rbt.at̠rt ym. | rbt.ilm.l ḥkmt. | šbt.dqn k.l tsr k. | rḥntt.d[-].l irt k. | wn ap.'dn.mṭr h. | b'l.y'dn.'dn.t̠kt.b glt̠. 4[51].5.66
.brḥ. | tkly.btn.'qltn. | šlyṭ.d šb'y.rašm. | t̠tkḥ.ttrp.šmm.k rs. | ipd k.ank.ispi.utm. | d̠rqm.amt m.l yrt. | b npš.bn ilm. 5[67].1.4
.tkly. | [btn.'qltn.]šlyṭ. | [d šb't.rašm].t̠tkḥ. | [ttrp.šmm.k rks.ipd]k. | [-----]. 5[67].1.31
k.y[--]. | šm' k.l arḫ.w bn.[--]. | limm.ql.b udn.k w[-]. | k rtqt mr[.---]. | k d lbšt.bir.mlak. | šmm.tmr.zbl.mlk. | šmm. 13[6].24
[---.--]d.'m y. | [--.]spr.lm.likt. | [--]y.k išal hm. | [--.'š]rm.kkr.t̠lt̠. | [--.]t̠lt̠m.kkr.t̠lt̠. | [--.]aštn.l k. | [- 1022.3
tpt̠.nhr. | b šm.tg'r m.'t̠trt.bt̠ l aliyn.[b'l.] | bt̠.l rkb.'rpt.k šby n.zb[l.ym.k] | šby n.tpt̠.nhr.w yṣa b[.---]. | ybt̠.nn.aliyn 2.4[68].29
'r m.'t̠trt.bt̠ l aliyn.[b'l.] | bt̠.l rkb.'rpt.k šby n.zb[l.ym.k] | šby n.tpt̠.nhr.w yṣa b[.--].. | ybt̠.nn.aliyn.b'l.w [---]. | ym.l 2.4[68].29
yn.iš[ryt.-]lnr. | spr.[--]ḫ[-] k.šb't. | ghl.ph.t̠mnt. | nblu h.špš.ymp. | hlkt.tdr[--]. | špš.b'd h 27[8].2
k.bt.[b'l.w mnt k]. | bt il.aḫd.yd k.b [škrn]. | m'ms k.k šb't.yn.t̠[ḫ]. | gg k.b ym.t̠it̠.rḥṣ. | npṣ k.b ym rt̠.b uni[l]. | pn 17[2AQHT].2.6

q.lḥt.|niṣ h.grš d.‘šy.ln h.|aḫd.yd h.b škrn.m‘ms h.|[k]šb‘ yn.spu.ksm h.bt.b‘l.|[w m]nt h bt.il.ṯḫ.gg h.b ym.|[ṭi 17[2AQHT].1.32
].|ṭbq lḥt.niṣ y.grš.|d ‘šy.ln.aḫd.yd y.b š|krn m‘ms y k šb‘t yn.|spu.ksm y.bt.b‘l.[w]mn[t].|y.bt.il.ṯḫ.gg y.b ym.ṯi 17[2AQHT].2.20
.nqpnt.‘d.|k lbš.km.lpš.dm a[ḫ h].|km.all.dm.ary h.|k šb‘t.l šb‘m.aḫ h.ym[.--].|w ṯmnt.l ṯmnym.|šr.aḫy h.mẓa h 12[75].2.49
.b ḫrt.|ilm.arṣ.w at.qḥ.|‘rpt k.rḥ k.mdl k.|mṭrt k.‘m k.šb‘t.|ǵlm k.ṯmn.ḫnzr k.|‘m k.pdry.bt.ar.|‘m k.ṭṭly.bt.rb.i 5[67].5.8
aḫt h l a|bn mznm.nkl w ib.|d ašr.ar yrḫ.w y|rḫ yar k.|[ašr ilht kṯrt bn]|t hll.snnt.bnt h|ll b‘l gml.yrdt.|b ‘rgz 24[77].39
r.|ṯmn.[---.]btlt.[‘]nt.|ṯṯb.[---.--]ša.|tlm.km[.---.]yd h.k šr.|knr.uṣb‘t h ḥrṣ.abn.|p h.tiḫd.šnt h.w akl.bqmm.|tšt ḥ 19[1AQHT].1.7
i[n.b ilht].|qlṣ k.tb‘.bt.ḫnp.lb[k.--.ti]|ḫd.d iṯ.b kbd k.tšt.b [---].|irt k.dṯ.ydṯ.m‘qb k.[ttb‘].|[bt]lt.‘nt.idk.l ttn.[pn 18[3AQHT].1.18
.l y.aliyn.b‘l.|tšm‘.nrt.ilm.špš.|tšu.aliyn.b‘l.l ktp.|‘nt.k tšt h.tš‘lyn h.|b ṣrrt.ṣpn.tbkyn h.|w tqbrn h.tštnn.b ḫrt.|i 6[62].1.15
ištir.b ḏdm.w n‘rs[.---].|w t‘n.btlt.‘nt.ṯb.yṯp.w[---].|l k.ašt k.km.nšr.b ḥb[š y].|km.diy.b t‘rt y.aqht.[km.yṯb].|l lḥ 18[3AQHT].4.17
tḥm iwrḏr.|l iwrpḫn.|bn y.aḫ y.rgm.|ilm.tǵr k.|tšlm k.|ik y.lḥt.|spr.d likt.|‘m.ṯryl.|mh y.rgmt.|w ht.a 138.4
tḥm.iwrḏr.|l iwrpḫn.|bn y.aḫ y.rgm.|ilm.tǵr k.|tšlm k.|iky.lḥt.|spr.d likt.|‘m.ṯryl.|mh y.rgmt.|w ht.aḫ 138.4
ḥm[.t]lm[yn].|l ṯryl.um y.|rgm.|ugrt.tǵr k.|ugrt.tǵr k.|tšlm k.um y.|td‘.ky.‘rbt.|l pn.špš.|w pn.špš.nr.|b y.mid 1015.5
bn [k].|[l].p‘n.um [y].|qlt[.l um] y.|yšlm.il[m].|tǵ[r] k.tš[lm] k.|[h]l ny.‘m n[.š]lm.|w.ṯm [ny.‘m.mlkt.u]m y.|m 1013.7
m.mlk.|bn k.|l.p‘n.um y.|qlt.l.um y.|yšlm.ilm.|tǵr k.tšlm k.|hl ny.‘m n[y].|kll.šlm.|ṯm ny.‘m.um y.|mnm.šlm 50[117].8
[yš]lm[.ilm].|tǵr k[.tšlm k].|hl ny.[---].|w.pdr[--.---].|tmǵyn[.---].|w.mli[.---] 57[101].2
tḥm.pgn.|l.mlk.ugrt.|rgm.|yšlm.l k.[il]m.|tǵr k.tšlm k.|hn ny.‘m n.š[l]m.|ṯm ny.‘[m.]bn y.|mnm.[šl]m[.r 2061.5
grt.|aḫ y.rgm.|tḥm.mlk.ṣr.aḫ k.|y[š]lm.l k.ilm.|tǵr k.tšlm k.|hn ny.‘m n.|šlm.ṯm ny.|‘m k.mnm[.š]lm.|rgm.ṯṯ 2059.5
.aḫtmlk ‘bd k.|l.p‘n.adt ny.|mrḥqtm.|qlny.ilm.|tǵr k.|tšlm k.|hn ny.‘m ny.|kll.mid.|šlm.|w.ap.ank.|nḫt.ṯm n 51[95].8
tḥm.mlk.|l.ṯryl.um y.rgm.|yšlm.l k.ilm.|tǵr k.tšlm k.|lḥt.šlm.k.lik[t].|um y.‘m y.ht.‘m[ny].|kll.šlm.ṯm 2009.1.4
ml]k.[b‘l y].|rg[m].|tḥm.wr[--].|yšlm.[l] k.|ilm.t[ǵ]r k.|tšlm k.|lm[.l.]likt.|ši[l.š]lm y.|[‘]d.r[-]š.|[-]ly.l.likt.|[a]n 2010.5
y[šlm.l k.ilm].|tǵ[r k.tšlm k].|‘bd[.---]y.|‘m[.---]y.|šk[--.--.]kll.|šk[--.--.]hm.|w. 2065.2
[t]ḥm.iṯtl.|l mnn.ilm.|tǵr k.tšlm k.|t‘zz k.alp ymm.|w rbt.šnt.|b ‘d ‘lm...gn‘.|iršt.arš 1019.1.3
].|l pḫry.a[ḫ y].|w l g.p[-]r[--].|yšlm[.l k].|[i]lm[.tǵr k].|[t]š[lm k.---].|[-----].|[-----].|h[--.---].|[-----].|w [----].|w 56[21].5
l.mlk.ugrt.|aḫ y.rgm.|tḥm.mlk.ṣr.aḫ k.|y[š]lm.l k.ilm.|tǵr k.tšlm k.|hn ny.‘m n.|šlm.ṯm ny.|‘m 2059.3
.b‘l.hwt.aliy.qrdm.|bhṯ.bn.ilm.mt.‘bd k.an.|w d ‘lm k.šmḫ.bn.ilm.mt.|[---.]g h.w aṣḥ.ik.yṣḥn.|[b‘l.‘m.aḫ y.ik].y 5[67].2.20
l.l ẓr.[mg]dl.|w ‘l.l ẓr.[mg]dl.rkb.|ṯkmm.ḥm[t].ša.yd k.|šmm.dbḥ.l ṯr.|ab k.il.šrd.b‘l.|b dbḥ k.bn.dgn.|b mṣd k. 14[KRT].2.75
gn h.|lk.l ab k.yṣb.lk.|l[ab]k.w rgm.‘ny.|l k[rt.adn k.]ištm[‘].|w tqǵ[.udn.k ǵz.ǵzm].|tdbr.w[ǵ]rm[.ṯṯwy].|šqlt 16.6[127].29
.s]glt h.at.|ht[.---.]špš.b‘l k.|yd‘m.l.yd‘t.|‘m y.špš.b‘l k.|šnt.šntm.lm.l.tlk.|w.lḥt.akl.ky.|likt.‘m.špš.|b‘l k.ky.akl. 2060.15
[---].aliyn.|[b‘l.---.-]ip.dpr k.|[---.-]mn k.ššrt.|[---.--]t.npš.‘gl.|[---.-]nk.aštn.b ḫrt.|ilm.arṣ.w at.qḥ. 5[67].5.3
‘l.|w t‘n.btlt.‘nt.|an.l an.y špš.|an.l an.il.yǵr[.-].|tǵr k.š[---.---].|yštd[.---].|dr[.---].|r[--.---]. 6[49].4.48
y‘n.lṭpn.il d p[id].|yd‘t k.bt.k anšt.w i[n.b ilht].|qlṣ k.tb‘.bt.ḫnp.lb[k.--.ti]|ḫd.d iṯ.b kbd k.tšt.b [---].|irt k.dṯ.yd 18[3AQHT].1.17
b[k.--.ti]|ḫd.d iṯ.b kbd k.tšt.b [---].|irt k.dṯ.ydṯ.m‘qb k.[ttb‘].|[bt]lt.‘nt.idk.l ttn.[pnm].|[‘m.a]qht.ǵzr.b alp.š[d].| 18[3AQHT].1.19
b‘l.hwt.aliy.|qrdm.bhṯ.l bn.ilm mt.|‘bd k.an.w d.‘lm k.|tb‘.w l.yṯb.ilm.idk.|l ytn.pn.‘m.bn.ilm.mt.|tk.qrt h.hmr 5[67].2.12
y w l k.|[---]m.l aqry k.b ntb.pš‘.|[---].b ntb.gan.ašql k.tḥt.|[p‘n y.a]nk.n‘mn.‘mq.nšm.|[td‘ṣ.p‘n]m.w tr.arṣ.idk.| 17[2AQHT].6.44
m.ḥš k.|[‘ṣ k.‘bṣ k.‘m y.p‘]n k.tlsmn.|[‘m y.twtḥ.išd] k.tk.ḫršn.|[---.-]bd k.spr.|[---.-]nk. 1[‘NT.IX].2.23
[ḥš k.‘ṣ k.‘bṣ k.‘]m y.p[‘]n k.|[tlsmn.‘m y.twt]ḥ.išd k.|[tk.ḫršn.---]r.[-]ḥm k.w št.|[---.]ẓ[--.-]rdy ḳ.|[---.i]qnim. 1[‘NT.IX].2.2
--].|ḥš k.‘ṣ k.‘[bṣ k.‘m y.p‘n k.tlsmn].|‘m y twtḥ.i[šd k.tk.ḫršn.-------------].|ǵr.ks.dm.r[gm.iṯ.l y.w argm k].|hwt. 1[‘NT.IX].3.11
b‘l.ib.hdt.lm.tḥš.|lm.tḥš.nṯq.dmrn.|‘n.b‘l.qdm.yd h.|k tǵḏ.arz.b ymn h.|bkm.yṯb.b‘l.l bht h.|u mlk.u bl mlk.|ar 4[51].7.41
]n.|‘n ha l yd h.tzd[.--].|pt l bšr h.dm a[--.--]ḥ.|w yn.k mtrḫt[.---]h.|šm‘ ilht kṯr[t.--]mm.|nh l yd h tzdn[.---]n.| 24[77].10
[tṣḥ].|‘n.mkṯr.ap.t[---].|dgy.rbt.aṯr[t.ym].|qḥ.rṯt.b d k t[---].|rbt.‘l.ydm[.---].|b mdd.il.y[--.---].|b ym.il.d[--.---.n] 4[51].2.32
|w [k]l hm.b d.|rb.tmtt.lqḥt.|w.ṯṯb.ank.l hm.|w.any k.ṯt.|by.‘ky.‘ryt.|w.aḫ y.mhk.|b lb h.al.yšt. 2059.24
bn k.hn[.---].|bn bn.aṯr k.hn[.---].|yd k.ṣǵr.tnšq.špt k.ṯm.|ṯkm.bm ṯkm.aḫm.qym.il.|b lsmt.ṯm.yṯbš.šm.il.mt m. 22.2[124].4
rṣ.w at.qḥ.|‘rpt k.rḥ k.mdl k.|mṭrt k.‘m k.šb‘t.|ǵlm k.ṯmn.ḫnzr k.|‘m k.pdry.bt.ar.|‘m k.ṭṭly.bt.rb.idk.|pn k.al 5[67].5.9
h.qrn[m].|dt.‘l h.riš h.b glṯ.b šm[m].|[---.i]l.ṯr.iṯ.p h.k ṯt.ǵlt[.--].|[---.--] k yn.ddm.l b[--.---].|[---.-]yt š[--.---].|[--- UG5.3.1.8
tišr.|[---.šm]m h.nšat ẓl h kbkbm.|[---.]b km kbkbt k ṯn.|[---.]b‘l yḥmdn h.yrṯ y.|[---.]dmrn.l pn h yrd.|[---.]b‘l 2001.2.6
m‘.|l bn.ilm.mt.ik.tmt[ḫ]|ṣ.‘m.aliyn.b‘l.|ik.al.yšm[‘] k.ṯr.|il.ab k.l ys‘.alt.|ṯbt k.l yhpk.ksa.mlk k.|l yṯbr.ḫṭ.mṯpṭ 6[49].6.26
ṯ]ir ṯr.il.ab k.l pn.zbl.ym.l pn[.ṯ]pṭ[.n]hr.|[ik.a]l.yšm‘ k.ṯr.[i]l.ab k.l ys‘.[alt.]ṯ[bt |k.l y]hpk.|[ksa.]mlk k.l yṯbr.ḫṭ. 2.3[129].17
.w tmt[.---].|[---.]k.w tṯ[--.---].|[---.]k.w ṯ[--.---].|[---.]k ṯrm.l p[--.---].|[---.]l.[--.]rlg[-.---].|[---.]bn.w [---].|[---.--]ṯ. 2125.9
[-----].|[-----].|il.šm‘.amr k.ph[.-].|k il.ḥkmt.k ṯr.lṭpn.|ṣḥ.ngr.il.ilš.il[š].|w aṯt h.ngrt[.i]lht.|kḥṣ.k m‘r[.-- 16[126].4.3
.]ilm[.w] ḥẓr[.k bn].|[qd]š.lbum.trd.b n[p]šn y.trḥṣn.k ṯrm.|[--]b b[ht].|[zbl.]ym.b hkł.ṯpṭ.nh[r].yṯir.ṯr.il.ab h l p 2.3[129].20
.al.|tdm.l y.al tkl.bn.|qr.‘n k.mḫ.riš k.|udm‘t.ṣḥ.aḫt k.|ṯtmnt.bt.ḥmḥ h.|d[-]n.tbkn.w tdm.l y.[--].|[---].al.trgm.l 16.1[125].28
š h.|[-]mt[-].ṣba.rbt.|špš.w tgh.nyr.|rbt.w rgm.l aḫt k.|ṯtmnt.krt n.dbḥ.|dbḥ.mlk.‘šr.|‘šrt.qḥ.tp k.b yd.|[-]r[-]k 16.1[125].38
[---.]l mdgkbr.|[---] y.‘m k.|[-]tn.l.stn.|[--.]d.n‘m.lbš k.|[-]dm.ṯn id.|[--]m.d.l.n‘mm.|[lm.]l.likt.‘m y.|[---.]‘bd.an 2128.1.4
w.drm.‘tr[--.---].|w ap.ht.k[--.]škn.|w.mṯnn[.---.]‘mn k.|[-]štš.[---.]rgm y.|[-]wd.r[-.]pǵt.|[---.--]t.yd‘t.|[----.r]gm. 54.1.21[13.2.6]
[---.]l mdgkbr.|[---] y.‘m k.|[-]tn.l.stn.|[--.]d.n‘m.lbš k.|[-]dm.ṯn id.|[--]m.d.l.n‘mm. 2128.1.2
id].|yd‘t k.bt.k anšt.w i[n.b ilht].|qlṣ k.tb‘.bt.ḫnp.lb[k.--.ti]|ḫd.d iṯ.b kbd k.tšt.b [---].|irt k.dṯ.ydṯ.m‘qb k.[ttb‘].| 18[3AQHT].1.17
--].|[---].w t‘n.[btlt.‘nt.---].|[bnt.bht]k.y ilm[.bnt.bht k.--].|[al.tšmḫ.]al.tš[mḫ.b rm.h]|[kl k.al.]aḫd hm.[---].|[---. 18[3AQHT].1.7
m.|a[-]ḥ.hy.mḫ.tmḫṣ.mḫṣ[.aḫ k].|tkl.m[k]ly.‘l.umt[k.--].|d ttql.b ym.trtḥ[ṣ.--].|[----.a]dm.tium.b ǵlp y[m.--].|d 19[1AQHT].4.202
.adn k.|[w y‘ny.]ǵzr.ilḥu.|[---.]mrṣ.mlk.|[--.k]rt.adn k.|[--.d]bḥ.dbḥ.|[--.‘]šr.‘šrt.|‘[---.---].|b[---.---].|t[--.---].|w[16.1[125].60
-.]uḫd.[b‘]l m.‘[--].yd k.amṣ.yd[.--].|[---.]ḥš[.-]nm[.--.]k.[--].w yḫnp[.---].|[---.]ylm.b[n.‘]n k.ṣmdm.špk[.---].|[---.] 1001.1.15
[--].|d [--].|ypḫ[--].|w s[--].|[---].|qrd ga[n.--].|b bt k.[--].|w l dbḥ[--].|ṭ[--].|[--] aṯt yqḥ ‘z.|[---]ḏ.|[---].|[---].| RS61[24.277.22]
r.klyt h.w lb h.|[ṯ]n.p k.b ǵr.ṯn.p k.b ḫlb.k tgwln.šnt k.|[--.]w špt k.l tššy.hm.tqrm.l mt.b rn k.|[--]ḫp.an.arnn.ql 1001.1.4
.ṯn.ym.|tš[.---.]ymm.lk.|hrg.ar[b‘.]ymm.bṣr.|kp.šsk k.[--].l ḥbš k.|‘tk.ri[š.]l mhr k.|w ‘p.l dr[‘].nšr k.|w rbṣ.l ǵr 13[6].6

b.k tgwln.šnt k.|[--.]w špt k.l tššy.hm.tqrm.l mt.b rn k.|[--]ẖp.an.arnn.ql.špš.ḥw.btnm.uẖd.bʻlm.|[--.a]ṯm.prṯl.l r 1001.1.5
-].|[l.---].|[a]ẖt y.rgm.|[y]šlm.l k.|[il]m.tšlm k.|[tǵ]r k.|[--]y.ibr[-].|[--]wy.rgm l.|mlkt.ugrt.|[--]kt.rgmt.|[--]y.l.i 1016.6
išal hm.|[--.ʻš]rm.kkr.ṯlṯ.|[--.]ṯlṯm.kkr.ṯlṯ.|[--.]aštn.l k.|[--]y.kl.dbrm.hm[.--].|[--]l.w.kl.mẖr k.|[--]tir.aštn.l [k].| 1022.6
l[m.---].|[--]ḏyn.bʻd.[--]ḏyn.w l.|[--]k bʻlt bhtm[.--]tn k.|[--]y.l ihbt.yb[--].rgm y.|[---.]škb.w m[--.]mlakt.|[---.]ʻl. 1002.45
lṯ.|[--.]aštn.l k.|[--]y.kl.dbrm.hm[.--].|[--]l.w.kl.mẖr k.|[--]tir.aštn.l [k].|[---].kkr.ṯl[ṯ]. 1022.8
[---.a]dt y.|[---].irrṯwm.ʻbd k.|[---.a]dt y.mrḥqm.|[---].adt y.yšlm.|[---.]mlk n.amṣ.|[.-- 1012.2
wt]ḥ.išd k.|[tk.ẖršn.---]r.[-]ḥm k.w št.|[---.]ẓ[--.-]rdy k.|[---.i]qnim.|[---.-]šu.b qrb.|[---].asr.|[---.--]m.ymt m.|[-- 1[ʻNT.IX].2.4
[---.--]b.|[---.r]iš k.|[---.]bn ʻn km.|[---.]alp.|[---.]ym.rbt.|[---.]b nhrm.|[ʻb]r. 3[ʻNT.VI].6.2
pẖr k ʻnt tqm.ʻnt.tqm.|[---.p]ẖr k.ygrš k.qr.bt k.ygrš k.|[---].bnt.ṣʻṣ.bnt.mʻmʻ.ʻbd.ḥrn.[--.]k.|[---].aǵwyn.ʻn k.ẓẓ. 1001.2.10
]w mlk.w rg[m.---].|[--.rg]m.ank.[b]ʻr.[--]ny.|[--]n.bt k.[---.]bʻ[r.---].|[--]my.b d[-.--]y.[---].|[---.]ʻm.w hm[.--]yt.w. 1002.55
l ri[š.---].|ypt.ʻṣ[--.---].|p šlm.[---].|bt k.b[--.--.m]|ǵy k[.---].|bt.[---]. 58[20].5
---].|y.arṣ.ḥšn[.---].|tʻtd.tkl.[---].|tkn.lbn[.---].|dt.lbn k[.---].|dk k.kbkb[.---].|dm.mt.aṣḥ[.---].|ydd.b qr[b.---].|al. 5[67].3.7
.---].|ṣḥ.il.yṯb.b[mrzḥ.---].|bṯt.ʻllm n.[---].|ilm.bt.bʻl k.[---].|dl.ylkn.ḥš.b a[rṣ.---].|b ʻpr.ḥbl ṭtm.[---.]|šqy.rṯa.tn 1[ʻNT.X].4.6
bʻl.ʻbd[.---].|ṯr ab h il.ṯtrm[.---].|tšlḥm yrẖ.ggn[.---].|k[.---.ẖ]mš.ẖssm[.---].|[---.--]m ʻṯtr[t.---].|[---.]n[--.---]. 2001.1.17
ṯny.l hyn].|d ḥrš.y[dm.ṯḥm.ṯr.il.ab k.]|hwt.lṭpn[.ḥtk k.---].|yh.kṯr.b[---].|št.lskt.n[--.---].|ʻdb.bǵrt.ṯ[--. --].|ḥš k.ʻ 1[ʻNT.IX].3.6
.|[---.i]b.hn[.w.]ht.ank.|[---.--]š[-.--].w.ašt.|[---].amr k.|[---].k.ybt.mlk.|[---].w.ap.ank.|[---].l.ǵr.amn.|[---.-]ktt.h 1012.13
[--]y.kl.dbrm.hm[.--].|[--]l.w.kl.mẖr k.|[--]tir.aštn.l [k].|[---].kkr.ṯl[ṯ]. 1022.9
t.ḥmḥ h.|d[-]n.tbkn.w tdm.l y.[--].|[---].al.trgm.l aẖt k.|[---.]l [ ]dm.aẖt k.|ydʻt.k rḥmt.|al.tšt.b šdm.mm h.|b s 16.1[125].31
|rgm.|ṯḥm.[---].|yšlm[.l k.ilm].|tšlm[k.tǵr] k.|tʻzz[k.---.]lm.|w t[--.--]ṣm k.|[-----].|[-----.]šil.|[-----.]šilt.|[-----]. 55[18].6
ʻm aẖ y.lḥm.|w št m.ʻm.a[ẖ] yn.|p nšt.bʻl.[ṭ]ʻn.iṭʻn k.|[---.]ma[---] k.k tmẖṣ.|[ltn.bṯn.br]ḥ.tkly.|[bṯn.ʻqltn.]šlyṭ. 5[67].1.26
[-----].|[---.]ṯty.|[---.-]rd y.|[---.]bʻl.|[---].plz.|[---.-]tt k.|[---.]mlk. 2159.18
š[t.---].|p ʻn.bʻl.aẖd[.---].|w ṣmt.ǵllm[.---].|aẖd.aklm.k [---].|npl.b mšmš[.---].|anp n m yḥr[r.---].|bmt n m.yšẖn. 12[75].2.36
m špš.kll.mid m.|šlm.|l.[--]n.špš.|ad[.ʻ]bd h.uk.škn.|k.[---.]sglt h.hw.|w.b[.---.]uk.nǵr.|w.[---].adny.l.yẖsr.|w.[a 2060.7
[k.---.]šš[w.---].|[---.w]yṣq b a[p h].|[k ẖr š]šw mǵmǵ w b[ṣ 160[55].2
t.mhr h.[---].|aqht.w tbk.y[---.---].|abn.ank.w ʻl.[qšt k.---.ʻl].|qṣʻt k.at.l ḥ[---.---].|w ẖlq.ʻpmm[.---]. 18[3AQHT].4.40
rš k.qr.bt k.ygrš k.|[---].bnt.ṣʻṣ.bnt.mʻmʻ.ʻbd.ḥrn.[--.]k.|[---].aǵwyn.ʻn k.ẓẓ.w k mǵ.ilm.|[--.]k ʻṣm.k ʻšm.l ttn.k a 1001.2.11
t[wtḥ.išd k.dm.rgm.iṯ.l y.d argmn k].|[h]wt.d aṯ[ny k.---.rgm.ʻṣ].|w lḥšt.abn[.tant.šmm.ʻm.arṣ.thmt].|ʻm kbkb 7.2[130].18
[tšu.]g h.w tṣḥ.šmʻ.m[ʻ.l a]|[qht.ǵ]zr.at.aẖ.w an.a[ẖt k].|[---].šbʻ.ṯir k.[---].|[---.]ab y.ndt.ank[.---].|[---.--]l.mlk.tl 18[3AQHT].1.24
.|w rbṣ.l ǵr k.inbb.|kt ǵr k.ank.ydʻt.|[-]n.atn.at.mṯb k[.---].|[š]mm.rm.lk.prẓ kt.|[k]bkbm.ṯm.tpl k.lbnt.|[-.]rgm 13[6].11
k[ṯ]r w [ẖss.t]bn.bht zbl ym.|[trm]m.hk[l.ṯpṭ].nhr.bt k.[---.]šp[-.---].|[ḥš.bh]t h.tbn[n.h]š.trm[mn.hkl h.---.]bt.|[- 2.3[129].9
|lk[.---].|ki[--.---].|w ẖ[--.---].|my[.---].|aṯ[t.---].|aẖ k[.---].|tr.ḥ[---].|w tṣḥ[.---].|tšqy[.---].|tr.ḥt[-.---].|w msk.tr 16.2[125].73
--].|ʻr[.---].|ʻr[.---].|w y[---].|bʻd[.---].|yatr[.---].|b d k.[---].|ṯnnt h[.---].|ṯlṯt h[.-.w yʻn].|lṭpn.[il.d pid.my].|b il 16[126].5.7
[---].aliyn.|[bʻl.---.-]ip.dpr k.|[---.-]mn k.ššrt.|[---.--]t.npš.ʻgl.|[---.-]nk.aštn.b ẖrt.|ilm. 5[67].5.2
tr[--.--]l.aṯrt y.|[--]ptm.ṣḥq.|[---.]rgm.hy.[-]ẖ[-]y.ilak k.|[---.--]g k.yritn.mǵy.hy.w kn.|[---].ḥln.d b.dmt.um.il[m.- 1002.41
mlit.t[--.---].|ymǵy k.bnm.ta[--.---].|[b]nm.w bnt.ytn k[.---].|[--]l.bn y.šḥt.w [---].|[--]tt.msgr.bn k[.---].|[--]n.ṯḥm 59[100].9
]m.d.l.nʻmm.|[lm.]l.likt.ʻm y.|[---.]ʻbd.ank.|[---.ʻb]d k.|[---.--]l y.ʻm.|[---.]ʻm.|[---.--]y.w.lm.|[---.]il.šlm.|[---.]an 2128.2.1
w bnt.ytn k[.---].|[--]l.bn y.šḥt.w [---].|[--]tt.msgr.bn k[.---].|[--]n.ṯḥm.bʻl[.---]. 59[100].11
-.--]dn.|[---.--]dd.|[---.--]n.kb|[--.---.]al.yns.|[---.]ysd k.|[---.--]r.dr.dr.|[---.--]y k.w rḥd.|[---]y ilm.d mlk.|y[ṯ]b.al 4[51].3.6
|riš k.ʻṯtrt.[šm.bʻl.qdqd k.---].|[--]t.mṭ.tpln.b g[bl.šnt k.---].|[--]šnm.aṯtm.t[--.---].|[m]lakm.ylak.ym.[tʻdt.ṯpṭ.nhr] 2.1[137].9
nhr.yṯb[r.ḥrn.y ym.yṯbr.ḥrn].|riš k.ʻṯtrt.[šm.bʻl.qdqd k.---].|[--]t.mṭ.tpln.b g[bl.šnt k.---].|[--]šnm.aṯtm.t[--.---].|[2.1[137].8
.šmʻ.m[ʻ.l a]|[qht.ǵ]zr.at.aẖ.w an.a[ẖt k].|[---].šbʻ.ṯir k.[---].|[---.]ab y.ndt.ank[.---].|[---.--]l.mlk.tlk.b ṣd[.---].|[--- 18[3AQHT].1.25
].nk.[---].|[---.--]ḥ.an[--.---].|[---.]ʻly k[.---].|[---.]at.bt k[.---].|[---.]ank[.---].|[---.-]hn.[---].|[---.--]pp h.w[.---].|[---. 1002.4
[--].nk.[---].|[---.--]ḥ.an[--.---].|[---.]ʻly k[.---].|[---.]at.bt k[.---].|[---.]ank[.---].|[---.-]hn.[---].|[---.--] 1002.3
l.[--].|[---.]ʻnt.šzrm.tštšḥ.km.ḥ[--].|[---].ʻpr.bt k.ygr[š k.---].|[---.]y.ḥr.ḥr.bnt.ḥ[---].|[--.]uẖd.[bʻ]l m.ʻ[--].yd k.amṣ. 1001.1.12
--.]plnt.[---].|[---.]ʻmt.l ql.rpi[.---].|[---.-]llm.abl.mṣrp k.[---].|[---.]y.mṭnt.w ṯḥ.ṯbt.n[--].|[---.b]ṯnm w ṯṯb.ʻl.bṯnt.trt 1001.2.3
|[---.b]n.qdš.k[--.---].|[---.]ʻsb.[-]ẖ[-.---].|[---.]b[-.]mṯt k.[---].|[---.]k.w tmt[.---].|[---.]k.w tt[--.---].|[---.]k.w ṯ[--.--- 2125.5
[--.]l mlk [---].|[---].aẖ y[.---].|[--]q lpš[.---].|[---] y št k[.---].|[---.]l m[lk]. 2130.2.2
-]l.mlk.tlk.b ṣd[.---].|[---.]mt.išryt[.---].|[---.--]r.almd k.[---].|[---.]qrt.ablm.a[blm].|[qrt.zbl.]yrẖ.d mgdl.š[---].|[-- 18[3AQHT].1.29
ẖ y].|w l g.p[-]r[--].|yšlm[.l k].|[i]lm[.tǵr k].|[t]š[lm k.---].|[-----].|[-----].|h[--.---].|[-----].|w [----].|w [----].|w [- 56[21].6
---.]ank[.---].|[---.-]hn.[---].|[---.--]pp h.w[.---].|[---.]l k[.---].|[-----].|[-----].|[-----].|[---].al.tš[--.---].|[---.]l ksi y.w 1002.8
.rgmt.|[--]y.l.ilak.|[---].ʻm y.|[---]m.w.lm.|[---.]w.ʻm k.|[---]m.ksp.|[---].ʻm.|[---.-]n[-].|[---.]l km.|[---.-]lk.|[---.-- 1016.14
.tṣḥq.ʻnt.w b lb.tqny.|[---.]ṯb l y.l aqht.ǵzr.ṯb l y w l k.|[---]m.l aqry k.b ntb.pšʻ.|[---].b ntb.gan.ašql k.ṯḥt.|[pʻn 17[2AQHT].6.42
ym.kp.---.k br]k.tǵll.b dm.|[ḏmr.---.]td[-.]rǵb.|[----]k.|[----] h. 7.1[131].11
k[.----].|y[---.---].|rb[-.---].|šr[-.---].|[-.]ʻl[.---].|rʻm[-.---].|m 9[33].1.1
[.l k.ilm].|tšlm[k.tǵr] k.|tʻzz[k.---.]lm.|w t[--.--]ṣm k.|[-----].|[-----.]šil.|[-----.]šilt.|[-----].|[-----.š]ilt.|[---.--]m.l 55[18].7
y.rgm.|[ṯ]ḥ]m.m[lk.-]bl[-].|yšlm.l[k].ilm.|tǵr.tšl[m] k.|[-----].|[-----].|[--].bt.gb[-.--].|[--]k[-].w.špš.|[---.b].ṣp[n]. 2159.5
.ʻqltn.]šlyṭ.|[d šbʻt.rašm].ṯṯkḥ.|[ttrp.šmm.k rks.ipd]k.|[-----]. 5[67].1.31
ḥqtm.|qlt.ʻm.|bʻl y.mnm.|šlm.|[r]gm[.ṯṯb].|[l.]ʻbd[k]. 2115.2.12
nk.|nẖt.ṯm ny.|ʻm.adt ny.|mnm.šlm.|rgm.ṯṯb.|l.ʻbd k. 51[95].18
l h[-] yʻl m.|bn y.yšal.|tryl.w rgm.|ṯṯb.l aẖ k.|l adn k. 138.19
h[t] aẖ y.|bn y.yšal.|tryl.w rgm[.-].|ṯṯb.l aẖ k.|l adn k. 138.19
k.ybl.šd.|a[--].dʻ.k.|šld.ašld.|hn.mrṯ.d.štt.|ašld b ldt k. 2009.3.2

kat

.ṯnt.alpm.|ʻšrm.hbn.|ṯlṯ.mat.dd.|šʻrm.|mit.šmn.|ʻšr.kat.|ẓrw. 2102.10

kbby

n.|tdn.bn.ddy.|ʻbdil[.b]n ṣdqn.|bnšm.h[-]mt.ypḥm.|kbby.yd.bt.amt.|ilmlk. 2045.7

kbd

at.kbd.|pwt.|ṯmn.mat.pṯtm.|kkrm.alpm.|ḫmš.mat.kbd.|abn.ṣrp. 2051.9
dqtm.w ynt.qr[t].|w mtntm.š l rmš.|w kbd.w š.l šlm kbd.|alp.w š.l bʻl ṣpn.|dqt l ṣpn.šrp.w šlmm.|kmm.w bbt.b UG5.13.8
m.w y[nt] qrt.|[w mtmt]m.[š.l] rm[š.]kbd.w š.|[l šlm.kbd.al]p.w š.[l] bʻl.ṣpn.|[dqt.l.ṣpn.šrp].w š[l]mm.kmm.|[w 36[9].1.14
dqt.ṯʻ.ynt.ṯʻm.dqt.ṯʻm.|mtntm nkbd.alp.š.l il.|gdlt.ilhm.ṯkmn.w šnm dqt.|ršp.dqt.šrp w šl 34[1].2
qrdm.qryy.b arṣ.mlḥmt.šṯ].|[b ʻ]pr[m.ddym.sk.šlm.l kbd.arṣ.arbdd].|l kbd.š[dm.ḥš k.ʻṣ k.ʻbṣ k.ʻm y.pʻn k.tls]|[7.2[130].15
liy.qrdm.qry.b arṣ.|mlḥmt št.b ʻpr m.ddym.|sk.šlm.l kbd.arṣ.|arbdd.l kbd.šdm.|ḥš k.ʻṣ k.ʻbṣ k.|ʻm y.pʻn k.tlsmn 3[ʻNT].3.13
tk k.|[qryy.b arṣ.mlḥ]mt.št b ʻp|[r m.ddym.sk.šlm].l kbd.arṣ.|[arbdd.l kbd.š]dm.ḥš k.|[ʻṣ k.ʻbṣ k.ʻm y.pʻ]n k.tls 1[ʻNT.IX].2.20
|qrdm.qry.b arṣ.mlḥmt.|št.b ʻp[r] m.ddym.sk.šlm.|l kbd.arṣ.arbdd.l kbd.šdm.|[ḥ]š k.[ʻ]ṣ k.ʻbṣ k.ʻm y.pʻn k.|[tls] 3[ʻNT].4.54
.|[---.]b a[r]ṣ.mlḥmt.|ašṯ[.b ʻ]p[r] m.ddym.ask.|šlm.l kb[d].awṣ.arbdd.|l kbd.š[d]m.ap.mṯn.rgmm.|argmn.lk.lk.ʻ 3[ʻNT].4.74
.aqry.|[b arṣ].mlḥmt.[aš]t.b ʻpr m.|ddym.ask[.šlm.]l kbd.arṣ.|ar[bdd.]l kb[d.š]dm.yšt.|[----.]bʻl.mdl h.ybʻr.|[---. 3[ʻNT].4.68
.my.hmlt.aṯr.|bʻl.ard.b arṣ.ap.|ʻnt.ttlk.w tṣd.kl.ġr.|l kbd.arṣ.kl.gbʻ.|l [k]bd.šdm.tmġ.l nʻm[y].|[arṣ.]dbr.ysmt.šd 5[67].6.27
.bn.ilm.mt.mh.|taršn.l btlt.ʻnt.|an.itlk.w aṣd.kl.|ġr.l kbd.arṣ.kl.gbʻ.|l kbd.šdm.npš.ḫsrt.|bn.nšm.npš.hmlt.|arṣ. 6[49].2.16
bʻm[.--].|pd[.---.ḫm]šm.kb[d].|ġb[-.---.]kbd.|m[--.---.k]bd.|a[--.---.]kbd.|m[--.---.]kb[d].|[---.kb]d.|š[--.---.k]bd.| 2042.5
.ṣm[d].|bn abbly.|ytʻd.ṣm[d].|bn.liy.|ʻšrm.ṣ[md].|ṯṯ kbd.b ḫ[--].|w.arbʻ.ḫ[mrm].|b m[ʻ]rby.|ṯmn.ṣmd.[---].|b d. 2113.28
alpm.pḥm.ḫm[š].mat.kbd.|b d.tt.w.ṯlṯ.ktnt.b dm.tt.|w.ṯmnt.ksp.hn.|ktn.d.ṣr.pḥ 1110.1
ṯlṯm.|[---].šbʻt.ʻšrt.|[---.-]kyn.ʻšrt.|b.bn.ʻsl.ʻšrm.ṯqlm kbd.|b.ṯmq.ḫmšt.l.ʻšrt.|b.[---].šbʻt.ʻšrt.|b.bn.pdrn.ʻšrm.|d. 2054.1.6
.|yky.ʻšrt.ṯṯt šlm.ʻšrt.|bn.ḫgby.ṯmnt.l ʻšrm.ʻšrt.ḫmš.kbd.|bn.ilṣdq.šbʻt ṯlṯt šlm.|bn.ṯmq.arbʻt ṯqlm šlmm. 1131.8
.a]bṣdq.|[---.--]š.|[---.ṣ]dq.|tgmr.|yṣḥm.|ṯlṯm.|aḥd.|kbd.|bnš.mlk. 1055.2.5
ʻbd[.-]r[-.-]š[-.---].|w kšt.[--]šq h[.---].|bnš rʻym.[---].|kbdt.bnš[.---].|šin.[---].|b ḥlm.[---].|pnt[.---]. 2158.2.7
---].dt.iṯ.|[---].ṯlṯ.kbd.|[---].alpm.ḫmš.mat.|šbʻm[.t]šʻ.kbd.|tgmr.uz.ġrn.arbʻ.mat.|tgmr.uz.aḫmn.arbʻ.mat.|arbʻm 1129.4
ḏrġlm.|ʻšrm.aḥd.kbd.ḫsnm.|ubnyn.|ṯṯm[.l.]mit.ṯlṯ.|kbd[.tg]mr.bnš.|l.b.bt.mlk. 1028.13
apṯ.|šbn.|gbrn.|ṯbʻm.|kyn.|bʻln.|ytršp.|ḫmšm.ṯmn.kbd.|tgmr.bnš.mlk.|d.b d.adnʻm.|[š]bʻ.b.ḥrṯm.|[ṯ]lṯ.b.ṯġr 1024.2.25
prš.glbm.l.bt.|tgmġ.kšmm.b.yrḫ.iṯtbnm.|šbʻm.dd.ṯn.kbd.|tgmr.ḥṯm.šbʻ.ddm.|ḫmš.dd.šʻrm.|kdm.yn.|kdm.ṣmṣ. 1099.31
mrynm.|ṯlṯ.ʻšr.|hbṯnm.|ṯmn.|mḏrġlm.|ṯmnym.ṯmn.kbd.|tgmr.ḫrd.|arbʻm.l.mit.|ṯn.kbd. 1031.14
ht [-]t.|w.bn.mṣrym.|arbʻm.yn.|l.ḫrd.|ḫmšm.ḫmš.|kbd.tgmr.|yn.d.nkly. 1089.14
.mḏrġlm.|arbʻ.l ʻšrm.ḫsnm.|ʻšr.hbṯnm.|ṯṯm.l.mit.ṯn.kbd.|tgmr. 1030.10
d w [---].|[--].p il[.---].|[i]l mt mr[b-].|qdš mlk [---].|kbd d ilgb[-].|mrmnmn.|brrn aryn.|a[-]ḥn tlyn.|atdb w ʻr. UG5.1.70
ṯn.ʻšr.yn.[kps]lnm.|arbʻ.mat[.arb]ʻm.[k]bd.|d ntn.d.ksp.|arbʻ.l.ḫlby.|[---].l.bt.|arbʻ.l.kpslnm.|kd 1087.2
l.bn.yšmʻ.|mit.arbʻm.kbd.|l.liy.bn.ʻmyn.|mit.ḫmšm.kbd.|d.škn.l.ks.ilm. 1143.13
w.ṯn.irpm.w.ṯn.trqm.|w.qpt.w.mqḥm.|w.ṯlṯm.yn šbʻ.kbd d ṯbṯ.|w.ḫmšm.yn.d iḫ h. 1103.22
ṯlṯ.mat[.---.]kbd.|ṯṯ.ddm.k[--.b]rqd.|mit.tšʻm.[kb]d.ddm.|b.gt.bir. 2168.3
ly.l.rʻym.šbʻm.l.mitm.dd.|[---.--]d.šbʻm.kbd.drʻ.|[---.]kbd.ddm.kbd[.---].|[---.]ʻm.kbd.l.rʻ[ym.---].|[---].kbd.ṯmn.k 1098.46
].ḫm[šm].|kdm.kbd.yn.b.gt.[---].|[mi]tm.ḫmšm.ḫmš.k[bd].|[dd].kšmm.tšʻ[.---].|[š]ʻrm.ṯṯ.ʻ[šr].|[dd].ḥṯm.w.ḫ[mš 2092.6
d].ḥṯm.w.ḫ[mšm].|[ṯ]lṯ kbd.yn.b [gt.---].|mit.[---].ṯlṯ.kb[d].|[dd.--]m.šbʻ.[---].|[---].ʻšr.dd[.---].|[---]mn.arbʻm.y[n 2092.11
|[---.yn.d.]nkly.l.rʻym.šbʻm.l.mitm.dd.|[---.--]d.šbʻm.kbd.drʻ.|[---.]kbd.ddm.kbd[.---].|[---.]ʻm.kbd.l.rʻ[ym.---].|[- 1098.45
alpm.arbʻ.mat.k[bd].|mit.b d.yd[r]m.|alp ḫmš mat.kbd.d[--]. 2109.3
.|[špt.l a]rṣ.špt.l šmm.|[---.l]šn.l kbkbm.yʻrb.|[bʻ]l.b kbd h.b p h yrd.|k ḥrr.zt.ybl.arṣ.w pr.|ʻṣm.yraun.aliyn.bʻl. 5[67].2.4
m.l ġzrm.mid.tmtḫṣn.w t]ʻn.tḫtṣb.|[w tḥdy.ʻnt.tġdd.kbd h.b ṣḥ]q.ymlu.lb h.|[b šmḫt.kbd.ʻnt.tšyt.tḥt h.k]kdrt.ri 7.1[131].7
m.l ġzrm.|mid.tmtḫṣn.w tʻn.|tḫtṣb.w tḥdy.ʻnt.|tġdd.kbd h.b ṣḥq.ymlu.|lb h.b šmḫt.kbd.ʻnt.|tšyt.k brkm.tġll b 3[ʻNT].2.25
w tbu.|qrš.mlk.ab.šnm.|l pʻn.il.thbr.w tql.|tštḥwy.w tkbd h.|hlm.il.k yphn h.|yprq.lṣb.w yṣḥq.|pʻn h.l hdm.ytp 4[51].4.26
np.hrgb.bʻl.ṯbr.|bʻl.ṯbr.diy.hwt.w yql.|tḥt.pʻn h.ybqʻ.kbd h.w yḥd.|[i]n.šmt.in.ʻẓm.yšu.g[h].|w yṣḥ.knp.hrgb.bʻl. 19[1AQHT].3.130
t h.knp.ṣml.bʻ[l].|bʻl.ṯbr.diy.hyt.tq[l.tḥt].|pʻn h.ybqʻ.kbd h.w yḥd.|iṯ.šmt.iṯ.ʻẓm.w yqḥ b hm.|aqht.ybl.l qẓ.ybky. 19[1AQHT].3.144
.knp.ṣml.|bʻl.yṯbr.bʻl.yṯbr.diy.|hyt.tql.tḥt.pʻn y.ibqʻ.|kbd h.w aḥd.hm.iṯ.šmt.iṯ.|ʻẓm.abky w aqbrn h.aštn.|b ḫrt.i 19[1AQHT].3.139
[g]b.|bʻl.yṯb.bʻl.y[ṯb]r.diy[.h]wt.|w yql.tḥt.pʻn y.ibqʻ.kbd[h].|w aḥd.hm.iṯ.šmt.hm.iṯ[.ʻẓm].|abky.w aqbrn.ašt.b 19[1AQHT].3.124
bk[r.z]bl.am..|rkm.agzrt[.--].arḫ..|bʻl.azrt.ʻnt.[-]ld.|kbd h.l ydʻ hr h.[---]d[-].|tnq[.---.]in[b]b.pʻr.|yd h[.--.]ṣʻr.gl 13[6].31
tbu.qr]š.mlk.ab.šnm.|[l pʻn.il.t]hbr.w tql.tštḥ|[wy.w tkbd]n h.tlšn.aqht.ġzr.|[---.kdd.dn]il.mt.rpi.w tʻn.|[btlt.ʻnt. 17[2AQHT].6.51
alp ḥẓr.|[rbt.kmn.l pʻ]n.ʻnt.|[yhbr.w yql.yšt]ḥwyn.w y|[kbdn h.yšu.g h.w y]ṣḥ.tḥm.|[ṯr.il.ab k.hwt.l]ṯpn.ḥtk k.|[1[ʻNT.IX].2.16
tbu.qrš..|mlk.ab.šnm.l pʻn.|il.thbr.w tql.|tštḥwy.w tkbdn h.|tšu.g h.w tṣḥ.tšmḫ ht.|aṯrt.w bn h.ilt.w ṣb|rt.ary 6.1.38[49.1.10]
q]rš.mlk[.ab.šnm.l pʻn.il.]|[yhbr.]w yql[.y]štḥw[y.]w ykb[dn h.--]r y[---].|[---.k]ṯr.w ḫ[ss.t]bʻ.b[n.]bht.ym[.rm]m. 2.3[129].6
bu.qrš.mlk].|ab.šnm.l [pʻn.il.yhbr.w yql].|yštḥwy.[w ykbdn h.---].|ṯr.il[.ab h.---].|ḥš b[ht m.tbnn.ḥš.trmmn.hkl 1[ʻNT.IX].3.25
.mt.b a|lp.šd.rbt.k|mn.l pʻn.mt.|hbr.w ql.|tštḥwy.w k|bd hwt.w rgm.|l bn.ilm.mt.|ṯny.l ydd.|il.ġzr.tḥm.|aliyn. 4[51].8.28
lt h.|b alp.šd.rbt.|kmn.l pʻn.kṯ.|hbr.w ql.tštḥ|wy.w kbd hwt.|w rgm.l kṯr.|w ḫss.ṯny.l h|yn.d ḥrš.ydm.|tḥm.al 3[ʻNT.VI].6.20
h].|b alp.šd.r[bt.kmn.l pʻn.kṯr].|hbr.w ql.t[štḥwy.w kbd.hwt].|w rgm l k[ṯr.w ḫss.ṯny.l hyn].|d ḥrš.y[dm.tḥm.ṯr 1[ʻNT.IX].3.3
t.yʻbdr.km ġlmm.|w ʻrb n.l pʻn.ʻnt.hbr.|w ql.tštḥwy.kbd hyt.|w rgm.l btlt.ʻnt.|ṯny.l ymmt.limm.|tḥm.aliyn.bʻl. 3[ʻNT].3.7
np.nšrm.bʻl.yṯbr.|bʻl.ṯbr.diy hmt.tqln.|tḥt.pʻn h.ybqʻ.kbdt hm.w[yḥd].|in.šmt.in.ʻẓm.yšu.g h.|w yṣḥ.knp.nšrm.y 19[1AQHT].3.116
.nšrm].|bʻl.yṯb.bʻl.yṯb[r.diy.hmt].|tqln.tḥ pʻn y.ibq[ʻ.kbd hm.w] |aḥd.hm.iṯ.šmt.hm.i[t].|ʻẓm.abky.w aqbrn h.|a 19[1AQHT].3.109

pš.kṭr.|w ḫss.l brlt.hyn d.|ḥrš yd.šlḥm.ššqy.|ilm sad.kbd.hmt.bʿl.|ḥkpt.il.kl h.tšmʿ.|mṯt.dnty.tʿdb.imr.|b pḏd.l 17[2AQHT].5.20
rk h.yʿdb.|qṣʿt.apnk.mṯt.dnty.|tšlḥm.tššqy ilm.|tsad.tkbd.hmt.bʿl.|ḥkpt il.kl h.tbʿ.kṯr.|l ahl h.hyn.tbʿ.l mš|knt h 17[2AQHT].5.30
.l[.---].|pamt.w bt.[---].|rmm.w ʿl[y.---].|bt.il.ṯq[l.---.kbd].|w bdḥ.k[--.---].|ʿṣrm.l i[nš.ilm.ṯb.md]|bḥ.bʿl.[gdlt.---. APP.II[173].42
.]l.ri[--.---].|[--]t.bʿlt.bt[.---].|[md]bḥt.b.ḫmš[.---].|[-.]kbd.w.db[ḥ.---].|[--].aṯrt.ʿṣr[m.l inš.ilm].|[t]ṯb.mdbḥ.bʿl.g[d 35[3].39
spr.npṣm.d yṣa.b milḫ.|ʿšrm.ḫpn.ḫmš.|kbd.w lpš.|ḫmš.mispt.|mṯ.|w lpš.d sgr b h.|b d.anrmy. 1109.3
[l bʿl.ṣ]pn.[dq]tm.w y[nt] qrt.|[w mtmt]m.[š.l] rm[š.]kbd.w š.|[l šlm.kbd.al]p.w š.[l] bʿl.ṣpn.|[dqt.l.ṣpn.šrp].w š[l 36[9].1.13
rḥ.ʿšrt.l bʿ[l].|dqtm.w ynt.qr[t].|w mtntm.š l rmš.|w kbd.w š.l šlm kbd.|alp.w š.l bʿl ṣpn.|dqt l ṣpn.šrp.w šlmm. UG5.13.8
-.---].|[ṯ]lṯm.w b[--.---].|l il limm[.---].|w ṯt.npš[.---].|kbd.w [---].|l ṣp[n.---].|š.[---].|w [----].|k[--.---].|ʿn[t.---]. 40[134].10
m.dd.dd.kbd.|[l].mḏr[ġ]lm.|b yrḫ[ri]šyn.|šb[ʿ.--]n.[k]bd.|w[.---.]qmʿt.|[---.]mḏrġlm.|[---.]mdm.|[w].ʿšr.dd.l n 2012.22
kb[d].|ḫmš.kbd.l.mdʿ.|b yr[ḫ.iṯtb]nm.|ṯlṯ[.mat.a]rbʿ.kbd.|w.[---.-]mʿt.|ṯlṯ[m.---.-]rm.|ʿšr[.---].alpm.|arbʿ.ddm.l. 2012.14
ṯlṯ.mat.|šbʿm kbd.|zt.ubdym.|b mlk. 1095.2
kšmm.b.mṣbt.|mit.ʿšrm.ṯn kbd.|[kš]mm.|[ʿ]š[r]m.ṯn.kbd.ḥtm.|[-]m[-.-]ʿ[-.-]ag šʿrm.|[---.--]mi.|[--.]ṯt[m] šbʿ.k[b 2091.5
.bnšm.|b.gt.ṯrmn.arbʿm.drʿ.w.ʿšrm.drt.|w.ṯlṯm.dd.ṯt.kbd.ḥpr.bnšm.|b.gt.ḥdṯt.arbʿm.drʿ.w.ṯlṯm.drt.|[w].šbʿm.dd 1098.21
pr.bnšm.|b.gt.knpy.mit.drʿ.ṯṯm.drt.w.šbʿm.dd.arbʿ.|kbd.ḥpr.bnšm.|b.gt.ṯrmn.arbʿm.drʿ.w.ʿšrm.drt.|w.ṯlṯm.dd.ṯ 1098.19
nšm.|b.gt.ḥdṯt.arbʿm.drʿ.w.ṯlṯm.drt.|[w].šbʿm.dd.ṯn.kbd.ḥpr.bnšm.|b.nzl.ʿšrm.l.mit.drʿ.w.šbʿm.drt.|w.ʿšrm.l.mi 1098.23
ḥpr.bnšm.|b.yʿny.arbʿm.drʿ.w.ʿšrm.drt.|w.ṯlṯm.dd.ṯt.kbd.ḥpr.bnšm.|b.ʿnmky.ʿšrm.drʿ[.---.d]rt.|w.ṯn.ʿšr h.dd.[--- 1098.27
-.]knm.ṯṯm.l.mit.drʿ.w.mit.drt.|w[.---.]ʿm.l.mit.dd.ṯn.kbd.ḥpr.bnšm.ṯmnym.dd.|l u[-]m.|b.ṭbq.arbʿm.drʿ.w.ʿšr.dd 1098.8
.ʿšrm[.---].|ṯmnym.drt.a[--].|drt.l.alpm[.---].|šbʿm.ṯn.kbd[.ḥpr.ʿb]dm.|tg[mr.---].|[-]m.m[--.---].|[m]itm.dr[t.---]. 2013.19
--].|tgm[r.ak]l.b.gt.ḫldy.|ṯlṯ.ma[t].ʿšr.kbd.|šbʿ m[at].kbd.ḥpr.ʿbdm.|mit[.d]rt.arbʿm.drt.|[---]m.|t[gm]r.akl.b.gt. 2013.12
ym.drt.|tgmr.akl.b.gt[.b]ʿln.|ṯlṯ.mat.ṯṯm.kbd.|ṯṯm.ṯt.kbd.ḥpr.ʿbdm.|šbʿm.drt.arbʿm.drt.|l.a[--.---].|tgm[r.ak]l.b. 2013.7
ʿšr.|qmy.arbʿ.ʿšr.|ṣʿq.arbʿ ʿšr.|ṣʿ.ṯmn.|šḥq.ʿšrm.arbʿ.kbd.|ḫlb rpš arbʿ.ʿšr.|bqʿt ṯt.|irab ṯn.ʿšr.|ḥbš.ṯmn.|amḏy.a 67[110].6
km.birtym.|b d.urtn.w.ṯt.mat.brr.|b.ṯmnym.ksp.ṯlṯt.kbd.|ḫmš.alp.ṯlṯ.l.ḫlby.|b d.tlmi.b.ʿšrm.ḫmšt.|kbd.ksp.|kk 2101.5
d.---].|ṯṯm.dd.dd[.---].|l.mḏrġlm[.---].|ṯlṯ.mat.ḫmšm.kb[d].|ḫmš.kbd.l.mdʿ.|b yr[ḫ.iṯtb]nm.|ṯlṯ[.mat.a]rbʿ.kbd.| 2012.11
.šl[m.---].|iwrpzn.ʿšrm ʿšrm š[lm.---].|ilabn.ʿšrt ṯqlm kbd.ḫmš.šl[m.---].|tlmyn.šbʿt.ʿšrt ʿšrt[.šlm.---].|ybn.ṯmnt.ʿš 1131.3
[---.-]kn.|[---.]ṯlṯm.|kuwṯ.ṯlṯ.kbd.|m[i]t.arbʿt.kbd.|ḫ[mš.]šʿrt.|[---.]tšʿ.kbd.skm.|[arb]ʿm.ḫpnt.ptṯ.|[-]r.pl 1111.4
ʿšr.mrum.|šbʿ.ḫsnm.|tšʿm.ṯt.kbd.mḏrġlm.|ʿšrm.aḥd.kbd.ḫsnm.|ubnyn.|ṯṯm[.l.]mit.ṯlṯ.|kbd[.tg]mr.bnš.|l.b.bt.m 1028.10
qḥ.iwrpzn.|argḏḏ.|ttkn.|ybrk.|ntbt.|b.mitm.|ʿšrm.|kbd.ḫrṣ. 2006.10
.k]bd.|a[--.---.]kbd.|m[--.---.]kb[d].|[---.kb]d.|š[--.---.k]bd.|ḫ[--.---.kb]d.|šr[-.---].|mʿr[-.---].|bqʿt.[---].|šḥq[.---].| 2042.9
l[.ṭb].b.gt.ipṯl.|ṯmnym.[yn].ṭb.b.gt.š[---].|tšʿm.[ḫ]mš[.kbd].yn.b gt[.-]n.|arbʿm.kbd.yn.ṭb.w.[--].|ṯmn.kbd.yn.d.l.ṭ 1084.21
--].|mit.ʿšr.[---.]dd[.--].|tšʿ.dd.ḥ[ṭm.w].ḫm[šm].|kdm.kbd.yn.b.gt.[---].|[mi]tm.ḫmšm.ḫmš.k[bd].|[dd].kšmm.tšʿ[. 2092.5
m.tšʿ[.---].|[š]ʿrm.ṯt.ʿ[šr].|[dd].ḥṭm.w.ḫ[mšm].|[t]lṯ kbd.yn.b [gt.---].|mit.[---].ṯlṯ.kb[d].|[dd.--]m.šbʿ.[---].|[---].ʿ 2092.10
ḫ]mš[.kbd].yn.b gt[.-]n.|arbʿm.kbd.yn.ṭb.w.[--].|ṯmn.kbd.yn.d.l.ṭb.b.gnʿ[y].|mitm.yn.ḥsp.d.nkly.b.db[ḥ.--].|mit. 1084.23
.ṭb.|w.ḫmšm.k[dm.]kbd.yn.d.l.ṭb.|b.gt.gwl.|ṯlṯm.tšʿ[.kbd.yn].d.l[.ṭb].b.gt.ipṯl.|ṯmnym.[yn].ṭb.b.gt.š[---].|tšʿm.[ḫ] 1084.19
.l.ṭb.b.gt.sġy.|arbʿm.kdm.kbd.yn.ṭb.|w.ḫmšm.k[dm.]kbd.yn.d.l.ṭb.|b.gt.gwl.|ṯlṯm.tšʿ[.kbd.yn].d.l[.ṭb].b.gt.ipṯl.|ṯ 1084.17
.ṭb.w.ḫmš.l.ʿšrm.|yn.d.l.ṭb.b.ulm.|mit.yn.ṭb.w.ṯṯm.ṯt.kbd.|yn.d.l.ṭb.b.gt.ḥdṯt.|tšʿm.yn.d.l.ṭb.b.zbl.|ʿšrm.yn.ṭb.w. 1084.11
.kbd.|yn.d.l.ṭb.gt.ṭbq.|mit.ʿšr.kbd.yn.ṭb.|w.ṯṯm.arbʿ.kbd.yn.d.l.ṭb.|b.gt.mʿrby.|ṯṯm.yn.ṭb.w.ḫmš.l.ʿšrm.|yn.d.l.ṭ 1084.7
b.gt.ḥdṯt.|tšʿm.yn.d.l.ṭb.b.zbl.|ʿšrm.yn.ṭb.w.ṯṯm.ḫmš.k[b]d.|yn.d.l.ṭb.b.gt.sġy.|arbʿm.kdm.kbd.yn.ṭb.|w.ḫmšm.k 1084.14
b.|w.arbʿm.yn.ḫlq.b.gt.sknm.|ʿšr.yn.ṭb.w.arbʿm.ḫmš.kbd.|yn.d.l.ṭb.gt.ṭbq.|mit.ʿšr.kbd.yn.ṭb.|w.ṯṯm.arbʿ.kbd.yn. 1084.4
ḫmš.ʿšr.yn.ṭb.|w.tšʿm.kdm.kbd.yn.d.l.ṭb.|w.arbʿm.yn.ḫlq.b.gt.sknm.|ʿšr.yn.ṭb.w.arbʿm 1084.2
y.b.db[ḥ.--].|mit.arbʿm.kbd.yn.ḥsp.l.m[--].|mit.ʿšrm.[k]bd.yn.ḥsp.l.y[--].|ʿšrm.yn.ḥsp.l.ql.d.tbʿ.mṣ[r]m.|mit.arbʿ 1084.26
b.b.gnʿ[y].|mitm.yn.ḥsp.d.nkly.b.db[ḥ.--].|mit.arbʿm.kbd.yn.ḥsp.l.m[--].|mit.ʿšrm.[k]bd.yn.ḥsp.l.y[--].|ʿšrm.yn.ḥ 1084.25
n.ṭb.w.ṯṯm.ḫmš.k[b]d.|yn.d.l.ṭb.b.gt.sġy.|arbʿm.kdm.kbd.yn.ṭb.|w.ḫmšm.k[dm.]kbd.yn.d.l.ṭb.|b.gt.gwl.|ṯlṯm.tšʿ 1084.16
|ʿšr.yn.ṭb.w.arbʿm.ḫmš.kbd.|yn.d.l.ṭb.gt.ṭbq.|mit.ʿšr.kbd.yn.ṭb.|w.ṯṯm.arbʿ.kbd.yn.d.l.ṭb.|b.gt.mʿrby.|ṯṯm.yn.ṭb. 1084.6
n].ṭb.b.gt.š[---].|tšʿm.[ḫ]mš[.kbd].yn.b gt[.-]n.|arbʿm.kbd.yn.ṭb.w.[--].|ṯmn.kbd.yn.d.l.ṭb.b.gnʿ[y].|mitm.yn.ḥsp. 1084.22
.ḥsp.l.y[--].|ʿšrm.yn.ḥsp.l.ql.d.tbʿ.mṣ[r]m.|mit.arbʿm.kbd.yn.mṣb.|l.mḏrġlm.|ʿšrn ʿšr.yn.mṣb.[-]ḥ[-].l.gzzm. 1084.28
ln.|ṯd n.km.mrm.tqrṣn.|il.yẓḥq.bm.|lb.w ygmḏ.bm kbd.|ẓi.at.l tlš.|amt.yrḫ.|l dmgy.amt.|aṯrt.qḥ.|ksan k.ḥdg 12[75].1.13
-.]hr n.km.šḥr.|[---.y]lt n.km.qdm.|[-.k]bd n.il.ab n.|kbd k iš.tikln.|ṯd n.km.mrm.tqrṣn.|il.yẓḥq.bm.|lb.w ygmḏ 12[75].1.10
nšt.w i[n.b ilht].|qlṣ k.tbʿ.bt.ḫnp.lb[k.--.ti]|ḫd.d iṯ.b kbd k.tšt.b [---].|irt k.dṯ.ydṯ.mʿqb k.[ttbʿ].|[bt]lt.ʿnt.idk.l tt 18[3AQHT].1.18
rgmn.d [ybl.n]qmd.|l špš.arn.ṯn[.ʿšr h.]mn.|ʿṣrm.ṯql.kbd[.ks].mn.ḫrṣ.|w arbʿ.ktnt.w [---]b.|[ḫm]š.mat pḥm.|[ḫ 64[118].20
mitm.ʿšr kbd.|kšmm.b.mṣbt.|mit.ʿšrm.ṯn kbd.|[kš]mm.|[ʿ]š[r]m.ṯn. 2091.1
mitm.ʿšr kbd.|kšmm.b.mṣbt.|mit.ʿšrm.ṯn kbd.|[kš]mm.|[ʿ]š[r]m.ṯn.kbd.ḥtm.|[-]m[-.-]ʿ[-.-]ag šʿrm.|[- 2091.3
ʿl.|ṣry.|iršy.|yʿḏrd.|ayaḫ.|bn.aylt.|ḫmš.mat.arbʿm.|kbd.ksp.anyt.|d.ʿrb.b.anyt.|l.mlk.gbl.|w.ḫmšm.ksp.|lqḥ.m 2106.11
k.|ṯlṯ.mat.ksp.d.šb[n].|mit.ksp.d.ṭbq.|ṯmnym.arbʿt.|kbd.ksp.|d.nqdm.|ḫmšm.l mit.|ksp.d.mkr.ar.|arbʿm ksp d 2107.7
sp.ṯlṯt.kbd.|ḫmš.alp.ṯlṯ.l.ḫlby.|b d.tlmi.b.ʿšrm.ḫmšt.|kbd.ksp.|kkrm.šʿrt.štt.b d.gg[ʿt].|b.ʿšrt.ksp.|ṯlṯ.uṭbm.b d.al 2101.8
mšq.mlkt.|mitm.ṯṯm.|kbd.ks[p].|ksp.|ṯmnym.|ḫrṣ. 1157.3
[ʿ]l [-]g[-.---].|w ni[t.w.mʿṣd].|w ḫrmṯt.|ṯlṯm.ar[bʿ].|kbd.ksp.|ʿl.tgyn.|w ʿl.aṯt h.|ypḫ.mʿnt.|bn.lbn. 2053.19
m.b.ṯmnt.ʿšrt.ksp.|šbʿm.lbš.d.ʿrb.bt.mlk.|b.mit.ḫmšt.kbd.ksp.|ṯlṯ.ktnt.b d.an[r]my.|b.ʿšrt.ksp.b.a[--].|ṯqlm.ḫr[ṣ.] 2101.17
š.mat.kbd.|arbʿ.alpm.iqni.|ḫmš.mat.kbd.|ṯlṯm.ḫmš kbd ktn.|ḫmš.rṭm.|ḫmš.ṯnt.d ḫmšm w.|ḫmš.ṯnt.d mit.|ḫm 1130.7
t[.---].|l.ilt.[---].|l.ḥtk[.---].|l.ršp[.---].|[l].ršp.[---.--]g.kbd.|[l.i]lt.qb[-.---].|[l.a]rṣy.|[l.--]r[-.---].|[l.--]ḥl.|[l.--.]mg 1004.11
.nkly.b.šd.|mit.ḫmšt.kbd.|[l.]gmn.bn.usyy.|mit.ṯṯm.kbd.|l.bn.yšmʿ.|mit.arbʿm.kbd.|l.liy.bn.ʿmyn.|mit.ḫmšm.k 1143.9
n.|bn.ulbtyn.|w.kkr.ṯlṯ.|ksp.d.nkly.b.šd.|mit.ḫmšt.kbd.|[l.]gmn.bn.usyy.|mit.ṯṯm.kbd.|l.bn.yšmʿ.|mit.arbʿm. 1143.7
[l.]gmn.bn.usyy.|mit.ṯṯm.kbd.|l.bn.yšmʿ.|mit.arbʿm.kbd.|l.liy.bn.ʿmyn.|mit.ḫmšm.kbd.|d.škn.l.ks.ilm. 1143.11
d.dd[.---].|l.mḏrġlm[.---].|ṯlṯ.mat.ḫmšm.kb[d].|ḫmš.kbd.l.mdʿ.|b yr[ḫ.iṯtb]nm.|ṯlṯ[.mat.a]rbʿ.kbd.|w.[---.-]mʿt.| 2012.12

.-]rm. | ‘šr[.---].alpm. | arb‘.ddm.l.k[-]ẖ. | t̲mnym.dd.dd.kbd. | [l].md̲r[ǵ]lm. | b yrẖ[ri]šyn. | šb[‘.--]n.[k]bd. | w[.---.]q 2012.19

]it.t̲lt̲m.kbd.šmn. | [l.]abrm.mšrm. | [mi]tm.arb‘m.t̲mn.kbd. | [l.]sbrdnm. | m[i]t.l.bn.‘ẓmt.rišy. | mit.l.tlmyn.bn.‘dy. | [2095.5

--.--]d.šb‘m.kbd.dr‘. | [---.]kbd.ddm.kbd[.---]. | [---.]‘m.kbd.l.r‘[ym.---]. | [---].kbd.t̲mn.kb[d.---]. 1098.47

alpm.arb‘.mat.k[bd]. | mit.b d.yd[r]m. | alp ẖmš mat.kbd.d[--]. 2109.1

.d yṣa. | b d.šmmn. | l argmn. | l nskm. | t̲mn.kkrm. | alp.kbd. | [m]itm.kbd. 147[90].6

[---.-]kn. | [---.]t̲lt̲m. | kuwt̲.t̲lt̲.kbd. | m[i]t.arb‘t.kbd. | ẖ[mš.]š‘rt. | [---.]tš‘.kbd.skm. | [arb]‘m. 1111.3

m. | t̲lt̲.bn.mrynm. | arb‘.t̲rtnm. | tš‘.ẖbṭnm. | t̲mnym.t̲lt̲.kbd. | md̲rǵlm. | w.šb‘.‘šr.ẖsnm. | ẖmšm.l.mit. | bnš.l.d. | yškb.l 1029.11

‘šr[.m]krm. | tš‘.hbṭnm. | ‘šr.mrum. | šb‘.ẖsnm. | tš‘m.t̲t̲.kbd.md̲rǵlm. | ‘šrm.aḥd.kbd.ẖsnm. | ubnyn. | t̲t̲m[.l.]mit.t̲lt̲. | 1028.9

m.trẖ[p]n. | ybṣr.ḥbl.diym. | tbky.pǵt.bm.lb. | tdm‘.bm.kbd. | tmz‘.kst.dnil.mt. | rpi.al.ǵzr.mt.hrnmy. | apnk.dnil.mt. 19[1AQHT].1.35

šm. | ṣṣ yrpi m[it.---]. | ṣṣ bn.š[m]mn ‘[šr.---]. | alp.t̲t̲m. | kbd.mlḥt. 2097.21

[ṭm].‘l.šrn. | ‘šrt.ksp.‘l.[-]lpy. | bn.ady.kkr.š‘rt. | nt̲k h. | kb[d.]mn.‘l.abršn. | b[n.---].kršu.nt̲k h. | [---.--]mm.b.krsi. 1146.11

bd.skm. | [arb]‘m.ẖpnt.pt̲t. | [-]r.pldm.dt.š‘rt. | t̲lt̲m.t̲lt̲.kbd.mṣrrt. | ‘šr.t̲n.kbd.pǵdrm. | t̲mn.mrbdt.mlk. | ‘šr.pld.š‘rt. 1111.9

ẖrd.arr. | ap arb‘m[.--]. | pd[.---.ẖm]šm.kb[d]. | ǵb[-.---.]kbd. | m[--.---.k]bd. | a[--.---.]kbd. | m[--.---.]kb[d]. | [---.kb]d. | 2042.4

--.ẖm]šm.kb[d]. | ǵb[-.---.]kbd. | m[--.---.k]bd. | a[--.---.]kbd. | m[--.---.]kb[d]. | [---.kb]d. | š[--.---.k]bd. | ẖ[--.---.kb]d. | š 2042.6

. | [---.-]kn. | [---.]hr n.km.šḥr. | [---.y]lt n.km.qdm. | [-.k]bd n.il.ab n. | kbd k iš.tikln. | t̲d n.km.mrm.tqrṣn. | il.yẓḥq. 12[75].1.9

. | kuwt̲.t̲lt̲.kbd. | m[i]t.arb‘t.kbd. | ẖ[mš.]š‘rt. | [---.]tš‘.kbd.skm. | [arb]‘m.ẖpnt.pt̲t. | [-]r.pldm.dt.š‘rt. | t̲lt̲m.t̲lt̲.kbd. 1111.6

š‘rt. | anntn. | ‘dn. | sdwn. | mztn. | ẖyrn. | šdn. | [‘š]rm.t̲n kbd. | šǵrm. | lqḥ.ššlmt. 2098.9

tṣb.w tḥdy.‘nt. | tǵdd.kbd h.b ṣḥq.ymlu. | lb h.b šmẖt.kbd.‘nt. | tšyt.k brkm.tǵll b dm. | d̲mr.ḥlqm.b mm‘.mhrm. | ‘ 3[‘NT].2.26

b. | [w tḥdy.‘nt.tǵdd.kbd h.b ṣḥ]q.ymlu.lb h. | [b šmẖt.kbd.‘nt.tšyt.tḥt h.k]kdrt.riš. | [‘l h.k irbym.kp.---.k br]k.tǵll. 7.1[131].8

šš[r]t.ẖrṣ.t̲qlm.kbd.‘šrt.mzn h. | b [ar]b‘m.ksp. | b d[.‘b]dym.t̲lt̲.kkr š‘rt. | iqn 2100.1

spr.ẖrd.arr. | ap arb‘m[.--]. | pd[.---.ẖm]šm.kb[d]. | ǵb[-.---.]kbd. | m[--.---.k]bd. | a[--.---.]kbd. | m[--.---.]k 2042.3

ṣḥm. | arb‘.alpm. | mitm.kbd.t̲lt̲. | arb‘.kkrm. | t̲mn.mat.kbd. | pwt. | t̲mn.mat.pt̲tm. | kkrm.alpm. | ẖmš.mat.kbd. | abn. 2051.5

ẖpnt.pt̲t. | [-]r.pldm.dt.š‘rt. | tlt̲m.t̲lt̲.kbd.mṣrrt. | ‘šr.t̲n.kbd.pǵdrm. | t̲mn.mrbdt.mlk. | ‘šr.pld.š‘rt. 1111.10

.alp. | [---.-]rbd.kbd.t̲nm kbd. | [---.-]nnm t̲rm. | [---.]t̲lt̲ kbd.ṣin. | [---.--]a.t̲[l]t̲.d.a[--]. | [---].mrn. | [---.]bn pnt̲bl. | [---.- 1145.1.9

ṣṣ mr‘m ẖmšm ẖmš kbd. | ṣṣ ubn ẖmš ‘šr h. | ṣṣ ‘myd ẖmšm. | ṣṣ tmn.ẖmšm. | [ṣṣ] ‘ 2097.1

iytlm mit t̲lt̲m kbd. | ṣṣ m[l]k ‘šrm. | ṣṣ abš[-] mit [‘š]r kbd. | ṣṣ yd̲rd ‘šrm. | ṣṣ bn aglby t̲lt̲[m]. | ṣṣ bn.šrš‘m.[---]. | ṣṣ 2097.11

ṣṣ bn adty ẖmšm. | ṣṣ amtrn arb‘m. | ṣṣ iytlm mit t̲lt̲m kbd. | ṣṣ m[l]k ‘šrm. | ṣṣ abš[-] mit [‘š]r kbd. | ṣṣ yd̲rd ‘šrm. | ṣṣ 2097.9

t̲mn.kkr.t̲lt̲. | t̲mn.kkr.brr. | arb‘.alpm.pḥm. | ẖmš.mat.kbd. | arb‘.alpm.iqni. | ẖmš.mat.kbd. | t̲lt̲m.ẖmš kbd ktn. | ẖm 1130.4

aḥd.kbd. | arb‘m.b ẖzr. | lqḥ š‘rt. | t̲t̲ ‘šr h.lqḥ. | ẖlpnt. | t̲t̲.ḥrt̲m. | lq 2052.1

t̲lt̲m.ktn. | ẖmšm.izml. | ẖmš.kbd.arb‘m. | dd.akl. | t̲t̲.‘šr h.yn. | kd.šmn.l.nr.ilm. | kdm.dǵm. 1126.3

| ‘šr.kkr.š‘rt. | b d.urtn.b.arb‘m. | arb‘t.‘šrt.ẖrṣ. | b.t̲qlm.kbd.arb‘m. | ‘šrt.ẖrṣ.b.arb‘ṃ. | mit.ẖršẖ.b.t̲qlm. | w.šb‘.‘šr.šm 2100.17

t̲t̲m.t̲lt̲.kb[d]. | arb‘m.t̲p[rt]. | ksp h. | t̲mn.dd[.--]. | t̲lt̲.dd.p[--]. | šb‘t.p[2120.1

šurt l b[nš.---]. | arb‘ šurt [---]. | t̲t̲ šurt l bnš [---]. | ẖmš kbd arb‘[.---]. | t̲t̲ šurt l tg[-.---]. | arb‘ šurt [---]. | [ẖm]šm šurt 137.1[92].12

b‘m.drt. | l.a[--.---]. | tgm[r.ak]l.b.gt.ẖldy. | t̲lt̲.ma[t].‘šr.kbd. | šb‘ m[at].kbd.ḥpr.‘bdm. | mit[.d]rt.arb‘m.drt. | [---]m. | 2013.11

. | ašt[.b ‘]p[r] m.ddym.ask. | šlm.l kb[d].awṣ.arbdd. | l kbd.š[d]m.ap.mt̲n.rgmm. | argmn.lk.lk.‘nn.ilm. | atm.bštm.w 3[‘NT].4.75

.mlḥmt. | št.b ‘p[r] m.ddym.sk.šlm. | l kbd.arṣ.arbdd.l kbd.šdm. | [ḥ]š k.[‘]ṣ k.‘bṣ k.‘m y.p‘n k. | [tls]mn.[‘]m y.twtḥ. 3[‘NT].4.54

lḥmt.št]. | [b ‘]pr[m.ddym.sk.šlm.l kbd.arṣ.arbdd]. | l kbd.š[dm.ḥš k.‘ṣ k.‘bṣ k.‘m y.p‘n k.tls] | [m]n ‘m y t[wtḥ.išd 7.2[130].16

lḥ]mt.št b ‘p | [r m.ddym.sk.šlm].l kbd.arṣ. | [arbdd.l kbd.š]dm.ḥš k. | [‘ṣ k.‘bṣ k.‘m y.p‘]n k.tlsmn. | [‘m y.twtḥ.išd 1[‘NT.IX].2.21

ṣ. | mlḥmt št.b ‘pr m.ddym. | sk.šlm.l kbd.arṣ. | arbdd.l kbd.šdm. | ḥš k.‘ṣ k.‘bṣ k. | ‘m y.p‘n k.tlsmn.‘m y. | twtḥ.išd k 3[‘NT].3.14

.ard.b arṣ.ap. | ‘nt.ttlk.w tṣd.kl.ǵr. | l kbd.arṣ.kl.gb‘. | l [k]bd.šdm.tmǵ.l n‘m[y]. | [arṣ.]dbr.ysmt.šd. | [šḥl]mmt.t[mǵ. 5[67].6.28

aršn.l btlt.‘nt. | an.itlk.w aṣd.kl. | ǵr.l kbd.arṣ.kl.gb‘. | l kbd.šdm.npš.ẖsrt. | bn.nšm.npš.hmlt. | arṣ.mǵt.l n‘m y.arṣ. | 6[49].2.17

t.[aš]t.b ‘pr m. | ddym.ask[.šlm.]l kbd.arṣ. | ar[bdd.]l kb[d.š]dm.yšt. | [----.]b‘l.mdl h.yb‘r. | [---.]rn h.aqry. | [---.]b 3[‘NT].4.69

t̲t̲.mat.t̲t̲m.kbd šmn. | l.abrm.alt̲yy. | [m]it.t̲lt̲m.kbd.šmn. | [l.]abrm.mšr 2095.1

t̲t̲.mat.t̲t̲m.kbd šmn. | l.abrm.alt̲yy. | [m]it.t̲lt̲m.kbd.šmn. | [l.]abrm.mšrm. | [mi]tm.arb‘m.t̲mn.kbd. | [l.]sbrd 2095.3

t̲lt̲.mat.t̲lt̲m. | kbd.šmn. | l kny. | t̲mnym.šmn. | b d.adnn‘m. 1094.2

.]kbd. | m[--.---.]kb[d]. | [---.kb]d. | š[--.---.k]bd. | ẖ[--.---.kb]d. | šr[-.---]. | m‘r[-.---]. | bq‘t.[---]. | šḥq[.---]. | rkby ar[b‘m]. 2042.10

kbd. | m[--.---.k]bd. | a[--.---.]kbd. | m[--.---.]kb[d]. | [---.kb]d. | š[--.---.k]bd. | ẖ[--.---.kb]d. | šr[-.---]. | m‘r[-.---]. | bq‘t.[-- 2042.8

bš.t̲rmnm. | [---.iqn]i.lbš.al[l.---]. | [---].t̲t̲.lbš[.---]. | [---.]kbd.t̲t̲.i[qnu.---]. | [---.]ǵprt.‘š[r.---]. | [---.p]t̲tm.l.ip[--.---]. | [--- 1106.23

t̲lt̲.mat[.---.]kbd. | t̲t̲.ddm.k[--.b]rqd. | mit.tš‘m.[kb]d.ddm. | b.gt.bir. 2168.1

pls. | kd.‘l.ynḥm. | tgrm.šmn.d.bn.kwy. | ‘l.šlmym.t̲mn.kbd. | t̲t̲m.šmn. 1082.2.9

itm.drt.t̲mnym.drt. | tgmr.akl.b.gt[.b]‘ln. | t̲lt̲.mat.t̲t̲m.kbd. | t̲t̲m.t̲t̲.kbd.ḥpr.‘bdm. | šb‘m.drt.arb‘m.drt. | l.a[--.---]. | t 2013.6

mr.uz.ǵrn.arb‘.mat. | tgmr.uz.aẖmn.arb‘.mat. | arb‘m.kbd. | t̲lt̲.alp.ṣpr.dt.aẖd. | ḥrt̲ h.aḥd.b gt.nẖl. | aḥd.b gt.knpy. 1129.7

| ẖmš.kkr.brr. | kkr.ẖmš.mat.kbd.t̲lt̲.šm[n]. | alp.mitm.kbd.t̲lt̲.ḥlb. | šb‘.l.‘šrm.kkr.t̲lt̲. | d.ybl.blym. 1135.5

.alpm.pḥm. | ẖmš.mat.kbd. | arb‘.alpm.iqni. | ẖmš.mat.kbd. | t̲lt̲m.ẖmš kbd ktn. | ẖmš.rṭm. | ẖmš.t̲nt.d ẖmšm w. | ẖm 1130.6

spr.ḥt̲bn.sbrdnm. | ẖmš.kkrm.alp kb[d]. | t̲lt̲.l.nskm.birtym. | b d.urtn.w.t̲t̲.mat.brr. | b.t̲mnym. 2101.2

iršt.yṣḥm. | arb‘.alpm. | mitm.kbd.t̲lt̲. | arb‘.kkrm. | t̲mn.mat.kbd. | pwt. | t̲mn.mat.pt̲tm. | kk 2051.3

.mzy.alzy. | ẖmš.kkr.ḥlb. | ẖmš.kkr.brr. | kkr.ẖmš.mat.kbd.t̲lt̲.šm[n]. | alp.mitm.kbd.t̲lt̲.ḥlb. | šb‘.l.‘šrm.kkr.t̲lt̲. | d.yb 1135.4

[---.]kbd.ddm.kbd[.---]. | [---.]‘m.kbd.l.r‘[ym.---]. | [---].kbd.t̲mn.kb[d.---]. 1098.48

ḥm. | [---.--]t.‘šr rmǵt.[--]. | [---].alp.[---].alp. | [---.-]rbd.kbd.t̲nm kbd. | [---.-]nnm t̲rm. | [---.]t̲lt̲ kbd.ṣin. | [---.--]a.t̲[l]t̲. 1145.1.7

‘šrm ddm kbd[.-] l alpm mrim. | t̲t̲ ddm l ṣin mrat. | ‘šr ddm.l šm‘rgm. | 1100.1

l.bn.ḥrn. | aẖty.bt.abm. | [-]rbn.‘dd.nryn. | [ab]r[p]u.bn.kbd. | [-]m[-].bn.ṣmrt. | liy.bn.yṣi. | d̲mrhd.bn.srt. | [---.--]m. | ‘ 102[322].6.4

n[-.]l ks[p.-]m. | l.mri[.--]. | t̲mn kbd[.--]i. | arb‘m[.--]. | l apy.mr[i.--]. | [---.--]d. | [-----]. 1133.3

[---].dt.it̲. | [---].t̲lt̲.kbd. | [---].alpm.ẖmš.mat. | šb‘m[.t]š‘.kbd. | tgmr.uz.ǵrn.arb‘. 1129.2

dm.|tg[mr.---].|[-]m.m[--.---].|[m]itm.dr[t.---].|[ʿš]r.[k]bd[.---].|[a]lpm[.---].|tg[m]r.[---].|ṯlṯ ma[t.---].|ṯmnym[.- 2013.23
[---]h.lbš.allm.lbnm.|[---].all.šmt.|[---].all.iqni.arbʿm.kbl.|[---].iqni.ʿšrm.ǵprt.|[---.š]pšg.iqni.mit.pṯtm.|[---].mitm 1106.6
n.dd[.--].|ṯlṯ.dd.p[--].|šbʿt.p[--].|tšʿt.k[bd.---].|ḫmšt.k[bd.---].|tgmr k[--.---].|ḫmšm a[--.---].|kbd [---].|d[.a]ǵlkz 2120.8
d.---].|ḫmšt.k[bd.---].|tgmr k[--.---].|ḫmšm a[--.---].|kbd [---].|d[.a]ǵlkz[.---]. 2120.11
y.ṯṯ.krmm.šl[-.---].|[---.]ʿšrm.krm.[---].|[ṯ]lrby.ʿšr.ṯn.kb[d.---].|ḫmrm.ṯṯ.krm[m.---].|krm.ǵlkz.b.p[--.---].|krm.ily 1081.21
p[rt].|ksp h.|ṯmn.dd[.--].|ṯlṯ.dd.p[--].|šbʿt.p[--].|tšʿt.k[bd.---].|ḫmšt.k[bd.---].|tgmr k[--.---].|ḫmšm a[--.---].|kb 2120.7
[---].yryt.|[---.a]drt.|[--.ṯṯ]m.ṯmn.k[bd].|[---.yr]yt.dq[-].|[--.ṯ]lṯm.l.mi[t].|[---.]arbʿ.kbd. 2170.3
|bn.ytrm.|bn.ḫgbt.|mtn.|mḫtn.|[p]lsy.|bn.ḥrš.|[--.]kbd.|[---].|y[---].|bn.ǵlyn.|bdl.ar.|bn.šyn.|bn.ubrš.|bn.d[- 1035.2.16
].|ǵb[-.---.]kbd.|m[--.---.k]bd.|a[--.---.]kbd.|m[--.---.]kb[d].|[---.kb]d.|š[--.---.k]bd.|ḫ[--.---.kb]d.|šr[-.---].|mʿr[-.- 2042.7
š[r]m.|arbʿ.b.arbʿm.|ṯṯm.[---.p]rm.|[-]l.b[--.---].|[---].kbd.|[---].kb[d.---].|[t]šʿm. 1138.6
ʿ.b.arbʿm.|ṯṯm.[---.p]rm.|[-]l.b[--.---].|[---].kbd.|[---].kb[d.---].|[t]šʿm. 1138.7
[--]t.ilhnm.b šnt.|[---.]šbʿ.mat.šʿrt.ḫmšm.kbd.|[---.-]nd.l.mlbš.ṯrmnm.|[---]h.lbš.allm.lbnm.|[---].all.š 1106.2
--]t.ʿšr rmǵt.[--].|[---].alp.[---].alp.|[---.-]rbd.kbd.ṯnm kbd.|[---.-]nnm ṯrm.|[---.]ṯlṯ kbd.ṣin.|[---.--]a.ṯ[l]ṯ.d.a[--].|[1145.1.7
kl.krm.[---].|gdn.krm.aḫ[d.--]r.krm.[---].|ary.ʿšr.arbʿ.kbd.[---].|[--]yy.ṯṯ.krmm.šl[-.---].|[---.]ʿšrm.krm.[---].|[ṯ]lrb 1081.18
[---.--]ṯ.slḫ.npš.ṯʿ w[.--.k]bdm.|[---.--]mm.ṯn.šm.w alp.l[--]n.|[---.]š.il š.bʿl š.dgn š.| 36[9].1.1
bʿm.l.mitm.dd.|[---.--]d.šbʿm.kbd.drʿ.|[---.]kbd.ddm.kbd[.---].|[---.]ʿm.kbd.l.rʿ[ym.---].|[---].kbd.ṯmn.kb[d.---]. 1098.46
]šm.ksp.ʿl.gd[--].|[---].ypḫ.ʿbdršp.b[--.--].|[ar]bʿt.ʿšrt.kbd[.---].|[---.-]rwd.šmbnš[.---].|[---].ksp.ʿl.k[--].|[---.--]k.|[1144.6
ddm.kbd[.---].|[---.]ʿm.kbd.l.rʿ[ym.---].|[---].kbd.ṯmn.kb[d.---]. 1098.48
[---].|[-----].|[---]lb[--].|[---]m[.---].|[---.]d nkly.|[---.]kbd[.---]. 1049.3.4
d.ḥtm.|[-]m[-.-]ʿ[-.-]ag šʿrm.|[---.--]mi.|[--.]ṯṯ[m] šbʿ.k[bd].|[---]m.b.mril. 2091.8
mn.|l argmn.|l nskm.|ṯmn.kkrm.|alp.kbd.|[m]itm.kbd. 147[90].7
.šbʿ.ʿšr.šmn.|d.l.yṣa.bt.mlk.|tgmr.ksp.mitm.|ḫmšm.kbd. 2100.23
ʿšrm.kkr.kkrm.|alp.ṯṯ.mat.kbd. 2111.2
npṣm.|b d.mri.|skn.|ʿšrm.|ḫmš.|kbd. 157[116].6
ḥbn.|ḫmšm.l.mitm.zt.|w.b d.krd.|ḫmšm.l.mit.|arbʿ.kbd. 1096.5
ṯlṯm.|ṣṣ.bn.ʿbd.ʿšrm.|ṣṣ.bn.mṣḫ[n].ʿšrm.|šbʿ.mat.ṯṯm kbd. 2096.20
.aḥd.d bnš.|arbʿ.ṣmdm.apnt.|w ḥrṣ.|tšʿm.mrḥ.aḥd.|kbd. 1123.10
ḏrǵlm.|ṯmnym.ṯmn.kbd.|tgmr.ḥrd.|arbʿm.l.mit.|ṯn.kbd. 1031.17
lbš.aḥd.b.ṯqlm.|ḫpn.pṯtm.b ʿšr.|tgmr.ksp.ṯlṯm.|ṯqlm.kbd. 1115.6
prs.|bt.mrkbt.w l šant.ṯṯ.|l bt.ʿšrm.|bt alḫnm.ṯlṯm ṯṯ kbd. 2105.4
ṯmn.k[bd].|[---.yr]yt.dq[-].|[--.ṯ]lṯm.l.mi[t].|[---.]arbʿ.kbd. 2170.6

kbdy

.kyn.|bn.ʿbdḥr.|[-]prm ḫlq.|[---]n ḫlq.|bn mʿnt.|bn kbdy.|bn krk.|bn srty.|bn lṯḥ ḫlq.|bn ytr.|bn ilšpš.|ubrš.| 2016.2.11

kbkb

t.rpi npš ṯḥ[.pǵt].|ṯ[km]t.mym.ḥspt.l šʿr.|ṭl.ydʿt.hlk.kbkbm.|a[-]ḥ.hy.mḫ.tmḫṣ.mḫṣ[.aḫ k].|tkl.m[k]ly.ʿl.umt[k. 19[1AQHT].4.200
m.w l t]bn.|[hmlt.a]rṣ.[tant.šmm.ʿm.ar]ṣ.|thmt.[ʿmn.kbkbm.abn.brq].|d l t[dʿ.šmm.at m.w ank].|ibǵ[y h.b tk.ǵ]r 3[ʿNT].4.61
k.---.rgm.ʿṣ].|w lḫšt.abn[.tant.šmm.ʿm.arṣ.thmt].|ʿm kbkbm[.abn.brq.d l tdʿ.šmm.at m].|w ank.ib[ǵy h.---].|[-].l 7.2[130].20
y k.rgm.|ʿṣ.w lḫšt.abn.|tant.šmm.ʿm.arṣ.|thmt.ʿmn.kbkbm.|abn.brq.d l.tdʿ.šmm.|rgm l tdʿ.nšm.w l tbn.|hmlt. 3[ʿNT].3.22
q.nqbn y.tš[mʿ].|pǵt.ṯkmt.my.ḥspt.l[š]ʿr.ṭl.|ydʿt.hlk.kbkbm.|bkm.tmdln.ʿr.|bkm.tṣmd.pḥl.bkm.|tšu.ab h.tštnn. 19[1AQHT].2.56
.ušpǵt tišr.|[---.šm]m h.nšat ẓl h kbkbm.|[---.]b km kbkbt k ṯn.|[---.]bʿl yḫmdn h.yrṯ y.|[---.]dmrn.l pn h yrd.|[2001.2.6
].|il.ylt.mh.ylt.yld y.šḥr.w šl[m].|šu.ʿdb.l špš.rbt.w l kbkbm.kn[-].|yhbr.špt hm.yšq.hn.[š]pt hm.mtqtm.|bm.nšq 23[52].54
qrym.ab.dbḥ.l ilm.|šʿly.dǵṯ h.b šmym.|dǵṯ.hrnmy.d kbkbm.|l tbrkn.alk brkt.|tmrn.alk.nmr[rt].|imḫṣ.mḫṣ.aḫ y 19[1AQHT].4.193
bmt.ʿr.|l ysmsmt.bmt.pḥl.|qdš.yuḫdm.šbʿr.|amrr.k kbkb.l pnm.|aṯr.btlt.ʿnt.|w bʿl.tbʿ.mrym.ṣpn.|idk.l ttn.pnm 4[51].4.17
il.k yṣḥ].|šmʿ.pǵt.ṯkmt[.my].|ḥspt.l šʿr.ṭl.yd[ʿt].|hlk.kbkbm.mdl.ʿr.|ṣmd.pḥl.št.gpn y dt ksp.|dt.yrq.nqbn y.tš[m 19[1AQHT].2.52
.|[---]m.ʿẓpn.l pit.|m[--]m[.--]tm.w mdbḥt.|ḥr[.---.]ʿl.kbkbt.|nʿm.[--.-]llm.trṯḥṣ.|btlt.ʿn[t].tptrʿ ṯd[h].|limm.w tʿl. 13[6].17
.ǵr.w yq.|dbḥ.ilm.yšʿly.dǵṯ h.|b šmym.dǵṯ hrnmy[.d k]|bkbm.ʿ[l.---].|[-]l h.yd ʿd[.---].|ltm.mrqdm.d š[-]l[-].|w t 19[1AQHT].4.186
[-----].|[špt.l a]rṣ.špt.l šmm.|[---.l]šn.l kbkbm.yʿrb.|[bʿ]l.b kbd h.b p h yrd.|k ḥrr.zt.ybl.arṣ.w pr.| 5[67].2.3
y k[.rgm.ʿṣ.w lḫšt.abn].|tunt.šmm.ʿm[.arṣ.thmt.ʿmn.kbkbm].|rgm.l tdʿ.nš[m.w l tbn.hmlt.arṣ].|at.w ank.ib[ǵy h 1[ʿNT.IX].3.14
h.w trḥṣ.|ṭl.šmm.šmn.arṣ.ṭl.šm[m.t]sk h.|rbb.nsk h.kbkbm.|ttpp.anhbm.d alp.šd[.ẓu h.b ym].|ṭl[.---]. 3[ʿNT].4.88
k.ydʿt.|[-]n.atn.at.mṯb k[.---].|[š]mm.rm.lk.prẓ kt.|[k]bkbm.ṯm.tpl k.lbnt.|[-.]rgm.k yrkt.ʿṯqbm.|[---]m.ʿẓpn.l pi 13[6].13
ḥtrt.pṯtm.|[---.-]t h.ušpǵt tišr.|[---.šm]m h.nšat ẓl h kbkbm.|[---.]b km kbkbt k ṯn.|[---.]bʿl yḫmdn h.yrṯ y.|[---. 2001.2.5
[.---].|tʿtd.tkl.[---].|tkn.lbn[.---].|dt.lbn k[.---].|dk k.kbkb[.---].|dm.mt.aṣḥ[.---].|ydd.b qr[b.---].|al.ašt.b[---].|a 5[67].3.8
---.]btlt.ʿnt.|[---.]pp.hrm.|[---].d l ydʿ bn il.|[---.]pḫr kkbm.|[---.]dr dt.šmm.|[---.al]iyn bʿl.|[---].rkb.ʿrpt.|[---.]ǵ 10[76].1.4
ṣrt.npš kn.u b]qṯt.|[tqṯṯn.ušn.yp kn.---.-]gym.|[---.]l kbkb.|[-----]. APP.I[-].2.17
m.šmn.arṣ.rbb.|[r]kb ʿrpt.ṭl.šmm.tsk h.|[rb]b.nsk h.kbkbm. 3[ʿNT].2.41

kbkbn

.|bn.asr[-].|bn.ḏr[--].|bn.ṣl[--].|bn.ḫd[--].|bn.ʿ[---].|kbkbn bn[.---].|bn.k[--].|bn.pdr[n.].|bn.ʿn[--].|nḥl h[.---].|[2014.57

kbl

n.|mrynm.|ʿzn.|ḥyn.|ʿmyn.|ilyn.|yrbʿm.|nʿmn.|bn.kbl.|knʿm.|bdlm.|bn.ṣǵr.|klb.|bn.mnḥm.|bn.brqn.|bn.ʿn. 1046.3.40

kblbn

kd.bt ilm. | rbm. | kd l ištnm. | kd l ḫty. | maḫdh. | kd l kblbn. | kdm.mṭḫ. | l.alṯy. | kd.l mrynm. | šbʿ yn. | l mrynm. | b 1090.6
n.a[--]. | [------]. | [------]. | [------]. | [------]. | [------]. | [bn.]kblbn[.---]. | [bn] uškny. | bn.krny[-]. | bn.mt. | bn.nzʿn. | bn.sl 2021.1.13

kbln

ʿzn.bn.irbn. | bn.mglb. | bn.ntp. | ʿmyn.bn ǵḥpn. | bn.kbln. | bn.bly. | bn.ṯʿy. | bn.nṣdn. | klby. 104[316].5
[---.]dd. | [---]n.dd. | [---.]dd. | bn.arwdn.dd. | mnḥm.w.kbln. | bn.ǵlm.dd. | bn.tbšn.dd. | bn.ḫran.w[.---]. | [-]n.yʿrtym. 131[309].5
. | [---]m. | [bn.]ulnhr. | [bn.p]rn. | [bn.a]nny. | [---]n. | bn.kbln. | bn.pdy. | bn.ṯpdn. 1075.2.1
bnš.kld. | kbln.ʿbdyrǵ.ilgt. | ǵyrn.ybnn qrwn. | ypltn.ʿbdnt. | klby.aḫrṯp. 1045.2
bly. | bn.apṯ. | bn.ysd. | bn.pl[-]. | bn.ṯbʿnq. | brqd. | bnn. | kbln.ṣ[md]. | bn gmrt. | bn.il.ṣm[d]. | bn abbly. | yṯʿd.ṣm[d]. | b 2113.17

kbm

t.prqt.pṯt. | lbš.psm.rq. | ṯn.mrdt.az. | ṯlṯ.pld.šʿrt. | ṯ[---].kbm. | p[---]r.aḥd. | [-----]. | [-----]. | [---.--]y. | [---.-]tt. | [---.]w.s 1112.8

kbs

. | [-----]. | [bnš.g]t.ir. | bnš.gt.rb[--]. | gpny. | bnš.mǵrt. | kbsm. | armsǵ. 1040.19
[---.--]ḥy. | [---.--]t. | [-----]. | [---.]l[--]. | [bn.]ubn. | kbs̀m. | bn.abḏr. | bn.kpltn. | bn.prn. | ʿbdm. | bn.kḏǵbr. | bn.mṣ 114[324].2.5
dm.l šmʿrgm. | ʿšr ddm.l bt. | ʿšrm.dd.l mḫṣm. | ddm l kbs. | dd l prgṯ. | dd.l mri. | dd.l ṯnǵly. | dd.l krwn. | dd.l ṯǵr. | d 1100.6
ṯlṯ. | [---].bty.ksp.ʿšr[t]. | [---.-]mbʿl.[---].ʿšrt. | [---.]ḥgbn.kbs.ks[p]. | [---].ḏmrd.bn.ḥrmn. | [---.-]ǵn.ksp.ṯṯt. | [---.]ygry.ṯ 2153.9
. | bʿl.šlm.ʿbd. | awr.ṯǵrn.ʿbd. | ʿbd.ḫmn.šmʿ.rgm. | s̀dn.[k]bs̀. | šdyn.mḫ[ṣ]. | aṯry.mḫṣ. | bʿln.mḫṣ. | y[ḥ]ṣdq.mḫṣ. | ṣp[r] 2084.13
[ʿ]b[dm]. | ʿšrm. | inšt. | mdm. | gt.mlkym. | yqšm. | kbs̀m. | trrm. | khnm. | kzym. | yṣrm. | mru.ibrn. | mru.skn. | ns 74[115].7

kbs̀

[---.--]ḥy. | [---.--]t. | [-----]. | [---.]l[--]. | [bn.]ubn. | kbs̀m. | bn.abḏr. | bn.kpltn. | bn.prn. | ʿbdm. | bn.kḏǵbr. | bn.mṣ 114[324].2.5
. | bʿl.šlm.ʿbd. | awr.ṯǵrn.ʿbd. | ʿbd.ḫmn.šmʿ.rgm. | s̀dn.[k]bs̀. | šdyn.mḫ[ṣ]. | aṯry.mḫṣ. | bʿln.mḫṣ. | y[ḥ]ṣdq.mḫṣ. | ṣp[r] 2084.13
[ʿ]b[dm]. | ʿšrm. | inšt. | mdm. | gt.mlkym. | yqšm. | kbs̀m. | trrm. | khnm. | kzym. | yṣrm. | mru.ibrn. | mru.skn. | ns 74[115].7

kbr

tnn. | bn gš[-]. | bn gbrn. | bn uldy. | synn.bn knʿm. | bn kbr. | bn iytlm. | bn ayln. | bn.kln. | bn.ʿlln. | bn.liy. | bn.nqṭn. | 1064.20
tlm. | šd.bn.nbʿm.l.ṯpṭbʿl. | šd.bn mšrn.l.ilšpš. | [šd.bn].kbr.l.snrn. | [---.--]k.l.gmrd. | [---.--]ṯ.l.yšn. | [šd.--]ln. | b d.trǵ 2030.1.6

kbrt

| pht.šrp.b išt. | ʿl k.[pht.ṯḥ]n.b rḥ | m.ʿ[l k.]pht[.dr]y.b kbrt. | ʿl k.pht.[-]l[-]. | b šdm.ʿl k.pht. | drʿ.b ym.tn.aḥd. | b aḫ 6[49].5.16

kbšy

[---.]nnd[-]. | [-]gbt. | [--]y bnš kb[š]y. | krmpy.b.bṣm. | [-]mrn.ṣd.b gl[-]. 2169.3

kd

. | ʿ[---]ʿm.kd. | a[----]ḥr.ṯlṯ. | y[---.bn.]kran.ḫmš. | ʿ[---].kd. | amry.kdm. | mnn.bn.gṯtn.kdm. | ynḥm.bn[.-]r[-]t.ṯlṯ. | pl 136[84].7
m k.mdd.i[l.---]. | bt ksp y.d[--.---]. | b d.aliyn b[ʿl.---]. | kd.ynaṣn[.---]. | gršnn.l k[si.mlk h.l nḫt.l kḥṯ]. | drkt h.š[--.--] 1[ʿNT.X].4.23
šlmym.lqḥ.akl. | yḥmn.ṯlṯ.šmn. | a[---.]kdm. | ʿ[---]ʿm.kd. | a[----]ḥr.ṯlṯ. | y[---.bn.]kran.ḫmš. | ʿ[---].kd. | amry.kdm. | 136[84].4
arbʿ.ʿšr h.šmn. | d.lqḥt.ṯlǵdy. | w.kd.ištir.ʿm.qrt. | ʿšt.ʿšr h.šmn. | ʿmn.bn.aǵlmn. | arbʿm.ksp.ʿl.q 1083.3
tt.[---]n. | kdm.l.mḏrǵlm. | kd.l.mṣrym. | kd.mštt.mlk. | kd.bn.amht [-]t. | w.bn.mṣrym. | arbʿm.yn. | l.ḫrd. | ḫmšm.ḫm 1089.9
iš ḫry. | ḫmš yn.b d. | bḥ mlkt. | b mdrʿ. | ṯlṯ bt.il | ann. | kd.bt.ilann. 1090.19
kd.bt ilm. | rbm. | kd l ištnm. | kd l ḫty. | maḫdh. | kd l kblbn. | 1090.1
d. | d ntn.d.ksp. | arbʿ.l.ḫlby. | [---].l.bt. | arbʿ.l.kpslnm. | kdm.b[t.]mlk. 1087.7
mš.kbd.arbʿm. | dd.akl. | ṯṯ.ʿšr h.yn. | kd.šmn.l.nr.ilm. | kdm.dǵm. | ṯṯ.kdm.ztm. 1126.7
[-] ym.prʿ d nkly yn kd w kd. | w ʿl ym kdm. | w b ṯlṯ.kd yn w krsnm. | w b rbʿ kdm yn. | w b ḫmš kd 1086.2
[-] ym.prʿ d nkly yn kd w kd. | w ʿl ym kdm. | w b ṯlṯ.kd yn w krsnm. | w b rbʿ kd 1086.1
ṣpn. | [dqt.l.ṣpn.šrp].w š[l]mm.kmm. | [w bbt.bʿl.ugrt.]kdm.w npš. | [ilib.gdlt.il.š.b]ʿ[l.]š.ʿnt ṣpn. | [---.]w [n]p[š.---]. | 36[9].1.16
l ṣpn. | dqt l ṣpn.šrp.w šlmm. | kmm.w bbt.bʿl.ugrt. | w kdm.w npš ilib. | gdlt.il š.bʿl š.ʿnt. | ṣpn.alp.w š.pdry.š. | šrp.w UG5.13.12
[-] ym.prʿ d nkly yn kd w kd. | w ʿl ym kdm. | w b ṯlṯ.kd yn w krsnm. | w b rbʿ kdm yn. 1086.1
. | dd.akl. | ṯṯ.ʿšr h.yn. | kd.šmn.l.nr.ilm. | kdm.dǵm. | ṯṯ.kdm.ztm. 1126.8
r.ḥṭb. | dd.ḥṭm.l.ḫḏǵb. | ṯṯ.ddm.l.gzzm. | kd yn.l.ḫtn.w.kd.ḥmṣ.w.[lt]ḥ.ʿšdm. | kd yn.l.ḫḏǵb.w.kd.ḥmṣ. | prs̀.glbm.l.b 1099.27
| kd yn.l.ḫtn.w.kd.ḥmṣ.w.[lt]ḥ.ʿšdm. | kd yn.l.ḫḏǵb.w.kd.ḥmṣ. | prs̀.glbm.l.bt. | tgmǵ.ks̀mm.b.yrḫ.ittbnm. | šbʿm.dd. 1099.28
| kd.[ʿl.---]. | [--.--]ḫ.bn.ag[--]. | [---.--]m[.---]. | [kd.]šš. | [k]d.ykn.bn.ʿbdṯrm. | kd.ʿbdil. | ṯlṯ.ʿl.bn.srt. | kd.ʿl.ẓrm. | kd.ʿl.š 1082.2.2
ʿšr.yn. | nnu arbʿ.yn. | šql ṯlṯ.yn. | šmny.kdm.yn. | šmgy.kd.yn. | hzp.tšʿ.yn. | [b]ir.ʿšr[.---]m ḥsp. | ḫpty.kdm[.---]. | [a]g 2004.27
w kd. | w ʿl ym kdm. | w b ṯlṯ.kd yn w krsnm. | w b rbʿ kdm yn. | w b ḫmš kd yn. 1086.4
[-] ym.prʿ d nkly yn kd w kd. | w ʿl ym kdm. | w b ṯlṯ.kd yn w krsnm. | w b rbʿ kdm yn. | w b ḫmš kd yn. 1086.3
spr[.---]. | ybnil[.---.]kd yn.w š. | spr.m[--]. | spr d[---]b.w š. | tt.ḫmš.[---]. | skn.ul[m 1093.2
. | šbʿm.dd.ṯn.kbd. | tgmr.ḥṭm.šbʿ.ddm. | ḫmš.dd.šʿrm. | kdm.yn. | kdm.ṣmṣ. 1099.34
| ṯṯ.ddm.l.gzzm. | kd yn.l.ḫtn.w.kd.ḥmṣ.w.[lt]ḥ.ʿšdm. | kd yn.l.ḫḏǵb.w.kd.ḥmṣ. | prs̀.glbm.l.bt. | tgmǵ.ks̀mm.b.yrḫ.iṯ 1099.28
. | dd.šʿrm.l.ḥmr.ḥṭb. | dd.ḥṭm.l.ḫḏǵb. | ṯṯ.ddm.l.gzzm. | kd yn.l.ḫtn.w.kd.ḥmṣ.w.[lt]ḥ.ʿšdm. | kd yn.l.ḫḏǵb.w.kd.ḥmṣ 1099.27
kd.yn. | l prṯ. 159[59].1
b yrḫ.[---]. | šbʿ.yn[.---]. | mlkt[.---]. | kd.yn.l.[---]. | armwl w [--]. | arbʿ.yn.[--]. | l adrm.b[--]. | šqym. 1092.4
[---.-]ṯr.kdm.yn. | [-]dyn.arbʿ.yn. | abškn.kdm.yn. | šbn.kdm.yn. | ʿbdiltp.ṯm[n].y[n]. | qṣn.ḫ[---]. | arny.[---]. | aǵltn.ḫ 1085.8

n.rqḥ.bt].|mtnt.w ynt.[qrt.w ṯn.ḥṯm].|w bǵr.arb‘.[---.kdm.yn].|prs.qmḥ.m‘[--.---].|mdbḥt.bt.i[lt.‘ṣrm.l].|ṣpn š.l ǵ APP.II[173].24
qḥ[.-]bt.mtnt[.w ynt.qrt].|w ṯn ḥṯm.w bǵr.arb[‘.---].|kdm.yn.prs.qmḥ.[---].|mdbḥt.bt.ilt.‘ṣr[m.l ṣpn.š].|l ǵlmt.š. 35[3].23
[---].ṯmn.yn.|[---.-]ṯr.kdm.yn.|[-]dyn.arb‘.yn.|abškn.kdm.yn.|šbn.kdm.yn.|‘bdiltp.ṯm[n].y[n].|qṣn.ḫ[---].|arny.[1085.7
nt.ṯlṯ.y[n].|bṣr.‘šr.yn.|nnu arb‘.yn.|šql ṯlṯ.yn.|šmny.kdm.yn.|šmgy.kd.yn.|hzp.tš‘.yn.|[b]ir.‘šr[.---]m ḥsp.|ḫpty 2004.26
.yn.|[---.a]rb‘.yn.|[---.arb]‘.yn.|[---].ṯmn.yn.|[---.-]ṯr.kdm.yn.|[-]dyn.arb‘.yn.|abškn.kdm.yn.|šbn.kdm.yn.|‘bdil 1085.5
.|w b ṯlṯ.kd yn w krsnm.|w b rb‘ kdm yn.|w b ḫmš kd yn. 1086.5
---.bn.]kran.ḫmš.|‘[---].kd.|amry.kdm.|mnn.bn.gṯtn.kdm.|ynḥm.bn[.-]r[-]t.ṯlṯ.|plwn.kdm.|tmyn.bn.ubrš.kd. 136[84].9
ṣb[-.---].|mit.‘šr.[---.]dd[.--].|tš‘.dd.ḥ[ṭm.w].ḫm[šm].|kdm.kbd.yn.b.gt.[---].|[mi]tm.ḫmšm.ḫmš.k[bd].|[dd].kšm 2092.5
.|yn.d.l.ṭb.b.gt.sǵy.|arb‘m.kdm.kbd.yn.ṭb.|w.ḫmšm.k[dm.]kbd.yn.d.l.ṭb.|b.gt.gwl.|ṯlṯm.tš‘[.kbd.yn].d.l[.ṭb].b.gt 1084.17
ḫmš.‘šr.yn.ṭb.|w.tš‘m.kdm.kbd.yn.d.l.ṭb.|w.arb‘m.yn.ḫlq.b.gt.sknm.|‘šr.yn.ṭb.w. 1084.2
rm.yn.ṭb.w.ṯṯm.ḫmš.k[b]d.|yn.d.l.ṭb.b.gt.sǵy.|arb‘m.kdm.kbd.yn.ṭb.|w.ḫmšm.k[dm.]kbd.yn.d.l.ṭb.|b.gt.gwl.|ṯlṯ 1084.16
šp.gn.|arb‘.b d.b[n].ušryn.|kdm.l.urtn.|kdm.l.ilšpš.|kd.l.annṯb.|kd.l.iwrmḏ.|kd.l.ydn.|[---.y]rḫ.ḫyr.|[---.]yn.l. 1088.7
arb‘.yn.l.mrynm.ḥ[--].kl h.|kdm.l.zn[-.---].|kd.l.aṯr[y]m.|kdm.‘m.[--]n.|kd.mštt.[---]n.|kdm.l.mḏrǵlm. 1089.3
b d.b[n].ušryn.|kdm.l.urtn.|kdm.l.ilšpš.|kd.l.annṯb.|kd.l.iwrmḏ.|kd.l.ydn.|[---.y]rḫ.ḫyr.|[---.]yn.l.mlkt.|[---.yrḫ 1088.8
]lṯ.‘šr h.[b]t.ršp.gn.|arb‘.b d.b[n].ušryn.|kdm.l.urtn.|kdm.l.ilšpš.|kd.l.annṯb.|kd.l.iwrmḏ.|kd.l.ydn.|[---.y]rḫ.ḫy 1088.6
kd.bt ilm.|rbm.|kd l ištnm.|kd l ḫty.|maḫdh.|kd l kblbn.|kdm.mṭḫ.|l.alṯy. 1090.3
.l.b]t.‘ṯtrt.|[ṯ]lṯ.‘šr h.[b]t.ršp.gn.|arb‘.b d.b[n].ušryn.|kdm.l.urtn.|kdm.l.ilšpš.|kd.l.annṯb.|kd.l.iwrmḏ.|kd.l.ydn. 1088.5
arb‘.yn.l.mrynm.ḥ[--].kl h.|kdm.l.zn[-.---].|kd.l.aṯr[y]m.|kdm.‘m.[--]n.|kd.mštt.[---]n. 1089.2
--].|ṯṯ[.l.]mštt[.---].|ṯlṯ.l.mḏr[ǵlm].|kd[.--].lm[d.---].|kd[.l.]ḫzr[m.---].|kd[.l.]ṯrtn[m].|arb‘ l.mry[nm].|kdm l.ḫty 1091.6
kd.bt ilm.|rbm.|kd l ištnm.|kd l ḫty.|maḫdh.|kd l kblbn.|kdm.mṭḫ.|l.alṯy.|kd.l mryn 1090.4
-].|kd[.l.]ḫzr[m.---].|kd[.l.]ṯrtn[m].|arb‘ l.mry[nm].|kdm l.ḫty.[---].|kdm l.‘ṯtr[t].|kd l.m[ḏ]rǵl[m].|kd l.mryn[1091.9
.|kdm.l.urtn.|kdm.l.ilšpš.|kd.l.annṯb.|kd.l.iwrmḏ.|kd.l.ydn.|[---.y]rḫ.ḫyr.|[---.]yn.l.mlkt.|[---.yrḫ.]ḥlt.šb‘.[---]. 1088.9
kd.bt ilm.|rbm.|kd l ištnm.|kd l ḫty.|maḫdh.|kd l kblbn.|kdm.mṭḫ.|l.alṯy.|kd.l mrynm.|šb‘ yn.|l mryn 1090.6
zn[-.---].|kd.l.aṯr[y]m.|kdm.‘m.[--]n.|kd.mštt.[---]n.|kdm.l.mḏrǵlm.|kd.l.mṣrym.|kd.mštt.mlk.|kd.bn.amht [-]t 1089.6
n[m].|arb‘ l.mry[nm].|kdm l.ḫty.[---].|kdm l.‘ṯtr[t].|kd l.m[ḏ]rǵl[m].|kd l.mryn[m]. 1091.11
[y]m.|kdm.‘m.[--]n.|kd.mštt.[---]n.|kdm.l.mḏrǵlm.|kd.l.mṣrym.|kd.mštt.mlk.|kd.bn.amht [-]t.|w.bn.mṣrym.| 1089.7
m.|kd l ḫty.|maḫdh.|kd l kblbn.|kdm.mṭḫ.|l.alṯy.|kd.l mrynm.|šb‘ yn.|l mrynm.|b yṯbmlk.|kdm.ǵbiš ḫry.|ḫ 1090.9
nm].|kdm l.ḫty.[---].|kdm l.‘ṯtr[t].|kd l.m[ḏ]rǵl[m].|kd l.mryn[m]. 1091.12
.---].|kd[.l.]ṯrtn[m].|arb‘ l.mry[nm].|kdm l.ḫty.[---].|kdm l.‘ṯtr[t].|kd l.m[ḏ]rǵl[m].|kd l.mryn[m]. 1091.10
].|ṯlṯ.l.mḏr[ǵlm].|kd[.--].lm[d.---].|kd[.l.]ḫzr[m.---].|kd[.l.]ṯrtn[m].|arb‘ l.mry[nm].|kdm l.ḫty.[---].|kdm l.‘ṯtr[t 1091.7
n.|mt.šmm.ks.qdš.|l tphn h.aṯt.krpn.|l t‘n.aṯrt.alp.|kd.yqḥ.b ḫmr.|rbt.ymsk.b msk h.|qm.ybd.w yšr.|mṣltm.b 3['NT].1.16
lm.|rbm.|kd l ištnm.|kd l ḫty.|maḫdh.|kd l kblbn.|kdm.mṭḫ.|l.alṯy.|kd.l mrynm.|šb‘ yn.|l mrynm.|b yṯbmlk. 1090.7
.kd.|a[----]ḥr.ṯlṯ.|y[---.bn.]kran.ḫmš.|‘[---].kd.|amry.kdm.|mnn.bn.gṯtn.kdm.|ynḥm.bn[.-]r[-]t.ṯlṯ.|plwn.kdm.|t 136[84].8
.[--]n.|kd.mštt.[---]n.|kdm.l.mḏrǵlm.|kd.l.mṣrym.|kd.mštt.mlk.|kd.bn.amht [-]t.|w.bn.mṣrym.|arb‘m.yn.|l.ḫ 1089.8
--].kl h.|kdm.l.zn[-.---].|kd.l.aṯr[y]m.|kdm.‘m.[--]n.|kd.mštt.[---]n.|kdm.l.mḏrǵlm.|kd.l.mṣrym.|kd.mštt.mlk.| 1089.5
[---.]ṯṯ.dd.gdl.ṯṯ.dd.š‘rm.|[---.-]hn.w.alp.kd.nbt.kd.šmn.mr.|[---.]arb‘.mat.ḫswn.ltḥ.aqhr.|[---.ltḥ.]sb 142[12].2
m.ḥm]r.škm.|[---.ṯṯ.dd.]gdl.ṯṯ.dd.š‘rm.|[---.hn.w.al]p.kd.nbt.kd.šmn.mr.|[---].kmn.ltḥ.sbbyn.|[---.-]‘t.ltḥ.ššmn.|[142[12].8
.|[---.ṯṯ.dd.]gdl.ṯṯ.dd.š‘rm.|[---.a]lp.arb‘.mat.tyt.|[---.kd.]nbt.k[d.]šmn.mr.|[---.l]tḥ.sb[by]n.ltḥ.šḥ[lt].|[---.l]tḥ.db 142[12].15
n.ag[--].|[---.--]m[.---].|[kd.]šš.|[k]d.ykn.bn.‘bdṯrm.|kd.‘bdil.|ṯlṯ.‘l.bn.srt.|kd.‘l.ẓrm.|kd.‘l.šz.bn pls.|kd.‘l.ynḥm 1082.2.3
[k]d.‘l.[---].|kd.‘l.[---].|ṯlṯ.‘l.gmrš[.---].|kd.‘l.‘bd[--].|kd.‘l.aǵlt[n].|ṯlṯ.‘l.a[b]m[n].|arb‘.‘l[.--]ly.|kd.[‘l.--]ẓ.|kd.[‘l. 1082.1.20
--].|kd.šmn.‘l.yddn.|kd.‘l.ššy.|kd.‘l.nḏbn.bn.agmn.|[k]d.‘l.brq.|[kd]m.[‘l].kṯr.|[kd]m[.---].ḥ[--].|[-----].|[kd.]‘l[.- 1082.1.9
.|[kd.]šš.|[k]d.ykn.bn.‘bdṯrm.|kd.‘bdil.|ṯlṯ.‘l.bn.srt.|kd.‘l.ẓrm.|kd.‘l.šz.bn pls.|kd.‘l.ynḥm.|tgrm.šmn.d.bn.kwy. 1082.2.5
rm.|kd.‘bdil.|ṯlṯ.‘l.bn.srt.|kd.‘l.ẓrm.|kd.‘l.šz.bn pls.|kd.‘l.ynḥm.|tgrm.šmn.d.bn.kwy.|‘l.šlmym.ṯmn.kbd.|ṯṯm.š 1082.2.7
‘l.yddn.|kd.‘l.ššy.|kd.‘l.nḏbn.bn.agmn.|[k]d.‘l.brq.|[kd]m.[‘l].kṯr.|[kd]m[.---].ḥ[--].|[-----].|[kd.]‘l[.---].|[kd.]‘[l.- 1082.1.10
kdm.šmn.‘l.ilršp.bn[.---].|kd.šmn.‘l.yddn.|kd.‘l.ššy.|kd.‘l.nḏbn.bn.agmn.|[k]d.‘l.brq.|[kd]m.[‘l].kṯr.|[kd]m[.---]. 1082.1.8
k]d.ykn.bn.‘bdṯrm.|kd.‘bdil.|ṯlṯ.‘l.bn.srt.|kd.‘l.ẓrm.|kd.‘l.šz.bn pls.|kd.‘l.ynḥm.|tgrm.šmn.d.bn.kwy.|‘l.šlmym. 1082.2.6
.|[k]d.‘l[.---].|[k]d.‘l.[---].|kd.‘l.[---].|ṯlṯ.‘l.gmrš[.---].|kd.‘l.‘bd[--].|kd.‘l.aǵlt[n].|ṯlṯ.‘l.a[b]m[n].|arb‘.‘l[.--]ly.|kd.[1082.1.19
n.w.[---].|kdm.šmn.‘l.ilršp.bn[.---].|kd.šmn.‘l.yddn.|kd.‘l.ššy.|kd.‘l.nḏbn.bn.agmn.|[k]d.‘l.brq.|[kd]m.[‘l].kṯr.|[1082.1.7
.‘l.‘bd[--].|kd.‘l.aǵlt[n].|ṯlṯ.‘l.a[b]m[n].|arb‘.‘l[.--]ly.|kd.[‘l.--]ẓ.|kd.[‘l.---].|[--.--]ḫ.bn.ag[--].|[---.--]m[.---].|[kd.]š 1082.1.23
[k]d.‘l.brq.|[kd]m.[‘l].kṯr.|[kd]m[.---].ḥ[--].|[-----].|[kd.]‘l[.---].|[kd.]‘[l.---].|[k]d.‘l[.---].|[k]d.‘l.[---].|kd.‘l.[---].| 1082.1.13
r.|[kd]m[.---].ḥ[--].|[-----].|[kd.]‘l[.---].|[kd.]‘[l.---].|[k]d.‘l[.---].|[k]d.‘l.[---].|kd.‘l.[---].|ṯlṯ.‘l.gmrš[.---].|kd.‘l.‘bd 1082.1.15
[kd]m.[‘l].kṯr.|[kd]m[.---].ḥ[--].|[-----].|[kd.]‘l[.---].|[kd.]‘[l.---].|[k]d.‘l[.---].|[k]d.‘l.[---].|kd.‘l.[---].|ṯlṯ.‘l.gmrš[.- 1082.1.14
-].ḥ[--].|[-----].|[kd.]‘l[.---].|[kd.]‘[l.---].|[k]d.‘l[.---].|[k]d.‘l.[---].|kd.‘l.[---].|ṯlṯ.‘l.gmrš[.---].|kd.‘l.‘bd[--].|kd.‘l.aǵ 1082.1.16
-].|[kd.]‘l[.---].|[kd.]‘[l.---].|[k]d.‘l[.---].|[k]d.‘l.[---].|kd.‘l.[---].|ṯlṯ.‘l.gmrš[.---].|kd.‘l.‘bd[--].|kd.‘l.aǵlt[n].|ṯlṯ.‘l. 1082.1.17
kd.‘l.aǵlt[n].|ṯlṯ.‘l.a[b]m[n].|arb‘.‘l[.--]ly.|kd.[‘l.--]ẓ.|kd.[‘l.---].|[--.--]ḫ.bn.ag[--].|[---.--]m[.---].|[kd.]šš.|[k]d.ykn 1082.1.24
yn.l.mrynm.ḥ[--].kl h.|kdm.l.zn[-.---].|kd.l.aṯr[y]m.|kdm.‘m.[--]n.|kd.mštt.[---]n.|kdm.l.mḏrǵlm.|kd.l.mṣrym.| 1089.4
šlmym.lqḥ.akl.|yḥmn.ṯlṯ.šmn.|a[---.]kdm.|‘[---]‘m.kd.|a[----]ḥr.ṯlṯ.|y[---.bn.]kran.ḫmš.|‘[---].kd 136[84].3
ḫ.|l.alṯy.|kd.l mrynm.|šb‘ yn.|l mrynm.|b yṯbmlk.|kdm.ǵbiš ḫry.|ḫmš yn.b d.|bḥ mlkt.|b mdr‘.|ṯlṯ bt.il|ann. 1090.13
.ṯn.kbd.|tgmr.ḥṭm.šb‘.ddm.|ḫmš.dd.š‘rm.|kdm.yn.|kdm.ṣmṣ. 1099.35
rm[m.---].|krm.ǵlkz.b.p[--.---].|krm.ilyy.b.m[--.---].|kd.šb‘.krmm.[---].|ṯn.krm[m.i]wrǵl[.---].|ṯn.krm.[-]myn.[--- 1081.25
lqḥ.š‘rt.|urḫ.ln.kkrm.|w.rḥd.kd.šmn.|drt.b.kkr.|ubn.ḫṣḥ.kkr.|kkr.lqḥ.ršpy.|tmtrn.bn.p 1118.3
kd.šmn.‘l.hbm.šlmy.|kd.šmn.ṯbil.|kd.šmn.ymtšr.|arb‘.šmn.‘l.‘bdn.w.[---].|kdm.šmn.‘l.ilršp.bn 1082.1.3
n.|ḫmšm.izml.|ḫmš.kbd.arb‘m.|dd.akl.|ṯṯ.‘šr h.yn.|kd.šmn.l.nr.ilm.|kdm.dǵm.|ṯṯ.kdm.ztm. 1126.6

.škm. | [---.ṯṯ.dd.]gdl.ṯṯ.dd.š'rm. | [---.hn.w.al]p.kd.nbt.kd.šmn.mr. | [---].kmn.lṯḥ.sbbyn. | [---.-]'t.lṯḥ.ššmn. | [---].ẖšw 142[12].8
dd.]gdl.ṯṯ.dd.š'rm. | [---.a]lp.arb'.mat.tyt. | [---.kd.]nbt.k[d.]šmn.mr. | [---.l]ṯḥ.sb[by]n.lṯḥ.šḥ[lt]. | [---.l]ṯḥ.dblt.lṯḥ.ṣm 142[12].15
[---.]ṯṯ.dd.gdl.ṯṯ.dd.š'rm. | [---.-]hn.w.alp.kd.nbt.kd.šmn.mr. | [---.]arb'.mat.ẖswn.lṯḥ.aqhr. | [---.lṯḥ.]sbbyn.lṯḥ 142[12].2
kd.šmn.ṯbil. | kd.šmn.ymtšr. | arb'.šmn.'l.'bdn.w.[---]. | kdm.šmn.'l.ilršp.bn[.---]. | kd.šmn.'l.yddn. | kd.'l.ššy. | kd.'l.n 1082.1.5
kd.šmn.'l.hbm.šlmy. | kd.šmn.ṯbil. | kd.šmn.ymtšr. | arb'.šmn 1082.1.1
r. | arb'.šmn.'l.'bdn.w.[---]. | kdm.šmn.'l.ilršp.bn[.---]. | kd.šmn.'l.yddn. | kd.'l.ššy. | kd.'l.nḏbn.bn.agmn. | [k]d.'l.brq. 1082.1.6
kd.šmn.'l.hbm.šlmy. | kd.šmn.ṯbil. | kd.šmn.ymtšr. | arb'.šmn.'l.'bdn.w.[---]. | kdm.š 1082.1.2
d.['l.--]ẓ. | kd.['l.---]. | [--.--]ẖ.bn.ag[--]. | [---.--]m[.---]. | [kd.]šš. | [k]d.ykn.bn.'bdṯrm. | kd.'bdil. | ṯlṯ.'l.bn.srt. | kd.'l.ẓr 1082.2.1
.kdm. | mnn.bn.gṯtn.kdm. | ynḥm.bn[.-]r[-]t.ṯlṯ. | plwn.kdm. | tmyn.bn.ubrš.kd. 136[84].11
l [----]. | w l [---]. | kd.[---]. | kd.t[---.ym.ymm]. | y'tqn.w[rḥm.'nt]. | tngṯ h.k lb.a[rẖ]. | l 'g 6[49].2.4
.l [---]. | ṯlṯ.l ḥr[š.---]. | ṯṯ[.l.]mštt[.---]. | ṯlṯ.l.mḏr[ġlm]. | kd[.--].lm[d.---]. | kd[.l.]ẖzr[m.---]. | kd[.l.]ṯrtn[m]. | arb' l.mr 1091.5
q[-]dr.g[--]. | q[--.---]. | kd[.--]ḥp. | dd '[--]ṯr. | [-]tm[-.--]n. | mq[--.---]. 153[335].3
n. | šmgy.kd.yn. | hzp.tš'.yn. | [b]ir.'šr[.---]m ḥsp. | ẖpty.kdm[.---]. | [a]gm.arb'[.---]. | šrš.šb'.mṣb. | rqd.ṯlṯ.mṣb.w.[---]. 2004.30
[---].i[y]tl[m]. | [---.--]y. | [-----]. | [---.k]d. | [---.]b gt.ḥgb[-]. | [--.]b gt.nṯt[-]. 2166.4
šy. | kd.'l.nḏbn.bn.agmn. | [k]d.'l.brq. | [kd]m.['l].kṯr. | [kd]m[.---].ḥ[--]. | [-----]. | [kd.]'l[.---]. | [kd.]'[l.---]. | [k]d.'l[.---] 1082.1.11
l [----]. | w l [---]. | kd.[---]. | kd.t[---.ym.ymm]. | y'tqn.w[rḥm.'nt]. | tngṯ h.k lb.a 6[49].2.3
kdm. | ynḥm.bn[.-]r[-]t.ṯlṯ. | plwn.kdm. | tmyn.bn.ubrš.kd. 136[84].12
.[---]. | uẖnp.ṯṯ.mṣb. | tgmr.[y]n.mṣb š[b']. | w ḥs[p] ṯn.k[dm]. 2004.36

kdgdl

rtn. | bn.ḥrẓn. | bn.bddn. | bn.anny. | ytršp. | bn.szn. | bn.kdgdl. | bn.gl'd. | bn.ktln. | [bn].ġrgn. | bn.pb[-]. | bn.[---]. | bn.[115[301].1.13
| bn.'bl. | bn.[-]rṯn. | bn[.---]. | bn u[l]pm. | bn '[p]ty. | bn.kdgdl. | bn.smyy. | bn.lbn. | bn.šlmn. | bn.mly. | pslm. | bn.annd 2163.3.4
---]. | [bn.]nnr. | [bn.]aglby. | [bn.]b'ly. | [mḏ]rġlm. | [bn.]kdgdl. | [b]n.qṭn. | [b]n.ġrgn. | [b]n.tgḏn. | bn.ẖdyn. | bn.sgr. | b 104[316].9
. | bn.alṯn. | bn.dly. | bn.btry. | bn.ẖdmn. | [bn].šty. | [bn].kdgdl. | [---.-]y[-.] 2018.7

kdd

.il.t]hbr.w tql.tšṯḥ | [wy.w tkbd]n h.tlšn.aqht.ġzr. | [---.kdd.dn]il.mt.rpi.w t'n. | [btlt.'nt.tšu.g]h.w tṣḥ.hwt. | [---.]aq 17[2AQHT].6.52
kl h.mšspdt.b ḥẓr h. | pẓġm.ġr.ybk.l aqht. | ġzr.ydm'.l kdd.dnil. | mt.rpi.l ymm.l yrẖm. | l yrẖm.l šnt.'d. | šb't.šnt.yb 19[1AQHT].4.174
ẖm. | l yrẖm.l šnt.'d. | šb't.šnt.ybk.l aq | ht.ġzr.yd[m'.]l kdd. | dnil.mt.r[pi.mk].b šb'. | šnt.w y'n[.dnil.mt.]rpi. | yṯb.ġz 19[1AQHT].4.178

kdwṯ

ẖmš.mat.šmt. | b.'šrt.ksp. | 'šr.ṣin.b.ṯṯt.w.kmsk. | arb'[.k]dwṯm.w.ṯt.ṯprtm. | b.'šr[m.]ksp. | ẖmš.kkr.ṣml. | b.'šrt.b d.b 2100.10
ṯt. | [---.]w.sbsg. | [-----]. | [-----]. | [---.--]ṯ. | [---.-]b.m.lk. | kdwṯ.ḥdṯ. | b d 'lpy. 1112.19
.b.alp.[b d].bn.[---]. | tš'.ṣin.b.tš't.ksp. | mšlt.b.ṯql.ksp. | kdwṯ.l.grgyn.b.ṯq[l]. | ẖmšm.šmt.b.ṯql. | kkr.w.[ml]ṯḥ.tyt.[---] 2101.24
[---.-]kn. | [---.]ṯlṯm. | kuwṯ.ṯlṯ.kbd. | m[i]t.arb't.kbd. | ẖ[mš.]š'rt. | [---.]tš'.kbd.skm. 1111.3
| 'šr[.---]. | ud[-.---]. | ṯn pld mẖ[--.---]. | ṯ[--] ẖpnt. | [---] kdwṯm.[---]. | ẖmš.pld š'rt. | ṯṯ pld pṯt. | arb' ẖpnt pṯt. | ẖmš ẖ 1113.6
š'rt. | ṯṯ pld pṯt. | arb' ẖpnt pṯt. | ẖmš ẖpnt.š'rt. | ṯlṯ.'šr kdwṯm. 1113.11

kdl

. | [bn].ẖdmn.qšt.[w.u]ṯp[t].ṯ[--]. | [---].arb'.[---]. | [---].kdl[.---.mr]ḥm.w.ṯ[t.---]. | [---.mr]ḥm.w.ṯ[t.---]. | [---].ql'[.---]. 2047.11

kdln

ryn. | ẖbsn. | ulmk. | 'dršp. | bn.knn. | pdyn. | bn.aṯtl.ṯn. | kdln.akdṯb. | ṯn.b gt ykn'm. 1061.21

kdn

n[.---]. | bn [-]'y. | [b]n [i]lmd. | bn [t]bdn. | bn štn. | b[n] kdn. | bn dwn. | bn ḏrn. 2088.6
i. | ḏmrhd.bn.srt. | [---.--]m. | 'bdmlk.bn.šrn. | 'bdb'l.bn.kdn. | gzl.bn.qldn. | gld.bt.klb. | l[---].bt.ẖzli. | bn.iẖyn. | ṣdqn. 102[323].3.3
qrṯym.mddb'l. | kdn.zlyy. | krwn.arty. | tlmu.zlyy. | pdu.qmnzy. | bdl.qrṯy. | trg 89[312].2
.ubr. | bn.'pṯb. | ṯbry. | bn.ymn. | krty. | bn.abr[-]. | yrpu. | kdn. | p'ṣ. | bn.liy. | yd'. | šmn. | 'dy. | 'nbr. | aẖrm. | bn.qrdy. | bn 2117.1.23

kdr

m.w [---]. | kmm.w.in.'ṣr[.---]. | w mit.š'rt.[-]y[-.---]. | w.kdr.w.npt t[--.---]. | w.ksp.y'db.[---]. 38[23].10
--].ṯnn. | [---.--]b.kdr. | [---.--]m n'rt. | [---].qt.b[--]. | [---.]kd[r]. | [---.]ṯpr. | [---.]prš. | [---.]šdm. | [---.-]nm.prš.glbm. | [---. 1142.3
nḥm.arb' š[mn]. | w 'l bn a[--.-]yn ṯqlm. | [--] ksp [---] kdr [---]. | [-]ṯrn [k]sp [-]al[.-]r[-]. | [--]dšq krsnm. | ẖmšm [-]t 1103.11
[---.]d.mškbt. | [---.--]m. | [---].ṯlḥn. | [---].ṯnn. | [---.--]b.kdr. | [---.--]m n'rt. | [---].qt.b[--]. | [---.]kd[r]. | [---.]ṯpr. | [---.]p 1142.1

kdrl

'd[rš]p. | pqr. | ṯġr. | ttġl. | ṯn.yṣḥm. | slṯmg. | kdrl. | wql. | adrdn. | prn. | 'bdil. | ušy.šbn[-]. | aẖt.ab. | krwn. | n 1069.7
spr.updt. | d b d.mlkytn. | kdrl. | slṯmg. | adrdn. | l[l]wn. | ydln. | ldn. | tdġl. | ibrkyṯ. 1034.3

kdrn

. | arsw. | dqn. | ṯlṯ.klbm. | ẖmn. | [---.-]rsd. | bn[.-]pṯ. | bn kdrn. | awldn. | arswn.y'r[ty.--]. | bn.ugr. | gny. | ṯn.mdm. 86[305].8
---.ub]r'y. | [bn.---.ubr]'y. | b[n.---]. | bn[.---.ušk]ny. | bn.kdrn.uškny. | bn.lgn.uškny. | bn.abn.uškny. | bn.arz.š'rty. | bn 87[64].22
.sdy.bn.ṯty. | bn.ḥyn.bn.ġlm. | bn.yyn.w.bn.au[pš]. | bn.kdrn. | 'rgzy.w.bn.'dy. | bn.gmḥn.w.ḥgbt. | bn.tgḏn. | yny. | [b] 131[309].26

kdrš

ḫrny.w.rʿ h. | klbr.w.rʿ h. | tškrǵ.w.rʿ h. | ǵlwš.w.rʿ h. | kdrš.w.rʿ h. | ṯrm[-].w[.rʿ h]. | [ʾ]ṯtr[-].w.[rʿ h]. | ḫlly[-].w.rʿ[h 2083.1.5

kdrt

kbd h.b ṣḥ]q.ymlu.lb h. | [b šmḫt.kbd.ʿnt.tšyt.tḥt h.k]kdrt.riš. | [ʿl h.k irbym.kp.---.k br]k.tǵll.b dm. | [ḏmr.---.]td[- 7.1[131].8

rytm tmḫṣ.lim.ḫp y[m]. | tṣmt.adm.ṣat.š[p]š. | tḥt h.k kdrt.ri[š]. | ʿl h.k irbym.kp.k.qṣm. | ǵrmn.kp.mhr.ʿtkt. | rišt.l 3[ʿNT].2.9

kḏd

. | thw.hm.brlt.anḫr. | b ym.hm.brk y.tkšd. | rumm.ʿn.kḏd.aylt. | hm.imt.imt.npš.blt. | ḫmr.p imt.b klt. | yd y.ilḫm.h 5[67].1.17

. | thw.w npš. | anḫr.b ym. | brkt.šbšt. | k rumm.hm. | ʿn.kḏd.aylt. | mt hm.ks.ym | sk.nhr hm. | šbʿ.ydt y.b ṣʿ. | [--.]šbʿ.r UG5.4.8

kḏyn

ddy. | ypʿ.aḏddy. | abǵl.aḏ[ddy]. | abǵl.a[---]. | rbil.[---]. | kḏyn.[---.-]gṯ. | šmrm.a[ḏdd]y.tb[--]. | ynḥm.aḏddy. | ǵdǵd.aḏ 2014.28

kḏǵbr

.]ubn. | kbšm. | bn.abḏr. | bn.kpltn. | bn.prn. | ʿbdm. | bn.kḏǵbr. | bn.mṣrn. | bn.[-]dr[-]. | [---]l[-]. | [--]ym. | [--]rm. | [bn.] 114[324].2.11

kḏǵdl

l ym hnd. | ʿmṯtmr.bn. | nqmpʿ.ml[k]. | ugrt.ytn. | šd.kḏǵdl[.bn]. | [-]š[-]y.d.b š[-]y. | [---.y]d gt h[.--]. | [---.]yd. | [k]r 1008.5

]drdn. | [---]n. | pǵdn. | ṯṯpḥ. | ḥgbn. | šrm. | bn.ymil. | bn.kḏǵdl. | [-]mn. | [--]n. | [ḫr]š.qṭn. | [---]n. | [-----]. | [--]dd. | [bʿ]l.t 1039.2.4

khn

mrynm. | mrum. | ʿšrm. | ṯnnm. | nq[dm]. | kh[nm]. | inšt. 2019.6

bn.yšmʿ. | bdl.mḏrǵlm. | bn.mmy. | bn.ḫnyn. | bn.knn. | khnm. | bn.ṯʿy. | w.nḥl h. | w.nḥl hm. | bn.nqly. | bn.snrn. | bn.ṯ 104[316].9

. | ʿšrm. | inšt. | mdm. | gt.mlkym. | yqšm. | kbšm. | trrm. | khnm. | kzym. | yṣrm. | mru.ibrn. | mru.skn. | nsk.ksp | mḫṣm. 74[115].9

khnm. | qdšm. | mkrm. | mdm. | inšt. | ḫrš.bhtm. 75[81].1

khnm. | qdšm. | m[ru.]škn. | mkrm. 76[82].1

rn. | pslm. | šrm. | yṣḥm. | ʿšrm. | mrum. | ṯnnm. | mqdm. | khnm. | qdšm. | nsk.ksp. | mkrm. 71[113].72

mrynm. | mrum. | ʿšrm. | ṯnnm. | nqdm. | khnm. | qdšm. | pslm. | mkrm. | yṣḥm. | šrm. | nʿrm. | ʿbdm. | kz 1026.1.6

.yd. | ytr.kṯr.w ḫss. | spr.ilmlk šbny. | lmd.atn.prln.rb. | khnm rb.nqdm. | ṯʿy.nqmd.mlk ugr[t]. | adn.yrgb.bʿl.ṯrmn. 6.6[62.2].55

l.rb.khnm. | rgm. | tḥm.[---]. | yšlm[.l k.ilm]. | tšlm[k.tǵr] k. | tʿzz[55[18].1

. | šd.b d.ytpr. | šd.b d.krb[-]. | šd.b d.bn.ptḏ. | šd.b d.dr.khnm. | šd.b d.bn.ʿmy. | šd.b d.bn.ʿyn. | ṯn.šdm.b d.klṯtb. | šd. 2090.17

khnm.tšʿ. | bnšm.w.ḥmr. | qdšm.tšʿ. | bnšm.w.ḥmr. 77[63].1

.d.iwrkl. | ṯlṯ.šd.d.bn.mlkyy. | kmsk.šd.iḥmn. | širm.šd.khn. | ṯlṯ.šd.w.krm.šir.d.ḫli. | širm.šd.šd.ʿšy. | w.šir.šd.krm. | d 1079.5

[-----]. | bn.[---]. | bn.il[--]. | khnm[.--]. | bn.ṯ[--]. | bn.[---]. | bn.ṯʿl[-]. | bn.nq[ly]. | bn.snr[n]. 2020.4

n[-.---.--]n.nmr. | [--.]l ytk.bl[-.---.]m[--.]hwt. | [---].ṯllt.khn[m.---.]k pʿn. | [---.--]y.yd.nšy.[---.--]š.l mdb. | [---] h.mḫl UG5.8.47

. | [---.]šrt.aḥt. | [---.]šrt.aḥ. | [---.]šr.aḥt. | [---].šr[t]. | [---.k]hnm. | [---.š]rt.aḥt. | [---.šr]tm. | [---.]šrtm. | [---.šrt.]aḥt. 2162.C.7

ḫrṣn rb khnm. A.1

rb khnm. B.1

khp

----]. | [-----]. | [---.-]rb. | [-----]. | [-----]. | [-----]. | k yraš w ykhp mid. | dblt yṯnt w ṣmqm yṯn[m]. | w qmḥ bql yṣq aḥd h 160[55].23

ǵ[n.ḥmr.ydk]. | aḥd[h.w.yṣq.b.ap h]. | k yr[a]š.šš[w.w.ykhp]. | mid.dblt.yṯ[nt.w]. | ṣmq[m].yṯnm.w[.qmḥ.bql]. | tdkn 161[56].32

kwy

d.ʿl.ẓrm. | kd.ʿl.šz.bn pls. | kd.ʿl.ynḥm. | tgrm.šmn.d.bn.kwy. | ʿl.šlmym.ṯmn.kbd. | ṯṯm.šmn. 1082.2.8

kwn

lik.bn y. | lḥt.akl.ʿm y. | mid y w ǵbn y. | w.bn y.hn kt. | yškn.anyt. | ym.yšrr. | w.ak[l.---]. | [--].š[--.--]. 2061.13

.d šbʿ. | [a]ḫm.l h.ṯmnt.bn um. | krt.htk n.rš. | krt.grdš.mknt. | aṯt.ṣdq h.l ypq. | mtrḫt.yšr h. | aṯt.trḫ.w tbʿt. | ṯar um.t 14[KRT].1.11

.yṣq.ksp. | l alpm.ḫrṣ.yṣq | m.l rbbt. | yṣq-ḫym.w tbṯḫ. | kt.il.dt.rbtm. | kt.il.nbt.b ksp. | šmrgt.b dm.ḫrṣ. | kḥṯ.il.nḫt. | b 4[51].1.31

m.ḫrṣ.yṣq | m.l rbbt. | yṣq-ḫym.w tbṯḫ. | kt.il.dt.rbtm. | kt.il.nbt.b ksp. | šmrgt.b dm.ḫrṣ. | kḥṯ.il.nḫt. | b ẓr.hdm.id. | d 4[51].1.32

]b ḥbq h.ḥmḥmt. | [---.--] n.ylt.ḥmḥmt. | [---.mt.r]pi.w ykn.bn h. | [b bt.šrš.]b qrb.hkl h. | [nṣb.skn.i]lib h.b qdš. | [ztr 17[2AQHT].1.43

y.bn.qdš. | l tbrknn l ṯr.il ab y. | tmrnn.l bny.bnwt. | w ykn.bn h b bt.šrš.b qrb. | hkl h.nṣb.skn.ilib h.b qdš. | ztr.ʿm h 17[2AQHT].1.26

-]. | [---.--]y. | [-----]. | [any.l yṣ]ḥ.ṯr. | [il.ab h.i]l.mlk. | [d yknn h.yṣ]ḥ.aṯ | [rt.w bn h.]ilt. | [w ṣbrt.ary]h. | [wn.in.bt.l bʿ 4[51].1.7

h. | nbln.klny y.nbl.ks h. | any.l yṣḥ.ṯr.il.ab h.il. | mlk.d yknn h.yṣḥ.aṯrt. | w bn h.ilt.w ṣbrt.arḫ h. | wn.in.bt.l bʿl.km.i 3[ʿNT.VI].5.44

]. | klny n[.n]bl.ks h. | [an]y.l yṣḥ.ṯr il.ab h. | [i]l.mlk.d yknn h.yṣḥ. | aṯrt.w bn h.ilt.w ṣbrt. | ary h.wn.in.bt.l bʿl. | km 4[51].4.48

tḥm.ydn.ʿm.mlk. | bʿl h.nǵr.ḥwt k. | w l.a[--]t.tšknn. | ḫmšm.l mi[t].any. | tškn[n.--]h.k[--]. | w šnm[.--.]w[.-- 2062.1.3

r k.ank.ydʿt. | [-]n.atn.at.mṯb k[.---]. | [š]mm.rm.lk.prẓ kt. | [k]bkbm.ṯm.tpl k.lbnt. | [-.]rgm.k yrkt.ʿtqbm. | [---]m.ʿẓp 13[6].12

. | aṯt.ṣdq h.l ypq. | mtrḫt.yšr h. | aṯt.trḫ.w tbʿt. | ṯar um.tkn l h. | mṯlṯt.kṯrm.tmt. | mrbʿt.zblnm. | mḫmšt.yitsp. | ršp.nṯ 14[KRT].1.15

.ḥwt.ṯt h. | w.mnm.šalm. | dt.tknn. | ʿl.ʿrbnm. | hn hmt. | tknn. | mtn.bn.ʿbdym. | ilrb.bn.ilyn. | ʿbdadt.bn ʿbdkb. | gnʿym 1161.9

[nq]dm.dt.kn.npṣ hm. | [bn].lbn.arbʿ.qšt.w.ar[bʿ]. | [u]ṯpt.qlʿ.w.ṯt.mr[ḥ] 2047.1

. | b.mtn.bn.ayaḫ. | b.ḥbṯ h.ḥwt.ṯt h. | w.mnm.šalm. | dt.tknn. | ʿl.ʿrbnm. | hn hmt. | tknn. | mtn.bn.ʿbdym. | ilrb.bn.ilyn 1161.6

. | bn.ṯmq. | bn.agmn. | bn.uṣb. | bn.yzg. | bn.anntn. | bn.kwn. | ǵmšd. | bn.ʿbdḥy. | bn.ubyn. | slpd. | bn.atnb. | bn.ktmn. 115[301].4.8

tk.ri[š.]l mhr k. | w ʿp.l dr[ʿ].nšr k. | w rbṣ.l ǵr k.inbb. | kt ǵr k.ank.ydʿt. | [-]n.atn.at.mṯb k[.---]. | [š]mm.rm.lk.prẓ kt 13[6].10

m]. | w yʿny.aliyn[.bʿl]. | lm.k qnym.ʿl[m.--]. | k dr d.d yknn[.--]. | bʿl.yṣǵd.mli[.--]. | il hd.mla.u[--.--]. | blt.p btlt.ʿn[t] 10[76].3.7

kwn

b‘l h.nǵr.ḥwt k. | w l.a[--]t.tšknn. | ḫmšm.l mi[t].any. | tškn[n.--]h.k[--]. | w šnm[.--.]w[.--]. | w ‘prm.a[--.--]n. | [--.]ḫ[- 2062.1.5

kwsgt

l ydn.‘bd.mlk. | d št.‘l.ḫrd h. | špḥ.al.thbṭ. | ḫrd.‘ps.aḫd.kw | sgt. | ḫrd ksp.[--]r. | ymm.w[.---]. | [-----]. | w[.-----]. | [-----] 2062.2.6

kzbn

.b d.pln.nḥl h. | šd.irdyn.bn.ḫrǵš[-].l.qrt. | šd.iǵlyn.bn.kzbn.l.qr[t]. | šd.pln.bn.tiyn.b d.ilmhr nḥl h. | šd knn.bn.ann. 2029.17

kzy

inšt. | mdm. | gt.mlkym. | yqšm. | kbšm. | trrm. | khnm. | kzym. | yṣrm. | mru.ibrn. | mru.skn. | nsk.ksp | mḫṣm. | ksdm. | 74[115].10

m. | qdšm. | pslm. | mkrm. | yṣḥm. | šrm. | n‘rm. | ‘bdm. | kzym. | ksdm. | [nsk].ṯlṯ. | gt.mlkym. | tmrym. | ṯnqym. | ṯǵrm. 1026.1.14

bq. | hzp. | gn‘y. | m‘rby. | [ṣ]‘q. | [š]ḥq. | n‘rm. | mḫrǵlm. | kzym. | mru.skn. | mru.ibrn. | pslm. | šrm. | yṣḥm. | ‘šrm. | mru 71[113].62

[---.--]l[-.---]. | [---.]ypl[ṯ].---]. | [---.--]l.rb.kzym. | [---]y. | [-----]. | [-----]. | [--]dt.nsk.ṯlṯ. | [‘b]dršp.nsk.ṯlṯ. | 1102.3

kzn

. | bn.ḫzrn. | bn.iǵyn. | w.nḥl h. | bn.ksd. | bn.bršm. | bn.kzn. | w.nḥl h. | w.nḥl hm. | w.[n]ḥl hm. | b[n.---]. | bn.gzry. | b 113[400].2.20

ṣṣ.bn.ilyn.ṯlṯm. | ṣṣ.bn.kzn.ṯlṯm. | ṣṣ.bn.tlmyn.‘šrm. | ṣṣ.bn.krwn.‘š[rm]. | ṣṣ.bn.iršyn. 2096.2

kzǵb

n. | prn. | ‘bdil. | ušy.šbn[-]. | aḫt.ab. | krwn. | nnḏ. | mkl. | kzǵb. | iyrḏ. 1069.17

kḥṣ

y.rṯa.tnm y.ytn.[ks.b yd]. | krpn.b klat yd.[---]. | km ll.kḥṣ.tusp[.---]. | tgr.il.bn h.ṯr[.---]. | w y‘n.lṭpn.il.d p[id.---]. | š 1[‘NT.X].4.11

.ḥkmt.k ṯr.lṭpn. | ṣḥ.ngr.il.ilš.il[š]. | w aṯt h.ngrt[.i]lht. | kḥṣ.k m‘r[.---]. | yṣḥ.ngr il.ilš. | ilš.ngr.bt.b‘l. | w aṯt h.ngrt.ilh 16[126].4.6

kḥṯ

h.w y‘n.‘ṯtr.‘rẓ. | l amlk.b ṣrrt.ṣpn. | yrd.‘ṯtr.‘rẓ.yrd. | l kḥṯ.aliyn.b‘l. | w ymlk.b arṣ.il.kl h. | [---] š abn.b rḥbt. | [---] š 6.1.64[49.1.36]

.‘rẓ. | ymlk.‘ṯtr.‘rẓ. | apnk.‘ṯtr.‘rẓ. | y‘l.b ṣrrt.ṣpn. | yṯb.l kḥṯ.aliyn. | b‘l.p‘n h.l tmǵyn. | hdm.riš h.l ymǵy. | aps h.w y‘ 6.1.58[49.1.30]

tbṯḫ. | kt.il.dt.rbtm. | kt.il.nbt.b ksp. | šmrgt.b dm.ḫrṣ. | kḥṯ.il.nḫt. | b ẓr.hdm.id. | d prša.b br. | n‘l.il.d qblbl. | ‘ln.ybl 4[51].1.34

ṯrm.hn.ym. | w ṯn.yṯb.krt.l ‘d h. | yṯb.l ksi mlk. | l nḫt.l kḥṯ.drkt. | ap.yṣb.yṯb.b hkl. | w ywsrnn.ggn h. | lk.l ab k.yṣb.l 16.6[127].24

[.---]. | ydr.hm.ym[.---]. | ‘l amr.yu[ḫd.ksa.mlk h]. | nḫt.kḥṯ.d[rkt h.b bt y]. | aṣḥ.rpi[m.iqra.ilnym]. | b qrb.h[kl y.aṯr 22.1[123].18

---]. | w bn.dgn.b š[---]. | b‘l.yṯb.l ks[i.mlk h]. | bn.dgn.l kḥ[ṯ.drkt h]. | l alp.ql.ẓ[--.---]. | l np ql.nd.[----]. | tlk.w tr.b[ḫl 10[76].3.15

md. | ṣḥr mt.ymṣḫ.l arṣ. | [yṯb.]b[‘]l.l ksi.mlk h. | [---].l kḥṯ.drkt h. | l [ym]m.l yrḫm.l yrḫm. | l šnt.[m]k.b šb‘. | šnt.w 6[49].5.6

ym.ṣpn.mšṣṣ.[-]k‘[-]. | udn h.grš h.l ksi.mlk h. | l nḫt.l kḥṯ.drkt h. | mn m.ib.yp‘.l b‘l.ṣrt.l rkb.‘rpt. | [-]‘n.ǵlmm.y‘ny 3[‘NT].4.47

hm. | šm k.at.aymr.aymr.mr.ym.mr.ym. | l ksi h.nhr l kḥṯ.drkt h.trtqṣ. | b d b‘l.km.nšr b uṣb‘t h.hlm.qdq | d zbl y 2.4[68].20

hm.šm k at. | ygrš.ygrš.grš ym grš ym.l ksi h. | [n]hr l kḥṯ drkt h.trtqṣ.b d b‘l km nš | r.b uṣb‘t h.hlm.ktp.zbl ym.b 2.4[68].13

iyn b[‘l.---]. | kd.ynaṣn[.---]. | gršnn.l k[si.mlk h.l nḫt.l kḥṯ]. | drkt h.š[--.--]. | w hm.ap.l[--.---]. | ymḫṣ k.k[--.---]. | il.d 1[‘NT.X].4.24

‘r.mt. | b ql h.y[---.---]. | b‘l.yṯṯbn[.l ksi]. | mlk h.l[nḫt.l kḥṯ]. | drkt h[.---]. | [---.]d[--.---]. | [---].hn[.---]. | [---.]šn[.---]. 6[49].6.34

lak.ym.t‘dt.ṯpṭ.nhr. | tšu ilm rašt hm.l ẓr.brkt hm.ln.kḥṯ.zbl hm. | aḫr.tmǵyn.mlak ym.t‘dt.ṯpṭ.nhr.l p‘n.il. | [l t]pl 2.1[137].29

ym.t‘dt.ṯpṭ[.nhr]. | t[ǵ]ly.hlm.rišt hm.l ẓr.brkt hm.w l kḥṯ. | zbl hm.b hm.yg‘r.b‘l.lm.ǵltm.ilm.rišt. | km l ẓr brkt k 2.1[137].23

ilm.‘ny h. | w y‘n.lṭpn.il.b pid. | ṯb.bn y.lm ṯb[t] km. | l kḥṯ.zbl k[m.a]nk. | iḥtrš.w [a]škn. | aškn.ydt.[m]rṣ gršt. | zbln 16[126].5.25

.mlak.ym.t‘dt.ṯpṭ.nhr. | šu.ilm.rašt km.l ẓr.brkt km.ln.kḥṯ. | zbl km.w ank.‘ny.mlak.ym.t‘dt.ṯpṭ.nhr. | tšu ilm rašt h 2.1[137].27

.b hm.yg‘r.b‘l.lm.ǵltm.ilm.rišt. | km l ẓr brkt km.w ln.kḥṯ.zbl km.aḥd. | ilm.t‘ny lḥt.mlak.ym.t‘dt.ṯpṭ.nhr. | šu.ilm.r 2.1[137].25

[.yn]. | špq.ilm.alpm.y[n]. | špq.ilht.arḫt[.yn]. | špq.ilm.kḥṯm.yn. | špq.ilht.ksat[.yn]. | špq.ilm.rḥbt yn. | špq.ilht.dkrt[4[51].6.51

ky

k. | šnt.šntm.lm.l.tlk. | w.lḥt.akl.ky. | likt.‘m.špš. | b‘l k.ky.akl. | b.ḥwt k.inn. | špš n.[---]. | hm.al[k.--]. | ytnt[.---]. | ṯn[. 2060.19

b gt prn. | šd.bn.gby.gt.prn. | šd.bn.kryn.gt.prn. | šd.bn.ky.gt.prn. | šd.hwil.gt.prn. | šd.ḫr.gt.prn. | šd.bn.ṯbǵl.gt.prn. | 1104.6

[-----]. | dd l krwn. | dd l [--]n. | dd l ky. | dd l ‘bdkṯr. | dd[m] l r‘y. | [--] šmḫ[.---]. | ddm gt dprnm. 1101.4

m n.š[l]m. | ṯm ny.‘[m.]bn y. | mnm.[šl]m[.r]gm[.ṯṯb]. | ky.lik.bn y. | lḥt.akl.‘m y. | mid y w ǵbn y. | w.bn y.hn kt. | yš 2061.9

‘m.l.yd‘t. | ‘m y.špš.b‘l k. | šnt.šntm.lm.l.tlk. | w.lḥt.akl.ky. | likt.‘m.špš. | b‘l k.ky.akl. | b.ḥwt k.inn. | špš n.[---]. | hm.a 2060.17

rgm h. | w ht ab y ǵm[--]. | t[--.---]. | ls[--.---]. | ṣḥ[.---]. | ky.m[--.---]. | w pr[--.---]. | tštil[.---]. | ‘mn.bn[.---]. 1021.13

um y. | rgm. | ugrt.tǵr k. | ugrt.tǵr k. | tšlm k.um y. | td‘.ky.‘rbt. | l pn.špš. | w pn.špš.nr. | b y.mid.w um. | tšmḫ.m ab. | 1015.7

‘l y.u. | ‘[--.]mlakt.‘bd h. | [---.]b‘l k.yḫpn. | [---.]‘m h.u ky. | [---.--]d k.k.tmǵy. | ml[--.--]š[.ml]k.rb. | b[‘l y.---]. | yd[--.] 1018.5

kyn

b. | bn.b‘ltn ḫlq. | bn.mlkbn. | bn.asyy ḫlq. | bn.kṯly. | bn.kyn. | bn.‘bdḫr. | [-]prm ḫlq. | [---]n ḫlq. | bn m‘nt. | bn kbdy. | 2016.2.6

[---]. | tsn. | rpiy. | mrṯn. | ṯnyn. | apṯ. | šbn. | gbrn. | ṯb‘m. | kyn. | b‘ln. | ytršp. | ḫmšm.ṯmn.kbd. | tgmr.bnš.mlk. | d.b d.ad 1024.2.22

--.]d.bn.[---.]l.dqn. | [---.--]‘.šdyn.l ytršn. | [---.--]ṯ.‘bd.l.kyn. | k[rm.--.]l.i[w]rtdl. | ḥl.d[--.‘bd]yrḫ.b d.apn. | krm.i[--].l. 2027.2.9

w.ṯt.ṯprtm. | b.‘šr[m.]ksp. | ḫmš.kkr.ṣml. | b.‘šrt.b d.bn.kyn. | ‘šr.kkr.š‘rt. | b d.urtn.b.arb‘m. | arb‘t.‘šrt.ḫrṣ. | b.ṯqlm.k 2100.13

kky

bn.ǵs.ḥrš.š‘ty. | ‘dy.bn.sl‘y.gbly. | yrm.b‘l.bn.kky. 2121.3

kkln

]yn. | pǵdn.ilb‘l.krwn.lbn.‘dn. | ḫyrn.md‘. | šm‘n.rb ‘šrt.kkln.‘bd.absn. | šdyn.unn.dqn. | ‘bd‘nt.rb ‘šrt.mnḥm.ṯb‘m.sḫ 2011.5

‘bdyrḫ. | ubn.ḫyrn. | ybnil.adrdn. | klyn.kkln. | ‘dmlk.tdn. | ‘zn.pǵdn. | [a]nndn. | [r]špab. | [-]glm. 1070.4

.bn.ʿẓmt.rišy. | mit.l.tlmyn.bn.ʿdy. | [---.]l.ad̲dy. | [--.]l.kkln. 2095.10

kkn

šd.snrym.dt.ʿqb. | b.ayly. | šd.abršn. | šd.kkn.[bn].ubyn. | šd.bn.li[y]. | šd.bn.š[--]y. | šd.bn.t̲[---]. | šd.ʿd 2026.4

kknt

| w ymlk.b arṣ.il.kl h. | [---] š abn.b rḥbt. | [---] š abn.b kknt. 6.1.67[49.1.39]

kkr

ṣml. | ʿšrt.ksp h. | ḫmš.kkr.qnm. | t̲lt̲t.w.t̲lt̲t.ksp h. | arbʿ.kkr. | algbt̲.arbʿt. | ksp h. | kkr.šʿrt. | šbʿt.ksp h. | ḫmš.mqdm.d 1127.14
.t̲lt̲. | arbʿ.kkrm. | t̲mn.mat.kbd. | pwt. | t̲mn.mat.pt̲tm. | kkrm.alpm. | ḫmš.mat.kbd. | abn.ṣrp. 2051.8
t̲lt̲.d yṣa. | b d.šmmn. | l argmn. | l nskm. | t̲mn.kkrm. | alp.kbd. | [m]itm.kbd. 147[90].5
spr.ḥt̲bn.sbrdnm. | ḫmš.kkrm.alp kb[d]. | t̲lt̲.l.nskm.birtym. | b d.urtn.w.t̲t̲.mat.brr. | 2101.2
ʿšrm.kkr.kkrm. | alp.t̲t̲.mat.kbd. 2111.1
.kkr. | kkr.lqḥ.ršpy. | tmtrn.bn.pnmn. | kkr. | bn.sgt̲tn. | kkr. | ilšpš.kkr. | bn.d̲ltn. | kkr.w[.--]. | ḫ[--.---]. 1118.10
lqḥ.šʿrt. | urḫ.ln.kkrm. | w.rḥd.kd.šmn. | drt.b.kkr. | ubn.ḫṣḥ.kkr. | kkr.lqḥ.ršpy. | tmtrn.bn.pnmn. | kkr. | bn. 1118.4
lqḥ.ršpy. | tmtrn.bn.pnmn. | kkr. | bn.sgt̲tn. | kkr. | ilšpš.kkr. | bn.d̲ltn. | kkr.w[.--]. | ḫ[--.---]. 1118.11
.b.kkr. | ubn.ḫṣḥ.kkr. | kkr.lqḥ.ršpy. | tmtrn.bn.pnmn. | kkr. | bn.sgt̲tn. | kkr. | ilšpš.kkr. | bn.d̲ltn. | kkr.w[.--]. | ḫ[--.---]. 1118.8
skn.ʿšrm kk[r.---]. | mšrn.t̲lt̲.ʿš[r.kkr]. | bn.šw.šbʿ.kk[r.---]. | arbʿm.kkr.[---]. | b d.mtn.[l].šlm. 2108.2
d.ybnn. | arbʿ.mat. | l.alp.šmn. | nḥ.t̲t̲.mat. | šm[n].rqḥ. | kkrm.brd̲l. | mit.tišrm. | t̲lt̲m.almg. | ḫmšm.kkr. | qnm. | ʿšrm. 141[120].6
mit.šmn.d.nm[-.]b d.mzy.alzy. | ḫmš.kkr.ḥlb. | ḫmš.kkr.brr. | kkr.ḫmš.mat.kbd.t̲lt̲.šm[n]. | alp.mitm.kbd.t̲lt̲.ḥlb. | 1135.3
.brd̲l. | mit.tišrm. | t̲lt̲m.almg. | ḫmšm.kkr. | qnm. | ʿšrm.kk[r]. | brr. | [ʿ]šrm.npš. | ʿšrm.zt.mm. | ʿrbʿm. | šmn.mr. 141[120].11
t̲mn.kkr.t̲lt̲. | t̲mn.kkr.brr. | arbʿ.alpm.pḥm. | ḫmš.mat.kbd. | arbʿ.alpm.iqni. | ḫ 1130.2
šlt.b.t̲ql.ksp. | kdwt̲.l.grgyn.b.t̲q[l]. | ḫmšm.šmt.b.t̲ql. | kkr.w.[ml]th.tyt.[---]. | [b]šbʿ[m.w.n]ṣp.ksp. | [tgm]r.[alp.w.] 2101.26
lqḥ.šʿrt. | urḫ.ln.kkrm. | w.rḥd.kd.šmn. | drt.b.kkr. | ubn.ḫṣḥ.kkr. | kkr.lqḥ.ršp 1118.2
n.bn.pnmn. | kkr. | bn.sgt̲tn. | kkr. | ilšpš.kkr. | bn.d̲ltn. | kkr.w[.--]. | ḫ[--.---]. 1118.13
mit.šmn.d.nm[-.]b d.mzy.alzy. | ḫmš.kkr.ḥlb. | ḫmš.kkr.brr. | kkr.ḫmš.mat.kbd.t̲lt̲.šm[n]. | alp.mit 1135.2
n.d.nm[-.]b d.mzy.alzy. | ḫmš.kkr.ḥlb. | ḫmš.kkr.brr. | kkr.ḫmš.mat.kbd.t̲lt̲.šm[n]. | alp.mitm.kbd.t̲lt̲.ḥlb. | šbʿ.l.ʿšrm 1135.4
ʿšrm.kkr.kkrm. | alp.t̲t̲.mat.kbd. 2111.1
rt. | urḫ.ln.kkrm. | w.rḥd.kd.šmn. | drt.b.kkr. | ubn.ḫṣḥ.kkr. | kkr.lqḥ.ršpy. | tmtrn.bn.pnmn. | kkr. | bn.sgt̲tn. | kkr. | ilš 1118.5
rḫ.ln.kkrm. | w.rḥd.kd.šmn. | drt.b.kkr. | ubn.ḫṣḥ.kkr. | kkr.lqḥ.ršpy. | tmtrn.bn.pnmn. | kkr. | bn.sgt̲tn. | kkr. | ilšpš.kk 1118.6
[---.]ḫ[---.]tmnym[.k]sp ḫmšt. | [w a]rbʿ kkr ʿl bn[.--]. | [w] t̲lt̲ šmn. | [w a]r[bʿ] ksp ʿl bn ymn. | šb šr š 1103.2
.kmsk. | arbʿ[.k]dwtm.w.t̲t̲.tprtm. | b.ʿšr[m.]ksp. | ḫmš.kkr.ṣml. | b.ʿšrt.b d.bn.kyn. | ʿšr.kkr.šʿrt. | b d.urtn.b.arbʿm. | a 2100.12
t̲.mat.trm.b.ʿšrt. | mit.adrm.b.ʿšrt. | ʿšr.ydt.b.ʿšrt. | ḫmš.kkrm.ṣml. | ʿšrt.ksp h. | ḫmš.kkr.qnm. | t̲lt̲t.w.t̲lt̲t.ksp h. | arbʿ. 1127.10
šm[n].rqḥ. | kkrm.brd̲l. | mit.tišrm. | t̲lt̲m.almg. | ḫmšm.kkr. | qnm. | ʿšrm.kk[r]. | brr. | [ʿ]šrm.npš. | ʿšrm.zt.mm. | ʿrbʿm 141[120].9
b.ʿšrt. | ʿšr.ydt.b.ʿšrt. | ḫmš.kkrm.ṣml. | ʿšrt.ksp h. | ḫmš.kkr.qnm. | t̲lt̲t.w.t̲lt̲t.ksp h. | arbʿ.kkr. | algbt̲.arbʿt. | ksp h. | kk 1127.12
]. | t̲n.ḫblm.alp.alp.am[-]. | t̲mn.ḫblm.šbʿ.šbʿ.ma[-]. | ʿšr.kkr.rtn. | b d.šmʿy.bn.bdn. 1128.32
.t̲ql]m.kbd.ʿšrt.mzn h. | b [ar]bʿm.ksp. | b d[.ʿb]dym.t̲lt̲.kkr šʿrt. | iqn[i]m.t̲t̲t.ʿšrt.ksp h. | ḫmšt.ḫrṣ.bt.il. | b.ḫmšt.ʿšrt.k 2100.3
m. | b.ʿšr[m.]ksp. | ḫmš.kkr.ṣml. | b.ʿšrt.b d.bn.kyn. | ʿšr.kkr.šʿrt. | b d.urtn.b.arbʿm. | arbʿt.ʿšrt.ḫrṣ. | b.t̲qlm.kbd.arbʿm 2100.14
n.t̲dnyn. | ddm.ḫ[t̲m].ʿl.šrn. | ʿšrt.ksp.ʿl.[-]lpy. | bn.ady.kkr.šʿrt. | nt̲k h. | kb[d.]mn.ʿl.abršn. | b[n.---].kršu.nt̲k h. | [---. 1146.9
. | ḫmš.alp.t̲lt̲.l.ḫlby. | b d.tlmi.b.ʿšrm.ḫmšt. | kbd.ksp. | kkrm.šʿrt.št̲t.b d.gg[ʿt]. | b.ʿšrt.ksp. | t̲lt̲.ut̲bm.b d.alḫn.b.ʿšrt[. 2101.9
.qnm. | t̲lt̲t.w.t̲lt̲t.ksp h. | arbʿ.kkr. | algbt̲.arbʿt. | ksp h. | kkr.šʿrt. | šbʿt.ksp h. | ḫmš.mqdm.dnyn. | b.t̲ql.dprn.aḥd. | b.t̲ 1127.17
mš.t̲nt.d t̲l | t̲ mat. | t̲t̲.t̲nt.d alp | alpm.t̲lt̲ ktt. | alp.brr. | kkr.tznt. | ḫmšt.kkr tyt. 1130.16
at. | t̲t̲.t̲nt.d alp | alpm.t̲lt̲ ktt. | alp.brr. | kkr.tznt. | ḫmšt.kkr tyt. 1130.17
spr.irgmn. | t̲lt̲.ḫmš.alpm. | b d.brq.maḫdy. | kkr.t̲lt̲. | b d.bn.by.ar[y]. | alpm.t̲lt̲. | b d.šim.il[š]tmʿy. 1134.4
š.mat.kbd.t̲lt̲.šm[n]. | alp.mitm.kbd.t̲lt̲.ḥlb. | šbʿ.l.ʿšrm.kkr.t̲lt̲. | d.ybl.blym. 1135.6
n.b[n].ṣdqn. | w.kkrm.t̲lt̲. | mit.ksp.ʿmn. | bn.ulbtyn. | w.kkr.t̲lt̲. | ksp.d.nkly.b.šd. | mit.ḫmšt.kbd. | [l.]gmn.bn.usyy. | 1143.5
mitm.ksp.ʿmn.b[n].ṣdqn. | w.kkrm.t̲lt̲. | mit.ksp.ʿmn. | bn.ulbtyn. | w.kkr.t̲lt̲. | ksp.d.nkly.b. 1143.2
t̲mn.kkr.t̲lt̲. | t̲mn.kkr.brr. | arbʿ.alpm.pḥm. | ḫmš.mat.kbd. | arbʿ.a 1130.1
any.al[t̲y]. | d b atlg[.---]. | ḫmš ʿš[r]. | kkr.t̲[lt̲]. | t̲t hrt[m]. | t̲n mq[pm]. | ult.t̲l[t̲]. | krk.kly[.--]. | ḫmš. 2056.4
pr.lm.likt. | [--]y.k išal hm. | [--.ʿš]rm.kkr.t̲lt̲. | [--.]t̲lt̲m.kkr.t̲lt̲. | [--.]aštn.l k. | [--]y.kl.dbrm.hm[.--]. | [--]l.w.kl.mḫr k. 1022.5
--.--]d.ʿm y. | [--.]spr.lm.likt. | [--]y.k išal hm. | [--.ʿš]rm.kkr.t̲lt̲. | [--.]t̲lt̲m.kkr.t̲lt̲. | [--.]aštn.l k. | [--]y.kl.dbrm.hm[.--]. 1022.4
dbrm.hm[.--]. | [--]l.w.kl.mḫr k. | [--]tir.aštn.l [k]. | [---].kkr.t̲l[t̲]. 1022.10
iršt.yṣḥm. | arbʿ.alpm. | mitm.kbd.t̲lt̲. | arbʿ.kkrm. | t̲mn.mat.kbd. | pwt. | t̲mn.mat.pt̲tm. | kkrm.alpm. | ḫ 2051.4
ʿšr.ktnt. | ʿšr.rt̲m. | kkr[.-].ḫt. | mitm[.p]t̲tm. | t̲lt̲m[.---].kst. | alp.a[bn.ṣ]rp. 1114.3
k[r.---]. | mšrn.t̲lt̲.ʿš[r.kkr]. | bn.šw.šbʿ.kk[r.---]. | arbʿm.kkr.[---]. | b d.mtn.[l].šlm. 2108.4
ʿrm. | [---.]r[--.]ḫtm. | kr[--.]tp[n]. | kkr[.---]. | kkr[.---]. | kkr[.---]. | kkr[.---]. | k[kr.---]. | k[kr.---]. | [---.-]krr. | [---.]tmt̲tb 2037.1.8
smm. | [---.-]rbr dd šʿrm. | [---.]r[--.]ḫtm. | kr[--.]tp[n]. | kkr[.---]. | kkr[.---]. | kkr[.---]. | kkr[.---]. | k[kr.---]. | k[kr.---]. | [2037.1.6
]r[--.]ḫtm. | kr[--.]tp[n]. | kkr[.---]. | kkr[.---]. | kkr[.---]. | kkr[.---]. | k[kr.---]. | k[kr.---]. | [---.-]krr. | [---.]tmt̲tb. | [---.-]dy 2037.1.9
.-]rbr dd šʿrm. | [---.]r[--.]ḫtm. | kr[--.]tp[n]. | kkr[.---]. | kkr[.---]. | kkr[.---]. | kkr[.---]. | k[kr.---]. | k[kr.---]. | [---.-]krr. | 2037.1.7
| kr[--.]tp[n]. | kkr[.---]. | kkr[.---]. | kkr[.---]. | kkr[.---]. | k[kr.---]. | k[kr.---]. | [---.-]krr. | [---.]tmt̲tb. | [---.-]dy. | [---.]ʿdyi 2037.1.10
skn.ʿšrm kk[r.---]. | mšrn.t̲lt̲.ʿš[r.kkr]. | bn.šw.šbʿ.kk[r.---]. | arbʿm.kkr.[2108.1
skn.ʿšrm kk[r.---]. | mšrn.t̲lt̲.ʿš[r.kkr]. | bn.šw.šbʿ.kk[r.---]. | arbʿm.kkr.[---]. | b d.mtn.[l].šlm. 2108.3
n]. | kkr[.---]. | kkr[.---]. | kkr[.---]. | kkr[.---]. | k[kr.---]. | k[kr.---]. | [---.-]krr. | [---.]tmt̲tb. | [---.-]dy. | [---.]ʿdyin. | [---.]ʿb 2037.1.11

rn.ṯq[lm].|pdy.[----].|[i]lmlk.bn.[---].|[--]‘[-.---].|[---.k]kr.|[-----].|[---.k]kr. 122[308].2.1
----].|[i]lmlk.bn.[---].|[--]‘[-.---].|[---.k]kr.|[-----].|[---.k]kr. 122[308].2.3

kkrdn

m.|ṯnqym.|ṯǵrm.|mru.skn.|mru.ibrn.|yqšm.|trrm.|kkrdnm.|yṣrm.|ktrm.|mṣlm.|tkn[m].|ǵ[---].|ǵm[--]. 1026.2.10

kl

mn.|tlk.škn.‘l.ṣrrt.|adn k.šqrb.[---].|b mgn k.w ḫrṣ.l kl.|apnk.ǵzr.ilḥu.|[m]rḥ h.yiḫd.b yd.|[g]rgr h.bm.ymn.|[16.1[125].45
m.dlt.tlk.km.p[---].|[---.]bt.tḥbṭ.km.ṣq.ṣdr[.---].|[---.]kl.b kl.l pgm.pgm.l.b[---].|[---.]mdbm.l ḥrn.ḥr[n.---].|[---.--] 1001.1.26
lt.aṯr.|b‘l.ard.b arṣ.ap.|‘nt.ttlk.w tṣd.kl.ǵr.|l kbd.arṣ.kl.gb‘.|l [k]bd.šdm.tmǵ.l n‘m[y].|[arṣ.]dbr.ysmt.šd.|[šḥl] 5[67].6.27
mt.mh.|taršn.l btlt.‘nt.|an.itlk.w aṣd.kl.|ǵr.l kbd.arṣ.kl.gb‘.|l kbd.šdm.npš.ḫsrt.|bn.nšm.npš.hmlt.|arṣ.mǵt.l n‘ 6[49].2.16
y.aṯrt.|mǵ.l qdš.amrr.|idk.al.tnn.|pnm.tk.ḥqkpt.|il.kl h.kptr.|ksu.ṯbt h.ḥkpt.|arṣ.nḥlt h.|b alp.šd.rbt.|kmn.l p 3['NT.VI].6.14
[idk.al.ttn.pnm.tk.ḥkpt.il.kl h].|[kptr.]ks[u.ṯbt h.ḥkpt.arṣ.nḥlt h].|b alp.šd.r[bt.kmn.l 1['NT.IX].3.01
yn d.|ḥrš yd.šlḥm.ššqy.|ilm sad.kbd.hmt.b‘l.|ḥkpt.il.kl h.tšm‘.|mṯt.dnty.t‘db.imr.|b pḫd.l npš.kṯr.w ḫss.|l brlt. 17[2AQHT].5.21
ṯt.dnty.|tšlḥm.tššqy ilm.|tsad.tkbd.hmt.b‘l.|ḥkpt il.kl h.tb‘.kṯr.|l ahl h.hyn.tb‘.l mš|knt h.apnk.dnil.m[t].|rpi.a 17[2AQHT].5.31
.ṣpn.|yrd.‘ṯtr.‘rẓ.yrd.|l kḥṯ.aliyn.b‘l.|w ymlk.b arṣ.il.kl h.|[---] š abn.b rḥbt.|[---] š abn.b kknt. 6.1.65[49.1.37]
.|hlk.l alpm.ḫdd.|w l.rbt.kmyr.|aṯr.ṯn.ṯn.hlk.|aṯr.ṯlṯ.kl hm.|aḥd.bt h.ysgr.|almnt.škr.|tškr.zbl.‘ršm.|yšu.‘wr.| 14[KRT].4.183
hlk.l alpm.ḫdd.|w l rbt.kmyr.|[a]ṯr.ṯn.ṯn.hlk.|aṯr.ṯlṯ.kl hm.|yḥd.bt h.sgr.|almnt.škr.|tškr.zbl.‘ršm.|yšu.‘wr.mzl 14[KRT].2.95
dbḥ klyrḫ.|ndr.|dbḥ.|dt nat.|w ytnt.|ṯrmn w.|dbḥ kl.|kl ykly.|dbḥ k.sprt.|dt nat.|w qrwn.|l k dbḥ.|[--]r bt [- RS61[24.277.7]
klyrḫ.|ndr.|dbḥ.|dt nat.|w ytnt.|ṯrmn w.|dbḥ kl.|kl ykly.|dbḥ k.sprt.|dt nat.|w qrwn.|l k dbḥ.|[--]r bt [--].| RS61[24.277.8]
lt.tlk.km.p[---].|[---.]bt.tḥbṭ.km.ṣq.ṣdr[.---].|[---.]kl.b kl.l pgm.pgm.l.b[---].|[---.]mdbm.l ḥrn.ḥr[n.---].|[---.--]m.q 1001.1.26
yqḥ.mt.aṯryt.spsg.ysk.|[l]riš.ḫrṣ.l ẓr.qdqd y.|[--.]mt.kl.amt.w an.mtm.amt.|[ap.m]ṯn.rgmm.argm.qštm.|[----.]m 17[2AQHT].6.38
bn.|dgn.my.hmlt.aṯr.|b‘l.ard.b arṣ.ap.|‘nt.ttlk.w tṣd.kl.ǵr.|l kbd.arṣ.kl.gb‘.|l [k]bd.šdm.tmǵ.l n‘m[y].|[arṣ.]dbr. 5[67].6.26
y.|w ‘n.bn.ilm.mt.mh.|taršn.l btlt.‘nt.|an.itlk.w aṣd.kl.|ǵr.l kbd.arṣ.kl.gb‘.|l kbd.šdm.npš.ḫsrt.|bn.nšm.npš.hm 6[49].2.15

klat

t.|qṣ.mri.ndd.|y‘šr.w yšqyn h.|ytn.ks.b d h.|krpn.b klat.yd h.|b krb.‘ẓm.ridn.|mt.šmm.ks.qdš.|l tphn h.aṯt.krp 3['NT].1.11
rumm.‘n.kḏd.aylt.|hm.imt.imt.npš.blt.|ḥmr.p imt.b klt.|yd y.ilḥm.hm.šb‘.|ydt y.b ṣ‘.hm.ks.ymsk.|nhr.k[--].ṣḥ 5[67].1.19
‘pr.ḫbl ṯtm.[---.]|šqy.rṯa.tnm y.ytn.[ks.b yd].|krpn.b klat yd.[---].|km ll.kḥṣ.tusp[.---].|tgr.il.bn h.ṯr[.---].|w y‘n.l 1['NT.X].4.10
uṣb‘t h.‘d.ṯkm.|‘rb.b ẓl.ḫmt.lqḥ.|imr.dbḥ.b yd h.|lla.klatnm.|klt.lḥm h.d nzl.|lqḥ.msrr.‘ṣr.db[ḥ].|yṣq.b gl.ḥṯt.y 14[KRT].3.161
[.b ẓl.ḫmt].|qḥ im[r.b yd k].|imr.d[bḥ.bm].ymn.|lla.kl[atn]m.|klt.l[ḥm k.d]nzl.|qḥ.ms[rr.]‘ṣr.|dbḥ.ṣ[q.b g]l.ḥṯt 14[KRT].2.68
.[b]ḥbq.w ḥ[m]ḥmt.ytb[n].|yspr.l ḫmš.l ṣ[---.]šr.pḫr.klat.|tqtnṣn.w tldn.tld.[ilm.]n‘mm.agzr ym.|bn.ym.ynqm.b 23[52].57
n[--.---.-]š[--].|kpr.šb‘.bnt.rḥ.gdm.|w anhbm.klat.ṯǵrt.|bht.‘nt.w tqry.ǵlmm.|b št.ǵr.w hln.‘nt.tm|tḥṣ.b ‘ 3['NT].2.3
[-].l y‘mdn.i[---.---].|kpr.šb‘ bn[t.rḥ.gdm.w anhbm].|kla[t.ṯǵ]r[t.bht.‘nt.w tqry.ǵlmm.b št.ǵr].|ap ‘nt tm[tḥṣ.b ‘m 7.2[130].24

kli

tldn.|ṯrkn.|kli.|plǵn.|apšny.|‘rb[.---].|w.b.p[.--].|apš[ny].|b.yṣi h.|ḥw 2116.3

klb

yšnn.ytn.g h.|bky.b ḥy k.ab n.ašmḫ.|b l.mt k.ngln.k klb.|b bt k.n‘tq.k inr.|ap.ḫšt k.ap.ab.k mtm.|tmtn.u ḫšt k.l 16.1[125].15
.[tt]n.|g h.bky.b ḥ[y k.a]b n.|nšmḫ.b l.mt k.ngln.|k klb.[b]bt k.n‘tq.|k inr[.ap.]ḫšt k.|ap.ab.k mtm.tmtn.|u ḫšt 16.2[125].100
[l]krt.|k [k]lb.b bt k.n‘tq.k inr.|ap.ḫšt k.ap.ab.ik mtm.|tmtn.u ḫšt k.l 16.1[125].2
.|ilyn.|yrb‘m.|n‘mn.|bn.kbl.|kn‘m.|bdlm.|bn.ṣǵr.|klb.|bn.mnḥm.|bn.brqn.|bn.‘n.|bn.‘bdy.|‘bd‘ttr. 1046.3.44
.]arb‘.mṯbt.azmr.b h.š.šr[-].|al[p.w].š.šlmm.pamt.šb‘.klb h.|yr[--.]mlk.ṣbu.špš.w.ḥl.mlk.|w.[---].ypm.w.mḥ[--].t[ṯ 35[3].52
b hm.tṯṯb[.--]d h.|km trpa.hn n‘r.|d yšt.l.lṣb h ḫš‘r klb.|[w]riš.pqq.w šr h.|yšt.aḥd h.dm zt.ḫrpnt. UG5.1.2.4
mdrǵlm.d.b.i[-]‘lt.mlk.|arsw.|dqn.|ṯlṯ.klbm.|ḫmn.|[---.-]rsd.|bn[.-]pṯ.|bn kdrn.|awldn.|arswn.y‘ 86[305].4
.|‘bdmlk.bn.šrn.|‘bdb‘l.bn.kdn.|gzl.bn.qldn.|gld.bt.klb.|l[---].bt.ḫzli.|bn.iḫyn.|ṣdqn.bn.ass.|b‘lyskn.bn.ss.|ṣdq 102[323].3.5
r.]ṯiqt.|ibr h[.l]ql.nhqt.|ḥmr[h.l g‘t.]alp.|ḥrṯ[.l z]ǵt.klb.|[ṣ]pr[.apn]k.|[pb]l[.mlk.g]m.l aṯt |[h.k]y[ṣḥ.]šm‘.m‘.| 14[KRT].5.226
mlk.l qr.ṯigt.ibr h.|l ql.nhqt.ḥmr h.|l g‘t.alp.ḥrṯ.zǵt.|klb.ṣpr.w ylak.|mlakm.l k.‘m.krt.|mswn h.ṯḥm.pbl.mlk.|q 14[KRT].3.123
.|šd.b d[.---]im.|šd.b d[.bn.--]n.|šd.b d.iwrkl.|šd.b d.klb.|šd.b d.klby.|šd.b d.iytlm.|ṯn.šdm.b d.amtrn.|šd.b d.i 2090.9

klby

kld.|kbln.‘bdyrǵ.ilgt.|ǵyrn.ybnn qrwn.|ypltn.‘bdnt.|klby.aḥrṯp.|ilyn.‘lby.ṣdkn.|gmrt.ṯlmyn.|‘bdnt.|bdy.ḥrš ark 1045.5
-].|ḥy bn.dnn.ṯkt.|ilṯḥm.bn.dnn.ṯkt.|šb‘l.bn.aly.ṯkt.|klby.bn.iḥy.ṯkt.|psš.bn.buly.ṯkt.|‘pṣpn.bn.‘dy.ṯkt.|n‘mn.bn 2085.7
ṯn.bn.klby.|bn.iytr.|[‘]bdyrḫ.|[b]n.gg‘t.|[‘]dy.|armwl.|uwaḫ.|y 2086.1
mil.bn.[---].|dly.bn[.---].|ynḥm.bn[.---].|gn.bn[.---].|klby.[bn.---].|šmmlk bn[.---].|‘myn.bn.[---].|mtb‘l.bn[.---].| 102[322].5.8
.‘bd.[---].|nsk.ḥdm.klyn[.ṣd]qn.‘bdilt.b‘l.|annmn.‘dy.klby.dqn.|ḥrtm.ḥgbn.‘dn.ynḥm[.---].|ḥrš.mrkbt.‘zn.[b]‘ln.ṯ 2011.26
m[.---].|ḥrš.mrkbt.‘zn.[b]‘ln.ṯb[--.-]nb.trtn.|[---]mm.klby.kl[--].dqn[.---].|[-]ntn.artn.b d[.--]nr[.---].|‘zn.w ymd.š 2011.29
---.--]m.|[šd.---.b d.]ṯpṭb‘l.|[šd.---.]b d.ymz.|[šd.b d].klby.psl.|[ub]dy.mri.ibrn.|[š]d.bn.bri.b d.bn.ydln.|[u]bdy.ṯ 82[300].2.4
w.ql‘.|t[t]n.qšt.w.ql‘.|u[l]n.qšt.w.ql‘.|y‘rn.qšt.w.ql‘.|klby.qšt.w.ql‘.|bq‘t.|ily.qšt.w.ql‘.|bn.ḥrẓn.qšt.w.ql‘.|tgrš.q 119[321].2.19
]im.|šd.b d[.bn.--]n.|šd.b d.iwrkl.|šd.b d.klb.|šd.b d.klby.|šd.b d.iytlm.|ṯn.šdm.b d.amtrn.|šd.b d.iwrm[--].|šd. 2090.10
tḥm.iwrdr.|l.plsy.|rgm.|yšlm.l k.|l.trǵds.|w.l.klby.|šm‘t.ḫti.|nḥtu.ht.|hm.in mm.|nḥtu.w.lak.|‘m y.w.y 53[54].6
dg.|bn.ḥgbn.|bn.tmr.|bn.prsn.|bn.ršpy.|[‘]bdḥgb.|[k]lby.|[-]ḥmn.|[š]pšyn.|[‘b]dmlk.|[---]yn.|bn.ṯ[--].|bn.idr 113[400].1.24
ṯ.|ḥrš.btm.|ršpab.|[r]ṣn.|[a]ǵlmn.|[a]ḫyn.|[k]rwn.|[k]l[by].|[--]ṯn.|[---]d.|a[ǵ]ltn.|[-----].|[--]ny.|kn‘m.|[-]p[-]. 2060.13
.|‘myn.bn ǵḥpn.|bn.kbln.|bn.bly.|bn.ṯ‘y.|bn.nṣdn.|klby. 104[316].9

klbr

ḫrny.w.r‘ h. | klbr.w.r‘ h. | tškrǵ.w.r‘ h. | ǵlwš.w.r‘ h. | kdrš.w.r‘ h. | ṯrm[-]. 2083.1.2

klbt

šb‘t.rašm. | mḫšt.mdd ilm.ar[š]. | ṣmt.‘gl.il.‘tk. | mḫšt.klbt.ilm išt. | klt.bt.il.ḏbb.imtḫṣ.ksp. | itrṯ.ḫrṣ.ṭrd.b‘l. | b mry 3['NT].3.42

kld

bnš.kld. | kbln.‘bdyrǵ.ilgt. | ǵyrn.ybnn qrwn. | ypltn.‘bdnt. | klby.a 1045.1

kly

qmḥ.d.kly.b bt.skn. | l.illḏrm. | ltḥ.ḫsr.b.šb‘.ddm. 2093.1
yn.d.ykl.b d.[---]. | b.dbḥ.mlk. | dbḥ ṣpn. | [-]zǵm. | [i]lib. | [i]lbldn. | 2004.1
šph.lṭpn.l yḥ. | w y‘ny.krt.ṯ‘. | bn.al.tbkn.al. | tdm.l y.al tkl.bn. | qr.‘n k.mḫ.riš k. | udm‘t.ṣḥ.aḫt k. | ṯtmnt.bt.ḥmḥ h. | 16.1[125].26
mḫšt.mdd ilm.ar[š]. | ṣmt.‘gl.il.‘tk. | mḫšt.klbt.ilm išt. | klt.bt.il.ḏbb.imtḫṣ.ksp. | itrṯ.ḫrṣ.ṭrd.b‘l. | b mrym.ṣpn.mšṣṣ.[- 3['NT].3.43
št.b‘l.[ṭ]‘n.iṭ‘n k. | [---.]ma[---] k.k tmḫṣ. | [ltn.bṯn.br]ḥ.tkly. | [bṯn.‘qltn.]šlyṭ. | [d šb‘t.rašm].ṯtkḥ. | [ttrp.šmm.k rks.ip 5[67].1.28
k tmḫṣ.ltn.bṯn.brḥ. | tkly.bṯn.‘qltn. | šlyṭ.d šb‘y.rašm. | ṯtkḥ.ttrp.šmm.k rs. | ipd k. 5[67].1.2
lyrḫ. | ndr. | dbḥ. | dt nat. | w ytnt. | ṯrmn w. | dbḥ kl. | kl ykly. | dbḥ k.sprt. | dt nat. | w qrwn. | l k dbḥ. | [--]r bt [--]. | [-- RS61[24.277.8]
ḥd.b aḫ k.l[--]n. | hn[-.]aḥẓ[.---]l[-]. | [‘]nt.akl[y.nšm]. | akly.hml[t.arṣ]. | w y[-]l.a[---]. | š[--.---]. | bl[.---]. 6[49].5.25
pn.yšu g h.w yṣḥ. | aḫ y m.ytnt.b‘l. | spu y.bn m.um y.kl | y y.yt‘n.k gmrm. | mt.‘z.b‘l.‘z.ynghn. | k rumm.mt.‘z.b‘l. | 6[49].6.15
].bn.ilm.mt. | p[-]n.aḫ y m.ytn.b‘l. | [s]pu y.bn m.um y.kly y. | ytb.‘m.b‘l.ṣrrt. | ṣpn.yšu g h.w yṣḥ. | aḫ y m.ytnt.b‘l. | s 6[49].6.11
rm. | nšu.[r]iš.ḥrṯm. | l ẓr.‘db.dgn kly. | lḥm.[b]‘dn hm.kly. | yn.b ḥmt hm.k[l]y. | šmn.b q[b‘t hm.---]. | bt.krt.t[--]. 16[126].3.14
qmḥ.d.kly.k ṣḥ.illḏrm. | b d.zlb[n.--]. | arb‘.‘š[r.]dd.n‘r. | d.apy[.--]. | 2094.1
. | l tbrkn.alk brkt. | tmrn.alk.nmr[rt]. | imḫṣ.mḫṣ.aḫ y.akl[.m] | kly[.‘]l.umt y.w y‘n[.dn] | il.mt.rpi npš ṯḥ[.pǵt]. | ṯ[k 19[1AQHT].4.196
‘r. | ṯl.yd‘t.hlk.kbkbm. | a[-]ḥ.hy.mḫ.tmḫṣ.mḫṣ[.aḫ k]. | tkl.m[k]ly.‘l.umt[k.--]. | d ttql.b ym.trtḥ[ṣ.--]. | [----.a]dm.tiu 19[1AQHT].4.202
t.ksmm. | ‘l.tl[-]k.‘ṭrtrm. | nšu.[r]iš.ḥrṯm. | l ẓr.‘db.dgn kly. | lḥm.[b]‘dn hm.kly. | yn.b ḥmt hm.k[l]y. | šmn.b q[b‘t h 16[126].3.13
n. | b rḥm.ttḥnn.b šd. | tdr‘nn.šir h.l tikl. | ‘ṣrm.mnt h.l tkly. | npr[m.]šir.l šir.yṣḥ. 6[49].2.36
anšt.im[-]. | aḥd.b aḫ k.l[--]n. | hn[-.]aḥẓ[.---]l[-]. | [‘]nt.akl[y.nšm]. | akly.hml[t.arṣ]. | w y[-]l.a[---]. | š[--.---]. | bl[.---]. 6[49].5.24
rkn.alk brkt. | tmrn.alk.nmr[rt]. | imḫṣ.mḫṣ.aḫ y.akl[.m] | kly[.‘]l.umt y.w y‘n[.dn] | il.mt.rpi npš ṯḥ[.pǵt]. | ṯ[km]t. 19[1AQHT].4.196
ṯl.yd‘t.hlk.kbkbm. | a[-]ḥ.hy.mḫ.tmḫṣ.mḫṣ[.aḫ k]. | tkl.m[k]ly.‘l.umt[k.--]. | d ttql.b ym.trtḥ[ṣ.--]. | [----.a]dm.tium.b 19[1AQHT].4.202
n.b]‘l. | ik.mǵyt.b[t]lt. | ‘nt.mḫṣ y hm[.m]ḫṣ. | bn y.hm[.mkly.ṣ]brt. | ary y[.ẓl].ksp.[a]ṭrt. | k t‘n.ẓl.ksp.w n[-]t. | ḫrṣ.š 4[51].2.25
. | l ẓr.‘db.dgn kly. | lḥm.[b]‘dn hm.kly. | yn.b ḥmt hm.k[l]y. | šmn.b q[b‘t hm.---]. | bt.krt.t[--]. 16[126].3.15
ql. | l arṣ.tngṣn.pnt h.w ydlp.tmn h. | yqṯ b‘l.w yšt.ym.ykly.ṯpṭ.nhr. | b šm.tg‘r m.‘ṯtrt.bṯ l aliyn.[b‘l.] | bṯ.l rkb.‘rpt.k 2.4[68].27
š ‘š[r]. | kkr.ṯ[lṯ]. | ṯt hrt[m]. | ṯn mq[pm]. | ulṯ.ṯl[ṯ]. | krk.kly[.--]. | ḥmš.mr[kbt]. | ṯṯ [-]az[-]. | ‘št[--.---]. | irg[mn.---]. | kr 2056.8
bm]. | w tqr[y.ǵlmm.b št.ǵr.---]. | [‘]d tš[b‘.tmtḫṣ.---]. | klyn[.---]. | špk.l[---]. | trḥṣ.yd[h.---]. | [--.]yṣt ḏm[r.---]. | tšt[. 7.2[130].6
| [-.]rbt.ṯbt.[---]. | rbt.ṯbt.ḫš[n.---]. | y.arṣ.ḫšn[.---]. | t‘td.tkl.[---]. | tkn.lbn[.---]. | dt.lbn k[.---]. | dk k.kbkb[.---]. | dm.m 5[67].3.5

klyn

b[---.---]. | b tn[--.---]. | swn.qrty[.---]. | uḫ h.w.‘šr[.---]. | klyn.apsn[y.---]. | plzn.qrty[.---]. | w.klt h.b.t[--.---]. | b‘l y.ml 81[329].10
ar. | bn.šyn. | bn.ubrš. | bn.d[--]b. | abrpu. | bn.k[n]y. | bn.klyn. | bn.gmḥn. | ḥnn. | ayab. | bn.gm[--]. | bn.[---]. | g[---]. | p[- 1035.3.7
. | adr[dn]. | krwn. | arkdn. | ilmn. | abškn. | ykn. | ršpab. | klyn. | ḥgbn. | ḥṯṯn. | ‘bdmlk. | y[--]k. | [-----]. | pǵdn. | [--]n. | [--] 1024.1.17
‘bdyrḫ. | ubn.ḫyrn. | ybnil.adrdn. | klyn.kkln. | ‘dmlk.tdn. | ‘zn.pǵdn. | [a]nndn. | [r]špab. | [-]glm. 1070.4
‘.skn.qrt. | nǵr krm.‘bdadt.b‘ln.yp‘mlk. | ṯǵrm.mnḥm.klyn.‘dršp.ǵlmn. | [a]bǵl.ṣṣn.ǵrn. | šib.mqdšt.‘b[dml]k.ṯtpḥ.m 2011.13
[bd]g. | ḥrš qṭn[.---.]dqn.b‘ln. | ǵltn.‘bd.[---]. | nsk.ḥdm.klyn[.ṣd]qn.‘bdilt.b‘l. | annmn.‘dy.klby.dqn. | ḥrṯm.ḥgbn.‘dn. 2011.25

klyrḫ

dbḥ klyrḫ. | ndr. | dbḥ. | dt nat. | w ytnt. | ṯrmn w. | dbḥ kl. | kl ykly. RS61[24.277.1]

klyt

.id]y.alt.l aḫš.idy.alt.in l y. | [--]t.b‘l.ḥẓ.ršp.b[n].km.yr.klyt h.w lb h. | [ṯ]n.p k.b ǵr.ṯn.p k.b ḫlb.k tgwln.šnt k. | [--.] 1001.1.3

klkl

[-]y.d.b š[-]y. | [---.y]d gt h[.--]. | [---.]yd. | [k]rm h.yd. | [k]lkl h. | [w] ytn.nn. | l.b‘ln.bn. | kltn.w l. | bn h.‘d.‘lm. | šḫr.‘l 1008.10
r. | [---.]ṯn.alpm. | [---.ṯ]n alpm. | [---.--]r[.‘]šr.ṣin. | [---.]klkl. 1142.8

kll

.šb‘[d.qlt]. | ankn.rgmt.l.b‘l y. | l.špš.‘lm.l.‘ṯtrt. | l.‘nt.l.kl.il.alṯ[y]. | nmry.mlk.‘lm. | mlk n.b‘l y.ḥw[t.--]. | yšhr k.w.‘ 2008.1.8
š h d.ytn.ṣṭqn. | ṭut ṭbḫ ṣṭq[n]. | b bz ‘zm ṭbḫ š[h]. | b kl ygz ḥḫ š h. 1153.5
. | [--.‘š]rm.kkr.ṯlṯ. | [--.]ṯlṯm.kkr.ṯlṯ. | [--.]aštn.l k. | [--]y.kl.dbrm.hm[.--]. | [--]l.w.kl.mḫr k. | [--]tir.aštn.l [k]. | [---].kkr 1022.7
| hn dt.b.ṣr. | mtt.by. | gšm.adr. | nškḥ.w. | rb.tmtt. | lqḥ.kl.ḏr‘. | b d a[-]m.w.ank. | k[l.]ḏr‘ hm. | [--.n]pš[.-]. | w [k]l hm 2059.17
.adr. | nškḥ.w. | rb.tmtt. | lqḥ.kl.ḏr‘. | b d a[-]m.w.ank. | k[l.]ḏr‘ hm. | [--.n]pš[.-]. | w [k]l hm.b d. | rb.tmtt.lqḥt. | w.ṯṯb. 2059.19
n.ṯkt.b glṯ. | w tn.ql h.b ‘rpt. | šrh.l arṣ.brqm. | bt.arzm.yklln h. | hm.bt.lbnt.y‘msn h. | l yrgm.l aliyn b‘l. | ṣḥ.ḫrn.b b 4[51].5.72
arb‘.yn.l.mrynm.ḥ[--].kl h. | kdm.l.zn[-.---]. | kd.l.aṯr[y]m. | kdm.‘m.[--]n. | kd.mštt.[1089.1
.]rgm y. | [-]wd.r[-.]pǵt. | [---.--]t.yd‘t. | [----.r]gm. | [---].kll h. | [---.--]l y. | [---.--]r. | [--.]wk[--.---]. | [--].lm.l[--.---]. | [-] 54.1.26[43.9]
[-----]. | [---.--]ty.l[--.---]. | [--.--]tm.w ‘[--.--]. | [---].w kl.hw[.---]. | w [--].brt.lb[--.---]. | u[-]šhr.nuš[-.---]. | b [u]grt.w 54.1.4[13.1.1]
.kl.ḏr‘. | b d a[-]m.w.ank. | k[l.]ḏr‘ hm. | [--.n]pš[.-]. | w [k]l hm.b d. | rb.tmtt.lqḥt. | w.ṯṯb.ank.l hm. | w.any k.ṯt. | by.‘k 2059.21
ḥ.ilm. | aṯr.ilm.ylk.p‘nm. | mlk.p‘nm.yl[k]. | šb‘.pamt.l kl hm. 33[5].26

m.|tšmḫ.m ab.|w al.trḥln.|‘tn.ḫrd.ank.|‘m ny.šlm.|kll.|w mnm.|šlm ‘m.|um y.|‘m y.ṯṯb.|rgm. 1015.15
|w š ḥll ydm.|b qdš il bt.|w tlḥm aṯt.|š l ilbt.šlmm.|kll ylḥm b h.|w l bbt šqym.|š l uḫr ḫlmṭ.|w tr l qlḥ.|ym a UG5.11.10
tḥm.špš.|l.‘mrpi.rgm.|‘m špš.kll.mid m.|šlm.|l.[--]n.špš.|ad[.‘]bd h.uk.škn.|k.[---.]sglt h. 2060.3
ny.|mrḥqtm.|qlny.ilm.|tǵr k.|tšlm k.|hn ny.‘m ny.|kll.mid.|šlm.|w.ap.ank.|nḫt.ṯm ny.|‘m.adt ny.|mnm.šlm. 51[95].11
m.kkr.ṯlṯ.|[--.]aštn.l k.|[--]y.kl.dbrm.hm[.--].|[--]l.w.kl.mḫr k.|[--]tir.aštn.l [k].|[---].kkr.ṯl[ṯ]. 1022.8
l k.ilm].|tǵ[r k.tšlm k].|‘bd[.---]y.|‘m[.---]y.|šk[--.--.]kll.|šk[--.--.]hm.|w.k[b--.---].|‘m[.---]m ib.|[---.--]m.|[-----]. 2065.5
.|qlt.l.um y.|yšlm.ilm.|tǵr k.tšlm k.|hl ny.‘m n[y].|kll.šlm.|ṯm ny.‘m.um y.|mnm.šlm.|w.rgm.ṯṯb.l y.|bm.ṯy.n 50[117].10
tǵr k.tšlm k.|lḥt.šlm.k.lik[t].|um y.‘m y.ht.‘m[ny].|kll.šlm.ṯm ny.|‘m.um y.mnm.šlm.|w.rgm.ṯṯb.l y.|w.mnd‘. 2009.1.7
[---.--]y.hnn.|[---.kll].šlm.|[---.ṯ]mn.‘m k.|[m]nm.šlm.|[---.w.r]gm.ṯṯb. 2171.2
qbr.tṣr.q[br].|tṣr.trm.tnq[--].|km.nkyt.tǵr[.---].|km.škllt.[---].|‘r.ym.l bl[.---].|b[---.]ny[.--].|l bl.sk.w [---] h.|yb 16.2[125].90
[.---].|[---].yṯbr[.---].|[---.]uṭm.ḏr[qm.---].|[btl]t.‘nt.l kl.[---].|[tt]b‘.btlt.‘nt[.idk.l ttn.pnm].|‘m.yṭpn.mhr.š[t.tšu.g 18[3AQHT].4.4
|[-----].|[-----].|[---].ḫmš[.---].|[---.]urš[-.---].|[---.]yd.kl.[---]. 2156.10

kln

uldy.|synn.bn kn‘m.|bn kbr.|bn iytlm.|bn ayln.|bn.kln.|bn.‘lln.|bn.liy.|bn.nqṭn.|bn abrḫṭ.|bn.grdy.|bn.ṣlpn.| 1064.23

klny

k.|mlk n.aliyn.b‘l.ṯpṭ n.|in.d ‘ln h.klny y.qš h.|nbln.klny y.nbl.ks h.|any.l yṣḥ.ṯr.il.ab h.il.|mlk.d yknn h.yṣḥ.aṯ 3[‘NT.VI].5.42
.‘lm.ḥyt.ḥẓt.ṯḥm k.|mlk n.aliyn.b‘l.ṯpṭ n.|in.d ‘ln h.klny y.qš h.|nbln.klny y.nbl.ks h.|any.l yṣḥ.ṯr.il.ab h.il.|ml 3[‘NT.VI].5.41
n.aliy[n.]b‘l.|ṯpṭ n.w in.d ‘ln h.|klny n.q[š] h.n[bln].|klny n[.n]bl.ks h.|[an]y.l yṣḥ.ṯr il.ab h.|[i]l.mlk.d yknn h.y 4[51].4.46
.ḥyt.ḥẓt.|ṯḥm k.mlk n.aliy[n.]b‘l.|ṯpṭ n.w in.d ‘ln h.|klny n.q[š] h.n[bln].|klny n[.n]bl.ks h.|[an]y.l yṣḥ.ṯr il.ab h 4[51].4.45

klnmw

sp.l bnš tpnr.|arb‘.spm.l.lbnš prwsdy.|ṯṯ spm.l bnš klnmw.|l yarš ḫswn.|ḫmš ‘šr.sp.|l bnš tpnr d yaḫd l g ynm 137.2[93].8
urtm l [---].|[-----.]a[---].|[---.--]ln.|[---.]kqmṯn.|[---.]klnmw.|[---.]w yky.|ṯlṯm sp.l bnš tpnr.|arb‘.spm.l.lbnš pr 137.2[93].4

klt

spr.tbṣr.|klt.bt špš. 1175.2
.|uḫ h.w.‘šr[.---].|klyn.apsn[y.---].|plzn.qrty[.---].|w.klt h.b.t[--.---].|b‘l y.mlk[y.---].|yd.bt h.yd[.---].|ary.yd.t[-- 81[329].12
|ary.yd.t[--.---].|ḫtn h.šb‘l[.---].|ṯlḥny.yd[.---].|yd.ṯlṯ.kl[t h.---].|w.ṯtm.ṣi[n.---].|tn[--].|agyn.[---].|[w].ṯn.[---]. 81[329].18
ḥdd.ar[y.---].|b‘lsip.a[ry.---].|klt h.[---].|tty.ary.m[--.---].|nrn.arny[.---].|w.ṯn.bn h.w.b[-- 81[329].3
pdr[y.bt.ar.mẓll].|ṭly.bt.r[b.mṯb.arṣy].|bt.y‘bdr[.mṯb.klt].|knyt.w t‘n[.btlt.‘nt].|yṯb l y.ṯr.il[.ab y.---].|yṯb.l y.w l 3[‘NT.VI].4.5
n.aṯ]r[t].|m[ṯ]b.il.mẓll.|bn h.mṯb.rbt.|aṯrt.ym.mṯb.|klt.knyt.|mṯb.pdry.b ar.|mẓll.ṭly.bt rb.|mṯb.arṣy.bt.y‘bdr. 4[51].1.16
ẓr.k bn.aṯrt.|mṯb il.mẓll.bn h.|mṯb rbt.aṯrt.ym.|mṯb.klt.knyt.|mṯb.pdry.bt.ar.|mẓll.ṭly.bt rb.|mṯb.arṣ.bt y‘bdr.| 4[51].4.54
]y.bt.ar.|[mẓll.]ṭly[.bt.]rb.mṯb.|[arṣy.bt.y‘bdr.mṯb].|[klt.knyt]. 3[‘NT.VI].5.52
.ṯkm.|‘rb.b ẓl.ḫmt.lqḥ.|imr.dbḥ.b yd h.|lla.klatnm.|klt.lḥm h.d nzl.|lqḥ.msrr.‘ṣr.db[ḥ].|yṣq.b gl.ḥṯṯ.yn.|b gl.ḫr 14[KRT].3.162
.|qḥ im[r.b yd k].|imr.d[bḥ.bm].ymn.|lla.kl[atn]m.|klt.l[ḥm k.d]nzl.|qḥ.ms[rr.]‘ṣr.|dbḥ.ṣ[q.b g]l.ḥṯṯ.|yn.b gl[. 14[KRT].2.69
gr.|mn.ib.yp‘.l b‘l.ṣrt.|l rkb.‘rpt.l mḫšt.mdd.|il ym.l klt.nhr.il.rbm.|l ištbm.tnn.ištml h.|mḫšt.bṯn.‘qltn.|šlyṭ.d š 3[‘NT].3.36

kltn

n h.‘d.‘lm.|šḥr.‘lmt.|bnš bnšm.|l.yqḥnn.b d.|b‘ln.bn.kltn.|w.b d.bn h.‘d.|‘lm.w unṯ.|in.b h. 1008.18
[---.]yd.|[k]rm h.yd.|[k]lkl h.|[w] ytn.nn.|l.b‘ln.bn.|kltn.w l.|bn h.‘d.‘lm.|šḥr.‘lmt.|bnš bnšm.|l.yqḥnn.b d.|b‘l 1008.13

klṯb

zn.ḫmš.|ubr‘ym.ḫmš.|[----].|[bn] itn.|[bn] il.|[---]ṯ.|klṯb.|gsn.|arm[w]l.|bn.ṣdqn.|ḫlbn.|tbq.alp. 2039.12
[u]bdy.nqdm.|[ṯlṯ].šdm.d.n‘rb.gt.npk.|[š]d.rpan.b d.klṯb.|[š]d.ilšy.b d.‘bdym.|[ub]dy.trrm.|[šd.]bn.ṯqdy.b d.g 82[300].2.14
.dr.khnm.|šd.b d.bn.‘my.|šd.b d.bn.‘yn.|ṯn.šdm.b d.klṯb.|šd.b d.krz[n].|ṯlṯ.šdm.b d.amtr[n].|ṯn.šdm.b d.skn.| 2090.20
pk.|[---.]l.bn.ydln.|[---].l.blkn.|[---].l.bn.k[--].|[---].l.klṯb. 2136.6

km

.yitmr.ḥrb.ltšt.|[--]n hm.rgm.l ṯr.ab h.il.ṯḥm.ym.b‘l km.|[adn]km.ṯpṭ.nhr.tn.il m.d tq h.d tqyn h.|[hml]t.tn.b‘l. 2.1[137].33
.d‘t km.w rgm.l ṯr.a[b.-.il.ṯny.l pḫr].|m‘d.ṯḥm.ym.b‘l km.adn km.ṯ[pṭ.nhr].|tn.il m.d tq h.d tqyn.hmlt.tn.b‘l.[w ‘ 2.1[137].17
]dm.mlak.ym.t‘dt.ṯpṭ.nh[r.---].|[---].an.rgmt.l ym.b‘l km.ad[n km.ṯpṭ].|[nhr.---.]hwt.gmr.hd.l wny[-.---].|[---.]iyr 2.1[137].45
my.d in.bn.l h.|km.aḫ h.w šrš.km.ary h.|bl.iṯ.bn.l h.km aḫ h.w šrš.|km.ary h.uzrm.ilm.ylḥm.|uzrm.yšqy.bn.qd 17[2AQHT].1.21
bynt.|[d]nil.mt.rpi anḫ.ǵzr.|[mt.]hrnmy.d in.bn.l h.|km.aḫ h.w šrš.km.ary h.|bl.iṯ.bn.l h.km aḫ h.w šrš.|km.ary 17[2AQHT].1.20
yṣḥ.aṯbn.ank.|w anḫn.w tnḫ.b irt y.|npš.k yld.bn.l y.km.|aḫ y.w šrš.km ary y.|nṣb.skn.ilib y.b qdš.|ztr.‘m y.l ‘p 17[2AQHT].2.14
lt.‘nt.tšu.|g h.w tṣḥ.tbšr b‘l.|bšrt k.yblt.y[b]n.|bt.l k.km.aḫ k.w ḥẓr.|km.ary k.ṣḥ.ḫrn.|b bht k.‘ḏbt.b qrb.|hkl k. 4[51].5.90
š.l tdy.|ṯšm.‘l.dl.l pn k.|l tšlḥm.ytm.b‘d.|ksl k.almnt.km.|aḫt.‘rš.mdw.anšt.|‘rš.zbln.rd.l mlk.|amlk.l drkt k.aṯb. 16.6[127].50
].|šqlt.b ǵlt.yd k.|l tdn.dn.almnt.|l ṯṯpṭ.ṯpṭ.qṣr.npš.|km.aḫt.‘rš.mdw.|anšt.‘rš.zbln.|rd.l mlk.amlk.|l drkt.k aṯb. 16.6[127].35
.il.mla.[-].|w ṯmn.nqpnt.‘d.|k lbš.km.lpš.dm a[ḫ h].|km.all.dm.ary h.|k šb‘t.l šb‘m.aḫ h.ym[.--].|w ṯmnt.l ṯmny 12[75].2.48
h.|w y‘n.lṭpn.il.b pid.|ṯb.bn y.lm ṯb[t] km.|l kḥṯ.zbl k[m.a]nk.|iḥtrš.w [a]škn.|aškn.ydt.[m]rṣ gršt.|zbln.r[---].y 16[126].5.25
km.aḫ h.w šrš.km.ary h.|bl.iṯ.bn.l h.km aḫ h.w šrš.|km.ary h.uzrm.ilm.ylḥm.|uzrm.yšqy.bn.qdš.|l tbrknn l ṯr.i 17[2AQHT].1.22
t.rpi anḫ.ǵzr.|[mt.]hrnmy.d in.bn.l h.|km.aḫ h.w šrš.km.ary h.|bl.iṯ.bn.l h.km aḫ h.w šrš.|km.ary h.uzrm.ilm.yl 17[2AQHT].1.20
anḫn.w tnḫ.b irt y.|npš.k yld.bn.l y.km.|aḫ y.w šrš.km ary y.|nṣb.skn.ilib y.b qdš.|ztr.‘m y.l ‘pr.ḏmr.aṯr[y].|ṭ 17[2AQHT].2.15
tṣḥ.tbšr b‘l.|bšrt k.yblt.y[b]n.|bt.l k.km.aḫ k.w ḥẓr.|km.ary k.ṣḥ.ḫrn.|b bht k.‘ḏbt.b qrb.|hkl k.tbl k.ǵrm.|mid. 4[51].5.91

knm.b ‘dn. | ‘dnm.kn.npl.b‘l. | km ṯr.w tkms.hd.p[.-]. | km.ibr.b tk.mšmš d[--]. | ittpq.l awl. | išttk.lm.ttkn. | štk.mlk. 12[75].2.56
m. | ilm.yp‘r. | šmt hm. | b hm.qrnm. | km.ṯrm.w gbṯt. | km.ibrm. | w b hm.pn.b‘l. | b‘l.ytlk.w yṣd. | yḥ pat.mlbr. | wn. 12[75].1.32
nn h.yṣḥ. | aṯrt.w bn h.ilt.w ṣbrt. | ary h.wn.in.bt.l b‘l. | km.ilm.w ḥẓr.k bn.aṯrt. | mṯb il.mẓll.bn h. | mṯb rbt.aṯrt.ym. 4[51].4.51
[---.wn.in]. | [bt].l [b‘l.km.ilm.w ḥẓr]. | k bn.[aṯrt.mṯb.il.mẓll]. | bn h.m[ṯb.rbt.aṯrt.y 3['NT.VI].4.01
‘bd.ank.aḫd.ulṯ. | hm.amt.aṯrt.tlbn. | lbnt.ybn.bt.l b‘l. | km ilm.w ḥẓr.k bn.aṯrt. | w t‘n.rbt.aṯrt ym. | rbt.ilm.l ḥkmt. | 4[51].5.63
[i]k.mgn.rbt.aṯrt. | [ym].mǵẓ.qnyt.ilm. | w tn.bt.l b‘l.km. | [i]lm.w ḥẓr.k bn. | [a]ṯrt.gm.l ǵlm h. | b‘l.yṣḥ.‘n.gpn. | w 8[51FRAG].3
y‘n[.‘ṯtr].dm[-]k[-]. | [--]ḥ.b y.ṯr.il.ab y.ank.in.bt[.l] y[.km.]ilm[.w] ḥẓr[.k bn]. | [qd]š.lbum.trd.b n[p]šn y.trḥṣn.k ṯr 2.3[129].19
]. | [l pn.ṯp]ṭ[.nhr.]mlkt.[--]pm.l mlkt.wn.in.aṯt. | [l]k.k[m.ilm]. | [w ǵlmt.k bn.qdš.]w y[--.]zbl.ym.y‘[--.]ṯpṭ.nhr. | [-
nn h.yṣḥ.aṯrt. | w bn h.ilt.w ṣbrt.arḫ h. | wn.in.bt.l b‘l.km.ilm. | ḥẓr.k b[n.a]ṯrt.mṯb.il. | mṯll.b[n h.m]ṯb.rbt.aṯrt. | y 3['NT.VI].5.46
.il. | [---.mrz‘]y.lk.bt y.rpim. | [rpim.bt y.aṣ]ḥ km.iqra km. | [ilnym.b hkl]y.aṯr h.rpum. | [l tdd.aṯr]h.l tdd.i[lnym]. 21[122].1.10
hkl y.[---]. | lk bt y.r[pim.rpim.b bt y.aṣḥ]. | km.iqr[a km.ilnym.b hkl y]. | aṯr h.r[pum.l tdd.aṯr h]. | l tdd.il[nym.-- 22.1[123].4
[---.m]rz‘y.lk.bt y. | [rpim.rpim.b]t y.aṣḥ km.iqra. | [km.ilnym.b h]kl y.aṯr h.rpum. | [l tdd.aṯr h].l tdd.ilnym. | [-- 21[122].1.3
---.mhr]. | ‘nt.lk b[t y.rpim.rpim.b bt y]. | aṣḥ.km.[iqra km.ilnym.b] | hkl y.aṯr[h.rpum.l tdd]. | aṯr h.l t[dd.ilnym.ṯ 22.1[123].9
l.ymzl. | w ybl.trḫ.ḥdṯ. | yb‘r.l ṯn.aṯt h. | w l nkr.mddt. | km irby.tškn. | šd.k ḥsn.pat. | mdbr.tlkn. | ym.w ṯn.aḫr. | šp[š] 14[KRT].4.192
š.w.ḥl.mlk. | w.[---].ypm.w.mḥ[--].t[t]ṯbn.[-]. | b.[--].w.km.iṯ.y[--.]šqm.yd[-]. 35[3].55
.udn.špk.km.šiy. | dm.km.šḫṭ.l brk h.tṣi.km. | rḥ.npš h.km.iṯl.brlt h.km. | qṭr.b ap h.b ap.mhr h.ank. | l aḥwy.tqḥ.yṭ 18[3AQHT].4.25
k.km]. | šiy.dm h.km.šḫ[ṭ.l brk h]. | yṣat.km.rḥ.npš[h.km.iṯl]. | brlt h.km.qṭr.[b ap h.---]. | ‘nt.b ṣmt.mhr h.[---]. | aq 18[3AQHT].4.36
p.ǵbr.]ulp. | ḫbt km.ulp.m[dl]l km.ulp.qr zbl.u[š]n yp km. | u b ap km.u b q[ṣ]rt.npš km.u b qṭt.tqṭṭ. | ušn yp km.l 32[2].1.22
.mdll km.ulp.qr zbl]. | [u tḫṭu.u b ap km.u b qṣrt.npš km.u b qṭt]. | [tqṭṭ.u tḫṭu.l dbḥm.w l.ṯ‘.dbḥ n.ndb]ḥ. | [hw.ṯ‘. 32[2].1.8A
km.ulp.qr zbl.u[š]n yp km. | u b ap km.u b q[ṣ]rt.npš km.u b qṭt.tqṭṭ. | ušn yp km.l d[b]ḥm.w l.ṯ‘.dbḥ n.ndbḥ.hw.ṯ 32[2].1.23
ll km.ulp]. | [qr zbl.ušn.yp km.b ap km.u b qṣrt.np]št km. | [u b qṭt.tqṭṭ.ušn.yp km.---.-]yt km. | [---.]km. | [-----]. | [- APP.I[-].1.17
lp.ḫbt km.ulp.mdll km.ulp]. | [qr zbl.ušn.yp km.b ap km.u b qṣrt.np]št km. | [u b qṭt.tqṭṭ.ušn.yp km.---.-]yt km. | [APP.I[-].1.17
| [ulp.ḫbt km.ulp.mdll km.ulp.qr zbl]. | [u tḫṭu.u b ap km.u b qṣrt.npš km.u b qṭt]. | [tqṭṭ.u tḫṭu.l dbḥm.w l.ṯ‘.dbḥ 32[2].1.8A
ḫbt km.ulp.m[dl]l km.ulp.qr zbl.u[š]n yp km. | u b ap km.u b q[ṣ]rt.npš km.u b qṭt.tqṭṭ. | ušn yp km.l d[b]ḥm.w l.ṯ 32[2].1.23
.ddm]y. | ulp.ḫry.ulp.ḫ[t]y.ulp.alṯy.ul[p.ǵbr.]ulp. | ḫbt km.ulp.m[dl]l km.ulp.qr zbl.u[š]n yp km. | u b ap km.u b q[32[2].1.22
.ddm]y. | [ulp.ḫry.ulp.ḫty.ulp.alṯy.ulp.ǵbr]. | [ulp.ḫbt km.ulp.mdll km.ulp.qr zbl]. | [u tḫṭu.u b ap km.u b qṣrt.npš 32[2].1.8
ulp.ddmy.ulp.ḫry.ulp.ḫty.u]lp.alṯy. | [ulp.ǵbr.ulp.ḫbt km.ulp.mdll km.ulp]. | [qr zbl.ušn.yp km.b ap km.u b qṣrt.n APP.I[-].1.16
yt.ugrt.w npy.yman.w npy.‘r]mt.w npy. | [---.ušn.yp km.ulp.]qṭy. | [ulp.ddmy.ulp.ḫry.ulp.ḫty.u]lp.alṯy. | [ulp.ǵbr. APP.I[-].1.14
y.yman.w npy.‘rmt.w npy.[---]. | w npy.nqmd.ušn.yp km.ulp.q[ṭy.ulp.ddm]y. | ulp.ḫry.ulp.ḫ[t]y.ulp.alṯy.ul[p.ǵbr. 32[2].1.20
.ḫry.ulp.ḫty.ulp.alṯy.ulp.ǵbr]. | [ulp.ḫbt km.ulp.mdll km.ulp.qr zbl]. | [u tḫṭu.u b ap km.u b qṣrt.npš km.u b qṭt]. 32[2].1.8
ry.ulp.ḫ[t]y.ulp.alṯy.ul[p.ǵbr.]ulp. | ḫbt km.ulp.m[dl]l km.ulp.qr zbl.u[š]n yp km. | u b ap km.u b q[ṣ]rt.npš km.u 32[2].1.22
.ḫry.ulp.ḫty.u]lp.alṯy. | [ulp.ǵbr.ulp.ḫbt km.ulp.mdll km.ulp]. | [qr zbl.ušn.yp km.b ap km.u b qṣrt.np]št km. | [u APP.I[-].1.16
ulp.ǵbr.ulp.ḫbt km.ulp.mdll km.ulp]. | [qr zbl.ušn.yp km.b ap km.u b qṣrt.np]št km. | [u b qṭt.tqṭṭ.ušn.yp km.---.-] APP.I[-].1.17
l.yi[--.-]m[---]. | b unṯ.km.špš. | d brt.kmt. | br.ṣṭqšlm. | b unṯ.‘d ‘lm. | mišmn.nqmd. | mlk ugrt. | nq 1005.3
ḫṣ.alpm.ib.št[-.]št. | ḥršm l ahlm p[---.]km. | [-]bl lb h.km.bṯn.y[--.-]ah. | ṯnm.tšqy msk.hwt.tšqy[.-.]w [---]. | w hn d 19[1AQHT].4.223
]q. | [---.]m[-]ǵ[-].thmt.brq. | [---].tṣb.qšt.bnt. | [---.‘]n h.km.bṯn.yqr. | [krpn h.-.l]arṣ.ks h.tšpk m. | [l ‘pr.tšu.g h.]w tṣ 17[2AQHT].6.14
[.ps]ltm[.b y‘r]. | thdy.lḥm.w dqn[.ṯlṯ]. | qn.ḏr‘ h.tḥrṯ.km.gn. | ap lb.k ‘mq.ṯlṯ.bmt. | b‘l.mt.my.lim.bn dgn. | my.h 6[62].1.4
.yzbrnn.zbrm.gpn. | yṣmdnn.ṣmdm.gpn.yšql.šdmt h. | km gpn. | šb‘ d.yrgm.‘l.‘d.w ‘rbm.t‘nyn. | w šd.šd ilm.šd aṯrt. 23[52].11
hr h.ank. | l aḥwy.tqḥ.yṭpn.mhr.št. | tštn.k nšr.b ḥbš h.km.diy. | b t‘rt h.aqht.km.yṯb.l lḥ[m]. | bn.dnil.l ṯrm.‘l h.nšr[18[3AQHT].4.28
t‘n.btlt.‘nt.ṯb.yṭp.w[---]. | l k.ašt k.km.nšr.b ḥb[š y]. | km.diy.b t‘rt y.aqht.[km.yṯb]. | l lḥm.w bn.dnil.l ṯrm[.‘l h]. | 18[3AQHT].4.18
m. | ‘dm.[lḥ]m.tšty. | w t‘n.mṯt ḥry. | l l[ḥ]m.l š[ty].ṣḥt km. | db[ḥ.l krt.a]dn km. | ‘l.krt.tbun.km. | rgm.ṯ[rm.]rgm h 15[128].6.4
tlk.[---].bm[.---]. | [---.-]qp.bn.ḥtt.bn ḥtt[.---]. | [---.--]p.km.dlt.tlk.km.p[---]. | [---.]bt.tḥbṭ.km.ṣq.ṣdr[.---]. | [---.]kl.b 1001.1.24
ṣpn hm.tliy m[.--.ṣ]pn hm. | nṣḥy.šrr.m[---.--]ay. | nbšr km.dnil.[--] h[.---]. | riš.r[--.--]ḥ[.---]y[.---.-]nt.[š]ṣat[k.]rḥ.np 19[1AQHT].2.86
b h.il.‘bd k.b‘l.y ym m.‘bd k.b‘l. | [--.--]m.bn.dgn.a[s]r km.hw ybl.argmn k.k ilm. | [---.]ybl.k bn.qdš.mnḥy k.ap.anš 2.1[137].37
nt.l h. | mk.b šb‘.šnt. | bn.krt.km hm.tdr. | ap.bnt.ḥry. | km hm.w tḫss.aṯrt. | ndr h.w ilt.p[--]. | w tšu.g h.w [tṣḥ]. | ph 15[128].3.25
ld.bn.l h. | w tqrb.w ld.bnt.l h. | mk.b šb‘.šnt. | bn.krt.km hm.tdr. | ap.bnt.ḥry. | km hm.w tḫss.aṯrt. | ndr h.w ilt.p[- 15[128].3.23
.t‘dt.ṯpṭ.nhr. | šu.ilm.rašt km.l ẓr.brkt km.ln.kḥṯ. | zbl km.w ank.‘ny.mlak.ym.t‘dt.ṯpṭ.nhr. | tšu ilm rašt hm.l ẓr.br 2.1[137].28
. | zbl hm.b hm.yg‘r.b‘l.lm.ǵltm.ilm.rišt. | km l ẓr brkt km.w ln.kḥṯ.zbl km.aḥd. | ilm.t‘ny lḥt.mlak.ym.t‘dt.ṯpṭ.nhr. 2.1[137].25
.il]. | al.tpl.al.tštḥwy.pḫr [m‘d.qmm.a--.am] | r ṯny.d‘t km.w rgm.l ṯr.a[b.-.il.ṯny.l pḫr]. | m‘d.tḥm.ym.b‘l km.adn k 2.1[137].16
bu.pnm. | ‘rm.tdu.mh. | pdrm.tdu.šrr. | ḥṭ m.t‘mt.[‘]ṭr.[k]m. | zbln.‘l.riš h. | w ttb.trḥṣ.nn.b d‘t. | npš h.l lḥm.tptḥ. | br 16.6[127].8
g‘r.b‘l.lm.ǵltm.ilm.rišt. | km l ẓr brkt km.w ln.kḥṯ.zbl km.aḥd. | ilm.t‘ny lḥt.mlak.ym.t‘dt.ṯpṭ.nhr. | šu.ilm.rašt km.l 2.1[137].25
dṯ.yb‘r.l ṯn. | aṯt h.lm.nkr. | mddt h.k irby. | [t]škn.šd. | km.ḥsn.pat.mdbr. | lk.ym.w ṯn.ṯlṯ.rb‘ ym. | ḫmš.ṯdṯ.ym.mk.š 14[KRT].2.105
ḥr[r.---]. | bmt n m.yšḫn.[---]. | qrn h.km.ǵb[-.---]. | hw km.ḥrr[.---]. | šnmtm.dbṭ[.---]. | tr‘.tr‘n.a[--.---]. | bnt.šdm.ṣḥr[12[75].2.41
. | u---].‘lt.b k.lk.l pn y.yrk.b‘l.[--]. | [---.]‘nt.šzrm.tštšḥ.km.ḥ[--]. | [---].‘pr.bt k.ygr[š k.---]. | [---.]y.ḥr.ḥr.bnt.ḥ[---]. | [- 1001.1.11
ṯn.[-]gmm.w ydm‘. | tntkn.udm‘t h. | km.ṯqlm.arṣ h. | km ḫmšt.mṭt h. | bm.bky h.w yšn. | b dm‘ h.nhmmt. | šnt.tlua 14[KRT].1.30
.tn. | l y.mṯt.ḥry. | n‘mt.šbḥ.bkr k. | d k n‘m.‘nt. | n‘m h.km.tsm. | ‘ṯtrt.tsm h. | d ‘q h.ib.iqni. | ‘p‘p h.sp.ṯrml. | d b ḥlm 14[KRT].6.292
. | tn.l y.mṯt.ḥry. | n‘mt.špḥ.bkr k. | d k.n‘m.‘nt.n‘m h. | km.tsm.‘ṯtrt.ts[m h]. | d ‘q h.ib.iqni.‘p[‘p] h. | sp.ṯrml.tḥgrn.[14[KRT].3.146
.l arṣ[.id]y.alt.l aḥš.idy.alt.in l y. | [--]t.b‘l.ḥẓ.ršp.b[n].km.yr.klyt h.w lb h. | [ṯ]n.p k.b ǵr.ṯn.p k.b ḫlb.k tgwln.šnt k 1001.1.3
yṭpn.mhr.št. | tštn.k nšr.b ḥbš h.km.diy. | b t‘rt h.aqht.km.yṯb.l lḥ[m]. | bn.dnil.l ṯrm.‘l h.nšr[m]. | trḫpn.ybṣr.ḥbl.di 18[3AQHT].4.29
---]. | l k.ašt k.km.nšr.b ḥb[š y]. | km.diy.b t‘rt y.aqht.[km.yṯb]. | l lḥm.w bn.dnil.l ṯrm[.‘l h]. | nšrm.trḫpn.ybṣr.[ḥbl. 18[3AQHT].4.18
[---.--]k.mdd il. | y[m.---.]l ṯr.qdqd h. | il[.--.]rḥq.b ǵr. | km.y[--.]ilm.b ṣpn. | ‘dr.l[‘r].‘rm. | ṯb.l pd[r.]pdrm. | ṯṯ.l ṯṯm.a 4[51].7.6
. | nḥlt h.w nǵr. | ‘nn.ilm.al. | tqrb.l bn.ilm. | mt.al.y‘db km. | k imr.b p h. | k lli.b ṯbrn. | qn h.tḫtan. | nrt.ilm.špš. | ṣḥrr 4[51].8.17
t.bir.mlak. | šmm.tmr.zbl.mlk. | šmm.tlak.ṭl.amr.. | bn km k bk[r.z]bl.am.. | rkm.agzrt[.--].arḫ.. | b‘l.azrt.‘nt.[-]ld. | k 13[6].28

-]t h.ušpǵt tišr.|[---.šm]m h.nšat ẓl h kbkbm.|[---.]b km kbkbt k t̲n.|[---.]b‘l yḥmdn h.yrt̲ y.|[---.]dmrn.l pn h yr 2001.2.6
].|w qbr.tṣr.q[br].|tṣr.trm.tnq[--].|km.nkyt.t̲ǵr[.---].|km.škllt.[---].|‘r.ym.l bl[.---].|b[---.]ny[.--].|l bl.sk.w [---] h. 16.2[125].90
m.|u b ap km.u b q[ṣ]rt.npš km.u b qt̲t.tqt̲t.|ušn yp km.l d[b]ḥm.w l.t̲‘.dbḥ n.ndbḥ.hw.t̲‘ |nt̲‘y.|hw.nkt.nkt.y[t] 32[2].1.24
t hm.w l kḥt̲.|zbl hm.b hm.yg‘r.b‘l.lm.ǵltm.ilm.rišt.|km l ẓr brkt km.w ln.kḥt̲.zbl km.aḥd.|ilm.t‘ny lḥt.mlak.ym 2.1[137].25
.aḥd.|ilm.t‘ny lḥt.mlak.ym.t‘dt.t̲pṭ.nhr.|šu.ilm.rašt km.l ẓr.brkt km.ln.kḥt̲.|zbl km.w ank.‘ny.mlak.ym.t‘dt.t̲pṭ. 2.1[137].27
.|in.b ilm.‘ny h.|w y‘n.lṭpn.il.b pid.|t̲b.bn y.lm t̲b[t] km.|l kḥt̲.zbl k[m.a]nk.|iḥtrš.w [a]škn.|aškn.ydt.[m]rṣ gršt 16[126].5.24
ny lḥt.mlak.ym.t‘dt.t̲pṭ.nhr.|šu.ilm.rašt km.l ẓr.brkt km.ln.kḥt̲.|zbl km.w ank.‘ny.mlak.ym.t‘dt.t̲pṭ.nhr.|tšu ilm 2.1[137].27
l.‘b]dmlk.|[--.-]m[-]r.|[w.l.]bn h.‘d.|[‘l]m.mn k.|mn km l.yqḥ.|bt.hnd.b d.|[‘b]dmlk.|[-]k.am‘[--].|[w.b] d.bn h[1009.13
.ugrt.|ktb.spr hnd.|dt brrt.ṣṭqšlm.|‘bd h.hnd.|w mn km.l yqḥ.|spr.mlk.hnd.|b yd.ṣṭqšlm.|‘d ‘lm. 1005.12
yrḫm.rḥm.‘nt.tngt̲ h.|k lb.arḫ.l ‘gl h.k lb.|t̲at.l imr h.km.lb.|‘nt.at̲r.b‘l.tiḫd.|bn.ilm.mt.b ḥrb.|tbq‘nn.b ḫt̲r.tdry| 6[49].2.29
rḥm.‘nt].|tngt̲ h.k lb.a[rḫ].|l ‘gl h.k lb.t̲a[t].|l imr h.km.lb.‘n[t].|at̲r.b‘l.tiḫd.m[t].|b sin.lpš.tšṣq[n h].|b qṣ.all.tš 6[49].2.8
--.]|šqy.rt̲a.tnm y.ytn.[ks.b yd].|krpn.b klat yd.[---].|km ll.kḥṣ.tusp[.---].|tgr.il.bn h.t̲r[.---].|w y‘n.lṭpn.il.d p[id.- 1[‘NT.X].4.11
m.ṣḥr[.---].|šb‘.šnt.il.mla.[-].|w t̲mn.nqpnt.‘d.|k lbš.km.lpš.dm a[ḫ h].|km.all.dm.ary h.|k šb‘t.l šb‘m.aḫ h.ym[. 12[75].2.47
nt.|ptḥ.bt.w ubn.hkl.w ištql šql.|tn.km.nḥšm.yḥr.tn.km.|mhr y.w bn.bt̲n.itnn y.|ytt.nḥšm.mhr k.bn bt̲n.|itnn k UG5.7.73
[---.rp]um.tdbḥn.|[----.]‘d.ilnym.|[---.--]l km amt m.|[---.]b w t‘rb.sd.|[---.--]n b ym.qẓ.|[---.]ym.tlḥ 20[121].1.3
y]lt n.km.qdm.|[-.k]bd n.il.ab n.|kbd k iš.tikln.|t̲d n.km.mrm.tqrṣn.|il.yẓḥq.bm.|lb.w ygmd̲.bm kbd.|ẓi.at.l tlš. 12[75].1.11
b‘l.mhr b‘l.|w mhr.‘nt.t̲m.yḥpn.ḥyl|y.zbl.mlk.‘llm y.km.tdd.|‘nt.ṣd.tštr.‘pt.šmm.|ṭbḫ.alpm.ap ṣin.šql.t̲rm.|w m 22.2[124].10
.‘dbt.t̲lt̲.ptḥ.bt.mnt.|ptḥ.bt.w ubn.hkl.w ištql šql.|tn.km.nḥšm.yḥr.tn.km.|mhr y.w bn.bt̲n.itnn y.|ytt.nḥšm.mhr UG5.7.73
.yb|ltm.ybln h.mǵy.ḥrn.l bt h.w.|yštql.l ḥtr h.tlu ḥt.km.nḫl.|tplg.km.plg.|b‘d h.bhtm.mnt.b‘d h.bhtm.sgrt.|b‘d UG5.7.68
mnd‘.krt.mǵ[y.---].|w qbr.tṣr.q[br].|tṣr.trm.tnq[--].|km.nkyt.t̲ǵr[.---].|km.škllt.[---].|‘r.ym.l bl[.---].|b[---.]ny[.-- 16.2[125].89
šmm.tqru.|[---.]nplt.y[--].md‘.nplt.bšr.|[---].w tpky.k[m.]n‘r.tdm‘.km.|[ṣǵ]r.bkm.y‘ny[.---.bn]wt h.|[--]nn.bnt y UG5.8.40
t.|[---.--]n h.ḥmt.w t‘btn h.abd y.|[---.ǵ]r.šrǵzz.ybky.km.n‘r.|[w ydm‘.k]m.ṣǵr.špš.b šmm.tqru.|[---.]nplt.y[--].m UG5.8.37
.hlm.ktp.zbl ym.bn ydm.|[t̲p]ṭ nhr.yrtqṣ.ṣmd.b d b‘l.km.nšr.|b[u]ṣb‘t h.ylm.ktp.zbl ym.bn ydm.t̲pṭ.|nhr.‘z.ym.l 2.4[68].15
grš ym grš ym.l ksi h.|[n]hr l kḥt̲ drkt h.trtqṣ.b d b‘l km nš|r.b uṣb‘t h.hlm.ktp.zbl ym.bn ydm.|[t̲p]ṭ nhr.yrtqṣ.ṣ 2.4[68].13
.t̲pṭ.nhr.yprsḥ ym.|w yql.l arṣ.w trtqṣ.ṣmd.b d b‘l.|[km.]nšr.b uṣb‘t h.ylm.qdqd.zbl.|[ym.]bn.‘nm.t̲pṭ.nhr.yprsḥ 2.4[68].24
.mr.ym.mr.ym.|l ksi h.nhr l kḥt̲.drkt h.trtqṣ.|b d b‘l.km.nšr b uṣb‘t h.hlm.qdq|d zbl ym.bn.‘nm.t̲pṭ.nhr.yprsḥ y 2.4[68].21
dm.w n‘rs[.---].|w t‘n.btlt.‘nt.t̲b.yṭp.w[---].|l k.ašt k.km.nšr.b ḥb[š y].|km.diy.b t‘rt y.aqht.[km.yt̲b].|l lḥm.w b 18[3AQHT].4.17
.|il.hr[r.---].|kb[-.---].|ym.[---].|yšḥr[.---].|yikl[.---].|km.s[--.---].|tš[.---].|t[---.---].|[-----].|[-----].|b [----].|w [--- 12[75].2.15
w t‘n.mt̲t ḥry.|l l[ḥ]m.l š[ty].ṣḥt km.|db[ḥ.l krt.a]dn km.|‘l.krt.tbun.km.|rgm.t̲[rm.]rgm hm.|b d̲rt[.---.]krt.|[--- 15[128].6.5
pš.|[---.h]d.tngt̲n h.|[---].b ṣpn.|[---].nšb.b ‘n.|[---.]b km.y‘n.|[---.yd‘.l] yd‘t.|[---.t]asrn.|[---.]trks.|[---.]abnm.up 1[‘NT.X].5.7
tngt̲m h.|[---.-]ḥm k b ṣpn.|[---.]išqb.aylt.|[---.--]m.b km.y‘n.|[---].yd‘.l yd‘t.|[---.]tasrn.t̲r il.|[---.]rks.bn.abnm.|[1[‘NT.X].5.20
š[.---].|anp n m yḥr[r.---].|bmt n m.yšḫn.[---].|qrn h.km.ǵb[-.---].|hw km.ḥrr[.---].|šnmtm.dbṭ[.---].|tr‘.tr‘n.a[--. 12[75].2.40
n.|b‘l.yd.pdry.bt.ar.|ahbt.ṭly.bt.rb.dd.arṣy.|bt.y‘bdr.km ǵlmm.|w ‘rb n.l p‘n.‘nt.hbr.|w ql.tštḥwy.kbd hyt.|w rg 3[‘NT].3.5
h.mǵy.ḥrn.l bt h.w.|yštql.l ḥtr h.tlu ḥt.km.nḫl.|tplg.km.plg.|b‘d h.bhtm.mnt.b‘d h.bhtm.sgrt.|b‘d h.‘dbt.t̲lt̲.ptḥ UG5.7.69
[.---].|[---.-]qp.bn.ḥtt.bn ḥtt[.---].|[---.--]p.km.dlt.tlk.km.p[---].|[---.]bt.tḥbṭ.km.ṣq.ṣdr[.---].|[---.]kl.b kl.l pgm.pg 1001.1.24
--.]nplt.y[--].md‘.nplt.bšr.|[---].w tpky.k[m.]n‘r.tdm‘.km.|[ṣǵ]r.bkm.y‘ny[.---.bn]wt h.|[--]nn.bnt yš[--.---.-]lk.|[-- UG5.8.40
w t‘btn h.abd y.|[---.ǵ]r.šrǵzz.ybky.km.n‘r.|[w ydm‘.k]m.ṣǵr.špš.b šmm.tqru.|[---.]nplt.y[--].md‘.nplt.bšr.|[---]. UG5.8.38
n ḥtt[.---].|[---.--]p.km.dlt.tlk.km.p[---].|[---.]bt.tḥbṭ.km.ṣq.ṣdr[.---].|[---.]kl.b kl.l pgm.pgm.l.b[---].|[---.]mdbm.l 1001.1.25
.|[---.]nb hm.|[---.-]kn.|[---.]hr n.km.šḥr.|[---.y]lt n.km.qdm.|[-.k]bd n.il.ab n.|kbd k iš.tikln.|t̲d n.km.mrm.tq 12[75].1.8
šiy.|dm.km.šḫṭ.l brk h.tṣi.km.|rḥ.npš h.km.it̲l.brlt h.km.|qṭr.b ap h.b ap.mhr h.ank.|l aḥwy.tqḥ.yṭpn.mhr.št.|tš 18[3AQHT].4.25
h.km.šḫ[ṭ.l brk h].|yṣat.km.rḥ.npš[h.km.it̲l].|brlt h.km.qṭr.[b ap h.---].|‘nt.b ṣmt.mhr h.[---].|aqht.w tbk.y[---.- 18[3AQHT].4.37
n.‘l.qbr.bn y.|tšḫṭann.b šnt h.qr.[mym].|mlk.yṣm.y l km.qr.mym.d ‘[l k].|mḫṣ.aqht.ǵzr.amd.gr bt il.|‘nt.brḥ.p ‘l 19[1AQHT].3.152
[---.m]rz‘y.lk.bt y.|[rpim.rpim.b]t y.aṣḥ km.iqra.|[km.ilnym.b h]kl y.at̲r h.rpum.|[l tdd.at̲r h].l tdd. 21[122].1.2
mhr.b‘l[.---.mhr].|‘nt.lk b[t y.rpim.rpim.b bt y].|aṣḥ.km.[iqra km.ilnym.b] |hkl y.at̲r[h.rpum.l tdd].|at̲r h.l t[dd 22.1[123].9
[--.b qr]|b hkl y.[---].|lk bt y.r[pim.rpim.b bt y.aṣḥ].|km.iqr[a km.ilnym.b hkl y].|at̲r h.r[pum.l tdd.at̲r h].|l tdd. 22.1[123].4
l y.w y‘n.il.|[---.mrz‘]y.lk.bt y.rpim.|[rpim.bt y.aṣ]ḥ km.iqra km.|[ilnym.b hkl]y.at̲r h.rpum.|[l tdd.at̲r]h.l tdd. 21[122].1.10
h[m.---].|‘l.pd.asr.[---.]l[.---].|mḫlpt.w l.ytk.[d]m[‘t.]km.|rb‘t.t̲qlm.t̲tp[.---.]bm.|yd.ṣpn hm.tliy m[.--.ṣ]pn hm.|n 19[1AQHT].2.82
l[ḥ]m.l š[ty].ṣḥt km.|db[ḥ.l krt.a]dn km.|‘l.krt.tbun.km.|rgm.t̲[rm.]rgm hm.|b d̲rt[.---.]krt.|[----]. 15[128].6.6
qdqd.|t̲lt̲ id.‘l.udn.špk.km.šiy.|dm.km.šḫṭ.l brk h.tṣi.km.|rḥ.npš h.km.it̲l.brlt h.km.|qṭr.b ap h.b ap.mhr h.ank.| 18[3AQHT].4.24
lt̲ id.‘l.udn.š[pk.km].|šiy.dm h.km.šḫ[ṭ.l brk h].|yṣat.km.rḥ.npš[h.km.it̲l].|brlt h.km.qṭr.[b ap h.---].|‘nt.b ṣmt. 18[3AQHT].4.36
[l tdd.at̲r h].l tdd.ilnym.|[---.m]rz‘y.apnnk.yrp.|[---.]km.r‘y.ht.alk.|[---.]t̲lt̲t.amǵy.l bt.|[y.---.b qrb].hkl y.w y‘n.i 21[122].1.6
.|[---.-]b[-.---].|[‘t̲]trt w ‘nt[.---].|w b hm.tt̲t̲b[.--]d h.|km trpa.hn n‘r.|d yšt.l.lṣb h ḫš‘r klb.|[w]riš.pqq.w šr h.|y UG5.1.2.3
km.r[--].|amr.[---].|ḫṭ.t̲k[l.---].|[-]l[--.---]. 2002.1
‘l[.aqht].|t‘dbn h.hlmn.t̲nm[.qdqd].|t̲lt̲ id.‘l.udn.š[pk.km].|šiy.dm h.km.šḫ[ṭ.l brk h].|yṣat.km.rḥ.npš[h.km.it̲l].| 18[3AQHT].4.34
an[k.‘]l.|aqht.‘db k.hlmn.t̲nm.qdqd.|t̲lt̲ id.‘l.udn.špk.km.šiy.|dm.km.šḫṭ.l brk h.tṣi.km.|rḥ.npš h.km.it̲l.brlt h.k 18[3AQHT].4.23
[---.]d arṣ.|[---.]ln.|[---.]nb hm.|[---.-]kn.|[---.]hr n.km.šḥr.|[---.y]lt n.km.qdm.|[-.k]bd n.il.ab n.|kbd k iš.tikln 12[75].1.7
h.hlmn.t̲nm[.qdqd].|t̲lt̲ id.‘l.udn.š[pk.km].|šiy.dm h.km.šḫ[ṭ.l brk h].|yṣat.km.rḥ.npš[h.km.it̲l].|brlt h.km.qṭr.[18[3AQHT].4.35
t.‘db k.hlmn.t̲nm.qdqd.|t̲lt̲ id.‘l.udn.špk.km.šiy.|dm.km.šḫṭ.l brk h.tṣi.km.|rḥ.npš h.km.it̲l.brlt h.km.|qṭr.b ap h 18[3AQHT].4.24
l.yi[--.-]m[---].|b unt̲.km.špš.|d brt.kmt.|br.ṣṭqšlm.|b unt̲.‘d ‘lm.|mišmn.nqmd. 1001.1.19
[---.]km.t[--.---].|[--.n]pš.ttn[.---].|[---.]yd‘t.k[---].|[---].w hm.|[- 61[-].1
rgm.l t̲r.a[b.-.il.t̲ny.l pḫr].|m‘d.tḥm.ym.b‘l km.adn km.t̲[pṭ.nhr].|tn.il m.d tq h.d tqyn.hmlt.tn.b‘l.[w ‘nn h].|b 2.1[137].17
.ltšt.|[--]n hm.rgm.l t̲r.ab h.il.tḥm.ym.b‘l km.|[adn]km.t̲pṭ.nhr.tn.il m.d tq h.d tqyn h.|[hml]t.tn.b‘l.w ‘nn h.bn 2.1[137].34
.ym.t‘dt.t̲pṭ.nh[r.---].|[---].an.rgmt.l ym.b‘l km.ad[n km.t̲pṭ].|[nhr.---.]hwt.gmr.hd.l wny[-.---].|[---.]iyr h.g[-.]th 2.1[137].45

.b ḥdr h.ybky.|b ṯn.[-]gmm.w ydmʻ.|tntkn.udmʻt h.|km.ṯqlm.arṣ h.|km ḫmšt.mṯt h.|bm.bky h.w yšn.|b dmʻ h. 14[KRT].1.29
.tbrk k.|w ld ʻqqm.|ilm.ypʻr.|šmt hm.|b hm.qrnm.|km.ṯrm.w gbṯt.|km.ibrm.|w b hm.pn.bʻl.|bʻl.ytlk.w yṣd.|y 12[75].1.31
mẓa h.šr.yly h.|b skn.sknm.b ʻdn.|ʻdnm.kn.npl.bʻl.|km ṯr.w tkms.hd.p[.-].|km.ibr.b tk.mšmš d[--].|ittpq.l awl. 12[75].2.55
.a[qh]t.ǵ|zr.tmḫṣ.alpm.ib.št[-.]št.|ḥršm l ahlm p[---.]km.|[-]bl lb h.km.bṯn.y[--.-]ah.|ṯnm.tšqy msk.hwt.tšqy[.-.] 19[1AQHT].4.222
šlḥ.|ḥrb.b bšr.tštn.|[w t]ʻn.mṯt.ḥry.|[l lḥ]m.l šty.ṣḥt km.|[--.dbḥ.l]krt.bʻl km. 15[128].4.27
[---.--]b.|[---.r]iš k.|[---.]bn ʻn km.|[---.]alp.|[---.]ym.rbt.|[---.]b nhrm.|[ʻb]r.gbl.ʻbr.|qʻl.ʻb 3[ʻNT.VI].6.3
.|[ḥrb.b]bš[r].tštn.|[w tʻn].mṯt.ḥry.|[l lḥ]m.l šty.ṣḥt k[m].|[---.]brk.t[---].|[ʻl.]krt.tbkn.|[--.]rgm.ṯrm.|[--.]mtm.t 15[128].5.10
qšt[.---]r.y[t]br.|ṯmn.[---.]btlt.[ʻ]nt.|ṯṯb.[---.--]ša.|tlm.km[.---.]yd h.k šr.|knr.uṣbʻt h ḥrṣ.abn.|p h.tiḫd.šnt h.w akl 19[1AQHT].1.7
km.u b qṣrt.np]št km.|[u b qṭt.tqṭṭ.ušn.yp km.---.-]yt km.|[---.]km.|[-----].|[---.]ugrt.|[---].l.lim.|[---.mšr m]šr.|[APP.I[-].1.18
.---].|l ytn.w rgm[.---].|w yrdnn.an[--.---].|[---].ank.l km[.---].|l y.ank.ašṣu[.---.]w[.---].|w hm.at.tr[gm.---].|w.dr 54.1.16[13.2.1]
|ilm.w tštn.tštn y[n] ʻd šbʻ.|trṯ.ʻd.škr.yʻdb.yrḫ.|gb h.km.[---.]yqṭqṭ.tḥt.|ṯlḥnt.il.d ydʻnn.|yʻdb.lḥm.l h.w d l ydʻn UG5.1.1.5
p km.b ap km.u b qṣrt.np]št km.|[u b qṭt.tqṭṭ.ušn.yp km.---.-]yt km.|[---.]km.|[-----].|[---.]ugrt.|[---].l.lim.|[---. APP.I[-].1.18
.|[---.]w.ʻm k.|[---]m.ksp.|[---].ʻm.|[---.-]n[-].|[---.]l km.|[---.-]lk.|[---.--]m.|t[--.---].t[-]ṯm.|i[---.--]d.[-]t.|y[---.-] 1016.18
rt.np]št km.|[u b qṭt.tqṭṭ.ušn.yp km.---.-]yt km.|[---.]km.|[-----].|[---.]ugrt.|[---].l.lim.|[---.mšr m]šr.|[bn.ugrt.--- APP.I[-].1.19
w t]ʻn.mṯt.ḥry.|[l lḥ]m.l šty.ṣḥt km.|[--.dbḥ.l]krt.bʻl km. 15[128].4.28

kmy

w.qlʻ.|bn.ḫršn.qšt.w.qlʻ.|ilrb.qšt.w.qlʻ.|psḫn.qšt.|bn.kmy.qšt.|bn.ilḫbn.qšt.w.q[lʻ].|ršpab.qšt.w.qlʻ.|pdrn.qšt.w. 119[321].3.43

kmyr

ṣ]bu h.u[l.mad].|ṯlṯ.mat.rbt.|hlk.l alpm.ḫdd.|w l.rbt.kmyr.|aṯr.ṯn.ṯn.hlk.|aṯr.ṯlṯ.kl hm.|aḥd.bt h.ysgr.|almnt.šk 14[KRT].4.181
t.|ḫpṯ.d bl.spr.|ṯnn.d bl.hg.|hlk.l alpm.ḫdd.|w l rbt.kmyr.|[a]ṯr.ṯn.ṯn.hlk.|aṯr.ṯlṯ.kl hm.|yḥd.bt h.sgr.|almnt.šk 14[KRT].2.93

kmkty

.--]y.|[---.yr]ml.|[---.--]y.|[---.yr]ml.|[---.y]rml.|[---.]kmkty.|[---].b.kmkty.|[---].b.ndb.|[---].b.ndb.|[---].b.ndb.| 2119.11
l.|[---.--]y.|[---.yr]ml.|[---.y]rml.|[---.]kmkty.|[---].b.kmkty.|[---].b.ndb.|[---].b.ndb.|[---].b.ndb.|[---].b.kmkty.| 2119.12
.b.kmkty.|[---].b.ndb.|[---].b.ndb.|[---].b.ndb.|[---].b.kmkty.|[---.]yrmly.qrtym.|[---].b.yrml.|[---.]b.yrml.|[---.]b 2119.16

kmm

.ṣpn.al[p].|pḫr.ilm.š.ym.š[.k]nr.š.[--.]ʻṣrm gdlt.|bʻlm.kmm.bʻlm.kmm[.bʻlm].kmm.bʻlm.kmm.|bʻlm.kmm.bʻlm.k UG5.9.1.11
.š[.k]nr.š.[--.]ʻṣrm gdlt.|bʻlm.kmm.bʻlm.kmm[.bʻlm].kmm.bʻlm.kmm.|bʻlm.kmm.bʻlm.kmm.|k tʻrb.ʻṯtrt.šd.bt.m UG5.9.1.11
pḫr.ilm.š.ym.š[.k]nr.š.[--.]ʻṣrm gdlt.|bʻlm.kmm.bʻlm.kmm[.bʻlm].kmm.bʻlm.kmm.|bʻlm.kmm.bʻlm.kmm.|k tʻrb UG5.9.1.11
--.]ʻṣrm gdlt.|bʻlm.kmm.bʻlm.kmm[.bʻlm].kmm.bʻlm.kmm.|bʻlm.kmm.bʻlm.kmm.|k tʻrb.ʻṯtrt.šd.bt.mlk[.---].|ṯn. UG5.9.1.11
|bʻlm.kmm.bʻlm.kmm[.bʻlm].kmm.bʻlm.kmm.|bʻlm.kmm.bʻlm.kmm.|k tʻrb.ʻṯtrt.šd.bt.mlk[.---].|ṯn.skm.šbʻ.mšl UG5.9.1.12
[d]qt.ṯkmn.w [šnm.dqt.--].|[--]t.dqtm.[b nbk.---].|[--.k]mm.gdlt.l.b[ʻl.---].|[dq]t.l.ṣpn.gdlt.l[.---].|u[gr]t.š.l.[il]ib.ǵ 35[3].33
d]lt.i[l.dqt.ṯkm]|n.w šnm.dqt[.---].|bqtm.b nbk.[---].|kmm.gdlt.l b[ʻl.--.dqt].|l ṣpn.gdlt.[l.---].|ugrt.š l ili[b.---].|r APP.II[173].36
r ṯṯ.ṣ[in.---].|tšnpn.ʻlm.km[m.---].|w.l ll.ʻṣrm.w [---].|kmm.w.in.ʻṣr[.---].|w mit.šʻrt.[-]y[-.---].|w.kdr.w.npt t[--.--- 38[23].8
š.l šlm kbd.|alp.w š.l bʻl ṣpn.|dqt l ṣpn.šrp.w šlmm.|kmm.w bbt.bʻl.ugrt.|w kdm.w npš ilib.|gdlt.il š.bʻl š.ʻnt.|ṣ UG5.13.11
šlm.kbd.al]p.w š.[l] bʻl.ṣpn.|[dqt.l.ṣpn.šrp].w š[l]mm.kmm.|[w bbt.bʻl.ugrt.]kdm.w npš.|[ilib.gdlt.il.š.b]ʻ[l.]š.ʻnt ṣ 36[9].1.15
.bʻlm.kmm[.bʻlm].kmm.bʻlm.kmm.|bʻlm.kmm.bʻlm.kmm.|k tʻrb.ʻṯtrt.šd.bt.mlk[.---].|ṯn.skm.šbʻ.mšlt.arbʻ.ḫpnt. UG5.9.1.12
m.|l gtrm.ǵṣ b šmal.|d alpm.w alp w š.|šrp.w šlmm kmm.|l bʻl.ṣpn b ʻrʻr.|pamt ṯlṯm š l qrnt.|ṯlḥn.bʻlt.bhtm.|ʻl UG5.13.28
r.bkm.yʻny[.---.bn]wt h.|[--]nn.bnt yš[--.---.-]lk.|[--]b.kmm.l k[--].|[šp]š.b šmm.tq[ru.---.-]rt.|[---.]mn mn[-.---.--] UG5.8.43
w aṯt k.ngrt.il[ht].|ʻl.l ṯkm.bnw n.|l nḫnpt.mšpy.|ṯlṯ.kmm.ṯrr y.|[---.]l ǵr.gm.ṣḥ.|[---.]r[-]m. 16[126].4.16
.---].|[---.]l pdr[-.---].|ṣin aḥd h[.---].|l ʻṯtrt[.---].|ʻlm.kmm[.---].|w b ṯlṯ.ṣ[in.---].|l ll.pr[-.---].|mit šʻ[rt.---].|ptr.k 37[22].7
[--.]l ilt.š l ʻṯt[rt.---].|[ʻ]ṣr.l pdr ṯṯ.ṣ[in.---].|tšnpn.ʻlm.km[m.---].|w.l ll.ʻṣrm.w [---].|kmm.w.in.ʻṣr[.---].|w mit.šʻrt 38[23].6

kmn

dnn.ṯlṯ.ṣmdm.|bn.ʻmnr.|bn.kmn.|bn.ibyn.|bn.mryn.ṣmd.w.ḥrṣ.|bn.prsn.ṣmd.w.ḥrṣ.|b 2113.3
[-----].|[-----].|ynḥm.|iḫy.|bn.mšt.|ʻpsn.|bn.ṣpr.|kmn.|bn.ršp.|tmn.|šmmn.|bn.rmy.|bn.aky.|ʻbdḫmn.|bn.ʻ 1047.8
|ḥš.trmmn.hk[l m].|b tk.ṣrrt.ṣpn.|alp.šd.aḫd bt.|rbt.kmn.hkl.|w yʻn.kṯr.w ḫss.|šmʻ.l aliyn bʻl.|bn.l rkb.ʻrpt.|bl. 4[51].5.119
ḥ.ǵyrm.|idk.l ttn pnm.ʻm.bʻl.|mrym.ṣpn.b alp.šd.rbt.kmn.|hlk.aḫt h.bʻl.yʻn.tdrq.|ybnt.ab h.šrḥq.aṯt.l pnn h.|št. 3[ʻNT].4.82
.almnt.yṯpṭ.ṯpṭ.ytm.|b nši ʻn h.w yphn.b alp.|šd.rbt.kmn.hlk.kṯr.|k yʻn.w yʻn.tdrq.ḫss.|hlk.qšt.ybln.hl.yš|rbʻ.qṣ 17[2AQHT].5.10
]lt.ʻnt.idk.l ttn.[pnm].|[ʻm.a]qht.ǵzr.b alp.š[d].|[rbt.]kmn.w ṣḥq.btlt.[ʻnt].|[tšu.]g h.w tṣḥ.šmʻ.m[ʻ.l a]|[qht.ǵ]zr. 18[3AQHT].1.22
il.kl h.kptr.|ksu.ṯbt h.ḥkpt.|arṣ.nḥlt h.|b alp.šd.rbt.|kmn.l pʻn.kṯ.|hbr.w ql.tšth|wy.w kbd hwt.|w rgm.l kṯr.|w 3[ʻNT.VI].6.18
l h].|[kptr.]ks[u.ṯbt h.ḥkpt.arṣ.nḥlt h].|b alp.šd.r[bt.kmn.l pʻn.kṯr].|hbr.w ql.t[šthwy.w kbd.hwt].|w rgm l k[ṯr. 1[ʻNT.IX].3.2
.špš.|ṣḥrrt.la.|šmm.b yd.md|d.ilm.mt.b a|lp.šd.rbt.k|mn.l pʻn.mt.|hbr.w ql.|tšthwy.w k|bd hwt.w rgm.|l bn.i 4[51].8.25
tqn.|[---.-]ʻb.idk.|[l ytn.pnm.tk.]in.bb.b alp ḥzr.|[rbt.kmn.l pʻ]n.ʻnt.|[yhbr.w yql.yšt]ḥwyn.w y|[kbdn h.yšu.g h. 1[ʻNT.IX].2.15
dl.ṯṯ.dd.šʻrm.|[---.hn.w.al]p.kd.nbt.kd.šmn.mr.|[---].kmn.lṯḥ.sbbyn.|[---.-]ʻt.lṯḥ.ššmn.|[---].ḫšwn.ṯṯ.mat.nṣ.|[---]. 142[12].9
tr.arṣ.|idk.l ttn.pnm.|ʻm.bʻl.mrym.ṣpn.|b alp.šd.rbt.kmn.|ṣḥq.btlt.ʻnt.tšu.|g h.w tṣḥ.tbšr bʻl.|bšrt k.yblt.y[b]n.| 4[51].5.86

kms

r.yly h.|b skn.sknm.b ʻdn.|ʻdnm.kn.npl.bʻl.|km ṯr.w tkms.hd.p[.-].|km.ibr.b tk.mšmš d[--].|ittpq.l awl.|išttk.lm 12[75].2.55

kmsk

arbʻ.ʻšr h.šd.|w.kmsk.d.iwrkl.|ṯlṯ.šd.d.bn.mlkyy.|kmsk.šd.iḫmn.|širm.šd.k 1079.2
mšt.ʻšrt.ksp.|ḫmš.mat.šmt.|b.ʻšrt.ksp.|ʻšr.ṣin.b.ṯṯt.w.kmsk.|arbʻ[.k]dwṯm.w.ṯt.ṯprtm.|b.ʻšr[m.]ksp.|ḫmš.kkr.ṣml 2100.9
arbʻ.ʻšr h.šd.|w.kmsk.d.iwrkl.|ṯlṯ.šd.d.bn.mlkyy.|kmsk.šd.iḫmn.|širm.šd.khn.|ṯlṯ.šd.w.krm.šir.d.ḫli.|širm.šd 1079.4

kmr

.|tšt ḥrṣ.k lb ilnm.|w ṯn.gprm.mn gpr h.šr.|aqht.yʻn.kmr.kmr[.--].|k apʻ.il.b gdrt.k lb.l |ḥṯ h.imḫṣ h.k d.ʻl.qšt h. 19[1AQHT].1.12
.ḥrṣ.k lb ilnm.|w ṯn.gprm.mn gpr h.šr.|aqht.yʻn.kmr.kmr[.--].|k apʻ.il.b gdrt.k lb.l |ḥṯ h.imḫṣ h.k d.ʻl.qšt h.|imḫ 19[1AQHT].1.12

kmry

.ǵr[--].|d.b[n.---].|d.bn.[---].|d.bn.š[--].|d.bn.ṯn[r].|d.kmry. 2164.B.5

kmrn

pll.b d.qrt.|š[d].anndr.b d.bdn.nḥ[l h].|[šd.]agyn.b d.kmrn.n[ḥl] h.|[š]d.nbzn.[-]l.qrt.|[š]d.agpṯr.b d.sḫrn.nḥl h.| 2029.8

kmrṯn

[u]lm.|mṯpṭ.ṯt.qštm.w.ṯn.q[l]ʻm.|kmrṯn.ṯt.qštm.ṯn.[q]lʻm.|ǵdyn.qšt.w.qlʻ.|bn.gzl.qšt.w.qlʻ.|[119[321].1.3
spr.mr[ynm].|[bʻ]l.[---].|mr[--.---].|hm.[---].|kmrṯn[.---].|bn.ṯbln[.---].|bn.pndr[.---].|bn.idr[-.---].|bn.ḥd 2070.2.3

kmṯ

mt.y[r]ḫ.w.ršp.yisp.ḥmt.|[ʻṯt]r.w ʻṯpr.yisp.ḥmt.ṯṯ.w kṯṯ.|[yus]p.ḥmt.mlk.b ʻṯrt.yisp.ḥmt.|[kṯ]r w ḫss.y[i]sp.ḥmt UG5.8.16
ʻdb.ksa w yṯb.|tqru l špš.um h.špš.um.ql bl ʻm.|ṯṯ.w kmṯ.ḥryt h.mnt.nṯk.nḥš.šm|rr.nḥš.ʻq šr.ln h.mlḫš abd.ln h. UG5.7.36
.w il[--].|[--] šlm.šlm i[l].|[š]lm.il.šr.|dgn.w bʻl.|ʻṯ w kmṯ.|yrḫ w ksa.|yrḫ mkty.|ṯkmn w šnm.|kṯr w ḫss.|ʻṯtr ʻṯ UG5.10.1.5

kn

[ulp.ǵbr.ulp.ḫbt kn.ulp.mdll kn.ulp.]qr zbl.|[ušn.yp kn.u b ap kn.u b qṣrt.npš kn.u b]qṭt.|[tqṭṭn.ušn.yp kn.---.-] APP.I[-].2.15
.ulp.ǵbr.ul]p.ḫbt kn.|[ulp.mdll kn.ulp.qr zbl.ušn.y]p kn.|[u b ap kn.u b qṣrt.npšt kn.u b qṭ]t tqṭṭ.|[ušn.yp kn.---. APP.I[-].1.6
md[ll k]n.ulp.q[r zbl].|u tḫṭin.b ap kn.u b [q]ṣrt.npš[kn.u b qṭt].|tqṭṭn u tḫṭin.l bḥm.w l ṯʻ.d[bḥ n.ndbḥ].|hw.ṯʻ.n 32[2].1.14
mdll kn.ulp qr z[bl].|lšn yp kn.b ap [kn.u b qṣ]rt.npš kn.u b qṭt.|tqṭṭn.ušn y[p kn.l dbḥm.]w l ṯʻ dbḥ n.|ndbḥ.hw 32[2].1.31
dll kn.ulp.]qr zbl.|[ušn.yp kn.u b ap kn.u b qṣrt.npš kn.u b]qṭt.|[tqṭṭn.ušn.yp kn.---.-]gym.|[---.]l kbkb.|[-----]. APP.I[-].2.15
dll kn.ulp.qr zbl.ušn.y]p kn.|[u b ap kn.u b qṣrt.npšt kn.u b qṭ]t tqṭṭ.|[ušn.yp kn.---.--]l.il.tʻḏr bʻl.|[-----.]lšnt.|[-- APP.I[-].1.7
.ḫbt kn.|[ulp.mdll kn.ulp.qr zbl.ušn.y]p kn.|[u b ap kn.u b qṣrt.npšt kn.u b qṭ]t tqṭṭ.|[ušn.yp kn.---.--]l.il.tʻḏr bʻl APP.I[-].1.7
lp.ḫbt kn.ulp.mdll kn.ulp.]qr zbl.|[ušn.yp kn.u b ap kn.u b qṣrt.npš kn.u b]qṭt.|[tqṭṭn.ušn.yp kn.---.-]gym.|[---. APP.I[-].2.15
r.|ulp.ḫbt kn.ulp.md[ll k]n.ulp.q[r zbl].|u tḫṭin.b ap kn.u b [q]ṣrt.npš[kn.u b qṭt].|tqṭṭn u tḫṭin.l bḥm.w l ṯʻ.d[b 32[2].1.14
p.[ḫbt] kn[.u]lp.mdll kn.ulp qr z[bl].|lšn yp kn.b ap [kn.u b qṣ]rt.npš kn.u b qṭt.|tqṭṭn.ušn y[p kn.l dbḥm.]w l ṯʻ 32[2].1.31
lp.ddmy.ul[p.ḫ]ry.ulp.ḫty.ulp.alṯy.|ulp.ǵbr.ulp.[ḫbt] kn[.u]lp.mdll kn.ulp qr z[bl].|lšn yp kn.b ap [kn.u b qṣ]rt.n 32[2].1.30
lp.ddmy.ul[p.ḫry.u]lp.ḫty.ulp[.alṯy.ulp.]ǵbr.|ulp.ḫbt kn.ulp.md[ll k]n.ulp.q[r zbl].|u tḫṭin.b ap kn.u b [q]ṣrt.npš 32[2].1.13
ulp.ddmy.ulp.ḫry.ulp.ḫty.ulp.alṯy].|[ulp.ǵbr.ulp.ḫbt kn.ulp.mdll kn.ulp.]qr zbl.|[ušn.yp kn.u b ap kn.u b [q]ṣrt.npš 32[2].1.13
lp.]ddmy.ulp ḫry.|[ulp.ḫty.ulp.alṯy.ulp.ǵbr.ul]p.ḫbt kn.|[ulp.mdll kn.ulp.qr zbl.ušn.y]p kn.|[u b ap kn.u b qṣrt.n APP.I[-].2.14
]py.yman.|[w npy.ʻrmt.---.w]npy.annpdgl.|[ušn.yp kn.ulp.qṭy.ulp.]ddmy.ulp ḫry.|[ulp.ḫty.ulp.alṯy.ulp.ǵbr.ulp.ḫbt kn.|[u b ap kn.u b qṣrt. APP.I[-].1.5
ʻḏ]r bʻl.|[-----].|[-----].|[---.--]r.|[---.]npy.|[---.ušn.yp kn.ulp.q]ṭy.|[ulp.ddmy.ulp.ḫry.ulp.ḫty.ulp.alṯy].|[ulp.ǵbr.ul] APP.I[-].1.4
mšr.bt.ugrt.w npy.gr.|ḥmyt.ugrt.w [np]y.nṭt.ušn.yp kn.ulp qṭy.|ulp.ddmy.ul[p.ḫ]ry.ulp.ḫty.ulp.alṯy.|[ulp.ǵbr. APP.I[-].2.12
.ḫry.u]lp.ḫty.ulp[.alṯy.ulp.]ǵbr.|ulp.ḫbt kn.ulp.md[ll k]n.ulp.q[r zbl].|u tḫṭin.b ap kn.u b [q]ṣrt.npš[kn.u b qṭt]. 32[2].1.28
ḫ]ry.ulp.ḫty.ulp.alṯy.|ulp.ǵbr.ulp.[ḫbt] kn[.u]lp.mdll kn.ulp qr z[bl].|lšn yp kn.b ap [kn.u b qṣ]rt.npš kn.u b qṭt. 32[2].1.13
p.ḫry.ulp.ḫty.ulp.alṯy].|[ulp.ǵbr.ulp.ḫbt kn.ulp.mdll kn.ulp.]qr zbl.|[ušn.yp kn.u b ap kn.u b qṣrt.npš kn.u b qṭt. 32[2].1.30
ḫry.|[ulp.ḫty.ulp.alṯy.ulp.ǵbr.ul]p.ḫbt kn.|[ulp.mdll kn.ulp.qr zbl.ušn.y]p kn.|[u b ap kn.u b qṣrt.npš kn.u b]qṭ APP.I[-].2.14
lp.ǵbr.ulp.[ḫbt] kn[.u]lp.mdll kn.ulp qr z[bl].|lšn yp kn.b ap [kn.u b qṣ]rt.npš kn.u b qṭt.|tqṭṭn.ušn y[p kn.l dbḥ 32[2].1.31
y.ʻm n.|šlm.ṯm ny.|ʻm k.mnm[.š]lm.|rgm.ṯṯ[b].|any kn.dt.|likt.mṣrm.|hn dt.b.ṣr.|mtt.by.|gšm.adr.|nškḥ.w.|r 2059.10
|b ql[.-----].|w tštqdn[.-----].|hm.|w yḫ.mlk.|w ik m.kn.w [---].|tšknnnn[.---]. 62[26].10
p kn.b ap [kn.u b qṣ]rt.npš kn.u b qṭt.|tqṭṭn.ušn y[p kn.l dbḥm.]w l ṯʻ dbḥ n.|ndbḥ.hw.ṯʻ n[ṯʻy.hw.nkt.nk]t.ytši.l 32[2].1.32
h.mẓa h.|w mẓa h.šr.yly h.|b skn.sknm.b ʻdn.|ʻdnm.kn.npl.bʻl.|km ṯr.w tkms.hd.p[.-].|km.ibr.b tk.mšmš d[--].| 12[75].2.54
[---.]rgm.hy.[-]ḫ[-]y.ilak k.|[---.--]g k.yritn.mǵy.hy.w kn.|[---].ḥln.d b.dmt.um.il[m.---].|[--]dyn.bʻd.[--]dyn.w l.|[1002.42
kn.u b ap kn.u b qṣrt.npš kn.u b]qṭt.|[tqṭṭn.ušn.yp kn.---.-]gym.|[---.]l kbkb.|[-----]. APP.I[-].2.16
kn.|[u b ap kn.u b qṣrt.npšt kn.u b qṭ]t tqṭṭ.|[ušn.yp kn.---.--]l.il.tʻḏr bʻl.|[-----.]lšnt.|[---.--]yp.tḥt.|[-----].|[---.]w APP.I[-].1.8

knd

ṯn pǵn.[-]dr|m.ṯn kndwm adrm.|w knd pnṯ.dq.|ṯn ḫpnm.ṯn pldm ǵlmm.|kpld.b[-.-]r[--].|w bl 140[98].3

kndw

ṯn pǵn.[-]dr|m.ṯn kndwm adrm.|w knd pnṯ.dq.|ṯn ḫpnm.ṯn pldm ǵlmm.|kpl 140[98].2

kny

ǵlyn.|bdl.ar.|bn.šyn.|bn.ubrš.|bn.d[--]b.|abrpu.|bn.k[n]y.|bn.klyn.|bn.gmḥn.|ḥnn.|ayab.|bn.gm[--].|bn.[---]. 1035.3.6
.bt.ar.mẓll].|ṭly.bt.r[b.mṯb.arṣy].|bt.y bdr[.mṯb.klt].|knyt.w tʻn[.btlt.ʻnt].|yṯb l y.ṯr.il[.ab y.---].|yṯb.l y.w l h.[---] 3[ʻNT.VI].4.6
bn.aṯrt.|mṯb il.mẓll.bn h.|mṯb rbt.aṯrt.ym.|mṯb.klt.knyt.|mṯb.pdry.bt.ar.|mẓll.ṭly.bt rb.|mṯb.arṣ.bt yʻbdr.|w y 4[51].4.54
ṯ]r[t].|m[ṯ]b.il.mẓll.|bn h.mṯb.rbt.|aṯrt.ym.mṯb.|klt.knyt.|mṯb.pdry.b ar.|mẓll.ṭly.bt rb.|mṯb.arṣy.bt.yʻbdr.|ap. 4[51].1.16

tlṯ.mat.ṯlṯm. | kbd.šmn. | l kny. | ṯmnym.šmn. | b d.adnn'm. 1094.3
t.ar. | [mẓll.]ṯly[.bt.]rb.mṯb. | [arṣy.bt.y'bdr.mṯb]. | [klt.knyt]. 3['NT.VI].5.52

knys

[---.]liy. | [---.]nrn. | [---.-]pṯ. | [---.]knys.[---]. | [---.--]by. | [---.-]ṯby[.---]. | [---].abb[.---]. | [---.-]k[-. 2134.4

knkny

k.pdry.bt.ar. | 'm k.ṯṯly.bt.rb.idk. | pn k.al ttn.tk.ǵr. | knkny.ša.ǵr.'l ydm. | ẖlb.l ẓr.rḥtm w rd. | bt ẖpṯt.arṣ.tspr b y 5[67].5.13

knm

]šb'm.dr'.w.arb'm.drt.mit.dd. | [---].ḥpr.bn.šm. | [b.---.]knm.ṯṯm.l.mit.dr'.w.mit.drt. | w[.---.]'m.l.mit.dd.ṯn.kbd.ḥpr. 1098.7

knn

ḏddy. | ildy.aḏddy. | gr'.aḏddy. | 'bd.ršp aḏddy. | 'dn.bn.knn. | iwrẖz.b d.skn. | škny.aḏddy. | mšu.aḏddy. | plsy.aḏddy. 2014.36
bn.d'm[-]. | bn.ppṯ.b[--]. | b[n.---]. | šm[-.---]. | tkn[.---]. | knn.b.ẖ[lb]. | bn mṯ.b.qmy. | n'r.b.ulm. 2046.2.4
n.bn.kzbn.l.qr[t]. | šd.pln.bn.tiyn.b d.ilmhr nḥl h. | šd knn.bn.ann.'db. | šd.iln[-].bn.irṯr.l.šẖrn.nḥl h. | šd[.ag]pṯn.b[2029.19
-]. | bn.gld. | bn.ṣmy. | bn.mry[n]. | bn.mgn. | bn.'dn. | bn.knn. | bn.py. | bn.mk[-]. | bn.by[--]. | bn.a[--]. | bn.iy[--]. | bn.ḥ[- 2117.1.8
'gwn. | bn.yšm'. | bdl.mḏrǵlm. | bn.mmy. | bn.ẖnyn. | bn.knn. | khnm. | bn.ṯ'y. | w.nḥl h. | w.nḥl hm. | bn.nqly. | bn.snrn. 104[316].9
bldn. | [-]ln. | [-]ldn. | [i]wryn. | ẖbsn. | ulmk. | 'dršp. | bn.knn. | pdyn. | bn.aṯtl.ṯn. | kdln.akdṯb. | ṯn.b gt ykn'm. 1061.18
rt.qšt. | ǵmrm. | bn.qṯn.qšt.w.ql'. | mrṯd.qšt. | ssw.qšt. | knn.qšt. | bn.ṯlln.qšt. | bn.šyn.qšt. | 'bd.qšt. | bn.ulmy.qšt. | ṯqb 119[321].1.15
l'. | ẖlb.rpš. | abmn.qšt. | ẓẓn.qšt. | dqry.qš[t]. | rkby. | bn.knn.qšt. | pbyn.qšt. | yddn.qšt.w.ql'. | š'rt. | bn.il.qšt.w.ql'. | ar 119[321].2.36
hbṯn. | bn.m[--.]skn. | bn.s[--.b]d.skn. | bn.ur[-.---]. | bn.knn[.---]y. | bn.ymlk[.b]d.skn. | bn.yẖnn.aḏddy. | bn.pdǵy.m 2014.14

kn'm

bnš.mlk. | d taršn.'msn. | bṣr.abn.špšyn. | dqn. | aǵlmn. | kn'm. | aẖršp. | anntn. | b'lrm. | [-]ral. | šḏn. | [-]ǵl. | bn.b'ltǵpṯ. | 2067.1.6
rynm. | 'zn. | ḥyn. | 'myn. | ilyn. | yrb'm. | n'mn. | bn.kbl. | kn'm. | bdlm. | bn.ṣǵr. | klb. | bn.mnḥm. | bn.brqn. | bn.'n. | bn.' 1046.3.41
d.'[ṯr]t. | ydy. | bn.škn. | bn.mdt. | bn.ẖ[--]y. | bn.'[-]y. | kn'm. | bn.yš[-]n. | bn.pd[y]. | ttn. | md.'ṯt[rt]. | kṯkt. | bn.ṯtn[--] 1054.1.7
n.srwd. | mtnn. | bn gš[-]. | bn gbrn. | bn uldy. | synn.bn kn'm. | bn kbr. | bn iytlm. | bn ayln. | bn.kln. | bn.'lln. | bn.liy. | 1064.19
šm [---]. | kn'm.bn.[---]. | plšb'l.bn.n[--]. | ḥy bn.dnn.ṯkt. | ilṯḥm.bn.dnn. 2085.2
n.ṭbrn. | šd.bn.ḥtb.l bn.y'ḏrd. | šd.gl.b'lz.l.bn.'mnr. | šd.kn'm.l.bn.'mnr. | šd.bn.krwn.l bn.'myn. | šd.bn.prmn.l aẖny. 2089.4
pṯr. | šb'l.mlky. | n'mn.mṣry. | y'l.kn'ny. | gdn.bn.umy. | kn'm.š'rty. | abrpu.ubr'y. | b.gt.bn.ṯlṯ. | ilḏ.b.gt.psḥn. 91[311].9
]rwn. | [k]l[by]. | [--]ṯn. | [---]d. | a[ǵ]lṯn. | [-----]. | [--]ny. | kn'm. | [-]p[-]. | 'pṯn. | pslm.ṣnr. 2060.13
ẖmṯ 'ṯr[.---]. | [-----]. | [---.-]y[-.---]. | w bn 'ṯl.[---]. | ypḥ kn'm[.---]. | aẖmn bt[.---]. | b ẖmṯ 'ṯr ṯmn[.---]. 207[57].9

kn'ny

'rty. | aryn.aḏddy. | agpṯr. | šb'l.mlky. | n'mn.mṣry. | y'l.kn'ny. | gdn.bn.umy. | kn'm.š'rty. | abrpu.ubr'y. | b.gt.bn.ṯlṯ. | i 91[311].7

knp

| tbky k.ab.ǵr.b'l. | ṣpn.ḥlm.qdš. | any.ḥlm.adr.ḥl. | rḥb.mknpt.ap. | [k]rt.bnm.il.špḥ. | lṭpn.w qdš.'l. | ab h.y'rb.ybky. | 16.1[125].9
ky k. | ab.ǵr.b'l.ṣ[p]n.ḥlm. | qdš.nny.ḥ[l]m.adr. | ḥl.rḥb.mk[npt]. | ap.krt bn[m.il]. | špḥ.lṭpn[.w qdš]. | bkm.t'r[b.'l.ab 16.2[125].109
.ymn h. | idk.l ytn pnm. | tk.aẖ.šmk.mla[t.r]umm. | tšu knp.btlt.'n[t]. | tšu.knp.w tr.b 'p. | tk.aẖ šmk.mlat rumm. | w 10[76].2.10
.ybq'.kbd h.w yḥd. | [i]n.šmt.in.'ẓm.yšu.g[h]. | w yṣḥ.knp.hrgb.b'l.ybn. | [b]'l.ybn.diy.hwt.hrg[b]. | tpr.w du.b nši.' 19[1AQHT].3.132
.b nši.'n h.w ypn. | yḥd.hrgb.ab.nšrm. | yšu.g h.w yṣḥ.knp.hr[g]b. | b'l.yṯb.b'l.y[ṯb]r.diy[.h]wt. | w yql.tḥt.p'n y.ibq' 19[1AQHT].3.122
rn.ašt.b ẖrt. | i[lm.arṣ.b p h.rgm.l yṣa.b šp]| t h.hwt h.knp.hrgb.b'l.ṯbr. | b'l.ṯbr.diy.hwt.w yql. | tḥt.p'n h.ybq'.kbd 19[1AQHT].3.128
nm. | tk.aẖ.šmk.mla[t.r]umm. | tšu knp.btlt.'n[t]. | tšu.knp.w tr.b 'p. | tk.aẖ šmk.mlat rumm. | w yšu.'n h.aliyn.b'l. | 10[76].2.11
.ybq'.kbdt hm.w[yḥd]. | in.šmt.in.'ẓm.yšu.g h. | w yṣḥ.knp.nšrm.ybn. | b'l.ybn.diy hmt nšrm. | tpr.w du.b nši.'n h.w 19[1AQHT].3.118
ši[.'n h.w yphn.yḥd]. | b 'rpt[.nšrm.yšu]. | [g h.]w yṣḥ[.knp.nšrm]. | b'l.yṯb.b'l.yṯb[r.diy.hmt]. | tqln.tḥ p'n y.ibq['.kb 19[1AQHT].3.107
y.w yqbr. | yqbr.nn.b mdgt.b knk[-]. | w yšu.g h.w yṣḥ.knp.nšrm. | b'l.yṯbr.b'l.yṯbr.diy. | hmt.hm.t'pn.'l.qbr.bn y. | tš 19[1AQHT].3.148
h. | ašt.b ẖrt.ilm.arṣ. | b p h.rgm.l yṣa.b špt h.hwt[h]. | knp.nšrm.b'l.yṯbr. | b'l.ṯbr.diy hmt.tqln. | tḥt.p'n h.ybq'.kbdt 19[1AQHT].3.114
h.aštn. | b ẖrt.ilm.arṣ.b p h.rgm.l[yṣ]a. | b špt h.hwt h.knp.ṣml.b'[l]. | b'l.ṯbr.diy.hyt.tq[l.tḥt]. | p'n h.ybq'.kbd h.w y 19[1AQHT].3.142
nši.'n h. | [w]yphn.yḥd.ṣml.um.nšrm. | yšu.g h.w yṣḥ.knp.ṣml. | b'l.yṯbr.b'l.yṯbr.diy. | hyt.tql.tḥt.p'n y.ibq'. | kbd h. 19[1AQHT].3.136
al]p 'nt.gdlt.b ṯlṯt mrm. | [---.i]l š.b'l š.aṯrt.š.ym š.[b']l knp. | [---.g]dlt.ṣpn.dqt.šrp.w [š]lmm. | [---.a]lp.l b'l.w aṯrt.'ṣr 36[9].1.6

knpy

.kbd. | ṯlṯ.alp.ṣpr.dt.aḥd. | ḥrṯ h.aḥd.b gt.nḥl. | aḥd.b gt.knpy.w.aḥd.b gt.ṯrmn. | aḥd.alp.idṯn.d aḥd.b.'nqpat. | [aḥd.a 1129.10
.alẖb.ṯṯm.dr'.w.ẖmšm.drt.w.ṯṯm.dd. | ḥpr.bnšm. | b.gt.knpy.mit.dr'.ṯṯm.drt.w.šb'm.dd.arb'. | kbd.ḥpr.bnšm. | b.gt.ṯ 1098.18

knr

n.[---.]btlt.[']nt. | ṯṯb.[---.--]ša. | tlm.km[.---.]yd h.k šr. | knr.uṣb't h ḥrṣ.abn. | p h.tiẖd.šnt h.w akl.bqmm. | tšt ḥrṣ.k l 19[1AQHT].1.8
m.b ṣ['.trḥṣ]. | yd h.btlt.'nt.uṣb't[h.ybmt]. | limm.tiẖd.knr h.b yd[h.tšt]. | rimt.l irt h.tšr.dd.al[iyn]. | b'l.ahbt. UG5.3.2.6
ṯr.w yqr.il.yṯb.b.'ṯtrt. | il.ṯpṭ.b hd r'y.d yšr.w yḏmr. | b knr.w ṯlb.b tp.w mṣltm.b m | rqdm.dšn.b.ḥbr.kṯr.ṭbm. | w tšt UG5.2.1.4
| [']ṯtrt. | i[l t]'ḏr b'l. | ršp. | ddmš. | pẖr ilm. | ym. | uṯẖt. | knr. | mlkm. | šlm. 29[17].2.10
w šlmm.ilib.š.i[l.--]m d gbl.ṣpn.al[p]. | pẖr.ilm.š.ym.š[.k]nr.š.[--.]'ṣrm gdlt. | b'lm.kmm.b'lm.kmm[.b'lm].kmm.b'l UG5.9.1.9

knt

grt. | b mrḥ il. | b nit il. | b ṣmd il. | b dṯn il. | b šrp il. | b knt il. | b ǵdyn il. | [b]n [---]. 30[107].17

ks

‘.l lṭpn.|[il.d]pid.l tbrk.|[krt.]ṯ‘.l tmr.n‘mn.|[ǵlm.]il.ks.yiḫd.|[il.b]yd.krpn.bm.|[ymn.]brkm.ybrk.|[‘bd h.]ybrk 15[128].2.16
it.arb‘m.kbd.|l.liy.bn.‘myn.|mit.ḫmšm.kbd.|d.škn.l.ks.ilm. 1143.14
nw h.|b ḥrb.mlḥt.|qṣ.mri.ndd.|y‘šr.w yšqyn h.|ytn.ks.b d h.|krpn.b klat.yd h.|b krb.‘ẓm.ridn.|mt.šmm.ks.qdš 3[‘NT].1.10
.qḥ.|ks.b d y.qb‘t.b ymn y[.t]q|ḥ.pǵt.w tšqyn h.tq[ḥ.ks.]b d h.|qb‘t.b ymn h.w y‘n.yṭ[p]n[.mh]r.|št.b yn.yšt.ila.i 19[1AQHT].4.217
|bat.b hlm w y‘n.yṭpn[.mhr].|št.qḥn.w tšqyn.yn.qḥ.|ks.b d y.qb‘t.b ymn y[.t]q|ḥ.pǵt.w tšqyn h.tq[ḥ.ks.]b d h.|q 19[1AQHT].4.216
.ḥš.b a[rṣ.---].|b ‘pr.ḫbl ṭtm.[---.]|šqy.rṯa.tnm y.ytn.[ks.b yd].|krpn.b klat yd.[---].|km ll.kḥṣ.tusp[.---].|tgr.il.bn 1[‘NT.X].4.9
rm.idk.l yt[n.pnm.‘m.lṭpn].|il d pid.tk ḫrš[n.---.tk.ǵr.ks].|ygly ḏd.i[l.w ybu.qrš.mlk].|ab.šnm.l [p‘n.il.yhbr.w yql 1[‘NT.IX].3.22
‘n k.tlsmn].|‘m y twtḥ.i[šd k.tk.ḫršn.-------------].|ǵr.ks.dm.r[gm.iṯ.l y.w argm k].|hwt.w aṯny k[.rgm.‘ṣ.w lḫšt.a 1[‘NT.IX].3.12
liyn.b‘l.ṯpṭ n.|in.d ‘ln h.klny y.qš h.|nbln.klny y.nbl.ks h.|any.l yṣḥ.ṯr.il.ab h.il.|mlk.d yknn h.yṣḥ.aṯrt.|w bn h. 3[‘NT.VI].5.42
|ṯpṭ n.w in.d ‘ln h.|klny n.q[š] h.n[bln].|klny n[.n]bl.ks h.|[an]y.l yṣḥ.ṯr il.ab h.|[i]l.mlk.d yknn h.yṣḥ.|aṯrt.w b 4[51].4.46
---].ṯṣb.qšt.bnt.|[---.‘]n h.km.bṯn.yqr.|[krpn h.-.l]arṣ.ks h.tšpk m.|[l ‘pr.tšu.g h.]w tṣḥ.šm‘.m‘.|[l aqht.ǵzr.i]rš.ks 17[2AQHT].6.15
m.b[‘l.---].|bn.dgn[.---].|‘ḏbm.[---].|uḫry.l[---].|mṣt.ks h.t[--.---].|idm.adr[.---].|idm.‘rẓ.t‘r[ẓ.---].|‘n.b‘l.a[ḫ]ḏ[.-- 12[75].2.29
b‘l.|gdlt.šlm.gdlt.w burm.[l]b.|rmṣt.ilhm.b‘lm.dṯt.w kšm.ḫmš.|‘ṯr h.mlun.šnpt.ḫṣt h.b‘l.ṣpn š.|[--]ṯ š.ilt.mgdl š.il 34[1].9
.|lḥm.hm.štym.lḥ[m].|b ṯlḥnt.lḥm št.|b krpnm.yn.b k.ḫrṣ.|dm.‘ṣm.hm.yd.il mlk.|yḫss k.ahbt.ṯr.t‘rr k.|w t‘n.rb 4[51].4.37
m.ṯd.---].|b ḥrb.[mlḥt.qṣ.mri].|šty.kr[pnm.yn.---].|b ks.ḫr[ṣ.dm.‘ṣm.---].|ks.ksp[.---].|krpn.[---].|w ṯṯn.[---].|t‘l. 5[67].4.16
mrǵtm.ṯd.|b ḥrb.mlḥt.qṣ[.m]r|i.tšty.krp[nm.y]n.|[b k]s.ḫrṣ.d[m.‘ṣm].|[---.--]n.|[---.---]t.|[---.--]ṯ.|[---.--]n. 4[51].6.59
ay š[---].|[---.b ḥ]rb.mlḥ[t.qṣ].|[mri.tšty.krpnm].yn.b ks.ḫ[rṣ].|[dm.‘ṣm.---]n.krpn.‘l.[k]rpn.|[---.]ym.w t‘l.trṯ.|[--- 17[2AQHT].6.5
.mrǵtm.|[ṯd.b ḥrb.m]lḥt.qṣ.|[mri.tšty.k]rpnm yn.|[b ks.ḫrṣ.dm].‘ṣm. 4[51].3.44
u.|argmn.nqmd.mlk.|ugrt.d ybl.l špš.|mlk.rb.b‘l h.|ks.ḫrṣ.ktn.mit.pḥm.|mit.iqni.l mlkt.|ks.ḫrṣ.ktn.mit.pḥm.| 64[118].27
.|mlk.rb.b‘l h.|ks.ḫrṣ.ktn.mit.pḥm.|mit.iqni.l mlkt.|ks.ḫrṣ.ktn.mit.pḥm.|mit.iqni.l uṯryn.|ks.ksp.ktn.mit.pḥm.| 64[118].29
.|l aḫ h.l r‘ h.|r‘ ‘lm.|ttn.w tn.|w l ttn.|w al ttn.|tn ks yn.|w ištn.|‘bd.prṯ.ṯḥm.|qrq.pt.ḏmn.|l iṯtl. 1019.1.15
rtn[r].|[ks.ksp.ktn.mit.pḥ]m.|[mit.iqni.l ḫbrtn]r ṯn.|[ks.ksp.ktn.mit.pḥm].|[mit.iqn]i.l skl.[--].|[---.m]it pḥm.l š[- 64[118].37
it.iqni.l mlkt.|ks.ḫrṣ.ktn.mit.pḥm.|mit.iqni.l uṯryn.|ks.ksp.ktn.mit.pḥm.|mit.iqni.l tpnr.|[ks.ksp.kt]n.mit.pḥ[m 64[118].31
tpnr.|[ks.ksp.kt]n.mit.pḥ[m].|[mit.iqni.l]ḫbrtn[r].|[ks.ksp.ktn.mit.pḥ]m.|[mit.iqni.l ḫbrtn]r ṯn.|[ks.ksp.ktn.mi 64[118].35
it.iqni.l uṯryn.|ks.ksp.ktn.mit.pḥm.|mit.iqni.l tpnr.|[ks.ksp.kt]n.mit.pḥ[m].|[mit.iqni.l]ḫbrtn[r].|[ks.ksp.ktn.mi 64[118].33
t.qṣ.mri].|šty.kr[pnm.yn.---].|b ks.ḫr[ṣ.dm.‘ṣm.---].|ks.ksp[.---].|krpn.[---].|w ṯṯn.[---].|t‘l.tr[-.---].|bt.il.li[mm.- 5[67].4.17
.d [ybl.n]qmd.|l špš.arn.ṯn[.‘šr h.]mn.|‘ṣrm.ṯql.kbd[.ks].mn.ḫrṣ.|w arb‘.ktnt.w [---]b.|[ḫm]š.mat pḥm.|[ḫm]š[. 64[118].20
r.b ym.|brkt.šbšt.|k rumm.hm.|‘n.kḏd.aylt.|mt hm.ks.ym|sk.nhr hm.|šb‘.ydt y.b ṣ‘.|[--.]šb‘.rbt.|[---.]qbt.ṯm.|[UG5.4.9
lt.|ḥmr.p imt.b klt.|yd y.ilḥm.hm.šb‘.|ydt y.b ṣ‘.hm.ks.ymsk.|nhr.k[--].ṣḥn.b‘l.‘m.|aḫ y.qran.hd.‘m.ary y.|w lḥ 5[67].1.21
t.|tp.aḫ.h.k.ysmsm.|tspi.šir.h.l.bl.ḥrb.|tšt.dm.h.l.bl.ks.|tpnn.‘n.bṯy.‘n.bṯt.tpnn.|‘n.mḫr.‘n.pḫr.‘n.ṯǵr.|‘n.ṯǵr.l.ṯǵ RS225.4
ks.b d h.|krpn.b klat.yd h.|b krb.‘ẓm.ridn.|mt.šmm.ks.qdš.|l tphn h.aṯt.krpn.|l t‘n.aṯrt.alp.|kd.yqḥ.b ḫmr.|rbt. 3[‘NT].1.13
.w ywpṯn.b tk.|p[ḫ]r.bn.ilm.štt.|p[--].b ṯlḥn y.qlt.|b ks.ištyn h.|dm.ṯn.dbḥm.šna.b‘l.ṯlṯ.|rkb.‘rpt.dbḥ.|bṯt.w dbḥ 4[51].3.16
lt.šlm.gdlt].|w burm.l[b.rmṣt.ilhm].|b‘lm.w mlu[.---.ksm].|ṯlṯm.w m‘rb[.---].|dbḥ šmn mr[.šmn.rqḥ.bt].|mtnt.w APP.II[173].20
b‘l].|gdlt.šlm[.gdlt.w burm.lb].|rmṣt.ilh[m.b‘lm.---].|ksm.ṯlṯm.[---].|d yqḥ bt[.--]r.dbḥ[.šmn.mr].|šmn.rqḥ[.-]bt. 35[3].19
b i[--.---].|l ṯ[--.---].|ks[.---].|kr[pn.---].|at.š[‘tqt.---].|š‘d[.---].|rt.[---].|‘ṯr[.---].| 16[126].5.40

ksa

[---.]‘ṯ[trt.---].|[-.k]su.ilt[.---].|[ṯl]ṯ.l ‘ṯtrt[.---].|[--.]l ilt.š l ‘ṯt[rt.---].|[‘]ṣr.l pdr 38[23].2
[---.]mṯbt.ilm.w.b.[---].|[---.]ṯṯbn.ilm.w.[---].|[---.]w.ksu.b‘lt.b[htm.---].|[---.]il.bt.gdlt.[---].|[---.]hkl[.---]. 47[33].7
w yp‘r.šmt hm.|šm k.at.aymr.aymr.mr.ym.mr.ym.|l ksi h.nhr l kḥṯ.drkt h.trtqṣ.|b d b‘l.km.nšr b uṣb‘t h.hlm.qd 2.4[68].20
ḥt.w yp‘r.šmt hm.šm k at.|ygrš.ygrš.grš ym grš ym.l ksi h.|[n]hr l kḥṯ drkt h.trtqṣ.b d b‘l km nš|r.b uṣb‘t h.hlm. 2.4[68].12
[---.--]y.npš[.---].|[---.k]si h.|[---.--]y.rb.šm[.---]. 2160.2
ḫr.mǵy.kṯr.w ḫss.|št.alp.qdm h.mra.|w tk.pn h.t‘db.ksu.|w yṯtb.l ymn.aliyn.|b‘l.‘d.lḥm.št[y.ilm].|[w]y‘n.aliy[n 4[51].5.108
bd.ln h.ydy.|ḥmt.hlm.ytq.nḥš.yšlḥm.nḥš.|‘q šr.y‘db.ksa.w ytb.|tqru.l špš.um h.špš.um.ql b.‘m.|ršp.bbt h.mnt.n UG5.7.29
bd.ln h.|ydy.ḥmt.hlm.ytq nḥš yšlḥm.nḥš.|‘q.šr.y‘db.ksa.w ytb.|tqru l špš um h.špš um ql.bl.‘m.|mlk.‘ṯtrt h.mnt UG5.7.39
.ln h.ydy.|ḥmt.hlm.ytq ytqšqy.nḥš.yšlḥm.‘q šr.|y‘db.ksa.w.ytb.|tqru.l špš.um h.špš.um.ql bl.|‘m b‘l.mrym.ṣpn. UG5.7.7
bd.|ln h.ydy.ḥmt.hlm ytq.nḥš.|yšlḥm.nḥš.‘q šr.y‘db ksa.|w ytb.|tqru l špš.um h.špš.um.ql bl ‘m.|šḥr.w šlm šm UG5.7.49
.abd.ln h.ydy.|ḥmt.hlm.ytq.nḥš.yšlḥm.nḥš ‘q.|š.y‘db.ksa w ytb.|tqru l špš.um h.špš.um.ql bl ‘m.|ṯṯ.w kmṯ.ḥryt UG5.7.34
š.abd.ln h.ydy.ḥmt.hlm.ytq.|nḥš.yšlḥm.nḥš.‘q šr.ydb.ksa.|w ytb.|tqru.l špš.u h.špš.um.ql.bl.‘m.|dgn.ttl h.mnt.nṯ UG5.7.12
ln h.ydy ḥmt.hlm.ytq šqy.|nḥš.yšlḥm.nḥš.‘q šr.y‘db.|ksa.w ytb.|tqru l špš.um h.špš.um.ql bl.|‘m ḥrn.mṣd h.mnt UG5.7.56
bd.ln h.ydy.|ḥmt.hlm.ytq.nḥš.yšlḥm.nḥš.|‘q šr.y‘db.ksa.w ytb.|tqru.l špš.um.ql bl.‘m|kṯr.w ḫss.kptr h.mnt.ntk. UG5.7.44
bd.ln h.|ydy.ḥmt.hlm.ytq.nḥš.yšlḥm.|nḥš.‘q šr.y‘db.ksa.w ytb.|tqru l špš.um h.špš.um.ql.bl.‘m.|‘nt w ‘ṯtrt inbb UG5.7.18
|[-]htm.l arṣ.ypl.ul ny.w l.‘pr.‘ẓm ny.|l b‘l[-.---].|tḥt.ksi.zbl.ym.w ‘n.kṯr.w ḫss.l rgmt.|l k.l zbl.b‘l.ṯnt.l rkb.‘rpt.h 2.4[68].7
l k[.---].|[-----].|[-----].|[-----].|[---].al.tš[--.---].|[---.]l ksi y.w pr[‘].|[---].pr‘.ank.[---].|[---.]ank.nši[.---].|[---.ṯ]br.ḫ 1002.13
.y[n].|špq.ilht.arḫt[.yn].|špq.ilm.kḥtm.yn.|špq.ilht.ksat[.yn].|špq.ilm.rḥbt yn.|špq.ilht.dkrt[.yn].|‘d.lḥm.šty.il 4[51].6.52
šlm.šlm i[l].|[š]lm.il.šr.|dgn.w b‘l.|‘ṯ w kmṯ.|yrḫ w ksa.|yrḫ mkty.|ṯkmn w šnm.|kṯr w ḫss.|‘ṯr ‘ṯpr.|šḥr w šl UG5.10.1.6
.l qdš.amrr.|idk.al.tnn.|pnm.tk.ḥqkpt.|il.kl h.kptr.|ksu.ṯbt h.ḥkpt.|arṣ.nḥlt h.|b alp.šd.rbt.|kmn.l p‘n.kṯ.|hbr. 3[‘NT.VI].6.15
[idk.al.ttn.pnm.tk.ḥkpt.il.kl h].|[kptr.]ks[u.ṯbt h.ḥkpt.arṣ.nḥlt h].|b alp.šd.r[bt.kmn.l p‘n.kṯr].|hb 1[‘NT.IX].3.1
spr.b y|rdm.arṣ.|idk.al.ttn.|pnm.tk.qrt h.|hmry.mk.ksu.|ṯbt h.ḫḫ.arṣ.|nḥlt h.w nǵr.|‘nn.ilm.al.|tqrb.l bn.ilm.| 4[51].8.12
ṯb.ilm.idk.|l ytn.pn.‘m.bn.ilm.mt.|tk.qrt h.hmry.mk.ksu.|ṯbt.ḫḫ.arṣ.nḥlt h.tša.|g hm.w tṣḥ.ṯḥm.aliyn.|bn.b‘l.hw 5[67].2.15
mt.aliyn.b‘l.|ḫlq.zbl.b‘l.arṣ.|apnk.lṭpn.il.|d pid.yrd.l ksi.ytb.|l hdm[.w] l.hdm.ytb.|l arṣ.yṣq.‘mr.|un.l riš h.‘pr.p 5[67].6.12
.bm kbd.|ẓi.at.l tlš.|amt.yrḫ.|l dmgy.amt.|aṯrt.qḥ.|ksan k.ḥdg k.|ḥtl k.w ẓi.|b aln.tk m.|b tk.mlbr.|ilšiy.|kry 12[75].1.18

. | [t]rḥṣ.yd h.b dm.ḏmr. | [u]ṣb‘t h.b mm‘.mhrm. | [ṯ]‘r.ksat.l ksat.ṯlḥnt. | [l]ṯlḥn.hdmm.tṯ‘r.l hdmm. | [t]ḥspn.m h. 3['NT].2.36
t.l hkl h. | w l.šb‘t.tmtḫṣ h.b ‘mq. | tḫtṣb.bn.qrtm.tṯ‘r. | ksat.l mhr.ṯ‘r.ṯlḥnt. | l ṣbim.hdmm.l ġzrm. | mid.tmtḫṣn.w t‘ 3['NT].2.21
aḫt[.b‘l]. | y‘l.b‘l.b ǵ[r.---]. | w bn.dgn.b š[---]. | b‘l.yṯb.l ks[i.mlk h]. | bn.dgn.l kḥ[ṯ.drkt h]. | l alp.ql.ẓ[--.---]. | l np ql. 10[76].3.14
t.ṯt‘.y | dd.il.ǵzr.y‘r.mt. | b ql h.y[---.---]. | b‘l.yṯṯbn[.l ksi]. | mlk h.l[nḫt.l kḥṯ]. | drkt h[.---]. | [---.]d[--.---]. | [---].hn[6[49].6.33
ṯ.ḥrṣ.ṯrd.b‘l. | b mrym.ṣpn.mšṣṣ.[-]k‘[-]. | udn h.grš h.l ksi.mlk h. | l nḫt.l kḥṯ.drkt h. | mn m.ib.yp‘.l b‘l.ṣrt.l rkb.‘rpt 3['NT].4.46
y.d[--.---]. | b d.aliyn b['l.---]. | kd.ynaṣn[.---]. | gršnn.l k[si.mlk h.l nḫt.l kḥṯ]. | drkt h.š[--.--]. | w hm.ap.l[--.---]. | ym 1['NT.X].4.24
[.---]. | šmn.prst[.---]. | ydr.hm.ym[.---]. | ‘l amr.yu[ḫd.ksa.mlk h]. | nḫt.kḥṯ.d[rkt h.b bt y]. | aṣḥ.rpi[m.iqra.ilnym]. 22.1[123].17
. | dk ym.ymḫṣ.b ṣmd. | ṣḥr mt.ymṣḫ.l arṣ. | [yṯb.]b[‘]l.l ksi.mlk h. | [---].l kḥṯ.drkt h. | l [ym]m.l yrḫm.l yrḫm. | l šnt.[6[49].5.5
yn.b‘l. | ik.al.yšm[‘] k.ṯr. | il.ab k.l ys‘.alt. | ṯbt k.l yhpk.ksa.mlk k. | l yṯbr.ḫṭ.mṯpṭ k. | yru.bn ilm t.ṯt‘.y | dd.il.ǵzr.y‘r. 6[49].6.28
. | [ik.a]l.yšm‘ k.ṯr.[i]l.ab k.l ys‘.[alt.]ṯ[bt | k.l y]hpk. | [ksa.]mlk k.l yṯbr.ḫṭ.mṯpṭ k.w y‘n[.‘ṯtr].dm[-]k[-]. | [--]ḥ.b y.ṯ 2.3[129].18
lḥm. | mgṯ.w yṯrm.hn.ym. | w ṯn.yṯb.krt.l ‘d h. | yṯb.l ksi mlk. | l nḫt.l kḥṯ.drkt. | ap.yṣb.yṯb.b hkl. | w ywsrnn.ggn 16.6[127].23
‘nt w ‘ṯtrt inbb h.mnt.nṯk. | nḥš.šlḥm.nḥš.‘q šr[.y‘]db.ksa. | nḥš.šmrr.nḥš.‘q šr.ln h.ml | ḫš.abd.ln h.ydy.ḥmt.hlm.yṯ UG5.7.23
---.gd]ltm.p[--.---]. | [---.]arb‘t[.---]. | [---.]qdš[.---]. | [---.k]su.p[--.---]. | [---.]agn[.---]. | [---.b‘lt.b]htm[.---]. | [---.--]by.ṯ[45[45].4
ṣ.yd h.b dm.ḏmr. | [u]ṣb‘t h.b mm‘.mhrm. | [ṯ]‘r.ksat.l ksat.ṯlḥnt. | [l]ṯlḥn.hdmm.tṯ‘r.l hdmm. | [t]ḥspn.m h.w trḥṣ. 3['NT].2.36

ksd

n. | bn.‘zn. | bn.aršw. | bn.ḫzrn. | bn.iǵyn. | w.nḥl h. | bn.ksd. | bn.bršm. | bn.kzn. | w.nḥl h. | w.nḥl hm. | w.[n]ḥl hm. | b 113[400].2.18
dyn.mḫ[ṣ]. | aṯry.mḫṣ. | b‘ln.mḫṣ. | y[ḫ]ṣdq.mḫṣ. | ṣp[r].ks[d]. | b‘l.š[lm]. | ḫyrn[.---]. | a[--.---]. | ‘[--.---]. | š[--.---]. | [-----] 2084.18
š.gt.ngr. | r‘ym. | bn.ḫri[-]. | bnš.gt.‘ṯtrt. | ad[-]l[-]m. | ‘šr.ksdm.yd.lmd hm.lqḥ. | ‘šr.mḫṣm.yd.lmd hm. | apym. | [bn]š 1040.8
| kzym. | yṣrm. | mru.ibrn. | mru.skn. | nsk.ksp | mḫṣm. | ksdm. | mdrǵlm. | pslm. | yṣḥm. 74[115].16
šm. | pslm. | mkrm. | yṣḥm. | šrm. | n‘rm. | ‘bdm. | kzym. | ksdm. | [nsk].ṯlṯ. | gt.mlkym. | tmrym. | ṯnqym. | ṯǵrm. | mru.sk 1026.1.15
ksdm. | ṣdqn. | nwrḏr. | ṯrin. | ‘dršp. | pqr. | agbṯr. | ‘bd. | ksd. 1044.1
ksdm. | ṣdqn. | nwrḏr. | ṯrin. | ‘dršp. | pqr. | agbṯr. | ‘bd. | ksd. 1044.9

ksy

m.yṯb. | l arṣ.yṣq.‘mr. | un.l riš h.‘pr.plṯt. | l qdqd h.lpš.yks. | mizrtm.ǵr.b abn. | ydy.psltm.b y‘r. | yhdy.lḥm.w dqn. | 5[67].6.16
]dbr.ysmt.šd. | [šḥl]mmt.t[mǵ.]l b‘l.np[l]. | [l a]rṣ[.lpš].tks.miz[rtm]. 5[67].6.31
‘šr.ktnt. | ‘šr.rṭm. | kkr[.-].ḫt. | mitm[.p]ttm. | ṯlṯm[.---].kst. | alp.a[bn.ṣ]rp. 1114.5
n[.---]. | aḫdt.plk h[.b yd h]. | plk.qlt.b ymn h. | npyn h.mks.bšr h. | tmt‘.md h.b ym.ṯn. | npyn h.b nhrm. | štt.ḫptr.l i 4[51].2.5
d[.l b‘l]. | w rum.l[rkb.‘rpt]. | tḥbq.[---]. | tḥbq[.---]. | w tksynn.bṯn[-.] | y[--.]šr h.w šḫp h. | [--.]šḫp.ṣǵrt h. | yrk.t‘l.b ǵ 10[76].3.25
. | ‘rpt.bl.ṭl.bl rbb. | bl.šr‘.thmtm.bl. | ṭbn.ql.b‘l.k tmz‘. | kst.dnil.mt.rpi. | all.ǵzr.m[t.]hr[nmy]. | gm.l bt[h.dnil.k yṣḥ] 19[1AQHT].1.47
| ybṣr.ḥbl.diym. | tbky.pǵt.bm.lb. | tdm‘.bm.kbd. | tmz‘.kst.dnil.mt. | rpi.al.ǵzr.mt.hrnmy. | apnk.dnil.mt. | rpi.yṣly.‘r 19[1AQHT].1.36
spr.npṣ.krw. | tt.ḫtrm.ṯn.kst. | spl.mšlt.w.mqḥm. | w md h. | arn.w mznm. | ṯn.ḫlpnm. | 2050.2

ksyn

gyn. | ullym.bn.abynm. | antn.bn.iwr[n]r. | pwn.ṯmry. | ksyn.bn.lḥsn. | [-]kyn.ṯmry. 94[313].9

ksl

.[b h.p‘nm]. | tṭṭ.‘l[n.pn h.td‘.b ‘dn]. | ksl.y[ṯbr.yǵṣ.pnt.ksl h]. | anš.[dt.ẓr h.yšu.g h]. | w yṣ[ḥ.---]. | mḫṣ[.---]. | š[--.---]. 19[1AQHT].2.95
h.p‘nm. | [tṭṭ.b ‘]dn.ksl. | [tṯbr.‘ln.p]n h.td[‘]. | tǵṣ[.pnt.ks]l h. | anš.dt.ẓr.[h]. | tšu.g h.w tṣḥ[.i]k. | mǵy.aliy[n.b]‘l. | ik. 4[51].2.19
ilm.b h.p‘nm. | tṭṭ.b‘d n.ksl.tṯbr. | ‘ln.pn h.td‘.tǵṣ.pnt. | ksl h.anš.dt.ẓr h.tšu. | g h.w tṣḥ.ik.mǵy.gpn.w ugr. | mn.ib.y 3['NT].3.32
--.]ḥtn.qn.yṣbt. | [---.--]m.b nši.‘n h.w tphn. | [---.--]ml.ksl h.k b[r]q. | [---.]m[-]ǵ[-].thmt.brq. | [---].tṣb.qšt.bnt. | [---.‘ 17[2AQHT].6.11
šib.yṣat.mrḥ h. | l tl.yṣb.pn h.tǵr. | yṣu.hlm.aḫ h.tph. | [ksl]h.l arṣ.tṯbr. | [---.]aḫ h.tbky. | [--.m]rṣ.mlk. | [---.]krt.adn 16.1[125].54
. | ṯpṭ qṣr.npš.l tdy. | ṯšm.‘l.dl.l pn k. | l tšlḥm.ytm.b‘d. | ksl k.almnt.km. | aḫt.‘rš.mdw.anšt. | ‘rš.zbln.rd.l mlk. | amlk. 16.6[127].50
]. | b dm.ḏmr.hlqm.b mm[‘]. | mhrm.mṭm.tgrš. | šbm.b ksl.qšt h.mdnt. | w hln.‘nt.l bt h.tmǵyn. | tštql.ilt.l hkl h. | w l 3['NT].2.16
pš h]. | k iṭl.brlt h.[b h.p‘nm]. | tṭṭ.‘l[n.pn h.td‘.b ‘dn]. | ksl.y[ṯbr.yǵṣ.pnt.ksl h]. | anš.[dt.ẓr h.yšu.g h]. | w yṣ[ḥ.---]. | 19[1AQHT].2.95
b n‘m.b gb‘.tliyt. | hlm.‘nt.tph.ilm.b h.p‘nm. | tṭṭ.b‘d n.ksl.tṯbr. | ‘ln.pn h.td‘.tǵṣ.pnt. | ksl h.anš.dt.ẓr h.tšu. | g h.w tṣ 3['NT].3.30
hlk.btlt. | ‘nt.tdrq.ybmt. | [limm].b h.p‘nm. | [tṭṭ.b ‘]dn.ksl. | [tṯbr.‘ln.p]n h.td[‘]. | tǵṣ[.pnt.ks]l h. | anš.dt.ẓr.[h]. | tšu. 4[51].2.17
qnu.---]. | [---.]ǵprt.‘š[r.---]. | [---.p]ttm.l.ip[--.---]. | [---.]ksl.ṯlṯ.m[at.---]. | [---].abn.ṣr[p.---]. | [---.-]rt.ṯlṯm[.---]. | [--]l.ṯr 1106.26
-].iqni.‘šrm.ǵprt. | [---.š]pšg.iqni.mit.pṯtm. | [---].mitm.kslm. | [---].pwt.ṯlṯ.mat.abn.ṣrp. | [---.-]qt.l.ṯrmnm. | [---].ṯlṯm. 1106.9

ksln

tn. | [--]ṯm.b.gt.irbṣ. | [--]šmyn. | [w.]nḥl h. | bn.qṣn. | bn.ksln. | bn.ṣrym. | bn.ṯmq. | bn.ntp. | bn.mlk. | bn.ṯ‘[-]. | bn.km[- 1073.1.6
[---]y. | [---.]w.nḥl h. | bn ksln.ṯlṯḫ. | bn yṣmḫ.bn.ṯrn w nḥl h. | bn srd.bn agmn. | bn [-]l 101[10].3

ksm

.‘šdm. | kd yn.l.ḫdǵb.w.kd.ḥmṣ. | prš.glbm.l.bt. | tgmǵ.kšmm.b.yrḫ.iṭtbnm. | šb‘m.dd.ṯn.kbd. | tgmr.ḥṭm.šb‘.ddm. | ḫ 1099.30
mitm.‘šr kbd. | kšmm.b.mṣbt. | mit.‘šrm.ṯn kbd. | [kš]mm. | [‘]š[r]m.ṯn.kbd.ḥ 2091.2
rš d.‘šy.ln h. | aḫd.yd h.b škrn.m‘ms h. | [k]šb‘ yn.spu.ksm h.bt.b‘l. | [w m]nt h bt.il.ṯḥ.gg h.b ym. | [ti]ṭ.rḥṣ.npṣ h.b 17[2AQHT].1.32
.grš. | d ‘šy.ln.aḫd.yd y.b š | krn m‘ms y k šb‘t yn. | spu.ksm y.bt.b‘l.[w]mn[t]. | y.bt.il.ṯḥ.gg y.b ym.ṭiṭ. | rḥṣ.npṣ y.b 17[2AQHT].2.21
]. | l ‘pr.ḏm[r.aṯr k.ṭbq]. | lḥt.niṣ k.gr[š.d ‘šy.ln k]. | spu.ksm k.bt.[b‘l.w mnt k]. | bt il.aḫd.yd k.b [škrn]. | m‘ms k.k š 17[2AQHT].2.4
t.k[--]. | tš‘.‘šr h.dd.l.b[t.--]. | ḫmš.ddm.l.ḥtyt. | ṯlṯm.dd.kšmn.l.gzzm. | yyn. | ṣdqn. | ‘bd.pdr. | myṣm. | tgt. | w.lmd h. | y 1099.4
pu. | w.lmd h. | ‘dršp. | w.lmd h. | krwn b.gt.nbk. | ddm.kšmm.l.ḫtn. | ddm.l.trbnn. | ddm.š‘rm.l.trbnn. | ddm.š‘rm.l.ḫ 1099.20
qrš.mlk.ab.]šnm. | [tša.g hm.w tṣ]ḥ.sbn. | [---]l[.---.]‘d. | ksm.mhyt[.m]ǵny. | l n‘m y.arṣ.dbr. | l ysmt.šd.šḥlmmt. | mǵ 5[67].6.5
-----]. | yṣq.šm[n.---]. | ‘n.tr.arṣ.w šmm. | sb.l qṣm.arṣ. | l ksm.mhyt.‘n. | l arṣ.m[t]r.b‘l. | w l šd.mṭr.‘ly. | n‘m.l arṣ.mṭr. 16[126].3.4

.l arṣ.mṭr.b‘l. | w l šd.mṭr.‘ly. | n‘m.l ḥṭt.b gn. | bm.nrt.ksmm. | ‘l.tl[-]k.‘ṭrṭrm. | nšu.[r]iš.ḥrṭm. | l ẓr.‘db.dgn kly. | lḥ 16[126].3.10
mitm.‘šr kbd. | kšmm.b.mṣbt. | mit.‘šrm.ṯn kbd. | [kš]mm. | [‘]š[r]m.ṯn.kbd.ḥṭm. | [-]m[-.-]‘[-.-]ag š‘rm. | [---.--]m 2091.4
dm.kbd.yn.b.gt.[---]. | [mi]tm.ḫmšm.ḫmš.k[bd]. | [dd].kšmm.tš‘[.---]. | [š]‘rm.ṯṯ.‘[šr]. | [dd].ḥṭm.w.ḫ[mšm]. | [ṯ]lṯ kb 2092.7
.dd[.---]. | [---]mn.arb‘m.y[n]. | b.gt.trǵnds. | tš‘.‘šr.[dd].kšmm. | ṯn.‘šr[.dd.ḥ]ṭm. | w.šb[‘.---]. 2092.16
[---.]ksp dd qmḥ. | [---.]ṯlṯ dd ksmm. | [---.-]rbr dd š‘rm. | [---.]r[--.]ḥṭm. | kr[--.]tp[n]. | kkr[. 2037.1.2

ksn

[-----]. | [-----]. | ḥd[-.---]. | ṯlṯm.[---]. | ksn.[---]. | u[--.---]. | [-----]. | a[--.---]. 155[-].5

ksp

y. | iršy. | y‘ḏrd. | ayaḫ. | bn.aylt. | ḫmš.mat.arb‘m. | kbd.ksp.anyt. | d.‘rb.b.anyt. | l.mlk.gbl. | w.ḫmšm.ksp. | lqḥ.mlk.g 2106.11
‘nt.mḫṣ y hm[.m]ḫṣ. | bn y.hm[.mkly.ṣ]brt. | ary y[.ẓl].ksp.[a]ṯrt. | k t‘n.ẓl.ksp.w n[-]t. | ḫrṣ.šmḫ.rbt.a[ṯrt]. | ym.gm.l 4[51].2.26
.mit. | ksp.b y[d]. | birtym. | [un]ṯ inn. | l [h]m ‘d ṯṯtbn. | ksp.iwrkl. | w ṯb.l unṯ hm. 1006.18
m. | agmy. | ‘dyn. | ‘bdb‘l. | ‘bdkṯr.‘bd. | tdǵl. | b‘lsn. | nsk.ksp. | iwrtn. | ydln. | ‘bdilm. | dqn. | nsk.ṯlṯ. | ‘bdadt. | bṣmn.spr. 1039.2.23
qrht.b[--.---]. | ksp.iš[-.---]. | art.[---]. | [-----]. | [-----]. | l [----]. | b[--.---]. | ḫl[--.- 1147.2
[r]my. | b.‘šrt.ksp.b.a[--]. | ṯqlm.ḫr[ṣ.]b.ṯmnt.ksp. | ‘šrt.ksp.b.alp.[b d].bn.[---]. | tš‘.ṣin.b.tš‘t.ksp. | mšlt.b.ṯql.ksp. | kd 2101.21
lk. | b.mit.ḫmšt.kbd.ksp. | ṯlṯ.ktnt.b d.an[r]my. | b.‘šrt.ksp.b.a[--]. | ṯqlm.ḫr[ṣ.]b.ṯmnt.ksp. | ‘šrt.ksp.b.alp.[b d].bn.[-- 2101.19
bt.‘bd mlk. | w.snt. | bt.ugrt. | w.pdy h[m]. | iwrkl.mit. | ksp.b y[d]. | birtym. | [un]ṯ inn. | l [h]m ‘d ṯṯtbn. | ksp.iwrkl. | 1006.14
šš[r]t.ḫrṣ.ṯqlm.kbd.‘šrt.mzn h. | b [ar]b‘m.ksp. | b d[.‘b]dym.ṯlṯ.kkr š‘rt. | iqn[i]m.ṯṯt.‘šrt.ksp h. | ḫmšt.ḫ 2100.2
| [---].ḏmrd.bn.ḥrmn. | [---.-]ǵn.ksp.ṯṯt. | [---.]ygry.ṯlṯm.ksp.b[--]. 2153.12
dy. | [---.šd] u[b]dy. | [---.]šd.ubdy. | [---.]bn.k[--.]ṯ[l]ṯm ksp b[---]. | [---.]šd b‘ly. | [---.]šd ubdy. | [---.š]d ubdy. | [---.šd] 2031.6
y k.ṣḥ.ḫrn. | b bht k.‘ḏbt.b qrb. | hkl k.tbl k.ǵrm. | mid.ksp.gb‘m.mḥmd.. | ḫrṣ.w bn.bht.ksp. | w ḫrṣ.bht.ṭhrm. | iqni 4[51].5.94
b‘l.ṣḥ.ḫrn.b bht h. | ‘ḏbt.b qrb hkl h. | yblnn ǵrm.mid.ksp. | gb‘m lḥmd.ḫrṣ. | yblnn.udr.ilqṣm. | yak.l kṯr.w ḫss. | w ṯ 4[51].5.100
b‘l. | ṣḥ.ḫrn.b bhm k. | ‘ḏbt.b qrb.hkl k. | tbl k.ǵrm.mid.ksp. | gb‘m.mḥmd.ḫrṣ. | ybl k.udr.ilqṣm. | w bn.bht.ksp.w ḫrṣ 4[51].5.77
m.šmt.b.ṯql. | kkr.w.[ml]tḥ.tyt.[---]. | [b]šb‘[m.w.n]ṣp.ksp. | [tgm]r.[alp.w.]ṯlṯ.mat. 2101.27
ǵzr.ṭḥm. | aliyn.b‘l. | [hw]t.aliy.q | [rdm.]bht y.bnt. | [dt.ksp.dtm]. | [ḫrṣ.hk]l y. | [---.]aḫ y. | [---.]aḫ y. | [----]y. | [---.]r 4[51].8.36
nm. | ‘šrm.ksp.d mkr. | mlk. | ṯlṯ.mat.ksp.d.šb[n]. | mit.ksp.d.ṭbq. | ṯmnym.arb‘t. | kbd.ksp. | d.nqdm. | ḫmšm.l mit. | k 2107.5
l š‘r.ṭl.yd[‘t]. | hlk.kbkbm.mdl.‘r. | ṣmd.pḥl.št.gpn y dt ksp. | dt.yrq.nqbn y.tš[m‘]. | pǵt.ṯkmt.my.ḫspt.l[š‘]r.ṭl. | yd‘t. 19[1AQHT].2.53
t[y]. | yšm‘.qd.w amr[r]. | mdl.‘r.ṣmd.pḥl. | št.gpnm.dt.ksp. | dt.yrq.nqbnm. | ‘db.gpn.atnt h. | yḥbq.qdš.w amrr. | yšt 4[51].4.10
r.l dgy.rbt]. | aṯrt.ym[.mdl.‘r]. | ṣmd.pḥl[.št.gpnm.dt]. | ksp.dt.yr[q.nqbnm]. | ‘db.gpn.atnt[y]. | yšm‘.qd.w amr[r]. | 4[51].4.6
.ṭbq. | ṯmnym.arb‘t. | kbd.ksp. | d.nqdm. | ḫmšm.l mit. | ksp.d.mkr.ar. | arb‘m ksp d mkr. | atlg. | mit.ksp.d mkr. | ilšt 2107.10
bd.ksp. | d.nqdm. | ḫmšm.l mit. | ksp.d.mkr.ar. | arb‘m ksp d mkr. | atlg. | mit.ksp.d mkr. | ilštm‘. | ‘šrm.l mit.ksp. | ‘l. 2107.11
šm.l mit. | ksp.d.mkr.ar. | arb‘m ksp d mkr. | atlg. | mit.ksp.d mkr. | ilštm‘. | ‘šrm.l mit.ksp. | ‘l.bn.alkbl.šb[ny]. | ‘šrm 2107.13
spr.argmnm. | ‘šrm.ksp.d mkr. | mlk. | ṯlṯ.mat.ksp.d.šb[n]. | mit.ksp.d.ṭbq. | ṯmny 2107.2
qn. | w.kkrm.ṯlṯ. | mit.ksp.‘mn. | bn.ulbtyn. | w.kkr.ṯlṯ. | ksp.d.nkly.b.šd. | mit.ḫmšt.kbd. | [l.]gmn.bn.usyy. | mit.ṯṯm.k 1143.6
lṯ.mat.ksp.d.šb[n]. | mit.ksp.d.ṭbq. | ṯmnym.arb‘t. | kbd.ksp. | d.nqdm. | ḫmšm.l mit. | ksp.d.mkr.ar. | arb‘m ksp d mk 2107.7
spr.argmnm. | ‘šrm.ksp.d mkr. | mlk. | ṯlṯ.mat.ksp.d.šb[n]. | mit.ksp.d.ṭbq. | ṯmnym.arb‘t. | kbd.ksp. | d.nqd 2107.4
[---.]ksp dd qmḥ. | [---.]ṯlṯ dd ksmm. | [---.-]rbr dd š‘rm. | [---.]r[--. 2037.1.1
[ar]b‘m.ksp. | b d[.‘b]dym.ṯlṯ.kkr š‘rt. | iqn[i]m.ṯṯt.‘šrt.ksp h. | ḫmšt.ḫrṣ.bt.il. | b.ḫmšt.‘šrt.ksp. | ḫmš.mat.šmt. | b.‘šrt 2100.4
. | mit.adrm.b.‘šrt. | ‘šr.ydt.b.‘šrt. | ḫmš.kkrm.ṣml. | ‘šrt.ksp h. | ḫmš.kkr.qnm. | ṯlṯt.w.ṯlṯt.ksp h. | arb‘.kkr. | algbṯ.arb‘ 1127.11
lṯt.ksp h. | arb‘.kkr. | algbṯ.arb‘t. | ksp h. | kkr.š‘rt. | šb‘t.ksp h. | ḫmš.mqdm.dnyn. | b.ṯql.dprn.aḥd. | b.ṯql. | ḫmšm.‘rgz 1127.18
mš.kkr.qnm. | ṯlṯt.w.ṯlṯt.ksp h. | arb‘.kkr. | algbṯ.arb‘t. | ksp h. | kkr.š‘rt. | šb‘t.ksp h. | ḫmš.mqdm.dnyn. | b.ṯql.dprn.a 1127.16
b‘ld‘.yd[.---.‘]šrt.ksp h. | lbiy.pdy.[---.k]sp h. 2112.1
t.b dm.tt. | w.ṯmnt.ksp.hn. | ktn.d.ṣr.pḥm.b h.w.ṯqlm. | ksp h.mitm.pḥm.b d.skn. | w.ṯṯ.ktnm.ḫmšt.w.nṣp.ksp.hn. 1110.5
ḫmš.kkrm.ṣml. | ‘šrt.ksp h. | ḫmš.kkr.qnm. | ṯlṯt.w.ṯlṯt.ksp h. | arb‘.kkr. | algbṯ.arb‘t. | ksp h. | kkr.š‘rt. | šb‘t.ksp h. | ḫ 1127.13
ṯṯm.ṯlṯ.kb[d]. | arb‘m.ṯp[rt]. | ksp h. | ṯmn.dd[.--]. | ṯlṯ.dd.p[--]. | šb‘t.p[--]. | tš‘t.k[bd.---]. | ḫ 2120.3
b‘ld‘.yd[.---.‘]šrt.ksp h. | lbiy.pdy.[---.k]sp h. 2112.2
.ksp.l rqm.ḫrṣ. | nṣb.l lbnt.šmḫ. | aliyn.b‘l.ht y.bnt. | dt.ksp.hkl y.dtm. | ḫrṣ.‘dbt.bht[h.b‘]l. | y‘db.hd.‘db[.‘d]bt. | hkl 4[51].6.37
l yblt.ḫbṭm. | ap ksp hm. | l yblt. | w ht.luk ‘m ml[kt]. | tǵsdb.šmlšn. | w tb‘ ank 1021.2
‘m.l.mit.šmn. | arb‘m.l.mit.tišr. | ṯṯ.ṯṯ.b [ṯ]ql.ṯlṯt.l.‘šrm.ksp hm. | sstm.b.šb‘m. | ṯlṯ.mat.trm.b.‘šrt. | mit.adrm.b.‘šrt. | ‘ 1127.5
m.ḫm[š].mat.kbd. | b d.tt.w.ṯlṯ.ktnt.b dm.tt. | w.ṯmnt.ksp.hn. | ktn.d.ṣr.pḥm.b h.w.ṯqlm. | ksp h.mitm.pḥm.b d.skn 1127.5
lm. | ksp h.mitm.pḥm.b d.skn. | w.ṯṯ.ktnm.ḫmšt.w.nṣp.ksp.hn. 1110.6
kl k.tbl k.ǵrm. | mid.ksp.gb‘m.mḥmd.. | ḫrṣ.w bn.bht.ksp. | w ḫrṣ.bht.ṭhrm. | iqnim.šmḫ.aliyn. | b‘l.ṣḥ.ḫrn.b bht h. | 4[51].5.95
id.ksp. | gb‘m.mḥmd.ḫrṣ. | ybl k.udr.ilqṣm. | w bn.bht.ksp.w ḫrṣ. | bht.ṭhrm.iqnim. | šmḫ.btlt.‘nt.td‘ṣ. | p‘nm.w tr.ar 4[51].5.80
id.yph.mlk. | r[š]p.ḥgb.ap. | w[.n]pš.ksp. | w ḫrṣ.km[-]. | w.ḥ[--.-]lp. | w.š.l[--]p. | w[.--.-]nš. | i[--.---] 2005.1.3
. | b ṯmnt.‘šrt.yr | ṯḥṣ.mlk.brr. | ‘lm.tzǵ.b ǵb.ṣpn. | nḥkt.ksp.w ḫrṣ ṯ‘ ṯn šm l btbt. | alp.w š šrp.alp šlmm. | l b‘l.‘ṣr l ṣp UG5.12.A.8
w ylak. | mlakm.l k.‘m.krt. | mswn h.ṯḥm.pbl.mlk. | qḥ.ksp.w yrq.ḫrṣ. | yd.mqm h.w ‘bd.‘lm. | ṯlṯ.sswm.mrkbt. | b trb 14[KRT].3.126
dm.ytnt.il w ušn. | ab.adm.w ṯtb. | mlakm.l h.lm.ank. | ksp.w yrq.ḫrṣ. | yd.mqm h.w ‘bd. | ‘lm.ṯlṯ.sswm.mrkbt. | b trb 14[KRT].3.138
rt.mswn h]. | tš[an.g hm.w tṣḥn]. | ṯḥ[m.pbl.mlk]. | qḥ[.ksp.w yrq]. | ḫrṣ.[yd.mqm h]. | w ‘bd[.‘lm.ṯlṯ]. | sswm.m[rkbt] 14[KRT].6.269
‘m.[krt.msw]n. | w r[gm.l krt.]ṯ‘. | ṯḥm[.pbl.mlk]. | qḥ.[ksp.w yr]q. | ḫrṣ[.yd.mqm] h. | ‘bd[.‘lm.ṯlṯ]. | ss[wm.mrkbt]. | 14[KRT].5.250
lk.l bt y. | n[g.]krt.l ḥẓ[r y]. | w y‘n[y.k]rt[.ṯ]‘. | lm.ank.ksp. | w yr[q.ḫrṣ]. | yd.mqm h.w ‘bd. | ‘lm.ṯlṯ.sswm. | mrkbt.b 14[KRT].6.282
[-----]. | [-----]. | [-----.lm]. | [ank.ksp.w yrq]. | [ḫrṣ.]yd.mqm h. | [w ‘b]d.‘lm.ṯlṯ. | [ssw]m.mrkbt 14[KRT].1.53
.tšpk m. | [l ‘pr.tšu.g h.]w tṣḥ.šm‘.m‘. | [l aqht.ǵzr.i]rš.ksp.w atn k. | [ḫrṣ.w aš]lḥ k.w tn.qšt k.[l]. | [‘nt.tq]ḥ[.q]ṣ‘t k. 17[2AQHT].6.17

ṣ.|bn y.hm[.mkly.ṣ]brt.|ary y[.ẓl].ksp.[a]ṯrt.|k ṯ'n.ẓl.ksp.w n[-]t.|ḫrṣ.šmḫ.rbt.a[ṯrt].|ym.gm.l ġlm h.k [ṯṣḥ].|'n. 4[51].2.27
y|rḫ ytrḫ.ib t'rb m b bh|t h.w atn mhr h l a|b h.alp ksp w rbt ḫ|rṣ.išlḥ ẓhrm iq|nim.atn šd h krm[m].|šd dd h 24[77].20
ṯṯ.mat.ksp.|ḫṯbn.ybnn.|arb'm.l.mit.šmn.|arb'm.l.mit.tišr.|ṯṯ.ṯṯ.b [1127.1
[---.]ḫ[---.]ṯmnym[.k]sp ḫmšt.|[w a]rb' kkr 'l bn[.--].|[w] ṯlṯ šmn.|[w a]r[b'] ks 1103.1
.ṣin.b.ṯṯt.w.kmsk.|arb'[.k]dwṯm.w.ṯṯ.ṯprtm.|b.'šr[m.]ksp.|ḫmš.kkr.ṣml.|b.'šrt.b d.bn.kyn.|'šr.kkr.š'rt.|b d.urtn. 2100.11
'rt.|iqn[i]m.ṯṯt.'šrt.ksp h.|ḫmšt.ḫrṣ.bt.il.|b.ḫmšt.'šrt.ksp.|ḫmš.mat.šmt.|b.'šrt.ksp.|'šr.ṣin.b.ṯṯt.w.kmsk.|arb'[.k 2100.6
'lm.t'rbn.gṯrm.|bt.mlk.ṯql.ḫrṣ.|l špš.w yrḫ.l gṯr.|ṯql.ksp.ṯb.ap w np[š].|l 'nt h.ṯql.ḫrṣ.|l špš[.w y]rḫ.l gṯr.ṯn.|[ṯql 33[5].12
ap w np[š].|l 'nt h.ṯql.ḫrṣ.|l špš[.w y]rḫ.l gṯr.ṯn.|[ṯql.ksp].ṯb.ap.w npš.|[---].bt.alp w š.|[---.--]m.l gṯrm.|[---.]l 'nt 33[5].15
n.il[.d pid.---].|'l.ydm.p'rt[.---].|šm k.mdd.i[l.---].|bt ksp y.d[--.---].|b d.aliyn b['l.---].|kd.ynaṣn[.---].|gršnn.l k[s 1['NT.X].4.21
qd[šm].|mru s[kn].|mru ib[rn].|mdm.|inšt.|nsk ksp.|yṣḥm.|ḥrš mrkbt.|ḥrš qṭn.|ḥrš bhtm. 73[114].6
].|ṣmt.'gl.il.'tk.|mḫšt.klbt.ilm išt.|klt.bt.il.ḏbb.imtḫṣ.ksp.|itrṯ.ḫrṣ.ṭrd.b'l.|b mrym.ṣpn.mšṣṣ.[-]k'[-].|udn h.grš h. 3['NT].3.43
ilt.ṣdynm.|hm.ḥry.bt y.|iqḥ.aš'rb.ġlmt.|ḥẓr y.ṯn h.wspm.|atn.w ṯlṯ h.ḫrṣm.|ylk ym.w ṯn.|ṯlṯ.rb'.ym.|aḫr.špš 14[KRT].4.205
t.ksp.b.alp.[b d].bn.[---].|ṯš'.ṣin.b.ṯš't.ksp.|mšlt.b.ṯql.ksp.|kdwṯ.l.grgyn.b.ṯq[l].|ḫmšm.šmt.b.ṯql.|kkr.w.[ml]ṭḥ.ty 2101.23
t.kbd.|ḫmš.alp.ṯlṯ.l.ḫlby.|b d.tlmi.b.'šrm.ḫmšt.|kbd.ksp.|kkrm.š'rt.šṯt.b d.gg['t].|b.'šrt.ksp.|ṯlṯ.uṭbm.b d.alḫn.b 2101.8
mšq.mlkt.|mitm.ṯṯm.|kbd.ks[p].|ksp.|ṯmnym.|ḫrṣ. 1157.3
[r].|[ks.ksp.ktn.mit.pḥ]m.|[mit.iqni.l ḫbrtn]r ṯn.|[ks.ksp.ktn.mit.pḥm].|[mit.iqn]i.l skl.[--].|[---.m]it pḥm.l š[--]. 64[118].37
qni.l uṯryn.|ks.ksp.ktn.mit.pḥm.|mit.iqni.l tpnr.|[ks.ksp.kt]n.mit.pḥ[m].|[mit.iqni.l]ḫbrtn[r].|[ks.ksp.ktn.mit.p 64[118].33
nr.|[ks.ksp.kt]n.mit.pḥ[m].|[mit.iqni.l]ḫbrtn[r].|[ks.ksp.ktn.mit.pḥ]m.|[mit.iqni.l ḫbrtn]r ṯn.|[ks.ksp.ktn.mit.p 64[118].35
iqni.l mlkt.|ks.ḫrṣ.ktn.mit.pḥm.|mit.iqni.l uṯryn.|ks.ksp.ktn.mit.pḥm.|mit.iqni.l tpnr.|[ks.ksp.kt]n.mit.pḥ[m].| 64[118].31
n.'ly.l mpḫm.|b d.ḫss.mṣbṭm.|yṣq.ksp.yšl|ḥ.ḫrṣ.yṣq.ksp.|l alpm.ḫrṣ.yṣq|m.l rbbt.|yṣq-ḫym.w tbṯḫ.|kt.il.dt.rbt 4[51].1.27
mlk[.---].|w.'l.ap.s[--.---].|b hm.w.rgm.hw.al[--].|atn.ksp.l hm.'d.|ilak.'m.mlk.|ht.lik[t.--.]mlk[.--].|w.mlk.yštal. 2008.2.7
p ṣin.šql.ṯrm.|w mri ilm.'glm.dt.šnt.|imr.qmṣ.llim.k ksp.|l 'brm.zt.ḫrṣ.l 'brm.kš.|dpr.ṯlḥn.b q'l.b q'l.|mlkm.hn. 22.2[124].14
k.|b šb['.]y[mm].td.išt.|b bht m.n[bl]at.b hkl m.|sb.ksp.l rqm.ḫrṣ.|nṣb.l lbnt.šmḫ.|aliyn.b'l.ht y.bnt.|dt.ksp.hk 4[51].6.34
'm.|kbd.ksp.anyt.|d.'rb.b.anyt.|l.mlk.gbl.|w.ḫmšm.ksp.|lqḥ.mlk.gbl.|lbš.anyt h.|b'rm.ksp.|mḫr.hn. 2106.14
mit.ḫršḫ.b.ṯqlm.|w.šb'.'šr.šmn.|d.l.yṣa.bt.mlk.|tgmr.ksp.mitm.|ḫmšm.kbd. 2100.22
lk.gbl.|w.ḫmšm.ksp.|lqḥ.mlk.gbl.|lbš.anyt h.|b'rm.ksp.|mḫr.hn. 2106.17
m.|'šrm.|mrum.|ṯnnm.|mqdm.|khnm.|qdšm.|nsk.ksp.|mkrm. 71[113].74
|m.l rbbt.|yṣq-ḫym.w tbṯḫ.|kt.il.dt.rbtm.|kt.il.nbt.b ksp.|šmrgt.b dm.ḫrṣ.|kḥt.il.nḥt.|b ẓr.hdm.id.|d prša.b br. 4[51].1.32
]b.ṯmnt.ksp.|'šrt.ksp.b.alp.[b d].bn.[---].|ṯš'.ṣin.b.ṯš't.ksp.|mšlt.b.ṯql.ksp.|kdwṯ.l.grgyn.b.ṯq[l].|ḫmšm.šmt.b.ṯql. 2101.22
ṣr[.---].|w mit.š'rt.[-]y[-.---].|w.kdr.w.npt t[--.---].|w.ksp.y'db.[---]. 38[23].11
ḫmšt.'š[rt].|ksp.'l.agd[ṯb].|w nit w m'ṣd.|w ḫrmṯt.|'šrt.ksp.|'l.ḫ[z]rn.| 2053.2
].|[-]šy[.---] h.|[-]kt[.---.]nrn.|[b]n.nmq[.---].|[ḫm]št.ksp.'l.aṯt.|[-]ṯd[.bn.]štn. 2055.19
[.--].|[-]ḥ[-.---].|[-]p[-.---.-]ny.|[-]ḥ[-.---.-]dn.|arb'[m.ksp.]'l.|il[m]l[k.a]rgnd.|uškny[.w]mit.|zt.b d hm.rib.|w [- 2055.10
ksp d mkr.|atlg.|mit.ksp.d mkr.|ilštm'.|'šrm.l mit.ksp.|'l.bn.alkbl.šb[ny].|'šrm ksp.'l.|wrt.mtny.w 'l.|prdny.a 2107.15
[ṯl]ṯm.ksp.'[l].|[b]n.bly.gb'ly.|[šp]ḥ.a[n]ntb.|w.m[--.u]škny.|[']š[r 2055.1
ḫmšt.|[w a]rb' kkr 'l bn[.--].|[w] ṯlṯ šmn.|[w a]r[b'] ksp 'l bn ymn.|šb šr šmn [--] ṯryn.|ḫm[š]m l 'šr ksp 'l bn lli 1103.4
r[b'] ksp 'l bn ymn.|šb šr šmn [--] ṯryn.|ḫm[š]m l 'šr ksp 'l bn llit.|[--]l[-.-]p 'l [---.-]b'm arny.|w 'l [---.]rb'm ṯql 1103.6
[---.-]rwd.šmbnš[.---].|[---].ksp.'l.k[--].|[---.--]k.|[---.]ksp.'l.bn[.---].|[---].ksp[.---].|[---.--]ir[.---].|[---].'l.ynḥ[m].|[1144.10
[-----].|[---.]'l.ṯny[.---]|[---.]pḫyr.bt h.[---].|[ḫm]šm.ksp.'l.gd[--].|[---].ypḥ.'bdršp.b[--.--].|[ar]b't.'šrt.kbd[.---].|[1144.4
mkr.|ilštm'.|'šrm.l mit.ksp.|'l.bn.alkbl.šb[ny].|'šrm ksp.'l.|wrt.mtny.w 'l.|prdny.aṯt h. 2107.17
št.'š[rt].|ksp.'l.agd[ṯb].|w nit w m'ṣd.|w ḫrmṯt.|'šrt.ksp.|'l.ḫ[z]rn.|w.nit.w[.m'ṣd].|w.ḫ[rmṯt].|'š[r.---].|'l[.---].| 2053.5
-.--].|[ar]b't.'šrt.kbd[.---].|[---.-]rwd.šmbnš[.---].|[---].ksp.'l.k[--].|[---.--]k.|[---.]ksp.'l.bn[.---].|[---].ksp[.---].|[---.- 1144.8
'šrm.ksp.|'l.šknt.syny. 1132.1
.kd.ištir.'m.qrt.|'št.'šr h.šmn.|'mn.bn.aġlmn.|arb'm.ksp.'l.qrt.|b.šd.bn.[u]brš.|ḫmšt.'šrt.|b.šd.bn.[-]n.|tl[ṯt].'šr[1083.6
[-]g[-.---].|w ni[t.w.m'ṣd].|w ḫrmṯt.|ṯlṯm.ar[b'].|kbd.ksp.|'l.tgyn.|w 'l.aṯt h.|ypḥ.m'nt.|bn.lbn. 2053.19
--].prš.ḥtm.|ṯlṯ[.---].bn.ṯdnyn.|ddm.ḥ[ṭm].'l.šrn.|'šrt.ksp.'l.[-]lpy.|bn.ady.kkr.š'rt.|nṯk h.|kb[d.]mn.'l.abršn.|b[n 1146.8
n.bly.gb'ly.|[šp]ḥ.a[n]nṯb.|w.m[--.u]škny.|[']š[r.---]t.ksp.|['l.---]b bn[.--].|[-]ḥ[-.---].|[-]p[-.---.-]ny.|[-]ḥ[-.---.-]dn 2055.5
---].|rg[m].|hn.i[---].|ds[-.---].|t[--.---].|a[--.---].|[---].ksp.'m[.---].|[---.]ilṯḥm.w.[---].|šm't.ḥwt[.---].|[---].nzdt.qr[2127.2.1
mitm.ksp.'mn.b[n].ṣdqn.|w.kkrm.ṯlṯ.|mit.ksp.'mn.|bn.ulbtyn.|w.kkr.ṯlṯ.|ksp.d.nkly.b.šd.|mit.ḫmšt. 1143.3
mitm.ksp.'mn.b[n].ṣdqn.|w.kkrm.ṯlṯ.|mit.ksp.'mn.|bn.ulbtyn.|w 1143.1
nsk k[sp].|'šrt.|w nṣ[p]. 1164.1
tnt.b d.an[r]my.|b.'šrt.ksp.b.a[--].|ṯqlm.ḫr[ṣ.]b.ṯmnt.ksp.|'šrt.ksp.b.alp.[b d].bn.[---].|ṯš'.ṣin.b.ṯš't.ksp.|mšlt.b.ṯq 2101.20
ḫmšt.ḫrṣ.bt.il.|b.ḫmšt.'šrt.ksp.|ḫmš.mat.šmt.|b.'šrt.ksp.|'šr.ṣin.b.ṯṯt.w.kmsk.|arb'[.k]dwṯm.w.ṯṯ.ṯprtm.|b.'šr[m 2100.8
.|[---.]šb'm.|[---.]ḫrg.'šrm.|[---.]abn.ksp.ṯlṯ.|[---].bty.ksp.'šr[t].|[---.-]mb'l.[---].'šrt.|[---.]ḫgbn.kbs.ks[p].|[---].ḏm 2153.7
ṯn.'šr.yn.[kps]lnm.|arb'.mat[.arb]'m.[k]bd.|d ntn.d.ksp.|arb'.l.ḫlby.|[---].l.bt.|arb'.l.kpslnm.|kdm.b[t.]mlk. 1087.3
š'rt.šṯt.b d.gg['t].|b.'šrt.ksp.|ṯlṯ.uṭbm.b d.alḫn.b.'šrt[.k]sp.|rṯ.l.ql.d.ybl.prd.|b.ṯql.w.nṣp.ksp.|ṯmn.lbšm.w.mšlt.|l 2101.11
l.w.nṣp.ksp.|ṯmn.lbšm.w.mšlt.|l.udmym.b.ṯmnt.'šrt.ksp.|šb'm.lbš.d.'rb.bt.mlk.|b.mit.ḫmšt.kbd.ksp.|ṯlṯ.ktnt.b 2101.15
mġẓ.qnyt.ilm.|hyn.'ly.l mpḫm.|b d.ḫss.mṣbṭm.|yṣq.ksp.yšl|ḥ.ḫrṣ.yṣq.ksp.|l alpm.ḫrṣ.yṣq|m.l rbbt.|yṣq-ḫym.w 4[51].1.26
]ṯtmn.|šnl.bn.ṣ[q]n.š[--].|yittm.w.b[--].|yšlm.|[']šrm.ks[p].yš[lm].|[il]ṯḥm.b d[.---].|[---].ṯl[l]m.[---].|[--].r[-]y[.--- 2104.7
.|'rb[.---].|w.b.p[.--].|apš[ny].|b.yṣi h.|ḥwt.[---].|alp.k[sp].|tš'n.|w.hm.al[-].|l.tš'n.|mṣrm.|tmkrn.|ypḥ.'bdilt.| 2116.11
t.|[---.]ḫgbn.kbs.ks[p].|[---].ḏmrd.bn.ḥrmn.|[---.-]ġn.ksp.ṯṯt.|[---.]ygry.ṯlṯm.ksp.b[--]. 2153.11
b.'šrm.ḫmšt.|kbd.ksp.|kkrm.š'rt.šṯt.b d.gg['t].|b.'šrt.ksp.|ṯlṯ.uṭbm.b d.alḫn.b.'šrt[.k]sp.|rṯ.l.ql.d.ybl.prd.|b.ṯql. 2101.10
.|ṯlṯ.l.nskm.birtym.|b d.urtn.w.ṯṯ.mat.brr.|b.ṯmnym.ksp.ṯlṯt.kbd.|ḫmš.alp.ṯlṯ.l.ḫlby.|b d.tlmi.b.'šrm.ḫmšt.|kbd. 2101.5

ksp

ṯmnt.ʿšrt.ksp.|šbʿm.lbš.d.ʿrb.bt.mlk.|b.mit.ḫmšt.kbd.ksp.|ṯlṯ.ktnt.b d.an[r]my.|b.ʿšrt.ksp.b.a[--].|ṯqlm.ḫr[ṣ.]b.ṯ 2101.17
annṯb.ḫmšm.ksp ṯlṯm.šl[m.---].|iwrpzn.ʿšrm ʿšrm š[lm.---].|ilabn.ʿšrt ṯql 1131.1
n.aḥd.b.ṯqlm.|lbš.aḥd.b.ṯqlm.|ḫpn.pṯtm.b ʿšr.|tgmr.ksp.ṯlṯm.|ṯqlm.kbd. 1115.5
.]mlkr[-] h.b.nṯk.|[---.]šbʿm.|[---.]ḫrg.ʿšrm.|[---.]abn.ksp.ṯlṯ.|[---].bty.ksp.ʿšr[t].|[---.-]mbʿl.[---].ʿšrt.|[---.]ḥgbn.k 2153.6
mšq.mlkt.|mitm.ṯṯm.|kbd.ks[p].|ksp.|ṯmnym.|ḫrṣ. 1157.4
[--].d.ntn[.d.]ksp.|[ṯ]mn.l.ʿšrm[.l.b]t.ʿṯtrt.|[ṯ]lṯ.ʿšr h.[b]t.ršp.gn.|arbʿ.b d. 1088.1
m.b d.alḫn.b.ʿšrt[.k]sp.|rṭ.l.ql.d.ybl.prd.|b.ṯql.w.nṣp.ksp.|ṯmn.lbšm.w.mšlt.|l.udmym.b.ṯmnt.ʿšrt.ksp.|šbʿm.lbš. 2101.13
.|w ʿl bn a[--.-]yn ṯqlm.|[--] ksp [---] kdr [---].|[-]ṯrn [k]sp [-]al[.-]r[-].|[--]dšq krsnm.|ḫmšm [-]t ṯlṯ ty[--].|bn.grg 1103.12
n[-.]l ks[p.-]m.|l.mri[.--].|ṯmn kbd[.--]i.|arbʿm[.--].|l apy.mr[i.--] 1133.1
[-]tm.iph.adt y.w.[---].|tšṣḥq.hn.aṯt.l.ʿbd.|šbʿt.w.nṣp.ksp.|[-]tm.rb[.--.a]ḫd.|[---.--]t.b[-].|[---.-]y[-]. 1017.5
[---.-]grm.|[---.-]n.ʿšrt.ksp.|[--.--]n.šbʿt.l ṯlṯm.|[---].šbʿt.ʿšrt.|[---.-]kyn.ʿšrt.|b.bn.ʿs 2054.1.2
.]b gt.[--].|[---.--]n.[--].|[--.--]ǵm.rm[-].|[---.-]ʿm.|[---.k]sp.[--]. 1148.A.2
ntn.artn.b d[.--]nr[.---].|ʿzn.w ymd.šr.b d ansny.|nsk.ks[p.--]mrtn.kṯrmlk.|yḥmn.aḥm[l]k.ʿbdrpu.adn.ṯ[--].|bdn.q 2011.32
.|d št.ʿl.ḫrd h.|špḥ.al.thbṭ.|ḫrd.ʿps.aḥd.kw|sgt.|ḫrd ksp.[--]r.|ymm.w[.---].|[-----].|w[.-----].|[-----]. 2062.2.8
[---].bty.ksp.ʿšr[t].|[---.-]mbʿl.[---].ʿšrt.|[---.]ḥgbn.kbs.ks[p].|[---].ḏmrd.bn.ḥrmn.|[---.-]ǵn.ksp.ṯṯt.|[---.]ygry.ṯlṯm. 2153.9
n.|w ʿl.mnḥm.arbʿ š[mn].|w ʿl bn a[--.-]yn ṯqlm.|[--] ksp [---] kdr [---].|[-]ṯrn [k]sp [-]al[.-]r[-].|[--]dšq krsnm.|ḫ 1103.11
ṣ.mri].|šty.kr[pnm.yn.---].|b ks.ḫr[ṣ.dm.ʿṣm.---].|ks.ksp[.---].|krpn.[---].|w ṯṯn.[---].|tʿl.tr[-.---].|bt.il.li[mm.---] 5[67].4.17
|mat[.---].|ḫrṣ[.---].|ṯlṯ.k[---].|ṯlṯ.a[--.---].|ḫmš[.---].|ksp[.---].|k[--.---].|ar[bʿ.---].|ṯmn[.---].|[-]r[-.---].|w ṯṯ.[---]. 148[96].7
t.|b.[šd.--]n.|ḫ[m]št[.ʿ]šrt.|[ar]bʿm.ksp.|[---]yn.|[---.]ksp.|[---.]mit.|[-----]. 1083.17
[---.]l mitm.ksp.|[---.]skn.|[---.-]im.bṯd.|[---.b]šḫr.atlgn.|[---].b šḫr.|[-- 2167.1
]y.l.ilak.|[---].ʿm y.|[---]m.w.lm.|[---.]w.ʿm k.|[---]m.ksp.|[---].ʿm.|[---.-]n[-].|[---.]l km.|[---.-]lk.|[---.--]m.|t[--.- 1016.15
-].|[---].ksp.ʿl.k[--].|[---.--]k.|[---.]ksp.ʿl.bn[.---].|[---].ksp[.---].|[---.--]ir[.---].|[---].ʿl.ynḥ[m].|[---.]ʿl.ab.b[---].|[---. 1144.11
[d].bn.ʿmyn.|ḫmšt.|b.[šd.--]n.|ḫ[m]št[.ʿ]šrt.|[ar]bʿm.ksp.|[---]yn.|[---.]ksp.|[---.]mit.|[-----]. 1083.15
.|[---.b]šḫr.atlgn.|[---].b šḫr.|[---.]bn h.|[-]k[--]g hn.ksp. 2167.7
d.|ʿl atlg.|w l.ʿṣm.|tspr.|nrn.al.tud|ad.at.l hm.|ṯṯm.ksp. 1010.21

kst

w sip.u hw[.---].|w ank.u šbt[--.---].|ank.n[--]n[.---].|kst.l[--.---].|w.hw.uy.ʿn[--.---].|l ytn.w rgm[.---].|w yrdnn.a 54.1.12[13.1.9]
dk[.-]it[.---].|trgm[.-]dk[.---].|mʿbd[.-]r[-.-]š[-.---].|w kšt.[--]šq h[.---].|bnš rʿym.[---].|kbdt.bnš[.---].|šin.[---].|b ḥ 2158.2.5

kšm

.ʿšdm.|kd yn.l.ḫḏǵb.w.kd.ḥmṣ.|prš.glbm.l.bt.|tgmǵ.kšmm.b.yrḫ.iṯtbnm.|šbʿm.dd.ṯn.kbd.|tgmr.ḥṭm.šbʿ.ddm.|ḫ 1099.30
mitm.ʿšr kbd.|kšmm.b.mṣbt.|mit.ʿšrm.ṯn kbd.|[kš]mm.|[ʿ]š[r]m.ṯn.kbd.ḥ 2091.2
pu.|w.lmd h.|ʿdršp.|w.lmd h.|krwn b.gt.nbk.|ddm.kšmm.l.ḫtn.|ddm.l.trbnn.|ddm.šʿrm.l.trbnn.|ddm.šʿrm.l.ḫ 1099.20
mitm.ʿšr kbd.|kšmm.b.mṣbt.|mit.ʿšrm.ṯn kbd.|[kš]mm.|[ʿ]š[r]m.ṯn.kbd.ḥṭm.|[-]m[-.-]ʿ[-.-]ag šʿrm.|[---.--]m 2091.4
dm.kbd.yn.b.gt.[---].|[mi]tm.ḫmšm.ḫmš.k[bd].|[dd].kšmm.tšʿ[.---].|[š]ʿrm.ṯṯ.ʿ[šr].|[dd].ḥṭm.w.ḫ[mšm].|[ṯ]lṯ kb 2092.7
.dd[.---].|[---]mn.arbʿm.y[n].|b.gt.trǵnds.|tšʿ.ʿšr.[dd].kšmm.|ṯn.ʿšr[.dd.ḥ]ṭm.|w.šb[ʿ.---]. 2092.16

kšmn

t.k[--].|tšʿ.ʿšr h.dd.l.b[t.--].|ḫmš.ddm.l.ḫtyt.|ṯlṯm.dd.kšmn.l.gzzm.|yyn.|ṣdqn.|ʿbd.pdr.|myṣm.|tgt.|w.lmd h.|y 1099.4

kšt

dk[.-]it[.---].|trgm[.-]dk[.---].|mʿbd[.-]r[-.-]š[-.---].|w kšt.[--]šq h[.---].|bnš rʿym.[---].|kbdt.bnš[.---].|šin.[---].|b ḥ 2158.2.5

kp

bym.kp.k.qṣm.|ǵrmn.kp.mhr.ʿtkt.|rišt.l bmt h.šnst.|kpt.b ḥbš h.brkm.tǵl[l].|b dm.ḏmr.ḥlqm.b mm[ʿ].|mhrm. 3[ʿNT].2.13
[---.šnst.kpt.b ḥb]š h.ʿtkt r[išt].|[l bmt h.---.]hy bt h tʿrb.|[---.tm]tḫ 7.1[131].2
].|tṣmt.adm.ṣat.š[p]š.|tḥt h.k kdrt.ri[š].|ʿl h.k irbym.kp.k.qṣm.|ǵrmn.kp.mhr.ʿtkt.|rišt.l bmt h.šnst.|kpt.b ḥbš h 3[ʿNT].2.10
[p]š.|tḥt h.k kdrt.ri[š].|ʿl h.k irbym.kp.k.qṣm.|ǵrmn.kp.mhr.ʿtkt.|rišt.l bmt h.šnst.|kpt.b ḥbš h.brkm.tǵl[l].|b d 3[ʿNT].2.11
n y.a[ḫ]r.|nkl yrḫ ytrḫ.adn h.|yšt mṣb.mznm.um h.|kp mznm.iḫ h ytʿr.|mšrrm.aḫt h l a|bn mznm.nkl w ib.|d 24[77].35
--.]ḫrm.ṯn.ym.|tš[.---.]ymm.lk.|hrg.ar[bʿ.]ymm.bṣr.|kp.šsk k.[--.]l ḥbš k.|ʿtk.ri[š.]l mhr k.|w ʿp.l dr[ʿ].nšr k.|w 13[6].6
.|[b šmḫt.kbd.ʿnt.tšyt.tḥt h.k]kdrt.riš.|[ʿl h.k irbym.kp.---.k br]k.tǵll.b dm.|[ḏmr.---.]td[-.]rǵb.|[----]k.|[----] h. 7.1[131].9
-].|[-----].|[---.]mrkbt.|[---.--]a.nrm.|[---.--]y.lm[.-.]b k[p].|[---].tr[--.]gpn lk.|[---].km[-.---].|[---.--]k yṣunn[.---].| 1002.31

kpld

dwm adrm.|w knd pnṯ.dq.|ṯn ḫpnm.ṯn pldm ǵlmm.|kpld.b[-.-]r[--].|w blḫ br[-]m p[-].|b[--.]l[-.]mat[.-]y.|ḫmšm 140[98].5

kpltn

.--]t.|[-----].|[---.]l[--].|[bn.]ubn.|kbšm.|bn.abḏr.|bn.kpltn.|bn.prn.|ʿbdm.|bn.kḏǵbr.|bn.mṣrn.|bn.[-]dr[-].|[---] 114[324].2.7

kpslnm

b]ʿm.[k]bd.|d ntn.d.ksp.|arbʿ.l.ḫlby.|[---].l.bt.|arbʿ.l.kpslnm.|kdm.b[t.]mlk. 1087.6
ṯn.ʿšr.yn.[kps]lnm.|arbʿ.mat[.arb]ʿm.[k]bd.|d ntn.d.ksp.|arbʿ.l.ḫlby.| 1087.1

kpr

.šmm.at m]. | w ank.ib[ǵy h.---]. | [-].l y'mdn.i[---.---]. | kpr.šb' bn[t.rḥ.gdm.w anhbm]. | kla[t.ṯǵ]r[t.bht.'nt.w tqry.ǵl 7.2[130].23
[-]p[-]l[.---]. | k lli.[---]. | kpr.[šb'.bnt.rḥ.gdm.w anhbm]. | w tqr[y.ǵlmm.b št.ǵr.---]. | [7.2[130].3
n[--.---.-]š[--]. | kpr.šb'.bnt.rḥ.gdm. | w anhbm.klat.ṯǵrt. | bht.'nt.w tqry.ǵlm 3['NT].2.2

kpt

--]. | [---.]ylm.b[n.']n k.ṣmdm.špk[.---]. | [---.]nt[-.]mbk kpt.w[.--].b g[--]. | [---.]ḥ[--.]bnt.ṣ'ṣ.bnt.ẖkp[.---]. | [---].aḫw.a 1001.1.17

kptr

q šr.y'db.ksa.w yṯb. | tqru.l špš.um.ql bl.'m | kṯr.w ẖss.kptr h.mnt.nṯk.nḥš. | šmrr.nḥš.'q šr.ln h.mlẖš.abd. | ln h.ydy UG5.7.46
[idk.al.ttn.pnm.tk.ḥkpt.il.kl h]. | [kptr.]ks[u.ṯbt h.ḥkpt.arṣ.nḥlt h]. | b alp.šd.r[bt.kmn.l p'n.kṯr 1['NT.IX].3.1
rt. | mǵ.l qdš.amrr. | idk.al.tnn. | pnm.tk.ḥqkpt. | il.kl h.kptr. | ksu.ṯbt h.ḥkpt. | arṣ.nḥlt h. | b alp.šd.rbt. | kmn.l p'n.kṯ 3['NT.VI].6.14
[---.]n[--.---]. | [---.kpt]r.l r[ḥq.ilm.ḥkpt.l rḥq]. | [ilnym.ṯn.mṯpd]m.t[ḥt.'nt.arṣ.ṯ 2.3[129].2
. | w y'n.kṯr.w ẖss[.lk.lk.'nn.ilm.] | atm.bštm.w an[.šnt.kptr]. | l rḥq.ilm.ḥkp[t.l rḥq.ilnym]. | ṯn.mṯpdm.tḥt.['nt.arṣ.ṯl 1['NT.IX].3.18

kpṯ

w tšt.'nt.gṯr.b'lt.mlk.b' | lt.drkt.b'lt.šmm.rmm. | [b'l]t.kpṯ.w 'nt.di.dit.rẖpt. | [---.-]rm.aklt.'gl.'l.mšt. | [---.--]r.špr.w UG5.2.1.8

kqmṯn

rt l [---]. | ṯn šurtm l [---]. | [-----.]a[---]. | [---.--]ln. | [---.]kqmṯn. | [---.]klnmw. | [---.]w yky. | ṯlṯm sp.l bnš tpnr. | arb'.s 137.2[93].3

kr

lm.il.k yphn h. | yprq.lṣb.w yṣḥq. | p'n h.l hdm.yṯpd.w ykrkr. | uṣb't h.yšu.g h.w y[ṣḥ]. | ik.mǵyt.rbt.aṯr[t.y]m. | ik.at 4[51].4.29

kran

ṯ.šmn. | a[---.]kdm. | '[---]'m.kd. | a[----]ḥr.ṯlṯ. | y[---.bn.]kran.ẖmš. | '[---].kd. | amry.kdm. | mnn.bn.gṯtn.kdm. | ynḥm. 136[84].6

krb

d. | y'šr.w yšqyn h. | ytn.ks.b d h. | krpn.b klat.yd h. | b krb.'ẓm.ridn. | mt.šmm.ks.qdš. | l tphn h.aṯt.krpn. | l t'n.aṯrt. 3['NT].1.12
[l a]q[h]t. | [t]krb.[---.]l qrb.mym. | tql.[---.]lb.tṯ[b]r. | qšt[.---]r.y[ṯ]br. | ṯm 19[1AQHT].1.2

krgmš

[---.k]rgmš. | [l.m]lk.ugrt.rgm[.-]y. | [---.--]m.rgm. | [---.]šknt. | [--- 1011.1

krd

š[--.---]. | ṣ'[-.---]. | ṣ'q[.---]. | ẖlb.k[rd]. | uškn. | 'nqp[at]. | ubr'[y]. | ilšt[m']. | šbn. | ṭbq. 2146.4
r.[---]. | arny.[---]. | š'rt.ṯn[.---]. | bq't.[--].ḥ[mr.---]. | ẖlb krd.ḥ[mr.---]. | ṣ'.ḥmr.w[.---]. | ṣ'q.ḥmr.w.[---]. | ẖlb 'prm.am 2040.13
b.gt.mlkt.b.rḥbn. | ẖmšm.l.mitm.zt. | w.b d.krd. | ẖmšm.l.mit. | arb'.kbd. 1096.3
šrš. | lbnm. | ẖlb.krd. | ṣ'. | mlk. | gb'ly. | ypr. | ary. | ẓrn. | art. | ṯlḥny. | ṯlrby. | dmt 71[113].3
ẖlb k[rd]. | ṣ'q. | š[---]. 1178.1
ẖlb 'prm.ṯṯ. | ẖlb krd.ṯn 'šr. | qmy.arb'.'šr. | ṣ'q.arb' 'šr. | ṣ'.ṯmn. | šḥq.'šrm.arb'. 67[110].2
il[štm']. | šbn. | ṭbq. | rqd. | uškn. | ẖbt. | [ẖlb].kr[d]. 1177.7

krw

.ṯṯ mat. | ušknym. | yp'.alpm. | aḫ[m]lk.bn.nskn.alpm. | krw.šlmy. | alpm. | atn.bṣry.alpm. | lbnym. | ṯm[n.]alp mitm. | 1060.2.4
spr.npṣ.krw. | ṯt.ẖtrm.ṯn.kst. | spl.mšlt.w.mqḥm. | w md h. | arn.w mz 2050.1

krwn

. | ilb'l. | 'bdyr[ẖ]. | ṯtpḥ. | artn. | ybnil. | brqn. | adr[dn]. | krwn. | arkdn. | ilmn. | abškn. | ykn. | ršpab. | klyn. | ḥgbn. | ḥtṯn 1024.1.11
qrṭym.mddb'l. | kdn.zlyy. | krwn.arty. | tlmu.zlyy. | pdu.qmnzy. | bdl.qrṭy. | trgn.bn.tǵḥ. | 89[312].3
n.ṯ[--]. | bdn.qln.mtn.ydln. | b'ltdtt.tlgn.ytn. | b'ltǵpṯm.krwn.ilšn.agyn. | mnn.šr.ugrt.ḏkr.yṣr. | tǵǵln.ẖmš.ddm. | [---] 2011.36
| rpan. | w.lmd h. | 'bdrpu. | w.lmd h. | 'dršp. | w.lmd h. | krwn b.gt.nbk. | ddm.kšmm.l.ḫtn. | ddm.l.trbnn. | ddm.š'rm.l 1099.19
rǵlm.dt.inn. | b d.tlmyn. | b d.gln.ary. | tgyn.y'rty. | bn.krwn.b.yny.iytlm. | sgryn.ary.b.yny. | bn.yddn.b.rkby. | agyn. 2071.5
šyn. | bn.prtn. | bn.ypr. | mrum. | bn.'[--]t. | bn.adty. | bn.krwn. | bn.ngsk. | bn.qnd. | bn.pity. | w.nḥl h. | bn.rt. | bn.l[--]. | 113[400].3.14
n.'mtdl. | bn.'myn. | bn.alz. | bn.birtn. | [bn.]ylkn. | [bn.]krwn. | [bn.-]ty. | [bn.]iršn. | bn.[---]. | bn.b[--]. | bn.š[--]. | bn.a[- 117[325].1.15
[--]ǵyn.b[n.---]. | krwn.b[n.---]. | tgyn.m'[---]. | w.agpṯn[.---]. | tyndr[-.---]. | gt.tg 103[334].2
ṣm. | ddm l kbs. | dd l prgṯ. | dd.l mri. | dd.l ṯngly. | dd.l krwn. | dd.l ṯǵr. | dd.l rmt.r[---]. 1100.10
[-----]. | dd l krwn. | dd l [--]n. | dd l ky. | dd l 'bdkṯr. | dd[m] l r'y. | [--] šm 1101.2
| [--]n. | [ḥr]š.qṯn. | [---]n. | [-----]. | [--]dd. | [b']l.tǵpṯm. | [k]rwn. | ḥrš.mrkbt. | mnḥm. | mṣrn. | mdrǵlm. | agmy. | 'dyn. | ' 1039.2.12
n.b'ltǵpṯ. | ḥrš.btm. | ršpab. | [r]ṣn. | [a]ǵlmn. | [a]ẖyn. | [k]rwn. | [k]l[by]. | [--]ṯn. | [---]d. | a[ǵ]ltn. | [-----]. | [--]ny. | kn'm 2060.13
.l bn.'mlbi. | šd.ṯpḫln.l bn.ǵl. | w dṯn.nḥl h.l bn.pl. | šd.krwn.l aḫn. | šd.'yy.l aḫn. | šd.brdn.l bn.bly. | šd gzl.l.bn.ṯbr[2089.11
'ḏrd. | šd.gl.b'lz.l.bn.'mnr. | šd.kn'm.l.bn.'mnr. | šd.bn.krwn.l bn.'myn. | šd.bn.prmn.l aḫny. | šd.bn ḥnn.l bn.adlḏn. 2089.5
mlk.b yrḫ iṯt[bnm]. | ršpab.rb 'šrt.m[r]yn. | pǵdn.ilb'l.krwn.lbn.'dn. | ẖyrn.md'. | šm'n.rb 'šrt.kkln.'bd.abṣn. | šdyn. 2011.3
.ṣnr. | iḫy.[b]n[.--]l[-]. | 'bdy[rḫ].bn.gttn. | yrmn.bn.'n. | krwn.nḥl h. | ttn.[n]ḥl h. | bn.b[r]zn. | [---.-]ḥn. 85[80].4.10
. | kdrl. | wql. | adrdn. | prn. | 'bdil. | ušy.šbn[-]. | aḫt.ab. | krwn. | nnḏ. | mkl. | kzǵb. | iyrḏ. 1069.14
št. | w.nḥl h.ẖm[š]t. | bn.unp.arb't. | 'bdbn.ytrš ẖmšt. | krwn.'šrt. | bn.ulb ẖmšt. | bn.ḥry.ẖmšt. | swn.ẖmšt. | bn.[-]r[-.] 1062.12
n.ilyn.ṯlṯm. | ṣṣ.bn.kzn.ṯlṯm. | ṣṣ.bn.tlmyn.'šrm. | ṣṣ.bn.krwn.'š[rm]. | ṣṣ.bn.iršyn.[---]. | [ṣṣ].bn.ilb'l.ṯl[ṯ]m. | ṣṣ.bn.ptḏ 2096.4

krwn

lṯ.šd.w.krm.šir.d.ḫli. | širm.šd.šd.ʻšy. | w.šir.šd.krm. | d.krwn. | šir.šd.šd.ʻšy. | d.abmn. | šir.šd.krm. | d.yrmn. | šir.[š]d. 1079.9
sḫr.ʻzn.ilhd. | bnil.rb ʻšrt.lkn.ypʻn.ṯ[--]. | yṣḥm.b d.ubn.krwn.tǵd.[m]nḥm. | ʻpṯrm.šmʻrgm.skn.qrt. | ḥgbn.šmʻ.skn.qr 2011.9
[s]pr.bnš.mlk.d.b.tbq. | [kr]wn. | [--]n. | [q]ṣy. | ṯn.bn.iwrḫz.[n]ʻrm. | yṣr[.-]qb. | w.ṯn.bn 2066.2.1
| s[d]rn [w].ṯn.šǵr h. | [---.]w.šǵr h. | [---.]w.šǵr h. | [---.]krwn. | [---].ḫzmyn. | [---.]bn.dll. | r[--.--]km. | w.spr h. 2072.11

krws

bnšm.dt.[---]. | krws.l.y[--.---]. | ypʻ.l[.---]. | šmr[m.---]. | [-----]. | bn.g[r.---]. | ḏ 2122.2

krz

[aṯt.w].bn h.b.bt.krz. | [aṯt.]w.pǵt.b.bt.gg. | [ǵz]r.aḥd.b.bt.nwrḏ. | [aṯ]t.adrt.b.b 80[119].1
n.b d.tyn.nḥl h. | šd.pǵyn[.b] d.krmn.l.ty[n.n]ḥl h. | šd.krz.[b]n.ann.ʻ[db]. | šd.ṯ[r]yn.bn.tkn.b d.qrt. | šd[.-].dyn.b d. 2029.13

krzn

mlk.ʻšr.ṣin. | mlknʻm.ʻšr. | bn.adty.ʻšr. | [ṣ]dqšlm ḫmš. | krzn.ḫmš. | ubrʻym.ḫmš. | [----]. | [bn] itn. | [bn] il. | [---]ṯ. | klṯṯ 2039.6
.b d.bn.ʻmy. | šd.b d.bn.ʻyn. | ṯn.šdm.b d.klṯṯb. | šd.b d.krz[n]. | ṯlṯ.šdm.b d.amtr[n]. | ṯn.šdm.b d.skn. | šd.b d[.ʻb]dyr 2090.21

kry

an k.ḥdg k. | ḥtl k.w ẓi. | b aln.tk m. | b tk.mlbr. | ilšiy. | kry amt. | ʻpr.ʻẓm yd. | ugrm.ḫl.ld. | aklm.tbrk k. | w ld ʻqqm. 12[75].1.23
i[ytlm.---]. | wr[t.---.]b d.yḫmn. | yry[.---.]br. | ydn[.---].kry. | bn.ydd[.---.b]r. | prkl.bʻl.any.d.b d.abr[-]. 2123.5
y. | [--]ṯy. | bn.ǵdʻ. | bn.ʻyn. | bn.grb[n]. | yṯtn. | bn.ab[l]. | kry. | psš. | ilṯḥm. | ḥrm. | bn.bty. | ʻby. | šm[n].bn.apn. | krty. | b 2078.11

kryn

d.skn. | šd.bn.ubrʻn b gt prn. | šd.bn.gby.gt.prn. | šd.bn.kryn.gt.prn. | šd.bn.ky.gt.prn. | šd.hwil.gt.prn. | šd.ḥr.gt.prn. 1104.5

krk

. | b.ulm.ṯṯ.ʻšr h.ḫrmṯt. | ṯt.nitm.ṯn.mʻṣdm.ṯn.mqbm. | krk.aḥt. | b.sǵy.ḫmš.ḫrmṯt.nit. | krk.mʻṣd.mqb. | b.gt.ʻmq.ḫm 2048.6
ḫlq. | bn ʻgy. | bn zlbn. | bn.aḫ[--]. | bn[.---]. | [-----]. | bn kr[k]. | bn ḫtyn. | w nḥl h. | bn ṯgrb. | bn ṯdnyn. | bn pbn. 2016.3.2
ʻbdḫr. | [-]prm ḫlq. | [---]n ḫlq. | bn mʻnt. | bn kbdy. | bn krk. | bn srty. | bn ltḥ ḫlq. | bn ytr. | bn ilšpš. | ubrš. | bn gmš ḫl 2016.2.12
ḫmš ʻš[r]. | kkr.ṯ[lṯ]. | ṯt hrt[m]. | ṯn mq[pm]. | ulṯ.ṯl[t]. | krk.kly[.--]. | ḫmš.mr[kbt]. | ṯṯ [-]az[-]. | ʻšt[--.---]. | irg[mn.---]. 2056.8
b.atlg.ṯlṯ.ḫrmṯt.ṯṯm. | mḫrhn.nit.mit.krk.mit. | mʻṣd.ḫmšm.mqb.[ʻ]šrm. | b.ulm.ṯṯ.ʻšr h.ḫrmṯt. | ṯt.n 2048.2
ḫrmṯt.nit. | krk.mʻṣd.mqb. | b.gt.ʻmq.ḫmš.ḫrmṯt.n[it]. | krk.mʻṣd.mqb. | b.gwl.ṯmn.ḫrmṯt.[nit]. | krk.mʻṣd.mqb. | [b] g 2048.10
š.ḫrmṯt.n[it]. | krk.mʻṣd.mqb. | b.gwl.ṯmn.ḫrmṯt.[nit]. | krk.mʻṣd.mqb. | [b] gt.ipṯl.ṯṯ.ḫrmṯ[t.nit]. | [k]rk.mʻṣd.mqb. | [2048.12
rmṯt.[nit]. | krk.mʻṣd.mqb. | [b] gt.ipṯl.ṯṯ.ḫrmṯ[t.nit]. | [k]rk.mʻṣd.mqb. | [b.g]t.bir.ʻš[r.---]. | [---].krk.mʻ[ṣd.---]. | [b.]g 2048.14
.ṯn.mʻṣdm.ṯn.mqbm. | krk.aḥt. | b.sǵy.ḫmš.ḫrmṯt.nit. | krk.mʻṣd.mqb. | b.gt.ʻmq.ḫmš.ḫrmṯt.n[it]. | krk.mʻṣd.mqb. | b 2048.8
.ḫrmṯ[t.nit]. | [k]rk.mʻṣd.mqb. | [b.g]t.bir.ʻš[r.---]. | [---].krk.mʻ[ṣd.---]. | [b.]gt.ḥrṯm.ḫm[š.---]. | [n]it.krk.mʻṣ[d.---]. | b. 2048.16
r.---]. | [---].krk.mʻ[ṣd.---]. | [b.]gt.ḥrṯm.ḫm[š.---]. | [n]it.krk.mʻṣ[d.---]. | b.ḫrbǵlm.ǵlm[n]. | w.trhy.aṯt h. | w.mlky.b[n] 2048.18
[.--]. | ḫmš.mr[kbt]. | ṯṯ [-]az[-]. | ʻšt[--.---]. | irg[mn.---]. | krk[.---]. 2056.13

krm

[.---]. | aupṯ.krm.aḥd.nšpin.kr[m.]aḥd[.---]. | dmt.lḫsn.krm.aḥd.annḏr.kr[m.---]. | aǵt.mryn.ary[.]yukl.krm.[---]. | gd 1081.15
.aḫ[d.---]. | krm.uḫn.b.šdmy.ṯlṯ.bzl[.d]prn[.---]. | aupṯ.krm.aḥd.nšpin.kr[m.]aḥd[.---]. | dmt.lḫsn.krm.aḥd.annḏr.kr 1081.14
.annḏr.kr[m.---]. | aǵt.mryn.ary[.]yukl.krm.[---]. | gdn.krm.aḫ[d.--]r.krm.[---]. | ary.ʻšr.arbʻ.kbd.[---]. | [--]yy.ṯṯ.krm 1081.17
.uḫn.b.šdmy.ṯlṯ.bzl[.d]prn[.---]. | aupṯ.krm.aḥd.nšpin.kr[m.]aḥd[.---]. | dmt.lḫsn.krm.aḥd.annḏr.kr[m.---]. | aǵt.mr 1081.14
-]. | ṯmry.ʻšr.ṯn.k[rmm.---]. | liy.krm.aḥd[.---]. | ʻbdmlk.krm.aḫ[d.---]. | krm.ubdy.b d.ǵ[--.---]. | krm.pyn.arty[.---]. | ṯl 1081.6
nz.ṯṯ.krm.yknʻm.ṯmn.krm[.---]. | krm.nʻmn.b.ḫly.ull.krm.aḫ[d.---]. | krm.uḫn.b.šdmy.ṯlṯ.bzl[.d]prn[.---]. | aupṯ.kr 1081.12
]rbʻ[.---]. | ʻnmky.ʻšr.[---]. | ṯmry.ʻšr.ṯn.k[rmm.---]. | liy.krm.aḥd[.---]. | ʻbdmlk.krm.aḫ[d.---]. | krm.ubdy.b d.ǵ[--.---]. 1081.5
[---.]ktb nǵr krm. | [---].ab h.krm ar. | [---.]h.mḫtrt.pṯtm. | [---.-]t h.ušpǵt tišr. | [---.šm]m h 2001.2.2
.p[--.---]. | krm.ilyy.b.m[--.---]. | kd.šbʻ.krmm.[---]. | ṯn.krm[m.i]wrǵl[.---]. | ṯn.krm.[-]myn.[---]. | ṯn.krm[.---]. | krm.[1081.26
.kb[d.---]. | ḫmrm.ṯṯ.krm[m.---]. | krm.ǵlkz.b.p[--.---]. | krm.ilyy.b.m[--.---]. | kd.šbʻ.krmm.[---]. | ṯn.krm[m.i]wrǵl[.-- 1081.24
d.l.kyn. | k[rm.--.]l.i[w]rtḏl. | ḥl.d[--.ʻbd]yrḫ.b d.apn. | krm.i[--].l.[---.]a[-]bn. 2027.2.12
k[rmm.---]. | liy.krm.aḥd[.---]. | ʻbdmlk.krm.aḫ[d.---]. | krm.ubdy.b d.ǵ[--.---]. | krm.pyn.arty[.---]. | ṯlṯ.krm.ubdym.l 1081.7
[d.---]. | krm.ubdy.b d.ǵ[--.---]. | krm.pyn.arty[.---]. | ṯlṯ.krm.ubdym.l mlkt.b.ʻnmky[.---]. | mgdly.ǵlpṯr.ṯn.krmm.w.ṯl 1081.9
ʻm.ṯmn.krm[.---]. | krm.nʻmn.b.ḫly.ull.krm.aḫ[d.---]. | krm.uḫn.b.šdmy.ṯlṯ.bzl[.d]prn[.---]. | aupṯ.krm.aḥd.nšpin.kr 1081.13
r šd.ri[šym]. | kr[-].šdm.ʻ[--]. | b gt ṯm[--] yn[.--]. | [---].krm.b ypʻl.yʻdd. | [---.]krm.b [-]dn.l.bn.[-]kn. | šd[.---.-]ʻn. | šd 2027.1.4
m.ʻ[--]. | b gt ṯm[--] yn[.--]. | [---].krm.b ypʻl.yʻdd. | [---.]krm.b [-]dn.l.bn.[-]kn. | šd[.---.-]ʻn. | šd[.---.-]šm.l.dqn. | š[d.-- 2027.1.5
| w.šir.šd.krm. | d.krwn. | šir.šd.šd.ʻšy. | d.abmn. | šir.šd.krm. | d.yrmn. | šir.[š]d.mltḥ.šd.ʻšy. | d.ynḥm. | tgmr.šd.ṯlṯm.š 1079.12
.khn. | ṯlṯ.šd.w.krm.šir.d.ḫli. | širm.šd.šd.ʻšy. | w.šir.šd.krm. | d.krwn. | šir.šd.šd.ʻšy. | d.abmn. | šir.šd.krm. | d.yrmn. | 1079.8
dl[.bn]. | [-]š[-]y.d.b š[-]y. | [---.y]d gt h[.--]. | [---.]yd. | [k]rm h.yd. | [k]lkl h. | [w] ytn.nn. | l.bʻln.bn. | kltn.w l. | bn h.ʻ 1008.9
| ṯlṯ.krm.ubdym.l mlkt.b.ʻnmky[.---]. | mgdly.ǵlpṯr.ṯn.krmm.w.ṯlṯ.ub[dym.---]. | qmnz.ṯṯ.krm.yknʻm.ṯmn.krm[.---]. 1081.10
. | hbṭ.hw. | ḫrd.w.šl hw. | qr[-]. | akl n.b.grnt. | l.bʻr. | ap.krmm. | ḫlq. | qrt n.ḫlq. | w.dʻ.dʻ. 2114.10
--]. | mgdly.ǵlpṯr.ṯn.krmm.w.ṯlṯ.ub[dym.---]. | qmnz.ṯṯ.krm.yknʻm.ṯmn.krm[.---]. | krm.nʻmn.b.ḫly.ull.krm.aḫ[d.--- 1081.11
bht h.a[r]y h. | b qrb hkl h.ṣḥ. | šbʻm.bn.aṯrt. | špq.ilm.krm.y[n]. | špq.ilht.ḫprt[.yn]. | špq.ilm.alpm.y[n]. | špq.ilht.ar 4[51].6.47
ṯ.ṯmṯ. | [--.]ydbr.ṯrmt.al m.qḥn y.š y.qḥn y. | [--.]šir.b krm.nṭṭt.dm.ʻlt.b ab y. | u---].ʻlt.b k.lk.l pn y.yrk.bʻl.[--]. | [--- 1001.1.9
.ṯlṯ.ub[dym.---]. | qmnz.ṯṯ.krm.yknʻm.ṯmn.krm[.---]. | krm.nʻmn.b.ḫly.ull.krm.aḫ[d.---]. | krm.uḫn.b.šdmy.ṯlṯ.bzl[. 1081.12
]nḥm. | ʻpṯrm.šmʻrgm.skn.qrt. | ḥgbn.šmʻ.skn.qrt. | nǵr krm.ʻbdadt.bʻln.ypʻmlk. | ṯǵrm.mnḥm.klyn.ʻdršp.ǵlmn. | [a]b 2011.12

m.[---].|[t̠]lrby.ʻšr.t̠n.kb[d.---].|ẖmrm.t̠t̠.krm[m.---].|krm.ǵlkz.b.p[--.---].|krm.ilyy.b.m[--.---].|kd.šbʻ.krmm.[---]. 1081.23
d[.---].|ʻbdmlk.krm.aḥ[d.---].|krm.ubdy.b d.ǵ[--.---].|krm.pyn.arty[.---].|t̠lt̠.krm.ubdym.l mlkt.b.ʻnmky[.---].|mg 1081.8
d.d.bn.mlkyy.|kmsk.šd.iẖmn.|širm.šd.khn.|t̠lt̠.šd.w.krm.šir.d.ẖli.|širm.šd.šd.ʻšy.|w.šir.šd.krm.|d.krwn.|šir.šd. 1079.6
l a|b h.alp ksp w rbt ẖ|rṣ.išlḥ ẓhrm iq|nim.atn šd h krm[m].|šd dd h ḥrnqm.w |yʻn ẖrẖb mlk qẓ [l].|nʻmn.ilm 24[77].22
rm.aḥ[d.--]r.krm.[---].|ary.ʻšr.arbʻ.kbd.[---].|[--]yy.t̠t̠.krmm.šl[-.---].|[---.]ʻšrm.krm.[---].|[t̠]lrby.ʻšr.t̠n.kb[d.---].| 1081.19
w at̠t̠ k.ngrt.il[ht].|ʻl.l t̠km.bnw n.|l nẖnpt.mšpy.|t̠lt̠.kmm.t̠rr y.|[---.]l ǵr.gm.ṣḥ.|[---.]r[-]m. 16[126].4.16
[--.---].|kd.šbʻ.krmm.[---].|t̠n.krm[m.i]wrǵl[.---].|t̠n.krm.[-]myn.[---].|t̠n.krm[.---].|krm.[---].|[--].kr[m.---].|ar[- 1081.27
n.[---.]l.dqn.|[---.--]ʻ.šdyn.l ytršn.|[---.--]t̠.ʻbd.l.kyn.|k[rm.--.]l.i[w]rtd̠l.|ḥl.d[--.ʻbd]yrẖ.b d.apn.|krm.i[--].l.[---.]a 2027.2.10
[---.]ktb nǵr krm.|[---].ab h.krm ar.|[---.]h.mḥtrt.pt̠tm.|[---.-]t h.ušpǵt t 2001.2.1
.aḥd.nšpin.kr[m.]aḥd[.---].|dmt.lẖsn.krm.aḥd.annd̠r.kr[m.---].|aǵt.mryn.ary[.]yukl.krm.[---].|gdn.krm.aḥ[d.--]r. 1081.15
--].|aǵt.mryn.ary[.]yukl.krm.[---].|gdn.krm.aḥ[d.--]r.krm.[---].|ary.ʻšr.arbʻ.kbd.[---].|[--]yy.t̠t̠.krmm.šl[-.---].|[--- 1081.17
---].|t̠n.krm.[-]myn.[---].|t̠n.krm[.---].|krm.[---].|[--].kr[m.---].|ar[--.---].|yp[-.---].|ẖr[-.---].|[-----]. 1081.30
t.lẖsn.krm.aḥd.annd̠r.kr[m.---].|aǵt.mryn.ary[.]yukl.krm.[---].|gdn.krm.aḥ[d.--]r.krm.[---].|ary.ʻšr.arbʻ.kbd.[---] 1081.16
t̠n.krmm.w.t̠lt̠.ub[dym.---].|qmnz.t̠t̠.krm.yknʻm.t̠mn.krm[.---].|krm.nʻmn.b.ẖly.ull.krm.aḥ[d.---].|krm.uẖn.b.šd 1081.11
|[---.]ʻšrm.krm.[---].|[t̠]lrby.ʻšr.t̠n.kb[d.---].|ẖmrm.t̠t̠.krm[m.---].|krm.ǵlkz.b.p[--.---].|krm.ilyy.b.m[--.---].|kd.šb 1081.22
.[---].|t̠n.krm[m.i]wrǵl[.---].|t̠n.krm.[-]myn.[---].|t̠n.krm[.---].|krm.[---].|[--].kr[m.---].|ar[--.---].|yp[-.---].|ẖr[-. 1081.28
.bt.alp w š.|[---.--]m.l gt̠rm.|[---.]l ʻnt m.|[---.--]rm.d krm.|[---].l ʻnt m.|[---.]l šlm.|[-]l[-.-]ry.ylbš.|mlk.ylk.lqḥ.il 33[5].19
-]n.ʻš[r.]|[a]rt[.a]rbʻ[.---].|ʻnmky.ʻšr.[---].|t̠mry.ʻšr.t̠n.k[rmm.---].|liy.krm.aḥd[.---].|ʻbdmlk.krm.aḥ[d.---].|krm.u 1081.4
y.ʻšr.arbʻ.kbd.[---].|[--]yy.t̠t̠.krmm.šl[-.---].|[---.]ʻšrm.krm.[---].|[t̠]lrby.ʻšr.t̠n.kb[d.---].|ẖmrm.t̠t̠.krm[m.---].|krm 1081.20
---].|krm.ǵlkz.b.p[--.---].|krm.ilyy.b.m[--.---].|kd.šbʻ.krmm.[---].|t̠n.krm[m.i]wrǵl[.---].|t̠n.krm.[-]myn.[---].|t̠n.k 1081.25
rm[m.i]wrǵl[.---].|t̠n.krm.[-]myn.[---].|t̠n.krm[.---].|krm.[---].|[--].kr[m.---].|ar[--.---].|yp[-.---].|ẖr[-.---].|[-----]. 1081.29
[---.mr]zḥ.ʻn[.---].|[---.]šir.šd.kr[m.---].|[---.]l.mrzḥ.ʻn[.---].|[---].mrzḥ.ʻn[.---].|[---].mrzḥ. 2032.2

krmn

ag]dtb.bn[.---].|ʻbdil.bn.[---].|ʻpt̠n.bn.t̠sq[-].|mnn.bn.krmn.|bn.umẖ.|yky.bn.slyn.|ypln.bn.ylḥn.|ʻzn.bn.mll.|šr 85[80].1.5
n.arm.|bn.bʻl.ṣdq.|bn.army.|bn.rpiyn.|bn.army.|bn.krmn.|bn.ykn.|bn.ʻt̠trab.|uṣn[-].|bn.alt̠n.|bn.aš[-]š.|bn.štn 1046.1.10
d.šẖrn.nẖl h.|šd.annmn.b d.tyn.nẖl h.|šd.pǵyn[.b] d.krmn.l.ty[n.n]ẖl h.|šd.krz.[b]n.ann.ʻ[db].|šd.t̠[r]yn.bn.tkn. 2029.12
h].|ẖlly[-].w.rʻ[h].|ilmškl.w.rʻ[h].|ššw[.--].w.r[ʻ h].|kr[mn.--.]w.r[ʻ h].|šd.[--.w.]r[ʻ h].|ẖla[n.---].|w lšt̠r[.---]. 2083.2.4

krmnpy

[šp].|bn.y[k]n.|ynḥm.|bn.abd.bʻ[l].|mnḥm.bn[.---].|krmn[py].|bn.[--]m.|bn.asr[-].|bn.d̠r[--].|bn.ṣl[--].|bn.ẖd[- 2014.50

krmpy

[---.]nnd[-].|[-]gbt.|[--]y bnš kb[š]y.|krmpy.b.bṣm.|[-]mrn.ṣd.b gl[-]. 2169.4
rmwl.|uwaẖ.|ypln.w.t̠n.bn h.|ydln.|anr[my].|mld.|krmp[y].|bṣmn. 2086.12

krsa

.|bn.ady.kkr.šʻrt.|nt̠k h.|kb[d.]mn.ʻl.abršn.|b[n.---].kr̀su.nt̠k h.|[---.--]mm.b.krsi. 1146.12
.|kb[d.]mn.ʻl.abršn.|b[n.---].kr̀su.nt̠k h.|[---.--]mm.b.krsi. 1146.13

krsn

[--] ksp [---] kdr [---].|[-]t̠rn [k]sp [-]al[.-]r[-].|[--]dšq krsnm.|ẖmšm [-]t t̠lt̠ ty[--].|bn.grgš.|w.npṣ bt t̠n.t̠lt̠ mat.| 1103.13

krsnm

rʻ d nkly yn kd w kd.|w ʻl ym kdm.|w b t̠lt̠.kd yn w krsnm.|w b rbʻ kdm yn.|w b ẖmš kd yn. 1086.3

kr̀sa

.|bn.ady.kkr.šʻrt.|nt̠k h.|kb[d.]mn.ʻl.abršn.|b[n.---].kr̀su.nt̠k h.|[---.--]mm.b.krsi. 1146.12

krʻ

btlt.ʻnt.|nʻmt.bn.aẖt.bʻl.|l pnn h.ydd.w yqm.|l pʻn h.ykrʻ.w yql.|w yšu.g h.w yṣḥ.|ḥwt.aẖt.w nar[-].|qrn.d bat k 10[76].2.18

krpn

.l tbrk.|[krt.]t̠ʻ.l tmr.nʻmn.|[ǵlm.]il.ks.yiḫd.|[il.b]yd.krpn.bm.|[ymn.]brkm.ybrk.|[ʻbd h.]ybrk.il.krt.|[t̠ʻ.ymr]m 15[128].2.17
ḥrb.mlḥt.|qṣ.mri.ndd.|yʻšr.w yšqyn h.|ytn.ks.b d h.|krpn.b klat.yd h.|b krb.ʻẓm.ridn.|mt.šmm.ks.qdš.|l tphn h 3[ʻNT].1.11
.---].|b ʻpr.ẖbl t̠tm.[---.]|šqy.rt̠a.tnm y.ytn.[ks.b yd].|krpn.b klat yd.[---].|km ll.kẖṣ.tusp[.---].|tgr.il.bn h.t̠r[.---]. 1[ʻNT.X].4.10
[-].thmt.brq.|[---].t̠ṣb.qšt.bnt.|[---.ʻ]n h.km.bt̠n.yqr.|[krpn h.-.l]arṣ.ks h.tšpk m.|[l ʻpr.tšu.g h.]w tṣḥ.šmʻ.mʻ.|[l a 17[2AQHT].6.15
m[.---].|[---].ay š[---].|[---.b ḥ]rb.mlḥ[t.qṣ].|[mri.tšty.krpnm].yn.b ks.ẖ[rṣ].|[dm.ʻṣm.---]n.krpn.ʻl.[k]rpn.|[---.]ym 17[2AQHT].6.5
.ǵmit.w ʻs[--].|lḥm.hm.štym.lḥ[m].|b t̠lḥnt.lḥm št.|b krpnm.yn.b k.ẖrṣ.|dm.ʻṣm.hm.yd.il mlk.|yẖss k.ahbt.t̠r.tʻr 4[51].4.37
.šty.ilm.|w pq mrǵtm.t̠d.|b ḥrb.mlḥt.qṣ[.m]r|i.tšty.krp[nm.y]n.|[b k]s.ẖrṣ.d[m.ʻṣm].|[---.--]n.|[---.---]t.|[---.--]t̠ 4[51].6.58
ty.|[ilm.w tp]q.mrǵtm.|[t̠d.b ḥrb.m]lḥt.qṣ.|[mri.tšty.k]rpnm yn.|[b ks.ẖrṣ.dm].ʻṣm. 4[51].3.43
.ilm].|w pq.mr[ǵtm.t̠d.---].|b ḥrb.[mlḥt.qṣ.mri].|šty.kr[pnm.yn.---].|b ks.ẖr[ṣ.dm.ʻṣm.---].|ks.ksp[.---].|krpn.[--- 5[67].4.15
t.yd h.|b krb.ʻẓm.ridn.|mt.šmm.ks.qdš.|l tphn h.at̠t̠.krpn.|l tʻn.atrt.alp.|kd.yqḥ.b ẖmr.|rbt.ymsk.b msk h.|qm. 3[ʻNT].1.14
[t.qṣ].|[mri.tšty.krpnm].yn.b ks.ẖ[rṣ].|[dm.ʻṣm.---]n.krpn.ʻl.[k]rpn.|[---.]ym.w tʻl.trt̠.|[---].yn.ʻšy l ḥbš.|[---.]ḥtn. 17[2AQHT].6.6
b i[--.---].|l t̠[--.---].|ks[.---].|kr[pn.---].|at.š[ʻtqt.---].|šʻd[.---].|rt.[---].|ʻt̠r[.---].|b p.š[---]. 16[126].5.41
y.kr[pnm.yn.---].|b ks.ẖr[ṣ.dm.ʻṣm.---].|ks.ksp[.---].|krpn.[---].|w t̠t̠n.[---].|tʻl.tr[-.---].|bt.il.li[mm.---].|ʻl.ḥbš.[-- 5[67].4.18

krpn

mri.tšty.krpnm].yn.b ks.ḫ[rṣ]. | [dm.ʻṣm.---]n.krpn.ʻl.[k]rpn. | [---.]ym.w tʻl.trṯ. | [---].yn.ʻšy l ḥbš. | [---.]ḥtn.qn.yṣbt. 17[2AQHT].6.6

krr

[---.]ḥlmt.alp.šnt.w[.---]. | šntm.alp.d krr[.---]. | alp.pr.bʻl.[---]. | w prt.tkt.[---]. | šnt.[---]. | ššw.ʻṯtrt. 2158.1.2

krt

| [ksl]h.l arṣ.ṯṯbr. | [---.]aḫ h.tbky. | [--.m]rṣ.mlk. | [---.]krt.adn k. | [w yʻny.]ġzr.ilḥu. | [---.]mrṣ.mlk. | [--.k]rt.adn k. | 16.1[125].57

ywsrnn.ggn h. | lk.l ab k.yṣb.lk. | l[ab]k.w rgm.ʻny. | l k[rt.adn k.]ištm[ʻ]. | w tqġ[.udn.k ġz.ġzm]. | tdbr.w[ġ]rm[.ṯṯ 16.6[127].29

| [---.]krt.adn k. | [w yʻny.]ġzr.ilḥu. | [---.]mrṣ.mlk. | [--.k]rt.adn k. | [--.d]bḥ.dbḥ. | [--.ʻ]šr.ʻšrt. | ʻ[---.---]. | b[---.---]. | t[- 16.1[125].60

]m.tšty. | w tʻn.mṯt ḥry. | l l[ḥ]m.l š[ty].ṣḥt km. | db[ḥ.l krt.a]dn km. | ʻl.krt.tbun.km. | rgm.ṯ[rm.]rgm hm. | b ḏrt[.---. 15[128].6.5

d h.]ybrk.il.krt. | [ṯʻ.ymr]m.nʻm[n.]ġlm.il. | a[ṯt.tq]ḥ.y krt.aṯt. | tqḥ.bt k.ġlmt.tšʻrb. | ḥqr k.tld.šbʻ.bnm.l k. | w ṯmn.ṯṯ 15[128].2.21

.aqny. | [tn.ṯa]rm.amid. | [w yʻn].ṯr.ab h.il. | d[--].b bk.krt. | b dmʻ.nʻmn.ġlm. | il.trḥṣ.w tadm. | rḥṣ[.y]d k.amt. | uṣb[ʻ 14[KRT].2.60

.---]. | tld.pġ[t.---]. | tld.pġ[t.---]. | tld.p[ġt.---]. | mid.rm[.krt]. | b tk.rpi.ar[ṣ]. | b pḫr.qbṣ.dtn. | ṣġrt hn.abkrn. | tbrk.ilm. 15[128].3.13

[-----]. | [---.mid.rm.]krt. | [b tk.rpi.]arṣ. | [b pḫr].qbṣ.dtn. | [w t]qrb.w ld. | bn.tl k. | 15[128].3.2

[m]t.dm.ḫt.šʻtqt dm. | li.w ttbʻ.šʻtqt. | bt.krt.bu.tbu. | bkt.tgly.w tbu. | nṣrt.tbu.pnm. | ʻrm.tdu.mh. | pdr 16.6[127].3

ṯt ḥry. | l l[ḥ]m.l š[ty].ṣḥt km. | db[ḥ.l krt.a]dn km. | ʻl.krt.tbun.km. | rgm.ṯ[rm.]rgm hm. | b ḏrt[.---.]krt. | [----]. 15[128].6.6

h.ṯr h.tšʻrb. | ʻl h.tšʻrb.ẓby h. | ṯr.ḫbr.rbt. | ḫbr.ṯrrt. | bt.krt.tbun. | lm.mṯb[.---]. | w lḥm mr.tqdm. | yd.b ṣʻ.tšlḥ. | ḥrb.b 15[128].4.21

n].mṯt.ḥry. | [l lḥ]m.l šty.ṣḥt k[m]. | [---.]brk.t[---]. | [ʻl.]krt.tbkn. | [--.]rgm.ṯrm. | [--.]mtm.tbkn. | [--]t.w b lb.tqb[-]. | [15[128].5.12

r.bʻl. | ṣpn.ḥlm.qdš. | any.ḥlm.adr.ḥl. | rḥb.mknpt.ap. | [k]rt.bnm.il.špḥ. | lṭpn.w qdš.ʻl. | ab h.yʻrb.ybky. | w yšnn.ytn. 16.1[125].10

ʻl.ṣ[p]n.ḥlm. | qdš.nny.ḥ[l]m.adr. | ḥl.rḥb.mk[npt]. | ap.krt bn[m.il]. | špḥ.lṭpn[.w qdš]. | bkm.tʻr[b.ʻl.ab h]. | tʻrb.ḥ[--]. 16.2[125].110

.tštn. | [w t]ʻn.mṯt.ḥry. | [l lḥ]m.l šty.ṣḥt km. | [--.dbḥ.l]krt.bʻl km. 15[128].4.28

m]lk.itdb.d šbʻ. | [a]ḫm.l h.ṯmnt.bn um. | krt.ḥtk n.rš. | krt.grdš.mknt. | aṯt.ṣdq h.l ypq. | mtrḫt.yšr h. | aṯt.trḫ.w tbʻt. 14[KRT].1.11

.w tṣḥ]. | lm.tbʻrn[.---]. | mn.yrḫ.k m[rṣ.---]. | mn.k dw.kr[t]. | w yʻny.ġzr[.ilḥu]. | ṯlṯ.yrḫm.k m[rṣ]. | arbʻ.k dw.k[rt]. | 16.2[125].82

ṣp.ʻn h. | d b ḥlm y.il.ytn. | b ḏrt y.ab.adm. | w ld.špḥ.l krt. | w ġlm.l ʻbd.il. | krt.yḫṭ.w ḥlm. | ʻbd.il.w hdrt. | yrtḥṣ.w y 14[KRT].3.152

sp.ṯrml. | d b ḥlm y.il.ytn. | b ḏrt y.ab.adm. | w ld.špḥ.l krk | t.w ġlm.l ʻbd. | il.ttbʻ.mlakm. | l yṯb.idk.pnm. | l ytn.ʻmm 14[KRT].6.298

---.]rpat.bt. | [m]lk.itdb.d šbʻ. | [a]ḫm.l h.ṯmnt.bn um. | krt.ḥtk n.rš. | krt.grdš.mknt. | aṯt.ṣdq h.l ypq. | mtrḫt.yšr h. | 14[KRT].1.10

l.ytn. | b ḏrt y.ab.adm. | w ld.špḥ.l krt. | w ġlm.l ʻbd.il. | krt.yḫṭ.w ḥlm. | ʻbd.il.w hdrt. | yrtḥṣ.w yadm. | yrḥṣ.yd h.amt 14[KRT].3.154

h. | il.yrd.b ḏhrt h. | ab adm.w yqrb. | b šal.krt.m at. | krt.k ybky. | ydmʻ.nʻmn.ġlm. | il.mlk[.ṯ]r ab h. | yarš.hm.drk[14[KRT].1.39

[l]krt. | k [k]lb.b bt k.nʻtq.k inr. | ap.ḫšt k.ap.ab.ik mtm. | tmtn. 16.1[125].1

rb.w ld.bn.l h. | w tqrb.w ld.bnt.l h. | mk.b šbʻ.šnt. | bn.krt.km hm.tdr. | ap.bnt.ḥry. | km hm.w ṯḫss.aṯrt. | ndr h.w ilt 15[128].3.23

l ṯr. | ab k.il.šrd.bʻl. | b dbḥ k.bn.dgn. | b mṣd k.w yrd. | krt.l ggt.ʻdb. | akl.l qryt. | ḥṭt.l bt.ḫbr. | yip.lḥm.d ḫmš. | mġd. 14[KRT].2.80

. | l ṯr.ab h.il.šrd. | [bʻl].b dbḥ h.bn dgn. | [b m]ṣd h.yrd.krt. | [l g]gt.ʻdb.akl.l qryt. | ḥṭt.l bt.ḫbr. | yip.lḥm.d ḫmš. | [mġ 14[KRT].4.171

bṣ.bn.amt. | qḥ.krt.šlmm. | šlmm.w ng.mlk. | l bt y.rḥq.krt. | l ḥẓr y.al.tṣr. | udm.rbt.w udm ṯrrt. | udm.ytnt.il w ušn. 14[KRT].3.132

t.udm.y[t]n[t]. | il.ušn.ab[.ad]m. | rḥq.mlk.l bt y. | n[g.]krt.l ḥẓ[r y]. | w yʻn[y.k]rt[.ṯ]ʻ. | lm.ank.ksp. | w yr[q.ḫrṣ]. | yd 14[KRT].6.280

.udm.ytnt]. | [il.w ušn.ab.adm]. | [rḥq.mlk.l bt y]. | [ng.kr]t.l ḥ[ẓ]r y. | [-----]. | [---.ttbʻ]. | [mlakm.l yṯb]. | [idk.pnm.l y 14[KRT].5.261

t.ḥry. | ṯṭbḫ.imr.w lḥm. | mgṯ.w yṯrm.hn.ym. | w ṯn.yṯb.krt.l ʻd h. | yṯb.l ksi mlk. | l nḫt.l kḥṯ.drkt. | ap.yṣb.yṯb.b hkl. | 16.6[127].22

ṣ.w b ḥlm h. | il.yrd.b ḏhrt h. | ab adm.w yqrb. | b šal.krt.m at. | krt.k ybky. | ydmʻ.nʻmn.ġlm. | il.mlk[.ṯ]r ab h. | yar 14[KRT].1.38

kr[t]. | w yʻny.ġzr[.ilḥu]. | ṯlṯ.yrḫm.k m[rṣ]. | arbʻ.k dw.k[rt]. | mndʻ.krt.mġ[y.---]. | w qbr.tṣr.q[br]. | tṣr.trm.tnq[--]. | 16.2[125].85

[mrġ]b.yd.m[tkt]. | mẓma.yd.mṯkt. | ṯṯkr.[--]dn. | ʻm.krt.mswn h. | arḫ.tzġ.l ʻgl h. | bn.ḫpṯ.l umht hm. | k tnḥn.ud 15[128].1.4

---]. | [---.ttbʻ]. | [mlakm.l yṯb]. | [idk.pnm.l ytn]. | [ʻ]m[.krt.mswn h]. | tš[an.g hm.w tṣḥn]. | tḥ[m.pbl.mlk]. | qḥ[.ksp. 14[KRT].6.266

r h. | l gʻt.alp.ḥrṯ.zġt. | klb.ṣpr.w ylak. | mlakm.l k.ʻm.krt. | mswn h.tḥm.pbl.mlk. | qḥ.ksp.w yrq.ḫrṣ. | yd.mqm h.w 14[KRT].3.124

m y. | [---.--]p. | [---.d]bḥ. | t[---.id]k. | pn[m.al.ttn]. | ʻm.[krt.msw]n. | w r[gm.l krt.]ṯʻ. | tḥm[.pbl.mlk]. | qḥ.[ksp.w yr]q 14[KRT].5.247

y.ġzr[.ilḥu]. | ṯlṯ.yrḫm.k m[rṣ]. | arbʻ.k dw.k[rt]. | mndʻ.krt.mġ[y.---]. | w qbr.tṣr.q[br]. | tṣr.trm.tnq[--]. | km.nkyt.ṯġr[16.2[125].86

t[-].ṣba.rbt. | špš.w tgh.nyr. | rbt.w rgm.l aḫt k. | ṯtmnt.krt n.dbḥ. | dbḥ.mlk.ʻšr. | ʻšrt.qḥ.tp k.b yd. | [-]r[-]k.bm.ymn. 16.1[125].39

p. | ršp.nṯdṯt.ġlm. | ym.mšbʻt hn.b šlḥ. | ttpl.yʻn.ḥtk h. | krt yʻn.ḥtk h.rš. | mid.grdš.ṯbt h. | w b tm hn.špḥ.yitbd. | w b. 14[KRT].1.22

b[-]. | [--]m[-].mtm.uṣbʻ[t]. | [-]tr.šrk.il. | ʻrb.špš.l ymġ. | krt.ṣbia.špš. | bʻl ny.w ymlk. | [y]ṣb.ʻln.w y[-]y. | [kr]t.ṯʻ.ʻln.bḫ 15[128].5.19

| w ʻbd[.ʻlm.ṯlṯ]. | sswm.m[rkbt]. | b trbṣ.[bn.amt]. | q[ḥ.kr]t[.šlmm]. | š[lmm.]al.t[ṣr]. | udm[.r]bt.w u[dm]. | [ṯ]rrt.ud 14[KRT].6.274

h. | ʻbd[.ʻlm.ṯlṯ]. | ss[wm.mrkbt]. | b[trbṣ.bn.amt]. | [qḥ.krt.šlmm]. | [šlmm.al.tṣr]. | [udm.rbt.w udm]. | [ṯrrt.udm.ytnt 14[KRT].5.255

qm h.w ʻbd.ʻlm. | ṯlṯ.sswm.mrkbt. | b trbṣ.bn.amt. | qḥ.krt.šlmm. | šlmm.w ng.mlk. | l bt y.rḥq.krt. | l ḥẓr y.al.tṣr. | u 14[KRT].3.130

tn.u ḫšt k.l ntn. | ʻtq.b d.aṯt.ab.ṣrry. | ik m.yrgm.bn.il. | krt.špḥ.lṭpn. | w qdš.u ilm.tmtn. | špḥ.lṭpn.l yḥ. | w yʻny.krt.ṯʻ 16.1[125].21

hm.kly. | yn.b ḥmt hm.k[l]y. | šmn.b q[bʻt hm.---]. | bt.krt.t[--]. 16[126].3.17

ṯ. | ym[ġy.]l qdš. | a[ṯrt.]ṣrm.w l ilt. | ṣd[yn]m.ṯm. | yd[r.k]rt.ṯʻ. | i.iṯt.aṯrt.ṣrm. | w ilt.ṣdynm. | hm.ḥry.bt y. | iqḥ.ašʻrb.ġ 14[KRT].4.200

rt.špḥ.lṭpn. | w qdš.u ilm.tmtn. | špḥ.lṭpn.l yḥ. | w yʻny.krt.ṯʻ. | bn.al.tbkn.al. | tdm.l y.al tkl.bn. | qr.ʻn k.mḫ.riš k. | ud 16.1[125].24

k.pnm. | l ytn.ʻmm.pbl. | mlk.tšan. | g hm.w tṣḥn. | tḥm.krt.ṯ[ʻ]. | hwt.[n]ʻmn.[ġlm.il]. 14[KRT].6.305

. | [w]yʻn.aliy[n.]bʻl. | [---.]tbʻ.l lṭpn. | [il.d]pid.l tbrk. | [krt.]ṯʻ.l tmr.nʻmn. | [ġlm.]il.ks.yiḫd. | [il.b]yd.krpn.bm. | [ym 15[128].2.15

.ab[.ad]m. | rḥq.mlk.l bt y. | n[g.]krt.l ḥẓ[r y]. | w yʻn[y.k]rt[.ṯ]ʻ. | lm.ank.ksp. | w yr[q.ḫrṣ]. | yd.mqm h.w ʻbd. | ʻlm.ṯlṯ 14[KRT].6.281

[il.b]yd.krpn.bm. | [ymn.]brkm.ybrk. | [ʻbd h.]ybrk.il.krt. | [ṯʻ.ymr]m.nʻm[n.]ġlm.il. | a[ṯt.tq]ḥ.y krt.aṯt. | tqḥ.bt k.ġ 15[128].2.19

.tpṯḥ. | brlt h.l trm. | mt.dm.ḫt.šʻtqt. | dm.lan.w ypqd. | krt.ṯʻ.yšu.g h. | w yṣḥ.šmʻ.l mṯt. | ḥry.ṯbḫ.imr. | w ilḥm.mgṯ.w 16.6[127].15

ymġ. | krt.ṣbia.špš. | bʻl ny.w ymlk. | [y]ṣb.ʻln.w y[-]y. | [kr]t.ṯʻ.ʻln.bḫr. | [---].aṯt k.ʻl. | [---] k.yšṣi. | [---.]ḫbr.rbt. | [ḫbr.ṯ 15[128].5.22

w ḫss. | [---]n.rḥm y.ršp zbl. | [w ʻd]t.ilm.ṯlṯ h. | [ap]nk.krt.ṯʻ.ʻ[-]r. | [--.]b bt h.yšt.ʻrb. | [--] h.ytn.w [--]u.l ytn. | [aḫ]r. 15[128].2.8

n. | ytbʻ.yṣb ġlm.ʻl. | ab h.yʻrb.yšu g h. | w yṣḥ.šmʻ mʻ.l krt. | ṯʻ.ištmʻ.w tqġ udn. | k ġz.ġzm.tdbr. | w ġrm.ṯṯwy.šqlt. | b 16.6[127].41

ḥ. | t[---.id]k. | pn[m.al.ttn]. | ʻm.[krt.msw]n. | w r[gm.l krt.]ṯʻ. | tḥm[.pbl.mlk]. | qḥ.[ksp.w yr]q. | ḫrṣ[.yd.mqm] h. | ʻb 14[KRT].5.248

anšt. | ʻrš.zbln.rd.l mlk. | amlk.l drkt k.aṯb. | an.w yʻny.krt ṯʻ.yṯbr. | ḥrn.y bn.yṯbr.ḥrn. | riš k.ʻṯtrt.šm.bʻl. | qdqd k.tql 16.6[127].54

zǵ.l ʿgl h. | bn.ḫpṯ.l umht hm. | k tnḥn.udmm. | w yʿny.krt.ṯʿ. 15[128].1.8
[l k]rt. | [--].ml[k.---]. | [---]m.k[---]. | [-----]. | [---]m.il[.---]. | [---] 14[KRT].1.1
ss.aṯrt. | ndr h.w ilt.p[--]. | w tšu.g h.w [tṣḥ]. | ph mʿ.ap.k[rt.--]. | u ṯn.ndr[.---]. | apr.[---]. | [-----]. 15[128].3.28
n km. | ʿl.krt.tbun.km. | rgm.ṯ[rm.]rgm hm. | b ḏrt[.---.]krt. | [----]. 15[128].6.8

krty

]. | bn.ḥ[---]. | bn.plš. | bn.ubr. | bn.ʿpṯb. | ṯbry. | bn.ymn. | krty. | bn.abr[-]. | yrpu. | kdn. | pʿṣ. | bn.liy. | ydʿ. | šmn. | ʿdy. | ʿn 2117.1.20
. | kry. | psš. | ilṯhm. | ḥrm. | bn.bty. | ʿby. | šm[n].bn.apn. | krty. | bn.ubr. | [bn] mdḫl. | bn.sy[n]n. | bn.šrn. 2078.18
bn.šmʿn. | bn.ǵlmy. | ǵly. | bn.dnn. | bn.rmy. | dll. | mny. | krty. | bn.ʿbṣ. | bn.argb. | ydn. | ilʿnt. | bn.urt. | ydn. | qṯn. | bn.as 2117.3.39

kš

ʿglm.dt.šnt. | imr.qmṣ.llim.k ksp. | l ʿbrm.zt.ḫrṣ.l ʿbrm.kš. | dpr.ṯlḥn.b qʿl.b qʿl. | mlkm.hn.ym.yṣq.yn.ṯmk. | mrṯ.yn.s 22.2[124].15

kšd

. | thw.hm.brlt.anḫr. | b ym.hm.brk y.tkšd. | rumm.ʿn.kḏd.aylt. | hm.imt.imt.npš.blt. | ḥmr.p imt.b klt. | yd y.ilḥm.h 5[67].1.17
. | thw.w npš. | anḫr.b ym. | brkt.šbšt. | k rumm.hm. | ʿn.kḏd.aylt. | mt hm.ks.ym | sk.nhr hm. | šbʿ.ydt y.b ṣʿ. | [--.]šbʿ.r UG5.4.8
r.p np.š.npš.lbim. | thw.hm.brlt.anḫr. | b ym.hm.brk y.tkšd. | rumm.ʿn.kḏd.aylt. | hm.imt.imt.npš.blt. | ḥmr.p imt.b 5[67].1.16

kt

ṯ.l.yšn. | [šd.--]ln. | b d.trǵds. | šd.ṯʿlb. | b d.bn.pl. | šd.bn.kt. | b d.pdy. | šd.ḫzr. | [b d].ḏ[---]. 2030.2.5
[sp]r.bnš.ml[k.d.b] d adn[ʿm]. | [---].riš[.---].kt. | [y]nḥm. | ilbʿl. | ʿbdyr[ḫ]. | ṯtpḥ. | artn. | ybnil. | brqn. | adr[d 1024.1.2
r k.ank.ydʿt. | [-]n.atn.at.mṯb k[.---]. | [š]mm.rm.lk.prẓ kt. | [k]bkbm.ṯm.tpl k.lbnt. | [-.]rgm.k yrkt.ʿtqbm. | [---]m.ʿẓp 13[6].12
ky.lik.bn y. | lḥt.akl.ʿm y. | mid y w ǵbn y. | w.bn y.hn kt. | yškn.anyt. | ym.yšrr. | w.ak[l.---]. | [--].š[--.--]. 2061.12
tk.ri[š.]l mhr k. | w ʿp.l dr[ʿ].nšr k. | w rbṣ.l ǵr k.inbb. | kt ǵr k.ank.ydʿt. | [-]n.atn.at.mṯb k[.---]. | [š]mm.rm.lk.prẓ kt 13[6].10

ktb

[---.]ktb nǵr krm. | [---].ab h.krm ar. | [---.]h.mḥtrt.pṯtm. | [---.-]t 2001.2.1
nṯ.ʿd ʿlm. | mišmn.nqmd. | mlk ugrt. | nqmd.mlk.ugrt. | ktb.spr hnd. | dt brrt.ṣṭqšlm. | ʿbd h.hnd. | w mn km.l yqḥ. | s 1005.9

ktkt

.ršp.ary. | bn.ǵlmn ary. | bn.ḥṣbn ary. | bn.šdy ary. | bn.ktkt.mʿqby. | bn.[---.]ṯlḥny. | b[n.---.ub]rʿy. | [bn.---.ubr]ʿy. | b[87[64].16

ktl

.abd[.---]. | [---.]anyt[.---]. | [-----]. | ʿšrm.l.umdym. | ʿšr.l.ktl. 2110.6

ktln

b]n.ǵrgn. | [b]n.tgdn. | bn.ḫdyn. | bn.sgr. | bn.aǵltn. | bn.ktln. | bn.ʿgwn. | bn.yšmʿ. | bdl.mḏrǵlm. | bn.mmy. | bn.ḫnyn. | 104[316].9
dn. | bn.anny. | ytršp. | bn.szn. | bn.kdgdl. | bn.glʿd. | bn.ktln. | [bn].ǵrgn. | bn.pb[-]. | bn.[---]. | bn.[---]. | bn.[---]. | bn.[--- 115[301].1.15

ktmn

.kwn. | ǵmšd. | bn.ʿbdḫy. | bn.ubyn. | slpd. | bn.atnb. | bn.ktmn. | bn.pity. | bn.iryn. | bn.ʿbl. | bn.grbn. | bn.iršyn. | bn.nkl 115[301].4.14
dy. | bʿl.bt.nqly. | bʿl.bt.ʿlr. | bʿl.bt.ssl. | bʿl.bt.ṯrn. | bʿl.bt.ktmn. | bʿl.bt.ndbd. | [--].ṣnr. | [bʿl].bt.bsn. | [-----]. | b[--.---]. 31[14].8
.--]n. | [-----]. | [---.-]bd. | [---]ybʿ.bʿl.ḫr[-]. | pqr.yḫd. | bn.ktmn.ṯǵr.hk[l]. | bn.ṯgbr.ṯǵr.hk[l]. | bn.ydln. | bn.ktmn. 1056.8
d. | bn.ktmn.ṯǵr.hk[l]. | bn.ṯgbr.ṯǵr.hk[l]. | bn.ydln. | bn.ktmn. 1056.11

ktn

t.ksp. | šbʿm.lbš.d.ʿrb.bt.mlk. | b.mit.ḫmšt.kbd.ksp. | ṯlṯ.ktnt.b d.an[r]my. | b.ʿšrt.ksp.b.a[--]. | ṯqlm.ḫr[ṣ.]b.ṯmnt.ksp. | 2101.18
alpm.pḥm.ḫm[š].mat.kbd. | b d.tt.w.ṯlṯ.ktnt.b dm.tt. | w.ṯmnt.ksp.hn. | ktn.d.ṣr.pḥm.b h.w.ṯqlm. | ks 1110.2
].mat.kbd. | b d.tt.w.ṯlṯ.ktnt.b dm.tt. | w.ṯmnt.ksp.hn. | ktn.d.ṣr.pḥm.b h.w.ṯqlm. | ksp h.mitm.pḥm.b d.skn. | w.tt.kt 1110.4
š.arn.ṯn[.ʿšr h.]mn. | ʿṣrm.ṯql.kbd[.ks].mn.ḫrṣ. | w arbʿ.ktnt.w [---]b. | [ḫm]š.mat pḥm. | [ḫm]š[.m]at.iqnu. | argmn.n 64[118].21
ṯlṯm.ktn. | ḫmšm.izml. | ḫmš.kbd.arbʿm. | dd.akl. | ṯṯ.ʿšr h.yn. | kd.š 1126.1
d.ṣr.pḥm.b h.w.ṯqlm. | ksp h.mitm.pḥm.b d.skn. | w.ṯt.ktnm.ḫmšt.w.nṣp.ksp.hn. 1110.6
at.kbd. | arbʿ.alpm.iqni. | ḫmš.mat.kbd. | ṯlṯm.ḫmš kbd ktn. | ḫmš.rṭm. | ḫmš.ṯnt.d ḫmšm w. | ḫmš.ṯnt.d mit. | ḫmš.ṯnt 1130.7
ḫmšm.dd. | nʿr. | ḫmšm.tišr. | ḫmš.ktnt. | ḫmš.ṯnt.alpm. | ʿšrm.hbn. | ṯlṯ.mat.dd. | šʿrm. | mit.šmn. 2102.4
[ks.ksp.kt]n.mit.pḥ[m]. | [mit.iqni.l]ḫbrtn[r]. | [ks.ksp.ktn.mit.pḥ]m. | [mit.iqni.l ḫbrtn]r ṯn. | [ks.ksp.ktn.mit.pḥm]. 64[118].35
rb.bʿl h. | ks.ḫrṣ.ktn.mit.pḥm. | mit.iqni.l mlkt. | ks.ḫrṣ.ktn.mit.pḥm. | mit.iqni.l uṯryn. | ks.ksp.ktn.mit.pḥm. | mit.iq 64[118].29
[ks.ksp.ktn.mit.pḥ]m. | [mit.iqni.l ḫbrtn]r ṯn. | [ks.ksp.ktn.mit.pḥm]. | [mit.iqn]i.l skl.[--]. | [---.m]it pḥm.l š[--]. | [---. 64[118].37
uṯryn. | ks.ksp.ktn.mit.pḥm. | mit.iqni.l tpnr. | [ks.ksp.kt]n.mit.pḥ[m]. | [mit.iqni.l]ḫbrtn[r]. | [ks.ksp.ktn.mit.pḥ]m 64[118].33
mn.nqmd.mlk. | ugrt.d ybl.l špš. | mlk.rb.bʿl h. | ks.ḫrṣ.ktn.mit.pḥm. | mit.iqni.l mlkt. | ks.ḫrṣ.ktn.mit.pḥm. | mit.iqn 64[118].27
l mlkt. | ks.ḫrṣ.ktn.mit.pḥm. | mit.iqni.l uṯryn. | ks.ksp.ktn.mit.pḥm. | mit.iqni.l tpnr. | [ks.ksp.kt]n.mit.pḥ[m]. | [mit 64[118].31
ʿšr.ktnt. | ʿšr.rṭm. | kkr[.-].ḫt. | mitm[.p]ṯtm. | ṯlṯm[.---].kst. | alp.a[1114.1

ktp

b hm.ygʿr.ṯǵr. | bt.il.pn.l mgr lb.tʿdbn. | nšb.l inr.tʿdbn.ktp. | b il ab h.gʿr.yṯb.il.kb[-]. | aṯ[rt.]il.yṯb.b mrzḥ h. | yšt[.il. UG5.1.1.13
ṯlḥn. | b qrʿ. | ʿṯtrt.w ʿnt.ymǵy. | ʿṯtrt.tʿdb.nšb l h. | w ʿnt.ktp.b hm.ygʿr.ṯǵr. | bt.il.pn.l mgr lb.tʿdbn. | nšb.l inr.tʿdbn.kt UG5.1.1.11
yiḫd.bʿl.bn.aṯrt. | rbm.ymḫṣ.b ktp. | dk ym.ymḫṣ.b ṣmd. | ṣḥr mt.ymṣḫ.l arṣ. | [yṯb.]b[ʿ]l.l ks 6[49].5.2
[n]hr l kḥṯ drkt h.trtqṣ.b d bʿl km nš | r.b uṣbʿt h.hlm.ktp.zbl ym.bn ydm. | [tp]ṭ nhr.yrtqṣ.ṣmd.b d bʿl.km.nšr. | b[2.4[68].14

. | [ṯp]ṭ nhr.yrtqṣ.ṣmd.b d bʿl.km.nšr. | b[u]ṣbʿt h.ylm.ktp.zbl ym.bn ydm.ṯpṭ. | nhr.ʿz.ym.l ymk.l tnǵṣn.pnt h.l ydl 2.4[68].16
. | ʿms mʿ.l y.aliyn.bʿl. | tšmʿ.nrt.ilm.špš. | tšu.aliyn.bʿl.l ktp. | ʿnt.k tšt h.tšʿlyn h. | b ṣrrt.ṣpn.tbkyn h. | w tqbrn h.tštn 6[62].1.14
.ym.tʿ]dt.ṯpṭ.nhr.mlak.mṯḫr.yḥb[-.---.] | [---].mlak.bn.ktpm.rgm.bʿl h.w y[--.---]. | [---].ap.anš.zbl.bʿl.šdmt.bg[--.---] 2.1[137].42

ktr

dmlk. | y[--]k. | [-----]. | pǵḏn. | [--]n. | [--]ntn. | ʿdn. | lkn. | ktr. | ubn. | dqn. | ḥṯṯn. | [--]n. | [---]. | tsn. | rpiy. | mrṯn. | ṯnyn. | a 1024.2.8
. | mru.skn. | mru.ibrn. | yqšm. | trrm. | kkrdnm. | yṣrm. | ktrm. | mṣlm. | tkn[m]. | ǵ[---]. | ǵm[--]. 1026.2.12

ktt

š.ṯnt.d mit. | ḫmš.ṯnt.d ṯl | ṯ mat. | ṯt.ṯnt.d alp | alpm.ṯlṯ ktt. | alp.brr. | kkr.tznt. | ḫmšt.kkr tyt. 1130.14
brʿ. | skn ḫrṣbʿ. | rb.ntbtš. | [---].ʿbd.r[--]. | arbʿ.k[--]. | ṯlṯ.ktt. 1033.9

kṯ

[--.m]itm.nṣ.l bn[.---]. | [-]l[-.---]. | [-]ṯ.[---]. | mṣb[-.---]. | kṯ.aqh[r.---]. | l bn[.---]. | [ṯ]lṯ.[---]. | [---.--]yn.š.aḫ[--]. | [---.]š.n 143[-].2.4
b.ntn.ṯlṯ.mat.[---]. | lg.šmn.rqḥ.šrʿm.ušpǵtm.p[--.---]. | kṯ.ẓrw.kṯ.nbt.ḏnt.w [-]n[-.---]. | il.ḫyr.ilib.š. | arṣ w šmm.š. | il. UG5.9.1.22
lṯ.mat.[---]. | lg.šmn.rqḥ.šrʿm.ušpǵtm.p[--.---]. | kṯ.ẓrw.kṯ.nbt.ḏnt.w [-]n[-.---]. | il.ḫyr.ilib.š. | arṣ w šmm.š. | il.š.kṯrt.š UG5.9.1.22
.---]. | [---].mit.ḫsw.[---]. | [----]d.nʿr.ṯ[--]d[.---]. | [---.]ṯlṯ.kṯt[.-]d.[---]. | [---.a]rbʿ.dblt.m[--.---]. | [--.mi]tm nṣ.[-]ṯ[-.]gr[- 143[-].1.4
ʿšr. | kṯt. | [--]š ʿšr. | lg. 158[58].2

kṯan

. | mʿq[bym]. | tšʿ.ʿ[šr.bnš]. | ǵr.ṯ[--.---]. | ṣbu.any[t]. | bn.kṯan. | ǵr.tšʿ[.ʿšr.b]nš. | ṣbu.any[t]. | bn abdḫ[r]. | pdym. | ḫmš. 79[83].8

kṯy

šp. | tmn. | šmmn. | bn.rmy. | bn.aky. | ʿbdḫmn. | bn.ʿdṯ. | kṯy. | bn.ḫny. | bn.ssm. | bn.ḫnn. | [--]ny. | [bn].ṯrdnt. | [bn].hya 1047.16
[-----]. | ʿbd[--]. | bn.i[--]. | ʿd[--]. | ild[--]. | bn.qṣn. | ʿlpy. | kṯy. | bn.ẓmn. | bn.trdn. | ypq. | ʿbd. | qrḥ. | abšr. | bn.bdn. | ḏmr 2117.2.22
bly.dbḥn š[p]š pgr. | [g]dlt iltm ḫnqtm.d[q]tm. | [yr]ḫ.kṯy gdlt.w l ǵlmt š. | [w]pamt ṯlṯm.w yrdt.[m]dbḥt. | gdlt.l bʿ 34[1].19
y. | dqt. | trṯ. | ršp. | ʿnt ḫbly. | špš pgr. | iltm ḫnqtm. | yrḫ kṯy. | ygb hd. | yrgb bʿl. | ydb il. | yarš il. | yrǵm il. | ʿmtr. | ydb i UG5.14.A.14
lʿn.qšt.w.qlʿ. | bn.tmy.qšt.w.qlʿ. | ʿky.qšt. | ʿbdlbit.qšt. | kṯy.qšt.w.qlʿ. | bn.ḫršn.qšt.w.qlʿ. | ilrb.qšt.w.qlʿ. | pšḫn.qšt. | b 119[321].3.39
i[l]. | [š]lm.il.šr. | dgn.w bʿl. | ʿṯ w kmṯ. | yrḫ w ksa. | yrḫ mkṯy. | ṯkmn w šnm. | kṯr w ḫss. | ʿṯtr ʿṯtpr. | šḥr w šlm. | ngh UG5.10.1.7

kṯky

l.rb. | kṯkym. 1163.2

kṯkt

bn.ʿ[-]y. | knʿm. | bn.yš[-]n. | bn.pd[y]. | ttn. | md.ʿṯt[rt]. | kṯkt. | bn.ṯtn[--]. | [m]d.m[--]. | [b]n.annḏ[r]. | bn.ṯḏyy. | bn.grb 1054.1.12

kṯl

-]nbbl. | bn bl. | bn dkn. | bn ils. | bn ḥšbn. | bn uryy. | bn kṯl. | bn army. | bn gln. | bn abg. | bn.nǵry. | bn.srwd. | mtnn. | b 1064.9

kṯly

]n. | bn.ṣṣb. | bn.bʿltn ḫlq. | bn.mlkbn. | bn.asyy ḫlq. | bn.kṯly. | bn.kyn. | bn.ʿbdḥr. | [-]prm ḫlq. | [---]n ḫlq. | bn mʿnt. | b 2016.2.5

kṯn

. | bn.kʿ[--]. | bn.y[---]. | [-----]. | [bn.a]mdy. | bn.ḫlln. | bn.kṯn. | bn.abn. | bn.nskn. | bn.gmrn. | bn[.-]škn. | [---.--]n. | [---.-- 2021.2.4

kṯp

[n.l]azd.ʿr.qdm. | [---].ʿẓ q[dm.--.šp]š. | [---.šm]n.mšḥt.kṯpm.a[-]ṯ[-]. | [---.--]ḥ b ym.tld[---.]b[-.]y[--.---]. | [---.il]m.rb UG5.8.23

kṯr

n[-]t. | ḫrṣ.šmḫ.rbt.a[ṯrt]. | ym.gm.l ǵlm h.k [ṯṣḥ]. | ʿn.mkṯr.ap.ṯ[---]. | dgy.rbt.aṯr[t.ym]. | qḥ.rṯt.b d k t[---]. | rbt.ʿl.y 4[51].2.30
. | d ḥrš.y[dm.tḥm.ṯr.il.ab k.] | hwt.lṭpn[.ḥtk k.---]. | yh.kṯr.b[---]. | št.lskt.n[--.---]. | ʿdb.bǵrt.ṯ[--. --]. | ḥš k.ʿṣ k.ʿ[bṣ k.ʿ 1[ʿNT.IX].3.7
.bʿl.mr[-]. | bt[.--]b bʿl.b qrb. | bt.w yʿn.aliyn. | bʿl.ašt m.kṯr bn. | ym.kṯr.bnm.ʿdt. | ypth.ḥln.b bht m. | urbt.b qrb.[h]kl 4[51].7.15
t[.--]b bʿl.b qrb. | bt.w yʿn.aliyn. | bʿl.ašt m.kṯr bn. | ym.kṯr.bnm.ʿdt. | ypth.ḥln.b bht m. | urbt.b qrb.[h]kl | m.w y[p]t 4[51].7.16
. | ksu.ṯbt h.ḥkpt. | arṣ.nḥlt h. | b alp.šd.rbt. | kmn.l pʿn.kṯ. | hbr.w ql.tštḥ | wy.w kbd hwt. | w rgm.l kṯr. | w ḫss.ṯny.l 3[ʿNT.VI].6.18
r.]ks[u.ṯbt h.ḥkpt.arṣ.nḥlt h]. | b alp.šd.r[bt.kmn.l pʿn.kṯr]. | hbr.w ql.t[štḥwy.w kbd.hwt]. | w rgm l k[ṯr.w ḫss.ṯny.l 1[ʿNT.IX].3.2
.yisp.ḥmt.ṯṯ.w kṯt. | [yus]p.ḥmt.mlk.b ʿṯtrt.yisp.ḥmt. | [kṯ]r w ḫss.y[i]sp.ḥmt.šḥr.w šlm. | [yis]p.ḥmt.isp.[šp]š l hrm. UG5.8.18
pḫd.l npš.kṯr.w ḫss. | l brlt.hyn.d ḥrš. | ydm.aḫr.ymǵy.kṯr. | w ḫss.b d.dnil.ytnn. | qšt.l brk h.yʿdb. | qṣʿt.apnk.mṯt.dn 17[2AQHT].5.25
.b[n.]bht.ym[.rm]m.hkl.ṯpṭ nh[r]. | [---.]hrn.w[---.]tbʿ.k[ṯ]r w [ḫss.t]bn.bht zbl ym. | [trm]m.hk[l.ṯpṭ].nhr.bt k.[---.] 2.3[129].8
adr.qrnt.b yʿlm.mtnm. | b ʿqbt.ṯr.adr.b ǵlil.qnm. | tn.l kṯr.w ḫss.ybʿl.qšt l ʿnt. | qṣʿt.l ybmt.limm.w tʿn.btlt. | ʿnt.irš ḥ 17[2AQHT].6.24
ʿ.nš[m.w l tbn.hmlt.arṣ]. | at.w ank.ib[ǵy h.---]. | w yʿn.kṯr.w ḫss[.lk.lk.ʿnn.ilm.] | atm.bštm.w an[.šnt.kptr]. | l rḥq.il 1[ʿNT.IX].3.17
rm.mid.ksp. | gbʿm lḥmd.ḥrṣ. | yblnn.udr.ilqṣm. | yak.l kṯr.w ḫss. | w ṯb l mspr..k tlakn. | ǵlmm. | aḫr.mǵy.kṯr.w ḫss. 4[51].5.103
tm. | ʿd k.kṯr m.ḥbr k. | w ḫss.dʿt k. | b ym.arš.w tnn. | kṯr.w ḫss.yd. | ytr.kṯr.w ḫss. | spr.ilmlk šbny. | lmd.atn.prln.r 6.6[62.2].51
m.l aṯt h.k yṣḥ. | šmʿ.mtt.dnty.ʿd[b]. | imr.b pḫd.l npš.kṯr. | w ḫss.l brlt.hyn d. | ḥrš yd.šlḥm.ššqy. | ilm sad.kbd.hmt 17[2AQHT].5.17
bʿl. | ḥkpt.il.kl h.tšmʿ. | mtt.dnty.tʿdb.imr. | b pḫd.l npš.kṯr.w ḫss. | l brlt.hyn.d ḥrš. | ydm.aḫr.ymǵy.kṯr. | w ḫss.b d.d 17[2AQHT].5.23
l.ul ny.w l.ʿpr.ʿẓm ny. | l bʿl[-.---]. | tḥt.ksi.zbl.ym.w ʿn.kṯr.w ḫss.l rgmt. | l k.l zbl.bʿl.ṯnt.l rkb.ʿrpt.ht.ib k. | bʿl m.ht. 2.4[68].7
.[h]kl | m.w y[p]tḥ.b dqt.ʿrpt. | ʿl h[wt].kṯr.w ḫss. | ṣḥq.kṯr.w ḫss. | yšu.g h.w yṣḥ. | l rgmt.l k.l ali | yn.bʿl.ṯtbn.bʿl. | l h 4[51].7.21
br k. | w ḫss.dʿt k. | b ym.arš.w tnn. | kṯr.w ḫss.yd. | ytr.kṯr.w ḫss. | spr.ilmlk šbny. | lmd.atn.prln.rb. | khnm rb.nqdm 6.6[62.2].52

b‘l.|‘ṭ w kmṯ.|yrḫ w ksa.|yrḫ mkṯy.|ṯkmn w šnm.|kṯr w ḫss.|‘ṯtr ‘ṯtpr.|šḥr w šlm.|ngh w srr.|‘dw šr.|ṣdqm š UG5.10.1.9
m.|urbt.b qrb.[h]kl |m.w y[p]tḥ.b dqt.‘rpt.|‘l h[wt].kṯr.w ḫss.|ṣḥq.kṯr.w ḫss.|yšu.g h.w yṣḥ.|l rgmt.l k.l ali|yn. 4[51].7.20
k.l kṯr.w ḫss.|w ṯb l mspr..k tlakn.|ǵlmm.|aḫr.mǵy.kṯr.w ḫss.|št.alp.qdm h.mra.|w tk.pn h.t‘db.ksu.|w yṯṯb.l y 4[51].5.106
m].|b tk.ṣrrt.ṣpn.|alp.šd.aḫd bt.|rbt.kmn.hkl.|w y‘n.kṯr.w ḫss.|šm‘.l aliyn b‘l.|bn.l rkb.‘rpt.|bl.ašt.urbt.b bh[t] 4[51].5.120
w y‘n.k[ṯr.w ḫs]s.|ṯṯb.b‘l.l[hwt y].|ṯn.rgm.k[ṯr.w]ḫss.|šm‘.m‘.l al[iy]n b‘l.|bl.ašt.ur[bt.]b bht m.|ḥln. 4[51].6.3
.]|[yhbr.]w yql[.y]štḥw[y.]w ykb[dn h.--]r y[---].|[---.k]ṯr.w ḫ[ss.t]b‘.b[n.]bht.ym[.rm]m.hkl.ṯpṭ nh[r].|[---.]hrn.w 2.3[129].7
w y‘n.k[ṯr.w ḫs]s.|ṯṯb.b‘l.l[hwt y].|ṯn.rgm.k[ṯr.w]ḫss.|šm‘.m‘.l a 4[51].6.1
.bt.rb.|[---.m]dd.il ym.|[---.-]qlṣn.wpṯ m.|[---.]w y‘n.kṯr.|[w ḫss.]ṯṯb.b‘l.l hwt y.|[ḥš.]bht h.tbnn.|[ḥš.]trmm.hkl 4[51].6.14
kmn.l p‘n.kṯ.|hbr.w ql.tšth|wy.w kbd hwt.|w rgm.l kṯr.|w ḫss.ṯny.l h|yn.d ḥrš.ydm.|tḥm.al[iyn.b‘l].|h[wt.aliy. 3[‘NT.VI].6.21
mn.l p‘n.kṯr].|hbr.w ql.t[štḥwy.w kbd.hwt].|w rgm l k[ṯr.w ḫss.ṯny.l hyn].|d ḥrš.y[dm.tḥm.ṯr.il.ab k.]|hwt.lṭpn[. 1[‘NT.IX].3.4
[-----].|[------.]ṯr.|[---.aliy]n.b‘l.|[------.]yrḫ.zbl.|[--.kṯ]r w ḫss.|[---]n.rḥm y.ršp zbl.|[w ‘d]t.ilm.ṯlṯ h.|[ap]nk.kr 15[128].2.5
ḥm.št[y.ilm].|[w]y‘n.aliy[n.b‘l].|[--]b[.---].|ḥš.bht m.k[ṯr].|ḥš.rmm.hk[l m].|ḥš.bht m.tbn[n].|ḥš.trmmn.hk[l m] 4[51].5.113
ryn.|a[-]ḥn tlyn.|atdb w ‘r.|qdš w amrr.|ṯḫr w bd.|[k]ṯr ḫss šlm.|šlm il bt.|šlm il ḫš[t].|ršp inšt.|[--]rm il [---].| UG5.7.71
ḏmr.|b knr.w ṯlb.b tp.w mṣltm.b m|rqdm.dšn.b.ḥbr.kṯr.ṭbm.|w tšt.‘nt.gṯr.b‘lt.mlk.b‘|lt.drkt.b‘lt.šmm.rmm.|[b‘ UG5.2.1.5
ṯpṭ.ṯpṭ.ytm.|b nši ‘n h.w yphn.b alp.|šd.rbt.kmn.hlk.kṯr.|k y‘n.w y‘n.tdrq.ḫss.|hlk.qšt.ybln.hl.yš|rb‘.qṣ‘t.apnk.d 17[2AQHT].5.10
d.‘l.ššy.|kd.‘l.nḏbn.bn.agmn.|[k]d.‘l.brq.|[kd]m.[‘l].kṯr.|[kd]m[.---].ḥ[--].|[-----].|[kd.]‘l[.---].|[kd.]‘[l.---].|[k]d.‘ 1082.1.10
.|tšlḥm.tššqy ilm.|tsad.tkbd.hmt.b‘l.|ḥkpt il.kl h.tb‘.kṯr.|l ahl h.hyn.tb‘.l mš|knt h.apnk.dnil.m[t].|rpi.aphn.ǵzr 17[2AQHT].5.31
š.|rpim.tḥtk.|špš.tḥtk.ilnym.|‘d k.ilm.hn.mtm.|‘d k.kṯr m.ḥbr k.|w ḫss.d‘t k.|b ym.arš.w tnn.|kṯr.w ḫss.yd.|yt 6.6[62.2].48
q.|mtrḫt.yšr h.|aṯt.trḫ.w tb‘t.|ṯar um.tkn l h.|mṯlṯt.kṯrm.tmt.|mrb‘t.zblnm.|mḫmšt.yitsp.|ršp.nṯdṯt.ǵlm.|ym. 14[KRT].1.16
zn.|drk.š.alp.w ṯlṯ.|ṣin.šlm[m.]šb‘ pamt.|l ilm.šb[‘.]l kṯr.|‘lm.t‘rbn.gṯrm.|bt.mlk.ṯql.ḫrṣ.|l špš.w yrḫ.l gṯr.|ṯql.ks 33[5].8
dm.ṯpṭ.|nhr.‘z.ym.l ymk.l tnǵṣn.pnt h.l ydlp.|tmn h.kṯr.ṣmdm.ynḥt.w yp‘r.šmt hm.|šm k.at.aymr.aymr.mr.ym. 2.4[68].18
k.tmḫṣ.ht.tṣmt.ṣrt k.|tqḥ.mlk.‘lm k.drkt.dt dr dr k.|kṯr ṣmdm.ynḥt.w yp‘r.šmt hm.šm k at.|ygrš.ygrš.grš ym gr 2.4[68].11
lb alp w š.|b‘l ṣpn alp.w.š.|ṯrṯy.alp.w.š.|yrḫ.š.ṣpn.š.|kṯr š ‘ṯtr.š.|[‘ṯt]rt.š.šgr w iṯm š.|[---.]š.ršp.idrp.š.|[---.il.t‘]ḏr UG5.9.2.8
‘lm.alp.w š[.---].|arṣ.w šmm.š.kṯr[t] š.yrḫ[.---].|ṣpn.š.kṯr.š.pdry.š.ǵrm.š[.---].|aṯrt.š.‘nt.š.špš.š.arṣy.š.‘ṯtrt.š.|ušḫry UG5.9.1.6
.l b‘lt.|bwrm š.iṯtqb.|w š.nbk m w.š.|gt mlk š.‘lm.|l kṯr.ṯn.‘lm.|tzǵ[.---.]nšm.pr. UG5.12.B.12
ilbt.|ušḫry.|ym.b‘l.|yrḫ.|kṯr.|ṯrmn.|pdry.|dqt.|trṯ.|ršp.|‘nt ḫbly.|špš pgr.|iltm ḫn UG5.14.A.5
l[--.]‘rb.šp|š.w ḥl[.ml]k.|bn.aup[š.--].bsbn hzpḫ ṯlṯt.|kṯr[.---.--]trt ḫmšt.bn gda[.-.]mḏ‘.|kl[--.---.]ṯmnt.[--.]w[.---]. APP.II[173].59

kṯrmlk

l.ṣ[--].š‘[rt].|l.‘dy.š[‘]r[t].|ṯlṯ.l.‘d.ab[ǵ]l.|l.ydln.š‘rt.|l.kṯrmlk.ḫpn.|l.‘bdil[m].ḫpn.|tmrtn.š‘rt.|lmd.n.rn.|[---].ḫpn 1117.9
.--]nr[.---].|‘zn.w ymd.šr.b d ansny.|nsk.ks[p.--]mrtn.kṯrmlk.|yḥmn.aḫm[l]k.‘bdrpu.adn.ṯ[--].|bdn.qln.mtn.ydln. 2011.32
-].|str[-.---].|bdlm.d[t.---].|‘dn.[---].|aḫqm bir[-.---].|kṯrmlk.ns[--.---].|bn.tbd.ilšt[m‘y.---].|mty.ilšt[m‘y.---].|bn. 90[314].2.5
t h.arb‘m.|[--.-]dn.‘šrm.|[--.-]dwn.ṯlṯm.w.šb‘.alpm.|[kṯ]rmlk.‘šrm.|[--]ny.‘šrt.trbyt.|[--.]‘bd.ṯlṯm.|[---].ṯlṯm.|[--. 2054.2.24

kṯrn

bnšm.dt.l.u[--]ṯṯb.|kṯ[r]n.|w.aṯt h.w.n‘r h.|bn.ḫby.w.[a]ṯt h.|ynḥm.ulmy.|[--] 2068.2

kṯrt

.sny.|bn.ablḥ.|[-----].|w [---].|bn.[---].|bn.yr[--].|bn.kṯr[t].|bn.šml.|bn.arnbt.|qdšm.|b[-.--]t.|[---.-]l[--].|[---.]pr 2163.2.5
m.rṯ.|dn.il.bt h.ymǵyn.|yštql.dnil.l hkl h.|‘rb.b bt h.kṯrt.bnt.|hll.snnt.apnk.dnil.|mt.rpi.ap.hn.ǵzr.mt.|hrnmy.a 17[2AQHT].2.26
mznm.nkl w ib.|d ašr.ar yrḫ.w y|rḫ yar k.|[ašr ilht kṯrt bn]|t hll.snnt.bnt h|ll b‘l gml.yrdt.|b ‘rgzm.b bz tdm. 24[77].40
rt.|w y[ššq].bnt.hll.snnt.|mk.b šb[‘.]ymm.tb‘.b bt h.|kṯrt.bnt.hll.snnt.|[-]d[-]t.n‘m y.‘rš.h[--]m.|ysmsmt.‘rš.ḫlln. 17[2AQHT].2.40
nh l yd h tzdn[.---]n.|l ad[n h.---].|dgn tt[--.---.-]l|‘.l kṯrt hl[l.sn]nt.|ylak yrḫ ny[r] šmm.‘m.|ḫr[ḫ]b mlk qẓ.tn n 24[77].15
šlḥm.kṯrt.w y|ššq.bnt.[hl]l.snnt.|hn.ym.w ṯn.yšlḥm.|kṯrt.w yš[š]q.bnt.hl[l].|snnt.ṯlṯ[.r]b‘ ym.yšl|ḥm kṯrt.w yššq. 17[2AQHT].2.33
.|mt.rpi.ap.hn.ǵzr.mt.|hrnmy.alp.yṭbḫ.l kṯ|rt.yšlḥm.kṯrt.w y|ššq.bnt.[hl]l.snnt.|hn.ym.w ṯn.yšlḥm.|kṯrt.w yš[š] 17[2AQHT].2.30
ḥm.|kṯrt.w yš[š]q.bnt.hl[l].|snnt.ṯlṯ[.r]b‘ ym.yšl|ḥm kṯrt.w yššq.|bnt hll.snnt.ḫmš.|ṯdṯ.ym.yšlḥm.k[ṯ]rt.|w y[šš 17[2AQHT].2.35
yšl|ḥm kṯrt.w yššq.|bnt hll.snnt.ḫmš.|ṯdṯ.ym.yšlḥm.k[ṯ]rt.|w y[ššq].bnt.hll.snnt.|mk.b šb[‘.]ymm.tb‘.b bt h.|kṯ 17[2AQHT].2.37
ǵzt.b sǵ[--.]špš.|yrḫ yṯkḥ yḥ[bq] [-].|tld bt.[--]t.ḫ[--.l k]|ṯrt.l bnt.hll[.snnt].|hl ǵlmt tld b[n.--]n.|‘n ha l yd h.tzd[24[77].5
nt.apnk.dnil.|mt.rpi.ap.hn.ǵzr.mt.|hrnmy.alp.yṭbḫ.l kṯ|rt.yšlḥm.kṯrt.w y|ššq.bnt.[hl]l.snnt.|hn.ym.w ṯn.yšlḥm. 17[2AQHT].2.29
ṯ.nbt.ḏnt.w [-]n[-.---].|il.ḫyr.ilib.š.|arṣ w šmm.š.|il.š.kṯrt.š.|dgn.š.b‘l.ḫlb alp w š.|b‘l ṣpn alp.w.š.|ṯrṯy.alp.w.š.|y UG5.9.2.3
-].|b‘lm.alp.w š[.---].|b‘lm.alp.w š[.---].|arṣ.w šmm.š.kṯr[t] š.yrḫ[.---].|ṣpn.š.kṯr.š.pdry.š.ǵrm.š[.---].|aṯrt.š.‘nt.š.š UG5.9.1.5
pt l bšr h.dm a[--.--]ḥ.|w yn.k mtrḫt[.---]h.|šm‘ ilht kṯr[t.--]mm.|nh l yd h tzdn[.---]n.|l ad[n h.---].|dgn tt[--.--- 24[77].11
.yabd.l alp.|[---.bt]lt.‘nt.|[---]q.hry.w yld.|[---]m.ḥbl.kṯ[r]t.|[---.bt]lt.‘nt.|[---.ali]yn.b‘l.|[---.]m‘n.|[-----].|[-----].| 11[132].1.6
w mlg h y|ṯtqt ‘m h b q‘t.|tq‘t ‘m prbḫṯ.|dmqt ṣǵrt kṯrt. 24[77].50

kṯtǵl

mit.ṯlṯ.mḫsrn.|‘l.nsk.kṯtǵlm.|arb‘m.ṯlṯ.mḫsrn.|mtb‘l.rišy.|ṯlṯm.ṯlṯ.‘l.nsk.|arym. 1137.2

kṯtǵlm

]ty.|[---.-]i[-.--].|[-----].|[---.--]y.|[---.--]lm.|ḫdmdr.b.kṯ[t]ǵlm.|mḏl.b.kṯtǵlm. 2118.23
[-----].|[---.--]y.|[---.--]lm.|ḫdmdr.b.kṯ[t]ǵlm.|mḏl.b.kṯtǵlm. 2118.24

l

l

.|d[-]n.tbkn.w tdm.l y.[--].|[---].al.trgm.l aẖt k.|[---.]l [ ]dm.aẖt k.|yd‘t.k rḥmt.|al.tšt.b šdm.mm h.|b smkt.ṣat. 16.1[125].32
bḥm.w l.ṯ‘.dbḥ n.ndb]ḥ.|[hw.ṯ‘.nṯ‘y.hw.nkt.nkt.]yt[ši.l ab.bn.il].|[ytši.l dr.bn.il.l mpẖ]rt.[bn.il.l ṯkmn.w šn]m hn 32[2].1.9A
[---.hw.ṯ‘.nṯ‘]y.|[hw.nkt.nkt.ytši.l ab.bn.il.ytši.l d]r.bn[.il].|[l mpẖrt.bn.il.l ṯkmn.w šnm.hn š 32[2].1.2
ḥm.w l ṯ‘.d[bḥ n.ndbḥ].|hw.ṯ‘.nṯ‘y.hw.nkt.n[k]t.ytši[.l ab.bn.il].|ytši.l dr.bn.il.l mpẖrt.bn.i[l.l ṯkmn.w š]nm hn š. 32[2].1.16
]ḥm.w l.ṯ‘.dbḥ n.ndbḥ.hw.ṯ‘ |nṯ‘y.|hw.nkt.nkt.y[t]ši.l ab.bn.il.ytši.l dr.|bn il.l mpẖrt.bn.il.l ṯkmn[.w]šnm.hn.‘r. 32[2].1.25
bḥm.]w l ṯ‘ dbḥ n.|ndbḥ.hw.ṯ‘ n[ṯ‘y.hw.nkt.nk]t.ytši.l ab bn il.|ytši.l d[r.bn il.l]mpḥrt.bn il.|l ṯkm[n.w šnm.]hn 32[2].1.33
k qẓ.tn nkl y|rẖ ytrẖ.ib t‘rb m b bh|t h.w atn mhr h l a|b h.alp ksp w rbt ẖ|rṣ.išlḥ ẓhrm iq|nim.atn šd h krm[m 24[77].19
|ap.yṣb.yṯb.b hkl.|w ywsrnn.ggn h.|lk.l ab k.yṣb.lk.|l[ab]k.w rgm.‘ny.|l k[rt.adn k.]ištm[‘].|w tqǵ[.udn.k ǵz.ǵz 16.6[127].28
ẖt.l kẖṯ.drkt.|ap.yṣb.yṯb.b hkl.|w ywsrnn.ggn h.|lk.l ab k.yṣb.lk.|l[ab]k.w rgm.‘ny.|l k[rt.adn k.]ištm[‘].|w tq 16.6[127].27
.|[--.]ḥy[--.--.]l aššṣi.hm.ap.amr[--].|[---].w b ym.mnẖ l abd.b ym.irtm.m[--].|[ṯpṯ].nhr.tl‘m.ṯm.ḥrbm.its.anšq.|[-]h 2.4[68].3
‘n y.aṯt.itrẖ.|y bn.ašld.šu.‘db.tk.mdbr qdš.|ṯm tgrgr.l abnm.w l.‘ṣm.šb‘.šnt.|tmt.ṯmn.nqpt.‘d.ilm.n‘mm.ttlkn.|šd 23[52].66
t mṣb.mznm.um h.|kp mznm.iẖ h yṯ‘r.|mšrrm.aẖt h l a|bn mznm.nkl w ib.|d ašr.ar yrẖ.w y|rẖ yar k.|[ašr ilht 24[77].36
[-----].|l abn[.---].|aḥdt.plk h[.b yd h].|plk.qlt.b ymn h.|npyn h.m 4[51].2.2
ṯṯ.mat.ṯṯm.kbd šmn.|l.abrm.alṯyy.|[m]it.ṯlṯm.kbd.šmn.|[l.]abrm.mšrm.|[mi]tm. 2095.2
at.ṯṯm.kbd šmn.|l.abrm.alṯyy.|[m]it.ṯlṯm.kbd.šmn.|[l.]abrm.mšrm.|[mi]tm.arb‘m.ṯmn.kbd.|[l.]sbrdnm.|m[i]t.l. 2095.4
t[.---]h.|šm‘ ilht kṯr[t.--]mm.|nh l yd h tzdn[.---]n.|l ad[n h.---].|dgn tt[--.---.-]l|‘.l kṯrt hl[l.sn]nt.|ylak yrẖ ny[24[77].13
[---.]b[--].|[---].šḥr.[---].|[---].al ytb‘[.--].|[---.]l adn.ḥwt[.--].|[--]h.w yššil[.--].|[---.]lp[--]. 1023.4
y.|w l h[-] y‘l m.|bn y.yšal.|ṯryl.w rgm.|ṯṯb.l aẖ k.|l adn k. 138.19
.|w h[t] aẖ y.|bn y.yšal.|ṯryl.w rgm[.-].|ṯṯb.l aẖ k.|l adn k. 138.19
.|mlkt[.---].|kd.yn.l.[---].|armwl w [--].|arb‘.yn.[--].|l adrm.b[--].|šqym. 1092.7
.---].|w tglṯ thmt.‘[--.---].|yṣi.ǵl h ṯḥm b[.---].|mrẖ h l adrt[.---].|ṯṯb ‘ṯtrt b ǵl[.---].|qrẓ tšt.l šmal[.---].|arbẖ.‘n h 2001.1.7
rdnm.|m[i]t.l.bn.‘ẓmt.rišy.|mit.l.tlmyn.bn.‘dy.|[---.]l.adddy.|[--.]l.kkln. 2095.9
[--]ḏyn.b‘d.[--]ḏyn.w l.|[--]k b‘lt bhtm[.--]tn k.|[--]y.l ihbt.yb[--].rgm y.|[---.]škb.w m[--.]mlakt.|[---.]‘l.w tš‘[d]n 1002.46
m.tššqy ilm.|tsad.tkbd.hmt.b‘l.|ḥkpt il.kl h.tb‘.kṯr.|l ahl h.hyn.tb‘.l mš|knt h.apnk.dnil.m[t].|rpi.aphn.ǵzr.m[t 17[2AQHT].5.32
b pẖr.qbṣ.dtn.|ṣǵrt hn.abkrn.|tbrk.ilm.tity.|tity.ilm.l ahl hm.|dr il.l mšknt hm.|w tqrb.w ld.bn.l h.|w tqrb.w ld 15[128].3.18
ḏdm.yd.mḫṣt.a[qh]t.ǵ|zr.tmḫṣ.alpm.ib.št[-.]št.|ḥršm l ahlm p[---.]km.|[-]bl lb h.km.bṯn.y[--.-]ah.|ṯnm.tšqy msk. 19[1AQHT].4.222
r[--].|pǵt.minš.šdm l m‘[rb].|nrt.ilm.špš.mǵy[t].|pǵt.l ahlm.rgm.l yṯ[pn.y]|bl.agrtn.bat.b ḏd k.[pǵt].|bat.b hlm 19[1AQHT].4.212
km ṯr.w tkms.hd.p[.-].|km.ibr.b tk.mšmš d[--].|ittpq.l awl.|išttk.lm.ttkn.|štk.mlk.dn.|štk.šibt.‘n.|štk.qr.bt.il.|w 12[75].2.57
[l a]n ḥmt.l p[.n]ṯk.abd.l p.akl ṯm.dl.|[---.q]l.bl.tbḥ[n.l]azd.‘r.qdm.|[---].‘ẓ q[dm.--.šp]š.|[---.šm]n.mšḥt.kṯpm.a[- UG5.8.21
‘ṯtrt.šd.|[---.-]rt.mḫṣ.bnš.mlk.yb‘l hm.|[---.--]t.w.ẖpn.l.azzlt.|[---.]l.‘ṯtrt.šd.|[---].yb‘lnn.|[---.--]n.b.ṯlṯ.šnt.l.nṣd.|[- 1106.54
---].|ẖmš[.---]t.ḥdrm.|w.[---.a]ḥd.d.sgrm.|w p[tḥ.---.]l.aḥd.adr.|[---.--]t.b[ḥd]r.mškb.|ṯl[l.---.-]ḥ.|b lṯk.bt.|[pt]ḥ 1151.5
nt.|b ‘d ‘lm...gn‘.|iršt.aršt.|l aẖ y.l r‘ y.dt.|w ytnnn.|l aẖ h.l r‘ h.|r‘ ‘lm.|ttn.w tn.|w l ttn.|w al ttn.|tn ks yn.|w 1019.1.10
k hwt.|[y]rš.‘m y.|mnm.iršt k.|d ẖsrt.w.ank.|aštn..l.iẖ y.|w.ap.ank.mnm.|[ẖ]s[r]t.w.uẖ y.|[y]‘msn.ṯmn.|w.[u] 2065.17
.|t‘zz k.alp ymm.|w rbt.šnt.|b ‘d ‘lm...gn‘.|iršt.aršt.|l aẖ y.l r‘ y.dt.|w ytnnn.|l aẖ h.l r‘ h.|r‘ ‘lm.|ttn.w tn.|w l 1019.1.8
l h.y‘l m.|w h[t] aẖ y.|bn y.yšal.|ṯryl.w rgm[.-].|ṯṯb.l aẖ k.|l adn k. 138.18
mlk.šm y.|w l h[-] y‘l m.|bn y.yšal.|ṯryl.w rgm.|ṯṯb.l aẖ k.|l adn k. 138.18
ln.l bn.ǵl.|w dṯn.nḥl h.l bn.pl.|šd.krwn.l aẖn.|šd.‘yy.l aẖn.|šd.brdn.l bn.bly.|šd gzl.l.bn.ṯbr[n].|šd.ẖzmyn.l a[--]. 2089.12
‘mlbi.|šd.ṯpḥln.l bn.ǵl.|w dṯn.nḥl h.l bn.pl.|šd.krwn.l aẖn.|šd.‘yy.l aẖn.|šd.brdn.l bn.bly.|šd gzl.l.bn.ṯbr[n].|šd. 2089.11
.kn‘m.l.bn.‘mnr.|šd.bn.krwn.l bn.‘myn.|šd.bn.prmn.l aẖny.|šd.bn ḥnn.l bn.adlḏn.|šd.bn.nṣdn.l bn.‘mlbi.|šd.ṯp 2089.6
ṣat.npš h.|[-]mt[-].ṣba.rbt.|špš.w tgh.nyr.|rbt.w rgm.l aẖt k.|ṯtmnt.krt n.dbḥ.|dbḥ.mlk.‘šr.|‘šrt.qḥ.ṯp k.b yd.|[-] 16.1[125].38
nt.bt.ḥmḥ h.|d[-]n.tbkn.w tdm.l y.[--].|[---].al.trgm.l aẖt k.|[---.]l [ ]dm.aẖt k.|yd‘t.k rḥmt.|al.tšt.b šdm.mm h. 16.1[125].31
[--].w rbb.|š[---]npš išt.|w.l.tikl w l tš[t]. 2003.3
.tdry|nn.b išt.tšrpnn.|b rḥm.tṭḥnn.b šd.|tdr‘nn.šir h.l tikl.|‘ṣrm.mnt h.l tkly.|npr[m.]šir.l šir.yṣḥ. 6[49].2.35
n.|alp.šd.aḥd bt.|rbt.kmn.hkl.|w y‘n.kṯr.w ẖss.|šm‘.l aliyn b‘l.|bn.l rkb.‘rpt.|bl.ašt.urbt.b bh[t] m.|ḥln.b qrb.h 4[51].5.121
.w ẖs]s.|ṯṯb.b‘l.l[hwt y].|ṯn.rgm.k[ṯr.w]ẖss.|šm‘.m‘.l al[iy]n b‘l.|bl.ašt.ur[bt.]b bht m.|ḥln.b qr[b.hk]l m.|w ‘n. 4[51].6.4
h.|yqṯ b‘l.w yšt.ym.ykly.ṯpṭ.nhr.|b šm.tg‘r m.‘ṯtrt.bṯ l aliyn.[b‘l.]|bṯ.l rkb.‘rpt.k šby n.zb[l.ym.k] |šby n.ṯpṭ.nhr. 2.4[68].28
.brqm.|bt.arzm.yklln h.|hm.bt.lbnt.y‘msn h.|l yrgm.l aliyn b‘l.|ṣḥ.ẖrn.b bhm k.|‘dbt.b qrb.hkl k.|tbl k.ǵrm.mi 4[51].5.74
].kṯr.w ẖss.|ṣḥq.kṯr.w ẖss.|yšu.g h.w yṣḥ.|l rgmt.l k.l ali|yn.b‘l.ṯtbn.b‘l.|l hwt y.yptḥ.ḥ|ln.b bht m.urbt.|b qrb. 4[51].7.23
-.]b‘lt h w yn.|[---.rk]b ‘rpt.|[---.--]n.w mnu dg.|[---.]l aliyn b‘l.|[---].rkb ‘rpt. 2001.2.17
y.bly m.|alpm.aršt.l k.w.l y.|mn.bnš.d.l.i[--].‘[m k].|l.alpm.w.l.y[n.--]t.|w.bl.bnš.hw[-.--]y.|w.k.at.trg[m.--].|w.[2064.25
g[b.w yṣi.‘dn].|m‘[.ṣ]bu h.u[l.mad].|ṯlṯ.mat.rbt.|hlk.l alpm.ẖdd.|w l.rbt.kmyr.|aṯr.ṯn.ṯn.hlk.|aṯr.ṯlṯ.kl hm.|aḥd 14[KRT].4.180
k.ul.mad.|ṯlṯ.mat.rbt.|ẖpṯ.d bl.spr.|ṯnn.d bl.hg.|hlk.l alpm.ẖdd.|w l rbt.kmyr.|[a]ṯr.ṯn.ṯn.hlk.|aṯr.ṯlṯ.kl hm.|yḥ 14[KRT].2.92
l mpẖm.|b d.ẖss.mṣbṭm.|yṣq.ksp.yšl|ḥ.ẖrṣ.yṣq.ksp.|l alpm.ẖrṣ.yṣq|m.l rbbt.|yṣq-ḥym.w tbṯḥ.|kt.il.dt.rbtm.|kt 4[51].1.28
‘šrm ddm kbd[.-] l alpm mrim.|ṯṯ ddm l ṣin mrat.|‘šr ddm.l šm‘rgm.|‘šr dd 1100.1
.b š[---].|b‘l.yṯb.l ks[i.mlk h].|bn.dgn.l kḥ[ṯ.drkt h].|l alp.ql.ẓ[--.---].|l np ql.nd.[----].|tlk.w tr.b[ḥl].|b n‘mm.b 10[76].3.16
l ks[i.mlk h].|bn.dgn.l kḥ[ṯ.drkt h].|l alp.ql.ẓ[--.---].|l np ql.nd.[----].|tlk.w tr.b[ḥl].|b n‘mm.b ys[mm.---].|arẖ. 10[76].3.17
mnḥ.b d.ybnn.|arb‘.mat.|l.alp.šmn.|nḥ.ṯṯ.mat.|šm[n].rqḥ.|kkrm.brdl.|mit.tišrm.|ṯlṯ 141[120].3
yiẖd.b qrb[.-].|[--.t]ṯkḥ.w tiẖd.b uš[k.--].|[-.b]‘l.yabd.l alp.|[---.bt]lt.‘nt.|[---]q.hry.w yld.|[---]m.ḥbl.kṯ[r]t.|[---.b 11[132].1.3

.akl.b.gt.ǵ[l].|tlṯ.mat.‘šrm[.---].|ṯmnym.drt.a[--].|drt.l.alpm[.---].|šb‘m.ṯn.kbd[.ḥpr.‘b]dm.|tg[mr.---].|[-]m.m[--.- 2013.18
d l ištnm.|kd l ẖty.|maẖdh.|kd l kblbn.|kdm.mṯẖ.|l.alṯy.|kd.l mrynm.|šb‘ yn.|l mrynm.|b yṯbmlk.|kdm.ǵbiš 1090.8
-] šmḥ[.---].|ddm gt dprnm.|l ḥršm.|ddm l ‘nqt.|dd l alṯt.w l lmdt h.|dd l iẖyn.|dd l [---]. 1101.11
t k.|w abqṯ.aliyn.b‘l.|w t‘n.btlt.‘nt.|an.l an.y špš.|an.l an.il.yǵr[.-].|tǵr k.š[---.---].|yštd[.---].|dr[.---].|r[---.---]. 6[49].4.47
p.ḥ[mt.---.-]hm.yasp.ḥmt.|[---.š]pš.l [hrm.ǵrpl].‘l.arṣ.l an.|[ḥ]mt.i[l.w] ḥrn.yisp.ḥmt.|[b‘l.w]dgn[.yi]sp.ḥmt.‘nt. UG5.8.12
mt.šḥr.w šlm.|[yis]p.ḥmt.isp.[šp]š l hrm.ǵrpl.‘l arṣ.|[l a]n ḥmt.l p[.n]ṯk.abd.l p.akl ṯm.dl.|[---.q]l.bl.tbḥ[n.l]azd.‘ UG5.8.20
t]|bl lyt.‘l.umt k.|w abqṯ.aliyn.b‘l.|w t‘n.btlt.‘nt.|an.l an.y špš.|an.l an.il.yǵr[.-].|tǵr k.š[---.---].|yštd[.---].|dr[. 6[49].4.46
gn.|arb‘.b d.b[n].ušryn.|kdm.l.urtn.|kdm.l.ilšpš.|kd.l.annṯb.|kd.l.iwrmḏ.|kd.l.ydn.|[---.y]rẖ.ẖyr.|[---.]yn.l.mlkt 1088.7
p[----].|gm.l[aṯt h k.yṣḥ].|šm‘[.l mṯt.ḥry].|ṭbẖ.š[mn].mri k.|ptḥ.[rḥ]bt 15[128].4.2
g‘t.]alp.|ḥrṯ[.l z]ǵt.klb.|[ṣ]pr[.apn]k.|[pb]l[.mlk.g]m.l aṯt |[h.k]y[ṣḥ.]šm‘.m‘.|[--.]‘m[.-.]aṯt y[.-].|[---.]tḥm.|[---] 14[KRT].5.228
š|rb‘.qṣ‘t.apnk.dnil.|mt.rpi.aphn.ǵzr.mt.|hrnmy.gm.l aṯt h.k yṣḥ.|šm‘.mṯt.dnty.‘d[b].|imr.b pẖd.l npš.kṯr.|w ẖs 17[2AQHT].5.15
n[-.]l ks[p.-]m.|l.mri[.--].|ṯmn kbd[.--]i.|arb‘m[.--].|l apy.mr[i.--].|[---.--]d.|[-----]. 1133.5
[l a]q[h]t.|[t]krb.[---.]l qrb.mym.|tql.[---.]lb.tṯ[b]r.|qšt[.---]r. 19[1AQHT].1.1
b‘l.qšt l ‘nt.|qṣ‘t.l ybmt.limm.w t‘n.btlt.|‘nt.irš ḥym.l aqht.ǵzr.|irš ḥym.w atn k.bl mt.|w ašlḥ k.ašspr k.‘m.b‘l.| 17[2AQHT].6.26
n h.-.l]arṣ.ks h.tšpk m.|[l ‘pr.tšu.g h.]w tṣḥ.šm‘.m‘.|[l aqht.ǵzr.i]rš.ksp.w atn k.|[ẖrṣ.w aš]lḥ k.w tn.qšt k.[l].|[‘n 17[2AQHT].6.17
].|[rbt.]kmn.w ṣḥq.btlt.[‘nt].|[tšu.]g h.w tṣḥ.šm‘.m[‘.l a]|[qht.ǵ]zr.at.aẖ.w an.a[ẖt k].|[---].šb‘.ṯir k.[---].|[---.]ab 18[3AQHT].1.23
hkl h.‘rb.b|kyt.b hkl h.mšspdt.b ḥẓr h.|pẓǵm.ǵr.ybk.l aqht.|ǵzr.ydm‘.l kdd.dnil.|mt.rpi.l ymm.l yrẖm.|l yrẖm.l 19[1AQHT].4.173
l.|mt.rpi.l ymm.l yrẖm.|l yrẖm.l šnt.‘d.|šb‘t.šnt.ybk.l aq|ht.ǵzr.yd[m‘.]l kdd.|dnil.mt.r[pi.mk].b šb‘.|šnt.w y‘n[. 19[1AQHT].4.177
.ht.tṣdn.tinṯt.|[---]m.tṣḥq.‘nt.w b lb.tqny.|[---.]ṯb l y.l aqht.ǵzr.ṯb l y w l k.|[---]m.l aqry k.b ntb.pš‘.|[---].b ntb.g 17[2AQHT].6.42
ṯlṯ.d yṣa.|b d.šmmn.|l argmn.|l nskm.|ṯmn.kkrm.|alp.kbd.|[m]itm.kbd. 147[90].3
r‘ ṯd[h].|limm.w t‘l.‘m.il.|ab h.ḥpr.p‘l k.y[--].|šm‘ k.l arẖ.w bn.[--].|limm.ql.b udn.k w[-].|k rtqt mr[.---].|k d l 13[6].22
[k.ym]ẖṣ.b‘l m[.--]y.tnn.w ygl.w ynsk.‘[-].|[--]y.l arṣ[.id]y.alt.l aḥš.idy.alt.in l y.|[--]t.b‘l.ḥẓ.ršp.b[n].km.yr. 1001.1.2
dn.mṭr h.|b‘l.y‘dn.‘dn.ṯkt.b glṯ.|w tn.ql h.b ‘rpt.|šrh.l arṣ.brqm.|bt.arzm.yklln h.|hm.bt.lbnt.y‘msn h.|l yrgm.l 4[51].5.71
y.ṯr.il[.ab y.---].|yṯb.l y.w l h.[---].|[--.i]mṣẖ.nn.k imr.l arṣ.|[ašh!k].šbt h.dmm.šbt.dqn h.|[mm‘m.-]d.l ytn.bt.l b‘l 3[‘NT.VI].5.9
.hlm.qdq|d zbl ym.bn.‘nm.ṯpṭ.nhr.yprsḥ ym.|w yql.l arṣ.w trtqṣ.ṣmd.b d b‘l.|[km.]nšr.b uṣb‘t h.ylm.qdqd.zbl.| 2.4[68].23
h b bt.šrš.b qrb.|hkl h.nṣb.skn.ilib h.b qdš.|ztr.‘m h.l arṣ.mšṣu.qṭr h.|l ‘pr.ḏmr.aṯr h.ṭbq.lḥt.|niṣ h.grš d.‘šy.ln h 17[2AQHT].1.28
bt.šrš.]b qrb.hkl h.|[nṣb.skn.i]lib h.b qdš.|[ztr.‘m h.l a]rṣ.mšṣu.|[qṭr h.l ‘pr.ḏ]mr.a[ṯ]r h.|[ṭbq.lḥt.niṣ h.gr]š.d ‘š 17[2AQHT].1.46
.a[ṯ]r h.|[ṭbq.lḥt.niṣ h.gr]š.d ‘šy.|[ln h.---].|z[tr.‘m k.l arṣ.mšṣu.qṭr k].|l ‘pr.ḏm[r.aṯr k.ṭbq].|lḥt.niṣ k.gr[š.d ‘šy.l 17[2AQHT].2.1
nk.lṭpn.il.|d pid.yrd.l ksi.yṯb.|l hdm[.w] l.hdm.yṯb.|l arṣ.yṣq.‘mr.|un.l riš h.‘pr.plṯt.|l qdqd h.lpš.yks.|mizrtm. 5[67].6.14
|rbm.ymẖṣ.b ktp.|dk ym.ymẖṣ.b ṣmd.|ṣḥr mt.ymṣḥ.l arṣ.|[yṯb.]b[‘]l.l ksi.mlk h.|[---].l kḥṯ.drkt h.|l [ym]m.l yr 6[49].5.4
rq.|[---].tṣb.qšt.bnt.|[---.‘]n h.km.bṯn.yqr.|[krpn h.-.l]arṣ.ks h.tšpk m.|[l ‘pr.tšu.g h.]w tṣḥ.šm‘.m‘.|[l aqht.ǵzr.i 17[2AQHT].6.15
[y].|[arṣ.]dbr.ysmt.šd.|[šḥl]mmt.t[mǵ.]l b‘l.np[l].|[l a]rṣ[.lpš].tks.miz[rtm]. 5[67].6.31
y.|l n‘m y.arṣ.dbr.|l ysmt.šd.šḥlmmt.|mǵny.l b‘l.npl.l a|rṣ.mt.aliyn.b‘l.|ẖlq.zbl.b‘l.arṣ.|apnk.lṭpn.il.|d pid.yrd.l 5[67].6.8
.---].|‘n.tr.arṣ.w šmm.|sb.l qṣm.arṣ.|l ksm.mhyt.‘n.|l arṣ.m[ṭ]r.b‘l.|w l šd.mṭr.‘ly.|n‘m.l arṣ.mṭr.b‘l.|w l šd.mṭr. 16[126].3.5
ṣ.|l ksm.mhyt.‘n.|l arṣ.m[ṭ]r.b‘l.|w l šd.mṭr.‘ly.|n‘m.l arṣ.mṭr.b‘l.|w l šd.mṭr.‘ly.|n‘m.l ḥṭt.b gn.|bm.nrt.ksmm. 16[126].3.7
h.ylm.qdqd.zbl.|[ym.]bn.‘nm.ṯpṭ.nhr.yprsḥ.ym.yql.|l arṣ.tnǵṣn.pnt h.w ydlp.tmn h.|yqṯ b‘l.w yšt.ym.ykly.ṯpṭ.n 2.4[68].26
.irtm.m[--].|[ṯpṭ].nhr.tl‘m.ṯm.ḥrbm.its.anšq.|[-]htm.l arṣ.ypl.ul ny.w l.‘pr.‘ẓm ny.|l b‘l[-.---].|tḥt.ksi.zbl.ym.w ‘ 2.4[68].5
ylt.ilmy n‘mm.|agzr ym.bn ym.ynqm.b ap.ḏd.št.špt.|l arṣ.špt l šmm.w ‘rb.b p hm.‘ṣr.šmm.|w dg b ym.w ndd.gz 23[52].62
[-----].|[špt.l a]rṣ.špt.l šmm.|[---.l]šn.l kbkbm.y‘rb.|[b‘]l.b kbd h.b p h 5[67].2.2
t.mrḥ h.|l tl.yṣb.pn h.tǵr.|yṣu.hlm.aẖ h.tph.|[ksl]h.l arṣ.ṯṯbr.|[---.]aẖ h.tbky.|[--.m]rṣ.mlk.|[---.]krt.adn k.|[w 16.1[125].54
--.al]iyn b‘l.|[---].rkb.‘rpt.|[---.]ǵš.l limm.|[---.]l yṯb.l arṣ.|[---].mtm.|[---.--]d mhr.ur.|[---.]yḥnnn.|[---.--]t.ytn.| 10[76].1.9
rb.|[---].asr.|[---.--]m.ymt m.|[---].k iṯl.|[---.--]m.‘db.l arṣ.|[---.]špm.‘db.|[---].t‘tqn.|[---.-]‘b.idk.|[l ytn.pnm.tk.]i 1[‘NT.IX].2.10
---.btlt.]‘nt.|[---.ybmt.]limm.|[---.---]l.limm.|[---.yṯ]b.l arṣ.|[---.--]l.šir.|[---.-]tm.|[---.]yd y.|[----]y.|[---.-]lm.|[--- 10[76].1.17
[---.--]r.pn[.---].|[---.-]ḏi.u[--.---].|[---].l.ar[ṣ.---].|[---.--]g.irb[-.---].|[---.-]rd.pn.[---].|[---.--]r.ṯṯ d.[-- 2157.3
um.|[l tdd.aṯr]h.l tdd.i[lnym].|[---.]r[--.---].|[---.yṯ]b.l arṣ. 21[122].2.1
.mtn y at zd.|[---.]t‘rb.bši.|[---.]l tzd.l tptq.|[---].g[--.]l arṣ. 1[‘NT.X].5.28
[.---].|l.ršp[.---].|[l].ršp.[---.--]g.kbd.|[l.i]lt.qb[-.---].|[l.a]rṣy.|[l.--]r[-.---].|[l.--]ḥl.|[l.--.]mgmr.|[l.-.]qdšt.|l.‘ṯtrt.n 1001.1.11
h.|[---.-]rš.l b‘l.|[---.-]ǵk.rpu mlk.|[‘lm.---.--]k.l tšt k.l iršt.|[‘lm.---.--]k.l tšt k.liršt.|[---.]rpi.mlk ‘lm.b ‘z.|[rpu.m UG5.2.2.5
ṯmn ‘šr šurt l [---].|ṯmn šurt l ar[--.---].|ṯn šurtm l bnš [---].|arb‘ šurt l bn[š.---].|arb‘ šur 137.1[92].2
arb‘.yn.l.mrynm.ḥ[--].kl h.|kdm.l.zn[-.---].|kd.l.aṯr[y]m.|kdm.‘m.[--]n.|kd.mštt.[---]n.|kdm.l.mḏrǵlm.|kd 1089.3
l aẖn.|šd.brdn.l bn.bly.|šd gzl.l.bn.ṭbr[n].|šd.ẖzmyn.l a[--].|ṯn šdm b uš[kn]. 2089.15
.ṯṯm.kbd.|ṯṯm.ṯṯ.kbd.ḥpr.‘bdm.|šb‘m.drt.arb‘m.drt.|l.a[--.---].|tgm[r.ak]l.b.gt.ẖldy.|tlṯ.ma[t].‘šr.kbd.|šb‘ m[at]. 2013.9
tḥm.ydn.‘m.mlk.|b‘l h.nǵr.ḥwt k.|w l.a[--]t.tšknn.|ẖmšm.l mi[t].any.|tškn[n.--]h.k[--].|w šnm[. 2062.1.3
t h.|mn m.ib.yp‘.l b‘l.ṣrt.l rkb.‘rpt.|[-]‘n.ǵlmm.y‘nyn.l ib.yp‘.|l b‘l.ṣrt.l rkb.‘rpt.|tḥm.aliyn.b‘l.hwt.aliy.|qrdm.qr 3[‘NT].4.49
.b[n].ušryn.|kdm.l.urtn.|kdm.l.ilšpš.|kd.l.annṯb.|kd.l.iwrmḏ.|kd.i.ydn.|[---.y]rẖ.ẖyr.|[---.]yn.l.mlkt.|[---.yrẖ.]ḥ 1088.8
tḥm.iwrḏr.|l iwrpẖn.|bn y.aẖ y.rgm.|ilm.tǵr k.|tšlm k.|iky.lḥt.|spr.d l 138.2
tḥm iwrḏr.|l iwrpẖn.|bn y.aẖ y.rgm.|ilm.tǵr k.|tšlm k.|ik y.lḥt.|spr.d 138.2
dqn.|[---.--]‘.šdyn.l ytršn.|[---.--]ṯ.‘bd.l.kyn.|k[rm.--.]l.i[w]rtḏl.|ḥl.d[--.‘bd]yrẖ.b d.apn.|krm.i[--].l.[---.]a[-]bn. 2027.2.10
dprnm.|l ḥršm.|ddm l ‘nqt.|dd l alṯt.w l lmdt h.|dd l iẖyn.|dd l [---]. 1101.12
ẖpn.d.iqni.w.šmt.|l.iyb‘l.|ṯlṯm.l.mit.š‘rt.|l.šr.‘ṯtrt.|mlbš.ṯrmnm.|k.yṯn.w.b.bt. 1107.2
[-----].|šd.prsn.l.[---].|šd.bddn.l.iytlm.|šd.bn.nb‘m.l.ṯpṭb‘l.|šd.bn mšrn.l.ilšpš.|[šd.bn].kbr. 2030.1.3
].ṯp[--.---].|[---.a]ḥt.b d[.---].|[---.]b d.rb.[m]dlm.|[---.l i]ytlm.|[---].gmn.|[---].l.urǵṯṯb.|[---.]l.‘ṯtrum.|[---.]l.brqn. 2162.B.3
[--]n.bu[-]bd.ubln.|[---].l.ubl[n].|[--.]tbq.l.iytlm.|[---].l.iytlm.|[---.]‘bdilm.l.iytlm.|[---.n]ḥl h.lm.iytl 1076.3

---].l.ubl[n].|[--.]ṭbq.l.iytlm.|[---].l.iytlm.|[---.]‘bdilm.l.iytlm.|[---.n]ḥl h.lm.iytlm. 1076.5
[--]n.bu[-]bd.ubln.|[---].l.ubl[n].|[--.]ṭbq.l.iytlm.|[---].l.iytlm.|[---.]‘bdilm.l.iytlm.|[---.n]ḥl h.lm.iytlm. 1076.4
.l.iytlm.|[---].l.iytlm.|[---.]‘bdilm.l.iytlm.|[---.n]ḥl h.lm.iytlm. 1076.6
|l.[----].|l.‘ṯ[trt.---].|l.mš[--.---].|l.ilt[.---].|l.b‘lt[.---].|l.il.bt[.---].|l.ilt.[---].|l.ḥtk[.---].|l.ršp[.---].|[l].ršp.[---.--]g.k 1004.7
dqt.ṯ‘.ynt.ṯ‘m.dqt.ṯ‘m.|mtntm nkbd.alp.š.l il.|gdlt.ilhm.ṯkmn.w šnm dqt.|ršp.dqt.šrp w šlmm.dqtm. 34[1].2
‘[--.---].|[--.-]g[-.-]s w [---].|w yn[t.q]rt.y[---].|w al[p.l]il.w bu[rm.---].|ytk.gdlt.ilhm.[ṯkmn.w šnm].|dqt.ršp.šrp. 35[3].11
-].|t.k[-]ml.[---].|l[---].w y[nt.qrt.---].|[---.--]n[.w alp.l il.w bu]|[rm.---.ytk.gdlt.ilhm].|ṯkmn.w [šnm.dqt.ršp.šrp]. APP.II[173].12
nšq.w hr.b ḥbq.ḥmḥmt.tqt[nṣn].|tldn.šḥr.w šlm.rgm.l il.ybl.a[ṯt y].|il.ylt.mh.ylt.yld y.šḥr.w šl[m].|šu.‘db.l špš.r 23[52].52
d.[ilm.]n‘mm.agzr ym.|bn.ym.ynqm.b a[p.]ḏ[d.r]gm.l il.ybl.|aṯt y.il.ylt.mh.ylt.ilmy n‘mm.|agzr ym.bn ym.ynq 23[52].59
r[t.---].|w ‘ṣrm[.---].|ṣlyh šr[-.---].|[ṯ]lṯm.w b[--.---].|l il limm[.---].|w ṯt.npš[.---].|kbd.w [---].|l ṣp[n.---].|š.[---]. 40[134].8
b yrḫ.[rišyn.b ym.ḥdṯ].|šmtr.[uṯkl.l il.šlmm].|b ṯlṯt ‘[šrt.yrtḥṣ.mlk.brr].|b arb‘[t.‘šrt.riš.argmn 35[3].2
[b yr]ḫ[.r]išyn.b ym.ḥdṯ.|[šmtr].uṯkl.l il.šlmm.|b [ṯlṯt].‘šrt.yrtḥṣ.mlk.|br[r.]b a[r]b‘t.‘šrt.riš.|arg[APP.II[173].2
[-----].|[---.--]t.š l i[l.---].|[--.aṯ]rt.š[.---].|[---.]l pdr[-.---].|ṣin aḥd h[.---].|l ‘ṯt 37[22].2
-.k]mm.gdlt.l.b[‘l.---].|[dq]t.l.ṣpn.gdlt.l[.---].|u[gr]t.š.l.[il]ib.ǵ[--.--rt].|w [‘ṣrm.]l.ri[--.---].|[--]t.b‘lt.bt[.---].|[md]b 35[3].35
.[---].|kmm.gdlt.l b[‘l.--.dqt].|l ṣpn.gdlt.[l.---].|ugrt.š l ili[b.---].|rt.w ‘ṣrm.l[.---].|pamt.w bt.[---].|rmm.w ‘l[y.---]. APP.II[173].38
ṭ.|w tr l qlḥ.|w š ḥll ydm.|b qdš il bt.|w tlḥm aṯt.|š l ilbt.šlmm.|kll ylḥm b h.|w l bbt šqym.|š l uḫr ḫlmṭ.|w tr UG5.11.9
qmḥ.d.kly.b bt.skn.|l.illḏrm.|ltḥ.ḫṣr.b.šb‘.ddm. 2093.2
gm]n.al[i]yn.b[‘l].|[---]ḥ h.tšt bm.‘[--].|[---.]zr h.ybm.l ilm.|[id]k.l ttn.pnm.‘m.|[il.]mbk nhrm.qrb.|[a]pq.thmtm. 6.1.31[49.1.3]
rqdm.d š[-]l[-].|w t‘n.pǵt.ṯkmt.mym.|qrym.ab.dbḥ.l ilm.|š‘ly.dǵṯ h.b šmym.|dǵṯ.hrnmy.d kbkbm.|l tbrkn.alk 19[1AQHT].4.191
ḫr[-].ṯlṯt.mzn.|drk.š.alp.w ṯlṯ.|ṣin.šlm[m.]šb‘ pamt.|l ilm.šb[‘.]l kṯr.|‘lm.t‘rbn.gṯrm.|bt.mlk.ṯql.ḫrṣ.|l špš.w yrḫ. 33[5].8
h.[b]t.ršp.gn.|arb‘.b d.b[n].ušryn.|kdm.l.urtn.|kdm.l.ilšpš.|kd.l.annṯb.|kd.l.iwrmḏ.|kd.l.ydn.|[---.y]rḫ.ḫyr.|[-- 1088.6
--].|šd.bddn.l.iytlm.|šd.bn.nb‘m.l.ṯpṭb‘l.|šd.bn mšrn.l.ilšpš.|[šd.bn].kbr.l.snrn.|[---.--]k.l.gmrd.|[---.--]ṯ.l.yšn.|[š 2030.1.5
.w ṯn.aḫr.|šp[š]m.b [ṯ]lṯ.|ym[ǵy.]l qdš.|a[ṯrt.]ṣrm.w l ilt.|ṣd[yn]m.ṯm.|yd[r.k]rt.ṯ‘.|i.iṯt.aṯrt.ṣrm.|w ilt.ṣdynm.| 14[KRT].4.198
|l.ilt.[---].|l.ḥtk[.---].|l.ršp[.---].|[l].ršp.[---.--]g.kbd.|[l.i]lt.qb[-.---].|[l.a]rṣy.|[l.--]r[-.---].|[l.--]ḥl.|[l.--.]mgmr.|[l.- 1004.1.10
[---.]‘ṯ[trt.---].|[-.k]su.ilt[.---].|[ṯl]ṯ.l ‘ṯtrt[.---].|[--.]l ilt.š l ‘ṯt[rt.---].|[‘]ṣr.l pdr ṯṯ.ṣ[in.---].|tšnpn.‘lm.km[m.---]. 38[23].4
-.]mgmr.|[l.-.]qdšt.|l.‘ṯtrt.ndrgd.|l.‘ṯtrt.abḏr.|l.dml.|l.ilt[.-]pn.|l.uš[ḫr]y.|[---.-]mrn.|l ṯwl.|[--]ḏ[--]. 1001.1.13
l.[----].|l.[----].|l.‘ṯ[trt.---].|l.mš[--.---].|l.ilt[.---].|l.b‘lt[.---].|l.il.bt[.---].|l.ilt.[---].|l.ḥtk[.---].|l.ršp[.- 1004.5
[trt.---].|l.mš[--.---].|l.ilt[.---].|l.b‘lt[.---].|l.il.bt[.---].|l.ilt.[---].|l.ḥtk[.---].|l.ršp[.---].|[l].ršp.[---.--]g.kbd.|[l.i]lt.qb 1004.8
‘tqn.w[rḥm.‘nt].|tngṯ h.k lb.a[rḫ].|l ‘gl h.k lb.ṯa[t].|l imr h.km.lb.‘n[t].|aṯr.b‘l.ṯiḫd.m[t].|b sin.lpš.tšṣq[n h].|b 6[49].2.8
mm.|l yrḫm.rḥm.‘nt.tngṯ h.|k lb.arḫ.l ‘gl h.k lb.|ṯat.l imr h.km.lb.|‘nt.aṯr.b‘l.tiḫd.|bn.ilm.mt.b ḥrb.|tbq‘nn.b ḫ 6[49].2.29
|w ‘nt.ktp.b hm.yg‘r.ṯǵr.|bt.il.pn.l mgr lb.t‘dbn.|nšb.l inr.t‘dbn.ktp.|b il ab h.g‘r.yṯb.il.kb[-].|aṯ[rt.]il.yṯb.b mrzḥ UG5.1.1.13
]b a[r]b‘t.‘šrt.riš.|arg[mn.w ṯn.]šm.l b‘lt.|bhtm.‘ṣ[rm.l in]š ilm.w š.|dd ilš.š[.---.]mlk.yṯb br|r.w mḥ[--.---.]w q[--] APP.II[173].6
r].|b arb‘[t.‘šrt.riš.argmn].|w ṯn šm.l [b‘lt.bhtm.‘ṣrm.l inš].|ilm.w š d[d.ilš.š.--.mlk].|yṯb.brr[.w mḥ-.---].|ym.[‘]l 35[3].5
d]bḥt.b.ḫmš[.---].|[-.]kbd.w.db[ḥ.---].|[--].aṯrt.‘ṣr[m.l inš.ilm].|[ṯ]ṯb.mdbḥ.b‘l.g[dlt.---].|dqt.l.ṣpn.w.dqt[.---].|ṯn 35[3].40
m.w ‘l[y.---].|bt.il.ṯq[l.---.kbd].|w bdḥ.k[--.---].|‘ṣrm.l i[nš.ilm.ṯb.md]|bḥ.b‘l.[gdlt.---.dqt].|l ṣpn.w [dqt.---.ṯn.l ‘š APP.II[173].44
š.w l.---].|l yrḫ.gdlt.l [nkl.gdlt.l b‘]|[lt].bht[m].[‘]ṣrm l [inš.ilm].|[---.]ilh[m.dqt.š.--].|[---.--]t.r[šp.šrp.w šl]|[mm.- APP.II[173].29
.š.w l [---.l yrḫ].|gd[lt].l nkl[.gdlt.l b‘lt.bhtm].|‘š[rm.]l inš[.ilm.---].|il[hm.]dqt.š[.---.rš]|[p.š]rp.w šl[mm.--.dqt].|[35[3].27
]dlt.ṣpn.dqt.šrp.w [š]lmm.|[---.a]lp.l b‘l.w aṯrt.‘ṣr[m] l inš.|[ilm.---].lbbmm.gdlt.‘rb špš w ḥl.|[mlk.b ar]b‘t.‘[š]rt. 36[9].1.8
w]pamt ṯlṯm.w yrdt.[m]dbḥt.|gdlt.l b‘lt bhtm.‘ṣrm.|l inš ilm. 34[1].22
-].|[---.]kbd.ṯṯ.i[qnu.---].|[---.]ǵprt.‘š[r.---].|[---.p]ṯtm.l.ip[--.---].|[---.]ksl.ṯlṯ.m[at.---].|[---].abn.ṣr[p.---].|[---.-]rt.ṯl 1106.25
tldn mṯ.|al[iyn.b‘]l šlbšn.|i[---.---.--]l h.mǵẓ.|y[--.---.]l irt h.|n[--.---]. 5[67].5.25
nt.uṣb‘t[h.ybmt].|limm.tiḫd.knr h.b yd[h.tšt].|rimt.l irt h.tšr.dd.al[iyn].|b‘l.ahbt. UG5.3.2.7
k.l[---].|trḥṣ.yd[h.---].|[--.]yṣt ḏm[r.---].|tšt[.r]imt.[l irt h.tšr.l dd.aliyn.b‘l].|[ahb]t pdr[y.bt.ar.ahbt.ṭly.bt.rb.dd 7.2[130].10
[---.t]št.rimt.|l irt h.mšr.l.dd.aliyn.|b‘l.yd.pdry.bt.ar.|ahbt.ṭly.bt.rb.dd.ar 3[‘NT].3.2
aṯrt ym.|rbt.ilm.l ḥkmt.|šbt.dqn k.l tsr k.|rḫntt.d[-].l irt k.|wn ap.‘dn.mṭr h.|b‘l.y‘dn.‘dn.ṯkt.b glṯ.|w tn.ql h.b ‘ 4[51].5.67
ḥn y.mt mt.|nḥtm.ḫṭ k.mmnnm.mṭ yd k.hl.‘ṣr.|tḥrr.l išt.w ṣḥrt.l pḥmm.aṯtm.a[ṯt.il].|aṯt.il.w ‘lm h.yhbr.špt hm. 23[52].48
.tṣḥn y.ad ad.nḥtm.ḫṭ k.|mmnnm.mṭ yd k.hl.‘ṣr.tḥrr.l išt.|w ṣḥrrt.l pḥmm.btm.bt.il.bt.il.|w ‘lm h.w hn.aṯtm.tṣḥ 23[52].44
.bšr h.|tmt‘.md h.b ym.ṯn.|npyn h.b nhrm.|štt.ḫptr.l išt.|ḫbrṯ.l ẓr.pḥmm.|t‘pp.ṯr.il.d pid.|tǵẓy.bny.bnwt.|b nši 4[51].2.8
n.|y mt.mt.nḥtm.ḫṭ k.mmnnm.mṭ.yd k.|h[l.]‘ṣr.tḥrr.l išt.ṣḥrrt.l pḥmm.|a[ṯ]tm.aṯt.il.aṯt.il.w ‘lm h.w hm.|aṯtm.t 23[52].41
kd.bt ilm.|rbm.|kd l ištnm.|kd l ḫty.|maḫdh.|kd l kblbn.|kdm.mṯḫ.|l.alṯy.|k 1090.3
al ttn.|tn ks yn.|w ištn.|‘bd.prṯ.ṯḥm.|qrq.pṯ.ḏmn.|l iṯtl. 1019.2.3
šm.|k.rgmt.l y.bly m.|alpm.aršt.l k.w.l y.|mn.bnš.d.l.i[--].‘[m k].|l.alpm.w.l.y[n.--]t.|w.bl.bnš.hw[-.--]y.|w.k.at. 2064.24
[--]n.bu[-]bd.ubln.|[---].l.ubl[n].|[--.]ṭbq.l.iytlm.|[---].l.iytlm.|[---.]‘bdilm.l.iytlm.|[- 1076.2
rṣm.|ylk ym.w ṯn.|ṯlṯ.rb‘.ym.|aḫr.špšm.b rb‘.|ymǵy.l udm.rbt.|w udm[.ṯr]rt.|grnn.‘rm.|šrnn.pdrm.|s‘t.b šdm. 14[KRT].4.210
.w ṯn.ṯlṯ.rb‘ ym.|ḫmš.ṯdṯ.ym.mk.špšm.|b šb‘.w tmǵy.l udm.|rbm.w l.udm.ṯrrt.|w gr.nn.‘rm.šrn.|pdrm.s‘t.b šdm 14[KRT].3.108
.|ḫmš.ṯdṯ.ym.mk.špšm.|b šb‘.w tmǵy.l udm.|rbm.w l.udm.ṯrrt.|w gr.nn.‘rm.šrn.|pdrm.s‘t.b šdm.|ḥṭb h.b grnt. 14[KRT].3.109
rṭ.l.ql.d.ybl.prd.|b.ṯql.w.nṣp.ksp.|ṯmn.lbšm.w.mšlt.|l.udmym.b.ṯmnt.‘šrt.ksp.|šb‘m.lbš.d.‘rb.bt.mlk.|b.mit.ḫmš 2101.15
|ṯṯkr.[--]dn.|‘m.krt.mswn h.|arḫ.tzǵ.l ‘gl h.|bn.ḫpṯ.l umht hm.|k tnḥn.udmm.|w y‘ny.krt.ṯ‘. 15[128].1.6
l um y.adt ny.|rgm.|tḥm.tlmyn.|w.aḫtmlk ‘bd k.|l.p‘n.adt 51[95].1
l.mlkt.|um y.rgm.|tḥm.mlk.|bn k.|l.p‘n.um y.|qlt.l.um y.|yšlm.ilm.|tǵr k.tšlm k.|hl ny.‘m n[y].|kll.šlm.|ṯm 50[117].6
m] y.|[rg]m[.]t[ḥm].|mlk.bn [k].|[l].p‘n.um [y].|qlt[.l um] y.|yšlm.il[m].|tǵ[r] k.tš[lm] k.|[h]l ny.‘m n[.š]lm.|w. 1013.5
it.‘[šr.---].|[t]lṯ.abd[.---].|[---.]anyt[.---].|[-----].|‘šrm.l.umdym.|‘šr.l.ktl. 2110.5
.|birtym.|[un]ṯ inn.|l [h]m ‘d ṯṯbn.|ksp.iwrkl.|w ṯb.l unṯ hm. 1006.19

---].|[---.]b d.rb.[m]dlm.|[---.l i]ytlm.|[---].gmn.|[---].l.urǵṯtb.|[---.]l.ʿṯtrum.|[---.]l.brqn.|[---].skn.|[---.ʿg]ltn.|[--- 2162.B.5
ʿṯtrt.|[t]lṯ.ʿšr h.[b]t.ršp.gn.|arbʿ.b d.b[n].ušryn.|kdm.l.urtn.|kdm.l.ilšpš.|kd.l.annṯb.|kd.l.iwrmḏ.|kd.l.ydn.|[---. 1088.5
ḥm aṯt.|š l ilbt.šlmm.|kll ylḥm b h.|w l bbt šqym.|š l uḫr ḫlmṭ.|w tr l qlḥ.|ym aḥd. UG5.11.12
id ydbḥ mlk.|l ušḫ[r] ḫlmṭ.|l bbt il bt.|š l ḫlmṭ.|w tr l qlḥ.|w š ḥll ydm.| UG5.7.TR3
.|k.yṯn.w.b.bt.|mlk.mlbš.|yṯn.l hm.|šbʿ.lbšm.allm.|l ušḫry.|ṯlṯ.mat.pṯtm.|l.mgmr.b.ṯlṯ.|šnt. 1107.10
l.-.]qdšt.|l.ʿṯtrt.ndrgd.|l.ʿṯtrt.abdr.|l.dml.|l.ilt[.-]pn.|l.uš[ḫr]y.|[---.-]mrn.|l ṯwl.|[--]ḏ[--]. 1001.1.14
.pḥm.|mit.iqni.l mlkt.|ks.ḫrṣ.ktn.mit.pḥm.|mit.iqni.l uṯryn.|ks.ksp.ktn.mit.pḥm.|mit.iqni.l tpnr.|[ks.ksp.kt]n. 64[118].30
drt.|w[.---.]ʿm.l.mit.dd.ṯn.kbd.ḥpr.bnšm.ṯmnym.dd.|l u[-]m.|b.ṯbq.arbʿm.drʿ.w.ʿšr.dd.drt.|w[.a]rbʿ.l.ʿšrm.dd.l.y 1098.9
.bʿlsr.|yd.ṯdn.ʿšr.|[ḫ]mrm.|ddm.l.ybr[k].|bdmr.prs.l.u[-]m[-].|ṯmn.l.ʿšrm.|dmd.b d.mry[n]m. 2102.8
bnšm.dt.l.u[--]ṯtb.|kṯ[r]n.|w.aṯt h.w.nʿr h.|bn.ḫby.w.[a]ṯt h.|ynḥm. 2068.1
mḏrǵlm.|w.šbʿ.ʿšr.ḫsnm.|ḫmšm.l.mit.|bnš.l.d.|yškb.l.b.bt.mlk. 1029.16
.kbd.ḫsnm.|ubnyn.|ṯtm[.l.]mit.ṯlṯ.|kbd[.tg]mr.bnš.|l.b.bt.mlk. 1028.14
id ydbḥ mlk.|l ušḫ[r] ḫlmṭ.|l bbt il bt.|š l ḫlmṭ.|w tr l qlḥ.|w š ḥll ydm.|b qdš il bt.|w UG5.7.TR3
qdš il bt.|w tlḥm aṯt.|š l ilbt.šlmm.|kll ylḥm b h.|w l bbt šqym.|š l uḫr ḫlmṭ.|w tr l qlḥ.|ym aḥd. UG5.11.11
|bṯt.w dbḥ.w dbḥ.|dnt.w dbḥ.tdmm.|amht.k b h.bṯt.l tbṯ.|w b h.tdmmt.amht.|aḫr.mǵy.aliyn.bʿl.|mǵyt.btlt.ʿnt. 4[51].3.21
t.ʿmn.kbkbm.|abn.brq.d l.tdʿ.šmm.|rgm l tdʿ.nšm.w l tbn.|hmlt.arṣ.at m.w ank.|ibǵy h.b tk.ǵr y.il.ṣpn.|b qdš.b 3[ʿNT].3.24
nt.šmm.ʿm[.arṣ.thmt.ʿmn.kbkbm].|rgm.l tdʿ.nš[m.w l tbn.hmlt.arṣ].|at.w ank.ib[ǵy h.---].|w yʿn.kṯr.w ḫss[.lk.lk 1[ʿNT.IX].3.15
wt.|[w aṯny k.rgm.]ʿṣ.w lḫšt.|[abn.rgm.l td]ʿ.nš[m.w l t]bn.|[hmlt.a]rṣ.[tant.šmm.ʿm.ar]ṣ.|thmt.[ʿmn.kbkbm.abn 3[ʿNT].4.59
t k.nʿtq.|k inr[.ap.]ḫšt k.|ap.ab.k mtm.tmtn.|u ḫšt k.l bky.ʿtq.|b d.aṯt ab.ṣrry.|u ilm.tmtn.špḥ.|[l]ṭpn.l yḥ.t[b]ky 16.2[125].103
ʿnt.hlkt.w.šnwt.|tp.aḫ.h.k.ysmsm.|tspi.šir.h.l.bl.ḥrb.|tšt.dm.h.l.bl.ks.|tpnn.ʿn.bṯy.ʿn.bṯt.tpnn.|ʿn.mḫr.ʿn RS225.3
.šnwt.|tp.aḫ.h.k.ysmsm.|tspi.šir.h.l.bl.ḥrb.|tšt.dm.h.l.bl.ks.|tpnn.ʿn.bṯy.ʿn.bṯt.tpnn.|ʿn.mḫr.ʿn.pḫr.ʿn.ṯǵr.|ʿn.ṯǵr. RS225.4
ṯǵr[.---].|km.škllt.[---].|ʿr.ym.l bl[.---].|b[---.]ny[.--].|l bl.sk.w [---] h.|ybm h.šbʿ[.---].|ǵzr.ilḥu.t[---]l.|trm.ṯṣr.trm 16.2[125].93
r.trm.tnq[--].|km.nkyt.ṯǵr[.---].|km.škllt.[---].|ʿr.ym.l bl[.---].|b[---.]ny[.--].|l bl.sk.w [---] h.|ybm h.šbʿ[.---].|ǵzr 16.2[125].91
[---.]yplṭ.|[---].l.[-]npk.|[---.]l.bn.ydln.|[---].l.blkn.|[---].l.bn.k[--].|[---].l.klṯtb. 2136.4
.ri[š].|ʿl h.k irbym.kp.k.qṣm.|ǵrmn.kp.mhr.ʿtkt.|rišt.l bmt h.šnst.|kpt.b ḥbš h.brkm.tǵl[l].|b dm.ḏmr.ḥlqm.b m 3[ʿNT].2.12
[---.šnst.kpt.b ḥb]š h.ʿtkt r[išt].|[l bmt h.---.]hy bt h tʿrb.|[---.tm]tḫṣ b ʿmq.|[tḫtṣb.bn.qrtm. 7.1[131].3
.nqbnm.|ʿdb.gpn.atnt h.|yḥbq.qdš.w amrr.|yštn.aṯrt.l bmt.ʿr.|l ysmsmt.bmt.pḥl.|qdš.yuḫdm.šbʿr.|amrr.k kbkb. 4[51].4.14
.|bkm.tmdln.ʿr.|bkm.tṣmd.pḥl.bkm.|tšu.ab h.tštnn.l[b]mt ʿr.|l ysmsm.bmt.pḥl.|y dnil.ysb.palt h.|bṣql.yph.b 19[1AQHT].2.59
d.bn.krwn.l bn.ʿmyn.|šd.bn.prmn.l aḫny.|šd.bn ḥnn.l bn.adlḏn.|šd.bn.nṣdn.l bn.ʿmlbi.|šd.ṯpḫln.l bn.ǵl.|w dṯn.n 2089.7
.|[---.--]mm.hlkt.|[---.]b qrb.ʿr.|[---.m]lakm l h.|[---.]l.bn.il.|[---.--]a.ʿd h.|[---.--]rh.|[---.--]y.špš.|[---.--]h.|[---.--] 26[135].7
mk.ksu.|ṯbt h.ḫḫ.arṣ.|nhlt h.w nǵr.|ʿnn.ilm.al.|tqrb.l bn.ilm.|mt.al.yʿdb km.|k imr.b p h.|k lli.b ṯbrn.|qn h.tḥt 4[51].8.16
mṣḫn.|k lsmm.mt.ql.|bʿl.ql.ʿln.špš.|tṣḥ.l mt.šmʿ.mʿ.|l bn.ilm.mt.ik.tmt[ḫ]|ṣ.ʿm.aliyn.bʿl.|ik.al.yšm[ʿ] k.ṯr.|il.ab 6[49].6.24
t.|ṯny.l ydd.il ǵzr.|ṯḥm.aliyn.bʿl.hwt.aliy.|qrdm.bht.l bn.ilm mt.|ʿbd k.an.w d.ʿlm k.|tbʿ.w l.yṯb.ilm.idk.|l ytn.p 5[67].2.11
ʿl.l bht h.|u mlk.u bl mlk.|arṣ.drkt.yštkn.|dll.al.ilak.l bn.|ilm.mt.ʿdd.l ydd.|il.ǵzr.yqra.mt.|b npš h.ystrn ydd.| 4[51].7.45
|mn.l pʿn.mt.|hbr.w ql.|tštḥwy.w k|bd hwt.w rgm.|l bn.ilm.mt.|ṯny.l ydd.|il.ǵzr.ṯḥm.|aliyn.bʿl.|[hw]t.aliy.q|[4[51].8.30
rṣ.w pr.|ʿṣm.yraun.aliyn.bʿl.|ṯtʿ.nn.rkb.ʿrpt.|tbʿ.rgm.l bn.ilm.mt.|ṯny.l ydd.il ǵzr.|ṯḥm.aliyn.bʿl.hwt.aliy.|qrdm. 5[67].2.8
n.nḥl h.l bn.pl.|šd.krwn.l aḫn.|šd.ʿyy.l aḫn.|šd.brdn.l bn.bly.|šd gzl.l.bn.ṯbr[n].|šd.ḫzmyn.l a[--].|ṯn šdm b uš[k 2089.13
nš.|[ml]k.d.b riš.|[--.-]nt.|[l.ʿb]dmlk.|[--.-]m[-]r.|[w.l.]bn h.ʿd.|[ʿl]m.mn k.|mn km l.yqḥ.|bt.hnd.b d.|[ʿb]dmlk. 1009.11
.|[k]rm h.yd.|[k]lkl h.|[w] ytn.nn.|l.bʿln.bn.|kltn.w l.|bn h.ʿd.ʿlm.|šḫr.ʿlmt.|bnš bnšm.|l.yqḥnn.b d.|bʿln.bn.kl 1008.13
--]sp.mr[y-.---].|[--]l.ṯtm sp[m.---].|[p]drn.ḫm[š.---].|l bn ḫdnr[.---].|ṯtm sp.km[-.---].|ʿšrm.sp[.---].|ʿšr sp.m[ry-.- 139[310].5
dpdr.|šd.iyry.l.ʿbdbʿl.|šd.šmmn.l.bn.šty.|šd.bn.arws.l.bn.ḫlan.|šd.bn.ibryn.l.bn.ʿmnr. 1102.19
šd.bn.šty.l.bn.ṯbrn.|šd.bn.ḫtb.l bn.yʿḏrd.|šd.gl.bʿlz.l.bn.ʿmnr.|šd.knʿ 2089.1
šd.krwn.l aḫn.|šd.ʿyy.l aḫn.|šd.brdn.l bn.bly.|šd gzl.l.bn.ṯbr[n].|šd.ḫzmyn.l a[--].|ṯn šdm b uš[kn]. 2089.14
[---.]yplṭ.|[---].l.[-]npk.|[---.]l.bn.ydln.|[---].l.blkn.|[---].l.bn.k[--].|[---].l.klṯtb. 2136.3
šd.bn.šty.l.bn.ṯbrn.|šd.bn.ḫtb.l bn.yʿḏrd.|šd.gl.bʿlz.l.bn.ʿmnr.|šd.knʿm.l.bn.ʿmnr.|šd.bn.k 2089.2
.b.šd.|mit.ḫmšt.kbd.|[l.]gmn.bn.usyy.|mit.ṯtm.kbd.|l.bn.yšmʿ.|mit.arbʿm.kbd.|l.liy.bn.ʿmyn.|mit.ḫmšm.kbd.|d 1143.10
.]yplṭ.|[---].l.[-]npk.|[---.]l.bn.ydln.|[---].l.blkn.|[---].l.bn.k[--].|[---].l.klṯtb. 2136.5
]np bl.hn.|[---].ḥ[m]t.pṯr.w.p nḥš.|[---.--]q.n[t]k.l ydʿ.l bn.l pq ḥmt.|[---.--]n h.ḥmt.w tʿbtn h.abd y.|[---.ǵ]r.šrǵzz. UG5.8.35
rm.mšrm.|[mi]tm.arbʿm.ṯmn.kbd.|[l.]sbrdnm.|m[i]t.l.bn.ʿẓmt.rišy.|mit.l.tlmyn.bn.ʿdy.|[---.]l.adddy.|[--.]l.kkln. 2095.7
šd.gl.bʿlz.l.bn.ʿmnr.|šd.knʿm.l.bn.ʿmnr.|šd.bn.krwn.l bn.ʿmyn.|šd.bn.prmn.l aḫny.|šd.bn ḥnn.l bn.adlḏn.|šd.bn 2089.5
d.bn.prmn.l aḫny.|šd.bn ḥnn.l bn.adlḏn.|šd.bn.nṣdn.l bn.ʿmlbi.|šd.ṯpḫln.l bn.ǵl.|w dṯn.nḥl h.l bn.pl.|šd.krwn.l 2089.8
.|šd.bn.ḫtb.l bn.yʿḏrd.|šd.gl.bʿlz.l.bn.ʿmnr.|šd.knʿm.l.bn.ʿmnr.|šd.bn.krwn.l bn.ʿmyn.|šd.bn.prmn.l aḫny.|šd.b 2089.4
šd.bn.šty.l.bn.ṯbrn.|šd.bn.ḫtb.l bn.yʿḏrd.|šd.gl.bʿlz.l.bn.ʿmnr.|šd.knʿm.l.bn.ʿmnr.|šd.bn.krwn.l bn.ʿmyn.|šd.bn 2089.3
šd.šmmn.l.bn.šty.|šd.bn.arws.l.bn.ḫlan.|šd.bn.ibryn.l.bn.ʿmnr. 1102.20
d.bn ḥnn.l bn.adlḏn.|šd.bn.nṣdn.l bn.ʿmlbi.|šd.ṯpḫln.l bn.ǵl.|w dṯn.nḥl h.l bn.pl.|šd.krwn.l aḫn.|šd.ʿyy.l aḫn.|š 2089.9
|šd.bn.nṣdn.l bn.ʿmlbi.|šd.ṯpḫln.l bn.ǵl.|w dṯn.nḥl h.l bn.pl.|šd.krwn.l aḫn.|šd.ʿyy.l aḫn.|šd.brdn.l bn.bly.|šd g 2089.10
.ands.|bn.ann.|bn.ʿbdpdr.|šd.iyry.l.ʿbdbʿl.|šd.šmmn.l.bn.šty.|šd.bn.arws.l.bn.ḫlan.|šd.bn.ibryn.l.bn.ʿmnr. 1102.18
ṯm[--] yn[.--].|[---].krm.b ypʿl.yʿdd.|[---.]krm.b [-]dn.l.bn.[-]kn.|šd[.---.-]ʿn.|šd[.---.-]šm.l.dqn.|š[d.---.--]d.pdy.|[- 2027.1.5
-.---].|apnm.l.ʿ[--].|apnm.l.[---].|apnm.l.d[--].|apnm.l.bn[.---].|apnm.l.[b]n[.---].|apnm.l.bn[.---].|ṯlṯ.ṣmdm[.---]. 145[318].6
-].|apnm.l.[---].|apnm.l.d[--].|apnm.l.bn[.---].|apnm.l.[b]n[.---].|apnm.l.bn[.---].|ṯlṯ.ṣmdm[.---].|mṣ[r]n[.---]. 145[318].7
pnm.l.d[--].|apnm.l.bn[.---].|apnm.l.[b]n[.---].|apnm.l.bn[.---].|ṯlṯ.ṣmdm[.---].|mṣ[r]n[.---]. 145[318].8
bn[.---].|[-]l[-.---].|[-]ṭ.[---].|mṣb[-.---].|kṯ.aqh[r.---].|l bn[.---].|[t]lṯ.[---].|[---.--]yn.š.aḫ[--].|[---.]š.nṣ[.-]al[-].|[---. 143[-].2.5
š[šm]n.k[--.---].|[---.ar]bʿ.dblt.ḏr[--.---].|[--.m]itm.nṣ.l bn[.---].|[-]l[-.---].|[-]ṭ.[---].|mṣb[-.---].|kṯ.aqh[r.---].|l bn[143[-].1.10

l

lḥm.|uzrm.yšqy.bn.qdš.|l tbrknn l ṯr.il ab y.|tmrnn.l bny.bnwt.|w ykn.bn h b bt.šrš.b qrb.|hkl h.nṣb.skn.ilib h. 17[2AQHT].1.25

.|ṯlṯm sp.l bnš tpnr.|arb‘.spm.l.lbnš prwsdy.|ṯṯ spm.l bnš klnmw.|l yarš ẖswn.|ẖmš ‘šr.sp.|l bnš tpnr d yaẖd l g 137.2[93].8

---.]klnmw.|[---.]w yky.|ṯlṯm sp.l bnš tpnr.|arb‘.spm.l.lbnš prwsdy.|ṯṯ spm.l bnš klnmw.|l yarš ẖswn.|ẖmš ‘šr.s 137.2[93].7

.---].|[-]r.l šlmt.šl[m.---.--]|r h.p šlmt.p šlm[.---].|bt.l bnš.trg[m.---].|l šlmt.l šlm.b[--.---]|b y.šnt.mlit.t[--.---].|y 59[100].5

wsdy.|ṯṯ spm.l bnš klnmw.|l yarš ẖswn.|ẖmš ‘šr.sp.|l bnš tpnr d yaẖd l g ynm.|ṯṯ spm l tgyn.|arb‘ spm l ll[-].|ṯ 137.2[93].11

.--]ln.|[---.]kqmṭn.|[---.]klnmw.|[---.]w yky.|ṯlṯm sp.l bnš tpnr.|arb‘.spm.l.lbnš prwsdy.|ṯṯ spm.l bnš klnmw.|l 137.2[93].6

l bn[š.---].|ṯlṯm šurt l b[nš.---].|arb‘ šurt [---].|ṯṯ šurt l bnš [---].|ẖmš kbd arb‘[.---].|ṯṯ šurt l tg[-.---].|arb‘ šurt [-- 137.1[92].11

ṯmn ‘šr šurt l [---].|ṯmn šurt l ar[--.---].|ṯn šurtm l bnš [---].|arb‘ šurt l bn[š.---].|arb‘ šurt l q[--.---].|ṯlṯ šurt l 137.1[92].3

-].|ṯmn šurt l ar[--.---].|ṯn šurtm l bnš [---].|arb‘ šurt l bn[š.---].|arb‘ šurt l q[--.---].|ṯlṯ šurt l bnš [---].|ṯṯ šurt.l b 137.1[92].4

[---].|ṯṯ šurt.l bnš[.---].|ṯn šurtm l bn[š.---].|ṯlṯm šurt l b[nš.---].|arb‘ šurt [---].|ṯṯ šurt l bnš [---].|ẖmš kbd arb‘[.- 137.1[92].9

[---].|arb‘ šurt l bn[š.---].|arb‘ šurt l q[--.---].|ṯlṯ šurt l bnš [---].|ṯṯ šurt.l bnš[.---].|ṯn šurtm l bn[š.---].|ṯlṯm šurt l 137.1[92].6

[--.---].|ṯlṯ šurt l bnš [---].|ṯṯ šurt.l bnš[.---].|ṯn šurtm l bn[š.---].|ṯlṯm šurt l b[nš.---].|arb‘ šurt [---].|ṯṯ šurt l bnš [137.1[92].8

n[š.---].|arb‘ šurt l q[--.---].|ṯlṯ šurt l bnš [---].|ṯṯ šurt.l bnš[.---].|ṯn šurtm l bn[š.---].|ṯlṯm šurt l b[nš.---].|arb‘ šur 137.1[92].7

b‘l.k tmz‘.|kst.dnil.mt.rpi.|all.ǵzr.m[t.]hr[nmy].|gm.l bt[h.dnil.k yṣḥ].|šm‘.pǵt.ṯkmt[.my].|ḥspt.l š‘r.ṭl.yd[‘t].|h 19[1AQHT].1.49

ǵ[--.]špš.|yrẖ yṯkḥ yḥ[bq] [-].|tld bt.[--]t.ẖ[--.l k]|ṯrt.l bnt.hll[.snnt].|hl ǵlmt tld b[n.--]n.|‘n ha l yd h.tzd[.--].|p 24[77].6

.--].|t‘ny.n[---.-]ṯq.|w š[--.---].|ḥdṯ[.---.]ḥ[--].|b bt.[-.]l bnt.q[-].|w št.b bt.ṯap[.--].|hy.yd h.w ym[ǵ].|mlak k.‘m d UG5.6.8

[t].|yrtḥṣ.mlk.b[rr].|b ym.mlat.|tqln.alpm.|yrẖ.‘šrt.l b‘[l].|dqtm.w ynt.qr[t].|w mtntm.š l rmš.|w kbd.w š.l šl UG5.13.5

š.[b‘]l knp.|[---.g]dlt.ṣpn.dqt.šrp.w [š]lmm.|[---.a]lp.l b‘l.w aṯrt.‘ṣr[m] l inš.|[ilm.---].lbbmm.gdlt.‘rb špš w ḥl.|[36[9].1.8

[ẖl].|b n‘mm.b ys[mm.---].|arẖ.arẖ.[---.tld].|ibr.tld[.l b‘l].|w rum.l[rkb.‘rpt].|tḥbq.[---].|tḥbq[.---].|w tksynn.bṯ 10[76].3.21

|l.p‘n.b‘l y[.mrḥqtm].|šb‘ d.w.šb‘[d.qlt].|ankn.rgmt.l.b‘l y.|l.špš.‘lm.l.‘ṯtrt.|l.‘nt.l.kl.il.alṯ[y].|nmry.mlk.‘lm.|ml 2008.1.6

t.|ql.l b‘l.ttnn.|bšrt.il.bš[r.b‘]l.|w bšr.ḥtk.dgn.|k.ibr.l b‘l[.yl]d.|w rum.l rkb.‘rpt.|yšmẖ.aliyn.b‘l. 10[76].3.36

t‘l.bkm.b arr.|bm.arr.w b ṣpn.|b n‘m.b ǵr.t[l]iyt.|ql.l b‘l.ttnn.|bšrt.il.bš[r.b‘]l.|w bšr.ḥtk.dgn.|k.ibr.l b‘l[.yl]d.| 10[76].3.33

rṣ.|[ašhlk].šbt h.dmm.šbt.dqn h.|[mm‘m.-]d.l ytn.bt.l b‘l.k ilm.|[w ḥẓ]r.k bn.aṯrt[.td‘ṣ.]p‘n.|[w tr.a]rṣ.id[k.l ttn. 3[‘NT.VI].5.11

[---.wn.in].|[bt].l [b‘l.km.ilm.w ḥẓr].|k bn.[aṯrt.mṯb.il.mẓll].|bn h.m[ṯb.rbt. 3[‘NT.VI].4.01

.d yknn h.yṣḥ.|aṯrt.w bn h.ilt.w ṣbrt.|ary h.wn.in.bt.l b‘l.|km.ilm.w ḥẓr.k bn.aṯrt.|mṯb il.mẓll.bn h.|mṯb rbt.aṯr 4[51].4.50

rt.|p.‘bd.ank.aẖd.ulṯ.|hm.amt.aṯrt.tlbn.|lbnt.ybn.bt.l b‘l.|km ilm.w ḥẓr.k bn.aṯrt.|w t‘n.rbt.aṯrt ym.|rbt.ilm.l ḥ 4[51].4.62

n h.yṣ]ḥ.aṯ|[rt.w bn h.]ilt.|[w ṣbrt.ary]h.|[wn.in.bt.l b‘l.]|[km.ilm.w ḥẓr].|[k bn.aṯ]r[t].|m[ṯ]b.il.mẓll.|bn h.mṯ 4[51].1.10

[i]k.mgn.rbt.aṯrt.|[ym].mǵẓ.qnyt.ilm.|w tn.bt.l b‘l.km.|[i]lm.w ḥẓr.k bn.|[a]ṯrt.gm.l ǵlm h.|b‘l.yṣḥ.‘n.gp 8[51FRAG].3

.d yknn h.yṣḥ.aṯrt.|w bn h.ilt.w ṣbrt.arẖ h.|wn.in.bt.l b‘l.km.ilm.|ḥẓr.k b[n.a]ṯrt.mṯb.il.|mṯll.b[n h.m]ṯb.rbt.aṯrt 3[‘NT.VI].5.46

m.tmǵ.l n‘m[y].|[arṣ.]dbr.ysmt.šd.|[šḥl]mmt.t[mǵ.]l b‘l.np[l].|[l a]rṣ[.lpš].tks.miz[rtm]. 5[67].6.30

t[.m]ǵny.|l n‘m y.arṣ.dbr.|l ysmt.šd.šḥlmmt.|mǵny.l b‘l.npl.l a|rṣ.mt.aliyn.b‘l.|ẖlq.zbl.b‘l.arṣ.|apnk.lṭpn.il.|d 5[67].6.8

b]r.mrḥ h.ti[ẖd.b yd h].|š[g]r h bm ymn.t[--.---].|[--.]l b‘l.‘bd[.---].|ṯr ab h il.tṯrm[.---].|tšlḥm yrẖ.ggn[.---].|k[.--- 2001.1.14

|tr.b lkt.w tr.b ẖl.|[b]n‘mm.b ysmm.ḥ[--]k.ǵrt.|[ql].l b‘l.‘nt.ttnn.|[---].b‘l m.d ip[---].|[il.]hd.d ‘nn.n[--].|[----.]al 10[76].2.31

nḥkt.ksp.w ẖrṣ ṯ‘ ṯn šm l btbt.|alp.w š šrp.alp šlmm.|l b‘l.‘ṣr l ṣpn.|npš.w.š.l ršp bbt.|[‘]ṣrm l h.ršp [-]m.|[---.]bq UG5.12.A.10

l b‘l.|ǵr.b ab.td[.ps]ltm[.b y‘r].|thdy.lḥm.w dqn[.ṯṯlṯ].|qn.ḏ 6[62].1.1

‘r‘r.|pamt ṯlṯm š l qrnt.|ṯlḥn.b‘lt.bhtm.|‘lm.‘lm.gdlt l b‘l.|ṣpn.ilbt[.---.]d[--].|l ṣpn[.---.-]lu.|ilib[.---.b]‘l.|ugrt[.--- UG5.13.32

rm.ǵṣ b šmal.|d alpm.w alp w š.|šrp.w šlmm kmm.|l b‘l.ṣpn b ‘r‘r.|pamt ṯlṯm š l qrnt.|ṯlḥn.b‘lt.bhtm.|‘lm.‘lm. UG5.13.29

t.yrtḥṣ.mlk.brr.|[b ym.ml]at.y[ql]n.al[p]m.yrẖ.‘šrt.|[l b‘l.ṣ]pn.[dq]tm.w y[nt] qrt.|[w mtmt]m.[š.l] rm[š.]kbd.w š 36[9].1.12

|[w mtmt]m.[š.l] rm[š.]kbd.w š.|[l šlm.kbd.al]p.w š.[l] b‘l.ṣpn.|[dqt.l.ṣpn.šrp].w š[l]mm.kmm.|[w bbt.b‘l.ugrt.]k 36[9].1.14

r[t].|w mtntm.š l rmš.|w kbd.w š.l šlm kbd.|alp.w š.l b‘l ṣpn.|dqt l ṣpn.šrp.w šlmm.|kmm.w bbt.b‘l.ugrt.|w kd UG5.13.9

š.dt.ẓr h.tšu.|g h.w tṣḥ.ik.mǵy.gpn.w ugr.|mn.ib.yp‘.l b‘l.ṣrt.|l rkb.‘rpt.l mẖšt.mdd.|il ym.l klt.nhr.il.rbm.|l ištb 3[‘NT].3.34

.ib.yp‘.l b‘l.ṣrt.l rkb.‘rpt.|[-]‘n.ǵlmm.y‘nyn.l ib.yp‘.|l b‘l.ṣrt.l rkb.‘rpt.|tḥm.aliyn.b‘l.hwt.aliy.|qrdm.qry.b arṣ.m 3[‘NT].4.50

n h.grš h.l ksi.mlk h.|l nẖt.l kḥṯ.drkt h.|mn m.ib.yp‘.l b‘l.ṣrt.l rkb.‘rpt.|[-]‘n.ǵlmm.y‘nyn.l ib.yp‘.|l b‘l.ṣrt.l rkb.‘r 3[‘NT].4.48

ṯkm]|n.w šnm.dqt[.---].|bqtm.b nbk.[---].|kmm.gdlt.l b[‘l.--.dqt].|l ṣpn.gdlt.[l.---].|ugrt.š l ili[b.---].|rt.w ‘ṣrm.l[. APP.II[173].36

.w [šnm.dqt.--].|[--]t.dqtm.[b nbk.---].|[--.k]mm.gdlt.l.b[‘l.---].|[dq]t.l.ṣpn.gdlt.l[.---].|u[gr]t.š.l.[il]ib.ǵ[--.--rt].|w 35[3].33

--].yšt.il h.|[---.]iṯm h.|[---.y]mǵy.|[---.]dr h.|[---.-]rš.l b‘l.|[---.-]ǵk.rpu mlk.|[‘lm.---.--]k.l tšt k.l iršt.|[‘lm.---.--] UG5.2.2.3

gt h[.--].|[---.]yd.|[k]rm h.yd.|[k]lkl h.|[w] ytn.nn.|l.b‘ln.bn.|kltn.w l.|bn h.‘d.‘lm.|šḥr.‘lmt.|bnš bnšm.|l.yqḥ 1008.12

yrẖ ẖyr.b ym ḥdṯ.|alp.w š.l b‘lt bhtm.|b arb‘t ‘šrt.b‘l.|‘rkm.|b ṯmnt.‘šrt.yr|tḥṣ.mlk.br UG5.12.A.2

rt.yrtḥṣ.mlk.|br[r.]b a[r]b‘t.‘šrt.riš.|arg[mn.w ṯn.]šm.l b‘lt.|bhtm.‘ṣ[rm.l in]š ilm.w š.|dd ilš.š[.---.]mlk.yṯb br|r. APP.II[173].5

t.‘ṣrm.l].|ṣpn š.l ǵlm[t.š.w l.---].|l yrẖ.gdlt.l [nkl.gdlt.l b‘]|[lt].bht[m].[‘]ṣrm l [inš.ilm].|[---.]ilh[m.dqt.š.--].|[---.- APP.II[173].28

‘[šrt.yrtḥṣ.mlk.brr].|b arb‘[t.‘šrt.riš.argmn].|w ṯn šm.l [b‘lt.bhtm.‘ṣrm.l inš].|ilm.w š d[d.ilš.š.--.mlk].|yṯb.brr[.w 35[3].5

r[m.l ṣpn.š].|l ǵlmt.š.w l [---.l yrẖ].|gd[lt].l nkl[.gdlt.l b‘lt.bhtm].|‘š[rm.]l inš[.ilm.---].|il[hm.]dqt.š[.---.rš]|[p.š]r 35[3].26

gdlt.w l ǵlmt š.|[w]pamt ṯlṯm.w yrdt.[m]dbḥt.|gdlt.l b‘lt bhtm.‘ṣrm.|l inš ilm. 34[1].21

.|šb‘.alpm.|bt b‘l.ugrt.ṯn šm.|‘lm.l ršp.mlk.|alp w.š.l b‘lt.|bwrm š.iṯtqb.|w š.nbk m w.š.|gt mlk š.‘lm.|l kṯr.ṯn.‘ UG5.12.B.8

l.[----].|l.[----].|l.‘ṯ[trt.---].|l.mš[--.---].|l.ilt[.---].|l.b‘lt[.---].|l.il.bt[.---].|l.ilt.[---].|l.ḥtk[.---].|l.ršp[.---].|[l].rš 1004.6

.ḥrbm.its.anšq.|[-]htm.l arṣ.ypl.ul ny.w l.‘pr.‘ẓm ny.|l b‘l[-.---].|tḥt.ksi.zbl.ym.w ‘n.kṯr.w ẖss.l rgmt.|l k.l zbl.b‘l. 2.4[68].6

k.|mǵy.|hbṭ.hw.|ẖrd.w.šl hw.|qr[-].|akl n.b.grnt.|l.b‘r.|ap.krmm.|ẖlq.|qrt n.ẖlq.|w.d‘.d‘. 2114.9

hlmn.ṯnm.qdqd.|ṯlṯ id.‘l.udn.špk.km.šiy.|dm.km.šẖṭ.l brk h.tṣi.km.|rḥ.npš h.km.iṯl.brlt h.km.|qṭr.b ap h.b ap.m 18[3AQHT].4.24

ṯnm[.qdqd].|ṯlṯ id.‘l.udn.š[pk.km].|šiy.dm h.km.šẖ[ṭ.l brk h].|yṣat.km.rḥ.npš[h.km.iṯl].|brlt h.km.qṭr.[b ap h.-- 18[3AQHT].4.35

n.d ḥrš.|ydm.aẖr.ymǵy.kṯr.|w ẖss.b d.dnil.ytnn.|qšt.l brk h.y‘db.|qṣ‘t.apnk.mṯt.dnty.|tšlḥm.tššqy ilm.|tsad.tkb 17[2AQHT].5.27

.dbḥ.l ilm.|š‘ly.dǵṯ h.b šmym.|dǵṯ.hrnmy.d kbkbm.|l tbrkn.alk brkt.|tmrn.alk.nmr[rt].|imẖṣ.mẖṣ.aẖ y.akl[.m]| 19[1AQHT].4.194

‘[d]t.ilm.|[w]y‘n.aliy[n.]b‘l.|[---.]tb‘.l lṭpn.|[il.d]pid.l tbrk.|[krt.]ṯ‘.l tmr.n‘mn.|[ǵlm.]il.ks.yiẖd.|[il.b]yd.krpn.b 15[128].2.14

w šrš.|km.ary h.uzrm.ilm.ylḥm.|uzrm.yšqy.bn.qdš.|l tbrknn l ṯr.il ab y.|tmrnn.l bny.bnwt.|w ykn.bn h b bt.šrš. 17[2AQHT].1.24

.kl h.tšm‘. | mṯt.dnty.t‘db.imr. | b pẖḏ.l npš.kṯr.w ẖss. | l brlt.hyn.d ḥrš. | ydm.aẖr.ymǵy.kṯr. | w ẖss.b d.dnil.ytnn. | q 17[2AQHT].5.24
yṣḥ. | šm‘.mṯt.dnty.‘d[b]. | imr.b pẖḏ.l npš.kṯr. | w ẖss.l brlt.hyn d. | ḥrš yd.šlḥm.ššqy. | ilm sad.kbd.hmt.b‘l. | ḥkpt.i 17[2AQHT].5.18
.l i]ytlm. | [---].gmn. | [---].l.urǵṯṯb. | [---.]l.‘ṯtrum. | [---.]l.brqn. | [---].skn. | [---.‘g]ltn. | [---].‘gltn. | [---.]‘gltn. | [---.šr]t.a 2162.B.7
arb‘.ḥm[r.---]. | l ṯlṯ. | ṯn.l.brr[.---]. | arb‘.ḥmr[.---]. | l.pḥ[-.]w.[---]. | w.l.k[--]. | w.l.k[--]. 1139.3
l[.snnt]. | hl ǵlmt tld b[n.--]n. | ‘n ha l yd h.tzd[.--]. | pt l bšr h.dm a[--.--]ḥ. | w yn.k mtrẖt[.---]h. | šm‘ ilht kṯr[t.--]m 24[77].9
ḥmṣ.w.[lt]ḥ.‘šdm. | kd yn.l.ẖḏǵb.w.kd.ḥmṣ. | prš.glbm.l.bt. | tgmǵ.kšmm.b.yrẖ.iṯtbnm. | šb‘m.dd.ṯn.kbd. | tgmr.ḥṭm. 1099.29
tḥm.rgm. | mlk. | l ḥyil. | lm.tlik.‘m y. | ik y.aškn. | ‘ṣm.l bt.dml. | p ank.atn. | ‘ṣm.l k. | arb‘.‘ṣm. | ‘l.ar. | w.ṯlṯ. | ‘l.ubr‘y. 1010.6
rn. | ‘n.b‘l.qdm.yd h. | k tǵḏ.arz.b ymn h. | bkm.yṯb.b‘l.l bht h. | u mlk.u bl mlk. | arṣ.drkt.yštkn. | dll.al.ilak.l bn. | il 4[51].7.42
h. | ssnm.ysyn h.‘dtm.y‘dyn h.yb | ltm.ybln h.mǵy.ḥrn.l bt h.w. | yštql.l ḥṭr h.tlu ḥt.km.nẖl. | tplg.km.plg. | b‘d h.bht UG5.7.67
]. | mhrm.mṭm.tgrš. | šbm.b ksl.qšt h.mdnt. | w hln.‘nt.l bt h.tmǵyn. | tštql.ilt.l hkl h. | w l.šb‘t.tmtẖṣ h.b ‘mq. | tẖtṣb 3[‘NT].2.17
[rt.]il.yṯb.b mrzḥ h. | yšt[.il.y]n.‘d šb‘.trṯ.‘d škr. | il.hlk.l bt h.yštql. | l ḥṭr h.y‘msn.nn.ṯkmn. | w šnm.w ngšnn.ḥby. | b UG5.1.1.17
.bn dgn. | [b m]ṣd h.yrd.krt. | [l g]gt.‘db.akl.l qryt. | ḥṭt.l bt.ẖbr. | yip.lḥm.d ẖmš. | [mǵ]d.ṯdṯ.yr[ẖm]. | ‘dn.ngb.w [yṣi. 14[KRT].4.173
bn.dgn. | b mṣd k.w yrd. | krt.l ggt.‘db. | akl.l qryt. | ḥṭt.l bt.ẖbr. | yip.lḥm.d ẖmš. | mǵd.ṯdṯ.yrẖm. | ‘dn.ngb.w yṣi. | ṣb 14[KRT].2.82
u[dm]. | [ṯ]rrt.udm.y[t]n[t]. | il.ušn.ab[.ad]m. | rḥq.mlk.l bt y. | n[g.]krt.l ḥẓ[r y]. | w y‘n[y.k]rt[.ṯ]‘. | lm.ank.ksp. | w y 14[KRT].6.279
udm]. | [ṯrrt.udm.ytnt]. | [il.w ušn.ab.adm]. | [rḥq.mlk.l bt y]. | [ng.kr]t.l ḥ[ẓ]r y. | [-----]. | [---.ttb‘]. | [mlakm.l yṯb]. | [14[KRT].5.260
rkbt. | b trbṣ.bn.amt. | qḥ.krt.šlmm. | šlmm.w ng.mlk. | l bt y.rḥq.krt. | l ḥẓr y.al.tṣr. | udm.rbt.w udm ṯrrt. | udm.ytn 14[KRT].3.132
m]rz‘y.apnnk.yrp. | [---.]km.r‘y.ht.alk. | [---.]ṯlṯt.amǵy.l bt. | [y.---.b qrb].hkl y.w y‘n.il. | [---.mrz‘]y.lk.bt y.rpim. | [r 21[122].1.7
[---.--]t.b[ḥd]r.mškb. | ṯl[l.---.--]ḥ. | b lṯk.bt. | [pt]ḥ.aḥd.l.bt.‘bdm. | [ṯ]n.ptḥ msb.bt.tu. | w.ptḥ[.aḥ]d.mmt. | ṯṯ.pt[ḥ.---] 1151.9
l ẖmš.mrkbt.ẖmš.‘šr h.prs. | bt.mrkbt.w l šant.ṯṯ. | l bt.‘šrm. | bt alẖnm.ṯlṯm ṯṯ kbd. 2105.3
rim. | ṯṯ ddm l ṣin mrat. | ‘šr ddm.l šm‘rgm. | ‘šr ddm.l bt. | ‘šrm.dd.l mẖṣm. | ddm l kbs. | dd l prgṯ. | dd.l mri. | dd.l 1100.4
[--].d.ntn[.d.]ksp. | [ṯ]mn.l.‘šrm[.l.b]t.‘ṯtrt. | [ṯ]lṯ.‘šr h.[b]t.ršp.gn. | arb‘.b d.b[n].ušryn. | kdm.l. 1088.2
rb‘.mat[.arb]‘m.[k]bd. | d ntn.d.ksp. | arb‘.l.ẖlby. | [---].l.bt. | arb‘.l.kpslnm. | kdm.b[t.]mlk. 1087.5
spr.ḥpr.bt.k[--]. | tš‘.‘šr h.dd.l.b[t.--]. | ẖmš.ddm.l.ẖtyt. | ṯlṯm.dd.kšmn.l.gzzm. | yyn. | ṣdqn 1099.2
ug[r.---]. | ‘nt[.---]. | tmm l bt[.---]. | b[‘]l.ugr[t.---]. | w ‘ṣrm[.---]. | ṣlyh šr[-.---]. | [ṯ]lṯm. 40[134].3
. | šmm.tṯrp. | ym.ḏnbtm. | tnn.l šbm. | tšt.trks. | l mrym.l bt[.---]. | p l.tb‘[.---]. | hmlt ẖt.[---]. | l.tp[-]m.[---]. | n[-]m[.---] 1003.10
ṣ.mlk.brr. | ‘lm.tzǵ.b ǵb.ṣpn. | nḥkt.ksp.w ẖrṣ ṯ‘ ṯn šm l btbt. | alp.w š šrp.alp šlmm. | l b‘l.‘ṣr l ṣpn. | npš.w.š.l ršp bb UG5.12.A.8
h.w[tṣ] | ḥ.at.mt.tn.aẖ y. | w ‘n.bn.ilm.mt.mh. | taršn.l btlt.‘nt. | an.itlk.w aṣd.kl. | ǵr.l kbd.arṣ.kl.gb‘. | l kbd.šdm.n 6[49].2.14
.ymn h.b anšt[.---]. | qdqd h.w y‘n.ytpn.[mhr.št]. | šm‘.l btlt.‘nt.at.‘[l.qšt h]. | tmẖṣ h.qṣ‘t h.hwt.l t[ḥwy]. | n‘mn.ǵzr. 18[3AQHT].4.12
[---.]arẖt.tld[n]. | a[lp].l btlt.‘nt. | w ypt l ybmt.li[mm]. | w y‘ny.aliyn[.b‘l]. | lm.k qn 10[76].3.3
grt.yd‘[t k.]bt.k an[št]. | k in.b ilht.ql[ṣ] k.mh.tarš[n]. | l btlt.‘nt.w t[‘]n.btlt.‘n[t]. | tḥm k.il.ḥkm.ḥkm k. | ‘m.‘lm.ḥyt. 3[‘NT.VI].5.37
ḥy.aliyn.b‘l. | k iṯ.zbl.b‘l.arṣ. | gm.yṣḥ.il.l btlt. | ‘nt.šm‘.l btlt.‘n[t]. | rgm.l nrt.il.šp[š]. | pl.‘nt.šdm.y špš. | pl.‘nt.šdm.il 6[49].3.23
.b irt y.npš. | k ḥy.aliyn.b‘l. | k iṯ.zbl.b‘l.arṣ. | gm.yṣḥ.il.l btlt. | ‘nt.šm‘.l btlt.‘n[t]. | rgm.l nrt.il.šp[š]. | pl.‘nt.šdm.y špš 6[49].3.22
dr[y.bt.ar.ahbt.ṭly.bt.rb.dd]. | arṣy bt.y[‘bdr.---]. | rgm l btl[t.‘nt.ṯny.l ybmt.limm.tḥm.aliyn.b‘l]. | hw[t.aliy.qrdm.q 7.2[130].13
. | w ‘rb n.l p‘n.‘nt.hbr. | w ql.tštḥwy.kbd hyt. | w rgm.l btlt.‘nt. | ṯny.l ymmt.limm. | tḥm.aliyn.b‘l.hwt. | aliy.qrdm.q 3[‘NT].3.8
ẖr.l.pẖr.tṯb. | ‘n.mẖr.l.mẖr.tṯb. | ‘n.bṯy.l.bṯy.tṯb. | ‘n.bṯt.l.bṯt.tṯb. RS225.11
r.l.ṯǵr.tṯb. | ‘n.pẖr.l.pẖr.tṯb. | ‘n.mẖr.l.mẖr.tṯb. | ‘n.bṯy.l.bṯy.tṯb. | ‘n.bṯt.l.bṯt.tṯb. RS225.10
šm[m]. | [---.i]l.ṯr.iṯ.p h.k ṯt.ǵlt[.--]. | [---.--] k yn.ddm.l b[--.---]. | [---.-]yt š[--.---]. | [---.]hl[-.---]. | [---.-]yṯr.ur[--.---]. | UG5.3.1.9
. | [---.]bt.tḥbṭ.km.ṣq.ṣdr[.---]. | [---.]kl.b kl.l pgm.pgm.l.b[---]. | [---.]mdbm.l ḥrn.ḥr[n.---]. | [---.--]m.ql.hm[.---]. | [--- 1001.1.26
ṯr. | [--]ḥ[d].šd.hwt. | [--.]iḥd.šd.gṯr. | [w]ht.yšm‘.uẖ y. | l g y.w yhbṭ.bnš. | w ytn.ilm.b d hm. | b d.iẖqm.gṯr. | w b d.yt 55[18].18
š klnmw. | l yarš ẖswn. | ẖmš ‘šr.sp. | l bnš tpnr d yaẖd l g ynm. | ṯṯ spm l tgyn. | arb‘ spm l ll[-]. | ṯn spm.l slyy. | ṯlṯ s 137.2[93].11
tḥm.hl[--]. | l pẖry.a[ẖ y]. | w l g.p[-]r[--]. | yšlm[.l k]. | [i]lm[.tǵr k]. | [t]š[lm k.---]. | [-----]. | [56[21].3
ab h.il.šrd. | [b‘l].b dbḥ h.bn dgn. | [b m]ṣd h.yrd.krt. | [l g]gt.‘db.akl.l qryt. | ḥṭt.l bt.ẖbr. | yip.lḥm.d ẖmš. | [mǵ]d.ṯdṯ 14[KRT].4.172
| ab k.il.šrd.b‘l. | b dbḥ k.bn.dgn. | b mṣd k.w yrd. | krt.l ggt.‘db. | akl.l qryt. | ḥṭt.l bt.ẖbr. | yip.lḥm.d ẖmš. | mǵd.ṯdṯ. 14[KRT].2.80
. | tš‘.‘šr h.dd.l.b[t.--]. | ẖmš.ddm.l.ẖtyt. | ṯlṯm.dd.kšmn.l.gzzm. | yyn. | ṣdqn. | ‘bd.pdr. | myṣm. | ṯgt. | w.lmd h. | yṯil. | w 1099.4
rm.l.ẖtn. | dd.š‘rm.l.ḥmr.ḥṭb. | dd.ḥṭm.l.ẖḏǵb. | ṯṯ.ddm.l.gzzm. | kd yn.l.ẖtn.w.kd.ḥmṣ.w.[lt]ḥ.‘šdm. | kd yn.l.ẖḏǵb.w 1099.26
arb‘m.kbd.yn.mṣb. | l.mḏrǵlm. | ‘šrn ‘šr.yn.mṣb.[-]ḥ[-].l.gzzm. 1084.30
t l šmm.w ‘rb.b p hm.‘ṣr.šmm. | w dg b ym.w ndd.gzr.l zr.y‘db.u ymn. | u šmal.b p hm.w l.tšb‘n y.aṯt.itrẖ. | y bn.aš 23[52].63
.ulbtyn. | w.kkr.ṯlṯ. | ksp.d.nkly.b.šd. | mit.ẖmšt.kbd. | [l.]gmn.bn.usyy. | mit.ṯṯm.kbd. | l.bn.yšm‘. | mit.arb‘m.kbd. | l. 1143.8
pṭb‘l. | šd.bn mšrn.l.ilšpš. | [šd.bn].kbr.l.snrn. | [---.--]k.l.gmrd. | [---.--]ṯ.l.yšn. | [šd.--]ln. | b d.trǵds. | šd.ṯ‘lb. | b d.bn.p 2030.1.7
šb‘.w l.yšn.pbl. | mlk.l qr.ṯigt.ibr h. | l ql.nhqt.ḥmr h. | l g‘t.alp.ḥrṯ.zǵt. | klb.ṣpr.w ylak. | mlakm.l k.‘m.krt. | mswn 14[KRT].3.122
w l.yšn.pbl. | mlk.l [qr.]ṯiqt. | ibr h[.l]ql.nhqt. | ḥmr[h.l g‘t.]alp. | ḥrṯ[.l z]ǵt.klb. | [ṣ]pr[.apn]k. | [pb]l[.mlk.g]m.l aṯt 14[KRT].5.225
.[b d].bn.[---]. | tš‘.ṣin.b.tš‘t.ksp. | mšlt.b.ṯql.ksp. | kdwṯ.l.grgyn.b.ṯq[l]. | ẖmšm.šmt.b.ṯql. | kkr.w.[ml]tḥ.tyt.[---]. | [b] 2101.24
y.l ‘r hm]. | tlkn.ym.w ṯa aẖr.š[pšm.b ṯlṯ]. | mǵy.rpum.l grnt.i[lnym.l] | mṭ‘t.w y‘n.dnil.[mt.rpi]. | yṯb.ǵzr.mt hrnmy 20[121].2.6
.l] | ‘r hm.tl[kn.ym.w ṯn.aẖr.špšm]. | b ṯlṯ.mǵy[.rpum.l grnt]. | i[ln]y[m].l mṭ‘t[.---]. | [-]m[.---]. | h.hn bn k.hn[.---]. | 22.1[123].25
[šd.---.]gt.prn. | [š]d.bn.š[p]šn l gt pr[n]. | šd bn.ilšḥr. | l.gt.mzln. | šd.gldy. | l.gt.mzln. | šd.glln.l.gt.mz[l]n. | šd.hyabn 1104.16
.bn.š[p]šn l gt pr[n]. | šd bn.ilšḥr. | l.gt.mzln. | šd.gldy. | l.gt.mzln. | šd.glln.l.gt.mz[l]n. | šd.hyabn[.l.]gt.mzln. | šd.‘bdb 1104.18
]. | šd bn.ilšḥr. | l.gt.mzln. | šd.gldy. | l.gt.mzln. | šd.glln.l.gt.mz[l]n. | šd.hyabn[.l.]gt.mzln. | šd.‘bdb‘l. | l.gt.mzln. 1104.19
n. | šd.gldy. | l.gt.mzln. | šd.glln.l.gt.mz[l]n. | šd.hyabn[.l.]gt.mzln. | šd.‘bdb‘l. | l.gt.mzln. 1104.20
| šd.glln.l.gt.mz[l]n. | šd.hyabn[.l.]gt.mzln. | šd.‘bdb‘l. | l.gt.mzln. 1104.22
]gt.prn. | [šd.---.]gt.prn. | [šd.---.]gt.prn. | [š]d.bn.š[p]šn l gt pr[n]. | šd bn.ilšḥr. | l.gt.mzln. | šd.gldy. | l.gt.mzln. | šd.gll 1104.14
. | b‘l š.‘nt š.ršp š. | šlmm. | w šnpt.il š. | l ‘nt.ḥl š.ṯn šm. | l gṯrm.ǵṣ b šmal. | d alpm.w alp w š. | šrp.w šlmm kmm. | l b‘ UG5.13.26
r. | ṯql.ksp.ṭb.ap w np[š]. | l ‘nt h.ṯql.ẖrṣ. | l špš[.w y]rẖ.l gṯr.ṯn. | [ṯql.ksp].ṭb.ap.w npš. | [---].bt.alp w š. | [---.--]m.l gṯ 33[5].14
b[‘.]l kṯr. | ‘lm.t‘rbn.gṯrm. | bt.mlk.ṯql.ẖrṣ. | l špš.w yrẖ.l gṯr. | ṯql.ksp.ṭb.ap w np[š]. | l ‘nt h.ṯql.ẖrṣ. | l špš[.w y]rẖ.l gṯ 33[5].11

ṯr.ṯn. | [ṯql.ksp].ṯb.ap.w npš. | [---].bt.alp w š. | [---.--]m.l gṯrm. | [---.]l ʿnt m. | [---.--]rm.d krm. | [---].l ʿnt m. | [---.]l šl 33[5].17
.ṯlṯ.kbd. | mdrǵlm. | w.šbʿ.ʿšr.ḫsnm. | ḫmšm.l.mit. | bnš.l.d. | yškb.l.b.bt.mlk. 1029.15
ṯḫṯu.u b ap km.u b qṣrt.npš km.u b qṭt]. | [tqṭt.u ṯḫṭu.l dbḥm.w l.ṯʿ.dbḥ n.ndb]ḫ. | [hw.ṯʿ.nṯʿy.hw.nkt.nkt.]yt[ši.l a 32[2].1.9
ḫṭin.b ap kn.u b [q]ṣrt.npš[kn.u b qṭt]. | tqṭṭn u ṯḫṭin.l bḥm.w l ṯʿ.d[bḥ n.ndbḥ]. | hw.ṯʿ.nṯʿy.hw.nkt.n[k]t.ytši[.l ab 32[2].1.15
u b ap km.u b q[ṣ]rt.npš km.u b qṭt.tqṭṭ. | ušn yp km.l d[b]ḥm.w l.ṯʿ.dbḥ n.ndbḥ.hw.ṯʿ | nṯʿy. | hw.nkt.nkt.y[t]ši.l 32[2].1.24
n.b ap [kn.u b qṣ]rt.npš kn.u b qṭt. | tqṭṭn.ušn y[p kn.l dbḥm.]w l ṯʿ dbḥ n. | ndbḥ.hw.ṯʿ n[ṯʿy.hw.nkt.nk]t.ytši.l ab 32[2].1.32
]. | ypḫ[--]. | w s[--]. | [---]. | qrd ga[n.--]. | b bt k.[--]. | w l dbḥ[--]. | ṯ[--]. | [--] aṯt yqḥ ʿz. | [---]ḏ. | [---]. | [---]. | hm qrt tu RS61[24.277.23]
ak k.ʿm dt[n]. | lqḥ.mṯpṭ. | w yʿny.nn. | dtn.bt n.mḫ[-]. | l dg.w [-]kl. | w aṯr.hn.mr[-]. UG5.6.15
[---.]b nhrm. | [ʿb]r.gbl.ʿbr. | qʿl.ʿbr.iht. | np šmm.šmšr. | l dgy.aṯrt. | mǵ.l qdš.amrr. | idk.al.tnn. | pnm.tk.ḥqkpt. | il.kl 3[ʿNT.VI].6.10
ṯr[.il.ab -.w ṯʿn.rbt]. | aṯr[t.ym.šmʿ.l qdš]. | w am[rr.l dgy.rbt]. | aṯrt.ym[.mdl.ʿr]. | ṣmd.pḥl[.št.gpnm.dt]. | ksp.dt. 4[51].4.3
-.ʿ]ṣrm. | [--]ṯpḫ bʿl. | [ṯl]ṯ.ʿṣrm. | [w]bʿlt btm. | [---.--]ṣn.l.dgn. | [---.--]m. | [---].pi[--.-]qš. | [--]pš.šn[--]. | ṯ[-]r.b iš[-]. | bʿl 39[19].5
trḥṣ.yd[h.---]. | [--.]yṣt ḏm[r.---]. | tšt[.r]imt.[l irt h.tšr.l dd.aliyn.bʿl]. | [ahb]t pdr[y.bt.ar.ahbt.ṭly.bt.rb.dd]. | arṣy bt 7.2[130].10
[---.t]št.rimt. | l irt h.mšr.l.dd.aliyn. | bʿl.yd.pdry.bt.ar. | ahbt.ṭly.bt.rb.dd.arṣy. | bt.yʿbd 3[ʿNT].3.2
tqǵ udn. | k ǵz.ǵzm.tdbr. | w ǵrm.ṯṯwy.šqlt. | b ǵlt.yd k.l tdn. | dn.almnt.l ṯpṭ. | ṯpṭ qṣr.npš.l tdy. | ṯšm.ʿl.dl.l pn k. | l t 16.6[127].45
udn.k ǵz.ǵzm]. | tdbr.w[ǵ]rm[.ṯṯwy]. | šqlt.b ǵlt.yd k. | l tdn.dn.almnt. | l ṯpṭ.ṯpṭ.qṣr.npš. | km.aḫt.ʿrš.mdw. | anšt.ʿrš 16.6[127].33
tp.zbl ym.bn ydm.ṯpṭ. | nhr.ʿz.ym.l ymk.l tnǵṣn.pnt h.l ydlp. | tmn h.kṯr.ṣmdm.ynḥt.w ypʿr.šmt hm. | šm k.at.aymr 2.4[68].17
ṯṯ spm l tgyn. | arbʿ spm l ll[-]. | ṯn spm.l slyy. | ṯlṯ spm l dlšpš amry. 137.2[93].15
il.yẓḥq.bm. | lb.w ygmḏ.bm kbd. | ẓi.at.l tlš. | amt.yrḫ. | l dmgy.amt. | aṯrt.qḥ. | ksan k.ḥdg k. | ḥtl k.w ẓi. | b aln.tk m. 12[75].1.16
ḥl. | [l.--.]mgmr. | [l.-.]qdšt. | l.ʿṯtrt.ndrgd. | l.ʿṯtrt.abḏr. | l.dml. | l.ilt[.-]pn. | l.uš[ḫr]y. | [---.-]mrn. | l ṯwl. | [--]ḏ[--]. 1001.1.13
]. | [b.yr]ḫ.riš.yn.[---]. | [---.bʿ]lt.bhtm.š[--.---]. | [---.-]rt.l.dml[.---]. | [b.yrḫ].nql.ṯn.ḫpn[.---]. | [---].aḥd.ḥmš.am[--.---]. 1106.34
l.brlt n[-.k qṭr.b ap -]. | tmǵyn.tša.g h[m.w tṣḥn]. | šmʿ.l dnil.[mt.rpi]. | mt.aqht.ǵzr.[šṣat]. | btlt.ʿnt.k [rḥ.npš h]. | k iṯ 19[1AQHT].2.90
. | [---.]krm.b [-]dn.l.bn.[-]kn. | šd[.---.-]ʿn. | šd[.---.-]ṣm.l.dqn. | š[d.---.--]d.pdy. | [---.dq]n. | [---.d]qn. | [---.--]b[.---]. | [-- 2027.1.7
zn. | [---.]yn.l.m[---]. | [---.]yn.l.m[--]m. | [---.]d.bn.[---.]l.dqn. | [---.--]ʿ.šdyn.l ytršn. | [---.--]ṯ.ʿbd.l.kyn. | k[rm.--.]l.i[w 2027.2.7
ḥ n. | ndbḥ.hw.ṯʿ n[ṯʿy.hw.nkt.nk]t.ytši.l ab bn il. | ytši.l d[r.bn il.l]mpḫrt.bn il. | l ṯkm[n.w šnm.]hn ʿ[r]. | [---.]w np 32[2].1.34
ḥ n.ndbḥ.hw.ṯʿ | nṯʿy. | hw.nkt.nkt.y[t]ši.l ab.bn.il.ytši.l dr. | bn il.l mpḫrt.bn.il.l ṯkmn[.w]šnm.hn.ʿr. | w.ṯb.l mspr. 32[2].1.25
.ndb]ḥ. | [hw.ṯʿ.nṯʿy.hw.nkt.nkt.]yt[ši.l ab.bn.il]. | [ytši.l dr.bn.il.l mpḫ]rt.[bn.il.l ṯkmn.w šn]m hn š. | [---.w n]py.gr[32[2].1.9B
[---.hw.ṯʿ.nṯʿ]y. | [hw.nkt.nkt.ytši.l ab.bn.il.ytši.l d]r.bn[.il]. | [l mpḫrt.bn.il.l ṯkmn.w šnm.hn š]. | [w šqrb.š. 32[2].1.2
.ndbḥ]. | hw.ṯʿ.nṯʿy.hw.nkt.n[k]t.ytši[.l ab.bn.il]. | ytši.l dr.bn.il.l mpḫrt.bn.i[l.l ṯkmn.w š]nm hn š. | w šqrb.ʿr.mšr 32[2].1.17
lmnt.km. | aḫt.ʿrš.mdw.anšt. | ʿrš.zbln.rd.l mlk. | amlk.l drkt k.aṯb. | an.w yʿny.krt ṯʿ.yṯbr. | ḥrn.y bn.yṯbr.ḥrn. | riš k. 16.6[127].53
.npš. | km.aḫt.ʿrš.mdw. | anšt.ʿrš.zbln. | rd.l mlk.amlk. | l drkt.k aṯb.an. | yṯbʿ.yṣb ǵlm.ʿl. | ab h.yʿrb.yšu g h. | w yṣḥ.š 16.6[127].38
mm.bṣr. | kp.šsk k.[--].l ḥbš k. | ʿtk.ri[š.]l mhr k. | w ʿp.l dr[ʿ].nšr k. | w rbṣ.l ǵr k.inbb. | kt ǵr k.ank.ydʿt. | [-]n.atn.at. 13[6].8
-.---]. | b d.prḫ[-.---]. | apnm.l.ʿ[--]. | apnm.l.[---]. | apnm.l.d[--]. | apnm.l.bn[.---]. | apnm.l.[b]n[.---]. | apnm.l.bn[.---]. | ṯ 145[318].5
l.ḏrdn. | bʿl y.rgm. | bn.ḥrn k. | mǵy. | hbṭ.hw. | ḥrd.w.šl hw. | q 2114.1
. | gb h.km.[---.]yqṭqṭ.ṯḥt. | ṯlḥnt.il.d ydʿnn. | yʿdb.lḥm.l h.w d l ydʿnn. | d.mṣd. | ylmn.ḫṭ.ṯḥt.ṯlḥn. | b qrʿ. | ʿṯtrt.w ʿnt. UG5.1.1.7
mn.ḫṭ.ṯḥt.ṯlḥn. | b qrʿ. | ʿṯtrt.w ʿnt.ymǵy. | ʿṯtrt.ṯʿdb.nšb l h. | w ʿnt.ktp.b hm.ygʿr.ṯǵr. | bt.il.pn.l mgr lb.ṯʿdbn. | nšb.l i UG5.1.1.10
. | tity.ilm.l ahl hm. | dr il.l mšknt hm. | w tqrb.w ld.bn.l h. | w tqrb.w ld.bnt.l h. | mk.b šbʿ.šnt. | bn.krt.km hm.tdr. | a 15[128].3.20
n.mṣd h.mnt.nṯk nḥš. | šmrr.nḥš.ʿq šr.ln h.mlḫš. | abd.ln h.ydy.ḥmt. | b ḥrn.pnm.trǵnw.w ṯṯkl. | bnwt h.ykr.ʿr.d qd UG5.7.60
š.ʿq šr[.yʿ]db.ksa. | nḥš.šmrr.nḥš.ʿq šr.ln h.ml | ḫš.abd.ln h.ydy.ḥmt.hlm.ytq. | w yṯb. | tqru.l špš.um h.špš.[um.q]l b UG5.7.22
t.thmtm. | mnt.nṯk.nḥš.šmrr.nḥš. | ʿq šr.ln h.mlḫš abd.ln h.ydy. | ḥmt.hlm.ytq ytqšqy.nḥš.yšlḥm.ʿq šr. | yʿdb.ksa.w. UG5.7.5
| dgn.ttl h.mnt.nṯk.nḥš.šmrr. | nḥš.ʿq šr.ln h.mlḫš.abd.ln h. | ydy.ḥmt.hlm.ytq.nḥš.yšlḥm. | nḥš.ʿq šr.yʿdb.ksa.w yṯb UG5.7.16
ʿm. | ršp.bbt h.mnt.nḥš.šmrr. | nḥš.ʿq šr.ln h.mlḫš.abd.ln h.ydy. | ḥmt.hlm.ytq.nḥš.yšlḥm.nḥš ʿq. | š.yʿdb.ksa w yṯb. UG5.7.32
lk.ʿṯtrt h.mnt.nṯk.nḥš.šmrr. | nḥš.ʿq šr.ln h.mlḫš abd.ln h.ydy. | ḥmt.hlm.ytq.nḥš.yšlḥm.nḥš. | ʿq šr.yʿdb.ksa.w yṯb UG5.7.42
m.ṣpn.mnt y.nṯk. | nḥš.šmrr.nḥš.ʿq šr ln h. | mlḫš.abd.ln h.ydy.ḥmt.hlm.ytq. | nḥš.yšlḥm.nḥš.ʿq šr.ydb.ksa. | w yṯb. UG5.7.11
ss.kptr h.mnt.nṯk.nḥš. | šmrr.nḥš.ʿq šr.ln h.mlḫš.abd. | ln h.ydy.ḥmt.hlm ytq.nḥš. | yšlḥm.nḥš.ʿq šr.yʿdb ksa. | w yṯb UG5.7.48
mṯ.ḥryt h.mnt.nṯk.nḥš.šm | rr.nḥš.ʿq šr.ln h.mlḫš abd.ln h. | ydy.ḥmt.hlm.ytq nḥš yšlḥm.nḥš. | ʿq.šr.yʿdb.ksa.w yṯb UG5.7.37
ḫ.lrgt h.mnt.nṯk.n[ḥš].šmrr. | nḥš.ʿq šr.ln h.mlḫš.abd.ln h.ydy. | ḥmt.hlm.ytq.nḥš.yšlḥm.nḥš. | ʿq šr.yʿdb.ksa.w yṯb UG5.7.27
šmm h mnt.nṯk.nḥš. | šmrr.nḥš ʿq šr.ln h.mlḫš. | abd.ln h.ydy ḥmt.hlm.ytq šqy. | nḥš.yšlḥm.nḥš.ʿq šr.yʿdb. | ksa.w UG5.7.54
hrnmy.d in.bn.l h. | km.aḫ h.w šrš.km.ary h. | bl.iṯ.bn.l h.km aḫ h.w šrš. | km.ary h.uzrm.ilm.ylḥm. | uzrm.yšqy.bn 17[2AQHT].1.21
t h.abynt. | [d]nil.mt.rpi anḫ.ǵzr. | [mt.]hrnmy.d in.bn.l h. | km.aḫ h.w šrš.km.ary h. | bl.iṯ.bn.l h.km aḫ h.w šrš. | k 17[2AQHT].1.19
l bl.ʿm | kṯr.w ḫss.kptr h.mnt.nṯk.nḥš. | šmrr.nḥš.ʿq šr.ln h.mlḫš.abd. | ln h.ydy.ḥmt.hlm ytq.nḥš. | yšlḥm.nḥš.ʿq šr. UG5.7.47
bl ʿm. | šḥr.w šlm šmm h mnt.nṯk.nḥš. | šmrr.nḥš ʿq šr.ln h.mlḫš. | abd.ln h.ydy ḥmt.hlm.ytq šqy. | nḥš.yšlḥm.nḥš.ʿ UG5.7.53
bk nhrm.b ʿdt.thmtm. | mnt.nṯk.nḥš.šmrr.nḥš. | ʿq šr.ln h.mlḫš abd.ln h.ydy. | ḥmt.hlm.ytq ytqšqy.nḥš.yšlḥm.ʿq š UG5.7.5
š.um.ql.bl.ʿm. | dgn.ttl h.mnt.nṯk.nḥš.šmrr. | nḥš.ʿq šr.ln h.mlḫš.abd.ln h. | ydy.ḥmt.hlm.ytq.nḥš.yšlḥm. | nḥš.ʿq šr. UG5.7.16
tk. | nḥš.šlḥm.nḥš.ʿq šr[.yʿ]db.ksa. | nḥš.šmrr.nḥš.ʿq šr.ln h.ml | ḫš.abd.ln h.ydy.ḥmt.hlm.ytq. | w yṯb. | tqru.l špš.um UG5.7.21
l bl. | ʿm bʿl.mrym.ṣpn.mnt y.nṯk. | nḥš.šmrr.nḥš.ʿq šr ln h. | mlḫš.abd.ln h.ydy.ḥmt.hlm.ytq. | nḥš.yšlḥm.nḥš.ʿq šr. UG5.7.10
m.q]l bl.ʿm. | yrḫ.lrgt h.mnt.nṯk.n[ḥš].šmrr. | nḥš.ʿq šr.ln h.mlḫš.abd.ln h.ydy. | ḥmt.hlm.ytq.nḥš.yšlḥm.nḥš. | ʿq šr. UG5.7.27
h.špš.um.ql b.ʿm. | ršp.bbt h.mnt.nḥš.šmrr. | nḥš.ʿq šr.ln h.mlḫš.abd.ln h.ydy. | ḥmt.hlm.ytq.nḥš.yšlḥm.nḥš ʿq. | š.y UG5.7.32
um ql.bl.ʿm. | mlk.ʿṯtrt h.mnt.nṯk.nḥš.šmrr. | nḥš.ʿq šr.ln h.mlḫš abd.ln h.ydy. | ḥmt.hlm.ytq.nḥš.yšlḥm.nḥš. | ʿq šr. UG5.7.42
l bl ʿm. | ṯṯ.w kmṯ.ḥryt h.mnt.nṯk.nḥš.šm | rr.nḥš.ʿq šr.ln h.mlḫš abd.ln h. | ydy.ḥmt.hlm.ytq nḥš yšlḥm.nḥš. | ʿq.šr. UG5.7.37
um.ql bl. | ʿm ḥrn.mṣd h.mnt.nṯk nḥš. | šmrr.nḥš.ʿq šr.ln h.mlḫš. | abd.ln h.ydy.ḥmt. | b ḥrn.pnm.trǵnw.w ṯṯkl. | bn UG5.7.59
udm ṯrrt. | udm.ytnt.il w ušn. | ab.adm.w ṯṯb. | mlakm.l h.lm.ank. | ksp.w yrq.ḫrṣ. | yd.mqm h.w ʿbd. | ʿlm.ṯlṯ.sswm. 14[KRT].3.137
r il.l mšknt hm. | w tqrb.w ld.bn.l h. | w tqrb.w ld.bnt.l h. | mk.b šbʿ.šnt. | bn.krt.km hm.tdr. | ap.bnt.ḥry. | km hm. 15[128].3.21
mt. | w ht.aḫ y. | bn y.yšal. | ṯryl.p rgm. | l mlk.šm y. | w l h.yʿl m. | w h[t] aḫ y. | bn y.yšal. | ṯryl.w rgm[.-]. | ṯṯb.l aḫ k. 138.14

--.---].|yrmm h[--.---].|mlk.gbʻ h d [---].|ibr.k l hm.d l h q[--.---].|l ytn.l hm.tḥt bʻl[.---].|h.u qšt pn hdd.b y[.----] 9[33].2.4
rp.alp šlmm.|l bʻl.ʻṣr l ṣpn.|npš.w.š.l ršp bbt.|[ʻ]ṣrm l h.ršp [-]m.|[---.]bqt[-].|[b] ǵb.ršp mh bnš.|šrp.w ṣp ḫršḫ. UG5.12.A.12
.ṣdq h.l ypq.|mtrḫt.yšr h.|aṯt.trḫ.w tbʻt.|ṯar um.tkn l h.|mṯlṯt.kṯrm.tmt.|mrbʻt.zblnm.|mḫmšt.yitsp.|ršp.nṯdṯt. 14[KRT].1.15
[---]d nhr.umt.|[---.]rpat.bt.|[m]lk.itdb.d šbʻ.|[a]ḫm.l h.ṯmnt.bn um.|krt.ḥtk n.rš.|krt.grdš.mknt.|aṯt.ṣdq h.l yp 14[KRT].1.9
[---]m.d.yṯ[--.]l[-].|ršp.ḫmš.[m]šl[t].|[--]arš[p.-]š.l[h].|[-]ṯl[.--]š.l h.|[---]l[.--] h.|mtn[.---.]l h.|[---.]l h.|[---.-- 2133.3
.|[---]l[.--] h.|mtn[.---.]l h.|[---.]l h.|[---.--]š.l h.|[---].l h.|[--.]spr[.---].|[--.]ḫrd[.---].|[---.]l h. 2133.9
[-----].|w.[-----].|w.abǵl.nḥ[l h.--].|w.unṯ.aḫd.l h[.---].|dnn.bn.yṣr[.---].|sln.bn.ʻṯt[-.---].|pdy.bn.nr[-.---].| 90[314].1.4
.--]mr.ph.|[---.--]mm.hlkt.|[---.]b qrb.ʻr.|[---.m]lakm l h.|[---.]l.bn.il.|[---.--]a.ʻd h.|[---.--]rh.|[---.--]y.špš.|[---.--] 26[135].6
ṯl[.--]š.l h.|[---]l[.--] h.|mtn[.---.]l h.|[---.]l h.|[---.--]š.l h.|[---].l h.|[--.]spr[.---].|[--.]ḫrd[.---].|[---.]l h. 2133.8
[--]arš[p.-]š.l[h].|[-]ṯl[.--]š.l h.|[---]l[.--] h.|mtn[.---.]l h.|[---.]l h.|[---.--]š.l h.|[---].l h.|[--.]spr[.---].|[--.]ḫrd[.---] 2133.6
|knyt.w tʻn[.btlt.ʻnt].|yṯb l y.ṯr.il[.ab y.---].|yṯb.l y.w l h.[---].|[--.i]mṣḫ.nn.k imr.l arṣ.|[ašhlk].šbt h.dmm.šbt.dq 3[ʻNT.VI].4.8
.-]š.l[h].|[-]ṯl[.--]š.l h.|[---]l[.--] h.|mtn[.---.]l h.|[---.]l h.|[---.--]š.l h.|[---].l h.|[--.]spr[.---].|[--.]ḫrd[.---].|[---.]l h 2133.7
[--.]l[-].|ršp.ḫmš.[m]šl[t].|[--]arš[p.-]š.l[h].|[-]ṯl[.--]š.l h.|[---]l[.--] h.|mtn[.---.]l h.|[---.]l h.|[---.--]š.l h.|[---].l h. 2133.4
k.ytn.mlbš.|[---.-]rn.k.ypdd.mlbš h.|[---.]mlk.ytn.lbš.l h. 1106.61
r[.---].|[--]šy.w ydn.bʻ[l.---]n.|[--]ʻ.k yn.hm.l.atn.bt y.l h. 1002.62
|[---.--]š.l h.|[---].l h.|[--.]spr[.---].|[--.]ḫrd[.---].|[---.]l h. 2133.12
yn.ʻn k.ẓẓ.w k mǵ.ilm.|[--.]k ʻṣm.k ʻšm.l ttn.k abnm.l thggn. 1001.2.13
bʻl.|ḫlq.zbl.bʻl.arṣ.|apnk.lṭpn.il.|d pid.yrd.l ksi.yṯb.|l hdm[.w] l.hdm.yṯb.|l arṣ.yṣq.ʻmr.|un.l riš h.ʻpr.plṯt.|l qd 5[67].6.13
mʻ.mhrm.|[ṯ]ʻr.ksat.l ksat.ṯlḥnt.|[l]ṯlḥn.hdmm.ṯṯʻr.l hdmm.|[t]ḥspn.m h.w trḥṣ.|[ṭ]l.šmm.šmn.arṣ.rbb.|[r]kb ʻ 3[ʻNT].2.37
l.bʻl.arṣ.|apnk.lṭpn.il.|d pid.yrd.l ksi.yṯb.|l hdm[.w] l.hdm.yṯb.|l arṣ.yṣq.ʻmr.|un.l riš h.ʻpr.plṯt.|l qdqd h.lpš.yk 5[67].6.13
y.w tkbd h.|hlm.il.k yphn h.|yprq.lṣb.w yṣḥq.|pʻn h.l hdm.yṯpd.w ykrkr.|uṣbʻt h.yšu.g h.w y[ṣḥ].|ik.mǵyt.rbt.a 4[51].4.29
šmn.tmṭrn.|nḫlm.tlk.nbtm.|šmḫ.lṭpn.il.d pid.|pʻn h.l hdm.yṯpd.|w yprq.lṣb w yṣḥq.|yšu.g h.w yṣḥ.|aṯbn.ank.w 6[49].3.15
ni[l].|pnm.tšmḫ.w ʻl yṣhl pi[t].|yprq.lṣb.w yṣḥq.|pʻn.l hdm.yṯpd.yšu.|g h.w yṣḥ.aṯbn.ank.|w anḫn.w tnḫ.b irt y. 17[2AQHT].2.11
ym.|[---.-]qlṣn.wpṯ m.|[---.]w yʻn.kṯr.|[w ḫss.]ṯṯb.bʻl.l hwt y.|[ḥš.]bht h.tbnn.|[ḥš.]trmm.hkl h.|y[tl]k.l lbnn.w ʻ 4[51].6.15
w ḫss.|yšu.g h.w yṣḥ.|l rgmt.l k.l ali|yn.bʻl.ṯṯbn.bʻl.|l hwt y.ypth.ḥ|ln.b bht m.urbt.|b qrb.hk[l m.yp]tḥ.|bʻl.b d 4[51].7.25
w yʻn.k[ṯr.w ḫs]s.|ṯṯb.bʻl.l[hwt y].|ṯn.rgm.k[ṯr.w]ḫss.|šmʻ.mʻ.l al[iy]n bʻl.|bl.ašt.ur[4[51].6.2
hbr.w ql.tšṯḥ|wy.w kbd hwt.|w rgm.l kṯr.|w ḫss.ṯny.l h|yn.d ḥrš.ydm.|tḥm.al[iyn.bʻl].|h[wt.aliy.qrdm]. 3[ʻNT.VI].6.22
hbr.w ql.t[šṯḥwy.w kbd.hwt].|w rgm l k[ṯr.w ḫss.ṯny.l hyn].|d ḥrš.y[dm.tḥm.ṯr.il.ab k.]|hwt.lṭpn[.ḥtk k.---].|yh. 1[ʻNT.IX].3.4
m.b ksl.qšt h.mdnt.|w hln.ʻnt.l bt h.tmǵyn.|tštql.ilt.l hkl h.|w l.šbʻt.tmtḫṣ h.b ʻmq.|tḫtṣb.bn.qrtm.tṯʻr.|ksat.l m 3[ʻNT].2.18
.ṯiṭ.|rḥṣ.npṣ y.b ym.rṯ.|dn.il.bt h.ymǵyn.|yštql.dnil.l hkl h.|ʻrb.b bt h.kṯrt.bnt.|hll.snnt.apnk.dnil.|mt.rpi.ap.h 17[2AQHT].2.25
r.dr.|ʻdb.uḫry.mṭ.yd h.|dnil.bt h.ymǵyn.yšt|ql.dnil.l hkl h.ʻrb.b|kyt.b hkl h.mšspdt.b ḥẓr h.|pẓǵm.ǵr.ybk.l aq 19[1AQHT].4.171
--.]špš.bʻl k.|ydʻm.l.ydʻt.|ʻm y.špš.bʻl k.|šnt.šntm.lm.l.tlk.|w.lḥt.akl.ky.|likt.ʻm.špš.|bʻl k.ky.akl.|b.ḥwt k.inn.|š 2060.16
bnšm.dt.iṯ.alpm.l hm.|bn.niršn.|bn.adty.|bn.alz.|bn.birtn.|bn.mlṣ.|bn.q[-- 2023.1.1
yrm.h[--.---].|yrmm h[--.---].|mlk.gbʻ h d [---].|ibr.k l hm.d l h q[--.---].|l ytn.l hm.tḥt bʻl[.---].|h.u qšt pn hdd.b 9[33].2.4
.|[--.n]pš[.-].|w [k]l hm.b d.|rb.tmtt.lqḥt.|w.ṯṯb.ank.l hm.|w.any k.ṯt.|by.ʻky.ʻryt.|w.aḫ y.mhk.|b lb h.al.yšt. 2059.23
.---].|w.ʻl.ap.s[--.---].|b hm.w.rgm.hw.al[--].|atn.ksp.l hm.ʻd.|ilak.ʻm.mlk.|ht.lik[t.--.]mlk[.--].|w.mlk.yštal.b.hn 2008.2.7
pdy h[m].|iwrkl.mit.|ksp.b y[d].|birtym.|[un]ṯ inn.|l [h]m ʻd tṯṯbn.|ksp.iwrkl.|w ṯb.l unṯ hm. 1006.17
mdrǵlm.d inn.|msgm.l hm.|pʻṣ.ḫbty.|artyn.ary.|brqn.ṯlḥy.|bn.aryn.|bn.lgn.|bn. 118[306].2
l.šr.ʻṯtrt.|mlbš.ṯrmnm.|k.yṯn.w.b.bt.|mlk.mlbš.|ytn.l hm.|šbʻ.lbšm.allm.|l ušḫry.|ṯlṯ.mat.pṯtm.|l.mgmr.b.ṯlṯ.|š 1107.8
.---].|mlk.gbʻ h d [---].|ibr.k l hm.d l h q[--.---].|l ytn.l hm.tḥt bʻl[.---].|h.u qšt pn hdd.b y[.----].|ʻm.b ym bʻl ysy 9[33].2.5
mlk.|w.aḥd.|ʻl atlg.|w l.ʻṣm.|tspr.|nrn.al.tud|ad.at.l hm.|ṯṯm.ksp. 1010.20
[---].in ḥẓm.l hm.|[---.--]ḏn.|mrkbt.mtrt.|ngršp.|ngǵln.|ilṯḥm.|bʻlṣdq. 1125.1.1
hm.nǵr mdrʻ[.iṯ.lḥm.---].|iṯ.yn.d ʻrb.bṯk[.---].|mǵ hw.l hn.lg yn h[.---].|w ḥbr h.mla yn.[---]. 23[52].75
ṣ.ʻm.aliyn.bʻl.|ik.al.yšm[ʻ] k.ṯr.|il.ab k.l ysʻ.alt.|ṯbt k.l yhpk.ksa.mlk k.|l yṯbr.ḫṭ.mṯpṭ k.|yru.bn ilm t.ṯṯʻ.y|dd.il. 6[49].6.28
.ṯ]pṭ[.n]hr.|[ik.a]l.yšmʻ k.ṯr.[i]l.ab k.l ysʻ.[alt.]ṯ[bt |k.l y]hpk.|[ksa.]mlk k.l yṯbr.ḫṭ.mṯpṭ k.w yʻn[.ʻṯtr].dm[-]k[-].|
[kṯ]r w ḫss.y[i]sp.ḥmt.šḥr.w šlm.|[yis]p.ḥmt.isp.[šp]š l hrm.ǵrpl.ʻl arṣ.|[l a]n ḥmt.l p[.n]ṯk.abd.l p.akl ṯm.dl.|[---. UG5.8.19
p.ak[l].|[ṯm.dl.]isp.ḥ[mt.---.-]hm.yasp.ḥmt.|[---.š]pš.l [hrm.ǵrpl].ʻl.arṣ.l an.|[ḥ]mt.i[l.w] ḥrn.yisp.ḥmt.|[bʻl.w]d UG5.8.12
p h.ḫ[--.---.šp]š.l hrm.|[ǵrpl.]ʻl.ar[ṣ.---.ḥ]mt.|[---.šp]š.l [hrm.ǵ]rpl.ʻl.arṣ.|[---.]ḥmt.l p[.nṯ]k.abd.l p.ak[l].|[ṯm.dl.]i UG5.8.9
.ḥ[--.---.-]lk.|[-]sr.n[--.---.]ḥrn.|[--]p.ḫp h.ḫ[--.---.šp]š.l hrm.|[ǵrpl.]ʻl.ar[ṣ.---.ḥ]mt.|[---.šp]š.l [hrm.ǵ]rpl.ʻl.arṣ.|[-- UG5.8.7
bn.qrrn.|bn.dnt.|bn.ṯʻl[-].|bdl.ar.dt.inn.|mhr l ht.|artyn.|ʻdmlk.|bn.alt[-].|iḫy[-].|ʻbdgṯr.|ḥrr.|bn.s[-]p[- 1035.1.5
ṣḥ.y l k.qrt.ablm.|d ʻl k.mḫṣ.aqht.ǵzr.|ʻwrt.yšt k.bʻl.l ht.|w ʻlm h.l ʻnt.p dr.dr.|ʻdb.uḫry.mṭ.yd h.|dnil.bt h.ymǵ 19[1AQHT].4.167
mt.|w ht.aḫ y.|bn y.yšal.|ṯryl.p rgm.|l mlk.šm y.|w l h[-] yʻl m.|bn y.yšal.|ṯryl.w rgm.|ṯṯb.l aḫ k.|l adn k. 138.15
ʻ.l] ydʻt.|[---.t]asrn.|[---.]trks.|[---.]abnm.upqt.|[---.]l w ǵr mtn y.|[---.]rq.gb.|[---.--]kl.tǵr.mtn h.|[---.--]b.w ym 1[ʻNT.X].5.12
rgmt.l ym.bʻl km.ad[n km.ṯpṭ].|[nhr.---.]hwt.gmr.hd.l wny[-.---].|[---.]iyr h.g[-.]thbr[.---]. 2.1[137].46
.|[ṯ]n.p k.b ǵr.ṯn.p k.b ḫlb.k tgwln.šnt k.|[--.]w špt k.l tššy.hm.tqrm.l mt.b rn k.|[--]ḫp.an.arnn.ql.špš.ḥw.bṯnm.u 1001.1.5
.|l bʻl[-.---].|tḥt.ksi.zbl.ym.w ʻn.kṯr.w ḫss.l rgmt.|l k.l zbl.bʻl.ṯnt.l rkb.ʻrpt.ht.ib k.|bʻl m.ht.ib k.tmḫṣ.ht.tṣmt.ṣrt 2.4[68].8
--.]upqt.ʻrb.|[---.w ẓ]r.mtn y at zd.|[---.]tʻrb.bši.|[---.]l tzd.l tptq.|[---].g[--.]l arṣ. 1[ʻNT.X].5.27
id.---].|šm.bn y.yw.ilt.[---].|w pʻr.šm.ym[-.---].|tʻnyn.l zn.tn[.---].|at.adn.tpʻr[.---].|ank.lṭpn.il[.d pid.---].|ʻl.ydm. 1[ʻNT.X].4.16
arbʻ.yn.l.mrynm.ḥ[--].kl h.|kdm.l.zn[-.---].|kd.l.aṯr[y]m.|kdm.ʻm.[--]n.|kd.mštt.[---]n.|kdm 1089.2
lk.l [qr.]ṯiqt.|ibr h[.l]ql.nhqt.|ḥmr[h.l gʻt.]alp.|ḥrṯ[.l z]ǵt.klb.|[ṣ]pr[.apn]k.|[pb]l[.mlk.g]m.l aṯt |[h.k]y[ṣḥ.]šm 14[KRT].5.226
.|tš[.---.]ymm.lk.|hrg.ar[bʻ.]ymm.bṣr.|kp.šsk k.[--].l ḥbš k.|ʻtk.ri[š.]l mhr k.|w ʻp.l dr[ʻ].nšr k.|w rbṣ.l ǵr k.inb 13[6].6
ʻṣm.---]n.krpn.ʻl.[k]rpn.|[---.]ym.w tʻl.trṯ.|[---].yn.ʻšy l ḥbš.|[---.]ḥtn.qn.yṣbt.|[---.--]m.b nši.ʻn h.w tphn.|[---.--]m 17[2AQHT].6.8
l hm.|aḫr.tmǵyn.mlak ym.tʻdt.ṯpṭ.nhr.l pʻn.il.|[l t]pl.l tšṯḥwy.pḫr.mʻd.qmm.a[--].amr.|[ṯn]y.dʻt hm.išt.ištm.yitm 2.1[137].31

rzḥ h. | yšt[.il.y]n.ʿd šbʿ.trṯ.ʿd škr. | il.hlk.l bt h.yštql. | l ḥṭr h.yʿmsn.nn.ṯkmn. | w šnm.w ngšnn.ḥby. | bʿl.qrnm w ḏ UG5.1.1.18
.ʿdtm.yʿdyn h.yb | ltm.ybln h.mǵy.ḥrn.l bt h.w. | yštql.l ḥṭr h.tlu ḥt.km.nḫl. | tplg.km.plg. | bʿd h.bhtm.mnt.bʿd h.b UG5.7.68
.amt. | qḥ.krt.šlmm. | šlmm.w ng.mlk. | l bt y.rḥq.krᵗt. | l ḥẓr y.al.tṣr. | udm.rbt.w udm ṯrrt. | udm.ytnt.il w ušn. | ab.a 14[KRT].3.133
m.y[t]n[t]. | il.ušn.ab[.ad]m. | rḥq.mlk.l bt y. | n[g.]krt.l ḥẓ[r y]. | w yʿn[y.k]rt[.ṯ]ʿ. | lm.ank.ksp. | w yr[q.ḫrṣ]. | yd.mq 14[KRT].6.280
.ytnt]. | [il.w ušn.ab.adm]. | [rḥq.mlk.l bt y]. | [ng.kr]t.l ḥ[ẓ]r y. | [-----]. | [---.ttbʿ]. | [mlakm.l yṯb]. | [idk.pnm.l ytn]. | 14[KRT].5.261
ṯḥm.rgm. | mlk. | l ḥyil. | lm.tlik.ʿm y. | ik y.aškn. | ʿṣm.l bt.dml. | p ank.atn. | ʿṣ 1010.3
.k lb.l | ḥṯ h.imḫṣ h.k d.ʿl.qšt h. | imḫṣ h.ʿl.qṣʿt h.hwt. | l aḥw.ap.qšt h.l ttn. | l y.w b mt[.-]ḥ.mṣṣ[-]t[.--]. | prʿ.qẓ.y[bl] 19[1AQHT].1.16
št k.l bky.ʿtq. | b d.aṯt ab.ṣrry. | u ilm.tmtn.šph. | [l]ṭpn.l yḥ.t[b]ky k. | ab.ǵr.bʿl.ṣ[p]n.ḥlm. | qdš.nny.ḥ[l]m.adr. | ḥl.rḥ 16.2[125].106
ṣ. | [.---].nn. | [---.]qrt.dt. | [---.--]sʿ.hn.mlk. | [---.l]qḥ.hn.l.ḥwt h. | [---.--]p.hn.ib.d.b.mgšḫ. | [---.i]b.hn[.w.]ht.ank. | [--- 1012.9
rgm.bn.il. | krt.šph.lṭpn. | w qdš.u ilm.tmtn. | šph.lṭpn.l yḥ. | w yʿny.krt.ṯʿ. | bn.al.tbkn.al. | tdm.l y.al tkl.bn. | qr.ʿn k. 16.1[125].23
.npš h.km.iṯl.brlt h.km. | qṭr.b ap h.b ap.mhr h.ank. | l aḥwy.tqḥ.yṭpn.mhr.št. | tštn.k nšr.b ḥbš h.km.diy. | b tʿrt h. 18[3AQHT].4.27
mhr.št]. | šmʿ.l btlt.ʿnt.at.ʿ[l.qšt h]. | tmḫṣ h.qṣʿt h.hwt.l t[ḥwy]. | nʿmn.ǵzr.št.ṯrm.w[---]. | ištir.b ddm.w nʿrs[.---]. | 18[3AQHT].4.13
]. | rb[.bʿl y.---]. | w.an[k.---]. | arš[.---]. | mlk.r[b.bʿ]l y.p.l. | ḥy.np[š.a]rš. | l.pn.bʿ[l y.l].pn.bʿl y. | w.urk.ym.bʿl y. | l.pn. 1018.17
l. | km ilm.w ḥẓr.k bn.aṯrt. | w tʿn.rbt.aṯrt ym. | rbt.ilm.l ḥkmt. | šbt.dqn k.l tsr k. | rḥntt.d[-].l irt k. | wn ap.ʿdn.mṭr 4[51].5.65
.l.trbnn. | ddm.šʿrm.l.trbnn. | ddm.šʿrm.l.ḫtn. | dd.šʿrm.l.ḥmr.ḥṭb. | dd.ḥṭm.l.ḫdǵb. | ṯṯ.ddm.l.gzzm. | kd yn.l.ḫtn.w.k 1099.24
ṯmn.ddm šʿrm.l ḥmrm. 1165.1
w l šd.mṭr.ʿly. | nʿm.l arṣ.mṭr.bʿl. | w l šd.mṭr.ʿly. | nʿm.l ḥṭt.b gn. | bm.nrt.ksmm. | ʿl.tl[-]k.ʿṭrtrm. | nšu.[r]iš.ḥrṯm. | l 16[126].3.9
.ṣdr[.---]. | [---.]kl.b kl.l pgm.pgm.l.b[---]. | [---.]mdbm.l ḥrn.ḥr[n.---]. | [---.--]m.ql.hm[.---]. | [---].aṯt n.r[---]. | [---.]ḥr 1001.1.27
l ʿbdkṯr. | dd[m] l rʿy. | [--] šmḫ[.---]. | ddm gt dprnm. | l ḥršm. | ddm l ʿnqt. | dd l alṯt.w l lmdt h. | dd l iḫyn. | dd l [-- 1101.9
[---.---.]l.mit.drʿ.w.šbʿm.drt. | [---.ḥpr.]bnšm.w.l.ḥrš.ʿrq.ṯn.ʿšr h. | [---.d]rʿ.w.mit.drt.w.ʿšrm.l.mit. | [drt.ḥpr.b 1098.2
šbʿ.yn.l [---]. | ṯlṯ.l ḥr[š.---]. | ṯṯ[.l.]mštt[.---]. | ṯlṯ.l.mdr[ǵlm]. | kd[.--].lm[d.---]. | 1091.2
ṣ.bʿl m[.--]y.tnn.w ygl.w ynsk.ʿ[-]. | [--]y.l arṣ[.id]y.alt.l aḫš.idy.alt.in l y. | [--]t.bʿl.ḥẓ.ršp.b[n].km.yr.klyt h.w lb h. | 1001.1.2
.mš[--.---]. | l.ilt[.---]. | l.bʿlt[.---]. | l.il.bt[.---]. | l.ilt.[---]. | l.ḥtk[.---]. | l.ršp[.---]. | [l].ršp.[---.--]g.kbd. | [l.i]lt.qb[-.---]. | [l. 1004.9
t.w tbk.y[---.---]. | abn.ank.w ʿl.[qšt k.---.ʿl]. | qṣʿt k.at.l ḥ[---.---]. | w ḫlq.ʿpmm[.---]. 18[3AQHT].4.41
m. | mit.iqni.l tpnr. | [ks.ksp.kt]n.mit.pḥ[m]. | [mit.iqni.l]ḫbrtn[r]. | [ks.ksp.ktn.mit.pḥ]m. | [mit.iqni.l ḫbrtn]r ṯn. | [k 64[118].34
[mit.iqni.l]ḫbrtn[r]. | [ks.ksp.ktn.mit.pḥ]m. | [mit.iqni.l ḫbrtn]r ṯn. | [ks.ksp.ktn.mit.pḥm]. | [mit.iqn]i.l skl.[--]. | [---. 64[118].36
m.l.gzzm. | kd yn.l.ḫtn.w.kd.ḥmṣ.w.[lt]ḥ.ʿšdm. | kd yn.l.ḫdǵb.w.kd.ḥmṣ. | prš.glbm.l.bt. | tgmǵ.kšmm.b.yrḫ.iṯtbnm. 1099.28
l.trbnn. | ddm.šʿrm.l.ḫtn. | dd.šʿrm.l.ḥmr.ḥṭb. | dd.ḥṭm.l.ḫdǵb. | ṯṯ.ddm.l.gzzm. | kd yn.l.ḫtn.w.kd.ḥmṣ.w.[lt]ḥ.ʿšdm. 1099.25
ṯṯ[.l.]mštt[.---]. | ṯlṯ.l.mdr[ǵlm]. | kd[.--].lm[d.---]. | kd[.l.]ḫzr[m.---]. | kd[.l.]ṯrtn[m]. | arbʿ l.mry[nm]. | kdm l.ḫty.[--- 1091.6
gpr h.šr. | aqht.yʿn.kmr.kmr[.--]. | k apʿ.il.b gdrt.k lb.l | ḥṯ h.imḫṣ h.k d.ʿl.qšt h. | imḫṣ h.ʿl.qṣʿt h.hwt. | l aḥw.ap.q 19[1AQHT].1.13
rtn.w.ṯṯ.mat.brr. | b.ṯmnym.ksp.ṯlṯt.kbd. | ḥmš.alp.ṯlṯ.l.ḫlby. | b d.tlmi.b.ʿšrm.ḥmšt. | kbd.ksp. | kkrm.šʿrt.štt.b d.gg[2101.6
.[kps]lnm. | arbʿ.mat[.arb]ʿm.[k]bd. | d ntn.d.ksp. | arbʿ.l.ḫlby. | [---].l.bt. | arbʿ.l.kpslnm. | kdm.b[t.]mlk. 1087.4
id ydbḥ mlk. | l ušḫ[r] ḫlmṭ. | l bbt il bt. | š l ḫlmṭ. | w tr l qlḥ. | w š ḥll ydm. | b qdš il bt. | w tlḥm aṯt. | š l UG5.7.TR3
tqtm. | bm.nšq.w hr.[b]ḥbq.w ḥ[m]ḥmt.ytb[n]. | yspr.l ḥmš.l ṣ[---.]šr.pḫr.klat. | tqtnṣn.w tldn.tld.[ilm.]nʿmm.agzr 23[52].57
l ḥmš.mrkbt.ḥmš.ʿšr h.prs. | bt.mrkbt.w l šant.ṯṯ. | l bt.ʿšrm. | 2105.1
[š]. | ilš.ngr bt bʿl. | w aṯt k.ngrt.il[ht]. | ʿl.l ṯkm.bnw n. | l nḫnpt.mšpy. | ṯlṯ.kmm.ṯrr y. | [---.]l ǵr.gm.ṣḥ. | [---.]r[-]m. 16[126].4.15
.škn. | k.[---.]sglt h.hw. | w.b[.---.]uk.ngr. | w.[---].adny.l.yḫsr. | w.[ank.yd]ʿ.l.ydʿt. | h[t.---.]l.špš.bʿl k. | ʿ[--.s]glt h.at. | 2060.9
]ššw ḫndrṯ w ṯ[qd m]r. | [ydk aḥd h w yṣq b ap h. | [k l yḫru w]l yttn mss št qlql. | [w št ʿrgz y]dk aḥd h w yṣq b a 160[55].8
šw.ḫndrṯ]. | w.ṯ[qd.mr.ydk.aḥd h]. | w.y[ṣq.b.ap h]. | k.l.ḫ[ru.w.l.yttn.ššw]. | mss.[št.qlql.w.št]. | ʿrgz[.ydk.aḥd h]. | w 161[56].8
mštt.mlk. | kd.bn.amht [-]t. | w.bn.mṣrym. | arbʿm.yn. | l.ḫrd. | ḫmšm.ḫmš. | kbd.tgmr. | yn.d.nkly. 1089.12
[---.-]ḥ[-]. | [---.--]r. | [---.--]ṣ. | [-----]. | [--]lm.aḥd. | [--]l.l ḥr[-.---]. | [--]m.dt nšu. | [---.]d[--.---]. | [---.--]m aḥ[d]. | [-----] 156[-].6
kd.bt ilm. | rbm. | kd l ištnm. | kd l ḫty. | maḫdh. | kd l kblbn. | kdm.mṭḫ. | l.alṯy. | kd.l mrynm. | 1090.4
d[.l.]ḫzr[m.---]. | kd[.l.]ṯrtn[m]. | arbʿ l.mry[nm]. | kdm l.ḫty.[---]. | kdm l.ʿṯr[t]. | kd l m[d]rǵl[m]. | kd l.mryn[m]. 1091.9
spr.ḥpr.bt.k[--]. | tšʿ.ʿšr h.dd.l.b[t.--]. | ḥmš.ddm.l.ḫtyt. | ṯlṯm.dd.kšmn.l.gzzm. | yyn. | ṣdqn. | ʿbd.pdr. | myṣm. | 1099.3
.lmd h. | ʿdršp. | w.lmd h. | krwn b.gt.nbk. | ddm.kšmm.l.ḫtn. | ddm.l.trbnn. | ddm.šʿrm.l.trbnn. | ddm.šʿrm.l.ḫtn. | dd. 1099.20
m.l.ḫtn. | ddm.l.trbnn. | ddm.šʿrm.l.ḫtn. | dd.šʿrm.l.ḥmr.ḥṭb. | dd.ḥṭm.l.ḫdǵb. | ṯṯ.ddm.l.gzzm. | k 1099.23
rm.l.ḥmr.ḥṭb. | dd.ḥṭm.l.ḫdǵb. | ṯṯ.ddm.l.gzzm. | kd yn.l.ḫtn.w.kd.ḥmṣ.w.[lt]ḥ.ʿšdm. | kd yn.l.ḫdǵb.w.kd.ḥmṣ. | prš.g 1099.27
]. | šd dd h ḥrnqm.w | yʿn ḥrḫb mlk qẓ [l]. | nʿmn.ilm l ḥt[n]. | m.bʿl trḫ pdry b[t h]. | aqrb k ab h bʿ[l]. | yǵtr.ʿṯtr t | r 24[77].25
.yn.d.l.ṭb. | b.gt.mʿrby. | ṯṯm.yn.ṭb.w.ḫmš.l.ʿšrm. | yn.d.l.ṭb.b.ulm. | mit.yn.ṭb.w.ṯṯm.ṯṯ.kbd. | yn.d.l.ṭb.b.gt.ḥdṯt. | tšʿm 1084.10
].yn.b gt[.-]n. | arbʿm.kbd.yn.ṭb.w.[--]. | ṯmn.kbd.yn.d.l.ṭb.b.gnʿ[y]. | mitm.yn.ḥsp.d.nkly.b.db[ḫ.--]. | mit.arbʿm.kbd 1084.23
m.k[dm.]kbd.yn.d.l.ṭb. | b.gt.gwl. | ṯlṯm.tšʿ[.kbd.yn].d.l[.ṭb].b.gt.iptl. | ṯmnym.[yn].ṭb.b.gt.š[---]. | tšʿm.[ḫ]mš[.kbd]. 1084.19
ǵy. | arbʿm.kdm.kbd.yn.ṭb. | w.ḫmšm.k[dm.]kbd.yn.d.l.ṭb. | b.gt.gwl. | ṯlṯm.tšʿ[.kbd.yn].d.l[.ṭb].b.gt.iptl. | ṯmnym.[y 1084.17
l.ʿšrm. | yn.d.l.ṭb.b.ulm. | mit.yn.ṭb.w.ṯṯm.ṯṯ.kbd. | yn.d.l.ṭb.b.gt.ḥdṯt. | tšʿm.yn.d.l.ṭb.b.zbl. | ʿšrm.yn.ṭb.w.ṯṯm.ḫmš.k[1084.12
.d.l.ṭb.gt.ṭbq. | mit.ʿšr.kbd.yn.ṭb. | w.ṯṯm.arbʿ.kbd.yn.d.l.ṭb. | b.gt.mʿrby. | ṯṯm.yn.ṭb.w.ḫmš.l.ʿšrm. | yn.d.l.ṭb.b.ulm. | 1084.7
ʿm.yn.d.l.ṭb.b.zbl. | ʿšrm.yn.ṭb.w.ṯṯm.ḫmš.k[b]d. | yn.d.l.ṭb.b.gt.sǵy. | arbʿm.kdm.kbd.yn.ṭb. | w.ḫmšm.k[dm.]kbd.yn 1084.15
it.yn.ṭb.w.ṯṯm.ṯṯ.kbd. | yn.d.l.ṭb.b.gt.ḥdṯt. | tšʿm.yn.d.l.ṭb.b.zbl. | ʿšrm.yn.ṭb.w.ṯṯm.ḫmš.k[b]d. | yn.d.l.ṭb.b.gt.sǵy. | 1084.13
.yn.ḫlq.b.gt.sknm. | ʿšr.yn.ṭb.w.arbʿm.ḫmš.kbd. | yn.d.l.ṭb.gt.ṭbq. | mit.ʿšr.kbd.yn.ṭb. | w.ṯṯm.arbʿ.kbd.yn.d.l.ṭb. | b.g 1084.5
ḫmš.ʿšr.yn.ṭb. | w.tšʿm.kdm.kbd.yn.d.l.ṭb. | w.arbʿm.yn.ḫlq.b.gt.sknm. | ʿšr.yn.ṭb.w.arbʿm.ḫmš.kbd 1084.2
.w lk[.---]. | [--]ṯ.lk[.---]. | [--]kṯ.i[---.---]. | p.šn[-.---]. | w l ṯlb.[---]. | mit.rḥ[.---]. | ṯṯlb.a[--.---]. | yšu.g h[.---]. | i.ap.bʿ[l.- 5[67].4.2
t.dt. | [---.]šbʿ.l šbʿm.aṯr. | [---.--]ldm.dt ymtm. | [--.--]r.l ẓpn. | [---.]pn.ym.y[--]. | [---].bʿl.tdd. | [---.]hkl. | [---.]yd h. | [- 25[136].5
hm.tphn.mlak.ym.tʿdt.ṯpṭ[.nhr]. | t[ǵ]ly.hlm.rišt hm.l ẓr.brkt hm.w l kḥṯ. | zbl hm.b hm.ygʿr.bʿl.lm.ǵltm.ilm.rišt. 2.1[137].23
km.w ank.ʿny.mlak.ym.tʿdt.ṯpṭ.nhr. | tšu ilm rašt hm.l ẓr.brkt hm.ln.kḥṯ.zbl hm. | aḫr.tmǵyn.mlak ym.tʿdt.ṯpṭ.nh 2.1[137].29
.w l kḥṯ. | zbl hm.b hm.ygʿr.bʿl.lm.ǵltm.ilm.rišt. | km l ẓr brkt km.w ln.kḥṯ.zbl km.aḥd. | ilm.tʿny lḥt.mlak.ym.tʿd 2.1[137].25

d.|ilm.t'ny lḥt.mlak.ym.t'dt.ṯpṭ.nhr.|šu.ilm.rašt km.l ẓr.brkt km.ln.kḥṯ.|zbl km.w ank.'ny.mlak.ym.t'dt.ṯpṭ.nhr 2.1[137].27
|qḥ.ms[rr.]'ṣr.|dbḥ.ṣ[q.b g]l.ḥtṯ.|yn.b gl[.ḫ]rṣ.nbt.|'l.l ẓr.[mg]dl.|w 'l.l ẓr.[mg]dl.rkb.|ṯkmm.ḥm[t].ša.yd k.|šm 14[KRT].2.73
ḥ.msrr.'ṣr.db[ḥ].|yṣq.b gl.ḥtṯ.yn.|b gl.ḫrṣ.nbt.w 'ly.|l ẓr.mgdl.rkb.|ṯkmm.ḥmt.nša.|[y]d h.šmmh.dbḥ.|l ṯr.ab h. 14[KRT].4.166
bḥ.ṣ[q.b g]l.ḥtṯ.|yn.b gl[.ḫ]rṣ.nbt.|'l.l ẓr.[mg]dl.|w 'l.l ẓr.[mg]dl.rkb.|ṯkmm.ḥm[t].ša.yd k.|šmm.dbḥ.l ṯr.|ab k.il 14[KRT].2.74
.b gn.|bm.nrt.ksmm.|'l.tl[-]k.'ṭrṭrm.|nšu.[r]iš.ḥrṯm.|l ẓr.'db.dgn kly.|lḥm.[b]'dn hm.kly.|yn.b ḥmt hm.k[l]y.|š 16[126].3.13
t'.md h.b ym.ṯn.|npyn h.b nhrm.|štt.ḫptr.l išt.|ḫbrt.l ẓr.pḥmm.|t'pp.ṯr.il.d pid.|tǵẓy.bny.bnwt.|b nši.'n h.w tp 4[51].2.9
.uḫryt.mh.yqḥ.|mh.yqḥ.mt.aṯryt.spsg.ysk.|[l]riš.ḥrṣ.l ẓr.qdqd y.|[--.]mt.kl.amt.w an.mtm.amt.|[ap.m]ṯn.rgmm. 17[2AQHT].6.37
trǵzz.|'m.ǵr.ṯrmg.|'m.tlm.ǵṣr.arṣ.|ša.ǵr.'l.ydm.|ḫlb.l ẓr.rḥtm.|w rd.bt ḫpṯt.|arṣ.tspr.b y|rdm.arṣ.|idk.al.ttn.|p 4[51].8.6
.bt.rb.idk.|pn k.al ttn.tk.ǵr.|knkny.ša.ǵr.'l ydm.|ḫlb.l ẓr.rḥtm w rd.|bt ḫpṯt.arṣ.tspr b y|rdm.arṣ.w td' ilm.|k m 5[67].5.14
tn.|šṗḥ.lṯpn.l yḥ.|w y'ny.krt.ṯ'.|bn.al.tbkn.al.|tdm.l y.al tkl.bn.|qr.'n k.mḫ.riš k.|udm't.ṣḥ.aḫt k.|ṯtmnt.bt.ḥm 16.1[125].26
tšb'.bk.|tšt.k yn.udm't.gm.|tṣḥ.l nrt.ilm.špš.|'ms m'.l y.aliyn.b'l.|tšm'.nrt.ilm.špš.|tšu.aliyn.b'l.l ktp.|'nt.k tšt h 6[62].1.12
.w rgm[.---].|w yrdnn.an[--.---].|[---].ank.l km[.---].|l y.ank.aššu[.---.]w[.---].|w hm.at.tr[gm.---].|w.drm.'tr[--.-- 54.1.17[13.2.2]
n[y].|kll.šlm.|ṯm ny.'m.um y.|mnm.šlm.|w.rgm.ṯṯb.l y.|bm.ṯy.ndr.|iṯt.'mn.mlkt.|w.rgm y.l[--].|lqt.w.pn.|mlk. 50[117].13
m.w.at.|nǵṯ.w.ytn.hm.l k.|w.lḥt.alpm.ḫršm.|k.rgmt.l y.bly m.|alpm.aršt.l k.w.l y.|mn.bnš.d.l.i[--].'[m k].|l.alp 2064.22
'bṣ k.'m y.p'n k.tls]|[m]n 'm y t[wtḥ.išd k.dm.rgm.iṯ.l y.d argmn k].|[h]wt.d aṯ[ny k.---.rgm.'ṣ].|w lḫšt.abn[.tant 7.2[130].17
.|w.ṯm [ny.'m.mlkt.u]m y.|mnm[.šlm].|w.rgm[.ṯṯb.l] y.|hl ny.'mn.|mlk.b.ṯy ndr.|iṯt.w.ht.|[-]sny.udr h.|w.hm 1013.11
d.'l.qšt h.|imḫṣ h.'l.qṣ't h.hwt.|l aḥw.ap.qšt h.l ttn.|l y.w b mt[.-]ḥ.mṣṣ[-]t[.--].|pr'.qẓ.y[bl].šblt.|b ǵlp h.apnk.d 19[1AQHT].1.17
[ny].|kll.šlm.ṯm ny.|'m.um y.mnm.šlm.|w.rgm.ṯṯb.l y.|w.mnd'.k.ank.|aḥš.mǵy.mnd'.|k.igr.w.u.[--].|'m.špš.[- 2009.1.9
.klt].|knyt.w t'n[.btlt.'nt].|ytb l y.ṯr.il[.ab y.---].|ytb.l y.w l h.[---].|[--.i]mṣḫ.nn.k imr.l arṣ.|[ašhlk].šbt h.dmm.š 3['NT.VI].4.8
.|[---]m.tṣḥq.'nt.w b lb.tqny.|[---.]tb l y.l aqht.ǵzr.ṯb l y w l k.|[---]m.l aqry k.b ntb.pš'.|[---].b ntb.gan.ašql k.tḥt 17[2AQHT].6.42
ṣ k.'m y.p'n k.|[tls]mn.['m y.twtḥ.išd k.|[dm.rgm.iṯ.l y.]w argm k.hwt.|[w aṯny k.rgm.]'ṣ.w lḫšt.|[abn.rgm.l td] 3['NT].4.57
m y twtḥ.i[šd k.tk.ḫršn.-------------].|ǵr.ks.dm.r[gm.iṯ.l y.]w argm k].|hwt.w aṯny k[.rgm.'ṣ.w lḫšt.abn].|tunt.šmm 1['NT.IX].3.12
.'bṣ k.|'m y.p'n k.tlsmn.'m y.|twtḥ.išd k.dm.rgm.|iṯ.l y.w argm k.|hwt.w aṯny k.rgm.|'ṣ.w lḫšt.abn.|tant.šmm.' 3['NT].3.18
'lgt.b lšn[y].|ǵr[.---]b.b pš y.t[--].|hwt.b'l.iš[--].|šm' l y.ypš.[---].|ḥkr[.---].|'ṣr[.--.]tb[-].|ṭat[.---].|yn[-.---].|i[--.-- 2124.5
.w yṣḥ.aṯbn.ank.|w anḫn.w tnḫ.b irt y.|npš.k yld.bn.l y.km.|aḫ l y.w šrš.km ary y.|nṣb.skn.ilib y.b qdš.|ztr.'m y. 17[2AQHT].2.14
k.w y'n[.'ṯtr].dm[-]k[-].|[--]ḥ.b y.ṯr.il.ab y.ank.in.bt[.l] y[.km.]ilm[.w] ḥẓr[.k bn].|[qd]š.lbum.trd.b n[p]šn y.trḥṣ 2.3[129].19
rm.ht.tṣdn.tinṯt.|[---]m.tṣḥq.'nt.w b lb.tqny.|[---.]tb l y.l aqht.ǵzr.ṯb l y w l k.|[---]m.l aqry k.b ntb.pš'.|[---].b nt 17[2AQHT].6.42
yn.|l mlkytn.|ḥnn y l pn mlk.|šin k itn.|r' y šṣa idn l y.|l šmn iṯr hw.|p iḫdn gnryn.|im mlkytn yrgm.|aḥnnn.| 1020.5
[---].ap[.---].|[---].l y.l [---].|[---] ny.ṯp[--.---].|[---.--]zn.a[--.---].|[---.--]y.ns[--.- 63[26].1.2
|w.lḥt.alpm.ḫršm.|k.rgmt.l y.bly m.|alpm.aršt.l k.w.l y.|mn.bnš.d.l.i[--].'[m k].|l.alpm.w.l.y[n.--]t.|w.bl.bnš.hw 2064.23
.sswm.|mrkbt.b trbṣ.|bn.amt.p d.[i]n.|b bt y.ttn.tn.|l y.mṯt.ḥry.|n'mt.šbḥ.bkr k.|d k n'm.'nt.|n'm h.km.tsm.|'ṯ 14[KRT].6.289
ṯlṯ.sswm.mrkbt.|b trbṣt.bn.amt.|p d.in.b bt y.ttn.|tn.l y.mṯt.ḥry.|n'mt.špḥ.bkr k.|d k.n'm.'nt.n'm h.|km.tsm.'ṯt 14[KRT].3.143
.|rgmt.'ly.ṯh.lm.|l.ytn.hm.mlk.[b]'l y.|w.hn.ibm.šṣq l y.|p.l.ašt.aṯt y.|n'r y.ṯh.l pn.ib.|hn.hm.yrgm.mlk.|b'l y.t 1012.27
'ryt k.k qlt[.---].|[--]at.brt.lb k.'nn.[---].|[--.]šdq.k ttn.l y.šn[.---].|[---.]bn.rgm.w yd'[.---]. 60[32].5
b.arṣy].|bt.y'bdr[.mṯb.klt].|knyt.w t'n[.btlt.'nt].|ytb l y.ṯr.il[.ab y.---].|ytb.l y.w l h.[---].|[--.i]mṣḫ.nn.k imr.l arṣ. 3['NT.VI].4.7
.|udm't.ṣḥ.aḫt k.|ṯtmnt.bt.ḥmḥ h.|d[-]n.tbkn.w tdm.l y.[--].|[---].al.trgm.l aḫt k.|[---.]l [ ]dm.aḫt k.|yd't.k rḥmt 16.1[125].30
.w ygl.w ynsk.'[-].|[--]y.l arṣ[.id]y.alt.l aḥš.idy.alt.in l y.|[--]t.b'l.ḥẓ.ršp.b[n].km.yr.klyt h.w lb h.|[ṯ]n.p k.b ǵr.ṯn 1001.1.2
-]y.|w.spr.in[.-.]'d m.|spr n.ṯhr[.--].|aṯr.iṯ.bqṯ.|w.štn.l y. 2060.35
š tpnr.|arb'.spm.l.lbnš prwsdy.|ṯṯ spm.l bnš klnmw.|l yarš ḫswn.|ḫmš 'šr.sp.|l bnš tpnr d yaḫd l g ynm.|ṯṯ spm 137.2[93].9
l.yi[--.-]m[---].|b unṯ.km.špš.|d brt.kmt.|br.ṣṯqšlm.|b unṯ.' 1001.1.18
l yblt.ḫbṭm.|ap ksp hm.|l yblt.|w ht.luk 'm ml[kt].|tǵsdb.šmlšn.|w tb' ank.|'m mla 1021.3
l yblt.ḫbṭm.|ap ksp hm.|l yblt.|w ht.luk 'm ml[kt].|tǵsdb.š 1021.1
[---.]arḫt.tld[n].|a[lp].l btlt.'nt.|w ypt l ybmt.li[mm].|w y'ny.aliyn[.b'l].|lm.k qnym.'l[m.--].|k dr 10[76].3.4
bt.ṯr.adr.b ǵlil.qnm.|tn.l kṯr.w ḫss.yb'l.qšt l 'nt.|qṣ't.l ybmt.limm.w t'n.btlt.|'nt.irš ḥym.l aqht.ǵzr.|irš ḥym.w a 17[2AQHT].6.25
t.ṯly.bt.rb.dd].|arṣy bt.y['bdr.---].|rgm l btl[t.'nt.ṯny.l ybmt.limm.tḥm.aliyn.b'l].|hw[t.aliy.qrdm.qryy.b arṣ.mlḥ 7.2[130].13
n.'nt.hbr.|w ql.tštḥwy.kbd hyt.|w rgm.l btlt.'nt.|ṯny.l ymmt.limm.|tḥm.aliyn.b'l.hwt.|aliy.qrdm.qry.b arṣ.|mlḥ 3['NT].3.9
l.ybnn.|adn y.|rgm.|tḥm.t[g]yn.|bn k.|l.p['n.adn y].|q[lt.- 2115.1.1
n y.|rgm.|tḥm.t[g]yn.|bn k.|l.p['n.adn y].|q[lt.---].|l.yb[nn].|b'l y.r[gm].|tḥm.'bd[--].|'bd k.|l p'n.b'l y.|ṯn id.š 2115.2.1
.|ṯmn.ṣmd.[---].|b d.b'lsr.|yd.ṯdn.'šr.|[ḥ]mrm.|ddm.l.ybr[k].|bdmr.prs.l.u[-]m[-].|ṯmn.l.'šrm.|dmd.b d.mry[n] 2102.6
[--.l k]|ṯrt.l bnt.hll[.snnt].|hl ǵlmt tld b[n.--]n.|'n ha l yd h.tzd[.--].|pt l bšr h.dm a[--.--]ḥ.|w yn.k mtrḫt[.---]h. 24[77].8
-.--]ḥ.|w yn.k mtrḫt[.---]h.|šm' ilht kṯr[t.--]mm.|nh l yd h tzdn[.---]n.|l ad[n h.---].|dgn tt[--.---.-]l|'.l kṯrt hl[l.s 24[77].12
u bl mlk.|arṣ.drkt.yštkn.|dll.al.ilak.l bn.|ilm.mt.'dd.l ydd.|il.ǵzr.yqra.mt.|b npš h.ystrn ydd.|b gngn h.aḥd y.d 4[51].7.46
n.aliyn.b'l.|ṯt'.nn.rkb.'rpt.|tb'.rgm.l bn.ilm.mt.|ṯny.l ydd.il ǵzr.|tḥm.aliyn.b'l.hwt.aliy.|qrdm.bḥt.l bn.ilm mt.| 5[67].2.9
r.w ql.|tštḥwy.w k|bd hwt.w rgm.|l bn.ilm.mt.|ṯny.l ydd.|il.ǵzr.tḥm.|aliyn.b'l.|[hw]t.aliy.q|[rdm.]bht y.bnt.|[4[51].8.31
spr.rpš d l y[dy].|atlg.|ulm.|izly.|uḫnp.|bn sḫrn.|m'qb.|tpn.|m'r.| 2075.1
y.šqlt.|b ǵlt.yd k.l tdn.|dn.almnt.l ṯpṭ.|ṯpṭ qṣr.npš.l tdy.|ṯšm.'l.dl.l pn k.|l tšlḥm.ytm.b'd.|ksl k.almnt.km.|aḫ 16.6[127].47
l.k[-]w.ḫpn.|l.ṣ[--].š'[rt].|l.'dy.š[']r[t].|ṯlṯ.l.'d.ab[ǵ]l.|l.ydln.š'rt.|l.kṯrmlk.ḫpn.|l.'bdil[m].ḫpn.|tmrtn.š'rt.|lmd.n 1117.8
[---.]š[--].|w ym ym.yš|al.|w mlk.d mlk.|b ḥwt.špḥ.|l ydn.'bd.mlk.|d št.'l.ḫrd h.|špḥ.al.thbṭ.|ḫrd.'ps.aḫd.kw|s 2062.2.3
dm.l.urtn.|kdm.l.ilšpš.|kd.l.anntb.|kd.l.iwrmd.|kd.l.ydn.|[---.y]rḫ.ḫyr.|[---.]yn.l.mlkt.|[---.yrḫ.]ḫlt.šb'.[---].ml 1088.9
[---.]btlt.'nt.|[---.]pp.hrm.|[---].d l yd' bn il.|[---.]pḫr kkbm.|[---.]dr dt.šmm.|[---.al]iyn b'l.|[10[76].1.3
km.[---.]yqṯqṭ.tḥt.|ṯlḥnt.il.d yd'nn.|y'db.lḥm.l h.w d l yd'nn.|d.mṣd.|ylmn.ḫt.tḥt.ṯlḥn.|b qr'.|'ṯtrt.w 'nt.ymǵy.|' UG5.1.1.7
]bl.am..|rkm.agzrt[.--].arḫ..|b'l.azrt.'nt.[-]ld.|kbd h.l yd' hr h.[---]d[-].|tnq[.---.]in[b]b.p'r.|yd h[.--.]ṣ'r.glgl.|a[- 13[6].31
w.|w.b[.---.]uk.nǵr.|w.[---].adny.l.yḫsr.|w.[ank.yd]'.l.yd't.|h[t.---.]l.špš.b'l k.|'[--.s]glt h.at.|ht[.---.]špš.b'l k.|yd 2060.10

ṯk[.--]np bl.hn. | [---].ḥ[m]t.pṭr.w.p nḥš. | [---.--]q.n[ṯ]k.l yd‘.l bn.l pq ḥmt. | [---.--]n h.ḥmt.w t‘btn h.abd y. | [---.ǵ]r.š UG5.8.35

.]w argm k.hwt. | [w aṯny k.rgm.]‘ṣ.w lḫšt. | [abn.rgm.l td]‘.nš[m.w l t]bn. | [hmlt.a]rṣ.[tant.šmm.‘m.ar]ṣ. | thmt.[‘ 3[‘NT].4.59

‘m.arṣ. | thmt.‘mn.kbkbm. | abn.brq.d l.td‘.šmm. | rgm l td‘.nšm.w l tbn. | hmlt.arṣ.at m.w ank. | ibǵy h.b tk.ǵr y.il.ṣ 3[‘NT].3.24

lḫšt.abn]. | tunt.šmm.‘m[.arṣ.thmt.‘mn.kbkbm]. | rgm.l td‘.nš[m.w l tbn.hmlt.arṣ]. | at.w ank.ib[ǵy h.---]. | w y‘n.kṯ 1[‘NT.IX].3.15

.---.]l.špš.b‘l k. | ‘[--.s]glt h.at. | ht[.---.]špš.b‘l k. | yd‘m.l.yd‘t. | ‘m y.špš.b‘l k. | šnt.šntm.lm.l.tlk. | w.lḥt.akl.ky. | likt.‘ 2060.14

rṣ.[tant.šmm.‘m.ar]ṣ. | thmt.[‘mn.kbkbm.abn.brq]. | d l t[d‘.šmm.at m.w ank]. | ibǵ[y h.b tk.ǵ]r y.il.ṣpn. | b q[dš.b ǵ 3[‘NT].4.62

t.abn[.tant.šmm.‘m.arṣ.thmt]. | ‘m kbkbm[.abn.brq.d l td‘.šmm.at m]. | w ank.ib[ǵy h.---]. | [-].l y‘mdn.i[---.---]. | kp 7.2[130].20

.abn. | tant.šmm.‘m.arṣ. | thmt.‘mn.kbkbm. | abn.brq.d l.td‘.šmm. | rgm l td‘.nšm.w l tbn. | hmlt.arṣ.at m.w ank. | ibǵ 3[‘NT].3.23

k b ṣpn. | [---.]išqb.aylt. | [---.--]m.b km.y‘n. | [---].yd‘.l yd‘t. | [---.]tasrn.ṯr il. | [---.]rks.bn.abnm. | [---.]upqt.‘rb. | [--- 1[‘NT.X].5.21

h. | [---].b ṣpn. | [---].nšb.b ‘n. | [---.]b km.y‘n. | [---.yd‘.l] yd‘t. | [---.t]asrn. | [---.]trks. | [---.]abnm.upqt. | [---.]l w ǵr m 1[‘NT.X].5.8

[-]m. | b.ṭbq.arb‘m.dr‘.w.‘šr.dd.drt. | w[.a]rb‘.l.‘šrm.dd.l.yḥšr.bl.bn h. | b.gt.m‘br.arb‘m.l.mit.dr‘.w.ṯmnym[.drt]. | w. 1098.11

inš.šdm l m‘[rb]. | nrt.ilm.špš.mǵy[t]. | pǵt.l ahlm.rgm.l yṭ[pn.y] | bl.agrtn.bat.b ḏd k.[pǵt]. | bat.b hlm w y‘n.yṭpn[. 19[1AQHT].4.212

--]. | [---.-]dm.mlak.ym.t‘dt.ṯpṭ.nh[r.---]. | [---].an.rgmt.l ym.b‘l km.ad[n km.ṯpṭ]. | [nhr.---.]hwt.gmr.hd.l wny[-.---]. 2.1[137].45

l ym hnd. | iwr[k]l.pdy. | agdn.bn.nrgn. | w ynḥm.aḫ h. | w.b‘l 1006.1

l ym hnd. | ‘mṯtmr.bn. | nqmp‘.ml[k]. | ugrt.ytn. | šd.kḏǵdl[.b 1008.1

l ym.hnd. | ‘mṯtmr. | bn.nqmp‘. | mlk.ugrt. | ytn.bt.annḏr. | bn. 1009.1

.ymṣḫ.l arṣ. | [yṯb.]b[‘]l.l ksi.mlk h. | [---].l kḥṯ.drkt h. | l [ym]m.l yrḫm.l yrḫm. | l šnt.[m]k.b šb‘. | šnt.w [--].bn.ilm. 6[49].5.7

h. | pẓǵm.ǵr.ybk.l aqht. | ǵzr.ydm‘.l kdd.dnil. | mt.rpi.l ymm.l yrḫm. | l yrḫm.l šnt.‘d. | šb‘t.šnt.ybk.l aq | ht.ǵzr.yd[19[1AQHT].4.175

m.špš.ṣḥrrt. | la.šmm.b yd.bn ilm.mt. | ym.ymm.y‘tqn.l ymm. | l yrḫm.rḥm.‘nt.tngṯ h. | k lb.arḫ.l ‘gl h.k lb. | ṯat.l im 6[49].2.26

w ḫss. | št.alp.qdm h.mra. | w tk.pn h.t‘db.ksu. | w yṯṯb.l ymn.aliyn. | b‘l.‘d.lḥm.št[y.ilm]. | [w]y‘n.aliy[n.b‘l]. | [--]b[.- 4[51].5.109

alpm.aršt.l k.w.l y. | mn.bnš.d.l.i[--].‘[m k]. | l.alpm.w.l.y[n.--]t. | w.bl.bnš.hw[-.--]y. | w.k.at.trg[m.--]. | w.[---]n.w.s[2064.25

dln.‘r. | bkm.tṣmd.pḥl.bkm. | tšu.ab h.tštnn.l[b]mt ‘r. | l ysmsm.bmt.pḥl. | y dnil.ysb.palt h. | bṣql.yph.b palt.bṣ[q]l. | 19[1AQHT].2.60

‘db.gpn.atnt h. | yḥbq.qdš.w amrr. | yštn.aṯrt.l bmt.‘r. | l ysmsmt.bmt.pḥl. | qdš.yuḫdm.šb‘r. | amrr.k kbkb.l pnm. | aṯ 4[51].4.15

n. | [---]l[.---.]‘d. | ksm.mhyt[.m]ǵny. | l n‘m y.arṣ.dbr. | l ysmt.šd.šḥlmmt. | mǵny.l b‘l.npl.l a | rṣ.mt.aliyn.b‘l. | ḫlq.zb 5[67].6.7

bn.aṯrt. | w t‘n.rbt.aṯrt ym. | rbt.ilm.l ḥkmt. | šbt.dqn k.l tsr k. | rḫntt.d[-].l irt k. | wn ap.‘dn.mṭr h. | b‘l.y‘dn.‘dn.ṯkt. 4[51].5.66

[-----]. | [--.]l tṣi.b b[--].bm.k[--]. | [--]ṯb.‘ryt k.k qlt[.---]. | [--]at.brt.lb k.‘n 60[32].2

.tisp k.yd.aqht.ǵz[r]. | tšt k.bm.qrb m.asm. | b p h.rgm.l yṣa.b špt h[.hwt h]. | b nši ‘n h.w tphn.in.[---]. | [-.]hlk.ǵlm 19[1AQHT].2.75

ṯ]. | ‘ẓm.abky.w aqbrn h. | ašt.b ḫrt.ilm.arṣ. | b p h.rgm.l yṣa.b špt h.hwt[h]. | knp.nšrm.b‘l.yṯbr. | b‘l.ṯbr.diy hmt.tql 19[1AQHT].3.113

.iṯ[.‘ẓm]. | abky.w aqbrn.ašt.b ḫrt. | i[lm.arṣ.b p h.rgm.l yṣa.b šp] | t h.hwt h.knp.hrgb.b‘l.ṯbr. | b‘l.ṯbr.diy.hwt.w yql 19[1AQHT].3.127

iṯ. | ‘ẓm.abky w aqbrn h.aštn. | b ḫrt.ilm.arṣ.b p h.rgm.l[yṣ]a. | b špt h.hwt h.knp.ṣml.b‘[l]. | b‘l.ṯbr.diy.hyt.tq[l.tḥt]. 19[1AQHT].3.141

. | ‘šrt.ḫrṣ.b.arb‘m. | mit.ḫršḫ.b.ṯqlm. | w.šb‘.‘šr.šmn. | d.l.yṣa.bt.mlk. | tgmr.ksp.mitm. | ḫmšm.kbd. 2100.21

.w tphn.in.[---]. | [-.]hlk.ǵlmm b dd y.yṣ[--]. | [-.]yṣa.w l.yṣa.hlm.[ṯnm]. | [q]dqd.ṯlṯ id.‘l.ud[n]. | [---.-]sr.pdm.riš h[m 19[1AQHT].2.78

[---.]y[--].ḫtt.mtt[--]. | [--.]ḥy[--.--.]l ašṣi.hm.ap.amr[--]. | [---].w b ym.mnḫ l abd.b ym.irtm.m[- 2.4[68].2

ṯkḥ.ttrp.šmm.k rs. | ipd k.ank.ispi.uṭm. | ḏrqm.amt m.l yrt. | b npš.bn ilm.mt.b mh | mrt.ydd.il.ǵzr. | tb‘.w l.yṯb ilm. 5[67].1.6

mḥ.[---]. | mdbḥt.bt.ilt.‘ṣr[m.l ṣpn.š]. | l ǵlmt.š.w l [---.l yrḫ]. | gd[lt].l nkl[.gdlt.l b‘lt.bhtm]. | ‘š[rm.]l inš[.ilm.---]. | il 35[3].25

‘[--.---]. | mdbḥt.bt.i[lt.‘ṣrm.l]. | ṣpn š.l ǵlm[t.š.w l.---]. | l yrḫ.gdlt.l [nkl.gdlt.l b‘] | [lt].bht[m].[‘]ṣrm l [inš.ilm]. | [---.] APP.II[173].28

rṣ. | [yṯb.]b[‘]l.l ksi.mlk h. | [---].l kḥṯ.drkt h. | l [ym]m.l yrḫm.l yrḫm. | l šnt.[m]k.b šb‘. | šnt.w [--].bn.ilm.mt. | ‘m.al 6[49].5.7

m.ǵr.ybk.l aqht. | ǵzr.ydm‘.l kdd.dnil. | mt.rpi.l ymm.l yrḫm. | l yrḫm.l šnt.‘d. | šb‘t.šnt.ybk.l aq | ht.ǵzr.yd[m‘.]l kd 19[1AQHT].4.175

.]b[‘]l.l ksi.mlk h. | [---].l kḥṯ.drkt h. | l [ym]m.l yrḫm.l yrḫm. | l šnt.[m]k.b šb‘. | šnt.w [--].bn.ilm.mt. | ‘m.aliyn.b‘l. 6[49].5.7

k.l aqht. | ǵzr.ydm‘.l kdd.dnil. | mt.rpi.l ymm.l yrḫm. | l yrḫm.l šnt.‘d. | šb‘t.šnt.ybk.l aq | ht.ǵzr.yd[m‘.]l kdd. | dnil. 19[1AQHT].4.176

rrt. | la.šmm.b yd.bn ilm.mt. | ym.ymm.y‘tqn.l ymm. | l yrḫm.rḥm.‘nt.tngṯ h. | k lb.arḫ.l ‘gl h.k lb. | ṯat.l imr h.km.l 6[49].2.27

k.al.tš‘l. | qrt h.abn.yd k. | mšdpt.w hn.špšm. | b šb‘.w l.yšn.pbl. | mlk.l qr.ṯigt.ibr h. | l ql.nhqt.ḥmr h. | l g‘t.alp.ḥrṯ. 14[KRT].3.119

ym.w ṯn. | ṯlṯ.rb‘.ym. | ḫmš.ṯdṯ.ym. | mk.špšm.b šb‘. | w l.yšn.pbl. | mlk.l [qr.]ṯiqt. | ibr h[.l]ql.nhqt. | ḥmr[h.l g‘t.]alp 14[KRT].5.222

rn.l.ilšpš. | [šd.bn].kbr.l.snrn. | [---.--]k.l.gmrd. | [---.--]ṯ.l.yšn. | [šd.--]ln. | b d.trǵds. | šd.ṯ‘lb. | b d.bn.pl. | šd.bn.kt. | b d. 2030.1.8

ap]nk.krt.ṯ‘.‘[-]r. | [--.]b bt h.yšt.‘rb. | [--] h.ytn.w [--]u.l ytn. | [aḫ]r.mǵy.‘[d]t.ilm. | [w]y‘n.aliy[n.]b‘l. | [---.]tb‘.l lṭpn 15[128].2.10

.hm.[-.]aṯr[.---]. | [--]šy.w ydn.b‘[l.---]n. | [--]‘.k yn.hm.l.atn.bt y.l h. 1002.62

imr.l arṣ. | [ašhlk].šbt h.dmm.šbt.dqn h. | [mm‘m.-]d.l ytn.bt.l b‘l.k ilm. | [w ḥẓ]r.k bn.aṯrt[.td‘ṣ.]p‘n. | [w tr.a]rṣ.id 3[‘NT.VI].5.11

. | lm.škn.hnk. | l ‘bd h.alpm.š[šw]m. | rgmt.‘ly.ṯh.lm. | l.ytn.hm.mlk.[b]‘l y. | w.hn.ibm.šṣq l y. | p.l.ašt.aṯt y. | n‘r y.ṯ 1012.26

.l r‘ y.dt. | w ytnnn. | l aḫ h.l r‘ h. | r‘ ‘lm. | ttn.w tn. | w l ttn. | w al ttn. | tn ks yn. | w ištn. | ‘bd.prṯ.ṯḥm. | qrq.pṯ.ḏmn. 1019.1.13

.---]. | ank.n[--]n[.---]. | kst.l[--.---]. | w.hw.uy.‘n[--.---]. | l ytn.w rgm[.---]. | w yrdnn.an[--.---]. | [---].ank.l km[.---]. | l y 54.1.14[13.1.11]

[---.]gtn ṯṯ. | [---.]tḥr l ytn ḫs[n]. | ‘bd ulm ṯn un ḫsn. | gdy lqḥ ṣtqn gt bn ndr. | um 1154.2

-.]k. | [---].aǵwyn.‘n k.ẓẓ.w k mǵ.ilm. | [--.]k ‘ṣm.k ‘šm.l ttn.k abnm.l thggn. 1001.2.13

h[--.---]. | mlk.gb‘ h d [---]. | ibr.k l hm.d l h q[--.---]. | l ytn.l hm.tḥt b‘l[.---]. | h.u qšt pn hdd.b y[.----]. | ‘m.b ym b‘ 9[33].2.5

ḫṣ h.k d.‘l.qšt h. | imḫṣ h.‘l.qṣ‘t h.hwt. | l aḥw.ap.qšt h.l ttn. | l y.w b mt[.-]ḥ.mṣṣ[-]t[.--]. | pr‘.qẓ.y[bl].šblt. | b ǵlp h.a 19[1AQHT].1.16

n un ḫsn. | gdy lqḥ ṣtqn gt bn ndr. | um r[-] gtn ṯṯ ḫsn l ytn. | l rḥt lqḥ ṣtqn. | bt qbṣ urt ilštm‘ dbḥ ṣtqn l. | ršp. 1154.5

.l ḥ[ẓ]r y. | [-----]. | [---.ttb‘]. | [mlakm.l yṯb]. | [idk.pnm.l ytn]. | [‘]m[.krt.mswn h]. | tš[an.g hm.w tṣḥn]. | tḥ[m.pbl.ml 14[KRT].6.265

ḥ.l krk | t.w ǵlm.l ‘bd. | il.ttb‘.mlakm. | l yṯb.idk.pnm. | l ytn.‘mm.pbl. | mlk.tšan. | g hm.w tṣḥn. | tḥm.krt.ṯ[‘]. | hwt.[14[KRT].6.302

d k.tšt.b [---]. | irt k.dṯ.ydṯ.m‘qb k.[ttb‘]. | [bt]lt.‘nt.idk.l ttn.[pnm]. | [‘m.a]qht.ǵzr.b alp.š[d]. | [rbt.]kmn.w ṣḥq.btlt.[18[3AQHT].1.20

p‘n y.a]nk.n‘mn.‘mq.nšm. | [td‘ṣ.p‘n]m.w tr.arṣ.idk. | [l ttn.pn]m.‘m il.mbk.nhrm. | [qrb.ap]q.thmtm tgly.ḏd il. | [w 17[2AQHT].6.47

.b[‘l]. | [---]ḥ h.tšt bm.‘[--]. | [---.]zr h.ybm.l ilm. | [id]k.l ttn.pnm.‘m. | [il.]mbk nhrm.qrb. | [a]pq.thmtm.tgly.ḏd. | il. 6.1.32[49.1.4]

[idk.l ttn.pnm]. | [‘m.il.mbk.nhrm]. | [qrb.apq.thmtm]. | [tgly.ḏd.il 5[67].6.03

b‘l.k ilm. | [w ḥẓ]r.k bn.aṯrt[.td‘ṣ.]p‘n. | [w tr.a]rṣ.id[k.l ttn.p]nm. | [‘m.i]l.mbk.nhr[m.qr]b.[ap]q. | [thm]tm.tgl.ḏ[d.] 3[‘NT.VI].5.13

.k kbkb.l pnm. | aṯr.btlt.‘nt. | w b‘l.tb‘.mrym.ṣpn. | idk.l ttn.pnm. | ‘m.il.mbk.nhrm. | qrb.apq.thmtm. | tgly.ḏd.il.w t 4[51].4.20

].|[ilnym.ṯn.mṯpd]m.t[ḥt.ʿnt.arṣ.ṯlṯ.mtḥ.ǵyrm].|[idk.]l ytn.pnm.ʿm.[i]l.mbk.[nhrm.qrb.apq.thmtm].|[ygly.]ḏl i[l]. 2.3[129].4
.l bn.ilm mt.|ʿbd k.an.w d.ʿlm k.|tbʿ.w l.yṯb.ilm.idk.|l ytn.pn.ʿm.bn.ilm.mt.|tk.qrt h.hmry.mk.ksu.|ṯbt.ḫḫ.arṣ.n 5[67].2.14
ht.ṯhrm.iqnim.|šmḫ.btlt.ʿnt.tdʿṣ.|pʿnm.w tr.arṣ.|idk.l ttn.pnm.|ʿm.bʿl.mrym.ṣpn.|b alp.šd.rbt.kmn.|ṣḥq.btlt.ʿnt. 4[51].5.84
.bn ilm.mt.b mh|mrt.ydd.il.ǵzr.|tbʿ.w l.yṯb ilm.idk.|l ytn.pnm.ʿm.bʿl.|mrym.ṣpn.w yʿn.|gpn.w ugr.tḥm.bn ilm. 5[67].1.10
l rḥq.ilnym.ṯn.mṯpdm.|tḥt.ʿnt.arṣ.ṯlṯ.mtḥ.ǵyrm.|idk.l ttn pnm.ʿm.bʿl.|mrym.ṣpn.b alp.šd.rbt.kmn.|hlk.aḫt h.bʿl 3[ʿNT].4.81
]uṯm.ḏr[qm.---].|[btl]t.ʿnt.l kl.[---].|[tt]bʿ.btlt.ʿnt[.idk.l ttn.pnm].|ʿm.yṭpn.mhr.š[t.tšu.g h].|w tṣḥ.yṯb.yṭp.[---].|qr 18[3AQHT].4.5
ḥq.ilnym].|ṯn.mṯpdm.tḥt.[ʿnt.arṣ.ṯlṯ.mtḥ].|ǵyrm.idk.l yt[n.pnm.ʿm.lṭpn].|il d pid.tk ḥrš[n.---.tk.ǵr.ks].|ygly ḏd.i 1[ʿNT.IX].3.21
nt.mhrtt.|iy.aliyn.bʿl.|iy.zbl.bʿl.arṣ.|ttbʿ.btlt.ʿnt.|idk.l ttn.pnm.|ʿm.nrt.ilm.špš.|tšu.g h.w tṣḥ.|tḥm.ṯr.il.ab k.|h 6[49].4.31
b.hkl h.|qšt hn.aḫd.b yd h.|w qṣʿt h.bm.ymn h.|idk.l ytn pnm.|tk.aḫ.šmk.mla[t.r]umm.|tšu knp.btlt.ʿn[t].|tšu. 10[76].2.8
-]m.ʿdb.l arṣ.|[---.]špm.ʿdb.|[---].t'tqn.|[---.-]ʿb.idk.|[l ytn.pnm.tk.]in.bb.b alp ḥzr.|[rbt.kmn.l pʿ]n.ʿnt.|[yhbr.w 1[ʿNT.IX].2.14
n.pnm.trǵnw.w ttkl.|bnwt h.ykr.ʿr.d qdm.|idk.pnm.l ytn.tk aršḫ.rbt.|w aršḫ.ṯrrt.ydy.b ʿṣm.ʿrʿr.|w b šḥt.ʿs.mt.ʿr UG5.7.63
ʿnn h].|bn.dgn.arṯ m.pḏ h.tbʿ.ǵlmm.l ttb.[idk.pnm].|l ytn.tk.ǵr.ll.ʿm.phr.mʿd.ap.ilm.l lḥ[m].|yṯb.bn qdš.l ṯrm.bʿl 2.1[137].20
.|[---.]yn.l.m[--]m.|[---.]d.bn.[---.]l.dqn.|[---.--]ʿ.šdyn.l ytršn.|[---.--]ṯ.ʿbd.l.kyn.|k[rm.--.]l.i[w]rtḏl.|ḥl.d[--.ʿbd]yr 2027.2.8
k.l bt y].|[ng.kr]t.l ḥ[z]r y.|[-----].|[---.ttbʿ].|[mlakm.l yṯb].|[idk.pnm.l ytn].|[ʿ]m[.krt.mswn h].|tš[an.g hm.w tṣ 14[KRT].6.264
b.adm.|w ld.špḥ.l krk|t.w ǵlm.l ʿbd.|il.ttbʿ.mlakm.|l yṯb.idk.pnm.|l ytn.ʿmm.pbl.|mlk.tšan.|g hm.w tṣḥn.|tḥ 14[KRT].6.301
m.l yrt.|b npš.bn ilm.mt.b mh|mrt.ydd.il.ǵzr.|tbʿ.w l.yṯb ilm.idk.|l ytn.pnm.ʿm.bʿl.|mrym.ṣpn.w yʿn.|gpn.w ug 5[67].1.9
liy.|qrdm.bhṯ.l bn.ilm mt.|ʿbd k.an.w d.ʿlm k.|tbʿ.w l.yṯb.ilm.idk.|l ytn.pn.ʿm.bn.ilm.mt.|tk.qrt h.hmry.mk.ksu 5[67].2.13
]bt.[yn].|[---.]rp[.---].|[---.ḫ]br[.---].|bḫr[.--]t[.----].|l mṯb[.--]t[.---].|[tqdm.]yd.b ṣʿ.t[šl]ḥ.|[ḥrb.b]bš[r].tštn.|[w 15[128].5.6
b.|ʿl h.tšʿrb.ẓby h.|ṯr.ḫbr.rbt.|ḫbr.ṯrrt.|bt.krt.tbun.|lm.mṯb[.---].|w lḥm mr.tqdm.|yd.b ṣʿ.tšlḥ.|ḥrb.b bšr.tštn.| 15[128].4.22
mit.arbʿm.kbd.yn.ḥsp.l.m[--].|mit.ʿšrm.[k]bd.yn.ḥsp.l.y[--].|ʿšrm.yn.ḥsp.l.ql.d.tbʿ.mṣ[r]m.|mit.arbʿm.kbd.yn.mṣ 1084.26
bnšm.dt.[---].|krws.l.y[--.---].|ypʿ.l[.---].|šmr[m.---].|[-----].|bn.g[r.---].|ḏmry[.- 2122.2
[---.-]lk[.---].|[---.ʿ]šr.ym[.---].|[---].hm.l y[--.---].|[---].mṣrm[.---].|[---.--]n mkr[.---].|[---].ank.[---]. 2126.3
l.mlk.ugrt.|aḫ y.rgm.|tḥm.mlk.ṣr.aḫ k.|y[š]lm.l k.ilm.|tǵr k.tšlm k.|hn ny.ʿm n.|šlm.ṯm ny.|ʿm k.mnm[.š 2059.4
tḥm.pgn.|l.mlk.ugrt.|rgm.|yšlm.l k.[il]m.|tǵr k.tšlm k.|hn ny.ʿm n.š[l]m.|ṯm ny.ʿ[m.]bn y.| 2061.4
tḥm.mlk.|l.ṯryl.um y.rgm.|yšlm.l k.ilm.|tǵr k.tšlm k.|lḥt.šlm.k.lik[t].|um y.ʿm y.ht.ʿm[ny]. 2009.1.3
[l.ml]k.[bʿl y].|rg[m].|tḥm.wr[--].|yšlm.[l] k.|ilm.t[ǵ]r k.|tšlm k.|lm[.l.]likt.|ši[l.š]lm y.|[ʿ]d.r[-]š.|[2010.4
y[šlm.l k.ilm].|tǵ[r k.tšlm k].|ʿbd[.---]y.|ʿm[.---]y.|šk[--.--.]kll.|š 2065.1
tḥm.hl[--].|l pḫry.a[ḫ y].|w l g.p[-]r[--].|yšlm[.l k].|[i]lm[.tǵr k].|[t]š[lm k.---].|[-----].|[-----].|h[--.---].|[--- 56[21].4
l.mlk[.u]grt.|iḫ y.rgm.|[tḥ]m.m[lk.-]bl[-].|yšlm l[k].ilm.|tǵr.tšl[m] k.|[-----].|[-----].|[--].bt.gb[-.--].|[--]k[-] 2159.4
l.rb.khnm.|rgm.|tḥm.[---].|yšlm[.l k.ilm].|tšlm[k.tǵr] k.|tʿzz[k.---.]lm.|w t[--.--]ṣm k.|[----- 55[18].4
[tḥm.---].|[l.---].|[a]ḫt y.rgm.|[y]šlm.l k.|[il]m.tšlm k.|[tǵ]r k.|[--]y.ibr[-].|[--]wy.rgm l.|mlkt.u 1016.4
n w.|dbḥ kl.|kl ykly.|dbḥ k.sprt.|dt nat.|w qrwn.|l k dbḥ.|[--]r bt [--].|[--]bnš [--].|š š[--].|w [--].|d [--].|ypḫ RS61[24.277.12]
.l k.|w.lḥt.alpm.ḫršm.|k.rgmt.l y.bly m.|alpm.aršt.l k.w.l y.|mn.bnš.d.l.i[--].ʿ[m k].|l.alpm.w.l.y[n.--]t.|w.bl.b 2064.23
lk.z[--.--]n.ššwm.|nʿmm.[--].ṯtm.w.at.|nǵt.w.ytn.hm.l k.|w.lḥt.alpm.ḫršm.|k.rgmt.l y.bly m.|alpm.aršt.l k.w.l y 2064.20
.tq]ḥ.y krt.aṯt.|tqḥ.bt k.ǵlmt.tšʿrb.|ḥqr k.tld.šbʿ.bnm.l k.|w ṯmn.tṯtmnm.|l k.tld.yṣb.ǵlm.|ynq.ḥlb.a[ṯ]rt.|mṣṣ.ṯd. 15[128].2.23
m.bʿl trḫ pdry b[t h].|aqrb k ab h bʿ[l].|ygtr.ʿṯtr t|rḫ l k ybrdmy.b[t.a]|b h lb[u] yʿrr.w yʿ[n].|yrḫ nyr šmm.w nʿ[24[77].29
k.ǵlmt.tšʿrb.|ḥqr k.tld.šbʿ.bnm.l k.|w ṯmn.tṯtmnm.|l k.tld.yṣb.ǵlm.|ynq.ḥlb.a[ṯ]rt.|mṣṣ.ṯd.btlt.[ʿnt].|mšnq.[---]. 15[128].2.25
rt.|[b tk.rpi.]arṣ.|[b pḫr].qbṣ.dtn.|[w t]qrb.w ld.|bn.tl k.|tld.pǵt.t[--]t.|tld.pǵt[.---].|tld.pǵ[t.---].|tld.pǵ[t.---].|tl 15[128].3.6
q.btlt.ʿnt.tšu.|g h.w tṣḥ.tbšr bʿl.|bšrt k.yblt.y[b]n.|bt.l k.km.aḫ k.w ḥẓr.|km.ary k.ṣḥ.ḥrn.|b bht k.ʿḏbt.b qrb.|hk 4[51].5.90
y[m].|[l pn.ṯp]ṭ[.nhr.]mlkt.[--]pm.l mlkt.wn.in.aṯt.|[l]k.k[m.ilm].|[w ǵlmt.k bn.qdš.]w y[--.]zbl.ym.yʿ[--.]ṯpṭ.nh
[wt].kṯr.w ḫss.|ṣḥq.kṯr.w ḫss.|yšu.g h.w yṣḥ.|l rgmt.l k.l ali|yn.bʿl.ttbn.bʿl.|l hwt y.yptḥ.ḥ|ln.b bht m.urbt.|b q 4[51].7.23
ny.|l bʿl[-.---].|tḥt.ksi.zbl.ym.w ʿn.kṯr.w ḫss.l rgmt.|l k.l zbl.bʿl.ṯnt.l rkb.ʿrpt.ht.ib k.|bʿl m.ht.ib k.tmḫṣ.ht.tṣmt. 2.4[68].8
tḥm.iwrḏr.|l.plsy.|rgm.|yšlm.l k.|l.trǵds.|w.l.klby.|šmʿt.ḫti.|nḫtu.ht.|hm.in mm.|nḫtu. 53[54].4
.uḫry mṯ.yd h.|ymǵ.l mrrt.tǵll.b nr.|yšu.g h.w yṣḥ.y l k.mrrt.|tǵll.b nr.d ʿl k.mḫṣ.aqht.|ǵzr.šrš k.b arṣ.al.|ypʿ.ri 19[1AQHT].3.157
hqt.hmr h.|l gʿt.alp.ḥrṯ.zǵt.|klb.ṣpr.w ylak.|mlakm.l k.ʿm.krt.|mswn h.tḥm.pbl.mlk.|qḥ.ksp.w yrq.ḫrṣ.|yd.mq 14[KRT].3.124
ymǵ.l qrt.ablm.abl[m].|qrt.zbl.yrḫ.yšu g h.|w yṣḥ.y l k.qrt.ablm.|d ʿl k.mḫṣ.aqht.ǵzr.|ʿwrt.yšt k.bʿl.l ht.|w ʿlm 19[1AQHT].4.165
m.tlik.ʿm y.|ik y.aškn.|ʿṣm.l bt.dml.|p ank.atn.|ʿṣm.l k.|arbʿ.ʿṣm.|ʿl.ar.|w.ṯlṯ.|ʿl.ubrʿy.|w.ṯn.ʿl.|mlk.|w.aḥd.|ʿl 1010.8
|ištir.b ḏdm.w nʿrs[.---].|w tʿn.btlt.ʿnt.ṯb.ytp.w[---].|l k.ašt k.km.nšr.b ḥbl[š y].|km.diy.b tʿrt y.aqht.[km.yṯb].|l l 18[3AQHT].4.17
k išal hm.|[--.ʿš]rm.kkr.ṯlṯ.|[--.]ṯlṯm.kkr.ṯlṯ.|[--.]aštn.l k.|[--]y.kl.dbrm.hm[.--].|[--]l.w.kl.mḫr k.|[--]tir.aštn.l [k] 1022.6
.|[--]y.kl.dbrm.hm[.--].|[--]l.w.kl.mḫr k.|[--]tir.aštn.l [k].|[---].kkr.ṯl[ṯ]. 1022.9
[---.]ank[.---].|[---.-]hn.[---].|[---.--]pp h.w[.---].|[---.]l k[.---].|[-----].|[-----].|[-----].|[---].al.tš[--.---].|[---.]l ksi y. 1002.8
]m.tṣḥq.ʿnt.w b lb.tqny.|[---.]ṯb l y.l aqht.ǵzr.ṯb l y w l k.|[---]m.l aqry k.b ntb.pšʿ.|[---].b ntb.gan.ašql k.tḥt.|[pʿn 17[2AQHT].6.42
.|qrdm.qry.b arṣ.mlḥmt.|št.b ʿp[r] m.ddym.sk.šlm.|l kbd.arṣ.arbdd.l kbd.šdm.|[ḥ]š k.[ʿ]ṣ k.ʿbṣ k.ʿm y.pʿn k.|[tl 3[ʿNT].4.54
y.|[---.]b a[r]ṣ.mlḥmt.|ašt[.b ʿ]p[r] m.ddym.ask.|šlm.l kb[d].awṣ.arbdd.|l kbd.š[d]m.ap.mṯn.rgmm.|argmn.lk.lk. 3[ʿNT].4.74
n.aqry.|[b arṣ].mlḥmt.[aš]t.b ʿpr m.|ddym.ask[.šlm.]l kbd.arṣ.|ar[bdd.]l kb[d.š]dm.yšt.|[----.]bʿl.mdl h.ybʿr.|[--- 3[ʿNT].4.68
aliy.qrdm.qry.b arṣ.|mlḥmt št.b ʿpr m.ddym.|sk.šlm.l kbd.arṣ.|arbdd.l kbd.šdm.|ḥš k.ʿṣ k.ʿbṣ k.|ʿm y.pʿn k.tlsm 3[ʿNT].3.13
ḥtk k.|[qryy.b arṣ.mlḥ]mt.št b ʿp|[r m.ddym.sk.šlm].l kbd.arṣ.|[arbdd.l kbd.š]dm.ḥš k.|[ʿṣ k.ʿbṣ k.ʿm y.pʿ]n k.tls 1[ʿNT.IX].2.20
.qrdm.qryy.b arṣ.mlḥmt.št].|[b ʿ]pr[m.ddym.sk.šlm.l kbd.arṣ.arbdd].|l kbd.š[dm.ḥš k.ʿṣ k.ʿbṣ k.ʿm y.pʿn k.tls]|[7.2[130].15
n.bn.ilm.mt.mh.|taršn.l btlt.ʿnt.|an.itlk.w aṣd.kl.|ǵr.l kbd.arṣ.kl.gbʿ.|l kbd.šdm.npš.ḫsrt.|bn.nšm.npš.hmlt.|arṣ. 6[49].2.16
n.my.hmlt.aṯr.|bʿl.ard.b arṣ.ap.|ʿnt.ttlk.w tṣd.kl.ǵr.|l kbd.arṣ.kl.gbʿ.|l [k]bd.šdm.tmǵ.l nʿm[y].|[arṣ.]dbr.ysmt.š 5[67].6.27
t.|ašt[.b ʿ]p[r] m.ddym.ask.|šlm.l kb[d].awṣ.arbdd.|l kbd.š[d]m.ap.mṯn.rgmm.|argmn.lk.lk.ʿnn.ilm.|atm.bštm. 3[ʿNT].4.75
rṣ.|mlḥmt št.b ʿpr m.ddym.|sk.šlm.l kbd.arṣ.|arbdd.l kbd.šdm.|ḥš k.ʿṣ k.ʿbṣ k.|ʿm y.pʿn k.tlsmn.ʿm y.|twtḥ.išd 3[ʿNT].3.14
rṣ.mlḥmt.|št.b ʿp[r] m.ddym.sk.šlm.|l kbd.arṣ.arbdd.l kbd.šdm.|[ḥ]š k.[ʿ]ṣ k.ʿbṣ k.ʿm y.pʿn k.|[tls]mn.[ʿ]m y.twt 3[ʿNT].4.54

.mlḥ]mt.št b ʻp | [r m.ddym.sk.šlm].l kbd.arṣ. | [arbdd.l kbd.š]dm.ḥš k. | [ʻṣ k.ʻbṣ k.ʻm y.pʻ]n k.tlsmn. | [ʻm y.twtḥ.iš 1[ʻNT.IX].2.21
mlḥmt.št]. | [b ʻ]pr[m.ddym.sk.šlm.l kbd.arṣ.arbdd]. | l kbd.š[dm.ḥš k.ʻṣ k.ʻbṣ k.ʻm y.pʻn k.tls] | [m]n ʻm y t[wtḥ.iš 7.2[130].16
ʻl.ard.b arṣ.ap. | ʻnt.ttlk.w tṣd.kl.ǵr. | l kbd.arṣ.kl.gbʻ. | l [k]bd.šdm.tmǵ.l nʻm[y]. | [arṣ.]dbr.ysmt.šd. | [šḥl]mmt.t[m 5[67].6.28
taršn.l btlt.ʻnt. | an.itlk.w aṣd.kl. | ǵr.l kbd.arṣ.kl.gbʻ. | l kbd.šdm.npš.ḫsrt. | bn.nšm.npš.hmlt. | arṣ.mǵt.l nʻm y.arṣ. 6[49].2.17
mt.[aš]t.b ʻpr m. | ddym.ask[.šlm.]l kbd.arṣ. | ar[bdd.]l kb[d.š]dm.yšt. | [----.]bʻl.mdl h.ybʻr. | [---.]rn h.aqry. | [---.]b 3[ʻNT].4.69
y]. | il.ylt.mh.ylt.yld y.šḥr.w šl[m]. | šu.ʻdb.l špš.rbt.w l kbkbm.kn[-]. | yhbr.špt hm.yšq.hn.[š]pt hm.mtqtm. | bm.nš 23[52].54
[-----]. | [špt.l a]rṣ.špt.l šmm. | [---.l]šn.l kbkbm.yʻrb. | [bʻ]l.b kbd h.b p h yrd. | k ḥrr.zt.ybl.arṣ.w pr. 5[67].2.3
qṣrt.npš kn.u b]qṯt. | [tqṯṯn.ušn.yp kn.---.-]gym. | [---.]l kbkb. | [-----]. APP.I[-].2.17
kd.bt ilm. | rbm. | kd l ištnm. | kd l ḫty. | maḫdh. | kd l kblbn. | kdm.mṯḫ. | l.alṯy. | kd.l mrynm. | šbʻ yn. | l mrynm. | 1090.6
ddm.l šmʻrgm. | ʻšr ddm.l bt. | ʻšrm.dd.l mḫṣm. | ddm l kbs. | dd l prgṯ. | dd.l mri. | dd.l ṯnǵly. | dd.l krwn. | dd.l ṯǵr. | 1100.6
hkl h.mšspdt.b ḥẓr h. | pẓǵm.ǵr.ybk.l aqht. | ǵzr.ydmʻ.l kdd.dnil. | mt.rpi.l ymm.l yrḫm. | l yrḫm.l šnt.ʻd. | šbʻt.šnt.y 19[1AQHT].4.174
rḫm. | l yrḫm.l šnt.ʻd. | šbʻt.šnt.ybk.l aq | ht.ǵzr.yd[mʻ.]l kdd. | dnil.mt.r[pi.mk].b šbʻ. | šnt.w yʻn[.dnil.mt.]rpi. | yṯb.ǵ 19[1AQHT].4.178
s h.w yʻn.ʻṯtr.ʻrẓ. | l amlk.b ṣrrt.ṣpn. | yrd.ʻṯtr.ʻrẓ.yrd. | l kḥṯ.aliyn.bʻl. | w ymlk.b arṣ.il.kl h. | [---] š abn.b rḥbt. | [---] 6.1.64[49.1.36]
tr.ʻrẓ. | ymlk.ʻṯtr.ʻrẓ. | apnk.ʻṯtr.ʻrẓ. | yʻl.b ṣrrt.ṣpn. | yṯb.l kḥṯ.aliyn. | bʻl.pʻn h.l tmǵyn. | hdm.riš h.l ymǵy. | aps h.w y 6.1.58[49.1.30]
yṯrm.hn.ym. | w ṯn.yṯb.krt.l ʻd h. | yṯb.l ksi mlk. | l nḫt.l kḥṯ.drkt. | ap.yṣb.yṯb.b hkl. | w ywsrnn.ggn h. | lk.l ab k.yṣb 16.6[127].24
r.---]. | w bn.dgn.b š[---]. | bʻl.yṯb.l ks[i.mlk h]. | bn.dgn.l kḥ[ṯ.drkt h]. | l alp.ql.ẓ[--.---]. | l np ql.nd.[----]. | tlk.w tr.b[10[76].3.15
ṣmd. | ṣḥr mt.ymṣḫ.l arṣ. | [yṯb.]b[ʻ]l.l ksi.mlk h. | [---].l kḥṯ.drkt h. | l [ym]m.l yrḫm.l yrḫm. | l šnt.[m]k.b šbʻ. | šnt. 6[49].5.6
rym.ṣpn.mšṣṣ.[-]kʻ[-]. | udn h.grš h.l ksi.mlk h. | l nḫt.l kḥṯ.drkt h. | mn m.ib.ypʻ.l bʻl.ṣrt.l rkb.ʻrpt. | [-]ʻn.ǵlmm.yʻn 3[ʻNT].4.47
t hm. | šm k.at.aymr.aymr.mr.ym.mr.ym. | l ksi h.nhr l kḥṯ.drkt h.trtqṣ. | b d bʻl.km.nšr b uṣbʻt h.hlm.qdq | d zbl y 2.4[68].20
t hm.šm k at. | ygrš.ygrš.grš ym grš ym.l ksi h. | [n]hr l kḥṯ drkt h.trtqṣ.b d bʻl km nš | r.b uṣbʻt h.hlm.ktp.zbl ym. 2.4[68].13
aliyn b[ʻl.---]. | kd.ynaṣn[.---]. | gršnn.l k[si.mlk h.l nḫt.l kḥṯ]. | drkt h.š[--.--]. | w hm.ap.l[--.---]. | ymḫṣ k.k[--.---]. | il. 1[ʻNT.X].4.24
yʻr.mt. | b ql h.y[---.---]. | bʻl.yṯṯbn[.l ksi]. | mlk h.l[nḫt.l kḥṯ]. | drkt h[.---]. | [---.]d[--.---]. | [---].hn[.---]. | [---.]šn[.---] 6[49].6.34
y.mlak.ym.tʻdt.ṯpṭ.nhr. | tšu ilm rašt hm.l ẓr.brkt hm.ln.kḥṯ.zbl hm. | aḫr.tmǵyn.mlak ym.tʻdt.ṯpṭ.nhr.l pʻn.il. | [l t 2.1[137].29
.ym.tʻdt.ṯpṭ[.nhr]. | t[ǵ]ly.hlm.rišt hm.l ẓr.brkt hm.w l kḥṯ. | zbl hm.b hm.ygʻr.bʻl.lm.ǵltm.ilm.rišt. | km l ẓr brkt k 2.1[137].23
b ilm.ʻny h. | w yʻn.lṭpn.il.b pid. | ṯb.bn y.lm ṯb[t] km. | l kḥṯ.zbl k[m.a]nk. | iḥtrš.w [a]škn. | aškn.ydt.[m]rṣ gršt. | zbl 16[126].5.25
ḥt.mlak.ym.tʻdt.ṯpṭ.nhr. | šu.ilm.rašt km.l ẓr.brkt km.ln.kḥṯ. | zbl km.w ank.ʻny.mlak.ym.tʻdt.ṯpṭ.nhr. | tšu ilm rašt 2.1[137].27
m.b hm.ygʻr.bʻl.lm.ǵltm.ilm.rišt. | km l ẓr brkt km.w ln.kḥṯ.zbl km.aḥd. | ilm.tʻny lḥt.mlak.ym.tʻdt.ṯpṭ.nhr. | šu.il 2.1[137].25
[-----]. | dd l krwn. | dd l [--]n. | dd l ky. | dd l ʻbdkṯr. | dd[m] l rʻy. | [--] šmḥ[.---]. | ddm gt dprnm 1101.4
[---.]d.bn.[---.]l.dqn. | [---.--]ʻ.šdyn.l ytršn. | [---.--]ṯ.ʻbd.l.kyn. | k[rm.--.]l.i[w]rtḏl. | ḥl.d[--.ʻbd]yrḫ.b d.apn. | krm.i[--]. 2027.2.9
.l.bn.ʻẓmt.rišy. | mit.l.tlmyn.bn.ʻdy. | [---.]l.aḏddy. | [--.]l.kkln. 2095.10
ymn. | tlk.škn.ʻl.ṣrrt. | adn k.šqrb.[---]. | b mgn k.w ḫrṣ.l kl. | apnk.ǵzr.ilḥu. | [m]rḥ h.yiḫd.b yd. | [g]rgr h.bm.ymn. | [16.1[125].45
tḥm.iwrḏr. | l.plsy. | rgm. | yšlm.l k. | l.trǵds. | w.l.klby. | šmʻt.ḫti. | nḫtu.ht. | hm.in mm. | nḫtu.w.lak. | ʻm y.w. 53[54].6
nn. | b rḥm.tṭḥnn.b šd. | tdrʻnn.šir h.l tikl. | ʻṣrm.mnt h.l tkly. | npr[m.]šir.l šir.yṣḥ. 6[49].2.36
w.šbʻ[d.qlt]. | ankn.rgmt.l.bʻl y. | l.špš.ʻlm.l.ʻṯtrt. | l.ʻnt.l.kl.il.alṯ[y]. | nmry.mlk.ʻlm. | mlk n.bʻl y.ḥw[t.--]. | yšhr k.w.ʻ 2008.1.8
lqḥ.ilm. | aṯr.ilm.ylk.pʻnm. | mlk.pʻnm.yl[k]. | šbʻ.pamt.l kl hm. 33[5].26
s[.---]. | [---].yṯbr[.---]. | [---.]uṭm.ḏr[qm.---]. | [btl]t.ʻnt.l kl.[---]. | [tt]bʻ.btlt.ʻnt[.idk.l ttn.pnm]. | ʻm.yṭpn.mhr.š[t.tšu. 18[3AQHT].4.4
ugr. | mn.ib.ypʻ.l bʻl.ṣrt. | l rkb.ʻrpt.l mḫšt.mdd. | il ym.l klt.nhr.il.rbm. | l ištbm.tnn.ištml h. | mḫšt.bṯn.ʻqltn. | šlyṭ.d 3[ʻNT].3.36
]npk. | [---.]l.bn.ydln. | [---].l.blkn. | [---].l.bn.k[--]. | [---].l.klṯṯb. 2136.6
pn.ʻl.qbr.bn y. | tšḫṭann.b šnt h.qr.[mym]. | mlk.yṣm.y l km.qr.mym.d ʻ[l k]. | mḫṣ.aqht.ǵzr.amd.gr bt il. | ʻnt.brḥ.p 19[1AQHT].3.152
--.---]. | l ytn.w rgm[.---]. | w yrdnn.an[--.---]. | [---].ank.l km[.---]. | l y.ank.ašṣu[.---.]w[.---]. | w hm.at.tr[gm.---]. | w.d 54.1.16[13.2.1]
lm. | [---.]w.ʻm k. | [---]m.ksp. | [---].ʻm. | [---.-]n[-]. | [---.]l km. | [---.-]lk. | [---.--]m. | t[--.---].t[-]ṯm. | i[---.--]d.[-]t. | y[---.- 1016.18
ṯlṯ.mat.ṯlṯm. | kbd.šmn. | l kny. | ṯmnym.šmn. | b d.adnnʻm. 1094.3
mit.arbʻm.kbd. | l.liy.bn.ʻmyn. | mit.ḫmšm.kbd. | d.škn.l.ks.ilm. 1143.14
nḥt.w ypʻr.šmt hm.šm k at. | ygrš.ygrš.grš ym grš ym.l ksi h. | [n]hr l kḥṯ drkt h.trtqṣ.b d bʻl km nš | r.b uṣbʻt h.hl 2.4[68].12
t.w ypʻr.šmt hm. | šm k.at.aymr.aymr.mr.ym.mr.ym. | l ksi h.nhr l kḥṯ.drkt h.trtqṣ. | b d bʻl.km.nšr b uṣbʻt h.hlm.q 2.4[68].20
.]l k[.---]. | [-----]. | [-----]. | [-----]. | [---].al.tš[--.---]. | [---.]l ksi y.w pr[ʻ]. | [---].prʻ.ank.[---]. | [---.]ank.nši[.---]. | [---.ṯ]br. 1002.13
.mt.aliyn.bʻl. | ḫlq.zbl.bʻl.arṣ. | apnk.lṭpn.il. | d pid.yrd.l ksi.yṯb. | l hdm[.w] l.hdm.yṯb. | l arṣ.yṣq.ʻmr. | un.l riš h.ʻpr. 5[67].6.12
t.aḫt[.bʻl]. | yʻl.bʻl.b ǵ[r.---]. | w bn.dgn.b š[---]. | bʻl.yṯb.l ks[i.mlk h]. | bn.dgn.l kḥ[ṯ.drkt h]. | l alp.ql.ẓ[--.---]. | l np ql 10[76].3.14
lm t.ṯtʻ.y | dd.il.ǵzr.yʻr.mt. | b ql h.y[---.---]. | bʻl.yṯṯbn[.l ksi]. | mlk h.l[nḫt.l kḥṯ]. | drkt h[.---]. | [---.]d[--.---]. | [---].h 6[49].6.33
trṯ.ḫrṣ.ṭrd.bʻl. | b mrym.ṣpn.mšṣṣ.[-]kʻ[-]. | udn h.grš h.l ksi.mlk h. | l nḫt.l kḥṯ.drkt h. | mn m.ib.ypʻ.l bʻl.ṣrt.l rkb.ʻr 3[ʻNT].4.46
p y.d[--.---]. | b d.aliyn b[ʻl.---]. | kd.ynaṣn[.---]. | gršnn.l k[si.mlk h.l nḫt.l kḥṯ]. | drkt h.š[--.--]. | w hm.ap.l[--.---]. | y 1[ʻNT.X].4.24
p. | dk ym.ymḫṣ.b ṣmd. | ṣḥr mt.ymṣḫ.l arṣ. | [yṯb.]b[ʻ]l.l ksi.mlk h. | [---].l kḥṯ.drkt h. | l [ym]m.l yrḫm.l yrḫm. | l šnt 6[49].5.5
.w lḥm. | mgṯ.w yṯrm.hn.ym. | w ṯn.yṯb.krt.l ʻd h. | yṯb.l ksi mlk. | l nḫt.l kḥṯ.drkt. | ap.yṣb.yṯb.b hkl. | w ywsrnn.ggn 16.6[127].23
ḥṣ.yd h.b dm.ḏmr. | [u]ṣbʻt h.b mmʻ.mhrm. | [ṯ]ʻr.ksat.l ksat.ṯlḥnt. | [l]ṯlḥn.hdmm.ṯṯʻr.l hdmm. | [t]ḥspn.m h.w trḥ 3[ʻNT].2.36
[-----]. | yṣq.šm[n.---]. | ʻn.tr.arṣ.w šmm. | sb.l qṣm.arṣ. | l ksm.mhyt.ʻn. | l arṣ.m[ṭ]r.bʻl. | w l šd.mṭr.ʻly. | nʻm.l arṣ.mṭr 16[126].3.4
n[-.]l ks[p.-]m. | l.mri[.--]. | ṯmn kbd[.--]i. | arbʻm[.--]. | l apy.mr[i.- 1133.1
rb]ʻm.[k]bd. | d ntn.d.ksp. | arbʻ.l.ḫlby. | [---].l.bt. | arbʻ.l.kpslnm. | kdm.b[t.]mlk. 1087.6
ḫṣm. | ddm l kbs. | dd l prgṯ. | dd.l mri. | dd.l ṯnǵly. | dd.l krwn. | dd.l ṯǵr. | dd.l rmt.r[---]. 1100.10
[-----]. | dd l krwn. | dd l [--]n. | dd l ky. | dd l ʻbdkṯr. | dd[m] l rʻy. | [--] š 1101.2
ywsrnn.ggn h. | lk.l ab k.yṣb.lk. | l[ab]k.w rgm.ʻny. | l k[rt.adn k.]ištm[ʻ]. | w tqǵ[.udn.k ǵz.ǵzm]. | tdbr.w[ǵ]rm[.t 16.6[127].29
ḥ]m.tšty. | w tʻn.mtt ḥry. | l l[ḥ]m.l š[ty].ṣḥt km. | db[ḥ.l krt.a]dn km. | ʻl.krt.tbun.km. | rgm.ṯ[rm.]rgm hm. | b ḏrt[.-- 15[128].6.5
šr.tštn. | [w t]ʻn.mtt.ḥry. | [l lḥ]m.l šty.ṣḥt km. | [--.dbḥ.l]krt.bʻl km. 15[128].4.28
b ṣp.ʻn h. | d b ḥlm y.il.ytn. | b ḏrt y.ab.adm. | w ld.špḥ.l krt. | w ǵlm.l ʻbd.il. | krt.yḫṯ.w ḥlm. | ʻbd.il.w hdrt. | yrtḥṣ.w 14[KRT].3.152

.sp.ṯrml. | d b ḥlm y.il.ytn. | b ḏrt y.ab.adm. | w ld.šph.l krk | t.w ǵlm.l ʿbd. | il.ttbʿ.mlakm. | l ytb.idk.pnm. | l ytn.ʿm 14[KRT].6.298
[l]krt. | k [k]lb.b bt k.nʿtq.k inr. | ap.ḫšt k.ap.ab.ik mtm. | tmt 16.1[125].1
.an. | ytbʿ.yṣb ǵlm.ʿl. | ab h.yʿrb.yšu g h. | w yṣḥ.šmʿ mʿ.l krt. | tʿ.ištmʿ.w tqǵ udn. | k ǵz.ǵzm.tdbr. | w ǵrm.ṯṯwy.šqlt. | 16.6[127].41
]bḥ. | t[---.id]k. | pn[m.al.ttn]. | ʿm.[krt.msw]n. | w r[gm.l krt.]ṯʿ. | ṯhm[.pbl.mlk]. | qḥ.[ksp.w yr]q. | ḫrṣ[.yd.mqm] h. | ʿ 14[KRT].5.248
[l k]rt. | [--].ml[k.---]. | [---]m.k[---]. | [-----]. | [---]m.il[.---]. | [-- 14[KRT].1.1
ṯ.abd[.---]. | [---.]anyt[.---]. | [-----]. | ʿšrm.l.umdym. | ʿšr.l.ktl. 2110.6
š. | ʿms mʿ.l y.aliyn.bʿl. | tšmʿ.nrt.ilm.špš. | tšu.aliyn.bʿl.l ktp. | ʿnt.k tšt h.tšʿlyn h. | b ṣrrt.ṣpn.tbkyn h. | w tqbrn h.tšt 6[62].1.14
. | adr.qrnt.b yʿlm.mtnm. | b ʿqbt.ṯr.adr.b ǵlil.qnm. | tn.l kṯr.w ḫss.ybʿl.qšt l ʿnt. | qṣʿt.l ybmt.limm.w tʿn.btlt. | ʿnt.irš 17[2AQHT].6.24
ǵrm.mid.ksp. | gbʿm lḥmd.ḫrṣ. | yblnn.udr.ilqṣm. | yak.l kṯr.w ḫss. | w ṯb l mspr..k tlakn. | ǵlmm. | aḫr.mǵy.kṯr.w ḫss 4[51].5.103
. | kmn.l pʿn.kṯ. | hbr.w ql.tšṯḥ | wy.w kbd hwt. | w rgm.l kṯr. | w ḫss.ṯny.l h | yn.d ḥrš.ydm. | ṯḥm.al[iyn.bʿl]. | h[wt.ali 3[ʿNT.VI].6.21
kmn.l pʿn.kṯr]. | hbr.w ql.t[šṯḥwy.w kbd.hwt]. | w rgm l k[ṯr.w ḫss.ṯny.l hyn]. | d ḥrš.y[dm.ṯḥm.ṯr.il.ab k.]| hwt.lṭpn 1[ʿNT.IX].3.4
zn. | drk.š.alp.w ṯlṯ. | ṣin.šlm[m.]šbʿ pamt. | l ilm.šb[ʿ.]l kṯr. | ʿlm.tʿrbn.gṯrm. | bt.mlk.ṯql.ḫrṣ. | l špš.w yrḫ.l gṯr. | ṯql. 33[5].8
.š.l bʿlt. | bwrm š.iṯṯqb. | w š.nbk m w.š. | gt mlk š.ʿlm. | l kṯr.ṯn.ʿlm. | tzǵ[.---.]nšm.pr. UG5.12.B.12
. | l.ṣ[--].šʿ[rt]. | l.ʿdy.š[ʿ]r[t]. | ṯlṯ.l.ʿd.ab[ǵ]l. | l.ydln.šʿrt. | l.kṯrmlk.ḫpn. | l.ʿbdil[m].ḫpn. | tmrtn.šʿrt. | lmd.n.rn. | [---].ḫp 1117.9
. | nh l yd h tzdn[.---]n. | l ad[n h.---]. | dgn tt[--.---.-]l | ʿ.l kṯrt hl[l.sn]nt. | ylak yrḫ ny[r] šmm.ʿm. | ḫr[ḫ]b mlk qẓ.tn 24[77].15
aǵzt.b sǵ[--.]špš. | yrḫ ytkḥ yḥ[bq] [-]. | tld bt.[--]t.ḫ[--.l k] | ṯrt.l bnt.hll[.snnt]. | hl ǵlmt tld b[n.--]n. | ʿn ha l yd h.tz 24[77].5
nnt.apnk.dnil. | mt.rpi.ap.hn.ǵzr.mt. | hrnmy.alp.yṭbḫ.l kṯ | rt.yšlḥm.kṯrt.w y | ššq.bnt.[hl]l.snnt. | hn.ym.w ṯn.yšlḥ 17[2AQHT].2.29
šbʿ.ḫdǵlm. | l.[---]mn ḫpn. | l[.--.]škn.ḫpn. | l.k[-]w.ḫpn. | l.ṣ[--].šʿ[rt]. | l.ʿdy.š[ʿ]r[t]. | ṯlṯ.l.ʿd.ab[ǵ]l. | l.ydln. 1117.4
| w.[---.-]mʿt. | ṯlṯ[m.---.-]rm. | ʿšr[.---].alpm. | arbʿ.ddm.l.k[-]ḫ. | ṯmnym.dd.dd.kbd. | [l].mdr[ǵ]lm. | b yrḫ[ri]šyn. | šb[2012.18
. | l ṯlṯ. | ṯn.l.brr[.---]. | arbʿ.ḥmr[.---]. | l.pḫ[-.]w.[---]. | w.l.k[--]. | w.l.k[--]. 1139.6
.yʿny[.---.bn]wt h. | [--]nn.bnt yš[--.---.-]lk. | [--]b.kmm.l k[--]. | [šp]š.b šmm.tq[ru.---.-]rt. | [---.]mn mn[-.---.--]n.nmr UG5.8.43
l.brr[.---]. | arbʿ.ḥmr[.---]. | l.pḫ[-.]w.[---]. | w.l.k[--]. | w.l.k[--]. 1139.7
[ǵ]r k. | tšlm k. | lm[.l.]likt. | ši[l.š]lm y. | [ʿ]d.r[-]š. | [-]ly.l.likt. | [a]nk.[---]. | šil.[šlm y]. | [l]m.li[kt]. | [-]t.ʿ[--]. 2010.10
. | [--.]d.nʿm.lbš k. | [-]dm.ṯn id. | [--]m.d.l.nʿmm. | [lm.]l.likt.ʿm y. | [---.]ʿbd.ank. | [---.ʿb]d k. | [---.--]l y.ʿm. | [---.]ʿm. | 2128.1.7
[m]. | ṯḥm.wr[--]. | yšlm.[l] k. | ilm.t[ǵ]r k. | tšlm k. | lm[.l.]likt. | ši[l.š]lm y. | [ʿ]d.r[-]š. | [-]ly.l.likt. | [a]nk.[---]. | šil.[šlm 2010.7
-]y.ibr[-]. | [--]wy.rgm l. | mlkt.ugrt. | [--]kt.rgmt. | [--]y.l.ilak. | [---].ʿm y. | [---]m.w.lm. | [---.]w.ʿm k. | [---]m.ksp. | [--- 1016.11
n.bn.usyy. | mit.ṯṯm.kbd. | l.bn.yšmʿ. | mit.arbʿm.kbd. | l.liy.bn.ʿmyn. | mit.ḫmšm.kbd. | d.škn.l.ks.ilm. 1143.12
[---.]dr dt.šmm. | [---.al]iyn bʿl. | [---.]rkb.ʿrpt. | [---.]ǵš.l limm. | [---.]l yṯb.l arṣ. | [---].mtm. | [---.--]d mhr.ur. | [---.]yḥ 10[76].1.8
n.yp km.---.-]yt km. | [---.]km. | [-----]. | [---.]ugrt. | [---].l.lim. | [---.mšr m]šr. | [bn.ugrt.---.--]y. | [---.np]y nqmd. | [---.] APP.I[-].1.22
d.išt. | b bht m.n[bl]at.b hkl m. | sb.ksp.l rqm.ḫrṣ. | nṣb.l lbnt.šmḫ. | aliyn.bʿl.ht y.bnt. | dt.ksp.hkl y.dtm. | ḫrṣ.ʿdbt.b 4[51].6.35
.bʿl.l hwt y. | [ḫš.]bht h.tbnn. | [ḫš.]trmm.hkl h. | y[tl]k.l lbnn.w ʿṣ h. | l[šr]yn.mḥmd.arz h. | h[n.l]bnn.w ʿṣ h. | š[r]yn 4[51].6.18
-]t.ilhnm.b šnt. | [---.]šbʿ.mat.šʿrt.ḫmšm.kbd. | [---.-]nd.l.mlbš.trmnm. | [---]h.lbš.allm.lbnm. | [---].all.šmt. | [---].all.iq 1106.3
r.št. | tštn.k nšr.b ḥbš h.km.diy. | b tʿrt h.aqht.km.yṯb.l lḥ[m]. | bn.dnil.l trm.ʿl h.nšr[m]. | trḫpn.ybṣr.ḥbl.diy[m.bn] 18[3AQHT].4.29
št k.km.nšr.b ḥb[š y]. | km.diy.b tʿrt y.aqht.[km.yṯb]. | l lḥm.w bn.dnil.l trm[.ʿl h]. | nšrm.trḫpn.ybṣr.[ḥbl.d] | iym.b 18[3AQHT].4.19
. | dn.almnt.l ṯpṭ. | ṯpṭ qṣr.npš.l tdy. | ṯšm.ʿl.dl.l pn k. | l tšlḥm.ytm.bʿd. | ksl k.almnt.km. | aḫt.ʿrš.mdw.anšt. | ʿrš.zbl 16.6[127].49
lmm.l ṯtb.[idk.pnm]. | l ytn.tk.ǵr.ll.ʿm.phr.mʿd.ap.ilm.l lḥ[m]. | ytb.bn qdš.l trm.bʿl.qm.ʿl.il.hlm. | ilm.tph hm.tphn. 2.1[137].20
.l [-]mt[.-]m.l[-]ṯnm. | ʿdm.[lḥ]m.tšty. | w tʿn.mṯt ḥry. | l l[ḥ]m.l š[ty].ṣḥt km. | db[ḥ.l krt.a]dn km. | ʿl.krt.tbun.km. | 15[128].6.4
.tqdm. | yd.b ṣʿ.tšlḥ. | ḥrb.b bšr.tštn. | [w t]ʿn.mṯt.ḥry. | [l lḥ]m.l šty.ṣḥt km. | [--.dbḥ.l]krt.bʿl km. 15[128].4.27
m.]yd.b ṣʿ.t[šl]ḥ. | [ḥrb.b]bš[r].tštn. | [w tʿn].mṯt.ḥry. | [l lḥ]m.l šty.ṣḥt k[m]. | [---.]brk.t[---]. | [ʿl.]krt.tbkn. | [--.]rgm.ṯ 15[128].5.10
[---].pit. | [---.]qbat. | [---.]inšt. | [--]u.l tštql. | [---].ṯry.ap.l tlḥm. | [l]ḥm.trmmt.l tšt. | yn.tǵzyt.špš. | rpim.tḥtk. | špš.tḥt 6.6[62.2].42
t.[ʿ]ṯr.[k]m. | zbln.ʿl.riš h. | w ttb.trḥṣ.nn.b dʿt. | npš h.l lḥm.tptḥ. | brlt h.l trm. | mt.dm.ḫt.šʿtqt. | dm.lan.w ypqd. | k 16.6[127].11
ytn. | [aḫ]r.mǵy.ʿ[d]t.ilm. | [w]yʿn.aliy[n.]bʿl. | [---.]tbʿ.l lṭpn. | [il.d]pid.l tbrk. | [krt.]ṯʿ.l tmr.nʿmn. | [ǵlm.]il.ks.yiḫd. 15[128].2.13
rt.---]. | [ʿ]ṣr.l pdr ṯṯ.ṣ[in.---]. | tšnpn.ʿlm.km[m.---]. | w.l ll.ʿṣrm.w [---]. | kmm.w.in.ʿṣr[.---]. | w mit.šʿrt.[-]y[-.---]. | w. 38[23].7
d h[.---]. | l ʿṯrt[.---]. | ʿlm.kmm[.---]. | w b ṯlṯ.ṣ[in.---]. | l ll.pr[-.---]. | mit šʿ[rt.---]. | ptr.k[--.---]. | [-]yu[-.---]. 37[22].9
un.šnpt.ḫṣt h.bʿl.ṣpn š. | [--]ṯ š.ilt.mgdl š.ilt.asrm š. | w l ll.šp. pgr.w trmnm.bt mlk. | il[bt].gdlt.ušḫry.gdlt.ym gdlt. 34[1].12
. | l bnš tpnr d yaḫd l g ynm. | ṯṯ spm l tgyn. | arbʿ spm l ll[-]. | ṯn spm.l slyy. | ṯlṯ spm l dlšpš amry. 137.2[93].13
.---]. | ddm gt dprnm. | l ḥršm. | ddm l ʿnqt. | dd l alṯt.w l lmdt h. | dd l iḫyn. | dd l [---]. 1101.11
ʿnt[.---]. | w b hm.ṯṯṯb[.--]d h. | km trpa.hn nʿr. | d yšt.l.lṣb h ḫšʿr klb. | [w]riš.pqq.w šr h. | yšt.aḥd h.dm zt.ḫrpnt. UG5.1.2.4
l.bʿln.bn. | kltn.w l. | bn h.ʿd.ʿlm. | šḫr.ʿlmt. | bnš bnšm. | l.yqḥnn.b d. | bʿln.bn.kltn. | w.b d.bn h.ʿd. | ʿlm.w unṯ. | in.b h. 1008.17
dmlk. | [--.-]m[-]r. | [w.l.]bn h.ʿd. | [ʿl]m.mn k. | mn km l.yqḥ. | bt.hnd.b d. | [ʿb]dmlk. | [-]k.amʿ[--]. | [w.b] d.bn h[.ʿ]d 1009.13
pn. | dqn.šʿrt. | [lm]d.yrṯ. | [-.]ynḥm.ḫpn. | ṯṯ.lmd.bʿln. | l.qḥ.ḫpnt. | ṯṯ[.-]l.md.ʿṯtr[t]. | l.qḥ.ḫpnt. 1117.18
]ynḥm.ḫpn. | ṯṯ.lmd.bʿln. | l.qḥ.ḫpnt. | ṯṯ[.-]l.md.ʿṯtr[t]. | l.qḥ.ḫpnt. 1117.20
t. | ktb.spr hnd. | dt brrt.ṣṭqšlm. | ʿbd h.hnd. | w mn km.l yqḥ. | spr.mlk.hnd. | b yd.ṣṭqšlm. | ʿd ʿlm. 1005.12
dn.ʿm.mlk. | bʿl h.nǵr.ḥwt k. | w l.a[--]t.tšknn. | ḫmšm.l mi[t].any. | tškn[n.--]h.k[--]. | w šnm[.--.]w[.--]. | w ʿprm.a[-- 2062.1.4
m. | ṯmnym.ṯlṯ.kbd. | mdrǵlm. | w.šbʿ.ʿšr.ḫsnm. | ḫmšm.l.mit. | bnš.l.d. | yškb.l.b.bt.mlk. 1029.14
.]bnšm. | b.gt.ǵl.ʿšrm.l.mit.drʿ.w.tšʿm.drt. | [w].ṯmnym.l.mit.dd.ḥpr.bnšm. | b.gt.alḫb.ṯṯm.drʿ.w.ḫmšm.drt.w.ṯṯm.dd 1098.15
h. | b.gt.mʿbr.arbʿm.l.mit.drʿ.w.ṯmnym[.drt]. | w.ʿšrm.l.mit.dd.ḥp[r.]bnšm. | b.gt.ǵl.ʿšrm.l.mit.drʿ.w.tšʿm.drt. | [w].ṯ 1098.13
d.ḥpr.bnšm. | b.nzl.ʿšrm.l.mit.drʿ.w.šbʿm.drt. | w.ʿšrm.l.mit.dd.ḥpr.bnšm. | b.yʿny.arbʿm.drʿ.w.ʿšrm.drt. | w.ṯlṯm.dd. 1098.25
n.šm. | [b.---.]knm.ṯṯm.l.mit.drʿ.w.mit.drt. | w[.---.]ʿm.l.mit.dd.ṯn.kbd.ḥpr.bnšm.ṯmnym.dd. | l u[-]m. | b.ṯbq.arbʿm. 1098.8
-.--]r h.ʿšr[m.---.ʿ]šrm.dd. | [---.yn.d.]nkly.l.rʿym.šbʿm.l.mitm.dd. | [---.--]d.šbʿm.kbd.drʿ. | [---.]kbd.ddm.kbd[.---]. | [1098.44
w.arbʿm.drt.mit.dd. | [---].ḥpr.bn.šm. | [b.---.]knm.ṯṯm.l.mit.drʿ.w.mit.drt. | w[.---.]ʿm.l.mit.dd.ṯn.kbd.ḥpr.bnšm.ṯm 1098.7
.ṯlṯm.drt. | [w].šbʿm.dd.ṯn.kbd.ḥpr.bnšm. | b.nzl.ʿšrm.l.mit.drʿ.w.šbʿm.drt. | w.ʿšrm.l.mit.dd.ḥpr.bnšm. | b.yʿny.arbʿ 1098.24
[---.---.]l.mit.drʿ.w.šbʿm.drt. | [---.ḥpr.]bnšm.w.l.ḥrš.ʿrq.ṯn.ʿšr h. | [--- 1098.1

nym[.drt]. | w.ʿšrm.l.mit.dd.ḥp[r.]bnšm. | b.gt.ǵl.ʿšrm.l.mit.drʿ.w.tšʿm.drt. | [w].ṯmnym.l.mit.dd.ḥpr.bnšm. | b.gt.al 1098.14

rt. | w[.a]rbʿ.l.ʿšrm.dd.l.yḥšr.bl.bn h. | b.gt.mʿbr.arbʿm.l.mit.drʿ.w.ṯmnym[.drt]. | w.ʿšrm.l.mit.dd.ḥp[r.]bnšm. | b.gt. 1098.12

.]bnšm.w.l.ḥrš.ʿrq.ṯn.ʿšr h. | [---.d]rʿ.w.mit.drt.w.ʿšrm.l.mit. | [drt.ḥpr.b]nšm.w.ṯn.ʿšr h.dd.l.rpš. | [---.]šbʿm.drʿ.w.ar 1098.3

b.gt.mlkt.b.rḥbn. | ẖmšm.l.mitm.zt. | w.b d.krd. | ẖmšm.l.mit. | arbʿ.kbd. 1096.2

[sp]r.akl[.---].ṯryn. | [tg]mr.akl.b.g[t.b]ir.alp. | [ʿ]šrm.l.mit.ḥ[p]r.ʿbdm. | mitm.drt.ṯmnym.drt. | tgmr.akl.b.gt[.b]ʿln 2013.3

t.ksp.d.ṭbq. | ṯmnym.arbʿt. | kbd.ksp. | d.nqdm. | ẖmšm.l mit. | ksp.d.mkr.ar. | arbʿm ksp d mkr. | atlg. | mit.ksp.d mk 2107.9

arbʿm ksp d mkr. | atlg. | mit.ksp.d mkr. | ilštmʿ. | ʿšrm.l mit.ksp. | ʿl.bn.alkbl.šb[ny]. | ʿšrm ksp.ʿl. | wrt.mtny.w ʿl. | pr 2107.15

[---.]l mitm.ksp. | [---.]skn. | [---.-]im.bṯd. | [---.b]šḥr.atlgn. | [---].b 2167.1

.gt.mlkt.b.rḥbn. | ẖmšm.l.mitm.zt. | w.b d.krd. | ẖmšm.l.mit. | arbʿ.kbd. 1096.4

ṯṯ.mat.ksp. | ḥṯbn.ybnn. | arbʿm.l.mit.šmn. | arbʿm.l.mit.tišr. | ṯṯ.ṯṯ.b [ṯ]ql.ṯlṯt.l.ʿšrm.ksp hm. | 1127.3

ẖpn.d.iqni.w.šmt. | l.iybʿl. | ṯlṯm.l.mit.šʿrt. | l.šr.ʿṯtrt. | mlbš.ṯrmnm. | k.yṯn.w.b.bt. | mlk.mlbš. | 1107.3

ṯṯ.mat.ksp. | ḥṯbn.ybnn. | arbʿm.l.mit.šmn. | arbʿm.l.mit.tišr. | ṯṯ.ṯṯ.b [ṯ]ql.ṯlṯt.l.ʿšrm.ksp hm. | šstm.b.šbʿm. | ṯlṯ.m 1127.4

m.ṯṯ.kbd.mḏrǵlm. | ʿšrm.aḥd.kbd.ẖsnm. | ubnyn. | ṯṯm[.l.]mit.ṯlṯ. | kbd[.tg]mr.bnš. | l.b.bt.mlk. 1028.12

m. | tšʿm.mḏrǵlm. | arbʿ.l ʿšrm.ẖsnm. | ʿšr.hbṭnm. | ṯṯm.l.mit.ṯn.kbd. | tgmr. 1030.10

. | ṯmn. | mḏrǵlm. | ṯmnym.ṯmn.kbd. | tgmr.ẖrd. | arbʿm.l.mit. | ṯn.kbd. 1031.16

--.a]drt. | [--.ṯṯ]m.ṯmn.k[bd]. | [---.yr]yt.dq[-]. | [--.ṯ]lṯm.l.mi[t]. | [---.]arbʿ.kbd. 2170.5

spr.gt.r[---]. | ʿšrm.l.m[it.---]. | šd.dr[-.---]. 1105.2

lbš. | ytn.l hm. | šbʿ.lbšm.allm. | l ušẖry. | ṯlṯ.mat.pṯtm. | l.mgmr.b.ṯlṯ. | šnt. 1107.12

y. | ʿṯtrt.tʿdb.nšb l h. | w ʿnt.ktp.b hm.ygʿr.ṯǵr. | bt.il.pn.l mgr lb.tʿdbn. | nšb.l inr.tʿdbn.ktp. | b il ab h.gʿr.yṯb.il.kb[-]. UG5.1.1.12

wt. | [---].ṯllt.khn[m.---.]k pʿn. | [---.--]y.yd.nšy.[---.--]š.l mdb. | [---] h.mẖlpt[.---.--]r. | [---.]nʿlm.[---]. | [---].hn.al[-.--- UG5.8.48

[---.]l mdgkbr. | [---] y.ʿm k. | [-]tn.l.stn. | [--.]d.nʿm.lbš k. | [-]dm.ṯ 2128.1.1

r[.---]. | w mʿn[.---]. | w bn[š.---]. | d bnš.ḥm[r.---]. | w d.l mdl.r[--.---]. | w ṣin.ʿz.b[ʿl.---]. | llu.bn[š.---]. | imr.ẖ[--.---]. | [- 2158.1.13

[.---]. | l.mḏrǵlm[.---]. | ṯlṯ.mat.ẖmšm.kb[d]. | ẖmš.kbd.l.mdʿ. | b yr[ẖ.iṯtb]nm. | ṯlṯ[.mat.a]rbʿ.kbd. | w.[---.-]mʿt. | ṯlṯ[2012.12

ʿšr[.---].alpm. | arbʿ.ddm.l.k[-]ẖ. | ṯmnym.dd.dd.kbd. | [l].mḏr[ǵ]lm. | b yrẖ[ri]šyn. | šb[ʿ.--]n.[k]bd. | w[.---.]qmʿt. | [-- 2012.20

--]. | kd.l.aṯr[y]m. | kdm.ʿm.[--]n. | kd.mštt.[---]n. | kdm.l.mḏrǵlm. | kd.l.mṣrym. | kd.mštt.mlk. | kd.bn.amht [-]t. | w.b 1089.6

]. | arbʿ l.mry[nm]. | kdm l.ẖty.[---]. | kdm l.ʿṯtr[t]. | kd l.m[ḏ]rǵl[m]. | kd l.mryn[m]. 1091.11

šbʿ.yn.l [---]. | ṯlṯ.l ḥr[š.---]. | ṯṯ[.l.]mštt[.---]. | ṯlṯ.l.mḏr[ǵlm]. | kd[.--].lm[d.---]. | kd[.l.]ẖzr[m.---]. | kd[.l.]ṯrtn[1091.4

rm.yn.ḥsp.l.ql.d.tbʿ.mṣ[r]m. | mit.arbʿm.kbd.yn.mṣb. | l.mḏrǵlm. | ʿšrn ʿšr.yn.mṣb.[-]ḥ[-].l.gzzm. 1084.29

]prš. | [-----]. | l.mšḥ[.---]. | ʿšr.d[d.---]. | ṯṯm.dd.dd[.---]. | l.mḏrǵlm[.---]. | ṯlṯ.mat.ẖmšm.kb[d]. | ẖmš.kbd.l.mdʿ. | b yr[ẖ 2012.10

k. | hrg.ar[bʿ.]ymm.bṣr. | kp.šsk k.[--].l ḥbš k. | ʿtk.ri[š.]l mhr k. | w ʿp.l dr[ʿ].nšr k. | w rbṣ.l ǵr k.inbb. | kt ǵr k.ank.y 13[6].7

l h. | w l.šbʿt.tmtẖṣ h.b ʿmq. | tẖtṣb.bn.qrtm.tṯʿr. | ksat.l mhr.ṯʿr.ṯlḥnt. | l ṣbim.hdmm.l ǵzrm. | mid.tmtẖṣn.w tʿn. | tẖ 3[ʿNT].2.21

y n.ṯpṭ.nhr.w yṣa b[.--]. | ybṯ.nn.aliyn.bʿl.w [---]. | ym.l mt.bʿl m.ym l[--.---]. | ḥm.l šrr.w [---]. | yʿn.ym.l mt[.---]. | l š 2.4[68].32

yʿrb.ybky. | w yšnn.ytn.g h. | bky.b ḥy k.ab n.ašmẖ. | b l.mt k.ngln.k klb. | b bt k.nʿtq.k inr. | ap.ẖšt k.ap.ab.k mtm. | 16.1[125].15

qt. | tbky.w tšnn.[tt]n. | g h.bky.b ḥ[y k.a]b n. | nšmẖ.b l.mt k.ngln. | k klb.[b]bt k.nʿtq. | k inr[.ap.]ẖšt k. | ap.ab.k m 16.2[125].99

r | [--.]arṣ.ʿz k.ḏmr k.l[-] | n k.ḥtk k.nmrt k.b tk. | ugrt.l ymt.špš.w yrẖ. | w nʿmt.šnt.il. UG5.2.2.11

]. | ym.l mt.bʿl m.ym l[--.---]. | ḥm.l šrr.w [---]. | yʿn.ym.l mt[.---]. | l šrr.w tʿ[n.ʿṯtrt.---]. | bʿl m.hmt.[---]. | l šrr.št[.---]. 2.4[68].34

---]. | ṯn.pt[ḥ.---]. | w.pt[ḥ.--]r.ṯǵr. | ṯmn.ḥlnm. | ṯt.tẖ[--].l.mtm. 1151.16

--.ṯq]l rb. | ṯl[ṯ.---]. | aḥt.ẖm[-.---]. | b ym.dbḥ.ṯp[-]. | aḥt.l mzy.bn[--]. | aḥt.l mkt.ǵr. | aḥt.l ʿṯtrt. | arbʿ.ʿṣrm. | gt.ṯrmn. | 39[19].14

.mlk. | [---.--]ḥ.uẖd. | [---.-]luẖ. | [---.-]tn.b d.mlkt. | [---.]l.mẖṣ. | ab[---.]aḏddy.bn.skn. | bn.[---.]uẖd. | bn.n[---.]hbṭn. | b 2014.7

l ṣin mrat. | ʿšr ddm.l šmʿrgm. | ʿšr ddm.l bt. | ʿšrm.dd.l mẖṣm. | ddm l kbs. | dd l prgṯ. | dd.l mri. | dd.l ṯnǵly. | dd.l k 1100.5

n.pẖr.ʿn.ṯǵr. | ʿn.ṯǵr.l.ṯǵr.ṯṯb. | ʿn.pẖr.l.pẖr.ṯṯb. | ʿn.mẖr.l.mẖr.ṯṯb. | ʿn.bṯy.l.bṯy.ṯṯb. | ʿn.bṯt.l.bṯt.ṯṯb. RS225.9

tṣḥ.ik.mǵy.gpn.w ugr. | mn.ib.ypʿ.l bʿl.ṣrt. | l rkb.ʿrpt.l mẖšt.mdd. | il ym.l klt.nhr.il.rbm. | l ištbm.tnn.ištml h. | mẖ 3[ʿNT].3.35

r. | b[u]ṣbʿt h.ylm.ktp.zbl ym.bn ydm.ṯpṭ. | nhr.ʿz.ym.l ymk.l tnǵṣn.pnt h.l ydlp. | tmn h.kṯr.ṣmdm.ynḥt.w ypʿr.šm 2.4[68].17

| aḥt.ẖm[-.---]. | b ym.dbḥ.ṯp[-]. | aḥt.l mzy.bn[--]. | aḥt.l mkt.ǵr. | aḥt.l ʿṯtrt. | arbʿ.ʿṣrm. | gt.ṯrmn. | aḥt.slẖu. 39[19].15

l.mlkt. | adt y. | rgm. | tḥm.tlmyn. | ʿbd k. | l.pʿn. | adt y. | šbʿ d. 52[89].1

l.mlk[.u]grt. | iẖ y.rgm. | [tḥ]m.m[lk.-]bl[-]. | yšlm.l[k].ilm. | t 2159.1

l.mlk.ugrt. | aẖ y.rgm. | tḥm.mlk.ṣr.aẖ k. | y[š]lm.l k.ilm. | ṯǵr 2059.1

tḥm.pgn. | l.mlk.ugrt. | rgm. | yšlm.l k.[il]m. | ṯǵr k.tšlm k. | hn ny.ʿm n.š 2061.2

[---.k]rgmš. | [l.m]lk.ugrt.rgm[.-]y. | [---.--]m.rgm. | [---.]šknt. | [---.--]dy. 1011.2

spr ʿpsm. | dt.št. | uryn. | l mlk.ugrt. 1171.4

l.mlkt. | um y.rgm. | tḥm.mlk. | bn k. | l.pʿn.um y. | qlt.l.um y. 50[117].1

ʿn h.l tmǵyn. | hdm.riš h.l ymǵy. | aps h.w yʿn.ʿṯtr.ʿrẓ. | l amlk.b ṣrrt.ṣpn. | yrd.ʿṯtr.ʿrẓ.yrd. | l kḥṯ.aliyn.bʿl. | w ymlk.b 6.1.62[49.1.34]

[l.ml]k.[bʿl y]. | rg[m]. | tḥm.wr[--]. | yšlm.[l] k. | ilm.t[ǵ]r k. | tš 2010.1

l.mlk.b[ʿl y]. | r[gm]. | tḥm.rb.mi[--.ʿ]bd k. | l.pʿn.bʿl y[.mrḥqt 2008.1.1

l.mlk.bʿ[l] y. | rgm. | tḥm.ṯpṭb[ʿl]. | [ʿ]bd k. | [l.p]ʿn.bʿl y. | [šbʿ] 2063.1

n.aylt. | ẖmš.mat.arbʿm. | kbd.ksp.anyt. | d.ʿrb.b.anyt. | l.mlk.gbl. | w.ẖmšm.ksp. | lqḥ.mlk.gbl. | lbš.anyt h. | bʿrm.ksp 2106.13

ṯr.il.ab h l pn[.zb]l y[m]. | [l pn.ṯp]ṭ[.nhr.]mlkt.[--]pm.l mlkt.wn.in.aṯt. | [l]k.k[m.ilm]. | [w ǵlmt.k bn.qdš.]w y[--.]z 2.3[129].22

l ṯṯpṭ.ṯpṭ.qṣr.npš. | km.aẖt.ʿrš.mdw. | anšt.ʿrš.zbln. | rd.l mlk.amlk. | l drkt.k aṯb.an. | ytbʿ.yṣb ǵlm.ʿl. | ab h.yʿrb.yšu 16.6[127].37

.bʿd. | ksl k.almnt.km. | aẖt.ʿrš.mdw.anšt. | ʿrš.zbln.rd.l mlk. | amlk.l drkt k.aṯb. | an.w yʿny.krt ṯʿ.yṯbr. | ḥrn.y bn.yṯ 16.6[127].52

.ṯny.uškny. | mnn.w.aṯt h. | slmu.ḥrš.mrkbt. | bnšm.dt.l.mlk. | ʿbdyrẖ.bn.ṯyl. | ʿbdn.w.aṯt h.w.bn h. | gpn.bn[.a]ly. | b 2068.17

.ṯryl. | mh y.rgmt. | w ht.aẖ y. | bn y.yšal. | ṯryl.p rgm. | l mlk.šm y. | w l h.yʿl m. | w h[t] aẖ y. | bn y.yšal. | ṯryl.w rgm 138.13

.ṯryl. | mh y.rgmt. | w ht.aẖ y. | bn y.yšal. | ṯryl.p rgm. | l mlk.šm y. | w l h[-] yʿl m. | bn y.yšal. | ṯryl.w rgm. | ṯṯb.l aẖ k 138.13

]. | l pʿn.bʿl y[.---]. | qlt. | [--]t.mlk.d.y[mlk]. | [--.]ʿbdyrẖ.l.ml[k]. | [--]t.w.lqḥ. | yn[.--].b dn h. | w.ml[k].šswm.nʿmm. | y 2064.13

tḫm.ml[k.---].|l.mlk.[---].|rg[m].|hn.i[---].|ds[-.---].|t[--.---].|a[--.---].|[---] 2127.1.2
[t]ḫm.uṯryn[.---].|[g]rgš ʻbdy[--].|[--.]l mlk [---].|[---].aḫ y[.---].|[--]q lpš[.---].|[---] y št k[.---].|[-- 2130.1.3
-].|[---].aḫ y[.---].|[--]q lpš[.---].|[---] y št k[.---].|[---.]l m[lk]. 2130.2.3
gnryn.|l mlkytn.|ḥnn y l pn mlk.|šin k itn.|rʻ y šṣa idn l y.|l šmn i 1020.2
l.mlkt.|adt y.rgm.|tḥm.illḏr.|ʻbd k..|l.pʻn a[dt y].|šbʻ d[.w 1014.1
lm.l k.|[il]m.tšlm k.|[tǵ]r k.|[--]y.ibr[-].|[--]wy.rgm l.|mlkt.ugrt.|[--]kt.rgmt.|[--]y.l.ilak.|[---].ʻm y.|[---]m.w.l 1016.8
l mlkt.u[m] y.|[rg]m[.]t[ḥm].|mlk.bn [k].|[l].pʻn.um [y].|q 1013.1
ubdy.b d.ǵ[--.---].|krm.pyn.arty[.---].|ṯlṯ.krm.ubdym.l mlkt.b.ʻnmky[.---].|mgdly.ǵlptr.ṯn.krmm.w.ṯlṯ.ub[dym.--- 1081.9
ybl.l špš.|mlk.rb.bʻl h.|ks.ḫrṣ.ktn.mit.pḥm.|mit.iqni.l mlkt.|ks.ḫrṣ.ktn.mit.pḥm.|mit.iqni.l uṯryn.|ks.ksp.ktn.mi 64[118].28
l.annṯb.|kd.l.iwrmḏ.|kd.l.ydn.|[---.y]rḫ.ḫyr.|[---.]yn.l.mlkt.|[---.yrḫ.]ḥlt.šbʻ.[---].mlkt.|[---.yrḫ.]gn.šbʻ[.--].|[---.y 1088.12
[t]ḥm.iṯtl.|l mnn.ilm.|tǵr k.tšlm k.|tʻzz k.alp ymm.|w rbt.šnt.|b ʻd ʻl 1019.1.2
rrt.ṣpn.|yṯb.l kḥṯ.aliyn.|bʻl.pʻn h.l tmǵyn.|hdm.riš h.l ymǵy.|aps h.w yʻn.ʻṯtr.ʻrẓ.|l amlk.b ṣrrt.ṣpn.|yrd.ʻṯtr.ʻrẓ. 6.1.60[49.1.32]
apnk.ʻṯtr.ʻrẓ.|yʻl.b ṣrrt.ṣpn.|yṯb.l kḥṯ.aliyn.|bʻl.pʻn h.l tmǵyn.|hdm.riš h.l ymǵy.|aps h.w yʻn.ʻṯtr.ʻrẓ.|l amlk.b ṣr 6.1.59[49.1.31]
b lb.tqb[-].|[--]m[-].mtm.uṣbʻ[t].|[-]tr.šrk.il.|ʻrb.špš.l ymǵ.|krt.ṣbia.špš.|bʻl ny.w ymlk.|[y]ṣb.ʻln.w y[-]y.|[kr]t. 15[128].5.18
m.|kdm.ʻm.[--]n.|kd.mštt.[---]n.|kdm.l.mdrǵlm.|kd.l.mṣrym.|kd.mštt.mlk.|kd.bn.amht [-]t.|w.bn.mṣrym.|arbʻ 1089.7
t.|b npš h.ystrn ydd.|b gngn h.aḥd y.d ym|lk.ʻl.ilm.l ymru.|ilm.w nšm.d yšb|[ʻ].hmlt.arṣ.gm.l ǵ|[lm] h.bʻl k.yṣ 4[51].7.50
ddm.l bt.|ʻšrm.dd.l mḫṣm.|ddm l kbs.|dd l prgṭ.|dd.l mri.|dd.l tnǵly.|dd.l krwn.|dd.l tǵr.|dd.l rmt.r[---]. 1100.8
n[-.]l ks[p.-]m.|l.mri[.--].|tmn kbd[.--]i.|arbʻm[.--].|l apy.mr[i.--].|[---.--]d. 1133.2
[---.mr]zḥ.ʻn[.---].|[---.]šir.šd.kr[m.---].|[---.]l.mrzḥ.ʻn[.---].|[---].mrzḥ.ʻn[.---].|[---].mrzḥ.ʻn[.---].|[---.mr 2032.3
.|kd l kblbn.|kdm.mṯḫ.|l.alṯy.|kd.l mrynm.|šbʻ yn.|l mrynm.|b yṯbmlk.|kdm.ǵbiš ḫry.|ḫmš yn.b d.|bḥ mlkt.| 1090.11
arbʻ.yn.l.mrynm.ḫ[--].kl h.|kdm.l.zn[-.---].|kd.l.aṯr[y]m.|kdm.ʻm.[1089.1
d[.--].lm[d.---].|kd[.l.]ḫzr[m.---].|kd[.l.]trtn[m].|arbʻ l.mry[nm].|kdm l.ḫty.[---].|kdm l.ʻṯtr[t].|kd l.m[ḏ]rǵl[m].| 1091.8
|kd l ḫty.|maḫdh.|kd l kblbn.|kdm.mṯḫ.|l.alṯy.|kd.l mrynm.|šbʻ yn.|l mrynm.|b yṯbmlk.|kdm.ǵbiš ḫry.|ḫmš 1090.9
].|kdm l.ḫty.[---].|kdm l.ʻṯtr[t].|kd l.m[ḏ]rǵl[m].|kd l.mryn[m]. 1091.12
rpum.l] |tdd.aṯr[h.l tdd.ilnym].|asr.mr[kbt.---].|tʻln.l mr[kbt hm.tity.l] |ʻr hm.tl[kn.ym.w ṯn.aḫr.špšm].|b ṯlṯ.m 22.1[123].23
d.aṯr h.tdd.iln[ym.---].|asr.sswm.tṣmd.dg[-.---].|tʻln.l mrkbt hm.ti[ty.l ʻr hm].|tlkn.ym.w ṯa aḫr.š[pšm.b ṯlṯ].|m 20[121].2.4
ʻn.aliy[n.]bʻl.|[---.]tbʻ.l lṯpn.|[il.d]pid.l tbrk.|[krt.]ṯʻ.l tmr.nʻmn.|[ǵlm.]il.ks.yiḫd.|[il.b]yd.krpn.bm.|[ymn.]brk 15[128].2.15
ʻnt.brḥ.p ʻlm h.ʻnt.p dr[.dr].|ʻdb.uḫry mṭ.yd h.|ymǵ.l mrrt.tǵll.b nr.|yšu.g h.w yṣḥ.y l k.mrrt.|tǵll.b nr.d ʻl k.m 19[1AQHT].3.156
.---].|ʻš[r.---].|ḫm[š.---].|b[yrḫ.---].|[---.]prš.|[-----].|l.mšḥ[.---].|ʻšr.d[d.---].|ṯṯm.dd.dd[.---].|l.mdrǵlm[.---].|ṯlṯ. 2012.7
sad.tkbd.hmt.bʻl.|ḥkpt il.kl h.tbʻ.kṯr.|l ahl h.hyn.tbʻ.l mš|knt h.apnk.dnil.m[t].|rpi.aphn.ǵzr.m[t].|hrnmy.qšt.y 17[2AQHT].5.32
ṣǵrt hn.abkrn.|tbrk.ilm.tity.|tity.ilm.l ahl hm.|dr il.l mšknt hm.|w tqrb.w ld.bn.l h.|w tqrb.w ld.bnt.l h.|mk.b 15[128].3.19
šbʻ.yn.l [---].|ṯlṯ.l ḥr[š.---].|ṯṯ[.l.]mštt[.---].|ṯlṯ.l.mdr[ǵlm].|kd[.--].lm[d.---].|kd[.l.]ḫzr[m.- 1091.3
l.[----].|l.[----].|l.ʻṯ[trt.---].|l.mš[--.---].|l.ilt[.---].|l.bʻlt[.---].|l.il.bt[.---].|l.ilt.[---].|l.ḥtk[1004.4
n.p k.b ḫlb.k tgwln.šnt k.|[--.]w špt k.l tššy.hm.tqrm.l mt.b rn k.|[--]ḫp.an.arnn.ql.špš.ḥw.bṯnm.uḫd.bʻlm.|[--.a]ṯ 1001.1.5
mt.ʻz.bʻl.ʻz.ymšḫn.|k lsmm.mt.ql.|bʻl.ql.ʻln.špš.|tṣḥ.l mt.šmʻ.mʻ.|l bn.ilm.mt.ik.tmt[ḫ]|ṣ.ʻm.aliyn.bʻl.|ik.al.yšm 6[49].6.23
.ḥt.šʻtqt.|dm.lan.w ypqd.|krt.ṯʻ.yšu.g h.|w yṣḥ.šmʻ.l mtt.|ḥry.ṭbḫ.imr.|w ilḥm.mgt.w iṯrm.|tšmʻ.mtt.ḥry.|tṭbḫ 16.6[127].16
p[----].|gm.l[aṯt h k.yṣḥ].|šmʻ[.l mtt.ḥry].|ṭbḫ.š[mn].mri k.|ptḥ.[rḥ]bt.yn.|ṣḥ.šbʻm.ṯr y.|ṯ 15[128].4.3
itm.yn.ḥsp.d.nkly.b.db[ḥ.--].|mit.arbʻm.kbd.yn.ḥsp.l.m[--].|mit.ʻšrm.[k]bd.yn.ḥsp.l.y[--].|ʻšrm.yn.ḥsp.l.ql.d.tbʻ. 1084.25
[---.--]b[.---].|[---.]y[--.-]kzn.|[---.]yn.l.m[---].|[---.]yn.l.m[--]m.|[---.]d.bn.[---.]l.dqn.|[---.--]ʻ.šdyn.l ytršn.|[---.--]ṯ. 2027.2.6
--].|[---.--]l[.--].|[---.--]b[.---].|[---.]y[--.-]kzn.|[---.]yn.l.m[---].|[---.]yn.l.m[--]m.|[---.]d.bn.[---.]l.dqn.|[---.--]ʻ.šdy 2027.2.5
w yrmy[.q]rn h.|[---.-]ny h pdr.ttǵr.|[---.n]šr k.al ttn.l n.|[---.]tn l rbd.|[---.]bʻlt h w yn.|[---.rk]b ʻrpt.|[---.--]n.w 2001.2.12
gr.bt.bʻl.|w aṯt h.ngrt.ilht.|w yʻn.lṯpn.il d pi[d].|šmʻ.l ngr.il il[š].|ilš.ngr bt bʻl.|w aṯt k.ngrt.il[ht].|ʻl.l ṯkm.bnw 16[126].4.11
.bt y.aṣ]ḥ km.iqra km.|[ilnym.b hkl]y.aṯr h.rpum.|[l tdd.aṯr]h.l tdd.i[lnym].|[---.]r[--.---].|[---.yṯ]b.l arṣ. 21[122].1.12
.b]t y.aṣḥ km.iqra.|[km.ilnym.b h]kl y.aṯr h.rpum.|[l tdd.aṯr h].l tdd.ilnym.|[---.m]rzʻy.apnnk.yrp.|[---.]km.rʻy. 21[122].1.4
bt y.aṣḥ].|km.iqr[a km.ilnym.b hkl y].|aṯr h.r[pum.l tdd.aṯr h].|l tdd.il[nym.---].|mhr.bʻl[.---.mhr].|ʻnt.lk b[t y 22.1[123].5
bt y].|aṣḥ.km.[iqra km.ilnym.b] |hkl y.aṯr[h.rpum.l tdd].|aṯr h.l t[dd.ilnym.ṯm].|yḥpn.ḥy[ly.zbl.mlk.ʻllm y].|š 22.1[123].10
t y].|aṣḥ.rpi[m.iqra.ilnym].|b qrb.h[kl y.aṯr h.rpum.l] |tdd.aṯr[h.l tdd.ilnym].|asr.mr[kbt.---].|tʻln.l mr[kbt hm 22.1[123].20
m.iqra.ilnym].|b qrb.h[kl y.aṯr h.rpum.l] |tdd.aṯr[h.l tdd.ilnym].|asr.mr[kbt.---].|tʻln.l mr[kbt hm.tity.l] |ʻr hm 22.1[123].21
m.[iqra km.ilnym.b] |hkl y.aṯr[h.rpum.l tdd].|aṯr h.l t[dd.ilnym.ṯm].|yḥpn.ḥy[ly.zbl.mlk.ʻllm y].|šmʻ.atm[.---]. 22.1[123].11
m.iqr[a km.ilnym.b hkl y].|aṯr h.r[pum.l tdd.aṯr h].|l tdd.il[nym.---].|mhr.bʻl[.---.mhr].|ʻnt.lk b[t y.rpim.rpim.b 22.1[123].6
m.iqra.|[km.ilnym.b h]kl y.aṯr h.rpum.|[l tdd.aṯr h].l tdd.ilnym.|[---.m]rzʻy.apnnk.yrp.|[---.]km.rʻy.ht.alk.|[---. 21[122].1.4
m.iqra km.|[ilnym.b hkl]y.aṯr h.rpum.|[l tdd.aṯr]h.l tdd.i[lnym].|[---.]r[--.---].|[---.yṯ]b.l arṣ. 21[122].1.12
k.nhr.ibr[.---].|zbl bʻl.ǵlm.[---].|ṣǵr hd w r[---.---].|w l nhr nd[-.---].|[---.--]l. 9[33].2.12
gt.w yṯrm.hn.ym.|w ṯn.yṯb.krt.l ʻd h.|yṯb.l ksi mlk.|l nḫt.l kḥṯ.drkt.|ap.yṣb.yṯb.b hkl.|w ywsrnn.ggn h.|lk.l ab 16.6[127].24
l.|b mrym.ṣpn.mšṣṣ.[-]kʻ[-].|udn h.grš h.l ksi.mlk h.|l nḫt.l kḥṯ.drkt h.|mn m.ib.ypʻ.l bʻl.ṣrt.l rkb.ʻrpt.|[-]ʻn.ǵlm 3[ʻNT].4.47
|b d.aliyn b[ʻl.---].|kd.ynaṣn[.---].|gršnn.l k[si.mlk h.l nḫt.l kḥṯ].|drkt h.š[--.--].|w hm.ap.l[--.---].|ymḫṣ k.k[--.-- 1[ʻNT.X].4.24
il.ǵzr.yʻr.mt.|b ql h.y[---.---].|bʻl.yṯtbn[.l ksi].|mlk h.l[nḫt.l kḥṯ].|drkt h[.---].|[---.]d[--.---].|[---].hn[.---].|[---.]š 6[49].6.34
n.ym.w ṯa aḫr.š[pšm.b ṯlṯ].|mǵy.rpum.l grnt.i[lnym.l] |mṭʻt.w yʻn.dnil.[mt.rpi].|yṯb.ǵzr.mt hrnmy[.---].|b grnt. 20[121].2.6
.w ṯn.aḫr.špšm].|b ṯlṯ.mǵy[.rpum.l grnt].|i[ln]y[m].l mṭʻt[.---].|[-]m[.---].|h.hn bn k.hn[.---].|bn bn.aṯr k.hn[.--- 22.1[123].26
.izml.|ḫmš.kbd.arbʻm.|dd.akl.|ṯṯ.ʻšr h.yn.|kd.šmn.l.nr.ilm.|kdm.dǵm.|ṯṯ.kdm.ztm. 1126.6
bḥt.bt.ilt.ʻṣr[m.l ṣpn.š].|l ǵlmt.š.w l [---.l yrḫ].|gd[lt].l nkl[.gdlt.l bʻlt.bhtm].|ʻš[rm.]l inš[.ilm.---].|il[hm.]dqt.š[.-- 35[3].26
dbḥt.bt.i[lt.ʻṣrm.l].|ṣpn š.l ǵlm[t.š.w l.---].|l yrḫ.gdlt.l [nkl.gdlt.l bʻ]|[lt].bht[m].[ʻ]ṣrm l [inš.ilm].|[---.]ilh[m.dqt. APP.II[173].28
yšu.ʻwr.|mzl.ymzl.|w ybl.trḫ.ḥdṯ.|ybʻr.l ṯn.aṯt h.|w l nkr.mddt.|km irby.tškn.|šd.k ḥsn.pat.|mdbr.tlkn.|ym.w 14[KRT].4.191

spr.ḥṯbn.sbrdnm.|ḫmš.kkrm.alp kb[d].|ṯlṯ.l.nskm.birtym.|b d.urtn.w.ṯṯ.mat.brr.|b.ṯmnym.ksp.ṯlṯt.kb 2101.3
ṯlṯ.d yṣa.|b d.šmmn.|l argmn.|l nskm.|ṯmn.kkrm.|alp.kbd.|[m]itm.kbd. 147[90].4
.mt.ik.tmt[ḫ]|ṣ.ʿm.aliyn.bʿl.|ik.al.yšm[ʿ] k.ṯr.|il.ab k.l ysʿ.alt.|ṯbt k.l yhpk.ksa.mlk k.|l yṯbr.ḫṭ.mṯpṭ k.|yru.bn il 6[49].6.27
l pn.zbl.ym.l pn[.ṯ]pṭ[.n]hr.|[ik.a]l.yšmʿ k.ṯr.[i]l.ab k.l ysʿ.[alt.]ṯ[bt |k.l y]hpk.|[ksa.]mlk k.l yṯbr.ḫṭ.mṯpṭ k.w yʿn 2.3[129].17
l.gbʿ.|l kbd.šdm.npš.ḫsrt.|bn.nšm.npš.hmlt.|arṣ.mǵt.l nʿm y.arṣ.|dbr.ysmt.šd.šḥlmmt.|ngš.ank.aliyn bʿl.|ʿdbnn 6[49].2.19
ʿnt.ttlk.w tṣd.kl.ǵr.|l kbd.arṣ.kl.gbʿ.|l [k]bd.šdm.tmǵ.l nʿm[y].|[arṣ.]dbr.ysmt.šd.|[šḥl]mmt.t[mǵ.]l bʿl.np[l].|[l a 5[67].6.28
a.g hm.w tṣ]ḥ.sbn.|[---]l[.---.]ʿd.|ksm.mhyt[.m]ǵny.|l nʿm y.arṣ.dbr.|l ysmt.šd.šḥlmmt.|mǵny.l bʿl.npl.l a|rṣ.mt 5[67].6.6
k.|[-]tn.l.stn.|[--.]d.nʿm.lbš k.|[-]dm.ṯn id.|[--]m.d.l.nʿmm.|[lm.]l.likt.ʿm y.|[---.]ʿbd.ank.|[---.ʿb]d k.|[---.--]l y 2128.1.6
[---.]w rm tp h.|[---.-]lu mm l nʿm.|[---.]w rm ṯlbm ṯlb.|[---.-]pr l nʿm.|[---.-]mt w rm tp UG5.5.2
lbm ṯlb.|[---.-]pr l nʿm.|[---.-]mt w rm tp h.|[---.-]ḫb l nʿm.|[---.]ymǵy.|[---.]rm ṯlbm.|[---.--]m.|[---.--]ḫ nʿm. UG5.5.6
p h.|[---.-]lu mm l nʿm.|[---.]w rm ṯlbm ṯlb.|[---.-]pr l nʿm.|[---.-]mt w rm tp h.|[---.-]ḫb l nʿm.|[---.]ymǵy.|[---.] UG5.5.4
n šd h krm[m].|šd dd h ḥrnqm.w |yʿn ḫrḫb mlk qẓ [l].|nʿmn.ilm l ḫt[n].|m.bʿl trḫ pdry b[t h].|aqrb k ab h bʿ[l] 24[77].24
]ṣbʿt h.ylm.ktp.zbl ym.bn ydm.ṯpṭ.|nhr.ʿz.ym.l ymk.l tngṣn.pnt h.l ydlp.|tmn h.kṯr.ṣmdm.ynḥt.w ypʿr.šmt hm. 2.4[68].17
k.šskn mʿ.|mgn.rbt.aṯrt ym.|mǵẓ.qnyt.ilm.|hyn.ʿly.l mpḫm.|b d.ḫss.mṣbṭm.|yṣq.ksp.yšl|ḥ.ḫrṣ.yṣq.ksp.|l alpm 4[51].1.24
ḫṭ.zbl hm.|aḫr.tmǵyn.mlak ym.tʿdt.ṯpṭ.nhr.l pʿn.il.|[l t]pl.l tštḥwy.pḫr.mʿd.qmm.a[--].amr.|[ṯn]y.dʿt hm.išt.ištm 2.1[137].31
d.|w[.---.]qmʿt.|[---.]mdrǵlm.|[---.]mdm.|[w].ʿšr.dd.l np[l].|r[p]š. 2012.26
.hmt.bʿl.|ḥkpt.il.kl h.tšmʿ.|mṯt.dnty.tʿdb.imr.|b pḫd.l npš.kṯr.w ḫss.|l brlt.hyn.d ḥrš.|ydm.aḫr.ymǵy.kṯr.|w ḫss. 17[2AQHT].5.23
nmy.gm.l aṯt h.k yṣḥ.|šmʿ.mṯt.dnty.ʿd[b].|imr.b pḫd.l npš.kṯr.|w ḫss.l brlt.hyn d.|ḥrš yd.šlḥm.ššqy.|ilm sad.kb 17[2AQHT].5.17
n.l.azzlt.|[---.]l.ʿṯtrt.šd.|[---].ybʿlnn.|[---.--]n.b.ṯlṯ.šnt.l.nṣd.|[---.--]ršp.mlk.k.ypdd.mlbš.|u---].mlk.ytn.mlbš.|[---. 1106.57
-].|w mlk[.nhš.w mlk.mg]šḫ.|ʿmn.[---].|ik y.[---].|w l n[qmd.---].|[w]nqmd.[---].|[-.]ʿmn.šp[š.mlk.rb].|bʿl h.šlm 64[118].9
nqmd.mlk.ugr[t.--].|phy.|w ṯpllm.mlk.r[b.--].|mṣmt.l nqmd.[---.-]št.|hl ny.argmn.d [ybl.n]qmd.|l špš.arn.ṯn[.ʿšr 64[118].17
h.trd.nrt.|ilm.špš.ʿd.tšbʿ.bk.|tšt.k yn.udmʿt.gm.|tṣḥ.l nrt.ilm.špš.|ʿms mʿ.l y.aliyn.bʿl.|tšmʿ.nrt.ilm.špš.|tšu.aliy 6[62].1.11
ṯ.zbl.bʿl.arṣ.|gm.yṣḥ.il.l btlt.|ʿnt.šmʿ.l btlt.ʿn[t].|rgm.l nrt.il.šp[š].|pl.ʿnt.šdm.y špš.|pl.ʿnt.šdm.il.yšt k.|[b]ʿl.ʿnt. 6[49].3.24
.|[---.t]ṯb h.aḫt.ppšr.w ppšrt[.---].|[---.]k.drḫm.w aṯb.l ntbt.k.ʿṣm l t[--].|[---.]drk.brḥ.arṣ.lk pn h.yrk.bʿ[l].|[---.]bt 1001.2.7
š.b šmm.tq[ru.---.-]rt.|[---.]mn mn[-.---.--]n.nmr.|[--.]l ytk.bl[-.---.]m[--.]hwt.|[---].ṯllt.khn[m.---.]k pʿn.|[---.--]y.y UG5.8.46
--.-]sr.pdm.riš h[m.---].|ʿl.pd.asr.[---.]l[.---].|mḫlpt.w l.ytk.[d]m[ʿt.]km.|rbʿt.ṯqlm.ṯtp[.---.]bm.|yd.ṣpn hm.tliy m[19[1AQHT].2.82
s.hd.p[.-].|km.ibr.b tk.mšmš d[--].|ittpq.l awl.|išttk.lm.ttkn.|štk.mlk.dn.|štk.šibt.ʿn.|štk.qr.bt.il.|w mṣlt.bt.ḥr[š 12[75].2.58
bt k.nʿtq.k inr.|ap.ḫšt k.ap.ab.ik mtm.|tmtn.u ḫšt k.l ntn.|ʿtq.b d.aṯt.ab ṣrry.|tbky k.ab.ǵr.bʿl.|ṣpn.ḥlm.qdš.|an 16.1[125].4
bt k.nʿtq.k inr.|ap.ḫšt k.ap.ab.k mtm.|tmtn.u ḫšt k.l ntn.|ʿtq.b d.aṯt.ab.ṣrry.|ik m.yrgm.bn.il.|krt.šph.lṭpn.|w 16.1[125].18
.kbd.šmn.|[l.]abrm.mšrm.|[mi]tm.arbʿm.ṯmn.kbd.|[l.]sbrdnm.|m[i]t.l.bn.ʿẓmt.rišy.|mit.l.tlmyn.bn.ʿdy.|[---.]l.a 2095.6
.b d.ilmhr nḥl h.|šd knn.bn.ann.ʿdb.|šd.iln[-].bn.irṯr.l.šḫrn.nḥl h.|šd[.ag]pṯn.b[n.]brrn.l.qrt.|šd[.--]dy.bn.brzn.|l 2029.20
it.iqni.l ḫbrtn]r ṯn.|[ks.ksp.ktn.mit.pḥm].|[mit.iqn]i.l skl.[--].|[---.m]it pḥm.l š[--].|[---.]a[--.--.]hn[--]. 64[118].38
yaḫd l g ynm.|ṯṯ spm l tgyn.|arbʿ spm l ll[-].|ṯn spm.l slyy.|ṯlṯ spm l dlšpš amry. 137.2[93].14
.|šd.bn.nbʿm.l.ṯpṭbʿl.|šd.bn mšrn.l.ilšpš.|[šd.bn].kbr.l.snrn.|[---.--]k.l.gmrd.|[---.--]ṯ.l.yšn.|[šd.--]ln.|b d.trǵds.|š 2030.1.6
ʿm lḥmd.ḫrṣ.|yblnn.udr.ilqṣm.|yak.l kṯr.w ḫss.|w ṯb l mspr..k tlakn.|ǵlmm.|aḫr.mǵy.kṯr.w ḫss.|št.alp.qdm h.m 4[51].5.104
]d[-]t.nʿm y.ʿrš.h[--]m.|ysmsmt.ʿrš.ḫlln.[-].|ytb.dnil.[l s]pr yrḫ h.|yrs.y[---.]y[--] h.|ṯlṯ.rb[ʿ.yrḫ.--]r[.--].|yrḫm.y 17[2AQHT].2.43
i.l dr.|bn il.l mpḫrt.bn.il.l ṯkmn[.w]šnm.hn.ʿr.|w.ṯb.l mspr.m[šr] mšr.bt.ugrt.w npy.gr.|ḥmyt.ugrt.w [np]y.nṯt.u 32[2].1.27
.-]ah.|ṯnm.tšqy msk.hwt.tšqy[.-.]w [---].|w hn dt.yṯb.l mspr. 19[1AQHT].5.1
[---.]l mdgkbr.|[---] y.ʿm k.|[-]tn.l.stn.|[--.]d.nʿm.lbš k.|[-]dm.ṯn id.|[--]m.d.l.nʿmm.|[lm.]l.li 2128.1.3
ḥlm y.il.ytn.|b ḏrt y.ab.adm.|w ld.šph.l krt.|w ǵlm.l ʿbd.il.|krt.yḫṯ.w ḥlm.|ʿbd.il.w hdrt.|yrtḥṣ.w yadm.|yrḥṣ. 14[KRT].3.153
ḥlm y.il.ytn.|b ḏrt y.ab.adm.|w ld.šph.l krk|t.w ǵlm.l ʿbd.|il.ttbʿ.mlakm.|l yṯb.idk.pnm.|l ytn.ʿmm.pbl.|mlk.tša 14[KRT].6.299
lk.ud[r].|[-]dʿ.k.iḫd.[---].|w.mlk.bʿl y.|lm.škn.hnk.|l ʿbd h.alpm.š[šw]m.|rgmt.ʿly.ṯh.lm.|l.ytn.hm.mlk.[b]ʿl y.| 1012.24
šbʿ id.|mrḥqtm.|qlt.|ʿm.adt y.|mnm.šlm.|rgm.ṯṯb.|l.ʿbd h. 52[89].15
.ap.ank.|nḫt.ṯm ny.|ʿm.adt ny.|mnm.šlm.|rgm.ṯṯb.|l.ʿbd k. 51[95].18
d.|mrḥqtm.|qlt.ʿm.|bʿl y.mnm.|šlm.|[r]gm[.ṯṯb].|[l.]ʿbd[k]. 2115.2.12
b.ab[d k].al[.---].|[-]tm.iph.adt y.w.[---].|tšṣḥq.hn.aṯt.l.ʿbd.|šbʿt.w.nṣp.ksp.|[-]tm.rb[.--.a]ḥd.|[---.--]t.b[-].|[---.-]y 1017.4
.]dd.nʿr.|d.apy[.--].|w.arb[ʿ.--]d.apy.ʿbd h.|w.mrbʿ[t.l ʿ]bdm. 2094.6
.ʿdy.š[ʿ]r[t].|ṯlṯ.l.ʿd.ab[ǵ]l.|l.ydln.šʿrt.|l.kṯrmlk.ḫpn.|l.ʿbdil[m].ḫpn.|tmrtn.šʿrt.|lmd.n.rn.|[---].ḫpn.|dqn.šʿrt.|[l 1117.10
ny.|ḫršn.|ldn.|bn.ands.|bn.ann.|bn.ʿbdpdr.|šd.iyry.l.ʿbdbʿl.|šd.šmmn.l.bn.šty.|šd.bn.arws.l.bn.ḫlan.|šd.bn.ibr 1102.17
[--]t.w.lqḥ.|yn[.--].b dn h.|w.ml[k].sswm.nʿmm.|ytn.l.ʿbdyrḫ.|w.mlk.z[--.--]n.sswm.|nʿmm.[--].ṯṯm.w.at.|nǵṯ.w. 2064.17
[-----].|dd l krwn.|dd l [--]n.|dd l ky.|dd l ʿbdkṯr.|dd[m] l rʿy.|[--] šmḫ[.---].|ddm gt dprnm.|l ḥršm 1101.5
t.|ytn.bt.anndr.|bn.ytn.bnš.|[ml]k.d.b riš.|[--.-]nt.|[l.ʿb]dmlk.|[--.-]m[-]r.|[w.l.]bn h.ʿd.|[ʿl]m.mn k.|mn km l.y 1009.9
.šql.ṯrm.|w mri ilm.ʿglm.dt.šnt.|imr.qmṣ.llim.k ksp.|l ʿbrm.zt.ḫrṣ.l ʿbrm.kš.|dpr.ṯlḥn.b qʿl.b qʿl.|mlkm.hn.ym.yṣ 22.2[124].15
ri ilm.ʿglm.dt.šnt.|imr.qmṣ.llim.k ksp.|l ʿbrm.zt.ḫrṣ.l ʿbrm.kš.|dpr.ṯlḥn.b qʿl.b qʿl.|mlkm.hn.ym.yṣq.yn.ṯmk.|m 22.2[124].15
ẓma.yd.mṯkt.|ṯṯkr.[--]dn.|ʿm.krt.mswn h.|arḫ.tzǵ.l ʿgl h.|bn.ḫpṯ.l umht hm.|k tnḥn.udmm.|w yʿny.krt.ṯʿ. 15[128].1.5
t[---.ym.ymm].|yʿtqn.w[rḥm.ʿnt].|tngṯ h.k lb.a[rḫ].|l ʿgl h.k lb.ṯa[t].|l imr h.km.lb.ʿn[t].|aṯr.bʿl.tiḫd.m[t].|b sin. 6[49].2.7
.ymm.yʿtqn.l ymm.|l yrḫm.rḥm.ʿnt.tngṯ h.|k lb.arḫ.l ʿgl h.k lb.|ṯat.l imr h.km.lb.|ʿnt.aṯr.bʿl.tiḫd.|bn.ilm.mt.b 6[49].2.28
.]škn.ḫpn.|l.k[-]w.ḫpn.|l.ṣ[--].šʿ[rt].|l.ʿdy.š[ʿ]r[t].|ṯlṯ.l.ʿd.ab[ǵ]l.|l.ydln.šʿrt.|l.kṯrmlk.ḫpn.|l.ʿbdil[m].ḫpn.|tmrtn. 1117.7
y.|ṯṯbḫ.imr.w lḥm.|mgṯ.w yṯrm.hn.ym.|w ṯn.yṯb.krt.l ʿd h.|yṯb.l ksi mlk.|l nḫt.l kḥṯ.drkt.|ap.yṣb.yṯb.b hkl.|w y 16.6[127].22
lk.ydʿ.ylḥn.|w yʿn.lṭpn.il d pi|d dq.anm.l yrẓ.|ʿm.bʿl.l yʿdb.mrḥ.|ʿm.bn.dgn.k tms m.|w ʿn.rbt.aṯrt ym.|blt.nmlk 6.1.51[49.1.23]
.]ʿm[.-.]aṯt y[.-].|[---.]ṯḥm.|[---]t.[ ]r.|[---.--]n.|[---] h.l ʿdb.|[---]n.yd h.|[---].bl.išlḥ.|[---] h.gm.|[l --- k.]yṣḥ.|[---] 14[KRT].5.234
---]mn ḫpn.|l[.--.]škn.ḫpn.|l.k[-]w.ḫpn.|l.ṣ[--].šʿ[rt].|l.ʿdy.š[ʿ]r[t].|ṯlṯ.l.ʿd.ab[ǵ]l.|l.ydln.šʿrt.|l.kṯrmlk.ḫpn.|l.ʿbdil 1117.6
|b krb.ʿẓm.ridn.|mt.šmm.ks.qdš.|l tphn h.aṯt.krpn.|l tʿn.aṯrt.alp.|kd.yqḥ.b ḫmr.|rbt.ymsk.b msk h.|qm.ybd.w 3[ʿNT].1.15

.w.ht. | [-]sny.udr h. | w.hm.ḫt. | ʻl.w.likt. | ʻm k.w.hm. | l.ʻl.w.lakm. | ilak.w.at. | um y.al.tdḥṣ. | w.ap.mhkm. | b.lb k.al 1013.19
iqra.ilm.n[ʻmm.---]. | w ysmm.bn.š[--]. | ytnm.qrt.l ʻly[.---]. | b mdbr.špm.yd[.---.---]r. | l riš hm.w yš[--.--]m. | lḥ 23[52].3
m[.abn.brq.d l tdʻ.šmm.at m]. | w ank.ib[ǵy h.---]. | [-].l yʻmdn.i[---.---]. | kpr.šbʻ bn[t.rḥ.gdm.w anhbm]. | kla[t.tǵ]r[7.2[130].22
tḫm.špš. | l.ʻmrpi.rgm. | ʻm špš.kll.mid m. | šlm. | l.[--]n.špš. | ad[.ʻ]bd h. 2060.2
m] l rʻy. | [--] šmḫ[.---]. | ddm gt dprnm. | l ḥršm. | ddm l ʻnqt. | dd l altt.w l lmdt h. | dd l iḫyn. | dd l [---]. 1101.10
.mlk.tql.ḫrṣ. | l špš.w yrḫ.l gtr. | tql.ksp.tb.ap w np[š]. | l ʻnt h.tql.ḫrṣ. | l špš[.w y]rḫ.l gtr.tn. | [tql.ksp].tb.ap.w npš. | 33[5].13
š. | dgn.š.il tʻdr.š. | bʻl š.ʻnt š.ršp š. | šlmm. | w šnpt.il š. | l ʻnt.ḥl š.tn šm. | l gtrm.ǵṣ b šmal. | d alpm.w alp w š. | šrp.w UG5.13.25
bʻ d.w.šbʻ[d.qlt]. | ankn.rgmt.l.bʻl y. | l.špš.ʻlm.l.ʻttrt. | l.ʻnt.l.kl.il.alt[y]. | nmry.mlk.ʻlm. | mlk n.bʻl y.ḥw[t.--]. | yšhr 2008.1.8
l aqht.ǵzr.i]rš.ksp.w atn k. | [ḫrṣ.w aš]lḥ k.w tn.qšt k.[l]. | [ʻnt.tq]ḥ[.q]ṣʻt k.ybmt.limm. | w yʻn.aqht.ǵzr.adr.tqbm. | 17[2AQHT].6.18
. | [---.--]m.l gtrm. | [---.]l ʻnt m. | [---.--]rm.d krm. | [---].l ʻnt m. | [---.]l šlm. | [-]l[-.-]ry.ylbš. | mlk.ylk.lqḥ.ilm. | atr.ilm 33[5].20
p].tb.ap.w npš. | [---].bt.alp w š. | [---.--]m.l gtrm. | [---.]l ʻnt m. | [---.--]rm.d krm. | [---].l ʻnt m. | [---.]l šlm. | [-]l[-.-]ry. 33[5].18
blm. | d ʻl k.mḫṣ.aqht.ǵzr. | ʻwrt.yšt k.bʻl.l ht. | w ʻlm h.l ʻnt.p dr.dr. | ʻdb.uḫry.mt.yd h. | dnil.bt h.ymǵyn.yšt | ql.dnil 19[1AQHT].4.168
tnm. | b ʻqbt.tr.adr.b ǵlil.qnm. | tn.l ktr.w ḫss.ybʻl.qšt l ʻnt. | qṣʻt.l ybmt.limm.w tʻn.btlt. | ʻnt.irš ḥym.l aqht.ǵzr. | ir 17[2AQHT].6.24
hkl h.nṣb.skn.ilib h.b qdš. | ztr.ʻm h.l arṣ.mšṣu.qtr h. | l ʻpr.dmr.atr h.tbq.lḥt. | niṣ h.grš d.ʻšy.ln h. | aḥd.yd h.b škrn 17[2AQHT].1.29
. | [nṣb.skn.i]lib h.b qdš. | [ztr.ʻm h.l a]rṣ.mšṣu. | [qtr h.l ʻpr.d]mr.a[t]r h. | [tbq.lḥt.niṣ h.gr]š.d ʻšy. | [ln h.---]. | z[tr.ʻ 17[2AQHT].1.47
. | aḫ y.w šrš.km ary y. | nṣb.skn.ilib y.b qdš. | ztr.ʻm y.l ʻpr.dmr.atr[y]. | tbq lḥt.niṣ y.grš. | d ʻšy.ln.aḥd.yd y.b š | kr 17[2AQHT].2.17
iṣ h.gr]š.d ʻšy. | [ln h.---]. | z[tr.ʻm k.l arṣ.mšṣu.qtr k]. | l ʻpr.dm[r.atr k.tbq]. | lḥt.niṣ k.gr[š.d ʻšy.ln k]. | spu.ksm k.bt 17[2AQHT].2.2
. | [---.ʻ]n h.km.btn.yqr. | [krpn h.-.l]arṣ.ks h.tšpk m. | [l ʻpr.tšu.g h.]w tṣḥ.šmʻ.mʻ. | [l aqht.ǵzr.i]rš.ksp.w atn k. | [ḫr 17[2AQHT].6.16
].nhr.tlʻm.tm.ḥrbm.its.anšq. | [-]htm.l arṣ.ypl.ul ny.w l.ʻpr.ʻzm ny. | l bʻl[-.---]. | tḥt.ksi.zbl.ym.w ʻn.ktr.w ḫss.l rgm 2.4[68].5
ʻl.ar. | w.tlt. | ʻl.ubrʻy. | w.tn.ʻl. | mlk. | w.aḥd. | ʻl atlg. | w l.ʻṣm. | tspr. | nrn.al.tud | ad.at.l hm. | ttm.ksp. 1010.17
rḫ. | y bn.ašld.šu.ʻdb.tk.mdbr qdš. | tm tgrgr.l abnm.w l.ʻṣm.šbʻ.šnt. | tmt.tmn.nqpt.ʻd.ilm.nʻmm.ttlkn. | šd.tṣdn.pat. 23[52].66
m.---]. | asr.sswm.tṣmd.dg[-.---]. | tʻln.l mrkbt hm.ti[ty.l ʻr hm]. | tlkn.ym.w ta aḫr.š[pšm.b tlt]. | mǵy.rpum.l grnt.i[l 20[121].2.4
h.l tdd.ilnym]. | asr.mr[kbt.---]. | tʻln.l mr[kbt hm.tity.l] | ʻr hm.tl[kn.ym.w tn.aḫr.špšm]. | b tlt.mǵy[.rpum.l grnt]. 22.1[123].23
.]l tr.qdqd h. | il[.--.]rḥq.b ǵr. | km.y[--.]ilm.b ṣpn. | ʻdr.l[ʻr].ʻrm. | tb.l pd[r.]pdrm. | tt.l ttm.aḥd.ʻr. | šbʻm.šbʻ.pdr. | t 4[51].7.7
lbš.npṣ.att.[--]. | ṣbi nrt.ilm.špš.[-]r[--]. | pǵt.minš.šdm l mʻ[rb]. | nrt.ilm.špš.mǵy[t]. | pǵt.l ahlm.rgm.l yt[pn.y] | bl.a 19[1AQHT].4.210
pš.yḥ.dnil. | [mt.rp]i.brlt.ǵzr.mt hrnmy. | [---].hw.mḫ.l ʻrš h.yʻl. | [---].bm.nšq.att h. | [---.]b ḥbq h.ḥmḥmt. | [---.--] n 17[2AQHT].1.39
b.rpan.bn.yyn.ʻšrt. | b.ypʻr.ʻšrm. | b.nʻmn.bn.ply.ḫmšt.l.ʻšrm. | b.gdn.bn.uss.ʻšrm. | b.ʻdn.bn.tt.ʻšrt. | b.bn.qrdmn.tlt 2054.1.17
t. | [---.-]kyn.ʻšrt. | b.bn.ʻsl.ʻšrm.tqlm kbd. | b.tmq.ḫmšt.l.ʻšrt. | b.[---].šbʻt.ʻšrt. | b.bn.pdrn.ʻšrm. | d.bn.šbʻl.uḫnpy.ḫmš 2054.1.7
n.šr.ugrt.dkr.yṣr. | tgǵln.ḫmš.ddm. | [---].ḫmš.ddm. | tt.l.ʻšrm.bn[š.mlk.---].ḫzr.lqḥ.ḥp[r]. | ʻšt.ʻšr h.bn[.---.--]ḫ.zr. | bʻ 2011.40
.dd. | l u[-]m. | b.tbq.arbʻm.drʻ.w.ʻšr.dd.drt. | w[.a]rbʻ.l.ʻšrm.dd.l.yḥšr.bl.bn h. | b.gt.mʻbr.arbʻm.l.mit.drʻ.w.tmnym 1098.11
šr. | [h]mrm. | ddm.l.ybr[k]. | bdmr.prs.l.u[-]m[-]. | tmn.l.ʻšrm. | dmd.b d.mry[n]m. 2102.9
.mrynm. | ʻšr.mrum.w.šbʻ.hsnm. | tšʻm.mdrǵlm. | arbʻ.l ʻšrm.ḫsnm. | ʻšr.hbtnm. | ttm.l.mit.tn.kbd. | tgmr. 1030.8
w.tn.ʻšr h.ḫpnt. | [š]šwm.amtm.ʻkyt. | yd.llḥ hm. | w.tlt.l.ʻšrm. | ḫpnt.ššwm.tn. | pddm.w.d.tt. | [mr]kbt.w.ḥrṣ. 2049.6
.ttm.arbʻ.kbd.yn.d.l.tb. | b.gt.mʻrby. | ttm.yn.tb.w.ḫmš.l.ʻšrm. | yn.d.l.tb.b.ulm. | mit.yn.tb.w.ttm.tt.kbd. | yn.d.l.tb.b. 1084.9
kr.ḫmš.mat.kbd.tlt.šm[n]. | alp.mitm.kbd.tlt.hlb. | šbʻ.l.ʻšrm.kkr.tlt. | d.ybl.blym. 1135.6
n. | arbʻm.l.mit.šmn. | arbʻm.l.mit.tišr. | tt.tt.b [t]ql.tltt.l.ʻšrm.ksp hm. | šstm.b.šbʻm. | tlt.mat.trm.b.ʻšrt. | mit.adrm.b 1127.5
w a]r[bʻ] ksp ʻl bn ymn. | šb šr šmn [--] tryn. | ḫm[š]m l ʻšr ksp ʻl bn llit. | [--]l[-.-]p ʻl [---.-]bʻm arny. | w ʻl [---.]rbʻm 1103.6
[--].d.ntn[.d.]ksp. | [t]mn.l.ʻšrm[.l.b]t.ʻttrt. | [t]lt.ʻšr h.[b]t.ršp.gn. | arbʻ.b d.b[n].ušryn. 1088.2
spr.bnš.mlk. | d.b d.prt. | tšʻ.l.ʻšrm. | lqḥ.ššlmt. | tmn.l.arbʻm. | lqḥ.š'rt. 1025.3
[---.ʻ]šrt. | ḫlb.ḫmšt.l.ʻšrm. | mril.ʻšrt. | glbty.arbʻt. | [--]tb.ʻšrt. 1180.2
.šbʻt.ʻšrt ʻšrt.šlm. | yky.ʻšrt.ttt šlm.ʻšrt. | bn.ḫgby.tmnt.l ʻšrm.ʻšrt.ḫmš.kbd. | bn.ilṣdq.šbʻt tltt šlm. | bn.tmq.arbʻt tql 1131.8
]. | [t]tb.mdbḥ.bʻl.g[dlt.---]. | dqt.l.ṣpn.w.dqt[.---]. | tn.l.ʻšrm.pamt.[---]. | š.dd.šmn.gdlt.w.[---.brr]. | rgm.yttb.b.tdt.t 35[3].43
nš.ilm.tb.md] | bḥ.bʻl.[gdlt.---.dqt]. | l ṣpn.w [dqt.---.tn.l ʻš] | rm.pam[t.---]. | š dd šmn[.gdlt.w.---]. | brr.r[gm.yttb.b t APP.II[173].46
yd ḫmšm. | ṣṣ tmn.ḫmšm. | [ṣṣ] ʻmtdl tltm. | ṣṣ ʻmlbi tt l ʻšrm. | ṣṣ bn adty ḫmšm. | ṣṣ amtrn arbʻm. | ṣṣ iytlm mit tlt 2097.6
b.ann[.---.-]ny[-]. | b.ḫqn.[---]m.ṣ[-]n. | [b].bn.ay[--.---].l.ʻšrm. | [-]gp[.---.]ʻrny.ttm. | [---.]dyn.ḫmšt.ʻšrt. | [---.-]til.ḫmš 2054.2.17
[ḫm]š l ʻšrm. | [-]dmm. | b.ubn. 1167.1
[-]gp[.---.]ʻrny.ttm. | [---.]dyn.ḫmšt.ʻšrt. | [---.-]til.ḫmšt.l ʻšrm. | [--.-]n.w.aḫt h.arbʻm. | [--.-]dn.ʻšrm. | [--.-]dwn.tltm. 2054.2.20
dbḥt.byy.bn. | šry.l ʻtt. RS61[24.323.2]
b.[m]dlm. | [---.l i]ytlm. | [---].gmn. | [---].l.urǵttb. | [---.]l.ʻttrum. | [---.]l.brqn. | [---].skn. | [---.ʻg]ltn. | [---].ʻgltn. | [---.]ʻ 2162.B.6
r[-.---]. | [l.--]ḥl. | [l.--.]mgmr. | [l.-.]qdšt. | l.ʻttrt.ndrgd. | l.ʻttrt.abdr. | l.dml. | l.ilt[.-]pn. | l.uš[ḫr]y. | [---.-]mrn. | l twl. | [1001.1.12
kd[.l.]trtn[m]. | arbʻ l.mry[nm]. | kdm l.ḥty.[---]. | kdm l.ʻtr[t]. | kd l.m[d]rǵl[m]. | kd l.mryn[m]. 1091.10
qtm]. | šbʻ d.w.šbʻ[d.qlt]. | ankn.rgmt.l.bʻl y. | l.špš.ʻlm.l.ʻttrt. | l.ʻnt.l.kl.il.alt[y]. | nmry.mlk.ʻlm. | mlk n.bʻl y.ḥw[t.--] 2008.1.7
[l.a]rṣy. | [l.--]r[-.---]. | [l.--]ḥl. | [l.--.]mgmr. | [l.-.]qdšt. | l.ʻttrt.ndrgd. | l.ʻttrt.abdr. | l.dml. | l.ilt[.-]pn. | l.uš[ḫr]y. | [---.-] 1001.1.12
. | b ym.dbḥ.tp[-]. | aḥt.l mzy.bn[--]. | aḥt.l mkt.ǵr. | aḥt.l ʻttrt. | arbʻ.ʻṣrm. | gt.trmn. | aḥt.slḫu. 39[19].16
]rt.mḫṣ.bnš.mlk.ybʻl hm. | [---.--]t.w.ḫpn.l.azzlt. | [---.]l.ʻttrt.šd. | [---].ybʻlnn. | [---.--]n.b.tlt.šnt.l.nṣd. | [---.--]ršp.mlk 1106.55
---.š]mt. | [---].y[--.--]m. | [---.--]n.d[--.--]i. | [--]t.mdt h[.l.]ʻttrt.šd. | [---.-]rt.mḫṣ.bnš.mlk.ybʻl hm. | [---.--]t.w.ḫpn.l.az 1106.52
l.[----]. | l.[----]. | l.ʻt[trt.---]. | l.mš[--.---]. | l.ilt[.---]. | l.bʻlt[.---]. | l.il.bt[.---]. | l.ilt 1004.3
l.---]. | [--.at]rt.š[.---]. | [---.]l pdr[-.---]. | ṣin aḥd h[.---]. | l ʻttrt[.---]. | ʻlm.kmm[.---]. | w b tlt.ṣ[in.---]. | l ll.pr[-.---]. | mit 37[22].6
-.]ʻt[trt.---]. | [-.k]su.ilt[.---]. | [tl]t.l ʻttrt[.---]. | [--.]l ilt.š l ʻtt[rt.---]. | [ʻ]ṣr.l pdr tt.ṣ[in.---]. | tšnpn.ʻlm.km[m.---]. | w.l l 38[23].4
[---.]ʻt[trt.---]. | [-.k]su.ilt[.---]. | [tl]t.l ʻttrt[.---]. | [--.]l ilt.š l ʻtt[rt.---]. | [ʻ]ṣr.l pdr tt.ṣ[in.---]. | tšnpn 38[23].3
ṣmdm.a[--.---]. | b d.prḫ[-.---]. | apnm.l.ʻ[--]. | apnm.l.[---]. | apnm.l.d[--]. | apnm.l.bn[.---]. | apnm.l.[145[318].3
ḫtṣb.bn.qrtm.ttʻr. | ksat.l mhr.tʻr.tlḥnt. | l ṣbim.hdmm.l ǵzrm. | mid.tmtḫṣn.w tʻn. | tḫtṣb.w tḥdy.ʻnt. | tǵdd.kbd h.b 3[ʻNT].2.22
]tḫṣ b ʻmq. | [tḫtṣb.bn.qrtm.ttʻr.tlḥnt.]l ṣbim. | [hdmm.l ǵzrm.mid.tmtḫṣn.w t]ʻn.tḫtṣb. | [w tḥdy.ʻnt.tǵdd.kbd h.b ṣ 7.1[131].6

wy. | aqht[.ġz]r.w y‘n.aqht.ġzr. | al.tšrgn.y btlt m.dm.l ġzr. | šrg k.ḫḫm.mt.uḫryt.mh.yqḥ. | mh.yqḥ.mt.aṯryt.spsg.y 17[2AQHT].6.34
m | lk.‘l.ilm.l ymru. | ilm.w nšm.d yšb | [‘].hmlt.arṣ.gm.l ġ | [lm] h.b‘l k.yṣḥ.‘n. | [gpn].w ugr.b ġlmt. | [‘mm.]ym.bn.ẓl 4[51].7.52
yt.ilm. | w tn.bt.l b‘l.km. | [i]lm.w ḥẓr.k bn. | [a]ṯrt.gm.l ġlm h. | b‘l.yṣḥ.‘n.gpn. | w ugr.bn.ġlmt. | ‘mm ym.bn.ẓlm[t]. 8[51FRAG].5
a]ṯrt. | k t‘n.ẓl.ksp.w n[-]t. | ḫrṣ.šmḫ.rbt.a[ṯrt]. | ym.gm.l ġlm h.k [tṣḥ]. | ‘n.mkṯr.ap.t[---]. | dgy.rbt.aṯr[t.ym]. | qḥ.rṯt. 4[51].2.29
]. | kdm.yn.prs.qmḥ.[---]. | mdbḥt.bt.ilt.‘ṣr[m.l ṣpn.š]. | l ġlmt.š.w l [---.l yrḫ]. | gd[lt].l nkl[.gdlt.l b‘lt.bhtm]. | ‘š[rm.] 35[3].25
.yn]. | prs.qmḥ.m‘[--.---]. | mdbḥt.bt.i[lt.‘ṣrm.l]. | ṣpn š.l ġlm[t.š.w l.---]. | l yrḫ.gdlt.l [nkl.gdlt.l b‘] | [lt].bht[m].[‘]ṣr APP.II[173].27
[p]š pgr. | [g]dlt iltm ḫnqtm.d[q]tm. | [yr]ḫ.kṯy gdlt.w l ġlmt š. | [w]pamt ṯlṯm.w yrdt.[m]dbḥt. | gdlt.l b‘lt bhtm.‘ṣr 34[1].19
.mt. | rpi.yṣly.‘rpt.b | ḥm.un.yr.‘rpt. | tmṭr.b qẓ.ṭl.yṭll. | l ġnbm.šb‘.šnt. | yṣr k.b‘l.ṯmn.rkb. | ‘rpt.bl.ṭl.bl rbb. | bl.šr‘.th 19[1AQHT].1.42
.ašt. | [---].amr k. | [---].k.ybt.mlk. | [---].w.ap.ank. | [---].l.ġr.amn. | [---.-]ktt.hn.ib. | [---.]mlk. | [---.]adt y.td‘. | w.ap.ml 1012.16
]. | ‘l.l ṯkm.bnw n. | l nḫnpt.mšpy. | ṯlṯ.kmm.ṯrr y. | [---.]l ġr.gm.ṣḥ. | [---.]r[-]m. 16[126].4.17
--].l ḥbš k. | ‘tk.ri[š.]l mhr k. | w ‘p.l dr[‘].nšr k. | w rbṣ.l ġr k.inbb. | kt ġr k.ank.yd‘t. | [-]n.atn.at.mṯb k[.---]. | [š]mm. 13[6].9
t. | [---.šp]š.l [hrm.ġ]rpl.‘l.arṣ. | [---.]ḥmt.l p[.nṯ]k.abd.l p.ak[l]. | [ṯm.dl.]isp.ḥ[mt.---.-]hm.yasp.ḥmt. | [---.š]pš.l [hr UG5.8.10
mt.isp.[šp]š l hrm.ġrpl.‘l arṣ. | [l a]n ḥmt.l p[.n]ṯk.abd.l p.akl ṯm.dl. | [---.q]l.bl.tbḥ[n.l]azd.‘r.qdm. | [---].‘ẓ q[dm.--. UG5.8.20
šlm. | [yis]p.ḥmt.isp.[šp]š l hrm.ġrpl.‘l arṣ. | [l a]n ḥmt.l p[.n]ṯk.abd.l p.akl ṯm.dl. | [---.q]l.bl.tbḥ[n.l]azd.‘r.qdm. | [- UG5.8.20
]‘l.ar[ṣ.---.ḥ]mt. | [---.šp]š.l [hrm.ġ]rpl.‘l.arṣ. | [---.]ḥmt.l p[.nṯ]k.abd.l p.ak[l]. | [ṯm.dl.]isp.ḥ[mt.---.-]hm.yasp.ḥmt. | [UG5.8.10
kbm.ṯm.tpl k.lbnt. | [-.]rgm.k yrkt.‘ṯqbm. | [---]m.‘ẓpn.l pit. | m[--]m[.--]tm.w mdbḥt. | ḥr[.---.]‘l.kbkbt. | n‘m.[--.-]ll 13[6].15
lk.km.p[---]. | [---.]bt.tḥbṭ.km.ṣq.ṣdr[.---]. | [---.]kl.b kl.l pgm.pgm.l.b[---]. | [---.]mdbm.l ḥrn.ḥr[n.---]. | [---.--]m.ql.h 1001.1.26
| il[.--.]rḥq.b ġr. | km.y[--.]ilm.b ṣpn. | ‘dr.l[‘ r].‘rm. | ṯb.l pd[r.]pdrm. | ṯṯ.l ṯṯm.aḥd.‘r. | šb‘m.šb‘.pdr. | ṯmnym.b‘l.[----] 4[51].7.8
su.ilt[.---]. | [ṯl]ṯ.l ‘ttrt[.---]. | [--.]l ilt.š l ‘ṯt[rt.---]. | [‘]ṣr.l pdr ṯṯ.ṣ[in.---]. | tšnpn.‘lm.km[m.---]. | w.l ll.‘ṣrm.w [---]. | k 38[23].5
[-----]. | [---.--]t.š l i[l.---]. | [--.aṯ]rt.š[.---]. | [---.]l pdr[-.---]. | ṣin aḥd h[.---]. | l ‘ṯtrt[.---]. | ‘lm.kmm[.---]. | w b ṯ 37[22].4
. | krpn.b klat.yd h. | b krb.‘ẓm.ridn. | mt.šmm.ks.qdš. | l tphn h.aṯt.krpn. | l t‘n.aṯrt.alp. | kd.yqḥ.b ḫmr. | rbt.ymsk.b 3[‘NT].1.14
. | nḫtm.ḫt k.mmnnm.mṭ yd k.hl.‘ṣr. | tḥrr.l išt.w ṣḥrt.l pḥmm.aṯtm.a[ṯt.il]. | aṯt.il.w ‘lm h.yhbr.špt hm.yš[q]. | hn.š 23[52].48
t.nḫtm.ḫt k.mmnnm.mṭ.yd k. | h[l.]‘ṣr.tḥrr.l išt.ṣḥrrt.l pḥmm. | a[ṯ]tm.aṯt.il.aṯt.il.w ‘lm h.w hm. | aṯtm.tṣḥn y.ad a 23[52].41
ymnn.mṭ.yd h.yšu. | yr.šmm h.yr.b šmm.‘ṣr.yḫrṭ yšt. | l pḥm.il.aṯtm.k ypt.hm.aṯtm.tṣḥn. | y mt.mt.nḫtm.ḫṭ k.mmn 23[52].39
nḫtm.ḫṭ k. | mmnnm.mṭ yd k.hl.‘ṣr.tḥrr.l išt. | w ṣḥrrt.l pḥmm.btm.bt.il.bt.il. | w ‘lm h.w hn.aṯtm.tṣḥn y.mt mt. | n 23[52].45
.hw.ṯ‘ n[ṯ‘y.hw.nkt.nk]t.ytši.l ab bn il. | ytši.l d[r.bn il.l]mpḫrt.bn il. | l ṯkm[n.w šnm.]hn ‘[r]. | [---.]w npy[.---]. | [--- 32[2].1.34
arb‘.ḥm[r.---]. | l ṯlṯ. | tn.l.brr[.---]. | arb‘.ḥmr[.---]. | l.pḫ[-.]w.[---]. | w.l.k[--]. | w.l.k[--]. 1139.5
hw.ṯ‘.nṯ‘y.hw.nkt.nkt.]yt[ši.l ab.bn.il]. | [ytši.l dr.bn.il.l mpḫ]rt.[bn.il.l ṯkmn.w šn]m hn š. | [---.w n]py.gr[.ḥmyt.ug 32[2].1.9B
w.ṯ‘ | nṯ‘y. | hw.nkt.nkt.y[t]ši.l ab.bn.il.ytši.l dr. | bn il.l mpḫrt.bn.il.l ṯkmn[.w]šnm.hn.‘r. | w.ṯb.l mspr.m[šr] mšr. 32[2].1.26
hw.ṯ‘.nṯ‘y.hw.nkt.n[k]t.ytši[.l ab.bn.il]. | ytši.l dr.bn.il.l mpḫrt.bn.i[l.l ṯkmn.w š]nm hn š. | w šqrb.‘r.mšr mšr bn.ug 32[2].1.17
.ṯ‘.nṯ‘]y. | [hw.nkt.nkt.ytši.l ab.bn.il.ytši.l d]r.bn[.il]. | [l mpḫrt.bn.il.l ṯkmn.w šnm.hn š]. | [w šqrb.š.mšr mšr.bn.ug 32[2].1.3
l t[--]. | [---.]drk.brḥ.arṣ.lk pn h.yrk.b‘[l]. | [---.]bt k.ap.l pḫr k ‘nt tqm.‘nt.tqm. | [---.p]ḫr k.ygrš k.qr.bt k.ygrš k. | [-- 1001.2.9
m‘d.qmm.a--.am] | r ṯny.d‘t km.w rgm.l ṯr.a[b.-.il.ṯny.l pḫr]. | m‘d.tḥm.ym.b‘l km.adn km.ṯ[pṭ.nhr]. | tn.il m.d tq h 2.1[137].16
ṯt.tpnn. | ‘n.mḫr.‘n.pḫr.‘n.ṯġr. | ‘n.ṯġr.l.ṯġr.ṯṯb. | ‘n.pḫr.l.pḫr.ṯṯb. | ‘n.mḫr.l.mḫr.ṯṯb. | ‘n.bṯy.l.bṯy.ṯṯb. | ‘n.bṯt.l.bṯt.ṯṯb. RS225.8
tḥm.hl[--]. | l pḫry.a[ḫ y]. | w l g.p[-]r[--]. | yšlm[.l k]. | [i]lm[.ṯġr k]. | [t]š[l 56[21].2
tḥm.iwrdr. | l.plsy. | rgm. | yšlm.l k. | l.trġds. | w.l.klby. | šm‘t.ḫti. | nḫtu.ht. 53[54].2
| ḥy.np[š.a]rš. | l.pn.b‘[l y.l].pn.b‘l y. | w.urk.ym.b‘l y. | l.pn.amn.w.l.pn. | il.mṣrm.dt.ṯġrn. | npš.špš.mlk. | rb.b‘l y. 1018.21
‘r. | l ysmsmt.bmt.pḫl. | qdš.yuḫdm.šb‘r. | amrr.k kbkb.l pnm. | aṯr.btlt.‘nt. | w b‘l.tb‘.mrym.ṣpn. | idk.l ttn.pnm. | ‘m.i 4[51].4.17
.mlk.[b]‘l y. | w.hn.ibm.šṣq l y. | p.l.ašt.aṯt y. | n‘r y.ṯh.l pn.ib. | hn.hm.yrgm.mlk. | b‘l y.tmġyy.hn. | alpm.šswm.hnd 1012.29
š. | l.pn.b‘[l y.l].pn.b‘l y. | w.urk.ym.b‘l y. | l.pn.amn.w.l.pn. | il.mṣrm.dt.ṯġrn. | npš.špš.mlk. | rb.b‘l y. 1018.21
. | arš[.---]. | mlk.r[b.b‘]l y.p.l. | ḥy.np[š.a]rš. | l.pn.b‘[l y.l].pn.b‘l y. | w.urk.ym.b‘l y. | l.pn.amn.w.l.pn. | il.mṣrm.dt.ṯġr 1018.21
.an[k.---]. | arš[.---]. | mlk.r[b.b‘]l y.p.l. | ḥy.np[š.a]rš. | l.pn.b‘[l y.l].pn.b‘l y. | w.urk.ym.b‘l y. | l.pn.amn.w.l.pn. 1018.19
n]. | b‘l.sid.zbl.b‘l. | arṣ.qm.yṯ‘r. | w yšlḥmn h. | ybrd.ṯd.l pnw h. | b ḥrb.mlḥt. | qṣ.mri.ndd. | y‘šr.w yšqyn h. | ytn.ks.b 3[‘NT].1.6
‘l. | w yšu.‘n h.w y‘n. | w y‘n.btlt.‘nt. | n‘mt.bn.aḫt.b‘l. | l pnn h.ydd.w yqm. | l p‘n h.ykr‘.w yql. | w yšu.g h.w yṣḥ. | ḥ 10[76].2.17
]b km kbkbt k ṯn. | [---.]b‘l yḥmdn h.yrṯ y. | [---.]dmrn.l pn h yrd. | [---.]b‘l.šm[.--.]rgbt yu. | [---]w yrmy[.q]rn h. | [-- 2001.2.8
d.rbt.kmn. | hlk.aḫt h.b‘l.y‘n.tdrq. | ybnt.ab h.šrḥq.aṯt.l pnn h. | št.alp.qdm h.mria.w tk. | pn h.tḥspn.m h.w trḥṣ. | ṭl 3[‘NT].4.84
m. | [--]b b[ht]. | [zbl.]ym.b hkl.ṯpṭ.nh[r].ytir.ṯr.il.ab h l pn[.zb]l y[m]. | [l pn.ṯp]ṭ[.nhr.]mlkt.[--]pm.l mlkt.wn.in.aṯt 2.3[129].21
n.nrt.ilm.špš.tšu.g h.w t[ṣḥ.šm]‘.m‘. | [-.yṯ]ir ṯr.il.ab k.l pn.zbl.ym.l pn[.ṯ]pṭ[.n]hr. | [ik.a]l.yšm‘ k.ṯr.[i]l.ab k.l ys‘.[a 2.3[129].16
ḥn y. | [--.]šir.b krm.nṭṭt.dm.‘lt.b ab y. | u---].‘lt.b k.lk.l pn y.yrk.b‘l.[--]. | [---.]‘nt.šzrm.tštšḥ.km.ḥ[--]. | [---].‘pr.bt k 1001.1.10
d k.l tdn. | dn.almnt.l ṯpṭ. | ṯpṭ qṣr.npš.l tdy. | ṯšm.‘l.dl.l pn k. | l tšlḥm.ytm.b‘d. | ksl k.almnt.km. | aḫt.‘rš.mdw.anšt. 16.6[127].48
gnryn. | l mlkytn. | ḥnn y l pn mlk. | šin k itn. | r‘ y šṣa idn l y. | l šmn iṯr hw. | p iḫdn gn 1020.3
m. | ugrt.ṯġr k. | ugrt.ṯġr k. | tšlm k.um y. | td‘.ky.‘rbt. | l pn.špš. | w pn.špš.nr. | b y.mid.w um. | tšmḫ.m ab. | w al.trḥl 1015.8
š.tšu.g h.w t[ṣḥ.šm]‘.m‘. | [-.yṯ]ir ṯr.il.ab k.l pn.zbl.ym.l pn[.ṯ]pṭ[.n]hr. | [ik.a]l.yšm‘ k.ṯr.[i]l.ab k.l ys‘.[alt.]ṯ[bt | k.l 2.3[129].16
bl.]ym.b hkl.ṯpṭ.nh[r].ytir.ṯr.il.ab h l pn[.zb]l y[m]. | [l pn.ṯp]ṭ[.nhr.]mlkt.[--]pm.l mlkt.wn.in.aṯt. | [l]k.k[m.ilm]. | 2.3[129].22
l.ybnn. | adn y. | rgm. | tḥm.t[g]yn. | bn k. | l.p[‘n.adn y]. | q[lt.---]. | l.yb[nn]. | b‘l y.r[gm]. | tḥm.‘bd[--]. | ‘ 2115.1.6
l.mlkt. | adt y.rgm. | tḥm.illdr. | ‘bd k.. | l.p‘n a[dt y]. | šb‘ d[.w šb‘ d]. | mrḥq[tm.qlt]. | mn[m.šlm]. 1014.5
l.mlkt. | adt y. | rgm. | tḥm.tlmyn. | ‘bd k. | l.p‘n. | adt y. | šb‘ d. | w.šb‘ id. | mrḥqtm. | qlt. | ‘m.adt y. | mnm 52[89].6
l um y.adt ny. | rgm. | tḥm.tlmyn. | w.aḫtmlk ‘bd k. | l.p‘n.adt ny. | mrḥqtm. | qlny.ilm. | ṯġr k. | tšlm k. | hn ny.‘m n 51[95].5
tb‘.ġlm[m.al.ṯṯb.idk.pnm]. | al.ttn.‘m.pḫr.m‘d.t[k.ġr.ll.l p‘n.il]. | al.tpl.al.tštḥwy.pḫr [m‘d.qmm.a--.am] | r ṯny.d‘t k 2.1[137].14
b.apq.thmtm]. | [ygly.]ḏl i[l].w ybu[.q]rš.mlk[.ab.šnm.l p‘n.il.] | [yhbr.]w yql[.y]štḥw[y.]w ykb[dn h.--]r y[---]. | [---. 2.3[129].5
rš[n.---.tk.ġr.ks]. | ygly ḏd.i[l.w ybu.qrš.mlk]. | ab.šnm.l [p‘n.il.yhbr.w yql]. | yštḥwy.[w ykbdn h.---]. | ṯr.il[.ab h.---] 1[‘NT.IX].3.24
rb. | [a]pq.thmtm.tgly.ḏd. | il.w tbu.qrš.. | mlk.ab.šnm.l p‘n. | il.thbr.w tql. | tštḥwy.w tkbdn h. | tšu.g h.w tṣḥ.tšmḫ 6.1.36[49.1.8]
. | qrb.apq.thmtm. | tgly.ḏd.il.w tbu. | qrš.mlk.ab.šnm. | l p‘n.il.thbr.w tql. | tštḥwy.w tkbd h. | hlm.il.k yphn h. | yprq 4[51].4.25

qrb.ap]q.thmtm tgly.dd il. | [w tbu.qr]š.mlk.ab.šnm. | [l pʻn.il.t]hbr.w tql.tštḥ | [wy.w tkbd]n h.tlšn.aqht.ǵzr. | [---.k 17[2AQHT].6.50
t hm.ln.kḫṯ.zbl hm. | aḫr.tmǵyn.mlak ym.tʻdt.ṯpṭ.nhr.l pʻn.il. | [l t]pl.l tštḥwy.pḫr.mʻd.qmm.a[--].amr. | [ṯn]y.dʻt h 2.1[137].30
l.mlkt. | um y.rgm. | ṯhm.mlk. | bn k. | l.pʻn.um y. | qlt.l.um y. | yšlm.ilm. | tǵr k.tšlm k. | hl ny.ʻm n[50[117].5
l mlkt.u[m] y. | [rg]m[.]t[ḥm]. | mlk.bn [k]. | [l].pʻn.um [y]. | qlt[.l um] y. | yšlm.il[m]. | tǵ[r] k.tš[lm] k. | [h] 1013.4
l.mlk.b[ʻl y]. | r[gm]. | ṯhm.rb.mi[--.ʻ]bd k. | l.pʻn.bʻl y[.mrḥqtm]. | šbʻ d.w.šbʻ[d.qlt]. | ankn.rgmt.l.bʻl y. | 2008.1.4
l.mlk.bʻ[l] y. | rgm. | ṯhm.ṯpṭb[ʻl]. | [ʻ]bd k. | [l.p]ʻn.bʻl y. | [šbʻ] d.šbʻ [d]. | [mr]ḥqtm. | qlt. | ʻbd k.b. | lwsnd. 2063.5
]. | q[lt.---]. | l.yb[nn]. | bʻl y.r[gm]. | ṯhm.ʻbd[--]. | ʻbd k. | l pʻn.bʻl y. | ṯn id.šbʻ d. | mrḥqtm. | qlt.ʻm. | bʻl y.mnm. | šlm. | [2115.2.5
--]. | hm.ṯn.[---]. | hn dt.[---]. | [-----]. | [-----]. | ṯhm[.---]. | l pʻn.bʻl y[.---]. | qlt. | [--]t.mlk.d.y[mlk]. | [--.]ʻbdyrḫ.l.ml[k]. | 2064.10
| w yʻn.btlt.ʻnt. | nʻmt.bn.aḫt.bʻl. | l pnn h.ydd.w yqm. | l pʻn h.ykrʻ.w yql. | w yšu.g h.w yṣḥ. | ḥwt.aḫt.w nar[-]. | qrn. 10[76].2.18
| [kptr.]ks[u.ṯbt h.ḥkpt.arṣ.nḥlt h]. | b alp.šd.r[bt.kmn.l pʻn.kṯr]. | hbr.w ql.t[štḥwy.w kbd.hwt]. | w rgm l k[ṯr.w ḫss 1[ʻNT.IX].3.2
.kptr. | ksu.ṯbt h.ḥkpt. | arṣ.nḥlt h. | b alp.šd.rbt. | kmn.l pʻn.kṯ. | hbr.w ql.tštḥ | wy.w kbd hwt. | w rgm.l kṯr. | w ḫss.ṯ 3[ʻNT.VI].6.18
ṣḥrrt.la. | šmm.b yd.md | d.ilm.mt.b a | lp.šd.rbt.k | mn.l pʻn.mt. | hbr.w ql. | tštḥwy.w k | bd hwt.w rgm. | l bn.ilm.mt 4[51].8.26
[---.-]ʻb.idk. | [l ytn.pnm.tk.]in.bb.b alp ḥzr. | [rbt.kmn.l pʻ]n.ʻnt. | [yhbr.w yql.yšt]ḥwyn.w y | [kbdn h.yšu.g h.w y]ṣ 1[ʻNT.IX].2.15
. | ahbt.ṭly.bt.rb.dd.arṣy. | bt.yʻbdr.km ǵlmm. | w ʻrb n.l pʻn.ʻnt.hbr. | w ql.tštḥwy.kbd hyt. | w rgm.l btlt.ʻnt. | ṯny.l y 3[ʻNT].3.6
ap]. | sgrt.g[-].[-]ẓ[.---] h[.---]. | ʻn.ṯk[.---]. | ʻln.ṭ[--.---]. | l pʻn.ǵl[m]m[.---]. | mid.an[--.]ṣn[--]. | nrt.ilm.špš[.ṣḥrr]t. | la.š 3[ʻNT.VI].5.23
t.ṣʻṣ.bnt.ḫkp[.---]. | [---].aḥw.aṭm.prṭl[.---]. | [---.]mnt.[l]pʻn[.-.-]bd h.aqšr[.---]. | [---].ptḥ y.a[--.]dt[.---].ml[--]. | [---. 1001.1.20
l.hn. | [---].ḫ[m]t.pṭr.w.p nḥš. | [---.--]q.n[t]k.l ydʻ.l bn.l pq ḥmt. | [---.--]n h.ḥmt.w tʻbtn h.abd y. | [---.ǵ]r.šrǵzz.ybk UG5.8.35
.ṯmnt.bn um. | krt.ḥtk n.rš. | krt.grdš.mknt. | aṯt.ṣdq h.l ypq. | mtrḫt.yšr h. | aṯt.trḫ.w tbʻt. | ṯar um.tkn l h. | mṯlṯt.kṯr 14[KRT].1.12
[ḥl.]mlk.[w.]b.ym.ḥdṯ.ṯn.šm. | l.[---]t. | i[d.yd]bḥ.mlk.l.prgl.ṣqrn.b.gg. | ar[bʻ.]arbʻ.mṯbt.azmr.b h.š.šr[-]. | al[p.w].š. 35[3].50
ʻrgm. | ʻšr ddm.l bt. | ʻšrm.dd.l mḫṣm. | ddm l kbs. | dd l prgṭ. | dd.l mri. | dd.l ṯnǵly. | dd.l krwn. | dd.l ṯǵr. | dd.l rmt.r 1100.7
kd.yn. | l prṭ. 159[59].2
qt.ʻrb. | [---.w ẓ]r.mtn y at zd. | [---.]tʻrb.bši. | [---.]l tzd.l tptq. | [---].g[--.]l arṣ. 1[ʻNT.X].5.27
[--]m.[---.] | gm.ṣḥ.l q[ṣ.ilm.---]. | l rḥqm.l p[-.---]. | ṣḥ.il.ytb.b[mrzḥ.---]. | bṯt.ʻllm n.[---]. | ilm.bt.bʻl k. 1[ʻNT.X].4.3
t[.---]. | [---.]k.w tt[--.---]. | [---.]k.w ṯ[--.---]. | [---.]k ṯrm.l p[--.---]. | [---.]l.[--.]rlg[-.---]. | [---.]bn.w [---]. | [---.--]ṭ.kn[-.-- 2125.9
ʻšrm ddm kbd[.-] l alpm mrim. | ṯṯ ddm l ṣin mrat. | ʻšr ddm.l šmʻrgm. | ʻšr ddm.l bt. | ʻšrm.dd.l mḫṣ 1100.2
ṯḫṣ h.b ʻmq. | ṯḫtṣb.bn.qrtm.ṯṭʻr. | ksat.l mhr.ṯʻr.ṯlḥnt. | l ṣbim.hdmm.l ǵzrm. | mid.tmtḫṣn.w tʻn. | ṯḫtṣb.w ṯḥdy.ʻnt. | 3[ʻNT].2.22
t h tʻrb. | [---.tm]ṯḫṣ b ʻmq. | [ṯḫtṣb.bn.qrtm.ṯṭʻr.ṯlḥnt.]l ṣbim. | [hdmm.l ǵzrm.mid.tmtḫṣn.w t]ʻn.ṯḫtṣb. | [w ṯḥdy.ʻn 7.1[131].5
[-----]. | [---.--]y. | [-----]. | [any.l yṣ]ḥ.ṯr. | [il.ab h.i]l.mlk. | [d yknn h.yṣ]ḥ.aṯ | [rt.w bn h.]ilt. | 4[51].1.4
ṯ n. | in.d ʻln h.klny y.qš h. | nbln.klny y.nbl.ks h. | any.l yṣḥ.ṯr.il.ab h.il. | mlk.d yknn h.yṣḥ.aṯrt. | w bn h.ilt.w ṣbrt. 3[ʻNT.VI].5.43
ʻln h. | klny n.q[š] h.n[bln]. | klny n[.n]bl.ks h. | [an]y.l yṣḥ.ṯr il.ab h. | [i]l.mlk.d yknn h.yṣḥ. | aṯrt.w bn h.ilt.w ṣbrt 4[51].4.47
trm.d [ṣ]py. | w.trm.aḥdm. | ṣpym. | ṯlṯ mrkbt mlk. | d.l.ṣpy. | [---.t]r hm. | [---].ššb. | [---.]tr h. | [a]rbʻ.qlʻm. | arbʻ.mḏr 1122.6
| [--]t.dqtm.[b nbk.---]. | [--.k]mm.gdlt.l.b[ʻl.---]. | [dq]t.l.ṣpn.gdlt.l[.---]. | u[gr]t.š.l.[il]ib.ǵ[--.--rt]. | w [ʻṣrm.]l.ri[--.---] 35[3].34
.dqt[.---]. | bqtm.b nbk.[---]. | kmm.gdlt.l b[ʻl.--.dqt]. | l ṣpn.gdlt.[l.---]. | ugrt.š l ili[b.---]. | rt.w ʻṣrm.l[.---]. | pamt.w APP.II[173].37
.k[--.---]. | ʻṣrm.l i[nš.ilm.ṯb.md] | bḥ.bʻl.[gdlt.---.dqt]. | l ṣpn.w [dqt.---.ṯn.l ʻš] | rm.pam[t.---]. | š dd šmn[.gdlt.w.---]. APP.II[173].46
[--].aṯrt.ʻṣr[m.l inš.ilm]. | [ṯ]ṯb.mdbḥ.bʻl.g[dlt.---]. | dqt.l.ṣpn.w.dqt[.---]. | ṯn.l.ʻšrm.pamt.[---]. | š.dd.šmn.gdlt.w.[---.b 35[3].42
.w ḫrṣ ṯʻ ṯn šm l btbt. | alp.w š šrp.alp šlmm. | l bʻl.ʻṣr l ṣpn. | npš.w.š.l ršp bbt. | [ʻ]ṣrm l h.ršp [-]m. | [---.]bqt[-]. | [b] UG5.12.A.10
r.arb[ʻ.---]. | kdm.yn.prs.qmḥ.[---]. | mdbḥt.bt.ilt.ʻṣr[m.l ṣpn.š]. | l ǵlmt.š.w l [---.l yrḫ]. | gd[lt].l nkl[.gdlt.l bʻlt.bhtm 35[3].24
ʻ.[---.kdm.yn]. | prs.qmḥ.m[--.---]. | mdbḥt.bt.i[lt.ʻṣrm.l]. | ṣpn š.l ǵlm[t.š.w l.---]. | l yrḫ.gdlt.l [nkl.gdlt.l bʻ] | [lt].bht APP.II[173].26
.l] rm[š.]kbd.w š. | [l šlm.kbd.al]p.w š.[l] bʻl.ṣpn. | [dqt.l.ṣpn.šrp].w š[l]mm.kmm. | [w bbt.bʻl.ugrt.]kdm.w npš. | [ili 36[9].1.15
.š l rmš. | w kbd.w š.l šlm kbd. | alp.w š.l bʻl ṣpn. | dqt l ṣpn.šrp.w šlmm. | kmm.w bbt.bʻl.ugrt. | w kdm.w npš ilib. | UG5.13.10
w b[--.---]. | l il limm[.---]. | w ṯt.npš[.---]. | kbd.w [---]. | l ṣp[n.---]. | š.[---]. | w [----]. | k[--.---]. | ʻn[t.---]. 40[134].11
ṯlḥn.bʻlt.bhtm. | ʻlm.ʻlm.gdlt l bʻl. | ṣpn.ilbt[.---.]d[--]. | l ṣpn[.---.-]lu. | ilib[.---.b]ʻl. | ugrt[.---.--]n. | [w] š l [---]. UG5.13.34
bʻ.ḫdǵlm. | l.[---]mn ḫpn. | l[.--.]škn.ḫpn. | l.k[-]w.ḫpn. | l.ṣ[--].šʻ[rt]. | l.ʻdy.š[ʻ]r[t]. | ṯlṯ.l.ʻd.ab[ǵ]l. | l.ydln.šʻrt. | l.kṯrml 1117.5
| bm.nšq.w hr.[b]ḥbq.w ḥ[m]ḥmt.ytb[n]. | yspr.l ḫmš.l ṣ[---.]šr.pḫr.klat. | tqtnṣn.w tldn.tld.[ilm.]nʻmm.agzr ym. | 23[52].57
.tm]. | yḥpn.ḥy[ly.zbl.mlk.ʻllm y]. | šmʻ.atm[.---]. | ym.lm.qd[.---]. | šmn.prst[.---]. | ydr.hm.ym[.---]. | ʻl amr.yu[ḫd. 22.1[123].14
hdm[.w] l.hdm.ytb. | l arṣ.yṣq.ʻmr. | un.l riš h.ʻpr.plṭt. | l qdqd h.lpš.yks. | mizrtm.ǵr.b abn. | ydy.psltm.b yʻr. | yhdy.l 5[67].6.16
b]r.gbl.ʻbr. | qʻl.ʻbr.iht. | np šmm.šmšr. | l dgy.aṯrt. | mǵ.l qdš.amrr. | idk.al.tnn. | pnm.tk.ḥqkpt. | il.kl l h.kptr. | ksu.ṯbt 3[ʻNT.VI].6.11
at. | mdbr.tlkn. | ym.w ṯn.aḥr. | šp[š]m.b [ṯ]lṯ. | ym[ǵy.]l qdš. | a[ṯrt.]ṣrm.w l ilt. | ṣd[yn]m.ṯm. | yd[r.k]rt.ṯʻ. | i.iṯt.aṯrt. 14[KRT].4.197
ṯr[.il.ab -.w tʻn.rbt]. | aṯr[t.ym.šmʻ.l qdš]. | w am[rr.l dgy.rbt]. | aṯrt.ym[.mdl.ʻr]. | ṣmd.pḥl[.št.gp 4[51].4.2
qʻ.kbd h.w yhd. | iṯ.šmt.iṯ.ʻẓm.w yqḥ b hm. | aqht.ybl.l qẓ.ybky.w yqbr. | yqbr.nn.b mdgt.b knk[-]. | w yšu.g h.w yṣ 19[1AQHT].3.146
d.gg[ʻt]. | b.ʻšrt.ksp. | ṯlṯ.uṯbm.b d.alḫn.b.ʻšrt[.k]sp. | rṯ.l.ql.d.ybl.prd. | b.ṯql.w.nṣp.ksp. | ṯmn.lbšm.w.mšlt. | l.udmym 2101.12
sp.l.m[--]. | mit.ʻšrm.[k]bd.yn.ḥsp.l.y[--]. | ʻšrm.yn.ḥsp.l.ql.d.tbʻ.mṣ[r]m. | mit.arbʻm.kbd.yn.mṣb. | l.mdrǵlm. | ʻšrn ʻš 1084.27
. | mk.špšm.b šbʻ. | w l.yšn.pbl. | mlk.l [qr.]ṯiqt. | ibr h[.l]ql.nhqt. | ḥmr[h.l gʻt.]alp. | ḥrṯ[.l z]ǵt.klb. | [ṣ]pr[.apn]k. | [14[KRT].5.224
pt.w hn.špšm. | b šbʻ.w l.yšn.pbl. | mlk.l qr.ṯigt.ibr h. | l ql.nhqt.ḥmr h. | l gʻt.alp.ḥrṯ.zǵt. | klb.ṣpr.w ylak. | mlakm.l 14[KRT].3.121
[---].aṯt n.r[---]. | [---.]ḫr[-.--]. | [---.]plnt.[---]. | [---.]ʻmt.l ql.rpi[.---]. | [---.-]llm.abl.mṣrp k.[---]. | [---.]y.mṯnt.w ṯḥ.ṯbt. 1001.2.2
d ydbḥ mlk. | l ušḫ[r] ḫlmṭ. | l bbt il bt. | š l ḫlmṭ. | w tr l qlḥ. | w š ḥll ydm. | b qdš il bt. | w ṯlḥm aṯt. | š l ilbt.šlmm. | k UG5.7.TR3
mm. | kll ylḥm b h. | w l bbt šqym. | š l uḫr ḫlmṭ. | w tr l qlḥ. | ym aḥd. UG5.11.13
[-----]. | yṣq.šm[n.---]. | ʻn.tr.arṣ.w šmm. | sb.l qṣm.arṣ. | l ksm.mhyt.ʻn. | l arṣ.m[ṭ]r.bʻl. | w l šd.mṭr.ʻly. | nʻ 16[126].3.3
il dbḥ.b bt h.mṣd.ṣd.b qrb | hkl [h].ṣḥ.l qṣ.ilm.tlḥmn. | ilm.w tštn.tštn y[n] ʻd šbʻ. | trṯ.ʻd.škr.yʻdb.yr UG5.1.1.2
[--]m.[---.] | gm.ṣḥ.l q[ṣ.ilm.---]. | l rḥqm.l p[-.---]. | ṣḥ.il.ytb.b[mrzḥ.---]. | bṯt.ʻll 1[ʻNT.X].4.2
.abn.yd k. | mšdpt.w hn.špšm. | b šbʻ.w l.yšn.pbl. | mlk.l qr.ṯigt.ibr h. | l ql.nhqt.ḥmr h. | l gʻt.alp.ḥrṯ.zǵt. | klb.ṣpr.w 14[KRT].3.120
ʻ.ym. | ḫmš.ṯdṯ.ym. | mk.špšm.b šbʻ. | w l.yšn.pbl. | mlk.l [qr.]ṯiqt. | ibr h[.l]ql.nhqt. | ḥmr[h.l gʻt.]alp. | ḥrṯ[.l z]ǵt.klb 14[KRT].5.223
[l a]q[h]t. | [t]krb.[---.]l qrb.mym. | tql.[---.]lb.ṯt[b]r. | qšt[.---]r.y[ṯ]br. | ṯmn.[---.]btlt. 19[1AQHT].1.2

.w b lb.tqny. | [---.]ṯb l y.l aqht.ġzr.ṯb l y w l k. | [---]m.l aqry k.b ntb.pš‘. | [---].b ntb.gan.ašql k.tḥt. | [p‘n y.a]nk.n‘ 17[2AQHT].6.43
w š. | šrp.w šlmm kmm. | l b‘l.ṣpn b ‘r‘r. | pamt ṯlṯm š l qrnt. | ṯlḥn.b‘lt.bhtm. | ‘lm.‘lm.gdlt l b‘l. | ṣpn.ilbt[.---.]d[--]. UG5.13.30
. | ‘nt.brḥ.p ‘lm h. | ‘nt.p dr.dr.‘db.uḫry mṭ yd h. | ymġ.l qrt.ablm.abl[m]. | qrt.zbl.yrḫ.yšu g h. | w yṣḥ.y l k.qrt.ablm 19[1AQHT].4.163
l. | b dbḥ k.bn.dgn. | b mṣd k.w yrd. | krt.l ggt.‘db. | akl.l qryt. | ḥṭt.l bt.ḫbr. | yip.lḥm.d ḫmš. | mġd.ṯdṯ.yrḫm. | ‘dn.ng 14[KRT].2.81
‘l].b dbḥ h.bn dgn. | [b m]ṣd h.yrd.krt. | [l g]gt.‘db.akl.l qryt. | ḥṭt.l bt.ḫbr. | yip.lḥm.d ḫmš. | [mġ]d.ṯdṯ.yr[ḫm]. | ‘dn. 14[KRT].4.172
.b d.qrt. | šd[.-].dyn.b d.pln.nḥl h. | šd.irdyn.bn.ḫrġš[-].l.qrt. | šd.iġlyn.bn.kzbn.l.qr[t]. | šd.pln.bn.tiyn.b d.ilmhr nḥl 2029.16
ln.nḥl h. | šd.irdyn.bn.ḫrġš[-].l.qrt. | šd.iġlyn.bn.kzbn.l.qr[t]. | šd.pln.bn.tiyn.b d.ilmhr nḥl h. | šd knn.bn.ann.‘db. | 2029.17
b. | šd.iln[-].bn.irṯr.l.sḫrn.nḥl h. | šd[.ag]pṯn.b[n.]brrn.l.qrt. | šd[.--]dy.bn.brzn. | l.qrt. 2029.21
.nḥl h. | šd[.ag]pṯn.b[n.]brrn.l.qrt. | šd[.--]dy.bn.brzn. | l.qrt. 2029.23
-]. | ṯn šurtm l bnš [---]. | arb‘ šurt l bn[š.---]. | arb‘ šurt l q[--.---]. | ṯlṯ šurt l bnš [---]. | ṯṯ šurt.l bnš[.---]. | ṯn šurtm l b 137.1[92].5
--]p.gp ym.w yṣġd.gp..thm. | [yqḥ.]il.mšt‘ltm.mšt‘ltm.l riš.agn. | hl h.[t]špl.hl h.trm.hl h.tṣḥ.ad ad. | w hl h.tṣḥ.um. 23[52].31
k.yd.il.k ym. | w yd.il.k mdb.yqḥ.il.mšt‘ltm. | mšt‘ltm.l riš.agn.yqḥ.tš.b bt h. | il.ḫṭ h.nḥt.il.ymnn.mṭ.yd h.yšu. | yr.š 23[52].36
--]ḫp.an.arnn.ql.špš.ḥw.bṯnm.uḫd.b‘lm. | [--.a]ṭm.prṯl.l riš h.ḥmṯ.ṭmṯ. | [--.]ydbr.ṯrmt.al m.qḥn y.š y.qḥn y. | [--.]šir 1001.1.7
yrd.l ksi.yṯb. | l hdm[.w] l.hdm.yṯb. | l arṣ.yṣq.‘mr. | un.l riš h.‘pr.plṯt. | l qdqd h.lpš.yks. | mizrtm.ġr.b abn. | ydy.pslt 5[67].6.15
.š[---]. | ytnm.qrt.l ‘ly[.---]. | b mdbr.špm.yd[.---.---]r. | l riš hm.w yš[--.--]m. | lḥm.b lḥm ay.w šty.b ḫmr yn ay. | šlm 23[52].5
.ḫḫm.mt.uḫryt.mh.yqḥ. | mh.yqḥ.mt.aṯryt.spsg.ysk. | [l]riš.ḥrṣ.l ẓr.qdqd y. | [--.]mt.kl.amt.w an.mtm.amt. | [ap.m] 17[2AQHT].6.37
[l r]iš.r‘y.y[šlm.---]. | [š]lm.bnš.yš[lm.---]. | [-]r.l šlmt.šl[m.---.- 59[100].1
l ri[š.---]. | ypt.‘ṣ[--.---]. | p šlm.[---]. | bt k.b[--.--.m] | ġy k[.---]. 58[20].1
]t.l.ṣpn.gdlt.l[.---]. | u[gr]t.š.l.[il]ib.ġ[--.--rt]. | w [‘ṣrm.]l.ri[--.---]. | [--]t.b‘lt.bt[.---]. | [md]bḥt.b.ḫmš[.---]. | [-.]kbd.w. 35[3].36
l.rb.khnm. | rgm. | tḥm.[---]. | yšlm[.l k.ilm]. | tšlm[k.tġr] k. | t 55[18].1
l.rb. | kṯkym. 1163.1
ṣbṭm. | yṣq.ksp.yšl | ḥ.ḫrṣ.yṣq.ksp. | l alpm.ḫrṣ.yṣq | m.l rbbt. | yṣq-ḫym.w tbṯḫ. | kt.il.dt.rbtm. | kt.il.nbt.b ksp. | šmr 4[51].1.29
m‘[.ṣ]bu h.u[l.mad]. | ṯlṯ.mat.rbt. | hlk.l alpm.ḫḏḏ. | w l.rbt.kmyr. | aṯr.ṯn.ṯn.hlk. | aṯr.ṯlṯ.kl hm. | aḥd.bt h.ysgr. | alm 14[KRT].4.181
at.rbt. | ḫpṯ.d bl.spr. | ṯnn.d bl.hg. | hlk.l alpm.ḫḏḏ. | w l rbt.kmyr. | [a]ṯr.ṯn.ṯn.hlk. | aṯr.ṯlṯ.kl hm. | yḥd.bt h.sgr. | alm 14[KRT].2.93
t.arṣ. | s‘.il.dqt.k amr. | sknt.k ḥwt.yman. | d b h.rumm.l rbbt. 4[51].1.44
n h. | [---.-]ny h pdr.ttġr. | [---.n]šr k.al ttn.l n. | [---.]tn l rbd. | [---.]b‘lt h w yn. | [---.rk]b ‘rpt. | [---.--]n.w mnu dg. | [- 2001.2.13
spr.bnš.mlk. | d.b d.prṯ. | tš‘.l.‘šrm. | lqḥ.ššlmt. | ṯmn.l.arb‘m. | lqḥ.š‘rt. 1025.5
ṯ.alp h.[---]. | swn.qrty.w.[b]n h[.---]. | w.alp h.w.a[r]b‘.l.arb‘[m.---]. | pln.ṯmry.w.ṯn.bn h.w[.---]. | ymrn.apsny.w.aṯt 2044.7
n. | b‘l.k ḫlq.zbl.b‘l. | arṣ.gm.yṣḥ il. | l rbt.aṯrt ym.šm‘. | l rbt.aṯr[t] ym.tn. | aḥd.b bn k.amlkn. | w t‘n.rbt.aṯrt ym. | bl. 6.1.45[49.1.17]
| rt.ary h.k mt.aliyn. | b‘l.k ḫlq.zbl.b‘l. | arṣ.gm.yṣḥ il. | l rbt.aṯrt ym.šm‘. | l rbt.aṯr[t] ym.tn. | aḥd.b bn k.amlkn. | w t 6.1.44[49.1.16]
rh.l arṣ.brqm. | bt.arzm.yklln h. | hm.bt.lbnt.y‘msn h. | l yrgm.l aliyn b‘l. | ṣḥ.ḫrn.b bhm k. | ‘ḏbt.b qrb.hkl k. | tbl k.ġ 4[51].5.74
pt. | ‘l h[wt].kṯr.w ḫss. | ṣḥq.kṯr.w ḫss. | yšu.g h.w yṣḥ. | l rgmt.l k.l ali | yn.b‘l.ṯṯbn.b‘l. | l hwt y.ypth.ḥ | ln.b bht m.ur 4[51].7.23
l.‘pr.‘ẓm ny. | l b‘l[-.---]. | tḥt.ksi.zbl.ym.w ‘n.kṯr.w ḫss.l rgmt. | l k.l zbl.b‘l.ṯnt.l rkb.‘rpt.ht.ib k. | b‘l m.ht.ib k.tmḫṣ. 2.4[68].7
t ym. | bl.nmlk.yd‘.ylḥn. | w y‘n.lṭpn.il d pi | d dq.anm.l yrẓ. | ‘m.b‘l.l y‘db.mrḥ. | ‘m.bn.dgn.k tms m. | w ‘n.rbt.aṯrt 6.1.50[49.1.22]
nṁ.tlḥk. | šmm.ṯtrp. | ym.ḏnbtm. | tnn.l šbm. | tšt.trks. | l mrym.l bt[.---]. | p l.tb‘[.---]. | hmlt ḫt.[---]. | l.tp[-]m.[---]. | n 1003.10
gmm. | argmn.lk.lk.‘nn.ilm. | atm.bštm.w an.šnt. | uġr.l rḥq.ilm.inbb. | l rḥq.ilnym.ṯn.mṯpdm. | tḥt.‘nt.arṣ.ṯlṯ.mtḥ.ġ 3[‘NT].4.78
[---.]n[--.---]. | [---.kpt]r.l r[ḥq.ilm.ḥkpt.l rḥq]. | [ilnym.ṯn.mṯpd]m.t[ḥt.‘nt.arṣ.ṯlṯ.mt 2.3[129].2
.kṯr.w ḫss[.lk.lk.‘nn.ilm.] | atm.bštm.w an[.šnt.kptr]. | l rḥq.ilm.ḥkp[t.l rḥq.ilnym]. | ṯn.mṯpdm.tḥt.[‘nt.arṣ.ṯlṯ.mtḥ]. 1[‘NT.IX].3.19
.‘nn.ilm.] | atm.bštm.w an[.šnt.kptr]. | l rḥq.ilm.ḥkp[t.l rḥq.ilnym]. | ṯn.mṯpdm.tḥt.[‘nt.arṣ.ṯlṯ.mtḥ]. | ġyrm.idk.l yt[1[‘NT.IX].3.19
[---.]n[--.---]. | [---.kpt]r.l r[ḥq.ilm.ḥkpt.l rḥq]. | [ilnym.ṯn.mṯpd]m.t[ḥt.‘nt.arṣ.ṯlṯ.mtḥ.ġyrm]. | [idk.]l 2.3[129].2
k.lk.‘nn.ilm. | atm.bštm.w an.šnt. | uġr.l rḥq.ilm.inbb. | l rḥq.ilnym.ṯn.mṯpdm. | tḥt.‘nt.arṣ.ṯlṯ.mtḥ.ġyrm. | idk.l ttn p 3[‘NT].4.79
[--]m.[---.] | gm.ṣḥ.l q[ṣ.ilm.---]. | l rḥqm.l p[-.---]. | ṣḥ.il.yṯb.b[mrzḥ.---]. | bṯt.‘llm n.[---]. | ilm. 1[‘NT.X].4.3
sn. | gdy lqḥ ṣtqn gt bn ndr. | um r[-] gtn ṯṯ ḫsn l ytn. | l rḥt lqḥ ṣtqn. | bt qbṣ urt ilštm‘ dbḥ ṣtqn l. | ršp. 1154.6
bt. | rbt.kmn.hkl. | w y‘n.kṯr.w ḫss. | šm‘.l aliyn b‘l. | bn.l rkb.‘rpt. | bl.ašt.urbt.b bh[t] m. | ḥln.b qrb.hkl m. | w y‘n.ali 4[51].5.122
| tḥt.ksi.zbl.ym.w ‘n.kṯr.w ḫss.l rgmt. | l k.l zbl.b‘l.ṯnt.l rkb.‘rpt.ht.ib k. | b‘l m.ht.ib k.tmḫṣ.ht.tṣmt.ṣrt k. | tqḥ.mlk. 2.4[68].8
.b ys[mm.---]. | arḫ.arḫ.[---.tld]. | ibr.tld[.l b‘l]. | w rum.l[rkb.‘rpt]. | tḥbq.[---]. | tḥbq[.---]. | w tksynn.bṯn[-.] | y[--.]šr 10[76].3.22
.ym.ykly.ṯpṭ.nhr. | b šm.tg‘r m.‘ṯtrt.bṯ l aliyn.[b‘l.] | bṯ.l rkb.‘rpt.k šby n.zb[l.ym.k] | šby n.ṯpṭ.nhr.w yṣa b[.--]. | yb 2.4[68].29
tšu. | g h.w tṣḥ.ik.mġy.gpn.w ugr. | mn.ib.yp‘.l b‘l.ṣrt. | l rkb.‘rpt.l mḫšt.mdd. | il ym.l klt.nhr.il.rbm. | l ištbm.tnn.išt 3[‘NT].3.35
rt.il.bš[r.b‘]l. | w bšr.ḥtk.dgn. | k.ibr.l b‘l[.yl]d. | w rum.l rkb.‘rpt. | yšmḫ.aliyn.b‘l. 10[76].3.37
.l b‘l.ṣrt.l rkb.‘rpt. | [-]‘n.ġlmm.y‘nyn.l ib.yp‘. | l b‘l.ṣrt.l rkb.‘rpt. | tḥm.aliyn.b‘l.hwt.aliy. | qrdm.qry.b arṣ.mlḥmt. | š 3[‘NT].4.50
.l ksi.mlk h. | l nḫt.l kḥṯ.drkt h. | mn m.ib.yp‘.l b‘l.ṣrt.l rkb.‘rpt. | [-]‘n.ġlmm.y‘nyn.l ib.yp‘. | l b‘l.ṣrt.l rkb.‘rpt. | tḥ 3[‘NT].4.48
.alpm. | yrḫ.‘šrt.l b‘[l]. | dqtm.w ynt.qr[t]. | w mtntm.š l rmš. | w kbd.w š.l šlm kbd. | alp.w š.l b‘l ṣpn. | dqt l ṣpn.šrp. UG5.13.7
rḫ.‘šrt. | [l b‘l.ṣ]pn.[dq]tm.w y[nt] qrt. | [w mtmt]m.[š.l] rm[š.]kbd.w š. | [l šlm.kbd.al]p.w š.[l] b‘l.ṣpn. | [dqt.l.ṣpn.š 36[9].1.13
l prgṯ. | dd.l mri. | dd.l ṯnġly. | dd.l krwn. | dd.l ṯġr. | dd.l rmt.r[---]. 1100.12
d ‘lm...gn‘. | iršt.aršt. | l aḫ y.l r‘ y.dt. | w ytnnn. | l aḫ h.l r‘ h. | r‘ ‘lm. | ttn.w tn. | w l ttn. | w al ttn. | tn ks yn. | w ištn. | 1019.1.10
.alp ymm. | w rbt.šnt. | b ‘d ‘lm...gn‘. | iršt.aršt. | l aḫ y.l r‘ y.dt. | w ytnnn. | l aḫ h.l r‘ h. | r‘ ‘lm. | ttn.w tn. | w l ttn. | w 1019.1.8
yd.sġr h. | [---.--]r h.‘šr[m.---.‘]šrm.dd. | [---.yn.d.]nkly.l.r‘ym.šb‘m.l.mitm.dd. | [---.--]d.šb‘m.kbd.dr‘. | [---.]kbd.dd 1098.44
]. | dd l krwn. | dd l [--]n. | dd l ky. | dd l ‘bdkṯr. | dd[m] l r‘y. | [--] šmḥ[.---]. | ddm gt dprnm. | l ḥršm. | ddm l ‘nqt. | d 1101.6
d.šb‘m.kbd.dr‘. | [---.]kbd.ddm.kbd[.---]. | [---.]‘m.kbd.l.r‘[ym.---]. | [---].kbd.ṯmn.kb[d.---]. 1098.47
.w.mit.drt.w.‘šrm.l.mit. | [drt.ḥpr.b]nšm.w.ṯn.‘šr h.dd.l.rpš. | [---.]šb‘m.dr‘.w.arb‘m.drt.mit.dd. | [---].ḥpr.bn.šm. | [b 1098.4
b šb[‘.]y[mm].td.išt. | b bht m.n[bl]at.b hkl m. | sb.ksp.l rqm.ḫrṣ. | nṣb.l lbnt.šmḫ. | aliyn.b‘l.ht y.bnt. | dt.ksp.hkl y.d 4[51].6.34
l btbt. | alp.w š šrp.alp šlmm. | l b‘l.‘ṣr l ṣpn. | npš.w.š.l ršp bbt. | [‘]ṣrm l h.ršp [-]m. | [---.]bqt[-]. | [b] ġb.ršp mh bnš UG5.12.A.11
ḫyr. | ṯmn l ṯlṯm ṣin. | šb‘.alpm. | bt b‘l.ugrt.ṯn šm. | ‘lm.l ršp.mlk. | alp w.š.l b‘lt. | bwrm š.iṯtqb. | w š.nbk m w.š. | gt UG5.12.B.7

l.ilt[.---].|l.b‘lt[.---].|l.il.bt[.---].|l.ilt.[---].|l.ḥtk[.---].|l.ršp[.---].|[l].ršp.[---.--]g.kbd.|[l.i]lt.qb[-.---].|[l.a]rṣy.|[l.--] 1004.10
b‘lt[.---].|l.il.bt[.---].|l.ilt.[---].|l.ḥtk[.---].|l.ršp[.---].|[l].ršp.[---.--]g.kbd.|[l.i]lt.qb[-.---].|[l.a]rṣy.|[l.--]r[-.---].|[l.-- 1004.11
ṯ ḫsn l ytn.|l rḥt lqḥ ṣtqn.|bt qbṣ urt ilštm‘ dbḥ ṣtqn l.|ršp. 1154.7
‘z.|[rpu.m]lk.‘lm.b ḏmr h.bl.|[---].b ḥtk h.b nmrt h.l r|[--.]arṣ.‘z k.ḏmr k.l[-]|n k.ḥtk k.nmrt k.b tk.|ugrt.l ymt UG5.2.2.8
l ḫmš.mrkbt.ḫmš.‘šr h.prs.|bt.mrkbt.w l šant.ṯṯ.|l bt.‘šrm.|bt alḫnm.ṯlṯm ṯṯ kbd. 2105.2
šd.|tdr‘nn.šir h.l tikl.|‘ṣrm.mnt h.l tkly.|npr[m.]šir.l šir.yṣḥ. 6[49].2.37
ḫnm.ṯrp ym.|lšnm.tlḥk.|šmm.tṯrp.|ym.ḏnbtm.|tnn.l šbm.|tšt.trks.|l mrym.l bt[.---].|p l.tb‘[.---].|hmlt ḫt.[---]. 1003.8
b‘l.ṣrt.|l rkb.‘rpt.l mḫšt.mdd.|il ym.l klt.nhr.il.rbm.|l ištbm.tnn.ištml h.|mḫšt.bṯn.‘qltn.|šlyṭ.d šb‘t.rašm.|mḫšt. 3['NT].3.37
.‘d.|k lbš.km.lpš.dm a[ḫ h].|km.all.dm.ary h.|k šb‘t.l šb‘m.aḫ h.ym[.--].|w ṯmnt.l ṯmnym.|šr.aḫy h.mẓa h.|w 12[75].2.49
[---.--]i[-.]a[--.---].|[---.]ilm.w ilht.dt.|[---.]šb‘.l šb‘m.aṯr.|[---.--]ldm.dt ymtm.|[--.--]r.l ẓpn.|[---.]pn.ym.y[25[136].3
g b ym.w ndd.gzr.l zr.y‘db.u ymn.|u šmal.b p hm.w l.tšb‘n y.aṯt.itrḫ.|y bn.ašld.šu.‘db.tk.mdbr qdš.|ṯm tgrgr.l a 23[52].64
t h.mdnt.|w hln.‘nt.l bt h.tmǵyn.|tštql.ilt.l hkl h.|w l.šb‘t.tmtḫṣ h.b ‘mq.|tḫtṣb.bn.qrtm.tṯ‘r.|ksat.l mhr.ṯ‘r.ṯlḥnt 3['NT].2.19
.b‘l.|yuhb.‘glt.b dbr.prt.|b šd.šḥlmmt.škb.|‘mn h.šb‘.l šb‘m.|tš[‘]ly.ṯmn.l ṯmnym.|w [th]rn.w tldn mṯ.|al[iyn.b‘]l 5[67].5.20
mm.|sb.l qṣm.arṣ.|l ksm.mhyt.‘n.|l arṣ.m[ṭ]r.b‘l.|w l šd.mṭr.‘ly.|n‘m.l arṣ.mṭr.b‘l.|w l šd.mṭr.‘ly.|n‘m.l ḥṭt.b g 16[126].3.6
.|l arṣ.m[ṭ]r.b‘l.|w l šd.mṭr.‘ly.|n‘m.l arṣ.mṭr.b‘l.|w l šd.mṭr.‘ly.|n‘m.l ḥṭt.b gn.|bm.nrt.ksmm.|‘l.tl[-]k.‘ṭrṭrm.| 16[126].3.8
[--.]a[--.---].|[--.-]bt.np[-.---].|[-] l šd.ql.[---.---].aṯr.|[--.]ǵrm.y[--.---.ḥ]rn.|[-]rk.ḥ[--.---.-]lk.|[UG5.8.3
m[mn.hkl h.---.]bt.|[---.-]k.mnh[-.---.-]š bš[-.]t[-].ǵlm.l šdt[.-.]ymm.|[---.]b ym.ym.y[--].yš[ ]n.ap k.‘ṯtr.dm[.---.]|[2.3[129].11
ḫpn.d.iqni.w.šmt.|l.iyb‘l.|ṯlṯm.l.mit.š‘rt.|l.šr.‘ṯtrt.|mlbš.ṯrmnm.|k.yṯn.w.b.bt.|mlk.mlbš.|ytn.l hm.| 1107.4
t.‘ly.ṯh.lm.|l.ytn.hm.mlk.[b]‘l y.|w.hn.ibm.šṣq l y.|p.l.ašt.aṯt y.|n‘r y.ṯh.l pn.ib.|hn.hm.yrgm.mlk.|b‘l y.tmǵyy.h 1012.28
spr.npš.d.|‘rb.bt.mlk.|w.b.spr.l.št.|yrm‘l.|ṣry.|iršy.|y‘ḏrd.|ayaḫ.|bn.aylt.|ḫmš.mat.arb‘ 2106.3
--.--]|r h.p šlmt.p šlm[.---].|bt.l bnš.trg[m.---].|l šlmt.l šlm.b[--.---]|b y.šnt.mlit.t[--.---].|ymǵy k.bnm.ta[--.---].|[b 59[100].6
.[dq]tm.w y[nt] qrt.|[w mtmt]m.[š.l] rm[š.]kbd.w š.|[l šlm.kbd.al]p.w š.[l] b‘l.ṣpn.|[dqt.l.ṣpn.šrp].w š[l]mm.kmm 36[9].1.14
b‘[l].|dqtm.w ynt.qr[t].|w mtntm.š l rmš.|w kbd.w š.l šlm kbd.|alp.w š.l b‘l ṣpn.|dqt l ṣpn.šrp.w šlmm.|kmm.w UG5.13.8
.šl[m.---.--]|r h.p šlmt.p šlm[.---].|bt.l bnš.trg[m.---].|l šlmt.l šlm.b[--.---]|b y.šnt.mlit.t[--.---].|ymǵy k.bnm.ta[--. 59[100].6
[l r]iš.r‘y.y[šlm.---].|[š]lm.bnš.yš[lm.---].|[-]r.l šlmt.šl[m.---.--]|r h.p šlmt.p šlm[.---].|bt.l bnš.trg[m.---].| 59[100].3
ṯrm.|[---.]l ‘nt m.|[---.--]rm.d krm.|[---].l ‘nt m.|[---.]l šlm.|[-]l[-.-]ry.ylbš.|mlk.ylk.lqḥ.ilm.|aṯr.ilm.ylk.p‘nm.|m 33[5].21
r.kkr].|bn.šw.šb‘.kk[r.---].|arb‘m.kkr.[---].|b d.mtn.[l].šlm. 2108.5
b[.---].|mrḥ h l adrt[.---].|tṯb ‘ṯtrt b ǵl[.---].|qrẓ tšt.l šmal[.---].|arbḫ.‘n h tšu w[.---].|aylt tǵpy ṯr.‘n[.---].|b[b]r 2001.1.9
‘mm.|agzr ym.bn ym.ynqm.b ap.ḏd.št.špt.|l arṣ.špt l šmm.w ‘rb.b p hm.‘ṣr.šmm.|w dg b ym.w ndd.gzr.l zr.y‘d 23[52].62
[-----].|[špt.l a]rṣ.špt.l šmm.|[---.l]šn.l kbkbm.y‘rb.|[b‘]l.b kbd h.b p h yrd.|k ḥr 5[67].2.2
l mlkytn.|ḥnn y l pn mlk.|šin k itn.|r‘ y šṣa idn l y.|l šmn iṯr hw.|p iḫdn gnryn.|im mlkytn yrgm.|aḫnnn.|w iḫ 1020.6
[t.---].|š dd šmn[.gdlt.w.---].|brr.r[gm.yṯṯb.b ṯdṯ.ṯn].|l šmn.‘[ly h.gdlt.rgm.yṯṯb].|brr.b šb‘[.ṣbu.špš.w ḥl]|yt.‘rb š APP.II[173].50
dm kbd[.-] l alpm mrim.|ṯṯ ddm l ṣin mrat.|‘šr ddm.l šm‘rgm.|‘šr ddm.l bt.|‘šrm.dd.l mḫṣm.|ddm l kbs.|dd l p 1100.3
si.mlk h.|[---].l kḥṯ.drkt h.|l [ym]m.l yrḫm.l yrḫm.|l šnt.[m]k.b šb‘.|šnt.w [--].bn.ilm.mt.|‘m.aliyn.b‘l.yšu.|g h. 6[49].5.8
.|ǵzr.ydm‘.l kdd.dnil.|mt.rpi.l ymm.l yrḫm.|l yrḫm.l šnt.‘d.|šb‘t.šnt.ybk.l aq|ht.ǵzr.yd[m‘.]l kdd.|dnil.mt.r[pi. 19[1AQHT].4.176
[ny].|b.yṣi h.|ḥwt.[---].|alp.k[sp].|tš‘n.|w.hm.al[-].|l.tš‘n.|mṣrm.|tmkrn.|ypḥ.‘bdilt.|bn.m.|ypḥ.ilšlm.|bn.prq 2116.14
y.w y‘n[.dn]|il.mt.rpi npš tḥ[.pǵt].|ṯ[km]t.mym.ḥspt.l š‘r.|ṭl.yd‘t.hlk.kbkbm.|a[-]ḥ.hy.mḫ.tmḫṣ.mḫṣ[.aḫ k].|tkl. 19[1AQHT].4.199
pn y dt ksp.|dt.yrq.nqbn y.tš[m‘].|pǵt.ṯkmt.my.ḥspt.l[š‘]r.ṭl.|yd‘t.hlk.kbkbm.|bkm.tmdln.‘r.|bkm.tṣmd.pḥl.bk 19[1AQHT].2.55
y].|gm.l bt[h.dnil.k yṣḥ].|šm‘.pǵt.ṯkmt[.my].|ḥspt.l š‘r.ṭl.yd[‘t].|hlk.kbkbm.mdl.‘r.|ṣmd.pḥl.št.gpn y dt ksp.| 19[1AQHT].2.51
].|mṣmt.l nqmd.[---.-]št.|hl ny.argmn.d [ybl.n]qmd.|l špš.arn.ṯn[.‘šr h.]mn.|‘ṣrm.ṯql.kbd[.ks].mn.ḫrṣ.|w arb‘.kt 64[118].19
t.hlm.yṯq.|nḥš.yšlḥm.nḥš.‘q šr.ydb.ksa.|w yṯb.|tqru.l špš.u h.špš.um.ql.bl.‘m.|dgn.ttl h.mnt.nṯk.nḥš.šmrr.|nḥš.‘ UG5.7.14
t.hlm.yṯq.nḥš.yšlḥm.|nḥš.‘q šr.y‘db.ksa.w yṯb.|tqru l špš.um h.špš.um.ql.bl.‘m.|‘nt w ‘ṯtrt inbb h.mnt.nṯk.|nḥš. UG5.7.19
lm.yṯq yṯqšqy.nḥš.yšlḥm.‘q šr.|y‘db.ksa.w.yṯb.|tqru.l špš.um h.špš.um.ql bl.|‘m b‘l.mrym.ṣpn.mnt y.nṯk.|nḥš.š UG5.7.8
.hlm yṯq.nḥš.|yšlḥm.nḥš.‘q šr.y‘db ksa.|w yṯb.|tqru l špš.um h.špš.um.ql bl ‘m.|šḥr.w šlm šmm h mnt.nṯk.nḥš. UG5.7.51
um.pḥl.pḥlt.bt.abn.bt šmm w thm.|qrit.l špš.um h.špš.um.ql.bl.‘m.|il.mbk nhrm.b ‘dt.thmtm.|mnt UG5.7.2
t.hlm.yṯq.nḥš.yšlḥm.nḥš.|‘q šr.y‘db.ksa.w yṯb.|tqru.l špš.um h.špš.um.ql b.‘m.|ršp.bbt h.mnt.nḥš.šmrr.|nḥš.‘q UG5.7.30
.yṯq šqy.|nḥš.yšlḥm.nḥš.‘q šr.y‘db.|ksa.w yṯb.|tqru l špš.um h.špš.um.ql bl.|‘m ḥrn.mṣd h.mnt.nṯk nḥš.|šmrr. UG5.7.57
r.ln h.ml|ḫš.abd.ln h.ydy.ḥmt.hlm.yṯq.|w yṯb.|tqru.l špš.um h.špš.[um.q]l bl.‘m.|yrḫ.lrgt h.mnt.nṯk.n[ḥš].šmrr. UG5.7.25
t.hlm.yṯq nḥš yšlḥm.nḥš.|‘q.šr.y‘db.ksa.w yṯb.|tqru l špš um h.špš um ql.bl.‘m.|mlk.‘ṯtrt h.mnt.nṯk.nḥš.šmrr.| UG5.7.40
mt.hlm.yṯq.nḥš.yšlḥm.nḥš ‘q.|š.y‘db.ksa w yṯb.|tqru l špš.um h.špš.um.ql bl ‘m.|ṭṭ.w kmṯ.ḥryt h.mnt.nṯk.nḥš.š UG5.7.35
t.hlm.yṯq.nḥš.yšlḥm.nḥš.|‘q šr.y‘db.ksa.w yṯb.|tqru.l špš.um.ql bl.‘m|kṯr.w ḫss.kptr h.mnt.nṯk.nḥš.|šmrr.nḥš.‘ UG5.7.45
k.nǵr.|w.[---].adny.l.yḫsr.|w.[ank.yd]‘.l.yd‘t.|h[t.---.]l.špš.b‘l k.|‘[--.s]glt h.at.|ht[.---.]špš.b‘l k.|yd‘m.l.yd‘t.|‘m 2060.11
pš.w yrḫ.l gṯr.|ṯql.ksp.ṭb.ap w np[š].|l ‘nt h.ṯql.ḫrṣ.|l špš[.w y]rḫ.l gṯr.ṯn.|[ṯql.ksp].ṭb.ap.w npš.|[---].bt.alp w š. 33[5].14
mt.|l ilm.šb[‘.]l kṯr.|‘lm.t‘rbn.gṯrm.|bt.mlk.ṯql.ḫrṣ.|l špš.w yrḫ.l gṯr.|ṯql.ksp.ṭb.ap w np[š].|l ‘nt h.ṯql.ḫrṣ.|l špš 33[5].11
m.|[ḫm]š[.m]at.iqnu.|argmn.nqmd.mlk.|ugrt.d ybl.l špš.|mlk.rb.b‘l h.|ks.ḫrṣ.ktn.mit.pḥm.|mit.iqni.l mlkt.|ks 64[118].25
‘l y[.mrḥqtm].|šb‘ d.w.šb‘[d.qlt].|ankn.rgmt.l.b‘l y.|l.špš.‘lm.l.‘ṯtrt.|l.‘nt.l.kl.il.alṯ[y].|nmry.mlk.‘lm.|mlk n.b‘l 2008.1.7
.l il.ybl.a[ṯt y].|il.ylt.mh.ylt.yld y.šḥr.w šl[m].|šu.‘db.l špš.rbt.w l kbkbm.kn[-].|yhbr.špt hm.yšq.hn.[š]pt hm.mt 23[52].54
[---.a]rb‘m.|[---.tš]‘m.|[---.t]š‘m.|[---.--]y arb‘m.|[---.]l špš ṯmny[m].|[---.]dbr h l šp[š].|[---.]dbr h l šp[š].|[---.]np 41[71].7
t]š‘m.|[---.--]y arb‘m.|[---.]l špš ṯmny[m].|[---.]dbr h l šp[š].|[---.]dbr h l šp[š].|[---.]npṭry ṯ[--].|[---.--]urm.|[----- 41[71].8
‘m.|[---.]l špš ṯmny[m].|[---.]dbr h l šp[š].|[---.]dbr h l šp[š].|[---.]npṭry ṯ[--].|[---.--]urm.|[-----]. 41[71].9
[-----.]w[.---].|[---.]l špš[.---]. 42[-].2
---].|[---.]šn[.---].|[---].pit.|[---.]qbat.|[---.]inšt.|[--]u.l tštql.|[---].ṭry.ap.l tlḥm.|[l]ḥm.trmmt.l tšt.|yn.tǵẓyt.špš.| 6.6[62.2].41
š.]bht h.tbnn.|[ḥš.]trmm.hkl h.|y[tl]k.l lbnn.w ‘ṣ h.|l[šr]yn.mḥmd.arz h.|h[n.l]bnn.w ‘ṣ h.|š[r]yn.mḥmd.arz h. 4[51].6.19

.b‘l m.ym l[--.---].|ḥm.l šrr.w [---].|y‘n.ym.l mt[.---].|l šrr.w t‘[n.‘ṯtrt.---].|b‘l m.hmt.[---].|l šrr.št[.---].|b riš h.[--- 2.4[68].35
bṯ.nn.aliyn.b‘l.w [---].|ym.l mt.b‘l m.ym l[--.---].|ḥm.l šrr.w [---].|y‘n.ym.l mt[.---].|l šrr.w t‘[n.‘ṯtrt.---].|b‘l m.h 2.4[68].33
n.ym.l mt[.---].|l šrr.w t‘[n.‘ṯtrt.---].|b‘l m.hmt.[---].|l šrr.št[.---].|b riš h.[---].|ib h.mš[--.---].|[b]n.‘n h[.---]. 2.4[68].37
--.]inšt.|[--]u.l tštql.|[---].ṭry.ap.l tlḥm.|[l]ḥm.trmmt.l tšt.|yn.tǵẓyt.špš.|rpim.tḥtk.|špš.tḥtk.ilnym.|‘d k.ilm.hn. 6.6[62.2].43
--.-]ǵk.rpu mlk.|[‘lm.---.--]k.l tšt k.l iršt.|[‘lm.---.--]k.l tšt k.liršt.|[---.]rpi.mlk ‘lm.b ‘z.|[rpu.m]lk.‘lm.b ḏmr h.bl. UG5.2.2.5
---.]dr h.|[---.-]rš.l b‘l.|[---.-]ǵk.rpu mlk.|[‘lm.---.--]k.l tšt k.l iršt.|[‘lm.---.--]k.l tšt k.liršt.|[---.]rpi.mlk ‘lm.b ‘z.|[UG5.2.2.5
.-]m.l[-]ṯnm.|‘dm.[lḥ]m.tšty.|w t‘n.mṯt ḥry.|l l[ḥ]m.l š[ty].ṣḥt km.|db[ḥ.l krt.a]dn km.|‘l.krt.tbun.km.|rgm.ṯ[r 15[128].6.4
|yd.b ṣ‘.tšlḥ.|ḥrb.b bšr.tštn.|[w t]‘n.mṯt.ḥry.|[l lḥ]m.l šty.ṣḥt km.|[--.dbḥ.l]krt.b‘l km. 15[128].4.27
ṣ‘.t[šl]ḥ.|[ḥrb.b]bš[r].tštn.|[w t‘n].mṯt.ḥry.|[l lḥ]m.l šty.ṣḥt k[m].|[---.]brk.t[---].|[‘l.]krt.tbkn.|[--.]rgm.ṯrm.|[- 15[128].5.10
[--.]w rbb.|š[---]npš išt.|w.l.tikl w l tš[t]. 2003.3
.ksp.ktn.mit.pḥm].|[mit.iqn]i.l skl.[--].|[---.m]it pḥm.l š[--].|[---.]a[--.--.]hn[--]. 64[118].39
|ym.ḏnbtm.|tnn.l šbm.|tšt.trks.|l mrym.l bt[.---].|p l.tb‘[.---].|hmlt ḫt.[---].|l.tp[-]m.[---].|n[-]m[.---]. 1003.11
ḫswn.|ḫmš ‘šr.sp.|l bnš tpnr d yaḫd l g ynm.|ṯṯ spm l tgyn.|arb‘ spm l ll[-].|ṯn spm.l slyy.|ṯlṯ spm l dlšpš amry. 137.2[93].12
urt [---].|ṯṯ šurt l bnš [---].|ḫmš kbd arb‘[.---].|ṯṯ šurt l tg[-.---].|arb‘ šurt [---].|[ḫm]šm šurt [---].|ṯlṯ šurt l [---].|ṯ 137.1[92].13
.nḥl h.|šd.annmn.b d.tyn.nḥl h.|šd.pǵyn[.b] d.krmn.l.ty[n.n]ḥl h.|šd.krz.[b]n.ann.‘[db].|šd.ṯ[r]yn.bn.tkn.b d.qrt 2029.12
rb.trẓẓ h.|[---].mǵy h.w ǵlm.|[a]ḫt h.šib.yṣat.mrḥ h.|l tl.yṣb.pn h.ṯǵr.|yṣu.hlm.aḫ h.tph.|[ksl]h.l arṣ.ṯṯbr.|[---.]a 16.1[125].52
rb‘m.ṯmn.kbd.|[l.]sbrdnm.|m[i]t.l.bn.‘ẓmt.rišy.|mit.l.tlmyn.bn.‘dy.|[---.]l.aḏddy.|[--.]l.kkln. 2095.8
m.mrm.tqrṣn.|il.yẓḥq.bm.|lb.w ygmḏ.bm kbd.|ẓi.at.l tlš.|amt.yrḫ.|l dmgy.amt.|aṯrt.qḥ.|ksan k.ḥdg k.|ḥtl k.w 12[75].1.14
pḥm.|mit.iqni.l uṯryn.|ks.ksp.ktn.mit.pḥm.|mit.iqni.l tpnr.|[ks.ksp.kt]n.mit.pḥ[m].|[mit.iqni.l]ḫbrtn[r].|[ks.ks 64[118].32
tšt.trks.|l mrym.l bt[.---].|p l.tb‘[.---].|hmlt ḫt.[---].|l.tp[-]m.[---].|n[-]m[.---]. 1003.13
b.gt.nbk.|ddm.kšmm.l.ḫtn.|ddm.l.trbnn.|ddm.š‘rm.l.trbnn.|ddm.š‘rm.l.ḫtn.|dd.š‘rm.l.ḥmr.ḥṯb.|dd.ḥṭm.l.ḫḏǵb 1099.22
p.|w.lmd h.|krwn b.gt.nbk.|ddm.kšmm.l.ḫtn.|ddm.l.trbnn.|ddm.š‘rm.l.trbnn.|ddm.š‘rm.l.ḫtn.|dd.š‘rm.l.ḥmr. 1099.21
tḥm.iwrḏr.|l.plsy.|rgm.|yšlm.l k.|l.trǵds.|w.l.klby.|šm‘t.ḫti.|nḫtu.ht.|hm.in mm.|nḫtu.w.la 53[54].5
n.hmlt.tn.b‘l.[w ‘nn h].|bn.dgn.arṯ m.pḏ h.tb‘.ǵlmm.l ṯṯb.[idk.pnm].|l ytn.tk.ǵr.ll.‘m.phr.m‘d.ap.ilm.l lḥ[m].|yṯ 2.1[137].19
ḫt.ppšr.w ppšrt[.---].|[---.]k.drḥm.w aṯb.l ntbt.k.‘šm l t[--].|[---.]drk.brḥ.arṣ.lk pn h.yrk.b‘[l].|[---.]bt k.ap.l pḫr 1001.2.7
‘ k.ṭr.[i]l.ab k.l ys‘.[alt.]ṯ[bt |k.l y]hpk.|[ksa.]mlk k.l ytbr.ḫṭ.mṯpṭ k.w y‘n[.‘ttr].dm[-]k[-].|[--]ḫ.b y.ṭr.il.ab y.an 2.3[129].18
.yšm[‘] k.ṭr.|il.ab k.l ys‘.alt.|ṯbt k.l yhpk.ksa.mlk k.|l yṯbr.ḫṭ.mṯpṭ k.|yru.bn ilm t.ṯṯ‘.y|dd.il.ǵzr.y‘r.mt.|b ql h. 6[49].6.29
km.y[--.]ilm.b ṣpn.|‘dr.l[‘r].‘rm.|ṯb.l pd[r.]pdrm.|ṯṯ.l ṯṯm.aḥd.‘r.|šb‘m.šb‘.pdr.|ṯmnym.b‘l.[----].|tš‘m.b‘l.mr[-]. 4[51].7.9
m.|[---.al]iyn b‘l.|[---].rkb.‘rpt.|[---.]ǵš.l limm.|[---.]l ytb.l arṣ.|[---].mtm.|[---.--]d mhr.ur.|[---.]yḥnnn.|[---.--]t. 10[76].1.9
|l.‘ṯtrt.abḏr.|l.dml.|l.ilt[.-]pn.|l.uš[ḫr]y.|[---.-]mrn.|l twl.|[--]ḏ[--]. 1001.1.14
rṯ w ṯ[qd m]r.|[ydk aḥd h w yṣq b ap h.|[k l yḫru w]l yttn mss št qlql.|[w št ‘rgz y]dk aḥd h w yṣq b ap h.|[k.yi 160[55].8
ṯ].|w.ṯ[qd.mr.ydk.aḥd h].|w.y[ṣq.b.ap h].|k.l.ḫ[ru.w.l.yttn.ššw].|mss.[št.qlql.w.št].|‘rgz[.ydk.aḥd h].|w.yṣq[.b.a 161[56].8
|šm‘.l ngr.il il[š].|ilš.ngr bt b‘l.|w aṯt k.ngrt.il[ht].|‘l.l ṯkm.bnw n.|l nḫnpt.mšpy.|ṯlṯ.kmm.ṯrr y.|[---.]l ǵr.gm.ṣḥ. 16[126].4.14
w.nkt.nkt.y[t]ši.l ab.bn.il.ytši.l dr.|bn il.l mpḫrt.bn.il.l ṯkmn[.w]šnm.hn.‘r.|w.ṯb.l mspr.m[šr] mšr.bt.ugrt.w npy. 32[2].1.26
nkt.nk]t.ytši.l ab bn il.|ytši.l d[r.bn il.l]mpḫrt.bn il.|l ṯkm[n.w šnm.]hn ‘[r].|[---.]w npy[.---].|[---.]w npy.u[grt.-- 32[2].1.35
.nkt.nkt.ytši.l ab.bn.il.ytši.l d]r.bn[.il].|[l mpḫrt.bn.il.l ṯkmn.w šnm.hn š].|[w šqrb.š.mšr mšr.bn.ugrt.w npy.---.] 32[2].1.3
nkt.n[k]t.ytši[.l ab.bn.il].|ytši.l dr.bn.il.l mpḫrt.bn.i[l.l ṯkmn.w š]nm hn š.|w šqrb.‘r.mšr mšr bn.ugrt.w [npy.---.] 32[2].1.17
kt.nkt.]yt[ši.l ab.bn.il].|[ytši.l dr.bn.il.l mpḫ]rt.[bn.il.l ṯkmn.w šn]m hn š.|[---.w n]py.gr[.ḥmyt.ugrt.w np]y.|[---] 32[2].1.9B
yky msg.|ynḥm.msg.|bn.ugr.msg.|bn.ǵlṣ msg.|arb‘ l ṯkṣ[-].|nn.arspy.ms[g].|[---.ms]g.|bn.[gr]gs.msg.|bn[.--]a 133[-].1.10
ḏmr.|[u]šb‘t h.b mm‘.mhrm.|[ṭ]‘r.ksat.l ksat.ṯlḥnt.|[l]ṯlḥn.hdmm.ṭṭ‘r.l hdmm.|[t]ḥspn.m h.w trḥṣ.|[ṭ]l.šmm.š 3[‘NT].2.37
[b] ǵb.ršp mh bnš.|šrp.w ṣp ḫršḥ.|‘lm b ǵb ḫyr.|ṯmn l ṯlṯm ṣin.|šb‘.alpm.|bt b‘l.ugrt.ṯn šm.|‘lm.l ršp.mlk.|alp w UG5.12.B.4
arb‘.ḥm[r.---].|l ṯlṯ.|ṯn.l.brr[.---].|arb‘.ḥmr[.---].|l.pḫ[-.]w.[---].|w.l.k[--].| 1139.2
[---.-]grm.|[---.-]n.‘šrt.ksp.|[--.--]n.šb‘t.l ṯlṯm.|[---].šb‘t.‘šrt.|[---.-]kyn.‘šrt.|b.bn.‘sl.‘šrm.ṯqlm kbd. 2054.1.3
r.prt.|b šd.šḥlmmt.škb.|‘mn h.šb‘.l šb‘m.|tš[‘]ly.ṯmn.l ṯmnym.|w [th]rn.w tldn mṯ.|al[iyn.b‘]l šlbšn.|i[---.---.--]l 5[67].5.21
|km.all.dm.ary h.|k šb‘t.l šb‘m.aḫ h.ym[.--].|w ṯmnt.l ṯmnym.|šr.aḫy h.mẓa h.|w mẓa h.šr.yly h.|b skn.sknm.b 12[75].2.50
kr.zbl.‘ršm.|yšu.‘wr.|mzl.ymzl.|w ybl.trḫ.ḥdṯ.|yb‘r.l ṯn.aṯt h.|w l nkr.mddt.|km irby.tškn.|šd.k ḥsn.pat.|mdbr 14[KRT].4.190
tškr.zbl.‘ršm.|yšu.‘wr.mzl.|ymzl.w yṣi.trḫ.|ḥdṯ.yb‘r.l ṯn.|aṯt h.lm.nkr.|mddt h.k irby.|[t]škn.šd.|km.ḥsn.pat.m 14[KRT].2.101
t.dt.|‘rb.bt.mlk.|yd.apnt hn.|yd.ḥẓ hn.|yd.tr hn.|w.l.ṯt.mrkbtm.|inn.uṯpt.|w.ṯlṯ.ṣmdm.w.ḥrṣ.|apnt.b d.rb.ḥrš 1121.6
‘šrm.dd.l mḫṣm.|ddm l kbs.|dd l prgṭ.|dd.l mri.|dd.l ṯngly.|dd.l krwn.|dd.l ṯǵr.|dd.l rmt.r[---]. 1100.9
p km.u b qṣrt.npš km.u b qṭṭ].|[tqṭṭ.u ṯḥṭu.l dbḥm.w l.ṯ‘.dbḥ n.ndb]ḥ.|[hw.ṯ‘.nṯ‘y.hw.nkt.nkt.]yt[ši.l ab.bn.il].|[y 32[2].1.9
u b q[ṣ]rt.npš km.u b qṭt.tqṭṭ.|ušn yp km.l d[b]ḥm.w l.ṯ‘.dbḥ n.ndbḥ.hw.ṯ‘ |nṯ‘y.|hw.nkt.nkt.y[t]ši.l ab.bn.il.ytši. 32[2].1.24
kn.u b [q]ṣrt.npš[kn.u b qṭt].|tqṭṭn u ṯḥṭin.l bḥm.w l ṯ‘.d[bḥ n.ndbḥ].|hw.ṯ‘.nṯ‘y.hw.nkt.n[k]t.ytši[.l ab.bn.il].|y 32[2].1.15
.u b qṣ]rt.npš kn.u b qṭt.|tqṭṭn.ušn y[p kn.l dbḥm.]w l ṯ‘ dbḥ n.|ndbḥ.hw.ṯ‘ n[ṯ‘y.hw.nkt.nk]t.ytši.l ab bn il.|ytši. 32[2].1.32
-.]šlm.|[---.--]š.lalit.|[---.]bt šp.š.|y[-]lm.w mlk.|ynṣl.l ṯ‘y. 2005.2.8
l kbs.|dd l prgṭ.|dd.l mri.|dd.l ṯngly.|dd.l krwn.|dd.l ṯǵr.|dd.l rmt.r[---]. 1100.11
|tpnn.‘n.bty.‘n.bṯt.tpnn.|‘n.mḫr.‘n.pḫr.‘n.ṯǵr.|‘n.ṯǵr.l.ṯǵr.ttb.|‘n.pḫr.l.pḫr.ttb.|‘n.mḫr.l.mḫr.ttb.|‘n.bty.l.bty.ttb. RS225.7
tdbr.w[ǵ]rm[.ṯṯwy].|šqlt.b ǵlt.yd k.|l tdn.dn.almnt.|l ṯṯpṭ.ṯpṭ.qṣr.npš.|km.aḫt.‘rš.mdw.|anšt.‘rš.zbln.|rd.l mlk. 16.6[127].34
m.tdbr.|w ǵrm.ṯṯwy.šqlt.|b ǵlt.yd k.l tdn.|dn.almnt.l ṯṯpṭ.|ṯpṭ qṣr.npš.l tdy.|tšm.‘l.dl.l pn k.|l tšlḥm.ytm.b‘d.|k 16.6[127].46
[-----].|šd.prsn.l.[---].|šd.bddn.l.iytlm.|šd.bn.nb‘m.l.ṯpṯb‘l.|šd.bn mšrn.l.ilšpš.|[šd.bn].kbr.l.snrn.|[---.--]k.l.gm 2030.1.4
.|l ẓr.mgdl.rkb.|ṯkmm.ḥmt.nša.|[y]d h.šmmh.dbḥ.|l ṯr.ab h.il.šrd.|[b‘l].b dbḥ h.bn dgn.|[b m]ṣd h.yrd.krt.|[l g 14[KRT].4.169
r.|[ṯn]y.d‘t hm.išt.ištm.yitmr.ḥrb.ltšt.|[--]n hm.rgm.l ṯr.ab h.il.ṯḥm.ym.b‘l km.|[adn]km.ṯpṭ.nhr.tn.il m.d tq h. 2.1[137].33
w ‘l.l ẓr.[mg]dl.rkb.|ṯkmm.ḥm[t].ša.yd k.|šmm.dbḥ.l ṯr.|ab k.il.šrd.b‘l.|b dbḥ k.bn.dgn.|b mṣd k.w yrd.|krt.l g 14[KRT].2.76
al.tšṯḥwy.pḫr [m‘d.qmm.a--.am]|r ṯny.d‘t km.w rgm.l ṯr.a[b.-.il.ṯny.l pḫr].|m‘d.ṯḥm.ym.b‘l km.adn km.ṯ[pṭ.nhr] 2.1[137].16

.ary h.uzrm.ilm.ylḥm.|uzrm.yšqy.bn.qdš.|l tbrknn l t̠r.il ab y.|tmrnn.l bny.bnwt.|w ykn.bn h b bt.šrš.b qrb.|h 17[2AQHT].1.24
--.i]qnim.[--].|[---.]aliyn.b'l.|[---.--]k.mdd il.|y[m.---.]l t̠r.qdqd h.|il[.--.]rḥq.b ǵr.|km.y[--.]ilm.b ṣpn.|'dr.l['r].'r 4[51].7.4
t̠ḥm[.t]lm[yn].|l t̠ryl.um y.|rgm.|ugrt.tǵr k.|ugrt.tǵr k.|tšlm k.um y.|td'. 1015.2
t̠ḥm.mlk.|l.t̠ryl.um y.rgm.|yšlm.l k.ilm.|tǵr k.tšlm k.|lḥt.šlm.k.lik[t]. 2009.1.2
.|l ytn.tk.ǵr.ll.'m.phr.m'd.ap.ilm.l lḥ[m].|yt̠b.bn qdš.l t̠rm.b'l.qm.'l.il.hlm.|ilm.tph hm.tphn.mlak.ym.t'dt.t̠pt̠[.n 2.1[137].21
.'l.riš h.|w t̠t̠b.trḥṣ.nn.b d't.|npš h.l lḥm.tptḥ.|brlt h.l t̠rm.|mt.dm.ḫt.š'tqt.|dm.lan.w ypqd.|krt.t̠'.yšu.g h.|w yṣ 16.6[127].12
[š y].|km.diy.b t'rt y.aqht.[km.yt̠b].|l lḥm.w bn.dnil.l t̠rm[.'l h].|nšrm.trḫpn.ybṣr.[ḥbl.d]|iym.bn.nšrm.arḫp.an[18[3AQHT].4.19
ḥbš h.km.diy.|b t'rt h.aqht.km.yt̠b.l lḥ[m].|bn.dnil.l t̠rm.'l h.nšr[m].|trḫpn.ybṣr.ḥbl.diy[m.bn].|nšrm.trḫp.'nt.' 18[3AQHT].4.30
[.---].|[--]l.t̠rmn.m[lk.---].|[---.--]rt.š'rt[.---].|[---.i]qni.l.t̠r[mn.art.---].|[b.yr]ḫ.riš.yn.[---].|[---.b']lt.bhtm.š[--.---].|[1106.31
lt̠.mat.abn.ṣrp.|[---.-]qt.l.t̠rmnm.|[---].t̠lt̠m.iqnu.|[---.l.]t̠rmn.mlk.|[---.]š'rt.šb'.'šr h.|[---.iqn]i.l.t̠rmn.qrt.|[---.]lbš 1106.13
m.iqnu.|[---.l.]t̠rmn.mlk.|[---.]š'rt.šb'.'šr h.|[---.iqn]i.l.t̠rmn.qrt.|[---.]lbš.ḫmšm.iqnu.|[---].šmt.ḫmšt.ḫndlt.|[---.i 1106.15
.iqnu.|[---].šmt.ḫmšt.ḫndlt.|[---.iqn]i.l.[-]k.btbt.|[---.l.t̠rm]nm.š[b'].mat.š'rt.|[---.]iqnu.[---.]lbš.t̠rmnm.|[---.iqn]i. 1106.19
.|[---].mitm.kslm.|[---].pwt.t̠lt̠.mat.abn.ṣrp.|[---.-]qt.l.t̠rmnm.|[---].t̠lt̠m.iqnu.|[---.l.]t̠rmn.mlk.|[---.]š'rt.šb'.'šr h 1106.11
t̠.l.md̠r[ǵlm].|kd[.--].lm[d.---].|kd[.l.]ḫzr[m.---].|kd[.l.]t̠rtn[m].|arb' l.mry[nm].|kdm l.ḫty.[---].|kdm l.'t̠tr[t].|k 1091.7
b i[--.---].|l t̠[--.---].|ks[.---].|kr[pn.---].|at.š['tqt.---].|š'd[.---].|rt.[---]. 16[126].5.39
.qb[-.---].|[l.a]rṣy.|[l.--]r[-.---].|[l.--]ḥl.|[l.--.]mgmr.|[l.-.]qdšt.|l.'t̠trt.ndrgd.|l.'t̠trt.abd̠r.|l.dml.|l.ilt[.-]pn.|l.uš[ḫ 1001.1.11
lt̠ spm w 'šr lḥm.|[--.]w nṣp w t̠lt̠ spm w 'šrm lḥ[m].|l[.-]dt ḫnd[r]t̠ ar' s[p]m w 'š[r].|[---.]ḫndrt̠m t̠t̠ spm [w] t̠lt̠ 134[-].5
[-----].|šm'.l [-]mt[.-]m.l[-]t̠nm.|'dm.[lḥ]m.tšty.|w t'n.mt̠t̠ ḥry.|l l[ḥ]m.l š[ty].ṣḥt 15[128].6.1
.|[---.]lbš.ḫmšm.iqnu.|[---].šmt.ḫmšt.ḫndlt.|[---.iqn]i.l.[-]k.btbt.|[---.l.t̠rm]nm.š[b'].mat.š'rt.|[---.]iqnu.[---.]lbš.t̠r 1106.18
[-----].|šm'.l [-]mt[.-]m.l[-]t̠nm.|'dm.[lḥ]m.tšty.|w t'n.mt̠t̠ ḥry.|l l[ḥ]m 15[128].6.1
[---.]yplt̠.|[---].l.[-]npk.|[---.]l.bn.ydln.|[---].l.blkn.|[---].l.bn.k[--].|[---].l.kl 2136.2
[-]b[-.---.--]|r t̠t̠m lḥm.|l[.-]ry t̠lt̠ spm w 'šr lḥm.|[--.]w nṣp w t̠lt̠ spm w 'šrm lḥ[m]. 134[-].3
g.kbd.|[l.i]lt.qb[-.---].|[l.a]rṣy.|[l.--]r[-.---].|[l.--]ḥl.|[l.--.]mgmr.|[l.-.]qdšt.|l.'t̠trt.ndrgd.|l.'t̠trt.abd̠r.|l.dml.|l.ilt 1001.1.11
t̠t̠[--.---].|[---.]k.w t̠[--.---].|[---.]k t̠rm.l p[--.---].|[---.]l.[--.]rlg[-.---].|[---.]bn.w [---].|[---.--]t̠.kn[-.---].|[---.--]tm.n[2125.10
šb'.ḫdǵlm.|l.[---]mn ḫpn.|l[.--.]škn.ḫpn.|l.k[-]w.ḫpn.|l.ṣ[--].š'[rt].|l.'dy.š[']r[t].|t̠lt̠.l.' 1117.3
.npṣ h.|[---.]rgm.hn.[--]n.w aspt.[q]l h.|[---.rg]m.ank l[.--.--]rny.|[---.]t̠m.hw.i[--]ty.|[---].ib'r.a[--.]d̠mr.|[---.]w m 1002.50
šp.[---.--]g.kbd.|[l.i]lt.qb[-.---].|[l.a]rṣy.|[l.--]r[-.---].|[l.--]ḥl.|[l.--.]mgmr.|[l.-.]qdšt.|l.'t̠trt.ndrgd.|l.'t̠trt.abd̠r.|l.d 1001.1.11
.|[---].ḥln.d b.dmt.um.il[m.---].|[--]d̠yn.b'd.[--]d̠yn.w l.|[--]k b'lt bhtm[.--]tn k.|[--]y.l ihbt.yb[--].rgm y.|[---.]škb. 1002.44
[-----].|dd l krwn.|dd l [--]n.|dd l ky.|dd l 'bdkt̠r.|dd[m] l r'y.|[--] šmḫ[.---].|dd 1101.3
t̠ḥm.špš.|l.'mrpi.rgm.|'m špš.kll.mid m.|šlm.|l.[--]n.špš.|ad[.']bd h.uk.škn.|k.[---.]sglt h.hw.|w.b[.---.]uk. 2060.5
šp[.---].|[l].ršp.[---.--]g.kbd.|[l.i]lt.qb[-.---].|[l.a]rṣy.|[l.--]r[-.---].|[l.--]ḥl.|[l.--.]mgmr.|[l.-.]qdšt.|l.'t̠trt.ndrgd.|l.'t̠ 1001.1.11
[t̠ḥm.---].|[l.---].|[a]ḫt y.rgm.|[y]šlm.l k.|[il]m.tšlm k.|[tǵ]r k.|[--]y.ib 1016.2
ṣmdm.a[--.---].|b d.prḫ[-.---].|apnm.l.'[--].|apnm.l.[---].|apnm.l.d[--].|apnm.l.bn[.---].|apnm.l.[b]n[.---].|apn 145[318].4
b yrḫ.[---].|šb'.yn[.---].|mlkt[.---].|kd.yn.l.[---].|armwl w [--].|arb'.yn.[--].|l adrm.b[--].|šqym. 1092.4
k[rm.--.]l.i[w]rtd̠l.|ḥl.d[--.'bd]yrḫ.b d.apn.|krm.i[--].l.[---.]a[-]bn. 2027.2.12
a[t.---].|t̠mnym[.---].|[t̠]mny[m.---].|[-]r[-.---].|[--]m.l.[---].|a[---.---].|'šrm.drt[.---]. 2013.30
.[b nbk.---].|[--.k]mm.gdlt.l.b['l.---].|[dq]t.l.ṣpn.gdlt.l[.---].|u[gr]t.š.l.[il]ib.ǵ[--.--rt].|w ['ṣrm.]l.ri[--.---].|[--]t.b'lt 35[3].34
bqtm.b nbk.[---].|kmm.gdlt.l b['l.--.dqt].|l ṣpn.gdlt.[l.---].|ugrt.š l ili[b.---].|rt.w 'ṣrm.l[.---].|pamt.w bt.[---].|rm APP.II[173].37
dm.mt.aṣ[ḫ.---].|yd.b qrb[.---].|w lk.ilm.[---].|w rgm.l [---].|b mud.ṣin[.---].|mud.ṣin[.---].|it̠m.mui[-.---].|dm.mt 5[67].3.21
--.--]b.|[---.--]a h.|[---.--]d.|[---].umt n.|[---.--]yh.wn l.|[---].bt b'l.|[---.--]y.|[---.--]nt. 28[-].11
lt̠ id.'l.ud[n].|[---.-]sr.pdm.riš h[m.---].|'l.pd.asr.[---.]l[.---].|mḫlpt.w l.ytk.[d]m['t.]km.|rb't.t̠qlm.t̠tp[.---.]bm.|y 19[1AQHT].2.81
]n.|[---] h.l 'db.|[---]n.yd h.|[---].bl.išlḥ.|[---] h.gm.|[l --- k.]yṣḥ.|[---]d.'r.|[----.-]bb.|[----.]lm y.|[---.--]p.|[---.d] 14[KRT].5.238
l [----].|w l [---].|kd.[---].|kd.t[---.ym.ymm].|y'tqn.w[rḥm.'nt].|tngt̠ 6[49].2.2
.prs.qmḥ.[---].|mdbḥt.bt.ilt.'ṣr[m.l ṣpn.š].|l ǵlmt.š.w l [---.l yrḫ].|gd[lt].l nkl[.gdlt.l b'lt.bhtm].|'ṣ[rm.]l inš[.ilm.- 35[3].25
mḫ.m'[--.---].|mdbḥt.bt.i[lt.'ṣrm.l].|ṣpn š.l ǵlm[t.š.w l.---].|l yrḫ.gdlt.l [nkl.gdlt.l b']|[lt].bht[m].[']ṣrm l [inš.ilm] APP.II[173].27
[---].|yisp hm.b['l.---].|bn.dgn[.---].|'d̠bm.[---].|uḫry.l[---].|mṣt.ks h.t[--.---].|idm.adr[.---].|idm.'rẓ.t'r[ẓ.---].|'n. 12[75].2.28
l.--.dqt].|l ṣpn.gdlt.[l.---].|ugrt.š l ili[b.---].|rt.w 'ṣrm.l[.---].|pamt.w bt.[---].|rmm.w 'l[y.---].|bt.il.t̠q[l.---.kbd].| APP.II[173].39
lmm.b št.ǵr.---].|[']d tš[b'.tmtḫṣ.---].|klyn[.---].|špk.l[---].|trḥṣ.yd[h.---].|[--.]yṣt d̠m[r.---].|tšt[.r]imt.[l irt h.tšr 7.2[130].7
[-----].|šd.prsn.l.[---].|šd.bddn.l.iytlm.|šd.bn.nb'm.l.t̠pt̠b'l.|šd.bn mšrn.l.ilš 2030.1.2
bnšm.dt.[---].|krws.l.y[--.---].|yp'.l[.---].|šmr[m.---].|[-----].|bn.g[r.---].|d̠mry[.---].|bn.pdr.l.[2122.3
šb'.yn.l [---].|t̠lt̠.l ḥr[š.---].|t̠t̠[.l.]mšt̠t[.---].|t̠lt̠.l.md̠r[ǵlm].|kd[.--]. 1091.1
t̠mn 'šr šurt l [---].|t̠mn šurt l ar[--.---].|t̠n šurtm l bnš [---].|arb' šurt l b 137.1[92].1
t l tg[-.---].|arb' šurt [---].|[ḫm]šm šurt [---].|t̠lt̠ šurt l [---].|t̠n šurtm l [---].|[-----.]a[---].|[---.--]ln.|[---.]kqmt̠n.|[137.1[92].16
[---.]l[.---].|[---.]l[.---].|[---].tbt̠t̠[b.---].|[---].bn.b[--.---].|[---].bn.a 2162.A.1
[---].ap[.---].|[---].l y.l [---].|[---] ny.t̠p[--.---].|[---.--]zn.a[--.---].|[---.--]y.ns[--.---]. 63[26].1.2
[---.]l[.---].|[---.]l[.---].|[---].tbt̠t̠[b.---].|[---].bn.b[--.---].|[---].bn.ab[--.---].|[-- 2162.A.2
šurt [---].|[ḫm]šm šurt [---].|t̠lt̠ šurt l [---].|t̠n šurtm l [---].|[-----.]a[---].|[---.--]ln.|[---.]kqmt̠n.|[---.]klnmw.|[---. 137.1[92].17
ršm.|ddm l 'nqt.|dd l alt̠t.w l lmdt h.|dd l iḫyn.|dd l [---]. 1101.13
-].|šmr[m.---].|[-----].|bn.g[r.---].|d̠mry[.---].|bn.pdr.l.[---]. 2122.8
t̠tpp.anhb[m.d alp.šd].|ẓu h.b ym[.---].|[--]rn.l [---]. 3['NT].3.01
d[--].|l ṣpn[.---.-]lu.|ilib[.---.b]'l.|ugrt[.---.--]n.|[w] š l [---]. UG5.13.37
šb'.ḫdǵlm.|l.[---]mn ḫpn.|l[.--.]škn.ḫpn.|l.k[-]w.ḫpn.|l.ṣ[--].š'[rt].|l.'dy 1117.2
.ḥly[t].'[r]b[.š]p[š].|w [ḥl.]mlk.[w.]b.ym.ḥdt̠.t̠n.šm.|l.[---]t.|i[d.yd]bḥ.mlk.l.prgl.ṣqrn.b.gg.|ar[b'.]arb'.mt̠bt.azm 35[3].49

qrht.b[--.---].|ksp.iš[-.---].|art.[---].|[-----].|[-----].|l [----].|b[--.---].|ẖl[--.---].|ẖp[ty.---]. 1147.6
l [----].|w l [---].|kd.[---].|kd.t[---.ym.ymm].|y‘tqn.w[rḥm. 6[49].2.1
l.[----].|l.[----].|l.‘ṯ[trt.---].|l.mš[--.---].|l.ilt[.---].|l.b‘lt[.---].|l.il.bt[.- 1004.2
l.[----].|l.[----].|l.‘ṯ[trt.---].|l.mš[--.---].|l.ilt[.---].|l.b‘lt[.---]. 1004.1
|špš n.[---].|hm.al[k.--].|ytnt[.---].|ṯn[.---].|w[.-----].|l[.-----].|h[--.---].|šp[š.---].|‘m.k[--.lḥt].|akl.yṯ[ṯb.--]pt.|ib.‘l 2060.26

la

n.ǵl[m]m[.---].|mid.an[--.]ṣn[--].|nrt.ilm.špš[.ṣḥrr]t.|la.šmm.b y[d.bn.ilm.m]t.|w t‘n.btlt.‘n[t.bnt.]bht |k.y ilm.b 3[‘NT.VI].5.26
imr.b p y.|k lli.b ṯbrn q y.ẖtu hw.|nrt.ilm.špš.ṣḥrrt.|la.šmm.b yd.bn ilm.mt.|ym.ymm.y‘tqn.l ymm.|l yrẖm.rḥ 6[49].2.25
mr.b p h.|k lli.b ṯbrn.|qn h.ṯẖtan.|nrt.ilm.špš.|ṣḥrrt.la.|šmm.b yd.md|d.ilm.mt.b a|lp.šd.rbt.k|mn.l p‘n.mt.|h 4[51].8.22

laa

.|npš h.l lḥm.tptḥ.|brlt h.l ṯrm.|mt.dm.ẖt.š‘tqt.|dm.lan.w ypqd.|krt.ṯ‘.yšu.g h.|w yṣḥ.šm‘.l mṯt.|ḥry.ṭbẖ.imr.| 16.6[127].14
ẖmšt.mṯt h.|bm.bky h.w yšn.|b dm‘ h.nhmmt.|šnt.tluan.|w yškb.nhmmt.|w yqmṣ.w b ḥlm h.|il.yrd.b ḏhrt h. 14[KRT].1.33
[m]t.dm.ẖt.š‘tqt dm.|li.w ttb‘.š‘tqt.|bt.krt.bu.tbu.|bkt.tgly.w tbu.|nṣrt.tbu.pnm. 16.6[127].2

lay

‘dyn h.yb|ltm.ybln h.mǵy.ḥrn.l bt h.w.|yštql.l ḥṭr h.tlu ḥt.km.nẖl.|tplg.km.plg.|b‘d h.bhtm.mnt.b‘d h.bhtm.sgr UG5.7.68
l.ytk.[d]m[‘t.]km.|rb‘t.ṯqlm.ṯṯp[.---.]bm.|yd.ṣpn hm.tliy m[.--.ṣ]pn hm.|nṣḥy.šrr.m[---.--]ay.|nbšr km.dnil.[--] h 19[1AQHT].2.84

lak

]r k.|tšlm k.|lm[.l.]likt.|ši[l.š]lm y.|[‘]d.r[-]š.|[-]ly.l.likt.|[a]nk.[---].|šil.[šlm y].|[l]m.li[kt].|[-]t.‘[--]. 2010.10
.ṯryl.um y.rgm.|yšlm.l k.ilm.|tǵr k.tšlm k.|lḥt.šlm.k.lik[t].|um y.‘m y.ht.‘m[ny].|kll.šlm.ṯm ny.|‘m.um y.mnm. 2009.1.5
n.š[l]m.|ṯm ny.‘[m.]bn y.|mnm.[šl]m[.r]gm[.ṯṯb].|ky.lik.bn y.|lḥt.akl.‘m y.|mid y w ǵbn y.|w.bn y.hn kt.|yškn. 2061.9
.uḏr h.|w.hm.ẖt.|‘l.w.likt.|‘m k.w.hm.|l.‘l.w.lakm.|ilak.w.at.|um y.al.tdḥṣ.|w.ap.mhkm.|b.lb k.al.|tšt. 1013.20
mr[.---].|k d lbšt.bir.mlak.|šmm.tmr.zbl.mlk.|šmm.tlak.ṭl.amr..|bn km k bk[r.z]bl.am..|rkm.agzrt[.--].arẖ..|b‘l 13[6].27
.tpln.b g[bl.šnt k.---].|[--]šnm.aṯtm.t[--.---].|[m]lakm.ylak.ym.[t‘dt.ṯpṭ.nhr].|b ‘lṣ.‘lṣm.npr.š[--.---].|uṭ.ṯbr.ap hm. 2.1[137].11
.---]n.|l ad[n h.---].|dgn tt[--.---.-]l|‘.l kṯrt hl[l.sn]nt.|ylak yrẖ ny[r] šmm.‘m.|ẖr[ẖ]b mlk qẓ.tn nkl y|rẖ ytrẖ.ib t 24[77].16
hdd tr[--.--]l.aṯrt y.|[--]ptm.ṣḥq.|[---.]rgm.hy.[-]ẖ[-]y.ilak k.|[---.--]g k.yritn.mǵy.hy.w kn.|[---].ḥln.d b.dmt.um.i 1002.41
ṯb.b‘l.l bht h.|u mlk.u bl mlk.|arṣ.drkt.yštkn.|dll.al.ilak.l bn.|ilm.mt.‘dd.l ydd.|il.ǵzr.yqra.mt.|b npš h.ystrn y 4[51].7.45
lnn ǵrm.mid.ksp.|gb‘m lḥmd.ẖrṣ.|yblnn.udr.ilqṣm.|yak.l kṯr.w ẖss.|w ṯb l mspr..k tiakn.|ǵlmm.|aẖr.mǵy.kṯr. 4[51].5.103
|[--]t.mṭ.tpln.b g[bl.šnt k.---].|[--]šnm.aṯtm.t[--.---].|[m]lakm.ylak.ym.[t‘dt.ṯpṭ.nhr].|b ‘lṣ.‘lṣm.npr.š[--.---].|uṭ.ṯb 2.1[137].11
|t‘l.tr[-.---].|bt.il.li[mm.---].|‘l.ḥbš.[---].|mn.lik.[---].|lik.tl[ak.---].|t‘ddn[.---].|niṣ.p[---.---]. 5[67].4.24
gt.ibr h.|l ql.nhqt.ḥmr h.|l g‘t.alp.ḥrṯ.zǵt.|klb.ṣpr.w ylak.|mlakm.l k.‘m.krt.|mswn h.tḥm.pbl.mlk.|qḥ.ksp.w yr 14[KRT].3.123
|šlm.ṯm ny.|‘m k.mnm[.š]lm.|rgm.ṯṯ[b].|any kn.dt.|likt.mṣrm.|hn dt.b.ṣr.|mtt.by.|gšm.adr.|nškḥ.w.|rb.tmtt.| 2059.11
tḥm.rgm.|mlk.|l ḥyil.|lm.tlik.‘m y.|ik y.aškn.|‘ṣm.l bt.dml.|p ank.atn.|‘ṣm.l k.|arb‘. 1010.4
ds.|w.l.klby.|šm‘t.ẖti.|nẖtu.ht.|hm.in mm.|nẖtu.w.lak.|‘m y.w.yd.|ilm.p.k mtm.|‘z.mid.|hm.nṯkp.|m‘n k.|w. 53[54].10
śwm.hnd.|w.mlk.b‘l y.bnš.|bnny.‘mn.|mlakty.hnd.|ylak ‘m y.|w.t‘l.ṯh.hn.|[a]lpm.śśwm.|[---].w.ṯb. 1012.36
|[--.]d.n‘m.lbš k.|[-]dm.ṯn id.|[--]m.d.l.n‘mm.|[lm.]l.likt.‘m y.|[---.]‘bd.ank.|[---.‘b]d k.|[---.--]l y.‘m.|[---.]‘m.|[- 2128.1.7
|mlk.b.ṯy ndr.|iṯt.w.ht.|[-]sny.uḏr h.|w.hm.ẖt.|‘l.w.likt.|‘m k.w.hm.|l.‘l.w.lakm.|ilak.w.at.|um y.al.tdḥṣ.|w.a 1013.17
l.ap.s[--.---].|b hm.w.rgm.hw.al[--].|atn.ksp.l hm.‘d.|ilak.‘m.mlk.|ht.lik[t.--.]mlk[.--].|w.mlk.yštal.b.hn[--].|hmt. 2008.2.8
l yblt.ẖbṯm.|ap ksp hm.|l yblt.|w ht.luk ‘m ml[kt].|tǵsdb.šmlšn.|w tb‘ ank.|‘m mlakt h šm‘ h.| 1021.4
yd‘t.|‘m y.špš.b‘l k.|šnt.šntm.lm.l.tlk.|w.lḥt.akl.ky.|likt.‘m.špš.|b‘l k.ky.akl.|b.ḥwt k.inn.|špš n.[---].|hm.al[k.- 2060.18
ẖn.|bn y.aẖ y.rgm.|ilm.tǵr k.|tšlm k.|iky.lḥt.|spr.d likt.|‘m.ṯryl.|mh y.rgmt.|w ht.aẖ y.|bn y.yšal.|ṯryl.p rgm. 138.7
n.|bn y.aẖ y.rgm.|ilm.tǵr k.|tšlm k.|ik y.lḥt.|spr.d likt.|‘m.ṯryl.|mh y.rgmt.|w ht.aẖ y.|bn y.yšal.|ṯryl.p rgm. 138.7
rṣ.|yblnn.udr.ilqṣm.|yak.l kṯr.w ẖss.|w ṯb l mspr..k tlakn.|ǵlmm.|aẖr.mǵy.kṯr.w ẖss.|št.alp.qdm h.mra.|w tk. 4[51].5.104
].|tḥm.wr[--].|yšlm.[l] k.|ilm.t[ǵ]r k.|tšlm k.|lm[.l.]likt.|ši[l.š]lm y.|[‘]d.r[-]š.|[-]ly.l.likt.|[a]nk.[---].|šil.[šlm y] 2010.7
y.|[‘]d.r[-]š.|[-]ly.l.likt.|[a]nk.[---].|šil.[šlm y].|[l]m.li[kt].|[-]t.‘[--]. 2010.13
m.w.rgm.hw.al[--].|atn.ksp.l hm.‘d.|ilak.‘m.mlk.|ht.lik[t.--.]mlk[.--].|w.mlk.yštal.b.hn[--].|hmt.w.anyt.hm.t‘[rb 2008.2.9
[---.--]d.‘m y.|[--.]spr.lm.likt.|[--]y.k išal hm.|[--.‘š]rm.kkr.ṯlṯ.|[--.]ṯlṯm.kkr.ṯlṯ.|[--.] 1022.2
lm.|mlk n.b‘l y.ḥw[t.--].|yšhr k.w.‘m.ṣ[--].|‘š[--.---]d.lik[t.---].|w [----].|k[--.---].|‘šrm[.---].|tšt.tb‘[.---].|qrt.mlk[. 2008.1.12
tṯn.[---].|t‘l.tr[-.---].|bt.il.li[mm.---].|‘l.ḥbš.[---].|mn.lik.[---].|lik.tl[ak.---].|t‘ddn[.---].|niṣ.p[---.---]. 5[67].4.23
.tr[-.---].|bt.il.li[mm.---].|‘l.ḥbš.[---].|mn.lik.[---].|lik.tl[ak.---].|t‘ddn[.---].|niṣ.p[---.---]. 5[67].4.24
y.ibr[-].|[--]wy.rgm l.|mlkt.ugrt.|[--]kt.rgmt.|[--]y.l.ilak.|[---].‘m y.|[---]m.w.lm.|[---.]w.‘m k.|[---]m.ksp.|[---].‘ 1016.11

lalit

[---.]šlm.|[---.--]š.lalit.|[---.]bt šp.š.|y[-]lm.w mlk.|ynṣl.l ṯ‘y. 2005.2.5

liy

|[-]rbn.‘dd.nryn.|[ab]r[p]u.bn.kbd.|[-]m[-].bn.ṣmrt.|liy.bn.yṣi.|ḏmrhd.bn.srt.|[---.--]m.|‘bdmlk.bn.śrn.|‘bdb‘l.b 102[322].6.6
n‘m.|bn kbr.|bn iytlm.|bn ayln.|bn.kln.|bn.‘lln.|bn.liy.|bn.nqṭn.|bn abrẖṭ.|bn.grdy.|bn.ṣlpn.|bn ǵlmn.|bn sgl 1064.25
.bn.usyy.|mit.ṯṯm.kbd.|l.bn.yšm‘.|mit.arb‘m.kbd.|l.liy.bn.‘myn.|mit.ẖmšm.kbd.|d.škn.l.ks.ilm. 1143.12
m.|[ar]swn.bn.qqln.|m[--].bn.qqln.|‘bdil[-].bn.qqln.|liy.bn.qqln.|mnn.bn.ṣnr.|iẖy.[b]n[.--]l[-].|‘bdy[rẖ].bn.gṯtn. 85[80].4.5
spr.ḥršm.|liy.bn.qqln.|[---.a]lṯy.|[-----].|[---]tl.|[---]‘bl.|[---]bln.|[---]d 1036.2
-].bn.mryn.|[---].bn.ṯyl.|annmt.nḥl h.|abmn.bn.‘bd.|liy.bn.rqdy.|bn.ršp. 1036.14

|tbry.|bn.ymn.|krty.|bn.abr[-].|yrpu.|kdn.|p'ṣ.|bn.liy.|yd'.|šmn.|'dy.|'nbr.|aḫrm.|bn.qrdy.|bn.šm'n.|bn.ġl 2117.1.25
t[.a]rb'[.---].|'nmky.'šr.[---].|ṯmry.'šr.ṯn.k[rmm.---].|liy.krm.aḥd[.---].|'bdmlk.krm.aḥ[d.---].|krm.ubdy.b d.ġ[--. 1081.5
d].|bn gmrt.|bn.il.ṣm[d].|bn abbly.|yṯ'd.ṣm[d].|bn.liy.|'šrm.ṣ[md].|ṯṯ kbd.b ḥ[--].|w.arb'.ḥ[mrm].|b m[']rby.| 2113.22
m.dt.'qb.|b.ayly.|šd.abršn.|šd.kkn.[bn].ubyn.|šd.bn.li[y].|šd.bn.š[--]y.|šd.bn.ṯ[---].|šd.'dmn[.bn.]ynḥm.|šd.bn.ṯ 2026.5
[---.]liy.|[---.]nrn.|[---.-]pṯ.|[---.]knys.[---].|[---.--]by.|[---.-]ṯby[. 2134.1

lim

yṣq šmn.šlm.b ṣ['.trḥṣ].|yd h.btlt.'nt.uṣb't[h.ybmt].|limm.tiḫd.knr h.b yd[h.tšt].|rimt.l irt h.tšr.dd.al[iyn].|b'l. UG5.3.2.6
ṣpn.|b q[dš.b ġr.nḥ]lt y.|w t['n].btlt.[']nt.ṯṯb.|[ybmt.]limm.[a]n.aqry.|[b arṣ].mlḥmt.[aš]t.b 'pr m.|ddym.ask[.šl 3['NT].4.66
.w tphn.|hlk.b'l.aṯtrt.|k t'n.hlk.btlt.|'nt.tdrq.ybmt.|[limm].b h.p'nm.|[ṯṭ.b ']dn.ksl.|[ṯṯbr.'ln.p]n h.td['].|tġṣ[.p 4[51].2.16
qn.ḏr' h.tḥrṯ.km.gn.|ap lb.k 'mq.ṯṯlṯ.bmt.|b'l.mt.my.lim.bn dgn.|my.hmlt.aṯr.b'l.nrd.|b arṣ.'m h.trd.nrt.|ilm.šp 6[62].1.6
k gn.ap lb.k 'mq.yṯlṯ.|bmt.yšu.g h.w yṣḥ.|b'l.mt.my.lim.bn.|dgn.my.hmlt.aṯr.|b'l.ard.b arṣ.ap.|'nt.ttlk.w tṣd.kl. 5[67].6.23
-.]'l.kbkbt.|n'm.[--.-]llm.trḥṣ.|btlt.'n[t].tptr' ṯd[h].|limm.w t'l.'m.il.|ab h.ḥpr.p'l k.y[--].|šm' k.l arḫ.w bn.[--].| 13[6].20
[---.]arḫt.tld[n].|a[lp].l btlt.'nt.|w ypt l ybmt.li[mm].|w y'ny.aliyn[.b'l].|lm.k qnym.'l[m.--].|k dr d.d yk 10[76].3.4
.|[ḫrṣ.w aš]lḥ k.w tn.qšt k.[l].|['nt.tq]ḥ[.q]ṣ't k.ybmt.limm.|w y'n.aqht.ġzr.adr.ṯqbm.|[d]lbnn.adr.gdm.b rumm. 17[2AQHT].6.19
r.b ġlil.qnm.|tn.l kṯr.w ḫss.yb'l.qšt l 'nt.|qṣ't.l ybmt.limm.w t'n.btlt.|'nt.irš ḥym.l aqht.ġzr.|irš ḥym.w atn k.bl 17[2AQHT].6.25
b št.ġr.w hln.'nt.tm|tḫṣ.b 'mq.tḫtṣb.bn.|qrytm tmḫṣ.lim.ḫp y[m].|tṣmt.adm.ṣat.š[p]š.|tḥt h.k kdrt.ri[š].|'l h.k ir 3['NT].2.7
.b št.ġr].|ap 'nt tm[tḫṣ.b 'mq.tḫtṣb.bn.qrytm.tmḫṣ].|lim ḫ[p.ym.---].|[--]m.t[-]t[.---].|m[-]mt[.---].|[-----].|t[---.-- 7.2[130].26
yrgb b'l.|ydb il.|yarš il.|yrġm il.|'mtr.|ydb il.|yrgb lim.|'mtr.|yarš il.|ydb b'l.|yrġm b'l.|'z b'l.|ydb hd. UG5.14.B.8
t'l.'m.il.|ab h.ḥpr.p'l k.y[--].|šm' k.l arḫ.w bn.[--].|limm.ql.b udn.k w[-].|k rtqt mr[.---].|k d lbšt.bir.mlak.|š 13[6].23
r.yṣq.šmn.|šlm.b ṣ'.trḥṣ.yd h.bt|[l]t.'nt.uṣb't h.ybmt.limm.|[t]rḥṣ.yd h.b dm.ḏmr.|[u]ṣb't h.b mm'.mhrm.|[ṯ]'r. 3['NT].2.33
r.|w ql.tštḥwy.kbd hyt.|w rgm.l btlt.'nt.|ṯny.l ymmt.limm.|tḥm.aliyn.b'l.hwt.|aliy.qrdm.qry.b arṣ.|mlḥmt št.b ' 3['NT].3.9
.rb.dd].|arṣy bt.y['bdr.---].|rgm l btl[t.'nt.ṯny.l ybmt.limm.tḥm.aliyn.b'l].|hw[t.aliy.qrdm.qryy.b arṣ.mlḥmt.št].| 7.2[130].13
h.|[---.yg]rš h.|[---.]ru.|[----] h.|[---.--]mt.|[---.--]mr.limm.|[---.]bn.ilm.mt.|[--]u.šb't.ġlm h.|[---].bn.ilm.mt.|p[- 6[49].6.6
.---].|w 'ṣrm[.---].|ṣlyh šr[-.---].|[ṯ]lṯm.w b[--.---].|l il limm[.---].|w ṯt.npš[.---].|kbd.w [---].|l ṣp[n.---].|š.[---].|w 40[134].8
--.]dr dt.šmm.|[---.al]iyn b'l.|[---].rkb.'rpt.|[---.]ġš.l limm.|[---.]l ytb.l arṣ.|[---].mtm.|[---.--]d mhr.ur.|[---.]yḫn 10[76].1.8
.yp km.---.-]yt km.|[---.]km.|[-----].|[---.]ugrt.|[---].l.lim.|[---.mšr m]šr.|[bn.ugrt.---.--]y.|[---.np]y nqmd.|[---.]p APP.I[-].1.22
|ks.ksp[.---].|krpn.[---].|w ṯṯn.[---].|t'l.tr[-.---].|bt.il.li[mm.---].|'l.ḥbš.[---].|mn.lik.[---].|lik.tl[ak.---].|t'ddn[.---] 5[67].4.21
.|[---.--]t.ytn.|[---.btlt.]'nt.|[---.ybmt.]limm.|[---.---]l.limm.|[---.yṯ]b.l arṣ.|[---.--]l.šir.|[---.-]tm.|[---.]yd y.|[----] 10[76].1.16
.ur.|[---.]yḫnnn.|[---.--]t.ytn.|[---.btlt.]'nt.|[---.ybmt.]limm.|[---.---]l.limm.|[---.yṯ]b.l arṣ.|[---.--]l.šir.|[---.-]tm.|[10[76].1.15

lb

adt y.[---].|lb.ab[d k].al[.---].|[-]tm.iph.adt y.w.[---].|tšṣḥq.hn.aṯt.l.'bd. 1017.2
.[---].|kd.t[---.ym.ymm].|y'tqn.w[rḥm.'nt].|tngṯ h.k lb.a[rḫ].|l 'gl h.k lb.ṯa[t].|l imr h.km.lb.'n[t].|aṯr.b'l.tiḫd.m 6[49].2.6
t.|ym.ymm.y'tqn.l ymm.|l yrḥm.rḥm.'nt.tngṯ h.|k lb.arḫ.l 'gl h.k lb.|ṯat.l imr h.km.lb.|'nt.aṯr.b'l.tiḫd.|bn.ilm 6[49].2.28
ṣb't h ḥrṣ.abn.|p h.tiḫd.šnt h.w akl.bqmm.|tšt ḥrṣ.k lb ilnm.|w ṯn.gprm.mn gpr h.šr.|aqht.y'n.kmr.kmr[.--].|k 19[1AQHT].1.10
'l.bt.ab h.nšrm.trḫ[p]n.|ybṣr.ḥbl.diym.|tbky.pġt.bm.lb.|tdm'.bm.kbd.|tmz'.kst.dnil.mt.|rpi.al.ġzr.mt.hrnmy.|a 19[1AQHT].1.34
ṯb.ank.l hm.|w.any k.ṯt.|by.'ky.'ryt.|w.aḫ y.mhk.|b lb h.al.yšt. 2059.27
ḫṣn.w t'n.|tḫtṣb.w tḥdy.'nt.|tġdd.kbd h.b ṣḥq.ymlu.|lb h.b šmḫt.kbd.'nt.|tšyt.k brkm.tġll b dm.|ḏmr.ḥlqm.b m 3['NT].2.26
ḫṣn.w t]'n.tḫtṣb.|[w tḥdy.'nt.tġdd.kbd h.b ṣḥ]q.ymlu.lb h.|[b šmḫt.kbd.'nt.tšyt.tḥt h.k]kdrt.riš.|['l h.k irbym.kp 7.1[131].7
zr.tmḫṣ.alpm.ib.št[-.]št.|ḥršm l ahlm p[---.]km.|[-]bl lb h.km.btn.y[--.-]ah.|ṯnm.tšqy msk.hwt.tšqy[.-.]w [---].|w 19[1AQHT].4.223
aḫš.idy.alt.in l y.|[--]t.b'l.ḥẓ.ršp.b[n].km.yr.klyt h.w lb h.|[t]n.p k.b ġr.ṯn.p k.b ḫlb.k tgwln.šnt k.|[--.]w špt k.l t 1001.1.3
n.|kbd k iš.tikln.|td n.km.mrm.tqrṣn.|il.yẓḥq.bm.|lb.w ygmḏ.bm kbd.|ẓi.at.l tlš.|amt.yrḫ.|l dmgy.amt.|aṯrt. 12[75].1.13
l.'l.w.lakm.|ilak.w.at.|um y.al.tdḥṣ.|w.ap.mhkm.|b.lb k.al.|tšt. 1013.23
y'r].|tḥdy.lḥm.w dqn[.ṯṯlṯ].|qn.ḏr' h.tḥrṯ.km.gn.|ap lb.k 'mq.ṯṯlṯ.bmt.|b'l.mt.my.lim.bn dgn.|my.hmlt.aṯr.b'l.nr 6[62].1.5
.b y'r.|yhdy.lḥm.w dqn.|yṯlṯ.qn.ḏr' h.yḥrṯ.|k gn.ap lb.k 'mq.yṯlṯ.|bmt.yšu.g h.w yṣḥ.|b'l.mt.my.lim.bn.|dgn.m 5[67].6.21
l tṣi.b b[--].bm.k[--].|[--]ṯb.'ryt k.k qlt[.---].|[--]at.brt.lb k.'nn.[---].|[--.]šdq.k ttn.l y.šn[.---].|[---.]bn.rgm.w yd'[.-- 60[32].4
p[id].|yd't k.bt.k anšt.w i[n.b ilht].|qlṣ k.tb'.bt.ḫnp.lb[k.--.ti]|ḫd.d iṯ.b kbd k.tšt.b [---].|irt k.dṯ.ydṯ.m'qb k.[ttb 18[3AQHT].1.17
mn gpr h.šr.|aqht.y'n.kmr.kmr[.--].|k ap'.il.b gdrt.k lb.l |ḥṯ h.imḫṣ h.k d.'l.qšt h.|imḫṣ h.'l.qṣ't h.hwt.|l aḥw.ap 19[1AQHT].1.13
[mlk.]ugrt.|b'l ṣdq.|skn.bt.|mlk.ṯġr.|[m]lk.bny.|[--].lb.mlk.|[---.]ṣmḫ. 1007.8
t.t'db.nšb l h.|w 'nt.ktp.b hm.yg'r.ṯġr.|bt.il.pn.l mgr lb.t'dbn.|nšb.l inr.t'dbn.ktp.|b il ab h.g'r.ytb.il.kb[-].|aṯ[rt. UG5.1.1.12
.rḥm.'nt.tngṯ h.|k lb.arḫ.l 'gl h.k lb.|ṯat.l imr h.km.lb.|'nt.aṯr.b'l.tiḫd.|bn.ilm.mt.b ḥrb.|tbq'nn.b ḫṯr.tdry|nn. 6[49].2.29
.'nt].|tngṯ h.k lb.a[rḫ].|l 'gl h.k lb.ṯa[t].|l imr h.km.lb.'n[t].|aṯr.b'l.tiḫd.m[t].|b sin.lpš.tšṣq[n h].|b qṣ.all.tšu.g 6[49].2.8
.qštm.|[----.]mhrm.ht.tṣdn.tintt.|[---]m.tṣḥq.'nt.w b lb.tqny.|[---.]ṯb l y.l aqht.ġzr.ṯb l y w l k.|[---]m.l aqry k.b 17[2AQHT].6.41
.š.|'nt.š.ršp.š.dr il w p[ḫ]r b'l.|gdlt.šlm.gdlt.w burm.[l]b.|rmṣt.ilhm.b'lm.dṯt.w kšm.ḥmš.|'ṯr h.mlun.šnpt.ḥṣt h.b 34[1].8
.š.'nt.š.ršp.š.dr].|il.w pḫr[.b'l.gdlt.šlm.gdlt].|w burm.l[b.rmṣt.ilhm].|b'lm.w mlu[.---.ksm].|ṯlṯm.w m'rb[.---].|db APP.II[173].19
š].|'nt š ršp š[.dr.il.w pḫr.b'l].|gdlt.šlm[.gdlt.w burm.lb].|rmṣt.ilh[m.b'lm.---].|ksm.ṯlṯm.[---].|d yqḥ bt[.--]r.dbḥ[35[3].17
|['l.]krt.tbkn.|[--.]rgm.trm.|[--.]mtm.tbkn.|[--]t.w b lb.tqb[-].|[--]m[-].mtm.uṣb'[t].|[-]tr.šrk.il.|'rb.špš.l ymġ.|k 15[128].5.15
ymm].|y'tqn.w[rḥm.'nt].|tngṯ h.k lb.a[rḫ].|l 'gl h.k lb.ṯa[t].|l imr h.km.lb.'n[t].|aṯr.b'l.tiḫd.m[t].|b sin.lpš.tšṣq[6[49].2.7
'tqn.l ymm.|l yrḥm.rḥm.'nt.tngṯ h.|k lb.arḫ.l 'gl h.k lb.|ṯat.l imr h.km.lb.|'nt.aṯr.b'l.tiḫd.|bn.ilm.mt.b ḥrb.|tbq' 6[49].2.28
[l a]q[h]t.|[t]krb.[---.]l qrb.mym.|tql.[---.]lb.ṯṯ[b]r.|qšt[.---]r.y[ṯ]br.|ṯmn.[---.]btlt.[']nt.|ṯṯb.[---.--]ša.| 19[1AQHT].1.3

lba

.w ugr.ṯhm.bn ilm.|mt.hwt.ydd.bn.il.|ǵzr.p np.š.npš.lbim.|thw.hm.brlt.anḫr.|b ym.hm.brk y.tkšd.|rumm.ʻn.kḏ 5[67].1.14
w yʻny.bn.|ilm.mt.npš[.-].|npš.lbun.|thw.w npš.|anḫr.b ym.|brkt.šbšt.|k rumm.hm.|ʻn.k UG5.4.3
aqrb k ab h bʻ[l].|yǵtr.ʻṯtr t|rḫ l k ybrdmy.b[t.a]|b h lb[u] yʻrr.w yʻ[n].|yrḫ nyr šmm.w nʻ[n].|ʻma nkl ḫtn y.a[ḫ] 24[77].30

lbiy

bʻldʻ.yd[.---.ʻ]šrt.ksp h.|lbiy.pdy.[---.k]sp h. 2112.2

lbum

r.il.ab y.ank.in.bt[.l] y[.km.]ilm[.w] ḥẓr[.k bn].|[qd]š.lbum.trd.b n[p]šn y.trḥṣn.k ṯrm.|[--]b b[ht].|[zbl.]ym.b hkl 2.3[129].20

lbbmm

p.w [š]lmm.|[---.a]lp.l bʻl.w aṯrt.ʻṣr[m] l inš.|[ilm.---].lbbmm.gdlt.ʻrb špš w ḥl.|[mlk.b ar]bʻt.ʻ[š]rt.yrtḥṣ.mlk.brr.| 36[9].1.9

lbn

[.---].|bn u[l]pm.|bn ʻ[p]ty.|bn.kdgdl.|bn.smyy.|bn.lbn.|bn.šlmn.|bn.mly.|pslm.|bn.annd.|bn.glʻd.|w.nḥl h.| 2163.3.6
bd.an.ʻnn.aṯrt.|p.ʻbd.ank.aḫd.ulṯ.|hm.amt.aṯrt.tlbn.|lbnt.ybn.bt.l bʻl.|km ilm.w ḥẓr.k bn.aṯrt.|w tʻn.rbt.aṯrt ym. 4[51].4.62
š[n.---].|y.arṣ.ḥšn[.---].|tʻtd.tkl.[---].|tkn.lbn[.---].|dt.lbn k[.---].|dk k.kbkb[.---].|dm.mt.aṣḥ[.---].|ydd.b qr[b.---]. 5[67].3.7
d.|p ʻbd.an.ʻnn.aṯrt.|p.ʻbd.ank.aḫd.ulṯ.|hm.amt.aṯrt.tlbn.|lbnt.ybn.bt.l bʻl.|km ilm.w ḥẓr.k bn.aṯrt.|w tʻn.rbt.aṯ 4[51].4.61
yrḫ iṯt[bnm].|ršpab.rb ʻšrt.m[r]yn.|pǵdn.ilbʻl.krwn.lbn.ʻdn.|ḫyrn.mdʻ.|šmʻn.rb ʻšrt.kkln.ʻbd.abṣn.|šdyn.unn.d 2011.3
.ql h.b ʻrpt.|šrh.l arṣ.brqm.|bt.arzm.yklln h.|hm.bt.lbnt.yʻmsn h.|l yrgm.l aliyn bʻl.|ṣḥ.ḫrn.b bhm k.|ʻḏbt.b qr 4[51].5.73
[nq]dm.dt.kn.npṣ hm.|[bn].lbn.arbʻ.qšt.w.ar[bʻ].|[u]ṯpt.qlʻ.w.ṯt.mr[ḥ]m.|[bn].smyy.qšt. 2047.2
.išt.|b bht m.n[bl]at.b hkl m.|sb.ksp.l rqm.ḫrṣ.|nṣb.l lbnt.šmḫ.|aliyn.bʻl.ht y.bnt.|dt.ksp.hkl y.dtm.|ḫrṣ.ʻdbt.bht 4[51].6.35
t.mṯb k[.---].|[š]mm.rm.lk.prẓ kt.|[k]bkbm.ṯm.tpl k.lbnt.|[-.]rgm.k yrkt.ʻṯqbm.|[---]m.ʻẓpn.l pit.|m[--]m[.--]tm. 13[6].13
rt.ḫmšm.kbd.|[---.-]nd.l.mlbš.ṯrmnm.|[---]h.lbš.allm.lbnm.|[---].all.šmt.|[---].all.iqni.arbʻm.kbl.|[---].iqni.ʻšrm.ǵ 1106.4
--].|rbt.ṯbt.ḥš[n.---].|y.arṣ.ḥšn[.---].|tʻtd.tkl.[---].|tkn.lbn[.---].|dt.lbn k[.---].|dk k.kbkb[.---].|dm.mt.aṣḥ[.---].|yd 5[67].3.6
m.ar[bʻ].|kbd.ksp.|ʻl.tgyn.|w ʻl.aṯt h.|yph.mʻnt.|bn.lbn. 2053.23

lbny

h.b d.ṯtmd.|[š]d.b d.iwrḫṭ.|[ṯn].šdm.b d.gmrd.|[šd.]lbny.b d.tbṯṯb.|[š]d.bn.ṯ[-]rn.b d.ʻdbmlk.|[šd.]bn.brzn.b d.n 82[300].1.15
šn.[---].|bn.ʻbdy.[---].|bn.dmtn.[---].|[b]n.gʻyn.ḫr[-].|lbnym.|grgš.[---].|bn.ǵrn.[---].|bn.agyn[.---].|iyṯ[-.---]. 93[328].13
]lk.bn.nskn.alpm.|krw.šlmy.|alpm.|atn.bṣry.alpm.|lbnym.|ṯm[n.]alp mitm.|ilbʻl ḫmš m[at].|ʻdn.ḫmš.mat.|bn. 1060.2.7

lbnm

šrš.|lbnm.|ḫlb.krd.|ṣʻ.|mlk.|gbʻly.|ypr.|ary.|ẓrn.|art.|ṯlḥny.| 71[113].2
].|atlg.|ulm.|izly.|uḫnp.|bn sḫrn.|mʻqb.|ṯpn.|mʻr.|lbnm.|nḫl.|yʻny.|atn.|utly.|bn.alz.|bn ḫlm.|bn.ḏmr.|bn.ʻ 2075.10
l[b]nm.|nnu.|ʻrm.|bṣr.|mʻr.|ḫlby.|mṣbt.|snr.|ṯm.|ubš.|gl 2041.1
[-----].|bṣr[.---].|lbn[m].|ʻr[.---].|nnu[.---].|šq[--.---].|[-]r[-.---].|[-----].|[-----] 2145.3
[---].|q[---].|ʻm[--].|ar[--].|ykn[ʻm].|ṣlyy.|ʻnm[ky].|l[bnm].|ʻr[--]. 2133.8
]m.|[---.]piln.|[---].ṣmd[.---.]pd[ry].|[-----].|[---.b]ʻlt.|lbnm.ʻšr.yn.|ḫlb.gngnt.ṯlṯ.y[n].|bṣr.ʻšr.yn.|nnu arbʻ.yn.|šql 2004.21
.b.nni.|ṯn.bnšm.b.slḫ.|[---].bnšm.b.yny.|[--.]bnšm.b.lbnm.|arbʻ.bnšm.b.ypr.|[---.]bnšm.b.šbn.|[---.b]nšm.b.šmn 2076.21
ʻ.|uḫnp.|art.|[--]n.|[-----].|[-----].|nnu.|šmg.|šmn.|lbnm.|ṯrm.|bṣr.|y[--].|y[--].|snr.|midḫ.|ḥ[lym].|[ḫ]lby.|ʻ 2058.2.14

lbnn

]ḥ[.q]ṣʻt k.ybmt.limm.|w yʻn.aqht.ǵzr.adr.ṯqbm.|[d]lbnn.adr.gdm.b rumm.|adr.qrnt.b yʻlm.mtnm.|b ʻqbt.ṯr.ad 17[2AQHT].6.21
ʻl.l hwt y.|[ḥš.]bht h.tbnn.|[ḥš.]trmm.hkl h.|y[tl]k.l lbnn.w ʻṣ h.|l[šr]yn.mḥmd.arz h.|h[n.l]bnn.w ʻṣ h.|š[r]yn. 4[51].6.18
hkl h.|y[tl]k.l lbnn.w ʻṣ h.|l[šr]yn.mḥmd.arz h.|h[n.l]bnn.w ʻṣ h.|š[r]yn.mḥmd.arz h.|tšt.išt.b bht m.|nb[l]at.b 4[51].6.20
q.yn.ṯmk.|mrṯ.yn.srnm.yn.bld.|ǵll.yn.išryt.ʻnq.smd.|lbnn.ṯl mrṯ.yḫrt.il.|hn.ym.w ṯn.tlḥmn.rpum.|tštyn.ṯlṯ.rbʻ.y 22.2[124].20
mš.|ṯdṯ.ym.tlḥmn.rpum.|tštyn.bt.ikl.b prʻ.|yṣq.b irt.lbnn.mk.b šbʻ.|[ymm.---]k.aliyn.bʻl.|[---].rʻ h ab y.|[---.]ʻ[-- 22.2[124].25
ḫrṯm[.---].|bn.ṯmq[-.---].|bn.ntp.[---].|bn.lbnn.[----].|ady.ḥ[--.---].|[-]b[-]n.[---].|bn.atnb.mr[--.---].|b 88[304].4

lbš

lbš.aḥd.|b.ʻšrt.|w.ṯn.b.ḫmšt.|ṯprt.b.ṯlṯt.|mṯyn.b.ṯṯt.|ṯn.lbš 1108.1
[-----].|[ḫ]pn.aḥd.b.ṯqlm.|lbš.aḥd.b.ṯqlm.|ḫpn.pṯtm.b ʻšr.|tgmr.ksp.ṯlṯm.|ṯqlm.kbd. 1115.3
mlbš.ṯrmnm.|k.yṯn.w.b.bt.|mlk.mlbš.|ytn.l hm.|šbʻ.lbšm.allm.|l ušḫry.|ṯlṯ.mat.pṯtm.|l.mgmr.b.ṯlṯ.|šnt. 1107.9
bʻ.mat.šʻrt.ḫmšm.kbd.|[---.-]nd.l.mlbš.ṯrmnm.|[---]h.lbš.allm.lbnm.|[---].all.šmt.|[---].all.iqni.arbʻm.kbl.|[---].iq 1106.4
m.š[bʻ].mat.šʻrt.|[---.]iqnu.[---.]lbš.ṯrmnm.|[---.iqn]i.lbš.al[l.---].|[---].ṯṯ.lbš[.---].|[---.]kbd.ṯṯ.i[qnu.---].|[---.]ǵprt. 1106.21
|d.ʻrb.b.anyt.|l.mlk.gbl.|w.ḫmšm.ksp.|lqḥ.mlk.gbl.|lbš.anyt h.|bʻrm.ksp.|mḫr.hn. 2106.16
|tš[ʻ]ly.ṯmn.l ṯmnym.|w [th]rn.w tldn mṯ.|al[iyn.bʻ]l šlbšn.|i[---.---.--]l h.mǵẓ.|y[--.---.]l irt h.|n[--.---]. 5[67].5.23
ybʻlnn.|[---.--]n.b.ṯlṯ.šnt.l.nṣd.|[---.--]ršp.mlk.k.ypdd.mlbš.|u---].mlk.ytn.mlbš.|[---.-]rn.k.ypdd.mlbš h.|[---.]mlk 1106.58
.aḥd.|b.ʻšrt.|w.ṯn.b.ḫmšt.|ṯprt.b.ṯlṯt.|mṯyn.b.ṯṯt.|ṯn.lbšm.b.ʻšrt.|pld.b.arbʻt.|lbš.ṯn.b.ṯnt.ʻšrt. 1108.6
w bn.[--].|limm.ql.b udn.k w[-].|k rtqt mr[.---].|k d lbšt.bir.mlak.|šmm.tmr.zbl.mlk.|šmm.tlak.ṭl.amr..|bn km 13[6].25
[--.l]bš.mtn.b.arʻt.|[--.l]bš.bn.yknʻ.b.arʻt.|[--.l]bš.bn.grbn.b.ṯqlm.|[--.lb]š.bn.sgryn.b[.ṯ]qlm.|[---.]bn.ully. 135[330].3
[--.l]bš.mtn.b.arʻt.|[--.l]bš.bn.yknʻ.b.arʻt.|[--.l]bš.bn.grbn.b.ṯqlm.|[--.lb]š.bn.sgryn 135[330].2
ʻt.|[--.l]bš.bn.yknʻ.b.arʻt.|[--.l]bš.bn.grbn.b.ṯqlm.|[--.lb]š.bn.sgryn.b[.ṯ]qlm.|[---.]bn.ully.b.ṯ[qlm].|[---.]bn.anndy 135[330].4
p.|ṯmn.lbšm.w.mšlt.|l.udmym.b.ṯmnt.ʻšrt.ksp.|šbʻm.lbš.d.ʻrb.bt.mlk.|b.mit.ḫmšt.kbd.ksp.|ṯlṯ.ktnt.b d.an[r]my. 2101.16

lk.k.ypdd.mlbš. | u---].mlk.ytn.mlbš. | [---.-]rn.k.ypdd.mlbš h. | [---.]mlk.ytn.lbš.l h. 1106.60
n.b.ʿšrt[.k]sp. | rṭ.l.ql.d.ybl.prd. | b.ṯql.w.nṣp.ksp. | ṯmn.lbšm.w.mšlt. | l.udmym.b.ṯmnt.ʿšrt.ksp. | šbʿm.lbš.d.ʿrb.bt.ml 2101.14
.ʿṯtrt.ḫr[-]. | bt mlk.ʿšr.ʿšr.[--].bt ilm. | kbr[-]m.[-]trmt. | lbš.w [-]tn.ušpǵt. | ḫr[-].ṯlṯt.mzn. | drk.š.alp.w ṯlṯ. | ṣin.šlm[m. 33[5].4
mn.mlk. | [---.]šʿrt.šbʿ.ʿšr h. | [---.iqn]i.l.ṯrmn.qrt. | [---.]lbš.ḫmšm.iqnu. | [---].šmt.ḫmšt.ḫndlt. | [---.iqn]i.l.[-]k.btbt. | [1106.16
.l.mit.šʿrt. | l.šr.ʿṯtrt. | mlbš.ṯrmnm. | k.yṯn.w.b.bt. | mlk.mlbš. | ytn.l hm. | šbʿ.lbšm.allm. | l ušḫry. | ṯlṯ.mat.pṯtm. | l.mg 1107.7
[---.]l mdgkbr. | [---] y.ʿm k. | [-]tn.l.stn. | [--.]d.nʿm.lbš k. | [-]dm.ṯn id. | [--]m.d.l.nʿmm. | [lm.]l.likt.ʿm y. | [---.]ʿb 2128.1.4
t.šdm.ṣḥr[.---]. | šbʿ.šnt.il.mla.[-]. | w ṯmn.nqpnt.ʿd. | k lbš.km.lpš.dm a[ḫ h]. | km.all.dm.ary h. | k šbʿt.l šbʿm.aḫ h.y 12[75].2.47
.mlk.ytn.mlbš. | [---.-]rn.k.ypdd.mlbš h. | [---.]mlk.ytn.lbš.l h. 1106.61
. | [---.--]rm.d krm. | [---].l ʿnt m. | [---.]l šlm. | [-]l[-.-]ry.ylbš. | mlk.ylk.lqḥ.ilm. | aṯr.ilm.ylk.pʿnm. | mlk.pʿnm.yl[k]. | š 33[5].22
[--.l]bš.mtn.b.arʿt. | [--.l]bš.bn.yknʿ.b.arʿt. | [--.l]bš.bn.grbn.b.ṯql 135[330].1
| tlbš.npṣ.ǵzr.tšt.ḫ[---.b] | nšg h.ḥrb.tšt.b tʿr[t h]. | w ʿl.tlbš.npṣ.aṯt.[--]. | ṣbi nrt.ilm.špš.[-]r[--]. | pǵt.minš.šdm l mʿ[r 19[1AQHT].4.208
--.a]dm.tium.b ǵlp y[m.--]. | d alp šd.ẓu h.b ym.t[---]. | tlbš.npṣ.ǵzr.tšt.ḫ[---.b] | nšg h.ḥrb.tšt.b tʿr[t h]. | w ʿl.tlbš.np 19[1AQHT].4.206
ṯn.pld.pṯt[.-]r. | lpš.sgr.rq. | ṯṯ.prqt. | w.mrdt.prqt.pṯt. | lbš.psm.rq. | ṯn.mrdt.az. | ṯlṯ.pld.šʿrt. | ṯ[---].kbm. | p[---]r.aḥd. 1112.5
t. | ṯprt.b.ṯlṯt. | mṯyn.b.ṯṯt. | ṯn.lbšm.b.ʿšrt. | pld.b.arbʿt. | lbš.ṯn.b.ṯnt.ʿšrt. 1108.8
ḫpn.d.iqni.w.šmt. | l.iybʿl. | ṯlṯm.l.mit.šʿrt. | l.šr.ʿṯtrt. | mlbš.ṯrmnm. | k.yṯn.w.b.bt. | mlk.mlbš. | ytn.l hm. | šbʿ.lbšm.a 1107.5
l.[-]k.btbt. | [---.l.ṯrm]nm.š[bʿ].mat.šʿrt. | [---.]iqnu.[---.]lbš.ṯrmnm. | [---.iqn]i.lbš.al[l.---]. | [---].ṯṯ.lbš[.---]. | [---.]kbd.ṯ 1106.20
t.ilhnm.b šnt. | [---.]šbʿ.mat.šʿrt.ḫmšm.kbd. | [---.-]nd.l.mlbš.ṯrmnm. | [---]h.lbš.allm.lbnm. | [---].all.šmt. | [---].all.iqn 1106.3
.šnt.l.nṣd. | [---.--]ršp.mlk.k.ypdd.mlbš. | u---].mlk.ytn.mlbš. | [---.-]rn.k.ypdd.mlbš h. | [---.]mlk.ytn.lbš.l h. 1106.59
---.]iqnu.[---.]lbš.ṯrmnm. | [---.iqn]i.lbš.al[l.---]. | [---].ṯṯ.lbš[.---]. | [---.]kbd.ṯṯ.i[qnu.---]. | [---.]ǵprt.ʿš[r.---]. | [---.p]ṯtm. 1106.22

lg

ǵr mdrʿ[.iṯ.lḥm.---]. | iṯ.yn.d ʿrb.bṯk[.---]. | mǵ hw.l hn.lg yn h[.---]. | w ḥbr h.mla yn.[---]. 23[52].75
ʿ.mšlt.arbʿ.ḫpnt.[---]. | ḫmšm.ṯlṯ.rkb.ntn.ṯlṯ.mat.[---]. | lg.šmn.rqḥ.šrʿm.ušpǵtm.p[--.---]. | kṯ.ẓrw.kṯ.nbt.dnt.w [-]n[-. UG5.9.1.21
.bʿlm. | bn.bʿly.ṯlṯtm.bʿlm. | w.aḥd.ḫbṯ. | w.arbʿ.aṯt. | bn.lg.ṯn.bn h. | bʿlm.w.aḫt h. | b.šrt. | šty.w.bn h. 2080.10
ʿšr. | kṯt. | [--]š ʿšr. | lg. 158[58].4

lgn

-.ubr]ʿy. | b[n.---]. | bn[.---.ušk]ny. | bn.kdrn.uškny. | bn.lgn.uškny. | bn.abn.uškny. | bn.arz.šʿrty. | bn.ibrd.mʿrby. | ṣdq 87[64].23
.l hm. | pʿṣ.ḫbty. | artyn.ary. | brqn.ṯlḥy. | bn.aryn. | bn.lgn. | bn.bʿyn. | šdyn. | ary. | brqn. | bn.ḫlln. | bn.mṣry. | ṯmn.qšt 118[306].7

ldn

.nsk.ṯlṯ. | [-]lkynt.nsk.ṯlṯ. | [-]by.nsk.ṯlṯ. | šmny. | ḫršn. | ldn. | bn.ands. | bn.ann. | bn.ʿbdpdr. | šd.iyry.l.ʿbdbʿl. | šd.šmm 1102.13
t. | d b d.mlkytn. | kdrl. | slṯmg. | adrdn. | l[l]wn. | ydln. | ldn. | tdǵl. | ibrkyṯ. 1034.8

lwn

nt h. | yrḫm.yd.ṯn.bn h. | bʿlm.w.ṯlṯ.nʿrm.w.bt.aḥt. | bn.lwn.ṯlṯtm.bʿlm. | bn.bʿly.ṯlṯtm.bʿlm. | w.aḥd.ḫbṯ. | w.arbʿ.aṯt. | 2080.6

lwsnd

[l.p]ʿn.bʿl y. | [šbʿ] d.šbʿ [d]. | [mr]ḥqtm. | qlt. | ʿbd k.b. | lwsnd. | [w] b ṣr. | ʿm.mlk. | w.ht. | mlk.syr. | ns.w.ṯm. | ydbḥ. | 2063.10

lwš

msn.nn.ṯkmn. | w šnm.w ngšnn.ḥby. | bʿl.qrnm w ḏnb.ylšn. | b ḫri h.w ṯnt h.ql.il.[--]. | il.k yrdm.arṣ.ʿnt. | w ʿṯtrt.ṭṣd UG5.1.1.20

lzn

l h. | bn nʿmyn. | bn aṯtyy. | bn ḫlp. | bn.ẓll. | bn ydy. | bn lzn. | bn.ṯyn. | bn gʿr. | bn.prtn. | bn ḫnn. | b[n.-]n. | bn.ṣṣb. | bn. 2016.1.14

lḥ

l[.-]ry ṯlṯ spm w ʿšr lḥm. | [--.]w nṣp w ṯlṯ spm w ʿšrm lḥ[m]. | l[.-]dt ḫnd[r]ṯ arʿ s[p]m w ʿš[r]. | [---.]ḫndrṯm ṯṯ spm 134[-].4
[-]b[-.---.--] | r ṯṯm lḥm. | l[.-]ry ṯlṯ spm w ʿšr lḥm. | [--.]w nṣp w ṯlṯ spm w ʿšrm l 134[-].2
[-]b[-.---.--] | r ṯṯm lḥm. | l[.-]ry ṯlṯ spm w ʿšr lḥm. | [--.]w nṣp w ṯlṯ spm w ʿšrm lḥ[m]. | l[.-]dt ḫnd[r]ṯ arʿ s 134[-].3
nd[r]ṯ arʿ s[p]m w ʿš[r]. | [---.]ḫndrṯm ṯṯ spm [w] ṯlṯm l[ḥm]. | [---.]arʿ spm w [---]. | [---]š[.---.--]b[.---]. | [--.]sp[m.w - 134[-].6
---.]arʿ spm w [---]. | [---]š[.---.--]b[.---]. | [--.]sp[m.w ---.l]ḥm. 134[-].9

lḫk

.[---]. | [---.]il.[---]. | [ṯs]un.b arṣ. | mḫnm.ṯrp ym. | lšnm.tlḫk. | šmm.ṯtrp. | ym.ḏnbtm. | tnn.l šbm. | tšt.trks. | l mrym.l 1003.5

lḥm

mdbr.špm.yd[.---.---]r. | l riš hm.w yš[--.--]m. | lḥm.b lḥm ay.w šty.b ḫmr yn ay. | šlm.mlk.šlm.mlkt.ʿrbm m.ṯnnm 23[52].6
l bt. | š l ḫlmṭ. | w tr l qlḥ. | w š ḥll ydm. | b qdš il bt. | w tlḥm aṯt. | š l ilbt.šlmm. | kll ylḥm b h. | w l bbt šqym. | š l uḫr UG5.7.TR3
il dbḥ.b bt h.mṣd.ṣd.b qrb | hkl [h].ṣḥ.l qṣ.ilm.tlḥmn. | ilm.w tštn.tštn y[n] ʿd šbʿ. | trṯ.ʿd.škr.yʿdb.yrḫ. | gb h. UG5.1.1.2
zr.yšqy bn. | [qdš.ḫ]mš.ṯdṯ.ym.uzr. | [ilm].dnil.uzr.ilm.ylḥm. | [uzr.]yšqy.bn qdš.yd.ṣṯ h. | [dn]il.yd.ṣṯ h.yʿl.w yškb. | 17[2AQHT].1.13
-.apnk]. | [dnil.mt.rp]i.apn.ǵz[r]. | [mt.hrnmy.]uzr.ilm.ylḥm. | [uzr.yšqy.]bn.qdš.yd. | [ṣṯ h.yʿl.]w yškb.yd. | [mizrt.]p 17[2AQHT].1.3
zr. | [yšqy.b]n.qdš ṯlṯ rbʿ ym. | [uzr.i]lm.dnil.uzr. | [ilm.y]lḥm.uzr.yšqy bn. | [qdš.ḫ]mš.ṯdṯ.ym.uzr. | [ilm].dnil.uzr.il 17[2AQHT].1.11
ry h. | bl.iṯ.bn.l h.km aḫ h.w šrš. | km.ary h.uzrm.ilm.ylḥm. | uzrm.yšqy.bn.qdš. | l tbrknn l ṯr.il ab y. | tmrnn.l bny. 17[2AQHT].1.22
. | [mizrt.]p ynl.hn.ym. | [w ṯn.uzr.]ilm.dnil. | [uzr.ilm.]ylḥm.uzr. | [yšqy.b]n.qdš ṯlṯ rbʿ ym. | [uzr.i]lm.dnil.uzr. | [ilm 17[2AQHT].1.8
š ḥll ydm. | b qdš il bt. | w tlḥm aṯt. | š l ilbt.šlmm. | kll ylḥm b h. | w l bbt šqym. | š l uḫr ḫlmṭ. | w tr l qlḥ. | ym aḥd. UG5.11.10
.---]. | b mdbr.špm.yd[.---.---]r. | l riš hm.w yš[--.--]m. | lḥm.b lḥm ay.w šty.b ḫmr yn ay. | šlm.mlk.šlm.mlkt.ʿrbm m 23[52].6

lḥm

m.|ʻl.tl[-]k.ʻṯrṯrm.|nšu.[r]iš.ḥrṯm.|l ẓr.ʻdb.dgn kly.|lḥm.[b]ʻdn hm.kly.|yn.b ḥmt hm.k[l]y.|šmn.b q[bʻt hm.--- 16[126].3.14
.rġbt.w tġt[--].|hm.ġmu.ġmit.w ʻs[--].|lḥm.hm.štym.lḥ[m].|b ṯlḥnt.lḥm št.|b krpnm.yn.b k.ḫrṣ.|dm.ʻṣm.hm.yd. 4[51].4.35
.št.|tštn.k nšr.b ḥbš h.km.diy.|b tʻrt h.aqht.km.yṯb.l lḥ[m].|bn.dnil.l ṯrm.ʻl h.nšr[m].|trḫpn.ybṣr.ḥbl.diy[m.bn]. 18[3AQHT].4.29
]ṣd h.yrd.krt.|[l g]gt.ʻdb.akl.l qryt.|ḥṭt.l bt.ḫbr.|yip.lḥm.d ḫmš.|[mġ]d.ṯdṯ.yr[ḫm].|ʻdn.ngb.w [yṣi.ṣbu].|ṣbi.ng[14[KRT].4.174
d k.w yrd.|krt.l ggt.ʻdb.|akl.l qryt.|ḥṭt.l bt.ḫbr.|yip.lḥm.d ḫmš.|mġd.ṯdṯ.yrḫm.|ʻdn.ngb.w yṣi.|ṣbu.ṣbi.ngb.|w 14[KRT].2.83
-].|prdmn.ʻbd.ali[yn].|bʻl.sid.zbl.bʻl.|arṣ.qm.yṯʻr.|w yšlḥmn h.|ybrd.ṯd.l pnw h.|b ḥrb.mlḥt.|qṣ.mri.ndd.|yʻšr. 3[ʻNT].1.5
.|ʻrb.b ẓl.ḫmt.lqḥ.|imr.dbḥ.b yd h.|lla.klatnm.|klt.lḥm h.d nzl.|lqḥ.msrr.ʻṣr.db[ḥ].|yṣq.b gl.ḥṭt.yn.|b gl.ḫrṣ.n 14[KRT].3.162
ṯḥ hw.prṣ.bʻd hm.|w ʻrb.hm.hm[.iṯ.--.l]ḥm.w t[n].|w nlḥm.hm.iṯ[.--.yn.w t]n.w nšt.|w ʻn hm.nġr mdrʻ[.iṯ.lḥm.--- 23[52].72
kḏd.aylt.|hm.imt.imt.npš.blt.|ḥmr.p imt.b klt.|yd y.ilḥm.hm.šbʻ.|ydt y.b ṣʻ.hm.ks.ymsk.|nhr.k[--].ṣḥn.bʻl.ʻm.|a 5[67].1.20
nyt.i[lm].|rġb.rġbt.w tġt[--].|hm.ġmu.ġmit.w ʻs[--].|lḥm.hm.štym.lḥ[m].|b ṯlḥnt.lḥm št.|b krpnm.yn.b k.ḫrṣ.|d 4[51].4.35
k.km.nšr.b ḥb[š y].|km.diy.b tʻrt y.aqht.[km.yṯb].|l lḥm.w bn.dnil.l ṯrm[.ʻl h].|nšrm.trḫpn.ybṣr.[ḥbl.d]|iym.bn. 18[3AQHT].4.19
d h.lpš.yks.|mizrtm.ġr.b abn.|ydy.psltm.b yʻr.|yhdy.lḥm.w dqn.|yṯlṯ.qn.ḏrʻ h.yḥrṯ.|k gn.ap lb.k ʻmq.yṯlṯ.|bmt.y 5[67].6.19
l bʻl.|ġr.b ab.td[.ps]ltm[.b yʻr].|thdy.lḥm.w dqn[.ṯṯlṯ].|qn.ḏrʻ h.tḥrṯ.km.gn.|ap lb.k ʻmq.ṯṯlṯ.bmt. 6[62].1.3
ġr.|nġr.ptḥ.w ptḥ hw.prṣ.bʻd hm.|w ʻrb.hm.hm[.iṯ.--.l]ḥm.w t[n].|w nlḥm.hm.iṯ[.--.yn.w t]n.w nšt.|w ʻn hm.nġr 23[52].71
ṣḥn.bʻl.ʻm.|aḫ y.qran.hd.ʻm.ary y.|w lḥm m ʻm aḫ y.lḥm.|w št m.ʻm.a[ḫ] yn.|p nšt.bʻl.[t]ʻn.iṯʻn k.|[---.]ma[---] k 5[67].1.24
.ik.yṣḥn.|[bʻl.ʻm.aḫ y.ik].yqrun.hd.|[ʻm.ary y.---.--]p.mlḥm y.|[---.---]lt.qẓb.|[---.]šmḫ y.|[---.]tbʻ.|[---.-]nnm. 5[67].2.23
ymn.t[--.---].|[--.]l bʻl.ʻbd[.---].|ṯr ab h il.ṯṯrm[.---].|tšlḥm yrḫ.ggn[.---].|k[.---.ḫ]mš.ḫssm[.---].|[---.--]m ʻṯtr[t.--- 2001.1.16
|dn.almnt.l ṯṯpṭ.|ṯpṭ qṣr.npš.l tdy.|ṯšm.ʻl.dl.l pn k.|l tšlḥm.ytm.bʻd.|ksl k.almnt.km.|aḫt.ʻrš.mdw.anšt.|ʻrš.zbln. 16.6[127].49
m.l ṯṯb.[idk.pnm].|l ytn.tk.ġr.ll.ʻm.phr.mʻd.ap.ilm.l lḥ[m].|ytb.bn qdš.l ṯrm.bʻl.qm.ʻl.il.hlm.|ilm.tph hm.tphn. 2.1[137].20
ḥ im[r.b yd k].|imr.d[bḥ.bm].ymn.|lla.kl[atn]m.|klt.l[ḥm k.d]nzl.|qḥ.ms[rr.]ʻṣr.|dbḥ.ṣ[q.b g]l.ḥṭt.|yn.b gl[.ḫ]rṣ 14[KRT].2.69
.w ṯn.yšlḥm.|kṯrt.w yš[š]q.bnt.hl[l].|snnt.ṯlṯ[.r]bʻ ym.yšl|ḥm kṯrt.w yššq.|bnt hll.snnt.ḫmš.|ṯdṯ.ym.yšlḥm.k[ṯ]rt. 17[2AQHT].2.34
k.dnil.|mt.rpi.ap.hn.ġzr.mt.|hrnmy.alp.ytbḫ.l kṯ|rt.yšlḥm.kṯrt.w y|ššq.bnt.[hl]l.snnt.|hn.ym.w ṯn.yšlḥm.|kṯrt. 17[2AQHT].2.30
kṯ|rt.yšlḥm.kṯrt.w y|ššq.bnt.[hl]l.snnt.|hn.ym.w ṯn.yšlḥm.|kṯrt.w yš[š]q.bnt.hl[l].|snnt.ṯlṯ[.r]bʻ ym.yšl|ḥm kṯrt 17[2AQHT].2.32
]bʻ ym.yšl|ḥm kṯrt.w yššq.|bnt hll.snnt.ḫmš.|ṯdṯ.ym.yšlḥm.k[ṯ]rt.|w y[ššq].bnt.hll.snnt.|mk.b šb[ʻ.]ymm.tbʻ.b b 17[2AQHT].2.37
b.yrḫ.|gb h.km.[---.]yqṯqṭ.tḥt.|ṯlḥnt.il.d ydʻnn.|yʻdb.lḥm.l h.w d l ydʻnn.|d.mṣd.|ylmn.ḥṭ.tḥt.ṯlḥn.|b qrʻ.|ʻṯtrt. UG5.1.1.7
[-]mt[-]m.l[-]ṯnm.|ʻdm.[lḥ]m.tšty.|w tʻn.mṯt ḥry.|l l[ḥ]m.l š[ty].ṣḥt km.|db[ḥ.l krt.a]dn km.|ʻl.krt.tbun.km.|r 15[128].6.4
qdm.|yd.b ṣʻ.tšlḥ.|ḥrb.b bšr.tštn.|[w t]ʻn.mṯt.ḥry.|[l lḥ]m.l šty.ṣḥt km.|[--.dbḥ.l]krt.bʻl km. 15[128].4.27
.]yd.b ṣʻ.t[šl]ḥ.|[ḥrb.b]bš[r].tštn.|[w tʻn].mṯt.ḥry.|[l lḥ]m.l šty.ṣḥt k[m].|[---.]brk.t[---].|[ʻl.]krt.tbkn.|[--.]rgm.ṯr 15[128].5.10
--].pit.|[---.]qbat.|[---.]inšt.|[--]u.l tštql.|[---].ṯry.ap.l tlḥm.|[l]ḥm.trmmt.l tšt.|yn.tġẓyt.špš.|rpim.tḥtk.|špš.tḥtk. 6.6[62.2].42
msk.|nhr.k[--].ṣḥn.bʻl.ʻm.|aḫ y.qran.hd.ʻm.ary y.|w lḥm m ʻm aḫ y.lḥm.|w št m.ʻm.a[ḫ] yn.|p nšt.bʻl.[t]ʻn.iṯʻn k 5[67].1.24
.imr.|w ilḥm.mgṯ.w iṯrm.|tšmʻ.mṯt.ḥry.|ṯṭbḫ.imr.w lḥm.|mgṯ.w yṯrm.hn.ym.|w ṯn.yṯb.krt.l ʻd h.|yṯb.l ksi mlk. 16.6[127].20
pqd.|krt.ṯʻ.yšu.g h.|w yṣḥ.šmʻ.l mṯt.|ḥry.ṭbḫ.imr.|w ilḥm.mgṯ.w iṯrm.|tšmʻ.mṯt.ḥry.|ṯṭbḫ.imr.w lḥm.|mgṯ.w yṯ 16.6[127].18
|i.hd.d[---.---].|ynpʻ.bʻ[l.---].|b ṯmnt.[---].|yqrb.[---].|lḥm.m[---.---].|[ʻ]d.lḥm[.šty.ilm].|w pq.mr[ġṯm.ṯd.---].|b ḥr 5[67].4.11
.|nḥš.ʻq šr.ln h.mlḫš abd.ln h.ydy.|ḥmt.hlm.ytq.nḥš.yšlḥm.nḥš.|ʻq šr.yʻdb.ksa.w yṯb.|tqru.l špš.um.ql bl.ʻm|kṯr UG5.7.43
.|nḥš.ʻq šr.ln h.mlḫš.abd.ln h.|ydy.ḥmt.hlm.ytq.nḥš.yšlḥm.|nḥš.ʻq šr.yʻdb.ksa.w yṯb.|tqru l špš.um h.špš.um.ql. UG5.7.17
.|nḥš.ʻq šr.ln h.mlḫš.abd.ln h.ydy.|ḥmt.hlm.ytq.nḥš.yšlḥm.nḥš ʻq.|š.yʻdb.ksa w yṯb.|tqru l špš.um h.špš.um.ql UG5.7.33
ʻq šr.ln h.mlḫš.|abd.ln h.ydy ḥmt.hlm.ytq šqy.|nḥš.yšlḥm.nḥš.ʻq šr.yʻdb.|ksa.w yṯb.|tqru l špš.um h.špš.um.ql UG5.7.55
.nḥš.ʻq šr.ln h.mlḫš.abd.|ln h.ydy.ḥmt.hlm ytq.nḥš.|yšlḥm.nḥš.ʻq šr.yʻdb ksa.|w yṯb.|tqru l špš.um h.špš.um.ql UG5.7.49
.|nḥš.ʻq šr.ln h.mlḫš.abd.ln h.ydy.|ḥmt.hlm.ytq.nḥš.yšlḥm.nḥš.|ʻq šr.yʻdb.ksa.w yṯb.|tqru.l špš.um h.špš.um.ql UG5.7.28
rr.nḥš.ʻq šr.ln h.mlḫš abd.ln h.|ydy.ḥmt.hlm.ytq nḥš yšlḥm.nḥš.|ʻq.šr.yʻdb.ksa.w yṯb.|tqru l špš um h.špš um ql. UG5.7.38
.nḥš.ʻq šr ln h.|mlḫš.abd.ln h.ydy.ḥmt.hlm.ytq.|nḥš.yšlḥm.nḥš.ʻq šr.ydb.ksa.|w yṯb.|tqru.l špš.u h.špš.um.ql.bl. UG5.7.12
m h.špš.um.ql.bl.ʻm.|ʻnt w ʻṯtrt inbb h.mnt.nṯk.|nḥš.šlḥm.nḥš.ʻq šr[.yʻ]db.ksa.|nḥš.šmrr.nḥš.ʻq šr.ln h.ml|ḫš.ab UG5.7.23
šr.ln h.mlḫš abd.ln h.ydy.|ḥmt.hlm.ytq ytqšqy.nḥš. yšlḥm.ʻq šr.|yʻdb.ksa.w.yṯb.|tqru.l špš.um h.špš.um.ql bl.|ʻ UG5.7.6
t.[ʻ]ṯr.[k]m.|zbln.ʻl.riš h.|w ṯṯb.trḥṣ.nn.b dʻt.|npš h.l lḥm.tptḥ.|brlt h.l ṯrm.|mt.dm.ḥt.š ʻtqt.|dm.lan.w ypqd.|kr 16.6[127].11
[---.]qbat.|[---.]inšt.|[--]u.l tštql.|[---].ṯry.ap.l tlḥm.|[l]ḥm.trmmt.l tšt.|yn.tġẓyt.špš.|rpim.tḥtk.|špš.tḥtk.ilnym.| 6.6[62.2].43
.ym.w ṯn.tlḥmn.rpum.|tštyn.ṯlṯ.rbʻ.ym.ḫmš.|ṯdṯ.ym.tlḥmn.rpum.|tštyn.bt.ikl.b prʻ.|yṣq.b irt.lbnn.mk.b šbʻ.|[y 22.2[124].23
ġll.yn.išryt.ʻnq.smd.|lbnn.ṯl mrṯ.yḥrṯ.il.|hn.ym.w ṯn.tlḥmn.rpum.|tštyn.ṯlṯ.rbʻ.ym.ḫmš.|ṯdṯ.ym.tlḥmn.rpum.|tšt 22.2[124].21
.b d.dnil.ytnn.|qšt.l brk h.yʻdb.|qṣʻt.apnk.mṯt.dnty.|tšlḥm.tššqy ilm.|tsad.tkbd.hmt.bʻl.|ḥkpt il.kl h.tbʻ.kṯr.|l a 17[2AQHT].5.29
d[b].|imr.b pḫd.l npš.kṯr.|w ḫss.l brlt.hyn d.|ḥrš yd.šlḥm.ššqy.|ilm sad.kbd.hmt.bʻl.|ḥkpt.il.kl h.tšmʻ.|mṯt.dnt 17[2AQHT].5.19
.mra.|w tk.pn h.tʻdb.ksu.|w yṯṯb.l ymn.aliyn.|bʻl.ʻd.lḥm.št[y.ilm].|[w]yʻn.aliy[n.bʻl].|[--]b[.---].|ḥš.bht m.k[ṯr]. 4[51].5.110
ilht.ksat[.yn].|špq.ilm.rḥbt yn.|špq.ilht.dkrt[.yn].|ʻd.lḥm.šty.ilm.|w pq mrġṯm.ṯd.|b ḥrb.mlḥt.qṣ[.m]r|i.tšty.krp 4[51].6.55
.hwt.|[--].aliyn.bʻl.|[--.]rbt.aṯrt.ym.|[---.]btlt.ʻnt.|[--.tl]ḥm.tšty.|[ilm.w tp]q.mrġṯm.|[ṯd.b ḥrb.m]lḥt.qṣ.|[mri.tšt 4[51].3.40
ʻ.bʻ[l.---].|b ṯmnt.[---].|yqrb.[---].|lḥm.m[---.---].|[ʻ]d.lḥm[.šty.ilm].|w pq.mr[ġṯm.ṯd.---].|b ḥrb.[mlḥt.qṣ.mri].|št 5[67].4.12
|hm.ġmu.ġmit.w ʻs[--].|lḥm.hm.štym.lḥ[m].|b ṯlḥnt.lḥm št.|b krpnm.yn.b k.ḫrṣ.|dm.ʻṣm.hm.yd.il mlk.|yḫss k. 4[51].4.36
[-----].|šmʻ.l [-]mt[.-]m.l[-]ṯnm.|ʻdm.[lḥ]m.tšty.|w tʻn.mṯt ḥry.|l l[ḥ]m.l š[ty].ṣḥt km.|db[ḥ.l krt. 15[128].6.2
nlḥm.hm.iṯ[.--.yn.w t]n.w nšt.|w ʻn hm.nġr mdrʻ[.iṯ.lḥm.---].|iṯ.yn.d ʻrb.bṯk[.---].|mġ hw.l hn.lg yn h[.---].|w ḥ 23[52].73
amt m.|[---.]b w tʻrb.sd.|[---.--]n b ym.qẓ.|[---.]ym.tlḥmn.|[---.rp]um.tštyn.|[---.]il.d ʻrgzm.|[---.]dt.ʻl.lty.|[---.] 20[121].1.6
[-----].|[-----].|[-----].|[-----].|[-----].|alp[.---.--]r.|mit.lḥ[m.---.-]dyt.|ṣlʻt.alp.mri.|ʻšr.bmt.alp.mri.|ṯn.nšbm.|ṯmn 1128.15
-].|prʻm.ṣd k.hn pr[ʻ.--].|ṣd.b hkl h[.---].|[------].|[---.l]ḥm[.---].|[---].ay š[---].|[---.b ḥ]rb.mlḥ[t.qṣ].|[mri.tšty.krp 17[2AQHT].6.2

lḫn

n.|aḥd.b bn k.amlkn.|w tʻn.rbt.aṯrt ym.|bl.nmlk.ydʻ.ylḥn.|w yʻn.lṭpn.il d pi|d dq.anm.l yrẓ.|ʻm.bʻl.l yʻdb.mrḥ.| 6.1.48[49.1.20]
[.ṯrrt].|[-]ʻb[-].š[--]m.|[----]r[.---]š[.--]qm.|id.u [---]t.|lḫn š[-]ʻ[--.]aḥd[.-].|tšmʻ.mṯt.[ḥ]ry.|ṯṭbḫ.šmn.[m]ri h.|t[p]t 15[128].4.13

lḥt

l k.|yd'm.l.yd't.|'m y.špš.b'l k.|šnt.šntm.lm.l.tlk.|w.lḥt.akl.ky.|likt.'m.špš.|b'l k.ky.akl.|b.ḫwt k.inn.|špš n.[---] 2060.17
m ny.'[m.]bn y.|mnm.[šl]m[.r]gm[.ṯṯb].|ky.lik.bn y.|lḥt.akl.'m y.|mid y w ǵbn y.|w.bn y.hn kt.|yškn.anyt.|ym. 2061.10
ṯn[.---].|w[.-----].|l[.-----].|h[--.---].|šp[š.---].|'m.k[--.lḥt].|akl.yṯ[ṯb.--]pt.|ib.'ltn.a[--.--]y.|w.spr.in[.-.]'d m.|spr 2060.29
--]n.ššwm.|n'mm.[--].ṯṯm.w.at.|nǵṯ.w.ytn.hm.l k.|w.lḥt.alpm.ḫršm.|k.rgmt.l y.bly m.|alpm.aršt.l k.w.l y.|mn.b 2064.21
.rišt.|km l ẓr brkt km.w ln.kḥṯ.zbl km.aḥd.|ilm.t'ny lḥt.mlak.ym.t'dt.ṯpṭ.nhr.|šu.ilm.rašt km.l ẓr.brkt km.ln.kḥ 2.1[137].26
.b qdš.|ztr.'m h.l arṣ.mšṣu.qṭr h.|l 'pr.ḏmr.aṯr h.ṭbq.lḥt.|niṣ h.grš d.'šy.ln h.|aḫd.yd h.b škrn.m'ms h.|[k]šb' y 17[2AQHT].1.29
.|[ztr.'m h.l a]rṣ.mšṣu.|[qṭr h.l 'pr.ḏ]mr.a[ṯ]r h.|[ṭbq.lḥt.niṣ h.gr]š.d 'šy.|[ln h.---].|z[tr.'m k.l arṣ.mšṣu.qṭr k].|l ' 17[2AQHT].1.48
.|nṣb.skn.ilib y.b qdš.|ztr.'m y.l 'pr.ḏmr.aṯr[y].|ṭbq lḥt.niṣ y.grš.|d 'šy.ln.aḫd.yd y.b š|krn m'ms y k šb't yn.|sp 17[2AQHT].2.18
--].|z[tr.'m k.l arṣ.mšṣu.qṭr k].|l 'pr.ḏm[r.aṯr k.ṭbq].|lḥt.niṣ k.gr[š.d 'šy.ln k].|spu.ksm k.bt.[b'l.w mnt k].|bt il.a 17[2AQHT].2.3
ḏr.|l iwrpḫn.|bn y.aḫ y.rgm.|ilm.tǵr k.|tšlm k.|iky.lḥt.|spr.d likt.|'m.tryl.|mh y.rgmt.|w ht.aḫ y.|bn y.yšal.|ṯ 138.6
ḏr.|l iwrpḫn.|bn y.aḫ y.rgm.|ilm.tǵr k.|tšlm k.|ik y.lḥt.|spr.d likt.|'m.tryl.|mh y.rgmt.|w ht.aḫ y.|bn y.yšal.|ṯ 138.6
m.mlk.|l.ṯryl.um y.rgm.|yšlm.l k.ilm.|tǵr k.tšlm k.|lḥt.šlm.k.lik[t].|um y.'m y.ht.'m[ny].|kll.šlm.ṯm ny.|'m.u 2009.1.5

lḫm

h.|ṯr.ḫbr.rbt.|ḫbr.ṯrrt.|bt.krt.tbun.|lm.mṯb[.---].|w lḫm mr.tqdm.|yd.b ṣ'.tšlḥ.|ḥrb.b bšr.tštn.|[w t]'n.mṯt.ḥry. 15[128].4.23

lḫsn

ṯrn.d[d].|tg d[d].|ḥdyn.d[d].|[-]ḏḏn.d[d].|qṭn.d[d].|lḫsn.d[d].|lsn.d[d].|and[--.---]. 132[331].10
d]prn[.---].|aupṯ.krm.aḥd.nšpin.kr[m.]aḥd[.---].|dmt.lḫsn.krm.aḥd.annḏr.kr[m.---].|aǵt.mryn.ary[.]yukl.krm.[--- 1081.15
ym.bn.abynm.|antn.bn.iwr[n]r.|pwn.ṯmry.|ksyn.bn.lḫsn.|[-]kyn.ṯmry. 94[313].9

lḫš

l bl.|'m ḥrn.mṣd h.mnt.nṯk nḥš.|šmrr.nḥš.'q šr.ln h.mlḫš.|abd.ln h.ydy.ḥmt.|b ḥrn.pnm.trǵnw.w ṯṯkl.|bnwt h. UG5.7.59
nhrm.b 'dt.thmtm.|mnt.nṯk.nḥš.šmrr.nḥš.|'q šr.ln h.mlḫš abd.ln h.ydy.|ḥmt.hlm.ytq yṯqšqy.nḥš.yšlḥm.'q šr.|y' UG5.7.5
l.bl.'m.|mlk.'ṯtrt h.mnt.nṯk.nḥš.šmrr.|nḥš.'q šr.ln h.mlḫš abd.ln h.ydy.|ḥmt.hlm.ytq.nḥš.yšlḥm.nḥš.|'q šr.y'db. UG5.7.42
'm b'l.mrym.ṣpn.mnt y.nṯk.|nḥš.šmrr.nḥš.'q šr ln h.|mlḫš.abd.ln h.ydy.ḥmt.hlm.ytq.|nḥš.yšlḥm.nḥš.'q šr.ydb.k UG5.7.11
m|kṯr.w ḫss.kptr h.mnt.nṯk.nḥš.|šmrr.nḥš.'q šr.ln h.mlḫš.abd.|ln h.ydy.ḥmt.hlm ytq.nḥš.|yšlḥm.nḥš.'q šr.y'db UG5.7.47
l bl.'m.|yrḫ.lrgt h.mnt.nṯk.n[ḥš].šmrr.|nḥš.'q šr.ln h.mlḫš.abd.ln h.ydy.|ḥmt.hlm.ytq.nḥš.yšlḥm.nḥš.|'q šr.y'db. UG5.7.27
.ql.bl.'m.|dgn.ttl h.mnt.nṯk.nḥš.šmrr.|nḥš.'q šr.ln h.mlḫš.abd.ln h.|ydy.ḥmt.hlm.ytq.nḥš.yšlḥm.|nḥš.'q šr.y'db. UG5.7.16
š.um.ql b.'m.|ršp.bbt h.mnt.nḥš.šmrr.|nḥš.'q šr.ln h.mlḫš.abd.ln h.ydy.|ḥmt.hlm.ytq.nḥš.yšlḥm.nḥš 'q.|š.y'db.k UG5.7.32
.|šḥr.w šlm šmm h mnt.nṯk.nḥš.|šmrr.nḥš 'q šr.ln h.mlḫš.|abd.ln h.ydy ḥmt.hlm.ytq šqy.|nḥš.yšlḥm.nḥš.'q šr.y UG5.7.53
m.|ṯṯ.w kmṯ.ḥryt h.mnt.nṯk.nḥš.šm|rr.nḥš.'q šr.ln h.mlḫš abd.ln h.|ydy.ḥmt.hlm.ytq nḥš yšlḥm.nḥš.|'q.šr.y'db. UG5.7.37
ḫš.šlḥm.nḥš.'q šr[.y']db.ksa.|nḥš.šmrr.nḥš.'q šr.ln h.ml|ḫš.abd.ln h.ydy.ḥmt.hlm.ytq.|w yṯb.|tqru.l špš.um h.š UG5.7.21
.|[dm.rgm.iṯ.l y.]w argm k.hwt.|[w aṯny k.rgm.]'ṣ.w lḫšt.|[abn.rgm.l td]'.nš[m.w l t]bn.|[hmlt.a]rṣ.[tant.šmm.' 3['NT].4.58
k.dm.rgm.|iṯ.l y.w argm k.|hwt.w aṯny k.rgm.|'ṣ.w lḫšt.abn.|tant.šmm.'m.arṣ.|thmt.'mn.kbkbm.|abn.brq.d l.t 3['NT].3.20
ks.dm.r[gm.iṯ.l y.w argm k].|hwt.w aṯny k[.rgm.'ṣ.w lḫšt.abn].|tunt.šmm.'m[.arṣ.thmt.'mn.kbkbm].|rgm.l td'.n 1['NT.IX].3.13
.rgm.iṯ.l y.d argmn k].|[h]wt.d aṯ[ny k.---.rgm.'ṣ].|w lḫšt.abn[.tant.šmm.'m.arṣ.thmt].|'m kbkbm[.abn.brq.d l td 7.2[130].19

lṭpn

tlk.nbtm.|w id'.k ḥy.aliyn.b'l.|k iṯ.zbl.b'l.arṣ.|b ḥlm.lṭpn.il d pid.|b ḏrt.bny.bnwt.|šmm.šmn.tmṭrn.|nḫlm.tlk.n 6[49].3.10
rṣ].|w hm.ḥy.a[liyn.b'l].|w hm.iṯ.zbl.b'[l.arṣ].|b ḥlm.lṭpn.il.d pid.|b ḏrt.bny.bnwt.|šmm.šmn.tmṭrn.|nḫlm.tlk.n 6[49].3.4
k.amlkn.|w t'n.rbt.aṯrt ym.|bl.nmlk.yd'.ylḥn.|w y'n.lṭpn.il d pi|d dq.anm.l yrẓ.|'m.b'l.l y'db.mrḥ.|'m.bn.dgn.k 6.1.49[49.1.21]
nnt.bnt h|ll b'l gml.yrdt.|b 'rgzm.b bz tdm.|lla y.'m lẓpn i|l ḏ.pid.hn b p y sp|r hn.b špt y mn|t hn ṯlḥ h w mlg 24[77].44
.w yplṭ k.bn[.dnil.---].|w y'ḏr k.b yd.btlt.['nt].|w y'n.lṭpn.il d p[id].|yd't k.bt.k anšt.w i[n.b ilht].|qlṣ k.tb'.bt.ḫn 18[3AQHT].1.15
ǵny.l b'l.npl.l a|rṣ.mt.aliyn.b'l.|ḫlq.zbl.b'l.arṣ.|apnk.lṭpn.il.|d pid.yrd.l ksi.ytb.|l hdm[.w] l.hdm.yṯb.|l arṣ.yṣq.' 5[67].6.11
my.]b ilm.|ydy.mrṣ.gršm zbln.|in.b ilm.'ny h.|w y'n.lṭpn.il.b pid.|ṯb.bn y.lm ṯb[t] km.|l kḥṯ.zbl k[m.a]nk.|iḥtrš 16[126].5.23
tn.|[aḫ]r.mǵy.'[d]t.ilm.|[w]y'n.aliy[n.]b'l.|[---.]tb'.l lṭpn.|[il.d]pid.l tbrk.|[krt.]ṯ'.l tmr.n'mn.|[ǵlm.]il.ks.yiḫd.| 15[128].2.13
-].|yaṯr[.---].|b d k.[---].|ṯnnt h[.---].|ṯlṯt h[.-.w y'n].|lṭpn.[il.d pid.my].|b ilm.[ydy.mrṣ].|gršm.z[bln.in.b ilm].|' 16[126].5.10
b.pdry.bt.ar.|mẓll.ṭly.bt rb.|mṯb.arṣ.bt y'bdr.|w y'n lṭpn il d pid.|p 'bd.an.'nn.aṯrt.|p.'bd.ank.aḫd.ulṯ.|hm.amt. 4[51].4.58
rt.bny.bnwt.|šmm.šmn.tmṭrn.|nḫlm.tlk.nbtm.|šmḫ.lṭpn.il.d pid.|p'n h.l hdm.yṯpd.|w yprq.lṣb w yṣḥq.|yšu.g h 6[49].3.14
|yṣḥ.ngr il.ilš.|ilš.ngr.bt.b'l.|w aṯt h.ngrt.ilht.|w y'n.lṭpn.il d pi[d].|šm'.l ngr.il il[š].|ilš.ngr bt b'l.|w aṯt k.ngrt.i 16[126].4.10
mṯpdm.tḥt.['nt.arṣ.ṯlṯ.mtḥ].|ǵyrm.idk.l yt[n.pnm.'m.lṭpn].|il d pid.tk ḫrš[n.---.tk.ǵr.ks].|ygly ḏd.i[l.w ybu.qrš.m 1['NT.IX].3.21
m.ym[-.---].|t'nyn.l zn.tn[.---].|at.adn.tp'r[.---].|ank.lṭpn.il[.d pid.---].|'l.ydm.p'rt[.---].|šm k.mdd.i[l.---].|bt ksp 1['NT.X].4.18
d.[---].|km ll.kḥṣ.tusp[.---].|tgr.il.bn h.ṯr[.---].|w y'n.lṭpn.il.d p[id.---].|šm.bn y.yw.ilt.[---].|w p'r.šm.ym[-.---].|t' 1['NT.X].4.13
k.l ntn.|'tq.b d.aṯt.ab.ṣrry.|ik m.yrgm.bn.il.|krt.šph.lṭpn.|w qdš.u ilm.tmtn.|šph.lṭpn.l yḥ.|w y'ny.krt.ṯ'.|bn.al. 16.1[125].21
nny.ḥ[l]m.adr.|ḥl.rḥb.mk[npt].|ap.krt bn[m.il].|šph.lṭpn[.w qdš].|bkm.t'r[b.'l.ab h].|t'rb.ḥ[--].|b ṯtm.t[---].|škn 16.2[125].111
š.|any.ḥlm.adr.ḥl.|rḥb.mknpt.ap.|[k]rt.bnm.il.šph.|lṭpn.w qdš.'l.|ab h.y'rb.ybky.|w yšnn.ytn.g h.|bky.b ḥy k.a 16.1[125].11
.|'m.nrt.ilm.špš.|tšu.g h.w tṣḥ.|ṯḥm.ṯr.il.ab k.|hwt.lṭpn.ḥtk k.|pl.'nt.šdm.y špš.|pl.'nt.šdm.il.yš[t k].|b'l.'nt.m 6[49].4.35
wyn.w y|[kbdn h.yšu.g h.w y]ṣḥ.ṯḥm.|[ṯr.il.ab k.hwt.l]ṭpn.ḥtk k.|[qryy.b arṣ.mlḥ]mt.št b 'p|[r m.ddym.sk.šlm].l 1['NT.IX].2.18
[ṯr.w ḫss.ṯny.l hyn].|d ḥrš.y[dm.ṯḥm.ṯr.il.ab k.]|hwt.lṭpn[.ḥtk k.---].|yh.kṯr.b[---].|št.lskt.n[--.---].|'db.bǵrt.ṯ[--. 1['NT.IX].3.6
.|u ḫšt k.l bky.'tq.|b d.aṯt ab.ṣrry.|u ilm.tmtn.šph.|[l]ṭpn.l yḥ.t[b]ky k.|ab.ǵr.b'l.ṣ[p]n.ḥlm.|qdš.nny.ḥ[l]m.adr. 16.2[125].106
m.yrgm.bn.il.|krt.šph.lṭpn.|w qdš.u ilm.tmtn.|šph.lṭpn.l yḥ.|w y'ny.krt.ṯ'.|bn.al.tbkn.al.|tdm.l y.al tkl.bn.|qr 16.1[125].23
[-----].|[-----].|il.šm'.amr k.ph[.-].|k il.ḥkmt.k ṯr.lṭpn.|ṣḥ.ngr.il.ilš.il[š].|w aṯt h.ngrt[.i]lht.|kḥṣ.k m'r[.---].|y 16[126].4.3

lyt

.zbl.b'l.arṣ. | w t'n.nrt.ilm.š[p]š. | šd yn.'n.b qbt[.t] | bl lyt.'l.umt k. | w abqṯ.aliyn.b'l. | w t'n.btlt.'nt. | an.l an.y špš. | 6[49].4.43

lk

['l]. | [---.btl]t.'n[t.-.]p h. | [---.---]n. | [-----]. | [-----]. | [---.]lk[.--]t. 10[76].2.39
r.'šrt. | '[---.---]. | b[---.---]. | t[--.---]. | w[----]. | pǵ[t.---]. | lk[.---]. | ki[--.---]. | w ẖ[--.---]. | my[.---]. | aṯ[t.---]. | aẖ k[.---]. | 16.2[125].68
dm.mt.aṣ[ḥ.---]. | ydd.b qr[b.---]. | ṯmm.w lk[.---]. | [--]ṯ.lk[.---]. | [--]kṯ.i[---.---]. | p.šn[-.---]. | w l ṯlb.[---]. | mit.rḥ[.---] 5[67].3.28
--.-]ṯt. | [---.]w.sbsg. | [-----]. | [-----]. | [---.--]ṯ. | [---.-]b.m.lk. | kdwṯ.ḥdṯ. | b d 'lpy. 1112.18

lky

.ǵb.qšt. | bn.ytrm.qšt.w.ql'. | bn.'bdyrẖ.qšt.w.q[l']. | bn.lky.qšt. | bn.dll.qšt.w.ql[']. | bn.pǵyn.qšt.w[.q]l'. | bn.bdn.qšt. 119[321].3.27

lkn

n. | 'bd'nt.rb 'šrt.mnḥm.ṯb'm.šẖr.'zn.ilhd. | bnil.rb 'šrt.lkn.yp'n.ṯ[--]. | yṣḥm.b d.ubn.krwn.tǵd.[m]nḥm. | 'pṯrm.šm'r 2011.8
n. | 'bdmlk. | y[--]k. | [-----]. | pǵdn. | [--]n. | [--]ntn. | 'dn. | lkn. | ktr. | ubn. | dqn. | ḥṯṯn. | [--]n. | [---]. | tsn. | rpiy. | mrṯn. | ṯn 1024.2.7

ll

šqy.rṯa.tnm y.ytn.[ks.b yd]. | krpn.b klat yd.[---]. | km ll.kḥṣ.tusp[.---]. | tgr.il.bn h.ṯr[.---]. | w y'n.lṭpn.il.d p[id.---]. | 1['NT.X].4.11
.tb'.ǵlm[m.al.ttb.idk.pnm]. | al.ttn.'m.pẖr.m'd.t[k.ǵr.ll.l p'n.il]. | al.tpl.al.tšthwy.pẖr [m'd.qmm.a--.am] | r ṯny.d't 2.1[137].14
.dgn.arṯ m.pḏ h.tb'.ǵlmm.l ṯṯb.[idk.pnm]. | l ytn.tk.ǵr.ll.'m.phr.m'd.ap.ilm.l lḥ[m]. | yṯb.bn qdš.l ṯrm.b'l.qm.'l.il.hl 2.1[137].20
t.---]. | [']ṣr.l pdr ṯṯ.ṣ[in.---]. | tšnpn.'lm.km[m.---]. | w.l ll.'ṣrm.w [---]. | kmm.w.in.'ṣr[.---]. | w mit.š'rt.[-]y[-.---]. | w.k 38[23].7
h[.---]. | l 'ṯtrt[.---]. | 'lm.kmm[.---]. | w b ṯlṯ.ṣ[in.---]. | l ll.pr[-.---]. | mit š'[rt.---]. | ptr.k[--.---]. | [-]yu[-.---]. 37[22].9
n.šnpt.ḥṣt h.b'l.ṣpn š. | [--]ṯ š.ilt.mgdl š.ilt.asrm š. | w l ll.šp. pgr.w ṯrmnm.bt mlk. | il[bt].gdlt.ušẖry.gdlt.ym gdlt. | b 34[1].12

lla

.ilm.al. | tqrb.l bn.ilm. | mt.al.y'db km. | k imr.b p h. | k lli.b ṯbrn. | qn h.ṯḫtan. | nrt.ilm.špš. | ṣḥrrt.la. | šmm.b yd.md | 4[51].8.19
d.šḥlmmt. | ngš.ank.aliyn b'l. | 'dbnn ank.imr.b p y. | k lli.b ṯbrn q y.ḫtu hw. | nrt.ilm.špš.ṣḥrrt. | la.šmm.b yd.bn ilm 6[49].2.23
d bnš.ḥm[r.---]. | w d.l mdl.r[--.---]. | w ṣin.'z.b['l.---]. | llu.bn[š.---]. | imr.ẖ[--.---]. | [--]n.b'[l.---]. | w [--]d.[---]. | idk[.-] 2158.1.15
] | t hll.snnt.bnt h | ll b'l gml.yrdt. | b 'rgzm.b bz tdm. | lla y.'m lẓpn i | l ḏ.pid.hn b p y sp | r hn.b špt y mn | t hn ṯlḥ 24[77].44
alpm.ap ṣin.šql.ṯrm. | w mri ilm.'glm.dt.šnt. | imr.qmṣ.llim.k ksp. | l 'brm.zt.ẖrṣ.l 'brm.kš. | dpr.ṯlḥn.b q'l.b q'l. | mlk 22.2[124].14
h. | uṣb't h.'d.ṯkm. | 'rb.b ẓl.ḫmt.lqḥ. | imr.dbḥ.b yd h. | lla.klatnm. | klt.lḥm h.d nzl. | lqḥ.msrr.'ṣr.db[ḥ]. | yṣq.b gl.ḥt 14[KRT].3.161
'rb[.b ẓl.ḫmt]. | qḥ im[r.b yd k]. | imr.d[bḥ.bm].ymn. | lla.kl[atn]m. | klt.l[ḥm k.d]nzl. | qḥ.ms[rr.]'ṣr. | dbḥ.ṣ[q.b g]l. 14[KRT].2.68
[.ap]. | ṣin.šql.ṯrm[.w]m | ria.il.'glm.d[t]. | šnt.imr.qmṣ.l[l]im. | ṣḥ.aẖ h.b bht h.a[r]y h. | b qrb hkl h.ṣḥ. | šb'm.bn.aṯrt 4[51].6.43
[-]p[-]l[.---]. | k lli.[---]. | kpr.[šb'.bnt.rḥ.gdm.w anhbm]. | w tqr[y.ǵlmm.b št. 7.2[130].2
m.ap.ṣin.šql]. | ṯrm.w [mri.ilm.'glm.dt.šnt]. | imr.[qmṣ.llim.---]. 1['NT.X].4.32

llit

'l bn ymn. | šb šr šmn [--] ṯryn. | ḫm[š]m l 'šr ksp 'l bn llit. | [--]l[-.-]p 'l [---.-]b'm arny. | w 'l [---.]rb'm ṯqlm.w [---] a 1103.6

llwn

zln. | ṯn.b ulm. | abmn.b gt.m'rb. | atn. | ḫryn. | bn.'nt. | llwn. | agdṯb. | aǵltn. | [-]wn. | bldn. | [-]ln. | [-]ldn. | [i]wryn. | ḫb 1061.7
spr.updt. | d b d.mlkytn. | kdrl. | slṯmg. | adrdn. | l[l]wn. | ydln. | ldn. | tdǵl. | ibrkyṯ. 1034.6

llẖ

.yd.grbs hm. | w.ṯn.'šr h.ẖpnt. | [š]šwm.amtm.'kyt. | yd.llẖ hm. | w.ṯlṯ.l.'šrm. | ẖpnt.ššwm.ṯn. | pddm.w.d.ṯṯ. | [mr]kbt. 2049.5

lm

[-----]. | [-----]. | [-----.lm]. | [ank.ksp.w yrq]. | [ẖrṣ.]yd.mqm h. | [w 'b]d.'lm.ṯlṯ. | [ss 14[KRT].1.52
m ṯrrt. | udm.ytnt.il w ušn. | ab.adm.w ṯṯb. | mlakm.l h.lm.ank. | ksp.w yrq.ẖrṣ. | yd.mqm h.w 'bd. | 'lm.ṯlṯ.sswm.mr 14[KRT].3.137
. | rḥq.mlk.l bt y. | n[g.]krt.l ḥẓ[r y]. | w y'n[y.k]rt[.ṯ]'. | lm.ank.ksp. | w yr[q.ẖrṣ]. | yd.mqm h.w 'bd. | 'lm.ṯlṯ.sswm. | 14[KRT].6.282
y[.---]. | tr.ḥt[-.---]. | w msk.tr[.---]. | tqrb.aẖ[h.w tṣḥ]. | lm.tb'rn[.---]. | mn.yrẖ.k m[rṣ.---]. | mn.k dw.kr[t]. | w y'ny.ǵ 16.2[125].80
. | ṯḥm.[---]. | yšlm[.l k.ilm]. | tšlm[k.tǵr] k. | t'zz[k.---.]lm. | w t[--.--]ṣm k. | [-----]. | [-----.]šil. | [-----.]šilt. | [-----]. | [----- 55[18].6
.b'l.tiẖd. | y'rm.šnu.hd.gpt. | ǵr.w y'n.aliyn. | b'l.ib.hdt.lm.ṯḥš. | lm.ṯḥš.nṯq.dmrn. | 'n.b'l.qdm.yd h. | k tǵḏ.arz.b ymn 4[51].7.38
. | y'rm.šnu.hd.gpt. | ǵr.w y'n.aliyn. | b'l.ib.hdt.lm.ṯḥš. | lm.ṯḥš.nṯq.dmrn. | 'n.b'l.qdm.yd h. | k tǵḏ.arz.b ymn h. | bkm 4[51].7.39
ḥ. | [---] h.gm. | [l --- k.]yṣḥ. | [---]d.'r. | [----.-]bb. | [----.]lm y. | [---.--]p. | [---.d]bḥ. | t[---.id]k. | pn[m.al.ttn]. | 'm.[krt.m 14[KRT].5.241
ršm zbln. | in.b ilm.'ny h. | w y'n.lṭpn.il.b pid. | ṯb.bn y.lm ṯb[t] km. | l kḥṯ.zbl k[m.a]nk. | iḥtrš.w [a]škn. | aškn.ydt.[16[126].5.24
p].l btlt.'nt. | w ypt l ybmt.li[mm]. | w y'ny.aliyn[.b'l]. | lm.k qnym.'l[m.--]. | k dr d.d yknn[.--]. | b'l.yṣǵd.mli[.--]. | il 10[76].3.6
t[.---.]špš.b'l k. | yd'm.l.yd't. | 'm y.špš.b'l k. | šnt.šntm.lm.l.tlk. | w.lḥt.akl.ky. | likt.'m.špš. | b'l k.ky.akl. | b.ḥwt k.in 2060.16
.b'l y. | lm.škn.hnk. | l 'bd h.alpm.š[šw]m. | rgmt.'ly.ṯh.lm. | l.ytn.hm.mlk.[b]'l y. | w.hn.ibm.šṣq l y. | p.l.ašt.aṯt y. | n' 1012.25
l.stn. | [--.]d.n'm.lbš k. | [-]dm.ṯn id. | [--]m.d.l.n'mm. | [lm.]l.likt.'m y. | [---.]'bd.ank. | [---.'b]d k. | [---.--]l y.'m. | [---.]' 2128.1.7
. | rg[m]. | ṯḥm.wr[--]. | yšlm.[l] k. | ilm.t[ǵ]r k. | tšlm k. | lm[.l.]likt. | ši[l.š]lm y. | [']d.r[-]š. | [-]ly.l.likt. | [a]nk.[---]. | šil.[2010.7
ṯḥm.rgm. | mlk. | l ḥyil. | lm.tlik.'m y. | ik y.aškn. | 'ṣm.l bt.dml. | p ank.atn. | 'ṣm.l k. | a 1010.4
š]lm y. | [']d.r[-]š. | [-]ly.l.likt. | [a]nk.[---]. | šil.[šlm y]. | [l]m.li[kt]. | [-]t.'[--]. 2010.13
[---.--]d.'m y. | [--.]spr.lm.likt. | [--]y.k išal hm. | [--.'š]rm.kkr.ṯlṯ. | [--.]ṯlṯm.kkr.ṯlṯ. | [1022.2
gm. | [---].kll h. | [---.--]l y. | [---.--]r. | [--.]wk[--.---]. | [--].lm.l[--.---]. | [-]m.in[.---]. | [--.]s'.[---]. | [---.]n[--.---]. | [--.]aw[-- 45[45].1
m. | yšu.'wr.mzl. | ymzl.w yṣi.trẖ. | ḥdṯ.yb'r.l ṯn. | aṯt h.lm.nkr. | mddt h.k irby. | [t]škn.šd. | km.ḥsn.pat.mdbr. | lk.y 14[KRT].2.102

m.rišt hm.l ẓr.brkt hm.w l kḥṯ.|zbl hm.b hm.yg‘r.b‘l.lm.ǵltm.ilm.rišt.|km l ẓr brkt km.w ln.kḥṯ.zbl km.aḥd.|ilm 2.1[137].24

y.td‘.|w.ap.mlk.ud̲[r].|[-]d‘.k.ih̲d.[---].|w.mlk.b‘l y.|lm.škn.hnk.|l ‘bd h.alpm.š[šw]m.|rgmt.‘ly.ṯh.lm.|l.ytn.hm 1012.23

--].|[-----].|[-----].|[---.]mrkbt.|[---.--]a.nrm.|[---.--]y.lm[.-.]b k[p].|[---].tr[--.]gpn lk.|[---].km[-.---].|[---.--]k yṣun 1002.31

‘bd.ank.|[---.‘b]d k.|[---.--]l y.‘m.|[---.]‘m.|[---.--]y.w.lm.|[---.]il.šlm.|[---.]ank.|[---].mly. 2128.2.4

lkt.ugrt.|[--]kt.rgmt.|[--]y.l.ilak.|[---].‘m y.|[---]m.w.lm.|[---.]w.‘m k.|[---]m.ksp.|[---].‘m.|[---.-]n[-].|[---.]l km. 1016.13

----].|[-----.]šil.|[-----.]šilt.|[-----].|[-----.š]ilt.|[---.--]m.lm.|[---.š]d.gṯr.|[--]ḥ[d].šd.hwt.|[--.]iḥd.šd.gṯr.|[w]ht.yšm‘ 55[18].13

lmd

d.b d.yr[š].|lmd.aḥd.b d.yḥ[--].|ṯlṯ.lmdm.b d.nḥ[--].|lmd.aḥd.b d.ar[--].|ṯlṯ.lmdm.b d.[---].|ṯlṯ.lmdm.b d.[---]. 1050.7

lm.b d.[---].|šb‘.lmdm.b d.s[n]rn.|lmd.aḥd.b d.yr[š].|lmd.aḥd.b d.yḥ[--].|ṯlṯ.lmdm.b d.nḥ[--].|lmd.aḥd.b d.ar[--]. 1050.5

mš.bnšm[.---].|h̲d̲ǵlm.b d.[---].|šb‘.lmdm.b d.s[n]rn.|lmd.aḥd.b d.yr[š].|lmd.aḥd.b d.yḥ[--].|ṯlṯ.lmdm.b d.nḥ[--]. 1050.4

--.]lmdm.b d.snrn.|[---.lm]dm.b d.nrn.|[---.h̲]d̲ǵlm.|[lmd.]aḥd.b d.yrš. 1051.6

.w tnn.|kṯr.w h̲ss.yd.|ytr.kṯr.w h̲ss.|spr.ilmlk šbny.|lmd.atn.prln.rb.|khnm rb.nqdm.|ṯ‘y.nqmd.mlk ugr[t].|ad 6.6[62.2].54

hwt.|[---.]aqht.yd̲[--].|[---.--]n.ṣ[---].|[spr.ilmlk.šbny.lmd.atn.]prln. 17[2AQHT].7.1

d.s[n]rn.|lmd.aḥd.b d.yr[š].|lmd.aḥd.b d.yḥ[--].|ṯlṯ.lmdm.b d.nḥ[--].|lmd.aḥd.b d.ar[--].|ṯlṯ.lmdm.b d.[---].|ṯlṯ. 1050.6

[---]‘.lmdm.|[---.b]‘ln.|[---.]lmdm.b d.snrn.|[---.lm]dm.b d.nrn.|[---.h̲]d̲ǵlm.|[lmd.]aḥd.b d.yrš. 1051.4

h̲mš.bnšm[.---].|h̲d̲ǵlm.b d.[---].|šb‘.lmdm.b d.s[n]rn.|lmd.aḥd.b d.yr[š].|lmd.aḥd.b d.yḥ[--].|ṯl 1050.3

[---]‘.lmdm.|[---.b]‘ln.|[---.]lmdm.b d.snrn.|[---.lm]dm.b d.nrn.|[---.h̲]d̲ǵlm.|[lmd.]aḥd 1051.3

d.yḥ[--].|ṯlṯ.lmdm.b d.nḥ[--].|lmd.aḥd.b d.ar[--].|ṯlṯ.lmdm.b d.[---].|ṯlṯ.lmdm.b d.[---]. 1050.8

.b d.nḥ[--].|lmd.aḥd.b d.ar[--].|ṯlṯ.lmdm.b d.[---].|ṯlṯ.lmdm.b d.[---]. 1050.9

.rn.|[---].h̲pn.|dqn.š‘rt.|[lm]d.yrṯ.|[-.]ynḥm.h̲pn.|ṯṯ.lmd.b‘ln.|l.qḥ.h̲pnt.|ṯṯ[.-]l.md.‘ṯtr[t].|l.qḥ.h̲pnt. 1117.17

grgš.|w.lmd h.|aršmg.|w.lmd h.|iyṯr.|[w].lmd h.|[yn]ḥm.|[w.]lm 1048.2

d h.|aršmg.|w.lmd h.|iyṯr.|[w].lmd h.|[yn]ḥm.|[w.]lmd h.|[i]wrmh̲.|[w.]lmd h. 1048.8

grgš.|w.lmd h.|aršmg.|w.lmd h.|iyṯr.|[w].lmd h.|[yn]ḥm.|[w.]lmd h.|[i]wrmh̲.|[w.] 1048.4

n.špš.|[w.l]m[d h].|yṣ[---].|‘bd[--].|pr[--].|‘dr[--].|w.lm[d h].|ily[---].|[-----].|[---]lb[--].|[---]m[.---].|[---.]d nkly. 1049.2.10

.|w.lmd h.|ymn.|w.lmd h.|y‘d̲rn.|w.lmd h.|‘dn.|w.lmd h.|bn.špš.|[w.l]m[d h].|yṣ[---].|‘bd[--].|pr[--].|‘dr[--]. 1049.1.10

--].|ddm gt dprnm.|l ḥršm.|ddm l ‘nqt.|dd l alṯt.w l lmdt h.|dd l ih̲yn.|dd l [---]. 1101.11

[-----].|w.lmd h.|mtn.|w.lmd h.|ymn.|w.lmd h.|y‘d̲rn.|w.lmd h.|‘dn.|w.lmd h.|bn 1049.1.4

grgš.|w.lmd h.|aršmg.|w.lmd h.|iyṯr.|[w].lmd h.|[yn]ḥm.|[w.]lmd h.|[i]wrmh̲.|[w.]lmd h. 1048.6

[-----].|w.lmd h.|mtn.|w.lmd h.|ymn.|w.lmd h.|y‘d̲rn.|w.lmd h.|‘dn.|w.lmd h.|bn.špš.|[w.l]m[d h] 1049.1.6

.lmd h.|y‘d̲rn.|w.lmd h.|‘dn.|w.lmd h.|bn.špš.|[w.l]m[d h].|yṣ[---].|‘bd[--].|pr[--].|‘dr[--].|w.lm[d h].|ily[---]. 1049.1.12

d.kšmn.l.gzzm.|yyn.|ṣdqn.|‘bd.pdr.|myṣm.|ṯgt.|w.lmd h.|yṯil.|w.lmd h.|rpan.|w.lmd h.|‘bdrpu.|w.lmd h.|‘ 1099.10

.lmd h.|rpan.|w.lmd h.|‘bdrpu.|w.lmd h.|‘dršp.|w.lmd h.|krwn b.gt.nbk.|ddm.kšmm.l.h̲tn.|ddm.l.trbnn.|dd 1099.18

[-----].|w.lmd h.|mtn.|w.lmd h.|ymn.|w.lmd h.|y‘d̲rn.|w.lmd h.|‘d 1049.1.2

.pdr.|myṣm.|ṯgt.|w.lmd h.|yṯil.|w.lmd h.|rpan.|w.lmd h.|‘bdrpu.|w.lmd h.|‘dršp.|w.lmd h.|krwn b.gt.nbk.| 1099.14

|w.lmd h.|mtn.|w.lmd h.|ymn.|w.lmd h.|y‘d̲rn.|w.lmd h.|‘dn.|w.lmd h.|bn.špš.|[w.l]m[d h].|yṣ[---].|‘bd[--]. 1049.1.8

w.lmd h.|yṯil.|w.lmd h.|rpan.|w.lmd h.|‘bdrpu.|w.lmd h.|‘dršp.|w.lmd h.|krwn b.gt.nbk.|ddm.kšmm.l.h̲tn.| 1099.16

.|yyn.|ṣdqn.|‘bd.pdr.|myṣm.|ṯgt.|w.lmd h.|yṯil.|w.lmd h.|rpan.|w.lmd h.|‘bdrpu.|w.lmd h.|‘dršp.|w.lmd h. 1099.12

|iyṯr.|[w].lmd h.|[yn]ḥm.|[w.]lmd h.|[i]wrmh̲.|[w.]lmd h. 1048.10

t.|ad[-]l[-]m.|‘šr.ksdm.yd.lmd hm.lqḥ.|‘šr.mh̲ṣm.yd.lmd hm.|apym.|[bn]š gt.ipṯl.|[---]ym.|[----]m.|[-----].|[bnš 1040.9

r‘ym.|bn.h̲ri[-].|bnš.gt.‘ṯtrt.|ad[-]l[-]m.|‘šr.ksdm.yd.lmd hm.lqḥ.|‘šr.mh̲ṣm.yd.lmd hm.|apym.|[bn]š gt.ipṯl.|[-- 1040.8

yn.‘lby.ṣdkn.|gmrt.ṭlmyn.|‘bdnt.|bdy.ḥrš arkd.|blšš lmd.|ḥṯṯn.tqn.|ydd.idṯn.|šǵr.ilgdn. 1045.10

lm.|[--.š]dm.b.m‘rby.|[--.šd]m.b.uškn.|[---.--]n.|[---].tlmdm.|[y]bnn.ṣmdm.|ṯp[ṭ]b‘l.ṣmdm.|[---.ṣ]mdm.w.ḥrṣ.|[- 2033.2.2

l[m].h̲pn.|tmrṯn.š‘rt.|lmd.n.rn.|[---].h̲pn.|dqn.š‘rt.|[lm]d.yrṯ.|[-.]ynḥm.h̲pn.|ṯṯ.lmd.b‘ln.|l.qḥ.h̲pnt.|ṯṯ[.-]l.md.‘ 1117.15

|[---.--]l.mlk.tlk.b ṣd[.---].|[---.]mt.išryt[.---].|[---.--]r.almd k.[---].|[---.]qrt.ablm.a[blm].|[qrt.zbl.]yrh̲.d mgdl.š[-- 18[3AQHT].1.29

l.ydln.š‘rt.|l.kṯrmlk.h̲pn.|l.‘bdil[m].h̲pn.|tmrtn.š‘rt.|lmd.n.rn.|[---].h̲pn.|dqn.š‘rt.|[lm]d.yrṯ.|[-.]ynḥm.h̲pn.|ṯṯ.l 1117.12

]d.yrṯ.|[-.]ynḥm.h̲pn.|ṯṯ.lmd.b‘ln.|l.qḥ.h̲pnt.|ṯṯ[.-]l.md.‘ṯtr[t].|l.qḥ.h̲pnt. 1117.19

[---]‘.lmdm.|[---.b]‘ln.|[---.]lmdm.b d.snrn.|[---.lm]dm.b d.nrn.| 1051.1

|ṯlṯ.l ḥr[š.---].|ṯṯ[.l.]mštt[.---].|ṯlṯ.l.md̲r[ǵlm].|kd[.--].lm[d.---].|kd[.l.]h̲zr[m.---].|kd[.l.]ṯrtn[m].|arb‘ l.mry[nm]. 1091.5

lmn

t.|ṯlḥnt.il.d yd‘nn.|y‘db.lḥm.l h.w d l yd‘nn.|d.mṣd.|ylmn.h̲ṭ.tḥt.ṯlḥn.|b qr‘.|‘ṯtrt.w ‘nt.ymǵy.|‘ṯtrt.t‘db.nšb l h. UG5.1.1.8

ln

dš.|ztr.‘m y.l ‘pr.d̲mr.aṯr[y].|ṭbq lḥt.niṣ y.grš.|d ‘šy.ln.ah̲d.yd y.b š|krn m‘ms y k šb‘t yn.|spu.ksm y.bt.b‘l.[w] 17[2AQHT].2.19

rṣ.mšṣu.qṭr h.|l ‘pr.d̲mr.aṯr h.ṭbq.lḥt.|niṣ h.grš d.‘šy.ln h.|ah̲d.yd h.b škrn.m‘ms h.|[k]šb‘ yn.spu.ksm h.bt.b‘l.| 17[2AQHT].1.30

u.|[qṭr h.l ‘pr.d̲]mr.a[ṯ]r h.|[ṭbq.lḥt.niṣ h.gr]š.d ‘šy.|[ln h.---].|z[tr.‘m k.l arṣ.mšṣu.qṭr k].|l ‘pr.d̲m[r.aṯr k.ṭbq].|l 17[2AQHT].1.49

mšṣu.qṭr k].|l ‘pr.d̲m[r.aṯr k.ṭbq].|lḥt.niṣ k.gr[š.d ‘šy.ln k].|spu.ksm k.bt.[b‘l.w mnt k].|bt il.ah̲d.yd k.b [škrn].| 17[2AQHT].2.3

lqḥ.š‘rt.|urh̲.ln.kkrm.|w.rḥd.kd.šmn.|drt.b.kkr.|ubn.h̲ṣḥ.kkr.|kkr.lqḥ.r 1118.2

[---.--]m.|[-----].|[---.]d arṣ.|[---.]ln.|[---.]nb hm.|[---.-]kn.|[---.]hr n.km.šḥr.|[---.y]lt n.km. 12[75].1.4

lnn

[---.]iy[t]r.|[---.‘bd.y]rh̲.|[---.b]n.mšrn.|[---].bn.lnn.|[-----].|[---.-]lyr. 2135.4

lskt

tḥm.ṯr.il.ab k.] | hwt.lṭpn[.ḥtk k.---]. | yh.kṯr.b[---]. | št.lskt.n[--.---]. | ‘db.bǵrt.ṯ[--. --]. | ḥš k.‘ṣ k.‘[bṣ k.‘m y.p‘n k.tls 1[‘NT.IX].3.8

lsm

m.mt.‘z.b‘l. | ‘z.ynṯkn.k bṯnm. | mt.‘z.b‘l.‘z.ymṣẖn. | k lsmm.mt.ql. | b‘l.ql.‘ln.špš. | tṣḥ.l mt.šm‘.m‘. | l bn.ilm.mt.ik.t 6[49].6.21

kbd.arṣ.arbdd]. | l kbd.š[dm.ḥš k.‘ṣ k.‘bṣ k.‘m y.p‘n k.tls] | [m]n ‘m y t[wtḥ.išd k.dm.rgm.iṯ.l y.d argmn k]. | [h]wt. 7.2[130].16

.arṣ.arbdd.l kbd.šdm. | [ḥ]š k.[‘]ṣ k.‘bṣ k.‘m y.p‘n k. | [tls]mn.[‘]m y.twtḥ.išd k. | [dm.rgm.iṯ.l y.]w argm k.hwt. | [w 3[‘NT].4.56

bd.arṣ. | arbdd.l kbd.šdm. | ḥš k.‘ṣ k.‘bṣ k. | ‘m y.p‘n k.tlsmn.‘m y. | twtḥ.išd k.dm.rgm. | iṯ.l y.w argm k. | hwt.w aṯn 3[‘NT].3.16

d.arṣ. | [arbdd.l kbd.š]dm.ḥš k. | [‘ṣ k.‘bṣ k.‘m y.p‘]n k.tlsmn. | [‘m y.twtḥ.išd] k.tk.ẖršn. | [---.-]bd k.spr. | [---.-]nk. 1[‘NT.IX].2.22

[ḥš k.‘ṣ k.‘bṣ k.‘]m y.p[‘]n k. | [tlsmn.‘m y.twt]ḥ.išd k. | [tk.ẖršn.---]r.[-]ḥm k.w št. | [---.]ẓ[-- 1[‘NT.IX].2.2

t.n[--.---]. | ‘db.bǵrt.ṯ[--. --]. | ḥš k.‘ṣ k.‘[bṣ k.‘m y.p‘n k.tlsmn]. | ‘m y twtḥ.i[šd k.tk.ẖršn.-------------]. | ǵr.ks.dm.r[gm 1[‘NT.IX].3.10

| yd k.ṣǵr.tnšq.špt k.ṯm. | ṯkm.bm ṯkm.aẖm.qym.il. | b lsmt.ṯm.yṯbš.šm.il.mt m. | y‘bš.brk n.šm.il.ǵzrm. | ṯm.ṯmq.rp 22.2[124].6

lsn

g d[d]. | ḥdyn.d[d]. | [-]dḏn.d[d]. | qṭn.d[d]. | lẖsn.d[d]. | lsn.d[d]. | and[--.---]. 132[331].11

l‘m

-]. | [---].w b ym.mnẖ l abd.b ym.irtm.m[--]. | [ṯpṭ].nhr.tl‘m.ṯm.ḥrbm.its.anšq. | [-]htm.l arṣ.ypl.ul ny.w l.‘pr.‘ẓm ny. 2.4[68].4

l‘q

ṯn.nḥl h. | šd.śẁn.b d.ttyn.nḥl [h]. | šd.tṯyn[.b]n.arkšt. | l‘q[.---]. | šd.pll.b d.qrt. | š[d].annḏr.b d.bdn.nḥ[l h]. | [šd.]agy 2029.5

lpš

milẖ. | ‘šrm.ẖpn.ẖmš. | kbd.w lpš. | ẖmš.mispt. | mṭ. | w lpš.d sgr b h. | b d.anrmy. 1109.6

ḥr[.---]. | šb‘.šnt.il.mla.[-]. | w ṯmn.nqpnt.‘d. | k lbš.km.lpš.dm a[ẖ h]. | km.all.dm.ary h. | k šb‘t.l šb‘m.aẖ h.ym[.--]. | 12[75].2.47

spr.npṣm.d yṣa.b milẖ. | ‘šrm.ẖpn.ẖmš. | kbd.w lpš. | ẖmš.mispt. | mṭ. | w lpš.d sgr b h. | b d.anrmy. 1109.3

l.hdm.yṯb. | l arṣ.yṣq.‘mr. | un.l riš h.‘pr.plṯt. | l qdqd h.lpš.yks. | mizrtm.ǵr.b abn. | ydy.psltm.b y‘r. | yhdy.lḥm.w dq 5[67].6.16

[arṣ.]dbr.ysmt.šd. | [šḥl]mmt.t[mǵ.]l b‘l.np[l]. | [l a]rṣ[.lpš].tks.miz[rtm]. 5[67].6.31

ṯn.pld.pṯt[.-]r. | lpš.sgr.rq. | ṯṯ.prqt. | w.mrdt.prqt.pṯt. | lbš.psm.rq. | ṯn.mrdt.a 1112.2

k lb.ṯa[t]. | l imr h.km.lb.‘n[t]. | aṯr.b‘l.tiẖd.m[t]. | b sin.lpš.tšṣq[n h]. | b qṣ.all.tšu.g h.w[tṣ] | ḥ.at.mt.tn.aẖ y. | w ‘n.b 6[49].2.10

. | [g]rgš ‘bdy[--]. | [--.]l mlk [---]. | [---].aẖ y[.---]. | [--]q lpš[.---]. | [---] y št k[.---]. | [---.]l m[lk]. 2130.2.1

lṣb

‘nt[.---]. | w b hm.tṯṯb[.--]d h. | km trpa.hn n‘r. | d yšt.l.lṣb h ẖš‘r klb. | [w]riš.pqq.w šr h. | yšt.aḥd h.dm zt.ẖrpnt. UG5.1.2.4

.nbtm. | šmẖ.lṭpn.il.d pid. | p‘n h.l hdm.yṯpd. | w yprq.lṣb w yṣḥq. | yšu.g h.w yṣḥ. | aṯbn.ank.w anẖn. | w tnẖ.b irt y. 6[49].3.16

.thbr.w tql. | tštḥwy.w tkbd h. | hlm.il.k yphn h. | yprq.lṣb.w yṣḥq. | p‘n h.l hdm.yṯpd.w ykrkr. | uṣb‘t h.yšu.g h.w y[4[51].4.28

pṣ k.b ym rṯ.b uni[l]. | pnm.tšmẖ.w ‘l yṣhl pi[t]. | yprq.lṣb.w yṣḥq. | p‘n.l hdm.yṯpd.yšu. | g h.w yṣḥ.aṯbn.ank. | w an 17[2AQHT].2.10

lṣn

]. | lt.hlk.b[.---]. | bn.b‘yn.š[--.---]. | aǵltn.mid[-.---]. | bn.lṣn.‘rm[y]. | arśw.bṣry. | arpṯr.y‘rty. | bn.ẖdyn.ugrty. | bn.tgḏn 87[64].5

lšt‘y. | bn grgs. | bn.ẖran. | bn.arś[w.b]ṣry. | bn.ykn. | bn.lṣn.‘rmy. | bn.b‘yn.šly. | bn.ynḥn. | bn.‘bdilm.hzpy. 99[327].2.3

lqḥ

šlmym.lqḥ.akl. | yḥmn.ṯlṯ.šmn. | a[---.]kdm. | ‘[---]‘m.kd. | a[----]ḥr.ṯlṯ 136[84].1

b ym ḥdṯ. | b.yrẖ.pgrm. | lqḥ.iwrpzn. | argḏḏ. | ṯṯkn. | ybrk. | ntbt. | b.mitm. | ‘šrm. | kbd. 2006.3

t.w rḥmy. | [---].y[t]b. | [---]p.gp ym.w yṣǵd.gp..thm. | [yqḥ.]il.mšt‘ltm.mšt‘ltm.l riš.agn. | hl h.[t]špl.hl h.trm.hl h.tṣ 23[52].31

l.k ym. | w yd il.k mdb.ark.yd.il.k ym. | w yd.il.k mdb.yqḥ.il.mšt‘ltm. | mšt‘ltm.l riš.agn.yqḥ.tš.b bt h. | il.ẖṭ h.nḥt.il 23[52].35

rm. | [---].l ‘nt m. | [---.]l šlm. | [-]l[-.-]ry.ylbš. | mlk.ylk.lqḥ.ilm. | aṯr.ilm.ylk.p‘nm. | mlk.p‘nm.yl[k]. | šb‘.pamt.l kl h 33[5].23

. | rḥṣ[.y]d k.amt. | uṣb[‘t k.]‘d[.ṯ]km. | ‘rb[.b ẓl.ẖmt]. | qḥ im[r.b yd k]. | imr.d[bḥ.bm].ymn. | lla.kl[atn]m. | klt.l[ḥm 14[KRT].2.66

yadm. | yrḥṣ.yd h.amt h. | uṣb‘t h.‘d.ṯkm. | ‘rb.b ẓl.ẖmt.lqḥ. | imr.dbḥ.b yd h. | lla.klatnm. | klt.lḥm h.d nzl. | lqḥ.msrr 14[KRT].3.159

yt.tq[l.tḥt]. | p‘n h.ybq‘.kbd h.w yḥd. | iṯ.šmt.iṯ.‘ẓm.w yqḥ b hm. | aqht.ybl.l qẓ.ybky.w yqbr. | yqbr.nn.b mdgt.b kn 19[1AQHT].3.145

mt.šmm.ks.qdš. | l tphn h.aṯt.krpn. | l t‘n.aṯrt.alp. | kd.yqḥ.b ẖmr. | rbt.ymsk.b msk h. | qm.ybd.w yšr. | mṣltm.bd.n‘ 3[‘NT].1.16

b‘ln.bn. | kltn.w l. | bn h.‘d.‘lm. | šḥr.‘lmt. | bnš bnšm. | l.yqḥnn.b d. | b‘ln.bn.kltn. | w.b d.bn h.‘d. | ‘lm.w unṯ. | in.b h. 1008.17

[---.]ṯlṯm.d.nlqḥt. | [bn.ẖ]tyn.yd.bt h. | [aǵ]ltn. | tdn.bn.ddy. | ‘bdil[.b]n ṣd 2045.1

b.ym.ḥdṯ. | b.yr.pgrm. | lqḥ.b‘lmḏr. | w.bn.ẖlp. | miẖd. | b.arb‘. | mat.ẖrṣ. 1156.3

b.ym.ḥdṯ. | b.yrẖ.pgrm. | lqḥ.b‘lm‘ḏr. | w bn.ẖlp. | w[--]y.d.b‘l. | miẖd.b. | arb‘.mat. | ẖrṣ 1155.3

mlk. | [--.-]m[-]r. | [w.l.]bn h.‘d. | [‘l]m.mn k. | mn km l.yqḥ. | bt.hnd.b d. | [‘b]dmlk. | [-]k.am‘[--]. | [w.b] d.bn h[.‘]d ‘l 1009.13

k.il.krt. | [ṯ‘.ymr]m.n‘m[n.]ǵlm.il. | a[ṯt.tq]ḥ.y krt.aṯt. | tqḥ.bt k.ǵlmt.tš‘rb. | ḥqr k.tld.šb‘.bnm.l k. | w ṯmn.tṯtmnm. | 15[128].2.22

t.w burm.lb]. | rmṣt.ilh[m.b‘lm.---]. | ksm.ṯlṯm.[---]. | d yqḥ bt[.--]r.dbḥ[.šmn.mr]. | šmn.rqḥ[.-]bt.mtnt[.w ynt.qrt]. | 35[3].20

lk n.amṣ. | [.---].nn. | [---.]qrt.dt. | [---.--]s‘.hn.mlk. | [---.l]qḥ.hn.l.ḥwt h. | [---.--]p.hn.ib.d.b.mgšẖ. | [---.i]b.hn[.w.]ht.a 1012.9

spr.npṣ.krw. | ṯt.ẖṭrm.ṯn.kst. | spl.mšlt.w.mqḥm. | w md h. | arn.w mznm. | ṯn.ẖlpnm. | ṯt.mrḥm. | drb. | 2050.3

rtn.bat.b ḏd k.[pǵt]. | bat.b hlm w y‘n.yṭpn[.mhr]. | št.qḥn.w tšqyn.yn.qḥ. | ks.b d y.qb‘t.b ymn y[.t]q | ḥ.pǵt.w tšqy 19[1AQHT].4.215

ank. | k[l.]ḏr‘ hm. | [--.n]pš[.-]. | w [k]l hm.b d. | rb.tmtt.lqḥt. | w.ṯṯb.ank.l hm. | w.any k.ṯt. | by.‘ky.‘ryt. | w.aẖ y.mhk. 2059.22

.ẖmš.ddm. | [---].ẖmš.ddm. | ṯṯ.l.‘šrm.bn[š.mlk.---].ẖzr.lqḥ.ḥp[r]. | ‘št.‘šr h.bn[.---.--]ẖ.zr. | b‘l.šd. 2011.40

aḥd.kbd. | arb‘m.b ẖzr. | lqḥ š‘rt. | ṯṯ ‘šr h.lqḥ. | ẖlpnt. | ṯṯ.ḥrṯm. | lqḥ.š‘rt. | ‘šr.ḥrš. | bhtm.lqḥ. | š‘rt. | arb‘. 2052.4

n. | dqn.š‘rt. | [lm]d.yrṯ. | [-.]ynḥm.ẖpn. | ṯṯ.lmd.b‘ln. | l.qḥ.ẖpnt. | ṯṯ[.-]l.md.‘ṯtr[t]. | l.qḥ.ẖpnt. 1117.18

nḥm.ḫpn. | ṯṯ.lmd.bʿln. | l.qḥ.ḫpnt. | ṯṯ[.-]l.md.ʿṯtr[t]. | l.qḥ.ḫpnt. 1117.20
rk. | [ʿbd h.]ybrk.il.krt. | [ṯʿ.ymr]m.nʿm[n.]ǵlm.il. | a[ṯt.tq]ḥ.y krt.aṯt. | tqḥ.bt k.ǵlmt.tšʿrb. | ḥqr k.tld.šbʿ.bnm.l k. | w 15[128].2.21
ʿlm. | [--.a]ṯm.prṯl.l riš h.ḥmṯ.ṯmṯ. | [--.]ydbr.ṯrmt.al m.qḥn y.š y.qḥn y. | [--.]šir.b krm.nṭṯt.dm.ʿlt.b ab y. | u---].ʿlt.b 1001.1.8
ṯm.prṯl.l riš h.ḥmṯ.ṯmṯ. | [--.]ydbr.ṯrmt.al m.qḥn y.š y.qḥn y. | [--.]šir.b krm.nṭṯt.dm.ʿlt.b ab y. | u---].ʿlt.b k.lk.l pn y 1001.1.8
km.iṯl.brlt h.km. | qṭr.b ap h.b ap.mhr h.ank. | l aḥwy.tqḥ.yṭpn.mhr.št. | tštn.k nšr.b ḥbš h.km.diy. | b tʿrt h.aqht.k 18[3AQHT].4.27
]. | qlt. | [--]t.mlk.d.y[mlk]. | [--.]ʿbdyrḫ.l.ml[k]. | [--]t.w.lqḥ. | yn[.--].b dn h. | w.ml[k].ššwm.nʿmm. | ytn.l.ʿbdyrḫ. | w. 2064.14
ṣrm. | hn dt.b.ṣr. | mtt.by. | gšm.adr. | nškḥ.w. | rb.tmtt. | lqḥ.kl.ḏrʿ. | b d a[-]m.w.ank. | k[l.]ḏrʿ hm. | [--.n]pš[.-]. | w [k]l 2059.17
yn.yn.qḥ. | ks.b d y.qbʿt.b ymn y[.t]q | ḥ.pǵt.w tšqyn h.tq[ḥ.ks.]b d h. | qbʿt.b ymn h.w yʿn.yṭ[p]n[.mh]r. | št.b yn.yšt 19[1AQHT].4.217
pǵt]. | bat.b hlm w yʿn.yṭpn[.mhr]. | št.qḥn.w tšqyn.yn.qḥ. | ks.b d y.qbʿt.b ymn y[.t]q | ḥ.pǵt.w tšqyn h.tq[ḥ.ks.]b d 19[1AQHT].4.215
gmḏ.bm kbd. | ẓi.at.l tlš. | amt.yrḫ. | l dmgy.amt. | aṯrt.qḥ. | ksan k.ḥdg k. | ḥtl k.w ẓi. | b aln.tk m. | b tk.mlbr. | ilšiy. | 12[75].1.17
[.krt.mswn h]. | tš[an.g hm.w tṣḥn]. | ṯḥ[m.pbl.mlk]. | qḥ[.ksp.w yrq]. | ḫrṣ.[yd.mqm h]. | w ʿbd[.ʿlm.ṯlṯ]. | sswm.m[r 14[KRT].6.269
pr.w ylak. | mlakm.l k.ʿm.krt. | mswn h.ṯḥm.pbl.mlk. | qḥ.ksp.w yrq.ḫrṣ. | yd.mqm h.w ʿbd.ʿlm. | ṯlṯ.sswm.mrkbt. | b 14[KRT].3.126
tn]. | ʿm.[krt.msw]n. | w r[gm.l krt.]ṯʿ. | ṯḥm[.pbl.mlk]. | qḥ.[ksp.w yr]q. | ḫrṣ[.yd.mqm] h. | ʿbd[.ʿlm.ṯlṯ]. | ss[wm.mrkb 14[KRT].5.250
m] h. | ʿbd[.ʿlm.ṯlṯ]. | ss[wm.mrkbt]. | b[trbṣ.bn.amt]. | [qḥ.krt.šlmm]. | [šlmm.al.tṣr]. | [udm.rbt.w udm]. | [ṯrrt.udm. 14[KRT].5.255
h]. | w ʿbd[.ʿlm.ṯlṯ]. | sswm.m[rkbt]. | b trbṣ.[bn.amt]. | q[ḥ.kr]t[.šlmm]. | š[lmm.]al.t[ṣr]. | udm[.r]bt.w u[dm]. | [ṯ]rrt 14[KRT].6.274
d.mqm h.w ʿbd.ʿlm. | ṯlṯ.sswm.mrkbt. | b trbṣ.bn.amt. | qḥ.krt.šlmm. | šlmm.w ng.mlk. | l bt y.rḥq.krt. | l ḥẓr y.al.tṣr. 14[KRT].3.130
sb[--]. | yqḥ.mi[t]. | b.ḥwt. 1174.2
. | al.tšrgn.y btlt m.dm.l ǵzr. | šrg k.ḫḫm.mt.uḫryt.mh.yqḥ. | mh.yqḥ.mt.aṯryt.spsg.ysk. | [l]riš.ḥrṣ.l ẓr.qdqd y. | [--.] 17[2AQHT].6.35
kbd.ksp.anyt. | d.ʿrb.b.anyt. | l.mlk.gbl. | w.ḥmšm.ksp. | lqḥ.mlk.gbl. | lbš.anyt h. | bʿrm.ksp. | mḫr.hn. 2106.15
nt.l rkb.ʿrpt.ht.ib k. | bʿl m.ht.ib k.tmḫṣ.ht.tṣmt.ṣrt k. | tqḥ.mlk.ʿlm k.drkt.dt dr dr k. | kṯr ṣmdm.ynḥt.w ypʿr.šmt h 2.4[68].10
| imr.d[bḥ.bm].ymn. | lla.kl[atn]m. | klt.l[ḥm k.d]nzl. | qḥ.ms[rr.]ʿṣr. | dbḥ.ṣ[q.b g]l.ḥtt. | yn.b gl[.ḫ]rṣ.nbt. | ʿl.l ẓr.[m 14[KRT].2.70
t.lqḥ. | imr.dbḥ.b yd h. | lla.klatnm. | klt.lḥm h.d nzl. | lqḥ.msrr.ʿṣr.db[ḥ]. | yṣq.b gl.ḥtt.yn. | b gl.ḫrṣ.nbt.w ʿly. | l ẓr. 14[KRT].3.163
.y btlt m.dm.l ǵzr. | šrg k.ḫḫm.mt.uḫryt.mh.yqḥ. | mh.yqḥ.mt.aṯryt.spsg.ysk. | [l]riš.ḥrṣ.l ẓr.qdqd y. | [--.]mt.kl.amt 17[2AQHT].6.36
| ktb.spr hnd. | dt brrt.ṣṭqšlm. | ʿbd h.hnd. | w mn km.l yqḥ. | spr.mlk.hnd. | b yd.ṣṭqšlm. | ʿd ʿlm. 1005.12
ḏ. | [---]. | [---]. | hm qrt tuḫd.hm mt yʿl bnš. | bt bn bnš yqḥ ʿz. | w yḥdy mrḥqm. RS61[24.277.30]
]. | qrd ga[n.--]. | b bt k.[--]. | w l dbḥ[--]. | t[--]. | [--] aṯt yqḥ ʿz. | [---]ḏ. | [---]. | [---]. | hm qrt tuḫd.hm mt yʿl bnš. | bt b RS61[24.277.25]
d[r.k]rt.ṯʿ. | i.iṯt.aṯrt.ṣrm. | w ilt.ṣdynm. | hm.ḥry.bt y. | iqḥ.ašʿrb.ǵlmt. | ḥẓr y.ṯn h.wspm. | atn.w ṯlṯ h.ḫrṣm. | ylk ym. 14[KRT].4.204
šrt. | [---.--]t.npš.ʿgl. | [---.-]nk.aštn.b ḫrt. | ilm.arṣ.w at.qḥ. | ʿrpt k.rḥ k.mdl k. | mṭrt k.ʿm k.šbʿt. | ǵlm k.ṯmn.ḫnzr k. 5[67].5.6
.ḫri[-]. | bnš.gt.ʿttrt. | ad[-]l[-]m. | ʿšr.ksdm.yd.lmd hm.lqḥ. | ʿšr.mḫṣm.yd.lmd hm. | apym. | [bn]š gt.iptl. | [---]ym. | [- 1040.8
.mhr]. | št.qḥn.w tšqyn.yn.qḥ. | ks.b d y.qbʿt.b ymn y[.t]q | ḥ.pǵt.w tšqyn h.tq[ḥ.ks.]b d h. | qbʿt.b ymn h.w yʿn.yṭ[p 19[1AQHT].4.216
dy lqḥ ṣtqn gt bn ndr. | um r[-] gtn ṯṯ ḫsn l ytn. | l rḥt lqḥ ṣtqn. | bt qbṣ urt ilštmʿ dbḥ ṣtqn l. | ršp. 1154.6
.]gtn ṯṯ. | [---.]thr l ytn ḫs[n]. | ʿbd ulm ṯn un ḫsn. | gdy lqḥ ṣtqn gt bn ndr. | um r[-] gtn ṯṯ ḫsn l ytn. | l rḥt lqḥ ṣtqn. | 1154.4
zr.i]rš.ksp.w atn k. | [ḫrṣ.w aš]lḥ k.w tn.qšt k.[l]. | [ʿnt.tq]ḥ[.q]ṣʿt k.ybmt.limm. | w yʿn.aqht.ǵzr.adr.ṯqbm. | [d]lbnn 17[2AQHT].6.19
.kkrm. | w.rḥd.kd.šmn. | drt.b.kkr. | ubn.ḫṣḥ.kkr. | kkr.lqḥ.ršpy. | tmtrn.bn.pnmn. | kkr. | bn.sgttn. | kkr. | ilšpš.kkr. | b 1118.6
.l ǵlm h.k [tṣḥ]. | ʿn.mkṯr.ap.t[---]. | dgy.rbt.aṯr[t.ym]. | qḥ.rtt.b d k t[---]. | rbt.ʿl.ydm[.---]. | b mdd.il.y[--.---]. | b ym.i 4[51].2.32
ym. | w yd.il.k mdb.yqḥ.il.mštʿltm. | mštʿltm.l riš.agn.yqḥ.tš.b bt h. | il.ḥṭ h.nḥt.il.ymnn.mṭ.yd h.yšu. | yr.šmm h.yr 23[52].36
spr.bnš.mlk. | d.b d.prṯ. | tšʿ.l.ʿšrm. | lqḥ.ššlmt. | ṯmn.l.arbʿm. | lqḥ.šʿrt. 1025.4
ʿdn. | sdwn. | mztn. | ḫyrn. | šdn. | [ʿš]rm.ṯn kbd. | šǵrm. | lqḥ.ššlmt. 2098.11
bnšm.d.bu. | tšʿ.dt.tq[ḥn]. | šʿrt. | šbʿ dt tqḥn. | ššlmt. 2099.4
spr.rʿym. | lqḥ.šʿrt. | anntn. | ʿdn. | sdwn. | mztn. | ḫyrn. | šdn. | [ʿš]rm.ṯn kb 2098.2
lqḥ.šʿrt. | urḫ.ln.kkrm. | w.rḥd.kd.šmn. | drt.b.kkr. | ubn.ḫṣḥ.k 1118.1
. | arbʿm.b ḫzr. | lqḥ šʿrt. | ṯṯ ʿšr h.lqḥ. | ḫlpnt. | ṯṯ.ḥrṯm. | lqḥ.šʿrt. | ʿšr.ḥrš. | bhtm.lqḥ. | šʿrt. | arbʿ. | ḥrš qṭn. | lqḥ šʿrt. | ṯṯ 2052.7
. | ṯṯ ʿšr h.lqḥ. | ḫlpnt. | ṯṯ.ḥrṯm. | lqḥ.šʿrt. | ʿšr.ḥrš. | bhtm.lqḥ. | šʿrt. | arbʿ. | ḥrš qṭn. | lqḥ šʿrt. | ṯṯ nsk.ḥdm. | lqḥ.šʿrt. 2052.9
bnšm.d.bu. | tšʿ.dt.tq[ḥn]. | šʿrt. | šbʿ dt tqḥn. | ššlmt. 2099.2
rṯm. | lqḥ.šʿrt. | ʿšr.ḥrš. | bhtm.lqḥ. | šʿrt. | arbʿ. | ḥrš qṭn. | lqḥ šʿrt. | ṯṯ nsk.ḥdm. | lqḥ.šʿrt. 2052.13
aḥd.kbd. | arbʿm.b ḫzr. | lqḥ šʿrt. | ṯṯ ʿšr h.lqḥ. | ḫlpnt. | ṯṯ.ḥrṯm. | lqḥ.šʿrt. | ʿšr.ḥrš. | bht 2052.3
bhtm.lqḥ. | šʿrt. | arbʿ. | ḥrš qṭn. | lqḥ šʿrt. | ṯṯ nsk.ḥdm. | lqḥ.šʿrt. 2052.15
š.mlk. | d.b d.prṯ. | tšʿ.l.ʿšrm. | lqḥ.ššlmt. | ṯmn.l.arbʿm. | lqḥ.šʿrt. 1025.6
bt.w rgm.l aḫt k. | ṯtmnt.krt n.dbḥ. | dbḥ.mlk.ʿšr. | ʿšrt.qḥ.tp k.b yd. | [-]r[-]k.bm.ymn. | tlk.škn.ʿl.ṣrrt. | adn k.šqrb.[16.1[125].41
arbʿ.ʿšr h.šmn. | d.lqḥt.ṯlǵdy. | w.kd.ištir.ʿm.qrt. | ʿšt.ʿšr h.šmn. | ʿmn.bn.aǵlmn. | 1083.2
št.b bt.ṯap[.--]. | hy.yd h.w ym[ǵ]. | mlak k.ʿm dt[n]. | lqḥ.mṯpṭ. | w yʿny.nn. | dtn.bt n.mḫ[-]. | l dg.w [-]kl. | w aṯr.h UG5.6.12
-]. | bnš[-] mdy[-]. | w.b.glb. | phnn.w. | mndym. | bdnh. | l[q]ḥt. | [--]km.ʿm.mlk. | [b]ǵl hm.w.iblbl hm. | w.b.ṯb h.[---]. 2129.8
n[--.---]. | rg[m.---]. | nǵt[.---]. | d.yqḥ[.---]. | hm.ṯn.[---]. | hn dt.[---]. | [-----]. | [-----]. | ṯḥm[.---]. | l 2064.4
.w.iblbl hm. | w.b.ṯb h.[---]. | spr ḥ[--.---]. | w.ʿm[.---]. | yqḥ[.---]. | w.n[--.---]. 2129.14

lqt

.rgm.ṯṯb.l y. | bm.ṯy.ndr. | iṯt.ʿmn.mlkt. | w.rgm y.l[--]. | lqt.w.pn. | mlk.nr b n. 50[117].17

lrgt

.yṯq. | w yṯb. | tqru.l špš.um h.špš.[um.q]l bl.ʿm. | yrḫ.lrgt h.mnt.nṯk.n[ḥš].šmrr. | nḥš.ʿq šr.ln h.mlḫš.abd.ln h.ydy. UG5.7.26

lrmn

ʿlm h.yhbr.špt hm.yš[q]. | hn.špt hm.mtqtm.mtqtm.k lrmn[.--]. | bm.nšq.w hr.b ḥbq.ḥmḥmt.tqt[nṣn]. | tldn.šḥr.w š 23[52].50

lšn

lk.ab.šnm. | [l p'n.il.t]hbr.w tql.tštḥ | [wy.w tkbd]n h.tlšn.aqht.ǵzr. | [---.kdd.dn]il.mt.rpi.w t'n. | [btlt.'nt.tšu.g]h. 17[2AQHT].6.51
arḫ.td.rgm.b ǵr. | b p y.t'lgt.b lšn[y]. | ǵr[.---]b.b pš y.t[--]. | hwt.b'l.iš[--]. | šm' l y.ypš.[---]. 2124.2
[-----]. | [špt.l a]rṣ.špt.l šmm. | [---.l]šn.l kbkbm.y'rb. | [b']l.b kbd h.b p h yrd. | k ḫrr.zt.ybl.arṣ. 5[67].2.3
[--]r.[---]. | [---.]il.[---]. | [tṣ]un.b arṣ. | mḫnm.ṭrp ym. | lšnm.tlḥk. | šmm.tṯrp. | ym.ḏnbtm. | tnn.l šbm. | tšt.trks. | l mr 1003.5
št kn.u b qṯ]t tqṯṯ. | [ušn.yp kn.---.--]l.il.t'ḏr b'l. | [-----.]lšnt. | [---.--]yp.tḥt. | [-----]. | [---.]w npy gr. | [ḥmyt.ugrt.w npy APP.I[-].1.9

lšṯr

' h]. | kr[mn.--.]w.r[' h]. | šd.[--.w.]r[' h]. | ḫla[n.---]. | w lšṯr[.---]. 2083.2.7

ltḥ

---.-]hn.w.alp.kd.nbt.kd.šmn.mr. | [---.]arb'.mat.ḫswn.ltḥ.aqhr. | [---.ltḥ.]sbbyn.ltḥ.ššmn.ltḥ.šḥlt. | [---.ltḥ.]ṣmqm.[t] 142[12].3
| ykn.ltḥ. | ḥgbn.ltḥ. | spr.mkrm. | bn.sl'n.prs. | bn.ṯpdn.ltḥ. | bn.urm.ltḥ. 1059.8
.kd.]nbt.k[d.]šmn.mr. | [---.l]tḥ.sb[by]n.ltḥ.šḥ[lt]. | [---.l]tḥ.dblt.ltḥ.ṣmqm. | [---.--]m.[ḫ]mšm.ḥmr.škm. 142[12].17
maḫdym. | grbn.ltḥ. | srn.ltḥ. | ykn.ltḥ. | ḥgbn.ltḥ. | spr.mkrm. | bn.sl'n.prs. | bn.ṯpdn.ltḥ. | bn.urm 1059.4
. | [---]n ḫlq. | bn m'nt. | bn kbdy. | bn krk. | bn srty. | bn ltḥ ḫlq. | bn ytr. | bn ilšpš. | ubrš. | bn gmš ḫlq. | bn 'gy. | bn zlb 2016.2.14
qmḥ.d.kly.b bt.skn. | l.illḏrm. | ltḥ.ḫṣr.b.šb'.ddm. 2093.3
maḫdym. | grbn.ltḥ. | srn.ltḥ. | ykn.ltḥ. | ḥgbn.ltḥ. | spr.mkrm. | bn.sl'n.prs. | bn.ṯpdn.ltḥ 1059.3
. | [---.a]lp.arb'.mat.tyt. | [---.kd.]nbt.k[d.]šmn.mr. | [---.l]tḥ.sb[by]n.ltḥ.šḥ[lt]. | [---.l]tḥ.dblt.ltḥ.ṣmqm. | [---.--]m.[ḫ] 142[12].16
kd.nbt.kd.šmn.mr. | [---.]arb'.mat.ḫswn.ltḥ.aqhr. | [---.ltḥ.]sbbyn.ltḥ.ššmn.ltḥ.šḥlt. | [---.ltḥ.]ṣmqm.[t]t.mat.nṣ.ṯlṯm. 142[12].4
.dd.š'rm. | [---.hn.w.al]p.kd.nbt.kd.šmn.mr. | [---].kmn.ltḥ.sbbyn. | [---.-]'t.ltḥ.ššmn. | [---].ḫswn.ṯṯ.mat.nṣ. | [---].ḫmš 142[12].9
maḫdym. | grbn.ltḥ. | srn.ltḥ. | ykn.ltḥ. | ḥgbn.ltḥ. | spr.mkrm. | bn.sl'n.prs. | bn.ṯpdn.ltḥ. | bn.urm.ltḥ. 1059.5
maḫdym. | grbn.ltḥ. | srn.ltḥ. | ykn.ltḥ. | ḥgbn.ltḥ. | spr.mkrm. | bn.sl'n.prs. | bn. 1059.2
ṭm.l.ḫḏǵb. | ṯṯ.ddm.l.gzzm. | kd yn.l.ḫtn.w.kd.ḥmṣ.w.[lt]ḥ.'šdm. | kd yn.l.ḫḏǵb.w.kd.ḥmṣ. | prš.glbm.l.bt. | tgmǵ.kš 1099.27
t.ḫswn.ltḥ.aqhr. | [---.ltḥ.]sbbyn.ltḥ.ššmn.ltḥ.šḥlt. | [---.ltḥ.]ṣmqm.[t]t.mat.nṣ.ṯlṯm.'ṣr. | [---].ḫmš[m.ḥm]r.škm. | [---.ṯ 142[12].5
k[d.]šmn.mr. | [---.l]tḥ.sb[by]n.ltḥ.šḥ[lt]. | [---.l]tḥ.dblt.ltḥ.ṣmqm. | [---.--]m.[ḫ]mšm.ḥmr.škm. 142[12].17
b'.mat.tyt. | [---.kd.]nbt.k[d.]šmn.mr. | [---.l]tḥ.sb[by]n.ltḥ.šḥ[lt]. | [---.l]tḥ.dblt.ltḥ.ṣmqm. | [---.--]m.[ḫ]mšm.ḥmr.šk 142[12].16
[---.]arb'.mat.ḫswn.ltḥ.aqhr. | [---.ltḥ.]sbbyn.ltḥ.ššmn.ltḥ.šḥlt. | [---.ltḥ.]ṣmqm.[t]t.mat.nṣ.ṯlṯm.'ṣr. | [---].ḫmš[m.ḥm 142[12].4
šmn.mr. | [---.]arb'.mat.ḫswn.ltḥ.aqhr. | [---.ltḥ.]sbbyn.ltḥ.ššmn.ltḥ.šḥlt. | [---.ltḥ.]ṣmqm.[t]t.mat.nṣ.ṯlṯm.'ṣr. | [---].ḫ 142[12].4
.al]p.kd.nbt.kd.šmn.mr. | [---].kmn.ltḥ.sbbyn. | [---.-]'t.ltḥ.ššmn. | [---].ḫswn.ṯṯ.mat.nṣ. | [---].ḫmšm.ḥmr.škm. | [---.ṯṯ. 142[12].10
bn.ltḥ. | spr.mkrm. | bn.sl'n.prs. | bn.ṯpdn.ltḥ. | bn.urm.ltḥ. 1059.9

lty

m.tlḥmn. | [---.rp]um.tštyn. | [---.]il.d 'rgzm. | [---.]dt.'l.lty. | [---.]tdbḥ.amr. | ṯmn.b qrb.hkl y.[aṯr h.rpum]. | tdd.aṯr h 20[121].1.9

ltm

ym.dǵṯ hrnmy[.d k] | bkbm.'[l.---]. | [-]l h.yd 'd[.---]. | ltm.mrqdm.d š[-]l[-]. | w t'n.pǵt.ṯkmt.mym. | qrym.ab.dbḥ.l i 19[1AQHT].4.189

ltn

a[ḫ] yn. | p nšt.b'l.[ṭ]'n.iṭ'n k. | [---.]ma[---] k.k tmḫṣ. | [ltn.bṯn.br]ḥ.tkly. | [bṯn.'qltn.]šlyṭ. | [d šb't.rašm].ṭṭkḥ. | [ttrp.š 5[67].1.28
k tmḫṣ.ltn.bṯn.brḥ. | tkly.bṯn.'qltn. | šlyṭ.d šb'y.rašm. | ṯṯkḥ.ttrp.šmm 5[67].1.1

ltšt

.m'd.qmm.a[--].amr. | [ṯn]y.d't hm.išt.ištm.yitmr.ḥrb.ltšt. | [--]n hm.rgm.l ṯr.ab h.il.tḥm.ym.b'l km. | [adn]km.ṯpṭ. 2.1[137].32

lṯk

tḥ.---.]l.aḥd.adr. | [---.--]t.b[ḥd]r.mškb. | tl[l.---.--]ḥ. | b lṯk.bt. | [pt]ḥ.aḥd.l.bt.'bdm. | [ṯ]n.ptḥ msb.bt.tu. | w.ptḥ[.aḥ]d 1151.8

m

m

.ky.‘rbt. | l pn.špš. | w pn.špš.nr. | b y.mid.w um. | tšmẖ.m ab. | w al.trḥln. | ‘tn.ẖrd.ank. | ‘m ny.šlm. | kll. | w mnm. | šl 1015.11
w ‘n.ali[yn.]b‘l. | al.tšt.u[rb]t.b bht m. | ḥln.b q[rb.hk]l m. | al td[.pdr]y.bt ar. | [---.ṭl]y.bt.rb. | [---.m]dd.il ym. | [---.-] 4[51].6.9
. | nǵṯ.w.ytn.hm.l k. | w.lḥt.alpm.ḥršm. | k.rgmt.l y.bly m. | alpm.aršt.l k.w.l y. | mn.bnš.d.l.i[--].‘[m k]. | l.alpm.w.l.y 2064.22
t.tp‘[.b ḥm]drt. | ur.tisp k.yd.aqht.ǵz[r]. | tšt k.bm.qrb m.asm. | b p h.rgm.l yṣa.b špt h[.hwt h]. | b nši ‘n h.w tphn.i 19[1AQHT].2.74
lt.bṣql yp‘ b yǵlm. | ur.tisp k.yd.aqht. | ǵzr.tšt k.b qrb m.asm. | y.dnh.ysb.aklt h.yph. | šblt.b akt.šblt.yp‘. | b ḥmdrt. 19[1AQHT].2.67
k‘[-]. | udn h.grš h.l ksi.mlk h. | l nẖt.l kḥṯ.drkt h. | mn m.ib.yp‘.l b‘l.ṣrt.l rkb.‘rpt. | [-]‘n.ǵlmm.y‘nyn.l ib.yp‘. | l b‘l.ṣ 3[‘NT].4.48
‘l.ṣrrt. | ṣpn.yšu g h.w yṣḥ. | aẖ y m.ytnt.b‘l. | spu y.bn m.um y.kl | y y.yt‘n.k gmrm. | mt.‘z.b‘l.‘z.ynghn. | k rumm.m 6[49].6.15
h. | [---].bn.ilm.mt. | p[-]n.aẖ y m.ytn.b‘l. | [s]pu y.bn m.um y.kly y. | yṯb.‘m.b‘l.ṣrrt. | ṣpn.yšu g h.w yṣḥ. | aẖ y m.y 6[49].6.11
n. | b‘l.ašt m.kṯr bn. | ym.kṯr.bnm.‘dt. | ypth.ḥln.b bht m. | urbt.b qrb.[h]kl | m.w y[p]tḥ.b dqt.‘rpt. | ‘l h[wt].kṯr.w ẖ 4[51].7.17
rgmt.l k.l ali | yn.b‘l.ṯṯbn.b‘l. | l hwt y.ypth.ḥ | ln.b bht m.urbt. | b qrb.hk[l m.yp]tḥ. | b‘l.b dqt[.‘rp]t. | ql h.qdš.b[‘l.y] 4[51].7.26
y[r] šmm.‘m. | ẖr[ẖ]b mlk qẓ.tn nkl y | rẖ ytrẖ.ib t‘rb m b bh | t h.w atn mhr h l a | b h.alp ksp w rbt ẖ | rṣ.išlẖ ẓhr 24[77].18
gy.amt. | aṯrt.qḥ. | ksan k.ḥdg k. | ḥtl k.w ẓi. | b aln.tk m. | b tk.mlbr. | ilšiy. | kry amt. | ‘pr.‘ẓm yd. | ugrm.ẖl.ld. | akl 12[75].1.20
]. | ḥš.rmm.hk[l m]. | ḥš.bht m.tbn[n]. | ḥš.trmmn.hk[l m]. | b tk.ṣrrt.ṣpn. | alp.šd.aẖd bt. | rbt.kmn.hkl. | w y‘n.kṯr.w 4[51].5.116
h.---]. | ṯr.il[.ab h.---]. | ḥš b[ht m.tbnn.ḥš.trmmn.hkl m]. | b tk.[---]. | bn.[---]. | a[--.---.] 1[‘NT.IX].3.27
br. | wn.ymǵy.aklm. | w ymẓa.‘qqm. | b‘l.ḥmd m.yḥmd m. | bn.dgn.yhrr m. | b‘l.ngṯ hm.b p‘n h. | w il hd.b ẖrẓ‘ h. | [-- 12[75].1.38
.aẖ y. | bn y.yšal. | tryl.p rgm. | l mlk.šm y. | w l h[-] y‘l m. | bn y.yšal. | tryl.w rgm. | ṯṯb.l aẖ k. | l adn k. 138.15
yql]. | yšthwy.[w ykbdn h.---]. | ṯr.il[.ab h.---]. | ḥš b[ht m.tbnn.ḥš.trmmn.hkl m]. | b tk.[---]. | bn.[---]. | a[--.---.] 1[‘NT.IX].3.27
]. | [--]b[.---]. | ḥš.bht m.k[ṯr]. | ḥš.rmm.hk[l m]. | ḥš.bht m.tbn[n]. | ḥš.trmmn.hk[l m]. | b tk.ṣrrt.ṣpn. | alp.šd.aẖd bt. | 4[51].5.115
m. | w ymẓa.‘qqm. | b‘l.ḥmd m.yḥmd m. | bn.dgn.yhrr m. | b‘l.ngṯ hm.b p‘n h. | w il hd.b ẖrẓ‘ h. | [-----]. | [--]t.[---]. | [12[75].1.39
d h ḥrnqm.w | y‘n ẖrẖb mlk qẓ [l]. | n‘mn.ilm l ẖt[n]. | m.b‘l trẖ pdry b[t h]. | aqrb k ab h b‘[l]. | yǵtr.‘ṯtr t | rẖ l k yb 24[77].26
. | [-]lp.izr. | [a]rz. | k.t‘rb.‘ṯtrt.šd.bt[.m]lk. | k.t‘rbn.ršp m.bt.mlk. | ẖlu.dg. | ḥdṯm. | dbḥ.b‘l.k.tdd.b‘lt.bhtm. | b.[-]ǵb.r 2004.11
]n‘mm.b ysmm.ḥ[--]k.ǵrt. | [ql].l b‘l.‘nt.ttnn. | [---].b‘l m.d ip[---]. | [il.]hd.d ‘nn.n[--]. | [----.]aliyn.b[‘l]. | [---.btl]t.‘n[10[76].2.32
gm.l ṯr.ab h.il.ṯḥm.ym.b‘l km. | [adn]km.ṯpṭ.nhr.tn.il m.d tq h.d tqyn h. | [hml]t.tn.b‘l.w ‘nn h.bn.dgn.arṯ m.pḏ h. 2.1[137].34
y.l pẖr]. | m‘d.ṯḥm.ym.b‘l km.adn km.ṯ[pṭ.nhr]. | tn.il m.d tq h.d tqyn.hmlt.tn.b‘l.[w ‘nn h]. | bn.dgn.arṯ m.pḏ h.tb 2.1[137].18
b‘r. | [---.]rn h.aqry. | [---.]b a[r]ṣ.mlḥmt. | ašt[.b ‘]p[r] m.ddym.ask. | šlm.l kb[d].awṣ.arbdd. | l kbd.š[d]m.ap.mṯn.r 3[‘NT].4.73
.aliyn.b‘l.hwt.aliy. | qrdm.qry.b arṣ.mlḥmt. | št.b ‘p[r] m.ddym.sk.šlm. | l kbd.arṣ.arbdd.l kbd.šdm. | [ḥ]š k.[‘]ṣ k.‘bṣ 3[‘NT].4.53
m.aliyn.b‘l.hwt. | aliy.qrdm.qry.b arṣ. | mlḥmt št.b ‘pr m.ddym. | sk.šlm.l kbd.arṣ. | arbdd.l kbd.šdm. | ḥš k.‘ṣ k.‘bṣ k 3[‘NT].3.12
ṯb. | [ybmt.]limm.[a]n.aqry. | [b arṣ].mlḥmt.[aš]t.b ‘pr m. | ddym.ask[.šlm.]l kbd.arṣ. | ar[bdd.]l kb[d.š]dm.yšt. | [---- 3[‘NT].4.67
il.ab k.hwt.l]ṯpn.ḥtk k. | [qryy.b arṣ.mlḥ]mt.št b ‘p | [r m.ddym.sk.šlm].l kbd.arṣ. | [arbdd.l kbd.š]dm.ḥš k. | [‘ṣ k.‘bṣ 1[‘NT.IX].2.20
n.b‘l]. | hw[t.aliy.qrdm.qryy.b arṣ.mlḥmt.št]. | [b ‘]pr[m.ddym.sk.šlm.l kbd.arṣ.arbdd]. | l kbd.š[dm.ḥš k.‘ṣ k.‘bṣ k. 7.2[130].15
ank.aḥwy. | aqht[.ǵz]r.w y‘n.aqht.ǵzr. | al.tšrgn.y btlt m.dm.l ǵzr. | šrg k.ẖḫm.mt.uẖryt.mh.yqḥ. | mh.yqḥ.mt.aṯryt 17[2AQHT].6.34
.šb‘ d.ǵzrm.ṭb.[g]d.b ḥlb.annẖ b ẖmat. | w ‘l.agn.šb‘ d m.dǵ[ṯ.---]t. | tlk m.rḥmy.w tṣd[.---]. | ṯḥgrn.ǵzr.n‘m.[---]. | w 23[52].15
šrr.w [---]. | y‘n.ym.l mt[.---]. | l šrr.w t‘[n.‘ṯtrt.---]. | b‘l m.hmt.[---]. | l šrr.št[.---]. | b riš h.[---]. | ib h.mš[--.---]. | [b]n.‘ 2.4[68].36
h. | š[r]yn.mḥmd.arz h. | tšt.išt.b bht m. | nb[l]at.b hkl m. | hn.ym.w ṯn.tikl. | išt.b bht m.nblat. | b hk[l] m.ṯlṯ.kb‘ ym 4[51].6.23
ṯr.w ẖss.l rgmt. | l k.l zbl.b‘l.ṯnt.l rkb.‘rpt.ht.ib k. | b‘l m.ht.ib k.tmẖṣ.ht.tṣmt.ṣrt k. | tqḥ.mlk.‘lm k.drkt.dt dr dr k. 2.4[68].9
‘m.ar]ṣ. | thmt.[‘mn.kbkbm.abn.brq]. | d l t[d‘.šmm.at m.w ank]. | ibǵ[y h.b tk.ǵ]r y.il.ṣpn. | b q[dš.b ǵr.nḥ]lt y. | w t 3[‘NT].4.62
.brq.d l.td‘.šmm. | rgm l td‘.nšm.w l tbn. | hmlt.arṣ.at m.w ank. | ibǵy h.b tk.ǵr y.il.ṣpn. | b qdš.b ǵr.nḥlt y. | b n‘m.b 3[‘NT].3.25
mm.‘m.arṣ.thmt]. | ‘m kbkbm[.abn.brq.d l td‘.šmm.at m]. | w ank.ib[ǵy h.---]. | [-].l y‘mdn.i[---.---]. | kpr.šb‘ bn[t.rḥ. 7.2[130].20
ht.aẖ y. | bn y.yšal. | tryl.p rgm. | l mlk.šm y. | w l h.y‘l m. | w h[t] aẖ y. | bn y.yšal. | tryl.w rgm[.-]. | ṯṯb.l aẖ k. | l adn 138.14
m‘.l al[iy]n b‘l. | bl.ašt.ur[bt.]b bht m. | ḥln.b qr[b.hk]l m. | w ‘n.ali[yn.]b‘l. | al.tšt.u[rb]t.b bht m. | ḥln.b q[rb.hk]l m 4[51].6.6
‘l. | bn.l rkb.‘rpt. | bl.ašt.urbt.b bh[t] m. | ḥln.b qrb.hkl m. | w y‘n.aliyn b‘l. | al.tšt.urbt.b[bhtm]. | [ḥln].b qrb.hk[l m] 4[51].5.124
| d dq.anm.l yrẓ. | ‘m.b‘l.l y‘db.mrḥ. | ‘m.bn.dgn.k tms m. | w ‘n.rbt.aṯrt ym. | blt.nmlk.‘ṯtr.‘rẓ. | ymlk.‘ṯtr.‘rẓ. | apnk.‘ 6.1.52[49.1.24]
ym.kṯr.bnm.‘dt. | ypth.ḥln.b bht m. | urbt.b qrb.[h]kl | m.w y[p]tḥ.b dqt.‘rpt. | ‘l h[wt].kṯr.w ẖss. | ṣḥq.kṯr.w ẖss. | yš 4[51].7.19
| ‘lm.l ršp.mlk. | alp w.š.l b‘lt. | bwrm š.iṯtqb. | w š.nbk m w.š. | gt mlk š.‘lm. | l kṯr.ṯn.‘lm. | tzǵ[.---.]nšm.pr. UG5.12.B.10
pim.ṯḥtk. | špš.ṯḥtk.ilnym. | ‘d k.ilm.hn.mtm. | ‘d k.kṯr m.ḥbr k. | w ẖss.d‘t k. | b ym.arš.w tnn. | kṯr.w ẖss.yd. | ytr.kṯ 6.6[62.2].48
ḥln.b qr[b.hk]l m. | w ‘n.ali[yn.]b‘l. | al.tšt.u[rb]t.b bht m. | ḥln.b q[rb.hk]l m. | al td[.pdr]y.bt ar. | [---.ṭl]y.bt.rb. | [---. 4[51].6.8
ẖss. | šm‘.l aliyn b‘l. | bn.l rkb.‘rpt. | bl.ašt.urbt.b bh[t] m. | ḥln.b qrb.hkl m. | w y‘n.aliyn b‘l. | al.tšt.urbt.b[bhtm]. | [4[51].5.123
.k[ṯr.w]ẖss. | šm‘.m‘.l al[iy]n b‘l. | bl.ašt.ur[bt.]b bht m. | ḥln.b qr[b.hk]l m. | w ‘n.ali[yn.]b‘l. | al.tšt.u[rb]t.b bht m 4[51].6.5
ḥ pat.mlbr. | wn.ymǵy.aklm. | w ymẓa.‘qqm. | b‘l.ḥmd m.yḥmd m. | bn.dgn.yhrr m. | b‘l.ngṯ hm.b p‘n h. | w il hd.b 12[75].1.38
.ǵllm[.---]. | aẖd.aklm.k [---]. | npl.b mšmš[.---]. | anp n m yḥr[r.---]. | bmt n m.yšẖn.[---]. | qrn h.km.ǵb[-.---]. | hw k 12[75].2.38
n.aliy[n.b‘l]. | [--]b[.---]. | ḥš.bht m.k[ṯr]. | ḥš.rmm.hk[l m]. | ḥš.bht m.tbn[n]. | ḥš.trmmn.hk[l m]. | b tk.ṣrrt.ṣpn. | alp. 4[51].5.114
b hk[l] m.ṯlṯ.kb‘ ym. | tikl[.i]št.b bht m. | nbla[t.]b hkl m. | ẖmš.ṯ[d]ṯ.ym.tikl. | išt.[b]bht m.nblat. | b[qrb.hk]l m.m 4[51].6.28
[t]špl.hl h.trm.hl h.tṣḥ.ad ad. | w hl h.tṣḥ.um.um.tirk m.yd.il.k ym. | w yd il.k mdb.ark.yd.il.k ym. | w yd.il.k mdb. 23[52].33
nhr.w yṣa b[.--]. | ybṯ.nn.aliyn.b‘l.w [---]. | ym.l mt.b‘l m.ym l[--.---]. | ḥm.l šrr.w [---]. | y‘n.ym.l mt[.---]. | l šrr.w t‘[2.4[68].32
‘n. | w.hm.al[-]. | l.tš‘n. | mṣrm. | tmkrn. | ypḥ.‘bdilt. | bn.m. | ypḥ.ilšlm. | bn.prqdš. | ypḥ.mnḥm. | bn.ḥnn. | brqn.spr. 2116.18
.um y.kly y. | yṯb.‘m.b‘l.ṣrrt. | ṣpn.yšu g h.w yṣḥ. | aẖ y m.ytnt.b‘l. | spu y.bn m.um y.kl | y y.yt‘n.k gmrm. | mt.‘z.b‘l. 6[49].6.14
.ilm.mt. | [--]u.šb‘t.ǵlm h. | [---].bn.ilm.mt. | p[-]n.aẖ y m.ytn.b‘l. | [s]pu y.bn m.um y.kly y. | yṯb.‘m.b‘l.ṣrrt. | ṣpn.yš 6[49].6.10
-]. | b ql[.-----]. | w tštqdn[.-----]. | hm. | w yḥ.mlk. | w ik m.kn.w [---]. | tšknnnn[.---]. 62[26].10

‘m.b‘l.mr[-]. | bt[.--]b b‘l.b qrb. | bt.w y‘n.aliyn. | b‘l.ašt m.kṯr bn. | ym.kṯr.bnm.‘dt. | ypth̬.ḥln.b bht m. | urbt.b qrb.[h 4[51].7.15
d.lḥm.št[y.ilm]. | [w]y‘n.aliy[n.b‘l]. | [--]b[.---]. | ḥš.bht m.k[ṯr]. | ḥš.rmm.hk[l m]. | ḥš.bht m.tbn[n]. | ḥš.trmmn.hk[l 4[51].5.113
. | ṯṯkḥ.ttrp.šmm.k rs. | ipd k.ank.ispi.uṭm. | ḏrqm.amt m.l yrt. | b npš.bn ilm.mt.b mh | mrt.ydd.il.ġzr. | tb‘.w l.yṯb il 5[67].1.6
t.bnt. | [---.‘]n h.km.bṯn.yqr. | [krpn h.-.l]arṣ.ks h.tšpk m. | [l ‘pr.tšu.g h.]w tṣḥ.šm‘.m‘. | [l aqht.ġzr.i]rš.ksp.w atn k. 17[2AQHT].6.15
| [---.-]ṯt. | [---.]w.sbsg. | [-----]. | [-----]. | [---.--]ṯ. | [---.-]b.m.lk. | kdwṯ.ḥdṯ. | b d ‘lpy. 1112.18
.b‘lm. | [--.a]ṯm.prṭl.l riš h.ḥmṯ.ṯmṯ. | [--.]ydbr.ṯrmt.al m.qḥn y.š y.qḥn y. | [--.]šir.b krm.nṭṭt.dm.‘lt.b ab y. | u---].‘lt 1001.1.8
. | ḫmš.ṯ[d]ṯ.ym.tikl. | išt.[b]bht m.nblat. | b[qrb.hk]l m.mk. | b šb[‘.]y[mm].td.išt. | b bht m.n[bl]at.b hkl m. | sb.ks 4[51].6.31
h. | h[n.l]bnn.w ‘ṣ h. | š[r]yn.mḥmd.arz h. | tšt.išt.b bht m. | nb[l]at.b hkl m. | hn.ym.w ṯn.tikl. | išt.b bht m.nblat. | b h 4[51].6.22
t.b bht m.nblat. | b hk[l] m.ṯlṯ.kb‘ ym. | tikl[.i]št.b bht m. | nbla[t.]b hkl m. | ḫmš.ṯ[d]ṯ.ym.tikl. | išt.[b]bht m.nblat. | 4[51].6.27
.nblat. | b[qrb.hk]l m.mk. | b šb[‘.]y[mm].td.išt. | b bht m.n[bl]at.b hkl m. | sb.ksp.l rqm.ḫrṣ. | nṣb.l lbnt.šmḫ. | aliyn. 4[51].6.33
.b bht m. | nb[l]at.b hkl m. | hn.ym.w ṯn.tikl. | išt.b bht m.nblat. | b hk[l] m.ṯlṯ.kb‘ ym. | tikl[.i]št.b bht m. | nbla[t.]b 4[51].6.25
ht m. | nbla[t.]b hkl m. | ḫmš.ṯ[d]ṯ.ym.tikl. | išt.[b]bht m.nblat. | b[qrb.hk]l m.mk. | b šb[‘.]y[mm].td.išt. | b bht m.n 4[51].6.30
.bm. | [ymn.]brkm.ybrk. | [‘bd h.]ybrk.il.krt. | [ṯ‘.ymr]m.n‘m[n.]ġlm.il. | a[ṯt.tq]ḥ.y krt.aṯt. | tqḥ.bt k.ġlmt.tš‘rb. | ḥq 15[128].2.20
]l m.mk. | b šb[‘.]y[mm].td.išt. | b bht m.n[bl]at.b hkl m. | sb.ksp.l rqm.ḫrṣ. | nṣb.l lbnt.šmḫ. | aliyn.b‘l.ht y.bnt. | dt. 4[51].6.33
--.lḥt]. | akl.yṯ[ṯb.--]pt. | ib.‘ltn.a[--.--]y. | w.spr.in[.-.]‘d m. | spr n.ṯhr[.--]. | aṯr.iṯ.bqṯ. | w.štn.l y. 2060.32
h.bn.dgn.arṯ m.pḏ h. | [w y‘n.]ṯr.ab h.il.‘bd k.b‘l.y ym m.‘bd k.b‘l. | [--.--]m.bn.dgn.a[s]r km.hw ybl.argmn k.k ilm. 2.1[137].36
[.---]m ib. | [---.--]m. | [-----]. | [-]š[--.---]. | [-]r[--.--]y. | in m.‘bd k hwt. | [y]rš.‘m y. | mnm.iršt k. | d ḫsrt.w.ank. | aštn..l. 2065.13
. | ṯkm.bm ṯkm.aḫm.qym.il. | b lsmt.ṯm.yṯbš.šm.il.mt m. | y‘bš.brk n.šm.il.ġzrm. | ṯm.ṯmq.rpu.b‘l.mhr b‘l. | w mhr.‘ 22.2[124].6
. | nhr.k[--].ṣḥn.b‘l.‘m. | aḫ y.qran.hd.‘m.ary y. | w lḥm m ‘m aḫ y.lḥm. | w št m.‘m.a[ḫ] yn. | p nšt.b‘l.[ṭ]‘n.iṭ‘n k. | [-- 5[67].1.24
| aḫ y.qran.hd.‘m.ary y. | w lḥm m ‘m aḫ y.lḥm. | w št m.‘m.a[ḫ] yn. | p nšt.b‘l.[ṭ]‘n.iṭ‘n k. | [---.]ma[---] k.k tmḫṣ. | [l 5[67].1.25
ydlp.tmn h. | yqṯ b‘l.w yšt.ym.ykly.ṯpṭ.nhr. | b šm.tg‘r m.‘ṯtrt.bṯ l aliyn.[b‘l.] | bṯ.l rkb.‘rpt.k šby n.zb[l.ym.k] | šby 2.4[68].28
bt k.ygr[š k.---]. | [---.]y.ḥr.ḥr.bnt.ḥ[---]. | [--.]uḫd.[b‘]l m.‘[--].yd k.amṣ.yd[.--]. | [---.]ḥš[.-]nm[.--.]k.[--].w yḫnp[.---] 1001.1.14
il m.d tq h.d tqyn h. | [hml]t.tn.b‘l.w ‘nn h.bn.dgn.arṯ m.pḏ h. | [w y‘n.]ṯr.ab h.il.‘bd k.b‘l.y ym m.‘bd k.b‘l. | [--.--] 2.1[137].35
n.il m.d tq h.d tqyn.hmlt.tn.b‘l.[w ‘nn h]. | bn.dgn.arṯ m.pḏ h.tb‘.ġlmm.l ṯṯb.[idk.pnm]. | l ytn.tk.ġr.ll.‘m.phr.m‘d. 2.1[137].19
[--].bn.ilm.mt. | ‘m.aliyn.b‘l.yšu. | g h.w yṣḥ.‘l k.b[‘]l m. | pht.qlt.‘l k.pht. | dry.b ḥrb.‘l k. | pht.šrp.b išt. | ‘l k.[pht.ṯ 6[49].5.11
l.ṯṯbn.b‘l. | l hwt y.ypth̬.ḥ | ln.b bht m.urbt. | b qrb.hk[l m.yp]tḥ. | b‘l.b dqt[.‘rp]t. | ql h.qdš.b[‘l.y]tn. | yṯny.b‘l.ṣ[---.-] 4[51].7.27
.ab.k mtm. | tmtn.u ḫšt k.l ntn. | ‘tq.b d.aṯt.ab.ṣrry. | ik m.yrgm.bn.il. | krt.špḥ.lṭpn. | w qdš.u ilm.tmtn. | špḥ.lṭpn.l y 16.1[125].20
]d.b ḥlb.annḫ b ḫmat. | w ‘l.agn.šb‘ d m.dġ[ṯ.---]t. | tlk m.rḥmy.w tṣd[.---]. | ṯḥgrn.ġzr.n‘m.[---]. | w šm.‘rbm.yr[.---] 23[52].16
.k [---]. | npl.b mšmš[.---]. | anp n m yḫr[r.---]. | bmt n m.yšḫn.[---]. | qrn h.km.ġb[-.---]. | hw km.ḥrr[.---]. | šnmtm.d 12[75].2.39
ṯḥm.špš. | l.‘mrpi.rgm. | ‘m špš.kll.mid m. | šlm. | l.[--]n.špš. | ad[.‘]bd h.uk.škn. | k.[---.]sglt h.hw. | w. 2060.3
w tbu. | nṣrt.tbu.pnm. | ‘rm.tdu.mh. | pdrm.tdu.šrr. | ḥṯ m.t‘mt.[‘]ṭr.[k]m. | zbln.‘l.riš h. | w ṯṯb.trḥṣ.nn.b d‘t. | npš h.l 16.6[127].8
.b hkl m. | hn.ym.w ṯn.tikl. | išt.b bht m.nblat. | b hk[l] m.ṯlṯ.kb‘ ym. | tikl[.i]št.b bht m. | nbla[t.]b hkl m. | ḫmš.ṯ[d]ṯ. 4[51].6.26
b lḥm ay.w šty.b ḫmr yn ay. | šlm.mlk.šlm.mlkt.‘rbm m.ṯnnm. | mt.w šr.yṯb.b d h.ḥṭ.ṯkl.b d h. | ḥṭ.ulmn.yzbrnn.zb 23[52].7
k.[d]m[‘t.]km. | rb‘t.ṯqlm.ṯtp[.---.]bm. | yd.ṣpn hm.tliy m[.--.ṣ]pn hm. | nṣḥy.šrr.m[---.--]ay. | nbšr km.dnil.[--] h[.---] 19[1AQHT].2.84
[k.ym]ḫṣ.b‘l m[.--]y.tnn.w ygl.w ynsk.‘[-]. | [--]y.l arṣ[.id]y.alt.l aḫš.idy.al 1001.1.1
pnm[.---]. | b‘l.n[--.---]. | il.hd[.---]. | at.bl[.at.---]. | ḥmd m.[---]. | il.hr[r.---]. | kb[-.---]. | ym.[---]. | yšḫr[.---]. | yikl[.---]. | 12[75].2.9
[---.rp]um.tdbḥn. | [----.]‘d.ilnym. | [---.--]l km amt m. | [---.]b w t‘rb.sd. | [---.--]n b ym.qẓ. | [---.]ym.tlḫmn. | [---.r 20[121].1.3
.bt ar. | [---.ṯl]y.bt.rb. | [---.m]dd.il ym. | [---.-]qlṣn.wpṯ m. | [---.]w y‘n.kṯr. | [w ḫss.]ṯṯb.b‘l.l hwt y. | [ḥš.]bht h.tbnn. | 4[51].6.13
k. | [---.i]qnim. | [---.-]šu.b qrb. | [---].asr. | [---.--]m.ymt m. | [---.]k iṯl. | [---.--]m.‘db.l arṣ. | [---.]špm.‘db. | [---].t‘tqn. | [- 1[‘NT.IX].2.8
.--]m.l gṯrm. | [---.]l ‘nt m. | [---.--]rm.d krm. | [---].l ‘nt m. | [---.]l šlm. | [-]l[-.-]ry.ylbš. | mlk.ylk.lqḥ.ilm. | aṯr.ilm.ylk. 33[5].20
.tḥt.[---] | m ‘ṣrm.ḥ[---]. | glṯ.isr[.---] | m.brt[.---]. | ymt m.[---]. | ši[.---]. | m[---.---]. 8[51FRAG].15
.ap.w npš. | [---].bt.alp w š. | [---.--]m.l gṯrm. | [---.]l ‘nt m. | [---.--]rm.d krm. | [---].l ‘nt m. | [---.]l šlm. | [-]l[-.-]ry.ylbš. 33[5].18
w y‘n.aliyn b‘l. | al.tšt.urbt.b[bhtm]. | [ḥln].b qrb.hk[l m]. 4[51].5.127

mad

n.ngb.w [yṣi.ṣbu]. | ṣbi.ng[b.w yṣi.‘dn]. | m‘[.ṣ]bu h.u[l.mad]. | ṯlṯ.mat.rbt. | hlk.l alpm.ḫḏḏ. | w l.rbt.kmyr. | aṯr.ṯn.ṯn. 14[KRT].4.178
. | ‘dn.ngb.w yṣi. | ṣbu.ṣbi.ngb. | w yṣi.‘dn.m‘. | ṣbu k.ul.mad. | ṯlṯ.mat.rbt. | ḫpṯ.d bl.spr. | ṯnn.d bl.hg. | hlk.l alpm.ḫḏḏ 14[KRT].2.88

maḫdh

kd.bt ilm. | rbm. | kd l ištnm. | kd l ḫty. | maḫdh. | kd l kblbn. | kdm.mṭḫ. | l.alṯy. | kd.l mrynm. | šb‘ yn. 1090.5

maḫdy

maḫdym. | grbn.ltḥ. | srn.ltḥ. | ykn.ltḥ. | ḥgbn.ltḥ. | spr.mkrm. 1059.1
spr.irgmn. | ṯlṯ.ḫmš.alpm. | b d.brq.maḫdy. | kkr.ṯlṯ. | b d.bn.by.ar[y]. | alpm.ṯlṯ. | b d.šim.il[š]tm‘ 1134.3

maḫdt

bt šbn. | iy‘dm.w b‘l h. | ddy. | ‘my. | iwrnr. | alnr. | maḫdt. | aby. | [-----]. | [-]nt. | ydn. | mnn.w bn h. | ṯkn. 107[15].7

mašmn

mašmn. | ytn. 1182.1

mat

---.š]pšg.iqni.mit.pṯtm. | [---].mitm.kslm. | [---].pwt.ṯlṯ.mat.abn.ṣrp. | [---.-]qt.l.ṯrmnm. | [---].ṯlṯm.iqnu. | [---.l.]ṯrmn. 1106.10
‘]t.šmn.uz. | mi[t].ygb.bq‘. | a[--].‘ṭ. | a[l]pm.alpnm. | ṯlṯ.m[a]t.art.ḥkpt. | mit.dnn. | mitm.iqnu. | ḫmš.‘šr.qn.n‘m.‘n[m] 1128.26
n.ḫrṣ. | w arb‘.ktnt.w [---]b. | [ḫm]š.mat pḥm. | [ḫm]š[.m]at.iqnu. | argmn.nqmd.mlk. | ugrt.d ybl.l špš. | mlk.rb.b‘l h 64[118].23

| [-----]. | ilmlk ṯṯ mat. | ʿbdilm.ṯṯ mat. | šmmn.bn.ʿdš.ṯṯ mat. | ušknym. | ypʿ.alpm. | aḫ[m]lk.bn.nskn.alpm. | krw.šlmy 1060.1.12

. | lbnym. | ṯm[n.]alp mitm. | ilbʿl ḫmš m[at]. | ʿdn.ḫmš.mat. | bn.[-]d.alp. | bn.[-]pn.ṯṯ mat. 1060.2.10

mš.kkrm.alp kb[d]. | ṯlṯ.l.nskm.birtym. | b d.urtn.w.ṯṯ.mat.brr. | b.ṯmnym.ksp.ṯlṯt.kbd. | ḫmš.alp.ṯlṯ.l.ḥlby. | b d.tlmi 2101.4

[---].alpm.ḫmš.mat. | šbʿm[.t]šʿ.kbd. | tgmr.uz.ǵrn.arbʿ.mat. | tgmr.uz.aḫmn.arbʿ.mat. | arbʿm.kbd. | ṯlṯ.alp.ṣpr.dt.aḫ 1129.5

. | ḫmšm.tišr. | ḫmš.ktnt. | ḫmš.ṯnt.alpm. | ʿšrm.hbn. | ṯlṯ.mat.dd. | šʿrm. | mit.šmn. | ʿšr.kat. | ẓrw. 2102.7

spr.argmn.nskm. | rqdym. | šṭšm.ṯṯ mat. | ṣprn.ṯṯ mat. | ḏkry.ṯṯ mat. | [p]lsy.ṯṯ mat. | ʿdn.ḫmš [m]at. | [--]kbʿl ṯṯ 1060.1.4

[-]t ṯlṯ ty[--]. | bn.grgš. | w.npṣ bt ṯn.ṯlṯ mat. | w spl ṯlṯ.mat. | w mmskn. | w.ṯṯ.mqrtm. | w.ṯn.irpm.w.ṯn.trqm. | w.qpt. 1103.17

krsnm. | ḫmšm [-]t ṯlṯ ty[--]. | bn.grgš. | w.npṣ bt ṯn.ṯlṯ mat. | w spl ṯlṯ.mat. | w mmskn. | w.ṯṯ.mqrtm. | w.ṯn.irpm.w.ṯ 1103.16

[.---]. | ʿšr.d[d.---]. | ṯṯm.dd.dd[.---]. | l.mdrǵlm[.---]. | ṯlṯ.mat.ḫmšm.kb[d]. | ḫmš.kbd.l.mdʿ. | b yr[ḫ.iṯtb]nm. | ṯlṯ[.mat. 2012.11

dd.šʿrm. | [---.-]hn.w.alp.kd.nbt.kd.šmn.mr. | [---.]arbʿ.mat.ḫswn.lṯḥ.aqhr. | [---.lṯḥ.]sbbyn.lṯḥ.ššmn.lṯḥ.šḥlt. | [---.lṯḥ 142[12].3

w blḫ br[-]m p[-]. | b[--.]l[-.]mat[.-]y. | ḫmšm[.--]i. | ṯlṯ m[at] ḫswn. | ṯlṯ ṯ[-].ṯṯ ḥ[--]. 140[98].9

--]. | bn[.---]. | w.yn[.---]. | bn.ʿdr[.---]. | ntb[t]. | b.arb[ʿ]. | mat.ḫr[ṣ]. 2007.12

. | lqḥ.bʿlmʿḏr. | w bn.ḥlp. | w[--]y.d.bʿl. | miḥd.b. | arbʿ.mat. | ḫrṣ. 1155.7

dṯ. | b.yr.pgrm. | lqḥ.bʿlmḏr. | w.bn.ḥlp. | miḥd. | b.arbʿ. | mat.ḫrṣ. 1156.7

mn.mat.kbd. | pwt. | ṯmn.mat.pṯtm. | kkrm.alpm. | ḫmš.mat.kbd. | abn.ṣrp. 2051.9

alpm.pḥm.ḫm[š].mat.kbd. | b d.tt.w.ṯlṯ.ktnt.b dm.tt. | w.ṯmnt.ksp.hn. | ktn.d.ṣr 1110.1

alpm.arbʿ.mat.k[bd]. | mit.b d.yd[r]m. | alp ḫmš mat.kbd.d[--]. 2109.3

l.a[--.---]. | tgm[r.ak]l.b.gt.ḫldy. | ṯlṯ.ma[t].ʿšr.kbd. | šbʿ m[at].kbd.ḥpr.ʿbdm. | mit[.d]rt.arbʿm.drt. | [---]m. | t[gm]r.ak 2013.12

alpm.arbʿ.mat.k[bd]. | mit.b d.yd[r]m. | alp ḫmš mat.kbd.d[--]. 2109.1

ršt.yṣḥm. | arbʿ.alpm. | mitm.kbd.ṯlṯ. | arbʿ.kkrm. | ṯmn.mat.kbd. | pwt. | ṯmn.mat.pṯtm. | kkrm.alpm. | ḫmš.mat.kbd. 2051.5

ṯmn.kkr.ṯlṯ. | ṯmn.kkr.brr. | arbʿ.alpm.pḥm. | ḫmš.mat.kbd. | arbʿ.alpm.iqni. | ḫmš.mat.kbd. | ṯlṯm.ḫmš kbd ktn. 1130.4

arbʿ.alpm.pḥm. | ḫmš.mat.kbd. | arbʿ.alpm.iqni. | ḫmš.mat.kbd. | ṯlṯm.ḫmš kbd ktn. | ḫmš.rṭm. | ḫmš.ṯnt.d ḫmšm w. 1130.6

.]b d.mzy.alzy. | ḫmš.kkr.ḥlb. | ḫmš.kkr.brr. | kkr.ḫmš.mat.kbd.ṯlṯ.šm[n]. | alp.mitm.kbd.ṯlṯ.ḥlb. | šbʿ.l.ʿšrm.kkr.ṯlṯ. | 1135.4

ʿšrm.kkr.kkrm. | alp.ṯṯ.mat.kbd. 2111.2

spr.argmnm. | ʿšrm.ksp.d mkr. | mlk. | ṯlṯ.mat.ksp.d.šb[n]. | mit.ksp.d.ṭbq. | ṯmnym.arbʿt. | kbd.ksp. | d. 2107.4

ṯṯ.mat.ksp. | ḥṯbn.ybnn. | arbʿm.l.mit.šmn. | arbʿm.l.mit.tišr. | ṯṯ. 1127.1

mnḥ.b d.ybnn. | arbʿ.mat. | l.alp.šmn. | nḥ.ṯṯ.mat. | šm[n].rqḥ. | kkrm.brḏl. | mit.tišr 141[120].2

. | [---.lṯḥ.]sbbyn.lṯḥ.ššmn.lṯḥ.šḥlt. | [---.lṯḥ.]ṣmqm.[t]ṯ.mat.nṣ.ṯlṯm.ʿṣr. | [---].ḫmš[m.ḥm]r.škm. | [---.ṯṯ.dd.]gdl.ṯṯ.dd. 142[12].5

. | [---].kmn.lṯḥ.sbbyn. | [---.-]ʿt.lṯḥ.ššmn. | [---].ḫšwn.ṯṯ.mat.nṣ. | [---].ḫmšm.ḥmr.škm. | [---.ṯṯ.dd.]gdl.ṯṯ.dd.šʿrm. | [--- 142[12].11

at. | ʿdn.ḫmš [m]at. | [--]kbʿl ṯṯ [mat]. | [-----]. | ilmlk ṯṯ mat. | ʿbdilm.ṯṯ mat. | šmmn.bn.ʿdš.ṯṯ mat. | ušknym. | ypʿ.alp 1060.1.10

. | atn.bṣry.alpm. | lbnym. | ṯm[n.]alp mitm. | ilbʿl ḫmš m[at]. | ʿdn.ḫmš.mat. | bn.[-]d.alp. | bn.[-]pn.ṯṯ mat. 1060.2.9

ym. | šṭšm.ṯṯ mat. | ṣprn.ṯṯ mat. | ḏkry.ṯṯ mat. | [p]lsy.ṯṯ mat. | ʿdn.ḫmš [m]at. | [--]kbʿl ṯṯ [mat]. | [-----]. | ilmlk ṯṯ mat. 1060.1.6

ʿm.drt.arbʿm.drt. | l.a[--.---]. | tgm[r.ak]l.b.gt.ḫldy. | ṯlṯ.ma[t].ʿšr.kbd. | šbʿ m[at].kbd.ḥpr.ʿbdm. | mit[.d]rt.arbʿm.drt. 2013.11

. | mit[.d]rt.arbʿm.drt. | [---]m. | t[gm]r.akl.b.gt.ǵ[l]. | ṯlṯ.mat.ʿšrm[.---]. | ṯmnym.drt.a[--]. | drt.l.alpm[.---]. | šbʿm.ṯn.k 2013.16

ʿṣrm.ṯql.kbd[.ks].mn.ḫrṣ. | w arbʿ.ktnt.w [---]b. | [ḫm]š.mat pḥm. | [ḫm]š[.m]at.iqnu. | argmn.nqmd.mlk. | ugrt.d ybl. 64[118].22

mn.nskm. | rqdym. | šṭšm.ṯṯ mat. | ṣprn.ṯṯ mat. | ḏkry.ṯṯ mat. | [p]lsy.ṯṯ mat. | ʿdn.ḫmš [m]at. | [--]kbʿl ṯṯ [mat]. | [-----]. 1060.1.5

. | mitm.kbd.ṯlṯ. | arbʿ.kkrm. | ṯmn.mat.kbd. | pwt. | ṯmn.mat.pṯtm. | kkrm.alpm. | ḫmš.mat.kbd. | abn.ṣrp. 2051.7

.bt. | mlk.mlbš. | ytn.l hm. | šbʿ.lbšm.allm. | l ušḫry. | ṯlṯ.mat.pṯtm. | l.mgmr.b.ṯlṯ. | šnt. 1107.11

spr.argmn.nskm. | rqdym. | šṭšm.ṯṯ mat. | ṣprn.ṯṯ mat. | ḏkry.ṯṯ mat. | [p]lsy.ṯṯ mat. | ʿdn.ḫmš [m]a 1060.1.3

ṣi.ṣbu]. | ṣbi.ng[b.w ysi.ʿdn]. | mʿ[.ṣ]bu h.u[l.mad]. | ṯlṯ.mat.rbt. | hlk.l alpm.ḫdd. | w l.rbt.kmyr. | aṯr.ṯn.ṯn.hlk. | aṯr.ṯl 14[KRT].4.179

.w yṣi. | ṣbu.ṣbi.ngb. | w yṣi.ʿdn.mʿ. | ṣbu k.ul.mad. | ṯlṯ.mat.rbt. | ḫpt.d bl.spr. | ṯnn.d bl.hg. | hlk.l alpm.ḫdd. | w l rbt. 14[KRT].2.89

ṯn.ʿšr.yn.[kps]lnm. | arbʿ.mat[.arb]ʿm.[k]bd. | d ntn.d.ksp. | arbʿ.l.ḥlby. | [---].l.bt. | arbʿ. 1087.2

at.ḫmšm.kb[d]. | ḫmš.kbd.l.mdʿ. | b yr[ḫ.iṯtb]nm. | ṯlṯ[.mat.a]rbʿ.kbd. | w.[---.-]mʿt. | ṯlṯ[m.---.-]rm. | ʿšr[.---].alpm. | a 2012.14

pr.l.št. | yrmʿl. | ṣry. | iršy. | yʿḏrd. | ayaḫ. | bn.aylt. | ḫmš.mat.arbʿm. | kbd.ksp.anyt. | d.ʿrb.b.anyt. | l.mlk.gbl. | w.ḫmš 2106.10

[.t]šʿ.kbd. | tgmr.uz.ǵrn.arbʿ.mat. | tgmr.uz.aḫmn.arbʿ.mat. | arbʿm.kbd. | ṯlṯ.alp.ṣpr.dt.aḥd. | ḥrt h.aḥd.b gt.nḥl. | aḥ 1129.6

ṯlṯ.mat. | šbʿm kbd. | zt.ubdym. | b mlk. 1095.1

[---].dt.iṯ. | [---].ṯlṯ.kbd. | [---].alpm.ḫmš.mat. | šbʿm[.t]šʿ.kbd. | tgmr.uz.ǵrn.arbʿ.mat. | tgmr.uz.aḫmn. 1129.3

[---.]ṯlṯm. | [---.n]ḥl. | [---.ṯ]lṯ.mat.šbʿm[.---]. | [---.--]mm.b.mṣbt[.---]. | [---.ṯl]ṯ.mat.ṯmny[m 2149.3

]at. | [--]kbʿl ṯṯ [mat]. | [-----]. | ilmlk ṯṯ mat. | ʿbdilm.ṯṯ mat. | šmmn.bn.ʿdš.ṯṯ mat. | ušknym. | ypʿ.alpm. | aḫ[m]lk.bn. 1060.1.11

mnḥ.b d.ybnn. | arbʿ.mat. | l.alp.šmn. | nḥ.ṯṯ.mat. | šm[n].rqḥ. | kkrm.brḏl. | mit.tišrm. | ṯlṯm.almg. | ḫmšm. 141[120].4

.ṯṯt.ʿšrt.ksp h. | ḫmšt.ḫrṣ.bt.il. | b.ḫmšt.ʿšrt.ksp. | ḫmš.mat.šmt. | b.ʿšrt.ksp. | ʿšr.ṣin.b.ṯṯt.w.kmsk. | arbʿ[.k]dwṯm.w.ṯ 2100.7

[--]t.ilhnm.b šnt. | [---.]šbʿ.mat.šʿrt.ḫmšm.kbd. | [---.-]nd.l.mlbš.ṯrmnm. | [---]h.lbš.allm. 1106.2

t.ḫmšt.ḫndlt. | [---.iqn]i.l.[-]k.btbt. | [---.l.trm]nm.š[bʿ].mat.šʿrt. | [---.]iqnu.[---.]lbš.ṯrmnm. | [---.iqn]i.lbš.al[l.---]. | [-- 1106.19

k.igr.w.u.[--]. | ʿm.špš.[---]. | nšlḥ[.---]. | [---.m]at. | [---.]mat. | š[--].išal. | ʿm k.ybl.šd. | a[--].dʿ.k. | šld.ašld. | hn.mrṯ.d.št 2009.2.2

šm.ḥmr.škm. | [---.ṯṯ.dd.]gdl.ṯṯ.dd.šʿrm. | [---.a]lp.arbʿ.mat.tyt. | [---.kd.]nbt.k[d.]šmn.mr. | [---.l]ṯḥ.sb[by]n.lṯḥ.šḥ[lt 142[12].14

.tišr. | ṯṯ.ṯṯ.b [t]ql.ṯlṯt.l.ʿšrm.ksp hm. | sstm.b.šbʿm. | ṯlṯ.mat.trm.b.ʿšrt. | mit.adrm.b.ʿšrt. | ʿšr.ydt.b.ʿšrt. | ḫmš.kkrm.ṣ 1127.7

ṯṯ.mat.ṯṯm.kbd šmn. | l.abrm.altyy. | [m]it.ṯlṯm.kbd.šmn. | [l.]ab 2095.1

ʿbdm. | mitm.drt.ṯmnym.drt. | tgmr.akl.b.gt[.b]ʿln. | ṯlṯ.mat.ṯṯm.kbd. | ṯṯm.ṯṯ.kbd.ḥpr.ʿbdm. | šbʿm.drt.arbʿm.drt. | l.a 2013.6

ṣ.bn.ʿglt.ṯlṯm. | ṣṣ.bn.ʿbd.ʿšrm. | ṣṣ.bn.mṣḥ[n].ʿšrm. | šbʿ.mat.ṯṯm kbd. 2096.20

mḫsrn.d.[--.]ušknym. | brq.ṯlṯ.[mat.ṯ]lṯ. | bsn.mi[t.--]. | ar[--.---]. | k[--.---]. 1136.2

ṯlṯ.mat.ṯlṯm. | kbd.šmn. | l kny. | ṯmnym.šmn. | b d.adnnʿm. 1094.1

ʿl.rišy. | ṯlṯm.ṯlṯ.ʿl.nsk. | arym. | alp.ṯlṯ.ʿl. | nsk.art. | ḫmš.mat.ṯlṯ. | ʿl.mtn.rišy. 1137.9

---.ṯ]lṯ.mat.šbʿm[.---]. | [---.--]mm.b.mṣbt[.---]. | [---.ṯl]ṯ.mat.ṯmny[m.---]. 2149.5

.|ḫmš.ṯnt.d ḫmšm w.|ḫmš.ṯnt.d mit.|ḫmš.ṯnt.d ṯl|ṯ mat.|ṯt.ṯnt.d alp|alpm.ṯlṯ ktt.|alp.brr.|kkr.tznt.|ḫmšt.kkr 1130.12
m ǵlmm.|kpld.b[-.-]r[--].|w blḫ br[-]m p[-].|b[--.]l[-.]mat[.-]y.|ḫmšm[.--]i.|ṯlṯ m[at] ḫswn.|ṯlṯ ṯ[-].ṯṯ ḥ[--]. 140[98].7
t.|ṣprn.ṯṯ mat.|ḏkry.ṯṯ mat.|[p]lsy.ṯṯ mat.|ʿdn.ḫmš [m]at.|[--]kbʿl ṯṯ [mat].|[-----].|ilmlk ṯṯ mat.|ʿbdilm.ṯṯ mat.| 1060.1.7
alp[.---].|mat[.---].|ḫrṣ[.---].|ṯlṯ.k[---].|ṯlṯ.a[--.---].|ḫmš[.---].|ksp[.--- 148[96].2
ṯlṯ.mat[.---.]kbd.|ṯṯ.ddm.k[--.b]rqd.|mit.tšʿm.[kb]d.ddm.|b.gt 2168.1
|ṯn.skm.šbʿ.mšlt.arbʿ.ḫpnt.[---].|ḫmšm.ṯlṯ.rkb.ntn.ṯlṯ.mat.[---].|lg.šmn.rqḥ.šrʿm.ušpǵtm.p[--.---].|kṯ.ẓrw.kṯ.nbt.ḏ UG5.9.1.20
mǵy.mndʿ.|k.igr.w.u.[--].|ʿm.špš.[---].|nšlḥ[.---].|[---.m]at.|[---.]mat.|š[--].išal.|ʿm k.ybl.šd.|a[--].dʿ.k.|šld.ašld.| 2009.2.1
[---.ṯ]lṯ.mat.|[---.m]itm.mqp.m[---].|[---.ṯmn]ym.mgnm ar[bʿ].|[---. 1145.1.1
ṯlṯ.mat.[---].|ṯmnt.k[---]. 1149.1
r[t.---].|[ʿš]r.[k]bd[.---].|[a]lpm[.---].|tg[m]r.[---].|ṯlṯ ma[t.---].|ṯmnym[.---].|[ṯ]mny[m.---].|[-]r[-.---].|[--]m.l.[--- 2013.26
-].|[---.]ǵprt.ʿš[r.---].|[---.p]ṯtm.l.ip[--.---].|[---.]ksl.ṯlṯ.m[at.---].|[---].abn.ṣr[p.---].|[---.-]rt.ṯlṯm[.---].|[--]l.ṯrmn.m[1106.26
kry.ṯṯ mat.|[p]lsy.ṯṯ mat.|ʿdn.ḫmš [m]at.|[--]kbʿl ṯṯ [mat].|[-----].|ilmlk ṯṯ mat.|ʿbdilm.ṯṯ mat.|šmmn.bn.ʿdš.ṯṯ 1060.1.8
bʿl ḫmš m[at].|ʿdn.ḫmš.mat.|bn.[-]d.alp.|bn.[-]pn.ṯṯ mat. 1060.2.12
l]ṯḥ.tyt.[---].|[b]šbʿ[m.w.n]ṣp.ksp.|[tgm]r.[alp.w.]ṯlṯ.mat. 2101.28

mid

--] h[.---].|ʿn.ṯk[.---].|ʿln.ṯ[--.---].|l pʿn.ǵl[m]m[.---].|mid.an[--.]ṣn[--].|nrt.ilm.špš[.ṣḥrr]t.|la.šmm.b y[d.bn.ilm. 3[ʿNT.VI].5.24
|ym.mšbʿt hn.b šlḥ.|ttpl.yʿn.ḥtk h.|krt yʿn.ḥtk h.rš.|mid.grdš.ṯbt h.|w b tm hn.špḥ.yitbd.|w b.pḫyr h.yrṯ.|yʿrb. 14[KRT].1.23
[-----].|[---.-]rb.|[-----].|[-----].|[-----].|k yraš w ykhp mid.|dblt yṯnt w ṣmqm yṯn[m].|w qmḥ bql yṣq aḥd h.|b a 160[55].23
r.ydk].|aḥd[h.w.yṣq.b.ap h].|k yr[a]š.šš[w.w.ykhp].|mid.dblt.yṯ[nt.w].|ṣmq[m].yṯnm.w[.qmḥ.bql].|tdkn.aḥd h. 161[56].33
hm.in mm.|nḫtu.w.lak.|ʿm y.w.yd.|ilm.p.k mtm.|ʿz.mid.|hm.nṯkp.|mʿn k.|w.mnm.|rgm.d.tšmʿ.|ṯmt.w.št.|b.s 53[54].13
|tšlm k.um y.|tdʿ.ky.ʿrbt.|l pn.špš.|w pn.špš.nr.|b y.mid.w um.|tšmḫ.m ab.|w al.trḫln.|ʿtn.ḫrd.ank.|ʿm ny.šlm 1015.10
w]m.mrkbt b trbṣ bn.amt.|[tn.b]nm.aqny.|[tn.ṯa]rm.amid.|[w yʿn].ṯr.ab h.il.|d[--].b bk.krt.|b dmʿ.nʿmn.ǵlm.|il. 14[KRT].2.58
y.|mnm.[šl]m[.r]gm[.ṯṯb].|ky.lik.bn y.|lḥt.akl.ʿm y.|mid y w ǵbn y.|w.bn y.hn kt.|yškn.anyt.|ym.yšrr.|w.ak[l.- 2061.11
m.ary k.ṣḥ.ḫrn.|b bht k.ʿḏbt.b qrb.|hkl k.tbl k.ǵrm.|mid.ksp.gbʿm.mḥmd..|ḫrṣ.w bn.bht.ksp.|w ḫrṣ.bht.ṯhrm.|i 4[51].5.94
liyn.|bʿl.ṣḥ.ḫrn.b bht h.|ʿḏbt.b qrb hkl h.|yblnn ǵrm.mid.ksp.|gbʿm lḥmd.ḫrṣ.|yblnn.udr.ilqṣm.|yak.l kṯr.w ḫss. 4[51].5.100
liyn bʿl.|ṣḥ.ḫrn.b bhm k.|ʿḏbt.b qrb.hkl k.|tbl k.ǵrm.mid.ksp.|gbʿm.mḥmd.ḫrṣ.|ybl k.udr.ilqṣm.|w bn.bht.ksp. 4[51].5.77
ṯḥm.špš.|l.ʿmrpi.rgm.|ʿm špš.kll.mid m.|šlm.|l.[--]n.špš.|ad[.ʿ]bd h.uk.škn.|k.[---.]sglt h.hw 2060.3
qrtm.ṯṯʿr.|ksat.l mhr.ṯʿr.ṯlḥnt.|l ṣbim.hdmm.l ǵzrm.|mid.tmtḫṣn.w tʿn.|ṯḫtṣb.w ṯḥdy.ʿnt.|tǵdd.kbd h.b ṣḥq.yml 3[ʿNT].2.23
mq.|[ṯḫtṣb.bn.qrtm.ṯṯʿr.ṯlḥnt.]l ṣbim.|[hdmm.l ǵzrm.mid.tmtḫṣn.w t]ʿn.ṯḫtṣb.|[w ṯḥdy.ʿnt.tǵdd.kbd h.b ṣḥ]q.yml 7.1[131].6
[-----].|[---.mid.rm.]krt.|[b tk.rpi.]arṣ.|[b pḫr].qbṣ.dtn.|[w t]qrb.w ld. 15[128].3.2
|tld.pǵ[t.---].|tld.pǵ[t.---].|tld.pǵ[t.---].|tld.p[ǵt.---].|mid.rm[.krt].|b tk.rpi.ar[ṣ].|b pḫr.qbṣ.dtn.|ṣǵrt hn.abkrn.| 15[128].3.13
|mrḥqtm.|qlny.ilm.|tǵr k.|tšlm k.|hn ny.ʿm ny.|kll.mid.|šlm.|w.ap.ank.|nḫt.ṯm ny.|ʿm.adt ny.|mnm.šlm.|rg 51[95].11
.b]nšm.b.šmny.|[---.b]nšm.b.šmngy.|[---.]bnšm.b.snr.mid.|[---.bn]šm.b.tkn.|[---.bn]šm.b.tmrm.|[---.bn]šm.b.ṯnq. 2076.26

midḫ

nnu.|šmg.|šmn.|lbnm.|ṯrm.|bṣr.|y[--].|y[--].|snr.|midḫ.|ḥ[lym].|[ḫ]lby.|ʿr.|ʿnq[pat].|glbty.|[-----].|[-----].|[- 2058.2.20
u.|ʿrm.|bṣr.|mʿr.|ḫlby.|mṣbt.|snr.|ṯm.|ubš.|glbt.|mi[d]ḫ.|mr[i]l.|ḫlb.|šld.|ʿrgz.|[-----]. 2041.12
[-].uḫ.pdm.b.yʿrt.|pǵyn.b.tpḥ.|amri[l].b.šrš.|aǵltn.b.midḫ.|[--]n.b.ayly.|[-]lyn.b.ngḥt.|[---.]b.nh[-]t.|[---.]almš.| 2118.13

midḫy

š[--]y.|šd.bn.ṯ[---].|šd.ʿdmn[.bn.]ynḥm.|šd.bn.ṯmr[n.m]idḫy.|šd.ṯbʿm[.--]y. 2026.9

miḫd

ṯ.|b.yrḫ.pgrm.|lqḥ.bʿlmʿdr.|w bn.ḫlp.|w[--]y.d.bʿl.|miḫd.b.|arbʿ.mat.|ḫrṣ. 1155.6
b.ym.ḥdṯ.|b.yr.pgrm.|lqḥ.bʿlmḏr.|w.bn.ḫlp.|miḫd.|b.arbʿ.|mat.ḫrṣ. 1156.5
mr[il.---].|ub[rʿy.---].|mi[ḫd.---].|snr[.---].|ṯm[--.---]. 2144.3

miḫdy

miḫdy[m].|bn.ḥgb[n].|bn.ulbt[-].|ḏkry[-].|bn.tlm[yn].|bn. 2017.1
miḫdym.|bn.ḥṭb.|bn abyt.|bn ḫdl.|bn ṣdqn.|bn ayy.|bn d 2016.1.1

milḫ

spr.npṣm.d yṣa.b milḫ.|ʿšrm.ḫpn.ḫmš.|kbd.w lpš.|ḫmš.mispt.|mṭ.|w lpš.d s 1109.1

mispt

.npṣm.d yṣa.b milḫ.|ʿšrm.ḫpn.ḫmš.|kbd.w lpš.|ḫmš.mispt.|mṭ.|w lpš.d sgr b h.|b d.anrmy. 1109.4

mišmn

].|b unṯ.km.špš.|d brt.kmt.|br.ṣṭqšlm.|b unṯ.ʿd ʿlm.|mišmn.nqmd.|mlk ugrt.|nqmd.mlk.ugrt.|ktb.spr hnd.|dt 1005.6

mit

l.ṯlṯt.l.ʿšrm.ksp hm.|šstm.b.šbʿm.|ṯlṯ.mat.trm.b.ʿšrt.|mit.adrm.b.ʿšrt.|ʿšr.ydt.b.ʿšrt.|ḫmš.kkrm.ṣml.|ʿšrt.ksp h.| 1127.8
n.ʿm.mlk.|bʿl h.ngr.ḥwt k.|w l.a[--]t.tšknn.|ḫmšm.l mi[t].any.|tškn[n.--]h.k[--].|w šnm[.--.]w[.--].|w ʿprm.a[--.- 2062.1.4
|krw.šlmy.|alpm.|atn.bṣry.alpm.|lbnym.|ṯm[n.]alp mitm.|ilbʿl ḫmš m[at].|ʿdn.ḫmš.mat.|bn.[-]d.alp.|bn.[-]pn. 1060.2.8
|a[--].ʿṯ.|a[l]pm.alpnm.|ṯlṯ.m[a]t.art.ḥkpt.|mit.dnn.|mitm.iqnu.|ḫmš.ʿšr.qn.nʿm.ʿn[m].|ṯn.ḥblm.alp.alp.am[-].|ṯ 1128.28

ṣ.ktn.mit.pḥm. | mit.iqni.l mlkt. | ks.ḫrṣ.ktn.mit.pḥm. | mit.iqni.l uṯryn. | ks.ksp.ktn.mit.pḥm. | mit.iqni.l tpnr. | [ks.k 64[118].30
.mit.pḥm. | mit.iqni.l tpnr. | [ks.ksp.kt]n.mit.pḥ[m]. | [mit.iqni.l]ḫbrtn[r]. | [ks.ksp.ktn.mit.pḥ]m. | [mit.iqni.l ḫbrtn 64[118].34
.pḥ[m]. | [mit.iqni.l]ḫbrtn[r]. | [ks.ksp.ktn.mit.pḥ]m. | [mit.iqni.l ḫbrtn]r ṯn. | [ks.ksp.ktn.mit.pḥm]. | [mit.iqn]i.l skl. 64[118].36
. | ugrt.d ybl.l špš. | mlk.rb.b'l h. | ks.ḫrṣ.ktn.mit.pḥm. | mit.iqni.l mlkt. | ks.ḫrṣ.ktn.mit.pḥm. | mit.iqni.l uṯryn. | ks.ks 64[118].28
pḥ]m. | [mit.iqni.l ḫbrtn]r ṯn. | [ks.ksp.ktn.mit.pḥm]. | [mit.iqn]i.l skl.[--]. | [---.m]it pḥm.l š[--]. | [---.]a[--.--.]hn[--]. 64[118].38
ktn.mit.pḥm. | mit.iqni.l uṯryn. | ks.ksp.ktn.mit.pḥm. | mit.iqni.l tpnr. | [ks.ksp.kt]n.mit.pḥ[m]. | [mit.iqni.l]ḫbrtn[r 64[118].32
sb[--]. | yqḥ.mi[t]. | b.ḥwt. 1174.2
alpm.arb'.mat.k[bd]. | mit.b d.yd[r]m. | alp ḫmš mat.kbd.d[--]. 2109.2
. | ṯmnym.ṯlṯ.kbd. | mdrǵlm. | w.šb'.'šr.ḫsnm. | ḫmšm.l.mit. | bnš.l.d. | yškb.l.b.bt.mlk. 1029.14
bnšm. | b.gt.ǵl.'šrm.l.mit.dr'.w.tš'm.drt. | [w].ṯmnym.l.mit.dd.ḥpr.bnšm. | b.gt.alḫb.ṯṯm.dr'.w.ḫmšm.drt.w.ṯṯm.dd. | 1098.15
. | b.gt.m'br.arb'm.l.mit.dr'.w.ṯmnym[.drt]. | w.'šrm.l.mit.dd.ḥp[r.]bnšm. | b.gt.ǵl.'šrm.l.mit.dr'.w.tš'm.drt. | [w].ṯ 1098.13
.ḥpr.bnšm. | b.nzl.'šrm.l.mit.dr'.w.šb'm.drt. | w.'šrm.l.mit.dd.ḥpr.bnšm. | b.y'ny.arb'm.dr'.w.'šrm.drt. | w.ṯlṯm.dd.ṯ 1098.25
.šm. | [b.---.]knm.ṯṯm.l.mit.dr'.w.mit.drt. | w[.---.]'m.l.mit.dd.ṯn.kbd.ḥpr.bnšm.ṯmnym.dd. | l u[-]m. | b.ṯbq.arb'm.d 1098.8
.b]nšm.w.ṯn.'šr h.dd.l.rpš. | [---.]šb'm.dr'.w.arb'm.drt.mit.dd. | [---].ḥpr.bn.šm. | [b.---.]knm.ṯṯm.l.mit.dr'.w.mit.drt. 1098.5
.--]r h.'šr[m.---.']šrm.dd. | [---.yn.d.]nkly.l.r'ym.šb'm.l.mitm.dd. | [---.--]d.šb'm.kbd.dr'. | [---.]kbd.ddm.kbd[.---]. | [-- 1098.44
].ygb.bq'. | a[--].'ṭ. | a[l]pm.alpnm. | ṯlṯ.m[a]t.art.ḥkpt. | mit.dnn. | mitm.iqnu. | ḫmš.'šr.qn.n'm.'n[m]. | ṯn.ḥblm.alp.al 1128.27
.arb'm.drt.mit.dd. | [---].ḥpr.bn.šm. | [b.---.]knm.ṯṯm.l.mit.dr'.w.mit.drt. | w[.---.]'m.l.mit.dd.ṯn.kbd.ḥpr.bnšm.ṯmn 1098.7
.ṯlṯm.drt. | [w].šb'm.dd.ṯn.kbd.ḥpr.bnšm. | b.nzl.'šrm.l.mit.dr'.w.šb'm.drt. | w.'šrm.l.mit.dd.ḥpr.bnšm. | b.y'ny.arb' 1098.24
[---.---.]l.mit.dr'.w.šb'm.drt. | [---.ḥpr.]bnšm.w.l.ḥrš.'rq.ṯn.'šr h. | [---. 1098.1
ym[.drt]. | w.'šrm.l.mit.dd.ḥp[r.]bnšm. | b.gt.ǵl.'šrm.l.mit.dr'.w.tš'm.drt. | [w].ṯmnym.l.mit.dd.ḥpr.bnšm. | b.gt.alḫ 1098.14
t. | w[.a]rb'.l.'šrm.dd.l.yḫšr.bl.bn h. | b.gt.m'br.arb'm.l.mit.dr'.w.ṯmnym[.drt]. | w.'šrm.l.mit.dd.ḥp[r.]bnšm. | b.gt.ǵl 1098.12
ṯṯm.dr'.w.ḫmšm.drt.w.ṯṯm.dd. | ḥpr.bnšm. | b.gt.knpy.mit.dr'.ṯṯm.drt.w.šb'm.dd.arb'. | kbd.ḥpr.bnšm. | b.gt.ṯrmn.a 1098.18
'm.drt. | [---.ḥpr.]bnšm.w.l.ḥrš.'rq.ṯn.'šr h. | [---.d]r'.w.mit.drt.w.'šrm.l.mit. | [drt.ḥpr.b]nšm.w.ṯn.'šr h.dd.l.rpš. | [-- 1098.3
t.mit.dd. | [---].ḥpr.bn.šm. | [b.---.]knm.ṯṯm.l.mit.dr'.w.mit.drt. | w[.---.]'m.l.mit.dd.ṯn.kbd.ḥpr.bnšm.ṯmnym.dd. | l 1098.7
]bnšm.w.l.ḥrš.'rq.ṯn.'šr h. | [---.d]r'.w.mit.drt.w.'šrm.l.mit. | [drt.ḥpr.b]nšm.w.ṯn.'šr h.dd.l.rpš. | [---.]šb'm.dr'.w.arb 1098.3
b.gt.ḫldy. | ṯlṯ.ma[t].'šr.kbd. | šb' m[at].kbd.ḥpr.'bdm. | mit[.d]rt.arb'm.drt. | [---]m. | t[gm]r.akl.b.gt.ǵ[l]. | ṯlṯ.mat.'šr 2013.13
n. | [tg]mr.akl.b.g[t.b]ir.alp. | [']šrm.l.mit.ḥ[p]r.'bdm. | mitm.drt.ṯmnym.drt. | tgmr.akl.b.gt[.b]'ln. | ṯlṯ.mat.ṯṯm.kbd. 2013.4
| šb'm.ṯn.kbd[.ḥpr.'b]dm. | tg[mr.---]. | [-]m.m[--.---]. | [m]itm.dr[t.---]. | [š]r.[k]bd[.---]. | [a]lpm[.---]. | tg[m]r.[---]. | ṯl 2013.22
-.---.-]dn. | arb'[m.ksp.]'l. | il[m]l[k.a]rgnd. | uškny[.w]mit. | zt.b d hm.rib. | w [---]. | [-----]. | [-]šy[.---] h. | [-]kt[.---.]n 2055.12
b.gt.mlkt.b.rḥbn. | ḫmšm.l.mitm.zt. | w.b d.krd. | ḫmšm.l.mit. | arb'.kbd. 1096.2
[sp]r.akl[.---].ṯryn. | [tg]mr.akl.b.g[t.b]ir.alp. | [']šrm.l.mit.ḥ[p]r.'bdm. | mitm.drt.ṯmnym.drt. | tgmr.akl.b.gt[.b]'ln. 2013.3
.--]. | tš'.dd.ḥ[tm.w].ḫm[šm]. | kdm.kbd.yn.b.gt.[---]. | [mi]tm.ḫmšm.ḫmš.k[bd]. | [dd].kšmm.tš'[.---]. | [š]'rm.ṯṯ.'[šr]. 2092.6
t.ṯṯm.kbd. | l.bn.yšm'. | mit.arb'm.kbd. | l.liy.bn.'myn. | mit.ḫmšm.kbd. | d.škn.l.ks.ilm. 1143.13
t. | l.udmym.b.ṯmnt.'šrt.ksp. | šb'm.lbš.d.'rb.bt.mlk. | b.mit.ḫmšt.kbd.ksp. | ṯlṯ.ktnt.b d.an[r]my. | b.'šrt.ksp.b.a[--]. | ṯ 2101.17
mit.ksp.'mn. | bn.ulbtyn. | w.kkr.ṯlṯ. | ksp.d.nkly.b.šd. | mit.ḫmšt.kbd. | [l.]gmn.bn.usyy. | mit.ṯṯm.kbd. | l.bn.yšm'. | 1143.7
ḥršḫ.b.tqlm. | w.šb'.'šr.šmn. | d.l.yṣa.bt.mlk. | tgmr.ksp.mitm. | ḫmšm.kbd. 2100.22
š kbd ktn. | ḫmš.rṭm. | ḫmš.ṯnt.d ḫmšm w. | ḫmš.ṯnt.d mit. | ḫmš.ṯnt.d ṯl | ṯ mat. | ṯṯ.ṯnt.d alp | alpm.ṯlṯ ktt. | alp.brr. | 1130.10
[---]t.ddm.š'r[m.---]. | [---].mit.ḫsw.[---]. | [----]d.n'r.ṯ[--]d[.---]. | [---.]ṯlṯ.kṯt[.-]d.[---]. | [-- 143[-].1.2
. | arb't.'šrt.ḫrṣ. | b.ṯqlm.kbd.arb'm. | 'šrt.ḫrṣ.b.arb'm. | mit.ḥršḫ.b.ṯqlm. | w.šb'.'šr.šmn. | d.l.yṣa.bt.mlk. | tgmr.ksp.m 2100.19
rat.mlḥt. | arb'.uzm.mrat.bq'. | ṯlṯ.[-]ṯt.aš[']t.šmn.uz. | mi[t].ygb.bq'. | a[--].'ṭ. | a[l]pm.alpnm. | ṯlṯ.m[a]t.art.ḥkpt. | m 1128.23
. | arb'm.kbd.yn.ṭb.w.[--]. | ṯmn.kbd.yn.d.l.ṭb.b.gn'[y]. | mitm.yn.ḥsp.d.nkly.b.db[ḥ.--]. | mit.arb'm.kbd.yn.ḥsp.l.m[-- 1084.24
.gt.m'rby. | ṯṯm.yn.ṭb.w.ḫmš.l.'šrm. | yn.d.l.ṭb.b.ulm. | mit.yn.ṭb.w.ṯṯm.ṯṯ.kbd. | yn.d.l.ṭb.b.gt.ḥdṯt. | tš'm.yn.d.l.ṭb.b. 1084.11
r.ḥlb. | ḫmš.kkr.brr. | kkr.ḫmš.mat.kbd.ṯlṯ.šm[n]. | alp.mitm.kbd.ṯlṯ.ḥlb. | šb'.l.'šrm.kkr.ṯlṯ. | d.ybl.blym. 1135.5
iršt.yṣḥm. | arb'.alpm. | mitm.kbd.ṯlṯ. | arb'.kkrm. | ṯmn.mat.kbd. | pwt. | ṯmn.mat.pṯt 2051.3
| b d.šmmn. | l argmn. | l nskm. | ṯmn.kkrm. | alp.kbd. | [m]itm.kbd. 147[90].7
bl. | [---].iqni.'šrm.ǵprt. | [---.š]pšg.iqni.mit.pṯtm. | [---].mitm.kslm. | [---].pwt.ṯlṯ.mat.abn.ṣrp. | [---.-]qt.l.ṯrmnm. | [--- 1106.9
rmy. | bt.'bd mlk. | w.snt. | bt.ugrt. | w.pdy h[m]. | iwrkl.mit. | ksp.b y[d]. | birtym. | [un]ṯ inn. | l [h]m 'd tṯtbn. | ksp.iw 1006.13
argmnm. | 'šrm.ksp.d mkr. | mlk. | ṯlṯ.mat.ksp.d.šb[n]. | mit.ksp.d.ṯbq. | ṯmnym.arb't. | kbd.ksp. | d.nqdm. | ḫmšm.l mi 2107.5
ksp.d.ṯbq. | ṯmnym.arb't. | kbd.ksp. | d.nqdm. | ḫmšm.l mit. | ksp.d.mkr.ar. | arb'm ksp d mkr. | atlg. | mit.ksp.d mkr. 2107.9
| ḫmšm.l mit. | ksp.d.mkr.ar. | arb'm ksp d mkr. | atlg. | mit.ksp.d mkr. | ilštm'. | 'šrm.l mit.ksp. | 'l.bn.alkbl.šb[ny]. | 'š 2107.13
rb'm ksp d mkr. | atlg. | mit.ksp.d mkr. | ilštm'. | 'šrm.l mit.ksp. | 'l.bn.alkbl.šb[ny]. | 'šrm ksp.'l. | wrt.mtny.w 'l. | prd 2107.15
mitm.ksp.'mn.b[n].ṣdqn. | w.kkrm.ṯlṯ. | mit.ksp.'mn. | bn.ulbtyn. | w.kkr.ṯlṯ. | ksp.d.nkly.b.šd. | mit.ḫ 1143.3
mitm.ksp.'mn.b[n].ṣdqn. | w.kkrm.ṯlṯ. | mit.ksp.'mn. | bn.ulbt 1143.1
[---.]l mitm.ksp. | [---.]skn. | [---.-]im.bṯd. | [---.b]šḥr.atlgn. | [---].b š 2167.1
b.atlg.ṯlṯ.ḫrmṯt.ṯṯm. | mḫrhn.nit.mit.krk.mit. | m'ṣd.ḫmšm.mqb.[']šrm. | b.ulm.ṯṯ.'šr h.ḫrmṯt. 2048.2
[l.]abrm.mšrm. | [mi]tm.arb'm.ṯmn.kbd. | [l.]sbrdnm. | m[i]t.l.bn.'ẓmt.rišy. | mit.l.tlmyn.bn.'dy. | [---.]l.adddy. | [--.]l. 2095.7
tm.arb'm.ṯmn.kbd. | [l.]sbrdnm. | m[i]t.l.bn.'ẓmt.rišy. | mit.l.tlmyn.bn.'dy. | [---.]l.adddy. | [--.]l.kkln. 2095.8
--]. | [-----]. | [-----]. | [-----]. | [-----]. | alp[.---.--]r. | mit.lḥ[m.---.-]dyt. | ṣl't.alp.mri. | 'šr.bmt.alp.mri. | ṯn.nšbm. | ṯ 1128.15
b.atlg.ṯlṯ.ḫrmṯt.ṯṯm. | mḫrhn.nit.mit.krk.mit. | m'ṣd.ḫmšm.mqb.[']šrm. | b.ulm.ṯṯ.'šr h.ḫrmṯt. | ṯṯ.nitm. 2048.2
[---.ṯ]lṯ.mat. | [---.m]itm.mqp.m[---]. | [---.ṯmn]ym.mgnm ar[b']. | [---.-]aḫ.mqḥ 1145.1.2
| [--.-]rṯm š[šm]n.k[--.---]. | [---.ar]b'.dblt.ḏr[--.---]. | [--.m]itm.nṣ.l bn[.---]. | [-]l[-.---]. | [-]ṯ.[---]. | mṣb[-.---]. | kṯ.aqḥ[r. 143[-].1.10
[.---]. | [---.]ṯlṯ.kṯt[.-]d.[---]. | [---.a]rb'.dblt.m[--.---]. | [--.mi]tm nṣ.[-]ṯ[-.]gr[-.---]. | [---].arb['.d]d.š['rm.---]. | [--.-]rṯm š 143[-].1.6
.yrḫ.pgrm. | lqḥ.iwrpzn. | argdd. | ṯṯkn. | ybrk. | ntbt. | b.mitm. | 'šrm. | kbd.ḫrṣ. 2006.8

.ḫsp.d.nkly.b.db[ḫ.--]. | mit.arbʻm.kbd.yn.ḫsp.l.m[--]. | mit.ʻšrm.[k]bd.yn.ḫsp.l.y[--]. | ʻšrm.yn.ḫsp.l.ql.d.tbʻ.mṣ[r]m. 1084.26
.sknm. | ʻšr.yn.ṭb.w.arbʻm.ḫmš.kbd. | yn.d.l.ṭb.gt.ṭbq. | mit.ʻšr.kbd.yn.ṭb. | w.ṯṯm.arbʻ.kbd.yn.d.l.ṭb. | b.gt.mʻrby. | ṯṯ 1084.6
mitm.ʻšr kbd. | kšmm.b.mṣbt. | mit.ʻšrm.ṯn kbd. | [kš]mm. | [ʻ] 2091.1
rbʻm. | ṣṣ iytlm mit ṯlṯm kbd. | ṣṣ m[l]k ʻšrm. | ṣṣ abš[-] mit [ʻš]r kbd. | ṣṣ yd̠rd ʻšrm. | ṣṣ bn aglby ṯlṯ[m]. | ṣṣ bn.šršʻm. 2097.11
mitm.ʻšr kbd. | kšmm.b.mṣbt. | mit.ʻšrm.ṯn kbd. | [kš]mm. | [ʻ]š[r]m.ṯn.kbd.ḥṭm. | [-]m[-.-]ʻ[-. 2091.3
ṯlṯm.dd[.---]. | b.gt.ṣb[-.---]. | mit.ʻšr.[---.]dd[.--]. | tšʻ.dd.ḥ[ṭm.w].ḫm[šm]. | kdm.kbd.yn.b. 2092.3
mit.ʻ[šr.---]. | [ṯ]lṯ.abd[.---]. | [---.]anyt[.---]. | [-----]. | ʻšrm.l.um 2110.1
.tt. | w.ṯmnt.ksp.hn. | ktn.d.ṣr.pḥm.b h.w.ṯqlm. | ksp h.mitm.pḥm.b d.skn. | w.ṯt.ktnm.ḫmšt.w.nṣp.ksp.hn. 1110.5
]r ṯn. | [ks.ksp.ktn.mit.pḥm]. | [mit.iqn]i.l skl.[--]. | [---.m]it pḥm.l š[--]. | [---.]a[--.--.]hn[--]. 64[118].39
ʻl h. | ks.ḫrṣ.ktn.mit.pḥm. | mit.iqni.l mlkt. | ks.ḫrṣ.ktn.mit.pḥm. | mit.iqni.l uṯryn. | ks.ksp.ktn.mit.pḥm. | mit.iqni.l t 64[118].29
sp.kt]n.mit.pḫ[m]. | [mit.iqni.l]ḫbrtn[r]. | [ks.ksp.ktn.mit.pḫ]m. | [mit.iqni.l ḫbrtn]r ṯn. | [ks.ksp.ktn.mit.pḥm]. | [m 64[118].35
n. | ks.ksp.ktn.mit.pḥm. | mit.iqni.l tpnr. | [ks.ksp.kt]n.mit.pḫ[m]. | [mit.iqni.l]ḫbrtn[r]. | [ks.ksp.ktn.mit.pḫ]m. | [mi 64[118].33
nqmd.mlk. | ugrt.d ybl.l špš. | mlk.rb.bʻl h. | ks.ḫrṣ.ktn.mit.pḥm. | mit.iqni.l mlkt. | ks.ḫrṣ.ktn.mit.pḥm. | mit.iqni.l u 64[118].27
ksp.ktn.mit.pḫ]m. | [mit.iqni.l ḫbrtn]r ṯn. | [ks.ksp.ktn.mit.pḥm]. | [mit.iqn]i.l skl.[--]. | [---.m]it pḥm.l š[--]. | [---.]a[- 64[118].37
kt. | ks.ḫrṣ.ktn.mit.pḥm. | mit.iqni.l uṯryn. | ks.ksp.ktn.mit.pḥm. | mit.iqni.l tpnr. | [ks.ksp.kt]n.mit.pḫ[m]. | [mit.iqni 64[118].31
ʻšr.ktnt. | ʻšr.rṯm. | kkr[.-].ḫt. | mitm[.p]ṯtm. | ṯlṯm[.---].kst. | alp.a[bn.ṣ]rp. 1114.4
all.iqni.arbʻm.kbl. | [---].iqni.ʻšrm.ǵprt. | [---.š]pšg.iqni.mit.pṯtm. | [---].mitm.kslm. | [---].pwt.ṯlṯ.mat.abn.ṣrp. | [---.-] 1106.8
[---.-]kn. | [---.]ṯlṯm. | kuwṯ.ṯlṯ.kbd. | m[i]t.arbʻt.kbd. | ḫ[mš.]šʻrt. | [---.]tšʻ.kbd.skm. | [arb]ʻm.ḫpnt. 1111.4
bd.yn.d.l.ṭb.b.gnʻ[y]. | mitm.yn.ḫsp.d.nkly.b.db[ḫ.--]. | mit.arbʻm.kbd.yn.ḫsp.l.m[--]. | mit.ʻšrm.[k]bd.yn.ḫsp.l.y[--]. 1084.25
.[k]bd.yn.ḫsp.l.y[--]. | ʻšrm.yn.ḫsp.l.ql.d.tbʻ.mṣ[r]m. | mit.arbʻm.kbd.yn.mṣb. | l.md̠rǵlm. | ʻšrn ʻšr.yn.mṣb.[-]ḫ[-].l. 1084.28
mšt.kbd. | [l.]gmn.bn.usyy. | mit.ṯṯm.kbd. | l.bn.yšmʻ. | mit.arbʻm.kbd. | l.liy.bn.ʻmyn. | mit.ḫmšm.kbd. | d.škn.l.ks.il 1143.11
t.mlkt.b.rḥbn. | ḫmšm.l.mitm.zt. | w.b d.krd. | ḫmšm.l.mit. | arbʻ.kbd. 1096.4
| l.abrm.alṯyy. | [m]it.ṯlṯm.kbd.šmn. | [l.]abrm.mšrm. | [mi]tm.arbʻm.ṯmn.kbd. | [l.]sbrdnm. | m[i]t.l.bn.ʻẓmt.rišy. | mi 2095.5
| [--]ṯ.lk[.---]. | [--]kṯ.i[---.---]. | p.šn[-.---]. | w l ṯlb.[---]. | mit.rḫ[.---]. | ṯṯlb.a[--.---]. | yšu.g h[.---]. | i.ap.bʻ[l.---]. | i.hd.d[5[67].4.3
mit.šmn.d.nm[-.]b d.mzy.alzy. | ḫmš.kkr.ḥlb. | ḫmš.kkr.brr. | 1135.1
š.ktnt. | ḫmš.ṯnt.alpm. | ʻšrm.hbn. | ṯlṯ.mat.dd. | šʻrm. | mit.šmn. | ʻšr.kat. | ẓrw. 2102.9
ṯṯ.mat.ksp. | ḥṭbn.ybnn. | arbʻm.l.mit.šmn. | arbʻm.l.mit.tišr. | ṯṯ.ṯṯ.b [ṯ]ql.ṯlṯt.l.ʻšrm.ksp hm. | šs 1127.3
ḫpn.d.iqni.w.šmt. | l.iybʻl. | ṯlṯm.l.mit.šʻrt. | l.šr.ʻṯtrt. | mlbš.ṯrmnm. | k.ytn.w.b.bt. | mlk.mlbš. | y 1107.3
.km[m.---]. | w.l ll.ʻṣrm.w [---]. | kmm.w.in.ʻṣr[.---]. | w mit.šʻrt.[-]y[-.---]. | w.kdr.w.npt t[--.---]. | w.ksp.yʻdb.[---]. 38[23].9
trt[.---]. | ʻlm.kmm[.---]. | w b ṯlṯ.ṣ[in.---]. | l ll.pr[-.---]. | mit šʻ[rt.---]. | ptr.k[--.---]. | [-]yu[-.---]. 37[22].10
ṯṯ.mat.ksp. | ḥṭbn.ybnn. | arbʻm.l.mit.šmn. | arbʻm.l.mit.tišr. | ṯṯ.ṯṯ.b [ṯ]ql.ṯlṯt.l.ʻšrm.ksp hm. | šstm.b.šbʻm. | ṯlṯ.ma 1127.4
ʻ.mat. | l.alp.šmn. | nḥ.ṯṯ.mat. | šm[n].rqḥ. | kkrm.brd̠l. | mit.tišrm. | ṯlṯm.almg. | ḫmšm.kkr. | qnm. | ʻšrm.kk[r]. | brr. | [ʻ 141[120].7
ṯlṯ.mat[.---.]kbd. | ṯṯ.ddm.k[--.b]rqd. | mit.tšʻm.[kb]d.ddm. | b.gt.bir. 2168.3
mšq.mlkt. | mitm.ṯṯm. | kbd.ks[p]. | ksp. | ṯmnym. | ḫrṣ. 1157.2
lṯ. | ksp.d.nkly.b.šd. | mit.ḫmšt.kbd. | [l.]gmn.bn.usyy. | mit.ṯṯm.kbd. | l.bn.yšmʻ. | mit.arbʻm.kbd. | l.liy.bn.ʻmyn. | mit 1143.9
ṯṯ.kbd.md̠rǵlm. | ʻšrm.aḥd.kbd.ḫsnm. | ubnyn. | ṯṯm[.l.]mit.ṯlṯ. | kbd[.tg]mr.bnš. | l.b.bt.mlk. 1028.12
ṯ l ʻšrm. | ṣṣ bn adty ḫmšm. | ṣṣ amtrn arbʻm. | ṣṣ iytlm mit ṯlṯm kbd. | ṣṣ m[l]k ʻšrm. | ṣṣ abš[-] mit [ʻš]r kbd. | ṣṣ yd̠rd 2097.9
ṯṯ.mat.ṯṯm.kbd šmn. | l.abrm.alṯyy. | [m]it.ṯlṯm.kbd.šmn. | [l.]abrm.mšrm. | [mi]tm.arbʻm.ṯmn.kbd 2095.3
mit.ṯlṯ.mḫsrn. | ʻl.nsk.kttǵlm. | arbʻm.ṯlṯ.mḫsrn. | mtbʻl.rišy. | 1137.1
. | tšʻm.md̠rǵlm. | arbʻ.l ʻšrm.ḫsnm. | ʻšr.hbṭnm. | ṯṯm.l.mit.ṯn.kbd. | tgmr. 1030.10
ṯmn. | md̠rǵlm. | ṯmnym.ṯmn.kbd. | tgmr.ḫrd. | arbʻm.l.mit. | ṯn.kbd. 1031.16
mḫsrn.d.[--.]ušknym. | brq.ṯlṯ.[mat.ṯ]lṯ. | bsn.mi[t.--]. | ar[--.---]. | k[--.---]. 1136.3
ṯlṯ[m]. | ṣṣ bn.šršʻm.[---]. | ṣṣ mlknʻm.a[rbʻm]. | ṣṣ mlk mit[.---]. | ṣṣ igy.ḫmšm. | ṣṣ yrpi m[it.---]. | ṣṣ bn.š[m]mn ʻ[šr.- 2097.16
knʻm.a[rbʻm]. | ṣṣ mlk mit[.---]. | ṣṣ igy.ḫmšm. | ṣṣ yrpi m[it.---]. | ṣṣ bn.š[m]mn ʻ[šr.---]. | alp.ṯṯm. | kbd.mlḥt. 2097.18
.a]drt. | [--.ṯṯ]m.ṯmn.k[bd]. | [---.yr]yt.dq[-]. | [--.ṯ]lṯm.l.mi[t]. | [---.]arbʻ.kbd. 2170.5
spr.gt.r[---]. | ʻšrm.l.m[it.---]. | šd.dr[-.---]. 1105.2
.ṯṯ.ʻ[šr]. | [dd].ḥṭm.w.ḫ[mšm]. | [ṯ]lṯ kbd.yn.b [gt.---]. | mit.[---].ṯlṯ.kb[d]. | [dd.--]m.šbʻ.[---]. | [---].ʻšr.dd[.---]. | [---]m 2092.11
m[.---]. | [---.--]m.bn l[---]. | [---].bn ṣd[-.---]. | [---.--]mn.mi[t.---]. | [---.ṯm]nym[.---]. | [---.-]dn.ṯlṯ[m.---]. | [---].mitm[.-- 149[99].9
n.mi[t.---]. | [---.ṯm]nym[.---]. | [---.-]dn.ṯlṯ[m.---]. | [---].mitm[.---]. | [---.--]m.mšrn[.---]. 149[99].12
[-----]. | [---.ʻ]šr[.---]. | [---.-]ʻrm. | [---.--]n.ʻšrm. | [---.-]rn.mit.[---]. | [---.--]t. | [---.]ḫmšt.ʻšrt. | [---.]ʻšrm. | [---.--]št.ʻšrt. | [- 2054.2.5
mš[.---]. | [--.-]rn.ʻrbt[.---]. | [---].ṯmnym[.---]. | [---.--]p.mit[.---]. 151[25].6
n. | ḫ[m]št[.ʻ]šrt. | [ar]bʻm.ksp. | [---]yn. | [---.]ksp. | [---.]mit. | [-----]. 1083.18

mud

rb[.---]. | w lk.ilm.[---]. | w rgm.l [---]. | b mud.ṣin[.---]. | mud.ṣin[.---]. | iṯm.mui[-.---]. | dm.mt.aṣ[ḫ.---]. | ydd.b qr[b.-- 5[67].3.23
[ḫ.---]. | yd.b qrb[.---]. | w lk.ilm.[---]. | w rgm.l [---]. | b mud.ṣin[.---]. | mud.ṣin[.---]. | iṯm.mui[-.---]. | dm.mt.aṣ[ḫ.---]. 5[67].3.22
[.---]. | w lk.ilm[.---]. | nʻm.ilm[.---]. | šgr.mu[d.---]. | šgr.mud[.---]. | dm.mt.aṣ[ḫ.---]. | yd.b qrb[.---]. | w lk.ilm.[---]. | w 5[67].3.17
---]. | ṯmm.w lk[.---]. | w lk.ilm[.---]. | nʻm.ilm[.---]. | šgr.mu[d.---]. | šgr.mud[.---]. | dm.mt.aṣ[ḫ.---]. | yd.b qrb[.---]. | w 5[67].3.16

mbk

np[.---]. | [---.]ylm.b[n.ʻ]n k.ṣmdm.špk[.---]. | [---.]nt[-.]mbk kpt.w[.--].b g[--]. | [---.]ḫ[--.]bnt.ṣʻṣ.bnt.ḫkp[.---]. | [---].a 1001.1.17
n.bt šmm w thm. | qrit.l špš.um h.špš.um.ql.bl.ʻm. | il.mbk nhrm.b ʻdt.thmtm. | mnt.nṯk.nḥš.šmrr.nḥš. | ʻq šr.ln h. UG5.7.3
]m.t[ḥt.ʻnt.arṣ.ṯlṯ.mtḥ.ǵyrm]. | [idk.]l ytn.pnm.ʻm.[i]l.mbk.[nhrm.qrb.apq.thmtm]. | [ygly.]d̠l i[l].w ybu[.q]rš.mlk[2.3[129].4

k bn.aṯrt[.td‘ṣ.]p‘n.|[w tr.a]rṣ.id[k.l ttn.p]nm.|[‘m.i]l.mbk.nhr[m.qr]b.[ap]q.|[thm]tm.tgl.ḏ[d.]i[l.]w tbu.|[qr]š.m 3[‘NT.VI].5.14
aṯr.btlt.‘nt.|w b‘l.tb‘.mrym.ṣpn.|idk.l ttn.pnm.|‘m.il.mbk.nhrm.|qrb.apq.thmtm.|tgly.ḏd.il.w tbu.|qrš.mlk.ab.š 4[51].4.21
[idk.l ttn.pnm].|[‘m.il.mbk.nhrm].|[qrb.apq.thmtm].|[tgly.ḏd.il.w]tb[a].|[qrš.ml 5[67].6.02
bm.‘[--].|[---.]zr h.ybm.l ilm.|[id]k.l ttn.pnm.‘m.|[il.]mbk nhrm.qrb.|[a]pq.thmtm.tgly.ḏd.|il.w tbu.qrš..|mlk.ab 6.1.33[49.1.5]
.‘mq.nšm.|[td‘ṣ.p‘n]m.w tr.arṣ.idk.|[l ttn.pn]m.‘m il.mbk.nhrm.|[qrb.ap]q.thmtm tgly.ḏd il.|[w tbu.qr]š.mlk.ab 17[2AQHT].6.47

mgdl

s[rr.]‘ṣr.|dbḥ.ṣ[q.b gl]l.ḥtṯ.|yn.b gl[.ḫ]rṣ.nbt.|‘l.l ẓr.[mg]dl.|w ‘l.l ẓr.[mg]dl.rkb.|ṯkmm.ḥm[t].ša.yd k.|šmm.db 14[KRT].2.73
q.b g]l.ḥtṯ.|yn.b gl[.ḫ]rṣ.nbt.|‘l.l ẓr.[mg]dl.|w ‘l.l ẓr.[mg]dl.rkb.|ṯkmm.ḥm[t].ša.yd k.|šmm.dbḥ.l ṯr.|ab k.il.šrd. 14[KRT].2.74
srr.‘ṣr.db[ḥ].|yṣq.b gl.ḥtṯ.yn.|b gl.ḫrṣ.nbt.w ‘ly.|l ẓr.mgdl.rkb.|ṯkmm.ḥmt.nša.|[y]d h.šmmh.dbḥ.|l ṯr.ab h.il.šr 14[KRT].4.166
-]r.almd k.[---].|[---.]qrt.ablm.a[blm].|[qrt.zbl.]yrḫ.d mgdl.š[---].|[---.]mn.‘r hm[.---].|[---.]it[.---].|[---.]‘p[.---]. 18[3AQHT].1.31

mgdly

.pyn.arty[.---].|ṯlṯ.krm.ubdym.l mlkt.b.‘nmky[.---].|mgdly.ǵlpṯr.ṯn.krmm.w.ṯlṯ.ub[dym.---].|qmnz.ṯṯ.krm.ykn‘ 1081.10
ny.w.aṯt h..b[n.---].|prd.m‘qby[.w.---.a]ṯt h[.---].|prṯ.mgd[ly.---.]aṯ[t h].|‘dyn[.---].|w.ṯn[.bn h.---].|iwrm[-.]b[n.- 2044.11

mglb

n.[---].|bn.ṯ‘l[-].|bn.nq[ly].|bn.snr[n].|bn.pzn[y].|bn.mg[lb].|bn.db[--].|bn.amd[n].|annš[-]. 2020.11
‘zn.bn.irbn.|bn.mglb.|bn.ntp.|‘myn.bn ǵḥpn.|bn.kbln.|bn.bly.|bn.ṯ‘y.|bn. 104[316].2
|bn.tgd.|bn.d[-]n.|bn.amdn.|bn.ṯmrn.|bn.pzny.|bn.mglb.|bn.[--]b.|bn.[---].|bn.[---]. 113[400].6.32
].|bn.prsn.|bn.mtyn.|bn.ḫlpn.|bn.ḥgbn.|bn.szn.|bn.mglb. 117[325].2.10

mgmr

š.|ytn.l hm.|šb‘.lbšm.allm.|l ušḫry.|ṯlṯ.mat.pṯtm.|l.mgmr.b.ṯlṯ.|šnt. 1107.12
d.|[l.i]lt.qb[-.---].|[l.a]rṣy.|[l.--]r[-.---].|[l.--]ḥl.|[l.--.]mgmr.|[l.-.]qdšt.|l.‘ṯtrt.ndrgd.|l.‘ṯtrt.abḏr.|l.dml.|l.ilt[.-]p 1001.1.11
.ḫmš.am[--.---].|[---.--]m.qmṣ.ṯlṯm.i[qnu.---].|[b.yr]ḫ.mgmr.mš[--.---].|[---].iqnu.ḫmš[.---].|[b.yr]ḫ.pgrm[.---]. 1106.38
b yrḫ.mgm[r.---].|yṣu.ḫlpn[.---].|ṯlṯ.dt.p[--.---].|dt.ṯgmi.[---].|b d 1159.1
[---.y]rḫ.n[ql.---].|[---.]m[---].|[---.yr]ḫ.mgm[r.---].|[---.--]š.b d.h[--.---].|[---.y]rḫ.dbḥ[.---].|[---.-]pn 1160.3

mgn

t.iš[--].|[b]n.b‘l[--].|bn.gld.|bn.ṣmy.|bn.mry[n].|bn.mgn.|bn.‘dn.|bn.knn.|bn.py.|bn.mk[-].|bn.by[--].|bn.a[--] 2117.1.6
btlt.‘nt.nmgn.|[-]m.rbt.aṯrt.ym.|[nǵ]ẓ.qnyt.ilm.|[---].nmgn.hwt.|[--].aliyn.b‘l.|[--.]rbt.aṯrt.ym.|[---.]btlt.‘nt.|[--.t 4[51].3.36
|[-]r[-]k.bm.ymn.|tlk.škn.‘l.ṣrrt.|adn k.šqrb.[---].|b mgn k.w ḫrṣ.l kl.|apnk.ǵzr.ilḥu.|[m]rḫ h.yiḫd.b yd.|[g]rgr 16.1[125].45
[---.ṯ]lṯ.mat.|[---.m]itm.mqp.m[---].|[---.ṯmn]ym.mgnm ar[b‘].|[---.-]aḫ.mqḥ mqḥm.|[---.--]t.‘šr rmǵt.[--].|[-- 1145.1.3
.rbt[.a]ṯrt ym.|tǵẓyn.qnyt.ilm.|w t‘n.rbt.aṯrt ym.|ik.tmgnn.rbt.|aṯrt.ym.tǵẓyn.|qnyt.ilm.mgntm.|ṯr.il.d pid.hm. 4[51].3.28
b h.tdmmt.amht.|aḫr.mǵy.aliyn.b‘l.|mǵyt.btlt.‘nt.|tmgnn.rbt[.a]ṯrt ym.|tǵẓyn.qnyt.ilm.|w t‘n.rbt.aṯrt ym.|ik. 4[51].3.25
|mṯb.arṣy.bt.y‘bdr.|ap.mṯn.rgmm.|argm k.šskn m‘.|mgn.rbt.aṯrt ym.|mǵẓ.qnyt.ilm.|hyn.‘ly.l mpḫm.|b d.ḫss. 4[51].1.22
[i]k.mgn.rbt.aṯrt.|[ym].mǵẓ.qnyt.ilm.|w tn.bt.l b‘l.km.|[i]lm.w 8[51FRAG].1
.rbt.aṯrt ym.|ik.tmgnn.rbt.|aṯrt.ym.tǵẓyn.|qnyt.ilm.mgntm.|ṯr.il.d pid.hm.ǵẓtm.|bny.bnwt w t‘n.|btlt.‘nt.nmg 4[51].3.30
gntm.|ṯr.il.d pid.hm.ǵẓtm.|bny.bnwt w t‘n.|btlt.‘nt.nmgn.|[-]m.rbt.aṯrt.ym.|[nǵ]ẓ.qnyt.ilm.|[---].nmgn.hwt.|[- 4[51].3.33

mgr

.|‘ṯtrt.t‘db.nšb l h.|w ‘nt.ktp.b hm.yg‘r.ṯǵr.|bt.il.pn.l mgr lb.t‘dbn.|nšb.l inr.t‘dbn.ktp.|b il ab h.g‘r.yṯb.il.kb[-].| UG5.1.1.12

mgšḫ

-.---].|mǵ[-.---].|šp[š.---].|ql.[---].|w mlk[.nhš.w mlk.mg]šḫ.|‘mn.[---].|ik y.[---].|w l n[qmd.---].|[w]nqmd.[---]. 64[118].6
-.--]s‘.hn.mlk.|[---.l]qḥ.hn.l.ḥwt h.|[---.--]p.hn.ib.d.b.mgšḫ.|[---.i]b.hn[.w.]ht.ank.|[---.--]š[-.--].w.ašt.|[---].amr k 1012.10

mgṯ

|w ilḥm.mgṯ.w iṯrm.|tšm‘.mtt.ḥry.|ṭṭbḫ.imr.w lḥm.|mgṯ.w yṯrm.hn.ym.|w ṯn.yṯb.krt.l ‘d h.|yṯb.l ksi mlk.|l nḫt 16.6[127].21
krt.ṯ‘.yšu.g h.|w yṣḥ.šm‘.l mtt.|ḥry.ṭbḫ.imr.|w ilḥm.mgṯ.w iṯrm.|tšm‘.mtt.ḥry.|ṭṭbḫ.imr.w lḥm.|mgṯ.w yṯrm.h 16.6[127].18

md

khnm.|qdšm.|mkrm.|mdm.|inšt.|ḥrš.bhtm. 75[81].4
qd[šm].|mru s[kn].|mru ib[rn].|mdm.|inšt.|nsk ksp.|yṣḥm.|ḥrš mrkbt.|ḥrš qṭn.|ḥrš bhtm 73[114].4
[‘]b[dm].|‘šrm.|inšt.|mdm.|gt.mlkym.|yqšm.|kbšm.|trrm.|khnm.|kzym.|yṣrm 74[115].4
spr.npṣ.krw.|ṯt.ḫtrm.ṯn.kst.|spl.mšlt.w.mqḥm.|w md h.|arn.w mznm.|ṯn.ḫlpnm.|ṯt.mrḥm.|drb.|mrbd.|mš 2050.4
h[.b yd h].|plk.qlt.b ymn h.|npyn h.mks.bšr h.|tmt‘.md h.b ym.ṯn.|npyn h.b nhrm.|štt.ḫptr.l išt.|ḫbrt.l ẓr.pḥm 4[51].2.6
šyn.|šb[‘.--]n.[k]bd.|w[.---.]qm‘t.|[---.]mdrǵlm.|[---.]mdm.|[w].‘šr.dd.l np[l].|r[p]š. 2012.25
n.yš[-]n.|bn.pd[y].|ttn.|md.‘ṯt[rt].|kṯkt.|bn.ṯtn[--].|[m]d.m[--].|[b]n.annḏ[r].|bn.ṯdyy.|bn.grbn.|[--.]ully.|[--]ṯi 1054.2.1
[---].md.‘[ṯtr]t.|ydy.|bn.škn.|bn.mdt.|bn.ḫ[--]y.|bn.‘[-]y.|kn‘m 1054.1.1
bn.ḫ[--]y.|bn.‘[-]y.|kn‘m.|bn.yš[-]n.|bn.pd[y].|ttn.|md.‘ṯt[rt].|kṯkt.|bn.ṯtn[--].|[m]d.m[--].|[b]n.annḏ[r].|bn.ṯ 1054.1.11
ubdy.mdm.|šd.b d.‘bdmlk.|šd.b d.yšn.ḥrš.|šd.b d.aupš.|šd.b d.r 82[300].1.1
.|bn kdrn.|awldn.|arswn.y‘r[ty.--].|bn.ugr.|gny.|ṯn.mdm. 86[305].13

mdb

d ad. | w hl h.tṣḥ.um.um.tirk m.yd.il.k ym. | w yd il.k mdb.ark.yd.il.k ym. | w yd.il.k mdb.yqḥ.il.mšt'ltm. | mšt'ltm 23[52].34

b'l.yṯb.k tbt.ġr.hd.r['y]. | k mdb.b tk.ġr h.il ṣpn.b [tk]. | ġr.tliyt.šb't.brqm.[---]. | ṯmnt.iṣr UG5.3.1.2

ṭ.km.ṣq.ṣdr[.---]. | [---.]kl.b kl.l pgm.pgm.l.b[---]. | [---.]mdbm.l ḫrn.ḫr[n.---]. | [---.--]m.ql.hm[.---]. | [---].aṯt n.r[---]. | 1001.1.27

.yd.il.k ym. | w yd il.k mdb.ark.yd.il.k ym. | w yd.il.k mdb.yqḥ.il.mšt'ltm. | mšt'ltm.l riš.agn.yqḥ.tš.b bt h. | il.ḥṭ h. 23[52].35

t. | [---].ṯllt.khn[m.---.]k p'n. | [---.--]y.yd.nšy.[---.--]š.l mdb. | [---] h.mẖlpt[.---.--]r. | [---.]n'lm.[---]. | [---].hn.al[-.---]. UG5.8.48

mdbr

. | aṯrt.qḥ. | ksan k.ḥdg k. | ḥtl k.w ẓi. | b aln.tk m. | b tk.mlbr. | ilšiy. | kry amt. | 'pr.'ẓm yd. | ugrm.ḫl.ld. | aklm.tbrk k. 12[75].1.21

ṯn.aṯt h. | w l nkr.mddt. | km irby.tškn. | šd.k ḥsn.pat. | mdbr.tlkn. | ym.w ṯn.aḫr. | šp[š]m.b [ṯ]lṯ. | ym[ġy.]l qdš. | a[ṯrt 14[KRT].4.194

| aṯt h.lm.nkr. | mddt h.k irby. | [t]škn.šd. | km.ḥsn.pat.mdbr. | lk.ym.w ṯn.ṯlṯ.rb' ym. | ḫmš.ṯdṯ.ym.mk.špšm. | b šb'. 14[KRT].2.105

b'.šnt. | tmt.ṯmn.nqpt.'d.ilm.n'mm.ttlkn. | šd.tṣdn.pat.mdbr.w ngš.hm.nġr. | mdr'.w ṣḥ hm.'m.nġr.mdr' y.nġr. | nġr 23[52].68

bṯt. | km.ibrm. | w b hm.pn.b'l. | b'l.ytlk.w yṣd. | yḥ pat.mlbr. | wn.ymġy.aklm. | w ymẓa.'qqm. | b'l.ḥmd m.yḥmd m. 12[75].1.35

šmal.b p hm.w l.tšb'n y.aṯt.itrḫ. | y bn.ašld.šu.'db.tk.mdbr qdš. | ṯm tgrgr.l abnm.w l.'ṣm.šb'.šnt. | tmt.ṯmn.nqpt.' 23[52].65

.n['mm.---]. | w ysmm.bn.š[---]. | ytnm.qrt.l 'ly[.---]. | b mdbr.špm.yd[.---.---]r. | l riš hm.w yš[--.--]m. | lḥm.b lḥm ay. 23[52].4

d ṯbil. | 'ṯtrt ṣwd[t.---]. | tlk b mdb[r.---]. | ṯḥdṯn w hl[.---]. | w tglṯ thmt.'[--.---]. | yṣi.ġl h tḥ 2001.1.3

mdgkbr

[---.]l mdgkbr. | [---] y.'m k. | [-]tn.l.stn. | [--.]d.n'm.lbš k. | [-]dm.ṯn 2128.1.1

mdgt

.w yqḥ b hm. | aqht.ybl.l qẓ.ybky.w yqbr. | yqbr.nn.b mdgt.b knk[-]. | w yšu.g h.w yṣḥ.knp.nšrm. | b'l.yṯbr.b'l.yṯbr. 19[1AQHT].3.147

mddb'l

qrṭym.mddb'l. | kdn.zlyy. | krwn.arty. | tlmu.zlyy. | pdu.qmnzy. | bdl. 89[312].1

[---]ym.mddb'l. | [---]n.bn.agyn. | [--]ṯn. | [--]tn.bn.aḏmṯn. | [-]tn bn.ag 94[313].1

mdẖl

ḥrm. | bn.bty. | 'by. | šm[n].bn.apn. | krty. | bn.ubr. | [bn] mdẖl. | bn.sy[n]n. | bn.śrn. 2078.20

mdl

sk[.šlm.]l kbd.arṣ. | ar[bdd.]l kb[d.š]dm.yšt. | [----.]b'l.mdl h.yb'r. | [---.]rn h.aqry. | [---.]b a[r]ṣ.mlḥmt. | ašt[.b ']p[r 3['NT].4.70

.'gl. | [---.-]nk.aštn.b ḫrt. | ilm.arṣ.w at.qḥ. | 'rpt k.rḥ k.mdl k. | mṭrt k.'m k.šb't. | ġlm k.ṯmn.ḫnzr k. | 'm k.pdry.bt.a 5[67].5.7

']. | pġt.ṯkmt.my.ḥspt.l[š']r.ṭl. | yd't.hlk.kbkbm. | bkm.tmdln.'r. | bkm.tṣmd.pḥl.bkm. | tšu.ab h.tštnn.l[b]mt 'r. | l ys 19[1AQHT].2.57

]. | šm'.pġt.ṯkmt[.my]. | ḥspt.l š'r.ṭl.yd['t]. | hlk.kbkbm.mdl.'r. | ṣmd.pḥl.št.gpn y dt ksp. | dt.yrq.nqbn y.tš[m']. | pġt. 19[1AQHT].2.52

t.yr[q.nqbnm]. | 'db.gpn.atnt[y]. | yšm'.qd.w amr[r]. | mdl.'r.ṣmd.pḥl. | št.gpnm.dt.ksp. | dt.yrq.nqbnm. | 'db.gpn.at 4[51].4.9

t]. | aṯr[t.ym.šm'.l qdš]. | w am[rr.l dgy.rbt]. | aṯrt.ym[.mdl.'r]. | ṣmd.pḥl[.št.gpnm.dt]. | ksp.dt.yr[q.nqbnm]. | 'db.gp 4[51].4.4

[.---]. | w m'n[.---]. | w bn[š.---]. | d bnš.ḥm[r.---]. | w d.l mdl.r[--.---]. | w ṣin.'z.b['l.---]. | llu.bn[š.---]. | imr.ḫ[--.---]. | [-- 2158.1.13

.i[--.---]. | [---].ṭp[--.---]. | [---.a]ḥt.b d[.---]. | [---.]b d.rb.[m]dlm. | [---.l i]ytlm. | [---].gmn. | [---].l.urġṯṯb. | [---.]l.'ṯtrum. 2162.B.2

mdn

b'lm'ḏr. | bn.mdn. | mkrm. 1168.2

mdnt

mr.ḥlqm.b mm[']. | mhrm.mṭm.tgrš. | šbm.b ksl.qšt h.mdnt. | w hln.'nt.l bt h.tmġyn. | tštql.ilt.l hkl h. | w l.šb't.tmt 3['NT].2.16

md'

.---]. | l.mḏrġlm[.---]. | ṯlṯ.mat.ḫmšm.kb[d]. | ḫmš.kbd.l.md'. | b yr[ḫ.iṯtb]nm. | ṯlṯ[.mat.a]rb'.kbd. | w.[---.-]m't. | ṯlṯ[m. 2012.12

| ršpab.rb 'šrt.m[r]yn. | pġḏn.ilb'l.krwn.lbn.'dn. | ḫyrn.md'. | šm'n.rb 'šrt.kkln.'bd.abṣn. | šdyn.unn.dqn. | 'bd'nt.rb 'š 2011.4

mdr'

.ḥmrm. | b.gt.gwl.ṯmn.ṣmdm. | w.arb'.'šr.bnš. | yd.nġr.mdr'.yd.š[--]m. | [b.]gt.ipṯl.ṯṯ.ṣmdm. | [w.']šr.bn[š]m.y[d].š[-- 2038.6

. | b yṯbmlk. | kdm.ġbiš ḫry. | ḫmš yn.b d. | bḥ mlkt. | b mdr'. | ṯlṯ bt.il | ann. | kd.bt.ilann. 1090.16

t.ḥršm. | ṯn.ḥršm. | [-]nbkm. | ṯn.ḥršm. | b.gt.ġl. | [-.]nġr.mdr'. | [-].nġr[.--]m. | [--.]psl.qšt. | [ṯl]ṯ.psl.ḥẓm. | [---.ḥ]rš.mr[1024.3.16

mdt

[---].md.'[ṯtr]t. | ydy. | bn.škn. | bn.mdt. | bn.ḫ[--]y. | bn.'[-]y. | kn'm. | bn.yš[-]n. | bn.pd[y]. | ttn. | 1054.1.4

].ḥdṯ. | [---.š]mt. | [---].y[--.--]m. | [---.--]n.d[--.--]i. | [--]t.mdt h[.l.]'ṯtrt.šd. | [---.-]rt.mḫṣ.bnš.mlk.yb'l hm. | [---.--]t.w. 1106.52

mdṯn

[---].ydm. | [---].ṯdr. | [---.]mdṯn.ipd. | [---.]m[---.]d.mškbt. | [---.--]m. | [---].ṯlḥn. | [---].ṯn 1152.1.3

mḏl

i[-.--]. | [-----]. | [---.--]y. | [---.--]lm. | ḫḏmḏr.b.kṯ[t]ġlm. | mḏl.b.kṯtġlm. 2118.24

mḏ'

up[š.--].bsbn hzpḫ ṯlṯt. | kṯr[.---.--]trt ḫmšt.bn gda[.-.]mḏ'. | kl[--.---.]ṯmnt.[--.]w[.---]. | [-]m[.---.]ṣpiry[.ṯ]lṯt[.---]. APP.II[173].59

mḏrn

]r hm. | [---].ššb. | [---.]tr h. | [a]rbʻ.qlʻm. | arbʻ.mḏrnm. | mḏrn.w.mšḫṭ. | d.mrkbt. | mlk. | mšḫṭ.w.msg. | d.tbk. 1122.12
py. | [---.t]r hm. | [---].ššb. | [---.]tr h. | [a]rbʻ.qlʻm. | arbʻ.mḏrnm. | mḏrn.w.mšḫṭ. | d.mrkbt. | mlk. | mšḫṭ.w.msg. | d.tbk 1122.11

mḏrǵl

dd. | [bʻ]l.tǵpṯm. | [k]rwn. | ḥrš.mrkbt. | mnḥm. | mṣrn. | mḏrǵlm. | agmy. | ʻdyn. | ʻbdbʻl. | ʻbdkṯr.ʻbd. | tdǵl. | bʻlṣn. | nsk. 1039.2.16
[.---].alpm. | arbʻ.ddm.l.k[-]ḫ. | ṯmnym.dd.dd.kbd. | [l].mḏr[ǵ]lm. | b yrḫ[ri]šyn. | šb[ʻ.--]n.[k]bd. | w[.---.]qmʻt. | [---.] 2012.20
]. | bn.ild[-]. | [-----]. | [bn.]nnr. | [bn.]aglby. | [bn.]bʻly. | [mḏ]rǵlm. | [bn.]kdgdl. | [b]n.qṭn. | [b]n.ǵrgn. | [b]n.tgḏn. | bn.ḫ 104[316].8
. | bn.sgr. | bn.aǵltn. | bn.ktln. | bn.ʻgwn. | bn.yšmʻ. | bdl.mḏrǵlm. | bn.mmy. | bn.ḫnyn. | bn.knn. | khnm. | bn.ṯʻy. | w.nḥ 104[316].9
k[.b]d.skn. | bn.yḥnn.aḏddy. | bn.pdǵy.mḫdy. | bn.yyn.mḏrǵl. | bn.ʻlr. | ḫṭpy.aḏddy. | ynḥm.aḏddy. | ykny.aḏddy. | m[2014.18
mṣry.d.ʻrb.b.unṯ. | bn.qrrn.mḏrǵl. | bn.tran.mḏrǵl | bn.ilh.mḏrǵl | špšyn.b.ulm. | bn.qṭn.b 2046.1.2
mḏrǵlm.dt.inn. | b d.tlmyn. | b d.gln.ary. | tgyn.yʻrty. | bn.krw 2071.1
mḏrǵlm.d inn. | msgm.l hm. | pʻṣ.ḫbty. | artyn.ary. | brqn.ṯlḥy 118[306].1
mḏrǵlm.d.b.i[-]ʻlt.mlk. | arsw. | dqn. | ṯlṯ.klbm. | ḫmn. | [---.-]rs 86[305].1
spr.mḏr[ǵlm]. | lt.hlk.b[.---]. | bn.bʻyn.š[--.---]. | aǵltn.mid[-.---]. | 87[64].1
.bn.mrynm. | arbʻ.ṯrtnm. | tšʻ.ḫbṭnm. | ṯmnym.ṯlṯ.kbd. | mḏrǵlm. | w.šbʻ.ʻšr.ḫsnm. | ḫmšm.l.mit. | bnš.l.d. | yškb.l.b.bt. 1029.12
]. | kd.l.aṯr[y]m. | kdm.ʻm.[--]n. | kd.mštt.[---]n. | kdm.l.mḏrǵlm. | kd.l.mṣrym. | kd.mštt.mlk. | kd.bn.amht [-]t. | w.bn 1089.6
. | arbʻ l.mry[nm]. | kdm l.ḫty.[---]. | kdm l.ʻṯr[t]. | kd l.m[ḏ]rǵl[m]. | kd l.mryn[m]. 1091.11
šbʻ.yn.l [---]. | ṯlṯ.l ḥr[š.---]. | ṯṯ[.l.]mštt[.---]. | ṯlṯ.l.mḏr[ǵlm]. | kd[.--].lm[d.---]. | kd[.l.]ḫzr[m.---]. | kd[.l.]ṯrtn[m 1091.4
ʻnqpat. | ṭbq. | hzp. | gnʻy. | mʻrby. | [ṣ]ʻq. | [š]ḥq. | nʻrm. | mḫrǵlm. | kzym. | mru.skn. | mru.ibrn. | pslm. | šrm. | yṣḥm. | ʻš 71[113].61
]krm. | tšʻ.hbṭnm. | ʻšr.mrum. | šbʻ.ḫsnm. | tšʻm.ṯṯ.kbd.mḏrǵlm. | ʻšrm.aḥd.kbd.ḫsnm. | ubnyn. | ṯṯm[.l.]mit.ṯlṯ. | kbd[. 1028.9
m.yn.ḥsp.l.ql.d.tbʻ.mṣ[r]m. | mit.arbʻm.kbd.yn.mṣb. | l.mḏrǵlm. | ʻšrn ʻšr.yn.mṣb.[-]ḫ[-].l.gzzm. 1084.29
| yṣrm. | mru.ibrn. | mru.skn. | nsk.ksp | mḫṣm. | ksdm. | mḏrǵlm. | pslm. | yṣḥm. 74[115].17
.ṯrtnm. | ḫmš.bn.mrynm. | ʻšr.mrum.w.šbʻ.ḫsnm. | tšʻm.mḏrǵlm. | arbʻ.l ʻšrm.ḫsnm. | ʻšr.hbṭnm. | ṯṯm.l.mit.ṯn.kbd. | tg 1030.7
[šd.]bn.ṯṯrn.b d.bnš.aǵlkz. | [šd.b]d.b[n].tkwn. | [ubdy.mḏ]rǵlm. | [šd.bn.--]n.b d.aḫny. | [šd.bn.--]rt.b d.ṭpṭbʻl. | [ubd 82[300].2.22
šr. | šbʻ.ḫsnm. | mkrm. | mrynm. | ṯlṯ.ʻšr. | hbṭnm. | ṯmn. | mḏrǵlm. | ṯmnym.ṯmn.kbd. | tgmr.ḫrd. | arbʻm.l.mit. | ṯn.kbd. 1031.13
b bt.[-]r[-]. | [aṯ]t.b.bt.aupš. | [aṯ]t.b.bt.ṭpṭbʻl. | [---.]n[--.mḏ]rǵlm. | [---.]b.bt[.---]l. | [ṯ]lṯ.aṯt.adrt.w.ṯlṯ.ǵzr[m]. | w.ḫmš. 80[119].14
]lm. | b yrḫ[ri]šyn. | šb[ʻ.--]n.[k]bd. | w[.---.]qmʻt. | [---.]mḏrǵlm. | [---.]mdm. | [w].ʻšr.dd.l np[l]. | r[p]š. 2012.24
rš. | [-----]. | l.mšḥ[.---]. | ʻšr.d[d.---]. | ṯṯm.dd.dd[.---]. | l.mḏrǵlm[.---]. | ṯlṯ.mat.ḫmšm.kb[d]. | ḫmš.kbd.l.mdʻ. | b yr[ḫ.i 2012.10

mḏrǵlbn

mṣry.d.ʻrb.b.unṯ. | bn.qrrn.mḏrǵl. | bn.tran.mḏrǵl | bn.ilh.mḏrǵl | špšyn.b.ulm. | bn.qṭn.b.ulm. | bn.gdrn.b 2046.1.3

mḏrǵlšpšyn

ry.d.ʻrb.b.unṯ. | bn.qrrn.mḏrǵl. | bn.tran.mḏrǵl | bn.ilh.mḏrǵl | špšyn.b.ulm. | bn.qṭn.b.ulm. | bn.gdrn.b.mʻr[by]. | [w]. 2046.1.4

mh

qṣ.all.tšu.g h.w[tṣ] | ḥ.at.mt.tn.aḫ y. | w ʻn.bn.ilm.mt.mh. | taršn.l btlt.ʻnt. | an.itlk.w aṣd.kl. | ǵr.l kbd.arṣ.kl.gbʻ. | l 6[49].2.13
b ṯmnt. | ap.sgrt.ydʻ[t k.]bt.k an[št]. | k in.b ilht.ql[ṣ] k.mh.tarš[n]. | l btlt.ʻnt.w t[ʻ]n.btlt.ʻn[t]. | ṯḥm k.il.ḥkm.ḥkm k. 3[ʻNT.VI].5.36
b ḥlm h. | il.yrd.b ḏhrt h. | ab adm.w yqrb. | b šal.krt.m at. | krt.k ybky. | ydmʻ.nʻmn.ǵlm. | il.mlk[.ṯ]r ab h. | yarš.h 14[KRT].1.38
š.l ršp bbt. | [ʻ]ṣrm l h.ršp [-]m. | [---.]bqt[-]. | [b] ǵb.ršp mh bnš. | šrp.w ṣp ḫršḫ. | ʻlm b ǵb ḫyr. | ṯmn l ṯlṯm ṣin. | šbʻ.al UG5.12.B.1
.rgm. | ilm.tǵr k. | tšlm k. | iky.lḥt. | spr.d likt. | ʻm.ṯryl. | mh y.rgmt. | w ht.aḫ y. | bn y.yšal. | ṯryl.p rgm. | l mlk.šm y. | 138.9
rgm. | ilm.tǵr k. | tšlm k. | ik y.lḥt. | spr.d likt. | ʻm.ṯryl. | mh y.rgmt. | w ht.aḫ y. | bn y.yšal. | ṯryl.p rgm. | l mlk.šm y. | 138.9
ym. | bn.ym.ynqm.b a[p.]ḏ[d.r]gm.l il.ybl. | aṯt y.il.ylt.mh.ylt.ilmy nʻmm. | agzr ym.bn ym.ynqm.b ap.ḏd.št.špt. | l 23[52].60
mt.tqt[nṣn]. | tldn.šḥr.w šlm.rgm.l il.ybl.a[ṯt y]. | il.ylt.mh.ylt.yld y.šḥr.w šl[m]. | šu.ʻdb.l špš.rbt.w l kbkbm.kn[-]. | 23[52].53
l.d[--.---.n] | hr.il.y[--.---]. | aliyn.[bʻl.---]. | btlt.[ʻnt.---]. | mh.k[--.---]. | w at[--.---]. | aṯr[t.---]. | b im[--.---]. | bl.l[---.---]. | 4[51].2.39
.ǵzr. | al.tšrgn.y btlt m.dm.l ǵzr. | šrg k.ḫḫm.mt.uḫryt.mh.yqḥ. | mh.yqḥ.mt.aṯryt.spsg.ysk. | [l]riš.ḥrṣ.l ẓr.qdqd y. | 17[2AQHT].6.35
rgn.y btlt m.dm.l ǵzr. | šrg k.ḫḫm.mt.uḫryt.mh.yqḥ. | mh.yqḥ.mt.aṯryt.spsg.ysk. | [l]riš.ḥrṣ.l ẓr.qdqd y. | [--.]mt.kl. 17[2AQHT].6.36
t.krt.bu.tbu. | bkt.tgly.w tbu. | nṣrt.tbu.pnm. | ʻrm.tdu.mh. | pdrm.tdu.šrr. | ḫṭ m.tʻmt.[ʻ]ṭr.[k]m. | zbln.ʻl.riš h. | w ṯṯb 16.6[127].6
[.---]. | rt.[---]. | ʻṭr.[---]. | b p.š[---]. | il.p.d[---]. | ʻrm.[di.mh.pdrm]. | di.š[rr.---]. | mr[ṣ.---]. | zb[ln.---]. | t[--.---]. | [-----]. 16[126].5.48

mhyt

lk.ab.]šnm. | [tša.g hm.w tṣ]ḥ.sbn. | [---]l[.---.]ʻd. | ksm.mhyt[.m]ǵny. | l nʻm y.arṣ.dbr. | l ysmt.šd.šḥlmmt. | mǵny.l b 5[67].6.5
| yṣq.šm[n.---]. | ʻn.tr.arṣ.w šmm. | sb.l qṣm.arṣ. | l ksm.mhyt.ʻn. | l arṣ.m[ṭ]r.bʻl. | w l šd.mṭr.ʻly. | nʻm.l arṣ.mṭr.bʻl. | 16[126].3.4

mhk

qḥt. | w.ṯṯb.ank.l hm. | w.any k.ṯt. | by.ʻky.ʻryt. | w.aḫ y.mhk. | b lb h.al.yšt. 2059.26
k.w.hm. | l.ʻl.w.lakm. | ilak.w.at. | um y.al.tdḥṣ. | w.ap.mhkm. | b.lb k.al. | tšt. 1013.22

mhr

. | [---.]ǵš.l limm. | [---.]l yṯb.l arṣ. | [---].mtm. | [---.--]d mhr.ur. | [---.]yḥnnn. | [---.--]t.ytn. | [---.btlt.]ʻnt. | [---.ybmt.]li 10[76].1.11
š.šm.il.mt m. | yʻbš.brk n.šm.il.ǵzrm. | ṯm.ṯmq.rpu.bʻl.mhr bʻl. | w mhr.ʻnt.ṯm.yḥpn.ḥyl | y.zbl.mlk.ʻllm y.km.tdd. | ʻ 22.2[124].8
.b hkl y]. | aṯr h.r[pum.l tdd.aṯr h]. | l tdd.il[nym.---]. | mhr.bʻl[.---.mhr]. | ʻnt.lk b[t y.rpim.rpim.b bt y]. | aṣḥ.km.[iq 22.1[123].7
h.tṣi.km. | rḥ.npš h.km.iṯl.brlt h.km. | qṭr.b ap h.b ap.mhr h.ank. | l aḥwy.tqḥ.yṭpn.mhr.št. | tštn.k nšr.b ḥbš h.km. 18[3AQHT].4.26
ḫ]b mlk qẓ.tn nkl y | rḫ ytrḫ.ib tʻrb m b bh | t h.w atn mhr h l a | b h.alp ksp w rbt ḫ | rṣ.išlḥ ẓhrm iq | nim.atn šd h 24[77].19

ḥ.npš[h.km.iṯl].|brlt h.km.qṭr.[b ap h.---].|ʻnt.b ṣmt.mhr h.[---].|aqht.w tbk.y[---.---].|abn.ank.w ʻl.[qšt k.---.ʻl]. 18[3AQHT].4.38
t.w an.mtm.amt.|[ap.m]ṯn.rgmm.argm.qštm.|[----.]mhrm.ht.tṣdn.tintt.|[---]m.tṣḥq.ʻnt.w b lb.tqny.|[---.]ṯb l y.l 17[2AQHT].6.40
tḥ.bt.w ubn.hkl.w ištql šql.|tn.km.nḥšm.yḥr.tn.km.|mhr y.w bn.bṯn.itnn y.|ytt.nḥšm.mhr k.bn bṯn.|itnn k.|aṯr UG5.7.74
.nḥšm.yḥr.tn.km.|mhr y.w bn.bṯn.itnn y.|ytt.nḥšm.mhr k.bn bṯn.|itnn k.|aṯr ršp.ʻṯtrt.|ʻm ʻṯtrt.mr h.|mnt.nṯk. UG5.7.75
.|hrg.ar[bʻ.]ymm.bṣr.|kp.šsk k.[--].l ḥbš k.|ʻtk.ri[š.]l mhr k.|w ʻp.l dr[ʻ].nšr k.|w rbṣ.l ǵr k.inbb.|kt ǵr k.ank.ydʻ 13[6].7
bn.qrrn.|bn.dnt.|bn.ṯʻl[-].|bdl.ar.dt.inn.|mhr l ht.|artyn.|ʻdmlk.|bn.alt[-].|iḫy[-].|ʻbdgtr.|ḥrr.|bn.s 1035.1.5
t.|kpt.b ḥbš h.brkm.tǵl[l].|b dm.ḏmr.ḥlqm.b mm[ʻ].|mhrm.mṭm.tgrš.|šbm.b ksl.qšt h.mdnt.|w hln.ʻnt.l bt h.tm 3[ʻNT].2.15
ḫt.kbd.ʻnt.|tšyt.k brkm.tǵll b dm.|ḏmr.ḥlqm.b mmʻ.mhrm.|ʻd.tšbʻ.tmtḫṣ.b bt.|tḫṣb.bn.ṯlḥnm.ymḥ.|[b]bt.dm.ḏ 3[ʻNT].2.28
ṯr h.r[pum.l tdd.aṯr h].|l tdd.il[nym.---].|mhr.bʻl[.---.mhr].|ʻnt.lk b[t y.rpim.rpim.b bt y].|aṣḥ.km.[iqra km.ilny 22.1[123].7
.|yʻbš.brk n.šm.il.ǵzrm.|ṯm.ṯmq.rpu.bʻl.mhr bʻl.|w mhr.ʻnt.ṯm.yḥpn.ḥyl|y.zbl.mlk.ʻllm y.km.tdd.|ʻnt.ṣd.tštr.ʻp 22.2[124].9
.|tḥt h.k kdrt.ri[š].|ʻl h.k irbym.kp.k.qṣm.|ǵrmn.kp.mhr.ʻtkt.|rišt.l bmt h.šnst.|kpt.b ḥbš h.brkm.tǵl[l].|b dm.ḏ 3[ʻNT].2.11
.w tšqyn h.tq[ḥ.ks.]b d h.|qbʻt.b ymn h.w yʻn.yṯ[p]n[.mh]r.|št.b yn.yšt.ila.il š[--.]il.|d yqny.ḏdm.yd.mḫṣt.a[qh]t. 19[1AQHT].4.218
n.y]|bl.agrtn.bat.b ḏd k.[pǵt].|bat.b hlm w yʻn.yṯpn[.mhr].|št.qḥn.w tšqyn.yn.qḥ.|ks.b d y.qbʻt.b ymn y[.t]q|ḥ.p 19[1AQHT].4.214
]t.ʻnt.l kl.[---].|[tt]bʻ.btlt.ʻnt[.idk.l ttn.pnm].|ʻm.yṯpn.mhr.š[t.tšu.g h].|w tṣḥ.yṯb.yṯp.[---].|qrt.ablm.ablm.[qrt.zbl 18[3AQHT].4.6
lt h.km.|qṭr.b ap h.b ap.mhr h.ank.|l aḥwy.tqḥ.yṯpn.mhr.št.|tštn.k nšr.b ḥbš h.km.diy.|b tʻrt h.aqht.km.yṯb.l lḥ 18[3AQHT].4.27
.b[---].|b qrn.ymn h.b anšt[.---].|qdqd h.w yʻn.yṯpn.[mhr.št].|šmʻ.l btlt.ʻnt.at.ʻ[l.qšt h].|tmḫṣ h.qṣʻt h.hwt.l t[ḥw 18[3AQHT].4.11
.ybmt.limm.|[t]rḥṣ.yd h.b dm.ḏmr.|[u]ṣbʻt h.b mmʻ.mhrm.|[ṯ]ʻr.ksat.l ksat.ṯlḥnt.|[l]ṯlḥn.hdmm.ṯʻr.l hdmm.|[3[ʻNT].2.35
h.|w l.šbʻ.tmtḫṣ h.b ʻmq.|tḫtṣb.bn.qrtm.ṯʻr.|ksat.l mhr.ṯʻr.ṯlḥnt.|l ṣbim.hdmm.l ǵzrm.|mid.tmtḫṣn.w tʻn.|tḫt 3[ʻNT].2.21

mwt

m y.arṣ.dbr.|l ysmt.šd.šḥlmmt.|mǵny.l bʻl.npl.l a|rṣ.mt.aliyn.bʻl.|ḫlq.zbl.bʻl.arṣ.|apnk.lṭpn.il.|d pid.yrd.l ksi.yṯ 5[67].6.9
[k mt.aliyn.bʻl].|k ḫlq.z[bl.bʻl.arṣ].|w hm.ḥy.a[liyn.bʻl].|w hm 6[49].3.01
tšu.g h.w tṣḥ.tšmḫ ht.|aṯrt.w bn h.ilt.w ṣb|rt.ary h.k mt.aliyn.|bʻl.k ḫlq.zbl.bʻl.|arṣ.gm.yṣḥ il.|l rbt.aṯrt ym.šmʻ. 6.1.41[49.1.13]
.ysk.|[l]riš.ḥrṣ.l ẓr.qdqd y.|[--.]mt.kl.amt.w an.mtm.amt.|[ap.m]ṯn.rgmm.argm.qštm.|[----.]mhrm.ht.tṣdn.tintt. 17[2AQHT].6.38
ap -].|tmǵyn.tša.g h[m.w tṣḥn].|šmʻ.l dnil.[mt.rpi].|mt.aqht.ǵzr.[šṣat].|btlt.ʻnt.k [rḥ.npš h].|k iṯl.brlt h.[b h.pʻn 19[1AQHT].2.91
[---.]ab y.ndt.ank[.---].|[---.--]l.mlk.tlk.b ṣd[.---].|[---.]mt.išryt[.---].|[---.--]r.almd k.[---].|[---.]qrt.ablm.a[blm].|[q 18[3AQHT].1.28
ln.|k klb.[b]bt k.nʻtq.|k inr[.ap.]ḫšt k.|ap.ab.k mtm.tmtn.|u ḫšt k.l bky.ʻtq.|b d.aṯt ab.ṣrry.|u ilm.tmtn.špḥ.|[l] 16.2[125].102
krt.|k [k]lb.b bt k.nʻtq.k inr.|ap.ḫšt k.ap.ab.ik mtm.|tmtn.u ḫšt k.l ntn.|ʻtq.b d.aṯt.ab ṣrry.|tbky k.ab.ǵr.bʻl.|ṣpn 16.1[125].4
.ngln.k klb.|b bt k.nʻtq.k inr.|ap.ḫšt k.ap.ab.k mtm.|tmtn.u ḫšt k.l ntn.|ʻtq.b d.aṯt.ab.ṣrry.|ik m.yrgm.bn.il.|krt 16.1[125].18
]rgm.ṯrm.|[--.]mtm.tbkn.|[--]t.w b lb.tqb[-].|[--]m[-].mtm.uṣbʻ[t].|[-]tr.šrk.il.|ʻrb.špš.l ymǵ.|krt.ṣbia.špš.|bʻl ny. 15[128].5.16
[.š]lm.|rgm.ṯṯ[b].|any kn.dt.|likt.mṣrm.|hn dt.b.ṣr.|mtt.by.|gšm.adr.|nškḥ.w.|rb.tmtt.|lqḥ.kl.ḏrʻ.|b d a[-]m.w 2059.13
k[m].|[---.]brk.t[---].|[ʻl.]krt.tbkn.|[--.]rgm.ṯrm.|[--.]mtm.tbkn.|[--]t.w b lb.tqb[-].|[--]m[-].mtm.uṣb[ʻt].|[-]tr.šr 15[128].5.14
n.ṯpṭ.nhr.w yṣa b[.--].|ybṯ.nn.aliyn.bʻl.w [---].|ym.l mt.bʻl m.ym l[--.---].|ḥm.l šrr.w [---].|yʻn.ym.l mt[.---].|l šr 2.4[68].32
[m]t.dm.ḫt.šʻtqt dm.|li.w ttbʻ.šʻtqt.|bt.krt.bu.tbu.|bkt.tgly. 16.6[127].1
.|w ṯṯb.trḥṣ.nn.b dʻt.|npš h.l lḥm.tpṯḥ.|brlt h.l trm.|mt.dm.ḫt.šʻtqt.|dm.lan.w ypqd.|krt.ṯʻ.yšu.g h.|w yṣḥ.šmʻ.l 16.6[127].13
ḥ.mt.aṯryt.spsg.ysk.|[l]riš.ḥrṣ.l ẓr.qdqd y.|[--.]mt.kl.amt.w an.mtm.amt.|[ap.m]ṯn.rgmm.argm.qštm.|[----.]mhr 17[2AQHT].6.38
w tʻn.btlt.|ʻnt.irš ḥym.l aqht.ǵzr.|irš ḥym.w atn k.bl mt.|w ašlḥ k.ašspr k.ʻm.bʻl.|šnt.ʻm.bn il.tspr.yrḫm.|k bʻl.k 17[2AQHT].6.27
ʻrb.ybky.|w yšnn.ytn.g h.|bky.b ḥy k.ab n.ašmḫ.|b l.mt k.ngln.k klb.|b bt k.nʻtq.k inr.|ap.ḫšt k.ap.ab.k mtm.|t 16.1[125].15
t.|tbky.w tšnn.[tt]n.|g h.bky.b ḥ[y k.a]b n.|nšmḫ.b l.mt k.ngln.|k klb.[b]bt k.nʻtq.|k inr[.ap.]ḫšt k.|ap.ab.k mt 16.2[125].99
h.yqḥ.mt.aṯryt.spsg.ysk.|[l]riš.ḥrṣ.l ẓr.qdqd y.|[--.]mt.kl.amt.w an.mtm.amt.|[ap.m]ṯn.rgmm.argm.qštm.|[---- 17[2AQHT].6.38
m.w.ank.|k[l.]ḏrʻ hm.|[--.n]pš[.-].|w [k]l hm.b d.|rb.tmtt.lqḥt.|w.ṯṯb.ank.l hm.|w.any k.ṯt.|by.ʻky.ʻryt.|w.aḫ y. 2059.22
likt.mṣrm.|hn dt.b.ṣr.|mtt.by.|gšm.adr.|nškḥ.w.|rb.tmtt.|lqḥ.kl.ḏrʻ.|b d a[-]m.w.ank.|k[l.]ḏrʻ hm.|[--.n]pš[.-]. 2059.16
rašm.|ṯṯkḥ.ttrp.šmm.k rs.|ipd k.ank.ispi.uṭm.|ḏrqm.amt m.l yrt.|b npš.bn ilm.mt.b mh|mrt.ydd.il.ǵzr.|tbʻ.w l. 5[67].1.6
[---.rp]um.tdbḥn.|[----.]ʻd.ilnym.|[---.--]l km amt m.|[---.]b w tʻrb.sd.|[---.--]n b ym.qẓ.|[---.]ym.tlḥmn.| 20[121].1.3
]rdy k.|[---.i]qnim.|[---.-]šu.b qrb.|[---].asr.|[---.--]m.ymt m.|[---].k iṯl.|[---.--]m.ʻdb.l arṣ.|[---.]špm.ʻdb.|[---].tʻtq 1[ʻNT.IX].2.8
|ʻrpt.tḥt.[---]|m ʻṣrm.ḥ[---].|glt.isr[.---]|m.brt[.---].|ymt m.[---].|ši[.---].|m[---.---]. 8[51FRAG].15
.spsg.ysk.|[l]riš.ḥrṣ.l ẓr.qdqd y.|[--.]mt.kl.amt.w an.mtm.amt.|[ap.m]ṯn.rgmm.argm.qštm.|[----.]mhrm.ht.tṣdn. 17[2AQHT].6.38
k.ngln.|k klb.[b]bt k.nʻtq.|k inr[.ap.]ḫšt k.|ap.ab.k mtm.tmtn.|u ḫšt k.l bky.ʻtq.|b d.aṯt ab.ṣrry.|u ilm.tmtn.šp 16.2[125].102
l.mt k.ngln.k klb.|b bt k.nʻtq.k inr.|ap.ḫšt k.ap.ab.k mtm.|tmtn.u ḫšt k.l ntn.|ʻtq.b d.aṯt.ab.ṣrry.|ik m.yrgm.bn. 16.1[125].17
[l]krt.|k [k]lb.b bt k.nʻtq.k inr.|ap.ḫšt k.ap.ab.ik mtm.|tmtn.u ḫšt k.l ntn.|ʻtq.b d.aṯt.ab ṣrry.|tbky k.ab.ǵr.b 16.1[125].3
h.yḥrṯ.|k gn.ap lb.k ʻmq.ytlṯ.|bmt.yšu.g h.w yṣḥ.|bʻl.mt.my.lim.bn.|dgn.my.hmlt.aṯr.|bʻl.ard.b arṣ.ap.|ʻnt.ttlk. 5[67].6.23
[.ṯṯlṯ].|qn.ḏrʻ h.tḥrṯ.km.gn.|ap lb.k ʻmq.ṯṯlṯ.bmt.|bʻl.mt.my.lim.bn dgn.|my.hmlt.aṯr.bʻl.nrd.|b arṣ.ʻm h.trd.nrt. 6[62].1.6
yn.tǵẓyt.špš.|rpim.tḥtk.|špš.tḥtk.ilnym.|ʻd k.ilm.hn.mtm.|ʻd k.kṯr m.ḥbr k.|w ḫss.dʻt k.|b ym.arš.w tnn.|kṯr.w 6.6[62.2].47
ḫtu.ht.|hm.in mm.|nḫtu.w.lak.|ʻm y.w.yd.|ilm.p.k mtm.|ʻz.mid.|hm.nṯkp.|mʻn k.|w.mnm.|rgm.d.tšmʻ.|ṯmt. 53[54].12
ytn.tk aršḫ.rbt.|w aršḫ.ṯrrt.ydy.b ʻṣm.ʻrʻr.|w b šḫt.ʻs.mt.ʻrʻrm.ynʻrn h.|ssnm.ysyn h.ʻdtm.yʻdyn h.yb|ltm.ybln h. UG5.7.65
trḫt.yšr h.|aṯt.trḫ.w tbʻt.|ṯar um.tkn l h.|mṯlṯt.kṯrm.tmt.|mrbʻt.zblnm.|mḫmšt.yitsp.|ršp.nṯdṯt.ǵlm.|ym.mšbʻt 14[KRT].1.16
rḥtm w rd.|bt ḫpṯt.arṣ.tspr b y|rdm.arṣ.w tdʻ ilm.|k mtt.yšmʻ.aliyn.bʻl.|yuhb.ʻglt.b dbr.prt.|b šd.šḥlmmt.škb.|ʻ 5[67].5.17
k mtm.tmtn.|u ḫšt k.l bky.ʻtq.|b d.aṯt ab.ṣrry.|u ilm.tmtn.špḥ.|[l]ṭpn.l yḥ.t[b]ky k.|ab.ǵr.bʻl.ṣ[p]n.ḥlm.|qdš.nny 16.2[125].105
.ab.ṣrry.|ik m.yrgm.bn.il.|krt.špḥ.lṭpn.|w qdš.u ilm.tmtn.|špḥ.lṭpn.l yḥ.|w yʻny.krt.ṯʻ.|bn.al.tbkn.al.|tdm.l y.al 16.1[125].22
|[--.]arṣ.ʻz k.ḏmr k.l[-]|n k.ḥtk k.nmrt k.b tk.|ugrt.l ymt.špš.w yrḫ.|w nʻmt.šnt.il. UG5.2.2.11
h.|imḫṣ h.ʻl.qṣʻt h.hwt.|l aḥw.ap.qšt h.l ttn.|l y.w b mt[.-]ḥ.mṣṣ[-]t[.--].|prʻ.qẓ.y[bl].šblt.|b ǵlp h.apnk.dnil.|[m 19[1AQHT].1.17
.|[---.]ilm.w ilht.dt.|[---.]šbʻ.l šbʻm.aṯr.|[---.--]ldm.dt ymtm.|[--.--]r.l ẓpn.|[---.]pn.ym.y[--].|[---].bʻl.tdd.|[---.]hkl 25[136].4
|ym.l mt.bʻl m.ym l[--.---].|ḥm.l šrr.w [---].|yʻn.ym.l mt[.---].|l šrr.w tʻ[n.ʻṯtrt.---].|bʻl m.hmt.[---].|l šrr.št[.---].| 2.4[68].34

l. | [---].rkb.ʻrpt. | [---.]ġš.l limm. | [---.]l yṯb.l arṣ. | [---].mtm. | [---.--]d mhr.ur. | [---.]yḥnnn. | [---.--]t.ytn. | [---.btlt.]ʻn 10[76].1.10
.---]. | [---.]ʻsb.[-]ḥ[-.---]. | [---.]b[-.]mṯt k.[---]. | [---.]k.w tmt[.---]. | [---.]k.w ṯt[--.---]. | [---.]k.w ṯ[--.---]. | [---.]k ṯrm.l p[2125.6
-.]pn.ym.y[--]. | [---].bʻl.tdd. | [---.]hkl. | [---.]yd h. | [---.]tmt. 25[136].10
--]. | ṯn.pt[ḥ.---]. | w.pt[ḥ.--]r.ṯġr. | ṯmn.ḥlnm. | ṯt.ṯḫ[--].l.mtm. 1151.16

mzy

mit.šmn.d.nm[-.]b d.mzy.alzy. | ḫmš.kkr.ḥlb. | ḫmš.kkr.brr. | kkr.ḫmš.mat.kbd.ṯlṯ. 1135.1
.ṯq]l rb. | ṯl[ṯ.---]. | aḥt.ḫm[-.---]. | b ym.dbḥ.ṯp[-]. | aḥt.l mzy.bn[--]. | aḥt.l mkt.ġr. | aḥt.l ʻṯtrt. | arbʻ.ʻṣrm. | gt.ṯrmn. | a 39[19].14

mzl

ḥd.bt h.ysgr. | almnt.škr. | tškr.zbl.ʻršm. | yšu.ʻwr. | mzl.ymzl. | w ybl.trḫ.ḥdṯ. | ybʻr.l ṯn.aṯt h. | w l nkr.mddt. | km irb 14[KRT].4.188
yḥd.bt h.sgr. | almnt.škr. | tškr.zbl.ʻršm. | yšu.ʻwr.mzl. | ymzl.w yṣi.trḫ. | ḥdṯ.ybʻr.l ṯn. | aṯt h.lm.nkr. | mddt h.k irby. 14[KRT].2.100
. | aḥd.bt h.ysgr. | almnt.škr. | tškr.zbl.ʻršm. | yšu.ʻwr. | mzl.ymzl. | w ybl.trḫ.ḥdṯ. | ybʻr.l ṯn.aṯt h. | w l nkr.mddt. | km 14[KRT].4.188
hm. | yḥd.bt h.sgr. | almnt.škr. | tškr.zbl.ʻršm. | yšu.ʻwr.mzl. | ymzl.w yṣi.trḫ. | ḥdṯ.ybʻr.l ṯn. | aṯt h.lm.nkr. | mddt h.k 14[KRT].2.99

mzln

.---.]gt.prn. | [š]d.bn.š[p]šn l gt pr[n]. | šd bn.ilšḥr. | l.gt.mzln. | šd.gldy. | l.gt.mzln. | šd.glln.l.gt.mz[l]n. | šd.hyabn[.l.] 1104.16
š[p]šn l gt pr[n]. | šd bn.ilšḥr. | l.gt.mzln. | šd.gldy. | l.gt.mzln. | šd.glln.l.gt.mz[l]n. | šd.hyabn[.l.]gt.mzln. | šd.ʻbdbʻl. | l 1104.18
d bn.ilšḥr. | l.gt.mzln. | šd.gldy. | l.gt.mzln. | šd.glln.l.gt.mz[l]n. | šd.hyabn[.l.]gt.mzln. | šd.ʻbdbʻl. | l.gt.mzln. 1104.19
.gldy. | l.gt.mzln. | šd.glln.l.gt.mz[l]n. | šd.hyabn[.l.]gt.mzln. | šd.ʻbdbʻl. | l.gt.mzln. 1104.20
ṯn.b gt.mzln. | ṯn.b ulm. | abmn.b gt.mʻrb. | atn. | ḫryn. | bn.ʻnt. | llwn. 1061.1
glln.l.gt.mz[l]n. | šd.hyabn[.l.]gt.mzln. | šd.ʻbdbʻl. | l.gt.mzln. 1104.22

mzn

.a[ḫ]r. | nkl yrḫ ytrḫ.adn h. | yšt mṣb.mznm.um h. | kp mznm.iḫ h ytʻr. | mšrrm.aḫt h l a | bn mznm.nkl w ib. | d ašr. 24[77].35
n]. | ʻma nkl ḫtn y.a[ḫ]r. | nkl yrḫ ytrḫ.adn h. | yšt mṣb.mznm.um h. | kp mznm.iḫ h ytʻr. | mšrrm.aḫt h l a | bn mzn 24[77].34
].bt ilm. | kbr[-]m.[-]trmt. | lbš.w [-]tn.ušpġt. | ḫr[-].ṯlṯt.mzn. | drk.š.alp.w ṯlṯ. | ṣin.šlm[m.]šbʻ pamt. | l ilm.šb[ʻ.]l kṯr. 33[5].5
šš[r]t.ḫrṣ.ṯqlm.kbd.ʻšrt.mzn h. | b [ar]bʻm.ksp. | b d[.ʻb]dym.ṯlṯ.kkr šʻrt. | iqn[i]m.ṯṯt.ʻ 2100.1
znm.um h. | kp mznm.iḫ h ytʻr. | mšrrm.aḫt h l a | bn mznm.nkl w ib. | d ašr.ar yrḫ.w y | rḫ yar k. | [ašr ilht kṯrt bn 24[77].37
. | ṯt.ḫṯrm.ṯn.kst. | spl.mšlt.w.mqḥm. | w md h. | arn.w mznm. | ṯn.ḫlpnm. | ṯt.mrḥm. | drb. | mrbd. | mškbt. 2050.5

mzʻ

n.rkb. | ʻrpt.bl.ṭl.bl rbb. | bl.šrʻ.thmtm.bl. | ṭbn.ql.bʻl.k tmzʻ. | kst.dnil.mt.rpi. | all.ġzr.m[t.]hr[nmy]. | gm.l bt[h.dnil. 19[1AQHT].1.46
[p]n. | ybṣr.ḥbl.diym. | tbky.pġt.bm.lb. | tdmʻ.bm.kbd. | tmzʻ.kst.dnil.mt. | rpi.al.ġzr.mt.hrnmy. | apnk.dnil.mt. | rpi.y 19[1AQHT].1.36

mzt

t. | qdšm. | b[-.--]t. | [---.-]l[--]. | [---.]pr[--]. | [-.a]pln. | bn.mzt. | bn.ṯrn. | w.nḥl h. | [--.-]hs. | [--.--]nyn. | [-----]. | [-----]. | bn 2163.2.13

mztn

mlk. | [---]yn. | bn.ṯ[--]. | bn.idrm. | bn.ymn. | bn.ṣry. | bn.mztn. | bn.šlgyn. | bn.[-]gštn. | bn[.n]klb. | b[n.]dtn. | w.nḥl h. | 113[400].2.5
m. | ḫyrn.w.šġr h. | šġr.bn.prsn. | agpṯr.w.šġ[r h]. | ṯʻln. | mztn.w.šġr [h]. | šġr.plṭ. | s[d]rn [w].ṯn.šġr h. | [---.]w.šġr h. | [2072.6
spr.rʻym. | lqḥ.šʻrt. | anntn. | ʻdn. | sdwn. | mztn. | ḫyrn. | šdn. | [ʻš]rm.ṯn kbd. | šġrm. | lqḥ.ššlmt. 2098.6

mḫ

my npš.yḥ.dnil. | [mt.rp]i.brlt.ġzr.mt hrnmy. | [---].hw.mḫ.l ʻrš h.yʻl. | [---].bm.nšq.aṯt h. | [---.]b ḥbq h.ḥmḥmt. | [---. 17[2AQHT].1.39
. | ṯ[km]t.mym.ḥspt.l šʻr. | ṭl.ydʻt.hlk.kbkbm. | a[-]ḥ.hy.mḫ.tmḫṣ.mḫṣ[.aḫ k]. | tkl.m[k]ly.ʻl.umt[k.--]. | d ttql.b ym.t 19[1AQHT].4.201
yʻny.krt.ṯʻ. | bn.al.tbkn.al. | tdm.l y.al tkl.bn. | qr.ʻn k.mḫ.riš k. | udmʻt.ṣḥ.aḫt k. | ṯtmnt.bt.ḥmḥ h. | d[-]n.tbkn.w td 16.1[125].27

mḫdy

[.---]y. | bn.ymlk[.b]d.skn. | bn.yḥnn.aḏddy. | bn.pdġy.mḫdy. | bn.yyn.mḏrġl. | bn.ʻlr. | ḫtpy.aḏddy. | ynḥm.aḏddy. | y 2014.17

mḫl

hdd.b y[.----]. | ʻm.b ym bʻl ysy ym[.---]. | rmm.ḫnpm.mḫl[.---]. | mlk.nhr.ibr[.---]. | zbl bʻl.ġlm.[---]. | ṣġr hd w r[---. 9[33].2.8

mḫnm

[--]r.[---]. | [---.]il.[---]. | [ṯṣ]un.b arṣ. | mḫnm.ṯrp ym. | lšnm.tlḥk. | šmm.ttrp. | ym.ḏnbtm. | tnn.l šb 1003.4

mḫsrn

mḫsrn.d.[--.]ušknym. | brq.ṯlṯ.[mat.ṯ]lṯ. | bsn.mi[t.--]. | ar[--.-- 1136.1
mit.ṯlṯ.mḫsrn. | ʻl.nsk.kṯṯġlm. | arbʻm.ṯlṯ.mḫsrn. | mtbʻl.rišy. | ṯlṯm.ṯlṯ.ʻl.nsk. | arym. | alp.ṯlṯ.ʻl. | nsk.art. 1137.3
mit.ṯlṯ.mḫsrn. | ʻl.nsk.kṯṯġlm. | arbʻm.ṯlṯ.mḫsrn. | mtbʻl.rišy. | ṯlṯm.ṯlṯ 1137.1

mḫṣ

lk. | [---.--]ḥ.uḫd. | [---.-]luḫ. | [---.-]tn.b d.mlkt. | [---.]l.mḫṣ. | ab[---.]aḏddy.bn.skn. | bn.[---.]uḫd. | bn.n[---.]hbṯn. | bn 2014.7
.d kbkbm. | l tbrkn.alk brkt. | tmrn.alk.nmr[rt]. | imḫṣ.mḫṣ.aḫ y.akl[.m] | kly[.ʻ]l.umt y.w yʻn[.dn] | il.mt.rpi npš ṯḥ[19[1AQHT].4.196
ym.ḥspt.l šʻr. | ṭl.ydʻt.hlk.kbkbm. | a[-]ḥ.hy.mḫ.tmḫṣ.mḫṣ[.aḫ k]. | tkl.m[k]ly.ʻl.umt[k.--]. | d ttql.b ym.trtḥ[ṣ.--]. | [19[1AQHT].4.201
yn.yšt.ila.il š[--.]il. | d yqny.ḏdm.yd.mḫṣt.a[qh]t.ġ | zr.tmḫṣ.alpm.ib.št[-.]št. | ḥršm l ahlm p[---.]km. | [-]bl lb h.km. 19[1AQHT].4.221
.b šnt h.qr.[mym]. | mlk.yṣm.y l km.qr.mym.d ʻ[l k]. | mḫṣ.aqht.ġzr.amd.gr bt il. | ʻnt.brḥ.p ʻlm h.ʻnt.p dr[.dr]. | ʻdb 19[1AQHT].3.153

ṯ[p]n[.mh]r.|št.b yn.yšt.ila.il š[--.]il.|d yqny.ḏdm.yd.mḫṣt.a[qh]t.ǵ|zr.tmḫṣ.alpm.ib.št[-.]št.|ḥršm l ahlm p[---.]k 19[1AQHT].4.220
[m].|qrt.zbl.yrḫ.yšu g h.|w yṣḥ.y l k.qrt.ablm.|d ʿl k.mḫṣ.aqht.ǵzr.|ʿwrt.yšt k.bʿl.l ht.|w ʿlm h.l ʿnt.p dr.dr.|ʿdb. 19[1AQHT].4.166
rrt.tǵll.b nr.|yšu.g h.w yṣḥ.y l k.mrrt.|tǵll.b nr.d ʿl k.mḫṣ.aqht.|ǵzr.šrš k.b arṣ.al.|ypʿ.riš.ǵly.b d.nsʿ k.|ʿnt.brḥ.p 19[1AQHT].3.158
d.|awr.ṯǵrn.ʿbd.|ʿbd.ḫmn.šmʿ.rgm.|s̀dn.[k]bs̀.|šdyn.mḫ[ṣ].|aṯry.mḫṣ.|bʿln.mḫṣ.|y[ḥ]ṣdq.mḫṣ.|ṣp[r].ks[d].|bʿl.š 2084.14
mḫṣm.|irpbn.|grgš.|[--]yn.|[---]n.|[--]mrt. 1042.1
t.k brkm.tǵll b dm.|ḏmr.ḥlqm.b mmʿ.mhrm.|ʿd.tšbʿ.tmtḫṣ.b bt.|tḫṣb.bn.ṯlḥnm.ymḥ.|[b]bt.dm.ḏmr.yṣq.šmn.|šl 3[ʿNT].2.29
yiḫd.bʿl.bn.aṯrt.|rbm.ymḫṣ.b ktp.|dk ym.ymḫṣ.b ṣmd.|ṣḥr mt.ymṣḫ.l arṣ.|[yṯb.] 6[49].5.2
bm].|kla[t.ṯǵ]r[t.bht.ʿnt.w tqry.ǵlmm.b št.ǵr].|ap ʿnt tm[tḫṣ.b ʿmq.tḫtṣb.bn.qrytm.tmḫṣ].|lim ḫ[p.ym.---].|[--]m. 7.2[130].25
kpt.b ḥb]š h.ʿtkt r[išt].|[l bmt h.---.]hy bt h tʿrb.|[---.tm]tḫṣ b ʿmq.|[tḫtṣb.bn.qrtm.tṯʿr.ṯlḥnt.]l ṣbim.|[hdmm.l ǵz 7.1[131].4
bm.klat.ṯǵrt.|bht.ʿnt.w tqry.ǵlmm.|b št.ǵr.w hln.ʿnt.tm|tḫṣ.b ʿmq.tḫtṣb.bn.|qrytm tmḫṣ.lim.ḫp y[m].|tṣmt.adm 3[ʿNT].2.5
yiḫd.bʿl.bn.aṯrt.|rbm.ymḫṣ.b ktp.|dk ym.ymḫṣ.b ṣmd.|ṣḥr mt.ymṣḫ.l arṣ.|[yṯb.]b[ʿ]l.l ksi.mlk h.|[--- 6[49].5.3
spr.mḫṣm.|bn.ḫps̀ry.b.šbn.|ilštmʿym.|y[---.]bn.ʿšq.|[---.]bn.tqy 1041.1
[.i]k.|mǵy.aliy[n.b]ʿl.|ik.mǵyt.b[t]lt.|ʿnt.mḫṣ y hm[.m]ḫṣ.|bn y.hm[.mkly.ṣ]brt.|ary y[.ẓl].ksp.[a]ṯrt.|k tʿn.ẓl.ks 4[51].2.24
--]m.|[---.--]n.d[--.--]i.|[--]t.mdt h[.l.]ʿṯtrt.šd.|[---.-]rt.mḫṣ.bnš.mlk.ybʿl hm.|[---.--]t.w.ḫpn.l.azzlt.|[---.]l.ʿṯtrt.šd.| 1106.53
[k.ym]ḫṣ.bʿl m[.--]y.tnn.w ygl.w ynsk.ʿ[-].|[--]y.l arṣ[.id]y.alt.l 1001.1.1
.ʿbd.|ʿbd.ḫmn.šmʿ.rgm.|s̀dn.[k]bs̀.|šdyn.mḫ[ṣ].|aṯry.mḫṣ.|bʿln.mḫṣ.|y[ḥ]ṣdq.mḫṣ.|ṣp[r].ks[d].|bʿl.š[lm].|ḫyrn[. 2084.15
ṣin mrat.|ʿšr ddm.l šmʿrgm.|ʿšr ddm.l bt.|ʿšrm.dd.l mḫṣm.|ddm l kbs.|dd l prgṯ.|dd.l mri.|dd.l ṯnǵly.|dd.l kr 1100.5
dnt.|w hln.ʿnt.l bt h.tmǵyn.|tštql.ilt.l hkl h.|w l.šbʿt.tmtḫṣ h.b ʿmq.|tḫtṣb.bn.qrtm.tṯʿr.|ksat.l mhr.ṯʿr.ṯlḥnt.|l ṣb 3[ʿNT].2.19
šr.|aqht.yʿn.kmr.kmr[.--].|k apʿ.il.b gdrt.k lb.l |ḫṭ h.imḫṣ h.k d.ʿl.qšt h.|imḫṣ h.ʿl.qṣʿt h.hwt.|l aḥw.ap.qšt h.l tt 19[1AQHT].1.14
r[.--].|k apʿ.il.b gdrt.k lb.l |ḫṭ h.imḫṣ h.k d.ʿl.qšt h.|imḫṣ h.ʿl.qṣʿt h.hwt.|l aḥw.ap.qšt h.l ttn.|l y.w b mt[.-]ḥ.m 19[1AQHT].1.15
dqd h.w yʿn.yṭpn.[mhr.št].|šmʿ.l btlt.ʿnt.at.ʿ[l.qšt h].|tmḫṣ h.qṣʿt h.hwt.l t[ḥwy].|nʿmn.ǵzr.št.ṯrm.w[---].|ištir.b 18[3AQHT].4.13
rgmt.|l k.l zbl.bʿl.ṯnt.l rkb.ʿrpt.ht.ib k.|bʿl m.ht.ib k.tmḫṣ.ht.tṣmt.ṣrt k.|tqḥ.mlk.ʿlm k.drkt.dt dr dr k.|kṯr ṣmd 2.4[68].9
.tṯʿr.|ksat.l mhr.ṯʿr.ṯlḥnt.|l ṣbim.hdmm.l ǵzrm.|mid.tmtḫṣn.w tʿn.|tḫtṣb.w tḥdy.ʿnt.|tǵdd.kbd h.b ṣḥq.ymlu.|lb 3[ʿNT].2.23
[tḫtṣb.bn.qrtm.tṯʿr.ṯlḥnt.]l ṣbim.|[hdmm.l ǵzrm.mid.tmtḫṣn.w t]ʿn.tḫtṣb.|[w tḥdy.ʿnt.tǵdd.kbd h.b ṣḥ]q.ymlu.lb 7.1[131].6
šu.g h.w tṣḥ[.i]k.|mǵy.aliy[n.b]ʿl.|ik.mǵyt.b[t]lt.|ʿnt.mḫṣ y hm[.m]ḫṣ.|bn y.hm[.mkly.ṣ]brt.|ary y[.ẓl].ksp.[a]ṯrt 4[51].2.24
bnš.gt.ʿṯtrt.|ad[-]l[-]m.|ʿšr.ksdm.yd.lmd hm.lqḥ.|ʿšr.mḫṣm.yd.lmd hm.|apym.|[bn]š gt.ipṯl.|[---]ym.|[----]m.|[- 1040.9
mn.šmʿ.rgm.|s̀dn.[k]bs̀.|šdyn.mḫ[ṣ].|aṯry.mḫṣ.|bʿln.mḫṣ.|y[ḥ]ṣdq.mḫṣ.|ṣp[r].ks[d].|bʿl.š[lm].|ḫyrn[.---].|a[--.-- 2084.16
i.mlk h.l nḫt.l kḥṯ].|drkt h.š[--.--].|w hm.ap.l[--.---].|ymḫṣ k.k[--.---].|il.dbḥ.[---].|pʿr.b[--.---].|ṭbḫ.alp[m.ap.ṣin.š 1[ʿNT.X].4.27
trrm.|khnm.|kzym.|yṣrm.|mru.ibrn.|mru.skn.|nsk.ksp|mḫṣm.|ksdm.|mḏrǵlm.|pslm.|yṣḥm. 74[115].14
.ar[š].|ṣmt.ʿgl.il.ʿtk.|mḫšt.klbt.ilm išt.|klt.bt.il.ḏbb.imtḫṣ.ksp.|itrṯ.ḫrṣ.ṭrd.bʿl.|b mrym.ṣpn.mšṣṣ.[-]kʿ[-].|udn h 3[ʿNT].3.43
mm.|b št.ǵr.w hln.ʿnt.tm|tḫṣ.b ʿmq.tḫtṣb.bn.|qrytm tmḫṣ.lim.ḫp y[m].|tṣmt.adm.ṣat.š[p]š.|tḥt h.k kdrt.ri[š].|ʿl 3[ʿNT].2.7
y.ǵlmm.b št.ǵr].|ap ʿnt tm[tḫṣ.b ʿmq.tḫtṣb.bn.qrytm.tmḫṣ].|lim ḫ[p.ym.---].|[--]m.t[-]t[.---].|m[-]mt[.---].|[-----]. 7.2[130].25
k tmḫṣ.ltn.bṯn.brḥ.|tkly.bṯn.ʿqltn.|šlyṭ.d šbʿy.rašm.|ṯṯkḥ.ttrp 5[67].1.1
t m.ʿm.a[ḫ] yn.|p nšt.bʿl.[ṭ]ʿn.iṭʿn k.|[---.]ma[---] k.k tmḫṣ.|[ltn.bṯn.br]ḥ.tkly.|[bṯn.ʿqltn.]šlyṭ.|[d šbʿt.rašm].ṯṯkḥ 5[67].1.27
rnmy.d kbkbm.|l tbrkn.alk brkt.|tmrn.alk.nmr[rt].|imḫṣ.mḫṣ.aḫ y.akl[.m]|kly[.ʿ]l.umt y.w yʿn[.dn]|il.mt.rpi n 19[1AQHT].4.196
m]t.mym.ḥspt.l šʿr.|ṭl.ydʿt.hlk.kbkbm.|a[-]ḥ.hy.mḫ.tmḫṣ.mḫṣ[.aḫ k].|tkl.m[k]ly.ʿl.umt[k.--].|d ttql.b ym.trtḥ[ṣ 19[1AQHT].4.201
ḫṣ.ǵlmm.yš[--].|[ymn h.ʿn]t.tuḫd.šmal h.tuḫd.ʿṯtrt.ik.m[ḫṣt.ml]|[ak.ym.tʿ]dt.ṯpṭ.nhr.mlak.mṯḫr.yḥb[-.---.]|[---]. 2.1[137].40
.mt.ql.|bʿl.ql.ʿln.špš.|tṣḥ.l mt.šmʿ.mʿ.|l bn.ilm.mt.ik.tmt[ḫ]|ṣ.ʿm.aliyn.bʿl.|ik.al.yšm[ʿ] k.ṯr.|il.ab k.l ysʿ.alt.|ṯbt 6[49].6.24
mnḥy k.ap.anš.zbl.bʿ[l].|[-.yuḫ]d.b yd.mšḫṭ.bm.ymn.mḫṣ.ǵlmm.yš[--].|[ymn h.ʿn]t.tuḫd.šmal h.tuḫd.ʿṯtrt.ik.m[ḫ 2.1[137].39
s̀dn.[k]bs̀.|šdyn.mḫ[ṣ].|aṯry.mḫṣ.|bʿln.mḫṣ.|y[ḥ]ṣdq.mḫṣ.|ṣp[r].ks[d].|bʿl.š[lm].|ḫyrn[.---].|a[--.---].|ʿ[--.---].|š[- 2084.17
.|[šd.bn.--]n.b d.aḫny.|[šd.bn.--]rt.b d.ṯpṭbʿl.|[ubdy.]mḫ[ṣ]m.|[šd.bn.]uzpy.b d.yšn.ḥrš.|[-----].|[-----].|[šd.b d.--] 82[300].2.25
.gdm.w anhbm].|w tqr[y.ǵlmm.b št.ǵr.---].|[ʿ]d tš[bʿ.tmtḫṣ.---].|klyn[.---].|špk.l[---].|trḥṣ.yd[h.---].|[--.]yṣt ḏm 7.2[130].5
ṯbr.yǵṣ.pnt.ksl h].|anš.[dt.ẓr h.yšu.g h].|w yṣ[ḥ.---].|mḫṣ[.---].|š[--.---]. 19[1AQHT].2.98

mḫr

l.|w.ḫmšm.ksp.|lqḥ.mlk.gbl.|lbš.anyt h.|bʿrm.ksp.|mḫr.hn. 2106.18
.kkr.ṯlṯ.|[--.]aštn.l k.|[--]y.kl.dbrm.hm[.--].|[--]l.w.kl.mḫr k.|[--]tir.aštn.l [k].|[---].kkr.ṯl[ṯ]. 1022.8
ḫr.ʿn.pḫr.ʿn.ṯǵr.|ʿn.ṯǵr.l.ṯǵr.ṯṯb.|ʿn.pḫr.l.pḫr.ṯṯb.|ʿn.mḫr.l.mḫr.ṯṯb.|ʿn.bṯy.l.bṯy.ṯṯb.|ʿn.bṯt.l.bṯt.ṯṯb. RS225.9
.l.bl.ḥrb.|tšt.dm.h.l.bl.ks.|tpnn.ʿn.bṯy.ʿn.bṯt.tpnn.|ʿn.mḫr.ʿn.pḫr.ʿn.ṯǵr.|ʿn.ṯǵr.l.ṯǵr.ṯṯb.|ʿn.pḫr.l.pḫr.ṯṯb.|ʿn.mḫr.l RS225.6
.pḫr.ʿn.ṯǵr.|ʿn.ṯǵr.l.ṯǵr.ṯṯb.|ʿn.pḫr.l.pḫr.ṯṯb.|ʿn.mḫr.l.mḫr.ṯṯb.|ʿn.bṯy.l.bṯy.ṯṯb.|ʿn.bṯt.l.bṯt.ṯṯb. RS225.9
ubrʿy.|arny.|mʿr.|šʿrt.|ḫlb rpš.|bqʿt.|šḥq.|yʿby.|mḫr. 65[108].9

mḫrhn

b.atlg.ṯlṯ.ḫrmṯt.ṯṯm.|mḫrhn.nit.mit.krk.mit.|mʿṣd.ḫmšm.mqb.[ʿ]šrm.|b.ulm.ṯṯ.ʿš 2048.2

mḫš

ḫšt.mdd.|il ym.l klt.nhr.il.rbm.|l ištbm.tnn.ištml h.|mḫšt.bṯn.ʿqltn.|šlyṭ.d šbʿt.rašm.|mḫšt.mdd ilm.ar[š].|ṣmt.ʿ 3[ʿNT].3.38
tṣḥ.ik.mǵy.gpn.w ugr.|mn.ib.ypʿ.l bʿl.ṣrt.|l rkb.ʿrpt.l mḫšt.mdd.|il ym.l klt.nhr.il.rbm.|l ištbm.tnn.ištml h.|mḫš 3[ʿNT].3.35
l ištbm.tnn.ištml h.|mḫšt.bṯn.ʿqltn.|šlyṭ.d šbʿt.rašm.|mḫšt.mdd ilm.ar[š].|ṣmt.ʿgl.il.ʿtk.|mḫšt.klbt.ilm išt.|klt.bt. 3[ʿNT].3.40
|šlyṭ.d šbʿt.rašm.|mḫšt.mdd ilm.ar[š].|ṣmt.ʿgl.il.ʿtk.|mḫšt.klbt.ilm išt.|klt.bt.il.ḏbb.imtḫṣ.ksp.|itrṯ.ḫrṣ.ṭrd.bʿl.|b 3[ʿNT].3.42

mḫt

t.|zbln.r[---].ymlu.|nʿm.[-]ṯ[-.--.]yqrṣ.|d[-] b pḫ[-.--.]mḫt.|[---.]tnn.|[---.]tnn. 16[126].5.30

mḫtn

bn].ayḫ.|[---]rn.|ill.|ǵlmn.|bn.ytrm.|bn.ḫgbt.|mtn.|mḫtn.|[p]lsy.|bn.ḥrš.|[--.]kbd.|[---].|y[---].|bn.ǵlyn.|bdl.a 1035.2.13

mṭ

ḫbš h.brkm.tǵl[l].|b dm.ḏmr.ḥlqm.b mm[ʻ].|mhrm.mṭm.tgrš.|šbm.b ksl.qšt h.mdnt.|w hln.ʻnt.l bt h.tmǵyn.|tš 3[ʻNT].2.15
yṣa.b milḫ.|ʻšrm.ḫpn.ḫmš.|kbd.w lpš.|ḫmš.mispt.|mṭ.|w lpš.d sgr b h.|b d.anrmy. 1109.5
zr.|ʻwrt.yšt k.bʻl.l ht.|w ʻlm h.l ʻnt.p dr.dr.|ʻdb.uḫry.mṭ.yd h.|dnil.bt h.ymǵyn.yšt|ql.dnil.l hkl h.ʻrb.b|kyt.b hkl 19[1AQHT].4.169
r.amd.gr bt il.|ʻnt.brḥ.p ʻlm h.ʻnt.p dr[.dr].|ʻdb.uḫry mṭ.yd h.|ymǵ.l mrrt.tǵll.b nr.|yšu.g h.w yṣḥ.y l k.mrrt.|tǵl 19[1AQHT].3.155
iš.ǵly.b d.nsʻ k.|ʻnt.brḥ.p ʻlm h.|ʻnt.p dr.dr.ʻdb.uḫry mṭ yd h.|ymǵ.l qrt.ablm.abl[m].|qrt.zbl.yrḫ.yšu g h.|w yṣ 19[1AQHT].3.162
.|mštʻltm.l riš.agn.yqḥ.tš.b bt h.|il.ḥṭ h.nḥt.il.ymnn.mṭ.yd h.yšu.|yr.šmm h.yr.b šmm.ʻṣr.yḫrṯ yšt.|l pḥm.il.aṯt 23[52].37
ʻlm h.w hn.aṯtm.tṣḥn y.mt mt.|nḥtm.ḥṭ k.mmnnm.mṭ yd k.hl.ʻṣr.|tḥrr.l išt.w ṣḥrt.l pḥmm.aṯtm.a[ṯt.il].|aṯt.il. 23[52].47
tm.k ypt.hm.aṯtm.tṣḥn.|y mt.mt.nḥtm.ḥṭ k.mmnnm.mṭ.yd k.|h[l.]ʻṣr.tḥrr.l išt.ṣḥrrt.l pḥmm.|a[ṯ]tm.aṯt.il.aṯt.il. 23[52].40
ʻlm h.w hm.|aṯtm.tṣḥn y.ad ad.nḥtm.ḥṭ k.|mmnnm.mṭ yd k.hl.ʻṣr.tḥrr.l išt.|w ṣḥrrt.l pḥmm.btm.bt.il.bt.il.|w ʻl 23[52].44
n.y ym.yṯbr.ḥrn].|riš k.ʻṯtrt.[šm.bʻl.qdqd k.---].|[--]t.mṭ.tpln.b g[bl.šnt k.---].|[--]šnm.aṯtm.t[--.---].|[m]lakm.yla 2.1[137].9

mṭḫ

bm.|kd l ištnm.|kd l ḫty.|maḫdh.|kd l kblbn.|kdm.mṭḫ.|l.alṯy.|kd.l mrynm.|šbʻ yn.|l mrynm.|b yṯbmlk.|kd 1090.7

mṭnt

---.]ʻmt.l ql.rpi[.---].|[---.-]llm.abl.mṣrp k.[---].|[---.]y.mṭnt.w tḥ.ṭbt.n[--].|[---.b]ṯnm w ṯṯb.ʻl.bṯnt.trtḥ[ṣ.---].|[---.t] 1001.2.4

mṭr

rnmy.|apnk.dnil.mt.|rpi.yṣly.ʻrpt.b |ḥm.un.yr.ʻrpt.|tmṭr.b qẓ.ṭl.ytll.|l ǵnbm.šbʻ.šnt.|yṣr k.bʻl.ṯmn.rkb.|ʻrpt.bl.ṭ 19[1AQHT].1.41
|ʻn.tr.arṣ.w šmm.|sb.l qṣm.arṣ.|l ksm.mhyt.ʻn.|l arṣ.m[ṭ]r.bʻl.|w l šd.mṭr.ʻly.|nʻm.l arṣ.mṭr.bʻl.|w l šd.mṭr.ʻly.| 16[126].3.5
sm.mhyt.ʻn.|l arṣ.m[ṭ]r.bʻl.|w l šd.mṭr.ʻly.|nʻm.l arṣ.mṭr.bʻl.|w l šd.mṭr.ʻly.|nʻm.l ḥṭt.b gn.|bm.nrt.ksmm.|ʻl.tl[16[126].3.7
ḫkmt.|šbt.dqn k.l tsr k.|rḫntt.d[-].l irt k.|wn ap.ʻdn.mṭr h.|bʻl.yʻdn.ʻdn.ṯkt.b glṯ.|w tn.ql h.b ʻrpt.|šrh.l arṣ.brq 4[51].5.68
-.-]nk.aštn.b ḫrt.|ilm.arṣ.w at.qḥ.|ʻrpt k.rḥ k.mdl k.|mṭrt k.ʻm k.šbʻt.|ǵlm k.ṯmn.ḫnzr k.|ʻm k.pdry.bt.ar.|ʻm k. 5[67].5.8
.arṣ].|b ḥlm.lṭpn.il.d pid.|b ḏrt.bny.bnwt.|šmm.šmn.tmṭrn.|nḫlm.tlk.nbtm.|w idʻ.k ḥy.aliyn.bʻl.|k iṯ.zbl.bʻl.arṣ. 6[49].3.6
l.arṣ.|b ḥlm.lṭpn.il d pid.|b ḏrt.bny.bnwt.|šmm.šmn.tmṭrn.|nḫlm.tlk.nbtm.|šmḫ.lṭpn.il.d pid.|pʻn h.l hdm.yṯpd 6[49].3.12
.|sb.l qṣm.arṣ.|l ksm.mhyt.ʻn.|l arṣ.m[ṭ]r.bʻl.|w l šd.mṭr.ʻly.|nʻm.l arṣ.mṭr.bʻl.|w l šd.mṭr.ʻly.|nʻm.l ḥṭt.b gn.|b 16[126].3.6
rṣ.m[ṭ]r.bʻl.|w l šd.mṭr.ʻly.|nʻm.l arṣ.mṭr.bʻl.|w l šd.mṭr.ʻly.|nʻm.l ḥṭt.b gn.|bm.nrt.ksmm.|ʻl.tl[-]k.ʻṭrṭrm.|nšu. 16[126].3.8

mṭt

m.w ydmʻ.|tntkn.udmʻt h.|km.ṯqlm.arṣ h.|km ḫmšt.mṭt h.|bm.bky h.w yšn.|b dmʻ h.nhmmt.|šnt.tluan.|w yšk 14[KRT].1.30

my

].|mrṣ.grš[m.zbln].|in.b ilm.ʻ[ny h.yrbʻ].|yḫmš.rgm.[my.b ilm].|ydy.mrṣ.g[ršm.zbln].|in.b ilm.ʻn[y h.]yṯdṯ.|yšbʻ 16[126].5.17
y.mrṣ].|gršm.z[bln.in.b ilm].|ʻny h.y[ṯny.yṯlṯ].|rgm.my.b[ilm.ydy].|mrṣ.grš[m.zbln].|in.b ilm.ʻ[ny h.yrbʻ].|yḫ 16[126].5.14
dy.mrṣ.g[ršm.zbln].|in.b ilm.ʻn[y h.]yṯdṯ.|yšbʻ.rgm.[my.]b ilm.|ydy.mrṣ.gršm zbln.|in.b ilm.ʻny h.|w yʻn.lṭpn.il 16[126].5.20
b d k.[---].|ṯnnt h[.---].|ṯlṯt h[.-.w yʻn].|lṭpn.[il.d pid.my].|b ilm.[ydy.mrṣ].|gršm.z[bln.in.b ilm].|ʻny h.y[ṯny.yṯl 16[126].5.10
.bn y.|tšḫṭann.b šnt h.qr.[mym].|mlk.yṣm.y l km.qr.mym.d ʻ[l k].|mḫṣ.aqht.ǵzr.amd.gr bt il.|ʻnt.brḥ.p ʻlm h.ʻnt 19[1AQHT].3.152
.l aḫt k.|[---.]l [ ]dm.aḫt k.|ydʻt.k rḥmt.|al.tšt.b šdm.mm h.|b smkt.ṣat.npš h.|[-]mt[-].ṣba.rbt.|špš.w tgh.nyr.|r 16.1[125].34
šrḥq.aṯt.l pnn h.|št.alp.qdm h.mria.w tk.|pn h.tḥspn.m h.w trḥṣ.|ṭl.šmm.šmn.arṣ.ṭl.šm[m.t]sk h.|rbb.nsk h.kbk 3[ʻNT].4.86
sat.l ksat.ṯlḥnt.|[l]ṯlḥn.hdmm.ttʻr.l hdmm.|[t]ḥspn.m h.w trḥṣ.|[ṭ]l.šmm.šmn.arṣ.rbb.|[r]kb ʻrpt.ṭl.šmm.tsk h. 3[ʻNT].2.38
ʻmq.yṯlṯ.|bmt.yšu.g h.w yṣḥ.|bʻl.mt.my.lim.bn.|dgn.my.hmlt.aṯr.|bʻl.ard.b arṣ.ap.|ʻnt.ttlk.w tṣd.kl.ǵr.|l kbd.arṣ 5[67].6.24
.km.gn.|ap lb.k ʻmq.ṯtlṯ.bmt.|bʻl.mt.my.lim.bn dgn.|my.hmlt.aṯr.bʻl.nrd.|b arṣ.ʻm h.trd.nrt.|ilm.špš.ʻd.tšbʻ.bk.| 6[62].1.7
.m[t.]hr[nmy].|gm.l bt[h.dnil.k yṣḥ].|šmʻ.pǵt.ṯkmt[.my].|ḥspt.l šʻr.ṭl.yd[ʻt].|hlk.kbkbm.mdl.ʻr.|ṣmd.pḥl.št.gpn 19[1AQHT].2.50
ly[.ʻ]l.umt y.w yʻn[.dn]|il.mt.rpi npš tḥ[.pǵt].|t[km]t.mym.ḥspt.l šʻr.|ṭl.ydʻt.hlk.kbkbm.|a[-]ḥ.hy.mḫ.tmḫṣ.mḫṣ[. 19[1AQHT].4.199
.pḥl.št.gpn y dt ksp.|dt.yrq.nqbn y.tš[mʻ].|pǵt.ṯkmt.my.ḥspt.l[š]ʻr.ṭl.|ydʻt.hlk.kbkbm.|bkm.tmdln.ʻr.|bkm.tṣm 19[1AQHT].2.55
d.sǵr[.---.--]r h.|aḥ[d.---.ʻ]šrm.d[d.---].|ʻš[r.---.--]r h.|my y[--.---.--]d.|ʻšrm[.---.--]r h.|[-]wyn.yd[-.---.]dd.|[---]n.y 1098.38
[---.]w rm tp h.|[---.-]lu mm l nʻm.|[---.]w rm ṯlbm ṯlb.|[---.-]pr l nʻm.|[---.-]mt w r UG5.5.2
lṯ].|qn.ḏrʻ h.tḥrṯ.km.gn.|ap lb.k ʻmq.ṯtlṯ.bmt.|bʻl.mt.my.lim.bn dgn.|my.hmlt.aṯr.bʻl.nrd.|b arṣ.ʻm h.trd.nrt.|il 6[62].1.6
rṭ.|k gn.ap lb.k ʻmq.yṯlṯ.|bmt.yšu.g h.w yṣḥ.|bʻl.mt.my.lim.bn.|dgn.my.hmlt.aṯr.|bʻl.ard.b arṣ.ap.|ʻnt.ttlk.w tṣ 5[67].6.23
ṯbr.diy.|hmt.hm.tʻpn.ʻl.qbr.bn y.|tšḫṭann.b šnt h.qr.[mym].|mlk.yṣm.y l km.qr.mym.d ʻ[l k].|mḫṣ.aqht.ǵzr.amd 19[1AQHT].3.151
[l a]q[h]t.|[t]krb.[---.]l qrb.mym.|tql.[---.]lb.tt[b]r.|qšt[.---]r.y[t]br.|tmn.[---.]btlt.[ʻ]nt. 19[1AQHT].1.2
-]l h.yd ʻd[.---].|ltm.mrqdm.d š[-]l[-].|w tʻn.pǵt.ṯkmt.mym.|qrym.ab.dbḥ.l ilm.|šʻly.dǵt h.b šmym.|dǵt.hrnmy.d 19[1AQHT].4.190
---].|w[----].|pǵ[t.---].|lk[.---].|ki[--.---].|w ḫ[--.---].|my[.---].|aṯ[t.---].|aḫ k[.---].|tr.ḥ[---].|w tṣḥ[.---].|tšqy[.---]. 16.2[125].71

myn

ilʻnt.|bn.urt.|ydn.|qṭn.|bn.asr.|bn.ʻdy.|bn.amt[m].|myn.|šr.|bn.zql.|bn.iḫy.|bn.iyṯr.|bn.ʻyn.|bn.ǵzl.|bn.ṣmy. 2117.3.50

myṣ

.l.ḫtyt.|ṯlṯm.dd.ksmn.l.gzzm.|yyn.|ṣdqn.|ʻbd.pdr.|myṣm.|tgt.|w.lmd h.|ytil.|w.lmd h.|rpan.|w.lmd h.|ʻbdr 1099.8

mk

dš.yd.ṣt h. | [dn]il.yd.ṣt h.y'l.w yškb. | [yd.]mizrt.p yln.mk.b šb'.ymm. | [w]yqrb.b'l.b ḥnt h.abynt. | [d]nil.mt.rpi an 17[2AQHT].1.16
ḫmš.ṯ[d]ṯ.ym.tikl. | išt.[b]bht m.nblat. | b[qrb.hk]l m.mk. | b šb['.]y[mm].td.išt. | b bht m.n[bl]at.b hkl m. | sb.ksp.l 4[51].6.31
nnt.ḫmš. | ṯdṯ.ym.yšlḥm.k[ṯ]rt. | w y[ššq].bnt.hll.snnt. | mk.b šb['.]ymm.tb'.b bt h. | kṯrt.bnt.hll.snnt. | [-]d[-]t.n'm y.' 17[2AQHT].2.39
ṯdṯ.ym.tlḥmn.rpum. | tštyn.bt.ikl.b pr'. | yṣq.b irt.lbnn.mk.b šb'. | [ymm.---]k.aliyn.b'l. | [---].r' h ab y. | [---.]'[---]. 22.2[124].25
mšknt hm. | w tqrb.w ld.bn.l h. | w tqrb.w ld.bnt.l h. | mk.b šb'.šnt. | bn.krt.km hm.tdr. | ap.bnt.ḥry. | km hm.w tḫs 15[128].3.22
d. | šb't.šnt.ybk.l aq | ht.ġzr.yd[m'.]l kdd. | dnil.mt.r[pi.mk].b šb'. | šnt.w y'n[.dnil.mt.]rpi. | yṯb.ġzr.m[t.hrnmy.y]šu. 19[1AQHT].4.179
k h. | [---].l kḥṯ.drkt h. | l [ym]m.l yrḫm.l yrḫm. | l šnt.[m]k.b šb'. | šnt.w [--].bn.ilm.mt. | 'm.aliyn.b'l.yšu. | g h.w yṣḥ 6[49].5.8
rṣ.tspr.b y | rdm.arṣ. | idk.al.ttn. | pnm.tk.qrt h. | hmry.mk.ksu. | ṯbt h.ḫḫ.arṣ. | nḫlt h.w nġr. | 'nn.ilm.al. | tqrb.l bn.il 4[51].8.12
l.yṯb.ilm.idk. | l ytn.pn.'m.bn.ilm.mt. | tk.qrt h.hmry.mk.ksu. | ṯbt.ḫḫ.arṣ.nḫlt h.tša. | g hm.w tṣḥ.ṯḥm.aliyn. | bn.b' 5[67].2.15
. | b[u]ṣb't h.ylm.ktp.zbl ym.bn ydm.ṯpṭ. | nhr.'z.ym.l ymk.l tnġṣn.pnt h.l ydlp. | tmn h.kṯr.ṣmdm.ynḥt.w yp'r.šmt 2.4[68].17
mqr.mmlat. | d[m].ym.w ṯn. | ṯlṯ.rb'.ym. | ḫmš.ṯdṯ.ym. | mk.špšm.b šb'. | w l.yšn.pbl. | mlk.l [qr.]ṯiqt. | ibr h[.l]ql.nhq 14[KRT].5.221
m.ḥsn.pat.mdbr. | lk.ym.w ṯn.ṯlṯ.rb' ym. | ḫmš.ṯdṯ.ym.mk.špšm. | b šb'.w tmġy.l udm. | rbm.w l.udm.ṯrrt. | w gr.nn. 14[KRT].3.107

mkl

| adrdn. | prn. | 'bdil. | ušy.šbn[-]. | aḫt.ab. | krwn. | nnḏ. | mkl. | kzġb. | iyrḏ. 1069.16

mkr

ṯmnym.arb't. | kbd.ksp. | d.nqdm. | ḫmšm.l mit. | ksp.d.mkr.ar. | arb'm ksp d mkr. | atlg. | mit.ksp.d mkr. | ilštm'. | 'šr 2107.10
p. | d.nqdm. | ḫmšm.l mit. | ksp.d.mkr.ar. | arb'm ksp d mkr. | atlg. | mit.ksp.d mkr. | ilštm'. | 'šrm.l mit.ksp. | 'l.bn.alk 2107.11
it. | ksp.d.mkr.ar. | arb'm ksp d mkr. | atlg. | mit.ksp.d mkr. | ilštm'. | 'šrm.l mit.ksp. | 'l.bn.alkbl.šb[ny]. | 'šrm ksp.'l. 2107.13
maḫdym. | grbn.ltḥ. | srn.ltḥ. | ykn.ltḥ. | ḥgbn.ltḥ. | spr.mkrm. | bn.sl'n.prs. | bn.ṯpdn.ltḥ. | bn.urm.ltḥ. 1059.6
lk[.--]. | w.mlk.yštal.b.hn[--]. | hmt.w.anyt.hm.t'[rb]. | mkr.hn d.w.rgm.ank[.--]. | mlkt.ybqš.anyt.w.at[--]. | w mkr n 2008.2.12
šb'.ṯnnm.w.šb'.ḫsnm. | ṯmn.'šr h.mrynm. | 'šr.mkrm. | ḫmš.ṯrtnm. | ḫmš.bn.mrynm. | 'šr.mrum.w.šb'.ḫsnm. 1030.3
ḥwt.[---]. | alp.k[sp]. | tš'n. | w.hm.al[-]. | l.tš'n. | mṣrm. | tmkrn. | ypḥ.'bdilt. | bn.m. | ypḥ.ilšlm. | bn.prqdš. | ypḥ.mnḥm 2116.16
. | mrum. | 'šrm. | ṯnnm. | nqdm. | khnm. | qdšm. | pslm. | mkrm. | yṣḥm. | šrm. | n'rm. | 'bdm. | kzym. | ksdm. | [nsk].ṯlṯ. | 1026.1.9
khnm. | qdšm. | mkrm. | mdm. | inšt. | ḥrš.bhtm. 75[81].3
spr.argmnm. | 'šrm.ksp.d mkr. | mlk. | ṯlṯ.mat.ksp.d.šb[n]. | mit.ksp.d.ṯbq. | ṯmnym.arb' 2107.2
n'r.mrynm. | ḫmš. | ṯrtnm.ḫmš. | mrum.'šr. | šb'.ḫsnm. | mkrm. | mrynm. | ṯlṯ.'šr. | hbṭnm. | ṯmn. | mḏrġlm. | ṯmnym.ṯm 1031.8
mkr.hn d.w.rgm.ank[.--]. | mlkt.ybqš.anyt.w.at[--]. | w mkr n.mlk[.---]. 2008.2.14
. | [---]. | bn[.---]y. | yr[---]. | ḫdyn. | grgš. | b[n.]tlš. | ḏmr. | mkrm. | 'zn. | yplṭ. | 'bdmlk. | ynḥm. | aḏddn. | mtn. | plsy. | qṭn. 1035.4.2
. | ṯlṯ.'šr.mrynm. | ḫmš.[ṯr]tnm. | ṯlṯ.b[n.]mrynm. | 'šr[.m]krm. | tš'.hbṭnm. | 'šr.mrum. | šb'.ḫsnm. | tš'm.ṯṯ.kbd.mḏrġ 1028.5
snm. | 'šr.mrum. | w.šb'.ḫsnm. | tš'.'šr. | mrynm. | ṯlṯ.'šr.mkrm. | ṯlṯ.bn.mrynm. | arb'.ṯrtnm. | tš'.ḫbṭnm. | ṯmnym.ṯlṯ.k 1029.7
---]. | [-]mn.n[--]. | ḥrš.d.[---]. | mrum.[---]. | yṣḥm[.---]. | mkrm[.---]. | pslm[.---]. 1038.6
.ym[.---]. | [---].hm.l y[--.---]. | [---].mṣrm[.---]. | [---.--]n mkr[.---]. | [---].ank.[---]. | [---.]tny.[---]. | [---.]mlk[.---]. | [---.-- 2126.5
khnm. | qdšm. | m[ru.]škn. | mkrm. 76[82].4
b'lm'ḏr. | bn.mdn. | mkrm. 1168.3
rm. | mrum. | ṯnnm. | mqdm. | khnm. | qdšm. | nsk.ksp. | mkrm. 71[113].75

mkšr

št 'rgz y]dk aḥd h w yṣq b ap h. | [k.yiḫd akl š]šw št mkšr grn. | [w št aškrr w p]r ḥḏrt. | [-----]. | [---.-]n[-]. | [k yraš 160[55].10
rgz[.ydk.aḥd h]. | w.yṣq[.b.ap h]. | k.yiḫd[.akl.ššw]. | št.mkš[r.grn]. | w.št.ašk[rr]. | w.pr.ḥḏr[t.ydk]. | aḥd h.w.yṣq[.b.a 161[56].13

mkšt

k]. | aḥd h.w.yṣq[.b.ap h]. | k.yiḫd.akl.š[šw]. | št.nni.št.mk[št.grn]. | št.irġn.ḥmr[.ydk]. | aḥd h.w.yṣq.b[.ap h]. | k.yra 161[56].18

mkt

aḥt.ḫm[-.---]. | b ym.dbḥ.ṯp[-]. | aḥt.l mzy.bn[--]. | aḥt.l mkt.ġr. | aḥt.l 'ṯtrt. | arb'.'ṣrm. | gt.ṯrmn. | aḥt.slḫu. 39[19].15

mkṯy

i[l]. | [š]lm.il.šr. | dgn.w b'l. | 'ṯ w kmṯ. | yrḫ w ksa. | yrḫ mkṯy. | ṯkmn w šnm. | kṯr w ḫss. | 'ṯtr 'ṯtpr. | šḥr w šlm. | ngh UG5.10.1.7

mla

m.'l[m.--]. | k dr d.d yknn[.--]. | b'l.yṣġd.mli[.--]. | il hd.mla.u[--.--]. | blt.p btlt.'n[t]. | w p.n'mt.aḫt[.b'l]. | y'l.b'l.b ġ[r. 10[76].3.9
't.b šdm.ḥṭb. | w b grnt.ḥpšt. | s't.b npk.šibt.w b | mqr.mmlat. | d[m].ym.w ṯn. | ṯlṯ.rb'.ym. | ḫmš.ṯdṯ.ym. | mk.špšm.b 14[KRT].5.217
rm.s't.b šdm. | ḥṭb h.b grnt.ḥpšt. | s't.b nk.šibt.b bqr. | mmlat.dm.ym.w ṯn. | ṯlṯ.rb'.ym.ymš. | ṯdṯ.ym.ḥẓ k.al.tš'l. | qr 14[KRT].3.114
ṯ.yn.d 'rb.bṯk[.---]. | mġ hw.l hn.lg yn h[.---]. | w ḥbr h.mla yn.[---]. 23[52].76
d.tmtḫṣn.w t]'n.tḫtṣb. | [w tḥdy.'nt.tġdd.kbd h.b ṣḥ]q.ymlu.lb h. | [b šmḫt.kbd.'nt.tšyt.tḥt h.k]kdrt.riš. | ['l h.k irb 7.1[131].7
id.tmtḫṣn.w t'n. | tḫtṣb.w tḥdy.'nt. | tġdd.kbd h.b ṣḥq.ymlu. | lb h.b šmḫt.kbd.'nt. | tšyt.k brkm.tġll b dm. | ḏmr.ḥlq 3['NT].2.25
. | d pršа.b br. | n'l.il.d qblbl. | 'ln.ybl hm.ḫrṣ. | tlḥn.il.d mla. | mnm.dbbm.d | msdt.arṣ. | s'.il.dqt.k amr. | sknt.k ḥwt. 4[51].1.39
a]nk. | iḥtrš.w [a]škn. | aškn.ydt.[m]rṣ gršt. | zbln.r[---].ymlu. | n'm.[-]ṯ[-.--.]yqrṣ. | d[-] b pḫ[-.--.]mḫt. | [---.]tnn. | [---. 16[126].5.28
b arb't.'šr[t]. | yrtḥṣ.mlk.b[rr]. | b ym.mlat. | tqln.alpm. | yrḫ.'šrt.l b'[l]. | dqtm.w ynt.qr[t]. | w mtnt UG5.13.3
rb špš w ḥl. | [mlk.b ar]b't.'[š]rt.yrtḥṣ.mlk.brr. | [b ym.ml]at.y[ql]n.al[p]m.yrḫ.'šrt. | [l b'l.ṣ]pn.[dq]tm.w y[nt] qrt. | 36[9].1.11
mm. | tšu knp.btlt.'n[t]. | tšu.knp.w tr.b 'p. | tk.aḫ šmk.mlat rumm. | w yšu.'n h.aliyn.b'l. | w yšu.'n h.w y'n. | w y'n.b 10[76].2.12
yd h. | w qṣ't h.bm.ymn h. | idk.l ytn pnm. | tk.aḫ.šmk.mla[t.r]umm. | tšu knp.btlt.'n[t]. | tšu.knp.w tr.b 'p. | tk.aḫ š 10[76].2.9

lt.w burm.[l]b. | rmṣt.ilhm.b'lm.dṯt.w kšm.ḫmš. | 'ṯr h.mlun.šnpt.ḫṣt h.b'l.ṣpn š. | [--]ṯ š.ilt.mgdl š.ilt.asrm š. | w l ll. 34[1].10
[.---]. | bt.l bnš.trg[m.---]. | l šlmt.l šlm.b[--.---] | b y.šnt.mlit.t[--.---]. | ymǵy k.bnm.ta[--.---]. | [b]nm.w bnt.ytn k[.---]. 59[100].7
dbṯ[.---]. | tr'.tr'n.a[--.---]. | bnt.šdm.ṣḥr[.---]. | šb'.šnt.il.mla.[-]. | w ṯmn.nqpnt.'d. | k lbš.km.lpš.dm a[ḫ h]. | km.all.d 12[75].2.45
b'l]. | lm.k qnym.'l[m.--]. | k dr d.d yknn[.--]. | b'l.yṣǵd.mli[.--]. | il hd.mla.u[--.--]. | blt.p btlt.'n[t]. | w p.n'mt.aḫt[.b'l 10[76].3.8
.t[--]. | aṯr.aṯrm[.---]. | aṯr.aṯrm[.---]. | išdym.t[---]. | b k.mla[.---]. | udm't.d[m'.---]. | [---].bn.[---]. | [-----]. 27[8].10
r[.b'l.gdlt.šlm.gdlt]. | w burm.l[b.rmṣt.ilhm]. | b'lm.w mlu[.---.ksm]. | ṯlṯm.w m'rb[.---]. | dbḥ šmn mr[.šmn.rqḥ.bt]. APP.II[173].20
r k[.tšlm k]. | hl ny.[---]. | w.pdr[--.---]. | tmǵyn[.---]. | w.mli[.---]. | [-]kl.w [---]. | 'd.mǵt[.---]. 57[101].6
šṣi. | [---.]ḫbr.rbt. | [ḫbr.ṯrr]t.il d. | [pid.---].b anšt. | [---.]mlu. | [---.--]tm. 15[128].5.28

mlak

t.ml] | [ak.ym.t']dt.ṯpṭ.nhr.mlak.mṯḫr.yḥb[-.---.] | [---].mlak.bn.ktpm.rgm.b'l h.w y[--.---]. | [---].ap.anš.zbl.b'l.šdmt 2.1[137].42
blt. | w ht.luk 'm ml[kt]. | tǵsdb.šmlšn. | w tb' ank. | 'm mlakt h šm' h. | w b.'ly skn.yd' rgm h. | w ht ab y ǵm[--]. | t[- 1021.7
y.hn. | alpm.ššwm.hnd. | w.mlk.b'l y.bnš. | bnny.'mn. | mlakty.hnd. | ylak 'm y. | w.t'l.ṯh.hn. | [a]lpm.šśwm. | [---].w.ṯ 1012.35
d.šmal h.tuḫd.'ttrt.ik.m[ḫṣt.ml] | [ak.ym.t']dt.ṯpṭ.nhr.mlak.mṯḫr.yḥb[-.---.] | [---].mlak.bn.ktpm.rgm.b'l h.w y[--.-- 2.1[137].41
u ilm rašt hm.l ẓr.brkt hm.ln.kḥṯ.zbl hm. | aḫr.tmǵyn.mlak ym.t'dt.ṯpṭ.nhr.l p'n.il. | [l t]pl.l tšṯḥwy.pḫr.m'd.qmm. 2.1[137].30
m.yš[--]. | [ymn h.'n]t.tuḫd.šmal h.tuḫd.'ṯtrt.ik.m[ḫṣt.ml] | [ak.ym.t']dt.ṯpṭ.nhr.mlak.mṯḫr.yḥb[-.---.] | [---].mlak.b 2.1[137].40
u.ilm.rašt km.l ẓr.brkt km.ln.kḥṯ. | zbl km.w ank.'ny.mlak.ym.t'dt.ṯpṭ.nhr. | tšu ilm rašt hm.l ẓr.brkt hm.ln.kḥṯ.z 2.1[137].28
t. | km l ẓr brkt km.w ln.kḥṯ.zbl km.aḥd. | ilm.t'ny lḥt.mlak.ym.t'dt.ṯpṭ.nhr. | šu.ilm.rašt km.l ẓr.brkt km.ln.kḥṯ. | z 2.1[137].26
]. | yṯb.bn qdš.l ṯrm.b'l.qm.'l.il.hlm. | ilm.tph hm.tphn.mlak.ym.t'dt.ṯpṭ[.nhr]. | t[ǵ]ly.hlm.rišt hm.l ẓr.brkt hm.w l 2.1[137].22
y[--.---]. | [---].ap.anš.zbl.b'l.šdmt.bg[--.---]. | [---.-]dm.mlak.ym.t'dt.ṯpṭ.nh[r.---]. | [---].an.rgmt.l ym.b'l km.ad[n k 2.1[137].44
bt.[-.]l bnt.q[-]. | w št.b bt.ṯap[.--]. | hy.yd h.w ym[ǵ]. | mlak k.'m dt[n]. | lqḥ.mṯpṭ. | w y'ny.nn. | dtn.bt n.mḫ[-]. | l d UG5.6.11
.rbt.w udm ṯrrt. | udm.ytnt.il w ušn. | ab.adm.w ṯṯb. | mlakm.l h.lm.ank. | ksp.w yrq.ḫrṣ. | yd.mqm h.w 'bd. | 'lm.ṯlṯ 14[KRT].3.137
.---]. | [---.--]mr.ph. | [---.--]mm.hlkt. | [---.]b qrb.'r. | [---.m]lakm l h. | [---.]l.bn.il. | [---.--]a.'d h. | [---.--]rh. | [---.--]y.špš 26[135].6
| b ḏrt y.ab.adm. | w ld.šph.l krk | t.w ǵlm.l 'bd. | il.ttb'.mlakm. | l yṯb.idk.pnm. | l ytn.'mm.pbl. | mlk.tšan. | g hm.w t 14[KRT].6.300
[rḥq.mlk.l bt y]. | [ng.kr]t.l ḥ[ẓ]r y. | [-----]. | [---.ttb']. | [mlakm.l yṯb]. | [idk.pnm.l ytn]. | [']m[.krt.mswn h]. | tš[an.g 14[KRT].6.264
h. | l ql.nhqt.ḥmr h. | l g't.alp.ḥrṯ.zǵt. | klb.ṣpr.w ylak. | mlakm.l k.'m.krt. | mswn h.tḥm.pbl.mlk. | qḥ.ksp.w yrq.ḫrṣ. 14[KRT].3.124
. | [-]sny.uḏr h. | w.hm.ḫt. | 'l.w.likt. | 'm k.w.hm. | l.'l.w.lakm. | ilak.w.at. | um y.al.tdḥṣ. | w.ap.mhkm. | b.lb k.al. | tšt. 1013.19
w.k.rgm.špš. | mlk.rb.b'l y.u. | '[--.]mlakt.'bd h. | [---.]b'l k.yḥpn. | [---.]'m h.u ky. | [---.--]d k.k.t 1018.3
]. | limm.ql.b udn.k w[-]. | k rtqt mr[.---]. | k d lbšt.bir.mlak. | šmm.tmr.zbl.mlk. | šmm.tlak.ṭl.amr.. | bn km k bk[r.z 13[6].25
m[.--]tn k. | [--]y.l ihbt.yb[--].rgm y. | [---.]škb.w m[--.]mlakt. | [---.]'l.w tš'[d]n.npṣ h. | [---.]rgm.hn.[--]n.w aspt.[q]l 1002.47

mlg

pn i | l ḏ.pid.hn b p y sp | r hn.b špt y mn | t hn ṯlḫ h w mlg h y | ṯtqt 'm h b q't. | tq't 'm prbḫt. | dmqt ṣǵrt kṯrt. 24[77].47

mld

rkby. | šḥq. | ǵn. | ṣ'. | mld. | amḏy. | ḫlb'prm. | ḫpty. | [ḫr]ṣb'. | [m']rb. 2077.5
]dy. | armwl. | uwaḫ. | ypln.w.ṯn.bn h. | ydln. | anr[my]. | mld. | krmp[y]. | bṣmn. 2086.11
[---]. | 'bd.[---]. | mtn[.---]. | ṯdpṯn[.--]. | tny[.--]. | sll[.--]. | mld[.--]. | yqš[.--]. | [-----]. | inš[r.---]. | ršp[.---]. | iḫy[-.--]. | iwr[- 1074.7

mldy

| šgryn.ary.b.yny. | bn.yddn.b.rkby. | agyn.agny. | ṯqbn.mldy. 2071.9

mlḥ

'l. | arṣ.qm.yṯ'r. | w yšlḥmn h. | ybrd.ṯd.l pnw h. | b ḥrb.mlḥt. | qṣ.mri.ndd. | y'šr.w yšqyn h. | ytn.ks.b d h. | krpn.b kl 3['NT].1.7
lht.dkrt[.yn]. | 'd.lḥm.šty.ilm. | w pq mrǵtm.ṯd. | b ḥrb.mlḥt.qṣ[.m]r | i.tšty.krp[nm.y]n. | [b k]s.ḫrṣ.d[m.'ṣm]. | [---.--] 4[51].6.57
-.---]. | [']d.lḥm[.šty.ilm]. | w pq.mr[ǵtm.ṯd.---]. | b ḥrb.[mlḥt.qṣ.mri]. | šty.kr[pnm.yn.---]. | b ks.ḫr[ṣ.dm.'ṣm.---]. | ks. 5[67].4.14
.---]. | [------]. | [---.l]ḥm[.---]. | [---].ay š[---]. | [---.b ḥ]rb.mlḥ[t.qṣ]. | [mri.tšty.krpnm].yn.b ks.ḫ[rṣ]. | [dm.'ṣm.---]n.kr 17[2AQHT].6.4
btlt.'nt. | [--.tl]ḥm.tšty. | [ilm.w tp]q.mrǵtm. | [ṯd.b ḥrb.m]lḥt.qṣ. | [mri.tšty.k]rpnm yn. | [b ks.ḫrṣ.dm].'ṣm. 4[51].3.42
'šr.bmt.alp.mri. | ṯn.nšbm. | ṯmnym.tbṯḫ.alp. | uz.mrat.mlḥt. | arb'.uzm.mrat.bq'. | ṯlṯ.[-]ṯt.aš[']t.šmn.uz. | mi[t].ygb. 1128.20

mlḥmt

ṣrt.l rkb.'rpt. | ṯḥm.aliyn.b'l.hwt.aliy. | qrdm.qry.b arṣ.mlḥmt. | št.b 'p[r] m.ddym.sk.šlm. | l kbd.arṣ.arbdd.l kbd.šd 3['NT].4.52
.w y]ṣḥ.ṯḥm. | [ṯr.il.ab k.hwt.l]ṯpn.ḥtk k. | [qryy.b arṣ.mlḥ]mt.št b 'p | [r m.ddym.sk.šlm].l kbd.arṣ. | [arbdd.l kbd.š 1['NT.IX].2.19
mmt.limm. | ṯḥm.aliyn.b'l.hwt. | aliy.qrdm.qry.b arṣ. | mlḥmt št.b 'pr m.ddym. | sk.šlm.l kbd.arṣ. | arbdd.l kbd.šdm 3['NT].3.12
yšt. | [----.]b'l.mdl h.yb'r. | [---.]rn h.aqry. | [---.]b a[r]ṣ.mlḥmt. | ašt[.b ']p[r] m.ddym.ask. | šlm.l kb[d].awṣ.arbdd. | l 3['NT].4.72
| w t['n].btlt.[']nt.ṯṯb. | [ybmt.]limm.[a]n.aqry. | [b arṣ].mlḥmt.[aš]t.b 'pr m. | ddym.ask[.šlm.]l kbd.arṣ. | ar[bdd.]l k 3['NT].4.67
ybmt.limm.ṯḥm.aliyn.b'l]. | hw[t.aliy.qrdm.qryy.b arṣ.mlḥmt.št]. | [b ']pr[m.ddym.sk.šlm.l kbd.arṣ.arbdd]. | l kbd. 7.2[130].14

mlḥt

ṣṣ yrpi m[it.---]. | ṣṣ bn.š[m]mn '[šr.---]. | alp.ṯṯm. | kbd.mlḥt. 2097.21

mly

bn '[p]ty. | bn.kdgdl. | bn.smyy. | bn.lbn. | bn.šlmn. | bn.mly. | pslm. | bn.annd. | bn.gl'd. | w.nḥl h. | bn.mlkyy. | [bn].b 2163.3.8
. | [---.]'m. | [---.--]y.w.lm. | [---.]il.šlm. | [---.]ank. | [---].mly. 2128.2.7

mlk

]mbk nhrm.qrb.|[a]pq.thmtm.tgly.ḏd.|il.w tbu.qrš..|mlk.ab.šnm.l p‘n.|il.thbr.w tql.|tštḥwy.w tkbdn h.|tšu.g h. 6.1.36[49.1.8]
].|il d pid.tk ḫrš[n.---.tk.ǵr.ks].|ygly ḏd.i[l.w ybu.qrš.mlk].|ab.šnm.l [p‘n.il.yhbr.w yql].|yštḥwy.[w ykbdn h.---]. 1['NT.IX].3.23
bk.[nhrm.qrb.apq.thmtm].|[ygly.]ḏl i[l].w ybu[.q]rš.mlk[.ab.šnm.l p‘n.il.]|[yhbr.]w yql[.y]štḥw[y.]w ykb[dn h.-- 2.3[129].5
.il.mbk.nhrm.|qrb.apq.thmtm.|tgly.ḏd.il.w tbu.|qrš.mlk.ab.šnm.|l p‘n.il.thbr.w tql.|tštḥwy.w tkbd h.|hlm.il.k 4[51].4.24
.mbk.nhrm.|[qrb.ap]q.thmtm tgly.ḏd il.|[w tbu.qr]š.mlk.ab.šnm.|[l p‘n.il.t]hbr.w tql.tštḥ|[wy.w tkbd]n h.tlšn.a 17[2AQHT].6.49
.nhr[m.qr]b.[ap]q.|[thm]tm.tgl.ḏ[d.]i[l.]w tbu.|[qr]š.m[l]k.ab[.šnm.]mṣr.|[t]bu.ḏdm.qn[-.-]n[-.-]lt.|ql h.yš[m‘].ṯr 3['NT.VI].5.16
k.nhrm].|[qrb.apq.thmtm].|[tgly.ḏd.il.w]tb[a].|[qrš.mlk.ab.]šnm.|[tša.g hm.w tṣ]ḥ.sbn.|[---]l[.---.]‘d.|ksm.mhy 5[67].6.2
.|[-----].|[---]m.il[.---].|[---]d nhr.umt.|[---.]rpat.bt.|[m]lk.itdb.d šb‘.|[a]ḫm.l h.ṯmnt.bn um.|krt.ḥtk n.rš.|krt.gr 14[KRT].1.8
l.mlkt.|adt y.|rgm.|tḥm.tlmyn.|‘bd k.|l.p‘n.|adt y.|šb‘ d.| 52[89].1
[---.--]n.aḥd.|[p]dr.ḫsyn.aḥd.|pdr.mlk.aḥd. 130[29].3
ṯmn l ṯlṯm ṣin.|šb‘.alpm.|bt b‘l.ugrt.ṯn šm.|‘lm.l ršp.mlk.|alp w.š.l b‘lt.|bwrm š.iṯtqb.|w š.nbk m w.š.|gt mlk š. UG5.12.B.7
ašr nkl w ib[.bt].|ḫrḫb.mlk qẓ ḫrḫb m|lk aǵzt.b sǵ[--.]špš.|yrḫ ytkḥ yḥ[bq] [-].|tld bt.[--]t.ḫ[--.l 24[77].2
ap.|pd.|mlk.|ar.|atlg.|gb‘ly.|ulm.|m‘rby.|m‘r.|arny.|š‘rt.|ḫlbrpš. 2074.3
mdrǵlm.d.b.i[-]‘lt.mlk.|arsw.|dqn.|ṯlṯ.klbm.|ḫmn.|[---.-]rsd.|bn[.-]pṯ.|bn kd 86[305].1
.|k tǵḏ.arz.b ymn h.|bkm.yṯb.b‘l.l bht h.|u mlk.u bl mlk.|arṣ.drkt.yštkn.|dll.al.ilak.l bn.|ilm.mt.‘dd.l ydd.|il.ǵ 4[51].7.43
[--]ṯ š.ilt.mgdl š.ilt.asrm š.|w l ll.šp. pgr.w ṯrmnm.bt mlk.|il[bt].gdlt.ušḫry.gdlt.ym gdlt.|b‘l gdlt.yrḫ.gdlt.|gdlt.ṯ 34[1].12
dm.yd h.|k tǵḏ.arz.b ymn h.|bkm.yṯb.b‘l.l bht h.|u mlk.u bl mlk.|arṣ.drkt.yštkn.|dll.al.ilak.l bn.|ilm.mt.‘dd.l 4[51].7.43
lk šbny.|lmd.atn.prln.rb.|khnm rb.nqdm.|ṯ‘y.nqmd.mlk ugr[t].|adn.yrgb.b‘l.ṯrmn. 6.6[62.2].56
l.mlk[.u]grt.|iḫ y.rgm.|[tḥ]m.m[lk.-]bl[-].|yšlm.l[k].ilm.|tǵ 2159.1
l.mlk.ugrt.|aḫ y.rgm.|tḥm.mlk.ṣr.aḫ k.|y[š]lm.l k.ilm.|tǵr k 2059.1
[šmt.n]qmp‘.|[bn.nq]md.|[mlk.]ugrt.|b‘l ṣdq.|skn.bt.|mlk.ṯǵr.|[m]lk.bny.|[--].lb.mlk. 1007.3
b.|[ḫm]š.mat pḥm.|[ḫm]š[.m]at.iqnu.|argmn.nqmd.mlk.|ugrt.d ybl.l špš.|mlk.rb.b‘l h.|ks.ḫrṣ.ktn.mit.pḥm.|m 64[118].24
l ym.hnd.|‘mṯtmr.|bn.nqmp‘.|mlk.ugrt.|ytn.bt.annḏr.|bn.ytn.bnš.|[ml]k.d.b riš.|[--.-]nt. 1009.4
l ym hnd.|‘mṯtmr.bn.|nqmp‘.ml[k].|ugrt.ytn.|šd.kḏǵdl[.bn].|[-]š[-]y.d.b š[-]y.|[---.y]d gt 1008.3
ṭqšlm.|b unṯ.‘d ‘lm.|mišmn.nqmd.|mlk ugrt.|nqmd.mlk.ugrt.|ktb.spr hnd.|dt brrt.ṣṭqšlm.|‘bd h.hnd.|w mn k 1005.8
.|d brt.kmt.|br.ṣṭqšlm.|b unṯ.‘d ‘lm.|mišmn.nqmd.|mlk ugrt.|nqmd.mlk.ugrt.|ktb.spr hnd.|dt brrt.ṣṭqšlm.|‘b 1005.7
tḥm.pgn.|l.mlk.ugrt.|rgm.|yšlm.l k.[il]m.|tǵr k.tšlm k.|hn ny.‘m n.š[l 2061.2
[---.k]rgmš.|[l.m]lk.ugrt.rgm[.-]y.|[---.--]m.rgm.|[---.]šknt.|[---.--]dy. 1011.2
.mlk.rb].|b‘l h.šlm.[w spš].|mlk.rb.b‘l h.[---].|nqmd.mlk.ugr[t.--].|phy.|w ṯpllm.mlk.r[b.--].|mṣmt.l nqmd.[---.- 64[118].14
spr ‘psm.|dt.št.|uryn.|l mlk.ugrt. 1171.4
[spr.ilmlk.ṯ‘]y.nqmd.mlk.ugrt. 4[51].9.1
.amn.|[---.-]ktt.hn.ib.|[---.]mlk.|[---.]adt y.td‘.|w.ap.mlk.uḏ[r].|[-]d‘.k.iḫd.[---].|w.mlk.b‘l y.|lm.škn.hnk.|l ‘bd 1012.20
l.mlkt.|um y.rgm.|tḥm.mlk.|bn k.|l.p‘n.um y.|qlt.l.um y.| 50[117].1
l amlk.b ṣrrt.ṣpn.|yrd.‘ṯtr.‘rẓ.yrd.|l kḥṯ.aliyn.b‘l.|w ymlk.b arṣ.il.kl h.|[---] š abn.b rḥbt.|[---] š abn.b kknt. 6.1.65[49.1.37]
t.|[---.]ḫw[t.---].|[---.]š[--].|w ym ym.yš|al.|w mlk.d mlk.|b ḫwt.špḥ.|l ydn.‘bd.mlk.|d št.‘l.ḫrd h.|špḥ.al.thbṭ.| 2062.2.1
spr.ḥpr.bnš mlk.b yrḫ iṯt[bnm].|ršpab.rb ‘šrt.m[r]yn.|pǵdn.ilb‘l.krwn.l 2011.1
.w.mšlt.|l.udmym.b.ṯmnt.‘šrt.ksp.|šb‘m.lbš.d.‘rb.bt.mlk.|b.mit.ḫmšt.kbd.ksp.|ṯlṯ.ktnt.b d.an[r]my.|b.‘šrt.ksp.b 2101.16
isp.ḥmt.|[‘ṯ]r.w ‘ṯtpr.yisp.ḥmt.ṯṯ.w kṯṯ.|[yus]p.ḥmt.mlk.b ‘ṯtrt.yisp.ḥmt.|[kṯ]r w ḫss.y[i]sp.ḥmt.šḥr.w šlm.|[yis UG5.8.17
w.b.glb.|phnn.w.|mndym.|bdnh.|l[q]ḥt.|[--]km.‘m.mlk.|[b]ǵl hm.w.iblbl hm.|w.b.ṯb h.[---].|spr ḥ[--.---].|w.‘ 2129.9
h.l tmǵyn.|hdm.riš h.l ymǵy.|aps h.w y‘n.‘ṯtr.‘rẓ.|l amlk.b ṣrrt.ṣpn.|yrd.‘ṯtr.‘rẓ.yrd.|l kḥṯ.aliyn.b‘l.|w ymlk.b 6.1.62[49.1.34]
aṯrt.‘ṣr[m] l inš.|[ilm.---].lbbmm.gdlt.‘rb špš w ḥl.|[mlk.b ar]b‘t.‘[š]rt.yrtḥṣ.mlk.brr.|[b ym.ml]at.y[ql]n.al[p]m. 36[9].1.10
lkt.u]m y.|mnm[.šlm].|w.rgm[.ṯṯb.l] y.|hl ny.‘mn.|mlk.b.ṯy ndr.|iṯt.w.ht.|[-]sny.uḏr h.|w.hm.ḫt.|‘l.w.likt.|‘m 1013.13
‘t.‘š|rt.yr[tḥṣ.ml]k.brr.|‘lm.š.š[--].l[--.]‘rb.šp|š.w ḥl[.ml]k.|bn.aup[š.--].bsbn hzpḫ tlṯt.|kṯr[.---.--]trt ḫmšt.bn gd APP.II[173].57
bn.bly.|bn.ṯbrn.|bn.ḥgby.|bn.pity.|bn.slgyn.|‘zn.bn.mlk.|bn.alṯn.|bn.ṯmyr.|ẓbr.|bn.ṯdṯb.|bn.‘rmn.|bn.alz.|bn. 115[301].2.8
.|bn.gṯprg.|gṯpbn.|bn.b[--].|[b]n.[---].|bn.a[--].|bn.ml[k].|bn.glyn.|bn.‘dr.|bn.ṯmq.|bn.ntp.|bn.‘grt. 1057.17
l mlkt.u[m] y.|[rg]m[.]t[ḥm].|mlk.bn [k].|[l].p‘n.um [y].|qlt[.l um] y.|yšlm.il[m].|tǵ[r] k 1013.3
l.mlkt.|um y.rgm.|tḥm.mlk.|bn k.|l.p‘n.um y.|qlt.l.um y.|yšlm.ilm.|tǵr k.tšlm k. 50[117].3
l h.|bn.qṣn.|bn.ksln.|bn.ṣrym.|bn.ṯmq.|bn.ntp.|bn.mlk.|bn.ṯ‘[-].|bn.km[-].|bn.r[--].|[bn.]‘[---].|[bn.]r[---].|[bn 1073.1.10
‘.|[bn.nq]md.|[mlk.]ugrt.|b‘l ṣdq.|skn.bt.|mlk.ṯǵr.|[m]lk.bny.|[--].lb.mlk.|[---.]ṣmḫ. 1007.7
tḥm.ydn.‘m.mlk.|b‘l h.nǵr.ḥwt k.|w l.a[--]t.tšknn.|ḫmšm.l mi[t].any.|t 2062.1.1
.--]n.d[--.--]i.|[--]t.mdt h[.l.]‘ṯtrt.šd.|[---.-]rt.mḫṣ.bnš.mlk.yb‘l hm.|[---.--]t.w.ḫpn.l.azzlt.|[---.]l.‘ṯtrt.šd.|[---].yb‘l 2062.1.1
.hm.yrgm.mlk.|b‘l y.tmǵyy.hn.|alpm.ššwm.hnd.|w.mlk.b‘l y.bnš.|bnny.‘mn.|mlakty.hnd.|ylak ‘m y.|w.t‘l.ṯh. 1106.53
.hnk.|l ‘bd h.alpm.š[šw]m.|rgmt.‘ly.ṯh.lm.|l.ytn.hm.mlk.[b]‘l y.|w.hn.ibm.šṣq l y.|p.l.ašt.aṯt y.|n‘r y.ṯh.l pn.ib. 1012.33
k.|[---.]adt y.td‘.|w.ap.mlk.uḏ[r].|[-]d‘.k.iḫd.[---].|w.mlk.b‘l y.|lm.škn.hnk.|l ‘bd h.alpm.š[šw]m.|rgmt.‘ly.ṯh.lm 1012.26
m.šṣq l y.|p.l.ašt.aṯt y.|n‘r y.ṯh.l pn.ib.|hn.hm.yrgm.mlk.|b‘l y.tmǵyy.hn.|alpm.ššwm.hnd.|w.mlk.b‘l y.bnš.|bn 1012.22
[l.ml]k.[b‘l y].|rg[m].|tḥm.wr[--].|yšlm.[l] k.|ilm.t[ǵ]r k.|tšl 1012.30
l.mlk.b[‘l y].|r[gm].|tḥm.rb.mi[--.‘]bd k.|l.p‘n.b‘l y[.mrḥqtm 2010.1
l.mlk.b‘[l] y.|rgm.|tḥm.ṯpṭb[‘l].|[‘]bd k.|[l.p]‘n.b‘l y.|[šb‘] d 2008.1.1
ṣltm.b m|rqdm.dšn.b.ḥbr.kṯr.ṭbm.|w tšt.‘nt.gṯr.b‘lt.mlk.b‘|lt.drkt.b‘lt.šmm.rmm.|[b‘l]t.kpṯ.w ‘nt.di.dit.rḫpt.|[- 2063.1
--].|hmt.w.anyt.hm.t‘[rb].|mkr.hn d.w.rgm.ank[.--].|mlkt.ybqš.anyt.w.at[--].|w mkr n.mlk[.---]. UG5.2.1.6
b arb‘t.‘šr[t].|yrtḥṣ.mlk.b[rr].|b ym.mlat.|tqln.alpm.|yrḫ.‘šrt.l b‘[l].|dqtm.w y 2008.2.13

UG5.13.2

--].lbbmm.gdlt.ʻrb špš w ḥl. | [mlk.b ar]bʻt.ʻ[š]rt.yrtḥṣ.mlk.brr. | [b ym.ml]at.y[ql]n.al[p]m.yrḫ.ʻšrt. | [l bʻl.ṣ]pn.[dq] 36[9].1.10

yn.b ym.ḥdṯ]. | šmtr.[uṯkl.l il.šlmm]. | b ṯlṯt ʻ[šrt.yrtḥṣ.mlk.brr]. | b arbʻ[t.ʻšrt.riš.argmn]. | w ṯn šm.l [bʻlt.bhtm.ʻṣrm 35[3].3

yn.b ym.ḥdṯ. | [šmtr].uṯkl.l il.šlmm. | b [ṯlṯt].ʻšrt.yrtḥṣ.mlk. | br[r.]b a[r]bʻt.ʻšrt.riš. | arg[mn.w ṯn.]šm.l bʻlt. | bhtm.ʻṣ APP.II[173].3

.l bʻlt bhtm. | b arbʻt ʻšrt.bʻl. | ʻrkm. | b ṯmnt.ʻšrt.yr | tḥṣ.mlk.brr. | ʻlm.tzǵ.b ǵb.ṣpn. | nḥkt.ksp.w ḫrṣ ṯʻ ṯn šm l btbt. | a UG5.12.A.6

] | m.ḥdṯ.ṯn šm[.---.--]t. | b yrḫ.ši[-.b ar]bʻt.ʻš | rt.yr[tḥṣ.ml]k.brr. | ʻlm.š.š[--].l[--.]ʻrb.šp | š.w ḥl[.ml]k. | bn.aup[š.--].bs APP.II[173].55

.aylt. | ḫmš.mat.arbʻm. | kbd.ksp.anyt. | d.ʻrb.b.anyt. | l.mlk.gbl. | w.ḫmšm.ksp. | lqḥ.mlk.gbl. | lbš.anyt h. | bʻrm.ksp. | 2106.13

ksp.anyt. | d.ʻrb.b.anyt. | l.mlk.gbl. | w.ḫmšm.ksp. | lqḥ.mlk.gbl. | lbš.anyt h. | bʻrm.ksp. | mḫr.hn. 2106.15

| rʻm[-.---]. | mn[-.---]. | hyrm.h[--.---]. | yrmm h[--.---]. | mlk.gbʻ h d [---]. | ibr.k l hm.d l h q[--.---]. | l ytn.l hm.tḥt bʻl 9[33].2.3

šrš. | lbnm. | ḫlb.krd. | ṣʻ. | mlk. | gbʻly. | ypr. | ary. | ẓrn. | art. | ṯlḥny. | ṯlrby. | dmt. | aǵt. | w 71[113].5

z. | bn ḫlm. | bn.ḏmr. | bn.ʻyn. | ubnyn. | rpš d ydy. | ǵbl. | mlk. | gwl. | rqd. | ḫlby. | ʻn[q]pat. | m[ʼ]rb. | ʻrm. | bn.ḥgby. | mr 2075.22

ḥmr[h.l gʻt.]alp. | ḥrṯ[.l z]ǵt.klb. | [ṣ]pr[.apn]k. | [pb]l[.mlk.g]m.l aṯt | [h.k]y[ṣḥ.]šmʻ.mʻ. | [--.]ʻm[.-.]aṯt y[.-]. | [---.]t 14[KRT].5.228

ṣ.b.arbʻm. | mit.ḫršḫ.b.ṯqlm. | w.šbʻ.ʻšr.šmn. | d.l.yṣa.bt.mlk. | tgmr.ksp.mitm. | ḫmšm.kbd. 2100.21

. | ṯbʻm. | kyn. | bʻln. | ytršp. | ḥmšm.ṯmn.kbd. | tgmr.bnš.mlk. | d.b d.adnʻm. | [š]bʻ.b.ḥrṯm. | [ṯ]lṯ.b.ṯǵrm. | rb qrt.aḫd. | ṯ 1024.2.26

[sp]r.bnš.ml[k.d.b] d adn[ʻm]. | [---].riš[.---].kt. | [y]nḥm. | ilbʻl. | ʻbdyr[1024.1.1

spr.bnš.mlk. | d.b d.prṯ. | tšʻ.l.ʻšrm. | lqḥ.ššlmt. | ṯmn.l.arbʻm. | lqḥ.šʻrt. 1025.1

r. | bn.nqmpʻ. | mlk.ugrt. | ytn.bt.annḏr. | bn.ytn.bnš. | [ml]k.d.b riš. | [--.-]nt. | [l.ʻb]dmlk. | [--.-]m[-]r. | [w.l.]bn h.ʻd. | 1009.7

[s]pr.bnš.mlk.d.b.tbq. | [kr]wn. | [--]n. | [q]ṣy. | ṯn.bn.iwrḫz.[n]ʻrm. | yṣr[2066.1.1

h.n[bln]. | klny n[.n]bl.ks h. | [an]y.l yṣḥ.ṯr il.ab h. | [i]l.mlk.d yknn h.yṣḥ. | aṯrt.w bn h.ilt.w ṣbrt. | ary h.wn.in.bt.l b 4[51].4.48

[-----]. | [---.--]y. | [-----]. | [any.l yṣ]ḥ.ṯr. | [il.ab h.i]l.mlk. | [d yknn h.yṣ]ḥ.aṯ | [rt.w bn h.]ilt. | [w ṣbrt.ary]h. | [wn. 4[51].1.5

y y.qš h. | nbln.klny y.nbl.ks h. | any.l yṣḥ.ṯr.il.ab h.il. | mlk.d yknn h.yṣḥ.aṯrt. | w bn h.ilt.w ṣbrt.arḫ h. | wn.in.bt.l b 3[ʻNT.VI].5.44

] ṣmdm trm.d [ṣ]py. | w.trm.aḥdm. | ṣpym. | ṯlṯ mrkbt mlk. | d.l.ṣpy. | [---.t]r hm. | [---].ššb. | [---.]tr h. | [a]rbʻ.qlʻm. | a 1122.5

-.]d[--]t. | [---.]ḥw[t.---]. | [---.]š[--]. | w ym ym.yš | al. | w mlk.d mlk. | b ḥwt.špḥ. | l ydn.ʻbd.mlk. | d št.ʻl.ḫrd h. | špḥ.al. 2062.2.1

-]. | [-----]. | [-----]. | tḥm[.---]. | l pʻn.bʻl y[.---]. | qlt. | [--]t.mlk.d.y[mlk]. | [--.]ʻbdyrḫ.l.ml[k]. | [--]t.w.lqḥ. | yn[.--].b dn 2064.12

w ym ym.yš | al. | w mlk.d mlk. | b ḥwt.špḥ. | l ydn.ʻbd.mlk. | d št.ʻl.ḫrd h. | špḥ.al.thbṭ. | ḫrd.ʻps.aḫd.kw | sgt. | ḫrd ks 2062.2.3

spr.bnš.mlk. | d taršn.ʻmsn. | bṣr.abn.špšyn. | dqn. | aǵlmn. | knʻm. | aḫr 2067.1.1

yn.d.ykl.b d.[---]. | b.dbḥ.mlk. | dbḥ ṣpn. | [-]zǵm. | [i]lib. | [i]lbldn. | [p]dry.bt.mlk. | [-]lp 2004.2

m.ibr.b tk.mšmš d[--]. | ittpq.l awl. | išttk.lm.ttkn. | štk.mlk.dn. | štk.šibt.ʻn. | štk.qr.bt.il. | w mṣlt.bt.ḥr[š]. 12[75].2.59

.bʻl]. | yʻl.bʻl.b ǵ[r.---]. | w bn.dgn.b š[---]. | bʻl.yṯb.l ks[i.mlk h]. | bn.dgn.l kḥ[ṯ.drkt h]. | l alp.ql.ẓ[--.---]. | l np ql.nd.[- 10[76].3.14

ʻ.y | dd.il.ǵzr.yʻr.mt. | b ql h.y[---.---]. | bʻl.yṯṯbn[.l ksi]. | mlk h.l[nḫt.l kḥṯ]. | drkt h[.---]. | [---.]d[--.---]. | [---].hn[.---]. 6[49].6.34

[--.---]. | b d.aliyn b[ʻl.---]. | kd.ynaṣn[.---]. | gršnn.l k[si.mlk h.l nḫt.l kḥṯ]. | drkt h.š[--.--]. | w hm.ap.l[--.---]. | ymḫṣ k 1[ʻNT.X].4.24

ṣ.ṭrd.bʻl. | b mrym.ṣpn.mšṣṣ.[-]kʻ[-]. | udn h.grš h.l ksi.mlk h. | l nḫt.l kḥṯ.drkt h. | mn m.ib.ypʻ.l bʻl.ṣrt.l rkb.ʻrpt. | [- 3[ʻNT].4.46

-]. | šmn.prst[.---]. | ydr.hm.ym[.---]. | ʻl amr.yu[ḫd.ksa.mlk h]. | nḫt.kḥṯ.d[rkt h.b bt y]. | aṣḥ.rpi[m.iqra.ilnym]. | b q 22.1[123].17

ym.ymḫṣ.b ṣmd. | ṣḥr mt.ymṣḫ.l arṣ. | [yṯb.]b[ʻ]l.l ksi.mlk h. | [---].l kḥṯ.drkt h. | l [ym]m.l yrḫm.l yrḫm. | l šnt.[m] 6[49].5.5

k]. | [---].šbʻ.ṯir k.[---]. | [---.]ab y.ndt.ank[.---]. | [---.--]l.mlk.tlk.b ṣd[.---]. | [---.]mt.išryt[.---]. | [---.--]r.almd k.[---]. | [- 18[3AQHT].1.27

--]rm.d krm. | [---].l ʻnt m. | [---.]l šlm. | [-]l[-.-]ry.ylbš. | mlk.ylk.lqḥ.ilm. | aṯr.ilm.ylk.pʻnm. | mlk.pʻnm.yl[k]. | šbʻ.pa 33[5].23

.k ksp. | l ʻbrm.zt.ḫrṣ.l ʻbrm.kš. | dpr.ṯlḥn.b qʻl.b qʻl. | mlkm.hn.ym.yṣq.yn.ṯmk. | mrṯ.yn.srnm.yn.bld. | ǵll.yn.išryt. 22.2[124].17

nd. | dt brrt.ṣṭqšlm. | ʻbd h.hnd. | w mn km.l yqḥ. | spr.mlk.hnd. | b yd.ṣṭqšlm. | ʻd ʻlm. 1005.13

.---]. | b hm.w.rgm.hw.al[--]. | atn.ksp.l hm.ʻd. | ilak.ʻm.mlk. | ht.lik[t.--.]mlk[.--]. | w.mlk.yštal.b.hn[--]. | hmt.w.anyt. 2008.2.8

atn. | ʻṣm.l k. | arbʻ.ʻṣm. | ʻl.ar. | w.ṯlṯ. | ʻl.ubrʻy. | w.ṯn.ʻl. | mlk. | w.aḥd. | ʻl atlg. | w l.ʻṣm. | tspr. | nrn.al.tud | ad.at.l hm. | 1010.14

[---].d[--.---]. | b ql[.-----]. | w tštqdn[.-----]. | hm. | w yḥ.mlk. | w ik m.kn.w [---]. | tšknnnn[.---]. 62[26].9

[ṯb.brr]. | b.[šb]ʻ.ṣbu.[š]pš.w.ḥly[t].ʻ[r]b[.š]p[š]. | w [ḥl.]mlk.[w.]b.ym.ḥdṯ.ṯn.šm. | l.[---]t. | i[d.yd]bḥ.mlk.l.prgl.ṣqrn. 35[3].48

lt.rgm.yṯṯb]. | brr.b šbʻ[.ṣbu.špš.w ḥl] | yt.ʻrb špš[.w ḥl.mlk.w.b y] | m.ḥdṯ.ṯn šm[.---.--]t. | b yrḫ.ši[-.b ar]bʻt.ʻš | rt.yr[APP.II[173].52

spr.npš.d. | ʻrb.bt.mlk. | w.b.spr.l.št. | yrmʻl. | ṣry. | iršy. | yʻḏrd. | ayaḫ. | bn.aylt. | 2106.2

šbʻ [d]. | [mr]ḥqtm. | qlt. | ʻbd k.b. | lwsnd. | [w] b ṣr. | ʻm.mlk. | w.ht. | mlk.syr. | ns.w.ṯm. | ydbḥ. | mlǵ[.---]. | w.m[--.--]y 2063.12

ʻln aḫ h. | w.ḥṯṯn bn h. | w.btšy.bt h. | w.ištrmy. | bt.ʻbd mlk. | w.snt. | bt.ugrt. | w.pdy h[m]. | iwrkl.mit. | ksp.b y[d]. | b 1006.9

ḥ il. | l rbt.aṯrt ym.šmʻ. | l rbt.aṯr[t] ym.tn. | aḥd.b bn k.amlkn. | w tʻn.rbt.aṯrt ym. | bl.nmlk.ydʻ.ylḥn. | w yʻn.lṭpn.il d 6.1.46[49.1.18]

.um y. | mnm.šlm. | w.rgm.ṯṯb.l y. | bm.ṯy.ndr. | iṯt.ʻmn.mlkt. | w.rgm y.l[--]. | lqt.w.pn. | mlk.nr b n. 50[117].15

--]rny. | [---.]ṯm.hw.i[--]ty. | [---].ibʻr.a[--.]ḏmr. | [---.]w mlk.w rg[m.---]. | [--.rg]m.ank.[b]ʻr.[--]ny. | [--]n.bt k.[---.]bʻ[1002.53

[p.w].š.šlmm.pamt.šbʻ.klb h. | yr[--.]mlk.ṣbu.špš.w.ḥl.mlk. | w.[---].ypm.w.mḫ[--].t[ṯ]ṯbn.[-]. | b.[--].w.km.iṯ.y[--.]šq 35[3].53

.il.ab h l pn[.zb]l y[m]. | [l pn.ṯp]ṭ[.nhr.]mlkt.[--]pm.l mlkt.wn.in.aṯt. | [l]k.k[m.ilm]. | [w ǵlmt.k bn.qdš.]w y[--.]zb 2.3[129].22

yn[.--].b dn h. | w.ml[k].ššwm.nʻmm. | ytn.l.ʻbdyrḫ. | w.mlk.z[--.--]n.ššwm. | nʻmm.[--].ṯṯm.w.at. | nǵṯ.w.ytn.hm.l k. | 2064.18

p.izr. | [a]rz. | k.tʻrb.ʻṯtrt.šd.bt[.m]lk. | k.tʻrbn.ršp m.bt.mlk. | ḫlu.dg. | ḥdṯm. | dbḥ.bʻl.k.tdd.bʻlt.bhtm. | b.[-]ǵb.ršp.ṣbi 2004.11

ṯlḥnt.lḥm št. | b krpnm.yn.b k.ḫrṣ. | dm.ʻṣm.hm.yd.il mlk. | yḫss k.ahbt.ṯr.tʻrr k. | w tʻn.rbt.aṯrt ym. | tḥm k.il.ḥkm. 4[51].4.38

n.apsn[y.---]. | plzn.qrty[.---]. | w.klt h.b.t[--.---]. | bʻl y.mlk[y.---]. | yd.bt h.yd[.---]. | ary.yd.t[--.---]. | ḫtn h.šbʻl[.---]. 81[329].13

ṯmn.mrkbt.dt. | ʻrb.bt.mlk. | yd.apnt hn. | yd.ḥẓ hn. | yd.tr hn. | w.l.ṯt.mrkbtm. | inn. 1121.2

ṯr[t] ym.tn. | aḥd.b bn k.amlkn. | w tʻn.rbt.aṯrt ym. | bl.nmlk.ydʻ.ylḥn. | w yʻn.lṭpn.il d pi | d dq.anm.l yrẓ. | ʻm.bʻl.l y 6.1.48[49.1.20]

ʻ[t]. | [-]tr.šrk.il. | ʻrb.špš.l ymǵ. | krt.ṣbia.špš. | bʻl ny.w ymlk. | [y]ṣb.ʻln.w y[-]y. | [kr]t.ṯʻ.ʻln.bḫr. | [---].aṯt k.ʻl. | [---] k. 15[128].5.20

bš. | u---].mlk.ytn.mlbš. | [---.-]rn.k.ypdd.mlbš h. | [---.]mlk.ytn.lbš.l h. 1106.61

.--]n.b.ṯlṯ.šnt.l.nṣd. | [---.--]ršp.mlk.k.ypdd.mlbš. | u---].mlk.ytn.mlbš. | [---.-]rn.k.ypdd.mlbš h. | [---.]mlk.ytn.lbš.l h. 1106.59

-.]ysd k. | [---.--]r.dr.dr. | [---.--]y k.w rḥd. | [---]y ilm.d mlk. | y[ṯ]b.aliyn.bʻl. | ytʻdd.rkb.ʻrpt. | [--].ydd.w yqlṣn. | yqm. 4[51].3.9

]. | w ṯn šm.l [bʻlt.bhtm.ʻṣrm.l inš]. | ilm.w š d[d.ilš.š.--.mlk]. | yṯb.brr[.w mḥ-.---]. | ym.[ʼ]lm.yʻ[--.---]. | [--.-]g[-.-]s w 35[3].6

.a]l.yšmʻ k.ṯr.[i]l.ab k.l ysʻ.[alt.]ṯ[bt | k.l y]hpk. | [ksa.]mlk k.l yṯbr.ḫṭ.mṯpṭ k.w yʻn[.ʻṯtr].dm[-]k[-]. | [--]ḥ.b y.ṯr.il.a 2.3[129].18

ʻl. | ik.al.yšm[ʻ] k.ṯr. | il.ab k.l ysʻ.alt. | ṯbt k.l yhpk.ksa.mlk k. | l yṯbr.ḫṭ.mṯpṭ k. | yru.bn ilm t.ṯtʻ.y | dd.il.ǵzr.yʻr.mt. 6[49].6.28

ldn.|[p]dry.bt.mlk.|[-]lp.izr.|[a]rz.|k.t‘rb.‘ṯtrt.šd.bt[.m]lk.|k.t‘rbn.ršp m.bt.mlk.|ḫlu.dg.|ḥdṯm.|dbḥ.b‘l.k.tdd.b‘ 2004.10
ṯtrt.šd.|[---].yb‘lnn.|[---.--]n.b.ṯlṯ.šnt.l.nṣd.|[---.--]ršp.mlk.k.ypdd.mlbš.|u---].mlk.ytn.mlbš.|[---.-]rn.k.ypdd.mlbš 1106.58
kd.mštt.[---]n.|kdm.l.mḏrǵlm.|kd.l.mṣrym.|kd.mštt.mlk.|kd.bn.amht [-]t.|w.bn.mṣrym.|arb‘m.yn.|l.ḫrd.|ḫmš 1089.8
id ydbḥ mlk.|l ušḫ[r] ḫlmṭ.|l bbt il bt.|š l ḫlmṭ.|w tr l qlḥ.|w š ḥll UG5.7.TR3
t.w u[dm].|[ṯ]rrt.udm.y[t]n[t].|il.ušn.ab[.ad]m.|rḥq.mlk.l bt y.|n[g.]krt.l ḥẓ[r y].|w y‘n[y.k]rt[.ṯ]‘.|lm.ank.ksp. 14[KRT].6.279
bt.w udm].|[ṯrrt.udm.ytnt].|[il.w ušn.ab.adm].|[rḥq.mlk.l bt y].|[ng.kr]t.l ḥ[ẓ]r y.|[-----].|[---.ttb‘].|[mlakm.l yṯ 14[KRT].5.260
wm.mrkbt.|b trbṣ.bn.amt.|qḥ.krt.šlmm.|šlmm.w ng.mlk.|l bt y.rḥq.krt.|l ḥẓr y.al.tṣr.|udm.rbt.w udm ṯrrt.|ud 14[KRT].3.131
sl k.almnt.km.|aḫt.‘rš.mdw.anšt.|‘rš.zbln.rd.l mlk.|amlk.l drkt k.aṯb.|an.w y‘ny.krt ṯ‘.yṯbr.|ḥrn.y bn.yṯbr.ḥrn. 16.6[127].53
ṯpṭ.qṣr.npš.|km.aḫt.‘rš.mdw.|anšt.‘rš.zbln.|rd.l mlk.amlk.|l drkt.k aṯb.an.|ytb‘.yṣb ǵlm.‘l.|ab h.y‘rb.yšu g h.|w 16.6[127].37
tḥm.rgm.|mlk.|l ḥyil.|lm.tlik.‘m y.|ik y.aškn.|‘ṣm.l bt.dml.|p ank.at 1010.2
m.|mgṯ.w yṯrm.hn.ym.|w ṯn.yṯb.krt.l ‘d h.|yṯb.l ksi mlk.|l nḫt.l kḥṯ.drkt.|ap.yṣb.yṯb.b hkl.|w ywsrnn.ggn h.|l 16.6[127].23
š].|w [ḥl.]mlk.[w.]b.ym.ḥdṯ.ṯn.šm.|l.[---]t.|i[d.yd]bḥ.mlk.l.prgl.ṣqrn.b.gg.|ar[b‘.]arb‘.mṯbt.azmr.b h.š.šr[-].|al[p. 35[3].50
ṯlṯ.rb‘.ym.|ḫmš.ṯdṯ.ym.|mk.špšm.b šb‘.|w l.yšn.pbl.|mlk.l [qr.]ṯiqt.|ibr h[.l]ql.nhqt.|ḥmr[h.l g‘t.]alp.|ḥrṯ[.l z]ǵ 14[KRT].5.223
qrt h.abn.yd k.|mšdpt.w hn.špšm.|b šb‘.w l.yšn.pbl.|mlk.l qr.ṯigt.ibr h.|l ql.nhqt.ḥmr h.|l g‘t.alp.ḥrṯ.zǵt.|klb.ṣp 14[KRT].3.120
tḥm.mlk.|l.ṯryl.um y.rgm.|yšlm.l k.ilm.|tǵr k.tšlm k.|lḥt.šlm.k 2009.1.1
ṯlṯm.l.mit.š‘rt.|l.šr.‘ṯtrt.|mlbš.ṯrmnm.|k.yṯn.w.b.bt.|mlk.mlbš.|ytn.l hm.|šb‘.lbšm.allm.|l ušḫry.|ṯlṯ.mat.pṯtm.| 1107.7
|klb.ṣpr.w ylak.|mlakm.l k.‘m.krt.|mswn h.tḥm.pbl.mlk.|qḥ.ksp.w yrq.ḫrṣ.|yd.mqm h.w ‘bd.‘lm.|ṯlṯ.sswm.mr 14[KRT].3.125
n].|[‘]m[.krt.mswn h].|tš[an.g hm.w tṣḥn].|tḥ[m.pbl.mlk].|qḥ[.ksp.w yrq].|ḫrṣ.[yd.mqm h].|w ‘bd[.‘lm.ṯlṯ].|ssw 14[KRT].6.268
m.al.ttn].|‘m.[krt.msw]n.|w r[gm.l krt.]ṯ‘.|tḥm[.pbl.mlk].|qḥ.[ksp.w yr]q.|ḫrṣ[.yd.mqm] h.|‘bd[.‘lm.ṯlṯ].|ss[w 14[KRT].5.249
glby ṯlṯ[m].|ṣṣ bn.šrš‘m.[---].|ṣṣ mlkn‘m.a[rb‘m].|ṣṣ mlk mit[.---].|ṣṣ igy.ḫmšm.|ṣṣ yrpi m[it.---].|ṣṣ bn.š[m]mn 2097.16
|‘m[-.---].|mǵ[-.---].|šp[š.---].|ql.[---].|w mlk[.nhš.w mlk.mg]šḫ.|‘mn.[---].|ik y.[---].|w l n[qmd.---].|[w]nqmd. 64[118].6
.b‘d.|ksl k.almnt.km.|aḫt.‘rš.mdw.anšt.|‘rš.zbln.rd.l mlk.|amlk.l drkt k.aṯb.|an.w y‘ny.krt ṯ‘.yṯbr.|ḥrn.y bn.yṯb 16.6[127].52
ṯṯpṭ.ṯpṭ.qṣr.npš.|km.aḫt.‘rš.mdw.|anšt.‘rš.zbln.|rd.l mlk.amlk.|l drkt.k aṯb.an.|ytb‘.yṣb ǵlm.‘l.|ab h.y‘rb.yšu g 16.6[127].37
.|[a]rb‘.ql‘m.|arb‘.mḏrnm.|mḏrn.w.mšḫṭ.|d.mrkbt.|mlk.|mšḫṭ.w.msg.|d.tbk. 1122.14
lt.‘n[t].|tḥm k.il.ḥkm.ḥkm k.|‘m.‘lm.ḥyt.ḥẓt.tḥm k.|mlk n.aliyn.b‘l.ṯpṭ n.|in.d ‘ln h.klny y.qš h.|nbln.klny y.nbl 3[‘NT.VI].5.40
aṯrt ym.|tḥm k.il.ḥkm.ḥkmt.|‘m ‘lm.ḥyt.ḥẓt.|tḥm k.mlk n.aliy[n.]b‘l.|ṯpṭ n.w in.d ‘ln h.|klny n.q[š] h.n[bln].|k 4[51].4.43
ṯwm.‘bd k.|[---.a]dt y.mrḥqm.|[---].adt y.yšlm.|[---.]mlk n.amṣ.|[.---].nn.|[---.]qrt.dt.|[---.--]s‘.hn.mlk.|[---.l]qḥ. 1012.5
y.|l.špš.‘lm.l.‘ṯtrt.|l.‘nt.l.kl.il.alṯ[y].|nmry.mlk.‘lm.|mlk n.b‘l y.ḥw[t.--].|yšhr k.w.‘m.ṣ[--].|‘š[--.---]d.lik[t.---].| 2008.1.10
----].|‘m.b ym b‘l ysy ym[.---].|rmm.ḫnpm.mḫl[.---].|mlk.nhr.ibr[.---].|zbl b‘l.ǵlm.[---].|ṣǵr hd w r[---.---].|w l n 9[33].2.9
[-----].|‘m[-.---].|mǵ[-.---].|šp[š.---].|ql.[---].|w mlk[.nhš.w mlk.mg]šḫ.|‘mn.[---].|ik y.[---].|w l n[qmd.---]. 64[118].6
y.|bm.ṯy.ndr.|iṯt.‘mn.mlkt.|w.rgm y.l[--].|lqt.w.pn.|mlk.nr b n. 50[117].18
[---.]šlm.|[---.--]š.lalit.|[---.]bt šp.š.|y[-]lm.w mlk.|ynṣl.l ṯ‘y. 2005.2.7
.l ‘bd.|il.ttb‘.mlakm.|l yṯb.idk.pnm.|l ytn.‘mm.pbl.|mlk.tšan.|g hm.w tṣḥn.|tḥm.krt.ṯ[‘].|hwt.[n]‘mn.[ǵlm.il]. 14[KRT].6.303
ḥqtm.|qlt.|‘bd k.b.|lwsnd.|[w] b ṣr.|‘m.mlk.|w.ht.|mlk.syr.|ns.w.ṯm.|ydbḥ.|mlǵ[.---].|w.m[--.--]y.|y[--.---]. 2063.14
lk].|[--.]‘bdyrḫ.l.ml[k].|[--]t.w.lqḥ.|yn[.--].b dn h.|w.ml[k].šswm.n‘mm.|ytn.l.‘bdyrḫ.|w.mlk.z[--.--]n.šswm.|n‘ 2064.16
ṯny.uškny.|mnn.w.aṯt h.|slmu.ḥrš.mrkbt.|bnšm.dt.l.mlk.|‘bdyrḫ.bn.ṯyl.|‘bdn.w.aṯt h.w.bn h.|gpn.bn[.a]ly.|bn. 2068.17
il.ǵzr.yqra.mt.|b npš h.ystrn ydd.|b gngn h.aḥd y.d ym|lk.‘l.ilm.l ymru.|ilm.w nšm.d yšb|[‘].hmlt.arṣ.gm.l ǵ|[l 4[51].7.49
m.ṯmq.rpu.b‘l.mhr b‘l.|w mhr.‘nt.ṯm.yḥpn.ḥyl|y.zbl.mlk.‘llm y.km.tdd.|‘nt.ṣd.tštr.‘pt.šmm.|ṭbḫ.alpm.ap ṣin.šql 22.2[124].10
.rpum.l tdd].|aṯr h.l t[dd.ilnym.ṯm].|yḥpn.ḥy[ly.zbl.mlk.‘llm y].|šm‘.atm[.---].|ym.lm.qd[.---].|šmn.prst[.---].| 22.1[123].12
t.|[‘lm.---.--]k.l tšt k.liršt.|[---.]rpi.mlk ‘lm.b ‘z.|[rpu.m]lk.‘lm.b ḏmr h.bl.|[---].b ḥtk h.b nmrt h.l r|[--.]arṣ.‘z k. UG5.2.2.7
.---.--]k.l tšt k.l iršt.|[‘lm.---.--]k.l tšt k.liršt.|[---.]rpi.mlk ‘lm.b ‘z.|[rpu.m]lk.‘lm.b ḏmr h.bl.|[---].b ḥtk h.b nmrt UG5.2.2.6
[---]n.yšt.rpu.mlk.‘lm.w yšt.|[--.]gṯr.w yqr.il.yṯb.b.‘ṯtrt.|il.ṯpṭ.b hd r‘y.d UG5.2.1.1
rkb.‘rpt.ht.ib k.|b‘l m.ht.ib k.tmḫṣ.ht.tṣmt.ṣrt k.|tqḥ.mlk.‘lm k.drkt.dt dr dr k.|kṯr ṣmdm.ynḥt.w yp‘r.šmt hm.š 2.4[68].10
.rgmt.l.b‘l y.|l.špš.‘lm.l.‘ṯtrt.|l.‘nt.l.kl.il.alṯ[y].|nmry.mlk.‘lm.|mlk n.b‘l y.ḥw[t.--].|yšhr k.w.‘m.ṣ[--].|‘š[--.---]d.li 2008.1.9
h.|[---.y]mǵy.|[---.]dr h.|[---.-]rš.l b‘l.|[---.-]ǵk.rpu mlk.|[‘lm.---.--]k.l tšt k.l iršt.|[‘lm.---.--]k.l tšt k.liršt.|[---.] UG5.2.2.4
.w tgh.nyr.|rbt.w rgm.l aḫt k.|ṯtmnt.krt n.dbḥ.|dbḥ.mlk.‘šr.|‘šrt.qḥ.tp k.b yd.|[-]r[-]k.bm.ymn.|tlk.škn.‘l.ṣrrt. 16.1[125].40
k t‘rb.‘ṯtrt.ḫr[-].|bt mlk.‘šr.‘šr.[--].bt ilm.|kbr[-]m.[-]trmt.|lbš.w [-]tn.ušpǵt.|ḫr 33[5].2
rt.|ṯlṯm.ṯlṯ.kbd.mṣrrt.|‘šr.ṯn.kbd.pǵdrm.|ṯmn.mrbdt.mlk.|‘šr.pld.š‘rt. 1111.11
ty ḫmšm.|ṣṣ amtrn arb‘m.|ṣṣ iytlm mit ṯlṯm kbd.|ṣṣ m[l]k ‘šrm.|ṣṣ abš[-] mit [‘š]r kbd.|ṣṣ yḏrd ‘šrm.|ṣṣ bn aglb 2097.10
.bn.dgn.k tms m.|w ‘n.rbt.aṯrt ym.|blt.nmlk.‘ṯtr.‘rẓ.|ymlk.‘ṯtr.‘rẓ.|apnk.‘ṯtr.‘rẓ.|y‘l.b ṣrrt.ṣpn.|yṯb.l kḥṯ.aliyn.|b 6.1.55[49.1.27]
y‘db.mrḥ.|‘m.bn.dgn.k tms m.|w ‘n.rbt.aṯrt ym.|blt.nmlk.‘ṯtr.‘rẓ.|ymlk.‘ṯtr.‘rẓ.|apnk.‘ṯtr.‘rẓ.|y‘l.b ṣrrt.ṣpn.|yṯ 6.1.54[49.1.26]
.šr.y‘db.ksa.w yṯb.|tqru l špš um h.špš um ql.bl.‘m.|mlk.‘ṯtrt h.mnt.nṯk.nḥš.šmrr.|nḥš.‘q šr.ln h.mlḫš abd.ln h. UG5.7.41
.|[-]l[-.-]ry.ylbš.|mlk.ylk.lqḥ.ilm.|aṯr.ilm.ylk.p‘nm.|mlk.p‘nm.yl[k].|šb‘.pamt.l kl hm. 33[5].25
zmr.b h.š.šr[-].|al[p.w].š.šlmm.pamt.šb‘.klb h.|yr[--.]mlk.ṣbu.špš.w.ḥl.mlk.|w.[---].ypm.w.mḥ[--].t[ṯ]ṯbn.[-].|b.[- 35[3].53
ṯn.ṣbrm.|b.uškn.|ṣbr.aḥd.|b.ar.|ṣbr.aḥd.|b.mlk.|ṣbr.aḥd.|b.m‘rby.|ṣbr.aḥd.|b.ulm.|ṣbr.aḥd.|b.ubr‘y. 2073.6
hmt.hm.t‘pn.‘l.qbr.bn y.|tšḫṭann.b šnt h.qr.[mym].|mlk.yṣm.y l km.qr.mym.d ‘[l k].|mḫṣ.aqht.ǵzr.amd.gr bt il. 19[1AQHT].3.152
l.mlk.ugrt.|aḫ y.rgm.|tḥm.mlk.ṣr.aḫ k.|y[š]lm.l k.ilm.|tǵr k.tšlm k.|hn ny.‘m n.|šlm. 2059.3
ašr nkl w ib[.bt].|ḫrḫb.mlk qẓ ḫrḫb m|lk aǵzt.b sǵ[--.]špš.|yrḫ yṯkḥ yḥ[bq] [-].|tld 24[77].2
-]l|‘.l kṯrt hl[l.sn]nt.|ylak yrḫ ny[r] šmm.‘m.|ḫr[ḫ]b mlk qẓ.tn nkl y|rḫ ytrḫ.ib t‘rb m b bh|t h.w atn mhr h l a| 24[77].17
q|nim.atn šd h krm[m].|šd dd h ḥrnqm.w |y‘n ḫrḫb mlk qẓ [l].|n‘mn.ilm l ḫt[n].|m.b‘l trḫ pdry b[t h].|aqrb k 24[77].24
m]š[.m]at.iqnu.|argmn.nqmd.mlk.|ugrt.d ybl.l špš.|mlk.rb.b‘l h.|ks.ḫrṣ.ktn.mit.pḥm.|mit.iqni.l mlkt.|ks.ḫrṣ.k 64[118].26
k y.[---].|w l n[qmd.---].|[w]nqmd.[---].|[-.]‘mn.šp[š.mlk.rb].|b‘l h.šlm.[w spš].|mlk.rb.b‘l h.[---].|nqmd.mlk.ug 64[118].11
]nqmd.[---].|[-.]‘mn.šp[š.mlk.rb].|b‘l h.šlm.[w spš].|mlk.rb.b‘l h.[---].|nqmd.mlk.ugr[t.--].|phy.|w ṯpllm.mlk.r[64[118].13

w.k.rgm.špš. | mlk.rb.b'l y.u. | '[--.]mlakt.'bd h. | [---.]b'l k.yḫpn. | [---.]'m h. 1018.2
.---]. | b.[---.mlk]. | rb[.b'l y.---]. | w.an[k.---]. | arš[.---]. | mlk.r[b.b']l y.p.l. | ḥy.np[š.a]rš. | l.pn.b'[l y.l].pn.b'l y. | w.urk 1018.17
.---]. | yd[--.]mlk. | rb.b['l y.---]. | [-----]. | r[--.---]. | b.[---.mlk]. | rb[.b'l y.---]. | w.an[k.---]. | arš[.---]. | mlk.r[b.b']l y.p.l. 1018.13
.yḫpn. | [---.]'m h.u ky. | [---.--]d k.k.tmǵy. | ml[--.--]š[.ml]k.rb. | b['l y.---]. | yd[--.]mlk. | rb.b['l y.---]. | [-----]. | r[--.---] 1018.7
-.--]d k.k.tmǵy. | ml[--.--]š[.ml]k.rb. | b['l y.---]. | yd[--.]mlk. | rb.b['l y.---]. | [-----]. | r[--.---]. | b.[---.mlk]. | rb[.b'l y.---]. 1018.9
.ym.b'l y. | l.pn.amn.w.l.pn. | il.mṣrm.dt.tǵrn. | npš.špš.mlk. | rb.b'l y. 1018.23
mlk.rb.b'l h.[---]. | nqmd.mlk.ugr[t.--]. | phy. | w ṯpllm.mlk.r[b.--]. | mṣmt.l nqmd.[---.-]št. | hl ny.argmn.d [ybl.n]q 64[118].16
.b.y'rt. | ṯn.bnšm.b.'rmt. | arb'.bnšm.b.šrš. | ṯṯ.bnšm.b.mlk. | arb'.bnšm.b.bṣr. | ṯn.bnšm.[b.]rqd. | ṯn.b[nšm.b.---]y. | [- 2076.38
ap. | pd. | mlk.arb'.ḫm[rm.w.arb]'.bnšm. | ar.ḫmš.ḥmr[m.w.ḫm]š.bnš 2040.3
mrkm. | bir.ḫmš. | uškn.arb'. | ubr'y.ṯlṯ. | ar.ṯmn 'šr h. | mlk.arb'. | ǵbl.ḫmš. | atlg.ḫmš 'šr[h]. | ulm ṯ[ṯ]. | m'rby.ḫmš. | 68[65].1.6
id.yph.mlk. | r[š]p.ḫgb.ap. | w[.n]pš.ksp. | w ḫrṣ.km[-]. | w.ḥ[--.-]lp. | 2005.1.1
mlk. | alp w.š.l b'lt. | bwrm š.iṯtqb. | w š.nbk m w.š. | gt mlk š.'lm. | l kṯr.ṯn.'lm. | tzǵ[.---.]nšm.pr. UG5.12.B.11
atn.ksp.l hm.'d. | ilak.'m.mlk. | ht.lik[t.--.]mlk[.--]. | w.mlk.yštal.b.hn[--]. | hmt.w.anyt.hm.t'[rb]. | mkr.hn d.w.rgm. 2008.2.10
gnryn. | l mlkytn. | ḥnn y l pn mlk. | šin k itn. | r' y šṣa idn l y. | l šmn iṯr hw. | p iḫdn gnryn. 1020.3
.w yš[--.--]m. | lḥm.b lḥm ay.w šty.b ḫmr yn ay. | šlm.mlk.šlm.mlkt.'rbm m.ṯnnm. | mt.w šr.ytb.b d h.ḫṭ.ṯkl.b d h. 23[52].7
ṯryl. | mh y.rgmt. | w ht.aḫ y. | bn y.yšal. | ṯryl.p rgm. | l mlk.šm y. | w l h.y'l m. | w h[t] aḫ y. | bn y.yšal. | ṯryl.w rgm[. 138.13
ṯryl. | mh y.rgmt. | w ht.aḫ y. | bn y.yšal. | ṯryl.p rgm. | l mlk.šm y. | w l h[-] y'l m. | bn y.yšal. | ṯryl.w rgm. | ṯṯb.l aḫ k. 138.13
[-]. | k rtqt mr[.---]. | k d lbšt.bir.mlak. | šmm.tmr.zbl.mlk. | šmm.tlak.ṭl.amr.. | bn km k bk[r.z]bl.am.. | rkm.agzrt[. 13[6].26
ṯn.]šm.l b'lt. | bhtm.'ṣ[rm.l in]š ilm.w š. | dd ilš.š[.---.]mlk.ytb br | r.w mḫ[--.---.]w q[--]. | ym.'lm.y[---.---]. | t.k[-]ml APP.II[173].7
spr.argmnm. | 'šrm.ksp.d mkr. | mlk. | ṯlṯ.mat.ksp.d.šb[n]. | mit.ksp.d.ṯbq. | ṯmnym.arb't. | kbd 2107.3
ṯn.ḫ[---].pgam. | ṯn[.---.b]n.mlk. | ṯ[n.---.]gpn. | [-----]. | [---.--]b. | b[--.---.b]n.'my. 1150.2
mt.n]qmp'. | [bn.nq]md. | [mlk.]ugrt. | b'l ṣdq. | skn.bt. | mlk.ṯǵr. | [m]lk.bny. | [--].lb.mlk. | [---.]ṣmḫ. 1007.6
šlm[m.]šb' pamt. | l ilm.šb['.]l kṯr. | 'lm.t'rbn.gṯrm. | bt.mlk.ṯql.ḫrṣ. | l špš.w yrḫ.l gṯr. | ṯql.ksp.ṯb.ap w np[š]. | l 'nt h. 33[5].10
yqrb. | b šal.krt.m at. | krt.k ybky. | ydm'.n'mn.ǵlm. | il.mlk[.ṯ]r ab h. | yarš.hm.drk[t]. | k ab.adm. | [-----]. 14[KRT].1.41
l.mlk[.u]grt. | iḫ y.rgm. | [ṯḥ]m.m[lk.-]bl[-]. | yšlm.l[k].ilm. | tǵr.tšl[m] k. | [-----]. | [-----]. | [--]. 2159.3
bḫ.mlk. | dbḫ ṣpn. | [-]zǵm. | [i]lib. | [i]lbldn. | [p]dry.bt.mlk. | [-]lp.izr. | [a]rz. | k.t'rb.'ṯtrt.šd.bt[.m]lk. | k.t'rbn.ršp m. 2004.7
.hw.al[--]. | atn.ksp.l hm.'d. | ilak.'m.mlk. | ht.lik[t.--.]mlk[.--]. | w.mlk.yštal.b.hn[--]. | hmt.w.anyt.hm.t'[rb]. | mkr. 2008.2.9
]rṣ.mlk. | [---.]krt.adn k. | [w y'ny.]ǵzr.ilḥu. | [---.]mrṣ.mlk. | [--.k]rt.adn k. | [--.d]bḫ.dbḫ. | [--.']šr.'šrt. | '[---.---]. | b[-- 16.1[125].59
--]. | [-----]. | ṯḥm[.---]. | l p'n.b'l y[.---]. | qlt. | [--]t.mlk.d.y[mlk]. | [--.]'bdyrḫ.l.ml[k]. | [--]t.w.lqḥ. | yn[.--].b dn h. | w.m 2064.12
[š]šw[.i]ryn.arr. | [š]dm.b.mlk. | [--.š]dm.b.ar. | [--.š]dm.b.ulm. | [--.š]dm.b.m'rby. | [--.šd 2033.1.2
pt.nh[r].yṯir.ṯr.il.ab h l pn[.zb]l y[m]. | [l pn.ṯp]ṭ[.nhr.]mlkt.[--]pm.l mlkt.wn.in.aṯt. | [l]k.k[m.ilm]. | [w ǵlmt.k bn. 2.3[129].22
| l p'n.b'l y[.---]. | qlt. | [--]t.mlk.d.y[mlk]. | [--.]'bdyrḫ.l.ml[k]. | [--]t.w.lqḥ. | yn[.--].b dn h. | w.ml[k].ššwm.n'mm. | yt 2064.13
k. | [---].w.ap.ank. | [---].l.ǵr.amn. | [---.-]ktt.hn.ib. | [---.]mlk. | [---.]adt y.td'. | w.ap.mlk.ud[r]. | [-]d'.k.iḫd.[---]. | w.ml 1012.18
[bnšm.dt.]b d.mlk. | [---.b]d.mlkt. | [---.b]d.mlk. | [---.--]ḫ.uḫd. | [---.-]luḫ. | [2014.1
--.---]. | w at[--.---]. | aṯr[t.---]. | b im[--.---]. | bl.l[---.---]. | mlk.[---]. | dt [---]. | b ṯ[--.---]. | gm[.---]. | y[--.---]. 4[51].2.44
w.]ht.ank. | [---.--]š[-.--].w.ašt. | [---].amr k. | [---].k.ybt.mlk. | [---].w.ap.ank. | [---].l.ǵr.amn. | [---.-]ktt.hn.ib. | [---.]ml 1012.14
.w.[---]. | šm't.ḫwt[.---]. | [---].nzdt.qr[t]. | [---.]dt nzdt.m[lk]. | [---.]w.ap.bṯn[.---]. | [---.]b'l y.y[--]. | [---.-]l[-.---]. 2127.2.5
ik[t.---]. | w [----]. | k[--.---]. | 'šrm[.---]. | tšt.tb'[.---]. | qrt.mlk[.---]. | w.'l.ap.s[--.---]. | b hm.w.rgm.hw.al[--]. | atn.ksp.l 2008.2.4
an[y]t.mlk[.---]. | w.[ṯ]lṯ.brm.[---]. | arb' 'tkm[.---]. 2057.1
r.yṣr. | tgǵln.ḫmš.ddm. | [---].ḫmš.ddm. | ṯṯ.l.'šrm.bn[š.mlk.---].ḫzr.lqḥ.ḥp[r]. | 'št.'šr h.bn[.---.--]ḫ.zr. | b'l.šd. 2011.40
l d[n]. | [-]bd w [---]. | [--].p il[.---]. | [i]l mt mr[b-]. | qdš mlk [---]. | kbd d ilgb[-]. | mrmnmn. | brrn aryn. | a[-]ḥn tlyn. UG5.10.2.3
.aḫ h.tph. | [ksl]h.l arṣ.ṯṯbr. | [---.]aḫ h.tbky. | [--.m]rṣ.mlk. | [---.]krt.adn k. | [w y'ny.]ǵzr.ilḥu. | [---.]mrṣ.mlk. | [--.k] 16.1[125].56
ṯḥm.ml[k.---]. | l.mlk.[---]. | rg[m]. | hn.i[---]. | ds[-.---]. | t[--.---]. | a[- 2127.1.1
. | [---.]mlk n.amṣ. | [.---].nn. | [---.]qrt.dt. | [---.--]s'.hn.mlk. | [---.l]qḥ.hn.l.ḥwt h. | [---.--]p.hn.ib.d.b.mgšḫ. | [---.i]b.h 1012.8
tkm[.---]. | uḫnp[.---]. | ušk[n.---]. | ubr['y.---]. | ar[.---]. | mlk[.---]. | ǵbl[.---]. | atl[g.---]. | u[lm.---]. | m['rby.---]. | ṯ[bq.--- 68[65].2.6
lk.]ugrt. | b'l ṣdq. | skn.bt. | mlk.ṯǵr. | [m]lk.bny. | [--].lb.mlk. | [---.]ṣmḫ. 1007.8
ṯḥm.ml[k.---]. | l.mlk.[---]. | rg[m]. | hn.i[---]. | ds[-.---]. | t[--.---]. | a[--.---]. | [---]. 2127.1.2
bn.ṣrp. | [---.-]qt.l.ṯrmnm. | [---].ṯlṯm.iqnu. | [---.l.]ṯrmn.mlk. | [---.]š'rt.šb'.'šr h. | [---.iqn]i.l.ṯrmn.qrt. | [---.]lbš.ḫmšm. 1106.13
-]r.špr.w yšt.il. | [---.--]n.il ǵnt.'gl il. | [---.--]d.il.šd yṣd mlk. | [---].yšt.il h. | [---.]iṯm h. | [---.y]mǵy. | [---.]dr h. | [---.-]r UG5.2.1.12
.b'lm.kmm. | b'lm.kmm.b'lm.kmm. | k t'rb.'ṯtrt.šd.bt.mlk[.---]. | ṯn.skm.šb'.mšlt.arb'.ḫpnt.[---]. | ḫmšm.ṯlṯ.rkb.ntn. UG5.9.1.18
[bnšm.dt.]b d.mlk. | [---.b]d.mlkt. | [---.b]d.mlk. | [---.--]ḫ.uḫd. | [---.-]luḫ. | [---.-]tn.b d.mlkt. | [---.]l.mḫṣ. 2014.3
[t]ḫm.utryn[.---]. | [g]rgš 'bdy[--]. | [--.]l mlk [---]. | [---].aḫ y[.---]. | [--]q lpš[.---]. | [---] y št k[.---]. | [---. 2130.1.3
. | [---.--]n mkr[.---]. | [---].ank.[---]. | [---.]tny.[---]. | [---.]mlk[.---]. | [---.--]m.'[-.---]. 2126.8
t.---]. | [---].abn.ṣr[p.---]. | [---.-]rt.ṯlṯm[.---]. | [--]l.ṯrmn.m[lk.---]. | [---.--]rt.š'rt[.---]. | [---.i]qni.l.ṯr[mn.art.---]. | [b.yr] 1106.29
[l k]rt. | [--].ml[k.---]. | [---]m.k[---]. | [-----]. | [---]m.il[.---]. | [---]d nhr.umt 14[KRT].1.2
d.w.rgm.ank[.--]. | mlkt.ybqš.anyt.w.at[--]. | w mkr n.mlk[.---]. 2008.2.14
ṯlṯ.mat. | šb'm kbd. | zt.ubdym. | b mlk. 1095.4
---.--]š. | [---.ṣ]dq. | tgmr. | yṣḥm. | ṯlṯm. | aḥd. | kbd. | bnš.mlk. 1055.2.6
d.ksp. | arb'.l.ḫlby. | [---].l.bt. | arb'.l.kpslnm. | kdm.b[t.]mlk. 1087.7
[---.]ṯty. | [---.-]rd y. | [---.]b'l. | [---].plz. | [---.-]tt k. | [---.]mlk. 2159.19
. | [---].aḫ y[.---]. | [--]q lpš[.---]. | [---] y št k[.---]. | [---.]l m[lk]. 2130.2.3
ḫsnm. | ubnyn. | ṯṯm[.l.]mit.ṯlṯ. | kbd[.tg]mr.bnš. | l.b.bt.mlk. 1028.14
m. | w.šb'.'šr.ḫsnm. | ḫmšm.l.mit. | bnš.l.d. | yškb.l.b.bt.mlk. 1029.16

mlkbn

.|bn.prtn.|bn ḫnn.|b[n.-]n.|bn.ṣṣb.|bn.b'ltn ḫlq.|bn.mlkbn.|bn.asyy ḫlq.|bn.kṯly.|bn.kyn.|bn.'bdḥr.|[-]prm ḫl 2016.2.3

mlky

]it.krk.m'ṣ[d.---].|b.ḫrbǵlm.ǵlm[n].|w.trhy.aṯt h.|w.mlky.b[n] h.|ily.mrily.tdgr. 2048.21
[']b[dm].|'šrm.|inšt.|mdm.|gt.mlkym.|yqšm.|kbśm.|trrm.|khnm.|kzym.|yṣrm.|mru.ibr 74[115].5
l.gt.bn.tbšn.|bn.mnyy.š'rty.|aryn.adddy.|agptr.|šb'l.mlky.|n'mn.mṣry.|y'l.kn'ny.|gdn.bn.umy.|kn'm.š'rty.|abr 91[311].5
ṣḥm.|šrm.|n'rm.|'bdm.|kzym.|ksdm.|[nsk].ṯlṯ.|gt.mlkym.|tmrym.|ṯnqym.|ṯǵrm.|mru.skn.|mru.ibrn.|yqšm. 1026.2.2

mlkyy

n.[---].|bn.[---].|bn.[---].|bn.[---].|[-----].|bn[---].|bn.mlkyy.|bn.atn.|bn.bly.|bn.ṯbrn.|bn.ḥgby.|bn.pity.|bn.slg 115[301].2.1
lmn.|bn.mly.|pslm.|bn.annd.|bn.gl'd.|w.nḥl h.|bn.mlkyy.|[bn].bm[--].|['š]rm.|[-----].|[-----].|bn.p[--].|bn.'bd 2163.3.13
arb'.'šr h.šd.|w.kmsk.d.iwrkl.|ṯlṯ.šd.d.bn.mlkyy.|kmsk.šd.iḫmn.|širm.šd.khn.|ṯlṯ.šd.w.krm.šir.d.ḫli. 1079.3

mlkym

bn[.---].|[---.]nḥl h.|[---.b]n.špš.|[---.b]n.mradn.|[---.m]lkym.|[---.--]d. 2137.6

mlkytn

gnryn.|l mlkytn.|ḥnn y l pn mlk.|šin k itn.|r' y šṣa idn l y.|l šmn iṯ 1020.2
spr.updt.|d b d.mlkytn.|kdrl.|slṯmg.|adrdn.|l[l]wn.|ydln.|ldn.|tdǵl.|ibrk 1034.2
itn.|r' y šṣa idn l y.|l šmn iṯr hw.|p iḫdn gnryn.|im mlkytn yrgm.|aḫnnn.|w iḫd. 1020.8

mlkm

t.|i[l t]'ḏr b'l.|ršp.|ddmš.|pḫr ilm.|ym.|uṯḫt.|knr.|mlkm.|šlm. 29[17].2.11

mlkn'm

b ṯlṯ.|ilmlk.'šr.ṣin.|mlkn'm.'šr.|bn.adty.'šr.|[ṣ]dqšlm ḫmš.|krzn.ḫmš.|ubr'ym 2039.3
skn.ṯlṯm.|iytlm.ṯlṯm.|ḫyml.ṯlṯm.|ǵlkz.ṯlṯm.|mlkn'm.'šrm.|mr'm.'šrm.|'mlbu.'šrm.|'mtḏl.'šrm.|y'ḏrd.' 1116.5
ṣṣ yḏrd 'šrm.|ṣṣ bn aglby ṯlṯ[m].|ṣṣ bn.šrš'm.[---].|ṣṣ mlkn'm.a[rb'm].|ṣṣ mlk mit[.---].|ṣṣ igy.ḫmšm.|ṣṣ yrpi m[i 2097.15
[---.]ybnn.|[---.]mlkn'm.|[---.]tǵpṯn.|[--.]ubln.|[--.-]ḥ[-].|[--.-]s[-]n.|[--.-]ny 123[326].1.2

mlkršp

ḏdy.|aḫyn.|ygmr.aḏddy.|gln.aṯṯ.|ddy.[a]ḏddy.|bn.mlkr[šp].|bn.y[k]n.|ynḥm.|bn.abd.b'[l].|mnḥm.bn[.---].|k 2014.45

mlkt

l.mlkt.|adt y.rgm.|tḥm.illḏr.|'bd k..|l.p'n a[dt y].|šb' d[.w š 1014.1
.l k.|[il]m.tšlm k.|[tǵ]r k.|[--]y.ibr[-].|[--]wy.rgm l.|mlkt.ugrt.|[--]kt.rgmt.|[--]y.l.ilak.|[---].'m y.|[---]m.w.lm. 1016.9
m].|tǵ[r] k.tš[lm] k.|[h]l ny.'m n[.š]lm.|w.ṯm [ny.'m.mlkt.u]m y.|mnm[.šlm].|w.rgm[.ṯṯb.l] y.|hl ny.'mn.|mlk.b 1013.9
l mlkt.u[m] y.|[rg]m[.]t[ḥm].|mlk.bn [k].|[l].p'n.um [y].|qlt 1013.1
l mrynm.|b yṯbmlk.|kdm.ǵbiš ḫry.|ḫmš yn.b d.|bḥ mlkt.|b mdr'.|ṯlṯ bt.il|ann.|kd.bt.ilann. 1090.15
bdy.b d.ǵ[--.---].|krm.pyn.arty[.---].|ṯlṯ.krm.ubdym.l mlkt.b.'nmky[.---].|mgdly.ǵlpṯr.ṯn.krmm.w.ṯlṯ.ub[dym.---]. 1081.9
b.gt.mlkt.b.rḥbn.|ḫmšm.l.mitm.zt.|w.b d.krd.|ḫmšm.l.mit.|ar 1096.1
bl.l špš.|mlk.rb.b'l h.|ks.ḫrṣ.ktn.mit.pḥm.|mit.iqni.l mlkt.|ks.ḫrṣ.ktn.mit.pḥm.|mit.iqni.l uṯryn.|ks.ksp.ktn.mit 64[118].28
mšq.mlkt.|mitm.ṯṯm.|kbd.ks[p].|ksp.|ṯmnym.|ḫrṣ. 1157.1
--]m.|lḥm.b lḥm ay.w šty.b ḫmr yn ay.|šlm.mlk.šlm.mlkt.'rbm m.ṯnnm.|mt.w šr.yṯb.b d h.ḫṭ.ṯkl.b d h.|ḫṭ.ulmn 23[52].7
[---.--]š.|[---.a]rb'm.|b'lyn.bnš.|mlkt.|'šrm.|[---.--]t. 138[41].4
l yblt.ḫbṯm.|ap ksp hm.|l yblt.|w ht.luk 'm ml[kt].|tǵsdb.šmlšn.|w tb' ank.|'m mlakt h šm' h.|w b.'ly 1021.4
[bnšm.dt.]b d.mlk.|[---.b]d.mlkt.|[---.b]d.mlk.|[---.--]ḫ.uḫd.|[---.-]luḫ.|[---.-]tn.b d.ml 2014.2
[---.--]y.bṭr.b d.mlkt.|[---.]bṭr.b d.mlkt.|[---].b d.mršp.|[---.m]rbṣ.|[---.r]b.ṯnnm.|[---.]asrm.|[2015.1.2
[---.--]y.bṭr.b d.mlkt.|[---.]bṭr.b d.mlkt.|[---].b d.mršp.|[---.m]rbṣ.|[---.r]b.ṯ 2015.1.1
n.|[---.y]rḫ.ḫyr.|[---.]yn.l.mlkt.|[---.yrḫ.]ḫlt.šb'.[---].mlkt.|[---.yrḫ.]gn.šb'[.--].|[---.yrḫ.]iṯb.šb['.---].|[-----]. 1088.13
annṯb.|kd.l.iwrmḏ.|kd.l.ydn.|[---.y]rḫ.ḫyr.|[---.]yn.l.mlkt.|[---.yrḫ.]ḫlt.šb'.[---].mlkt.|[---.yrḫ.]gn.šb'[.--].|[---.yr 1088.12
b yrḫ.[---].|šb'.yn[.---].|mlkt[.---].|kd.yn.l.[---].|armwl w [--].|arb'.yn.[--].|l adrm. 1092.3
t.|[---.b]d.mlk.|[---.--]ḫ.uḫd.|[---.-]luḫ.|[---.-]tn.b d.mlkt.|[---.]l.mḫṣ.|ab[---.]aḏddy.bn.skn.|bn.[---.]uḫd.|bn.n[2014.6

mll

---].|ṯmnt.iṣr r't.'ṣ brq y.|riš h.tply.ṭly.bn.'n h.|uz'rt.tmll.išd h.qrn[m].|dt.'l h.riš h.b glṯ.b šm[m].|[---.i]l.ṯr.iṯ.p UG5.3.1.6
.krmn.|bn.umḫ.|yky.bn.slyn.|ypln.bn.ylḥn.|'zn.bn.mll.|šrm.|[b]n.špš[yn].|[b]n.ḫrmln.|bn.tnn.|bn.pndr.|bn. 85[80].1.9

ml'n

rm.|[-]lhd.ṯt.qštm.w.ṯn.ql'm.|ulšn.ṯt.qšm.w.ql'.|bn.ml'n.qšt.w.ql'.|bn.tmy.qšt.w.ql'.|'ky.qšt.|'bdlbit.qšt.|kṯy.q 119[321].3.35

mlǵ

.|[w] b ṣr.|'m.mlk.|w.ht.|mlk.syr.|ns.w.ṯm.|ydbḥ.|mlǵ[.---].|w.m[--.--]y.|y[--.---]. 2063.17

mlṣ

.alpm.l hm. | bn.niršn. | bn.adty. | bn.alz. | bn.birtn. | bn.mlṣ. | bn.q[--]. | bn.[---]. | bn.ṯ[-]r. | bn.grdn. | [bn.-]ẖr. | [--.-]nb. 2023.1.6
ṯpt]. | [w.q]l'.w.ṯt.mrḥm. | [bn].šlmn.ql'.w.ṯ[t.---]. | [bn].mlṣ.qštm.w.uṯp[t]. | [--.q]l'.w[.---.m]rḥm. | [bn].ẖdmn.qšt.[w. 2047.7

mltḥ

. | šir.šd.šd.'šy. | d.abmn. | šir.šd.krm. | d.yrmn. | šir.[š]d.mltḥ.šd.'šy. | d.ynḥm. | tgmr.šd.ṯlṯm.šd. | w.tr[--.---]. 1079.14
l.ksp. | kdwṯ.l.grgyn.b.ṯq[l]. | ẖmšm.šmt.b.ṯql. | kkr.w.[ml]tḥ.tyt.[---]. | [b]šb'[m.w.n]ṣp.ksp. | [tgm]r.[alp.w.]ṯlṯ.mat. 2101.26

mm

yšlm.l k. | l.trǵds. | w.l.klby. | šm't.ẖti. | nẖtu.ht. | hm.in mm. | nẖtu.w.lak. | 'm y.w.yd. | ilm.p.k mtm. | 'z.mid. | hm.nṯ 53[54].9
šm.kkr. | qnm. | 'šrm.kk[r]. | brr. | [']šrm.npš. | 'šrm.zt.mm. | 'rb'm. | šmn.mr. 141[120].14

mmy

.aǵltn. | bn.ktln. | bn.'gwn. | bn.yšm'. | bdl.mḏrǵlm. | bn.mmy. | bn.ẖnyn. | bn.knn. | khnm. | bn.ṯ'y. | w.nḥl h. | w.nḥl h 104[316].9

mmskn

ty[--]. | bn.grgš. | w.npṣ bt ṯn.ṯlṯ mat. | w spl ṯlṯ.mat. | w mmskn. | w.ṯt.mqrtm. | w.ṯn.irpm.w.ṯn.trqm. | w.qpt.w.mqḥ 1103.18

mm'

y.am--]. | [---.qdq]d k.ašhlk[.šbt k.dmm]. | [šbt.dq]n k.mm'm.w[---]. | aqht.w yplṭ k.bn[.dnil.---]. | w y'ḏr k.b yd.btl 18[3AQHT].1.12
t h.šnst. | kpt.b ḥbš h.brkm.tǵl[l]. | b dm.ḏmr.ḥlqm.b mm[']. | mhrm.mṭm.tgrš. | šbm.b ksl.qšt h.mdnt. | w hln.'nt.l 3['NT].2.14
.b šmẖt.kbd.'nt. | tšyt.k brkm.tǵll b dm. | ḏmr.ḥlqm.b mm'.mhrm. | 'd.tšb'.tmtẖṣ.b bt. | tẖṣb.bn.ṯlḥnm.ymḥ. | [b]bt. 3['NT].2.28
ṣb't h.ybmt.limm. | [t]rḥṣ.yd h.b dm.ḏmr. | [u]ṣb't h.b mm'.mhrm. | [ṯ]'r.ksat.l ksat.ṯlḥnt. | [l]ṯlḥn.hdmm.ṯṯ'r.l hd 3['NT].2.35
rkt y.am[---]. | qdqd k.ašhlk.šbt[k.dmm]. | [šbt.dqn k.mm'm.]y'ny. | il.b šb't.ḥdrm.b ṯmnt. | ap.sgrt.yd'[t k.]bt.k an 3['NT.VI].5.33
.i]mṣẖ.nn.k imr.l arṣ. | [ašhlk].šbt h.dmm.šbt.dqn h. | [mm'm.-]d.l ytn.bt.l b'l.k ilm. | [w ḥẓ]r.k bn.aṯrt[.td'ṣ.]p'n. | [3['NT.VI].5.11

mmt

[pt]ḥ.aḥd.l.bt.'bdm. | [ṯ]n.ptḥ msb.bt.tu. | w.ptḥ[.aḥ]d.mmt. | ṯṯ.pt[ḥ.---]. | ṯn.pt[ḥ.---]. | w.pt[ḥ.--]r.ṯǵr. | ṯmn.ḥlnm. | ṯ 1151.11

mn

. | ksl h.anš.dt.ẓr h.tšu. | g h.w tṣḥ.ik.mǵy.gpn.w ugr. | mn.ib.yp'.l b'l.ṣrt. | l rkb.'rpt.l mẖšt.mdd. | il ym.l klt.nhr.il.r 3['NT].3.34
ḥt.alpm.ḥršm. | k.rgmt.l y.bly m. | alpm.aršt.l k.w.l y. | mn.bnš.d.l.i[--].'[m k]. | l.alpm.w.l.y[n.--]t. | w.bl.bnš.hw[-.--] 2064.24
tiẖd.šnt h.w akl.bqmm. | tšt ḥrṣ.k lb ilnm. | w ṯn.gprm.mn gpr h.šr. | aqht.y'n.kmr.kmr[.--]. | k ap'.il.b gdrt.k lb.l | ẖ 19[1AQHT].1.11
ybl.n]qmd. | l špš.arn.ṯn[.'šr h.]mn. | 'ṣrm.ṯql.kbd[.ks].mn.ẖrṣ. | w arb'.ktnt.w [---]b. | [ẖm]š.mat pḥm. | [ẖm]š[.m]at. 64[118].20
---]. | w msk.tr[.---]. | tqrb.aẖ[h.w tṣḥ]. | lm.tb'rn[.---]. | mn.yrẖ.k m[rṣ.---]. | mn.k dw.kr[t]. | w y'ny.ǵzr[.ilḥu]. | ṯlṯ.yr 16.2[125].81
tqrb.aẖ[h.w tṣḥ]. | lm.tb'rn[.---]. | mn.yrẖ.k m[rṣ.---]. | mn.k dw.kr[t]. | w y'ny.ǵzr[.ilḥu]. | ṯlṯ.yrẖm.k m[rṣ]. | arb'.k 16.2[125].82
. | [--.-]nt. | [l.'b]dmlk. | [--.-]m[-]r. | [w.l.]bn h.'d. | [']m.mn k. | mn km l.yqḥ. | bt.hnd.b d. | ['b]dmlk. | [-]k.am'[--]. | [1009.12
t. | [l.'b]dmlk. | [--.-]m[-]r. | [w.l.]bn h.'d. | [']m.mn k. | mn km l.yqḥ. | bt.hnd.b d. | ['b]dmlk. | [-]k.am'[--]. | [w.b] d.b 1009.13
mlk.ugrt. | ktb.spr hnd. | dt brrt.ṣṭqšlm. | 'bd h.hnd. | w mn km.l yqḥ. | spr.mlk.hnd. | b yd.ṣṭqšlm. | 'd 'lm. 1005.12
| w ṯṯtn.[---]. | t'l.tr[-.---]. | bt.il.li[mm.---]. | 'l.ḥbš.[---]. | mn.lik.[---]. | lik.tl[ak.---]. | t'ddn[.---]. | niṣ.p[---.---]. 5[67].4.23
ṣ.[-]k'[-]. | udn h.grš h.l ksi.mlk h. | l nẖt.l kḥṯ.drkt h. | mn m.ib.yp'.l b'l.ṣrt.l rkb.'rpt. | [-]'n.ǵlmm.y'nyn.l ib.yp'. | l 3['NT].4.48
lk. | [--]b.kmm.l k[--]. | [šp]š.b šmm.tq[ru.---.-]rt. | [---.]mn mn[-.---.--]n.nmr. | [--.]l ytk.bl[-.---.]m[--.]hwt. | [---].ṯllt. UG5.8.45
l.šrn. | 'šrt.ksp.'l.[-]lpy. | bn.ady.kkr.š'rt. | nṯk h. | kb[d.]mn.'l.abršn. | b[n.---].kršu.nṯk h. | [---.--]mm.b.krsi. 1146.11
--.-]št. | hl ny.argmn.d [ybl.n]qmd. | l špš.arn.ṯn[.'šr h.]mn. | 'ṣrm.ṯql.kbd[.ks].mn.ẖrṣ. | w arb'.ktnt.w [---]b. | [ẖm]š. 64[118].19
---.]qrt.ablm.a[blm]. | [qrt.zbl.]yrẖ.d mgdl.š[---]. | [---.]mn.'r hm[.---]. | [---.]it[.---]. | [---.]'p[.---]. 18[3AQHT].1.32
b. | bn.'rmn. | bn.alz. | bn.mṣrn. | bn.'dy. | bn.ršpy. | [---.]mn. | [--.-]sn. | [bn.-]ny. | [b]n.ẖnyn. | [bn].nbq. | [bn.]snrn. | [b 115[301].2.18
[---.b]n.[y]drn. | [---.]bn.ẖlan. | [--]r bn.mn. | [--]ry. | [--]lim bn.brq. | [--.]qtn bn.drṣy. | [--]kn bn.pri. | [2087.3

mna

-.]tn l rbd. | [---.]b'lt h w yn. | [---.rk]b 'rpt. | [---.--]n.w mnu dg. | [---.]l aliyn b'l. | [---].rkb 'rpt. 2001.2.16

mnip'l

. | šmb'l. | ykr. | bly. | ṯb'm. | ḥdṯn. | rpty. | ilym. | bn.'br. | mnip'l. | amrb'l. | dqry. | ṯdy. | yp'b'l. | bdlm. | bn.pḏ[-]. | bn.[--- 1058.15

mnd'

w y'ny.ǵzr[.ilḥu]. | ṯlṯ.yrẖm.k m[rṣ]. | arb'.k dw.k[rt]. | mnd'.krt.mǵ[y.---]. | w qbr.tṣr.q[br]. | tṣr.trm.tnq[--]. | km.nk 16.2[125].86

mnḥ

mnḥ.b d.ybnn. | arb'.mat. | l.alp.šmn. | nḥ.ṯṯ.mat. | šm[n].rqḥ. 141[120].1

mnḥy

gn.a[s]r km.hw ybl.argmn k.k ilm. | [---.]ybl.k bn.qdš.mnḥy k.ap.anš.zbl.b'[l]. | [-.yuẖ]d.b yd.mšẖṭ.bm.ymn.mẖṣ.ǵ 2.1[137].38

mnḥm

yrb'm. | n'mn. | bn.kbl. | kn'm. | bdlm. | bn.ṣǵr. | klb. | bn.mnḥm. | bn.brqn. | bn.'n. | bn.'bdy. | 'bd'ṯtr. 1046.3.45
tmkrn. | ypḥ.'bdilt. | bn.m. | ypḥ.ilšlm. | bn.prqdš. | ypḥ.mnḥm. | bn.ḥnn. | brqn.spr. 2116.21
| bn.iẖyn. | ṣdqn.bn.ass. | b'lyskn.bn.ss. | ṣdqn.bn.imrt. | mnḥm.bn.ẖyrn. | [-]yn.bn.arkbt. | [--]zbl.bt.mrnn. | a[--.---.-]' 102[323].3.11
]ḏdy. | bn.mlkr[šp]. | bn.y[k]n. | ynḥm. | bn.abd.b'[l]. | mnḥm.bn[.---]. | krmn[py]. | bn.[--]m. | bn.asr[-]. | bn.ḏr[--]. | b 2014.49

mnḥm

[---.]dd. | [---]n.dd. | [---.]dd. | bn.arwdn.dd. | mnḥm.w.kbln. | bn.ǵlm.dd. | bn.tbšn.dd. | bn.ḫran.w[.---]. | [-] 131[309].5
ḫgbn.šmʻ.skn.qrt. | nǵr krm.ʻbdadt.bʻln.ypʻmlk. | t̠ǵrm.mnḥm.klyn.ʻdršp.ǵlmn. | [a]bǵl.ṣṣn.ǵrn. | šib.mqdšt.ʻb[dml]k 2011.13
--]n. | [-----]. | [--]dd. | [bʻ]l.tǵpt̠m. | [k]rwn. | ḫrš.mrkbt. | mnḥm. | mṣrn. | md̠rǵlm. | agmy. | ʻdyn. | ʻbdbʻl. | ʻbdkt̠r.ʻbd. | t 1039.2.14
. | bnil.rb ʻšrt.lkn.ypʻn.t̠[--]. | yṣḥm.b d.ubn.krwn.tǵd.[m]nḥm. | ʻpt̠rm.šmʻrgm.skn.qrt. | ḫgbn.šmʻ.skn.qrt. | nǵr krm 2011.9
--.-]bʻm arny. | w ʻl [---.]rbʻm t̠qlm.w [---] arbʻyn. | w ʻl.mnḥm.arbʻ š[mn]. | w ʻl bn a[--.-]yn t̠qlm. | [--] ksp [---] kdr [1103.9
ʻn.rb ʻšrt.kkln.ʻbd.abṣn. | šdyn.unn.dqn. | ʻbdʻnt.rb ʻšrt.mnḥm.t̠bʻm.sḫr.ʻzn.ilhd. | bnil.rb ʻšrt.lkn.ypʻn.t̠[--]. | yṣḥm.b 2011.7

mnḫ

tt[--]. | [--.]ḫy[--.--.]l aššì.hm.ap.amr[--]. | [---].w b ym.mnḫ l abd.b ym.irtm.m[--]. | [t̠pt̠].nhr.tlʻm.t̠m.ḥrbm.its.anšq 2.4[68].3

mny

rdy. | bn.šmʻn. | bn.ǵlmy. | ǵly. | bn.dnn. | bn.rmy. | dll. | mny. | krty. | bn.ʻbṣ. | bn.argb. | ydn. | ilʻnt. | bn.urt. | ydn. | qt̠n. 2117.3.38

mnyy

bdl.gt.bn.tbšn. | bn.mnyy.šʻrty. | aryn.ad̠ddy. | agpt̠r. | šbʻl.mlky. | nʻmn.mṣry. | yʻl 91[311].2

mnm

]. | [-]š[--.---]. | [-]r[--.--]y. | in m.ʻbd k hwt. | [y]rš.ʻm y. | mnm.iršt k. | d ḫsrt.w.ank. | aštn..l.iḫ y. | w.ap.ank.mnm. | [ḫ] 2065.15
ša.b br. | nʻl.il.d qblbl. | ʻln.ybl hm.ḫrṣ. | t̠lḥn.il.d mla. | mnm.dbbm.d | msdt.arṣ. | sʻ.il.dqt.k amr. | sknt.k ḥwt.yman. 4[51].1.40
y. | mnm.iršt k. | d ḫsrt.w.ank. | aštn..l.iḫ y. | w.ap.ank.mnm. | [ḫ]s[r]t.w.uḫ y. | [y]ʻmsn.t̠mn. | w.[u]ḫ y.al ybʻrn. 2065.18
y.w.yd. | ilm.p.k mtm. | ʻz.mid. | hm.nt̠kp. | mʻn k. | w.mnm. | rgm.d.tšmʻ. | t̠mt.w.št. | b.spr.ʻm y. 53[54].16
r.ʻrbnm. | dt.ʻrb. | b.mtn.bn.ayaḫ. | b.ḫbt̠ h.ḥwt.tt h. | w.mnm.šalm. | dt.tknn. | ʻl.ʻrbnm. | hn hmt. | tknn. | mtn.bn.ʻbdy 1161.5
ǵr k.tšlm k. | hl ny.ʻm n[y]. | kll.šlm. | t̠m ny.ʻm.um y. | mnm.šlm. | w.rgm.t̠t̠b.l y. | bm.t̠y.ndr. | it̠t.ʻmn.mlkt. | w.rgm 50[117].12
[lm] k. | [h]l ny.ʻm n[.š]lm. | w.t̠m [ny.ʻm.mlkt.u]m y. | mnm[.šlm]. | w.rgm[.t̠t̠b.l] y. | hl ny.ʻmn. | mlk.b.t̠y ndr. | it̠t. 1013.10
ik[t]. | um y.ʻm y.ht.ʻm[ny]. | kll.šlm.t̠m ny. | ʻm.um y.mnm.šlm. | w.rgm.t̠t̠b.l y. | w.mndʻ.k.ank. | aḫš.mǵy.mndʻ. | k 2009.1.8
ḫ.m ab. | w al.trḫln. | ʻtn.ḫrd.ank. | ʻm ny.šlm. | kll. | w mnm. | šlm ʻm. | um y. | ʻm y.t̠t̠t̠b. | rgm. 1015.16
.l k.ilm. | tǵr k.tšlm k. | hn ny.ʻm n. | šlm.t̠m ny. | ʻm k.mnm[.š]lm. | rgm.t̠t̠[b]. | any kn.dt. | likt.mṣrm. | hn dt.b.ṣr. | 2059.8
m. | tǵr k.tšlm k. | hn ny.ʻm n.š[l]m. | t̠m ny.ʻ[m.]bn y. | mnm.[šl]m[.r]gm[.t̠t̠b]. | ky.lik.bn y. | lḥt.akl.ʻm y. | mid y w 2061.8
.pʻn. | adt y. | šbʻ d. | w.šbʻ id. | mrḫqtm. | qlt. | ʻm.adt y. | mnm.šlm. | rgm.t̠t̠t̠b. | l.ʻbd h. 52[89].13
ny. | kll.mid. | šlm. | w.ap.ank. | nḫt.t̠m ny. | ʻm.adt ny. | mnm.šlm. | rgm.t̠t̠b. | l.ʻbd k. 51[95].16
ʻbd k. | l pʻn.bʻl y. | t̠n id.šbʻ d. | mrḫqtm. | qlt.ʻm. | bʻl y.mnm. | šlm. | [r]gm[.t̠t̠t̠b]. | [l.]ʻbd[k]. 2115.2.9
[---.--]y.hnn. | [---.kll].šlm. | [---.t̠]mn.ʻm k. | [m]nm.šlm. | [---.w.r]gm.t̠t̠b. 2171.4
| ʻbd k.. | l.pʻn a[dt y]. | šbʻ d[.w šbʻ d]. | mrḫq[tm.qlt]. | mn[m.šlm]. 1014.11

mnn

[t]ḥm.it̠tl. | l mnn.ilm. | tǵr k.tšlm k. | tʻzz k.alp ymm. | w rbt.šnt. | b ʻd ʻlm 1019.1.2
----]ḫr.t̠lt̠. | y[---.bn.]kran.ḫmš. | ʻ[---].kd. | amry.kdm. | mnn.bn.gt̠tn.kdm. | ynḥm.bn[.-]r[-]t.t̠lt̠. | plwn.kdm. | tmyn.b 136[84].9
n[.---]. | [ag]dt̠b.bn[.---]. | ʻbdil.bn.[---]. | ʻpt̠n.bn.t̠sq[-]. | mnn.bn.krmn. | bn.umḫ. | yky.bn.slyn. | ypln.bn.ylḥn. | ʻzn.bn 85[80].1.5
dn. | bn.ummt. | bn.t̠b[-]. | bn.[-]r[-]. | bn.tgn. | bn.id̠rn. | mnn. | b[n].skn. | bn.pʻṣ. | bn.d̠rm. | [bn.-]ln. | [bn.-]d̠prd. 124[-].6.9
n.qqln. | m[--].bn.qqln. | ʻbdil[-].bn.qqln. | liy.bn.qqln. | mnn.bn.ṣnr. | iḫy.[b]n[.--]l[-]. | ʻbdy[rḫ].bn.gt̠tn. | yrmn.bn.ʻn. 85[80].4.6
| aršmg. | ršpy.w.at̠t h. | bn.glgl.uškny. | bn.t̠ny.uškny. | mnn.w.at̠t h. | slmu.ḫrš.mrkbt. | bnšm.dt.l.mlk. | ʻbdyrḫ.bn.t̠y 2068.15
| ʻmy. | iwrnr. | alnr. | maḫdt. | aby. | [-----]. | [-]nt. | ydn. | mnn.w bn h. | t̠kn. 107[15].12
štʻltm. | mštʻltm.l riš.agn.yqḥ.tš.b bt h. | il.ḥt̠ h.nḥt.il.ymnn.mṭ.yd h.yšu. | yr.šmm h.yr.b šmm.ʻṣr.yḫrṭ yšt. | l pḥm 23[52].37
pḥm.il.at̠tm.k ypt.hm.at̠tm.tṣḥn. | y mt.mt.nḥtm.ḥt̠ k.mmnnm.mṭ.yd k. | h[l.]ʻṣr.tḥrr.l išt.ṣḥrrt.l pḥmm. | a[t̠]tm.at̠ 23[52].40
il.at̠t.il.w ʻlm h.w hm. | at̠tm.tṣḥn y.ad ad.nḥtm.ḥt̠ k. | mmnnm.mṭ yd k.hl.ʻṣr.tḥrr.l išt. | w ṣḥrrt.l pḥmm.btm.bt.il. 23[52].44
.il.bt.il. | w ʻlm h.w hn.at̠tm.tṣḥn y.mt mt. | nḥtm.ḥt̠ k.mmnnm.mṭ yd k.hl.ʻṣr. | tḥrr.l išt.w ṣḥrt.l pḥmm.at̠tm.a[t̠t.il 23[52].47
mtn.ydln. | bʻltdtt.tlgn.ytn. | bʻltǵpt̠m.krwn.ilšn.agyn. | mnn.šr.ugrt.d̠kr.yṣr. | tǵǵln.ḫmš.ddm. | [---].ḫmš.ddm. | t̠t̠.l.ʻš 2011.37
l[--.š]šlmt. | šdyn.ššlmt. | prtwn.šʻrt. | t̠t̠n.šʻrt. | ʻdn.šʻrt. | mnn.šʻrt. | bdn.šʻrt. | ʻpt̠n.šʻrt. | ʻbd.yrḫ šʻrt. | ḫbd.t̠r yṣr šʻr. | p 97[315].7
.t̠tm.t̠lt̠m. | b.bn.agdt̠b.ʻšrm. | b.bn.ibn.arbʻt.ʻšrt. | b.bn.mnn.t̠t̠m. | b.rpan.bn.yyn.ʻšrt. | b.ypʻr.ʻšrm. | b.nʻmn.bn.ply.ḫ 2054.1.14

mnt

yštql.l ḥtr h.tlu ḥt.km.nḫl. | tplg.km.plg. | bʻd h.bhtm.mnt.bʻd h.bhtm.sgrt. | bʻd h.ʻdbt.t̠lt̠.ptḥ.bt.mnt. | ptḥ.bt.w ub UG5.7.70
.yd h.b škrn.mʻms h. | [k]šbʻ yn.spu.ksm h.bt.bʻl. | [w m]nt h bt.il.t̠ḥ.gg h.b ym. | [ti]t̠.rḥṣ.npṣ h.b ym.rt̠. | [--.y]iḫd.i 17[2AQHT].1.33
št.tšrpnn. | b rḥm.tṭḥnn.b šd. | tdrʻnn.šir h.l tikl. | ʻṣrm.mnt h.l tkly. | npr[m.]šir.l šir.yṣḥ. 6[49].2.36
tdm. | lla y.ʻm lẓpn i | l d̠.pid.hn b p y sp | r hn.b špt y mn | t hn t̠lḫ h w mlg h y | t̠t̠qt ʻm h b qʻt. | tqʻt ʻm prbḫt̠. | dm 24[77].46
.yd y.b š | krn mʻms y k šbʻt yn. | spu.ksm y.bt.bʻl.[w]mn[t]. | y.bt.il.t̠ḥ.gg y.b ym.t̠it̠. | rḥṣ.npṣ y.b ym.rt̠. | dn.il.bt h 17[2AQHT].2.21
.yt̠b. | tqru.l špš.um h.špš.um.ql bl. | ʻm bʻl.mrym.ṣpn.mnt y.nt̠k. | nḫš.šmrr.nḫš.ʻq šr ln h. | mlḫš.abd.ln h.ydy.ḥmt. UG5.7.9
k.t̠bq]. | lḥt.niṣ k.gr[š.d ʻšy.ln k]. | spu.ksm k.bt.[bʻl.w mnt k]. | bt il.aḫd.yd k.b [škrn]. | mʻms k.k šbʻt.yn.t̠[ḫ]. | gg k 17[2AQHT].2.4
[--.]bnt.ṣʻṣ.bnt.ḫkp[.---]. | [---].aḥw.at̠m.prt̠l[.---]. | [---.]mnt.[l]pʻn[.-.-]bd h.aqšr[.---]. | [---].ptḥ y.a[--.]dt[.---].ml[--]. 1001.1.20
ksa.w yt̠b. | tqru.l špš.um h.špš.um.ql b.ʻm. | ršp.bbt h.mnt.nḫš.šmrr. | nḫš.ʻq šr.ln h.mlḫš.abd.ln h.ydy. | ḥmt.hlm.y UG5.7.31
b. | tqru l špš.um h.špš.um.ql.bl.ʻm. | ʻnt w ʻt̠trt inbb h.mnt.nt̠k. | nḫš.šlḥm.nḫš.ʻq šr[.yʻ]db.ksa. | nḫš.šmrr.nḫš.ʻq šr. UG5.7.20
.ksa. | w yt̠b. | tqru.l špš.u h.špš.um.ql.bl.ʻm. | dgn.ttl h.mnt.nt̠k.nḫš.šmrr. | nḫš.ʻq šr.ln h.mlḫš.abd.ln h. | ydy.ḥmt.h UG5.7.15
b.ksa.w yt̠b. | tqru.l špš.um.ql bl.ʻm | kt̠r.w ḫss.kptr h.mnt.nt̠k.nḫš. | šmrr.nḫš.ʻq šr.ln h.mlḫš.abd. | ln h.ydy.ḥmt.h UG5.7.46
| w yt̠b. | tqru.l špš.um h.špš.[um.q]l bl.ʻm. | yrḫ.lrgt h.mnt.nt̠k.n[ḫš].šmrr. | nḫš.ʻq šr.ln h.mlḫš.abd.ln h.ydy. | ḥmt. UG5.7.26
a.w yt̠b. | tqru l špš um h.špš um ql.bl.ʻm. | mlk.ʻt̠trt h.mnt.nt̠k.nḫš.šmrr. | nḫš.ʻq šr.ln h.mlḫš abd.ln h.ydy. | ḥmt.h UG5.7.41

a.w yṯb. | tqru l špš.um h.špš.um.ql bl. | ʿm ḥrn.mṣd h.mnt.nṯk nḥš. | šmrr.nḥš.ʿq šr.ln h.mlḫš. | abd.ln h.ydy.ḥmt. | UG5.7.58
ṯb. | tqru l špš.um h.špš.um.ql bl ʿm. | ṯṯ.w kmṯ.ḥryt h.mnt.nṯk.nḥš.šm | rr.nḥš.ʿq šr.ln h.mlḫš abd.ln h. | ydy.ḥmt.h UG5.7.36
. | tqru l špš.um h.špš.um.ql bl ʿm. | šḥr.w šlm šmm h mnt.nṯk.nḥš. | šmrr.nḥš ʿq šr.ln h.mlḫš. | abd.ln h.ydy ḥmt.h UG5.7.52
pš.um h.špš.um.ql.bl.ʿm. | il.mbk nhrm.b ʿdt.thmtm. | mnt.nṯk.nḥš.šmrr.nḥš. | ʿq šr.ln h.mlḫš abd.ln h.ydy. | ḥmt.h UG5.7.4
m.mhr k.bn bṯn. | itnn k. | aṯr ršp.ʿṯtrt. | ʿm ʿṯtrt.mr h. | mnt.nṯk.nḥš. UG5.7.TR3
ʿd h.bhtm.mnt.bʿd h.bhtm.sgrt. | bʿd h.ʿdbt.ṯlṯ.ptḥ.bt.mnt. | ptḥ.bt.w ubn.hkl.w ištql šql. | tn.km.nḥšm.yḥr.tn.km. UG5.7.71
pn. | w ugr.bn.ǵlmt. | ʿmm ym.bn.ẓlm[t]. | rmt.prʿt.ibr[.mnt]. | ṣḥrrm.ḥbl[.--]. | ʿrpt.ṯḥt.[---] | m ʿṣrm.ḥ[---]. | glṯ.isr[.- 8[51FRAG].9
pn].w ugr.b ǵlmt. | [ʿmm.]ym.bn.ẓlmt.r | [mt.prʿ]t.ibr.mnt. | [ṣḥrrm.ḥbl.ʿ]rpt. | [---.---.-]ḥt. | [---.---]m. | [----] h. 4[51].7.56
. | [---.bn]šm.b.ǵbl. | [---.b]nšm.b.mʿr.arr. | arbʿ.bnšm.b.mnt. | arbʿ.bnšm.b.irbn. | ṯn.bnšm.b.yʿrt. | ṯn.bnšm.b.ʿrmt. | ar 2076.33
[-.---]. | [---.--]ḫ[.---]. | [---.]dt[-.---]. | [---.]ksḥ[-.--]. | [---.]mnty[.-]. | [---.]rb spr ḫbb. | [---.--]n.dbḥm. | [---].ʿbdssm. 49[73].2.3

mnṯ

spr.bdlm. | nʿmn. | rbil. | plsy. | ygmr. | mnṯ. | prḫ. | ʿdršp. | ršpab. | ṯnw. | abmn. | abǵl. | bʿldn. | ypʿ. 1032.6

msb

b. | ṯl[l.---.--]ḥ. | b lṯk.bt. | [pt]ḥ.aḥd.l.bt.ʿbdm. | [ṯ]n.ptḥ msb.bt.tu. | w.ptḥ[.aḥ]d.mmt. | ṯṯ.pt[ḥ.---]. | ṯn.pt[ḥ.---]. | w.pt 1151.10

msg

g]. | pyn.yny.[msg]. | bn.mṣrn m[sg]. | yky msg. | ynḥm.msg. | bn.ugr.msg. | bn.ǵlṣ msg. | arbʿ l ṯkṣ[-]. | nn.arspy.ms[g] 133[-].1.7
r.msg. | bn.ǵlṣ msg. | arbʿ l ṯkṣ[-]. | nn.arspy.ms[g]. | [---.ms]g. | bn.[gr]gs.msg. | bn[.--]an.msg. | bn[.--].m[sg]. | b[--]n.q 133[-].2.1
nb[.msg]. | bn.twyn[.msg]. | bn.ʿdrš[p.msg]. | pyn.yny.[msg]. | bn.mṣrn m[sg]. | yky msg. | ynḥm.msg. | bn.ugr.msg. | 133[-].1.4
bn.gnb[.msg]. | bn.twyn[.msg]. | bn.ʿdrš[p.msg]. | pyn.yny.[msg]. | bn.mṣrn m[sg]. | yky 133[-].1.2
msg]. | bn.mṣrn m[sg]. | yky msg. | ynḥm.msg. | bn.ugr.msg. | bn.ǵlṣ msg. | arbʿ l ṯkṣ[-]. | nn.arspy.ms[g]. | [---.ms]g. | 133[-].1.8
bn.gnb[.msg]. | bn.twyn[.msg]. | bn.ʿdrš[p.msg]. | pyn.yny.[msg]. | bn. 133[-].1.1
| nn.arspy.ms[g]. | [---.ms]g. | bn.[gr]gs.msg. | bn[.--]an.msg. | bn[.--].m[sg]. | b[--]n.qmy.msg. | [---]n.msg. | [----].msg. 133[-].2.3
g. | arbʿ l ṯkṣ[-]. | nn.arspy.ms[g]. | [---.ms]g. | bn.[gr]gs.msg. | bn[.--]an.msg. | bn[.--].m[sg]. | b[--]n.qmy.msg. | [---]n. 133[-].2.2
s[g]. | [---.ms]g. | bn.[gr]gs.msg. | bn[.--]an.msg. | bn[.--].m[sg]. | b[--]n.qmy.msg. | [---]n.msg. | [----].msg. | [---].ms[g]. 133[-].2.4
arbʿ.mdrnm. | mdrn.w.mšḫṯ. | d.mrkbt. | mlk. | mšḫṯ.w.msg. | d.tbk. 1122.15
yn[.msg]. | bn.ʿdrš[p.msg]. | pyn.yny.[msg]. | bn.mṣrn m[sg]. | yky msg. | ynḥm.msg. | bn.ugr.msg. | bn.ǵlṣ msg. | arbʿ 133[-].1.5
bn.ʿdrš[p.msg]. | pyn.yny.[msg]. | bn.mṣrn m[sg]. | yky msg. | ynḥm.msg. | bn.ugr.msg. | bn.ǵlṣ msg. | arbʿ l ṯkṣ[-]. | nn 133[-].1.6
mdrǵlm.d inn. | msgm.l hm. | pʿṣ.ḫbty. | artyn.ary. | brqn.ṯlḥy. | bn.aryn. | bn.l 118[306].2
bn.gnb[.msg]. | bn.twyn[.msg]. | bn.ʿdrš[p.msg]. | pyn.yny.[msg]. | bn.mṣrn m[sg]. | yky msg. | ynḥm.ms 133[-].1.3
ṣrn m[sg]. | yky msg. | ynḥm.msg. | bn.ugr.msg. | bn.ǵlṣ msg. | arbʿ l ṯkṣ[-]. | nn.arspy.ms[g]. | [---.ms]g. | bn.[gr]gs.msg 133[-].1.9
sg. | bn.ugr.msg. | bn.ǵlṣ msg. | arbʿ l ṯkṣ[-]. | nn.arspy.ms[g]. | [---.ms]g. | bn.[gr]gs.msg. | bn[.--]an.msg. | bn[.--].m[s 133[-].1.11
sg. | bn[.--].m[sg]. | b[--]n.qmy.msg. | [---]n.msg. | [----].msg. | [---].ms[g]. 133[-].2.7
[gr]gs.msg. | bn[.--]an.msg. | bn[.--].m[sg]. | b[--]n.qmy.msg. | [---]n.msg. | [----].msg. | [---].ms[g]. 133[-].2.5
bn[.--]an.msg. | bn[.--].m[sg]. | b[--]n.qmy.msg. | [---]n.msg. | [----].msg. | [---].ms[g]. 133[-].2.6
].m[sg]. | b[--]n.qmy.msg. | [---]n.msg. | [----].msg. | [---].ms[g]. 133[-].2.8

mswn

rǵ]b.yd.m[ṯkt]. | mẓma.yd.mṯkt. | ṯṯkr.[--]dn. | ʿm.krt.mswn h. | arḫ.tẓǵ.l ʿgl h. | bn.ḫpṯ.l umht hm. | k tnḥn.udmm. 15[128].1.4
. | [---.ttbʿ]. | [mlakm.l yṯb]. | [idk.pnm.l ytn]. | [ʿ]m[.krt.mswn h]. | tš[an.g hm.w tṣḥn]. | ṯḥ[m.pbl.mlk]. | qḥ[.ksp.w yr 14[KRT].6.266
| l gʿt.alp.ḥrṯ.zǵt. | klb.ṣpr.w ylak. | mlakm.l k.ʿm.krt. | mswn h.ṯḥm.pbl.mlk. | qḥ.ksp.w yrq.ḫrṣ. | yd.mqm h.w ʿbd.ʿ 14[KRT].3.125
. | [---.--]p. | [---.d]bḥ. | t[---.id]k. | pn[m.al.ttn]. | ʿm.[krt.msw]n. | w r[gm.l krt.]ṯʿ. | ṯḥm[.pbl.mlk]. | qḥ.[ksp.w yr]q. | ḫ 14[KRT].5.247

msy

d pi | d dq.anm.l yrẓ. | ʿm.bʿl.l yʿdb.mrḥ. | ʿm.bn.dgn.k tms m. | w ʿn.rbt.aṯrt ym. | blt.nmlk.ʿṯtr.ʿrẓ. | ymlk.ʿṯtr.ʿrẓ. | a 6.1.52[49.1.24]

msk

. | l tphn h.aṯṯ.krpn. | l tʿn.aṯrt.alp. | kd.yqḥ.b ḫmr. | rbt.ymsk.b msk h. | qm.ybd.w yšr. | mṣltm.bd.nʿm. | yšr.ǵzr.ṭb.ql 3[ʿNT].1.17
h.aṯṯ.krpn. | l tʿn.aṯrt.alp. | kd.yqḥ.b ḫmr. | rbt.ymsk.b msk h. | qm.ybd.w yšr. | mṣltm.bd.nʿm. | yšr.ǵzr.ṭb.ql. | ʿl.bʿl.b 3[ʿNT].1.17
ahlm p[---.]km. | [-]bl lb h.km.bṯn.y[--.-]ah. | ṯnm.tšqy msk.hwt.tšqy[.-.]w [---]. | w hn dt.yṯb.l mspr. 19[1AQHT].4.224
ym. | brkt.šbšt. | k rumm.hm. | ʿn.kdd.aylt. | mt hm.ks.ym | sk.nhr hm. | šbʿ.ydt y.b ṣʿ. | [--.]šbʿ.rbt. | [---.]qbṯ.ṯm. | [---. UG5.4.9
ḥmr.p imt.b klt. | yd y.ilḥm.hm.šbʿ. | ydt y.b ṣʿ.hm.ks.ymsk. | nhr.k[--].ṣḥn.bʿl.ʿm. | aḫ y.qran.hd.ʿm.ary y. | w lḥm 5[67].1.21
k[.---]. | tr.ḥ[---]. | w tṣḥ[.---]. | tšqy[.---]. | tr.ḥt[-.---]. | w msk.tr[.---]. | tqrb.aḫ[h.w tṣḥ]. | lm.tbʿrn[.---]. | mn.yrḫ.k m[r 16.2[125].78

mss

qd m]r. | [ydk aḥd h w yṣq b ap h. | [k l yḫru w]l yṯtn mss št qlql. | [w št ʿrgz y]dk aḥd h w yṣq b ap h. | [k.yiḫd akl 160[55].8
r.ydk.aḥd h]. | w.y[ṣq.b.ap h]. | k.l.ḫ[ru.w.l.yṯtn.ššw]. | mss.[št.qlql.w.št]. | ʿrgz[.ydk.aḥd h]. | w.yṣq[.b.ap h]. | k.yiḫd 161[56].9

msrr

ḥ. | imr.dbḥ.b yd h. | lla.klatnm. | klt.lḥm h.d nzl. | lqḥ.msrr.ʿṣr.db[ḥ]. | yṣq.b gl.ḥṯṯ.yn. | b gl.ḫrṣ.nbt.w ʿly. | l ẓr.mgd 14[KRT].3.163
r.d[bḥ.bm].ymn. | lla.kl[atn]m. | klt.l[ḥm k.d]nzl. | qḥ.ms[rr.]ʿṣr. | dbḥ.ṣ[q.b g]l.ḥṯṯ. | yn.b gl[.ḫ]rṣ.nbt. | ʿl.l ẓr.[mg]d 14[KRT].2.70

m‘

.w tẖss.aṯrt.|ndr h.w ilt.p[--].|w tšu.g h.w [tṣḥ].|ph m‘.ap.k[rt.--].|u ṯn.ndr[.---].|apr.[---].|[-----]. 15[128].3.28
[ṯr.w ẖs]s.|ṯtb.b‘l.l[hwt y].|ṯn.rgm.k[ṯr.w]ẖss.|šm‘.m‘.l al[iy]n b‘l.|bl.ašt.ur[bt.]b bht m.|ḥln.b qr[b.hk]l m.|w 4[51].6.4
[krpn h.-.l]arṣ.ks h.tšpk m.|[l ‘pr.tšu.g h.]w tṣḥ.šm‘.m‘.|[l aqht.ǵzr.i]rš.ksp.w atn k.|[ẖrṣ.w aš]lḥ k.w tn.qšt k.[l 17[2AQHT].6.16
.š[d].|[rbt.]kmn.w ṣḥq.btlt.[‘nt].|[tšu.]g h.w tṣḥ.šm‘.m[‘.l a]|[qht.ǵ]zr.at.aẖ.w an.a[ẖt k].|[---].šb‘.ṯir k.[---].|[---. 18[3AQHT].1.23
.‘z.ymṣẖn.|k lsmm.mt.ql.|b‘l.ql.‘ln.špš.|tṣḥ.l mt.šm‘.m‘.|l bn.ilm.mt.ik.tmt[ẖ]|ṣ.‘m.aliyn.b‘l.|ik.al.yšm[‘] k.ṯr.|i 6[49].6.23
.‘d.tšb‘.bk.|tšt.k yn.udm‘t.gm.|tṣḥ.l nrt.ilm.špš.|‘ms m‘.l y.aliyn.b‘l.|tšm‘.nrt.ilm.špš.|tšu.aliyn.b‘l.l ktp.|‘nt.k tš 6[62].1.12
aṯb.an.|ytb‘.yṣb ǵlm.‘l.|ab h.y‘rb.yšu g h.|w yṣḥ.šm‘ m‘.l krt.|ṯ‘.ištm‘.w tqǵ udn.|k ǵz.ǵzm.tdbr.|w ǵrm.ṯṯwy.šq 16.6[127].41
t rb.|mṯb.arṣy.bt.y‘bdr.|ap.mṯn.rgmm.|argm k.šskn m‘.|mgn.rbt.aṯrt ym.|mǵẓ.qnyt.ilm.|hyn.‘ly.l mpẖm.|b d. 4[51].1.21
ṯdṯ.yr[ẖm].|‘dn.ngb.w [yṣi.ṣbu].|ṣbi.ng[b.w yṣi.‘dn].|m‘[.ṣ]bu h.u[l.mad].|ṯlṯ.mat.rbt.|hlk.l alpm.ẖḏḏ.|w l.rbt.k 14[KRT].4.178
ǵd.ṯdṯ.yrẖm.|‘dn.ngb.w yṣi.|ṣbu.ṣbi.ngb.|w yṣi.‘dn.m‘.|ṣbu k.ul.mad.|ṯlṯ.mat.rbt.|ẖpṯ.d bl.spr.|ṯnn.d bl.hg.|h 14[KRT].2.87
.--.]i[---]n.bn.|[---.-]nn.nrt.ilm.špš.tšu.g h.w t[ṣḥ.šm]‘.m‘.|[-.yṯ]ir ṯr.il.ab k.l pn.zbl.ym.l pn[.ṯ]pṭ[.n]hr.|[ik.a]l.yš 2.3[129].15
b.|[ṣ]pr[.apn]k.|[pb]l[.mlk.g]m.l aṯt |[h.k]y[ṣḥ.]šm‘.m‘.|[--.]‘m[.-.]aṯt y[.-].|[---.]tḥm.|[---]t.[ ]r.|[---.--]n.|[---] h 14[KRT].5.229

m‘bd

.b‘[l.---].|w [--]d.[---].|idk[.-]it[.---].|trgm[.-]dk[.---].|m‘bd[.-]r[-.-]š[-.---].|w kšt.[--]šq h[.---].|bnš r‘ym.[---].|kbd 2158.2.4

m‘br

r‘.w.‘šr.dd.drt.|w[.a]rb‘.l.‘šrm.dd.l.yḥšr.bl.bn h.|b.gt.m‘br.arb‘m.l.mit.dr‘.w.ṯmnym[.drt].|w.‘šrm.l.mit.dd.ḥp[r.] 1098.12

m‘d

.pḏ h.tb‘.ǵlmm.l ṯṯb.[idk.pnm].|l ytn.tk.ǵr.ll.‘m.phr.m‘d.ap.ilm.l lḥ[m].|yṯb.bn qdš.l ṯrm.b‘l.qm.‘l.il.hlm.|ilm.tp 2.1[137].20
ttn.‘m.pẖr.m‘d.t[k.ǵr.ll.l p‘n.il].|al.tpl.al.tšthwy.pẖr [m‘d.qmm.a--.am]|r ṯny.d‘t km.w rgm.l ṯr.a[b.-.il.ṯny.l pẖr]. 2.1[137].15
ǵyn.mlak ym.t‘dt.ṯpṭ.nhr.l p‘n.il.|[l t]pl.l tšthwy.pẖr.m‘d.qmm.a[--].amr.|[ṯn]y.d‘t hm.išt.ištm.yitmr.ḥrb.ltšt.|[-- 2.1[137].31
m.a--.am]|r ṯny.d‘t km.w rgm.l ṯr.a[b.-.il.ṯny.l pẖr].|m‘d.tḥm.ym.b‘l km.adn km.ṯ[pṭ.nhr].|tn.il m.d tq h.d tqyn 2.1[137].17
ṭ.ṯbr.ap hm.tb‘.ǵlm[m.al.ṯṯb.idk.pnm].|al.ttn.‘m.pẖr.m‘d.t[k.ǵr.ll.l p‘n.il].|al.tpl.al.tšthwy.pẖr [m‘d.qmm.a--.am 2.1[137].14

m‘m‘

qm.|[---.p]ẖr k.ygrš k.qr.bt k.ygrš k.|[---].bnt.ṣ‘ṣ.bnt.m‘m‘.‘bd.ḥrn.[--.]k.|[---].aǵwyn.‘n k.ẓẓ.w k mǵ.ilm.|[--.]k ‘ 1001.2.11

m‘n

-]k.šsw[.-]rym[.---].|d ymǵy.bnš[.---].|w ḥmr[.---].|w m‘n[.---].|w bn[š.---].|d bnš.ḥm[r.---].|w d.l mdl.r[--.---].|w 2158.1.10
ld.|[---]m.ḥbl.kṯ[r]t.|[---.bt]lt.‘nt.|[---.ali]yn.b‘l.|[---.]m‘n.|[-----].|[-----].|[---.--]r.|[---.--]qk.|[---.--]ik.|[-----].|[--- 11[132].1.9

m‘nt

bn[.---].|bn.qdšt.|bn.m‘nt.|bn.g[--]n.|bn[.---].|[-----].|b[n.---].|b[n.---].|bn.[---].| 2163.1.3
n.kṯly.|bn.kyn.|bn.‘bdḥr.|[-]prm ẖlq.|[---]n ẖlq.|bn m‘nt.|bn kbdy.|bn krk.|bn srty.|bn lṯḥ ẖlq.|bn ytr.|bn ilš 2016.2.10
ẖrmṯt.|ṯlṯm.ar[b‘].|kbd.ksp.|‘l.tgyn.|w ‘l.aṯt h.|ypḥ.m‘nt.|bn.lbn. 2053.22

m‘ṣd

ẖmšt.‘š[rt].|ksp.‘l.agd[ṯb].|w nit w m‘ṣd.|w ẖrmṯt.|‘šrt.ksp.|‘l.ẖ[z]rn.|w.nit.w[.m‘ṣd].|w.ẖ[rm 2053.3
w[.m‘ṣd].|w.ẖ[rmṯt].|‘š[r.---].|‘l[.---].|w.ni[t.---].|w[.m‘ṣd].|w ẖr[mṯt].|[‘]šr[.---].|[‘]l [-]g[-.---].|w ni[t.w.m‘ṣd].| 2053.12
w nit w m‘ṣd.|w ẖrmṯt.|‘šrt.ksp.|‘l.ẖ[z]rn.|w.nit.w[.m‘ṣd].|w.ẖ[rmṯt].|‘š[r.---].|‘l[.---].|w.ni[t.---].|w[.m‘ṣd].|w 2053.7
.m‘ṣd].|w ẖr[mṯt].|[‘]šr[.---].|[‘]l [-]g[-.---].|w ni[t.w.m‘ṣd].|w ẖrmṯt.|ṯlṯm.ar[b‘].|kbd.ksp.|‘l.tgyn.|w ‘l.aṯt h.|y 2053.16
b.atlg.ṯlṯ.ẖrmṯt.ṯṯm.|mẖrhn.nit.mit.krk.mit.|m‘ṣd.ẖmšm.mqb.[‘]šrm.|b.ulm.ṯṯ.‘šr h.ẖrmṯt.|ṯt.nitm.ṯn.m‘ 2048.3
ṯt.nit.|krk.m‘ṣd.mqb.|b.gt.‘mq.ẖmš.ẖrmṯt.n[it].|krk.m‘ṣd.mqb.|b.gwl.ṯmn.ẖrmṯt.[nit].|krk.m‘ṣd.mqb.|[b] gt.ipṯ 2048.10
ṯt.n[it].|krk.m‘ṣd.mqb.|b.gwl.ṯmn.ẖrmṯt.[nit].|krk.m‘ṣd.mqb.|[b] gt.ipṯl.ṯṯ.ẖrmṯ[t.nit].|[k]rk.m‘ṣd.mqb.|[b.g]t 2048.12
.[nit].|krk.m‘ṣd.mqb.|[b] gt.ipṯl.ṯṯ.ẖrmṯ[t.nit].|[k]rk.m‘ṣd.mqb.|[b.g]t.bir.‘š[r.---].|[---].krk.m‘[ṣd.---].|[b.]gt.ḥrṯ 2048.14
m‘ṣdm.ṯn.mqbm.|krk.aḥt.|b.sǵy.ẖmš.ẖrmṯt.nit.|krk.m‘ṣd.mqb.|b.gt.‘mq.ẖmš.ẖrmṯt.n[it].|krk.m‘ṣd.mqb.|b.gwl 2048.8
d.ẖmšm.mqb.[‘]šrm.|b.ulm.ṯṯ.‘šr h.ẖrmṯt.|ṯt.nitm.ṯn.m‘ṣdm.ṯn.mqbm.|krk.aḥt.|b.sǵy.ẖmš.ẖrmṯt.nit.|krk.m‘ṣd. 2048.5
ṯ[t.nit].|[k]rk.m‘ṣd.mqb.|[b.g]t.bir.‘š[r.---].|[---].krk.m‘[ṣd.---].|[b.]gt.ḥrṯm.ẖm[š.---].|[n]it.krk.m‘ṣ[d.---].|b.ẖrb 2048.16
.|[---].krk.m‘[ṣd.---].|[b.]gt.ḥrṯm.ẖm[š.---].|[n]it.krk.m‘ṣ[d.---].|b.ẖrbǵlm.ǵlm[n].|w.trhy.aṯt h.|w.mlky.b[n] h.| 2048.18

m‘qb

‘rt.|uškn.|‘nqpat.|ilštm‘.|šbn.|ṭbq.|rqd.|šrš.|gn‘y.|m‘qb.|agm.|bir.|ypr.|hzp.|šql.|m‘rḥ[-].|sl[ẖ].|snr.|‘rgz.| 2074.27
|[-----].|[ẖl]bkrd.|[ẖl]b‘prm.|[q]dš.|[a]mḏy.|[gn]‘y.|m‘qb.|agm.|ẖpty.|ypr.|ẖrṣb‘.|uẖnp.|art.|[--]n.|[-----].|[-- 2058.2.1
[---.ṣ]mdm[.---].|[ul]l.aḥdm.w[.---].|[m‘q]b.aḥdm.w[.---].|[‘r]gz.ṯlṯ.ṣmd[m.---].|[m]ṣbt.ṣmdm.[--- 1179.3
ag[--].|ẖp[--].|m‘q[b].|ar[--].|ẓr[n].|ṯlḥ[n].|ṯlr[by].|qm[--].|šl[--].|a[---].| 2147.3
‘rm.|nnu.|[--].|[---].|m‘r.|arny.|ubr‘y.|ilštm‘.|bir.|m‘qb.|uškn.|snr.|rq[d].|[---].|[---].|mid[-].|ubš.|mṣb[t].| 71[113].31
šbn aḥd.|ṭbq aḥd.|šrš aḥd.|bir aḥd.|uẖnp.|hzp ṯn.|m‘qb arb‘. 2040.34
spr.rpš d l y[dy].|atlg.|ulm.|izly.|uẖnp.|bn sẖrn.|m‘qb.|ṯpn.|m‘r.|lbnm.|nẖl.|y‘ny.|atn.|utly.|bn.alz.|bn ẖ 2075.7

m‘qby

ary.|bn.ǵlmn ary.|bn.ḥṣbn ary.|bn.šdy ary.|bn.ktkt.m‘qby.|bn.[---.]ṯlḥny.|b[n.---.ub]r‘y.|[bn.---.ubr]‘y.|b[n.---] 87[64].16
.w.ṯn.bn h.w[.---].|ymrn.apsny.w.aṯt h..b[n.---].|prd.m‘qby[.w.---.a]ṯt h[.---].|prṯ.mgd[ly.---.]aṯ[t h].|‘dyn[.---].| 2044.10
ṣb[u.anyt].|‘dn.|ṭbq[ym].|m‘q[bym].|tš‘.‘[šr.bnš].|ǵr.ṯ[--.---].|ṣbu.any[t].|bn.kṯan.|ǵr 79[83].4

w.bn h.w.alp.w.[---]. | [-]ln.[---]. | w.ṯn.bn [h.---]. | [--]d mʻqby[.---]. | swn.qrty.w[.aṯt h]. | [w].bn h.w.ṯn.alpm. | [w.]ṯlṯ 1080.11

mʻr

nʻm. | šlmy. | w.ull. | ṯmry. | qrt. | ʻrm. | nnu. | [--]. | [---]. | mʻr. | arny. | ubrʻy. | ilštmʻ. | bir. | mʻqb. | uškn. | snr. | rq[d]. | [--- 71[113].26
[-----]. | [-----]. | [----] h. | [-----]. | [-]bʻl. | [--]m. | [mʻ]rby. | mʻr. | arny. | ʻnqpat. | šʻrt. | ubrʻy. | ilštmʻ. | šbn. | tbq. | rqd. | [š]r 2058.1.10
ap. | pd. | mlk. | ar. | atlg. | gbʻly. | ulm. | mʻrby. | mʻr. | arny. | šʻrt. | ḫlbrpš. | hry. | qmṣ. | ṣʻq. | qmy. | ḫlbkrd. | yʻrt 2074.9
ṯnq. | [---.b]nšm.b.ugrt. | [---.bn]šm.b.ǵbl. | [---.b]nšm.b.mʻr.arr. | arbʻ.bnšm.b.mnt. | arbʻ.bnšm.b.irbn. | ṯn.bnšm.b.yʻr 2076.32
l[b]nm. | nnu. | ʻrm. | bṣr. | mʻr. | ḫlby. | mṣbt. | snr. | ṯm. | ubš. | glbt. | mi[d]ḫ. | mr[i]l. | ḫlb. 2041.5
y[dy]. | atlg. | ulm. | izly. | uḫnp. | bn sḫrn. | mʻqb. | ṯpn. | mʻr. | lbnm. | nḫl. | yʻny. | atn. | utly. | bn.alz. | bn ḫlm. | bn.ḏmr. 2075.9
ʻ. | uln.qšt. | bn.blẓn.qšt.w.qlʻ. | gbʻ.qšt.w.qlʻ. | nṣṣn.qšt. | mʻr. | [ʻ]dyn.ṯt.qštm.w.qlʻ. | [-]lrš.qšt.w.qlʻ. | t[t]n.qšt.w.qlʻ. | u 119[321].2.13
ubrʻy. | arny. | mʻr. | šʻrt. | ḫlb rpš. | bqʻt. | šḥq. | yʻby. | mḫr. 65[108].3
--.b]nšm. | ulm.ṯn.[---.]bnšm. | mʻrby.[---.--]m.ṯn[.---]. | mʻr.[---]. | arny.[---]. | šʻrt.ṯn[.---]. | bqʻt.[--].ḫ[mr.---]. | ḫlb krd 2040.9
.k ṯr.lṭpn. | ṣḥ.ngr.il.ilš.il[š]. | w aṯt h.ngrt[.i]lht. | kḥṣ.k mʻr[.---]. | yṣḥ.ngr il.ilš. | ilš.ngr.bt.bʻl. | w aṯt h.ngrt.ilht. | w y 16[126].4.6

mʻrb

ṯn.b gt.mzln. | ṯn.b ulm. | abmn.b gt.mʻrb. | atn. | ḫryn. | bn.ʻnt. | llwn. | agdṯb. | aǵltn. | [-]wn. | bldn. 1061.3
yn. | rpš d ydy. | ǵbl. | mlk. | gwl. | rqd. | ḫlby. | ʻn[q]pat. | m[ʻ]rb. | ʻrm. | bn.ḥgby. | mrat. 2075.27
| šḥq. | ǵn. | ṣʻ. | mld. | amḏy. | ḫlbʻprm. | ḫpty. | [ḫr]ṣbʻ. | [mʻ]rb. 2077.10

mʻrby

bn.ilh.mḏrǵl | špšyn.b.ulm. | bn.qṭn.b.ulm. | bn.gdrn.b.mʻr[by]. | [w].bn.dʻm[-]. | bn.ppṯ.b[--]. | b[n.---]. | šm[-.---]. | tk 2046.1.7
ʻšr h. | mlk.arbʻ. | ǵbl.ḫmš. | atlg.ḫmš ʻšr[h]. | ulm ṯ[ṯ]. | mʻrby.ḫmš. | ṭbq.arbʻ. | tkm[.---]. | uḫnp[.---]. |ušk[n.---]. | ubr[68[65].1.10
. | [-----]. | [-----]. | [-----]. | [----] h. | [-----]. | [-]bʻl. | [--]m. | [mʻ]rby. | mʻr. | arny. | ʻnqpat. | šʻrt. | ubrʻy. | ilštmʻ. | šbn. | tbq. | r 2058.1.9
ap. | pd. | mlk. | ar. | atlg. | gbʻly. | ulm. | mʻrby. | mʻr. | arny. | šʻrt. | ḫlbrpš. | hry. | qmṣ. | ṣʻq. | qmy. | ḫlbk 2074.8
my.qšt. | ṯqbn.qšt. | bn.qnmlk.qšt. | ytḥm.qšt. | grp.qšt. | mʻrby. | nʻmn.ṯt.qštm.w.qlʻ. | gln.ṯt.qštm.w.qlʻ. | gtn.qšt. | pm 104[316].9
. | b.uškn. | ṣbr.aḥd. | b.ar. | ṣbr.aḥd. | b.mlk. | ṣbr.aḥd. | b.mʻrby. | ṣbr.aḥd. | b.ulm. | ṣbr.aḥd. | b.ubrʻy. 2073.8
. | bn.lgn.uškny. | bn.abn.uškny. | bn.arz.šʻrty. | bn.ibrd.mʻrby. | ṣdqn.gbʻly. | bn.ypy.gbʻly. | bn.grgs.ilštmʻy. | bn.ḫran. 87[64].26
ty. | ḫlb.ṣpn. | mril. | ʻnmky. | ʻnqpat. | ṭbq. | hzp. | gnʻy. | mʻrby. | [ṣ]ʻq. | [š]ḥq. | nʻrm. | mḫrǵlm. | kzym. | mru.skn. | mru 71[113].57
i[l]štmʻym. | bn.ṯk. | bn.arwdn. | tmrtn. | šdʻl.bn aḫyn. | mʻrbym. | rpan. | abršn. | atlgy. | šršn. 95[91].6
bq. | mit.ʻšr.kbd.yn.ṭb. | w.ṯṯm.arbʻ.kbd.yn.d.l.ṭb. | b.gt.mʻrby. | ṯṯm.yn.ṭb.w.ḫmš.l.ʻšrm. | yn.d.l.ṭb.b.ulm. | mit.yn.ṭb. 1084.8
bn.liy. | ʻšrm.ṣ[md]. | ṯṯ kbd.b ḥ[--]. | w.arbʻ.ḥ[mrm]. | b m[ʻ]rby. | ṯmn.ṣmd.[---]. | b d.bʻlsr. | yd.ṯdn.ʻšr. | [ḥ]mrm. | dd 2102.1
]dm.b.mlk. | [--.š]dm.b.ar. | [--.š]dm.b.ulm. | [--.š]dm.b.mʻrby. | [--.šd]m.b.uškn. | [---.--]n. | [---].tlmdm. | [y]bnn.ṣmd 2033.1.5
---]. | ar[.---]. | mlk[.---]. | ǵbl[.---]. | atl[g.---]. | u[lm.---]. | m[ʻrby.---]. | ṭ[bq.---]. 68[65].2.10
.---.]bnšm. | gbʻly.ḥmr š[--.b]nšm. | ulm.ṯn.[---.]bnšm. | mʻrby.[---.--]m.ṯn[.---]. | mʻr.[---]. | arny.[---]. | šʻrt.ṯn[.---]. | bq 2040.8

mʻry

w.bnš.aḥd. | [---.--]m. | [---].ʻtgrm. | [---.-]ṣbm. | [---.]nrn.mʻry. | [---.--]r. | [---.]w.ṯn.bn h. | [---.b]t h.ʻtgrm. 2043.9

mʻrt

bdadt.ḫmšt. | abmn.ilštmʻy.ḫmš[t]. | ʻzn.bn.brn.ḫmšt. | mʻrt.ḫmšt. | arṯtb.bn.ḫmšt. | bn.ysr[.ḫmš]t. | ṣ[-]r.ḫ[mšt]. | ʻzn. 1062.27

mǵd

rt.l ggt.ʻdb. | akl.l qryt. | ḥṭt.l bt.ḫbr. | yip.lḥm.d ḫmš. | mǵd.ṯdṯ.yrḫm. | ʻdn.ngb.w yṣi. | ṣbu.ṣbi.ngb. | w yṣi.ʻdn.mʻ. | ṣ 14[KRT].2.84
. | [l g]gt.ʻdb.akl.l qryt. | ḥṭt.l bt.ḫbr. | yip.lḥm.d ḫmš. | [mǵ]d.ṯdṯ.yr[ḫm]. | ʻdn.ngb.w [yṣi.ṣbu]. | ṣbi.ng[b.w yṣi.ʻdn]. | 14[KRT].4.175

mǵy

k ymǵy.adn. | ilm.rbm ʻm dtn. | w yšal.mṯpṭ.yld. | w yʻny.nn[.-- UG5.6.1
rm. | w b hm.pn.bʻl. | bʻl.ytlk.w yṣd. | yḥ pat.mlbr. | wn.ymǵy.aklm. | w ymẓa.ʻqqm. | bʻl.ḥmd m.yḥmd m. | bn.dgn.y 12[75].1.36
[ʻ]. | tǵṣ[.pnt.ks]l h. | anš.dt.ẓr.[h]. | tšu.g h.w tṣḥ[.i]k. | mǵy.aliy[n.b]ʻl. | ik.mǵyt.b[t]lt. | ʻnt.mḫṣ y hm[.m]ḫṣ. | bn y.h 4[51].2.22
dmm. | amht.k b h.bṯt.l tbṯ. | w b h.tdmmt.amht. | aḫr.mǵy.aliyn.bʻl. | mǵyt.btlt.ʻnt. | tmgnn.rbt[.a]ṯrt ym. | tǵẓyn.q 4[51].3.23
t.ṣpn. | yṯb.l kḥṯ.aliyn. | bʻl.pʻn h.l tmǵyn. | hdm.riš h.l ymǵy. | aps h.w yʻn.ʻṯtr.ʻrẓ. | l amlk.b ṣrrt.ṣpn. | yrd.ʻṯtr.ʻrẓ.yr 6.1.60[49.1.32]
t.ṣʻṣ.bnt.mʻmʻ.ʻbd.ḥrn.[--.]k. | [---].aǵwyn.ʻn k.ẓẓ.w k mǵ.ilm. | [--.]k ʻṣm.k ʻšm.l ttn.k abnm.l thggn. 1001.2.12
ššw.ʻṯtrt.w ššw.ʻ[nt.---]. | w ht.[--]k.ššw[.-]rym[.---]. | d ymǵy.bnš[.---]. | w ḥmr[.---]. | w mʻn[.---]. | w bn[š.---]. | d bnš. 2158.1.8
b h.bṯt.l tbṯ. | w b h.tdmmt.amht. | aḫr.mǵy.aliyn.bʻl. | mǵyt.btlt.ʻnt. | tmgnn.rbt[.a]ṯrt ym. | tǵẓyn.qnyt.ilm. | w tʻn.r 4[51].3.24
| anš.dt.ẓr.[h]. | tšu.g h.w tṣḥ[.i]k. | mǵy.aliy[n.b]ʻl. | ik.mǵyt.b[t]lt. | ʻnt.mḫṣ y hm[.m]ḫṣ. | bn y.hm[.mkly.ṣ]brt. | ary 4[51].2.23
n.pn h.tdʻ.tǵṣ.pnt. | ksl h.anš.dt.ẓr h.tšu. | g h.w tṣḥ.ik.mǵy.gpn.w ugr. | mn.ib.ypʻ.l bʻl.ṣrt. | l rkb.ʻrpt.l mḫšt.mdd. | 3[ʻNT].3.33
h.yiḫd.b yd. | [g]rgr h.bm.ymn. | [w]yqrb.trẓẓ h. | [---].mǵy h.w ǵlm. | [a]ḫt h.šib.yṣat.mrḥ h. | l tl.yṣb.pn h.tǵr. | yṣu 16.1[125].50
l.ḏrdn. | bʻl y.rgm. | bn.ḫrn k. | mǵy. | hbṭ.hw. | ḫrd.w.šl hw. | qr[-]. | akl n.b.grnt. | l.bʻr. | ap.k 2114.4
pnk.ʻṯtr.ʻrẓ. | yʻl.b ṣrrt.ṣpn. | yṯb.l kḥṯ.aliyn. | bʻl.pʻn h.l tmǵyn. | hdm.riš h.l ymǵy. | aps h.w yʻn.ʻṯtr.ʻrẓ. | l amlk.b ṣrr 6.1.59[49.1.31]
t. | w ʻn hm.ngr mdrʻ[.iṯ.lḥm.---]. | iṯ.yn.d ʻrb.bṭk[.---]. | mǵ hw.l hn.lg yn h[.---]. | w ḥbr h.mla yn.[---]. 23[52].75
ptm.ṣḥq. | [---.]rgm.hy.[-]ḫ[-]y.ilak k. | [---.--]g k.yritn.mǵy.hy.w kn. | [---].ḥln.d b.dmt.um.il[m.---]. | [--]ḏyn.bʻd.[-- 1002.42
p.l.ašt.aṯt y. | nʻr y.ṯḥ.l pn.ib. | hn.hm.yrgm.mlk. | bʻl y.tmǵyy.hn. | alpm.ššwm.hnd. | w.mlk.bʻl y.bnš. | bnny.ʻmn. | m 1012.31
m.ynʻrn h. | ssnm.ysyn h.ʻdtm.yʻdyn h.yb | ltm.ybln h.mǵy.ḥrn.l bt h.w. | yštql.l ḥṭr h.tlu ḥt.km.nḫl. | tplg.km.plg. | UG5.7.67
.um y.mnm.šlm. | w.rgm.ṯṯb.l y. | w.mndʻ.k.ank. | aḥš.mǵy.mndʻ. | k.igr.w.u.[--]. | ʻm.špš.[---]. | nšlḥ[.---]. | [---.m]at. 2009.1.11
.trg[m.---]. | l šlmt.l šlm.b[--.---] | b y.šnt.mlit.t[--.---]. | ymǵy k.bnm.ta[--.---]. | [b]nm.w bnt.ytn k[.---]. | [--]l.bn y.šḥ 59[100].8

mǵy

l ri[š.---].|ypt.‘ṣ[--.---].|p šlm.[---].|bt k.b[--.--.m]|ǵy k[.---].|bt.[---]. 58[20].4
b lb.tqb[-].|[--]m[-].mtm.uṣb‘[t].|[-]tr.šrk.il.|‘rb.špš.l ymǵ.|krt.ṣbia.špš.|b‘l ny.w ymlk.|[y]ṣb.‘ln.w y[-]y.|[kr]t.ṯ‘ 15[128].5.18
r.|b pẖd.l npš.kṯr.w ẖss.|l brlt.hyn.d ḥrš.|ydm.aẖr.ymǵy.kṯr.|w ẖss.b d.dnil.ytnn.|qšt.l brk h.y‘db.|qṣ‘t.apnk. 17[2AQHT].5.25
.|yak.l kṯr.w ẖss.|w ṯb l mspr..k tlakn.|ǵlmm.|aẖr.mǵy.kṯr.w ẖss.|št.alp.qdm h.mra.|w tk.pn h.t‘db.ksu.|w yṯ 4[51].5.106
ṯlṯ h.ẖrṣm.|ylk ym.w ṯn.|ṯlṯ.rb‘.ym.|aẖr.špšm.b rb‘.|ymǵy.l udm.rbt.|w udm[.ṯr]rt.|grnn.‘rm.|šrnn.pdrm.|s‘t.b 14[KRT].4.210
lk.ym.w ṯn.ṯlṯ.rb‘ ym.|ẖmš.ṯdṯ.ym.mk.špšm.|b šb‘.w tmǵy.l udm.|rbm.w l.udm.ṯrrt.|w gr.nn.‘rm.šrn.|pdrm.s‘t. 14[KRT].3.108
]bd.šdm.tmǵ.l n‘m[y].|[arṣ.]dbr.ysmt.šd.|[šḥl]mmt.t[mǵ.]l b‘l.np[l].|[l a]rṣ[.lpš].tks.miz[rtm]. 5[67].6.30
m.mhyt[.m]ǵny.|l n‘m y.arṣ.dbr.|l ysmt.šd.šḥlmmt.|mǵny.l b‘l.npl.l a|rṣ.mt.aliyn.b‘l.|ẖlq.zbl.b‘l.arṣ.|apnk.lṭpn 5[67].6.8
.|[---.m]rz‘y.apnnk.yrp.|[---.]km.r‘y.ht.alk.|[---.]ṯlṯt.amǵy.l bt.|[y.---.b qrb].hkl y.w y‘n.il.|[---.mrz‘]y.lk.bt y.rpi 21[122].1.7
t il.|‘nt.brḥ.p ‘lm h.‘nt.p dr[.dr].|‘db.uẖry mṭ.yd h.|ymǵ.l mrrt.tǵll.b nr.|yšu.g h.w yṣḥ.y l k.mrrt.|tǵll.b nr.d ‘l 19[1AQHT].3.156
ap.|‘nt.ttlk.w tṣd.kl.ǵr.|l kbd.arṣ.kl.gb‘.|l [k]bd.šdm.tmǵ.l n‘m[y].|[arṣ.]dbr.ysmt.šd.|[šḥl]mmt.t[mǵ.]l b‘l.np[l]. 5[67].6.28
rṣ.kl.gb‘.|l kbd.šdm.npš.ẖsrt.|bn.nšm.npš.hmlt.|arṣ.mǵt.l n‘m y.arṣ.|dbr.ysmt.šd.šḥlmmt.|ngš.ank.aliyn b‘l.|‘d 6[49].2.19
šnm.|[tša.g hm.w tṣ]ḥ.sbn.|[---]l[.---.]‘d.|ksm.mhyt[.m]ǵny.|l n‘m y.arṣ.dbr.|l ysmt.šd.šḥlmmt.|mǵny.l b‘l.npl.l 5[67].6.5
.|[‘b]r.gbl.‘br.|q‘l.‘br.iht.|np šmm.šmšr.|l dgy.aṯrt.|mǵ.l qdš.amrr.|idk.al.tnn.|pnm.tk.ḥqkpt.|il.kl h.kptr.|ksu 3[‘NT.VI].6.11
.k ḥsn.pat.|mdbr.tlkn.|ym.w ṯn.aẖr.|šp[š]m.b [ṯ]lṯ.|ym[ǵy.]l qdš.|a[ṯrt.]ṣrm.w l ilt.|ṣd[yn]m.ṯm.|yd[r.k]rt.ṯ‘.|i. 14[KRT].4.197
.ns‘ k.|‘nt.brḥ.p ‘lm h.|‘nt.p dr.dr.‘db.uẖry mṭ yd h.|ymǵ.l qrt.ablm.abl[m].|qrt.zbl.yrẖ.yšu g h.|w yṣḥ.y l k.qrt. 19[1AQHT].4.163
nhr.|tšu ilm rašt hm.l ẓr.brkt hm.ln.kḥṯ.zbl hm.|aẖr.tmǵyn.mlak ym.t‘dt.ṯpṭ.nhr.l p‘n.il.|[l t]pl.l tšṯḥwy.pẖr.m‘d 2.1[137].30
ḥ[--].|b bt.[-.]l bnt.q[-].|w št.b bt.ṯap[.--].|hy.yd h.w ym[ǵ].|mlak k.‘m dt[n].|lqḥ.mṯpṭ.|w y‘ny.nn.|dtn.bt n.mḥ UG5.6.10
t.‘bd h.|[---.]b‘l k.yẖpn.|[---.]‘m h.u ky.|[---.--]d k.k.tmǵy.|ml[--.--]š[.ml]k.rb.|b[‘l y.---].|yd[--.]mlk.|rb.b[‘l y.-- 1018.6
[---.--]b.|[---.w ym.ym]m.|[y‘tqn.---.ymǵy.]npš.|[---.h]d.tngṯn h.|[---].b ṣpn.|[---].nšb.b ‘n.|[---.] 1[‘NT.X].5.3
.|[---.--]kl.tǵr.mtn h.|[---.--]b.w ym ymm.|[y‘tqn.---].ymǵy.npš.|[---.--]t.hd.tngṯm h.|[---.-]ḥm k b ṣpn.|[---.]išqb. 1[‘NT.X].5.16
-.-]nt.[š]ṣat[k.]rḥ.npš.hm.|k.iṯl.brlt n[-.k qṭr.b ap -].|tmǵyn.tša.g h[m.w tṣḥn].|šm‘.l dnil.[mt.rpi].|mt.aqht.ǵzr.[19[1AQHT].2.89
‘[-]r.|[--.]b bt h.yšt.‘rb.|[--] h.ytn.w [--]u.l ytn.|[aẖ]r.mǵy.‘[d]t.ilm.|[w]y‘n.aliy[n.]b‘l.|[---.]tb‘.l lṭpn.|[il.d]pid.l 15[128].2.11
d l yd‘nn.|d.mṣd.|ylmn.ḥṭ.tḥt.ṯlḥn.|b qr‘.|‘ṯtrt.w ‘nt.ymǵy.|‘ṯtrt.t‘db.nšb l h.|w ‘nt.ktp.b hm.yg‘r.ṯǵr.|bt.il.pn.l UG5.1.1.9
rt.ilm.špš.[-]r[--].|pǵt.minš.šdm l m‘[rb].|nrt.ilm.špš.mǵy[t].|pǵt.l ahlm.rgm.l yṯ[pn.y]|bl.agrtn.bat.b ḏd k.[pǵt]. 19[1AQHT].4.211
‘n h.l hdm.yṯpd.w ykrkr.|uṣb‘t h.yšu.g h.w y[ṣḥ].|ik.mǵyt.rbt.aṯr[t.y]m.|ik.atwt.qnyt.i[lm].|rǵb.rǵbt.w tǵt[--].| 4[51].4.31
kbt hm.ti[ty.l ‘r hm].|tlkn.ym.w ṯa aẖr.š[pšm.b ṯlṯ].|mǵy.rpum.l grnt.i[lnym.l] |mṭ‘t.w y‘n.dnil.[mt.rpi].|yṯb.ǵz 20[121].2.6
[kbt hm.tity.l] |‘r hm.tl[kn.ym.w ṯn.aẖr.špšm].|b ṯlṯ.mǵy[.rpum.l grnt].|i[ln]y[m].l mṭ‘t[.---].|[-]m[.---].|h.hn bn 22.1[123].25
rm.mṭm.tgrš.|šbm.b ksl.qšt h.mdnt.|w hln.‘nt.l bt h.tmǵyn.|tštql.ilt.l hkl h.|w l.šb‘t.tmtḫṣ h.b ‘mq.|tḫtṣb.bn.qr 3[‘NT].2.17
t.|w ‘lm h.l ‘nt.p dr.dr.|‘db.uẖry.mṭ.yd h.|dnil.bt h.ymǵyn.yšt|ql.dnil.l hkl h.‘rb.b|kyt.b hkl h.mšspdt.b ḥẓr h. 19[1AQHT].4.170
y.bt.il.ṯẖ.gg y.b ym.ṯiṭ.|rḥṣ.npṣ y.b ym.rṯ.|dn.il.bt h.ymǵyn.|yštql.dnil.l hkl h.|‘rb.b bt h.kṯrt.bnt.|hll.snnt.apn 17[2AQHT].2.24
.|[---.--]d.il.šd yṣd mlk.|[---].yšt.il h.|[---.]iṯm h.|[---.y]mǵy.|[---.]dr h.|[---.-]rš.l b‘l.|[---.-]ǵk.rpu mlk.|[‘lm.---.-- UG5.2.2.1
yš]lm[.ilm].|tǵr k[.tšlm k].|hl ny.[---].|w.pdr[--.---].|tmǵyn[.---].|w.mli[.---].|[-]kl.w [---].|‘d.mǵt[.---]. 57[101].5
r[.ilḥu].|ṯlṯ.yrẖm.k m[rṣ].|arb‘.k dw.k[rt].|mnd‘.krt.mǵ[y.---].|w qbr.tṣr.q[br].|tṣr.trm.tnq[--].|km.nkyt.ṯǵr[.---] 16.2[125].86
r yrẖ h.|yrs.y[---.]y[--] h.|ṯlṯ.rb[‘.yrẖ.--]r[.--].|yrẖm.ymǵy[.---].|ẖ[--.]r[---]. 17[2AQHT].2.46
-.-]pr l n‘m.|[---.-]mt w rm tp h.|[---.-]ḥb l n‘m.|[---.]ymǵy.|[---.]rm ṯlbm.|[---.--]m.|[---.--]ḥ n‘m. UG5.5.7
.pdr[--.---].|tmǵyn[.---].|w.mli[.---].|[-]kl.w [---].|‘d.mǵt[.---]. 57[101].8

mǵln

.|sǵr.irgn.aḥd.¦sǵr.ršpab.aḥd.|sǵr.arwṯ.aḥd.|sǵr.bn.mǵln.|aḥd. 1140.12

mǵmǵ

[k.---.]šš[w.---].|[---.w]yṣq b a[p h].|[k ẖr š]šw mǵmǵ w b[ṣql ‘rgz].|[ydk aḥ]d h w yṣq b ap h.|[k ẖr]ššw 160[55].4
k [ẖr ššw mǵmǵ].|w [bṣql.‘rgz.ydk].|a[ḥd h.w.yṣq.b.ap h].|k.[ẖr.ššw. 161[56].2
p h].|k yg‘r[.ššw.---].|dprn[.---].|dr‘.[---].|tmṯl[.---].|mǵm[ǵ.---].|w.š[t.nni.w.pr.‘bk].|w.pr[.ḥḏrt.w.št].|irǵ[n.ḥm 161[56].27

mǵrt

|[----]m.|[-----].|[bnš.g]t.ir.|bnš.gt.rb[--].|gpny.|bnš.mǵrt.|kbsm.|armsǵ. 1040.18

mṣa

k šb‘t.l šb‘m.aẖ h.ym[.--].|w ṯmnt.l ṯmnym.|šr.aẖy h.mẓa h.|w mẓa h.šr.yly h.|b skn.sknm.b ‘dn.|‘dnm.kn.npl.b 12[75].2.51
.aẖ h.ym[.--].|w ṯmnt.l ṯmnym.|šr.aẖy h.mẓa h.|w mẓa h.šr.yly h.|b skn.sknm.b ‘dn.|‘dnm.kn.npl.b‘l.|km ṯr. 12[75].2.52
n.aṯrt.|rbm.ymẖṣ.b ktp.|dk ym.ymẖṣ.b ṣmd.|ṣḥr mt.ymṣẖ.l arṣ.|[yṯb.]b[‘]l.l ksi.mlk h.|[---].l kḥṯ.drkt h.|l [ym] 6[49].5.4
.b‘l.|b‘l.ytlk.w yṣd.|yḥ pat.mlbr.|wn.ymǵy.aklm.|w ymẓa.‘qqm.|b‘l.ḥmd m.yḥmd m.|bn.dgn.yhrr m.|b‘l.ngṯ h 12[75].1.37

mṣb

m.arb‘[.---].|šrš.šb‘.mṣb.|rqd.ṯlṯ.mṣb.w.[---].|uẖnp.ṯṯ.mṣb.|tgmr.[y]n.mṣb š[b‘].|w ḥs[p] ṯn.k[dm]. 2004.34
ẖpty.kdm[.---].|[a]gm.arb‘[.---].|šrš.šb‘.mṣb.|rqd.ṯlṯ.mṣb.w.[---].|uẖnp.ṯṯ.mṣb.|tgmr.[y]n.mṣb š[b‘].|w ḥs[p] ṯn. 2004.33
--].|‘šrm.yn.ḥsp.l.ql.d.tb‘.mṣ[r]m.|mit.arb‘m.kbd.yn.mṣb.|l.mḏrǵlm.|‘šrn ‘šr.yn.mṣb.[-]ḥ[-].l.gzzm. 1084.28
r[.---]m ḥsp.|ẖpty.kdm[.---].|[a]gm.arb‘[.---].|šrš.šb‘.mṣb.|rqd.ṯlṯ.mṣb.w.[---].|uẖnp.ṯṯ.mṣb.|tgmr.[y]n.mṣb š[b‘]. 2004.32
ṣ[r]m.|mit.arb‘m.kbd.yn.mṣb.|l.mḏrǵlm.|‘šrn ‘šr.yn.mṣb.[-]ḥ[-].l.gzzm. 1084.30

mṣbt

ir.|m‘qb.|uškn.|snr.|rq[d].|[---].|[---].|mid[-].|ubš.|mṣb[t].|ḥl.y[---].|‘rg[z].|y‘r[t].|amḏ[y].|atl[g].|bṣr[y].|[---] 71[113].39
mitm.‘šr kbd.|kšmm.b.mṣbt.|mit.‘šrm.ṯn kbd.|[kš]mm.|[‘]š[r]m.ṯn.kbd.ḥṭm.|[-]m 2091.2

l[b]nm. | nnu. | ʻrm. | bṣr. | mʻr. | ḫlby. | mṣbt. | snr. | ṯm. | ubš. | glbt. | mi[d]ḫ. | mr[i]l. | ḫlb. | šld. | ʻrgz. | 2041.7
.w[.---]. | [mʻq]b.aḥdm.w[.---]. | [ʻr]gz.ṯlṯ.ṣmd[m.---]. | [m]ṣbt.ṣmdm.[---]. | [--]nr.arbʻ.[---]. | [--]idḫ.ṣmd[.---]. | [u]bš.[- 1179.5
-.]ṯlṯm. | [---.n]ḫl. | [---.ṯ]lṯ.mat.šbʻm[.---]. | [---.--]mm.b.mṣbt[.---]. | [---.ṯl]ṯ.mat.ṯmny[m.---]. 2149.4

mṣbty

du.qmnzy. | bdl.qrṭy. | trgn.bn.tǵh. | aupš.qmnzy. | ṯrry.mṣbty. | prn.nǵty. | ṯrdn.zlyy. 89[312].9

mṣḥn

.bn.adldn.ṯlṯm. | ṣṣ.bn.ʻglt.ṯlṯm. | ṣṣ.bn.ʻbd.ʻšrm. | ṣṣ.bn.mṣḥ[n].ʻšrm. | šbʻ.mat.ṯṯm kbd. 2096.19

mṣḫ

ḥn. | k rumm.mt.ʻz.bʻl. | ʻz.ynṯkn.k bṯnm. | mt.ʻz.bʻl.ʻz.ymṣḫn. | k lsmm.mt.ql. | bʻl.ql.ʻln.špš. | tṣḫ.l mt.šmʻ.mʻ. | l bn. 6[49].6.20
n.aṯrt. | rbm.ymḫṣ.b ktp. | dk ym.ymḫṣ.b ṣmd. | ṣḥr mt.ymṣḫ.l arṣ. | [yṯb.]b[ʻ]l.l ksi.mlk h. | [---].l kḥṯ.drkt h. | l [ym] 6[49].5.4
.btlt.ʻnt]. | yṯb l y.ṯr.il[.ab y.---]. | yṯb.l y.w l h.[---]. | [--.i]mṣḫ.nn.k imr.l arṣ. | [ašhlk].šbt h.dmm.šbt.dqn h. | [mmʻm 3[ʻNT.VI].5.9

mṣy

isp hm.b[ʻl.---]. | bn.dgn[.---]. | ʻḏbm.[---]. | uḫry.l[---]. | mṣt.ks h.t[--.---]. | idm.adr[.---]. | idm.ʻrẓ.tʻr[ẓ.---]. | ʻn.bʻl.a[ḫ] 12[75].2.29

mṣl

[---.ʻ]ttry. | [-----.]yn. | [----.-]mn. | [---.--]m.mṣl. | [---].prš.ḥtm. | ṯlṯ[.---].bn.ṯdnyn. | ddm.ḥ[ṭm].ʻl.šrn. | ʻšrt 1146.4

mṣṣ

.l k. | w ṯmn.ṯṯmnm. | l k.tld.yṣb.ǵlm. | ynq.ḥlb.a[ṯ]rt. | mṣṣ.ṯd.btlt.[ʻnt]. | mšnq.[---]. 15[128].2.27

mṣr

]q. | [thm]tm.tgl.ḏ[d.]i[l.]w tbu. | [qr]š.m[l]k.ab[.šnm.]mṣr. | [t]bu.ḏdm.qn[-.-]n[-.-]lt. | ql h.yš[mʻ].ṯr.[il].ab h.[---]l. | 3[ʻNT.VI].5.16

mṣry

mṣry.d.ʻrb.b.unṯ. | bn.qrrn.mḏrǵl. | bn.tran.mḏrǵl | bn.ilh.mḏ 2046.1.1
bn.mnyy.šʻrty. | aryn.aḏddy. | agpṯr. | šbʻl.mlky. | nʻmn.mṣry. | yʻl.knʻny. | gdn.bn.umy. | knʻm.šʻrty. | abrpu.ubrʻy. | b. 91[311].6
. | kdm.ʻm.[--]n. | kd.mštt.[---]n. | kdm.l.mḏrǵlm. | kd.l.mṣrym. | kd.mštt.mlk. | kd.bn.amht [-]t. | w.bn.mṣrym. | arbʻ 1089.7
t. | bn.gdrn.qšt. | prpr.qšt. | ugry.qšt. | bn.ṣrptn.qšt. | bn.mṣry.qšt. | arny. | abm.qšt. | ḥdṯn.qlʻ. | yṯpṭ.qšt. | ilthm.qšt.w.q 119[321].1.47
. | kd.l.mṣrym. | kd.mštt.mlk. | kd.bn.amht [-]t. | w.bn.mṣrym. | arbʻm.yn. | l.ḫrd. | ḫmšm.ḫmš. | kbd.tgmr. | yn.d.nkl 1089.10
ryn. | bn.lgn. | bn.bʻyn. | šdyn. | ary. | brqn. | bn.ḫlln. | bn.mṣry. | ṯmn.qšt. | w ʻšr.uṯpt. | upšt irš[-]. 118[306].13

mṣrm

bʻ[l y.l].pn.bʻl y. | w.urk.ym.bʻl y. | l.pn.amn.w.l.pn. | il.mṣrm.dt.tǵrn. | npš.špš.mlk. | rb.bʻl y. 1018.22
.ṯm ny. | ʻm k.mnm[.š]lm. | rgm.ṯṯ[b]. | any kn.dt. | likt.mṣrm. | hn dt.b.ṣr. | mtt.by. | gšm.adr. | nškḥ.w. | rb.tmtt. | lqḥ. 2059.11
. | mit.ʻšrm.[k]bd.yn.ḥsp.l.y[--]. | ʻšrm.yn.ḥsp.l.ql.d.tbʻ.mṣ[r]m. | mit.arbʻm.kbd.yn.mṣb. | l.mḏrǵlm. | ʻšrn ʻšr.yn.mṣb 1084.27
.yṣi h. | ḥwt.[---]. | alp.k[sp]. | tšʻn. | w.hm.al[-]. | l.tšʻn. | mṣrm. | tmkrn. | ypḥ.ʻbdilt. | bn.m. | ypḥ.ilšlm. | bn.prqdš. | yp 2116.15
---.-]lk[.---]. | [---.ʻ]šr.ym[.---]. | [---].hm.l y[--.---]. | [---].mṣrm[.---]. | [---.--]n mkr[.---]. | [---].ank.[---]. | [---.]tny.[---]. | 2126.4

mṣrn

n.ʻbd. | [-----]. | [---.n]ḥ[l h]. | [-]ntm[.---]. | [ʻ]bdm. | [bn].mṣrn. | [a]ršwn. | ʻb[d]. | w nḥl h. | atn.bn.ap[s]n. | nsk.ṯlṯ. | bn.[85[80].3.3
n.alṯn. | bn.ṯmyr. | ẓbr. | bn.ṯdṯb. | bn.ʻrmn. | bn.alz. | bn.mṣrn. | bn.ʻdy. | bn.ršpy. | [---.]mn. | [--.-]sn. | [bn.-]ny. | [b]n.ḫn 115[301].2.15
m. | bn.abḏr. | bn.kpltn. | bn.prn. | ʻbdm. | bn.kḏǵbr. | bn.mṣrn. | bn.[-]dr[-]. | [---]l[-]. | [--]ym. | [--]rm. | [bn.]aǵld. | [w.n 114[324].2.12
n.bn.ubn.ṯql[m]. | yšn.ḥrš.mrkbt.ṯq[lm]. | bn.pʻṣ.ṯqlm. | mṣrn.ḥrš.mrkbt.ṯqlm. | ʻpṯn.ḥrš.qṭn.ṯqlm. | bn.pǵdn.ṯqlm. | b 122[308].1.8
--]. | [--]dd. | [bʻ]l.tǵpṭm. | [k]rwn. | ḥrš.mrkbt. | mnḥm. | mṣrn. | mḏrǵlm. | agmy. | ʻdyn. | ʻbdbʻl. | ʻbdkṯr.ʻbd. | tdǵl. | bʻlṣ 1039.2.15
| bn.twyn[.msg]. | bn.ʻdrš[p.msg]. | pyn.yny.[msg]. | bn.mṣrn m[sg]. | yky msg. | ynḥm.msg. | bn.ugr.msg. | bn.ǵlṣ msg 133[-].1.5
-]. | apnm.l.[b]n[.---]. | apnm.l.bn[.---]. | ṯlṯ.ṣmdm[.---]. | mṣ[r]n[.---]. 145[318].10

mṣrrt

km. | [arb]ʻm.ḫpnt.pṯt. | [-]r.pldm.dt.šʻrt. | ṯlṯm.ṯlṯ.kbd.mṣrrt. | ʻšr.ṯn.kbd.pǵdrm. | ṯmn.mrbdt.mlk. | ʻšr.pld.šʻrt. 1111.9

mqb

| krk.mʻṣd.mqb. | b.gt.ʻmq.ḫmš.ḫrmṯt.n[it]. | krk.mʻṣd.mqb. | b.gwl.ṯmn.ḫrmṯt.[nit]. | krk.mʻṣd.mqb. | [b] gt.ipṯl.ṯṯ.ḫ 2048.10
it]. | krk.mʻṣd.mqb. | b.gwl.ṯmn.ḫrmṯt.[nit]. | krk.mʻṣd.mqb. | [b] gt.ipṯl.ṯṯ.ḫrmṯ[t.nit]. | [k]rk.mʻṣd.mqb. | [b.g]t.bir.ʻš 2048.12
| krk.mʻṣd.mqb. | [b] gt.ipṯl.ṯṯ.ḫrmṯ[t.nit]. | [k]rk.mʻṣd.mqb. | [b.g]t.bir.ʻš[r.---]. | [---].krk.mʻ[ṣd.---]. | [b.]gt.ḫrṯm.ḫm 2048.14
.ṯn.mqbm. | krk.aḥt. | b.sǵy.ḫmš.ḫrmṯt.nit. | krk.mʻṣd.mqb. | b.gt.ʻmq.ḫmš.ḫrmṯt.n[it]. | krk.mʻṣd.mqb. | b.gwl.ṯmn. 2048.8
qb.[ʻ]šrm. | b.ulm.ṯṯ.ʻšr h.ḫrmṯt. | ṯt.nitm.ṯn.mʻṣdm.ṯn.mqbm. | krk.aḥt. | b.sǵy.ḫmš.ḫrmṯt.nit. | krk.mʻṣd.mqb. | b.gt. 2048.5
g.ṯlṯ.ḫrmṯt.ṯṯm. | mḫrhn.nit.mit.krk.mit. | mʻṣd.ḫmšm.mqb.[ʻ]šrm. | b.ulm.ṯṯ.ʻšr h.ḫrmṯt. | ṯt.nitm.ṯn.mʻṣdm.ṯn.mqb 2048.3

mqd

bʻ.kkr. | algbṯ.arbʻt. | ksp h. | kkr.šʻrt. | šbʻt.ksp h. | ḫmš.mqdm.dnyn. | b.ṯql.dprn.aḥd. | b.ṯql. | ḫmšm.ʻrgz.b.ḫmšt. 1127.19

mqwṭ

bdlḥn[-]. | bn.mqwṭ. | bn.bsn. | bn.inr[-]. | bn.ṯbil. | bn.iryn. | ṯṯl. | bn.nṣdn. | b 1071.2

mqḥ

mskn. | w.t̲t.mqrtm. | w.t̲n.irpm.w.t̲n.trqm. | w.qpt.w.mqḥm. | w.t̲lt̲m.yn šbʿ.kbd d t̲bt̲. | w.ḫmšm.yn.d iḫ h. 1103.21
]itm.mqp.m[---]. | [---.t̲mn]ym.mgnm ar[bʿ]. | [---.-]aḫ.mqḥ mqḥm. | [---.--]t.ʿšr rmǵt.[--]. | [---].alp.[---].alp. | [---.-]rb 1145.1.4
mqp.m[---]. | [---.t̲mn]ym.mgnm ar[bʿ]. | [---.-]aḫ.mqḥ mqḥm. | [---.--]t.ʿšr rmǵt.[--]. | [---].alp.[---].alp. | [---.-]rbd.kb 1145.1.4

mqp

[t̲y]. | d b atlg[.---]. | ḫmš ʿš[r]. | kkr.t̲[lt̲]. | t̲t hrt[m]. | t̲n mq[pm]. | ult̲.t̲l[t̲]. | krk.kly[.--]. | ḫmš.mr[kbt]. | t̲t [-]az[-]. | ʿšt 2056.6
[---.t̲]lt̲.mat. | [---.m]itm.mqp.m[---]. | [---.t̲mn]ym.mgnm ar[bʿ]. | [---.-]aḫ.mqḥ mqḥm 1145.1.2

mqr

m. | sʿt.b šdm.ḥt̲b. | w b grnt.ḥpšt. | sʿt.b npk.šibt.w b | mqr.mmlat. | d[m].ym.w t̲n. | t̲lt̲.rbʿ.ym. | ḫmš.t̲dt̲.ym. | mk.šp 14[KRT].5.217
n. | pdrm.sʿt.b šdm. | ḥt̲b h.b grnt.ḥpšt. | sʿt.b nk.šibt.b bqr. | mmlat.dm.ym.w t̲n. | t̲lt̲.rbʿ.ym.ymš. | t̲dt̲.ym.ḥẓ k.al.tšʿ 14[KRT].3.113

mqrt

. | w.npṣ bt t̲n.t̲lt̲ mat. | w spl t̲lt̲.mat. | w mmskn. | w.t̲t.mqrtm. | w.t̲n.irpm.w.t̲n.trqm. | w.qpt.w.mqḥm. | w.t̲lt̲m.yn š 1103.19

mr

]. | šmʿ k.l arḫ.w bn.[--]. | limm.ql.b udn.k w[-]. | k rtqt mr[.---]. | k d lbšt.bir.mlak. | šmm.tmr.zbl.mlk. | šmm.tlak.t̲l. 13[6].24
m[t̲ʿ.ilnym]. | d tit.yspi.spu.q[--.---]. | tpḥ.t̲ṣr.shr[.---]. | mr[.---]. 20[121].2.12
]. | [ydk aḥ]d h w yṣq b ap h. | [k ḫr]ššw ḫndrt w t̲[qd m]r. | [ydk aḥd h w yṣq b ap h. | [k l yḫru w]l yt̲tn mss št ql 160[55].6
dk]. | a[ḥd h.w.yṣq.b.ap h]. | k.[ḫr.ššw.ḫndrt̲]. | w.t̲[qd.mr.ydk.aḥd h]. | w.y[ṣq.b.ap h]. | k.l.ḫ[ru.w.l.yt̲tn.ššw]. | mss. 161[56].6
yt̲t.nḫšm.mhr k.bn bt̲n. | itnn k. | at̲r ršp.ʿt̲trt. | ʿm ʿt̲trt.mr h. | mnt.nt̲k.nḫš. UG5.7.TR2
dm.ynḥt.w ypʿr.šmt hm. | šm k.at.aymr.aymr.mr.ym.mr.ym. | l ksi h.nhr l kḥt̲.drkt h.trtqṣ. | b d bʿl.km.nšr b uṣbʿt 2.4[68].19
.kt̲r.ṣmdm.ynḥt.w ypʿr.šmt hm. | šm k.at.aymr.aymr.mr.ym.mr.ym. | l ksi h.nhr l kḥt̲.drkt h.trtqṣ. | b d bʿl.km.nšr 2.4[68].19
r.ḫbr.rbt. | ḫbr.t̲rrt. | bt.krt.tbun. | lm.mt̲b[.---]. | w lḥm mr.tqdm. | yd.b ṣʿ.tšlḥ. | ḥrb.b bšr.tštn. | [w t]ʿn.mt̲t.ḥry. | [l lḥ 15[128].4.23
]. | bʿlm.w mlu[.---.ksm]. | t̲lt̲m.w mʿrb[.---]. | dbḥ šmn mr[.šmn.rqḥ.bt]. | mtnt.w ynt.[qrt.w t̲n.ḥt̲m]. | w bǵr.arbʿ.[-- APP.II[173].22
[m.bʿlm.---]. | ksm.t̲lt̲m.[---]. | d yqḥ bt[.--]r.dbḥ[.šmn.mr]. | šmn.rqḥ[.-]bt.mtnt[.w ynt.qrt]. | w t̲n ḥt̲m.w bǵr.arb[ʿ. 35[3].20
[---.]y[--].ḫtt.mtt[--]. | [--.]ḥy[--.--.]l aššị.hm.ap.amr[--]. | [---].w b ym.mnḫ l abd.b ym.irtm.m[--]. | [t̲pt̲].nhr. 2.4[68].2
--.t̲t̲.dd.]gdl.t̲t̲.dd.šʿrm. | [---.hn.w.al]p.kd.nbt.kd.šmn.mr. | [---].kmn.lth̲.sbbyn. | [---.-]ʿt.lth̲.ššmn. | [---].ḫšwn.t̲t̲.ma 142[12].8
.dd.šʿrm. | [---.a]lp.arbʿ.mat.tyt. | [---.kd.]nbt.k[d.]šmn.mr. | [---.l]th̲.sb[by]n.lth̲.šḫ[lt]. | [---.l]th̲.dblt.lth̲.ṣmqm. | [---.- 142[12].15
-.]t̲t̲.dd.gdl.t̲t̲.dd.šʿrm. | [---.-]hn.w.alp.kd.nbt.kd.šmn.mr. | [---.]arbʿ.mat.ḫswn.lth̲.aqhr. | [---.lth̲.]sbbyn.lth̲.ššmn.lt 142[12].2
rm.kk[r]. | brr. | [ʿ]šrm.npš. | ʿšrm.zt.mm. | ʿrbʿm. | šmn.mr. 141[120].16

mra

rẓn. | bn.qdšt. | bn.nt̲ǵ[-]. | bn.gr[--]. | bn.[---]. | bn.[---]. | mr[u.ibrn]. | bn.i[---]. | bn.n[---]. | bn.b[---]. | bn.iš[--]. | bn.ab[-- 113[400].5.17
sk].t̲lt̲. | gt.mlkym. | tmrym. | t̲nqym. | t̲ǵrm. | mru.skn. | mru.ibrn. | yqšm. | trrm. | kkrdnm. | yṣrm. | ktrm. | mṣlm. | tkn[1026.2.7
qd[šm]. | mru s[kn]. | mru ib[rn]. | mdm. | inšt. | nsk ksp. | yṣḥm. | ḥrš mrkbt. | ḥrš qṭ 73[114].3
t.mlkym. | yqšm. | kbšm. | trrm. | khnm. | kzym. | yṣrm. | mru.ibrn. | mru.skn. | nsk.ksp | mḫṣm. | ksdm. | mdrǵlm. | psl 74[115].12
ʿrby. | [ṣ]ʿq. | [š]ḥq. | nʿrm. | mḫrǵlm. | kzym. | mru.skn. | mru.ibrn. | pslm. | šrm. | yṣḥm. | ʿšrm. | mrum. | t̲nnm. | mqdm. 71[113].64
d.]t̲pt̲bʿl. | [šd.---.]b d.ymz. | [šd.b d].klby.psl. | [ub]dy.mri.ibrn. | [š]d.bn.bri.b d.bn.ydln. | [u]bdy.t̲ǵrm. | [š]d.t̲ǵr.mt̲ 82[300].2.5
[---.]mru ib[rn.---]. | [---.]yṣḥm[.---]. | [---.]ʿbd[m.---]. | [---.-]ḫy[-.--- 1027.1
. | b npš h.ystrn ydd. | b gngn h.aḥd y.d ym | lk.ʿl.ilm.l ymru. | ilm.w nšm.d yšb | [ʿ].hmlt.arṣ.gm.l ǵ | [lm] h.bʿl k.yṣḥ 4[51].7.50
b.hd.ʿdb[.ʿd]bt. | hkl h.t̲bḫ.alpm[.ap]. | ṣin.šql.t̲rm[.w]m | ria.il.ʿglm.d[t]. | šnt.imr.qmṣ.l[l]im. | ṣḥ.aḫ h.b bht h.a[r]y 4[51].6.41
.dbḥ.[---]. | pʿr.b[--.---]. | t̲bḫ.alp[m.ap.ṣin.šql]. | t̲rm.w [mri.ilm.ʿglm.dt.šnt]. | imr.[qmṣ.llim.---]. 1[ʿNT.X].4.31
tdd. | ʿnt.ṣd.tštr.ʿpt.šmm. | t̲bḫ.alpm.ap ṣin.šql.t̲rm. | w mri ilm.ʿglm.dt.šnt. | imr.qmṣ.llim.k ksp. | l ʿbrm.zt.ḫrṣ.l ʿbr 22.2[124].13
yn. | bdl.mrynm. | bn.ṣqn. | bn.šyn. | bn.prtn. | bn.ypr. | mrum. | bn.ʿ[--]t. | bn.adty. | bn.krwn. | bn.nǵsk. | bn.qnd̲. | bn. 113[400].3.11
rt[.---]. | t̲nǵrn.[---]. | w.bn h.n[--.---]. | ḥnil.[---]. | aršmg.mru. | bʿl.šlm.ʿbd. | awr.t̲ǵrn.ʿbd. | ʿbd.ḫmn.šmʿ.rgm. | šdn.[k] 2084.9
| t̲n.nšbm. | t̲mnym.tbtḫ.alp. | uz.mrat.mlḥt. | arbʿ.uzm.mrat.bqʿ. | t̲lt̲.[-]t̲t.aš[ʿ]t.šmn.uz. | mi[t].ygb.bqʿ. | a[--].ʿt̲. | a[l] 1128.21
.b.šb[n]. | bn.pr[-.]d.y[t̲b.b].šlmy. | tlš.w[.n]ḥl h[.-].t̲gd.mrum. | bt.[-]b[-.-]sy[-]h. | nn[-].b[n].py[-.d.]yt̲b.b.gt.aǵld. | šg 2015.2.3
[---]t. | lḥn š[-]ʿ[--.]aḫd[.-]. | tšmʿ.mt̲t.[ḥ]ry. | t̲t̲bḫ.šmn.[m]ri h. | t[p]tḥ.rḥbt.yn. | ʿl h.t̲r h.tšʿrb. | ʿl h.tšʿrb.ẓby h. | t̲r.ḫb 15[128].4.15
[-----]. | [t̲t̲bḫ.šm]n.[mri h]. | [t̲ptḥ.rḥ]bt.[yn]. | [---.]rp[.---]. | [---.ḫ]br[.---]. | bḫr[.-- 15[128].5.1
mrynm. | ʿšr.mkrm. | ḫmš.t̲rtnm. | ḫmš.bn.mrynm. | ʿšr.mrum.w.šbʿ.ḫsnm. | tšʿm.mdrǵlm. | arbʿ.l ʿšrm.ḫsnm. | ʿšr.hbt̲ 1030.6
tšʿ.t̲nnm. | w.arbʿ.ḫsnm. | ʿšr.mrum. | w.šbʿ.ḫsnm. | tšʿ.ʿšr. | mrynm. | t̲lt̲.ʿšr.mkrm. | t̲lt̲.bn.m 1029.3
ʿl.yʿn.tdrq. | ybnt.ab h.šrḥq.at̲t.l pnn h. | št.alp.qdm h.mria.w tk. | pn h.tḥspn.m h.w trḥṣ. | t̲l.šmm.šmn.arṣ.t̲l.šm[m 3[ʿNT].4.85
pr..k tlakn. | ǵlmm. | aḫr.mǵy.kt̲r.w ḫss. | št.alp.qdm h.mra. | w tk.pn h.tʿdb.ksu. | w yt̲t̲b.l ymn.aliyn. | bʿl.ʿd.lḥm.št[4[51].5.107
m. | t̲lḥny.yrḫ.w.ḫm[š.ymm]. | ẓrn.yrḫ.w.ḫmš.y[m]m. | mrat.ḫmš.ʿšr.ymm. | qmnz.yrḫ.w.ḫmš.ymm. | ʿnmk.yrḫ. | ypr 66[109].7
[----]. | gm.l[at̲t h k.yṣḥ]. | šmʿ[.l mt̲t.ḥry]. | t̲bḫ.š[mn].mri k. | ptḥ.[rḥ]bt.yn. | ṣḥ.šbʿm.t̲r y. | t̲mnym.[ẓ]by y. | t̲r.ḫbr[. 15[128].4.4
.mri. | ʿšr.bmt.alp.mri. | t̲n.nšbm. | t̲mnym.tbtḫ.alp. | uz.mrat.mlḥt. | arbʿ.uzm.mrat.bqʿ. | t̲lt̲.[-]t̲t.aš[ʿ]t.šmn.uz. | mi[t] 1128.20
.yt̲ʿr. | w yšlḥmn h. | ybrd.t̲d.l pnw h. | b ḥrb.mlḥt. | qṣ.mri.ndd. | yʿšr.w yšqyn h. | ytn.ks.b d h. | krpn.b klat.yd h. | b 3[ʿNT].1.8
[-----]. | bn.[---]. | bn.[---]. | w.nḥ[l h]. | bn.ẓr[-]. | mru.skn. | bn.bddn. | bn.ǵrgn. | bn.tgtn. | bn.ḥrẓn. | bn.qdšt. | b 113[400].5.6
khnm. | qdšm. | m[ru.]škn. | mkrm. 76[82].3
ksdm. | [nsk].t̲lt̲. | gt.mlkym. | tmrym. | t̲nqym. | t̲ǵrm. | mru.skn. | mru.ibrn. | yqšm. | trrm. | kkrdnm. | yṣrm. | ktrm. | 1026.2.6
qd[šm]. | mru s[kn]. | mru ib[rn]. | mdm. | inšt. | nsk ksp. | yṣḥm. | ḥrš m 73[114].2
. | gnʿy. | mʿrby. | [ṣ]ʿq. | [š]ḥq. | nʿrm. | mḫrǵlm. | kzym. | mru.skn. | mru.ibrn. | pslm. | šrm. | yṣḥm. | ʿšrm. | mrum. | t̲nn 71[113].63

qšm. | kbšm. | trrm. | khnm. | kzym. | yṣrm. | mru.ibrn. | mru.skn. | nsk.ksp | mẖṣm. | ksdm. | mḏrǵlm. | pslm. | yṣḥm. 74[115].13
[t]. | dm[t]. | šl[-]. | [---]m. | [-]rm. | [-]dm. | [-]m. | [--]m. | [m]ru skn. | šrm. | [--]m. | [i]nšt. 2058.4.1
[-----]. | [-----]. | alp[.---.--]r. | mit.lḥ[m.---.-]dyt. | ṣlʻt.alp.mri. | ʻšr.bmt.alp.mri. | ṯn.nšbm. | ṯmnym.tbtẖ.alp. | uz.mrat. 1128.16
ʻšrm ddm kbd[.-] l alpm mrim. | ṯṯ ddm l ṣin mrat. | ʻšr ddm.l šmʻrgm. | ʻšr ddm.l bt. | ʻšrm.dd.l mẖṣm. | dd 1100.2
ṯnnm.ṯṯ. | ʻšr.ẖsnm. | nʻr.mrynm. | ẖmš. | ṯrtnm.ẖmš. | mrum.ʻšr. | šbʻ.ẖsnm. | mkrm. | mrynm. | ṯlṯ.ʻšr. | hbṭnm. | ṯmn. 1031.6
mrynm. | mrum. | ʻšrm. | ṯnnm. | nq[dm]. | kh[nm]. | inšt. 2019.2
mrynm. | mrum. | ʻšrm. | ṯnnm. | nqdm. | khnm. | qdšm. | pslm. | mkrm. | 1026.1.2
[ṯr]tnm. | ṯlṯ.b[n.]mrynm. | ʻšr[.m]krm. | tšʻ.hbṭnm. | ʻšr.mrum. | šbʻ.ẖsnm. | tšʻm.ṯṯ.kbd.mḏrǵlm. | ʻšrm.aḥd.kbd.ẖsnm 1028.7
. | [šd.]bn.nḥbl.b d.ʻdbym. | [šd.b]n.qṭy.b d.tt. | [ubd]y.mrim. | [šd.b]n.ṯpdn.b d.bn.gʻr. | [šd.b]n.ṯqrn.b d.ẖby. | [ṯn.š] 82[300].1.20
.tl]ḥm.tšty. | [ilm.w tp]q.mrǵṯm. | [td.b ḥrb.m]lḥt.qṣ. | [mri.tšty.k]rpnm yn. | [b ks.ẖrṣ.dm].ʻṣm. 4[51].3.43
.yn]. | ʻd.lḥm.šty.ilm. | w pq mrǵṯm.td. | b ḥrb.mlḥt.qṣ[.m]r | i.tšty.krp[nm.y]n. | [b k]s.ẖrṣ.d[m.ʻṣm]. | [---.--]n. | [---.--
. | [---.l]ḥm[.---]. | [---].ay š[---]. | [---.b ḥ]rb.mlḥ[t.qṣ]. | [mri.tšty.krpnm].yn.b ks.ẖ[rṣ]. | [dm.ʻṣm.---]n.krpn.ʻl.[k]rpn. 17[2AQHT].6.5
d.lḥm[.šty.ilm]. | w pq.mr[ǵṯm.ṯd.---]. | b ḥrb.[mlḥt.qṣ.mri]. | šty.kr[pnm.yn.---]. | b ks.ẖr[ṣ.dm.ʻṣm.---]. | ks.ksp[.---]. 5[67].4.14
ʻšrm ddm kbd[.-] l alpm mrim. | ṯṯ ddm l ṣin mrat. | ʻšr ddm.l šmʻrgm. | ʻšr ddm.l bt. | ʻ 1100.1
[.---.--]r. | mit.lḥ[m.---.-]dyt. | ṣlʻt.alp.mri. | ʻšr.bmt.alp.mri. | ṯn.nšbm. | ṯmnym.tbtẖ.alp. | uz.mrat.mlḥt. | arbʻ.uzm.m 1128.17
zym. | mru.skn. | mru.ibrn. | pslm. | šrm. | yṣḥm. | ʻšrm. | mrum. | ṯnnm. | mqdm. | khnm. | qdšm. | nsk.ksp. | mkrm. 71[113].69
ks[p.-]m. | l.mri[.--]. | ṯmn kbd[.--]i. | arbʻm[.--]. | l apy.mr[i.--]. | [---.--]d. | [-----]. 1133.5
[s]pr.ḥ[rš.---]. | [-]mn.n[--]. | ḥrš.d.[---]. | mrum.[---]. | yṣḥm[.---]. | mkrm[.---]. | pslm[.---]. 1038.4
k. | gwl. | rqd. | ẖlby. | ʻn[q]pat. | m[ʻ]rb. | ʻrm. | bn.ḥgby. | mrat. 2075.30

mradn

n[.---]. | [---.]bn[.---]. | [---.]nḥl h. | [---.b]n.špš. | [---.b]n.mradn. | [---.m]lkym. | [---.--]d. 2137.5

mri

dm.l bt. | ʻšrm.dd.l mẖṣm. | ddm l kbs. | dd l prgṯ. | dd.l mri. | dd.l ṯnǵly. | dd.l krwn. | dd.l ṯǵr. | dd.l rmt.r[---]. 1100.8
npṣm. | b d.mri. | skn. | ʻšrm. | ẖmš. | kbd. 157[116].2
n[-.]l ks[p.-]m. | l.mri[.--]. | ṯmn kbd[.--]i. | arbʻm[.--]. | l apy.mr[i.--]. | [---.--]d. | 1133.2

mril

bṣr. | mʻr. | ẖlby. | mṣbt. | snr. | ṯm. | ubš. | glbt. | mi[d]ẖ. | mr[i]l. | ẖlb. | šld. | ʻrgz. | [-----]. 2041.13
tl[g]. | bṣr[y]. | [---]. | [---]y. | ar. | agm.w.ẖpty. | ẖlb.ṣpn. | mril. | ʻnmky. | ʻnqpat. | ṭbq. | hzp. | gnʻy. | mʻrby. | [ṣ]ʻq. | [š]ḥq. 71[113].51
[---.ʻ]šrt. | ẖlb.ẖmšt.l.ʻšrm. | mril.ʻšrt. | glbty.arbʻt. | [--]ṯb.ʻšrt. 1180.3
mr[il.---]. | ub[rʻy.---]. | mi[ẖd.---]. | snr[.---]. | ṯm[--.---]. 2144.1
]ʻ[-.-]ag šʻrm. | [---.--]mi. | [--.]ṯṯ[m] šbʻ.k[bd]. | [---]m.b.mril. 2091.9

mrily

. | b.ẖrbǵlm.ǵlm[n]. | w.trhy.aṯt h. | w.mlky.b[n] h. | ily.mrily.tdgr. 2048.22

mrbd

. | w md h. | arn.w mznm. | ṯn.ẖlpnm. | ṯṯ.mrḥm. | drb. | mrbd. | mškbt. 2050.9

mrbdt

m.dt.šʻrt. | ṯlṯm.ṯlṯ.kbd.mṣrrt. | ʻšr.ṯn.kbd.pǵdrm. | ṯmn.mrbdt.mlk. | ʻšr.pld.šʻrt. 1111.11

mrbṣ

y.bṭr.b d.mlkt. | [---.]bṭr.b d.mlkt. | [---].b d.mršp. | [---.m]rbṣ. | [---.r]b.ṯnnm. | [---.]asrm. | [---.--]kn. | [-----]. | [-----]. | [2015.1.4

mrg

rbbt. | yṣq-ẖym.w tbṯẖ. | kt.il.dt.rbtm. | kt.il.nbt.b ksp. | šmrgt.b dm.ẖrṣ. | kḥṯ.il.nḥṯ. | b ẓr.hdm.id. | d prša.b br. | nʻl.il 4[51].1.33

mrdt

| lpš.sgr.rq. | ṯṯ.prqt. | w.mrdt.prqt.pṯt. | lbš.psm.rq. | ṯn.mrdt.az. | ṯlṯ.pld.šʻrt. | ṯ[---].kbm. | p[---]r.aḥd. | [-----]. | [-----]. 1112.6
ṯn.pld.pṯt[.-]r. | lpš.sgr.rq. | ṯṯ.prqt. | w.mrdt.prqt.pṯt. | lbš.psm.rq. | ṯn.mrdt.az. | ṯlṯ.pld.šʻrt. | ṯ[---].kb 1112.4

mrzḥ

inr.tʻdbn.ktp. | b il ab h.gʻr.yṯb.il.kb[-]. | aṯ[rt.]il.yṯb.b mrzḥ h. | yšt[.il.y]n.ʻd šbʻ.trṯ.ʻd škr. | il.hlk.l bt h.yštql. | l ḥṭr UG5.1.1.15
r[m.---]. | [---.]l.mrzḥ.ʻn[.---]. | [---].mrzḥ.ʻn[.---]. | [---].mrzḥ.ʻn[.---]. | [---.mr]zḥ.ʻn[.---]. 2032.5
[---.mr]zḥ.ʻn[.---]. | [---.]šir.šd.kr[m.---]. | [---.]l.mrzḥ.ʻn[.---]. | [---].mrzḥ.ʻn[.---]. | [---].mrzḥ.ʻn[.---]. | [---.mr] 2032.3
n[.---]. | [---.]šir.šd.kr[m.---]. | [---.]l.mrzḥ.ʻn[.---]. | [---].mrzḥ.ʻn[.---]. | [---].mrzḥ.ʻn[.---]. | [---.mr]zḥ.ʻn[.---]. 2032.4
[---.mr]zḥ.ʻn[.---]. | [---.]šir.šd.kr[m.---]. | [---.]l.mrzḥ.ʻn[.---]. | [--- 2032.1
rzḥ.ʻn[.---]. | [---].mrzḥ.ʻn[.---]. | [---].mrzḥ.ʻn[.---]. | [---.mr]zḥ.ʻn[.---]. 2032.6
--.] | gm.ṣḥ.l q[ṣ.ilm.---]. | l rḥqm.l p[-.---]. | ṣḥ.il.yṯb.b[mrzḥ.---]. | bṯt.ʻllm n.[---]. | ilm.bt.bʻl k.[---]. | dl.ylkn.ḥš.b a[r 1[ʻNT.X].4.4

mrzʻy

m.b h]kl y.aṯr h.rpum. | [l tdd.aṯr h].l tdd.ilnym. | [---.m]rzʻy.apnnk.yrp. | [---.]km.rʻy.ht.alk. | [---.]ṯlṯt.amǵy.l bt. | [21[122].1.5
k. | [---.]ṯlṯt.amǵy.l bt. | [y.---.b qrb].hkl y.w yʻn.il. | [---.mrzʻ]y.lk.bt y.rpim. | [rpim.bt y.aṣ]ḥ km.iqra km. | [ilnym.b 21[122].1.9
[---.m]rzʻy.lk.bt y. | [rpim.rpim.b]t y.aṣḥ km.iqra. | [km.ilnym.b 21[122].1.1

mrḥ

šwm.|tryn.aḥd.d bnš.|arbʿ.ṣmdm.apnt.|w ḥrṣ.|tšʿm.mrḥ.aḥd.|kbd. 1123.9
n il.|nṣbt il.|šlm il.|il ḥš il add.|bʿl ṣpn bʿl.|ugrt.|b mrḥ il.|b nit il.|b ṣmd il.|b dṯn il.|b šrp il.|b knt il.|b ǵdy 30[107].12
n.qlʿ.w.ṯ[t.---].|[bn].mlṣ.qštm.w.uṯp[t].|[--.q]lʿ.w[.---.m]rḥm.|[bn].ḫdmn.qšt.[w.u]ṯp[t].ṯ[--].|[---].arbʿ.[---].|[---]. 2047.8
.kn.npṣ hm.|[bn].lbn.arbʿ.qšt.w.ar[bʿ].|[u]ṯpt.qlʿ.w.ṯt.mr[ḥ]m.|[bn].smyy.qšt.w.u[ṯpt].|[w.q]lʿ.w.ṯt.mrḥm.|[bn].š 2047.3
qlʿ.w.ṯt.mr[ḥ]m.|[bn].smyy.qšt.w.u[ṯpt].|[w.q]lʿ.w.ṯt.mrḥm.|[bn].šlmn.qlʿ.w.ṯ[t.---].|[bn].mlṣ.qštm.w.uṯp[t].|[--. 2047.5
mšlt.w.mqḥm.|w md h.|arn.w mznm.|ṯn.ḫlpnm.|ṯt.mrḥm.|drb.|mrbd.|mškbt. 2050.7
adn k.šqrb.[---].|b mgn k.w ḫrṣ.l kl.|apnk.ǵzr.ilḥu.|[m]rḥ h.yiḫd.b yd.|[g]rgr h.bm.ymn.|[w]yqrb.trẓẓ h.|[---]. 16.1[125].47
.---].|arbḫ.ʿn h tšu w[.---].|aylt tǵpy tr.ʿn[.---].|b[b]r.mrḥ h.ti[ḫd.b yd h].|š[g]r h bm ymn.t[--.---].|[--.]l bʿl.ʿbd[.- 2001.1.12
n w hl[.---].|w tglṯ thmt.ʿ[--.---].|yṣi.ǵl h tḥm b[.---].|mrḥ h l adrt[.---].|ṯṯb ʿṯtrt b ǵl[.---].|qrẓ tšt.l šmal[.---].|arb 2001.1.7
|[w]yqrb.trẓẓ h.|[---].mǵy h.w ǵlm.|[a]ḫt h.šib.yṣat.mrḥ h.|l tl.yṣb.pn h.tǵr.|yṣu.hlm.aḫ h.tph.|[ksl]h.l arṣ.ṯṯb 16.1[125].51
.ḫdmn.qšt.[w.u]ṯp[t].ṯ[--].|[---].arbʿ.[---].|[---].kdl[.---.mr]ḥm.w.ṯ[t.---].|[---.mr]ḥm.w.ṯ[t.---].|[---].qlʿ[.---].|[---.a]r 2047.11
[--].|[---].arbʿ.[---].|[---].kdl[.---.mr]ḥm.w.ṯ[t.---].|[---.mr]ḥm.w.ṯ[t.---].|[---].qlʿ[.---].|[---.a]rbʿ[.---]. 2047.12
ylḥn.|w yʿn.lṭpn.il d pi|d dq.anm.l yrẓ.|ʿm.bʿl.l yʿdb.mrḥ.|ʿm.bn.dgn.k tms m.|w ʿn.rbt.aṯrt ym.|blt.nmlk.ʿṯtr.ʿr 6.1.51[49.1.23]

mrṭn

.ʿdršp.ǵlmn.|[a]bǵl.ṣṣn.ǵrn.|šib.mqdšt.ʿb[dml]k.ṯṯpḥ.mrṭn.|ḫdǵlm.i[---]n.pbn.ndbn.sbd.|šrm.[---].ḫpn.|ḥrš[bht 2011.15
n.|lkn.|ktr.|ubn.|dqn.|ḥṯṯn.|[--]n.|[---].|tsn.|rpiy.|mrṭn.|ṯnyn.|apṯ.|šbn.|gbrn.|ṯbʿm.|kyn.|bʿln.|ytršp.|ḫmš 1024.2.16
[-----].|[---.]ršy.[---].|[---.-]mdr.|[---.]bty.|[---.] mrṭn.[--].|[---.]d[.---]. 2172.5

mryn

m.]aḥd[.---].|dmt.lḫsn.krm.aḥd.anndr.kr[m.---].|aǵt.mryn.ary[.]yukl.krm.[---].|gdn.krm.aḫ[d.--]r.krm.[---].|ary 1081.16
kd l kblbn.|kdm.mṯḫ.|l.alṯy.|kd.l mrynm.|šbʿ yn.|l mrynm.|b ytbmlk.|kdm.ǵbiš ḫry.|ḫmš yn.b d.|bḥ mlkt.|b 1090.11
mryn[m].|bn.bly.|nrn.|w.nḥl h.|bn.rmyy.|bn.tlmyn.|w.n 113[400].1.1
ity.|bn.iryn.|bn.ʿbl.|bn.grbn.|bn.iršyn.|bn.nklb.|bn.mryn.|[bn.]b[--].|bn.ẓrl.|bn.illm[-].|bn.š[---].|bn.ṣ[---].|bn 115[301].4.21
[bn]šm.dt.iš[--].|[b]n.bʿl[--].|bn.gld.|bn.ṣmy.|bn.mry[n].|bn.mgn.|bn.ʿdn.|bn.knn.|bn.py.|bn.mk[-].|bn.by 2117.1.5
-].|bn.gzry.|bn.atyn.|bn.ttn.|bn.rwy.|bn.ʿmyn.|bdl.mrynm.|bn.ṣqn.|bn.šyn.|bn.prtn.|bn.ypr.|mrum.|bn.ʿ[--]t 113[400].3.6
mry[n]m.|bn rmy[y].|yšril[.---].|anntn bn[.---].|bn.brzn [-- 2069.1
spr.mr[ynm].|[bʿ]l.[---].|mr[--.---].|hm.[---].|kmrṭn[.---].|bn.ṯb 2070.1.1
arbʿ.yn.l.mrynm.ḫ[--].kl h.|kdm.l.zn[-.---].|kd.l.aṯr[y]m.|kdm.ʿm.[-- 1089.1
ṯnnm.ṯṯ.|ʿšr.ḫsnm.|nʿr.mrynm.|ḫmš.|ṯrtnm.ḫmš.|mrum.ʿšr.|šbʿ.ḫsnm.|mkrm.|m 1031.3
ḫmš.ṯnnm.ʿšr.ḫsnm.|ṯlṯ.ʿšr.mrynm.|ḫmš.[ṯr]tnm.|ṯlṯ.b[n.]mrynm.|ʿšr[.m]krm.|tšʿ.hbṭ 1028.2
[.--].lm[d.---].|kd[.l.]ḫzr[m.---].|kd[.l.]ṯrtn[m].|arbʿ l.mry[nm].|kdm l.ḫty.[---].|kdm l.ʿṯtr[t].|kd l.m[d]rǵl[m].|k 1091.8
mrynm.|mrum.|ʿšrm.|ṯnnm.|nqdm.|khnm.|qdšm.|pslm. 1026.1.1
mrynm.|mrum.|ʿšrm.|ṯnnm.|nq[dm].|kh[nm].|inšt. 2019.1
mn.|bn.gṯrn.|bn.arpḫn.|bn.ṯryn.|bn.dll.|bn.ḫswn.|mrynm.|ʿzn.|ḥyn.|ʿmyn.|ilyn.|yrbʿm.|nʿmn.|bn.kbl.|knʿ 1046.3.33
šbʿ.ṯnnm.w.šbʿ.ḫsnm.|ṯmn.ʿšr h.mrynm.|ʿšr.mkrm.|ḫmš.ṯrtnm.|ḫmš.bn.mrynm.|ʿšr.mrum 1030.2
ṯnnm.ʿšr.ḫsnm.|ṯlṯ.ʿšr.mrynm.|ḫmš.[ṯr]tnm.|ṯlṯ.b[n.]mrynm.|ʿšr[.m]krm.|tšʿ.hbṭnm.|ʿšr.mrum.|šbʿ.ḫsnm.|tšʿm 1028.4
.|ṯmn.ʿšr h.mrynm.|ʿšr.mkrm.|ḫmš.ṯrtnm.|ḫmš.bn.mrynm.|ʿšr.mrum.w.šbʿ.ḫsnm.|tšʿm.mdrǵlm.|arbʿ.l ʿšrm.ḫ 1030.5
spr.ḫpr.bnš mlk.b yrḫ iṯt[bnm].|ršpab.rb ʿšrt.m[r]yn.|pǵdn.ilbʿl.krwn.lbn.ʿdn.|ḫyrn.mdʿ.|šmʿn.rb ʿšrt.kk 2011.2
dnn.ṯlṯ.ṣmdm.|bn.ʿmnr.|bn.kmn.|bn.ibyn.|bn.mryn.ṣmd.w.ḥrṣ.|bn.prsn.ṣmd.w.ḥrṣ.|bn.ilbʿl.|bn.idrm.|b 2113.5
m.|w.šbʿ.ḫsnm.|tšʿ.ʿšr.|mrynm.|ṯlṯ.ʿšr.mkrm.|ṯlṯ.bn.mrynm.|arbʿ.ṯrtnm.|tšʿ.ḫbṭnm.|ṯmnym.ṯlṯ.kbd.|mdrǵlm.| 1029.8
kd l ḫty.|maḫdh.|kd l kblbn.|kdm.mṯḫ.|l.alṯy.|kd.l mrynm.|šbʿ yn.|l mrynm.|b yṯbmlk.|kdm.ǵbiš ḫry.|ḫmš y 1090.9
.aupš.|šd.b d.ršpab.aḫ.ubn.|šd.b d.bn.uṯryn.|[ubd]y.mrynm.|[š]d.bn.ṣnrn.b d.nrn.|[š]d.bn.rwy.b d.ydln.|[š].bn. 82[300].1.7
nm.|ḫmš.|ṯrtnm.ḫmš.|mrum.ʿšr.|šbʿ.ḫsnm.|mkrm.|mrynm.|ṯlṯ.ʿšr.|hbṭnm.|ṯmn.|mdrǵlm.|ṯmnym.ṯmn.kbd.|t 1031.9
ṯnnm.|w.arbʿ.ḫsnm.|ʿšr.mrum.|w.šbʿ.ḫsnm.|tšʿ.ʿšr.|mrynm.|ṯlṯ.ʿšr.mkrm.|ṯlṯ.bn.mrynm.|arbʿ.ṯrtnm.|tšʿ.ḫbṭn 1029.6
.|[---]tl.|[---]ʿbl.|[---]bln.|[---]dy.|[---.n]ḥl h.|[---].bn.mryn.|[---].bn.ṯyl.|annmt.nḥl h.|abmn.bn.ʿbd.|liy.bn.rqdy. 1036.10
.l.ybr[k].|bdmr.prs.l.u[-]m[-].|ṯmn.l.ʿšrm.|dmd.b d.mry[n]m. 2102.11
|kdm l.ḫty.[---].|kdm l.ʿṯtr[t].|kd l.m[d]rǵl[m].|kd l.mryn[m]. 1091.12

mrkbt

.|ʿrb.bt.mlk.|yd.apnt hn.|yd.ḥẓ hn.|yd.tr hn.|w.l.ṯt.mrkbtm.|inn.uṯpt.|w.ṯlṯ.ṣmdm.w.ḥrṣ.|apnt.b d.rb.ḥršm.|d 1121.6
ksp.w yrq].|[ḫrṣ.]yd.mqm h.|[w ʿb]d.ʿlm.ṯlṯ.|[ssw]m.mrkbt b trbṣ bn.amt.|[tn.b]nm.aqny.|[tn.ṯa]rm.amid.|[w y 14[KRT].2.56
ḥ.[ksp.w yr]q.|ḫrṣ[.yd.mqm] h.|ʿbd[.ʿlm.ṯlṯ].|ss[wm.mrkbt].|b[trbṣ.bn.amt].|[qḥ.krt.šlmm].|[šlmm.al.tṣr].|[ud 14[KRT].5.253
k.|qḥ.ksp.w yrq.ḫrṣ.|yd.mqm h.w ʿbd.ʿlm.|ṯlṯ.sswm.mrkbt.|b trbṣ.bn.amt.|qḥ.krt.šlmm.|šlmm.w ng.mlk.|l bt 14[KRT].3.128
[.ksp.w yrq].|ḫrṣ.[yd.mqm h].|w ʿbd[.ʿlm.ṯlṯ].|sswm.m[rkbt].|b trbṣ.[bn.amt].|q[ḥ.kr]t[.šlmm].|š[lmm.]al.t[ṣr]. 14[KRT].6.272
k.ksp.|w yr[q.ḫrṣ].|yd.mqm h.w ʿbd.|ʿlm.ṯlṯ.sswm.|mrkbt.b trbṣ.|bn.amt.p d.[i]n.|b bt y.ttn.tn.|l y.mṯt.ḥry.|nʿ 14[KRT].6.286
.ank.|ksp.w yrq.ḫrṣ.|yd.mqm h.w ʿbd.|ʿlm.ṯlṯ.sswm.mrkbt.|b trbṣt.bn.amt.|p d.in.b bt y.ttn.|tn.l y.mṯt.ḥry.|nʿ 14[KRT].3.140
n.glgl.uškny.|bn.ṯny.uškny.|mnn.w.aṯt h.|slmu.ḥrš.mrkbt.|bnšm.dt.l.mlk.|ʿbdyrḫ.bn.ṯyl.|ʿbdn.w.aṯt h.w.bn h. 2068.16
ṯmn.mrkbt.dt.|ʿrb.bt.mlk.|yd.apnt hn.|yd.ḥẓ hn.|yd.tr hn.|w.l. 1121.1
um.l] |tdd.aṯr[h.l tdd.ilnym].|asr.mr[kbt.---].|tʿln.l mr[kbt hm.tity.l] |ʿr hm.tl[kn.ym.w ṯn.aḫr.špšm].|b ṯlṯ.mǵ 22.1[123].23
.aṯr h.tdd.iln[ym.---].|asr.sswm.ṯṣmd.dg[-.---].|tʿln.l mrkbt hm.ti[ty.l ʿr hm].|tlkn.ym.w ṯa aḫr.š[pšm.b ṯlṯ].|mǵ 20[121].2.4
.llḫ hm.|w.ṯlṯ.l.ʿšrm.|ḫpnt.ššwm.ṯn.|pddm.w.d.ṯṯ.|[mr]kbt.w.ḥrṣ. 2049.9
l ḫmš.mrkbt.ḫmš.ʿšr h.prs.|bt.mrkbt.w l šant.ṯṯ.|l bt.ʿšrm.|bt alḫnm.ṯlṯm ṯṯ kbd. 2105.2

s[kn] | mru ib[rn]. | mdm. | inšt. | nsk ksp. | yṣḥm. | ḥrš mrkbt. | ḥrš qṭn. | ḥrš bhtm. 73[114].8
l ḫmš.mrkbt.ḫmš.ʿšr h.prs. | bt.mrkbt.w l šant.ṯṯ. | l bt.ʿšrm. | bt alḫ 2105.1
ḫrṣ[.w] ṣmdm trm.d [ṣ]py. | w.trm.aḫdm. | ṣpym. | ṯlṯ mrkbt mlk. | d.l.ṣpy. | [---.t]r hm. | [---].ššb. | [---.]tr h. | [a]rbʿ. 1122.5
---.]tr h. | [a]rbʿ.qlʿm. | arbʿ.mdrnm. | mdrn.w.mšḫṭ. | d.mrkbt. | mlk. | mšḫṭ.w.msg. | d.tbk. 1122.13
š.qṭn. | [---]n. | [-----]. | [--]dd. | [bʿ]l.ṯǵptm. | [k]rwn. | ḥrš.mrkbt. | mnḥm. | mṣrn. | mdrǵlm. | agmy. | ʿdyn. | ʿbdbʿl. | ʿbdkṯ 1039.2.13
annmn.ʿdy.klby.dqn. | ḥrṯm.ḥgbn.ʿdn.ynḥm[.---]. | ḥrš.mrkbt.ʿzn.[b]ʿln.ṯb[--.-]nb.trtn. | [---]mm.klby.kl[--].dqn[.---] 2011.28
ṯlṯ mrkb[t]. | ṣpyt b ḫrṣ[.w] ṣmdm trm.d [ṣ]py. | w.trm.aḫdm. | ṣ 1122.1
[---].in ḫẓm.l hm. | [---.--]dn. | mrkbt.mtrt. | ngršp. | ngǵln. | ilṯḥm. | bʿlṣdq. 1125.2.1
ṯ]. | ṯṯ hrt[m]. | ṯn mq[pm]. | ulṯ.ṯl[ṯ]. | krk.kly[.--]. | ḫmš.mr[kbt]. | ṯṯ [-]az[-]. | ʿšt[--.---]. | irg[mn.---]. | krk[.---]. 2056.9
gmy[.---]. | bn.dlq[-.---]. | ṯǵyn.bn.ubn.ṯql[m]. | yšn.ḥrš.mrkbt.ṯq[lm]. | bn.pʿṣ.ṯqlm. | mṣrn.ḥrš.mrkbt.ṯqlm. | ʿpṯn.ḥrš. 122[308].1.6
ṯql[m]. | yšn.ḥrš.mrkbt.ṯq[lm]. | bn.pʿṣ.ṯqlm. | mṣrn.ḥrš.mrkbt.ṯqlm. | ʿpṯn.ḥrš.qṭn.ṯqlm. | bn.pǵdn.ṯqlm. | bn.bʿln.ṯql 122[308].1.8
drʿ. | [-].nǵr[.--]m. | [--.]psl.qšt. | [ṯl]ṯ.psl.ḫẓm. | [---.ḥ]rš.mr[k]bt. | [--].ʿšr h[.---]. | [ḫm]š.ʿšr h[.---]. | ḫmš.ʿšr h. | šrm. 1024.3.20
qrb.h[kl y.aṯr h.rpum.l] | tdd.aṯr[h.l tdd.ilnym]. | asr.mr[kbt.---]. | tʿln.l mr[kbt hm.tity.l] | ʿr hm.tl[kn.ym.w ṯn.aḫ 22.1[123].22
.w šqr. | [---.--]b.b y[--.---]. | [-----]. | [-----]. | [-----]. | [---.]mrkbt. | [---.--]a.nrm. | [---.--]y.lm[.-.]b k[p]. | [---].tr[--.]gpn l 1002.29

mrm

n.km.qdm. | [-.k]bd n.il.ab n. | kbd k iš.tikln. | ṯd n.km.mrm.tqrṣn. | il.yẓḥq.bm. | lb.w ygmd.bm kbd. | ẓi.at.l tlš. | am 12[75].1.11

mrmnmn

p il[.---]. | [i]l mt mr[b-]. | qdš mlk [---]. | kbd d ilgb[-]. | mrmnmn. | brrn aryn. | a[-]ḥn tlyn. | atdb w ʿr. | qdš w amrr. | UG5.7.71

mrn

-]nnm ṯrm. | [---.]ṯlṯ kbd.ṣin. | [---.--]a.ṯ[l]ṯ.d.a[--]. | [---].mrn. | [---.]bn pnṯbl. | [---.-]py w.bn h. 1145.2.1

mrnn

n.bn.imrt. | mnḥm.bn.ḫyrn. | [-]yn.bn.arkbt. | [--]zbl.bt.mrnn. | a[--.---.-]ʿn. | ml[--.---]. | ar[--.---.--]l. | aty[n.bn.]šmʿnt. 102[323].3.13
šd.bn.adn. | [b] d.armwl. | [šd].mrnn. | b d.[-]tw[-]. | šd.bn[.---]. | b d.dd[--]. | šd.d[---]. | b d.d[- 2028.3
bn.]šmʿnt. | ḥnn[.bn].pls. | abrš[p.bn.]ḫrpn. | gmrš[.bn].mrnn. | ʿbdmlk.bn.ʿmyn. | agyn.rʿy. | abmlk.bn.ilrš. | iḫyn.bn. 102[323].4.7

mrʿm

ṣṣ mrʿm ḫmšm ḫmš kbd. | ṣṣ ubn ḫmš ʿšr h. | ṣṣ ʿmyd ḫmšm. | ṣṣ 2097.1
m. | iytlm.ṯlṯm. | ḫyml.ṯlṯm. | ǵlkz.ṯlṯm. | mlknʿm.ʿšrm. | mrʿm.ʿšrm. | ʿmlbu.ʿšrm. | ʿmtdl.ʿšrm. | yʿdrd.ʿšrm. | gmrd.ʿšr 1116.6

mrṣ

ln]. | in.b ilm.ʿ[ny h.yrbʿ]. | yḫmš.rgm.[my.b ilm]. | ydy.mrṣ.g[ršm.zbln]. | in.b ilm.ʿn[y h.]yṯdṯ. | yšbʿ.rgm.[my.]b ilm 16[126].5.18
bln]. | in.b ilm.ʿn[y h.]yṯdṯ. | yšbʿ.rgm.[my.]b ilm. | ydy.mrṣ.gršm zbln. | in.b ilm.ʿny h. | w yʿn.lṭpn.il.b pid. | ṯb.bn y.l 16[126].5.21
h[.---]. | ṯlṯt h[.-.w yʿn]. | lṭpn.[il.d pid.my]. | b ilm.[ydy.mrṣ]. | gršm.z[bln.in.b ilm]. | ʿny h.y[ṯny.yṯlṯ]. | rgm.my.b[il 16[126].5.11
bln.in.b ilm]. | ʿny h.y[ṯny.yṯlṯ]. | rgm.my.b[ilm.ydy]. | mrṣ.grš[m.zbln]. | in.b ilm.ʿ[ny h.yrbʿ]. | yḫmš.rgm.[my.b il 16[126].5.15
[t] km. | l kḥṯ.zbl k[m.a]nk. | iḥtrš.w [a]škn. | aškn.ydt.[m]rṣ gršt. | zbln.r[---].ymlu. | nʿm.[-]ṯ[-.--.]yqrṣ. | d[-] b pḫ[-.-- 16[126].5.27
[--.m]rṣ.mlk. | [---.]krt.adn k. | [w yʿny.]ǵzr.ilḥu. | [---.]mrṣ.mlk. | [--.k]rt.adn k. | [--.d]bḥ.dbḥ. | [--.ʿ]šr.ʿšrt. | ʿ[---.---]. 16.1[125].59
u.hlm.aḫ h.tph. | [ksl]h.l arṣ.ṯṯbr. | [---.]aḫ h.tbky. | [--.m]rṣ.mlk. | [---.]krt.adn k. | [w yʿny.]ǵzr.ilḥu. | [---.]mrṣ.mlk. 16.1[125].56
[rṣ.---]. | mn.k dw.kr[t]. | w yʿny.ǵzr[.ilḥu]. | ṯlṯ.yrḫm.k m[rṣ]. | arbʿ.k dw.k[rt]. | mndʿ.krt.mǵ[y.---]. | w qbr.tṣr.q[br]. 16.2[125].84
b p.š[---]. | il.p.d[---]. | ʿrm.[di.mh.pdrm]. | di.š[rr.---]. | mr[ṣ.---]. | zb[ln.---]. | t[--.---]. | [-----]. 16[126].5.50
k.tr[.---]. | tqrb.aḫ[h.w tṣḥ]. | lm.tbʿrn[.---]. | mn.yrḫ.k m[rṣ.---]. | mn.k dw.kr[t]. | w yʿny.ǵzr[.ilḥu]. | ṯlṯ.yrḫm.k m[r 16.2[125].81

mrr

lk ʿlm.b ʿz. | [rpu.m]lk.ʿlm.b dmr h.bl. | [---].b ḥtk h.b nmrt h.l r | [--.]arṣ.ʿz k.dmr k.l[-] | n k.ḥtk k.nmrt k.b tk. | ug UG5.2.2.8
ṯ h.b šmym. | dǵṯ.hrnmy.d kbkbm. | l tbrkn.alk brkt. | tmrn.alk.nmr[rt]. | imḫṣ.mḫṣ.aḫ y.akl[.m] | kly[.ʿ]l.umt y.w 19[1AQHT].4.195
udn.k w[-]. | k rtqt mr[.---]. | k d lbšt.bir.mlak. | šmm.tmr.zbl.mlk. | šmm.tlak.ṭl.amr.. | bn km k bk[r.z]bl.am.. | rk 13[6].26
b ḥtk h.b nmrt h.l r | [--.]arṣ.ʿz k.dmr k.l[-] | n k.ḥtk k.nmrt k.b tk. | ugrt.l ymt.špš.w yrḫ. | w nʿmt.šnt.il. UG5.2.2.10
mgšḫ. | [---.i]b.hn[.w.]ht.ank. | [---.--]š[-.-].w.ašt. | [---].amr k. | [---].k.ybt.mlk. | [---].w.ap.ank. | [---].l.ǵr.amn. | [---.-] 1012.13
.ilm.ylḥm. | uzrm.yšqy.bn.qdš. | l tbrknn l ṯr.il ab y. | tmrnn.l bny.bnwt. | w ykn.bn h b bt.šrš.b qrb. | hkl h.nṣb.sk 17[2AQHT].1.25
.krpn.bm. | [ymn.]brkm.ybrk. | [ʿbd h.]ybrk.il.krt. | [ṯʿ.ymr]m.n.ʿm[n.]ǵlm.il. | a[ṯt.tq]ḥ.y krt.aṯt. | tqḥ.bt k.ǵlmt.tšʿr 15[128].2.20
m. | dǵṯ.hrnmy.d kbkbm. | l tbrkn.alk brkt. | tmrn.alk.nmr[rt]. | imḫṣ.mḫṣ.aḫ y.akl[.m] | kly[.ʿ]l.umt y.w yʿn[.dn] | il 19[1AQHT].4.195
.um h.špš.um.ql bl. | ʿm bʿl.mrym.ṣpn.mnt y.nṯk. | nḥš.šmrr.nḥš.ʿq šr ln h. | mlḫš.abd.ln h.ydy.ḥmt.hlm.ytq. | nḥš.y UG5.7.10
tqru.l špš.u h.špš.um.ql.bl.ʿm. | dgn.ttl h.mnt.nṯk.nḥš.šmrr. | nḥš.ʿq šr.ln h.mlḫš.abd.ln h. | ydy.ḥmt.hlm.ytq.nḥš.y UG5.7.15
tqru.l špš.um.ql bl.ʿm | kṯr.w ḫss.kptr h.mnt.nṯk.nḥš. | šmrr.nḥš.ʿq šr.ln h.mlḫš.abd. | ln h.ydy.ḥmt.hlm ytq.nḥš. | y UG5.7.47
l špš.um h.špš.um.ql bl. | ʿm ḥrn.mṣd h.mnt.nṯk nḥš. | šmrr.nḥš.ʿq šr.ln h.mlḫš. | abd.ln h.ydy.ḥmt. | b ḥrn.pnm.trǵ UG5.7.59
um.ql.bl.ʿm. | il.mbk nhrm.b ʿdt.thmtm. | mnt.nṯk.nḥš.šmrr.nḥš. | ʿq šr.ln h.mlḫš abd.ln h.ydy. | ḥmt.hlm.ytq ytqšq UG5.7.4
t inbb h.mnt.nṯk. | nḥš.šlḥm.nḥš.ʿq šr[.yʿ]db.ksa. | nḥš.šmrr.nḥš.ʿq šr.ln h.ml | ḫš.abd.ln h.ydy.ḥmt.hlm.ytq. | w ytb. UG5.7.21
. | tqru.l špš.um h.špš.um.ql b.ʿm. | ršp.bbt h.mnt.nṯk.nḥš.šmrr. | nḥš.ʿq šr.ln h.mlḫš.abd.ln h.ydy. | ḥmt.hlm.ytq.nḥš.y UG5.7.31
š.um h.špš.um.ql bl ʿm. | ṯṯ.w kmṯ.ḥryt h.mnt.nṯk.nḥš.šm | rr.nḥš.ʿq šr.ln h.mlḫš abd.ln h. | ydy.ḥmt.hlm.ytq nḥš y UG5.7.36
h.špš.um.ql bl ʿm. | šḥr.w šlm šmm h mnt.nṯk.nḥš. | šmrr.nḥš ʿq šr.ln h.mlḫš. | abd.ln h.ydy ḥmt.hlm.ytq šqy. | n UG5.7.53
l špš um h.špš um ql.bl.ʿm. | mlk.ʿṯtrt h.mnt.nṯk.nḥš.šmrr. | nḥš.ʿq šr.ln h.mlḫš abd.ln h.ydy. | ḥmt.hlm.ytq.nḥš.y UG5.7.41
špš.um h.špš.[um.q]l bl.ʿm. | yrḫ.lrgt h.mnt.nṯk.n[ḥš].šmrr. | nḥš.ʿq šr.ln h.mlḫš.abd.ln h.ydy. | ḥmt.hlm.ytq.nḥš.y UG5.7.26

n.aliy[n.]b'l. | [---.]tb'.l lṭpn. | [il.d]pid.l tbrk. | [krt.]ṯ'.l tmr.n'mn. | [ǵlm.]il.ks.yiẖd. | [il.b]yd.krpn.bm. | [ymn.]brkm 15[128].2.15
ṣ.npṣ h.b ym.rṭ. | [--.y]iẖd.il.'bd h.ybrk. | [dni]l mt rpi.ymr.ǵzr. | [mt.hr]nmy npš.yḥ.dnil. | [mt.rp]i.brlt.ǵzr.mt hrn 17[2AQHT].1.36
ry mṭ.yd h. | ymǵ.l mrrt.tǵll.b nr. | yšu.g h.w yṣḥ.y l k.mrrt. | tǵll.b nr.d 'l k.mẖṣ.aqht. | ǵzr.šrš k.b arṣ.al. | yp'.riš.ǵl 19[1AQHT].3.157
nt.brḥ.p 'lm h.'nt.p dr[.dr]. | 'db.uẖry mṭ.yd h. | ymǵ.l mrrt.tǵll.b nr. | yšu.g h.w yṣḥ.y l k.mrrt. | tǵll.b nr.d 'l k.mẖṣ 19[1AQHT].3.156

mršp

[---.--]y.bṭr.b d.mlkt. | [---.]bṭr.b d.mlkt. | [---].b d.mršp. | [---.m]rbṣ. | [---.r]b.ṯnnm. | [---.]asrm. | [---.--]kn. | [----- 2015.1.3

mrṯ

.]mat. | š[--].išal. | 'm k.ybl.šd. | a[--].d'.k. | šld.ašld. | hn.mrṯ.d.štt. | ašld b ldt k. 2009.3.1
k. | mrṯ.yn.srnm.yn.bld. | ǵll.yn.išryt.'nq.smd. | lbnn.ṭl mrṯ.yḥrṯ.il. | hn.ym.w ṯn.tlḥmn.rpum. | tštyn.ṯlṯ.rb'.ym.ẖmš. 22.2[124].20
m.kš. | dpr.ṯlḥn.b q'l.b q'l. | mlkm.hn.ym.yṣq.yn.ṯmk. | mrṯ.yn.srnm.yn.bld. | ǵll.yn.išryt.'nq.smd. | lbnn.ṭl mrṯ.yḥrṯ. 22.2[124].18

mrṯd

hr.qšt.w.ql'. | bn.gmrt.qšt. | ǵmrm. | bn.qṯn.qšt.w.ql'. | mrṯd.qšt. | ssw.qšt. | knn.qšt. | bn.ṯlln.qšt. | bn.šyn.qšt. | 'bd.qšt 119[321].1.13

mšu

ršp aḏddy. | 'dn.bn.knn. | iwrẖz.b d.skn. | škny.aḏddy. | mšu.aḏddy. | plsy.aḏddy. | aẖyn. | ygmr.aḏddy. | gln.aṯṯ. | ddy. 2014.39
mšu. | ẖtpy. | ǵldy. | iẖǵl. | aby. | abmn. | ynḥm. | npl. | ynḥm. | m 1065.1

mšdpt

. | ṯlṯ.rb'.ym.ymš. | ṯdṯ.ym.ḥẓ k.al.tš'l. | qrt h.abn.yd k. | mšdpt.w hn.špšm. | b šb'.w l.yšn.pbl. | mlk.l qr.ṯigt.ibr h. | l q 14[KRT].3.118

mšḥ

ḥwt.aẖt.w nar[-]. | qrn.d bat k.btlt.'nt. | qrn.d bat k b'l.ymšḥ. | b'l.ymšḥ.hm.b 'p. | nṭ'n.b arṣ.ib y. | w b 'pr.qm.aẖ k. | 10[76].2.22
nar[-]. | qrn.d bat k.btlt.'nt. | qrn.d bat k b'l.ymšḥ. | b'l.ymšḥ.hm.b 'p. | nṭ'n.b arṣ.ib y. | w b 'pr.qm.aẖ k. | w tšu.'n h. 10[76].2.23
bl.tbḥ[n.l]azd.'r.qdm. | [---].'ẓ q[dm.--.šp]š. | [---.šm]n.mšḥt.kṭpm.a[-]ṯ[-]. | [---.--]ḥ b ym.tld[---.]b[-.]y[--.---]. | [---.il UG5.8.23
--]. | 'š[r.---]. | ẖm[š.---]. | b[yrẖ.---]. | [---.]prš. | [-----]. | l.mšḥ[.---]. | 'šr.d[d.---]. | ṯṯm.dd.dd[.---]. | l.mḏrǵlm[.---]. | ṯlṯ.m 2012.7

mšẖṭ

.]ybl.k bn.qdš.mnḥy k.ap.anš.zbl.b'[l]. | [-.yuẖ]d.b yd.mšẖṭ.bm.ymn.mẖṣ.ǵlmm.yš[--]. | [ymn h.'n]t.tuẖd.šmal h.tu 2.1[137].39
---].ššb. | [---.]tr h. | [a]rb'.ql'm. | arb'.mḏrnm. | mḏrn.w.mšẖṭ. | d.mrkbt. | mlk. | mšẖṭ.w.msg. | d.tbk. 1122.12
'.ql'm. | arb'.mḏrnm. | mḏrn.w.mšẖṭ. | d.mrkbt. | mlk. | mšẖṭ.w.msg. | d.tbk. 1122.15

mšknt

ad.tkbd.hmt.b'l. | ḥkpt il.kl h.tb'.kṯr. | l ahl h.hyn.tb'.l mš | knt h.apnk.dnil.m[t]. | rpi.aphn.ǵzr.m[t]. | hrnmy.qšt.yq 17[2AQHT].5.32
ǵrt hn.abkrn. | tbrk.ilm.tity. | tity.ilm.l ahl hm. | dr il.l mšknt hm. | w tqrb.w ld.bn.l h. | w tqrb.w ld.bnt.l h. | mk.b š 15[128].3.19

mšlt

nt.ksp. | 'šrt.ksp.b.alp.[b d].bn.[---]. | tš'.ṣin.b.tš't.ksp. | mšlt.b.ṯql.ksp. | kdwṯ.l.grgyn.b.ṯq[l]. | ẖmšm.šmt.b.ṯql. | kkr. 2101.23
spr.npṣ.krw. | tt.ẖṭrm.ṯn.kst. | spl.mšlt.w.mqḥm. | w md h. | arn.w mznm. | ṯn.ẖlpnm. | ṯṯ.mrḥm 2050.3
.k]sp. | rṯ.l.ql.d.ybl.prd. | b.ṯql.w.nṣp.ksp. | ṯmn.lbšm.w.mšlt. | l.udmym.b.ṯmnt.'šrt.ksp. | šb'm.lbš.d.'rb.bt.mlk. | b.mi 2101.14
m.b'lm.kmm. | k t'rb.'ṯtrt.šd.bt.mlk[.---]. | ṯn.skm.šb'.mšlt.arb'.ẖpnt.[---]. | ẖmšm.ṯlṯ.rkb.ntn.ṯlṯ.mat.[---]. | lg.šmn. UG5.9.1.19
[---]m.d.yṯ[--.]l[-]. | ršp.ẖmš.[m]šl[t]. | [--]arš[p.-]š.l[h]. | [-]ṯl[.--]š.l h. | [---]l[.--] h. | mtn[.--- 2133.2

mšmš

'dnm.kn.npl.b'l. | km ṯr.w tkms.hd.p[.-]. | km.ibr.b tk.mšmš d[--]. | ittpq.l awl. | išttk.lm.ttkn. | štk.mlk.dn. | štk.šibt. 12[75].2.56
'l.aẖd[.---]. | w ṣmt.ǵllm[.---]. | aẖd.aklm.k [---]. | npl.b mšmš[.---]. | anp n m yḥr[r.---]. | bmt n m.yšẖn.[---]. | qrn h.k 12[75].2.37

mšpy

gr bt b'l. | w aṯt k.ngrt.il[ht]. | 'l.l ṯkm.bnw n. | l nẖnpt.mšpy. | ṯlṯ.kmm.ṯrr y. | [---.]l ǵr.gm.ṣḥ. | [---.]r[-]m. 16[126].4.15

mšṣṣ

| klt.bt.il.ḏbb.imtẖṣ.ksp. | itrṯ.ẖrṣ.ṭrd.b'l. | b mrym.ṣpn.mšṣṣ.[-]k'[-]. | udn h.grš h.l ksi.mlk h. | l nẖt.l kḥṯ.drkt h. | m 3['NT].4.45

mšq

mšq.mlkt. | mitm.ṯṯm. | kbd.ks[p]. | ksp. | ṯmnym. | ẖrṣ. 1157.1

mšr

n.il.l mpẖrt.bn.i[l.l ṯkmn.w š]nm hn š. | w šqrb.'r.mšr mšr bn.ugrt.w [npy.---.]ugr. | w npy.yman.w npy.'rmt.w np 32[2].1.18
il]. | [l mpẖrt.bn.il.l ṯkmn.w šnm.hn š]. | [w šqrb.š.mšr mšr.bn.ugrt.w npy.---.]w npy. | [---.w np]y.ugrt. | [---.u ṯẖṭu. 32[2].1.4
t km. | [---.]km. | [-----]. | [---.]ugrt. | [---].l.lim. | [---.mšr m]šr. | [bn.ugrt.---.--]y. | [---.np]y nqmd. | [---.]pẖr. | [-----]. | [-- APP.I[-].2.1
mpẖrt.bn.il.l ṯkmn[.w]šnm.hn.'r. | w.ṯb.l mspr.m[šr] mšr.bt.ugrt.w npy.gr. | ḥmyt.ugrt.w [np]y.nṯt.ušn.yp kn.ulp 32[2].1.27
.rbt. | [---.]b nhrm. | ['b]r.gbl.'br. | q'l.'br.iht. | np šmm.šmšr. | l dgy.aṯrt. | mǵ.l qdš.amrr. | idk.al.tnn. | pnm.tk.ḥqkpt. 3['NT.VI].6.9
dr.bn.il.l mpẖrt.bn.i[l.l ṯkmn.w š]nm hn š. | w šqrb.'r.mšr mšr bn.ugrt.w [npy.---.]ugr. | w npy.yman.w npy.'rmt. 32[2].1.18
.bn[.il]. | [l mpẖrt.bn.il.l ṯkmn.w šnm.hn š]. | [w šqrb.š.mšr mšr.bn.ugrt.w npy.---.]w npy. | [---.w np]y.ugrt. | [---.u t 32[2].1.4
--.-]yt km. | [---.]km. | [-----]. | [---.]ugrt. | [---].l.lim. | [---.mšr m]šr. | [bn.ugrt.---.--]y. | [---.np]y nqmd. | [---.]pẖr. | [----- APP.I[-].2.1
bn il.l mpẖrt.bn.il.l ṯkmn[.w]šnm.hn.'r. | w.ṯb.l mspr.m[šr] mšr.bt.ugrt.w npy.gr. | ḥmyt.ugrt.w [np]y.nṯt.ušn.yp 32[2].1.27

mšrm

bd šmn. | l.abrm.altyy. | [m]it.tltm.kbd.šmn. | [l.]abrm.mšrm. | [mi]tm.arbʻm.tmn.kbd. | [l.]sbrdnm. | m[i]t.l.bn.ʻzmt. 2095.4

mšrn

sn.l.[---]. | šd.bddn.l.iytlm. | šd.bn.nbʻm.l.tptbʻl. | šd.bn mšrn.l.ilšpš. | [šd.bn].kbr.l.snrn. | [---.--]k.l.gmrd. | [---.--]t.l.y 2030.1.5
skn.ʻšrm kk[r.---]. | mšrn.tlt.ʻš[r.kkr]. | bn.šw.šbʻ.kk[r.---]. | arbʻm.kkr.[---]. | b d. 2108.2
[---.]iy[t]r. | [---.ʻbd.y]rh. | [---.b]n.mšrn. | [---].bn.lnn. | [-----]. | [---.-]lyr. 2135.3
ym[.---]. | [---.-]dn.tlt[m.---]. | [---].mitm[.---]. | [---.--]m.mšrn[.---]. 149[99].13

mšt

[-----]. | [-----]. | ynhm. | ihy. | bn.mšt. | ʻpsn. | bn.spr. | kmn. | bn.ršp. | tmn. | šmmn. | bn.rmy. | bn 1047.5

mštt

-]n. | kd.mštt.[---]n. | kdm.l.mdrǵlm. | kd.l.msrym. | kd.mštt.mlk. | kd.bn.amht [-]t. | w.bn.msrym. | arbʻm.yn. | l.hrd. 1089.8
šbʻ.yn.l [---]. | tlt.l hr[š.---]. | tt[.l.]mštt[.---]. | tlt.l.mdr[ǵlm]. | kd[.--].lm[d.---]. | kd[.l.]hzr[m.---] 1091.3
kl h. | kdm.l.zn[-.---]. | kd.l.atr[y]m. | kdm.ʻm.[--]n. | kd.mštt.[---]n. | kdm.l.mdrǵlm. | kd.l.msrym. | kd.mštt.mlk. | kd. 1089.5

mt

yʻn.aqht.ǵzr. | al.tšrgn.y btlt m.dm.l ǵzr. | šrg k.hhm.mt.uhryt.mh.yqh. | mh.yqh.mt.atryt.spsg.ysk. | [l]riš.hrs.l zr 17[2AQHT].6.35
bt h.hh.ars. | nhlt h.w nǵr. | ʻnn.ilm.al. | tqrb.l bn.ilm. | mt.al.yʻdb km. | k imr.b p h. | k lli.b tbrn. | qn h.tḫtan. | nrt.il 4[51].8.17
lt m.dm.l ǵzr. | šrg k.hhm.mt.uhryt.mh.yqh. | mh.yqh.mt.atryt.spsg.ysk. | [l]riš.hrs.l zr.qdqd y. | [--.]mt.kl.amt.w a 17[2AQHT].6.36
lsmm.mt.ql. | bʻl.ql.ʻln.špš. | tsh.l mt.šmʻ.mʻ. | l bn.ilm.mt.ik.tmt[h] | s.ʻm.aliyn.bʻl. | ik.al.yšm[ʻ] k.tr. | il.ab k.l ysʻ.al 6[49].6.24
h.tḫtan. | nrt.ilm.špš. | shrrt.la. | šmm.b yd.md | d.ilm.mt.b a | lp.šd.rbt.k | mn.l pʻn.mt. | hbr.w ql. | tšthwy.w k | bd h 4[51].8.24
ipd k.ank.ispi.utm. | drqm.amt m.l yrt. | b npš.bn ilm.mt.b mh | mrt.ydd.il.ǵzr. | tbʻ.w l.ytb ilm.idk. | l ytn.pnm.ʻm. 5[67].1.7
l ʻgl h.k lb. | tat.l imr h.km.lb. | ʻnt.atr.bʻl.tihd. | bn.ilm.mt.b hrb. | tbqʻnn.b htr.tdry | nn.b išt.tšrpnn. | b rhm.tthnn.b 6[49].2.31
.yštkn. | dll.al.ilak.l bn. | ilm.mt.ʻdd.l ydd. | il.ǵzr.yqra.mt. | b npš h.ystrn ydd. | b gngn h.ahd y.d ym | lk.ʻl.ilm.l ym 4[51].7.47
rh]. | l ʻgl h.k lb.ta[t]. | l imr h.km.lb.ʻn[t]. | atr.bʻl.tihd.m[t]. | b sin.lpš.tšsq[n h]. | b qs.all.tšu.g h.w[ts] | h.at.mt.tn.a 6[49].2.9
lk k. | l ytbr.ht.mtpt k. | yru.bn ilm t.ttʻ.y | dd.il.ǵzr.yʻr.mt. | b ql h.y[---.---]. | bʻl.yttbn[.l ksi]. | mlk h.l[nht.l kht]. | dr 6[49].6.31
.p k.b hlb.k tgwln.šnt k. | [--.]w špt k.l tššy.hm.tqrm.l mt.b rn k. | [--]hp.an.arnn.ql.špš.hw.btnm.uhd.bʻlm. | [--.a]t 1001.1.5
[------]. | [bn.]kblbn[.---]. | [bn] uškny. | bn.krny[-]. | bn.mt. | bn.nzʻn. | bn.slmz[-]. | bn.kʻ[--]. | bn.y[---]. | [-----]. | [bn.a] 2021.1.16
.la. | šmm.b yd.md | d.ilm.mt.b a | lp.šd.rbt.k | mn.l pʻn.mt. | hbr.w ql. | tšthwy.w k | bd hwt.w rgm. | l bn.ilm.mt. | tny 4[51].8.26
nm.ʻm.bʻl. | mrym.spn.w yʻn. | gpn.w ugr.thm.bn ilm. | mt.hwt.ydd.bn.il. | ǵzr.p np.š.npš.lbim. | thw.hm.brlt.anhr. | 5[67].1.13
pš. | anhr.b ym. | brkt.šbšt. | k rumm.hm. | ʻn.kdd.aylt. | mt hm.ks.ym | sk.nhr hm. | šbʻ.ydt y.b sʻ. | [--.]šbʻ.rbt. | [---.]q UG5.4.9
.b bt h.ktrt.bnt. | hll.snnt.apnk.dnil. | mt.rpi.ap.hn.ǵzr.mt. | hrnmy.alp.ytbh.l kt | rt.yšlhm.ktrt.w y | ššq.bnt.[hl]l.sn 17[2AQHT].2.28
ǵt.bm.lb. | tdmʻ.bm.kbd. | tmzʻ.kst.dnil.mt. | rpi.al.ǵzr.mt.hrnmy. | apnk.dnil.mt. | rpi.ysly.ʻrpt.b | hm.un.yr.ʻrpt. | t 19[1AQHT].1.37
[-----.apnk]. | [dnil.mt.rp]i.apn.ǵz[r]. | [mt.hrnmy.]uzr.ilm.ylhm. | [uzr.yšqy.]bn.qdš.yd. | [st h.yʻl.]w 17[2AQHT].1.3
lk.qšt.ybln.hl.yš | rbʻ.qsʻt.apnk.dnil. | mt.rpi.aphn.ǵzr.mt. | hrnmy.gm.l att h.k ysh. | šmʻ.mtt.dnty.ʻd[b]. | imr.b phd 17[2AQHT].5.14
.thmtm.bl. | tbn.ql.bʻl.k tmzʻ. | kst.dnil.mt.rpi. | all.ǵzr.m[t.]hr[nmy]. | gm.l bt[h.dnil.k ysh]. | šmʻ.pǵt.tkmt[.my]. | h 19[1AQHT].1.48
. | [w]yqrb.bʻl.b hnt h.abynt. | [d]nil.mt.rpi anh.ǵzr. | [mt.]hrnmy.d in.bn.l h. | km.ah h.w šrš.km.ary h. | bl.it.bn.l h 17[2AQHT].1.19
m.rt. | [--.y]ihd.il.ʻbd h.ybrk. | [dni]l mt rpi.ymr.ǵzr. | [mt.hr]nmy npš.yh.dnil. | [mt.rp]i.brlt.ǵzr.mt hrnmy. | [---].h 17[2AQHT].1.37
il.mt.r[pi.mk].b šbʻ. | šnt.w yʻn[.dnil.mt.]rpi. | ytb.ǵzr.m[t.hrnmy.y]šu. | g h.w ysh.t[bʻ.---]. | bkyt.b hk[l]y.msspdt. 19[1AQHT].4.181
z.y[bl].šblt. | b ǵlp h.apnk.dnil. | [m]t.rpi.ap[h]n.ǵzr. | [mt.hrn]my.ytšu. | [ytb.b ap.t]ǵr[.t]ht. | [adrm.d b grn.y]dn. | [19[1AQHT].1.21
bʻ.qsʻt.w hn šb[ʻ]. | b ymm.apnk.dnil.mt. | rpi.a hn.ǵzr.mt.hrnm[y]. | ytšu.ytb.b ap.tǵr.tht. | adrm.d b grn.ydn. | dn.a 17[2AQHT].5.5
hl h.hyn.tbʻ.l mš | knt h.apnk.dnil.m[t]. | rpi.aphn.ǵzr.m[t]. | hrnmy.qšt.yqb.[--] | rk.ʻl.aqht.k yq[--.---]. | prʻm.sd k.y 17[2AQHT].5.34
um.l grnt.i[lnym.l] | mtʻt.w yʻn.dnil.[mt.rpi]. | ytb.ǵzr.mt hrnmy[.---]. | b grnt.ilm.b qrb.m[tʻt.ilnym]. | d tit.yspi.sp 20[121].2.8
i.ymr.ǵzr. | [mt.hr]nmy npš.yh.dnil. | [mt.rp]i.brlt.ǵzr.mt hrnmy. | [---].hw.mh.l ʻrš h.yʻl. | [---].bm.nšq.att h. | [---.]b 17[2AQHT].1.38
n[--.]sn[--]. | nrt.ilm.špš[.shrr]t. | la.šmm.b y[d.bn.ilm.m]t. | w tʻn.btlt.ʻn[t.bnt.]bht | k.y ilm.bnt.bh[t k].a[l.tš]mh. | 3[ʻNT.VI].5.26
w šty.b hmr yn ay. | šlm.mlk.šlm.mlkt.ʻrbm m.tnnm. | mt.w šr.ytb.b d h.ht.tkl.b d h. | ht.ulmn.yzbrnn.zbrm.gpn. | 23[52].8
n q y.htu hw. | nrt.ilm.špš.shrrt. | la.šmm.b yd.bn ilm.mt. | ym.ymm.yʻtqn.l ymm. | l yrhm.rhm.ʻnt.tngt h. | k lb.arh 6[49].2.25
.m[t]. | b sin.lpš.tšsq[n h]. | b qs.all.tšu.g h.w[ts] | h.at.mt.tn.ah y. | w ʻn.bn.ilm.mt.mh. | taršn.l btlt.ʻnt. | an.itlk.w a 6[49].2.12
k.tm. | tkm.bm tkm.ahm.qym.il. | b lsmt.tm.ytbš.šm.il.mt m. | yʻbš.brk n.šm.il.ǵzrm. | tm.tmq.rpu.bʻl.mhr bʻl. | w m 22.2[124].6
]. | b qs.all.tšu.g h.w[ts] | h.at.mt.tn.ah y. | w ʻn.bn.ilm.mt.mh. | taršn.l btlt.ʻnt. | an.itlk.w asd.kl. | ǵr.l kbd.ars.kl.gbʻ 6[49].2.13
ʻl.bn.atrt. | rbm.ymhs.b ktp. | dk ym.ymhs.b smd. | shr mt.ymsh.l ars. | [ytb.]b[ʻ]l.l ksi.mlk h. | [---].l kht.drkt h. | l [y 6[49].5.4
dqm šr. | hnbn il d[n]. | [-]bd w [---]. | [--].p il[.---]. | [i]l mt mr[b-]. | qdš mlk [---]. | kbd d ilgb[-]. | mrmnmn. | brrn ar UG5.10.2.2
rrt.l phmm.btm.bt.il.bt.il. | w ʻlm h.w hn.attm.tshn y.mt mt. | nhtm.ht k.mmnnm.mt yd k.hl.ʻsr. | thrr.l išt.w shrt. 23[52].46
m.ʻsr.yhrt yšt. | l phm.il.attm.k ypt.hm.attm.tshn. | y mt.mt.nhtm.ht k.mmnnm.mt.yd k. | h[l.]ʻsr.thrr.l išt.shrrt.l 23[52].40
.l phmm.btm.bt.il.bt.il. | w ʻlm h.w hn.attm.tshn y.mt mt. | nhtm.ht k.mmnnm.mt yd k.hl.ʻsr. | thrr.l išt.w shrt.l ph 23[52].46
ʻsr.yhrt yšt. | l phm.il.attm.k ypt.hm.attm.tshn. | y mt.mt.nhtm.ht k.mmnnm.mt.yd k. | h[l.]ʻsr.thrr.l išt.shrrt.l ph 23[52].40
w yʻny.bn. | ilm.mt.npš[.-]. | npš.lbun. | thw.w npš. | anhr.b ym. | brkt.šbšt. | k UG5.4.2
.w tsh.thm.aliyn. | bn.bʻl.hwt.aliy.qrdm. | bht.bn.ilm.mt.ʻbd k.an. | w d ʻlm k.šmh.bn.ilm.mt. | [---.]g h.w ash.ik.ys 5[67].2.19
ydd.il ǵzr. | thm.aliyn.bʻl.hwt.aliy. | qrdm.bht.l bn.ilm mt. | ʻbd k.an.w d.ʻlm k. | tbʻ.w l.ytb.ilm.idk. | l ytn.pn.ʻm.bn. 5[67].2.11
| u mlk.u bl mlk. | ars.drkt.yštkn. | dll.al.ilak.l bn. | ilm.mt.ʻdd.l ydd. | il.ǵzr.yqra.mt. | b npš h.ystrn ydd. | b gngn h.a 4[51].7.46
.ʻz.bʻl.ʻz.ynghn. | k rumm.mt.ʻz.bʻl. | ʻz.yntkn.k btnm. | mt.ʻz.bʻl.ʻz.ymshn. | k lsmm.mt.ql. | bʻl.ql.ʻln.špš. | tsh.l mt.š 6[49].6.20
y m.ytnt.bʻl. | spu y.bn m.um y.kl | y y.ytʻn.k gmrm. | mt.ʻz.bʻl.ʻz.ynghn. | k rumm.mt.ʻz.bʻl. | ʻz.yntkn.k btnm. | mt. 6[49].6.17

y.kl|y y.yt‘n.k gmrm.|mt.‘z.b‘l.‘z.ynghn.|k rumm.mt.‘z.b‘l.|‘z.ynṯkn.k bṯnm.|mt.‘z.b‘l.‘z.ymṣẖn.|k lsmm.mt. 6[49].6.18
].|[--] aṯt yqḥ ‘z.|[---]ḏ.|[---].|[---].|hm qrt tuẖd.hm mt y‘l bnš.|bt bn bnš yqḥ ‘z.|w yḥdy mrḥqm. RS61[24.277.29]
]m.l yrẖm.l yrẖm.|l šnt.[m]k.b šb‘.|šnt.w [--].bn.ilm.mt.|‘m.aliyn.b‘l.yšu.|g h.w yṣḥ.‘l k.b[‘]l m.|pht.qlt.‘l k.pht. 6[49].5.9
r.limm.|[---.]bn.ilm.mt.|[--]u.šb‘t.ǵlm h.|[---].bn.ilm.mt.|p[-]n.aẖ y m.ytn.b‘l.|[s]pu y.bn m.um y.kly y.|yṯb.‘m. 6[49].6.9
[.---].|n‘m.ilm[.---].|šgr.mu[d.---].|šgr.mud[.---].|dm.mt.aṣ[ḥ.---].|yd.b qrb[.---].|w lk.ilm.[---].|w rgm.l [---].|b 5[67].3.18
---].|tkn.lbn[.---].|dt.lbn k[.---].|dk k.kbkb[.---].|dm.mt.aṣḥ[.---].|ydd.b qr[b.---].|al.ašt.b[---].|ahpk k.l[--.---].|ṯ 5[67].3.9
-].|b mud.ṣin[.---].|mud.ṣin[.---].|iṯm.mui[-.---].|dm.mt.aṣ[ḥ.---].|ydd.b qr[b.---].|ṯmm.w lk[.---].|[--]ṯ.lk[.---].|[5[67].3.25
.‘z.b‘l.|‘z.ynṯkn.k bṯnm.|mt.‘z.b‘l.‘z.ymṣẖn.|k lsmm.mt.ql.|b‘l.ql.‘ln.špš.|tṣḥ.l mt.šm‘.m‘.|l bn.ilm.mt.ik.tmt[ẖ] 6[49].6.21
.ṭl.bl rbb.|bl.šr‘.thmtm.bl.|ṭbn.ql.b‘l.k tmz‘.|kst.dnil.mt.rpi.|all.ǵzr.m[t.]hr[nmy].|gm.l bt[h.dnil.k yṣḥ].|šm‘.pǵ 19[1AQHT].1.47
l.diym.|tbky.pǵt.bm.lb.|tdm‘.bm.kbd.|tmz‘.kst.dnil.mt.|rpi.al.ǵzr.mt.hrnmy.|apnk.dnil.mt.|rpi.yṣly.‘rpt.b |ḥ 19[1AQHT].1.36
ln.mk.b šb‘.ymm.|[w]yqrb.b‘l.b ḥnt h.abynt.|[d]nil.mt.rpi anẖ.ǵzr.|[mt.]hrnmy.d in.bn.l h.|km.aẖ h.w šrš.km. 17[2AQHT].1.18
]abl.qšt ṯmn.|ašrb‘.qṣ‘t.w hn šb[‘].|b ymm.apnk.dnil.mt.|rpi.a hn.ǵzr.mt.hrnm[y].|ytšu.yṯb.b ap.ṯǵr.tḥt.|adrm.d 17[2AQHT].5.4
l.dnil.l hkl h.|‘rb.b bt h.kṯrt.bnt.|hll.snnt.apnk.dnil.|mt.rpi.ap.hn.ǵzr.mt.|hrnmy.alp.yṭbẖ.l kṯ|rt.yšlḥm.kṯrt.w y 17[2AQHT].2.28
.-]ḥ.mṣṣ[-]t[.--].|pr‘.qẓ.y[bl].šblt.|b ǵlp h.apnk.dnil.|[m]t.rpi.ap[h]n.ǵzr.|[mt.hrn]my.ytšu.|[yṯb.b ap.ṯ]ǵr[.t]ḥt.|[19[1AQHT].1.20
t il.kl h.tb‘.kṯr.|l ahl h.hyn.tb‘.l mš|knt h.apnk.dnil.m[t].|rpi.aphn.ǵzr.m[t].|hrnmy.qšt.yqb.[--]|rk.‘l.aqht.k yq 17[2AQHT].5.33
w y‘n.tdrq.ẖss.|hlk.qšt.ybln.hl.yš|rb‘.qṣ‘t.apnk.dnil.|mt.rpi.aphn.ǵzr.mt.|hrnmy.gm.l aṯt h.k yṣḥ.|šm‘.mṯt.dnty. 17[2AQHT].5.14
[-----.apnk].|[dnil.mt.rp]i.apn.ǵz[r].|[mt.hrnmy.]uzr.ilm.ylḥm.|[uzr.yšqy.]bn 17[2AQHT].1.2
rk.|[dni]l mt rpi.ymr.ǵzr.|[mt.hr]nmy npš.yḥ.dnil.|[mt.rp]i.brlt.ǵzr.mt hrnmy.|[---].hw.mẖ.l ‘rš h.y‘l.|[---].bm. 17[2AQHT].1.38
aṯt h.|[---.]b ḥbq h.ḥmḥmt.|[---.--] n.ylt.ḥmḥmt.|[---.mt.r]pi.w ykn.bn h.|[b bt.šrš.]b qrb.hkl h.|[nṣb.skn.i]lib h. 17[2AQHT].1.43
tql.tšth.|[wy.w tkbd]n h.tlšn.aqht.ǵzr.|[---.kdd.dn]il.mt.rpi.w t‘n.|[btlt.‘nt.tšu.g]h.w tṣḥ.hwt.|[---.]aqht.yḏ[--].| 17[2AQHT].6.52
t.b ḥẓr h.|pẓǵm.ǵr.ybk.l aqht.|ǵzr.ydm‘.l kdd.dnil.|mt.rpi.l ymm.l yrẖm.|l yrẖm.l šnt.‘d.|šb‘t.šnt.ybk.l aq|ht.ǵ 19[1AQHT].4.175
[-.k qṭr.b ap -].|tmǵyn.tša.g h[m.w tṣḥn].|šm‘.l dnil.[mt.rpi].|mt.aqht.ǵzr.[šṣat].|btlt.‘nt.k [rḥ.npš h].|k iṯl.brlt 19[1AQHT].2.90
.l šnt.‘d.|šb‘t.šnt.ybk.l aq|ht.ǵzr.yd[m‘.]l kdd.|dnil.mt.r[pi.mk].b šb‘.|šnt.w y‘n[.dnil.mt.]rpi.|yṯb.ǵzr.m[t.hrn 19[1AQHT].4.179
[ṯi]ṯ.rḥṣ.npṣ h.b ym.rṯ.|[--.y]iẖd.il.‘bd h.ybrk.|[dni]l mt rpi.ymr.ǵzr.|[mt.hr]nmy npš.yḥ.dnil.|[mt.rp]i.brlt.ǵzr. 17[2AQHT].1.36
].|imẖṣ.mẖṣ.aẖ y.akl[.m]|kly[.‘]l.umt y.w y‘n[.dn]|il.mt.rpi npš tḥ[.pǵt].|ṯ[km]t.mym.ḥspt.l š‘r.|ṭl.yd‘t.hlk.kbkb 19[1AQHT].4.198
d.|tmz‘.kst.dnil.mt.|rpi.al.ǵzr.mt.hrnmy.|apnk.dnil.mt.|rpi.yṣly.‘rpt.b |ḥm.un.ỵr.‘rpt.|tmṭr.b qẓ.ṭl.yṭll.|l ǵnbm 19[1AQHT].1.38
.yd[m‘.]l kdd.|dnil.mt.r[pi.mk].b šb‘.|šnt.w y‘n[.dnil.mt.]rpi.|yṯb.ǵzr.m[t.hrnmy.y]šu.|g h.w yṣḥ.t[b‘.---].|bkyt.b 19[1AQHT].4.180
m.b ṯlṯ].|mǵy.rpum.l grnt.i[lnym.l] |mṭ‘t.w y‘n.dnil.[mt.rpi].|yṯb.ǵzr.mt hrnmy[.---].|b grnt.ilm.b qrb.m[ṭ‘t.ilny 20[121].2.7
šb‘.ydt y.b ṣ‘.|[--.]šb‘.rbt.|[---.]qbṭ.ṯm.|[---.]bn.ilm.|[m]t.šmḥ.p ydd.|il[.ǵ]zr.|b [-]dn.‘.z.w.|rgbt.zbl. UG5.4.15
n h.|ytn.ks.b d h.|krpn.b klat.yd h.|b krb.‘ẓm.ridn.|mt.šmm.ks.qdš.|l tphn h.aṯt.krpn.|l t‘n.aṯrt.alp.|kd.yqḥ.b 3[‘NT].1.13
t.‘z.b‘l.‘z.ymṣẖn.|k lsmm.mt.ql.|b‘l.ql.‘ln.špš.|tṣḥ.l mt.šm‘.m‘.|l bn.ilm.mt.ik.tmt[ẖ]|ṣ.‘m.aliyn.b‘l.|ik.al.yšm[‘ 6[49].6.23
.an.w d.‘lm k.|tb‘.w l.yṯb.ilm.idk.|l ytn.pn.‘m.bn.ilm.mt.|tk.qrt h.hmry.mk.ksu.|ṯbt.ẖẖ.arṣ.nḥlt h.tša.|g hm.w tṣ 5[67].2.14
‘ṣm.yraun.aliyn.b‘l.|ṯt‘.nn.rkb.‘rpt.|tb‘.rgm.l bn.ilm.mt.|ṯny.l ydd.il ǵzr.|tḥm.aliyn.b‘l.hwt.aliy.|qrdm.bhṯ.l bn. 5[67].2.8
n.mt.|hbr.w ql.|tšthwy.w k|bd hwt.w rgm.|l bn.ilm.mt.|ṯny.l ydd.|il.ǵzr.tḥm.|aliyn.b‘l.|[hw]t.aliy.q|[rdm.]bht 4[51].8.30
ṯbt k.l yhpk.ksa.mlk k.|l yṯbr.ẖṭ.mṯpṭ k.|yru.bn ilm t.ṯt‘.y|dd.il.ǵzr.y‘r.mt.|b ql h.y[---.---].|b‘l.yṯṯbn[.l ksi].|ml 6[49].6.30
.]ru.|[----] h.|[---.--]mt.|[---.--]mr.limm.|[---.]bn.ilm.mt.|[--]u.šb‘t.ǵlm h.|[---].bn.ilm.mt.|p[-]n.aẖ y m.ytn.b‘l.|[6[49].6.7
rdm.|bhṯ.bn.ilm.mt.‘bd k.an.|w d ‘lm k.šmẖ.bn.ilm.mt.|[---.]g h.w aṣḥ.ik.yṣḥn.|[b‘l.‘m.aẖ y.ik].yqrun.hd.|[‘m. 5[67].2.20
n.mṣ[--.---].|[---.]b‘lš[-.---].|[---.]bn.zzb[-.---].|[---.]bn mt[.---].|[---.b]n r[--.---]. 2139.6

mtb‘l

.|ẖṯpy.|ǵldy.|iẖǵl.|aby.|abmn.|ynḥm.|npl.|ynḥm.|mtb‘l.|bn ǵlmn.|bn sgld. 1065.10
n[.---].|klby.[bn.---].|šmmlk bn[.---].|‘myn.bn.[---].|mtb‘l.bn[.---].|ymy.bn[.---].|‘bd‘n.p[--.---].|[-]d[-]l.bn.ḥrn.| 102[322].5.11
mit.ṯlṯ.mẖsrn.|‘l.nsk.kṯtǵlm.|arb‘m.ṯlṯ.mẖsrn.|mtb‘l.rišy.|ṯlṯm.ṯlṯ.‘l.nsk.|arym.|alp.ṯlṯ.‘l.|nsk.art.|ẖmš.m 1137.4

mtḥ

.l rḥq.ilm.inbb.|l rḥq.ilnym.ṯn.mṯpdm.|tḥt.‘nt.arṣ.ṯlṯ.mtḥ.ǵyrm.|idk.l ttn pnm.‘m.b‘l.|mrym.ṣpn.b alp.šd.rbt.km 3[‘NT].4.80
[ḥq.ilm.ḥkpt.l rḥq].|[ilnym.ṯn.mṯpd]m.t[ḥt.‘nt.arṣ.ṯlṯ.mtḥ.ǵyrm].|[idk.]l ytn.pnm.‘m.[i]l.mbk.[nhrm.qrb.apq.thm 2.3[129].3
rḥq.ilm.ḥkp[t.l rḥq.ilnym].|ṯn.mṯpdm.tḥt.[‘nt.arṣ.ṯlṯ.mtḥ].|ǵyrm.idk.l yt[n.pnm.‘m.lṭpn].|il d pid.tk ẖrš[n.---.tk. 1[‘NT.IX].3.20

mty

ẖqm bir[-.---].|kṯrmlk.ns[--.---].|bn.tbd.ilšt[m‘y.---].|mty.ilšt[m‘y.---].|bn.pynq.‘nqp[a]t[y.---].|ayiẖ.ilšt[m‘y.---]. 90[314].2.7

mtyn

n.|bn.[---].|bn.b[--].|bn.š[--].|bn.a[---].|bn.prsn.|bn.mtyn.|bn.ẖlpn.|bn.ḥgbn.|bn.szn.|bn.mglb. 117[325].2.6

mtn

dr.ṯqbm.|[d]lbnn.adr.gdm.b rumm.|adr.qrnt.b y‘lm.mtnm.|b ‘qbt.ṯr.adr.b ǵlil.qnm.|tn.l kṯr.w ẖss.yb‘l.qšt l ‘nt. 17[2AQHT].6.22
[--.l]bš.mtn.b.ar‘t.|[--.l]bš.bn.ykn‘.b.ar‘t.|[--.l]bš.bn.grbn.b.ṯqlm.|[135[330].1
spr.‘rbnm.|dt.‘rb.|b.mtn.bn.ayaẖ.|b.ẖbṯ h.ḥwt.ṯt h.|w.mnm.šalm.|dt.tknn.|‘l.‘r 1161.3
h.|w.mnm.šalm.|dt.tknn.|‘l.‘rbnm.|hn hmt.|tknn.|mtn.bn.‘bdym.|ilrb.bn.ilyn.|‘bdadt.bn ‘bdkb.|gn‘ym. 1161.10
nm.upqt.|[---.]l w ǵr mtn y.|[---.]rq.gb.|[---.--]kl.tǵr.mtn h.|[---.--]b.w ym ymm.|[y‘tqn.---].ymǵy.npš.|[---.--]t.h 1[‘NT.X].5.14
[-----].|w.lmd h.|mtn.|w.lmd h.|ymn.|w.lmd h.|y‘ḏrn.|w.lmd h.|‘dn.|w.l 1049.1.3
asrn.ṯr il.|[---.]rks.bn.abnm.|[---.]upqt.‘rb.|[---.w ẓ]r.mtn y at zd.|[---.]t‘rb.bši.|[---.]l tzd.l tptq.|[---].g[--.]l arṣ. 1[‘NT.X].5.25
‘t.|[---.t]asrn.|[---.]trks.|[---.]abnm.upqt.|[---.]l w ǵr mtn y.|[---.]rq.gb.|[---.--]kl.tǵr.mtn h.|[---.--]b.w ym ymm. 1[‘NT.X].5.12
rtn.kṯrmlk.|yḥmn.aẖm[l]k.‘bdrpu.adn.ṯ[--].|bdn.qln.mtn.ydln.|b‘ltdtt.tlgn.ytn.|b‘ltǵpṯm.krwn.ilšn.agyn.|mnn.š 2011.34

.ṯlṯ.ʿš[r.kkr]. | bn.św.šbʿ.kk[r.---]. | arbʿm.kkr.[---]. | b d.mtn.[l].šlm. 2108.5
ṯpṭ. | [bn].ayḫ. | [---]rn. | ill. | ǵlmn. | bn.ytrm. | bn.ḫgbt. | mtn. | mḫtn. | [p]lsy. | bn.ḥrš. | [--.]kbd. | [---]. | y[---]. | bn.ǵlyn. 1035.2.12
w.ildgn.ḥṭbm. | tdǵlm.iln.bʿ[l]n.alḏy. | tdn.ṣr[--.--]t.ʿzn.mtn.n[bd]g. | ḥrš qṭn[.---.]dqn.bʿln. | ǵltn.ʿbd.[---]. | nsk.ḥḏm. 2011.22
lš. | ḏmr. | mkrm. | ʿzn. | yplṭ. | ʿbdmlk. | ynḥm. | aḏddn. | mtn. | plsy. | qṭn. | ypr. | bn.ymy. | bn.ʿrd. | [-]b.da[-]. | [--]l[--]. | [1035.4.8
.ṯlṯ.ʿl.nsk. | arym. | alp.ṯlṯ.ʿl. | nsk.art. | ḫmš.mat.ṯlṯ. | ʿl.mtn.rišy. 1137.10
k[---]. | ʿbd.[---]. | mtn[.---]. | ṯdpṯn[.--]. | tny[.--]. | sll[.--]. | mld[.--]. | yqš[.--]. | [--- 1074.3

mtnbʿl

| ubn. | špšyn. | abmn. | [--]dn. | [ṯ]bʿm. | [--]mlk. | [--]ty. | mtnbʿl. | bn.ndbn. | bn irgn. 1072.11

mtny

ʿ. | ʿšrm.l mit.ksp. | ʿl.bn.alkbl.šb[ny]. | ʿšrm ksp.ʿl. | wrt.mtny.w ʿl. | prdny.aṯt h. 2107.18

mtnn

n kṯl. | bn army. | bn gln. | bn abg. | bn.nǵry. | bn.srwd. | mtnn. | bn gš[-]. | bn gbrn. | bn uldy. | synn.bn knʿm. | bn kbr. | 1064.15

mtʿ

.plk h[.b yd h]. | plk.qlt.b ymn h. | npyn h.mks.bšr h. | tmtʿ.md h.b ym.ṯn. | npyn h.b nhrm. | štt.ḫptr.l išt. | ḫbrṯ.l ẓr. 4[51].2.6

mtq

š.rbt.w l kbkbm.kn[-]. | yhbr.špt hm.yšq.hn.[š]pt hm.mtqtm. | bm.nšq.w hr.[b]ḥbq.w ḥ[m]ḥmt.yṯb[n]. | yspr.l ḫm 23[52].55
. | aṯt.il.w ʿlm h.yhbr.špt hm.yš[q]. | hn.špt hm.mtqtm.mtqtm.k lrmn[.--]. | bm.nšq.w hr.b ḥbq.ḥmḥmt.tqt[nṣn]. | tl 23[52].50
.a[ṯt.il]. | aṯt.il.w ʿlm h.yhbr.špt hm.yš[q]. | hn.špt hm.mtqtm.mtqtm.k lrmn[.--]. | bm.nšq.w hr.b ḥbq.ḥmḥmt.tqt[n 23[52].50

mṯ

n h.šbʿ.l šbʿm. | tš[ʿ]ly.ṯmn.l ṯmnym. | w [th]rn.w tldn mṯ. | al[iyn.bʿ]l šlbšn. | i[---.---.--]l h.mǵẓ. | y[--.---.]l irt h. | n[-- 5[67].5.22
pṭ.b[--]. | b[n.---]. | šm[-.---]. | tkn[.---]. | knn.b.ḫ[lb]. | bn mṯ.b.qmy. | nʿr.b.ulm. 2046.2.5
.at.tr[gm.---]. | w.drm.ʿtr[--.---]. | w ap.ht.k[--.]škn. | w.mṯnn[.---.]ʿmn k. | [-]štš.[---.]rgm y. | [-]wd.r[-.]pǵt. | [---.--]t.y 54.1.21[13.2.6]

mṯyn

lbš.aḥd. | b.ʿšrt. | w.ṯn.b.ḫmšt. | ṯprt.b.ṯlṯt. | mṯyn.b.ṯṯt. | ṯn.lbšm.b.ʿšrt. | pld.b.arbʿt. | lbš.ṯn.b.ṯnt.ʿšrt. 1108.5

mṯk

[mrǵ]b.yd.m[ṯkt]. | mẓma.yd.mṯkt. | ṯṯkr.[--]dn. | ʿm.krt.mswn h. | arḫ.t 15[128].1.1
[mrǵ]b.yd.m[ṯkt]. | mẓma.yd.mṯkt. | ṯṯkr.[--]dn. | ʿm.krt.mswn h. | arḫ.tzǵ.l ʿgl h. | bn.ḫpṯ.l 15[128].1.2

mṯpit

i.ibrn. | [š]d.bn.bri.b d.bn.ydln. | [u]bdy.ṯǵrm. | [š]d.ṯǵr.mṯpit.b d.bn.iryn. | [u]bdy.šrm. | [š]d.bn.ḫrmln.b d.bn.tnn. | [82[300].2.8

mṯpṭ

[u]lm. | mṯpṭ.ṯt.qštm.w.ṯn.q[l]ʿm. | kmrṯn.ṯt.qštm.ṯn.[q]lʿm. | ǵdyn.qš 119[321].1.2

mṯt

.kṯr. | w ḫss.b d.dnil.ytnn. | qšt.l brk h.yʿdb. | qṣʿt.apnk.mṯt.dnty. | tšlḥm.tššqy ilm. | tsad.tkbd.hmt.bʿl. | ḥkpt il.kl h.t 17[2AQHT].5.28
d.šlḥm.ššqy. | ilm sad.kbd.hmt.bʿl. | ḥkpt.il.kl h.tšmʿ. | mṯt.dnty.tʿdb.imr. | b pḫd.l npš.kṯr.w ḫss. | l brlt.hyn.d ḥrš. | 17[2AQHT].5.22
il. | mt.rpi.aphn.ǵzr.mt. | hrnmy.gm.l aṯt h.k yṣḥ. | šmʿ.mṯt.dnty.ʿd[b]. | imr.b pḫd.l npš.kṯr. | w ḫss.l brlt.hyn d. | ḥrš 17[2AQHT].5.16
.ḫt.šʿtqt. | dm.lan.w ypqd. | krt.ṯʿ.yšu.g h. | w yṣḥ.šmʿ.l mṯt. | ḥry.ṭbḫ.imr. | w ilḥm.mgṯ.w iṯrm. | tšmʿ.mṯt.ḥry. | tṭbḫ.i 16.6[127].16
ṣḥ.šmʿ.l mṯt. | ḥry.ṭbḫ.imr. | w ilḥm.mgṯ.w iṯrm. | tšmʿ.mṯt.ḥry. | tṭbḫ.imr.w lḥm. | mgṯ.w yṯrm.hn.ym. | w ṯn.yṯb.krt 16.6[127].19
--]r[.---]š[.--]qm. | id.u [---]t. | lḥn š[-]ʿ[--.]aḥd[.-]. | tšmʿ.mṯt.[ḥ]ry. | tṭbḫ.šmn.[m]ri h. | t[p]tḥ.rḥbt.yn. | ʿl h.ṯr h.tšʿrb. | 15[128].4.14
p[----]. | gm.l[aṯt h k.yṣḥ]. | šm[ʿ.l mṯt.ḥry]. | ṭbḫ.š[mn].mri k. | ptḥ.[rḥ]bt.yn. | ṣḥ.šbʿm.ṯr y. | ṯm 15[128].4.3
w lḥm mr.tqdm. | yd.b ṣʿ.tšlḥ. | ḥrb.b bšr.tštn. | [w t]ʿn.mṯt.ḥry. | [l lḥ]m.l šty.ṣḥt km. | [--.dbḥ.l]krt.bʿl km. 15[128].4.26
.---]. | [tqdm.]yd.b ṣʿ.t[šl]ḥ. | [ḥrb.b]bš[r].tštn. | [w tʿn].mṯt.ḥry. | [l lḥ]m.l šty.ṣḥt k[m]. | [---.]brk.t[---]. | [ʿl.]krt.tbkn. 15[128].5.9
----]. | šmʿ.l [-]mt[.-]m.l[-]ṯnm. | ʿdm.[lḥ]m.tšty. | w tʿn.mṯt ḥry. | l l[ḥ]m.l š[ty].ṣḥt km. | db[ḥ.l krt.a]dn km. | ʿl.krt.t 15[128].6.3
m. | mrkbt.b trbṣ. | bn.amt.p d.[i]n. | b bt y.ttn.tn. | l y.mṯt.ḥry. | nʿmt.šbḥ.bkr k. | d k nʿm.ʿnt. | nʿm h.km.tsm. | ʿṯtrt. 14[KRT].6.289
swm.mrkbt. | b trbṣt.bn.amt. | p d.in.b bt y.ttn. | tn.l y.mṯt.ḥry. | nʿmt.špḥ.bkr k. | d k.nʿm.ʿnt.nʿm h. | km.tsm.ʿṯtrt.t 14[KRT].3.143
---]. | [---.b]n.qdš.k[--.---]. | [---.]ʿsb.[-]ḫ[-.---]. | [---.]b[-.]mṯt k.[---]. | [---.]k.w tmt[.---]. | [---.]k.w ṯt[--.---]. | [---.]k.w ṯ[- 2125.5

n

n

t]. | tḥm k.il.ḥkm.ḥkm k. | ‘m.‘lm.ḥyt.ḥẓt.tḥm k. | mlk n.aliyn.b‘l.ṯpṭ n. | in.d ‘ln h.klny y.qš h. | nbln.klny y.nbl.ks 3['NT.VI].5.40
ym. | tḥm k.il.ḥkm.ḥkmt. | ‘m ‘lm.ḥyt.ḥẓt. | tḥm k.mlk n.aliy[n.]b‘l. | ṯpṭ n.w in.d ‘ln h. | klny n.q[š] h.n[bln]. | klny n 4[51].4.43
.‘bd k. | [---.a]dt y.mrḥqm. | [---].adt y.yšlm. | [---.]mlk n.amṣ. | [.---].nn. | [---.]qrt.dt. | [---.--]s‘.hn.mlk. | [---.l]qḥ.hn.l. 1012.5
š bš[-.]t[-].ǵlm.l šdt[.-.]ymm. | [---.]b ym.ym.y[--].yš[ ]n.ap k.‘ṯtr.dm[.---.] | [---.]ḥrḥrtm.w[--.]n[--.]iš[--.]h[---.]išt. | 2.3[129].12
-.-]kn. | [---.]hr n.km.šḥr. | [---.y]lt n.km.qdm. | [-.k]bd n.il.ab n. | kbd k iš.tikln. | ṯd n.km.mrm.tqrṣn. | il.yẓḥq.bm. | l 12[75].1.9
m.ḥkm k. | ‘m.‘lm.ḥyt.ḥẓt.tḥm k. | mlk n.aliyn.b‘l.ṯpṭ n. | in.d ‘ln h.klny y.qš h. | nbln.klny y.nbl.ks h. | any.l yṣḥ.ṯr. 3['NT.VI].5.40
m. | bn.ḫrn k. | mǵy. | hbṭ.hw. | ḫrd.w.šl hw. | qr[-]. | akl n.b.grnt. | l.b‘r. | ap.krmm. | ḫlq. | qrt n.ḫlq. | w.d‘.d‘. 2114.8
.špš.‘lm.l.‘ṯtrt. | l.‘nt.l.kl.il.alṯ[y]. | nmry.mlk.‘lm. | mlk n.b‘l y.ḥw[t.--]. | yšhr k.w.‘m.ṣ[--]. | ‘š[--.---]d.lik[t.---]. | w [--- 2008.1.10
.ṣba.rbt. | špš.w tgh.nyr. | rbt.w rgm.l aḫt k. | ṯtmnt.krt n.dbḥ. | dbḥ.mlk.‘šr. | ‘šrt.qḥ.tp k.b yd. | [-]r[-]k.bm.ymn. | tl 16.1[125].39
t.npš kn.u b qṯt. | tqṯṯn.ušn y[p kn.l dbḥm.]w l ṯ‘ dbḥ n. | ndbḥ.hw.ṯ‘ n[ṯ‘y.hw.nkt.nk]t.ytši.l ab bn il. | ytši.l d[r.bn 32[2].1.32
t.npš km.u b qṯt.tqṯṯ. | ušn yp km.l d[b]ḥm.w l.ṯ‘.dbḥ n.ndbḥ.hw.ṯ‘ | nṯ‘y. | hw.nkt.nkt.y[t]ši.l ab.bn.il.ytši.l dr. | bn 32[2].1.24
b qṣrt.npš km.u b qṯt]. | [tqṯṯ.u ṯḫṯu.l dbḥm.w l.ṯ‘.dbḥ n.ndb]ḥ. | [hw.ṯ‘.nṯ‘y.hw.nkt.nkt.]yt[ši.l ab.bn.il]. | [ytši.l dr. 32[2].1.9
q]ṣrt.npš[kn.u b qṯt]. | tqṯṯn u ṯḫṯin.l bḥm.w l ṯ‘.d[bḥ n.ndbḥ]. | hw.ṯ‘.nṯ‘y.hw.nkt.n[k]t.ytši[.l ab.bn.il]. | ytši.l dr.b 32[2].1.15
.ḥkmt. | ‘m ‘lm.ḥyt.ḥẓt. | tḥm k.mlk n.aliy[n.]b‘l. | ṯpṭ n.w in.d ‘ln h. | klny n.q[š] h.n[bln]. | klny n[.n]bl.ks h. | [an] 4[51].4.44
t.š.--]. | [---.--]t.r[šp.šrp.w šl] | [mm.---].dq[t.ilh.gdlt]. | n.w šnm.dqt[.---]. | [i]lh[m.gd]lt.i[l.dqt.ṯkm] | n.w šnm.dqt[.- APP.II[173].34
r. | b šm.tg‘r m.‘ṯtrt.bṯ l aliyn.[b‘l.] | bṯ.l rkb.‘rpt.k šby n.zb[l.ym.k] | šby n.ṯpṭ.nhr.w yṣa b[.--]. | ybṯ.nn.aliyn.b‘l.w 2.4[68].29
.šl hw. | qr[-]. | akl n.b.grnt. | l.b‘r. | ap.krmm. | ḫlq. | qrt n.ḫlq. | w.d‘.d‘. 2114.12
akl.yt[ṯb.--]pt. | ib.‘ltn.a[--.--]y. | w.spr.in[.-.]‘d m. | spr n.ṯhr[.--]. | aṯr.iṯ.bqṯ. | w.štn.l y. 2060.33
.y‘l. | [---].bm.nšq.aṯt h. | [---.]b ḥbq h.ḥmḥmt. | [---.--] n.ylt.ḥmḥmt. | [---.mt.r]pi.w ykn.bn h. | [b bt.šrš.]b qrb.hkl h 17[2AQHT].1.42
[---.]hr n.km.šḥr. | [---.y]lt n.km.qdm. | [-.k]bd n.il.ab n. | kbd k iš.tikln. | ṯd n.km.mrm.tqrṣn. | il.yẓḥq.bm. | lb.w yg 12[75].1.9
-.y]lt n.km.qdm. | [-.k]bd n.il.ab n. | kbd k iš.tikln. | ṯd n.km.mrm.tqrṣn. | il.yẓḥq.bm. | lb.w ygmḏ.bm kbd. | ẓi.at.l tl 12[75].1.11
ln. | [---.]nb hm. | [---.-]kn. | [---.]hr n.km.šḥr. | [---.y]lt n.km.qdm. | [-.k]bd n.il.ab n. | kbd k iš.tikln. | ṯd n.km.mrm.t 12[75].1.8
]. | [---.]d arṣ. | [---.]ln. | [---.]nb hm. | [---.-]kn. | [---.]hr n.km.šḥr. | [---.y]lt n.km.qdm. | [-.k]bd n.il.ab n. | kbd k iš.tik 12[75].1.7
. | b n‘m.b gb‘.tliyt. | hlm.‘nt.tph.ilm.b h.p‘nm. | ṭṭṭ.b‘d n.ksl.ṯṯbr. | ‘ln.pn h.td‘.tǵṣ.pnt. | ksl h.anš.dt.ẓr h.tšu. | g h.w 3['NT].3.30
l il[š]. | ilš.ngr bt b‘l. | w aṯt k.ngrt.il[ht]. | ‘l.l ṯkm.bnw n. | l nḫnpt.mšpy. | ṯlṯ.kmm.ṯrr y. | [---.]l ǵr.gm.ṣḥ. | [---.]r[-]m 16[126].4.14
.ar. | ahbt.ṭly.bt.rb.dd.arṣy. | bt.y‘bdr.km ǵlmm. | w ‘rb n.l p‘n.‘nt.hbr. | w ql.tšṯḥwy.kbd hyt. | w rgm.l btlt.‘nt. | ṯny.l 3['NT].3.6
t.ǵllm[.---]. | aḫḏ.aklm.k [---]. | npl.b mšmš[.---]. | anp n m yḫr[r.---]. | bmt n m.yšḫn.[---]. | qrn h.km.ǵb[-.---]. | hw 12[75].2.38
lm.k [---]. | npl.b mšmš[.---]. | anp n m yḫr[r.---]. | bmt n m.yšḫn.[---]. | qrn h.km.ǵb[-.---]. | hw km.ḥrr[.---]. | šnmtm 12[75].2.39
m[ǵ]. | mlak k.‘m dt[n]. | lqḥ.mṯpṭ. | w y‘ny.nn. | dtn.bt n.mḫ[-]. | l dg.w [-]kl. | w aṯr.hn.mr[-]. UG5.6.14
hn d.w.rgm.ank[.--]. | mlkt.ybqš.anyt.w.at[--]. | w mkr n.mlk[.---]. 2008.2.14
[n.]b‘l. | ṯpṭ n.w in.d ‘ln h. | klny n.q[š] h.n[bln]. | klny n[.n]bl.ks h. | [an]y.l yṣḥ.ṯr il.ab h. | [i]l.mlk.d yknn h.yṣḥ. | a 4[51].4.46
n.š‘rt. | l.kṯrmlk.ḫpn. | l.‘bdil[m].ḫpn. | tmrtn.š‘rt. | lmd.n.rn. | [---].ḫpn. | dqn.š‘rt. | [lm]d.yrṯ. | [-.]ynḥm.ḫpn. | ṯṯ.lmd. 1117.12
ḥẓt. | tḥm k.mlk n.aliy[n.]b‘l. | ṯpṭ n.w in.d ‘ln h. | klny n.q[š] h.n[bln]. | klny n[.n]bl.ks h. | [an]y.l yṣḥ.ṯr il.ab h. | [i]l. 4[51].4.45
.bt. | [m]lk.itdb.d šb‘. | [a]ḫm.l h.ṯmnt.bn um. | krt.ḥtk n.rš. | krt.grdš.mknt. | aṯt.ṣdq h.l ypq. | mtrḫt.yšr h. | aṯt.trḫ. 14[KRT].1.10
-.]mdbm.l ḥrn.ḥr[n.---]. | [---.--]m.ql.hm[.---]. | [---].aṯt n.r[---]. | [---.]ḥr[-.--]. | [---.]plnt.[---]. | [---.]‘mt.l ql.rpi[.---]. | [- 1001.1.29
qlt[.l um] y. | yšlm.il[m]. | tǵ[r] k.tš[lm] k. | [h]l ny.‘m n[.š]lm. | w.ṯm [ny.‘m.mlkt.u]m y. | mnm[.šlm]. | w.rgm[.ṯṯb.l 1013.8
lk.ugrt. | rgm. | yšlm.l k.[il]m. | tǵr k.tšlm k. | hn ny.‘m n.š[l]m. | ṯm ny.‘[m.]bn y. | mnm.[šl]m[.r]gm[.ṯṯb]. | ky.lik.bn 2061.6
.mlk.ṣr.aḫ k. | y[š]lm.l k.ilm. | tǵr k.tšlm k. | hn ny.‘m n. | šlm.ṯm ny. | ‘m k.mnm[.š]lm. | rgm.ṯṯ[b]. | any kn.dt. | likt. 2059.6
km.aḫm.qym.il. | b lsmt.ṯm.yṯbš.šm.il.mt m. | y‘bš.brk n.šm.il.ǵzrm. | ṯm.ṯmq.rpu.b‘l.mhr b‘l. | w mhr.‘nt.ṯm.yḥpn. 22.2[124].7
dš.‘l. | ab h.y‘rb.ybky. | w yšnn.ytn.g h. | bky.b ḥy k.ab n.ašmḫ. | b l.mt k.ngln.k klb. | b bt k.n‘tq.k inr. | ap.ḫšt k.ap. 16.1[125].14
.ṭṣr.trm[.‘]tqt. | tbky.w tšnn.[tt]n. | g h.bky.b ḥ[y k.a]b n. | nšmḫ.b l.mt k.ngln. | k klb.[b]bt k.n‘tq. | k inr[.ap.]ḫšt k. 16.2[125].98
t.bṯ l aliyn.[b‘l.] | bṯ.l rkb.‘rpt.k šby n.zb[l.ym.k] | šby n.ṯpṭ.nhr.w yṣa b[.--]. | ybṯ.nn.aliyn.b‘l.w [---]. | ym.l mt.b‘l 2.4[68].30
.---]. | l rḥqm.l p[-.---]. | ṣḥ.il.ytb.b[mrzḥ.---]. | bṯt.‘llm n.[---]. | ilm.bt.b‘l k.[---]. | dl.ylkn.ḥš.b a[rṣ.---]. | b ‘pr.ḫbl ṭtm 1['NT.X].4.5
-]n.d[--.]bnš[.---]. | [---.]idmt.n[--.]t[--]. | [---.--]r.dlt.tḥt n. | [---.]dlt. | [---.b]nš. | [---.]yp‘. | [---.]b[--]. 2158B.3
ḥt.akl.ky. | likt.‘m.špš. | b‘l k.ky.akl. | b.ḥwt k.inn. | špš n.[---]. | hm.al[k.--]. | ytnt[.---]. | ṯn[.---]. | w[.-----]. | l[.-----]. | h[2060.21
yrmy[.q]rn h. | [---.-]ny h pdr.ttǵr. | [---.n]šr k.al ttn.l n. | [---.]tn l rbd. | [---.]b‘lt h w yn. | [---.rk]b ‘rpt. | [---.--]n.w 2001.2.12
n. | [---.]bšr y. | [---.--]b. | [---.--]a h. | [---.--]d. | [---].umt n. | [---.--]yh.wn l. | [---].bt b‘l. | [---.--]y. | [---.--]nt. 28[-].10
ndr. | iṯt.‘mn.mlkt. | w.rgm y.l[--]. | lqt.w.pn. | mlk.nr b n. 50[117].18

naṣ

š. | ẓtr.‘m h.l arṣ.mšṣu.qṭr h. | l ‘pr.ḏmr.aṯr h.ṭbq.lḥt. | niṣ h.grš d.‘šy.ln h. | aḫḏ.yd h.b škrn.m‘ms h. | [k]šb‘ yn.spu 17[2AQHT].1.30
tr.‘m h.l a]rṣ.mšṣu. | [qṭr h.l ‘pr.ḏ]mr.a[ṯ]r h. | [ṭbq.lḥt.niṣ h.gr]š.d ‘šy. | [ln h.---]. | z[tr.‘m k.l arṣ.mšṣu.qṭr k]. | l ‘pr. 17[2AQHT].1.48
ṣb.skn.ilib y.b qdš. | ẓtr.‘m y.l ‘pr.ḏmr.aṯr[y]. | ṭbq lḥt.niṣ y.grš. | d ‘šy.ln.aḫḏ.yd y.b š | krn m‘ms y k šb‘t yn. | spu.k 17[2AQHT].2.18
z[tr.‘m k.l arṣ.mšṣu.qṭr k]. | l ‘pr.ḏm[r.aṯr k.ṭbq]. | lḥt.niṣ k.gr[š.d ‘šy.ln k]. | spu.ksm k.bt.[b‘l.w mnt k]. | bt il.aḫḏ. 17[2AQHT].2.3
-]. | ‘l.ḥbš.[---]. | mn.lik.[---]. | lik.tl[ak.---]. | t‘ddn[.---]. | niṣ.p[---.---]. 5[67].4.26

nat

dbḥ klyrḫ. | ndr. | dbḥ. | dt nat. | w ytnt. | ṯrmn w. | dbḥ kl. | kl ykly. | dbḥ k.sprt. | dt nat. | RS61[24.277.4]
at. | w ytnt. | ṯrmn w. | dbḥ kl. | kl ykly. | dbḥ k.sprt. | dt nat. | w qrwn. | l k dbḥ. | [--]r bt [--]. | [--]bnš [--]. | š š[--]. | w [- RS61[24.277.10]

niršn

bnšm.dt.iṯ.alpm.l hm. | bn.niršn. | bn.adty. | bn.alz. | bn.birtn. | bn.mlṣ. | bn.q[--]. | bn.[---]. 2023.1.2

nit

il. | šlm il. | il ḥš il add. | bʻl ṣpn bʻl. | ugrt. | b mrḥ il. | b nit il. | b ṣmd il. | b dṯn il. | b šrp il. | b knt il. | b ǵdyn il. | [b]n [30[107].13
d[ṯb]. | w nit w mʻṣd. | w ẖrmṯt. | ʻšrt.ksp. | ʻl.ẖ[z]rn. | w.nit.w[.mʻṣd]. | w.ẖ[rmṯt]. | ʻš[r.---]. | ʻl[.---]. | w.ni[t.---]. | w[.mʻ 2053.7
ẖmšt.ʻš[rt]. | ksp.ʻl.agd[ṯb]. | w nit w mʻṣd. | w ẖrmṯt. | ʻšrt.ksp. | ʻl.ẖ[z]rn. | w.nit.w[.mʻṣd]. | w 2053.3
--]. | w[.mʻṣd]. | w ẖr[mṯt]. | [ʻ]šr[.---]. | [ʻ]l [-]g[-.---]. | w ni[t.w.mʻṣd]. | w ẖrmṯt. | ṯlṯm.ar[bʻ]. | kbd.ksp. | ʻl.tgyn. | w ʻl.a 2053.16
.ẖmš.ẖrmṯt.nit. | krk.mʻṣd.mqb. | b.gt.ʻmq.ẖmš.ẖrmṯt.n[it]. | krk.mʻṣd.mqb. | b.gwl.ṯmn.ẖrmṯt.[nit]. | krk.mʻṣd.mqb 2048.9
q.ẖmš.ẖrmṯt.n[it]. | krk.mʻṣd.mqb. | b.gwl.ṯmn.ẖrmṯt.[nit]. | krk.mʻṣd.mqb. | [b] gt.ipṯl.ṯṯ.ẖrmṯ[t.nit]. | [k]rk.mʻṣd.m 2048.11
.ṯmn.ẖrmṯt.[nit]. | krk.mʻṣd.mqb. | [b] gt.ipṯl.ṯṯ.ẖrmṯ[t.nit]. | [k]rk.mʻṣd.mqb. | [b.g]t.bir.ʻš[r.---]. | [---].krk.mʻ[ṣd.---]. 2048.13
.nitm.ṯn.mʻṣdm.ṯn.mqbm. | krk.aḥt. | b.sǵy.ẖmš.ẖrmṯt.nit. | krk.mʻṣd.mqb. | b.gt.ʻmq.ẖmš.ẖrmṯt.n[it]. | krk.mʻṣd.mq 2048.7
r.ʻš[r.---]. | [---].krk.mʻ[ṣd.---]. | [b.]gt.ẖrṯm.ẖm[š.---]. | [n]it.krk.mʻṣ[d.---]. | b.ẖrbǵlm.ǵlm[n]. | w.trhy.aṯt h. | w.mlky. 2048.18
b.atlg.ṯlṯ.ẖrmṯt.ṯṯm. | mẖrhn.nit.mit.krk.mit. | mʻṣd.ẖmšm.mqb.[ʻ]šrm. | b.ulm.ṯṯ.ʻšr h.ẖr 2048.2
it. | mʻṣd.ẖmšm.mqb.[ʻ]šrm. | b.ulm.ṯṯ.ʻšr h.ẖrmṯt. | ṯt.nitm.ṯn.mʻṣdm.ṯn.mqbm. | krk.aḥt. | b.sǵy.ẖmš.ẖrmṯt.nit. | kr 2048.5
[z]rn. | w.nit.w[.mʻṣd]. | w.ẖ[rmṯt]. | ʻš[r.---]. | ʻl[.---]. | w.ni[t.---]. | w[.mʻṣd]. | w ẖr[mṯt]. | [ʻ]šr[.---]. | [ʻ]l [-]g[-.---]. | w n 2053.11

nb

[---.--]m. | [-----]. | [---.]d arṣ. | [---.]ln. | [---.]nb hm. | [---.-]kn. | [---.]hr n.km.šḥr. | [---.y]lt n.km.qdm. | [-.k 12[75].1.5

nbd

kḥ.w yiẖd.b qrb[.-]. | [--.t]tkḥ.w tiẖd.b uš[k.--]. | [-.b]ʻl.yabd.l alp. | [---.bt]lt.ʻnt. | [---]q.hry.w yld. | [---]m.ḥbl.kṯ[r]t. | 11[132].1.3

nbdg

bn.n[---]. | bn.b[---]. | bn.iš[--]. | bn.ab[--]. | bn.al[--]. | bn.nb[dg]. | bn.ild[-]. | [-----]. | [bn.]nnr. | [bn.]aglby. | [bn.]bʻly. | [113[416].4
n. | bn.šbl. | bn.ẖnzr. | bn.arwṯ. | bn.ṯbtnq. | bn.pṯdn. | bn.nbdg. | bn.ḥgbn. | bn.tmr. | bn.prsn. | bn.ršpy. | [ʻ]bdḥgb. | [k]lb 113[400].1.18
gn.ḥṭbm. | tdǵlm.iln.bʻ[l]n.alḏy. | tdn.ṣr[--.--]t.ʻzn.mtn.n[bd]g. | ḥrš qṭn[.---.]dqn.bʻln. | ǵltn.ʻbd.[---]. | nsk.ḥḏm.klyn[2011.22

nbzn

ḏr.b d.bdn.nḥ[l h]. | [šd.]agyn.b d.kmrn.n[ḥl] h. | [š]d.nbzn.[-]l.qrt. | [š]d.agpṯr.b d.sḫrn.nḥl h. | šd.annmn.b d.tyn. 2029.9

nbk

md h. | ʻbdrpu. | w.lmd h. | ʻdršp. | w.lmd h. | krwn b.gt.nbk. | ddm.kšmm.l.ḥtn. | ddm.l.trbnn. | ddm.šʻrm.l.trbnn. | dd 1099.19
šm. | ʻlm.l ršp.mlk. | alp w.š.l bʻlt. | bwrm š.iṯtqb. | w š.nbk m w.š. | gt mlk š.ʻlm. | l kṯr.ṯn.ʻlm. | tzǵ[.---.]nšm.pr. UG5.12.B.10
| [i]lh[m.gd]lt.i[l.dqt.ṯkm] | n.w šnm.dqt[.---]. | bqtm.b nbk.[---]. | kmm.gdlt.l b[ʻl.--.dqt]. | l ṣpn.gdlt.[l.---]. | ugrt.š l i APP.II[173].35
hm.gdlt.il]. | [d]qt.ṯkmn.w [šnm.dqt.--]. | [--]t.dqtm.[b nbk.---]. | [--.k]mm.gdlt.l.b[ʻl.---]. | [dq]t.l.ṣpn.gdlt.l[.---]. | u[g 35[3].32

nbl

.ṯḥm k. | mlk n.aliyn.bʻl.ṯpṭ n. | in.d ʻln h.klny y.qš h. | nbln.klny y.nbl.ks h. | any.l yṣḥ.ṯr.il.ab h.il. | mlk.d yknn h.y 3[ʻNT.VI].5.42
k.mlk n.aliy[n.]bʻl. | ṯpṭ n.w in.d ʻln h. | klny n.q[š] h.n[bln]. | klny n[.n]bl.ks h. | [an]y.l yṣḥ.ṯr il.ab h. | [i]l.mlk.d y 4[51].4.45
n.aliyn.bʻl.ṯpṭ n. | in.d ʻln h.klny y.qš h. | nbln.klny y.nbl.ks h. | any.l yṣḥ.ṯr.il.ab h.il. | mlk.d yknn h.yṣḥ.aṯrt. | w b 3[ʻNT.VI].5.42
.]bʻl. | ṯpṭ n.w in.d ʻln h. | klny n.q[š] h.n[bln]. | klny n[.n]bl.ks h. | [an]y.l yṣḥ.ṯr il.ab h. | [i]l.mlk.d yknn h.yṣḥ. | aṯrt. 4[51].4.46
.---]. | [---.]hl[-.---]. | [---.-]yṯr.ur[--.---]. | [---.n]skt.nʻmn.nbl[.---]. | [--.]yṣq šmn.šlm.b ṣ[ʻ.trḥṣ]. | yd h.btlt.ʻnt.uṣbʻt[h.y UG5.3.2.3

nbla

yn.iš[ryt.-]lnr. | spr.[--]ḥ[-] k.šbʻt. | ghl.ph.ṯmnt. | nblu h.špš.ymp. | hlkt.tdr[--]. | špš.bʻd h.t[--]. | aṯr.aṯrm[.---]. | 27[8].4

nblat

[n.l]bnn.w ʻṣ h. | š[r]yn.mḥmd.arz h. | tšt.išt.b bht m. | nb[l]at.b hkl m. | hn.ym.w ṯn.tikl. | išt.b bht m.nblat. | b hk[l] 4[51].6.23
bht m.nblat. | b hk[l] m.ṯlṯ.kbʻ ym. | tikl[.i]št.b bht m. | nbla[t.]b hkl m. | ẖmš.ṯ[d]ṯ.ym.tikl. | išt.[b]bht m.nblat. | b[q 4[51].6.28
lat. | b[qrb.hk]l m.mk. | b šb[ʻ.]y[mm].td.išt. | b bht m.n[bl]at.b hkl m. | sb.ksp.l rqm.ẖrṣ. | nṣb.l lbnt.šmẖ. | aliyn.bʻl. 4[51].6.33
bht m. | nb[l]at.b hkl m. | hn.ym.w ṯn.tikl. | išt.b bht m.nblat. | b hk[l] m.ṯlṯ.kbʻ ym. | tikl[.i]št.b bht m. | nbla[t.]b hkl 4[51].6.25
m. | nbla[t.]b hkl m. | ẖmš.ṯ[d]ṯ.ym.tikl. | išt.[b]bht m.nblat. | b[qrb.hk]l m.mk. | b šb[ʻ.]y[mm].td.išt. | b bht m.n[bl 4[51].6.30

nbʻm

[-----]. | šd.prsn.l.[---]. | šd.bddn.l.iytlm. | šd.bn.nbʻm.l.ṯpṯbʻl. | šd.bn mšrn.l.ilšpš. | [šd.bn].kbr.l.snrn. | [---.--] 2030.1.4

nbq

n.ršpy. | [---.]mn. | [--.-]sn. | [bn.-]ny. | [b]n.ẖnyn. | [bn].nbq. | [bn.]snrn. | [bn.-]lṣ. | bn.[---]ym. 115[301].3.3

nbt

rṣ.yṣq | m.l rbbt. | yṣq-ẖym.w tbṯẖ. | kt.il.dt.rbtm. | kt.il.nbt.b ksp. | šmrgt.b dm.ẖrṣ. | kḥṯ.il.nḥt. | b ẓr.hdm.id. | d prša 4[51].1.32
at.[---]. | lg.šmn.rqḥ.šrʻm.ušpǵtm.p[--.---]. | kṯ.ẓrw.kṯ.nbt.ḏnt.w [-]n[-.---]. | il.ẖyr.ilib.š. | arṣ w šmm.š. | il.š.kṯrt.š. | UG5.9.1.22
il.d pid. | b ḏrt.bny.bnwt. | šmm.šmn.tmṭrn. | nḥlm.tlk.nbtm. | w idʻ.k ḥy.aliyn.bʻl. | k iṯ.zbl.bʻl.arṣ. | b hlm.ltpn.il d p 6[49].3.7
h.d nzl. | lqḥ.msrr.ʻṣr.db[ḥ]. | yṣq.b gl.ḥtt.yn. | b gl.ẖrṣ.nbt.w ʻly. | l ẓr.mgdl.rkb. | ṯkmm.ḥmt.nša. | [y]d h.šmmh.dbḥ 14[KRT].4.165
m]r.škm. | [---.ṯṯ.dd.]gdl.ṯṯ.dd.šʻrm. | [---.hn.w.al]p.kd.nbt.kd.šmn.mr. | [---].kmn.lṯḥ.sbbyn. | [---.-]ʻt.lṯḥ.ššmn. | [---]. 142[12].8
--.ṯṯ.dd.]gdl.ṯṯ.dd.šʻrm. | [---.a]lp.arbʻ.mat.tyt. | [---.kd.]nbt.k[d.]šmn.mr. | [---.l]ṯḥ.sb[by]n.lṯḥ.šḥ[lt]. | [---.l]ṯḥ.dblt.lt 142[12].15

[---.]ṯṯ.dd.gdl.ṯṯ.dd.š‘rm.|[---.-]hn.w.alp.kd.nbt.kd.šmn.mr.|[---.]arb‘.mat.ḫswn.lṯḥ.aqhr.|[---.lṯḥ.]sbby 142[12].2
.d]nzl.|qḥ.ms[rr.]‘ṣr.|dbḥ.ṣ[q.b g]l.ḥṯṯ.|yn.b gl[.ḫ]rṣ.nbt.|‘l.l ẓr.[mg]dl.|w ‘l.l ẓr.[mg]dl.rkb.|ṯkmm.ḥm[t].ša.yd 14[KRT].2.72
il d pid.|b ḏrt.bny.bnwt.|šmm.šmn.tmṭrn.|nḫlm.tlk.nbtm.|šmḫ.lṭpn.il.d pid.|p‘n h.l hdm.yṯpd.|w yprq.lṣb w y 6[49].3.13

ngb

.d ḫmš.|[mġ]d.ṯdṯ.yr[ḫm].|‘dn.ngb.w [yṣi.ṣbu].|ṣbi.ng[b.w yṣi.‘dn].|m‘[.ṣ]bu h.u[l.mad].|ṯlṯ.mat.rbt.|hlk.l alp 14[KRT].4.177
p.lḥm.d ḫmš.|mġd.ṯdṯ.yrḫm.|‘dn.ngb.w yṣi.|ṣbu.ṣbi.ngb.|w yṣi.‘dn.m‘.|ṣbu k.ul.mad.|ṯlṯ.mat.rbt.|ḫpṯ.d bl.spr. 14[KRT].2.86
yt.|ḥṯt.l bt.ḫbr.|yip.lḥm.d ḫmš.|mġd.ṯdṯ.yrḫm.|‘dn.ngb.w yṣi.|ṣbu.ṣbi.ngb.|w yṣi.‘dn.m‘.|ṣbu k.ul.mad.|ṯlṯ.ma 14[KRT].2.85
|ḥṯt.l bt.ḫbr.|yip.lḥm.d ḫmš.|[mġ]d.ṯdṯ.yr[ḫm].|‘dn.ngb.w [yṣi.ṣbu].|ṣbi.ng[b.w yṣi.‘dn].|m‘[.ṣ]bu h.u[l.mad].|ṯl 14[KRT].4.176

ngh

kṯy.|ṯkmn w šnm.|kṯr w ḫss.|‘ṯtr ‘ṯtpr.|šḫr w šlm.|ngh w srr.|‘dw šr.|ṣdqm šr.|ḥnbn il d[n].|[-]bd w [---].|[--] UG5.10.1.12
dm.mm h.|b smkt.ṣat.npš h.|[-]mt[-].ṣba.rbt.|špš.w tgh.nyr.|rbt.w rgm.l aḫt k.|ṯtmnt.krt n.dbḥ.|dbḥ.mlk.‘šr.|‘ 16.1[125].37

ngzḥn

.b]n.ṯpdn.b d.bn.g‘r.|[šd.b]n.ṯqrn.b d.ḫby.|[ṯn.š]d.bn.ngzḥn.b d.gmrd.|[šd.bn].pll.b d.gmrd.|[šd.bn.-]ll.b d.iwrḫṯ 82[300].1.23

ngḥ

‘l.|spu y.bn m.um y.kl|y y.yt‘n.k gmrm.|mt.‘z.b‘l.‘z.ynghn.|k rumm.mt.‘z.b‘l.|‘z.ynṯkn.k bṯnm.|mt.‘z.b‘l.‘z.ym 6[49].6.17

ngḥt

ḥ.|amri[l].b.šrš.|aġltn.b.midḫ.|[--]n.b.ayly.|[-]lyn.b.ngḥt.|[---.]b.nh[-]t.|[---.]almš.|[---.--]ty.|[---.-]i[-.--].|[-----]. 2118.15

ngy

[ṯ]rrt.udm.y[t]n[t].|il.ušn.ab[.ad]m.|rḥq.mlk.l bt y.|n[g.]krt.l ḥẓ[r y].|w y‘n[y.k]rt[.ṯ]‘.|lm.ank.ksp.|w yr[q.ḫrṣ] 14[KRT].6.280
ṯrrt.udm.ytnt].|[il.w ušn.ab.adm].|[rḥq.mlk.l bt y].|[ng.kr]t.l ḥ[ẓ]r y.|[-----].|[---.ttb‘].|[mlakm.l yṯb].|[idk.pnm 14[KRT].5.261
.sswm.mrkbt.|b trbṣ.bn.amt.|qḥ.krt.šlmm.|šlmm.w ng.mlk.|l bt y.rḥq.krt.|l ḥẓr y.al.tṣr.|udm.rbt.w udm ṯrrt.| 14[KRT].3.131

ngġln

[---].in ḥẓm.l hm.|[---.--]ḏn.|mrkbt.mtrt.|ngršp.|ngġln.|ilṯḥm.|b‘lṣdq. 1125.2.3

ngr

-].|[-----].|il.šm‘.amr k.ph[.-].|k il.ḥkmt.k ṯr.lṭpn.|ṣḥ.ngr.il.ilš.il[š].|w aṯt h.ngrt[.i]lht.|kḥṣ.k m‘r[.---].|yṣḥ.ngr il 16[126].4.4
gr.il.ilš.il[š].|w aṯt h.ngrt[.i]lht.|kḥṣ.k m‘r[.---].|yṣḥ.ngr il.ilš.|ilš.ngr.bt.b‘l.|w aṯt h.ngrt.ilht.|w y‘n.lṭpn.il d pi[16[126].4.7
r.bt.b‘l.|w aṯt h.ngrt.ilht.|w y‘n.lṭpn.il d pi[d].|šm‘.l ngr.il il[š].|ilš.ngr bt b‘l.|w aṯt k.ngrt.il[ht].|‘l.l ṯkm.bnw n. 16[126].4.11
|w aṯt h.ngrt[.i]lht.|kḥṣ.k m‘r[.---].|yṣḥ.ngr il.ilš.|ilš.ngr.bt.b‘l.|w aṯt h.ngrt.ilht.|w y‘n.lṭpn.il d pi[d].|šm‘.l ngr. 16[126].4.8
h.ngrt.ilht.|w y‘n.lṭpn.il d pi[d].|šm‘.l ngr.il il[š].|ilš.ngr bt b‘l.|w aṯt k.ngrt.il[ht].|‘l.l ṯkm.bnw n.|l nḫnpt.mšpy 16[126].4.12
ḥrš.anyt.|bnš.gt.gl‘d.|bnš.gt.ngr.|r‘ym.|bn.ḫri[-].|bnš.gt.‘ṯtrt.|ad[-]l[-]m.|‘šr.ksdm.yd.l 1040.3

ngršp

[---].in ḥẓm.l hm.|[---.--]ḏn.|mrkbt.mtrt.|ngršp.|ngġln.|ilṯḥm.|b‘lṣdq. 1125.2.2

ngrt

.|kḥṣ.k m‘r[.---].|yṣḥ.ngr il.ilš.|ilš.ngr.bt.b‘l.|w aṯt h.ngrt.ilht.|w y‘n.lṭpn.il d pi[d].|šm‘.l ngr.il il[š].|ilš.ngr bt b 16[126].4.9
.ph[.-].|k il.ḥkmt.k ṯr.lṭpn.|ṣḥ.ngr.il.ilš.il[š].|w aṯt h.ngrt[.i]lht.|kḥṣ.k m‘r[.---].|yṣḥ.ngr il.ilš.|ilš.ngr.bt.b‘l.|w a 16[126].4.5
ṭpn.il d pi[d].|šm‘.l ngr.il il[š].|ilš.ngr bt b‘l.|w aṯt k.ngrt.il[ht].|‘l.l ṯkm.bnw n.|l nḫnpt.mšpy.|ṯlṯ.kmm.ṯrr y.|[- 16[126].4.13

ngš

npš.hmlt.|arṣ.mġt.l n‘m y.arṣ.|dbr.ysmt.šd.šḥlmmt.|ngš.ank.aliyn b‘l.|‘dbnn ank.imr.b p y.|k lli.b ṯbrn q y.ḫtu 6[49].2.21
mt.ṯmn.nqpt.‘d.ilm.n‘mm.ttlkn.|šd.tṣdn.pat.mdbr.w ngš.hm.nġr.|mdr‘.w ṣḥ hm.‘m.nġr.mdr‘ y.nġr.|nġr.ptḥ.w p 23[52].68
|il.hlk.l bt h.yštql.|l ḥṭr h.y‘msn.nn.ṯkmn.|w šnm.w ngšnn.ḥby.|b‘l.qrnm w ḏnb.ylšn.|b ḫri h.w ṯnt h.ql.il.[--].|i UG5.1.1.19

ngṯ

d.bn ilm.mt.|ym.ymm.y‘tqn.l ymm.|l yrḫm.rḥm.‘nt.tngṯ h.|k lb.arḫ.l ‘gl h.k lb.|ṯat.l imr h.km.lb.|‘nt.aṯr.b‘l.tiḫd 6[49].2.27
[---].|kd.[---].|kd.t[---.ym.ymm].|y‘tqn.w[rḥm.‘nt].|tngṯ h.k lb.a[rḫ].|l ‘gl h.k lb.ṯa[t].|l imr h.km.lb.‘n[t].|aṯr.b 6[49].2.6
.--]b.|[---.w ym.ym]m.|[y‘tqn.---.ymġy.]npš.|[---.h]d.tngṯn h.|[---].b ṣpn.|[---].nšb.b ‘n.|[---.]b km.y‘n.|[---.yd‘.l] 1['NT.X].5.4
[---.--]b.w ym ymm.|[y‘tqn.---].ymġy.npš.|[---.--]t.hd.tngṯm h.|[---.-]ḥm k b ṣpn.|[---.]išqb.aylt.|[---.--]m.b km.y‘ 1['NT.X].5.17
mẓa.‘qqm.|b‘l.ḥmd m.yḥmd m.|bn.dgn.yhrr m.|b‘l.ngṯ hm.b p‘n h.|w il hd.b ḫrẓ‘ h.|[-----].|[--]t.[---].|[---.]‘n[. 12[75].1.40

nd

lk h].|bn.dgn.l kḥ[ṯ.drkt h].|l alp.ql.ẓ[--.---].|l np ql.nd.[----].|tlk.w tr.b[ḫl].|b n‘mm.b ys[mm.---].|arḫ.arḫ.[---. 10[76].3.17

ndb

kmkty.|[---].b.kmkty.|[---].b.ndb.|[---].b.ndb.|[---].b.ndb.|[---].b.kmkty.|[---.]yrmly.qrtym.|[---].b.yrml.|[---.]b. 2119.15
y]rml.|[---.]kmkty.|[---].b.kmkty.|[---].b.ndb.|[---].b.ndb.|[---].b.ndb.|[---].b.kmkty.|[---.]yrmly.qrtym.|[---].b.y 2119.14
.yr]ml.|[---.y]rml.|[---.]kmkty.|[---].b.kmkty.|[---].b.ndb.|[---].b.ndb.|[---].b.ndb.|[---].b.kmkty.|[---.]yrmly.qrty 2119.13

ndbd

ly. | b'l.bt.'lr. | b'l.bt.ssl. | b'l.bt.ṯrn. | b'l.bt.ktmn. | b'l.bt.ndbd. | [--].ṣnr. | [b'l].bt.bsn. | [-----]. | b[--.---]. 31[14].9

ndbn

n. | abmn. | [--]dn. | [ṯ]b'm. | [--]mlk. | [--]ty. | mtnb'l. | bn.ndbn. | bn irgn. 1072.12

ndd

]. | aṣḥ.rpi[m.iqra.ilnym]. | b qrb.h[kl y.aṯr h.rpum.l] | tdd.aṯr[h.l tdd.ilnym]. | asr.mr[kbt.---]. | t'ln.l mr[kbt hm.tit 22.1[123].21
bt y]. | aṣḥ.km.[iqra km.ilnym.b] | hkl y.aṯr[h.rpum.l tdd]. | aṯr h.l t[dd.ilnym.ṯm]. | yḥpn.ḥy[ly.zbl.mlk.'llm y]. | š 22.1[123].10
b]t y.aṣḥ km.iqra. | [km.ilnym.b h]kl y.aṯr h.rpum. | [l tdd.aṯr h].l tdd.ilnym. | [---.m]rz'y.apnnk.yrp. | [---.]km.r'y.h 21[122].1.4
bt y.aṣ]ḥ km.iqra km. | [ilnym.b hkl]y.aṯr h.rpum. | [l tdd.aṯr]h.l tdd.i[lnym]. | [---.]r[--.---]. | [---.yṯ]b.l arṣ. 21[122].1.12
bt y.aṣḥ]. | km.iqr[a km.ilnym.b hkl y]. | aṯr h.r[pum.l tdd.aṯr h]. | l tdd.il[nym.---]. | mhr.b'l[.---.mhr]. | 'nt.lk b[t y.r 22.1[123].5
.'l.lty. | [---.]tdbḥ.amr. | ṯmn.b qrb.hkl y.[aṯr h.rpum]. | tdd.aṯr h.tdd.iln[ym.---]. | asr.sswm.ṯṣmd.dg[-.---]. | t'ln.l mr 20[121].2.2
.iqra.ilnym]. | b qrb.h[kl y.aṯr h.rpum.l] | tdd.aṯr[h.l tdd.ilnym]. | asr.mr[kbt.---]. | t'ln.l mr[kbt hm.tity.l] | 'r hm. 22.1[123].21
.[iqra km.ilnym.b] | hkl y.aṯr[h.rpum.l tdd]. | aṯr h.l t[dd.ilnym.ṯm]. | yḥpn.ḥy[ly.zbl.mlk.'llm y]. | šm'.atm[.---]. | 22.1[123].11
-.]tdbḥ.amr. | ṯmn.b qrb.hkl y.[aṯr h.rpum]. | tdd.aṯr h.tdd.iln[ym.---]. | asr.sswm.ṯṣmd.dg[-.---]. | t'ln.l mrkbt hm.ti[20[121].2.2
.iqr[a km.ilnym.b hkl y]. | aṯr h.r[pum.l tdd.aṯr h]. | l tdd.il[nym.---]. | mhr.b'l[.---.mhr]. | 'nt.lk b[t y.rpim.rpim.b 22.1[123].6
.iqra. | [km.ilnym.b h]kl y.aṯr h.rpum. | [l tdd.aṯr h].l tdd.ilnym. | [---.m]rz'y.apnnk.yrp. | [---.]km.r'y.ht.alk. | [---.]ṯ 21[122].1.4
.iqra km. | [ilnym.b hkl]y.aṯr h.rpum. | [l tdd.aṯr]h.l tdd.i[lnym]. | [---.]r[--.---]. | [---.yṯ]b.l arṣ. 21[122].1.12
išt.[b]bht m.nblat. | b[qrb.hk]l m.mk. | b šb['.]y[mm].td.išt. | b bht m.n[bl]at.b hkl m. | sb.ksp.l rqm.ḫrṣ. | nṣb.l lbnt 4[51].6.32
]lk. | k.t'rbn.ršp m.bt.mlk. | ḫlu.dg. | ḥdṯm. | dbḥ.b'l.k.tdd.b'lt.bhtm. | b.[-]ǵb.ršp.ṣbi. | [---.--]m. | [---.]piln. | [---].ṣmd 2004.14
| l arṣ.špt l šmm.w 'rb.b p hm.'ṣr.šmm. | w dg b ym.w ndd.gzr.l zr.y'db.u ymn. | u šmal.b p hm.w l.tšb'n y.aṯt.itrḫ. 23[52].63
hr b'l. | w mhr.'nt.ṯm.yḥpn.ḥyl | y.zbl.mlk.'llm y.km.tdd. | 'nt.ṣd.tštr.'pt.šmm. | ṭbḫ.alpm.ap ṣin.šql.ṯrm. | w mri il 22.2[124].10
r. | w yšlḥmn h. | ybrd.ṯd.l pnw h. | b ḥrb.mlḥt. | qṣ.mri.ndd. | y'šr.w yšqyn h. | ytn.ks.b d h. | krpn.b klat.yd h. | b krb 3['NT].1.8
dm.dt ymtm. | [--.--]r.l ẓpn. | [---.]pn.ym.y[--]. | [---].b'l.tdd. | [---.]hkl. | [---.]yd h. | [---.]tmt. 25[136].7

ndy

zr.ilm.ylḥm. | [uzr.yšqy.]bn.qdš.yd. | [ṣt h.y'l.]w yškb.yd. | [mizrt.]p ynl.hn.ym. | [w ṯn.uzr.]ilm.dnil. | [uzr.ilm.]ylḥ 17[2AQHT].1.5
[uzr.]yšqy.bn qdš.yd.ṣt h. | [dn]il.yd.ṣt h.y'l.w yškb. | [yd.]mizrt.p yln.mk.b šb'.ymm. | [w]yqrb.b'l.b ḥnt h.abynt. | 17[2AQHT].1.16
t.ǵ]zr.at.aḫ.w an.a[ḫt k]. | [---].šb'.ṯir k.[---]. | [---.]ab y.ndt.ank[.---]. | [---.--]l.mlk.tlk.b ṣd[.---]. | [---.]mt.išryt[.---]. | [18[3AQHT].1.26
i[--.---]. | d.[---]. | bnš[-] mdy[-]. | w.b.glb. | phnn.w. | mndym. | bdnh. | l[q]ḥt. | [--]km.'m.mlk. | [b]ǵl hm.w.iblbl h 2129.6
ṯ.ym.uzr. | [ilm].dnil.uzr.ilm.ylḥm. | [uzr.]yšqy.bn qdš.yd.ṣt h. | [dn]il.yd.ṣt h.y'l.w yškb. | [yd.]mizrt.p yln.mk.b šb' 17[2AQHT].1.14
.dnil.uzr.ilm.ylḥm. | [uzr.]yšqy.bn qdš.yd.ṣt h. | [dn]il.yd.ṣt h.y'l.w yškb. | [yd.]mizrt.p yln.mk.b šb'.ymm. | [w]yqr 17[2AQHT].1.15
.ǵz[r]. | [mt.hrnmy.]uzr.ilm.ylḥm. | [uzr.yšqy.]bn.qdš.yd. | [ṣt h.y'l.]w yškb.yd. | [mizrt.]p ynl.hn.ym. | [w ṯn.uzr.]il 17[2AQHT].1.4
arḫ.td.rgm.b ǵr. | b p y.t'lgt.b lšn[y]. | ǵr[.---]b.b pš y.t[--]. | hwt. 2124.1

ndr

h. | w tqrb.w ld.bnt.l h. | mk.b šb'.šnt. | bn.krt.km hm.tdr. | ap.bnt.ḥry. | km hm.w ṯḫss.aṯrt. | ndr h.w ilt.p[--]. | w tš 15[128].3.23
y. | mnm[.šlm]. | w.rgm[.ṯṯb.l] y. | hl ny.'mn. | mlk.b.ṯy ndr. | iṯt.w.ht. | [-]sny.uḏr h. | w.hm.ḫt. | 'l.w.likt. | 'm k.w.hm. 1013.13
m. | ṯm ny.'m.um y. | mnm.šlm. | w.rgm.ṯṯb.l y. | bm.ṯy.ndr. | iṯt.'mn.mlkt. | w.rgm y.l[--]. | lqt.w.pn. | mlk.nr b n. 50[117].14
r l ytn ḫs[n]. | 'bd ulm ṯn un ḫsn. | gdy lqḥ ṣtqn gt bn ndr. | um r[-] gtn ṯṯ ḫsn l ytn. | l rḥt lqḥ ṣtqn. | bt qbṣ urt ilšt 1154.4
dbḥ klyrḫ. | ndr. | dbḥ. | dt nat. | w ytnt. | ṯrmn w. | dbḥ kl. | kl ykly. | dbḥ k RS61[24.277.2]
| bn.krt.km hm.tdr. | ap.bnt.ḥry. | km hm.w ṯḫss.aṯrt. | ndr h.w ilt.p[--]. | w tšu.g h.w [tṣḥ]. | ph m'.ap.k[rt.--]. | u ṯn. 15[128].3.26
lm y]. | šm'.atm[.---]. | ym.lm.qd[.---]. | šmn.prst[.---]. | ydr.hm.ym[.---]. | 'l amr.yu[ḫd.ksa.mlk h]. | nḫt.kḥṯ.d[rkt h. 22.1[123].16
b [ṯ]lṯ. | ym[ǵy.]l qdš. | a[ṯrt.]ṣrm.w l ilt. | ṣd[yn]m.ṯm. | yd[r.k]rt.ṯ'. | i.iṯt.aṯrt.ṣrm. | w ilt.ṣdynm. | hm.ḥry.bt y. | iqḥ.a 14[KRT].4.200
.w ilt.p[--]. | w tšu.g h.w [tṣḥ]. | ph m'.ap.k[rt.--]. | u ṯn.ndr[.---]. | apr.[---]. | [-----]. 15[128].3.29

ndrgd

y. | [l.--]r[-.---]. | [l.--]ḫl. | [l.--.]mgmr. | [l.-.]qdšt. | l.'ṯtrt.ndrgd. | l.'ṯtrt.abḏr. | l.dml. | l.ilt[.-]pn. | l.uš[ḫr]y. | [---.-]mrn. | 1001.1.12

nḏbn

.šmn.'l.ilršp.bn[.---]. | kd.šmn.'l.yddn. | kd.'l.ššy. | kd.'l.nḏbn.bn.agmn. | [k]d.'l.brq. | [kd]m.['l].kṯr. | [kd]m[.---].ḫ[--]. 1082.1.8
ḫl h. | [---]n. | [--]ly. | [iw]ryn. | [--.w.n]ḫl h. | [-]ibln. | bn.nḏbn. | bn.'bl. | bn.tlšn. | bn.sln. | w nḫl h. 1063.11
rn. | šib.mqdšt.'b[dml]k.ṯṯpḥ.mrṯn. | ḫḏǵlm.i[---]n.pbn.nḏbn.sbd. | šrm.[---].ḫpn. | ḥrš[bhtm.--]n.'bdyrḫ.ḥḏṯn.y'r. | a 2011.16

nh

a[--.--]ḥ. | w yn.k mtrḫt[.---]h. | šm' ilht kṯr[t.--]mm. | nh l yd h tzdn[.---]n. | l ad[n h.---]. | dgn tt[--.---.-]l | '.l kṯrt hl 24[77].12

nhq

k.špšm.b šb'. | w l.yšn.pbl. | mlk.l [qr.]ṯiqt. | ibr h[.l]ql.nhqt. | ḥmr[h.l g't.]alp. | ḥrṯ[.l z]ǵt.klb. | [ṣ]pr[.apn]k. | [pb]l[. 14[KRT].5.224
hn.špšm. | b šb'.w l.yšn.pbl. | mlk.l qr.ṯigt.ibr h. | l ql.nhqt.ḥmr h. | l g't.alp.ḥrṯ.zǵt. | klb.ṣpr.w ylak. | mlakm.l k.'m 14[KRT].3.121

nhr

'm.b ym b'l ysy ym[.---]. | rmm.ḫnpm.mḫl[.---]. | mlk.nhr.ibr[.---]. | zbl b'l.ǵlm.[---]. | ṣǵr hd w r[---.---]. | w l nhr nd 9[33].2.9
ṯ[ṣḥ.šm]'.m'. | [-.yṯ]ir ṯr.il.ab k.l pn.zbl.ym.l pn[.ṯ]pṭ[.n]hr. | [ik.a]l.yšm' k.ṯr.[i]l.ab k.l ys'.[alt.]ṯ[bt | k.l y]hpk. | [ks 2.3[129].16
--]. | rbt.'l.ydm[.---]. | b mdd.il.y[--.---]. | b ym.il.d[--.---.n] | hr.il.y[--.---]. | aliyn.[b'l.---]. | btlt.['nt.---]. | mh.k[--.---]. | w 4[51].2.35

nhr

mn.ib.yp‘.l b‘l.ṣrt. | l rkb.‘rpt.l mḫšt.mdd. | il ym.l klt.nhr.il.rbm. | l ištbm.tnn.ištml h. | mḫšt.btn.‘qltn. | šlyṭ.d šb‘t. 3['NT].3.36
].ml[k.---]. | [---]m.k[---]. | [-----]. | [---]m.il[.---]. | [---]d nhr.umt. | [---.]rpat.bt. | [m]lk.itdb.d šb‘. | [a]ḫm.l h.ṯmnt.bn 14[KRT].1.6
šmm w thm. | qrit.l špš.um h.špš.um.ql.bl.‘m. | il.mbk nhrm.b ‘dt.thmtm. | mnt.nṯk.nḥš.šmrr.nḥš. | ‘q šr.ln h.mlḫš UG5.7.3
---]. | [--]šnm.aṯtm.t[--.---]. | [m]lakm.ylak.ym.[t‘dt.ṯpṭ.nhr]. | b ‘lṣ.‘lṣm.npr.š[--.---]. | uṯ.ṯbr.ap hm.tb‘.ǵlm[m.al.ṯṯb.i 2.1[137].11
.tnǵṣn.pnt h.w ydlp.tmn h. | yqṯ b‘l.w yšt.ym.ykly.ṯpṭ.nhr. | b šm.tg‘r m.‘ṯtrt.bṯ l aliyn.[b‘l.] | bṯ.l rkb.‘rpt.k šby n.z 2.4[68].27
---.]tb‘.k[ṯ]r w [ḫss.t]bn.bht zbl ym. | [trm]m.hk[l.ṯpṭ].nhr.bt k.[---.]šp[-.---]. | [ḥš.bh]t h.tbn[n.ḥ]š.trm[mn.hkl h.---. 2.3[129].9
rkt.šbšt. | k rumm.hm. | ‘n.kdd.aylt. | mt hm.ks.ym | sk.nhr hm. | šb‘.ydt y.b ṣ‘. | [--.]šb‘.rbt. | [---.]qbṭ.ṯm. | [---.]bn.ilm UG5.4.10
aliyn.[b‘l.] | bṯ.l rkb.‘rpt.k šby n.zb[l.ym.k] | šby n.ṯpṭ.nhr.w yṣa b[.--]. | ybṯ.nn.aliyn.b‘l.w [---]. | ym.l mt.b‘l m.ym 2.4[68].30
--]n hm.rgm.l ṯr.ab h.il.ṯḥm.ym.b‘l km. | [adn]km.ṯpṭ.nhr.tn.il m.d tq h.d tqyn h. | [hml]t.tn.b‘l.w ‘nn h.bn.dgn.ar 2.1[137].34
ṯr.a[b.-.il.ṯny.l pḫr]. | m‘d.ṯḥm.ym.b‘l km.adn km.ṯ[pṭ.nhr]. | tn.il m.d tq h.d tqyn.hmlt.tn.b‘l.[w ‘nn h]. | bn.dgn.ar 2.1[137].17
imt.b klt. | yd y.ilḫm.hm.šb‘. | ydt y.b ṣ‘.hm.ks.ymsk. | nhr.k[--].ṣḥn.b‘l.‘m. | aḫ y.qran.hd.‘m.ary y. | w lḥm m ‘m a 5[67].1.22
r.šmt hm. | šm k.at.aymr.aymr.mr.ym.mr.ym. | l ksi h.nhr l kḥṯ.drkt h.trtqṣ. | b d b‘l.km.nšr b uṣb‘t h.hlm.qdq | d z 2.4[68].20
‘r.šmt hm.šm k at. | ygrš.ygrš.grš ym grš ym.l ksi h. | [n]hr l kḥṯ drkt h.trtqṣ.b d b‘l km nš | r.b uṣb‘t h.hlm.ktp.zbl 2.4[68].13
.brkt hm.ln.kḥṯ.zbl hm. | aḫr.tmǵyn.mlak ym.t‘dt.ṯpṭ.nhr.l p‘n.il. | [l t]pl.l tšṯḥwy.pḫr.m‘d.qmm.a[--].amr. | [ṯn]y.d 2.1[137].30
r[--]. | [---].w b ym.mnḫ l abd.b ym.irtm.m[--]. | [ṯpṭ].nhr.tl‘m.ṯm.ḥrbm.its.anšq. | [-]htm.l arṣ.ypl.ul ny.w l.‘pr.‘ẓ 2.4[68].4
.tuḥd.šmal h.tuḥd.‘ṯtrt.ik.m[ḫṣt.ml] | [ak.ym.t‘]dt.ṯpṭ.nhr.mlak.mṯḫr.yḥb[-.---.] | [---].mlak.bn.ktpm.rgm.b‘l h.w y 2.1[137].41
hkl.ṯpṭ.nh[r].yṯir.ṯr.il.ab h l pn[.zb]l y[m]. | [l pn.ṯp]ṭ[.nhr.]mlkt.[--]pm.l mlkt.wn.in.aṯt. | [l]k.k[m.ilm]. | [w ǵlmt.k 2.3[129].22
.nhr.ibr[.---]. | zbl b‘l.ǵlm.[---]. | ṣǵr hd w r[---.---]. | w l nhr nd[-.---]. | [---.--]l. 9[33].2.12
b]r.arṣ. | [---.]ǵrm[.t]ḫšn. | rḥq[.---.td‘]. | qdm ym.bmt.[nhr]. | ṯṯn.ib.b‘l.tiḥd. | y‘rm.šnu.hd.gpt. | ǵr.w y‘n.aliyn. | b‘l.i 4[51].7.34
r.brkt km.ln.kḥṯ. | zbl km.w ank.‘ny.mlak.ym.t‘dt.ṯpṭ.nhr. | tšu ilm rašt hm.l ẓr.brkt hm.ln.kḥṯ.zbl hm. | aḫr.tmǵy 2.1[137].28
.w ln.kḥṯ.zbl km.aḥd. | ilm.t‘ny lḥt.mlak.ym.t‘dt.ṯpṭ.nhr. | šu.ilm.rašt km.l ẓr.brkt km.ln.kḥṯ. | zbl km.w ank.‘ny. 2.1[137].26
--.r]iš k. | [---.]bn ‘n km. | [---.]alp. | [---.]ym.rbt. | [---.]b nhrm. | [‘b]r.gbl.‘br. | q‘l.‘br.iht. | np šmm.šmšr. | l dgy.aṯrt. | 3['NT.VI].6.6
b‘l.km.nšr. | b[u]ṣb‘t h.ylm.ktp.zbl ym.bn ydm.ṯpṭ. | nhr.‘z.ym.l ymk.l tnǵṣn.pnt h.l ydlp. | tmn h.kṯr.ṣmdm.ynḥt 2.4[68].17
.b‘l.qm.‘l.il.hlm. | ilm.tph hm.tphn.mlak.ym.t‘dt.ṯpṭ[.nhr]. | t[ǵ]ly.hlm.rišt hm.l ẓr.brkt hm.w l kḥṯ. | zbl hm.b hm. 2.1[137].22
d b‘l.km.nšr b uṣb‘t h.hlm.qdq | d zbl ym.bn.‘nm.ṯpṭ.nhr.yprsḥ ym. | w yql.l arṣ.w trtqṣ.ṣmd.b d b‘l. | [km.]nšr.b u 2.4[68].22
‘l. | [km.]nšr.b uṣb‘t h.ylm.qdqd.zbl. | [ym.]bn.‘nm.ṯpṭ.nhr.yprsḥ.ym.yql. | l arṣ.tnǵṣn.pnt h.w ydlp.tmn h. | yqṯ b‘l. 2.4[68].25
t.‘nt.arṣ.ṯlṯ.mṯḥ.ǵyrm]. | [idk.]l ytn.pnm.‘m.[i]l.mbk.[nhrm.qrb.apq.thmtm]. | [ygly.]ḏl i[l].w ybu[.q]rš.mlk[.ab.šn 2.3[129].4
lt.‘nt. | w b‘l.tb‘.mrym.ṣpn. | idk.l ttn.pnm. | ‘m.il.mbk.nhrm. | qrb.apq.thmtm. | tgly.ḏd.il.w tbu. | qrš.mlk.ab.šnm. | l 4[51].4.21
aṯrt[.td‘ṣ.]p‘n. | [w tr.a]rṣ.id[k.l ttn.p]nm. | [‘m.i]l.mbk.nhr[m.qr]b.[ap]q. | [thm]tm.tgl.ḏ[d.]i[l.]w tbu. | [qr]š.m[l]k.a 3['NT.VI].5.14
--]. | [---.]zr h.ybm.l ilm. | [id]k.l ttn.pnm.‘m. | [il.]mbk nhrm.qrb. | [a]pq.thmtm.tgly.ḏd. | il.w tbu.qrš.. | mlk.ab.šnm 6.1.33[49.1.5]
[idk.l ttn.pnm]. | [‘m.il.mbk.nhrm]. | [qrb.apq.thmtm]. | [tgly.ḏd.il.w]tb[a]. | [qrš.mlk.ab.] 5[67].6.02
.nšm. | [td‘ṣ.p‘n]m.w tr.arṣ.idk. | [l ttn.pn]m.‘m il.mbk.nhrm. | [qrb.ap]q.thmtm tgly.ḏd il. | [w tbu.qr]š.mlk.ab.šnm. 17[2AQHT].6.47
b‘l km nš | r.b uṣb‘t h.hlm.ktp.zbl ym.bn ydm. | [ṯp]ṭ nhr.yrtqṣ.ṣmd.b d b‘l.km.nšr. | b[u]ṣb‘t h.ylm.ktp.zbl ym.b 2.4[68].15
h. | npyn h.mks.bšr h. | tmt‘.md h.b ym.ṯn. | npyn h.b nhrm. | šṯt.ḫptr.l išt. | ḫbrt.l ẓr.pḥmm. | t‘pp.ṯr.il.d pid. | tǵẓy. 4[51].2.7
n[p]šn y.trḥṣn.k trm. | [--]b b[ht]. | [zbl.]ym.b hkl.ṯpṭ.nh[r].yṯir.ṯr.il.ab h l pn[.zb]l y[m]. | [l pn.ṯp]ṭ[.nhr.]mlkt.[--] 2.3[129].21
liyn.b‘l[.---]. | drkt k.mšl[-.---]. | b riš k.aymr[.---]. | ṯpṭ.nhr.ytb[r.ḥrn.y ym.ytbr.ḥrn]. | riš k.‘ṯtrt.[šm.b‘l.qdqd k.---]. 2.1[137].7
pṭ.nh[r.---]. | [---].an.rgmt.l ym.b‘l km.ad[n km.ṯpṭ]. | [nhr.---.]hwt.gmr.hd.l wny[-.---]. | [---.]iyr h.g[-.]thbr[.---]. 2.1[137].46
y[---]. | [---.k]ṯr.w ḫ[ss.t]b‘.b[n.]bht.ym[.rm]m.hkl.ṯpṭ nh[r]. | [---.]hrn.w[---.]tb‘.k[ṯ]r w [ḫss.t]bn.bht zbl ym. | [trm 2.3[129].7
[---.]ydm ym. | [---.]ydm nhr. | [---.]trǵt. | [---.]h aḫd[.--]. | [---.]iln[-.---]. | [---.--]ḫ[.---]. | 49[73].1.2
anš.zbl.b‘l.šdmt.bg[--.---]. | [---.-]dm.mlak.ym.t‘dt.ṯpṭ.nh[r.---]. | [---].an.rgmt.l ym.b‘l km.ad[n km.ṯpṭ]. | [nhr.---.]h 2.1[137].44
.k[m.ilm]. | [w ǵlmt.k bn.qdš.]w y[--.]zbl.ym.y‘[--.]ṯpṭ.nhr. | [-------.]yšlḥn.w y‘n ‘ṯtr[.-]. 2.3[129].23

nhš

[-----]. | ‘m[-.---]. | mǵ[-.---]. | šp[š.---]. | ql.[---]. | w mlk[.nhš.w mlk.mg]šḫ. | ‘mn.[---]. | ik y.[---]. | w l n[qmd.---]. | [w] 64[118].6

nwḫ

prq.lṣb w yṣḥq. | yšu.g h.w yṣḥ. | aṯbn.ank.w anḫn. | w tnḫ.b irt y.npš. | k ḥy.aliyn.b‘l. | k iṯ.zbl.b‘l.arṣ. | gm.yṣḥ.il.l b 6[49].3.19
| p‘n.l hdm.ytpd.yšu. | g h.w yṣḥ.aṯbn.ank. | w anḫn.w tnḫ.b irt y. | npš.k yld.bn.l y.km. | aḫ y.w šrš.km ary y. | nṣb.s 17[2AQHT].2.13
kt.il.dt.rbtm. | kt.il.nbt.b ksp. | šmrgt.b dm.ḫrṣ. | kḥṯ.il.nḫt. | b ẓr.hdm.id. | d prša.b br. | n‘l.il.d qblbl. | ‘ln.ybl hm.ḫrṣ 4[51].1.34
.w yṣḥq. | p‘n.l hdm.ytpd.yšu. | g h.w yṣḥ.aṯbn.ank. | w anḫn.w tnḫ.b irt y. | npš.k yld.bn.l y.km. | aḫ y.w šrš.km ary 17[2AQHT].2.13
ṯpd. | w yprq.lṣb w yṣḥq. | yšu.g h.w yṣḥ. | aṯbn.ank.w anḫn. | w tnḫ.b irt y.npš. | k ḥy.aliyn.b‘l. | k iṯ.zbl.b‘l.arṣ. | gm 6[49].3.18
prst[.---]. | ydr.hm.ym[.---]. | ‘l amr.yu[ḫd.ksa.mlk h]. | nḫt.kḥṯ.d[rkt h.b bt y]. | aṣḥ.rpi[m.iqra.ilnym]. | b qrb.h[kl y 22.1[123].18
ṯ.w ytrm.hn.ym. | w ṯn.ytb.krt.l ‘d h. | ytb.l ksi mlk. | l nḫt.l kḥṯ.drkt. | ap.yṣb.ytb.b hkl. | w ywsrnn.ggn h. | lk.l ab k 16.6[127].24
| b mrym.ṣpn.mšṣṣ.[-]k‘[-]. | udn h.grš h.l ksi.mlk h. | l nḫt.l kḥṯ.drkt h. | mn m.ib.yp‘.l b‘l.ṣrt.l rkb.‘rpt. | [-]‘n.ǵlmm 3['NT].4.47
b d.aliyn b[‘l.---]. | kd.ynaṣn[.---]. | gršnn.l k[si.mlk h.l nḫt.l kḥṯ]. | drkt h.š[--.--]. | w hm.ap.l[--.---]. | ymḫṣ k.k[--.---] 1['NT.X].4.24
ǵzr.y‘r.mt. | b ql h.y[---.---]. | b‘l.yṯṯbn[.l ksi]. | mlk h.l[nḫt.l kḥṯ]. | drkt h[.---]. | [---.]d[--.---]. | [---].hn[.---]. | [---.]šn[6[49].6.34
ǵr k. | tšlm k. | hn ny.‘m ny. | kll.mid. | šlm. | w.ap.ank. | nḫt.ṯm ny. | ‘m.adt ny. | mnm.šlm. | rgm.ṯṯb. | l.‘bd k. 51[95].14

nwm

m.bky h.w yšn. | b dm‘ h.nhmmt. | šnt.tluan. | w yškb.nhmmt. | w yqmṣ.w b ḥlm h. | il.yrd.b ḏhrt h. | ab adm.w yqr 14[KRT].1.34
lm.arṣ h. | km ḫmšt.mṯt h. | bm.bky h.w yšn. | b dm‘ h.nhmmt. | šnt.tluan. | w yškb.nhmmt. | w yqmṣ.w b ḥlm h. | il. 14[KRT].1.32

nws

t. | ʻbd k.b. | lwsnd. | [w] b ṣr. | ʻm.mlk. | w.ht. | mlk.syr. | ns.w.ṯm. | ydbḥ. | mlǵ[.---]. | w.m[--.--]y. | y[--.---]. 2063.15
[-----]. | [---.--]dn. | [---.--]dd. | [---.--]n.kb | [--.---.]al.yns. | [---.]ysd k. | [---.--]r.dr.dr. | [---.--]y k.w rḥd. | [---]y ilm. 4[51].3.5

nwrd̲

t.w].bn h.b.bt.krz. | [aṯt.]w.pǵt.b.bt.gg. | [ǵz]r.aḥd.b.bt.nwrd̲. | [aṯ]t.adrt.b.bt.arttb. | aṯt.w.ṯn.bn h.b.bt.iwwpzn. | aṯt. 80[119].3
b d.tbṯtb. | [š]d.bn.ṯ[-]rn.b d.ʻdbmlk. | [šd.]bn.brzn.b d.nwrd̲. | [šd.]bn.nḥbl.b d.ʻdbym. | [šd.b]n.qṭy.b d.tt. | [ubd]y.m 82[300].1.17

nwrd̲r

ksdm. | ṣdqn. | nwrd̲r. | ṯrin. | ʻdršp. | pqr. | agbṯr. | ʻbd. | ksd. 1044.3

nzdt

]ilṯḥm.w.[---]. | šmʻt.ḥwt[.---]. | [---].nzdt.qr[t]. | [---.]dt nzdt.m[lk]. | [---.]w.ap.bṯn[.---]. | [---.]bʻl y.y[--]. | [---.-]l[-.---]. 2127.2.5
-].ksp.ʻm[.---]. | [---.]ilṯḥm.w.[---]. | šmʻt.ḥwt[.---]. | [---].nzdt.qr[t]. | [---.]dt nzdt.m[lk]. | [---.]w.ap.bṯn[.---]. | [---.]bʻl y 2127.2.4

nzl

d k]. | imr.d[bḥ.bm].ymn. | lla.kl[atn]m. | klt.l[ḥm k.d]nzl. | qḥ.ms[rr.]ʻṣr. | dbḥ.ṣ[q.b g]l.ḥtt. | yn.b gl[.ḫ]rṣ.nbt. | ʻl.l ẓ 14[KRT].2.69
ẓl.ḫmt.lqḥ. | imr.dbḥ.b yd h. | lla.klatnm. | klt.lḥm h.d nzl. | lqḥ.msrr.ʻṣr.db[ḥ]. | yṣq.b gl.ḥtt.yn. | b gl.ḫrṣ.nbt.w ʻly. | 14[KRT].3.162
bʻm.drʻ.w.ṯlṯm.drt. | [w].šbʻm.dd.ṯn.kbd.ḥpr.bnšm. | b.nzl.ʻšrm.l.mit.drʻ.w.šbʻm.drt. | w.ʻšrm.l.mit.dd.ḥpr.bnšm. | b. 1098.24

nzʻn

| [bn.]kblbn[.---]. | [bn] uškny. | bn.krny[-]. | bn.mt. | bn.nzʻn. | bn.slmz[-]. | bn.kʻ[--]. | bn.y[---]. | [-----]. | [bn.a]mdy. | b 2021.1.17

nḥ

mnḥ.b d.ybnn. | arbʻ.mat. | l.alp.šmn. | nḥ.ṯṯ.mat. | šm[n].rqḥ. | kkrm.brd̲l. | mit.tišrm. | ṯlṯm.almg. | ḫ 141[120].4

nḥbl

bn.ṯ[-]rn.b d.ʻdbmlk. | [šd.]bn.brzn.b d.nwrd̲. | [šd.]bn.nḥbl.b d.ʻdbym. | [šd.b]n.qṭy.b d.tt. | [ubd]y.mrim. | [šd.b]n.ṯ 82[300].1.18

nḥw

rm.w gbṯt. | km.ibrm. | w b hm.pn.bʻl. | bʻl.ytlk.w yṣd. | yḥ pat.mlbr. | wn.ymǵy.aklm. | w ymẓa.ʻqqm. | bʻl.ḥmd m.yḥ 12[75].1.35

nḥk

| ʻrkm. | b ṯmnt.ʻšrt.yr | ṯḥṣ.mlk.brr. | ʻlm.tzǵ.b ǵb.ṣpn. | nḥkt.ksp.w ḫrṣ ṯʻ ṯn šm l btbt. | alp.w š šrp.alp šlmm. | l bʻl.ʻṣ UG5.12.A.8

nḥl

---]dy. | [---.n]ḥl h. | [---].bn.mryn. | [---].bn.ṯyl. | annmt.nḥl h. | abmn.bn.ʻbd. | liy.bn.rqdy. | bn.ršp. 1036.12
. | [-]ntm[.---]. | [ʻ]bdm. | [bn].mṣrn. | [a]ršwn. | ʻb[d]. | w nḥl h. | atn.bn.ap[s]n. | nsk.ṯlṯ. | bn.[--.]m[-]ḫr. | bn.šmrm. | ṯn 85[80].3.6
| [š].bn.trn.b d.ibrmd̲. | [š]d.bn.ilṯtmr.b d.tbbr. | [w.]šd.nḥl h.b d.ṯtmd. | [š]d.b d.iwrḫṭ. | [ṯn].šdm.b d.gmrd. | [šd.]lbn 82[300].1.12
bn.tlmyn. | w.nḥl h. | w.nḥl hm. | bn.ḥrm. | bn.brzn. | w.nḥl h. | bn.adld̲n. | bn.šbl. | bn.ḫnzr. | bn.arwṭ. | bn.ṯbtnq. | bn.p 113[400].1.11
n[.---]. | [-----]. | b[n.---]. | b[n.---]. | bn.[---]. | bn.a[--]. | w.nḥl h. | bn.alz. | w.nḥl h. | bn.sny. | bn.ablḥ. | [-----]. | w [---]. | b 2163.1.11
[w]nḥ[l h]. | [bn].amd[-]. | [bn].ṣbṭ[--]. | [bn].ḫla[n]. | [bn].ǵr[--]. | 2164.A.1
l[-]. | ʻbdy[rḫ].bn.gṯtn. | yrmn.bn.ʻn. | krwn.nḥl h. | ttn.[n]ḥl h. | bn.b[r]zn. | [---.-]ḫn. 85[80].4.11
.izl. | bn.ibln. | bn.ilt. | špšyn.nḥl h. | nʻmn.bn.iryn. | nrn.nḥl h. | bn.ḫsn. | bn.ʻbd. | [-----]. | [---.n]ḥ[l h]. | [-]ntm[.---]. | [ʻ] 85[80].2.8
[-----]. | bn.[---]. | bn.[---]. | w.nḥ[l h]. | bn.ẓr[-]. | mru.skn. | bn.bddn. | bn.ǵrgn. | bn.tgtn. | bn 113[400].5.3
m. | bn.iršyn. | bn.ʻzn. | bn.aršw. | bn.ḫzrn. | bn.iǵyn. | w.nḥl h. | bn.ksd. | bn.bršm. | bn.kzn. | w.nḥl h. | w.nḥl hm. | w.[n 113[400].2.17
[---]y. | [---.]w.nḥl h. | bn ksln.ṯlṯḫ. | bn yṣmḫ.bn.ṯrn w nḥl h. | bn srd.bn ag 101[10].2
bn.brzn. | bn.ḫtr[-]. | bn.yd[--]. | bn.ʻ[---]. | w.nḥ[l h]. | w.nḥ[l h]. | bn.k[---]. | bn.y[---]. | [bn].i[---]. 116[303].11
n.lbn. | bn.šlmn. | bn.mly. | pslm. | bn.annd. | bn.glʻd. | w.nḥl h. | bn.mlkyy. | [bn].bm[--]. | [ʻš]rm. | [-----]. | [-----]. | bn.p[- 2163.3.12
.ḥṭb. | bn abyt. | bn ḫdl. | bn ṣdqn. | bn ayy. | bn dbb. | w nḥl h. | bn nʻmyn. | bn aṯtyy. | bn ḫlp. | bn.ẓll. | bn ydy. | bn lzn 2016.1.8
n.---]. | b[n.---]. | bn.[---]. | bn.a[--]. | w.nḥl h. | bn.alz. | w.nḥl h. | bn.sny. | bn.ablḥ. | [-----]. | w [---]. | bn.[---]. | bn.yr[--]. | 2163.1.13
[---]y. | [---.]w.nḥl h. | bn ksln.ṯlṯḫ. | bn yṣmḫ.bn.ṯrn w nḥl h. | bn srd.bn agmn. | bn [-]ln.bn.ṯbil. | bn is.bn tbdn. | bn 101[10].4
.nḥl h. | [--.-]hs. | [--.--]nyn. | [-----]. | [-----]. | bn.ʻdy. | w.nḥl h. | bn.ʻbl. | bn.[-]rṯn. | bn[.---]. | bn u[l]pm. | bn ʻ[p]ty. | bn. 2163.2.20
[aǵ]ltn. | [--]ṯm.b.gt.irbṣ. | [--]šmyn. | [w.]nḥl h. | bn.qṣn. | bn.ksln. | bn.ṣrym. | bn.ṯmq. | bn.ntp. | bn.mlk 1073.1.4
mryn[m]. | bn.bly. | nrn. | w.nḥl h. | bn.rmyy. | bn.tlmyn. | w.nḥl h. | w.nḥl hm. | bn.ḥrm. | b 113[400].1.4
]t. | bn.adty. | bn.krwn. | bn.nǵsk. | bn.qnd̲. | bn.pity. | w.nḥl h. | bn.rt. | bn.l[--]. | bn.[---]. | [---.--]y. | [--.-]d̲rm. | [--.--]y. | 113[400].3.18
ṯnnm. | bn.qqln. | w.nḥl h. | w.nḥl h. | bn.šml[-]. | bn.brzn. | bn.ḫtr[-]. | bn.yd[--]. | bn.ʻ[---]. | w 116[303].4
bn. | bn.aḫ[--]. | bn[.---]. | [-----]. | bn kr[k]. | bn ḫtyn. | w nḥl h. | bn ṯgrb. | bn ṯdnyn. | bn pbn. 2016.3.4
bn.šml[-]. | bn.brzn. | bn.ḫtr[-]. | bn.yd[--]. | bn.ʻ[---]. | w.nḥ[l h]. | w.nḥ[l h]. | bn.k[---]. | bn.y[---]. | [bn].i[---]. 116[303].10
ṯnnm. | bn.qqln. | w.nḥl h. | w.nḥl h. | bn.šml[-]. | bn.brzn. | bn.ḫtr[-]. | bn.yd[--]. | b 116[303].3
n. | bn.[-]dr[-]. | [---]l[-]. | [--]ym. | [--]rm. | [bn.]aǵld. | [w.nḥ]l h. | [w.nḥ]l h[.-]. 114[324].3.5
.mztn. | bn.šlgyn. | bn.[-]gštn. | bn[.n]klb. | b[n.]dtn. | w.nḥl h. | w.nḥl hm. | bn.iršyn. | bn.ʻzn. | bn.aršw. | bn.ḫzrn. | bn. 113[400].2.10
n[m]. | bn.bly. | nrn. | w.nḥl h. | bn.rmyy. | bn.tlmyn. | w.nḥl h. | w.nḥl hm. | bn.ḥrm. | bn.brzn. | w.nḥl h. | bn.adld̲n. | b 113[400].1.7
rǵlm. | bn.mmy. | bn.ḫnyn. | bn.knn. | khnm. | bn.ṯʻy. | w.nḥl h. | w.nḥl hm. | bn.nqly. | bn.snrn. | bn.ṯgd. | bn.d[-]n. | bn. 105[86].1
-]. | bn.[---]. | bn.[---]. | bn.yk[--]. | bn.šmm. | bn.irgy. | w.nḥl h. | w.nḥl hm. | [bn].pmn. | bn.gtrn. | bn.arpḫn. | bn.ṯryn. | 1046.2.11
zrn. | bn.iǵyn. | w.nḥl h. | bn.ksd. | bn.bršm. | bn.kzn. | w.nḥl h. | w.nḥl hm. | w.[n]ḥl hm. | b[n.---]. | bn.gzry. | bn.atyn. | 113[400].2.21

rsw ʻ[šr]m. | ʻšdyn.ḫmš[t]. | abršn.ʻšr[t]. | bʻln.ḫmšt. | w.nḫl h.ḫm[š]t. | bn.unp.arbʻt. | ʻbdbn.ytrš ḫmšt. | krwn.ʻšrt. | bn 1062.9
[--.]ṯbq.l.iytlm. | [---].l.iytlm. | [---.]ʻbdilm.l.iytlm. | [---.n]ḫl h.lm.iytlm. 1076.6
dlḏn. | šd.bn.nṣdn.l bn.ʻmlbi. | šd.ṯpḫln.l bn.ǵl. | w dṯn.nḫl h.l bn.pl. | šd.krwn.l aḫn. | šd.ʻyy.l aḫn. | šd.brdn.l bn.bly. 2089.10
bn.sḫr.mr[-.---]. | bn.idrn.ʻš[-.---]. | bn.bly.mr[-.---]. | w.nḫl h.mr[-.---]. | ilšpš.[---]. | iḫny.[---]. | bn.[---]. 88[304].11
dr. | bn.nqq. | ḫrš.bhtm. | bn.izl. | bn.ibln. | bn.ilt. | špšyn.nḫl h. | nʻmn.bn.iryn. | nrn.nḫl h. | bn.ḫsn. | bn.ʻbd. | [-----]. | [-- 85[80].2.6
[spr.----]m. | bn.pi[ty]. | w.nḫ[l h]. | ʻbd[--]. | bn.s[---]. | bn.at[--]. | bn.qnḏ. | ṣmq[-]. | bn.an 117[325].1.3
]n.arkšt. | lʻq[.---]. | šd.pll.b d.qrt. | š[d].annḏr.b d.bdn.nḫ[l h]. | [šd.]agyn.b d.kmrn.n[ḫl] h. | [š]d.nbzn.[-]l.qrt. | [š]d 2029.7
hr nḫl h. | šd knn.bn.ann.ʻdb. | šd.iln[-].bn.irṯr.l.sḫrn.nḫl h. | šd[.ag]pṯn.b[n.]brrn.l.qrt. | šd[.--]dy.bn.brzn. | l.qrt. 2029.20
.kmrn.n[ḫl] h. | [š]d.nbzn.[-]l.qrt. | [š]d.agpṯr.b d.sḫrn.nḫl h. | šd.annmn.b d.tyn.nḫl h. | šd.pǵyn[.b] d.krmn.l.ty[n.n 2029.10
nn.ʻ[db]. | šd.ṯ[r]yn.bn.tkn.b d.qrt. | šd[.-].dyn.b d.pln.nḫl h. | šd.irdyn.bn.ḫrǵš[-].l.qrt. | šd.iǵlyn.bn.kzbn.l.qr[t]. | šd 2029.15
rt. | šd.iǵlyn.bn.kzbn.l.qr[t]. | šd.pln.bn.tiyn.b d.ilmhr nḫl h. | šd knn.bn.ann.ʻdb. | šd.iln[-].bn.irṯr.l.sḫrn.nḫl h. | šd[. 2029.18
. | šd.annmn.b d.tyn.nḫl h. | šd.pǵyn[.b] d.krmn.l.ty[n.n]ḫl h. | šd.krz.[b]n.ann.ʻ[db]. | šd.ṯ[r]yn.bn.tkn.b d.qrt. | šd[.- 2029.12
.qrt. | š[d].annḏr.b d.bdn.nḫ[l h]. | [šd.]agyn.b d.kmrn.n[ḫl] h. | [š]d.nbzn.[-]l.qrt. | [š]d.agpṯr.b d.sḫrn.nḫl h. | šd.an 2029.8
spr.ubdy.art. | šd.prn.b d.agpṯn.nḫl h. | šd.šwn.b d.ttyn.nḫl [h]. | šd.ttyn[.b]n.arkšt. | lʻq[.---]. | 2029.2
[-]l.qrt. | [š]d.agpṯr.b d.sḫrn.nḫl h. | šd.annmn.b d.tyn.nḫl h. | šd.pǵyn[.b] d.krmn.l.ty[n.n]ḫl h. | šd.krz.[b]n.ann.ʻ[d 2029.11
pr.ubdy.art. | šd.prn.b d.agpṯn.nḫl h. | šd.šwn.b d.ttyn.nḫl [h]. | šd.ttyn[.b]n.arkšt. | lʻq[.---]. | šd.pll.b d.qrt. | š[d].ann 2029.3
iḫy.[b]n[.--]l[-]. | ʻbdy[rḫ].bn.gttn. | yrmn.bn.ʻn. | krwn.nḫl h. | ttn.[n]ḫl h. | bn.b[r]zn. | [---.-]ḫn. 85[80].4.10
--]kt.[--.d.]ytb.b.šb[n]. | bn.pr[-.]d.y[ṯb.b].šlmy. | tlš.w[.n]ḫl h[.-].ṯgd.mrum. | bt.[-]b[-.-]sy[-]h. | nn[-].b[n].py[-.d.]yṯ 2015.2.3
-]. | [---]l[-]. | [--]ym. | [--]rm. | [bn.]aǵld. | [w.nḫ]l h. | [w.nḫ]l h[.-]. 114[324].3.6
w.nḫl h. | [--]ilt.w.nḫl h. | [---]n. | [--]ly. | [iw]ryn. | [--.w.n]ḫl h. | [-]ibln. | bn.nḏbn. | bn.ʻbl. | bn.tlšn. | bn.sln. | w nḫl h. 1063.9
bn.ṣrṯn. | bn.ʻbd. | snb.w.nḫl h. | [-]by.w.nḫl h. | [--]ilt.w.nḫl h. | [---]n. | [--]ly. | [iw]ryn. 1063.3
ʻmn.bn.iryn. | nrn.nḫl h. | bn.ḫsn. | bn.ʻbd. | [-----]. | [---.n]ḫ[l h]. | [-]ntm[.---]. | [ʻ]bdm. | [bn].mṣrn. | [a]ršwn. | ʻb[d]. | 85[80].2.12
[-----]. | w.[-----]. | w.abǵl.nḫ[l h.--]. | w.unṯ.aḫd.l h[.---]. | dnn.bn.yṣr[.---]. | sln.bn.ʻtt[-.- 90[314].1.3
t. | [---.-]l[--]. | [---.]pr[--]. | [-.a]pln. | bn.mzt. | bn.ṯrn. | w.nḫl h. | [--.-]hs. | [--.--]nyn. | [-----]. | [-----]. | bn.ʻdy. | w.nḫl h. | 2163.2.15
-]. | [-----]. | [-----]. | [-----]. | [-----]. | [-----]. | [---.--]yn. | [w.nḫ]l h. | [--.---]n. | [-----]. | [-----]. | [-----]. | [-----]. | [--.-]gn. | [--.-- 113[400].4.18
bn.ṣrṯn. | bn.ʻbd. | snb.w.nḫl h. | [-]by.w.nḫl h. | [--]ilt.w.nḫl h. | [---]n. | [--]ly. | [iw]ryn. | [--.w.n]ḫl h. | [1063.4
[---.a]lty. | [-----]. | [---]tl. | [---]ʻbl. | [---]bln. | [---]dy. | [---.n]ḫl h. | [---].bn.mryn. | [---].bn.ṯyl. | annmt.nḫl h. | abmn.bn.ʻ 1036.9
[---.]bn[.---]. | [---.]bn[.---]. | [---.]nḫl h. | [---.b]n.špš. | [---.b]n.mradn. | [---.m]lkym. | [---.--]d. 2137.3
yṣr[.---]. | ʻdyn.bn.uḏr[-.---]. | w.ʻdʻ.nḫl h[.---]. | w.yknil.nḫl h[.---]. | w.iltm.nḫl h[.---]. | w.unṯm.nḫ[l h.---]. | [---.]ʻḏr[.- 90[314].1.15
ḏr[-.---]. | w.ʻdʻ.nḫl h[.---]. | w.yknil.nḫl h[.---]. | w.iltm.nḫl h[.---]. | w.unṯm.nḫ[l h.---]. | [---.]ʻḏr[.---]. | str[-.---]. | bdl 90[314].1.16
n.bʻly[.---]. | bnil.bn.yṣr[.---]. | ʻdyn.bn.uḏr[-.---]. | w.ʻdʻ.nḫl h[.---]. | w.yknil.nḫl h[.---]. | w.iltm.nḫl h[.---]. | w.unṯm.n 90[314].1.14
[--.-]ln. | [---.n]ḫl h. | [---.n]ḫl h. | [---.n]ḫl h. 126[-].2
[--.-]ln. | [---.n]ḫl h. | [---.n]ḫl h. | [---.n]ḫl h. 126[-].3
[.---]. | w.yknil.nḫl h[.---]. | w.iltm.nḫl h[.---]. | w.unṯm.nḫ[l h.---]. | [---.]ʻḏr[.---]. | str[-.---]. | bdlm.d[t.---]. | ʻdn.[---]. | 90[314].1.17
ʻ[---]. | kbkbn bn[.---]. | bn.k[--]. | bn.pdr[n.]. | bn.ʻn[--]. | nḫl h[.---]. | [-----]. 2014.61
n.ṣrṯn. | bn.ʻbd. | snb.w.nḫl h. | [-]by.w.nḫl h. | [--]ilt.w.nḫl h. | [---]n. | [--]ly. | [iw]ryn. | [--.w.n]ḫl h. | [-]ibln. | bn.nḏbn 1063.5
.n]ḫl h. | [-]ibln. | bn.nḏbn. | bn.ʻbl. | bn.tlšn. | bn.sln. | w nḫl h. 1063.15
[--.-]s[-]n. | [--.-]nyn. | [---].[-]ǵtyn. | [---].[-]tyn. | [---.w.]nḫl h. 123[326].2.6
[---.--]n. | [---.]rmṣm. | [---.]dyy. | [---.n]ḫl h. 2155.4
[--.-]ln. | [---.n]ḫl h. | [---.n]ḫl h. | [---.n]ḫl h. 126[-].4
n.šlgyn. | bn.[-]gštn. | bn[.n]klb. | b[n.]dtn. | w.nḫl h. | w.nḫl hm. | bn.iršyn. | bn.ʻzn. | bn.aršw. | bn.ḫzrn. | bn.iǵyn. | w.n 113[400].2.11
.bly. | nrn. | w.nḫl h. | bn.rmyy. | bn.tlmyn. | w.nḫl h. | w.nḫl hm. | bn.ḫrm. | bn.brzn. | w.nḫl h. | bn.adlḏn. | bn.šbl. | bn. 113[400].1.8
mmy. | bn.ḫnyn. | bn.knn. | khnm. | bn.ṯʻy. | w.nḫl h. | w.nḫl hm. | bn.nqly. | bn.snrn. | bn.ṯgd. | bn.d[-]n. | bn.amdn. | bn 105[86].1
-]. | bn.[---]. | bn.yk[--]. | bn.šmm. | bn.irgy. | w.nḫl h. | w.nḫl hm. | [bn].pmn. | bn.gṯrn. | bn.arpḫn. | bn.ṯryn. | bn.dll. | b 1046.2.12
. | bn.ksd. | bn.bršm. | bn.kzn. | w.nḫl h. | w.nḫl hm. | w.[n]ḫl hm. | b[n.---]. | bn.gzry. | bn.atyn. | bn.ttn. | bn.rwy. | bn.ʻ 113[400].2.23
yn. | w.nḫl h. | bn.ksd. | bn.bršm. | bn.kzn. | w.nḫl h. | w.nḫl hm. | w.[n]ḫl hm. | b[n.---]. | bn.gzry. | bn.atyn. | bn.ttn. | b 113[400].2.22
[---.]ṯlṯm. | [---.n]ḫl. | [---.ṯ]lṯ.mat.šbʻm[.---]. | [---.--]mm.b.mṣbt[.---]. | [---.ṯl]ṯ 2149.2

nḫlt

tnn. | pnm.tk.ḥqkpt. | il.kl h.kptr. | ksu.ṯbt h.ḥkpt. | arṣ.nḫlt h. | b alp.šd.rbt. | kmn.l pʻn.kṯ. | hbr.w ql.tšṯḥ | wy.w kbd 3[ʻNT.VI].6.16
al.ttn.pnm.tk.ḥkpt.il.kl h]. | [kptr.]ks[u.ṯbt h.ḥkpt.arṣ.nḫlt h]. | b alp.šd.r[bt.kmn.l pʻn.kṯr]. | hbr.w ql.t[šṯḥwy.w kb 1[ʻNT.IX].3.1
k.al.ttn. | pnm.tk.qrt h. | hmry.mk.ksu. | ṯbt h.ḫḫ.arṣ. | nḫlt h.w nǵr. | ʻnn.ilm.al. | tqrb.l bn.ilm. | mt.al.yʻdb km. | k i 4[51].8.14
.pn.ʻm.bn.ilm.mt. | tk.qrt h.hmry.mk.ksu. | ṯbt.ḫḫ.arṣ.nḫlt h.tša. | g hm.w tṣḥ.ṯḥm.aliyn. | bn.bʻl.hwt.aliy.qrdm. | bh 5[67].2.16
lt.arṣ.at m.w ank. | ibǵy h.b tk.ǵr y.il.ṣpn. | b qdš.b ǵr.nḫlt y. | b nʻm.b gbʻ.tliyt. | hlm.ʻnt.tph.ilm.b h.pʻnm. | ṯṭṭ.bʻd 3[ʻNT].3.27
m.at m.w ank]. | ibǵ[y h.b tk.ǵ]r y.il.ṣpn. | b q[dš.b ǵr.nḫ]lt y. | w t[ʻn].btlt.[ʻ]nt.ttb. | [ybmt.]limm.[a]n.aqry. | [b arṣ 3[ʻNT].4.64

nḫn

ʻm.krt.mswn h. | arḫ.tzǵ.l ʻgl h. | bn.ḫpṯ.l umht hm. | k tnḫn.udmm. | w yʻny.krt.ṯʻ. 15[128].1.7

nḫš

t.ṯlṯ.ptḥ.bt.mnt. | ptḥ.bt.w ubn.hkl.w ištql šql. | tn.km.nḥšm.yḥr.tn.km. | mhr y.w bn.bṯn.itnn y. | ytt.nḥšm.mhr k.b UG5.7.73
šmrr. | nḥš.ʻq šr.ln h.mlḫš.abd.ln h.ydy. | ḥmt.hlm.ytq.nḥš.yšlḥm.nḥš. | ʻq šr.yʻdb.ksa.w ytb. | tqru.l špš.um h.špš.u UG5.7.28
šmrr.nḥš.ʻq šr ln h. | mlḫš.abd.ln h.ydy.ḥmt.hlm.ytq. | nḥš.yšlḥm.nḥš.ʻq šr.ydb.ksa. | w ytb. | tqru.l špš.u h.špš.um. UG5.7.12
.nḥš ʻq šr.ln h.mlḫš. | abd.ln h.ydy ḥmt.hlm.ytq šqy. | nḥš.yšlḥm.nḥš.ʻq šr.yʻdb. | ksa.w ytb. | tqru l špš.um h.špš.u UG5.7.55

|šmrr.nḥš.ʿq šr.ln h.mlḫš.abd.|ln h.ydy.ḥmt.hlm yṯq.nḥš.|yšlḥm.nḥš.ʿq šr.yʿdb ksa.|w yṯb.|tqru l špš.um h.špš.u UG5.7.48
šmrr.|nḥš.ʿq šr.ln h.mlḫš abd.ln h.ydy.|ḥmt.hlm.yṯq.nḥš.yšlḥm.nḥš.|ʿq šr.yʿdb.ksa.w yṯb.|tqru.l špš.um.ql bl.ʿm UG5.7.43
šm|rr.nḥš.ʿq šr.ln h.mlḫš abd.ln h.|ydy.ḥmt.hlm.yṯq nḥš yšlḥm.nḥš.|ʿq.šr.yʿdb.ksa.w yṯb.|tqru l špš um h.špš u UG5.7.38
pš.um h.špš.um.ql.bl.ʿm.|ʿnt w ʿṯtrt inbb h.mnt.nṯk.|nḥš.šlḥm.nḥš.ʿq šr[.yʿ]db.ksa.|nḥš.šmrr.nḥš.ʿq šr.ln h.ml|ḫ UG5.7.23
šmrr.|nḥš.ʿq šr.ln h.mlḫš.abd.ln h.|ydy.ḥmt.hlm.yṯq.nḥš.yšlḥm.|nḥš.ʿq šr.yʿdb.ksa.w yṯb.|tqru l špš.um h.špš.u UG5.7.17
šmrr.|nḥš.ʿq šr.ln h.mlḫš.abd.ln h.ydy.|ḥmt.hlm.yṯq.nḥš.yšlḥm.nḥš ʿq.|š.yʿdb.ksa w yṯb.|tqru l špš.um h.špš.um UG5.7.33
š.|ʿq šr.ln h.mlḫš abd.ln h.ydy.|ḥmt.hlm.yṯq yṯqšqy.nḥš.yšlḥm.ʿq šr.|yʿdb.ksa.w.yṯb.|tqru.l špš.um h.špš.um.ql UG5.7.6
|tn.km.nḥšm.yḥr.tn.km.|mhr y.w bn.bṯn.itnn y.|ytt.nḥšm.mhr k.bn bṯn.|itnn k.|aṯr ršp.ʿṯtrt.|ʿm ʿṯtrt.mr h.|m UG5.7.75
tqru l špš um h.špš um ql.bl.ʿm.|mlk.ʿṯtrt h.mnt.nṯk.nḥš.šmrr.|nḥš.ʿq šr.ln h.mlḫš abd.ln h.ydy.|ḥmt.hlm.yṯq.n UG5.7.41
špš.um h.špš.um.ql bl.|ʿm bʿl.mrym.ṣpn.mnt y.nṯk.|nḥš.šmrr.nḥš.ʿq šr ln h.|mlḫš.abd.ln h.ydy.ḥmt.hlm.yṯq.|n UG5.7.10
l špš.um h.špš.um.ql bl ʿm.|ṯṯ.w kmṯ.ḥryt h.mnt.nṯk.nḥš.šm|rr.nḥš.ʿq šr.ln h.mlḫš abd.ln h.|ydy.ḥmt.hlm.yṯq n UG5.7.36
špš.um.ql.bl.ʿm.|il.mbk nhrm.b ʿdt.thmtm.|mnt.nṯk.nḥš.šmrr.nḥš.|ʿq šr.ln h.mlḫš abd.ln h.ydy.|ḥmt.hlm.yṯq yṯ UG5.7.4
ʿṯtrt inbb h.mnt.nṯk.|nḥš.šlḥm.nḥš.ʿq šr[.yʿ]db.ksa.|nḥš.šmrr.nḥš.ʿq šr.ln h.ml|ḫš.abd.ln h.ydy.ḥmt.hlm.yṯq.|w UG5.7.21
tqru.l špš.um h.špš.[um.q]l bl.ʿm.|yrḫ.lrgt h.mnt.nṯk.n[ḥš].šmrr.|nḥš.ʿq šr.ln h.mlḫš.abd.ln h.ydy.|ḥmt.hlm.yṯq. UG5.7.26
tqru l špš.um h.špš.um.ql bl.|ʿm ḥrn.mṣd h.mnt.nṯk nḥš.|šmrr.nḥš.ʿq šr.ln h.mlḫš.|abd.ln h.ydy.ḥmt.|b ḥrn.pn UG5.7.58
yṯb.|tqru.l špš.um.ql bl.ʿm|kṯr.w ḫss.kptr h.mnt.nṯk.nḥš.|šmrr.nḥš.ʿq šr.ln h.mlḫš.abd.|ln h.ydy.ḥmt.hlm yṯq.n UG5.7.46
yṯb.|tqru.l špš.um h.špš.um.ql b.ʿm.|ršp.bbt h.mnt.nḥš.šmrr.|nḥš.ʿq šr.ln h.mlḫš.abd.ln h.ydy.|ḥmt.hlm.yṯq.n UG5.7.31
ṯb.|tqru.l špš.u h.špš.um.ql.bl.ʿm.|dgn.ttl h.mnt.nṯk.nḥš.šmrr.|nḥš.ʿq šr.ln h.mlḫš.abd.ln h.|ydy.ḥmt.hlm.yṯq.n UG5.7.15
špš.um h.špš.um.ql bl ʿm.|šḥr.w šlm šmm h mnt.nṯk.nḥš.|šmrr.nḥš ʿq šr.ln h.mlḫš.|abd.ln h.ydy ḥmt.hlm.yṯq š UG5.7.52
.špš.um.ql bl ʿm.|ṯṯ.w kmṯ.ḥryt h.mnt.nṯk.nḥš.šm|rr.nḥš.ʿq šr.ln h.mlḫš abd.ln h.|ydy.ḥmt.hlm.yṯq nḥš yšlḥm.n UG5.7.37
špš.um.ql bl.ʿm|kṯr.w ḫss.kptr h.mnt.nṯk.nḥš.|šmrr.nḥš.ʿq šr.ln h.mlḫš.abd.|ln h.ydy.ḥmt.hlm yṯq.nḥš.|yšlḥm. UG5.7.47
.l špš.um h.špš.um.ql b.ʿm.|ršp.bbt h.mnt.nḥš.šmrr.|nḥš.ʿq šr.ln h.mlḫš.abd.ln h.ydy.|ḥmt.hlm.yṯq.nḥš.yšlḥm.n UG5.7.32
h.mnt.nṯk.|nḥš.šlḥm.nḥš.ʿq šr[.yʿ]db.ksa.|nḥš.šmrr.nḥš.ʿq šr.ln h.ml|ḫš.abd.ln h.ydy.ḥmt.hlm.yṯq.|w yṯb.|tqr UG5.7.21
špš.u h.špš.um.ql.bl.ʿm.|dgn.ttl h.mnt.nṯk.nḥš.šmrr.|nḥš.ʿq šr.ln h.mlḫš.abd.ln h.|ydy.ḥmt.hlm.yṯq.nḥš.yšlḥm.| UG5.7.16
m h.špš um ql.bl.ʿm.|mlk.ʿṯtrt h.mnt.nṯk.nḥš.šmrr.|nḥš.ʿq šr.ln h.mlḫš abd.ln h.ydy.|ḥmt.hlm.yṯq.nḥš.yšlḥm.n UG5.7.42
h.špš.[um.q]l bl.ʿm.|yrḫ.lrgt h.mnt.nṯk.n[ḥš].šmrr.|nḥš.ʿq šr.ln h.mlḫš.abd.ln h.ydy.|ḥmt.hlm.yṯq.nḥš.yšlḥm.n UG5.7.27
.bl.ʿm.|il.mbk nhrm.b ʿdt.thmtm.|mnt.nṯk.nḥš.šmrr.nḥš.|ʿq šr.ln h.mlḫš abd.ln h.ydy.|ḥmt.hlm.yṯq yṯqšqy.nḥš. UG5.7.4
pš.um.ql bl ʿm.|šḥr.w šlm šmm h mnt.nṯk.nḥš.|šmrr.nḥš ʿq šr.ln h.mlḫš.|abd.ln h.ydy ḥmt.hlm.yṯq šqy.|nḥš.yšl UG5.7.53
.špš.um.ql bl.|ʿm bʿl.mrym.ṣpn.mnt y.nṯk.|nḥš.šmrr.nḥš.ʿq šr ln h.|mlḫš.abd.ln h.ydy.ḥmt.hlm.yṯq.|nḥš.yšlḥm. UG5.7.10
um h.špš.um.ql bl.|ʿm ḥrn.mṣd h.mnt.nṯk nḥš.|šmrr.nḥš.ʿq šr.ln h.mlḫš.|abd.ln h.ydy.ḥmt.|b ḥrn.pnm.trǵnw.w UG5.7.59
ʿq šr.ln h.mlḫš abd.ln h.|ydy.ḥmt.hlm.yṯq nḥš yšlḥm.nḥš.|ʿq.šr.yʿdb.ksa.w yṯb.|tqru l špš um h.špš um ql.bl.ʿm.| UG5.7.38
ʿq šr.ln h.mlḫš.abd.ln h.ydy.|ḥmt.hlm.yṯq.nḥš.yšlḥm.nḥš.|ʿq šr.yʿdb.ksa.w yṯb.|tqru.l špš.um h.špš.um.ql b.ʿm.| UG5.7.28
šr.ln h.mlḫš.abd.|ln h.ydy.ḥmt.hlm yṯq.nḥš.|yšlḥm.nḥš.ʿq šr.yʿdb ksa.|w yṯb.|tqru l špš.um h.špš.um.ql bl ʿm.| UG5.7.49
šr.ln h.mlḫš.abd.ln h.|ydy.ḥmt.hlm.yṯq.nḥš.yšlḥm.|nḥš.ʿq šr.yʿdb.ksa.w yṯb.|tqru l špš.um h.špš.um.ql.bl.ʿm.|ʿ UG5.7.18
ʿq šr.ln h.mlḫš.abd.ln h.ydy.|ḥmt.hlm.yṯq.nḥš.yšlḥm.nḥš ʿq.|š.yʿdb.ksa w yṯb.|tqru l špš.um h.špš.um.ql bl ʿm.|ṯ UG5.7.33
šr ln h.|mlḫš.abd.ln h.ydy.ḥmt.hlm.yṯq.|nḥš.yšlḥm.nḥš.ʿq šr.ydb.ksa.|w yṯb.|tqru.l špš.u h.špš.um.ql.bl.ʿm.|dg UG5.7.12
ʿq šr.ln h.mlḫš abd.ln h.ydy.|ḥmt.hlm.yṯq.nḥš.yšlḥm.nḥš.|ʿq šr.yʿdb.ksa.w yṯb.|tqru.l špš.um.ql bl.ʿm|kṯr.w ḫss. UG5.7.43
n h.mlḫš.|abd.ln h.ydy ḥmt.hlm.yṯq šqy.|nḥš.yšlḥm.nḥš.ʿq šr.yʿdb.|ksa.w yṯb.|tqru l špš.um h.špš.um.ql bl.|ʿm UG5.7.55
pš.um.ql.bl.ʿm.|ʿnt w ʿṯtrt inbb h.mnt.nṯk.|nḥš.šlḥm.nḥš.ʿq šr[.yʿ]db.ksa.|nḥš.šmrr.nḥš.ʿq šr.ln h.ml|ḫš.abd.ln h. UG5.7.23
m.|[---.]iṯ[-].yšql.ytk[.--]np bl.hn.|[---].ḫ[m]t.pṭr.w.p nḥš.|[---.--]q.n[t]k.l ydʿ.l bn.l pq ḥmt.|[---.--]n h.ḥmt.w tʿbt UG5.8.34
.bn bṯn.|itnn k.|aṯr ršp.ʿṯtrt.|ʿm ʿṯtrt.mr h.|mnt.nṯk.nḥš. UG5.7.TR3

nḫt

qḫ.il.mštʿltm.|mštʿltm.l riš.agn.yqḫ.tš.b bt h.|il.ḫṭ h.nḫt.il.ymnn.mṭ.yd h.yšu.|yr.šmm h.yr.b šmm.ʿṣr.yḫrṭ yšt.| 23[52].37
hr.ʿz.ym.l ymk.l tngṣn.pnt h.l ydlp.|tmn h.kṯr.ṣmdm.ynḫt.w ypʿr.šmt hm.|šm k.at.aymr.aymr.mr.ym.mr.ym.|l 2.4[68].18
.tṣmt.ṣrt k.|tqḫ.mlk.ʿlm k.drkt.dt dr dr k.|kṯr ṣmdm.ynḫt.w ypʿr.šmt hm.šm k at.|ygrš.ygrš.grš ym grš ym.l ksi 2.4[68].11
yḫrṭ yšt.|l pḥm.il.aṯtm.k ypt.hm.aṯtm.tṣḥn.|y mt.mt.nḫtm.ḫṭ k.mmnnm.mṭ.yd k.|h[l.]ʿṣr.tḥrr.l išt.ṣḥrrt.l pḥmm. 23[52].40
m.btm.bt.il.bt.il.|w ʿlm h.w hn.aṯtm.tṣḥn y.mt mt.|nḫtm.ḫṭ k.mmnnm.mṭ yd k.hl.ʿṣr.|tḥrr.l išt.w ṣḥrt.l pḥmm. 23[52].47
.|a[t]tm.aṯt.il.aṯt.il.w ʿlm h.w hm.|aṯtm.tṣḥn y.ad ad.nḫtm.ḫṭ k.|mmnnm.mṭ yd k.hl.ʿṣr.tḥrr.l išt.|w ṣḥrrt.l pḥm 23[52].43

nḫl

bʿ.mat.|arbʿm.kbd.|ṯlṯ.alp.ṣpr.dt.aḥd.|ḥrṯ h.aḥd.b gt.nḫl.|aḥd.b gt.knpy.w.aḥd.b gt.ṯrmn.|aḥd.alp.idṯn.d aḥd.b.ʿ 1129.9
ḫlm.lṭpn.il.d pid.|b ḏrt.bny.bnwt.|šmm.šmn.tmṭrn.|nḫlm.tlk.nbtm.|w idʿ.k ḥy.aliyn.bʿl.|k iṯ.zbl.bʿl.arṣ.|b ḫlm. 6[49].3.7
ḫlm.lṭpn.il.d pid.|b ḏrt.bny.bnwt.|šmm.šmn.tmṭrn.|nḫlm.tlk.nbtm.|šmḫ.lṭpn.il.d pid.|pʿn h.l hdm.yṯpd.|w ypr 6[49].3.13
|ulm.|izly.|uḫnp.|bn sḫrn.|mʿqb.|ṯpn.|mʿr.|lbnm.|nḫl.|yʿny.|atn.|utly.|bn.alz.|bn ḫlm.|bn.ḏmr.|bn.ʿyn.|ub 2075.11
|ltm.ybln h.mǵy.ḥrn.l bt h.w.|yštql.l ḥṭr h.tlu ḥt.km.nḫl.|tplg.km.plg.|bʿd h.bhtm.mnt.bʿd h.bhtm.sgrt.|bʿd h.ʿ UG5.7.68

nḫry

ṯlṯ.ṣmdm.|b.nḫry.|ṣmdm.b.ṯp[--].|aḥdm.b.gm[--]. 144[317].2

nṯṯ

ṣ.|[---.]ǵrm[.t]ḫšn.|rḥq[.---.tdʿ].|qdm ym.bmt.[nhr].|tṯṯn.ib.bʿl.tiḫd.|yʿrm.šnu.hd.gpt.|ǵr.w yʿn.aliyn.|bʿl.ib.hdt. 4[51].7.35
trt.|k tʿn.hlk.btlt.|ʿnt.tdrq.ybmt.|[limm].b h.pʿnm.|[tṭṭ.b ʿ]dn.ksl.|[ṯṯbr.ʿln.p]n h.td[ʿ].|tǵṣ[.pnt.ks]l h.|anš.dt.ẓr. 4[51].2.17
.nḫlt y.|b nʿm.b gbʿ.tliyt.|hlm.ʿnt.tph.ilm.b h.pʿnm.|tṭṭ.bʿd n.ksl.ṯṯbr.|ʿln.pn h.tdʿ.tǵṣ.pnt.|ksl h.anš.dt.ẓr h.tšu. 3[ʿNT].3.30

ṯ.|[--.]ydbr.ṯrmt.al m.qḥn y.š y.qḥn y.|[--.]šir.b krm.nṭṭt.dm.ʻlt.b ab y.|u---].ʻlt.b k.lk.l pn y.yrk.bʻl.[--].|[---.]ʻnt. 1001.1.9
r.[šṣat].|btlt.ʻnt.k [rḥ.npš h].|k iṯl.brlt h.[b h.pʻnm].|tṭṭ.ʻl[n.pn h.tdʻ.b ʻdn].|ksl.y[ṯbr.yǵṣ.pnt.ksl h].|anš.[dt.ẓr h 19[1AQHT].2.94

nṭʻ

il.[mt.rpi].|yṯb.ǵzr.mt hrnmy[.---].|b grnt.ilm.b qrb.m[ṭʻt.ilnym].|d tit.yspi.spu.q[--.---].|tpḥ.ṯṣr.shr[.---].|mr[.- 20[121].2.9
t k.btlt.ʻnt.|qrn.d bat k bʻl.ymšḥ.|bʻl.ymšḥ.hm.b ʻp.|nṭʻn.b arṣ.ib y.|w b ʻpr.qm.aḫ k.|w tšu.ʻn h.btlt.ʻnt.|w tšu.ʻ 10[76].2.24
m.w ṯa aḫr.š[pšm.b ṯlṯ].|mǵy.rpum.l grnt.i[lnym.l] |mṭʻt.w yʻn.dnil.[mt.rpi].|yṯb.ǵzr.mt hrnmy[.---].|b grnt.ilm 20[121].2.7
.w ṯn.aḫr.špšm].|b ṯlṯ.mǵy[.rpum.l grnt].|i[ln]y[m].l mṭʻt[.---].|[-]m[.---].|h.hn bn k.hn[.---].|bn bn.aṯr k.hn[.---] 22.1[123].26

nẓǵil

.|bn štn.|bn annyn.|b[n] slg.|u[--] dit.|bn p[-]n.|bn nẓǵil. 101[10].16

ny

|phy.|w ṯpllm.mlk.r[b.--].|mṣmt.l nqmd.[---.-]št.|hl ny.argmn.d [ybl.n]qmd.|l špš.arn.ṯn[.ʻšr h.]mn.|ʻṣrm.ṯql.kb 64[118].18
.|[ṯpṭ].nhr.tlʻm.ṯm.ḥrbm.its.anšq.|[-]htm.l arṣ.ypl.ul ny.w l.ʻpr.ʻẓm ny.|l bʻl[-.---].|ṯḥt.ksi.zbl.ym.w ʻn.kṯr.w ḫss.l 2.4[68].5
m.uṣbʻ[t].|[-]tr.šrk.il.|ʻrb.špš.l ymǵ.|krt.ṣbia.špš.|bʻl ny.w ymlk.|[y]ṣb.ʻln.w y[-]y.|[kr]t.ṯʻ.ʻln.bḫr.|[---].aṯt k.ʻl.|[15[128].5.20
.adt ny.|mrḥqtm.|qlny.ilm.|tǵr k.|tšlm k.|hn ny.ʻm ny.|kll.mid.|šlm.|w.ap.ank.|nḫt.ṯm ny.|ʻm.adt ny.|mnm.š 51[95].10
n.um y.|qlt.l.um y.|yšlm.ilm.|tǵr k.tšlm k.|hl ny.ʻm n[y].|kll.šlm.|ṯm ny.ʻm.um y.|mnm.šlm.|w.rgm.ṯṯb.l y.|b 50[117].9
.ilm.|tǵr k.tšlm k.|lḥt.šlm.k.lik[t].|um y.ʻm y.ht.ʻm[ny].|kll.šlm.ṯm ny.|ʻm.um y.mnm.šlm.|w.rgm.ṯṯb.l y.|w. 2009.1.6
.ṯm.ḥrbm.its.anšq.|[-]htm.l arṣ.ypl.ul ny.w l.ʻpr.ʻẓm ny.|l bʻl[-.---].|ṯḥt.ksi.zbl.ym.w ʻn.kṯr.w ḫss.l rgmt.|l k.l zb 2.4[68].5
.ʻm ny.|kll.mid.|šlm.|w.ap.ank.|nḫt.ṯm ny.|ʻm.adt ny.|mnm.šlm.|rgm.ṯṯb.|l.ʻbd k. 51[95].15
lm k.|hn ny.ʻm ny.|kll.mid.|šlm.|w.ap.ank.|nḫt.ṯm ny.|ʻm.adt ny.|mnm.šlm.|rgm.ṯṯb.|l.ʻbd k. 51[95].14
.|yšlm.ilm.|tǵr k.tšlm k.|hl ny.ʻm n[y].|kll.šlm.|ṯm ny.ʻm.um y.|mnm.šlm.|w.rgm.ṯṯb.l y.|bm.ṯy.ndr.|iṯt.ʻmn. 50[117].11
k.|lḥt.šlm.k.lik[t].|um y.ʻm y.ht.ʻm[ny].|kll.šlm.ṯm ny.|ʻm.um y.mnm.šlm.|w.rgm.ṯṯb.l y.|w.mndʻ.k.ank.|aḥš. 2009.1.7
.|yšlm.l k.[il]m.|tǵr k.tšlm k.|hn ny.ʻm n.š[l]m.|ṯm ny.ʻ[m.]bn y.|mnm.[šl]m[.r]gm[.ṯṯb].|ky.lik.bn y.|lḥt.akl.ʻ 2061.7
k.|y[š]lm.l k.ilm.|tǵr k.tšlm k.|hn ny.ʻm n.|šlm.ṯm ny.|ʻm k.mnm[.š]lm.|rgm.ṯṯ[b].|any kn.dt.|likt.mṣrm.|hn 2059.7
šlm.il[m].|tǵ[r] k.tš[lm] k.|[h]l ny.ʻm n[.š]lm.|w.ṯm [ny.ʻm.mlkt.u]m y.|mnm[.šlm].|w.rgm[.ṯṯb.l] y.|hl ny.ʻmn. 1013.9
m [y].|qlt[.l um] y.|yšlm.il[m].|tǵ[r] k.tš[lm] k.|[h]l ny.ʻm n[.š]lm.|w.ṯm [ny.ʻm.mlkt.u]m y.|mnm[.šlm].|w.rg 1013.8
n.|l.mlk.ugrt.|rgm.|yšlm.l k.[il]m.|tǵr k.tšlm k.|hn ny.ʻm n.š[l]m.|ṯm ny.ʻ[m.]bn y.|mnm.[šl]m[.r]gm[.ṯṯb].|ky 2061.6
.|ṯḥm.mlk.ṣr.aḫ k.|y[š]lm.l k.ilm.|tǵr k.tšlm k.|hn ny.ʻm n.|šlm.ṯm ny.|ʻm k.mnm[.š]lm.|rgm.ṯṯ[b].|any kn.d 2059.6
.|l.pʻn.adt ny.|mrḥqtm.|qlny.ilm.|tǵr k.|tšlm k.|hn ny.ʻm ny.|kll.mid.|šlm.|w.ap.ank.|nḫt.ṯm ny.|ʻm.adt ny.| 51[95].10
k.|l.pʻn.um y.|qlt.l.um y.|yšlm.ilm.|tǵr k.tšlm k.|hl ny.ʻm n[y].|kll.šlm.|ṯm ny.ʻm.um y.|mnm.šlm.|w.rgm.ṯṯb. 50[117].9
[ny.ʻm.mlkt.u]m y.|mnm[.šlm].|w.rgm[.ṯṯb.l] y.|hl ny.ʻmn.|mlk.b.ṯy ndr.|iṯt.w.ht.|[-]sny.uḏr h.|w.hm.ḫt.|ʻl. 1013.12
l um y.adt ny.|rgm.|ṯḥm.tlmyn.|w.aḫtmlk ʻbd k.|l.pʻn.adt ny.|mrḥqt 51[95].1
.adt ny.|rgm.|ṯḥm.tlmyn.|w.aḫtmlk ʻbd k.|l.pʻn.adt ny.|mrḥqtm.|qlny.ilm.|tǵr k.|tšlm k.|hn ny.ʻm ny.|kll.mi 51[95].5
.mid.w um.|tšmḫ.m ab.|w al.trḥln.|ʻtn.ḫrd.ank.|ʻm ny.šlm.|kll.|w mnm.|šlm ʻm.|um y.|ʻm y.ṯṯb.|rgm. 1015.14
[---].ap[.---].|[---].l y.l [---].|[---] ny.ṯp[-.---].|[---.--]zn.a[--.---].|[---.--]y.ns[--.---].|[---.]trgm[63[26].1.3
m.nkyt.ṯǵr[.---].|km.škllt.[---].|ʻr.ym.l bl[.---].|b[---.]ny[.--].|l bl.sk.w [---] h.|ybm h.šbʻ[.---].|ǵzr.ilḥu.t[---]l.|tr 16.2[125].92
[yš]lm[.ilm].|tǵr k[.tšlm k].|hl ny.[---].|w.pdr[--.---].|tmǵyn[.---].|w.mli[.---].|[-]kl.w [---]. 57[101].3

nyr

.izml.|ḫmš.kbd.arbʻm.|dd.akl.|ṯṯ.ʻšr h.yn.|kd.šmn.l.nr.ilm.|kdm.dǵm.|ṯṯ.kdm.ztm. 1126.6
rt.tǵr k.|tšlm k.um y.|tdʻ.ky.ʻrbt.|l pn.špš.|w pn.špš.nr.|b y.mid.w um.|tšmḫ.m ab.|w al.trḥln.|ʻtn.ḫrd.ank.|ʻm 1015.9
.ṯy.ndr.|iṯt.ʻmn.mlkt.|w.rgm y.l[--].|lqt.w.pn.|mlk.nr b n. 50[117].18
.mm h.|b smkt.ṣat.npš h.|[-]mt[-].ṣba.rbt.|špš.w tgh.nyr.|rbt.w rgm.l aḫt k.|ṯtmnt.krt n.dbḥ.|dbḥ.mlk.ʻšr.|ʻšrt. 16.1[125].37
ʻṯtr t|rḫ l k ybrdmy.b[t.a]|b h lb[u] yʻrr.w yʻ[n].|yrḫ nyr šmm.w nʻ[n].|ʻma nkl ḫtn y.a[ḫ]r.|nkl yrḫ ytrḫ.adn h. 24[77].31
d[n h.---].|dgn tt[--.---.-]l|ʻ.l kṯrt hl[l.sn]nt.|ylak yrḫ ny[r] šmm.ʻm.|ḫr[ḫ]b mlk qẓ.tn nkl y|rḫ ytrḫ.ib tʻrb m b b 24[77].16
.b y[--.---].|[-----].|[-----].|[-----].|[---.]mrkbt.|[---.--]a.nrm.|[---.--]y.lm[.-.]b k[p].|[---].tr[--.]gpn lk.|[---].km[-.---]. 1002.30

nk

[--].nk.[---].|[---.--]ḥ.an[--.---].|[---.]ʻly k[.---].|[---.]at.bt k[.---].| 1002.1

nky

dʻ.krt.mǵ[y.---].|w qbr.tṣr.q[br].|tṣr.trm.tnq[--].|km.nkyt.ṯǵr[.---].|km.škllt.[---].|ʻr.ym.l bl[.---].|b[---.]ny[.--].|l 16.2[125].89

nkl

ḥt.bt.ilt.ʻṣr[m.l ṣpn.š].|l ǵlmt.š.w l [---.l yrḫ].|gd[lt].l nkl[.gdlt.l bʻlt.bhtm].|ʻš[rm.]l inš[.ilm.---].|il[hm.]dqt.š[.---. 35[3].26
ḥt.bt.i[lt.ʻṣrm.l].|ṣpn š.l ǵlm[t.š.w l.---].|l yrḫ.gdlt.l [nkl.gdlt.l bʻ]|[lt].bht[m].[ʻ]ṣrm l [inš.ilm].|[---.]ilh[m.dqt.š.- APP.II[173].28
ašr nkl w ib[.bt].|ḫrḫb.mlk qẓ ḫrḫb m|lk aǵzt.b sǵ[--.]špš.|yrḫ 24[77].1
m h.|kp mznm.iḫ h yṯʻr.|mšrrm.aḫt h l a|bn mznm.nkl w ib.|d ašr.ar yrḫ.w y|rḫ yar k.|[ašr ilht kṯrt bn]|t hll. 24[77].37
.a]|b h lb[u] yʻrr.w yʻ[n].|yrḫ nyr šmm.w nʻ[n].|ʻma nkl ḫtn y.a[ḫ]r.|nkl yrḫ ytrḫ.adn h.|yšt mṣb.mznm.um h.| 24[77].32
.w yʻ[n].|yrḫ nyr šmm.w nʻ[n].|ʻma nkl ḫtn y.a[ḫ]r.|nkl yrḫ ytrḫ.adn h.|yšt mṣb.mznm.um h.|kp mznm.iḫ h yṯ 24[77].33
hl[l.sn]nt.|ylak yrḫ ny[r] šmm.ʻm.|ḫr[ḫ]b mlk qẓ.tn nkl y|rḫ ytrḫ.ib tʻrb m b bh|t h.w atn mhr h l a|b h.alp ks 24[77].17
abršp.qšt.|ssg.qšt.|ynḥm.qšt.|pprn.qšt.|uln.qšt.|bn.nkl qšt.|ady.qšt.|bn.srn.qšt.|bn.gdrn.qšt.|prpr.qšt.|ugry.q 119[321].1.40

nklb

bn.ymn. | bn.ṣry. | bn.mztn. | bn.šlgyn. | bn.[-]gštn. | bn[.n]klb. | b[n.]dtn. | w.nḥl h. | w.nḥl hm. | bn.iršyn. | bn.ʿzn. | bn. 113[400].2.8

mn. | bn.pity. | bn.iryn. | bn.ʿbl. | bn.grbn. | bn.iršyn. | bn.nklb. | bn.mryn. | [bn.]b[--]. | bn.ẓrl. | bn.illm[-]. | bn.š[---]. | bn. 115[301].4.20

-]. | [bn.]r[---]. | [bn.]ḥ[---]. | [bn.]šbl. | [bn.]ḫdmn. | [bn.]nklb. | [---]dn. | [---]y. | [-----]. | [-----]. | bn.adn. | prtn. | bn.btry. 1073.2.6

nkly

.ṭb.w.[--]. | ṯmn.kbd.yn.d.l.ṭb.b.gnʿ[y]. | mitm.yn.ḥsp.d.nkly.b.db[ḥ.--]. | mit.arbʿm.kbd.yn.ḥsp.l.m[--]. | mit.ʿšrm.[k] 1084.24

.kkrm.ṯlṯ. | mit.ksp.ʿmn. | bn.ulbtyn. | w.kkr.ṯlṯ. | ksp.d.nkly.b.šd. | mit.ḫmšt.kbd. | [l.]gmn.bn.usyy. | mit.ṯṯm.kbd. | l. 1143.6

[-] ym.prʿ d nkly yn kd w kd. | w ʿl ym kdm. | w b ṯlṯ.kd yn w krsnm. | w 1086.1

.[---.]yd.sǵr h. | [---.--]r h.ʿšr[m.---.ʿ]šrm.dd. | [---.yn.d.]nkly.l.rʿym.šbʿm.l.mitm.dd. | [---.--]d.šbʿm.kbd.drʿ. | [---.]kbd 1098.44

m[d h]. | ily[---]. | [-----]. | [---]lb[--]. | [---]m[.---]. | [---.]d nkly. | [---.]kbd[.---]. 1049.3.3

ṣrym. | arbʿm.yn. | l.ḫrd. | ḫmšm.ḫmš. | kbd.tgmr. | yn.d.nkly. 1089.15

nkr

| yšu.ʿwr.mzl. | ymzl.w yṣi.trḫ. | ḥdṯ.ybʿr.l ṯn. | aṯt h.lm.nkr. | mddt h.k irby. | [t]škn.šd. | km.ḥsn.pat.mdbr. | lk.ym.w 14[KRT].2.102

šu.ʿwr. | mzl.ymzl. | w ybl.trḫ.ḥdṯ. | ybʿr.l ṯn.aṯt h. | w l nkr.mddt. | km irby.tškn. | šd.k ḥsn.pat. | mdbr.tlkn. | ym.w ṯ 14[KRT].4.191

| abd.ln h.ydy.ḥmt. | b ḥrn.pnm.trǵnw.w ṯtkl. | bnwt h.ykr.ʿr.d qdm. | idk.pnm.l ytn.tk aršḫ.rbt. | w aršḫ.ṯrrt.ydy.b ʿ UG5.7.62

nkt

qṯṯn u ṯḫṯin.l bḥm.w l ṯʿ.d[bḥ n.ndbḥ]. | hw.ṯʿ.nṯʿy.hw.nkt.n[k]t.ytši[.l ab.bn.il]. | ytši.l dr.bn.il.l mpḫrt.bn.i[l.l ṯkm 32[2].1.16

šn yp km.l d[b]ḥm.w l.ṯʿ.dbḥ n.ndbḥ.hw.ṯʿ | nṯʿy. | hw.nkt.nkt.y[t]ši.l ab.bn.il.ytši.l dr. | bn il.l mpḫrt.bn.il.l ṯkmn[. 32[2].1.25

[---.hw.ṯʿ.nṯʿ]y. | [hw.nkt.nkt.ytši.l ab.bn.il.ytši.l d]r.bn[.il]. | [l mpḫrt.bn.il.l ṯkmn 32[2].1.2

tqṯṯ.u ṯḫṯu.l dbḥm.w l.ṯʿ.dbḥ n.ndb]ḥ. | [hw.ṯʿ.nṯʿy.hw.nkt.nkt.]yt[ši.l ab.bn.il]. | [ytši.l dr.bn.il.l mpḫ]rt.[bn.il.l ṯkm 32[2].1.9A

šn y[p kn.l dbḥm.]w l ṯʿ dbḥ n. | ndbḥ.hw.ṯʿ n[ṯʿy.hw.nkt.nk]t.ytši.l ab bn il. | ytši.l d[r.bn il.l]mpḫrt.bn il. | l ṯkm[32[2].1.33

y[p kn.l dbḥm.]w l ṯʿ dbḥ n. | ndbḥ.hw.ṯʿ n[ṯʿy.hw.nkt.nk]t.ytši.l ab bn il. | ytši.l d[r.bn il.l]mpḫrt.bn il. | l ṯkm[n.w 32[2].1.33

[---.hw.ṯʿ.nṯʿ]y. | [hw.nkt.nkt.ytši.l ab.bn.il.ytši.l d]r.bn[.il]. | [l mpḫrt.bn.il.l ṯkmn.w š 32[2].1.2

p km.l d[b]ḥm.w l.ṯʿ.dbḥ n.ndbḥ.hw.ṯʿ | nṯʿy. | hw.nkt.nkt.y[t]ši.l ab.bn.il.ytši.l dr. | bn il.l mpḫrt.bn.il.l ṯkmn[.w]š 32[2].1.25

u ṯḫṯu.l dbḥm.w l.ṯʿ.dbḥ n.ndb]ḥ. | [hw.ṯʿ.nṯʿy.hw.nkt.nkt.]yt[ši.l ab.bn.il]. | [ytši.l dr.bn.il.l mpḫ]rt.[bn.il.l ṯkmn.w 32[2].1.9A

u ṯḫṯin.l bḥm.w l ṯʿ.d[bḥ n.ndbḥ]. | hw.ṯʿ.nṯʿy.hw.nkt.n[k]t.ytši[.l ab.bn.il]. | ytši.l dr.bn.il.l mpḫrt.bn.i[l.l ṯkmn.w 32[2].1.16

nt.w[.---]. | šntm.alp.d krr[.---]. | alp.pr.bʿl.[---]. | w prt.tkt.[---]. | šnt.[---]. | ššw.ʿṯtrt.w ššw.ʿ[nt.---]. | w ht.[--]k.ššw[.-] 2158.1.4

nmq

b. | [-]lpl. | bn.asrn. | bn.šḫyn. | bn.abdʿn. | bn.ḫnqn. | bn.nmq. | bn.amdn. | bn.špšn. 1067.7

bn.nkt[-]. | bn.abḏr. | bn.ḥrẓn. | bn.ḏqnt. | bn.gmrš. | bn.nmq. | bn.špš[yn]. | bn.ar[--]. | bn.gb[--]. | bn.ḥn[n]. | bn.gntn[-] 2023.3.13

.rib. | w [---]. | [-----]. | [-]šy[.---] h. | [-]kt[.---.]nrn. | [b]n.nmq[.---]. | [ḫm]št.ksp.ʿl.aṯt. | [-]td[.bn.]štn. 2055.18

nmr

[--]. | [šp]š.b šmm.tq[ru.---.-]rt. | [---.]mn mn[-.---.--]n.nmr. | [--.]l ytk.bl[-.---.]m[--.]hwt. | [---].ṯllt.khn[m.---.]k pʿn. UG5.8.45

nmry

| ankn.rgmt.l.bʿl y. | l.špš.ʿlm.l.ʿṯtrt. | l.ʿnt.l.kl.il.alṯ[y]. | nmry.mlk.ʿlm. | mlk n.bʿl y.ḥw[t.--]. | yšhr k.w.ʿm.ṣ[--]. | ʿš[--. 2008.1.9

nmš

qšt.w.qlʿ. | bn.šmlbi.qšt.w.qlʿ. | bn.yy.qšt. | ilrb.qšt. | bn.nmš.ṯt.qšt.w.qlʿ. | bʿl.qšt.w.qlʿ. 119[321].4.16

nn

t.k šby n.zb[l.ym.k] | šby n.ṯpṭ.nhr.w yṣa b[.--]. | ybṯ.nn.aliyn.bʿl.w [---]. | ym.l mt.bʿl m.ym l[--.---]. | ḥm.l šrr.w [- 2.4[68].31

. | ynḥm.msg. | bn.ugr.msg. | bn.ǵlṣ msg. | arbʿ l tkṣ[-]. | nn.arspy.ms[g]. | [---.ms]g. | bn.[gr]gs.msg. | bn[.--]an.msg. | b 133[-].1.11

tdu.šrr. | ḥt m.tʿmt.[ʿ]ṯr.[k]m. | zbln.ʿl.riš h. | w ttb.trḥṣ.nn.b dʿt. | npš h.l lḥm.tptḥ. | brlt h.l trm. | mt.dm.ḫt.šʿtqt. | d 16.6[127].10

iṯ.ʿẓm.w yqḥ b hm. | aqht.ybl.l qẓ.ybky.w yqbr. | yqbr.nn.b mdgt.b knk[-]. | w yšu.g h.w yṣḥ.knp.nšrm. | bʿl.yṯbr.bʿl 19[1AQHT].3.147

y.yd h.w ym[ǵ]. | mlak k.ʿm dt[n]. | lqḥ.mṯpṭ. | w yʿny.nn. | dtn.bt n.mḫ[-]. | l dg.w [-]kl. | w aṯr.hn.mr[-]. UG5.6.13

t]. | yṯb l y.ṯr.il[.ab y.---]. | yṯb.l y.w l h.[---]. | [--.i]msḫ.nn.k imr.l arṣ. | [ašhlk].šbt h.dmm.šbt.dqn h. | [mmʿm.-]d.l y 3[ʿNT.VI].5.9

-.y]d gt h[.--]. | [---.]yd. | [k]rm h.yd. | [k]lkl h. | [w] ytn.nn. | l.bʿln.bn. | kltn.w l. | bn h.ʿd.ʿlm. | šḫr.ʿlmt. | bnš bnšm. | l. 1008.11

.špšm. | b šbʿ.w tmǵy.l udm. | rbm.w l.udm.ṯrrt. | w gr.nn.ʿrm.šrn. | pdrm.sʿt.b šdm. | ḥṭb h.b grnt.ḥpšt. | sʿt.b nk.šib 14[KRT].3.110

h yrd. | k ḥrr.ẓt.ybl.arṣ.w pr. | ʿṣm.yraun.aliyn.bʿl. | ṯtʿ.nn.rkb.ʿrpt. | tbʿ.rgm.l bn.ilm.mt. | ṯny.l ydd.il ǵzr. | tḥm.aliy 5[67].2.7

.y]n.ʿd šbʿ.trṯ.ʿd škr. | il.hlk.l bt h.yštql. | l ḥṭr h.yʿmsn.nn.ṯkmn. | w šnm.w ngšnn.hby. | bʿl.qrnm w ḏnb.ylšn. | b ḫri UG5.1.1.18

mǵy.adn. | ilm.rbm ʿm dtn. | w yšal.mṯpṭ.yld. | w yʿny.nn[.--]. | tʿny.n[---.-]tq. | w š[--.---]. | ḥdṯ[.---.]ḥ[--]. | b bt.[-.]l b UG5.6.4

]dt y.mrḥqm. | [---].adt y.yšlm. | [---.]mlk n.amṣ. | [.---].nn. | [---.]qrt.dt. | [---.--]sʿ.hn.mlk. | [---.l]qḥ.hn.l.ḥwt h. | [---.-- 1012.6

nni

--]. | dprn[.---]. | drʿ.[---]. | tmṯl[.---]. | mǵm[ǵ.---]. | w.š[t.nni.w.pr.ʿbk]. | w.pr[.ḥḏrt.w.št]. | irǵ[n.ḥmr.ydk]. | aḥd[h.w. 161[56].28

ḏr[t.ydk]. | aḥd h.w.yṣq[.b.ap h]. | k.yiḫd.akl.š[šw]. | št.nni.št.mk[št.grn]. | št.irǵn.ḥmr[.ydk]. | aḥd h.w.yṣq.b[.ap h]. 161[56].18

rṣbʿ. | arbʿ.bnšm.b.hzp. | arbʿ.bnšm.b.šql. | arbʿ.bnšm.b.nni. | ṯn.bnšm.b.slḫ. | [---].bnšm.b.yny. | [--.]bnšm.b.lbnm. | ar 2076.18

nnu

l[b]nm.|nnu.|'rm.|bṣr.|m'r.|ḫlby.|mṣbt.|snr.|ṯm.|ubš.|glbt.|mi[d 2041.2
[---.b]'lt.|lbnm.'šr.yn.|ḫlb.gngnt.ṯlṯ.y[n].|bṣr.'šr.yn.|nnu arb'.yn.|šql ṯlṯ.yn.|šmny.kdm.yn.|šmgy.kd.yn.|hzp.tš 2004.24
.|ḫpty.|ypr.|ḫrṣb'.|uḫnp.|art.|[--]n.|[-----].|[-----].|nnu.|šmg.|šmn.|lbnm.|ṯrm.|bṣr.|y[--].|y[--].|snr.|midḫ.| 2058.2.11
w.qmnz.|slḫ.|ykn'm.|šlmy.|w.ull.|ṯmry.|qrt.|'rm.|nnu.|[--].|[---].|m'r.|arny.|ubr'y.|ilštm'.|bir.|m'qb.|uškn 71[113].23
[-----].|bṣr[.---].|lbn[m].|'r[.---].|nnu[.---].|šq[--.---].|[-]r[-.---].|[-----].|[-----].|mg[--.---]. 2145.5

nnḏ

|wql.|adrdn.|prn.|'bdil.|ušy.šbn[-].|aḫt.ab.|krwn.|nnḏ.|mkl.|kzǵb.|iyrḏ. 1069.15

nnr

n.ab[--].|bn.al[--].|bn.nb[dg].|bn.ild[-].|[-----].|[bn.]nnr.|[bn.]aglby.|[bn.]b'ly.|[mḏ]rǵlm.|[bn.]kdgdl.|[b]n.qṭn 104[316].5

nsy

ṯrrt.ydy.b 'ṣm.'r'r.|w b šḥt.'s.mt.'r'rm.yn'rn h.|ssnm.ysyn h.'dtm.y'dyn h.yb|ltm.ybln h.mǵy.ḥrn.l bt h.w.|yštql. UG5.7.66
m.tḥt b'l[.---].|h.u qšt pn hdd.b y[.----].|'m.b ym b'l ysy ym[.---].|rmm.ḫnpm.mḫl[.---].|mlk.nhr.ibr[.---].|zbl b' 9[33].2.7
[-----].|[---.--]dn.|[---.--]dd.|[---.--]n.kb|[--.---.]al.yns.|[---.]ysd k.|[---.--]r.dr.dr.|[---.--]y k.w rḥd.|[---]y ilm. 4[51].3.5

nsk

'l.nsk.kṯṯǵlm.|arb'm.ṯlṯ.mḫsrn.|mtb'l.rišy.|ṯlṯm.ṯlṯ.'l.nsk.|arym.|alp.ṯlṯ.'l.|nsk.art.|ḫmš.mat.ṯlṯ.|'l.mtn.rišy. 1137.5
ṯ.mḫsrn.|mtb'l.rišy.|ṯlṯm.ṯlṯ.'l.nsk.|arym.|alp.ṯlṯ.'l.|nsk.art.|ḫmš.mat.ṯlṯ.|'l.mtn.rišy. 1137.8
spr.ḥṭbn.sbrdnm.|ḫmš.kkrm.alp kb[d].|ṯlṯ.l.nskm.birtym.|b d.urtn.w.ṯṯ.mat.brr.|b.ṯmnym.ksp.ṯlṯt.kbd. 2101.3
spn.m h.w trḥṣ.|ṭl.šmm.šmn.arṣ.ṭl.šm[m.t]sk h.|rbb.nsk h.kbkbm.|ttpp.anhbm.d alp.šd[.ẓu h.b ym].|ṭl[.---]. 3['NT].4.88
[ṭ]l.šmm.šmn.arṣ.rbb.|[r]kb 'rpt.ṭl.šmm.tsk h.|[rb]b.nsk h.kbkbm. 3['NT].2.41
tk.|pn h.tḥspn.m h.w trḥṣ.|ṭl.šmm.šmn.arṣ.ṭl.šm[m.t]sk h.|rbb.nsk h.kbkbm.|ttpp.anhbm.d alp.šd[.ẓu h.b ym]. 3['NT].4.87
m h.w trḥṣ.|[ṭ]l.šmm.šmn.arṣ.rbb.|[r]kb 'rpt.ṭl.šmm.tsk h.|[rb]b.nsk h.kbkbm. 3['NT].2.40
.---].|km.škllt.[---].|'r.ym.l bl[.---].|b[---.]ny[.--].|l bl.sk.w [---] h.|ybm h.šb'[.---].|ǵzr.ilḥu.t[---]l.|trm.tṣr.trm[.']t 16.2[125].93
'zn.mtn.n[bd]g.|ḥrš qṭn[.---.]dqn.b'ln.|ǵltn.'bd.[---].|nsk.ḥdm.klyn[.ṣd]qn.'bdilt.b'l.|annmn.'dy.klby.dqn.|ḥrṯm. 2011.25
t.|'šr.ḥrš.|bhtm.lqḥ.|š'rt.|arb'.|ḥrš qṭn.|lqḥ š'rt.|ṯṯ nsk.ḥdm.|lqḥ.š'rt. 2052.14
ḏrǵlm.|agmy.|'dyn.|'bdb'l.|'bdkṯr.'bd.|tdǵl.|b'lṣn.|nsk.ksp.|iwrtn.|ydln.|'bdilm.|dqn.|nsk.ṯlṯ.|'bdadt.|bṣmn. 1039.2.23
qd[šm].|mru s[kn].|mru ib[rn].|mdm.|inšt.|nsk ksp.|yṣḥm.|ḥrš mrkbt.|ḥrš qṭn.|ḥrš bhtm. 73[114].6
|yṣḥm.|'šrm.|mrum.|ṯnnm.|mqdm.|khnm.|qdšm.|nsk.ksp.|mkrm. 71[113].74
nsk k[sp].|'šrt.|w nṣ[p]. 1164.1
.|[-]ntn.artn.b d[.--]nr[.---].|'zn.w ymd.šr.b d ansny.|nsk.ks[p.--]mrtn.kṯrmlk.|yḥmn.aḫm[l]k.'bdrpu.adn.ṯ[--].|b 2011.32
mit.ṯlṯ.mḫsrn.|'l.nsk.kṯṯǵlm.|arb'm.ṯlṯ.mḫsrn.|mtb'l.rišy.|ṯlṯm.ṯlṯ.'l.nsk.|ar 1137.2
|šrg k.ḫḫm.mt.uḫryt.mh.yqḥ.|mh.yqḥ.mt.aṯryt.spsg.ysk.|[l]riš.ḥrṣ.l ẓr.qdqd y.|[--.]mt.kl.amt.w an.mtm.amt.|[17[2AQHT].6.36
m.|trrm.|khnm.|kzym.|yṣrm.|mru.ibrn.|mru.skn.|nsk.ksp|mḫṣm.|ksdm.|mḏrǵlm.|pslm.|yṣḥm. 74[115].14
[---.-]yt š[--.---].|[---.]hl[-.---].|[---.-]ytr.ur[--.---].|[---.n]skt.n'mn.nbl[.---].|[--.]yṣq šmn.šlm.b ṣ['.trḥṣ].|yd h.btlt.' UG5.3.2.3
[k.ym]ḫṣ.b'l m[.--]y.tnn.w ygl.w ynsk.'[-].|[--]y.l arṣ[.id]y.alt.l aḫš.idy.alt.in l y.|[--]t.b'l.ḥẓ.r 1001.1.1
qlm.|bn.'my.ṯqlm.|bn.brq.ṯqlm.|bn.ḫnzr.ṯqlm.|dqn.nsk.arb't.|bn.ḫdyn.ṯqlm.|bn.'bd.šḫr.ṯqlm.|bn.ḫnqn.arb't.|[122[308].1.17
spr.argmn.nskm.|rqdym.|šṭšm.ṯṯ mat.|ṣprn.ṯṯ mat.|ḏkry.ṯṯ mat.|[p]l 1060.1.1
t.l]ṯpn.ḥtk k.|[qryy.b arṣ.mlḥ]mt.št b 'p|[r m.ddym.sk.šlm].l kbd.arṣ.|[arbdd.l kbd.š]dm.ḥš k.|['ṣ k.'bṣ k.'m y.p 1['NT.IX].2.20
]rn h.aqry.|[---.]b a[r]ṣ.mlḥmt.|ašt[.b ']p[r] m.ddym.ask.|šlm.l kb[d].awṣ.arbdd.|l kbd.š[d]m.ap.mṯn.rgmm.|ar 3['NT].4.73
.hwt.aliy.|qrdm.qry.b arṣ.mlḥmt.|št.b 'p[r] m.ddym.sk.šlm.|l kbd.arṣ.arbdd.l kbd.šdm.|[ḥ]š k.[']ṣ k.'bṣ k.'m y.p 3['NT].4.53
l.hwt.|aliy.qrdm.qry.b arṣ.|mlḥmt št.b 'pr m.ddym.|sk.šlm.l kbd.arṣ.|arbdd.l kbd.šdm.|ḥš k.'ṣ k.'bṣ k.|'m y.p'n 3['NT].3.13
.]limm.[a]n.aqry.|[b arṣ].mlḥmt.[aš]t.b 'pr m.|ddym.ask[.šlm.]l kbd.arṣ.|ar[bdd.]l kb[d.š]dm.yšt.|[----.]b'l.mdl h 3['NT].4.68
w[t.aliy.qrdm.qryy.b arṣ.mlḥmt.št].|[b ']pr[m.ddym.sk.šlm.l kbd.arṣ.arbdd].|l kbd.š[dm.ḥš k.'ṣ k.'bṣ k.'m y.p'n 7.2[130].15
|[bn].mṣrn.|[a]ršwn.|'b[d].|w nḥl h.|atn.bn.ap[s]n.|nsk.ṯlṯ.|bn.[--.]m[-]ḫr.|bn.šmrm.|ṯnnm.|[ar]swn.bn.qqln.| 85[80].3.8
.|mkrm.|yṣḥm.|šrm.|n'rm.|'bdm.|kzym.|ksdm.|[nsk].ṯlṯ.|gt.mlkym.|tmrym.|ṯnqym.|ṯǵrm.|mru.skn.|mru. 1026.2.1
d.|tdǵl.|b'lṣn.|nsk.ksp.|iwrtn.|ydln.|'bdilm.|dqn.|nsk.ṯlṯ.|'bdadt.|bṣmn.spr. 1039.2.28
lṯ[.---].|[---.--]l.rb.kzym.|[---]y.|[-----].|[-----].|[--]dt.nsk.ṯlṯ.|['b]dršp.nsk.ṯlṯ.|[-]lkynt.nsk.ṯlṯ.|[-]by.nsk.ṯlṯ.|šmn 1102.7
[--]dt.nsk.ṯlṯ.|['b]dršp.nsk.ṯlṯ.|[-]lkynt.nsk.ṯlṯ.|[-]by.nsk.ṯlṯ.|šmny.|ḫršn.|ldn.|bn.ands.|bn.ann.|bn.'bdpdr.|šd 1102.10
[-----].|[-----].|[--]dt.nsk.ṯlṯ.|['b]dršp.nsk.ṯlṯ.|[-]lkynt.nsk.ṯlṯ.|[-]by.nsk.ṯlṯ.|šmny.|ḫršn.|ldn.|bn.ands.|bn.ann.| 1102.9
b.kzym.|[---]y.|[-----].|[-----].|[--]dt.nsk.ṯlṯ.|['b]dršp.nsk.ṯlṯ.|[-]lkynt.nsk.ṯlṯ.|[-]by.nsk.ṯlṯ.|šmny.|ḫršn.|ldn.|bn 1102.8
ṯlṯ.d yṣa.|b d.šmmn.|l argmn.|l nskm.|ṯmn.kkrm.|alp.kbd.|[m]itm.kbd. 147[90].4
y'dd.tḥt.bn arbn.|'bdil.tḥt.ilmlk.|qly.tḥt b'ln.nsk. 1053.3

nskn

šmmn.bn.'dš.ṯṯ mat.|ušknym.|yp'.alpm.|aḫ[m]lk.bn.nskn.alpm.|krw.šlmy.|alpm.|atn.bṣry.alpm.|lbnym.|ṯm[n 1060.2.3
---].|[-----].|[bn.a]mdy.|bn.ḫlln.|bn.kṯn.|bn.abn.|bn.nskn.|bn.gmrn.|bn[.-]škn.|[---.--]n.|[---.--]n.|[--.]'[--].|[bn] 2021.2.6

nsl

spr.ḥrš.|qštiptl.|bn.anny.|ilṣdq.|ypltn.bn iln.|špšm.nsl h.|[-----]. 1037.6

ns'

t.ik.tmt[h̲] | ṣ.'m.aliyn.b'l. | ik.al.yšm['] k.t̲r. | il.ab k.l ys'.alt. | t̲bt k.l yhpk.ksa.mlk k. | l yt̲br.ḫṭ.mṯpṭ k. | yru.bn il 6[49].6.27
pn.zbl.ym.l pn[.t̲]pṭ[.n]hr. | [ik.a]l.yšm' k.t̲r.[i]l.ab k.l ys'.[alt.]t̲[bt | k.l y]hpk. | [ksa.]mlk k.l yt̲br.ḫṭ.mṯpṭ k.w y'n[. 2.3[129].17
nr.d 'l k.mh̲ṣ.aqht. | ǵzr.šrš k.b arṣ.al. | yp'.riš.ǵly.b d.ns' k. | 'nt.brḥ.p 'lm h. | 'nt.p dr.dr.'db.uh̲ry mṭ yd h. | ymǵ.l 19[1AQHT].3.160

nsš

rm.t̲n.ym. | tš[.---.]ymm.lk. | hrg.ar[b'.]ymm.bṣr. | kp.šsk k.[--].l ḥbš k. | 'tk.ri[š.]l mhr k. | w 'p.l dr['].nšr k. | w rbṣ. 13[6].6

n'l

rgt.b dm.h̲rṣ. | kḥt̲.il.nḥt̲. | b ẓr.hdm.id. | d pršа.b br. | n'l.il.d qblbl. | 'ln.ybl hm.h̲rṣ. | t̲lḥn.il.d mla. | mnm.dbbm.d | 4[51].1.37
-]. | [---.]akl[.---]. | [---.-]l[-.-]hg[.---]. | [---.-]r[-.il]m.rbm.n'l[.-]gr. | [---.]'ṣ.b d h.ydrm[.]pi[-.]adm. | [---.]it̲[-].yšql.ytk[.- UG5.8.31
.--]y.yd.nšy.[---.--]š.l mdb. | [---] h.mh̲lpt[.---.--]r. | [---.]n'lm.[---]. | [---].hn.al[-.---]. | [---]t.bn[.---]. UG5.8.50

n'm

[--.--]. | pamt.šb'. | iqnu.šmt[.---]. | [b]n.šrm. | iqran.ilm.n'mm[.agzry ym.bn]ym. | ynqm.b ap zd.at̲rt.[---]. | špš.mṣpr 23[52].23
[---]. | ahpk k.l[--.---]. | t̲mm.w lk[.---]. | w lk.ilm[.---]. | n'm.ilm[.---]. | šgr.mu[d.---]. | šgr.mud[.---]. | dm.mt.aṣ[ḥ.---]. 5[67].3.15
.w ank. | ibǵy h.b tk.ǵr y.il.ṣpn. | b qdš.b ǵr.nḥlt y. | b n'm.b gb'.tliyt. | hlm.'nt.tph.ilm.b h.p'nm. | tṭṭ.b'd n.ksl.t̲tbr. 3['NT].3.28
n h.w t'n. | w t'n.arh̲.w tr.b lkt. | tr.b lkt.w tr.b h̲l. | [b]n'mm.b ysmm.ḥ[--]k.ǵrt. | [ql].l b'l.'nt.ttnn. | [---].b'l m.d ip[10[76].2.30
]. | l alp.ql.ẓ[--.---]. | l np ql.nd.[----]. | tlk.w tr.b[h̲l]. | b n'mm.b ys[mm.---]. | arh̲.arh̲.[---.tld]. | ibr.tld[.l b'l]. | w rum. 10[76].3.19
mslmt.b ǵr.tliyt. | w t'l.bkm.b arr. | bm.arr.w b ṣpn. | b n'm.b ǵr.t[l]iyt. | ql.l b'l.ttnn. | bšrt.il.bš[r.b']l. | w bšr.ḥtk.dgn 10[76].3.32
ynqm.b a[p.]d̲[d.r]gm.l il.ybl. | at̲t y.il.ylt.mh.ylt.ilmy n'mm. | agzr ym.bn ym.ynqm.b ap.d̲d.št.špt. | l arṣ.špt l šm 23[52].60
spr.l h̲mš.l ṣ[---.]šr.ph̲r.klat. | tqtnṣn.w tldn.tld.[ilm.]n'mm.agzr ym. | bn.ym.ynqm.b a[p.]d̲[d.r]gm.l il.ybl. | at̲t y. 23[52].58
bt y.ttn. | tn.l y.mt̲t.ḥry. | n'mt.špḥ.bkr k. | d k.n'm.'nt.n'm h. | km.tsm.'t̲trt.ts[m h]. | d 'q h.ib.iqni.'p['p] h. | sp.t̲rml 14[KRT].3.145
t y.ttn.tn. | l y.mt̲t.ḥry. | n'mt.šbḥ.bkr k. | d k n'm.'nt. | n'm h.km.tsm. | 't̲trt.tsm h. | d 'q h.ib.iqni. | 'p'p h.sp.t̲rml. | d 14[KRT].6.292
t̲m tgrgr.l abnm.w l.'ṣm.šb'.šnt. | tmt.t̲mn.nqpt.'d.ilm.n'mm.ttlkn. | šd.tṣdn.pat.mdbr.w ngš.hm.nǵr. | mdr'.w ṣḥ h 23[52].67
t.ttlk.w tṣd.kl.ǵr. | l kbd.arṣ.kl.gb'. | l [k]bd.šdm.tmǵ.l n'm[y]. | [arṣ.]dbr.ysmt.šd. | [šḥl]mmt.t[mǵ.]l b'l.np[l]. | [l a] 5[67].6.28
gb'. | l kbd.šdm.npš.h̲srt. | bn.nšm.npš.hmlt. | arṣ.mǵt.l n'm y.arṣ. | dbr.ysmt.šd.šḥlmmt. | ngš.ank.aliyn b'l. | 'dbnn a 6[49].2.19
.g hm.w tṣ]ḥ.sbn. | [---]l[.---.]'d. | ksm.mhyt[.m]ǵny. | l n'm y.arṣ.dbr. | l ysmt.šd.šḥlmmt. | mǵny.l b'l.npl.l a | rṣ.mt. 5[67].6.6
mk.b šb['.]ymm.tb'.b bt h. | kt̲rt.bnt.hll.snnt. | [-]d[-]t.n'm y.'rš.h[--]m. | ysmsmt.'rš.h̲lln.[-]. | yt̲b.dnil.[l s]pr yrh̲ h. 17[2AQHT].2.41
rh̲.l.ml[k]. | [--]t.w.lqḥ. | yn[.--].b dn h. | w.ml[k].šswm.n'mm. | ytn.l.'bdyrh̲. | w.mlk.z[--.--]n.šswm. | n'mm.[--].t̲tm. 2064.16
m.arṣ. | l ksm.mhyt.'n. | l arṣ.m[t]r.b'l. | w l šd.mṭr.'ly. | n'm.l arṣ.mṭr.b'l. | w l šd.mṭr.'ly. | n'm.l ḥṭt.b gn. | bm.nrt.ks 16[126].3.7
.b'l. | w l šd.mṭr.'ly. | n'm.l arṣ.mṭr.b'l. | w l šd.mṭr.'ly. | n'm.l ḥṭt.b gn. | bm.nrt.ksmm. | 'l.tl[-]k.'ṭrṭrm. | nšu.[r]iš.ḥrt̲ 16[126].3.9
[---.]l mdgkbr. | [---] y.'m k. | [-]tn.l.stn. | [--.]d.n'm.lbš k. | [-]dm.t̲n id. | [--]m.d.l.n'mm. | [lm.]l.likt.'m y. | [-- 2128.1.4
k. | [-]tn.l.stn. | [--.]d.n'm.lbš k. | [-]dm.t̲n id. | [--]m.d.l.n'mm. | [lm.]l.likt.'m y. | [---.]'bd.ank. | [---.'b]d k. | [---.--]l y.' 2128.1.6
| t̲lt̲.m[a]t.art.ḥkpt. | mit.dnn. | mitm.iqnu. | h̲mš.'šr.qn.n'm.'n[m]. | t̲n.ḥblm.alp.alp.am[-]. | t̲mn.ḥblm.šb'.šb'.ma[-]. | 1128.29
.[i]n. | b bt y.ttn.tn. | l y.mt̲t.ḥry. | n'mt.šbḥ.bkr k. | d k n'm.'nt. | n'm h.km.tsm. | 't̲trt.tsm h. | d 'q h.ib.iqni. | 'p'p h.s 14[KRT].6.291
p d.in.b bt y.ttn. | tn.l y.mt̲t.ḥry. | n'mt.špḥ.bkr k. | d k.n'm.'nt.n'm h. | km.tsm.'t̲trt.ts[m h]. | d 'q h.ib.iqni.'p['p] h. 14[KRT].3.145
.b h̲mr. | rbt.ymsk.b msk h. | qm.ybd.w yšr. | mṣltm.bd.n'm. | yšr.ǵzr.ṭb.ql. | 'l.b'l.b ṣrrt. | ṣpn.ytmr.b'l. | bnt h.y'n.pdr 3['NT].1.19
.l[-] | n k.ḥtk k.nmrt k.b tk. | ugrt.l ymt.špš.w yrh̲. | w n'mt.šnt.il. UG5.2.2.12
ḥtrš.w [a]škn. | aškn.ydt.[m]rṣ gršt. | zbln.r[---].ymlu. | n'm.[-]t̲[-.--.]yqrṣ. | d[-] b pḥ[-.--.]mh̲t. | [---.]tnn. | [---.]tnn. 16[126].5.29
k].šswm.n'mm. | ytn.l.'bdyrh̲. | w.mlk.z[--.--]n.šswm. | n'mm.[--].t̲tm.w.at. | nǵt.w.ytn.hm.l k. | w.lḥt.alpm.ḥršm. | k. 2064.19
.'ẓpn.l pit. | m[--]m[.--]tm.w mdbḥt. | h̲r[.---.]'l.kbkbt. | n'm.[--.-]llm.trtḥṣ. | btlt.'n[t].tptr' t̲d[h]. | limm.w t'l.'m.il. | a 13[6].18
iqra.ilm.n['mm.---]. | w ysmm.bn.š[---]. | ytnm.qrt.l 'ly[.---]. | b mdbr.š 23[52].1
.šb' d m.dǵ[t̲.---]t. | tlk m.rḥmy.w tṣd[.---]. | tḥgrn.ǵzr.n'm.[---]. | w šm.'rbm.yr[.---]. | mt̲bt.ilm.t̲mn.t̲[--.--]. | pamt.š 23[52].17
[---.]w rm tp h. | [---.-]lu mm l n'm. | [---.]w rm t̲lbm t̲lb. | [---.-]pr l n'm. | [---.-]mt w rm tp h UG5.5.2
m t̲lb. | [---.-]pr l n'm. | [---.-]mt w rm tp h. | [---.-]h̲b l n'm. | [---.]ymǵy. | [---.]rm t̲lbm. | [---.--]m. | [---.--]ḥ n'm. UG5.5.6
h. | [---.-]lu mm l n'm. | [---.]w rm t̲lbm t̲lb. | [---.-]pr l n'm. | [---.-]mt w rm tp h. | [---.-]h̲b l n'm. | [---.]ymǵy. | [---.]r UG5.5.4
b l n'm. | [---.]ymǵy. | [---.]rm t̲lbm. | [---.--]m. | [---.--]ḥ n'm. UG5.5.10

n'my

[-----]. | [---.--]yn. | [---.]at̲rn. | [---.--]h̲t. | [---.]b'ly. | [---.]n'my. | [---.-]ml. | [---.-]mn. | [---.-]rn. | [---.--]n. 102.5B[323.5].6

n'myn

byt. | bn h̲dl. | bn ṣdqn. | bn ayy. | bn dbb. | w nḥl h. | bn n'myn. | bn at̲tyy. | bn h̲lp. | bn.ẓll. | bn ydy. | bn lzn. | bn.t̲yn. | 2016.1.9

n'mn

d h krm[m]. | šd dd h ḥrnqm.w | y'n h̲rh̲b mlk qẓ [l]. | n'mn.ilm l h̲t[n]. | m.b'l trh̲ pdry b[t h]. | aqrb k ab h b'[l]. | y 24[77].25
b[dym.---]. | qmnz.t̲t̲.krm.ykn'm.t̲mn.krm[.---]. | krm.n'mn.b.h̲ly.ull.krm.aḥ[d.---]. | krm.uh̲n.b.šdmy.t̲lt̲.bzl[.d]pr 1081.12
nqq. | ḥrš.bhtm. | bn.izl. | bn.ibln. | bn.ilt. | špšyn.nḥl h. | n'mn.bn.iryn. | nrn.nḥl h. | bn.ḥsn. | bn.'bd. | [-----]. | [---.n]ḥ[l 85[80].2.7
l. | bn.ḥswn. | mrynm. | 'zn. | ḥyn. | 'myn. | ilyn. | yrb'm. | n'mn. | bn.kbl. | kn'm. | bdlm. | bn.ṣǵr. | klb. | bn.mnḥm. | bn.br 1046.3.39
qn.šlmn. | prdn.ndb[--]. | [-]rn.h̲bty. | abmn.bn.qdmn. | n'mn.bn.'bdilm. 87[64].41
. | klby.bn.ih̲y.t̲kt. | psš.bn.buly.t̲kt. | 'pṣpn.bn.'dy.t̲kt. | n'mn.bn.'yn.t̲kt. | 'ptn.bn.ilrš.t̲kt. | ilt̲hm.bn.šrn.t̲kt. | šmlbu.b 2085.10
t. | b.bn.mnn.t̲t̲m. | b.rpan.bn.yyn.'šrt. | b.yp'r.'šrm. | b.n'mn.bn.ply.h̲mšt.l.'šrm. | b.gdn.bn.uss.'šrm. | b.'dn.bn.t̲t̲.'šr 2054.1.17
b'l.k yḥwy.y'šr.ḥwy.y'š. | r.w yšqyn h.ybd.w yšr.'l h. | n'm[n.w t]'nynn.ap ank.aḥwy. | aqht[.ǵz]r.w y'n.aqht.ǵzr. | a 17[2AQHT].6.32
tbšn. | bn.mnyy.š'rty. | aryn.ad̲ddy. | agptr. | šb'l.mlky. | n'mn.mṣry. | y'l.kn'ny. | gdn.bn.umy. | kn'm.š'rty. | abrpu.ubr 91[311].6

yt š[--.---].|[---.]hl[-.---].|[---.-]yṯr.ur[--.---].|[---.n]skt.n‘mn.nbl[.---].|[--.]yṣq šmn.šlm.b ṣ[‘.trḥṣ].|yd h.btlt.‘nt.uṣb UG5.3.2.3
ry k.b ntb.pš‘.|[---].b ntb.gan.ašql k.tḥt.|[p‘n y.a]nk.n‘mn.‘mq.nšm.|[td‘ṣ.p‘n]m.w tr.arṣ.idk.|[l ttn.pn]m.‘m il. 17[2AQHT].6.45
m‘.l btlt.‘nt.at.‘[l.qšt h].|tmḫṣ h.qṣ‘t h.hwt.l t[ḥwy].|n‘mn.ǵzr.št.ṯrm.w[---].|ištir.b ḏdm.w n‘rs[.---].|w t‘n.btlt.‘ 18[3AQHT].4.14
m.|[ymn.]brkm.ybrk.|[‘bd h.]ybrk.il.krt.|[ṯ‘.ymr]m.n‘m[n.]ǵlm.il.|a[ṯt.tq]ḥ.y krt.aṯt.|tqḥ.bt k.ǵlmt.tš‘rb.|ḥqr k 15[128].2.20
y[n.]b‘l.|[---.]tb‘.l ltpn.|[il.d]pid.l tbrk.|[krt.]ṯ‘.l tmr.n‘mn.|[ǵlm.]il.ks.yiḫd.|[il.b]yd.krpn.bm.|[ymn.]brkm.ybr 15[128].2.15
h.|ab adm.w yqrb.|b šal.krt.m at.|krt.k ybky.|ydm‘.n‘mn.ǵlm.|il.mlk[.ṯ]r ab h.|yarš.hm.drk[t].|k ab.adm.|[---- 14[KRT].1.40
.ṯa]rm.amid.|[w y‘n].ṯr.ab h.il.|d[--].b bk.krt.|b dm‘.n‘mn.ǵlm.|il.trḥṣ.w tadm.|rḥṣ[.y]d k.amt.|uṣb[‘t k.]‘d[.ṯ]k 14[KRT].2.61
‘mm.pbl.|mlk.tšan.|g hm.w tṣḥn.|ṯḥm.krt.ṯ[‘].|hwt.[n]‘mn.[ǵlm.il]. 14[KRT].6.306
ršpab.qšt.w.ql‘.|pdrn.qšt.w.ql‘.|bn.pǵm[-.qšt].w.ql‘.|n‘mn.q[št.w.]ql‘.|[t]tn.qš[t].|bn.ṯǵdy[.qšt.]w.ql‘.|ṯty.qšt[.w. 119[321].4.2
spr.bdlm.|n‘mn.|rbil.|plsy.|ygmr.|mnṯ.|prḫ.|‘dršp.|ršpab.|ṯnw.|ab 1032.2
ṯqbn.qšt.|bn.qnmlk.qšt.|ytḥm.qšt.|grp.qšt.|m‘rby.|n‘mn.ṯt.qštm.w.ql‘.|gln.ṯt.qštm.w.ql‘.|gtn.qšt.|pmn.ṯt.qšt. 104[316].9
twm.|[-]bln.|[-]bldn.|[-]bdy.|[b]‘ln.|[-]šdm.|iwryn.|n‘mn.|[-----].|b gt.yny.|agttp.|bn.‘nt.|ǵzldn.|ṯrn.|ḫdbṯ.|[- 1043.8

n‘mt

l.yṣǵd.mli[.--].|il hd.mla.u[--.--].|blt.p btlt.‘n[t].|w p.n‘mt.aḫt[.b‘l].|y‘l.b‘l.b ǵ[r.---].|w bn.dgn.b š[---].|b‘l.yṯb.l k 10[76].3.11
yšu.‘n h.aliyn.b‘l.|w yšu.‘n h.w y‘n.|w y‘n.btlt.‘nt.|n‘mt.bn.aḫt.b‘l.|l pnn h.ydd.w yqm.|l p‘n h.ykr‘.w yql.|w 10[76].2.16
bt.b trbṣ.|bn.amt.p d.[i]n.|b bt y.ttn.tn.|l y.mṯt.ḥry.|n‘mt.šbḥ.bkr k.|d k n‘m.‘nt.|n‘m h.km.tsm.|‘ṯtrt.tsm h.|d 14[KRT].6.290
dlt hm[.---].|w ǵnbm.šlm.‘rbm.ṯn[nm].|hlkm.b dbḥ n‘mt.|šd[.i]lm.šd.aṯrt.w rḥmy.|[---].y[ṯ]b.|[---]p.gp ym.w y 23[52].27
bt.|b trbṣt.bn.amt.|p d.in.b bt y.ttn.|tn.l y.mṯt.ḥry.|n‘mt.špḥ.bkr k.|d k.n‘m.‘nt.n‘m h.|km.tsm.‘ṯtrt.ts[m h].|d 14[KRT].3.144

n‘r

.---].|šm[-.---].|tkn[.---].|knn.b.ḫ[lb].|bn mṯ.b.qmy.|n‘r.b.ulm. 2046.2.6
bt.ydrm.|ṯt.aṯtm.adrtm.w.pǵt.aḥt.b[.bt.---].|aṯt.w ṯn.n‘rm.b.bt.ilsk.|aṯt.ad[r]t.b.bt.armwl.|aṯt.aḥt.b.bt.iwrpzn.|ṯ 80[119].8
qmḥ.d.kly.k ṣḥ.illdrm.|b d.zlb[n.--].|arb‘.‘š[r.]dd.n‘r.|d.apy[.--].|w.arb[‘.--]d.apy.‘bd h.|w.mrb‘[t.l ‘]bdm. 2094.3
-].|[‘ṯ]trt w ‘nt[.---].|w b hm.tṯtb[.--]d h.|km trpa.hn n‘r.|d yšt.l.lṣb h ḫš‘r klb.|[w]riš.pqq.w šr h.|yšt.aḥd h.dm UG5.1.2.3
.tqru.|[---.]nplt.y[--].md‘.nplt.bšr.|[---].w tpky.k[m.]n‘r.tdm‘.km.|[ṣǵ]r.bkm.y‘ny[.---.bn]wt h.|[--]nn.bnt yš[--.-- UG5.8.40
, bnšm.dt.l.u[--]ṯtb.|kṯ[r]n.|w.aṯt h.w.n‘r h.|bn.ḫby.w.[a]ṯt h.|ynḥm.ulmy.|[--]q.w.aṯt h.w.bn h.| 2068.3
šḫ.rbt.|w aršḫ.ṯrrt.ydy.b ‘ṣm.‘r‘r.|w b šḫt.‘s.mt.‘r‘rm.yn‘rn h.|ssnm.ysyn h.‘dtm.y‘dyn h.yb|ltm.ybln h.mǵy.ḥrn. UG5.7.65
y].ṯbǵ.|iḫmlk.|yp‘n w.aṯt h.|anntn.yṣr.|annmn.w.ṯlṯ.n‘[r] h.|rpan.w.ṯ[n.]bn h.|bn.ayln.w.ṯn.bn h.|yt. 2068.25
adn hm.ṯr.w.arb‘.bnt h.|yrḫm.yd.ṯn.bn h.|b‘lm.w.ṯlṯ.n‘rm.w.bt.aḥt.|bn.lwn.ṯlṯtm.b‘lm.|bn.b‘ly.ṯlṯtm.b‘lm.|w.aḥ 2080.5
---.--]n h.ḥmt.w t‘btn h.abd y.|[---.ǵ]r.šrǵzz.ybky.km.n‘r.|[w ydm‘.k]m.ṣǵr.špš.b šmm.tqru.|[---.]nplt.y[--].md‘.n UG5.8.37
ḫmšm.dd.|n‘r.|ḫmšm.tišr.|ḫmš.ktnt.|ḫmš.ṯnt.alpm.|‘šrm.hbn.|ṯlṯ.ma 2102.2
l.ytn.hm.mlk.[b]‘l y.|w.hn.ibm.šṣq l y.|p.l.ašt.aṯt y.|n‘r y.ṯh.l pn.ib.|hn.hm.yrgm.mlk.|b‘l y.tmǵyy.hn.|alpm.šš 1012.29
.bnš.mlk.d.b.tbq.|[kr]wn.|[--]n.|[q]ṣy.|ṯn.bn.iwrḫz.[n]‘rm.|yṣr[.-]qb.|w.ṯn.bnš.iytlm.|w.‘šrm.ṣmd.alpm. 2066.2.4
nmky.|‘nqpat.|ṭbq.|hzp.|gn‘y.|m‘rby.|[ṣ]‘q.|[š]ḥq.|n‘rm.|mḫrǵlm.|kzym.|mru.skn.|mru.ibrn.|pslm.|šrm.|yṣ 71[113].60
ṯnnm.ṯt.|‘šr.ḫsnm.|n‘r.mrynm.|ḫmš.|ṯrtnm.ḫmš.|mrum.‘šr.|šb‘.ḫsnm.|mkrm 1031.3
.|nqdm.|khnm.|qdšm.|pslm.|mkrm.|yṣḥm.|šrm.|n‘rm.|‘bdm.|kzym.|ksdm.|[nsk].ṯlṯ.|gt.mlkym.|tmrym.|ṯ 1026.1.12
[---]t.ddm.š‘r[m.---].|[---].mit.ḫsw.[---].|[----]d.n‘r.ṯ[--]d[.---].|[---.]ṯlṯ.kṯt[.-]d.[---].|[---.a]rb‘.dblt.m[--.---].| 143[-].1.3
[---.--]ǵz.|[---.]qrt.|[---].aṯt.|[---.]w arb‘.n‘r[m].|[---.a]ḥd.|[---.]ṯlṯ.aṯt. 2142.4
[--.‘]ṯtrum[.---].|[---.]ḥmr.y[--].|[---].n‘r[.---].|[---.]dd gdl[.---]. 2133.12

n‘rt

lm.|[---.]b.bt[.---]l.|[ṯ]lṯ.aṯt.adrt.w.ṯlṯ.ǵzr[m].|w.ḫmš.n‘rt.b.bt.sk[n].|ṯt.aṯtm.adrtm.w.pǵt.w ǵzr[.aḥd.b.bt.---].|aṯ 80[119].17
|[---.--]m.|[---].ṯlḥn.|[---].ṯnn.|[---.--]b.kdr.|[---.--]m n‘rt.|[---].qt.b[--].|[---.]kd[r].|[---.]ṯpr.|[---.]prš.|[---.]šdm.| 1142.1

nǵsk

tn.|bn.ypr.|mrum.|bn.‘[--]t.|bn.adty.|bn.krwn.|bn.nǵsk.|bn.qnḏ.|bn.pity.|w.nḥl h.|bn.rt.|bn.l[--].|bn.[---].|[- 113[400].3.15

nǵṣ

.qdqd.zbl.|[ym.]bn.‘nm.ṯpṭ.nhr.yprsḥ.ym.yql.|l arṣ.tnǵṣn.pnt h.w ydlp.tmn h.|yqṯ b‘l.w yšt.ym.ykly.ṯpṭ.nhr.|b 2.4[68].26
ṣb‘t h.ylm.ktp.zbl ym.bn ydm.ṯpṭ.|nhr.‘z.ym.l ymk.l tnǵṣn.pnt h.l ydlp.|tmn h.kṯr.ṣmdm.ynḥt.w yp‘r.šmt hm.|š 2.4[68].17
.‘nt.tph.ilm.b h.p‘nm.|ṭṭṭ.b‘d n.ksl.ṯṯbr.|‘ln.pn h.td‘.tǵṣ.pnt.|ksl h.anš.dt.ẓr h.tšu.|g h.w tṣḥ.ik.mǵy.gpn.w ugr.| 3[‘NT].3.31
limm].b h.p‘nm.|[ṭṭṭ.b ‘]dn.ksl.|[ṯṯbr.‘ln.p]n h.td[‘].|tǵṣ[.pnt.ks]l h.|anš.dt.ẓr.[h].|tšu.g h.w tṣḥ[.i]k.|mǵy.aliy[n 4[51].2.19
ṯl.brlt h.[b h.p‘nm].|ṭṭṭ.‘l[n.pn h.td‘.b ‘dn].|ksl.y[ṯbr.yǵṣ.pnt.ksl h].|anš.[dt.ẓr h.yšu.g h].|w yṣ[ḥ.---].|mḫṣ[.---]. 19[1AQHT].2.95

nǵr

m.w t[n].|w nlḥm.hm.iṯ[.--.yn.w t]n.w nšt.|w ‘n hm.nǵr mdr‘[.iṯ.lḥm.---].|iṯ.yn.d ‘rb.bṯk[.---].|mǵ hw.l hn.lg yn 23[52].73
.nqpt.‘d.ilm.n‘mm.ttlkn.|šd.tṣdn.pat.mdbr.w ngš.hm.nǵr.|mdr‘.w ṣḥ hm.‘m.nǵr.mdr‘ y.nǵr.|nǵr.ptḥ.w ptḥ hw.p 23[52].68
.|šd.tṣdn.pat.mdbr.w ngš.hm.nǵr.|mdr‘.w ṣḥ hm.‘m.nǵr.mdr‘ y.nǵr.|nǵr.ptḥ.w ptḥ hw.prṣ.b‘d hm.|w ‘rb.hm.h 23[52].69
špš.|ad[.‘]bd h.uk.škn.|k.[---.]sglt h.hw.|w.b[.---.]uk.nǵr.|w.[---].adny.l.yḥsr.|w.[ank.yd]‘.l.yd‘t.|h[t.---.]l.špš.b‘l 2060.8
ṯḥm.ydn.‘m.mlk.|b‘l h.nǵr.ḥwt k.|w l.a[--]t.tšknn.|ḫmšm.l mi[t].any.|tškn[n.--]h. 2062.1.2
ṯḥm[.t]lm[yn].|l ṯryl.um y.|rgm.|ugrt.tǵr k.|ugrt.tǵr k.|tšlm k.um y.|td‘.ky.‘rbt.|l pn.špš.|w pn. 1015.5
l.rb.khnm.|rgm.|ṯḥm.[---].|yšlm[.l k.ilm].|tšlm[k.tǵr] k.|t‘zz[k.---.]lm.|w t[--.--]ṣm k.|[-----].|[-----.]šil.|[----- 55[18].5
ṯḥm iwrḏr.|l iwrpḫn.|bn y.aḫ y.rgm.|ilm.tǵr k.|tšlm k.|ik y.lḥt.|spr.d likt.|‘m.ṯryl.|mh y.rgmt.|w h 138.4
mlk.bn [k].|[l].p‘n.um [y].|qlt[.l um] y.|yšlm.il[m].|tǵ[r] k.tš[lm] k.|[h]l ny.‘m n[.š]lm.|w.ṯm [ny.‘m.mlkt.u]m 1013.7

.|ṯḥm.mlk.|bn k.|l.p'n.um y.|qlt.l.um y.|yšlm.ilm.|tǵr k.tšlm k.|hl ny.'m n[y].|kll.šlm.|ṯm ny.'m.um y.|mnm. 50[117].8
[yš]lm[.ilm].|tǵr k[.tšlm k].|hl ny.[---].|w.pdr[--.---].|tmǵyn[.---].|w.mli[57[101].2
tḥm.pgn.|l.mlk.ugrt.|rgm.|yšlm.l k.[il]m.|tǵr k.tšlm k.|hn ny.'m n.š[l]m.|ṯm ny.'[m.]bn y.|mnm.[šl] 2061.5
lk.ugrt.|aḫ y.rgm.|tḥm.mlk.ṣr.aḫ k.|y[š]lm.l k.ilm.|tǵr k.tšlm k.|hn ny.'m n.|šlm.ṯm ny.|'m k.mnm[.š]lm.|rg 2059.5
.|w.aḫtmlk 'bd k.|l.p'n.adt ny.|mrḫqtm.|qlny.ilm.|tǵr k.|tšlm k.|hn ny.'m ny.|kll.mid.|šlm.|w.ap.ank.|nḫt.ṯ 51[95].8
tḥm.mlk.|l.ṯryl.um y.rgm.|yšlm.l k.ilm.|tǵr k.tšlm k.|lḥt.šlm.k.lik[t].|um y.'m y.ht.'m[ny].|kll.šlm 2009.1.4
[l.ml]k.[b'l y].|rg[m].|tḥm.wr[--].|yšlm.[l] k.|ilm.t[ǵ]r k.|tšlm k.|lm[.l.]likt.|ši[l.š]lm y.|[']d.r[-]š.|[-]ly.l.likt. 2010.5
y[šlm.l k.ilm].|tǵ[r k.tšlm k].|'bd[.---]y.|'m[.---]y.|šk[--.--.]kll.|šk[--.--.]h 2065.2
[t]ḥm.iṯtl.|l mnn.ilm.|tǵr k.tšlm k.|t'zz k.alp ymm.|w rbt.šnt.|b 'd 'lm...gn'.|iršt. 1019.1.3
l[--].|l pḫry.a[ḫ y].|w l g.p[-]r[--].|yšlm[.l k].|[i]lm[.tǵr k].|[t]š[lm k.---].|[-----].|[-----].|h[--.---].|[-----].|w [----] 56[21].5
yn.b'l.|w t'n.btlt.'nt.|an.l an.y špš.|an.l an.il.yǵr[.-].|tǵr k.š[---.---].|yštd[.---].|dr[.---].|r[---.---]. 6[49].4.48
m.---].|[l.---].|[a]ḫt y.rgm.|[y]šlm.l k.|[il]m.tšlm k.|[tǵ]r k.|[--]y.ibr[-].|[--]wy.rgm l.|mlkt.ugrt.|[--]kt.rgmt.|[-- 1016.6
.[m]nḥm.|'pṯrm.šm'rgm.skn.qrt.|ḥgbn.šm'.skn.qrt.|nǵr krm.'bdadt.b'ln.yp'mlk.|ṯǵrm.mnḥm.klyn.'dršp.ǵlmn.| 2011.12
[---.]ktb nǵr krm.|[---].ab h.krm ar.|[---.]h.mḫtrt.pṯtm.|[---.-]t h.uš 2001.2.1
d.r'y.ḥmrm.|b.gt.gwl.ṯmn.ṣmdm.|w.arb'.'šr.bnš.|yd.nǵr.mdr'.yd.š[--]m.|[b.]gt.ipṯl.ṯṯ.ṣmdm.|[w.']šr.bn[š]m.y[d] 2038.6
|b.gt.ḥršm.|ṯn.ḥršm.|[-]nbkm.|ṯn.ḥršm.|b.gt.ǵl.|[-.]nǵr.mdr'.|[-].nǵr[.--]m.|[--.]psl.qšt.|[ṯl]ṯ.psl.ḥẓm.|[---.ḫ]rš. 1024.3.16
at.mdbr.w ngš.hm.nǵr.|mdr'.w ṣḥ hm.'m.nǵr.mdr' y.nǵr.|nǵr.ptḥ.w ptḥ hw.prṣ.b'd hm.|w 'rb.hm.hm[.iṯ.--.l]ḥm 23[52].69
n.b'l y.|w.urk.ym.b'l y.|l.pn.amn.w.l.pn.|il.mṣrm.dt.tǵrn.|npš.špš.mlk.|rb.b'l y. 1018.22
pnm.tk.qrt h.|hmry.mk.ksu.|ṯbt h.ḫḫ.arṣ.|nḫlt h.w nǵr.|'nn.ilm.al.|tqrb.l bn.ilm.|mt.al.y'db km.|k imr.b p h. 4[51].8.14
[---.]m[--.---].|[---.']šrm[.---].|[---.]nǵr.'š[rm.---].|[---.-]yl.'š[rm.---].|[---.a]rb'[.---].|[---.ṯ]lṯm[.- 149[99].3
br.w ngš.hm.nǵr.|mdr'.w ṣḥ hm.'m.nǵr.mdr' y.nǵr.|nǵr.ptḥ.w ptḥ hw.prṣ.b'd hm.|w 'rb.hm.hm[.iṯ.--.l]ḥm.w t[23[52].70
[.u]grt.|iḫ y.rgm.|[tḥ]m.m[lk.-]bl[-].|yšlm.l[k].ilm.|tǵr.tšl[m] k.|[-----].|[-----].|[--].bt.gb[-.--].|[--]k[-].w.špš.|[-- 2159.5
abqṯ.aliyn.b'l.|w t'n.btlt.'nt.|an.l an.y špš.|an.l an.il.yǵr[.-].|tǵr k.š[---.---].|yštd[.---].|dr[.---].|r[---.---]. 6[49].4.47
n.ḥršm.|[-]nbkm.|ṯn.ḥršm.|b.gt.ǵl.|[-.]nǵr.mdr'.|[-].nǵr[.--]m.|[--.]psl.qšt.|[ṯl]ṯ.psl.ḥẓm.|[---.ḫ]rš.mr[k]bt.|[--].' 1024.3.17
l.šm[.--.]rgbt yu.|[---]w yrmy[.q]rn h.|[---.-]ny h pdr.ttǵr.|[---.n]šr k.al ttn.l n.|[---.]tn l rbd.|[---.]b'lt h w yn.|[-- 2001.2.11

nǵry

šbn.|bn uryy.|bn kṯl.|bn army.|bn gln.|bn abg.|bn.nǵry.|bn.srwd.|mtnn.|bn gš[-].|bn gbrn.|bn uldy.|synn.b 1064.13

nǵṯ

.l.'bdyrḫ.|w.mlk.z[--.--]n.ššwm.|n'mm.[--].ṯṯm.w.at.|nǵṯ.w.ytn.hm.l k.|w.lḥt.alpm.ḥršm.|k.rgmt.l y.bly m.|alp 2064.20
n[--.---].|rg[m.---].|nǵṯ[.---].|d.yqḥ[.---].|hm.ṯn.[---].|hn dt.[---].|[-----].|[-----]. 2064.3

nǵṯy

bdl.qrṭy.|trgn.bn.tǵḥ.|aupš.qmnzy.|ṯrry.mṣbty.|prn.nǵṯy.|ṯrd̲n.zlyy. 89[312].10

np

y'n.|gpn.w ugr.tḥm.bn ilm.|mt.hwt.ydd.bn.il.|ǵzr.p np.š.npš.lbim.|thw.hm.brlt.anḫr.|b ym.hm.brk y.tkšd.|ru 5[67].1.14
.|[---.]ym.rbt.|[---.]b nhrm.|['b]r.gbl.'br.|q'l.'br.iht.|np šmm.šmšr.|l dgy.aṯrt.|mǵ.l qdš.amrr.|idk.al.tnn.|pnm. 3['NT.VI].6.9

npḫ

k.šskn m'.|mgn.rbt.aṯrt ym.|mǵẓ.qnyt.ilm.|hyn.'ly.l mpḫm.|b d.ḫss.mṣbṭm.|yṣq.ksp.yšl|ḥ.ḫrṣ.yṣq.ksp.|l alpm. 4[51].1.24

npṭry

š ṯmny[m].|[---.]dbr h l šp[š].|[---.]dbr h l šp[š].|[---.]npṭry ṯ[--].|[---.--]urm.|[-----]. 41[71].10

npy

'nt.hlkt.w.šnwt.|tp.aḫ.h.k.ysmsm.|tspi.šir.h.l.bl.ḥrb.|tšt.dm.h.l.bl.ks.|tpnn. RS225.2
[---.--]t ugrt.|[---.w n]py.yman.|[w npy.'rmt.---.w]npy.annpdgl.|[ušn.yp kn.ulp.qṭy.ulp.]ddmy.ulp ḫry.|[ulp.ḫ APP.I[-].1.3
.|[w šqrb.š.mšr mšr.bn.ugrt.w npy.---.]w npy.|[---.w np]y.ugrt.|[---.u tḫṭu.ulp.qṭy.ulp.ddm]y.|[ulp.ḫry.ulp.ḫty.u 32[2].1.5
n il.|l ṯkm[n.w šnm.]hn '[r].|[---.]w npy[.---].|[---.]w npy.u[grt.---].|[---.--]y.ulp.[---].|[---.]ǵbr.u[lp.---].|[---.--]n[. 32[2].2.2
kmn[.w]šnm.hn.'r.|w.ṯb.l mspr.m[šr] mšr.bt.ugrt.w npy.gr.|ḥmyt.ugrt.w [np]y.nṯt.ušn.yp kn.ulp qṭy.|ulp.ddm 32[2].1.27
i.l dr.bn.il.l mpḫ]rt.[bn.il.l ṯkmn.w šn]m hn š.|[---.w n]py.gr[.ḥmyt.ugrt.w np]y.|[---].w n[py.---].u tḫṭi[n.ulp.qṭy 32[2].1.10
-]l.il.t'd̲r b'l.|[-----.]lšnt.|[---.--]yp.tḥt.|[-----].|[---.]w npy gr.|[ḥmyt.ugrt.w npy.yman.w npy.'r]mt.w npy.|[---.uš APP.I[-].1.12
qlt.b ymn h.|npyn h.mks.bšr h.|tmt'.md h.b ym.ṯn.|npyn h.b nhrm.|štt.ḫptr.l išt.|ḫbrt.l ẓr.pḥmm.|t'pp.ṯr.il.d 4[51].2.7
--].|l abn[.---].|aḫdt.plk h[.b yd h].|plk.qlt.b ymn h.|npyn h.mks.bšr h.|tmt'.md h.b ym.ṯn.|npyn h.b nhrm.|štt. 4[51].2.5
t.|[---.--]yp.tḥt.|[-----].|[---.]w npy gr.|[ḥmyt.ugrt.w npy.yman.w npy.'r]mt.w npy.|[---.ušn.yp km.ulp.]qṭy.|[ul APP.I[-].1.13
hn š.|w šqrb.'r.mšr mšr bn.ugrt.w [npy.---.]ugr.|w npy.yman.w npy.'rmt.w npy.[---].|w npy.nqmd.ušn.yp km. 32[2].1.19
[---.--]t ugrt.|[---.w n]py.yman.|[w npy.'rmt.---.w]npy.annpdgl.|[ušn.yp kn.ul APP.I[-].1.2
npy.---.]ugr.|w npy.yman.w npy.'rmt.w npy.[---].|w npy.nqmd.ušn.yp km.ulp.q[ṭy.ulp.ddm]y.|ulp.ḫry.ulp.ḫ[t]y 32[2].1.20
]ugrt.|[---].l.lim.|[---.mšr m]šr.|[bn.ugrt.---.--]y.|[---.np]y nqmd.|[---.]pḫr.|[-----].|[-----].|[---.t'd̲]r b'l.|[-----].|[- APP.I[-].2.3
.ṯb.l mspr.m[šr] mšr.bt.ugrt.w npy.gr.|ḥmyt.ugrt.w [np]y.nṯt.ušn.yp kn.ulp qṭy.|ulp.ddmy.ul[p.ḫ]ry.ulp.ḫty.ulp. 32[2].1.28
'ṯtrt[.---].|[--.]l ilt.š l 'ṯt[rt.---].|[']ṣr.l pdr ṯṯ.ṣ[in.---].|tšnpn.'lm.km[m.---].|w.l ll.'ṣrm.w [---].|kmm.w.in.'ṣr[.---]. 38[23].6
p.aḫ.h.k.ysmsm.|tspi.šir.h.l.bl.ḥrb.|tšt.dm.h.l.bl.ks.|tpnn.'n.bty.'n.bṯt.tpnn.|'n.mḫr.'n.pḫr.'n.tǵr.|'n.tǵr.l.tǵr.ttb RS225.5
tspi.šir.h.l.bl.ḥrb.|tšt.dm.h.l.bl.ks.|tpnn.'n.bty.'n.bṯt.tpnn.|'n.mḫr.'n.pḫr.'n.tǵr.|'n.tǵr.l.tǵr.ttb.|'n.pḫr.l.pḫr.ttb. RS225.5

npy

ḥt. | [-----]. | [---.]w npy gr. | [ḥmyt.ugrt.w npy.yman.w npy.ʿr]mt.w npy. | [---.ušn.yp km.ulp.]qṭy. | [ulp.ddmy.ulp.ḫ APP.I[-].1.13
b.ʿr.mšr mšr bn.ugrt.w [npy.---.]ugr. | w npy.yman.w npy.ʿrmt.w npy.[---]. | w npy.nqmd.ušn.yp km.ulp.q[ṭy.ulp. 32[2].1.19
[---.--]t ugrt. | [---.w n]py.yman. | [w npy.ʿrmt.---.w]npy.annpdgl. | [ušn.yp kn.ulp.qṭy.ulp.]ddmy APP.I[-].1.3
šn]m hn š. | [---.w n]py.gr[.ḥmyt.ugrt.w np]y. | [---].w n[py.---].u tḫṭi[n.ulp.qṭy]. | ulp.ddmy.ul[p.ḫry.u]lp.ḫty.ulp[. 32[2].1.11
i[l.l ṯkmn.w š]nm hn š. | w šqrb.ʿr.mšr mšr bn.ugrt.w [npy.---.]ugr. | w npy.yman.w npy.ʿrmt.w npy.[---]. | w npy.n 32[2].1.18
--.]w npy gr. | [ḥmyt.ugrt.w npy.yman.w npy.ʿr]mt.w npy. | [---.ušn.yp km.ulp.]qṭy. | [ulp.ddmy.ulp.ḫry.ulp.ḫty.u] APP.I[-].1.13
---]. | [-----]. | [---.tʿḏ]r bʿl. | [-----]. | [-----]. | [---.--]r. | [---.]npy. | [---.ušn.yp kn.ulp.q]ṭy. | [ulp.ddmy.ulp.ḫry.ulp.ḫty.ulp APP.I[-].2.11
w šnm.hn š]. | [w šqrb.š.mšr mšr.bn.ugrt.w npy.---.]w npy. | [---.w np]y.ugrt. | [---.u tḫṭu.ulp.qṭy.ulp.ddm]y. | [ulp.ḫ 32[2].1.4
r bn.ugrt.w [npy.---.]ugr. | w npy.yman.w npy.ʿrmt.w npy.[---]. | w npy.nqmd.ušn.yp km.ulp.q[ṭy.ulp.ddm]y. | ulp. 32[2].1.19
n.il.l ṯkmn.w šn]m hn š. | [---.w n]py.gr[.ḥmyt.ugrt.w np]y. | [---].w n[py.---].u tḫṭi[n.ulp.qṭy]. | ulp.ddmy.ul[p.ḫry. 32[2].1.10
.il.l ṯkmn.w šnm.hn š]. | [w šqrb.š.mšr mšr.bn.ugrt.w npy.---.]w npy. | [---.w np]y.ugrt. | [---.u tḫṭu.ulp.qṭy.ulp.dd 32[2].1.4
r.bn il.l]mpḫrt.bn il. | l ṯkm[n.w šnm.]hn ʿ[r]. | [---.]w npy[.---]. | [---.]w npy.u[grt.---]. | [---.--]y.ulp.[---]. | [---.]ǵbr.u 32[2].2.1

npk

nn.ʿrm.šrn. | pdrm.sʿt.b šdm. | ḥṭb h.b grnt.ḥpšt. | sʿt.b nk.šibt.b bqr. | mmlat.dm.ym.w ṯn. | ṯlṯ.rbʿ.ym.ymš. | ṯdṯ.ym. 14[KRT].3.113
.ʿrm. | šrnn.pdrm. | sʿt.b šdm.ḥṭb. | w b grnt.ḥpšt. | sʿt.b npk.šibt.w b | mqr.mmlat. | d[m].ym.w ṯn. | ṯlṯ.rbʿ.ym. | ḫmš. 14[KRT].5.216
ln.ṯn.b d.bn.ḫdmn. | [u]bdy.nqdm. | [ṯlṯ].šdm.d.nʿrb.gt.npk. | [š]d.rpan.b d.klṯṯb. | [š]d.ilṣy.b d.ʿbdym. | [ub]dy.trrm. 82[300].2.13

npl

l.ṯṯb.idk.pnm]. | al.ttn.ʿm.pḫr.mʿd.t[k.ǵr.ll.l pʿn.il]. | al.tpl.al.tštḥwy.pḫr [mʿd.qmm.a--.am] | r ṯny.dʿt km.w rgm.l ṯ 2.1[137].15
.m[--]. | [ṯpṭ].nhr.tlʿm.ṯm.ḥrbm.its.anšq. | [-]htm.l arṣ.ypl.ul ny.w l.ʿpr.ʿẓm ny. | l bʿl[-.---]. | tḥt.ksi.zbl.ym.w ʿn.kṯr. 2.4[68].5
ym.yṯbr.ḥrn]. | riš k.ʿṯrt.[šm.bʿl.qdqd k.---]. | [--]t.mṯ.tpln.b g[bl.šnt k.---]. | [--]šnm.aṯtm.t[--.---]. | [m]lakm.ylak.y 2.1[137].9
p ʿn.bʿl.aḫḏ[.---]. | w šmt.ǵllm[.---]. | aḫḏ.aklm.k [---]. | npl.b mšmš[.---]. | anp n m yḥr[r.---]. | bmt n m.yšḫn.[---]. | q 12[75].2.37
ẓa h. | w mẓa h.šr.yly h. | b skn.sknm.b ʿdn. | ʿdnm.kn.npl.bʿl. | km ṯr.w tkms.hd.p[.-]. | km.ibr.b tk.mšmš d[--]. | itt 12[75].2.54
[w ydmʿ.k]m.ṣǵr.špš.b šmm.tqru. | [---.]nplt.y[--].mdʿ.nplt.bšr. | [---].w tpky.k[m.]nʿr.tdmʿ.km. | [ṣǵ]r.bkm.yʿny[.--- UG5.8.39
mšu. | ḫtpy. | ǵldy. | iḫǵl. | aby. | abmn. | ynḥm. | npl. | ynḥm. | mtbʿl. | bn ǵlmn. | bn sgld. 1065.8
ybky.km.nʿr. | [w ydmʿ.k]m.ṣǵr.špš.b šmm.tqru. | [---.]nplt.y[--].mdʿ.nplt.bšr. | [---].w tpky.k[m.]nʿr.tdmʿ.km. | [ṣǵ]r UG5.8.39
.atn.at.mṯb k[.---]. | [š]mm.rm.lk.prẓ kt. | [k]bkbm.ṯm.tpl k.lbnt. | [-.]rgm.k yrkt.ʿṯqbm. | [---]m.ʿẓpn.l pit. | m[--]m[.- 13[6].13
mǵ.l nʿm[y]. | [arṣ.]dbr.ysmt.šd. | [šḥl]mmt.t[mǵ.]l bʿl.np[l]. | [l a]rṣ[.lpš].tks.miz[rtm]. 5[67].6.30
]ǵny. | l nʿm y.arṣ.dbr. | l ysmt.šd.šḥlmmt. | mǵny.l bʿl.npl.l a | rṣ.mt.aliyn.bʿl. | ḫlq.zbl.bʿl.arṣ. | apnk.lṭpn.il. | d pid.y 5[67].6.8
ṯ.zbl hm. | aḫr.tmǵyn.mlak ym.tʿdt.ṯpṭ.nhr.l pʿn.il. | [l t]pl.l tštḥwy.pḫr.mʿd.qmm.a[--].amr. | [ṯn]y.dʿt hm.išt.ištm. 2.1[137].31
m. | mḫmšt.yitsp. | ršp.nṯdṯt.ǵlm. | ym.mšbʿt hn.b šlḥ. | ttpl.yʿn.ḥtk h. | krt yʿn.ḥtk h.rš. | mid.grdš.ṯbt h. | w b tm hn. 14[KRT].1.21
. | w[.---.]qmʿt. | [---.]mḏrǵlm. | [---.]mdm. | [w].ʿšr.dd.l np[l]. | r[p]š. 2012.26

npʿ

. | w ṯn.gprm.mn gpr h.šr. | aqht.yʿn.kmr.kmr[.--]. | k apʿ.il.b gdrt.k lb.l | ḫṯ h.imḫṣ h.k d.ʿl.qšt h. | imḫṣ h.ʿl.qṣʿt h. 19[1AQHT].1.13
kt.šblt.ypʿ. | b ḥmdrt.šblt.yḥ[bq]. | w ynšq.aḥl.an.šblt. | tpʿ.b aklt.šblt.tpʿ[.b ḥm]drt. | ur.tisp k.yd.aqht.ǵz[r]. | tšt k.b 19[1AQHT].2.72
ḥmdrt.šblt.yḥ[bq]. | w ynšq.aḥl.an.šblt. | tpʿ.b aklt.šblt.tpʿ[.b ḥm]drt. | ur.tisp k.yd.aqht.ǵz[r]. | tšt k.bm.qrb m.asm. 19[1AQHT].2.72
k.b qrb m.asm. | y.dnh.ysb.aklt h.yph. | šblt.b akt.šblt.ypʿ. | b ḥmdrt.šblt.yḥ[bq]. | w ynšq.aḥl.an.šblt. | tpʿ.b aklt.šblt 19[1AQHT].2.69
.bṣql.y[hb]q. | w ynšq.aḥl.an bṣ[ql]. | ynpʿ.b palt.bṣql ypʿ b yǵlm. | ur.tisp k.yd.aqht. | ǵzr.tšt k.b qrb m.asm. | y.dn 19[1AQHT].2.65
ṣ[q]l. | yph.b yǵlm.bṣql.y[ḥb]q. | w ynšq.aḥl.an bṣ[ql]. | ynpʿ.b palt.bṣql ypʿ b yǵlm. | ur.tisp k.yd.aqht. | ǵzr.tšt k.b q 19[1AQHT].2.65
ṭlb.a[--.---]. | yšu.g h[.---]. | i.ap.bʿ[l.---]. | i.hd.d[---.---]. | ynpʿ.bʿ[l.---]. | b ṯmnt.[---]. | yqrb.[---]. | lḥm.m[---.---]. | [ʿ]d.lḥ 5[67].4.8
k.mrrt. | tǵll.b nr.d ʿl k.mḫṣ.aqht. | ǵzr.šrš k.b arṣ.al. | ypʿ.riš.ǵly.b d.ns' k. | ʿnt.brḥ.p ʿlm h. | ʿnt.p dr.dr.ʿdb.uḫry m 19[1AQHT].3.160

npṣ

.npṣ.ǵzr.tšt.ḫ[---.b] | nšg h.ḥrb.tšt.b tʿr[t h]. | w ʿl.tlbš.npṣ.aṯt.[--]. | ṣbi nrt.ilm.špš.[-]r[--]. | pǵt.minš.šdm l mʿ[rb]. | 19[1AQHT].4.208
npṣm. | b d.mri. | skn. | ʿšrm. | ḫmš. | kbd. 157[116].1
]r[-]. | [--]dšq krsnm. | ḫmšm [-]t ṯlṯ ty[--]. | bn.grgš. | w.npṣ bt ṯn.ṯlṯ mat. | w spl ṯlṯ.mat. | w mmskn. | w.ṯt.mqrtm. | w 1103.16
spr.npṣm.d yṣa.b milḫ. | ʿšrm.ḫpn.ḫmš. | kbd.w lpš. | ḫmš.mispt. | 1109.1
.ksm h.bt.bʿl. | [w m]nt h bt.il.ṯḫ.gg h.b ym. | [ṭi]ṭ.rḥṣ.npṣ h.b ym.rṯ. | [--.y]iḫd.il.ʿbd h.ybrk. | [dni]l mt rpi.ymr.ǵzr 17[2AQHT].1.34
[---.]yd.npṣ h. | [---.]yd.npṣ h. | [---.]yd.npṣ h. | [---.yd].npṣ h. | [---.yd.np]ṣ h. | [---.yd. 1119.2
[---.]yd.npṣ h. | [---.]yd.npṣ h. | [---.]yd.npṣ h. | [---.yd].npṣ h. | [---.yd.np]ṣ h. | [---.yd.np]ṣ h. | [---.yd.npṣ] h. | [---.-]n 1119.4
[---.]yd.npṣ h. | [---.]yd.npṣ h. | [---.]yd.npṣ h. | [---.yd].npṣ h. | [---.yd.np]ṣ h. | [---.yd.np]ṣ h. | [---.yd. 1119.3
[---.]yd.npṣ h. | [---.]yd.npṣ h. | [---.]yd.npṣ h. | [---.yd].npṣ h. | [---.yd. 1119.1
. | [---.]yd.npṣ h. | [---.]yd.npṣ h. | [---.yd].npṣ h. | [---.yd.np]ṣ h. | [---.yd.np]ṣ h. | [---.yd.npṣ] h. | [---.-]nm. | [---.--]ṯ. 1119.5
. | [---.]yd.npṣ h. | [---.yd].npṣ h. | [---.yd.np]ṣ h. | [---.yd.np]ṣ h. | [---.yd.npṣ] h. | [---.-]nm. | [---.--]ṯ. 1119.6
b[--].rgm y. | [---.]škb.w m[--.]mlakt. | [---.]ʿl.w tšʿ[d]n.npṣ h. | [---.]rgm.hn.[--]n.w aspt.[q]l h. | [---.rg]m.ank l[.--.--] 1002.48
. | [---.yd].npṣ h. | [---.yd.np]ṣ h. | [---.yd.np]ṣ h. | [---.yd.npṣ] h. | [---.-]nm. | [---.--]ṯ. 1119.7
[nq]dm.dt.kn.npṣ hm. | [bn].lbn.arbʿ.qšt.w.ar[bʿ]. | [u]ṯpt.qlʿ.w.ṯt.mr[ḥ]m. | 2047.1
u.ksm y.bt.bʿl.[w]mn[t]. | y.bt.il.ṯḫ.gg y.b ym.ṭiṭ. | rḥṣ.npṣ y.b ym.rṯ. | dn.il.bt h.ymǵyn. | yštql.dnil.l hkl h. | ʿrb.b bt 17[2AQHT].2.23
k.b [škrn]. | mʿms k.k šbʿt.yn.ṭ[ḫ]. | gg k.b ym.ṭiṭ.rḥṣ. | npṣ k.b ym rṯ.b uni[l]. | pnm.tšmḫ.w ʿl yṣhl pi[t]. | yprq.lṣb.w 17[2AQHT].2.8
spr.npṣ.krw. | ṯt.ḫṭrm.ṯn.kst. | spl.mšlt.w.mqḥm. | w md h. | arn.w 2050.1
npṣ.ʿ[--.---]. | d.b d.a[--.---]. | w.b d.b[--.---]. | udbr[.---]. | ʿrš[.-- 1120.1
dm.tium.b ǵlp y[m.--]. | d alp šd.ẓu h.b ym.t[---]. | tlbš.npṣ.ǵzr.tšt.ḫ[---.b] | nšg h.ḥrb.tšt.b tʿr[t h]. | w ʿl.tlbš.npṣ.aṯt. 19[1AQHT].4.206

[---.]npṣ ṯlṯ. | [---.-]kṣ. 154[-].1

npq

.bʻl. | km ṯr.w tkms.hd.p[.-]. | km.ibr.b tk.mšmš d[--]. | ittpq.l awl. | išttk.lm.ttkn. | štk.mlk.dn. | štk.šibt.ʻn. | štk.qr.bt. 12[75].2.57

npr

[s]ǵr.bn.bdn. | [sǵ]r.bn.psḥn. | alṯy. | sǵr.npr. | bn.ḫty. | ṯn.bnš ibrd̲r. | bnš tlmi. | sǵr.ḫryn. | ʻdn.w sǵr h. 2082.4

]. | w yṣḥ.knp.hrgb.bʻl.ybn. | [b]ʻl.ybn.diy.hwt.hrg[b]. | tpr.w du.b nši.ʻn h. | [w]yphn.yḥd.ṣml.um.nšrm. | yšu.g h.w 19[1AQHT].3.134

šu.g h. | w yṣḥ.knp.nšrm.ybn. | bʻl.ybn.diy hmt nšrm. | tpr.w du.b nši.ʻn h.w ypn. | yḥd.hrgb.ab.nšrm. | yšu.g h.w yṣ 19[1AQHT].3.120

-----]. | [-----]. | [-----]. | [-----]. | [ṣṣ].b[n].ṣd[-.---]. | [ṣṣ].bn.npr.ḫmšm. | ṣṣ.bn.adld̲n.ṯlṯm. | ṣṣ.bn.ʻglt.ṯlṯm. | ṣṣ.bn.ʻbd.ʻšrm 2096.15

ḥm.ṯṯḥnn.b šd. | tdrʻnn.šir h.l tikl. | ʻṣrm.mnt h.l tkly. | npr[m.]šir.l šir.yṣḥ. 6[49].2.37

m.t[--.---]. | [m]lakm.ylak.ym.[tʻdt.ṯpṭ.nhr]. | b ʻlṣ.ʻlṣm.npr.š[--.---]. | uṭ.ṯbr.ap hm.tbʻ.ǵlm[m.al.ṯṯb.idk.pnm]. | al.ttn. 2.1[137].12

npš

w yʻny.bn. | ilm.mt.npš[.-]. | npš.lbun. | thw.w npš. | anḫr.b ym. | brkt.šbšt. | k rumm.hm. | ʻn.kd̲d.aylt. | mt h UG5.4.4

bʻl y.---]. | w.an[k.---]. | arš[.---]. | mlk.r[b.bʻ]l y.p.l. | ḥy.np[š.a]rš. | l.pn.bʻ[l y.l].pn.bʻl y. | w.urk.ym.bʻl y. | l.pn.amn. 1018.18

qt l ṣpn.šrp.w šlmm. | kmm.w bbt.bʻl.ugrt. | w kdm.w npš ilib. | gdlt.il š.bʻl š.ʻnt. | ṣpn.alp.w š.pdry.š. | šrp.w šlmm i UG5.13.12

qt.l.ṣpn.šrp].w š[l]mm.kmm. | [w bbt.bʻl.ugrt.]kdm.w npš. | [ilib.gdlt.il.š.b]ʻ[l.]š.ʻnt ṣpn. | [---.]w [n]p[š.---]. | [---.--]t. 36[9].1.16

[--].w rbb. | š[---]npš išt. | w.l.tikl w l tš[t]. 2003.2

.bt.trǵds. | [---.]aṯt.adrt.w.pǵt.a[ḫt.b.bt.---]. | [---.ʻ]šrm.npš.b.bt.[---]. | [---.]w.pǵt.aḫt.b.bt.[---]. 80[119].29

b ym.hm.brk y.tkšd. | rumm.ʻn.kd̲d.aylt. | hm.imt.imt.npš.blt. | ḥmr.p imt.b klt. | yd y.ilḫm.hm.šbʻ. | ydt y.b ṣʻ.hm.k 5[67].1.18

.šmm.k rs. | ipd k.ank.ispi.uṭm. | d̲rqm.amt m.l yrt. | b npš.bn ilm.mt.b mh | mrt.ydd.il.ǵzr. | tbʻ.w l.yṯb ilm.idk. | l y 5[67].1.7

spr.npš.d. | ʻrb.bt.mlk. | w.b.spr.l.št. | yrmʻl. | ṣry. | iršy. | yʻd̲rd. | ay 2106.1

| šmʻ.l dnil.[mt.rpi]. | mt.aqht.ǵzr.[šṣat]. | btlt.ʻnt.k [rḥ.npš h]. | k iṯl.brlt h.[b h.pʻnm]. | ṭṭ.ʻl[n.pn h.tdʻ.b ʻdn]. | ksl.y 19[1AQHT].2.92

dn.š[pk.km]. | šiy.dm h.km.šḫ[ṭ.l brk h]. | yṣat.km.rḥ.npš[h.km.iṯl]. | brlt h.km.qṭr.[b ap h.---]. | ʻnt.b ṣmt.mhr h.[- 18[3AQHT].4.36

lṯ id.ʻl.udn.špk.km.šiy. | dm.km.šḫṭ.l brk h.tṣi.km. | rḥ.npš h.km.iṯl.brlt h.km. | qṭr.b ap h.b ap.mhr h.ank. | l aḥwy. 18[3AQHT].4.25

ṭ m.tʻmt.[ʻ]ṯr.[k]m. | zbln.ʻl.riš h. | w ṯṯb.trḥṣ.nn.b dʻt. | npš h.l lḥm.tpth. | brlt h.l ṯrm. | mt.dm.ḫt.šʻtqt. | dm.lan.w y 16.6[127].11

. | dll.al.ilak.l bn. | ilm.mt.ʻdd.l ydd. | il.ǵzr.yqra.mt. | b npš h.ystrn ydd. | b gngn h.aḥd y.d ym | lk.ʻl.ilm.l ymru. | il 4[51].7.48

.aḫt k. | ydʻt.k rḥmt. | al.tšt.b šdm.mm h. | b smkt.ṣat.npš h. | [-]mt[-].ṣba.rbt. | špš.w tgh.nyr. | rbt.w rgm.l aḫt k. | ṯ 16.1[125].35

dnil.[--] h[.---]. | riš.r[--.--]ḥ[.---]y[.---.-]nt.[š]ṣat[k.]rḥ.npš.hm. | k.iṯl.brlt n[-.k qṭr.b ap -]. | tmǵyn.tša.g h[m.w tṣḥn 19[1AQHT].2.87

.kl. | ǵr.l kbd.arṣ.kl.gbʻ. | l kbd.šdm.npš.ḫsrt. | bn.nšm.npš.hmlt. | arṣ.mǵt.l nʻm y.arṣ. | dbr.ysmt.šd.šḥlmmt. | ngš.a 6[49].2.18

ṯʻ tn šm l btbt. | alp.w š šrp.alp šlmm. | l bʻl.ʻṣr l ṣpn. | npš.w.š.l ršp bbt. | [ʻ]ṣrm l h.ršp [-]m. | [---.]bqt[-]. | [b] ǵb.ršp UG5.12.A.11

iḥd.il.ʻbd h.ybrk. | [dni]l mt rpi.ymr.ǵzr. | [mt.hr]nmy npš.yḥ.dnil. | [mt.rp]i.brlt.ǵzr.mt hrnmy. | [---].hw.mḫ.l ʻrš h 17[2AQHT].1.37

.mḫṣ.aḫ y.akl[.m] | kly[.ʻ]l.umt y.w yʻn[.dn] | il.mt.rpi npš tḥ[.pǵt]. | ṯ[km]t.mym.ḥspt.l šʻr. | ṭl.ydʻt.hlk.kbkbm. | a[-] 19[1AQHT].4.198

t.ʻnt. | an.itlk.w aṣd.kl. | ǵr.l kbd.arṣ.kl.gbʻ. | l kbd.šdm.npš.ḫsrt. | bn.nšm.npš.hmlt. | arṣ.mǵt.l nʻm y.arṣ. | dbr.ysmt. 6[49].2.17

.in.bt[.l] y[.km.]ilm[.w] ḥẓr[.k bn]. | [qd]š.lbum.trd.b n[p]šn y.trḥṣn.k ṯrm. | [--]b b[ht]. | [zbl.]ym.b hkl.ṯpṭ.nh[r].y 2.3[129].20

[---.]km.t[--.---]. | [--.n]pṣ.ttn[.---]. | [---.]ydʻt.k[---]. | [---].w hm. | [--]y.ṯb y.w [---]. | 61[-].2

ṣḥq. | yšu.g h.w yṣḥ. | aṯbn.ank.w anḫn. | w tnḫ.b irt y.npš. | k ḥy.aliyn.bʻl. | k iṯ.zbl.bʻl.arṣ. | gm.yṣḥ.il.l btlt. | ʻnt.šmʻ 6[49].3.19

ṯpd.yšu. | g h.w yṣḥ.aṯbn.ank. | w anḫn.w tnḫ.b irt y. | npš.k yld.bn.l y.km. | aḫ y.w šrš.km ary y. | nṣb.skn.ilib y.b q 17[2AQHT].2.14

[.ṯṯwy]. | šqlt.b ǵlt.yd k. | l tdn.dn.almnt. | l ṯpṭ.ṯpṭ.qṣr.npš. | km.aḫt.ʻrš.mdw. | anšt.ʻrš.zbln. | rd.l mlk.amlk. | l drkt. 16.6[127].34

.ulp.mdll km.ulp.qr zbl]. | [u ṯḫṭu.u b ap km.u b qṣrt.npš km.u b qṭt]. | [tqṭṭ.u ṯḫṭu.l dbḥm.w l.ṯʻ.dbḥ n.ndb]ḫ. | [h 32[2].1.8A

[dl]l km.ulp.qr zbl.u[š]n yp km. | u b ap km.u b q[ṣ]rt.npš km.u b qṭt.tqṭṭ. | ušn yp km.l d[b]ḥm.w l.ṯʻ.dbḥ n.ndbḥ. 32[2].1.23

lp.mdll km.ulp]. | [qr zbl.ušn.yp km.b ap km.u b qṣrt.np]št km. | [u b qṭt.tqṭṭ.ušn.yp km.---.-]yt km. | [---.]km. | [--- APP.I[-].1.17

.ulp.md[ll k]n.ulp.q[r zbl]. | u ṯḫṭin.b ap kn.u b [q]ṣrt.npš[kn.u b qṭt]. | tqṭṭn u ṯḫṭin.l bḥm.w l ṯʻ.d[bḥ n.ndbḥ]. | h 32[2].1.14

]lp.mdll kn.ulp qr z[bl]. | lšn yp kn.b ap [kn.u b qṣ]rt.npš kn.u b qṭt. | tqṭṭn.ušn y[p kn.l dbḥm.]w l ṯʻ dbḥ n. | ndbḥ 32[2].1.31

lp.mdll kn.ulp.]qr zbl. | [ušn.yp kn.u b ap kn.u b qṣrt.npš kn.u b]qṭt. | [tqṭṭn.ušn.yp kn.---.-]gym. | [---.]l kbkb. | [-- APP.I[-].2.15

lp.mdll kn.ulp.qr zbl.ušn.y]p kn. | [u b ap kn.u b qṣrt.npšt kn.u b qṭ]t tqṭṭ. | [ušn.yp kn.---.--]l.il.tʻd̲r bʻl. | [-----.]lšn APP.I[-].1.7

id.yph.mlk. | r[š]p.ḥgb.ap. | w[.n]pš.ksp. | w ḫrṣ.km[-]. | w.ḫ[--.-]lp. | w.š.l[--]p. | w[.--.-]nš. | i[- 2005.1.3

my.gm.l aṯt h.k yṣḥ. | šmʻ.mtt.dnty.ʻd[b]. | imr.b pḥd.l npš.kṯr. | w ḫss.l brlt.hyn d. | ḥrš yd.šlḥm.ššqy. | ilm sad.kbd. 17[2AQHT].5.17

mt.bʻl. | ḥkpt.il.kl h.tšmʻ. | mtt.dnty.tʻdb.imr. | b pḥd.l npš.kṯr.w ḫss. | l brlt.hyn.d ḥrš. | ydm.aḫr.ymǵy.kṯr. | w ḫss.b 17[2AQHT].5.23

.ṯṯwy.šqlt. | b ǵlt.yd k.l tdn. | dn.almnt.l ṯpṭ. | ṯpṭ qṣr.npš.l tdy. | ṯšm.ʻl.dl.l pn k. | l tšlḥm.ytm.bʻd. | ksl k.almnt.km 16.6[127].47

rm. | bt.mlk.ṯql.ḫrṣ. | l špš.w yrḫ.l gtr. | ṯql.ksp.ṯb.ap w np[š]. | l ʻnt h.ṯql.ḫrṣ. | l špš[.w y]rḫ.l gtr.ṯn. | [ṯql.ksp].ṯb.ap. 33[5].12

gpn.w ugr.tḥm.bn ilm. | mt.hwt.ydd.bn.il. | ǵzr.p np.š.npš.lbim. | thw.hm.brlt.anḫr. | b ym.hm.brk y.tkšd. | rumm.ʻ 5[67].1.14

w yʻny.bn. | ilm.mt.npš[.-]. | npš.lbun. | thw.w npš. | anḫr.b ym. | brkt.šbšt. | k rumm.hm. | UG5.4.3

. | gpn.w ugr.tḥm.bn ilm. | mt.hwt.ydd.bn.il. | ǵzr.p np.š.npš.lbim. | thw.hm.brlt.anḫr. | b ym.hm.brk y.tkšd. | rumm. 5[67].1.14

[---].aliyn. | [bʻl.---.-]ip.dpr k. | [---.-]mn k.ššrt. | [---.--]t.npš.ʻgl. | [---.-]nk.aštn.b ḫrt. | ilm.arṣ.w at.qḥ. | ʻrpt k.rḥ k.md 5[67].5.4

lṯm.almg. | ḫmšm.kkr. | qnm. | ʻšrm.kk[r]. | brr. | [ʻ]šrm.npš. | ʻšrm.zt.mm. | ʻrbʻm. | šmn.mr. 141[120].13

. | w.urk.ym.bʻl y. | l.pn.amn.w.l.pn. | il.mṣrm.dt.tǵrn. | npš.špš.mlk. | rb.bʻl y. 1018.23

[---.--]t.slḫ.npš.ṯʻ w[.--.k]bdm. | [---.--]mm.ṯn.šm.w alp.l[--]n. | [---.]š.il š. 36[9].1.1

b.tmtt. | lqḥ.kl.d̲rʻ. | b d a[-]m.w.ank. | k[l.]d̲rʻ hm. | [--.n]pš[.-]. | w [k]l hm.b d. | rb.tmtt.lqḥt. | w.ṯṯb.ank.l hm. | w.an 2059.20

w yʻny.bn. | ilm.mt.npš[.-]. | npš.lbun. | thw.w npš. | anḫr.b ym. | brkt.šbšt. | k ru UG5.4.2

| [---.-]bʻ.npš. | [---].npš. | [---.ḫm]š.npš. | [---].npš. | [---].npš. | [---.a]ḥd. 1142.7

ʻnt h.ṯql.ḫrṣ. | l špš[.w y]rḫ.l gtr.ṯn. | [ṯql.ksp].ṯb.ap.w npš. | [---].bt.alp w š. | [---.--]m.l gtrm. | [---.]l ʻnt m. | [---.--]r 33[5].15

[---.--]b. | [---.w ym.ym]m. | [yʻtqn.---.ymǵy.]npš. | [---.h]d.tngṯn h. | [---].b ṣpn. | [---].nšb.b ʻn. | [---.]b km.y 1[ʻNT.X].5.3

[---.n]pš. | [---.--]'.npš. | [---.-]b'.npš. | [---].npš. | [---.ḫm]š.npš. | [---].npš. | [---].npš. | [---.a]ḥd. 1142.4
. | ṣlyh šr[-.---]. | [ṯ]lṯm.w b[--.---]. | l il limm[.---]. | w ṯt.npš[.---]. | kbd.w [---]. | l ṣp[n.---]. | š.[---]. | w [----]. | k[--.---]. | ' 40[134].9
--.--]'.npš. | [---.-]b'.npš. | [---].npš. | [---.ḫm]š.npš. | [---].npš. | [---].npš. | [---.a]ḥd. 1142.6
[---.n]pš. | [---.--]'.npš. | [---.-]b'.npš. | [---].npš. | [---.ḫm]š.npš. | [---].npš. | [---].npš. | [---.a]ḥd. 1142.3
--.n]pš. | [---.--]'.npš. | [---.-]b'.npš. | [---].npš. | [---.ḫm]š.npš. | [---].npš. | [---].npš. | [---.a]ḥd. 1142.5
[---.n]pš. | [---.--]'.npš. | [---.-]b'.npš. | [---].npš. | [---.ḫm]š.npš. | [---].npš. | [---].n 1142.2
[---.n]pš. | [---.--]'.npš. | [---.-]b'.npš. | [---].npš. | [---.ḫm]š.npš. | [--- 1142.1
-]kl.tǵr.mtn h. | [---.--]b.w ym ymm. | [y'tqn.---].ymǵy.npš. | [---.--]t.hd.tngṯm h. | [---.-]ḥm k b ṣpn. | [---.]išqb.aylt. | [1['NT.X].5.16
[---.--]y.npš[.---]. | [---.k]si h. | [---.--]y.rb.šm[.---]. 2160.1
grt.]kdm.w npš. | [ilib.gdlt.il.š.b]'[l.]š.'nt ṣpn. | [---.]w [n]p[š.---]. | [---.--]t.w[.---]. | [---.--]pr.ṯ[--.---]. | [-----]. | [---.--]lk[36[9].1.18

npt

--]. | kmm.w.in.'ṣr[.---]. | w mit.š'rt.[-]y[-.---]. | w.kdr.w.npt t[--.---]. | w.ksp.y'db.[---]. 38[23].10

nṣ

bn.nṣ. | [b]n.'ṣr. | [---]m. | [bn.]ulnhr. | [bn.p]rn. | [bn.a]nny. | [---]n 1075.1.1
ṯm š[šm]n.k[--.---]. | [---.ar]b'.dblt.ḏr[--.---]. | [--.m]itm.nṣ.l bn[.---]. | [-]l[-.---]. | [-]ṯ.[---]. | mṣb[-.---]. | kṯ.aqh[r.---]. | l 143[-].1.10
-.ltḥ.]sbbyn.ltḥ.ššmn.ltḥ.šḥlt. | [---.ltḥ.]ṣmqm.[ṯ]ṯ.mat.nṣ.ṯlṯm.'ṣr. | [---].ḫmš[m.ḥm]r.škm. | [---.ṯṯ.dd.]gdl.ṯṯ.dd.š'rm 142[12].5
h[r.---]. | l bn[.---]. | [ṯ]lṯ.[---]. | [---.--]yn.š.aḫ[--]. | [---.]š.nṣ[.-]al[-]. | [---.---]m[.---]. 143[-].3.2
---.]ṯlṯ.kṯṯ[.-]d.[---]. | [---.a]rb'.dblt.m[--.---]. | [--.mi]tm nṣ.[-]ṯ[-.]gr[-.---]. | [---].arb['.d]d.š['rm.---]. | [--.-]rṯm š[šm]n. 143[-].1.6
-].kmn.ltḥ.sbbyn. | [---.-]'t.ltḥ.ššmn. | [---].ḫswn.ṯṯ.mat.nṣ. | [---].ḫmšm.ḥmr.škm. | [---.ṯṯ.dd.]gdl.ṯṯ.dd.š'rm. | [---.a]llp 142[12].11

nṣb

r bn il. | mpḫrt bn il. | ṯrmn w šnm. | il w aṯrt. | ḫnn il. | nṣbt il. | šlm il. | il ḥš il add. | b'l ṣpn b'l. | ugrt. | b mrḥ il. | b ni 30[107].7
].td.išt. | b bht m.n[bl]at.b hkl m. | sb.ksp.l rqm.ḫrṣ. | nṣb.l lbnt.šmḫ. | aliyn.b'l.ht y.bnt. | dt.ksp.hkl y.dtm. | ḫrṣ.'d 4[51].6.35
n'[n]. | 'ma nkl ḫtn y.a[ḫ]r. | nkl yrḫ ytrḫ.adn h. | yšt mṣb.mznm.um h. | kp mznm.iḫ h yṯ'r. | mšrrm.aḫt h l a | bn 24[77].34
| tmrnn.l bny.bnwt. | w ykn.bn h b bt.šrš.b qrb. | hkl h.nṣb.skn.ilib h.b qdš. | ztr.'m h.l arṣ.mšṣu.qṭr h. | l 'pr.ḏmr.aṯr 17[2AQHT].1.27
mt. | [---.mt.r]pi.w ykn.bn h. | [b bt.šrš.]b qrb.hkl h. | [nṣb.skn.i]lib h.b qdš. | [ztr.'m h.l a]rṣ.mšṣu. | [qṭr h.l 'pr.ḏ]m 17[2AQHT].1.45
ḫ.b irt y. | npš.k yld.bn.l y.km. | aḫ y.w šrš.km ary y. | nṣb.skn.ilib y.b qdš. | ztr.'m y.l 'pr.ḏmr.aṯr[y]. | ṭbq lḥt.niṣ y 17[2AQHT].2.16
rẓẓ h. | [---].mǵy h.w ǵlm. | [a]ḫt h.šib.yṣat.mrḥ h. | l tl.yṣb.pn h.tǵr. | yṣu.hlm.aḫ h.tph. | [ksl]h.l arṣ.ṯṯbr. | [---.]aḫ h 16.1[125].52
. | [---.--]ml.ksl h.k b[r]q. | [---.]m[-]ǵ[-].thmt.brq. | [---].tṣb.qšt.bnt. | [---.']n h.km.bṯn.yqr. | [krpn h.-.l]arṣ.ks h.tšpk 17[2AQHT].6.13
šb'.mṣb. | rqd.ṯlṯ.mṣb.w.[---]. | uḫnp.ṯṯ.mṣb. | tgmr.[y]n.mṣb š[b']. | w ḥs[p] ṯn.k[dm]. 2004.35
]rpn. | [---.]ym.w t'l.trṯ. | [---].yn.'šy l ḥbš. | [---.]ḥtn.qn.yṣbt. | [---.--]m.b nši.'n h.w tphn. | [---.--]ml.ksl h.k b[r]q. | [-- 17[2AQHT].6.9

nṣd

.l.azzlt. | [---.]l.'ṯtrt.šd. | [---].yb'lnn. | [---.--]n.b.ṯlṯ.šnt.l.nṣd. | [---.--]ršp.mlk.k.ypdd.mlbš. | u---].mlk.ytn.mlbš. | [---.-] 1106.57

nṣdn

n.mqwṭ. | bn.bsn. | bn.inr[-]. | bn.ṯbil. | bn.iryn. | ṯṯl. | bn.nṣdn. | bn.ydln. | [bn].'dy. | [bn].ilyn. 1071.8
[-----]. | ḏ[----]. | ab[--.---]. | bn.nṣdn[.ḫm]št. | bn.arsw '[šr]m. | 'šdyn.ḫmš[t]. | abršn.'šr[t]. | b' 1062.4
bn.ntp. | 'myn.bn ǵḥpn. | bn.kbln. | bn.bly. | bn.ṯ'y. | bn.nṣdn. | klby. 104[316].8
yn. | šd.bn.prmn.l aḫny. | šd.bn ḥnn.l bn.adlḏn. | šd.bn.nṣdn.l bn.'mlbi. | šd.ṯpḫln.l bn.ǵl. | w dṯn.nḥl h.l bn.pl. | šd.kr 2089.8

nṣl

[---.]šlm. | [---.--]š.lalit. | [---.]bt šp.š. | y[-]lm.w mlk. | ynṣl.l ṯ'y. 2005.2.8

nṣp

qrt ṯqlm.w nṣp. | šlmy.ṯql. | ary ṯql. | ṯmry ṯql.w.nṣp. | aǵt nṣp. | dmt ṯql. | ykn'm ṯql. 69[111].4
t ṯqlm.w nṣp. | šlmy.ṯql. | ary ṯql. | ṯmry ṯql.w.nṣp. | aǵt nṣp. | dmt ṯql. | ykn'm ṯql. 69[111].5
b[-.---.--] | r ṯṯm lḥm. | l[.-]ry ṯlṯ spm w 'šr lḥm. | [--.]w nṣp w ṯlṯ spm w 'šrm lḥ[m]. | l[.-]dt ḫnd[r]ṯ ar' s[p]m w 'š[r] 134[-].4
| ḫmšm.šmt.b.ṯql. | kkr.w.[ml]tḥ.tyt.[---]. | [b]šb'[m.w.n]ṣp.ksp. | [tgm]r.[alp.w.]ṯlṯ.mat. 2101.27
.ṯqlm. | ksp h.mitm.pḥm.b d.skn. | w.ṯṯ.ktnm.ḫmšt.w.nṣp.ksp.hn. 1110.6
.uṯbm.b d.alḫn.b.'šrt[.k]sp. | rṭ.l.ql.d.ybl.prd. | b.ṯql.w.nṣp.ksp. | ṯmn.lbšm.w.mšlt. | l.udmym.b.ṯmnt.'šrt.ksp. | šb'm 2101.13
---]. | [-]tm.iph.adt y.w.[---]. | tšṣḥq.hn.aṯt.l.'bd. | šb't.w.nṣp.ksp. | [-]tm.rb[.--.a]ḥd. | [---.--]t.b[-]. | [---.-]y[-]. 1017.5
qrt ṯqlm.w nṣp. | šlmy.ṯql. | ary ṯql. | ṯmry ṯql.w.nṣp. | aǵt nṣp. | dmt ṯql. | 69[111].1
nsk k[sp]. | 'šrt. | w nṣ[p]. 1164.3

nṣṣn

n.qšt.w.ql'. | uln.qšt. | bn.blẓn.qšt.w.ql'. | gb'.qšt.w.ql'. | nṣṣn.qšt. | m'r. | [']dyn.ṯt.qštm.w.ql'. | [-]lrš.qšt.w.ql'. | t[t]n.qš 119[321].2.11

nṣr

qt dm. | li.w ttb'.š'tqt. | bt.krt.bu.tbu. | bkt.tgly.w tbu. | nṣrt.tbu.pnm. | 'rm.tdu.mh. | pdrm.tdu.šrr. | ḫṭ m.t'mt.[']ṭr.[16.6[127].5

nqbn

. | hlk.kbkbm.mdl.'r. | ṣmd.pḥl.št.gpn y dt ksp. | dt.yrq.nqbn y.tš[m']. | pǵt.ṯkmt.my.ḥspt.l[š']r.ṭl. | yd't.hlk.kbkbm. 19[1AQHT].2.54
d.w amr[r]. | mdl.'r.ṣmd.pḥl. | št.gpnm.dt.ksp. | dt.yrq.nqbnm. | 'db.gpn.atnt h. | yḫbq.qdš.w amrr. | yštn.aṯrt.l bmt.' 4[51].4.11
| aṯrt.ym[.mdl.'r]. | ṣmd.pḥl[.št.gpnm.dt]. | ksp.dt.yr[q.nqbnm]. | 'db.gpn.atnt[y]. | yšm'.qd.w amr[r]. | mdl.'r.ṣmd.p 4[51].4.6

nqd

nqdm. | bn.alṯn. | bn.dly. | bn.btry. | bn.ḫdmn. | [bn].šty. | [bn]. 2018.1
[nq]dm.dt.kn.npṣ hm. | [bn].lbn.arb‘.qšt.w.ar[b‘]. | [u]ṯpt.ql‘. 2047.1
sp.d.šb[n]. | mit.ksp.d.ṯbq. | ṯmnym.arb‘t. | kbd.ksp. | d.nqdm. | ḫmšm.l mit. | ksp.d.mkr.ar. | arb‘m ksp d mkr. | atlg. 2107.8
mrynm. | mrum. | ‘šrm. | ṯnnm. | nq[dm]. | kh[nm]. | inšt. 2019.5
| mru.ibrn. | pslm. | šrm. | yṣḥm. | ‘šrm. | mrum. | ṯnnm. | mqdm. | khnm. | qdšm. | nsk.ksp. | mkrm. 71[113].71
mrynm. | mrum. | ‘šrm. | ṯnnm. | nqdm. | khnm. | qdšm. | pslm. | mkrm. | yṣḥm. | šrm. | n‘rm. | ‘b 1026.1.5
n.b d.bn.tnn. | [š]d.bn.ḫrmln.ṯn.b d.bn.ḫdmn. | [u]bdy.nqdm. | [ṯlṯ].šdm.d.n‘rb.gt.npk. | [š]d.rpan.b d.klṯṯb. | [š]d.ilṣ 82[300].2.12
ṯr.w ḫss. | spr.ilmlk šbny. | lmd.atn.prln.rb. | khnm rb.nqdm. | ṯ‘y.nqmd.mlk ugr[t]. | adn.yrgb.b‘l.ṯrmn. 6.6[62.2].55
n.ḥrš.qṭn.ṯqlm. | bn.pǵdn.ṯqlm. | bn.b‘ln.ṯqlm. | ‘bdyrḫ.nqd.ṯqlm. | bt.sgld.ṯqlm. | bn.‘my.ṯqlm. | bn.brq.ṯqlm. | bn.ḫnz 122[308].1.12
q[--.--]. | w [---.]rkb[.---]. | [---].d[--.---]. | b ql[.-----]. | w tštqdn[.-----]. | hm. | w yḥ.mlk. | w ik m.kn.w [---]. | tšknnnn[. 62[26].7

nqṯn

kbr. | bn iytlm. | bn ayln. | bn.kln. | bn.‘lln. | bn.liy. | bn.nqṯn. | bn abrḫṯ. | bn.grdy. | bn.ṣlpn. | bn ǵlmn. | bn sgld. 1064.26

nql

-]. | [---.b‘]lt.bhtm.š[--.---]. | [---.-]rt.l.dml[.---]. | [b.yrḫ].nql.ṯn.ḫpn[.---]. | [---].aḥd.ḫmš.am[--.---]. | [---.--]m.qmṣ.ṯlṯm 1106.35
[---.y]rḫ.n[ql.---]. | [---.]m[---]. | [---.yr]ḫ.mgm[r.---]. | [---.--]š.b d.h[--.- 1160.1

nqly

. | bn.il[--]. | khnm[.--]. | bn.ṯ[--]. | bn.[---]. | bn.ṯ‘l[-]. | bn.nq[ly]. | bn.snr[n]. | bn.pzn[y]. | bn.mg[lb]. | bn.db[--]. | bn.am 2020.8
yn. | bn.knn. | khnm. | bn.ṯ‘y. | w.nḥl h. | w.nḥl hm. | bn.nqly. | bn.snrn. | bn.tgd. | bn.d[-]n. | bn.amdn. | bn.ṯmrn. | bn.p 105[86].2
bt.il. | b‘l.bt.aḏmny. | b‘l.bt.pdy. | b‘l.bt.nqly. | b‘l.bt.‘lr. | b‘l.bt.ssl. | b‘l.bt.ṯrn. | b‘l.bt.ktmn. | b‘l.bt.ndb 31[14].4

nqmd

---.]ugr. | w npy.yman.w npy.‘rmt.w npy.[---]. | w npy.nqmd.ušn.yp km.ulp.q[ṭy.ulp.ddm]y. | ulp.ḫry.ulp.ḫ[t]y.ulp. 32[2].1.20
lk.r[b.--]. | mṣmt.l nqmd.[---.-]št. | hl ny.argmn.d [ybl.n]qmd. | l špš.arn.ṯn[.‘šr h.]mn. | ‘ṣrm.ṯql.kbd[.ks].mn.ḫrṣ. | 64[118].18
pr.ilmlk šbny. | lmd.atn.prln.rb. | khnm rb.nqdm. | ṯ‘y.nqmd.mlk ugr[t]. | adn.yrgb.b‘l.ṯrmn. 6.6[62.2].56
[šmt.n]qmp‘. | [bn.nq]md. | [mlk.]ugrt. | b‘l ṣdq. | skn.bt. | mlk.ṯǵr. | [m]lk.bny. | [- 1007.2
.w [---]b. | [ḫm]š.mat pḥm. | [ḫm]š[.m]at.iqnu. | argmn.nqmd.mlk. | ugrt.d ybl.l špš. | mlk.rb.b‘l h. | ks.ḫrṣ.ktn.mit.p 64[118].24
t. | br.ṣtqšlm. | b unṯ.‘d ‘lm. | mišmn.nqmd. | mlk ugrt. | nqmd.mlk.ugrt. | ktb.spr hnd. | dt brrt.ṣtqšlm. | ‘bd h.hnd. | w 1005.8
.km.špš. | d brt.kmt. | br.ṣtqšlm. | b unṯ.‘d ‘lm. | mišmn.nqmd. | mlk ugrt. | nqmd.mlk.ugrt. | ktb.spr hnd. | dt brrt.ṣtq 1005.6
n.šp[š.mlk.rb]. | b‘l h.šlm.[w spš]. | mlk.rb.b‘l h.[---]. | nqmd.mlk.ugr[t.--]. | phy. | w tpllm.mlk.r[b.--]. | mṣmt.l nqm 64[118].14
[spr.ilmlk.ṯ‘]y.nqmd.mlk.ugrt. 4[51].9.1
]. | w mlk[.nhš.w mlk.mg]šḫ. | ‘mn.[---]. | ik y.[---]. | w l n[qmd.---]. | [w]nqmd.[---]. | [-.]‘mn.šp[š.mlk.rb]. | b‘l h.šlm.[64[118].9
. | [---].l.lim. | [---.mšr m]šr. | [bn.ugrt.---.--]y. | [---.np]y nqmd. | [---.]pḫr. | [-----]. | [-----]. | [---.t‘ḏ]r b‘l. | [-----]. | [-----]. | APP.I[-].2.3
mlk.mg]šḫ. | ‘mn.[---]. | ik y.[---]. | w l n[qmd.---]. | [w]nqmd.[---]. | [-.]‘mn.šp[š.mlk.rb]. | b‘l h.šlm.[w spš]. | mlk.rb. 64[118].10
qmd.mlk.ugr[t.--]. | phy. | w tpllm.mlk.r[b.--]. | mṣmt.l nqmd.[---.-]št. | hl ny.argmn.d [ybl.n]qmd. | l špš.arn.ṯn[.‘šr 64[118].17

nqmp‘

[šmt.n]qmp‘. | [bn.nq]md. | [mlk.]ugrt. | b‘l ṣdq. | skn.bt. | mlk.ṯǵr. | 1007.1
l ym.hnd. | ‘mṯtmr. | bn.nqmp‘. | mlk.ugrt. | ytn.bt.anndr. | bn.ytn.bnš. | [ml]k.d.b riš. 1009.3
l ym hnd. | ‘mṯtmr.bn. | nqmp‘.ml[k]. | ugrt.ytn. | šd.kḏǵdl[.bn]. | [-]š[-]y.d.b š[-]y. | [-- 1008.3

nqp

mdbr qdš. | ṯm tgrgr.l abnm.w l.‘ṣm.šb‘.šnt. | tmt.ṯmn.nqpt.‘d.ilm.n‘mm.ttlkn. | šd.tṣdn.pat.mdbr.w ngš.hm.nǵr. | 23[52].67
.a[--.---]. | bnt.šdm.ṣḥr[.---]. | šb‘.šnt.il.mla.[-]. | w ṯmn.nqpnt.‘d. | k lbš.km.lpš.dm a[ḫ h]. | km.all.dm.ary h. | k šb‘t.l 12[75].2.46

nqq

šrm. | [b]n.špš[yn]. | [b]n.ḫrmln. | bn.tnn. | bn.pndr. | bn.nqq. | ḥrš.bhtm. | bn.izl. | bn.ibln. | bn.ilt. | špšyn.nḥl h. | n‘mn. 85[80].2.1

nr

ymǵ.l mrrt.tǵll.b nr. | yšu.g h.w yṣḥ.y l k.mrrt. | tǵll.b nr.d ‘l k.mḫṣ.aqht. | ǵzr.šrš k.b arṣ.al. | yp‘.riš.ǵly.b d.ns‘ k. | ‘ 19[1AQHT].3.158
h.‘nt.p dr[.dr]. | ‘db.uḫry mṭ.yd h. | ymǵ.l mrrt.tǵll.b nr. | yšu.g h.w yṣḥ.y l k.mrrt. | tǵll.b nr.d ‘l k.mḫṣ.aqht. | ǵzr. 19[1AQHT].3.156

nrgn

l ym hnd. | iwr[k]l.pdy. | agdn.bn.nrgn. | w ynḥm.aḫ h. | w.b‘ln aḫ h. | w.ḥttn bn h. | w.btšy.bt h 1006.3

nryn

d‘n.p[--.---]. | [-]d[-]l.bn.ḥrn. | aḫty.bt.abm. | [-]rbn.‘dd.nryn. | [ab]r[p]u.bn.kbd. | [-]m[-].bn.ṣmrt. | liy.bn.yṣi. | ḏmrhd 102[322].6.3
.y‘rty. | bn.ḫdyn.ugrty. | bn.tgdn.ugrty. | tgyn.arty. | bn.nryn.arty. | bn.ršp.ary. | bn.ǵlmn ary. | bn.ḥṣbn ary. | bn.šdy a 87[64].11

nrn

‘l.ubr‘y. | w.ṯn.‘l. | mlk. | w.aḥd. | ‘l atlg. | w l.‘ṣm. | tspr. | nrn.al.tud | ad.at.l hm. | ṯṯm.ksp. 1010.19
ar[y.---]. | b‘lsip.a[ry.---]. | klt h.[---]. | ṯty.ary.m[--.---]. | nrn.arny[.---]. | w.ṯn.bn h.w.b[---.---]. | b tn[--.---]. | swn.qrty[. 81[329].5
sln.bn.‘ṯt[-.---]. | pdy.bn.nr[-.---]. | abmlk.bn.un[-.---]. | nrn.bn.mtn[-.---]. | aḫyn.bn.nbk[-.---]. | ršpn.bn.b‘ly[.---]. | bni 90[314].1.9
zt.b d hm.rib. | w [---]. | [-----]. | [-]šy[.---] h. | [-]kt[.---.]nrn. | [b]n.nmq[.---]. | [ḫm]št.ksp.‘l.aṯt. | [-]ṯd[.bn.]štn. 2055.17

nrn

mryn[m]. | bn.bly. | nrn. | w.nḥl h. | bn.rmyy. | bn.tlmyn. | w.nḥl h. | w.nḥl hm. | bn 113[400].1.3
---.]w.bnš.aḥd. | [---.--]m. | [---].‘tgrm. | [---.-]ṣbm. | [---.]nrn.m‘ry. | [---.--]r. | [---.]w.ṯn.bn h. | [---.b]t h.‘tgrm. 2043.9
. | bn.izl. | bn.ibln. | bn.ilt. | špšyn.nḥl h. | n‘mn.bn.iryn. | nrn.nḥl h. | bn.ḫsn. | bn.‘bd. | [-----]. | [---.n]ḥ[l h]. | [-]ntm[.---] 85[80].2.8
n. | šd.b d.bn.uṯryn. | [ubd]y.mrynm. | [š]d.bn.ṣnrn.b d.nrn. | [š]d.bn.rwy.b d.ydln. | [š].bn.trn.b d.ibrmd̠. | [š]d.bn.ilṯt 82[300].1.8
mdm. | [---.b]‘ln. | [---.]lmdm.b d.snrn. | [---.lm]dm.b d.nrn. | [---.ḫ]d̠ǵlm. | [lmd.]aḥd.b d.yrš. 1051.4
š‘rt. | l.kṯrmlk.ḫpn. | l.‘bdil[m].ḫpn. | tmrtn.š‘rt. | lmd.n.rn. | [---].ḫpn. | dqn.š‘rt. | [lm]d.yrṯ. | [-.]ynḥm.ḫpn. | ṯṯ.lmd.b‘l 1117.12
[---.]liy. | [---.]nrn. | [---.-]pṯ. | [---.]knys.[---]. | [---.--]by. | [---.-]ṯby[.---]. | [---]. 2134.2

nrpd

‘dmlk. | bn.alt[-]. | iḫy[-]. | ‘bdgṯr. | ḥrr. | bn.s[-]p[-]. | bn.nrpd. | bn.ḥ[-]y. | b‘lskn. | bn.‘bd. | ḫyrn. | alpy. | bn.plsy. | bn.qr 1035.1.13

nrt

t.[--]. | ṣbi nrt.ilm.špš.[-]r[--]. | pǵt.minš.šdm l m‘[rb]. | nrt.ilm.špš.mǵy[t]. | pǵt.l ahlm.rgm.l yṯ[pn.y] | bl.agrtn.bat.b 19[1AQHT].4.211
dm‘t.gm. | tṣḥ.l nrt.ilm.špš. | ‘ms m‘.l y.aliyn.b‘l. | tšm‘.nrt.ilm.špš. | tšu.aliyn.b‘l.l ktp. | ‘nt.k tšt h.tš‘lyn h. | b ṣrrt.ṣp 6[62].1.13
iyn.b‘l. | iy.zbl.b‘l.arṣ. | ttb‘.btlt.‘nt. | idk.l ttn.pnm. | ‘m.nrt.ilm.špš. | tšu.g h.w tṣḥ. | tḥm.ṯr.il.ab k. | hwt.lṭpn.ḥtk k. | 6[49].4.32
išt. | [---]y.yblmm.u[---]k.yrd[.--.]i[---]n.bn. | [---.-]nn.nrt.ilm.špš.tšu.g h.w t[ṣḥ.šm]‘.m‘. | [-.yṯ]ir ṯr.il.ab k.l pn.zbl. 2.3[129].15
t.my.lim.bn dgn. | my.hmlt.aṯr.b‘l.nrd. | b arṣ.‘m h.trd.nrt. | ilm.špš.‘d.tšb‘.bk. | tšt.k yn.udm‘t.gm. | tṣḥ.l nrt.ilm.špš. 6[62].1.8
.trd.nrt. | ilm.špš.‘d.tšb‘.bk. | tšt.k yn.udm‘t.gm. | tṣḥ.l nrt.ilm.špš. | ‘ms m‘.l y.aliyn.b‘l. | tšm‘.nrt.ilm.špš. | tšu.aliyn. 6[62].1.11
zbl.b‘l.arṣ. | gm.yṣḥ.il.l btlt. | ‘nt.šm‘.l btlt.‘n[t]. | rgm.l nrt.il.šp[š]. | pl.‘nt.šdm.y špš. | pl.‘nt.šdm.il.yšt k. | [b]‘l.‘nt.m 6[49].3.24
yn b‘l. | ‘dbnn ank.imr.b p y. | k lli.b ṯbrn q y.ḫtu hw. | nrt.ilm.špš.ṣḥrrt. | la.šmm.b yd.bn ilm.mt. | ym.ymm.y‘tqn.l 6[49].2.24
---]. | ‘ln.ṯ[--.---]. | l p‘n.ǵl[m]m[.---]. | mid.an[--.]ṣn[--]. | nrt.ilm.špš[.ṣḥrr]t. | la.šmm.b y[d.bn.ilm.m]t. | w t‘n.btlt.‘n[t 3[‘NT.VI].5.25
t.al.y‘db km. | k imr.b p h. | k lli.b ṯbrn. | qn h.ṯḫtan. | nrt.ilm.špš. | ṣḥrrt.la. | šmm.b yd.md | d.ilm.mt.b a | lp.šd.rbt. 4[51].8.21
t k]. | b‘l.‘nt.mḥrṯ[-]. | iy.aliyn.b‘l. | iy.zbl.b‘l.arṣ. | w t‘n.nrt.ilm.š[p]š. | šd yn.‘n.b qbt[.t] | bl lyt.‘l.umt k. | w abqt.aliy 6[49].4.41
-.b] | nšg h.ḥrb.tšt.b t‘r[t h]. | w ‘l.tlbš.npṣ.aṯt.[--]. | ṣbi nrt.ilm.špš.[-]r[--]. | pǵt.minš.šdm l m‘[rb]. | nrt.ilm.špš.mǵy[19[1AQHT].4.209
n‘m.l arṣ.mṭr.b‘l. | w l šd.mṭr.‘ly. | n‘m.l ḥṭt.b gn. | bm.nrt.ksmm. | ‘l.tl[-]k.‘ṭrṭrm. | nšu.[r]iš.ḥrṯm. | l ẓr.‘db.dgn kly. 16[126].3.10

nš

b ym.tld[---.]b[-.]y[--.---]. | [---.il]m.rb[m.--]š[-]. | [---].nš.b [---]. | [---].tm[--.--]aṯ[.---]. | [---.]akl[.---]. | [---.-]l[-.-]hg[.- UG5.8.27

nša

yd‘t.hlk.kbkbm. | bkm.tmdln.‘r. | bkm.tṣmd.pḥl.bkm. | tšu.ab h.tštnn.l[b]mt ‘r. | l ysmsm.bmt.pḥl. | y dnil.ysb.palt 19[1AQHT].2.59
.l nrt.ilm.špš. | ‘ms m‘.l y.aliyn.b‘l. | tšm‘.nrt.ilm.špš. | tšu.aliyn.b‘l.l ktp. | ‘nt.k tšt h.tš‘lyn h. | b ṣrrt.ṣpn.tbkyn h. | 6[62].1.14
km.ln.kḥṯ. | zbl km.w ank.‘ny.mlak.ym.t‘dt.ṯpṭ.nhr. | tšu ilm rašt hm.l ẓr.brkt hm.ln.kḥṯ.zbl hm. | aḫr.tmǵyn.mla 2.1[137].29
n.kḥṯ.zbl km.aḥd. | ilm.t‘ny lḥt.mlak.ym.t‘dt.ṯpṭ.nhr. | šu.ilm.rašt km.l ẓr.brkt km.ln.kḥṯ. | zbl km.w ank.‘ny.mlak. 2.1[137].27
tn.b‘l. | [s]pu y.bn m.um y.kly y. | yṯb.‘m.b‘l.ṣrrt. | ṣpn.yšu g h.w yṣḥ. | aḫ y m.ytnt.b‘l. | spu y.bn m.um y.kl | y y.yt‘ 6[49].6.13
lb.‘n[t]. | aṯr.b‘l.tiḫd.m[t]. | b sin.lpš.tšṣq[n h]. | b qṣ.all.tšu.g h.w[tṣ] | ḥ.at.mt.tn.aḫ y. | w ‘n.bn.ilm.mt.mh. | taršn.l 6[49].2.11
l. | [ṯṯbr.‘ln.p]n h.td[‘]. | tǵṣ[.pnt.ks]l h. | anš.dt.ẓr.[h]. | tšu.g h.w tṣḥ[.i]k. | mǵy.aliy[n.b]‘l. | ik.mǵyt.b[t]lt. | ‘nt.mḫṣ 4[51].2.21
ṭ.b‘d n.ksl.ṯṯbr. | ‘ln.pn h.td‘.tǵṣ.pnt. | ksl h.anš.dt.ẓr h.tšu. | g h.w tṣḥ.ik.mǵy.gpn.w ugr. | mn.ib.yp‘.l b‘l.ṣrt. | l rkb.‘ 3[‘NT].3.32
yprq.lṣb.w yṣḥq. | p‘n h.l hdm.yṭpd.w ykrkr. | uṣb‘t h.yšu.g h.w y[ṣḥ]. | ik.mǵyt.rbt.aṯr[t.y]m. | ik.atwt.qnyt.i[lm]. | 4[51].4.30
dqn. | yṯlṯ.qn.d̠r‘ h.yḥrṯ. | k gn.ap lb.k ‘mq.yṯlṯ. | bmt.yšu.g h.w yṣḥ. | b‘l.mt.my.lim.bn. | dgn.my.hmlt.aṯr. | b‘l.ard. 5[67].6.22
nm. | ‘m.b‘l.mrym.ṣpn. | b alp.šd.rbt.kmn. | ṣḥq.btlt.‘nt.tšu. | g h.w tṣḥ.tbšr b‘l. | bšrt k.yblt.y[b]n. | bt.l k.km.aḫ k.w 4[51].5.87
h.tlšn.aqht.ǵzr. | [---.kdd.dn]il.mt.rpi.w t‘n. | [btlt.‘nt.tšu.g]h.w tṣḥ.hwt. | [---.]aqht.yd̠[--]. | [---.--]n.ṣ[---]. | [spr.ilm 17[2AQHT].6.53
n.aḫt.b‘l. | l pnn h.ydd.w yqm. | l p‘n h.ykr‘.w yql. | w yšu.g h.w yṣḥ. | ḥwt.aḫt.w nar[-]. | qrn.d bat k.btlt.‘nt. | qrn.d 10[76].2.19
nt.p dr[.dr]. | ‘db.uḫry mṭ.yd h. | ymǵ.l mrrt.tǵll.b nr. | yšu.g h.w yṣḥ.y l k.mrrt. | tǵll.b nr.d ‘l k.mḫṣ.aqht. | ǵzr.šrš 19[1AQHT].3.157
db.uḫry mṭ yd h. | ymǵ.l qrt.ablm.abl[m]. | qrt.zbl.yrḫ.yšu g h. | w yṣḥ.y l k.qrt.ablm. | d ‘l k.mḫṣ.aqht.ǵzr. | ‘wrt.yšt 19[1AQHT].4.164
.lṭpn.il.d pid. | p‘n h.l hdm.yṭpd. | w yprq.lṣb w yṣḥq. | yšu.g h.w yṣḥ. | aṯbn.ank.w anḫn. | w tnḫ.b irt y.npš. | k ḥy.al 6[49].3.17
šmḫ.w ‘l yṣhl pi[t]. | yprq.lṣb.w yṣḥq. | p‘n.l hdm.yṭpd.yšu. | g h.w yṣḥ.aṯbn.ank. | w anḫn.w tnḫ.b irt y. | npš.k yld.b 17[2AQHT].2.11
l.[---]. | [tt]b‘.btlt.‘nt[.idk.l ttn.pnm]. | ‘m.yṭpn.mhr.š[t.tšu.g h]. | w tṣḥ.ytb.yṭp.[---]. | qrt.ablm.ablm.[qrt.zbl.yrḫ]. | i 18[3AQHT].4.6
šrm. | tpr.w du.b nši.‘n h.w ypn. | yḥd.hrgb.ab.nšrm. | yšu.g h.w yṣḥ.knp.hr[g]b. | b‘l.yṯb.b‘l.y[ṯb]r.diy[.h]wt. | w yq 19[1AQHT].3.122
t.w yql. | tḥt.p‘n h.ybq‘.kbd h.w yḥd. | [i]n.šmt.in.‘ẓm.yšu.g[h]. | w yṣḥ.knp.hrgb.b‘l.ybn. | [b]‘l.ybn.diy.hwt.hrg[b]. 19[1AQHT].3.131
t.ybl.l qẓ.ybky.w yqbr. | yqbr.nn.b mdgt.b knk[-]. | w yšu.g h.w yṣḥ.knp.nšrm. | b‘l.yṯbr.b‘l.yṯbr.diy. | hmt.hm.t‘pn 19[1AQHT].3.148
b nši[.‘n h.w yphn.yḥd]. | b ‘rpt[.nšrm.yšu]. | [g h.]w yṣḥ[.knp.nšrm]. | b‘l.yṯb.b‘l.yṯb[r.diy.hmt]. | tql 19[1AQHT].2.106
.tqln. | tḥt.p‘n h.ybq‘.kbdt hm.w[yḥd]. | in.šmt.in.‘ẓm.yšu.g h. | w yṣḥ.knp.nšrm.ybn. | b‘l.ybn.diy hmt nšrm. | tpr.w 19[1AQHT].3.117
b]. | tpr.w du.b nši.‘n h. | [w]yphn.yḥd.ṣml.um.nšrm. | yšu.g h.w yṣḥ.knp.ṣml. | b‘l.yṯbr.b‘l.yṯbr.diy. | hyt.tql.tḥt.p‘n 19[1AQHT].3.136
y[p]tḥ.b dqt.‘rpt. | ‘l h[wt].kṯr.w ḫss. | ṣḥq.kṯr.w ḫss. | yšu.g h.w yṣḥ. | l rgmt.l k.l ali | yn.b‘l.ttbn.b‘l. | l hwt y.yptḥ. 4[51].7.22
. | l šnt.[m]k.b šb‘. | šnt.w [--].bn.ilm.mt. | ‘m.aliyn.b‘l.yšu. | g h.w yṣḥ.‘l k.b[‘]l m. | pht.qlt.‘l k.pht. | dry.b ḥrb.‘l k. | 6[49].5.10
| ap.bnt.ḥry. | km hm.w ṯbss.aṯrt. | ndr h.w ilt.p[--]. | w tšu.g h.w [tṣḥ]. | ph m‘.ap.k[rt.--]. | u ṯn.ndr[.---]. | apr.[---]. | [15[128].3.27
| mlk.ab.šnm.l p‘n. | il.thbr.w tql. | tštḥwy.w tkbdn h. | tšu.g h.w tṣḥ.tšmḫ ht. | aṯrt.w bn h.ilt.w ṣb | rt.ary h.k mt.ali 6.1.39[49.1.11]
| brlt h.l ṯrm. | mt.dm.ḫt.š‘tqt. | dm.lan.w ypqd. | krt.ṯ‘.yšu.g h. | w yṣḥ.šm‘.l mṯt. | ḥry.ṭbḫ.imr. | w ilḥm.mgt.w iṯrm. 16.6[127].15
.‘]n h.km.bṯn.yqr. | [krpn h.-.l]arṣ.ks h.tšpk m. | [l ‘pr.tšu.g h.]w tṣḥ.šm‘.m‘. | [l aqht.ǵzr.i]rš.ksp.w atn k. | [ḫrṣ.w a 17[2AQHT].6.16
[‘m.a]qht.ǵzr.b alp.š[d]. | [rbt.]kmn.w ṣḥq.btlt.[‘nt]. | [tšu.]g h.w tṣḥ.šm‘.m[‘.l a] | [qht.ǵ]zr.at.aḫ.w an.a[ḫt k]. | [---] 18[3AQHT].1.23
mlk.amlk. | l drkt.k aṯb.an. | ytb‘.yṣb ǵlm.‘l. | ab h.y‘rb.yšu g h. | w yṣḥ.šm‘ m‘.l krt. | ṯ‘.ištm‘.w tqǵ udn. | k ǵz.ǵzm.t 16.6[127].40
blmm.u[---]k.yrd[.--.]i[---]n.bn. | [---.-]nn.nrt.ilm.špš.tšu.g h.w t[ṣḥ.šm]‘.m‘. | [-.yṯ]ir ṯr.il.ab k.l pn.zbl.ym.l pn[.ṯ] 2.3[129].15
k].b šb‘. | šnt.w y‘n[.dnil.mt.]rpi. | yṯb.ǵzr.m[t.hrnmy.y]šu. | g h.w yṣḥ.t[b‘.---]. | bkyt.b hk[l]y.mšspdt. | b ḥẓr y pẓ 19[1AQHT].4.181

t.kmn.l p‘]n.‘nt. | [yhbr.w yql.yšt]ḥwyn.w y | [kbdn h.yšu.g h.w y]ṣḥ.tḥm. | [ṯr.il.ab k.hwt.l]ṭpn.ḥtk k. | [qryy.b arṣ. 1[‘NT.IX].2.17
l.b‘l.arṣ. | ttb‘.btlt.‘nt. | idk.l ttn.pnm. | ‘m.nrt.ilm.špš. | tšu.g h.w tṣḥ. | tḥm.ṯr.il.ab k. | hwt.lṭpn.ḥtk k. | pl.‘nt.šdm.y š 6[49].4.33
.pn h.td‘.b ‘dn]. | ksl.y[ṯbr.yǵṣ.pnt.ksl h]. | anš.[dt.ẓr h.yšu.g h]. | w yṣ[ḥ.---]. | mḫṣ[.---]. | š[--.---]. 19[1AQHT].2.96
]. | p.šn[-.---]. | w l ṯlb.[---]. | mit.rḥ[.---]. | ṯṯlb.a[--.---]. | yšu.g h[.---]. | i.ap.b‘[l.---]. | i.hd.d[---.---]. | ynp‘.b‘[l.---]. | b ṯm 5[67].4.5
apq.thmtm]. | [tgly.ḏd.il.w]tb[a]. | [qrš.mlk.ab.]šnm. | [tša.g hm.w tṣ]ḥ.sbn. | [---]l[.---.]‘d. | ksm.mhyt[.m]ǵny. | l n‘m 5[67].6.3
]ṣat[k.]rḥ.npš.hm. | k.iṯl.brlt n[-.k qṭr.b ap -]. | tmǵyn.tša.g h[m.w tṣḥn]. | šm‘.l dnil.[mt.rpi]. | mt.aqht.ǵzr.[ṣṣat]. | b 19[1AQHT].2.89
.bn.ilm.mt. | tk.qrt h.hmry.mk.ksu. | ṯbt.ḫḫ.arṣ.nḫlt h.tša. | g hm.w tṣḥ.tḥm.aliyn. | bn.b‘l.hwt.aliy.qrdm. | bhṯ.bn.il 5[67].2.16
d. | il.ttb‘.mlakm. | l ytb.idk.pnm. | l ytn.‘mm.pbl. | mlk.tšan. | g hm.w tṣḥn. | tḥm.krt.ṯ[‘]. | hwt.[n]‘mn.[ǵlm.il]. 14[KRT].6.303
| [mlakm.l yṯb]. | [idk.pnm.l ytn]. | [‘]m[.krt.mswn h]. | tš[an.g hm.w tṣḥn]. | tḥ[m.pbl.mlk]. | qḥ[.ksp.w yrq]. | ḫrṣ.[y 14[KRT].6.267
[.---]. | ṯṯb ‘ṯrt b ǵl[.---]. | qrẓ tšt.l šmal[.---]. | arbḫ.‘n h tšu w[.---]. | aylt tǵpy ṯr.‘n[.---]. | b[b]r.mrḥ h.ti[ḫd.b yd h]. | 2001.1.10
. | [---.]h.mḫtrt.pṯtm. | [---.-]t h.ušpǵt tišr. | [---.šm]m h.nšat ẓl h kbkbm. | [---.]b km kbkbt k ṯn. | [---.]b‘l yḥmdn h.y 2001.2.5
ḥtt.yn. | b gl.ḫrṣ.nbt.w ‘ly. | l ẓr.mgdl.rkb. | ṯkmm.ḥmt.nša. | [y]d h.šmmh.dbḥ. | l ṯr.ab h.il.šrd. | [b‘l].b dbḥ h.bn dg 14[KRT].4.167
nbt. | ‘l.l ẓr.[mg]dl. | w ‘l.l ẓr.[mg]dl.rkb. | ṯkmm.ḥm[t].ša.yd k. | šmm.dbḥ.l ṯr. | ab k.il.šrd.b‘l. | b dbḥ k.bn.dgn. | b m 14[KRT].2.75
m.l riš.agn.yqḥ.tš.b bt h. | il.ḥṭ h.nḥt.il.ymnn.mṭ.yd h.yšu. | yr.šmm h.yr.b šmm.‘ṣr.yḫrṭ yšt. | l pḥm.il.aṯtm.k ypt.h 23[52].37
| b ǵlp h.apnk.dnil. | [m]t.rpi.ap[h]n.ǵzr. | [mt.hrn]my.ytšu. | [yṯb.b ap.ṯ]ǵr[.t]ḥt. | [adrm.d b grn.y]dn. | [dn.almnt.y] 19[1AQHT].1.21
b[‘]. | b ymm.apnk.dnil.mt. | rpi.a hn.ǵzr.mt.hrnm[y]. | ytšu.ytb.b ap.ṯǵr.tḥt. | adrm.d b grn.ydn. | dn.almnt.yṯpṭ.ṯpṭ. 17[2AQHT].5.6
.bm.ymn h. | idk.l ytn pnm. | tk.aḫ.šmk.mla[t.r]umm. | tšu knp.btlt.‘n[t]. | tšu.knp.w tr.b ‘p. | tk.aḫ šmk.mlat rumm. 10[76].2.10
tn pnm. | tk.aḫ.šmk.mla[t.r]umm. | tšu knp.btlt.‘n[t]. | tšu.knp.w tr.b ‘p. | tk.aḫ šmk.mlat rumm. | w yšu.‘n h.aliyn. 10[76].2.11
u.l dbḥm.w l.ṯ‘.dbḥ n.ndbḥ]. | [hw.ṯ‘.nṯ‘y.hw.nkt.nkt.]yt[ši.l ab.bn.il]. | [ytši.l dr.bn.il.l mpḫ]rt.[bn.il.l ṯkmn.w šn] 32[2].1.9A
n.l dbḥm.]w l ṯ‘ dbḥ n. | ndbḥ.hw.ṯ‘ n[ṯ‘y.hw.nkt.nk]t.ytši.l ab bn il. | ytši.l d[r.bn il.l]mpḫrt.bn il. | l ṯkm[n.w šnm. 32[2].1.33
.l d[b]ḥm.w l.ṯ‘.dbḥ n.ndbḥ.hw.ṯ‘ | nṯ‘y. | hw.nkt.nkt.y[t]ši.l ab.bn.il.ytši.l dr. | bn il.l mpḫrt.bn.il.l ṯkmn[.w]šnm. 32[2].1.25
in.l bḥm.w l ṯ‘.d[bḥ n.ndbḥ]. | hw.ṯ‘.nṯ‘y.hw.nkt.n[k]t.ytši[.l ab.bn.il]. | ytši.l dr.bn.il.l mpḫrt.bn.i[l.l ṯkmn.w š]nm 32[2].1.16
[---.hw.ṯ‘.nṯ‘]y. | [hw.nkt.nkt.ytši.l ab.bn.il.ytši.l d]r.bn[.il]. | [l mpḫrt.bn.il.l ṯkmn.w šnm. 32[2].1.2
‘ dbḥ n. | ndbḥ.hw.ṯ‘ n[ṯ‘y.hw.nkt.nk]t.ytši.l ab bn il. | ytši.l d[r.bn il.l]mpḫrt.bn il. | l ṯkm[n.w šnm.]hn ‘[r]. | [---.] 32[2].1.34
[---.hw.ṯ‘.nṯ‘]y. | [hw.nkt.nkt.ytši.l ab.bn.il.ytši.l d]r.bn[.il]. | [l mpḫrt.bn.il.l ṯkmn.w šnm.hn š]. | [w šqr 32[2].1.2
bḥ n.ndb]ḥ. | [hw.ṯ‘.nṯ‘y.hw.nkt.nkt.]yt[ši.l ab.bn.il]. | [ytši.l dr.bn.il.l mpḫ]rt.[bn.il.l ṯkmn.w šn]m hn š. | [---.w n]p 32[2].1.9B
‘.dbḥ n.ndbḥ.hw.ṯ‘ | nṯ‘y. | hw.nkt.nkt.y[t]ši.l ab.bn.il.ytši.l dr. | bn il.l mpḫrt.bn.il.l ṯkmn[.w]šnm.hn.‘r. | w.ṯb.l m 32[2].1.25
[bḥ n.ndbḥ]. | hw.ṯ‘.nṯ‘y.hw.nkt.n[k]t.ytši[.l ab.bn.il]. | ytši.l dr.bn.il.l mpḫrt.bn.i[l.l ṯkmn.w š]nm hn š. | w šqrb.‘r. 32[2].1.17
m.rgm.l il.ybl.a[ṯt y]. | il.ylt.mh.ylt.yld y.šḥr.w šl[m]. | šu.‘db.l špš.rbt.w l kbkbm.kn[-]. | yhbr.špt hm.yšq.hn.[š]pt 23[52].54
.u ymn. | u šmal.b p hm.w l.tšb‘n y.aṯt.itrḫ. | y bn.ašld.šu.‘db.tk.mdbr qdš. | ṯm tgrgr.l abnm.w l.‘ṣm.šb‘.šnt. | tmt.ṯ 23[52].65
r.ṯlṯ.kl hm. | aḥd.bt h.ysgr. | almnt.škr. | tškr.zbl.‘ršm. | yšu.‘wr. | mzl.ymzl. | w ybl.trḫ.ḥdṯ. | yb‘r.l ṯn.aṯt h. | w l nkr. 14[KRT].4.187
ṯr.ṯlṯ.kl hm. | yḥd.bt h.sgr. | almnt.škr. | tškr.zbl.‘ršm. | yšu.‘wr.mzl. | ymzl.w yṣi.trḫ. | ḥdṯ.yb‘r.l ṯn. | aṯt h.lm.nkr. | m 14[KRT].2.99
lt.‘n[t]. | tšu.knp.w tr.b ‘p. | tk.aḫ šmk.mlat rumm. | w yšu.‘n h.aliyn.b‘l. | w yšu.‘n h.w y‘n. | w y‘n.btlt.‘nt. | n‘mt.bn 10[76].2.13
‘l.ymšḫ.hm.b ‘p. | nṭ‘n.b arṣ.ib y. | w b ‘pr.qm.aḫ k. | w tšu.‘n h.btlt.‘nt. | w tšu.‘n h.w t‘n. | w t‘n.arḫ.w tr.b lkt. | tr.b 10[76].2.26
‘n.b arṣ.ib y. | w b ‘pr.qm.aḫ k. | w tšu.‘n h.btlt.‘nt. | w tšu.‘n h.w t‘n. | w t‘n.arḫ.w tr.b lkt. | tr.b lkt.w tr.b ḫl. | [b]n‘ 10[76].2.27
.b ‘p. | tk.aḫ šmk.mlat rumm. | w yšu.‘n h.aliyn.b‘l. | w yšu.‘n h.w y‘n. | w y‘n.btlt.‘nt. | n‘mt.bn.aḫt.b‘l. | l pnn h.ydd. 10[76].2.14
k.bm.qrb m.asm. | b p h.rgm.l yṣa.b špt h[.hwt h]. | b nši ‘n h.w tphn.in.[---]. | [-.]hlk.ǵlmm b dd y.yṣ[--]. | [-.]yṣa. 19[1AQHT].2.76
ṯǵr.tḥt. | adrm.d b grn.ydn. | dn.almnt.yṯpṭ.ṯpṭ.ytm. | b nši ‘n h.w yphn.b alp. | šd.rbt.kmn.hlk.kṯr. | k y‘n.w y‘n.tdrq 17[2AQHT].5.9
. | ḫbrt.l ẓr.pḥmm. | t‘pp.ṯr.il.d pid. | tǵẓy.bny.bnwt. | b nši.‘n h.w tphn. | hlk.b‘l.aṯtrt. | k t‘n.hlk.btlt. | ‘nt.tdrq.ybmt. 4[51].2.12
b nši[.‘n h.w yphn.yḥd]. | b ‘rpt[.nšrm.yšu]. | [g h.]w yṣḥ[.knp. 19[1AQHT].2.105
ṣḥ.knp.nšrm.ybn. | b‘l.ybn.diy hmt nšrm. | tpr.w du.b nši.‘n h.w ypn. | yḥd.hrgb.ab.nšrm. | yšu.g h.w yṣḥ.knp.hr[g] 19[1AQHT].3.120
p.hrgb.b‘l.ybn. | [b]‘l.ybn.diy.hwt.hrg[b]. | tpr.w du.b nši.‘n h. | [w]yphn.yḥd.ṣml.um.nšrm. | yšu.g h.w yṣḥ.knp.ṣ 19[1AQHT].3.134
nt.y]ṯpṭ. | [ṯpṭ.ytm.---] h. | [---.---]n. | [-----]. | hlk.[---.b n]ši. | ‘n h.w tphn.[---]. | b grn.yḫrb[.---]. | yǵly.yḥsp.ib[.---]. | ‘ 19[1AQHT].1.28
t‘l.trṯ. | [---].yn.‘šy l ḥbš. | [---.]ḫtn.qn.yṣbt. | [---.--]m.b nši.‘n h.w tphn. | [---.--]ml.ksl h.k b[r]q. | [---.]m[-]ǵ[-].thmt. 17[2AQHT].6.10
l.ttn.pnm. | ‘m.ǵr.trǵzz. | ‘m.ǵr.ṯrmg. | ‘m.tlm.ǵṣr.arṣ. | ša.ǵr.‘l.ydm. | ḫlb.l ẓr.rḥtm. | w rd.bt ḫpṯt. | arṣ.tspr.b y | rdm. 4[51].8.5
y.bt.ar. | ‘m k.ṯṯly.bt.rb.idk. | pn k.al ttn.tk.ǵr. | knkny.ša.ǵr.‘l ydm. | ḫlb.l ẓr.rḥtm w rd. | bt ḫpṯt.arṣ.tspr b y | rdm.a 5[67].5.13
ṯr.‘ly. | n‘m.l ḥṭt.b gn. | bm.nrt.ksmm. | ‘l.tl[-]k.‘ṭrṭrm. | nšu.[r]iš.ḥrṯm. | l ẓr.‘db.dgn kly. | lḥm.[b]‘dn hm.kly. | yn.b 16[126].3.12
. | [---.--]ṣ. | [-----]. | [--]lm.aḥd. | [--]l.l ḫr[-.---]. | [--]m.dt nšu. | [---.]d[--.---]. | [---.--]m aḫ[d]. | [-----]. | [---.--]m. 156[-].7
--.---]. | [---.]l ksi y.w pr[‘]. | [---].pr‘.ank.[---]. | [---.]ank.nši[.---]. | [---.ṯ]br.ḫss.[---]. | [---.--]št.b [---]. | [---.--]b. | [---.--]k. 1002.15

nšb

‘tqn.---.ymǵy.]npš. | [---.h]d.tngṯn h. | [---].b ṣpn. | [---].nšb.b ‘n. | [---.]b km.y‘n. | [---.yd‘.l] yd‘t. | [---.t]asrn. | [---.]trk 1[‘NT.X].5.6
l h. | w ‘nt.ktp.b hm.yg‘r.ṯǵr. | bt.il.pn.l mgr lb.t‘dbn. | nšb.l inr.t‘dbn.ktp. | b il ab h.g‘r.ytb.il.kb[-]. | aṯ[rt.]il.ytb.b UG5.1.1.13
. | ylmn.ḥṭ.tḥt.ṯlḥn. | b qr‘. | ‘ṯtrt.w ‘nt.ymǵy. | ‘ṯtrt.t‘db.nšb l h. | w ‘nt.ktp.b hm.yg‘r.ṯǵr. | bt.il.pn.l mgr lb.t‘dbn. | nš UG5.1.1.10
. | mit.lḥ[m.---.-]dyt. | ṣl‘t.alp.mri. | ‘šr.bmt.alp.mri. | ṯn.nšbm. | ṯmnym.tbtḫ.alp. | uz.mrat.mlḥt. | arb‘.uzm.mrat.bq‘. 1128.18

nšg

-]. | d alp šd.ẓu h.b ym.t[---]. | tlbš.npṣ.ǵzr.tšt.ḫ[---.b] | nšg h.ḥrb.tšt.b t‘r[t h]. | w ‘l.tlbš.npṣ.aṯt.[--]. | ṣbi nrt.ilm.špš. 19[1AQHT].4.207

nšy

-.---.]m[--.]hwt. | [---].ṯllt.khn[m.---.]k p‘n. | [---.--]y.yd.nšy.[---.--]š.l mdb. | [---] h.mḫlpt[.---.--]r. | [---.]n‘lm.[---]. | [--- UG5.8.48

nšlm

--.nš]lm. | [---.nš]lm. | [---.nš]lm. | [---.nš]lm. | [---.pr]š.d.nšlm. | [---.]d.nšlm. 2036.7
[---].prš qmḫ.d.nšlm. | [---].prš.d.nšlm. | [---.nš]lm. | [---.nš]lm. | [---.nš]lm. | [---.nš]lm. | [---.pr]š. 2036.2
[---].prš qmḫ.d.nšlm. | [---].prš.d.nšlm. | [---.nš]lm. | [---.nš]lm. | [---.nš]lm. | [---.nš]lm. | [---.pr]š.d.nšlm. | [- 2036.3
---].prš qmḫ.d.nšlm. | [---].prš.d.nšlm. | [---.nš]lm. | [---.nš]lm. | [---.nš]lm. | [---.nš]lm. | [---.pr]š.d.nšlm. | [---.]d.nšlm. 2036.4
ḫ.d.nšlm. | [---].prš.d.nšlm. | [---.nš]lm. | [---.nš]lm. | [---.nš]lm. | [---.nš]lm. | [---.pr]š.d.nšlm. | [---.]d.nšlm. 2036.5
[---].prš qmḫ.d.nšlm. | [---].prš.d.nšlm. | [---.nš]lm. | [---.nš]lm. | [---.nš]lm. | [-- 2036.1
---].prš.d.nšlm. | [---.nš]lm. | [---.nš]lm. | [---.nš]lm. | [---.nš]lm. | [---.pr]š.d.nšlm. | [---.]d.nšlm. 2036.6
nš]lm. | [---.nš]lm. | [---.nš]lm. | [---.pr]š.d.nšlm. | [---.]d.nšlm. 2036.8

nšm

n ydd. | b gngn h.aḥd y.d ym | lk.ʻl.ilm.l ymru. | ilm.w nšm.d yšb | [ʻ].hmlt.arṣ.gm.l ǵ | [lm] h.bʻl k.yṣḥ.ʻn. | [gpn].w 4[51].7.51
.pšʻ. | [---].b ntb.gan.ašql k.tḥt. | [pʻn y.a]nk.nʻmn.ʻmq.nšm. | [tdʻṣ.pʻn]m.w tr.arṣ.idk. | [l ttn.pn]m.ʻm il.mbk.nhrm. 17[2AQHT].6.45
rṣ. | thmt.ʻmn.kbkbm. | abn.brq.d l.tdʻ.šmm. | rgm l tdʻ.nšm.w l tbn. | hmlt.arṣ.at m.w ank. | ibǵy h.b tk.ǵr y.il.ṣpn. | 3[ʻNT].3.24
abn]. | tunt.šmm.ʻm[.arṣ.thmt.ʻmn.kbkbm]. | rgm.l tdʻ.nš[m.w l tbn.hmlt.arṣ]. | at.w ank.ib[ǵy h.---]. | w yʻn.kṯr.w ḫ 1[ʻNT.IX].3.15
rgm k.hwt. | [w aṯny k.rgm.]ʻṣ.w lḫšt. | [abn.rgm.l td]ʻ.nš[m.w l t]bn. | [hmlt.a]rṣ.[tant.šmm.ʻm.ar]ṣ. | thmt.[ʻmn.kb 3[ʻNT].4.59
m[-]. | aḥd.b aḫ k.l[--]n. | hn[-.]aḥẓ[.---]l[-]. | [ʻ]nt.akl[y.nšm]. | akly.hml[t.arṣ]. | w y[-]l.a[---]. | š[--.---]. | bl[.---]. 6[49].5.24
w aṣd.kl. | ǵr.l kbd.arṣ.kl.gbʻ. | l kbd.šdm.npš.ḫsrt. | bn.nšm.npš.hmlt. | arṣ.mǵt.l nʻm y.arṣ. | dbr.ysmt.šd.šḥlmmt. | n 6[49].2.18
ṯ.---]t. | tlk m.rḥmy.w tṣd[.---]. | tḥgrn.ǵzr.nʻm.[---]. | w šm.ʻrbm.yr[.---]. | mṯbt.ilm.ṯmn.ṯ[--.--]. | pamt.šbʻ. | iqnu.šmt 23[52].18
. | w š.nbk m w.š. | gt mlk š.ʻlm. | l kṯr.ṯn.ʻlm. | tzǵ[.---.]nšm.pr. UG5.12.B.13

nšpin

]. | krm.uḫn.b.šdmy.ṯlṯ.bzl[.d]prn[.---]. | aupṯ.krm.aḥd.nšpin.kr[m.]aḥd[.---]. | dmt.lḫsn.krm.aḥd.annḏr.kr[m.---]. | a 1081.14

nšq

h. | bṣql.yph.b palt.bṣ[q]l. | yph.b yǵlm.bṣql.y[ḥb]q. | w ynšq.aḥl.an bṣ[ql]. | ynpʻ.b palt.bṣql ypʻ b yǵlm. | ur.tisp k.yd 19[1AQHT].2.64
lt h.yph. | šblt.b akt.šblt.ypʻ. | b ḥmdrt.šblt.yḥ[bq]. | w ynšq.aḥl.an.šblt. | tpʻ.b aklt.šblt.tpʻ[.b ḥm]drt. | ur.tisp k.yd.a 19[1AQHT].2.71
]i.brlt.ǵzr.mt hrnmy. | [---].hw.mḫ.l ʻrš h.yʻl. | [---].bm.nšq.aṯt h. | [---.]b ḥbq h.ḥmḥmt. | [---.--] n.ylt.ḥmḥmt. | [---.m 17[2AQHT].1.40
šl[m]. | šu.ʻdb.l špš.rbt.w l kbkbm.kn[-]. | yhbr.špt hm.yšq.hn.[š]pt hm.mtqtm. | bm.nšq.w hr.[b]ḥbq.w ḥ[m]ḥmt.y 23[52].55
ṣḥrt.l pḥmm.aṯtm.a[ṯt.il]. | aṯt.il.w ʻlm h.yhbr.špt hm.yš[q]. | hn.špt hm.mtqtm.mtqtm.k lrmn[.--]. | bm.nšq.w hr.b 23[52].49
kbm.kn[-]. | yhbr.špt hm.yšq.hn.[š]pt hm.mtqtm. | bm.nšq.w hr.[b]ḥbq.w ḥ[m]ḥmt.ytb[n]. | yspr.l ḫmš.l ṣ[---.]šr.p 23[52].56
hm.yš[q]. | hn.špt hm.mtqtm.mtqtm.k lrmn[.--]. | bm.nšq.w hr.b ḥbq.ḥmḥmt.tqt[nṣn]. | tldn.šḥr.w šlm.rgm.l il.ybl 23[52].51
---]. | h.hn bn k.hn[.---]. | bn bn.aṯr k.hn[.---]. | yd k.ṣǵr.tnšq.špt k.ṯm. | ṯkm.bm ṯkm.aḫm.qym.il. | b lsmt.ṯm.yṯbš.šm 22.2[124].4
nḫ l abd.b ym.irtm.m[--]. | [ṯpṯ].nhr.tlʻm.ṯm.ḥrbm.its.anšq. | [-]htm.l arṣ.ypl.ul ny.w l.ʻpr.ʻẓm ny. | l bʻl[-.---]. | tḥt.k 2.4[68].4

nšr

ym grš ym.l ksi h. | [n]hr l kḥṯ drkt h.trtqṣ.b d bʻl km nš | r.b uṣbʻt h.hlm.ktp.zbl ym.bn ydm. | [ṯp]ṭ nhr.yrtqṣ.ṣmd. 2.4[68].13
.ktp.zbl ym.bn ydm. | [ṯp]ṭ nhr.yrtqṣ.ṣmd.b d bʻl.km.nšr. | b[u]ṣbʻt h.ylm.ktp.zbl ym.bn ydm.ṯpṭ. | nhr.ʻz.ym.l ym 2.4[68].15
.ym.mr.ym. | l ksi h.nhr l kḥṯ.drkt h.trtqṣ. | b d bʻl.km.nšr b uṣbʻt h.hlm.qdq | d zbl ym.bn.ʻnm.ṯpṭ.nhr.yprsḥ ym. | 2.4[68].21
.nhr.yprsḥ ym. | w yql.l arṣ.w trtqṣ.ṣmd.b d bʻl. | [km.]nšr.b uṣbʻt h.ylm.qdqd.zbl. | [ym.]bn.ʻnm.ṯpṭ.nhr.yprsḥ.ym. 2.4[68].24
ap h.b ap.mhr h.ank. | l aḥwy.tqḥ.yṯpn.mhr.šṭ. | tštn.k nšr.b ḥbš h.km.diy. | b tʻrt h.aqht.km.yṯb.l lḥ[m]. | bn.dnil.l ṯ 18[3AQHT].4.28
.w nʻrs[.---]. | w tʻn.btlt.ʻnt.ṯb.ytp.w[---]. | l k.ašt k.km.nšr.b ḥb[š y]. | km.diy.b tʻrt y.aqht.[km.yṯb]. | l lḥm.w bn.dn 18[3AQHT].4.17
.kbdt hm.w[yḥd]. | in.šmt.in.ʻẓm.yšu.g h. | w yṣḥ.knp.nšrm.ybn. | bʻl.ybn.diy hmt nšrm. | tpr.w du.b nši.ʻn h.w ypn 19[1AQHT].3.118
h.w yphn.yḥd]. | b ʻrpt[.nšrm.yšu]. | [g h.]w yṣḥ[.knp.nšrm]. | bʻl.yṯb.bʻl.yṯb[r.diy.hmt]. | tqln.tḥ pʻn y.ibq[ʻ.kbd h 19[1AQHT].3.107
št.b ḫrt.ilm.arṣ. | b p h.rgm.l yṣa.b špt h.hwt[h]. | knp.nšrm.bʻl.yṯbr. | bʻl.ṯbr.diy hmt.tqln. | tḥt.pʻn h.ybqʻ.kbdt hm. 19[1AQHT].3.114
qbr. | yqbr.nn.b mdgt.b knk[-]. | w yšu.g h.w yṣḥ.knp.nšrm. | bʻl.yṯbr.bʻl.yṯbr.diy. | hmt.hm.tʻpn.ʻl.qbr.bn y. | tšḫṭan 19[1AQHT].3.148
gbt yu. | [---]w yrmy[.q]rn h. | [---.-]ny h pdr.ttǵr. | [---.n]šr k.al ttn.l n. | [---.]tn l rbd. | [---.]bʻlt h w yn. | [---.rk]b ʻrp 2001.2.12
ṣr. | kp.šsk k.[--].l ḥbš k. | ʻtk.ri[š.]l mhr k. | w ʻp.l dr[ʻ].nšr k. | w rbṣ.l ǵr k.inbb. | kt ǵr k.ank.ydʻt. | [-]n.atn.at.mṯb k 13[6].8
n.ʻẓm.yšu.g h. | w yṣḥ.knp.nšrm.ybn. | bʻl.ybn.diy hmt nšrm. | tpr.w du.b nši.ʻn h.w ypn. | yḥd.hrgb.ab.nšrm. | yšu.g 19[1AQHT].3.119
y hmt nšrm. | tpr.w du.b nši.ʻn h.w ypn. | yḥd.hrgb.ab.nšrm. | yšu.g h.w yṣḥ.knp.hr[g]b. | bʻl.yṯb.bʻl.y[ṯb]r.diy[.h]wt 19[1AQHT].3.121
b nši[.ʻn h.w yphn.yḥd]. | b ʻrpt[.nšrm.yšu]. | [g h.]w yṣḥ[.knp.nšrm]. | bʻl.yṯb.bʻl.yṯb[r.diy.hm 19[1AQHT].2.106
t.hrg[b]. | tpr.w du.b nši.ʻn h. | [w]yphn.yḥd.ṣml.um.nšrm. | yšu.g h.w yṣḥ.knp.ṣml. | bʻl.yṯbr.bʻl.yṯbr.diy. | hyt.tql. 19[1AQHT].3.135
bn.dnil.l ṯrm[.ʻl h]. | nšrm.trḫpn.ybṣr.[ḥbl.d] | iym.bn.nšrm.arḫp.an[k.ʻ]l. | aqht.ʻdb k.hlmn.ṯnm.qdqd. | ṯlṯ id.ʻl.ud 18[3AQHT].4.21
.diy. | b tʻrt h.aqht.km.yṯb.l lḥ[m]. | bn.dnil.l ṯrm.ʻl h.nšr[m]. | trḫpn.ybṣr.ḥbl.diy[m.bn]. | nšrm.trḫp.ʻnt.ʻl[.aqht]. | 18[3AQHT].4.30
y.b tʻrt y.aqht.[km.yṯb]. | l lḥm.w bn.dnil.l ṯrm[.ʻl h]. | nšrm.trḫpn.ybṣr.[ḥbl.d] | iym.bn.nšrm.arḫp.an[k.ʻ]l. | aqht.ʻd 18[3AQHT].4.20
n.[---]. | b grn.yḫrb[.---]. | yǵly.yḫsp.ib[.---]. | ʻl.bt.ab h.nšrm.trḫ[p]n. | ybṣr.ḥbl.diym. | tbky.pǵt.bm.lb. | tdmʻ.bm.kb 19[1AQHT].1.32
bn.dnil.l ṯrm.ʻl h.nšr[m]. | trḫpn.ybṣr.ḥbl.diy[m.bn]. | nšrm.trḫp.ʻnt.ʻl[.aqht]. | tʻdbn h.hlmn.ṯnm[.qdqd]. | ṯlṯ id.ʻl.u 18[3AQHT].4.32

ntb

aqht.ǵzr.ṯb l y w l k. | [---]m.l aqry k.b ntb.pšʻ. | [---].b ntb.gan.ašql k.tḥt. | [pʻn y.a]nk.nʻmn.ʻmq.nšm. | [tdʻṣ.pʻn]m. 17[2AQHT].6.44
[---.t]ṯb h.aḫt.ppšr.w ppšrt[.---]. | [---.]k.drḥm.w aṯb.l ntbt.k.ʻšm l t[--]. | [---.]drk.brḥ.arṣ.lk pn h.yrk.bʻ[l]. | [---.]bt 1001.2.7
y. | [---.]ṯb l y.l aqht.ǵzr.ṯb l y w l k. | [---]m.l aqry k.b ntb.pšʻ. | [---].b ntb.gan.ašql k.tḥt. | [pʻn y.a]nk.nʻmn.ʻmq.nš 17[2AQHT].6.43

ntbt

ḥdṯ. | b.yrḫ.pgrm. | lqḥ.iwrpzn. | argdd. | ttkn. | ybrk. | ntbt. | b.mitm. | ʿšrm. | kbd.ḫrṣ. 2006.7
. | m[--.---]. | bn[.---]. | bn[.---]. | w.yn[.---]. | bn.ʿdr[.---]. | ntb[t]. | b.arb[ʿ]. | mat.ḫr[ṣ]. 2007.10

ntbtš

r.blblm. | skn uškn. | skn šbn. | skn ubrʿ. | skn ḫrṣbʿ. | rb.ntbtš. | [---].ʿbd.r[--]. | arbʿ.k[--]. | ṯlṯ.ktt. 1033.6

ntk

pḫyr h.yrṯ. | yʿrb.b ḥdr h.ybky. | b ṯn.[-]gmm.w ydmʿ. | tntkn.udmʿt h. | km.ṯqlm.arṣ h. | km ḫmšt.mṭt h. | bm.bky h. 14[KRT].1.28
b šmm.tq[ru.---.-]rt. | [---.]mn mn[-.---.--]n.nmr. | [--.]l ytk.bl[-.---.]m[--.]hwt. | [---].ṯllt.khn[m.---.]k pʿn. | [---.--]y.yd UG5.8.46
s w [---]. | w yn[t.q]rt.y[---]. | w al[p.l]il.w bu[rm.---]. | ytk.gdlt.ilhm.[ṯkmn.w šnm]. | dqt.ršp.šrp.w š[lmm.dqtm]. | il 35[3].12
l[---].w y[nt.qrt.---]. | [---.--]n[.w alp.l il.w bu] | [rm.---.ytk.gdlt.ilhm]. | ṯkmn.w [šnm.dqt.ršp.šrp]. | w šlmm.[dqtm.il APP.II[173].13
.-]sr.pdm.riš h[m.---]. | ʿl.pd.asr.[---.]l[.---]. | mḫlpt.w l.ytk.[d]m[ʿt.]km. | rbʿt.ṯqlm.ṯtp[.---.]bm. | yd.ṣpn hm.tliy m[.- 19[1AQHT].2.82
tkms.hd.p[.-]. | km.ibr.b tk.mšmš d[--]. | ittpq.l awl. | išttk.lm.ttkn. | štk.mlk.dn. | štk.šibt.ʿn. | štk.qr.bt.il. | w mṣlt.b 12[75].2.58
]. | km.ibr.b tk.mšmš d[--]. | ittpq.l awl. | išttk.lm.ttkn. | štk.mlk.dn. | štk.šibt.ʿn. | štk.qr.bt.il. | w mṣlt.bt.ḥr[š]. 12[75].2.59
d.p[.-]. | km.ibr.b tk.mšmš d[--]. | ittpq.l awl. | išttk.lm.ttkn. | štk.mlk.dn. | štk.šibt.ʿn. | štk.qr.bt.il. | w mṣlt.bt.ḥr[š]. 12[75].2.58
]. | ittpq.l awl. | išttk.lm.ttkn. | štk.mlk.dn. | štk.šibt.ʿn. | štk.qr.bt.il. | w mṣlt.bt.ḥr[š]. 12[75].2.61
k.mšmš d[--]. | ittpq.l awl. | išttk.lm.ttkn. | štk.mlk.dn. | štk.šibṭ.ʿn. | štk.qr.bt.il. | w mṣlt.bt.ḥr[š]. 12[75].2.60

ntn

bt k.nʿtq.k inr. | ap.ḫštʿk.ap.ab.k mtm. | tmtn.u ḫšt k.l ntn. | ʿtq.b d.aṯt.ab.ṣrry. | ik m.yrgm.bn.il. | krt.špḥ.lṭpn. | w q 16.1[125].18
t k.nʿtq.k inr. | ap.ḫšt k.ap.ab.ik mtm. | tmtn.u ḫšt k.l ntn. | ʿtq.b d.aṯt.ab ṣrry. | tbky k.ab.ǵr.bʿl. | ṣpn.ḥlm.qdš. | any 16.1[125].4
lk[.---]. | ṯn.skm.šbʿ.mšlt.arbʿ.ḫpnt.[---]. | ḫmšm.ṯlṯ.rkb.ntn.ṯlṯ.mat.[---]. | lg.šmn.rqḥ.šrʿm.ušpǵtm.p[--.---]. | kṯ.ẓrw.k UG5.9.1.20

nts

.mnḫ l abd.b ym.irtm.m[--]. | [ṯpṭ].nhr.tlʿm.ṯm.ḥrbm.its.anšq. | [-]htm.l arṣ.ypl.ul ny.w l.ʿpr.ʿẓm ny. | l bʿl[-.---]. | t 2.4[68].4

ntp

. | [w.]nḥl h. | bn.qṣn. | bn.ksln. | bn.ṣrym. | bn.ṯmq. | bn.ntp. | bn.mlk. | bn.ṯʿ[-]. | bn.km[-]. | bn.r[--]. | [bn.]ʿ[---]. | [bn.]r 1073.1.9
--]. | bn.a[--]. | bn.ml[k]. | bn.glyn. | bn.ʿdr. | bn.ṯmq. | bn.ntp. | bn.ʿgrt. 1057.21
ʿzn.bn.irbn. | bn.mglb. | bn.ntp. | ʿmyn.bn ǵḥpn. | bn.kbln. | bn.bly. | bn.ṯʿy. | bn.nṣdn. | klb 104[316].3
ḥrṯm[.---]. | bn.ṯmq[-.---]. | bn.ntp.[---]. | bn.lbnn.[----]. | ady.ḥ[--.---]. | [-]b[-]n.[---]. | bn.atnb. 88[304].3

nṯk

| [yis]p.ḥmt.isp.[šp]š l hrm.ǵrpl.ʿl arṣ. | [l a]n ḥmt.l p[.n]ṯk.abd.l p.akl ṯm.dl. | [---.q]l.bl.tbḥ[n.l]azd.ʿr.qdm. | [---].ʿ UG5.8.20
r[ṣ.---.ḥ]mt. | [---.šp]š.l [hrm.ǵ]rpl.ʿl.arṣ. | [---.]ḥmt.l p[.nṯ]k.abd.l p.ak[l]. | [ṯm.dl.]isp.ḥ[mt.---.-]hm.yasp.ḥmt. | [---.š UG5.8.10
| ddm.ḥ[ṯm].ʿl.šrn. | ʿšrt.ksp.ʿl.[-]lpy. | bn.ady.kkr.šʿrt. | nṯk h. | kb[d.]mn.ʿl.abršn. | b[n.---].kršu.nṯk h. | [---.--]mm.b. 1146.10
.ady.kkr.šʿrt. | nṯk h. | kb[d.]mn.ʿl.abršn. | b[n.---].kršu.nṯk h. | [---.--]mm.b.krsi. 1146.12
ʿn.k gmrm. | mt.ʿz.bʿl.ʿz.ynghn. | k rumm.mt.ʿz.bʿl. | ʿz.ynṯkn.k bṯnm. | mt.ʿz.bʿl.ʿz.ymṣḥn. | k lsmm.mt.ql. | bʿl.ql.ʿln. 6[49].6.19
šql.yṯk[.--]np bl.hn. | [---].ḥ[m]t.pṭr.w.p nḥš. | [---.--]q.n[ṯ]k.l ydʿ.l bn.l pq ḥmt. | [---.--]n h.ḥmt.w tʿbtn h.abd y. | [-- UG5.8.35
ru l špš.um h.špš.um.ql.bl.ʿm. | ʿnt w ʿṯtrt inbb h.mnt.nṯk. | nḥš.šlḥm.nḥš.ʿq šr[.yʿ]db.ksa. | nḥš.šmrr.nḥš.ʿq šr.ln h. UG5.7.20
ṯb. | tqru.l špš.um h.špš.[um.q]l bl.ʿm. | yrḫ.lrgt h.mnt.nṯk.n[ḥš].šmrr. | nḥš.ʿq šr.ln h.mlḫš.abd.ln h.ydy. | ḥmt.hlm. UG5.7.26
tqru.l špš.um h.špš.um.ql bl. | ʿm bʿl.mrym.ṣpn.mnt y.nṯk. | nḥš.šmrr.nḥš.ʿq šr ln h. | mlḫš.abd.ln h.ydy.ḥmt.hlm.y UG5.7.9
m h.špš.um.ql.bl.ʿm. | il.mbk nhrm.b ʿdt.thmtm. | mnt.nṯk.nḥš.šmrr.nḥš. | ʿq šr.ln h.mlḫš abd.ln h.ydy. | ḥmt.hlm.y UG5.7.4
ru l špš.um h.špš.um.ql bl ʿm. | šḥr.w šlm šmm h mnt.nṯk.nḥš. | šmrr.nḥš ʿq šr.ln h.mlḫš. | abd.ln h.ydy ḥmt.hlm.y UG5.7.52
ṯb. | tqru l špš um h.špš um ql.bl.ʿm. | mlk.ʿṯtrt h.mnt.nṯk.nḥš.šmrr. | nḥš.ʿq šr.ln h.mlḫš abd.ln h.ydy. | ḥmt.hlm.y UG5.7.41
qru l špš.um h.špš.um.ql bl ʿm. | ṯṯ.w kmṯ.ḥryt h.mnt.nṯk.nḥš.šm | rr.nḥš.ʿq šr.ln h.mlḫš abd.ln h. | ydy.ḥmt.hlm.y UG5.7.36
a.w yṯb. | tqru.l špš.um.ql bl.ʿm | kṯr.w ḫss.kptr h.mnt.nṯk.nḥš. | šmrr.nḥš.ʿq šr.ln h.mlḫš.abd. | ln h.ydy.ḥmt.hlm y UG5.7.46
w yṯb. | tqru.l špš.u h.špš.um.ql.bl.ʿm. | dgn.ttl h.mnt.nṯk.nḥš.šmrr. | nḥš.ʿq šr.ln h.mlḫš.abd.ln h. | ydy.ḥmt.hlm.y UG5.7.15
ṯb. | tqru l špš.um h.špš.um.ql bl. | ʿm ḥrn.mṣd h.mnt.nṯk nḥš. | šmrr.nḥš.ʿq šr.ln h.mlḫš. | abd.ln h.ydy.ḥmt. | b ḥr UG5.7.58
hr k.bn bṯn. | itnn k. | aṯr ršp.ʿṯtrt. | ʿm ʿṯtrt.mr h. | mnt.nṯk.nḥš. UG5.7.TR3
ʿl[.-]gr. | [---.]ʿṣ.b d h.ydrm[.]pi[-.]adm. | [---.]iṯ[-].yšql.yṯk[.--]np bl.hn. | [---].ḥ[m]t.pṭr.w.p nḥš. | [---.--]q.n[ṯ]k.l ydʿ UG5.8.33
[---.-]bʿm. | [---.b]n.yšm[ʿ]. | [---.]mlkr[-] h.b.nṯk. | [---.]šbʿm. | [---.]ḫrg.ʿšrm. | [---.]abn.ksp.ṯlṯ. | [---].bty.ks 2153.3

ntq

šnu.hd.gpt. | ǵr.w yʿn.aliyn. | bʿl.ib.hdt.lm.tḫš. | lm.tḫš.ntq.dmrn. | ʿn.bʿl.qdm.yd h. | k tǵd.arz.b ymn h. | bkm.yṯb.bʿ 4[51].7.39
arbʿm.qšt. | alp ḥẓm.w alp. | ntq.ṯn.qlʿm. | ḫmš.ṣmdm.w ḥrṣ. | ṯryn.sswm. | ṯryn.aḥd.d bnš. 1123.3

nṯt

mspr.m[šr] mšr.bt.ugrt.w npy.gr. | ḥmyt.ugrt.w [np]y.nṯt.ušn.yp kn.ulp qṭy. | ulp.ddmy.ul[p.ḫ]ry.ulp.ḫty.ulp.alṯy. 32[2].1.28

S

sad

al.tǵl[.---].|prdmn.ʿbd.ali[yn].|bʿl.sid.zbl.bʿl.|arṣ.qm.yṯʿr.|w yšlḥmn h.|ybrd.ṯd.l pnw h.|b ḥr 3[ʿNT].1.3
št.l brk h.yʿdb.|qṣʿt.apnk.mṯt.dnty.|tšlḥm.tššqy ilm.|tsad.tkbd.hmt.bʿl.|ḥkpt il.kl h.tbʿ.kṯr.|l ahl h.hyn.tbʿ.l mš| 17[2AQHT].5.30
.l npš.kṯr.|w ḫss.l brlt.hyn d.|ḥrš yd.šlḥm.ššqy.|ilm sad.kbd.hmt.bʿl.|ḥkpt.il.kl h.tšmʿ.|mṯt.dnty.tʿdb.imr.|b pḫ 17[2AQHT].5.20

sap

.nuš[-.---].|b [u]grt.w ht.a[--].|w hm.at.trg[m.---].|w sip.u hw[.---].|w ank.u šbt[--.---].|ank.n[--]n[.---].|kst.l[--.-- 54.1.9[13.1.6]

sin

l h.k lb.ṯa[t].|l imr h.km.lb.ʿn[t].|aṯr.bʿl.tiḫd.m[t].|b sin.lpš.tšṣq[n h].|b qṣ.all.tšu.g h.w[tṣ]|ḥ.at.mt.tn.aḫ y.|w ʿ 6[49].2.10

sbb

lm.|ur.tisp k.yd.aqht.|ǵzr.tšt k.b qrb m.asm.|y.dnh.ysb.aklt h.yph.|šblt.b akt.šblt.ypʿ.|b ḥmdrt.šblt.yḫ[bq].|w 19[1AQHT].2.68
.mk.|b šb[ʿ.]y[mm].td.išt.|b bht m.n[bl]at.b hkl m.|sb.ksp.l rqm.ḫrṣ.|nṣb.l lbnt.šmḫ.|aliyn.bʿl.ht y.bnt.|dt.ksp. 4[51].6.34
[-----].|yṣq.šm[n.---].|ʿn.tr.arṣ.w šmm.|sb.l qṣm.arṣ.|l ksm.mhyt.ʿn.|l arṣ.m[ṭ]r.bʿl.|w l šd.mṭr.ʿly. 16[126].3.3
.|tšu.ab h.tštnn.l[b]mt ʿr.|l ysmsm.bmt.pḫl.|y dnil.ysb.palt h.|bṣql.yph.b palt.bṣ[q]l.|yph.b yǵlm.bṣql.y[ḥb]q.| 19[1AQHT].2.61
dm.|ṣpym.|ṯlṯ mrkbt mlk.|d.l.ṣpy.|[---.t]r hm.|[---].ššb.|[---.]tr h.|[a]rbʿ.qlʿm.|arbʿ.mḏrnm.|mḏrn.w.mšḫṭ.|d. 1122.8
ly.ḏd.il.w]tb[a].|[qrš.mlk.ab.]šnm.|[tša.g hm.w tṣ]ḥ.sbn.|[---]l[.---.]ʿd.|ksm.mhyt[.m]ǵny.|l nʿm y.arṣ.dbr.|l ys 5[67].6.3

sbbyn

-.a]lp.arbʿ.mat.tyt.|[---.kd.]nbt.k[d.]šmn.mr.|[---.l]tḥ.sb[by]n.ltḥ.šḥ[lt].|[---.l]tḥ.dblt.ltḥ.ṣmqm.|[---.--]m.[ḫ]mšm. 142[12].16
bt.kd.šmn.mr.|[---.]arbʿ.mat.ḫswn.ltḥ.aqhr.|[---.ltḥ.]sbbyn.ltḥ.ššmn.ltḥ.šḥlt.|[---.ltḥ.]ṣmqm.[t]t.mat.nṣ.ṯlṯm.ʿṣr.| 142[12].4
šʿrm.|[---.hn.w.al]p.kd.nbt.kd.šmn.mr.|[---].kmn.ltḥ.sbbyn.|[---.-]ʿt.ltḥ.ššmn.|[---].ḫswn.ṯṯ.mat.nṣ.|[---].ḫmšm.ḥ 142[12].9

sbd

b.mqdšt.ʿb[dml]k.ṯṯpḥ.mrṯn.|ḫḏǵlm.i[---]n.pbn.nḏbn.sbd.|šrm.[---].ḫpn.|ḥrš[bhtm.--]n.ʿbdyrḫ.ḥdṯn.yʿr.|adbʿl[.- 2011.16

sbsg

.|p[---]r.aḥd.|[-----].|[-----].|[---.--]y.|[---.-]ṯt.|[---.]w.sbsg.|[-----].|[-----].|[---.--]ṯ.|[---.-]b.m.lk.|kdwṯ.ḥdṯ.|b d ʿl 1112.14

sbrdn

spr.ḥṯbn.sbrdnm.|ḫmš.kkrm.alp kb[d].|ṯlṯ.l.nskm.birtym.|b d.urtn. 2101.1
bd.šmn.|[l.]abrm.mšrm.|[mi]tm.arbʿm.ṯmn.kbd.|[l.]sbrdnm.|m[i]t.l.bn.ʿẓmt.rišy.|mit.l.tlmyn.bn.ʿdy.|[---.]l.aḏ 2095.6

sgld

.|bn.pǵḏn.ṯqlm.|bn.bʿln.ṯqlm.|ʿbdyrḫ.nqd.ṯqlm.|bt.sgld.ṯqlm.|bn.ʿmy.ṯqlm.|bn.brq.ṯqlm.|bn.ḫnzr.ṯqlm.|dqn. 122[308].1.13
by.|abmn.|ynḥm.|npl.|ynḥm.|mtbʿl.|bn ǵlmn.|bn sgld. 1065.B.2
|bn.nqṭn.|bn abrḫṭ.|bn.grdy.|bn.ṣlpn.|bn ǵlmn.|bn sgld. 1064.B.2

sglt

dny.l.yḫsr.|w.[ank.yd]ʿ.l.ydʿt.|h[t.---.]l.špš.bʿl k.|ʿ[--.s]glt h.at.|ht[.---.]špš.bʿl k.|ydʿm.l.ydʿt.|ʿm y.špš.bʿl k.|šnt. 2060.12
kll.mid m.|šlm.|l.[--]n.špš.|ad[.ʿ]bd h.uk.škn.|k.[---.]sglt h.hw.|w.b[.---.]uk.nǵr.|w.[---].adny.l.yḫsr.|w.[ank.yd]ʿ 2060.7

sgn

m.|bt.[-]b[-.-]sy[-]h.|nn[-].b[n].py[-.d.]yṯb.b.gt.aǵld.|šgn.bn b[--.---].d.yṯb.b.ilštmʿ.|abmn.bn.r[---].b.syn.|bn.irṣ[- 2015.2.6

sgr

w l rbt.kmyr.|[a]ṯr.ṯn.ṯn.hlk.|aṯr.ṯlṯ.kl hm.|yḥd.bt h.sgr.|almnt.škr.|tškr.zbl.ʿršm.|yšu.ʿwr.mzl.|ymzl.w yṣi.trḫ. 14[KRT].2.96
.|w l.rbt.kmyr.|aṯr.ṯn.ṯn.hlk.|aṯr.ṯlṯ.kl hm.|aḥd.bt h.ysgr.|almnt.škr.|tškr.zbl.ʿršm.|yšu.ʿwr.|mzl.ymzl.|w ybl.t 14[KRT].4.184
|ʿšrm.ḫpn.ḫmš.|kbd.w lpš.|ḫmš.mispt.|mṯ.|w lpš.d sgr b h.|b d.anrmy. 1109.6
kdgdl.|[b]n.qṭn.|[b]n.ǵrgn.|[b]n.tgḏn.|bn.ḫdyn.|bn.sgr.|bn.aǵltn.|bn.ktln.|bn.ʿgwn.|bn.yšmʿ.|bdl.mḏrǵlm.|b 104[316].9
].|[b]nm.w bnt.ytn k[.---].|[--]l.bn y.šḥt.w [---].|[--]tt.msgr.bn k[.---].|[--]n.ṯḥm.bʿl[.---]. 59[100].11
ḥt.km.nḫl.|tplg.km.plg.|bʿd h.bhtm.mnt.bʿd h.bhtm.sgrt.|bʿd h.ʿdbt.ṯlṯ.ptḥ.bt.mnt.|ptḥ.bt.w ubn.hkl.w ištql šql. UG5.7.70
h.yš[mʿ].ṯr.[il].ab h.[---]l.|b šbʿt.ḥdrm.[b ṯ]mn[t.ap].|sgrt.g[-].[-]ẓ[.---] h[.---].|ʿn.ṯk[.---].|ʿln.ṯ[--.---].|l pʿn.ǵl[m] 3[ʿNT.VI].5.20
[---.--]t ḥ[dr].|[-----].|ḫmš[.---]t.ḥdrm.|w.[---.a]ḥd.d.sgrm.|w p[tḥ.---.]l.aḥd.adr.|[---.--]t.b[ḥd]r.mškb.|ṯl[l.---.--] 1151.4
].|[šbt.dqn k.mmʿm.]yʿny.|il.b šbʿt.ḥdrm.b ṯmnt.|ap.sgrt.ydʿ[t k.]bt.k an[št].|k in.b ilht.ql[ṣ] k.mh.tarš[n].|l btlt. 3[ʿNT.VI].5.35
ṯn.pld.ptṯ[.-]r.|lpš.sgr.rq.|ṯṯ.prqt.|w.mrdt.prqt.ptṯ.|lbš.psm.rq.|ṯn.mrdt.az.|ṯ 1112.2

sgryn

myn.|b d.gln.ary.|tgyn.yʿrty.|bn.krwn.b.yny.iytlm.|šgryn.ary.b.yny.|bn.yddn.b.rkby.|agyn.agny.|ṯqbn.mldy. 2071.6
]bš.bn.yknʿ.b.arʿt.|[--.l]bš.bn.grbn.b.ṯqlm.|[--.lb]š.bn.sgryn.b[.ṯ]qlm.|[---.]bn.ully.b.ṯ[qlm].|[---.]bn.annḏy.b[.---]. 135[330].4

sgṯtn

bn.ḫṣḥ.kkr. | kkr.lqḥ.ršpy. | tmtrn.bn.pnmn. | kkr. | bn.sgṯtn. | kkr. | ilšpš.kkr. | bn.ḏltn. | kkr.w[.--]. | ḫ[--.---]. 1118.9

sd

ḥn. | [----.]ʻd.ilnym. | [---.--]l km amt m. | [---.]b w tʻrb.sd. | [---.--]n b ym.qẓ. | [---.]ym.tlḥmn. | [---.rp]um.tštyn. | [---. 20[121].1.4

sdwn

spr.rʻym. | lqḥ.šʻrt. | anntn. | ʻdn. | sdwn. | mztn. | ḫyrn. | šdn. | [ʻš]rm.ṯn kbd. | šǵrm. | lqḥ.ššlmt. 2098.5

sdy

ryn.arty. | bn.ršp.ary. | bn.ǵlmn ary. | bn.ḥṣbn ary. | bn.šdy ary. | bn.ktkt.mʻqby. | bn.[---.]ṯlḥny. | b[n.---.ub]rʻy. | [bn.- 87[64].15

bn.ǵlmn.ary. | [bn].šdy. | [bn].gmḥ. | [---]ty. | [b]n.ypy.gbʻly. | b[n].ḥyn. | ḏmn.šʻrt 99[327].1.2

--]m. | [---]nb.w ykn. | [--]ndbym. | [ʻ]rmy.w snry. | [b]n.sdy.bn.ṯty. | bn.ḥyn.bn.ǵlm. | bn.yyn.w.bn.au[pš]. | bn.kdrn. | 131[309].23

sdrn

prsn. | agpṯr.w.šǵ[r h]. | ṯʻln. | mztn.w.šǵr [h]. | šǵr.plṭ. | s[d]rn [w].ṯn.šǵr h. | [---.]w.šǵr h. | [---.]w.šǵr h. | [---.]krwn. | 2072.8

shr

lm.b qrb.m[ṯʻt.ilnym]. | d tit.yspi.spu.q[--.---]. | tpḥ.ṭṣr.shr[.---]. | mr[.---]. 20[121].2.11

sw

ṯ. | šmrm.a[ḏḏd]y.tb[--]. | ynḥm.aḏḏdy. | ǵdǵd.aḏḏdy. | sw.aḏḏdy. | ildy.aḏḏdy. | grʻ.aḏḏdy. | ʻbd.ršp aḏḏdy. | ʻdn.bn.k 2014.32

skn.ʻšrm kk[r.---]. | mšrn.ṯlṯ.ʻš[r.kkr]. | bn.šw.šbʻ.kk[r.---]. | arbʻm.kkr.[---]. | b d.mtn.[l].šlm. 2108.3

swy

ilṣdq.bn.zry. | bʻlytn.bn.ulb. | ytrʻm.bn.swy. | ṣḥrn.bn.qrtm. | bn.špš.bn.ibrd. | ʻpṯrm.bn.ʻbdy. | n[--.]b 2024.3

swn

spr.ubdy.art. | šd.prn.b d.agpṯn.nḫl h. | šd.šwn.b d.ttyn.nḫl [h]. | šd.ṯtyn[.b]n.arkšt. | lʻq[.---]. | šd.pll.b d. 2029.3

bn.ytrš ḫmšt. | krwn.ʻšrt. | bn.ulb ḫmšt. | bn.ḥry.ḫmšt. | swn.ḫmšt. | bn.[-]r[-.]ḫmšt. | bn.ḥḏṯ.ʻšrt. | bn.ḫnyn.ʻšrt. | rpan. 1062.15

--]. | nrn.arny[.---]. | w.ṯn.bn h.w.b[---.---]. | b tn[--.---]. | swn.qrty[.---]. | uḫ h.w.ʻšr[.---]. | klyn.apsn[y.---]. | plzn.qrty[. 81[329].8

.yrml. | [---.]b.yrml. | [---.--]n.b.yrml. | [---.--]ny.yrml. | šwn.qrty. | b.šlmy. 2119.25

.w.[---]. | [-]ln.[---]. | w.ṯn.bn [h.---]. | [--]d mʻqby[.---]. | swn.qrty.w[.aṯt h]. | [w].bn h.w.ṯn.alpm. | [w.]ṯlṯm.ṣin. | annḏ 1080.12

.[---]. | w.a[ṯt] h.[---]. | ḫḏmtn.ṯn[.---]. | w.ṯlṯ.alp h.[---]. | swn.qrty.w.[b]n h[.---]. | w.alp h.w.a[r]bʻ.l.arbʻ[m.---]. | pln.ṯ 2044.6

swr

y[.---]. | šd.bn.ḫb[--.---]. | šd.srn[.---]. | šd.yʻḏr[.---]. | šd.swr.[---]. | šd.bn ppn[-.---]. | šd.bn.uḫn[.---]. 83[85].5

szn

y. | bn.birtn. | bn.ḥrẓn. | bn.bddn. | bn.anny. | ytršp. | bn.szn. | bn.kdgdl. | bn.glʻd. | bn.ktln. | [bn].ǵrgn. | bn.pb[-]. | bn.[- 115[301].1.12

bn.a[---]. | bn.prsn. | bn.mtyn. | bn.ḫlpn. | bn.ḥgbn. | bn.szn. | bn.mglb. 117[325].2.9

sḫr

--]. | ady.ḫ[--.---]. | [-]b[-]n.[---]. | bn.atnb.mr[--.---]. | bn.sḫr.mr[-.---]. | bn.idrn.ʻš[-.---]. | bn.bly.mr[-.---]. | w.nḥl h.mr[88[304].8

n.ʻbd.abṣn. | šdyn.unn.dqn. | ʻbdʻnt.rb ʻšrt.mnḥm.ṯbʻm.sḫr.ʻzn.ilhd. | bnil.rb ʻšrt.lkn.ypʻn.ṯ[--]. | yṣḥm.b d.ubn.krwn. 2011.7

sḫrn

spr.rpš d l y[dy]. | atlg. | ulm. | izly. | uḫnp. | bn sḫrn. | mʻqb. | ṯpn. | mʻr. | lbnm. | nḫl. | yʻny. | atn. | utly. | bn.alz. 2075.6

d.ilmhr nḫl h. | šd knn.bn.ann.ʻdb. | šd.iln[-].bn.irṯr.l.sḫrn.nḫl h. | šd[.ag]pṯn.b[n.]brrn.l.qrt. | šd[.--]dy.bn.brzn. | l. 2029.20

n.b d.kmrn.n[ḫl] h. | [š]d.nbzn.[-]l.qrt. | [š]d.agpṯr.b d.sḫrn.nḫl h. | šd.annmn.b d.tyn.nḫl h. | šd.pǵyn[.b] d.krmn.l.ṯ 2029.10

syn

aǵld. | šgn.bn b[--.---].d.yṯb.b.ilštmʻ. | abmn.bn.r[---].b.syn. | bn.irṣ[-.---.]h. | šdyn.b[n.---.--]n. 2015.2.7

syny

spr. | synym. 1170.2

ʻšrm.ksp. | ʻl.šknt.syny. 1132.2

synn

ʻbdym. | [ub]dy.trrm. | [šd.]bn.ṯqdy.b d.gmrd. | [š]d bn.synn.b d.gmrd. | [šd.]abyy.b d.ibrmḏ. | [šd.]bn.ṯṯrn.b d.bnš.a 82[300].2.18

.nǵry. | bn.srwd. | mtnn. | bn gš[-]. | bn gbrn. | bn uldy. | synn.bn knʻm. | bn kbr. | bn iytlm. | bn ayln. | bn.kln. | bn.ʻlln. 1064.19

ty. | ʻby. | šm[n].bn.apn. | krty. | bn.ubr. | [bn] mdḫl. | bn.sy[n]n. | bn.šrn. 2078.21

syr

. | qlt. | ʻbd k.b. | lwsnd. | [w] b ṣr. | ʻm.mlk. | w.ht. | mlk.syr. | ns.w.ṯm. | ydbḥ. | mlǵ[.---]. | w.m[--.--]y. | y[--.---]. 2063.14

sk

.---]. | km.škllt.[---]. | ʻr.ym.l bl[.---]. | b[---.]ny[.--]. | l bl.sk.w [---] h. | ybm h.šbʻ[.---]. | ǵzr.ilḥu.t[---]l. | trm.ṭṣr.trm[.ʻ]t 16.2[125].93

uwṯ.ṯlṯ.kbd. | m[i]t.arbʻt.kbd. | ḫ[mš.]šʻrt. | [---.]tšʻ.kbd.skm. | [arb]ʻm.ḫpnt.pṯt. | [-]r.pldm.dt.šʻrt. | ṯlṯm.ṯlṯ.kbd.mṣrrt 1111.6

sk

| bʿlm.kmm.bʿlm.kmm. | k tʿrb.ʿṯtrt.šd.bt.mlk[.---]. | ṯn.skm.šbʿ.mšlt.arbʿ.ḫpnt.[---]. | ḫmšm.ṯlṯ.rkb.ntn.ṯlṯ.mat.[---]. | UG5.9.1.19

skl

t.iqni.l ḫbrtn]r ṯn. | [ks.ksp.ktn.mit.pḥm]. | [mit.iqn]i.l skl.[--]. | [---.m]it pḥm.l š[--]. | [---.]a[--.--.]hn[--]. 64[118].38

skn

. | [---.mt.r]pi.w ykn.bn h. | [b bt.šrš.]b qrb.hkl h. | [nṣb.skn.i]lib h.b qdš. | [ztr.ʿm h.l a]rṣ.mšṣu. | [qṭr h.l ʿpr.ḏ]mr.a[ṯ 17[2AQHT].1.45
rnn.l bny.bnwt. | w ykn.bn h b bt.šrš.b qrb. | hkl h.nṣb.skn.ilib h.b qdš. | ztr.ʿm h.l arṣ.mšṣu.qṭr h. | l ʿpr.ḏmr.aṯr h.ṭ 17[2AQHT].1.27
irt y. | npš.k yld.bn.l y.km. | aḫ y.w šrš.km ary y. | nṣb.skn.ilib y.b qdš. | ztr.ʿm y.l ʿpr.ḏmr.aṯr[y]. | ṭbq lḥt.niṣ y.grš. 17[2AQHT].2.16
spr.blblm. | skn uškn. | skn šbn. | skn ubrʿ. | skn ḫrṣbʿ. | rb.ntbtš. | [---].ʿbd.r[--]. | arbʿ.k[--]. | ṯlṯ. 1033.4
-.]kd yn.w š. | spr.m[--]. | spr d[---]b.w š. | tt.ḫmš.[---]. | skn.ul[m.---]. | [---]š.[---]. | [---]y[.---]. | sk[n.---]. | u[---.]w š. | [- 1093.6
spr.blblm. | skn uškn. | skn šbn. | skn ubrʿ. | skn ḫrṣbʿ. | rb.ntbtš. | [---].ʿbd. 1033.2
t.l ṯmnym. | šr.aḫy h.mẓa h. | w mẓa h.šr.yly h. | b skn.sknm.b ʿdn. | ʿdnm.kn.npl.bʿl. | km ṯr.w tkms.hd.p[.-]. | km.ib 12[75].2.53
n.[---.]uḫd. | bn.n[---.]hbṭn. | bn.m[--.]skn. | bn.s[--.b]d.skn. | bn.ur[-.---]. | bn.knn[.---]y. | bn.ymlk[.b]d.skn. | bn.yḥn 2014.12
[-----]. | bn.[---]. | bn.[---]. | w.nḥ[l h]. | bn.ẓr[-]. | mru.skn. | bn.bddn. | bn.ǵrgn. | bn.tgtn. | bn.ḥrẓn. | bn.qdšt. | bn.nṯǵ 113[400].5.6
--.b]d.skn. | bn.ur[-.---]. | bn.knn[.---]y. | bn.ymlk[.b]d.skn. | bn.yḥnn.aḏddy. | bn.pdǵy.mḫdy. | bn.yyn.mḏrǵl. | bn.ʿlr 2014.15
aḏddy.bn.skn. | bn.[---.]uḫd. | bn.n[---.]hbṭn. | bn.m[--.]skn. | bn.s[--.b]d.skn. | bn.ur[-.---]. | bn.knn[.---]y. | bn.ymlk[. 2014.11
mt. | bn.ṯb[-]. | bn.[-]r[-]. | bn.tgn. | bn.iḏrn. | mnn. | b[n].skn. | bn.pʿṣ. | bn.ḏrm. | [bn.-]ln. | [bn.-]ḏprḏ. 124[-].6.10
]luḫ. | [---.-]tn.b d.mlkt. | [---.]l.mḫṣ. | ab[---.]aḏddy.bn.skn. | bn.[---.]uḫd. | bn.n[---.]hbṭn. | bn.m[--.]skn. | bn.s[--.b]d 2014.8
[šmt.n]qmpʿ. | [bn.nq]md. | [mlk.]ugrt. | bʿl ṣdq. | skn.bt. | mlk.ṯǵr. | [m]lk.bny. | [--].lb.mlk. | [---.]ṣmḫ. 1007.5
.hn. | ktn.d.ṣr.pḥm.b h.w.ṯqlm. | ksp h.mitm.pḥm.b d.skn. | w.ṯt.ktnm.ḫmšt.w.nṣp.ksp.hn. 1110.5
spr.blblm. | skn uškn. | skn šbn. | skn ubrʿ. | skn ḫrṣbʿ. | rb.ntbtš. | [---].ʿbd.r[--]. | arbʿ.k[--]. | ṯlṯ.ktt. 1033.5
. | ṯǵsdb.šmlšn. | w tbʿ ank. | ʿm mlakt h šmʿ h. | w b.ʿly skn.ydʿ rgm h. | w ht ab y ǵm[--]. | t[--.---]. | ls[--.---]. | ṣḥ[.---]. 1021.8
n.il.d mla. | mnm.dbbm.d | msdt.arṣ. | sʿ.il.dqt.k amr. | sknt.k ḥwt.yman. | d b h.rumm.l rbbt. 4[51].1.43
qmḥ.d.kly.b bt.skn. | l.illḏrm. | ltḥ.ḥsr.b.šbʿ.ddm. 2093.1
khnm. | qdšm. | m[ru.]škn. | mkrm. 76[82].3
.ṭly.bt rb. | mṯb.arṣy.bt.yʿbdr. | ap.mṯn.rgmm. | argm k.šskn mʿ. | mgn.rbt.aṯrt ym. | mǵẓ.qnyt.ilm. | hyn.ʿly.l mpḫm. 4[51].1.21
. | [nsk].ṯlṯ. | gt.mlkym. | tmrym. | ṯnqym. | ṯǵrm. | mru.skn. | mru.ibrn. | yqšm. | trrm. | kkrdnm. | yṣrm. | ktrm. | mṣlm. 1026.2.6
qd[šm]. | mru s[kn]. | mru ib[rn]. | mdm. ! inšt. | nsk ksp. | yṣḥm. | ḥrš mrkbt. 73[114].2
ʿy. | mʿrby. | [ṣ]ʿq. | [š]ḥq. | nʿrm. | mḫrǵlm. | kzym. | mru.skn. | mru.ibrn. | pslm. | šrm. | yṣḥm. | ʿšrm. | mrum. | ṯnnm. | m 71[113].63
. | kbšm. | trrm. | khnm. | kzym. | yṣrm. | mru.ibrn. | mru.skn. | nsk.ksp | mḫṣm. | ksdm. | mḏrǵlm. | pslm. | yṣḥm. 74[115].13
ʿšrm.ksp. | ʿl.šknt.syny. 1132.2
ṯmnt.l ṯmnym. | šr.aḫy h.mẓa h. | w mẓa h.šr.yly h. | b skn.sknm.b ʿdn. | ʿdnm.kn.npl.bʿl. | km ṯr.w tkms.hd.p[.-]. | k 12[75].2.53
npṣm. | b d.mri. | skn. | ʿšrm. | ḫmš. | kbd. 157[116].3
n.ṭb. | w.tšʿm.kdm.kbd.yn.d.l.ṭb. | w.arbʿm.yn.ḫlq.b.gt.sknm. | ʿšr.yn.ṭb.w.arbʿm.ḫmš.kbd. | yn.d.l.ṭb.gt.ṭbq. | mit.ʿšr. 1084.3
skn.ʿšrm kk[r.---]. | mšrn.ṯlṯ.ʿš[r.kkr]. | bn.šw.šbʿ.kk[r.---]. | ar 2108.1
[--]. | yṣḥm.b d.ubn.krwn.tǵd.[m]nḥm. | ʿpṯrm.šmʿrgm.skn.qrt. | ḥgbn.šmʿ.skn.qrt. | nǵr krm.ʿbdadt.bʿln.ypʿmlk. | ṯǵ 2011.10
krwn.tǵd.[m]nḥm. | ʿpṯrm.šmʿrgm.skn.qrt. | ḥgbn.šmʿ.skn.qrt. | nǵr krm.ʿbdadt.bʿln.ypʿmlk. | ṯǵrm.mnḥm.klyn.ʿdr 2011.11
spr.blblm. | skn uškn. | skn šbn. | skn ubrʿ. | skn ḫrṣbʿ. | rb.ntbtš. | [---].ʿbd.r[--]. | arbʿ. 1033.3
ltṯb. | šd.b d.krz[n]. | ṯlṯ.šdm.b d.amtr[n]. | ṯn.šdm.b d.skn. | šd.b d[.ʿb]dyrḫ. | šd.b [d.--]ṯtb. 2090.23
šd.ubdy.ilštmʿ. | dt b d.skn. | šd.bn.ubrʿn b gt prn. | šd.bn.gby.gt.prn. | šd.bn.kryn.gt. 1104.2
m[t]. | šl[-]. | [---]m. | [-]rm. | [-]dm. | [-]m. | [--]m. | [m]ru skn. | šrm. | [--]m. | [i]nšt. 2058.4.1
y. | grʿ.aḏddy. | ʿbd.ršp aḏddy. | ʿdn.bn.knn. | iwrḫz.b d.skn. | škny.aḏddy. | mšu.aḏddy. | plsy.aḏddy. | aḫyn. | ygmr.aḏ 2014.37
skn.ṯlṯm. | iytlm.ṯlṯm. | ḥyml.ṯlṯm. | ǵlkz.ṯlṯm. | mlknʿm.ʿšrm. 1116.1
b.bt[.---]l. | [ṯ]lṯ.aṯt.adrt.w.ṯlṯ.ǵzr[m]. | w.ḫmš.nʿrt.b.bt.sk[n]. | ṯt.aṯtm.adrtm.w.pǵt.w ǵzr[.aḥd.b.bt.---]. | aṯt.w.ṯt.pǵt 80[119].17
š. | tt.ḫmš.[---]. | skn.ul[m.---]. | [---]š.[---]. | [---]y[.---]. | sk[n.---]. | u[---.]w š. | [---].w š. | [--]b.šd.[---]. | [--]kz[--]. 1093.9
-].gmn. | [---].l.urǵṯtb. | [---.]l.ʿṯtrum. | [---.]l.brqn. | [---].skn. | [---.ʿg]ltn. | [---].ʿgltn. | [---.]ʿgltn. | [---.šr]t.aḥt. | [---].šrt. 2162.B.8
[---.]l mitm.ksp. | [---.]skn. | [---.-]im.bṯd. | [---.b]šḥr.atlgn. | [---].b šḥr. | [---.]bn h. | [2167.2
b ṯṯ ym ḥdṯ. | ḥyr.ʿrbt. | špš ṯǵr h. | ršp. | w ʿbdm tbqrn. | skn. 1162.6

slg

bn uryy. | bn abdʿn. | bn prkl. | bn štn. | bn annyn. | b[n] slg. | u[--] dit. | bn p[-]n. | bn nẓǵil. 101[10].13

slgyn

n. | bn.ṭ[--]. | bn.idrm. | bn.ymn. | bn.ṣry. | bn.mztn. | bn.šlgyn. | bn.[-]gštn. | bn[.n]klb. | b[n.]dtn. | w.nḥl h. | w.nḥl hm. 113[400].2.6
kyy. | bn.atn. | bn.bly. | bn.ṯbrn. | bn.ḥgby. | bn.pity. | bn.slgyn. | ʿzn.bn.mlk. | bn.alṯn. | bn.ṯmyr. | ẓbr. | bn.ṯdṯb. | bn.ʿrm 115[301].2.7

slḫ

pr. | ary. | ẓrn. | art. | ṯlḥny. | ṯlrby. | dmt. | aǵt. | w.qmnz. | slḫ. | yknʿm. | šlmy. | w.ull. | ṯmry. | qrt. | ʿrm. | nnu. | [--]. | [---]. | 71[113].16
[---.--]ṯ.slḫ.npš.ṭʿ w[.--.k]bdm. | [---.--]mm.ṯn.šm.w alp.l[--]n. | [---.]š. 36[9].1.1
šrš. | gnʿy. | mʿqb. | agm. | bir. | ypr. | hzp. | šql. | mʿrḫ[-]. | sl[ḫ]. | snr. | ʿrgz. | yknʿm. | ʿnmky. | ǵr. 2074.34
.b.hzp. | arbʿ.bnšm.b.šql. | arbʿ.bnšm.b.nni. | ṯn.bnšm.b.slḫ. | [---].bnšm.b.yny. | [--.]bnšm.b.lbnm. | arbʿ.bnšm.b.ypr. | 2076.19

slẖu

--].|aḥt.l mkt.ǵr.|aḥt.l ʻṯtrt.|arbʻ.ʻṣrm.|gt.ṯrmn.|aḥt.slẖu. 39[19].19

sly

yṯr.|bn.ʻyn.|bn.ǵzl.|bn.ṣmy.|bn.il[-]šy.|bn.ybšr.|bn.sly.|bn.ḫlbt.|bn.brzt.|bn.ayl.|[-----].|ʻbd[--].|bn.i[--].|ʻd[-- 2117.2.11

slyy

aḫd l g ynm.|ṯṯ spm l tgyn.|arbʻ spm l ll[-].|ṯn spm.l slyy.|ṯlṯ spm l dlšpš amry. 137.2[93].14

slyn

[---].|ʻpṯn.bn.ṯṣq[-].|mnn.bn.krmn.|bn.umḫ.|yky.bn.slyn.|ypln.bn.ylḥn.|ʻzn.bn.mll.|šrm.|[b]n.špš[yn].|[b]n.ḫr 85[80].1.7

sll

k[---].|ʻbd.[---].|mtn[.---].|ṯdpṯn[.--].|tny[.--].|sll[.--].|mld[.--].|yqš[.--].|[-----].|inš[r.---].|ršp[.---].|iḫy[-.- 1074.6

slm

ṯn[-.]|y[--.]šr h.w šḫp h.|[--.]šḫp.ṣǵrt h.|yrk.tʻl.b ǵr.|mslmt.b ǵr.tliyt.|w tʻl.bkm.b arr.|bm.arr.w b ṣpn.|b nʻm.b 10[76].3.29

slmu

w.aṯt h.|bn.glgl.uškny.|bn.ṯny.uškny.|mnn.w.aṯt h.|slmu.ḥrš.mrkbt.|bnšm.dt.l.mlk.|ʻbdyrḫ.bn.ṯyl.|ʻbdn.w.aṯt 2068.16

sln

.abǵl.nḥ[l h.--].|w.unṯ.aḫd.l h[.---].|dnn.bn.yṣr[.---].|sln.bn.ʻṯt[-.---].|pdy.bn.nr[-.---].|abmlk.bn.un[-.---].|nrn.bn 90[314].1.6
.|[--.w.n]ḥl h.|[-]ibln.|bn.nḏbn.|bn.ʻbl.|bn.tlšn.|bn.sln.|w nḥl h. 1063.14

slʻy

bn.ǵs.ḥrš.šʻty.|ʻdy.bn.slʻy.gbly.|yrm.bʻl.bn.kky. 2121.2

slʻn

grbn.ltḥ.|srn.ltḥ.|ykn.ltḥ.|ḥgbn.ltḥ.|spr.mkrm.|bn.slʻn.prs.|bn.ṯpdn.ltḥ.|bn.urm.ltḥ. 1059.7

slpd

yzg.|bn.anntn.|bn.kwn.|ǵmšd.|bn.ʻbdḥy.|bn.ubyn.|slpd.|bn.atnb.|bn.ktmn.|bn.pity.|bn.iryn.|bn.ʻbl.|bn.grbn 115[301].4.12

slṯmg

spr.updt.|d b d.mlkytn.|kdrl.|slṯmg.|adrdn.|l[l]wn.|ydln.|ldn.|tdǵl.|ibrkyṯ. 1034.4
ʻd[rš]p.|pqr.|ṯǵr.|ttǵl.|ṯn.yṣḥm.|slṯmg.|kdrl.|wql.|adrdn.|prn.|ʻbdil.|ušy.šbn[-].|aḫt.ab.|k 1069.6

smd

ym.yṣq.yn.ṯmk.|mrṯ.yn.srnm.yn.bld.|ǵll.yn.išryt.ʻnq.smd.|lbnn.ṯl mrṯ.yḥrṯ.il.|hn.ym.w ṯn.tlḥmn.rpum.|tštyn.ṯl 22.2[124].19

smyy

.[-]rṯn.|bn[.---].|bn u[l]pm.|bn ʻ[p]ty.|bn.kdgdl.|bn.smyy.|bn.lbn.|bn.šlmn.|bn.mly.|pslm.|bn.annd.|bn.glʻd.| 2163.3.5
n].lbn.arbʻ.qšt.w.ar[bʻ].|[u]ṯpt.qlʻ.w.ṯt.mr[ḥ]m.|[bn].smyy.qšt.w.u[ṯpt].|[w.q]lʻ.w.ṯt.mrḥm.|[bn].šlmn.qlʻ.w.ṯ[t.-- 2047.4

smkt

---.]l [ ]dm.aḫt k.|ydʻt.k rḥmt.|al.tšt.b šdm.mm h.|b smkt.ṣat.npš h.|[-]mt[-].ṣba.rbt.|špš.w tgh.nyr.|rbt.w rgm. 16.1[125].35

snb

bn.ṣrṯn.|bn.ʻbd.|snb.w.nḥl h.|[-]by.w.nḥl h.|[--]ilt.w.nḥl h.|[---]n.|[--]ly.|[i 1063.3

sndrn

.aḥd.|sǵr.ʻdn.aḥd.|sǵr.awldn.aḥd.|sǵr.idṯn.aḥd.|sǵr.sndrn.aḥd.|sǵr.adn.ṣdq.aḥd.|sǵr.irgn.aḥd.|sǵr.ršpab.aḥd.| 1140.7

sny

.---].|bn.[---].|bn.a[--].|w.nḥl h.|bn.alz.|w.nḥl h.|bn.sny.|bn.ablḥ.|[-----].|w [---].|bn.[---].|bn.yr[--].|bn.kṯr[t].| 2163.1.14

snn

t h.ymǵyn.|yštql.dnil.l hkl h.|ʻrb.b bt h.kṯrt.bnt.|hll.snnt.apnk.dnil.|mt.rpi.ap.hn.ǵzr.mt.|hrnmy.alp.yṭbḫ.l kṯ| 17[2AQHT].2.27
ib.|d ašr.ar yrḫ.w y|rḫ yar k.|[ašr ilht kṯrt bn]|t hll.snnt.bnt h|ll bʻl gml.yrdt.|b ʻrgzm.b bz tdm.|lla y.ʻm lẓpn 24[77].41
yrḫ ytkḥ yḥ[bq] [-].|tld bt.[--]t.ḫ[--.l k]|ṯrt.l bnt.hll[.snnt].|hl ǵlmt tld b[n.--]n.|ʻn ha l yd h.tzd[.--].|pt l bšr h.d 24[77].6
.|hrnmy.alp.yṭbḫ.l kṯ|rt.yšlḥm.kṯrt.w y|ššq.bnt.[hl]l.snnt.|hn.ym.w ṯn.yšlḥm.|kṯrt.w yš[š]q.bnt.hl[l].|snnt.ṯlṯ[.r 17[2AQHT].2.31
nt.hl[l].|snnt.ṯlṯ[.r]bʻ ym.yšl|ḥm kṯrt.w yššq.|bnt hll.snnt.ḫmš.|ṯdṯ.ym.yšlḥm.k[ṯ]rt.|w y[ššq].bnt.hll.snnt.|mk.b 17[2AQHT].2.36
tzdn[.---]n.|l ad[n h.---].|dgn tt[--.---.-]l|ʻ.l kṯrt hl[l.sn]nt.|ylak yrḫ ny[r] šmm.ʻm.|ḫr[ḫ]b mlk qẓ.tn nkl y|rḫ y 24[77].15
t hll.snnt.ḫmš.|ṯdṯ.ym.yšlḥm.k[ṯ]rt.|w y[ššq].bnt.hll.snnt.|mk.b šb[ʻ.]ymm.tbʻ.b bt h.|kṯrt.bnt.hll.snnt.|[-]d[-]t. 17[2AQHT].2.38
hl]l.snnt.|hn.ym.w ṯn.yšlḥm.|kṯrt.w yš[š]q.bnt.hl[l].|snnt.ṯlṯ[.r]bʻ ym.yšl|ḥm kṯrt.w yššq.|bnt hll.snnt.ḫmš.|ṯdṯ. 17[2AQHT].2.34
.bnt.hll.snnt.|mk.b šb[ʻ.]ymm.tbʻ.b bt h.|kṯrt.bnt.hll.snnt.|[-]d[-]t.nʻm y.ʻrš.h[--]m.|ysmsmt.ʻrš.ḫlln.[-].|yṯb.dnil 17[2AQHT].2.40

snr

[---.b]nšm.b.šmny. | [---.b]nšm.b.šmngy. | [---.]bnšm.b.snr.mid. | [---.bn]šm.b.tkn. | [---.bn]šm.b.tmrm. | [---.bn]šm.b. 2076.26
----]. | nnu. | šmg. | šmn. | lbnm. | ṯrm. | bṣr. | y[--]. | y[--]. | snr. | midḫ. | ḥ[lym]. | [ḫ]lby. | ʿr. | ʿnq[pat]. | glbty. | [-----]. | [---- 2058.2.19
nʿy. | mʿqb. | agm. | bir. | ypr. | hzp. | šql. | mʿrḥ[-]. | sl[ḫ]. | snr. | ʿrgz. | yknʿm. | ʿnmky. | ġr. 2074.35
]. | [---]. | mʿr. | arny. | ubrʿy. | ilštmʿ. | bir. | mʿqb. | uškn. | snr. | rq[d]. | [---]. | [---]. | mid[-]. | ubs̀. | mṣb[t]. | ḥl.y[---]. | ʿrg[z 71[113].33
l[b]nm. | nnu. | ʿrm. | bṣr. | mʿr. | ḫlby. | mṣbt. | snr. | ṯm. | ubs̀. | glbt. | mi[d]ḫ. | mr[i]l. | ḫlb. | s̀ld. | ʿrgz. | [-----]. 2041.8
mr[il.---]. | ub[rʿy.---]. | mi[ḫd.---]. | snr[.---]. | ṯm[--.---]. 2144.4

snry

--]ḫm. | [---.--]m. | [---]nb.w ykn. | [--]ndbym. | [ʿ]rmy.w snry. | [b]n.sdy.bn.ṯty. | bn.ḥyn.bn.ġlm. | bn.yyn.w.bn.au[pš]. 131[309].22
šd.snrym.dt.ʿqb. | b.ayly. | šd.abršn. | šd.kkn.[bn].ubyn. | šd.bn.li 2026.1
y. | bn.ʿn.rqdy. | bn.gʿyn. | bn.ġrn. | bn.agynt. | bn.abdḫr.snry. | dqn.šlmn. | prdn.ndb[--]. | [-]rn.ḫbty. | abmn.bn.qdmn. 87[64].36
ʿšr.b]nš. | ṣbu.any[t]. | bn abdḫ[r]. | pdym. | ḫmš.bnšm. | snrym. | tšʿ.bnš[m]. | gbʿlym. | arbʿ.b[nšm]. | ṯbqym. 79[83].14

snrn

khnm[.--]. | bn.ṯ[--]. | bn.[---]. | bn.ṯʿl[-]. | bn.nq[ly]. | bn.snr[n]. | bn.pzn[y]. | bn.mg[lb]. | bn.db[--]. | bn.amd[n]. | annš[2020.9
nn. | khnm. | bn.ṯʿy. | w.nḥl h. | w.nḥl hm. | bn.nqly. | bn.snrn. | bn.ṯgd. | bn.d[-]n. | bn.amdn. | bn.ṯmrn. | bn.pzny. | bn. 105[86].3
--.]mn. | [--.-]sn. | [bn.-]ny. | [b]n.ḫnyn. | [bn].nbq. | [bn.]snrn. | [bn.-]lṣ. | bn.[---]ym. 115[301].3.4
ḫmš.bnšm[.---]. | ḫdġlm.b d.[---]. | šbʿ.lmdm.b d.s[n]rn. | lmd.aḥd.b d.yr[š]. | lmd.aḥd.b d.yḥ[--]. | ṯlṯ.lmdm.b 1050.3
[---]ʿ.lmdm. | [---.b]ʿln. | [---.]lmdm.b d.snrn. | [---.lm]dm.b d.nrn. | [---.ḫ]dġlm. | [lmd.]aḥd.b d.yrš. 1051.3
šd.bn.nbʿm.l.ṯpṭbʿl. | šd.bn mšrn.l.ilšpš. | [šd.bn].kbr.l.snrn. | [---.--]k.l.gmrd. | [---.--]ṯ.l.yšn. | [šd.--]ln. | b d.trġds. | šd 2030.1.6

snt

. | w.ḥṯṯn bn h. | w.btšy.bt h. | w.ištrmy. | bt.ʿbd mlk. | w.snt. | bt.ugrt. | w.pdy h[m]. | iwrkl.mit. | ksp.b y[d]. | birtym. | [1006.10

ss

.klb. | l[---].bt.ḫzli. | bn.iḫyn. | ṣdqn.bn.ass. | bʿlyskn.bn.ss. | ṣdqn.bn.imrt. | mnḫm.bn.ḫyrn. | [-]yn.bn.arkbt. | [--]zbl.b 102[323].3.9

ssg

štm.w.qlʿ. | bn.ysd.qšt. | [ġ]mrm. | ilgn.qšt. | abršp.qšt. | ssg.qšt. | ynḥm.qšt. | pprn.qšt. | uln.qšt. | bn.nkl qšt. | ady.qšt. | 105[86].3

ssw

ṯ]lṯ.ʿš[r h.---]. | d bnšm.yd.grbs hm. | w.ṯn.ʿšr h.ḫpnt. | [s̀]s̀wm.amtm.ʿkyt. | yd.llḫ hm. | w.ṯlṯ.l.ʿšrm. | ḫpnt.s̀s̀wm.ṯn. | 2049.4
[s̀]s̀w[.i]ryn.arr. | [š]dm.b.mlk. | [--.š]dm.b.ar. | [--.š]dm.b.ulm. 2033.1.1
šmn. | arbʿm.l.mit.tišr. | ṯṯ.ṯṯ.b [ṯ]ql.ṯlṯt.l.ʿšrm.ksp hm. | s̀stm.b.šbʿm. | ṯlṯ.mat.trm.b.ʿšrt. | mit.adrm.b.ʿšrt. | ʿšr.ydt.b.ʿ 1127.6
.ṯh.l pn.ib. | hn.hm.yrgm.mlk. | bʿl y.tmġyy.hn. | alpm.s̀s̀wm.hnd. | w.mlk.bʿl y.bnš. | bnny.ʿmn. | mlakty.hnd. | ylak ʿ 1012.32
.št]. | irġ[n.ḥmr.ydk]. | aḥd[h.w.yṣq.b.ap h]. | k yr[a]š.s̀s̀[w.w.ykhp]. | mid.dblt.yṯ[nt.w]. | ṣmq[m].yṯnm.w[.qmḥ.bql 161[56].32
ġmġ]. | w [bṣql.ʿrgz.ydk]. | a[ḥd h.w.yṣq.b.ap h]. | k.[ḫr.s̀s̀w.ḫndrṯ]. | w.ṯ[qd.mr.ydk.aḥd h]. | w.y[ṣq.b.ap h]. | k.l.ḫ[ru 161[56].5
ġmġ w b[ṣql ʿrgz]. | [ydk aḥ]d h w yṣq b ap h. | [k ḫr]s̀s̀w ḫndrṯ w ṯ[qd m]r. | [ydk aḥd h w yṣq b ap h. | [k l yḫru 160[55].6
ṯ[qd.mr.ydk.aḥd h]. | w.y[ṣq.b.ap h]. | k.l.ḫ[ru.w.l.yṯtn.s̀s̀w]. | mss.[št.qlql.w.št]. | ʿrgz[.ydk.aḥd h]. | w.yṣq[.b.ap h]. | 161[56].8
[k.---.]s̀s̀[w.---]. | [---.w]yṣq b a[p h]. | [k ḫr s̀]s̀w mġmġ w b[ṣql ʿrgz]. | [ydk aḥ]d h w yṣq b ap h. | [k ḫr] 160[55].4
k [ḫr s̀s̀w mġmġ]. | w [bṣql.ʿrgz.ydk]. | a[ḥd h.w.yṣq.b.ap h]. | k.[ḫr. 161[56].2
pbl.mlk. | qḥ.ksp.w yrq.ḫrṣ. | yd.mqm h.w ʿbd.ʿlm. | ṯlṯ.sswm.mrkbt. | b trbṣ.bn.amt. | qḥ.krt.šlmm. | šlmm.w ng.mlk 14[KRT].3.128
. | [ank.ksp.w yrq]. | [ḫrṣ.]yd.mqm h. | [w ʿb]d.ʿlm.ṯlṯ. | [ssw]m.mrkbt b trbṣ bn.amt. | [tn.b]nm.aqny. | [tn.ṯa]rm.ami 14[KRT].2.56
ʿ. | lm.ank.ksp. | w yr[q.ḫrṣ]. | yd.mqm h.w ʿbd. | ʿlm.ṯlṯ.sswm. | mrkbt.b trbṣ. | bn.amt.p d.[i]n. | b bt y.ttn.tn. | l y.mṯt 14[KRT].6.285
.l h.lm.ank. | ksp.w yrq.ḫrṣ. | yd.mqm h.w ʿbd. | ʿlm.ṯlṯ.sswm.mrkbt. | b trbṣt.bn.amt. | p d.in.b bt y.ttn. | tn.l y.mṯt.ḥ 14[KRT].3.140
lk]. | qḥ.[ksp.w yr]q. | ḫrṣ[.yd.mqm] h. | ʿbd[.ʿlm.ṯlṯ]. | ss[wm.mrkbt]. | b[trbṣ.bn.amt]. | [qḥ.krt.šlmm]. | [šlmm.al.tṣ 14[KRT].5.253
k]. | qḥ[.ksp.w yrq]. | ḫrṣ.[yd.mqm h]. | w ʿbd[.ʿlm.ṯlṯ]. | sswm.m[rkbt]. | b trbṣ.[bn.amt]. | q[ḥ.kr]t[.šlmm]. | š[lmm.]al 14[KRT].6.272
-.]ʿbdyrḫ.l.ml[k]. | [--]t.w.lqḥ. | yn[.--].b dn h. | w.ml[k].s̀s̀wm.nʿmm. | ytn.l.ʿbdyrḫ. | w.mlk.z[--.--]n.s̀s̀wm. | nʿmm.[-- 2064.16
. | w.ml[k].s̀s̀wm.nʿmm. | ytn.l.ʿbdyrḫ. | w.mlk.z[--.--]n.s̀s̀wm. | nʿmm.[--].ṯṯm.w.at. | nġṯ.w.ytn.hm.l k. | w.lḥt.alpm.ḥ 2064.18
. | alp.pr.bʿl.[---]. | w prt.tkt.[---]. | šnt.[---]. | s̀s̀w.ʿṯtrt.w s̀s̀w.ʿ[nt.---]. | w ht.[--]k.s̀s̀w[.-]rym[.---]. | d ymġy.bnš[.---]. | 2158.1.6
p.d krr[.---]. | alp.pr.bʿl.[---]. | w prt.tkt.[---]. | šnt.[---]. | s̀s̀w.ʿṯtrt.w s̀s̀w.ʿ[nt.---]. | w ht.[--]k.s̀s̀w[.-]rym[.---]. | d ymġy. 2158.1.6
qrb.hkl y.[aṯr h.rpum]. | tdd.aṯr h.tdd.iln[ym.---]. | asr.sswm.tṣmd.dg[-.---]. | tʿln.l mrkbt hm.ti[ty.l ʿr hm]. | tlkn.ym 20[121].2.3
lʿ. | bn.gmrt.qšt. | ġmrm. | bn.qṭn.qšt.w.qlʿ. | mrṯd.qšt. | ssw.qšt. | knn.qšt. | bn.ṯlln.qšt. | bn.šyn.qšt. | ʿbd.qšt. | bn.ulmy 119[321].1.14
rn. | [w št aškrr w p]r ḥdrt. | [-----]. | [---.-]n[-]. | [k yraš s̀s̀w št bln q]ṭ ydk. | [w yṣq b ap h]. | [-----]. | [-----]. | [-----]. | [-- 160[55].14
rn]. | št.irġn.ḥmr[.ydk]. | aḥd h.w.yṣq.b[.ap h]. | k.yraš.s̀s̀w.[št]. | bln.qṭ.yṣq.b.a[p h]. | k ygʿr[.s̀s̀w.---]. | dprn[.---]. | dr 161[56].21
qlql. | [w št ʿrgz y]dk aḥd h w yṣq b ap h. | [k.yiḫd akl s̀]s̀w št mkšr grn. | [w št aškrr w p]r ḥdrt. | [-----]. | [---.-]n[-]. | 160[55].10
l.w.št]. | ʿrgz[.ydk.aḥd h]. | w.yṣq[.b.ap h]. | k.yiḫd[.akl.s̀s̀w]. | št.mkš[r.grn]. | w.št.ašk[rr]. | w.pr.ḥdr[t.ydk]. | aḥd h. 161[56].12
]. | w.pr.ḥdr[t.ydk]. | aḥd h.w.yṣq[.b.ap h]. | k.yiḫd.akl.s̀[s̀w]. | št.nni.št.mk[št.grn]. | št.irġn.ḥmr[.ydk]. | aḥd h.w.yṣq. 161[56].17
t. | [s̀]s̀wm.amtm.ʿkyt. | yd.llḫ hm. | w.ṯlṯ.l.ʿšrm. | ḫpnt.s̀s̀wm.ṯn. | pddm.w.d.ṯṯ. | [mr]kbt.w.ḥrṣ. 2049.7
alp ḥẓm.w alp. | ntq.ṯn.qlʿm. | ḫmš.ṣmdm.w ḥrṣ. | ṯryn.s̀s̀wm. | ṯryn.aḥd.d bnš. | arbʿ.ṣmdm.apnt. | w ḥrṣ. | tšʿm.mrḥ. 1123.5
tkt.[---]. | šnt.[---]. | s̀s̀w.ʿṯtrt.w s̀s̀w.ʿ[nt.---]. | w ht.[--]k.s̀s̀w[.-]rym[.---]. | d ymġy.bnš[.---]. | w ḥmr[.---]. | w mʿn[.---]. 2158.1.7
h]. | [ʿ]ṯtr[-].w.[rʿ h]. | ḫlly[-].w.rʿ[h]. | ilmškl.w.rʿ[h]. | s̀s̀w[.--].w.r[ʿ h]. | kr[mn.--.]w.r[ʿ h]. | šd.[--.w.]r[ʿ h]. | ḫla[n.-- 2083.2.3
b[.ap h]. | k.yraš.s̀s̀w.[št]. | bln.qṭ.yṣq.b.a[p h]. | k ygʿr[.s̀s̀w.---]. | dprn[.---]. | drʿ.[---]. | tmṯl[.---]. | mġm[ġ.---]. | w.š[t.n 161[56].23
ny.ʿmn. | mlakty.hnd. | ylak ʿm y. | w.tʿl.ṯh.hn. | [a]lpm.s̀s̀wm. | [---].w.ṯb. 1012.38

[k.---.]šš[w.---]. | [---.w]yṣq b a[p h]. | [k ẖr š]šw mǵmǵ w b[ṣql ʻrgz 160[55].2
]. | yly[.---]. | ykn[.---]. | rp[--]. | ṯṯw.[---]. | [---.ʻ]šrm.ṣmd.ššw. 2131.12

ssl

ʻl.bt.aḏmny. | bʻl.bt.pdy. | bʻl.bt.nqly. | bʻl.bt.ʻlr. | bʻl.bt.ssl. | bʻl.bt.ṯrn. | bʻl.bt.ktmn. | bʻl.bt.ndbd. | [--].ṣnr. | [bʻl].bt.bs 31[14].6

ssm

| bn.rmy. | bn.aky. | ʻbdḫmn. | bn.ʻdṯ. | kṯy. | bn.ḫny. | bn.ssm. | bn.ḫnn. | [--]ny. | [bn].ṯrdnt. | [bn].hyadt. | [--]lt. | šmrm. 1047.18

ssn

šlmt. | ṯtrn.bʻl ššlmt. | aršwn.bʻl ššlmt. | ḥdṯn.bʻl ššlmt. | ssn.bʻl ššlmt. 1077.11
aršḫ.ṯrrt.ydy.b ʻṣm.ʻrʻr. | w b šḥt.ʻs.mt.ʻrʻrm.ynʻrn h. | ssnm.ysyn h.ʻdtm.yʻdyn h.yb | ltm.ybln h.mǵy.ḥrn.l bt h.w. UG5.7.66

sʻ

.ybl hm.ḫrṣ. | ṯlḥn.il.d mla. | mnm.dbbm.d | msdt.arṣ. | sʻ.il.dqt.k amr. | sknt.k ḥwt.yman. ¦d b h.rumm.l rbbt. 4[51].1.42
-.--]r. | [--.]wk[--.---]. | [--].lm.l[--.---]. | [-]m.in[.---]. | [--.]sʻ.[---]. | [---.]n[--.---]. | [--.]aw[--.---]. | [---.]ʻl.y[--.---]. | [--.]dn[- 45[45].2

sʻt

w gr.nn.ʻrm.šrn. | pdrm.sʻt.b šdm. | ḥṭb h.b grnt.ḥpšt. | sʻt.b nk.šibt.b bqr. | mmlat.dm.ym.w ṯn. | ṯlṯ.rbʻ.ym.ymš. | ṯdṯ 14[KRT].3.113
grnn.ʻrm. | šrnn.pdrm. | sʻt.b šdm.ḥṭb. | w b grnt.ḥpšt. | sʻt.b npk.šibt.w b | mqr.mmlat. | d[m].ym.w ṯn. | ṯlṯ.rbʻ.ym. | 14[KRT].5.216
ǵy.l udm. | rbm.w l.udm.ṯrrt. | w gr.nn.ʻrm.šrn. | pdrm.sʻt.b šdm. | ḥṭb h.b grnt.ḥpšt. | sʻt.b nk.šibt.b bqr. | mmlat.dm 14[KRT].3.111
ǵy.l udm.rbt. | w udm[.ṯr]rt. | grnn.ʻrm. | šrnn.pdrm. | sʻt.b šdm.ḥṭb. | w b grnt.ḥpšt. | sʻt.b npk.šibt.w b | mqr.mmla 14[KRT].4.214

sǵy

.ʻšr h.ḫrmṯt. | ṯt.nitm.ṯn.mʻṣdm.ṯn.mqbm. | krk.aḥt. | b.sǵy.ḫmš.ḫrmṯt.nit. | krk.mʻṣd.mqb. | b.gt.ʻmq.ḫmš.ḫrmṯt.n[it 2048.7
.ṭb.b.zbl. | ʻšrm.yn.ṭb.w.ṯṯm.ḫmš.k[b]d. | yn.d.l.ṭb.b.gt.sǵy. | arbʻm.kdm.kbd.yn.ṭb. | w.ḫmšm.k[dm.]kbd.yn.d.l.ṭb. | 1084.15

sǵr

n.aḥd. | sǵr.awldn.aḥd. | sǵr.idṯn.aḥd. | sǵr.sndrn.aḥd. | sǵr.adn.ṣdq.aḥd. | sǵr.irgn.aḥd. | sǵr.ršpab.aḥd. | sǵr.arwṯ.aḥd 1140.8
.uzm. | sǵr.bn.ḫpsry.aḥd. | sǵr.artn.aḥd. | sǵr.ʻdn.aḥd. | sǵr.awldn.aḥd. | sǵr.idṯn.aḥd. | sǵr.sndrn.aḥd. | sǵr.adn.ṣdq.a 1140.5
.aḥd. | sǵr.adn.ṣdq.aḥd. | sǵr.irgn.aḥd. | sǵr.ršpab.aḥd. | sǵr.arwṯ.aḥd. | sǵr.bn.mǵln. | aḥd. 1140.11
ṯn.rʻy.uzm. | sǵr.bn.ḫpsry.aḥd. | sǵr.artn.aḥd. | sǵr.ʻdn.aḥd. | sǵr.awldn.aḥd. | sǵr.idṯn.aḥd. | sǵ 1140.3
sry.aḥd. | sǵr.artn.aḥd. | sǵr.ʻdn.aḥd. | sǵr.awldn.aḥd. | sǵr.idṯn.aḥd. | sǵr.sndrn.aḥd. | sǵr.adn.ṣdq.aḥd. | sǵr.irgn.aḥd 1140.6
| ʻbdnt. | bdy.ḥrš arkd. | blšš lmd. | ḥṯṯn.tqn. | ydd.idṯn. | šǵr.ilgdn. 1045.13
.aḥd. | sǵr.idṯn.aḥd. | sǵr.sndrn.aḥd. | sǵr.adn.ṣdq.aḥd. | sǵr.irgn.aḥd. | sǵr.ršpab.aḥd. | sǵr.arwṯ.aḥd. | sǵr.bn.mǵln. | a 1140.9
[s]ǵr.bn.bdn. | [sǵ]r.bn.psḥn. | alṯy. | sǵr.npr. | bn.ḫty. | ṯn.bnš i 2082.1
ṯn.rʻy.uzm. | sǵr.bn.ḫpsry.aḥd. | sǵr.artn.aḥd. | sǵr.ʻdn.aḥd. | sǵr.awldn.aḥ 1140.2
ṣdq.aḥd. | sǵr.irgn.aḥd. | sǵr.ršpab.aḥd. | sǵr.arwṯ.aḥd. | sǵr.bn.mǵln. | aḥd. 1140.12
[s]ǵr.bn.bdn. | [sǵ]r.bn.psḥn. | alṯy. | sǵr.npr. | bn.ḫty. | ṯn.bnš ibrdr. | bnš tlmi. 2082.2
rʻym.dt.b d.iytlm. | ḫyrn.w.šǵr h. | šǵr.bn.prsn. | agpṯr.w.šǵ[r h]. | ṯʻln. | mztn.w.šǵr [h]. | šǵr.plṭ. 2072.3
pr. | bn.ḫty. | ṯn.bnš ibrdr. | bnš tlmi. | sǵr.ḫryn. | ʻdn.w sǵr h. | bn.ḥgbn. 2082.9
rʻym.dt.b d.iytlm. | ḫyrn.w.šǵr h. | šǵr.bn.prsn. | agpṯr.w.šǵ[r h]. | ṯʻln. | mztn.w.šǵr [h]. | š 2072.2
.w.šǵr h. | šǵr.bn.prsn. | agpṯr.w.šǵ[r h]. | ṯʻln. | mztn.w.šǵr [h]. | šǵr.plṭ. | s[d]rn [w].ṯn.šǵr h. | [---.]w.šǵr h. | [---.]w.šǵ 2072.6
ym.dt.b d.iytlm. | ḫyrn.w.šǵr h. | šǵr.bn.prsn. | agpṯr.w.šǵ[r h]. | ṯʻln. | mztn.w.šǵr [h]. | šǵr.plṭ. | s[d]rn [w].ṯn.šǵr h. | [2072.4
.šǵ[r h]. | ṯʻln. | mztn.w.šǵr [h]. | šǵr.plṭ. | s[d]rn [w].ṯn.šǵr h. | [---.]w.šǵr h. | [---.]w.šǵr h. | [---.]krwn. | [---].ḫzmyn. | 2072.8
. | mztn.w.šǵr [h]. | šǵr.plṭ. | s[d]rn [w].ṯn.šǵr h. | [---.]w.šǵr h. | [---.]w.šǵr h. | [---.]krwn. | [---].ḫzmyn. | [---.]bn.dll. | r[2072.9
[h]. | šǵr.plṭ. | s[d]rn [w].ṯn.šǵr h. | [---.]w.šǵr h. | [---.]w.šǵr h. | [---.]krwn. | [---].ḫzmyn. | [---.]bn.dll. | r[--.--]km. | w.sp 2072.10
--.]dd. | [---]n.yd.sǵ[r.---.--]k.[--]. | [---.]dd.bn.š.[---.]yd.sǵr h. | [---.--]r h.ʻšr[m.---.ʻ]šrm.dd. | [---.yn.d.]nkly.l.rʻym.šbʻ 1098.42
psḥn. | alṯy. | sǵr.npr. | bn.ḫty. | ṯn.bnš ibrdr. | bnš tlmi. | sǵr.ḫryn. | ʻdn.w sǵr h. | bn.ḥgbn. 2082.8
nntn. | ʻdn. | sdwn. | mztn. | ḫyrn. | šdn. | [ʻš]rm.ṯn kbd. | šǵrm. | lqḥ.ššlmt. 2098.10
[s]ǵr.bn.bdn. | [sǵ]r.bn.psḥn. | alṯy. | sǵr.npr. | bn.ḫty. | ṯn.bnš ibrdr. | bnš tlmi. | sǵr.ḫryn. | ʻdn.w sǵ 2082.4
artn.aḥd. | sǵr.ʻdn.aḥd. | sǵr.awldn.aḥd. | sǵr.idṯn.aḥd. | sǵr.sndrn.aḥd. | sǵr.adn.ṣdq.aḥd. | sǵr.irgn.aḥd. | sǵr.ršpab.aḥ 1140.7
ṯn.rʻy.uzm. | sǵr.bn.ḫpsry.aḥd. | sǵr.artn.aḥd. | sǵr.ʻdn.aḥd. | sǵr.awldn.aḥd. | sǵr.idṯn.aḥd. | sǵr.sndrn.aḥd. | s 1140.4
. | šǵr.bn.prsn. | agpṯr.w.šǵ[r h]. | ṯʻln. | mztn.w.šǵr [h]. | šǵr.plṭ. | s[d]rn [w].ṯn.šǵr h. | [---.]w.šǵr h. | [---.]w.šǵr h. | [---. 2072.7
.aḥd. | sǵr.sndrn.aḥd. | sǵr.adn.ṣdq.aḥd. | sǵr.irgn.aḥd. | sǵr.ršpab.aḥd. | sǵr.arwṯ.aḥd. | sǵr.bn.mǵln. | aḥd. 1140.10
---.--]d. | ʻšrm[.---.--]r h. | [-]wyn.yd[-.---.]dd. | [---]n.yd.sǵ[r.---.--]k.[--]. | [---.]dd.bn.š.[---.]yd.sǵr h. | [---.--]r h.ʻšr[m.- 1098.41
--.--]n.ṯn.ʻšr h.d[--.---]. | [---.]ḥdṯn.ʻšr.dd[.---]. | [---.]yd.sǵr[.---.--]r h. | aḥ[d.---.ʻ]šrm.d[d.---]. | ʻš[r.---.--]r h. | my y[--. 1098.35

sp

r ṯṯm lḥm. | l[.-]ry ṯlṯ spm w ʻšr lḥm. | [--.]w nṣp w ṯlṯ spm w ʻšrm lḥ[m]. | l[.-]dt ḫnd[r]ṯ arʻ s[p]m w ʻš[r]. | [---.]ḫn 134[-].4
[-]b[-.---.--] | r ṯṯm lḥm. | l[.-]ry ṯlṯ spm w ʻšr lḥm. | [--.]w nṣp w ṯlṯ spm w ʻšrm lḥ[m]. | l[.-]dt ḫ 134[-].3
[--.]w nṣp w ṯlṯ spm w ʻšrm lḥ[m]. | l[.-]dt ḫnd[r]ṯ arʻ s[p]m w ʻš[r]. | [---.]ḫndrṯm ṯṯ spm [w] ṯlṯm l[ḥm]. | [---.]arʻ s 134[-].5
[m]. | l[.-]dt ḫnd[r]ṯ arʻ s[p]m w ʻš[r]. | [---.]ḫndrṯm ṯṯ spm [w] ṯlṯm l[ḥm]. | [---.]arʻ spm w [---]. | [---]š[.---.--]b[.---]. 134[-].6
m l[ḥm]. | [---.]arʻ spm w [---]. | [---]š[.---.--]b[.---]. | [--.]sp[m.w ---.l]ḥm. 134[-].9
w ʻš[r]. | [---.]ḫndrṯm ṯṯ spm [w] ṯlṯm l[ḥm]. | [---.]arʻ spm w [---]. | [---]š[.---.--]b[.---]. | [--.]sp[m.w ---.l]ḥm. 134[-].7
l.ṯṯm sp[m.---]. | [p]drn.ḫm[š.---]. | l bn ḥḏnr[.---]. | ṯṯm sp.km[-.---]. | ʻšrm.sp[.---]. | ʻšr sp.m[ry-.---]. | ʻšr sp.m[ry-.---] 139[310].6

yky.|ṯlṯm sp.l bnš tpnr.|arb‘.spm.l.lbnš prwsdy.|ṯṯ spm.l bnš klnmw.|l yarš ḫswn.|ḫmš ‘šr.sp.|l bnš tpnr d ya 137.2[93].8
ṯn.|[---.]klnmw.|[---.]w yky.|ṯlṯm sp.l bnš tpnr.|arb‘.spm.l.lbnš prwsdy.|ṯṯ spm.l bnš klnmw.|l yarš ḫswn.|ḫmš 137.2[93].7
š prwsdy.|ṯṯ spm.l bnš klnmw.|l yarš ḫswn.|ḫmš ‘šr.sp.|l bnš tpnr d yaḫd l g ynm.|ṯṯ spm l tgyn.|arb‘ spm l ll[- 137.2[93].10
[---.--]ln.|[---.]kqmṯn.|[---.]klnmw.|[---.]w yky.|ṯlṯm sp.l bnš tpnr.|arb‘.spm.l.lbnš prwsdy.|ṯṯ spm.l bnš klnmw. 137.2[93].6
nm.|ṯṯ spm l tgyn.|arb‘ spm l ll[-].|ṯn spm.l slyy.|ṯlṯ spm l dlšpš amry. 137.2[93].15
šr.sp.|l bnš tpnr d yaḫd l g ynm.|ṯṯ spm l tgyn.|arb‘ spm l ll[-].|ṯn spm.l slyy.|ṯlṯ spm l dlšpš amry. 137.2[93].13
nr d yaḫd l g ynm.|ṯṯ spm l tgyn.|arb‘ spm l ll[-].|ṯn spm.l slyy.|ṯlṯ spm l dlšpš amry. 137.2[93].14
yarš ḫswn.|ḫmš ‘šr.sp.|l bnš tpnr d yaḫd l g ynm.|ṯṯ spm l tgyn.|arb‘ spm l ll[-].|ṯn spm.l slyy.|ṯlṯ spm l dlšpš a 137.2[93].12
-].|‘šrm.sp[.---].|‘šr sp.m[ry-.---].|‘šr sp.m[ry-.---].|ṯṯ sp.mry[-.---].|‘šr sp.m[ry-.---].|tš‘m s[p.---].|tš‘[m.sp.---].|ṯṯ 139[310].10
-].|l bn ḫḏnr[.---].|ṯṯm sp.km[-.---].|‘šrm.sp[.---].|‘šr sp.m[ry-.---].|‘šr sp.m[ry-.---].|ṯṯ sp.mry[-.---].|‘šr sp.m[ry-. 139[310].8
šr sp.m[ry-.---].|‘šr sp.m[ry-.---].|ṯṯ sp.mry[-.---].|‘šr sp.m[ry-.---].|tš‘m s[p.---].|tš‘[m.sp.---].|ṯṯ[.---]. 139[310].11
.|ṯṯm sp.km[-.---].|‘šrm.sp[.---].|‘šr sp.m[ry-.---].|‘šr sp.m[ry-.---].|ṯṯ sp.mry[-.---].|‘šr sp.m[ry-.---].|tš‘m s[p.---]. 139[310].9
‘nt.|n‘m h.km.tsm.|‘ṯtrt.tsm h.|d ‘q h.ib.iqni.|‘p‘p h.sp.ṯrml.|d b ḥlm y.il.ytn.|b ḏrt y.ab.adm.|w ld.špḥ.l krk|t. 14[KRT].6.295
t.n‘m h.|km.tsm.‘ṯtrt.ts[m h].|d ‘q h.ib.iqni.‘p[‘p] h.|sp.ṯrml.ṯḫgrn.[-]dm[.-].|ašlw.b ṣp.‘n h.|d b ḥlm y.il.ytn.|b 14[KRT].3.148
]drn.ḫm[š.---].|l bn ḫḏnr[.---].|ṯṯm sp.km[-.---].|‘šrm.sp[.---].|‘šr sp.m[ry-.---].|‘šr sp.m[ry-.---].|ṯṯ sp.mry[-.---].|‘ 139[310].7
[---.]mr[y-.---].|[--]sp.mr[y-.---].|[--]l.ṯṯm sp[m.---].|[p]drn.ḫm[š.---].|l bn ḫḏnr[.---].|ṯṯm sp.km[-.---] 139[310].3
sp.m[ry-.---].|ṯṯ sp.mry[-.---].|‘šr sp.m[ry-.---].|tš‘m s[p.---].|tš‘[m.sp.---].|ṯṯ[.---]. 139[310].12
ṯṯ sp.mry[-.---].|‘šr sp.m[ry-.---].|tš‘m s[p.---].|tš‘[m.sp.---].|ṯṯ[.---]. 139[310].13

spa

ltn.|šlyṭ.d šb‘y.rašm.|ṯṯkḥ.ttrp.šmm.k rs.|ipd k.ank.ispi.uṭm.|ḏrqm.amt m.l yrt.|b npš.bn ilm.mt.b mh|mrt.yd 5[67].1.5
k.pht.[-]l[-].|b šdm.‘l k.pht.|dr‘.b ym.tn.aḥd.|b aḫ k.ispa.w ytb.|ap.d anšt.im[-].|aḥd.b aḫ k.l[--]n.|hn[-.]aḥẓ[.--- 6[49].5.20
-]u.šb‘t.ġlm h.|[---].bn.ilm.mt.|p[-]n.aḫ y m.ytn.b‘l.|[s]pu y.bn m.um y.kly y.|yṯb.‘m.b‘l.ṣrrt.|ṣpn.yšu g h.w yṣḥ. 6[49].6.11
|yṯb.‘m.b‘l.ṣrrt.|ṣpn.yšu g h.w yṣḥ.|aḫ y m.ytnt.b‘l.|spu y.bn m.um y.kl|y y.yt‘n.k gmrm.|mt.‘z.b‘l.‘z.ynghn.|k 6[49].6.15
h.grš d.‘šy.ln h.|aḥd.yd h.b škrn.m‘ms h.|[k]šb‘ yn.spu.ksm h.bt.b‘l.|[w m]nt h bt.il.ṯḥ.gg h.b ym.|[ṭi]ṭ.rḥṣ.npṣ 17[2AQHT].1.32
iṣ y.grš.|d ‘šy.ln.aḥd.yd y.b š|krn m‘ms y k šb‘t yn.|spu.ksm y.bt.b‘l.[w]mn[t].|y.bt.il.ṯḥ.gg y.b ym.ṭiṭ.|rḥṣ.npṣ 17[2AQHT].2.21
ṯr k].|l ‘pr.ḏm[r.aṯr k.ṭbq].|lḥt.niṣ k.gr[š.d ‘šy.ln k].|spu.ksm k.bt.[b‘l.w mnt k].|bt il.aḥd.yd k.b [škrn].|m‘ms k 17[2AQHT].2.4
r.mt hrnmy[.---].|b grnt.ilm.b qrb.m[ṭ‘t.ilnym].|d tit.yspi.spu.q[--.---].|tpḥ.ṭṣr.shr[.---].|mr[.---]. 20[121].2.10
hrnmy[.---].|b grnt.ilm.b qrb.m[ṭ‘t.ilnym].|d tit.yspi.spu.q[--.---].|tpḥ.ṭṣr.shr[.---].|mr[.---]. 20[121].2.10
‘nt.hlkt.w.šnwt.|tp.aḫ.h.k.ysmsm.|tspi.šir.h.l.bl.ḥrb.|tšt.dm.h.l.bl.ks.|tpnn.‘n.bṯy.‘n.bṯt.tpnn.| RS225.3

spd

dnil.bt h.ymġyn.yšt|ql.dnil.l hkl h.‘rb.b|kyt.b hkl h.mšspdt.b ḥẓr h.|pẓġm.ġr.ybk.l aqht.|ġzr.ydm‘.l kdd.dnil.| 19[1AQHT].4.172
r.m[t.hrnmy.y]šu.|g h.w yṣḥ.t[b‘.---].|bkyt.b hk[l]y.mšspdt.|b ḥẓr y pẓġm.ġr.w yq.|dbḥ.ilm.yš‘ly.dġṯ h.|b šmy 19[1AQHT].4.183

spḫy

].|bn.uḫn.|ybru.i[---].|[p]dyn.[---].|bnšm.d.b [d.---].|spḫy.[---].|[-----].|b[--.---].|n‘[--.---].|[-----].|ḫn[--.---].|tg[-- 2161.14

spl

spr.npṣ.krw.|ṯt.ḥṯrm.ṯn.kst.|spl.mšlt.w.mqḥm.|w md h.|arn.w mznm.|ṯn.ḫlpnm.|ṯṯ.mr 2050.3
ḫmšm [-]t ṯlṯ ty[--].|bn.grgš.|w.npṣ bt ṯn.ṯlṯ mat.|w spl ṯlṯ.mat.|w mmskn.|w.ṯṯ.mqrtm.|w.ṯn.irpm.w.ṯn.trqm.| 1103.17

spsg

.šmt.|[---].all.iqni.arb‘m.kbl.|[---].iqni.‘šrm.ġprt.|[---.š]pšg.iqni.mit.pṯtm.|[---].mitm.kslm.|[---].pwt.ṯlṯ.mat.abn.ṣ 1106.8
l ġzr.|šrg k.ḫḫm.mt.uḫryt.mh.yqḥ.|mh.yqḥ.mt.aṯryt.spsg.ysk.|[l]riš.ḥrṣ.l ẓr.qdqd y.|[--.]mt.kl.amt.w an.mtm.a 17[2AQHT].6.36

spr

lḥmd.ḫrṣ.|yblnn.udr.ilqṣm.|yak.l kṯr.w ḫss.|w ṯb l mspr..k tlakn.|ġlmm.|aḫr.mġy.kṯr.w ḫss.|št.alp.qdm h.mr 4[51].5.104
[sp]r.akl[.---].tryn.|[tg]mr.akl.b.g[t.b]ir.alp.|[‘]šrm.l.mit.ḫ[p 2013.1
spr.argmn.nskm.|rqdym.|šṯšm.ṯṯ mat.|ṣprn.ṯṯ mat.|dkry.ṯ 1060.1.1
spr.argmnm.|‘šrm.ksp.d mkr.|mlk.|ṯlṯ.mat.ksp.d.šb[n].|m 2107.1
.tšu.g]h.w tṣḥ.hwt.|[---.]aqht.yḏ[--].|[---.--]n.ṣ[---].|[spr.ilmlk.šbny.lmd.atn.]prln. 17[2AQHT].7.1
s.d‘t k.|b ym.arš.w tnn.|kṯr.w ḫss.yd.|ytr.kṯr.w ḫss.|spr.ilmlk šbny.|lmd.atn.prln.rb.|khnm rb.nqdm.|ṯ‘y.nqmd 6.6[62.2].53
[spr.ilmlk.ṯ‘]y.nqmd.mlk.ugrt. 4[51].9.1
.‘ṯtrt.šm.b‘l.|qdqd k.tqln.b gbl.|šnt k.b ḥpn k.w t‘n.|spr ilmlk ṯ‘y. 16[127]EDGE
š.---].|‘m.k[--.lḥt].|akl.yṯ[ṯb.--]pt.|ib.‘ltn.a[--.--]y.|w.spr.in[.-.]‘d m.|spr n.ṯhr[.--].|aṯr.iṯ.bqṯ.|w.štn.l y. 2060.32
spr.irgmn.|ṯlṯ.ḫmš.alpm.|b d.brq.maḫdy.|kkr.ṯlṯ.|b d.bn.b 1134.1
spr.ubdy.art.|šd.prn.b d.agpṯn.nḫl h.|šd.šwn.b d.ttyn.nḫl [2029.1
spr.updt.|d b d.mlkytn.|kdrl.|slṯmg.|adrdn.|l[l]wn.|ydln. 1034.1
[s]p[r] ušknym.dt.[b d.---].|bn.btr.|bn.‘ms.|bn.pṣn.|bn.agm 2021.1.1
ṣr.arṣ.|ša.ġr.‘l.ydm.|ḫlb.l ẓr.rḥtm.|w rd.bt ḫpṯt.|arṣ.tspr.b y|rdm.arṣ.|idk.al.ttn.|pnm.tk.qrt h.|hmry.mk.ksu.| 4[51].8.8
.|knkny.ša.ġr.‘l ydm.|ḫlb.l ẓr.rḥtm w rd.|bt ḫpṯt.arṣ.tspr b y|rdm.arṣ.w td‘ ilm.|k mtt.yšm‘.aliyn.b‘l.|yuhb.‘glt. 5[67].5.15
spr.bdlm.|n‘mn.|rbil.|plsy.|ygmr.|mnṯ.|prḫ.|‘dršp.|ršpa 1032.1
spr.blblm.|skn uškn.|skn šbn.|skn ubr‘.|skn ḫrṣb‘.|rb.ntbt 1033.1
[sp]r.bnš.ml[k.d.b] d adn[‘m].|[---].riš[.---].kt.|[y]nḥm.|ilb‘l 1024.1.1

spr.bnš.mlk. | d.b d.prṯ. | tš'.l.'šrm. | lqḥ.ššlmt. | ṯmn.l.arb'm. | 1025.1
[s]pr.bnš.mlk.d.b.tbq. | [kr]wn. | [--]n. | [q]ṣy. | ṯn.bn.iwrḫz.[n]' 2066.1.1
spr.bnš.mlk. | d taršn.'msn. | bṣr.abn.špšyn. | dqn. | aǵlmn. | kn 2067.1.1
spr.gt.r[---]. | 'šrm.l.m[it.---]. | šd.dr[-.---]. 1105.1
l iwrpḫn. | bn y.aḫ y.rgm. | ilm.tǵr k. | tšlm k. | iky.lḥt. | spr.d likt. | 'm.ṯryl. | mh y.rgmt. | w ht.aḫ y. | bn y.yšal. | ṯryl.p 138.7
iwrpḫn. | bn y.aḫ y.rgm. | ilm.tǵr k. | tšlm k. | ik y.lḥt. | spr.d likt. | 'm.ṯryl. | mh y.rgmt. | w ht.aḫ y. | bn y.yšal. | ṯryl.p 138.7
bḥ. | dt nat. | w ytnt. | ṯrmn w. | dbḥ kl. | kl ykly. | dbḥ k.sprt. | dt nat. | w qrwn. | l k dbḥ. | [--]r bt [--]. | [--]bnš [--]. | š š RS61[24.277.9]
spr[.---]. | ybnil[.---.]kd yn.w š. | spr.m[--]. | spr d[---]b.w š. | tt.ḫmš.[---]. | skn.ul[m.---]. | [---]š.[---]. | [---]y 1093.4
. | [---.]krwn. | [---].ḫzmyn. | [---.]bn.dll. | r[--.--]km. | w.spr h. 2072.15
t. | b 'rgzm.b bz tdm. | lla y.'m lẓpn i | l d.pid.hn b p y sp | r hn.b špt y mn | t hn ṯlḥ h w mlg h y | ṯtqt 'm h b q't. | tq 24[77].45
'lm. | mišmn.nqmd. | mlk ugrt. | nqmd.mlk.ugrt. | ktb.spr hnd. | dt brrt.ṣṯqšlm. | 'bd h.hnd. | w mn km.l yqḥ. | spr.m 1005.9
spr.ḥpr.bnš mlk.b yrḫ iṯt[bnm]. | ršpab.rb 'šrt.m[r]yn. | pǵdn 2011.1
spr.ḥpr.bt.k[--]. | tš'.'šr h.dd.l.b[t.--]. | ḫmš.ddm.l.ḥtyt. | ṯlṯm. 1099.1
spr.ḥršm. | liy.bn.qqln. | [---.a]lty. | [-----]. | [---]tl. | [---]'bl. | [--- 1036.1
spr.ḥrš. | qštiptl. | bn.anny. | ilṣdq. | ypltn.bn iln. | špšm.nsl h. | 1037.1
[s]pr.ḥ[rš.---]. | [-]mn.n[--]. | ḥrš.d.[---]. | mrum.[---]. | yṣḥm[.--- 1038.1
spr.ḥtbn.sbrdnm. | ḫmš.kkrm.alp kb[d]. | ṯlṯ.l.nskm.birtym. | 2101.1
[--]km.'m.mlk. | [b]ǵl hm.w.iblbl hm. | w.b.ṯb h.[---]. | spr ḥ[--.---]. | w.'m[.---]. | yqḥ[.---]. | w.n[--.---]. 2129.12
-]. | [---.]dt[-.---]. | [---.]ksḥ[-.--]. | [---.]mnty[.-]. | [---.]rb spr ḫbb. | [---.--]n.dbḥm. | [---].'bdssm. 49[73].2.4
spr.ḫrd.arr. | ap arb'm[.--]. | pd[.---.ḫm]šm.kb[d]. | ǵb[-.---.]k 2042.1
d[-]t.n'm y.'rš.h[--]m. | ysmsmt.'rš.ḫlln.[-]. | yṯb.dnil.[l s]pr yrḫ h. | yrs.y[---.]y[--] h. | ṯlṯ.rb['.yrḫ.--]r[.--]. | yrḫm.ymǵ 17[2AQHT].2.43
.w atn k.bl mt. | w ašlḥ k.ašspr k.'m.b'l. | šnt.'m.bn il.tspr.yrḫm. | k b'l.k yḥwy.y'šr.ḥwy.y'š. | r.w yšqyn h.ybd.w y 17[2AQHT].6.29
spr.ytnm. | bn.ḫlbym. | bn.ady. | bn.'ṯtry. | bn.ḫrẓn. | ady. | bn. 115[301].1.1
.irš ḥym.l aqht.ǵzr. | irš ḥym.w atn k.bl mt. | w ašlḥ k.ašspr k.'m.b'l. | šnt.'m.bn il.tspr.yrḫm. | k b'l.k yḥwy.y'šr.ḥw 17[2AQHT].6.28
[sp]r.k[--]. | ṯ[ṯ.bn]šm[.b.a]gmy. | ṯṯ.bn[šm.---]. | 'šr.b[nšm.---]. 2076.1
hm.mtqtm. | bm.nšq.w hr.[b]ḥbq.w ḥ[m]ḥmt.yṯb[n]. | yspr.l ḫmš.l ṣ[---.]šr.pḫr.klat. | tqtnṣn.w tldn.tld.[ilm.]n'mm 23[52].57
spr.npš.d. | 'rb.bt.mlk. | w.b.spr.l.št. | yrm'l. | ṣry. | iršy. | y'ḏrd. | ayaḫ. | bn.aylt. | ḫmš.mat.a 2106.3
[---.--]d.'m y. | [--.]spr.lm.likt. | [--]y.k išal hm. | [--.'š]rm.kkr.ṯlṯ. | [--.]ṯlṯm.kkr.ṯl 1022.2
spr.mdr[ǵlm]. | lt.hlk.b[.---]. | bn.b'yn.š[--.---]. | aǵltn.mid[-.-- 87[64].1
spr.mḫšm. | bn.ḫpṣry.b.šbn. | ilštm'ym. | y[---.]bn.'šq. | [---.]bn 1041.1
maḫdym. | grbn.lṯḥ. | srn.lṯḥ. | ykn.lṯḥ. | ḥgbn.lṯḥ. | spr.mkrm. | bn.sl'n.prs. | bn.ṯpdn.lṯḥ. | bn.urm.lṯḥ. 1059.6
pr hnd. | dt brrt.ṣṯqšlm. | 'bd h.hnd. | w mn km.l yqḥ. | spr.mlk.hnd. | b yd.ṣṯqšlm. | 'd 'lm. 1005.13
spr.mr[ynm]. | [b']l.[---]. | mr[--.---]. | hm.[---]. | kmrṯn[.---]. | b 2070.1.1
.l dr. | bn il.l mpḫrt.bn.il.l ṯkmn[.w]šnm.hn.'r. | w.ṯb.l mspr.m[šr] mšr.bt.ugrt.w npy.gr. | ḥmyt.ugrt.w [np]y.ntt.uš 32[2].1.27
spr[.---]. | ybnil[.---.]kd yn.w š. | spr.m[--]. | spr d[---]b.w š. | tt.ḫmš.[---]. | skn.ul[m.---]. | [---]š. 1093.3
t]. | akl.yṯ[ṯb.--]pt. | ib.'ltn.a[--.--]y. | w.spr.in[.-.]'d m. | spr n.ṯhr[.--]. | aṯr.iṯ.bqṯ. | w.štn.l y. 2060.33
spr.npṣm.d yṣa.b milḫ. | 'šrm.ḫpn.ḫmš. | kbd.w lpš. | ḫmš.mis 1109.1
spr.npṣ.krw. | tt.ḫtrm.ṯn.kst. | spl.mšlt.w.mqḥm. | w md h. | a 2050.1
spr.npš.d. | 'rb.bt.mlk. | w.b.spr.l.št. | yrm'l. | ṣry. | iršy. | y'ḏrd. 2106.1
.ṯlṯ. | 'l.ubr'y. | w.ṯn.'l. | mlk. | w.aḥd. | 'l atlg. | w l.'ṣm. | tspr. | nrn.al.tud | ad.at.l hm. | ṯṯm.ksp. 1010.18
spr. | synym. 1170.1
| hm.nṯkp. | m'n k. | w.mnm. | rgm.d.tšm'. | ṯmt.w.št. | b.spr.'m y. 53[54].19
spr 'psm. | dt.št. | uryn. | l mlk.ugrt. 1171.1
spr.'rbnm. | dt.'rb. | b.mtn.bn.ayaḫ. | b.ḫbṯ h.ḥwt.ṯt h. | w.mn 1161.1
spr.r'ym. | lqḥ.š'rt. | anntn. | 'dn. | sdwn. | mztn. | ḫyrn. | šdn. | [' 2098.1
spr.rpš d l y[dy]. | atlg. | ulm. | izly. | uḫnp. | bn sḫrn. | m'qb. | ṯ 2075.1
spr. | šal[m]. | mt[--]. 1172.1
spr šd.ri[šym]. | kr[-].šdm.'[--]. | b gt ṯm[--] yn[.--]. | [---].krm. 2027.1.1
spr.tbṣr. | klt.bt špš. 1175.1
b. | w yṣi.'dn.m'. | ṣbu k.ul.mad. | ṯlṯ.mat.rbt. | ḫpṯ.d bl.spr. | ṯnn.d bl.hg. | hlk.l alpm.ḫdd. | w l rbt.kmyr. | [a]ṯr.ṯn.ṯn. 14[KRT].2.90
yn.iš[ryt.-]lnr. | spr.[--]ḥ[-] k.šb't. | ghl.ph.ṯmnt. | nblu h.špš.ymp. | hlkt.tdr[-- 27[8].2
spr.[---]. | iytlm[.---]. | ybnn[.---]. | ilšp[š.---]. 2140.1
spr[.---]. | ḫmš.k[--.---]. | ḫmš[.---]. | 'š[r.---]. | [-----]. | [-----]. | [-- 1128.1
spr[.---]. | ybnil[.---.]kd yn.w š. | spr.m[--]. | spr d[---]b.w š. | tt 1093.1
spr.[---]. | ṯpṯb['l.---]. | mb[--.---]. | gmr[.---]. | [---]. 92[302].1
y.p']n k.tlsmn. | ['m y.twtḥ.išd] k.tk.ḫršn. | [---.-]bd k.spr. | [---.-]nk. 1['NT.IX].2.24
--] h. | mtn[.---.]l h. | [---.]l h. | [---.--]š.l h. | [---].l h. | [--.]spr[.---]. | [--.]ḫrd[.---]. | [---.]l h. 2133.10
[---.]spr[.---]. | [---.]yrd[.---]. 2154.1
[spr.----]m. | bn.pi[ty]. | w.nḥ[l h]. | 'bd[--]. | bn.s[---]. | bn.at[--]. 117[325].1.1
.m. | ypḥ.ilšlm. | bn.prqdš. | ypḥ.mnḥm. | bn.ḥnn. | brqn.spr. 2116.23
]ah. | ṯnm.tšqy msk.hwt.tšqy[.-.]w [---]. | w hn dt.yṯb.l mspr. 19[1AQHT].5.1
p. | iwrtn. | ydln. | 'bdilm. | dqn. | nsk.ṯlṯ. | 'bdadt. | bṣmn.spr. 1039.2.30

spš

-]. | [w]nqmd.[---]. | [-.]ʿmn.šp[š.mlk.rb]. | bʿl h.šlm.[w spš]. | mlk.rb.bʿl h.[---]. | nqmd.mlk.ugr[t.--]. | phy. | w ṯpllm. 64[118].12

srd

.]w.nḥl h. | bn ksln.ṯlṯḥ. | bn yṣmḫ.bn.ṯrn w nḥl h. | bn srd.bn agmn. | bn [-]ln.bn.ṯbil. | bn is.bn tbdn. | bn uryy. | bn a 101[10].5

srdnn

iḫyn.uṯpt.ḥẓm. | anšrm.uṯpt.ḥẓm. | w uṯpt.srdnnm. | awpn.uṯpt.ḥẓm. | w uṯpt.srdnnm. | rpan.uṯpt.srdnn 1124.3
. | rpan.uṯpt.srdnnm. | šbʿm.uṯpt.srdnnm. | bn.aǵli.uṯpt.srdnnm. | asrn.uṯpt.srdnnm. | bn.qṣn.uṯpt.srdnnm. | yly.uṯpt. 1124.8
m. | asrn.uṯpt.srdnnm. | bn.qṣn.uṯpt.srdnnm. | yly.uṯpt.srdnnm. | arṯṯb.uṯpt.srdnnm. 1124.11
.ḥẓm. | w uṯpt.srdnnm. | rpan.uṯpt.srdnnm. | šbʿm.uṯpt.srdnnm. | bn.aǵli.uṯpt.srdnnm. | asrn.uṯpt.srdnnm. | bn.qṣn.u 1124.7
. | šbʿm.uṯpt.srdnnm. | bn.aǵli.uṯpt.srdnnm. | asrn.uṯpt.srdnnm. | bn.qṣn.uṯpt.srdnnm. | yly.uṯpt.srdnnm. | arṯṯb.uṯpt. 1124.9
bn.aǵli.uṯpt.srdnnm. | asrn.uṯpt.srdnnm. | bn.qṣn.uṯpt.srdnnm. | yly.uṯpt.srdnnm. | arṯṯb.uṯpt.srdnnm. 1124.10
.uṯpt.ḥẓm. | w uṯpt.srdnnm. | awpn.uṯpt.ḥẓm. | w uṯpt.srdnnm. | rpan.uṯpt.srdnnm. | šbʿm.uṯpt.srdnnm. | bn.aǵli.uṯ 1124.5
srdnnm. | awpn.uṯpt.ḥẓm. | w uṯpt.srdnnm. | rpan.uṯpt.srdnnm. | šbʿm.uṯpt.srdnnm. | bn.aǵli.uṯpt.srdnnm. | asrn.uṯp 1124.6

srdnnm

. | bn.qṣn.uṯpt.srdnnm. | yly.uṯpt.srdnnm. | arṯṯb.uṯpt.srdnnm. 1124.12

srwd

ryy. | bn kṯl. | bn army. | bn gln. | bn abg. | bn.nǵry. | bn.srwd. | mtnn. | bn gš[-]. | bn gbrn. | bn uldy. | synn.bn knʿm. | b 1064.14

srn

pr.ṯlḥn.b qʿl.b qʿl. | mlkm.hn.ym.yṣq.yn.ṯmk. | mrṯ.yn.srnm.yn.bld. | ǵll.yn.išryt.ʿnq.smd. | lbnn.ṯl mrṯ.yḫrṯ.il. | hn.y 22.2[124].18
maḫdym. | grbn.lṯḥ. | srn.lṯḥ. | ykn.lṯḥ. | ḥgbn.lṯḥ. | spr.mkrm. | bn.slʿn.prs. | bn.ṯpdn 1059.3
ṣmrt. | liy.bn.yṣi. | ḏmrhd.bn.srt. | [---.--]m. | ʿbdmlk.bn.s̀rn. | ʿbdbʿl.bn.kdn. | gzl.bn.qldn. | gld.bt.klb. | l[---].bt.ḫzli. | b 102[323].3.2
.mṣl. | [---].prs̀.ḥtm. | ṯlṯ[.---].bn.ṯdnyn. | ddm.ḥ[ṯm].ʿl.s̀rn. | ʿs̀rt.ksp.ʿl.[-]lpy. | bn.ady.kkr.s̀ʿrt. | nṯk h. | kb[d.]mn.ʿl.a 1146.7
nḥm.qšt. | pprn.qšt. | uln.qšt. | bn.nkl qšt. | ady.qšt. | bn.srn.qšt. | bn.gdrn.qšt. | prpr.qšt. | ugry.qšt. | bn.ṣrptn.qšt. | bn. 119[321].1.42
n.ʿdy.ṯkt. | nʿmn.bn.ʿyn.ṯkt. | ʿpṯn.bn.ilrš.ṯkt. | ilṯḥm.bn.s̀rn.ṯkt. | šmlbu.bn.grb.ṯkt. | šmlbu.bn.ypʿ.ṯkt. | [---.--]m. 2085.12
šd.ubdy[.---]. | šd.bn.ḫb[--.---]. | šd.srn[.---]. | šd.yʿḏr[.---]. | šd.swr.[---]. | šd.bn ppn[-.---]. | šd.bn.u 83[85].3
[n].bn.apn. | krty. | bn.ubr. | [bn] mdḫl. | bn.sy[n]n. | bn.s̀rn. 2078.22

srr

l.ilak.l bn. | ilm.mt.ʿdd.l ydd. | il.ǵzr.yqra.mt. | b npš h.ystrn ydd. | b gngn h.aḥd y.d ym | lk.ʿl.ilm.l ymru. | ilm.w nš 4[51].7.48
kmn w šnm. | kṯr w ḫss. | ʿṯr ʿṯpr. | šḫr w šlm. | ngh w srr. | ʿdw šr. | ṣdqm šr. | ḥnbn il d[n]. | [-]bd w [---]. | [--].p il[.-- UG5.10.1.12

srt

bn.ḫran. | bn.srt. | bn.adn. | bn.ʿgw. | bn.urt. | aḫdbu. | pḥ[-]. | bn.ʿb . | bn.uḏn 121[307].2
[.---]. | [kd.]šš. | [k]d.ykn.bn.ʿbdṯrm. | kd.ʿbdil. | ṯlṯ.ʿl.bn.srt. | kd.ʿl.ẓrm. | kd.ʿl.šz.bn pls. | kd.ʿl.ynḥm. | tgrm.šmn.d.bn. 1082.2.4
r[p]u.bn.kbd. | [-]m[-].bn.ṣmrt. | liy.bn.yṣi. | ḏmrhd.bn.srt. | [---.--]m. | ʿbdmlk.bn.s̀rn. | ʿbdbʿl.bn.kdn. | gzl.bn.qldn. | g 102[322].6.7

srty

]prm ḫlq. | [---]n ḫlq. | bn mʿnt. | bn kbdy. | bn krk. | bn srty. | bn lṯḥ ḫlq. | bn ytr. | bn ilšpš. | ubrš. | bn gmš ḫlq. | bn ʿg 2016.2.13

stn

[---.]l mdgkbr. | [---] y.ʿm k. | [-]tn.l.stn. | [--.]d.nʿm.lbš k. | [-]dm.ṯn id. | [--]m.d.l.nʿmm. | [lm.]l.lik 2128.1.3

ś

śbb

dm. | ṣpym. | ṯlṯ mrkbt mlk. | d.l.ṣpy. | [---.t]r hm. | [---].śśb. | [---.]tr h. | [a]rbʿ.qlʿm. | arbʿ.mḏrnm. | mḏrn.w.mšḫṭ. | d. 1122.8

śbl

[-]. | bn.r[--]. | [bn.]ʿ[---]. | [bn.]r[---]. | [bn.]ḥ[---]. | [bn.]śbl. | [bn.]ḫdmn. | [bn.]nklb. | [---]dn. | [---]y. | [-----]. | [-----]. | b 1073.2.4
w.nḥl hm. | bn.ḥrm. | bn.brzn. | w.nḥl h. | bn.adlḏn. | bn.śbl. | bn.ḫnzr. | bn.arwṯ. | bn.ṯbtnq. | bn.pṯḏn. | bn.nbdg. | bn.ḥg 113[400].1.13

śgn

m. | bt.[-]b[-.-]sy[-]h. | nn[-].b[n].py[-.d.]yṯb.b.gt.aǵld. | śgn.bn b[--.---].d.yṯb.b.ilštmʿ. | abmn.bn.r[---].b.syn. | bn.irṣ[- 2015.2.6

śgryn

myn. | b d.gln.ary. | tgyn.yʿrty. | bn.krwn.b.yny.iytlm. | śgryn.ary.b.yny. | bn.yddn.b.rkby. | agyn.agny. | ṯqbn.mldy. 2071.6

śdy

ryn.arty. | bn.ršp.ary. | bn.ǵlmn ary. | bn.ḥṣbn ary. | bn.śdy ary. | bn.ktkt.mʿqby. | bn.[---.]ṯlḥny. | b[n.---.ub]rʿy. | [bn.- 87[64].15
bn.ǵlmn.ary. | [bn].śdy. | [bn].gmḥ. | [---]ty. | [b]n.ypy.gbʿly. | b[n].ḥyn. | ḏmn.šʿrt 99[327].1.2

śdn

g.mru. | bʿl.šlm.ʿbd. | awr.ṯǵrn.ʿbd. | ʿbd.ḫmn.šmʿ.rgm. | śdn.[k]bś. | śdyn.mḫ[ṣ]. | aṯry.mḫṣ. | bʿln.mḫṣ. | y[ḥ]ṣdq.mḫṣ. | 2084.13

św

skn.ʿšrm kk[r.---]. | mšrn.ṯlṯ.ʿš[r.kkr]. | bn.św.šbʿ.kk[r.---]. | arbʿm.kkr.[---]. | b d.mtn.[l].šlm. 2108.3

śwn

spr.ubdy.art. | šd.prn.b d.agpṯn.nḥl h. | šd.śwn.b d.ttyn.nḥl [h]. | šd.ṯtyn[.b]n.arkšt. | lʿq[.---]. | šd.pll.b d. 2029.3
.yrml. | [---.]b.yrml. | [---.--]n.b.yrml. | [---.--]ny.yrml. | śwn.qrty. | b.šlmy. 2119.25

śz

kn.bn.ʿbdṯrm. | kd.ʿbdil. | ṯlṯ.ʿl.bn.srt. | kd.ʿl.ẓrm. | kd.ʿl.śz.bn pls. | kd.ʿl.ynḥm. | tgrm.šmn.d.bn.kwy. | ʿl.šlmym.ṯmn. 1082.2.6

śkn

khnm. | qdšm. | m[ru.]śkn. | mkrm. 76[82].3
ʿšrm.ksp. | ʿl.śknt.syny. 1132.2

ślgyn

n. | bn.ṯ[--]. | bn.idrm. | bn.ymn. | bn.ṣry. | bn.mztn. | bn.ślgyn. | bn.[-]gštn. | bn[.n]klb. | b[n.]dtn. | w.nḥl h. | w.nḥl hm. 113[400].2.6

śld

by. | mṣbt. | snr. | ṯm. | ubś. | glbt. | mi[d]ḫ. | mr[i]l. | ḫlb. | śld. | ʿrgz. | [-----]. 2041.15

śnd

rn.bn.qrtm. | bn.špš.bn.ibrd. | ʿpṯrm.bn.ʿbdy. | n[--.]bn.śnd. | [---].bn.[---]. 2024.7

śśw

ṯ]lṯ.ʿš[r h.---]. | d bnšm.yd.grbs hm. | w.ṯn.ʿšr h.ḫpnt. | [s]śwm.amtm.ʿkyt. | yd.llḫ hm. | w.ṯlṯ.l.ʿšrm. | ḫpnt.śśwm.ṯn. | 2049.4
[s]św[.i]ryn.arr. | [š]dm.b.mlk. | [--.š]dm.b.ar. | [--.š]dm.b.ulm. 2033.1.1
šmn. | arbʿm.l.mit.tišr. | ṯt.ṯt.b [ṯ]ql.ṯlṯt.l.ʿšrm.ksp hm. | śstm.b.šbʿm. | ṯlṯ.mat.trm.b.ʿšrt. | mit.adrm.b.ʿšrt. | ʿšr.ydt.b.ʿ 1127.6
.ṯh.l pn.ib. | hn.hm.yrgm.mlk. | bʿl y.tmǵyy.hn. | alpm.śśwm.hnd. | w.mlk.bʿl y.bnš. | bnny.ʿmn. | mlakty.hnd. | ylak ʿ 1012.32
.št]. | irǵ[n.ḥmr.ydk]. | aḥd[h.w.yṣq.b.ap h]. | k yr[a]š.śś[w.w.ykhp]. | mid.dblt.yṯ[nt.w]. | ṣmq[m].yṯnm.w[.qmḥ.bql 161[56].32
ǵmǵ]. | w [bṣql.ʿrgz.ydk]. | a[ḥd h.w.yṣq.b.ap h]. | k.[ḫr.śśw.ḫndrṯ]. | w.ṯ[qd.mr.ydk.aḥd h]. | w.y[ṣq.b.ap h]. | k.l.ḫ[ru 161[56].5
ǵmǵ w b[ṣql ʿrgz]. | [ydk aḥ]d h w yṣq b ap h. | [k ḫr]śśw ḫndrṯ w ṯ[qd m]r. | [ydk aḥd h w yṣq b ap h. | [k l yḫru 160[55].6
ṯ[qd.mr.ydk.aḥd h]. | w.y[ṣq.b.ap h]. | k.l.ḫ[ru.w.l.yṯtn.śśw]. | mss.[št.qlql.w.št]. | ʿrgz[.ydk.aḥd h]. | w.yṣq[.b.ap h]. | 161[56].8
[k.---.]śś[w.---]. | [---.w]yṣq b a[p h]. | [k ḫr s]św mǵmǵ w b[ṣql ʿrgz]. | [ydk aḥ]d h w yṣq b ap h. | [k ḫr] 160[55].4
k [ḫr śśw mǵmǵ]. | w [bṣql.ʿrgz.ydk]. | a[ḥd h.w.yṣq.b.ap h]. | k.[ḫr. 161[56].2
-.]ʿbdyrḫ.l.ml[k]. | [--]t.w.lqḥ. | yn[.--].b dn h. | w.ml[k].śśwm.nʿmm. | ytn.l.ʿbdyrḫ. | w.mlk.z[--.--]n.śśwm. | nʿmm.[-- 2064.16
. | w.ml[k].śśwm.nʿmm. | ytn.l.ʿbdyrḫ. | w.mlk.z[--.--]n.śśwm. | nʿmm.[--].ṯtm.w.at. | nǵṯ.w.ytn.hm.l k. | w.lḥt.alpm.ḫ 2064.18
. | alp.pr.bʿl.[---]. | w prt.tkt.[---]. | šnt.[---]. | śśw.ʿṯtrt.w śśw.ʿ[nt.---]. | w ht.[--]k.śśw[.-]rym[.---]. | d ymǵy.bnš[.---]. | 2158.1.6
p.d krr[.---]. | alp.pr.bʿl.[---]. | w prt.tkt.[---]. | šnt.[---]. | śśw.ʿṯtrt.w śśw.ʿ[nt.---]. | w ht.[--]k.śśw[.-]rym[.---]. | d ymǵy. 2158.1.6
dʿ.k.iḫd.[---]. | w.mlk.bʿl y. | lm.škn.hnk. | l ʿbd h.alpm.ś[św]m. | rgmt.ʿly.ṯh.lm. | l.ytn.hm.mlk.[b]ʿl y. | w.hn.ibm.šṣq 1012.24
rn. | [w št ašk̀rr w p]r ḥḏrt. | [-----]. | [---.-]n[-]. | [k yraš śśw št bln q]ṭ ydk. | [w yṣq b ap h]. | [-----]. | [-----]. | [-----]. | [-- 160[55].14
rn]. | št.irǵn.ḥmr[.ydk]. | aḥd h.w.yṣq.b[.ap h]. | k.yraš.śśw.[št]. | bln.qṭ.yṣq.b.a[p h]. | k ygʿr[.śśw.---]. | dprn[.---]. | dr 161[56].21
qlql. | [w št ʿrgz y]dk aḥd h w yṣq b ap h. | [k.yiḫd akl s]św št mkšr grn. | [w št ašk̀rr w p]r ḥḏrt. | [-----]. | [---.-]n[-]. | 160[55].10
l.w.št]. | ʿrgz[.ydk.aḥd h]. | w.yṣq[.b.ap h]. | k.yiḫd[.akl.śśw]. | št.mkš[r.grn]. | w.št.ašk[rr]. | w.pr.ḥḏr[t.ydk]. | aḥd h. 161[56].12
]. | w.pr.ḥḏr[t.ydk]. | aḥd h.w.yṣq[.b.ap h]. | k.yiḫd.akl.s[św]. | št.nni.št.mk[št.grn]. | št.irǵn.ḥmr[.ydk]. | aḥd h.w.yṣq. 161[56].17

s̀s̀w

t. | [s̀]s̀wm.amtm.‘kyt. | yd.llẖ hm. | w.t̠lt̠.l.‘šrm. | ẖpnt.s̀s̀wm.t̠n. | pddm.w.d.t̠t̠. | [mr]kbt.w.ḥrṣ. 2049.7
alp ḥẓm.w alp. | nt̠q.t̠n.ql‘m. | ẖmš.ṣmdm.w ḥrṣ. | t̠ryn.s̀s̀wm. | t̠ryn.aḥd.d bnš. | arb‘.ṣmdm.apnt. | w ḥrṣ. | tš‘m.mrḥ. 1123.5
tkt.[---]. | šnt.[---]. | s̀s̀w.‘t̠trt.w s̀s̀w.‘[nt.---]. | w ht.[--]k.s̀s̀w[.-]rym[.---]. | d ymǵy.bnš[.---]. | w ḥmr[.---]. | w m‘n[.---]. 2158.1.7
h]. | [‘]t̠tr[-].w.[r‘ h]. | ẖlly[-].w.r‘[h]. | ilmškl.w.r‘[h]. | s̀s̀w[.--].w.r[‘ h]. | kr[mn.--.]w.r[‘ h]. | šd.[--.w.]r[‘ h]. | ẖla[n.-- 2083.2.3
b[.ap h]. | k.yraš.s̀s̀w.[št]. | bln.qṭ.yṣq.b.a[p h]. | k yg‘r[.s̀s̀w.---]. | dprn[.---]. | dr‘.[---]. | tmt̠l[.---]. | mǵm[ǵ.---]. | w.š[t.n 161[56].23
ny.‘mn. | mlakty.hnd. | ylak ‘m y. | w.t‘l.t̠h.hn. | [a]lpm.s̀s̀wm. | [---].w.t̠b. 1012.38
[k.---.]s̀s̀[w.---]. | [---.w]yṣq b a[p h]. | [k ẖr s̀]s̀w mǵmǵ w b[ṣql ‘rgz 160[55].2
]. | yly[.---]. | ykn[.---]. | rp[--]. | t̠t̠w.[---]. | [---.‘]šrm.ṣmd.s̀s̀w. 2131.12

s̀ǵr

| ‘bdnt. | bdy.ḥrš arkd. | blšš lmd. | ḥtt̠n.tqn. | ydd.idt̠n. | s̀ǵr.ilgdn. 1045.13
r‘ym.dt.b d.iytlm. | ẖyrn.w.s̀ǵr h. | s̀ǵr.bn.prsn. | agpt̠r.w.s̀ǵ[r h]. | t̠‘ln. | mztn.w.s̀ǵr [h]. | s̀ǵr.plṭ. 2072.3
r‘ym.dt.b d.iytlm. | ẖyrn.w.s̀ǵr h. | s̀ǵr.bn.prsn. | agpt̠r.w.s̀ǵ[r h]. | t̠‘ln. | mztn.w.s̀ǵr [h]. | s̀ 2072.2
.w.s̀ǵr h. | s̀ǵr.bn.prsn. | agpt̠r.w.s̀ǵ[r h]. | t̠‘ln. | mztn.w.s̀ǵr [h]. | s̀ǵr.plṭ. | s[d]rn [w].t̠n.s̀ǵr h. | [---.]w.s̀ǵr h. | [---.]w.s̀ǵ 2072.6
ym.dt.b d.iytlm. | ẖyrn.w.s̀ǵr h. | s̀ǵr.bn.prsn. | agpt̠r.w.s̀ǵ[r h]. | t̠‘ln. | mztn.w.s̀ǵr [h]. | s̀ǵr.plṭ. | s[d]rn [w].t̠n.s̀ǵr h. | [2072.4
.s̀ǵ[r h]. | t̠‘ln. | mztn.w.s̀ǵr [h]. | s̀ǵr.plṭ. | s[d]rn [w].t̠n.s̀ǵr h. | [---.]w.s̀ǵr h. | [---.]w.s̀ǵr h. | [---.]krwn. | [---].ẖzmyn. | 2072.8
. | mztn.w.s̀ǵr [h]. | s̀ǵr.plṭ. | s[d]rn [w].t̠n.s̀ǵr h. | [---.]w.s̀ǵr h. | [---.]w.s̀ǵr h. | [---.]krwn. | [---].ẖzmyn. | [---.]bn.dll. | r[2072.9
[h]. | s̀ǵr.plṭ. | s[d]rn [w].t̠n.s̀ǵr h. | [---.]w.s̀ǵr h. | [---.]w.s̀ǵr h. | [---.]krwn. | [---].ẖzmyn. | [---.]bn.dll. | r[--.--]km. | w.sp 2072.10
nntn. | ‘dn. | sdwn. | mztn. | ẖyrn. | šdn. | [‘š]rm.t̠n kbd. | s̀ǵrm. | lqḥ.ššlmt. 2098.10
. | s̀ǵr.bn.prsn. | agpt̠r.w.s̀ǵ[r h]. | t̠‘ln. | mztn.w.s̀ǵr [h]. | s̀ǵr.plṭ. | s[d]rn [w].t̠n.s̀ǵr h. | [---.]w.s̀ǵr h. | [---.]w.s̀ǵr h. | [---. 2072.7

s̀ps̀g

.šmt. | [---].all.iqni.arb‘m.kbl. | [---].iqni.‘šrm.ǵprt. | [---.s̀]ps̀g.iqni.mit.pt̠tm. | [---].mitm.kslm. | [---].pwt.t̠lt̠.mat.abn.ṣ 1106.8

s̀rn

ṣmrt. | liy.bn.yṣi. | ḏmrhd.bn.srt. | [---.--]m. | ‘bdmlk.bn.s̀rn. | ‘bdb‘l.bn.kdn. | gzl.bn.qldn. | gld.bt.klb. | l[---].bt.ẖzli. | b 102[323].3.2
.mṣl. | [---].prs̀.ḥtm. | t̠lt̠[.---].bn.t̠dnyn. | ddm.ḥ[t̠m].‘l.s̀rn. | ‘šrt.ksp.‘l.[-]lpy. | bn.ady.kkr.š‘rt. | nt̠k h. | kb[d.]mn.‘l.a 1146.7
n.‘dy.t̠kt. | n‘mn.bn.‘yn.t̠kt. | ‘pt̠n.bn.ilrš.t̠kt. | iltḥm.bn.s̀rn.t̠kt. | šmlbu.bn.grb.t̠kt. | šmlbu.bn.yp‘.t̠kt. | [---.--]m. 2085.12
[n].bn.apn. | krty. | bn.ubr. | [bn] mdẖl. | bn.sy[n]n. | bn.s̀rn. 2078.22

bṭ.ṯm. | [---.]bn.ilm. | [m]t.šmḫ.p ydd. | il[.ǵ]zr. | b [-]dn.‘.z.w. | rgbt.zbl. UG5.4.17

‘b

. | bn.srt. | bn.adn. | bn.‘gw. | bn.urt. | aḫdbu. | pḥ[-]. | bn.‘b . | bn.uḏn[-]. | bn.yṣr. 121[307].8

‘bd

pǵḏn.ilb‘l.krwn.lbn.‘dn. | ḫyrn.md‘. | šm‘n.rb ‘šrt.kkln.‘bd.abṣn. | šdyn.unn.dqn. | ‘bd‘nt.rb ‘šrt.mnḥm.ṯb‘m.sḫr.‘zn.i 2011.5
.[---]. | w.bn h.n[--.---]. | ḥnil.[---]. | aršmg.mru. | b‘l.šlm.‘bd. | awr.ṯǵrn.‘bd. | ‘bd.ḫmn.šm‘.rgm. | šdn.[k]bš. | šdyn.mḫ[ṣ 2084.10
al.ṯǵl[.---]. | prdmn.‘bd.ali[yn]. | b‘l.sid.zbl.b‘l. | arṣ.qm.yṯ‘r. | w yšlḥmn h. | ybrd.ṯ 3['NT].1.2
ẓll.ṭly.bt rb. | mṯb.arṣ.bt y‘bdr. | w y‘n lṭpn il d pid. | p ‘bd.an.‘nn.aṯrt. | p.‘bd.ank.aḫd.ulṯ. | hm.amt.aṯrt.tlbn. | lbnt.y 4[51].4.59
arṣ.bt y‘bdr. | w y‘n lṭpn il d pid. | p ‘bd.an.‘nn.aṯrt. | p.‘bd.ank.aḫd.ulṯ. | hm.amt.aṯrt.tlbn. | lbnt.ybn.bt.l b‘l. | km il 4[51].4.60
k. | [-]dm.ṯn id. | [--]m.d.l.n‘mm. | [lm.]l.likt.‘m y. | [---.]‘bd.ank. | [---.‘b]d k. | [---.--]l y.‘m. | [---.]‘m. | [---.--]y.w.lm. | [- 2128.1.8
.adm. | w ld.špḥ.l krt. | w ǵlm.l ‘bd.il. | krt.yḫṭ.w ḥlm. | ‘bd.il.w hdrt. | yrtḥṣ.w yadm. | yrḥṣ.yd h.amt h. | uṣb‘t h.‘d.ṯ 14[KRT].3.155
ḥlm y.il.ytn. | b ḏrt y.ab.adm. | w ld.špḥ.l krt. | w ǵlm.l ‘bd.il. | krt.yḫṭ.w ḥlm. | ‘bd.il.w hdrt. | yrtḥṣ.w yadm. | yrḥṣ.y 14[KRT].3.153
lm y.il.ytn. | b ḏrt y.ab.adm. | w ld.špḥ.l krk | t.w ǵlm.l ‘bd. | il.ttb‘.mlakm. | l yṯb.idk.pnm. | l ytn.‘mm.pbl. | mlk.tšan 14[KRT].6.299
[---.]š[---]. | [---.]‘bd.ilm[.---]. 110[-].2
[---.]gtn ṯṯ. | [---.]ṯhr l ytn ḫs[n]. | ‘bd ulm ṯn un ḫsn. | gdy lqḥ ṣṭqn gt bn ndr. | um r[-] gtn ṯṯ ḫ 1154.3
.]l[--]. | [bn.]ubn. | kbšm. | bn.abḏr. | bn.kpltn. | bn.prn. | ‘bdm. | bn.kḏǵbr. | bn.mṣrn. | bn.[-]dr[-]. | [---]l[-]. | [--]ym. | [-- 114[324].2.10
. | bn.ḫsn. | bn.‘bd. | [-----]. | [---.n]ḫ[l h]. | [-]ntm[.---]. | [‘]bdm. | [bn].mṣrn. | [a]ršwn. | ‘b[d]. | w nḫl h. | atn.bn.ap[s]n. 85[80].3.2
b ṯṯ ym ḥdṯ. | ḫyr.‘rbt. | špš ṯǵr h. | ršp. | w ‘bdm tbqrn. | skn. 1162.5
. | ṯmnym.drt.a[--]. | drt.l.alpm[.---]. | šb‘m.ṯn.kbd[.ḥpr.‘b]dm. | tg[mr.---]. | [-]m.m[--.---]. | [m]itm.dr[t.---]. | [‘š]r.[k]b 2013.19
lk.uḏ[r]. | [-]d‘.k.iḫd.[---]. | w.mlk.b‘l y. | lm.škn.hnk. | l ‘bd h.alpm.š[šw]m. | rgmt.‘ly.ṯh.lm. | l.ytn.hm.mlk.[b]‘l y. | w 1012.24
l.‘mrpi.rgm. | ‘m špš.kll.mid m. | šlm. | l.[--]n.špš. | ad[.‘]bd h.uk.škn. | k.[---.]sglt h.hw. | w.b[.---.]uk.nǵr. | w.[---].ad 2060.6
m.]il.ks.yiḫd. | [il.b]yd.krpn.bm. | [ymn.]brkm.ybrk. | [‘bd h.]ybrk.il.krt. | [ṯ‘.ymr]m.n‘m[n.]ǵlm.il. | a[ṯt.tq]ḥ.y krt. 15[128].2.19
bt.il.ṯḫ.gg h.b ym. | [ti]ṭ.rḥṣ.npṣ h.b ym.rṯ. | [--.y]iḫd.il.‘bd h.ybrk. | [dni]l mt rpi.ymr.ǵzr. | [mt.hr]nmy npš.yḥ.dnil. 17[2AQHT].1.35
ugrt. | nqmd.mlk.ugrt. | ktb.spr hnd. | dt brrt.ṣṭqšlm. | ‘bd h.hnd. | w mn km.l yqḥ. | spr.mlk.hnd. | b yd.ṣṭqšlm. | ‘d ‘ 1005.11
lb[n.--]. | arb‘.‘š[r.]dd.n‘r. | d.apy[.--]. | w.arb[‘.--]d.apy.‘bd h. | w.mrb‘[t.l ‘]bdm. 2094.5
w.k.rgm.špš. | mlk.rb.b‘l y.u. | ‘[--.]mlakt.‘bd h. | [---.]b‘l k.yḫpn. | [---.]‘m h.u ky. | [---.--]d k.k.tmǵy. | 1018.3
‘ id. | mrḥqtm. | qlt. | ‘m.adt y. | mnm.šlm. | rgm.ṯṯb. | l.‘bd h. 52[89].15
-.n]ḫ[l h]. | [-]ntm[.---]. | [‘]bdm. | [bn].mṣrn. | [a]ršwn. | ‘b[d]. | w nḫl h. | atn.bn.ap[s]n. | nsk.ṯlṯ. | bn.[--.]m[-]ḫr. | bn.š 85[80].3.5
---.p]ḫr k.ygrš k.qr.bt k.ygrš k. | [---].bnt.ṣ‘ṣ.bnt.m‘m‘.‘bd.ḥrn.[--.]k. | [---].aǵwyn.‘n k.ẓẓ.w k mǵ.ilm. | [--.]k ‘ṣm.k ‘ 1001.2.11
dgṯr. | ḫrr. | bn.s[-]p[-]. | bn.nrpd. | bn.ḥ[-]y. | b‘lskn. | bn.‘bd. | ḫyrn. | alpy. | bn.plsy. | bn.qrr[-]. | bn.ḥyl. | bn.g‘yn. | ḥyn. 1035.1.16
-]. | ḥnil.[---]. | aršmg.mru. | b‘l.šlm.‘bd. | awr.ṯǵrn.‘bd. | ‘bd.ḫmn.šm‘.rgm. | šdn.[k]bš. | šdyn.mḫ[ṣ]. | aṯry.mḫṣ. | b‘ln. 2084.12
[-]rm. | [‘b]dm. | [yṣ]rm. | [-]qy[m]. 78[-].2
.š‘rt. | ṯṯn.š‘rt. | ‘dn.š‘rt. | mnn.š‘rt. | bdn.š‘rt. | ‘pṯn.š‘rt. | ‘bd.yrḫ š‘rt. | ḫbd.ṯr yṣr š‘r. | pdy.yṣr š‘rt. | atnb.ḫr. | š‘rt.š‘rt. 97[315].10
[---.]iy[ṯ]r. | [---.‘bd.y]rḫ. | [---.b]n.mšrn. | [---].bn.lnn. | [-----]. | [---.-]lyr. 2135.2
l.mlkt. | adt y.rgm. | ṯḥm.illḏr. | ‘bd k.. | l.p‘n a[dt y]. | šb‘ d[.w šb‘ d]. | mrḥq[tm.qlt]. | mn[m.š 1014.4
tṣḥ.ṯḥm.aliyn. | bn.b‘l.hwt.aliy.qrdm. | bhṯ.bn.ilm.mt.‘bd k.an. | w d ‘lm k.šmḫ.bn.ilm.mt. | [---.]g h.w aṣḥ.ik.yṣḥn. 5[67].2.19
il ǵzr. | ṯḥm.aliyn.b‘l.hwt.aliy. | qrdm.bhṯ.l bn.ilm mt. | ‘bd k.an.w d.‘lm k. | tb‘.w l.yṯb.ilm.idk. | l ytn.pn.‘m.bn.ilm. 5[67].2.12
[‘]bd k. | [l.p]‘n.b‘l y. | [šb‘] d.šb‘ [d]. | [mr]ḥqtm. | qlt. | ‘bd k.b. | lwsnd. | [w] b ṣr. | ‘m.mlk. | w.ht. | mlk.syr. | ns.w.ṯm. 2063.9
]t.tn.b‘l.w ‘nn h.bn.dgn.arṯ m.pḏ h. | [w y‘n.]ṯr.ab h.il.‘bd k.b‘l.y ym m.‘bd k.b‘l. | [--.--]m.bn.dgn.a[s]r km.hw ybl. 2.1[137].36
n.dgn.arṯ m.pḏ h. | [w y‘n.]ṯr.ab h.il.‘bd k.b‘l.y ym m.‘bd k.b‘l. | [--.--]m.bn.dgn.a[s]r km.hw ybl.argmn k.k ilm. | [- 2.1[137].36
--]m ib. | [---.--]m. | [-----]. | [-]š[--.---]. | [-]r[--.--]y. | in m.‘bd k hwt. | [y]rš.‘m y. | mnm.iršt k. | d ḫsrt.w.ank. | aštn..l.iḫ 2065.13
l.mlkt. | adt y. | rgm. | ṯḥm.tlmyn. | ‘bd k. | l.p‘n. | adt y. | šb‘ d. | w.šb‘ id. | mrḥqtm. | qlt. | ‘m.adt y 52[89].5
l um y.adt ny. | rgm. | ṯḥm.tlmyn. | w.aḫtmlk ‘bd k. | l.p‘n.adt ny. | mrḥqtm. | qlny.ilm. | tǵr k. | tšlm k. | hn 51[95].4
l.mlk.b[‘l y]. | r[gm]. | ṯḥm.rb.mi[--.‘]bd k. | l.p‘n.b‘l y[.mrḥqtm]. | šb‘ d.w.šb‘[d.qlt]. | ankn.rgmt. 2008.1.3
l.mlk.b‘[l] y. | rgm. | ṯḥm.ṯpṭb[‘l]. | [‘]bd k. | [l.p]‘n.b‘l y. | [šb‘] d.šb‘ [d]. | [mr]ḥqtm. | qlt. | ‘bd k.b. 2063.4
.adn y]. | q[lt.---]. | l.yb[nn]. | b‘l y.r[gm]. | ṯḥm.‘bd[--]. | ‘bd k. | l p‘n.b‘l y. | ṯn id.šb‘ d. | mrḥqtm. | qlt.‘m. | b‘l y.mnm. 2115.2.4
[---.a]dt y. | [---].irrṯwm.‘bd k. | [---.a]dt y.mrḥqm. | [---].adt y.yšlm. | [---.]mlk n.amṣ. 1012.2
. | [--]m.d.l.n‘mm. | [lm.]l.likt.‘m y. | [---.]‘bd.ank. | [---.‘b]d k. | [---.--]l y.‘m. | [---.]‘m. | [---.--]y.w.lm. | [---.]il.šlm. | [-- 2128.2.1
. | mrḥqtm. | qlt.‘m. | b‘l y.mnm. | šlm. | [r]gm[.ṯṯb]. | [l.]‘bd[k]. 2115.2.12
p.ank. | nḫṯ.ṯm ny. | ‘m.adt ny. | mnm.šlm. | rgm.ṯṯb. | l.‘bd k. 51[95].18
m. | khnm. | qdšm. | pslm. | mkrm. | yṣḥm. | šrm. | n‘rm. | ‘bdm. | kzym. | ksdm. | [nsk].ṯlṯ. | gt.mlkym. | tmrym. | ṯnqym. 1026.1.13
ksdm. | ṣdqn. | nwrḏr. | ṯrin. | ‘dršp. | pqr. | agbṯr. | ‘bd. | ksd. 1044.8
m. | [---.]d.bn.[---.]l.dqn. | [---.--]‘.šdyn.l ytršn. | [---.--]ṯ.‘bd.l.kyn. | k[rm.--.]l.i[w]rtḏl. | ḥl.d[--.‘bd]yrḫ.b d.apn. | krm.i 2027.2.9
. | [---].bn.mryn. | [---].bn.ṭyl. | annmt.nḫl h. | abmn.bn.‘bd. | liy.bn.rqdy. | bn.ršp. 1036.13
[r.ak]l.b.gt.ḫldy. | ṯlṯ.ma[t].‘šr.kbd. | šb‘ m[at].kbd.ḥpr.‘bdm. | mit[.d]rt.arb‘m.drt. | [---]m. | t[gm]r.akl.b.gt.ǵ[l]. | ṯlṯ. 2013.12
.---].tryn. | [tg]mr.akl.b.g[t.b]ir.alp. | [‘]šrm.l.mit.ḥ[p]r.‘bdm. | mitm.drt.ṯmnym.drt. | tgmr.akl.b.gt[.b]‘ln. | ṯlṯ.mat.ṯṯ 2013.3
--]. | w ym ym.yš | al. | w mlk.d mlk. | b ḥwt.špḥ. | l ydn.‘bd.mlk. | d št.‘l.ḫrd h. | špḥ.al.thbṭ. | ḫrd.‘ps.aḫd.kw | sgt. | ḫr 2062.2.3

‘bd

w.b‘ln aẖ h. | w.ḥtṯn bn h. | w.btšy.bt h. | w.ištrmy. | bt.‘bd mlk. | w.snt. | bt.ugrt. | w.pdy h[m]. | iwrkl.mit. | ksp.b y[d 1006.9
bn.ṣrṯn. | bn.‘bd. | snb.w.nḥl h. | [-]by.w.nḥl h. | [--]ilt.w.nḥl h. | [---]n. | [--]l 1063.2
[--.---]. | ḫnil.[---]. | aršmg.mru. | b‘l.šlm.‘bd. | awr.ṯǵrn.‘bd. | ‘bα.ḫmn.šm‘.rgm. | šdn.[k]bš. | šdyn.mḫ[ṣ]. | aṯry.mḫṣ. | 2084.11
ṯtb. | mlakm.l h.lm.ank. | ksp.w yrq.ḫrṣ. | yd.mqm h.w ‘bd. | ‘lm.ṯlṯ.sswm.mrkbt. | b trbṣt.bn.amt. | p d.in.b bt y.ttn. | 14[KRT].3.139
--]. | [-----.lm]. | [ank.ksp.w yrq]. | [ḫrṣ.]yd.mqm h. | [w ‘b]d.‘lm.ṯlṯ. | [ssw]m.mrkbt b trbṣ bn.amt. | [tn.b]nm.aqny. | [14[KRT].2.55
swn h.tḥm.pbl.mlk. | qḥ.ksp.w yrq.ḫrṣ. | yd.mqm h.w ‘bd.‘lm. | ṯlṯ.sswm.mrkbt. | b trbṣ.bn.amt. | qḥ.krt.šlmm. | šlm 14[KRT].3.127
| tḥ[m.pbl.mlk]. | qḥ[.ksp.w yrq]. | ḫrṣ.[yd.mqm h]. | w ‘bd[.‘lm.ṯlṯ]. | sswm.m[rkbt]. | b trbṣ.[bn.amt]. | q[ḥ.kr]t[.šlm 14[KRT].6.271
ṯ‘. | tḥm[.pbl.mlk]. | qḥ.[ksp.w yr]q. | ḫrṣ[.yd.mqm] h. | ‘bd[.‘lm.ṯlṯ]. | ss[wm.mrkbt]. | b[trbṣ.bn.amt]. | [qḥ.krt.šlmm 14[KRT].5.252
‘n[y.k]rt[.ṯ]‘. | lm.ank.ksp. | w yr[q.ḫrṣ]. | yd.mqm h.w ‘bd. | ‘lm.ṯlṯ.sswm. | mrkbt.b trbṣ. | bn.amt.p d.[i]n. | b bt y.ttn 14[KRT].6.284
[‘]b[dm]. | ‘šrm. | inšt. | mdm. | gt.mlkym. | yqšm. | kbšm. | trrm. 74[115].1
n.npr.ḫmšm. | ṣṣ.bn.adlḏn.ṯlṯm. | ṣṣ.bn.‘glt.ṯlṯm. | ṣṣ.bn.‘bd.‘šrm. | ṣṣ.bn.mṣḥ[n].‘šrm. | šb‘.mat.ṯṯm kbd. 2096.18
| ḫmš.ddm.l.ḫtyt. | ṯlṯm.dd.kšmn.l.gzzm. | yyn. | ṣdqn. | ‘bd.pdr. | myṣm. | ṯgt. | w.lmd h. | yṯil. | w.lmd h. | rpan. | w.lm 1099.7
r‘ ‘lm. | ttn.w tn. | w l ttn. | w al ttn. | tn ks yn. | w ištn. | ‘bd.prṯ.ṯḥm. | qrq.pṯ.ḏmn. | l iṯtl. 1019.2.1
. | ild[--]. | bn.qṣn. | ‘lpy. | kṯy. | bn.ẓmn. | bn.trdn. | ypq. | ‘bd. | qrḥ. | abšr. | bn.bdn. | ḏmry. | bn.pndr. | bn.aḫt. | bn.‘dn. | 2117.2.26
mrṯd.qšt. | ssw.qšt. | knn.qšt. | bn.ṯlln.qšt. | bn.šyn.qšt. | ‘bd.qšt. | bn.ulmy.qšt. | ṯqbn.qšt. | bn.qnmlk.qšt. | yṯhm.qšt. | g 104[316].5
dy. | ǵdǵd.aḏddy. | sw.aḏddy. | ildy.aḏddy. | gr‘.aḏddy. | ‘bd.ršp aḏddy. | ‘dn.bn.knn. | iwrḫz.b d.skn. | škny.aḏddy. | m 2014.35
n uškn. | skn šbn. | skn ubr‘. | skn ḫrṣb‘. | rb.ntbtš. | [---].‘bd.r[--]. | arb‘.k[--]. | ṯlṯ.ktt. 1033.7
tgmr.akl.b.gt[.b]‘ln. | ṯlṯ.mat.ṯṯm.kbd. | ṯṯm.ṯṯ.kbd.ḥpr.‘bdm. | šb‘m.drt.arb‘m.drt. | l.a[--.---]. | tgm[r.ak]l.b.gt.ḫldy. | 2013.7
.ab[d k].al[.---]. | [-]tm.iph.adt y.w.[---]. | tšṣḥq.hn.aṯt.l.‘bd. | šb‘t.w.nṣp.ksp. | [-]tm.rb[.--.a]ḥd. | [---.--]t.b[-]. | [---.-]y[- 1017.4
lm. | bn.ḫnzr.ṯqlm. | dqn.nsk.arb‘t. | bn.ḫdyn.ṯqlm. | bn.‘bd.šḫr.ṯqlm. | bn.ḫnqn.arb‘t. | [b]n.ṯrk.ṯqlm. | [b]n.pdrn.ṯq[l 122[308].1.19
[-----]. | [-]mn. | b‘ly. | rpan. | ‘pṯrm. | bn.‘bd. | šmb‘l. | ykr. | bly. | ṯb‘m. | ḥdṯn. | rpty. | ilym. | bn.‘br. | mni 1058.6
mnḥm. | mṣrn. | mḏrǵlm. | agmy. | ‘dyn. | ‘bdb‘l. | ‘bdkṯr.‘bd. | tdǵl. | b‘lṣn. | nsk.ksp. | iwrtn. | ydln. | ‘bdilm. | dqn. | nsk.ṯ 1039.2.20
ṯlṯm.w.šb‘.alpm. | [kṯ]rmlk.‘šrm. | [--]ny.‘šrt.trbyt. | [--.]‘bd.ṯlṯm. | [---].ṯlṯm. | [--.p]ndyn.ṯlṯm. 2054.2.26
--]t.b[ḥd]r.mškb. | ṯl[l.---.--]ḥ. | b lṯk.bt. | [pt]ḥ.aḥd.l.bt.‘bdm. | [ṯ]n.ptḥ msb.bt.tu. | w.ptḥ[.aḥ]d.mmt. | ṯṯ.pt[ḥ.---]. | tn 1151.9
k[---]. | ‘bd.[---]. | mtn[.---]. | ṯdpṯn[.--]. | tny[.--]. | sll[.--]. | mld[.--]. | yq 1074.2
.ṣr[--.--]t.‘zn.mtn.n[bd]g. | ḥrš qtn[.---.]dqn.b‘ln. | ǵltn.‘bd.[---]. | nsk.ḥdm.klyn[.ṣd]qn.‘bdilt.b‘l. | annmn.‘dy.klby.d 2011.24
rḥ h.ti[ḫd.b yd h]. | š[g]r h bm ymn.t[--.---]. | [--.]l b‘l.‘bd[.---]. | ṯr ab h il.ṯṯrm[.---]. | tšlḥm yrḫ.ggn[.---]. | k[.---.ḫ]m 2001.1.14
[---.]mru ib[rn.---]. | [---.]yṣḥm[.---]. | [---.]‘bd[m.---]. | [---.-]ḫy[-.---]. | [---.-]ml[-.---]. | [---.-]š[-.---]. 1027.3
y[šlm.l k.ilm]. | ṯǵ[r k.tšlm k]. | ‘bd[.---]y. | ‘m[.---]y. | šk[--.--.]kll. | šk[--.--.]hm. | w.k[b--.---]. | 2065.3
. | špšyn.nḥl h. | n‘mn.bn.iryn. | nrn.nḥl h. | bn.ḫsn. | bn.‘bd. | [-----]. | [---.n]ḥ[l h]. | [-]ntm[.---]. | [‘]bdm. | [bn].mṣrn. | [85[80].2.10
]dd.n‘r. | d.apy[.--]. | w.arb[‘.--]d.apy.‘bd h. | w.mrb‘[t.l ‘]bdm. 2094.6

‘bdadt

.‘rbnm. | hn hmt. | tknn. | mtn.bn.‘bdym. | ilrb.bn.ilyn. | ‘bdadt.bn ‘bdkb. | gn‘ym. 1161.12
. | ‘pṯrm.šm‘rgm.skn.qrt. | ḥgbn.šm‘.skn.qrt. | nǵr krm.‘bdadt.b‘ln.yp‘mlk. | ṯǵrm.mnḥm.klyn.‘dršp.ǵlmn. | [a]bǵl.ṣṣ 2011.12
| b‘lṣn. | nsk.ksp. | iwrtn. | ydln. | ‘bdilm. | dqn. | nsk.ṯlṯ. | ‘bdadt. | bṣmn.spr. 1039.2.29
št. | abǵl.ḫmšt. | bn.aḫdy.‘šrt. | ṯṯn.‘ṣrt. | bn.pnmn.‘šrt. | ‘bdadt.ḫmšt. | abmn.ilštm‘y.ḫmš[t]. | ‘zn.bn.brn.ḫmšt. | m‘rt. 1062.24

‘bdil

| ṯǵr. | ttǵl. | ṯn.yṣḥm. | slṯmg. | kdrl. | wql. | adrdn. | prn. | ‘bdil. | ušy.šbn[-]. | aḫt.ab. | krwn. | nnḏ. | mkl. | kzǵb. | iyrḏ. 1069.11
lṯm.d.nlqḥt. | [bn.ḫ]tyn.yd.bt h. | [aǵ]ltn. | tdn.bn.ddy. | ‘bdil[.b]n ṣdqn. | bnšm.h[-]mt.ypḥm. | kbby.yd.bt.amt. | ilmlk 2045.5
[---]n[.---]. | [ag]dṯb.bn[.---]. | ‘bdil.bn.[---]. | ‘pṯn.bn.ṯsq[-]. | mnn.bn.krmn. | bn.umḫ. | yky.b 85[80].1.3
y‘dd.tḥt.bn arbn. | ‘bdil.tḥt.ilmlk. | qly.tḥt b‘ln.nsk. 1053.2
g[--]. | [---.--]m[.---]. | [kd.]šš. | [k]d.ykn.bn.‘bdṯrm. | kd.‘bdil. | ṯlṯ.‘l.bn.srt. | kd.‘l.ẓrm. | kd.‘l.šz.bn pls. | kd.‘l.ynḥm. | t 1082.2.3

‘bdilm

db‘l. | ‘bdkṯr.‘bd. | tdǵl. | b‘lṣn. | nsk.ksp. | iwrtn. | ydln. | ‘bdilm. | dqn. | nsk.ṯlṯ. | ‘bdadt. | bṣmn.spr. 1039.2.26
ṣry. | bn.ykn. | bn.lṣn.‘rmy. | bn.b‘yn.šly. | bn.ynḥn. | bn.‘bdilm.hzpy. 99[327].2.6
dy.š[‘]r[t]. | ṯlṯ.l.‘d.ab[ǵ]l. | l.ydln.š‘rt. | l.kṯrmlk.ḫpn. | l.‘bdil[m].ḫpn. | tmrtn.š‘rt. | lmd.n.rn. | [---].ḫpn. | dqn.š‘rt. | [l 1117.10
ubln. | [---].l.ubl[n]. | [--.]ṯbq.l.iytlm. | [---].l.iytlm. | [---.]‘bdilm.l.iytlm. | [---.n]ḥl h.lm.iytlm. 1076.5
dn.ḫmš [m]at. | [--]kb‘l ṯṯ [mat]. | [-----]. | ilmlk ṯṯ mat. | ‘bdilm.ṯṯ mat. | šmmn.bn.‘dš.ṯṯ mat. | ušknym. | yp‘.alpm. | aḫ 1060.1.11
| prdn.ndb[--]. | [-]rn.ḫbty. | abmn.bn.qdmn. | n‘mn.bn.‘bdilm. 87[64].41

‘bdilt

p.k[sp]. | tš‘n. | w.hm.al[-]. | l.tš‘n. | mṣrm. | tmkrn. | ypḥ.‘bdilt. | bn.m. | ypḥ.ilšlm. | bn.prqdš. | ypḥ.mnḥm. | bn.ḥnn. | b 2116.17
ṯn[.---.]dqn.b‘ln. | ǵltn.‘bd.[---]. | nsk.ḥdm.klyn[.ṣd]qn.‘bdilt.b‘l. | annmn.‘dy.klby.dqn. | ḥrṯm.ḥgbn.‘dn.ynḥm[.---]. | 2011.25
dkṯr. | [---.‘]bdgṯr. | [---.--]n. | [---.‘]bd‘nt. | [---.-]šn. | [---.‘]bdilt. | [---.-]lgn. | [---.--]gbn. | [---.a]bṣdq. | [---.--]š. | [---.ṣ]dq. 1055.1.8

‘bdiltp

dm.yn. | [-]dyn.arb‘.yn. | abškn.kdm.yn. | šbn.kdm.yn. | ‘bdiltp.ṯm[n].y[n]. | qṣn.ḫ[---]. | arny.[---]. | aǵltn.ḫmš[.yn]. 1085.9

‘bdbn

ršn.‘šr[t]. | b‘ln.ḫmšt. | w.nḥl h.ḫm[š]t. | bn.unp.arb‘t. | ‘bdbn.ytrš ḫmšt. | krwn.‘šrt. | bn.ulb ḫmšt. | bn.ḥry.ḫmšt. | sw 1062.11

‘bdb‘l

. | liy.bn.yṣi. | ḏmrhd.bn.srt. | [---.--]m. | ‘bdmlk.bn.šrn. | ‘bdb‘l.bn.kdn. | gzl.bn.qldn. | gld.bt.klb. | l[---].bt.ḫzli. | bn.iḫy 102[323].3.3
t.mzln. | šd.glln.l.gt.mz[l]n. | šd.hyabn[.l.]gt.mzln. | šd.‘bdb‘l. | l.gt.mzln. 1104.21
. | ḥrš.mrkbt. | mnḥm. | mṣrn. | mdrǵlm. | agmy. | ‘dyn. | ‘bdb‘l. | ‘bdkṯr.‘bd. | tdǵl. | b‘lṣn. | nsk.ksp. | iwrtn. | ydln. | ‘bdil 1039.2.19
y. | ḫršn. | ldn. | bn.ands. | bn.ann. | bn.‘bdpdr. | šd.iyry.l.‘bdb‘l. | šd.šmmn.l.bn.šty. | šd.bn.arws.l.bn.ḫlan. | šd.bn.ibry 1102.17
]. | bdil[.---]. | abǵl.[---]. | [.---]. | ḏmrb‘[l.---]. | iḫyn.[---]. | ‘bdb‘[l.---]. | uwil[.---]. | ušry[n.---]. | y‘ḏrn[.---]. | [‘]bdyr[ḫ.---]. 102[322].2.7

‘bdgṯr

.ar.dt.inn. | mhr l ht. | artyn. | ‘dmlk. | bn.alt[-]. | iḫy[-]. | ‘bdgṯr. | ḥrr. | bn.s[-]p[-]. | bn.nrpd. | bn.ḥ[-]y. | b‘lskn. | bn.‘bd. 1035.1.10
[---.‘ṯt]rab. | [---.ar]šmg. | [---.‘]bdkṯr. | [---.‘]bdgṯr. | [---.--]n. | [---.‘]bd‘nt. | [---.-]šn. | [---.‘]bdilt. | [---.-]lgn 1055.1.4

‘bdḥgb

ṯdn. | bn.nbdg. | bn.ḥgbn. | bn.tmr. | bn.prsn. | bn.ršpy. | [‘]bdḥgb. | [k]lby. | [-]ḥmn. | [š]pšyn. | [‘b]dmlk. | [---]yn. | bn.ṯ[- 113[400].1.23

‘bdḥy

mn. | bn.uṣb. | bn.yzg. | bn.anntn. | bn.kwn. | ǵmšd. | bn.‘bdḥy. | bn.ubyn. | slpd. | bn.atnb. | bn.ktmn. | bn.pity. | bn.iryn 115[301].4.10

‘bdḥr

tn ḫlq. | bn.mlkbn. | bn.asyy ḫlq. | bn.kṯly. | bn.kyn. | bn.‘bdḥr. | [-]prm ḫlq. | [---]n ḫlq. | bn m‘nt. | bn kbdy. | bn krk. | 2016.2.7

‘bdḫmn

n.ṣpr. | kmn. | bn.ršp. | tmn. | šmmn. | bn.rmy. | bn.aky. | ‘bdḫmn. | bn.‘dṯ. | kṯy. | bn.ḫny. | bn.ssm. | bn.ḫnn. | [--]ny. | [bn 1047.14
ḥrm.b[n].ng[-]n. | atyn.š[r]šy. | ‘bdḫmn[.bn.-]bdn. | ḥṣmn.[bn.---]ln. | [--]dm.[bn.---]n. | b‘ly.[102[322].1.3
[---].b d.š[--]mlk. | [---.b] d.gb‘ly. | [---.b] d.‘bdḫmn. | [---.b] d.ṯbq. | [---.b] d.šbn. | [---.b] d.ulm. | [---.b] d. 1052.3

‘bdy

r‘m.bn.swy. | ṣḥrn.bn.qrtm. | bn.špš.bn.ibrd. | ‘pṯrm.bn.‘bdy. | n[--.]bn.šnd. | [---].bn.[---]. 2024.6
. | bdlm. | bn.ṣǵr. | klb. | bn.mnḥm. | bn.brqn. | bn.‘n. | bn.‘bdy. | ‘bd‘ṯtr. 1046.3.48
--.---]. | yšr[-.---]. | bn.gnb[-.---]. | hzpym. | rišn.[---]. | bn.‘bdy.[---]. | bn.dmtn.[---]. | [b]n.g‘yn.ḫr[-]. | lbnym. | grgš.[---]. 93[328].10

‘bdym

nm.šalm. | dt.tknn. | ‘l.‘rbnm. | hn hmt. | tknn. | mtn.bn.‘bdym. | ilrb.bn.ilyn. | ‘bdadt.bn ‘bdkb. | gn‘ym. 1161.10
].šdm.d.n‘rb.gt.npk. | [š]d.rpan.b d.klṯṯb. | [š]d.ilṣy.b d.‘bdym. | [ub]dy.trrm. | [šd.]bn.ṯqdy.b d.gmrd. | [š]d bn.synn. 82[300].2.15
šš[r]t.ḫrṣ.ṯqlm.kbd.‘šrt.mzn h. | b [ar]b‘m.ksp. | b d[.‘b]dym.ṯlṯ.kkr š‘rt. | iqn[i]m.ṯṯṯ.‘šrt.ksp h. | ḫmšt.ḫrṣ.bt.il. | b. 2100.3

‘bdyrḫ

‘bdyrḫ. | ubn.ḫyrn. | ybnil.adrdn. | klyn.kkln. | ‘dmlk.tdn. | ‘zn 1070.1
.l ytršn. | [---.--]ṯ.‘bd.l.kyn. | k[rm.--.]l.i[w]rtdl. | ḥl.d[--.‘bd]yrḫ.b d.apn. | krm.i[--].l.[---.]a[-]bn. 2027.2.11
ṯn.bn.klby. | bn.iyṯr. | [‘]bdyrḫ. | [b]n.gg‘t. | [‘]dy. | armwl. | uwaḫ. | ypln.w.ṯn.bn h. | y 2086.3
].bn.qqln. | liy.bn.qqln. | mnn.bn.ṣnr. | iḫy.[b]n[.--]l[-]. | ‘bdy[rḫ].bn.gṯtn. | yrmn.bn.‘n. | krwn.nḥl h. | ttn.[n]ḥl h. | bn. 86[80].4.8
kny. | mnn.w.aṯt h. | slmu.ḥrš.mrkbt. | bnšm.dt.l.mlk. | ‘bdyrḫ.bn.ṯyl. | ‘bdn.w.aṯt h.w.bn h. | gpn.bn[.a]ly. | bn.rqd[y] 2068.18
-]t.w.lqḥ. | yn[.--].b dn h. | w.ml[k].ššwm.n‘mm. | ytn.l.‘bdyrḫ. | w.mlk.z[--.--]n.ššwm. | n‘mm.[--].ṯṯm.w.at. | nǵṯ.w.y 2064.17
.i[---]n.pbn.ndbn.sbd. | šrm.[---].ḫpn. | ḥrš[bhtm.--]n.‘bdyrḫ.ḥdtn.y‘r. | adb‘l[.---].ḥdtn.yḥmn.bnil. | ‘dn.w.ildgn.ḥṯ 2011.18
ḥm[.---]. | l p‘n.b‘l y[.---]. | qlt. | [--]t.mlk.d.y[mlk]. | [--.]‘bdyrḫ.l.ml[k]. | [--]t.w.lqḥ. | yn[.--].b dn h. | w.ml[k].ššwm.n‘ 2064.13
lm. | ‘pṯn.ḥrš.qṭn.ṯqlm. | bn.pǵdn.ṯqlm. | bn.b‘ln.ṯqlm. | ‘bdyrḫ.nqd.ṯqlm. | bt.sgld.ṯqlm. | bn.‘my.ṯqlm. | bn.brq.ṯqlm. 122[308].1.12
]. | bn.rpš.qšt.w.ql‘. | bn.ǵb.qšt. | bn.ytrm.qšt.w.ql‘. | bn.‘bdyrḫ.qšt.w.q[l‘]. | bn.lky.qšt. | bn.dll.qšt.w.ql[‘]. | bn.pǵyn.q 119[321].3.26
. | tlmyn.šb‘t.‘šrt ‘šrt[.šlm.---]. | ybn.ṯmnt.‘šrt ‘šrt.šlm. | ‘bdyrḫ.šb‘t.‘šrt ‘šrt.šlm. | yky.‘šrt.ṯṯṯ šlm.‘šrt. | bn.ḥgby.ṯmnt. 1131.6
krz[n]. | ṯlṯ.šdm.b d.amtr[n]. | ṯn.šdm.b d.skn. | šd.b d[.‘b]dyrḫ. | šd.b [d.--]ṯṯb. 2090.24
h.w.bn h. | [--]an.w.aṯt h. | [--]y.w.aṯt h. | [--]r.w.aṯt h. | ‘bdyrḫ.ṯn ǵlyt h. | aršmg. | ršpy.w.aṯt h. | bn.glgl.uškny. | bn.ṯ 2068.10
.ml[k.d.b] d adn[‘m]. | [---].riš[.---].kt. | [y]nḥm. | ilb‘l. | ‘bdyr[ḫ]. | ṯtpḥ. | artn. | ybnil. | brqn. | adr[dn]. | krwn. | arkdn. | 1024.1.5
.bn].ḥrtn.‘[--]. | b.t[--.---] h.[---]. | [-----]. | [--]ly.ḫmšm.b.‘bdyr[ḫ]. | [---].‘šrm. | [-----]. | [---.‘]šr[.---]. | [---.-]‘rm. | [---.--]n 2054.1.24
.[---]. | ‘bdb‘[l.---]. | uwil[.---]. | ušry[n.---]. | y‘ḏrn[.---]. | [‘]bdyr[ḫ.---]. | [---]mlk[.---]. | [-----]. | ilb‘l[.---]. | ḫluy.bn[.---]. | 102[322].2.11

‘bdyrǵ

bnš.kld. | kbln.‘bdyrǵ.ilgt. | ǵyrn.ybnn qrwn. | ypltn.‘bdnt. | klby.aḥrṯp. | ilyn 1045.2

‘bdkb

n hmt. | tknn. | mtn.bn.‘bdym. | ilrb.bn.ilyn. | ‘bdadt.bn ‘bdkb. | gn‘ym. 1161.12

‘bdkṯr

[-----]. | dd l krwn. | dd l [--]n. | dd l ky. | dd l ‘bdkṯr. | dd[m] l r‘y. | [--] šmḥ[.---]. | ddm gt dprnm. | l ḥršm. | 1101.5
rkbt. | mnḥm. | mṣrn. | mdrǵlm. | agmy. | ‘dyn. | ‘bdb‘l. | ‘bdkṯr.‘bd. | tdǵl. | b‘lṣn. | nsk.ksp. | iwrtn. | ydln. | ‘bdilm. | dqn 1039.2.20
bq. | [---.b] d.šbn. | [---.b] d.ulm. | [---.b] d.ǵbl. | [---.b] d.‘bdkṯr. | [---.b] d.urǵnr. 1052.8
[---.‘ṯt]rab. | [---.ar]šmg. | [---.‘]bdkṯr. | [---.‘]bdgṯr. | [---.--]n. | [---.‘]bd‘nt. | [---.-]šn. | [---.‘]bd 1055.1.3

'bdlbit

.w.ql'. | bn.ml'n.qšt.w.ql'. | bn.tmy.qšt.w.ql'. | 'ky.qšt. | 'bdlbit.qšt. | kṯy.qšt.w.ql'. | bn.ẖršn.qšt.w.ql'. | ilrb.qšt.w.ql'. | 119[321].3.38

'bdmlk

[-]m[-].bn.ṣmrt. | liy.bn.yṣi. | ḏmrhd.bn.srt. | [---.--]m. | 'bdmlk.bn.šrn. | 'bdb'l.bn.kdn. | gzl.bn.qldn. | gld.bt.klb. | l[--- 102[323].3.2
nt. | ḥnn[.bn].pls. | abrš[p.bn.]ẖrpn. | gmrš[.bn].mrnn. | 'bdmlk.bn.'myn. | agyn.r'y. | abmlk.bn.ilrš. | iẖyn.bn.ẖryn. | [102[323].4.8
r[---]. | ẖdyn. | grgš. | b[n.]tlš. | ḏmr. | mkrm. | 'zn. | yplṭ. | 'bdmlk. | ynḥm. | aḏddn. | mtn. | plsy. | qṭn. | ypr. | bn.ymy. | bn. 1035.4.5
rkḏn. | ilmn. | abškn. | ykn. | ršpab. | klyn. | ẖgbn. | ḥṯṯn. | 'bdmlk. | y[--]k. | [-----]. | pǵḏn. | [--]n. | [--]ntn. | 'dn. | lkn. | ktr. 1024.1.20
y.'šr.[---]. | ṯmry.'šr.ṯn.k[rmm.---]. | liy.krm.aḥd[.---]. | 'bdmlk.krm.aḥ[d.---]. | krm.ubdy.b d.ǵ[--.---]. | krm.pyn.arty 1081.6
ubdy.mdm. | šd.b d.'bdmlk. | šd.b d.yšn.ḥrš. | šd.b d.aupš. | šd.b d.ršpab.aẖ.ubn. | 82[300].1.2
m.mnḥm.klyn.'dršp.ǵlmn. | [a]bǵl.ṣṣn.ǵrn. | šib.mqdšt.'b[dml]k.ṯṯpḥ.mrṯn. | ẖḏǵlm.i[---]n.pbn.nḏbn.sbd. | šrm.[---]. 2011.15
w.l.]bn h.'d. | ['l]m.mn k. | mn km l.yqẖ. | bt.hnd.b d. | ['b]dmlk. | [-]k.am'[--]. | [w.b] d.bn h[.']d 'lm. | [w.un]ṯ.in[n.]b 1009.15
. | ytn.bt.annḏr. | bn.ytn.bnš. | [ml]k.d.b riš. | [--.-]nt. | [l.'b]dmlk. | [--.-]m[-]r. | [w.l.]bn h.'d. | ['l]m.mn k. | mn km l.yq 1009.9
'[l.---]. | br.dmty[.---]. | ṯkt.ydln[.---]. | ṯkt.ṯryn[.---]. | br.'bdm[lk.---]. | wry[.---]. | ṯkt[.---]. | ṯk[t.---]. | br[.---]. | br[.---]. | 84[319].1.6
.prsn. | bn.ršpy. | [']bdẖgb. | [k]lby. | [-]ḥmn. | [š]pšyn. | ['b]dmlk. | [---]yn. | bn.ṭ[--]. | bn.idrm. | bn.ymn. | bn.ṣry. | bn.m 113[400].1.27
kyy. | [bn].bm[--]. | ['š]rm. | [-----]. | [-----]. | bn.p[--]. | bn.'bdmlk. 2163.3.19

'bdn

ṯt h. | slmu.ḥrš.mrkbt. | bnšm.dt.l.mlk. | 'bdyrẖ.bn.ṯyl. | 'bdn.w.aṯt h.w.bn h. | gpn.bn[.a]ly. | bn.rqd[y].ṯbg. | iẖmlk. | y 2068.19
l.hbm.šlmy. | kd.šmn.ṯbil. | kd.šmn.ymtšr. | arb'.šmn.'l.'bdn.w.[---]. | kdm.šmn.'l.ilršp.bn[.---]. | kd.šmn.'l.yddn. | kd. 1082.1.4

'bdnkl

ddn.qšt.w.ql'. | š'rt. | bn.il.qšt.w.ql'. | ark.qšt.w.ql'. | bn.'bdnkl.qšt.w.ql'. | bn.znan.qšt. | bn.arz.[ar]b'.qšt.w.arb['.]ql' 119[321].2.43

'bdnt

pltn.'bdnt. | klby.aḥrṯp. | ilyn.'lby.ṣdkn. | gmrt.ṭlmyn. | 'bdnt. | bdy.ḥrš arkd. | blšš lmd. | ḥṯṯn.tqn. | ydd.idṯn. | šǵr.ilgd 1045.8
bnš.kld. | kbln.'bdyrǵ.ilgt. | ǵyrn.ybnn qrwn. | ypltn.'bdnt. | klby.aḥrṯp. | ilyn.'lby.ṣdkn. | gmrt.ṭlmyn. | 'bdnt. | bdy. 1045.4

'bdssm

. | [---.]mnty[.-]. | [---.]rb spr ẖbb. | [---.--]n.dbḥm. | [---].'bdssm. 49[73].2.6

'bd'n

bn[.---]. | 'myn.bn.[---]. | mtb'l.bn[.---]. | ymy.bn[.---]. | 'bd'n.p[--.---]. | [-]d[-]l.bn.ḥrn. | aẖty.bt.abm. | [-]rbn.'dd.nryn 102[322].5.13

'bd'nt

yrn.md'. | šm'n.rb 'šrt.kkln.'bd.abṣn. | šdyn.unn.dqn. | 'bd'nt.rb 'šrt.mnḥm.ṯb'm.sẖr.'zn.ilhd. | bnil.rb 'šrt.lkn.yp'n. 2011.7
b. | [---.ar]šmg. | [---.']bdkṯr. | [---.']bdgṯr. | [---.--]n. | [---.']bd'nt. | [---.-]šn. | [---.']bdilt. | [---.-]lgn. | [---.--]gbn. | [---.a]bṣ 1055.1.6

'bd'ṯtr

---]n. | b'ly.[bn.---]n. | krr[-.---]. | špš[yn.---]. | [--]b[.---]. | 'bd'ṯ[tr.---]. | bdil[.---]. | abǵl.[---]. | [.---]. | ḏmrb'[l.---]. | iẖyn.[- 102[322].2.1
. | bn.ṣǵr. | klb. | bn.mnḥm. | bn.brqn. | bn.'n. | bn.'bdy. | 'bd'ṯtr. 1046.3.49

'bdpdr

-]by.nsk.ṯlṯ. | šmny. | ẖršn. | ldn. | bn.ands. | bn.ann. | bn.'bdpdr. | šd.iyry.l.'bdb'l. | šd.šmmn.l.bn.šty. | šd.bn.arws.l.bn. 1102.16

'bdrpu

.b d ansny. | nsk.ks[p.--]mrtn.kṭrmlk. | yḥmn.aẖm[l]k.'bdrpu.adn.ṯ[--]. | bdn.qln.mtn.ydln. | b'ltdtt.tlgn.ytn. | b'ltǵp 2011.33
yṣm. | ṯgt. | w.lmd h. | yṯil. | w.lmd h. | rpan. | w.lmd h. | 'bdrpu. | w.lmd h. | 'dršp. | w.lmd h. | krwn b.gt.nbk. | ddm.kš 1099.15

'bdršp

] | [---.]pẖyr.bt h.[---]. | [ẖm]šm.ksp.'l.gd[--]. | [---].ypḥ.'bdršp.b[--.--]. | [ar]b't.'šrt.kbd[.---]. | [---.-]rwd.šmbnš[.---]. | [1144.5
---.--]l.rb.kzym. | [---]y. | [-----]. | [-----]. | [--]dt.nsk.ṯlṯ. | ['b]dršp.nsk.ṯlṯ. | [-]lkynt.nsk.ṯlṯ. | [-]by.nsk.ṯlṯ. | šmny. | ẖršn. | 1102.8

'bdrṯb

'bdrṯ[b.---]. | b ṯṯ 'ṯr ṯmn.r[qẖ.---]. | p bn btb[-.---]. | b ẖmṯ 'ṯr 207[57].1

'bdṯrm

[--.--]ẖ.bn.ag[--]. | [---.--]m[.---]. | [kd.]šš. | [k]d.ykn.bn.'bdṯrm. | kd.'bdil. | ṯlṯ.'l.bn.srt. | kd.'l.ẓrm. | kd.'l.šz.bn pls. | k 1082.2.2

'by

b[n]. | yṯtn. | bn.ab[l]. | kry. | psš. | ilṯḥm. | ḥrm. | bn.bty. | 'by. | šm[n].bn.apn. | krty. | bn.ubr. | [bn] mdẖl. | bn.sy[n]n. | b 2078.16

'bk

[.---]. | dr'.[---]. | tmṯl[.---]. | mǵm[ǵ.---]. | w.š[t.nni.w.pr.'bk]. | w.pr[.ḥdrt.w.št]. | irǵ[n.ḥmr.ydk]. | aḥd[h.w.yṣq.b.ap 161[56].28

'bl

byn. | slpd. | bn.atnb. | bn.ktmn. | bn.pity. | bn.iryn. | bn.'bl. | bn.grbn. | bn.iršyn. | bn.nklb. | bn.mryn. | [bn.]b[--]. | bn.ẓ 115[301].4.17
. | [--]ly. | [iw]ryn. | [--.w.n]ḥl h. | [-]ibln. | bn.nḏbn. | bn.'bl. | bn.tlšn. | bn.sln. | w nḥl h. 1063.12
-.-]hs. | [--.--]nyn. | [-----]. | [-----]. | bn.'dy. | w.nḥl h. | bn.'bl. | bn.[-]rṯn. | bn[.---]. | bn u[l]pm. | bn '[p]ty. | bn.kdgdl. | bn. 2163.2.21

ʿbs

mṣmt.ʿbs. | arr.d.qr | ht. 1173.1

ʿbṣ

bn.ǵlmy. | ǵly. | bn.dnn. | bn.rmy. | dll. | mny. | krty. | bn.ʿbṣ. | bn.argb. | ydn. | ilʿnt. | bn.urt. | ydn. | qṯn. | bn.asr. | bn.ʿdy. 2117.3.40
.ddym.sk.šlm.l kbd.arṣ.arbdd]. | l kbd.š[dm.ḥš k.ʿṣ k.ʿbṣ k.ʿm y.pʿn k.tls] | [m]n ʿm y t[wtḥ.išd k.dm.rgm.iṯ.l y.d a 7.2[130].16
.ddym. | sk.šlm.l kbd.arṣ. | arbdd.l kbd.šdm. | ḥš k.ʿṣ k.ʿbṣ k. | ʿm y.pʿn k.tlsmn.ʿm y. | twtḥ.išd k.dm.rgm. | iṯ.l y.w a 3[ʿNT].3.15
dym.sk.šlm].l kbd.arṣ. | [arbdd.l kbd.š]dm.ḥš k. | [ʿṣ k.ʿbṣ k.ʿm y.pʿ]n k.tlsmn. | [ʿm y.twtḥ.išd] k.tk.ḫršn. | [---.-]bd 1[ʿNT.IX].2.22
[ḥš k.ʿṣ k.ʿbṣ k.ʿ]m y.p[ʿ]n k. | [tlsmn.ʿm y.twt]ḥ.išd k. | [tk.ḫršn.---]r.[- 1[ʿNT.IX].2.1
.kṯr.b[---]. | št.lskt.n[--.---]. | ʿdb.bǵrt.ṯ[--. --]. | ḥš k.ʿṣ k.ʿ[bṣ k.ʿm y.pʿn k.tlsmn]. | ʿm y twtḥ.i[šd k.tk.ḫršn.------------ 1[ʿNT.IX].3.10
dym.sk.šlm. | l kbd.arṣ.arbdd.l kbd.šdm. | [ḥ]š k.[ʿ]ṣ k.ʿbṣ k.ʿm y.pʿn k. | [tls]mn.[ʿ]m y.twtḥ.išd k. | [dm.rgm.iṯ.l y.] 3[ʿNT].4.55

ʿbr

[---.]alp. | [---.]ym.rbt. | [---.]b nhrm. | [ʿb]r.gbl.ʿbr. | qʿl.ʿbr.iht. | np šmm.šmšr. | l dgy.aṯrt. | mǵ.l qdš.amrr. | idk.al.tn 3[ʿNT.VI].6.8
| [---.]bn ʿn km. | [---.]alp. | [---.]ym.rbt. | [---.]b nhrm. | [ʿb]r.gbl.ʿbr. | qʿl.ʿbr.iht. | np šmm.šmšr. | l dgy.aṯrt. | mǵ.l qdš. 3[ʿNT.VI].6.7
ql.ṯrm. | w mri ilm.ʿglm.dt.šnt. | imr.qmṣ.llim.k ksp. | l ʿbrm.zt.ḫrṣ.l ʿbrm.kš. | dpr.ṯlḥn.b qʿl.b qʿl. | mlkm.hn.ym.yṣq 22.2[124].15
i ilm.ʿglm.dt.šnt. | imr.qmṣ.llim.k ksp. | l ʿbrm.zt.ḫrṣ.l ʿbrm.kš. | dpr.ṯlḥn.b qʿl.b qʿl. | mlkm.hn.ym.yṣq.yn.ṯmk. | mr 22.2[124].15
n.ʿbd. | šmbʿl. | ykr. | bly. | ṯbʿm. | ḥdṯn. | rpty. | ilym. | bn.ʿbr. | mnipʿl. | amrbʿl. | dqry. | ṯdy. | ypʿbʿl. | bdlm. | bn.pd̠[-]. | b 1058.14
ʿn km. | [---.]alp. | [---.]ym.rbt. | [---.]b nhrm. | [ʿb]r.gbl.ʿbr. | qʿl.ʿbr.iht. | np šmm.šmšr. | l dgy.aṯrt. | mǵ.l qdš.amrr. | i 3[ʿNT.VI].6.7

ʿbš

km.bm ṯkm.aḫm.qym.il. | b lsmt.ṯm.yṯbš.šm.il.mt m. | yʿbš.brk n.šm.il.ǵzrm. | ṯm.ṯmq.rpu.bʿl.mhr bʿl. | w mhr.ʿnt.ṯ 22.2[124].7

ʿbt

š. | [---.--]q.n[t]k.l ydʿ.l bn.l pq ḥmt. | [---.--]n h.ḥmt.w tʿbtn h.abd y. | [---.ǵ]r.šrǵzz.ybky.km.nʿr. | [w ydmʿ.k]m.ṣǵr. UG5.8.36

ʿgd

---.]ṯpr. | [---.]prš. | [---.]šdm. | [---.-]nm.prš.glbm. | [---.]ʿgd.dqr. | [---.]ṯn.alpm. | [---.ṯ]n alpm. | [---.--]r[.ʿ]šr.ṣin. | [---.] 1142.8

ʿgw

bn.ḫran. | bn.srt. | bn.adn. | bn.ʿgw. | bn.urt. | aḫdbu. | pḥ[-]. | bn.ʿb . | bn.ud̠n[-]. | bn.yṣr. 121[307].4
pṯr.ṯt.qštm.[w].qlʿ. | bn.aǵlyn.ṯt.qštm[.w.ṯl]ṯ.qlʿm. | bn.ʿgw.qšt.w qlʿ. | bn.tbšn.ṯlṯ.qšt.w.[ṯlṯ.]qlʿm. | bn.army.ṯt.qštm. 119[321].3.20
| bn.ṯǵd̠y[.qšt.]w.qlʿ. | ṯṯy.qšt[.w.]qlʿ. | bn.šp[š.]qšt. | bn.ʿg[w.]qšt.w qlʿ. | ḥd[ṯ]n.qšt.w.qlʿ. | bn.bb.qšt.w[.ql]ʿ. | bn.akt 119[321].4.7

ʿgwn

. | [b]n.tgd̠n. | bn.ḫdyn. | bn.sgr. | bn.aǵltn. | bn.ktln. | bn.ʿgwn. | bn.yšmʿ. | bdl.md̠rǵlm. | bn.mmy. | bn.ḫnyn. | bn.knn. | 104[316].9

ʿgy

. | bn lṯḥ ḫlq. | bn ytr. | bn ilšpš. | ubrš. | bn gmš ḫlq. | bn ʿgy. | bn zlbn. | bn.aḫ[--]. | bn[.---]. | [-----]. | bn kr[k]. | bn ḫtyn. 2016.2.19

ʿgl

bṯn.ʿqltn. | šlyṭ.d šbʿt.rašm. | mḫšt.mdd ilm.ar[š]. | ṣmt.ʿgl.il.ʿtk. | mḫšt.klbt.ilm išt. | klt.bt.il.d̠bb.imtḫṣ.ksp. | itrṯ.ḫrṣ. 3[ʿNT].3.41
rm.aklt.ʿgl.ʿl.mšt. | [---.--]r.špr.w yšt.il. | [---.--]n.il ǵnṯ.ʿgl il. | [---.--]d.il.šd yṣd mlk. | [---].yšt.il h. | [---.]iṯm h. | [---.y] UG5.2.1.11
.ṣd.tštr.ʿpt.šmm. | ṭbḫ.alpm.ap ṣin.šql.ṯrm. | w mri ilm.ʿglm.dt.šnt. | imr.qmṣ.llim.k ksp. | l ʿbrm.zt.ḫrṣ.l ʿbrm.kš. | d 22.2[124].13
[.ʿd]bt. | hkl h.ṭbḫ.alpm[.ap]. | ṣin.šql.ṯrm[.w]m | ria.il.ʿglm.d[t]. | šnt.imr.qmṣ.l[l]im. | ṣḥ.aḫ h.b bht h.a[r]y h. | b qr 4[51].6.42
]. | pʿr.b[--.---]. | ṭbḫ.alp[m.ap.ṣin.šql]. | ṯrm.w [mri.ilm.ʿglm.dt.šnt]. | imr.[qmṣ.llim.---]. 1[ʿNT.X].4.31
ẓma.yd.mṯkt. | ṯṯkr.[--]dn. | ʿm.krt.mswn h. | arḫ.tzǵ.l ʿgl h. | bn.ḫpt.l umht hm. | k tnḥn.udmm. | w yʿny.krt.ṯʿ. 15[128].1.5
ymm.yʿtqn.l ymm. | l yrḫm.rḥm.ʿnt.tngṯ h. | k lb.arḫ.l ʿgl h.k lb. | ṯat.l imr h.km.lb. | ʿnt.aṯr.bʿl.tiḫd. | bn.ilm.mt.b ḥr 6[49].2.28
---.ym.ymm]. | yʿtqn.w[rḥm.ʿnt]. | tngṯ h.k lb.a[rḫ]. | l ʿgl h.k lb.ṯa[t]. | l imr h.km.lb.ʿn[t]. | aṯr.bʿl.tiḫd.m[t]. | b sin.l 6[49].2.7
.šmm.rmm. | [bʿl]t.kpṯ.w ʿnt.di.dit.rḫpt. | [---.-]rm.aklt.ʿgl.ʿl.mšt. | [---.--]r.špr.w yšt.il. | [---.--]n.il ǵnṯ.ʿgl il. | [---.--]d.i UG5.2.1.9
aliyn. | [bʿl.---.-]ip.dpr k. | [---.-]mn k.ššrt. | [---.--]t.npš.ʿgl. | [---.-]nk.aštn.b ḫrt. | ilm.arṣ.w at.qḥ. | ʿrpt k.rḥ k.mdl k. 5[67].5.4

ʿglt

pr b y | rdm.arṣ.w tdʿ ilm. | k mtt.yšmʿ.aliyn.bʿl. | yuhb.ʿglt.b dbr.prt. | b šd.šḫlmmt.škb. | ʿmn h.šbʿ.l šbʿm. | tš[ʿ]ly.ṯ 5[67].5.18
.ṣd[-.---]. | [ṣṣ].bn.npr.ḫmšm. | ṣṣ.bn.adld̠n.ṯlṯm. | ṣṣ.bn.ʿglt.ṯlṯm. | ṣṣ.bn.ʿbd.ʿšrm. | ṣṣ.bn.mṣḥ[n].ʿšrm. | šbʿ.mat.ṯṯm k 2096.17

ʿgltn

---].l.urǵṯṯb. | [---.]l.ʿṯtrum. | [---.]l.brqn. | [---].skn. | [---.ʿg]ltn. | [---].ʿgltn. | [---.]ʿgltn. | [---.šr]t.aḥt. | [---].šrt.aḥt. | [---]. 2162.B.9
. | [---.]l.ʿṯtrum. | [---.]l.brqn. | [---].skn. | [---.ʿg]ltn. | [---].ʿgltn. | [---.]ʿgltn. | [---.šr]t.aḥt. | [---].šrt.aḥt. | [---].šrt.aḥt. | [---. 2162.B.10
um. | [---.]l.brqn. | [---].skn. | [---.ʿg]ltn. | [---].ʿgltn. | [---.]ʿgltn. | [---.šr]t.aḥt. | [---].šrt.aḥt. | [---].šrt.aḥt. | [---.]šrt.aḥt. | [- 2162.B.11

ʿgrt

[--]. | bn.ml[k]. | bn.glyn. | bn.ʿdr. | bn.ṯmq. | bn.ntp. | bn.ʿgrt. 1057.22

ʿd

škn.ḫpn. | l.k[-]w.ḫpn. | l.ṣ[--].šʿ[rt]. | l.ʿdy.š[ʿ]r[t]. | ṯlṯ.l.ʿd.ab[ǵ]l. | l.ydln.šʿrt. | l.kṯrmlk.ḫpn. | l.ʿbdil[m].ḫpn. | tmrtn.š 1117.7
[---.]unṯ[.---]. | [---.]šrq[-.---]. | [---.]ʿd ʿlm[.---]. | [---.]ʿd.admn[.---]. | [---.--]d.ytr.mṯ[--]. | [-----]. | [-----]. | [---].ḫmš[.- 2156.4
qdš. | ṯm tgrgr.l abnm.w l.ʿṣm.šbʿ.šnt. | tmt.ṯmn.nqpt.ʿd.ilm.nʿmm.ttlkn. | šd.tṣdn.pat.mdbr.w ngš.hm.nǵr. | mdrʿ. 23[52].67

[---.rp]um.tdbḥn.|[----.]ʿd.ilnym.|[---.--]l km amt m.|[---.]b w tʿrb.sd.|[---.--]n b ym
|tṯbḫ.imr.w lḥm.|mgṯ.w yṯrm.hn.ym.|w ṯn.ytb.krt.l ʿd h.|ytb.l ksi mlk.|l nḫt.l kḥṯ.drkt.|ap.yṣb.ytb.b hkl.|w y 20[121].1.2
t.|[---.]b qrb.ʿr.|[---.m]lakm l h.|[---.]l.bn.il.|[---.--]a.ʿd h.|[---.--]rh.|[---.--]y.špš.|[---.--]h.|[---.--]th. 16.6[127].22
dnn.ṣmdm.gpn.yšql.šdmt h.|km gpn.|šbʿ d.yrgm.ʿl.ʿd.w ʿrbm.tʿnyn.|w šd.šd ilm.šd aṯrt.w rḥm.|ʿl.išt.šbʿ d.ǵzr 26[135].8
rmmt.l tšt.|yn.tǵzyt.špš.|rpim.tḥtk.|špš.tḥtk.ilnym.|ʿd k.ilm.hn.mtm.|ʿd k.kṯr m.ḫbr k.|w ḫss.dʿt k.|b ym.arš. 23[52].12
yt.špš.|rpim.tḥtk.|špš.tḥtk.ilnym.|ʿd k.ilm.hn.mtm.|ʿd k.kṯr m.ḫbr k.|w ḫss.dʿt k.|b ym.arš.w tnn.|kṯr.w ḫss.yd 6.6[62.2].47
-].|bnt.šdm.ṣḥr[.---].|šbʿ.šnt.il.mla.[-].|w ṯmn.nqpnt.ʿd.|k lbš.km.lpš.dm a[ḫ h].|km.all.dm.ary h.|k šbʿt.l šbʿm. 6.6[62.2].48
].|[qrš.mlk.ab.]šnm.|[tša.g hm.w tṣ]ḥ.sbn.|[---]l[.---.]ʿd.|ksm.mhyt[.m]ǵny.|l nʿm y.arṣ.dbr.|l ysmt.šd.šḥlmmt.| 12[75].2.46
w.ʿl.ap.s[--.---].|b hm.w.rgm.hw.al[--].|atn.ksp.l hm.ʿd.|ilak.ʿm.mlk.|ht.lik[t.--.]mlk[.--].|w.mlk.yštal.b.hn[--].| 5[67].6.4
h.mra.|w tk.pn h.tʿdb.ksu.|w yṯṯb.l ymn.aliyn.|bʿl.ʿd.lḥm.št[y.ilm].|[w]yʿn.aliy[n.bʿl].|[--]b[.---].|ḥš.bht m.k[ṯ 2008.2.7
npʿ.bʿ[l.---].|b ṯmnt.[---].|yqrb.[---].|lḥm.m[---.---].|[ʿ]d.lḥm[.šty.ilm].|w pq.mr[ǵtm.ṯd.---].|b ḥrb.[mlḥt.qṣ.mri]. 4[51].5.110
q.ilht.ksat[.yn].|špq.ilm.rḥbt yn.|špq.ilht.dkrt[.yn].|ʿd.lḥm.šty.ilm.|w pq mrǵtm.ṯd.|b ḥrb.mlḥt.qṣ[.m]r|i.tšty.k 5[67].4.12
.k[--.lḥt].|akl.yṯ[ṯb.--]pt.|ib.ʿltn.a[--.--]y.|w.spr.in[.-.]ʿd m.|spr n.ṯhr[.--].|aṯr.iṯ.bqṯ.|w.štn.l y. 4[51].6.55
.|w.pdr[--.---].|tmǵyn[.---].|w.mli[.---].|[-]kl.w [---].|ʿd.mǵt[.---]. 2060.32
mnn.ilm.|tǵr k.tšlm k.|tʿzz k.alp ymm.|w rbt.šnt.|b ʿd ʿlm...gnʿ.|iršt.aršt.|l aḫ y.l rʿ y.dt.|w ytnnn.|l aḫ h.l rʿ h. 57[101].8
qḥ.|bt.hnd.b d.|[ʿb]dmlk.|[-]k.amʿ[--].|[w.b] d.bn h[.ʿ]d ʿlm.|[w.un]ṯ.in[n.]b h.|[---.]nʿm[-]. 1019.1.6
t.|bnš bnšm.|l.yqḥnn.b d.|bʿln.bn.kltn.|w.b d.bn h.ʿd.|ʿlm.w unṯ.|in.b h. 1009.17
.-]m[---].|b unṯ.km.špš.|d brt.kmt.|br.ṣṭqšlm.|b unṯ.ʿd ʿlm.|mišmn.nqmd.|mlk ugrt.|nqmd.mlk.ugrt.|ktb.spr h 1008.19
l]k.d.b riš.|[--.-]nt.|[l.ʿb]dmlk.|[--.-]m[-]r.|[w.l.]bn h.ʿd.|[ʿl]m.mn k.|mn km l.yqḥ.|bt.hnd.b d.|[ʿb]dmlk.|[-]k.a 1005.5
h.yd.|[k]lkl h.|[w] ytn.nn.|l.bʿln.bn.|kltn.w l.|bn h.ʿd.ʿlm.|šḥr.ʿlmt.|bnš bnšm.|l.yqḥnn.b d.|bʿln.bn.kltn.|w.b 1009.11
[---.]unṯ[.---].|[---.]šrq[-.---].|[---.]ʿd ʿlm[.---].|[---.]ʿd.admn[.---].|[---.--]d.ytr.mṯ[--].|[-----].|[- 1008.14
h.hnd.|w mn km.l yqḥ.|spr.mlk.hnd.|b yd.ṣṭqšlm.|ʿd ʿlm. 2156.3
lm.[l] k.|ilm.t[ǵ]r k.|tšlm k.|lm[.l.]likt.|ši[l.š]lm y.|[ʿ]d.r[-]š.|[-]ly.l.likt.|[a]nk.[---].|šil.[šlm y].|[l]m.li[kt].|[-]t. 1005.15
gn.|my.hmlt.aṯr.bʿl.nrd.|b arṣ.ʿm h.trd.nrt.|ilm.špš.ʿd.tšbʿ.bk.|tšt.k yn.udmʿt.gm.|tṣḥ.l nrt.ilm.špš.|ʿms mʿ.l y. 2010.9
nt.|tšyt.k brkm.tǵll b dm.|ḏmr.ḥlqm.b mmʿ.mhrm.|ʿd.tšbʿ.tmtḫṣ.b bt.|tḫṣb.bn.ṯlḥnm.ymḫ.|[b]bt.dm.ḏmr.yṣq.š 6[62].1.9
bʿ.bnt.rḥ.gdm.w anhbm].|w tqr[y.ǵlmm.b št.ǵr.---].|[ʿ]d tš[bʿ.tmtḫṣ.---].|klyn[.---].|špk.l[---].|trḥṣ.yd[h.---].|[-- 3[ʿNT].2.29
.ydmʿ.l kdd.dnil.|mt.rpi.l ymm.l yrḫm.|l yrḫm.l šnt.ʿd.|šbʿt.šnt.ybk.l aq|ht.ǵzr.yd[mʿ.]l kdd.|dnil.mt.r[pi.mk]. 7.2[130].5
b h.gʿr.yṯb.il.kb[-].|aṯ[rt.]il.yṯb.b mrzḥ h.|yšt[.il.y]n.ʿd šbʿ.trṯ.ʿd škr.|il.hlk.l bt h.yštql.|l ḥṭr h.yʿmsn.nn.ṯkmn.| 19[1AQHT].4.176
.b qrb|hkl [h].ṣḥ.l qṣ.ilm.tlḥmn.|ilm.w tštn.tštn y[n] ʿd šbʿ.|trṯ.ʿd.škr.yʿdb.yrḫ.|gb h.km.[---.]yqṭqṭ.tḥt.|ṯlḥnt.il. UG5.1.1.16
ṯb.il.kb[-].|aṯ[rt.]il.yṯb.b mrzḥ h.|yšt[.il.y]n.ʿd šbʿ.trṯ.ʿd škr.|il.hlk.l bt h.yštql.|l ḥṭr h.yʿmsn.nn.ṯkmn.|w šnm.w UG5.1.1.3
[h].ṣḥ.l qṣ.ilm.tlḥmn.|ilm.w tštn.tštn y[n] ʿd šbʿ.|trṯ.ʿd.škr.yʿdb.yrḫ.|gb h.km.[---.]yqṭqṭ.tḥt.|ṯlḥnt.il.d ydʿnn.|yʿ UG5.1.1.16
].|iwrkl.mit.|ksp.b y[d].|birtym.|[un]ṯ inn.|l [h]m ʿd ṯṯtbn.|ksp.iwrkl.|w ṯb.l unṯ hm. UG5.1.1.4
d.il.w hdrt.|yrtḥṣ.w yadm.|yrḥṣ.yd h.amt h.|uṣbʿt h.ʿd.ṯkm.|ʿrb.b ẓl.ḫmt.lqḥ.|imr.dbḥ.b yd h.|lla.klatnm.|klt.l 1006.17
.nʿmn.ǵlm.|il.trḥṣ.w tadm.|rḥṣ[.y]d k.amt.|uṣb[ʿt k.]ʿd[.ṯ]km.|ʿrb[.b ẓl.ḫmt].|qḥ im[r.b yd k].|imr.d[bḥ.bm].ym 14[KRT].3.158
ṯ h.|b šmym.dǵṯ hrnmy[.d k]|bkbm.ʿ[l.---].|[-]l h.yd ʿd[.---].|ltm.mrqdm.d š[-]l[-].|w tʿn.pǵt.ṯkmt.mym.|qrym.a 14[KRT].2.64

ʿdb

19[1AQHT].4.188
ḫṣ.aqht.ǵzr.|ʿwrt.yšt k.bʿl.l ht.|w ʿlm h.l ʿnt.p dr.dr.|ʿdb.uḫry.mṭ.yd h.|dnil.bt h.ymǵyn.yšt|ql.dnil.l hkl h.ʿrb.b
ṣ.aqht.ǵzr.amd.gr bt il.|ʿnt.brḥ.p ʿlm h.ʿnt.p dr[.dr].|ʿdb.uḫry mṭ.yd h.|ymǵ.l mrrt.tǵll.b nr.|yšu.g h.w yṣḥ.y l k. 19[1AQHT].4.169
ṣ.al.|ypʿ.riš.ǵly.b d.nsʿ k.|ʿnt.brḥ.p ʿlm h.|ʿnt.p dr.dr.ʿdb.uḫry mṭ yd h.|ymǵ.l qrt.ablm.abl[m].|qrt.zbl.yrḫ.yšu g 19[1AQHT].3.155
.šrd.|[bʿl].b dbḥ h.bn dgn.|[b m]ṣd h.yrd.krt.|[l g]gt.ʿdb.akl.l qryt.|ḥṭt.l bt.ḫbr.|yip.lḥm.d ḫmš.|[mǵ]d.ṯdṯ.yr[ḫ 19[1AQHT].3.162
.il.šrd.bʿl.|b dbḥ k.bn.dgn.|b mṣd k.w yrd.|krt.l ggt.ʿdb.|akl.l qryt.|ḥṭt.l bt.ḫbr.|yip.lḥm.d ḫmš.|mǵd.ṯdṯ.yrḫm 14[KRT].4.172
.l nʿm y.arṣ.|dbr.ysmt.šd.šḥlmmt.|ngš.ank.aliyn bʿl.|ʿdbnn ank.imr.b p y.|k lli.b ṯbrn q y.ḫṭu hw.|nrt.ilm.špš.ṣḥ 14[KRT].2.80
.aphn.ǵzr.mt.|hrnmy.gm.l aṯt h.k yṣḥ.|šmʿ.mtt.dnty.ʿd[b].|imr.b pḥd.l npš.kṯr.|w ḫss.l brlt.hyn d.|ḥrš yd.šlḥm. 6[49].2.22
qy.|ilm sad.kbd.hmt.bʿl.|ḥkpt.il.kl h.tšmʿ.|mtt.dnty.tʿdb.imr.|b pḥd.l npš.kṯr.w ḫss.|l brlt.hyn.d ḥrš.|ydm.aḫr. 17[2AQHT].5.16
m.w ʿrb.b p hm.ʿṣr.šmm.|w dg b ym.w ndd.gzr.l zr.yʿdb.u ymn.|u šmal.b p hm.w l.tšbʿn y.aṯt.itrḫ.|y bn.ašld.š 17[2AQHT].5.22
.]|hwt.lṭpn[.ḥtk k.---].|yh.kṯr.b[---].|št.lskt.n[--.---].|ʿdb.bǵrt.ṯ[--. --].|ḥš k.ʿṣ k.ʿ[bṣ k.ʿm y.pʿn k.tlsmn].|ʿm y twt 23[52].63
.l lbnt.šmḫ.|aliyn.bʿl.ht y.bnt.|dt.ksp.hkl y.dtm.|ḫrṣ.ʿdbt.bht[h.bʿ]l.|yʿdb.hd.ʿdb[.ʿd]bt.|hkl h.ṭbḫ.alpm[.ap].|ṣi 1[ʿNT.IX].3.9
[r].|mdl.ʿr.ṣmd.pḥl.|št.gpnm.dt.ksp.|dt.yrq.nqbnm.|ʿdb.gpn.atnt h.|yḫbq.qdš.w amrr.|yštn.aṯrt.l bmt.ʿr.|l ysms 4[51].6.38
.mdl.ʿr].|ṣmd.pḥl[.št.gpnm.dt].|ksp.dt.yr[q.nqbnm].|ʿdb.gpn.atnt[y].|yšmʿ.qd.w amr[r].|mdl.ʿr.ṣmd.pḥl.|št.gpn 4[51].4.12
.|bm.nrt.ksmm.|ʿl.tl[-]k.ʿṭrṭrm.|nšu.[r]iš.ḥrṭm.|l ẓr.ʿdb.dgn kly.|lḥm.[b]ʿdn hm.kly.|yn.b ḫmt hm.k[l]y.|šmn. 4[51].4.7
].|trḫpn.ybṣr.ḥbl.diy[m.bn].|nšrm.trḫp.ʿnt.ʿl[.aqht].|tʿdbn h.hlmn.ṯnm[.qdqd].|ṯlṯ id.ʿl.udn.š[pk.km].|šiy.dm h. 16[126].3.13
n.bʿl.ht y.bnt.|dt.ksp.hkl y.dtm.|ḫrṣ.ʿdbt.bht[h.bʿ]l.|yʿdb.hd.ʿdb[.ʿd]bt.|hkl h.ṭbḫ.alpm[.ap].|ṣin.šql.ṯrm[.w]m| 18[3AQHT].4.33
.|dt.ksp.hkl y.dtm.|ḫrṣ.ʿdbt.bht[h.bʿ]l.|yʿdb.hd.ʿdb[.ʿd]bt.|hkl h.ṭbḫ.alpm[.ap].|ṣin.šql.ṯrm[.w]m|ria.il.ʿglm.d[t 4[51].6.39
.l qṣ.ilm.tlḥmn.|ilm.w tštn.tštn y[n] ʿd šbʿ.|trṯ.ʿd.škr.yʿdb.yrḫ.|gb h.km.[---.]yqṭqṭ.tḥt.|ṯlḥnt.il.d ydʿnn.|yʿdb.lḥ 4[51].6.39
.trḫpn.ybṣr.[ḥbl.d]|iym.bn.nšrm.arḫp.an[k.ʿ]l.|aqht.ʿdb k.hlmn.ṯnm.qdqd.|ṯlṯ id.ʿl.udn.špk.km.šiy.|dm.km.šḥṭ. UG5.1.1.4
ḫ.arṣ.|nḫlt h.w nǵr.|ʿnn.ilm.al.|tqrb.l bn.ilm.|mt.al.yʿdb km.|k imr.b p h.|k lli.b ṯbrn.|qn h.tḫtan.|nrt.ilm.špš. 18[3AQHT].4.22
m.|aḫr.mǵy.kṯr.w ḫss.|št.alp.qdm h.mra.|w tk.pn h.tʿdb.ksu.|w yṯṯb.l ymn.aliyn.|bʿl.ʿd.lḥm.št[y.ilm].|[w]yʿn.a 4[51].8.17
lḫš.abd.ln h.|ydy.ḥmt.hlm.ytq.nḫš.yšlḥm.|nḫš.ʿq šr.yʿdb.ksa.w ytb.|tqru l špš.um h.špš.um.ql.bl.ʿm.|ʿnt w ʿṯtrt 4[51].5.108
š abd.ln h.ydy.|ḥmt.hlm.ytq ytqšqy.nḫš.yšlḥm.ʿq šr.|yʿdb.ksa.w.ytb.|tqru.l špš.um h.špš.um.ql bl.|ʿm bʿl.mrym. UG5.7.18
mlḫš.abd.ln h.ydy.ḥmt.hlm.ytq.|nḫš.yšlḥm.nḫš.ʿq šr.ydb.ksa.|w ytb.|tqru.l špš.u h.špš.um.ql.bl.ʿm.|dgn.ttl h.m UG5.7.7
lḫš abd.ln h.ydy.|ḥmt.hlm.ytq.nḫš.yšlḥm.nḫš.|ʿq šr.yʿdb.ksa.w ytb.|tqru l špš.um.ql bl.ʿm|kṯr.w ḫss.kptr h.mn UG5.7.12
mlḫš.abd.ln h.ydy.|ḥmt.hlm.ytq.nḫš.yšlḥm.nḫš ʿq.|š.yʿdb.ksa w ytb.|tqru l špš.um h.špš.um.ql bl ʿm.|ṯṯ.w kmṯ. UG5.7.44
UG5.7.34

.|abd.ln h.ydy ḥmt.hlm.yṯq šqy.|nḥš.yšlḥm.nḥš.ʿq šr.yʿdb.|ksa.w yṯb.|tqru l špš.um h.špš.um.ql bl.|ʿm ḥrn.mṣd UG5.7.55
lḫš abd.ln h.|ydy.ḥmt.hlm.yṯq nḥš yšlḥm.nḥš.|ʿq.šr.yʿdb.ksa.w yṯb.|tqru l špš um h.špš um ql.bl.ʿm.|mlk.ʿṯtrt UG5.7.39
lḫš.abd.ln h.ydy.|ḥmt.hlm.yṯq.nḥš.yšlḥm.nḥš.|ʿq šr.yʿdb.ksa.w yṯb.|tqru.l špš.um h.špš.um.ql b.ʿm.|ršp.bbt h. UG5.7.29
lḫš.abd.|ln h.ydy.ḥmt.hlm yṯq.nḥš.|yšlḥm.nḥš.ʿq šr.yʿdb ksa.|w yṯb.|tqru l špš.um h.špš.um.ql bl ʿm.|šḥr.w šl UG5.7.49
l.ʿm.|ʿnt w ʿṯtrt inbb h.mnt.nṯk.|nḥš.šlḥm.nḥš.ʿq šr[.yʿ]db.ksa.|nḥš.šmrr.nḥš.ʿq šr.ln h.ml|ḫš.abd.ln h.ydy.ḥmt. UG5.7.23
t.ktp.b hm.ygʿr.ṯǵr.|bt.il.pn.l mgr lb.tʿdbn.|nšb.l inr.tʿdbn.ktp.|b il ab h.gʿr.yṯb.il.kb[-].|aṯ[rt.]il.yṯb.b mrzḥ h.|y UG5.1.1.13
.b qrb.|[---].asr.|[---.--]m.ymt m.|[---].k iṯl.|[---.--]m.ʿdb.l arṣ.|[---.]špm.ʿdb.|[---].tʿtqn.|[---.-]ʿb.idk.|[l ytn.pnm. 1[ʿNT.IX].2.10
gm.l il.ybl.a[ṯt y].|il.ylt.mh.ylt.yld y.šḥr.w šl[m].|šu.ʿdb.l špš.rbt.w l kbkbm.kn[-].|yhbr.špt hm.yšq.hn.[š]pt hm. 23[52].54
r.yʿdb.yrḫ.|gb h.km.[---.]yqṯqṭ.tḥt.|ṯlḥnt.il.d ydʿnn.|yʿdb.lḥm.l h.w d l ydʿnn.|d.mṣd.|ylmn.ḥṭ.tḥt.ṯlḥn.|b qrʿ.|ʿ UG5.1.1.7
.ydʿ.ylḥn.|w yʿn.lṭpn.il d pi|d dq.anm.l yrẓ.|ʿm.bʿl.l yʿdb.mrḥ.|ʿm.bn.dgn.k tms m.|w ʿn.rbt.aṯrt ym.|blt.nmlk.ʿ 6.1.51[49.1.23]
ʿdb.nšb l h.|w ʿnt.ktp.b hm.ygʿr.ṯǵr.|bt.il.pn.l mgr lb.tʿdbn.|nšb.l inr.tʿdbn.ktp.|b il ab h.gʿr.yṯb.il.kb[-].|aṯ[rt.]il. UG5.1.1.12
.mṣd.|ylmn.ḥṭ.tḥt.ṯlḥn.|b qrʿ.|ʿṯtrt.w ʿnt.ymǵy.|ʿṯtrt.tʿdb.nšb l h.|w ʿnt.ktp.b hm.ygʿr.ṯǵr.|bt.il.pn.l mgr lb.tʿdbn UG5.1.1.10
.bnt.|dt.ksp.hkl y.dtm.|ḫrṣ.ʿdbt.bht[h.bʿ]l.|yʿdb.hd.ʿdb[.ʿd]bt.|hkl h.ṭbḫ.alpm[.ap].|ṣin.šql.ṯrm[.w]m|ria.il.ʿgl 4[51].6.39
|ydm.aḫr.ymǵy.kṯr.|w ḫss.b d.dnil.ytnn.|qšt.l brk h.yʿdb.|qṣʿt.apnk.mṯt.dnty.|tšlḥm.tššqy ilm.|tsad.tkbd.hmt. 17[2AQHT].5.27
.qr[t].|šd.pln.bn.tiyn.b d.ilmhr nḥl h.|šd knn.bn.ann.ʿdb.|šd.iln[-].bn.irṯr.l.šḥrn.nḥl h.|šd[.ag]pṯn.b[n.]brrn.l.qrt. 2029.19
h.|šd.pǵyn[.b] d.krmn.l.ty[n.n]ḥl h.|šd.krz.[b]n.ann.ʿ[db].|šd.ṯ[r]yn.bn.tkn.b d.qrt.|šd[.-].dyn.b d.pln.nḥl h.|šd. 2029.13
mn.|u šmal.b p hm.w l.tšbʿn y.aṯt.itrḫ.|y bn.ašld.šu.ʿdb.tk.mdbr qdš.|ṯm tgrgr.l abnm.w l.ʿṣm.šbʿ.šnt.|tmt.ṯmn. 23[52].65
tplg.km.plg.|bʿd h.bhtm.mnt.bʿd h.bhtm.sgrt.|bʿd h.ʿdbt.ṯlṯ.ptḥ.bt.mnt.|ptḥ.bt.w ubn.hkl.w ištql šql.|tn.km.nḥš UG5.7.71
-.--]m.ymt m.|[---].k iṯl.|[---.--]m.ʿdb.l arṣ.|[---.]špm.ʿdb.|[---].tʿtqn.|[---.-]ʿb.idk.|[l ytn.pnm.tk.]in.bb.b alp ḥẓr. 1[ʿNT.IX].2.11
--].|w mit.šʿrt.[-]y[-.---].|w.kdr.w.npt t[--.---].|w.ksp.yʿdb.[---]. 38[23].11
ʿm[.-.]aṯt y[.-].|[---.]tḥm.|[---]t.[ ]r.|[---.--]n.|[---] h.l ʿdb.|[---]n.yd h.|[---].bl.išlḥ.|[---] h.gm.|[l --- k.]yṣḥ.|[---]d. 14[KRT].5.234

ʿdbym

.b d.ʿdbmlk.|[šd.]bn.brzn.b d.nwrḏ.|[šd.]bn.nḥbl.b d.ʿdbym.|[šd.b]n.qṭy.b d.tt.|[ubd]y.mrim.|[šd.b]n.ṯpdn.b d.b 82[300].1.18

ʿdbmlk

šdm.b d.gmrd.|[šd.]lbny.b d.tbtṯb.|[š]d.bn.ṯ[-]rn.b d.ʿdbmlk.|[šd.]bn.brzn.b d.nwrḏ.|[šd.]bn.nḥbl.b d.ʿdbym.|[š 82[300].1.16

ʿdd

lk.u bl mlk.|arṣ.drkt.yštkn.|dll.al.ilak.l bn.|ilm.mt.ʿdd.l ydd.|il.ǵzr.yqra.mt.|b npš h.ystrn ydd.|b gngn h.aḥd 4[51].7.46
].|ʿbdʿn.p[--.---].|[-]d[-]l.bn.ḥrn.|aḥty.bt.abm.|[-]rbn.ʿdd.nryn.|[ab]r[p]u.bn.kbd.|[-]m[-].bn.ṣmrt.|liy.bn.yṣi.|ḏ 102[322].6.3
r.|[---.--]y k.w rḥd.|[---]y ilm.d mlk.|y[ṯ]b.aliyn.bʿl.|ytʿdd.rkb.ʿrpt.|[--].ydd.w yqlṣn.|yqm.w ywpṯn.b tk.|p[ḫ]r. 4[51].3.11
t.il.li[mm.---].|ʿl.ḥbš.[---].|mn.lik.[---].|lik.tl[ak.---].|tʿddn[.---].|niṣ.p[---.---]. 5[67].4.25

ʿdw

w šnm.|kṯr w ḫss.|ʿṯtr ʿṯpr.|šḥr w šlm.|ngh w srr.|ʿdw šr.|ṣdqm šr.|ḥnbn il d[n].|[-]bd w [---].|[--].p il[.---].|[i UG5.10.1.13

ʿdy

ṯn.bn.klby.|bn.iyṯr.|[ʿ]bdyrḫ.|[b]n.ggʿt.|[ʿ]dy.|armwl.|uwaḫ.|ypln.w.ṯn.bn h.|ydln.|anr[my].|mld. 2086.5
.|bn.argb.|ydn.|ilʿnt.|bn.urt.|ydn.|qṭn.|bn.asr.|bn.ʿdy.|bn.amt[m].|myn.|šr.|bn.zql.|bn.iḫy.|bn.iyṯr.|bn.ʿyn. 2117.3.48
.inr[-].|bn.ṯbil.|bn.iryn.|ṯtl.|bn.nṣdn.|bn.ydln.|[bn].ʿdy.|[bn].ilyn. 1071.10
n.bn.ǵlm.|bn.yyn.w.bn.au[pš].|bn.kdrn.|ʿrgzy.w.bn.ʿdy.|bn.gmḥn.w.ḥgbt.|bn.tgḏn.|yny.|[b]n.gʿyn dd.|[-]n.dd 131[309].27
bn.ǵs.ḥrš.šʿty.|ʿdy.bn.slʿy.gbly.|yrm.bʿl.bn.kky. 2121.2
.ṯmyr.|ẓbr.|bn.ṯdṯb.|bn.ʿrmn.|bn.alz.|bn.mṣrn.|bn.ʿdy.|bn.ršpy.|[---.]mn.|[--.-]sn.|[bn.-]ny.|[b]n.ḫnyn.|[bn]. 115[301].2.16
.ʿrʿr.|w b šḥt.ʿs.mt.ʿrʿrm.ynʿrn h.|ssnm.ysyn h.ʿdtm.yʿdyn h.yb|ltm.ybln h.mǵy.ḥrn.l bt h.w.|yštql.l ḥṭr h.tlu ḥt UG5.7.66
n.ṯrn.|w.nḥl h.|[--.-]hs.|[--.--]nyn.|[-----].|[-----].|bn.ʿdy.|w.nḥl h.|bn.ʿbl.|bn.[-]rṯn.|bn[.---].|bn u[l]pm.|bn ʿ[p] 2163.2.19
ǵltn.ʿbd.[---].|nsk.ḥḏm.klyn[.ṣd]qn.ʿbdilt.bʿl.|annmn.ʿdy.klby.dqn.|ḥrṯm.ḥgbn.ʿdn.ynḥm[.---].|ḥrš.mrkbt.ʿzn.[b]ʿ 2011.26
.b ʿṣm.ʿrʿr.|w b šḥt.ʿs.mt.ʿrʿrm.ynʿrn h.|ssnm.ysyn h.ʿdtm.yʿdyn h.yb|ltm.ybln h.mǵy.ḥrn.l bt h.w.|yštql.l ḥṭr h. UG5.7.66
|krty.|bn.abr[-].|yrpu.|kdn.|pʿṣ.|bn.liy.|ydʿ.|šmn.|ʿdy.|ʿnbr.|aḫrm.|bn.qrdy.|bn.šmʿn.|bn.ǵlmy.|ǵly.|bn.dnn 2117.3.28
-]mn ḫpn.|l[.--.]škn.ḫpn.|l.k[-]w.ḫpn.|l.ṣ[--].šʿ[rt].|l.ʿdy.š[ʿ]r[t].|ṯlṯ.l.ʿd.ab[ǵ]l.|l.ydln.šʿrt.|l.kṯrmlk.ḫpn.|l.ʿbdil[1117.6
n.aly.ṯkt.|klby.bn.iḫy.ṯkt.|psš.bn.buly.ṯkt.|ʿpṣpn.bn.ʿdy.ṯkt.|nʿmn.bn.ʿyn.ṯkt.|ʿpṯn.bn.ilrš.ṯkt.|ilṯḥm.bn.šrn.ṯkt. 2085.9
bd.|[l.]sbrdnm.|m[i]t.l.bn.ʿẓmt.rišy.|mit.l.tlmyn.bn.ʿdy.|[---.]l.adddy.|[--.]l.kkln. 2095.8
.|[---].gwl.|[---]ady.|[---]ṣry.|miḫ[-]m.|ṣdqm.|dnn.|ʿdy. 1041.15

ʿdyin

r.---].|k[kr.---].|[---.-]krr.|[---.]tmtṯb.|[---.-]dy.|[---.]ʿdyin.|[---.]ʿbdḫ[-]m. 2037.2.8

ʿdyn

bʿln.|yrmn.|ʿnil.|pmlk.|aby.|ʿdyn.|aǵlyn.|[--]rd.|[--]qrd.|[--]r. 1066.6
yn.bn.nbk[-.---].|ršpn.bn.bʿly[.---].|bnil.bn.yṣr[.---].|ʿdyn.bn.udr[-.---].|w.ʿdʿ.nḥl h[.---].|w.yknil.nḥl h[.---].|w.il 90[314].1.13
[k]rwn.|ḥrš.mrkbt.|mnḥm.|mṣrn.|mdrǵlm.|agmy.|ʿdyn.|ʿbdbʿl.|ʿbdkṯr.ʿbd.|tdǵl.|bʿlṣn.|nsk.ksp.|iwrtn.|ydln 1039.2.18
qšt.|bn.blẓn.qšt.w.qlʿ.|gbʿ.qšt.w.qlʿ.|nṣṣn.qšt.|mʿr.|[ʿ]dyn.ṯt.qštm.w.qlʿ.|[-]lrš.qšt.w.qlʿ.|t[t]n.qšt.w.qlʿ.|u[l]n.qš 119[321].2.14
|prd.mʿqby[.w.---.a]ṯt h[.---].|prṯ.mgd[ly.---.]aṯ[t h].|ʿdyn[.---].|w.ṯn[.bn h.---].|iwrm[-.]b[n.---].|annt[n.]w[.---]. 2044.12

‘dm

[-----]. | šm‘.l [-]mt[.-]m.l[-]ṯnm. | ‘dm.[lḥ]m.tšty. | w t‘n.mṯt ḥry. | l l[ḥ]m.l š[ty].ṣḥt km. | db[ḥ. 15[128].6.2

‘dmlk

rn. | bn.dnt. | bn.ṯ‘l[-]. | bdl.ar.dt.inn. | mhr l ht. | artyn. | ‘dmlk. | bn.alt[-]. | iḫy[-]. | ‘bdgṯr. | ḥrr. | bn.s[-]p[-]. | bn.nrpd. | 1035.1.7
‘bdyrḫ. | ubn.ḫyrn. | ybnil.adrdn. | klyn.kkln. | ‘dmlk.tdn. | ‘zn.pǵdn. | [a]nndn. | [r]špab. | [-]glm. 1070.5

‘dmn

.[bn].ubyn. | šd.bn.li[y]. | šd.bn.š[--]y. | šd.bn.ṯ[---]. | šd.‘dmn[.bn.]ynḥm. | šd.bn.ṯmr[n.m]idḫy. | šd.ṯb‘m[.--]y. 2026.8

‘dn

ṯn.r‘y.uzm. | sǵr.bn.ḫpsry.aḥd. | sǵr.artn.aḥd. | sǵr.‘dn.aḥd. | sǵr.awldn.aḥd. | sǵr.idṯn.aḥd. | sǵr.sndrn.aḥd. | sǵr. 1140.4
bd. | qrḥ. | abšr. | bn.bdn. | ḏmry. | bn.pndr. | bn.aḫt. | bn.‘dn. | bn.išb‘[l]. 2117.4.33
. | sw.aḏddy. | ildy.aḏddy. | gr‘.aḏddy. | ‘bd.ršp aḏddy. | ‘dn.bn.knn. | iwrḫz.b d.skn. | škny.aḏddy. | mšu.aḏddy. | plsy. 2014.36
b]n.b‘l[--]. | bn.gld. | bn.ṣmy. | bn.mry[n]. | bn.mgn. | bn.‘dn. | bn.knn. | bn.py. | bn.mk[-]. | bn.by[--]. | bn.a[--]. | bn.iy[-- 2117.1.7
m. | b.n‘mn.bn.ply.ḫmšt.l.‘šrm. | b.gdn.bn.uss.‘šrm. | b.‘dn.bn.ṯṯ.‘šrt. | b.bn.qrdmn.ṯlṯm. | b.bṣmn[.bn].ḥrtn.‘[--]. | b.ṯ[2054.1.19
[ily.w].ḏmry.‘rb. | b.ṯb‘m. | ydn.bn.ilrpi. | w.ṯb‘m.‘rb.b.‘[d]n. | ḏmry.bn.yrm. | ‘rb.b.ad‘y. 2079.8
[-]k.‘ṯrṯrm. | nšu.[r]iš.ḥrṯm. | l ẓr.‘db.dgn kly. | lḥm.[b]‘dn hm.kly. | yn.b ḥmt hm.k[l]y. | šmn.b q[b‘t hm.---]. | bt.krt 16[126].3.14
tm.--]n.‘bdyrḫ.ḥdṯn.y‘r. | adb‘l[.---].ḥdṯn.yḥmn.bnil. | ‘dn.w.ildgn.ḥṯbm. | tdǵlm.iln.b‘[l]n.alḏy. | tdn.ṣr[--.--]t.‘zn.m 2011.20
h. | mtn. | w.lmd h. | ymn. | w.lmd h. | y‘drn. | w.lmd h. | ‘dn. | w.lmd h. | bn.špš. | [w.l]m[d h]. | yṣ[---]. | ‘bd[--]. | pr[--]. | 1049.1.9
. | sǵr.npr. | bn.ḫty. | ṯn.bnš ibrḏr. | bnš tlmi. | sǵr.ḫryn. | ‘dn.w sǵr h. | bn.ḥgbn. 2082.9
iṯt[bnm]. | ršpab.rb ‘šrt.m[r]yn. | pǵdn.ilb‘l.krwn.lbn.‘dn. | ḫyrn.md‘. | šm‘n.rb ‘šrt.kkln.‘bd.abṣn. | šdyn.unn.dqn. | 2011.3
ṣry.alpm. | lbnym. | ṯm[n.]alp mitm. | ilb‘l ḫmš m[at]. | ‘dn.ḫmš.mat. | bn.[-]d.alp. | bn.[-]pn.ṯṯ mat. 1060.2.10
ṯšm.ṯṯ mat. | ṣprn.ṯṯ mat. | ḏkry.ṯṯ mat. | [p]lsy.ṯṯ mat. | ‘dn.ḫmš [m]at. | [--]kb‘l ṯṯ [mat]. | [-----]. | ilmlk ṯṯ mat. | ‘bdil 1060.1.7
ṣb[u.anyt]. | ‘dn. | ṯbq[ym]. | m‘q[bym]. | ṯš‘.‘[šr.bnš]. | ǵr.ṯ[--.---]. | ṣbu.any[79[83].2
n[.ṣd]qn.‘bdilt.b‘l. | annmn.‘dy.klby.dqn. | ḥrṯm.ḥgbn.‘dn.ynḥm[.---]. | ḥrš.mrkbt.‘zn.[b]‘ln.ṯb[--.-]nb.trtn. | [---]mm 2011.27
r.aḫy h.mẓa h. | w mẓa h.šr.yly h. | b skn.sknm.b ‘dn. | ‘dnm.kn.npl.b‘l. | km ṯr.w tkms.hd.p[.-]. | km.ibr.b tk.mšmš 12[75].2.54
[rḥ.npš h]. | k iṯl.brlt h.[b h.p‘nm]. | ṯṭṭ.‘l[n.pn h.td‘.b ‘dn]. | ksl.y[ṯbr.yǵṣ.pnt.ksl h]. | anš.[dt.ẓr h.yšu.g h]. | w yṣ[ḥ. 19[1AQHT].2.94
t‘n.hlk.btlt. | ‘nt.tdrq.ybmt. | [limm].b h.p‘nm. | [ṭṭṭ.b ‘]dn.ksl. | [ṯṯbr.‘ln.p]n h.td[‘]. | tǵṣ[.pnt.ks]l h. | anš.dt.ẓr.[h]. | 4[51].2.17
. | ḥṯṯn. | ‘bdmlk. | y[--]k. | [-----]. | pǵdn. | [--]n. | [--]ntn. | ‘dn. | lkn. | ktr. | ubn. | dqn. | ḥṯṯn. | [--]n. | [---]. | tsn. | rpiy. | mrṯ 1024.2.6
m.l ḥkmt. | šbt.dqn k.l tsr k. | rḫntt.d[-].l irt k. | wn ap.‘dn.mṭr h. | b‘l.y‘dn.‘dn.ṯkt.b glṯ. | w tn.ql h.b ‘rpt. | šrh.l arṣ. 4[51].5.68
mǵ]d.ṯdṯ.yr[ḫm]. | ‘dn.ngb.w [yṣi.ṣbu]. | ṣbi.ng[b.w yṣi.‘dn]. | m‘[.ṣ]bu h.u[l.mad]. | ṯlṯ.mat.rbt. | hlk.l alpm.ḫḏd. | w l. 14[KRT].4.177
š. | mǵd.ṯdṯ.yrḫm. | ‘dn.ngb.w yṣi. | ṣbu.ṣbi.ngb. | w yṣi.‘dn.m‘. | ṣbu k.ul.mad. | ṯlṯ.mat.rbt. | ḫpṯ.d bl.spr. | ṯnn.d bl.h 14[KRT].2.87
ryt. | ḥṯt.l bt.ḫbr. | yip.lḥm.d ḫmš. | [mǵ]d.ṯdṯ.yr[ḫm]. | ‘dn.ngb.w [yṣi.ṣbu]. | ṣbi.ng[b.w yṣi.‘dn]. | m‘[.ṣ]bu h.u[l.mad 14[KRT].4.176
.l qryt. | ḥṯt.l bt.ḫbr. | yip.lḥm.d ḫmš. | mǵd.ṯdṯ.yrḫm. | ‘dn.ngb.w yṣi. | ṣbu.ṣbi.ngb. | w yṣi.‘dn.m‘. | ṣbu k.ul.mad. | ṯlṯ 14[KRT].2.85
spr.r‘ym. | lqḥ.š‘rt. | anntn. | ‘dn. | sdwn. | mztn. | ḫyrn. | šdn. | [‘š]rm.ṯn kbd. | šǵrm. | lqḥ.ššl 2098.4
m. | šr.aḫy h.mẓa h. | w mẓa h.šr.yly h. | b skn.sknm.b ‘dn. | ‘dnm.kn.npl.b‘l. | km ṯr.w tkms.hd.p[.-]. | km.ibr.b tk.m 12[75].2.53
.dqn k.l tsr k. | rḫntt.d[-].l irt k. | wn ap.‘dn.mṭr h. | b‘l.y‘dn.‘dn.ṯkt.b glṯ. | w tn.ql h.b ‘rpt. | šrh.l arṣ.brqm. | bt.arzm 4[51].5.69
ǵdyn.qšt.w.ql‘. | bn.gzl.qšt.w.ql‘. | [---]n.qšt. | ilhd.qšt. | ‘dn.qšt.w.ql‘. | ilmhr.qšt.w.ql‘. | bn.gmrt.qšt. | ǵmrm. | bn.qtn. 119[321].1.8
--]. | ṯn.‘šr.b.gt.ir[bṣ]. | arb‘.b.gt.b‘ln. | ‘št.‘šr.b.gpn. | yd.‘dnm. | arb‘.ǵzlm. | ṯn.yṣrm. 2103.8
]. | bnš.iwl[--.š]šlmt. | šdyn.ššlmt. | prtwn.š‘rt. | ṯṯn.š‘rt. | ‘dn.š‘rt. | mnn.š‘rt. | bdn.š‘rt. | ‘pṯn.š‘rt. | ‘bd.yrḫ š‘rt. | ḫbd.ṯr y 97[315].6
k.l tsr k. | rḫntt.d[-].l irt k. | wn ap.‘dn.mṭr h. | b‘l.y‘dn.‘dn.ṯkt.b glṯ. | w tn.ql h.b ‘rpt. | šrh.l arṣ.brqm. | bt.arzm.ykll 4[51].5.69
ṯm.nḥ[l h.---]. | [---.]‘ḏr[.---]. | str[-.---]. | bdlm.d[t.---]. | ‘dn.[---]. | aḫqm bir[-.---]. | kṯrmlk.ns[--.---]. | bn.tbd.ilšt[m‘y.- 90[314].2.3
[-]ay[.---]. | [a]rš[mg.---]. | urt[n.---]. | ‘dn[.---]. | bqrt[.---]. | ṯnǵrn.[---]. | w.bn h.n[--.---]. | ḥnil.[---]. | 2084.4
.b d[.---]. | [---].ṯl[l]m.[---]. | [--].r[-]y[.---]. | ‘l.[--]l[-] h. | ‘dn.[---]. | d.u[--.---]. 2104.12

‘d‘

n.bn.b‘ly[.---]. | bnil.bn.yṣr[.---]. | ‘dyn.bn.uḏr[-.---]. | w.‘d‘.nḥl h[.---]. | w.yknil.nḥl h[.---]. | w.iltm.nḥl h[.---]. | w.unṯ 90[314].1.14

‘dr

| bn.b[--]. | [b]n.[---]. | bn.a[--]. | bn.ml[k]. | bn.glyn. | bn.‘dr. | bn.ṯmq. | bn.ntp. | bn.‘grt. 1057.19
.---.]l ṯr.qdqd h. | il[.--.]rḥq.b ǵr. | km.y[--.]ilm.b ṣpn. | ‘dr.l[‘r].‘rm. | ṯb.l pd[r.]pdrm. | ṯṯ.l ṯṯm.aḥd.‘r. | šb‘m.šb‘.pdr. 4[51].7.7
ilm[.---]. | ṯš‘.‘š[r.---]. | bn ‘dr[.---]. | ḫmš ‘l.bn[.---]. | ḫmš ‘l r‘l[-]. | ḫmš ‘l ykn[.--]. | ḫ[mš 2034.2.3
]. | l[--.---]. | m[--.---]. | bn[.---]. | bn[.---]. | w.yn[.---]. | bn.‘dr[.---]. | ntb[t]. | b.arb[‘]. | mat.ḫr[ṣ]. 2007.9

‘dršp

n. | [-]wn. | bldn. | [-]ln. | [-]ldn. | [i]wryn. | ḫbsn. | ulmk. | ‘dršp. | bn.knn. | pdyn. | bn.aṯtl.ṯn. | kdln.akdṯb. | ṯn.b gt ykn‘ 1061.17
. | ttḫ.b‘l aṯt. | ayab.b‘l aṯt. | iyṯr.b‘l aṯt. | ptm.b‘l ššlmt. | ‘dršp.b‘l ššlmt. | ttrn.b‘l ššlmt. | aršwn.b‘l ššlmt. | ḥdṯn.b‘l ššl 1077.7
. | yṯil. | w.lmd h. | rpan. | w.lmd h. | ‘bdrpu. | w.lmd h. | ‘dršp. | w.lmd h. | krwn b.gt.nbk. | ddm.ksmm.l.ḫtn. | ddm.l.t 1099.17
bn.gnb[.msg]. | bn.twyn[.msg]. | bn.‘drš[p.msg]. | pyn.yny.[msg]. | bn.mṣrn m[sg]. | yky msg. | yn 133[-].1.3
.qrt. | nǵr krm.‘bdadt.b‘ln.yp‘mlk. | ṯǵrm.mnḥm.klyn.‘dršp.ǵlmn. | [a]bǵl.ṣṣn.ǵrn. | šib.mqdšt.‘b[dml]k.ṯṯpḥ.mrṯn. | 2011.13
ksdm. | ṣdqn. | nwrḏr. | ṯrin. | ‘dršp. | pqr. | agbṯr. | ‘bd. | ksd. 1044.5
‘d[rš]p. | pqr. | ṯǵr. | ttǵl. | ṯn.yṣḥm. | slṯmg. | kdrl. | wql. | adrdn. 1069.1
spr.bdlm. | n‘mn. | rbil. | plsy. | ygmr. | mnṯ. | prḫ. | ‘dršp. | ršpab. | ṯnw. | abmn. | abǵl. | b‘ldn. | yp‘. 1032.8

ʻdš

[mat].|[-----].|ilmlk ṯṯ mat.|ʻbdilm.ṯṯ mat.|šmmn.bn.ʻdš.ṯṯ mat.|ušknym.|ypʻ.alpm.|aḫ[m]lk.bn.nskn.alpm.|kr 1060.1.12

ʻdt

|[--.]b bt h.yšt.ʻrb.|[--] h.ytn.w [--]u.l ytn.|[aḫ]r.mǵy.ʻ[d]t.ilm.|[w]yʻn.aliy[n.]bʻl.|[---.]tbʻ.l lṭpn.|[il.d]pid.l tbrk. 15[128].2.11
-----.]yrḫ.zbl.|[--.kṯ]r w ḫss.|[---]n.rḥm y.ršp zbl.|[w ʻd]t.ilm.ṯlṯ h.|[ap]nk.krt.ṯʻ.ʻ[-]r.|[--.]b bt h.yšt.ʻrb.|[--] h.yt 15[128].2.7
.b qrb.|bt.w yʻn.aliyn.|bʻl.ašt m.kṯr bn.|ym.kṯr.bnm.ʻdt.|ypth.ḫln.b bht m.|urbt.b qrb.[h]kl |m.w y[p]tḥ.b dqt.ʻ 4[51].7.16
thm.|qrit.l špš.um h.špš.um.ql.bl.ʻm.|il.mbk nhrm.b ʻdt.thmtm.|mnt.nṯk.nḥš.šmrr.nḥš.|ʻq šr.ln h.mlḫš abd.ln h. UG5.7.3

ʻdṯ

bn.ršp.|tmn.|šmmn.|bn.rmy.|bn.aky.|ʻbdḫmn.|bn.ʻdṯ.|kṯy.|bn.ḫny.|bn.ssm.|bn.ḫnn.|[--]ny.|[bn].ṯrdnt.|[bn] 1047.15

ʻḏb

ḫrṣ.bht.ṯhrm.|iqnim.šmḫ.aliyn.|bʻl.ṣḥ.ḫrn.b bht h.|ʻḏbt.b qrb hkl h.|yblnn ǵrm.mid.ksp.|gbʻm lḥmd.ḫrṣ.|ybln 4[51].5.99
.bt.lbnt.yʻmsn h.|l yrgm.l aliyn bʻl.|ṣḥ.ḫrn.b bhm k.|ʻḏbt.b qrb.hkl k.|tbl k.ǵrm.mid.ksp.|gbʻm.mḥmd.ḫrṣ.|ybl 4[51].5.76
b]n.|bt.l k.km.aḫ k.w ḥẓr.|km.ary k.ṣḥ.ḫrn.|b bht k.ʻḏbt.b qrb.|hkl k.tbl k.ǵrm.|mid.ksp.gbʻm.mḥmd..|ḫrṣ.w b 4[51].5.92
d.b[---].|at.bl.at.[---].|yisp hm.b[ʻl.---].|bn.dgn[.---].|ʻḏbm.[---].|uḫry.l[---].|mṣt.ks h.t[--.---].|idm.adr[.---].|id 12[75].2.27

ʻḏr

t.dq]n k.mmʻm.w[---].|aqht.w yplṭ k.bn[.dnil.---].|w yʻḏr k.b yd.btlt.[ʻnt].|w yʻn.lṭpn.il d p[id].|ydʻt k.bt.k anšt. 18[3AQHT].1.14
ḥl h[.---].|w.iltm.nḥl h[.---].|w.unṯm.nḥ[l h.---].|[---.]ʻḏr[.---].|str[-.---].|bdlm.d[t.---].|ʻdn.[---].|aḫqm bir[-.---].| 90[314].1.18

ʻwd

.l ihbt.yb[--].rgm y.|[---.]škb.w m[--.]mlakt.|[---.]ʻl.w tšʻ[d]n.npṣ h.|[---.]rgm.hn.[--]n.w aspt.[q]l h.|[---.rg]m.ank 1002.48

ʻwr

.kl hm.|aḥd.bt h.ysgr.|almnt.škr.|tškr.zbl.ʻršm.|yšu.ʻwr.|mzl.ymzl.|w ybl.trḫ.ḥdṯ.|ybʻr.l ṯn.aṯt h.|w l nkr.mddt 14[KRT].4.187
ṯ.kl hm.|yḥd.bt h.sgr.|almnt.škr.|tškr.zbl.ʻršm.|yšu.ʻwr.mzl.|ymzl.w yṣi.trḫ.|ḥdṯ.ybʻr.l ṯn.|aṯt h.lm.nkr.|mddt 14[KRT].2.99
.yšu g h.|w yṣḥ.y l k.qrt.ablm.|d ʻl k.mḫṣ.aqht.ǵzr.|ʻwrt.yšt k.bʻl.l ht.|w ʻlm h.l ʻnt.p dr.dr.|ʻdb.uḫry.mṭ.yd h.| 19[1AQHT].4.167

ʻz

.|ydb il.|yrgb lim.|ʻmtr.|yarš il.|ydb bʻl.|yrǵm bʻl.|ʻz bʻl.|ydb hd. UG5.14.B.13
ʻl.ʻz.ynghn.|k rumm.mt.ʻz.bʻl.|ʻz.ynṯkn.k bṯnm.|mt.ʻz.bʻl.ʻz.ymṣḫn.|k lsmm.mt.ql.|bʻl.ql.ʻln.špš.|tṣḥ.l mt.šmʻ. 6[49].6.20
.ytnt.bʻl.|spu y.bn m.um y.kl|y y.ytʻn.k gmrm.|mt.ʻz.bʻl.ʻz.ynghn.|k rumm.mt.ʻz.bʻl.|ʻz.ynṯkn.k bṯnm.|mt.ʻz. 6[49].6.17
.kl|y y.ytʻn.k gmrm.|mt.ʻz.bʻl.ʻz.ynghn.|k rumm.mt.ʻz.bʻl.|ʻz.ynṯkn.k bṯnm.|mt.ʻz.bʻl.ʻz.ymṣḫn.|k lsmm.mt.ql.| 6[49].6.18
w bn[š.---].|d bnš.ḥm[r.---].|w d.l mdl.r[--.---].|w ṣin.ʻz.b[ʻl.---].|llu.bn[š.---].|imr.ḫ[--.---].|[--]n.bʻ[l.---].|w [--]d.[2158.1.14
---].|[---].|hm qrt tuḫd.hm mt yʻl bnš.|bt bn bnš yqḥ ʻz.|w yḥdy mrḥqm. RS61[24.277.30]
ilštmʻ.|bt ubnyn š h d.ytn.ṣtqn.|tut ṭbḫ ṣtq[n].|b bz ʻzm ṭbḫ š[h].|b kl ygz ḥḫ š h. 1153.4
.km.nšr.|b[u]ṣbʻt h.ylm.ktp.zbl ym.bn ydm.ṭpṭ.|nhr.ʻz.ym.l ymk.l tnǵṣn.pnt h.l ydlp.|tmn h.kṯr.ṣmdm.ynḥt.w y 2.4[68].17
]lk.ʻlm.b ḏmr h.bl.|[---].b ḥtk h.b nmrt h.l r|[--.]arṣ.ʻz k.ḏmr k.l[-]|n k.ḥtk k.nmrt k.b tk.|ugrt.l ymt.špš.w yrḫ. UG5.2.2.9
.|hm.in mm.|nḫtu.w.lak.|ʻm y.w.yd.|ilm.p.k mtm.|ʻz.mid.|hm.ntkp.|mʻn k.|w.mnm.|rgm.d.tšmʻ.|ṭmt.w.št.| 53[54].13
nghn.|k rumm.mt.ʻz.bʻl.|ʻz.ynṯkn.k bṯnm.|mt.ʻz.bʻl.ʻz.ymṣḫn.|k lsmm.mt.ql.|bʻl.ql.ʻln.špš.|tṣḥ.l mt.šmʻ.mʻ.|l b 6[49].6.20
t.bʻl.|spu y.bn m.um y.kl|y y.ytʻn.k gmrm.|mt.ʻz.bʻl.ʻz.ynghn.|k rumm.mt.ʻz.bʻl.|ʻz.ynṯkn.k bṯnm.|mt.ʻz.bʻl.ʻz. 6[49].6.17
.ytʻn.k gmrm.|mt.ʻz.bʻl.ʻz.ynghn.|k rumm.mt.ʻz.bʻl.|ʻz.ynṯkn.k bṯnm.|mt.ʻz.bʻl.ʻz.ymṣḫn.|k lsmm.mt.ql.|bʻl.ql.ʻ 6[49].6.19
št k.l iršt.|[ʻlm.---.--]k.l tšt k.liršt.|[---.]rpi.mlk ʻlm.b ʻz.|[rpu.m]lk.ʻlm.b ḏmr h.bl.|[---].b ḥtk h.b nmrt h.l r|[--.] UG5.2.2.6
d ga[n.--].|b bt k.[--].|w l dbḥ[--].|ṯ[--].|[--] aṯt yqḥ ʻz.|[---]ḏ.|[---].|[---].|hm qrt tuḫd.hm mt yʻl bnš.|bt bn bn RS61[24.277.25]

ʻzz

[t]ḥm.iṯtl.|l mnn.ilm.|tǵr k.tšlm k.|tʻzz k.alp ymm.|w rbt.šnt.|b ʻd ʻlm...gnʻ.|iršt.aršt.|l aḫ y.l 1019.1.4
hnm.|rgm.|tḥm.[---].|yšlm[.l k.ilm].|tšlm[k.tǵr] k.|tʻzz[k.---.]lm.|w t[--.--]ṣm k.|[-----].|[-----.]šil.|[-----.]šilt.|[55[18].6

ʻzn

d.abṣn.|šdyn.unn.dqn.|ʻbdʻnt.rb ʻšrt.mnḥm.ṭbʻm.sḫr.ʻzn.ilhd.|bnil.rb ʻšrt.lkn.ypʻn.ṯ[--].|yṣḥm.b d.ubn.krwn.tǵd. 2011.7
[.n]klb.|b[n.]dtn.|w.nḥl h.|w.nḥl hm.|bn.iršyn.|bn.ʻzn.|bn.aršw.|bn.ḫzrn.|bn.iǵyn.|w.nḥl h.|bn.ksd.|bn.brš 113[400].2.13
ʻzn.bn.irbn.|bn.mglb.|bn.ntp.|ʻmyn.bn ǵḫpn.|bn.kbln.|bn. 104[316].1
t.|bn.pnmn.ʻšrt.|ʻbdadt.ḫmšt.|abmn.ilštmʻy.ḫmš[t].|ʻzn.bn.brn.ḫmšt.|mʻrt.ḫmšt.|arṯṯb.bn.ḫmšt.|bn.ysr[.ḫmš]t. 1062.26
n.atn.|bn.bly.|bn.ṯbrn.|bn.ḥgby.|bn.pity.|bn.slgyn.|ʻzn.bn.mlk.|bn.altn.|bn.ṯmyr.|ẓbr.|bn.ṯdṯb.|bn.ʻrmn.|bn. 115[301].2.8
mnn.bn.krmn.|bn.umḫ.|yky.bn.slyn.|ypln.bn.ylḥn.|ʻzn.bn.mll.|šrm.|[b]n.špš[yn].|[b]n.ḫrmln.|bn.tnn.|bn.pnd 85[80].1.9
.ʻdy.klby.dqn.|ḥrṯm.ḥgbn.ʻdn.ynḥm[.---].|ḥrš.mrkbt.ʻzn.[b]ʻln.ṯb[--.-]nb.trtn.|[---]mm.klby.kl[--].dqn[.---].|[-]nt 2011.28
-]mm.klby.kl[--].dqn[.---].|[-]ntn.artn.b d[.--]nr[.---].|ʻzn.w ymd.šr.b d ansny.|nsk.ks[p.--]mrtn.kṯrmlk.|yḥmn.aḫ 2011.31
gṯrn.|bn.arpḫn.|bn.ṯryn.|bn.dll.|bn.ḫswn.|mrynm.|ʻzn.|ḥyn.|ʻmyn.|ilyn.|yrbʻm.|nʻmn.|bn.kbl.|knʻm.|bdlm. 1046.3.34
rt.ḫmšt.|arṯṯb.bn.ḫmšt.|bn.ysr[.ḫmš]t.|ṣ[-]r.ḫ[mšt].|ʻzn.ḫ[mšt]. 1062.31
n[.---]y.|yr[---].|ḫdyn.|grgš.|b[n.]tlš.|ḏmr.|mkrm.|ʻzn.|yplṭ.|ʻbdmlk.|ynḥm.|adddn.|mtn.|plsy.|qṭn.|ypr.|b 1035.4.3
dn.w.ildgn.ḥṭbm.|tdǵlm.iln.bʻ[l]n.aldy.|tdn.ṣr[--.--]t.ʻzn.mtn.n[bd]g.|ḥrš qṭn[.---.]dqn.bʻln.|ǵltn.ʻbd.[---].|nsk.ḥ 2011.22
yrḫ.|ubn.ḫyrn.|ybnil.adrdn.|klyn.kkln.|ʻdmlk.tdn.|ʻzn.pǵdn.|[a]nndn.|[r]špab.|[-]glm. 1070.6
t.|ǵzldn.|ṭrn.|ḫdbṭ.|[-]ḫl.aǵltn.|[-]n.|[-]mṭ.|[--.]bn.[ʻ]zn.|[--]yn. 1043.19

ʻṭ

.mrat.bqʻ. | ṯlṯ.[-]ṯt.aš[ʻ]t.šmn.uz. | mi[t].ygb.bqʻ. | a[--].ʻṭ. | a[l]pm.alpnm. | ṯlṯ.m[a]t.art.ḫkpt. | mit.dnn. | mitm.iqnu. 1128.24
-.]ab.w il[--]. | [--] šlm.šlm i[l]. | [š]lm.il.šr. | dgn.w bʻl. | ʻṭ w kmṯ. | yrḫ w ksa. | yrḫ mkṯy. | ṯkmn w šnm. | kṯr w ḫss. | ʻ UG5.10.1.5

ʻṭl

ṯr k[--.---]. | b ḫmṯ ʻṯr[.---]. | [-----]. | [---.-]y[-.---]. | w bn ʻṭl.[---]. | ypḫ knʻm[.---]. | aḫmn bt[.---]. | b ḫmṯ ʻṯr ṯmn[.---]. 207[57].8

ʻṭr

ṣrt.tbu.pnm. | ʻrm.tdu.mh. | pdrm.tdu.šrr. | ḫṭ m.tʻmt.[ʻ]ṭr.[k]m. | zbln.ʻl.riš h. | w ṯṯb.trḥṣ.nn.b dʻt. | npš h.l lḥm.tpt 16.6[127].8
-]. | ks[.---]. | kr[pn.---]. | at.š[ʻtqt.---]. | šʻd[.---]. | rt.[---]. | ʻṭr[.---]. | b p.š[---]. | il.p.d[---]. | ʻrm.[di.mh.pdrm]. | di.š[rr.--- 16[126].5.45

ʻṭrṭr

l šd.mṭr.ʻly. | nʻm.l ḥṭt.b gn. | bm.nrt.ksmm. | ʻl.tl[-]k.ʻṭrṭrm. | nšu.[r]iš.ḥrṯm. | l ẓr.ʻdb.dgn kly. | lḥm.[b]ʻdn hm.kly 16[126].3.11

ʻẓ

abd.l p.akl ṯm.dl. | [---.q]l.bl.tbḥ[n.l]azd.ʻr.qdm. | [---].ʻẓ q[dm.--.šp]š. | [---.šm]n.mšḥt.kṯpm.a[-]ṯ[-]. | [---.--]ḥ b ym. UG5.8.22

ʻẓm

ln.ṯḥ pʻn y.ibq[ʻ.kbd hm.w] | aḥd.hm.iṯ.šmt.hm.i[ṯ]. | ʻẓm.abky.w aqbrn h. | ašt.b ḫrt.ilm.arṣ. | b p h.rgm.l yṣa.b šp 19[1AQHT].3.111
iy. | hyt.tql.ṯḥt.pʻn y.ibqʻ. | kbd h.w aḥd.hm.iṯ.šmt.iṯ. | ʻẓm.abky w aqbrn h.aštn. | b ḫrt.ilm.arṣ.b p h.rgm.l[yṣ]a. | b 19[1AQHT].3.140
w yql.ṯḥt.pʻn y.ibqʻ.kbd[h]. | w aḥd.hm.iṯ.šmt.hm.iṯ[.ʻẓm]. | abky.w aqbrn.ašt.b ḫrt. | i[lm.arṣ.b p h.rgm.l yṣa.b šp] 19[1AQHT].3.125
r.diy.hyt.tq[l.ṯḥt]. | pʻn h.ybqʻ.kbd h.w yḥd. | iṯ.šmt.iṯ.ʻẓm.w yqḥ b hm. | aqht.ybl.l qẓ.ybky.w yqbr. | yqbr.nn.b md 19[1AQHT].3.145
tl k.w ẓi. | b aln.tk m. | b tk.mlbr. | ilšiy. | kry amt. | ʻpr.ʻẓm yd. | ugrm.ḫl.ld. | aklm.tbrk k. | w ld ʻqqm. | ilm.ypʻr. | šm 12[75].1.24
.tlʻm.ṯm.ḥrbm.its.anšq. | [-]htm.l arṣ.ypl.ul ny.w l.ʻpr.ʻẓm ny. | l bʻl[-.---]. | ṯḥt.ksi.zbl.ym.w ʻn.kṯr.w ḫss.l rgmt. | l k 2.4[68].5
y.hwt.w yql. | ṯḥt.pʻn h.ybqʻ.kbd h.w yḥd. | [i]n.šmt.in.ʻẓm.yšu.g[h]. | w yṣḥ.knp.hrgb.bʻl.ybn. | [b]ʻl.ybn.diy.hwt.hr 19[1AQHT].3.131
hmt.tqln. | ṯḥt.pʻn h.ybqʻ.kbdt hm.w[yḥd]. | in.šmt.in.ʻẓm.yšu.g h. | w yṣḥ.knp.nšrm.ybn. | bʻl.ybn.diy hmt nšrm. | t 19[1AQHT].3.117
ʻšr.w yšqyn h. | ytn.ks.b d h. | krpn.b klat.yd h. | b krb.ʻẓm.ridn. | mt.šmm.ks.qdš. | l tphn h.aṯt.krpn. | l tʻn.aṯrt.alp. 3[ʻNT].1.12

ʻẓmt

šrm. | [mi]tm.arbʻm.ṯmn.kbd. | [l.]sbrdnm. | m[i]t.l.bn.ʻẓmt.rišy. | mit.l.tlmyn.bn.ʻdy. | [---.]l.adddy. | [--.]l.kkln. 2095.7

ʻẓpn

| [k]bkbm.ṯm.tpl k.lbnt. | [-.]rgm.k yrkt.ʻṯqbm. | [---]m.ʻẓpn.l pit. | m[--]m[.--]tm.w mdbḥt. | ḫr[.---.]ʻl.kbkbt. | nʻm.[-- 13[6].15

ʻyy

ṯpḫln.l bn.ǵl. | w dṯn.nḥl h.l bn.pl. | šd.krwn.l aḫn. | šd.ʻyy.l aḫn. | šd.brdn.l bn.bly. | šd gzl.l.bn.ṭbr[n]. | šd.ḫzmyn.l a 2089.12

ʻyn

ʻpr.qm.aḫ k. | w tšu.ʻn h.btlt.ʻnt. | w tšu.ʻn h.w tʻn. | w tʻn.arḫ.w tr.b lkt. | tr.b lkt.w tr.b ḫl. | [b]nʻmm.b ysmm.ḫ[-- 10[76].2.28
b krb.ʻẓm.ridn. | mt.šmm.ks.qdš. | l tphn h.aṯt.krpn. | l tʻn.aṯrt.alp. | kd.yqḥ.b ḫmr. | rbt.ymsk.b msk h. | qm.ybd.w y 3[ʻNT].1.15
. | nḫl. | yʻny. | atn. | utly. | bn.alz. | bn ḫlm. | bn.ḏmr. | bn.ʻyn. | ubnyn. | rpš d ydy. | ǵbl. | mlk. | gwl. | rqd. | ḫlby. | ʻn[q]pa 2075.18
.qnum. | bn.ilrš. | ʻ[p]ṯn. | b[n.ʻr]my. | [--]ṯy. | bn.ǵdʻ. | bn.ʻyn. | bn.grb[n]. | yṯtn. | bn.ab[l]. | kry. | psš. | ilṯḥm. | ḥrm. | bn.b 2078.7
.ḥn[n]. | bn.gntn[-]. | [--.]nqq[-]. | b[n.---]. | bn.[---]. | bn.ʻyn. | bn.dtn. 2023.4.3
y. | bn.amt[m]. | myn. | šr. | bn.zql. | bn.iḫy. | bn.iytr. | bn.ʻyn. | bn.ǵzl. | bn.ṣmy. | bn.il[-]šy. | bn.ybšr. | bn.sly. | bn.ḫlbt. | 2117.2.6
m.ʻrẓ.tʻr[ẓ.---]. | ʻn.bʻl.a[ḫ]ḏ[.---]. | ẓr h.aḫḏ.qš[t.---]. | p ʻn.bʻl.aḫḏ[.---]. | w ṣmt.ǵllm[.---]. | aḫḏ.aklm.k [---]. | npl.b mš 12[75].2.34
-]. | mṣt.ks h.t[--.---]. | idm.adr[.---]. | idm.ʻrẓ.tʻr[ẓ.---]. | ʻn.bʻl.a[ḫ]ḏ[.---]. | ẓr h.aḫḏ.qš[t.---]. | p ʻn.bʻl.aḫḏ[.---]. | w ṣmt 12[75].2.32
| ǵr.w yʻn.aliyn. | bʻl.ib.hdt.lm.ṯḥš. | lm.ṯḥš.nṯq.dmrn. | ʻn.bʻl.qdm.yd h. | k tǵd.arz.b ymn h. | bkm.yṯb.bʻl.l bht h. | u 4[51].7.40
lat rumm. | w yšu.ʻn h.aliyn.bʻl. | w yšu.ʻn h.w yʻn. | w yʻn.btlt.ʻnt. | nʻmt.bn.aḫt.bʻl. | l pnn h.ydd.w yqm. | l pʻn h.yk 10[76].2.15
l bʻl.km. | [i]lm.w ḥẓr.k bn. | [a]ṯrt.gm.l ǵlm h. | bʻl.yṣḥ.ʻn.gpn. | w ugr.bn.ǵlmt. | ʻmm ym.bn.ẓlm[t]. | rmt.prʻt.ibr[.m 8[51FRAG].6
ilm.w nšm.d yšb | [ʻ].hmlt.arṣ.gm.l ǵ | [lm] h.bʻl k.yṣḥ.ʻn. | [gpn].w ugr.b ǵlmt. | [ʻmm.]ym.bn.ẓlmt.r | [mt.prʻ]t.ibr. 4[51].7.53
m.ʻm.bʻl. | mrym.ṣpn.b alp.šd.rbt.kmn. | hlk.aḫt h.bʻl.yʻn.tdrq. | ybnt.ab h.šrḥq.aṯt.l pnn h. | št.alp.qdm h.mria.w t 3[ʻNT].4.83
b nši ʻn h.w yphn.b alp. | šd.rbt.kmn.hlk.kṯr. | k yʻn.w yʻn.tdrq.ḫss. | hlk.qšt.ybln.hl.yš | rbʻ.qṣʻt.apnk.dnil. | mt.rpi.a 17[2AQHT].5.11
d. | tǵẓy.bny.bnwt. | b nši.ʻn h.w tphn. | hlk.bʻl.aṯtrt. | k tʻn.hlk.btlt. | ʻnt.tdrq.ybmt. | [limm].b h.pʻnm. | [ṭṭṭ.b ʻ]dn.ksl 4[51].2.14
y. | w b ʻpr.qm.aḫ k. | w tšu.ʻn h.btlt.ʻnt. | w tšu.ʻn h.w tʻn. | w tʻn.arḫ.w tr.b lkt. | tr.b lkt.w tr.b ḫl. | [b]nʻmm.b ysm 10[76].2.27
šmk.mlat rumm. | w yšu.ʻn h.aliyn.bʻl. | w yšu.ʻn h.w yʻn. | w yʻn.btlt.ʻnt. | nʻmt.bn.aḫt.bʻl. | l pnn h.ydd.w yqm. | l 10[76].2.14
.ytm. | b nši ʻn h.w yphn.b alp. | šd.rbt.kmn.hlk.kṯr. | k yʻn.w yʻn.tdrq.ḫss. | hlk.qšt.ybln.hl.yš | rbʻ.qṣʻt.apnk.dnil. | m 17[2AQHT].5.11
mḫmšt.yitsp. | ršp.nṯdṯt.ǵlm. | ym.mšbʻt hn.b šlḥ. | ttpl.yʻn.ḥtk h. | krt yʻn.ḥtk h.rš. | mid.grdš.ṯbt h. | w b tm hn.špḥ. 14[KRT].1.21
šp.nṯdṯt.ǵlm. | ym.mšbʻt hn.b šlḥ. | ttpl.yʻn.ḥtk h. | krt yʻn.ḥtk h.rš. | mid.grdš.ṯbt h. | w b tm hn.šph.yitbd. | w b.pḫy 14[KRT].1.22
qrtm.tṯʻr.ṯlḥnt.]l ṣbim. | [hdmm.l ǵzrm.mid.tmtḫṣn.w t]ʻn.ṯḫtṣb. | [w thdy.ʻnt.tǵdd.kbd h.b ṣḥ]q.ymlu.lb h. | [b šmḫ 7.1[131].6
.l mhr.tṯʻr.ṯlḥnt. | l ṣbim.hdmm.l ǵzrm. | mid.tmtḫṣn.w tʻn. | ṯḫtṣb.w thdy.ʻnt. | tǵdd.kbd h.b ṣḥq.ymlu. | lb h.b šmḫt. 3[ʻNT].2.23
[.m]ḫṣ. | bn y.hm[.mkly.ṣ]brt. | ary y[.ẓl].ksp.[a]ṯrt. | k tʻn.ẓl.ksp.w n[-]t. | ḫrṣ.šmḫ.rbt.a[ṯrt]. | ym.gm.l ǵlm h.k [ṯṣḥ] 4[51].2.27
ʻl.w [---]. | ym.l mt.bʻl m.ym l[--.---]. | ḥm.l šrr.w [---]. | yʻn.ym.l mt[.---]. | l šrr.w tʻ[n.ʻṯtrt.---]. | bʻl m.hmt.[---]. | l šrr. 2.4[68].34
p.w n[-]t. | ḫrṣ.šmḫ.rbt.a[ṯrt]. | ym.gm.l ǵlm h.k [ṯṣḥ]. | ʻn.mktr.ap.t[---]. | dgy.rbt.aṯr[t.ym]. | qḥ.rṯt.b d k t[---]. | rbt.ʻ 4[51].2.30
.nʻm. | yšr.ǵzr.ṭb.ql. | ʻl.bʻl.b ṣrrt. | ṣpn.ytmr.bʻl. | bnt h.yʻn.pdry. | bt.ar.apn.ṯly. | [bt.r]b.pdr.ydʻ. | [---]t.im[-]lt. | [-----] 3[ʻNT].1.23
. | b šbʻt.ḫdrm.[b ṯ]mn[t.ap]. | sgrt.g[-].[-]ẓ[.---] h[.---]. | ʻn.ṯk[.---]. | ʻln.ṯ[--.---]. | l pʻn.ǵl[m]m[.---]. | mid.an[--.]ṣn[--]. 3[ʻNT.VI].5.21
.iḫy.ṯkt. | psš.bn.buly.ṯkt. | ʻpṣpn.bn.ʻdy.ṯkt. | nʻmn.bn.ʻyn.ṯkt. | ʻpṯn.bn.ilrš.ṯkt. | ilṯḥm.bn.šrn.ṯkt. | šmlbu.bn.grb.ṯkt 2085.10

d.bn.pṭḏ.|šd.b d.dr.khnm.|šd.b d.bn.‘my.|šd.b d.bn.‘yn.|ṯn.šdm.b d.klṯṯb.|šd.b d.krz[n].|ṯlṯ.šdm.b d.amtr[n].|ṯ 2090.19
[---.h]d.tngṯn h.|[---].b ṣpn.|[---].nšb.b ‘n.|[---.]b km.y‘n.|[---.yd‘.l] yd‘t.|[---.t]asrn.|[---.]trks.|[---.]abnm.upqt.| 1[‘NT.X].5.7
m h.|[---.-]ḥm k b ṣpn.|[---.]išqb.aylt.|[---.--]m.b km.y‘n.|[---].yd‘.l yd‘t.|[---.]tasrn.ṯr il.|[---.]rks.bn.abnm.|[---.] 1[‘NT.X].5.20

‘ky

m.b d.|rb.tmtt.lqḥt.|w.ṯṯb.ank.l hm.|w.any k.ṯt.|by.‘ky.‘ryt.|w.aẖ y.mhk.|b lb h.al.yšt. 2059.25
šn.ṯt.qšm.w.ql‘.|bn.ml‘n.qšt.w.ql‘.|bn.tmy.qšt.w.ql‘.|‘ky.qšt.|‘bdlbit.qšt.|kṯy.qšt.w.ql‘.|bn.ẖršn.qšt.w.ql‘.|ilrb.qš 119[321].3.37

‘kyt

|d bnšm.yd.grbs hm.|w.ṯn.‘šr h.ẖpnt.|[s̀]s̀wm.amtm.‘kyt.|yd.llẖ hm.|w.ṯlṯ.l.‘šrm.|ẖpnt.s̀s̀wm.ṯn.|pddm.w.d.ṯṯ. 2049.4

‘l

---].|[---].ksp[.---].|[---.--]ir[.---].|[---].‘l.ynḥ[m].|[---.]‘l.ab.b[---].|[---.]‘l.‘[--].|[---.‘]l.‘[--]. 1144.14
.adr.ḥl.|rḥb.mknpt.ap.|[k]rt.bnm.il.špḥ.|lṭpn.w qdš.‘l.|ab h.y‘rb.ybky.|w yšnn.ytn.g h.|bky.b ḥy k.ab n.ašmẖ.| 16.1[125].11
k[npt].|ap.krt bn[m.il].|špḥ.lṭpn[.w qdš].|bkm.t‘r[b.‘l.ab h].|t‘rb.ḥ[--].|b ṯtm.t[---].|šknt.[---].|bkym[.---].|ǵr.y[16.2[125].112
rš.zbln.|rd.l mlk.amlk.|l drkt.k aṯb.an.|ytb‘.yṣb ǵlm.‘l.|ab h.y‘rb.yšu g h.|w yṣḥ.šm‘ m‘.l krt.|ṯ‘.ištm‘.w tqǵ udn 16.6[127].39
‘l.[---].|ṯlṯ.‘l.gmrš[.---].|kd.‘l.‘bd[--].|kd.‘l.aǵlt[n].|ṯlṯ.‘l.a[b]m[n].|arb‘.‘l[.--]ly.|kd.[‘l.--]ẓ.|kd.[‘l.---].|[--.--]ẖ.bn.a 1082.1.21
.|ẖmš ‘l.bn[.---].|ẖmš ‘l r‘l[-].|ẖmš ‘l ykn[.--].|ẖ[mš] ‘l abǵ[l].|ẖmš ‘l ilb[‘l].|‘šr ‘l [---]. 2034.2.7
.|‘šrt.ksp.‘l.[-]lpy.|bn.ady.kkr.š‘rt.|nṯk h.|kb[d.]mn.‘l.abršn.|b[n.---].krs̀u.nṯk h.|[---.--]mm.b.krsi. 1146.11
ẖmšt.‘š[rt].|ksp.‘l.agd[ṯb].|w nit w m‘ṣd.|w ẖrmṯt.|‘šrt.ksp.|‘l.ẖ[z]rn.|w.ni 2053.2
rḥm.|‘l.išt.šb‘ d.ǵzrm.ṭb.[g]d.b ḥlb.annẖ b ẖmat.|w ‘l.agn.šb‘ d m.dǵ[ṯ.---]t.|tlk m.rḥmy.w tṣd[.---].|tḥgrn.ǵzr.n 23[52].15
‘l.alpm.bnš.yd.|titṯm[n].w.‘l.[---].|[-]rym.t[i]ṯṯmn.|šnl.bn.ṣ[2104.1
--].|ym.lm.qd[.---].|šmn.prst[.---].|ydr.hm.ym[.---].|‘l amr.yu[ẖd.ksa.mlk h].|nẖt.kḥṯ.d[rkt h.b bt y].|aṣḥ.rpi[m 22.1[123].17
.w.m‘ṣd].|w ẖrmṯt.|ṯlṯm.ar[b‘].|kbd.ksp.|‘l.tgyn.|w ‘l.aṯt h.|ypḥ.m‘nt.|bn.lbn. 2053.21
]šy[.---] h.|[-]kt[.---.]nrn.|[b]n.nmq[.---].|[ẖm]št.ksp.‘l.aṯt.|[-]ṯd[.bn.]štn. 2055.19
d.‘l.[---].|kd.‘l.[---].|ṯlṯ.‘l.gmrš[.---].|kd.‘l.‘bd[--].|kd.‘l.aǵlt[n].|ṯlṯ.‘l.a[b]m[n].|arb‘.‘l[.--]ly.|kd.[‘l.--]ẓ.|kd.[‘l.---] 1082.1.20
---].|k[--.---].|‘šrm[.---].|tšt.tb‘[.---].|qrt.mlk[.---].|w.‘l.ap.s[--.---].|b hm.w.rgm.hw.al[--].|atn.ksp.l hm.‘d.|ilak.‘ 2008.2.5
.dnil.m[t].|rpi.aphn.ǵzr.m[t].|hrnmy.qšt.yqb.[--]|rk.‘l.aqht.k yq[--.---].|pr‘m.ṣd k.y bn[.---].|pr‘m.ṣd k.hn pr[‘.-- 17[2AQHT].5.36
‘l h.nšr[m].|trẖpn.ybṣr.ḥbl.diy[m.bn].|nšrm.trẖp.‘nt.‘l[.aqht].|t‘dbn h.hlmn.ṯnm[.qdqd].|ṯlṯ id.‘l.udn.š[pk.km].| 18[3AQHT].4.32
h].|nšrm.trẖpn.ybṣr.[ḥbl.d]|iym.bn.nšrm.arẖp.an[k.‘]l.|aqht.‘db k.hlmn.ṯnm.qdqd.|ṯlṯ id.‘l.udn.špk.km.šiy.|d 18[3AQHT].4.21
y.aškn.|‘ṣm.l bt.dml.|p ank.atn.|‘ṣm.l k.|arb‘.‘ṣm.|‘l.ar.|w.ṯlṯ.|‘l.ubr‘y.|w.ṯn.‘l.|mlk.|w.aḥd.|‘l atlg.|w l.‘ṣm. 1010.10
.dl.]isp.ḥ[mt.---.-]hm.yasp.ḥmt.|[---.š]pš.l [hrm.ǵrpl].‘l.arṣ.l an.|[ḥ]mt.i[l.w] ḥrn.yisp.ḥmt.|[b‘l.w]dgn[.yi]sp.ḥm UG5.8.12
y[i]sp.ḥmt.šḥr.w šlm.|[yis]p.ḥmt.isp.[šp]š l hrm.ǵrpl.‘l arṣ.|[l a]n ḥmt.l p[.n]ṯk.abd.l p.akl ṯm.dl.|[---.q]l.bl.tbḥ[n UG5.8.19
]š.l hrm.|[ǵrpl.]‘l.ar[ṣ.---.ḥ]mt.|[---.šp]š.l [hrm.ǵ]rpl.‘l.arṣ.|[---.]ḥmt.l p[.nṯ]k.abd.l p.ak[l].|[ṯm.dl.]isp.ḥ[mt.---.-] UG5.8.9
-]sr.n[--.---.]ḥrn.|[--]p.ẖp h.ẖ[--.---.šp]š.l hrm.|[ǵrpl.]‘l.ar[ṣ.---.ḥ]mt.|[---.šp]š.l [hrm.ǵ]rpl.‘l.arṣ.|[---.]ḥmt.l p[.nṯ] UG5.8.8
arb‘.‘ṣm.|‘l.ar.|w.ṯlṯ.|‘l.ubr‘y.|w.ṯn.‘l.|mlk.|w.aḥd.|‘l atlg.|w l.‘ṣm.|tspr.|nrn.al.tud|ad.at.l hm.|ṯṯm.ksp. 1010.16
ll.‘m.phr.m‘d.ap.ilm.l lḥ[m].|yṯb.bn qdš.l ṯrm.b‘l.qm.‘l.il.hlm.|ilm.tph hm.tphn.mlak.ym.t‘dt.ṯpṭ[.nhr].|t[ǵ]ly.hl 2.1[137].21
-].|ẖmš ‘l r‘l[-].|ẖmš ‘l ykn[.--].|ẖ[mš] ‘l abǵ[l].|ẖmš ‘l ilb[‘l].|‘šr ‘l [---]. 2034.2.8
qra.mt.|b npš h.ystrn ydd.|b gngn h.aḥd y.d ym|lk.‘l.ilm.l ymru.|ilm.w nšm.d yšb|[‘].hmlt.arṣ.gm.l ǵ|[lm] h.b 4[51].7.50
|[-]ḥ[-.---].|[-]p[-.---.-]ny.|[-]ḥ[-.---.-]dn.|arb‘[m.ksp.]‘l.|il[m]l[k.a]rgnd.|uškny[.w]mit.|zt.b d hm.rib.|w [---].|[2055.10
il.|kd.šmn.ymtšr.|arb‘.šmn.‘l.‘bdn.w.[---].|kdm.šmn.‘l.ilršp.bn[.---].|kd.šmn.‘l.yddn.|kd.‘l.ššy.|kd.‘l.nḏbn.bn.ag 1082.1.5
.yrgm.‘l.‘d.w ‘rbm.t‘nyn.|w šd.šd ilm.šd aṯrt.w rḥm.|‘l.išt.šb‘ d.ǵzrm.ṭb.[g]d.b ḥlb.annẖ b ẖmat.|w ‘l.agn.šb‘ d m 23[52].14
.l bt.dml.|p ank.atn.|‘ṣm.l k.|arb‘.‘ṣm.|‘l.ar.|w.ṯlṯ.|‘l.ubr‘y.|w.ṯn.‘l.|mlk.|w.aḥd.|‘l atlg.|w l.‘ṣm.|tspr.|nrn.al 1010.12
m.trẖp.‘nt.‘l[.aqht].|t‘dbn h.hlmn.ṯnm[.qdqd].|ṯlṯ id.‘l.udn.š[pk.km].|šiy.dm h.km.šẖ[ṭ.l brk h].|yṣat.km.rḥ.npš 18[3AQHT].4.34
šrm.arẖp.an[k.‘]l.|aqht.‘db k.hlmn.ṯnm.qdqd.|ṯlṯ id.‘l.udn.špk.km.šiy.|dm.km.šẖṭ.l brk h.tṣi.km.|rḥ.npš h.km.i 18[3AQHT].4.23
b dd y.yṣ[--].|[-.]yṣa.w l.yṣa.hlm.[ṯnm].|[q]dqd.ṯlṯ id.‘l.ud[n].|[---.-]sr.pdm.riš h[m.---].|‘l.pd.asr.[---.]l[.---].|mẖl 19[1AQHT].2.79
brkt.|tmrn.alk.nmr[rt].|imẖṣ.mẖṣ.aẖ y.akl[.m]|kly[.‘]l.umt y.w y‘n[.dn]|il.mt.rpi npš tḥ[.pǵt].|ṯ[km]t.mym.ḥsp 19[1AQHT].4.197
l.b‘l.arṣ.|w t‘n.nrt.ilm.š[p]š.|šd yn.‘n.b qbt[.t]|bl lyt.‘l.umt k.|w abqṯ.aliyn.b‘l.|w t‘n.btlt.‘nt.|an.l an.y špš.|an.l 6[49].4.43
lk.kbkbm.|a[-]ḥ.hy.mẖ.tmẖṣ.mẖṣ[.aẖ k].|tkl.m[k]ly.‘l.umt[k.--].|d ttql.b ym.trtḥ[ṣ.--].|[----.a]dm.tium.b ǵlp y[19[1AQHT].4.202
d mkr.|atlg.|mit.ksp.d mkr.|ilštm‘.|‘šrm.l mit.ksp.|‘l.bn.alkbl.šb[ny].|‘šrm ksp.‘l.|wrt.mtny.w ‘l.|prdny.aṯt h. 2107.16
.]rb‘m ṯqlm.w [---] arb‘yn.|w ‘l.mnḥm.arb‘ š[mn].|w ‘l bn a[--.-]yn ṯqlm.|[--] ksp [---] kdr [---].|[-]ṯrn [k]sp [-]al[. 1103.10
[ṯl]ṯm.ksp.‘[l].|[b]n.bly.gb‘ly.|[šp]ḥ.a[n]nṯb.|w.m[--.u]škny.|[‘]š[r.---] 2055.1
št.|[w a]rb‘ kkr ‘l bn[.--].|[w] ṯlṯ šmn.|[w a]r[b‘] ksp ‘l bn ymn.|šb šr šmn [--] ṯryn.|ẖm[š]m l ‘šr ksp ‘l bn llit.|[- 1103.4
ksp ‘l bn ymn.|šb šr šmn [--] ṯryn.|ẖm[š]m l ‘šr ksp ‘l bn llit.|[--]l[-.-]p ‘l [---.-]b‘m arny.|w ‘l [---.]rb‘m ṯqlm.w 1103.6
.--]m[.---].|[kd.]šš.|[k]d.ykn.bn.‘bdṯrm.|kd.‘bdil.|ṯlṯ.‘l.bn.srt.|kd.‘l.ẓrm.|kd.‘l.s̀z.bn pls.|kd.‘l.ynḥm.|tgrm.šmn. 1082.2.4
[---.]ẖ[---.]ṯmnym[.k]sp ẖmšt.|[w a]rb‘ kkr ‘l bn[.--].|[w] ṯlṯ šmn.|[w a]r[b‘] ksp ‘l bn ymn.|šb šr šmn [1103.2
ilm[.---].|tš‘.‘š[r.---].|bn ‘dr[.---].|ẖmš ‘l.bn[.---].|ẖmš ‘l r‘l[-].|ẖmš ‘l ykn[.--].|ẖ[mš] ‘l abǵ[l].|ẖm 2034.2.4
-]rwd.šmbnš[.---].|[---].ksp.‘l.k[--].|[---.--]k.|[---.]ksp.‘l.bn[.---].|[---].ksp[.---].|[---.--]ir[.---].|[---].‘l.ynḥ[m].|[---.]‘ 1144.10
msk h.|qm.ybd.w yšr.|mṣltm.bd.n‘m.|yšr.ǵzr.ṭb.ql.|‘l.b‘l.b ṣrrt.|ṣpn.ytmr.b‘l.|bnt h.y‘n.pdry.|bt.ar.apn.ṭly.|[bt 3[‘NT].1.21
kd.šmn.‘l.yddn.|kd.‘l.ššy.|kd.‘l.nḏbn.bn.agmn.|[k]d.‘l.brq.|[kd]m.[‘l].kṯr.|[kd]m[.---].ḥ[--].|[-----].|[kd.]‘l[.---].| 1082.1.9
‘n h.w tphn.[---].|b grn.yẖrb[.---].|yǵly.yẖsp.ib[.---].|‘l.bt.ab h.nšrm.trẖ[p]n.|ybṣr.ḥbl.diym.|tbky.pǵt.bm.lb.|td 19[1AQHT].1.32
rp k.[---].|[---.]y.mṭnt.w tḥ.ṭbt.n[--].|[---.b]ṯnm w ṯṯb.‘l.bṯnt.trtḥ[ṣ.---].|[---.t]ṯb h.aẖt.ppšr.w ppšrt[.---].|[---.]k.dr 1001.2.5
---].|[---.]‘l.ṯny[.---]|[---.]pẖyr.bt h.[---].|[ẖm]šm.ksp.‘l.gd[--].|[---].ypḥ.‘bdršp.b[--.--].|[ar]b‘t.‘šrt.kbd[.---].|[---.-] 1144.4
].|[kd.]‘[l.---].|[k]d.‘l[.---].|[k]d.‘l.[---].|kd.‘l.[---].|ṯlṯ.‘l.gmrš[.---].|kd.‘l.‘bd[--].|kd.‘l.aǵlt[n].|ṯlṯ.‘l.a[b]m[n].|arb‘ 1082.1.18

ǵlt.yd k.l tdn.|dn.almnt.l ṯpṭ.|ṯpṭ qṣr.npš.l tdy.|ṯšm.‘l.dl.l pn k.|l tšlḥm.ytm.b‘d.|ksl k.almnt.km.|aḫt.‘rš.mdw. 16.6[127].48
.lim.ḫp y[m].|tṣmt.adm.ṣat.š[p]š.|tḥt h.k kdrt.ri[š].|‘l h.k irbym.kp.k.qṣm.|ǵrmn.kp.mhr.‘tkt.|rišt.l bmt h.šnst. 3[‘NT].2.10
]q.ymlu.lb h.|[b šmḫt.kbd.‘nt.tšyt.tḥt h.k]kdrt.riš.|[‘l h.k irbym.kp.---.k br]k.tǵll.b dm.|[ḏmr.---.]td[-.]rǵb.|[---- 7.1[131].9
m.|k b‘l.k yḥwy.y‘šr.ḥwy.y‘š.|r.w yšqyn h.ybd.w yšr.‘l h.|n‘m[n.w t]‘nynn.ap ank.aḥwy.|aqht[.ǵz]r.w y‘n.aqht.ǵ 17[2AQHT].6.31
km.diy.b t‘rt y.aqht.[km.yṯb].|l lḥm.w bn.dnil.l ṯrm[.‘l h].|nšrm.trḫpn.ybṣr.[ḥbl.d]|iym.bn.nšrm.arḫp.an[k.‘]l.|a 18[3AQHT].4.19
h.km.diy.|b t‘rt h.aqht.km.yṯb.l lḥ[m].|bn.dnil.l ṯrm.‘l h.nšr[m].|trḫpn.ybṣr.ḥbl.diy[m.bn].|nšrm.trḫp.‘nt.‘l[.aqh 18[3AQHT].4.30
]ry.|tṭbḫ.šmn.[m]ri h.|t[p]tḥ.rḥbt.yn.|‘l h.ṯr h.tš‘rb.|‘l h.tš‘rb.ẓby h.|ṯr.ḫbr.rbt.|ḫbr.ṯrrt.|bt.krt.tbun.|lm.mṯb[.- 15[128].4.18
y.|riš h.tply.ṭly.bn.‘n h.|uz‘rt.tmll.išd h.qrn[m].|dt.‘l h.riš h.b glṯ.b šm[m].|[---.i]l.ṯr.iṯ.p h.k ṯt.ǵlt[.--].|[---.--] k UG5.3.1.7
-].|tšm‘.mṯt.[ḥ]ry.|tṭbḫ.šmn.[m]ri h.|t[p]tḥ.rḥbt.yn.|‘l h.ṯr h.tš‘rb.|‘l h.tš‘rb.ẓby h.|ṯr.ḫbr.rbt.|ḫbr.ṯrrt.|bt.krt.t 15[128].4.17
kd.šmn.‘l.hbm.šlmy.|kd.šmn.ṯbil.|kd.šmn.ymtšr.|arb‘.šmn.‘l.‘bdn. 1082.1.1
ln.b bht m.|urbt.b qrb.[h]kl |m.w y[p]tḥ.b dqt.‘rpt.|‘l h[wt].kṯr.w ḫss.|ṣḥq.kṯr.w ḫss.|yšu.g h.w yṣḥ.|l rgmt.l k. 4[51].7.20
[--]y.l ihbt.yb[--].rgm y.|[---.]škb.w m[--.]mlakt.|[---.]‘l.w tš‘[d]n.npṣ h.|[---.]rgm.hn.[--]n.w aspt.[q]l h.|[---.rg]m 1002.48
.|ilštm‘.|‘šrm.l mit.ksp.|‘l.bn.alkbl.šb[ny].|‘šrm ksp.‘l.|wrt.mtny.w ‘l.|prdny.aṯt h. 2107.17
.|krpn.[---].|w ṯṯn.[---].|t‘l.tr[-.---].|bt.il.li[mm.---].|‘l.ḥbš.[---].|mn.lik.[---].|lik.tl[ak.---].|t‘ddn[.---].|niṣ.p[---.-- 5[67].4.22
rt].|ksp.‘l.agd[ṯb].|w nit w m‘ṣd.|w ḫrmṯt.|‘šrt.ksp.|‘l.ḫ[z]rn.|w.nit.w[.m‘ṣd].|w.ḫ[rmṯt].|‘š[r.---].|‘l[.---].|w.ni[2053.6
.yš|al.|w mlk.d mlk.|b ḥwt.špḥ.|l ydn.‘bd.mlk.|d št.‘l.ḫrd h.|špḥ.al.thbṭ.|ḫrd.‘ps.aḫd.kw|sgt.|ḫrd ksp.[--]r.|y 2062.2.4
d.]šš.|[k]d.ykn.bn.‘bdṯrm.|kd.‘bdil.|ṯlṯ.‘l.bn.srt.|kd.‘l.ẓrm.|kd.‘l.šz.bn pls.|kd.‘l.ynḥm.|tgrm.šmn.d.bn.kwy.|‘l. 1082.2.5
r.|‘m k.ṭṭly.bt.rb.idk.|pn k.al ttn.tk.ǵr.|knkny.ša.ǵr.‘l ydm.|ḫlb.l ẓr.rḥtm w rd.|bt ḫpṯt.arṣ.tspr b y|rdm.arṣ.w t 5[67].5.13
pnm.|‘m.ǵr.trǵzz.|‘m.ǵr.ṯrmg.|‘m.tlm.ǵṣr.arṣ.|ša.ǵr.‘l.ydm.|ḫlb.l ẓr.rḥtm.|w rd.bt ḫpṯt.|arṣ.tspr.b y|rdm.arṣ.|i 4[51].8.5
.l zn.tn[.---].|at.adn.tp‘r[.---].|ank.lṭpn.il[.d pid.---].|‘l.ydm.p‘rt[.---].|šm k.mdd.i[l.---].|bt ksp y.d[--.---].|b d.ali 1[‘NT.X].4.19
ṯr.ap.t[---].|dgy.rbt.aṯr[t.ym].|qḥ.rṯt.b d k t[---].|rbt.‘l.ydm[.---].|b mdd.il.y[--.---].|b ym.il.d[--.---.n]|hr.il.y[--.-- 4[51].2.33
mn.‘l.‘bdn.w.[---].|kdm.šmn.‘l.ilršp.bn[.---].|kd.šmn.‘l.yddn.|kd.‘l.ššy.|kd.‘l.nḏbn.bn.agmn.|[k]d.‘l.brq.|[kd]m. 1082.1.6
[r.---].|bn ‘dr[.---].|ḫmš ‘l.bn[.---].|ḫmš ‘l r‘l[-].|ḫmš ‘l ykn[.--].|ḫ[mš] ‘l abǵ[l].|ḫmš ‘l ilb[‘l].|‘šr ‘l [---]. 2034.2.6
[-] ym.pr‘ d nkly yn kd w kd.|w ‘l ym kdm.|w b ṯlṯ.kd yn w krsnm.|w b rb‘ kdm yn.|w b ḫ 1086.2
|kd.‘bdil.|ṯlṯ.‘l.bn.srt.|kd.‘l.ẓrm.|kd.‘l.šz.bn pls.|kd.‘l.ynḥm.|tgrm.šmn.d.bn.kwy.|‘l.šlmym.ṯmn.kbd.|ṯṯm.šmn. 1082.2.7
|[---.]ksp.‘l.bn[.---].|[---].ksp[.---].|[---.--]ir[.---].|[---].‘l.ynḥ[m].|[---.]‘l.ab.b[---].|[---.]‘l.‘[--].|[---.‘]l.‘[--]. 1144.13
.in[.---].|[--.]s‘.[---].|[---.]n[--.---].|[--.]aw[--.---].|[---.]‘l.y[--.---].|[--.]dn[--.---].|[--.]lq[--.---].|[--.]g[--.---].|[--.]w[.- 45[45].5
šb‘.|šnt.w [--].bn.ilm.mt.|‘m.aliyn.b‘l.yšu.|g h.w yṣḥ.‘l k.b[‘]l m.|pht.qlt.‘l k.pht.|dry.b ḥrb.‘l k.|pht.šrp.b išt.|‘l 6[49].5.11
šḫṭann.b šnt h.qr.[mym].|mlk.yṣm.y l km.qr.mym.d ‘[l k].|mḫṣ.aqht.ǵzr.amd.gr bt il.|‘nt.brḥ.p ‘lm h.‘nt.p dr[.d 19[1AQHT].3.152
.abl[m].|qrt.zbl.yrḫ.yšu g h.|w yṣḥ.y l k.qrt.ablm.|d ‘l k.mḫṣ.aqht.ǵzr.|‘wrt.yšt k.b‘l.l ht.|w ‘lm h.l ‘nt.p dr.dr.| 19[1AQHT].4.166
.l mrrt.tǵll.b nr.|yšu.g h.w yṣḥ.y l k.mrrt.|tǵll.b nr.d ‘l k.mḫṣ.aqht.|ǵzr.šrš k.b arṣ.al.|yp‘.riš.ǵly.b d.ns‘ k.|‘nt.b 19[1AQHT].3.158
.mt.|‘m.aliyn.b‘l.yšu.|g h.w yṣḥ.‘l k.b[‘]l m.|pht.qlt.‘l k.pht.|dry.b ḥrb.‘l k.|pht.šrp.b išt.|‘l k.[pht.ṭḥ]n.b rḥ|m. 6[49].5.12
t.|dry.b ḥrb.‘l k.|pht.šrp.b išt.|‘l k.[pht.ṭḥ]n.b rḥ|m.‘[l k.]pht[.dr]y.b kbrt.|‘l k.pht.[-]l[-].|b šdm.‘l k.pht.|dr‘.b 6[49].5.16
.b rḥ|m.‘[l k.]pht[.dr]y.b kbrt.|‘l k.pht.[-]l[-].|b šdm.‘l k.pht.|dr‘.b ym.tn.aḥd.|b aḫ k.ispa.w yṯb.|ap.d anšt.im[- 6[49].5.18
[‘]l m.|pht.qlt.‘l k.pht.|dry.b ḥrb.‘l k.|pht.šrp.b išt.|‘l k.[pht.ṭḥ]n.b rḥ|m.‘[l k.]pht[.dr]y.b kbrt.|‘l k.pht.[-]l[-].| 6[49].5.15
šu.|g h.w yṣḥ.‘l k.b[‘]l m.|pht.qlt.‘l k.pht.|dry.b ḥrb.‘l k.|pht.šrp.b išt.|‘l k.[pht.ṭḥ]n.b rḥ|m.‘[l k.]pht[.dr]y.b kb 6[49].5.13
rp.b išt.|‘l k.[pht.ṭḥ]n.b rḥ|m.‘[l k.]pht[.dr]y.b kbrt.|‘l k.pht.[-]l[-].|b šdm.‘l k.pht.|dr‘.b ym.tn.aḥd.|b aḫ k.ispa. 6[49].5.17
m.|[---]m.‘ẓpn.l pit.|m[--]m[.--]tm.w mdbḥt.|ḫr[.---.]‘l.kbkbt.|n‘m.[--.-]llm.trtḥṣ.|btlt.‘n[t].tptr‘ ṯd[h].|limm.w t 13[6].17
.|[mri.tšty.krpnm].yn.b ks.ḫ[rṣ].|[dm.‘ṣm.---]n.krpn.‘l.[k]rpn.|[---.]ym.w t‘l.trṯ.|[---].yn.‘šy l ḥbš.|[---.]ḥtn.qn.yṣ 17[2AQHT].6.6
.mṯt ḥry.|l l[ḥ]m.l š[ty].ṣḥt km.|db[ḥ.l krt.a]dn km.|‘l.krt.tbun.km.|rgm.ṯ[rm.]rgm hm.|b ḏrt[.---.]krt.|[----]. 15[128].6.6
t‘n].mṯt.ḥry.|[l lḥ]m.l šty.ṣḥt k[m].|[---.]brk.t[---].|[‘l.]krt.tbkn.|[--.]rgm.ṯrm.|[--.]mtm.tbkn.|[--]t.w b lb.tqb[-] 15[128].5.12
.|kd.‘l.ššy.|kd.‘l.nḏbn.bn.agmn.|[k]d.‘l.brq.|[kd]m.[‘l].kṯr.|[kd]m[.---].ḥ[--].|[-----].|[kd.]‘l[.---].|[kd.]‘[l.---].|[k 1082.1.10
|[ar]b‘t.‘šrt.kbd[.---].|[---.-]rwd.šmbnš[.---].|[---].ksp.‘l.k[--].|[---.--]k.|[---.]ksp.‘l.bn[.---].|[---].ksp[.---].|[---.--]ir[1144.8
].|šm‘.l ngr.il il[š].|ilš.ngr bt b‘l.|w aṯt k.ngrt.il[ht].|‘l.l ṯkm.bnw n.|l nḫnpt.mšpy.|ṯlṯ.kmm.ṯrr y.|[---.]l ǵr.gm.ṣ 16[126].4.14
-].|tlbš.npṣ.ǵzr.tšt.ḫ[---.b] |nšg h.ḥrb.tšt.b t‘r[t h].|w ‘l.tlbš.npṣ.aṯt.[--].|ṣbi nrt.ilm.špš.[-]r[--].|pǵt.minš.šdm l m‘ 19[1AQHT].4.208
]ym.tlḥmn.|[---.rp]um.tštyn.|[---.]il.d ‘rgzm.|[---.]dt.‘l.lty.|[---.]tdbḥ.amr.|ṯmn.b qrb.hkl y.[aṯr h.rpum].|tdd.aṯr 20[121].1.9
nk.atn.|‘ṣm.l k.|arb‘.‘ṣm.|‘l.ar.|w.ṯlṯ.|‘l.ubr‘y.|w.ṯn.‘l.|mlk.|w.aḥd.|‘l atlg.|w l.‘ṣm.|tspr.|nrn.al.tud|ad.at.l h 1010.13
[---.-]b‘m arny.|w ‘l [---.]rb‘m ṯqlm.w [---] arb‘yn.|w ‘l.mnḥm.arb‘ š[mn].|w ‘l bn a[--.-]yn ṯqlm.|[--] ksp [---] kd 1103.9
lṯm.ṯlṯ.‘l.nsk.|arym.|alp.ṯlṯ.‘l.|nsk.art.|ḫmš.mat.ṯlṯ.|‘l.mtn.rišy. 1137.10
m.šmn.‘l.ilršp.bn[.---].|kd.šmn.‘l.yddn.|kd.‘l.ššy.|kd.‘l.nḏbn.bn.agmn.|[k]d.‘l.brq.|[kd]m.[‘l].kṯr.|[kd]m[.---].ḥ[- 1082.1.8
.|‘l.nsk.kṯtǵlm.|arb‘m.ṯlṯ.mḫsrn.|mtb‘l.rišy.|ṯlṯm.ṯlṯ.‘l.nsk.|arym.|alp.ṯlṯ.‘l.|nsk.art.|ḫmš.mat.ṯlṯ.|‘l.mtn.rišy. 1137.5
.ṯlṯ.mḫsrn.|mtb‘l.rišy.|ṯlṯm.ṯlṯ.‘l.nsk.|arym.|alp.ṯlṯ.‘l.|nsk.art.|ḫmš.mat.ṯlṯ.|‘l.mtn.rišy. 1137.7
mit.ṯlṯ.mḫsrn.|‘l.nsk.kṯtǵlm.|arb‘m.ṯlṯ.mḫsrn.|mtb‘l.rišy.|ṯlṯm.ṯlṯ.‘l.nsk.| 1137.2
‘šrm.ksp.|‘l.šknt.syny. 1132.2
-]m.mṣl.|[---].pršं.ḥtm.|ṯlṯ[.---].bn.ṯdnyn.|ddm.ḥ[ṭm].‘l.šrn.|‘šrt.ksp.‘l.[-]lpy.|bn.ady.kkr.š‘rt.|nṯk h.|kb[d.]mn.‘l 1146.7
.ykn.bn.‘bdṯrm.|kd.‘bdil.|ṯlṯ.‘l.bn.srt.|kd.‘l.ẓrm.|kd.‘l.šz.bn pls.|kd.‘l.ynḥm.|tgrm.šmn.d.bn.kwy.|‘l.šlmym.ṯm 1082.2.6
.‘l.hbm.šlmy.|kd.šmn.ṯbil.|kd.šmn.ymtšr.|arb‘.šmn.‘l.‘bdn.w.[---].|kdm.šmn.‘l.ilršp.bn[.---].|kd.šmn.‘l.yddn.|k 1082.1.4
]d.‘l[.---].|[k]d.‘l.[---].|kd.‘l.[---].|ṯlṯ.‘l.gmrš[.---].|kd.‘l.‘bd[--].|kd.‘l.aǵlt[n].|ṯlṯ.‘l.a[b]m[n].|arb‘.‘l[.--]ly.|kd.[‘l.-- 1082.1.19
ṣmdnn.ṣmdm.gpn.yšql.šdmt h.|km gpn.|šb‘ d.yrgm.‘l.‘d.w ‘rbm.t‘nyn.|w šd.šd ilm.šd aṯrt.w rḥm.|‘l.išt.šb‘ d.ǵz 23[52].12
n.bn.ayaḫ.|b.ḫbṯ h.ḥwt.ṯt h.|w.mnm.šalm.|dt.tknn.|‘l.‘rbnm.|hn hmt.|tknn.|mtn.bn.‘bdym.|ilrb.bn.ilyn.|‘bda 1161.7
].|[---.--]ir[.---].|[---].‘l.ynḥ[m].|[---.]‘l.ab.b[---].|[---.]‘l.‘[--].|[---.‘]l.‘[--]. 1144.15
.---].|[---].‘l.ynḥ[m].|[---.]‘l.ab.b[---].|[---.]‘l.‘[--].|[---.‘]l.‘[--]. 1144.16
nm].|[q]dqd.ṯlṯ id.‘l.ud[n].|[---.-]sr.pdm.riš h[m.---].|‘l.pd.asr.[---.]l[.---].|mḫlpt.w l.ytk.[d]m[‘t.]km.|rb‘t.ṯqlm.ṯṯ 19[1AQHT].2.81

mit.ksp. | ‘l.bn.alkbl.šb[ny]. | ‘šrm ksp.‘l. | wrt.mtny.w ‘l. | prdny.aṯt h. 2107.18
k.b ym.ṯiṯ.rḥṣ. | npṣ k.b ym rṯ.b uni[l]. | pnm.tšmḫ.w ‘l yṣhl pi[t]. | yprq.lṣb.w yṣḥq. | p‘n.l hdm.yṯpd.yšu. | g h.w yṣ 17[2AQHT].2.9
.mlk.‘šr. | ‘šrt.qḥ.tp k.b yd. | [-]r[-]k.bm.ymn. | tlk.škn.‘l.ṣrrt. | adn k.šqrb.[---]. | b mgn k.w ḫrṣ.l kl. | apnk.ǵzr.ilḥu. | 16.1[125].43
.w yṣḥ.knp.nšrm. | b‘l.yṯbr.b‘l.yṯbr.diy. | hmt.hm.t‘pn.‘l.qbr.bn y. | tšḫṭann.b šnt h.qr.[mym]. | mlk.yṣm.y l km.qr. 19[1AQHT].3.150
k ap‘.il.b gdrt.k lb.l | ḫṭ h.imḫṣ h.k d.‘l.qšt h. | imḫṣ h.‘l.qṣ‘t h.hwt. | l aḥw.ap.qšt h.l ttn. | l y.w b mt[.-]ḥ.mṣṣ[-]t[.-- 19[1AQHT].1.15
r h.[---]. | aqht.w tbk.y[---.---]. | abn.ank.w ‘l.[qšt k.---.‘l]. | qṣ‘t k.at.l ḥ[---.---]. | w ḫlq.‘pmm[.---]. 18[3AQHT].4.40
ištir.‘m.qrt. | ‘št.‘šr h.šmn. | ‘mn.bn.aǵlmn. | arb‘m.ksp.‘l.qrt. | b.šd.bn.[u]brš. | ḫmšt.‘šrt. | b.šd.bn.[-]n. | ṯl[ṯt].‘šr[t]. | b 1083.6
.kmr.kmr[.--]. | k ap‘.il.b gdrt.k lb.l | ḫṭ h.imḫṣ h.k d.‘l.qšt h. | imḫṣ h.‘l.qṣ‘t h.hwt. | l aḥw.ap.qšt h.l ttn. | l y.w b 19[1AQHT].1.14
št[.---]. | qdqd h.w y‘n.yṭpn.[mhr.št]. | šm‘.l btlt.‘nt.at.‘[l.qšt h]. | tmḫṣ h.qṣ‘t h.hwt.l t[ḥwy]. | n‘mn.ǵzr.št.ṯrm.w[-- 18[3AQHT].4.12
t.b ṣmt.mhr h.[---]. | aqht.w tbk.y[---.---]. | abn.ank.w ‘l.[qšt k.---.‘l]. | qṣ‘t k.at.l ḥ[---.---]. | w ḫlq.‘pmm[.---]. 18[3AQHT].4.40
m.tdu.mh. | pdrm.tdu.šrr. | ḫṭ m.t‘mt.[‘]ṭr.[k]m. | zbln.‘l.riš h. | w tṯb.trḥṣ.nn.b d‘t. | npš h.l lḥm.tpṯḥ. | brlt h.l ṯrm. | 16.6[127].9
lm[.---]. | tš‘.‘š[r.---]. | bn ‘dr[.---]. | ḫmš ‘l.bn[.---]. | ḫmš ‘l r‘l[-]. | ḫmš ‘l ykn[.--]. | ḫ[mš] ‘l abǵ[l]. | ḫmš ‘l ilb[‘l]. | ‘šr ‘l 2034.2.5
. | kd.‘l.ṡz.bn pls. | kd.‘l.ynḥm. | tgrm.šmn.d.bn.kwy. | ‘l.šlmym.ṯmn.kbd. | ṯṯm.šmn. 1082.2.9
.[---]. | kdm.šmn.‘l.ilršp.bn[.---]. | kd.šmn.‘l.yddn. | kd.‘l.ššy. | kd.‘l.nḏbn.bn.agmn. | [k]d.‘l.brq. | [kd]m.[‘l].kṯr. | [kd] 1082.1.7
m.rmm. | [b‘l]t.kpṯ.w ‘nt.di.dit.rḫpt. | [---.-]rm.aklt.‘gl.‘l.mšt. | [---.--]r.špr.w yšt.il. | [---.--]n.il ǵnṯ.‘gl il. | [---.--]d.il.š UG5.2.1.9
---]. | w ni[t.w.m‘ṣd]. | w ḫrmṯt. | ṯlṯm.ar[b‘]. | kbd.ksp. | ‘l.tgyn. | w ‘l.aṯt h. | ypḥ.m‘nt. | bn.lbn. 2053.20
ṭr.b‘l. | w l šd.mṭr.‘ly. | n‘m.l ḥṭt.b gn. | bm.nrt.ksmm. | ‘l.tl[-]k.‘ṭrṭrm. | nšu.[r]iš.ḥrṯm. | l ẓr.‘db.dgn kly. | lḥm.[b]‘dn 16[126].3.11
[-----]. | [---.]‘l.ṯny[.---] | [---.]pḫyr.bt h.[---]. | [ḫm]šm.ksp.‘l.gd[--]. | [---].y 1144.2
| ‘l[.---]. | w.ni[t.---]. | w[.m‘ṣd]. | w ḫr[mṯt]. | [‘]šr[.---]. | [‘]l [-]g[-.---]. | w ni[t.w.m‘ṣd]. | w ḫrmṯt. | ṯlṯm.ar[b‘]. | kbd.ksp 2053.15
rṡ.ḥtm. | ṯlṯ[.---].bn.ṯdnyn. | ddm.ḥ[ṭm].‘l.ṡrn. | ‘šrt.ksp.‘l.[-]lpy. | bn.ady.kkr.š‘rt. | nṯk h. | kb[d.]mn.‘l.abršn. | b[n.---] 1146.8
d[--]. | kd.‘l.aǵlt[n]. | ṯlṯ.‘l.a[b]m[n]. | arb‘.‘l[.--]ly. | kd.[‘l.--]ẓ. | kd.[‘l.---]. | [--.--]ḫ.bn.ag[--]. | [---.--]m[.---]. | [kd.]šš. | [1082.1.23
[.---]. | kd.‘l.‘bd[--]. | kd.‘l.aǵlt[n]. | ṯlṯ.‘l.a[b]m[n]. | arb‘.‘l[.--]ly. | kd.[‘l.--]ẓ. | kd.[‘l.---]. | [--.--]ḫ.bn.ag[--]. | [---.--]m[.-- 1082.1.22
lm]. | [il]tḥm.b d[.---]. | [---].ṯl[l]m.[---]. | [--].r[-]y[.---]. | ‘l.[--]l[-] h. | ‘dn.[---]. | d.u[--.---]. 2104.11
t.ksp. | ‘l.ḫ[z]rn. | w.nit.w[.m‘ṣd]. | w.ḫ[rmṯt]. | ‘š[r.---]. | ‘l[.---]. | w.ni[t.---]. | w[.m‘ṣd]. | w ḫr[mṯt]. | [‘]šr[.---]. | [‘]l [-]g[2053.10
.w ymlk. | [y]ṣb.‘ln.w y[-]y. | [kr]t.ṯ‘.‘ln.bḫr. | [---].aṯt k.‘l. | [---] k.yšši. | [---.]ḫbr.rbt. | [ḫbr.ṯrr]t.il d. | [pid.---].b anšt. | 15[128].5.23
.‘l.brq. | [kd]m.[‘l].kṯr. | [kd]m[.---].ḥ[--]. | [-----]. | [kd.]‘l[.---]. | [kd.]‘[l.---]. | [k]d.‘l[.---]. | [k]d.‘l.[---]. | kd.‘l.[---]. | ṯlṯ.‘ 1082.1.13
]m.[‘l].kṯr. | [kd]m[.---].ḥ[--]. | [-----]. | [kd.]‘l[.---]. | [kd.]‘[l.---]. | [k]d.‘l[.---]. | [k]d.‘l.[---]. | kd.‘l.[---]. | ṯlṯ.‘l.gmrš[.---]. | 1082.1.14
kd]m[.---].ḥ[--]. | [-----]. | [kd.]‘l[.---]. | [kd.]‘[l.---]. | [k]d.‘l[.---]. | [k]d.‘l.[---]. | kd.‘l.[---]. | ṯlṯ.‘l.gmrš[.---]. | kd.‘l.‘bd[--]. 1082.1.15
--]. | [-----]. | [kd.]‘l[.---]. | [kd.]‘[l.---]. | [k]d.‘l[.---]. | [k]d.‘l.[---]. | kd.‘l.[---]. | ṯlṯ.‘l.gmrš[.---]. | kd.‘l.‘bd[--]. | kd.‘l.aǵlt[n] 1082.1.16
[š]m l ‘šr ksp ‘l bn llit. | [--]l[-.-]p ‘l [---.-]b‘m arny. | w ‘l [---.]rb‘m ṯqlm.w [---] arb‘yn. | w ‘l.mnḥm.arb‘ š[mn]. | w ‘l 1103.8
k[.----]. | y[---.---]. | rb[-.---]. | šr[-.---]. | [-.]‘l[.---]. | r‘m[-.---]. | mn[-.---]. | hyrm.h[--.---]. | yrmm h[--.---]. 9[33].1.5
[kd.]‘l[.---]. | [kd.]‘[l.---]. | [k]d.‘l[.---]. | [k]d.‘l.[---]. | kd.‘l.[---]. | ṯlṯ.‘l.gmrš[.---]. | kd.‘l.‘bd[--]. | kd.‘l.aǵlt[n]. | ṯlṯ.‘l.a[b] 1082.1.17
šr šmn [--] ṯryn. | ḫm[š]m l ‘šr ksp ‘l bn llit. | [--]l[-.-]p ‘l [---.-]b‘m arny. | w ‘l [---.]rb‘m ṯqlm.w [---] arb‘yn. | w ‘l.m 1103.7
dbḥ.ilm.yš‘ly.dǵṯ h. | b šmym.dǵṯ hrnmy[.d k] | bkbm.‘[l.---]. | [-]l h.yd ‘d[.---]. | ltm.mrqdm.d š[-]l[-]. | w t‘n.pǵt.ṯk 19[1AQHT].4.187
‘l.alpm.bnš.yd. | titṯm[n].w.‘l.[---]. | [-]rym.t[i]ṯṯmn. | šnl.bn.ṣ[q]n.ṡ[--]. | yitṯm.w.b[--]. | yš 2104.2
l.aǵlt[n]. | ṯlṯ.‘l.a[b]m[n]. | arb‘.‘l[.--]ly. | kd.[‘l.--]ẓ. | kd.[‘l.---]. | [--.--]ḫ.bn.ag[--]. | [---.--]m[.---]. | [kd.]šš. | [k]d.ykn.bn. 1082.1.24
[-]. | ḫmš ‘l ykn[.--]. | ḫ[mš] ‘l abǵ[l]. | ḫmš ‘l ilb[‘l]. | ‘šr ‘l [---]. 2034.2.9
gb‘ly. | [šp]ḥ.a[n]nṯb. | w.m[--.u]škny. | [‘]š[r.---]t.ksp. | [‘l.---]b bn[.--]. | [-]ḥ[-.---]. | [-]p[-.---.-]ny. | [-]ḥ[-.---.-]dn. | arb‘[2055.6

‘lby

.ilgt. | ǵyrn.ybnn qrwn. | ypltn.‘bdnt. | klby.aḥrṯp. | ilyn.‘lby.ṣdkn. | gmrt.ṭlmyn. | ‘bdnt. | bdy.ḥrš arkd. | blšš lmd. | ḥtṯ 1045.6

‘ly

--]. | h[--.---]. | šp[š.---]. | ‘m.k[--.lḥt]. | akl.yṯ[ṯb.--]pt. | ib.‘ltn.a[--.--]y. | w.spr.in[.-.]‘d m. | spr n.ṯhr[.--]. | aṯr.iṯ.bqṯ. | w.š 2060.31
dbr.ṯrmt.al m.qḥn y.š y.qḥn y. | [--.]šir.b krm.nṭṭt.dm.‘lt.b ab y. | u---].‘lt.b k.lk.l pn y.yrk.b‘l.[--]. | [---.]‘nt.šzrm.tšt 1001.1.9
ḥn y.š y.qḥn y. | [--.]šir.b krm.nṭṭt.dm.‘lt.b ab y. | u---].‘lt.b k.lk.l pn y.yrk.b‘l.[--]. | [---.]‘nt.šzrm.tštšḥ.km.ḥ[--]. | [--- 1001.1.10
tksynn.bṯn[-.] | y[--.]šr h.w šḫp h. | [--.]šḫp.ṣǵrt h. | yrk.t‘l.b ǵr. | mslmt.b ǵr.tliyt. | w t‘l.bkm.b arr. | bm.arr.w b ṣpn. 10[76].3.28
rt ym. | blt.nmlk.‘ṯtr.‘rẓ. | ymlk.‘ṯtr.‘rẓ. | apnk.‘ṯtr.‘rẓ. | y‘l.b ṣrrt.ṣpn. | yṯb.l kḥṯ.aliyn. | b‘l.p‘n h.l tmǵyn. | hdm.riš h. 6.1.57[49.1.29]
p h. | [--.]šḫp.ṣǵrt h. | yrk.t‘l.b ǵr. | mslmt.b ǵr.tliyt. | w t‘l.bkm.b arr. | bm.arr.w b ṣpn. | b n‘m.b ǵr.t[l]iyt. | ql.l b‘l.tt 10[76].3.30
--] aṯt yqḥ ‘z. | [---]ḏ. | [---]. | [---]. | hm qrt tuḫd.hm mt y‘l bnš. | bt bn bnš yqḥ ‘z. | w yḥdy mrḥqm. RS61[24.277.29]
il hd.mla.u[--.--]. | blt.p btlt.‘n[t]. | w p.n‘mt.aḫt[.b‘l]. | y‘l.b‘l.b ǵ[r.---]. | w bn.dgn.b š[---]. | b‘l.yṯb.l ks[i.mlk h]. | bn. 10[76].3.12
yt.b hk[l]y.mšspdt. | b ḥẓr y pẓǵm.ǵr.w yq. | dbḥ.ilm.yš‘ly.dǵṯ h. | b šmym.dǵṯ hrnmy[.d k] | bkbm.‘[l.---]. | [-]l h.y 19[1AQHT].4.185
.d š[-]l[-]. | w t‘n.pǵt.ṯkmt.mym. | qrym.ab.dbḥ.l ilm. | š‘ly.dǵṯ h.b šmym. | dǵṯ.hrnmy.d kbkbm. | l tbrkn.alk brkt. | 19[1AQHT].4.192
n.b‘l. | tšm‘.nrt.ilm.špš. | tšu.aliyn.b‘l.l ktp. | ‘nt.k tšt h.tš‘lyn h. | b ṣrrt.ṣpn.tbkyn h. | w tqbrn h.tštnn.b ḫrt. | ilm.arṣ. 6[62].1.15
| š dd šmn[.gdlt.w.---]. | brr.r[gm.yṯṯb.b ṯdṯ.ṯn]. | l šmn.‘[ly h.gdlt.rgm.yṯṯb]. | brr.b šb‘[.ṣbu.špš.w ḥl] | yt.‘rb špš[.w APP.II[173].50
š.dd.šmn.gdlt.w.[---.brr]. | rgm.yṯṯb.b.ṯdṯ.ṯn[.--.šmn]. | ‘ly h.gdlt.rgm.yṯ[ṯb.brr]. | b.[šb]‘.ṣbu.[š]pš.w.ḥly[t].‘[r]b[.š]p[35[3].46
‘mn. | mlk.b.ṯy ndr. | iṯt.w.ht. | [-]sny.udr h. | w.hm.ḫt. | ‘l.w.likt. | ‘m k.w.hm. | l.‘l.w.lakm. | ilak.w.at. | um y.al.tdḥṣ. | 1013.17
.ht. | [-]sny.udr h. | w.hm.ḫt. | ‘l.w.likt. | ‘m k.w.hm. | l.‘l.w.lakm. | ilak.w.at. | um y.al.tdḥṣ. | w.ap.mhkm. | b.lb k.al. 1013.19
t.hrnmy.]uzr.ilm.ylḥm. | [uzr.yšqy.]bn.qdš.yd. | [ṣt h.y‘l.]w yškb.yd. | [mizrt.]p ynl.hn.ym. | [w ṯn.uzr.]ilm.dnil. | [17[2AQHT].1.5
r.ilm.ylḥm. | [uzr.]yšqy.bn qdš.yd.ṣt h. | [dn]il.yd.ṣt h.y‘l.w yškb. | [yd.]mizrt.p yln.mk.b šb‘.ymm. | [w]yqrb.b‘l.b 17[2AQHT].1.15
[--].nk.[---]. | [---.--]ḥ.an[--.---]. | [---.]‘ly k[.---]. | [---.]at.bt k[.---]. | [---.]ank[.---]. | [---.-]hn.[---]. | [-- 1002.3
l. | qḥ.ms[rr.]‘ṣr. | dbḥ.ṣ[q.b g]l.ḥtṯ. | yn.b gl[.ḫ]rṣ.nbt. | ‘l.l ẓr.[mg]dl. | w ‘l.l ẓr.[mg]dl.rkb. | ṯkmm.ḥm[t].ša.yd k. | š 14[KRT].2.73
l. | lqḥ.msrr.‘ṣr.db[ḥ]. | yṣq.b gl.ḥtṯ.yn. | b gl.ḫrṣ.nbt.w ‘ly. | l ẓr.mgdl.rkb. | ṯkmm.ḥmt.nša. | [y]d h.šmmh.dbḥ. | l ṯr. 14[KRT].4.165

‘ly

dbḥ.ṣ[q.b g]l.ḥtṯ.|yn.b gl[.ḫ]rṣ.nbt.|‘l.l ẓr.[mg]dl.|w ‘l.l ẓr.[mg]dl.rkb.|ṯkmm.ḥm[t].ša.yd k.|šmm.dbḥ.l ṯr.|ab k 14[KRT].2.74
r h.rpum.l] |tdd.aṯr[h.l tdd.ilnym].|asr.mr[kbt.---].|t‘ln.l mr[kbt hm.tity.l] |‘r hm.tl[kn.ym.w ṯn.aḫr.špšm].|b ṯ 22.1[123].23
].|tdd.aṯr h.tdd.iln[ym.---].|asr.sswm.tṣmd.dg[-.---].|t‘ln.l mrkbt hm.ti[ty.l ‘r hm].|tlkn.ym.w ṯa aḫr.š[pšm.b ṯlṯ] 20[121].2.4
gm k.šskn m‘.|mgn.rbt.aṯrt ym.|mǵẓ.qnyt.ilm.|hyn.‘ly.l mpḫm.|b d.ḫss.mṣbṭm.|yṣq.ksp.yšl|ḥ.ḫrṣ.yṣq.ksp.|l al 4[51].1.24
ht.aḫ y.|bn y.yšal.|ṯryl.p rgm.|l mlk.šm y.|w l h[-] y‘l m.|bn y.yšal.|ṯryl.w rgm.|ṯṯb.l aḫ k.|l adn k. 138.15
|w ht.aḫ y.|bn y.yšal.|ṯryl.p rgm.|l mlk.šm y.|w l h.y‘l m.|w h[t] aḫ y.|bn y.yšal.|ṯryl.w rgm[.-].|ṯṯb.l aḫ k.|l a 138.14
.l qṣm.arṣ.|l ksm.mhyt.‘n.|l arṣ.m[ṭ]r.b‘l.|w l šd.mṭr.‘ly.|n‘m.l arṣ.mṭr.b‘l.|w l šd.mṭr.‘ly.|n‘m.l ḥṭt.b gn.|bm.nr 16[126].3.6
[ṭ]r.b‘l.|w l šd.mṭr.‘ly.|n‘m.l arṣ.mṭr.b‘l.|w l šd.mṭr.‘ly.|n‘m.l ḥṭt.b gn.|bm.nrt.ksmm.|‘l.tl[-]k.‘ṭrṭrm.|nšu.[r]iš. 16[126].3.8
[kt].|tǵsdb.šmlšn.|w tb‘ ank.|‘m mlakt h šm‘ h.|w b.‘ly skn.yd‘ rgm h.|w ht ab y ǵm[--].|t[--.---].|ls[--.---].|ṣḥ[.- 1021.8
bt.|n‘m.[--.-]llm.trtḥṣ.|btlt.‘n[t].tptr‘ ṭd[h].|limm.w t‘l.‘m.il.|ab h.ḥpr.p‘l k.y[--].|šm‘ k.l arḫ.w bn.[--].|limm.ql 13[6].20
|mmlat.dm.ym.w ṯn.|ṯlṯ.rb‘.ym.ymš.|ṯdṯ.ym.ḥẓ k.al.tš‘l.|qrt h.abn.yd k.|mšdpt.w hn.špšm.|b šb‘.w l.yšn.pbl.| 14[KRT].3.116
n.b ks.ḫ[rṣ].|[dm.‘ṣm.---]n.krpn.‘l.[k]rpn.|[---.]ym.w t‘l.trṯ.|[---].yn.‘šy l ḥbš.|[---.]ḥtn.qn.yṣbt.|[---.--]m.b nši.‘n 17[2AQHT].6.7
r[ṣ.dm.‘ṣm.---].|ks.ksp[.---].|krpn.[---].|w tṯtn.[---].|t‘l.tr[-.---].|bt.il.li[mm.---].|‘l.ḥbš.[---].|mn.lik.[---].|lik.tl[a 5[67].4.20
mlk.b‘l y.bnš.|bnny.‘mn.|mlakty.hnd.|ylak ‘m y.|w.t‘l.ṯh.hn.|[a]lpm.s̀swm.|[---].w.ṯb. 1012.37
w.mlk.b‘l y.|lm.škn.hnk.|l ‘bd h.alpm.s̀[s̀w]m.|rgmt.‘ly.ṯh.lm.|l.ytn.hm.mlk.[b]‘l y.|w.hn.ibm.šṣq l y.|p.l.ašt.aṯt 1012.25
b.‘glt.b dbr.prt.|b šd.šḥlmmt.škb.|‘mn h.šb‘.l šb‘m.|tš[‘]ly.ṯmn.l ṯmnym.|w [th]rn.w tldn mṯ.|al[iyn.b‘]l šlbšn.| 5[67].5.21
iqra.ilm.n[‘mm.---].|w ysmm.bn.š[---].|ytnm.qrt.l ‘ly[.---].|b mdbr.špm.yd[.---.---]r.|l riš hm.w yš[--.--]m.|lḥ 23[52].3
.dnil.|[mt.rp]i.brlt.ǵzr.mt hrnmy.|[---].hw.mḫ.l ‘rš h.y‘l.|[---].bm.nšq.aṯt h.|[---.]b ḥbq h.ḥmḥmt.|[---.--] n.ylt.ḥ 17[2AQHT].1.39
š l ili[b.---].|rt.w ‘ṣrm.l[.---].|pamt.w bt.[---].|rmm.w ‘l[y.---].|bt.il.ṯq[l.---.kbd].|w bdḥ.k[--.---].|‘ṣrm.l i[nš.ilm.ṯb APP.II[173].41

‘llm

q.rpu.b‘l.mhr b‘l.|w mhr.‘nt.ṯm.yḥpn.ḥyl|y.zbl.mlk.‘llm y.km.tdd.|‘nt.ṣd.tštr.‘pt.šmm.|ṭbḫ.alpm.ap ṣin.šql.ṯrm 22.2[124].10
m.l tdd].|aṯr h.l t[dd.ilnym.ṯm].|yḥpn.ḥy[ly.zbl.mlk.‘llm y].|šm‘.atm[.---].|ym.lm.qd[.---].|šmn.prst[.---].|ydr. 22.1[123].12
ṣ.ilm.---].|l rḥqm.l p[-.---].|ṣḥ.il.yṯb.b[mrzḥ.---].|bṯt.‘llm n.[---].|ilm.bt.b‘l k.[---].|dl.ylkn.ḥš.b a[rṣ.---].|b ‘pr.ḫb 1[‘NT.X].4.5

‘lln

nn.bn kn‘m.|bn kbr.|bn iytlm.|bn ayln.|bn.kln.|bn.‘lln.|bn.liy.|bn.nqṭn.|bn abrḫṭ.|bn.grdy.|bn.ṣlpn.|bn ǵlm 1064.24

‘lm

n.ilm.|tǵr k.tšlm k.|t‘zz k.alp ymm.|w rbt.šnt.|b ‘d ‘lm...gn‘.|iršt.aršt.|l aḫ y.l r‘ y.dt.|w ytnnn.|l aḫ h.l r‘ h.|r 1019.1.6
.---.--]k.l tšt k.liršt.|[---.]rpi.mlk ‘lm.b ‘z.|[rpu.m]lk.‘lm.b ḏmr h.bl.|[---].b ḥtk h.b nmrt h.l r|[--.]arṣ.‘z k.ḏmr k UG5.2.2.7
--]k.l tšt k.l iršt.|[‘lm.---.--]k.l tšt k.liršt.|[---.]rpi.mlk ‘lm.b ‘z.|[rpu.m]lk.‘lm.b ḏmr h.bl.|[---].b ḥtk h.b nmrt h.l UG5.2.2.6
[-]m.|[---.]bqt[-].|[b] ǵb.ršp mh bnš.|šrp.w ṣp ḫršḫ.|‘lm b ǵb ḫyr.|ṯmn l ṯlṯm ṣin.|šb‘.alpm.|bt b‘l.ugrt.ṯn šm.|‘l UG5.12.B.3
l h.|[w] ytn.nn.|l.b‘ln.bn.|kltn.w l.|bn h.‘d.‘lm.|šḥr.‘lmt.|bnš bnšm.|l.yqḥnn.b d.|b‘ln.bn.kltn.|w.b d.bn h.‘d.|‘ 1008.15
b‘l.ṣpn b ‘r‘r.|pamt ṯlṯm š l qrnt.|ṯlḥn.b‘lt.bhtm.|‘lm.‘lm.gdlt l b‘l.|ṣpn.ilbt[.---.]d[--].|l ṣpn[.---.-]lu.|ilib[.---.b]‘l. UG5.13.32
.hl.‘ṣr.|tḥrr.l išt.w ṣḥrt.l pḥmm.aṯtm.a[ṯt.il].|aṯt.il.w ‘lm h.yhbr.špt hm.yš[q].|hn.špt hm.mtqtm.mtqtm.k lrmn[. 23[52].49
.|h[l.]‘ṣr.tḥrr.l išt.ṣḥrrt.l pḥmm.|a[ṯ]tm.aṯt.il.aṯt.il.w ‘lm h.w hm.|aṯtm.tṣḥn y.ad ad.nḥtm.ḫṭ k.|mmnnm.mṭ yd 23[52].42
d k.hl.‘ṣr.tḥrr.l išt.|w ṣḥrrt.l pḥmm.btm.bt.il.bt.il.|w ‘lm h.w hn.aṯtm.tṣḥn y.mt mt.|nḥtm.ḫṭ k.mmnnm.mṭ yd k 23[52].46
.qrt.ablm.|d ‘l k.mḫṣ.aqht.ǵzr.|‘wrt.yšt k.b‘l.l ht.|w ‘lm h.l ‘nt.p dr.dr.|‘db.uḫry.mṭ.yd h.|dnil.bt h.ymǵyn.yšt| 19[1AQHT].4.168
r.mym.d ‘[l k].|mḫṣ.aqht.ǵzr.amd.gr bt il.|‘nt.brḥ.p ‘lm h.‘nt.p dr[.dr].|‘db.uḫry mṭ.yd h.|ymǵ.l mrrt.tǵll.b nr. 19[1AQHT].3.154
ht.|ǵzr.šrš k.b arṣ.al.|yp‘.riš.ǵly.b d.ns‘ k.|‘nt.brḥ.p ‘lm h.|‘nt.p dr.dr.‘db.uḫry mṭ yd h.|ymǵ.l qrt.ablm.abl[m]. 19[1AQHT].3.161
bt.hnd.b d.|[‘b]dmlk.|[-]k.am‘[--].|[w.b] d.bn h[.‘]d ‘lm.|[w.un]ṯ.in[n.]b h.|[---.]n‘m[-]. 1009.17
bnš bnšm.|l.yqḥnn.b d.|b‘ln.bn.kltn.|w.b d.bn h.‘d.|‘lm.w unṯ.|in.b h. 1008.20
[---]n.yšt.rpu.mlk.‘lm.w yšt.|[--.]gṯr.w yqr.il.yṯb.b.‘ṯtrt.|il.ṯpṭ.b hd r‘y.d yšr.w UG5.2.1.1
.|b arb‘t ‘šrt.b‘l.|‘rkm.|b ṯmnt.‘šrt.yr|tḥṣ.mlk.brr.|‘lm.tzǵ.b ǵb.ṣpn.|nḥkt.ksp.w ḫrṣ ṯ‘ ṯn šm l btbt.|alp.w š šrp UG5.12.A.7
|bwrm š.iṯtqb.|w š.nbk m w.š.|gt mlk š.‘lm.|l kṯr.ṯn.‘lm.|tzǵ[.---.]nšm.pr. UG5.12.B.12
.ṯr.t‘rr k.|w t‘n.rbt.aṯrt ym.|tḥm k.il.ḥkm.ḥkmt.|‘m ‘lm.ḥyt.ḥẓt.|tḥm k.mlk n.aliy[n.]b‘l.|ṯpṭ n.w in.d ‘ln h.|kln 4[51].4.42
.|l btlt.‘nt.w t[‘]n.btlt.‘n[t].|tḥm k.il.ḥkm.ḥkm k.|‘m.‘lm.ḥyt.ḥẓt.tḥm k.|mlk n.aliyn.b‘l.ṯpṭ n.|in.d ‘ln h.klny y.q 3[‘NT.VI].5.39
š].|ilm.w š d[d.ilš.š.--.mlk].|yṯb.brr[.w mḥ-.---].|ym.[‘]lm.y‘[--.---].|[--.-]g[-.-]s w [---].|w yn[t.q]rt.y[---].|w al[p.l 35[3].8
‘.|iršt.aršt.|l aḫ y.l r‘ y.dt.|w ytnnn.|l aḫ h.l r‘ h.|r‘ ‘lm.|ttn.w tn.|w l ttn.|w al ttn.|tn ks yn.|w ištn.|‘bd.prṯ.t 1019.1.11
š.|dd ilš.š[.---.]mlk.yṯb br|r.w mḥ[--.---.]w q[--].|ym.‘lm.y[---.---].|t.k[-]ml.[---].|l[---].w y[nt.qrt.---].|[---.--]n[.w APP.II[173].9
rpt.ht.ib k.|b‘l m.ht.ib k.tmḫṣ.ht.tṣmt.ṣrt k.|tqḥ.mlk.‘lm k.drkt.dt dr dr k.|kṯr ṣmdm.ynḥt.w yp‘r.šmt hm.šm k 2.4[68].10
.|bn.b‘l.hwt.aliy.qrdm.|bhṯ.bn.ilm.mt.‘bd k.an.|w d ‘lm k.šmḫ.bn.ilm.mt.|[---.]g h.w aṣḥ.ik.yṣḥn.|[b‘l.‘m.aḫ y.i 5[67].2.20
iyn.b‘l.hwt.aliy.|qrdm.bhṯ.l bn.ilm mt.|‘bd k.an.w d.‘lm k.|tb‘.w l.yṯb.ilm.idk.|l ytn.pn.‘m.bn.ilm.mt.|tk.qrt h. 5[67].2.12
rt.š[.---].|[---.]l pdr[-.---].|ṣin aḥd h[.---].|l ‘ṯtrt[.---].|‘lm.kmm[.---].|w b ṯlṯ.ṣ[in.---].|l ll.pr[-.---].|mit š‘[rt.---].|p 37[22].7
---].|[--.]l ilt.š l ‘ṯt[rt.---].|[‘]ṣr.l pdr ṯṯ.ṣ[in.---].|tšnpn.‘lm.km[m.---].|w.l ll.‘ṣrm.w [---].|kmm.w.in.‘ṣr[.---].|w mit 38[23].6
alp w.š.l b‘lt.|bwrm š.iṯtqb.|w š.nbk m w.š.|gt mlk š.‘lm.|l kṯr.ṯn.‘lm.|tzǵ[.---.]nšm.pr. UG5.12.B.11
rḥqtm].|šb‘ d.w.šb‘[d.qlt].|ankn.rgmt.l.b‘l y.|l.špš.‘lm.l.‘ṯtrt.|l.‘nt.l.kl.il.alṯ[y].|nmry.mlk.‘lm.|mlk n.b‘l y.ḥw[2008.1.7
ǵb ḫyr.|ṯmn l ṯlṯm ṣin.|šb‘.alpm.|bt b‘l.ugrt.ṯn šm.|‘lm.l ršp.mlk.|alp w.š.l b‘lt.|bwrm š.iṯtqb.|w š.nbk m w.š.| UG5.12.B.7
m[---].|b unṯ.km.špš.|d brt.kmt.|br.ṣṭqšlm.|b unṯ.‘d ‘lm.|mišmn.nqmd.|mlk ugrt.|nqmd.mlk.ugrt.|ktb.spr hnd 1005.5
t.l.b‘l y.|l.špš.‘lm.l.‘ṯtrt.|l.‘nt.l.kl.il.alṯ[y].|nmry.mlk.‘lm.|mlk n.b‘l y.ḥw[t.--].|yšhr k.w.‘m.ṣ[--].|‘š[--.---]d.lik[t.- 2008.1.9
.b riš.|[--.-]nt.|[l.‘b]dmlk.|[--.-]m[-]r.|[w.l.]bn h.‘d.|[‘l]m.mn k.|mn km l.yqḥ.|bt.hnd.b d.|[‘b]dmlk.|[-]k.am‘[-- 1009.12
.|l b‘l.ṣpn b ‘r‘r.|pamt ṯlṯm š l qrnt.|ṯlḥn.b‘lt.bhtm.|‘lm.‘lm.gdlt l b‘l.|ṣpn.ilbt[.---.]d[--].|l ṣpn[.---.-]lu.|ilib[.---. UG5.13.32
rk.š.alp.w ṯlṯ.|ṣin.šlm[m.]šb‘ pamt.|l ilm.šb[‘.]l kṯr.|‘lm.t‘rbn.gṯrm.|bt.mlk.ṯql.ḫrṣ.|l špš.w yrḫ.l gṯr.|ṯql.ksp.ṭb. 33[5].9

šm[.---.--]t. | b yrḫ.ši[-.b ar]b‘t.‘š | rt.yr[tḥṣ.ml]k.brr. | ‘lm.š.š[--].l[--.]‘rb.šp | š.w ḥl[.ml]k. | bn.aup[š.--].bsbn hzpḫ ṯl APP.II[173].56
yd. | [k]lkl h. | [w] ytn.nn. | l.b‘ln.bn. | kltn.w l. | bn h.‘d.‘lm. | šḥr.‘lmt. | bnš bnšm. | l.yqḥnn.b d. | b‘ln.bn.kltn. | w.b d. 1008.14
mlakm.l h.lm.ank. | ksp.w yrq.ḫrṣ. | yd.mqm h.w ‘bd. | ‘lm.ṯlṯ.sswm.mrkbt. | b trbṣt.bn.amt. | p d.in.b bt y.ttn. | tn.l 14[KRT].3.140
.pbl.mlk]. | qḥ[.ksp.w yrq]. | ḫrṣ.[yd.mqm h]. | w ‘bd[.‘lm.ṯlṯ]. | sswm.m[rkbt]. | b trbṣ.[bn.amt]. | q[ḥ.kr]t[.šlmm]. | š 14[KRT].6.271
ḥm[.pbl.mlk]. | qḥ.[ksp.w yr]q. | ḫrṣ[.yd.mqm] h. | ‘bd[.‘lm.ṯlṯ]. | ss[wm.mrkbt]. | b[trbṣ.bn.amt]. | [qḥ.krt.šlmm]. | [šl 14[KRT].5.252
k]rt[.ṯ]‘. | lm.ank.ksp. | w yr[q.ḫrṣ]. | yd.mqm h.w ‘bd. | ‘lm.ṯlṯ.sswm. | mrkbt.b trbṣ. | bn.amt.p d.[i]n. | b bt y.ttn.tn. | 14[KRT].6.285
h.tḥm.pbl.mlk. | qḥ.ksp.w yrq.ḫrṣ. | yd.mqm h.w ‘bd.‘lm. | ṯlṯ.sswm.mrkbt. | b trbṣ.bn.amt. | qḥ.krt.šlmm. | šlmm.w 14[KRT].3.127
[-----.lm]. | [ank.ksp.w yrq]. | [ḫrṣ.]yd.mqm h. | [w ‘b]d.‘lm.ṯlṯ. | [ssw]m.mrkbt b trbṣ bn.amt. | [tn.b]nm.aqny. | [tn.ṯa 14[KRT].2.55
w ypt l ybmt.li[mm]. | w y‘ny.aliyn[.b‘l]. | lm.k qnym.‘l[m.--]. | k dr d.d yknn[.--]. | b‘l.yṣǵd.mli[.--]. | il hd.mla.u[--. 10[76].3.6
--.y]mǵy. | [---.]dr h. | [---.-]rš.l b‘l. | [---.-]ǵk.rpu mlk. | [‘lm.---.--]k.l tšt k.l iršt. | [‘lm.---.--]k.l tšt k.liršt. | [---.]rpi.ml UG5.2.2.5
-]rš.l b‘l. | [---.-]ǵk.rpu mlk. | [‘lm.---.--]k.l tšt k.l iršt. | [‘lm.---.--]k.l tšt k.liršt. | [---.]rpi.mlk ‘lm.b ‘z. | [rpu.m]lk.‘lm. UG5.2.2.5
[---.]unṯ[.---]. | [---.]šrq[-.---]. | [---.]‘d ‘lm[.---]. | [---.]‘d.admn[.---]. | [---.--]d.ytr.mṯ[--]. | [-----]. | [---- 2156.3
.hnd. | w mn km.l yqḥ. | spr.mlk.hnd. | b yd.ṣṭqšlm. | ‘d ‘lm. 1005.15

‘ln

rt.ṣbia.špš. | b‘l ny.w ymlk. | [y]ṣb.‘ln.w y[-]y. | [kr]t.ṯ‘.‘ln.bḫr. | [---].aṯt k.‘l. | [---] k.yššṣi. | [---.]ḫbr.rbt. | [ḫbr.ṯrr]t.il 15[128].5.22
k. | ‘m.‘lm.ḥyt.ḥẓt.tḥm k. | mlk n.aliyn.b‘l.ṯpṭ n. | in.d ‘ln h.klny y.qš h. | nbln.klny y.nbl.ks h. | any.l yṣḥ.ṯr.il.ab h.i 3[‘NT.VI].5.41
‘m ‘lm.ḥyt.ḥẓt. | tḥm k.mlk n.aliy[n.]b‘l. | ṯpṭ n.w in.d ‘ln h. | klny n.q[š] h.n[bln]. | klny n[.n]bl.ks h. | [an]y.l yṣḥ.ṯr 4[51].4.44
.il. | ‘rb.špš.l ymǵ. | krt.ṣbia.špš. | b‘l ny.w ymlk. | [y]ṣb.‘ln.w y[-]y. | [kr]t.ṯ‘.‘ln.bḫr. | [---].aṯt k.‘l. | [---] k.yššṣi. | [---.]ḫ 15[128].5.21
. | kḥṯ.il.nḥt. | b ẓr.hdm.id. | d pršа.b br. | n‘l.il.d qblbl. | ‘ln.ybl hm.ḫrṣ. | ṯlḥn.il.d mla. | mnm.dbbm.d | msdt.arṣ. | s‘.il 4[51].1.38
ṣat]. | btlt.‘nt.k [rḥ.npš h]. | k iṯl.brlt h.[b h.p‘nm]. | ṭṭṭ.‘l[n.pn h.td‘.b ‘dn]. | ksl.y[ṯbr.yǵṣ.pnt.ksl h]. | anš.[dt.ẓr h.yš 19[1AQHT].2.94
nt.tdrq.ybmt. | [limm].b h.p‘nm. | [ṭṭṭ.b ‘]dn.ksl. | [ṯṯbr.‘ln.p]n h.td[‘]. | tǵṣ[.pnt.ks]l h. | anš.dt.ẓr.[h]. | tšu.g h.w tṣḥ[. 4[51].2.18
b‘.tliyt. | hlm.‘nt.tph.ilm.b h.p‘nm. | ṭṭṭ.b‘d n.ksl.ṯṯbr. | ‘ln.pn h.td‘.tǵṣ.pnt. | ksl h.anš.dt.ẓr h.tšu. | g h.w tṣḥ.ik.mǵy. 3[‘NT].3.31
kn.k bṯnm. | mt.‘z.b‘l.‘z.ymṣḫn. | k lsmm.mt.ql. | b‘l.ql.‘ln.špš. | tṣḥ.l mt.šm‘.m‘. | l bn.ilm.mt.ik.tmt[ḫ]. | ṣ.‘m.aliyn.b‘ 6[49].6.22
.[b ṯ]mn[t.ap]. | sgrt.g[-].[-]ẓ[.---] h[.---]. | ‘n.ṯk[.---]. | ‘ln.ṯ[--.---]. | l p‘n.ǵl[m]m[.---]. | mid.an[--.]ṣn[--]. | nrt.ilm.špš 3[‘NT.VI].5.22
[---.]‘ln. | [---.--]ln. 4[51].3.52

‘lpy

.ayl. | [-----]. | ‘bd[--]. | bn.i[--]. | ‘d[--]. | ild[--]. | bn.qṣn. | ‘lpy. | kṯy. | bn.ẓmn. | bn.trdn. | ypq. | ‘bd. | qrḥ. | abšr. | bn.bdn. 2117.2.21
. | [-----]. | [-----]. | [---.--]ṯ. | [---.-]b.m.lk. | kdwṯ.ḥdṯ. | b d ‘lpy. 1112.20

‘lṣ

.aṯtm.t[--.---]. | [m]lakm.ylak.ym.[t‘dt.ṯpṭ.nhr]. | b ‘lṣ.‘lṣm.npr.š[--.---]. | uṭ.ṯbr.ap hm.tb‘.ǵlm[m.al.ṯṯb.idk.pnm]. | a 2.1[137].12
šnm.aṯtm.t[--.---]. | [m]lakm.ylak.ym.[t‘dt.ṯpṭ.nhr]. | b ‘lṣ.‘lṣm.npr.š[--.---]. | uṭ.ṯbr.ap hm.tb‘.ǵlm[m.al.ṯṯb.idk.pnm] 2.1[137].12

‘lr

bt.il. | b‘l.bt.admny. | b‘l.bt.pdy. | b‘l.bt.nqly. | b‘l.bt.‘lr. | b‘l.bt.ssl. | b‘l.bt.ṯrn. | b‘l.bt.ktmn. | b‘l.bt.ndbd. | [--].ṣnr. | 31[14].5
| bn.yḥnn.aḏddy. | bn.pdǵy.mḫdy. | bn.yyn.mḏrǵl. | bn.‘lr. | ḫṯpy.aḏddy. | ynḥm.aḏddy. | ykny.aḏddy. | m[--].aḏddy. | 2014.19

‘m

. | ‘bd k. | l.p‘n. | adt y. | šb‘ d. | w.šb‘ id. | mrḥqtm. | qlt. | ‘m.adt y. | mnm.šlm. | rgm.ṯṯb. | l.‘bd h. 52[89].12
. | hn ny.‘m ny. | kll.mid. | šlm. | w.ap.ank. | nḫt.ṯm ny. | ‘m.adt ny. | mnm.šlm. | rgm.ṯṯb. | l.‘bd k. 51[95].15
d ‘lm k.šmḫ.bn.ilm.mt. | [---.]g h.w aṣḥ.ik.yṣḥn. | [b‘l.‘m.aḫ y.ik].yqrun.hd. | [‘m.ary y.---.--]p.mlḥm y. | [---.---]lt.q 5[67].2.22
hr.k[--].ṣḥn.b‘l.‘m. | aḫ y.qran.hd.‘m.ary y. | w lḥm m ‘m aḫ y.lḥm. | w šṯ m.‘m.a[ḫ] yn. | p nšt.b‘l.[ṭ]‘n.iṭ‘n k. | [---.] 5[67].1.24
lḥm.hm.šb‘. | ydt y.b ṣ‘.hm.ks.ymsk. | nhr.k[--].ṣḥn.b‘l.‘m. | aḫ y.qran.hd.‘m.ary y. | w lḥm m ‘m aḫ y.lḥm. | w šṯ m.‘ 5[67].1.22
ḫ y.qran.hd.‘m.ary y. | w lḥm m ‘m aḫ y.lḥm. | w šṯ m.‘m.a[ḫ] yn. | p nšt.b‘l.[ṭ]‘n.iṭ‘n k. | [---.]ma[---] k.k tmḫṣ. | [ltn 5[67].1.25
‘l.ql.‘ln.špš. | tṣḥ.l mt.šm‘.m‘. | l bn.ilm.mt.ik.tmt[ḫ] | ṣ.‘m.aliyn.b‘l. | ik.al.yšm[‘] k.ṯr. | il.ab k.l ys‘.alt. | ṯbt k.l yhpk. 6[49].6.25
yrḫm.l yrḫm. | l šnt.[m]k.b šb‘. | šnt.w [--].bn.ilm.mt. | ‘m.aliyn.b‘l.yšu. | g h.w yṣḥ.‘l k.b[‘]l m. | pht.qlt.‘l k.pht. | dry 6[49].5.10
irt k.dṯ.ydṯ.m‘qb k.[ttb‘]. | [bt]lt.‘nt.idk.l ttn.[pnm]. | [‘m.a]qht.ǵzr.b alp.š[d]. | [rbt.]kmn.w ṣḥq.btlt.[‘nt]. | [tšu.]g h 18[3AQHT].1.21
.b ṣ‘.hm.ks.ymsk. | nhr.k[--].ṣḥn.b‘l.‘m. | aḫ y.qran.hd.‘m.ary y. | w lḥm m ‘m aḫ y.lḥm. | w šṯ m.‘m.a[ḫ] yn. | p nšt. 5[67].1.23
. | [---.]g h.w aṣḥ.ik.yṣḥn. | [b‘l.‘m.aḫ y.ik].yqrun.hd. | [‘m.ary y.---.--]p.mlḥm y. | [---.---]lt.qẓb. | [---.]šmḫ y. | [---.]tb‘ 5[67].2.23
| [abn.rgm.l td]‘.nš[m.w l t]bn. | [hmlt.a]rṣ.[tant.šmm.‘m.ar]ṣ. | thmt.[‘mn.kbkbm.abn.brq]. | d l t[d‘.šmm.at m.w a 3[‘NT].4.60
k]. | [h]wt.d aṯ[ny k.---.rgm.‘ṣ]. | w lḫšt.abn[.tant.šmm.‘m.arṣ.thmt]. | ‘m kbkbm[.abn.brq.d l td‘.šmm.at m]. | w ank 7.2[130].19
argm k. | hwt.w aṯny k.rgm. | ‘ṣ.w lḫšt.abn. | tant.šmm.‘m.arṣ. | thmt.‘mn.kbkbm. | abn.brq.d l.td‘.šmm. | rgm l td‘.n 3[‘NT].3.21
rgm k]. | hwt.w aṯny k[.rgm.‘ṣ.w lḫšt.abn]. | tunt.šmm.‘m[.arṣ.thmt.‘mn.kbkbm]. | rgm.l td‘.nš[m.w l tbn.hmlt.arṣ]. 1[‘NT.IX].3.14
| n‘m.[--.-]llm.trtḥṣ. | btlt.‘n[t].tptr‘ ṭd[h]. | limm.w t‘l.‘m.il. | ab h.ḥpr.p‘l k.y[--]. | šm‘ k.l arḫ.w bn.[--]. | limm.ql.b 13[6].20
lt.bt.abn.bt šmm w thm. | qrit.l špš.um h.špš.um.ql.bl.‘m. | il.mbk nhrm.b ‘dt.thmtm. | mnt.nṯk.nḫš.šmrr.nḫš. | ‘q šr UG5.7.2
]ḫ h.tšt bm.‘[--]. | [---.]zr h.ybm.l ilm. | [id]k.l ttn.pnm.‘m. | [il.]mbk nhrm.qrb. | [a]pq.thmtm.tgly.ḏd. | il.w tbu.qrš.. 6.1.32[49.1.4]
n.mtpd]m.t[ḥt.‘nt.arṣ.ṯlṯ.mtḥ.ǵyrm]. | [idk.]l ytn.pnm.‘m.[i]l.mbk.[nhrm.qrb.apq.thmtm]. | [ygly.]ḏl i[l].w ybu[.q]r 2.3[129].4
ḥẓ]r.k bn.aṯrt[.td‘ṣ.]p‘n. | [w tr.a]rṣ.id[k.l ttn.p]nm. | [‘m.i]l.mbk.nhr[m.qr]b.[ap]q. | [thm]tm.tgl.ḏ[d.]i[l.]w tbu. | [3[‘NT.VI].5.14
nm. | aṯr.btlt.‘nt. | w b‘l.tb‘.mrym.ṣpn. | idk.l ttn.pnm. | ‘m.il.mbk.nhrm. | qrb.apq.thmtm. | tgly.ḏd.il.w tbu. | qrš.mlk 4[51].4.21
[idk.l ttn.pnm]. | [‘m.il.mbk.nhrm]. | [qrb.apq.thmtm]. | [tgly.ḏd.il.w]tb[a]. | [q 5[67].6.02
.n‘mn.‘mq.nšm. | [td‘ṣ.p‘n]m.w tr.arṣ.idk. | [l ttn.pn]m.‘m il.mbk.nhrm. | [qrb.ap]q.thmtm tgly.ḏd il. | [w tbu.qr]š.m 17[2AQHT].6.47
šlm.ilm. | tǵr k.tšlm k. | hl ny.‘m n[y]. | kll.šlm. | ṯm ny.‘m.um y. | mnm.šlm. | w.rgm.ṯṯb.l y. | bm.ṯy.ndr. | iṯt.‘mn.mlk 50[117].11
ḥt.šlm.k.lik[t]. | um y.‘m y.ht.‘m[ny]. | kll.šlm.ṯm ny. | ‘m.um y.mnm.šlm. | w.rgm.ṯṯb.l y. | w.mnd‘.k.ank. | aḫš.mǵy 2009.1.8

al.trḫln.|‘tn.ḫrd.ank.|‘m ny.šlm.|kll.|w mnm.|šlm ‘m.|um y.|‘m y.ṯṯb.|rgm. 1015.17
--].|l ytn.l hm.ṯḥt b‘l[.---].|h.u qšt pn hdd.b y[.----].|‘m.b ym b‘l ysy ym[.---].|rmm.ḫnpm.mḫl[.---].|mlk.nhr.ibr 9[33].2.7
.|irš ḥym.w atn k.bl mt.|w ašlḥ k.ašspr k.‘m.b‘l.|šnt.‘m.bn il.tspr.yrḫm.|k b‘l.k yḥwy.y‘šr.ḥwy.y‘š.|r.w yšqyn h. 17[2AQHT].6.29
mt.|‘bd k.an.w d.‘lm k.|tb‘.w l.yṯb.ilm.idk.|l ytn.pn.‘m.bn.ilm.mt.|tk.qrt h.hmry.mk.ksu.|ṯbt.ḫḫ.arṣ.nḫlt h.tša. 5[67].2.14
w y‘n.lṭpn.il d pi|d dq.anm.l yrẓ.|‘m.b‘l.l y‘db.mrḥ.|‘m.bn.dgn.k tms m.|w ‘n.rbt.aṯrt ym.|blt.nmlk.‘ṯtr.‘rẓ.|ym 6.1.52[49.1.24]
šlm.l k.[il]m.|tǵr k.tšlm k.|hn ny.‘m n.š[l]m.|ṯm ny.‘[m.]bn y.|mnm.[šl]m[.r]gm[.ṯṯb].|ky.lik.bn y.|lḥt.akl.‘m y 2061.7
.‘bd[--].|‘bd k.|l p‘n.b‘l y.|ṯn id.šb‘ d.|mrḥqtm.|qlt.‘m.|b‘l y.mnm.|šlm.|[r]gm[.ṯṯb].|[l.]‘bd[k]. 2115.2.8
bl.nmlk.yd‘.ylḥn.|w y‘n.lṭpn.il d pi|d dq.anm.l yrẓ.|‘m.b‘l.l y‘db.mrḥ.|‘m.bn.dgn.k tms m.|w ‘n.rbt.aṯrt ym.|bl 6.1.51[49.1.23]
.|p[-]n.aḫ y m.ytn.b‘l.|[s]pu y.bn m.um y.kly y.|yṯb.‘m.b‘l.ṣrrt.|ṣpn.yšu g h.w yṣḥ.|aḫ y m.ytnt.b‘l.|spu y.bn m. 6[49].6.12
.ṯn.mṯpdm.|ṯḥt.‘nt.arṣ.ṯlṯ.mtḥ.ǵyrm.|idk.l ttn pnm.‘m.b‘l.|mrym.ṣpn.b alp.šd.rbt.kmn.|hlk.aḫt h.b‘l.y‘n.tdrq.| 3[‘NT].4.81
im.|šmḫ.btlt.‘nt.td‘ṣ.|p‘nm.w tr.arṣ.|idk.l ttn.pnm.|‘m.b‘l.mrym.ṣpn.|b alp.šd.rbt.kmn.|ṣḥq.btlt.‘nt.tšu.|g h.w 4[51].5.85
.b mh|mrt.ydd.il.ǵzr.|tb‘.w l.yṯb ilm.idk.|l ytn.pnm.‘m.b‘l.|mrym.ṣpn.w y‘n.|gpn.w ugr.ṯḥm.bn ilm.|mt.hwt.y 5[67].1.10
.‘q šr.|y‘db.ksa.w.yṯb.|tqru.l špš.um h.špš.um.ql bl.|‘m b‘l.mrym.ṣpn.mnt y.nṯk.|nḥš.šmrr.nḥš.‘q šr ln h.|mlḫš. UG5.7.9
.l aqht.ǵzr.|irš ḥym.w atn k.bl mt.|w ašlḥ k.ašspr k.‘m.b‘l.|šnt.‘m.bn il.tspr.yrḫm.|k b‘l.k yḥwy.y‘šr.ḥwy.y‘š.|r 17[2AQHT].6.28
.nḥš.‘q šr.ydb.ksa.|w yṯb.|tqru.l špš.u h.špš.um.ql.bl.‘m.|dgn.ttl h.mnt.nṯk.nḥš.šmrr.|nḥš.‘q šr.ln h.mlḫš.abd.ln UG5.7.14
k ymǵy.adn.|ilm.rbm ‘m dtn.|w yšal.mṯpṭ.yld.|w y‘ny.nn[.--].|t‘ny.n[---.-]ṯq.|w š UG5.6.2
bnt.q[-].|w št.b bt.ṯap[.--].|hy.yd h.w ym[ǵ].|mlak k.‘m dt[n].|lqḥ.mṯpṭ.|w y‘ny.nn.|dtn.bt n.mḥ[-].|l dg.w [-]kl UG5.6.11
lk.rb.b‘l y.u.|‘[--.]mlakt.‘bd h.|[---.]b‘l k.yḥpn.|[---.]‘m h.u ky.|[---.--]d k.k.tmǵy.|ml[--.--]š[.ml]k.rb.|b[‘l y.---]. 1018.5
n b p y sp|r hn.b špt y mn|t hn ṯlḥ h w mlg h y|ṯṯqt ‘m h b q‘t.|tq‘t ‘m prbḫt.|dmqt ṣǵrt kṯrt. 24[77].48
t.|b‘l.mt.my.lim.bn dgn.|my.hmlt.aṯr.b‘l.nrd.|b arṣ.‘m h.trd.nrt.|ilm.špš.‘d.tšb‘.bk.|tšt.k yn.udm‘t.gm.|tṣḥ.l nr 6[62].1.8
n.bn h b bt.šrš.b qrb.|hkl h.nṣb.skn.ilib h.b qdš.|ztr.‘m h.l arṣ.mšṣu.qṭr h.|l ‘pr.ḏmr.aṯr h.ṭbq.lḥt.|niṣ h.grš d.‘š 17[2AQHT].1.28
h.|[b bt.šrš.]b qrb.hkl h.|[nṣb.skn.i]lib h.b qdš.|[ztr.‘m h.l a]rṣ.mšṣu.|[qṭr h.l ‘pr.ḏ]mr.a[ṯ]r h.|[ṭbq.lḥt.niṣ h.gr] 17[2AQHT].1.46
šm‘.aliyn.b‘l.|yuhb.‘glt.b dbr.prt.|b šd.šḥlmmt.škb.|‘mn h.šb‘.l šb‘m.|tš[‘]ly.ṯmn.l ṯmnym.|w [th]rn.w tldn mṯ. 5[67].5.20
y.|[--]n.bt k.[---.]b‘[r.---].|[--]my.b d[-.--]y.[---].|[---.]‘m.w hm[.--]yt.w.[---].|[---.ṯ]y.al.an[k.--.]il[m.--]y.|[--.m]ṣl 1002.57
.‘q šr.y‘db.|ksa.w yṯb.|tqru l špš.um h.špš.um.ql bl.|‘m ḥrn.mṣd h.mnt.nṯk nḥš.|šmrr.nḥš.‘q šr.ln h.mlḫš.|abd.l UG5.7.58
dgn tt[--.---.-]l|‘.l kṯrt hl[l.sn]nt.|ylak yrḫ ny[r] šmm.‘m.|ḫr[ḫ]b mlk qẓ.tn nkl y|rḫ ytrḫ.ib t‘rb m b bh|t h.w atn 24[77].16
ḥš ‘q.|š.y‘db.ksa w yṯb.|tqru l špš.um h.špš.um.ql bl ‘m.|ṯṯ.w kmṯ.ḥryt h.mnt.nṯk.nḥš.šm|rr.nḥš.‘q šr.ln h.mlḫš UG5.7.35
ṯḥm.rgm.|mlk.|l ḥyil.|lm.tlik.‘m y.|ik y.aškn.|‘ṣm.l bt.dml.|p ank.atn.|‘ṣm.l k.|arb‘.‘ṣm. 1010.4
m.|yšlm.l k.ilm.|tǵr k.tšlm k.|lḥt.šlm.k.lik[t].|um y.‘m y.ht.‘m[ny].|kll.šlm.ṯm ny.|‘m.um y.mnm.šlm.|w.rgm. 2009.1.6
.l.klby.|šm‘t.ḫti.|nḫtu.ht.|hm.in mm.|nḫtu.w.lak.|‘m y.w.yd.|ilm.p.k mtm.|‘z.mid.|hm.nṯkp.|m‘n k.|w.mn 53[54].11
.hnd.|w.mlk.b‘l y.bnš.|bnny.‘mn.|mlakty.hnd.|ylak ‘m y.|w.t‘l.ṯḥ.hn.|[a]lpm.šswm.|[---].w.ṯb. 1012.36
dd.l kbd.šdm.|[ḥ]š k.[‘]ṣ k.‘bṣ k.‘m y.p‘n k.|[tls]mn.[‘]m y.twtḥ.išd k.|[dm.rgm.iṯ.l y.]w argm k.hwt.|[w aṯny k. 3[‘NT].4.56
rbdd].|l kbd.š[dm.ḥš k.‘ṣ k.‘bṣ k.‘m y.p‘n k.tls]|[m]n ‘m y t[wtḥ.išd k.dm.rgm.iṯ.l y.d argmn k].|[h]wt.d aṯ[ny k. 7.2[130].17
ṣ.|arbdd.l kbd.šdm.|ḥš k.‘ṣ k.‘bṣ k.|‘m y.p‘n k.tlsmn.‘m y.|twtḥ.išd k.dm.rgm.|iṯ.l y.w argm k.|hwt.w aṯny k.rg 3[‘NT].3.16
[ḥš k.‘ṣ k.‘bṣ k.‘]m y.p[‘]n k.|[tlsmn.‘m y.twt]ḥ.išd k.|[tk.ḫršn.---]r.[-]ḥm k.w št.|[---.]ẓ[--.-]rdy 1[‘NT.IX].2.2
.|‘db.bǵrt.ṯ[--. --].|ḥš k.‘ṣ k.‘[bṣ k.‘m y.p‘n k.tlsmn].|‘m y twtḥ.i[šd k.tk.ḫršn.-------------].|ǵr.ks.dm.r[gm.iṯ.l y.w 1[‘NT.IX].3.11
rbdd.l kbd.š]dm.ḥš k.|[‘ṣ k.‘bṣ k.‘m y.p‘]n k.tlsmn.|[‘m y.twtḥ.išd] k.tk.ḫršn.|[---.-]bd k.spr.|[---.-]nk. 1[‘NT.IX].2.23
y.km.|aḫ y.w šrš.km ary y.|nṣb.skn.ilib y.b qdš.|ztr.‘m y.l ‘pr.ḏmr.aṯr[y].|ṭbq lḥt.niṣ y.grš.|d ‘šy.ln.aḫd.yd y.b 17[2AQHT].2.17
m.]bn y.|mnm.[šl]m[.r]gm[.ṯṯb].|ky.lik.bn y.|lḥt.akl.‘m y.|mid y w ǵbn y.|w.bn y.hn kt.|yškn.anyt.|ym.yšrr.| 2061.10
.|[-----].|[-]š[--.---].|[-]r[--.--]y.|in m.‘bd k hwt.|[y]rš.‘m y.|mnm.iršt k.|d ḫsrt.w.ank.|aštn..l.iḫ y.|w.ap.ank.mn 2065.14
sk.šlm].l kbd.arṣ.|[arbdd.l kbd.š]dm.ḥš k.|[‘ṣ k.‘bṣ k.‘m y.p‘]n k.tlsmn.|[‘m y.twtḥ.išd] k.tk.ḫršn.|[---.-]bd k.spr. 1[‘NT.IX].2.22
---].|št.lskt.n[--.---].|‘db.bǵrt.ṯ[--. --].|ḥš k.‘ṣ k.‘[bṣ k.‘m y.p‘n k.tlsmn].|‘m y twtḥ.i[šd k.tk.ḫršn.-------------].|ǵr. 1[‘NT.IX].3.10
[ḥš k.‘ṣ k.‘bṣ k.‘]m y.p[‘]n k.|[tlsmn.‘m y.twt]ḥ.išd k.|[tk.ḫršn.---]r.[-]ḥm 1[‘NT.IX].2.1
.|sk.šlm.l kbd.arṣ.|arbdd.l kbd.šdm.|ḥš k.‘ṣ k.‘bṣ k.|‘m y.p‘n k.tlsmn.‘m y.|twtḥ.išd k.dm.rgm.|iṯ.l y.w argm k. 3[‘NT].3.16
m.sk.šlm.l kbd.arṣ.arbdd].|l kbd.š[dm.ḥš k.‘ṣ k.‘bṣ k.‘m y.p‘n k.tls]|[m]n ‘m y t[wtḥ.išd k.dm.rgm.iṯ.l y.d argmn 7.2[130].16
sk.šlm.|l kbd.arṣ.arbdd.l kbd.šdm.|[ḥ]š k.[‘]ṣ k.‘bṣ k.‘m y.p‘n k.|[tls]mn.[‘]m y.twtḥ.išd k.|[dm.rgm.iṯ.l y.]w arg 3[‘NT].4.55
pš.b‘l k.|‘[--.s]glt h.at.|ht[.---.]špš.b‘l k.|yd‘m.l.yd‘t.|‘m y.špš.b‘l k.|šnt.šntm.lm.l.tlk.|w.lḥt.akl.ky.|likt.‘m.špš.| 2060.15
n.ḫrd.ank.|‘m ny.šlm.|kll.|w mnm.|šlm ‘m.|um y.|‘m y.ṯṯb.|rgm. 1015.19
[---.--]d.‘m y.|[--.]spr.lm.likt.|[--]y.k išal hm.|[--.‘š]rm.kkr.ṯlṯ.|[--.] 1022.1
]d.n‘m.lbš k.|[-]dm.ṯn id.|[--]m.d.l.n‘mm.|[lm.]l.likt.‘m y.|[---.]‘bd.ank.|[---.‘b]d k.|[---.--]l y.‘m.|[---.]‘m.|[---.-- 2128.1.7
--]wy.rgm l.|mlkt.ugrt.|[--]kt.rgmt.|[--]y.l.ilak.|[---].‘m y.|[---]m.w.lm.|[---.]w.‘m k.|[---]m.ksp.|[---].‘m.|[---.-] 1016.12
.nṯkp.|m‘n k.|w.mnm.|rgm.d.tšm‘.|ṯmt.w.št.|b.spr.‘m y. 53[54].19
---].|[btl]t.‘nt.l kl.[---].|[tt]b‘.btlt.‘nt[.idk.l ttn.pnm].|‘m.yṭpn.mhr.š[t.tšu.g h].|w tṣḥ.yṯb.yṭp.[---].|qrt.ablm.ablm 18[3AQHT].4.6
.ḥmt.hlm.ytq.|w yṯb.|tqru.l špš.um h.špš.[um.q]l bl.‘m.|yrḫ.lrgt h.mnt.nṯk.n[ḥš].šmrr.|nḥš.‘q šr.ln h.mlḫš.abd. UG5.7.25
.b.ty ndr.|iṯt.w.ht.|[-]sny.uḏr h.|w.hm.ḫt.|‘l.w.likt.|‘m k.w.hm.|l.‘l.w.lakm.|ilak.w.at.|um y.al.tdḥṣ.|w.ap.mh 1013.18
ṯrt k.‘m k.šb‘t.|ǵlm k.ṯmn.ḫnzr k.|‘m k.pdry.bt.ar.|‘m k.ṭṭly.bt.rb.idk.|pn k.al ttn.tk.ǵr.|knkny.ša.ǵr.‘l ydm.|ḫ 5[67].5.11
‘m.špš.[---].|nšlḥ[.---].|[---.m]at.|[---.]mat.|š[--].išal.|‘m k.ybl.šd.|a[--].d‘.k.|šld.ašld.|hn.mrṯ.d.štt.|ašld b ldt k. 2009.2.4
.rgmt.l y.bly m.|alpm.arštl k.w.l y.|mn.bnš.d.l.i[--].‘[m k].|l.alpm.w.l.y[n.--]t.|w.bl.bnš.hw[-.--]y.|w.k.at.trg[m 2064.24
.ḏ]mr.a[ṯ]r h.|[ṭbq.lḥt.niṣ h.gr]š.d ‘šy.|[ln h.---].|z[tr.‘m k.l arṣ.mšṣu.qṭr k].|l ‘pr.ḏm[r.aṯr k.ṭbq].|lḥt.niṣ k.gr[š.d 17[2AQHT].2.1
y[š]lm.l k.ilm.|tǵr k.tšlm k.|hn ny.‘m n.|šlm.ṯm ny.|‘m k.mnm[.š]lm.|rgm.ṯṯ[b].|any kn.dt.|likt.mṣrm.|hn dt.b 2059.8
[---.--]y.hnn.|[---.kll].šlm.|[---.ṯ]mn.‘m k.|[m]nm.šlm.|[---.w.r]gm.ṯṯb. 2171.3
t k.rḥ k.mdl k.|mṭrt k.‘m k.šb‘t.|ǵlm k.ṯmn.ḫnzr k.|‘m k.pdry.bt.ar.|‘m k.ṭṭly.bt.rb.idk.|pn k.al ttn.tk.ǵr.|knkn 5[67].5.10
štn.b ḫrt.|ilm.arṣ.w at.qḥ.|‘rpt k.rḥ k.mdl k.|mṭrt k.‘m k.šb‘t.|ǵlm k.ṯmn.ḫnzr k.|‘m k.pdry.bt.ar.|‘m k.ṭṭly.bt. 5[67].5.8

[---.]l mdgkbr. | [---] y.‘m k. | [-]tn.l.stn. | [--.]d.n‘m.lbš k. | [-]dm.ṯn id. | [--]m.d.l.n‘ 2128.1.2
]kt.rgmt. | [--]y.l.ilak. | [---].‘m y. | [---]m.w.lm. | [---.]w.‘m k. | [---]m.ksp. | [---].‘m. | [---.-]n[-]. | [---.]l km. | [---.-]lk. | [- 1016.14
. | [---.--]d.šb‘m.kbd.dr‘. | [---.]kbd.ddm.kbd[.---]. | [---.]‘m.kbd.l.r‘[ym.---]. | [---].kbd.ṯmn.kb[d.---]. 1098.47
‘.nš[m.w l t]bn. | [hmlt.a]rṣ.[tant.šmm.‘m.ar]ṣ. | thmt.[‘mn.kbkbm.abn.brq]. | d l t[d‘.šmm.at m.w ank]. | ibǵ[y h.b t 3[‘NT].4.61
ny k.---.rgm.‘ṣ]. | w lḫšt.abn[.tant.šmm.‘m.arṣ.thmt]. | ‘m kbkbm[.abn.brq.d l td‘.šmm.at m]. | w ank.ib[ǵy h.---]. | [7.2[130].20
w aṯny k.rgm. | ‘ṣ.w lḫšt.abn. | tant.šmm.‘m.arṣ. | thmt.‘mn.kbkbm. | abn.brq.d l.td‘.šmm. | rgm l td‘.nšm.w l tbn. | h 3[‘NT].3.22
w aṯny k[.rgm.‘ṣ.w lḫšt.abn]. | tunt.šmm.‘m[.arṣ.thmt.‘mn.kbkbm]. | rgm.l td‘.nš[m.w l tbn.hmlt.arṣ]. | at.w ank.ib[1[‘NT.IX].3.14
[mrǵ]b.yd.m[ṯkt]. | mẓma.yd.mṯkt. | ṯṯkr.[--]dn. | ‘m.krt.mswn h. | arḫ.tẓǵ.l ‘gl h. | bn.ḫpt.l umht hm. | k tnḥn. 15[128].1.4
y. | [-----]. | [---.ttb‘]. | [mlakm.l yṯb]. | [idk.pnm.l ytn]. | [‘]m[.krt.mswn h]. | tš[an.g hm.w tṣḥn]. | tḥ[m.pbl.mlk]. | qḥ[. 14[KRT].6.266
t.ḥmr h. | l g‘t.alp.ḥrṯ.zǵt. | klb.ṣpr.w ylak. | mlakm.l k.‘m.krt. | mswn h.tḥm.pbl.mlk. | qḥ.ksp.w yrq.ḫrṣ. | yd.mqm 14[KRT].3.124
--.]lm y. | [---.--]p. | [---.d]bḥ. | t[---.id]k. | pn[m.al.ttn]. | ‘m.[krt.msw]n. | w r[gm.l krt.]ṯ‘. | tḥm[.pbl.mlk]. | qḥ.[ksp.w 14[KRT].5.247
nt[.---]. | ṯn[.---]. | w[.-----]. | l[.-----]. | h[--.---]. | šp[š.---]. | ‘m.k[--.lḥt]. | akl.yṯ[ṯb.--]pt. | ib.‘ltn.a[--.--]y. | w.spr.in[.-.]‘d 2060.29
pr.bn.šm. | [b.---.]knm.ṯṯm.l.mit.dr‘.w.mit.drt. | w[.---.]‘m.l.mit.dd.ṯn.kbd.ḥpr.bnšm.ṯmnym.dd. | l u[-]m. | b.ṯbq.arb 1098.8
ll.snnt.bnt h | ll b‘l gml.yrdt. | b ‘rgzm.b bz tdm. | lla y.‘m lẓpn i | l ḏ.pid.hn b p y sp | r hn.b špt y mn | t hn ṯlḫ h w 24[77].44
ṯn.mṯpdm.tḥt.[‘nt.arṣ.ṯlṯ.mtḥ]. | ǵyrm.idk.l yt[n.pnm.‘m.lṭpn]. | il d pid.tk ḫrš[n.---.tk.ǵr.ks]. | ygly ḏd.i[l.w ybu.qr 1[‘NT.IX].3.21
| l yblt. | w ht.luk ‘m ml[kt]. | tǵsdb.šmlšn. | w tb‘ ank. | ‘m mlakt h šm‘ h. | w b.‘ly skn.yd‘ rgm h. | w ht ab y ǵm[--]. 1021.7
-]. | w.b.glb. | phnn.w. | mndym. | bdnh. | l[q]ḥt. | [--]km.‘m.mlk. | [b]ǵl hm.w.iblbl hm. | w.b.ṯb h.[---]. | spr ḥ[--.---]. | 2129.9
tḥm.ydn.‘m.mlk. | b‘l h.nǵr.ḥwt k. | w l.a[--]t.tšknn. | ḫmšm.l mi[t].an 2062.1.1
s[--.---]. | b hm.w.rgm.hw.al[--]. | atn.ksp.l hm.‘d. | ilak.‘m.mlk. | ht.lik[t.--.]mlk[.--]. | w.mlk.yštal.b.hn[--]. | hmt.w.a 2008.2.8
] d.šb‘ [d]. | [mr]ḥqtm. | qlt. | ‘bd k.b. | lwsnd. | [w] b ṣr. | ‘m.mlk. | w.ht. | mlk.syr. | ns.w.ṯm. | ydbḥ. | mlǵ[.---]. | w.m[--.- 2063.12
y.‘m.um y. | mnm.šlm. | w.rgm.ṯṯb.l y. | bm.ṯy.ndr. | iṯt.‘mn.mlkt. | w.rgm y.l[--]. | lqt.w.pn. | mlk.nr b n. 50[117].15
š. | ‘q.šr.y‘db.ksa.w yṯb. | tqru l špš um h.špš um ql.bl.‘m. | mlk.‘ṯtrt h.mnt.nṯk.nḥš.šmrr. | nḥš.‘q šr.ln h.mlḫš abd.l UG5.7.40
.il[m]. | tǵ[r] k.tš[lm] k. | [h]l ny.‘m n[.š]lm. | w.ṯm [ny.‘m.mlkt.u]m y. | mnm[.šlm]. | w.rgm[.ṯṯb.l] y. | hl ny.‘mn. | ml 1013.9
l yblt.ḫbṯm. | ap ksp hm. | l yblt. | w ht.luk ‘m ml[kt]. | tǵsdb.šmlšn. | w tb‘ ank. | ‘m mlakt h šm‘ h. | w b. 1021.4
y]. | qlt[.l um] y. | yšlm.il[m]. | tǵ[r] k.tš[lm] k. | [h]l ny.‘m n[.š]lm. | w.ṯm [ny.‘m.mlkt.u]m y. | mnm[.šlm]. | w.rgm[.ṯ 1013.8
l.mlk.ugrt. | rgm. | yšlm.l k.[il]m. | tǵr k.tšlm k. | hn ny.‘m n.š[l]m. | ṯm ny.‘[m.]bn y. | mnm.[šl]m[.r]gm[.ṯṯb]. | ky.lik 2061.6
tḥm.mlk.ṣr.aḫ k. | y[š]lm.l k.ilm. | tǵr k.tšlm k. | hn ny.‘m n. | šlm.ṯm ny. | ‘m k.mnm[.š]lm. | rgm.ṯṯ[b]. | any kn.dt. | l 2059.6
p‘n.adt ny. | mrḥqtm. | qlny.ilm. | tǵr k. | tšlm k. | hn ny.‘m ny. | kll.mid. | šlm. | w.ap.ank. | nḫt.ṯm ny. | ‘m.adt ny. | mn 51[95].10
l.p‘n.um y. | qlt.l.um y. | yšlm.ilm. | tǵr k.tšlm k. | hl ny.‘m n[y]. | kll.šlm. | ṯm ny.‘m.um y. | mnm.šlm. | w.rgm.ṯṯb.l y. 50[117].9
.l k.ilm. | tǵr k.tšlm k. | lḥt.šlm.k.lik[t]. | um y.‘m y.ht.‘m[ny]. | kll.šlm.ṯm ny. | ‘m.um y.mnm.šlm. | w.rgm.ṯṯb.l y. | 2009.1.6
b y.mid.w um. | tšmḫ.m ab. | w al.trḥln. | ‘tn.ḫrd.ank. | ‘m ny.šlm. | kll. | w mnm. | šlm ‘m. | um y. | ‘m y.ṯṯb. | rgm. 1015.14
y.b[t.a] | b h lb[u] y‘rr.w y‘[n]. | yrḫ nyr šmm.w n‘[n]. | ‘ma nkl ḫtn y.a[ḫ]r. | nkl yrḫ ytrḫ.adn h. | yšt mṣb.mznm.u 24[77].32
lkn. | šd.tṣdn.pat.mdbr.w ngš.hm.nǵr. | mdr‘.w ṣḥ hm.‘m.nǵr.mdr‘ y.nǵr. | nǵr.ptḥ.w ptḥ hw.prṣ.b‘d hm. | w ‘rb.h 23[52].69
.aliyn.b‘l. | iy.zbl.b‘l.arṣ. | ttb‘.btlt.‘nt. | idk.l ttn.pnm. | ‘m.nrt.ilm.špš. | tšu.g h.w tṣḥ. | tḥm.ṯr.il.ab k. | hwt.lṭpn.ḥtk 6[49].4.32
hbt.ṯr.t‘rr k. | w t‘n.rbt.aṯrt ym. | tḥm k.il.ḥkm.ḥkmt. | ‘m ‘lm.ḥyt.ḥẓt. | tḥm k.mlk n.aliy[n.]b‘l. | ṯpṭ n.w in.d ‘ln h. | 4[51].4.42
[n]. | l btlt.‘nt.w t[‘]n.btlt.‘n[t]. | tḥm k.il.ḥkm.ḥkm k. | ‘m.‘lm.ḥyt.ḥẓt.tḥm k. | mlk n.aliyn.b‘l.ṯpṭ n. | in.d ‘ln h.klny 3[‘NT.VI].5.39
ḥš.‘q šr.y‘db.ksa.w yṯb. | tqru l špš.um h.špš.um.ql.bl.‘m. | ‘nt w ‘ṯtrt inbb h.mnt.nṯk. | nḥš.šlḥm.nḥš.‘q šr[.y‘]db.ks UG5.7.19
itnn y. | ytt.nḥšm.mhr k.bn bṯn. | itnn k. | aṯr ršp.‘ṯtrt. | ‘m ‘ṯtrt.mr h. | mnt.nṯk.nḥš. UG5.7.TR2
idk.al.ttn.pnm. | ‘m.ǵr.trǵzz. | ‘m.ǵr.ṯrmg. | ‘m.tlm.ǵṣr.arṣ. | ša.ǵr.‘l.ydm. | ḫlb.l 4[51].8.2
idk.al.ttn.pnm. | ‘m.ǵr.trǵzz. | ‘m.ǵr.ṯrmg. | ‘m.tlm.ǵṣr.arṣ. | ša.ǵr.‘l.ydm. | ḫlb.l ẓr.rḥtm. | w 4[51].8.3
rk | t.w ǵlm.l ‘bd. | il.ttb‘.mlakm. | l yṯb.idk.pnm. | l ytn.‘mm.pbl. | mlk.tšan. | g hm.w tṣḥn. | tḥm.krt.ṯ[‘]. | hwt.[n]‘mn 14[KRT].6.302
gn.art m.pḏ h.tb‘.ǵlmm.l ṯṯb.[idk.pnm]. | l ytn.tk.ǵr.ll.‘m.phr.m‘d.ap.ilm.l lḥ[m]. | yṯb.bn qdš.l ṯrm.b‘l.qm.‘l.il.hlm 2.1[137].20
-.---]. | uṯ.ṯbr.ap hm.tb‘.ǵlm[m.al.ṯṯb.idk.pnm]. | al.ttn.‘m.pḫr.m‘d.t[k.ǵr.ll.l p‘n.il]. | al.tpl.al.tštḥwy.pḫr [m‘d.qmm 2.1[137].14
.b špt y mn | t hn ṯlḫ h w mlg h y | ṯtqt ‘m h b q‘t. | tq‘t ‘m prbḫt. | dmqt ṣǵrt kṯrt. 24[77].49
alṯ[y]. | nmry.mlk.‘lm. | mlk n.b‘l y.ḥw[t.--]. | yšhr k.w.‘m.ṣ[--]. | ‘š[--.---]d.lik[t.---]. | w [----]. | k[--.---]. | ‘šrm[.---]. | tšt 2008.1.11
arb‘.‘šr h.šmn. | d.lqḥt.ṯlǵdy. | w.kd.ištir.‘m.qrt. | ‘št.‘šr h.šmn. | ‘mn.bn.aǵlmn. | arb‘m.ksp.‘l.qrt. | b.šd 1083.3
ḥš. | ‘q šr.y‘db.ksa.w yṯb. | tqru.l špš.um h.špš.um.ql b.‘m. | ršp.bbt h.mnt.nḥš.šmrr. | nḥš.‘q šr.ln h.mlḫš.abd.ln h.y UG5.7.30
š.‘q šr.y‘db ksa. | w yṯb. | tqru l špš.um h.špš.um.ql bl ‘m. | šḥr.w šlm šmm h mnt.nṯk.nḥš. | šmrr.nḥš ‘q šr.ln h.mlḫ UG5.7.51
. | ‘m y.špš.b‘l k. | šnt.šntm.lm.l.tlk. | w.lḥt.akl.ky. | likt.‘m.špš. | b‘l k.ky.akl. | b.ḥwt k.inn. | špš n.[---]. | hm.al[k.--]. | y 2060.18
tḥm.špš. | l.‘mrpi.rgm. | ‘m špš.kll.mid m. | šlm. | l.[--]n.špš. | ad[.‘]bd h.uk.škn. | k.[--- 2060.3
ṯb.l y. | w.mnd‘.k.ank. | aḥš.mǵy.mnd‘. | k.igr.w.u.[--]. | ‘m.špš.[---]. | nšlḥ[.---]. | [---.m]at. | [---.]mat. | š[--].išal. | ‘m k. 2009.1.13
idk.al.ttn.pnm. | ‘m.ǵr.trǵzz. | ‘m.ǵr.ṯrmg. | ‘m.tlm.ǵṣr.arṣ. | ša.ǵr.‘l.ydm. | ḫlb.l ẓr.rḥtm. | w rd.bt ḫpṯt. | a 4[51].8.4
n y.aḫ y.rgm. | ilm.tǵr k. | tšlm k. | iky.lḥt. | spr.d likt. | ‘m.ṯryl. | mh y.rgmt. | w ht.aḫ y. | bn y.yšal. | ṯryl.p rgm. | l ml 138.8
n y.aḫ y.rgm. | ilm.tǵr k. | tšlm k. | ik y.lḥt. | spr.d likt. | ‘m.ṯryl. | mh y.rgmt. | w ht.aḫ y. | bn y.yšal. | ṯryl.p rgm. | l ml 138.8
[.apn]k. | [pb]l[.mlk.g]m.l att | [h.k]y[ṣḥ.]šm‘.m‘. | [--.]‘m[.-.]att y[.-]. | [---.]tḥm. | [---]t.[ ]r. | [---.--]n. | [---] h.l ‘db. | [- 14[KRT].5.230
rynm.ḥ[--].kl h. | kdm.l.zn[-.---]. | kd.l.aṯr[y]m. | kdm.‘m.[--]n. | kd.mštt.[---]n. | kdm.l.mḏrǵlm. | kd.l.mṣrym. | kd.m 1089.4
| [b]ǵl hm.w.iblbl hm. | w.b.ṯb h.[---]. | spr ḥ[--.---]. | w.‘m[.---]. | yqḥ[.---]. | w.n[--.---]. 2129.13
. | [lm.]l.likt.‘m y. | [---.]‘bd.ank. | [---.‘b]d k. | [---.--]l y.‘m. | [---.]‘m. | [---.--]y.w.lm. | [---.]il.šlm. | [---.]ank. | [---].mly. 2128.2.2
[---].‘m y. | [---]m.w.lm. | [---.]w.‘m k. | [---]m.ksp. | [---].‘m. | [---.-]n[-]. | [---.]l km. | [---.-]lk. | [---.--]m. | t[--.---].t[-]ṯm. 1016.16
likt.‘m y. | [---.]‘bd.ank. | [---.‘b]d k. | [---.--]l y.‘m. | [---.]‘m. | [---.--]y.w.lm. | [---.]il.šlm. | [---.]ank. | [---].mly. 2128.2.3
rg[m]. | hn.i[---]. | ds[-.---]. | t[--.---]. | a[--.---]. | [---].ksp.‘m[.---]. | [---.]iltḥm.w.[---]. | šm‘t.ḥwt[.---]. | [---].nzdt.qr[t]. | [2127.2.1
y[šlm.l k.ilm]. | tǵ[r k.tšlm k]. | ‘bd[.---]y. | ‘m[.---]y. | šk[--.--.]kll. | šk[--.--.]hm. | w.k[b--.---]. | ‘m[.---]m i 2065.4
-]y. | ‘m[.---]y. | šk[--.--.]kll. | šk[--.--.]hm. | w.k[b--.---]. | ‘m[.---]m ib. | [---.--]m. | [-----]. | [-]š[--.---]. | [-]r[--.--]y. | in m.‘ 2065.8

‘md

[.abn.brq.d l td‘.šmm.at m]. | w ank.ib[ǵy h.---]. | [-].l y‘mdn.i[---.---]. | kpr.šb‘ bn[t.rḥ.gdm.w anhbm]. | kla[t.ṯǵ]r[t. 7.2[130].22

‘my

bt šbn. | iy‘dm.w b‘l h. | ddy. | ‘my. | iwrnr. | alnr. | maẖdt. | aby. | [-----]. | [-]nt. | ydn. | mnn.w 107[15].4
b d.krb[-]. | šd.b d.bn.pṯd̲. | šd.b d.dr.khnm. | šd.b d.bn.‘my. | šd.b d.bn.‘yn. | ṯn.šdm.b d.klṯtb. | šd.b d.krz[n]. | ṯlṯ.šd 2090.18
m. | bn.b‘ln.ṯqlm. | ‘bdyrẖ.nqd.ṯqlm. | bt.sgld.ṯqlm. | bn.‘my.ṯqlm. | bn.brq.ṯqlm. | bn.ẖnzr.ṯqlm. | dqn.nsk.arb‘t. | bn.ẖ 122[308].1.14
.---.b]n.mlk. | ṯ[n.---.]gpn. | [-----]. | [---.--]b. | b[--.---.b]n.‘my. 1150.6

‘myd

ṣṣ mr‘m ẖmšm ẖmš kbd. | ṣṣ ubn ẖmš ‘šr h. | ṣṣ ‘myd ẖmšm. | ṣṣ tmn.ẖmšm. | [ṣṣ] ‘mtd̲l ṯlṯm. | ṣṣ ‘mlbi ṯṯ l ‘šr 2097.3

‘myn

n].pls. | abrš[p.bn.]ẖrpn. | gmrš[.bn].mrnn. | ‘bdmlk.bn.‘myn. | agyn.r‘y. | abmlk.bn.ilrš. | iḫyn.bn.ẖryn. | [ab]ǵl.bn.gd 102[323].4.8
pẖn. | bn.ṯryn. | bn.dll. | bn.ẖswn. | mrynm. | ‘zn. | ḥyn. | ‘myn. | ilyn. | yrb‘m. | n‘mn. | bn.kbl. | kn‘m. | bdlm. | bn.ṣǵr. | kl 1046.3.36
hm. | b[n.---]. | bn.gzry. | bn.atyn. | bn.ttn. | bn.rwy. | bn.‘myn. | bdl.mrynm. | bn.ṣqn. | bn.šyn. | bn.prtn. | bn.ypr. | mru 113[400].3.5
]. | bn.at[--]. | bn.qnd̲. | ṣmq[-]. | bn.anny. | bn.‘mtd̲l. | bn.‘myn. | bn.alz. | bn.birtn. | [bn.]ylkn. | [bn.]krwn. | [bn.-]ty. | [b 117[325].1.11
‘zn.bn.irbn. | bn.mglb. | bn.ntp. | ‘myn.bn ǵḫpn. | bn.kbln. | bn.bly. | bn.ṯ‘y. | bn.nṣdn. | klby. 104[316].4
m.bn[.---]. | gn.bn[.---]. | klby.[bn.---]. | šmmlk bn[.---]. | ‘myn.bn.[---]. | mtb‘l.bn[.---]. | ymy.bn[.---]. | ‘bd‘n.p[--.---]. | [- 102[322].5.10
[u]brš. | ẖmšt.‘šrt. | b.šd.bn.[-]n. | ṯl[ṯt].‘šr[t]. | b.š[d].bn.‘myn. | ẖmšt. | b.[šd.--]n. | ẖ[m]št[.‘]šrt. | [ar]b‘m.ksp. | [---]yn. 1083.11
yy. | mit.ṯṯm.kbd. | l.bn.yšm‘. | mit.arb‘m.kbd. | l.liy.bn.‘myn. | mit.ẖmšm.kbd. | d.škn.l.ks.ilm. 1143.12
l.b‘lz.l.bn.‘mnr. | šd.kn‘m.l.bn.‘mnr. | šd.bn.krwn.l bn.‘myn. | šd.bn.prmn.l aẖny. | šd.bn ḥnn.l bn.adld̲n. | šd.bn.nṣd 2089.5
[-]k[-.---]. | ar[--.---]. | yrt.[---]. | ṯṯ.prš[.---]. | bn.‘myn[.---]. 2152.5

‘mkṯr

.yšlḥm.nḥš. | ‘q šr.y‘db.ksa.w yṯb. | tqru.l špš.um.ql bl.‘m | kṯr.w ẖss.kptr h.mnt.nṯk.nḥš. | šmrr.nḥš.‘q šr.ln h.mlẖš. UG5.7.45

‘mlbi

.prmn.l aẖny. | šd.bn ḥnn.l bn.adld̲n. | šd.bn.nṣdn.l bn.‘mlbi. | šd.ṯpẖln.l bn.ǵl. | w dṯn.nḥl h.l bn.pl. | šd.krwn.l aẖn. 2089.8
h. | ṣṣ ‘myd ẖmšm. | ṣṣ tmn.ẖmšm. | [ṣṣ] ‘mtd̲l ṯlṯm. | ṣṣ ‘mlbi ṯṯ l ‘šrm. | ṣṣ bn adty ẖmšm. | ṣṣ amtrn arb‘m. | ṣṣ iytlm 2097.6

‘mlbu

. | ẖyml.ṯlṯm. | ǵlkz.ṯlṯm. | mlkn‘m.‘šrm. | mr‘m.‘šrm. | ‘mlbu.‘šrm. | ‘mtd̲l.‘šrm. | y‘d̲rd.‘šrm. | gmrd.‘šrm. | ṣdqšlm.‘š 1116.7

‘mm

n. | [a]ṯrt.gm.l ǵlm h. | b‘l.yṣḥ.‘n.gpn. | w ugr.bn.ǵlmt. | ‘mm ym.bn.ẓlm[t]. | rmt.pr‘t.ibr[.mnt]. | ṣḥrrm.ḥbl[.--]. | ‘rpt 8[51FRAG].8
.arṣ.gm.l ǵ | [lm] h.b‘l k.yṣḥ.‘n. | [gpn].w ugr.b ǵlmt. | [‘mm.]ym.bn.ẓlmt.r | [mt.pr‘]t.ibr.mnt. | [ṣḥrrm.ḥbl.‘]rpt. | [--- 4[51].7.55

‘mn

.šmn. | d.lqḥt.ṯlǵdy. | w.kd.ištir.‘m.qrt. | ‘št.‘šr h.šmn. | ‘mn.bn.aǵlmn. | arb‘m.ksp.‘l.qrt. | b.šd.bn.[u]brš. | ẖmšt.‘šrt. | 1083.5
mitm.ksp.‘mn.b[n].ṣdqn. | w.kkrm.ṯlṯ. | mit.ksp.‘mn. | bn.ulbtyn. | w.kkr.ṯlṯ. | ksp.d.nkly.b.šd. | mit.ẖmšt.kbd. 1143.3
mitm.ksp.‘mn.b[n].ṣdqn. | w.kkrm.ṯlṯ. | mit.ksp.‘mn. | bn.ulbtyn. | w.kkr 1143.1
ls[--.---]. | ṣḥ[.---]. | ky.m[--.---]. | w pr[--.---]. | tštil[.---]. | ‘mn.bn[.---]. 1021.16
--]. | w.drm.‘tr[--.---]. | w ap.ht.k[--.]škn. | w.mṯnn[.---.]‘mn k. | [-]štš.[---.]rgm y. | [-]wd.r[-.]pǵt. | [---.--]t.yd‘t. | [----.r 54.1.21[13.2.6]
.tmǵyy.hn. | alpm.ššwm.hnd. | w.mlk.b‘l y.bnš. | bnny.‘mn. | mlakty.hnd. | ylak ‘m y. | w.t‘l.ṯh.hn. | [a]lpm.ššwm. | [-- 1012.34
y.‘m.mlkt.u]m y. | mnm[.šlm]. | w.rgm[.ṯṯb.l] y. | hl ny.‘mn. | mlk.b.ṯy ndr. | iṯt.w.ht. | [-]sny.ud̲r h. | w.hm.ẖt. | ‘l.w.li 1013.12
n.[---]. | ik y.[---]. | w l n[qmd.---]. | [w]nqmd.[---]. | [-.]‘mn.šp[š.mlk.rb]. | b‘l h.šlm.[w spš]. | mlk.rb.b‘l h.[---]. | nqm 64[118].11
ǵ[-.---]. | šp[š.---]. | ql.[---]. | w mlk[.nhš.w mlk.mg]šẖ. | ‘mn.[---]. | ik y.[---]. | w l n[qmd.---]. | [w]nqmd.[---]. | [-.]‘mn. 64[118].7

‘mnr

dnn.ṯlṯ.ṣmdm. | bn.‘mnr. | bn.kmn. | bn.ibyn. | bn.mryn.ṣmd.w.ḥrṣ. | bn.prsn.ṣmd 2113.2
.bn.ẖtb.l bn.y‘d̲rd. | šd.gl.b‘lz.l.bn.‘mnr. | šd.kn‘m.l.bn.‘mnr. | šd.bn.krwn.l bn.‘myn. | šd.bn.prmn.l aẖny. | šd.bn ḥn 2089.4
bn.šty.l.bn.ṯbrn. | šd.bn.ẖtb.l bn.y‘d̲rd. | šd.gl.b‘lz.l.bn.‘mnr. | šd.kn‘m.l.bn.‘mnr. | šd.bn.krwn.l bn.‘myn. | šd.bn.pr 2089.3
mn.l.bn.šty. | šd.bn.arws.l.bn.ẖlan. | šd.bn.ibryn.l.bn.‘mnr. 1102.20

‘ms

[s]p[r] ušknym.dt.[b d.---]. | bn.btr. | bn.‘ms. | bn.pṣn. | bn.agmz. | bn.[--]n. | bn.a[--]. | [------]. | [------]. | [2021.1.3
r.aṯr h.ṭbq.lḥt. | niṣ h.grš d.‘šy.ln h. | aẖd.yd h.b škrn.m‘ms h. | [k]šb‘ yn.spu.ksm h.bt.b‘l. | [w m]nt h bt.il.ṯḥ.gg h 17[2AQHT].1.31
.b ‘rpt. | šrh.l arṣ.brqm. | bt.arzm.yklln h. | hm.bt.lbnt.y‘msn h. | l yrgm.l aliyn b‘l. | ṣḥ.ẖrn.b bhm k. | ‘d̲bt.b qrb.hkl 4[51].5.73
r.aṯr[y]. | ṭbq lḥt.niṣ y.grš. | d ‘šy.ln.aẖd.yd y.b š | krn m‘ms y k šb‘t yn. | spu.ksm y.bt.b‘l.[w]mn[t]. | y.bt.il.ṯḥ.gg y 17[2AQHT].2.20
| spu.ksm k.bt.[b‘l.w mnt k]. | bt il.aẖd.yd k.b [škrn]. | m‘ms k.k šb‘t.yn.ṭ[ẖ]. | gg k.b ym.ṭiṭ.rḥṣ. | npṣ k.b ym rṭ.b un 17[2AQHT].2.6
.špš.‘d.tšb‘.bk. | tšt.k yn.udm‘t.gm. | tṣḥ.l nrt.ilm.špš. | ‘ms m‘.l y.aliyn.b‘l. | tšm‘.nrt.ilm.špš. | tšu.aliyn.b‘l.l ktp. | ‘nt 6[62].1.12
| yšt[.il.y]n.‘d šb‘.trṯ.‘d škr. | il.hlk.l bt h.yštql. | l ḥṭr h.y‘msn.nn.ṯkmn. | w šnm.w ngšnn.ḥby. | b‘l.qrnm w d̲nb.ylšn. UG5.1.1.18
.ank. | aštn..l.iẖ y. | w.ap.ank.mnm. | [ẖ]s[r]t.w.uẖ y. | [y]‘msn.ṯmn. | w.[u]ẖ y.al yb‘rn. 2065.20

ʿmsn

spr.bnš.mlk. | d taršn.ʿmsn. | bṣr.abn.špšyn. | dqn. | aǵlmn. | knʿm. | aḫršp. | anntn. | b 2067.1.2

ʿmq

. | krk.aḥt. | b.sǵy.ḫmš.ḫrmṯt.nit. | krk.mʿṣd.mqb. | b.gt.ʿmq.ḫmš.ḫrmṯt.n[it]. | krk.mʿṣd.mqb. | b.gwl.ṯmn.ḫrmṯt.[nit] 2048.9
[t.ṯǵ]r[t.bht.ʿnt.w tqry.ǵlmm.b št.ǵr]. | ap ʿnt tm[ṯḫṣ.b ʿmq.tḫtṣb.bn.qrytm.tmḫṣ]. | lim ḫ[p.ym.---]. | [--]m.t[-]t[.---]. 7.2[130].25
ǵrt. | bht.ʿnt.w tqry.ǵlmm. | b št.ǵr.w hln.ʿnt.tm | ṯḫṣ.b ʿmq.tḫtṣb.bn. | qrytm tmḫṣ.lim.ḫp y[m]. | tṣmt.adm.ṣat.š[p]š. 3[ʿNT].2.6
.ʿnt.l bt h.tmǵyn. | tštql.ilt.l hkl h. | w l.šbʿt.tmtḫṣ h.b ʿmq. | tḫtṣb.bn.qrtm.ṯṯʿr. | ksat.l mhr.ṯʿr.ṯlḥnt. | l ṣbim.hdmm. 3[ʿNT].2.19
š h.ʿtkt r[išt]. | [l bmt h.---.]hy bt h tʿrb. | [---.tm]tḫṣ b ʿmq. | [tḫtṣb.bn.qrtm.ṯṯʿr.ṯlḥnt.]l ṣbim. | [hdmm.l ǵzrm.mid.t 7.1[131].4
ntb.pšʿ. | [---].b ntb.gan.ašql k.tḥt. | [pʿn y.a]nk.nʿmn.ʿmq.nšm. | [tdʿṣ.pʿn]m.w tr.arṣ.idk. | [l ttn.pn]m.ʿm il.mbk.n 17[2AQHT].6.45
| thdy.lḥm.w dqn[.ṯṯlt]. | qn.ḏrʿ h.tḥrṯ.km.gn. | ap lb.k ʿmq.ṯṯlt.bmt. | bʿl.mt.my.lim.bn dgn. | my.hmlt.aṯr.bʿl.nrd. | b 6[62].1.5
ʿr. | yhdy.lḥm.w dqn. | yṯlṯ.qn.ḏrʿ h.yḥrṯ. | k gn.ap lb.k ʿmq.yṯlṯ. | bmt.yšu.g h.w yṣḥ. | bʿl.mt.my.lim.bn. | dgn.my.h 5[67].6.21

ʿmr

l. | d pid.yrd.l ksi.yṯb. | l hdm[.w] l.hdm.yṯb. | l arṣ.yṣq.ʿmr. | un.l riš h.ʿpr.pltt. | l qdqd h.lpš.yks. | mizrtm.ǵr.b abn. 5[67].6.14

ʿmrpi

ṯḥm.špš. | l.ʿmrpi.rgm. | ʿm špš.kll.mid m. | šlm. | l.[--]n.špš. | ad[.ʿ]bd h.u 2060.2

ʿmt

--]. | [---].aṯt n.r[---]. | [---.]ḫr[-.--]. | [---.]plnt.[---]. | [---.]ʿmt.l ql.rpi[.---]. | [---.-]llm.abl.mṣrp k.[---]. | [---.]y.mṯnt.w tḥ 1001.2.2

ʿmtḏl

-]. | bn.s[---]. | bn.at[--]. | bn.qnḏ. | ṣmq[-]. | bn.anny. | bn.ʿmtḏl. | bn.ʿmyn. | bn.alz. | bn.birtn. | [bn.]ylkn. | [bn.]krwn. | [117[325].1.10
. | ǵlkz.ṯlṯm. | mlknʿm.ʿšrm. | mrʿm.ʿšrm. | ʿmlbu.ʿšrm. | ʿmtḏl.ʿšrm. | yʿḏrd.ʿšrm. | gmrd.ʿšrm. | ṣdqšlm.ʿšr[m]. | yknil.ḫ 1116.8
ṣṣ ubn ḫmš ʿšr h. | ṣṣ ʿmyd ḫmšm. | ṣṣ tmn.ḫmšm. | [ṣṣ] ʿmtḏl ṯlṯm. | ṣṣ ʿmlbi ṯṯ l ʿšrm. | ṣṣ bn adty ḫmšm. | ṣṣ amtrn a 2097.5

ʿmtr

bʿl. | ydb il. | yarš il. | yrǵm il. | ʿmtr. | ydb il. | yrgb lim. | ʿmtr. | yarš il. | ydb bʿl. | yrǵm bʿl. | ʿz bʿl. | ydb hd. UG5.14.B.9
| yrḫ kṯy. | ygb hd. | yrgb bʿl. | ydb il. | yarš il. | yrǵm il. | ʿmtr. | ydb il. | yrgb lim. | ʿmtr. | yarš il. | ydb bʿl. | yrǵm bʿl. | ʿz UG5.14.B.6

ʿmṯtmr

l ym.hnd. | ʿmṯtmr. | bn.nqmpʿ. | mlk.ugrt. | ytn.bt.annḏr. | bn.ytn.bnš. | [1009.2
l ym hnd. | ʿmṯtmr.bn. | nqmpʿ.ml[k]. | ugrt.ytn. | šd.kḏǵdl[.bn]. | [-]š[-]y. 1008.2

ʿn

| iy.aliyn.bʿl. | iy.zbl.bʿl.arṣ. | w tʿn.nrt.ilm.š[p]š. | šd yn.ʿn.b qbt[.t] | bl lyt.ʿl.umt k. | w abqṯ.aliyn.bʿl. | w tʿn.btlt.ʿnt. | 6[49].4.42
. | knʿm. | bdlm. | bn.ṣǵr. | klb. | bn.mnḥm. | bn.brqn. | bn.ʿn. | bn.ʿbdy. | ʿbdʿṯtr. 1046.3.47
| ǵr.w yʿn.aliyn. | bʿl.ib.hdt.lm.tḫš. | lm.tḫš.ntq.dmrn. | ʿn.bʿl.qdm.yd h. | k tǵḏ.arz.b ymn h. | bkm.yṯb.bʿl.l bht h. | u 4[51].7.40
. | ʿn.pḫr.l.pḫr.ṯṯb. | ʿn.mḫr.l.mḫr.ṯṯb. | ʿn.bṯy.l.bṯy.ṯṯb. | ʿn.bṯt.l.bṯt.ṯṯb. RS225.11
sm. | tspi.šir.h.l.bl.ḥrb. | tšt.dm.h.l.bl.ks. | tpnn.ʿn.bṯy.ʿn.bṯt.tpnn. | ʿn.mḫr.ʿn.pḫr.ʿn.ṯǵr. | ʿn.ṯǵr.l.ṯǵr.ṯṯb. | ʿn.pḫr.l.p RS225.5
r. | ʿn.ṯǵr.l.ṯǵr.ṯṯb. | ʿn.pḫr.l.pḫr.ṯṯb. | ʿn.mḫr.l.mḫr.ṯṯb. | ʿn.bṯy.l.bṯy.ṯṯb. | ʿn.bṯt.l.bṯt.ṯṯb. RS225.10
h.k.ysmsm. | tspi.šir.h.l.bl.ḥrb. | tšt.dm.h.l.bl.ks. | tpnn.ʿn.bṯy.ʿn.bṯt.tpnn. | ʿn.mḫr.ʿn.pḫr.ʿn.ṯǵr. | ʿn.ṯǵr.l.ṯǵr.ṯṯb. | ʿn. RS225.5
[t]. | tšu.knp.w tr.b ʿp. | tk.aḫ šmk.mlat rumm. | w yšu.ʿn h.aliyn.bʿl. | w yšu.ʿn h.w yʿn. | w yʿn.btlt.ʿnt. | nʿmt.bn.aḫt 10[76].2.13
.šbʿt.brqm.[---]. | ṯmnt.iṣr rʿt.ʿṣ brq y. | riš h.tply.ṭly.bn.ʿn h. | uzʿrt.tmll.išd h.qrn[m]. | dt.ʿl h.riš h.b glṯ.b šm[m]. | [-- UG5.3.1.5
šḥ.hm.b ʿp. | nṭʿn.b arṣ.ib y. | w b ʿpr.qm.aḫ k. | w tšu.ʿn h.btlt.ʿnt. | w tšu.ʿn h.w tʿn. | w tʿn.arḫ.w tr.b lkt. | tr.b lkt. 10[76].2.26
h.ib.iqni.ʿp[ʿp] h. | sp.ṯrml.ṯhgrn.[-]dm[.-]. | ašlw.b ṣp.ʿn h. | d b ḥlm y.il.ytn. | b ḏrt y.ab.adm. | w ld.špḥ.l krt. | w ǵl 14[KRT].3.149
arṣ.ib y. | w b ʿpr.qm.aḫ k. | w tšu.ʿn h.btlt.ʿnt. | w tšu.ʿn h.w tʿn. | w tʿn.arḫ.w tr.b lkt. | tr.b lkt.w tr.b ḫl. | [b]nʿmm 10[76].2.27
. | tk.aḫ šmk.mlat rumm. | w yšu.ʿn h.aliyn.bʿl. | w yšu.ʿn h.w yʿn. | w yʿn.btlt.ʿnt. | nʿmt.bn.aḫt.bʿl. | l pnn h.ydd.w y 10[76].2.14
m.qrb m.asm. | b p h.rgm.l yṣa.b špt h[.hwt h]. | b nši ʿn h.w tphn.in.[---]. | [-.]hlk.ǵlmm b dd y.yṣ[--]. | [-.]yṣa.w l.y 19[1AQHT].2.76
ṯḥt. | adrm.d b grn.ydn. | dn.almnt.yṯpṭ.ṯpṭ.ytm. | b nši ʿn h.w yphn.b alp. | šd.rbt.kmn.hlk.kṯr. | k yʿn.w yʿn.tdrq.ḫss 17[2AQHT].5.9
brṯ.l ẓr.pḥmm. | tʿpp.ṯr.il.d pid. | tǵẓy.bny.bnwt. | b nši.ʿn h.w tphn. | hlk.bʿl.aṯtrt. | k tʿn.hlk.btlt. | ʿnt.tdrq.ybmt. | [li 4[51].2.12
b nši[.ʿn h.w yphn.yḥd]. | b ʿrpt[.nšrm.yšu]. | [g h.]w yṣḥ[.knp.nšr 19[1AQHT].2.105
knp.nšrm.ybn. | bʿl.ybn.diy hmt nšrm. | tpr.w du.b nši.ʿn h.w ypn. | yḥd.hrgb.ab.nšrm. | yšu.g h.w yṣḥ.knp.hr[g]b. | 19[1AQHT].3.120
rgb.bʿl.ybn. | [b]ʿl.ybn.diy.hwt.hrg[b]. | tpr.w du.b nši.ʿn h. | [w]yphn.yḥd.ṣml.um.nšrm. | yšu.g h.w yṣḥ.knp.ṣml. | 19[1AQHT].3.134
]ṯpṭ. | [ṯpṭ.ytm.---] h. | [---.---]n. | [-----]. | hlk.[---.b n]ši. | ʿn h.w tphn.[---]. | b grn.yḥrb[.---]. | yǵly.yḥsp.ib[.---]. | ʿl.bt.a 19[1AQHT].1.29
rt. | [---].yn.ʿšy l ḥbš. | [---.]ḥtn.qn.yṣbt. | [---.--]m.b nši.ʿn h.w tphn. | [---.--]ml.ksl h.k b[r]q. | [---.]m[-]ǵ[-].thmt.brq. 17[2AQHT].6.10
.k b[r]q. | [---.]m[-]ǵ[-].thmt.brq. | [---].tṣb.qšt.bnt. | [---.ʿ]n h.km.btn.yqr. | [krpn h.-.l]arṣ.ks h.tšpk m. | [l ʿpr.tšu.g h 17[2AQHT].6.14
adrt[.---]. | ṯṯb ʿṯtrt b ǵl[.---]. | qrẓ tšt.l šmal[.---]. | arbḫ.ʿn h tšu w[.---]. | aylt tǵpy ṯr.ʿn[.---]. | b[b]r.mrḥ h.ti[ḥd.b yd 2001.1.10
t.[---]. | l šrr.št[.---]. | b riš h.[---]. | ib h.mš[--.---]. | [b]n.ʿn h[.---]. 2.4[68].40
[--]t.ḫ[--.l k] | ṯrt.l bnt.hll[.snnt]. | hl ǵlmt tld b[n.--]n. | ʿn ha l yd h.tzd[.--]. | pt l bšr h.dm a[--.--]ḫ. | w yn.k mtrḫt[.- 24[77].8
rš k. | [---].bnt.ṣʿṣ.bnt.mʿmʿ.ʿbd.ḥrn.[--.]k. | [---].aǵwyn.ʿn k.ẓẓ.w k mǵ.ilm. | [--.]k ʿṣm.k ʿšm.l ttn.k abnm.l thggn. 1001.2.12
ḥ. | w yʿny.krt.ṯʿ. | bn.al.tbkn.al. | tdm.l y.al tkl.bn. | qr.ʿn k.mḫ.riš k. | udmʿt.ṣḥ.aḫt k. | ṯtmnt.bt.ḥmḥ h. | d[-]n.tbkn. 16.1[125].27
-]. | [---.]ḥš[.-]nm[.--.]k.[--].w yḫnp[.---]. | [---.]ylm.b[n.ʿ]n k.ṣmdm.špk[.---]. | [---.]nt[-.]mbk kpt.w[.--].b g[--]. | [---.] 1001.1.16
bim. | thw.hm.brlt.anḫr. | b ym.hm.brk y.tkšd. | rumm.ʿn.kdd.aylt. | hm.imt.imt.npš.blt. | ḥmr.p imt.b klt. | yd y.ilḥ 5[67].1.17
un. | thw.w npš. | anḫr.b ym. | brkt.šbšt. | k rumm.hm. | ʿn.kdd.aylt. | mt hm.ks.ym | sk.nhr hm. | šbʿ.ydt y.b ṣʿ. | [--.]šb UG5.4.8

ʻn

[---.--]b. | [---.r]iš k. | [---.]bn ʻn km. | [---.]alp. | [---.]ym.rbt. | [---.]b nhrm. | [ʻb]r.gbl.ʻbr. | qʻl 3[ʻNT.VI].6.3
n.bn.ṣnr. | iẖy.[b]n[.--]l[-]. | ʻbdy[rẖ].bn.gṯtn. | yrmn.bn.ʻn. | krwn.nḥl h. | ttn.[n]ḥl h. | bn.b[r]zn. | [---.-]ḥn. 85[80].4.9
m[n.---]. | ʻn.tr.arṣ.w šmm. | sb.l qṣm.arṣ. | l ksm.mhyt.ʻn. | l arṣ.m[ṯ]r.bʻl. | w l šd.mṯr.ʻly. | nʻm.l arṣ.mṯr.bʻl. | w l šd. 16[126].3.4
n.mẖr.ʻn.pẖr.ʻn.ṯǵr. | ʻn.ṯǵr.l.ṯǵr.ṯṯb. | ʻn.pẖr.l.pẖr.ṯṯb. | ʻn.mẖr.l.mẖr.ṯṯb. | ʻn.bṯy.l.bṯy.ṯṯb. | ʻn.bṯt.l.bṯt.ṯṯb. RS225.9
.h.l.bl.ẖrb. | tšt.dm.h.l.bl.ks. | tpnn.ʻn.bṯy.ʻn.bṯt.tpnn. | ʻn.mẖr.ʻn.pẖr.ʻn.ṯǵr. | ʻn.ṯǵr.l.ṯǵr.ṯṯb. | ʻn.pẖr.l.pẖr.ṯṯb. | ʻn.m RS225.6
d[--]. | ittpq.l awl. | išttk.lm.ttkn. | štk.mlk.dn. | štk.šibt.ʻn. | štk.qr.bt.il. | w mṣlt.bt.ḥr[š]. 12[75].2.60
bṯy.ʻn.bṯt.tpnn. | ʻn.mẖr.ʻn.pẖr.ʻn.ṯǵr. | ʻn.ṯǵr.l.ṯǵr.ṯṯb. | ʻn.pẖr.l.pẖr.ṯṯb. | ʻn.mẖr.l.mẖr.ṯṯb. | ʻn.bṯy.l.bṯy.ṯṯb. | ʻn.bṯt.l. RS225.8
rb. | tšt.dm.h.l.bl.ks. | tpnn.ʻn.bṯy.ʻn.bṯt.tpnn. | ʻn.mẖr.ʻn.pẖr.ʻn.ṯǵr. | ʻn.ṯǵr.l.ṯǵr.ṯṯb. | ʻn.pẖr.l.pẖr.ṯṯb. | ʻn.mẖr.l.mẖr RS225.6
.grgs.ilštmʻy. | bn.ẖran.ilštmʻy. | bn.abdʻn.ilštmʻy. | bn.ʻn.rqdy. | bn.gʻyn. | bn.ǵrn. | bn.agynt. | bn.abdẖr.snry. | dqn.šl 87[64].32
[-----]. | yṣq.šm[n.---]. | ʻn.tr.arṣ.w šmm. | sb.l qṣm.arṣ. | l ksm.mhyt.ʻn. | l arṣ.m[ṯ]r.bʻ 16[126].3.2
[a]t.art.ḥkpt. | mit.dnn. | mitm.iqnu. | ẖmš.ʻšr.qn.nʻm.ʻn[m]. | ṯn.ḥblm.alp.alp.am[-]. | ṯmn.ḥblm.šbʻ.šbʻ.ma[-]. | ʻšr.k 1128.29
l.bl.ks. | tpnn.ʻn.bṯy.ʻn.bṯt.tpnn. | ʻn.mẖr.ʻn.pẖr.ʻn.ṯǵr. | ʻn.ṯǵr.l.ṯǵr.ṯṯb. | ʻn.pẖr.l.pẖr.ṯṯb. | ʻn.mẖr.l.mẖr.ṯṯb. | ʻn.bṯy.l.b RS225.7
t.dm.h.l.bl.ks. | tpnn.ʻn.bṯy.ʻn.bṯt.tpnn. | ʻn.mẖr.ʻn.pẖr.ʻn.ṯǵr. | ʻn.ṯǵr.l.ṯǵr.ṯṯb. | ʻn.pẖr.l.pẖr.ṯṯb. | ʻn.mẖr.l.mẖr.ṯṯb. | ʻ RS225.6
.trtqṣ. | b d bʻl.km.nšr b uṣbʻt h.hlm.qdq | d zbl ym.bn.ʻnm.ṯpṭ.nhr.yprsḥ ym. | w yql.l arṣ.w trtqṣ.ṣmd.b d bʻl. | [km 2.4[68].22
d.b d bʻl. | [km.]nšr.b uṣbʻt h.ylm.qdqd.zbl. | [ym.]bn.ʻnm.ṯpṭ.nhr.yprsḥ.ym.yql. | l arṣ.tnǵṣn.pnt h.w ydlp.tmn h. | 2.4[68].25
qrẓ tšt.l šmal[.---]. | arbẖ.ʻn h tšu w[.---]. | aylt tǵpy ṯr.ʻn[.---]. | b[b]r.mrḥ h.ti[ẖd.b yd h]. | š[g]r h bm ymn.t[--.---]. 2001.1.11
--.ymǵy.]npš. | [---.h]d.tngṯn h. | [---].b ṣpn. | [---].nšb.b ʻn. | [---.]b km.yʻn. | [---.ydʻ.l] ydʻt. | [---.t]asrn. | [---.]trks. | [---. 1[ʻNT.X].5.6
ṯ hm.b pʻn h. | w il hd.b ẖrẓʻ h. | [-----]. | [--]t.[---]. | [---.]ʻn[.---]. | pnm[.---]. | bʻl.n[--.---]. | il.hd[.---]. | at.bl[.at.---]. | ḥm 12[75].2.3
[---.mr]zḥ.ʻn[.---]. | [---.]šir.šd.kr[m.---]. | [---.]l.mrzḥ.ʻn[.---]. | [---].mrzḥ.ʻn[.---]. | [---].mrzḥ.ʻn[.---]. | [---.mr]zḥ.ʻn[. 2032.3
--]. | [---.]l.mrzḥ.ʻn[.---]. | [---].mrzḥ.ʻn[.---]. | [---].mrzḥ.ʻn[.---]. | [---.mr]zḥ.ʻn[.---]. 2032.5
. | [---.]šir.šd.kr[m.---]. | [---.]l.mrzḥ.ʻn[.---]. | [---].mrzḥ.ʻn[.---]. | [---].mrzḥ.ʻn[.---]. | [---.mr]zḥ.ʻn[.---]. 2032.4
[---.mr]zḥ.ʻn[.---]. | [---.]šir.šd.kr[m.---]. | [---.]l.mrzḥ.ʻn[.---]. | [---].mrzḥ. 2032.1
.---]. | [---].mrzḥ.ʻn[.---]. | [---].mrzḥ.ʻn[.---]. | [---.mr]zḥ.ʻn[.---]. 2032.6

ʻnil

bʻln. | yrmn. | ʻnil. | pmlk. | aby. | ʻdyn. | aǵlyn. | [--]rd. | [--]qrd. | [--]r. 1066.3

ʻnbr

. | bn.abr[-]. | yrpu. | kdn. | pʻṣ. | bn.liy. | ydʻ. | šmn. | ʻdy. | ʻnbr. | aẖrm. | bn.qrdy. | bn.šmʻn. | bn.ǵlmy. | ǵly. | bn.dnn. | bn. 2117.3.29

ʻny

[iy]n bʻl. | bl.ašt.ur[bt.]b bht m. | ḥln.b qr[b.hk]l m. | w ʻn.ali[yn.]bʻl. | al.tšt.u[rb]t.b bht m. | ḥln.b q[rb.hk]l m. | al td 4[51].6.7
.l rkb.ʻrpt. | bl.ašt.urbt.b bh[t] m. | ḥln.b qrb.hkl m. | w yʻn.aliyn bʻl. | al.tšt.urbt.b[bhtm]. | [ḥln].b qrb.hk[l m]. 4[51].5.125
m.bmt.[nhr]. | ṯṯtn.ib.bʻl.tiẖd. | yʻrm.šnu.hd.gpt. | ǵr.w yʻn.aliyn. | bʻl.ib.hdt.lm.ṯḥš. | lm.ṯḥš.nṯq.dmrn. | ʻn.bʻl.qdm.y 4[51].7.37
.]arẖt.tld[n]. | a[lp].l btlt.ʻnt. | w ypt l ybmt.li[mm]. | w yʻny.aliyn[.bʻl]. | lm.k qnym.ʻl[m.--]. | k dr d.d yknn[.--]. | bʻl. 10[76].3.5
nym.bʻl.[----]. | tšʻm.bʻl.mr[-]. | bt[.--]b bʻl.b qrb. | bt.w yʻn.aliyn. | bʻl.ašt m.kṯr bn. | ym.kṯr.bnm.ʻdt. | ypth.ḥln.b bht 4[51].7.14
db.ksu. | w yṯtb.l ymn.aliyn. | bʻl.ʻd.lḥm.št[y.ilm]. | [w]yʻn.aliy[n.bʻl]. | [--]b[.---]. | ḥš.bht m.k[ṯr]. | ḥš.rmm.hk[l m]. | 4[51].5.111
.ʻrb. | [--] h.ytn.w [--]u.l ytn. | [aẖ]r.mǵy.ʻ[d]t.ilm. | [w]yʻn.aliy[n.]bʻl. | [---.]tbʻ.l lṯpn. | [il.d]pid.l tbrk. | [krt.]ṭʻ.l tmr 15[128].2.12
y.yʻšr.ḥwy.yʻš. | r.w yšqyn h.ybd.w yšr.ʻl h. | nʻm[n.w t]ʻnynn.ap ank.aḥwy. | aqht[.ǵz]r.w yʻn.aqht.ǵzr. | al.tšrgn.y 17[2AQHT].6.32
š]lḥ k.w tn.qšt k.[l]. | [ʻnt.tq]ḥ[.q]ṣʻt k.ybmt.limm. | w yʻn.aqht.ǵzr.adr.ṯqbm. | [d]lbnn.adr.gdm.b rumm. | adr.qrnt 17[2AQHT].6.20
yšr.ʻl h. | nʻm[n.w t]ʻnynn.ap ank.aḥwy. | aqht[.ǵz]r.w yʻn.aqht.ǵzr. | al.tšrgn.y btlt m.dm.l ǵzr. | šrg k.ẖḫm.mt.uẖr 17[2AQHT].6.33
[---]. | qdqd k.ašhlk.šbt[k.dmm]. | [šbt.dqn k.mmʻm.]yʻny. | il.b šbʻt.ḥdrm.b ṯmnt. | ap.sgrt.ydʻ[t k.]bt.k an[št]. | k i 3[ʻNT.VI].5.33
m.rʻy.ht.alk. | [---.]ṯlṯt.amǵy.l bt. | [y.---.b qrb].hkl y.w yʻn.il. | [---.mrzʻ]y.lk.bt y.rpim. | [rpim.bt y.aṣ]ḥ km.iqra km. 21[122].1.8
š.tšṣq[n h]. | b qṣ.all.tšu.g h.w[tṣ] | ḥ.at.mt.tn.aẖ y. | w ʻn.bn.ilm.mt.mh. | taršn.l btlt.ʻnt. | an.itlk.w aṣd.kl. | ǵr.l kbd. 6[49].2.13
w yʻny.bn. | ilm.mt.npš[.-]. | npš.lbun. | thw.w npš. | anẖr.b ym. UG5.4.1
šd yn.ʻn.b qbt[.t] | bl lyt.ʻl.umt k. | w abqṯ.aliyn.bʻl. | w tʻn.btlt.ʻnt. | an.l an.y špš. | an.l an.il.yǵr[.-]. | ṯǵr k.š[---.---]. | 6[49].4.45
nm. | tn.l kṯr.w ẖss.ybʻl.qšt l ʻnt. | qṣʻt.l ybmt.limm.w tʻn.btlt. | ʻnt.irš ḥym.l aqht.ǵzr. | irš ḥym.w atn k.bl mt. | w a 17[2AQHT].6.25
[--]. | nrt.ilm.špš[.ṣḥrr]t. | la.šmm.b y[d.bn.ilm.m]t. | w tʻn.btlt.ʻn[t.bnt.]bht | k.y ilm.bnt.bh[t k].a[l.tš]mẖ. | al.tšmẖ. 3[ʻNT.VI].5.27
. | qnyt.ilm.mgntm. | ṯr.il.d pid.hm.ǵẓtm. | bny.bnwt w tʻn. | btlt.ʻnt.nmgn. | [-]m.rbt.aṯrt.ym. | [nǵ]ẓ.qnyt.ilm. | [---].n 4[51].3.32
[wy.w tkbd]n h.tlšn.aqht.ǵzr. | [---.kdd.dn]il.mt.rpi.w tʻn. | [btlt.ʻnt.tšu.g]h.w tṣḥ.hwt. | [---.]aqht.yd[--]. | [---.--]n.ṣ[17[2AQHT].6.52
bt.k an[št]. | k in.b ilht.ql[ṣ] k.mh.tarš[n]. | l btlt.ʻnt.w t[ʻ]n.btlt.ʻn[t]. | ṯḥm k.il.ḥkm.ḥkm k. | ʻm.ʻlm.ḥyt.ḥẓt.ṯḥm k. 3[ʻNT.VI].5.37
ank]. | ibǵ[y h.b tk.ǵ]r y.il.ṣpn. | b q[dš.b ǵr.nḥ]lt y. | w t[ʻn].btlt.[ʻ]nt.ṯṯb. | [ybmt.]limm.[a]n.aqry. | [b arṣ].mlḥmt.[a 3[ʻNT].4.65
]. | nʻmn.ǵzr.št.ṯrm.w[---]. | ištir.b ḏdm.w nʻrs[.---]. | w tʻn.btlt.ʻnt.ṯb.ytp.w[---]. | l k.ašt k.km.nšr.b ḥb[š y]. | km.diy 18[3AQHT].4.16
ẓll]. | ṯly.bt.r[b.mṯb.arṣy]. | bt.y.ʻbdr[.mṯb.klt]. | knyt.w tʻn[.btlt.ʻnt]. | yṯb l y.ṯr.il[.ab y.---]. | yṯb.l y.w l h.[---]. | [--.i] 3[ʻNT.VI].4.6
[-----]. | [---].at[--.---]. | [---] h.ap.[---]. | [---].w tʻn.[btlt.ʻnt.---]. | [bnt.bht]k.y ilm[.bnt.bht k.--]. | [al.tšmẖ.]a 18[3AQHT].1.6
. | tbʻ.w l.yṯb ilm.idk. | l ytn.pnm.ʻm.bʻl. | mrym.ṣpn.w yʻn. | gpn.w ugr.ṯḥm.bn ilm. | mt.hwt.ydd.bn.il. | ǵzr.p np.š.n 5[67].1.11
.alk.nmr[rt]. | imḥṣ.mḥṣ.aẖ y.akl[.m] | kly[.ʻ]l.umt y.w yʻn[.dn] | il.mt.rpi npš ṯḥ[.pǵt]. | t[km]t.mym.ḥspt.l šʻr. | ṯl.yd 19[1AQHT].4.197
aẖr.š[pšm.b ṯlṯ]. | mǵy.rpum.l grnt.i[lnym.l] | mṯʻt.w yʻn.dnil.[mt.rpi]. | yṯb.ǵzr.mt hrnmy[.---]. | b grnt.ilm.b qrb. 20[121].2.7
q | ht.ǵzr.yd[mʻ.]l kdd. | dnil.mt.r[pi.mk].b šbʻ. | šnt.w yʻn[.dnil.mt.]rpi. | yṯb.ǵzr.m[t.hrnmy.y]šu. | g h.w yṣḥ.t[bʻ.-- 19[1AQHT].4.180
ṯ. | yšbʻ.rgm.[my.]b ilm. | ydy.mrṣ.gršm zbln. | in.b ilm.ʻny h. | w yʻn.lṯpn.il.b pid. | ṯb.bn y.lm ṯb[t] km. | l kḥṯ.zbl k[16[126].5.22
ṯlṯ]. | rgm.my.b[ilm.ydy]. | mrṣ.grš[m.zbln]. | in.b ilm.ʻ[ny h.yrbʻ]. | yẖmš.rgm.[my.b ilm]. | ydy.mrṣ.g[ršm.zbln]. | i 16[126].5.16
ẖmš.rgm.[my.b ilm]. | ydy.mrṣ.g[ršm.zbln]. | in.b ilm.ʻn[y h.]ytdṯ. | yšbʻ.rgm.[my.]b ilm. | ydy.mrṣ.gršm zbln. | in.b 16[126].5.19
[il.d pid.my]. | b ilm.[ydy.mrṣ]. | gršm.z[bln.in.b ilm]. | ʻny h.y[ṯny.yṯlṯ]. | rgm.my.b[ilm.ydy]. | mrṣ.grš[m.zbln]. | in. 16[126].5.13
iṯ.--.l]ḥm.w t[n]. | w nlḥm.hm.iṯ[.--.yn.w t]n.w nšt. | w ʻn hm.nǵr mdrʻ[.iṯ.lḥm.---]. | iṯ.yn.d ʻrb.bṯk[.---]. | mǵ hw.l h 23[52].73

m.gpn.yšql.šdmt h.|km gpn.|šb‘ d.yrgm.‘l.‘d.w ‘rbm.t‘nyn.|w šd.šd ilm.šd aṯrt.w rḥm.|‘l.išt.šb‘ d.ǵzrm.ṭb.[g]d.b 23[52].12
lḥ ẓhrm iq|nim.atn šd h krm[m].|šd dd h ḥrnqm.w |y‘n ḫrḫb mlk qẓ [l].|n‘mn.ilm l ḫt[n].|m.b‘l trḫ pdry b[t h]. 24[77].24
[.t]q|ḥ.pǵt.w tšqyn h.tq[ḥ.ks.]b d h.|qb‘t.b ymn h.w y‘n.yṭ[p]n[.mh]r.|št.b yn.yšt.ila.il š[--.]il.|d yqny.ḏdm.yd.m 19[1AQHT].4.218
gm.l yṭ[pn.y]|bl.agrtn.bat.b ḏd k.[pǵt].|bat.b hlm w y‘n.yṭpn[.mhr].|št.qḥn.w tšqyn.yn.qḥ.|ks.b d y.qb‘t.b ymn 19[1AQHT].4.214
l.yḥdṯ.yrḫ.b[---].|b qrn.ymn h.b anšt[.---].|qdqd h.w y‘n.yṭpn.[mhr.št].|šm‘.l btlt.‘nt.at.‘[l.qšt h].|tmḫṣ h.qṣ‘t h.h 18[3AQHT].4.11
‘l.w [---].|ym.l mt.b‘l m.ym l[--.---].|ḥm.l šrr.w [---].|y‘n.ym.l mt[.---].|l šrr.w t‘[n.‘ṯtrt.---].|b‘l m.hmt.[---].|l šrr. 2.4[68].34
b‘[l].|yǵtr.‘ṯtr t|rḫ l k ybrdmy.b[t.a]|b h lb[u] y‘rr.w y‘[n].|yrḫ nyr šmm.w n‘[n].|‘ma nkl ḫtn y.a[ḫ]r.|nkl yrḫ y 24[77].30
g h.w yṣḥ.|aḫ y m.ytnt.b‘l.|spu y.bn m.um y.kl|y y.yt‘n.k gmrm.|mt.‘z.b‘l.‘z.ynghn.|k rumm.mt.‘z.b‘l.|‘z.ynṯk 6[49].6.16
.w.lak.|‘m y.w.yd.|ilm.p.k mtm.|‘z.mid.|hm.nṯkp.|m‘n k.|w.mnm.|rgm.d.tšm‘.|ṯmt.w.št.|b.spr.‘m y. 53[54].15
mm.|tšt ḥrṣ.k lb ilnm.|w ṯn.gprm.mn gpr h.šr.|aqht.y‘n.kmr.kmr[.--].|k ap‘.il.b gdrt.k lb.l |ḫṯ h.imḫṣ h.k d.‘l.qš 19[1AQHT].1.12
.il.|krt.špḥ.lṭpn.|w qdš.u ilm.tmtn.|špḥ.lṭpn.l yḥ.|w y‘ny.krt.ṯ‘.|bn.al.tbkn.al.|tdm.l y.al tkl.bn.|qr.‘n k.mḫ.riš 16.1[125].24
il.ušn.ab[.ad]m.|rḥq.mlk.l bt y.|n[g.]krt.l ḥẓ[r y].|w y‘n[y.k]rt[.ṯ]‘.|lm.ank.ksp.|w yr[q.ḫrṣ].|yd.mqm h.w ‘bd.|‘ 14[KRT].6.281
dw.anšt.|‘rš.zbln.rd.l mlk.|amlk.l drkt k.aṯb.|an.w y‘ny.krt ṯ‘.yṯbr.|ḥrn.y bn.yṯbr.ḥrn.|riš k.‘ṯtrt.šm.b‘l.|qdqd 16.6[127].54
arḫ.tzǵ.l ‘gl h.|bn.ḫpṯ.l umht hm.|k tnḥn.udmm.|w y‘ny.krt.ṯ‘. 15[128].1.8
l td‘.nš[m.w l tbn.hmlt.arṣ].|at.w ank.ib[ǵy h.---].|w y‘n.kṯr.w ḫss[.lk.lk.‘nn.ilm.]|atm.bštm.w an[.šnt.kptr].|l rḥ 1[‘NT.IX].3.17
ypl.ul ny.w l.‘pr.‘ẓm ny.|l b‘l[-.---].|tḥt.ksi.zbl.ym.w ‘n.kṯr.w ḫss.l rgmt.|l k.l zbl.b‘l.ṯnt.l rkb.‘rpt.ht.ib k.|b‘l m. 2.4[68].7
k[l m].|b tk.ṣrrt.ṣpn.|alp.šd.aḫd bt.|rbt.kmn.hkl.|w y‘n.kṯr.w ḫss.|šm‘.l aliyn b‘l.|bn.l rkb.‘rpt.|bl.ašt.urbt.b bh 4[51].5.120
.ṭl]y.bt.rb.|[---.m]dd.il ym.|[---.-]qlṣn.wpṯ m.|[---.]w y‘n.kṯr.|[w ḫss.]tṯb.b‘l.l hwt y.|[ḥš.]bht h.tbnn.|[ḥš.]trmm. 4[51].6.14
w y‘n.k[ṯr.w ḫs]s.|tṯb.b‘l.l[hwt y].|ṯn.rgm.k[ṯr.w]ḫss.|šm‘.m 4[51].6.1
ḥṯ.drkt h.|mn m.ib.yp‘.l b‘l.ṣrt.l rkb.‘rpt.|[-]‘n.ǵlmm.y‘nyn.l ib.yp‘.|l b‘l.ṣrt.l rkb.‘rpt.|tḥm.aliyn.b‘l.hwt.aliy.|qr 3[‘NT].4.49
il.d p[id.---].|šm.bn y.yw.ilt.[---].|w p‘r.šm.ym[-.---].|t‘nyn.l zn.tn[.---].|at.adn.tp‘r[.---].|ank.lṭpn.il[.d pid.---].|‘l 1[‘NT.X].4.16
kl.|w ywsrnn.ggn h.|lk.l ab k.yṣb.lk.|l[ab]k.w rgm.‘ny.|l k[rt.adn k.]ištm[‘].|w tqǵ[.udn.k ǵz.ǵzm].|tdbr.w[ǵ] 16.6[127].28
.ilm.rišt.|km l ẓr brkt km.w ln.kḥṯ.zbl km.aḥd.|ilm.t‘ny lḥt.mlak.ym.t‘dt.ṯpṭ.nhr.|šu.ilm.rašt km.l ẓr.brkt km.l 2.1[137].26
bn k.amlkn.|w t‘n.rbt.aṯrt ym.|bl.nmlk.yd‘.ylḥn.|w y‘n.lṭpn.il d pi|d dq.anm.l yrẓ.|‘m.b‘l.l y‘db.mrḥ.|‘m.bn.dg 6.1.49[49.1.21]
qht.w ypltṭ k.bn[.dnil.---].|w y‘ḏr k.b yd.btlt.[‘nt].|w y‘n.lṭpn.il d p[id].|yd‘t k.bt.k anšt.w i[n.b ilht].|qlṣ k.tb‘.bt. 18[3AQHT].1.15
m.[my.]b ilm.|ydy.mrṣ.gršm zbln.|in.b ilm.‘ny h.|w y‘n.lṭpn.il.b pid.|ṯb.bn y.lm ṯb[t] km.|l kḥṯ.zbl k[m.a]nk.|i 16[126].5.23
‘d[.---].|yaṯr[.---].|b d k.[---].|ṯnnt h[.---].|ṯlṯt h[.-.w y‘n].|lṭpn.[il.d pid.my].|b ilm.[ydy.mrṣ].|gršm.z[bln.in.b il 16[126].5.9
|mṯb.pdry.bt.ar.|mẓll.ṭly.bt rb.|mṯb.arṣ.bt y‘bdr.|w y‘n lṭpn il d pid.|p ‘bd.an.‘nn.aṯrt.|p.‘bd.ank.aḫd.ulṯ.|hm.a 4[51].4.58
---].|yṣḥ.ngr il.ilš.|ilš.ngr.bt.b‘l.|w aṯt h.ngrt.ilht.|w y‘n.lṭpn.il d pi[d].|šm‘.l ngr.il il[š].|ilš.ngr bt b‘l.|w aṯt k.n 16[126].4.10
at yd.[---].|km ll.kḥṣ.tusp[.---].|tgr.il.bn h.ṯr[.---].|w y‘n.lṭpn.il.d p[id.---].|šm.bn y.yw.ilt.[---].|w p‘r.šm.ym[-.--- 1[‘NT.X].4.13
r.|šu.ilm.rašt km.l ẓr.brkt km.ln.kḥṯ.|zbl km.w ank.‘ny.mlak.ym.t‘dt.ṯpṭ.nhr.|tšu ilm rašt hm.l ẓr.brkt hm.ln.k 2.1[137].28
.--]t[.---].|[tqdm.]yd.b ṣ‘.t[šl]ḥ.|[ḥrb.b]bš[r].tštn.|[w t‘n].mṯt.ḥry.|[l lḥ]m.l šty.ṣḥt k[m].|[---.]brk.t[---].|[‘l.]krt.t 15[128].5.9
--].|w lḫm mr.tqdm.|yd.b ṣ‘.tšlḥ.|ḥrb.b bšr.tštn.|[w t]‘n.mṯt.ḥry.|[l lḥ]m.l šty.ṣḥt km.|[--.dbḥ.l]krt.b‘l km. 15[128].4.26
[-----].|šm‘.l [-]mt[.-]m.l[-]ṯnm.|‘dm.[lḥ]m.tšty.|w t‘n.mṯt ḥry.|l l[ḥ]m.l š[ty].ṣḥt km.|db[ḥ.l krt.a]dn km.|‘l.k 15[128].6.3
--].|hy.yd h.w ym[ǵ].|mlak k.‘m dt[n].|lqḥ.mṯpṭ.|w y‘ny.nn.|dtn.bt n.mḫ[-].|l dg.w [-]kl.|w aṯr.hn.mr[-]. UG5.6.13
k ymǵy.adn.|ilm.rbm ‘m dtn.|w yšal.mṯpṭ.yld.|w y‘ny.nn[.--].|t‘ny.n[---.-]ṯq.|w š[--.---].|ḥdṯ[.---.]ḥ[--].|b bt.[UG5.6.4
.yš[t k].|b‘l.‘nt.mḥrṯ[-].|iy.aliyn.b‘l.|iy.zbl.b‘l.arṣ.|w t‘n.nrt.ilm.š[p]š.|šd yn.‘n.b qbt[.t]|bl lyt.‘l.umt k.|w abqṯ.a 6[49].4.41
n.|ilm.rbm ‘m dtn.|w yšal.mṯpṭ.yld.|w y‘ny.nn[.--].|t‘ny.n[---.-]ṯq.|w š[--.---].|ḥdṯ[.---.]ḥ[--].|b bt.[-.]l bnt.q[-].| UG5.6.5
riš k.‘ṯtrt.šm.b‘l.|qdqd k.tqln.b gbl.|šnt k.b ḥpn k.w t‘n.|spr ilmlk ṯ‘y. 16.6[127].58
ybrdmy.b[t.a]|b h lb[u] y‘rr.w y‘[n].|yrḫ nyr šmm.w n‘[n].|‘ma nkl ḫtn y.a[ḫ]r.|nkl yrḫ ytrḫ.adn h.|yšt mṣb.mz 24[77].31
‘.[alt.]ṯ[bt |k.l y]hpk.|[ksa.]mlk k.l yṯbr.ḫṭ.mṯpṭ k.w y‘n[.‘ṯtr].dm[-]k[-].|[--]ḥ.b y.ṯr.il.ab y.ank.in.bt[.l] y[.km.]il 2.3[129].18
.aliyn.|b‘l.p‘n h.l tmǵyn.|hdm.riš h.l ymǵy.|aps h.w y‘n.‘ṯtr.‘rẓ.|l amlk.b ṣrrt.ṣpn.|yrd.‘ṯtr.‘rẓ.yrd.|l kḥṯ.aliyn.b‘ 6.1.61[49.1.33]
bn.qdš.]w y[--.]zbl.ym.y‘[--.]ṯpṭ.nhr.|[-------.]yšlḥn.w y‘n ‘ṯtr[.-]. 2.3[129].24
m l[--.---].|ḥm.l šrr.w [---].|y‘n.ym.l mt[.---].|l šrr.w t‘[n.‘ṯtrt.---].|b‘l m.hmt.[---].|l šrr.št[.---].|b riš h.[---].|ib h. 2.4[68].35
lm.tb‘rn[.---].|mn.yrḫ.k m[rṣ.---].|mn.k dw.kr[t].|w y‘ny.ǵzr[.ilḥu].|ṯlṯ.yrḫm.k m[rṣ].|arb‘.k dw.k[rt].|mnd‘.krt 16.2[125].83
ṯbr.|[---.]aḫ h.tbky.|[--.m]rṣ.mlk.|[---.]krt.adn k.|[w y‘ny.]ǵzr.ilḥu.|[---.]mrṣ.mlk.|[--.k]rt.adn k.|[--.d]bḥ.dbḥ.|[16.1[125].58
[---.b‘l.b bht h].|[il.hd.b qr]b.hkl h.|w t‘nyn.ǵlm.b‘l.|in.b‘l.b bht ht.|il hd.b qrb.hkl h.|qšt hn.aḫd. 10[76].2.3
bm.‘[l.---].|[-]l h.yd ‘d[.---].|ltm.mrqdm.d š[-]l[-].|w t‘n.pǵt.ṯkmt.mym.|qrym.ab.dbḥ.l ilm.|š‘ly.dǵṯ h.b šmym.| 19[1AQHT].4.190
ǵyt.btlt.‘nt.|tmgnn.rbt[.a]ṯrt ym.|tǵẓyn.qnyt.ilm.|w t‘n.rbt.aṯrt ym.|ik.tmgnn.rbt.|aṯrt.ym.tǵẓyn.|qnyt.ilm.mg 4[51].3.27
ṯrt ym.šm‘.|l rbt.aṯr[t] ym.tn.|aḥd.b bn k.amlkn.|w t‘n.rbt.aṯrt ym.|bl.nmlk.yd‘.ylḥn.|w y‘n.lṭpn.il d pi|d dq.a 6.1.47[49.1.19]
anm.l yrẓ.|‘m.b‘l.l y‘db.mrḥ.|‘m.bn.dgn.k tms m.|w ‘n.rbt.aṯrt ym.|blt.nmlk.‘ṯtr.‘rẓ.|ymlk.‘ṯtr.‘rẓ.|apnk.‘ṯtr.‘rẓ. 6.1.53[49.1.25]
ṯrt.tlbn.|lbnt.ybn.bt.l b‘l.|km ilm.w ḥẓr.k bn.aṯrt.|w t‘n.rbt.aṯrt ym.|rbt.ilm.l ḥkmt.|šbt.dqn k.l tsr k.|rḫntt.d[-] 4[51].5.64
ṯr[.il.ab -.w t‘n.rbt].|aṯr[t.ym.šm‘.l qdš].|w am[rr.l dgy.rbt].|aṯrt.ym[. 4[51].4.1
k.ḫrṣ.|dm.‘ṣm.hm.yd.il mlk.|yḫss k.ahbt.ṯr.t‘rr k.|w t‘n.rbt.aṯrt ym.|tḥm k.il.ḥkm.ḥkmt.|‘m ‘lm.ḥyt.ḥẓt.|tḥm k 4[51].4.40
.|b šb‘t.ḥdrm.[b ṯ]mn[t.ap].|sgrt.g[-].[-]ẓ[.---] h[.---].|‘n.ṯk[.---].|‘ln.ṯ[--.---].|l p‘n.ǵl[m]m[.---].|mid.an[--.]ṣn[--]. 3[‘NT.VI].5.21
t b trbṣ bn.amt.|[tn.b]nm.aqny.|[tn.ṯa]rm.amid.|[w y‘n].ṯr.ab h.il.|d[--].b bk.krt.|b dm‘.n‘mn.ǵlm.|il.trḥṣ.w ta 14[KRT].2.59
tqyn h.|[hml]t.tn.b‘l.w ‘nn h.bn.dgn.arṯ m.pḏ h.|[w y‘n.]ṯr.ab h.il.‘bd k.b‘l.y ym m.‘bd k.b‘l.|[--.--]m.bn.dgn.a[s 2.1[137].36
‘.nplt.bšr.|[---].w tpky.k[m.]n‘r.tdm‘.km.|[ṣǵ]r.bkm.y‘ny[.---.bn]wt h.|[--]nn.bnt yš[--.---.-]lk.|[--]b.kmm.l k[--]. UG5.8.41
[---.h]d.tngṯn h.|[---].b ṣpn.|[---].nšb.b ‘n.|[---.]b km.y‘n.|[---.yd‘.l] yd‘t.|[---.t]asrn.|[---.]trks.|[---.]abnm.upqt.| 1[‘NT.X].5.7
m h.|[---.-]ḥm k b ṣpn.|[---.]išqb.aylt.|[---.--]m.b km.y‘n.|[---].yd‘.l yd‘t.|[---.]tasrn.ṯr il.|[---.]rks.bn.abnm.|[---.] 1[‘NT.X].5.20

‘nmk

y[m]m. | mrat.ḫmš.‘šr.ymm. | qmnz.yrḫ.w.ḫmš.ymm. | ‘nmk.yrḫ. | ypr.yrḫ.w.ḫmš.ymm. 66[109].9
k[-.---]. | [-]rn[.---]. | [-----]. | yt[--.---]. | ṯl[ṯ.---]. | ṯl[ṯ.---]. | ‘nmk[.---]. | ykn‘m[.---]. | qm[n]z[---]. | šl[-.---]. | ar[--.---]. | qrt[1181.7

‘nmky

š.bnšm. | ǵr. | ary.ḥmr w.bnš. | qmy.ḥmr.w.bnš. | ṯbil. | ‘nmky.ḥmr.w.bnš. | rqd arb‘. | šbn aḥd. | ṭbq aḥd. | šrš aḥd. | bi 2040.26
]. | a[---]. | d[---]. | q[---]. | ‘m[--]. | ar[--]. | ykn[‘m]. | ṣlyy. | ‘nm[ky]. | l[bnm]. | ‘r[--]. 2133.8
bṣr[y]. | [---]. | [---]y. | ar. | agm.w.ḫpty. | ḫlb.ṣpn. | mril. | ‘nmky. | ‘nqpat. | ṭbq. | hzp. | gn‘y. | m‘rby. | [ṣ]‘q. | [š]ḥq. | n‘rm. 71[113].52
.arb‘m.dr‘.w.‘šrm.drt. | w.ṯlṯm.dd.ṯṯ.kbd.ḥpr.bnšm. | b.‘nmky.‘šrm.dr‘[.---.d]rt. | w.ṯn.‘šr h.dd.[---]. | iwrḏn.ḥ[--.---]. 1098.28
[--]n.‘š[r.] | [a]rt[.a]rb‘[.---]. | ‘nmky.‘šr.[---]. | ṯmry.‘šr.ṯn.k[rmm.---]. | liy.krm.aḥd[.---]. | ‘b 1081.3
ir. | ypr. | hzp. | šql. | m‘rḫ[-]. | sl[ḫ]. | snr. | ‘rgz. | ykn‘m. | ‘nmky. | ǵr. 2074.38
mt ṯlṯ. | qmnz ṯql. | zlyy ṯql. | ary ḫmšt. | ykn‘m ḫmšt. | ‘nmky ṯqlm. | [-]kt ‘šrt. | qrn šb‘t. 1176.6
.ǵ[--.---]. | krm.pyn.arty[.---]. | ṯlṯ.krm.ubdym.l mlkt.b.‘nmky[.---]. | mgdly.ǵlpṯr.ṯn.krmm.w.ṯlṯ.ub[dym.---]. | qmnz. 1081.9

‘nn

bt rb. | mṯb.arṣ.bt y‘bdr. | w y‘n lṭpn il d pid. | p ‘bd.an.‘nn.aṯrt. | p.‘bd.ank.aḫd.ulṯ. | hm.amt.aṯrt.tlbn. | lbnt.ybn.bt.l 4[51].4.59
.tk.qrt h. | hmry.mk.ksu. | ṯbt h.ḫḫ.arṣ. | nḫlt h.w nǵr. | ‘nn.ilm.al. | tqrb.l bn.ilm. | mt.al.y‘db km. | k imr.b p h. | k lli. 4[51].8.15
.awṣ.arbdd. | l kbd.š[d]m.ap.mṯn.rgmm. | argmn.lk.lk.‘nn.ilm. | atm.bštm.w an.šnt. | uǵr.l rḥq.ilm.inbb. | l rḥq.ilny 3[‘NT].4.76
mlt.arṣ]. | at.w ank.ib[ǵy h.---]. | w y‘n.kṯr.w ḫss[.lk.lk.‘nn.ilm.] | atm.bštm.w an[.šnt.kptr]. | l rḥq.ilm.ḥkp[t.l rḥq.il 1[‘NT.IX].3.17
n]km.ṯpṭ.nhr.tn.il m.d tq h.d tqyn h. | [hml]t.tn.b‘l.w ‘nn h.bn.dgn.arṯ m.pḏ h. | [w y‘n.]ṯr.ab h.il.‘bd k.b‘l.y ym m 2.1[137].35
dn km.ṯ[pṭ.nhr]. | tn.il m.d tq h.d tqyn.hmlt.tn.b‘l.[w ‘nn h]. | bn.dgn.arṯ m.pḏ h.tb‘.ǵlmm.l ṯṯb.[idk.pnm]. | l ytn.t 2.1[137].18
k.ǵrt. | [ql].l b‘l.‘nt.ttnn. | [---].b‘l m.d ip[---]. | [il.]hd.d ‘nn.n[--]. | [----.]aliyn.b[‘l]. | [---.btl]t.‘n[t.-.]p h. | [---.---]n. | [-- 10[76].2.33
b b[--].bm.k[--]. | [--]ṯb.‘ryt k.k qlt[.---]. | [--]at.brt.lb k.‘nn.[---]. | [--.]šdq.k ttn.l y.šn[.---]. | [---.]bn.rgm.w yd‘[.---]. 60[32].4

‘nq

.hn.ym.yṣq.yn.ṯmk. | mrṯ.yn.srnm.yn.bld. | ǵll.yn.išryt.‘nq.smd. | lbnn.ṯl mrṯ.yḥrṯ.il. | hn.ym.w ṯn.tlḥmn.rpum. | tšty 22.2[124].19

‘nqpat

aḥd.b gt.knpy.w.aḥd.b gt.ṯrmn. | aḥd.alp.idṯn.d aḥd.b.‘nqpat. | [aḥd.al]p.d aǵlmn. | [d aḥd b.g]t gbry. | [---].aḥd.aḥd 1129.11
. | ḫlbrpš. | hry. | qmṣ. | ṣ‘q. | qmy. | ḫlbkrd. | y‘rt. | uškn. | ‘nqpat. | ilštm‘. | šbn. | ṭbq. | rqd. | šrš. | gn‘y. | m‘qb. | agm. | bir. 2074.20
š[--.---]. | ṣ‘[-.---]. | ṣ‘q[.---]. | ḫlb.k[rd]. | uškn. | ‘nqp[at]. | ubr‘[y]. | ilšt[m‘]. | šbn. | ṭbq. 2146.6
m. | bṣr. | y[--]. | y[--]. | snr. | midḫ. | ḥ[lym]. | [ḫ]lby. | ‘r. | ‘nq[pat]. | glbty. | [-----]. | [-----]. | [-----]. | [-----]. | ykn‘m. | šlmy. 2058.2.24
---]. | [---]y. | ar. | agm.w.ḫpty. | ḫlb.ṣpn. | mril. | ‘nmky. | ‘nqpat. | ṭbq. | hzp. | gn‘y. | m‘rby. | [ṣ]‘q. | [š]ḥq. | n‘rm. | mḫrǵl 71[113].53
.‘yn. | ubnyn. | rpš d ydy. | ǵbl. | mlk. | gwl. | rqd. | ḫlby. | ‘n[q]pat. | m[‘]rb. | ‘rm. | bn.ḥgby. | mrat. 2075.26
]. | [----] h. | [-----]. | [-]b‘l. | [--]m. | [m‘]rby. | m‘r. | arny. | ‘nqpat. | š‘rt. | ubr‘y. | ilštm‘. | šbn. | ṭbq. | rqd. | [š]rš. | [-----]. | [-- 2058.1.12
y.[ḫm]r.w bn[š]. | gn‘y.[---.bn]š. | uškn[.---].‘šr.bnšm. | ‘nqpat[.---].bnš. | ubr‘y.ar[b‘.]ḥm[r]m.w[.---.]bnšm. | ilštm‘.ar 2040.19
‘r[-.---]. | bq‘t.[---]. | šḥq[.---]. | rkby ar[b‘m]. | bir ṯ[--]. | ‘nqpat [---]. | m[--.---]. | [-----]. | k[--.---]. | [-----]. | ḫmrn.‘š[r.---] 2042.17

‘nqpaty

-.---]. | bn.tbd.ilšt[m‘y.---]. | mty.ilšt[m‘y.---]. | bn.pynq.‘nqp[a]t[y.---]. | ayiḫ.ilšt[m‘y.---]. | [b]dlm.dt.yṯb[.---]. | [-]y[-- 90[314].2.8
t[y.---]. | ayiḫ.ilšt[m‘y.---]. | [b]dlm.dt.yṯb[.---]. | [-]y[--].‘nqp[aty.---]. | ‘ṯt[r]n.[-]bṭ[-.---]. | [---]n.š[--.---]. | [---]n.[---]. | [- 90[314].2.11

‘nqt

] l r‘y. | [--] šmḫ[.---]. | ddm gt dprnm. | l ḥršm. | ddm l ‘nqt. | dd l alṯt.w l lmdt h. | dd l iḫyn. | dd l [---]. 1101.10

‘nt

.yuḫ]d.b yd.mšḫṭ.bm.ymn.mḫṣ.ǵlmm.yš[--]. | [ymn h.‘n]t.tuḫd.šmal h.tuḫd.‘ṯtrt.ik.m[ḫṣt.ml] | [ak.ym.t‘]dt.ṯpṭ.nh 2.1[137].40
[tṣ] | ḥ.at.mt.tn.aḫ y. | w ‘n.bn.ilm.mt.mh. | taršn.l btlt.‘nt. | an.itlk.w aṣd.kl. | ǵr.l kbd.arṣ.kl.gb‘. | l kbd.šdm.npš.ḫsr 6[49].2.14
.b qbt[.t] | bl lyt.‘l.umt k. | w abqt.aliyn.b‘l. | w t‘n.btlt.‘nt. | an.l an.y špš. | an.l an.il.yǵr[.-]. | tǵr k.š[---.---]. | yštd[.-- 6[49].4.45
-.kpt]r.l r[ḥq.ilm.ḥkpt.l rḥq]. | [ilnym.ṯn.mṯpd]m.t[ḥt.‘nt.arṣ.ṯlṯ.mtḥ.ǵyrm]. | [idk.]l ytn.pnm.‘m.[i]l.mbk.[nhrm.qr 2.3[129].3
t.kptr]. | l rḥq.ilm.ḥkp[t.l rḥq.ilnym]. | ṯn.mṯpdm.tḥt.[‘nt.arṣ.ṯlṯ.mtḥ]. | ǵyrm.idk.l yt[n.pnm.‘m.lṭpn]. | il d pid.tk ḫ 1[‘NT.IX].3.20
.šnt. | uǵr.l rḥq.ilm.inbb. | l rḥq.ilnym.ṯn.mṯpdm. | tḥt.‘nt.arṣ.ṯlṯ.mtḥ.ǵyrm. | idk.l ttn pnm.‘m.b‘l. | mrym.ṣpn.b alp. 3[‘NT].4.80
l kṯr.w ḫss.yb‘l.qšt l ‘nt. | qṣ‘t.l ybmt.limm.w t‘n.btlt. | ‘nt.irš ḥym.l aqht.ǵzr. | irš ḥym.w atn k.bl mt. | w ašlḥ k.ašs 17[2AQHT].6.26
h.b anšt[.---]. | qdqd h.w y‘n.ytpn.[mhr.št]. | šm‘.l btlt.‘nt.at.‘[l.qšt h]. | tmḫṣ h.qṣ‘t h.hwt.l t[ḥwy]. | n‘mn.ǵzr.št.ṯr 18[3AQHT].4.12
m.‘nt.tngṯ h. | k lb.arḫ.l ‘gl h.k lb. | ṯat.l imr h.km.lb. | ‘nt.aṯr.b‘l.tiḫd. | bn.ilm.mt.b ḥrb. | tbq‘nn.b ḫṯr.tdry | nn.b išt 6[49].2.30
nt]. | tngṯ h.k lb.a[rḫ]. | l ‘gl h.k lb.ṯa[t]. | l imr h.km.lb.‘n[t]. | aṯr.b‘l.tiḫd.m[t]. | b sin.lpš.tšṣq[n h]. | b qṣ.all.tšu.g h. 6[49].2.8
iṯ.b kbd k.tšt.b [---]. | irt k.dṯ.ydṯ.m‘qb k.[ttb‘]. | [bt]lt.‘nt.idk.l ttn.[pnm]. | [‘m.a]qht.ǵzr.b alp.š[d]. | [rbt.]kmn.w ṣ 18[3AQHT].1.20
--]. | [---.]uṯm.ḏr[qm.---]. | [btl]t.‘nt.l kl.[---]. | [tt]b‘.btlt.‘nt[.idk.l ttn.pnm]. | ‘m.ytpn.mhr.š[t.tšu.g h]. | w tṣḥ.yṯb.ytp. 18[3AQHT].4.5
k. | [b]‘l.‘nt.mḥrṯt. | iy.aliyn.b‘l. | iy.zbl.b‘l.arṣ. | ttb‘.btlt.‘nt. | idk.l ttn.pnm. | ‘m.nrt.ilm.špš. | tšu.g h.w tṣḥ. | tḥm.ṯr.il. 6[49].4.30
.n‘mn.nbl[.---]. | [--.]yṣq šmn.šlm.b ṣ[‘.trḥṣ]. | yd h.btlt.‘nt.uṣb‘t[h.ybmt]. | limm.tiḫd.knr h.b yd[h.tšt]. | rimt.l irt h UG5.3.2.5
ḥ. | [b]bt.dm.ḏmr.yṣq.šmn. | šlm.b ṣ‘.trḥṣ.yd h.bt | [l]t.‘nt.uṣb‘t h.ybmt.limm. | [t]rḥṣ.yd h.b dm.ḏmr. | [u]ṣb‘t h.b m 3[‘NT].2.33
yṣat.km.rḥ.npš[h.km.iṯl]. | brlt h.km.qṭr.[b ap h.---]. | ‘nt.b ṣmt.mhr h.[---]. | aqht.w tbk.y[---.---]. | abn.ank.w ‘l.[qš 18[3AQHT].4.38
t.ilm.špš[.ṣḥrr]t. | la.šmm.b y[d.bn.ilm.m]t. | w t‘n.btlt.‘n[t.bnt.]bht | k.y ilm.bnt.bh[t k].a[l.tš]mḫ. | al.tšmḫ.b r[m.h 3[‘NT.VI].5.27
.y l km.qr.mym.d ‘[l k]. | mḫṣ.aqht.ǵzr.amd.gr bt il. | ‘nt.brḥ.p ‘lm h.‘nt.p dr[.dr]. | ‘db.uḫry mṭ.yd h. | ymǵ.l mrrt. 19[1AQHT].3.154
k.mḫṣ.aqht. | ǵzr.šrš k.b arṣ.al. | yp‘.riš.ǵly.b d.ns‘ k. | ‘nt.brḥ.p ‘lm h. | ‘nt.p dr.dr.‘db.uḫry mṭ yd h. | ymǵ.l qrt.abl 19[1AQHT].3.161

l š.b‘l š.dgn š.|[---.--]r.w t̲t pl.gdlt.[ṣ]pn.dqt.|[---.al]p ‘nt.gdlt.b t̲lt̲t mrm.|[---.i]l š.b‘l š.at̲rt.š.ym š.[b‘]l knp.|[---.g 36[9].1.5
t̲lb.b tp.w mṣltm.b m|rqdm.dšn.b.ḥbr.kt̲r.t̲bm.|w tšt.‘nt.gt̲r.b‘lt.mlk.b‘|lt.drkt.b‘lt.šmm.rmm.|[b‘l]t.kpt̲.w ‘nt.di. UG5.2.1.6
‘nt.gt̲r.b‘lt.mlk.b‘|lt.drkt.b‘lt.šmm.rmm.|[b‘l]t.kpt̲.w ‘nt.di.dit.rḫpt.|[---.-]rm.aklt.‘gl.‘l.mšt.|[---.--]r.špr.w yšt.il. UG5.2.1.8
qṣm.|w bn.bht.ksp.w ḫrṣ.|bht.t̲hrm.iqnim.|šmḫ.btlt.‘nt.td‘ṣ.|p‘nm.w tr.arṣ.|idk.l ttn.pnm.|‘m.b‘l.mrym.ṣpn.|b 4[51].5.82
bnwt.|b nši.‘n h.w tphn.|hlk.b‘l.at̲trt.|k t‘n.hlk.btlt.|‘nt.tdrq.ybmt.|[limm].b h.p‘nm.|[t̲t̲t.b ‘]dn.ksl.|[t̲t̲br.‘ln.p] 4[51].2.15
lk.t̲ql.ḫrṣ.|l špš.w yrḫ.l gt̲r.|t̲ql.ksp.t̲b.ap w np[š].|l ‘nt h.t̲ql.ḫrṣ.|l špš[.w y]rḫ.l gt̲r.t̲n.|[t̲ql.ksp].t̲b.ap.w npš.|[- 33[5].13
b.idk.|[l ytn.pnm.tk.]in.bb.b alp ḥẓr.|[rbt.kmn.l p‘]n.‘nt.|[yhbr.w yql.yšt]ḥwyn.w y|[kbdn h.yšu.g h.w y]ṣḥ.t̲hm. 1[‘NT.IX].2.15
t.t̲ly.bt.rb.dd.arṣy.|bt.y‘bdr.km ǵlmm.|w ‘rb n.l p‘n.‘nt.hbr.|w ql.tšt̲ḥwy.kbd hyt.|w rgm.l btlt.‘nt.|t̲ny.l ymmt. 3[‘NT].3.6
um.l tdd.at̲r h].|l tdd.il[nym.---].|mhr.b‘l[.---.mhr].|‘nt.lk b[t y.rpim.rpim.b bt y].|aṣḥ.km.[iqra km.ilnym.b] |h 22.1[123].8
‘l.mt.my.lim.bn.|dgn.my.hmlt.at̲r.|b‘l.ard.b arṣ.ap.|‘nt.ttlk.w tṣd.kl.ǵr.|l kbd.arṣ.kl.gb‘.|l [k]bd.šdm.tmǵ.l n‘m[5[67].6.26
‘nt.hlkt.w.šnwt.|tp.aḫ.h.k.ysmsm.|tspi.šir.h.l.bl.ḫrb.|tšt.d RS225.1
m.argm.qštm.|[----.]mhrm.ht.tṣdn.tint̲t.|[---]m.tṣḥq.‘nt.w b lb.tqny.|[---.]t̲b l y.l aqht.ǵzr.t̲b l y w l k.|[---]m.l a 17[2AQHT].6.41
t.pḫl.|qdš.yuḫdm.šb‘r.|amrr.k kbkb.l pnm.|at̲r.btlt.‘nt.|w b‘l.tb‘.mrym.ṣpn.|idk.l ttn.pnm.|‘m.il.mbk.nhrm.|q 4[51].4.18
[---.]arḫt.tld[n].|a[lp].l btlt.‘nt.|w ypt l ybmt.li[mm].|w y‘ny.aliyn[.b‘l].|lm.k qnym.‘l[10[76].3.3
‘p.|nt‘n.b arṣ.ib y.|w b ‘pr.qm.aḫ k.|w tšu.‘n h.btlt.‘nt.|w tšu.‘n h.w t‘n.|w t‘n.arḫ.w tr.b lkt.|tr.b lkt.w tr.b ḫl. 10[76].2.26
‘[t k.]bt.k an[št].|k in.b ilht.ql[ṣ] k.mh.tarš[n].|l btlt.‘nt.w t[‘]n.btlt.‘n[t].|t̲hm k.il.ḥkm.ḥkm k.|‘m.‘lm.ḥyt.ḥẓt.t 3[‘NT.VI].5.37
[---].|aqht.w yplṭ k.bn[.dnil.---].|w y‘d̲r k.b yd.btlt.[‘nt].|w y‘n.lṭpn.il d p[id].|yd‘t k.bt.k anšt.w i[n.b ilht].|qlṣ 18[3AQHT].1.14
n.|[ḫ]mt.i[l.w] ḥrn.yisp.ḥmt.|[b‘l.w]dgn[.yi]sp.ḥmt.‘nt.w ‘t̲trt.|[ti]sp.ḥmt.y[r]ḫ.w.ršp.yisp.ḥmt.|[‘t̲]r.w ‘t̲tpr.yi UG5.8.14
šr.y‘db.ksa.w yt̲b.|tqru l špš.um h.špš.um.ql.bl.‘m.|‘nt w ‘t̲trt inbb h.mnt.nt̲k.|nhš.šlḥm.nhš.‘q šr[.y‘]db.ksa.|n UG5.7.20
m w d̲nb.ylšn.|b ḫri h.w t̲nt h.ql.il.[--].|il.k yrdm.arṣ.‘nt.|w ‘t̲trt.tṣdn.[---].|[---.-]b[-.---].|[‘t̲]trt w ‘nt[.---].|w b h UG5.1.1.22
nn[.--].|b‘l.yṣǵd.mli[.--].|il hd.mla.u[--.--].|blt.p btlt.‘n[t].|w p.n‘mt.aḫt[.b‘l].|y‘l.b‘l.b ǵ[r.---].|w bn.dgn.b š[---]. 10[76].3.10
.---].|kpr.šb‘ bn[t.rḥ.gdm.w anhbm].|kla[t.t̲ǵ]r[t.bht.‘nt.w tqry.ǵlmm.b št.ǵr].|ap ‘nt tm[t̲ḫṣ.b ‘mq.t̲ḫtṣb.bn.qryt 7.2[130].24
-.-]š[--].|kpr.šb‘.bnt.rḥ.gdm.|w anhbm.klat.t̲ǵrt.|bht.‘nt.w tqry.ǵlmm.|b št.ǵr.w hln.‘nt.tm|t̲ḫṣ.b ‘mq.t̲ḫtṣb.bn.| 3[‘NT].2.4
w t̲ḥdy.‘nt.|tǵdd.kbd h.b ṣḥq.ymlu.|lb h.b šmḫt.kbd.‘nt.|tšyt.k brkm.tǵll b dm.|d̲mr.ḥlqm.b mm‘.mhrm.|‘d.tšb‘ 3[‘NT].2.26
t.dm.‘lt.b ab y.|u---].‘lt.b k.lk.l pn y.yrk.b‘l.[--].|[---.]‘nt.šzrm.tštšḥ.km.ḥ[--].|[---].‘pr.bt k.ygr[š k.---].|[---.]y.ḥr. 1001.1.11
.|dgn.š.il t‘d̲r.š.|b‘l š.‘nt š.ršp š.|šlmm.|w šnpt.il š.|l ‘nt.ḥl š.t̲n šm.|l gt̲rm.ǵṣ b šmal.|d alpm.w alp w š.|šrp.w šl UG5.13.25
lṭpn.ḥtk k.|pl.‘nt.šdm.y špš.|pl.‘nt.šdm.il.yš[t k].|b‘l.‘nt.mḥrt̲[-].|iy.aliyn.b‘l.|iy.zbl.b‘l.arṣ.|w t‘n.nrt.ilm.š[p]š.| 6[49].4.38
rt.il.šp[š].|pl.‘nt.šdm.y špš.|pl.‘nt.šdm.il.yšt k.|[b]‘l.‘nt.mḥrt̲t.|iy.aliyn.b‘l.|iy.zbl.b‘l.arṣ.|ttb‘.btlt.‘nt.|idk.l ttn. 6[49].4.27
gdlt.|gdlt.t̲rmn.gdlt.pdry.gdlt dqt.|dqt.trt̲.dqt.|[rš]p.‘nt.ḫbly.dbḥn š[p]š pgr.|[g]dlt iltm ḫnqtm.d[q]tm.|[yr]ḫ.kt̲ 34[1].17
šḫry.|ym.b‘l.|yrḫ.|kt̲r.|t̲rmn.|pdry.|dqt.|trt̲.|ršp.|‘nt ḫbly.|špš pgr.|iltm ḫnqtm.|yrḫ kty.|ygb hd.|yrgb b‘l.| UG5.14.A.11
.|bn km k bk[r.z]bl.am..|rkm.agzrt[.--].arḫ..|b‘l.azrt.‘nt.[-]ld.|kbd h.l yd‘ hr h.[---]d[-].|tnq[.---.]in[b]b.p‘r.|yd h 13[6].30
t̲t̲mnm.|l k.tld.yṣb.ǵlm.|ynq.ḥlb.a[t̲]rt.|mṣṣ.t̲d.btlt.[‘nt].|mšnq.[---]. 15[128].2.27
lkt.w tr.b ḫl.|[b]n‘mm.b ysmm.ḥ[--]k.ǵrt.|[ql].l b‘l.‘nt.ttnn.|[---].b‘l m.d ip[---].|[il.]hd.d ‘nn.n[--].|[----.]aliyn. 10[76].2.31
ym.|tql.[---.]lb.tt̲[b]r.|qšt[.---]r.y[t̲]br.|t̲mn.[---.]btlt.[‘]nt.|tt̲b.[---.--]ša.|tlm.km[.---.]yd h.k šr.|knr.uṣb‘t h ḫrṣ.ab 19[1AQHT].1.5
.w tṣḥn].|šm‘.l dnil.[mt.rpi].|mt.aqht.ǵzr.[šṣat].|btlt.‘nt.k [rḥ.npš h].|k it̲l.brlt h.[b h.p‘nm].|tt̲t.‘l[n.pn h.td‘.b ‘d 19[1AQHT].2.92
m‘.l y.aliyn.b‘l.|tšm‘.nrt.ilm.špš.|tšu.aliyn.b‘l.l ktp.|‘nt.k tšt h.tš‘lyn h.|b ṣrrt.ṣpn.tbkyn h.|w tqbrn h.tštnn.b ḫ 6[62].1.15
p.d anšt.im[-].|aḥd.b aḫ k.l[--]n.|hn[-.]aḥẓ[.---]l[-].|[‘]nt.akl[y.nšm].|akly.hml[t.arṣ].|w y[-]l.a[---].|š[--.---].|bl[6[49].5.24
ḥt.t̲lḥn.|b qr‘.|‘t̲trt.w ‘nt.ymǵy.|‘t̲trt.t‘db.nšb l h.|w ‘nt.ktp.b hm.yg‘r.t̲ǵr.|bt.il.pn.l mgr lb.t‘dbn.|nšb.l inr.t‘db UG5.1.1.11
m[‘].|mhrm.mt̲m.tgrš.|šbm.b ksl.qšt h.mdnt.|w hln.‘nt.l bt h.tmǵyn.|tštql.ilt.l hkl h.|w l.šb‘t.tmt̲ḫṣ h.b ‘mq.|t̲ḫ 3[‘NT].2.17
‘ d.w.šb‘[d.qlt].|ankn.rgmt.l.b‘l y.|l.špš.‘lm.l.‘t̲trt.|l.‘nt.l.kl.il.alt̲[y].|nmry.mlk.‘lm.|mlk n.b‘l y.ḥw[t.--].|yšhr k 2008.1.8
-.]ps[.---].|[---].ytbr[.---].|[---.]uṭm.d̲r[qm.---].|[btl]t.‘nt.l kl.[---].|[tt]b‘.btlt.‘nt[.idk.l ttn.pnm].|‘m.ytpn.mhr.š[t. 18[3AQHT].4.4
gt.mzln.|t̲n.b ulm.|abmn.b gt.m‘rb.|atn.|ḫryn.|bn.‘nt.|llwn.|agdt̲b.|aǵltn.|[-]wn.|bldn.|[-]ln.|[-]ldn.|[i]wryn 1061.6
t.ǵzr.i]rš.ksp.w atn k.|[ḫrṣ.w aš]lḥ k.w tn.qšt k.[l].|[‘nt.tq]ḥ[.q]ṣ‘t k.ybmt.limm.|w y‘n.aqht.ǵzr.adr.t̲qbm.|[d]l 17[2AQHT].6.19
[---.--]m.l gt̲rm.|[---.]l ‘nt m.|[---.--]rm.d krm.|[---].l ‘nt m.|[---.]l šlm.|[-]l[-.-]ry.ylbš.|mlk.ylk.lqḥ.ilm.|at̲r.ilm.y 33[5].20
].t̲b.ap.w npš.|[---].bt.alp w š.|[---.--]m.l gt̲rm.|[---.]l ‘nt m.|[---.--]rm.d krm.|[---].l ‘nt m.|[---.]l šlm.|[-]l[-.-]ry.y 33[5].18
bṭ.|w b h.tdmmt.amht.|aḫr.mǵy.aliyn.b‘l.|mǵyt.btlt.‘nt.|tmgnn.rbt[.a]t̲rt ym.|tǵzyn.qnyt.ilm.|w t‘n.rbt.at̲rt ym 4[51].3.24
.mgntm.|t̲r.il.d pid.hm.ǵztm.|bny.bnwt w t‘n.|btlt.‘nt.nmgn.|[-]m.rbt.at̲rt.ym.|[nǵ]ẓ.qnyt.ilm.|[---].nmgn.hwt 4[51].3.33
anhbm.klat.t̲ǵrt.|bht.‘nt.w tqry.ǵlmm.|b št.ǵr.w hln.‘nt.tm|t̲ḫṣ.b ‘mq.t̲ḫtṣb.bn.|qrytm tmḫṣ.lim.ḫp y[m].|tṣmt. 3[‘NT].2.5
nhbm].|kla[t.t̲ǵ]r[t.bht.‘nt.w tqry.ǵlmm.b št.ǵr].|ap ‘nt tm[t̲ḫṣ.b ‘mq.t̲ḫtṣb.bn.qrytm.tmḫṣ].|lim ḫ[p.ym.---].|[-- 7.2[130].25
].|tšu.g h.w tṣḥ[.i]k.|mǵy.aliy[n.b]‘l.|ik.mǵyt.b[t̲]lt.|‘nt.mḫṣ y hm[.m]ḫṣ.|bn y.hm[.mkly.ṣ]brt.|ary y[.ẓl].ksp.[a 4[51].2.24
.w d l yd‘nn.|d.mṣd.|ylmn.ḫt̲.t̲ḥt.t̲lḥn.|b qr‘.|‘t̲trt.w ‘nt.ymǵy.|‘t̲trt.t‘db.nšb l h.|w ‘nt.ktp.b hm.yg‘r.t̲ǵr.|bt.il.p UG5.1.1.9
.b yd.bn ilm.mt.|ym.ymm.y‘tqn.l ymm.|l yrḫm.rḥm.‘nt.tngt̲ h.|k lb.arḫ.l ‘gl h.k lb.|t̲at.l imr h.km.lb.|‘nt.at̲r.b‘l 6[49].2.27
.|w l [---].|kd.[---].|kd.t[---.ym.ymm].|y‘tqn.w[rḥm.‘nt].|tngt̲ h.k lb.a[rḫ].|l ‘gl h.k lb.t̲a[t].|l imr h.km.lb.‘n[t]. 6[49].2.5
.|b bt y.ttn.tn.|l y.mt̲t.ḥry.|n‘mt.šbḥ.bkr k.|d k n‘m.‘nt.|n‘m h.km.tsm.|‘t̲trt.tsm h.|d ‘q h.ib.iqni.|‘p‘p h.sp.t̲r 14[KRT].6.291
n.b bt y.ttn.|tn.l y.mt̲t.ḥry.|n‘mt.špḥ.bkr k.|d k.n‘m.‘nt.n‘m h.|km.tsm.‘t̲trt.ts[m h].|d ‘q h.ib.iqni.‘p[‘p] h.|sp.t̲ 14[KRT].3.145
m.|w yšu.‘n h.aliyn.b‘l.|w yšu.‘n h.w y‘n.|w y‘n.btlt.‘nt.|n‘mt.bn.aḫt.b‘l.|l pnn h.ydd.w yqm.|l p‘n h.ykr‘.w yql 10[76].2.15
n.pnm.|‘m.b‘l.mrym.ṣpn.|b alp.šd.rbt.kmn.|ṣḥq.btlt.‘nt.tšu.|g h.w tṣḥ.tbšr b‘l.|bšrt k.yblt.y[b]n.|bt.l k.km.aḫ k. 4[51].5.87
d]n h.tlšn.aqht.ǵzr.|[---.kdd.dn]il.mt.rpi.w t‘n.|[btlt.‘nt.tšu.g]h.w tṣḥ.hwt.|[---.]aqht.yd̲[--].|[---.--]n.ṣ[---].|[spr. 17[2AQHT].6.53
nm].|[‘m.a]qht.ǵzr.b alp.š[d].|[rbt.]kmn.w ṣḥq.btlt.[‘nt].|[tšu.]g h.w tṣḥ.šm‘.m[‘.l a]|[qht.ǵ]zr.at.aḫ.w an.a[ḫt k 18[3AQHT].1.22
idk.l ytn pnm.|tk.aḫ.šmk.mla[t.r]umm.|tšu knp.btlt.‘n[t].|tšu.knp.w tr.b ‘p.|tk.aḫ šmk.mlat rumm.|w yšu.‘n h. 10[76].2.10
rm.‘l h.nšr[m].|trḫpn.ybṣr.ḥbl.diy[m.bn].|nšrm.trḫp.‘nt.‘l[.aqht].|t‘dbn h.hlmn.t̲nm[.qdqd].|t̲lt̲ id.‘l.udn.š[pk.k 18[3AQHT].4.32
m.|[hdmm.l ǵzrm.mid.tmt̲ḫṣn.w t]‘n.t̲ḫtṣb.|[w t̲ḥdy.‘nt.tǵdd.kbd h.b ṣḥ]q.ymlu.lb h.|[b šmḫt.kbd.‘nt.tšyt.t̲ḥt h. 7.1[131].7
ṣbim.hdmm.l ǵzrm.|mid.tmt̲ḫṣn.w t‘n.|t̲ḫtṣb.w t̲ḥdy.‘nt.|tǵdd.kbd h.b ṣḥq.ymlu.|lb h.b šmḫt.kbd.‘nt.|tšyt.k br 3[‘NT].2.24

‘nt

.|[-]šdm.|iwryn.|n‘mn.|[-----].|b gt.yny.|agttp.|bn.‘nt.|ǵzldn.|ṯrn.|ẖdbṯ.|[-]ḥl.aǵltn.|[-]n.|[-]mṯ.|[--.]bn.[‘]zn. 1043.12
r.šrš k.b arṣ.al.|yp‘.riš.ǵly.b d.ns‘ k.|‘nt.brḥ.p ‘lm h.|‘nt.p dr.dr.‘db.uẖry mṭ yd h.|ymǵ.l qrt.ablm.abl[m].|qrt.z 19[1AQHT].3.162
lm.|d ‘l k.mẖṣ.aqht.ǵzr.|‘wrt.yšt k.b‘l.l ht.|w ‘lm h.l ‘nt.p dr.dr.|‘db.uẖry.mṭ.yd h.|dnil.bt h.ymǵyn.yšt|ql.dnil.l 19[1AQHT].4.168
.d ‘[l k].|mẖṣ.aqht.ǵzr.amd.gr bt il.|‘nt.brḥ.p ‘lm h.‘nt.p dr[.dr].|‘db.uẖry mṭ.yd h.|ymǵ.l mrrt.tǵll.b nr.|yšu.g 19[1AQHT].3.154
.ǵr y.il.ṣpn.|b qdš.b ǵr.nḥlt y.|b n‘m.b gb‘.tliyt.|hlm.‘nt.tph.ilm.b h.p‘nm.|tṭṭ.b‘d n.ksl.ṯṯbr.|‘ln.pn h.td‘.tǵṣ.pnt. 3[‘NT].3.29
.w mdbḥt.|ẖr[.---.]‘l.kbkbt.|n‘m.[--.-]llm.trtḥṣ.|btlt.‘n[t].tptr‘ ṯd[h].|limm.w t‘l.‘m.il.|ab h.ḥpr.p‘l k.y[--].|šm‘ 13[6].19
‘l.|w mhr.‘nt.ṯm.yḥpn.ḥyl|y.zbl.mlk.‘llm y.km.tdd.|‘nt.ṣd.tštr.‘pt.šmm.|ṭbẖ.alpm.ap ṣin.šql.ṯrm.|w mri ilm.‘gl 22.2[124].11
kmm.w bbt.b‘l.ugrt.|w kdm.w npš ilib.|gdlt.il š.b‘l š.‘nt.|ṣpn.alp.w š.pdry.š.|šrp.w šlmm ilib š.|b‘l ugrt š.b‘l ẖlb UG5.13.13
š.pdry.š.|šrp.w šlmm ilib š.|b‘l ugrt š.b‘l ẖlb š.|yrẖ š.‘nt ṣpn.alp.|w š.pdry š.ddmš š.|w b urbt.ilib š.|b‘l alp w š. UG5.13.17
m.|[w bbt.b‘l.ugrt.]kdm.w npš.|[ilib.gdlt.il.š.b]‘[l.]š.‘nt ṣpn.|[---.]w [n]p[š.---].|[---.--]t.w[.---].|[---.--]pr.ṯ[--.---]. 36[9].1.17
[---.]drk.brḥ.arṣ.lk pn h.yrk.b‘[l].|[---.]bt k.ap.l pẖr k ‘nt tqm.‘nt.tqm.|[---.p]ẖr k.ygrš k.qr.bt k.ygrš k.|[---].bnt.ṣ 1001.2.9
.brḥ.arṣ.lk pn h.yrk.b‘[l].|[---.]bt k.ap.l pẖr k ‘nt tqm.‘nt.tqm.|[---.p]ẖr k.ygrš k.qr.bt k.ygrš k.|[---].bnt.ṣ‘ṣ.bnt.m 1001.2.9
nm.|b ‘qbt.ṯr.adr.b ǵlil.qnm.|tn.l kṯr.w ẖss.yb‘l.qšt l ‘nt.|qṣ‘t.l ybmt.limm.w t‘n.btlt.|‘nt.irš ḥym.l aqht.ǵzr.|irš 17[2AQHT].6.24
|w yšu.g h.w yṣḥ.|ḥwt.aẖt.w nar[-].|qrn.d bat k.btlt.‘nt.|qrn.d bat k b‘l.ymšḥ.|b‘l.ymšḥ.hm.b ‘p.|nṭ‘n.b arṣ.ib y 10[76].2.21
iyn.b‘l.|k iṯ.zbl.b‘l.arṣ.|gm.yṣḥ.il.l btlt.|‘nt.šm‘.l btlt.‘n[t].|rgm.l nrt.il.šp[š].|pl.‘nt.šdm.y špš.|pl.‘nt.šdm.il.yšt k 6[49].3.23
alp.w š].|ilhm.gd[lt.ilhm.b‘l.š.aṯrt.š].|ṯkmn.w š[nm.š.‘nt.š.ršp.š.dr].|il.w pẖr[.b‘l.gdlt.šlm.gdlt].|w burm.l[b.rmṣt APP.II[173].17
š[.il]hm.[gdlt.ilhm].|b‘[l.š].aṯrt[.š.ṯkm]n w [šnm.š].|‘nt š ršp š[.dr.il.w pẖr.b‘l].|gdlt.šlm[.gdlt.w burm.lb].|rmṣt 35[3].16
alp w š ilhm.gdl[t.]ilhm.|[b]‘l š.aṯrt.š.ṯkmn w šnm.š.|‘nt.š.ršp.š.dr il w p[ẖ]r b‘l.|gdlt.šlm.gdlt.w burm.[l]b.|rmṣt 34[1].7
š š.|w b urbt.ilib š.|b‘l alp w š.|dgn.š.il t‘ḏr.š.|b‘l š.‘nt š.ršp š.|šlmm.|w šnpt.il š.|l ‘nt.ḥl š.ṯn šm.|l gṯrm.ǵṣ b š UG5.13.22
.kṯr[t] š.yrẖ[.---].|ṣpn.š.kṯr.š.pdry.š.ǵrm.š[.---].|aṯrt.š.‘nt.š.špš.š.arṣy.š.‘ṯtrt.š.|ušẖry.š.il.t‘ḏr.b‘l.š.ršp.š.ddmš.š.|w UG5.9.1.7
.|ṯḥm.ṯr.il.ab k.|hwt.lṭpn.ḥtk k.|pl.‘nt.šdm.y špš.|pl.‘nt.šdm.il.yš[t k].|b‘l.‘nt.mḥrṯ[-].|iy.aliyn.b‘l.|iy.zbl.b‘l.arṣ. 6[49].4.37
m‘.l btlt.‘n[t].|rgm.l nrt.il.šp[š].|pl.‘nt.šdm.y špš.|pl.‘nt.šdm.il.yšt k.|[b]‘l.‘nt.mḥrṯt.|iy.aliyn.b‘l.|iy.zbl.b‘l.arṣ.| 6[49].4.26
pš.|tšu.g h.w tṣḥ.|ṯḥm.ṯr.il.ab k.|hwt.lṭpn.ḥtk k.|pl.‘nt.šdm.y špš.|pl.‘nt.šdm.il.yš[t k].|b‘l.‘nt.mḥrṯ[-].|iy.aliyn. 6[49].4.36
.yṣḥ.il.l btlt.|‘nt.šm‘.l btlt.‘n[t].|rgm.l nrt.il.šp[š].|pl.‘nt.šdm.y špš.|pl.‘nt.šdm.il.yšt k.|[b]‘l.‘nt.mḥrṯt.|iy.aliyn.b 6[49].4.25
w tḥdy.‘nt.tǵdd.kbd h.b ṣḥ]q.ymlu.lb h.|[b šmẖt.kbd.‘nt.tšyt.tḥt h.k]kdrt.riš.|[‘l h.k irbym.kp.---.k br]k.tǵll.b d 7.1[131].8
.npš.|k ḥy.aliyn.b‘l.|k iṯ.zbl.b‘l.arṣ.|gm.yṣḥ.il.l btlt.|‘nt.šm‘.l btlt.‘n[t].|rgm.l nrt.il.šp[š].|pl.‘nt.šdm.y špš.|pl.‘n 6[49].3.23
t].|k in.b ilht.ql[ṣ] k.mh.tarš[n].|l btlt.‘nt.w t[‘]n.btlt.‘n[t].|ṯḥm k.il.ḥkm.ḥkm k.|‘m.‘lm.ḥyt.ḥẓt.ṯḥm k.|mlk n.al 3[‘NT.VI].5.37
y h.b tk.ǵ]r y.il.ṣpn.|b q[dš.b ǵr.nḥ]lt y.|w t[‘n].btlt.[‘]nt.ṯṯb.|[ybmt.]limm.[a]n.aqry.|[b arṣ].mlḥmt.[aš]t.b ‘pr 3[‘NT].4.65
.ǵzr.št.ṯrm.w[---].|ištir.b ḏdm.w n‘rs[.---].|w t‘n.btlt.‘nt.ṯb.yṭp.w[---].|l k.ašt k.km.nšr.b ḥb[š y].|km.diy.b t‘rt y 18[3AQHT].4.16
.bt.r[b.mṯb.arṣy].|bt.y‘bdr[.mṯb.klt].|knyt.w t‘n[.btlt.‘nt].|yṯb l y.ṯr.il[.ab y.---].|yṯb.l y.w l h.[---].|[--.i]mṣẖ.nn.k 3[‘NT.VI].4.6
bš.brk n.šm.il.ǵzrm.|ṯm.ṯmq.rpu.b‘l.mhr b‘l.|w mhr.‘nt.ṯm.yḥpn.ḥyl|y.zbl.mlk.‘llm y.km.tdd.|‘nt.ṣd.tštr.‘pt.šm 22.2[124].9
t.ar.ahbt.ṭly.bt.rb.dd].|arṣy bt.y[‘bdr.---].|rgm l btl[t.‘nt.ṯny.l ybmt.limm.ṯḥm.aliyn.b‘l].|hw[t.aliy.qrdm.qryy.b a 7.2[130].13
rb n.l p‘n.‘nt.hbr.|w ql.tšthwy.kbd hyt.|w rgm.l btlt.‘nt.|ṯny.l ymmt.limm.|ṯḥm.aliyn.b‘l.hwt.|aliy.qrdm.qry.b 3[‘NT].3.8
ip[---].|[il.]hd.d ‘nn.n[--].|[----.]aliyn.b[‘l].|[---.btl]t.‘n[t.-.]p h.|[---.---]n.|[-----].|[-----].|[---.]lk[.--]t. 10[76].2.35
-].nmgn.hwt.|[--].aliyn.b‘l.|[--.]rbt.aṯrt.ym.|[---.]btlt.‘nt.|[--.tl]ḥm.tšty.|[ilm.w tp]q.mrǵṯm.|[ṯd.b ḥrb.m]lḥt.qṣ.| 4[51].3.39
[---.]btlt.‘nt.|[---.]pp.hrm.|[---].d l yd‘ bn il.|[---.]pẖr kkbm.|[---.]dr 10[76].1.1
.bt]lt.‘nt.|[---]q.hry.w yld.|[---]m.ḥbl.kṯ[r]t.|[---.bt]lt.‘nt.|[---.ali]yn.b‘l.|[---.]m‘n.|[-----].|[-----].|[---.--]r.|[---.--] 11[132].1.7
[-----].|[---].aṯ[--.---].|[---] h.ap.[---].|[---].w t‘n.[btlt.‘nt.---].|[bnt.bht]k.y ilm[.bnt.bht k.--].|[al.tšmẖ.]al.tš[mẖ. 18[3AQHT].1.6
rdm.arṣ.‘nt.|w ‘ṯtrt.tṣdn.[---].|[---.-]b[-.---].|[‘t]trt w ‘nt[.---].|w b hm.tṯṯb[.--]d h.|km trpa.hn n‘r.|d yšt.l.lṣb h ẖ UG5.1.2.1
p.pr.b‘l.[---].|w prt.tkt.[---].|šnt.[---].|ššw.‘ṯtrt.w ššw.‘[nt.---].|w ht.[--]k.ššw[.-]rym[.---].|d ymǵy.bnš[.---].|w ḥm 2158.1.6
.|[---.--]d mhr.ur.|[---.]yḥnnn.|[---.--]t.ytn.|[---.btlt.]‘nt.|[---.ybmt.]limm.|[---.---]l.limm.|[---.yṯ]b.l arṣ.|[---.--]l. 10[76].1.14
.|b ym.il.d[--.---.n]|hr.il.y[--.---].|aliyn.[b‘l.---].|btlt.[‘nt.---].|mh.k[--.---].|w at[--.---].|aṯr[t.---].|b im[--.---].|bl.l 4[51].2.38
ug[r.---].|‘nt[.---].|tmm l bt[.---].|b[‘]l.ugr[t.---].|w ‘ṣrm[.---].|ṣlyh šr 40[134].2
--].|kbd.w [---].|l ṣp[n.---].|š.[---].|w [----].|k[--.---].|‘n[t.---]. 40[134].15
[--.t]ṯkḥ.w tiẖd.b uš[k.--].|[-.b]‘l.yabd.l alp.|[---.bt]lt.‘nt.|[---]q.hry.w yld.|[---]m.ḥbl.kṯ[r]t.|[---.bt]lt.‘nt.|[---.ali] 11[132].1.4

‘ntn

[b]n ‘ntn.[---].|bn agyn[.---].|b[n] ‘ṯlṯ[.---].|bn qṭy[.---].|bn yp‘[.- 105[86].1

‘s

.l ytn.tk aršẖ.rbt.|w aršẖ.ṯrrt.ydy.b ‘ṣm.‘r‘r.|w b šḥt.‘s.mt.‘r‘rm.yn‘rn h.|ssnm.ysyn h.‘dtm.y‘dyn h.yb|ltm.ybln UG5.7.65

‘sb

--].|[---.--]t btm.qdš.il[.---].|[---.b]n.qdš.k[--.---].|[---.]‘sb.[-]ḥ[-.---].|[---.]b[-.]mṯt k.[---].|[---.]k.w tmt[.---].|[---.]k. 2125.4

‘sl

|[--.--]n.šb‘t.l ṯlṯm.|[---].šb‘t.‘šrt.|[---.-]kyn.‘šrt.|b.bn.‘sl.‘šrm.ṯqlm kbd.|b.ṯmq.ẖmšt.l.‘šrt.|b.[---].šb‘t.‘šrt.|b.bn.p 2054.1.6

‘p

.d mgdl.š[---].|[---.]mn.‘r hm[.---].|[---.]it[.---].|[---.]‘p[.---]. 18[3AQHT].1.34
‘.]ymm.bṣr.|kp.šsk k.[--].l ḥbš k.|‘tk.ri[š.]l mhr k.|w ‘p.l dr[‘].nšr k.|w rbṣ.l ǵr k.inbb.|kt ǵr k.ank.yd‘t.|[-]n.atn. 13[6].8
d bat k.btlt.‘nt.|qrn.d bat k b‘l.ymšḥ.|b‘l.ymšḥ.hm.b ‘p.|nṭ‘n.b arṣ.ib y.|w b ‘pr.qm.aẖ k.|w tšu.‘n h.btlt.‘nt.|w t 10[76].2.23
u.g h.w yṣḥ.knp.nšrm.|b‘l.yṯbr.b‘l.yṯbr.diy.|hmt.hm.t‘pn.‘l.qbr.bn y.|tšẖṭann.b šnt h.qr.[mym].|mlk.yṣm.y l km 19[1AQHT].3.150
.‘nt.ṯm.yḥpn.ḥyl|y.zbl.mlk.‘llm y.km.tdd.|‘nt.ṣd.tštr.‘pt.šmm.|ṭbẖ.alpm.ap ṣin.šql.ṯrm.|w mri ilm.‘glm.dt.šnt.|i 22.2[124].11
.šmk.mla[t.r]umm.|tšu knp.btlt.‘n[t].|tšu.knp.w tr.b ‘p.|tk.aẖ šmk.mlat rumm.|w yšu.‘n h.aliyn.b‘l.|w yšu.‘n h. 10[76].2.11

|abn.ank.w ‘l.[qšt k.---.‘l].|qṣ‘t k.at.l ḥ[---.---].|w ḫlq.‘pmm[.---]. 18[3AQHT].4.42

‘ps

t.špḥ.|l ydn.‘bd.mlk.|d št.‘l.ḫrd h.|špḥ.al.thbṭ.|ḫrd.‘ps.aḫd.kw|sgt.|ḫrd ksp.[--]r.|ymm.w[.---].|[-----].|w[.----- 2062.2.6
spr ‘psm.|dt.št.|uryn.|l mlk.ugrt. 1171.1

‘psn

[-----].|[-----].|ynḥm.|iḫy.|bn.mšt.|‘psn.|bn.ṣpr.|kmn.|bn.ršp.|tmn.|šmmn.|bn.rmy.|bn.aky. 1047.6

‘p‘p

k n‘m.‘nt.|n‘m h.km.tsm.|‘ṯtrt.tsm h.|d ‘q h.ib.iqni.|‘p‘p h.sp.ṯrml.|d b ḥlm y.il.ytn.|b ḏrt y.ab.adm.|w ld.špḥ.l 14[KRT].6.295
k.n‘m.‘nt.n‘m h.|km.tsm.‘ṯtrt.ts[m h].|d ‘q h.ib.iqni.‘p[‘p] h.|sp.ṯrml.thgrn.[-]dm[.-].|ašlw.b ṣp.‘n h.|d b ḥlm y. 14[KRT].3.147

‘pp

.ṯn.|npyn h.b nhrm.|štt.ḫptr.l išt.|ḫbrṯ.l ẓr.pḥmm.|t‘pp.ṯr.il.d pid.|tǵẓy.bny.bnwt.|b nši.‘n h.w tphn.|hlk.b‘l.a 4[51].2.10

‘pṣpn

kt.|šb‘l.bn.aly.ṯkt.|klby.bn.iḫy.ṯkt.|psš.bn.buly.ṯkt.|‘pṣpn.bn.‘dy.ṯkt.|n‘mn.bn.‘yn.ṯkt.|‘pṯn.bn.ilrš.ṯkt.|ilṯḥm.b 2085.9

‘pr

lb krd.ḥ[mr.---].|ṣ‘.ḥmr.w[.---].|ṣ‘q.ḥmr.w.[---].|ḫlb ‘prm.amḏy.[ḥm]r.w bn[š].|gn‘y.[---.bn]š.|uškn[.---].‘šr.bnš 2040.16
m.l mi[t].any.|tškn[n.--]h.k[--].|w šnm[.--.]w[.--].|w ‘prm.a[--.--]n.|[--.]ḫ[--.]d[--]t.|[---.]ḥw[t.---].|[---.]š[--].|w y 2062.1.7
.l pn y.yrk.b‘l.[--].|[---.]‘nt.šzrm.tštšḫ.km.ḥ[--].|[---].‘pr.bt k.ygr[š k.---].|[---.]y.ḥr.ḥr.bnt.ḥ[---].|[--.]uḫd.[b‘]l m. 2062.1.12
kl h.nṣb.skn.ilib h.b qdš.|ztr.‘m h.l arṣ.mšṣu.qṭr h.|l ‘pr.ḏmr.aṯr h.ṭbq.lḥt.|niṣ h.grš d.‘šy.ln h.|aḫd.yd h.b škrn. 1001.1.12
[nṣb.skn.i]lib h.b qdš.|[ztr.‘m h.l a]rṣ.mšṣu.|[qṭr h.l ‘pr.ḏ]mr.a[ṯ]r h.|[ṭbq.lḥt.niṣ h.gr]š.d ‘šy.|[ln h.---].|z[tr.‘m 17[2AQHT].1.29
|aḫ y.w šrš.km ary y.|nṣb.skn.ilib y.b qdš.|ztr.‘m y.l ‘pr.ḏmr.aṯr[y].|ṭbq lḥt.niṣ y.grš.|d ‘šy.ln.aḫd.yd y.b š|krn 17[2AQHT].1.47
ṣ h.gr]š.d ‘šy.|[ln h.---].|z[tr.‘m k.l arṣ.mšṣu.qṭr k].|l ‘pr.ḏm[r.aṯr k.ṭbq].|lḥt.niṣ k.gr[š.d ‘šy.ln k].|spu.ksm k.bt.[17[2AQHT].2.17
‘llm n.[---].|ilm.bt.b‘l k.[---].|dl.ylkn.ḥš.b a[rṣ.---].|b ‘pr.ḫbl ṭtm.[---.]|šqy.rṯa.tnm y.ytn.[ks.b yd].|krpn.b klat y 17[2AQHT].2.2
|ṯḥm.aliyn.b‘l.hwt.aliy.|qrdm.qry.b arṣ.mlḥmt.|št.b ‘p[r] m.ddym.sk.šlm.|l kbd.arṣ.arbdd.l kbd.šdm.|[ḥ]š k.[‘]ṣ 1[‘NT.X].4.8
.|[ṯr.il.ab k.hwt.l]ṭpn.ḥtk k.|[qryy.b arṣ.mlḥ]mt.št b ‘p|[r m.ddym.sk.šlm].l kbd.arṣ.|[arbdd.l kbd.š]dm.ḥš k.|[‘ 3[‘NT].4.53
|ṯḥm.aliyn.b‘l.hwt.|aliy.qrdm.qry.b arṣ.|mlḥmt št.b ‘pr m.ddym.|sk.šlm.l kbd.arṣ.|arbdd.l kbd.šdm.|ḥš k.‘ṣ k.‘ 1[‘NT.IX].2.19
nt.ṯṯb.|[ybmt.]limm.[a]n.aqry.|[b arṣ].mlḥmt.[aš]t.b ‘pr m.|ddym.ask[.šlm.]l kbd.arṣ.|ar[bdd.]l kb[d.š]dm.yšt.|[3[‘NT].3.12
dl h.yb‘r.|[---.]rn h.aqry.|[---.]b a[r]ṣ.mlḥmt.|ašt[.b ‘]p[r] m.ddym.ask.|šlm.l kb[d].awṣ.arbdd.|l kbd.š[d]m.ap. 3[‘NT].4.67
.aliyn.b‘l].|hw[t.aliy.qrdm.qryy.b arṣ.mlḥmt.št].|[b ‘]pr[m.ddym.sk.šlm.l kbd.arṣ.arbdd].|l kbd.š[dm.ḥš k.‘ṣ k.‘ 3[‘NT].4.73
[---.‘]n h.km.bṯn.yqr.|[krpn h.-.l]arṣ.ks h.tšpk m.|[l ‘pr.tšu.g h.]w tṣḥ.šm‘.m‘.|[l aqht.ǵzr.i]rš.ksp.w atn k.|[ḥrṣ. 7.2[130].15
k.|ḥtl k.w ẓi.|b aln.tk m.|b tk.mlbr.|ilšiy.|kry amt.|‘pr.‘ẓm yd.|ugrm.ḫl.ld.|aklm.tbrk k.|w ld ‘qqm.|ilm.yp‘r. 17[2AQHT].6.16
nhr.tl‘m.ṯm.ḥrbm.its.anšq.|[-]htm.l arṣ.ypl.ul ny.w l.‘pr.‘ẓm ny.|l b‘l[-.---].|ṯḥt.ksi.zbl.ym.w ‘n.kṯr.w ḫss.l rgmt. 12[75].1.24
si.ytb.|l hdm[.w] l.hdm.ytb.|l arṣ.yṣq.‘mr.|un.l riš h.‘pr.plṯt.|l qdqd h.lpš.yks.|mizrtm.ǵr.b abn.|ydy.psltm.b y‘ 2.4[68].5
at k b‘l.ymšḫ.|b‘l.ymšḫ.hm.b ‘p.|nṭ‘n.b arṣ.ib y.|w b ‘pr.qm.aḫ k.|w tšu.‘n h.btlt.‘nt.|w tšu.‘n h.w t‘n.|w t‘n.arḫ 5[67].6.15
ḫlb ‘prm.ṯṯ.|ḫlb krd.ṯn ‘šr.|qmy.arb‘.‘šr.|ṣ‘q.arb‘ ‘šr.|ṣ‘.ṯmn.|š 10[76].2.25
z[p].ṯṯ.|ḫrṣb‘.aḥd.|ypr.arb.|m[-]qb.‘šr.|ṯn‘y.ṯlṯ.|ḫlb ‘prm.ṯn.|tmḏy.ṯlṯ.|[--]rt.arb‘.|[---].‘šr. 67[110].1
70[112].12

‘pty

.|w.nḥl h.|bn.‘bl.|bn.[-]rṯn.|bn[.---].|bn u[l]pm.|bn ‘[p]ty.|bn.kdgdl.|bn.smyy.|bn.lbn.|bn.šlmn.|bn.mly.|psl 2163.3.3

‘pṯb

--].|bn.a[--].|bn.iy[--].|bn.ḫ[---].|bn.plš.|bn.ubr.|bn.‘pṯb.|ṯbry.|bn.ymn.|krty.|bn.abr[-].|yrpu.|kdn.|p‘ṣ.|bn.li 2117.1.17

‘pṯn

.|psš.bn.buly.ṯkt.|‘pṣpn.bn.‘dy.ṯkt.|n‘mn.bn.‘yn.ṯkt.|‘pṯn.bn.ilrš.ṯkt.|ilṯḥm.bn.šrn.ṯkt.|šmlbu.bn.grb.ṯkt.|šmlbu. 2085.11
rišym.qnum.|bn.ilrš.|‘[p]ṯn.|b[n.‘r]my.|[--]ṯy.|bn.ǵd‘.|bn.‘yn.|bn.grb[n].|yṯtn.| 2078.3
[---]n[.---].|[ag]dṯb.bn[.---].|‘bdil.bn.[---].|‘pṯn.bn.ṯṣq[-].|mnn.bn.krmn.|bn.umḫ.|yky.bn.slyn.|ypln. 85[80].1.4
rš.mrkbt.ṯq[lm].|bn.p‘ṣ.ṯqlm.|mṣrn.ḥrš.mrkbt.ṯqlm.|‘pṯn.ḥrš.qṭn.ṯqlm.|bn.pǵdn.ṯqlm.|bn.b‘ln.ṯqlm.|‘bdyrḫ.nqd 122[308].1.9
|[--]ṯn.|[---]d.|a[ǵ]lṯn.|[-----].|[--]ny.|kn‘m.|[-]p[-].|‘pṯn.|pslm.ṣnr. 2060.14
t.|prtwn.š‘rt.|ṯṯn.š‘rt.|‘dn.š‘rt.|mnn.š‘rt.|bdn.š‘rt.|‘pṯn.š‘rt.|‘bd.yrḫ š‘rt.|ḫbd.ṯr yṣr š‘r.|pdy.yṣr š‘rt.|atnb.ḥr. 97[315].9

‘pṯr

‘šrt.lkn.yp‘n.ṯ[--].|yṣḥm.b d.ubn.krwn.tǵd.[m]nḥm.|‘pṯrm.šm‘rgm.skn.qrt.|ḥgbn.šm‘.skn.qrt.|nǵr krm.‘bdadt.b 2011.10

‘pṯrm

drṣy.|[--]kn bn.pri.|[r]špab bn.pni.|[ab]mn bn.qṣy.|[‘]pṯrm bn.agmz.|[-]n bn.iln.|[--]nn bn.ibm.|[-]n bn.ḥrn.|[š] 2087.10
[-----].|[-]mn.|b‘ly.|rpan.|‘pṯrm.|bn.‘bd.|šmb‘l.|ykr.|bly.|ṯb‘m.|ḥdṯn.|rpty.|ilym.|b 1058.5
n.ulb.|ytr‘m.bn.swy.|ṣḥrn.bn.qrtm.|bn.špš.bn.ibrd.|‘pṯrm.bn.‘bdy.|n[--.]bn.šnd.|[---].bn.[---]. 2024.6

‘ṣ

].|[---.-]l[-.-]hg[.---].|[---.-]r[-.il]m.rbm.n‘l[.-]gr.|[---.]‘ṣ.b d h.ydrm[.]pi[-.]adm.|[---.]iṯ[-].yšql.ytk[.--]np bl.hn.|[-- UG5.8.32
ǵr h.il ṣpn.b [tk].|ǵr.tliyt.šb‘t.brqm.[---].|ṯmnt.iṣr r‘t.‘ṣ brq y.|riš h.tply.ṯly.bn.‘n h.|uz‘rt.tmll.išd h.qrn[m].|dt.‘l UG5.3.1.4

‘ṣ

y. | [ḥš.]bht h.tbnn. | [ḥš.]trmm.hkl h. | y[tl]k.l lbnn.w ‘ṣ h. | l[šr]yn.mḥmd.arz h. | h[n.l]bnn.w ‘ṣ h. | š[r]yn.mḥmd. 4[51].6.18

[tl]k.l lbnn.w ‘ṣ h. | l[šr]yn.mḥmd.arz h. | h[n.l]bnn.w ‘ṣ h. | š[r]yn.mḥmd.arz h. | tšt.išt.b bht m. | nb[l]at.b hkl m. | 4[51].6.20

štym.lḥ[m]. | b ṯlḥnt.lḥm št. | b krpnm.yn.b k.ḫrṣ. | dm.‘ṣm.hm.yd.il mlk. | yḫss k.ahbt.ṯr.t‘rr k. | w t‘n.rbt.aṯrt ym. | 4[51].4.38

išd k. | [dm.rgm.iṯ.l y.]w argm k.hwt. | [w aṯny k.rgm.]‘ṣ.w lḫšt. | [abn.rgm.l td]‘.nš[m.w l t]bn. | [hmlt.a]rṣ.[tant.šm 3[‘NT].4.58

. | ǵr.ks.dm.r[gm.iṯ.l y.w argm k]. | hwt.w aṯny k[.rgm.‘ṣ.w lḫšt.abn]. | tunt.šmm.‘m[.arṣ.thmt.‘mn.kbkbm]. | rgm.l t 1[‘NT.IX].3.13

ḥ.išd k.dm.rgm. | iṯ.l y.w argm k. | hwt.w aṯny k.rgm. | ‘ṣ.w lḫšt.abn. | tant.šmm.‘m.arṣ. | thmt.‘mn.kbkbm. | abn.brq 3[‘NT].3.20

k.dm.rgm.iṯ.l y.d argmn k]. | [h]wt.d aṯ[ny k.---.rgm.‘ṣ]. | w lḫšt.abn[.tant.šmm.‘m.arṣ.thmt]. | ‘m kbkbm[.abn.br 7.2[130].18

.y‘rb. | [b‘]l.b kbd h.b p h yrd. | k ḥrr.zt.ybl.arṣ.w pr. | ‘ṣm.yraun.aliyn.b‘l. | ṯt‘.nn.rkb.‘rpt. | tb‘.rgm.l bn.ilm.mt. | ṯn 5[67].2.6

r[m.ddym.sk.šlm.l kbd.arṣ.arbdd]. | l kbd.š[dm.ḥš k.‘ṣ k.‘bṣ k.‘m y.p‘n k.tls] | [m]n ‘m y t[wtḥ.išd k.dm.rgm.iṯ.l y 7.2[130].16

r m.ddym. | sk.šlm.l kbd.arṣ. | arbdd.l kbd.šdm. | ḥš k.‘ṣ k.‘bṣ k. | ‘m y.p‘n k.tlsmn.‘m y. | twtḥ.išd k.dm.rgm. | iṯ.l y. 3[‘NT].3.15

] m.ddym.sk.šlm. | l kbd.arṣ.arbdd.l kbd.šdm. | [ḥ]š k.[‘]ṣ k.‘bṣ k.‘m y.p‘n k. | [tls]mn.[‘]m y.twtḥ.išd k. | [dm.rgm.iṯ 3[‘NT].4.55

m.ddym.sk.šlm].l kbd.arṣ. | [arbdd.l kbd.š]dm.ḥš k. | [‘ṣ k.‘bṣ k.‘m y.p‘]n k.tlsmn. | [‘m y.twtḥ.išd] k.tk.ḫršn. | [---.- 1[‘NT.IX].2.22

[ḥš k.‘ṣ k.‘bṣ k.‘]m y.p[‘]n k. | [tlsmn.‘m y.twt]ḥ.išd k. | [tk.ḫršn.--- 1[‘NT.IX].2.1

| yh.kṯr.b[---]. | št.lskt.n[--.---]. | ‘db.bǵrt.ṯ[--. --]. | ḥš k.‘ṣ k.‘[bṣ k.‘m y.p‘n k.tlsmn]. | ‘m y twtḥ.i[šd k.tk.ḫršn.-------- 1[‘NT.IX].3.10

tḥm.rgm. | mlk. | l ḥyil. | lm.tlik.‘m y. | ik y.aškn. | ‘ṣm.l bt.dml. | p ank.atn. | ‘ṣm.l k. | arb‘.‘ṣm. | ‘l.ar. | w.ṯlṯ. | ‘l.u 1010.6

il. | lm.tlik.‘m y. | ik y.aškn. | ‘ṣm.l bt.dml. | p ank.atn. | ‘ṣm.l k. | arb‘.‘ṣm. | ‘l.ar. | w.ṯlṯ. | ‘l.ubr‘y. | w.ṯn.‘l. | mlk. | w.aḥ 1010.8

b h.aḫt.ppšr.w ppšrt[.---]. | [---.]k.drḫm.w aṯb.l ntbt.k.‘ṣm l t[--]. | [---.]drk.brḥ.arṣ.lk pn h.yrk.b‘[l]. | [---.]bt k.ap.l 1001.2.7

.ar. | w.ṯlṯ. | ‘l.ubr‘y. | w.ṯn.‘l. | mlk. | w.aḥd. | ‘l atlg. | w l.‘ṣm. | tspr. | nrn.al.tud | ad.at.l hm. | ṯṯm.ksp. 1010.17

y. | ik y.aškn. | ‘ṣm.l bt.dml. | p ank.atn. | ‘ṣm.l k. | arb‘.‘ṣm. | ‘l.ar. | w.ṯlṯ. | ‘l.ubr‘y. | w.ṯn.‘l. | mlk. | w.aḥd. | ‘l atlg. | w l 1010.9

.d qdm. | idk.pnm.l ytn.tk aršḫ.rbt. | w aršḫ.ṯrrt.ydy.b ‘ṣm.‘r‘r. | w b šḥt.‘s.mt.‘r‘rm.yn‘rn h. | ssnm.ysyn h.‘dtm.y‘d UG5.7.64

. | y bn.ašld.šu.‘db.tk.mdbr qdš. | ṯm tgrgr.l abnm.w l.‘ṣm.šb‘.šnt. | tmt.ṯmn.nqpt.‘d.ilm.n‘mm.ttlkn. | šd.tṣdn.pat. 23[52].66

ḥrb.[mlḥt.qṣ.mri]. | šty.kr[pnm.yn.---]. | b ks.ḫr[ṣ.dm.‘ṣm.---]. | ks.ksp[.---]. | krpn.[---]. | w ṯṯn.[---]. | t‘l.tr[-.---]. | bt. 5[67].4.16

b ḥrb.mlḥt.qṣ[.m]r | i.tšty.krp[nm.y]n. | [b k]s.ḫrṣ.d[m.‘ṣm]. | [---.--]n. | [---.---]t. | [---.--]ṯ. | [---.--]n. 4[51].6.59

ḥ]rb.mlḥ[t.qṣ]. | [mri.tšty.krpnm].yn.b ks.ḫ[rṣ]. | [dm.‘ṣm.---]n.krpn.‘l.[k]rpn. | [---.]ym.w t‘l.trṯ. | [---].yn.‘šy l ḥbš. 17[2AQHT].6.6

.b ḥrb.m]lḥt.qṣ. | [mri.tšty.k]rpnm yn. | [b ks.ḫrṣ.dm].‘ṣm. 4[51].3.44

‘ṣm

.‘bd.ḥrn.[--.]k. | [---].aǵwyn.‘n k.ẓẓ.w k mǵ.ilm. | [--.]k ‘ṣm.k ‘šm.l ttn.k abnm.l thggn. 1001.2.13

‘ṣr

b.š.i[l.--]m d gbl.ṣpn.al[p]. | pḫr.ilm.š.ym.š[.k]nr.š.[--.]‘ṣrm gdlt. | b‘lm.kmm.b‘lm.kmm[.b‘lm].kmm.b‘lm.kmm. | b‘ UG5.9.1.9

ṯp[-]. | aḥt.l mzy.bn[--]. | aḥt.l mkt.ǵr. | aḥt.l ‘ṯtrt. | arb‘.‘ṣrm. | gt.ṯrmn. | aḥt.slḫu. 39[19].17

bm].ymn. | lla.kl[atn]m. | klt.l[ḥm k.d]nzl. | qḥ.ms[rr.]‘ṣr. | dbḥ.ṣ[q.b g]l.ḥtṯ. | yn.b gl[.ḫ]rṣ.nbt. | ‘l.l ẓr.[mg]dl. | w ‘l.l 14[KRT].2.70

r.dbḥ.b yd h. | lla.klatnm. | klt.lḥm h.d nzl. | lqḥ.msrr.‘ṣr.db[ḥ]. | yṣq.b gl.ḥtṯ.yn. | b gl.ḫrṣ.nbt.w ‘ly. | l ẓr.mgdl.rkb. 14[KRT].3.163

[---.‘]ṣrm. | [--]ṯpḥ b‘l. | [ṯl]ṯ.‘ṣrm. | [w]b‘lt btm. | [---.--]ṣn.l.dgn. | [---.--]m. | [---].pi[--.-]qš. 39[19].3

--]. | [‘]ṣr.l pdr ṯṯ.ṣ[in.---]. | tšnpn.‘lm.km[m.---]. | w.l ll.‘ṣrm.w [---]. | kmm.w.in.‘ṣr[.---]. | w mit.š‘rt.[-]y[-.---]. | w.kdr 38[23].7

. | aṯtm.tṣḥn y.ad ad.nḥtm.ḫṭ k. | mmnnm.mṭ yd k.hl.‘ṣr.tḥrr.l išt. | w ṣḥrrt.l pḥmm.btm.bt.il.bt.il. | w ‘lm h.w hn.a 23[52].44

n.aṯtm.tṣḥn y.mt mt. | nḥtm.ḫṭ k.mmnnm.mṭ yd k.hl.‘ṣr. | tḥrr.l išt.w ṣḥrt.l pḥmm.aṯtm.a[ṯt.il]. | aṯt.il.w ‘lm h.yhb 23[52].47

ṯtm.tṣḥn. | y mt.mt.nḥtm.ḫṭ k.mmnnm.mṭ.yd k. | h[l.]‘ṣr.tḥrr.l išt.ṣḥrrt.l pḥmm. | a[ṯ]tm.aṯt.il.aṯt.il.w ‘lm h.w hm. 23[52].41

. | rmt.pr‘t.ibr[.mnt]. | ṣḥrrm.ḥbl[.--]. | ‘rpt.tḥt.[---] | m ‘ṣrm.ḥ[---]. | glṯ.isr[.---] | m.brt[.---]. | ymt m.[---]. | ši[.---]. | 8[51FRAG].12

il.ḫṭ h.nḥt.il.ymnn.mṭ.yd h.yšu. | yr.šmm h.yr.b šmm.‘ṣr.yḫrṭ yšt. | l pḥm.il.aṯtm.k ypt.hm.aṯtm.tṣḥn. | y mt.mt.nḥ 23[52].38

lk.brr]. | b arb‘[t.‘šrt.riš.argmn]. | w ṯn šm.l [b‘lt.bhtm.‘ṣrm.l inš]. | ilm.w š d[d.ilš.š.--.mlk]. | yṯb.brr[.w mḥ-.---]. | y 35[3].5

| br[r.]b a[r]b‘t.‘šrt.riš. | arg[mn.w ṯn.]šm.l b‘lt. | bhtm.‘ṣ[rm.l in]š ilm.w š. | dd ilš.š[.---.]mlk.yṯb br | r.w mḥ[--.---.] APP.II[173].6

]. | rmm.w ‘l[y.---]. | bt.il.ṯq[l.---.kbd]. | w bdḥ.k[--.---]. | ‘ṣrm.l i[nš.ilm.ṯb.md] | bḥ.b‘l.[gdlt.---.dqt]. | l ṣpn.w [dqt.---.ṯ APP.II[173].44

--]. | [md]bḥt.b.ḫmš[.---]. | [-.]kbd.w.db[ḥ.---]. | [--].aṯrt.‘ṣr[m.l inš.ilm]. | [ṯ]ṯb.mdbḥ.b‘l.g[dlt.---]. | dqt.l.ṣpn.w.dqt[.-- 35[3].40

l ǵlmt.š.w l [---.l yrḫ]. | gd[lt].l nkl[.gdlt.l b‘lt.bhtm]. | ‘š[rm.]l inš[.ilm.---]. | il[hm.]dqt.š[.---.rš] | [p.š]rp.w šl[mm.--. 35[3].27

lm[t.š.w l.---]. | l yrḫ.gdlt.l [nkl.gdlt.l b‘] | [lt].bht[m].[‘]ṣrm l [inš.ilm]. | [---.]ilh[m.dqt.š.--]. | [---.--]t.r[šp.šrp.w šl] | APP.II[173].29

. | [---.g]dlt.ṣpn.dqt.šrp.w [š]lmm. | [---.a]lp.l b‘l.w aṯrt.‘ṣr[m] l inš. | [ilm.---].lbbmm.gdlt.‘rb špš w ḥl. | [mlk.b ar]b‘t 36[9].1.8

t š. | [w]pamt ṯlṯm.w yrdt.[m]dbḥt. | gdlt.l b‘lt bhtm.‘ṣrm. | l inš ilm. 34[1].21

.w š šrp.alp šlmm. | l b‘l.‘ṣr l ṣpn. | npš.w.š.l ršp bbt. | [‘]ṣrm l h.ršp [-]m. | [---.]bqt[-]. | [b] ǵb.ršp mh bnš. | šrp.w ṣp UG5.12.A.12

[-.k]su.ilt[.---]. | [ṯl]ṯ.l ‘ṯtrt[.---]. | [--.]l ilt.š l ‘ṯt[rt.---]. | [‘]ṣr.l pdr ṯṯ.ṣ[in.---]. | tšnpn.‘lm.km[m.---]. | w.l ll.‘ṣrm.w [---] 38[23].5

.ksp.w ḫrṣ ṯ‘ ṯn šm l btbt. | alp.w š šrp.alp šlmm. | l b‘l.‘ṣr l ṣpn. | npš.w.š.l ršp bbt. | [‘]ṣrm l h.ršp [-]m. | [---.]bqt[-]. | UG5.12.A.10

.w bǵr.arb[‘.---]. | kdm.yn.prs.qmḥ.[---]. | mdbḥt.bt.ilt.‘ṣr[m.l ṣpn.š]. | l ǵlmt.š.w l [---.l yrḫ]. | gd[lt].l nkl[.gdlt.l b‘lt. 35[3].24

r.arb‘.[---.kdm.yn]. | prs.qmḥ.m‘[--.---]. | mdbḥt.bt.i[lt.‘ṣrm.l]. | ṣpn š.l ǵlm[t.š.w l.---]. | l yrḫ.gdlt.l [nkl.gdlt.l b‘] | [lt APP.II[173].26

]. | [dq]t.l.ṣpn.gdlt.l[.---]. | u[gr]t.š.l.[il]ib.ǵ[--.--rt]. | w [‘ṣrm.]l.ri[--.---]. | [--]t.b‘lt.bt[.---]. | [md]bḥt.b.ḫmš[.---]. | [-.]k 35[3].36

.l b[‘l.--.dqt]. | l ṣpn.gdlt.[l.---]. | ugrt.š l ili[b.---]. | rt.w ‘ṣrm.l[.---]. | pamt.w bt.[---]. | rmm.w ‘l[y.---]. | bt.il.ṯq[l.---.kb APP.II[173].39

n.b išt.tšrpnn. | b rḥm.tṭḥnn.b šd. | tdr‘nn.šir h.l tikl. | ‘ṣrm.mnt h.l tkly. | npr[m.]šir.l šir.yṣḥ. 6[49].2.36

m.ynqm.b ap.ḏd.št.špt. | l arṣ.špt l šmm.w ‘rb.b p hm.‘ṣr.šmm. | w dg b ym.w ndd.gzr.l zr.y‘db.u ymn. | u šmal.b p 23[52].62

. | hl ny.argmn.d [ybl.n]qmd. | l špš.arn.ṯn[.‘šr h.]mn. | ‘ṣrm.ṯql.kbd[.ks].mn.ḫrṣ. | w arb‘.ktnt.w [---]b. | [ḫm]š.mat p 64[118].20

b pš y.t[--]. | hwt.b‘l.iš[--]. | šm‘ l y.ypš.[---]. | ḥkr[.---]. | ‘ṣr[.--.]tb[-]. | ṯat[.---]. | yn[-.---]. | i[--.---]. 2124.7

[---.‘]ṣrm. | [--]ṯpḥ b‘l. | [ṯl]ṯ.‘ṣrm. | [w]b‘lt btm. | [---.--]ṣn.l.dgn. | [39[19].1

. | tšnpn.‘lm.km[m.---]. | w.l ll.‘ṣrm.w [---]. | kmm.w.in.‘ṣr[.---]. | w mit.š‘rt.[-]y[-.---]. | w.kdr.w.npt t[--.---]. | w.ksp.y‘ 38[23].8

byn.ltḥ.ššmn.ltḥ.šḥlt. | [---.ltḥ.]ṣmqm.[ṯ]ṯ.mat.nṣ.ṯlṯm.‘ṣr. | [---].ḫmš[m.ḥm]r.škm. | [---.ṯṯ.dd.]gdl.ṯṯ.dd.š‘rm. | [---.h 142[12].5

ug[r.---].|‘nt[.---].|tmm l bt[.---].|b[‘]l.ugr[t.---].|w ‘ṣrm[.---].|ṣlyh šr[-.---].|[t]ltm.w b[--.---].|l il limm[.---].|w 40[134].5
bn.nṣ.|[b]n.‘ṣr.|[---]m.|[bn.]ulnhr.|[bn.p]rn.|[bn.a]nny.|[---]n.|bn.kbl 1075.1.2

‘q

bḫ.bkr k.|d k n‘m.‘nt.|n‘m h.km.tsm.|‘ṯtrt.tsm h.|d ‘q h.ib.iqni.|‘p‘p h.sp.ṯrml.|d b ḥlm y.il.ytn.|b ḏrt y.ab.ad 14[KRT].6.294
pḫ.bkr k.|d k.n‘m.‘nt.n‘m h.|km.tsm.‘ṯtrt.ts[m h].|d ‘q h.ib.iqni.‘p[‘p] h.|sp.ṯrml.ṯhgrn.[-]dm[.-].|ašlw.b ṣp.‘n h. 14[KRT].3.147
nt.nṯk.|nḥš.šlḥm.nḥš.‘q šr[.y‘]db.ksa.|nḥš.šmrr.nḥš.‘q šr.ln h.ml|ḫš.abd.ln h.ydy.ḥmt.hlm.yṯq.|w yṯb.|tqru.l šp UG5.7.21
um.ql bl.‘m|kṯr.w ḫss.kptr h.mnt.nṯk.nḥš.|šmrr.nḥš.‘q šr.ln h.mlḫš.abd.|ln h.ydy.ḥmt.hlm yṯq.nḥš.|yšlḥm.nḥš.‘ UG5.7.47
.um.ql bl.|‘m b‘l.mrym.ṣpn.mnt y.nṯk.|nḥš.šmrr.nḥš.‘q šr ln h.|mlḫš.abd.ln h.ydy.ḥmt.hlm.yṯq.|nḥš.yšlḥm.nḥš.‘ UG5.7.10
h.špš.um.ql.bl.‘m.|dgn.ttl h.mnt.nṯk.nḥš.šmrr.|nḥš.‘q šr.ln h.mlḫš.abd.ln h.|ydy.ḥmt.hlm.yṯq.nḥš.yšlḥm.|nḥš.‘ UG5.7.16
um.ql bl ‘m.|ṯṯ.w kmṯ.ḥryt h.mnt.nṯk.nḥš.šm|rr.nḥš.‘q šr.ln h.mlḫš abd.ln h.|ydy.ḥmt.hlm.yṯq nḥš yšlḥm.nḥš.|‘ UG5.7.37
š.um h.špš.um.ql b.‘m.|ršp.bbt h.mnt.nḥš.šmrr.|nḥš.‘q šr.ln h.mlḫš.abd.ln h.ydy.|ḥmt.hlm.yṯq.nḥš.yšlḥm.nḥš ‘q UG5.7.32
.|il.mbk nhrm.b ‘dt.thmtm.|mnt.nṯk.nḥš.šmrr.nḥš.|‘q šr.ln h.mlḫš abd.ln h.ydy.|ḥmt.hlm.yṯq yṯqšqy.nḥš.yšlḥ UG5.7.5
pš.[um.q]l bl.‘m.|yrḫ.lrgt h.mnt.nṯk.n[ḥš].šmrr.|nḥš.‘q šr.ln h.mlḫš.abd.ln h.ydy.|ḥmt.hlm.yṯq.nḥš.yšlḥm.nḥš.|‘ UG5.7.27
.špš um ql.bl.‘m.|mlk.‘ṯtrt h.mnt.nṯk.nḥš.šmrr.|nḥš.‘q šr.ln h.mlḫš abd.ln h.ydy.|ḥmt.hlm.yṯq.nḥš.yšlḥm.nḥš.|‘ UG5.7.42
.špš.um.ql bl.|‘m ḥrn.mṣd h.mnt.nṯk nḥš.|šmrr.nḥš.‘q šr.ln h.mlḫš.|abd.ln h.ydy.ḥmt.|b ḥrn.pnm.trġnw.w ṯṯkl UG5.7.59
.ql bl ‘m.|šḥr.w šlm šmm h mnt.nṯk.nḥš.|šmrr.nḥš ‘q šr.ln h.mlḫš.|abd.ln h.ydy ḥmt.hlm.yṯq šqy.|nḥš.yšlḥm. UG5.7.53
mlḫš.|abd.ln h.ydy ḥmt.hlm.yṯq šqy.|nḥš.yšlḥm.nḥš.‘q šr.y‘db.|ksa.w yṯb.|tqru l špš.um h.špš.um.ql bl.|‘m ḥrn UG5.7.55
.ln h.mlḫš.abd.ln h.ydy.|ḥmt.hlm.yṯq.nḥš.yšlḥm.nḥš ‘q.|š.y‘db.ksa w yṯb.|tqru l špš.um h.špš.um.ql bl ‘m.|ṯṯ.w UG5.7.33
h.mlḫš abd.ln h.ydy.|ḥmt.hlm.yṯq yṯqšqy.nḥš.yšlḥm.‘q šr.|y‘db.ksa.w.yṯb.|tqru.l špš.um h.špš.um.ql bl.|‘m b‘l. UG5.7.6
n h.mlḫš.abd.|ln h.ydy.ḥmt.hlm yṯq.nḥš.|yšlḥm.nḥš.‘q šr.y‘db ksa.|w yṯb.|tqru l špš.um h.špš.um.ql bl ‘m.|šḥr. UG5.7.49
n h.mlḫš.abd.ln h.ydy.|ḥmt.hlm.yṯq.nḥš.yšlḥm.nḥš.|‘q šr.y‘db.ksa.w yṯb.|tqru.l špš.um h.špš.um.ql b.‘m.|ršp.b UG5.7.29
n h.mlḫš abd.ln h.ydy.|ḥmt.hlm.yṯq.nḥš.yšlḥm.nḥš.|‘q šr.y‘db.ksa.w yṯb.|tqru.l špš.um.ql bl.‘m|kṯr.w ḫss.kptr UG5.7.44
n h.|mlḫš.abd.ln h.ydy.ḥmt.hlm.yṯq.|nḥš.yšlḥm.nḥš.‘q šr.ydb.ksa.|w yṯb.|tqru.l špš.u h.špš.um.ql.bl.‘m.|dgn.ttl UG5.7.12
n h.mlḫš.abd.ln h.|ydy.ḥmt.hlm.yṯq.nḥš.yšlḥm.|nḥš.‘q šr.y‘db.ksa.w yṯb.|tqru l špš.um h.špš.um.ql.bl.‘m.|‘nt w UG5.7.18
n h.mlḫš abd.ln h.|ydy.ḥmt.hlm.yṯq nḥš yšlḥm.nḥš.|‘q.šr.y‘db.ksa.w yṯb.|tqru l špš um h.špš um ql.bl.‘m.|mlk.‘ UG5.7.39
m.ql.bl.‘m.|‘nt w ‘ṯtrt inbb h.mnt.nṯk.|nḥš.šlḥm.nḥš.‘q šr[.y‘]db.ksa.|nḥš.šmrr.nḥš.‘q šr.ln h.ml|ḫš.abd.ln h.ydy UG5.7.23

‘qb

šd.snrym.dt.‘qb.|b.ayly.|šd.abršn.|šd.kkn.[bn].ubyn.|šd.bn.li[y].|šd.bn 2026.1
.[l].|[‘nt.tq]ḥ[.q]ṣ‘t k.ybmt.limm.|w y‘n.aqht.ġzr.adr.ṯqbm.|[d]lbnn.adr.gdm.b rumm.|adr.qrnt.b y‘lm.mtnm.|b 17[2AQHT].6.20
ḫnp.lb[k.--.ti]|ḫd.d iṯ.b kbd k.tšt.b [---].|irt k.dṯ.ydṯ.m‘qb k.[ttb‘].|[bt]lt.‘nt.idk.l ttn.[pnm].|[‘m.a]qht.ġzr.b alp. 18[3AQHT].1.19
[d]lbnn.adr.gdm.b rumm.|adr.qrnt.b y‘lm.mtnm.|b ‘qbt.ṯr.adr.b ġlil.qnm.|tn.l kṯr.w ḫss.yb‘l.qšt l ‘nt.|qṣ‘t.l yb 17[2AQHT].6.23

‘qltn

il ym.l klt.nhr.il.rbm.|l ištbm.tnn.ištml h.|mḫšt.bṯn.‘qltn.|šlyṭ.d šb‘t.rašm.|mḫšt.mdd ilm.ar[š].|ṣmt.‘gl.il.‘tk.| 3[‘NT].3.38
k tmḫṣ.ltn.bṯn.brḥ.|tkly.bṯn.‘qltn.|šlyṭ.d šb‘y.rašm.|ṯṯkḥ.ttrp.šmm.k rs.|ipd k.ank.ispi. 5[67].1.2
iṯ‘n k.|[---.]ma[---] k.k tmḫṣ.|[ltn.bṯn.br]ḥ.tkly.|[bṯn.‘qltn.]šlyṭ.|[d šb‘t.rašm].ṯṯkḥ.|[ttrp.šmm.k rks.ipd]k.|[----- 5[67].1.29

‘qqm

kry amt.|‘pr.‘ẓm yd.|ugrm.ḥl.ld.|aklm.tbrk k.|w ld ‘qqm.|ilm.yp‘r.|šmt hm.|b hm.qrnm.|km.ṯrm.w gbṯt.|km. 12[75].1.27
‘l.ytlk.w yṣd.|yḥ pat.mlbr.|wn.ymġy.aklm.|w ymẓa.‘qqm.|b‘l.ḥmd m.yḥmd m.|bn.dgn.yhrr m.|b‘l.ngṯ hm.b p‘ 12[75].1.37

‘r

.ṯkmt.my.ḫspt.l[š‘]r.ṭl.|yd‘t.hlk.kbkbm.|bkm.tmdln.‘r.|bkm.tṣmd.pḥl.bkm.|tšu.ab h.tštnn.l[b]mt ‘r.|l ysmsm.b 19[1AQHT].2.57
.ln h.ydy.ḥmt.|b ḥrn.pnm.trġnw.w ṯṯkl.|bnwt h.ykr.‘r.d qdm.|idk.pnm.l ytn.tk aršḫ.rbt.|w aršḫ.ṯrrt.ydy.b ‘ṣm.‘ UG5.7.62
‘.š‘tqt.|bt.krt.bu.tbu.|bkt.tgly.w tbu.|nṣrt.tbu.pnm.|‘rm.tdu.mh.|pdrm.tdu.šrr.|ḥṭ m.t‘mt.[‘]ṭr.[k]m.|zbln.‘l.riš 16.6[127].6
.---].|š‘d[.---].|rt.[---].|‘ṯr[.---].|b p.š[---].|il.p.d[---].|‘rm.[di.mh.pdrm].|di.š[rr.---].|mr[ṣ.---].|zb[ln.---].|t[--.---]. 16[126].5.48
.---].|asr.sswm.tṣmd.dg[-.---].|t‘ln.l mrkbt hm.ti[ty.l ‘r hm].|tlkn.ym.w ṯa aḫr.š[pšm.b ṯlṯ].|mġy.rpum.l grnt.i[ln 20[121].2.4
tdd.ilnym].|asr.mr[kbt.---].|t‘ln.l mr[kbt hm.tity.l] |‘r hm.tl[kn.ym.w ṯn.aḫr.špšm].|b ṯlṯ.mġy[.rpum.l grnt].|i[l 22.1[123].24
qrt.ablm.a[blm].|[qrt.zbl.]yrḫ.d mgdl.š[---].|[---.]mn.‘r hm[.---].|[---.]it[.---].|[---.]‘p[.---]. 18[3AQHT].1.32
.bn.il.ytši.l dr.|bn il.l mpḫrt.bn.il.l ṯkmn[.w]šnm.hn.‘r.|w.ṯb.l mspr.m[šr] mšr.bt.ugrt.w npy.gr.|ḥmyt.ugrt.w [n 32[2].1.26
br].|tṣr.trm.tnq[--].|km.nkyt.ṯġr[.---].|km.škllt.[---].|‘r.ym.l bl[.---].|b[---.]ny[.---].|l bl.sk.w [---] h.|ybm h.šb‘[.--- 16.2[125].91
.tmdln.‘r.|bkm.tṣmd.pḥl.bkm.|tšu.ab h.tštnn.l[b]mt ‘r.|l ysmsm.bmt.pḥl.|y dnil.ysb.palt h.|bṣql.yph.b palt.bṣ[19[1AQHT].2.59
.|‘db.gpn.atnt h.|yḥbq.qdš.w amrr.|yštn.aṯrt.l bmt.‘r.|l ysmsmt.bmt.pḥl.|qdš.yuḫdm.šb‘r.|amrr.k kbkb.l pnm 4[51].4.14
i.l dr.bn.il.l mpḫrt.bn.i[l.l ṯkmn.w š]nm hn š.|w šqrb.‘r.mšr mšr bn.ugrt.w [npy.---.]ugr.|w npy.yman.w npy.‘rm 32[2].1.18
.|ṯrm.|bṣr.|y[--].|y[--].|snr.|midḫ.|ḫ[lym].|[ḫ]lby.|‘r.|‘nq[pat].|glbty.|[-----].|[-----].|[-----].|ykn‘m.|šl 2058.2.23
ṯr.qdqd h.|il[.--.]rḥq.b ġr.|km.y[--.]ilm.b ṣpn.|‘dr.l[‘r].‘rm.|ṯb.l pd[r.]pdrm.|ṯṯ.l ṯṯm.aḥd.‘r.|šb‘m.šb‘.pdr.|ṯmn 4[51].7.7
[q.nqbnm].|‘db.gpn.atnt[y].|yšm‘.qd.w amr[r].|mdl.‘r.ṣmd.pḥl.|št.gpnm.dt.ksp.|dt.yrq.nqbnm.|‘db.gpn.atnt h. 4[51].4.9
ṯr[t.ym.šm‘.l qdš].|w am[rr.l dgy.rbt].|aṯrt.ym[.mdl.‘r].|ṣmd.pḥl[.št.gpnm.dt].|ksp.dt.yr[q.nqbnm].|‘db.gpn.at 4[51].4.4
‘.pġt.ṯkmt[.my].|ḥspt.l š‘r.ṭl.yd[‘t].|hlk.kbkbm.mdl.‘r.|ṣmd.pḥl.št.gpn y dt ksp.|dt.yrq.nqbn y.tš[m‘].|pġt.ṯkmt 19[1AQHT].2.52
mt.l p[.n]ṯk.abd.l p.akl ṯm.dl.|[---.q]l.bl.tbḥ[n.l]azd.‘r.qdm.|[---].‘ẓ q[dm.--.šp]š.|[---.šm]n.mšḥt.kṯpm.a[-]ṯ[-].|[UG5.8.21
d ilgb[-].|mrmnmn.|brrn aryn.|a[-]ḥn tlyn.|atdb w ‘r.|qdš w amrr.|ṯḥr w bd.|[k]ṯr ḫss šlm.|šlm il bt.|šlm il ḫ UG5.7.71
lm.b ṣpn.|‘dr.l[‘r].‘rm.|ṯb.l pd[r.]pdrm.|ṯṯ.l ṯṯm.aḥd.‘r.|šb‘m.šb‘.pdr.|ṯmnym.b‘l.[----].|tš‘m.b‘l.mr[-].|bt[.--]b b‘ 4[51].7.9
šm.|b šb‘.w tmġy.l udm.|rbm.w l.udm.ṯrrt.|w gr.nn.‘rm.šrn.|pdrm.s‘t.b šdm.|ḥṭb h.b grnt.ḥpšt.|s‘t.b nk.šibt.b 14[KRT].3.110

‘r

aẖr.špšm.b rb‘. | ymǵy.l udm.rbt. | w udm[.ṯr]rt. | grnn.‘rm. | šrnn.pdrm. | s‘t.b šdm.ḥṭb. | w b grnt.ḥpšt. | s‘t.b npk.ši 14[KRT].4.212

qdqd h. | il[.--.]rḥq.b ǵr. | km.y[--.]ilm.b ṣpn. | ‘dr.l[‘r].‘rm. | ṯb.l pd[r.]pdrm. | ṯṯ.l ṯṯm.aẖd.‘r. | šb‘m.šb‘.pdr. | ṯmnym 4[51].7.7

[-----]. | ‘r[.---]. | ‘r[.---]. | ‘r[.---]. | w y[---]. | b‘d[.---]. | yaṯr[.---]. | b d k.[---]. | ṯnnt h[.---]. 16[126].5.3

il. | ytši.l d[r.bn il.l]mpḥrt.bn il. | l ṯkm[n.w šnm.]hn ‘[r]. | [---.]w npy[.---]. | [---.]w npy.u[grt.---]. | [---.--]y.ulp.[---] 32[2].1.35

-]n.irš[.---]. | [---.--]mr.ph. | [---.--]mm.hlkt. | [---.]b qrb.‘r. | [---.m]lakm l h. | [---.]l.bn.il. | [---.--]a.‘d h. | [---.--]rh. | [---. 26[135].5

[-----]. | bṣr[.---]. | lbn[m]. | ‘r[.---]. | nnu[.---]. | šq[--.---]. | [-]r[-.---]. | [-----]. | [-----]. | mg[--. 2145.4

[-----]. | ‘r[.---]. | ‘r[.---]. | ‘r[.---]. | w y[---]. | b‘d[.---]. | yaṯr[.---]. | b d k.[---]. | ṯnn 16[126].5.2

[-----]. | ‘r[.---]. | ‘r[.---]. | ‘r[.---]. | w y[---]. | b‘d[.---]. | yaṯr[.---]. | b d k.[16[126].5.1

--]n.yd h. | [---].bl.išlḥ. | [---] h.gm. | [l --- k.]yṣḥ. | [---]d.‘r. | [----.-]bb. | [----.]lm y. | [---.--]p. | [---.d]bḥ. | t[---.id]k. | pn[14[KRT].5.239

‘rb

‘m. | ydn.bn.ilrpi. | w.ṯb‘m.‘rb.b.‘[d]n. | ḏmry.bn.yrm. | ‘rb.b.ad‘y. 2079.10

rd. | ayaẖ. | bn.aylt. | ẖmš.mat.arb‘m. | kbd.ksp.anyt. | d.‘rb.b.anyt. | l.mlk.gbl. | w.ẖmšm.ksp. | lqḥ.mlk.gbl. | lbš.anyt 2106.12

mṣry.d.‘rb.b.unṯ. | bn.qrrn.mḏrǵl. | bn.tran.mḏrǵl | bn.ilh.mḏrǵl | špš 2046.1.1

rišym.dt.‘rb. | b bnš hm. | ḏmry.w.pṯpṯ.‘rb. | b.yrm. | [ily.w].ḏmry.‘rb. | 2079.1

.npṣ y.b ym.rṯ. | dn.il.bt h.ymǵyn. | yštql.dnil.l hkl h. | ‘rb.b bt h.kṯrt.bnt. | hll.snnt.apnk.dnil. | mt.rpi.ap.hn.ǵzr.mt. 17[2AQHT].2.26

id.grdš.ṯbt h. | w b tm hn.špḥ.yitbd. | w b.pẖyr h.yrṯ. | y‘rb.b ḥdr h.ybky. | b ṯn.[-]gmm.w ydm‘. | tntkn.udm‘t h. | k 14[KRT].1.26

. | il.trḥṣ.w tadm. | rḥṣ[.y]d k.amt. | uṣb[‘t k.]‘d[.ṯ]km. | ‘rb[.b ẓl.ẖmt]. | qḥ im[r.b yd k]. | imr.d[bḥ.bm].ymn. | lla.kl[a 14[KRT].2.65

rt. | yrtḥṣ.w yadm. | yrḥṣ.yd h.amt h. | uṣb‘t h.‘d.ṯkm. | ‘rb.b ẓl.ẖmt.lqḥ. | imr.dbḥ.b yd h. | lla.klatnm. | klt.lḥm h.d n 14[KRT].3.159

rišym.dt.‘rb. | b bnš hm. | ḏmry.w.pṯpṯ.‘rb. | b.yrm. | [ily.w].ḏmry.‘rb. | b.ṯb‘m. | ydn.bn.ilrpi. | w.ṯb‘m 2079.3

spr.‘rbnm. | dt.‘rb. | b.mtn.bn.ayaẖ. | b.ẖbṯ h.ḥwt.ṯt h. | w.mnm.šalm. | dt.tkn 1161.2

yrm. | [ily.w].ḏmry.‘rb. | b.ṯb‘m. | ydn.bn.ilrpi. | w.ṯb‘m.‘rb.b.‘[d]n. | ḏmry.bn.yrm. | ‘rb.b.ad‘y. 2079.8

zr ym.bn ym.ynqm.b ap.ḏd.št.špt. | l arṣ.špt l šmm.w ‘rb.b p hm.‘ṣr.šmm. | w dg b ym.w ndd.gzr.l zr.y‘db.u ymn. 23[52].62

b. | b bnš hm. | ḏmry.w.pṯpṯ.‘rb. | b.yrm. | [ily.w].ḏmry.‘rb. | b.ṯb‘m. | ydn.bn.ilrpi. | w.ṯb‘m.‘rb.b.‘[d]n. | ḏmry.bn.yrm 2079.5

db.uẖry.mṭ.yd h. | dnil.bt h.ymǵyn.yšt | ql.dnil.l hkl h.‘rb.b | kyt.b hkl h.mšspdt.b ḥẓr h. | pẓǵm.ǵr.ybk.l aqht. | ǵzr. 19[1AQHT].4.171

rḥb.mknpt.ap. | [k]rt.bnm.il.špḥ. | lṭpn.w qdš.‘l. | ab h.y‘rb.ybky. | w yšnn.ytn.g h. | bky.b ḥy k.ab n.ašmẖ. | b l.mt k 16.1[125].12

[-----]. | [špt.l a]rṣ.špt.l šmm. | [---.l]šn.l kbkbm.y‘rb. | [b‘]l.b kbd h.b p h yrd. | k ḥrr.zt.ybl.arṣ.w pr. | ‘ṣm.yra 5[67].2.3

.bn.abnm. | [---.]upqt.‘rb. | [---.w ẓ]r.mtn y at zd. | [---.]t‘rb.bši. | [---.]l tzd.l tptq. | [---].g[--.]l arṣ. 1[‘NT.X].5.26

n.lbšm.w.mšlt. | l.udmym.b.ṯmnt.‘šrt.ksp. | šb‘m.lbš.d.‘rb.bt.mlk. | b.mit.ẖmšt.kbd.ksp. | ṯlṯ.ktnt.b d.an[r]my. | b.‘šrt 2101.16

spr.npš.d. | ‘rb.bt.mlk. | w.b.spr.l.št. | yrm‘l. | ṣry. | iršy. | y‘ḏrd. | ayaẖ. | bn. 2106.2

ṯmn.mrkbt.dt. | ‘rb.bt.mlk. | yd.apnt hn. | yd.ḥẓ hn. | yd.tr hn. | w.l.ṯt.mrkbtm 1121.2

n.w t]n.w nšt. | w ‘n hm.nǵr mdr‘[.iṯ.lḥm.---]. | iṯ.yn.d ‘rb.bṯk[.---]. | mǵ hw.l hn.lg yn h[.---]. | w ḥbr h.mla yn.[---]. 23[52].74

bn.ẖrmln.ṯn.b d.bn.ẖdmn. | [u]bdy.nqdm. | [ṯlṯ].šdm.d.n‘rb.gt.npk. | [š]d.rpan.b d.klṯṯb. | [š]d.ilṣy.b d.‘bdym. | [ub]d 82[300].2.13

š.alp.w ṯlṯ. | ṣin.šlm[m.]šb‘ pamt. | l ilm.šb[‘.]l kṯr. | ‘lm.t‘rbn.gṯrm. | bt.mlk.ṯql.ẖrṣ. | l špš.w yrẖ.l gṯr. | ṯql.ksp.ṭb.ap 33[5].9

‘m.nǵr.mdr‘ y.nǵr. | nǵr.ptḥ.w ptḥ hw.prṣ.b‘d hm. | w ‘rb.hm.hm[.iṯ.--.l]ḥm.w t[n]. | w nlḥm.hm.iṯ[.--.yn.w t]n.w n 23[52].71

r]m.n‘m[n.]ǵlm.il. | a[ṯt.tq]ḥ.y krt.aṯt. | tqḥ.bt k.ǵlmt.tš‘rb. | ḥqr k.tld.šb‘.bnm.l k. | w ṯmn.tṯtmnm. | l k.tld.yṣb.ǵlm 15[128].2.22

ap.krt bn[m.il]. | špḥ.lṭpn[.w qdš]. | bkm.t‘r[b.‘l.ab h]. | t‘rb.ḥ[--]. | b ṯtm.t[---]. | šknt.[---]. | bkym[.---]. | ǵr.y[----]. | yd 16.2[125].113

tṭbẖ.šmn.[m]ri h. | t[p]tḥ.rḥbt.yn. | ‘l h.ṯr h.tš‘rb. | ‘l h.tš‘rb.ẓby h. | ṯr.ẖbr.rbt. | ẖbr.ṯrrt. | bt.krt.tbun. | lm.mṯb[.---]. | 15[128].4.18

]t. | tlk m.rḥmy.w tṣd[.---]. | tḥgrn.ǵzr.n‘m.[---]. | w šm.‘rbm.yr[.---]. | mṯbt.ilm.ṯmn.ṯ[--.--]. | pamt.šb‘. | iqnu.šmt[.--- 23[52].18

y. | rgm. | ugrt.tǵr k. | ugrt.tǵr k. | tšlm k.um y. | td‘.ky.‘rbt. | l pn.špš. | w pn.špš.nr. | b y.mid.w um. | tšmẖ.m ab. | w 1015.7

yrẖ ny[r] šmm.‘m. | ẖr[ẖ]b mlk qẓ.tn nkl y | rẖ ytrẖ.ib t‘rb m b bh | t h.w atn mhr h l a | b h.alp ksp w rbt ẖ | rṣ.išlḥ 24[77].18

| lḥm.b lḥm ay.w šty.b ẖmr yn ay. | šlm.mlk.šlm.mlkt.‘rbm m.ṯnnm. | mt.w šr.yṯb.b d h.ẖṭ.ṯkl.b d h. | ẖṭ.ulmn.yzbr 23[52].7

[t.--.]mlk[.--]. | w.mlk.yštal.b.hn[--]. | hmt.w.anyt.hm.t‘[rb]. | mkr.hn d.w.rgm.ank[.--]. | mlkt.ybqš.anyt.w.at[--]. | 2008.2.11

.bt.ar. | ahbt.ṭly.bt.rb.dd.arṣy. | bt.y‘bdr.km ǵlmm. | w ‘rb n.l p‘n.‘nt.hbr. | w ql.tšthwy.kbd hyt. | w rgm.l btlt.‘nt. | ṯ 3[‘NT].3.6

bš.npṣ.aṯt.[--]. | ṣbi nrt.ilm.špš.[-]r[--]. | pǵt.minš.šdm l m‘[rb]. | nrt.ilm.špš.mǵy[t]. | pǵt.l ahlm.rgm.l yṯ[pn.y] | bl.ag 19[1AQHT].4.210

rd.l mlk.amlk. | l drkt.k aṯb.an. | ytb‘.yṣb ǵlm.‘l. | ab h.y‘rb.yšu g h. | w yṣḥ.šm‘ m‘.l krt. | ṯ‘.ištm‘.w tqǵ udn. | k ǵz.ǵ 16.6[127].40

.tdbḥn. | [----.]‘d.ilnym. | [---.--]l km amt m. | [---.]b w t‘rb.sd. | [---.--]n b ym.qẓ. | [---.]ym.tlḥmn. | [---.rp]um.tštyn. 20[121].1.4

ḥb.mk[npt]. | ap.krt bn[m.il]. | špḥ.lṭpn[.w qdš]. | bkm.t‘r[b.‘l.ab h]. | t‘rb.ḥ[--]. | b ṯtm.t[---]. | šknt.[---]. | bkym[.---]. | 16.2[125].112

mṯt.[ḥ]ry. | tṭbẖ.šmn.[m]ri h. | t[p]tḥ.rḥbt.yn. | ‘l h.ṯr h.tš‘rb. | ‘l h.tš‘rb.ẓby h. | ṯr.ẖbr.rbt. | ẖbr.ṯrrt. | bt.krt.tbun. | lm. 15[128].4.17

.ṣmdm.gpn.yšql.šdmt h. | km gpn. | šb‘ d.yrgm.‘l.‘d.w ‘rbm.t‘nyn. | w šd.šd ilm.šd aṯrt.w rḥm. | ‘l.išt.šb‘ d.ǵzrm.ṭb.[23[52].12

k t‘rb.‘ṯtrt.ẖr[-]. | bt mlk.‘šr.‘šr.[--].bt ilm. | kbr[-]m.[-]trmt. | lb 33[5].1

m. | [i]lib. | [i]lbldn. | [p]dry.bt.mlk. | [-]lp.izr. | [a]rz. | k.t‘rb.‘ṯtrt.šd.bt[.m]lk. | k.t‘rbn.ršp m.bt.mlk. | ẖlu.dg. | ḥdṯm. | 2004.10

m[.b‘lm].kmm.b‘lm.kmm. | b‘lm.kmm.b‘lm.kmm. | k t‘rb.‘ṯtrt.šd.bt.mlk[.---]. | ṯn.skm.šb‘.mšlt.arb‘.ẖpnt.[---]. | ẖm UG5.9.1.18

k]rt.ṯ‘. | i.iṯt.aṯrt.ṣrm. | w ilt.ṣdynm. | hm.ḥry.bt y. | iqḥ.aš‘rb.ǵlmt. | ḥẓr y.ṯn h.wspm. | atn.w ṯlṯ h.ẖrṣm. | ylk ym.w ṯ 14[KRT].4.204

ry.bt.mlk. | [-]lp.izr. | [a]rz. | k.t‘rb.‘ṯtrt.šd.bt[.m]lk. | k.t‘rbn.ršp m.bt.mlk. | ẖlu.dg. | ḥdṯm. | dbḥ.b‘l.k.tdd.b‘lt.bhtm. 2004.11

[---.a]lp.l b‘l.w aṯrt.‘ṣr[m] l inš. | [ilm.---].lbbmm.gdlt.‘rb špš w ḥl. | [mlk.b ar]b‘t.‘[š]rt.yrtḥṣ.mlk.brr. | [b ym.ml]at 36[9].1.9

yrẖ.ši[-.b ar]b‘t.‘š | rt.yr[tḥṣ.ml]k.brr. | ‘lm.š.š[--].l[--.]‘rb.šp | š.w ḥl[.ml]k. | bn.aup[š.--].bsbn hzpẖ ṯlṯt. | kṯr[.---.--]t APP.II[173].56

šmn.‘[ly h.gdlt.rgm.yṯṯb]. | brr.b šb‘[.ṣbu.špš.w ḥl] | yt.‘rb špš[.w ḥl.mlk.w.b y] | m.ḥdṯ.ṯn šm[.---.--]t. | b yrẖ.ši[-.b a APP.II[173].52

]. | ‘ly h.gdlt.rgm.yṯ[ṯb.brr]. | b.[šb]‘.ṣbu.[š]pš.w.ḥly[t].‘[r]b[.š]p[š]. | w [ḥl.]mlk.[w.]b.ym.ḥdṯ.ṯn.šm. | l.[---]t. | i[d.yd] 35[3].47

| [--]t.w b lb.tqb[-]. | [--]m[-].mtm.uṣb‘[t]. | [-]tr.šrk.il. | ‘rb.špš.l ymǵ. | krt.ṣbia.špš. | b‘l ny.w ymlk. | [y]ṣb.‘ln.w y[-]y 15[128].5.18

b ṯt ym ḥdṯ. | ẖyr.‘rbt. | špš tǵr h. | ršp. | w ‘bdm tbqrn. | skn. 1162.2

ap zd.aṯrt.[---]. | špš.mṣprt dlt hm[.---]. | w ǵnbm.šlm.‘rbm.ṯn[nm]. | hlkm.b dbḥ n‘mt. | šd[.i]lm.šd.aṯrt.w rḥmy. | [- 23[52].26

bl. | [w ‘d]t.ilm.ṯlṯ h. | [ap]nk.krt.ṯ‘.‘[-]r. | [--.]b bt h.yšt.‘rb. | [--] h.ytn.w [--]u.l ytn. | [aẖ]r.mǵy.‘[d]t.ilm. | [w]y‘n.ali 15[128].2.9

burm.l[b.rmṣt.ilhm].|bʻlm.w mlu[.---.ksm].|ṯlṯm.w mʻrb[.---].|dbḥ šmn mr[.šmn.rqḥ.bt].|mtnt.w ynt.[qrt.w ṯn. APP.II[173].21
tldn.|ṯrkn.|kli.|plǵn.|apšny.|ʻrb[.---].|w.b.p[.--].|apš[ny].|b.yṣi h.|ḥwt.[---].|alp.k[sp].|t 2116.6
ʻ.l ydʻt.|[---.]tasrn.ṯr il.|[---.]rks.bn.abnm.|[---.]upqt.ʻrb.|[---.w ẓ]r.mtn y at zd.|[---.]tʻrb.bši.|[---.]l tzd.l tptq.|[- 1[ʻNT.X].5.24
[---.šnst.kpt.b ḥb]š h.ʻtkt r[išt].|[l bmt h.---.]hy bt h tʻrb.|[---.tm]ṯḫṣ b ʻmq.|[ṯḫṭṣb.bn.qrtm.ṯtʻr.ṯlḥnt.]l ṣbim.|[h 7.1[131].3
---]t ṯm[n.---].|[--]l ḫmš[.---].|[----.]ḫmš[.---].|[--.-]rn.ʻrbt[.---].|[---].ṯmnym[.---].|[---.--]p.mit[.---]. 151[25].4
.w [---].|[---.--]ṯ.kn[-.---].|[---.--]tm.n[--.---].|[---.-]km.tʻrb[.---]. 2125.14

ʻrbn

spr.ʻrbnm.|dt.ʻrb.|b.mtn.bn.ayaḫ.|b.ḫbṯ h.ḥwt.ṯt h.|w.mnm.ša 1161.1
bn.ayaḫ.|b.ḫbṯ h.ḥwt.ṯt h.|w.mnm.šalm.|dt.tknn.|ʻl.ʻrbnm.|hn hmt.|tknn.|mtn.bn.ʻbdym.|ilrb.bn.ilyn.|ʻbdadt. 1161.7

ʻrgz

.|[ašr ilht kṯrt bn]|t hll.snnt.bnt h|ll bʻl gml.yrdt.|b ʻrgzm.b bz tdm.|lla y.ʻm lẓpn i|l ḏ.pid.hn b p y sp|r hn.b š 24[77].43
p h.|ḫmš.mqdm.dnyn.|b.ṯql.dprn.aḥd.|b.ṯql.|ḫmšm.ʻrgz.b.ḫmšt. 1127.22
h w yṣq b ap h.|[k l yḫru w]l yttn mss št qlql.|[w št ʻrgz y]dk aḥd h w yṣq b ap h.|[k.yiḫd akl s]šw št mkšr grn. 160[55].9
k [ḫr ššw mǵmǵ].|w [bṣql.ʻrgz.ydk].|a[ḥd h.w.yṣq.b.ap h].|k.[ḫr.ššw.ḫndrṯ].|w.ṯ[qd. 161[56].3
ṣq.b.ap h].|k.l.ḫ[ru.w.l.yttn.ššw].|mss.[št.qlql.w.št].|ʻrgz[.ydk.aḥd h].|w.yṣq[.b.ap h].|k.yiḫd[.akl.ššw].|št.mkš[161[56].10
w.---].|[---.w]yṣq b a[p h].|[k ḫr š]šw mǵmǵ w b[ṣql ʻrgz].|[ydk aḥ]d h w yṣq b ap h.|[k ḫr]ššw ḫndrṯ w ṯ[qd m 160[55].4
mʻqb.|agm.|bir.|ypr.|hzp.|šql.|mʻrḫ[-].|sl[ḫ].|snr.|ʻrgz.|yknʻm.|ʻnmky.|ǵr. 2074.36
nr.|rq[d].|[---].|[---].|mid[-].|ubš.|mṣb[t].|ḫl.y[---].|ʻrg[z].|yʻr[t].|amd[y].|atl[g].|bṣr[y].|[---].|[---]y.|ar.|agm. 71[113].41
mdm[.---].|[ul]l.aḥdm.w[.---].|[mʻq]b.aḥdm.w[.---].|[ʻr]gz.ṯlṯ.ṣmd[m.---].|[m]ṣbt.ṣmdm.[---].|[--]nr.arbʻ.[---].|[--] 1179.4
-.--]m.|[---.ḫlb.]rp[š].|[---.]bht[.---].|[---.]amr[-].|[---.ʻ]rg[z.-].|[---.ḫl]b ṣpn. 72[-].2.4
b ym.qẓ.|[---.]ym.tlḥmn.|[---.rp]um.tštyn.|[---.]il.d ʻrgzm.|[---.]dt.ʻl.lty.|[---.]tdbḥ.amr.|ṯmn.b qrb.hkl y.[aṯr h. 20[121].1.8
mṣbt.|snr.|ṯm.|ubš.|glbt.|mi[d]ḫ.|mr[i]l.|ḫlb.|šld.|ʻrgz.|[-----]. 2041.16

ʻrgzy

.ṯty.|bn.ḥyn.bn.ǵlm.|bn.yyn.w.bn.au[pš].|bn.kdrn.|ʻrgzy.w.bn.ʻdy.|bn.gmḥn.w.ḥgbt.|bn.tgḏn.|yny.|[b]n.gʻyn 131[309].27

ʻrd

.|ynḥm.|aḏddn.|mtn.|plsy.|qṯn.|ypr.|bn.ymy.|bn.ʻrd.|[-]b.da[-].|[--]l[--].|[-----]. 1035.4.13

ʻrẓ

tms m.|w ʻn.rbt.aṯrt ym.|blt.nmlk.ʻṯtr.ʻrẓ.|ymlk.ʻṯtr.ʻrẓ.|apnk.ʻṯtr.ʻrẓ.|yʻl.b ṣrrt.ṣpn.|yṯb.l kḥṯ.aliyn.|bʻl.pʻn h.l 6.1.55[49.1.27]
mǵy.|aps h.w yʻn.ʻṯtr.ʻrẓ.|l amlk.b ṣrrt.ṣpn.|yrd.ʻṯtr.ʻrẓ.yrd.|l kḥṯ.aliyn.bʻl.|w ymlk.b arṣ.il.kl h.|[---] š abn.b rḥ 6.1.63[49.1.35]
bʻl.pʻn h.l tmǵyn.|hdm.riš h.l ymǵy.|aps h.w yʻn.ʻṯtr.ʻrẓ.|l amlk.b ṣrrt.ṣpn.|yrd.ʻṯtr.ʻrẓ.yrd.|l kḥṯ.aliyn.bʻl.|w y 6.1.61[49.1.33]
.|ʻm.bn.dgn.k tms m.|w ʻn.rbt.aṯrt ym.|blt.nmlk.ʻṯtr.ʻrẓ.|ymlk.ʻṯtr.ʻrẓ.|apnk.ʻṯtr.ʻrẓ.|yʻl.b ṣrrt.ṣpn.|yṯb.l kḥṯ.ali 6.1.54[49.1.26]
bt.aṯrt ym.|blt.nmlk.ʻṯtr.ʻrẓ.|ymlk.ʻṯtr.ʻrẓ.|apnk.ʻṯtr.ʻrẓ.|yʻl.b ṣrrt.ṣpn.|yṯb.l kḥṯ.aliyn.|bʻl.pʻn h.l tmǵyn.|hdm. 6.1.56[49.1.28]
--].|uḫry.l[---].|mṣt.ks h.t[--.---].|idm.adr[.---].|idm.ʻrẓ.tʻr[ẓ.---].|ʻn.bʻl.a[ḫ]ḏ[.---].|ẓr h.aḫḏ.qš[t.---].|p ʻn.bʻl.aḫ 12[75].2.31
|uḫry.l[---].|mṣt.ks h.t[--.---].|idm.adr[.---].|idm.ʻrẓ.tʻr[ẓ.---].|ʻn.bʻl.a[ḫ]ḏ[.---].|ẓr h.aḫḏ.qš[t.---].|p ʻn.bʻl.aḫḏ[.- 12[75].2.31

ʻry

d.|rb.tmtt.lqḥt.|w.ṯṯb.ank.l hm.|w.any k.ṯt.|by.ʻky.ʻryt.|w.aḫ y.mhk.|b lb h.al.yšt. 2059.25
[-----].|[--.]l tṣi.b b[--].bm.k[--].|[--]ṯb.ʻryt k.k qlt[.---].|[--]at.brt.lb k.ʻnn.[---].|[--.]šdq.k ttn.l y.šn[60[32].3

ʻrk

rḫ ḫyr.b ym ḥdṯ.|alp.w š.l bʻlt bhtm.|b arbʻt ʻšrt.bʻl.|ʻrkm.|b ṯmnt.ʻšrt.yr|tḫṣ.mlk.brr.|ʻlm.tzǵ.b ǵb.ṣpn.|nḥkt.k UG5.12.A.4

ʻrm

d ydy.|ǵbl.|mlk.|gwl.|rqd.|ḫlby.|ʻn[q]pat.|m[ʻ]rb.|ʻrm.|bn.ḥgby.|mrat. 2075.28
l[b]nm.|nnu.|ʻrm.|bṣr.|mʻr.|ḫlby.|mṣbt.|snr.|ṯm.|ubš.|glbt.|mi[d]ḫ.| 2041.3
aǵt.|w.qmnz.|slḫ.|yknʻm.|šlmy.|w.ull.|ṯmry.|qrt.|ʻrm.|nnu.|[--].|[---].|mʻr.|arny.|ubrʻy.|ilštmʻ.|bir.|mʻqb.| 71[113].22

ʻrmy

t.hlk.b[.---].|bn.bʻyn.š[--.---].|aǵltn.mid[-.---].|bn.lṣn.ʻrm[y].|aršw.bṣry.|arpṯr.yʻrty.|bn.ḫdyn.ugrty.|bn.tgḏn.ug 87[64].5
y.|bn grgs.|bn.ḫran.|bn.arš[w.b]ṣry.|bn.ykn.|bn.lṣn.ʻrmy.|bn.bʻyn.šly.|bn.ynḥn.|bn.ʻbdilm.hzpy. 99[327].2.3
m.|[---.--]ḫm.|[---.--]m.|[---]nb.w ykn.|[--]ndbym.|[ʻ]rmy.w snry.|[b]n.sdy.bn.ṯty.|bn.ḥyn.bn.ǵlm.|bn.yyn.w.b 131[309].22
rišym.qnum.|bn.ilrš.|ʻ[p]ṯn.|b[n.ʻr]my.|[--]ṯy.|bn.ǵdʻ.|bn.ʻyn.|bn.grb[n].|yṯtn.|bn.ab[l].|kr 2078.4

ʻrmn

yn.|ʻzn.bn.mlk.|bn.alṯn.|bn.ṯmyr.|ẓbr.|bn.ṯdṯb.|bn.ʻrmn.|bn.alz.|bn.mṣrn.|bn.ʻdy.|bn.ršpy.|[---.]mn.|[--.-]sn. 115[301].2.13

ʻrmt

-----].|[---.]w npy gr.|[ḥmyt.ugrt.w npy.yman.w npy.ʻr]mt.w npy.|[---.ušn.yp km.ulp.]qṭy.|[ulp.ddmy.ulp.ḫry.ul APP.I[-].1.13
mšr mšr bn.ugrt.w [npy.---.]ugr.|w npy.yman.w npy.ʻrmt.w npy.[---].|w npy.nqmd.ušn.yp km.ulp.q[ṭy.ulp.ddm] 32[2].1.19
.b.mnt.|arbʻ.bnšm.b.irbn.|ṯn.bnšm.b.yʻrt.|ṯn.bnšm.b.ʻrmt.|arbʻ.bnšm.b.šrš.|ṯṯ.bnšm.b.mlk.|arbʻ.bnšm.b.bṣr.|ṯn. 2076.36
[---.--]t ugrt.|[---.w n]py.yman.|[w npy.ʻrmt.---.w]npy.annpdgl.|[ušn.yp kn.ulp.qṭy.ulp.]ddmy.ulp APP.I[-].1.3

ʻrny

|b.ḫqn.[---]m.ṣ[-]n.|[b].bn.ay[--.---].l.ʻšrm.|[-]gp[.---.]ʻrny.ṯṯm.|[---.]dyn.ḫmšt.ʻšrt.|[---.-]til.ḫmšt.l ʻšrm.|[--.-]n.w 2054.2.18

ʻrs

.hwt.l t[ḫwy].|nʻmn.ǵzr.št.ṯrm.w[---].|ištir.b ḏdm.w nʻrs[.---].|w tʻn.btlt.ʻnt.ṯb.yṯp.w[---].|l k.ašt k.km.nšr.b ḥb[18[3AQHT].4.15

ʻrʻr

dm.|idk.pnm.l ytn.tk aršḫ.rbt.|w aršḫ.ṯrrt.ydy.b ʻṣm.ʻrʻr.|w b šḫt.ʻs.mt.ʻrʻrm.ynʻrn h.|ssnm.ysyn h.ʻdtm.yʻdyn h UG5.7.64
.tk aršḫ.rbt.|w aršḫ.ṯrrt.ydy.b ʻṣm.ʻrʻr.|w b šḫt.ʻs.mt.ʻrʻrm.ynʻrn h.|ssnm.ysyn h.ʻdtm.yʻdyn h.yb|ltm.ybln h.mǵ UG5.7.65
al.|d alpm.w alp w š.|šrp.w šlmm kmm.|l bʻl.ṣpn b ʻrʻr.|pamt ṯlṯm š l qrnt.|ṯlḥn.bʻlt.bhtm.|ʻlm.ʻlm.gdlt l bʻl.|ṣ UG5.13.29

ʻrpt

nil.mt.|rpi.al.ǵzr.mt.hrnmy.|apnk.dnil.mt.|rpi.yṣly.ʻrpt.b |ḥm.un.yr.ʻrpt.|tmṭr.b qẓ.ṭl.yṭll.|l ǵnbm.šbʻ.šnt.|yṣr 19[1AQHT].1.39
|tmṭr.b qẓ.ṭl.yṭll.|l ǵnbm.šbʻ.šnt.|yṣr k.bʻl.ṯmn.rkb.|ʻrpt.bl.ṭl.bl rbb.|bl.šrʻ.thmtm.bl.|ṭbn.ql.bʻl.k tmzʻ.|kst.dnil. 19[1AQHT].1.44
t.kmn.hkl.|w yʻn.kṯr.w ḫss.|šmʻ.l aliyn bʻl.|bn.l rkb.ʻrpt.|bl.ašt.urbt.b bh[t] m.|ḥln.b qrb.hkl m.|w yʻn.aliyn bʻl 4[51].5.122
].|tnq[.---.]in[b]b.pʻr.|yd h[.--.]ṣʻr.glgl.|a[---]m.rḥ.ḥḏ ʻ[r]pt.|gl[.---.]yhpk.m[---]m.|sʻ[--.]k[--]t. 13[6].34
ṯlḥn y.qlt.|b ks.ištyn h.|dm.ṯn.dbḥm.šna.bʻl.ṯlṯ.|rkb.ʻrpt.dbḥ.|bṯt.w dbḥ.w dbḥ.|dnt.w dbḥ.tdmm.|amht.k b h. 4[51].3.18
si.zbl.ym.w ʻn.kṯr.w ḫss.l rgmt.|l k.l zbl.bʻl.ṯnt.l rkb.ʻrpt.ht.ib k.|bʻl m.ht.ib k.tmḫṣ.ht.tṣmt.ṣrt k.|tqḥ.mlk.ʻlm k 2.4[68].8
m.---].|arḫ.arḫ.[---.tld].|ibr.tld[.l bʻl].|w rum.l[rkb.ʻrpt].|tḥbq.[---].|tḥbq[.---].|w tksynn.bṯn[-.]|y[--.]šr h.w šḫ 10[76].3.22
m.|[t]ḫspn.m h.w trḥṣ.|[ṭ]l.šmm.šmn.arṣ.rbb.|[r]kb ʻrpt.ṭl.šmm.tsk h.|[rb]b.nsk h.kbkbm. 3[ʻNT].2.40
[---.--]t.npš.ʻgl.|[---.-]nk.aštn.b ḫrt.|ilm.arṣ.w at.qḥ.|ʻrpt k.rḥ k.mdl k.|mṭrt k.ʻm k.šbʻt.|ǵlm k.ṯmn.ḫnzr k.|ʻm 5[67].5.7
kly.ṯpṭ.nhr.|b šm.tgʻr m.ʻṯtrt.bṯ l aliyn.[bʻl.]|bṯ.l rkb.ʻrpt.k šby n.zb[l.ym.k] |šby n.ṯpṭ.nhr.w yṣa b[.--].|ybṯ.nn.a 2.4[68].29
h.w tṣḥ.ik.mǵy.gpn.w ugr.|mn.ib.ypʻ.l bʻl.ṣrt.|l rkb.ʻrpt.l mḫšt.mdd.|il ym.l klt.nhr.il.rbm.|l ištbm.tnn.ištml h. 3[ʻNT].3.35
.mt.hrnmy.|apnk.dnil.mt.|rpi.yṣly.ʻrpt.b |ḥm.un.yr.ʻrpt.|tmṭr.b qẓ.ṭl.yṭll.|l ǵnbm.šbʻ.šnt.|yṣr k.bʻl.ṯmn.rkb.|ʻr 19[1AQHT].1.40
b nši[.ʻn h.w yphn.yḥd].|b ʻrpt[.nšrm.yšu].|[g h.]w yṣḥ[.knp.nšrm].|bʻl.yṯb.bʻl.yṯb[r.di 19[1AQHT].2.106
ptḥ.ḥln.b bht m.|urbt.b qrb.[h]kl |m.w y[p]tḥ.b dqt.ʻrpt.|ʻl h[wt].kṯr.w ḫss.|ṣḥq.kṯr.w ḫss.|yšu.g h.w yṣḥ.|l rg 4[51].7.19
tḥ.ḥ|ln.b bht m.urbt.|b qrb.hk[l m.yp]tḥ.|bʻl.b dqt[.ʻrp]t.|ql h.qdš.b[ʻl.y]tn.|yṯny.bʻl.ṣ[---.-]pt h.|ql h.q[dš.ṯb]r. 4[51].7.28
š[r.bʻ]l.|w bšr.ḥtk.dgn.|k.ibr.l bʻl[.yl]d.|w rum.l rkb.ʻrpt.|yšmḫ.aliyn.bʻl. 10[76].3.37
.|wn ap.ʻdn.mṭr h.|bʻl.yʻdn.ʻdn.ṯkt.b glṯ.|w tn.ql h.b ʻrpt.|šrh.l arṣ.brqm.|bt.arzm.ykllnh.|hm.bt.lbnt.yʻmsn h. 4[51].5.70
k ḫrr.zt.ybl.arṣ.w pr.|ʻṣm.yraun.aliyn.bʻl.|ṯtʻ.nn.rkb.ʻrpt.|tbʻ.rgm.l bn.ilm.mt.|tny.l ydd.il ǵzr.|tḥm.aliyn.bʻl.hw 5[67].2.7
ṣrt.l rkb.ʻrpt.|[-]ʻn.ǵlmm.yʻnyn.l ib.ypʻ.|l bʻl.ṣrt.l rkb.ʻrpt.|tḥm.aliyn.bʻl.hwt.aliy.|qrdm.qry.b arṣ.mlḥmt.|št.b ʻp 3[ʻNT].4.50
m ym.bn.ẓlm[t].|rmt.prʻt.ibr[.mnt].|ṣḥrrm.ḥbl[.--].|ʻrpt.tḥt.[---]|m ʻṣrm.ḥ[---].|glṯ.isr[.---]|m.brt[.---].|ymt m. 8[51FRAG].11
.mlk h.|l nḥt.l kḥṯ.drkt h.|mn m.ib.ypʻ.l bʻl.ṣrt.l rkb.ʻrpt.|[-]ʻn.ǵlmm.yʻnyn.l ib.ypʻ.|l bʻl.ṣrt.l rkb.ʻrpt.|tḥm.aliy 3[ʻNT].4.48
k.w rḥd.|[---]y ilm.d mlk.|y[ṯ]b.aliyn.bʻl.|ytʻdd.rkb.ʻrpt.|[--].ydd.w yqlṣn.|yqm.w ywpṯn.b tk.|p[ḫ]r.bn.ilm.štt. 4[51].3.11
.]pḫr kkbm.|[---.]dr dt.šmm.|[---.al]iyn bʻl.|[---].rkb.ʻrpt.|[---.]ǵš.l limm.|[---.]l yṯb.l arṣ.|[---].mtm.|[---.--]d m 10[76].1.7
r k.al ttn.l n.|[---.]tn l rbd.|[---.]bʻlt h w yn.|[---.rk]b ʻrpt.|[---.--]n.w mnu dg.|[---.]l aliyn bʻl.|[---].rkb ʻrpt. 2001.2.15
.|[ʻmm.]ym.bn.ẓlmt.r|[mt.prʻ]t.ibr.mnt.|[ṣḥrrm.ḥbl.ʻ]rpt.|[---.---.-]ḥt.|[---.---]m.|[----] h. 4[51].7.57
k]b ʻrpt.|[---.--]n.w mnu dg.|[---.]l aliyn bʻl.|[---].rkb ʻrpt. 2001.2.18

ʻrq

[---.---.]l.mit.drʻ.w.šbʻm.drt.|[---.ḥpr.]bnšm.w.l.ḥrš.ʻrq.ṯn.ʻšr h.|[---.d]rʻ.w.mit.drt.w.ʻšrm.l.mit.|[drt.ḥpr.b]nšm 1098.2

ʻrr

ab h bʻ[l].|yǵtr.ʻṯtr t|rḫ l k ybrdmy.b[t.a]|b h lb[u] yʻrr.w yʻ[n].|yrḫ nyr šmm.w nʻ[n].|ʻma nkl ḫtn y.a[ḫ]r.|nk 24[77].30
nm.yn.b k.ḫrṣ.|dm.ʻṣm.hm.yd.il mlk.|yḫss k.ahbt.ṯr.tʻrr k.|w tʻn.rbt.aṯrt ym.|tḥm k.il.ḥkm.ḥkmt.|ʻm ʻlm.ḥyt.ḥ 4[51].4.39
.mlk k.|l yṯbr.ḫṭ.mṯpṭ k.|yru.bn ilm t.ṯtʻ.y|dd.il.ǵzr.yʻr.mt.|b ql h.y[---.---].|bʻl.yṯṯbn[.l ksi].|mlk h.l[nḥt.l kḥṯ]. 6[49].6.31

ʻrš

b ǵlt.yd k.|l tdn.dn.almnt.|l ṯpṭ.ṯpṭ.qṣr.npš.|km.aḫt.ʻrš.mdw.|anšt.ʻrš.zbln.|rd.l mlk.amlk.|l drkt.k aṯb.an.|ytbʻ 16.6[127].35
m.ʻl.dl.l pn k.|l tšlḥm.ytm.bʻd.|ksl k.almnt.km.|aḫt.ʻrš.mdw.anšt.|ʻrš.zbln.rd.l mlk.|amlk.l drkt k.aṯb.|an.w yʻ 16.6[127].51
š.yḥ.dnil.|[mt.rp]i.brlt.ǵzr.mt hrnmy.|[---].hw.mḫ.l ʻrš h.yʻl.|[---].bm.nšq.aṯt h.|[---.]b ḥbq h.ḥmḥmt.|[---.--] n. 17[2AQHT].1.39
šb[ʻ.]ymm.tbʻ.b bt h.|kṯrt.bnt.hll.snnt.|[-]d[-]t.nʻm y.ʻrš.h[--]m.|ysmsmt.ʻrš.ḫlln.[-].|yṯb.dnil.[l s]pr yrḫ h.|yrs.y[17[2AQHT].2.41
n.dn.almnt.|l ṯpṭ.ṯpṭ.qṣr.npš.|km.aḫt.ʻrš.mdw.|anšt.ʻrš.zbln.|rd.l mlk.amlk.|l drkt.k aṯb.an.|ytbʻ.yṣb ǵlm.ʻl.|ab 16.6[127].36
l tšlḥm.ytm.bʻd.|ksl k.almnt.km.|aḫt.ʻrš.mdw.anšt.|ʻrš.zbln.rd.l mlk.|amlk.l drkt k.aṯb.|an.w yʻny.krt ṯʻ.yṯbr.| 16.6[127].52
.|kṯrt.bnt.hll.snnt.|[-]d[-]t.nʻm y.ʻrš.h[--]m.|ysmsmt.ʻrš.ḫlln.[-].|yṯb.dnil.[l s]pr yrḫ h.|yrs.y[---.]y[--] h.|ṯlṯ.rb[ʻ. 17[2AQHT].2.42
lk.|aṯr.ṯlṯ.kl hm.|aḥd.bt h.ysgr.|almnt.škr.|tškr.zbl.ʻršm.|yšu.ʻwr.|mzl.ymzl.|w ybl.trḫ.ḥdṯ.|ybʻr.l ṯn.aṯt h.|w 14[KRT].4.186
.hlk.|aṯr.ṯlṯ.kl hm.|yḥd.bt h.sgr.|almnt.škr.|tškr.zbl.ʻršm.|yšu.ʻwr.mzl.|ymzl.w yṣi.trḫ.|ḥdṯ.ybʻr.l ṯn.|aṯt h.lm. 14[KRT].2.98
pṣ.ʻ[--.---].|d.b d.a[--.---].|w.b d.b[--.---].|udbr[.---].|ʻrš[.---].|ṯl[ḥn.---].|a[--.---].|ṯn[.---].|ptr[-.---].|yp[-.---].|b[- 1120.5

ʻšd

l.ḫḏǵb.|ṯṯ.ddm.l.gzzm.|kd yn.l.ḫtn.w.kd.ḥmṣ.w.[lt]ḥ.ʻšdm.|kd yn.l.ḫḏǵb.w.kd.ḥmṣ.|prš.glbm.l.bt.|tgmǵ.kšmm. 1099.27

ʻšdyn

.|d[----].|ab[--.---].|bn.nṣdn[.ḫm]št.|bn.arsw ʻ[šr]m.|ʻšdyn.ḫmš[t].|abršn.ʻšr[t].|bʻln.ḫmšt.|w.nḥl h.ḫm[š]t.|bn.u 1062.6

‘šy

.ḫli. | širm.šd.šd.‘šy. | w.šir.šd.krm. | d.krwn. | šir.šd.šd.‘šy. | d.abmn. | šir.šd.krm. | d.yrmn. | šir.[š]d.mlth.šd.‘šy. | d.y 1079.10
d.‘šy. | d.abmn. | šir.šd.krm. | d.yrmn. | šir.[š]d.mlth.šd.‘šy. | d.ynḫm. | tgmr.šd.ṯlṯm.šd. | w.tr[--.---]. 1079.14
ḫmn. | širm.šd.khn. | ṯlṯ.šd.w.krm.šir.d.ḫli. | širm.šd.šd.‘šy. | w.šir.šd.krm. | d.krwn. | šir.šd.šd.‘šy. | d.abmn. | šir.šd.kr 1079.7
m.‘ṣm.---]n.krpn.‘l.[k]rpn. | [---.]ym.w t‘l.trṯ. | [---].yn.‘šy l ḥbš. | [---.]ḫtn.qn.yṣbt. | [---.--]m.b nši.‘n h.w tphn. | [---.- 17[2AQHT].6.8
.b qdš. | ztr.‘m y.l ‘pr.ḏmr.aṯr[y]. | ṭbq lḥt.niṣ y.grš. | d ‘šy.ln.aḫd.yd y.b š | krn m‘ms y k šb‘t yn. | spu.ksm y.bt.b‘l.[17[2AQHT].2.19
.l arṣ.mšṣu.qṭr h. | l ‘pr.ḏmr.aṯr h.ṭbq.lḥt. | niṣ h.grš d.‘šy.ln h. | aḫd.yd h.b škrn.m‘ms h. | [k]šb‘ yn.spu.ksm h.bt.b 17[2AQHT].1.30
ṣ.mšṣu. | [qṭr h.l ‘pr.d]mr.a[ṯ]r h. | [ṭbq.lḥt.niṣ h.gr]š.d ‘šy. | [ln h.---]. | z[tr.‘m k.l arṣ.mšṣu.qṭr k]. | l ‘pr.ḏm[r.aṯr k.ṭ 17[2AQHT].1.48
rṣ.mšṣu.qṭr k]. | l ‘pr.ḏm[r.aṯr k.ṭbq]. | lḥt.niṣ k.gr[š.d ‘šy.ln k]. | spu.ksm k.bt.[b‘l.w mnt k]. | bt il.aḫd.yd k.b [škrn 17[2AQHT].2.3

‘šm

rn.[--.]k. | [---].aǵwyn.‘n k.ẓẓ.w k mǵ.ilm. | [--.]k ‘ṣm.k ‘šm.l ttn.k abnm.l thggn. 1001.2.13

‘šq

spr.mḫṣm. | bn.ḫpṣry.b.šbn. | ilštm‘ym. | y[---.]bn.‘šq. | [---.]bn.tqy. | [---.]bn.šlmy. | [-----]. | [---].ubr‘y. | [---].gwl. 1041.4

‘šr

‘.hbṭnm. | ‘šr.mrum. | šb‘.ḫsnm. | tš‘m.ṯṯ.kbd.mdrǵlm. | ‘šrm.aḥd.kbd.ḫsnm. | ubnyn. | ṯtm[.l.]mit.ṯlṯ. | kbd[.tg]mr.bnš 1028.10
[--]n.‘š[r.] | [a]rt[.a]rb‘[.---]. | ‘nmky.‘šr.[---]. | ṯmry.‘šr.ṯn.k[rmm.-- 1081.1
[‘]b[dm]. | ‘šrm. | inšt. | mdm. | gt.mlkym. | yqšm. | kbšm. | trrm. | khnm. | 74[115].2
rd.‘šrm. | ṣdqšlm.‘šr[m]. | yknil.ḫmš. | ilmlk.ḫmš. | prṯ.‘šr. | ubn.‘šr. 1116.14
yn. | šdyn. | ary. | brqn. | bn.ḫlln. | bn.mṣry. | ṯmn.qšt. | w ‘šr.uṯpt. | upšt irš[-]. 118[306].15
rmṯt.ṯṯm. | mḫrhn.nit.mit.krk.mit. | m‘ṣd.ḫmšm.mqb.[‘]šrm. | b.ulm.ṯṯ.‘šr h.ḫrmṯt. | ṯt.nitm.ṯn.m‘ṣdm.ṯn.mqbm. | kr 2048.3
. | d.bn.šb‘l.uḫnpy.ḫmšm. | b.bn.ṯtm.ṯlṯm. | b.bn.agdṯb.‘šrm. | b.bn.ibn.arb‘t.‘šrt. | b.bn.mnn.ṯṯm. | b.rpan.bn.yyn.‘šrt 2054.1.12
šm. | b.bn.ṯtm.ṯlṯm. | b.bn.agdṯb.‘šrm. | b.bn.ibn.arb‘t.‘šrt. | b.bn.mnn.ṯṯm. | b.rpan.bn.yyn.‘šrt. | b.yp‘r.‘šrm. | b.n‘m 2054.1.13
n.‘šrt.ksp. | [--.--]n.šb‘t.l ṯlṯm. | [---].šb‘t.‘šrt. | [---.-]kyn.‘šrt. | b.bn.‘sl.‘šrm.ṯqlm kbd. | b.ṯmq.ḫmšt.l.‘šrt. | b.[---].šb‘t.‘š 2054.1.5
b.bn.‘sl.‘šrm.ṯqlm kbd. | b.ṯmq.ḫmšt.l.‘šrt. | b.[---].šb‘t.‘šrt. | b.bn.pdrn.‘šrm. | d.bn.šb‘l.uḫnpy.ḫmšm. | b.bn.ṯtm.ṯlṯm 2054.1.8
n.bn.ply.ḫmšt.l.‘šrm. | b.gdn.bn.uss.‘šrm. | b.‘dn.bn.ṯṯ.‘šrt. | b.bn.qrdmn.ṯlṯm. | b.bṣmn[.bn].ḥrtn.‘[--]. | b.ṯ[--.---] h.[- 2054.1.19
.rpan.bn.yyn.‘šrt. | b.yp‘r.‘šrm. | b.n‘mn.bn.ply.ḫmšt.l.‘šrm. | b.gdn.bn.uss.‘šrm. | b.‘dn.bn.ṯṯ.‘šrt. | b.bn.qrdmn.ṯlṯm. 2054.1.17
---]. | ‘šr.b gt.[---]. | ṯn.‘šr.b.gt.ir[bṣ]. | arb‘.b.gt.b‘ln. | ‘št.‘šr.b.gpn. | yd.‘dnm. | arb‘.ǵzlm. | ṯn.yṣrm. 2103.7
bt.alpm. | ‘šr.bnšm. | ḫmš.bnši.ṯt[---]. | ‘šr.b gt.[---]. | ṯn.‘šr.b.gt.ir[bṣ]. | arb‘.b.gt.b‘ln. | ‘št.‘šr.b.gpn. | yd.‘dnm. | arb‘.ǵ 2103.5
bt.alpm. | ‘šr.bnšm. | ḫmš.bnši.ṯt[---]. | ‘šr.b gt.[---]. | ṯn.‘šr.b.gt.ir[bṣ]. | arb‘.b.gt.b‘ln. | ‘št.‘šr.b.gpn. | 2103.4
‘[.k]dwṯm.w.ṯṯ.ṯprtm. | b.‘šr[m.]ksp. | ḫmš.kkr.ṣml. | b.‘šrt.b d.bn.kyn. | ‘šr.kkr.š‘rt. | b d.urtn.b.arb‘m. | arb‘t.‘šrt.ḫrṣ 2100.13
m. | b.bn.ibn.arb‘t.‘šrt. | b.bn.mnn.ṯṯm. | b.rpan.bn.yyn.‘šrt. | b.yp‘r.‘šrm. | b.n‘mn.bn.ply.ḫmšt.l.‘šrm. | b.gdn.bn.uss.‘ 2054.1.15
.arb‘t.‘šrt. | b.bn.mnn.ṯṯm. | b.rpan.bn.yyn.‘šrt. | b.yp‘r.‘šrm. | b.n‘mn.bn.ply.ḫmšt.l.‘šrm. | b.gdn.bn.uss.‘šrm. | b.‘dn. 2054.1.16
.yp‘r.‘šrm. | b.n‘mn.bn.ply.ḫmšt.l.‘šrm. | b.gdn.bn.uss.‘šrm. | b.‘dn.bn.ṯṯ.‘šrt. | b.bn.qrdmn.ṯlṯm. | b.bṣmn[.bn].ḥrtn.‘ 2054.1.18
p.‘l.qrt. | b.šd.bn.[u]brš. | ḫmšt.‘šrt. | b.šd.bn.[-]n. | ṯl[ṯt].‘šr[t]. | b.š[d].bn.‘myn. | ḫmšt. | b.[šd.--]n. | ḫ[m]št[.‘]šrt. | [ar]b 1083.10
n.bn.aǵlmn. | arb‘m.ksp.‘l.qrt. | b.šd.bn.[u]brš. | ḫmšt.‘šrt. | b.šd.bn.[-]n. | ṯl[ṯt].‘šr[t]. | b.š[d].bn.‘myn. | ḫmšt. | b.[šd. 1083.8
| [---.-]kyn.‘šrt. | b.bn.‘sl.‘šrm.ṯqlm kbd. | b.ṯmq.ḫmšt.l.‘šrt. | b.[---].šb‘t.‘šrt. | b.bn.pdrn.‘šrm. | d.bn.šb‘l.uḫnpy.ḫmš 2054.1.7
. | [-----]. | alp[.---.--]r. | mit.lḥ[m.---.-]dyt. | ṣl‘t.alp.mri. | ‘šr.bmt.alp.mri. | ṯn.nšbm. | ṯmnym.ṯbṯḫ.alp. | uz.mrat.mlḥt. | 1128.17
b ṯlṯ. | ilmlk.‘šr.ṣin. | mlkn‘m.‘šr. | bn.adty.‘šr. | [ṣ]dqšlm ḫmš. | krzn.ḫmš. | ubr‘ym.ḫmš. | [-- 2039.3
.nḥl h.ḫm[š]t. | bn.unp.arb‘t. | ‘bdbn.ytrš ḫmšt. | krwn.‘šrt. | bn.ulb ḫmšt. | bn.ḫry.ḫmšt. | swn.ḫmšt. | bn.[-]r[-.]ḫmšt. 1062.12
‘šrt ‘šrt.šlm. | ‘bdyrḫ.šb‘t.‘šrt ‘šrt.šlm. | yky.‘šrt.ṯṯt šlm.‘šrt. | bn.ḫgby.ṯmnt.l ‘šrm.‘šrt.ḫmš.kbd. | bn.ilṣdq.šb‘t ṯlṯt šl 1131.7
št. | bn.ḫry.ḫmšt. | swn.ḫmšt. | bn.[-]r[-.]ḫmšt. | bn.ḥdṯ.‘šrt. | bn.ḫnyn.‘šrt. | rpan.ḫmšt. | abǵl.ḫmšt. | bn.aḫdy.‘šrt. | ṯṯn 1062.17
.ḫnyn.‘šrt. | rpan.ḫmšt. | abǵl.ḫmšt. | bn.aḫdy.‘šrt. | ṯṯn.‘šrt. | bn.pnmn.‘šrt. | ‘bdadt.ḫmšt. | abmn.ilštm‘y.ḫmš[t]. | ‘zn. 1062.22
. | ‘šr[.bn]šm[.---]. | ṯn.bnšm.b.š[--]. | arb‘.bnšm.b[.---]. | ‘šrm.bnšm.[b.]‘d[--]. | arb‘.bnšm.b.ag[m]y. | arb‘.bnšm.b.ḫpt 2076.10
bt.alpm. | ‘šr.bnšm. | ḫmš.bnši.ṯt[---]. | ‘šr.b gt.[---]. | ṯn.‘šr.b.gt.ir[bṣ]. | a 2103.2
[b.]gt.ṯpn.‘šr.ṣmdm. | w.ṯlṯ.‘šr.bnš. | yd.ytm.yd.r‘y.ḫmrm. | b.gt.gwl.ṯmn.ṣmdm. | w.arb‘.‘ 2038.2
š. | yd.ytm.yd.r‘y.ḫmrm. | b.gt.gwl.ṯmn.ṣmdm. | w.arb‘.‘šr.bnš. | yd.nǵr.mdr‘.yd.š[--]m. | [b.]gt.iptl.ṯṯ.ṣmdm. | [w.‘]šr. 2038.5
.bnš. | yd.nǵr.mdr‘.yd.š[--]m. | [b.]gt.iptl.ṯṯ.ṣmdm. | [w.‘]šr.bn[š]m.y[d].š[--]. | [-]lm.b d.r[-]m.l[-]m. | ṯṯ.‘šr.ṣ[mdm]. | 2038.8
.šr.ugrt.ḏkr.yṣr. | tgǵln.ḫmš.ddm. | [---].ḫmš.ddm. | ṯṯ.l.‘šrm.bn[š.mlk.---].ḫzr.lqḥ.ḫp[r]. | ‘št.‘šr h.bn[.---.--]ḫ.zr. | b‘l. 2011.40
‘prm.amdy.[ḫm]r.w bn[š]. | gn‘y.[---.bn]š. | uškn[.---].‘šr.bnšm. | ‘nqpat[.---].bnš. | ubr‘y.ar[b‘.]ḫm[r]m.w[.---.]bnš 2040.18
ṣb[u.anyt]. | ‘dn. | ṯbq[ym]. | m‘q[bym]. | tš‘.‘[šr.bnš]. | ǵr.ṯ[--.---]. | ṣbu.any[t]. | bn.kṯan. | ǵr.tš‘[.‘šr.b]nš. | ṣ 79[83].5
| tš‘.‘[šr.bnš]. | ǵr.ṯ[--.---]. | ṣbu.any[t]. | bn.kṯan. | ǵr.tš‘[.‘šr.b]nš. | ṣbu.any[t]. | bn abdḫ[r]. | pdym. | ḫmš.bnšm. | snrym 79[83].9
gmy. | ṯṯ.bn[šm.---]. | ‘šr.b[nšm.---]. | arb‘[.bnšm.---]. | ṯṯ.‘šr.bnš[m.---]. | ‘šr[.bn]šm[.---]. | ṯn.bnšm.b.š[--]. | arb‘.bnšm.b 2076.6
[sp]r.k[--]. | ṯ[ṯ.bn]šm[.b.a]gmy. | ṯṯ.bn[šm.---]. | ‘šr.b[nšm.---]. | arb‘[.bnšm.---]. | ṯṯ.‘šr.bnš[m.---]. | ‘šr[.bn]šm[. 2076.4
---]. | ‘šr.b[nšm.---]. | arb‘[.bnšm.---]. | ṯṯ.‘šr.bnš[m.---]. | ‘šr[.bn]šm[.---]. | ṯn.bnšm.b.š[--]. | arb‘.bnšm.b[.---]. | ‘šrm.bnš 2076.7
yrḫ ḫyr.b ym ḥdṯ. | alp.w š.l b‘lt bhtm. | b arb‘t ‘šrt.b‘l. | ‘rkm. | b ṯmnt.‘šrt.yr | ṯḥṣ.mlk.brr. | ‘lm.tzǵ.b ǵb.ṣpn. UG5.12.A.3
n.nṣdn[.ḫm]št. | bn.arsw ‘[šr]m. | ‘šdyn.ḫmš[t]. | abršn.‘šr[t]. | b‘ln.ḫmšt. | w.nḥl h.ḫm[š]t. | bn.unp.arb‘t. | ‘bdbn.ytrš 1062.7
| ṣ‘q.arb‘ ‘šr. | ṣ‘.ṯmn. | šḥq.‘šrm.arb‘.kbd. | ḫlb rpš arb‘.‘šr. | bq‘t ṯṯ. | irab ṯn.‘šr. | ḥbš.ṯmn. | amdy.arb‘.‘šr. | [-]n‘y.ṯṯ.‘š 67[110].7
l ḫmš.mrkbt.ḫmš.‘šr h.prs. | bt.mrkbt.w l šant.ṯṯ. | l bt.‘šrm. | bt alḫnm.ṯlṯm ṯt kbd. 2105.3
‘šr šṯpm. | b ḫmš.šmn. | ‘šrm.gdy. | b ḫmš.šmn. | w ḫmš t‘dt. 1097.3
[---.‘]šrt. | ḫlb.ḫmšt.l.‘šrm. | mril.‘šrt. | glbty.arb‘t. | [--]ṯb.‘šrt. 1180.3
-----]. | [ḫ]pn.aḥd.b.ṯqlm. | lbš.aḥd.b.ṯqlm. | ḫpn.pṯtm.b ‘šr. | tgmr.ksp.ṯlṯm. | ṯqlm.kbd. 1115.4

‘m.‘šrm.|mr‘m.‘šrm.|‘mlbu.‘šrm.|‘mtḏl.‘šrm.|y‘ḏrd.‘šrm.|gmrd.‘šrm.|ṣdqšlm.‘šr[m].|yknil.ḫmš.|ilmlk.ḫmš.|p 1116.9
m kbd.|b.ṯmq.ḫmšt.l.‘šrt.|b.[---].šb‘t.‘šrt.|b.bn.pdrn.‘šrm.|d.bn.šb‘l.uḫnpy.ḫmšm.|b.bn.ṯtm.ṯlṯm.|b.bn.agdṯb.‘šr 2054.1.9
bd.ḥpr.bnšm.ṯmnym.dd.|l u[-]m.|b.ṭbq.arb‘m.dr‘.w.‘šr.dd.drt.|w[.a]rb‘.l.‘šrm.dd.l.yḥšr.bl.bn h.|b.gt.m‘br.arb‘ 1098.10
i]tm.ḫmšm.ḫmš.k[bd].|[dd].ks̀mm.tš‘[.---].|[š]‘rm.ṯṯ.‘[šr].|[dd].ḥṭm.w.ḫ[mšm].|[ṯ]lṯ kbd.yn.b [gt.---].|mit.[---].ṯl 2092.8
--]mn.arb‘m.y[n].|b.gt.trǵnds.|tš‘.‘šr.[dd].ks̀mm.|ṯn.‘šr[.dd.ḥ]ṭm.|w.šb[‘.---]. 2092.17
‘šrm ddm kbd[.-] l alpm mrim.|ṯṯ ddm l ṣin mrat.|‘šr ddm. 1100.1
[---].‘šr.dd[.---].|[---]mn.arb‘m.y[n].|b.gt.trǵnds.|tš‘.‘šr.[dd].ks̀mm.|ṯn.‘šr[.dd.ḥ]ṭm.|w.šb[‘.---]. 2092.16
l alpm mrim.|ṯṯ ddm l ṣin mrat.|‘šr ddm.l šm‘rgm.|‘šr ddm.l bt.|‘šrm.dd.l mḫṣm.|ddm l kbs.|dd l prgṯ.|dd.l 1100.4
.dd.|l u[-]m.|b.ṭbq.arb‘m.dr‘.w.‘šr.dd.drt.|w[.a]rb‘.l.‘šrm.dd.l.yḥšr.bl.bn h.|b.gt.m‘br.arb‘m.l.mit.dr‘.w.ṯmnym[1098.11
.|ṯṯ ddm l ṣin mrat.|‘šr ddm.l šm‘rgm.|‘šr ddm.l bt.|‘šrm.dd.l mḫṣm.|ddm l kbs.|dd l prgṯ.|dd.l mri.|dd.l ṯnǵly 1100.5
]n.[k]bd.|w[.---.]qm‘t.|[---.]mḏrǵlm.|[---.]mdm.|[w].‘šr.dd.l np[l].|r[p]š. 2012.26
‘šrm ddm kbd[.-] l alpm mrim.|ṯṯ ddm l ṣin mrat.|‘šr ddm.l šm‘rgm.|‘šr ddm.l bt.|‘šrm.dd.l mḫṣm.|ddm l kb 1100.3
qmḥ.d.kly.k ṣḥ.illḏrm.|b d.zlb[n.--].|arb‘.‘š[r.]dd.n‘r.|d.apy[.--].|w.arb[‘.--]d.apy.‘bd h.|w.mrb‘[t.l ‘] 2094.3
-]k.[--].|[---.]dd.bn.š.[---.]yd.sǵr h.⌞⌞---.--]r h.‘šr[m.---.‘]šrm.dd.|[---.yn.d.]nkly.l.r‘ym.šb‘m.l.mitm.dd.|[---.--]d.šb‘ 1098.43
|[---.]ḥdṯn.‘šr.dd[.---].|[---.]yd.sǵr[.---.--]r h.|aḥ[d.---.‘]šrm.d[d.---].|‘š[r.---.--]r h.|my y[--.---.--]d.|‘šrm[.---.--]r h. 1098.36
].|ḫm[š.---].|b[yrḫ.---].|[---.]prš.|[-----].|l.mšḫ[.---].|‘šr.d[d.---].|ṯṯm.dd.dd[.---].|l.mḏrǵlm[.---].|ṯlṯ.mat.ḫmšm.k 2012.8
š[.š]dyn[.---].|agr.[---.--]n.ṯn.‘šr h.d[--.---].|[---.]ḥdṯn.‘šr.dd[.---].|[---.]yd.sǵr[.---.--]r h.|aḥ[d.---.‘]šrm.d[d.---].|‘š[1098.34
n.b [gt.---].|mit.[---].ṯlṯ.kb[d].|[dd.--]m.šb‘.[---].|[---].‘šr.dd[.---].|[---]mn.arb‘m.y[n].|b.gt.trǵnds.|tš‘.‘šr.[dd].ks̀ 2092.13
.|[ḫ]mrm.|ddm.l.ybr[k].|bdmr.prs.l.u[-]m[-].|ṯmn.l.‘šrm.|dmd.b d.mry[n]m. 2102.9
dr‘.w.‘šrm.drt.|w.ṯlṯm.dd.ṯṯ.kbd.ḥpr.bnšm.|b.‘nmky.‘šrm.dr‘[.---.d]rt.|w.ṯn.‘šr h.dd.[---].|iwrḏn.ḥ[--.---].|w.ṯlṯm 1098.28
.šb‘m.dd.arb‘.|kbd.ḥpr.bnšm.|b.gt.ṯrmn.arb‘m.dr‘.w.‘šrm.drt.|w.ṯlṯm.dd.ṯṯ.kbd.ḥpr.bnšm.|b.gt.ḥdṯt.arb‘m.dr‘.w 1098.20
.drt.|w.‘šrm.l.mit.dd.ḥpr.bnšm.|b.y‘ny.arb‘m.dr‘.w.‘šrm.drt.|w.ṯlṯm.dd.ṯṯ.kbd.ḥpr.bnšm.|b.‘nmky.‘šrm.dr‘[.---. 1098.26
.---].|[ṯ]mny[m.---].|[-]r[-.---].|[--]m.l.[---].|a[---.---].|‘šrm.drt[.---]. 2013.32
ubr‘y.ṯlṯ.|ar.ṯmn ‘šr h.|mlk.arb‘.|ǵbl.ḫmš.|atlg.ḫmš ‘šr[h].|ulm ṯ[ṯ].|m‘rby.ḫmš.|ṭbq.arb‘.|tkm[.---].|uḫnp[.--- 68[65].1.8
-].ḫmš.ddm.|ṯṯ.l.‘šrm.bn[š.mlk.---].ḫzr.lqḥ.ḥp[r].|‘št.‘šr h.bn[.---.--]ḫ.zr.|b‘l.šd. 2011.41
[--].d.ntn[.d.]ksp.|[ṯ]mn.l.‘šrm[.l.b]t.‘ṯtrt.|[ṯ]lṯ.‘šr h.[b]t.ršp.gn.|arb‘.b d.b[n].ušryn.|kdm.l.urtn.|kdm.l.ilš 1088.3
spr.ḥpr.bt.k[--].|tš‘.‘šr h.dd.l.b[t.--].|ḫmš.ddm.l.ḥtyt.|ṯlṯm.dd.ks̀mn.l.gzzm.|yy 1099.2
[---.d]r‘.w.mit.drt.w.‘šrm.l.mit.|[drt.ḥpr.b]nšm.w.ṯn.‘šr h.dd.l.rpš.|[---.]šb‘m.dr‘.w.arb‘m.drt.mit.dd.|[---].ḥpr.b 1098.4
dd.ṯṯ.kbd.ḥpr.bnšm.|b.‘nmky.‘šrm.dr‘[.---.d]rt.|w.ṯn.‘šr h.dd.[---].|iwrḏn.ḥ[--.---].|w.ṯlṯm.dd.[---.]n[---.---].|w.a[1098.29
[---.---].|w.a[r]b‘[.---].bnš[.š]dyn[.---].|agr.[---.--]n.ṯn.‘šr h.d[--.---].|[---.]ḥdṯn.‘šr.dd[.---].|[---.]yd.sǵr[.---.--]r h.|a 1098.33
[---.ṯ]lṯ.‘š[r h.---].|d bnšm.yd.grbs hm.|w.ṯn.‘šr h.ḫpnt.|[š]šwm.amtm.‘kyt.|yd.llḫ hm.|w.ṯlṯ.l.‘šrm.|ḫp 2049.3
n.nit.mit.krk.mit.|m‘ṣd.ḫmšm.mqb.[‘]šrm.|b.ulm.ṯṯ.‘šr h.ḫrmṯt.|ṯṯ.nitm.ṯn.m‘ṣdm.ṯn.mqbm.|krk.aḥt.|b.sǵy.ḫ 2048.4
ṯlṯm.ktn.|ḫmšm.izml.|ḫmš.kbd.arb‘m.|dd.akl.|ṯṯ.‘šr h.yn.|kd.šmn.l.nr.ilm.|kdm.dǵm.|ṯṯ.kdm.ztm. 1126.5
aḥd.kbd.|arb‘m.b ḫzr.|lqḥ š‘rt.|ṯṯ ‘šr h.lqḥ.|ḫlpnt.|ṯṯ.ḥrṯm.|lqḥ.š‘rt.|‘šr.ḥrš.|bhtm.lqḥ.|š‘rt.| 2052.4
[--.]wmrkm.|bir.ḫmš.|uškn.arb‘.|ubr‘y.ṯlṯ.|ar.ṯmn ‘šr h.|mlk.arb‘.|ǵbl.ḫmš.|atlg.ḫmš ‘šr[h].|ulm ṯ[ṯ].|m‘rby. 68[65].1.5
md.[---.-]št.|hl ny.argmn.d [ybl.n]qmd.|l špš.arn.ṯn[.‘šr h.]mn.|‘šrm.ṯql.kbd[.ks].mn.ḫrṣ.|w arb‘.ktnt.w [---]b.|[64[118].19
šb‘.ṯnnm.w.šb‘.ḫsnm.|ṯmn.‘šr h.mrynm.|‘šr.mkrm.|ḫmš.ṯrtnm.|ḫmš.bn.mrynm.|‘šr. 1030.2
l ḫmš.mrkbt.ḫmš.‘šr h.prs.|bt.mrkbt.w l šant.ṯṯ.|l bt.‘šrm.|bt alḫnm.ṯlṯm ṯṯ k 2105.1
ṣṣ mr‘m ḫmšm ḫmš kbd.|ṣṣ ubn ḫmš ‘šr h.|ṣṣ ‘myd ḫmšm.|ṣṣ tmn.ḫmšm.|[ṣṣ] ‘mtḏl ṯlṯm.|ṣṣ ‘ml 2097.2
arb‘.‘šr h.šd.|w.kmsk.d.iwrkl.|ṯlṯ.šd.d.bn.mlkyy.|kmsk.šd.iḫm 1079.1
---.ḫ]rš.mr[k]bt.|[--].‘šr h[.---].|[ḫm]š.‘šr h[.---].|ḫmš.‘šr h.|šrm. 1024.4.1
arb‘.‘šr h.šmn.|d.lqḥt.ṯlǵdy.|w.kd.ištir.‘m.qrt.|‘št.‘šr h.šmn.|‘m 1083.1
arb‘.‘šr h.šmn.|d.lqḥt.ṯlǵdy.|w.kd.ištir.‘m.qrt.|‘št.‘šr h.šmn.|‘mn.bn.aǵlmn.|arb‘m.ksp.‘l.qrt.|b.šd.bn.[u]brš. 1083.4
ṯrmnm.|[---].ṯlṯm.iqnu.|[---.l.]ṯrmn.mlk.|[---.]š‘rt.šb‘.‘šr h.|[---.iqn]i.l.ṯrmn.qrt.|[---.]lbš.ḫmšm.iqnu.|[---].šmt.ḫ 1106.14
[---.ṯ]lṯ.‘š[r h.---].|d bnšm.yd.grbs hm.|w.ṯn.‘šr h.ḫpnt.|[š]šwm.am 2049.1
---.]l.mit.dr‘.w.šb‘m.drt.|[---.ḥpr.]bnšm.w.l.ḥrš.‘rq.ṯn.‘šr h.|[---.d]r‘.w.mit.drt.w.‘šrm.l.mit.|[drt.ḥpr.b]nšm.w.ṯn.‘ 1098.2
[ṯl]ṯ.psl.ḥzm.|[---.ḫ]rš.mr[k]bt.|[--].‘šr h[.---].|[ḫm]š.‘šr h[.---].|ḫmš.‘šr h.|šrm. 1024.3.22
-]m.|[--.]psl.qšt.|[ṯl]ṯ.psl.ḥzm.|[---.ḫ]rš.mr[k]bt.|[--].‘šr h[.---].|[ḫm]š.‘šr h[.---].|ḫmš.‘šr h.|šrm. 1024.3.21
mrum.w.šb‘.ḫsnm.|tš‘m.mḏrǵlm.|arb‘.l ‘šrm.ḫsnm.|‘šr.hbṯnm.|ṯtm.l.mit.ṯn.kbd.|tgmr. 1030.9
tnm.ḫmš.|mrum.‘šr.|šb‘.ḫsnm.|mkrm.|mrynm.|ṯlṯ.‘šr.|hbṯnm.|ṯmn.|mḏrǵlm.|ṯmnym.ṯmn.kbd.|tgmr.ḫrd.|a 1031.10
mšm.dd.|n‘r.|ḫmšm.tišr.|ḫmš.ktnt.|ḫmš.ṯnt.alpm.|‘šrm.hbn.|ṯlṯ.mat.dd.|š‘rm.|mit.šmn.|‘šr.kat.|ẓrw. 2102.6
nsk k[sp].|‘šrt.|w nṣ[p]. 1164.2
l.|šnt.‘m.bn il.tspr.yrḫm.|k b‘l.k yḥwy.y‘šr.ḥwy.y‘š.|r.w yšqyn h.ybd.w yšr.‘l h.|n‘m[n.w t]‘nynn.ap ank.aḥwy.| 17[2AQHT].6.31
šlḥmn h.|ybrd.ṯd.l pnw h.|b ḥrb.mlḥt.|qṣ.mri.ndd.|y‘šr.w yšqyn h.|ytn.ks.b d h.|krpn.b klat.yd h.|b krb.‘ẓm.r 3[‘NT].1.9
lbš.aḥd.|b.‘šrt.|w.ṯn.b.ḫmšt.|ṯprt.b.ṯlṯt.|mṯyn.b.ṯṯt.|ṯn.lbšm.b.‘šrt.|pl 1108.2
lmg.|ḫmšm.kkr.|qnm.|‘šrm.kk[r].|brr.|[‘]šrm.npš.|‘šrm.zt.mm.|‘rb‘m.|šmn.mr. 141[120].14
.|šḥq.‘šrm.arb‘.kbd.|ḫlb rpš arb‘.‘šr.|bq‘t ṯṯ.|irab ṯn.‘šr.|ḫbš.ṯmn.|amḏy.arb‘.‘šr.|[-]n‘y.ṯṯ.‘šr. 67[110].9
.ašspr k.‘m.b‘l.|šnt.‘m.bn il.tspr.yrḫm.|k b‘l.k yḥwy.y‘šr.ḥwy.y‘š.|r.w yšqyn h.ybd.w yšr.‘l h.|n‘m[n.w t]‘nynn.a 17[2AQHT].6.30
ḫ[mrm].|b m[‘]rby.|ṯmn.ṣmd.[---].|b d.b‘lsr.|yd.ṯdn.‘šr.|[ḫ]mrm.|ddm.l.ybr[k].|bdmr.prs.l.u[-]m[-].|ṯmn.l.‘šr 2102.5
ḫzr.|lqḥ š‘rt.|ṯṯ ‘šr h.lqḥ.|ḫlpnt.|ṯṯ.ḥrṯm.|lqḥ.š‘rt.|‘šr.ḥrš.|bhtm.lqḥ.|š‘rt.|arb‘.|ḥrš qṭn.|lqḥ š‘rt.|ṯṯ nsk.ḥdm. 2052.8
mn.ḫzr.|w.arb‘.ḥršm.|dt.tb‘ln.b.pḫn.|ṯṯtm.ḫzr.w.‘št.‘šr.ḥrš.|dt.tb‘ln.b.ugrt.|ṯṯtm.ḫzr.|dt.tb‘ln.|b.gt.ḥršm.|ṯn.ḫ 1024.3.7
[---.‘]šrt.|ḫlb.ḫmšt.l.‘šrm.|mril.‘šrt.|glbty.arb‘t.|[--]ṯb.‘šrt. 1180.1
rt ‘šrt.šlm.|yky.‘šrt.ṯṯt šlm.‘šrt.|bn.ḥgby.ṯmnt.l ‘šrm.‘šrt.ḫmš.kbd.|bn.ilṣdq.šb‘t ṯlṯt šlm.|bn.ṯmq.arb‘t ṯqlm šlm 1131.8

b.ṯmnym.ksp.ṯlṯt.kbd. | ḫmš.alp.ṯlṯ.l.ḥlby. | b d.tlmi.b.‘šrm.ḫmšt. | kbd.ksp. | kkrm.š‘rt.štt.b d.gg[‘t]. | b.‘šrt.ksp. | ṯlṯ. 2101.7
npṣm. | b d.mri. | skn. | ‘šrm. | ḫmš. | kbd. 157[116].4
b.šb‘m. | ṯlṯ.mat.trm.b.‘šrt. | mit.adrm.b.‘šrt. | ‘šr.ydt.b.‘šrt. | ḫmš.kkrm.ṣml. | ‘šrt.ksp h. | ḫmš.kkr.qnm. | ṯlṯt.w.ṯlṯt.k 1127.9
‘.ṯrtnm. | tš‘.ḥbṯnm. | ṯmnym.ṯlṯ.kbd. | mdrġlm. | w.šb‘.‘šr.ḫsnm. | ḫmšm.l.mit. | bnš.l.d. | yškb.l.b.bt.mlk. 1029.13
ṯnnm.ṯṯ. | ‘šr.ḫsnm. | n‘r.mrynm. | ḫmš. | trtnm.ḫmš. | mrum.‘šr. | šb‘.ḫs 1031.2
mrynm. | ‘šr.mrum.w.šb‘.ḫsnm. | tš‘m.mdrġlm. | arb‘.l ‘šrm.ḫsnm. | ‘šr.hbṯnm. | ṯṯm.l.mit.ṯn.kbd. | tgmr. 1030.8
ḫmš.ṯnnm.‘šr.ḫsnm. | ṯlṯ.‘šr.mrynm. | ḫmš.[tr]tnm. | ṯlṯ.b[n.]mrynm. | ‘šr 1028.1
spr.npṣm.d yṣa.b milḫ. | ‘šrm.ḫpn.ḫmš. | kbd.w lpš. | ḫmš.mispt. | mṯ. | w lpš.d sgr b h. 1109.2
.ṯn.‘šr h.ḫpnt. | [š]šwm.amtm.‘kyt. | yd.llḫ hm. | w.ṯlṯ.l.‘šrm. | ḫpnt.ššwm.ṯn. | pddm.w.d.ṯṯ. | [mr]kbt.w.ḥrṣ. 2049.6
| b d.urtn.b.arb‘m. | arb‘t.‘šrt.ḥrṣ. | b.ṯqlm.kbd.arb‘m. | ‘šrt.ḥrṣ.b.arb‘m. | mit.ḥršḫ.b.ṯqlm. | w.šb‘.‘šr.šmn. | d.l.yṣa.bt. 2100.18
.‘šrt.b d.bn.kyn. | ‘šr.kkr.š‘rt. | b d.urtn.b.arb‘m. | arb‘t.‘šrt.ḥrṣ. | b.ṯqlm.kbd.arb‘m. | ‘šrt.ḥrṣ.b.arb‘m. | mit.ḥršḫ.b.ṯql 2100.16
m. | šstm.b.šb‘m. | ṯlṯ.mat.trm.b.‘šrt. | mit.adrm.b.‘šrt. | ‘šr.ydt.b.‘šrt. | ḫmš.kkrm.ṣml. | ‘šrt.ksp h. | ḫmš.kkr.qnm. | ṯlṯ 1127.9
u.‘šrm. | ‘mtdl.‘šrm. | y‘drd.‘šrm. | gmrd.‘šrm. | ṣdqšlm.‘šr[m]. | yknil.ḫmš. | ilmlk.ḫmš. | prṯ.‘šr. | ubn.‘šr. 1116.11
rḫ.w.ḫm[š.ymm]. | ẓrn.yrḫ.w.ḫmš.y[m]m. | mrat.ḫmš.‘šr.ymm. | qmnz.yrḫ.w.ḫmš.ymm. | ‘nmk.yrḫ. | ypr.yrḫ.w.ḫm 66[109].7
[---.-]lk[.---]. | [---.‘]šr.ym[.---]. | [---].hm.l y[--.---]. | [---].mṣrm[.---]. | [---.--]n m 2126.2
ṯm.arb‘.kbd.yn.d.l.ṭb. | b.gt.m‘rby. | ṯṯm.yn.ṭb.w.ḫmš.l.‘šrm. | yn.d.l.ṭb.b.ulm. | mit.yn.ṭb.w.ṯṯm.ṯṯ.kbd. | yn.d.l.ṭb.b.g 1084.9
‘m.kbd.yn.ḥsp.l.m[--]. | mit.‘šrm.[k]bd.yn.ḥsp.l.y[--]. | ‘šrm.yn.ḥsp.l.ql.d.tb‘.mṣ[r]m. | mit.arb‘m.kbd.yn.mṣb. | l.md 1084.27
--.]piln. | [---].ṣmd[.---.]pd[ry]. | [-----]. | [---.b]‘lt. | lbnm.‘šr.yn. | ḫlb.gngnt.ṯlṯ.y[n]. | bṣr.‘šr.yn. | nnu arb‘.yn. | šql ṯlṯ.y 2004.21
.tš‘m.kdm.kbd.yn.d.l.ṭb. | w.arb‘m.yn.ḫlq.b.gt.sknm. | ‘šr.yn.ṭb.w.arb‘m.ḫmš.kbd. | yn.d.l.ṭb.gt.ṭbq. | mit.‘šr.kbd.yn 1084.4
ḫmš.‘šr.yn.ṭb. | w.tš‘m.kdm.kbd.yn.d.l.ṭb. | w.arb‘m.yn.ḫlq.b.gt.s 1084.1
.ṯṯm.ṯṯ.kbd. | yn.d.l.ṭb.b.gt.ḥdṯt. | tš‘m.yn.d.l.ṭb.b.zbl. | ‘šrm.yn.ṭb.w.ṯṯm.ḫmš.k[b]d. | yn.d.l.ṭb.b.gt.sġy. | arb‘m.kdm 1084.14
ṯn.‘šr.yn.[kps]lnm. | arb‘.mat[.arb]‘m.[k]bd. | d ntn.d.ksp. | arb‘. 1087.1
.tb‘.mṣ[r]m. | mit.arb‘m.kbd.yn.mṣb. | l.mdrġlm. | ‘šrn ‘šr.yn.mṣb.[-]ḫ[-].l.gzzm. 1084.30
[-----]. | [---.b]‘lt. | lbnm.‘šr.yn. | ḫlb.gngnt.ṯlṯ.y[n]. | bṣr.‘šr.yn. | nnu arb‘.yn. | šql ṯlṯ.yn. | šmny.kdm.yn. | šmgy.kd.yn. 2004.23
.ṯlṯm. | mlkn‘m.‘šrm. | mr‘m.‘šrm. | ‘mlbu.‘šrm. | ‘mtdl.‘šrm. | y‘drd.‘šrm. | gmrd.‘šrm. | ṣdqšlm.‘šr[m]. | yknil.ḫmš. | il 1116.8
mš.ṯnt.alpm. | ‘šrm.hbn. | ṯlṯ.mat.dd. | š‘rm. | mit.šmn. | ‘šr.kat. | ẓrw. 2102.10
rm. | lqḥ.iwrpzn. | argdd. | ṯṯkn. | ybrk. | ntbt. | b.mitm. | ‘šrm. | kbd.ḥrṣ. 2006.9
.d.nkly.b.db[ḫ.--]. | mit.arb‘m.kbd.yn.ḥsp.l.m[--]. | mit.‘šrm.[k]bd.yn.ḥsp.l.y[--]. | ‘šrm.yn.ḥsp.l.ql.d.tb‘.mṣ[r]m. | mi 1084.26
m. | ‘šr.yn.ṭb.w.arb‘m.ḫmš.kbd. | yn.d.l.ṭb.gt.ṭbq. | mit.‘šr.kbd.yn.ṭb. | w.ṯṯm.arb‘.kbd.yn.d.l.ṭb. | b.gt.m‘rby. | ṯṯm.yn 1084.6
mitm.‘šr kbd. | kšmm.b.mṣbt. | mit.‘šrm.ṯn kbd. | [kš]mm. | [‘]š[r]m. 2091.1
. | ṣṣ iytlm mit ṯlṯm kbd. | ṣṣ m[l]k ‘šrm. | ṣṣ abš[-] mit [‘š]r kbd. | ṣṣ ydrd ‘šrm. | ṣṣ bn aglby ṯlṯ[m]. | ṣṣ bn.šrš‘m.[---]. 2097.11
.arb‘m.drt. | l.a[--.---]. | tgm[r.ak]l.b.gt.ḥldy. | ṯlṯ.ma[t].‘šr.kbd. | šb‘ m[at].kbd.ḥpr.‘bdm. | mit[.d]rt.arb‘m.drt. | [---] 2013.11
r.‘b]dm. | tg[mr.---]. | [-]m.m[--.---]. | [m]itm.dr[t.---]. | [‘š]r.[k]bd[.---]. | [a]lpm[.---]. | tg[m]r.[---]. | ṯlṯ ma[t.---]. | ṯmny 2013.23
[ḫm]šm.ksp.‘l.gd[--]. | [---].ypḥ.‘bdršp.b[--.--]. | [ar]b‘t.‘šrt.kbd[.---]. | [---.-]rwd.šmbnš[.---]. | [---].ksp.‘l.k[--]. | [---.--] 1144.6
.pld š‘rt. | ṯt pld pṯt. | arb‘ ḥpnt pṯt. | ḫmš ḥpnt.š‘rt. | ṯlṯ.‘šr kdwṯm. 1113.11
m[r]yn. | pġdn.ilb‘l.krwn.lbn.‘dn. | ḫyrn.md‘. | šm‘n.rb ‘šrt.kkln.‘bd.abṣn. | šdyn.unn.dqn. | ‘bd‘nt.rb ‘šrt.mnḥm.ṭb‘ 2011.5
skn.‘šrm kk[r.---]. | mšrn.ṯlṯ.‘š[r.kkr]. | bn.šw.šb‘.kk[r.---]. | arb‘m.kkr.[---]. | b d.mtn.[l].šl 2108.2
kkrm.brdl. | mit.tišrm. | ṯlṯm.almg. | ḫmšm.kkr. | qnm. | ‘šrm.kk[r]. | brr. | [‘]šrm.npš. | ‘šrm.zt.mm. | ‘rb‘m. | šmn.mr. 141[120].11
‘šrm.kkr.kkrm. | alp.ṯṯ.mat.kbd. 2111.1
[m]. | ṯn.ḥblm.alp.alp.am[-]. | ṯmn.ḥblm.šb‘.šb‘.ma[-]. | ‘šr.kkr.rtn. | b d.šm‘y.bn.bdn. 1128.32
prtm. | b.‘šr[m.]ksp. | ḫmš.kkr.ṣml. | b.‘šrt.b d.bn.kyn. | ‘šr.kkr.š‘rt. | b d.urtn.b.arb‘m. | arb‘t.‘šrt.ḥrṣ. | b.ṯqlm.kbd.ar 2100.14
r.ḫmš.mat.kbd.ṯlṯ.šm[n]. | alp.mitm.kbd.ṯlṯ.ḥlb. | šb‘.l.‘šrm.kkr.ṯlṯ. | d.ybl.blym. 1135.6
any.al[ty]. | d b atlg[.---]. | ḫmš ‘š[r]. | kkr.ṯ[lṯ]. | ṯt hrt[m]. | ṯn mq[pm]. | ulṯ.ṯl[ṯ]. | krk.kly[.--]. 2056.3
[---.--]d.‘m y. | [--.]spr.lm.likt. | [--]y.k išal hm. | [--.‘š]rm.kkr.ṯlṯ. | [--.]ṯlṯm.kkr.ṯlṯ. | [--.]aštn.l k. | [--]y.kl.dbrm.h 1022.4
skn.‘šrm kk[r.---]. | mšrn.ṯlṯ.‘š[r.kkr]. | bn.šw.šb‘.kk[r.---]. | arb‘m. 2108.1
bnš.gt.ngr. | r‘ym. | bn.ḫri[-]. | bnš.gt.‘ṯrt. | ad[-]l[-]m. | ‘šr.ksdm.yd.lmd hm.lqḥ. | ‘šr.mḫšm.yd.lmd hm. | apym. | [bn 1040.8
d.an[r]my. | b.‘šrt.ksp.b.a[--]. | ṯqlm.ḫr[ṣ.]b.ṯmnt.ksp. | ‘šrt.ksp.b.alp.[b d].bn.[---]. | tš‘.ṣin.b.tš‘t.ksp. | mšlt.b.ṯql.ksp. 2101.21
bt.mlk. | b.mit.ḫmšt.kbd.ksp. | ṯlṯ.ktnt.b d.an[r]my. | b.‘šrt.ksp.b.a[--]. | ṯqlm.ḫr[ṣ.]b.ṯmnt.ksp. | ‘šrt.ksp.b.alp.[b d].b 2101.19
spr.argmnm. | ‘šrm.ksp.d mkr. | mlk. | ṯlṯ.mat.ksp.d.šb[n]. | mit.ksp.d.ṯbq. | ṯ 2107.2
. | b [ar]b‘m.ksp. | b d[.‘b]dym.ṯlṯ.kkr š‘rt. | iqn[i]m.ṯṯt.‘šrt.ksp h. | ḫmšt.ḥrṣ.bt.il. | b.ḫmšt.‘šrt.ksp. | ḫmš.mat.šmt. | b 2100.4
.‘šrt. | mit.adrm.b.‘šrt. | ‘šr.ydt.b.‘šrt. | ḫmš.kkrm.ṣml. | ‘šrt.ksp h. | ḫmš.kkr.qnm. | ṯlṯt.w.ṯlṯt.ksp h. | arb‘.kkr. | algbṯ. 1127.11
b‘ld‘.yd[.---.‘]šrt.ksp h. | lbiy.pdy.[---.k]sp h. 2112.1
. | arb‘m.l.mit.šmn. | arb‘m.l.mit.tišr. | ṯt.ṯt.b [ṯ]ql.ṯlṯt.l.‘šrm.ksp hm. | šstm.b.šb‘m. | ṯlṯ.mat.trm.b.‘šrt. | mit.adrm.b.‘ 1127.5
sp. | ‘šr.ṣin.b.ṯṯt.w.kmsk. | arb‘[.k]dwṯm.w.ṯt.ṯprtm. | b.‘šr[m.]ksp. | ḫmš.kkr.ṣml. | b.‘šrt.b d.bn.kyn. | ‘šr.kkr.š‘rt. | b 2100.11
kr š‘rt. | iqn[i]m.ṯṯt.‘šrt.ksp h. | ḫmšt.ḥrṣ.bt.il. | b.ḫmšt.‘šrt.ksp. | ḫmš.mat.šmt. | b.‘šrt.ksp. | ‘šr.ṣin.b.ṯṯt.w.kmsk. | arb 2100.6
ḫmšt.‘š[rt]. | ksp.‘l.agd[ṯb]. | w nit w m‘ṣd. | w ḫrmṯt. | ‘šrt.ksp. | ‘l.ḫ[2053.1
a]r[b‘] ksp ‘l bn ymn. | šb šr šmn [--] ṯryn. | ḫm[š]m l ‘šr ksp ‘l bn llit. | [--]l[-.-]p ‘l [---.-]b‘m arny. | w ‘l [---.]rb‘m ṯ 1103.6
sp.d mkr. | ilštm‘. | ‘šrm.l mit.ksp. | ‘l.bn.alkbl.šb[ny]. | ‘šrm ksp.‘l. | wrt.mtny.w ‘l. | prdny.aṯt h. 2107.17
ḫmšt.‘š[rt]. | ksp.‘l.agd[ṯb]. | w nit w m‘ṣd. | w ḫrmṯt. | ‘šrt.ksp. | ‘l.ḫ[z]rn. | w.nit.w[.m‘ṣd]. | w.ḫ[rmṯt]. | ‘š[r.---]. | ‘l[.- 2053.5
‘šrm.ksp. | ‘l.šknt.syny. 1132.1
l. | [---].prš.ḥtm. | ṯlṯ[.---].bn.ṯdnyn. | ddm.ḥ[ṭm].‘l.šrn. | ‘šrt.ksp.‘l.[-]lpy. | bn.ady.kkr.š‘rt. | nṯk h. | kb[d.]mn.‘l.abršn. 1146.8
h. | ḫmšt.ḥrṣ.bt.il. | b.ḫmšt.‘šrt.ksp. | ḫmš.mat.šmt. | b.‘šrt.ksp. | ‘šr.ṣin.b.ṯṯt.w.kmsk. | arb‘[.k]dwṯm.w.ṯt.ṯprtm. | b.‘ 2100.8
krm.š‘rt.štt.b d.gg[‘t]. | b.‘šrt.ksp. | ṯlṯ.uṯbm.b d.alḫn.b.‘šrt[.k]sp. | rṯ.l.ql.d.ybl.prd. | b.ṯql.w.nṣp.ksp. | ṯmn.lbšm.w.m 2101.11

b.ṯql.w.nṣp.ksp. | ṯmn.lbšm.w.mšlt. | l.udmym.b.ṯmnt.‘šrt.ksp. | šb‘m.lbš.d.‘rb.bt.mlk. | b.mit.ḫmšt.kbd.ksp. | ṯlṯ.ktn 2101.15
m.t[i]ṯṯmn. | šnl.bn.ṣ[q]n.š̀[--]. | yiṯṯm.w.b[--]. | yšlm. | [‘]šrm.ks[p].yš[lm]. | [il]tḥm.b d[.---]. | [---].ṯl[l]m.[---]. | [--].r[- 2104.7
lmi.b.‘šrm.ḫmšt. | kbd.ksp. | kkrm.š‘rt.štt.b d.gg[‘t]. | b.‘šrt.ksp. | ṯlṯ.uṭbm.b d.alḫn.b.‘šrt[.k]sp. | rṭ.l.ql.d.ybl.prd. | b.ṯ 2101.10
[---.-]grm. | [---.-]n.‘šrt.ksp. | [--.--]n.šb‘t.l ṯlṯm. | [---].šb‘t.‘šrt. | [---.-]kyn.‘šrt. | b.b 2054.1.2
-]. | ary.‘šr.arb‘.kbd.[---]. | [--]yy.ṯṯ.krmm.šl[-.---]. | [---.]‘šrm.krm.[---]. | [ṯ]lrby.‘šr.ṯn.kb[d.---]. | ḫmrm.ṯṯ.krm[m.---]. 1081.20
‘šr.ktnt. | ‘šr.rṭm. | kkr[.-].ḫt. | mitm[.p]ṯtm. | ṯlṯm[.---].kst. | al 1114.1
‘šr. | kṯt. | [--]š ‘šr. | lg. 158[58].1
rṯ[b.---]. | b ṯṯ ‘ṯr ṯmn.r[qḫ.---]. | p bn btb[-.---]. | b ḫmṯ ‘ṯr k[--.---]. | b ḫmṯ ‘ṯr[.---]. | [-----]. | [---.-]y[-.---]. | w bn ‘ṭl.[--- 207[57].4
mit.‘[šr.---]. | [ṯ]lṯ.abd[.---]. | [---.]anyt[.---]. | [-----]. | ‘šrm.l.umdym. | ‘šr.l.ktl. 2110.5
‘t.‘šr[t]. | yrtḥṣ.mlk.b[rr]. | b ym.mlat. | tqln.alpm. | yrḫ.‘šrt.l b‘[l]. | dqtm.w ynt.qr[t]. | w mtntm.š l rmš. | w kbd.w š.l UG5.13.5
‘t.‘[š]rt.yrtḥṣ.mlk.brr. | [b ym.ml]at.y[ql]n.al[p]m.yrḫ.‘šrt. | [l b‘l.ṣ]pn.[dq]tm.w y[nt] qrt. | [w mtmt]m.[š.l] rm[š.]k 36[9].1.11
[--].d.ntn[.d.]ksp. | [ṯ]mn.l.‘šrm[.l.b]t.‘ṯtrt. | [ṯ]lṯ.‘šr h.[b]t.ršp.gn. | arb‘.b d.b[n].ušryn. | 1088.2
[ṯ]lṯ.abd[.---]. | [---.]anyt[.---]. | [-----]. | ‘šrm.l.umdym. | ‘šr.l.ktl. 2110.6
bl.bn h. | b.gt.m‘br.arb‘m.l.mit.dr‘.w.ṯmnym[.drt]. | w.‘šrm.l.mit.dd.ḥp[r.]bnšm. | b.gt.ǵl.‘šrm.l.mit.dr‘.w.tš‘m.drt. | 1098.13
ṯn.kbd.ḥpr.bnšm. | b.nzl.‘šrm.l.mit.dr‘.w.šb‘m.drt. | w.‘šrm.l.mit.dd.ḥpr.bnšm. | b.y‘ny.arb‘m.dr‘.w.‘šrm.drt. | w.ṯlṯ 1098.25
.dr‘.w.ṯlṯm.drt. | [w].šb‘m.dd.ṯn.kbd.ḥpr.bnšm. | b.nzl.‘šrm.l.mit.dr‘.w.šb‘m.drt. | w.‘šrm.l.mit.dd.ḥpr.bnšm. | b.y‘n 1098.24
.w.ṯmnym[.drt]. | w.‘šrm.l.mit.dd.ḥp[r.]bnšm. | b.gt.ǵl.‘šrm.l.mit.dr‘.w.tš‘m.drt. | [w].ṯmnym.l.mit.dd.ḥpr.bnšm. | b 1098.14
--.ḥpr.]bnšm.w.l.ḥrš.‘rq.ṯn.‘šr h. | [---.d]r‘.w.mit.drt.w.‘šrm.l.mit. | [drt.ḥpr.b]nšm.w.ṯn.‘šr h.dd.l.rpš. | [---.]šb‘m.dr‘ 1098.3
[sp]r.akl[.---].ṯryn. | [tg]mr.akl.b.g[t.b]ir.alp. | [‘]šrm.l.mit.ḥ[p]r.‘bdm. | mitm.drt.ṯmnym.drt. | tgmr.akl.b.gt 2013.3
r.ar. | arb‘m ksp d mkr. | atlg. | mit.ksp.d mkr. | ilštm‘. | ‘šrm.l mit.ksp. | ‘l.bn.alkbl.šb[ny]. | ‘šrm ksp.‘l. | wrt.mtny.w 2107.15
spr.gt.r[---]. | ‘šrm.l.m[it.---]. | šd.dr[-.---]. 1105.2
‘šr. | kṯt. | [--]š ‘šr. | lg. 158[58].3
ḥm. | l[.-]ry ṯlṯ spm w ‘šr lḥm. | [--.]w nṣp w ṯlṯ spm w ‘šrm lḥ[m]. | l[.-]dt ḫnd[r]ṯ ar‘ s[p]m w ‘š[r]. | [---.]ḫndrṯm ṯṯ 134[-].4
[-]b[-.---.--] | r ṯṯm lḥm. | l[.-]ry ṯlṯ spm w ‘šr lḥm. | [--.]w nṣp w ṯlṯ spm w ‘šrm lḥ[m]. | l[.-]dt ḫnd[r]ṯ a 134[-].3
.dqn. | ‘bd‘nt.rb ‘šrt.mnḥm.ṯb‘m.sḫr.‘zn.ilhd. | bnil.rb ‘šrt.lkn.yp‘n.ṯ[--]. | yṣḥm.b d.ubn.krwn.tǵd.[m]nḥm. | ‘pṯrm. 2011.8
spr.bnš.mlk. | d.b d.prṯ. | tš‘.l.‘šrm. | lqḥ.ššlmt. | ṯmn.l.arb‘m. | lqḥ.š‘rt. 1025.3
r. | rbt.w rgm.l aḫt k. | ṯtmnt.krt n.dbḥ. | dbḥ.mlk.‘šr. | ‘šrt.qḥ.tp k.b yd. | [-]r[-]k.bm.ymn. | tlk.škn.‘l.ṣrrt. | adn k.šq 16.1[125].41
b [ṯ]ql.ṯlṯt.l.‘šrm.ksp hm. | s̀stm.b.šb‘m. | ṯlṯ.mat.trm.b.‘šrt. | mit.adrm.b.‘šrt. | ‘šr.ydt.b.‘šrt. | ḫmš.kkrm.ṣml. | ‘šrt.ks 1127.7
šš[r]t.ḫrṣ.ṯqlm.kbd.‘šrt.mzn h. | b [ar]b‘m.ksp. | b d[.‘b]dym.ṯlṯ.kkr š‘rt. | iqn[i]m 2100.1
-]. | bnš.gt.‘ṯtrt. | ad[-]l[-]m. | ‘šr.ksdm.yd.lmd hm.lqḥ. | ‘šr.mḫṣm.yd.lmd hm. | apym. | [bn]š gt.ipṯl. | [---]ym. | [----]m 1040.9
šb‘.ṯnnm.w.šb‘.ḫsnm. | ṯmn.‘šr h.mrynm. | ‘šr.mkrm. | ḫmš.ṯrtnm. | ḫmš.bn.mrynm. | ‘šr.mrum.w.šb‘.ḫs 1030.3
ḫsnm. | ṯlṯ.‘šr.mrynm. | ḫmš.[ṯr]tnm. | ṯlṯ.b[n.]mrynm. | ‘šr[.m]krm. | tš‘.hbṭnm. | ‘šr.mrum. | šb‘.ḫsnm. | tš‘m.ṯṯ.kbd.m 1028.5
b‘.ḫsnm. | ‘šr.mrum. | w.šb‘.ḫsnm. | tš‘.‘šr. | mrynm. | ṯlṯ.‘šr.mkrm. | ṯlṯ.bn.mrynm. | arb‘.ṯrtnm. | tš‘.ḫbṭnm. | ṯmnym.ṯl 1029.7
šm‘n.rb ‘šrt.kkln.‘bd.abṣn. | šdyn.unn.dqn. | ‘bd‘nt.rb ‘šrt.mnḥm.ṯb‘m.sḫr.‘zn.ilhd. | bnil.rb ‘šrt.lkn.yp‘n.ṯ[--]. | yṣḥ 2011.7
h.mrynm. | ‘šr.mkrm. | ḫmš.ṯrtnm. | ḫmš.bn.mrynm. | ‘šr.mrum.w.šb‘.ḫsnm. | tš‘m.mḏrǵlm. | arb‘.l ‘šrm.ḫsnm. | ‘šr. 1030.6
tš‘.ṯnnm. | w.arb‘.ḫsnm. | ‘šr.mrum. | w.šb‘.ḫsnm. | tš‘.‘šr. | mrynm. | ṯlṯ.‘šr.mkrm. | ṯlṯ.b 1029.3
š.[ṯr]tnm. | ṯlṯ.b[n.]mrynm. | ‘šr[.m]krm. | tš‘.hbṭnm. | ‘šr.mrum. | šb‘.ḫsnm. | tš‘m.ṯṯ.kbd.mḏrǵlm. | ‘šrm.aḥd.kbd.ḫs 1028.7
lm. | kzym. | mru.skn. | mru.ibrn. | pslm. | šrm. | yṣḥm. | ‘šrm. | mrum. | ṯnnm. | mqdm. | khnm. | qdšm. | nsk.ksp. | mkr 71[113].68
[---.‘]šrt. | ḫlb.ḫmšt.l.‘šrm. | mril.‘šrt. | glbty.arb‘t. | [--]ṯb.‘šrt. 1180.2
ḫmš.ṯnnm.‘šr.ḫsnm. | ṯlṯ.‘šr.mrynm. | ḫmš.[ṯr]tnm. | ṯlṯ.b[n.]mrynm. | ‘šr[.m]krm. | tš‘. 1028.2
spr.ḥpr.bnš mlk.b yrḫ iṯt[bnm]. | ršpab.rb ‘šrt.m[r]yn. | pǵdn.ilb‘l.krwn.lbn.‘dn. | ḫyrn.md‘. | šm‘n.rb ‘šr 2011.2
tš‘.ṯnnm. | w.arb‘.ḫsnm. | ‘šr.mrum. | w.šb‘.ḫsnm. | tš‘.‘šr. | mrynm. | ṯlṯ.‘šr.mkrm. | ṯlṯ.bn.mrynm. | arb‘.ṯrtnm. | tš‘.ḫ 1029.5
skn.ṯlṯm. | iytlm.ṯlṯm. | ḫyml.ṯlṯm. | ǵlkz.ṯlṯm. | mlkn‘m.‘šrm. | mr‘m.‘šrm. | ‘mlbu.‘šrm. | ‘mtḏl.‘šrm. | y‘ḏrd.‘šrm. | gm 1116.5
]bt h.b.bt.trǵds. | [---.]aṯt.adrt.w.pǵt.a[ḥt.b.bt.---]. | [---.‘]šrm.npš.b.bt.[---]. | [---.]w.pǵt.aḥt.b.bt.[---]. 80[119].29
šrm. | ṯlṯm.almg. | ḫmšm.kkr. | qnm. | ‘šrm.kk[r]. | brr. | [‘]šrm.npš. | ‘šrm.zt.mm. | ‘rb‘m. | šmn.mr. 141[120].13
lbnš prwsdy. | ṯṯ spm.l bnš klnmw. | l yarš ḫswn. | ḫmš ‘šr.sp. | l bnš tpnr d yaḫd l g ynm. | ṯṯ spm l tgyn. | arb‘ spm l 137.2[93].10
š.---]. | l bn ḫḏnr[.---]. | ṯṯm sp.km[-.---]. | ‘šrm.sp[.---]. | ‘šr sp.m[ry-.---]. | ‘šr sp.m[ry-.---]. | ṯṯ sp.mry[-.---]. | ‘šr sp.m[139[310].8
]. | ‘šr sp.m[ry-.---]. | ‘šr sp.m[ry-.---]. | ṯṯ sp.mry[-.---]. | ‘šr sp.m[ry-.---]. | tš‘m s[p.---]. | tš‘[m.sp.---]. | ṯṯ[.---]. 139[310].11
---]. | ṯṯm sp.km[-.---]. | ‘šrm.sp[.---]. | ‘šr sp.m[ry-.---]. | ‘šr sp.m[ry-.---]. | ṯṯ sp.mry[-.---]. | ‘šr sp.m[ry-.---]. | tš‘m s[p. 139[310].9
]. | [p]drn.ḫm[š.---]. | l bn ḫḏnr[.---]. | ṯṯm sp.km[-.---]. | ‘šrm.sp[.---]. | ‘šr sp.m[ry-.---]. | ‘šr sp.m[ry-.---]. | ṯṯ sp.mry[-. 139[310].7
n.ḫmšt. | abǵl.ḫmšt. | bn.aḫdy.‘šrt. | ṯṯn.‘ṣrt. | bn.pnmn.‘šrt. | ‘bdadt.ḫmšt. | abmn.ilštm‘y.ḫmš[t]. | ‘zn.bn.brn.ḫmšt. | 1062.23
r‘l[-]. | ḫmš ‘l ykn[.--]. | ḫ[mš] ‘l abǵ[l]. | ḫmš ‘l ilb[‘l]. | ‘šr ‘l [---]. 2034.2.9
lm.ṯlṯm. | ḫyml.ṯlṯm. | ǵlkz.ṯlṯm. | mlkn‘m.‘šrm. | mr‘m.‘šrm. | ‘mlbu.‘šrm. | ‘mtḏl.‘šrm. | y‘ḏrd.‘šrm. | gmrd.‘šrm. | ṣdq 1116.6
l.ṯlṯm. | ǵlkz.ṯlṯm. | mlkn‘m.‘šrm. | mr‘m.‘šrm. | ‘mlbu.‘šrm. | ‘mtḏl.‘šrm. | y‘ḏrd.‘šrm. | gmrd.‘šrm. | ṣdqšlm.‘šr[m]. | 1116.7
[-----]. | ḏ[----]. | ab[--.---]. | bn.nṣdn[.ḫm]št. | bn.arsw ‘[šr]m. | ‘šdyn.ḫmš[t]. | abršn.‘šr[t]. | b‘ln.ḫmšt. | w.nḥl h.ḫm[š 1062.5
šb‘t.‘šrt ‘šrt.šlm. | yky.‘šrt.ṯṯt šlm.‘šrt. | bn.ḥgby.ṯmnt.l ‘šrm.‘šrt.ḫmš.kbd. | bn.ilṣdq.šb‘t ṯlṯt šlm. | bn.ṯmq.arb‘t ṯqlm 1131.8
ksp hm. | s̀stm.b.šb‘m. | ṯlṯ.mat.trm.b.‘šrt. | mit.adrm.b.‘šrt. | ‘šr.ydt.b.‘šrt. | ḫmš.kkrm.ṣml. | ‘šrt.ksp h. | ḫmš.kkr.qn 1127.8
h.nyr. | rbt.w rgm.l aḫt k. | ṯtmnt.krt n.dbḥ. | dbḥ.mlk.‘šr. | ‘šrt.qḥ.tp k.b yd. | [-]r[-]k.bm.ymn. | tlk.škn.‘l.ṣrrt. | adn 16.1[125].40
.ilḥu. | [---.]mrṣ.mlk. | [--.k]rt.adn k. | [--.d]bḥ.dbḥ. | [--.‘]šr.‘šrt. | ‘[---.---]. | b[---.---]. | t[--.---]. | w[----]. | pǵ[t.---]. | lk[. 16.1[125].62
.‘šrt ‘šrt[.šlm.---]. | ybn.ṯmnt.‘šrt ‘šrt.šlm. | ‘bdyrḫ.šb‘t.‘šrt ‘šrt.šlm. | yky.‘šrt.ṯṯt šlm.‘šrt. | bn.ḥgby.ṯmnt.l ‘šrm.‘šrt.ḫ 1131.6
ḫmš.šl[m.---]. | tlmyn.šb‘t.‘šrt ‘šrt[.šlm.---]. | ybn.ṯmnt.‘šrt ‘šrt.šlm. | ‘bdyrḫ.šb‘t.‘šrt ‘šrt.šlm. | yky.‘šrt.ṯṯt šlm.‘šrt. | b 1131.5
annṯb.ḫmšm.ksp ṯlṯm.šl[m.---]. | iwrpzn.‘šrm ‘šrm š[lm.---]. | ilabn.‘šrt ṯqlm kbd.ḫmš.šl[m.---]. | tlmy 1131.2
lm.---]. | ilabn.‘šrt ṯqlm kbd.ḫmš.šl[m.---]. | tlmyn.šb‘t.‘šrt ‘šrt[.šlm.---]. | ybn.ṯmnt.‘šrt ‘šrt.šlm. | ‘bdyrḫ.šb‘t.‘šrt ‘šrt 1131.4

k t‘rb.‘ṯtrt.ẖr[-].|bt mlk.‘šr.‘šr.[--].bt ilm.|kbr[-]m.[-]trmt.|lbš.w [-]tn.ušpǵt.|ẖr[-].ṯl 33[5].2
u.|[---.]mrṣ.mlk.|[--.k]rt.adn k.|[--.d]bḥ.dbḥ.|[--.‘]šr.‘šrt.|‘[---.---].|b[---.---].|t[--.---].|w[----].|pǵ[t.---].|lk[.---]. 16.1[125].62
arb‘.‘šr.ǵzrm.|arb‘.aṯt.|pǵt.aḥt.|w.pǵy.aḥ. 2081.1
.lbnm.|[---].all.šmt.|[---].all.iqni.arb‘m.kbl.|[---].iqni.‘šrm.ǵprt.|[---.š]pšg.iqni.mit.pṯtm.|[---].mitm.kslm.|[---].p 1106.7
š.ilm.ṯb.md]|bḥ.b‘l.[gdlt.---.dqt].|l ṣpn.w [dqt.---.ṯn.l ‘š]|rm.pam[t.---].|š dd šmn[.gdlt.w.---].|brr.r[gm.yṯṯb.b ṯdṯ APP.II[173].46
].|[t]ṯb.mdbḥ.b‘l.g[dlt.---].|dqt.l.ṣpn.w.dqt[.---].|ṯn.l.‘šrm.pamt.[---].|š.dd.šmn.gdlt.w.[---.brr].|rgm.yṯṯb.b.ṯdṯ.ṯn 35[3].43
.‘šrt.|w.ṯn.b.ẖmšt.|ṯprt.b.ṯlṯt.|mṯyn.b.ṯṯt.|ṯn.lbšm.b.‘šrt.|pld.b.arb‘t.|lbš.ṯn.b.ṯnt.‘šrt. 1108.6
m.ṯlṯ.kbd.mṣrrt.|‘šr.ṯn.kbd.pǵdrm.|ṯmn.mrbdt.mlk.|‘šr.pld.š‘rt. 1111.12
.ẖrṣ.bt.il.|b.ẖmšt.‘šrt.ksp.|ẖmš.mat.šmt.|b.‘šrt.ksp.|‘šr.ṣin.b.ṯṯt.w.kmsk.|arb‘[.k]dwṯm.w.ṯṯ.ṯprtm.|b.‘šr[m.]ksp. 2100.9
b ṯlṯ.|ilmlk.‘šr.ṣin.|mlkn‘m.‘šr.|bn.adty.‘šr.|[ṣ]dqšlm ẖmš.|krzn.ẖmš.| 2039.2
.|[---.]‘gd.dqr.|[---.]ṯn.alpm.|[---.ṯ]n alpm.|[---.--]r[.‘]šr.ṣin.|[---.]klkl. 1142.8
b ṯlṯ.|ilmlk.‘šr.ṣin.|mlkn‘m.‘šr.|bn.adty.‘šr.|[ṣ]dqšlm ẖmš.|krzn.ẖmš.|ubr‘ym.ẖmš.|[----].|[bn] itn. 2039.4
‘m.‘šrm.|‘mlbu.‘šrm.|‘mtdl.‘šrm.|y‘ḏrd.‘šrm.|gmrd.‘šrm.|ṣdqšlm.‘šr[m].|yknil.ẖmš.|ilmlk.ẖmš.|prṯ.‘šr.|ubn.‘š 1116.10
m.|[---.bn]šm.|[---.]ẖmš.ṣmd.alpm.|[---.bnš]m.|[---.]‘šr.ṣmd.alpm.|[---.bn]šm.|[---.--]m.ẖmš.ṣmdm.|[---.bnš]m. 2038.19
ṣy.|ṯn.bn.iwrẖz.[n]‘rm.|yṣr[.-]qb.|w.ṯn.bnš.iytlm.|w.‘šrm.ṣmd.alpm. 2066.2.7
m.|[w.‘]šr.bn[š]m.y[d].š[--].|[-]lm.b d.r[-]m.l[-]m.|ṯṯ.‘šr.ṣ[mdm].|w.tš‘.‘[šr.--]m.ḥr[š].|[---].ḥr[š.---].|[---.ṯ]lṯ.[---.] 2038.10
[b.]gt.ṯpn.‘šr.ṣmdm.|w.ṯlṯ.‘šr.bnš.|yd.ytm.yd.r‘y.ḥmrm.|b.gt.gwl.ṯm 2038.1
--].|bn.[---].|yly[.---].|ykn[.---].|rp[--].|ṯṯw.[---].|[---.‘]šrm.ṣmd.ššw. 2131.12
bn gmrt.|bn.il.ṣm[d].|bn abbly.|yt‘d.ṣm[d].|bn.liy.|‘šrm.ṣ[md].|ṯṯ kbd.b ḥ[--].|w.arb‘.ḥ[mrm].|b m[‘]rby.|ṯmn 2113.23
ẖlb ‘prm.ṯṯ.|ẖlb krd.ṯn ‘šr.|qmy.arb‘.‘šr.|ṣ‘q.arb‘ ‘šr.|ṣ‘.ṯmn.|šḥq.‘šrm.arb‘.kbd.|ẖlb rpš arb‘.‘šr.|bq‘t ṯṯ.|ira 67[110].4
ẖlb ‘prm.ṯṯ.|ẖlb krd.ṯn ‘šr.|qmy.arb‘.‘šr.|ṣ‘q.arb‘ ‘šr.|ṣ‘.ṯmn.|šḥq.‘šrm.arb‘.kbd.|ẖlb rpš arb‘.‘šr. 67[110].3
šm.|ṣṣ amtrn arb‘m.|ṣṣ iytlm mit ṯlṯm kbd.|ṣṣ m[l]k ‘šrm.|ṣṣ abš[-] mit [‘š]r kbd.|ṣṣ yḏrd ‘šrm.|ṣṣ bn aglby ṯlṯ[2097.10
kbd.|ṣṣ m[l]k ‘šrm.|ṣṣ abš[-] mit [‘š]r kbd.|ṣṣ yḏrd ‘šrm.|ṣṣ bn aglby ṯlṯ[m].|ṣṣ bn.šrš‘m.[---].|ṣṣ mlkn‘m.a[rb‘ 2097.12
d ẖmšm.|ṣṣ tmn.ẖmšm.|[ṣṣ] ‘mtḏl ṯlṯm.|ṣṣ ‘mlbi ṯṯ l ‘šrm.|ṣṣ bn adty ẖmšm.|ṣṣ amtrn arb‘m.|ṣṣ iytlm mit ṯlṯm 2097.6
.ṯlṯm.|ṣṣ.bn.kzn.ṯlṯm.|ṣṣ.bn.tlmyn.‘šrm.|ṣṣ.bn.krwn.‘š[rm].|ṣṣ.bn.iršyn.[---].|[ṣṣ].bn.ilb‘l.ṯl[ṯ]m.|ṣṣ.bn.pṯḏn.[--] 2096.4
ṣṣ.bn.ilyn.ṯlṯm.|ṣṣ.bn.kzn.ṯlṯm.|ṣṣ.bn.tlmyn.‘šrm.|ṣṣ.bn.krwn.‘š[rm].|ṣṣ.bn.iršyn.[---].|[ṣṣ].bn.ilb‘l.ṯl[ṯ] 2096.3
r.ẖmšm.|ṣṣ.bn.adlḏn.ṯlṯm.|ṣṣ.bn.‘glt.ṯlṯm.|ṣṣ.bn.‘bd.‘šrm.|ṣṣ.bn.mṣẖ[n].‘šrm.|šb‘.mat.ṯṯm kbd. 2096.18
ẖlb ‘prm.ṯṯ.|ẖlb krd.ṯn ‘šr.|qmy.arb‘.‘šr.|ṣ‘q.arb‘ ‘šr.|ṣ‘.ṯmn.|šḥq.‘šrm.arb‘.kbd.|ẖ 67[110].2
lpnm.|ṯlṯ.m[a]t.art.ḥkpt.|mit.dnn.|mitm.iqnu.|ẖmš.‘šr.qn.n‘m.‘n[m].|ṯn.ḥblm.alp.alp.am[-].|ṯmn.ḥblm.šb‘.šb‘. 1128.29
zlyy tql.|ary ẖmšt.|ykn‘m ẖmšt.|‘nmky tqlm.|[-]kt ‘šrt.|qrn šb‘t. 1176.7
].uṯkl.l il.šlmm.|b [ṯlṯt].‘šrt.yrtḥṣ.mlk.|br[r.]b a[r]b‘t.‘šrt.riš.|arg[mn.w ṯn.]šm.l b‘lt.|bhtm.‘ṣ[rm.l in]š ilm.w š.| APP.II[173].4
tr.[uṯkl.l il.šlmm].|b ṯlṯt ‘[šrt.yrtḥṣ.mlk.brr].|b arb‘[t.‘šrt.riš.argmn].|w ṯn šm.l [b‘lt.bhtm.‘ṣrm.l inš].|ilm.w š d[35[3].4
[ṯ]n.prm.b ‘šrm.|arb‘.prm.b.‘š[r]m.|arb‘.b.arb‘m.|ṯṯm.[---.p]rm.|[-]l.b[--.---].|[---].kbd.| 1138.2
ẖlb krd.ṯn ‘šr.|qmy.arb‘.‘šr.|ṣ‘q.arb‘ ‘šr.|ṣ‘.ṯmn.|šḥq.‘šrm.arb‘.kbd.|ẖlb rpš arb‘.‘šr.|bq‘t ṯṯ.|irab ṯn.‘šr.|ḥbš.ṯmn 67[110].6
ry[.]yukl.krm.[---].|gdn.krm.aḥ[d.--]r.krm.[---].|ary.‘šr.arb‘.kbd.[---].|[--]yy.ṯṯ.krmm.šl[-.---].|[---.]‘šrm.krm.[--- 1081.18
l[ṯṯ].‘šr[t].|b.š[d].bn.‘myn.|ẖmšt.|b.[šd.--]n.|ẖ[m]št[.‘]šrt.|[ar]b‘m.ksp.|[---]yn.|[---.]ksp.|[---.]mit.|[-----]. 1083.14
[ṯ]n.prm.b ‘šrm.|arb‘.prm.b.‘š[r]m.|arb‘.b.arb‘m.|ṯṯm.[---.p]rm.|[-]l.b 1138.1
l inš.|[ilm.---].lbbmm.gdlt.‘rb špš w ḥl.|[mlk.b ar]b‘t.‘[š]rt.yrtḥṣ.mlk.brr.|[b ym.ml]at.y[ql]n.al[p]m.yrẖ.‘šrt.|[l b 36[9].1.10
b arb‘t.‘šr[t].|yrtḥṣ.mlk.b[rr].|b ym.mlat.|tqln.alpm.|yrẖ.‘šrt.l b‘[UG5.13.1
b yrẖ.[rišyn.b ym.ḥdṯ].|šmtr.[uṯkl.l il.šlmm].|b ṯlṯt ‘[šrt.yrtḥṣ.mlk.brr].|b arb‘[t.‘šrt.riš.argmn].|w ṯn šm.l [b‘lt. 35[3].3
yr]ẖ[.r]išyn.b ym.ḥdṯ.|[šmtr].uṯkl.l il.šlmm.|b [ṯlṯt].‘šrt.yrtḥṣ.mlk.|br[r.]b a[r]b‘t.‘šrt.riš.|arg[mn.w ṯn.]šm.l b‘lt APP.II[173].3
dṯ.|alp.w š.l b‘lt bhtm.|b arb‘t ‘šrt.b‘l.|‘rkm.|b ṯmnt.‘šrt.yr|tḥṣ.mlk.brr.|‘lm.tzǵ.b ǵb.ṣpn.|nḥkt.ksp.w ẖrṣ ṭ‘ ṯn š UG5.12.A.5
l.mlk.w.b y]|m.ḥdṯ.ṯn šm[.---.--]t.|b yrẖ.ši[-.b ar]b‘t.‘š|rt.yr[tḥṣ.ml]k.brr.|‘lm.š.š[--].l[--.]‘rb.šp|š.w ḥl[.ml]k.|bn APP.II[173].54
‘šr.ktnt.|‘šr.rṯm.|kkr[.-].ḥt.|mitm[.p]ṯtm.|ṯlṯm[.---].kst.|alp.a[bn.ṣ]r 1114.2
.ṯmn]ym.mgnm ar[b‘].|[---.-]aḥ.mqḥ mqḥm.|[---.--]t.‘šr rmǵt.[--].|[---].alp.[---].alp.|[---.-]rbd.kbd.ṯnm kbd.|[---. 1145.1.5
št.|swn.ẖmšt.|bn.[-]r[-.]ẖmšt.|bn.ḥdṯ.‘šrt.|bn.ẖnyn.‘šrt.|rpan.ẖmšt.|abǵl.ẖmšt.|bn.aẖdy.‘šrt.|ṯṯn.‘ṣrt.|bn.pnm 1062.18
ṯmn ‘šr šurt l [---].|ṯmn šurt l ar[--.---].|ṯn šurtm l bnš [---].|arb‘ 137.1[92].1
.ṯṯ.|‘šr.ẖsnm.|n‘r.mrynm.|ẖmš.|trtnm.ẖmš.|mrum.‘šr.|šb‘.ẖsnm.|mkrm.|mrynm.|ṯlṯ.‘šr.|hbṭnm.|ṯmn.|mḏrǵ 1031.6
n.ṯlṯm.|ṣṣ.bn.‘glt.ṯlṯm.|ṣṣ.bn.‘bd.‘šrm.|ṣṣ.bn.mṣẖ[n].‘šrm.|šb‘.mat.ṯṯm kbd. 2096.19
ṯṯmd.|[šd.bn.-]rn.b d.ṣdqšlm.|[šd.b d.]bn.p‘ṣ.|[ubdy.‘]šrm.|[šd.---]n.b d.brdd.|[---.--]m.|[šd.---.b d.]ṯpṭb‘l.|[šd.-- 82[300].1.30
‘šr štpm.|b ẖmš.šmn.|‘šrm.gdy.|b ẖmš.šmn.|w ẖmš ṭ‘dt. 1097.1
‘šrt[.šlm.---].|ybn.ṯmnt.‘šrt ‘šrt.šlm.|‘bdyrẖ.šb‘t.‘šrt ‘šrt.šlm.|yky.‘šrt.ṯṯt šlm.‘šrt.|bn.ḥgby.ṯmnt.l ‘šrm.‘šrt.ẖmš. 1131.6
.šl[m.---].|tlmyn.šb‘t.‘šrt ‘šrt[.šlm.---].|ybn.ṯmnt.‘šrt ‘šrt.šlm.|‘bdyrẖ.šb‘t.‘šrt ‘šrt.šlm.|yky.‘šrt.ṯṯt šlm.‘šrt.|bn.ḥ 1131.5
annṯb.ẖmšm.ksp ṯlṯm.šl[m.---].|iwrpzn.‘šrm ‘šrm š[lm.---].|ilabn.‘šrt ṯqlm kbd.ẖmš.šl[m.---].|tlmyn.šb‘t 1131.2
--].|ilabn.‘šrt ṯqlm kbd.ẖmš.šl[m.---].|tlmyn.šb‘t.‘šrt ‘šrt[.šlm.---].|ybn.ṯmnt.‘šrt ‘šrt.šlm.|‘bdyrẖ.šb‘t.‘šrt ‘šrt.šlm 1131.4
.kbd.arb‘m.|‘šrt.ẖrṣ.b.arb‘m.|mit.ẖršẖ.b.ṯqlm.|w.šb‘.‘šr.šmn.|d.l.yṣa.bt.mlk.|tgmr.ksp.mitm.|ẖmšm.kbd. 2100.20
rm.|[--.-]dwn.ṯlṯm.w.šb‘.alpm.|[kṯ]rmlk.‘šrm.|[--]ny.‘šrt.trbyt.|[--.]‘bd.ṯlṯm.|[---].ṯlṯm.|[--.p]ndyn.ṯlṯm. 2054.2.25
ṯ.‘šrt.|bn.ẖnyn.‘šrt.|rpan.ẖmšt.|abǵl.ẖmšt.|bn.aẖdy.‘šrt.|ṯṯn.‘ṣrt.|bn.pnmn.‘šrt.|‘bdadt.ẖmšt.|abmn.ilštm‘y.ẖm 1062.21
|ybn.ṯmnt.‘šrt ‘šrt.šlm.|‘bdyrẖ.šb‘t.‘šrt ‘šrt.šlm.|yky.‘šrt.ṯṯt šlm.‘šrt.|bn.ḥgby.ṯmnt.l ‘šrm.‘šrt.ẖmš.kbd.|bn.ilṣdq 1131.7
‘bdrt[b.---].|b ṯṯ ‘tr ṯmn.r[qḥ.---].|p bn btb[-.---].|b ẖmṯ ‘tr k[--.---].|b ẖmṯ ‘ṯ 207[57].2
.|w bn ‘ṯl.[---].|ypẖ kn‘m[.---].|aẖmn bt[.---].|b ẖmṯ ‘tr ṯmn[.---]. 207[57].11
.‘šr kbd.|kšmm.b.mṣbt.|mit.‘šrm.ṯn kbd.|[kš]mm.|[‘]š[r]m.ṯn.kbd.ḥṭm.|[-]m[-.-]‘[-.-]ag š‘rm.|[---.--]mi.|[--.]ṯṯ[2091.5
mitm.‘šr kbd.|kšmm.b.mṣbt.|mit.‘šrm.ṯn kbd.|[kš]mm.|[‘]š[r]m.ṯn.kbd.ḥṭm.|[-]m[-.-]‘[-.-]ag 2091.3

ym. | lqḥ.š‘rt. | anntn. | ‘dn. | sdwn. | mztn. | ḫyrn. | šdn. | [‘š]rm.ṯn kbd. | šǵrm. | lqḥ.ššlmt. 2098.9
rb]‘m.ḫpnt.pṯt. | [-]r.pldm.dt.š‘rt. | ṯlṯm.ṯlṯ.kbd.mṣrrt. | ‘šr.ṯn.kbd.pǵdrm. | ṯmn.mrbdt.mlk. | ‘šr.pld.š‘rt. 1111.10
]. | [--]yy.ṯṯ.krmm.šl[-.---]. | [---.]‘šrm.krm.[---]. | [ṯ]lrby.‘šr.ṯn.kb[d.---]. | ḫmrm.ṯṯ.krm[m.---]. | krm.ǵlkz.b.p[--.---]. | k 1081.21
[--]n.‘š[r.] | [a]rt[.a]rb‘[.---]. | ‘nmky.‘šr.[---]. | ṯmry.‘šr.ṯn.k[rmm.---]. | liy.krm.aḥd[.---]. | ‘bdmlk.krm.aḥ[d.---]. | 1081.4
mrynm. | mrum. | ‘šrm. | ṯnnm. | nq[dm]. | kh[nm]. | inšt. 2019.3
mrynm. | mrum. | ‘šrm. | ṯnnm. | nqdm. | khnm. | qdšm. | pslm. | mkrm. | yṣḥm. | š 1026.1.3
].aḥd. | u[--].ṯn. | hz[p].ṯṯ. | ḫrṣb‘.aḥd. | ypr.arb. | m[-]qb.‘šr. | ṯn‘y.ṯlṯ. | ḫlb ‘prm.ṯn. | tmḏy.ṯlṯ. | [--]rt.arb‘. | [---].‘šr. 70[112].10
.--]n.šb‘t.l ṯlṯm. | [---].šb‘t.‘šrt. | [---.-]kyn.‘šrt. | b.bn.‘sl.‘šrm.ṯqlm kbd. | b.ṯmq.ḫmšt.l.‘šrt. | b.[---].šb‘t.‘šrt. | b.bn.pdr 2054.1.6
.ksp ṯlṯm.šl[m.---]. | iwrpzn.‘šrm ‘šrm š[lm.---]. | ilabn.‘šrt ṯqlm kbd.ḫmš.šl[m.---]. | tlmyn.šb‘t.‘šrt ‘šrt[.šlm.---]. | yb 1131.3
.ann[.---.-]ny[-]. | b.ḫqn.[---]m.ṣ[-]n. | [b].bn.ay[--.---].l.‘šrm. | [-]gp[.---.]‘rny.ṯṯm. | [---.]dyn.ḫmšt.‘šrt. | [---.-]til.ḫmšt. 2054.2.17
[ḫm]š l ‘šrm. | [-]dmm. | b.ubn. 1167.1
rpš arb‘.‘šr. | bq‘t ṯṯ. | irab ṯn.‘šr. | ḥbš.ṯmn. | amḏy.arb‘.‘šr. | [-]n‘y.ṯṯ.‘šr. 67[110].11
k t‘rb.‘ṯtrt.ḫr[-]. | bt mlk.‘šr.‘šr.[--].bt ilm. | kbr[-]m.[-]trmt. | lbš.w [-]tn.ušpǵt. | ḫr[-].ṯlṯt. 33[5].2
. | [---.-]til.ḫmšt.l ‘šrm. | [--.-]n.w.aḫt h.arb‘m. | [--.-]dn.‘šrm. | [--.-]dwn.ṯlṯm.w.šb‘.alpm. | [kṯ]rmlk.‘šrm. | [--]ny.‘šrt.t 2054.2.22
]gp[.---.]‘rny.ṯṯm. | [---.]dyn.ḫmšt.‘šrt. | [---.-]til.ḫmšt.l ‘šrm. | [--.-]n.w.aḫt h.arb‘m. | [--.-]dn.‘šrm. | [--.-]dwn.ṯlṯm.w. 2054.2.20
.y[d].š[--]. | [-]lm.b d.r[-]m.l[-]m. | ṯṯ.‘šr.ṣ[mdm]. | w.tš‘.‘[šr.--]m.ḥr[š]. | [---].ḥr[š.---]. | [---.ṯ]lṯ.[---.]dpm. | [---.]bnšn. | [2038.11
. | [--.-]dn.‘šrm. | [--.-]dwn.ṯlṯm.w.šb‘.alpm. | [kṯ]rmlk.‘šrm. | [--]ny.‘šrt.trbyt. | [--.]‘bd.ṯlṯm. | [---].ṯlṯm. | [--.p]ndyn.ṯl 2054.2.24
b]n.yšm[‘]. | [---.]mlkr[-] h.b.nṯk. | [---.]šb‘m. | [---.]ḫrg.‘šrm. | [---.]abn.ksp.ṯlṯ. | [---].bty.ksp.‘šr[t]. | [---.-]mb‘l.[---].‘šr 2153.5
]nm. | ṯlṯ[.mat.a]rb‘.kbd. | w.[---.-]m‘t. | ṯlṯ[m.---.-]rm. | ‘šr[.---].alpm. | arb‘.ddm.l.k[-]ḫ. | ṯmnym.dd.dd.kbd. | [l].mḏr 2012.17
iṯ[.---]. | ṣṣ igy.ḫmšm. | ṣṣ yrpi m[iṯ.---]. | ṣṣ bn.š[m]mn ‘[šr.---]. | alp.ṯṯm. | kbd.mlḥt. 2097.19
[-----]. | ‘šr[.---]. | ud[-.---]. | ṯn pld mḫ[--.---]. | ṯ[--] ḫpnt. | [---] kdwṯm. 1113.2
ilm[.---]. | tš‘.‘š[r.---]. | bn ‘dr[.---]. | ḫmš ‘l.bn[.---]. | ḫmš ‘l r‘l[-]. | ḫmš ‘l yk 2034.2.2
| ‘nqpat [---]. | m[--.---]. | [-----]. | k[--.---]. | [-----]. | ḫmrn.‘š[r.---]. | gll.tky.ṯlṯ[.---]. 2042.22
ṯlṯm.dd[.---]. | b.gt.ṣb[-.---]. | mit.‘šr.[---.]dd[.--]. | tš‘.dd.ḥ[ṯm.w].ḫm[šm]. | kdm.kbd.yn.b.gt.[-- 2092.3
. | [---.]abn.ksp.ṯlṯ. | [---].bty.ksp.‘šr[t]. | [---.-]mb‘l.[---].‘šrt. | [---.]ḫgbn.kbs.ks[p]. | [---].ḏmrd.bn.ḥrmn. | [---.-]ǵn.ksp 2153.8
b y[rḫ.---]. | ‘š[r.---]. | ḫm[š.---]. | b[yrḫ.---]. | [---.]prš. | [-----]. | l.mšḫ[.---]. | 2012.2
p w ṯlṯ spm w ‘šrm lḥ[m]. | l[.-]dt ḫnd[r]ṯ ar‘ s[p]m w ‘š[r]. | [---.]ḫndrṯm ṯṯ spm [w] ṯlṯm l[ḥm]. | [---.]ar‘ spm w [-- 134[-].5
.bn h.w.b[---.---]. | b tn[--.---]. | swn.qrty[.---]. | uḫ h.w.‘šr[.---]. | klyn.apsn[y.---]. | plzn.qrty[.---]. | w.klt h.b.t[--.---]. 81[329].9
]. | ‘š[r.---]. | ‘l[.---]. | w.ni[t.---]. | w[.m‘ṣd]. | w ḫr[mṯt]. | [‘]šr[.---]. | [‘]l [-]g[-.---]. | w ni[t.w.m‘ṣd]. | w ḫrmṯt. | ṯlṯm.ar[b‘ 2053.14
rmṯt. | ‘šrt.ksp. | ‘l.ḫ[z]rn. | w.nit.w[.m‘ṣd]. | w.ḫ[rmṯt]. | ‘š[r.---]. | ‘l[.---]. | w.ni[t.---]. | w[.m‘ṣd]. | w ḫr[mṯt]. | [‘]šr[.---]. 2053.9
.sǵ[r.---.--]k.[--]. | [---.]dd.bn.š.[---.]yd.sǵr h. | [---.--]r h.‘šr[m.---.‘]šrm.dd. | [---.yn.d.]nkly.l.r‘ym.šb‘m.l.mitm.dd. | [- 1098.43
. | [---.--]n.‘šrm. | [---.-]rn.mit.[---]. | [---.--]t. | [---.]ḫmšt.‘šrt. | [---.]‘šrm. | [---.--]št.‘šrt. | [---.--]m. | [---.--]ṯm. | [---.]‘šrt. | 2054.2.7
hr k.w.‘m.ṣ[--]. | ‘š[--.---]d.lik[t.---]. | w [----]. | k[--.---]. | ‘šrm[.---]. | tšt.tb‘[.---]. | qrt.mlk[.---]. | w.‘l.ap.s[--.---]. | b hm. 2008.2.2
mit.‘[šr.---]. | [ṯ]lṯ.abd[.---]. | [---.]anyt[.---]. | [-----]. | ‘šrm.l.umdy 2110.1
[---].‘šr. | [---].ṯlṯ. | [---].ṯmn. | [---].ṯlṯ. | [---].aḥd. | u[--].ṯn. | hz[p].ṯṯ. 70[112].1
[.d]rt.arb‘m.drt. | [---]m. | t[gm]r.akl.b.gt.ǵ[l]. | ṯlṯ.mat.‘šrm[.---]. | ṯmnym.drt.a[--]. | drt.l.alpm[.---]. | šb‘m.ṯn.kbd[.ḫ 2013.16
[--]n.‘š[r.] | [a]rt[.a]rb‘[.---]. | ‘nmky.‘šr.[---]. | ṯmry.‘šr.ṯn.k[rmm.---]. | liy.krm.aḥd[.---]. | ‘bdmlk.k 1081.3
--.-]grm. | [---.-]n.‘šrt.ksp. | [--.--]n.šb‘t.l ṯlṯm. | [---].šb‘t.‘šrt. | [---.-]kyn.‘šrt. | b.bn.‘sl.‘šrm.ṯqlm kbd. | b.ṯmq.ḫmšt.l.‘š 2054.1.4
-.]šb‘m. | [---.]ḫrg.‘šrm. | [---.]abn.ksp.ṯlṯ. | [---].bty.ksp.‘šr[t]. | [---.-]mb‘l.[---].‘šrt. | [---.]ḫgbn.kbs.ks[p]. | [---].ḏmrd.b 2153.7
]. | [---].‘šrm. | [-----]. | [---.‘]šr[.---]. | [---.-]‘rm. | [---.--]n.‘šrm. | [---.-]rn.mit.[---]. | [---.--]t. | [---.]ḫmšt.‘šrt. | [---.]‘šrm. | [2054.2.4
n.ay[--.---].l.‘šrm. | [-]gp[.---.]‘rny.ṯṯm. | [---.]dyn.ḫmšt.‘šrt. | [---.-]til.ḫmšt.l ‘šrm. | [--.-]n.w.aḫt h.arb‘m. | [--.-]dn.‘šr 2054.2.19
.mit.[---]. | [---.--]t. | [---.]ḫmšt.‘šrt. | [---.]‘šrm. | [---.--]št.‘šrt. | [---.--]m. | [---.--]ṯm. | [---.]‘šrt. | [-----]. | b.[---.---]r. | b.ann 2054.2.9
d[.---]. | [---.]yd.sǵr[.---.--]r h. | aḥ[d.---.‘]šrm.d[d.---]. | ‘š[r.---.--]r h. | my y[--.---.--]d. | ‘šrm[.---.--]r h. | [-]wyn.yd[-.-- 1098.37
aḥ[d.---.‘]šrm.d[d.---]. | ‘š[r.---.--]r h. | my y[--.---.--]d. | ‘šrm[.---.--]r h. | [-]wyn.yd[-.---.]dd. | [---]n.yd.sǵ[r.---.--]k.[--] 1098.39
.‘šrm. | [---.-]rn.mit.[---]. | [---.--]t. | [---.]ḫmšt.‘šrt. | [---.]‘šrm. | [---.--]št.‘šrt. | [---.--]m. | [---.--]ṯm. | [---.]‘šrt. | [-----]. | b.[2054.2.8
[---.--]š. | [---.a]rb‘m. | b‘lyn.bnš. | mlkt. | ‘šrm. | [---.--]t. 138[41].5
. | [b] gt.iptl.ṯṯ.ḫrmṯ[t.nit]. | [k]rk.m‘ṣd.mqb. | [b.g]t.bir.‘š[r.---]. | [---].krk.m‘[ṣd.---]. | [b.]gt.ḥrtm.ḫm[š.---]. | [n]it.krk 2048.15
[---.]m[--.---]. | [---.‘]šrm[.---]. | [---.]nǵr.‘š[rm.---]. | [---.-]yl.‘š[rm.---]. | [---.a]rb‘[. 149[99].2
l.---]. | [---].ṯṯ.lbš[.---]. | [---.]kbd.ṯṯ.i[qnu.---]. | [---.]ǵprt.‘š[r.---]. | [---.p]ṯtm.l.ip[--.---]. | [---.]ksl.ṯlṯ.m[at.---]. | [---].abn. 1106.24
.]m[--.---]. | [---.‘]šrm[.---]. | [---.]nǵr.‘š[rm.---]. | [---.-]yl.‘š[rm.---]. | [---.a]rb‘[.---]. | [---.ṯ]lṯm[.---]. | [---.--]m.bn l[---]. | [149[99].4
[---.]m[--.---]. | [---.‘]šrm[.---]. | [---.]nǵr.‘š[rm.---]. | [---.-]yl.‘š[rm.---]. | [---.a]rb‘[.---]. | [---.ṯ]lṯm[.---]. | 149[99].3
[-----]. | [--]ly.ḫmšm.b.‘bdyr[ḫ]. | [---].‘šrm. | [-----]. | [---.‘]šr[.---]. | [---.-]‘rm. | [---.--]n.‘šrm. | [---.-]rn.mit.[---]. | [---.--]t 2054.2.2
n.r[qḥ.---]. | p bn btb[-.---]. | b ḫmt ‘tr k[--.---]. | b ḫmt ‘tr[.---]. | [-----]. | [---.-]y[-.---]. | w bn ‘ṯl.[---]. | ypḫ kn‘m[.---]. | 207[57].5
spr[.---]. | ḫmš.k[--.---]. | ḫmš[.---]. | ‘š[r.---]. | [-----]. | [-----]. | [-----]. | [-----]. | [-----]. | [-----]. | [-----]. | 1128.4
ṯlṯ.yn. | šmny.kdm.yn. | šmgy.kd.yn. | hzp.tš‘.yn. | [b]ir.‘šr[.---]m ḥsp. | ḫpty.kdm[.---]. | [a]gm.arb‘[.---]. | šrš.šb‘.mṣb. 2004.29
p.‘[l]. | [b]n.bly.gb‘ly. | [šp]ḥ.a[n]nṯb. | w.m[--.u]škny. | [‘]š[r.---]t.ksp. | [‘l.---]b bn[.--]. | [-]ḫ[-.---]. | [-]p[-.---.-]ny. | [-]ḥ 2055.5
rt. | [---.]‘šrm. | [---.--]št.‘šrt. | [---.--]m. | [---.--]ṯm. | [---.]‘šrt. | [-----]. | b.[---.---]r. | b.ann[.---.-]ny[-]. | b.ḫqn.[---]m.ṣ[-]n 2054.2.12
b.t[--.---] h.[---]. | [-----]. | [--]ly.ḫmšm.b.‘bdyr[ḫ]. | [---].‘šrm. | [-----]. | [---.‘]šr[.---]. | [---.-]‘rm. | [---.--]n.‘šrm. | [---.-]rn 2054.1.25
bn.annd. | bn.gl‘d. | w.nḥl h. | bn.mlkyy. | [bn].bm[--]. | [‘š]rm. | [-----]. | [-----]. | bn.p[--]. | bn.‘bdmlk. 2163.3.15
. | ṣdqšlm.‘šr[m]. | yknil.ḫmš. | ilmlk.ḫmš. | prṯ.‘šr. | ubn.‘šr. 1116.15
ny. | [bn].ṯrdnt. | [bn].hyadt. | [--]lt. | šmrm. | p‘ṣ.bn.byy.‘šrt. 1047.25
t. | mṯyn.b.ṯṯt. | ṯn.lbšm.b.‘šrt. | pld.b.arb‘t. | lbš.ṯn.b.ṯnt.‘šrt. 1108.8
bq‘t ṯṯ. | irab ṯn.‘šr. | ḥbš.ṯmn. | amḏy.arb‘.‘šr. | [-]n‘y.ṯṯ.‘šr. 67[110].12

--.ʿ]šrt. | ḫlb.ḫmšt.l.ʿšrm. | mril.ʿšrt. | glbty.arbʿt. | [--]ṯb.ʿšrt. 1180.5
.ʿšr. | ṯnʿy.ṯlṯ. | ḫlb ʿprm.ṯn. | tmdy.ṯlṯ. | [--]rt.arbʿ. | [---].ʿšr. 70[112].15

ʿšrn

l.ql.d.tbʿ.mṣ[r]m. | mit.arbʿm.kbd.yn.mṣb. | l.mdrǵlm. | ʿšrn ʿšr.yn.mṣb.[-]ḥ[-].l.gzzm. 1084.30

ʿšt

.ṯt[---]. | ʿšr.b gt.[---]. | ṯn.ʿšr.b.gt.ir[bṣ]. | arbʿ.b.gt.bʿln. | ʿšt.ʿšr.b.gpn. | yd.ʿdnm. | arbʿ.ǵzlm. | ṯn.yṣrm. 2103.7
| [---].ḫmš.ddm. | ṯṯ.l.ʿšrm.bn[š.mlk.---].ḫzr.lqḥ.ḥp[r]. | ʿšt.ʿšr h.bn[.---.--]ḫ.zr. | bʿl.šd. 2011.41
arbʿ.ʿšr h.šmn. | d.lqḥt.ṯlǵdy. | w.kd.ištir.ʿm.qrt. | ʿšt.ʿšr h.šmn. | ʿmn.bn.aǵlmn. | arbʿm.ksp.ʿl.qrt. | b.šd.bn.[u]b 1083.4
. | ṯmn.ḫzr. | w.arbʿ.ḥršm. | dt.tbʿln.b.pḫn. | ṯṯtm.ḫzr.w.ʿšt.ʿšr.ḥrš. | dt.tbʿln.b.ugrt. | ṯṯtm.ḫzr. | dt.tbʿln. | b.gt.ḥršm. | ṯ 1024.3.7

ʿtgr

-]. | [-----]. | [---].ḥ[mr]. | [---.]w.bnš.aḥd. | [---.--]m. | [---].ʿtgrm. | [---.-]ṣbm. | [---.]nrn.mʿry. | [---.--]r. | [---.]w.ṯn.bn h. | [2043.7
m. | [---.]nrn.mʿry. | [---.--]r. | [---.]w.ṯn.bn h. | [---.b]t h.ʿtgrm. 2043.12

ʿtd

.---]. | [-.]rbt.ṯbt.[---]. | rbt.ṯbt.ḥš[n.---]. | y.arṣ.ḥšn[.---]. | tʿtd.tkl.[---]. | tkn.lbn[.---]. | dt.lbn k[.---]. | dk k.kbkb[.---]. | d 5[67].3.5

ʿtk

qltn. | šlyṭ.d šbʿt.rašm. | mḫšt.mdd ilm.ar[š]. | ṣmt.ʿgl.il.ʿtk. | mḫšt.klbt.ilm išt. | klt.bt.il.ḏbb.imtḫṣ.ksp. | itrṯ.ḫrṣ.ṭrd.b 3[ʿNT].3.41
h.k kdrt.ri[š]. | ʿl h.k irbym.kp.k.qṣm. | ǵrmn.kp.mhr.ʿtkt. | rišt.l bmt h.šnst. | kpt.b ḥbš h.brkm.tǵl[l]. | b dm.ḏmr.ḥ 3[ʿNT].2.11
[---.šnst.kpt.b ḥb]š h.ʿtkt r[išt]. | [l bmt h.---.]hy bt h tʿrb. | [---.tm]ṯḫṣ b ʿmq. | [ṯḫt 7.1[131].2
.]ymm.lk. | hrg.ar[bʿ.]ymm.bṣr. | kp.šsk k.[--].l ḥbš k. | ʿtk.ri[š.]l mhr k. | w ʿp.l dr[ʿ].nšr k. | w rbṣ.l ǵr k.inbb. | kt ǵr 13[6].7
an[y]t.mlk[.---]. | w.[ṯ]lṯ.brm.[---]. | arbʿ ʿtkm[.---]. 2057.3

ʿtn

w pn.špš.nr. | b y.mid.w um. | tšmḫ.m ab. | w al.trḥln. | ʿtn.ḫrd.ank. | ʿm ny.šlm. | kll. | w mnm. | šlm ʿm. | um y. | ʿm y. 1015.13

ʿtq

ʿtq.k inr. | ap.ḫšt k.ap.ab.k mtm. | tmtn.u ḫšt k.l ntn. | ʿtq.b d.aṯt.ab.ṣrry. | ik m.yrgm.bn.il. | krt.špḥ.lṭpn. | w qdš.u i 16.1[125].19
q. | k inr[.ap.]ḫšt k. | ap.ab.k mtm.tmtn. | u ḫšt k.l bky.ʿtq. | b d.aṯt ab.ṣrry. | u ilm.tmtn.špḥ. | [l]ṭpn.l yḥ.t[b]ky k. | a 16.2[125].103
tq.k inr. | ap.ḫšt k.ap.ab.ik mtm. | tmtn.u ḫšt k.l ntn. | ʿtq.b d.aṯt.ab ṣrry. | tbky k.ab.ǵr.bʿl. | ṣpn.ḥlm.qdš. | any.ḥlm. 16.1[125].5
[---] h. | ybm h.šbʿ[.---]. | ǵzr.ilḥu.t[---]l. | trm.tṣr.trm[.ʿ]tqt. | tbky.w tšnn.[tt]n. | g h.bky.b ḥ[y k.a]b n. | nšmḫ.b l.mt 16.2[125].96
l [----]. | w l [---]. | kd.[---]. | kd.t[---.ym.ymm]. | yʿtqn.w[rḥm.ʿnt]. | tngṯ h.k lb.a[rḫ]. | l ʿgl h.k lb.ṯa[t]. | l imr 6[49].2.5
bky.b ḥ[y k.a]b n. | nšmḫ.b l.mt k.ngln. | k klb.[b]bt k.nʿtq. | k inr[.ap.]ḫšt k. | ap.ab.k mtm.tmtn. | u ḫšt k.l bky.ʿtq. 16.2[125].100
h. | bky.b ḥy k.ab n.ašmḫ. | b l.mt k.ngln.k klb. | b bt k.nʿtq.k inr. | ap.ḫšt k.ap.ab.k mtm. | tmtn.u ḫšt k.l ntn. | ʿtq.b 16.1[125].16
[l]krt. | k [k]lb.b bt k.nʿtq.k inr. | ap.ḫšt k.ap.ab.ik mtm. | tmtn.u ḫšt k.l ntn. | ʿtq.b 16.1[125].2
| nrt.ilm.špš.ṣḥrrt. | la.šmm.b yd.bn ilm.mt. | ym.ymm.yʿtqn.l ymm. | l yrḫm.rḥm.ʿnt.tngṯ h. | k lb.arḫ.l ʿgl h.k lb. | ṯ 6[49].2.26
[---.--]b. | [---.w ym.ym]m. | [yʿtqn.---.ymǵy.]npš. | [---.h]d.tngṯn h. | [---].b ṣpn. | [---].nšb.b 1[ʿNT.X].5.3
[---.]rq.gb. | [---.--]kl.tǵr.mtn h. | [---.--]b.w ym ymm. | [yʿtqn.---.]ymǵy.npš. | [---.--]t.hd.tngṯm h. | [---.-]ḫm k b ṣpn. 1[ʿNT.X].5.16
t m. | [---].k iṯl. | [---.--]m.ʿdb.l arṣ. | [---.]špm.ʿdb. | [---].tʿtqn. | [---.-]ʿb.idk. | [l ytn.pnm.tk.]in.bb.b alp ḥzr. | [rbt.kmn 1[ʿNT.IX].2.12

ʿṯlṯ

[b]n ʿntn.[---]. | bn agyn[.---]. | b[n] ʿṯlṯ[.---]. | bn qṭy[.---]. | bn ypʿ[.---]. | [---]bʿm[.---]. | [-----]. 105[86].3

ʿṯqb

.rm.lk.prẓ kt. | [k]bkbm.ṯm.tpl k.lbnt. | [-.]rgm.k yrkt.ʿṯqbm. | [---]m.ʿẓpn.l pit. | m[--]m[.--]tm.w mdbḥt. | ḫr[.---.]ʿl. 13[6].14

ʿṯqbt

ʿ. | tgrš.qšt.w.qlʿ. | špšyn.qšt.w.qlʿ. | bn.ṯʿln.qš[t.w.q]lʿ. | ʿṯqbt.qšt. | [-]ll.qšt.w.qlʿ. | ḫlb.rpš. | abmn.qšt. | ẓẓn.qšt. | dqry. 119[321].2.27

ʿṯr

m.gdlt.w burm.[l]b. | rmṣt.ilhm.bʿlm.dṯt.w kšm.ḫmš. | ʿṯr h.mlun.šnpt.ḫṣt h.bʿl.ṣpn š. | [--]ṯ š.ilt.mgdl š.ilt.asrm š. | 34[1].10

ʿṯt

dbḥt.byy.bn. | šry.l ʿṯt. RS61[24.323.2]

ʿṯtpr

t.ʿnt.w ʿṯtrt. | [ti]sp.ḥmt.y[r]ḫ.w.ršp.yisp.ḥmt. | [ʿṯ]r.w ʿṯtpr.yisp.ḥmt.ṯṯ.w ktṯ. | [yus]p.ḥmt.mlk.b ʿṯtrt.yisp.ḥmt. | [k UG5.8.16
| yrḫ w ksa. | yrḫ mkṭy. | ṯkmn w šnm. | kṯr w ḫss. | ʿṯr ʿṯtpr. | šḥr w šlm. | ngh w srr. | ʿdw šr. | ṣdqm šr. | ḥnbn il d[n]. UG5.10.1.10

ʿṯtr

t[-].ǵlm.l šdt[.-.]ymm. | [---.]b ym.ym.y[--].yš[ ]n.ap k.ʿṯtr.dm[.---.]| [---.]ḥrḥrtm.w[--.]n[--.]iš[--.]h[---.]išt. | [---]y.y 2.3[129].12
.]ṯ[bt | k.l y]hpk. | [ksa.]mlk k.l ytbr.ḫṭ.mtpṭ k.w yʿn[.ʿṯtr].dm[-]k[-]. | [--]ḥ.b y.ṯr.il.ab y.ank.in.bt[.l] y[.km.]ilm[.w 2.3[129].18
]sp.ḥmt.ʿnt.w ʿṯtrt. | [ti]sp.ḥmt.y[r]ḫ.w.ršp.yisp.ḥmt. | [ʿṯ]r.w ʿṯtpr.yisp.ḥmt.ṯṯ.w ktṯ. | [yus]p.ḥmt.mlk.b ʿṯtrt.yisp.ḥ UG5.8.16
n.k tms m. | w ʿn.rbt.aṯrt ym. | blt.nmlk.ʿṯtr.ʿrẓ. | ymlk.ʿṯtr.ʿrẓ. | apnk.ʿṯtr.ʿrẓ. | yʿl.b ṣrrt.ṣpn. | yṯb.l kḥṯ.aliyn. | bʿl.pʿn 6.1.55[49.1.27]
h.l ymǵy. | aps h.w yʿn.ʿṯtr.ʿrẓ. | l amlk.b ṣrrt.ṣpn. | yrd.ʿṯtr.ʿrẓ.yrd. | l kḥṯ.aliyn.bʿl. | w ymlk.b arṣ.il.kl h. | [---] š abn. 6.1.63[49.1.35]

n.|b‘l.p‘n h.l tmǵyn.|hdm.riš h.l ymǵy.|aps h.w y‘n.‘ṯtr.‘rẓ.|l amlk.b ṣrrt.ṣpn.|yrd.‘ṯtr.‘rẓ.yrd.|l kḥṯ.aliyn.b‘l.| 6.1.61[49.1.33]
rḥ.|‘m.bn.dgn.k tms m.|w ‘n.rbt.aṯrt ym.|blt.nmlk.‘ṯtr.‘rẓ.|ymlk.‘ṯtr.‘rẓ.|apnk.‘ṯtr.‘rẓ.|y‘l.b ṣrrt.ṣpn.|yṯb.l kḥṯ 6.1.54[49.1.26]
‘n.rbt.aṯrt ym.|blt.nmlk.‘ṯtr.‘rẓ.|ymlk.‘ṯtr.‘rẓ.|apnk.‘ṯtr.‘rẓ.|y‘l.b ṣrrt.ṣpn.|yṯb.l kḥṯ.aliyn.|b‘l.p‘n h.l tmǵyn.|h 6.1.56[49.1.28]
mṯ.|yrḫ w ksa.|yrḫ mkṯy.|ṯkmn w šnm.|kṯr w ḫss.|‘ṯtr ‘ṯpr.|šḥr w šlm.|ngh w srr.|‘dw šr.|ṣdqm šr.|ḥnbn il UG5.10.1.10
w š.|b‘l ṣpn alp.w.š.|ṯrṯy.alp.w.š.|yrḫ.š.ṣpn.š.|kṯr š ‘ṯtr.š.|[‘ṯ]rt.š.šgr w iṯm š.|[---.]š.ršp.idrp.š.|[---.il.t‘]ḏr.š.|[- UG5.9.2.8
l ḫt[n].|m.b‘l trḫ pdry b[t h].|aqrb k ab h b‘[l].|yǵtr.‘ṯtr t|rḫ l k ybrdmy.b[t.a]|b h lb[u] y‘rr.w y‘[n].|yrḫ nyr š 24[77].28
dš.]w y[--.]zbl.ym.y‘[--.]ṯpṭ.nhr.|[-------.]yšlḥn.w y‘n ‘ṯtr[.-]. 2.3[129].24
ṯb[-.---].|ab[.---].|ḥyi[l.---].|iḫy[.---].|ar[.---].|‘ṯtr[.---].|bn.[---].|yly[.---].|ykn[.---].|rp[--].|ṯtw.[---].|[---.‘] 2131.6

‘ṯtrab

bn.army.|bn.rpiyn.|bn.army.|bn.krmn.|bn.ykn.|bn.‘ṯtrab.|uṣn[-].|bn.alṯn.|bn.aš[-]š.|bn.štn.|bn.ilš.|bn.tnabn. 1046.1.12
[---.‘ṯt]rab.|[---.ar]šmg.|[---.‘]bdkṯr.|[---.‘]bdgṯr.|[---.--]n.|[---.‘ 1055.1.1

‘ṯtrum

.[m]dlm.|[---.l i]ytlm.|[---].gmn.|[---].l.urǵṯṯb.|[---.]l.‘ṯtrum.|[---.]l.brqn.|[---].skn.|[---.‘g]ltn.|[---].‘gltn.|[---.]‘gl 2162.B.6
[--.‘]ṯtrum[.---].|[---.]ḥmr.y[--].|[---].n‘r[.---].|[---.]dd gdl[.---]. 2133.12

‘ṯtry

spr.ytnm.|bn.ḫlbym.|bn.ady.|bn.‘ṯtry.|bn.ḫrẓn.|ady.|bn.birtn.|bn.ḥrẓn.|bn.bddn.|bn.anny 115[301].1.4
[---.‘]ṯtry.|[-----.]yn.|[----.-]mn.|[---.--]m.mṣl.|[---].prš.ḥtm.|ṯlṯ[1146.1

‘ṯtrn

lšt[m‘y.---].|[b]dlm.dt.yṯb[.---].|[-]y[--].‘nqp[aty.---].|‘ṯt[r]n.[-]bṯ[-.---].|[---]n.š[--.---].|[---]n.[---].|[--]n[-].[---]. 90[314].2.12

‘ṯtrt

-.---].|[l.--]ḥl.|[l.--.]mgmr.|[l.-.]qdšt.|l.‘ṯtrt.ndrgd.|l.‘ṯtrt.abḏr.|l.dml.|l.ilt[.-]pn.|l.uš[ḫr]y.|[---.-]mrn.|l ṯwl.|[-- 1001.1.12
nyt.|bnš.gt.gl‘d.|bnš.gt.ngr.|r‘ym.|bn.ḫri[-].|bnš.gt.‘ṯtrt.|ad[-]l[-]m.|‘šr.ksdm.yd.lmd hm.lqḥ.|‘šr.mḫṣm.yd.lm 1040.6
]mt.i[l.w] ḥrn.yisp.ḥmt.|[b‘l.w]dgn[.yi]sp.ḥmt.‘nt.w ‘ṯtrt.|[ti]sp.ḥmt.y[r]ḫ.w.ršp.yisp.ḥmt.|[‘ṯt]r.w ‘ṯpr.yisp.ḥm UG5.8.14
t.|[‘ṯ]r.w ‘ṯpr.yisp.ḥmt.ṯṯ.w kṯṯ.|[yus]p.ḥmt.mlk.b ‘ṯtrt.yisp.ḥmt.|[kṯ]r w ḫss.y[i]sp.ḥmt.šḥr.w šlm.|[yis]p.ḥmt UG5.8.17
ymn.mḫṣ.ǵlmm.yš[--].|[ymn h.‘n]t.tuḫd.šmal h.tuḫd.‘ṯtrt.ik.m[ḫṣt.ml]|[ak.ym.t‘]dt.ṯpṭ.nhr.mlak.mṯḫr.yḥb[-.---.] 2.1[137].40
lm.|[b‘l]m.|[arṣ] w šm[m].|[-----].|[a]rṣ.|[u]šḫr[y].|[‘]ṯtrt.|i[l t]‘ḏr b‘l.|ršp.|ddmš.|pḫr ilm.|ym.|uṯḫt.|knr.|ml 29[17].2.3
[---]n.yšt.rpu.mlk.‘lm.w yšt.|[--.]gṯr.w yqr.il.ytb.b.‘ṯtrt.|il.ṯpṭ.b hd r‘y.d yšr.w yḏmr.|b knr.w ṯlb.b tp.w mṣlt UG5.2.1.2
db.ksa.w yṯb.|tqru l špš.um h.špš.um.ql.bl.‘m.|‘nt w ‘ṯtrt inbb h.mnt.nṯk.|nḥš.šlḥm.nḥš.‘q šr[.y‘]db.ksa.|nḥš.šm UG5.7.20
t.‘[--.---].|yṣi.ǵl h ṯḥm b[.---].|mrḥ h l adrt[.---].|ṯṯb ‘ṯtrt b ǵl[.---].|qrẓ tšt.l šmal[.---].|arbḫ.‘n h tšu w[.---].|aylt 2001.1.8
lp.tmn h.|yqṯ b‘l.w yšt.ym.ykly.ṯpṭ.nhr.|b šm.tg‘r m.‘ṯtrt.bṯ l aliyn.[b‘l.]|bṯ.l rkb.‘rpt.k šby n.zb[l.ym.k] |šby n.ṯ 2.4[68].28
‘db.ksa.w yṯb.|tqru l špš um h.špš um ql.bl.‘m.|mlk.‘ṯtrt h.mnt.nṯk.nḥš.šmrr.|nḥš.‘q šr.ln h.mlḫš abd.ln h.ydy.| UG5.7.41
rr[.---].|alp.pr.b‘l.[---].|w prt.tkt.[---].|šnt.[---].|ššw.‘ṯtrt.w ššw.‘[nt.---].|w ht.[--]k.ššw[.-]rym[.---].|d ymǵy.bnš[2158.1.6
lḥm.l h.w d l yd‘nn.|d.mṣd.|ylmn.ḫṯ.tḥt.ṯlḥn.|b qr‘.|‘ṯtrt.w ‘nt.ymǵy.|‘ṯtrt.t‘db.nšb l h.|w ‘nt.ktp.b hm.yg‘r.ṯǵr. UG5.1.1.9
-].|il.k yrdm.arṣ.‘nt.|w ‘ṯtrt.tṣdn.[---].|[---.-]b[-.---].|[‘ṯ]trt w ‘nt[.---].|w b hm.tṯṯb[.--]d h.|km trpa.hn n‘r.|d yšt. UG5.1.2.1
k t‘rb.‘ṯtrt.ḫr[-].|bt mlk.‘šr.‘šr.[--].bt ilm.|kbr[-]m.[-]trmt.|lbš.w [33[5].1
[---].md.‘[ṯtr]t.|ydy.|bn.škn.|bn.mdt.|bn.ḫ[--]y.|bn.‘[-]y.|kn‘m.|bn 1054.1.1
ṯt.ḥry.|n‘mt.šbḥ.bkr k.|d k n‘m.‘nt.|n‘m h.km.tsm.|‘ṯtrt.tsm h.|d ‘q h.ib.iqni.|‘p‘p h.sp.ṯrml.|d b ḥlm y.il.ytn.| 14[KRT].6.293
ṯt.ḥry.|n‘mt.špḥ.bkr k.|d k.n‘m.‘nt.n‘m h.|km.tsm.‘ṯtrt.ts[m h].|d ‘q h.ib.iqni.‘p[‘p] h.|sp.ṯrml.ṯḥgrn.[-]dm[.-]. 14[KRT].3.146
d[.l.]ṯrtn[m].|arb‘ l.mry[nm].|kdm l.ḫty.[---].|kdm l.‘ṯtr[t].|kd l.m[ḏ]rǵl[m].|kd l.mryn[m]. 1091.10
ḫ[--]y.|bn.‘[-]y.|kn‘m.|bn.yš[-]n.|bn.pd[y].|ttn.|md.‘ṯt[rt].|kṯkt.|bn.ṯtn[--].|[m]d.m[--].|[b]n.annḏ[r].|bn.ṯdyy. 1054.1.11
yrṯ.|[-.]ynḥm.ḫpn.|ṯṯ.lmd.b‘ln.|l.qḥ.ḫpnt.|ṯṯ[.-]l.md.‘ṯtr[t].|l.qḥ.ḫpnt. 1117.19
tm].|šb‘ d.w.šb‘[d.qlt].|ankn.rgmt.l.b‘l y.|l.špš.‘lm.l.‘ṯtrt.|l.‘nt.l.kl.il.alṯ[y].|nmry.mlk.‘lm.|mlk n.b‘l y.ḥw[t.--]. 2008.1.7
ḫpn.d.iqni.w.šmt.|l.iyb‘l.|ṯlṯm.l.mit.š‘rt.|l.šr.‘ṯtrt.|mlbš.ṯrmnm.|k.yṯn.w.b.bt.|mlk.mlbš.|ytn.l hm.|šb‘.l 1107.4
y.|ytt.nḫšm.mhr k.bn bṯn.|itnn k.|aṯr ršp.‘ṯtrt.|‘m ‘ṯtrt.mr h.|mnt.nṯk.nḥš. UG5.7.TR2
l.a]rṣy.|[l.--]r[-.---].|[l.--]ḥl.|[l.--.]mgmr.|[l.-.]qdšt.|l.‘ṯtrt.ndrgd.|l.‘ṯtrt.abḏr.|l.dml.|l.ilt[.-]pn.|l.uš[ḫr]y.|[---.-] 1001.1.12
n.|d.mṣd.|ylmn.ḫṯ.tḥt.ṯlḥn.|b qr‘.|‘ṯtrt.w ‘nt.ymǵy.|‘ṯtrt.t‘db.nšb l h.|w ‘nt.ktp.b hm.yg‘r.ṯǵr.|bt.il.pn.l mgr lb.t UG5.1.1.10
n.bṯn.itnn y.|ytt.nḫšm.mhr k.bn bṯn.|itnn k.|aṯr ršp.‘ṯtrt.|‘m ‘ṯtrt.mr h.|mnt.nṯk.nḥš. UG5.7.TR1
d ṯbil.|‘ṯtrt ṣwd[t.---].|tlk b mdb[r.---].|ṯḥdṯn w hl[.---].|w tglṯ th 2001.1.2
b.ylšn.|b ḫri h.w ṯnt h.ql.il.[--].|il.k yrdm.arṣ.‘nt.|w ‘ṯtrt.tṣdn.[---].|[---.-]b[-.---].|[‘ṯ]trt w ‘nt[.---].|w b hm.tṯṯb[. UG5.1.1.23
b ym.dbḥ.ṯp[-].|aḥt.l mzy.bn[--].|aḥt.l mkt.ǵr.|aḥt.l ‘ṯtrt.|arb‘.‘ṣrm.|gt.ṯrmn.|aḥt.slḫu. 39[19].16
|ṣpn.š.kṯr.š.pdry.š.ǵrm.š[.---].|aṯrt.š.‘nt.š.špš.š.arṣy.š.‘ṯtrt.š.|ušḫry.š.il.t‘ḏr.b‘l.š.ršp.š.ddmš.š.|w šlmm.ilib.š.i[l.--] UG5.9.1.7
‘l ṣpn alp.w.š.|ṯrṯy.alp.w.š.|yrḫ.š.ṣpn.š.|kṯr š ‘ṯtr.š.|[‘ṯt]rt.š.šgr w iṯm š.|[---.]š.ršp.idrp.š.|[---.il.t‘]ḏr.š.|[---.-]mt. UG5.9.2.9
[i]lib.|[i]lbldn.|[p]dry.bt.mlk.|[-]lp.izr.|[a]rz.|k.t‘rb.‘ṯtrt.šd.bt[.m]lk.|k.t‘rbn.ršp m.bt.mlk.|ḫlu.dg.|ḥdṯm.|dbḥ. 2004.10
b‘lm].kmm.b‘lm.kmm.|b‘lm.kmm.b‘lm.kmm.|k t‘rb.‘ṯtrt.šd.bt.mlk[.---].|ṯn.skm.šb‘.mšlt.arb‘.ḫpnt.[---].|ḫmšm.ṯ UG5.9.1.18
rt.mḫṣ.bnš.mlk.yb‘l hm.|[---.--]t.w.ḫpn.l.azzlt.|[---.]l.‘ṯtrt.šd.|[---].yb‘lnn.|[---.--]n.b.ṯlṯ.šnt.l.nṣd.|[---.--]ršp.mlk. 1106.55
-.š]mt.|[---].y[--.--]m.|[---.--]n.d[--.--]i.|[--]t.mdt h[.l.]‘ṯtrt.šd.|[---.-]rt.mḫṣ.bnš.mlk.yb‘l hm.|[---.--]t.w.ḫpn.l.azzlt 1106.52
k.aṯb.|an.w y‘ny.krt ṯ‘.yṯbr.|ḥrn.y bn.yṯbr.ḥrn.|riš k.‘ṯtrt.šm.b‘l.|qdqd k.tqln.b gbl.|šnt k.b ḥpn k.w t‘n.|spr ilm 16.6[127].56
k.aymr[.---].|ṯpṭ.nhr.yṯb[r.ḥrn.y ym.yṯbr.ḥrn].|riš k.‘ṯtrt.[šm.b‘l.qdqd k.---].|[--]t.mṯ.tpln.b g[bl.šnt k.---].|[--]šn 2.1[137].8
[--].d.ntn[.d.]ksp.|[ṯ]mn.l.‘šrm[.l.b]t.‘ṯtrt.|[ṯ]lṯ.‘šr h.[b]t.ršp.gn.|arb‘.b d.b[n].ušryn.|kdm.l.urtn. 1088.2
--.---].|ḥm.l šrr.w [---].|y‘n.ym.l mt[.---].|l šrr.w t‘[n.‘ṯtrt.---].|b‘l m.hmt.[---].|l šrr.št[.---].|b riš h.[---].|ib h.mš[2.4[68].35

l.[----].|l.[----].|l.‘ṯ[trt.---].|l.mš[--.---].|l.ilt[.---].|l.b‘lt[.---].|l.il.bt[.---].|l.ilt.[1004.3
---].|[--.aṯ]rt.š[.---].|[---.]l pdr[-.---].|ṣin aḥd h[.---].|l ‘ṯrt[.---].|‘lm.kmm[.---].|w b ṯlṯ.ṣ[in.---].|l ll.pr[-.---].|mit š 37[22].6
]‘ṯ[trt.---].|[-.k]su.ilt[.---].|[ṯl]ṯ.l ‘ṯrt[.---].|[--.]l ilt.š l ‘ṯt[rt.---].|[‘]ṣr.l pdr ṯṯ.ṣ[in.---].|tšnpn.‘lm.km[m.---].|w.l ll.‘ 38[23].4
[---.]‘ṯ[trt.---].|[-.k]su.ilt[.---].|[ṯl]ṯ.l ‘ṯrt[.---].|[--.]l ilt.š l ‘ṯt[rt.-- 38[23].1
[---.]‘ṯ[trt.---].|[-.k]su.ilt[.---].|[ṯl]ṯ.l ‘ṯrt[.---].|[--.]l ilt.š l ‘ṯt[rt.---].|[‘]ṣr.l pdr ṯṯ.ṣ[in.---].|tšnpn.‘ 38[23].3
.|tšlḥm yrẖ.ggn[.---].|k[.---.ẖ]mš.ẖssm[.---].|[---.--]m ‘ṯr[t.---].|[---.]n[--.---]. 2001.1.18

ǵ

ǵb

| [---.]bqt[-]. | [b] ǵb.ršp mh bnš. | šrp.w ṣp ḫršḫ. | ʻlm b ǵb ḫyr. | ṯmn l ṯlṯm ṣin. | šbʻ.alpm. | bt bʻl.ugrt.ṯn šm. | ʻlm.l rš UG5.12.B.3
ʻšrt.bʻl. | ʻrkm. | b ṯmnt.ʻšrt.yr | tḥṣ.mlk.brr. | ʻlm.tzǵ.b ǵb.ṣpn. | nḥkt.ksp.w ḫrṣ ṯʻ ṯn šm l btbt. | alp.w š šrp.alp šlm UG5.12.A.7
qlʻm. | bn.army.ṯt.qštm.w[.]q[lʻ]. | bn.rpš.qšt.w.qlʻ. | bn.ǵb.qšt. | bn.ytrm.qšt.w.qlʻ. | bn.ʻbdyrḫ.qšt.w.q[lʻ]. | bn.lky.qšt. 119[321].3.24
npš.w.š.l ršp bbt. | [ʻ]ṣrm l h.ršp [-]m. | [---.]bqt[-]. | [b] ǵb.ršp mh bnš. | šrp.w ṣp ḫršḫ. | ʻlm b ǵb ḫyr. | ṯmn l ṯlṯm ṣin UG5.12.B.1

ǵbiš

lṯy. | kd.l mrynm. | šbʻ yn. | l mrynm. | b yṯbmlk. | kdm.ǵbiš ḫry. | ḫmš yn.b d. | bḥ mlkt. | b mdrʻ. | ṯlṯ bt.il | ann. | kd.b 1090.13

ǵbl

ir.ḫmš. | uškn.arbʻ. | ubrʻy.ṯlṯ. | ar.ṯmn ʻšr h. | mlk.arbʻ. | ǵbl.ḫmš. | atlg.ḫmš ʻšr[h]. | ulm ṯ[ṯ]. | mʻrby.ḫmš. | ṭbq.arbʻ. | t 68[65].1.7
n.alz. | bn ḫlm. | bn.ḏmr. | bn.ʻyn. | ubnyn. | rpš d ydy. | ǵbl. | mlk. | gwl. | rqd. | ḫlby. | ʻn[q]pat. | m[ʻ]rb. | ʻrm. | bn.ḥgby. 2075.21
uḫnp[.---]. | ušk[n.---]. | ubr[ʻy.---]. | ar[.---]. | mlk[.---]. | ǵbl[.---]. | atl[g.---]. | u[lm.---]. | m[ʻrby.---]. | ṭ[bq.---]. 68[65].2.7
n. | [---.b] d.ṯbq. | [---.b] d.šbn. | [---.b] d.ulm. | [---.b] d.ǵbl. | [---.b] d.ʻbdkṯr. | [---.b] d.urǵnr. 1052.7
rm. | [---.bn]šm.b.ṯnq. | [---.b]nšm.b.ugrt. | [---.bn]šm.b.ǵbl. | [---.b]nšm.b.mʻr.arr. | arbʻ.bnšm.b.mnt. | arbʻ.bnšm.b.ir 2076.31

ǵbn

.[šl]m[.r]gm[.ṯṯb]. | ky.lik.bn y. | lḥt.akl.ʻm y. | mid y w ǵbn y. | w.bn y.hn kt. | yškn.anyt. | ym.yšrr. | w.ak[l.---]. | [--].š 2061.11

ǵbr

.ulp.]qṯy. | [ulp.ddmy.ulp.ḫry.ulp.ḫty.u]lp.alṯy. | [ulp.ǵbr.ulp.ḫbt km.ulp.mdll km.ulp]. | [qr zbl.ušn.yp km.b ap k APP.I[-].1.16
ḫṭu.ulp.qṯy.ulp.ddm]y. | [ulp.ḫry.ulp.ḫty.ulp.alṯy.ulp.ǵbr]. | [ulp.ḫbt km.ulp.mdll km.ulp.qr zbl]. | [u tḫṭu.u b ap k 32[2].1.7
.ulp.q[ṯy.ulp.ddm]y. | ulp.ḫry.ulp.ḫ[t]y.ulp.alṯy.ul[p.ǵbr.]ulp. | ḫbt km.ulp.m[dl]l km.ulp.qr zbl.u[š]n yp km. | u b 32[2].1.21
n.ulp.qṯy]. | ulp.ddmy.ul[p.ḫry.u]lp.ḫty.ulp[.alṯy.ulp.]ǵbr. | ulp.ḫbt kn.ulp.md[ll k]n.ulp.q[r zbl]. | u tḫṭin.b ap kn. 32[2].1.12
kn.ulp qṯy. | ulp.ddmy.ul[p.ḫ]ry.ulp.ḫty.ulp.alṯy. | ulp.ǵbr.ulp.[ḫbt] kn[.u]lp.mdll kn.ulp qr z[bl]. | lšn yp kn.b ap [32[2].1.30
n.ulp.q]ṯy. | [ulp.ddmy.ulp.ḫry.ulp.ḫty.ulp.alṯy]. | [ulp.ǵbr.ulp.ḫbt kn.ulp.mdll kn.ulp.]qr zbl. | [ušn.yp kn.u b ap k APP.I[-].2.14
kn.ulp.qṯy.ulp.]ddmy.ulp ḫry. | [ulp.ḫty.ulp.alṯy.ulp.ǵbr.ul]p.ḫbt kn. | [ulp.mdll kn.ulp.qr zbl.ušn.y]p kn. | [u b a APP.I[-].1.5
py[.---]. | [---.]w npy.u[grt.---]. | [---.--]y.ulp.[---]. | [---.]ǵbr.u[lp.---]. | [---.--]n[.---]. 32[2].2.4

ǵdd

.hdmm.l ǵzrm. | mid.tmtḫṣn.w tʻn. | tḫtṣb.w tḥdy.ʻnt. | tǵdd.kbd h.b ṣḥq.ymlu. | lb h.b šmḫt.kbd.ʻnt. | tšyt.k brkm.t 3[ʻNT].2.25
[hdmm.l ǵzrm.mid.tmtḫṣn.w t]ʻn.tḫtṣb. | [w tḥdy.ʻnt.tǵdd.kbd h.b ṣḥ]q.ymlu.lb h. | [b šmḫt.kbd.ʻnt.tšyt.tḥt h.k]k 7.1[131].7

ǵdyn

rḥ il. | b nit il. | b ṣmd il. | b dṯn il. | b šrp il. | b knt il. | b ǵdyn il. | [b]n [---]. 30[107].18
. | mṯpṭ.ṯt.qštm.w.ṯn.q[l]ʻm. | kmrṯn.ṯt.qštm.ṯn.[q]lʻm. | ǵdyn.qšt.w.qlʻ. | bn.gzl.qšt.w.qlʻ. | [---]n.qšt. | ilhd.qšt. | ʻdn.qš 119[321].1.4

ǵdʻ

rišym.qnum. | bn.ilrš. | ʻ[p]ṯn. | b[n.ʻr]my. | [--]ṯy. | bn.ǵdʻ. | bn.ʻyn. | bn.grb[n]. | yṯṯn. | bn.ab[l]. | kry. | pss. | ilṯḥm. | ḥr 2078.6

ǵdǵd

. | kḏyn.[---.-]gṯ. | šmrm.a[ḏdd]y.tb[--]. | ynḥm.aḏddy. | ǵdǵd.aḏddy. | sw.aḏddy. | ildy.aḏddy. | grʻ.aḏddy. | ʻbd.ršp aḏ 2014.31

ǵwy

bt k.ygrš k. | [---].bnt.ṣʻṣ.bnt.mʻmʻ.ʻbd.ḥrn.[--.]k. | [---].aǵwyn.ʻn k.ẓẓ.w k mǵ.ilm. | [--.]k ʻṣm.k ʻšm.l ttn.k abnm.l t 1001.2.12

ǵz

]k.w rgm.ʻny. | l k[rt.adn k.]ištm[ʻ]. | w tqǵ[.udn.k ǵz.ǵzm]. | tdbr.w[ǵ]rm[.ṯṯwy]. | šqlt.b ǵlt.yd k. | l tdn.dn.almnt. 16.6[127].30
yšu g h. | w yṣḥ.šmʻ mʻ.l krt. | ṯʻ.ištmʻ.w tqǵ udn. | k ǵz.ǵzm.tdbr. | w ǵrm.ṯṯwy.šqlt. | b ǵlt.yd k.l tdn. | dn.almnt.l ṯṯp 16.6[127].43
ab]k.w rgm.ʻny. | l k[rt.adn k.]ištm[ʻ]. | w tqǵ[.udn.k ǵz.ǵzm]. | tdbr.w[ǵ]rm[.ṯṯwy]. | šqlt.b ǵlt.yd k. | l tdn.dn.alm 16.6[127].30
rb.yšu g h. | w yṣḥ.šmʻ mʻ.l krt. | ṯʻ.ištmʻ.w tqǵ udn. | k ǵz.ǵzm.tdbr. | w ǵrm.ṯṯwy.šqlt. | b ǵlt.yd k.l tdn. | dn.almnt.l 16.6[127].43

ǵzl

t[m]. | myn. | šr. | bn.zql. | bn.iḫy. | bn.iyṯr. | bn.ʻyn. | bn.ǵzl. | bn.ṣmy. | bn.il[-]šy. | bn.ybšr. | bn.sly. | bn.ḫlbt. | bn.brzt. 2117.2.7
.gt.ir[bṣ]. | arbʻ.b.gt.bʻln. | ʻšt.ʻšr.b.gpn. | yd.ʻdnm. | arbʻ.ǵzlm. | ṯn.yṣrm. 2103.9

ǵzldn

]šdm. | iwryn. | nʻmn. | [-----]. | b gt.yny. | agttp. | bn.ʻnt. | ǵzldn. | ṯrn. | ḫdbṯ. | [-]ḫl.aǵltn. | [-]n. | [-]mṯ. | [--.]bn.[ʻ]zn. | [--] 1043.13

ǵzr

tn.qšt k.[l]. | [ʻnt.tq]ḥ[.q]ṣʻt k.ybmt.limm. | w yʻn.aqht.ǵzr.adr.ṯqbm. | [d]lbnn.adr.gdm.b rumm. | adr.qrnt.b yʻlm. 17[2AQHT].6.20
[aṯt.w].bn h.b.bt.krz. | [aṯt.]w.pǵt.b.bt.gg. | [ǵz]r.aḥd.b.bt.nwrḏ. | [aṯ]t.adrt.b.bt.arṯṯb. | aṯt.w.ṯn.bn h.b.bt. 80[119].3
zr[m]. | w.ḫmš.nʻrt.b.bt.sk[n]. | ṯt.aṯtm.adrtm.w.pǵt.w ǵzr[.aḥd.b.bt.---]. | aṯt.w.ṯt.pǵtm.w.ǵzr.aḥd.b.[bt.---]. | ṯt.aṯt 80[119].18
]. | aṯt.w.ṯt.pǵtm.w.ǵzr.aḥd.b.[bt.---]. | ṯt.aṯtm.w.pǵt.w.ǵzr.aḥd.b.[bt.---]. | aṯt.w.bn h.w.pǵt.aḥt.b.bt.m[--]. | aṯt.w.ṯt. 80[119].20

tm.adrtm.w.pǵt.w ǵzr[.aḥd.b.bt.---].|aṯt.w.ṯt.pǵtm.w.ǵzr.aḥd.b.[bt.---].|ṯt.aṯtm.w.pǵt.w.ǵzr.aḥd.b.[bt.---].|aṯt.w. 80[119].19
n'm[n.w t]'nynn.ap ank.aḥwy.|aqht[.ǵz]r.w y'n.aqht.ǵzr.|al.tšrgn.y btlt m.dm.l ǵzr.|šrg k.ḫḫm.mt.uḫryt.mh.yq 17[2AQHT].6.33
r.[mym].|mlk.yṣm.y l km.qr.mym.d '[l k].|mḫṣ.aqht.ǵzr.amd.gr bt il.|'nt.brḥ.p 'lm h.'nt.p dr[.dr].|'db.uḫry mṯ. 19[1AQHT].3.153
l 'nt.|qṣ't.l ybmt.limm.w t'n.btlt.|'nt.irš ḥym.l aqht.ǵzr.|irš ḥym.w atn k.bl mt.|w ašlḥ k.ašspr k.'m.b'l.|šnt.'m. 17[2AQHT].6.26
]arṣ.ks h.tšpk m.|[l 'pr.tšu.g h.]w tṣḥ.šm'.m'.|[l aqht.ǵzr.i]rš.ksp.w atn k.|[ḫrṣ.w aš]lḥ k.w tn.qšt k.[l].|['nt.tq]ḥ[17[2AQHT].6.17
mn.w ṣḥq.btlt.['nt].|[tšu.]g h.w tṣḥ.šm'.m['.l a]|[qht.ǵ]zr.at.aḫ.w an.a[ḫt k].|[---].šb'.ṯir k.[---].|[---.]ab y.ndt.an 18[3AQHT].1.24
kn.'l.ṣrrt.|adn k.šqrb.[---].|b mgn k.w ḫrṣ.l kl.|apnk.ǵzr.ilḥu.|[m]rḥ h.yiḫd.b yd.|[g]rgr h.bm.ymn.|[w]yqrb.tr 16.1[125].46
l[.---].|b[---.]ny[.--].|l bl.sk.w [---] h.|ybm h.šb'[.---].|ǵzr.ilḥu.t[---]l.|trm.tṣr.trm[.']tqt.|tbky.w tšnn.[tt]n.|g h.bk 16.2[125].95
'rn[.---].|mn.yrḫ.k m[rṣ.---].|mn.k dw.kr[t].|w y'ny.ǵzr[.ilḥu].|tlṯ.yrḫm.k m[rṣ].|arb'.k dw.k[rt].|mnd'.krt.mǵ[16.2[125].83
---.]aḫ h.tbky.|[--.m]rṣ.mlk.|[---.]krt.adn k.|[w y'ny.]ǵzr.ilḥu.|[---.]mrṣ.mlk.|[--.k]rt.adn k.|[--.d]bḥ.dbḥ.|[--.']šr 16.1[125].58
dṯ.m'qb k.[ttb'].|[bt]lt.'nt.idk.l ttn.[pnm].|['m.a]qht.ǵzr.b alp.š[d].|[rbt.]kmn.w ṣḥq.btlt.['nt].|[tšu.]g h.w tṣḥ.š 18[3AQHT].1.21
pǵt.aḥt.b.bt.m[--].|aṯt.w.ṯt.bt h.b.bt.ḫdmrd.|aṯt.w.ṯn.ǵzrm.b.bt.ṣdqš[lm].|[a]ṯt.aḥt.b.bt.rpi[--].|[aṯt.]w.bt h.b.bt.a 80[119].23
b'.rbt.|[---.]qbṯ.ṯm.|[---.]bn.ilm.|[m]t.šmḫ.p ydd.|il[.ǵ]zr.|b [-]dn.'.z.w.|rgbt.zbl. UG5.4.16
i.l ymm.l yrḫm.|l yrḫm.l šnt.'d.|šb't.šnt.ybk.l aq|ht.ǵzr.yd[m'.]l kdd.|dnil.mt.r[pi.mk].b šb'.|šnt.w y'n[.dnil.mt 19[1AQHT].4.178
.b|kyt.b hkl h.mšspdt.b ḥẓr h.|pẓǵm.ǵr.ybk.l aqht.|ǵzr.ydm'.l kdd.dnil.|mt.rpi.l ymm.l yrḫm.|l yrḫm.l šnt.'d. 19[1AQHT].4.174
[---.]n[--.mḏ]rǵlm.|[---.]b.bt[.---]l.|[ṯ]lṯ.aṯt.adrt.w.ṯlṯ.ǵzr[m].|w.ḫmš.n'rt.b.bt.sk[n].|ṯt.aṯtm.adrtm.w.pǵt.w ǵzr[. 80[119].16
.ybd.w yšr.'l h.|n'm[n.w t]'nynn.ap ank.aḥwy.|aqht[.ǵz]r.w y'n.aqht.ǵzr.|al.tšrgn.y btlt m.dm.l ǵzr.|šrg k.ḫḫm. 17[2AQHT].6.33
.w 'rbm.t'nyn.|w šd.šd ilm.šd aṯrt.w rḥm.|'l.išt.šb' d.ǵzrm.ṭb.[g]d.b ḥlb.annḫ b ḫmat.|w 'l.agn.šb' d m.dǵ[ṯ.---]t. 23[52].14
bt.ymsk.b msk h.|qm.ybd.w yšr.|mṣltm.bd.n'm.|yšr.ǵzr.ṭb.ql.|'l.b'l.b ṣrrt.|ṣpn.ytmr.b'l.|bnt h.y'n.pdry.|bt.ar.a 3['NT].1.20
ǵyn.tša.g h[m.w tṣḥn].|šm'.l dnil.[mt.rpi].|mt.aqht.ǵzr.[šṣat].|btlt.'nt.k [rḥ.npš h].|k iṯl.brlt h.[b h.p'nm].|ṭṭ.'l 19[1AQHT].2.91
tṣb.bn.qrtm.ṯṭ'r.|ksat.l mhr.ṯ'r.ṯlḥnt.|l ṣbim.hdmm.l ǵzrm.|mid.tmtḫṣn.w t'n.|tḫtṣb.w tḥdy.'nt.|tǵdd.kbd h.b ṣ 3['NT].2.22
ḫṣ b 'mq.|[tḫtṣb.bn.qrtm.ṯṭ'r.ṯlḥnt.]l ṣbim.|[hdmm.l ǵzrm.mid.tmtḫṣn.w t]'n.tḫtṣb.|[w tḥdy.'nt.tǵdd.kbd h.b ṣḥ] 7.1[131].6
|št.b yn.yšt.ila.il š[--.]il.|d yqny.ḏdm.yd.mḫṣt.a[qh]t.ǵ|zr.tmḫṣ.alpm.ib.št[-.]št.|ḥršm l ahlm p[---.]km.|[-]bl lb h 19[1AQHT].4.220
|'rb.b bt h.kṯrt.bnt.|hll.snnt.apnk.dnil.|mt.rpi.ap.hn.ǵzr.mt.|hrnmy.alp.yṭbḫ.l kṯ|rt.yšlḥm.kṯrt.w y|ššq.bnt.[hl]l 17[2AQHT].2.28
ky.pǵt.bm.lb.|tdm'.bm.kbd.|tmz'.kst.dnil.mt.|rpi.al.ǵzr.mt.hrnmy.|apnk.dnil.mt.|rpi.yṣly.'rpt.b|ḥm.un.yr.'rpt 19[1AQHT].1.37
[-----.apnk].|[dnil.mt.rp]i.apn.ǵz[r].|[mt.hrnmy.]uzr.ilm.ylḥm.|[uzr.yšqy.]bn.qdš.yd.|[ṣt 17[2AQHT].1.2
s.|hlk.qšt.ybln.hl.yš|rb'.qṣ't.apnk.dnil.|mt.rpi.aphn.ǵzr.mt.|hrnmy.gm.l aṯt h.k yṣḥ.|šm'.mṯt.dnty.'d[b].|imr.b 17[2AQHT].5.14
l.šr'.thmtm.bl.|ṭbn.ql.b'l.k tmz'.|kst.dnil.mt.rpi.|all.ǵzr.m[t.]hr[nmy].|gm.l bt[h.dnil.k yṣḥ].|šm'.pǵt.ṯkmt[.my 19[1AQHT].1.48
'.ymm.|[w]yqrb.b'l.b ḥnt h.abynt.|[d]nil.mt.rpi anḫ.ǵzr.|[mt.]hrnmy.d in.bn.l h.|km.aḫ h.w šrš.km.ary h.|bl.iṯ 17[2AQHT].1.18
ṣ h.b ym.rṯ.|[--.y]iḫd.il.'bd h.ybrk.|[dni]l mt rpi.ymr.ǵzr.|[mt.hr]nmy npš.yḥ.dnil.|[mt.rp]i.brlt.ǵzr.mt hrnmy.| 17[2AQHT].1.36
.|dnil.mt.r[pi.mk].b šb'.|šnt.w y'n[.dnil.mt.]rpi.|yṯb.ǵzr.m[t.hrnmy.y]šu.|g h.w yṣḥ.t[b'.---].|bkyt.b hk[l]y.mšs 19[1AQHT].4.181
ašrb'.qṣ't.w hn šb['].|b ymm.apnk.dnil.mt.|rpi.a hn.ǵzr.mt.hrnm[y].|ytšu.ytb.b ap.ṯǵr.tḥt.|adrm.d b grn.ydn.| 17[2AQHT].5.5
|pr'.qẓ.y[bl].šblt.|b ǵlp h.apnk.dnil.|[m]t.rpi.ap[h]n.ǵzr.|[mt.hrn]my.ytšu.|[ytb.b ap.ṯ]ǵr[.t]ḥt.|[adrm.d b grn.y 19[1AQHT].1.20
.|l ahl h.hyn.tb'.l mš|knt h.apnk.dnil.m[t].|rpi.aphn.ǵzr.m[t].|hrnmy.qšt.yqb.[--]|rk.'l.aqht.k yq[--.---].|pr'm.ṣd 17[2AQHT].5.34
.rpum.l grnt.i[lnym.l] |mṯ't.w y'n.dnil.[mt.rpi].|yṯb.ǵzr.mt hrnmy[.---].|b grnt.ilm.b qrb.m[ṯ't.ilnym].|d tit.yspi 20[121].2.8
t rpi.ymr.ǵzr.|[mt.hr]nmy npš.yḥ.dnil.|[mt.rp]i.brlt.ǵzr.mt hrnmy.|[---].hw.mḫ.l 'rš h.y'l.|[---].bm.nšq.aṯt h.|[- 17[2AQHT].1.38
.agn.šb' d m.dǵ[ṯ.---]t.|tlk m.rḥmy.w tṣd[.---].|tḥgrn.ǵzr.n'm.[---].|w šm.'rbm.yr[.---].|mṯbt.ilm.ṯmn.ṯ[--.--].|pa 23[52].17
bl.yrḫ.yšu g h.|w yṣḥ.y l k.qrt.ablm.|d 'l k.mḫṣ.aqht.ǵzr.|'wrt.yšt k.b'l.l ht.|w 'lm h.l 'nt.p dr.dr.|'db.uḫry.mṯ.y 19[1AQHT].4.166
.ksa.mlk k.|l ytbr.ḥṭ.mṯpṭ k.|yru.bn ilm t.ṯt'.y|dd.il.ǵzr.y'r.mt.|b ql h.y[---.---].|b'l.yṯṯbn[.l ksi].|mlk h.l[nḫt.l 6[49].6.31
pn.w y'n.|gpn.w ugr.tḥm.bn ilm.|mt.hwt.ydd.bn.il.|ǵzr.p np.š.npš.lbim.|thw.hm.brlt.anḫr.|b ym.hm.brk y.tkš 5[67].1.14
.|arṣ.drkt.yštkn.|dll.al.ilak.l bn.|ilm.mt.'dd.l ydd.|il.ǵzr.yqra.mt.|b npš h.ystrn ydd.|b gngn h.aḥd y.d ym|lk.'l. 4[51].7.47
arb'.'šr.ǵzrm.|arb'.aṯt.|pǵt.aḥt.|w.pǵy.aḥ. 2081.1
ium.b ǵlp y[m.--].|d alp šd.ẓu h.b ym.t[---].|tlbš.npṣ.ǵzr.tšt.ḫ[---.b] |nšg h.ḥrb.tšt.b t'r[t h].|w 'l.tlbš.npṣ.aṯt.[--]. 19[1AQHT].4.206
n.šblt.|tp'.b aklt.šblt.tp'[.b ḥm]drt.|ur.tisp k.yd.aqht.ǵz[r].|tšt k.bm.qrb m.asm.|b p h.rgm.l yṣa.b špt h[.hwt h]. 19[1AQHT].2.73
ṣ[ql].|ynp'.b palt.bṣql yp' b yǵlm.|ur.tisp k.yd.aqht.|ǵzr.tšt k.b qrb m.asm.|y.dnh.ysb.aklt h.yph.|šblt.b akt.šblt 19[1AQHT].2.67
tlt.'nt.at.'[l.qšt h].|tmḫṣ h.qṣ't h.hwt.l t[ḥwy].|n'mn.ǵzr.št.ṯrm.w[---].|ištir.b ḏdm.w n'rs[.---].|w t'n.btlt.'nt.ṯb. 18[3AQHT].4.14
y.|aqht[.ǵz]r.w y'n.aqht.ǵzr.|al.tšrgn.y btlt m.dm.l ǵzr.|šrg k.ḫḫm.mt.uḫryt.mh.yqḥ.|mh.yqḥ.mt.aṯryt.spsg.ys 17[2AQHT].6.34
.|yšu.g h.w yṣḥ.y l k.mrrt.|tǵll.b nr.d 'l k.mḫṣ.aqht.|ǵzr.šrš k.b arṣ.al.|yp'.riš.ǵly.b d.ns' k.|'nt.brḥ.p 'lm h.|'nt. 19[1AQHT].3.159
ḏrqm.amt m.l yrt.|b npš.bn ilm.mt.b mh|mrt.ydd.il.ǵzr.|tb'.w l.yṯb ilm.idk.|l ytn.pnm.'m.b'l.|mrym.ṣpn.w y'n 5[67].1.8
šṯḥwy.w k|bd hwt.w rgm.|l bn.ilm.mt.|ṯny.l ydd.|il.ǵzr.tḥm.|aliyn.b'l.|[hw]t.aliy.q|[rdm.]bht y.bnt.|[dt.ksp.dt 4[51].8.32
.b'l.|ṯt'.nn.rkb.'rpt.|tb'.rgm.l bn.ilm.mt.|ṯny.l ydd.il ǵzr.|tḥm.aliyn.b'l.hwt.aliy.|qrdm.bht.l bn.ilm mt.|'bd k.an 5[67].2.9
n.tinṯt.|[---]m.tṣḥq.'nt.w b lb.tqny.|[---.]tb l y.l aqht.ǵzr.ṯb l y w l k.|[---]m.l aqry k.b ntb.pš'.|[---].b ntb.gan.ašq 17[2AQHT].6.42
.qym.il.|b lsmt.ṯm.yṭbš.šm.il.mt m.|y'bš.brk n.šm.il.ǵzrm.|ṯm.ṯmq.rpu.b'l.mhr b'l.|w mhr.'nt.ṯm.yḥpn.ḥyl|y.z 22.2[124].7
m.|[l p'n.il.t]hbr.w tql.tštḥ|[wy.w tkbd]n h.tlšn.aqht.ǵzr.|[---.kdd.dn]il.mt.rpi.w t'n.|[btlt.'nt.tšu.g]h.w tṣḥ.hwt. 17[2AQHT].6.51

ǵḥpn

'zn.bn.irbn.|bn.mglb.|bn.ntp.|'myn.bn ǵḥpn.|bn.kbln.|bn.bly.|bn.ṯ'y.|bn.nṣdn.|klby. 104[316].4

ǵẓy

hrm.|štt.ḫptr.l išt.|ḫbrṯ.l ẓr.pḥmm.|t'pp.ṯr.il.d pid.|tǵẓy.bny.bnwt.|b nši.'n h.w tphn.|hlk.b'l.aṯtrt.|k t'n.hlk.bt 4[51].2.11
.rbt.|aṯrt.ym.tǵẓyn.|qnyt.ilm.mgntm.|ṯr.il.d pid.hm.ǵẓtm.|bny.bnwt w t'n.|btlt.'nt.nmgn.|[-]m.rbt.aṯrt.ym.|[n 4[51].3.31
.|w [th]rn.w tldn mṯ.|al[iyn.b']l šlbšn.|i[---.---.--]l h.mǵẓ.|y[--.---.]l irt h.|n[--.---]. 5[67].5.24
.|ap.mṯn.rgmm.|argm k.šskn m'.|mgn.rbt.aṯrt ym.|mǵẓ.qnyt.ilm.|hyn.'ly.l mpḫm.|b d.ḫss.mṣbṭm.|yṣq.ksp.yšl 4[51].1.23

ǵẓy

[i]k.mgn.rbt.aṯrt. | [ym].mǵẓ.qnyt.ilm. | w tn.bt.l bʿl.km. | [i]lm.w ḥẓr.k bn. | [a]ṯrt.gm 8[51FRAG].2
r.mǵy.aliyn.bʿl. | mǵyt.btlt.ʿnt. | tmgnn.rbt[.a]ṯrt ym. | tǵẓyn.qnyt.ilm. | w tʿn.rbt.aṯrt ym. | ik.tmgnn.rbt. | aṯrt.ym.t 4[51].3.26
n.qnyt.ilm. | w tʿn.rbt.aṯrt ym. | ik.tmgnn.rbt. | aṯrt.ym.tǵẓyn. | qnyt.ilm.mgntm. | ṯr.il.d pid.hm.ǵẓtm. | bny.bnwt w 4[51].3.29
. | bny.bnwt w tʿn. | btlt.ʿnt.nmgn. | [-]m.rbt.aṯrt.ym. | [nǵ]ẓ.qnyt.ilm. | [---].nmgn.hwt. | [--].aliyn.bʿl. | [--.]rbt.aṯrt.y 4[51].3.35
--]u.l tštql. | [---].ṯry.ap.l tlḥm. | [l]ḥm.trmmt.l tšt. | yn.tǵẓyt.špš. | rpim.tḥtk. | špš.tḥtk.ilnym. | ʿd k.ilm.hn.mtm. | ʿd 6.6[62.2].44

ǵyr

tḥm.iwrdr. | l iwrpẖn. | bn y.aẖ y.rgm. | ilm.tǵr k. | tšlm k. | iky.lḥt. | spr.d likt. | ʿm.ṯryl. | mh y.rgmt. | w ht 138.4
tḥm[.t]lm[yn]. | l ṯryl.um y. | rgm. | ugrt.tǵr k. | ugrt.tǵr k. | tšlm k.um y. | tdʿ.ky.ʿrbt. | l pn.špš. | w pn.špš.nr. | b y. 1015.5

ǵyrm

lm.ḥkpt.l rḥq]. | [ilnym.ṯn.mṯpd]m.t[ḥt.ʿnt.arṣ.ṯlṯ.mtḥ.ǵyrm]. | [idk.]l ytn.pnm.ʿm.[i]l.mbk.[nhrm.qrb.apq.thmtm]. 2.3[129].3
.ilm.inbb. | l rḥq.ilnym.ṯn.mṯpdm. | tḥt.ʿnt.arṣ.ṯlṯ.mtḥ.ǵyrm. | idk.l ttn pnm.ʿm.bʿl. | mrym.ṣpn.b alp.šd.rbt.kmn. | h 3[ʿNT].4.80
.ḥkp[t.l rḥq.ilnym]. | ṯn.mṯpdm.tḥt.[ʿnt.arṣ.ṯlṯ.mtḥ]. | ǵyrm.idk.l yt[n.pnm.ʿm.lṭpn]. | il d pid.tk ẖrš[n.---.tk.ǵr.ks]. 1[ʿNT.IX].3.21

ǵyrn

bnš.kld. | kbln.ʿbdyrǵ.ilgt. | ǵyrn.ybnn qrwn. | ypltn.ʿbdnt. | klby.aḥrṯp. | ilyn.ʿlby.ṣdkn. | 1045.3

ǵl

mdb[r.---]. | tḥdṯn w hl[.---]. | w tglṯ thmt.ʿ[--.---]. | yṣi.ǵl h tḥm b[.---]. | mrḥ h l adrt[.---]. | ṯṯb ʿṯtrt b ǵl[.---]. | qrẓ tš 2001.1.6
phnn.w. | mndym. | bdnh. | l[q]ḥt. | [--]km.ʿm.mlk. | [b]ǵl hm.w.iblbl hm. | w.b.ṯb h.[---]. | spr ḥ[--.---]. | w.ʿm[.---]. | y 2129.10
ḥnn.l bn.adlḏn. | šd.bn.nṣdn.l bn.ʿmlbi. | šd.ṯpẖln.l bn.ǵl. | w dṯn.nḥl h.l bn.pl. | šd.krwn.l aẖn. | šd.ʿyy.l aẖn. | šd.brd 2089.9
rʿ.w.ṯmnym[.drt]. | w.ʿšrm.l.mit.dd.ḥp[r.]bnšm. | b.gt.ǵl.ʿšrm.l.mit.drʿ.w.tšʿm.drt. | [w].ṯmnym.l.mit.dd.ḥpr.bnšm. 1098.14
pr.ʿbdm. | mit[.d]rt.arbʿm.drt. | [---]m. | t[gm]r.akl.b.gt.ǵ[l]. | ṯlṯ.mat.ʿšrm[.---]. | ṯmnym.drt.a[--]. | drt.l.alpm[.---]. | šb 2013.15
t.tbʿln. | b.gt.ḥršm. | ṯn.ḥršm. | [-]nbkm. | ṯn.ḥršm. | b.gt.ǵl. | [-.]nǵr.mdrʿ. | [-].nǵr[.--]m. | [--.]psl.qšt. | [ṯl]ṯ.psl.ḥẓm. | [- 1024.3.15
---]. | yṣi.ǵl h tḥm b[.---]. | mrḥ h l adrt[.---]. | ṯṯb ʿṯtrt b ǵl[.---]. | qrẓ tšt.l šmal[.---]. | arbẖ.ʿn h tšu w[.---]. | aylt tǵpy ṯ 2001.1.8

ǵlil

gdm.b rumm. | adr.qrnt.b yʿlm.mtnm. | b ʿqbt.ṯr.adr.b ǵlil.qnm. | tn.l kṯr.w ẖss.ybʿl.qšt l ʿnt. | qṣʿt.l ybmt.limm.w tʿ 17[2AQHT].6.23

ǵldy

mšu. | ẖṯpy. | ǵldy. | iẖǵl. | aby. | abmn. | ynḥm. | npl. | ynḥm. | mtbʿl. | bn ǵlm 1065.3

ǵlwš

ẖrny.w.rʿ h. | klbr.w.rʿ h. | tškrǵ.w.rʿ h. | ǵlwš.w.rʿ h. | kdrš.w.rʿ h. | ṯrm[-].w[.rʿ h]. | [ʿ]ṯtr[-].w.[rʿ h]. | 2083.1.4

ǵly

.ʿl.il.hlm. | ilm.tph hm.tphn.mlak.ym.tʿdt.ṯpṭ[.nhr]. | t[ǵ]ly.hlm.rišt hm.l ẓr.brkt hm.w l kḥṯ. | zbl hm.b hm.ygʿr.b 2.1[137].23
išt hm.l ẓr.brkt hm.w l kḥṯ. | zbl hm.b hm.ygʿr.bʿl.lm.ǵltm.ilm.rišt. | km l ẓr brkt km.w ln.kḥṯ.zbl km.aḥd. | ilm.tʿn 2.1[137].24
t. | tǵll.b nr.d ʿl k.mḫṣ.aqht. | ǵzr.šrš k.b arṣ.al. | ypʿ.riš.ǵly.b d.nsʿ k. | ʿnt.brḥ.p ʿlm h. | ʿnt.p dr.dr.ʿdb.uẖry mṭ yd h. 19[1AQHT].3.160
mn. | ʿdy. | ʿnbr. | aẖrm. | bn.qrdy. | bn.šmʿn. | bn.ǵlmy. | ǵly. | bn.dnn. | bn.rmy. | dll. | mny. | krty. | bn.ʿbṣ. | bn.argb. | yd 2117.3.34
-]. | hlk.[---.b n]ši. | ʿn h.w tphn.[---]. | b grn.yẖrb[.---]. | yǵly.yḫsp.ib[.---]. | ʿl.bt.ab h.nšrm.trẖ[p]n. | ybṣr.ḥbl.diym. | t 19[1AQHT].1.31
al.tǵl[.---]. | prdmn.ʿbd.ali[yn]. | bʿl.sid.zbl.bʿl. | arṣ.qm.yṯʿr. | w y 3[ʿNT].1.1

ǵlyn

tn. | mẖtn. | [p]lsy. | bn.ḥrš. | [--.]kbd. | [---]. | y[---]. | bn.ǵlyn. | bdl.ar. | bn.šyn. | bn.ubrš. | bn.d[--]b. | abrpu. | bn.k[n]y. 1035.2.19

ǵlyt

| [--]an.w.aṯt h. | [--]y.w.aṯt h. | [--]r.w.aṯt h. | ʿbdyrẖ.ṯn ǵlyt h. | aršmg. | ršpy.w.aṯt h. | bn.glgl.uškny. | bn.ṯny.uškny. | 2068.10

ǵlkz

--]. | [ṯ]lrby.ʿšr.ṯn.kb[d.---]. | ẖmrm.ṯṯ.krm[m.---]. | krm.ǵlkz.b.p[--.---]. | krm.ilyy.b.m[--.---]. | kd.šbʿ.krmm.[---]. | ṯn. 1081.23
skn.ṯlṯm. | iytlm.ṯlṯm. | ẖyml.ṯlṯm. | ǵlkz.ṯlṯm. | mlknʿm.ʿšrm. | mrʿm.ʿšrm. | ʿmlbu.ʿšrm. | ʿmtḏl.ʿšr 1116.4

ǵll

.kbd h.b ṣḥq.ymlu. | lb h.b šmẖt.kbd.ʿnt. | tšyt.k brkm.tǵll b dm. | ḏmr.ḥlqm.b mmʿ.mhrm. | ʿd.tšbʿ.tmtẖṣ.b bt. | tẖṣ 3[ʿNT].2.27
mn.kp.mhr.ʿtkt. | rišt.l bmt h.šnst. | kpt.b ḥbš h.brkm.tǵl[l]. | b dm.ḏmr.ḥlqm.b mm[ʿ]. | mhrm.mṭm.tgrš. | šbm.b ks 3[ʿNT].2.13
d.ʿnt.tšyt.tḥt h.k]kdrt.riš. | [ʿl h.k irbym.kp.---.k br]k.tǵll.b dm. | [ḏmr.---.]td[-.]rǵb. | [----]k. | [----] h. 7.1[131].9
yd h. | ymǵ.l mrrt.tǵll.b nr. | yšu.g h.w yṣḥ.y l k.mrrt. | tǵll.b nr.d ʿl k.mḫṣ.aqht. | ǵzr.šrš k.b arṣ.al. | ypʿ.riš.ǵly.b d.n 19[1AQHT].3.158
.p ʿlm h.ʿnt.p dr[.dr]. | ʿdb.uẖry mṭ.yd h. | ymǵ.l mrrt.tǵll.b nr. | yšu.g h.w yṣḥ.y l k.mrrt. | tǵll.b nr.d ʿl k.mḫṣ.aqht 19[1AQHT].3.156
qʿl. | mlkm.hn.ym.yṣq.yn.ṯmk. | mrṯ.yn.srnm.yn.bld. | ǵll.yn.išryt.ʿnq.smd. | lbnn.ṯl mrṯ.yḥrṯ.il. | hn.ym.w ṯn.tlḥmn 22.2[124].19
[ẖ]d[.---]. | ẓr h.aḥḏ.qš[t.---]. | p ʿn.b ʿl.aḥḏ[.---]. | w šmt.ǵllm[.---]. | aḥḏ.aklm.k [---]. | npl.b mšmš[.---]. | anp n m yḥr[12[75].2.35

ǵlm

lnn.udr.ilqṣm. | yak.l kṯr.w ẖss. | w ṯb l mspr..k tlakn. | ǵlmm. | aẖr.mǵy.kṯr.w ẖss. | št.alp.qdm h.mra. | w tk.pn h.tʿd 4[51].5.105
yd. | [g]rgr h.bm.ymn. | [w]yqrb.trẓẓ h. | [---].mǵy h.w ǵlm. | [a]ẖt h.šib.yṣat.mrḥ h. | l tl.yṣb.pn h.ṯǵr. | yṣu.hlm.aẖ h 16.1[125].50
tʿdt.ṯpṭ.nhr]. | b ʿlṣ.ʿlṣm.npr.š[--.---]. | uṯ.ṯbr.ap hm.tbʿ.ǵlm[m.al.ṯṯb.idk.pnm]. | al.ttn.ʿm.pẖr.mʿd.t[k.ǵr.ll.l pʿn.il]. | 2.1[137].13
n.]brkm.ybrk. | [ʿbd h.]ybrk.il.krt. | [ṯʿ.ymr]m.nʿm[n.]ǵlm.il. | a[ṯt.tq]ḥ.y krt.aṯt. | tqḥ.bt k.ǵlmt.tšʿrb. | ḥqr k.tld.šbʿ. 15[128].2.20

|[---.]tb‘.l lṭpn.|[il.d]pid.l tbrk.|[krt.]ṯ‘.l tmr.n‘mn.|[ǵlm.]il.ks.yiḫd.|[il.b]yd.krpn.bm.|[ymn.]brkm.ybrk.|[‘bd 15[128].2.16
adm.w yqrb.|b šal.krt.m at.|krt.k ybky.|ydm‘.n‘mn.ǵlm.|il.mlk[.ṯ]r ab h.|yarš.hm.drk[t].|k ab.adm.|[-----]. 14[KRT].1.40
.amid.|[w y‘n].ṯr.ab h.il.|d[--].b bk.krt.|b dm‘.n‘mn.ǵlm.|il.trḥṣ.w tadm.|rḥṣ[.y]d k.amt.|uṣb[‘t k.]‘d[.ṯ]km.|‘rb 14[KRT].2.61
l.|mlk.tšan.|g hm.w tṣḥn.|ṯḥm.krt.ṯ[‘].|hwt.[n]‘mn.[ǵlm.il]. 14[KRT].6.306
yṣa.b špt h[.hwt h].|b nši ‘n h.w tphn.in.[---].|[-.]hlk.ǵlmm b dd y.yṣ[--].|[-.]yṣa.w l.yṣa.hlm.[ṯnm].|[q]dqd.ṯlṯ id. 19[1AQHT].2.77
b‘ bn[t.rḥ.gdm.w anhbm].|kla[t.ṯǵ]r[t.bht.‘nt.w tqry.ǵlmm.b št.ǵr].|ap ‘nt tm[ṯḫṣ.b ‘mq.ṯḫtṣb.bn.qrytm.tmḫṣ].|l 7.2[130].24
r.šb‘.bnt.rḥ.gdm.|w anhbm.klat.ṯǵrt.|bht.‘nt.w tqry.ǵlmm.|b št.ǵr.w hln.‘nt.tm|ṯḫṣ.b ‘mq.ṯḫtṣb.bn.|qrytm tmḫ 3[‘NT].2.4
].|k lli.[---].|kpr.[šb‘.bnt.rḥ.gdm.w anhbm].|w tqr[y.ǵlmm.b št.ǵr.---].|[‘]d tš[b‘.tmṯḫṣ.---].|klyn[.---].|špk.l[---]. 7.2[130].4
-]ndbym.|[‘]rmy.w snry.|[b]n.sdy.bn.ṯty.|bn.ḥyn.bn.ǵlm.|bn.yyn.w.bn.au[pš].|bn.kdrn.|‘rgzy.w.bn.‘dy.|bn.gm 131[309].24
[---.b‘l.b bht h].|[il.hd.b qr]b.hkl h.|w t‘nyn.ǵlm.b‘l.|in.b‘l.b bht ht.|il hd.b qrb.hkl h.|qšt hn.aḫd.b yd 10[76].2.3
[---]n.dd.|[---.]dd.|bn.arwdn.dd.|mnḫm.w.kbln.|bn.ǵlm.dd.|bn.tbšn.dd.|bn.ḫran.w[.---].|[-]n.y‘rtym.|gmm.w. 131[309].6
|lk.‘l.ilm.l ymru.|ilm.w nšm.d yšb|[‘].hmlt.arṣ.gm.l ǵ|[lm] h.b‘l k.yṣḥ.‘n.|[gpn].w ugr.b ǵlmt.|[‘mm.]ym.bn.ẓl 4[51].7.52
t.ilm.|w tn.bt.l b‘l.km.|[i]lm.w ḥẓr.k bn.|[a]ṯrt.gm.l ǵlm h.|b‘l.yṣḥ.‘n.gpn.|w ugr.bn.ǵlmt.|‘mm ym.bn.ẓlm[t].| 8[51FRAG].5
ṯrt.|k t‘n.ẓl.ksp.w n[-]t.|ḫrṣ.šmḫ.rbt.a[ṯrt].|ym.gm.l ǵlm h.k [tṣḥ].|‘n.mkṯr.ap.t[---].|dgy.rbt.aṯr[t.ym].|qḥ.rṯt.b 4[51].2.29
[---.--]mt.|[---.--]mr.limm.|[---.]bn.ilm.mt.|[--]u.šb‘t.ǵlm h.|[---].bn.ilm.mt.|p[-]n.aḫ y m.ytn.b‘l.|[s]pu y.bn m.u 6[49].6.8
‘l.yd.pdry.bt.ar.|ahbt.ṭly.bt.rb.dd.arṣy.|bt.y‘bdr.km ǵlmm.|w ‘rb n.l p‘n.‘nt.hbr.|w ql.tšṯḥwy.kbd hyt.|w rgm.l 3[‘NT].3.5
ṯlṯt.kṯrm.tmt.|mrb‘t.zblnm.|mḫmšt.yitsp.|ršp.nṯdṯt.ǵlm.|ym.mšb‘t hn.b šlḥ.|ttpl.y‘n.ḥtk h.|krt y‘n.ḥtk h.rš.|m 14[KRT].1.19
rb.|ḥqr k.tld.šb‘.bnm.l k.|w ṯmn.tṯtmnm.|l k.tld.yṣb.ǵlm.|ynq.ḥlb.a[ṯ]rt.|mṣṣ.ṯd.btlt.[‘nt].|mšnq.[---]. 15[128].2.25
y k.ap.anš.zbl.b‘[l].|[-.yuḫ]d.b yd.mšḫṭ.bm.ymn.mḫṣ.ǵlmm.yš[--].|[ymn h.‘n]t.tuḫd.šmal h.tuḫd.‘ṯtrt.ik.m[ḫṣt.ml 2.1[137].39
ilm.arṣ.w at.qḥ.|‘rpt k.rḥ k.mdl k.|mṭrt k.‘m k.šb‘t.|ǵlm k.ṯmn.ḫnzr k.|‘m k.pdry.bt.ar.|‘m k.ṭly.bt.rb.idk.|pn 5[67].5.9
.ṯn kndwm adrm.|w knd pnt.dq.|ṯn ḫpnm.ṯn pldm ǵlmm.|kpld.b[-.-]r[--].|w blḫ br[-]m p[-].|b[--.]l[-.]mat[.-]y. 140[98].4
.|d b ḥlm y.il.ytn.|b ḏrt y.ab.adm.|w ld.šph.l krt.|w ǵlm.l ‘bd.il.|krt.yḫṭ.w ḥlm.|‘bd.il.w hdrt.|yrtḥṣ.w yadm.|y 14[KRT].3.153
d b ḥlm y.il.ytn.|b ḏrt y.ab.adm.|w ld.šph.l krk|t.w ǵlm.l ‘bd.|il.ttb‘.mlakm.|l ytb.idk.pnm.|l ytn.‘mm.pbl.|ml 14[KRT].6.299
]š.trm[mn.hkl h.---.]bt.|[---.-]k.mnh[-.---.-]š bš[-.]t[-].ǵlm.l šdt[.-.]ymm.|[---.]b ym.ym.y[--].yš[ ]n.ap k.‘ṯtr.dm[.-- 2.3[129].11
h.d tqyn.hmlt.tn.b‘l.[w ‘nn h].|bn.dgn.art m.pd h.tb‘.ǵlmm.l ttb.[idk.pnm].|l ytn.tk.ǵr.ll.‘m.phr.m‘d.ap.ilm.l lḥ[2.1[137].19
nšt.‘rš.zbln.|rd.l mlk.amlk.|l drkt.k aṯb.an.|ytb‘.yṣb ǵlm.‘l.|ab h.y‘rb.yšu g h.|w yṣḥ.šm‘ m‘.l krt.|ṯ‘.ištm‘.w tqǵ 16.6[127].39
ḫt.l kḫṯ.drkt h.|mn m.ib.yp‘.l b‘l.ṣrt.l rkb.‘rpt.|[-]‘n.ǵlmm.y‘nyn.l ib.yp‘.|l b‘l.ṣrt.l rkb.‘rpt.|ṯḥm.aliyn.b‘l.hwt.a 3[‘NT].4.49
sgrt.g[-].[-]ẓ[.---] h[.---].|‘n.ṯk[.---].|‘ln.ṯ[--.---].|l p‘n.ǵl[m]m[.---].|mid.an[--.]ṣn[--].|nrt.ilm.špš[.ṣḥrr]t.|la.šmm. 3[‘NT.VI].5.23
[.---].|rmm.ḫnpm.mḫl[.---].|mlk.nhr.ibr[.---].|zbl b‘l.ǵlm.[---].|ṣǵr hd w r[---.---].|w l nhr nd[-.---].|[---.--]l. 9[33].2.10

ǵlmy

|yd‘.|šmn.|‘dy.|‘nbr.|aḫrm.|bn.qrdy.|bn.šm‘n.|bn.ǵlmy.|ǵly.|bn.dnn.|bn.rmy.|dll.|mny.|krty.|bn.‘bṣ.|bn.ar 2117.3.33

ǵlmn

nǵr krm.‘bdadt.b‘ln.yp‘mlk.|ṯǵrm.mnḥm.klyn.‘dršp.ǵlmn.|[a]bǵl.ṣsn.ǵrn.|šib.mqdšt.‘b[dml]k.ṯṯph.mrṯn.|ḫdǵl 2011.13
tgdn.ugrty.|tgyn.arty.|bn.nryn.arty.|bn.ršp.ary.|bn.ǵlmn ary.|bn.ḥṣbn ary.|bn.šdy ary.|bn.ktkt.m‘qby.|bn.[--- 87[64].13
bn.ǵlmn.ary.|[bn].šdy.|[bn].gmḥ.|[---]ty.|[b]n.ypy.gb‘ly.|b[n] 99[327].1.1
n.|ḥyn.|bn.armg[-].|b‘lmṯpṭ.|[bn].ayḫ.|[---]rn.|ill.|ǵlmn.|bn.ytrm.|bn.ḫgbt.|mtn.|mḫtn.|[p]lsy.|bn.ḥrš.|[--.] 1035.2.9
ln.|bn.liy.|bn.nqtn.|bn abrḫṭ.|bn.grdy.|bn.ṣlpn.|bn ǵlmn.|bn sgld. 1064.B.1
dy.|iḫǵl.|aby.|abmn.|ynḥm.|npl.|ynḥm.|mtb‘l.|bn ǵlmn.|bn sgld. 1065.B.1
.ilš.|bn.tnabn.|bn.ḥṣn.|ṣprn.|bn.ašbḥ.|bn.qtnn.|bn.ǵlmn.|[bn].ṣwy.|[bn].ḫnq[n].|[-----].|[-----].|[-----].|[-----].| 1046.1.23
|[b.]gt.ḥrtm.ḫm[š.---].|[n]it.krk.m‘ṣ[d.---].|b.ḫrbǵlm.ǵlm[n].|w.trhy.aṯt h.|w.mlky.b[n] h.|ily.mrily.tdgr. 2048.19

ǵlmt

‘.|i.iṯt.aṯrt.ṣrm.|w ilt.ṣdynm.|hm.ḥry.bt y.|iqḥ.aš‘rb.ǵlmt.|ḥẓr y.ṯn h.wspm.|atn.w ṯlṯ h.ḫrṣm.|ylk ym.w ṯn.|ṯlṯ. 14[KRT].4.204
yḫ[bq] [-].|tld bt.[--]t.ḫ[--.l k]|ṯrt.l bnt.hll[.snnt].|hl ǵlmt tld b[n.--]n.|‘n ha l yd h.tzd[.--].|pt l bšr h.dm a[--.--] 24[77].7
nhr.]mlkt.[--]pm.l mlkt.wn.in.aṯt.|[l]k.k[m.ilm].|[w ǵlmt.k bn.qdš.]w y[--.]zbl.ym.y‘[--.]ṯpṭ.nhr.|[-------.]yšlḥn.w 2.3[129].23
ẓr.k bn.|[a]ṯrt.gm.l ǵlm h.|b‘l.yṣḥ.‘n.gpn.|w ugr.bn.ǵlmt.|‘mm ym.bn.ẓlm[t].|rmt.pr‘t.ibr[.mnt].|ṣḥrrm.ḥbl[.-- 8[51FRAG].7
[‘].hmlt.arṣ.gm.l ǵ|[lm] h.b‘l k.yṣḥ.‘n.|[gpn].w ugr.b ǵlmt.|[‘mm.]ym.bn.ẓlmt.r|[mt.pr‘]t.ibr.mnt.|[ṣḥrrm.ḥbl.‘] 4[51].7.54
[ṯ‘.ymr]m.n‘m[n.]ǵlm.il.|a[ṯt.tq]ḥ.y krt.aṯt.|tqḥ.bt k.ǵlmt.tš‘rb.|ḥqr k.tld.šb‘.bnm.l k.|w ṯmn.tṯtmnm.|l k.tld.yṣ 15[128].2.22
.|kdm.yn.prs.qmḥ.[---].|mdbḥt.bt.ilt.‘ṣr[m.l ṣpn.š].|l ǵlmt.š.w l [---.l yrḫ].|gd[lt].l nkl[.gdlt.l b‘lt.bhtm].|‘š[rm.]l 35[3].25
yn].|prs.qmḥ.m‘[--.---].|mdbḥt.bt.i[lt.‘ṣrm.l].|ṣpn š.l ǵlm[t.š.w l.---].|l yrḫ.gdlt.l [nkl.gdlt.l b‘]|[lt].bht[m].[‘]ṣrm APP.II[173].27
p]š pgr.|[g]dlt iltm ḫnqtm.d[q]tm.|[yr]ḫ.kty gdlt.w l ǵlmt š.|[w]pamt ṯlṯm.w yrdt.[m]dbḥt.|gdlt.l b‘lt bhtm.‘ṣr 34[1].19

ǵlp

.l ttn.|l y.w b mt[.-]ḫ.mṣṣ[-]t[.--].|pr‘.qẓ.y[bl].šblt.|b ǵlp h.apnk.dnil.|[m]t.rpi.ap[h]n.ǵzr.|[mt.hrn]my.ytšu.|[yṯ 19[1AQHT].1.19
‘l.umt[k.--].|d ttql.b ym.trth[ṣ.--].|[----.a]dm.tium.b ǵlp y[m.--].|d alp šd.ẓu h.b ym.t[---].|tlbš.npṣ.ǵzr.tšt.ḫ[---. 19[1AQHT].4.204

ǵlpṯr

rty[.---].|ṯlṯ.krm.ubdym.l mlkt.b.‘nmky[.---].|mgdly.ǵlpṯr.ṯn.krmm.w.ṯlṯ.ub[dym.---].|qmnz.ṯṯ.krm.ykn‘m.ṯmn. 1081.10

ǵlṣ

.mṣrn m[sg].|yky msg.|ynḥm.msg.|bn.ugr.msg.|bn.ǵlṣ msg.|arb‘ l ṯkṣ[-].|nn.arspy.ms[g].|[---.ms]g.|bn.[gr]gs. 133[-].1.9

ǵlṯ

.ištm'.w tqǵ udn.|k ǵz.ǵzm.tdbr.|w ǵrm.ṯṯwy.šqlt.|b ǵlṯ.yd k.l tdn.|dn.almnt.l ṯṯpṭ.|ṯpṭ qṣr.npš.l tdy.|ṯšm.'l.dl.l 16.6[127].45
].|w tqǵ[.udn.k ǵz.ǵzm].|tdbr.w[ǵ]rm[.ṯṯwy].|šqlt.b ǵlṯ.yd k.|l tdn.dn.almnt.|l ṯṯpṭ.ṯpṭ.qṣr.npš.|km.aḫt.'rš.md 16.6[127].32
rn[m].|dt.'l h.riš h.b glṯ.b šm[m].|[---.i]l.ṯr.iṯ.p h.k ṯt.ǵlṯ[.--].|[---.--] k yn.ddm.l b[--.---].|[---.-]yt š[--.---].|[---.]hl[UG5.3.1.8

ǵltn

.|tdn.ṣr[--.--]t.'zn.mtn.n[bd]g.|ḥrš qṯn[.---.]dqn.b'ln.|ǵltn.'bd.[---].|nsk.ḥḏm.klyn[.ṣd]qn.'bdilt.b'l.|annmn.'dy.kl 2011.24

ǵma

y]m.|ik.atwt.qnyt.i[lm].|rǵb.rǵbt.w tǵt[--].|hm.ǵmu.ǵmit.w 's[--].|lḥm.hm.štym.lḥ[m].|b ṯlḥnt.lḥm št.|b krpnm 4[51].4.34
aṯr[t.y]m.|ik.atwt.qnyt.i[lm].|rǵb.rǵbt.w tǵt[--].|hm.ǵmu.ǵmit.w 's[--].|lḥm.hm.štym.lḥ[m].|b ṯlḥnt.lḥm št.|b k 4[51].4.34

ǵmr

.zry.q[š]t.w.ql'.|bn.tlmyn.ṯt.qštm.w.ql'.|bn.ysd.qšt.|[ǵ]mrm.|ilgn.qšt.|abršp.qšt.|ssg.qšt.|ynḥm.qšt.|pprn.qšt.| 105[86].1
lhd.qšt.|'dn.qšt.w.ql'.|ilmhr.qšt.w.ql'.|bn.gmrt.qšt.|ǵmrm.|bn.qṯn.qšt.w.ql'.|mrṯd.qšt.|ssw.qšt.|knn.qšt.|bn.ṯll 119[321].1.11
.w.ql['].|bn.pǵyn.qšt.w[.q]l'.|bn.bdn.qšt.|bn.pls.qšt.|ǵmrm.|[-]lhd.ṯt.qštm.w.ṯn.ql'm.|ulšn.ṯt.qšm.w.ql'.|bn.ml'n 119[321].3.32

ǵmšd

ṯmq.|bn.agmn.|bn.uṣb.|bn.yzg.|bn.anntn.|bn.kwn.|ǵmšd.|bn.'bdḥy.|bn.ubyn.|slpd.|bn.atnb.|bn.ktmn.|bn.pit 115[301].4.9

ǵn

rkby.|šḥq.|ǵn.|ṣ'.|mld.|amḏy.|ḫlb'prm.|ḫpty.|[ḫr]ṣb'.|[m']rb. 2077.3

ǵnb

t.|rpi.yṣly.'rpt.b |ḥm.un.yr.'rpt.|tmṭr.b qẓ.ṭl.yṭll.|l ǵnbm.šb'.šnt.|yṣr k.b'l.ṯmn.rkb.|'rpt.bl.ṭl.bl rbb.|bl.šr'.thm 19[1AQHT].1.42
.|ynqm.b ap zd.aṯrt.[---].|špš.mṣprt dlt hm[.---].|w ǵnbm.šlm.'rbm.ṯn[nm].|hlkm.b dbḥ n'mt.|šd[.i]lm.šd.aṯrt. 23[52].26

ǵnbn

[-----].|ǵnbn[.---].|pdn[.---].|ṯr[--.---].|nn[-.---].|au[pš.---].|i[---.---] 2161.2

ǵnṯ

---.-]rm.aklt.'gl.'l.mšt.|[---.--]r.špr.w yšt.il.|[---.--]n.il ǵnṯ.'gl il.|[---.--]d.il.šd yṣd mlk.|[---].yšt.il h.|[---.]iṯm h.|[- UG5.2.1.11

ǵs

bn.ǵs.ḥrš.š'ty.|'dy.bn.sl'y.gbly.|yrm.b'l.bn.kky. 2121.1

ǵsdb

l yblt.ḫbṯm.|ap ksp hm.|l yblt.|w ht.luk 'm ml[kt].|tǵsdb.šmlšn.|w tb' ank.|'m mlakt h šm' h.|w b.'ly skn.yd' 1021.5

ǵpy

ǵl[.---].|qrẓ tšt.l šmal[.---].|arbḫ.'n h tšu w[.---].|aylt tǵpy ṯr.'n[.---].|b[b]r.mrḥ h.ti[ḫd.b yd h].|š[g]r h bm ymn. 2001.1.11

ǵprt

š.al[l.---].|[---].ṯṯ.lbš[.---].|[---.]kbd.ṯṯ.i[qnu.---].|[---.]ǵprt.'š[r.---].|[---.p]ttm.l.ip[--.---].|[---.]ksl.ṯlṯ.m[at.---].|[---] 1106.24
.|[---].all.šmt.|[---].all.iqni.arb'm.kbl.|[---].iqni.'šrm.ǵprt.|[---.š]pšg.iqni.mit.pṯtm.|[---].mitm.kslm.|[---].pwt.ṯlṯ. 1106.7

ǵṣ

nt š.ršp š.|šlmm.|w šnpt.il š.|l 'nt.ḥl š.ṯn šm.|l gṯrm.ǵṣ b šmal.|d alpm.w alp w š.|šrp.w šlmm kmm.|l b'l.ṣpn b UG5.13.26

ǵṣr

idk.al.ttn.pnm.|'m.ǵr.trǵzz.|'m.ǵr.ṯrmg.|'m.tlm.ǵṣr.arṣ.|ša.ǵr.'l.ydm.|ḫlb.l ẓr.rḥtm.|w rd.bt ḫpṯt.|arṣ.tspr. 4[51].8.4

ǵr

m[-.---].|b ym.dbḥ.ṯp[-].|aḥt.l mzy.bn[--].|aḥt.l mkt.ǵr.|aḥt.l 'ṯtrt.|arb'.'ṣrm.|gt.ṯrmn.|aḥt.slḫu. 39[19].15
št.|[---].amr k.|[---].k.ybt.mlk.|[---].w.ap.ank.|[---].l.ǵr.amn.|[---.-]ktt.hn.ib.|[---.]mlk.|[---.]adt y.td'.|w.ap.mlk. 1012.16
gdm.w anhbm].|kla[t.ṯǵ]r[t.bht.'nt.w tqry.ǵlmm.b št.ǵr].|ap 'nt tm[ṯḫṣ.b 'mq.tḫtṣb.bn.qrytm.tmḫṣ].|lim ḫ[p.ym. 7.2[130].24
m[r]m.w[.---.]bnšm.|ilštm'.arb'.ḥm[r]m.ḫmš.bnšm.|ǵr.|ary.ḥmr w.bnš.|qmy.ḥmr.w.bnš.|ṯbil.|'nmky.ḥmr.w.b 2040.22
l b'l.|ǵr.b ab.td[.ps]ltm[.b y'r].|thdy.lḥm.w dqn[.ṯṯlṯ].|qn.ḏr' h.t 6[62].1.2
ṣq.'mr.|un.l riš h.'pr.plṯt.|l qdqd h.lpš.yks.|mizrtm.ǵr.b abn.|ydy.psltm.b y'r.|yhdy.lḥm.w dqn.|yṯlṯ.qn.ḏr' h.y 5[67].6.17
arḫ.td.rgm.b ǵr.|b p y.t'lgt.b lšn[y].|ǵr[.---]b.b pš y.t[--].|hwt.b'l.iš[--].| 2124.1
l.dnil.l hkl h.'rb.b|kyt.b hkl h.mšspdt.b ḥẓr h.|pẓǵm.ǵr.ybk.l aqht.|ǵzr.ydm'.l kdd.dnil.|mt.rpi.l ymm.l yrḫm.|l 19[1AQHT].4.173
tm.|tmtn.u ḫšt k.l ntn.|'tq.b d.aṯt.ab ṣrry.|tbky k.ab.ǵr.b'l.|ṣpn.ḥlm.qdš.|any.ḥlm.adr.ḥl.|rḥb.mknpt.ap.|[k]rt. 16.1[125].6
.aṯt ab.ṣrry.|u ilm.tmtn.šph.|[l]ṭpn.l yḥ.t[b]ky k.|ab.ǵr.b'l.ṣ[p]n.ḥlm.|qdš.nny.ḥ[l]m.adr.|ḥl.rḥb.mk[npt].|ap.kr 16.2[125].107
|'l.l ṯkm.bnw n.|l nḫnpt.mšpy.|ṯlṯ.kmm.ṯrr y.|[---.]l ǵr.gm.ṣḥ.|[---.]r[-]m. 16[126].4.17
b'l.yṯb.k ṯbt.ǵr.hd.r['y].|k mdb.b tk.ǵr h.il ṣpn.b [tk].|ǵr.tliyt.šb't.brqm.[---].|ṯmnt.iṣr r't.'ṣ brq UG5.3.1.2
b'l.yṯb.k ṯbt.ǵr.hd.r['y].|k mdb.b tk.ǵr h.il ṣpn.b [tk].|ǵr.tliyt.šb't.brqm. UG5.3.1.1
.gdm.|w anhbm.klat.ṯǵrt.|bht.'nt.w tqry.ǵlmm.|b št.ǵr.w hln.'nt.tm|tḫṣ.b 'mq.tḫtṣb.bn.|qrytm tmḫṣ.lim.ḫp y[3['NT].2.5
dm ym.bmt.[nhr].|tṯṯn.ib.b'l.tiḫd.|y'rm.šnu.hd.gpt.|ǵr.w y'n.aliyn.|b'l.ib.hdt.lm.tḫš.|lm.tḫš.nṯq.dmrn.|'n.b'l.q 4[51].7.37

.w yṣḥ.t[bʻ.---]. | bkyt.b hk[l]y.mšspdt. | b ḥẓr y pẓǵm.ǵr.w yq. | dbḥ.ilm.yšʻly.dǵṯ h. | b šmym.dǵṯ hrnmy[.d k] | bkb 19[1AQHT].4.184
b[ʻl.y]tn. | yṯny.bʻl.ṣ[---.-]pt h. | ql h.q[dš.ṭb]r.arṣ. | [---.]ǵrm[.t]ḫšn. | rḥq[.---.tdʻ]. | qdm ym.bmt.[nhr]. | ṭṭṯn.ib.bʻl.tiḫ 4[51].7.32
l tdʻ.nšm.w l tbn. | hmlt.arṣ.at m.w ank. | ibǵy h.b tk.ǵr y.il.ṣpn. | b qdš.b ǵr.nḥlt y. | b nʻm.b gbʻ.tliyt. | hlm.ʻnt.tph 3[ʻNT].3.26
bm.abn.brq]. | d l t[dʻ.šmm.at m.w ank]. | ibǵ[y h.b tk.ǵ]r y.il.ṣpn. | b q[dš.b ǵr.nḥ]lt y. | w t[ʻn].btlt.[ʻ]nt.ṯṯb. | [ybmt 3[ʻNT].4.63
-.]a[--.---]. | [--.-]bt.np[-.---]. | [-] l šd.ql.[---.---].aṯr. | [--.]ǵrm.y[--.---.ḫ]rn. | [-]rk.ḫ[--.---.-]lk. | [-]sr.n[--.---.]ḫrn. | [--]p. UG5.8.4
.ab h]. | tʻrb.ḥ[--]. | b ṯtm.t[---]. | šknt.[---]. | bkym[.---]. | ǵr.y[----]. | ydm.[---]. | apn.[---]. | [--.]b[.---]. 16.2[125].117
ri[š.]l mhr k. | w ʻp.l dr[ʻ].nšr k. | w rbṣ.l ǵr k.inbb. | kt ǵr k.ank.ydʻt. | [-]n.atn.at.mṯb k[.---]. | [š]mm.rm.lk.prẓ kt. | [13[6].10
-].l ḥbš k. | ʻtk.ri[š.]l mhr k. | w ʻp.l dr[ʻ].nšr k. | w rbṣ.l ǵr k.inbb. | kt ǵr k.ank.ydʻt. | [-]n.atn.at.mṯb k[.---]. | [š]mm.r 13[6].9
bʻl. | [---.--]k.mdd il. | y[m.---.]l ṯr.qdqd h. | il[.--.]rḥq.b ǵr. | km.y[--.]ilm.b ṣpn. | ʻdr.l[ʻr].ʻrm. | ṯb.l pd[r.]pdrm. | ṯṯ.l ṯ 4[51].7.5
. | ʻm k.pdry.bt.ar. | ʻm k.ṭṭly.bt.rb.idk. | pn k.al ttn.tk.ǵr. | knkny.ša.ǵr.ʻl ydm. | ḫlb.l ẓr.rḥtm w rd. | bt ḫpṯt.arṣ.tspr 5[67].5.12
ǵyrm.idk.l yt[n.pnm.ʻm.lṭpn]. | il d pid.tk ḫrš[n.---.tk.ǵr.ks]. | ygly ḏd.i[l.w ybu.qrš.mlk]. | ab.šnm.l [pʻn.il.yhbr.w 1[ʻNT.IX].3.22
y.pʻn k.tlsmn]. | ʻm y twtḥ.i[šd k.tk.ḫršn.-------------]. | ǵr.ks.dm.r[gm.iṯ.l y.w argm k]. | hwt.w aṯny k[.rgm.ʻṣ.w lḫš 1[ʻNT.IX].3.12
w ʻn.bn.ilm.mt.mh. | taršn.l btlt.ʻnt. | an.itlk.w aṣd.kl. | ǵr.l kbd.arṣ.kl.gbʻ. | l kbd.šdm.npš.ḫsrt. | bn.nšm.npš.hmlt. | 6[49].2.16
. | dgn.my.hmlt.aṯr. | bʻl.ard.b arṣ.ap. | ʻnt.ttlk.w tṣd.kl.ǵr. | l kbd.arṣ.kl.gbʻ. | l [k]bd.šdm.tmǵ.l nʻm[y]. | [arṣ.]dbr.ys 5[67].6.26
hm.tbʻ.ǵlm[m.al.ṯṯb.idk.pnm]. | al.ttn.ʻm.pḫr.mʻd.t[k.ǵr.ll.l pʻn.il]. | al.tpl.al.tšthwy.pḫr [mʻd.qmm.a--.am] | r ṯny. 2.1[137].14
bn.dgn.arṯ m.pḏ h.tbʻ.ǵlmm.l ṯṯb.[idk.pnm]. | l ytn.tk.ǵr.ll.ʻm.phr.mʻd.ap.ilm.l lḥ[m]. | yṯb.bn qdš.l ṯrm.bʻl.qm.ʻl.il 2.1[137].20
ẓr. | km.ary k.ṣḥ.ḫrn. | b bht k.ʻḏbt.b qrb. | hkl k.tbl k.ǵrm. | mid.ksp.gbʻm.mḥmd.. | ḫrṣ.w bn.bht.ksp. | w ḫrṣ.bht.ṯ 4[51].5.93
.l aliyn bʻl. | ṣḥ.ḫrn.b bhm k. | ʻḏbt.b qrb.hkl k. | tbl k.ǵrm.mid.ksp. | gbʻm.mḥmd.ḫrṣ. | ybl k.udr.ilqṣm. | w bn.bht. 4[51].5.77
ḫ.aliyn. | bʻl.ṣḥ.ḫrn.b bht h. | ʻḏbt.b qrb hkl h. | yblnn ǵrm.mid.ksp. | gbʻm lḥmd.ḫrṣ. | yblnn.udr.ilqṣm. | yak.l kṯr. 4[51].5.100
.]abnm.upqt. | [---.]l w ǵr mtn y. | [---.]rq.gb. | [---.--]kl.tǵr.mtn h. | [---.--]b.w ym ymm. | [yʻtqn.---].ymǵy.npš. | [---.-- 1[ʻNT.X].5.14
ydʻt. | [---.t]asrn. | [---.]trks. | [---.]abnm.upqt. | [---.]l w ǵr mtn y. | [---.]rq.gb. | [---.--]kl.tǵr.mtn h. | [---.--]b.w ym ym 1[ʻNT.X].5.12
hmlt.arṣ.at m.w ank. | ibǵy h.b tk.ǵr y.il.ṣpn. | b qdš.b ǵr.nḥlt y. | b nʻm.b gbʻ.tliyt. | hlm.ʻnt.tph.ilm.b h.pʻnm. | ṭṭṭ.b 3[ʻNT].3.27
.šmm.at m.w ank]. | ibǵ[y h.b tk.ǵ]r y.il.ṣpn. | b q[dš.b ǵr.nḥ]lt y. | w t[ʻn].btlt.[ʻ]nt.ṯṯb. | [ybmt.]limm.[a]n.aqry. | [b 3[ʻNT].4.64
n.bṯn[-.] | y[--.]šr h.w šḫp h. | [--.]šḫp.ṣǵrt h. | yrk.tʻl.b ǵr. | mslmt.b ǵr.tliyt. | w tʻl.bkm.b arr. | bm.arr.w b ṣpn. | b nʻ 10[76].3.28
t.ar. | ʻm k.ṭṭly.bt.rb.idk. | pn k.al ttn.tk.ǵr. | knkny.ša.ǵr.ʻl ydm. | ḫlb.l ẓr.rḥtm w rd. | bt ḫpṯt.arṣ.tspr b y | rdm.arṣ. 5[67].5.13
tn.pnm. | ʻm.ǵr.trǵzz. | ʻm.ǵr.ṯrmg. | ʻm.tlm.ǵṣr.arṣ. | ša.ǵr.ʻl.ydm. | ḫlb.l ẓr.rḥtm. | w rd.bt ḫpṯt. | arṣ.tspr.b y | rdm.ar 4[51].8.5
---]. | arṣ.w šmm.š.kṯr[t] š.yrḫ[.---]. | ṣpn.š.kṯr.š.pdry.š.ǵrm.š[.---]. | aṯrt.š.ʻnt.š.špš.š.aršy.š.ʻṯtrt.š. | ušḫry.š.il.tʻḏr.bʻl. UG5.9.1.6
dʻ.l bn.l pq ḥmt. | [---.--]n h.ḥmt.w tʻbtn h.abd y. | [---.ǵ]r.šrǵzz.ybky.km.nʻr. | [w ydmʻ.k]m.ṣǵr.špš.b šmm.tqru. | [- UG5.8.37
-.]šr h.w šḫp h. | [--.]šḫp.ṣǵrt h. | yrk.tʻl.b ǵr. | mslmt.b ǵr.tliyt. | w tʻl.bkm.b arr. | bm.arr.w b ṣpn. | b nʻm.b ǵr.t[l]iyt 10[76].3.29
.b ǵr.tliyt. | w tʻl.bkm.b arr. | bm.arr.w b ṣpn. | b nʻm.b ǵr.t[l]iyt. | ql.l bʻl.ttnn. | bšrt.il.bš[r.bʻ]l. | w bšr.ḥtk.dgn. | k.ib 10[76].3.32
ʻl.yṯb.k ṯbt.ǵr.hd.r[ʻy]. | k mdb.b tk.ǵr h.il ṣpn.b [tk]. | ǵr.tliyt.šbʻt.brqm.[---]. | ṯmnt.iṣr rʻt.ʻṣ brq y. | riš h.tply.ṭly.b UG5.3.1.3
idk.al.ttn.pnm. | ʻm.ǵr.trǵzz. | ʻm.ǵr.ṯrmg. | ʻm.tlm.ǵṣr.arṣ. | ša.ǵr.ʻl.ydm. | ḫlb.l ẓr. 4[51].8.2
[bym]. | tšʻ.ʻ[šr.bnš]. | ǵr.ṯ[--.---]. | ṣbu.any[t]. | bn.kṯan. | ǵr.tšʻ[.ʻšr.b]nš. | ṣbu.any[t]. | bn abdḫ[r]. | pdym. | ḫmš.bnšm. | 79[83].9
| l k[rt.adn k.]ištm[ʻ]. | w tqǵ[.udn.k ǵz.ǵzm]. | tdbr.w[ǵ]rm[.ṯṯwy]. | šqlt.b ǵlt.yd k. | l tdn.dn.almnt. | l ṯpṭ.ṯpṭ.qṣr.n 16.6[127].31
ḥ.šmʻ mʻ.l krt. | ṯʻ.ištmʻ.w tqǵ udn. | k ǵz.ǵzm.tdbr. | w ǵrm.ṯṯwy.šqlt. | b ǵlt.yd k.l tdn. | dn.almnt.l ṯpṭ. | ṯpṭ qṣr.npš 16.6[127].44
y. | [--]t.bʻl.ḥẓ.ršp.b[n].km.yr.klyt h.w lb h. | [ṯ]n.p k.b ǵr.ṯn.p k.b ḫlb.k tgwln.šnt k. | [--.]w špt k.l tššy.hm.tqrm.l 1001.1.4
idk.al.ttn.pnm. | ʻm.ǵr.trǵzz. | ʻm.ǵr.ṯrmg. | ʻm.tlm.ǵṣr.arṣ. | ša.ǵr.ʻl.ydm. | ḫlb.l ẓr.rḥtm. | w rd. 4[51].8.3
ṣb[u.anyt]. | ʻdn. | ṭbq[ym]. | mʻq[bym]. | tšʻ.ʻ[šr.bnš]. | ǵr.ṯ[--.---]. | ṣbu.any[t]. | bn.kṯan. | ǵr.tšʻ[.ʻšr.b]nš. | ṣbu.any[t]. 79[83].6
a.u[--.--]. | blt.p btlt.ʻn[t]. | w p.nʻmt.aḫt[.bʻl]. | yʻl.bʻl.b ǵ[r.---]. | w bn.dgn.b š[---]. | bʻl.yṯb.l ks[i.mlk h]. | bn.dgn.l kḥ 10[76].3.12
]. | kpr.[šbʻ.bnt.rḥ.gdm.w anhbm]. | w tqr[y.ǵlmm.b št.ǵr.---]. | [ʻ]d tš[bʻ.tmtḫṣ.---]. | klyn[.---]. | špk.l[---]. | trḥṣ.yd[7.2[130].4
arḫ.td.rgm.b ǵr. | b p y.tʻlgt.b lšn[y]. | ǵr[.---]b.b pš y.t[--]. | hwt.bʻl.iš[--]. | šmʻ l y.ypš.[---]. | ḥkr[.--- 2124.3
hzp. | šql. | mʻrḫ[-]. | sl[ḫ]. | snr. | ʻrgz. | yknʻm. | ʻnmky. | ǵr. 2074.39

ǵrgn

ny. | ytršp. | bn.szn. | bn.kdgdl. | bn.glʻd. | bn.ktln. | [bn].ǵrgn. | bn.pb[-]. | bn.[---]. | bn.[---]. | bn.[---]. | bn.[---]. | bn.[---]. 115[301].1.16
lby. | [bn.]bʻly. | [mḏ]rǵlm. | [bn.]kdgdl. | [b]n.qṭn. | [b]n.ǵrgn. | [b]n.tgḏn. | bn.ḫdyn. | bn.sgr. | bn.aǵltn. | bn.ktln. | bn.ʻ 104[316].9
bn.[---]. | w.nḥ[l h]. | bn.ẓr[-]. | mru.skn. | bn.bddn. | bn.ǵrgn. | bn.tgtn. | bn.ḥrẓn. | bn.qdšt. | bn.nṯǵ[-]. | bn.gr[--]. | bn.[113[400].5.8

ǵrmn

.ṣat.š[p]š. | ṯḥt h.k kdrt.ri[š]. | ʻl h.k irbym.kp.k.qṣm. | ǵrmn.kp.mhr.ʻtkt. | rišt.l bmt h.šnst. | kpt.b ḥbš h.brkm.tǵl[l 3[ʻNT].2.11

ǵrn

n.ilštmʻy. | bn.abdʻn.ilštmʻy. | bn.ʻn.rqdy. | bn.gʻyn. | bn.ǵrn. | bn.agynt. | bn.abdḫr.snry. | dqn.šlmn. | prdn.ndb[--]. | [-] 87[64].34
ṯlṯ.kbd. | [---].alpm.ḥmš.mat. | šbʻm[.t]šʻ.kbd. | tgmr.uz.ǵrn.arbʻ.mat. | tgmr.uz.aḫmn.arbʻ.mat. | arbʻm.kbd. | ṯlṯ.alp.ṣ 1129.5
ʻln.ypʻmlk. | ṯǵrm.mnḥm.klyn.ʻdršp.ǵlmn. | [a]bǵl.ṣṣn.ǵrn. | šib.mqdšt.ʻb[dml]k.ṯṯpḥ.mrṭn. | ḫḏǵlm.i[---]n.pbn.nḏbn 2011.14
bn.dmtn.[---]. | [b]n.gʻyn.ḫr[-]. | lbnym. | grgš.[---]. | bn.ǵrn.[---]. | bn.agyn[.---]. | iyṯ[-.---]. 93[328].15

ǵrpl

. | [ṯm.dl.]isp.ḥ[mt.---.-]hm.yasp.ḥmt. | [---.š]pš.l [hrm.ǵrpl].ʻl.arṣ.l an. | [ḥ]mt.i[l.w] ḥrn.yisp.ḥmt. | [bʻl.w]dgn[.yi]s UG5.8.12
ḫss.y[i]sp.ḥmt.šḥr.w šlm. | [yis]p.ḥmt.isp.[šp]š l hrm.ǵrpl.ʻl arṣ. | [l a]n ḥmt.l p[.n]ṯk.abd.l p.akl ṯm.dl. | [---.q]l.bl.t UG5.8.19
.---.šp]š.l hrm. | [ǵrpl.]ʻl.ar[ṣ.---.ḥ]mt. | [---.šp]š.l [hrm.ǵ]rpl.ʻl.arṣ. | [---.]ḥmt.l p[.nṯ]k.abd.l p.ak[l]. | [ṯm.dl.]isp.ḥ[m UG5.8.9
-]lk. | [-]sr.n[--.---.]ḫrn. | [--]p.ḫp h.ḫ[--.---.šp]š.l hrm. | [ǵrpl.]ʻl.ar[ṣ.---.ḥ]mt. | [---.šp]š.l [hrm.ǵ]rpl.ʻl.arṣ. | [---.]ḥmt.l UG5.8.8

ǵrt

tr.b lkt. | tr.b lkt.w tr.b ẖl. | [b]n‘mm.b ysmm.ḥ[--]k.ǵrt. | [ql].l b‘l.‘nt.ttnn. | [---].b‘l m.d ip[---]. | [il.]hd.d ‘nn.n[--] 10[76].2.30

ǵš

. | [---.]dr dt.šmm. | [---.al]iyn b‘l. | [---].rkb.‘rpt. | [---.]ǵš.l limm. | [---.]l yṯb.l arṣ. | [---].mtm. | [---.--]d mhr.ur. | [---.] 10[76].1.8

ǵtr

.ilm l ẖt[n]. | m.b‘l trẖ pdry b[t h]. | aqrb k ab h b‘[l]. | yǵtr.‘ṯtr t | rẖ l k ybrdmy.b[t.a] | b h lb[u] y‘rr.w y‘[n]. | yrẖ n 24[77].28

p

p

y l pn mlk. | šin k itn. | r‘ y šṣa idn l y. | l šmn iṯr hw. | p iẖdn gnryn. | im mlkytn yrgm. | aẖnnn. | w iẖd. 1020.7
t. | [---.šp]š.l [hrm.ǵ]rpl.‘l.arṣ. | [---.]ḥmt.l p[.nṯ]k.abd.l p.ak[l]. | [ṯm.dl.]isp.ḥ[mt.---.-]hm.yasp.ḥmt. | [---.š]pš.l [hrm. UG5.8.10
t.isp.[šp]š l hrm.ǵrpl.‘l arṣ. | [l a]n ḥmt.l p[.n]ṯk.abd.l p.akl ṯm.dl. | [---.q]l.bl.tbḥ[n.l]azd.‘r.qdm. | [---].‘ẓ q[dm.--.š UG5.8.20
. | mlk. | l ḥyil. | lm.tlik.‘m y. | ik y.aškn. | ‘ṣm.l bt.dml. | p ank.atn. | ‘ṣm.l k. | arb‘.‘ṣm. | ‘l.ar. | w.ṯlṯ. | ‘l.ubr‘y. | w.ṯn.‘l. | 1010.7
srr. | ‘dw šr. | ṣdqm šr. | ḥnbn il d[n]. | [-]bd w [---]. | [--].p il[.---]. | [i]l mt mr[b-]. | qdš mlk [---]. | kbd d ilgb[-]. | mrmn UG5.10.2.1
y.tkšd. | rumm.‘n.kḏd.aylt. | hm.imt.imt.npš.blt. | ḥmr.p imt.b klt. | yd y.ilḥm.hm.šb‘. | ydt y.b ṣ‘.hm.ks.ymsk. | nhr. 5[67].1.19
‘bdrṯ[b.---]. | b ṯṯ ‘ṯr ṯmn.r[qḫ.---]. | p bn btb[-.---]. | b ḫmṯ ‘ṯr k[--.---]. | b ḫmṯ ‘ṯr[.---]. | [-----]. | [--- 207[57].3
d.d yknn[.--]. | b‘l.yṣǵd.mli[.--]. | il hd.mla.u[--.--]. | blt.p btlt.‘n[t]. | w p.n‘mt.aḫt[.b‘l]. | y‘l.b‘l.b ǵ[r.---]. | w bn.dgn.b 10[76].3.10
d.mqm h.w ‘bd. | ‘lm.ṯlṯ.sswm. | mrkbt.b trbṣ. | bn.amt.p d.[i]n. | b bt y.ttn.tn. | l y.mṯt.ḥry. | n‘mt.šbḥ.bkr k. | d k n‘ 14[KRT].6.287
.mqm h.w ‘bd. | ‘lm.ṯlṯ.sswm.mrkbt. | b trbṣt.bn.amt. | p d.in.b bt y.ttn. | tn.l y.mṯt.ḥry. | n‘mt.špḥ.bkr k. | d k.n‘m.‘ 14[KRT].3.142
. | at.š[‘tqt.---]. | š‘d[.---]. | rt.[---]. | ‘ṭr[.---]. | b p.š[---]. | il.p.d[---]. | ‘rm.[di.mh.pdrm]. | di.š[rr.---]. | mr[ṣ.---]. | zb[ln.---] 16[126].5.47
‘[l k]. | mḫṣ.aqht.ǵzr.amd.gr bt il. | ‘nt.brḥ.p ‘lm h.‘nt.p dr[.dr]. | ‘db.uḫry mṭ.yd h. | ymǵ.l mrrt.tǵll.b nr. | yšu.g h. 19[1AQHT].3.154
š k.b arṣ.al. | yp‘.riš.ǵly.b d.ns‘ k. | ‘nt.brḥ.p ‘lm h. | ‘nt.p dr.dr.‘db.uḫry mṭ yd h. | ymǵ.l qrt.ablm.abl[m]. | qrt.zbl.y 19[1AQHT].3.162
| d ‘l k.mḫṣ.aqht.ǵzr. | ‘wrt.yšt k.b‘l.l ht. | w ‘lm h.l ‘nt.p dr.dr. | ‘db.uḫry.mṭ.yd h. | dnil.bt h.ymǵyn.yšt | ql.dnil.l hk 19[1AQHT].4.168
---.--]ša. | tlm.km[.---.]yd h.k šr. | knr.uṣb‘t h ḥrṣ.abn. | p h.tiḫd.šnt h.w akl.bqmm. | tšt ḥrṣ.k lb ilnm. | w ṯn.gprm.m 19[1AQHT].1.9
a]rṣ.špt.l šmm. | [---.l]šn.l kbkbm.y‘rb. | [b‘]l.b kbd h.b p h yrd. | k ḥrr.zt.ybl.arṣ.w pr. | ‘ṣm.yraun.aliyn.b‘l. | ṯt‘.nn.r 5[67].2.4
r. | ‘nn.ilm.al. | tqrb.l bn.ilm. | mt.al.y‘db km. | k imr.b p h. | k lli.b ṯbrn. | qn h.tḫtan. | nrt.ilm.špš. | ṣḥrrt.la. | šmm.b 4[51].8.18
l.išd h.qrn[m]. | dt.‘l h.riš h.b glṯ.b šm[m]. | [---.i]l.ṯr.iṯ.p h.k ṯt.ǵlt[.--]. | [---.--] k yn.ddm.l b[--.---]. | [---.-]yt š[--.---]. UG5.3.1.8
.iṯ.šmt.iṯ. | ‘ẓm.abky w aqbrn h.aštn. | b ḫrt.ilm.arṣ.b p h.rgm.l[yṣ]a. | b špt h.hwt h.knp.ṣml.b‘[l]. | b‘l.ṯbr.diy.hyt. 19[1AQHT].3.141
t.hm.i[ṯ]. | ‘ẓm.abky.w aqbrn h. | ašt.b ḫrt.ilm.arṣ. | b p h.rgm.l yṣa.b špt h.hwt[h]. | knp.nšrm.b‘l.yṯbr. | b‘l.ṯbr.diy 19[1AQHT].3.113
]drt. | ur.tisp k.yd.aqht.ǵz[r]. | tšt k.bm.qrb m.asm. | b p h.rgm.l yṣa.b špt h[.hwt h]. | b nši ‘n h.w tphn.in.[---]. | [-.] 19[1AQHT].2.75
ṯ.šmt.hm.iṯ[.‘ẓm]. | abky.w aqbrn.ašt.b ḫrt. | i[lm.arṣ.b p h.rgm.l yṣa.b šp] | t h.hwt h.knp.hrgb.b‘l.ṯbr. | b‘l.ṯbr.diy.h 19[1AQHT].3.127
]. | [il.]hd.d ‘nn.n[--]. | [----.]aliyn.b[‘l]. | [---.btl]t.‘n[t.-.]p h. | [---.---]n. | [-----]. | [-----]. | [---.]lk[.--]t. 10[76].2.35
m. | w dg b ym.w ndd.gzr.l zr.y‘db.u ymn. | u šmal.b p hm.w l.tšb‘n y.aṯt.itrḫ. | y bn.ašld.šu.‘db.tk.mdbr qdš. | ṯm 23[52].64
.bn ym.ynqm.b ap.ḏd.št.špt. | l arṣ.špt l šmm.w ‘rb.b p hm.‘ṣr.šmm. | w dg b ym.w ndd.gzr.l zr.y‘db.u ymn. | u šm 23[52].62
ysmt.šd.šḥlmmt. | ngš.ank.aliyn b‘l. | ‘dbnn ank.imr.b p y. | k lli.b ṯbrn q y.ḫtu hw. | nrt.ilm.špš.ṣḥrrt. | la.šmm.b yd 6[49].2.22
.yrdt. | b ‘rgzm.b bz tdm. | lla y.‘m lẓpn i | l ḏ.pid.hn b p y sp | r hn.b špt y mn | t hn ṯlḫ h w mlg h y | ṯtqt ‘m h b q‘t. 24[77].45
arḫ.td.rgm.b ǵr. | b p y.t‘lgt.b lšn[y]. | ǵr[.---]b.b pš y.t[--]. | hwt.b‘l.iš[--]. | šm‘ l 2124.2
.b ṣ‘. | [--.]šb‘.rbt. | [---.]qbṭ.ṯm. | [---.]bn.ilm. | [m]t.šmḥ.p ydd. | il[.ǵ]zr. | b [-]dn.‘.z.w. | rgbt.zbl. UG5.4.15
. | [uzr.yšqy.]bn.qdš.yd. | [ṣt h.y‘l.]w yškb.yd. | [mizrt.]p ynl.hn.ym. | [w ṯn.uzr.]ilm.dnil. | [uzr.ilm.]ylḥm.uzr. | [yšq 17[2AQHT].1.6
.bn qdš.yd.ṣt h. | [dn]il.yd.ṣt h.y‘l.w yškb. | [yd.]mizrt.p yln.mk.b šb‘.ymm. | [w]yqrb.b‘l.b ḥnt h.abynt. | [d]nil.mt. 17[2AQHT].1.16
]t.b‘l.ḥẓ.ršp.b[n].km.yr.klyt h.w lb h. | [ṯ]n.p k.b ǵr.ṯn.p k.b ḫlb.k tgwln.šnt k. | [--.]w špt k.l tššy.hm.tqrm.l mt.b r 1001.1.4
t.in l y. | [--]t.b‘l.ḥẓ.ršp.b[n].km.yr.klyt h.w lb h. | [ṯ]n.p k.b ǵr.ṯn.p k.b ḫlb.k tgwln.šnt k. | [--.]w špt k.l tššy.hm.tq 1001.1.4
ti. | nḫtu.ht. | hm.in mm. | nḫtu.w.lak. | ‘m y.w.yd. | ilm.p.k mtm. | ‘z.mid. | hm.nṯkp. | m‘n k. | w.mnm. | rgm.d.tšm‘. | ṯ 53[54].12
k]. | rb[.b‘l y.---]. | w.an[k.---]. | arš[.---]. | mlk.r[b.b‘]l y.p.l. | ḥy.np[š.a]rš. | l.pn.b‘[l y.l].pn.b‘l y. | w.urk.ym.b‘l y. | l.p 1018.17
mt.‘ly.ṯh.lm. | l.ytn.hm.mlk.[b]‘l y. | w.hn.ibm.šṣq l y. | p.l.ašt.aṯt y. | n‘r y.ṯh.l pn.ib. | hn.hm.yrgm.mlk. | b‘l y.tmǵyy 1012.28
p. | ym.ḏnbtm. | tnn.l šbm. | tšt.trks. | l mrym.l bt[.---]. | p l.tb‘[.---]. | hmlt ẖt.[---]. | l.tp[-]m.[---]. | n[-]m[.---]. 1003.11
dm. | [---.]iṯ[-].yšql.ytk[.--]np bl.hn. | [---].ḥ[m]t.pṭr.w.p nḥš. | [---.--]q.n[ṯ]k.l yd‘.l bn.l pq ḥmt. | [---.--]n h.ḥmt.w t‘ UG5.8.34
b‘l.yṣǵd.mli[.--]. | il hd.mla.u[--.--]. | blt.p btlt.‘n[t]. | w p.n‘mt.aḫt[.b‘l]. | y‘l.b‘l.b ǵ[r.---]. | w bn.dgn.b š[---]. | b‘l.yṯb.l 10[76].3.11
y‘n. | gpn.w ugr.tḥm.bn ilm. | mt.hwt.ydd.bn.il. | ǵzr.p np.š.npš.lbim. | thw.hm.brlt.anḫr. | b ym.hm.brk y.tkšd. | r 5[67].1.14
l.ar[ṣ.---.ḥ]mt. | [---.šp]š.l [hrm.ǵ]rpl.‘l.arṣ. | [---.]ḥmt.l p[.nṯ]k.abd.l p.ak[l]. | [ṯm.dl.]isp.ḥ[mt.---.-]hm.yasp.ḥmt. | [- UG5.8.10
m. | [yis]p.ḥmt.isp.[šp]š l hrm.ǵrpl.‘l arṣ. | [l a]n ḥmt.l p[.n]ṯk.abd.l p.akl ṯm.dl. | [---.q]l.bl.tbḥ[n.l]azd.‘r.qdm. | [--- UG5.8.20
mẓll.ṭly.bt rb. | mṯb.arṣ.bt y‘bdr. | w y‘n lṭpn il d pid. | p ‘bd.an.‘nn.aṯrt. | p.‘bd.ank.aḫd.ulṯ. | hm.amt.aṯrt.tlbn. | lbnt 4[51].4.59
b.arṣ.bt y‘bdr. | w y‘n lṭpn il d pid. | p ‘bd.an.‘nn.aṯrt. | p.‘bd.ank.aḫd.ulṯ. | hm.amt.aṯrt.tlbn. | lbnt.ybn.bt.l b‘l. | km i 4[51].4.60
idm.‘rẓ.t‘r[ẓ.---]. | ‘n.b‘l.a[ḫ]ḏ[.---]. | ẓr h.aḫḏ.qš[t.---]. | p ‘n.b‘l.aḫḏ[.---]. | w ṣmt.ǵllm[.---]. | aḫḏ.aklm.k [---]. | npl.b 12[75].2.34
aqht. | ǵzr.šrš k.b arṣ.al. | yp‘.riš.ǵly.b d.ns‘ k. | ‘nt.brḥ.p ‘lm h. | ‘nt.p dr.dr.‘db.uḫry mṭ yd h. | ymǵ.l qrt.ablm.abl[19[1AQHT].3.161
.qr.mym.d ‘[l k]. | mḫṣ.aqht.ǵzr.amd.gr bt il. | ‘nt.brḥ.p ‘lm h.‘nt.p dr[.dr]. | ‘db.uḫry mṭ.yd h. | ymǵ.l mrrt.tǵll.b n 19[1AQHT].3.154
likt. | ‘m.ṯryl. | mh y.rgmt. | w ht.aḫ y. | bn y.yšal. | ṯryl.p rgm. | l mlk.šm y. | w l h.y‘l m. | w h[t] aḫ y. | bn y.yšal. | ṯry 138.12
likt. | ‘m.ṯryl. | mh y.rgmt. | w ht.aḫ y. | bn y.yšal. | ṯryl.p rgm. | l mlk.šm y. | w l h[-] y‘l m. | bn y.yšal. | ṯryl.w rgm. | ṯ 138.12
‘m.ary y. | w lḥm m ‘m aḫ y.lḥm. | w št m.‘m.a[ḫ] yn. | p nšt.b‘l.[ṭ]‘n.iṭ‘n k. | [---.]ma[---] k.k tmḫṣ. | [ltn.bṯn.br]ḥ.tkl 5[67].1.26
m.---]. | [š]lm.bnš.yš[lm.---]. | [-]r.l šlmt.šl[m.---.--] | r h.p šlmt.p šlm[.---]. | bt.l bnš.trg[m.---]. | l šlmt.l šlm.b[--.---] | b 59[100].4
l ri[š.---]. | ypt.‘ṣ[--.---]. | p šlm.[---]. | bt k.b[--.--.m] | ǵy k[.---]. | bt.[---]. 58[20].3
[š]lm.bnš.yš[lm.---]. | [-]r.l šlmt.šl[m.---.--] | r h.p šlmt.p šlm[.---]. | bt.l bnš.trg[m.---]. | l šlmt.l šlm.b[--.---] | b y.šnt. 59[100].4
r[b.---]. | ṯmm.w lk[.---]. | [--]ṯ.lk[.---]. | [--]kṯ.i[---.---]. | p.šn[-.---]. | w l ṭlb.[---]. | mit.rḥ[.---]. | ṭṭlb.a[--.---]. | yšu.g h[.- 5[67].4.1
| kr[pn.---]. | at.š[‘tqt.---]. | š‘d[.---]. | rt.[---]. | ‘ṭr[.---]. | b p.š[---]. | il.p.d[---]. | ‘rm.[di.mh.pdrm]. | di.š[rr.---]. | mr[ṣ.---] 16[126].5.46
skn.sknm.b ‘dn. | ‘dnm.kn.npl.b‘l. | km ṯr.w tkms.hd.p[.-]. | km.ibr.b tk.mšmš d[--]. | ittpq.l awl. | išttk.lm.ttkn. | št 12[75].2.55
tldn. | ṯrkn. | kli. | plǵn. | apsny. | ‘rb[.---]. | w.b.p[.--]. | aps[ny]. | b.yṣi h. | ḥwt.[---]. | alp.k[sp]. | tš‘n. | w.hm.al[2116.7

palt

ph.b yǵlm.bṣql.y[ḫb]q. | w ynšq.aḫl.an bṣ[ql]. | ynp'.b palt.bṣql yp' b yǵlm. | ur.tisp k.yd.aqht. | ǵzr.tšt k.b qrb m.as 19[1AQHT].2.65
t 'r. | l ysmsm.bmt.pḫl. | y dnil.ysb.palt h. | bṣql.yph.b palt.bṣ[q]l. | yph.b yǵlm.bṣql.y[ḫb]q. | w ynšq.aḫl.an bṣ[ql]. | 19[1AQHT].2.62
šu.ab h.tštnn.l[b]mt 'r. | l ysmsm.bmt.pḫl. | y dnil.ysb.palt h. | bṣql.yph.b palt.bṣ[q]l. | yph.b yǵlm.bṣql.y[ḫb]q. | w y 19[1AQHT].2.61

pam

. | l ṣpn.gdlt.[l.---]. | ugrt.š l ili[b.---]. | rt.w 'ṣrm.l[.---]. | pamt.w bt.[---]. | rmm.w 'l[y.---]. | bt.il.ṯq[l.---.kbd]. | w bdḥ.k APP.II[173].40
.ušpǵt. | ḫr[-].ṯlṯt.mzn. | drk.š.alp.w ṯlṯ. | ṣin.šlm[m.]šb' pamt. | l ilm.šb['.]l kṯr. | 'lm.t'rbn.gṯrm. | bt.mlk.ṯql.ḫrṣ. | l špš 33[5].7
k.ylk.lqḥ.ilm. | aṯr.ilm.ylk.p'nm. | mlk.p'nm.yl[k]. | šb'.pamt.l kl hm. 33[5].26
.gg. | ar[b'.]arb'.mṯbt.azmr.b h.š.šr[-]. | al[p.w].š.šlmm.pamt.šb'.klb h. | yr[--.]mlk.ṣbu.špš.w.ḫl.mlk. | w.[---].ypm.w. 35[3].52
.n'm.[---]. | w šm.'rbm.yr[.---]. | mṯbt.ilm.ṯmn.ṯ[--.--]. | pamt.šb'. | iqnu.šmt[.---]. | [b]n.šrm. | iqran.ilm.n'mm[.agzry 23[52].20
lt iltm ḫnqtm.d[q]tm. | [yr]ḫ.kty gdlt.w l ǵlmt š. | [w]pamt ṯlṯm.w yrdt.[m]dbḥt. | gdlt.l b'lt bhtm.'ṣrm. | l inš ilm. 34[1].20
d alpm.w alp w š. | šrp.w šlmm kmm. | l b'l.ṣpn b 'r'r. | pamt ṯlṯm š l qrnt. | ṭlḥn.b'lt.bhtm. | 'lm.'lm.gdlt l b'l. | ṣpn.il UG5.13.30
ṯb.mdbḥ.b'l.g[dlt.---]. | dqt.l.ṣpn.w.dqt[.---]. | ṯn.l.'šrm.pamt.[---]. | š.dd.šmn.gdlt.w.[---.brr]. | rgm.yṯṯb.b.ṯdṯ.ṯn[.--.š 35[3].43
.md] | bḥ.b'l.[gdlt.---.dqt]. | l ṣpn.w [dqt.---.ṯn.l 'š] | rm.pam[t.---]. | š dd šmn[.gdlt.w.---]. | brr.r[gm.yṯṯb.b ṯdṯ.ṯn]. | l APP.II[173].47

pat

tš'.ṣmdm. | ṯlṯm.b d. | ibrtlm. | w.pat.aḫt. | in.b hm. 1141.4
b'r.l ṯn.aṯt h. | w l nkr.mddt. | km irby.tškn. | šd.k ḥsn.pat. | mdbr.tlkn. | ym.w ṯn.aḫr. | šp[š]m.b [ṯ]lṯ. | ym[ǵy.]l qdš. 14[KRT].4.193
l ṯn. | aṯt h.lm.nkr. | mddt h.k irby. | [t]škn.šd. | km.ḥsn.pat.mdbr. | lk.ym.w ṯn.ṯlṯ.rb' ym. | ḫmš.ṯdṯ.ym.mk.špšm. | b š 14[KRT].2.105
ṣm.šb'.šnt. | tmt.ṯmn.nqpt.'d.ilm.n'mm.ttlkn. | šd.tṣdn.pat.mdbr.w ngš.hm.nǵr. | mdr'.w ṣḥ hm.'m.nǵr.mdr' y.nǵr. 23[52].68
.w gbṯt. | km.ibrm. | w b hm.pn.b'l. | b'l.ytlk.w yṣd. | yḥ pat.mlbr. | wn.ymǵy.aklm. | w ymẓa.'qqm. | b'l.ḥmd m.yḥmd 12[75].1.35

pid

. | w id'.k ḥy.aliyn.b'l. | k iṯ.zbl.b'l.arṣ. | b ḥlm.lṭpn.il d pid. | b ḏrt.bny.bnwt. | šmm.šmn.tmṭrn. | nḫlm.tlk.nbtm. | šm 6[49].3.10
.ḥy.a[liyn.b'l]. | w hm.iṯ.zbl.b'[l.arṣ]. | b ḥlm.lṭpn.il.d pid. | b ḏrt.bny.bnwt. | šmm.šmn.tmṭrn. | nḫlm.tlk.nbtm. | w i 6[49].3.4
| w t'n.rbt.aṯrt ym. | bl.nmlk.yd'.ylḥn. | w y'n.lṭpn.il d pi | d dq.anm.l yrẓ. | 'm.b'l.l y'db.mrḥ. | 'm.bn.dgn.k tms m. | 6.1.49[49.1.21]
.tmgnn.rbt. | aṯrt.ym.tǵẓyn. | qnyt.ilm.mgntm. | ṯr.il.d pid.hm.ǵẓtm. | bny.bnwt w t'n. | btlt.'nt.nmgn. | [-]m.rbt.aṯrt. 4[51].3.31
ll b'l gml.yrdt. | b 'rgzm.b bz tdm. | lla y.'m lẓpn i | l ḏ.pid.hn b p y sp | r hn.b špt y mn | t hn ṯlḥ h w mlg h y | ṯtqt ' 24[77].45
.bn[.dnil.---]. | w y'ḏr k.b yd.btlt.['nt]. | w y'n.lṭpn.il d p[id]. | yd't k.bt.k anšt.w i[n.b ilht]. | qlṣ k.tb'.bt.ḫnp.lb[k.--. 18[3AQHT].1.15
pl.l a | rṣ.mt.aliyn.b'l. | ḫlq.zbl.b'l.arṣ. | apnk.lṭpn.il. | d pid.yrd.l ksi.yṯb. | l hdm[.w] l.hdm.yṯb. | l arṣ.yṣq.'mr. | un.l r 5[67].6.12
. | ydy.mrṣ.gršm zbln. | in.b ilm.'ny h. | w y'n.lṭpn.il.b pid. | ṯb.bn y.lm ṯb[t] km. | l kḥṯ.zbl k[m.a]nk. | iḥtrš.w [a]šk 16[126].5.23
ǵy.'[d]t.ilm. | [w]y'n.aliy[n.]b'l. | [---.]tb'.l lṭpn. | [il.d]pid.l tbrk. | [krt.]ṯ'.l tmr.n'mn. | [ǵlm.]il.ks.yiḫd. | [il.b]yd.kr 15[128].2.14
--]. | b d k.[---]. | ṯnnt h[.---]. | ṯlṯt h[.-.w y'n]. | lṭpn.[il.d pid.my]. | b ilm.[ydy.mrṣ]. | gršm.z[bln.in.b ilm]. | 'ny h.y[ṯny 16[126].5.10
h.b nhrm. | štt.ḫptr.l išt. | ḫbrṯ.l ẓr.pḥmm. | t'pp.ṯr.il.d pid. | tǵẓy.bny.bnwt. | b nši.'n h.w tphn. | hlk.b'l.aṯtrt. | k t'n. 4[51].2.10
t.ar. | mẓll.ṯly.bt rb. | mṯb.arṣ.bt y'bdr. | w y'n lṭpn il d pid. | p 'bd.an.'nn.aṯrt. | p.'bd.ank.aḫd.ulṯ. | hm.amt.aṯrt.tlbn. 4[51].4.58
nwt. | šmm.šmn.tmṭrn. | nḫlm.tlk.nbtm. | šmḫ.lṭpn.il.d pid. | p'n h.l hdm.yṯpd. | w yprq.lṣb w yṣḥq. | yšu.g h.w yṣḥ. | 6[49].3.14
il.ilš. | ilš.ngr.bt.b'l. | w aṯt h.ngrt.ilht. | w y'n.lṭpn.il d pi[d]. | šm'.l ngr.il il[š]. | ilš.ngr bt b'l. | w aṯt k.ngrt.il[ht]. | 'l.l 16[126].4.10
t.['nt.arṣ.ṯlṯ.mth]. | ǵyrm.idk.l yt[n.pnm.'m.lṭpn]. | il d pid.tk ḫrš[n.---.tk.ǵr.ks]. | ygly ḏd.i[l.w ybu.qrš.mlk]. | ab.šn 1['NT.IX].3.22
---].aṯt k.'l. | [---] k.yššı. | [---.]ḫbr.rbt. | [ḫbr.ṯrr]t.il d. | [pid.---].b anšt. | [---.]mlu. | [---.--]tm. 15[128].5.27
--]. | t'nyn.l zn.tn[.---]. | at.adn.tp'r[.---]. | ank.lṭpn.il[.d pid.---]. | 'l.ydm.p'rt[.---]. | šm k.mdd.i[l.---]. | bt ksp y.d[--.--- 1['NT.X].4.18
m ll.kḥṣ.tusp[.---]. | tgr.il.bn h.ṯr[.---]. | w y'n.lṭpn.il.d p[id.---]. | šm.bn y.yw.ilt.[---]. | w p'r.šm.ym[-.---]. | t'nyn.l zn 1['NT.X].4.13

piln

bḥ.b'l.k.tdd.b'lt.bhtm. | b.[-]ǵb.ršp.ṣbi. | [---.--]m. | [---.]piln. | [---].ṣmd[.---.]pd[ry]. | [-----]. | [---.b]'lt. | lbnm.'šr.yn. | ḫ 2004.17

pit

bm.ṯm.tpl k.lbnt. | [-.]rgm.k yrkt.'ṯqbm. | [---]m.'ẓpn.l pit. | m[--]m[.--]tm.w mdbḥt. | ḫr[.---.]'l.kbkbt. | n'm.[--.-]llm. 13[6].15
m.ṯiṭ.rḥṣ. | npṣ k.b ym rṯ.b uni[l]. | pnm.tšmḫ.w 'l yṣhl pi[t]. | yprq.lṣb.w yṣḥq. | p'n.l hdm.yṯpd.yšu. | g h.w yṣḥ.aṯbn 17[2AQHT].2.9
h[.---]. | [---.]d[--.---]. | [---].hn[.---]. | [---.]šn[.---]. | [---].pit. | [---.]qbat. | [---.]inšt. | [--]u.l tštql. | [---].ṯry.ap.l tlḥm. | [l] 6.6.38A[62.2.38]

pity

d. | bn.'bdḥy. | bn.ubyn. | slpd. | bn.atnb. | bn.ktmn. | bn.pity. | bn.iryn. | bn.'bl. | bn.grbn. | bn.iršyn. | bn.nklb. | bn.mry 115[301].4.15
-]. | bn.mlkyy. | bn.atn. | bn.bly. | bn.ṯbrn. | bn.ḥgby. | bn.pity. | bn.slgyn. | 'zn.bn.mlk. | bn.alṯn. | bn.ṯmyr. | ẓbr. | bn.ṯdṯ 115[301].2.6
. | bn.'[--]t. | bn.adty. | bn.krwn. | bn.nǵsk. | bn.qnḏ. | bn.pity. | w.nḥl h. | bn.rt. | bn.l[--]. | bn.[---]. | [---.--]y. | [--.-]ḏrm. | 113[400].3.17
[spr.----]m. | bn.pi[ty]. | w.nḥ[l h]. | 'bd[--]. | bn.s[---]. | bn.at[--]. | bn.qnḏ. | ṣmq 117[325].1.2

pbyn

š. | abmn.qšt. | ẓẓn.qšt. | dqry.qš[t]. | rkby. | bn.knn.qšt. | pbyn.qšt. | yddn.qšt.w.ql'. | š'rt. | bn.il.qšt.w.ql'. | ark.qšt.w.ql' 119[321].2.37

pbl

hqt. | ḥmr[h.l g't.]alp. | ḥrṯ[.l z]ǵt.klb. | [ṣ]pr[.apn]k. | [pb]l[.mlk.g]m.l aṯt | [h.k]y[ṣḥ.]šm'.m'. | [--.]'m[.-.]aṯt y[.-]. | 14[KRT].5.228
tš'l. | qrt h.abn.yd k. | mšdpt.w hn.špšm. | b šb'.w l.yšn.pbl. | mlk.l qr.ṯigt.ibr h. | l ql.nhqt.ḥmr h. | l g't.alp.ḥrṯ.zǵt. | k 14[KRT].3.119
ṯn. | ṯlṯ.rb'.ym. | ḫmš.ṯdṯ.ym. | mk.špšm.b šb'. | w l.yšn.pbl. | mlk.l [qr.]ṯiqt. | ibr h[.l]ql.nhqt. | ḥmr[h.l g't.]alp. | ḥrṯ[14[KRT].5.222
l ytn]. | [']m[.krt.mswn h]. | tš[an.g hm.w tṣḥn]. | tḥ[m.pbl.mlk]. | qḥ[.ksp.w yrq]. | ḫrṣ.[yd.mqm h]. | w 'bd[.'lm.ṯlṯ]. 14[KRT].6.268
pn[m.al.ttn]. | 'm.[krt.msw]n. | w r[gm.l krt.]ṯ'. | tḥm[.pbl.mlk]. | qḥ.[ksp.w yr]q. | ḫrṣ[.yd.mqm] h. | 'bd[.'lm.ṯlṯ]. | ss 14[KRT].5.249

zǵt. | klb.ṣpr.w ylak. | mlakm.l k.ʻm.krt. | mswn h.tḥm.pbl.mlk. | qḥ.ksp.w yrq.ḫrṣ. | yd.mqm h.w ʻbd.ʻlm. | ṯlṯ.sswm. 14[KRT].3.125
ǵlm.l ʻbd. | il.ttbʻ.mlakm. | l yṯb.idk.pnm. | l ytn.ʻmm.pbl. | mlk.tšan. | g hm.w tṣḥn. | tḥm.krt.ṯ[ʻ]. | hwt.[n]ʻmn.[ǵlm 14[KRT].6.302

pbn

ṣn.ǵrn. | šib.mqdšt.ʻb[dml]k.ṯtpḥ.mrṯn. | ḫdǵlm.i[---]n.pbn.nḏbn.sbd. | šrm.[---].ḫpn. | ḥrš[bhtm.--]n.ʻbdyrḫ.ḥdṯn.yʻ 2011.16
| bn kr[k]. | bn ḫtyn. | w nḥl h. | bn ṯgrb. | bn ṯdnyn. | bn pbn. 2016.3.7

pgam

ṯn.ḥ[---].pgam. | ṯn[.---.b]n.mlk. | ṯ[n.---.]gpn. | [-----]. | [---.--]b. | b[--.--- 1150.1

pgm

.p[---]. | [---.]bt.tḥbṭ.km.ṣq.ṣdr[.---]. | [---.]kl.b kl.l pgm.pgm.l.b[---]. | [---.]mdbm.l ḥrn.ḥr[n.---]. | [---.--]m.ql.hm[.---] 1001.1.26
.km.p[---]. | [---.]bt.tḥbṭ.km.ṣq.ṣdr[.---]. | [---.]kl.b kl.l pgm.pgm.l.b[---]. | [---.]mdbm.l ḥrn.ḥr[n.---]. | [---.--]m.ql.h 1001.1.26

pgn

tḥm.pgn. | l.mlk.ugrt. | rgm. | yšlm.l k.[il]m. | tǵr k.tšlm k. | hn ny.ʻ 2061.1

pgr

. | yrḫ. | kṯr. | ṯrmn. | pdry. | dqt. | trṯ. | ršp. | ʻnt ḫbly. | špš pgr. | iltm ḫnqtm. | yrḫ kṯy. | ygb hd. | yrgb bʻl. | ydb il. | yarš il UG5.14.A.12
.pdry.gdlt dqt. | dqt.trṯ.dqt. | [rš]p.ʻnt.ḫbly.dbḥn š[p]š pgr. | [g]dlt iltm ḫnqtm.d[q]tm. | [yr]ḫ.kṯy gdlt.w l ǵlmt š. | [34[1].17
t.ḫṣt h.bʻl.ṣpn š. | [--]ṯ š.ilt.mgdl š.ilt.asrm š. | w l ll.šp. pgr.w ṯrmnm.bt mlk. | il[bt].gdlt.ušḫry.gdlt.ym gdlt. | bʻl gdl 34[1].12

pgrm

yr[ḫ]. | pgr[m]. | yṣa[.---]. | mšr[-]. | [-]b.m[--]. | b y[rḫ]. | pgr[m]. | yṣa[.---]. | lb[-.---]. | b d[.---]. 1158.2.2
b yr[ḫ]. | pgr[m]. | yṣa[.---]. | mšr[-]. | [-]b.m[--]. | b y[rḫ]. | pgr[m]. | yṣa[. 1158.1.2
b ym ḥdṯ. | b.yrḫ.pgrm. | lqḥ.iwrpzn. | argḏḏ. | ṯtkn. | ybrk. | ntbt. | b.mitm. | ʻšrm 2006.2
b.ym.ḥdṯ. | b.yr.pgrm. | lqḥ.bʻlmḏr. | w.bn.ḫlp. | miḫd. | b.arbʻ. | mat.ḫrṣ. 1156.2
b.ym.ḥdṯ. | b.yrḫ.pgrm. | lqḥ.bʻlmʻḏr. | w bn.ḫlp. | w[--]y.d.bʻl. | miḫd.b. | arbʻ. 1155.2
[b.yr]ḫ.mgmr.mš[--.---]. | [---].iqnu.ḫmš[.---]. | [b.yr]ḫ.pgrm[.---]. 1106.40

pd

]. | [q]dqd.ṯlṯ id.ʻl.ud[n]. | [---.-]sr.pdm.riš h[m.---]. | ʻl.pd.asr.[---.]l[.---]. | mḫlpt.w l.ytk.[d]m[ʻt.]km. | rbʻt.ṯqlm.ṯtp[19[1AQHT].2.81
ap. | pd. | mlk. | ar. | atlg. | gbʻly. | ulm. | mʻrby. | mʻr. | arny. | šʻrt. | ḫl 2074.2
ap. | pd. | mlk.arbʻ.ḥm[rm.w.arb]ʻ.bnšm. | ar.ḫmš.ḥmr[m.w.ḫm]š. 2040.2
yṣa.w l.yṣa.hlm.[ṯnm]. | [q]dqd.ṯlṯ id.ʻl.ud[n]. | [---.-]sr.pdm.riš h[m.---]. | ʻl.pd.asr.[---.]l[.---]. | mḫlpt.w l.ytk.[d]m[ʻt 19[1AQHT].2.80
spr.ḫrd.arr. | ap arbʻm[.--]. | pd[.---.ḫm]šm.kb[d]. | ǵb[-.---.]kbd. | m[--.---.k]bd. | a[--.---.]k 2042.3

pdu

qrṯym.mddbʻl. | kdn.zlyy. | krwn.arty. | tlmu.zlyy. | pdu.qmnzy. | bdl.qrṯy. | trgn.bn.tǵh. | aupš.qmnzy. | ṯrry.mṣbt 89[312].5

pdd

.amtm.ʻkyt. | yd.llḫ hm. | w.ṯlṯ.l.ʻšrm. | ḫpnt.ššwm.ṯn. | pddm.w.d.ṯṯ. | [mr]kbt.w.ḥrṣ. 2049.8
| [---].ybʻlnn. | [---.--]n.b.ṯlṯ.šnt.l.nṣd. | [---.--]ršp.mlk.k.ypdd.mlbš. | u---].mlk.ytn.mlbš. | [---.-]rn.k.ypdd.mlbš h. | [-- 1106.58
]ršp.mlk.k.ypdd.mlbš. | u---].mlk.ytn.mlbš. | [---.-]rn.k.ypdd.mlbš h. | [---.]mlk.ytn.lbš.l h. 1106.60

pdy

l ym hnd. | iwr[k]l.pdy. | agdn.bn.nrgn. | w ynḥm.aḫ h. | w.bʻln aḫ h. | w.ḥṯṯn bn 1006.2
w.unṯ.aḫd.l h[.---]. | dnn.bn.yṣr[.---]. | sln.bn.ʻṯt[-.---]. | pdy.bn.nr[-.---]. | abmlk.bn.un[-.---]. | nrn.bn.mtn[-.---]. | aḫy 90[314].1.7
[bn.]ulnhr. | [bn.p]rn. | [bn.a]nny. | [---]n. | bn.kbln. | bn.pdy. | bn.ṯpdn. 1075.2.2
bt.il. | bʻl.bt.aḏmny. | bʻl.bt.pdy. | bʻl.bt.nqly. | bʻl.bt.ʻlr. | bʻl.bt.ssl. | bʻl.bt.ṯrn. | bʻl.bt.ktmn 31[14].3
.btšy.bt h. | w.ištrmy. | bt.ʻbd mlk. | w.snt. | bt.ugrt. | w.pdy h[m]. | iwrkl.mit. | ksp.b y[d]. | birtym. | [un]ṯ inn. | l [h]m 1006.12
t]. | bn.kṯan. | ǵr.tšʻ[.ʻšr.b]nš. | ṣbu.any[t]. | bn abdḫ[r]. | pdym. | ḫmš.bnšm. | snrym. | tšʻ.bnš[m]. | gbʻlym. | arbʻ.b[nšm 79[83].12
.šʻrt. | bdn.šʻrt. | ʻpṯn.šʻrt. | ʻbd.yrḫ šʻrt. | ḫbd.ṯr yṣr šʻr. | pdy.yṣr šʻrt. | atnb.ḥr. | šʻrt.šʻrt. 97[315].12
[šd.--]ln. | b d.trǵds. | šd.ṯʻlb. | b d.bn.pl. | šd.bn.kt. | b d.pdy. | šd.ḫzr. | [b d].d[---]. 2030.2.6
n. | bn.mdt. | bn.ḫ[--]y. | bn.ʻ[-]y. | knʻm. | bn.yš[-]n. | bn.pd[y]. | ttn. | md.ʻṯt[rt]. | kṯkt. | bn.ṯtn[--]. | [m]d.m[--]. | [b]n.an 1054.1.9
.l.bn.[-]kn. | šd[.---.-]ʻn. | šd[.---.-]ṣm.l.dqn. | š[d.---.--]d.pdy. | [---.dq]n. | [---.d]qn. | [---.--]b[.---]. | [---.--]l[.--]. | [---.--]b 2027.1.8
bʻldʻ.yd[.---.ʻ]šrt.ksp h. | lbiy.pdy.[---.k]sp h. 2112.2
lm. | bn.ḫnqn.arbʻt. | [b]n.ṯrk.ṯqlm. | [b]n.pdrn.ṯq[lm]. | pdy.[----]. | [i]lmlk.bn.[---]. | [--]ʻ[-.---]. | [---.k]kr. | [-----]. | [---. 122[308].1.23

pdyn

| [-]ln. | [-]ldn. | [i]wryn. | ḫbsn. | ulmk. | ʻdršp. | bn.knn. | pdyn. | bn.aṯtl.ṯn. | kdln.akdṯb. | ṯn.b gt yknʻm. 1061.19
-]. | i[---.---]. | pgl[--.---]. | šy[.---]. | bn.uḫn. | ybru.i[---]. | [p]dyn.[---]. | bnšm.d.b [d.---]. | spḫy.[---]. | [-----]. | b[--.---]. | nʻ[2161.12

pdm

]in.b.trzy. | [--]yn.b.glltky. | ṯd[y]n.b.glltky. | lbw[-].uḫ.pdm.b.yʻrt. | pǵyn.b.tpḥ. | amri[l].b.šrš. | aǵltn.b.midḫ. | [--]n. 2118.10

pdn

š. | iḫyn.bn.ḫryn. | [ab]ǵl.bn.gdn. | [---].bn.bqš. | [---].bn.pdn. | [---.bn.-]ky. | [---.bn.--]r. | [-----]. | [---.--]yn. | [---.]aṯrn. | [102[323].4.14
[-----]. | ǵnbn[.---]. | pdn[.---]. | ṯr[--.---]. | nn[-.---]. | au[pš.---]. | i[---.---]. | pgl[--.---]. 2161.3

pdǵy

n.knn[.---]y. | bn.ymlk[.b]d.skn. | bn.yḥnn.aḏddy. | bn.pdǵy.mḫdy. | bn.yyn.mḏrǵl. | bn.ʻlr. | ḫṯpy.aḏddy. | ynḥm.aḏd 2014.17

pdr

.bu.tbu. | bkt.tgly.w tbu. | nṣrt.tbu.pnm. | ʻrm.tdu.mh. | pdrm.tdu.šrr. | ḫṯ m.tʻmt.[ʻ]ṯr.[k]m. | zbln.ʻl.riš h. | w ttb.trḥṣ. 16.6[127].7
-]. | rt.[---]. | ʻṯr[.---]. | b p.š[---]. | il.p.d[---]. | ʻrm.[di.mh.pdrm]. | di.š[rr.---]. | mr[ṣ.---]. | zb[ln.---]. | t[--.---]. | [-----]. 16[126].5.48
[---.--]n.aḥd. | [p]dr.ḫsyn.aḥd. | pdr.mlk.aḥd. 130[29].2
. | ṣpn.ytmr.bʻl. | bnt h.yʻn.pdry. | bt.ar.apn.ṭly. | [bt.r]b.pdr.ydʻ. | [---]t.im[-]lt. | [-----]. | [---.--]rt. 3[ʻNT].1.25
.l[.---]. | šmr[m.---]. | [-----]. | bn.g[r.---]. | ḏmry[.---]. | bn.pdr.l.[---]. 2122.8
š.ddm.l.ḫtyt. | ṯlṯm.dd.ksmn.l.gzzm. | yyn. | ṣdqn. | ʻbd.pdr. | myṣm. | ṯgt. | w.lmd h. | yṯil. | w.lmd h. | rpan. | w.lmd h. 1099.7
[---.--]n.aḥd. | [p]dr.ḫsyn.aḥd. | pdr.mlk.aḥd. 130[29].3
-.]bʻl.šm[.--.]rgbt yu. | [---]w yrmy[.q]rn h. | [---.-]ny h pdr.ttǵr. | [---.n]šr k.al ttn.l n. | [---.]tn l rbd. | [---.]bʻlt h w yn 2001.2.11
ʻ.w tmǵy.l udm. | rbm.w l.udm.ṯrrt. | w gr.nn.ʻrm.šrn. | pdrm.sʻt.b šdm. | ḥṭb h.b grnt.ḥpšt. | sʻt.b nk.šibt.b bqr. | mm 14[KRT].3.111
rbʻ. | ymǵy.l udm.rbt. | w udm[.ṯr]rt. | grnn.ʻrm. | šrnn.pdrm. | sʻt.b šdm.ḥṭb. | w b grnt.ḥpšt. | sʻt.b npk.šibt.w b | mq 14[KRT].4.213
il[.--.]rḥq.b ǵr. | km.y[--.]ilm.b ṣpn. | ʻdr.l[ʻr].ʻrm. | ṯb.l pd[r.]pdrm. | ṯṯ.l ṯṯm.aḫd.ʻr. | šbʻm.šbʻ.pdr. | ṯmnym.bʻl.[----]. 4[51].7.8
rḥq.b ǵr. | km.y[--.]ilm.b ṣpn. | ʻdr.l[ʻr].ʻrm. | ṯb.l pd[r.]pdrm. | ṯṯ.l ṯṯm.aḫd.ʻr. | šbʻm.šbʻ.pdr. | ṯmnym.bʻl.[----]. | tšʻm. 4[51].7.8
u.ilt[.---]. | [ṯl]ṯ.l ʻṯtrt[.---]. | [--.]l ilt.š l ʻṯt[rt.---]. | [ʻ]ṣr.l pdr ṯṯ.ṣ[in.---]. | tšnpn.ʻlm.km[m.---]. | w.l ll.ʻṣrm.w [---]. | km 38[23].5
r.l[ʻr].ʻrm. | ṯb.l pd[r.]pdrm. | ṯṯ.l ṯṯm.aḫd.ʻr. | šbʻm.šbʻ.pdr. | ṯmnym.bʻl.[----]. | tšʻm.bʻl.mr[-]. | bt[.--]b bʻl.b qrb. | bt. 4[51].7.10

pdry

ḏm[r.---]. | tšt[.r]imt.[l irt h.tšr.l dd.aliyn.bʻl]. | [ahb]t pdr[y.bt.ar.ahbt.ṭly.bt.rb.dd]. | arṣy bt.y[ʻbdr.---]. | rgm l btl[7.2[130].11
[---.t]št.rimt. | l irt h.mšr.l.dd.aliyn. | bʻl.yd.pdry.bt.ar. | ahbt.ṭly.bt.rb.dd.arṣy. | bt.yʻbdr.km ǵlmm. | w ʻr 3[ʻNT].3.3
. | yšr.ǵzr.ṭb.ql. | ʻl.bʻl.b ṣrrt. | ṣpn.ytmr.bʻl. | bnt h.yʻn.pdry. | bt.ar.apn.ṭly. | [bt.r]b.pdr.ydʻ. | [---]t.im[-]lt. | [-----]. | [- 3[ʻNT].1.23
k bn.[aṯrt.mṯb.il.mẓll]. | bn h.m[ṯb.rbt.aṯrt.ym]. | mṯb.pdr[y.bt.ar.mẓll]. | ṭly.bt.r[b.mṯb.arṣy]. | bt.yʻbdr[.mṯb.klt]. | 3[ʻNT.VI].4.3
b.il.mẓll. | bn h.mṯb.rbt. | aṯrt.ym.mṯb. | klt.knyt. | mṯb.pdry.b ar. | mẓll.ṭly.bt rb. | mṯb.arṣy.bt.yʻbdr. | ap.mṯn.rgmm 4[51].1.17
ṯb il.mẓll.bn h. | mṯb rbt.aṯrt.ym. | mṯb.klt.knyt. | mṯb.pdry.bt.ar. | mẓll.ṭly.bt rb. | mṯb.arṣ.bt yʻbdr. | w yʻn lṭpn il d 4[51].4.55
k b[n.a]ṯrt.mṯb.il. | mṯll.b[n h.m]ṯb.rbt.aṯrt. | ym.mṯb.[pdr]y.bt.ar. | [mẓll.]ṭly[.bt.]rb.mṯb. | [arṣy.bt.yʻbdr.mṯb]. | [klt 3[ʻNT.VI].5.49
k.mdl k. | mṭrt k.ʻm k.šbʻt. | ǵlm k.ṯmn.ḫnzr k. | ʻm k.pdry.bt.ar. | ʻm k.ṭṭly.bt.rb.idk. | pn k.al ttn.tk.ǵr. | knkny.ša. 5[67].5.10
.]bʻl. | al.tšt.u[rb]t.b bht m. | ḥln.b q[rb.hk]l m. | al td[.pdr]y.bt ar. | [---.ṭl]y.bt.rb. | [---.m]dd.il ym. | [---.-]qlṣn.wpṯ 4[51].6.10
.w | yʻn ḫrḫb mlk qẓ [l]. | nʻmn.ilm l ḫt[n]. | m.bʻl trḫ pdry b[t h]. | aqrb k ab h bʻ[l]. | ygtr.ʻṯtr t | rḫ l k ybrdmy.b[t. 24[77].26
.[---]. | b.dbḥ.mlk. | dbḥ ṣpn. | [-]zǵm. | [i]lib. | [i]lbldn. | [p]dry.bt.mlk. | [-]lp.izr. | [a]rz. | k.tʻrb.ʻṯtrt.šd.bt[.m]lk. | k.tʻrb 2004.7
.ušḫry.gdlt.ym gdlt. | bʻl gdlt.yrḫ.gdlt. | gdlt.ṯrmn.gdlt.pdry.gdlt dqt. | dqt.trṯ.dqt. | [rš]p.ʻnt.ḫbly.dbḥn š[p]š pgr. | [g 34[1].15
ilbt. | ušḫry. | ym.bʻl. | yrḫ. | kṯr. | ṯrmn. | pdry. | dqt. | trṯ. | ršp. | ʻnt ḫbly. | špš pgr. | iltm ḫnqtm. | yrḫ kṯ UG5.14.A.7
lmm ilib š. | bʻl ugrt š.bʻl ḫlb š. | yrḫ š.ʻnt ṣpn.alp. | w š.pdry š.ddmš š. | w b urbt.ilib š. | bʻl alp w š. | dgn.š.il tʻḏr.š. | b UG5.13.18
lp.w š[.---]. | arṣ.w šmm.š.kṯr[t] š.yrḫ[.---]. | ṣpn.š.kṯr.š.pdry.š.ǵrm.š[.---]. | aṯrt.š.ʻnt.š.špš.š.arṣy.š.ʻṯtrt.š. | ušḫry.š.il.t UG5.9.1.6
grt. | w kdm.w npš ilib. | gdlt.il š.bʻl š.ʻnt. | ṣpn.alp.w š.pdry.š. | šrp.w šlmm ilib š. | bʻl ugrt š.bʻl ḫlb š. | yrḫ š.ʻnt ṣpn. UG5.13.14
m. | b.[-]ǵb.ršp.ṣbi. | [---.--]m. | [---.]piln. | [---].ṣmd[.---.]pd[ry]. | [-----]. | [---.b]ʻlt. | lbnm.ʻšr.yn. | ḫlb.gngnt.ṯlṯ.y[n]. | bṣ 2004.18

pdrn

[--]. | bn.ḫd[--]. | bn.ʻ[---]. | kbkbn bn[.---]. | bn.k[--]. | bn.pdr[n.]. | bn.ʻn[--]. | nḥl h[.---]. | [-----]. 2014.59
[---.]mr[y-.---]. | [--]sp.mr[y-.---]. | [--]l.ṯṯm sp[m.---]. | [p]drn.ḫm[š.---]. | l bn ḥdnr[.---]. | ṯṯm sp.km[-.---]. | ʻšrm.sp[.- 139[310].4
m.ṯqlm kbd. | b.ṯmq.ḫmšt.l.ʻšrt. | b.[---].šbʻt.ʻšrt. | b.bn.pdrn.ʻšrm. | d.bn.šbʻl.uḫnpy.ḫmšm. | b.bn.ṯtm.ṯlṯm. | b.bn.ag 2054.1.9
t. | bn.kmy.qšt. | bn.ilḥbn.qšt.w.q[lʻ]. | ršpab.qšt.w.qlʻ. | pdrn.qšt.w.qlʻ. | bn.pǵm[-.qšt].w.qlʻ. | nʻmn.q[št.w.]qlʻ. | [t]tn. 119[321].3.46
bn.ʻbd.šḫr.ṯqlm. | bn.ḫnqn.arbʻt. | [b]n.ṯrk.ṯqlm. | [b]n.pdrn.ṯq[lm]. | pdy.[----]. | [i]lmlk.bn.[---]. | [--]ʻ[-.---]. | [---.k]kr 122[308].1.22

pḏ

.d tq h.d tqyn h. | [hml]t.tn.bʻl.w ʻnn h.bn.dgn.arṯ m.pḏ h. | [w yʻn.]ṯr.ab h.il.ʻbd k.bʻl.y ym m.ʻbd k.bʻl. | [--.--]m.b 2.1[137].35
l m.d tq h.d tqyn.hmlt.tn.bʻl.[w ʻnn h]. | bn.dgn.arṯ m.pḏ h.tbʻ.ǵlmm.l ṯṯb.[idk.pnm]. | l ytn.tk.ǵr.ll.ʻm.phr.mʻd.ap.i 2.1[137].19

ph

adt y.[---]. | lb.ab[d k].al[.---]. | [-]tm.iph.adt y.w.[---]. | tšṣḥq.hn.aṯṯ.l.ʻbd. | šbʻt.w.nṣp.ksp. | [-]tm.r 1017.3
y.il.ṣpn. | b qdš.b ǵr.nḥlt y. | b nʻm.b gbʻ.tliyt. | hlm.ʻnt.tph.ilm.b h.pʻnm. | ṭṭṭ.bʻd n.ksl.ṯṯbr. | ʻln.pn h.tdʻ.tǵṣ.pnt. | ks 3[ʻNT].3.29
m.asm. | b p h.rgm.l yṣa.b špt h[.hwt h]. | b nši ʻn h.w tphn.in.[---]. | [-]hlk.ǵlmm b dd y.yṣ[--]. | [-.]yṣa.w l.yṣa.hlm 19[1AQHT].2.76
rm.d b grn.ydn. | dn.almnt.yṯpṭ.ṯpṭ.ytm. | b nši ʻn h.w yphn.b alp. | šd.rbt.kmn.hlk.kṯr. | k yʻn.w yʻn.tdrq.ḫss. | hlk. 17[2AQHT].5.9
m.bmt.pḫl. | y dnil.ysb.palt h. | bṣql.yph.b palt.bṣ[q]l. | yph.b yǵlm.bṣql.y[ḫb]q. | w ynšq.aḥl.an bṣ[ql]. | ynpʻ.b palt.b 19[1AQHT].2.63
.l[b]mt ʻr. | l ysmsm.bmt.pḫl. | y dnil.ysb.palt h. | bṣql.yph.b palt.bṣ[q]l. | yph.b yǵlm.bṣql.y[ḫb]q. | w ynšq.aḥl.an b 19[1AQHT].2.62
. | ʻm.aliyn.bʻl.yšu. | g h.w yṣḥ.ʻl k.b[ʻ]l m. | pht.qlt.ʻl k.pht. | dry.b ḥrb.ʻl k. | pht.šrp.b išt. | ʻl k.[pht.ṭḥ]n.b rḥ | m.ʻ[l k 6[49].5.12
y.b ḥrb.ʻl k. | pht.šrp.b išt. | ʻl k.[pht.ṭḥ]n.b rḥ | m.ʻ[l k.]pht[.dr]y.b kbrt. | ʻl k.pht.[-]l[-]. | b šdm.ʻl k.pht. | drʻ.b ym.tn 6[49].5.16
| m.ʻ[l k.]pht[.dr]y.b kbrt. | ʻl k.pht.[-]l[-]. | b šdm.ʻl k.pht. | drʻ.b ym.tn.aḥd. | b aḫ k.ispa.w yṯb. | ap.d anšt.im[-]. | a 6[49].5.18
krpn.b klat.yd h. | b krb.ʻẓm.ridn. | mt.šmm.ks.qdš. | l tphn h.aṯt.krpn. | l tʻn.aṯrt.alp. | kd.yqḥ.b ḫmr. | rbt.ymsk.b 3[ʻNT].1.14
b.šnm. | l pʻn.il.thbr.w tql. | tšṭḥwy.w tkbd h. | hlm.il.k yphn h. | yprq.lṣb.w yṣḥq. | pʻn h.l hdm.yṯpd.w ykrkr. | uṣbʻt 4[51].4.27

.pḫmm.|t'pp.ṯr.il.d pid.|tǵẓy.bny.bnwt.|b nši.'n h.w tphn.|hlk.b'l.aṯtrt.|k t'n.hlk.btlt.|'nt.tdrq.ybmt.|[limm].b 4[51].2.12
ap.ilm.l lḥ[m].|yṯb.bn qdš.l ṯrm.b'l.qm.'l.il.hlm.|ilm.tph hm.tphn.mlak.ym.t'dt.ṯpṭ[.nhr].|t[ǵ]ly.hlm.rišt hm.l ẓr 2.1[137].22
i[--.---].|d.[---].|bnš[-] mdy[-].|w.b.glb.|phnn.w.|mndym.|bdnh.|l[q]ḥt.|[--]km.'m.mlk.|[b]ǵl hm. 2129.5
b nši[.'n h.w yphn.yḥd].|b 'rpt[.nšrm.yšu].|[g h.]w yṣḥ[.knp.nšrm].|b'l. 19[1AQHT].2.105
rm.ybn.|b'l.ybn.diy hmt nšrm.|tpr.w du.b nši.'n h.w ypn.|yḥd.hrgb.ab.nšrm.|yšu.g h.w yṣḥ.knp.hr[g]b.|b'l.yṯb. 19[1AQHT].3.120
n.|[b]'l.ybn.diy.hwt.hrg[b].|tpr.w du.b nši.'n h.|[w]yphn.yḥd.ṣml.um.nšrm.|yšu.g h.w yṣḥ.knp.ṣml.|b'l.yṯbr.b' 19[1AQHT].3.135
.|pht.qlt.'l k.pht.|dry.b ḥrb.'l k.|pht.šrp.b išt.|'l k.[pht.ṭḥ]n.b rḥ|m.'[l k.]pht[.dr]y.b kbrt.|'l k.pht.[-]l[-].|b šd 6[49].5.15
]ḫt h.šib.yṣat.mrḥ h.|l tl.yṣb.pn h.ṯǵr.|yṣu.hlm.aḫ h.tph.|[ksl]h.l arṣ.ṯṯbr.|[---.]aḫ h.tbky.|[--.m]rṣ.mlk.|[---.]kr 16.1[125].53
lḥ[m].|yṯb.bn qdš.l ṯrm.b'l.qm.'l.il.hlm.|ilm.tph hm.tphn.mlak.ym.t'dt.ṯpṭ[.nhr].|t[ǵ]ly.hlm.rišt hm.l ẓr.brkt h 2.1[137].22
id.yph.mlk.|r[š]p.ḥgb.ap.|w[.n]pš.ksp.|w ḫrṣ.km[-].|w.ḫ[--.-] 2005.1.1
hm.w ṯḫss.aṯrt.|ndr h.w ilt.p[--].|w tšu.g h.w [tṣḥ].|ph m'.ap.k[rt.--].|u ṯn.ndr[.---].|apr.[---].|[-----]. 15[128].3.28
].bn.ilm.mt.|'m.aliyn.b'l.yšu.|g h.w yṣḥ.'l k.b[']l m.|pht.qlt.'l k.pht.|dry.b ḥrb.'l k.|pht.šrp.b išt.|'l k.[pht.ṭḥ]n. 6[49].5.12
p k.yd.aqht.|ǵzr.tšt k.b qrb m.asm.|y.dnh.ysb.aklt h.yph.|šblt.b akt.šblt.yp'.|b ḥmdrt.šblt.yḥ[bq].|w ynšq.aḥl.a 19[1AQHT].2.68
h.w yṣḥ.'l k.b[']l m.|pht.qlt.'l k.pht.|dry.b ḥrb.'l k.|pht.šrp.b išt.|'l k.[pht.ṭḥ]n.b rḥ|m.'[l k.]pht[.dr]y.b kbrt.|'l 6[49].5.14
yn.iš[ryt.-]lnr.|spr.[--]ḥ[-] k.šb't.|ghl.ph.ṯmnt.|nblu h.špš.ymp.|hlkt.tdr[--].|špš.b'd h.t[--].|aṯr.a 27[8].3
[-----].|[-----].|il.šm'.amr k.ph[.-].|k il.ḥkmt.k ṯr.lṭpn.|ṣḥ.ngr.il.ilš.il[š].|w aṯt h.ngrt[.i] 16[126].4.2
išt.|'l k.[pht.ṭḥ]n.b rḥ|m.'[l k.]pht[.dr]y.b kbrt.|'l k.pht.[-]l[-].|b šdm.'l k.pht.|dr'.b ym.tn.aḥd.|b aḫ k.ispa.w y 6[49].5.17
yṣunn[.---].|[---.--]dy.w.pr'[.---].|[---.]ytn.ml[--].ank.iphn.|[---.a]nk.i[--.--]slm.w.yṯb.|[----.--]t.hw[-]y.h[--]r.w rg 1002.36
pṭ.ytm.---] h.|[---.---]n.|[-----].|hlk.[---.b n]ši.|'n h.w tphn.[---].|b grn.yḥrb[.---].|yǵly.yḥsp.ib[.---].|'l.bt.ab h.nšr 19[1AQHT].1.29
].yn.'šy l ḥbš.|[---.]ḥtn.qn.yṣbt.|[---.--]m.b nši.'n h.w tphn.|[---.--]ml.ksl h.k b[r]q.|[---.]m[-]ǵ[-].thmt.brq.|[---].t 17[2AQHT].6.10
[---.]h.yb[--].|[---.--]n.irš[.---].|[---.--]mr.ph.|[---.--]mm.hlkt.|[---.]b qrb.'r.|[---.m]lakm l h.|[---.]l.bn 26[135].3

phy

.šlm.[w spš].|mlk.rb.b'l h.[---].|nqmd.mlk.ugr[t.--].|phy.|w ṯpllm.mlk.r[b.--].|mṣmt.l nqmd.[---.-]št.|hl ny.arg 64[118].15

pwn

n.|[-]tn bn.agyn.|ullym.bn.abynm.|antn.bn.iwr[n]r.|pwn.ṯmry.|ksyn.bn.lḥsn.|[-]kyn.ṯmry. 94[313].8
gyn.m'[---].|w.agpṯn[.---].|ṯyndr[-.---].|gt.tg[yn.---].|pwn[.---]. 103[334].7

pwt

.ǵprt.|[---.š]pšg.iqni.mit.pṯtm.|[---].mitm.kslm.|[---].pwt.ṯlṯ.mat.abn.ṣrp.|[---.-]qt.l.ṯrmnm.|[---].ṯlṯm.iqnu.|[---.l 1106.10
arb'.alpm.|mitm.kbd.ṯlṯ.|arb'.kkrm.|ṯmn.mat.kbd.|pwt.|ṯmn.mat.pṯtm.|kkrm.alpm.|ḫmš.mat.kbd.|abn.ṣrp. 2051.6

pzny

|bn.ṯ[--].|bn.[---].|bn.ṯ'l[-].|bn.nq[ly].|bn.snr[n].|bn.pzn[y].|bn.mg[lb].|bn.db[--].|bn.amd[n].|annš[-]. 2020.10
.|bn.snrn.|bn.ṯgd.|bn.d[-]n.|bn.amdn.|bn.ṯmrn.|bn.pzny.|bn.mglb.|bn.[--]b.|bn.[---].|bn.[---]. 113[400].6.31

pḥ

d.|b d.tt.w.ṯlṯ.ktnt.b dm.tt.|w.ṯmnt.ksp.hn.|ktn.d.ṣr.pḥm.b h.w.ṯqlm.|ksp h.mitm.pḥm.b d.skn.|w.tt.ktnm.ḫmš 1110.4
.ṯmnt.ksp.hn.|ktn.d.ṣr.pḥm.b h.w.ṯqlm.|ksp h.mitm.pḥm.b d.skn.|w.tt.ktnm.ḫmšt.w.nṣp.ksp.hn. 1110.5
alpm.pḥm.ḫm[š].mat.kbd.|b d.tt.w.ṯlṯ.ktnt.b dm.tt.|w.ṯmnt.ksp. 1110.1

pḥl

.l[š']r.ṭl.|yd't.hlk.kbkbm.|bkm.tmdln.'r.|bkm.tṣmd.pḥl.bkm.|tšu.ab h.tštnn.l[b]mt 'r.|l ysmsm.bmt.pḥl.|y dni 19[1AQHT].2.58
md.pḥl.bkm.|tšu.ab h.tštnn.l[b]mt 'r.|l ysmsm.bmt.pḥl.|y dnil.ysb.palt h.|bṣql.yph.b palt.bṣ[q]l.|yph.b yǵlm.b 19[1AQHT].2.60
um.pḥl.pḥlt.bt.abn.bt šmm w thm.|qrit.l špš.um h.špš.um.ql.bl UG5.7.1
.|yḥbq.qdš.w amrr.|yštn.aṯrt.l bmt.'r.|l ysmsmt.bmt.pḥl.|qdš.yuḫdm.šb'r.|amrr.k kbkb.l pnm.|aṯr.btlt.'nt.|w b 4[51].4.15
m'.l qdš].|w am[rr.l dgy.rbt].|aṯrt.ym[.mdl.'r].|ṣmd.pḥl[.št.gpnm.dt].|ksp.dt.yr[q.nqbnm].|'db.gpn.atnt[y].|yš 4[51].4.5
m].|'db.gpn.atnt[y].|yšm'.qd.w amr[r].|mdl.'r.ṣmd.pḥl.|št.gpnm.dt.ksp.|dt.yrq.nqbnm.|'db.gpn.atnt h.|yḥbq. 4[51].4.9
mt[.my].|ḥspt.l š'r.ṭl.yd['t].|hlk.kbkbm.mdl.'r.|ṣmd.pḥl.št.gpn y dt ksp.|dt.yrq.nqbn y.tš[m'].|pǵt.ṯkmt.my.ḥsp 19[1AQHT].2.53

pḥlt

um.pḥl.pḥlt.bt.abn.bt šmm w thm.|qrit.l špš.um h.špš.um.ql.bl.'m. UG5.7.1

pḥm

nḥtm.ḫṭ k.mmnnm.mṭ yd k.hl.'ṣr.|tḥrr.l išt.w ṣḥrt.l pḥmm.aṯtm.a[ṯt.il].|aṯt.il.w 'lm h.yhbr.špt hm.yš[q].|hn.šp 23[52].48
.nḥtm.ḫṭ k.mmnnm.mṭ.yd k.|h[l.]'ṣr.tḥrr.l išt.ṣḥrrt.l pḥmm.|a[ṯ]tm.aṯt.il.aṯt.il.w 'lm h.w hm.|aṯtm.tṣḥn y.ad ad 23[52].41
mnn.mṭ.yd h.yšu.|yr.šmm h.yr.b šmm.'ṣr.yḥrṭ yšt.|l pḥm.il.aṯtm.k ypt.hm.aṯtm.tṣḥn.|y mt.mt.nḥtm.ḫṭ k.mmnn 23[52].39
ḥtm.ḫṭ k.|mmnnm.mṭ yd k.hl.'ṣr.tḥrr.l išt.|w ṣḥrrt.l pḥmm.btm.bt.il.bt.il.|w 'lm h.w hn.aṯtm.tṣḥn y.mt mt.|nḥt 23[52].45
ṯql.kbd[.ks].mn.ḫrṣ.|w arb'.ktnt.w [---]b.|[ḫm]š.mat pḥm.|[ḫm]š[.m]at.iqnu.|argmn.nqmd.mlk.|ugrt.d ybl.l špš 64[118].22
ṯmn.kkr.ṯlṯ.|ṯmn.kkr.brr.|arb'.alpm.pḥm.|ḫmš.mat.kbd.|arb'.alpm.iqni.|ḫmš.mat.kbd.|ṯlṯm.ḫ 1130.3
.|[ks.ksp.ktn.mit.pḥm].|[mit.iqn]i.l skl.[--].|[---.m]it pḥm.l š[--].|[---.]a[--.--.]hn[--]. 64[118].39
|ks.ḫrṣ.ktn.mit.pḥm.|mit.iqni.l mlkt.|ks.ḫrṣ.ktn.mit.pḥm.|mit.iqni.l uṯryn.|ks.ksp.ktn.mit.pḥm.|mit.iqni.l tpnr 64[118].29
s.ksp.ktn.mit.pḥm.|mit.iqni.l tpnr.|[ks.ksp.kt]n.mit.pḥ[m].|[mit.iqni.l]ḫbrtn[r].|[ks.ksp.ktn.mit.pḥ]m.|[mit.iq 64[118].33
t]n.mit.pḥ[m].|[mit.iqni.l]ḫbrtn[r].|[ks.ksp.ktn.mit.pḥ]m.|[mit.iqni.l ḫbrtn]r tn.|[ks.ksp.ktn.mit.pḥm].|[mit.iq 64[118].35
d.mlk.|ugrt.d ybl.l špš.|mlk.rb.b'l h.|ks.ḫrṣ.ktn.mit.pḥm.|mit.iqni.l mlkt.|ks.ḫrṣ.ktn.mit.pḥm.|mit.iqni.l uṯryn 64[118].27

pḥm

ktn.mit.pḫ]m.|[mit.iqni.l ḫbrtn]r ṯn.|[ks.ksp.ktn.mit.pḥm].|[mit.iqn]i.l skl.[--].|[---.m]it pḥm.l š[--].|[---.]a[--.--.] 64[118].37
ks.ḫrṣ.ktn.mit.pḥm.|mit.iqni.l uṯryn.|ks.ksp.ktn.mit.pḥm.|mit.iqni.l tpnr.|[ks.ksp.kt]n.mit.pḥ[m].|[mit.iqni.l]ḫ 64[118].31
d h.b ym.ṯn.|npyn h.b nhrm.|štt.ḫptr.l išt.|ḫbrṯ.l ẓr.pḥmm.|t'pp.ṯr.il.d pid.|tǵẓy.bny.bnwt.|b nši.'n h.w tphn.| 4[51].2.9

pḥr

w.ṯ' n[ṯ'y.hw.nkt.nk]t.ytši.l ab bn il.|ytši.l d[r.bn il.l]mpḥrt.bn il.|l ṯkm[n.w šnm.]hn '[r].|[---.]w npy[.---].|[---.] 32[2].1.34

pḫd

.|hrnmy.gm.l aṯt h.k yṣḥ.|šm'.mṯt.dnty.'d[b].|imr.b pḫd.l npš.kṯr.|w ḫss.l brlt.hyn d.|ḥrš yd.šlḥm.ššqy.|ilm sa 17[2AQHT].5.17
.kbd.hmt.b'l.|ḥkpt.il.kl h.tšm'.|mṯt.dnty.t'db.imr.|b pḫd.l npš.kṯr.w ḫss.|l brlt.hyn.d ḥrš.|ydm.aḫr.ymǵy.kṯr.| 17[2AQHT].5.23

pḫn

.ṯǵrm.|rb qrt.aḫd.|ṯmn.ḫzr.|w.arb'.ḥršm.|dt.tb'ln.b.pḫn.|ṯṯtm.ḫzr.w.'št.'šr.ḥrš.|dt.tb'ln.b.ugrt.|ṯṯtm.ḫzr.|dt.tb' 1024.3.6

pḫr

--].|[a]rṣ.|[u]šḫr[y].|[']ṯtrt.|i[l t]'ḏr b'l.|ršp.|ddmš.|pḫr ilm.|ym.|uṯḫt.|knr.|mlkm.|šlm. 29[17].2.7
š.ršp.š.ddmš.š.|w šlmm.ilib.š.i[l.--]m d gbl.ṣpn.al[p].|pḫr.ilm.š.ym.š[.k]nr.š.[--.]'ṣrm gdlt.|b'lm.kmm.b'lm.kmm[. UG5.9.1.9
w.ṯ'.nṯ'y.hw.nkt.n[k]t.ytši[.l ab.bn.il].|ytši.l dr.bn.il.l mpḫrt.bn.i[l.l ṯkmn.w š]nm hn š.|w šqrb.'r.mšr mšr bn.ugr 32[2].1.17
w.ṯ'.nṯ'y.hw.nkt.nkt.]yt[ši.l ab.bn.il].|[ytši.l dr.bn.il.l mpḫ]rt.[bn.il.l ṯkmn.w š]n]m hn š.|[---.w n]py.gr[.ḥmyt.ugr 32[2].1.9B
'.nṯ']y.|[hw.nkt.nkt.ytši.l ab.bn.il.ytši.l d]r.bn[.il].|[l mpḫrt.bn.il.l ṯkmn.w šnm.hn š].|[w šqrb.š.mšr mšr.bn.ugrt 32[2].1.3
.ṯ' |nṯ'y.|hw.nkt.nkt.y[t]ši.l ab.bn.il.ytši.l dr.|bn il.l mpḫrt.bn.il.l ṯkmn[.w]šnm.hn.'r.|w.ṯb.l mspr.m[šr] mšr.bt 32[2].1.26
il b[n] il.|dr bn il.|mpḫrt bn il.|ṯrmn w šnm.|il w aṯrt.|ḫnn il.|nṣbt il.|šlm il. 30[107].3
yt'dd.rkb.'rpt.|[--].ydd.w yqlṣn.|yqm.w ywpṯn.b tk.|p[ḫ]r.bn.ilm.štt.|p[--].b ṯlḥn y.qlt.|b ks.ištyn h.|dm.ṯn.dbḥ 4[51].3.14
].|b'[l.š].aṯrt[.š.ṯkm]n w [šnm.š].|'nt š ršp š[.dr.il.w pḫr.b'l].|gdlt.šlm[.gdlt.w burm.lb].|rmṣt.ilh[m.b'lm.---].|k 35[3].16
.]ilhm.|[b]'l š.aṯrt.š.ṯkmn w šnm.š.|'nt.š.ršp.š.dr il w p[ḫ]r b'l.|gdlt.šlm.gdlt.w burm.[l]b.|rmṣt.ilhm.b'lm.dṯt.w 34[1].7
.ilhm.b'l.š.aṯrt.š].|ṯkmn.w š[nm.š.'nt.š.ršp.š.dr].|il.w pḫr[.b'l.gdlt.šlm.gdlt].|w burm.l[b.rmṣt.ilhm].|b'lm.w mlu APP.II[173].18
[-----].|[---.]'l.ṯny[.---]|[---.]pḫyr.bt h.[---].|[ḫm]šm.ksp.'l.gd[--].|[---].ypḥ.'bdršp.b[--.-- 1144.3
.ḥtk h.rš.|mid.grdš.ṯbt h.|w b tm hn.špḥ.yitbd.|w b.pḫyr h.yrṯ.|y'rb.b ḥdr h.ybky.|b ṯn.[-]gmm.w ydm'.|tntkn. 14[KRT].1.25
h.yrk.b'[l].|[---.]bt k.ap.l pḫr k 'nt tqm.'nt.tqm.|[---.p]ḫr k.ygrš k.qr.bt k.ygrš k.|[---].bnt.ṣ'ṣ.bnt.m'm'.'bd.ḥrn.[1001.2.10
t[--].|[---.]drk.brḥ.arṣ.lk pn h.yrk.b'[l].|[---.]bt k.ap.l pḫr k 'nt tqm.'nt.tqm.|[---.p]ḫr k.ygrš k.qr.bt k.ygrš k.|[--- 1001.2.9
[---.]btlt.'nt.|[---.]pp.hrm.|[---].d l yd' bn il.|[---.]pḫr kkbm.|[---.]dr dt.šmm.|[---.al]iyn b'l.|[---].rkb.'rpt.|[-- 10[76].1.4
hr.[b]ḥbq.w ḥ[m]ḥmt.yṯb[n].|yspr.l ḫmš.l ṣ[---.]šr.pḫr.klat.|tqtnṣn.w tldn.tld.[ilm.]n'mm.agzr ym.|bn.ym.yn 23[52].57
.'n.bṯt.tpnn.|'n.mḫr.'n.pḫr.'n.ṯǵr.|'n.ṯǵr.l.ṯǵr.ttb.|'n.pḫr.l.pḫr.ttb.|'n.mḫr.l.mḫr.ttb.|'n.bty.l.bty.ttb.|'n.bṯt.l.bṯt. RS225.8
arṯ m.pḏ h.tb'.ǵlmm.l ttb.[idk.pnm].|l ytn.tk.ǵr.ll.'m.phr.m'd.ap.ilm.l lḥ[m].|yṯb.bn qdš.l ṯrm.b'l.qm.'l.il.hlm.|il 2.1[137].20
r.tmǵyn.mlak ym.t'dt.ṯpṭ.nhr.l p'n.il.|[l t]pl.l tštḥwy.pḫr.m'd.qmm.a[--].amr.|[ṯn]y.d't hm.išt.ištm.yitmr.ḥrb.lṭšt 2.1[137].31
].|al.ttn.'m.pḫr.m'd.t[k.ǵr.ll.l p'n.il].|al.tpl.al.tštḥwy.pḫr [m'd.qmm.a--.am]|r ṯny.d't km.w rgm.l ṯr.a[b.-.il.ṯny.l 2.1[137].15
'd.qmm.a--.am]|r ṯny.d't km.w rgm.l ṯr.a[b.-.il.ṯny.l pḫr].|m'd.ṯhm.ym.b'l km.adn km.ṯ[pṭ.nhr].|tn.il m.d tq h. 2.1[137].16
-].|uṯ.ṯbr.ap hm.tb'.ǵlm[m.al.ttb.idk.pnm].|al.ttn.'m.pḫr.m'd.t[k.ǵr.ll.l p'n.il].|al.tpl.al.tštḥwy.pḫr [m'd.qmm.a-- 2.1[137].14
.|tšt.dm.h.l.bl.ks.|tpnn.'n.bty.'n.bṯt.tpnn.|'n.mḫr.'n.pḫr.'n.ṯǵr.|'n.ṯǵr.l.ṯǵr.ttb.|'n.pḫr.l.pḫr.ttb.|'n.mḫr.l.mḫr.tt RS225.6
[-----].|[---.mid.rm.]krt.|[b tk.rpi.]arṣ.|[b pḫr].qbṣ.dtn.|[w t]qrb.w ld.|bn.tl k.|tld.pǵt.t[--]t.|tld.pǵt[. 15[128].3.4
pǵ[t.---].|tld.p[ǵt.---].|mid.rm[.krt].|b tk.rpi.ar[ṣ].|b pḫr.qbṣ.dtn.|ṣǵrt hn.abkrn.|tbrk.ilm.tity.|tity.ilm.l ahl hm 15[128].3.15
t.tpnn.|'n.mḫr.'n.pḫr.'n.ṯǵr.|'n.ṯǵr.l.ṯǵr.ttb.|'n.pḫr.l.pḫr.ttb.|'n.mḫr.l.mḫr.ttb.|'n.bty.l.bty.ttb.|'n.bṯt.l.bṯt.ttb. RS225.8
[---.mšr m]šr.|[bn.ugrt.---.--]y.|[---.np]y nqmd.|[---.]pḫr.|[-----].|[-----].|[---.t'ḏ]r b'l.|[-----].|[-----].|[---.--]r.|[--- APP.I[-].2.4

pḫry

tḥm.hl[--].|l pḫry.a[ḫ y].|w l g.p[-]r[--].|yšlm[.l k].|[i]lm[.ṯǵr k].|[t]š[lm 56[21].2

pṭḏ

šd.b d.iwrm[--].|šd.b d.yṯpr.|šd.b d.krb[-].|šd.b d.bn.pṭḏ.|šd.b d.dr.khnm.|šd.b d.bn.'my.|šd.b d.bn.'yn.|ṯn.šdm 2090.16

pṭḏn

.|bn.adlḏn.|bn.šbl.|bn.ḫnzr.|bn.arwṯ.|bn.ṯbtnq.|bn.pṭḏn.|bn.nbdg.|bn.ḥgbn.|bn.tmr.|bn.prsn.|bn.ršpy.|[']bd 113[400].1.17
wn.'š[rm].|ṣṣ.bn.iršyn.[---].|[ṣṣ].bn.ilb'l.ṯl[ṯ]m.|ṣṣ.bn.pṭḏn.[--]m.|ṣṣ.[bn].gyn.[---].|[-----].|[-----].|[-----].|[-----].|[2096.7

pṭr

]pi[-.]adm.|[---.]iṯ[-].yšql.ytk[.--]np bl.hn.|[---].ḥ[m]t.pṭr.w.p nḥš.|[---.--]q.n[ṯ]k.l yd'.l bn.l pq ḥmt.|[---.--]n h.ḥ UG5.8.34

pẓǵ

.yšt|ql.dnil.l hkl h.'rb.b|kyt.b hkl h.mššpdt.b ḥẓr h.|pẓǵm.ǵr.ybk.l aqht.|ǵzr.ydm'.l kdd.dnil.|mt.rpi.l ymm.l yr 19[1AQHT].4.173
u.|g h.w yṣḥ.t[b'.---].|bkyt.b hk[l]y.mššpdt.|b ḥẓr y pẓǵm.ǵr.w yq.|dbḥ.ilm.yš'ly.dǵṯ h.|b šmym.dǵṯ hrnmy[.d 19[1AQHT].4.184

py

.|bn.ṣmy.|bn.mry[n].|bn.mgn.|bn.'dn.|bn.knn.|bn.py.|bn.mk[-].|bn.by[--].|bn.a[--].|bn.iy[--].|bn.ḫ[---].|bn.p 2117.1.9

pyn

].|'bdmlk.krm.aḥ[d.---].|krm.ubdy.b d.ǵ[--.---].|krm.pyn.arty[.---].|ṯlṯ.krm.ubdym.l mlkt.b.'nmky[.---].|mgdly.ǵ 1081.8
bn.gnb[.msg].|bn.twyn[.msg].|bn.'drš[p.msg].|pyn.yny.[msg].|bn.mṣrn m[sg].|yky msg.|ynḥm.msg.|bn.u 133[-].1.4

pynq

k.ns[--.---]. | bn.tbd.ilšt[m'y.---]. | mty.ilšt[m'y.---]. | bn.pynq.'nqp[a]t[y.---]. | ayiḫ.ilšt[m'y.---]. | [b]dlm.dt.ytb[.---]. | [90[314].2.8

pky

.špš.b šmm.tqru. | [---.]nplt.y[--].md'.nplt.bšr. | [---].w tpky.k[m.]n'r.tdm'.km. | [ṣǵ]r.bkm.y'ny[.---.bn]wt h. | [--]nn. UG5.8.40

pl

.ṯn.šm.w alp.l[--]n. | [---.]š.il š.b'l š.dgn š. | [---.--]r.w ṯt pl.gdlt.[ṣ]pn.dqt. | [---.al]p 'nt.gdlt.b ṯlṯt mrm. | [---.i]l š.b'l š. 36[9].1.4
ṣḥ. | ṯḥm.ṯr.il.ab k. | hwt.lṭpn.ḥtk k. | pl.'nt.šdm.y špš. | pl.'nt.šdm.il.yš[t k]. | b'l.'nt.mḥrṯ[-]. | iy.aliyn.b'l. | iy.zbl.b'l.a 6[49].4.37
t.šm'.l btlt.'n[t]. | rgm.l nrt.il.šp[š]. | pl.'nt.šdm.y špš. | pl.'nt.šdm.il.yšt k. | [b]'l.'nt.mḥrṯt. | iy.aliyn.b'l. | iy.zbl.b'l.ar 6[49].4.26
.špš. | tšu.g h.w tṣḥ. | ṯḥm.ṯr.il.ab k. | hwt.lṭpn.ḥtk k. | pl.'nt.šdm.y špš. | pl.'nt.šdm.il.yš[t k]. | b'l.'nt.mḥrṯ[-]. | iy.ali 6[49].4.36
m.yṣḥ.il.l btlt. | 'nt.šm'.l btlt.'n[t]. | rgm.l nrt.il.šp[š]. | pl.'nt.šdm.y špš. | pl.'nt.šdm.il.yšt k. | [b]'l.'nt.mḥrṯt. | iy.aliy 6[49].4.25
rd. | [---.--]ṯ.l.yšn. | [šd.--]ln. | b d.trǵds. | šd.ṯ'lb. | b d.bn.pl. | šd.bn.kt. | b d.pdy. | šd.ḫzr. | [b d].d[---]. 2030.2.4
n.nṣdn.l bn.'mlbi. | šd.ṯpḫln.l bn.ǵl. | w dṯn.nḥl h.l bn.pl. | šd.krwn.l aḫn. | šd.'yy.l aḫn. | šd.brdn.l bn.bly. | šd gzl.l.b 2089.10

plg

ǵy.ḥrn.l bt h.w. | yštql.l ḥṭr h.tlu ḥt.km.nḫl. | tplg.km.plg. | b'd h.bhtm.mnt.b'd h.bhtm.sgrt. | b'd h.'dbt.ṯlṯ.ptḥ.bt. UG5.7.69
ybln h.mǵy.ḥrn.l bt h.w. | yštql.l ḥṭr h.tlu ḥt.km.nḫl. | tplg.km.plg. | b'd h.bhtm.mnt.b'd h.bhtm.sgrt. | b'd h.'dbt.ṯl UG5.7.69

pld

| w.ṯn.b.ḫmšt. | ṯprt.b.ṯlṯt. | mṯyn.b.ṯṯt. | ṯn.lbšm.b.'šrt. | pld.b.arb't. | lbš.ṯn.b.ṯnt.'šrt. 1108.7
. | ḫ[mš.]š'rt. | [---.]tš'.kbd.skm. | [arb]'m.ḫpnt.pṯt. | [-]r.pldm.dt.š'rt. | ṯlṯm.ṯlṯ.kbd.mṣrrt. | 'šr.ṯn.kbd.pǵdrm. | ṯmn.mr 1111.8
[-----]. | 'šr[.---]. | ud[-.---]. | ṯn pld mḫ[--.---]. | ṯ[--] ḫpnt. | [---] kdwṯm.[---]. | ḫmš.pld š'rt. | ṯṯ 1113.4
-]dr | m.ṯn kndwm adrm. | w knd pnṯ.dq. | ṯn ḫpnm.ṯn pldm ǵlmm. | kpld.b[-.-]r[--]. | w blḫ br[-]m p[-]. | b[--.]l[-.]m 140[98].4
[--.---]. | ṯ[--] ḫpnt. | [---] kdwṯm.[---]. | ḫmš.pld š'rt. | ṯṯ pld pṯt. | arb' ḫpnt pṯt. | ḫmš ḫpnt.š'rt. | ṯlṯ.'šr kdwṯm. 1113.8
ṯn.pld.pṯt[.-]r. | lpš.sgr.rq. | ṯṯ.prqt. | w.mrdt.prqt.pṯt. | lbš.psm.r 1112.1
. | ṯn pld mḫ[--.---]. | ṯ[--] ḫpnt. | [---] kdwṯm.[---]. | ḫmš.pld š'rt. | ṯṯ pld pṯt. | arb' ḫpnt pṯt. | ḫmš ḫpnt.š'rt. | ṯlṯ.'šr kd 1113.7
ṯṯ.prqt. | w.mrdt.prqt.pṯt. | lbš.psm.rq. | ṯn.mrdt.az. | ṯlṯ.pld.š'rt. | ṯ[---].kbm. | p[---]r.aḫd. | [-----]. | [-----]. | [---.--]y. | [--- 1112.7
lṯ.kbd.mṣrrt. | 'šr.ṯn.kbd.pǵdrm. | ṯmn.mrbdt.mlk. | 'šr.pld.š'rt. 1111.12

plwn

amry.kdm. | mnn.bn.gṯṯn.kdm. | ynḥm.bn[.-]r[-]t.ṯlṯ. | plwn.kdm. | tmyn.bn.ubrš.kd. 136[84].11

plz

[--]. | [-----]. | [-----]. | [---.]tty. | [---.-]rd y. | [---.]b'l. | [---].plz. | [---.-]tt k. | [---.]mlk. 2159.17

plzn

--]. | swn.qrty[.---]. | uḫ h.w.'šr[.---]. | klyn.apsn[y.---]. | plzn.qrty[.---]. | w.klt h.b.t[--.---]. | b'l y.mlk[y.---]. | yd.bt h.y 81[329].11

plṭ

šhlk[.šbt k.dmm]. | [šbt.dq]n k.mm'm.w[---]. | aqht.w yplṭ k.bn[.dnil.---]. | w y'ḏr k.b yd.btlt.['nt]. | w y'n.lṭpn.il d 18[3AQHT].1.13
r.bn.prsn. | agpṯr.w.šǵ[r h]. | ṯ'ln. | mztn.w.šǵr [h]. | šǵr.plṭ. | s[d]rn [w].ṯn.šǵr h. | [---.]w.šǵr h. | [---.]w.šǵr h. | [---.]kr 2072.7

ply

nn.ṯṯm. | b.rpan.bn.yyn.'šrt. | b.yp'r.'šrm. | b.n'mn.bn.ply.ḫmšt.l.'šrm. | b.gdn.bn.uss.'šrm. | b.'dn.bn.ṯṯ.'šrt. | b.bn.q 2054.1.17
k]. | ǵr.tliyt.šb't.brqm.[---]. | ṯmnt.iṣr r't.'ṣ brq y. | riš h.tply.ṭly.bn.'n h. | uz'rt.tmll.išd h.qrn[m]. | dt.'l h.riš h.b glṯ.b UG5.3.1.5

plk

[-----]. | l abn[.---]. | aḫdt.plk h[.b yd h]. | plk.qlt.b ymn h. | npyn h.mks.bšr h. | tmt'.m 4[51].2.3
[-----]. | l abn[.---]. | aḫdt.plk h[.b yd h]. | plk.qlt.b ymn h. | npyn h.mks.bšr h. | tmt'.md h.b ym.ṯn. | np 4[51].2.4

pll

]n.ṯqrn.b d.ḫby. | [ṯn.š]d.bn.ngzḫn.b d.gmrd. | [šd.bn].pll.b d.gmrd. | [šd.bn.-]ll.b d.iwrḫṯ. | [šd.bn.-]nn.b d.bn.šmr 82[300].1.24
.šwn.b d.ttyn.nḥl [h]. | šd.ttyn[.b]n.arkšt. | l'q[.---]. | šd.pll.b d.qrt. | š[d].annḏr.b d.bdn.nḥ[l h]. | [šd.]agyn.b d.kmrn. 2029.6

pln

šd.irdyn.bn.ḫrǵš[-].l.qrt. | šd.iǵlyn.bn.kzbn.l.qr[t]. | šd.pln.bn.tiyn.b d.ilmhr nḥl h. | šd knn.bn.ann.'db. | šd.iln[-].bn 2029.18
]n.ann.'[db]. | šd.ṯ[r]yn.bn.tkn.b d.qrt. | šd[.-]dyn.b d.pln.nḥl h. | šd.irdyn.bn.ḫrǵš[-].l.qrt. | šd.iǵlyn.bn.kzbn.l.qr[t] 2029.15
wn.qrty.w.[b]n h[.---]. | w.alp h.w.a[r]b'.l.arb'[m.---]. | pln.ṯmry.w.ṯn.bn h.w[.---]. | ymrn.apsny.w.aṯt h..b[n.---]. | pr 2044.8

plnt

--.--]m.ql.hm[.---]. | [---].aṯt n.r[---]. | [---.]ḫr[-.--]. | [---.]plnt.[---]. | [---.]'mt.l ql.rpi[.---]. | [---.-]llm.abl.mṣrp k.[---]. | [- 1001.2.1

pls

'n. | ml[--.---]. | ar[--.---.--]l. | aty[n.bn.]šm'nt. | ḥnn[.bn].pls. | abrš[p.bn.]ḫrpn. | gmrš[.bn].mrnn. | 'bdmlk.bn.'myn. | a 102[323].4.5
bn.mk[-]. | bn.by[--]. | bn.a[--]. | bn.iy[--]. | bn.ḫ[---]. | bn.pls. | bn.ubr. | bn.'ptb. | ṯbry. | bn.ymn. | krty. | bn.abr[-]. | yrpu. 2117.1.15
.'bdṯrm. | kd.'bdil. | ṭiṭ.'l.bn.srt. | kd.'l.zrm. | kd.'l.šz.bn pls. | kd.'l.ynḥm. | tgrm.šmn.d.bn.kwy. | 'l.šlmym.ṯmn.kbd. | ṯ 1082.2.6
n.dll.qšt.w.ql[']. | bn.pǵyn.qšt.w[.q]l'. | bn.bdn.qšt. | bn.pls.qšt. | ǵmrm. | [-]lhd.ṯt.qštm.w.ṯn.ql'm. | ulšn.ṯt.qšm.w.ql'. 119[321].3.31

plsy

n.bn.knn. | iwrḫz.b d.skn. | škny.adddy. | mšu.adddy. | plsy.adddy. | aḫyn. | ygmr.adddy. | gln.aṯṯ. | ddy.[a]dddy. | bn. 2014.40
| [---]rn. | ill. | ǵlmn. | bn.ytrm. | bn.ḫgbt. | mtn. | mḫtn. | [p]lsy. | bn.ḥrš. | [--.]kbd. | [---]. | y[---]. | bn.ǵlyn. | bdl.ar. | bn.šy 1035.2.14
. | bn.nrpd. | bn.ḥ[-]y. | b'lskn. | bn.'bd. | ḫyrn. | alpy. | bn.plsy. | bn.qrr[-]. | bn.ḥyl. | bn.g'yn. | ḥyn. | bn.armg[-]. | b'lmṯpṭ 1035.1.19
spr.bdlm. | n'mn. | rbil. | plsy. | ygmr. | mnṯ. | prḫ. | 'dršp. | ršpab. | ṯnw. | abmn. | abǵl. | b' 1032.4
r. | mkrm. | 'zn. | yplṭ. | 'bdmlk. | ynḥm. | adddn. | mtn. | plsy. | qṭn. | ypr. | bn.ymy. | bn.'rd. | [-]b.da[-]. | [--]l[--]. | [-----]. 1035.4.9
ṯḥm.iwrdr. | l.plsy. | rgm. | yšlm.l k. | l.trǵds. | w.l.klby. | šm't.ḫti. | nḫtu.ht. | 53[54].2
m. | rqdym. | šṭšm.ṯṯ mat. | ṣprn.ṯṯ mat. | dkry.ṯṯ mat. | [p]lsy.ṯṯ mat. | 'dn.ḫmš [m]at. | [--]kb'l ṯṯ [mat]. | [-----]. | ilmlk 1060.1.6

plš̀

bn.mk[-]. | bn.by[--]. | bn.a[--]. | bn.iy[--]. | bn.ḥ[---]. | bn.plš̀. | bn.ubr. | bn.'pṯb. | ṯbry. | bn.ymn. | krty. | bn.abr[-]. | yrpu. 2117.1.15

plš̀b'l

šm [---]. | kn'm.bn.[---]. | plš̀b'l.bn.n[--]. | ḥy bn.dnn.ṯkt. | ilṯḥm.bn.dnn.ṯkt. | šb'l.bn.aly 2085.3

plǵn

tldn. | ṯrkn. | kli. | plǵn. | apš̀ny. | 'rb[.---]. | w.b.p[.--]. | apš̀[ny]. | b.yṣi h. | ḥwt.[--- 2116.4

plṯ

ṯb. | l hdm[.w] l.hdm.yṯb. | l arṣ.yṣq.'mr. | un.l riš h.'pr.plṯt. | l qdqd h.lpš.yks. | mizrtm.ǵr.b abn. | ydy.psltm.b y'r. | y 5[67].6.15

pmlk

b'ln. | yrmn. | 'nil. | pmlk. | aby. | 'dyn. | aǵlyn. | [--]rd. | [--]qrd. | [--]r. 1066.4

pmn

.yk[--]. | bn.šmm. | bn.irgy. | w.nḥl h. | w.nḥl hm. | [bn].pmn. | bn.gṯrn. | bn.arpḫn. | bn.ṯryn. | bn.dll. | bn.ḫswn. | mryn 1046.3.27
'rby. | n'mn.ṯt.qštm.w.ql'. | gln.ṯt.qštm.w.ql'. | gtn.qšt. | pmn.ṯt.qšt.w.ql'. | bn.zry.q[š]t.w.ql'. | bn.tlmyn.ṯt.qštm.w.ql' 104[316].9

pn

| [----.-]bb. | [----.]lm y. | [---.--]p. | [---.d]bḥ. | t[---.id]k. | pn[m.al.ttn]. | 'm.[krt.msw]n. | w r[gm.l krt.]ṯ'. | ṯḥm[.pbl.ml 14[KRT].5.246
lṣ.'lṣm.npr.š[--.---]. | uṭ.ṯbr.ap hm.tb'.ǵlm[m.al.ṯṯb.idk.pnm]. | al.ttn.'m.pḫr.m'd.t[k.ǵr.ll.l p'n.il]. | al.tpl.al.tšṯḥwy.p 2.1[137].13
ḥy.np[š.a]rš. | l.pn.b'[l y.l].pn.b'l y. | w.urk.ym.b'l y. | l.pn.amn.w.l.pn. | il.mṣrm.dt.tǵrn. | npš.špš.mlk. | rb.b'l y. 1018.21
. | l ysmsmt.bmt.pḫl. | qdš.yuḫdm.šb'r. | amrr.k kbkb.l pnm. | aṯr.btlt.'nt. | w b'l.tb'.mrym.ṣpn. | idk.l ttn.pnm. | 'm.il. 4[51].4.17
.mlk.[b]'l y. | w.hn.ibm.šṣq l y. | p.l.ašt.aṯt y. | n'r y.ṯh.l pn.ib. | hn.hm.yrgm.mlk. | b'l y.tmǵyy.hn. | alpm.š̀šwm.hnd. 1012.29
. | l.pn.b'[l y.l].pn.b'l y. | w.urk.ym.b'l y. | l.pn.amn.w.l.pn. | il.mṣrm.dt.tǵrn. | npš.špš.mlk. | rb.b'l y. 1018.21
hm. | b hm.qrnm. | km.ṯrm.w gbṯt. | km.ibrm. | w b hm.pn.b'l. | b'l.ytlk.w yṣd. | yḥ pat.mlbr. | wn.ymǵy.aklm. | w ym 12[75].1.33
rš[.---]. | mlk.r[b.b']l y.p.l. | ḥy.np[š.a]rš. | l.pn.b'[l y.l].pn.b'l y. | w.urk.ym.b'l y. | l.pn.amn.w.l.pn. | il.mṣrm.dt.tǵrn. 1018.19
.an[k.---]. | arš[.---]. | mlk.r[b.b']l y.p.l. | ḥy.np[š.a]rš. | l.pn.b'[l y.l].pn.b'l y. | w.urk.ym.b'l y. | l.pn.amn.w.l.pn. | il.mṣ 1018.19
]. | b'l.sid.zbl.b'l. | arṣ.qm.yṯ'r. | w yšlḥmn h. | ybrd.ṯd.l pnw h. | b ḥrb.mlḥt. | qṣ.mri.ndd. | y'šr.w yšqyn h. | ytn.ks.b d 3['NT].1.6
. | btlt.'nt.k [rḥ.npš h]. | k iṯl.brlt h.[b h.p'nm]. | ṭṭṭ.'l[n.pn h.td'.b 'dn]. | ksl.y[ṯbr.ygṣ.pnt.ksl h]. | anš.[dt.ẓr h.yšu.g 19[1AQHT].2.94
liyt. | hlm.'nt.tph.ilm.b h.p'nm. | ṭṭṭ.b'd n.ksl.ṯṯbr. | 'ln.pn h.td'.tǵṣ.pnt. | ksl h.anš.dt.ẓr h.tšu. | g h.w tṣḥ.ik.mǵy.gp 3['NT].3.31
drq.ybmt. | [limm].b h.p'nm. | [ṭṭṭ.b ']dn.ksl. | [ṯṯbr.'ln.p]n h.td[']. | tǵṣ[.pnt.ks]l h. | anš.dt.ẓr.[h]. | tšu.g h.w tṣḥ[.i]k. 4[51].2.18
| ybnt.ab h.šrḥq.aṯt.l pnn h. | št.alp.qdm h.mria.w tk. | pn h.tḥspn.m h.w trḥṣ. | ṭl.šmm.šmn.arṣ.ṭl.šm[m.t]sk h. | rbb 3['NT].4.86
. | w yšu.'n h.w y'n. | w y'n.btlt.'nt. | n'mt.bn.aḫt.b'l. | l pnn h.ydd.w yqm. | l p'n h.ykr'.w yql. | w yšu.g h.w yṣḥ. | ḥw 10[76].2.17
km kbkbt k ṯn. | [---.]b'l yḥmdn h.yrṯ y. | [---.]dmrn.l pn h yrd. | [---.]b'l.šm[.--.]rgbt yu. | [---]w yrmy[.q]rn h. | [---. 2001.2.8
]k.drḫm.w aṯb.l ntbt.k.'ṣm l t[--]. | [---.]drk.brḥ.arṣ.lk pn h.yrk.b'[l]. | [---.]bt k.ap.l pḫr k 'nt tqm.'nt.tqm. | [---.p]ḫ 1001.2.8
| ǵlmm. | aḫr.mǵy.kṯr.w ḫss. | št.alp.qdm h.mra. | w tk.pn h.t'db.ksu. | w yṯṯb.l ymn.aliyn. | b'l.'d.lḥm.št[y.ilm]. | [w 4[51].5.108
.rbt.kmn. | hlk.aḫt h.b'l.y'n.tdrq. | ybnt.ab h.šrḥq.aṯt.l pnn h. | št.alp.qdm h.mria.w tk. | pn h.tḥspn.m h.w trḥṣ. | ṭl.š 3['NT].4.84
h. | [---].mǵy h.w ǵlm. | [a]ḫt h.šib.yṣat.mrḥ h. | l tl.yṣb.pn h.tǵr. | yṣu.hlm.aḫ h.tph. | [ksl]h.l arṣ.ṯṯbr. | [---.]aḫ h.tbk 16.1[125].52
r.k l hm.d l h q[--.---]. | l ytn.l hm.tḫt b'l[.---]. | h.u qšt pn hdd.b y[.----]. | 'm.b ym b'l ysy ym[.---]. | rmm.ḫnpm.mḫ 9[33].2.6
.nrt.ilm.špš.tšu.g h.w t[ṣḥ.šm]'.m'. | [-.yṯ]ir ṯr.il.ab k.l pn.zbl.ym.l pn[.ṯ]pṭ[.n]hr. | [ik.a]l.yšm' k.ṯr.[i]l.ab k.l ys'.[al 2.3[129].16
. | [--]b b[ht]. | [zbl.]ym.b hkl.ṯpṭ.nh[r].yṯir.ṯr.il.ab h l pn[.zb]l y[m]. | [l pn.ṯp]ṭ[.nhr.]mlkt.[--]pm.l mlkt.wn.in.aṯt. 2.3[129].21
n y. | [--.]šir.b krm.nṭṭt.dm.'lt.b ab y. | u---].'lt.b k.lk.l pn y.yrk.b'l.[--]. | [---.]'nt.šzrm.tštšḥ.km.ḥ[--]. | [---].'pr.bt k. 1001.1.10
[.--]yt.w.[---]. | [---.ṯ]y.al.an[k.---.]il[m.--]y. | [--.m]šlm.pn y[.-.]tlkn. | [---.]rḫbn.hm.[-.]aṯr[.---]. | [--]šy.w ydn.b'[l.---] 1002.59
b'.l šb'm.aṯr. | [---.--]ldm.dt ymtm. | [--.--]r.l ẓpn. | [---.]pn.ym.y[--]. | [---].b'l.tdd. | [---.]hkl. | [---.]yd h. | [---.]tmt. 25[136].6
k.ṯmn.ḫnzr k. | 'm k.pdry.bt.ar. | 'm k.ṭṭly.bt.rb.idk. | pn k.al ttn.tk.ǵr. | knkny.ša.ǵr.'l ydm. | ḫlb.l ẓr.rḥtm w rd. | b 5[67].5.12
k.l tdn. | dn.almnt.l ṯpṭ. | ṯpṭ qṣr.npš.l tdy. | ṯšm.'l.dl.l pn k. | l tšlḥm.ytm.b'd. | ksl k.almnt.km. | aḫt.'rš.mdw.anšt. | 16.6[127].48
g.kr]t.l ḥ[ẓ]r y. | [-----]. | [---.ttb']. | [mlakm.l yṯb]. | [idk.pnm.l ytn]. | [']m[.krt.mswn h]. | tš[an.g hm.w tṣḥn]. | ṯḥ[m.p 14[KRT].6.265
w ld.špḥ.l krk | t.w ǵlm.l 'bd. | il.ttb'.mlakm. | l yṯb.idk.pnm. | l ytn.'mm.pbl. | mlk.tšan. | g hm.w tṣḥn. | ṯḥm.krt.ṯ[']. 14[KRT].6.301
. | b ḥrn.pnm.trǵnw.w ṯtkl. | bnwt h.ykr.'r.d qdm. | idk.pnm.l ytn.tk aršḫ.rbt. | w aršḫ.ṯrrt.ydy.b 'ṣm.'r'r. | w b šḫt.'s. UG5.7.63
.b'l.[w 'nn h]. | bn.dgn.arṯ m.pd h.tb'.ǵlmm.l ṯṯb.[idk.pnm]. | l ytn.tk.ǵr.ll.'m.phr.m'd.ap.ilm.l lḥ[m]. | yṯb.bn qdš.l 2.1[137].19
ṯb.l y. | bm.ṯy.ndr. | iṯt.'mn.mlkt. | w.rgm y.l[--]. | lqt.w.pn. | mlk.nr b n. 50[117].17
gnryn. | l mlkytn. | ḥnn y l pn mlk. | šin k itn. | r' y šṣa idn l y. | l šmn iṯr hw. | p iḫdn gnr 1020.3
t.b [---]. | irt k.dṯ.ydṯ.m'qb k.[ttb']. | [bt]lt.'nt.idk.l ttn.[pnm]. | ['m.a]qht.ǵzr.b alp.š[d]. | [rbt.]kmn.w ṣḥq.btlt.['nt]. | 18[3AQHT].1.20
.a]nk.n'mn.'mq.nšm. | [td'ṣ.p'n]m.w tr.arṣ.idk. | [l ttn.pn]m.'m il.mbk.nhrm. | [qrb.ap]q.thmtm tgly.ḏd il. | [w tbu. 17[2AQHT].6.47

ym.ṯn.mṯpd]m.t[ḥt.ʿnt.arṣ.ṯlṯ.mtḥ.ǵyrm].|[idk.]l ytn.pnm.ʿm.[i]l.mbk.[nhrm.qrb.apq.thmtm].|[ygly.]ḏl i[l].w yb 2.3[129].4
ilm.|[w ḥẓ]r.k bn.aṯrt[.tdʿṣ.]pʿn.|[w tr.a]rṣ.id[k.l ttn.p]nm.|[ʿm.i]l.mbk.nhr[m.qr]b.[ap]q.|[thm]tm.tgl.ḏ[d.]i[l.] 3[ʿNT.VI].5.13
kb.l pnm.|aṯr.btlt.ʿnt.|w bʿl.tbʿ.mrym.ṣpn.|idk.l ttn.pnm.|ʿm.il.mbk.nhrm.|qrb.apq.thmtm.|tgly.ḏd.il.w tbu.|q 4[51].4.20
.|[---]ḥ h.tšt bm.ʿ[--].|[---.]zr h.ybm.l ilm.|[id]k.l ttn.pnm.ʿm.|[il.]mbk nhrm.qrb.|[a]pq.thmtm.tgly.ḏd.|il.w tbu 6.1.32[49.1.4]
[idk.l ttn.pnm].|[ʿm.il.mbk.nhrm].|[qrb.apq.thmtm].|[tgly.ḏd.il.w]t 5[67].6.03
lm mt.|ʿbd k.an.w d.ʿlm k.|tbʿ.w l.yṯb.ilm.idk.|l ytn.pn.ʿm.bn.ilm.mt.|tk.qrt h.hmry.mk.ksu.|ṯbt.ḫḫ.arṣ.nḥlt h.t 5[67].2.14
rm.iqnim.|šmḫ.btlt.ʿnt.tdʿṣ.|pʿnm.w tr.arṣ.|idk.l ttn.pnm.|ʿm.bʿl.mrym.ṣpn.|b alp.šd.rbt.kmn.|ṣḥq.btlt.ʿnt.tšu.| 4[51].5.84
.ilnym.ṯn.mṯpdm.|tḥt.ʿnt.arṣ.ṯlṯ.mtḥ.ǵyrm.|idk.l ttn pnm.ʿm.bʿl.|mrym.ṣpn.b alp.šd.rbt.kmn.|hlk.aḫt h.bʿl.yʿn.t 3[ʿNT].4.81
m.mt.b mh|mrt.ydd.il.ǵzr.|tbʿ.w l.yṯb ilm.idk.|l ytn.pnm.ʿm.bʿl.|mrym.ṣpn.w yʿn.|gpn.w ugr.ṯḥm.bn ilm.|mt.h 5[67].1.10
.ḏr[qm.---].|[btl]t.ʿnt.l kl.[---].|[tt]bʿ.btlt.ʿnt[.idk.l ttn.pnm].|ʿm.yṭpn.mhr.š[t.tšu.g h].|w tṣḥ.yṭb.yṭp.[---].|qrt.abl 18[3AQHT].4.5
ym].|ṯn.mṯpdm.tḥt.[ʿnt.arṣ.ṯlṯ.mtḥ].|ǵyrm.idk.l yt[n.pnm.ʿm.lṭpn].|il d pid.tk ḫrš[n.---.tk.ǵr.ks].|ygly ḏd.i[l.w y 1[ʿNT.IX].3.21
rṯt.|iy.aliyn.bʿl.|iy.zbl.bʿl.arṣ.|ttbʿ.btlt.ʿnt.|idk.l ttn.pnm.|ʿm.nrt.ilm.špš.|tšu.g h.w tṣḥ.|ṯḥm.ṯr.il.ab k.|hwt.lṭp 6[49].4.31
idk.al.ttn.pnm.|ʿm.ǵr.trǵzz.|ʿm.ǵr.ṯrmg.|ʿm.tlm.ǵṣr.arṣ.|ša.ǵr.ʿl.ydm 4[51].8.1
i.w ttbʿ.šʿtqt.|bt.krt.bu.tbu.|bkt.tgly.w tbu.|nṣrt.tbu.pnm.|ʿrm.tdu.mh.|pdrm.tdu.šrr.|ḥṭ m.tʿmt.[ʿ]ṭr.[k]m.|zbl 16.6[127].5
.|šmrr.nḥš.ʿq šr.ln h.mlḫš.|abd.ln h.ydy.ḥmt.|b ḥrn.pnm.trǵnw.w ṯtkl.|bnwt h.ykr.ʿr.d qdm.|idk.pnm.l ytn.tk UG5.7.61
bʿt.yn.ṯ[ḫ].|gg k.b ym.ṭiṭ.rḥṣ.|npṣ k.b ym rṯ.b uni[l].|pnm.tšmḫ.w ʿl yṣhl pi[t].|yprq.lṣb.w yṣḥq.|pʿn.l hdm.yṯpd. 17[2AQHT].2.9
.|ugrt.ṭǵr k.|ugrt.ṭǵr k.|tšlm k.um y.|tdʿ.ky.ʿrbt.|l pn.špš.|w pn.špš.nr.|b y.mid.w um.|tšmḫ.m ab.|w al.trḥln 1015.8
k.|ugrt.ṭǵr k.|tšlm k.um y.|tdʿ.ky.ʿrbt.|l pn.špš.|w pn.špš.nr.|b y.mid.w um.|tšmḫ.m ab.|w al.trḥln.|ʿtn.ḫrd.a 1015.9
l h.|qšt hn.aḫd.b yd h.|w qṣʿt h.bm.ymn h.|idk.l ytn pnm.|tk.aḫ.šmk.mla[t.r]umm.|tšu knp.btlt.ʿn[t].|tšu.knp. 10[76].2.8
db.l arṣ.|[---.]špm.ʿdb.|[---].tʿtqn.|[---.-]ʿb.idk.|[l ytn.pnm.tk.]in.bb.b alp ḥẓr.|[rbt.kmn.l pʿ]n.ʿnt.|[yhbr.w yql.yš 1[ʿNT.IX].2.14
[idk.al.ttn.pnm.tk.ḥkpt.il.kl h].|[kptr.]ks[u.ṯbt h.ḥkpt.arṣ.nḥlt h].|b al 1[ʿNT.IX].3.01
p šmm.šmšr.|l dgy.aṯrt.|mǵ.l qdš.amrr.|idk.al.tnn.|pnm.tk.ḥqkpt.|il.kl h.kptr.|ksu.ṯbt h.ḥkpt.|arṣ.nḥlt h.|b al 3[ʿNT.VI].6.13
ḥtm.|w rd.bt ḫpṯt.|arṣ.tspr.b y|rdm.arṣ.|idk.al.ttn.|pnm.tk.qrt h.|hmry.mk.ksu.|ṯbt h.ḫḫ.arṣ.|nḥlt h.w nǵr.|ʿn 4[51].8.11
tšu.g h.w t[ṣḥ.šm]ʿ.mʿ.|[-.yṯ]ir ṯr.il.ab k.l pn.zbl.ym.l pn[.ṯ]pṭ[.n]hr.|[ik.a]l.yšmʿ k.ṯr.[i]l.ab k.l ys[ʿ.[alt.]ṯ[bt |k.l y 2.3[129].16
l.]ym.b hkl.ṯpṭ.nh[r].yṯir.ṯr.il.ab h l pn[.zb]l y[m].|[l pn.ṯp]ṭ[.nhr.]mlkt.[--]pm.l mlkt.wn.in.aṯt.|[l]k.k[m.ilm].|[2.3[129].22
ʿn h.|w il hd.b ḫrẓʿ h.|[-----].|[--]t.[---].|[---.]ʿn[.---].|pnm[.---].|bʿl.n[--.---].|il.hd[.---].|at.bl[.at.---].|ḥmd m.[---] 12[75].2.4
[---.--]r.pn[.---].|[---.-]ḏi.u[--.---].|[---].l.ar[ṣ.---].|[---.--]g.irb[-.---].|[2157.1
]ḏi.u[--.---].|[---].l.ar[ṣ.---].|[---.--]g.irb[-.---].|[---.-]rd.pn.[---].|[---.--]r.ṯṯ d.[---].|[---.--]r.[---]. 2157.5

pni

m bn.brq.|[--.]qtn bn.drṣy.|[--]kn bn.pri.|[r]špab bn.pni.|[ab]mn bn.qṣy.|[ʿ]pṯrm bn.agmz.|[-]n bn.iln.|[--]nn b 2087.8

pndḏn

ilšt[mʿym].|yddt[.---].|ilšn.[---].|ṣdqn.[----].|pndḏn.b[n.---].|ayaḫ.b[n.---]. 96[333].5

pndyn

lk.ʿšrm.|[--]ny.ʿšrt.trbyt.|[--.]ʿbd.ṯlṯm.|[---].ṯlṯm.|[--.p]ndyn.ṯlṯm. 2054.2.28
w.[---].|ity[.---].|tlby[.---].|ir[--.---].|pndyn[.---].|w.idṯ[-.---].|b.gt.b[n.---].|yḫl[.---].|b.gt.[---].|[- 1078.5

pndr

.|bn.trdn.|ypq.|ʿbd.|qrḥ.|abšr.|bn.bdn.|ḏmry.|bn.pndr.|bn.aḫt.|bn.ʿdn.|bn.išbʿ[l]. 2117.4.31
.bn.mll.|šrm.|[b]n.špš[yn].|[b]n.ḫrmln.|bn.tnn.|bn.pndr.|bn.nqq.|ḫrš.bhtm.|bn.izl.|bn.ibln.|bn.ilt.|špšyn.nḥl 85[80].1.14
-].|mr[--.---].|hm.[---].|kmrṯn[.---].|bn.ṯbln[.---].|bn.pndr[.---].|bn.idr[-.---].|bn.ḥdn[-.---].|bn.ṯbi[l.---]. 2070.2.5

pny

mǵy.|ʿṯtrt.tʿdb.nšb l h.|w ʿnt.ktp.b hm.ygʿr.ṯǵr.|bt.il.pn.l mgr lb.tʿdbn.|nšb.l inr.tʿdbn.ktp.|b il ab h.gʿr.yṯb.il.kb UG5.1.1.12

pnmn

n.|drt.b.kkr.|ubn.ḫṣḥ.kkr.|kkr.lqḥ.ršpy.|tmtrn.bn.pnmn.|kkr.|bn.sgttn.|kkr.|ilšpš.kkr.|bn.ḏltn.|kkr.w[.--].| 1118.7
rt.|rpan.ḫmšt.|abǵl.ḫmšt.|bn.aḫdy.ʿšrt.|ṯṯn.ʿṣrt.|bn.pnmn.ʿšrt.|ʿbdadt.ḫmšt.|abmn.ilštmʿy.ḫmš[t].|ʿzn.bn.brn. 1062.23

pnt

.zbl.|[ym.]bn.ʿnm.ṯpṭ.nhr.yprsḥ.ym.yql.|l arṣ.tnǵṣn.pnt h.w ydlp.tmn h.|yqṯ bʿl.w yšt.ym.ykly.ṯpṭ.nhr.|b šm.tg 2.4[68].26
ylm.ktp.zbl ym.bn ydm.ṯpṭ.|nhr.ʿz.ym.l ymk.l tnǵṣn.pnt h.l ydlp.|tmn h.kṯr.ṣmdm.ynḥt.w ypʿr.šmt hm.|šm k.a 2.4[68].17
rlt h.[b h.pʿnm].|ṯṭṭ.ʿl[n.pn h.tdʿ.b ʿdn].|ksl.y[ṯbr.yǵṣ.pnt.ksl h].|anš.[dt.ẓr h.yšu.g h].|w yṣ[ḥ.---].|mḫṣ[.---].|š[-- 19[1AQHT].2.95
t.tph.ilm.b h.pʿnm.|ṯṭṭ.bʿd n.ksl.ṯṯbr.|ʿln.pn h.tdʿ.tǵṣ.pnt.|ksl h.anš.dt.ẓr h.tšu.|g h.w tṣḥ.ik.mǵy.gpn.w ugr.|mn 3[ʿNT].3.31
].b h.pʿnm.|[ṯṭṭ.b ʿ]dn.ksl.|[ṯṯbr.ʿln.p]n h.td[ʿ].|tǵṣ[.pnt.ks]l h.|anš.dt.ẓr.[h].|tšu.g h.w tṣḥ[.i]k.|mǵy.aliy[n.b]ʿl. 4[51].2.19
.|bnš rʿym.[---].|kbdt.bnš[.---].|šin.[---].|b ḥlm.[---].|pnt[.---]. 2158.2.10

pnṯ

ṯn pǵn.[-]dr|m.ṯn kndwm adrm.|w knd pnṯ.dq.|ṯn ḫpnm.ṯn pldm ǵlmm.|kpld.b[-.-]r[--].|w blḫ br[140[98].3

pnṯbl

--.]ṯlṯ kbd.ṣin.|[---.--]a.ṯ[l]ṯ.d.a[--].|[---].mrn.|[---.]bn pnṯbl.|[---.-]py w.bn h. 1145.2.2

ps

[---.]ps[.---].|[---].ytbr[.---].|[---.]uṭm.ḏr[qm.---].|[btl]t.ʻnt.l kl.[- 18[3AQHT].4.1
pld.pṯt[.-]r.|lpš.sgr.rq.|ṯṯ.prqt.|w.mrdt.prqt.pṯt.|lbš.psm.rq.|ṯn.mrdt.az.|ṯlṯ.pld.šʻrt.|ṯ[---].kbm.|p[---]r.aḥd.|[-- 1112.5

psḥn

[s]ǵr.bn.bdn.|[sǵ]r.bn.psḥn.|alṯy.|sǵr.npr.|bn.ḫty.|ṯn.bnš ibrḏr.|bnš tlmi.|sǵr.ḫr 2082.2
t.qšt.|kṯy.qšt.w.qlʻ.|bn.ḫršn.qšt.w.qlʻ.|ilrb.qšt.w.qlʻ.|psḥn.qšt.|bn.kmy.qšt.|bn.ilḥbn.qšt.w.q[lʻ].|ršpab.qšt.w.qlʻ. 119[321].3.42
n.umy.|knʻm.šʻrty.|abrpu.ubrʻy.|b.gt.bn.ṯlṯ.|ilḏ.b.gt.psḥn. 91[311].12

psl

]m.|[šd.---.b d.]ṯpṭbʻl.|[šd.---.]b d.ymz.|[šd.b d].klby.psl.|[ub]dy.mri.ibrn.|[š]d.bn.bri.b d.bn.ydln.|[u]bdy.ṯǵrm. 82[300].2.4
]ty.|bn.kdgdl.|bn.smyy.|bn.lbn.|bn.šlmn.|bn.mly.|pslm.|bn.annd.|bn.glʻd.|w.nḥl h.|bn.mlkyy.|[bn].bm[--].| 2163.3.9
|b.gt.ǵl.|[-.]nǵr.mdrʻ.|[-].nǵr[.--]m.|[--.]psl.qšt.|[ṯl]ṯ.psl.ḥẓm.|[---.ḥ]rš.mr[k]bt.|[--].ʻšr h[.---].|[ḫm]š.ʻšr h[.---].| 1024.3.19
ru.ibrn.|mru.skn.|nsk.ksp|mḫṣm.|ksdm.|mdrǵlm.|pslm.|yṣḥm. 74[115].18
mrynm.|mrum.|ʻšrm.|ṯnnm.|nqdm.|khnm.|qdšm.|pslm.|mkrm.|yṣḥm.|šrm.|nʻrm.|ʻbdm.|kzym.|ksdm.|[ns 1026.1.8
.|[---]d.|a[ǵ]ltn.|[-----].|[--]ny.|knʻm.|[-]p[-].|ʻpṯn.|pslm.ṣnr. 2060.14
m.|ṯn.ḥršm.|b.gt.ǵl.|[-.]nǵr.mdrʻ.|[-].nǵr[.--]m.|[--.]psl.qšt.|[ṯl]ṯ.psl.ḥẓm.|[---.ḥ]rš.mr[k]bt.|[--].ʻšr h[.---].|[ḫm] 1024.3.18
|[š]ḥq.|nʻrm.|mḫrǵlm.|kzym.|mru.skn.|mru.ibrn.|pslm.|šrm.|yṣḥm.|ʻšrm.|mrum.|ṯnnm.|mqdm.|khnm.|q 71[113].65
[--].|ḥrš.d.[---].|mrum.[---].|yṣḥm[.---].|mkrm[.---].|pslm[.---]. 1038.7

pslt

l bʻl.|ǵr.b ab.td[.ps]ltm[.b yʻr].|thdy.lḥm.w dqn[.ṯṯlṯ].|qn.ḏrʻ h.tḥrṯ.km.gn.| 6[62].1.2
iš h.ʻpr.plṯt.|l qdqd h.lpš.yks.|mizrtm.ǵr.b abn.|ydy.psltm.b yʻr.|yhdy.lḥm.w dqn.|yṯlṯ.qn.ḏrʻ h.yḥrṯ.|k gn.ap l 5[67].6.18

psʼ

-]ṯy.|bn.ǵdʻ.|bn.ʻyn.|bn.grb[n].|yṯtn.|bn.ab[l].|kry.|psʼ.|ilṯḥm.|ḥrm.|bn.bty.|ʻby.|šm[n].bn.apn.|krty.|bn.ubr 2078.12
t.|ilṯḥm.bn.dnn.ṯkt.|šbʻl.bn.aly.ṯkt.|klby.bn.iḫy.ṯkt.|psʼ.bn.buly.ṯkt.|ʻpṣpn.bn.ʻdy.ṯkt.|nʻmn.bn.ʻyn.ṯkt.|ʻpṯn.bn. 2085.8

pʻl

tḥṣ.|btlt.ʻn[t].tptrʻ ṯd[h].|limm.w tʻl.ʻm.il.|ab h.ḥpr.pʻl k.y[--].|šmʻ k.l arḫ.w bn.[--].|limm.ql.b udn.k w[-].|k rt 13[6].21

pʻn

l.ybnn.|adn y.|rgm.|tḥm.t[g]yn.|bn k.|l.p[ʻn.adn y].|q[lt.---].|l.yb[nn].|bʻl y.r[gm].|tḥm.ʻbd[--].|ʻb 2115.1.6
l.mlkt.|adt y.|rgm.|tḥm.tlmyn.|ʻbd k.|l.pʻn.|adt y.|šbʻ d.|w.šbʻ id.|mrḥqtm.|qlt.|ʻm.adt y.|mnm.š 52[89].6
l.mlkt.|adt y.rgm.|tḥm.illḏr.|ʻbd k..|l.pʻn a[dt y].|šbʻ d[.w šbʻ d].|mrḥq[tm.qlt].|mn[m.šlm]. 1014.5
l um y.adt ny.|rgm.|tḥm.tlmyn.|w.aḫtmlk ʻbd k.|l.pʻn.adt ny.|mrḥqtm.|qlny.ilm.|tǵr k.|tšlm k.|hn ny.ʻm ny 51[95].5
ʻ.ǵlm[m.al.tṯb.idk.pnm].|al.ttn.ʻm.pḫr.mʻd.t[k.ǵr.ll.l pʻn.il].|al.tpl.al.tštḥwy.pḫr [mʻd.qmm.a--.am]|r ṯny.dʻt km 2.1[137].14
.apq.thmtm].|[ygly.]ḏl i[l].w ybu[.q]rš.mlk[.ab.šnm.l pʻn.il.]|[yhbr.]w yql[.y]štḥw[y.]w ykb[dn h.--]r y[---].|[---.k 2.3[129].5
n.---.tk.ǵr.ks].|ygly ḏd.i[l.w ybu.qrš.mlk].|ab.šnm.l [pʻn.il.yhbr.w yql].|yštḥwy.[w ykbdn h.---].|ṯr.il[.ab h.---].| 1[ʻNT.IX].3.24
qrb.apq.thmtm.|tgly.ḏd.il.w tbu.|qrš.mlk.ab.šnm.|l pʻn.il.thbr.w tql.|tštḥwy.w tkbd h.|hlm.il.k yphn h.|yprq.l 4[51].4.25
b.|[a]pq.thmtm.tgly.ḏd.|il.w tbu.qrš..|mlk.ab.šnm.l pʻn.|il.thbr.w tql.|tštḥwy.w tkbdn h.|tšu.g h.w tṣḥ.tšmḫ ht 6.1.36[49.1.8]
rb.ap]q.thmtm tgly.ḏd il.|[w tbu.qr]š.mlk.ab.šnm.|[l pʻn.il.t]hbr.w tql.tštḥ|[wy.w tkbd]n h.tlšn.aqht.ǵzr.|[---.kd 17[2AQHT].6.50
hm.ln.kḥṯ.zbl hm.|aḫr.tmǵyn.mlak ym.tʻdt.ṯpṭ.nhr.l pʻn.il.|[l t]pl.l tštḥwy.pḫr.mʻd.qmm.a[--].amr.|[ṯn]y.dʻt hm 2.1[137].30
l.mlkt.|um y.rgm.|tḥm.mlk.|bn k.|l.pʻn.um y.|qlt.l.um y.|yšlm.ilm.|tǵr k.tšlm k.|hl ny.ʻm n[y] 50[117].5
l mlkt.u[m] y.|[rg]m[.]t[ḥm].|mlk.bn [k].|[l].pʻn.um [y].|qlt[.l um] y.|yšlm.il[m].|tǵ[r] k.tš[lm] k.|[h]l n 1013.4
l.mlk.b[ʻl y].|r[gm].|tḥm.rb.mi[--.ʻ]bd k.|l.pʻn.bʻl y[.mrḥqtm].|šbʻ d.w.šbʻ[d.qlt].|ankn.rgmt.l.bʻl y.|l. 2008.1.4
l.mlk.bʻ[l] y.|rgm.|tḥm.ṯpṭbʻ[l].|[ʻ]bd k.|[l.p]ʻn.bʻl y.|[šbʻ] d.šbʻ [d].|[mr]ḥqtm.|qlt.|ʻbd k.b.|lwsnd.|[2063.5
|q[lt.---].|l.yb[nn].|bʻl y.r[gm].|tḥm.ʻbd[--].|ʻbd k.|l pʻn.bʻl y.|ṯn id.šbʻ d.|mrḥqtm.|qlt.ʻm.|bʻl y.mnm.|šlm.|[r] 2115.2.5
-].|hm.ṯn.[---].|hn dt.[---].|[-----].|[-----].|tḥm[.---].|l pʻn.bʻl y[.---].|qlt.|[--]t.mlk.d.y[mlk].|[--.]ʻbdyrḫ.l.ml[k].|[- 2064.10
b špt h.hwt h.knp.ṣml.bʻ[l].|bʻl.ṯbr.diy.hyt.tq[l.tḥt].|pʻn h.ybqʻ.kbd h.w yḥd.|iṯ.šmt.iṯ.ʻẓm.w yqḫ b hm.|aqht.yb 19[1AQHT].3.144
t h.hwt h.knp.hrgb.bʻl.ṯbr.|bʻl.ṯbr.diy.hwt.w yql.|tḥt.pʻn h.ybqʻ.kbd h.w yḥd.|[i]n.šmt.in.ʻẓm.yšu.g[h].|w yṣḥ.k 19[1AQHT].3.130
hwt[h].|knp.nšrm.bʻl.yṯbr.|bʻl.ṯbr.diy hmt.tqln.|tḥt.pʻn h.ybqʻ.kbdt hm.w[yḥd].|in.šmt.in.ʻẓm.yšu.g h.|w yṣḥ. 19[1AQHT].3.116
.|bʻl.ḥmd m.yḥmd m.|bn.dgn.yhrr m.|bʻl.ngṯ hm.b pʻn h.|w il hd.b ḫrẓʻ h.|[-----].|[--]t.[---].|[---.]ʻn[.---].|pnm[12[75].1.40
yʻn.btlt.ʻnt.|nʻmt.bn.aḫt.bʻl.|l pnn h.ydd.w yqm.|l pʻn h.ykrʻ.w yql.|w yšu.g h.w yṣḥ.|hwt.aḫt.w nar[-].|qrn.d 10[76].2.18
tštḥwy.w tkbd h.|hlm.il.k yphn h.|yprq.lṣb.w yṣḥq.|pʻn h.l hdm.yṯpd.w ykrkr.|uṣbʻt h.yšu.g h.w y[ṣḥ].|ik.mǵyt 4[51].4.29
šmm.šmn.tmṭrn.|nḫlm.tlk.nbtm.|šmḫ.lṭpn.il.d pid.|pʻn h.l hdm.yṯpd.|w yprq.lṣb w yṣḥq.|yšu.g h.w yṣḥ.|aṯbn. 6[49].3.15
.ʻrẓ.|apnk.ʻṯtr.ʻrẓ.|yʻl.b ṣrrt.ṣpn.|yṯb.l kḥṯ.aliyn.|bʻl.pʻn h.l tmǵyn.|hdm.riš h.l ymǵy.|aps h.w yʻn.ʻṯtr.ʻrẓ.|l am 6.1.59[49.1.31]
l[-.-]ry.ylbš.|mlk.ylk.lqḥ.ilm.|aṯr.ilm.ylk.pʻnm.|mlk.pʻnm.yl[k].|šbʻ.pamt.l kl hm. 33[5].25
n.bht.ksp.w ḫrṣ.|bht.ṯhrm.iqnim.|šmḫ.btlt.ʻnt.tdʻṣ.|pʻnm.w tr.arṣ.|idk.l ttn.pnm.|ʻm.bʻl.mrym.ṣpn.|b alp.šd.rb 4[51].5.83
ntb.gan.ašql k.tḥt.|[pʻn y.a]nk.nʻmn.ʻmq.nšm.|[tdʻṣ.pʻn]m.w tr.arṣ.idk.|[l ttn.pn]m.ʻm il.mbk.nhrm.|[qrb.ap]q. 17[2AQHT].6.46
mmʻm.-]d.l ytn.bt.l bʻl.k ilm.|[w ḥẓ]r.k bn.aṯrt[.tdʻṣ.]pʻn.|[w tr.a]rṣ.id[k.l ttn.p]nm.|[ʻm.i]l.mbk.nhr[m.qr]b.[ap] 3[ʻNT.VI].5.12
|[---]m.l aqry k.b ntb.pšʻ.|[---].b ntb.gan.ašql k.tḥt.|[pʻn y.a]nk.nʻmn.ʻmq.nšm.|[tdʻṣ.pʻn]m.w tr.arṣ.idk.|[l ttn.p 17[2AQHT].6.45
ṣḥ.knp.hr[g]b.|bʻl.yṯb.bʻl.y[ṯb]r.diy[.h]wt.|w yql.tḥt.pʻn y.ibqʻ.kbd[h].|w aḥd.hm.iṯ.šmt.hm.iṯ[.ʻẓm].|abky.w aq 19[1AQHT].3.124
.g h.w yṣḥ.knp.šml.|bʻl.yṯbr.bʻl.yṯbr.diy.|hyt.tql.tḥt.pʻn y.ibqʻ.|kbd h.w aḥd.hm.iṯ.šmt.iṯ.|ʻẓm.abky w aqbrn h. 19[1AQHT].3.138
w yṣḥ[.knp.nšrm].|bʻl.yṯb.bʻl.yṯb[r.diy.hmt].|tqln.tḥ pʻn y.ibq[ʻ.kbd hm.w]|aḥd.hm.iṯ.šmt.hm.i[ṯ].|ʻẓm.abky.w 19[1AQHT].3.109

šlm.l kbd.arṣ.|arbdd.l kbd.šdm.|ḥš k.ʿṣ k.ʿbṣ k.|ʿm y.pʿn k.tlsmn.ʿm y.|twtḥ.išd k.dm.rgm.|iṯ.l y.w argm k.|hwt 3[ʿNT].3.16
.|l kbd.arṣ.arbdd.l kbd.šdm.|[ḥ]š k.[ʿ]ṣ k.ʿbṣ k.ʿm y.pʿn k.|[tls]mn.[ʿ]m y.twtḥ.išd k.|[dm.rgm.iṯ.l y.]w argm k. 3[ʿNT].4.55
].l kbd.arṣ.|[arbdd.l kbd.š]dm.ḥš k.|[ʿṣ k.ʿbṣ k.ʿm y.pʿ]n k.tlsmn.|[ʿm y.twtḥ.išd] k.tk.ḫršn.|[---.-]bd k.spr.|[---. 1[ʿNT.IX].2.22
[ḥš k.ʿṣ k.ʿbṣ k.ʿ]m y.p[ʿ]n k.|[tlsmn.ʿm y.twt]ḥ.išd k.|[tk.ḫršn.---]r.[-]ḥm k.w št. 1[ʿNT.IX].2.1
št.lskt.n[--.---].|ʿdb.bǵrt.ṯ[--. --].|ḥš k.ʿṣ k.ʿ[bṣ k.ʿm y.pʿn k.tlsmn].|ʿm y twtḥ.i[šd k.tk.ḫršn.-------------].|ǵr.ks.d 1[ʿNT.IX].3.10
.šlm.l kbd.arṣ.arbdd].|l kbd.š[dm.ḥš k.ʿṣ k.ʿbṣ k.ʿm y.pʿn k.tls]|[m]n ʿm y t[wtḥ.išd k.dm.rgm.iṯ.l y.d argmn k].|[7.2[130].16
kptr.]ks[u.ṯbt h.ḥkpt.arṣ.nḥlt h].|b alp.šd.r[bt.kmn.l pʿn.kṯr].|hbr.w ql.t[šṯḥwy.w kbd.hwt].|w rgm l k[ṯr.w ḫss.ṯ 1[ʿNT.IX].3.2
kptr.|ksu.ṯbt h.ḥkpt.|arṣ.nḥlt h.|b alp.šd.rbt.|kmn.l pʿn.kṯ.|hbr.w ql.tšṯḥ|wy.w kbd hwt.|w rgm.l kṯr.|w ḫss.ṯn 3[ʿNT.VI].6.18
.b uni[l].|pnm.tšmḫ.w ʿl yṣhl pi[t].|yprq.lṣb.w yṣḥq.|pʿn.l hdm.yṯpd.yšu.|g h.w yṣḥ.aṯbn.ank.|w anḫn.w tnḫ.b ir 17[2AQHT].2.11
--.]l šlm.|[-]l[-.-]ry.ylbš.|mlk.ylk.lqḥ.ilm.|aṯr.ilm.ylk.pʿnm.|mlk.pʿnm.yl[k].|šbʿ.pamt.l kl hm. 33[5].24
ḫrrt.la.|šmm.b yd.md|d.ilm.mt.b a|lp.šd.rbt.k|mn.l pʿn.mt.|hbr.w ql.|tšṯḥwy.w k|bd hwt.w rgm.|l bn.ilm.mt. 4[51].8.26
lk.bʿl.aṯtrt.|k tʿn.hlk.btlt.|ʿnt.tdrq.ybmt.|[limm].b h.pʿnm.|[ṭṭ].b ʿ]dn.ksl.|[ṯṯbr.ʿln.p]n h.td[ʿ].|tǵṣ[.pnt.ks]l h.|a 4[51].2.16
dš.b ǵr.nḥlt y.|b nʿm.b gbʿ.tliyt.|hlm.ʿnt.tph.ilm.b h.pʿnm.|ṭṭ.bʿd n.ksl.ṯṯbr.|ʿln.pn h.tdʿ.tǵṣ.pnt.|ksl h.anš.dt.ẓr 3[ʿNT].3.29
.aqht.ǵzr.[šṣat].|btlt.ʿnt.k [rḥ.npš h].|k iṯl.brlt h.[b h.pʿnm].|ṭṭ.ʿl[n.pn h.tdʿ.b ʿdn].|ksl.y[ṯbr.yǵṣ.pnt.ksl h].|anš. 19[1AQHT].2.93
--.-]ʿb.idk.|[l ytn.pnm.tk.]in.bb.b alp ḥẓr.|[rbt.kmn.l pʿ]n.ʿnt.|[yhbr.w yql.yšt]ḥwyn.w y|[kbdn h.yšu.g h.w y]ṣḥ. 1[ʿNT.IX].2.15
|ahbt.ṭly.bt.rb.dd.arṣy.|bt.yʿbdr.km ǵlmm.|w ʿrb n.l pʿn.ʿnt.hbr.|w ql.tšṯḥwy.kbd hyt.|w rgm.l btlt.ʿnt.|ṯny.l y 3[ʿNT].3.6
p].|sgrt.g[-].[-]ẓ[.---] h[.---].|ʿn.ṯk[.---].|ʿln.ṯ[--.---].|l pʿn.ǵl[m]m[.---].|mid.an[--.]ṣn[--].|nrt.ilm.špš[.ṣḥrr]t.|la.š 3[ʿNT.VI].5.23
ṣʿṣ.bnt.ḫkp[.---].|[---].aḫw.aṭm.prṭl[.---].|[---.]mnt.[l]pʿn[.-.-]bd h.aqšr[.---].|[---].ptḥ y.a[--.]dt[.---].ml[--].|[---.-]ṯ 1001.1.20
r.|[--.]l ytk.bl[-.---.]m[--.]hwt.|[---].ṯllt.khn[m.---.]k pʿn.|[---.--]y.yd.nšy.[---.--]š.l mdb.|[---] h.mḫlpt[.---.--]r.|[-- UG5.8.47

pʿṣ

-]ṯtayy.b d.ṯṯmd.|[šd.bn.-]rn.b d.ṣdqšlm.|[šd.b d.]bn.pʿṣ.|[ubdy.ʿ]šrm.|[šd.---]n.b d.brdd.|[---.--]m.|[šd.---.b d.]ṯ 82[300].1.29
n.ḫnn.|[--]ny.|[bn].ṯrdnt.|[bn].hyadt.|[--]lt.|šmrm.|pʿṣ.bn.byy.ʿšrt. 1047.25
b[-].|bn.[-]r[-].|bn.tgn.|bn.idrn.|mnn.|b[n].skn.|bn.pʿṣ.|bn.ḏrm.|[bn.-]ln.|[bn.-]ḏprḏ. 124[-].6.11
bn.ʿpṯb.|ṯbry.|bn.ymn.|krty.|bn.abr[-].|yrpu.|kdn.|pʿṣ.|bn.liy.|ydʿ.|šmn.|ʿdy.|ʿnbr.|aḫrm.|bn.qrdy.|bn.šmʿn. 2117.1.24
mḏrǵlm.d inn.|msgm.l hm.|pʿṣ.ḫbty.|artyn.ary.|brqn.ṯlḥy.|bn.aryn.|bn.lgn.|bn.bʿyn.| 118[306].3
-.---].|tǵyn.bn.ubn.ṯql[m].|yšn.ḥrš.mrkbt.ṯq[lm].|bn.pʿṣ.ṯqlm.|mṣrn.ḥrš.mrkbt.ṯqlm.|ʿpṯn.ḥrš.qṯn.ṯqlm.|bn.pǵḏ 122[308].1.7

pʿr

--.--].|w hm.ap.l[--.---].|ymḫṣ k.k[--.---].|il.dbḥ.[---].|pʿr.b[--.---].|ṯbḫ.alp[m.ap.ṣin.šql].|ṯrm.w [mri.ilm.ʿglm.dt.š 1[ʿNT.X].4.29
rt.ʿnt.[-]ld.|kbd h.l ydʿ hr h.[---]d[-].|tnq[.---.]in[b]b.pʿr.|yd h[.--.]ṣʿr.glgl.|a[---]m.rḥ.ḥḏ ʿ[r]pt.|gl[.---.]yhpk.m[- 13[6].32
pr.ʿẓm yd.|ugrm.ḫl.ld.|aklm.tbrk k.|w ld ʿqqm.|ilm.ypʿr.|šmt hm.|b hm.qrnm.|km.ṯrm.w gbṯt.|km.ibrm.|w b 12[75].1.28
.l ymk.l tnǵṣn.pnt h.l ydlp.|tmn h.kṯr.ṣmdm.ynḥt.w ypʿr.šmt hm.|šm k.at.aymr.aymr.mr.ym.mr.ym.|l ksi h.nh 2.4[68].18
t k.|tqḥ.mlk.ʿlm k.drkt.dt dr dr k.|kṯr ṣmdm.ynḥt.w ypʿr.šmt hm.šm k at.|ygrš.ygrš.grš ym grš ym.l ksi h.|[n]h 2.4[68].11
[.---].|w yʿn.lṭpn.il.d p[id.---].|šm.bn y.yw.ilt.[---].|w pʿr.šm.ym[-.---].|tʿnyn.l zn.tn[.---].|at.adn.tpʿr[.---].|ank.lṭ 1[ʿNT.X].4.15
lt.[---].|w pʿr.šm.ym[-.---].|tʿnyn.l zn.tn[.---].|at.adn.tpʿr[.---].|ank.lṭpn.il[.d pid.---].|ʿl.ydm.pʿrt[.---].|šm k.mdd 1[ʿNT.X].4.17
[.---].|at.adn.tpʿr[.---].|ank.lṭpn.il[.d pid.---].|ʿl.ydm.pʿrt[.---].|šm k.mdd.i[l.---].|bt ksp y.d[--.---].|b d.aliyn b[ʿl. 1[ʿNT.X].4.19

pǵdr

t.pṯt.|[-]r.pldm.dt.šʿrt.|ṯlṯm.ṯlṯ.kbd.mṣrrt.|ʿšr.ṯn.kbd.pǵdrm.|ṯmn.mrbdt.mlk.|ʿšr.pld.šʿrt. 1111.10

pǵḏn

.|ubn.ḫyrn.|ybnil.adrdn.|klyn.kkln.|ʿdmlk.tdn.|ʿzn.pǵḏn.|[a]nndn.|[r]špab.|[-]glm. 1070.6
pr.ḥpr.bnš mlk.b yrḫ iṯt[bnm].|ršpab.rb ʿšrt.m[r]yn.|pǵḏn.ilbʿl.krwn.lbn.ʿdn.|ḫyrn.mdʿ.|šmʿn.rb ʿšrt.kkln.ʿbd.ab 2011.3
ṣ.ṯqlm.|mṣrn.ḥrš.mrkbt.ṯqlm.|ʿpṯn.ḥrš.qṯn.ṯqlm.|bn.pǵḏn.ṯqlm.|bn.bʿln.ṯqlm.|ʿbdyrḫ.nqd.ṯqlm.|bt.sgld.ṯqlm.| 122[308].1.10
[ḥrš].bhtm.bʿl.šd.|[---d]nil.|[a]drdn.|[---]n.|pǵḏn.|ṯṯpḥ.|ḥgbn.|šrm.|bn.ymil.|bn.kḏǵdl.|[-]mn.|[--]n.| 1039.1.24
n.|ršpab.|klyn.|ḥgbn.|ḥṯṯn.|ʿbdmlk.|y[--]k.|[-----].|pǵḏn.|[--]n.|[--]ntn.|ʿdn.|lkn.|ktr.|ubn.|dqn.|ḥṯṯn.|[--]n. 1024.2.3

pǵy

arbʿ.ʿšr.ǵzrm.|arbʿ.aṯt.|pǵt.aḥt.|w.pǵy.aḥ. 2081.4

pǵyn

]d.agpṯr.b d.sḫrn.nḥl h.|šd.annmn.b d.tyn.nḥl h.|šd.pǵyn[.b] d.krmn.l.ty[n.n]ḥl h.|šd.krz.[b]n.ann.ʿ[db].|šd.ṯ[r] 2029.12
--]yn.b.glltky.|td[y]n.b.glltky.|lbw[-].uḫ.pdm.b.yʿrt.|pǵyn.b.tpḥ.|amri[l].b.šrš.|aǵltn.b.midḫ.|[--]n.b.ayly.|[-]ly 2118.11
.ʿbdyrḫ.qšt.w.q[lʿ].|bn.lky.qšt.|bn.dll.qšt.w.ql[ʿ].|bn.pǵyn.qšt.w[.q]lʿ.|bn.bdn.qšt.|bn.pls.qšt.|ǵmrm.|[-]lhd.ṯt.q 119[321].3.29

pǵn

ṯn pǵn.[-]dr|m.ṯn kndwm adrm.|w knd pnṯ.dq.|ṯn ḫpnm.ṯn p 140[98].1

pǵt

.---].|ṯt.aṯtm.w.pǵt.w.ǵzr.aḥd.b.[bt.---].|aṯt.w.bn h.w.pǵt.aḥt.b.bt.m[--].|aṯt.w.ṯt.bt h.b.bt.ḫdmrd.|aṯt.w.ṯn.ǵzrm. 80[119].21
].|[a]ṯt.aḥt.b.bt.rpi[--].|[aṯt.]w.bt h.b.bt.alḫn.|[aṯt.w.]pǵt.aḥt.b.bt.tt.|[aṯt.w.]bt h.b.bt.trǵds.|[---.]aṯt.adrt.w.pǵt.a 80[119].26
aṯt.ad[r]t.b.bt.armwl.|aṯt.aḥt.b.bt.iwrpzn.|ṯt.aṯtm.w.pǵt.aḥt.b bt.[-]r[-].|[aṯ]t.b.bt.aupš.|[aṯ]t.b.bt.ṯpṯbʿl.|[---.]n[- 80[119].11
.b.bt.iwwpzn.|aṯt.w.pǵt.b.bt.ydrm.|ṯt.aṯtm.adrtm.w.pǵt.aḥt.b[.bt.---].|aṯt.w ṯn.nʿrm.b.bt.ilsk.|aṯt.ad[r]t.b.bt.ar 80[119].7
ǵt.aḥt.b.bt.tt.|[aṯt.w.]bt h.b.bt.trǵds.|[---.]aṯt.adrt.w.pǵt.a[ḥt.b.bt.---].|[---.ʿ]šrm.npš.b.bt.[---].|[---.]w.pǵt.aḥt.b.b 80[119].28
rt.w.pǵt.a[ḥt.b.bt.---].|[---.ʿ]šrm.npš.b.bt.[---].|[---.]w.pǵt.aḥt.b.bt.[---]. 80[119].30

pǵt

arb‘.‘šr.ǵzrm.|arb‘.aṯt.|pǵt.aẖt.|w.pǵy.aẖ. 2081.3

t‘r[t h].|w ‘l.tlbš.npṣ.aṯt.[--].|ṣbi nrt.ilm.špš.[-]r[--].|pǵt.minš.šdm l m‘[rb].|nrt.ilm.špš.mǵy[t].|pǵt.l ahlm.rgm. 19[1AQHT].4.210

[aṯt.w].bn h.b.bt.krz.|[aṯt.]w.pǵt.b.bt.gg.|[ǵz]r.aḥd.b.bt.nwrḏ.|[aṯ]t.adrt.b.bt.arṯtb.|aṯt. 80[119].2

aṯ]t.adrt.b.bt.arṯtb.|aṯt.w.ṯn.bn h.b.bt.iwwpzn.|aṯt.w.pǵt.b.bt.ydrm.|ṯt.aṯtm.adrtm.w.pǵt.aẖt.b[.bt.---].|aṯt.w ṯn. 80[119].6

ib[.---].|‘l.bt.ab h.nšrm.trẖ[p]n.|ybṣr.ḥbl.diym.|tbky.pǵt.bm.lb.|tdm‘.bm.kbd.|tmz‘.kst.dnil.mt.|rpi.al.ǵzr.mt.hr 19[1AQHT].1.34

ǵy[t].|pǵt.l ahlm.rgm.l yṯ[pn.y]|bl.agrtn.bat.b ḏd k.[pǵt].|bat.b hlm w y‘n.yṯpn[.mhr].|št.qḥn.w tšqyn.yn.qḥ.|k 19[1AQHT].4.213

w.ṯlṯ.ǵzr[m].|w.ẖmš.n‘rt.b.bt.sk[n].|ṯt.aṯtm.adrtm.w.pǵt.w ǵzr[.aḥd.b.bt.---].|aṯt.w.ṯt.pǵtm.w.ǵzr.aḥd.b.[bt.---].| 80[119].18

n].|ṯt.aṯtm.adrtm.w.pǵt.w ǵzr[.aḥd.b.bt.---].|aṯt.w.ṯt.pǵtm.w.ǵzr.aḥd.b.[bt.---].|ṯt.aṯtm.w.pǵt.w.ǵzr.aḥd.b.[bt.---] 80[119].19

.bt.---].|aṯt.w.ṯt.pǵtm.w.ǵzr.aḥd.b.[bt.---].|ṯt.aṯtm.w.pǵt.w.ǵzr.aḥd.b.[bt.---].|aṯt.w.bn h.w.pǵt.aẖt.b.bt.m[--].|aṯ 80[119].20

.|št.qḥn.w tšqyn.yn.qḥ.|ks.b d y.qb‘t.b ymn y[.t]q|ḥ.pǵt.w tšqyn h.tq[ḥ.ks.]b d h.|qb‘t.b ymn h.w y‘n.yṯ[p]n[.m 19[1AQHT].4.217

š.[-]r[--].|pǵt.minš.šdm l m‘[rb].|nrt.ilm.špš.mǵy[t].|pǵt.l ahlm.rgm.l yṯ[pn.y]|bl.agrtn.bat.b ḏd k.[pǵt].|bat.b hl 19[1AQHT].4.212

.rpi.]arṣ.|[b pẖr].qbṣ.dtn.|[w t]qrb.w ld.|bn.tl k.|tld.pǵt.t[--]t.|tld.pǵt[.---].|tld.pǵ[t.---].|tld.pǵ[t.---].|tld.pǵ[t.--- 15[128].3.7

y.akl[.m]|kly[.‘]l.umt y.w y‘n[.dn]|il.mt.rpi npš ṯḥ[.pǵt].|ṯ[km]t.mym.ḥspt.l š‘r.|ṭl.yd‘t.hlk.kbkbm.|a[-]ḥ.hy.m 19[1AQHT].4.198

dl.‘r.|ṣmd.pḥl.št.gpn y dt ksp.|dt.yrq.nqbn y.tš[m‘].|pǵt.ṯkmt.my.ḥspt.l[š‘]r.ṭl.|yd‘t.hlk.kbkbm.|bkm.tmdln.‘r. 19[1AQHT].2.55

pi.|all.ǵzr.m[t.]hr[nmy].|gm.l bt[h.dnil.k yṣḥ].|šm‘.pǵt.ṯkmt[.my].|ḥspt.l š‘r.ṭl.yd[‘t].|hlk.kbkbm.mdl.‘r.|ṣmd. 19[1AQHT].2.50

.‘[l.---].|[-]l h.yd ‘d[.---].|ltm.mrqdm.d š[-]l[-].|w t‘n.pǵt.ṯkmt.mym.|qrym.ab.dbḥ.l ilm.|š‘ly.dǵṯ h.b šmym.|dǵṯ 19[1AQHT].4.190

ẖr].qbṣ.dtn.|[w t]qrb.w ld.|bn.tl k.|tld.pǵt.t[--]t.|tld.pǵt[.---].|tld.pǵ[t.---].|tld.pǵ[t.---].|tld.pǵ[t.---].|tld.p[ǵt.---] 15[128].3.8

.|bn.tl k.|tld.pǵt.t[--]t.|tld.pǵt[.---].|tld.pǵ[t.---].|tld.pǵ[t.---].|tld.pǵ[t.---].|tld.p[ǵt.---].|mid.rm[.krt].|b tk.rpi.a 15[128].3.10

[w t]qrb.w ld.|bn.tl k.|tld.pǵt.t[--]t.|tld.pǵt[.---].|tld.pǵ[t.---].|tld.pǵ[t.---].|tld.pǵ[t.---].|tld.p[ǵt.---].|mid.rm[.kr 15[128].3.9

.pǵt.t[--]t.|tld.pǵt[.---].|tld.pǵ[t.---].|tld.pǵ[t.---].|tld.pǵ[t.---].|tld.p[ǵt.---].|mid.rm[.krt].|b tk.rpi.ar[ṣ].|b pẖr.q 15[128].3.11

bḥ.|[--.‘]šr.‘šrt.|‘[--.---].|b[---.---].|t[--.---].|w[----].|pǵ[t.---].|lk[.---].|ki[--.---].|w ẖ[--.---].|my[.---].|aṯ[t.---].|a 16.2[125].67

.pǵt[.---].|tld.pǵ[t.---].|tld.pǵ[t.---].|tld.pǵ[t.---].|tld.p[ǵt.---].|mid.rm[.krt].|b tk.rpi.ar[ṣ].|b pẖr.qbṣ.dtn.|ṣǵrt h 15[128].3.12

škn.|w.mṯnn[.---.]‘mn k.|[-]štš.[---.]rgm y.|[-]wd.r[-.]pǵt.|[---.--]t.yd‘t.|[----.r]gm.|[---].kll h.|[---.--]l y.|[---.--]r.| 54.1.23[13.2.8]

pp

[---.]btlt.‘nt.|[---.]pp.hrm.|[---].d l yd‘ bn il.|[---.]pẖr kkbm.|[---.]dr dt.šmm. 10[76].1.2

pprn

št.|[ǵ]mrm.|ilgn.qšt.|abršp.qšt.|ssg.qšt.|ynḥm.qšt.|pprn.qšt.|uln.qšt.|bn.nkl qšt.|ady.qšt.|bn.srn.qšt.|bn.gdrn 105[86].4

ppšr

[--].|[---.b]ṯnm w ṯṯb.‘l.bṯnt.trtḥ[ṣ.---].|[---.t]ṯb h.aẖt.ppšr.w ppšrt[.---].|[---.]k.drẖm.w aṯb.l ntbt.k.‘ṣm l t[--].|[-- 1001.2.6

-.b]ṯnm w ṯṯb.‘l.bṯnt.trtḥ[ṣ.---].|[---.t]ṯb h.aẖt.ppšr.w ppšrt[.---].|[---.]k.drẖm.w aṯb.l ntbt.k.‘ṣm l t[--].|[---.]drk.b 1001.2.6

ppṯ

bn.qṭn.b.ulm.|bn.gdrn.b.m‘r[by].|[w].bn.d‘m[-].|bn.ppṯ.b[--].|b[n.---].|šm[-.---].|tkn[.---].|knn.b.ẖ[lb].|bn mṯ.b 2046.1.9

pṣn

[s]p[r] ušknym.dt.[b d.---].|bn.btr.|bn.‘ms.|bn.pṣn.|bn.agmz.|bn.[--]n.|bn.a[--].|[------].|[------].|[------].|[2021.1.4

pq

ilm.krm.y[n].|špq.ilht.ẖprt[.yn].|špq.ilm.alpm.y[n].|špq.ilht.arẖt[.yn].|špq.ilm.kḥṯm.yn.|špq.ilht.ksat[.yn].|špq 4[51].6.50

pq.ilm.kḥṯm.yn.|špq.ilht.ksat[.yn].|špq.ilm.rḥbt yn.|špq.ilht.dkrt[.yn].|‘d.lḥm.šty.ilm.|w pq mrǵtm.ṯd.|b ḥrb.m 4[51].6.54

y h.|b qrb hkl h.ṣḥ.|šb‘m.bn.aṯrt.|špq.ilm.krm.y[n].|špq.ilht.ẖprt[.yn].|špq.ilm.alpm.y[n].|špq.ilht.arẖt[.yn].|šp 4[51].6.48

.ilm.alpm.y[n].|špq.ilht.arẖt[.yn].|špq.ilm.kḥṯm.yn.|špq.ilht.ksat[.yn].|špq.ilm.rḥbt yn.|špq.ilht.dkrt[.yn].|‘d.lḥ 4[51].6.52

.|šb‘m.bn.aṯrt.|špq.ilm.krm.y[n].|špq.ilht.ẖprt[.yn].|špq.ilm.alpm.y[n].|špq.ilht.arẖt[.yn].|špq.ilm.kḥṯm.yn.|šp 4[51].6.49

ilht.ẖprt[.yn].|špq.ilm.alpm.y[n].|špq.ilht.arẖt[.yn].|špq.ilm.kḥṯm.yn.|špq.ilht.ksat[.yn].|špq.ilm.rḥbt yn.|špq.i 4[51].6.51

ḥ.aẖ h.b bht h.a[r]y h.|b qrb hkl h.ṣḥ.|šb‘m.bn.aṯrt.|špq.ilm.krm.y[n].|špq.ilht.ẖprt[.yn].|špq.ilm.alpm.y[n].|šp 4[51].6.47

.ilht.arẖt[.yn].|špq.ilm.kḥṯm.yn.|špq.ilht.ksat[.yn].|špq.ilm.rḥbt yn.|špq.ilht.dkrt[.yn].|‘d.lḥm.šty.ilm.|w pq m 4[51].6.53

.hn.|[---].ḥ[m]t.pṭr.w.p nḥš.|[---.--]q.n[t]k.l yd‘.l bn.l pq ḥmt.|[---.--]n h.ḥmt.w t‘btn h.abd y.|[---.ǵ]r.šrǵzz.ybky. UG5.8.35

pq.ilm.rḥbt yn.|špq.ilht.dkrt[.yn].|‘d.lḥm.šty.ilm.|w pq mrǵtm.ṯd.|b ḥrb.mlḥt.qṣ[.m]r|i.tšty.krp[nm.y]n.|[b k]s. 4[51].6.56

.|[--.]rbt.aṯrt.ym.|[---.]btlt.‘nt.|[--.tl]ḥm.tšty.|[ilm.w tp]q.mrǵtm.|[ṯd.b ḥrb.m]lḥt.qṣ.|[mri.tšty.k]rpnm yn.|[b ks 4[51].3.41

[---].|yqrb.[---].|lḥm.m[---.---].|[‘]d.lḥm[.šty.ilm].|w pq.mr[ǵtm.ṯd.---].|b ḥrb.[mlḥt.qṣ.mri].|šty.kr[pnm.yn.---]. 5[67].4.13

ṯmnt.bn um.|krt.ḥtk n.rš.|krt.grdš.mknt.|aṯt.ṣdq h.l ypq.|mtrẖt.yšr h.|aṯt.trẖ.w tb‘t.|ṯar um.tkn l h.|mṯlṯt.kṯr 14[KRT].1.12

pqd

h.l lḥm.tptḥ.|brlt h.l ṯrm.|mt.dm.ẖt.š‘tqt.|dm.lan.w ypqd.|krt.ṯ‘.yšu.g h.|w yṣḥ.šm‘.l mṯt.|ḥry.ṭbẖ.imr.|w ilḥm 16.6[127].14

pqq

.--]d h.|km trpa.hn n‘r.|d yšt.l.lṣb h ẖš‘r klb.|[w]riš.pqq.w šr h.|yšt.aḥd h.dm zt.ẖrpnt. UG5.1.2.5

pqr

ksdm.|ṣdqn.|nwrdr.|ṯrin.|‘dršp.|pqr.|agbṯr.|‘bd.|ksd. 1044.6

|[---.--]ḥ.|[---.--]n.|[-----].|[---.-]bd.|[---]yb‘.b‘l.ẖr[-].|pqr.yḥd.|bn.ktmn.ṯǵr.hk[l].|bn.ṯgbr.ṯǵr.hk[l].|bn.ydln.|bn 1056.7

‘d[rš]p.|pqr.|ṯǵr.|ttǵl.|ṯn.yṣḥm.|slṯmg.|kdrl.|wql.|adrdn.|prn.|‘b 1069.2

pr

[t̠]n.prm.b ʻšrm.|arbʻ.prm.b.ʻš[r]m.|arbʻ.b.arbʻm.|t̠t̠m.[---.p]rm.|[-]l.b[--.---].|[--- 1138.2
[t̠]n.prm.b ʻšrm.|arbʻ.prm.b.ʻš[r]m.|arbʻ.b.arbʻm.|t̠t̠m.[---.p]rm. 1138.1
[---.]ḫlmt.alp.šnt.w[.---].|šntm.alp.d krr[.---].|alp.pr.bʻl.[---].|w prt.tkt.[---].|šnt.[---].|ššw.ʻt̠rt.w ššw.ʻ[nt.---]. 2158.1.3
h].|k.yiḫd[.akl.ššw].|št.mkš[r.grn].|w.št.ašk[rr].|w.pr.ḥd̠r[t.ydk].|aḥd h.w.yṣq[.b.ap h].|k.yiḫd.akl.š[šw].|št.n 161[56].15
ʻ.[---].|tmt̠l[.---].|mǵm[ǵ.---].|w.š[t.nni.w.pr.ʻbk].|w.pr[.ḥd̠rt.w.št].|irǵ[n.ḥmr.ydk].|aḥd[h.w.yṣq.b.ap h].|k yr[161[56].29
q b ap h.|[k.yiḫd akl š]šw št mkšr grn.|[w št aškrr w p]r ḥd̠rt.|[-----].|[---.-]n[-].|[k yraš ššw št bln q]t̠ ydk.|[w y 160[55].11
rn[.---].|drʻ.[---].|tmt̠l[.---].|mǵm[ǵ.---].|w.š[t.nni.w.pr.ʻbk].|w.pr[.ḥd̠rt.w.št].|irǵ[n.ḥmr.ydk].|aḥd[h.w.yṣq.b.a 161[56].28
kbm.yʻrb.|[bʻ]l.b kbd h.b p h yrd.|k ḫrr.zt.ybl.arṣ.w pr.|ʻṣm.yraun.aliyn.bʻl.|t̠ʻ.nn.rkb.ʻrpt.|tbʻ.rgm.l bn.ilm.mt 5[67].2.5
rm.b ʻšrm.|arbʻ.prm.b.ʻš[r]m.|arbʻ.b.arbʻm.|t̠t̠m.[---.p]rm.|[-]l.b[--.---].|[---].kbd.|[---].kb[d.---].|[t]šʻm. 1138.4
š.nbk m w.š.|gt mlk š.ʻlm.|l kt̠r.t̠n.ʻlm.|tzǵ[.---.]nšm.pr. UG5.12.B.13

pri

n.|[--]ry.|[--]lim bn.brq.|[--.]qtn bn.drṣy.|[--]kn bn.pri.|[r]špab bn.pni.|[ab]mn bn.qṣy.|[ʻ]pt̠rm bn.agmz.|[-]n 2087.7

prbḫt̠

pt y mn|t hn t̠lḫ h w mlg h y|t̠tqt ʻm h b qʻt.|tqʻt ʻm prbḫt̠.|dmqt ṣǵrt kt̠rt. 24[77].49

prgl

[ḥl.]mlk.[w.]b.ym.ḥdt̠.t̠n.šm.|l.[---]t.|i[d.yd]bḥ.mlk.l.prgl.ṣqrn.b.gg.|ar[bʻ.]arbʻ.mt̠bt.azmr.b h.š.šr[-].|al[p.w].š.š 35[3].50

prgt̠

rgm.|ʻšr ddm.l bt.|ʻšrm.dd.l mḫṣm.|ddm l kbs.|dd l prgt̠.|dd.l mri.|dd.l t̠nǵly.|dd.l krwn.|dd.l t̠ǵr.|dd.l rmt.r[1100.7

prd

b.ʻšrt.ksp.|t̠lt̠.ut̠bm.b d.alḫn.b.ʻšrt[.k]sp.|rt̠.l.ql.d.ybl.prd.|b.t̠ql.w.nṣp.ksp.|t̠mn.lbšm.w.mšlt.|l.udmym.b.t̠mnt.ʻš 2101.12
t̠mry.w.t̠n.bn h.w[.---].|ymrn.apsny.w.at̠t h..b[n.---].|prd.mʻqby[.w.---.a]t̠t h[.---].|prt̠.mgd[ly.---.]at̠[t h].|ʻdyn[.-- 2044.10

prdmn

al.tǵl[.---].|prdmn.ʻbd.ali[yn].|bʻl.sid.zbl.bʻl.|arṣ.qm.yt̠ʻr.|w yšlḥmn h. 3[ʻNT].1.2

prdn

.gʻyn.|bn.ǵrn.|bn.agynt.|bn.abdḫr.snry.|dqn.šlmn.|prdn.ndb[--].|[-]rn.ḫbty.|abmn.bn.qdmn.|nʻmn.bn.ʻbdilm. 87[64].38

prdny

t.ksp.|ʻl.bn.alkbl.šb[ny].|ʻšrm ksp.ʻl.|wrt.mtny.w ʻl.|prdny.at̠t h. 2107.19

prwsdy

mw.|[---.]w yky.|t̠lt̠m sp.l bnš tpnr.|arbʻ.spm.l.lbnš prwsdy.|t̠t̠ spm.l bnš klnmw.|l yarš ḫswn.|ḫmš ʻšr.sp.|l bn 137.2[93].7

prḫ

spr.bdlm.|nʻmn.|rbil.|plsy.|ygmr.|mnt̠.|prḫ.|ʻdršp.|ršpab.|t̠nw.|abmn.|abǵl.|bʻldn.|ypʻ. 1032.7

prṭl

k.|[--]ḫp.an.arnn.ql.špš.ḥw.bt̠nm.uḫd.bʻlm.|[--.a]t̠m.prṭl.l riš h.ḥmt.t̠mt.|[--.]ydbr.t̠rmt.al m.qḥn y.š y.qḥn y.|[-- 1001.1.7
.b g[--].|[---.]ḥ[--.]bnt.ṣʻṣ.bnt.ḫkp[.---].|[---].aḥw.aṭm.prṭl[.---].|[---.]mnt.[l]pʻn[.-.-]bd h.aqšr[.---].|[---].ptḥ y.a[--. 1001.1.19

prẓ

kt ǵr k.ank.ydʻt.|[-]n.atn.at.mt̠b k[.---].|[š]mm.rm.lk.prẓ kt.|[k]bkbm.t̠m.tpl k.lbnt.|[-.]rgm.k yrkt.ʻt̠qbm.|[---]m 13[6].12

prkl

n [-]ln.bn.t̠bil.|bn is.bn tbdn.|bn uryy.|bn abdʻn.|bn prkl.|bn štn.|bn annyn.|b[n] slg.|u[--] dit.|bn p[-]n.|bn nẓ 101[10].10
d.yḥmn.|yry[.---.]br.|ydn[.---].kry.|bn.ydd[.---.b]r.|prkl.bʻl.any.d.b d.abr[-]. 2123.7

prln

kt̠r.w ḫss.yd.|ytr.kt̠r.w ḫss.|spr.ilmlk šbny.|lmd.atn.prln.rb.|khnm rb.nqdm.|t̠ʻy.nqmd.mlk ugr[t].|adn.yrgb.bʻ 6.6[62.2].54
.]aqht.yd̠[--].|[---.--]n.ṣ[---].|[spr.ilmlk.šbny.lmd.atn.]prln. 17[2AQHT].7.1

prmn

nr.|šd.knʻm.l.bn.ʻmnr.|šd.bn.krwn.l bn.ʻmyn.|šd.bn.prmn.l aḫny.|šd.bn ḥnn.l bn.adld̠n.|šd.bn.nṣdn.l bn.ʻmlbi.| 2089.6

prn

spr.ubdy.art.|šd.prn.b d.agpt̠n.nḫl h.|šd.šwn.b d.ttyn.nḫl [h].|šd.t̠tyn[.b]n.a 2029.2
bn.nṣ.|[b]n.ʻṣr.|[---]m.|[bn.]ulnhr.|[bn.p]rn.|[bn.a]nny.|[---]n.|bn.kbln.|bn.pdy.|bn.t̠pdn. 1075.1.5
zy.|bdl.qrt̠y.|trgn.bn.tǵḥ.|aupš.qmnzy.|t̠rry.mṣbty.|prn.ngt̠y.|t̠rd̠n.zlyy. 89[312].10
].|[---.]l[--].|[bn.]ubn.|kbšm.|bn.abd̠r.|bn.kpltn.|bn.prn.|ʻbdm.|bn.kd̠ǵbr.|bn.mṣrn.|bn.[-]dr[-].|[---]l[-].|[--]y 114[324].2.8
|pqr.|t̠ǵr.|ttǵl.|t̠n.yṣḥm.|slt̠mg.|kdrl.|wql.|adrdn.|prn.|ʻbdil.|ušy.šbn[-].|aḫt.ab.|krwn.|nnd̠.|mkl.|kzǵb.|iyr 1069.10
rn.|[šd.---.]gt.prn.|[šd.---.]gt.prn.|[š]d.bn.š[p]šn l gt pr[n].|šd bn.ilšḫr.|l.gt.mzln.|šd.gldy.|l.gt.mzln.|šd.glln.l.g 1104.14
y.gt.prn.|šd.hwil.gt.prn.|šd.ḥr.gt.prn.|šd.bn.t̠bǵl.gt.prn.|šd.bn.inšr.gt.prn.|šd.[---.]gt.prn.|[šd.---.]gt.prn.|[šd.-- 1104.9

prn

šd.ubdy.ilštm‘. | dt b d.skn. | šd.bn.ubr‘n b gt prn. | šd.bn.gby.gt.prn. | šd.bn.kryn.gt.prn. | šd.bn.ky.gt.prn. 1104.3
d.bn.ubr‘n b gt prn. | šd.bn.gby.gt.prn. | šd.bn.kryn.gt.prn. | šd.bn.ky.gt.prn. | šd.hwil.gt.prn. | šd.ḥr.gt.prn. | šd.bn.ṯ 1104.5
lštm‘. | dt b d.skn. | šd.bn.ubr‘n b gt prn. | šd.bn.gby.gt.prn. | šd.bn.kryn.gt.prn. | šd.bn.ky.gt.prn. | šd.hwil.gt.prn. | š 1104.4
.inšr.gt.prn. | šd.[---.]gt.prn. | [šd.---.]gt.prn. | [šd.---.]gt.prn. | [š]d.bn.š[p]šn l gt pr[n]. | šd bn.ilšḥr. | l.gt.mzln. | šd.gld 1104.13
ryn.gt.prn. | šd.bn.ky.gt.prn. | šd.hwil.gt.prn. | šd.ḥr.gt.prn. | šd.bn.ṯbǵl.gt.prn. | šd.bn.inšr.gt.prn. | šd.[---.]gt.prn. | [š 1104.8
rn. | šd.bn.gby.gt.prn. | šd.bn.kryn.gt.prn. | šd.bn.ky.gt.prn. | šd.hwil.gt.prn. | šd.ḥr.gt.prn. | šd.bn.ṯbǵl.gt.prn. | šd.bn. 1104.6
.prn. | šd.bn.kryn.gt.prn. | šd.bn.ky.gt.prn. | šd.hwil.gt.prn. | šd.ḥr.gt.prn. | šd.bn.ṯbǵl.gt.prn. | šd.bn.inšr.gt.prn. | šd.[1104.7
l.gt.prn. | šd.bn.inšr.gt.prn. | šd.[---.]gt.prn. | [šd.---.]gt.prn. | [šd.---.]gt.prn. | [š]d.bn.š[p]šn l gt pr[n]. | šd bn.ilšḥr. | l. 1104.12
t.prn. | šd.bn.ṯbǵl.gt.prn. | šd.bn.inšr.gt.prn. | šd.[---.]gt.prn. | [šd.---.]gt.prn. | [šd.---.]gt.prn. | [š]d.bn.š[p]šn l gt pr[n]. 1104.11
gt.prn. | šd.ḥr.gt.prn. | šd.bn.ṯbǵl.gt.prn. | šd.bn.inšr.gt.prn. | šd.[---.]gt.prn. | [šd.---.]gt.prn. | [šd.---.]gt.prn. | [š]d.bn.š 1104.10

prs

n.ltḥ. | srn.ltḥ. | ykn.ltḥ. | ḥgbn.ltḥ. | spr.mkrm. | bn.sl‘n.prs. | bn.ṯpdn.ltḥ. | bn.urm.ltḥ. 1059.7
l ḫmš.mrkbt.ḫmš.‘šr h.prs. | bt.mrkbt.w l šant.ṯṯ. | l bt.‘šrm. | bt alḫnm.ṯlṯm ṯṯ kbd. 2105.1
-]. | [---.]kd[r]. | [---.]ṯpr. | [---.]prš̀. | [---.]šdm. | [---.-]nm.prš̀.glbm. | [---.]‘gd.dqr. | [---.]ṯn.alpm. | [---.ṯ]n alpm. | [---.--]r 1142.8
ḫtn.w.kd.ḥmṣ.w.[lt]ḥ.‘šdm. | kd yn.l.ḫdǵb.w.kd.ḥmṣ. | prš̀.glbm.l.bt. | tgmǵ.kš̀mm.b.yrḫ.iṯtbnm. | šb‘m.dd.ṯn.kbd. | t 1099.29
lm. | [---.nš]lm. | [---.nš]lm. | [---.nš]lm. | [---.nš]lm. | [---.pr]š̀.d.nšlm. | [---.]d.nšlm. 2036.7
[---].prš̀ qmḥ.d.nšlm. | [---].prš̀.d.nšlm. | [---.nš]lm. | [---.nš]lm. | [---.nš]lm. | [---.nš]lm. | [-- 2036.2
[---.‘]ṯtry. | [-----.]yn. | [----.-]mn. | [---.--]m.mṣl. | [---].prš̀.ḥtm. | ṯlṯ[.---].bn.ṯdnyn. | ddm.ḥ[tm].‘l.šrn. | ‘šrt.ksp.‘l.[-]l 1146.5
. | b d.b‘lsr. | yd.ṯdn.‘šr. | [ḥ]mrm. | ddm.l.ybr[k]. | bdmr.prs.l.u[-]m[-]. | ṯmn.l.‘šrm. | dmd.b d.mry[n]m. 2102.7
[---].prš̀ qmḥ.d.nšlm. | [---].prš̀.d.nšlm. | [---.nš]lm. | [---.nš]lm. | [-- 2036.1
mtnt.w ynt.[qrt.w ṯn.ḥṯm]. | w bǵr.arb‘.[---.kdm.yn]. | prs.qmḥ.m‘[--.---]. | mdbḥt.bt.i[lt.‘ṣrm.l]. | ṣpn š.l ǵlm[t.š.w l. APP.II[173].25
.mtnt[.w ynt.qrt]. | w ṯn ḥṯm.w bǵr.arb[‘.---]. | kdm.yn.prs.qmḥ.[---]. | mdbḥt.bt.ilt.‘ṣr[m.l ṣpn.š]. | l ǵlmt.š.w l [---.l 35[3].23
[-]k[-.---]. | ar[--.---]. | yrt.[---]. | ṯṯ.prš̀[.---]. | bn.‘myn[.---]. 2152.6
.zbl.mlk.‘llm y]. | šm‘.atm[.---]. | ym.lm.qd[.---]. | šmn.prst[.---]. | ydr.hm.ym[.---]. | ‘l amr.yu[ḫd.ksa.mlk h]. | nḫt.k 22.1[123].15
[---.--]m n‘rt. | [---].qt.b[--]. | [---.]kd[r]. | [---.]ṯpr. | [---.]prš̀. | [---.]šdm. | [---.-]nm.prš̀.glbm. | [---.]‘gd.dqr. | [---.]ṯn.alp 1142.5
b y[rḫ.---]. | ‘š[r.---]. | ḫm[š.---]. | b[yrḫ.---]. | [---.]prš̀. | [-----]. | l.mšḫ[.---]. | ‘šr.d[d.---]. | ṯṯm.dd.dd[.---]. | l.mḏrǵ 2012.5

prsḥ

‘l.km.nšr b uṣb‘t h.hlm.qdq | d zbl ym.bn.‘nm.ṯpṭ.nhr.yprsḥ ym. | w yql.l arṣ.w trtqṣ.ṣmd.b d b‘l. | [km.]nšr.b uṣb‘t 2.4[68].22
km.]nšr.b uṣb‘t h.ylm.qdqd.zbl. | [ym.]bn.‘nm.ṯpṭ.nhr.yprsḥ.ym.yql. | l arṣ.tnǵṣn.pnt h.w ydlp.tmn h. | yqṯ b‘l.w yšt 2.4[68].25

prsn

r‘ym.dt.b d.iytlm. | ḫyrn.w.š̀ǵr h. | š̀ǵr.bn.prsn. | agpṯr.w.š̀ǵ[r h]. | ṯ‘ln. | mztn.w.š̀ǵr [h]. | š̀ǵr.plṭ. | s[d]rn 2072.3
. | [bn.]iršn. | bn.[---]. | bn.b[--]. | bn.š[--]. | bn.a[---]. | bn.prsn. | bn.mtyn. | bn.ḫlpn. | bn.ḥgbn. | bn.szn. | bn.mglb. 117[325].2.5
| bn.ṯbtnq. | bn.pṯdn. | bn.nbdg. | bn.ḥgbn. | bn.tmr. | bn.prsn. | bn.ršpy. | [‘]bdḥgb. | [k]lby. | [-]ḥmn. | [š]pšyn. | [‘b]dml 113[400].1.21
[-----]. | šd.prsn.l.[---]. | šd.bddn.l.iytlm. | šd.bn.nb‘m.l.ṯpṭb‘l. | šd.bn mšr 2030.1.2
bn.‘mnr. | bn.kmn. | bn.ibyn. | bn.mryn.ṣmd.w.ḥrṣ. | bn.prsn.ṣmd.w.ḥrṣ. | bn.ilb‘l. | bn.idrm. | bn.grgš. | bn.bly. | bn.apṯ 2113.6

prš̀

-]. | [---.]kd[r]. | [---.]ṯpr. | [---.]prš̀. | [---.]šdm. | [---.-]nm.prš̀.glbm. | [---.]‘gd.dqr. | [---.]ṯn.alpm. | [---.ṯ]n alpm. | [---.--]r 1142.8
ḫtn.w.kd.ḥmṣ.w.[lt]ḥ.‘šdm. | kd yn.l.ḫdǵb.w.kd.ḥmṣ. | prš̀.glbm.l.bt. | tgmǵ.kš̀mm.b.yrḫ.iṯtbnm. | šb‘m.dd.ṯn.kbd. | t 1099.29
lm. | [---.nš]lm. | [---.nš]lm. | [---.nš]lm. | [---.nš]lm. | [---.pr]š̀.d.nšlm. | [---.]d.nšlm. 2036.7
[---].prš̀ qmḥ.d.nšlm. | [---].prš̀.d.nšlm. | [---.nš]lm. | [---.nš]lm. | [---.nš]lm. | [---.nš]lm. | [-- 2036.2
[---.‘]ṯtry. | [-----.]yn. | [----.-]mn. | [---.--]m.mṣl. | [---].prš̀.ḥtm. | ṯlṯ[.---].bn.ṯdnyn. | ddm.ḥ[tm].‘l.šrn. | ‘šrt.ksp.‘l.[-]l 1146.5
[---].prš̀ qmḥ.d.nšlm. | [---].prš̀.d.nšlm. | [---.nš]lm. | [---.nš]lm. | [-- 2036.1
[-]k[-.---]. | ar[--.---]. | yrt.[---]. | ṯṯ.prš̀[.---]. | bn.‘myn[.---]. 2152.6
[---.--]m n‘rt. | [---].qt.b[--]. | [---.]kd[r]. | [---.]ṯpr. | [---.]prš̀. | [---.]šdm. | [---.-]nm.prš̀.glbm. | [---.]‘gd.dqr. | [---.]ṯn.alp 1142.5
b y[rḫ.---]. | ‘š[r.---]. | ḫm[š.---]. | b[yrḫ.---]. | [---.]prš̀. | [-----]. | l.mšḫ[.---]. | ‘šr.d[d.---]. | ṯṯm.dd.dd[.---]. | l.mḏrǵ 2012.5

pr‘

----]. | [-----]. | [---].al.tš[--.---]. | [---.]l ksi y.w pr[‘]. | [---].pr‘.ank.[---]. | [---.]ank.nši[.---]. | [---.ṯ]br.ḫss.[---]. | [---.--]št.b 1002.14
.yṣḥ.‘n.gpn. | w ugr.bn.ǵlmt. | ‘mm ym.bn.ẓlm[t]. | rmt.pr‘t.ibr[.mnt]. | ṣḥrrm.ḥbl[.--]. | ‘rpt.ṯḥt.[---] | m ‘ṣrm.ḥ[---]. | 8[51FRAG].9
ṣḥ.‘n. | [gpn].w ugr.b ǵlmt. | [‘mm.]ym.bn.ẓlmt.r | [mt.pr‘]t.ibr.mnt. | [ṣḥrrm.ḥbl.‘]rpt. | [---.---.-]ḥt. | [---.---]m. | [----] 4[51].7.56
[-] ym.pr‘ d nkly yn kd w kd. | w ‘l ym kdm. | w b ṯlṯ.kd yn w krsn 1086.1
n.ṯlṯ.rb‘.ym.ḫmš. | ṯdṯ.ym.tlḥmn.rpum. | tštyn.bt.ikl.b pr‘. | yṣq.b irt.lbnn.mk.b šb‘. | [ymm.---]k.aliyn.b‘l. | [---].r‘ h 22.2[124].24
t.yqb.[--] | rk.‘l.aqht.k yq[--.---]. | pr‘m.ṣd k.y bn[.---]. | pr‘m.ṣd k.hn pr[‘.--]. | ṣd.b hkl h[.---]. | [------]. | [---.l]ḫm[.---]. 17[2AQHT].5.38
.ǵzr.m[t]. | hrnmy.qšt.yqb.[--] | rk.‘l.aqht.k yq[--.---]. | pr‘m.ṣd k.y bn[.---]. | pr‘m.ṣd k.hn pr[‘.--]. | ṣd.b hkl h[.---]. | 17[2AQHT].5.37
wt. | l aḫw.ap.qšt h.l ttn. | l y.w b mt[.-]ḥ.mṣṣ[-]t[.--]. | pr‘.qẓ.y[bl].šblt. | b ǵlp h.apnk.dnil. | [m]t.rpi.ap[h]n.ǵzr. | [m 19[1AQHT].1.18
dbḥt. | ḫr[.---.]‘l.kbkbt. | n‘m.[--.-]llm.trtḥṣ. | btlt.‘n[t].tptr‘ ṭd[h]. | limm.w t‘l.‘m.il. | ab h.ḥpr.p‘l k.y[--]. | šm‘ k.l ar 13[6].19
l.aqht.k yq[--.---]. | pr‘m.ṣd k.y bn[.---]. | pr‘m.ṣd k.hn pr[‘.--]. | ṣd.b hkl h[.---]. | [------]. | [---.l]ḫm[.---]. | [---].ay š[---] 17[2AQHT].5.38
. | [-----]. | [-----]. | [-----]. | [---].al.tš[--.---]. | [---.]l ksi y.w pr[‘]. | [---].pr‘.ank.[---]. | [---.]ank.nši[.---]. | [---.ṯ]br.ḫss.[---]. 1002.13
n lk. | [---].km[-.---]. | [---.--]k yṣunn[.---]. | [---.--]dy.w.pr‘[.---]. | [---.]ytn.ml[--].ank.iphn. | [---.a]nk.i[--.--]slm.w.yṯb 1002.35

prpr

ln.qšt. | bn.nkl qšt. | ady.qšt. | bn.srn.qšt. | bn.gdrn.qšt. | prpr.qšt. | ugry.qšt. | bn.ṣrptn.qšt. | bn.mṣry.qšt. | arny. | abm. 119[321].1.44

prṣ

mdr'.w ṣḥ hm.'m.nǵr.mdr' y.nǵr. | nǵr.ptḥ.w ptḥ hw.prṣ.b'd hm. | w 'rb.hm.hm[.iṯ.--.l]ḥm.w t[n]. | w nlḥm.hm.iṯ[. 23[52].70

prq

lm.tlk.nbtm. | šmḫ.lṯpn.il.d pid. | p'n h.l hdm.yṯpd. | w yprq.lṣb w yṣḥq. | yšu.g h.w yṣḥ. | aṯbn.ank.w anḫn. | w tnḫ.b 6[49].3.16
p'n.il.thbr.w tql. | tštḥwy.w tkbd h. | hlm.il.k yphn h. | yprq.lṣb.w yṣḥq. | p'n h.l hdm.yṯpd.w ykrkr. | uṣb't h.yšu.g h 4[51].4.28
ḥṣ. | npṣ k.b ym rṯ.b uni[l]. | pnm.tšmḫ.w 'l yṣhl pi[t]. | yprq.lṣb.w yṣḥq. | p'n.l hdm.yṯpd.yšu. | g h.w yṣḥ.aṯbn.ank. | 17[2AQHT].2.10

prqdš

š'n. | mṣrm. | tmkrn. | ypḥ.'bdilt. | bn.m. | ypḥ.ilšlm. | bn.prqdš. | ypḥ.mnḥm. | bn.ḥnn. | brqn.spr. 2116.20

prqt

ṯn.pld.pṯt[.-]r. | lpš.sgr.rq. | ṯṯ.prqt. | w.mrdt.prqt.pṯt. | lbš.psm.rq. | ṯn.mrdt.az. | ṯlṯ.pld.š'rt. 1112.3
ṯn.pld.pṯt[.-]r. | lpš.sgr.rq. | ṯṯ.prqt. | w.mrdt.prqt.pṯt. | lbš.psm.rq. | ṯn.mrdt.az. | ṯlṯ.pld.š'rt. | ṯ[---].kbm. | p 1112.4

prr

. | w tšu.g h.w [tṣḥ]. | ph m'.ap.k[rt.--]. | u ṯn.ndr[.---]. | apr.[---]. | [-----]. 15[128].3.30

prša

t.b ksp. | šmrgt.b dm.ḫrṣ. | kḫṯ.il.nḫt. | b ẓr.hdm.id. | d prša.b br. | n'l.il.d qblbl. | 'ln.ybl hm.ḫrṣ. | ṯlḥn.il.d mla. | mn 4[51].1.36

prt

.arṣ.w td' ilm. | k mtt.yšm'.aliyn.b'l. | yuhb.'glt.b dbr.prt. | b šd.šḥlmmt.škb. | 'mn h.šb'.l šb'm. | tš[']ly.ṯmn.l ṯmny 5[67].5.18
lp.šnt.w[.---]. | šntm.alp.d krr[.---]. | alp.pr.b'l.[---]. | w prt.tkt.[---]. | šnt.[---]. | ššw.'ṯtrt.w ššw.'[nt.---]. | w ht.[--]k.šš 2158.1.4

prtwn

[--]an.š[šlmt]. | bnš.iwl[--.š]šlmt. | šdyn.ššlmt. | prtwn.š'rt. | ṯṯn.š'rt. | 'dn.š'rt. | mnn.š'rt. | bdn.š'rt. | 'pṯn.š'rt. | ' 97[315].4

prtn

n. | [bn.]nklb. | [---]dn. | [---]y. | [-----]. | [-----]. | bn.adn. | prtn. | bn.btry. 1073.3.4
. | bn ḫlp. | bn.ẓll. | bn ydy. | bn lzn. | bn.ṯyn. | bn g'r. | bn.prtn. | bn ḫnn. | b[n.-]n. | bn.ṣṣb. | bn.b'ltn ḫlq. | bn.mlkbn. | bn 2016.1.17
n.--]my. | [bn.b]rq. | [bn.--]r. | [bn.--]tn. | [bn.-]rmn. | bn.prtn. | bn.ymn. | bn.dby. | bn.ir[--]. | bn.kr[--]. | bn.nn[-]. | [-----] 124[-].5.8
| bn.rwy. | bn.'myn. | bdl.mrynm. | bn.ṣqn. | bn.šyn. | bn.prtn. | bn.ypr. | mrum. | bn.'[--]t. | bn.adty. | bn.krwn. | bn.nǵsk 113[400].3.9

prṯ

.apsny.w.aṯt h..b[n.---]. | prd.m'qby[.w.---.a]ṯt h[.---]. | prṯ.mgd[ly.---.]aṯ[t h]. | 'dyn[.---]. | w.ṯn[.bn h.---]. | iwrm[-.]b 2044.11
. | gmrd.'šrm. | ṣdqšlm.'šr[m]. | yknil.ḫmš. | ilmlk.ḫmš. | prṯ.'šr. | ubn.'šr. 1116.14
m. | ttn.w tn. | w l ttn. | w al ttn. | tn ks yn. | w ištn. | 'bd.prṯ.ṯḥm. | qrq.pṯ.ḏmn. | l iṯtl. 1019.2.1
spr.bnš.mlk. | d.b d.prṯ. | tš'.l.'šrm. | lqḥ.ššlmt. | ṯmn.l.arb'm. | lqḥ.š'rt. 1025.2
kd.yn. | l prṯ. 159[59].2

pš

arḫ.td.rgm.b ǵr. | b p y.t'lgt.b lšn[y]. | ǵr[.---]b.b pš y.t[--]. | hwt.b'l.iš[--]. | šm' l y.ypš.[---]. | ḥkr[.---]. | 'ṣr[.--.]t 2124.3

pš'

---.]ṯb l y.l aqht.ǵzr.ṯb l y w l k. | [---]m.l aqry k.b ntb.pš'. | [---].b ntb.gan.ašql k.tḥt. | [p'n y.a]nk.n'mn.'mq.nšm. | [17[2AQHT].6.43

pt

.hll[.snnt]. | hl ǵlmt tld b[n.--]n. | 'n ha l yd h.tzd[.--]. | pt l bšr h.dm a[--.--]ḥ. | w yn.k mtrḫt[.---]h. | šm' ilht kṯr[t.-- 24[77].9

pṯḥ

ḥd.adr. | [---.--]t.b[ḥd]r.mškb. | ṯl[l.---.--]ḥ. | b lṯk.bt. | [pt]ḥ.aḥd.l.bt.'bdm. | [ṯ]n.pṯḥ msb.bt.tu. | w.pṯḥ[.aḥ]d.mmt. | ṯ 1151.9
| b lṯk.bt. | [pt]ḥ.aḥd.l.bt.'bdm. | [ṯ]n.pṯḥ msb.bt.tu. | w.pṯḥ[.aḥ]d.mmt. | ṯṯ.pt[ḥ.---]. | ṯn.pt[ḥ.---]. | w.pt[ḥ.--]r.ṯǵr. | ṯm 1151.11
ṯr.bnm.'dt. | ypṯḥ.ḥln.b bht m. | urbt.b qrb.[h]kl | m.w y[p]tḥ.b dqt.'rpt. | 'l h[wt].kṯr.w ḫss. | ṣḥq.kṯr.w ḫss. | yšu.g h 4[51].7.19
bn.b'l. | l hwt y.ypṯḥ.ḥ | ln.b bht m.urbt. | b qrb.hk[l m.yp]tḥ. | b'l.b dqt[.'rp]t. | ql h.qdš.b['l.y]tn. | yṯny.b'l.ṣ[---.-]pt 4[51].7.27
r.[k]m. | zbln.'l.riš h. | w ṯṯb.trḥṣ.nn.b d't. | npš h.l lḥm.tpṯḥ. | brlt h.l ṯrm. | mt.dm.ḫt.š'tqt. | dm.lan.w ypqd. | krt.ṯ'.y 16.6[127].11
htm.mnt.b'd h.bhtm.sgrt. | b'd h.'dbt.ṯlṯ.pṯḥ.bt.mnt. | pṯḥ.bt.w ubn.hkl.w ištql šql. | tn.km.nḥšm.yḥr.tn.km. | mhr UG5.7.72
.plg. | b'd h.bhtm.mnt.b'd h.bhtm.sgrt. | b'd h.'dbt.ṯlṯ.pṯḥ.bt.mnt. | pṯḥ.bt.w ubn.hkl.w ištql šql. | tn.km.nḥšm.yḥr.t UG5.7.71
m.nǵr. | mdr'.w ṣḥ hm.'m.nǵr.mdr' y.nǵr. | nǵr.pṯḥ.w pṯḥ hw.prṣ.b'd hm. | w 'rb.hm.hm[.iṯ.--.l]ḥm.w t[n]. | w nlḥ 23[52].70
ngš.hm.nǵr. | mdr'.w ṣḥ hm.'m.nǵr.mdr' y.nǵr. | nǵr.pṯḥ.w pṯḥ hw.prṣ.b'd hm. | w 'rb.hm.hm[.iṯ.--.l]ḥm.w t[n]. | 23[52].70
b. | bt.w y'n.aliyn. | b'l.ašt m.kṯr bn. | ym.kṯr.bnm.'dt. | ypṯḥ.ḥln.b bht m. | urbt.b qrb.[h]kl | m.w y[p]tḥ.b dqt.'rpt. | 4[51].7.17
yšu.g h.w yṣḥ. | l rgmt.l k.l ali | yn.b'l.ṯṯbn.b'l. | l hwt y.ypṯḥ.ḥ | ln.b bht m.urbt. | b qrb.hk[l m.yp]tḥ. | b'l.b dqt[.'rp]t 4[51].7.25
ṯm.prṯl[.---]. | [---.]mnt.[l]p'n[.-.-]bd h.aqšr[.---]. | [---].pṯḥ y.a[--.]dt[.---].ml[--]. | [---.-]ṯk.ytmt.dlt tlk.[---].bm[.---]. 1001.1.21
mškb. | ṯl[l.---.--]ḥ. | b lṯk.bt. | [pt]ḥ.aḥd.l.bt.'bdm. | [ṯ]n.pṯḥ msb.bt.tu. | w.pṯḥ[.aḥ]d.mmt. | ṯṯ.pt[ḥ.---]. | ṯn.pt[ḥ.---]. | 1151.10
n š[-]'[--.]aḫd[.-]. | tšm'.mṯt.[ḥ]ry. | ṯṯbḫ.šmn.[m]ri h. | t[p]tḥ.rḥbt.yn. | 'l h.ṯr h.tš'rb. | 'l h.tš'rb.ẓby h. | ṯr.ḫbr.rbt. | ḫ 15[128].4.16

pṭḥ

gm.l[aṯt h k.yṣḥ].|šm'[.l mṯt.ḥry].|ṭbḫ.š[mn].mri k.|pṭḥ.[rḥ]bt.yn.|ṣḥ.šb'm.ṯr y.|ṯmnym.[ẓ]by y.|ṯr.ḫbr[.rb]t.|ḫ 15[128].4.5
[-----].|[tṭbḫ.šm]n.[mri h].|[tpṭḥ.rḥ]bt.[yn].|[---.]rp[.---].|[---.ḫ]br[.---].|bḫr[.--]t[.----].| 15[128].5.2
.bt.tu.|w.pṭḥ[.aḥ]d.mmt.|ṯṯ.pṭ[ḥ.---].|ṯn.pṭ[ḥ.---].|w.pṭ[ḥ.--]r.ṯǵr.|ṯmn.ḥlnm.|ṯt.tḫ[--].l.mtm. 1151.14
[ṯ]n.pṭḥ msb.bt.tu.|w.pṭḥ[.aḥ]d.mmt.|ṯṯ.pṭ[ḥ.---].|ṯn.pṭ[ḥ.---].|w.pṭ[ḥ.--]r.ṯǵr.|ṯmn.ḥlnm.|ṯt.tḫ[--].l.mtm. 1151.13
[dr].|[-----].|ḫmš[.---]t.ḥdrm.|w.[---.a]ḥd.d.sgrm.|w p[tḥ.---.]l.aḥd.adr.|[---.--]t.b[ḥd]r.mškb.|ṯl[l.---.--]ḥ.|b lṯk. 1151.5
.l.bt.'bdm.|[ṯ]n.pṭḥ msb.bt.tu.|w.pṭḥ[.aḥ]d.mmt.|ṯṯ.pṭ[ḥ.---].|ṯn.pṭ[ḥ.---].|w.pṭ[ḥ.--]r.ṯǵr.|ṯmn.ḥlnm.|ṯt.tḫ[--].l. 1151.12

pty

šu.|yr.šmm h.yr.b šmm.'ṣr.yḫrṭ yšt.|l pḥm.il.aṯtm.k ypt.hm.aṯtm.tṣḥn.|y mt.mt.nḥtm.ḫṭ k.mmnnm.mṭ.yd k.|h[23[52].39

ptm

.|aršm.b'l [aṯt].|ttḫ.b'l aṯt.|ayab.b'l aṯt.|iyṯr.b'l aṯt.|ptm.b'l ššlmt.|'dršp.b'l ššlmt.|ṯtrn.b'l ššlmt.|arŝwn.b'l ššl 1077.6

ptq

t.'rb.|[---.w ẓ]r.mtn y at zd.|[---.]t'rb.bši.|[---.]l tzd.l tptq.|[---].g[--.]l arṣ. 1['NT.X].5.27

ptr

mm[.---].|w b ṯlṯ.ṣ[in.---].|l ll.pr[-.---].|mit š'[rt.---].|ptr.k[--.---].|[-]yu[-.---]. 37[22].11

pṯ

w l ttn.|w al ttn.|tn ks yn.|w ištn.|'bd.prṯ.tḥm.|qrq.pṯ.ḏmn.|l iṯtl. 1019.2.2

pṯpṯ

rišym.dt.'rb.|b bnš hm.|ḏmry.w.pṯpṯ.'rb.|b.yrm.|[ily.w].ḏmry.'rb.|b.ṯb'm.|ydn.bn.ilrpi.|w. 2079.3

pṯt

[-----].|[ḫ]pn.aḥd.b.ṯqlm.|lbš.aḥd.b.ṯqlm.|ḫpn.pṯtm.b 'šr.|tgmr.ksp.ṯlṯm.|ṯqlm.kbd. 1115.4
[---] kdwṯm.[---].|ḫmš.pld š'rt.|ṯṯ pld pṯt.|arb' ḫpnt pṯt.|ḫmš ḫpnt.š'rt.|ṯlṯ.'šr kdwṯm. 1113.9
tm.kbd.ṯlṯ.|arb'.kkrm.|ṯmn.mat.kbd.|pwt.|ṯmn.mat.pṯtm.|kkrm.alpm.|ḫmš.mat.kbd.|abn.ṣrp. 2051.7
.lbš[.---].|[---.]kbd.ṯṯ.i[qnu.---].|[---.]ǵprt.'š[r.---].|[---.p]ṯtm.l.ip[--.---].|[---.]ksl.ṯlṯ.m[at.---].|[---].abn.ṣr[p.---].|[-- 1106.25
mlk.mlbš.|ytn.l hm.|šb'.lbšm.allm.|l ušḫry.|ṯlṯ.mat.pṯtm.|l.mgmr.b.ṯlṯ.|šnt. 1107.11
ṯn.pld.pṯt[.-]r.|lpš.sgr.rq.|ṯṯ.prqt.|w.mrdt.prqt.pṯt.|lbš.psm.rq.|ṯn.mrdt.az.|ṯlṯ.pld.š'rt.|ṯ[---].kbm.|p[---]r. 1112.4
--].|ṯ[--] ḫpnt.|[---] kdwṯm.[---].|ḫmš.pld š'rt.|ṯṯ pld pṯt.|arb' ḫpnt pṯt.|ḫmš ḫpnt.š'rt.|ṯlṯ.'šr kdwṯm. 1113.8
'šr.ktnt.|'šr.rṭm.|kkr[.-].ḫt.|mitm[.p]ṯtm.|ṯlṯm[.---].kst.|alp.a[bn.ṣ]rp. 1114.4
ṯn.pld.pṯt[.-]r.|lpš.sgr.rq.|ṯṯ.prqt.|w.mrdt.prqt.pṯt.|lbš.psm.rq.|ṯ 1112.1
rb't.kbd.|ḫ[mš.]š'rt.|[---.]tš'.kbd.skm.|[arb]'m.ḫpnt.pṯt.|[-]r.pldm.dt.š'rt.|ṯlṯm.ṯlṯ.kbd.mṣrrt.|'šr.ṯn.kbd.pǵdrm. 1111.7
qni.arb'm.kbl.|[---].iqni.'šrm.ǵprt.|[---.ŝ]pŝg.iqni.mit.pṯtm.|[---].mitm.kslm.|[---].pwt.ṯlṯ.mat.abn.ṣrp.|[---.-]qt.l.ṯ 1106.8
[---.]ktb nǵr krm.|[---].ab h.krm ar.|[---.]h.mḥtrt.pṯtm.|[---.-]t h.ušpǵt tišr.|[---.šm]m h.nšat ẓl h kbkbm.|[--- 2001.2.3

Ṣ

ṣin

-]. | [---.--]t.š l i[l.---]. | [--.aṯ]rt.š[.---]. | [---.]l pdr[-.---]. | ṣin aḥd h[.---]. | l ʿṯtrt[.---]. | ʿlm.kmm[.---]. | w b ṯlṯ.ṣ[in.---]. | l 37[22].5
-]. | swn.qrty.w[.aṯt h]. | [w].bn h.w.ṯn.alpm. | [w.]ṯlṯm.ṣin. | anndr.yknʿmy. | w.aṯt h.w.bn h. | w.alp.w.tš[ʿ.]ṣin. 1080.14
qlm.ḫr[ṣ.]b.ṯmnt.ksp. | ʿšrt.ksp.b.alp.[b d].bn.[---]. | tšʿ.ṣin.b.tšʿt.ksp. | mšlt.b.ṯql.ksp. | kdwṯ.l.grgyn.b.ṯq[l]. | ḫmšm.š 2101.22
ṣ.bt.il. | b.ḫmšt.ʿšrt.ksp. | ḫmš.mat.šmt. | b.ʿšrt.ksp. | ʿšr.ṣin.b.ṯṯt.w.kmsk. | arbʿ[.k]dwṯm.w.ṯt.ṯprtm. | b.ʿšr[m.]ksp. | ḫ 2100.9
nnt[n.]w[.---]. | w.ṯn.bn h.[---]. | aǵltn.ypr[y.---]. | w.šbʿ.ṣin h[.---]. 2044.18
| [b]ʿl.ṯṯbḫ.šbʿm.alpm. | [k g]mn.aliyn.bʿl. | [ṯṯ]bḫ.šbʿm.ṣin. | [k gm]n.aliyn.bʿl. | [ṯṯb]ḫ.šbʿm.aylm. | [k gmn.]aliyn.bʿl. 6[62].1.22
b ṯlṯ. | ilmlk.ʿšr.ṣin. | mlknʿm.ʿšr. | bn.adty.ʿšr. | [ṣ]dqšlm ḫmš. | krzn.ḫmš. | ub 2039.2
ʿšrm ddm kbd[.-] l alpm mrim. | ṯt ddm l ṣin mrat. | ʿšr ddm.l šmʿrgm. | ʿšr ddm.l bt. | ʿšrm.dd.l mḫṣm. 1100.2
-]. | w bn[š.---]. | d bnš.ḥm[r.---]. | w d.l mdl.r[--.---]. | w ṣin.ʿz.b[ʿl.---]. | llu.bn[š.---]. | imr.ḫ[--.---]. | [--]n.b[ʿl.---]. | w [-- 2158.1.14
ršp mh bnš. | šrp.w ṣp ḫršḫ. | ʿlm b ǵb ḥyr. | ṯmn l ṯlṯm ṣin. | šbʿ.alpm. | bt bʿl.ugrt.ṯn šm. | ʿlm.l ršp.mlk. | alp w.š.l bʿl UG5.12.B.4
t. | lbš.w [-]tn.ušpǵt. | ḫr[-].ṯlṯt.mzn. | drk.š.alp.w ṯlṯ. | ṣin.šlm[m.]šbʿ pamt. | l ilm.šb[ʿ.]l kṯr. | ʿlm.tʿrbn.gṯrm. | bt.ml 33[5].7
mlk.ʿllm y.km.tdd. | ʿnt.ṣd.tštr.ʿpt.šmm. | ṭbḫ.alpm.ap ṣin.šql.ṯrm. | w mri ilm.ʿglm.dt.šnt. | imr.qmṣ.llim.k ksp. | l ʿb 22.2[124].12
.bht[h.bʿ]l. | yʿdb.hd.ʿdb[.ʿd]bt. | hkl h.ṭbḫ.alpm[.ap]. | ṣin.šql.ṯrm[.w]m | ria.il.ʿglm.d[t]. | šnt.imr.qmṣ.l[l]im. | ṣḥ.aḫ 4[51].6.41
ḫṣ k.k[--.---]. | il.dbḥ.[---]. | pʿr.b[--.---]. | ṭbḫ.alp[m.ap.ṣin.šql]. | ṯrm.w [mri.ilm.ʿglm.dt.šnt]. | imr.[qmṣ.llim.---]. 1[ʿNT.X].4.30
[-]ḏmu.apsty.b[--]. | w.bn h.w aṯt h.w.alp.w ṯmn.ṣin. | [-]dln.qmnzy.w.a[ṯt h]. | wšṯn.bn h. | ṯmgdl.yknʿmy.w.aṯ 1080.2
-]. | w lk.ilm.[---]. | w rgm.l [---]. | b mud.ṣin[.---]. | mud.ṣin[.---]. | iṯm.mui[-.---]. | dm.mt.aṣ[ḫ.---]. | ydd.b qr[b.---]. | ṯ 5[67].3.23
[---.]šd ubdy. | [---.š]d ubdy. | [---.šd] ubdy. | [---.š]d.bn.ṣin. | [---].bn.dly. | [---.]ṯty[-.--]. 2031.11
---.]ʿgd.dqr. | [---.]ṯn.alpm. | [---.ṯ]n alpm. | [---.--]r[.ʿ]šr.ṣin. | [---.]klkl. 1142.8
-]. | ṣin aḥd h[.---]. | l ʿṯtrt[.---]. | ʿlm.kmm[.---]. | w b ṯlṯ.ṣ[in.---]. | l ll.pr[-.---]. | mit š[ʿrt.---]. | ptr.k[--.---]. | [-]yu[-.---]. 37[22].8
]. | yd.b qrb[.---]. | w lk.ilm.[---]. | w rgm.l [---]. | b mud.ṣin[.---]. | mud.ṣin[.---]. | iṯm.mui[-.---]. | dm.mt.aṣ[ḫ.---]. | ydd 5[67].3.22
--]. | [ṯl]ṯ.l ʿṯtrt[.---]. | [--.]l ilt.š l ʿṯt[rt.---]. | [ʿ]ṣr.l pdr ṯṯ.ṣ[in.---]. | tšnpn.ʿlm.km[m.---]. | w.l ll.ʿṣrm.w [---]. | kmm.w.i 38[23].5
tn h.šbʿl[.---]. | ṯlḥny.yd[.---]. | yd.ṯlṯ.kl[t h.---]. | w.ṯṯm.ṣi[n.---]. | tn[--]. | agyn.[---]. | [w].ṯn.[---]. 81[329].19
| [---.-]rbd.kbd.ṯnm kbd. | [---.-]nnm ṯrm. | [---.]ṯlṯ kbd.ṣin. | [---.--]a.ṯ[l]ṯ.d.a[--]. | [---].mrn. | [---.]bn pnṯbl. | [---.-]py 1145.1.9
ṯm.ṣin. | anndr.yknʿmy. | w.aṯt h.w.bn h. | w.alp.w.tš[ʿ.]ṣin. 1080.17

ṣba

nš]. | ǵr.ṯ[--.---]. | ṣbu.any[t]. | bn.kṯan. | ǵr.tš[ʿ.ʿšr.b]nš. | ṣbu.any[t]. | bn abdḫ[r]. | pdym. | ḫmš.bnšm. | snrym. | tšʿ.bnš[79[83].10
]. | ʿdn. | ṯbq[ym]. | mʿq[bym]. | tšʿ.ʿ[šr.bnš]. | ǵr.ṯ[--.---]. | ṣbu.any[t]. | bn.kṯan. | ǵr.tš[ʿ.ʿšr.b]nš. | ṣbu.any[t]. | bn abdḫ[r] 79[83].7
ṣb[u.anyt]. | ʿdn. | ṯbq[ym]. | mʿq[bym]. | tšʿ.ʿ[šr.bnš]. | ǵr.ṯ[--.-- 79[83].1
r[ḫm]. | ʿdn.ngb.w [yṣi.ṣbu]. | ṣbi.ng[b.w yṣi.ʿdn]. | mʿ[.ṣ]bu h.u[l.mad]. | ṯlṯ.mat.rbt. | hlk.l alpm.ḫḏḏ. | w l.rbt.kmyr. 14[KRT].4.178
h tʿrb. | [---.tm]tḫṣ b ʿmq. | [tḫtṣb.bn.qrtm.ttʿr.ṯlḥnt.]l ṣbim. | [hdmm.l ǵzrm.mid.tmtḫṣn.w t]ʿn.tḫtṣb. | [w tḥdy.ʿnt. 7.1[131].5
ṣ h.b ʿmq. | tḫtṣb.bn.qrtm.ttʿr. | ksat.l mhr.tʿr.ṯlḥnt. | l ṣbim.hdmm.l ǵzrm. | mid.tmtḫṣn.w tʿn. | tḫtṣb.w tḥdy.ʿnt. | t 3[ʿNT].2.22
ṯdṯ.yrḫm. | ʿdn.ngb.w yṣi. | ṣbu.ṣbi.ngb. | w yṣi.ʿdn.mʿ. | ṣbu k.ul.mad. | ṯlṯ.mat.rbt. | ḥpṯ.d bl.spr. | ṯnn.d bl.hg. | hlk.l a 14[KRT].2.88
.lḥm.d ḫmš. | [mǵ]d.ṯdṯ.yr[ḫm]. | ʿdn.ngb.w [yṣi.ṣbu]. | ṣbi.ng[b.w yṣi.ʿdn]. | mʿ[.ṣ]bu h.u[l.mad]. | ṯlṯ.mat.rbt. | hlk.l 14[KRT].4.177
. | yip.lḥm.d ḫmš. | mǵd.ṯdṯ.yrḫm. | ʿdn.ngb.w yṣi. | ṣbu.ṣbi.ngb. | w yṣi.ʿdn.mʿ. | ṣbu k.ul.mad. | ṯlṯ.mat.rbt. | ḥpṯ.d bl.s 14[KRT].2.86
ḫ[---.b] | nšg h.ḥrb.tšt.b tʿr[t h]. | w ʿl.tlbš.npṣ.aṯt.[--]. | ṣbi nrt.ilm.špš.[-]r[--]. | pǵt.minš.šdm l mʿ[rb]. | nrt.ilm.špš. 19[1AQHT].4.209
r. | yip.lḥm.d ḫmš. | [mǵ]d.ṯdṯ.yr[ḫm]. | ʿdn.ngb.w [yṣi.ṣbu]. | ṣbi.ng[b.w yṣi.ʿdn]. | mʿ[.ṣ]bu h.u[l.mad]. | ṯlṯ.mat.rbt. | 14[KRT].4.176
.ḥbr. | yip.lḥm.d ḫmš. | mǵd.ṯdṯ.yrḫm. | ʿdn.ngb.w yṣi. | ṣbu.ṣbi.ngb. | w yṣi.ʿdn.mʿ. | ṣbu k.ul.mad. | ṯlṯ.mat.rbt. | ḥpṯ.d 14[KRT].2.86
rḥmt. | al.tšt.b šdm.mm h. | b smkt.ṣat.npš h. | [-]mt[-].ṣba.rbt. | špš.w tgh.nyr. | rbt.w rgm.l aḫt k. | ṯtmnt.krt n.dbḥ. 16.1[125].36
. | [--]m[-].mtm.uṣbʿ[t]. | [-]tr.šrk.il. | ʿrb.špš.l ymǵ. | krt.ṣbia.špš. | bʿl ny.w ymlk. | [y]ṣb.ʿln.w y[-]y. | [kr]t.ṭʿ.ʿln.bḫr. | [15[128].5.19
b h.š.šr[-]. | al[p.w].š.šlmm.pamt.šbʿ.klb h. | yr[--.]mlk.ṣbu.špš.w.ḥl.mlk. | w.[---].ypm.w.mḥ[--].t[ṯ]tbn.[-]. | b.[--].w. 35[3].53
ṯb.b.ṯdṯ.ṯn[.--.šmn]. | ʿly h.gdlt.rgm.yṯ[tb.brr]. | b.[šb]ʿ.ṣbu.[š]pš.w.ḥly[t].ʿ[r]b[.š]p[š]. | w [ḥl.]mlk.[w.]b.ym.ḥdṯ.ṯn.š 35[3].47
.yṯtb.b ṯdṯ.ṯn]. | l šmn.ʿ[ly h.gdlt.rgm.yṯtb]. | brr.b šbʿ[.ṣbu.špš.w ḥl] | yt.ʿrb špš[.w ḥl.mlk.w.b y] | m.ḥdṯ.ṯn šm[.---.- APP.II[173].51
. | ḫlu.dg. | ḥdṯm. | dbḥ.bʿl.k.tdd.bʿlt.bhtm. | b.[-]ǵb.ršp.ṣbi. | [---.--]m. | [---.]piln. | [---].ṣmd[.---.]pd[ry]. | [-----]. | [---.b] 2004.15

ṣbṭ

rbt.aṯrt ym. | mǵẓ.qnyt.ilm. | hyn.ʿly.l mpḫm. | b d.ḫss.mṣbṭm. | yṣq.ksp.yšl | ḥ.ḫrṣ.yṣq.ksp. | l alpm.ḫrṣ.yṣq | m.l rbbt 4[51].1.25

ṣbr

ṯn.ṣbrm. | b.uškn. | ṣbr.aḥd. | b.ar. | ṣbr.aḥd. | b.mlk. | ṣbr.aḥd. | b.mʿrby. | ṣbr.aḥd. 2073.3
ṣbr.aḥd. | b.mlk. | ṣbr.aḥd. | b.mʿrby. | ṣbr.aḥd. | b.ulm. | ṣbr.aḥd. | b.ubrʿy. 2073.11
. | ṣbr.aḥd. | b.ar. | ṣbr.aḥd. | b.mlk. | ṣbr.aḥd. | b.mʿrby. | ṣbr.aḥd. | b.ulm. | ṣbr.aḥd. | b.ubrʿy. 2073.9
ṯn.ṣbrm. | b.uškn. | ṣbr.aḥd. | b.ar. | ṣbr.aḥd. | b.mlk. | ṣbr.aḥd. | b.mʿrby. | ṣbr.aḥd. | b.ulm. | ṣbr.aḥ 2073.5
ṯn.ṣbrm. | b.uškn. | ṣbr.aḥd. | b.ar. | ṣbr.aḥd. | b.mlk. | ṣbr.aḥd. | b.mʿrby. | ṣbr.aḥd. | b.ulm. | ṣbr.aḥd. | b.ubrʿy. 2073.7
[il.ab h.i]l.mlk. | [d yknn h.yṣ]ḥ.aṯ | [rt.w bn h.]ilt. | [w ṣbrt.ary]h. | [wn.in.bt.l bʿl.] | [km.ilm.w ḥẓr]. | [k bn.aṯ]r[t]. | 4[51].1.9
ṣḥ.ṯr il.ab h. | [i]l.mlk.d yknn h.yṣḥ. | aṯrt.w bn h.ilt.w ṣbrt. | ary h.wn.in.bt.l bʿl. | km.ilm.w ḥẓr.k bn.aṯrt. | mṯb il.m 4[51].4.49
yṣḥ.ṯr.il.ab h.il. | mlk.d yknn h.yṣḥ.aṯrt. | w bn h.ilt.w ṣbrt.arḫ h. | wn.in.bt.l bʿl.km.ilm. | ḥẓr.k b[n.a]ṯrt.mṯb.il. | mṯ 3[ʿNT.VI].5.45
.w tkbdn h. | tšu.g h.w tṣḥ.tšmḫ ht. | aṯrt.w bn h.ilt.w ṣb | rt.ary h.k mt.aliyn. | bʿl.k ḥlq.zbl.bʿl. | arṣ.gm.yṣḥ il. | l rbt 6.1.40[49.1.12]
| ik.mǵyt.b[t]lt. | ʿnt.mḫṣ y hm[.m]ḫṣ. | bn y.hm[.mkly.ṣ]brt. | ary y[.ẓl].ksp.[a]ṯrt. | k tʿn.ẓl.ksp.w n[-]t. | ḫrṣ.šmḫ.rbt 4[51].2.25

ṯn.ṣbrm. | b.uškn. | ṣbr.aḥd. | b.ar. | ṣbr.aḥd. | b.mlk. | ṣbr.aḥd. | b. 2073.1

ṣd

nd[-]. | [-]gbt. | [--]y bnš kb[š]y. | krmpy.b.bṣm. | [-]mrn.ṣd.b gl[-]. 2169.5

ṣdyn

.w l ilt. | ṣd[yn]m.ṯm. | yd[r.k]rt.ṯ'. | i.iṯt.aṯrt.ṣrm. | w ilt.ṣdynm. | hm.ḥry.bt y. | iqḥ.aš'rb.ǵlmt. | ḥẓr y.ṯn h.wspm. | atn 14[KRT].4.202
.aḫr. | šp[š]m.b [t]lṯ. | ym[ǵy.]l qdš. | a[ṯrt.]ṣrm.w l ilt. | ṣd[yn]m.ṯm. | yd[r.k]rt.ṯ'. | i.iṯt.aṯrt.ṣrm. | w ilt.ṣdynm. | hm.ḥ 14[KRT].4.199

ṣdkn

| ǵyrn.ybnn qrwn. | ypltn.'bdnt. | klby.aḥrṯp. | ilyn.'lby.ṣdkn. | gmrt.ṯlmyn. | 'bdnt. | bdy.ḥrš arkd. | blšš lmd. | ḥṯṯn.tq 1045.6

ṣdq

ǵr.awldn.aḥd. | sǵr.idṯn.aḥd. | sǵr.sndrn.aḥd. | sǵr.adn.ṣdq.aḥd. | sǵr.irgn.aḥd. | sǵr.ršpab.aḥd. | sǵr.arwṯ.aḥd. | sǵr.bn 1140.8
rqd. | bn.abdg. | ilyn. | bn.tan. | bn.arm. | bn.b'l.ṣdq. | bn.army. | bn.rpiyn. | bn.army. | bn.krmn. | bn.ykn. | bn.' 1046.1.6
bdilt. | [---.-]lgn. | [---.--]gbn. | [---.a]bṣdq. | [---.--]š. | [---.ṣ]dq. | tgmr. | yṣḥm. | ṯlṯm. | aḥd. | kbd. | bnš.mlk. 1055.1.13
ḫm.l h.ṯmnt.bn um. | krt.ḥtk n.rš. | krt.grdš.mknt. | aṯt.ṣdq h.l ypq. | mtrḫt.yšr h. | aṯt.trḫ.w tb't. | ṯar um.tkn l h. | mṯ 14[KRT].1.12
[šmt.n]qmp'. | [bn.nq]md. | [mlk.]ugrt. | b'l ṣdq. | skn.bt. | mlk.ṯǵr. | [m]lk.bny. | [--].lb.mlk. | [---.]ṣmḫ. 1007.4

ṣdqil

y. | abmn.qšt.w.ṯn.ql'm. | qdmn.ṯt.qštm.w.ṯlṯ.ql'm. | bn.ṣdqil.ṯt.qštm.w.ṯn.ql'm. | bn.ṯlṯ.ṯ[lṯ.]qšt.w.ṯn.ql'm. | qṣn.ṯt.qšt 119[321].3.4

ṣdqm

-]. | [---].ubr'y. | [---].gwl. | [---]ady. | [---]ṣry. | miḫ[-]m. | ṣdqm. | dnn. | 'dy. 1041.13
| arny. | abm.qšt. | ḥdṯn.ql'. | yṯpṭ.qšt. | ilṯḥm.qšt.w.ql'. | ṣdqm.qšt.w.ql'. | uln.qšt.w.ql'. | uln.qšt. | bn.blẓn.qšt.w.ql'. | g 119[321].2.6
| kṯr w ḫss. | 'ṯtr 'ṯtpr. | šḥr w šlm. | ngh w srr. | 'dw šr. | ṣdqm šr. | ḥnbn il d[n]. | [-]bd w [---]. | [--].p il[.---]. | [i]l mt m UG5.10.1.14

ṣdqn

miḫdym. | bn.ḥṭb. | bn abyt. | bn ḫdl. | bn ṣdqn. | bn ayy. | bn dbb. | w nḥl h. | bn n'myn. | bn aṯtyy. | bn ḫ 2016.1.5
kdn. | gzl.bn.qldn. | gld.bt.klb. | l[---].bt.ḫzli. | bn.iḫyn. | ṣdqn.bn.ass. | b'lyskn.bn.ss. | ṣdqn.bn.imrt. | mnḥm.bn.ḫyrn. 102[323].3.8
. | l[---].bt.ḫzli. | bn.iḫyn. | ṣdqn.bn.ass. | b'lyskn.bn.ss. | ṣdqn.bn.imrt. | mnḥm.bn.ḫyrn. | [-]yn.bn.arkbt. | [--]zbl.bt.m 102[323].3.10
t. | [bn.ḫ]tyn.yd.bt h. | [aǵ]ltn. | tdn.bn.ddy. | 'bdil[.b]n ṣdqn. | bnšm.h[-]mt.ypḥm. | kbby.yd.bt.amt. | ilmlk. 2045.5
.uškny. | bn.abn.uškny. | bn.arz.š'rty. | bn.ibrd.m'rby. | ṣdqn.gb'ly. | bn.ypy.gb'ly. | bn.grgs.ilštm'y. | bn.ḫran.ilštm'y. 87[64].27
mitm.ksp.'mn.b[n].ṣdqn. | w.kkrm.ṯlṯ. | mit.ksp.'mn. | bn.ulbtyn. | w.kkr.ṯlṯ. | ksp. 1143.1
---]. | [bn] itn. | [bn] il. | [---]ṯ. | klṯṯb. | gsn. | arm[w]l. | bn.ṣdqn. | ḫlbn. | tbq.alp. 2039.15
ksdm. | ṣdqn. | nwrḏr. | ṯrin. | 'dršp. | pqr. | agbṯr. | 'bd. | ksd. 1044.2
b[t.--]. | ḫmš.ddm.l.ḥtyt. | ṯlṯm.dd.kšmn.l.gzzm. | yyn. | ṣdqn. | 'bd.pdr. | myṣm. | tgt. | w.lmd h. | ytil. | w.lmd h. | rpan. 1099.6
. | ḥrš qṭn[.---.]dqn.b'ln. | ǵltn.'bd.[---]. | nsk.ḥḏm.klyn[.ṣd]qn.'bdilt.b'l. | annmn.'dy.klby.dqn. | ḥrṯm.ḥgbn.'dn.ynḥm 2011.25
[-]n. | [-----]. | m[--.---]. | [-]n.qrqr. | [--]n.ymn.y[--]. | ilḫr.ṣdqn[.--]. 2022.26
ilšt[m'ym]. | yddt[.---]. | ilšn.[---]. | ṣdqn.[----]. | pnddn.b[n.---]. | ayaḫ.b[n.---]. 96[333].4
y[-]. | bn.tlm[yn]. | bn.y'dd. | bn.idly[-]. | bn.'bd[--]. | bn.ṣd[qn]. 2017.9

ṣdqnšk

ṣdqn C.1

ṣdqšlm

t.m[--]. | aṯt.w.ṯt.bt h.b.bt.ḫdmrd. | aṯt.w.ṯn.ǵzrm.b.bt.ṣdqš[lm]. | [a]ṯt.aḥt.b.bt.rpi[--]. | [aṯt.]w.bt h.b.bt.alḫn. | [aṯt. 80[119].23
b ṯlṯ. | ilmlk.'šr.ṣin. | mlkn'm.'šr. | bn.adty.'šr. | [ṣ]dqšlm ḫmš. | krzn.ḫmš. | ubr'ym.ḫmš. | [----]. | [bn] itn. | [bn] 2039.5
m. | 'mlbu.'šrm. | 'mtdl.'šrm. | y'drd.'šrm. | gmrd.'šrm. | ṣdqšlm.'šr[m]. | yknil.ḫmš. | ilmlk.ḫmš. | prṯ.'šr. | ubn.'šr. 1116.11
d.bn.šmrm. | [šd.bn.-]ṯtayy.b d.ṯṯmd. | [šd.bn.-]rn.b d.ṣdqšlm. | [šd.b d.]bn.p'ṣ. | [ubdy.']šrm. | [šd.---]n.b d.brdd. | [-- 82[300].1.28

ṣdr

.---]. | [---.--]p.km.dlt.tlk.km.p[---]. | [---.]bt.tḥbṭ.km.ṣq.ṣdr[.---]. | [---.]kl.b kl.l pgm.pgm.l.b[---]. | [---.]mdbm.l ḥrn.ḥ 1001.1.25

ṣhl

.b ym.ṭiṭ.rḥṣ. | npṣ k.b ym rṯ.b uni[l]. | pnm.tšmḫ.w 'l yṣhl pi[t]. | yprq.lṣb.w yṣḥq. | p'n.l hdm.ytpd.yšu. | g h.w yṣḥ. 17[2AQHT].2.9

ṣwd

tm.amt. | [ap.m]ṯn.rgmm.argm.qštm. | [----.]mhrm.ht.tṣdn.tinṯt. | [---]m.tṣḥq.'nt.w b lb.tqny. | [---.]ṯb l y.l aqht.ǵzr. 17[2AQHT].6.40
yq[--.---]. | pr'm.ṣd k.y bn[.---]. | pr'm.ṣd k.hn pr['.--]. | ṣd.b hkl h[.---]. | [------]. | [---.l]ḫm[.---]. | [---].ay š[---]. | [---.b 17[2AQHT].5.39
il dbḥ.b bt h.mṣd.ṣd.b qrb | hkl [h].ṣḥ.l qṣ.ilm.tlḥmn. | ilm.w tštn.tštn y[n] 'd š UG5.1.1.1
.šmmh.dbḥ. | l ṯr.ab h.il.šrd. | [b'l].b dbḥ h.bn dgn. | [b m]ṣd h.yrd.krt. | [l g]gt.'db.akl.l qryt. | ḥṭt.l bt.ḫbr. | yip.lḥm. 14[KRT].4.171
'db. | ksa.w yṯb. | tqru l špš.um h.špš.um.ql bl. | 'm ḥrn.mṣd h.mnt.nṯk nḥš. | šmrr.nḥš.'q šr.ln h.mlḫš. | abd.ln h.ydy UG5.7.58
w mhr.'nt.ṯm.yḥpn.ḥyl | y.zbl.mlk.'llm y.km.tdd. | 'nt.ṣd.tštr.'pt.šmm. | ṭbḫ.alpm.ap ṣin.šql.ṯrm. | w mri ilm.'glm.d 22.2[124].11
.[--] | rk.'l.aqht.k yq[--.---]. | pr'm.ṣd k.y bn[.---]. | pr'm.ṣd k.hn pr['.--]. | ṣd.b hkl h[.---]. | [------]. | [---.l]ḫm[.---]. | [---] 17[2AQHT].5.38
k. | šmm.dbḥ.l ṯr. | ab k.il.šrd.b'l. | b dbḥ k.bn.dgn. | b mṣd k.w yrd. | krt.l ggt.'db. | akl.l qryt. | ḥṭt.l bt.ḫbr. | yip.lḥm 14[KRT].2.79
m[t]. | hrnmy.qšt.yqb.[--] | rk.'l.aqht.k yq[--.---]. | pr'm.ṣd k.y bn[.---]. | pr'm.ṣd k.hn pr['.--]. | ṣd.b hkl h[.---]. | [------] 17[2AQHT].5.37

lim.bn.|dgn.my.hmlt.aṯr.|b'l.ard.b arṣ.ap.|'nt.ttlk.w tṣd.kl.ǵr.|l kbd.arṣ.kl.gb'.|l [k]bd.šdm.tmǵ.l n'm[y].|[arṣ.] 5[67].6.26
.aḫ y.|w 'n.bn.ilm.mt.mh.|taršn.l btlt.'nt.|an.itlk.w aṣd.kl.|ǵr.l kbd.arṣ.kl.gb'.|l kbd.šdm.npš.ḫsrt.|bn.nšm.npš 6[49].2.15
ṯqt.tḥt.|ṯlḥnt.il.d yd'nn.|y'db.lḥm.l h.w d l yd'nn.|d.mṣd.|ylmn.ḥṭ.tḥt.ṯlḥn.|b qr'.|'ṯtrt.w 'nt.ymǵy.|'ṯtrt.t'db.nš UG5.1.1.7B
[---.--]r.špr.w yšt.il.|[---.--]n.il ǵnṯ.'gl il.|[---.--]d.il.šd yṣd mlk.|[---].yšt.il h.|[---.]iṯm h.|[---.y]mǵy.|[---.]dr h.|[-- UG5.2.1.12
km.ṯrm.w gbṯt.|km.ibrm.|w b hm.pn.b'l.|b'l.ytlk.w yṣd.|yḥ pat.mlbr.|wn.ymǵy.aklm.|w ymẓa.'qqm.|b'l.ḥmd 12[75].1.34
.w l.'ṣm.šb'.šnt.|tmt.ṯmn.nqpt.'d.ilm.n'mm.ttlkn.|šd.tṣdn.pat.mdbr.w ngš.hm.nǵr.|mdr'.w ṣḥ hm.'m.nǵr.mdr' y. 23[52].68
il dbḥ.b bt h.mṣd.ṣd.b qrb|hkl [h].ṣḥ.l qṣ.ilm.tlḥmn.|ilm.w tštn.tštn y[n] UG5.1.1.1
d ṯbil.|'ṯtrt ṣwd[t.---].|tlk b mdb[r.---].|tḥdṯn w hl[.---].|w tglṯ thmt.'[- 2001.1.2
nḫ b ḫmat.|w 'l.agn.šb' d m.dǵ[ṯ.---]t.|tlk m.rḥmy.w tṣd[.---].|tḥgrn.ǵzr.n'm.[---].|w šm.'rbm.yr[.---].|mṯbt.ilm. 23[52].16
b'.ṯir k.[---].|[---.]ab y.ndt.ank[.---].|[---.--]l.mlk.tlk.b ṣd[.---].|[---.]mt.išryt[.---].|[---.--]r.almd k.[---].|[---.]qrt.abl 18[3AQHT].1.27
n.|b ḫri h.w ṯnt h.ql.il.[--].|il.k yrdm.arṣ.'nt.|w 'ṯtrt.tṣdn.[---].|[---.-]b[-.---].|['ṯ]trt w 'nt[.---].|w b hm.tṯṯb[.--]d UG5.1.1.23

ṣwy

bn.|bn.ḥṣn.|ṣprn.|bn.ašbḥ.|bn.qṭnn.|bn.ǵlmn.|[bn].ṣwy.|[bn].ḫnq[n].|[-----].|[-----].|[-----].|[-----].|n[----].|bn.[1046.1.24

ṣwm

.hm.t'pn.'l.qbr.bn y.|tšḫṭann.b šnt h.qr.[mym].|mlk.yṣm.y l km.qr.mym.d '[l k].|mḫṣ.aqht.ǵzr.amd.gr bt il.|'nt. 19[1AQHT].3.152

ṣwq

]m.|rgmt.'ly.ṯh.lm.|l.ytn.hm.mlk.[b]'l y.|w.hn.ibm.šṣq l y.|p.l.ašt.aṯt y.|n'r y.ṯh.l pn.ib.|hn.hm.yrgm.mlk.|b'l 1012.27

ṣḥq

k]bd n.il.ab n.|kbd k iš.tikln.|td n.km.mrm.tqrṣn.|il.yẓḥq.bm.|lb.w ygmd.bm kbd.|ẓi.at.l tlš.|amt.yrḫ.|l dmgy. 12[75].1.12
dk.l ttn.[pnm].|['m.a]qht.ǵzr.b alp.š[d].|[rbt.]kmn.w ṣḥq.btlt.['nt].|[tšu.]g h.w tṣḥ.šm'.m['.l a]|[qht.ǵ]zr.at.aḫ.w 18[3AQHT].1.22
|idk.l ttn.pnm.|'m.b'l.mrym.ṣpn.|b alp.šd.rbt.kmn.|ṣḥq.btlt.'nt.tšu.|g h.w tṣḥ.tbšr b'l.|bšrt k.yblt.y[b]n.|bt.l k. 4[51].5.87
adt y.[---].|lb.ab[d k].al[.---].|[-]tm.iph.adt y.w.[---].|tšṣḥq.hn.aṯt.l.'bd.|šb't.w.nṣp.ksp.|[-]tm.rb[.--.a]ḫd.|[---.--]t 1017.4
qrb.[h]kl |m.w y[p]tḥ.b dqt.'rpt.|'l h[wt].kṯr.w ḫss.|ṣḥq.kṯr.w ḫss.|yšu.g h.w yṣḥ.|l rgmt.l k.l ali|yn.b'l.ṯtbn.b'l 4[51].7.21
m.mid.tmtḫṣn.w t]'n.tḫtṣb.|[w tḥdy.'nt.tǵdd.kbd h.b ṣḥ]q.ymlu.lb h.|[b šmḫt.kbd.'nt.tšyt.tḥt h.k]kdrt.riš.|['l h. 7.1[131].7
.|mid.tmtḫṣn.w t'n.|tḫtṣb.w tḥdy.'nt.|tǵdd.kbd h.b ṣḥq.ymlu.|lb h.b šmḫt.kbd.'nt.|tšyt.k brkm.tǵll b dm.|dmr 3['NT].2.25
.|šmḫ.ltpn.il.d pid.|p'n h.l hdm.ytpd.|w yprq.lṣb w yṣḥq.|yšu.g h.w yṣḥ.|aṯbn.ank.w anḫn.|w tnḫ.b irt y.npš.| 6[49].3.16
.rgmm.argm.qštm.|[----.]mhrm.ht.tṣdn.tinṯt.|[---]m.tṣḥq.'nt.w b lb.tqny.|[---.]tb l y.l aqht.ǵzr.tb l y w l k.|[---] 17[2AQHT].6.41
w tql.|tštḥwy.w tkbd h.|hlm.il.k yphn h.|yprq.lṣb.w yṣḥq.|p'n h.l hdm.ytpd.w ykrkr.|uṣb't h.yšu.g h.w y[ṣḥ].|i 4[51].4.28
ym rṯ.b uni[l].|pnm.tšmḫ.w 'l yṣhl pi[t].|yprq.lṣb.w yṣḥq.|p'n.l hdm.ytpd.yšu.|g h.w yṣḥ.aṯbn.ank.|w anḫn.w t 17[2AQHT].2.10
y.h[--]r.w rgm.ank.|[---.]hdd tr[--.--]l.aṯrt y.|[--]ptm.ṣḥq.|[---.]rgm.hy.[-]ḫ[-]y.ilak k.|[---.--]g k.yritn.mǵy.hy.w 1002.40

ṣḫr

d.b'l.bn.aṯrt.|rbm.ymḫṣ.b ktp.|dk ym.ymḫṣ.b ṣmd.|ṣḫr mt.ymṣḫ.l arṣ.|[ytb.]b[']l.l ksi.mlk h.|[---].l kḥṯ.drkt h. 6[49].5.4
.ḥrr[.---].|šnmtm.dbṭ[.---].|tr'.tr'n.a[--.---].|bnt.šdm.ṣḫr[.---].|šb'.šnt.il.mla.[-].|w ṯmn.nqpnt.'d.|k lbš.km.lpš.d 12[75].2.44

ṣḫrn

ilṣdq.bn.zry.|b'lytn.bn.ulb.|ytr'm.bn.swy.|ṣḫrn.bn.qrtm.|bn.špš.bn.ibrd.|'pṯrm.bn.'bdy.|n[--.]bn.šnd. 2024.4

ṣḫrr

ugr.bn.ǵlmt.|'mm ym.bn.ẓlm[t].|rmt.pr't.ibr[.mnt].|ṣḫrrm.ḥbl[.--].|'rpt.tḥt.[---]|m 'ṣrm.ḥ[---].|glṯ.isr[.---]|m.b 8[51FRAG].10
ugr.b ǵlmt.|['mm.]ym.bn.ẓlmt.r|[mt.pr']t.ibr.mnt.|[ṣḫrrm.ḥbl.']rpt.|[---.---.-]ḥt.|[---.---]m.|[----] h. 4[51].7.57
mt.mt.nḥtm.ḫṭ k.mmnnm.mṭ.yd k.|h[l.]'ṣr.tḥrr.l išt.ṣḫrrt.l pḥmm.|a[t]tm.aṯt.il.aṯt.il.w 'lm h.w hm.|aṯtm.tṣḥn 23[52].41
t mt.|nḥtm.ḫṭ k.mmnnm.mṭ yd k.hl.'ṣr.|tḥrr.l išt.w ṣḫrt.l pḥmm.aṯtm.a[ṯt.il].|aṯt.il.w 'lm h.yhbr.špt hm.yš[q].| 23[52].48
d ad.nḥtm.ḫṭ k.|mmnnm.mṭ yd k.hl.'ṣr.tḥrr.l išt.|w ṣḫrrt.l pḥmm.btm.bt.il.bt.il.|w 'lm h.w hn.aṯtm.tṣḥn y.mt 23[52].45
n ank.imr.b p y.|k lli.b ṯbrn q y.ḫtu hw.|nrt.ilm.špš.ṣḫrrt.|la.šmm.b yd.bn ilm.mt.|ym.ymm.y'tqn.l ymm.|l yr 6[49].2.24
--].|l p'n.ǵl[m]m[.---].|mid.an[--.]ṣn[--].|nrt.ilm.špš[.ṣḫrr]t.|la.šmm.b y[d.bn.ilm.m]t.|w t'n.btlt.'n[t.bnt.]bht |k. 3['NT.VI].5.25
.|k imr.b p h.|k lli.b ṯbrn.|qn h.tḫtan.|nrt.ilm.špš.|ṣḫrrt.la.|šmm.b yd.md|d.ilm.mt.b a|lp.šd.rbt.k|mn.l p'n. 4[51].8.22

ṣṭqšlm

l.yi[--.-]m[---].|b unṯ.km.špš.|d brt.kmt.|br.ṣṭqšlm.|b unṯ.'d 'lm.|mišmn.nqmd.|mlk ugrt.|nqmd.mlk. 1005.4
md.|mlk ugrt.|nqmd.mlk.ugrt.|ktb.spr hnd.|dt brrt.ṣṭqšlm.|'bd h.hnd.|w mn km.l yqḥ.|spr.mlk.hnd.|b yd.ṣṭq 1005.10
šlm.|'bd h.hnd.|w mn km.l yqḥ.|spr.mlk.hnd.|b yd.ṣṭqšlm.|'d 'lm. 1005.14

ṣyḥ

]il.mšt'ltm.mšt'ltm.l riš.agn.|hl h.[t]špl.hl h.trm.hl h.tṣḥ.ad ad.|w hl h.tṣḥ.um.um.tirk m.yd.il.k ym.|w yd il.k m 23[52].32
in.šql.ṯrm[.w]m|ria.il.'glm.d[t].|šnt.imr.qmṣ.l[l]im.|ṣḥ.aḫ h.b bht h.a[r]y h.|b qrb hkl h.ṣḥ.|šb'm.bn.aṯrt.|špq.il 4[51].6.44
pu y.bn m.um y.kly y.|ytb.'m.b'l.ṣrrt.|ṣpn.yšu g h.w yṣḥ.|aḫ y m.ytnt.b'l.|spu y.bn m.um y.kl|y y.yt'n.k gmrm. 6[49].6.13
al.tbkn.al.|tdm.l y.al tkl.bn.|qr.'n k.mḫ.riš k.|udm't.ṣḥ.aḫt k.|ṯtmnt.bt.ḥmḥ h.|d[-]n.tbkn.w tdm.l y.[--].|[---].al 16.1[125].28
r.b'l.tiḫd.m[t].|b sin.lpš.tšṣq[n h].|b qṣ.all.tšu.g h.w[tṣ]|ḥ.at.mt.tn.aḫ y.|w 'n.bn.ilm.mt.mh.|taršn.l btlt.'nt.|an 6[49].2.11
n[.n]bl.ks h.|[an]y.l yṣḥ.ṯr il.ab h.|[i]l.mlk.d yknn h.yṣḥ.|aṯrt.w bn h.ilt.w ṣbrt.|ary h.wn.in.bt.l b'l.|km.ilm.w 4[51].4.48
-]y.|[-----].|[any.l yṣ]ḥ.ṯr.|[il.ab h.i]l.mlk.|[d yknn h.yṣ]ḥ.aṯ|[rt.w bn h.]ilt.|[w ṣbrt.ary]h.|[wn.in.bt.l b'l.]|[km. 4[51].1.7
.klny y.nbl.ks h.|any.l yṣḥ.ṯr.il.ab h.il.|mlk.d yknn h.yṣḥ.aṯrt.|w bn h.ilt.w ṣbrt.arḫ h.|wn.in.bt.l b'l.km.ilm.|ḥẓr 3['NT.VI].5.44

n.p]n h.td[‘].|tǵṣ[.pnt.ks]l h.|anš.dt.ẓr.[h].|tšu.g h.w tṣḥ[.i]k.|mǵy.aliy[n.b]‘l.|ik.mǵyt.b[t]lt.|‘nt.mḫṣ y hm[.m]ḫ 4[51].2.21

ṯbr.|‘ln.pn h.td‘.tǵṣ.pnt.|ksl h.anš.dt.ẓr h.tšu.|g h.w tṣḥ.ik.mǵy.gpn.w ugr.|mn.ib.yp‘.l b‘l.ṣrt.|l rkb.‘rpt.l mḫšt. 3[‘NT].3.33

yṣḥq.|p‘n h.l hdm.yṯpd.w ykrkr.|uṣb‘t h.yšu.g h.w y[ṣḥ].|ik.mǵyt.rbt.aṯr[t.y]m.|ik.atwt.qnyt.i[lm].|rǵb.rǵbt.w 4[51].4.30

m.mt.‘bd k.an.|w d ‘lm k.šmḫ.bn.ilm.mt.|[---.]g h.w aṣḥ.ik.yṣḥn.|[b‘l.‘m.aḫ y.ik].yqrun.hd.|[‘m.ary y.---.--]p.ml 5[67].2.21

[--]m.[---.]|gm.ṣḥ.l q[ṣ.ilm.---].|l rḥqm.l p[-.---].|ṣḥ.il.yṯb.b[mrzḥ.---].|bṯt.‘llm n.[---].|ilm.bt.b‘l k.[---].|dl.yl 1[‘NT.X].4.4

w tnḫ.b irt y.npš.|k ḥy.aliyn.b‘l.|k iṯ.zbl.b‘l.arṣ.|gm.yṣḥ.il.l btlt.|‘nt.šm‘.l btlt.‘n[t].|rgm.l nrt.il.šp[š].|pl.‘nt.šd 6[49].3.22

ilt.w ṣb|rt.ary h.k mt.aliyn.|b‘l.k ḫlq.zbl.b‘l.|arṣ.gm.yṣḥ il.|l rbt.aṯrt ym.šm‘.|l rbt.aṯr[t] ym.tn.|aḥd.b bn k.aml 6.1.43[49.1.15]

qmḥ.d.kly.k ṣḥ.illḏrm.|b d.zlb[n.--].|arb‘.‘š[r.]dd.n‘r.|d.apy[.--].|w.arb[2094.1

.l riš.agn.|hl h.[t]špl.hl h.trm.hl h.tṣḥ.ad ad.|w hl h.tṣḥ.um.um.tirk m.yd.il.k ym.|w yd il.k mdb.ark.yd.il.k ym. 23[52].33

ṯ.qn.ḏr‘ h.yḥrṯ.|k gn.ap lb.k ‘mq.yṯlṯ.|bmt.yšu.g h.w yṣḥ.|b‘l.mt.my.lim.bn.|dgn.my.hmlt.aṯr.|b‘l.ard.b arṣ.ap.| 5[67].6.22

bd k.an.|w d ‘lm k.šmḫ.bn.ilm.mt.|[---.]g h.w aṣḥ.ik.yṣḥn.|[b‘l.‘m.aḫ y.ik].yqrun.hd.|[‘m.ary y.---.--]p.mlḥm y.| 5[67].2.21

.|yd y.ilḥm.hm.šb‘.|ydt y.b ṣ‘.hm.ks.ymsk.|nhr.k[--].ṣḥn.b‘l.‘m.|aḫ y.qran.hd.‘m.ary y.|w lḥm m ‘m aḫ y.lḥm.| 5[67].1.22

mrym.ṣpn.|b alp.šd.rbt.kmn.|ṣḥq.btlt.‘nt.tšu.|g h.w tṣḥ.tbšr b‘l.|bšrt k.yblt.y[b]n.|bt.l k.km.aḫ k.w ḥẓr.|km.ar 4[51].5.88

t.ǵzr.|[---.kdd.dn]il.mt.rpi.w t‘n.|[btlt.‘nt.tšu.g]h.w tṣḥ.hwt.|[---.]aqht.yḏ[--].|[---.--]n.ṣ[---].|[spr.ilmlk.šbny.lm 17[2AQHT].6.53

‘mm.ttlkn.|šd.tṣdn.pat.mdbr.w ngš.hm.nǵr.|mdr‘.w ṣḥ hm.‘m.nǵr.mdr‘ y.nǵr.|nǵr.ptḥ.w ptḥ hw.prṣ.b‘d hm.|w 23[52].69

l pnn h.ydd.w yqm.|l p‘n h.ykr‘.w yql.|w yšu.g h.w yṣḥ.|ḥwt.aḫt.w nar[-].|qrn.d bat k.btlt.‘nt.|qrn.d bat k b‘l. 10[76].2.19

w bn.bht.ksp.|w ḫrṣ.bht.ṯhrm.|iqnim.šmḫ.aliyn.|b‘l.ṣḥ.ḫrn.b bht h.|‘ḏbt.b qrb hkl h.|yblnn ǵrm.mid.ksp.|gb‘m 4[51].5.98

‘l.|bšrt k.yblt.y[b]n.|bt.l k.km.aḫ k.w ḥẓr.|km.ary k.ṣḥ.ḫrn.|b bht k.‘ḏbt.b qrb.|hkl k.tbl k.ǵrm.|mid.ksp.gb‘m. 4[51].5.91

rzm.yklln h.|hm.bt.lbnt.y‘msn h.|l yrgm.l aliyn b‘l.|ṣḥ.ḫrn.b bhm k.|‘ḏbt.b qrb.hkl k.|tbl k.ǵrm.mid.ksp.|gb‘m 4[51].5.75

ḥrrt.l pḥmm.|a[ṯ]tm.aṯt.il.aṯt.il.w ‘lm h.w hm.|aṯtm.tṣḥn y.ad ad.nḥtm.ḫṭ k.|mmnnm.mṭ yd k.hl.‘ṣr.tḥrr.l išt.| 23[52].43

].|‘db.uḫry mṭ.yd h.|ymǵ.l mrrt.tǵll.b nr.|yšu.g h.w yṣḥ.y l k.mrrt.|tǵll.b nr.d ‘l k.mḫṣ.aqht.|ǵzr.šrš k.b arṣ.al.| 19[1AQHT].3.157

yd h.|ymǵ.l qrt.ablm.abl[m].|qrt.zbl.yrḫ.yšu g h.|w yṣḥ.y l k.qrt.ablm.|d ‘l k.mḫṣ.aqht.ǵzr.|‘wrt.yšt k.b‘l.l ht.| 19[1AQHT].4.165

t.|w ṣḥrrt.l pḥmm.btm.bt.il.bt.il.|w ‘lm h.w hn.aṯtm.tṣḥn y.mt mt.|nḥtm.ḫṭ k.mmnnm.mṭ yd k.hl.‘ṣr.|tḥrr.l išt. 23[52].46

.yr.b šmm.‘ṣr.yḫrṭ yšt.|l pḥm.il.aṯtm.k ypt.hm.aṯtm.tṣḥn.|y mt.mt.nḥtm.ḫṭ k.mmnnm.mṭ.yd k.|h[l.]‘ṣr.tḥrr.l iš 23[52].39

hl pi[t].|yprq.lṣb.w yṣḥq.|p‘n.l hdm.yṯpd.yšu.|g h.w yṣḥ.aṯbn.ank.|w anḫn.w tnḫ.b irt y.|npš.k yld.bn.l y.km.|a 17[2AQHT].2.12

id.|p‘n h.l hdm.yṯpd.|w yprq.lṣb w yṣḥq.|yšu.g h.w yṣḥ.|aṯbn.ank.w anḫn.|w tnḫ.b irt y.npš.|k ḥy.aliyn.b‘l.|k 6[49].3.17

‘.btlt.‘nt[.idk.l ttn.pnm].|‘m.yṭpn.mhr.š[t.tšu.g h].|w tṣḥ.yṯb.yṭp.[---].|qrt.ablm.ablm.[qrt.zbl.yrḫ].|ik.al.yḥdṯ.yr 18[3AQHT].4.7

-]ṭnm.|‘dm.[lḥ]m.tšty.|w t‘n.mṯt ḥry.|l l[ḥ]m.l š[ty].ṣḥt km.|db[ḥ.l krt.a]dn km.|‘l.krt.tbun.km.|rgm.ṯ[rm.]rg 15[128].6.4

--].[-]l[--.b qr]|b hkl y.[---].|lk bt y.r[pim.rpim.b bt y.aṣḥ].|km.iqr[a km.ilnym.b hkl y].|aṯr h.r[pum.l tdd.aṯr h]. 22.1[123].3

[---.m]rz‘y.lk.bt y.|[rpim.rpim.b]t y.aṣḥ km.iqra.|[km.ilnym.b h]kl y.aṯr h.rpum.|[l tdd.aṯr h].l 21[122].1.2

b].hkl y.w y‘n.il.|[---.mrz‘]y.lk.bt y.rpim.|[rpim.bt y.aṣ]ḥ km.iqra km.|[ilnym.b hkl]y.aṯr h.rpum.|[l tdd.aṯr]h.l 21[122].1.10

--].|mhr.b‘l[.---.mhr].|‘nt.lk b[t y.rpim.rpim.b bt y].|aṣḥ.km.[iqra km.ilnym.b] |hkl y.aṯr[h.rpum.l tdd].|aṯr h.l 22.1[123].9

ṣ‘.tšlḥ.|ḥrb.b bšr.tštn.|[w t]‘n.mṯt.ḥry.|[l lḥ]m.l šty.ṣḥt km.|[--.dbḥ.l]krt.b‘l km. 15[128].4.27

šl]ḥ.|[ḥrb.b]bš[r].tštn.|[w t‘n].mṯt.ḥry.|[l lḥ]m.l šty.ṣḥt k[m].|[---.]brk.t[---].|[‘l.]krt.tbkn.|[--.]rgm.ṯrm.|[--.]mt 15[128].5.10

p‘n h.ybq‘.kbd h.w yḥd.|[i]n.šmt.in.‘ẓm.yšu.g[h].|w yṣḥ.knp.hrgb.b‘l.ybn.|[b]‘l.ybn.diy.hwt.hrg[b].|tpr.w du.b 19[1AQHT].3.132

w du.b nši.‘n h.w ypn.|yḥd.hrgb.ab.nšrm.|yšu.g h.w yṣḥ.knp.hr[g]b.|b‘l.yṯb.b‘l.y[ṯb]r.diy[.h]wt.|w yql.tḥt.p‘n y. 19[1AQHT].3.122

‘n h.ybq‘.kbdt hm.w[yḥd].|in.šmt.in.‘ẓm.yšu.g h.|w yṣḥ.knp.nšrm.ybn.|b‘l.ybn.diy hmt nšrm.|tpr.w du.b nši.‘n 19[1AQHT].3.118

b nši[.‘n h.w yphn.yḥd].|b ‘rpt[.nšrm.yšu].|[g h.]w yṣḥ[.knp.nšrm].|b‘l.yṯb.b‘l.yṯb[r.diy.hmt].|tqln.tḥ p‘n y.ibq 19[1AQHT].3.107

ybky.w yqbr.|yqbr.nn.b mdgt.b knk[-].|w yšu.g h.w yṣḥ.knp.nšrm.|b‘l.yṯbr.b‘l.yṯbr.diy.|hmt.hm.t‘pn.‘l.qbr.bn 19[1AQHT].3.148

u.b nši.‘n h.|[w]yphn.yḥd.ṣml.um.nšrm.|yšu.g h.w yṣḥ.knp.ṣml.|b‘l.yṯbr.b‘l.yṯbr.diy.|hyt.tql.tḥt.p‘n y.ibq‘.|kb 19[1AQHT].3.136

m.|mt.‘z.b‘l.‘z.ymṣḫn.|k lsmm.mt.ql.|b‘l.ql.‘ln.špš.|tṣḥ.l mt.šm‘.m‘.|l bn.ilm.mt.ik.tmt[ḫ]|ṣ.‘m.aliyn.b‘l.|ik.al. 6[49].6.23

.‘m h.trd.nrt.|ilm.špš.‘d.tšb‘.bk.|tšt.k yn.udm‘t.gm.|tṣḥ.l nrt.ilm.špš.|‘ms m‘.l y.aliyn.b‘l.|tšm‘.nrt.ilm.špš.|tšu. 6[62].1.11

il dbḥ.b bt h.mṣd.ṣd.b qrb|hkl [h].ṣḥ.l qṣ.ilm.tlḥmn.|ilm.w tštn.tštn y[n] ‘d šb‘.|trṯ.‘d.škr.y‘db UG5.1.1.2

[--]m.[---.]|gm.ṣḥ.l q[ṣ.ilm.---].|l rḥqm.l p[-.---].|ṣḥ.il.yṯb.b[mrzḥ.---].|bṯt. 1[‘NT.X].4.2

qt.‘rpt.|‘l h[wt].kṯr.w ḫss.|ṣḥq.kṯr.w ḫss.|yšu.g h.w yṣḥ.|l rgmt.l k.l ali|yn.b‘l.ṯṯbn.b‘l.|l hwt y.yptḥ.ḥ|ln.b bht 4[51].7.22

].|tšqy[.---].|tr.ḥt[-.---].|w msk.tr[.---].|tqrb.aḫ[h.w tṣḥ].|lm.tb‘rn[.---].|mn.yrḫ.k m[rṣ.---].|mn.k dw.kr[t].|w y 16.2[125].79

----].|[-----].|il.šm‘.amr k.ph[.-].|k il.ḥkmt.k ṯr.lṭpn.|ṣḥ.ngr.il.ilš.il[š].|w aṯt h.ngrt[.i]lht.|kḥṣ.k m‘r[.---].|yṣḥ.ng 16[126].4.4

ṣḥ.ngr.il.ilš.il[š].|w aṯt h.ngrt[.i]lht.|kḥṣ.k m‘r[.---].|yṣḥ.ngr il.ilš.|ilš.ngr.bt.b‘l.|w aṯt h.ngrt.ilht.|w y‘n.lṭpn.il 16[126].4.7

.|[tgly.ḏd.il.w]tb[a].|[qrš.mlk.ab.]šnm.|[tša.g hm.w tṣ]ḥ.sbn.|[---]l[.---.]‘d.|ksm.mhyt[.m]ǵny.|l n‘m y.arṣ.dbr.| 5[67].6.3

ru.|ilm.w nšm.d yšb|[‘].hmlt.arṣ.gm.l ǵ|[lm] h.b‘l k.yṣḥ.‘n.|[gpn].w ugr.b ǵlmt.|[‘mm.]ym.bn.ẓlmt.r|[mt.pr‘]t.i 4[51].7.53

.bt.l b‘l.km.|[i]lm.w ḥẓr.k bn.|[a]ṯrt.gm.l ǵlm h.|b‘l.yṣḥ.‘n.gpn.|w ugr.bn.ǵlmt.|‘mm ym.bn.ẓlm[t].|rmt.pr‘t.ib 8[51FRAG].6

.ẓl.ksp.w n[-]t.|ḫrṣ.šmḫ.rbt.a[ṯrt].|ym.gm.l ǵlm h.k [tṣḥ].|‘n.mkṯr.ap.t[---].|dgy.rbt.aṯr[t.ym].|qḥ.rṯt.b d k t[---]. 4[51].2.29

k.b šb‘.|šnt.w [--].bn.ilm.mt.|‘m.aliyn.b‘l.yšu.|g h.w yṣḥ.‘l k.b[‘]l m.|pht.qlt.‘l k.pht.|dry.b ḥrb.‘l k.|pht.šrp.b iš 6[49].5.11

.|km hm.w tḫss.aṯrt.|ndr h.w ilt.p[--].|w tšu.g h.w [tṣḥ].|ph m‘.ap.k[rt.--].|u ṯn.ndr[.---].|apr.[---].|[-----]. 15[128].3.27

-].|‘l amr.yu[ḫd.ksa.mlk h].|nḫt.kḥṯ.d[rkt h.b bt y].|aṣḥ.rpi[m.iqra.ilnym].|b qrb.h[kl y.aṯr h.rpum.l] |tdd.aṯr[22.1[123].19

.imr.qmṣ.l[l]im.|ṣḥ.aḫ h.b bht h.a[r]y h.|b qrb hkl h.ṣḥ.|šb‘m.bn.aṯrt.|špq.ilm.krm.y[n].|špq.ilht.ḫprt[.yn].|špq 4[51].6.45

ḥ].|šm‘[.l mṯt.ḥry].|ṭbḫ.š[mn].mri k.|ptḥ.[rḥ]bt.yn.|ṣḥ.šb‘m.ṯr y.|ṯmnym.[ẓ]by y.|ṯr.ḫbr[.rb]t.|ḫbr[.ṯrrt].|[-]‘b[15[128].4.6

nm.l p‘n.|il.thbr.w tql.|tštḥwy.w tkbdn h.|tšu.g h.w tṣḥ.tšmḫ ht.|aṯrt.w bn h.ilt.w ṣb|rt.ary h.k mt.aliyn.|b‘l.k 6.1.39[49.1.11]

pš.hm.|k.iṯl.brlt n[-.k qṭr.b ap -].|tmǵyn.tša.g h[m.w tṣḥn].|šm‘.l dnil.[mt.rpi].|mt.aqht.ǵzr.[šṣat].|btlt.‘nt.k [rḥ. 19[1AQHT].2.89

.|mt.dm.ḫt.š‘tqt.|dm.lan.w ypqd.|krt.ṯ‘.yšu.g h.|w yṣḥ.šm‘.l mṯt.|ḥry.ṭbḫ.imr.|w ilḥm.mgṯ.w iṯrm.|tšm‘.mṯt.ḥ 16.6[127].16

p[----].|gm.l[aṯt h k.yṣḥ].|šm‘[.l mṯt.ḥry].|ṭbḫ.š[mn].mri k.|ptḥ.[rḥ]bt.yn.|ṣḥ.š 15[128].4.2

ǵzr.b alp.š[d].|[rbt.]kmn.w ṣḥq.btlt.[‘nt].|[tšu.]g h.w tṣḥ.šm‘.m[‘.l a]|[qht.ǵ]zr.at.aḫ.w an.a[ḫt k].|[---].šb‘.ṯir k.[- 18[3AQHT].1.23

ṯn.yqr.|[krpn h.-.l]arṣ.ks h.tšpk m.|[l ‘pr.tšu.g h.]w tṣḥ.šm‘.m‘.|[l aqht.ǵzr.i]rš.ksp.w atn k.|[ḫrṣ.w aš]lḥ k.w tn 17[2AQHT].6.16

l drkt.k aṯb.an. | ytbʿ.yṣb ġlm.ʿl. | ab h.yʿrb.yšu g h. | w yṣḥ.šmʿ mʿ.l krt. | ṯʿ.ištmʿ.w tqġ udn. | k ġz.ġzm.tdbr. | w ġrm 16.6[127].41
--]k.yrd[.--.]i[---]n.bn. | [---.-]nn.nrt.ilm.špš.tšu.g h.w t[ṣḥ.šm]ʿ.mʿ. | [-.yṯ]ir ṯr.il.ab k.l pn.zbl.ym.l pn[.ṯ]pṭ[.n]hr. | [2.3[129].15
ṯ[.l z]ġt.klb. | [ṣ]pr[.apn]k. | [pb]l[.mlk.g]m.l aṯt | [h.k]y[ṣḥ.]šmʿ.mʿ. | [--.]ʿm[.-.]aṯt y[.-]. | [---.]ṯḥm. | [---]t.[ ]r. | [---.-- 14[KRT].5.229
t.apnk.dnil. | mt.rpi.aphn.ġzr.mt. | hrnmy.gm.l aṯt h.k yṣḥ. | šmʿ.mṯt.dnty.ʿd[b]. | imr.b pḫd.l npš.kṯr. | w ḫss.l brlt.h 17[2AQHT].5.15
t.dnil.mt.rpi. | all.ġzr.m[t.]hr[nmy]. | gm.l bt[h.dnil.k yṣḥ]. | šmʿ.pġt.ṯkmt[.my]. | ḥspt.l šʿr.ṭl.yd[ʿt]. | hlk.kbkbm.md 19[1AQHT].1.49
rbʿt.ṯqlm.ṯṯp[.---.]bm. | yd.ṣpn hm.tliy m[.--.ṣ]pn hm. | nṣḥy.šrr.m[---.--]ay. | nbšr km.dnil.[--] h[.---]. | riš.r[--.--]ḥ[.-- 19[1AQHT].2.85
t.w yʿn[.dnil.mt.]rpi. | yṯb.ġzr.m[t.hrnmy.y]šu. | g h.w yṣḥ.t[bʿ.---]. | bkyt.b hk[l]y.mšspdt. | b ḥẓr y pẓġm.ġr.w yq. | 19[1AQHT].4.182
tk.qrt h.hmry.mk.ksu. | ṯbt.ḫḫ.arṣ.nḫlt h.tša. | g hm.w tṣḥ.ṯḥm.aliyn. | bn.bʿl.hwt.aliy.qrdm. | bhṯ.bn.ilm.mt.ʿbd k.a 5[67].2.17
m. | l yṯb.idk.pnm. | l ytn.ʿmm.pbl. | mlk.tšan. | g hm.w tṣḥn. | ṯḥm.krt.ṯ[ʿ]. | hwt.[n]ʿmn.[ġlm.il]. 14[KRT].6.304
]. | [idk.pnm.l ytn]. | [ʿ]m[.krt.mswn h]. | tš[an.g hm.w tṣḥn]. | ṯḥ[m.pbl.mlk]. | qḥ[.ksp.w yrq]. | ḫrṣ.[yd.mqm h]. | w ʿ 14[KRT].6.267
ttbʿ.btlt.ʿnt. | idk.l ttn.pnm. | ʿm.nrt.ilm.špš. | tšu.g h.w tṣḥ. | ṯḥm.ṯr.il.ab k. | hwt.lṭpn.ḥtk k. | pl.ʿnt.šdm.y špš. | pl.ʿnt 6[49].4.33
ʿ]n.ʿnt. | [yhbr.w yql.yšt]ḥwyn.w y | [kbdn h.yšu.g h.w y]ṣḥ.ṯḥm. | [ṯr.il.ab k.hwt.l]ṭpn.ḥtk k. | [qryy.b arṣ.mlḥ]mt.št 1[ʿNT.IX].2.17
n. | in.d ʿln h.klny y.qš h. | nbln.klny y.nbl.ks h. | any.l yṣḥ.ṯr.il.ab h.il. | mlk.d yknn h.yṣḥ.aṯrt. | w bn h.ilt.w ṣbrt.ar 3[ʿNT.VI].5.43
ʿln h. | klny n.q[š] h.n[bln]. | klny n[.n]bl.ks h. | [an]y.l yṣḥ.ṯr il.ab h. | [i]l.mlk.d yknn h.yṣḥ. | aṯrt.w bn h.ilt.w ṣbrt. 4[51].4.47
[-----]. | [---.--]y. | [-----]. | [any.l yṣ]ḥ.ṯr. | [il.ab h.i]l.mlk. | [d yknn h.yṣ]ḥ.aṯ | [rt.w bn h.]ilt. | [4[51].1.4
. | tkn.lbn[.---]. | dt.lbn k[.---]. | dk k.kbkb[.---]. | dm.mt.aṣḫ[.---]. | ydd.b qr[b.---]. | al.ašt.b[---]. | ahpk k.l[--.---]. | ṯm 5[67].3.9
]. | nʿm.ilm[.---]. | šgr.mu[d.---]. | šgr.mud[.---]. | dm.mt.aṣ[ḫ.---]. | yd.b qrb[.---]. | w lk.ilm.[---]. | w rgm.l [---]. | b mud 5[67].3.18
b mud.ṣin[.---]. | mud.ṣin[.---]. | iṯm.mui[-.---]. | dm.mt.aṣ[ḫ.---]. | ydd.b qr[b.---]. | ṯmm.w lk[.---]. | [--]ṯ.lk[.---]. | [--]k 5[67].3.25
skn.ydʿ rgm h. | w ht ab y ġm[--]. | t[--.---]. | ls[--.---]. | ṣḥ[.---]. | ky.m[--.---]. | w pr[--.---]. | tštil[.---]. | ʿmn.bn[.---]. 1021.12
n]. | ksl.y[ṯbr.yġṣ.pnt.ksl h]. | anš.[dt.ẓr h.yšu.g h]. | w yṣ[ḥ.---]. | mḫṣ[.---]. | š[--.---]. 19[1AQHT].2.97
m.bnw n. | l nḫnpt.mšpy. | ṯlṯ.kmm.ṯrr y. | [---.]l ġr.gm.ṣḥ. | [---.]r[-]m. 16[126].4.17
w ḫ[--.---]. | my[.---]. | aṯ[t.---]. | aḫ k[.---]. | tr.ḥ[---]. | w tṣḥ[.---]. | tšqy[.---]. | tr.ḥt[-.---]. | w msk.tr[.---]. | tqrb.aḫ[h.w 16.2[125].75
rṣ.hk]l y. | [---.]aḫ y. | [---.]aḫ y. | [----]y. | [---.]rb. | [---].ṣḥt. | [---.--]t. | [---.]ilm. | [---.--]u.yd. | [---.--]k. | [---.gpn.]w ugr 4[51].8.42
] h.l ʿdb. | [---]n.yd h. | [---].bl.išlḥ. | [---] h.gm. | [l --- k.]yṣḥ. | [---]d.ʿr. | [----.-]bb. | [----.]lm y. | [---.--]p. | [---.d]bḥ. | t[-- 14[KRT].5.238
tdrʿnn.šir h.l tikl. | ʿṣrm.mnt h.l tkly. | npr[m.]šir.l šir.yṣḥ. 6[49].2.37

ṣly

.kst.dnil.mt. | rpi.al.ġzr.mt.hrnmy. | apnk.dnil.mt. | rpi.yṣly.ʿrpt.b | ḥm.un.yr.ʿrpt. | tmṭr.b qẓ.ṭl.yṭll. | l ġnbm.šbʿ.šnt. 19[1AQHT].1.39

ṣlyh

ʿnt[.---]. | tmm l bt[.---]. | b[ʿ]l.ugr[t.---]. | w ʿṣrm[.---]. | ṣlyh šr[-.---]. | [ṯ]lṯm.w b[--.---]. | l il limm[.---]. | w ṯt.npš[.---]. 40[134].6

ṣlyy

. | šl[--]. | a[---]. | d[---]. | q[---]. | ʿm[--]. | ar[--]. | ykn[ʿm]. | ṣlyy. | ʿnm[ky]. | l[bnm]. | ʿr[--]. 2133.8

ṣll

ttrt. | il.ṯpṭ.b hd rʿy.d yšr.w yḏmr. | b knr.w ṯlb.b tp.w mṣltm.b m | rqdm.dšn.b.ḥbr.kṯr.ṭbm. | w tšt.ʿnt.gṯr.bʿlt.mlk. UG5.2.1.4
p. | kd.yqḥ.b ḫmr. | rbt.ymsk.b msk h. | qm.ybd.w yšr. | mṣltm.bd.nʿm. | yšr.ġzr.ṭb.ql. | ʿl.bʿl.b ṣrrt. | ṣpn.ytmr.bʿl. | bnt 3[ʿNT].1.19
išttk.lm.ttkn. | štk.mlk.dn. | štk.šibt.ʿn. | štk.qr.bt.il. | w mṣlt.bt.ḥr[š]. 12[75].2.62
m.w hm[.--]yt.w.[---]. | [---.ṯ]y.al.an[k.--.]il[m.--]y. | [--.m]ṣlm.pn y[.-.]tlkn. | [---.]rḫbn.hm.[-.]aṯr[.---]. | [--]šy.w ydn. 1002.59
skn. | mru.ibrn. | yqšm. | trrm. | kkrdnm. | yṣrm. | ktrm. | mṣlm. | tkn[m]. | ġ[---]. | ġm[--]. 1026.2.13

ṣlʿ

[-----]. | [-----]. | [-----]. | alp[.---.--]r. | mit.lḥ[m.---.-]dyt. | ṣlʿt.alp.mri. | ʿšr.bmt.alp.mri. | ṯn.nšbm. | ṯmnym.tbth.alp. | uz 1128.16

ṣlpn

ln. | bn.ʿlln. | bn.liy. | bn.nqṯn. | bn abrḫṭ. | bn.grdy. | bn.ṣlpn. | bn ġlmn. | bn sgld. 1064.29

ṣmd

[---].ḥr[š.---]. | [---.ṯ]lṯ.[---.]dpm. | [---.]bnšn. | [---.ḫ]mš.ṣmd.alpm. | [---.bn]šm. | [---.]ḫmš.ṣmd.alpm. | [---.bnš]m. | [--- 2038.15
[---.]bnšn. | [---.ḫ]mš.ṣmd.alpm. | [---.bn]šm. | [---.]ḫmš.ṣmd.alpm. | [---.bnš]m. | [---.]ʿšr.ṣmd.alpm. | [---.bn]šm. | [---.- 2038.17
| [---.bn]šm. | [---.]ḫmš.ṣmd.alpm. | [---.bnš]m. | [---.]ʿšr.ṣmd.alpm. | [---.bn]šm. | [---.--]m.ḫmš.ṣmdm. | [---.bnš]m. 2038.19
.bn.iwrḫz.[n]ʿrm. | yṣr[.-]qb. | w.ṯn.bnš.iytlm. | w.ʿšrm.ṣmd.alpm. 2066.2.7
| ḫmš.ṣmdm.w ḥrṣ. | ṯryn.sswm. | ṯryn.aḥd.d bnš. | arbʿ.ṣmdm.apnt. | w ḥrṣ. | tšʿm.mrḥ.aḥd. | kbd. 1123.7
ṣmdm.a[--.---]. | b d.prḫ[-.---]. | apnm.l.ʿ[--]. | apnm.l.[---]. | ap 145[318].1
il. | il ḥš il add. | bʿl ṣpn bʿl. | ugrt. | b mrḥ il. | b nit il. | b ṣmd il. | b dṯn il. | b šrp il. | b knt il. | b ġdyn il. | [b]n [---]. 30[107].14
zbl ym.bn.ʿnm.ṯpṭ.nhr.yprsḥ ym. | w yql.l arṣ.w trtqṣ.ṣmd.b d bʿl. | [km.]nšr.b uṣbʿt h.ylm.qdqd.zbl. | [ym.]bn.ʿnm 2.4[68].23
š | r.b uṣbʿt h.hlm.ktp.zbl ym.bn ydm. | [ṯp]ṭ nhr.yrtqṣ.ṣmd.b d bʿl.km.nšr. | b[u]ṣbʿt h.ylm.ktp.zbl ym.bn ydm.ṯpṭ. 2.4[68].15
ṯlṯ.ṣmdm. | b.nḫry. | ṣmdm.b.ṯp[--]. | aḥdm.b.gm[--]. 144[317].1
ṯlṯ.ṣmdm. | b.nḫry. | ṣmdm.b.ṯp[--]. | aḥdm.b.gm[--]. 144[317].3
-]. | bn.ṯbʿnq. | brqd. | bnn. | kbln.ṣ[md]. | bn gmrt. | bn.il.ṣm[d]. | bn abbly. | yṯʿd.ṣm[d]. | bn.liy. | ʿšrm.ṣ[md]. | ṯṯ kbd.b 2113.19
bn.apṯ. | bn.ysd. | bn.pl[-]. | bn.ṯbʿnq. | brqd. | bnn. | kbln.ṣ[md]. | bn gmrt. | bn.il.ṣm[d]. | bn abbly. | yṯʿd.ṣm[d]. | bn.liy. 2113.17
n. | kbln.ṣ[md]. | bn gmrt. | bn.il.ṣm[d]. | bn abbly. | yṯʿd.ṣm[d]. | bn.liy. | ʿšrm.ṣ[md]. | ṯṯ kbd.b ḥ[--]. | w.arbʿ.ḥ[mrm]. | 2113.21

dnn.ṯlṯ.ṣmdm.|bn.ʿmnr.|bn.kmn.|bn.ibyn.|bn.mryn.ṣmd.w.ḥrṣ.|b 2113.1
d h.ḫṭ.ṯkl.b d h.|ḫṭ.ulmn.yzbrnn.zbrm.gpn.|yṣmdnn.ṣmdm.gpn.yšql.šdmt h.|km gpn.|šbʿ d.yrgm.ʿl.ʿd.w ʿrbm.tʿ 23[52].10
l y.[aṯr h.rpum].|tdd.aṯr h.tdd.iln[ym.---].|asr.sswm.tṣmd.dg[-.---].|tʿln.l mrkbt hm.ti[ty.l ʿr hm].|tlkn.ym.w ṯa 20[121].2.3
.|yd.ḥẓ hn.|yd.tr hn.|w.l.ṯt.mrkbtm.|inn.uṯpt.|w.ṯlṯ.ṣmdm.w.ḥrṣ.|apnt.b d.rb.ḥršm.|d.šṣa.ḥwy h. 1121.8
nr.|bn.kmn.|bn.ibyn.|bn.mryn.ṣmd.w.ḥrṣ.|bn.prsn.ṣmd.w.ḥrṣ.|bn.ilbʿl.|bn.idrm.|bn.grgš.|bn.bly.|bn.apṯ.|bn. 2113.6
dnn.ṯlṯ.ṣmdm.|bn.ʿmnr.|bn.kmn.|bn.ibyn.|bn.mryn.ṣmd.w.ḥrṣ.|bn.prsn.ṣmd.w.ḥrṣ.|bn.ilbʿl.|bn.idrm.|bn.grgš. 2113.5
arbʿm.qšt.|alp ḥẓm.w alp.|nṯq.ṯn.qlʿm.|ḫmš.ṣmdm.w ḥrṣ.|ṯryn.sswm.|ṯryn.aḥd.d bnš.|arbʿ.ṣmdm.apnt. 1123.4
--]n.|[---].tlmdm.|[y]bnn.ṣmdm.|ṯp[ṭ]bʿl.ṣmdm.|[---.ṣ]mdm.w.ḥrṣ.|[---].aḥdm.|[iwr]pzn.aḥdm.|[i]lšpš.aḥd. 2033.2.5
.|w.arbʿ.ʿšr.bnš.|yd.ngr.mdrʿ.yd.š[--]m.|[b.]gt.ipṯl.ṯt.ṣmdm.|[w.ʿ]šr.bn[š]m.y[d].š[--].|[-]lm.b d.r[-]m.l[-]m.|ṯt.ʿš 2038.7
m.|w.ṯlṯ.ʿšr.bnš.|yd.ytm.yd.rʿy.ḥmrm.|b.gt.gwl.ṯmn.ṣmdm.|w.arbʿ.ʿšr.bnš.|yd.ngr.mdrʿ.yd.š[--]m.|[b.]gt.ipṯl.ṯt. 2038.4
[w.ʿ]šr.bn[š]m.y[d].š[--].|[-]lm.b d.r[-]m.l[-]m.|ṯt.ʿšr.ṣ[mdm].|w.tšʿ.ʿ[šr.--]m.ḥr[š].|[---].ḥr[š.---].|[---.ṯ]lṯ.[---.]dp 2038.10
[b.]gt.ṯpn.ʿšr.ṣmdm.|w.ṯlṯ.ʿšr.bnš.|yd.ytm.yd.rʿy.ḥmrm.|b.gt.gwl.ṯmn.ṣ 2038.1
.ṯpṭ.|nhr.ʿz.ym.l ymk.l tngṣn.pnt h.l ydlp.|tmn h.kṯr.ṣmdm.ynḥt.w ypʿr.šmt hm.|šm k.at.aymr.aymr.mr.ym.mr. 2.4[68].18
ḫṣ.ht.tṣmt.ṣrt k.|tqḥ.mlk.ʿlm k.drkt.dt dr dr k.|kṯr ṣmdm.ynḥt.w ypʿr.šmt hm.šm k at.|ygrš.ygrš.grš ym grš y 2.4[68].11
n.[---].|yly[.---].|ykn[.---].|rp[--].|ṯtw.[---].|[---.ʿ]šrm.ṣmd.ššw. 2131.12
.ḥspt.l[šʿ]r.ṭl.|ydʿt.hlk.kbkbm.|bkm.tmdln.ʿr.|bkm.tṣmd.pḥl.bkm.|tšu.ab h.tštnn.l[b]mt ʿr.|l ysmsm.bmt.pḥl.| 19[1AQHT].2.58
.ym.šmʿ.l qdš].|w am[rr.l dgy.rbt].|aṯrt.ym[.mdl.ʿr].|ṣmd.pḥl[.št.gpnm.dt].|ksp.dt.yr[q.nqbnm].|ʿdb.gpn.atnt[y 4[51].4.5
nqbnm].|ʿdb.gpn.atnt[y].|yšmʿ.qd.w amr[r].|mdl.ʿr.ṣmd.pḥl.|št.gpnm.dt.ksp.|dt.yrq.nqbnm.|ʿdb.gpn.atnt h.|y 4[51].4.9
ǵt.ṯkmt[.my].|ḥspt.l šʿr.ṭl.yd[ʿt].|hlk.kbkbm.mdl.ʿr.|ṣmd.pḥl.št.gpn y dt ksp.|dt.yrq.nqbn y.tš[mʿ].|pǵt.ṯkmt.m 19[1AQHT].2.53
yiḫd.bʿl.bn.aṯrt.|rbm.ymḫṣ.b ktp.|dk ym.ymḫṣ.b ṣmd.|ṣḥr mt.ymṣḥ.l arṣ.|[yṯb.]b[ʿ]l.l ksi.mlk h.|[---].l kḥṯ.d 6[49].5.3
šr.yṯb.b d h.ḫṭ.ṯkl.b d h.|ḫṭ.ulmn.yzbrnn.zbrm.gpn.|yṣmdnn.ṣmdm.gpn.yšql.šdmt h.|km gpn.|šbʿ d.yrgm.ʿl.ʿd. 23[52].10
--.]ḥš[.-]nm[.--.]k.[--].w yḫnp[.---].|[---.]ylm.b[n.ʿ]n k.ṣmdm.špk[.---].|[---.]nt[-.]mbk kpt.w[.--].b g[--].|[---.]ḥ[--.] 1001.1.16
ṯlṯ mrkb[t].|ṣpyt b ḫrṣ[.w] ṣmdm trm.d [ṣ]py.|w.trm.aḥdm.|ṣpym.|ṯlṯ mrkbt mlk.|d.l 1122.2
mrt.|bn.il.ṣm[d].|bn abbly.|ytʿd.ṣm[d].|bn.liy.|ʿšrm.ṣ[md].|ṯt kbd.b ḥ[--].|w.arbʿ.ḥ[mrm].|b m[ʿ]rby.|ṯmn.ṣmd. 2113.23
tšʿ.ṣmdm.|ṯlṯm.b d.|ibrtlm.|w.pat.aḫt.|in.b hm. 1141.1
ʿrby.|[--.šd]m.b.uškn.|[---.--]n.|[---].tlmdm.|[y]bnn.ṣmdm.|ṯp[ṭ]bʿl.ṣmdm.|[---.ṣ]mdm.w.ḥrṣ.|[---].aḥdm.|[iwr] 2033.2.3
d[m.---].|[m]ṣbt.ṣmdm.[---].|[--]nr.arbʿ.[---].|[--]idḫ.ṣmd[.---].|[u]bṣ.[---]. 1179.7
[---.ṣ]mdm[.---].|[ul]l.aḥdm.w[.---].|[mʿq]b.aḥdm.w[.---].|[ʿr]gz 1179.1
md].|ṯt kbd.b ḥ[--].|w.arbʿ.ḥ[mrm].|b m[ʿ]rby.|ṯmn.ṣmd.[---].|b d.bʿlsr.|yd.ṯdn.ʿšr.|[ḥ]mrm.|ddm.l.ybr[k].|bd 2102.3
.bnš]m.|[---.]ʿšr.ṣmd.alpm.|[---.bn]šm.|[---.--]m.ḫmš.ṣmdm.|[---.bnš]m. 2038.21
-].|[ul]l.aḥdm.w[.---].|[mʿq]b.aḥdm.w[.---].|[ʿr]gz.ṯlṯ.ṣmd[m.---].|[m]ṣbt.ṣmdm.[---].|[--]nr.arbʿ.[---].|[--]idḫ.ṣmd 1179.4
pnm.l.bn[.---].|apnm.l.[b]n[.---].|apnm.l.bn[.---].|ṯlṯ.ṣmdm[.---].|mṣ[r]n[.---]. 145[318].9
d.bʿlt.bhtm.|b.[-]ǵb.ršp.ṣbi.|[---.--]m.|[---.]piln.|[---].ṣmd[.---.]pd[ry].|[-----].|[---.b]ʿlt.|lbnm.ʿšr.yn.|ḫlb.gngnt.ṯl 2004.18
b.uškn.|[---.--]n.|[---].tlmdm.|[y]bnn.ṣmdm.|ṯp[ṭ]bʿl.ṣmdm.|[---.ṣ]mdm.w.ḥrṣ.|[---].aḥdm.|[iwr]pzn.aḥdm.|[i]lš 2033.2.4
-].|[mʿq]b.aḥdm.w[.---].|[ʿr]gz.ṯlṯ.ṣmd[m.---].|[m]ṣbt.ṣmdm.[---].|[--]nr.arbʿ.[---].|[--]idḫ.ṣmd[.---].|[u]bṣ.[---]. 1179.5

ṣmḫ

ʿl ṣdq.|skn.bt.|mlk.ṯǵr.|[m]lk.bny.|[--].lb.mlk.|[---.]ṣmḫ. 1007.9

ṣmy

yn.|šr.|bn.zql.|bn.iḫy.|bn.iytr.|bn.ʿyn.|bn.ǵzl.|bn.ṣmy.|bn.il[-]šy.|bn.ybšr.|bn.sly.|bn.ḫlbt.|bn.brzt.|bn.ayl. 2117.2.8
[bn]šm.dt.iš[--].|[b]n.bʿl[--].|bn.gld.|bn.ṣmy.|bn.mry[n].|bn.mgn.|bn.ʿdn.|bn.knn.|bn.py.|bn.mk[2117.1.4

ṣml

n.diy.hwt.hrg[b].|tpr.w du.b nši.ʿn h.|[w]yphn.yḥd.ṣml.um.nšrm.|yšu.g h.w yṣḥ.knp.ṣml.|bʿl.yṯbr.bʿl.yṯbr.diy. 19[1AQHT].3.135
sk.|arbʿ[.k]dwṯm.w.ṯt.ṯprtm.|b.ʿšr[m.]ksp.|ḫmš.kkr.ṣml.|b.ʿšrt.b d.bn.kyn.|ʿšr.kkr.šʿrt.|b d.urtn.b.arbʿm.|arbʿt 2100.12
n.|b ḫrt.ilm.arṣ.b p h.rgm.l[yṣ]a.|b špt h.hwt h.knp.ṣml.bʿ[l].|bʿl.ṯbr.diy.hyt.tq[l.tḥt].|pʿn h.ybqʿ.kbd h.w yḥd.| 19[1AQHT].3.142
n h.|[w]yphn.yḥd.ṣml.um.nšrm.|yšu.g h.w yṣḥ.knp.ṣml.|bʿl.yṯbr.bʿl.yṯbr.diy.|hyt.tql.tḥt.pʿn y.ibqʿ.|kbd h.w aḥ 19[1AQHT].3.136
trm.b.ʿšrt.|mit.adrm.b.ʿšrt.|ʿšr.ydt.b.ʿšrt.|ḫmš.kkrm.ṣml.|ʿšrt.ksp h.|ḫmš.kkr.qnm.|ṯlṯt.w.ṯlṯt.ksp h.|arbʿ.kkr.| 1127.10

ṣmṣ

bd.|tgmr.ḥṭm.šbʿ.ddm.|ḫmš.dd.šʿrm.|kdm.yn.|kdm.ṣmṣ. 1099.35

ṣmq

q.b.ap h].|k yr[a]š.šš[w.w.ykhp].|mid.dblt.yṯ[nt.w].|ṣmq[m].yṯnm.w[.qmḥ.bql].|tdkn.aḥd h.w[.yṣq].|b.ap h. 161[56].34
-----].|[-----].|[-----].|k yraš w ykhp mid.|dblt yṯnt w ṣmqm yṯn[m].|w qmḥ bql yṣq aḥd h.|b ap h. 160[55].24
n.ltḥ.aqhr.|[---.ltḥ.]sbbyn.ltḥ.ššmn.ltḥ.šḥlt.|[---.ltḥ.]ṣmqm.[ṯ]t.mat.nṣ.ṯlṯm.ʿṣr.|[---].ḫmš[m.ḥm]r.škm.|[---.ṯt.dd 142[12].5
.]šmn.mr.|[---.l]tḥ.sb[by]n.ltḥ.šḥ[lt].|[---.l]tḥ.dblt.ltḥ.ṣmqm.|[---.--]m.[ḫ]mšm.ḥmr.škm. 142[12].17

ṣmrt

t.abm.|[-]rbn.ʿdd.nryn.|[ab]r[p]u.bn.kbd.|[-]m[-].bn.ṣmrt.|liy.bn.yṣi.|ḏmrhd.bn.srt.|[---.--]m.|ʿbdmlk.bn.šrn.|ʿ 102[322].6.5

ṣmt

ʿnt.tm|ṯḫṣ.b ʿmq.tḫtṣb.bn.|qrytm tmḫṣ.lim.ḫp y[m].|tṣmt.adm.ṣat.š[p]š.|tḥt h.k kdrt.ri[š].|ʿl h.k irbym.kp.k.qṣ 3[ʿNT].2.8
.[---].|nqmd.mlk.ugr[t.--].|phy.|w tpllm.mlk.r[b.--].|mṣmt.l nqmd.[---.-]št.|hl ny.argmn.d [ybl.n]qmd.|l špš.arn. 64[118].17

m.rḥ.npš[h.km.iṯl]. | brlt h.km.qṭr.[b ap h.---]. | ʻnt.b ṣmt.mhr h.[---]. | aqht.w tbk.y[---.---]. | abn.ank.w ʻl.[qšt k.--- 18[3AQHT].4.38
mṣmt.ʻbs. | arr.d.qr | ht. 1173.1
ḫšt.bṯn.ʻqltn. | šlyṭ.d šbʻt.rašm. | mḫšt.mdd ilm.ar[š]. | ṣmt.ʻgl.il.ʻtk. | mḫšt.klbt.ilm išt. | klt.bt.il.ḏbb.imtḫṣ.ksp. | itrṯ 3[ʻNT].3.41
bʻl.a[ḫ]ḏ[.---]. | ẓr h.aḥḏ.qš[t.---]. | p ʻn.bʻl.aḥḏ[.---]. | w ṣmt.ǵllm[.---]. | aḥḏ.aklm.k [---]. | npl.b mšmš[.---]. | anp n m 12[75].2.35
k.l zbl.bʻl.ṯnt.l rkb.ʻrpt.ht.ib k. | bʻl m.ht.ib k.tmḫṣ.ht.tṣmt.ṣrt k. | tqḥ.mlk.ʻlm k.drkt.dt dr dr k. | kṯr ṣmdm.ynḥt. 2.4[68].9

ṣnr

m[--].bn.qqln. | ʻbdil[-].bn.qqln. | liy.bn.qqln. | mnn.bn.ṣnr. | iḫy.[b]n[.--]l[-]. | ʻbdy[rḫ].bn.gṯtn. | yrmn.bn.ʻn. | krwn.n 85[80].4.6
r. | bʻl.bt.ssl. | bʻl.bt.ṯrn. | bʻl.bt.ktmn. | bʻl.bt.ndbd. | [--].ṣnr. | [bʻl].bt.bsn. | [-----]. | b[--.---]. 31[14].10
]d. | a[ǵ]ltn. | [-----]. | [--]ny. | knʻm. | [-]p[-]. | ʻpṯn. | pslm.ṣnr. 2060.15

ṣnrn

ab.aḫ.ubn. | šd.b d.bn.uṯryn. | [ubd]y.mrynm. | [š]d.bn.ṣnrn.b d.nrn. | [š]d.bn.rwy.b d.ydln. | [š].bn.trn.b d.ibrmḏ. | [š 82[300].1.8

ṣʻ

.npš.blt. | ḥmr.p imt.b klt. | yd y.ilḥm.hm.šbʻ. | ydt y.b ṣʻ.hm.ks.ymsk. | nhr.k[--].ṣḥn.bʻl.ʻm. | aḫ y.qran.hd.ʻm.ary y. 5[67].1.21
-]. | šʻrt.ṯn[.---]. | bqʻt.[--].ḫ[mr.---]. | ḫlb krd.ḫ[mr.---]. | ṣʻ.ḥmr.w[.---]. | ṣʻq.ḥmr.w.[---]. | ḫlb ʻprm.amḏy.[ḥm]r.w bn[2040.14
rkby. | šḥq. | ǵn. | ṣʻ. | mld. | amḏy. | ḫlbʻprm. | ḫpty. | [ḥr]ṣbʻ. | [mʻ]rb. 2077.4
šrš. | lbnm. | ḫlb.krd. | ṣʻ. | mlk. | gbʻly. | ypr. | ary. | ẓrn. | art. | ṯlḥny. | ṯlrby. | dmt. | aǵt. 71[113].4
| tḫṣb.bn.ṯlḥnm.ymḥ. | [b]bt.dm.ḏmr.yṣq.šmn. | šlm.b ṣʻ.trḥṣ.yd h.bt | [l]t.ʻnt.uṣbʻt h.ybmt.limm. | [t]rḥṣ.yd h.b dm. 3[ʻNT].2.32
ur[--.---]. | [---.n]skt.nʻmn.nbl[.---]. | [--.]yṣq šmn.šlm.b ṣ[ʻ.trḥṣ]. | yd h.btlt.ʻnt.uṣbʻt[h.ybmt]. | limm.tiḫd.knr h.b yd UG5.3.2.4
rrt. | bt.krt.tbun. | lm.mṯb[.---]. | w lḥm mr.tqdm. | yd.b ṣʻ.tšlḥ. | ḥrb.b bšr.tštn. | [w t]ʻn.mṯt.ḥry. | [l lḥ]m.l šty.ṣḥt km. 15[128].4.24
]br[.---]. | bḥr[.--]t[.----]. | l mṯb[.--]t[.---]. | [tqdm.]yd.b ṣʻ.t[šl]ḥ. | [ḥrb.b]bš[r].tštn. | [w tʻn].mṯt.ḥry. | [l lḥ]m.l šty.ṣḥ 15[128].5.7
lb ʻprm.ṯṯ. | ḫlb krd.ṯn ʻšr. | qmy.arbʻ.ʻšr. | ṣʻq.arbʻ ʻšr. | ṣʻ.ṯmn. | šḥq.ʻšrm.arbʻ.kbd. | ḫlb rpš arbʻ.ʻšr. | bqʻt ṯṯ. | irab ṯn. 67[110].5
. | ʻn.kḏd.aylt. | mt hm.ks.ym | sk.nhr hm. | šbʻ.ydt y.b ṣʻ. | [--.]šbʻ.rbt. | [---.]qbṭ.ṯm. | [---.]bn.ilm. | [m]t.šmḫ.p ydd. | il UG5.4.11

ṣʻṣ

[.---]. | [---.]nt[-.]mbk kpt.w[.--].b g[--]. | [---.]ḫ[--.]bnt.ṣʻṣ.bnt.ḫkp[.---]. | [---].aḥw.aṯm.prṯl[.---]. | [---.]mnt.[l]pʻn[.-. 1001.1.18
m.ʻnt.tqm. | [---.p]ḫr k.ygrš k.qr.bt k.ygrš k. | [---].bnt.ṣʻṣ.bnt.mʻmʻ.ʻbd.ḥrn.[--.]k. | [---].aǵwyn.ʻn k.ẓẓ.w k mǵ.ilm. 1001.2.11

ṣʻq

bqʻt.[--].ḫ[mr.---]. | ḫlb krd.ḫ[mr.---]. | ṣʻ.ḥmr.w[.---]. | ṣʻq.ḥmr.w.[---]. | ḫlb ʻprm.amḏy.[ḥm]r.w bn[š]. | gnʻy.[---.bn] 2040.15
y. | ulm. | mʻrby. | mʻr. | arny. | šʻrt. | ḫlbrpš. | ḥry. | qmṣ. | ṣʻq. | qmy. | ḫlbkrd. | yʻrt. | uškn. | ʻnqpat. | ilštmʻ. | šbn. | ṭbq. | r 2074.15
ḫlb ʻprm.ṯṯ. | ḫlb krd.ṯn ʻšr. | qmy.arbʻ.ʻšr. | ṣʻq.arbʻ ʻšr. | ṣʻ.ṯmn. | šḥq.ʻšrm.arbʻ.kbd. | ḫlb rpš arbʻ.ʻšr. | bqʻ 67[110].4
ṣpn. | mril. | ʻnmky. | ʻnqpat. | ṭbq. | hzp. | gnʻy. | mʻrby. | [ṣ]ʻq. | [š]ḥq. | nʻrm. | mḥrǵlm. | kzym. | mru.skn. | mru.ibrn. | ps 71[113].58
ḫlb k[rd]. | ṣʻq. | š[---]. 1178.2
š[--.---]. | ṣʻ[-.---]. | ṣʻq[.---]. | ḫlb.k[rd]. | uškn. | ʻnqp[at]. | ubrʻ[y]. | ilšt[mʻ]. | šbn. | 2146.3

ṣʻr

bd h.l ydʻ hr h.[---]d[-]. | tnq[.---.]in[b]b.pʻr. | yd h[.--.]ṣʻr.glgl. | a[---]m.rḥ.ḥḏ ʻ[r]pt. | gl[.---.]yhpk.m[---]m. | sʻ[--.]k[13[6].33

ṣǵd

. | šd[.i]lm.šd.aṯrt.w rḥmy. | [---].y[ṯ]b. | [---]p.gp ym.w yṣǵd.gp..thm. | [yqḥ.]il.mštʻltm.mštʻltm.l riš.agn. | hl h.[t]špl 23[52].30
liyn[.bʻl]. | lm.k qnym.ʻl[m.--]. | k dr d.d yknn[.--]. | bʻl.yṣǵd.mli[.--]. | il hd.mla.u[--.--]. | blt.p btlt.ʻn[t]. | w p.nʻmt.aḫ 10[76].3.8

ṣǵr

lt.y[--].mdʻ.nplt.bšr. | [---].w tpky.k[m.]nʻr.tdmʻ.km. | [ṣǵ]r.bkm.yʻny[.---.bn]wt h. | [--]nn.bnt yš[--.---.-]lk. | [--]b.km UG5.8.41
bq[.---]. | w tksynn.bṯn[-.] | y[--.]šr h.w šḫp h. | [--.]šḫp.ṣǵrt h. | yrk.tʻl.b ǵr. | mslmt.b ǵr.tliyt. | w tʻl.bkm.b arr. | bm.a 10[76].3.27
.ḫnpm.mḫl[.---]. | mlk.nhr.ibr[.---]. | zbl bʻl.ǵlm.[---]. | ṣǵr hd w r[---.---]. | w l nhr nd[-.---]. | [---.--]l. 9[33].2.11
[ǵt.---]. | mid.rm[.krt]. | b tk.rpi.ar[ṣ]. | b pḫr.qbṣ.dtn. | ṣǵrt hn.abkrn. | tbrk.ilm.tity. | tity.ilm.l ahl hm. | dr il.l mškn 15[128].3.16
ʻmyn. | ilyn. | yrbʻm. | nʻmn. | bn.kbl. | knʻm. | bdlm. | bn.ṣǵr. | klb. | bn.mnḥm. | bn.brqn. | bn.ʻn. | bn.ʻbdy. | ʻbdʻṯtr. 1046.3.43
ṯlḫ h w mlg h y | ṯtqt ʻm h b qʻt. | tqʻt ʻm prbḫṯ. | dmqt ṣǵrt kṯrt. 24[77].50
m[.---]. | h.hn bn k.hn[.---]. | bn bn.aṯr k.hn[.---]. | yd k.ṣǵr.tnšq.špt k.ṯm. | ṯkm.bm ṯkm.aḫm.qym.il. | b lsmt.ṯm.yṭbš 22.2[124].4
tn h.abd y. | [---.ǵ]r.šrǵzz.ybky.km.nʻr. | [w ydmʻ.k]m.ṣǵr.špš.b šmm.tqru. | [---.]nplt.y[--].mdʻ.nplt.bšr. | [---].w tpk UG5.8.38

ṣp

m l h.ršp [-]m. | [---.]bqt[-]. | [b] ǵb.ršp mh bnš. | šrp.w ṣp ḫršḫ. | ʻlm b ǵb ḫyr. | ṯmn l ṯlṯm ṣin. | šbʻ.alpm. | bt bʻl.ugrt UG5.12.B.2
ʻq h.ib.iqni.ʻp[ʻp] h. | sp.ṯrml.ṯḥgrn.[-]dm[.-]. | ašlw.b ṣp.ʻn h. | d b ḥlm y.il.ytn. | b ḏrt y.ab.adm. | w ld.šph.l krt. | w 14[KRT].3.149

ṣpiry

t.bn gda[.-.]mḏʻ. | kl[--.---.]ṯmnt.[--.]w[.---]. | [-]m[.---.]ṣpiry[.ṯ]lṯt[.---]. APP.II[173].61

ṣpy

ṯlṯ mrkb[t]. | ṣpyt b ḫrṣ[.w] ṣmdm trm.d [ṣ]py. | w.trm.aḥdm. | ṣpym. | ṯlṯ 1122.2
ṯlṯ mrkb[t]. | ṣpyt b ḫrṣ[.w] ṣmdm trm.d [ṣ]py. | w.trm.aḥdm. | ṣpym. | ṯlṯ mrkbt mlk. | d.l.ṣpy. | [---.t]r h 1122.2
[t]. | ṣpyt b ḫrṣ[.w] ṣmdm trm.d [ṣ]py. | w.trm.aḥdm. | ṣpym. | ṯlṯ mrkbt mlk. | d.l.ṣpy. | [---.t]r hm. | [---].ššb. | [---.]tr 1122.4
trm.d [ṣ]py. | w.trm.aḥdm. | ṣpym. | ṯlṯ mrkbt mlk. | d.l.ṣpy. | [---.t]r hm. | [---].ššb. | [---.]tr h. | [a]rbʻ.qlʻm. | arbʻ.mḏrn 1122.6

ṣpn

ry.š.|šrp.w šlmm ilib š.|b‘l ugrt š.b‘l ḫlb š.|yrḫ š.‘nt ṣpn.alp.|w š.pdry š.ddmš š.|w b urbt.ilib š.|b‘l alp w š.|dg UG5.13.17
.w bbt.b‘l.ugrt.|w kdm.w npš ilib.|gdlt.il š.b‘l š.‘nt.|ṣpn.alp.w š.pdry.š.|šrp.w šlmm ilib š.|b‘l ugrt š.b‘l ḫlb š.|y UG5.13.14
.š.|arṣ w šmm.š.|il.š.kṯrt.š.|dgn.š.b‘l.ḫlb alp w š.|b‘l ṣpn alp.w.š.|ṯrṯy.alp.w.š.|yrḫ.š.ṣpn.š.|kṯr š ‘ṯtr.š.|[‘ṯt]rt.š.š UG5.9.2.5
.il.t‘ḏr.b‘l.š.ršp.š.ddmš.š.|w šlmm.ilib.š.i[l.--]m d gbl.ṣpn.al[p].|pḫr.ilm.š.ym.š[.k]nr.š.[--.]‘ṣrm gdlt.|b‘lm.kmm.b UG5.9.1.10
[l m].|ḥš.bht m.tbn[n].|ḥš.trmmn.hk[l m].|b tk.ṣrrt.ṣpn.|alp.šd.aḫd bt.|rbt.kmn.hkl.|w y‘n.kṯr.w ḫss.|šm‘.l ali 4[51].5.117
bd.w yšr.|mṣltm.bd.n‘m.|yšr.ǵzr.ṭb.ql.|‘l.b‘l.b ṣrrt.|ṣpn.ytmr.b‘l.|bnt h.y‘n.pdry.|bt.ar.apn.ṭly.|[bt.r]b.pdr.yd‘. 3[‘NT].1.22
b‘r.|amrr.k kbkb.l pnm.|aṯr.btlt.‘nt.|w b‘l.tb‘.mrym.ṣpn.|idk.l ttn.pnm.|‘m.il.mbk.nhrm.|qrb.apq.thmtm.|tgly. 4[51].4.19
il ṣpn.|il[i]b.|i[l].|dgn.|b‘[l ṣ]pn.|b‘lm.|[b‘]lm.|[b‘]lm.|[b‘]l 29[17].1.1
pamt ṯlṯm š l qrnt.|ṯlḥn.b‘lt.bhtm.|‘lm.‘lm.gdlt l b‘l.|ṣpn.ilbt[.---.]d[--].|l ṣpn[.---.-]lu.|ilib[.---.b]‘l.|ugrt[.---.--]n. UG5.13.33
tḥt.‘nt.arṣ.ṯlṯ.mtḥ.ǵyrm.|idk.l ttn pnm.‘m.b‘l.|mrym.ṣpn.b alp.šd.rbt.kmn.|hlk.aḫt h.b‘l.y‘n.tdrq.|ybnt.ab h.šrḥ 3[‘NT].4.82
.‘nt.td‘ṣ.|p‘nm.w tr.arṣ.|idk.l ttn.pnm.|‘m.b‘l.mrym.ṣpn.|b alp.šd.rbt.kmn.|ṣḥq.btlt.‘nt.tšu.|g h.w tṣḥ.tbšr b‘l.| 4[51].5.85
l.b ǵr.|mslmt.b ǵr.tliyt.|w t‘l.bkm.b arr.|bm.arr.w b ṣpn.|b n‘m.b ǵr.t[l]iyt.|ql.l b‘l.ttnn.|bšrt.il.bš[r.b‘]l.|w bšr. 10[76].3.31
ṣ b šmal.|d alpm.w alp w š.|šrp.w šlmm kmm.|l b‘l.ṣpn b ‘r‘r.|pamt ṯlṯm š l qrnt.|ṯlḥn.b‘lt.bhtm.|‘lm.‘lm.gdlt l UG5.13.29
šm.w l tbn.|hmlt.arṣ.at m.w ank.|ibǵy h.b tk.ǵr y.il.ṣpn.|b qdš.b ǵr.nḥlt y.|b n‘m.b gb‘.tliyt.|hlm.‘nt.tph.ilm.b 3[‘NT].3.26
.brq].|d l t[d‘.šmm.at m.w ank].|ibǵ[y h.b tk.ǵ]r y.il.ṣpn.|b q[dš.b ǵr.nḥ]lt y.|w t[‘n].btlt.[‘]nt.tṯb.|[ybmt.]limm. 3[‘NT].4.63
b‘l.yṯb.k ṯbt.ǵr.hd.r[‘y].|k mdb.b tk.ǵr h.il ṣpn.b [tk].|ǵr.tliyt.šb‘t.brqm.[---].|ṯmnt.iṣr r‘t.‘ṣ brq y.|riš UG5.3.1.2
ilm.špš.|tšu.aliyn.b‘l.l ktp.|‘nt.k tšt h.tš‘lyn h.|b ṣrrt.ṣpn.tbkyn h.|w tqbrn h.tštnn.b ḫrt.|ilm.arṣ.ṭṭbḫ.šb‘m.|ru 6[62].1.16
nm.|il w aṯrt.|ḫnn il.|nṣbt il.|šlm il.|il ḥš il add.|b‘l ṣpn b‘l.|ugrt.|b mrḥ il.|b nit il.|b ṣmd il.|b dṯn il.|b šrp il. 30[107].10
il ṣpn.|il[i]b.|i[l].|dgn.|b‘[l ṣ]pn.|b‘lm.|[b‘]lm.|[b‘]lm.|[b‘]lm.|[b‘]lm.|[b‘l]m.|[arṣ] w 29[17].1.5
[--]t.dqtm.[b nbk.---].|[--.k]mm.gdlt.l.b[‘l.---].|[dq]t.l.ṣpn.gdlt.l[.---].|u[gr]t.š.l.[il]ib.ǵ[--.--rt].|w [‘ṣrm.]l.ri[--.---]. 35[3].34
.dqt[.---].|bqtm.b nbk.[---].|kmm.gdlt.l b[‘l.--.dqt].|l ṣpn.gdlt.[l.---].|ugrt.š l ili[b.---].|rt.w ‘ṣrm.l[.---].|pamt.w b APP.II[173].37
ḥṣ.mlk.brr.|[b ym.ml]at.y[ql]n.al[p]m.yrḫ.‘šrt.|[l b‘l.ṣ]pn.[dq]tm.w y[nt] qrt.|[w mtmt]m.[š.l] rm[š.]kbd.w š.|[l 36[9].1.12
tmt]m.[š.l] rm[š.]kbd.w š.|[l šlm.kbd.al]p.w š.[l] b‘l.ṣpn.|[dqt.l.ṣpn.šrp].w š[l]mm.kmm.|[w bbt.b‘l.ugrt.]kdm. 36[9].1.14
|w mtntm.š l rmš.|w kbd.w š.l šlm kbd.|alp.w š.l b‘l ṣpn.|dqt l ṣpn.šrp.w šlmm.|kmm.w bbt.b‘l.ugrt.|w kdm.w UG5.13.9
lṯt mrm.|[---.i]l š.b‘l š.aṯrt.š.ym š.[b‘]l knp.|[---.g]dlt.ṣpn.dqt.šrp.w [š]lmm.|[---.a]lp.l b‘l.w aṯrt.‘ṣr[m] l inš.|[ilm 36[9].1.7
alp.l[--]n.|[---.]š.il š.b‘l š.dgn š.|[---.--]r.w ṯt pl.gdlt.[ṣ]pn.dqt.|[---.al]p ‘nt.gdlt.b ṯlṯt mrm.|[---.i]l š.b‘l š.aṯrt.š.y 36[9].1.4
mḫlpt.w l.ytk.[d]m[‘t.]km.|rb‘t.ṯqlm.ṯṯp[.---.]bm.|yd.ṣpn hm.tliy m[.--.ṣ]pn hm.|nṣḥy.šrr.m[---.--]ay.|nbšr km.d 19[1AQHT].2.84
[‘t.]km.|rb‘t.ṯqlm.ṯṯp[.---.]bm.|yd.ṣpn hm.tliy m[.--.ṣ]pn hm.|nṣḥy.šrr.m[---.--]ay.|nbšr km.dnil.[--] h[.---].|riš. 19[1AQHT].2.84
-].aṯrt.‘ṣr[m.l inš.ilm].|[ṯ]ṯb.mdbḥ.b‘l.g[dlt.---].|dqt.l.ṣpn.w.dqt[.---].|ṯn.l.‘šrm.pamt.[---].|š.dd.šmn.gdlt.w.[---.br 35[3].42
k[--.---].|‘ṣrm.l i[nš.ilm.ṯb.md]|bḥ.b‘l.[gdlt.---.dqt].|l ṣpn.w [dqt.---.ṯn.l ‘š]|rm.pam[t.---].|š dd šmn[.gdlt.w.---].| APP.II[173].46
d.il.ǵzr.|tb‘.w l.yṯb ilm.idk.|l ytn.pnm.‘m.b‘l.|mrym.ṣpn.w y‘n.|gpn.w ugr.tḥm.bn ilm.|mt.hwt.ydd.bn.il.|ǵzr.p 5[67].1.11
tn.u ḫšt k.l ntn.|‘tq.b d.aṯt.ab ṣrry.|tbky k.ab.ǵr.b‘l.|ṣpn.ḥlm.qdš.|any.ḥlm.adr.ḥl.|rḥb.mknpt.ap.|[k]rt.bnm.il.š 16.1[125].7
.ṣrry.|u ilm.tmtn.špḥ.|[l]ṭpn.l yḥ.t[b]ky k.|ab.ǵr.b‘l.ṣ[p]n.ḥlm.|qdš.nny.ḥ[l]m.adr.|ḥl.rḥb.mk[npt].|ap.krt bn[16.2[125].107
hdm.riš h.l ymǵy.|aps h.w y‘n.‘ṯtr.‘rẓ.|l amlk.b ṣrrt.ṣpn.|yrd.‘ṯtr.‘rẓ.yrd.|l kḥṯ.aliyn.b‘l.|w ymlk.b arṣ.il.kl h.|[6.1.62[49.1.34]
lt.nmlk.‘ṯtr.‘rẓ.|ymlk.‘ṯtr.‘rẓ.|apnk.‘ṯtr.‘rẓ.|y‘l.b ṣrrt.ṣpn.|yṯb.l kḥṯ.aliyn.|b‘l.p‘n h.l tmǵyn.|hdm.riš h.l ymǵy.| 6.1.57[49.1.29]
sa.w.yṯb.|tqru.l špš.um h.špš.um.ql bl.|‘m b‘l.mrym.ṣpn.mnt y.nṯk.|nḥš.šmrr.nḥš.‘q šr ln h.|mlḫš.abd.ln h.ydy. UG5.7.9
[y].|atl[g].|bṣr[y].|[---].|[---]y.|ar.|agm.w.ḫpty.|ḫlb.ṣpn.|mril.|‘nmky.|‘nqpat.|ṭbq.|hzp.|gn‘y.|m‘rby.|[ṣ]‘q.|[71[113].50
išt.|klt.bt.il.ḏbb.imtḫṣ.ksp.|itrṯ.ḫrṣ.ṭrd.b‘l.|b mrym.ṣpn.mšṣṣ.[-]k‘[-].|udn h.grš h.l ksi.mlk h.|l nḫt.l kḥṯ.drkt h 3[‘NT].4.45
t.b‘l.|‘rkm.|b ṯmnt.‘šrt.yr|tḥṣ.mlk.brr.|‘lm.tzǵ.b ǵb.ṣpn.|nḥkt.ksp.w ḫrṣ ṭ‘ ṯn šm l btbt.|alp.w š šrp.alp šlmm.|l UG5.12.A.7
w ḫrṣ ṭ‘ ṯn šm l btbt.|alp.w š šrp.alp šlmm.|l b‘l.‘ṣr l ṣpn.|npš.w.š.l ršp bbt.|[‘]ṣrm l h.ršp [-]m.|[---.]bqt[-].|[b] UG5.12.A.10
m.ytn.b‘l.|[s]pu y.bn m.um y.kly y.|yṯb.‘m.b‘l.ṣrrt.|ṣpn.yšu g h.w yṣḥ.|aḫ y m.ytnt.b‘l.|spu y.bn m.um y.kl|y 6[49].6.13
l.|y[m.---.]l ṯr.qdqd h.|il[.--.]rḥq.b ǵr.|km.y[--.]ilm.b ṣpn.|‘dr.l[‘r].‘rm.|ṯb.l pd[r.]pdrm.|ṯṯ.l ṯṯm.aḫd.‘r.|šb‘m.šb 4[51].7.6
.š.b‘l.ḫlb alp w š.|b‘l ṣpn alp.w.š.|ṯrṯy.alp.w.š.|yrḫ.š.ṣpn.š.|kṯr š ‘ṯtr.š.|[‘ṯt]rt.š.šgr w iṯm š.|[---.]š.ršp.idrp.š.|[--- UG5.9.2.7
--].|b‘lm.alp.w š[.---].|arṣ.w šmm.š.kṯr[t] š.yrḫ[.---].|ṣpn.š.kṯr.š.pdry.š.ǵrm.š[.---].|aṯrt.š.‘nt.š.špš.š.arṣy.š.‘ṯtrt.š.| UG5.9.1.6
arb[‘.---].|kdm.yn.prs.qmḥ.[---].|mdbḥt.bt.ilt.‘ṣr[m.l ṣpn.š].|l ǵlmt.š.w l [---.l yrḫ].|gd[lt].l nkl[.gdlt.l b‘lt.bhtm]. 35[3].24
-.kdm.yn].|prs.qmḥ.m‘[--.---].|mdbḥt.bt.i[lt.‘ṣrm.l].|ṣpn š.l ǵlm[t.š.w l.---].|l yrḫ.gdlt.l [nkl.gdlt.l b‘]|[lt].bht[m] APP.II[173].27
t.ilhm.b‘lm.dṯt.w kšm.ḫmš.|‘ṯr h.mlun.šnpt.ḫṣt h.b‘l.ṣpn š.|[--]ṯ š.ilt.mgdl š.ilt.asrm š.|w l ll.šp. pgr.w ṯrmnm.bt 34[1].10
] rm[š.]kbd.w š.|[l šlm.kbd.al]p.w š.[l] b‘l.ṣpn.|[dqt.l.ṣpn.šrp].w š[l]mm.kmm.|[w bbt.b‘l.ugrt.]kdm.w npš.|[ilib. 36[9].1.15
š l rmš.|w kbd.w š.l šlm kbd.|alp.w š.l b‘l ṣpn.|dqt l ṣpn.šrp.w šlmm.|kmm.w bbt.b‘l.ugrt.|w kdm.w npš ilib.|g UG5.13.10
yn.d.ykl.b d.[---].|b.dbḥ.mlk.|dbḥ ṣpn.|[-]zǵm.|[i]lib.|[i]lbldn.|[p]dry.bt.mlk.|[-]lp.izr.|[a]rz. 2004.3
dbḥ.ṣp[n.---].|il.alp.w š[.---].|b‘lm.alp.w š[.---].|b‘lm.alp.w š[.--- UG5.9.1.1
.|[w bbt.b‘l.ugrt.]kdm.w npš.|[ilib.gdlt.il.š.b]‘[l.]š.‘nt ṣpn.|[---.]w [n]p[š.---].|[---.--]t.w[.---].|[---.--]pr.ṯ[--.---].|[--- 36[9].1.17
.ym]m.|[y‘tqn.---.ymǵy.]npš.|[---.h]d.tngṯn h.|[---].b ṣpn.|[---].nšb.b ‘n.|[---.]b km.y‘n.|[---.yd‘.l] yd‘t.|[---.t]asrn 1[‘NT.X].5.5
.dt.|[---.]šb‘.l šb‘m.aṯr.|[---.--]ldm.dt ymtm.|[--.--]r.l ẓpn.|[---.]pn.ym.y[--].|[---].b‘l.tdd.|[---.]hkl.|[---.]yd h.|[--- 25[136].5
b[--.---].|l il limm[.---].|w ṯt.npš[.---].|kbd.w [---].|l ṣp[n.---].|š.[---].|w [----].|k[--.---].|‘n[t.---]. 40[134].11
‘tqn.---].ymǵy.npš.|[---.--]t.hd.tngṯm h.|[---.-]ḥm k b ṣpn.|[---.]išqb.aylt.|[---.--]m.b km.y‘n.|[---].yd‘.l yd‘t.|[---.] 1[‘NT.X].5.18
.|[-----].|[-----].|[--].bt.gb[-.--].|[--]k[-].w.špš.|[---.b].ṣp[n].|[---.]š[--].|[-----].|[-----].|[---.]ṯty.|[---.-]rd y.|[---.]b‘l. 2159.10
lḥn.b‘lt.bhtm.|‘lm.‘lm.gdlt l b‘l.|ṣpn.ilbt[.---.]d[--].|l ṣpn[.---.-]lu.|ilib[.---.b]‘l.|ugrt[.---.--]n.|[w] š l [---]. UG5.13.34
[š].|[---.]bht[.---].|[---.]amr[-].|[---.‘]rg[z.-].|[---.ḫl]b ṣpn. 72[-].2.5

ṣpr

. | ibr h[.l]ql.nhqt. | ḥmr[h.l g‘t.]alp. | ḥrt[.l z]ǵt.klb. | [s]pr[.apn]k. | [pb]l[.mlk.g]m.l att | [h.k]y[ṣḥ.]šm‘.m‘. | [--.]‘ 14[KRT].5.227
rb‘.mat. | tgmr.uz.aḫmn.arb‘.mat. | arb‘m.kbd. | tlt.alp.ṣpr.dt.aḥd. | ḥrt h.aḥd.b gt.nḫl. | aḥd.b gt.knpy.w.aḥd.b gt.ṯr 1129.8
‘mm[.agzry ym.bn]ym. | ynqm.b ap zd.aṯrt.[---]. | špš.mṣprt dlt hm[.---]. | w ǵnbm.šlm.‘rbm.ṯn[nm]. | hlkm.b dbḥ 23[52].25
.l qr.ṯigt.ibr h. | l ql.nhqt.ḥmr h. | l g‘t.alp.ḥrṯ.zǵt. | klb.ṣpr.w ylak. | mlakm.l k.‘m.krt. | mswn h.tḥm.pbl.mlk. | qḥ.ks 14[KRT].3.123
[-----]. | [-----]. | ynḥm. | iḫy. | bn.mšt. | ‘psn. | bn.ṣpr. | kmn. | bn.ršp. | tmn. | šmmn. | bn.rmy. | bn.aky. | ‘bdḫmn. 1047.7
]bš. | šdyn.mḫ[ṣ]. | aṯry.mḫṣ. | b‘ln.mḫṣ. | y[ḫ]ṣdq.mḫṣ. | ṣp[r].ks[d]. | b‘l.š[lm]. | ḫyrn[.---]. | a[--.---]. | ‘[--.---]. | š[--.---]. | 2084.18

ṣprn

n.alṯn. | bn.aš[-]š. | bn.štn. | bn.ilš. | bn.tnabn. | bn.ḫṣn. | ṣprn. | bn.ašbḥ. | bn.qṭnn. | bn.ǵlmn. | [bn].ṣwy. | [bn].ḫnq[n]. | 1046.1.20
spr.argmn.nskm. | rqdym. | šṭšm.ṯṯ mat. | ṣprn.ṯṯ mat. | ḏkry.ṯṯ mat. | [p]lsy.ṯṯ mat. | ‘dn.ḫmš [m]at. | [--] 1060.1.4

ṣṣ

amtrn arb‘m. | ṣṣ iytlm mit ṯlṯm kbd. | ṣṣ m[l]k ‘šrm. | ṣṣ abš[-] mit [‘š]r kbd. | ṣṣ ydrd ‘šrm. | ṣṣ bn aglby ṯlṯ[m]. | ṣṣ 2097.11
[ṣṣ] ‘mtdl ṯlṯm. | ṣṣ ‘mlbi ṯṯ l ‘šrm. | ṣṣ bn adty ḫmšm. | ṣṣ amtrn arb‘m. | ṣṣ iytlm mit ṯlṯm kbd. | ṣṣ m[l]k ‘šrm. | ṣṣ ab 2097.8
ṣ bn.šrš‘m.[---]. | ṣṣ mlkn‘m.a[rb‘m]. | ṣṣ mlk mit[.---]. | ṣṣ igy.ḫmšm. | ṣṣ yrpi m[it.---]. | ṣṣ bn.š[m]mn ‘[šr.---]. | alp.ṯṯ 2097.17
ṣ ‘mlbi ṯṯ l ‘šrm. | ṣṣ bn adty ḫmšm. | ṣṣ amtrn arb‘m. | ṣṣ iytlm mit ṯlṯm kbd. | ṣṣ m[l]k ‘šrm. | ṣṣ abš[-] mit [‘š]r kbd. 2097.9
ṣṣ mr‘m ḫmšm ḫmš kbd. | ṣṣ ubn ḫmš ‘šr h. | ṣṣ ‘myd ḫmšm. | ṣṣ tmn.ḫmšm. | [ṣṣ] ‘mtdl 2097.2
| ṣṣ m[l]k ‘šrm. | ṣṣ abš[-] mit [‘š]r kbd. | ṣṣ ydrd ‘šrm. | ṣṣ bn aglby ṯlṯ[m]. | ṣṣ bn.šrš‘m.[---]. | ṣṣ mlkn‘m.a[rb‘m]. | ṣṣ 2097.13
| [-----]. | [-----]. | [ṣṣ].b[n].ṣd[-.---]. | [ṣṣ].bn.npr.ḫmšm. | ṣṣ.bn.adldn.ṯlṯm. | ṣṣ.bn.‘glt.ṯlṯm. | ṣṣ.bn.‘bd.‘šrm. | ṣṣ.bn.mṣḥ 2096.16
m. | ṣṣ tmn.ḫmšm. | [ṣṣ] ‘mtdl ṯlṯm. | ṣṣ ‘mlbi ṯṯ l ‘šrm. | ṣṣ bn adty ḫmšm. | ṣṣ amtrn arb‘m. | ṣṣ iytlm mit ṯlṯm kbd. | ṣ 2097.7
bn.tlmyn.‘šrm. | ṣṣ.bn.krwn.‘š[rm]. | ṣṣ.bn.iršyn.[---]. | [ṣṣ].bn.ilb‘l.ṯl[ṯ]m. | ṣṣ.bn.pṭdn.[--]m. | ṣṣ.[bn].gyn.[---]. | [-----]. 2096.6
ṣṣ.bn.ilyn.ṯlṯm. | ṣṣ.bn.kzn.ṯlṯm. | ṣṣ.bn.tlmyn.‘šrm. | ṣṣ.bn.kr 2096.1
ṣ.bn.kzn.ṯlṯm. | ṣṣ.bn.tlmyn.‘šrm. | ṣṣ.bn.krwn.‘š[rm]. | ṣṣ.bn.iršyn.[---]. | [ṣṣ].bn.ilb‘l.ṯl[ṯ]m. | ṣṣ.bn.pṭdn.[--]m. | ṣṣ.[b 2096.5
ṣ.bn.iršyn.[---]. | [ṣṣ].bn.ilb‘l.ṯl[ṯ]m. | ṣṣ.bn.pṭdn.[--]m. | ṣṣ.[bn].gyn.[---]. | [-----]. | [-----]. | [-----]. | [-----]. | [-----]. | [ṣṣ].b[2096.8
ṣṣ.bn.ilyn.ṯlṯm. | ṣṣ.bn.kzn.ṯlṯm. | ṣṣ.bn.tlmyn.‘šrm. | ṣṣ.bn.krwn.‘š[rm]. | ṣṣ.bn. 2096.2
ṣṣ.bn.ilyn.ṯlṯm. | ṣṣ.bn.kzn.ṯlṯm. | ṣṣ.bn.tlmyn.‘šrm. | ṣṣ.bn.krwn.‘š[rm]. | ṣṣ.bn.iršyn.[---]. | [ṣṣ].bn.ilb‘l.ṯl[ṯ]m. | ṣṣ.b 2096.4
m. | ṣṣ.bn.adldn.ṯlṯm. | ṣṣ.bn.‘glt.ṯlṯm. | ṣṣ.bn.‘bd.‘šrm. | ṣṣ.bn.mṣḥ[n].‘šrm. | šb‘.mat.ṯṯm kbd. 2096.19
----]. | [-----]. | [-----]. | [-----]. | [-----]. | [ṣṣ].b[n].ṣd[-.---]. | [ṣṣ].bn.npr.ḫmšm. | ṣṣ.bn.adldn.ṯlṯm. | ṣṣ.bn.‘glt.ṯlṯm. | ṣṣ.bn.‘b 2096.15
[ṣṣ].bn.npr.ḫmšm. | ṣṣ.bn.adldn.ṯlṯm. | ṣṣ.bn.‘glt.ṯlṯm. | ṣṣ.bn.‘bd.‘šrm. | ṣṣ.bn.mṣḥ[n].‘šrm. | šb‘.mat.ṯṯm kbd. 2096.18
].b[n].ṣd[-.---]. | [ṣṣ].bn.npr.ḫmšm. | ṣṣ.bn.adldn.ṯlṯm. | ṣṣ.bn.‘glt.ṯlṯm. | ṣṣ.bn.‘bd.‘šrm. | ṣṣ.bn.mṣḥ[n].‘šrm. | šb‘.mat.ṯ 2096.17
bn.krwn.‘š[rm]. | ṣṣ.bn.iršyn.[---]. | [ṣṣ].bn.ilb‘l.ṯl[ṯ]m. | ṣṣ.bn.pṭdn.[--]m. | ṣṣ.[bn].gyn.[---]. | [-----]. | [-----]. | [-----]. | [-- 2096.7
ṣ.[bn].gyn.[---]. | [-----]. | [-----]. | [-----]. | [-----]. | [-----]. | [ṣṣ].b[n].ṣd[-.---]. | [ṣṣ].bn.npr.ḫmšm. | ṣṣ.bn.adldn.ṯlṯm. | ṣṣ.bn 2096.14
‘m]. | ṣṣ mlk mit[.---]. | ṣṣ igy.ḫmšm. | ṣṣ yrpi m[it.---]. | ṣṣ bn.š[m]mn ‘[šr.---]. | alp.ṯṯm. | kbd.mlḥt. 2097.19
bš[-] mit [‘š]r kbd. | ṣṣ ydrd ‘šrm. | ṣṣ bn aglby ṯlṯ[m]. | ṣṣ bn.šrš‘m.[---]. | ṣṣ mlkn‘m.a[rb‘m]. | ṣṣ mlk mit[.---]. | ṣṣ ig 2097.14
ṣṣ.bn.ilyn.ṯlṯm. | ṣṣ.bn.kzn.ṯlṯm. | ṣṣ.bn.tlmyn.‘šrm. | ṣṣ.bn.krwn.‘š[rm]. | ṣṣ.bn.iršyn.[---]. | [ṣṣ]. 2096.3
mit ṯlṯm kbd. | ṣṣ m[l]k ‘šrm. | ṣṣ abš[-] mit [‘š]r kbd. | ṣṣ ydrd ‘šrm. | ṣṣ bn aglby ṯlṯ[m]. | ṣṣ bn.šrš‘m.[---]. | ṣṣ mlkn‘ 2097.12
. | ṣṣ mlkn‘m.a[rb‘m]. | ṣṣ mlk mit[.---]. | ṣṣ igy.ḫmšm. | ṣṣ yrpi m[it.---]. | ṣṣ bn.š[m]mn ‘[šr.---]. | alp.ṯṯm. | kbd.mlḥt. 2097.18
n aglby ṯlṯ[m]. | ṣṣ bn.šrš‘m.[---]. | ṣṣ mlkn‘m.a[rb‘m]. | ṣṣ mlk mit[.---]. | ṣṣ igy.ḫmšm. | ṣṣ yrpi m[it.---]. | ṣṣ bn.š[m] 2097.16
adty ḫmšm. | ṣṣ amtrn arb‘m. | ṣṣ iytlm mit ṯlṯm kbd. | ṣṣ m[l]k ‘šrm. | ṣṣ abš[-] mit [‘š]r kbd. | ṣṣ ydrd ‘šrm. | ṣṣ bn a 2097.10
. | ṣṣ ydrd ‘šrm. | ṣṣ bn aglby ṯlṯ[m]. | ṣṣ bn.šrš‘m.[---]. | ṣṣ mlkn‘m.a[rb‘m]. | ṣṣ mlk mit[.---]. | ṣṣ igy.ḫmšm. | ṣṣ yrpi 2097.15
ṣṣ mr‘m ḫmšm ḫmš kbd. | ṣṣ ubn ḫmš ‘šr h. | ṣṣ ‘myd ḫmšm. 2097.1
ṣṣ mr‘m ḫmšm ḫmš kbd. | ṣṣ ubn ḫmš ‘šr h. | ṣṣ ‘myd ḫmšm. | ṣṣ tmn.ḫmšm. | [ṣṣ] ‘mtdl ṯlṯm. | ṣṣ ‘mlbi ṯṯ l 2097.3
šr h. | ṣṣ ‘myd ḫmšm. | ṣṣ tmn.ḫmšm. | [ṣṣ] ‘mtdl ṯlṯm. | ṣṣ ‘mlbi ṯṯ l ‘šrm. | ṣṣ bn adty ḫmšm. | ṣṣ amtrn arb‘m. | ṣṣ iytl 2097.6
d. | ṣṣ ubn ḫmš ‘šr h. | ṣṣ ‘myd ḫmšm. | ṣṣ tmn.ḫmšm. | [ṣṣ] ‘mtdl ṯlṯm. | ṣṣ ‘mlbi ṯṯ l ‘šrm. | ṣṣ bn adty ḫmšm. | ṣṣ amtr 2097.5
ḫmšm ḫmš kbd. | ṣṣ ubn ḫmš ‘šr h. | ṣṣ ‘myd ḫmšm. | ṣṣ tmn.ḫmšm. | [ṣṣ] ‘mtdl ṯlṯm. | ṣṣ ‘mlbi ṯṯ l ‘šrm. | ṣṣ bn adty 2097.4

ṣṣb

n lzn. | bn.ṯyn. | bn g‘r. | bn.prtn. | bn ḫnn. | b[n.-]n. | bn.ṣṣb. | bn.b‘ltn ḫlq. | bn.mlkbn. | bn.asyy ḫlq. | bn.kṯly. | bn.kyn. 2016.2.1

ṣṣn

dt.b‘ln.yp‘mlk. | tǵrm.mnḥm.klyn.‘dršp.ǵlmn. | [a]bǵl.ṣṣn.ǵrn. | šib.mqdšt.‘b[dml]k.ṯtpḥ.mrṭn. | ḫdǵlm.i[---]n.pbn.n 2011.14

ṣq

.ṭa[t]. | l imr h.km.lb.‘n[t]. | aṯr.b‘l.tiḫd.m[t]. | b sin.lpš.tšṣq[n h]. | b qṣ.all.tšu.g h.w[tṣ] | ḥ.at.mt.tn.aḫ y. | w ‘n.bn.il 6[49].2.10
tt[.---]. | [---.--]p.km.dlt.tlk.km.p[---]. | [---.]bt.tḥbṭ.km.ṣq.ṣdr[.---]. | [---.]kl.b kl.l pgm.pgm.l.b[---]. | [---.]mdbm.l ḥr 1001.1.25

ṣqn

bn.atyn. | bn.ttn. | bn.rwy. | bn.‘myn. | bdl.mrynm. | bn.ṣqn. | bn.šyn. | bn.prtn. | bn.ypr. | mrum. | bn.‘[--]t. | bn.adty. | b 113[400].3.7
m.bnš.yd. | titṯm[n].w.‘l.[---]. | [-]rym.t[i]ṯtmn. | šnl.bn.ṣ[q]n.š[--]. | yitṯm.w.b[--]. | yšlm. | [‘]šrm.ks[p].yš[lm]. | [il]tḥ 2104.4

ṣqrn

lk.[w.]b.ym.ḥdṯ.ṯn.šm. | l.[---]t. | i[d.yd]bḥ.mlk.l.prgl.ṣqrn.b.gg. | ar[b‘.]arb‘.mṯbt.azmr.b h.š.šr[-]. | al[p.w].š.šlmm. 35[3].50

ṣr

l.mlk.ugrt. | aḫ y.rgm. | tḥm.mlk.ṣr.aḫ k. | y[š]lm.l k.ilm. | tǵr k.tšlm k. | hn ny.ʻm n. | šlm.ṯm n 2059.3
[rkbt]. | b trbṣ.[bn.amt]. | q[ḥ.kr]t[.šlmm]. | š[lmm.]al.t[ṣr]. | udm[.r]bt.w u[dm]. | [ṯ]rrt.udm.y[t]n[t]. | il.ušn.ab[.ad] 14[KRT].6.275
.krt.šlmm. | šlmm.w ng.mlk. | l bt y.rḥq.krt. | l ḥẓr y.al.tṣr. | udm.rbt.w udm ṯrrt. | udm.ytnt.il w ušn. | ab.adm.w ṯtb. 14[KRT].3.133
m.mrkbt]. | b[trbṣ.bn.amt]. | [qḥ.krt.šlmm]. | [šlmm.al.tṣr]. | [udm.rbt.w udm]. | [ṯrrt.udm.ytnt]. | [il.w ušn.ab.adm]. 14[KRT].5.256
| a[ṯrt.]ṣrm.w l ilt. | ṣd[yn]m.ṯm. | yd[r.k]rt.ṯʻ. | i.iṯt.aṯrt.ṣrm. | w ilt.ṣdynm. | hm.ḥry.bt y. | iqḥ.ašʻrb.ǵlmt. | ḥẓr y.ṯn h. 14[KRT].4.201
kn. | ym.w ṯn.aḫr. | šp[š]m.b [t]lṯ. | ym[ǵy.]l qdš. | a[ṯrt.]ṣrm.w l ilt. | ṣd[yn]m.ṯm. | yd[r.k]rt.ṯʻ. | i.iṯt.aṯrt.ṣrm. | w ilt.ṣd 14[KRT].4.198
nm[.š]lm. | rgm.ṯṯ[b]. | any kn.dt. | likt.mṣrm. | hn dt.b.ṣr. | mtt.by. | gšm.adr. | nškḥ.w. | rb.tmtt. | lqḥ.kl.ḏrʻ. | b d a[-] 2059.12
[šbʻ] d.šbʻ [d]. | [mr]ḥqtm. | qlt. | ʻbd k.b. | lwsnd. | [w] b ṣr. | ʻm.mlk. | w.ht. | mlk.syr. | ns.w.ṯm. | ydbḥ. | mlǵ[.---]. | w.m 2063.11
kbd. | b d.tt.w.ṯlṯ.ktnt.b dm.tt. | w.ṯmnt.ksp.hn. | ktn.d.ṣr.pḥm.b h.w.ṯqlm. | ksp h.mitm.pḥm.b d.skn. | w.ṯt.ktnm.ḫ 1110.4

ṣrṯn

bn.ṣrṯn. | bn.ʻbd. | snb.w.nḥl h. | [-]by.w.nḥl h. | [--]ilt.w.nḥl h. | [- 1063.1

ṣry

spr.npš.d. | ʻrb.bt.mlk. | w.b.spr.l.št. | yrmʻl. | ṣry. | iršy. | yʻḏrd. | ayaḫ. | bn.aylt. | ḫmš.mat.arbʻm. | kbd.ksp. 2106.5
n. | [ʻb]dmlk. | [---]yn. | bn.ṯ[--]. | bn.idrm. | bn.ymn. | bn.ṣry. | bn.mztn. | bn.šlgyn. | bn.[-]gštn. | bn[.n]klb. | b[n.]dtn. | w 113[400].2.4

ṣrym

.b.gt.irbṣ. | [--]šmyn. | [w.]nḥl h. | bn.qṣn. | bn.ksln. | bn.ṣrym. | bn.ṯmq. | bn.ntp. | bn.mlk. | bn.ṯʻ[-]. | bn.km[-]. | bn.r[--] 1073.1.7

ṣrp

--]. | [---.]plnt.[---]. | [---.]ʻmt.l ql.rpi[.---]. | [---.-]llm.abl.mṣrp k.[---]. | [---.]y.mṭnt.w tḥ.ṭbt.n[--]. | [---.b]ṯnm w ṯṯb.ʻl.b 1001.2.3
iqni.mit.pṯtm. | [---].mitm.kslm. | [---].pwt.ṯlṯ.mat.abn.ṣrp. | [---.-]qt.l.ṯrmnm. | [---].ṯlṯm.iqnu. | [---.l.]ṯrmn.mlk. | [---. 1106.10
]. | [---.p]ṯtm.l.ip[--.---]. | [---.]ksl.ṯlṯ.m[at.---]. | [---].abn.ṣr[p.---]. | [---.-]rt.ṯlṯm[.---]. | [--]l.ṯrmn.m[lk.---]. | [---.--]rt.šʻrt 1106.27
wt. | ṯmn.mat.pṯtm. | kkrm.alpm. | ḫmš.mat.kbd. | abn.ṣrp. 2051.10
ṭm. | kkr[.-].ḫt. | mitm[.p]ṯtm. | ṯlṯm[.---].kst. | alp.a[bn.ṣ]rp. 1114.6

ṣrptn

.qšt. | bn.srn.qšt. | bn.gdrn.qšt. | prpr.qšt. | ugry.qšt. | bn.ṣrptn.qšt. | bn.mṣry.qšt. | arny. | abm.qšt. | ḥdtn.qlʻ. | ytpt.qšt. | 119[321].1.46

ṣrr

ḫšt k.ap.ab.k mtm. | tmtn.u ḫšt k.l ntn. | ʻtq.b d.aṯt.ab.ṣrry. | ik m.yrgm.bn.il. | krt.špḥ.lṭpn. | w qdš.u ilm.tmtn. | špḥ 16.1[125].19
št k. | ap.ab.k mtm.tmtn. | u ḫšt k.l bky.ʻtq. | b d.aṯt ab.ṣrry. | u ilm.tmtn.špḥ. | [l]ṭpn.l yḥ.t[b]ky k. | ab.ǵr.bʻl.ṣ[p]n.ḥl 16.2[125].104
št k.ap.ab.ik mtm. | tmtn.u ḫšt k.l ntn. | ʻtq.b d.aṯt.ab ṣrry. | tbky k.ab.ǵr.bʻl. | ṣpn.ḥlm.qdš. | any.ḥlm.adr.ḥl. | rḥb. 16.1[125].5
t.b | ḥm.un.yr.ʻrpt. | tmṭr.b qẓ.ṭl.yṭll. | l ǵnbm.šbʻ.šnt. | yṣr k.bʻl.ṯmn.rkb. | ʻrpt.bl.ṭl.bl rbb. | bl.šrʻ.thmtm.bl. | ṭbn.ql. 19[1AQHT].1.43
l.bʻl.ṯnt.l rkb.ʻrpt.ht.ib k. | bʻl m.ht.ib k.tmḫṣ.ht.tṣmt.ṣrt k. | tqḥ.mlk.ʻlm k.drkt.dt dr dr k. | kṯr ṣmdm.ynḥt.w ypʻr 2.4[68].9
ẓr h.tšu. | g h.w tṣḥ.ik.mǵy.gpn.w ugr. | mn.ib.ypʻ.l bʻl.ṣrt. | l rkb.ʻrpt.l mḫšt.mdd. | il ym.l klt.nhr.il.rbm. | l ištbm.tn 3[ʻNT].3.34
ypʻ.l bʻl.ṣrt.l rkb.ʻrpt. | [-]ʻn.ǵlmm.yʻnyn.l ib.ypʻ. | l bʻl.ṣrt.l rkb.ʻrpt. | tḥm.aliyn.bʻl.hwt.aliy. | qrdm.qry.b arṣ.mlḥm 3[ʻNT].4.50
rš h.l ksi.mlk h. | l nḫt.l kḥṯ.drkt h. | mn m.ib.ypʻ.l bʻl.ṣrt.l rkb.ʻrpt. | [-]ʻn.ǵlmm.yʻnyn.l ib.ypʻ. | l bʻl.ṣrt.l rkb.ʻrpt. | 3[ʻNT].4.48
.k m[rṣ]. | arbʻ.k dw.k[rt]. | mndʻ.krt.mǵ[y.---]. | w qbr.tṣr.q[br]. | tṣr.trm.tnq[--]. | km.nkyt.ṯǵr[.---]. | km.škllt.[---]. | ʻ 16.2[125].87
l bl.sk.w [---] h. | ybm h.šbʻ[.---]. | ǵzr.ilḥu.t[---]l. | trm.tṣr.trm[.ʻ]tqt. | tbky.w tšnn.[tt]n. | g h.bky.b ḥ[y k.a]b n. | nš 16.2[125].96
arbʻ.k dw.k[rt]. | mndʻ.krt.mǵ[y.---]. | w qbr.tṣr.q[br]. | tṣr.trm.tnq[--]. | km.nkyt.ṯǵr[.---]. | km.škllt.[---]. | ʻr.ym.l bl[. 16.2[125].88

ṣrrt

lk.ʻšr. | ʻšrt.qḥ.tp k.b yd. | [-]r[-]k.bm.ymn. | tlk.škn.ʻl.ṣrrt. | adn k.šqrb.[---]. | b mgn k.w ḫrṣ.l kl. | apnk.ǵzr.ilḥu. | [16.1[125].43
.hk[l m]. | ḫš.bht m.tbn[n]. | ḫš.trmmn.hk[l m]. | b tk.ṣrrt.ṣpn. | alp.šd.aḫd bt. | rbt.kmn.hkl. | w yʻn.kṯr.w ḫss. | šmʻ. 4[51].5.117
| qm.ybd.w yšr. | mṣltm.bd.nʻm. | yšr.ǵzr.ṭb.ql. | ʻl.bʻl.b ṣrrt. | ṣpn.ytmr.bʻl. | bnt h.yʻn.pdry. | bt.ar.apn.ṭly. | [bt.r]b.pd 3[ʻNT].1.21
.nrt.ilm.špš. | tšu.aliyn.bʻl.l ktp. | ʻnt.k tšt h.tšʻlyn h. | b ṣrrt.ṣpn.tbkyn h. | w tqbrn h.tštnn.b ḫrt. | ilm.arṣ.ṯṭbḫ.šbʻm. 6[62].1.16
yn. | hdm.riš h.l ymǵy. | aps h.w yʻn.ʻṯtr.ʻrẓ. | l amlk.b ṣrrt.ṣpn. | yrd.ʻṯtr.ʻrẓ.yrd. | l kḥṯ.aliyn.bʻl. | w ymlk.b arṣ.il.kl 6.1.62[49.1.34]
. | blt.nmlk.ʻṯtr.ʻrẓ. | ymlk.ʻṯtr.ʻrẓ. | apnk.ʻṯtr.ʻrẓ. | yʻl.b ṣrrt.ṣpn. | yṯb.l kḥṯ.aliyn. | bʻl.pʻn h.l tmǵyn. | hdm.riš h.l ym 6.1.57[49.1.29]
.aḫ y m.ytn.bʻl. | [s]pu y.bn m.um y.kly y. | yṯb.ʻm.bʻl.ṣrrt. | ṣpn.yšu g h.w yṣḥ. | aḫ y m.ytnt.bʻl. | spu y.bn m.um y. 6[49].6.12

ṣt

.uzr. | [ilm].dnil.uzr.ilm.ylḥm. | [uzr.]yšqy.bn qdš.yd.ṣt h. | [dn]il.yd.ṣt h.yʻl.w yškb. | [yd.]mizrt.p yln.mk.b šbʻ.y 17[2AQHT].1.14
il.uzr.ilm.ylḥm. | [uzr.]yšqy.bn qdš.yd.ṣt h. | [dn]il.yd.ṣt h.yʻl.w yškb. | [yd.]mizrt.p yln.mk.b šbʻ.ymm. | [w]yqrb.b 17[2AQHT].1.15
]. | [mt.hrnmy.]uzr.ilm.ylḥm. | [uzr.yšqy.]bn.qdš.yd. | [ṣt h.yʻl.]w yškb.yd. | [mizrt.]p ynl.hn.ym. | [w ṯn.uzr.]ilm.dni 17[2AQHT].1.5

ṣtqn

b gt ilštmʻ. | bt ubnyn š h d.ytn.ṣtqn. | ṯut ṭbḫ ṣtq[n]. | b bz ʻzm ṭbḫ š[h]. | b kl ygz ḥḫ š h. 1153.3
lqḥ ṣtqn gt bn ndr. | um r[-] gtn ṯṯ ḫsn l ytn. | l rḥt lqḥ ṣtqn. | bt qbṣ urt ilštmʻ dbḥ ṣtqn l. | ršp. 1154.6
n ṯṯ. | [---.]ṯḥr l ytn ḫs[n]. | ʻbd ulm ṯn un ḫsn. | gdy lqḥ ṣtqn gt bn ndr. | um r[-] gtn ṯṯ ḫsn l ytn. | l rḥt lqḥ ṣtqn. | bt q 1154.4
gtn ṯṯ ḫsn l ytn. | l rḥt lqḥ ṣtqn. | bt qbṣ urt ilštmʻ dbḥ ṣtqn l. | ršp. 1154.7
b gt ilštmʻ. | bt ubnyn š h d.ytn.ṣtqn. | ṯut ṭbḫ ṣtq[n]. | b bz ʻzm ṭbḫ š[h]. | b kl ygz ḥḫ š h. 1153.2

q

qbat

--.]d[--.---].|[---].hn[.---].|[---.]šn[.---].|[---].pit.|[---.]qbat.|[---.]inšt.|[--]u.l tštql.|[---].ṯry.ap.l tlḥm.|[l]ḥm.trmm 6.6[62.2].39

qbṭ

m.ks.ym|sk.nhr hm.|šb'.ydt y.b ṣ'.|[--.]šb'.rbt.|[---.]qbṭ.ṯm.|[---.]bn.ilm.|[m]t.šmḥ.p ydd.|il[.ǵ]zr.|b [-]dn.'.z.w UG5.4.13

qbl

dm.ẖrṣ.|kḥṯ.il.nẖt.|b ẓr.hdm.id.|d pršа.b br.|n'l.il.d qblbl.|'ln.ybl hm.ẖrṣ.|ṯlḥn.il.d mla.|mnm.dbbm.d |msdt.a 4[51].1.37

qb't

d y.qb't.b ymn y[.t]q|ḥ.pǵt.w tšqyn h.tq[ḥ.ks.]b d h.|qb't.b ymn h.w y'n.yṭ[p]n[.mh]r.|št.b yn.yšt.ila.il š[--.]il.|d 19[1AQHT].4.218
lm w y'n.yṭpn[.mhr].|št.qḥn.w tšqyn.yn.qḥ.|ks.b d y.qb't.b ymn y[.t]q|ḥ.pǵt.w tšqyn h.tq[ḥ.ks.]b d h.|qb't.b ym 19[1AQHT].4.216
kly.|lḥm.[b]'dn hm.kly.|yn.b ḥmt hm.k[l]y.|šmn.b q[b't hm.---].|bt.krt.t[--]. 16[126].3.16

qbṣ

gt bn ndr.|um r[-] gtn ṯṯ ẖsn l ytn.|l rḥt lqḥ ṣtqn.|bt qbṣ urt ilštm' dbḥ ṣtqn l.|ršp. 1154.7
[-----].|[---.mid.rm.]krt.|[b tk.rpi.]arṣ.|[b pẖr].qbṣ.dtn.|[w t]qrb.w ld.|bn.tl k.|tld.pǵt.t[--]t.|tld.pǵt[.---].| 15[128].3.4
.---].|tld.p[ǵt.---].|mid.rm[.krt].|b tk.rpi.ar[ṣ].|b pẖr.qbṣ.dtn.|ṣǵrt hn.abkrn.|tbrk.ilm.tity.|tity.ilm.l ahl hm.|dr 15[128].3.15

qbr

yṣḥ.knp.nšrm.|b'l.yṯbr.b'l.yṯbr.diy.|hmt.hm.t'pn.'l.qbr.bn y.|tšẖṭann.b šnt h.qr.[mym].|mlk.yṣm.y l km.qr.my 19[1AQHT].3.150
ibq['.kbd hm.w] |aḥd.hm.iṯ.šmt.hm.i[ṯ].|'ẓm.abky.w aqbrn h.|ašt.b ẖrt.ilm.arṣ.|b p h.rgm.l yṣa.b špt h.hwt[h].| 19[1AQHT].3.111
ḥt.p'n y.ibq'.|kbd h.w aḥd.hm.iṯ.šmt.iṯ.|'ẓm.abky w aqbrn h.aštn.|b ẖrt.ilm.arṣ.b p h.rgm.l[yṣ]a.|b špt h.hwt h 19[1AQHT].3.140
n.b'l.l ktp.|'nt.k tšt h.tš'lyn h.|b ṣrrt.ṣpn.tbkyn h.|w tqbrn h.tštnn.b ẖrt.|ilm.arṣ.ṯṯbẖ.šb'm.|rumm.k gmn.aliyn. 6[62].1.17
ṯ.šmt.iṯ.'ẓm.w yqḥ b hm.|aqht.ybl.l qẓ.ybky.w yqbr.|yqbr.nn.b mdgt.b knk[-].|w yšu.g h.w yṣḥ.knp.nšrm.|b'l.yṯ 19[1AQHT].3.147
rḥm.k m[rṣ].|arb'.k dw.k[rt].|mnd'.krt.mǵ[y.---].|w qbr.tṣr.q[br].|tṣr.trm.tnq[--].|km.nkyt.tǵr[.---].|km.škllt.[-- 16.2[125].87
m[rṣ].|arb'.k dw.k[rt].|mnd'.krt.mǵ[y.---].|w qbr.tṣr.q[br].|tṣr.trm.tnq[--].|km.nkyt.tǵr[.---].|km.škllt.[---].|'r.y 16.2[125].87
yḥd.|iṯ.šmt.iṯ.'ẓm.w yqḥ b hm.|aqht.ybl.l qẓ.ybky.w yqbr.|yqbr.nn.b mdgt.b knk[-].|w yšu.g h.w yṣḥ.knp.nšrm. 19[1AQHT].3.146
y.ibq'.kbd[h].|w aḥd.hm.iṯ.šmt.hm.iṯ[.'ẓm].|abky.w aqbrn.ašt.b ẖrt.|i[lm.arṣ.b p h.rgm.l yṣa.b šp]|t h.hwt h.kn 19[1AQHT].3.126

qbt

liyn.b'l.|iy.zbl.b'l.arṣ.|w t'n.nrt.ilm.š[p]š.|šd yn.'n.b qbt[.t]|bl lyt.'l.umt k.|w abqṯ.aliyn.b'l.|w t'n.btlt.'nt.|an.l 6[49].4.42

qd

].|yḥpn.ḥy[ly.zbl.mlk.'llm y].|šm'.atm[.---].|ym.lm.qd[.---].|šmn.prst[.---].|ydr.hm.ym[.---].|'l amr.yu[ẖd.ksa. 22.1[123].14

qdm

.ydy.ḥmt.|b ḥrn.pnm.trǵnw.w ṯṯkl.|bnwt h.ykr.'r.d qdm.|idk.pnm.l ytn.tk aršẖ.rbt.|w aršẖ.ṯrrt.ydy.b 'ṣm.'r'r. UG5.7.62
.aẖt h.b'l.y'n.tdrq.|ybnt.ab h.šrḥq.aṯt.l pnn h.|št.alp.qdm h.mria.w tk.|pn h.tḥspn.m h.w trḥṣ.|ṭl.šmm.šmn.arṣ.ṭ 3['NT].4.85
ṭb l mspr..k tlakn.|ǵlmm.|aẖr.mǵy.kṯr.w ẖss.|št.alp.qdm h.mra.|w tk.pn h.t'db.ksu.|w yṯṯb.l ymn.aliyn.|b'l.'d. 4[51].5.107
r.rbt.|ẖbr.ṯrrt.|bt.krt.tbun.|lm.mṯb[.---].|w lḥm mr.tqdm.|yd.b ṣ'.tšlḥ.|ḥrb.b bšr.tštn.|[w t]'n.mṯt.ḥry.|[l lḥ]m. 15[128].4.23
[.---].|[---.ẖ]br[.---].|bẖr[.--]t[.----].|l mṯb[.--]t[.---].|[tqdm.]yd.b ṣ'.t[šl]ḥ.|[ḥrb.b]bš[r].tštn.|[w t'n].mṯt.ḥry.|[l l 15[128].5.7
y'n.aliyn.|b'l.ib.hdt.lm.tḥš.|lm.tḥš.ntq.dmrn.|'n.b'l.qdm.yd h.|k tǵd̲.arz.b ymn h.|bkm.yṯb.b'l.l bht h.|u mlk.u 4[51].7.40
t h.|ql h.q[dš.ṭb]r.arṣ.|[---.]ǵrm[.t]ẖšn.|rḥq[.---.td'].|qdm ym.bmt.[nhr].|tṭṭn.ib.b'l.tiḥd.|y'rm.šnu.hd.gpt.|ǵr.w 4[51].7.34
--.]nb hm.|[---.-]kn.|[---.]hr n.km.šḥr.|[---.y]lt n.km.qdm.|[-.k]bd n.il.ab n.|kbd k iš.tikln.|ṯd n.km.mrm.tqrṣn. 12[75].1.8
d.l p.akl ṯm.dl.|[---.q]l.bl.tbḥ[n.l]azd.'r.qdm.|[---].'ẓ q[dm.--.šp]š.|[---.šm]n.mšḥt.kṯpm.a[-]ṯ[-].|[---.--]ḥ b ym.tld UG5.8.22
t.l p[.n]ṯk.abd.l p.akl ṯm.dl.|[---.q]l.bl.tbḥ[n.l]azd.'r.qdm.|[---].'ẓ q[dm.--.šp]š.|[---.šm]n.mšḥt.kṯpm.a[-]ṯ[-].|[--- UG5.8.21

qdmn

.snry.|dqn.šlmn.|prdn.ndb[--].|[-]rn.ẖbty.|abmn.bn.qdmn.|n'mn.bn.'bdilm. 87[64].40
lyn.qšt.w.ql'.|šmrm.ql'.|ubr'y.|abmn.qšt.w.ṯn.ql'm.|qdmn.ṯṯ.qštm.w.ṯlṯ.ql'm.|bn.ṣdqil.ṯṯ.qštm.w.ṯn.ql'm.|bn.ṯlṯ 119[321].3.3
bn[.---].|ubr['ym.---].|qdm[n.---].|b'l[--.---].|šm[---.---].|yšr[-.---].|bn.gnb[-.---].|h 93[328].3

qdqd

qnim.[--].|[---.]aliyn.b'l.|[---.--]k.mdd il.|y[m.---.]l ṯr.qdqd h.|il[.--.]rḥq.b ǵr.|km.y[--.]ilm.b ṣpn.|'dr.l['r].'rm.|ṯ 4[51].7.4
.yrẖ].|ik.al.yḥdṯ.yrẖ.b[---].|b qrn.ymn h.b anšt[.---].|qdqd h.w y'n.yṭpn.[mhr.št].|šm'.l btlt.'nt.at.'[l.qšt h].|tmẖṣ 18[3AQHT].4.11
dm[.w] l.hdm.yṯb.|l arṣ.yṣq.'mr.|un.l riš h.'pr.plṯt.|l qdqd h.lpš.yks.|mizrtm.ǵr.b abn.|ydy.psltm.b y'r.|yhdy.lḥ 5[67].6.16
yql.l arṣ.w trtqṣ.ṣmd.b d b'l.|[km.]nšr.b uṣb't h.ylm.qdqd.zbl.|[ym.]bn.'nm.ṯpṭ.nhr.yprsḥ.ym.yql.|l arṣ.tnǵṣn.p 2.4[68].24
h.nhr l kḥṯ.drkt h.trtqṣ.|b d b'l.km.nšr b uṣb't h.hlm.qdq|d zbl ym.bn.'nm.ṯpṭ.nhr.yprsḥ ym.|w yql.l arṣ.w trtqṣ 2.4[68].21
yt.mh.yqḥ.|mh.yqḥ.mt.aṯryt.spsg.ysk.|[l]riš.ḥrṣ.l ẓr.qdqd y.|[--.]mt.kl.amt.w an.mtm.amt.|[ap.m]ṯn.rgmm.arg 17[2AQHT].6.37
|[kl k.al.]aḥd hm.[---].|[---.b]gdlt.ar[kt y.am--].|[---.qdq]d k.ašhlk[.šbt k.dmm].|[šbt.dq]n k.mm'm.w[---].|aqht 18[3AQHT].1.11
].|al.aḥd.hm.b y[--] y.[---]b[-].|b gdlt.arkt y.am[---].|qdqd k.ašhlk.šbt[k.dmm].|[šbt.dqn k.mm'm.]y'ny.|il.b šb' 3['NT.VI].5.32
y'ny.krt ṯ'.yṯbr.|ḥrn.y bn.yṯbr.ḥrn.|riš k.'ṯtrt.šm.b'l.|qdqd k.tqln.b gbl.|šnt k.b ḥpn k.w t'n.|spr ilmlk ṯ'y. 16.6[127].57

qdqd

.|ṯpṭ.nhr.yṯb[r.ḥrn.y ym.yṯbr.ḥrn].|riš k.ʿṯtrt.[šm.bʿl.qdqd k.---].|[--]t.mṭ.tpln.b g[bl.šnt k.---].|[--]šnm.aṯtm.t[--.- 2.1[137].8
.d]|iym.bn.nšrm.arḫp.an[k.ʿ]l.|aqht.ʿdb k.hlmn.ṯnm.qdqd.|ṯlṯ id.ʿl.udn.špk.km.šiy.|dm.km.šḫṭ.l brk h.tṣi.km.|r 18[3AQHT].4.22
iy[m.bn].|nšrm.trḫp.ʿnt.ʿl[.aqht].|tʿdbn h.hlmn.ṯnm[.qdqd].|ṯlṯ id.ʿl.udn.š[pk.km].|šiy.dm h.km.šḫ[ṭ.l brk h].|yṣ 18[3AQHT].4.33
.]hlk.ǵlmm b dd y.yṣ[--].|[-.]yṣa.w l.yṣa.hlm.[ṯnm].|[q]dqd.ṯlṯ id.ʿl.ud[n].|[---.-]sr.pdm.riš h[m.---].|ʿl.pd.asr.[---. 19[1AQHT].2.79

qdš

q.qdš.w amrr.|yštn.aṯrt.l bmt.ʿr.|l ysmsmt.bmt.pḫl.|qdš.yuḫdm.šbʿr.|amrr.k kbkb.l pnm.|aṯr.btlt.ʿnt.|w bʿl.tbʿ. 4[51].4.16
.|[-----].|[-----].|[-----].|[-----].|[ḫl]bkrd.|[ḫl]bʿprm.|[q]dš.|[a]mdy.|[gn]ʿy.|mʿqb.|agm.|ḫpty.|ypr.|ḫrṣbʿ.|uḫnp 2058.1.28
]r.gbl.ʿbr.|qʿl.ʿbr.iht.|np šmm.šmšr.|l dgy.aṯrt.|mǵ.l qdš.amrr.|idk.al.tnn.|pnm.tk.ḥqkpt.|il.kl h.kptr.|ksu.ṯbt h 3[ʿNT.VI].6.11
.tmtn.špḥ.|[l]ṭpn.l yḥ.t[b]ky k.|ab.ǵr.bʿl.ṣ[p]n.ḥlm.|qdš.nny.ḥ[l]m.adr.|ḥl.rḥb.mk[npt].|ap.krt bn[m.il].|špḥ.lṭ 16.2[125].108
k.l ntn.|ʿtq.b d.aṯt.ab ṣrry.|tbky k.ab.ǵr.bʿl.|ṣpn.ḥlm.qdš.|any.ḥlm.adr.ḥl.|rḥb.mknpt.ap.|[k]rt.bnm.il.špḥ.|lṭpn 16.1[125].7
t.|mdbr.tlkn.|ym.w ṯn.aḫr.|šp[š]m.b [ṯ]lṯ.|ym[ǵy.]l qdš.|a[ṯrt.]ṣrm.w l ilt.|ṣd[yn]m.ṯm.|yd[r.k]rt.ṯʿ.|i.iṯt.aṯrt.ṣr 14[KRT].4.197
ḫlmṭ.|l bbt il bt.|š l ḫlmṭ.|w tr l qlḥ.|w š ḥll ydm.|b qdš il bt.|w tlḥm aṯt.|š l ilbt.šlmm.|kll ylḥm b h.|w l bbt š UG5.7.TR3
[---].ybšr.qdš[.---].|[---.--]t btm.qdš.il[.---].|[---.b]n.qdš.k[--.---].|[---.]ʿsb.[-]ḥ[-.---].|[---.]b[-. 2125.2
ʿtq.b d.aṯt.ab.ṣrry.|ik m.yrgm.bn.il.|krt.špḥ.lṭpn.|w qdš.u ilm.tmtn.|špḥ.lṭpn.l yḥ.|w yʿny.krt.ṯʿ.|bn.al.tbkn.al. 16.1[125].22
tbn.|hmlt.arṣ.at m.w ank.|ibǵy h.b tk.ǵr y.il.ṣpn.|b qdš.b ǵr.nḥlt y.|b nʿm.b gbʿ.tliyt.|hlm.ʿnt.tph.ilm.b h.pʿnm 3[ʿNT].3.27
d l t[dʿ.šmm.at m.w ank].|ibǵ[y h.b tk.ǵ]r y.il.ṣpn.|b q[dš.b ǵr.nḥ]lt y.|w t[ʿn].btlt.[ʿ]nt.ṯṯb.|[ybmt.]limm.[a]n.aq 3[ʿNT].4.64
m.adr.|ḥl.rḥb.mk[npt].|ap.krt bn[m.il].|špḥ.lṭpn[.w qdš].|bkm.tʿr[b.ʿl.ab h].|tʿrb.ḥ[--].|b ṯtm.t[---].|šknt.[---].| 16.2[125].111
ht m.urbt.|b qrb.hk[l m.yp]tḥ.|bʿl.b dqt[.ʿrp]t.|ql h.qdš.b[ʿl.y]tn.|yṯny.bʿl.ṣ[---.-]pt h.|ql h.q[dš.ṯb]r.arṣ.|[---.]ǵr 4[51].7.29
---].|bn.[---].|bn.yr[--].|bn.kṯr[t].|bn.šml.|bn.arnbt.|qdšm.|b[-.--]t.|[---.-]l[--].|[---.]pr[--].|[-.a]pln.|bn.mzt.|bn. 2163.2.8
š.ṯdṯ.ym.uzr.|[ilm].dnil.uzr.ilm.ylḥm.|[uzr.]yšqy.bn qdš.yd.ṣt h.|[dn]il.yd.ṣt h.yʿl.w yškb.|[yd.]mizrt.p yln.mk. 17[2AQHT].1.14
i.apn.ǵz[r].|[mt.hrnmy.]uzr.ilm.ylḥm.|[uzr.yšqy.]bn.qdš.yd.|[ṣt h.yʿl.]w yškb.yd.|[mizrt.]p ynl.hn.ym.|[w ṯn.uz 17[2AQHT].1.4
ṯr[.il.ab -.w tʿn.rbt].|aṯr[t.ym.šmʿ.l qdš].|w am[rr.l dgy.rbt].|aṯrt.ym[.mdl.ʿr].|ṣmd.pḥl[.št.gpn 4[51].4.2
nm.dt].|ksp.dt.yr[q.nqbnm].|ʿdb.gpn.atnt[y].|yšmʿ.qd.w amr[r].|mdl.ʿr.ṣmd.pḥl.|št.gpnm.dt.ksp.|dt.yrq.nqbn 4[51].4.8
t.gpnm.dt.ksp.|dt.yrq.nqbnm.|ʿdb.gpn.atnt h.|yḥbq.qdš.w amrr.|yštn.aṯrt.l bmt.ʿr.|l ysmsmt.bmt.pḥl.|qdš.yuḫ 4[51].4.13
lgb[-].|mrmnmn.|brrn aryn.|a[-]ḥn tlyn.|atdb w ʿr.|qdš w amrr.|ṯḥr w bd.|[k]ṯr ḫss šlm.|šlm il bt.|šlm il ḫš[t]. UG5.7.71
[--]pm.l mlkt.wn.in.aṯt.|[l]k.k[m.ilm].|[w ǵlmt.k bn.qdš.]w y[--.]zbl.ym.yʿ[--.]ṯpṭ.nhr.|[-------.]yšlḥn.w yʿn ʿṯtr[.- 2.3[129].23
wt.|w ykn.bn h b bt.šrš.b qrb.|hkl h.nṣb.skn.ilib h.b qdš.|ztr.ʿm h.l arṣ.mšṣu.qṭr h.|l ʿpr.ḏmr.aṯr h.ṭbq.lḥt.|niṣ 17[2AQHT].1.27
.w ykn.bn h.|[b bt.šrš.]b qrb.hkl h.|[nṣb.skn.i]lib h.b qdš.|[ztr.ʿm h.l a]rṣ.mšṣu.|[qṭr h.l ʿpr.ḏ]mr.a[ṯ]r h.|[ṭbq.lḥ 17[2AQHT].1.45
yld.bn.l y.km.|aḫ y.w šrš.km ary y.|nṣb.skn.ilib y.b qdš.|ztr.ʿm y.l ʿpr.ḏmr.aṯr[y].|ṭbq lḥt.niṣ y.grš.|d ʿšy.ln.aḫ 17[2AQHT].2.16
rbʿ ym.|[uzr.i]lm.dnil.uzr.|[ilm.y]lḥm.uzr.yšqy bn.|[qdš.ḫ]mš.ṯdṯ.ym.uzr.|[ilm].dnil.uzr.ilm.ylḥm.|[uzr.]yšqy.b 17[2AQHT].1.12
[---].ybšr.qdš[.---].|[---.--]t btm.qdš.il[.---].|[---.b]n.qdš.k[--.---].|[---.]ʿsb.[-]ḥ[-.---].|[---.]b[-.]mṯt k.[---].|[---.]k. 2125.3
aḫ h.w šrš.|km.ary h.uzrm.ilm.ylḥm.|uzrm.yšqy.bn.qdš.|l tbrknn l ṯr.il ab y.|tmrnn.l bny.bnwt.|w ykn.bn h b 17[2AQHT].1.23
-.---].|[l.a]rṣy.|[l.--]r[-.---].|[l.--]ḫl.|[l.--.]mgmr.|[l.-.]qdšt.|l.ʿṯtrt.ndrgd.|l.ʿṯtrt.abdr.|l.dml.|l.ilt[.-]pn.|l.uš[ḫr]y. 1001.1.12
b d h.|krpn.b klat.yd h.|b krb.ʿẓm.ridn.|mt.šmm.ks.qdš.|l tphn h.aṯt.krpn.|l tʿn.aṯrt.alp.|kd.yqḥ.b ḫmr.|rbt.y 3[ʿNT].1.13
nm].|l ytn.tk.ǵr.ll.ʿm.phr.mʿd.ap.ilm.l lḥ[m].|yṯb.bn qdš.l ṯrm.bʿl.qm.ʿl.il.hlm.|ilm.tph hm.tphn.mlak.ym.tʿdt.ṯp 2.1[137].21
.b y.ṯr.il.ab y.ank.in.bt[.l] y[.km.]ilm[.w] ḥẓr[.k bn].|[qd]š.lbum.trd.b n[p]šn y.trḥṣn.k ṯrm.|[--]b b[ht].|[zbl.]ym. 2.3[129].20
khnm.|qdšm.|mkrm.|mdm.|inšt.|ḥrš.bhtm. 75[81].2
bn il d[n].|[-]bd w [---].|[--].p il[.---].|[i]l mt mr[b-].|qdš mlk [---].|kbd d ilgb[-].|mrmnmn.|brrn aryn.|a[-]ḥn tl UG5.10.2.3
bn.dgn.a[s]r km.hw ybl.argmn k.k ilm.|[---.]ybl.k bn.qdš.mnḥy k.ap.anš.zbl.bʿ[l].|[-.yuḫ]d.b yd.mšḫṭ.bm.ymn.m 2.1[137].38
khnm.|qdšm.|m[ru.]škn.|mkrm. 76[82].2
qd[šm].|mru s[kn].|mru ib[rn].|mdm.|inšt.|nsk ksp.|yṣḥ 73[114].1
.|šrm.|yṣḥm.|ʿšrm.|mrum.|ṯnnm.|mqdm.|khnm.|qdšm.|nsk.ksp.|mkrm. 71[113].73
lk.|ṯǵrm.mnḥm.klyn.ʿdršp.ǵlmn.|[a]bǵl.ṣṣn.ǵrn.|šib.mqdšt.ʿb[dml]k.ṯṯpḥ.mrṯn.|ḫdǵlm.i[---]n.pbn.ndbn.sbd.|šr 2011.15
.ḥlm.adr.ḥl.|rḥb.mknpt.ap.|[k]rt.bnm.il.špḥ.|lṭpn.w qdš.ʿl.|ab h.yʿrb.ybky.|w yšnn.ytn.g h.|bky.b ḥy k.ab n.aš 16.1[125].11
mrynm.|mrum.|ʿšrm.|ṯnnm.|nqdm.|khnm.|qdšm.|pslm.|mkrm.|yṣḥm.|šrm.|nʿrm.|ʿbdm.|kzym.|ksd 1026.1.7
khnm.tšʿ.|bnšm.w.ḥmr.|qdšm.tšʿ.|bnšm.w.ḥmr. 77[63].3
qt[.ʿrp]t.|ql h.qdš.b[ʿl.y]tn.|yṯny.bʿl.ṣ[---.-]pt h.|ql h.q[dš.ṯb]r.arṣ.|[---.]ǵrm[.t]ḫšn.|rḥq[.---.tdʿ].|qdm ym.bmt.[4[51].7.31
.|[w ṯn.uzr.]ilm.dnil.|[uzr.ilm.]ylḥm.uzr.|[yšqy.b]n.qdš ṯlṯ rbʿ ym.|[uzr.i]lm.dnil.uzr.|[ilm.y]lḥm.uzr.yšqy bn.| 17[2AQHT].1.9
.b p hm.w l.tšbʿn y.aṯt.itrḫ.|y bn.ašld.šu.ʿdb.tk.mdbr qdš.|ṯm tgrgr.l abnm.w l.ʿṣm.šbʿ.šnt.|tmt.ṯmn.nqpt.ʿd.ilm. 23[52].65
[---.dmt q]dš.|[---.d]mt qdš.|[---].b.dmt qdš.|[---].b.dmt qdš.|[---.--]n.b.anan.|[--]yl 2118.2
[---.dmt q]dš.|[---.d]mt qdš.|[---].b.dmt qdš.|[---].b.dmt qdš.|[---.--]n.b.anan.|[--]yl.b.bqʿt.b.gt.tgyn. 2118.3
[---.dmt q]dš.|[---.d]mt qdš.|[---].b.dmt qdš.|[---].b.dmt qdš.|[---.--] 2118.1
.dmt q]dš.|[---.d]mt qdš.|[---].b.dmt qdš.|[---].b.dmt qdš.|[---.--]n.b.anan.|[--]yl.b.bqʿt.b.gt.tgyn.|[--]in.b.trzy.|[- 2118.4
[---.gd]ltm.p[--.---].|[---.]arbʿt[.---].|[---.]qdš[.---].|[---.k]su.p[--.---].|[---.]agn[.---].|[---.bʿlt.b]htm[.--- 45[45].3
[---].ybšr.qdš[.---].|[---.--]t btm.qdš.il[.---].|[---.b]n.qdš.k[--.---].|[---.]ʿ 2125.1

qdšt

bn[.---].|bn.qdšt.|bn.mʿnt.|bn.g[--]n.|bn[.---].|[-----].|b[n.---].|b[n.---]. 2163.1.2
|mru.skn.|bn.bddn.|bn.ǵrgn.|bn.tgtn.|bn.ḥrzn.|bn.qdšt.|bn.ntǵ[-].|bn.gr[--].|bn.[---].|bn.[---].|mr[u.ibrn].|bn 113[400].5.11

qwm

bʿl.ymšḥ.|bʿl.ymšḥ.hm.b ʿp.|nṭʿn.b arṣ.ib y.|w b ʿpr.qm.aḫ k.|w tšu.ʿn h.btlt.ʿnt.|w tšu.ʿn h.w tʿn.|w tʿn.arḫ.w t 10[76].2.25
mlak ym.tʿdt.ṯpṭ.nhr.l pʿn.il.|[l t]pl.l tštḥwy.pḫr.mʿd.qmm.a[--].amr.|[ṯn]y.dʿt hm.išt.ištm.yitmr.ḥrb.ltšt.|[--]n h 2.1[137].31

.pẖr.m'd.t[k.ǵr.ll.l p'n.il]. | al.tpl.al.tšthwy.pẖr [m'd.qmm.a--.am] | r ṯny.d't km.w rgm.l ṯr.a[b.-.il.ṯny.l pẖr]. | m' 2.1[137].15
pn. | l t'n.aṯrt.alp. | kd.yqḥ.b ḫmr. | rbt.ymsk.b msk h. | qm.ybd.w yšr. | mṣltm.bd.n'm. | yšr.ǵzr.ṭb.ql. | 'l.b'l.b ṣrrt. | ṣ 3['NT].1.18
hm.w tṣḥn]. | tḥ[m.pbl.mlk]. | qḥ[.ksp.w yrq]. | ḫrṣ.[yd.mqm h]. | w 'bd[.'lm.ṯlṯ]. | sswm.m[rkbt]. | b trbṣ.[bn.amt]. | q 14[KRT].6.270
ab.adm.w ṯṯb. | mlakm.l h.lm.ank. | ksp.w yrq.ḫrṣ. | yd.mqm h.w 'bd. | 'lm.ṯlṯ.sswm.mrkbt. | b trbṣt.bn.amt. | p d.in. 14[KRT].3.139
ẓ[r y]. | w y'n[y.k]rt[.ṯ]'. | lm.ank.ksp. | w yr[q.ḫrṣ]. | yd.mqm h.w 'bd. | 'lm.ṯlṯ.sswm. | mrkbt.b trbṣ. | bn.amt.p d.[i]n. 14[KRT].6.284
[-----]. | [-----]. | [-----.lm]. | [ank.ksp.w yrq]. | [ḫrṣ.]yd.mqm h. | [w 'b]d.'lm.ṯlṯ. | [ssw]m.mrkbt b trbṣ bn.amt. | [tn.b 14[KRT].2.54
.'m.krt. | mswn h.tḥm.pbl.mlk. | qḥ.ksp.w yrq.ḫrṣ. | yd.mqm h.w 'bd.'lm. | ṯlṯ.sswm.mrkbt. | b trbṣ.bn.amt. | qḥ.krt.š 14[KRT].3.127
[gm.l krt.]ṯ'. | tḥm[.pbl.mlk]. | qḥ.[ksp.w yr]q. | ḫrṣ[.yd.mqm] h. | 'bd[.'lm.ṯlṯ]. | ss[wm.mrkbt]. | b[trbṣ.bn.amt]. | [qḥ. 14[KRT].5.251
lk. | y[ṯ]b.aliyn.b'l. | yt'dd.rkb.'rpt. | [--].ydd.w yqlṣn. | yqm.w ywpṯn.b tk. | p[ḫ]r.bn.ilm.štt. | p[--].b ṯlḥn y.qlt. | b ks 4[51].3.13
. | w.[---].ypm.w.mḫ[--].t[ṯ]tbn.[-]. | b.[--].w.km.iṯ.y[--.]šqm.yd[-]. 35[3].55
w y'n. | w y'n.btlt.'nt. | n'mt.bn.aḫt.b'l. | l pnn h.ydd.w yqm. | l p'n h.ykr'.w yql. | w yšu.g h.w yṣḥ. | ḥwt.aḫt.w nar[-] 10[76].2.17
.ǵr.ll.'m.phr.m'd.ap.ilm.l lḥ[m]. | yṯb.bn qdš.l ṯrm.b'l.qm.'l.il.hlm. | ilm.tph hm.tphn.mlak.ym.t'dt.ṯpṭ[.nhr]. | t[ǵ]l 2.1[137].21
]drk.brḥ.arṣ.lk pn h.yrk.b'[l]. | [---.]bt k.ap.l pẖr k 'nt tqm.'nt.tqm. | [---.p]ẖr k.ygrš k.qr.bt k.ygrš k. | [---].bnt.ṣ'ṣ.b 1001.2.9
al.tǵl[.---]. | prdmn.'bd.ali[yn]. | b'l.sid.zbl.b'l. | arṣ.qm.yṯ'r. | w yšlḥmn h. | ybrd.ṯd.l pnw h. | b ḥrb.mlḥt. | qṣ.mri 3['NT].1.4
.arṣ.lk pn h.yrk.b'[l]. | [---.]bt k.ap.l pẖr k 'nt tqm.'nt.tqm. | [---.p]ẖr k.ygrš k.qr.bt k.ygrš k. | [---].bnt.ṣ'ṣ.bnt.m'm' 1001.2.9

qṯ

škrr w p]r ḥdrt. | [-----]. | [---.-]n[-]. | [k yraš ššw št bln q]ṯ ydk. | [w yṣq b ap h]. | [-----]. | [-----]. | [-----]. | [---.-]rb. | [--- 160[55].14
mr[.ydk]. | aḥd h.w.yṣq.b[.ap h]. | k.yraš.ššw.[št]. | bln.qṯ.yṣq.b.a[p h]. | k yg'r[.ššw.---]. | dprn[.---]. | dr'.[---]. | tmṯl[.- 161[56].22

qṯṯ

.q[r zbl]. | u tḫṭin.b ap kn.u b [q]ṣrt.npš[kn.u b qṯt]. | tqṯṯn u tḫṭin.l bḥm.w l ṯ'.d[bḥ n.ndbḥ]. | hw.ṯ'.nṯ'y.hw.nkt.n 32[2].1.15
qr zbl]. | [u tḫṭu.u b ap km.u b qṣrt.npš km.u b qṯt]. | [tqṯṯ.u tḫṭu.l dbḥm.w l.ṯ'.dbḥ n.ndb]ḥ. | [hw.ṯ'.nṯ'y.hw.nkt.n 32[2].1.9
zbl.u[š]n yp km. | u b ap km.u b q[ṣ]rt.npš km.u b qṯt.tqṯṯ. | ušn yp km.l d[b]ḥm.w l.ṯ'.dbḥ n.ndbḥ.hw.ṯ' | nṯ'y. | hw 32[2].1.23
qr zbl.ušn.yp km.b ap km.u b qṣrt.np]št km. | [u b qṯt.tqṯṯ.ušn.yp km.---.-]yt km. | [---.]km. | [-----]. | [---.]ugrt. | [---]. APP.I[-].1.18
qr z[bl]. | lšn yp kn.b ap [kn.u b qṣ]rt.npš kn.u b qṯt. | tqṯṯn.ušn y[p kn.l dbḥm.]w l ṯ' dbḥ n. | ndbḥ.hw.ṯ' n[ṯ'y.hw. 32[2].1.32
r zbl. | [ušn.yp kn.u b ap kn.u b qṣrt.npš kn.u b]qṯt. | [tqṯṯn.ušn.yp kn.---.-]gym. | [---.]l kbkb. | [-----]. APP.I[-].2.16
r zbl.ušn.y]p kn. | [u b ap kn.u b qṣrt.npšt kn.u b qṯ]t tqṯṯ. | [ušn.yp kn.---.--]l.il.t'ḏr b'l. | [-----.]lšnt. | [---.--]yp.tḥt. | APP.I[-].1.7
m.ulp.qr zbl]. | [u tḫṭu.u b ap km.u b qṣrt.npš km.u b qṯt]. | [tqṯṯ.u tḫṭu.l dbḥm.w l.ṯ'.dbḥ n.ndb]ḥ. | [hw.ṯ'.nṯ'y.hw. 32[2].1.8A
]n.ulp.q[r zbl]. | u tḫṭin.b ap kn.u b [q]ṣrt.npš[kn.u b qṯt]. | tqṯṯn u tḫṭin.l bḥm.w l ṯ'.d[bḥ n.ndbḥ]. | hw.ṯ'.nṯ'y.hw. 32[2].1.14
.qr zbl.u[š]n yp km. | u b ap km.u b q[ṣ]rt.npš km.u b qṯt.tqṯṯ. | ušn yp km.l d[b]ḥm.w l.ṯ'.dbḥ n.ndbḥ.hw.ṯ' | nṯ'y. 32[2].1.23
]. | [qr zbl.ušn.yp km.b ap km.u b qṣrt.np]št km. | [u b qṯt.tqṯṯ.ušn.yp km.---.-]yt km. | [---.]km. | [-----]. | [---.]ugrt. | [APP.I[-].1.18
.ulp qr z[bl]. | lšn yp kn.b ap [kn.u b qṣ]rt.npš kn.u b qṯt. | tqṯṯn.ušn y[p kn.l dbḥm.]w l ṯ' dbḥ n. | ndbḥ.hw.ṯ' n[ṯ'y 32[2].1.31
lp.qr zbl.ušn.y]p kn. | [u b ap kn.u b qṣrt.npšt kn.u b qṯ]t tqṯṯ. | [ušn.yp kn.---.--]l.il.t'ḏr b'l. | [-----.]lšnt. | [---.--]yp.t APP.I[-].1.7
lp.]qr zbl. | [ušn.yp kn.u b ap kn.u b qṣrt.npš kn.u b]qṯt. | [tqṯṯn.ušn.yp kn.---.-]gym. | [---.]l kbkb. | [-----]. APP.I[-].2.15

qṯy

w npy.yman.w npy.'r]mt.w npy. | [---.ušn.yp km.ulp.]qṯy. | [ulp.ddmy.ulp.ḫry.ulp.ḫty.u]lp.alṯy. | [ulp.ǵbr.ulp.ḫbt APP.I[-].1.14
. | [-----]. | [-----]. | [---.--]r. | [---.]npy. | [---.ušn.yp kn.ulp.q]ṯy. | [ulp.ddmy.ulp.ḫry.ulp.ḫty.ulp.alṯy]. | [ulp.ǵbr.ulp.ḫbt APP.I[-].2.12
an. | [w npy.'rmt.---.w]npy.annpdgl. | [ušn.yp kn.ulp.qṯy.ulp.]ddmy.ulp ḫry. | [ulp.ḫty.ulp.alṯy.ulp.ǵbr.ul]p.ḫbt k APP.I[-].1.4
rt.w npy.---.]w npy. | [---.w np]y.ugrt. | [---.u tḫṭu.ulp.qṯy.ulp.ddm]y. | [ulp.ḫry.ulp.ḫty.ulp.alṯy.ulp.ǵbr]. | [ulp.ḫbt 32[2].1.6
y.gr[.ḥmyt.ugrt.w np]y. | [---].w n[py.---].u tḫṭi[n.ulp.qṯy]. | ulp.ddmy.ul[p.ḫry.u]lp.ḫty.ulp[.alṯy.ulp.]ǵbr. | ulp.ḫbt 32[2].1.11
.w npy.'rmt.w npy.[---]. | w npy.nqmd.ušn.yp km.ulp.q[ṯy.ulp.ddm]y. | ulp.ḫry.ulp.ḫ[ṭ]y.ulp.alṯy.ul[p.ǵbr.]ulp. | ḫb 32[2].1.20
.ugrt.w npy.gr. | ḥmyt.ugrt.w [np]y.nṯt.ušn.yp kn.ulp qṯy. | ulp.ddmy.ul[p.ḫ]ry.ulp.ḫty.ulp.alṯy. | ulp.ǵbr.ulp.[ḫbt] 32[2].1.28
.]bn.brzn.b d.nwrḏ. | [šd.]bn.nḥbl.b d.'dbym. | [šd.b]n.qṯy.b d.tt. | [ubd]y.mrim. | [šd.b]n.ṯpdn.b d.bn.g'r. | [šd.b]n.ṯq 82[300].1.19
[b]n 'ntn.[---]. | bn agyn[.---]. | b[n] 'ṯlṯ[.---]. | bn qṯy[.---]. | bn yp'[.---]. | [---]b'm[.---]. | [-----]. 105[86].4

qṯn

ḏrǵl. | bn.tran.mḏrǵl | bn.ilh.mḏrǵl | špšyn.b.ulm. | bn.qṯn.b.ulm. | bn.gdrn.b.m'r[by]. | [w].bn.d'm[-]. | bn.ppṯ.b[--]. 2046.1.6
ny. | krty. | bn.'bṣ. | bn.argb. | ydn. | il'nt. | bn.urt. | ydn. | qṯn. | bn.asr. | bn.'dy. | bn.amt[m]. | myn. | šr. | bn.zql. | bn.iḫy. 2117.3.46
r. | [bn.]aglby. | [bn.]b'ly. | [mḏ]rǵlm. | [bn.]kdgdl. | [b]n.qṯn. | [b]n.ǵrgn. | [b]n.tgdn. | bn.ḫdyn. | bn.sgr. | bn.aǵltn. | bn. 104[316].9
ilwn.[---]. | ṯrn.d[d]. | tg d[d]. | ḫdyn.d[d]. | [-]ḏdn.d[d]. | qṯn.d[d]. | lḫsn.d[d]. | lsn.d[d]. | and[--.---]. 132[331].9
ib[rn]. | mdm. | inšt. | nsk ksp. | yṣḥm. | ḥrš mrkbt. | ḥrš qṯn. | ḥrš bhtm. 73[114].9
krm. | 'zn. | yplṭ. | 'bdmlk. | ynḥm. | aḏddn. | mtn. | plsy. | qṯn. | ypr. | bn.ymy. | bn.'rd. | [-]b.da[-]. | [--]l[--]. | [-----]. 1035.4.10
| ṯṯ.ḥrtm. | lqḥ.š'rt. | 'šr.ḥrš. | bhtm.lqḥ. | š'rt. | arb'. | ḥrš qṯn. | lqḥ š'rt. | ṯṯ nsk.ḥḏm. | lqḥ.š'rt. 2052.12
n.qšt.w.ql'. | ilmhr.qšt.w.ql'. | bn.gmrt.qšt. | ǵmrm. | bn.qṯn.qšt.w.ql'. | mrṯd.qšt. | ssw.qšt. | knn.qšt. | bn.ṯlln.qšt. | bn.š 119[321].1.12
.ṯq[lm]. | bn.p'ṣ.ṯqlm. | mṣrn.ḥrš.mrkbt.ṯqlm. | 'pṯn.ḥrš.qṯn.ṯqlm. | bn.pǵdn.ṯqlm. | bn.b'ln.ṯqlm. | 'bdyrḫ.nqd.ṯqlm. | b 122[308].1.9
ǵlm.iln.b'[l]n.aldy. | tdn.ṣr[--.--]t.'zn.mtn.n[bd]g. | ḥrš qṯn[.---.]dqn.b'ln. | ǵltn.'bd.[---]. | nsk.ḥḏm.klyn[.ṣd]qn.'bdilt 2011.23
| ḥgbn. | šrm. | bn.ymil. | bn.kdǵdl. | [-]mn. | [--]n. | [ḥr]š.qṯn. | [---]n. | [-----]. | [--]dd. | [b']l.tǵpṯm. | [k]rwn. | ḥrš.mrkbt. 1039.2.7

qṯnn

bn.štn. | bn.ilš. | bn.tnabn. | bn.ḥṣn. | ṣprn. | bn.ašbḥ. | bn.qṯnn. | bn.ǵlmn. | [bn].ṣwy. | [bn].ḫnq[n]. | [-----]. | [-----]. | [----- 1046.1.22

qṭr

m.km.šḫṭ.l brk h.tṣi.km. | rḥ.npš h.km.iṭl.brlt h.km. | qṭr.b ap h.b ap.mhr h.ank. | l aḥwy.tqḥ.yṭpn.mhr.št. | tštn.k 18[3AQHT].4.26

m.šḫ[ṭ.l brk h]. | yṣat.km.rḥ.npš[h.km.iṭl]. | brlt h.km.qṭr.[b ap h.---]. | ʿnt.b ṣmt.mhr h.[---]. | aqht.w tbk.y[---.---]. | 18[3AQHT].4.37

-]ḥ[.---]y[.---.-]nt.[š]ṣat[k.]rḥ.npš.hm. | k.iṭl.brlt n[-.k qṭr.b ap -]. | tmǵyn.tša.g h[m.w tṣḥn]. | šmʿ.l dnil.[mt.rpi]. | 19[1AQHT].2.88

b qrb. | hkl h.nṣb.skn.ilib h.b qdš. | ztr.ʿm h.l arṣ.mšṣu.qṭr h. | l ʿpr.ḏmr.aṯr h.ṭbq.lḥt. | niṣ h.grš d.ʿšy.ln h. | aḥd.yd h 17[2AQHT].1.28

.hkl h. | [nṣb.skn.i]lib h.b qdš. | [ztr.ʿm h.l a]rṣ.mšṣu. | [qṭr h.l ʿpr.ḏ]mr.a[ṯ]r h. | [ṭbq.lḥt.niṣ h.gr]š.d ʿšy. | [ln h.---]. | 17[2AQHT].1.47

bq.lḥt.niṣ h.gr]š.d ʿšy. | [ln h.---]. | z[tr.ʿm k.l arṣ.mšṣu.qṭr k]. | l ʿpr.ḏm[r.aṯr k.ṭbq]. | lḥt.niṣ k.gr[š.d ʿšy.ln k]. | spu.k 17[2AQHT].2.1

qẓ

ʿ.kbd h.w yḥd. | iṯ.šmt.iṯ.ʿẓm.w yqḥ b hm. | aqht.ybl.l qẓ.ybky.w yqbr. | yqbr.nn.b mdgt.b knk[-]. | w yšu.g h.w yṣḥ 19[1AQHT].3.146

ašr nkl w ib[.bt]. | ḫrḫb.mlk qẓ ḫrḫb m | lk aǵzt.b sǵ[--.]špš. | yrḫ yṯkḥ yḥ[bq] [-]. | tld bt.[24[77].2

apnk.dnil.mt. | rpi.yṣly.ʿrpt.b | ḥm.un.yr.ʿrpt. | tmṭr.b qẓ.ṭl.yṭll. | l ǵnbm.šbʿ.šnt. | yṣr k.bʿl.ṯmn.rkb. | ʿrpt.bl.ṭl.bl rbb 19[1AQHT].1.41

. | l aḫw.ap.qšt h.l ttn. | l y.w b mt[.-]ḥ.mṣṣ[-]t[.--]. | prʿ.qẓ.y[bl].šblt. | b ǵlp h.apnk.dnil. | [m]t.rpi.ap[h]n.ǵzr. | [mt.h 19[1AQHT].1.18

.l kṯrt hl[l.sn]nt. | ylak yrḫ ny[r] šmm.ʿm. | ḫr[ḫ]b mlk qẓ.tn nkl y | rḫ ytrḫ.ib tʿrb m b bh | t h.w atn mhr h l a | b h. 24[77].17

.atn šd h krm[m]. | šd dd h ḥrnqm.w | yʿn ḫrḫb mlk qẓ [l]. | nʿmn.ilm l ḫt[n]. | m.bʿl trḫ pdry b[t h]. | aqrb k ab h 24[77].24

. | [---.--]l km amt m. | [---.]b w tʿrb.sd. | [---.--]n b ym.qẓ. | [---.]ym.tlḥmn. | [---.rp]um.tštyn. | [---.]il.d ʿrgzm. | [---.]d 20[121].1.5

qẓb

y.ik].yqrun.hd. | [ʿm.ary y.---.--]p.mlḥm y. | [---.---]lt.qẓb. | [---.]šmḥ y. | [---.]tbʿ. | [---.-]nnm. 5[67].2.24

qym

k.hn[.---]. | yd k.ṣǵr.tnšq.špt k.ṯm. | ṯkm.bm ṯkm.aḫm.qym.il. | b lsmt.ṯm.yṯbš.šm.il.mt m. | yʿbš.brk n.šm.il.ǵzrm. | 22.2[124].5

ql

.w ngšnn.ḥby. | bʿl.qrnm w ḏnb.ylšn. | b ḫri h.w ṯnt h.ql.il.[--]. | il.k yrdm.arṣ.ʿnt. | w ʿṯtrt.tṣdn.[---]. | [---.-]b[-.---]. | [UG5.1.1.21

.il. | ab h.ḥpr.pʿl k.y[--]. | šmʿ k.l arḫ.w bn.[--]. | limm.ql.b udn.k w[-]. | k rtqt mr[.---]. | k d lbšt.bir.mlak. | šmm.tm 13[6].23

ǵrpl.ʿl arṣ. | [l a]n ḥmt.l p[.n]ṯk.abd.l p.akl ṯm.dl. | [---.q]l.bl.tbḥ[n.l]azd.ʿr.qdm. | [---].ʿẓ q[dm.--.šp]š. | [---.šm]n.mš UG5.8.21

ḥl.pḥlt.bt.abn.bt šmm w thm. | qrit.l špš.um h.špš.um.ql.bl.ʿm. | il.mbk nhrm.b ʿdt.thmtm. | mnt.nṯk.nḥš.šmrr.nḥš. UG5.7.2

.yšlḥm.ʿq šr. | yʿdb.ksa.w.yṯb. | tqru.l špš.um h.špš.um.ql bl. | ʿm bʿl.mrym.ṣpn.mnt y.nṯk. | nḥš.šmrr.nḥš.ʿq šr ln h. UG5.7.8

šlḥm.nḥš.ʿq šr.ydb.ksa. | w yṯb. | tqru.l špš.u h.špš.um.ql.bl.ʿm. | dgn.ttl h.mnt.nṯk.nḥš.šmrr. | nḥš.ʿq šr.ln h.mlḫš.a UG5.7.14

m.nḥš.ʿq šr.yʿdb. | ksa.w yṯb. | tqru l špš.um h.špš.um.ql bl. | ʿm ḥrn.mṣd h.mnt.nṯk nḥš. | šmrr.nḥš.ʿq šr.ln h.mlḫš. UG5.7.57

ḥm.nḥš ʿq. | š.yʿdb.ksa w yṯb. | tqru l špš.um h.špš.um.ql bl ʿm. | ṯṯ.w kmṯ.ḥryt h.mnt.nṯk.nḥš.šm | rr.nḥš.ʿq šr.ln h. UG5.7.35

h.ydy.ḥmt.hlm.yṯq. | w yṯb. | tqru.l špš.um h.špš.[um.q]l bl.ʿm. | yrḫ.lrgt h.mnt.nṯk.n[ḥš].šmrr. | nḥš.ʿq šr.ln h.mlḫ UG5.7.25

m.nḥš. | ʿq.šr.yʿdb.ksa.w yṯb. | tqru l špš um h.špš um ql.bl.ʿm. | mlk.ʿṯtrt h.mnt.nṯk.nḥš.šmrr. | nḥš.ʿq šr.ln h.mlḫš UG5.7.40

m. | nḥš.ʿq šr.yʿdb.ksa.w yṯb. | tqru l špš.um h.špš.um.ql.bl.ʿm. | ʿnt w ʿṯtrt inbb h.mnt.nṯk. | nḥš.šlḥm.nḥš.ʿq šr[.yʿ] UG5.7.19

m.nḥš. | ʿq šr.yʿdb.ksa.w yṯb. | tqru.l špš.um h.špš.um.ql b.ʿm. | ršp.bbt h.mnt.nḥš.šmrr. | nḥš.ʿq šr.ln h.mlḫš.abd.ln UG5.7.30

m.nḥš.ʿq šr.yʿdb ksa. | w yṯb. | tqru l špš.um h.špš.um.ql bl ʿm. | šḥr.w šlm šmm h mnt.nṯk.nḥš. | šmrr.nḥš ʿq šr.ln UG5.7.51

q.nḥš.yšlḥm.nḥš. | ʿq šr.yʿdb.ksa.w yṯb. | tqru.l špš.um.ql bl.ʿm | kṯr.w ḫss.kptr h.mnt.nṯk.nḥš. | šmrr.nḥš.ʿq šr.ln h. UG5.7.45

.gg[ʿt]. | b.ʿšrt.ksp. | ṯlṯ.uṭbm.b d.alḫn.b.ʿšrt[.k]sp. | rṯ.l.ql.d.ybl.prd. | b.ṯql.w.nṣp.ksp. | ṯmn.lbšm.w.mšlt. | l.udmym. 2101.12

.l.m[--]. | mit.ʿšrm.[k]bd.yn.ḥsp.l.y[--]. | ʿšrm.yn.ḥsp.l.ql.d.tbʿ.mṣ[r]m. | mit.arbʿm.kbd.yn.mṣb. | l.mdrǵlm. | ʿšrn ʿšr 1084.27

.l irt k. | wn ap.ʿdn.mṭr h. | bʿl.y.ʿdn.ʿdn.ṯkt.b glṯ. | w tn.ql h.b ʿrpt. | šrh.l arṣ.brqm. | bt.arzm.yklln h. | hm.bt.lbnt.yʿ 4[51].5.70

ln.b bht m.urbt. | b qrb.hk[l m.yp]tḥ. | bʿl.b dqt[.ʿrp]t. | ql h.qdš.b[ʿl.y]tn. | yṯny.bʿl.ṣ[---.-]pt h. | ql h.q[dš.ṭb]r.arṣ. | [-- 4[51].7.29

ʿl.b dqt[.ʿrp]t. | ql h.qdš.b[ʿl.y]tn. | yṯny.bʿl.ṣ[---.-]pt h. | ql h.q[dš.ṭb]r.arṣ. | [---.]ǵrm[.t]ḫšn. | rḥq[.---.td ʿ]. | qdm ym.b 4[51].7.31

. | [qr]š.m[l]k.ab[.šnm.]mṣr. | [t]bu.ḏdm.qn[-.-]n[-.-]lt. | ql h.yš[mʿ].tr.[il].ab h.[---]l. | b šbʿt.ḫdrm.[b ṯ]mn[t.ap]. | sgrt 3[ʿNT.VI].5.18

akt. | [---.]ʿl.w tšʿ[d]n.npš h. | [---.]rgm.hn.[--]n.w aspt.[q]l h. | [---.rg]m.ank l[.--.--]rny. | [---.]ṯm.hw.i[--]ty. | [---.]ib ʿr. 1002.49

gm.pgm.l.b[---]. | [---.]mdbm.l ḥrn.ḥr[n.---]. | [---.--]m.ql.hm[.---]. | [---].aṯt n.r[---]. | [---.]ḥr[-.--]. | [---.]plnt.[---]. | [--- 1001.1.28

---]. | bʿl.yṯb.l ks[i.mlk h]. | bn.dgn.l kḥ[ṯ.drkt h]. | l alp.ql.ẓ[--.---]. | l np ql.nd.[----]. | tlk.w tr.b[ḫl]. | b nʿmm.b ys[m 10[76].3.16

w tʿl.bkm.b arr. | bm.arr.w b ṣpn. | b nʿm.b ǵr.t[l]iyt. | ql.l bʿl.ttnn. | bšrt.il.bš[r.bʿ]l. | w bšr.ḥtk.dgn. | k.ibr.l bʿl[.yl]d 10[76].3.33

lkt. | tr.b lkt.w tr.b ḫl. | [b]nʿmm.b ysmm.ḥ[--]k.ǵrt. | [ql].l bʿl.ʿnt.ttnn. | [---].bʿl m.d ip[---]. | [il.]hd.d ʿnn.n[--]. | [---- 10[76].2.31

i.mlk h]. | bn.dgn.l kḥ[ṯ.drkt h]. | l alp.ql.ẓ[--.---]. | l np ql.nd.[----]. | tlk.w tr.b[ḫl]. | b nʿmm.b ys[mm.---]. | arḫ.arḫ.[10[76].3.17

t.w hn.špšm. | b šbʿ.w l.yšn.pbl. | mlk.l qr.ṯigt.ibr h. | l ql.nhqt.ḥmr h. | l gʿt.alp.ḥrṯ.zǵt. | klb.ṣpr.w ylak. | mlakm.l k. 14[KRT].3.121

mk.špšm.b šbʿ. | w l.yšn.pbl. | mlk.l [qr.]ṯiqt. | ibr h[.l]ql.nhqt. | ḥmr[h.l gʿt.]alp. | ḥrṯ[.l z]ǵt.klb. | [ṣ]pr[.apn]k. | [pb 14[KRT].5.224

k.b msk h. | qm.ybd.w yšr. | mṣltm.bd.nʿm. | yšr.ǵzr.ṭb.ql. | ʿl.bʿl.b ṣrrt. | ṣpn.ytmr.bʿl. | bnt h.yʿn.pdry. | bt.ar.apn.ṭly. 3[ʿNT].1.20

---].aṯt n.r[---]. | [---.]ḥr[-.--]. | [---.]plnt.[---]. | [---.]ʿmt.l ql.rpi[.---]. | [---.-]llm.abl.mṣrp k.[---]. | [---.]y.mṯnt.w tḥ.ṭbt.n 1001.2.2

--.]w špt k.l tššy.hm.tqrm.l mt.b rn k. | [--]ḫp.an.arnn.ql.špš.ḥw.bṭnm.uḫd.bʿlm. | [--.a]ṯm.prṯl.l riš h.ḥmṯ.ṯmṯ. | [--.] 1001.1.6

[-----]. | ʿm[-.---]. | mǵ[-.---]. | šp[š.---]. | ql.[---]. | w mlk[.nḥš.w mlk.mg]šḫ. | ʿmn.[---]. | ik y.[---]. | w l 64[118].5

[--.]a[-.---]. | [--.-]bt.np[-.---]. | [-] l šd.ql.[---.---].aṯr. | [--.]ǵrm.y[--.---.ḥ]rn. | [-]rk.ḥ[--.---.-]lk. | [-]sr. UG5.8.3

-]. | bk[--.--].yq[--.--]. | w [---.]rkb[.---]. | [---].d[--.---]. | b ql[.-----]. | w tštqdn[.-----]. | hm. | w yḥ.mlk. | w ik m.kn.w [--- 62[26].6

qldn

.srt. | [---.--]m. | ʿbdmlk.bn.šrn. | ʿbdbʿl.bn.kdn. | gzl.bn.qldn. | gld.bt.klb. | l[---].bt.ḫzli. | bn.iḫyn. | ṣdqn.bn.ass. | bʿlys 102[323].3.4

qlḥ

ydbḥ mlk. | l ušḫ[r] ḫlmṭ. | l bbt il bt. | š l ḫlmṭ. | w tr l qlḥ. | w š ḥll ydm. | b qdš il bt. | w tlḥm aṯt. | š l ilbt.šlmm. | kll UG5.7.TR3

m. | kll ylḥm b h. | w l bbt šqym. | š l uḫr ḫlmṭ. | w tr l qlḥ. | ym aḥd. UG5.11.13

qly

y‘dd.tḥt.bn arbn. | ‘bdil.tḥt.ilmlk. | qly.tḥt b‘ln.nsk. 1053.3

qll

b arb‘t.‘šr[t]. | yrtḫṣ.mlk.b[rr]. | b ym.mlat. | tqln.alpm. | yrḫ.‘šrt.l b‘[l]. | dqtm.w ynt.qr[t]. | w mtntm.š l r UG5.13.4
w ḥl. | [mlk.b ar]b‘t.‘[š]rt.yrtḫṣ.mlk.brr. | [b ym.ml]at.y[ql]n.al[p]m.yrḫ.‘šrt. | [l b‘l.ṣ]pn.[dq]tm.w y[nt] qrt. | [w mt 36[9].1.11
.rb.mi[--.‘]bd k. | l.p‘n.b‘l y[.mrḥqtm]. | šb‘ d.w.šb‘[d.qlt]. | ankn.rgmt.l.b‘l y. | l.špš.‘lm.l.‘ttrt. | l.‘nt.l.kl.il.alt[y]. | n 2008.1.5
tḥm.tlmyn. | w.aḫtmlk ‘bd k. | l.p‘n.adt ny. | mrḥqtm. | qlny.ilm. | tǵr k. | tšlm k. | hn ny.‘m ny. | kll.mid. | šlm. | w.ap. 51[95].7
ṯ‘.yṯbr. | ḥrn.y bn.yṯbr.ḥrn. | riš k.‘ṯtrt.šm.b‘l. | qdqd k.tqln.b gbl. | šnt k.b ḥpn k.w t‘n. | spr ilmlk ṯ‘y. 16.6[127].57
ḥ.hy.mḫ.tmḫṣ.mḫṣ[.aḫ k]. | tkl.m[k]ly.‘l.umt[k.--]. | d ttql.b ym.trtḥ[ṣ.--]. | [----.a]dm.tium.b ǵlp y[m.--]. | d alp šd.ẓ 19[1AQHT].4.203
[-----]. | l abn[.---]. | aḫdt.plk h[.b yd h]. | plk.qlt.b ymn h. | npyn h.mks.bšr h. | tmt‘.md h.b ym.ṯn. | npyn 4[51].2.4
. | yqm.w ywptn.b tk. | p[ḫ]r.bn.ilm.štt. | p[--].b ṯlḥn y.qlt. | b ks.ištyn h. | dm.ṯn.dbḥm.šna.b‘l.ṯlṯ. | rkb.‘rpt.dbḥ. | bṯt. 4[51].3.15
ištm[‘]. | w tqǵ[.udn.k ǵz.ǵzm]. | tdbr.w[ǵ]rm[.ṯṯwy]. | šqlt.b ǵlt.yd k. | l tdn.dn.almnt. | l ṯpṭ.ṯpṭ.qṣr.npš. | km.aḫt.‘r 16.6[127].32
krt. | ṯ‘.ištm‘.w tqǵ udn. | k ǵz.ǵzm.tdbr. | w ǵrm.ṯṯwy.šqlt. | b ǵlt.yd k.l tdn. | dn.almnt.l ṯpṭ. | ṯpṭ qṣr.npš.l tdy. | ṯš 16.6[127].44
k.b‘l.ṯmn.rkb. | ‘rpt.bl.ṯl.bl rbb. | bl.šr‘.thmtm.bl. | ṭbn.ql.b‘l.k tmz‘. | kst.dnil.mt.rpi. | all.ǵzr.m[t.]hr[nmy]. | gm.l bt 19[1AQHT].1.46
‘l. | ‘z.ynṯkn.k bṯnm. | mt.‘z.b‘l.‘z.ymṣḫn. | k lsmm.mt.ql. | b‘l.ql.‘ln.špš. | tṣḥ.l mt.šm‘.m‘. | l bn.ilm.mt.ik.tmt[ḫ] | ṣ.‘ 6[49].6.21
yṯbr.ḫt.mṯpṭ k. | yru.bn ilm t.ṯt‘.y | dd.il.ǵzr.y‘r.mt. | b ql h.y[---.---]. | b‘l.yṯṯbn[.l ksi]. | mlk h.l[nḫt.l kḥt]. | drkt h[.- 6[49].6.32
. | n‘mt.bn.aḫt.b‘l. | l pnn h.ydd.w yqm. | l p‘n h.ykr‘.w yql. | w yšu.g h.w yṣḥ. | ḥwt.aḫt.w nar[-]. | qrn.d bat k.btlt.‘nt 10[76].2.18
tm. | tgly.ḏd.il.w tbu. | qrš.mlk.ab.šnm. | l p‘n.il.thbr.w tql. | tštḥwy.w tkbd h. | hlm.il.k yphn h. | yprq.lṣb.w yṣḥq. | p‘ 4[51].4.25
tgly.ḏd il. | [w tbu.qr]š.mlk.ab.šnm. | [l p‘n.il.t]hbr.w tql.tštḥ | [wy.w tkbd]n h.tlšn.aqht.ǵzr. | [---.kdd.dn]il.mt.rpi. 17[2AQHT].6.50
m.tgly.ḏd. | il.w tbu.qrš.. | mlk.ab.šnm.l p‘n. | il.thbr.w tql. | tštḥwy.w tkbdn h. | tšu.g h.w tṣḥ.tšmḫ ht. | aṯrt.w bn h.i 6.1.37[49.1.9]
pnm.tk.]in.bb.b alp ḥẓr. | [rbt.kmn.l p‘]n.‘nt. | [yhbr.w yql.yšt]ḥwyn.w y | [kbdn h.yšu.g h.w y]ṣḥ.tḥm. | [ṯr.il.ab k.h 1[‘NT.IX].2.16
ly.]ḏl i[l].w ybu[.q]rš.mlk[.ab.šnm.l p‘n.il.] | [yhbr.]w yql[.y]štḥw[y.]w ykb[dn h.--]r y[---]. | [---.k]ṯr.w ḫ[ss.t]b‘.b[2.3[129].6
. | ygly ḏd.i[l.w ybu.qrš.mlk]. | ab.šnm.l [p‘n.il.yhbr.w yql]. | yštḥwy.[w ykbdn h.---]. | ṯr.il[.ab h.---]. | ḥš b[ht m.tbn 1[‘NT.IX].3.24
.ḥkpt. | arṣ.nḥlt h. | b alp.šd.rbt. | kmn.l p‘n.kṯ. | hbr.w ql.tštḥ | wy.w kbd hwt. | w rgm.l kṯr. | w ḫss.ṯny.l h | yn.d ḥrš. 3[‘NT.VI].6.19
.ḥkpt.arṣ.nḥlt h]. | b alp.šd.r[bt.kmn.l p‘n.kṯr]. | hbr.w ql.t[štḥwy.w kbd.hwt]. | w rgm l k[ṯr.w ḫss.ṯny.l hyn]. | d ḥrš 1[‘NT.IX].3.3
yd.md | d.ilm.mt.b a | lp.šd.rbt.k | mn.l p‘n.mt. | hbr.w ql. | tštḥwy.w k | bd hwt.w rgm. | l bn.ilm.mt. | ṯny.l ydd. | il.ǵ 4[51].8.27
dd.arṣy. | bt.y‘bdr.km ǵlmm. | w ‘rb n.l p‘n.‘nt.hbr. | w ql.tštḥwy.kbd hyt. | w rgm.l btlt.‘nt. | ṯny.l ymmt.limm. | tḥm 3[‘NT].3.7
.ṭb l y w l k. | [---]m.l aqry k.b ntb.pš‘. | [---].b ntb.gan.ašql k.tḥt. | [p‘n y.a]nk.n‘mn.‘mq.nšm. | [td‘ṣ.p‘n]m.w tr.arṣ. 17[2AQHT].6.44
b‘t h.hlm.qdq | d zbl ym.bn.‘nm.ṯpṭ.nhr.yprsḥ ym. | w yql.l arṣ.w trtqṣ.ṣmd.b d b‘l. | [km.]nšr.b uṣb‘t h.ylm.qdqd.z 2.4[68].23
uṣb‘t h.ylm.qdqd.zbl. | [ym.]bn.‘nm.ṯpṭ.nhr.yprsḥ.ym.yql. | l arṣ.tnǵṣn.pnt h.w ydlp.tmn h. | yqt b‘l.w yšt.ym.ykly. 2.4[68].25
l.mlkt. | um y.rgm. | tḥm.mlk. | bn k. | l.p‘n.um y. | qlt.l.um y. | yšlm.ilm. | tǵr k.tšlm k. | hl ny.‘m n[y]. | kll.šlm. | 50[117].6
t.u[m] y. | [rg]m[.]t[ḥm]. | mlk.bn [k]. | [l].p‘n.um [y]. | qlt[.l um] y. | yšlm.il[m]. | tǵ[r] k.tš[lm] k. | [h]l ny.‘m n[.š]lm 1013.5
.illdr. | ‘bd k.. | l.p‘n a[dt y]. | šb‘ d[.w šb‘ d]. | mrḥq[tm.qlt]. | mn[m.šlm]. 1014.7
bm.n‘l[.-]gr. | [---.]‘ṣ.b d h.ydrm[.]pi[-.]adm. | [---.]iṯ[-].yšql.ytk[.--]np bl.hn. | [---].ḥ[m]t.pṭr.w.p nḥš. | [---.--]q.n[t]k. UG5.8.33
[‘l]. | [‘]bd k. | [l.p]‘n.b‘l y. | [šb‘] d.šb‘ [d]. | [mr]ḥqtm. | qlt. | ‘bd k.b. | lwsnd. | [w] b ṣr. | ‘m.mlk. | w.ht. | mlk.syr. | ns. 2063.8
.ilm.mt. | ‘m.aliyn.b‘l.yšu. | g h.w yṣḥ.‘l k.b[‘]l m. | pht.qlt.‘l k.pht. | dry.b ḥrb.‘l k. | pht.šrp.b išt. | ‘l k.[pht.ṭḥ]n.b rḥ 6[49].5.12
nṯkn.k bṯnm. | mt.‘z.b‘l.‘z.ymṣḫn. | k lsmm.mt.ql. | b‘l.ql.‘ln.špš. | tṣḥ.l mt.šm‘.m‘. | l bn.ilm.mt.ik.tmt[ḫ] | ṣ.‘m.aliyn 6[49].6.22
lmyn. | ‘bd k. | l.p‘n. | adt y. | šb‘ d. | w.šb‘ id. | mrḥqtm. | qlt. | ‘m.adt y. | mnm.šlm. | rgm.tṯṯb. | l.‘bd h. 52[89].11
tḥm.‘bd[--]. | ‘bd k. | l p‘n.b‘l y. | ṯn id.šb‘ d. | mrḥqtm. | qlt.‘m. | b‘l y.mnm. | šlm. | [r]gm[.tṯṯb]. | [l.]‘bd[k]. 2115.2.8
d h. | ḫṯ.ulmn.yzbrnn.zbrm.gpn. | yṣmdnn.ṣmdm.gpn.yšql.šdmt h. | km gpn. | šb‘ d.yrgm.‘l.‘d.w ‘rbm.t‘nyn. | w šd.š 23[52].10
a.b špt h.hwt[h]. | knp.nšrm.b‘l.yṯbr. | b‘l.ṯbr.diy hmt.tqln. | tḥt.p‘n h.ybq‘.kbdt hm.w[yḥd]. | in.šmt.in.‘ẓm.yšu.g 19[1AQHT].3.115
m.l[yṣ]a. | b špt h.hwt h.knp.ṣml.b‘[l]. | b‘l.ṯbr.diy.hyt.tq[l.tḥt]. | p‘n h.ybq‘.kbd h.w yḥd. | iṯ.šmt.iṯ.‘ẓm.w yqḥ b hm 19[1AQHT].3.143
a.b šp]t h.hwt h.knp.hrgb.b‘l.ṯbr. | b‘l.ṯbr.diy.hwt.w yql. | tḥt.p‘n h.ybq‘.kbd h.w yḥd. | [i]n.šmt.in.‘ẓm.yšu.g[h]. | 19[1AQHT].3.129
]. | [g h.]w yṣḥ[.knp.nšrm]. | b‘l.yṯb.b‘l.yṯb[r.diy.hmt]. | tqln.tḥ p‘n y.ibq[‘.kbd hm.w] | aḥd.hm.iṯ.šmt.hm.i[ṯ]. | ‘ẓm. 19[1AQHT].3.109
m. | yšu.g h.w yṣḥ.knp.ṣml. | b‘l.yṯbr.b‘l.yṯbr.diy. | hyt.tql.tḥt.p‘n y.ibq‘. | kbd h.w aḥd.hm.iṯ.šmt.iṯ. | ‘ẓm.abky w aq 19[1AQHT].3.138
.g h.w yṣḥ.knp.hr[g]b. | b‘l.yṯb.b‘l.y[ṯb]r.diy[.h]wt. | w yql.tḥt.p‘n y.ibq‘.kbd[h]. | w aḥd.hm.iṯ.šmt.hm.iṯ[.‘ẓm]. | ab 19[1AQHT].3.124
| hn dt.[---]. | [-----]. | [-----]. | tḥm[.---]. | l p‘n.b‘l y[.---]. | qlt. | [--]t.mlk.d.y[mlk]. | [--.]‘bdyrḫ.l.ml[k]. | [--]t.w lqḥ. | yn[. 2064.11
ybnn. | adn y. | rgm. | tḥm.t[g]yn. | bn k. | l.p[‘n.adn y]. | q[lt.---]. | l.yb[nn]. | b‘l y.r[gm]. | tḥm.‘bd[--]. | ‘bd k. | l p‘n.b‘l 2115.1.7
[l a]q[h]t. | [t]krb.[---.]l qrb.mym. | tql.[---.]lb.tṯ[b]r. | qšt[.---]r.y[t]br. | ṯmn.[---.]btlt.[‘]nt. | ṯṭb.[-- 19[1AQHT].1.3
[-----]. | [--.]l tṣi.b b[--].bm.k[--]. | [--]tb.‘ryt k.k qlt[.---]. | [--]at.brt.lb k.‘nn.[---]. | [--.]šdq.k ttn.l y.šn[.---]. | [-- 60[32].3
-]. | bk[--.--].yq[--.--]. | w [---.]rkb[.---]. | [---].d[--.---]. | b ql[.-----]. | w tštqdn[.-----]. | hm. | w yḥ.mlk. | w ik m.kn.w [--- 62[26].6

qln

--]mrtn.kṯrmlk. | yḥmn.aḫm[l]k.‘bdrpu.adn.ṯ[--]. | bdn.qln.mtn.ydln. | b‘ltdtt.tlgn.ytn. | b‘ltǵpṭm.krwn.ilšn.agyn. | m 2011.34

ql‘

.knn.qšt. | pbyn.qšt. | yddn.qšt.w.ql‘. | š‘rt. | bn.il.qšt.w.ql‘. | ark.qšt.w.ql‘. | bn.‘bdnkl.qšt.w.ql‘. | bn.znan.qšt. | bn.arz. 119[321].2.41
qṣn.ṯt.qštm.w.ql‘. | bn.gṯrn.q[š]t. | bn.ḫdi.ṯt.qštm.w.ṯn.ql‘m. | ildgn.qšt. | bn.y‘rn.ṯt.qštm w.ql‘. | bn.ḥṣn.qšt.w.ql‘. | bn 119[321].3.8
.ql‘. | bn.gzl.qšt.w.ql‘. | [---]n.qšt. | ilhd.qšt. | ‘dn.qšt.w.ql‘. | ilmhr.qšt.w.ql‘. | bn.gmrt.qšt. | ǵmrm. | bn.qṭn.qšt.w.ql‘. 119[321].1.8
ql‘. | ‘ky.qšt. | ‘bdlbit.qšt. | kṭy.qšt.w.ql‘. | bn.ḫršn.qšt.w.ql‘. | ilrb.qšt.w.ql‘. | pshn.qšt. | bn.kmy.qšt. | bn.ilḥbn.qšt.w.q[119[321].3.40
ql‘m. | b[n.]ad‘l.q[š]t.w.ql‘. | b[n].ilyn.qšt.w.ql‘. | šmrm.ql‘. | ubr‘y. | abmn.qšt.w.ṯn.ql‘m. | qdmn.ṯt.qštm.w.ṯlṯ.ql‘m. | 119[321].2.48
| yṯpṭ.qšt. | ilthm.qšt.w.ql‘. | ṣdqm.qšt.w.ql‘. | uln.qšt.w.ql‘. | uln.qšt. | bn.blẓn.qšt.w.ql‘. | gb‘.qšt.w.ql‘. | nṣṣn.qšt. | m‘r. 119[321].2.7
.qšt. | ḥdtn.ql‘. | yṯpṭ.qšt. | ilthm.qšt.w.ql‘. | ṣdqm.qšt.w.ql‘. | uln.qšt.w.ql‘. | uln.qšt. | bn.blẓn.qšt.w.ql‘. | gb‘.qšt.w.ql‘. 119[321].2.6

ql‘

m‘r. | [‘]dyn.ṯt.qštm.w.ql‘. | [-]lrš.qšt.w.ql‘. | t[t]n.qšt.w.ql‘. | u[l]n.qšt.w.ql‘. | y‘rn.qšt.w.ql‘. | klby.qšt.w.ql‘. | bq‘t. | ily. 119[321].2.16
‘. | bn.bdn.qšt. | bn.pls.qšt. | ǵmrm. | [-]lhd.ṯt.qštm.w.ṯn.ql‘m. | ulšn.ṯt.qšm.w.ql‘. | bn.ml‘n.qšt.w.ql‘. | bn.tmy.qšt.w.ql 119[321].3.33
nkl.qšt.w.ql‘. | bn.znan.qšt. | bn.arz.[ar]b‘.qšt.w.arb[‘.]ql‘m. | b[n.]ad‘l.q[š]t.w.ql‘. | b[n].ilyn.qšt.w.ql‘. | šmrm.ql‘. | u 119[321].2.45
št. | bn.‘g[w.]qšt.w ql‘. | ḥd[ṯ]n.qšt.w.ql‘. | bn.bb.qšt.w[.ql]‘. | bn.aktmy.qšt. | šdyn.qšt. | bdn.qšt.w.ql‘. | bn.šmlbi.qšt.w 119[321].4.9
-]rkṯ.ṯt.qštm.w.ql‘. | bn.ṯ‘l.qšt. | bn.[ḫ]dpṯr.ṯt.qštm.[w].ql‘. | bn.aǵlyn.ṯt.qštm[.w.ṯl]ṯ.ql‘m. | bn.‘gw.qšt.w ql‘. | bn.tbšn 119[321].3.18
[.w.ṯl]ṯ.ql‘m. | bn.‘gw.qšt.w ql‘. | bn.tbšn.ṯlṯ.qšt.w.[ṯlṯ.]ql‘m. | bn.army.ṯt.qštm.w[.]q[l‘]. | bn.rpš.qšt.w.ql‘. | bn.ǵb.qšt 119[321].3.21
.qšt. | bn.arz.[ar]b‘.qšt.w.arb[‘.]ql‘m. | b[n.]ad‘l.q[š]t.w.ql‘. | b[n].ilyn.qšt.w.ql‘. | šmrm.ql‘. | ubr‘y. | abmn.qšt.w.ṯn.ql‘ 119[321].2.46
.w.]ql‘. | bn.šp[š.]qšt. | bn.‘g[w.]qšt.w ql‘. | ḥd[ṯ]n.qšt.w.ql‘. | bn.bb.qšt.w[.ql]‘. | bn.aktmy.qšt. | šdyn.qšt. | bdn.qšt.w.q 119[321].4.8
.q[l‘]. | bn.lky.qšt. | bn.dll.qšt.w.ql[‘]. | bn.pǵyn.qšt.w[.q]l‘. | bn.bdn.qšt. | bn.pls.qšt. | ǵmrm. | [-]lhd.ṯt.qštm.w.ṯn.ql‘ 119[321].3.29
.ql‘m. | ildgn.qšt. | bn.y‘rn.ṯt.qštm w.ql‘. | bn.ḥṣn.qšt.w.ql‘. | bn.gdn.ṯt.qštm.w.ql‘. | bn.[-]q.qšt.w.ql‘. | gb[l]n.qšt.w.ql‘ 119[321].3.11
tm.w.ṯn.q[l]‘m. | kmrṯn.ṯt.qštm.ṯn.[q]l‘m. | ǵdyn.qšt.w.ql‘. | bn.gzl.qšt.w.ql‘. | [---]n.qšt. | ilhd.qšt. | ‘dn.qšt.w.ql‘. | ilm 119[321].1.4
w.ql‘. | [---]n.qšt. | ilhd.qšt. | ‘dn.qšt.w.ql‘. | ilmhr.qšt.w.ql‘. | bn.gmrt.qšt. | ǵmrm. | bn.qṭn.qšt.w.ql‘. | mrṯd.qšt. | ssw.q 119[321].1.9
.w.ṯn.ql‘m. | bn.ṯlṭ.ṯ[lṯ.]qšt.w.ṯn.ql‘m. | qṣn.ṯt.qštm.w.ql‘. | bn.gṯrn.q[š]t. | bn.ḫdi.ṯt.qštm.w.ṯn.ql‘m. | ildgn.qšt. | bn. 119[321].3.6
‘. | š‘rt. | bn.il.qšt.w.ql‘. | ark.qšt.w.ql‘. | bn.‘bdnkl.qšt.w.ql‘. | bn.znan.qšt. | bn.arz.[ar]b‘.qšt.w.arb[‘.]ql‘m. | b[n.]ad‘l.q 119[321].2.43
.qštm.w.ql‘. | gln.ṯt.qštm.w.ql‘. | gtn.qšt. | pmn.ṯt.qšt.w.ql‘. | bn.zry.q[š]t.w.ql‘. | bn.tlmyn.ṯt.qštm.w.ql‘. | bn.ysd.qšt. | 104[316].9
.ḫdi.ṯt.qštm.w.ṯn.ql‘m. | ildgn.qšt. | bn.y‘rn.ṯt.qštm w.ql‘. | bn.ḥṣn.qšt.w.ql‘. | bn.gdn.ṯt.qštm.w.ql‘. | bn.[-]q.qšt.w.ql 119[321].3.10
t.w.ql‘. | y‘rn.qšt.w.ql‘. | klby.qšt.w.ql‘. | bq‘t. | ily.qšt.w.ql‘. | bn.ḥrẓn.qšt.w.ql‘. | tgrš.qšt.w.ql‘. | špšyn.qšt.w.ql‘. | bn.ṯ‘ 119[321].2.22
.ql‘. | bn.tmy.qšt.w.ql‘. | ‘ky.qšt. | ‘bdlbit.qšt. | kṯy.qšt.w.ql‘. | bn.ḫršn.qšt.w.ql‘. | ilrb.qšt.w.ql‘. | psḥn.qšt. | bn.kmy.qšt. 119[321].3.39
.aktmy.qšt. | šdyn.qšt. | bdn.qšt.w.ql‘. | bn.šmlbi.qšt.w.ql‘. | bn.yy.qšt. | ilrb.qšt. | bn.nmš.ṯt.qšt.w.ql‘. | b‘l.qšt.w.ql‘. 119[321].4.13
n.ṯt.qšt.w.ql‘. | bn.zry.q[š]t.w.ql‘. | bn.tlmyn.ṯt.qštm.w.ql‘. | bn.ysd.qšt. | [ǵ]mrm. | ilgn.qšt. | abršp.qšt. | ssg.qšt. | ynḥ 104[316].9
w.ql‘. | bn.ǵb.qšt. | bn.ytrm.qšt.w.ql‘. | bn.‘bdyrḫ.qšt.w.q[l‘]. | bn.lky.qšt. | bn.dll.qšt.w.ql[‘]. | bn.pǵyn.qšt.w[.q]l‘. | bn 119[321].3.26
.qšt. | ǵmrm. | [-]lhd.ṯt.qštm.w.ṯn.ql‘m. | ulšn.ṯt.qšm.w.ql‘. | bn.ml‘n.qšt.w.ql‘. | bn.tmy.qšt.w.ql‘. | ‘ky.qšt. | ‘bdlbit.qš 119[321].3.34
.w[.]q[l‘]. | bn.rpš.qšt.w.ql‘. | bn.ǵb.qšt. | bn.ytrm.qšt.w.ql‘. | bn.‘bdyrḫ.qšt.w.q[l‘]. | bn.lky.qšt. | bn.dll.qšt.w.ql[‘]. | bn 119[321].3.25
n.qšt. | yddn.qšt.w.ql‘. | š‘rt. | bn.il.qšt.w.ql‘. | ark.qšt.w.ql‘. | bn.‘bdnkl.qšt.w.ql‘. | bn.znan.qšt. | bn.arz.[ar]b‘.qšt.w.ar 119[321].2.42
t. | bn.[ḫ]dpṯr.ṯt.qštm.[w].ql‘. | bn.aǵlyn.ṯt.qštm[.w.ṯl]ṯ.ql‘m. | bn.‘gw.qšt.w ql‘. | bn.tbšn.ṯlṯ.qšt.w.[ṯlṯ.]ql‘m. | bn.arm 119[321].3.19
.w.[ṯlṯ.]ql‘m. | bn.army.ṯt.qštm.w[.]q[l‘]. | bn.rpš.qšt.w.ql‘. | bn.ǵb.qšt. | bn.ytrm.qšt.w.ql‘. | bn.‘bdyrḫ.qšt.w.q[l‘]. | bn 119[321].3.23
w.ql‘. | bn.‘bdyrḫ.qšt.w.q[l‘]. | bn.lky.qšt. | bn.dll.qšt.w.ql[‘]. | bn.pǵyn.qšt.w[.q]l‘. | bn.bdn.qšt. | bn.pls.qšt. | ǵmrm. | [119[321].3.28
qšt. | bn.ilḥbn.qšt.w.q[l‘]. | ršpab.qšt.w.ql‘. | pdrn.qšt.w.ql‘. | bn.pǵm[-.qšt].w.ql‘. | n‘mn.q[št.w.]ql‘. | [t]tn.qš[t]. | bn.ṯǵ 119[321].3.46
.ql‘. | ubr‘y. | abmn.qšt.w.ṯn.ql‘m. | qdmn.ṯt.qštm.w.ṯlṯ.ql‘m. | bn.ṣdqil.ṯt.qštm.w.ṯn.ql‘m. | bn.ṯlṭ.ṯ[lṯ.]qšt.w.ṯn.ql‘m. | 119[321].3.3
ql‘. | bn.tbšn.ṯlṯ.qšt.w.[ṯlṯ.]ql‘m. | bn.army.ṯt.qštm.w[.]q[l‘]. | bn.rpš.qšt.w.ql‘. | bn.ǵb.qšt. | bn.ytrm.qšt.w.ql‘. | bn.‘bd 119[321].3.22
n.bb.qšt.w[.ql]‘. | bn.aktmy.qšt. | šdyn.qšt. | bdn.qšt.w.ql‘. | bn.šmlbi.qšt.w.ql‘. | bn.yy.qšt. | ilrb.qšt. | bn.nmš.ṯt.qšt.w 119[321].4.12
[št.w.]ql‘. | [t]tn.qš[t]. | bn.ṯǵḏy[.qšt.]w.ql‘. | ṯṯy.qšt[.w.]ql‘. | bn.šp[š.]qšt. | bn.‘g[w.]qšt.w ql‘. | ḥd[ṯ]n.qšt.w.ql‘. | bn.bb 119[321].4.5
.[w].ql‘. | bn.aǵlyn.ṯt.qštm[.w.ṯl]ṯ.ql‘m. | bn.‘gw.qšt.w ql‘. | bn.tbšn.ṯlṯ.qšt.w.[ṯlṯ.]ql‘m. | bn.army.ṯt.qštm.w[.]q[l‘]. | 119[321].3.20
qštm.w.ql‘. | gtn.qšt. | pmn.ṯt.qšt.w.ql‘. | bn.zry.q[š]t.w.ql‘. | bn.tlmyn.ṯt.qštm.w.ql‘. | bn.ysd.qšt. | [ǵ]mrm. | ilgn.qšt. | 104[316].9
.ṯt.qštm.w.ṯn.ql‘m. | ulšn.ṯt.qšm.w.ql‘. | bn.ml‘n.qšt.w.ql‘. | bn.tmy.qšt.w.ql‘. | ‘ky.qšt. | ‘bdlbit.qšt. | kṯy.qšt.w.ql‘. | b 119[321].3.35
l‘m. | qdmn.ṯt.qštm.w.ṯlṯ.ql‘m. | bn.ṣdqil.ṯt.qštm.w.ṯn.ql‘m. | bn.ṯlṭ.ṯ[lṯ.]qšt.w.ṯn.ql‘m. | qṣn.ṯt.qštm.w.ql‘. | bn.gṯrn. 119[321].3.4
w.ql‘. | bn.[-]bl.ṯt.qštm.w.ṯn.ql‘m. | bn.[-]rkṯ.ṯt.qštm.w.ql‘. | bn.ṯ‘l.qšt. | bn.[ḫ]dpṯr.ṯt.qštm.[w].ql‘. | bn.aǵlyn.ṯt.qštm[119[321].3.16
.w.ql‘. | bn.ḥrẓn.qšt.w.ql‘. | tgrš.qšt.w.ql‘. | špšyn.qšt.w.ql‘. | bn.ṯ‘ln.qš[t.w.q]l‘. | ‘ṯqbt.qšt. | [-]ll.qšt.w.ql‘. | ḫlb.rpš. | ab 119[321].2.25
| bn.gdn.ṯt.qštm.w.ql‘. | bn.[-]q.qšt.w.ql‘. | gb[l]n.qšt.w.ql‘. | bn.[-]bl.ṯt.qštm.w.ṯn.ql‘m. | bn.[-]rkṯ.ṯt.qštm.w.ql‘. | bn.ṯ 119[321].3.14
‘rn.ṯt.qštm w.ql‘. | bn.ḥṣn.qšt.w.ql‘. | bn.gdn.ṯt.qštm.w.ql‘. | bn.[-]q.qšt.w.ql‘. | gb[l]n.qšt.w.ql‘. | bn.[-]bl.ṯt.qštm.w.ṯn 119[321].3.12
.[-]q.qšt.w.ql‘. | gb[l]n.qšt.w.ql‘. | bn.[-]bl.ṯt.qštm.w.ṯn.ql‘m. | bn.[-]rkṯ.ṯt.qštm.w.ql‘. | bn.ṯ‘l.qšt. | bn.[ḫ]dpṯr.ṯt.qštm. 119[321].3.15
.šmlbi.qšt.w.ql‘. | bn.yy.qšt. | ilrb.qšt. | bn.nmš.ṯt.qšt.w.ql‘. | b‘l.qšt.w.ql‘. 119[321].4.16
.qšt.w.ql‘. | u[l]n.qšt.w.ql‘. | y‘rn.qšt.w.ql‘. | klby.qšt.w.ql‘. | bq‘t. | ily.qšt.w.ql‘. | bn.ḥrẓn.qšt.w.ql‘. | tgrš.qšt.w.ql‘. | šp 119[321].2.19
bn.ḥṣn.qšt.w.ql‘. | bn.gdn.ṯt.qštm.w.ql‘. | bn.[-]q.qšt.w.ql‘. | gb[l]n.qšt.w.ql‘. | bn.[-]bl.ṯt.qštm.w.ṯn.ql‘m. | bn.[-]rkṯ.ṯt 119[321].3.13
ṣdqm.qšt.w.ql‘. | uln.qšt.w.ql‘. | uln.qšt. | bn.blẓn.qšt.w.ql‘. | gb‘.qšt.w.ql‘. | nṣṣn.qšt. | m‘r. | [‘]dyn.ṯt.qštm.w.ql‘. | [-]lrš 119[321].2.9
mlk.qšt. | ytḥm.qšt. | grp.qšt. | m‘rby. | n‘mn.ṯt.qštm.w.ql‘. | gln.ṯt.qštm.w.ql‘. | gtn.qšt. | pmn.ṯt.qšt.w.ql‘. | bn.zry.q[š 104[316].9
t. | grp.qšt. | m‘rby. | n‘mn.ṯt.qštm.w.ql‘. | gln.ṯt.qštm.w.ql‘. | gtn.qšt. | pmn.ṯt.qšt.w.ql‘. | bn.zry.q[š]t.w.ql‘. | bn.tlmyn. 104[316].9
]dm.dt.kn.npṣ hm. | [bn].lbn.arb‘.qšt.w.ar[b‘]. | [u]ṯpt.ql‘.w.ṯt.mr[ḥ]m. | [bn].smyy.qšt.w.u[ṯpt]. | [w.q]l‘.w.ṯt.mrḥm 2047.3
]. | [u]ṯpt.ql‘.w.ṯt.mr[ḥ]m. | [bn].smyy.qšt.w.u[ṯpt]. | [w.q]l‘.w.ṯt.mrḥm. | [bn].šlmn.ql‘.w.ṯ[t.---]. | [bn].mlṣ.qštm.w.uṯ 2047.5
bn].smyy.qšt.w.u[ṯpt]. | [w.q]l‘.w.ṯt.mrḥm. | [bn].šlmn.ql‘.w.ṯ[t.---]. | [bn].mlṣ.qštm.w.uṯp[t]. | [--.q]l‘.w[.---.m]rḥm. | 2047.6
. | [bn].šlmn.ql‘.w.ṯ[t.---]. | [bn].mlṣ.qštm.w.uṯp[t]. | [--.q]l‘.w[.---.m]rḥm. | [bn].ḫdmn.qšt.[w.u]ṯp[t].ṯ[--]. | [---].arb‘.[2047.8
št.]w.ql‘. | ṯṯy.qšt[.w.]ql‘. | bn.šp[š.]qšt. | bn.‘g[w.]qšt.w ql‘. | ḥd[ṯ]n.qšt.w.ql‘. | bn.bb.qšt.w[.ql]‘. | bn.aktmy.qšt. | šdyn 119[321].4.7
yn.qšt.w.ql‘. | bn.ṯ‘ln.qš[t.w.q]l‘. | ‘ṯqbt.qšt. | [-]ll.qšt.w.ql‘. | ḫlb.rpš. | abmn.qšt. | ẓẓn.qšt. | dqry.qš[t]. | rkby. | bn.knn. 119[321].2.28
arb‘m.qšt. | alp ḥẓm.w alp. | nṯq.ṯn.ql‘m. | ḫmš.ṣmdm.w ḥrṣ. | ṯryn.ššwm. | ṯryn.aḥd.d bnš. | arb‘.ṣ 1123.3
tm.w.ql‘. | [-]lrš.qšt.w.ql‘. | t[t]n.qšt.w.ql‘. | u[l]n.qšt.w.ql‘. | y‘rn.qšt.w.ql‘. | klby.qšt.w.ql‘. | bq‘t. | ily.qšt.w.ql‘. | bn.ḥr 119[321].2.17
št. | bn.ṣrptn.qšt. | bn.mṣry.qšt. | arny. | abm.qšt. | ḥdṯn.ql‘. | yṯpṭ.qšt. | ilṯḥm.qšt.w.ql‘. | ṣdqm.qšt.w.ql‘. | uln.qšt.w.ql‘ 119[321].2.3
.qšt.w.ql‘. | t[t]n.qšt.w.ql‘. | u[l]n.qšt.w.ql‘. | y‘rn.qšt.w.ql‘. | klby.qšt.w.ql‘. | bq‘t. | ily.qšt.w.ql‘. | bn.ḥrẓn.qšt.w.ql‘. | t 119[321].2.18
[u]lm. | mṯpṭ.ṯt.qštm.w.ṯn.q[l]‘m. | kmrṯn.ṯt.qštm.ṯn.[q]l‘m. | ǵdyn.qšt.w.ql‘. | bn.gzl.qšt. 119[321].1.2
‘. | ilmhr.qšt.w.ql‘. | bn.gmrt.qšt. | ǵmrm. | bn.qṭn.qšt.w.ql‘. | mrṯd.qšt. | ssw.qšt. | knn.qšt. | bn.ṯlln.qšt. | bn.šyn.qšt. | ‘b 119[321].1.12
[l‘]. | ršpab.qšt.w.ql‘. | pdrn.qšt.w.ql‘. | bn.pǵm[-.qšt].w.ql‘. | n‘mn.q[št.w.]ql‘. | [t]tn.qš[t]. | bn.ṯǵḏy[.qšt.]w.ql‘. | ṯṯy.qš 119[321].4.1
‘. | uln.qšt.w.ql‘. | uln.qšt. | bn.blẓn.qšt.w.ql‘. | gb‘.qšt.w.ql‘. | nṣṣn.qšt. | m‘r. | [‘]dyn.ṯt.qštm.w.ql‘. | [-]lrš.qšt.w.ql‘. | t[t] 119[321].2.10
. | ulšn.ṯt.qšm.w.ql‘. | bn.ml‘n.qšt.w.ql‘. | bn.tmy.qšt.w.ql‘. | ‘ky.qšt. | ‘bdlbit.qšt. | kṯy.qšt.w.ql‘. | bn.ḫršn.qšt.w.ql‘. | il 119[321].3.36
t.w.ql‘. | tgrš.qšt.w.ql‘. | špšyn.qšt.w.ql‘. | bn.ṯ‘ln.qš[t.w.q]l‘. | ‘ṯqbt.qšt. | [-]ll.qšt.w.ql‘. | ḫlb.rpš. | abmn.qšt. | ẓẓn.qšt. | 119[321].2.26

[u]lm. | mṯpṯ.ṯt.qštm.w.ṯn.q[l]ʻm. | kmrṯn.ṯt.qštm.ṯn.[q]lʻm. | ǵdyn.qšt.w.qlʻ. | bn.gzl.qšt.w.qlʻ. | [---]n.qšt. | ilhd.qšt. 119[321].1.3
n.qšt. | bn.kmy.qšt. | bn.ilḥbn.qšt.w.q[lʻ]. | ršpab.qšt.w.qlʻ. | pdrn.qšt.w.qlʻ. | bn.pǵm[-.qšt].w.qlʻ. | nʻmn.q[št.w.]qlʻ. | [119[321].3.45
dlbit.qšt. | kṯy.qšt.w.qlʻ. | bn.ḫršn.qšt.w.qlʻ. | ilrb.qšt.w.qlʻ. | psḥn.qšt. | bn.kmy.qšt. | bn.ilḥbn.qšt.w.q[lʻ]. | ršpab.qšt. 119[321].3.41
.qšt. | arny. | abm.qšt. | ḥdṯn.qlʻ. | yṯpṭ.qšt. | ilṯhm.qšt.w.qlʻ. | ṣdqm.qšt.w.qlʻ. | uln.qšt.w.qlʻ. | uln.qšt. | bn.blẓn.qšt.w.q 119[321].2.5
b[n].ilyn.qšt.w.qlʻ. | šmrm.qlʻ. | ubrʻy. | abmn.qšt.w.ṯn.qlʻm. | qdmn.ṯt.qštm.w.ṯlṯ.qlʻm. | bn.ṣdqil.ṯt.qštm.w.ṯn.qlʻm. 119[321].3.2
qlʻm. | bn.ṣdqil.ṯt.qštm.w.ṯn.qlʻm. | bn.ṯlṯ.ṯ[lṯ.]qšt.w.ṯn.qlʻm. | qṣn.ṯt.qštm.w.qlʻ. | bn.gṯrn.q[š]t. | bn.ḫdi.ṯt.qštm.w.ṯn. 119[321].3.5
t mlk. | d.l.ṣpy. | [---.t]r hm. | [---].ššb. | [---.]tr h. | [a]rbʻ.qlʻm. | arbʻ.mdrnm. | mdrn.w.mšḫṭ. | d.mrkbt. | mlk. | mšḫṭ.w. 1122.10
ilrb.qšt.w.qlʻ. | psḥn.qšt. | bn.kmy.qšt. | bn.ilḥbn.qšt.w.q[lʻ]. | ršpab.qšt.w.qlʻ. | pdrn.qšt.w.qlʻ. | bn.pǵm[-.qšt].w.qlʻ. | 119[321].3.44
št.w.arb[ʻ.]qlʻm. | b[n.]adʻl.q[š]t.w.qlʻ. | b[n].ilyn.qšt.w.qlʻ. | šmrm.qlʻ. | ubrʻy. | abmn.qšt.w.ṯn.qlʻm. | qdmn.ṯt.qštm.w 119[321].2.47
dqry.qš[t]. | rkby. | bn.knn.qšt. | pbyn.qšt. | yddn.qšt.w.qlʻ. | šʻrt. | bn.il.qšt.w.qlʻ. | ark.qšt.w.qlʻ. | bn.ʻbdnkl.qšt.w.qlʻ. 119[321].2.38
.qlʻ. | bqʻt. | ily.qšt.w.qlʻ. | bn.ḫrẓn.qšt.w.qlʻ. | tgrš.qšt.w.qlʻ. | špšyn.qšt.w.qlʻ. | bn.ṯʻln.qš[t.w.q]lʻ. | ʻṯqbt.qšt. | [-]ll.qšt. 119[321].2.24
qlʻ. | klby.qšt.w.qlʻ. | bqʻt. | ily.qšt.w.qlʻ. | bn.ḫrẓn.qšt.w.qlʻ. | tgrš.qšt.w.qlʻ. | špšyn.qšt.w.qlʻ. | bn.ṯʻln.qš[t.w.q]lʻ. | ʻṯqbt 119[321].2.23
lʻ. | pdrn.qšt.w.qlʻ. | bn.pǵm[-.qšt].w.qlʻ. | nʻmn.q[št.w.]qlʻ. | [t]tn.qš[t]. | bn.ṯǵdy[.qšt.]w.qlʻ. | ṯṯy.qšt[.w.]qlʻ. | bn.šp[š.] 119[321].4.2
.qlʻ. | nṣṣn.qšt. | mʻr. | [ʻ]dyn.ṯt.qštm.w.qlʻ. | [-]lrš.qšt.w.qlʻ. | t[t]n.qšt.w.qlʻ. | u[l]n.qšt.w.qlʻ. | yʻrn.qšt.w.qlʻ. | klby.qšt. 119[321].2.15
].w.qlʻ. | nʻmn.q[št.w.]qlʻ. | [t]tn.qš[t]. | bn.ṯǵdy[.qšt.]w.qlʻ. | ṯṯy.qšt[.w.]qlʻ. | bn.šp[š.]qšt. | bn.ʻg[w.]qšt.w qlʻ. | ḥd[ṯ]n. 119[321].4.4
.w.qlʻ. | gbʻ.qšt.w.qlʻ. | nṣṣn.qšt. | mʻr. | [ʻ]dyn.ṯt.qštm.w.qlʻ. | [-]lrš.qšt.w.qlʻ. | t[t]n.qšt.w.qlʻ. | u[l]n.qšt.w.qlʻ. | yʻrn.qšt. 119[321].2.14
].kdl[.---.mr]ḫm.w.ṯ[t.---]. | [---.mr]ḫm.w.ṯ[t.---]. | [---].qlʻ[.---]. | [---.a]rbʻ[.---]. 2047.13
mrṯn.ṯt.qštm.ṯn.[q]lʻm. | ǵdyn.qšt.w.qlʻ. | bn.gzl.qšt.w.qlʻ. | [---]n.qšt. | ilhd.qšt. | ʻdn.qšt.w.qlʻ. | ilmhr.qšt.w.qlʻ. | bn.g 119[321].1.5
lʻ. | bn.yy.qšt. | ilrb.qšt. | bn.nmš.ṯt.qšt.w.qlʻ. | bʻl.qšt.w.qlʻ. 119[321].4.17

qlṣ

.ḥdrm.b ṯmnt. | ap.sgrt.ydʻ[t k.]bt.k an[št]. | k in.b ilht.ql[ṣ] k.mh.tarš[n]. | l btlt.ʻnt.w t[ʻ]n.btlt.ʻn[t]. | ṯhm k.il.ḥkm. 3[ʻNT.VI].5.36
]. | w yʻn.lṭpn.il d p[id]. | ydʻt k.bt.k anšt.w i[n.b ilht]. | qlṣ k.tbʻ.bt.ḫnp.lb[k.--.ti] | ḫd.d iṯ.b kbd k.tšt.b [---]. | irt k.d 18[3AQHT].1.17
ilm.d mlk. | y[t]b.aliyn.bʻl. | ytʻdd.rkb.ʻrpt. | [--].ydd.w yqlṣn. | yqm.w ywpṯn.b tk. | p[ḫ]r.bn.ilm.štt. | p[--].b ṯlḥn y.q 4[51].3.12

qlql

ḥd h]. | w.y[ṣq.b.ap h]. | k.l.ḫ[ru.w.l.yṯtn.ššw]. | mss.[št.qlql.w.št]. | ʻrgz[.ydk.aḥd h]. | w.yṣq[.b.ap h]. | k.yiḫd[.akl.šš 161[56].9
. | [ydk aḥd h w yṣq b ap h. | [k l yḫru w]l yṯtn mss št qlql. | [w št ʻrgz y]dk aḥd h w yṣq b ap h. | [k.yiḫd akl š]šw š 160[55].8

qmḥ

š.šš[w.w.ykhp]. | mid.dblt.yṯ[nt.w]. | ṣmq[m].yṯnm.w[.qmḥ.bql]. | tdkn.aḥd h.w[.yṣq]. | b.ap h. 161[56].34
-]. | k yraš w ykhp mid. | dblt yṯnt w ṣmqm yṯn[m]. | w qmḥ bql yṣq aḥd h. | b ap h. 160[55].25
qmḥ.d.kly.b bt.skn. | l.illdrm. | lṯḥ.ḥsr.b.šbʻ.ddm. 2093.1
qmḥ.d.kly.k šḥ.illdrm. | b d.zlb[n.--]. | arbʻ.ʻš[r.]dd.nʻr. | d.ap 2094.1
[---].prš qmḥ.d.nšlm. | [---].prš.d.nšlm. | [---.nš]lm. | [---.nš]lm. | [---.nš 2036.1
t.w ynt.[qrt.w ṯn.ḥṯm]. | w bǵr.arbʻ.[---.kdm.yn]. | prs.qmḥ.mʻ[--.---]. | mdbḥt.bt.i[lt.ʻṣrm.l]. | ṣpn š.l ǵlm[t.š.w l.---]. APP.II[173].25
t[.w ynt.qrt]. | w ṯn ḥṯm.w bǵr.arb[ʻ.---]. | kdm.yn.prs.qmḥ.[---]. | mdbḥt.bt.ilt.ʻṣr[m.l ṣpn.š]. | l ǵlmt.š.w l [---.l yrḫ] 35[3].23
[---.]ksp dd qmḥ. | [---.]ṯlṯ dd ksmm. | [---.-]rbr dd šʻrm. | [---.]r[--.]ḥṯm. | 2037.1.1

qmy

. | ilštmʻ.arbʻ.ḥm[r]m.ḫmš.bnšm. | ǵr. | ary.ḥmr w.bnš. | qmy.ḥmr.w.bnš. | ṯbil. | ʻnmky.ḥmr.w.bnš. | rqd arbʻ. | šbn aḥ 2040.24
lm. | mʻrby. | mʻr. | arny. | šʻrt. | ḫlbrpš. | hry. | qmṣ. | ṣʻq. | qmy. | ḫlbkrd. | yʻrt. | uškn. | ʻnqpat. | ilštmʻ. | šbn. | ṯbq. | rqd. | š 2074.16
. | bn.[gr]gs.msg. | bn[.--]an.msg. | bn[.--].m[sg]. | b[--]n.qmy.msg. | [---]n.msg. | [----].msg. | [---].ms[g]. 133[-].2.5
-]. | b[n.---]. | šm[-.---]. | tkn[.---]. | knn.b.ḫ[lb]. | bn mṯ.b.qmy. | nʻr.b.ulm. 2046.2.5
ḫlb ʻprm.ṯṯ. | ḫlb krd.ṯn ʻšr. | qmy.arbʻ.ʻšr. | ṣʻq.arbʻ ʻšr. | ṣʻ.ṯmn. | šḥq.ʻšrm.arbʻ.kbd. | ḫlb r 67[110].3
----]. | [---.--]k. | [---.q]rt. | [---.--]d.b.gnʻ. | [---].ḫbt. | [---].qmy. | [---.]qmy. | [---.--]b. | bn.t[--.---.a]ǵt. | špš[yn.---.u]brʻy. | 2015.1.16
]k. | [---.q]rt. | [---.--]d.b.gnʻ. | [---].ḫbt. | [---].qmy. | [---.]qmy. | [---.--]b. | bn.t[--.---.a]ǵt. | špš[yn.---.u]brʻy. | iln.[---]. | b 2015.1.17

qmnz

š.ymm]. | ẓrn.yrḫ.w.ḫmš.y[m]m. | mrat.ḫmš.ʻšr.ymm. | qmnz.yrḫ.w.ḫmš.ymm. | ʻnmk.yrḫ. | ypr.yrḫ.w.ḫmš.ymm. 66[109].8
bʻly. | ypr. | ary. | ẓrn. | art. | ṯlḥny. | ṯlrby. | dmt. | aǵt. | w.qmnz. | slḫ. | yknʻm. | šlmy. | w.ull. | ṯmry. | qrt. | ʻrm. | nnu. | [--] 71[113].15
ʻnmky[.---]. | mgdly.ǵlpṯr.ṯn.krmm.w.ṯlṯ.ub[dym.---]. | qmnz.ṯṯ.krm.yknʻm.ṯmn.krm[.---]. | krm.nʻmn.b.ḫly.ull.krm 1081.11
dmt ṯlṯ. | qmnz ṯql. | zlyy ṯql. | ary ḫmšt. | yknʻm ḫmšt. | ʻnmky ṯqlm. | [1176.2

qmnzy

rṭym.mddbʻl. | kdn.zlyy. | krwn.arty. | tlmu.zlyy. | pdu.qmnzy. | bdl.qrṭy. | trgn.bn.ṯǵh. | aupš.qmnzy. | ṯrry.mṣbty. | p 89[312].5
u.apsty.b[--]. | w.bn h.w aṯt h.w.alp.w ṯmn.ṣin. | [-]dln.qmnzy.w.a[ṯt h]. | wšṯn.bn h. | ṯmgdl.yknʻmy.w.aṯt h. | w.bn 1080.3
tlmu.zlyy. | pdu.qmnzy. | bdl.qrṭy. | trgn.bn.ṯǵh. | aupš.qmnzy. | ṯrry.mṣbty. | prn.nǵṭy. | ṯrdn.zlyy. 89[312].8

qmʻt

. | [l].mdr[ǵ]lm. | b yrḫ[ri]šyn. | šb[ʻ.--]n.[k]bd. | w[.---.]qmʻt. | [---.]mdrǵlm. | [---.]mdm. | [w].ʻšr.dd.l np[l]. | r[p]š. 2012.23

qmṣ

yšn. | b dmʻ h.nhmmt. | šnt.tluan. | w yškb.nhmmt. | w yqmṣ.w b ḥlm h. | il.yrd.b ḏhrt h. | ab adm.w yqrb. | b šal.krt. 14[KRT].1.35
ṭbḫ.alpm.ap ṣin.šql.ṯrm. | w mri ilm.ʻǵlm.dt.šnt. | imr.qmṣ.llim.k ksp. | l ʻbrm.zt.ḫrṣ.l ʻbrm.kš. | dpr.ṯlḥn.b qʻl.b qʻl. 22.2[124].14
alpm[.ap]. | ṣin.šql.ṯrm[.w]m | ria.il.ʻǵlm.d[t]. | šnt.imr.qmṣ.l[l]im. | ṣḥ.aḫ h.b bht h.a[r]y h. | b qrb hkl h.ṣḥ. | šbʻm.b 4[51].6.43

.alp[m.ap.ṣin.šql]. | ṯrm.w [mri.ilm.‘glm.dt.šnt]. | imr.[qmṣ.llim.---]. 1[‘NT.X].4.32
. | gb‘ly. | ulm. | m‘rby. | m‘r. | arny. | š‘rt. | ḫlbrpš. | hry. | qmṣ. | ṣ‘q. | qmy. | ḫlbkrd. | y‘rt. | uškn. | ‘nqpat. | ilštm‘. | šbn. | ṭ 2074.14
ḫ].nql.ṯn.ḫpn[.---]. | [---].aḥd.ḫmš.am[--.---]. | [---.--]m.qmṣ.ṯlṯm.i[qnu.---]. | [b.yr]ḫ.mgmr.mš[--.---]. | [---].iqnu.ḫmš 1106.37

qn

tm.ǵr.b abn. | ydy.psltm.b y‘r. | yhdy.lḥm.w dqn. | yṯlṯ.qn.ḏr‘ h.yḥrṯ. | k gn.ap lb.k ‘mq.yṯlṯ. | bmt.yšu.g h.w yṣḥ. | b‘l 5[67].6.20
‘l. | ǵr.b ab.td[.ps]ltm[.b y‘r]. | thdy.lḥm.w dqn[.ṯṯlṯ]. | qn.ḏr‘ h.tḥrṯ.km.gn. | ap lb.k ‘mq.ṯṯlṯ.bmt. | b‘l.mt.my.lim.bn 6[62].1.4
b.l bn.ilm. | mt.al.y‘db km. | k imr.b p h. | k lli.b ṯbrn. | qn h.ṯḫtan. | nrt.ilm.špš. | ṣḥrrt.la. | šmm.b yd.md | d.ilm.mt.b 4[51].8.20
. | ngš.ank.aliyn b‘l. | ‘dbnn ank.imr.b p y. | k lli.b ṯbrn q y.ḫtu hw. | nrt.ilm.špš.ṣḥrrt. | la.šmm.b yd.bn ilm.mt. | ym. 6[49].2.23
l.[k]rpn. | [---.]ym.w t‘l.trṯ. | [---].yn.‘šy l ḥbš. | [---.]ḥtn.qn.yṣbt. | [---.--]m.b nši.‘n h.w tphn. | [---.--]ml.ksl h.k b[r]q. 17[2AQHT].6.9
.b rumm. | adr.qrnt.b y‘lm.mtnm. | b ‘qbt.ṯr.adr.b ǵlil.qnm. | tn.l kṯr.w ḫss.yb‘l.qšt l ‘nt. | qṣ‘t.l ybmt.limm.w t‘n.btl 17[2AQHT].6.23
m. | ṯlṯ.m[a]t.art.ḥkpt. | mit.dnn. | mitm.iqnu. | ḫmš.‘šr.qn.n‘m.‘n[m]. | ṯn.ḥblm.alp.alp.am[-]. | ṯmn.ḥblm.šb‘.šb‘.ma[1128.29
.rqḥ. | kkrm.brḏl. | mit.tišrm. | ṯlṯm.almg. | ḫmšm.kkr. | qnm. | ‘šrm.kk[r]. | brr. | [‘]šrm.npš. | ‘šrm.zt.mm. | ‘rb‘m. | šm 141[120].10
t. | ‘šr.ydt.b.‘šrt. | ḫmš.kkrm.ṣml. | ‘šrt.ksp h. | ḫmš.kkr.qnm. | ṯlṯt.w.ṯlṯt.ksp h. | arb‘.kkr. | algbṯ.arb‘t. | ksp h. | kkr.š‘r 1127.12

qna

rišym.qnum. | bn.ilrš. | ‘[p]ṯn. | b[n.‘r]my. | [--]ṯy. | bn.ǵd‘. | bn.‘yn. | b 2078.1
w šm.‘rbm.yr[.---]. | mṯbt.ilm.ṯmn.ṯ[--.--]. | pamt.šb‘. | iqnu.šmt[.---]. | [b]n.šrm. | iqran.ilm.n‘mm[.agzry ym.bn]y 23[52].21

qnḏ

r. | mrum. | bn.‘[--]t. | bn.adty. | bn.krwn. | bn.nǵsk. | bn.qnḏ. | bn.pity. | w.nḥl h. | bn.rt. | bn.l[--]. | bn.[---]. | [---.--]y. | [- 113[400].3.16
bn.pi[ty]. | w.nḥ[l h]. | ‘bd[--]. | bn.s[---]. | bn.at[--]. | bn.qnḏ. | ṣmq[-]. | bn.anny. | bn.‘mtḏl. | bn.‘myn. | bn.alz. | bn.birt 117[325].1.7

qny

.mṯn.rgmm. | argm k.šskn m‘. | mgn.rbt.aṯrt ym. | mǵẓ.qnyt.ilm. | hyn.‘ly.l mpḫm. | b d.ḫss.mṣbṭm. | yṣq.ksp.yšl | ḥ.ḫ 4[51].1.23
[i]k.mgn.rbt.aṯrt. | [ym].mǵẓ.qnyt.ilm. | w tn.bt.l b‘l.km. | [i]lm.w ḥẓr.k bn. | [a]ṯrt.gm.l ǵl 8[51FRAG].2
.aliyn.b‘l. | mǵyt.btlt.‘nt. | tmgnn.rbt[.a]ṯrt ym. | tǵẓyn.qnyt.ilm. | w t‘n.rbt.aṯrt ym. | ik.tmgnn.rbt. | aṯrt.ym.tǵẓyn. | 4[51].3.26
lm. | w t‘n.rbt.aṯrt ym. | ik.tmgnn.rbt. | aṯrt.ym.tǵẓyn. | qnyt.ilm.mgntm. | ṯr.il.d pid.hm.ǵẓtm. | bny.bnwt w t‘n. | btlt 4[51].3.30
ṣb‘t h.yšu.g h.w y[ṣḥ]. | ik.mǵyt.rbt.aṯr[t.y]m. | ik.atwt.qnyt.i[lm]. | rǵb.rǵbt.w tǵt[--]. | hm.ǵmu.ǵmit.w ‘s[--]. | lḥm.h 4[51].4.32
y.bnwt w t‘n. | btlt.‘nt.nmgn. | [-]m.rbt.aṯrt.ym. | [nǵ]ẓ.qnyt.ilm. | [---].nmgn.hwt. | [--].aliyn.b‘l. | [--.]rbt.aṯrt.ym. | [-- 4[51].3.35
ymn h.w y‘n.yṯ[p]n[.mh]r. | št.b yn.yšt.ila.il š[--.]il. | d yqny.ḏdm.yd.mḫṣt.a[qh]t.ǵ | zr.tmḫṣ.alpm.ib.št[-.]št. | ḥršm 19[1AQHT].4.220
‘b]d.‘lm.ṯlṯ. | [ssw]m.mrkbt b trbṣ bn.amt. | [tn.b]nm.aqny. | [tn.ṯa]rm.amid. | [w y‘n].ṯr.ab h.il. | d[--].b bk.krt. | b d 14[KRT].2.57
tlt.‘nt. | w ypt l ybmt.li[mm]. | w y‘ny.aliyn[.b‘l]. | lm.k qnym.‘l[m.--]. | k dr d.d yknn[.--]. | b‘l.yṣǵd.mli[.--]. | il hd.ml 10[76].3.6
štm. | [----.]mhrm.ht.tṣdn.tinṯt. | [---]m.tṣḥq.‘nt.w b lb.tqny. | [---.]ṯb l y.l aqht.ǵzr.ṯb l y w l k. | [---]m.l aqry k.b ntb 17[2AQHT].6.41

qnmlk

.qšt. | bn.šyn.qšt. | ‘bd.qšt. | bn.ulmy.qšt. | ṯqbn.qšt. | bn.qnmlk.qšt. | ytḥm.qšt. | grp.qšt. | m‘rby. | n‘mn.ṯt.qštm.w.ql‘. | 104[316].5

qnṣ

q.w ḥ[m]ḥmt.yṯb[n]. | yspr.l ḫmš.l ṣ[---.]šr.pḫr.klat. | tqtnṣn.w tldn.tld.[ilm.]n‘mm.agzr ym. | bn.ym.ynqm.b a[p.] 23[52].58
tqtm.mtqtm.k lrmn[.--]. | bm.nšq.w hr.b ḥbq.ḥmḥmt.tqt[nṣn]. | tldn.šḥr.w šlm.rgm.l il.ybl.a[ṯt y]. | il.ylt.mh.ylt.yl 23[52].51

q‘l

r.qmṣ.llim.k ksp. | l ‘brm.zt.ḫrṣ.l ‘brm.kš. | dpr.ṯlḥn.b q‘l.b q‘l. | mlkm.hn.ym.yṣq.yn.ṯmk. | mrṯ.yn.srnm.yn.bld. | ǵl 22.2[124].16
ṣ.llim.k ksp. | l ‘brm.zt.ḫrṣ.l ‘brm.kš. | dpr.ṯlḥn.b q‘l.b q‘l. | mlkm.hn.ym.yṣq.yn.ṯmk. | mrṯ.yn.srnm.yn.bld. | ǵll.yn.i 22.2[124].16
m. | [---.]alp. | [---.]ym.rbt. | [---.]b nhrm. | [‘b]r.gbl.‘br. | q‘l.‘br.iht. | np šmm.šmšr. | l dgy.aṯrt. | mǵ.l qdš.amrr. | idk.al 3[‘NT.VI].6.8

q‘t

hn.b špt y mn | t hn ṯlḫ h w mlg h y | ṯtqt ‘m h b q‘t. | tq‘t ‘m prbḫt. | dmqt ṣǵrt kṯrt. 24[77].49
sp | r hn.b špt y mn | t hn ṯlḫ h w mlg h y | ṯtqt ‘m h b q‘t. | tq‘t ‘m prbḫt. | dmqt ṣǵrt kṯrt. 24[77].48

qpḥn

[---.]ṯrd. | [---.]qpḥn. | [---.a]ǵlṯr. | [---.]ṭml. | [---.]bn.ḥṣqt. | [---.]bn.udr[-]. 2132.2

qpt

at. | w mmskn. | w.ṯt.mqrtm. | w.ṯn.irpm.w.ṯn.trqm. | w.qpt.w.mqḥm. | w.ṯlṯm.yn šb‘.kbd d ṯbṭ. | w.ḫmšm.yn.d iḫ h. 1103.21

qṣ

h.km.lb.‘n[t]. | aṯr.b‘l.tiḫd.m[t]. | b sin.lpš.tšṣq[n h]. | b qṣ.all.tšu.g h.w[tṣ] | ḥ.at.mt.tn.aḫ y. | w ‘n.bn.ilm.mt.mh. | ta 6[49].2.11
[-----]. | yṣq.šm[n.---]. | ‘n.tr.arṣ.w šmm. | sb.l qṣm.arṣ. | l ksm.mhyt.‘n. | l arṣ.m[ṭ]r.b‘l. | w l šd.mṭr.‘ly. | n‘m 16[126].3.3
il dbḥ.b bt h.mṣd.ṣd.b qrb | hkl [h].ṣḥ.l qṣ.ilm.tlḥmn. | ilm.w tštn.tštn y[n] ‘d šb‘. | trṯ.‘d.škr.y‘db.yrḫ UG5.1.1.2
[--]m.[---.] | gm.ṣḥ.l q[ṣ.ilm.---]. | l rḥqm.l p[-.---]. | ṣḥ.il.ytb.b[mrzḥ.---]. | bṯt.‘llm 1[‘NT.X].4.2
.qm.yṯ‘r. | w yšlḥmn h. | ybrd.ṯd.l pnw h. | b ḥrb.mlḥt. | qṣ.mri.ndd. | y‘šr.w yšqyn h. | ytn.ks.b d h. | krpn.b klat.yd h. 3[‘NT].1.8
rt[.yn]. | ‘d.lḥm.šty.ilm. | w pq mrǵtm.ṯd. | b ḥrb.mlḥt.qṣ[.m]r | i.tšty.krp[nm.y]n. | [b k]s.ḫrṣ.d[m.‘ṣm]. | [---.--]n. | [-- 4[51].6.57
[------]. | [---.l]ḥm[.---]. | [---].ay š[---]. | [---.b ḥ]rb.mlḥ[t.qṣ]. | [mri.tšty.krpnm].yn.b ks.ḫ[rṣ]. | [dm.‘ṣm.---]n.krpn.‘l.[17[2AQHT].6.4
[‘]d.lḥm[.šty.ilm]. | w pq.mr[ǵtm.ṭd.---]. | b ḥrb.[mlḥt.qṣ.mri]. | šty.kr[pnm.yn.---]. | b ks.ḫr[ṣ.dm.‘ṣm.---]. | ks.ksp[.- 5[67].4.14

qṣy

tn bn.drṣy. | [--]kn bn.pri. | [r]špab bn.pni. | [ab]mn bn.qṣy. | [ʿ]pṯrm bn.agmz. | [-]n bn.iln. | [--]nn bn.ibm. | [-]n bn.ḥ 2087.9
[s]pr.bnš.mlk.d.b.tbq. | [kr]wn. | [--]n. | [q]ṣy. | ṯn.bn.iwrḫz.[n]ʿrm. | yṣr[.-]qb. | w.ṯn.bnš.iytlm. | w.ʿšr 2066.2.3

qṣm

t.adm.ṣat.š[p]š. | tḥt h.k kdrt.ri[š]. | ʿl h.k irbym.kp.k.qṣm. | ǵrmn.kp.mhr.ʿtkt. | rišt.l bmt h.šnst. | kpt.b ḥbš h.brk 3[ʿNT].2.10

qṣn

rdnnm. | bn.aǵli.uṯpt.srdnnm. | asrn.uṯpt.srdnnm. | bn.qṣn.uṯpt.srdnnm. | yly.uṯpt.srdnnm. | arṯṯb.uṯpt.srdnnm. 1124.10
[aǵ]ltn. | [--]ṯm.b.gt.irbṣ. | [--]šmyn. | [w.]nḥl h. | bn.qṣn. | bn.ksln. | bn.ṣrym. | bn.ṯmq. | bn.ntp. | bn.mlk. | bn.ṯʿ[-]. | 1073.1.5
yn. | abškn.kdm.yn. | šbn.kdm.yn. | ʿbdiltp.ṯm[n].y[n]. | qṣn.ḫ[---]. | arny.[---]. | aǵltn.ḫmš[.yn]. 1085.10
zt. | bn.ayl. | [-----]. | ʿbd[--]. | bn.i[--]. | ʿd[--]. | ild[--]. | bn.qṣn. | ʿlpy. | kṯy. | bn.ẓmn. | bn.trdn. | ypq. | ʿbd. | qrḥ. | abšr. | bn 2117.2.20
bn.ṣdqil.ṯt.qštm.w.ṯn.qlʿm. | bn.ṯlṯ.ṯ[lṯ.]qšt.w.ṯn.qlʿm. | qṣn.ṯt.qštm.w.qlʿ. | bn.gṯrn.q[š]t. | bn.ḫdi.ṯt.qštm.w.ṯn.qlʿm. | 119[321].3.6

qṣʿt

.hlk.kṯr. | k yʿn.w yʿn.tdrq.ḫss. | hlk.qšt.ybln.hl.yš | rbʿ.qṣʿt.apnk.dnil. | mt.rpi.aphn.ǵzr.mt. | hrnmy.gm.l aṯt h.k yṣ 17[2AQHT].5.13
aḫr.ymǵy.kṯr. | w ḫss.b d.dnil.ytnn. | qšt.l brk h.yʿdb. | qṣʿt.apnk.mṯt.dnty. | tšlḥm.tššqy ilm. | tsad.tkbd.hmt.bʿl. | ḥk 17[2AQHT].5.28
.bʿl.b bht ht. | il hd.b qrb.hkl h. | qšt hn.aḫd.b yd h. | w qṣʿt h.bm.ymn h. | idk.l ytn pnm. | tk.aḫ.šmk.mla[t.r]umm. | 10[76].2.7
apʿ.il.b gdrt.k lb.l | ḥṯ h.imḫṣ h.k d.ʿl.qšt h. | imḫṣ h.ʿl.qṣʿt h.hwt. | l aḥw.ap.qšt h.l ttn. | l y.w b mt[.-]ḫ.mṣṣ[-]t[.--]. 19[1AQHT].1.15
yʿn.ytpn.[mhr.št]. | šmʿ.l btlt.ʿnt.at.ʿ[l.qšt h]. | tmḫṣ h.qṣʿt h.hwt.l t[ḥwy]. | nʿmn.ǵzr.št.ṯrm.w[---]. | ištir.b ddm.w 18[3AQHT].4.13
[-----]. | [---.]abl.qšt ṯmn. | ašrb.ʿqṣʿt.w hn šb[ʿ]. | b ymm.apnk.dnil.mt. | rpi.a hn.ǵzr.mt.hrnm 17[2AQHT].5.3
[---]. | aqht.w tbk.y[---.---]. | abn.ank.w ʿl.[qšt k.---.ʿl]. | qṣʿt k.at.l ḥ[---.---]. | w ḫlq.ʿpmm[.---]. 18[3AQHT].4.41
š.ksp.w atn k. | [ḫrṣ.w aš]lḥ k.w tn.qšt k.[l]. | [ʿnt.tq]ḥ[.q]ṣʿt k.ybmt.limm. | w yʿn.aqht.ǵzr.adr.ṯqbm. | [d]lbnn.adr. 17[2AQHT].6.19
b ʿqbt.ṯr.adr.b ǵlil.qnm. | tn.l kṯr.w ḫss.ybʿl.qšt l ʿnt. | qṣʿt.l ybmt.limm.w tʿn.btlt. | ʿnt.irš ḥym.l aqht.ǵzr. | irš ḥym. 17[2AQHT].6.25

qṣṣ

t. | [--.tl]ḥm.tšty. | [ilm.w tp]q.mrǵtm. | [ṯd.b ḥrb.m]lḥt.qṣ. | [mri.tšty.k]rpnm yn. | [b ks.ḫrṣ.dm].ʿṣm. 4[51].3.42

qṣr

]rm[.ṯṯwy]. | šqlt.b ǵlt.yd k. | l tdn.dn.almnt. | l ṯpṭ.ṯpṭ.qṣr.npš. | km.aḫt.ʿrš.mdw. | anšt.ʿrš.zbln. | rd.l mlk.amlk. | l d 16.6[127].34
ulp.m[dl]l km.ulp.qr zbl.u[š]n yp km. | u b ap km.u b q[ṣ]rt.npš km.u b qṭt.tqṭṭ. | ušn yp km.l d[b]ḥm.w l.ṯʿ.dbḥ n. 32[2].1.23
t km.ulp.mdll km.ulp.qr zbl]. | [u ṯḥṭu.u b ap km.u b qṣrt.npš km.u b qṭt]. | [tqṭṭ.u ṯḥṭu.l dbḥm.w l.ṯʿ.dbḥ n.ndb]ḥ 32[2].1.8A
m.ulp.mdll km.ulp]. | [qr zbl.ušn.yp km.b ap km.u b qṣrt.np]št km. | [u b qṭt.tqṭṭ.ušn.yp km.---.-]yt km. | [---.]km. APP.I[-].1.17
. | [ulp.mdll kn.ulp.qr zbl.ušn.y]p kn. | [u b ap kn.u b qṣrt.npšt kn.u b qṭ]t tqṭṭ. | [ušn.yp kn.---.--]l.il.tʿḏr bʿl. | [----- APP.I[-].1.7
kn.ulp.mdll kn.ulp.]qr zbl. | [ušn.yp kn.u b ap kn.u b qṣrt.npš kn.u b]qṭt. | [tqṭṭn.ušn.yp kn.---.-]gym. | [---.]l kbkb APP.I[-].2.15
kn[.u]lp.mdll kn.ulp qr z[bl]. | lšn yp kn.b ap [kn.u b qṣ]rt.npš kn.u b qṭt. | tqṭṭn.ušn y[p kn.l dbḥm.]w l ṯʿ dbḥ n. 32[2].1.31
bt kn.ulp.md[ll k]n.ulp.q[r zbl]. | u ṯḥṭin.b ap kn.u b [q]ṣrt.npš[kn.u b qṭt]. | tqṭṭn u ṯḥṭin.l bḥm.w l ṯʿ.d[bḥ n.ndb 32[2].1.14
ǵrm.ṯṯwy.šqlt. | b ǵlt.yd k.l tdn. | dn.almnt.l ṯpṭ. | ṯpṭ qṣr.npš.l tdy. | ṯšm.ʿl.dl.l pn k. | l tšlḥm.ytm.bʿd. | ksl k.almnt 16.6[127].47

qqln

ṯnnm. | bn.qqln. | w.nḥl h. | w.nḥl h. | bn.šml[-]. | bn.brzn. | bn.ḫtr[-]. | bn. 116[303].2
. | ṯnnm. | [ar]swn.bn.qqln. | m[--].bn.qqln. | ʿbdil[-].bn.qqln. | liy.bn.qqln. | mnn.bn.ṣnr. | iḫy.[b]n[.--]l[-]. | ʿbdy[rḫ].b 85[80].4.4
]swn.bn.qqln. | m[--].bn.qqln. | ʿbdil[-].bn.qqln. | liy.bn.qqln. | mnn.bn.ṣnr. | iḫy.[b]n[.--]l[-]. | ʿbdy[rḫ].bn.gttn. | yrmn 85[80].4.5
nsk.ṯlṯ. | bn.[--.]m[-]ḫr. | bn.šmrm. | ṯnnm. | [ar]swn.bn.qqln. | m[--].bn.qqln. | ʿbdil[-].bn.qqln. | liy.bn.qqln. | mnn.bn. 85[80].4.2
m[-]ḫr. | bn.šmrm. | ṯnnm. | [ar]swn.bn.qqln. | m[--].bn.qqln. | ʿbdil[-].bn.qqln. | liy.bn.qqln. | mnn.bn.ṣnr. | iḫy.[b]n[.- 85[80].4.3
spr.ḥršm. | liy.bn.qqln. | [---.a]lṯy. | [-----]. | [---]tl. | [---]ʿbl. | [---]bln. | [---]dy. | [--- 1036.2

qr

tpq.l awl. | išttk.lm.ttkn. | štk.mlk.dn. | štk.šibt.ʿn. | štk.qr.bt.il. | w mṣlt.bt.ḥr[š]. 12[75].2.61
---.]bt k.ap.l pḫr k ʿnt tqm.ʿnt.tqm. | [---.p]ḫr k.ygrš k.qr.bt k.ygrš k. | [---].bnt.ṣʿṣ.bnt.mʿmʿ.ʿbd.ḥrn.[--.]k. | [---].aǵ 1001.2.10
p.ḫty.ulp.alṯy.ulp.ǵbr]. | [ulp.ḫbt km.ulp.mdll km.ulp.qr zbl]. | [u ṯḥṭu.u b ap km.u b qṣrt.npš km.u b qṭt]. | [tqṭṭ.u 32[2].1.8
.ḫty.ulp[.alṯy.ulp.]ǵbr. | ulp.ḫbt kn.ulp.md[ll k]n.ulp.q[r zbl]. | u ṯḥṭin.b ap kn.u b [q]ṣrt.npš[kn.u b qṭt]. | tqṭṭn u 32[2].1.13
[t]y.ulp.alṯy.ul[p.ǵbr.]ulp. | ḫbt km.ulp.m[dl]l km.ulp.qr zbl.u[š]n yp km. | u b ap km.u b q[ṣ]rt.npš km.u b qṭt.tqṭ 32[2].1.22
ty.u]lp.alṯy. | [ulp.ǵbr.ulp.ḫbt km.ulp.mdll km.ulp]. | [qr zbl.ušn.yp km.b ap km.u b qṣrt.np]št km. | [u b qṭt.tqṭṭ.u APP.I[-].1.17
lp.ḫty.ulp.alṯy]. | [ulp.ǵbr.ulp.ḫbt kn.ulp.mdll kn.ulp.]qr zbl. | [ušn.yp kn.u b ap kn.u b qṣrt.npš kn.u b]qṭt. | [tqṭṭn APP.I[-].2.14
lp.ḫty.ulp.alṯy.ulp.ǵbr.ul]p.ḫbt kn. | [ulp.mdll kn.ulp.qr zbl.ušn.y]p kn. | [u b ap kn.u b qṣrt.npšt kn.u b qṭ]t tqṭṭ. | APP.I[-].1.6
.ḫty.ulp.alṯy. | ulp.ǵbr.ulp.[ḫbt] kn[.u]lp.mdll kn.ulp qr z[bl]. | lšn yp kn.b ap [kn.u b qṣ]rt.npš kn.u b qṭt. | tqṭṭn.u 32[2].1.30
m[-]ǵ[-].thmt.brq. | [---].ṯṣb.qšt.bnt. | [---.ʿ]n h.km.bṯn.yqr. | [krpn h.-.l]arṣ.ks h.tšpk m. | [l ʿpr.tšu.g h.]w tṣḥ.šmʿ. 17[2AQHT].6.14
qbr.bn y. | tšḫṭann.b šnt h.qr.[mym]. | mlk.yṣm.y l km.qr.mym.d ʿ[l k]. | mḫṣ.aqht.ǵzr.amd.gr bt il. | ʿnt.brḥ.p ʿlm h 19[1AQHT].3.152
ʿl.ytbr.diy. | hmt.hm.tʿpn.ʿl.qbr.bn y. | tšḫṭann.b šnt h.qr.[mym]. | mlk.yṣm.y l km.qr.mym.d ʿ[l k]. | mḫṣ.aqht.ǵzr. 19[1AQHT].3.151
.l yḫ. | w yʿny.krt.ṯʿ. | bn.al.tbkn.al. | tdm.l y.al tkl.bn. | qr.ʿn k.mḫ.riš k. | udmʿt.ṣḥ.aḫt k. | ṯtmnt.bt.ḥmḥ h. | d[-]n.tb 16.1[125].27
bn.yd k. | mšdpt.w hn.špšm. | b šbʿ.w l.yšn.pbl. | mlk.l qr.ṯigt.ibr h. | l ql.nhqt.ḥmr h. | l gʿt.alp.ḥrṯ.zǵt. | klb.ṣpr.w yl 14[KRT].3.120
m. | ḫmš.ṯdṯ.ym. | mk.špšm.b šbʿ. | w l.yšn.pbl. | mlk.l [qr.]ṯiqt. | ibr h[.l]ql.nhqt. | ḥmr[h.l gʿt.]alp. | ḥrṯ[.l z]ǵt.klb. | 14[KRT].5.223

qra

.ilm.ṯmn.ṯ[--.--].|pamt.šbʻ.|iqnu.šmt[.---].|[b]n.šrm.|iqran.ilm.nʻmm[.agzry ym.bn]ym.|ynqm.b ap zd.aṯrt.[---]. 23[52].23
iqra.ilm.n[ʻmm.---].|w ysmm.bn.š[---].|ytnm.qrt.l ʻly[.---].| 23[52].1
yu[ḫd.ksa.mlk h].|nḫt.kḥṯ.d[rkt h.b bt y].|aṣḥ.rpi[m.iqra.ilnym].|b qrb.h[kl y.aṯr h.rpum.l] |tdd.aṯr[h.l tdd.ilny 22.1[123].19
bʻ.|ydt y.b ṣʻ.hm.ks.ymsk.|nhr.k[--].ṣḥn.bʻl.ʻm.|aḫ y.qran.hd.ʻm.ary y.|w lḥm m ʻm aḫ y.lḥm.|w št m.ʻm.a[ḫ] y 5[67].1.23
ḫ.bn.ilm.mt.|[---.]g h.w aṣḥ.ik.yṣḥn.|[bʻl.ʻm.aḫ y.ik].yqrun.hd.|[ʻm.ary y.---.--]p.mlḥm y.|[---.---]lt.qẓb.|[---.]šm 5[67].2.22
qr]|b hkl y.[---].|lk bt y.r[pim.rpim.b bt y.aṣḥ].|km.iqr[a km.ilnym.b hkl y].|aṯr h.r[pum.l tdd.aṯr h].|l tdd.il[n 22.1[123].4
[---.m]rzʻy.lk.bt y.|[rpim.rpim.b]t y.aṣḥ km.iqra.|[km.ilnym.b h]kl y.aṯr h.rpum.|[l tdd.aṯr h].l tdd.ilny 21[122].1.2
w yʻn.il.|[---.mrzʻ]y.lk.bt y.rpim.|[rpim.bt y.aṣ]ḥ km.iqra km.|[ilnym.b hkl]y.aṯr h.rpum.|[l tdd.aṯr]h.l tdd.i[ln 21[122].1.10
.bʻl[.---.mhr].|ʻnt.lk b[t y.rpim.rpim.b bt y].|aṣḥ.km.[iqra km.ilnym.b] |hkl y.aṯr[h.rpum.l tdd].|aṯr h.l t[dd.ilny 22.1[123].9
um.pḫl.pḫlt.bt.abn.bt šmm w thm.|qrit.l špš.um h.špš.um.ql.bl.ʻm.|il.mbk nhrm.b ʻdt.thmtm.| UG5.7.2
š.ʻq šr.ln h.ml|ḫš.abd.ln h.ydy.ḥmt.hlm.yṯq.|w yṯb.|tqru.l špš.um h.špš.[um.q]l bl.ʻm.|yrḫ.lrgt h.mnt.nṯk.n[ḥš]. UG5.7.25
.|ḥmt.hlm.yṯq.nḥš.yšlḥm.nḥš.|ʻq šr.yʻdb.ksa.w yṯb.|tqru.l špš.um h.špš.um.ql b.ʻm.|ršp.bbt h.mnt.nḥš.šmrr.|n UG5.7.30
y.ḥmt.hlm.yṯq.|nḥš.yšlḥm.nḥš.ʻq šr.ydb.ksa.|w yṯb.|tqru.l špš.u h.špš.um.ql.bl.ʻm.|dgn.ttl h.mnt.nṯk.nḥš.šmrr. UG5.7.14
y.ḥmt.hlm.yṯq.nḥš.yšlḥm.|nḥš.ʻq šr.yʻdb.ksa.w yṯb.|tqru l špš.um h.špš.um.ql.bl.ʻm.|ʻnt w ʻṯtrt inbb h.mnt.nṯk. UG5.7.19
y.|ḥmt.hlm.yṯq.nḥš.yšlḥm.nḥš ʻq.|š.yʻdb.ksa w yṯb.|tqru l špš.um h.špš.um.ql bl ʻm.|ṯṯ.w kmṯ.ḥryt h.mnt.nṯk.n UG5.7.35
t.hlm.yṯq šqy.|nḥš.yšlḥm.nḥš.ʻq šr.yʻdb.|ksa.w yṯb.|tqru.l špš.um h.špš.um.ql bl.|ʻm ḥrn.mṣd h.mnt.nṯk nḥš.|š UG5.7.57
.ḥmt.hlm yṯq.nḥš.|yšlḥm.nḥš.ʻq šr.yʻdb ksa.|w yṯb.|tqru l špš.um h.špš.um.ql bl ʻm.|šḥr.w šlm šmm h mnt.nṯk. UG5.7.51
mt.hlm.yṯq yṯqšqy.nḥš.yšlḥm.ʻq šr.|yʻdb.ksa.w.yṯb.|tqru.l špš.um h.špš.um.ql bl.|ʻm bʻl.mrym.ṣpn.mnt y.nṯk.| UG5.7.8
y.ḥmt.hlm.yṯq nḥš yšlḥm.nḥš.|ʻq.šr.yʻdb.ksa.w yṯb.|tqru l špš um h.špš um ql.bl.ʻm.|mlk.ʻṯtrt h.mnt.nṯk.nḥš.š UG5.7.40
.|ḥmt.hlm.yṯq.nḥš.yšlḥm.nḥš.|ʻq šr.yʻdb.ksa.w yṯb.|tqru.l špš.um.ql bl.ʻm|kṯr.w ḫss.kptr h.mnt.nṯk.nḥš.|šmrr. UG5.7.45
ṣ.drkt.yštkn.|dll.al.ilak.l bn.|ilm.mt.ʻdd.l ydd.|il.ǵzr.yqra.mt.|b npš h.ystrn ydd.|b gngn h.aḥd y.d ym|lk.ʻl.ilm. 4[51].7.47
-.ǵ]r.šrǵzz.ybky.km.nʻr.|[w ydmʻ.k]m.ṣǵr.špš.b šmm.tqru.|[---.]nplt.y[--].mdʻ.nplt.bšr.|[---].w tpky.k[m.]nʻr.tdm UG5.8.38
-]nn.bnt yš[--.---.-]lk.|[--]b.kmm.l k[--].|[šp]š.b šmm.tq[ru.---.-]rt.|[---.]mn mn[-.---.--]n.nmr.|[--.]l ytk.bl[-.---.]m UG5.8.44

qrb

--].|w tṣḥ[.---].|tšqy[.---].|tr.ḥt[-.---].|w msk.tr[.---].|tqrb.aḫ[h.w tṣḥ].|lm.tbʻrn[.---].|mn.yrḫ.k m[rṣ.---].|mn.k 16.2[125].79
bʻl.tbʻ.mrym.ṣpn.|idk.l ttn.pnm.|ʻm.il.mbk.nhrm.|qrb.apq.thmtm.|tgly.ḏd.il.w tbu.|qrš.mlk.ab.šnm.|l pʻn.il.t 4[51].4.22
-.]zr h.ybm.l ilm.|[id]k.l ttn.pnm.ʻm.|[il.]mbk nhrm.qrb.|[a]pq.thmtm.tgly.ḏd.|il.w tbu.qrš..|mlk.ab.šnm.l pʻn. 6.1.33[49.1.5]
[idk.l ttn.pnm].|[ʻm.il.mbk.nhrm].|[qrb.apq.thmtm].|[tgly.ḏd.il.w]tb[a].|[qrš.mlk.ab.]šnm.|[tš 5[67].6.01
dʻṣ.pʻn]m.w tr.arṣ.idk.|[l ttn.pn]m.ʻm il.mbk.nhrm.|[qrb.ap]q.thmtm tgly.ḏd il.|[w tbu.qr]š.mlk.ab.šnm.|[l pʻn.i 17[2AQHT].6.48
rṣ.ṯlṯ.mtḥ.ǵyrm].|[idk.]l ytn.pnm.ʻm.[i]l.mbk.[nhrm.qrb.apq.thmtm].|[ygly.]ḏl i[l].w ybu[.q]rš.mlk[.ab.šnm.l pʻ 2.3[129].4
ʻṣ.]pʻn.|[w tr.a]rṣ.id[k.l ttn.p]nm.|[ʻm.i]l.mbk.nhr[m.qr]b.[ap]q.|[thm]tm.tgl.ḏ[d.]i[l.]w tbu.|[qr]š.m[l]k.ab[.šnm 3[ʻNT.VI].5.14
mmt.|w yqmṣ.w b ḥlm h.|il.yrd.b ḏhrt h.|ab adm.w yqrb.|b šal.krt.m at.|krt.k ybky.|ydmʻ.nʻmn.ǵlm.|il.mlk[.ṯ 14[KRT].1.37
.ṣt h.yʻl.w yškb.|[yd.]mizrt.p yln.mk.b šbʻ.ymm.|[w]yqrb.bʻl.b ḥnt h.abynt.|[d]nil.mt.rpi anḫ.ǵzr.|[mt.]hrnmy. 17[2AQHT].1.17
bʻ.pdr.|ṯmnym.bʻl.[----].|tšʻm.bʻl.mr[-].|bt[.--]b bʻl.b qrb.|bt.w yʻn.aliyn.|bʻl.ašt m.kṯr bn.|ym.kṯr.bnm.ʻdt.|ypt 4[51].7.13
[---.bʻl.b bht h].|[il.hd.b qr]b.hkl h.|w tʻnyn.ǵlm.bʻl.|in.bʻl.b bht ht.|il hd.b qrb.hkl 10[76].2.2
ht.ṯhrm.|iqnim.šmḫ.aliyn.|bʻl.ṣḥ.ḫrn.b bht h.|ʻḏbt.b qrb hkl h.|yblnn ǵrm.mid.ksp.|gbʻm lḥmd.ḫrṣ.|yblnn.udr. 4[51].5.99
--] n.ylt.ḥmḥmt.|[---.mt.r]pi.w ykn.bn h.|[b bt.šrš.]b qrb.hkl h.|[nṣb.skn.i]lib h.b qdš.|[ẓtr.ʻm h.l a]rṣ.mšṣu.|[qṭr 17[2AQHT].1.44
l ṯr.il ab y.|tmrnn.l bny.bnwt.|w ykn.bn h b bt.šrš.b qrb.|hkl h.nṣb.skn.ilib h.b qdš.|ẓtr.ʻm h.l arṣ.mšṣu.qṭr h.|l 17[2AQHT].1.26
.d[t].|šnt.imr.qmṣ.l[l]im.|ṣḥ.aḫ h.b bht h.a[r]y h.|b qrb hkl h.ṣḥ.|šbʻm.bn.aṯrt.|špq.ilm.krm.y[n].|špq.ilht.ḫprt 4[51].6.45
b qr]b.hkl h.|w tʻnyn.ǵlm.bʻl.|in.bʻl.b bht ht.|il hd.b qrb.hkl h.|qšt hn.aḥd.b yd h.|w qṣʻt h.bm.ymn h.|idk.l ytn 10[76].2.5
h].|nḫt.kḥṯ.d[rkt h.b bt y].|aṣḥ.rpi[m.iqra.ilnym].|b qrb.h[kl y.aṯr h.rpum.l] |tdd.aṯr[h.l tdd.ilnym].|asr.mr[kb 22.1[123].20
|[---.]il.d ʻrgzm.|[---.]dt.ʻl.lty.|[---.]tdbḥ.amr.|ṯmn.b qrb.hkl y.[aṯr h.rpum].|tdd.aṯr h.tdd.iln[ym.---].|asr.sswm. 20[121].2.1
k.yrp.|[---.]km.rʻy.ht.alk.|[---.]ṯlṯt.amǵy.l bt.|[y.---.b qrb].hkl y.w yʻn.il.|[---.mrzʻ]y.lk.bt y.rpim.|[rpim.bt y.aṣ]ḥ 21[122].1.8
[--].[-]l[--.b qr]|b hkl y.[---].|lk bt y.r[pim.rpim.b bt y.aṣḥ].|km.iqr[a k 22.1[123].1
t.l k.km.aḫ k.w ḫẓr.|km.ary k.ṣḥ.ḫrn.|b bht k.ʻḏbt.b qrb.|hkl k.tbl k.ǵrm.|mid.ksp.gbʻm.mḥmd..|ḫrṣ.w bn.bht. 4[51].5.92
t.yʻmsn h.|l yrgm.l aliyn bʻl.|ṣḥ.ḫrn.b bhm k.|ʻḏbt.b qrb.hkl k.|tbl k.ǵrm.mid.ksp.|gbʻm.mḥmd.ḫrṣ.|ybl k.udr.i 4[51].5.76
.hk]l m.|w ʻn.ali[yn.]bʻl.|al.tšt.u[rb]t.b bht m.|ḥln.b q[rb.hk]l m.|al td[.pdr]y.bt ar.|[---.ṯl]y.bt.rb.|[---.m]dd.il y 4[51].6.9
l aliyn bʻl.|bn.l rkb.ʻrpt.|bl.ašt.urbt.b bh[t] m.|ḥln.b qrb.hkl m.|w yʻn.aliyn bʻl.|al.tšt.urbt.b[bhtm].|[ḥ]ln].b qrb 4[51].5.124
ḫss.|šmʻ.mʻ.l al[iy]n bʻl.|bl.ašt.ur[bt.]b bht m.|ḥln.b qr[b.hk]l m.|w ʻn.ali[yn.]bʻl.|al.tšt.u[rb]t.b bht m.|ḥln.b q[4[51].6.6
m.kṯr bn.|ym.kṯr.bnm.ʻdt.|ypth.ḥln.b bht m.|urbt.b qrb.[h]kl |m.w y[p]tḥ.b dqt.ʻrpt.|ʻl h[wt].kṯr.w ḫss.|ṣḥq.kṯ 4[51].7.18
t.]b hkl m.|ḫmš.ṯ[d]ṯ.ym.tikl.|išt.[b]bht m.nblat.|b[qrb.hk]l m.mk.|b šb[ʻ.]y[mm].td.išt.|b bht m.n[bl]at.b hkl 4[51].6.31
ali|yn.bʻl.ṯṯbn.bʻl.|l hwt y.ypth.ḥ|ln.b bht m.urbt.|b qrb.hk[l m.yp]tḥ.|bʻl.b dqt[.ʻrp]t.|ql h.qdš.b[ʻl.y]tn.|yṯny.b 4[51].7.27
.hkl m.|w yʻn.aliyn bʻl.|al.tšt.urbt.b[bhtm].|[ḥln].b qrb.hk[l m]. 4[51].5.127
tbrk.ilm.tity.|tity.ilm.l ahl hm.|dr il.l mšknt hm.|w tqrb.w ld.bn.l h.|w tqrb.w ld.bnt.l h.|mk.b šbʻ.šnt.|bn.krt. 15[128].3.20
m.l ahl hm.|dr il.l mšknt hm.|w tqrb.w ld.bn.l h.|w tqrb.w ld.bnt.l h.|mk.b šbʻ.šnt.|bn.krt.km hm.tdr.|ap.bnt. 15[128].3.21
|[---.mid.rm.]krt.|[b tk.rpi.]arṣ.|[b pḫr].qbṣ.dtn.|[w t]qrb.w ld.|bn.tl k.|tld.pǵt.t[--]t.|tld.pǵt[.---].|tld.pǵ[t.---]. 15[128].3.5
b mlk qẓ [l].|nʻmn.ilm l ḫt[n].|m.bʻl trḫ pdry b[t h].|aqrb k ab h bʻ[l].|yǵtr.ʻṯtr t|rḫ l k ybrdmy.b[t.a]|b h lb[u] 24[77].27
mry.mk.ksu.|ṯbt h.ḫḫ.arṣ.|nḥlt h.w nǵr.|ʻnn.ilm.al.|tqrb.l bn.ilm.|mt.al.yʻdb km.|k imr.b p h.|k lli.b ṯbrn.|qn 4[51].8.16
t.šblt.tpʻ[.b ḥm]drt.|ur.tisp k.yd.aqht.ǵz[r].|tšt k.bm.qrb m.asm.|b p h.rgm.l yṣa.b špt h[.hwt h].|b nši ʻn h.w tp 19[1AQHT].2.74
.b palt.bṣql ypʻ b yǵlm.|ur.tisp k.yd.aqht.|ǵzr.tšt k.b qrb m.asm.|y.dnh.ysb.aklt h.yph.|šblt.b akt.šblt.ypʻ.|b ḥm 19[1AQHT].2.67
[l a]q[h]t.|[t]krb.[---.]l qrb.mym.|tql.[---.]lb.ṯṯ[b]r.|qšt[.---]r.y[ṯ]br.|ṯmn.[---.]btlt.[19[1AQHT].1.2

'n.dnil.[mt.rpi].|ytb.ǵzr.mt hrnmy[.---].|b grnt.ilm.b qrb.m[ṯ't.ilnym].|d tit.yspi.spu.q[--.---].|tpḫ.ṯṣr.shr[.---].|m 20[121].2.9
.|ytši.l dr.bn.il.l mpḫrt.bn.i[l.l ṯkmn.w š]nm hn š.|w šqrb.'r.mšr mšr bn.ugrt.w [npy.---.]ugr.|w npy.yman.w np 32[2].1.18
---.--]n.irš[.---].|[---.--]mr.ph.|[---.--]mm.hlkt.|[---.]b qrb.'r.|[---.m]lakm l h.|[---.]l.bn.il.|[---.--]a.'d h.|[---.--]rh. 26[135].5
.ǵzr.ilḥu.|[m]rḥ h.yiḫd.b yd.|[g]rgr h.bm.ymn.|[w]yqrb.trẓẓ h.|[---].mǵy h.w ǵlm.|[a]ḫt h.šib.yṣat.mrḥ h.|l tl. 16.1[125].49
ši.l d]r.bn[.il].|[l mpḫrt.bn.il.l ṯkmn.w šnm.hn š].|[w šqrb.š.mšr mšr.bn.ugrt.w npy.---.]w npy.|[---.w np]y.ugrt.| 32[2].1.4
[--].yṯkḥ.w yiḫd.b qrb[.-].|[--.t]ṯkḥ.w tiḫd.b uš[k.--].|[-.b]'l.yabd.l alp.|[---.bt]l 11[132].1.1
t.lbn k[.---].|dk k.kbkb[.---].|dm.mt.aṣḥ[.---].|ydd.b qr[b.---].|al.ašt.b[---].|ahpk k.l[--.---].|ṯmm.w lk[.---].|w lk 5[67].3.10
[-]ḫm k.w št.|[---.]ẓ[--.-]rdy k.|[---.i]qnim.|[---.-]šu.b qrb.|[---].asr.|[---.--]m.ymt m.|[---].k iṯl.|[---.--]m.'db.l arṣ. 1['NT.IX].2.6
qḫ.tp k.b yd.|[-]r[-]k.bm.ymn.|tlk.škn.'l.ṣrrt.|adn k.šqrb.[---].|b mgn k.w ḫrṣ.l kl.|apnk.ǵzr.ilḥu.|[m]rḥ h.yiḫd. 16.1[125].44
.|šgr.mu[d.---].|šgr.mud[.---].|dm.mt.aṣ[ḥ.---].|yd.b qrb[.---].|w lk.ilm.[---].|w rgm.l [---].|b mud.ṣin[.---].|mud 5[67].3.19
ap.b'[l.---].|i.hd.d[---.---].|ynp'.b'[l.---].|b ṯmnt.[---].|yqrb.[---].|lḥm.m[---.---].|[']d.lḥm[.šty.ilm].|w pq.mr[ǵṯm.ṯ 5[67].4.10
mud.ṣin[.---].|iṯm.mui[-.---].|dm.mt.aṣ[ḥ.---].|ydd.b qr[b.---].|ṯmm.w lk[.---].|[--]ṯ.lk[.---].|[--]kṯ.i[---.---].|p.šn[5[67].3.26

qrbhkl

il dbḥ.b bt h.mṣd.ṣd.b qrb|hkl [h].ṣḥ.l qṣ.ilm.tlḥmn.|ilm.w tštn.tštn y[n] 'd šb'.|tr UG5.1.1.1

qrd

arṣ.nḥlt h.tša.|g hm.w tṣḥ.ṯḥm.aliyn.|bn.b'l.hwt.aliy.qrdm.|bhṯ.bn.ilm.mt.'bd k.an.|w d 'lm k.šmḫ.bn.ilm.mt.|[5[67].2.18
l bn.ilm.mt.|ṯny.l ydd.il ǵzr.|ṯḥm.aliyn.b'l.hwt.aliy.|qrdm.bhṯ.l bn.ilm mt.|'bd k.an.w d.'lm k.|tb'.w l.yṯb.ilm.i 5[67].2.11
n.ilm.mt.|ṯny.l ydd.|il.ǵzr.ṯḥm.|aliyn.b'l.|[hw]t.aliy.q|[rdm.]bht y.bnt.|[dt.ksp.dtm].|[ḫrṣ.hk]l y.|[---.]aḫ y.|[-- 4[51].8.34
nš [--].|š š[--].|w [--].|d [--].|ypḫ[--].|w s[--].|[---].|qrd ga[n.--].|b bt k.[--].|w l dbḥ[--].|ṯ[--].|[--] aṯt yqḥ 'z.|[RS61[24.277.21]
l btl[t.'nt.ṯny.l ybmt.limm.ṯḥm.aliyn.b'l].|hw[t.aliy.qrdm.qryy.b arṣ.mlḥmt.št].|[b ']pr[m.ddym.sk.šlm.l kbd.a 7.2[130].14
n.l ib.yp'.|l b'l.ṣrt.l rkb.'rpt.|ṯḥm.aliyn.b'l.hwt.aliy.|qrdm.qry.b arṣ.mlḥmt.|št.b 'p[r] m.ddym.sk.šlm.|l kbd.arṣ 3['NT].4.52
.l btlt.'nt.|ṯny.l ymmt.limm.|ṯḥm.aliyn.b'l.hwt.|aliy.qrdm.qry.b arṣ.|mlḥmt št.b 'pr m.ddym.|sk.šlm.l kbd.arṣ.| 3['NT].3.11
ḫss.ṯny.l h|yn.d ḥrš.ydm.|ṯḥm.al[iyn.b'l].|h[wt.aliy.qrdm]. 3['NT.VI].6.25

qrdy

u.|kdn.|p'ṣ.|bn.liy.|yd'.|šmn.|'dy.|'nbr.|aḫrm.|bn.qrdy.|bn.šm'n.|bn.ǵlmy.|ǵly.|bn.dnn.|bn.rmy.|dll.|mny. 2117.3.31

qrdmn

mšt.l.'šrm.|b.gdn.bn.uss.'šrm.|b.'dn.bn.ṯṯ.'šrt.|b.bn.qrdmn.ṯlṯm.|b.bṣmn[.bn].ḥrtn.'[--].|b.t[--.---] h.[---].|[-----]. 2054.1.20

qrwl

[n].|[---.--ṯ]lḥn.|[---.]ṯlḥn.|[---.]ṯlḥn.|bn adty ṯlḥn.bn qrwl ṯlḥn. 98[11].36

qrwn

bnš.kld.|kbln.'bdyrǵ.ilgt.|ǵyrn.ybnn qrwn.|ypltn.'bdnt.|klby.aḥrṯp.|ilyn.'lby.ṣdkn.|gmrt.ṯlmyn 1045.3
tnt.|ṯrmn w.|dbḥ kl.|kl ykly.|dbḥ k.sprt.|dt nat.|w qrwn.|l k dbḥ.|[--]r bt [--].|[--]bnš [--].|š š[--].|w [--].|d [- RS61[24.277.11]

qrḥ

[--].|bn.qṣn.|'lpy.|kṭy.|bn.ẓmn.|bn.trdn.|ypq.|'bd.|qrḥ.|abšr.|bn.bdn.|ḏmry.|bn.pndr.|bn.aḫt.|bn.'dn.|bn.išb 2117.4.27

qrṭy

qrṭym.mddb'l.|kdn.zlyy.|krwn.arty.|tlmu.zlyy.|pdu.qmnz 89[312].1
l.|kdn.zlyy.|krwn.arty.|tlmu.zlyy.|pdu.qmnzy.|bdl.qrṭy.|trgn.bn.tǵh.|aupš.qmnzy.|ṯrry.mṣbty.|prn.nǵṭy.|ṯrḏ 89[312].6

qrẓ

ǵl h ṯḥm b[.---].|mrḥ h l adrt[.---].|ṯṯb 'ṯtrt b ǵl[.---].|qrẓ tšt.l šmal[.---].|arbḫ.'n h tšu w[.---].|aylt tǵpy ṯr.'n[.---] 2001.1.9

qry

'd[.---].|ltm.mrqdm.d š[-]l[-].|w t'n.pǵt.ṯkmt.mym.|qrym.ab.dbḥ.l ilm.|š'ly.dǵṯ h.b šmym.|dǵṯ.hrnmy.d kbkb 19[1AQHT].4.191
n h.yšu.g h.w y]ṣḥ.ṯḥm.|[ṯr.il.ab k.hwt.l]ṭpn.ḥtk k.|[qryy.b arṣ.mlḥ]mt.št b 'p|[r m.ddym.sk.šlm].l kbd.arṣ.|[ar 1['NT.IX].2.19
š.b ǵr.nḥ]lt y.|w t['n].btlt.[']nt.ṯṯb.|[ybmt.]limm.[a]n.aqry.|[b arṣ].mlḥmt.[aš]t.b 'pr m.|ddym.ask[.šlm.]l kbd.ar 3['NT].4.66
yp'.|l b'l.ṣrt.l rkb.'rpt.|ṯḥm.aliyn.b'l.hwt.aliy.|qrdm.qry.b arṣ.mlḥmt.|št.b 'p[r] m.ddym.sk.šlm.|l kbd.arṣ.arbd 3['NT].4.52
'nt.|ṯny.l ymmt.limm.|ṯḥm.aliyn.b'l.hwt.|aliy.qrdm.qry.b arṣ.|mlḥmt št.b 'pr m.ddym.|sk.šlm.l kbd.arṣ.|arbdd 3['NT].3.11
t.'nt.ṯny.l ybmt.limm.ṯḥm.aliyn.b'l].|hw[t.aliy.qrdm.qryy.b arṣ.mlḥmt.št].|[b ']pr[m.ddym.sk.šlm.l kbd.arṣ.arb 7.2[130].14
ḥ.t[b'.---].|bkyt.b hk[l]y.mšspdt.|b ḥẓr y pẓǵm.ǵr.w yq.|dbḥ.ilm.yš'ly.dǵṯ h.|b šmym.dǵṯ hrnmy[.d k]|bkbm.'[l 19[1AQHT].4.184
b lb.tqny.|[---.]ṯb l y.l aqht.ǵzr.ṯb l y w l k.|[---]m.l aqry k.b ntb.pš'.|[---].b ntb.gan.ašql k.ṯḥt.|[p'n y.a]nk.n'm 17[2AQHT].6.43
kpr.šb' bn[t.rḥ.gdm.w anhbm].|kla[t.ṯǵ]r[t.bht.'nt.w tqry.ǵlmm.b št.ǵr].|ap 'nt tm[ṯḫṣ.b 'mq.ṯḫtṣb.bn.qrytm.tm 7.2[130].24
].|kpr.šb'.bnt.rḥ.gdm.|w anhbm.klat.ṯǵrt.|bht.'nt.w tqry.ǵlmm.|b št.ǵr.w hln.'nt.tm|ṯḫṣ.b 'mq.ṯḫtṣb.bn.|qrytm 3['NT].2.4
-]l[.---].|k lli.[---].|kpr.[šb'.bnt.rḥ.gdm.w anhbm].|w tqr[y.ǵlmm.b št.ǵr.---].|[']d tš[b'.tmtḫṣ.---].|klyn[.---].|špk. 7.2[130].4
[bdd.]l kb[d.š]dm.yšt.|[----.]b'l.mdl h.yb'r.|[---.]rn h.aqry.|[---.]b a[r]ṣ.mlḥmt.|ašt[.b ']p[r] m.ddym.ask.|šlm.l k 3['NT].4.71

qrm

b ǵr.ṯn.p k.b ḫlb.k tgwln.šnt k.|[--.]w špt k.l tššy.hm.tqrm.l mt.b rn k.|[--]ḫp.an.arnn.ql.špš.ḥw.bṯnm.uḫd.b'lm.| 1001.1.5

qrn

.aqht.ǵzr.adr.ṯqbm.|[d]lbnn.adr.gdm.b rumm.|adr.qrnt.b y‘lm.mtnm.|b ‘qbt.ṯr.adr.b ǵlil.qnm.|tn.l kṯr.w ḫss.y 17[2AQHT].6.22

šu.g h.w yṣḥ.|ḥwt.aḫt.w nar[-].|qrn.d bat k.btlt.‘nt.|qrn.d bat k b‘l.ymšḥ.|b‘l.ymšḥ.hm.b ‘p.|nṭ‘n.b arṣ.ib y.|w 10[76].2.22

‘n h.ykr‘.w yql.|w yšu.g h.w yṣḥ.|ḥwt.aḫt.w nar[-].|qrn.d bat k.btlt.‘nt.|qrn.d bat k b‘l.ymšḥ.|b‘l.ymšḥ.hm.b ‘p 10[76].2.21

.iṣr r‘t.‘ṣ brq y.|riš h.tply.ṭly.bn.‘n h.|uz‘rt.tmll.išd h.qrn[m].|dt.‘l h.riš h.b glṯ.b šm[m].|[---.i]l.ṯr.iṯ.p h.k ṭt.ǵlṯ[.- UG5.3.1.6

mšmš[.---].|anp n m yḥr[r.---].|bmt n m.yšḫn.[---].|qrn h.km.ǵb[-.---].|hw km.ḥrr[.---].|šnmtm.dbṭ[.---].|tr‘.tr‘ 12[75].2.40

mrn.l pn h yrd.|[---.]b‘l.šm[.--.]rgbt yu.|[---]w yrmy[.q]rn h.|[---.-]ny h pdr.ttǵr.|[---.n]šr k.al ttn.l n.|[---.]tn l rb 2001.2.10

tql.|l ḥṯr h.y‘msn.nn.ṯkmn.|w šnm.w ngšnn.ḥby.|b‘l.qrnm w ḏnb.ylšn.|b ḫri h.w ṯnt h.ql.il.[--].|il.k yrdm.arṣ.‘nt UG5.1.1.20

|qrt.ablm.ablm.[qrt.zbl.yrḫ].|ik.al.yḥdṯ.yrḫ.b[---].|b qrn.ymn h.b anšt[.---].|qdqd h.w y‘n.yṭpn.[mhr.št].|šm‘.l b 18[3AQHT].4.10

.|aklm.tbrk k.|w ld ‘qqm.|ilm.yp‘r.|šmt hm.|b hm.qrnm.|km.ṭrm.w gbṯt.|km.ibrm.|w b hm.pn.b‘l.|b‘l.ytlk.w 12[75].1.30

ṯql.|ary ḫmšt.|ykn‘m ḫmšt.|‘nmky tqlm.|[-]kt ‘šrt.|qrn šb‘t. 1176.8

w š.|šrp.w šlmm kmm.|l b‘l.ṣpn b ‘r‘r.|pamt ṯlṯm š l qrnt.|ṯlḥn.b‘lt.bhtm.|‘lm.‘lm.gdlt l b‘l.|ṣpn.ilbt[.---.]d[--].|l UG5.13.30

qr‘

‘db.lḥm.l h.w d l yd‘nn.|d.mṣd.|ylmn.ḫṭ.tḥt.ṯlḥn.|b qr‘.|‘ṯtrt.w ‘nt.ymǵy.|‘ṯtrt.t‘db.nšb l h.|w ‘nt.ktp.b hm.yg‘r UG5.1.1.8B

qrṣ

.qdm.|[-.k]bd n.il.ab n.|kbd k iš.tikln.|ṯd n.km.mrm.tqrṣn.|il.yẓḥq.bm.|lb.w ygmḏ.bm kbd.|ẓi.at.l tlš.|amt.yrḫ. 12[75].1.11

.|aškn.ydt.[m]rṣ gršt.|zbln.r[---].ymlu.|n‘m.[-]ṯ[-.--.]yqrṣ.|d[-] b pḫ[-.--.]mḫt.|[---.]tnn.|[---.]tnn. 16[126].5.29

qrq

tn.|w l ttn.|w al ttn.|tn ks yn.|w ištn.|‘bd.prṯ.ṯḥm.|qrq.pṯ.ḏmn.|l iṯtl. 1019.2.2

qrqr

|ibyn.|illḏrm.|iǵlkḏ.|[i]ly[-]n.|[-----].|m[--.---].|[-]n.qrqr.|[--]n.ymn.y[--].|ilḫr.ṣdqn[.--]. 2022.24

qrrn

bn.qrrn.|bn.dnt.|bn.ṯ‘l[-].|bdl.ar.dt.inn.|mhr l ht.|artyn.|‘dm 1035.1.1

mṣry.d.‘rb.b.unṯ.|bn.qrrn.mḏrǵl.|bn.tran.mḏrǵl|bn.ilh.mḏrǵl|špšyn.b.ulm.|bn. 2046.1.2

qrš

.|[il.]mbk nhrm.qrb.|[a]pq.thmtm.tgly.ḏd.|il.w tbu.qrš..|mlk.ab.šnm.l p‘n.|il.thbr.w tql.|tštḥwy.w tkbdn h.|tš 6.1.35[49.1.7]

|‘m.il.mbk.nhrm.|qrb.apq.thmtm.|tgly.ḏd.il.w tbu.|qrš.mlk.ab.šnm.|l p‘n.il.thbr.w tql.|tštḥwy.w tkbd h.|hlm.i 4[51].4.24

‘m il.mbk.nhrm.|[qrb.ap]q.thmtm tgly.ḏd il.|[w tbu.qr]š.mlk.ab.šnm.|[l p‘n.il.t]hbr.w tql.tštḥ|[wy.w tkbd]n h.t 17[2AQHT].6.49

[i]l.mbk.[nhrm.qrb.apq.thmtm].|[ygly.]ḏl i[l].w ybu[.q]rš.mlk[.ab.šnm.l p‘n.il.]|[yhbr.]w yql[.y]štḥw[y.]w ykb[d 2.3[129].5

ṭpn].|il d pid.tk ḫrš[n.---.tk.ǵr.ks].|ygly ḏd.i[l.w ybu.qrš.mlk].|ab.šnm.l [p‘n.il.yhbr.w yql].|yštḥwy.[w ykbdn h. 1['NT.IX].3.23

.mbk.nhr[m.qr]b.[ap]q.|[thm]tm.tgl.ḏ[d.]i[l.]w tbu.|[qr]š.m[l]k.ab[.šnm.]mṣr.|[t]bu.ḏdm.qn[-.-]n[-.-]lt.|ql h.yš[3['NT.VI].5.16

.mbk.nhrm].|[qrb.apq.thmtm].|[tgly.ḏd.il.w]tb[a].|[qrš.mlk.ab.]šnm.|[tša.g hm.w tṣ]ḥ.sbn.|[-.--]l[.---.]‘d.|ksm. 5[67].6.2

qrt

.pnm].|‘m.yṭpn.mhr.š[t.tšu.g h].|w tṣḥ.yṯb.yṯp.[---].|qrt.ablm.ablm.[qrt.zbl.yrḫ].|ik.al.yḥdṯ.yrḫ.b[---].|b qrn.ym 18[3AQHT].4.8

ṣd[.---].|[---.]mt.išryt[.---].|[---.--]r.almd k.[---].|[---.]qrt.ablm.a[blm].|[qrt.zbl.]yrḫ.d mgdl.š[---].|[---.]mn.‘r hm[18[3AQHT].1.30

‘nt.brḥ.p ‘lm h.|‘nt.p dr.dr.‘db.uḫry mṭ yd h.|ymǵ.l qrt.ablm.abl[m].|qrt.zbl.yrḫ.yšu g h.|w yṣḥ.y l k.qrt.ablm. 19[1AQHT].4.163

ǵ.l qrt.ablm.abl[m].|qrt.zbl.yrḫ.yšu g h.|w yṣḥ.y l k.qrt.ablm.|d ‘l k.mḫṣ.aqht.ǵzr.|‘wrt.yšt k.b‘l.l ht.|w ‘lm h.l 19[1AQHT].4.165

dbḥ[--].|ṯ[--].|[--] aṯt yqḥ ‘z.|[---]ḏ.|[---].|[---].|hm qrt tuḫd.hm mt y‘l bnš.|bt bn bnš yqḥ ‘z.|w yḥdy mrḥqm. RS61[24.277.29]

bnš.mlk.|d.b d.adn‘m.|[š]b‘.b.ḥrṯm.|[ṯ]lṯ.b.ṯǵrm.|rb qrt.aḥd.|ṯmn.ḫzr.|w.arb‘.ḥršm.|dt.tb‘ln.b.pḫn.|ṯṯtm.ḫzr.w 1024.3.3

tir.‘m.qrt.|‘št.‘šr h.šmn.|‘mn.bn.aǵlmn.|arb‘m.ksp.‘l.qrt.|b.šd.bn.[u]brš.|ḫmšt.‘šrt.|b.šd.bn.[-]n.|ṯl[ṯt].‘šr[t].|b.š 1083.6

qrht.b[--.---].|ksp.iš[-.---].|art.[---].|[-----].|[-----].|l [----].|b 1147.1

qrht.d.tššlmn.|ṯlrb h.|art.ṯn.yrḫm.|ṯlrby.yrḫ.w.ḫm[š.ym]m 66[109].1

qm.|[---].adt y.yšlm.|[---.]mlk n.amṣ.|[.---].nn.|[---.]qrt.dt.|[---.--]s‘.hn.mlk.|[---.l]qḥ.hn.l.ḥwt h.|[---.--]p.hn.ib. 1012.7

lat.dm.ym.w ṯn.|ṯlṯ.rb‘.ym.ymš.|ṯdṯ.ym.ḥẓ k.al.tš‘l.|qrt h.abn.yd k.|mšdpt.w hn.špšm.|b šb‘.w l.yšn.pbl.|mlk.l 14[KRT].3.117

rd.bt ḫpṯt.|arṣ.tspr.b y|rdm.arṣ.|idk.al.ttn.|pnm.tk.qrt h.|hmry.mk.ksu.|ṯbt h.ḫḫ.arṣ.|nḫlt h.w nǵr.|‘nn.ilm.al 4[51].8.11

.‘lm k.|tb‘.w l.yṯb.ilm.idk.|l ytn.pn.‘m.bn.ilm.mt.|tk.qrt h.hmry.mk.ksu.|ṯbt.ḫḫ.arṣ.nḫlt h.tša.|g hm.w tṣḥ.tḥm. 5[67].2.15

.|b ym.mlat.|tqln.alpm.|yrḫ.‘šrt.l b‘[l].|dqtm.w ynt.qr[t].|w mtntm.š l rmš.|w kbd.w š.l šlm kbd.|alp.w š.l b‘l ṣ UG5.13.6

l]at.y[ql]n.al[p]m.yrḫ.‘šrt.|[l b‘l.ṣ]pn.[dq]tm.w y[nt] qrt.|[w mtmt]m.[š.l] rm[š.]kbd.w š.|[l šlm.kbd.al]p.w š.[l] 36[9].1.12

qḥ bt[.--]r.dbḥ[.šmn.mr].|šmn.rqḥ[.-]bt.mtnt[.w ynt.qrt].|w ṯn ḥṯm.w bǵr.arb[‘.---].|kdm.yn.prs.qmḥ.[---].|mdb 35[3].21

w m‘rb[.---].|dbḥ šmn mr[.šmn.rqḥ.bt].|mtnt.w ynt.[qrt.w ṯn.ḥṯm].|w bǵr.arb‘.[---.kdm.yn].|prs.qmḥ.m‘[--.---].| APP.II[173].23

.mhr.š[t.tšu.g h].|w tṣḥ.yṯb.yṯp.[---].|qrt.ablm.ablm.[qrt.zbl.yrḫ].|ik.al.yḥdṯ.yrḫ.b[---].|b qrn.ymn h.b anšt[.---]. 18[3AQHT].4.8

ryt[.---].|[---.--]r.almd k.[---].|[---]qrt.ablm.a[blm].|[qrt.zbl.]yrḫ.d mgdl.š[---].|[---.]mn.‘r hm[.---].|[---.]it[.---].| 18[3AQHT].1.31

nt.p dr.dr.‘db.uḫry mṭ yd h.|ymǵ.l qrt.ablm.abl[m].|qrt.zbl.yrḫ.yšu g h.|w yṣḥ.y l k.qrt.ablm.|d ‘l k.mḫṣ.aqht.ǵ 19[1AQHT].4.164

yṣḥm.b d.ubn.krwn.tǵd.[m]nḥm.|‘pṯrm.šm‘rgm.skn.qrt.|ḥgbn.šm‘.skn.qrt.|nǵr krm.‘bdadt.b‘ln.yp‘mlk.|ṯǵrm. 2011.10

|b dbḥ k.bn.dgn.|b mṣd k.w yrd.|krt.l ggt.‘db.|akl.l qryt.|ḥṭt.l bt.ḫbr.|yip.lḥm.d ḫmš.|mǵd.ṯdṯ.yrḫm.|‘dn.ngb. 14[KRT].2.81

].b dbḥ h.bn dgn.|[b m]ṣd h.yrd.krt.|[l g]gt.‘db.akl.l qryt.|ḥṭt.l bt.ḫbr.|yip.lḥm.d ḫmš.|[mǵ]d.ṯdṯ.yr[ḫm].|‘dn.n 14[KRT].4.172

ḥ-.---].|ym.[‘]lm.y‘[--.---].|[--.-]g[-.-]s w [---].|w yn[t.q]rt.y[---].|w al[p.l]il.w bu[rm.---].|ytk.gdlt.ilhm.[ṯkmn.w 35[3].10

iqra.ilm.n[‘mm.---].|w ysmm.bn.š[---].|ytnm.qrt.l ‘ly[.---].|b mdbr.špm.yd[.---.---]r.|l riš hm.w yš[--.--]m 23[52].3

tqry.ǵlmm.|b št.ǵr.w hln.ʿnt.tm|tḫṣ.b ʿmq.tḫtṣb.bn.|qrytm tmḫṣ.lim.ḫp y[m].|tṣmt.adm.ṣat.š[p]š.|tḥt h.k kdrt.r 3[ʿNT].2.7
t.w tqry.ǵlmm.b št.ǵr].|ap ʿnt tm[tḫṣ.b ʿmq.tḫtṣb.bn.qrytm.tmḫṣ].|lim ḫ[p.ym.---].|[--]m.t[-]t[.---].|m[-]mt[.---]. 7.2[130].25
]d.lik[t.---].|w [----].|k[--.---].|ʿšrm[.---].|tšt.tbʿ[.---].|qrt.mlk[.---].|w.ʿl.ap.s[--.---].|b hm.w.rgm.hw.al[--].|atn.ks 2008.2.4
d.w.šl hw.|qr[-].|akl n.b.grnt.|l.bʿr.|ap.krmm.|ḫlq.|qrt n.ḫlq.|w.dʿ.dʿ. 2114.12
n.tǵd.[m]nḥm.|ʿpṯrm.šmʿrgm.skn.qrt.|ḥgbn.šmʿ.skn.qrt.|nǵr krm.ʿbdadt.bʿln.ypʿmlk.|ṯǵrm.mnḥm.klyn.ʿdršp.ǵl 2011.11
mt.|aǵt.|w.qmnz.|slḫ.|yknʿm.|šlmy.|w.ull.|ṯmry.|qrt.|ʿrm.|nnu.|[--].|[---].|mʿr.|arny.|ubrʿy.|ilštmʿ.|bir.|m 71[113].21
arbʿ.ʿšr h.šmn.|d.lqḥt.ṯlǵdy.|w.kd.ištir.ʿm.qrt.|ʿšt.ʿšr h.šmn.|ʿmn.bn.aǵlmn.|arbʿm.ksp.ʿl.qrt.|b.šd.bn 1083.3
n.nḥ[l h].|[šd.]agyn.b d.kmrn.n[ḥl] h.|[š]d.nbzn.[-]l.qrt.|[š]d.agpṯr.b d.šḫrn.nḥl h.|šd.annmn.b d.tyn.nḥl h.|šd. 2029.9
d.ttyn.nḥl [h].|šd.ttyn[.b]n.arkšt.|lʿq[.---].|šd.pll.b d.qrt.|š[d].anndr.b d.bdn.nḥ[l h].|[šd.]agyn.b d.kmrn.n[ḥl] h 2029.6
d.qrt.|šd[.-].dyn.b d.pln.nḥl h.|šd.irdyn.bn.ḫrǵš[-].l.qrt.|šd.iǵlyn.bn.kzbn.l.qr[t].|šd.pln.bn.tiyn.b d.ilmhr nḥl h 2029.16
n.nḥl h.|šd.irdyn.bn.ḫrǵš[-].l.qrt.|šd.iǵlyn.bn.kzbn.l.qr[t].|šd.pln.bn.tiyn.b d.ilmhr nḥl h.|šd knn.bn.ann.ʿdb.|š 2029.17
[n.n]ḥl h.|šd.krz.[b]n.ann.ʿ[db].|šd.ṯ[r]yn.bn.tkn.b d.qrt.|šd[.-].dyn.b d.pln.nḥl h.|šd.irdyn.bn.ḫrǵš[-].l.qrt.|šd.i 2029.14
.|šd.iln[-].bn.irṯr.l.šḫrn.nḥl h.|šd[.ag]pṯn.b[n.]brrn.l.qrt.|šd[.--]dy.bn.brzn.|l.qrt. 2029.21
yn.|tštql.ilt.l hkl h.|w l.šbʿt.tmtḫṣ h.b ʿmq.|tḫtṣb.bn.qrtm.ṯtʿr.|ksat.l mhr.ṯʿr.ṯlḥnt.|l ṣbim.hdmm.l ǵzrm.|mid.t 3[ʿNT].2.20
l bmt h.---.]hy bt h tʿrb.|[---.tm]tḫṣ b ʿmq.|[tḫtṣb.bn.qrtm.ṯtʿr.ṯlḥnt.]l ṣbim.|[hdmm.l ǵzrm.mid.tmtḫṣn.w t]ʿn.tḫ 7.1[131].5
qrt ṯqlm.w nṣp.|šlmy.ṯql.|ary ṯql.|ṯmry ṯql.w.nṣp.|aǵt nṣp. 69[111].1
rn.arny[.---].|w.ṯn.bn h.w.b[---.---].|b tn[--.---].|swn.qrty[.---].|uḫ h.w.ʿšr[.---].|klyn.apsn[y.---].|plzn.qrty[.---].| 81[329].8
[---.--]ǵz.|[---.]qrt.|[---].aṯt.|[---.]w arbʿ.nʿr[m].|[---.a]ḥd.|[---.]ṯlṯ.aṯt. 2142.2
.ʿm[.---].|[---.]ilṯḥm.w.[---].|šmʿt.ḥwt[.---].|[---].nzdt.qr[t].|[---.]dt nzdt.m[lk].|[---.]w.ap.bṯn[.---].|[---.]bʿl y.y[--] 2127.2.4
wn.qrty[.---].|uḫ h.w.ʿšr[.---].|klyn.apsn[y.---].|plzn.qrty[.---].|w.klt h.b.t[--.---].|bʿl y.mlk[y.---].|yd.bt h.yd[.-- 81[329].11
.|[---.l.]ṯrmn.mlk.|[---.]šʿrt.šbʿ.ʿšr h.|[---.iqn]i.l.ṯrmn.qrt.|[---.]lbš.ḫmšm.iqnu.|[---].šmt.ḫmšt.ḫndlt.|[---.iqn]i.l.[- 1106.15
k[.---].|yknʿm[.---].|qm[n]z[---].|šl[-.---].|ar[--.---].|qrt[.---].|ṯm[r.---].|dm[t.---].|gl[bt.---].|al[-.---]. 1181.12
.--]kn.|[-----].|[-----].|[-----.-]l[-].|[-----].|[---.--]k.|[---.q]rt.|[---.--]d.b.gnʿ.|[---].ḫbt.|[---].qmy.|[---.]qmy.|[---.--]b. 2015.1.13
]w q[--].|ym.ʿlm.y[---.---].|t.k[-]ml.[---].|l[---].w y[nt.qrt.---].|[---.--]n[.w alp.l il.w bu]|[rm.---.ytk.gdlt.ilhm].|ṯk APP.II[173].11
ḥl h.|šd[.ag]pṯn.b[n.]brrn.l.qrt.|šd[.--]dy.bn.brzn.|l.qrt. 2029.23
mṣmt.ʿbs.|arr.d.qr|ht. 1173.2

qrty

l.|[---.]b.yrml.|[---.--]n.b.yrml.|[---.--]ny.yrml.|šwn.qrty.|b.šlmy. 2119.25
--].|[-]ln.[---].|w.ṯn.bn [h.---].|[--]d mʿqby[.---].|swn.qrty.w[.aṯt h].|[w].bn h.w.ṯn.alpm.|[w.]ṯlṯm.ṣin.|anndr.yk 1080.12
|w.a[tt] h.[---].|ḫdmtn.ṯn[.---].|w.ṯlṯ.alp h.[---].|swn.qrty.w.[b]n h[.---].|w.alp h.w.a[r]bʿ.l.arbʿ[m.---].|pln.ṯmry. 2044.6
b.|[---].b.ndb.|[---].b.ndb.|[---].b.kmkty.|[---.]yrmly.qrtym.|[---].b.yrml.|[---.]b.yrml.|[---.]b.yrml.|[---.]b.yrml. 2119.17

qrtm *

ilṣdq.bn.zry.|bʿlytn.bn.ulb.|ytrʿm.bn.swy.|ṣḫrn.bn.qrtm.|bn.špš.bn.ibrd.|ʿpṯrm.bn.ʿbdy.|n[--.]bn.šnd.|[---].bn. 2024.4

qš

yt.ḥẓt.tḥm k.|mlk n.aliyn.bʿl.ṯpṭ n.|in.d ʿln h.klny y.qš h.|nbln.klny y.nbl.ks h.|any.l yṣḥ.ṯr.il.ab h.il.|mlk.d yk 3[ʿNT.VI].5.41
t.|tḥm k.mlk n.aliy[n.]bʿl.|ṯpṭ n.w in.d ʿln h.|klny n.q[š] h.n[bln].|klny n[.n]bl.ks h.|[an]y.l yṣḥ.ṯr il.ab h.|[i]l.m 4[51].4.45

qšr

---].|[---].aḥw.aṭm.prṭl[.---].|[---.]mnt.[l]pʿn[.-.-]bd h.aqšr[.---].|[---].ptḥ y.a[--.]dt[.---].ml[--].|[---.-]ṯk.ytmt.dlt tl 1001.1.20

qšt

lʿ.|bn.tlmyn.ṯt.qštm.w.qlʿ.|bn.ysd.qšt.|[ǵ]mrm.|ilgn.qšt.|abršp.qšt.|ssg.qšt.|ynḥm.qšt.|pprn.qšt.|uln.qšt.|bn.n 105[86].2
šp.qšt.|ssg.qšt.|ynḥm.qšt.|pprn.qšt.|uln.qšt.|bn.nkl qšt.|ady.qšt.|bn.srn.qšt.|bn.gdrn.qšt.|prpr.qšt.|ugry.qšt.| 119[321].1.40
arbʿm.qšt.|alp ḥzm.w alp.|ntq.ṯn.qlʿm.|ḫmš.ṣmdm.w ḥrṣ.|ṯryn.šš 1123.1
.gdrn.qšt.|prpr.qšt.|ugry.qšt.|bn.ṣrptn.qšt.|bn.mṣry.qšt.|arny.|abm.qšt.|ḥdṯn.qlʿ.|ytpṭ.qšt.|ilṯḥm.qšt.w.qlʿ.|ṣd 119[321].1.47
tm.ṯn.[q]lʿm.|ǵdyn.qšt.w.qlʿ.|bn.gzl.qšt.w.qlʿ.|[---]n.qšt.|ilhd.qšt.|ʿdn.qšt.w.qlʿ.|ilmhr.qšt.w.qlʿ.|bn.gmrt.qšt.|ǵ 119[321].1.6
t.|šdyn.qšt.|bdn.qšt.w.qlʿ.|bn.šmlbi.qšt.w.qlʿ.|bn.yy.qšt.|ilrb.qšt.|bn.nmš.ṯt.qšt.w.qlʿ.|bʿl.qšt.w.qlʿ. 119[321].4.14
ptn.qšt.|bn.mṣry.qšt.|arny.|abm.qšt.|ḥdṯn.qlʿ.|ytpṭ.qšt.|ilṯḥm.qšt.w.qlʿ.|ṣdqm.qšt.w.qlʿ.|uln.qšt.w.qlʿ.|uln.qšt. 119[321].2.4
.|bn.nkl qšt.|ady.qšt.|bn.srn.qšt.|bn.gdrn.qšt.|prpr.qšt.|ugry.qšt.|bn.ṣrptn.qšt.|bn.mṣry.qšt.|arny.|abm.qšt.| 119[321].1.44
]mrm.|ilgn.qšt.|abršp.qšt.|ssg.qšt.|ynḥm.qšt.|pprn.qšt.|uln.qšt.|bn.nkl qšt.|ady.qšt.|bn.srn.qšt.|bn.gdrn.qšt.| 105[86].4
[t]n.qšt.w.qlʿ.|bn.bb.qšt.w[.ql]ʿ.|bn.aktmy.qšt.|šdyn.qšt.|bdn.qšt.w.qlʿ.|bn.šmlbi.qšt.w.qlʿ.|bn.yy.qšt.|ilrb.qšt.| 119[321].4.11
št.w.qlʿ.|ark.qšt.w.qlʿ.|bn.ʿbdnkl.qšt.w.qlʿ.|bn.znan.qšt.|bn.arz.[ar]bʿ.qšt.w.arb[ʿ.]qlʿm.|b[n.]adʿl.q[š]t.w.qlʿ.|b[119[321].2.44
.|bn.ḫršn.qšt.w.qlʿ.|ilrb.qšt.w.qlʿ.|psḥn.qšt.|bn.kmy.qšt.|bn.ilḥbn.qšt.w.q[lʿ].|ršpab.qšt.w.qlʿ.|pdrn.qšt.w.qlʿ.|b 119[321].3.43
d.qšt.|ssw.qšt.|knn.qšt.|bn.ṯlln.qšt.|bn.šyn.qšt.|ʿbd.qšt.|bn.ulmy.qšt.|ṯqbn.qšt.|bn.qnmlk.qšt.|ytḥm.qšt.|grp.q 104[316].5
.|ilṯḥm.qšt.w.qlʿ.|ṣdqm.qšt.w.qlʿ.|uln.qšt.w.qlʿ.|uln.qšt.|bn.blẓn.qšt.w.qlʿ.|gbʿ.qšt.w.qlʿ.|nṣṣn.qšt.|mʿr.|[ʿ]dyn. 119[321].2.8
.qšt.|pprn.qšt.|uln.qšt.|bn.nkl qšt.|ady.qšt.|bn.srn.qšt.|bn.gdrn.qšt.|prpr.qšt.|ugry.qšt.|bn.ṣrptn.qšt.|bn.mṣr 119[321].1.42
qšt.|bn.ytrm.qšt.w.qlʿ.|bn.ʿbdyrḫ.qšt.w.q[lʿ].|bn.lky.qšt.|bn.dll.qšt.w.ql[ʿ].|bn.pǵyn.qšt.w[.q]lʿ.|bn.bdn.qšt.|bn. 119[321].3.27
|bn.ṯlṯ.ṯ[lṯ.]qšt.w.ṯn.qlʿm.|qṣn.ṯt.qštm.w.qlʿ.|bn.gtrn.q[š]t.|bn.ḫdi.ṯt.qštm.w.ṯn.qlʿm.|ildgn.qšt.|bn.yʿrn.ṯt.qštm 119[321].3.7
-]bl.ṯt.qštm.w.ṯn.qlʿm.|bn.[-]rkṭ.ṯt.qštm.w.qlʿ.|bn.ṯʿl.qšt.|bn.[ḫ]dpṯr.ṯt.qštm.[w].qlʿ.|bn.aǵlyn.ṯt.qštm[.w.ṯl]ṯ.qlʿ 119[321].3.17
w.qlʿ.|bn.gtrn.q[š]t.|bn.ḫdi.ṯt.qštm.w.ṯn.qlʿm.|ildgn.qšt.|bn.yʿrn.ṯt.qštm w.qlʿ.|bn.ḥṣn.qšt.w.qlʿ.|bn.gdn.ṯt.qštm 119[321].3.9
.|bn.army.ṯt.qštm.w[.]q[lʿ].|bn.rpš.qšt.w.qlʿ.|bn.ǵb.qšt.|bn.ytrm.qšt.w.qlʿ.|bn.ʿbdyrḫ.qšt.w.q[lʿ].|bn.lky.qšt.|b 119[321].3.24
kty.qšt.w.qlʿ.|bn.ḫršn.qšt.w.qlʿ.|ilrb.qšt.w.qlʿ.|psḥn.qšt.|bn.kmy.qšt.|bn.ilḥbn.qšt.w.q[lʿ].|ršpab.qšt.w.qlʿ.|pdr 119[321].3.42

n.srn.qšt. | bn.gdrn.qšt. | prpr.qšt. | ugry.qšt. | bn.ṣrptn.qšt. | bn.mṣry.qšt. | arny. | abm.qšt. | ḥdṯn.ql‘. | yṯpṭ.qšt. | ilṯḥm 119[321].1.46

lgn.qšt. | abršp.qšt. | ssg.qšt. | ynḥm.qšt. | pprn.qšt. | uln.qšt. | bn.nkl qšt. | ady.qšt. | bn.srn.qšt. | bn.gdrn.qšt. | prpr.qšt. 119[321].1.39

št. | bdn.qšt.w.ql‘. | bn.šmlbi.qšt.w.ql‘. | bn.yy.qšt. | ilrb.qšt. | bn.nmš.ṯt.qšt.w.ql‘. | b‘l.qšt.w.ql‘. 119[321].4.15

g.qšt. | ynḥm.qšt. | pprn.qšt. | uln.qšt. | bn.nkl qšt. | ady.qšt. | bn.srn.qšt. | bn.gdrn.qšt. | prpr.qšt. | ugry.qšt. | bn.ṣrptn. 119[321].1.41

tn.qš[t]. | bn.ṯǵd̠y[.qšt.]w.ql‘. | ṯṯy.qšt[.w.]ql‘. | bn.šp[š.]qšt. | bn.‘g[w.]qšt.w ql‘. | ḥd[ṯ]n.qšt.w.ql‘. | bn.bb.qšt.w[.ql]‘. | 119[321].4.6

y.qšt. | bn.dll.qšt.w.ql[‘]. | bn.pǵyn.qšt.w[.q]l‘. | bn.bdn.qšt. | bn.pls.qšt. | ǵmrm. | [-]lhd.ṯt.qštm.w.ṯn.ql‘m. | ulšn.ṯt.qš 119[321].3.30

št. | ady.qšt. | bn.srn.qšt. | bn.gdrn.qšt. | prpr.qšt. | ugry.qšt. | bn.ṣrptn.qšt. | bn.mṣry.qšt. | arny. | abm.qšt. | ḥdṯn.ql‘. | y 119[321].1.45

. | bn.ṯlln.qšt. | bn.šyn.qšt. | ‘bd.qšt. | bn.ulmy.qšt. | ṯqbn.qšt. | bn.qnmlk.qšt. | ytḥm.qšt. | grp.qšt. | m‘rby. | n‘mn.ṯt.qšt 104[316].5

bn.qṯn.qšt.w.ql‘. | mrṯd.qšt. | ssw.qšt. | knn.qšt. | bn.ṯlln.qšt. | bn.šyn.qšt. | ‘bd.qšt. | bn.ulmy.qšt. | ṯqbn.qšt. | bn.qnmlk. 119[316].4

št. | ǵmrm. | bn.qṯn.qšt.w.ql‘. | mrṯd.qšt. | ssw.qšt. | knn.qšt. | bn.ṯlln.qšt. | bn.šyn.qšt. | ‘bd.qšt. | bn.ulmy.qšt. | ṯqbn.qšt 119[321].1.15

št.w.ql‘. | bn.pǵm[-.qšt].w.ql‘. | n‘mn.q[št.w.]ql‘. | [t]tn.qš[t]. | bn.ṯǵd̠y[.qšt.]w.ql‘. | ṯṯy.qšt[.w.]ql‘. | bn.šp[š.]qšt. | bn.‘ 119[321].4.3

-.--]ml.ksl h.k b[r]q. | [---.]m[-]ǵ[-].thmt.brq. | [---].ṯṣb.qšt.bnt. | [---.‘]n h.km.bṯn.yqr. | [krpn h.-.l]arṣ.ks h.tšpk m. | 17[2AQHT].6.13

‘bd.qšt. | bn.ulmy.qšt. | ṯqbn.qšt. | bn.qnmlk.qšt. | ytḥm.qšt. | grp.qšt. | m‘rby. | n‘mn.ṯt.qštm.w.ql‘. | gln.ṯt.qštm.w.ql‘. 104[316].7

]l‘. | ‘ṯqbt.qšt. | [-]ll.qšt.w.ql‘. | ḫlb.rpš. | abmn.qšt. | ẓẓn.qšt. | dqry.qš[t]. | rkby. | bn.knn.qšt. | pbyn.qšt. | yddn.qšt.w.ql 119[321].2.32

h.imḫṣ h.k d.‘l.qšt h. | imḫṣ h.‘l.qṣ‘t h.hwt. | l aḥw.ap.qšt h.l ttn. | l y.w b mt[.-]ḥ.mṣṣ[-]t[.--]. | pr‘.qẓ.y[bl].šblt. | b ǵ 19[1AQHT].1.16

dm.d̠mr.ḥlqm.b mm[‘]. | mhrm.mṭm.tgrš. | šbm.b ksl.qšt h.mdnt. | w hln.‘nt.l bt h.tmǵyn. | tštql.ilt.l hkl h. | w l.šb‘ 3[‘NT].2.16

mr.kmr[.--]. | k ap‘.il.b gdrt.k lb.l | ḫṯ h.imḫṣ h.k d.‘l.qšt h. | imḫṣ h.‘l.qṣ‘t h.hwt. | l aḥw.ap.qšt h.l ttn. | l y.w b mt[19[1AQHT].1.14

[.---]. | qdqd h.w y‘n.ytpn.[mhr.št]. | šm‘.l btlt.‘nt.at.‘[l.qšt h]. | tmḫṣ h.qṣ‘t h.hwt.l t[ḥwy]. | n‘mn.ǵzr.št.ṯrm.w[---]. 18[3AQHT].4.12

. | w t‘nyn.ǵlm.b‘l. | in.b‘l.b bht ht. | il hd.b qrb.hkl h. | qšt hn.aḥd.b yd h. | w qṣ‘t h.bm.ymn h. | idk.l ytn pnm. | tk.a 10[76].2.6

.arb‘.qšt.w.ar[b‘]. | [u]ṯpt.ql‘.w.ṯt.mr[ḥ]m. | [bn].smyy.qšt.w.u[ṯpt]. | [w.q]l‘.w.ṯt.mrḥm. | [bn].šlmn.ql‘.w.ṯ[t.---]. | [b 2047.4

.mlṣ.qštm.w.uṯp[t]. | [--.q]l‘.w[.---.m]rḥm. | [bn].ḫdmn.qšt.[w.u]ṯp[t].ṯ[--]. | [---].arb‘.[---]. | [---].kdl[.---.mr]ḥm.w.ṯ[t. 2047.9

| [w.q]l‘.w.ṯt.mrḥm. | [bn].šlmn.ql‘.w.ṯ[t.---]. | [bn].mlṣ.qštm.w.uṯp[t]. | [--.q]l‘.w[.---.m]rḥm. | [bn].ḫdmn.qšt.[w.u]ṯp 2047.7

. | bn.b‘yn. | šdyn. | ary. | brqn. | bn.ḫlln. | bn.mṣry. | ṯmn.qšt. | w ‘šr.uṯpt. | upšt irš[-]. 118[306].14

by. | bn.knn.qšt. | pbyn.qšt. | yddn.qšt.w.ql‘. | š‘rt. | bn.il.qšt.w.ql‘. | ark.qšt.w.ql‘. | bn.‘bdnkl.qšt.w.ql‘. | bn.znan.qšt. | 119[321].2.41

n.qšt.w.ql‘. | bn.gzl.qšt.w.ql‘. | [---]n.qšt. | ilhd.qšt. | ‘dn.qšt.w.ql‘. | ilmhr.qšt.w.ql‘. | bn.gmrt.qšt. | ǵmrm. | bn.qṯn.qšt. 119[321].1.8

qšt.w.ql‘. | ‘ky.qšt. | ‘bdlbit.qšt. | kṯy.qšt.w.ql‘. | bn.ḫršn.qšt.w.ql‘. | ilrb.qšt.w.ql‘. | pshn.qšt. | bn.kmy.qšt. | bn.ilḥbn.qš 119[321].3.40

ṯn.ql‘. | yṯpṭ.qšt. | ilṯḥm.qšt.w.ql‘. | ṣdqm.qšt.w.ql‘. | uln.qšt.w.ql‘. | uln.qšt. | bn.blẓn.qšt.w.ql‘. | gb‘.qšt.w.ql‘. | nṣṣn.qšt 119[321].2.7

.qšt. | m‘r. | [‘]dyn.ṯt.qštm.w.ql‘. | [-]lrš.qšt.w.ql‘. | t[t]n.qšt.w.ql‘. | u[l]n.qšt.w.ql‘. | y‘rn.qšt.w.ql‘. | klby.qšt.w.ql‘. | bq‘ 119[321].2.16

. | abm.qšt. | ḥdṯn.ql‘. | yṯpṭ.qšt. | ilṯḥm.qšt.w.ql‘. | ṣdqm.qšt.w.ql‘. | uln.qšt.w.ql‘. | uln.qšt. | bn.blẓn.qšt.w.ql‘. | gb‘.qšt. 119[321].2.6

.šp[š.]qšt. | bn.‘g[w.]qšt.w ql‘. | ḥd[ṯ]n.qšt.w.ql‘. | bn.bb.qšt.w[.ql]‘. | bn.aktmy.qšt. | šdyn.qšt. | bdn.qšt.w.ql‘. | bn.šml 119[321].4.9

l‘m. | bn.[-]rkṯ.ṯt.qštm.w.ql‘. | bn.ṯ‘l.qšt. | bn.[ḫ]dpṯr.ṯt.qštm.[w].ql‘. | bn.aǵlyn.ṯt.qštm[.w.ṯl]ṯ.ql‘m. | bn.‘gw.qšt.w ql 119[321].3.18

n.znan.qšt. | bn.arz.[ar]b‘.qšt.w.arb[‘.]ql‘m. | b[n.]ad‘l.q[š]t.w.ql‘. | b[n].ilyn.qšt.w.ql‘. | šmrm.ql‘. | ubr‘y. | abmn.qšt. 119[321].2.46

y.qšt[.w.]ql‘. | bn.šp[š.]qšt. | bn.‘g[w.]qšt.w ql‘. | ḥd[ṯ]n.qšt.w.ql‘. | bn.bb.qšt.w[.ql]‘. | bn.aktmy.qšt. | šdyn.qšt. | bdn.q 119[321].4.8

ḫ.qšt.w.q[l‘]. | bn.lky.qšt. | bn.dll.qšt.w.ql[‘]. | bn.pǵyn.qšt.w[.q]l‘. | bn.bdn.qšt. | bn.pls.qšt. | ǵmrm. | [-]lhd.ṯt.qštm.w 119[321].3.29

.w.ṯn.ql‘m. | ildgn.qšt. | bn.y‘rn.ṯt.qštm w.ql‘. | bn.ḥṣn.qšt.w.ql‘. | bn.gdn.ṯt.qštm.w.ql‘. | bn.[-]q.qšt.w.ql‘. | gb[l]n.qšt 119[321].3.11

ṯ.ṯt.qštm.w.ṯn.q[l]‘m. | kmrṯn.ṯt.qštm.ṯn.[q]l‘m. | ǵdyn.qšt.w.ql‘. | bn.gzl.qšt.w.ql‘. | [---]n.qšt. | ilhd.qšt. | ‘dn.qšt.w.ql 119[321].1.4

zl.qšt.w.ql‘. | [---]n.qšt. | ilhd.qšt. | ‘dn.qšt.w.ql‘. | ilmhr.qšt.w.ql‘. | bn.gmrt.qšt. | ǵmrm. | bn.qṯn.qšt.w.ql‘. | mrṯd.qšt. | 119[321].1.9

il.ṯt.qštm.w.ṯn.ql‘m. | bn.ṯlṯ.ṯ[lṯ.]qšt.w.ṯn.ql‘m. | qṣn.ṯt.qštm.w.ql‘. | bn.gṯrn.q[š]t. | bn.ḫdi.ṯt.qštm.w.ṯn.ql‘m. | ildgn. 119[321].3.6

t.w.ql‘. | š‘rt. | bn.il.qšt.w.ql‘. | ark.qšt.w.ql‘. | bn.‘bdnkl.qšt.w.ql‘. | bn.znan.qšt. | bn.arz.[ar]b‘.qšt.w.arb[‘.]ql‘m. | b[n. 119[321].2.43

‘mn.ṯt.qštm.w.ql‘. | gln.ṯt.qštm.w.ql‘. | gtn.qšt. | pmn.ṯt.qšt.w.ql‘. | bn.zry.q[š]t.w.ql‘. | bn.tlmyn.ṯt.qštm.w.ql‘. | bn.ys 104[316].9

q[š]t. | bn.ḫdi.ṯt.qštm.w.ṯn.ql‘m. | ildgn.qšt. | bn.y‘rn.ṯt.qštm w.ql‘. | bn.ḥṣn.qšt.w.ql‘. | bn.gdn.ṯt.qštm.w.ql‘. | bn.[-]q. 119[321].3.10

l]n.qšt.w.ql‘. | y‘rn.qšt.w.ql‘. | klby.qšt.w.ql‘. | bq‘t. | ily.qšt.w.ql‘. | bn.ḥrẓn.qšt.w.ql‘. | tgrš.qšt.w.ql‘. | špšyn.qšt.w.ql‘. 119[321].2.22

.qšt.w.ql‘. | bn.tmy.qšt.w.ql‘. | ‘ky.qšt. | ‘bdlbit.qšt. | kṯy.qšt.w.ql‘. | bn.ḫršn.qšt.w.ql‘. | ilrb.qšt.w.ql‘. | pshn.qšt. | bn.k 119[321].3.39

l]‘. | bn.aktmy.qšt. | šdyn.qšt. | bdn.qšt.w.ql‘. | bn.šmlbi.qšt.w.ql‘. | bn.yy.qšt. | ilrb.qšt. | bn.nmš.ṯt.qšt.w.ql‘. | b‘l.qšt.w 119[321].4.13

qšt. | pmn.ṯt.qšt.w.ql‘. | bn.zry.q[š]t.w.ql‘. | bn.tlmyn.ṯt.qštm.w.ql‘. | bn.ysd.qšt. | [ǵ]mrm. | ilgn.qšt. | abršp.qšt. | ssg.q 104[316].9

š.qšt.w.ql‘. | bn.ǵb.qšt. | bn.ytrm.qšt.w.ql‘. | bn.‘bdyrḫ.qšt.w.q[l‘]. | bn.lky.qšt. | bn.dll.qšt.w.ql[‘]. | bn.pǵyn.qšt.w[.q] 119[321].3.26

| bn.pls.qšt. | ǵmrm. | [-]lhd.ṯt.qštm.w.ṯn.ql‘m. | ulšn.ṯt.qšm.w.ql‘. | bn.ml‘n.qšt.w.ql‘. | bn.tmy.qšt.w.ql‘. | ‘ky.qšt. | ‘b 119[321].3.34

.qštm.w[.]q[l‘]. | bn.rpš.qšt.w.ql‘. | bn.ǵb.qšt. | bn.ytrm.qšt.w.ql‘. | bn.‘bdyrḫ.qšt.w.q[l‘]. | bn.lky.qšt. | bn.dll.qšt.w.ql[119[321].3.25

. | pbyn.qšt. | yddn.qšt.w.ql‘. | š‘rt. | bn.il.qšt.w.ql‘. | ark.qšt.w.ql‘. | bn.‘bdnkl.qšt.w.ql‘. | bn.znan.qšt. | bn.arz.[ar]b‘.qš 119[321].2.42

ṯlṯ.qšt.w.[ṯlṯ.]ql‘m. | bn.army.ṯt.qštm.w[.]q[l‘]. | bn.rpš.qšt.w.ql‘. | bn.ǵb.qšt. | bn.ytrm.qšt.w.ql‘. | bn.‘bdyrḫ.qšt.w.q[l 119[321].3.23

m.qšt.w.ql‘. | bn.‘bdyrḫ.qšt.w.q[l‘]. | bn.lky.qšt. | bn.dll.qšt.w.ql[‘]. | bn.pǵyn.qšt.w[.q]l‘. | bn.bdn.qšt. | bn.pls.qšt. | ǵm 119[321].3.28

.kmy.qšt. | bn.ilḥbn.qšt.w.q[l‘]. | ršpab.qšt.w.ql‘. | pdrn.qšt.w.ql‘. | bn.pǵm[-.qšt].w.ql‘. | n‘mn.q[št.w.]ql‘. | [t]tn.qš[t]. 119[321].3.46

‘gw.qšt.w ql‘. | bn.tbšn.ṯlṯ.qšt.w.[ṯlṯ.]ql‘m. | bn.army.ṯt.qštm.w[.]q[l‘]. | bn.rpš.qšt.w.ql‘. | bn.ǵb.qšt. | bn.ytrm.qšt.w.q 119[321].3.22

.ql‘. | bn.bb.qšt.w[.ql]‘. | bn.aktmy.qšt. | šdyn.qšt. | bdn.qšt.w.ql‘. | bn.šmlbi.qšt.w.ql‘. | bn.yy.qšt. | ilrb.qšt. | bn.nmš.ṯt 119[321].4.12

n‘mn.q[št.w.]ql‘. | [t]tn.qš[t]. | bn.ṯǵd̠y[.qšt.]w.ql‘. | ṯṯy.qšt[.w.]ql‘. | bn.šp[š.]qšt. | bn.‘g[w.]qšt.w ql‘. | ḥd[ṯ]n.qšt.w.ql 119[321].4.5

t.qštm.[w].ql‘. | bn.aǵlyn.ṯt.qštm[.w.ṯl]ṯ.ql‘m. | bn.‘gw.qšt.w ql‘. | bn.tbšn.ṯlṯ.qšt.w.[ṯlṯ.]ql‘m. | bn.army.ṯt.qštm.w[.] 119[321].3.20

| gln.ṯt.qštm.w.ql‘. | gtn.qšt. | pmn.ṯt.qšt.w.ql‘. | bn.zry.q[š]t.w.ql‘. | bn.tlmyn.ṯt.qštm.w.ql‘. | bn.ysd.qšt. | [ǵ]mrm. | il 104[316].9

[-]lhd.ṯt.qštm.w.ṯn.ql‘m. | ulšn.ṯt.qšm.w.ql‘. | bn.ml‘n.qšt.w.ql‘. | bn.tmy.qšt.w.ql‘. | ‘ky.qšt. | ‘bdlbit.qšt. | kṯy.qšt.w. 119[321].3.35

[l]n.qšt.w.ql‘. | bn.[-]bl.ṯt.qštm.w.ṯn.ql‘m. | bn.[-]rkṯ.ṯt.qštm.w.ql‘. | bn.ṯ‘l.qšt. | bn.[ḫ]dpṯr.ṯt.qštm.[w].ql‘. | bn.aǵlyn. 119[321].3.16

ily.qšt.w.ql‘. | bn.ḥrẓn.qšt.w.ql‘. | tgrš.qšt.w.ql‘. | špšyn.qšt.w.ql‘. | bn.ṯ‘ln.qš[t.w.q]l‘. | ‘ṯqbt.qšt. | [-]ll.qšt.w.ql‘. | ḫlb.r 119[321].2.25

w.ql‘. | bn.gdn.ṯt.qštm.w.ql‘. | bn.[-]q.qšt.w.ql‘. | gb[l]n.qšt.w.ql‘. | bn.[-]bl.ṯt.qštm.w.ṯn.ql‘m. | bn.[-]rkṯ.ṯt.qštm.w.ql‘ 119[321].3.14

št. | bn.y‘rn.ṯt.qštm w.ql‘. | bn.ḥṣn.qšt.w.ql‘. | bn.gdn.ṯt.qštm.w.ql‘. | bn.[-]q.qšt.w.ql‘. | gb[l]n.qšt.w.ql‘. | bn.[-]bl.ṯt.qš 119[321].3.12

l‘. | bn.šmlbi.qšt.w.ql‘. | bn.yy.qšt. | ilrb.qšt. | bn.nmš.ṯt.qšt.w.ql‘. | b‘l.qšt.w.ql‘. 119[321].4.16

. | t[t]n.qšt.w.ql‘. | u[l]n.qšt.w.ql‘. | y‘rn.qšt.w.ql‘. | klby.qšt.w.ql‘. | bq‘t. | ily.qšt.w.ql‘. | bn.ḫrẓn.qšt.w.ql‘. | tgrš.qšt.w. 119[321].2.19
.ql‘. | bn.ḥṣn.qšt.w.ql‘. | bn.gdn.ṯt.qštm.w.ql‘. | bn.[-]q.qšt.w.ql‘. | gb[l]n.qšt.w.ql‘. | bn.[-]bl.ṯt.qštm.w.ṯn.ql‘m. | bn.[- 119[321].3.13
.ql‘. | ṣdqm.qšt.w.ql‘. | uln.qšt.w.ql‘. | uln.qšt. | bn.blẓn.qšt.w.ql‘. | gb‘.qšt.w.ql‘. | nṣṣn.qšt. | m‘r. | [‘]dyn.ṯt.qštm.w.ql‘. 119[321].2.9
t. | bn.qnmlk.qšt. | ytḥm.qšt. | grp.qšt. | m‘rby. | n‘mn.ṯt.qštm.w.ql‘. | gln.ṯt.qštm.w.ql‘. | gtn.qšt. | pmn.ṯt.qšt.w.ql‘. | bn 104[316].9
tḥm.qšt. | grp.qšt. | m‘rby. | n‘mn.ṯt.qštm.w.ql‘. | gln.ṯt.qštm.w.ql‘. | gtn.qšt. | pmn.ṯt.qšt.w.ql‘. | bn.zry.q[š]t.w.ql‘. | b 104[316].9
ḏy[.qšt.]w.ql‘. | ṯty.qšt[.w.]ql‘. | bn.šp[š.]qšt. | bn.‘g[w.]qšt.w ql‘. | ḥd[ṯ]n.qšt.w.ql‘. | bn.bb.qšt.w[.ql]‘. | bn.aktmy.qšt. 119[321].4.7
l‘. | špšyn.qšt.w.ql‘. | bn.ṯ‘ln.qš[t.w.q]l‘. | ‘ṯqbt.qšt. | [-]ll.qšt.w.ql‘. | ḥlb.rpš. | abmn.qšt. | ẓẓn.qšt. | dqry.qš[t]. | rkby. | b 119[321].2.28
n.ṯt.qštm.w.ql‘. | [-]lrš.qšt.w.ql‘. | t[t]n.qšt.w.ql‘. | u[l]n.qšt.w.ql‘. | y‘rn.qšt.w.ql‘. | klby.qšt.w.ql‘. | bq‘t. | ily.qšt.w.ql‘. 119[321].2.17
. | [-]lrš.qšt.w.ql‘. | t[t]n.qšt.w.ql‘. | u[l]n.qšt.w.ql‘. | y‘rn.qšt.w.ql‘. | klby.qšt.w.ql‘. | bq‘t. | ily.qšt.w.ql‘. | bn.ḫrẓn.qšt.w. 119[321].2.18
t.w.ql‘. | ilmhr.qšt.w.ql‘. | bn.gmrt.qšt. | ǵmrm. | bn.qṯn.qšt.w.ql‘. | mrṯd.qšt. | ssw.qšt. | knn.qšt. | bn.ṯlln.qšt. | bn.šyn.q 119[321].1.12
št.w.q[l‘]. | ršpab.qšt.w.ql‘. | pdrn.qšt.w.ql‘. | bn.pǵm[-.qšt].w.ql‘. | n‘mn.q[št.w.]ql‘. | [t]tn.qš[t]. | bn.ṯǵḏy[.qšt.]w.ql‘. 119[321].4.1
t.w.ql‘. | uln.qšt.w.ql‘. | uln.qšt. | bn.blẓn.qšt.w.ql‘. | gb‘.qšt.w.ql‘. | nṣṣn.qšt. | m‘r. | [‘]dyn.ṯt.qštm.w.ql‘. | [-]lrš.qšt.w.q 119[321].2.10
n.ql‘m. | ulšn.ṯt.qšm.w.ql‘. | bn.ml‘n.qšt.w.ql‘. | bn.tmy.qšt.w.ql‘. | ‘ky.qšt. | ‘bdlbit.qšt. | kṯy.qšt.w.ql‘. | bn.ḫršn.qšt.w. 119[321].3.36
rẓn.qšt.w.ql‘. | tgrš.qšt.w.ql‘. | špšyn.qšt.w.ql‘. | bn.ṯ‘ln.qš[t.w.q]l‘. | ‘ṯqbt.qšt. | [-]ll.qšt.w.ql‘. | ḥlb.rpš. | abmn.qšt. | ẓẓ 119[321].2.26
l‘. | psḥn.qšt. | bn.kmy.qšt. | bn.ilḥbn.qšt.w.q[l‘]. | ršpab.qšt.w.ql‘. | pdrn.qšt.w.ql‘. | bn.pǵm[-.qšt].w.ql‘. | n‘mn.q[št.w. 119[321].3.45
št. | ‘bdlbit.qšt. | kṯy.qšt.w.ql‘. | bn.ḫršn.qšt.w.ql‘. | ilrb.qšt.w.ql‘. | psḥn.qšt. | bn.kmy.qšt. | bn.ilḥbn.qšt.w.q[l‘]. | ršpa 119[321].3.41
.mṣry.qšt. | arny. | abm.qšt. | ḥdṯn.ql‘. | yṯpṯ.qšt. | ilṯḥm.qšt.w.ql‘. | ṣdqm.qšt.w.ql‘. | uln.qšt.w.ql‘. | uln.qšt. | bn.blẓn.q 119[321].2.5
w.ql‘. | ilrb.qšt.w.ql‘. | psḥn.qšt. | bn.kmy.qšt. | bn.ilḥbn.qšt.w.q[l‘]. | ršpab.qšt.w.ql‘. | pdrn.qšt.w.ql‘. | bn.pǵm[-.qšt]. 119[321].3.44
r]b‘.qšt.w.arb[‘.]ql‘m. | b[n.]ad‘l.q[š]t.w.ql‘. | b[n].ilyn.qšt.w.ql‘. | šmrm.ql‘. | ubr‘y. | abmn.qšt.w.ṯn.ql‘m. | qdmn.ṯt.q 119[321].2.47
n.qšt. | dqry.qš[t]. | rkby. | bn.knn.qšt. | pbyn.qšt. | yddn.qšt.w.ql‘. | š‘rt. | bn.il.qšt.w.ql‘. | ark.qšt.w.ql‘. | bn.‘bdnkl.qšt. 119[321].2.38
.qšt.w.ql‘. | bq‘t. | ily.qšt.w.ql‘. | bn.ḫrẓn.qšt.w.ql‘. | tgrš.qšt.w.ql‘. | špšyn.qšt.w.ql‘. | bn.ṯ‘ln.qš[t.w.q]l‘. | ‘ṯqbt.qšt. | [-]l 119[321].2.24
qšt.w.ql‘. | klby.qšt.w.ql‘. | bq‘t. | ily.qšt.w.ql‘. | bn.ḫrẓn.qšt.w.ql‘. | tgrš.qšt.w.ql‘. | špšyn.qšt.w.ql‘. | bn.ṯ‘ln.qš[t.w.q]l‘. 119[321].2.23
.qšt.w.ql‘. | pdrn.qšt.w.ql‘. | bn.pǵm[-.qšt].w.ql‘. | n‘mn.q[št.w.]ql‘. | [t]tn.qš[t]. | bn.ṯǵḏy[.qšt.]w.ql‘. | ṯty.qšt[.w.]ql‘. | 119[321].4.2
‘.qšt.w.ql‘. | nṣṣn.qšt. | m‘r. | [‘]dyn.ṯt.qštm.w.ql‘. | [-]lrš.qšt.w.ql‘. | t[t]n.qšt.w.ql‘. | u[l]n.qšt.w.ql‘. | y‘rn.qšt.w.ql‘. | kl 119[321].2.15
m[-.qšt].w.ql‘. | n‘mn.q[št.w.]ql‘. | [t]tn.qš[t]. | bn.ṯǵḏy[.qšt.]w.ql‘. | ṯty.qšt[.w.]ql‘. | bn.šp[š.]qšt. | bn.‘g[w.]qšt.w ql‘. | 119[321].4.4
blẓn.qšt.w.ql‘. | gb‘.qšt.w.ql‘. | nṣṣn.qšt. | m‘r. | [‘]dyn.ṯt.qštm.w.ql‘. | [-]lrš.qšt.w.ql‘. | t[t]n.qšt.w.ql‘. | u[l]n.qšt.w.ql‘. | 119[321].2.14
]‘m. | kmrṯn.ṯt.qštm.ṯn.[q]l‘m. | ǵdyn.qšt.w.ql‘. | bn.gzl.qšt.w.ql‘. | [---]n.qšt. | ilhd.qšt. | ‘dn.qšt.w.ql‘. | ilmhr.qšt.w.ql‘ 119[321].1.5
št.w.ql‘. | bn.yy.qšt. | ilrb.qšt. | bn.nmš.ṯt.qšt.w.ql‘. | b‘l.qšt.w.ql‘. 119[321].4.17
[nq]dm.dt.kn.npṣ hm. | [bn].lbn.arb‘.qšt.w.ar[b‘]. | [u]ṯpt.ql‘.w.ṯt.mr[ḥ]m. | [bn].smyy.qšt.w.u[ṯpt] 2047.2
.ql‘. | bn.‘bdnkl.qšt.w.ql‘. | bn.znan.qšt. | bn.arz.[ar]b‘.qšt.w.arb[‘.]ql‘m. | b[n.]ad‘l.q[š]t.w.ql‘. | b[n].ilyn.qšt.w.ql‘. | 119[321].2.45
lyn.ṯt.qštm[.w.ṯl]ṯ.ql‘m. | bn.‘gw.qšt.w ql‘. | bn.tbšn.ṯlṯ.qšt.w.[ṯlṯ.]ql‘m. | bn.army.ṯt.qštm.w[.]q[l‘]. | bn.rpš.qšt.w.ql‘. 119[321].3.21
l‘. | bn.ṯ‘l.qšt. | bn.[ḫ]dpṯr.ṯt.qštm.[w].ql‘. | bn.aǵlyn.ṯt.qštm[.w.ṯl]ṯ.ql‘m. | bn.‘gw.qšt.w ql‘. | bn.tbšn.ṯlṯ.qšt.w.[ṯlṯ.]ql 119[321].3.19
.ql‘. | šmrm.ql‘. | ubr‘y. | abmn.qšt.w.ṯn.ql‘m. | qdmn.ṯt.qštm.w.ṯlṯ.ql‘m. | bn.ṣdqil.ṯt.qštm.w.ṯn.ql‘m. | bn.ṯlṯ.ṯ[lṯ.]qšt. 119[321].3.3
.ṯn.ql‘m. | qṣn.ṯt.qštm.w.ql‘. | bn.gṯrn.q[š]t. | bn.ḫdi.ṯt.qštm.w.ṯn.ql‘m. | ildgn.qšt. | bn.y‘rn.ṯt.qštm w.ql‘. | bn.ḥṣn.qš 119[321].3.8
.qšt.w[.q]l‘. | bn.bdn.qšt. | bn.pls.qšt. | ǵmrm. | [-]lhd.ṯt.qštm.w.ṯn.ql‘m. | ulšn.ṯt.qšm.w.ql‘. | bn.ml‘n.qšt.w.ql‘. | bn.t 119[321].3.33
.qšt.w.ṯn.ql‘m. | qdmn.ṯt.qštm.w.ṯlṯ.ql‘m. | bn.ṣdqil.ṯt.qštm.w.ṯn.ql‘m. | bn.ṯlṯ.ṯ[lṯ.]qšt.w.ṯn.ql‘m. | qṣn.ṯt.qštm.w.ql‘ 119[321].3.4
.w.ql‘. | bn.[-]q.qšt.w.ql‘. | gb[l]n.qšt.w.ql‘. | bn.[-]bl.ṯt.qštm.w.ṯn.ql‘m. | bn.[-]rkṯ.ṯt.qštm.w.ql‘. | bn.ṯ‘l.qšt. | bn.[ḫ]d 119[321].3.15
[u]lm. | mṯpṯ.ṯt.qštm.w.ṯn.q[l]‘m. | kmrṯn.ṯt.qštm.ṯn.[q]l‘m. | ǵdyn.qšt.w.ql‘. 119[321].1.2
]t.w.ql‘. | b[n].ilyn.qšt.w.ql‘. | šmrm.ql‘. | ubr‘y. | abmn.qšt.w.ṯn.ql‘m. | qdmn.ṯt.qštm.w.ṯlṯ.ql‘m. | bn.ṣdqil.ṯt.qštm.w. 119[321].3.2
tm.w.ṯlṯ.ql‘m. | bn.ṣdqil.ṯt.qštm.w.ṯn.ql‘m. | bn.ṯlṯ.ṯ[lṯ.]qšt.w.ṯn.ql‘m. | qṣn.ṯt.qštm.w.ql‘. | bn.gṯrn.q[š]t. | bn.ḫdi.ṯt.qš 119[321].3.5
št. | ugry.qšt. | bn.ṣrptn.qšt. | bn.mṣry.qšt. | arny. | abm.qšt. | ḥdṯn.ql‘. | yṯpṯ.qšt. | ilṯḥm.qšt.w.ql‘. | ṣdqm.qšt.w.ql‘. | ul 119[321].2.2
.qš[t.w.q]l‘. | ‘ṯqbt.qšt. | [-]ll.qšt.w.ql‘. | ḥlb.rpš. | abmn.qšt. | ẓẓn.qšt. | dqry.qš[t]. | rkby. | bn.knn.qšt. | pbyn.qšt. | ydd 119[321].2.31
.b alp. | šd.rbt.kmn.hlk.kṯr. | k y‘n.w y‘n.tdrq.ḫss. | hlk.qšt.ybln.hl.yš | rb‘.qṣ‘t.apnk.dnil. | mt.rpi.aphn.ǵzr.mt. | hrn 17[2AQHT].5.12
n.qšt. | ẓẓn.qšt. | dqry.qš[t]. | rkby. | bn.knn.qšt. | pbyn.qšt. | yddn.qšt.w.ql‘. | š‘rt. | bn.il.qšt.w.ql‘. | ark.qšt.w.ql‘. | bn.‘ 119[321].2.37
.w.ql‘. | bn.ysd.qšt. | [ǵ]mrm. | ilgn.qšt. | abršp.qšt. | ssg.qšt. | ynḥm.qšt. | pprn.qšt. | uln.qšt. | bn.nkl qšt. | ady.qšt. | bn. 105[86].3
mš | knt h.apnk.dnil.m[t]. | rpi.aphn.ǵzr.m[t]. | hrnmy.qšt.yqb.[--] | rk.‘l.aqht.k yq[--.---]. | pr‘m.ṣd k.y bn[.---]. | pr‘ 17[2AQHT].5.35
n.šyn.qšt. | ‘bd.qšt. | bn.ulmy.qšt. | ṯqbn.qšt. | bn.qnmlk.qšt. | ytḥm.qšt. | grp.qšt. | m‘rby. | n‘mn.ṯt.qštm.w.ql‘. | gln.ṯt. 104[316].6
‘.m‘. | [l aqht.ǵzr.i]rš.ksp.w atn k. | [ḫrṣ.w aš]lḥ k.w tn.qšt k.[l]. | [‘nt.tq]ḥ[.q]ṣ‘t k.ybmt.limm. | w y‘n.aqht.ǵzr.adr.ṯ 17[2AQHT].6.18
ṣmt.mhr h.[---]. | aqht.w tbk.y[---.---]. | abn.ank.w ‘l.[qšt k.---.‘l]. | qṣ‘t k.at.l ḥ[---.---]. | w ḥlq.‘pmm[.---]. 18[3AQHT].4.40
bn.gmrt.qšt. | ǵmrm. | bn.qṯn.qšt.w.ql‘. | mrṯd.qšt. | ssw.qšt. | knn.qšt. | bn.ṯlln.qšt. | bn.šyn.qšt. | ‘bd.qšt. | bn.ulmy.qšt. 119[321].1.14
bn.ml‘n.qšt.w.ql‘. | bn.tmy.qšt.w.ql‘. | ‘ky.qšt. | ‘bdlbit.qšt. | kṯy.qšt.w.ql‘. | bn.ḫršn.qšt.w.ql‘. | ilrb.qšt.w.ql‘. | psḥn.q 119[321].3.38
.hyn.d ḥrš. | ydm.aḫr.ymǵy.kṯr. | w ḫss.b d.dnil.ytnn. | qšt.l brk h.y‘db. | qṣ‘t.apnk.mṯt.dnty. | tšlḥm.tššqy ilm. | tsad. 17[2AQHT].5.27
m.mtnm. | b ‘qbt.ṯr.adr.b ǵlil.qnm. | tn.l kṯr.w ḫss.yb‘l.qšt l ‘nt. | qṣ‘t.l ybmt.limm.w t‘n.btlt. | ‘nt.irš ḥym.l aqht.ǵzr. 17[2AQHT].6.24
w.ql‘. | uln.qšt. | bn.blẓn.qšt.w.ql‘. | gb‘.qšt.w.ql‘. | nṣṣn.qšt. | m‘r. | [‘]dyn.ṯt.qštm.w.ql‘. | [-]lrš.qšt.w.ql‘. | t[t]n.qšt.w.q 119[321].2.11
bn.ulmy.qšt. | ṯqbn.qšt. | bn.qnmlk.qšt. | ytḥm.qšt. | grp.qšt. | m‘rby. | n‘mn.ṯt.qštm.w.ql‘. | gln.ṯt.qštm.w.ql‘. | gtn.qšt. 104[316].8
n.ṯt.qštm.w.ql‘. | bn.ysd.qšt. | [ǵ]mrm. | ilgn.qšt. | abršp.qšt. | ssg.qšt. | ynḥm.qšt. | pprn.qšt. | uln.qšt. | bn.nkl qšt. | ady. 105[86].2
t.w.ql‘. | bn.gmrt.qšt. | ǵmrm. | bn.qṯn.qšt.w.ql‘. | mrṯd.qšt. | ssw.qšt. | knn.qšt. | bn.ṯlln.qšt. | bn.šyn.qšt. | ‘bd.qšt. | bn. 119[321].1.13
.ql‘. | mrṯd.qšt. | ssw.qšt. | knn.qšt. | bn.ṯlln.qšt. | bn.šyn.qšt. | ‘bd.qšt. | bn.ulmy.qšt. | ṯqbn.qšt. | bn.qnmlk.qšt. | ytḥm.q 104[316].5
t.qšm.w.ql‘. | bn.ml‘n.qšt.w.ql‘. | bn.tmy.qšt.w.ql‘. | ‘ky.qšt. | ‘bdlbit.qšt. | kṯy.qšt.w.ql‘. | bn.ḫršn.qšt.w.ql‘. | ilrb.qšt.w. 119[321].3.37
l‘m. | ǵdyn.qšt.w.ql‘. | bn.gzl.qšt.w.ql‘. | [---]n.qšt. | ilhd.qšt. | ‘dn.qšt.w.ql‘. | ilmhr.qšt.w.ql‘. | bn.gmrt.qšt. | ǵmrm. | bn 119[321].1.7
l‘. | bn.zry.q[š]t.w.ql‘. | bn.tlmyn.ṯt.qštm.w.ql‘. | bn.ysd.qšt. | [ǵ]mrm. | ilgn.qšt. | abršp.qšt. | ssg.qšt. | ynḥm.qšt. | pprn. 104[316].9
št. | ilhd.qšt. | ‘dn.qšt.w.ql‘. | ilmhr.qšt.w.ql‘. | bn.gmrt.qšt. | ǵmrm. | bn.qṯn.qšt.w.ql‘. | mrṯd.qšt. | ssw.qšt. | knn.qšt. | 119[321].1.10
ll.qšt.w.ql[‘]. | bn.pǵyn.qšt.w[.q]l‘. | bn.bdn.qšt. | bn.pls.qšt. | ǵmrm. | [-]lhd.ṯt.qštm.w.ṯn.ql‘m. | ulšn.ṯt.qšm.w.ql‘. | bn 119[321].3.31

qšt

lb.rpš. | abmn.qšt. | ẓẓn.qšt. | dqry.qš[t]. | rkby. | bn.knn.qšt. | pbyn.qšt. | yddn.qšt.w.ql‘. | š‘rt. | bn.il.qšt.w.ql‘. | ark.qšt. 119[321].2.36

t. | m‘rby. | n‘mn.ṯt.qštm.w.ql‘. | gln.ṯt.qštm.w.ql‘. | gtn.qšt. | pmn.ṯt.qšt.w.ql‘. | bn.zry.q[š]t.w.ql‘. | bn.tlmyn.ṯt.qštm. 104[316].9

. | ibr.k l hm.d l h q[--.---]. | l ytn.l hm.tḥt b‘l[.---]. | h.u qšt pn hdd.b y[.----]. | ‘m.b ym b‘l ysy ym[.---]. | rmm.ẖnpm. 9[33].2.6

ysd.qšt. | [ǵ]mrm. | ilgn.qšt. | abršp.qšt. | ssg.qšt. | ynḥm.qšt. | pprn.qšt. | uln.qšt. | bn.nkl qšt. | ady.qšt. | bn.srn.qšt. | bn. 105[86].3

št. | uln.qšt. | bn.nkl qšt. | ady.qšt. | bn.srn.qšt. | bn.gdrn.qšt. | prpr.qšt. | ugry.qšt. | bn.ṣrptn.qšt. | bn.mṣry.qšt. | arny. | a 119[321].1.43

št. | [-]ll.qšt.w.ql‘. | ẖlb.rpš. | abmn.qšt. | ẓẓn.qšt. | dqry.qš[t]. | rkby. | bn.knn.qšt. | pbyn.qšt. | yddn.qšt.w.ql‘. | š‘rt. | bn 119[321].2.33

.w ql‘. | ḥd[ṯ]n.qšt.w.ql‘. | bn.bb.qšt.w[.ql]‘. | bn.aktmy.qšt. | šdyn.qšt. | bdn.qšt.w.ql‘. | bn.šmlbi.qšt.w.ql‘. | bn.yy.qšt. 119[321].4.10

ṯn.ḥršm. | b.gt.ǵl. | [-.]nǵr.mdr‘. | [-].nǵr[.--]m. | [--.]psl.qšt. | [ṯl]ṯ.psl.ḥẓm. | [---.ḥ]rš.mr[k]bt. | [--].‘šr h[.---]. | [ẖm]š.‘š 1024.3.18

[-----]. | [---.]abl.qšt ṯmn. | ašrb‘.qṣ‘t.w hn šb[‘]. | b ymm.apnk.dnil.mt. | rpi.a 17[2AQHT].5.2

[u]lm. | mṯpṭ.ṯt.qštm.w.ṯn.q[l]‘m. | kmrṯn.ṯt.qštm.ṯn.[q]l‘m. | ǵdyn.qšt.w.ql‘. | bn.gzl.qšt.w.ql‘. | [---]n.qšt. 119[321].1.3

t. | knn.qšt. | bn.ṯlln.qšt. | bn.šyn.qšt. | ‘bd.qšt. | bn.ulmy.qšt. | ṯqbn.qšt. | bn.qnmlk.qšt. | ytḥm.qšt. | grp.qšt. | m‘rby. | n‘ 104[316].5

š.qšt.w.ql‘. | špšyn.qšt.w.ql‘. | bn.ṯ‘ln.qš[t.w.q]l‘. | ‘ṯqbt.qšt. | [-]ll.qšt.w.ql‘. | ẖlb.rpš. | abmn.qšt. | ẓẓn.qšt. | dqry.qš[t]. 119[321].2.27

dr[.---]. | idm.‘rẓ.t‘r[ẓ.---]. | ‘n.b‘l.a[ẖ]d̲[.---]. | ẓr h.aẖd̲.qš[t.---]. | p ‘n.b‘l.aẖd̲[.---]. | w ṣmt.ǵllm[.---]. | aẖd̲.aklm.k [--- 12[75].2.33

[l a]q[h]t. | [t]krb.[---.]l qrb.mym. | tql.[---.]lb.tṯ[b]r. | qšt[.---]r.y[ṯ]br. | ṯmn.[---.]btlt.[‘]nt. | tṯb.[---.--]ša. | tlm.km[.-- 19[1AQHT].1.4

[--.]mt.kl.amt.w an.mtm.amt. | [ap.m]ṯn.rgmm.argm.qštm. | [----.]mhrm.ht.tṣdn.tinṯt. | [---]m.tṣḥq.‘nt.w b lb.tqny. 17[2AQHT].6.39

qštipṯl

spr.ḥrš. | qštipṯl. | bn.anny. | ilṣdq. | yplṭn.bn iln. | špšm.nsl h. | [-----]. 1037.2

qt

| [---].ṯlḥn. | [---].ṯnn. | [---.--]b.kdr. | [---.--]m n‘rt. | [---].qt.b[--]. | [---.]kd[r]. | [---.]ṯpr. | [---.]prš. | [---.]šdm. | [---.-]nm. 1142.2

qtn

[---.]bn.ẖlan. | [--]r bn.mn. | [--]ry. | [--]lim bn.brq. | [--.]qtn bn.drṣy. | [--]kn bn.pri. | [r]špab bn.pni. | [ab]mn bn.qṣy. | 2087.6

qṯṯ

ṭ.nhr.yprsḥ.ym.yql. | l arṣ.tnǵṣn.pnt h.w ydlp.tmn h. | yqṯ b‘l.w yšt.ym.ykly.ṯpṭ.nhr. | b šm.tg‘r m.‘ṯtrt.bṯ l aliyn.[b‘ 2.4[68].27

štn.tštn y[n] ‘d šb‘. | trṯ.‘d.škr.y‘db.yrẖ. | gb h.km.[---.]yqṯqṯ.tḥt. | ṯlḥnt.il.d yd‘nn. | y‘db.lḥm.l h.w d l yd‘nn. | d.mṣ UG5.1.1.5

r

r

]y[ṣḥ.]šm‘.m‘.|[--.]‘m[.-.]att y[.-].|[---.]tḥm.|[---]t.[ ]r.|[---.--]n.|[---] h.l ‘db.|[---]n.yd h.|[---].bl.išlḥ.|[---] h.gm. 14[KRT].5.232

raš

----].|[-----].|[-----].|[---.-]rb.|[-----].|[-----].|[-----].|k yraš w ykhp mid.|dblt ytnt w ṣmqm ytn[m].|w qmḥ bql yṣ 160[55].23
.ḥdrt.w.št].|irǵ[n.ḥmr.ydk].|aḥd[h.w.yṣq.b.ap h].|k yr[a]š.ššw[w.w.ykhp].|mid.dblt.yt[nt.w].|ṣmq[m].ytnm.w[.q 161[56].32
kšr grn.|[w št aškrr w p]r ḥdrt.|[-----].|[---.-]n[-].|[k yraš ššw št bln q]t ydk.|[w yṣq b ap h].|[-----].|[-----].|[----- 160[55].14
[št.grn].|št.irǵn.ḥmr[.ydk].|aḥd h.w.yṣq.b[.ap h].|k.yraš.ššw.[št].|bln.qt.yṣq.b.a[p h].|k yg‘r[.ššw.---].|dprn[.--- 161[56].21

rib

m.ksp.]‘l.|il[m]l[k.a]rgnd.|uškny[.w]mit.|zt.b d hm.rib.|w [---].|[-----].|[-]šy[.---] h.|[-]kt[.---.]nrn.|[b]n.nmq[.-- 2055.13

ridn

yšqyn h.|ytn.ks.b d h.|krpn.b klat.yd h.|b krb.‘ẓm.ridn.|mt.šmm.ks.qdš.|l tphn h.att.krpn.|l t‘n.atrt.alp.|kd. 3[‘NT].1.12

rimt

btlt.‘nt.uṣb‘t[h.ybmt].|limm.tiḫd.knr h.b yd[h.tšt].|rimt.l irt h.tšr.dd.al[iyn].|b‘l.ahbt. UG5.3.2.7
---].|špk.l[---].|trḥṣ.yd[h.---].|[--.]yṣt ḏm[r.---].|tšt[.r]imt.[l irt h.tšr.l dd.aliyn.b‘l].|[ahb]t pdr[y.bt.ar.ahbt.ṭly.b 7.2[130].10

riš

-]p.gp ym.w yṣǵd.gp..thm.|[yqḥ.]il.mšt‘ltm.mšt‘ltm.l riš.agn.|hl h.[t]špl.hl h.trm.hl h.tṣḥ.ad ad.|w hl h.tṣḥ.um.u 23[52].31
.yd.il.k ym.|w yd.il.k mdb.yqḥ.il.mšt‘ltm.|mšt‘ltm.l riš.agn.yqḥ.tš.b bt h.|il.ḫṭ h.nḥt.il.ymnn.mṭ.yd h.yšu.|yr.š 23[52].36
ṯkl.l il.šlmm].|b ṯlṯt ‘[šrt.yrtḥṣ.mlk.brr].|b arb‘[t.‘šrt.riš.argmn].|w ṯn šm.l [b‘lt.bhtm.‘ṣrm.l inš].|ilm.w š d[d.ilš. 35[3].4
l.l il.šlmm.|b [ṯlṯt].‘šrt.yrtḥṣ.mlk.|br[r.]b a[r]b‘t.‘šrt.riš.|arg[mn.w ṯn.]šm.l b‘lt.|bhtm.‘ṣ[rm.l in]š ilm.w š.|dd il APP.II[173].4
riš h.tply.ṭly.bn.‘n h.|uz‘rt.tmll.išd h.qrn[m].|dt.‘l h.riš h.b glṯ.b šm[m].|[---.i]l.ṯr.iṯ.p h.k ṯt.ǵlṯ[.--].|[---.--] k yn. UG5.3.1.7
.tdu.mh.|pdrm.tdu.šrr.|ḥṭ m.t‘mt.[‘]ṯr.[k]m.|zbln.‘l.riš h.|w ṯṯb.trḥṣ.nn.b d‘t.|npš h.l lḥm.tpth.|brlt h.l ṯrm.|m 16.6[127].9
]ḫp.an.arnn.ql.špš.ḫw.bṯnm.uḫd.b‘lm.|[--.a]ṯm.prṯl.l riš h.ḥmṯ.ṯmṯ.|[--.]ydbr.ṯrmt.al m.qḥn y.š y.qḥn y.|[--.]šir. 1001.1.7
‘l.b ṣrrt.ṣpn.|yṯb.l kḥṯ.aliyn.|b‘l.p‘n h.l tmǵyn.|hdm.riš h.l ymǵy.|aps h.w y‘n.‘ṯtr.‘rẓ.|l amlk.b ṣrrt.ṣpn.|yrd.‘ṯt 6.1.60[49.1.32]
rd.l ksi.yṯb.|l hdm[.w] l.hdm.yṯb.|l arṣ.yṣq.‘mr.|un.l riš h.‘pr.plṯt.|l qdqd h.lpš.yks.|mizrtm.ǵr.b abn.|ydy.pslt 5[67].6.15
n.b [tk].|ǵr.tliyt.šb‘t.brqm.[---].|ṯmnt.iṣr r‘t.‘ṣ brq y.|riš h.tply.ṭly.bn.‘n h.|uz‘rt.tmll.išd h.qrn[m].|dt.‘l h.riš h.b UG5.3.1.5
.|l šrr.w t‘[n.‘ṯtrt.---].|b‘l m.hmt.[---].|l šrr.št[.---].|b riš h.[---].|ib h.mš[--.---].|[b]n.‘n h[.---]. 2.4[68].38
š[---].|ytnm.qrt.l ‘ly[.---].|b mdbr.špm.yd[.---.---]r.|l riš hm.w yš[--.--]m.|lḥm.b lḥm ay.w šty.b ḫmr yn ay.|šlm. 23[52].5
|ilm.tph hm.tphn.mlak.ym.t‘dt.ṯpṭ[.nhr].|t[ǵ]ly.hlm.rišt hm.l ẓr.brkt hm.w l kḥṯ.|zbl hm.b hm.yg‘r.b‘l.lm.ǵltm. 2.1[137].23
kḥṯ.|zbl km.w ank.‘ny.mlak.ym.t‘dt.ṯpṭ.nhr.|tšu ilm rašt hm.l ẓr.brkt hm.ln.kḥṯ.zbl hm.|aḫr.tmǵyn.mlak ym.t‘ 2.1[137].29
l.yṣa.hlm.[ṯnm].|[q]dqd.ṯlṯ id.‘l.ud[n].|[---.-]sr.pdm.riš h[m.---].|‘l.pd.asr.[---.]l[.---].|mḫlpt.w l.ytk.[d]m[‘t.]km. 19[1AQHT].2.80
ḫm.mt.uḫryt.mh.yqḥ.|mh.yqḥ.mt.atryt.spsg.ysk.|[l]riš.ḥrṣ.l ẓr.qdqd y.|[--.]mt.kl.amt.w an.mtm.amt.|[ap.m]ṯn 17[2AQHT].6.37
.|n‘m.l ḥtt.b gn.|bm.nrt.ksmm.|‘l.tl[-]k.‘ṭrtrm.|nšu.[r]iš.ḥrṯm.|l ẓr.‘db.dgn kly.|lḥm.[b]‘dn hm.kly.|yn.b ḥmt 16[126].3.12
].|[---.--]rt.š‘rt[.---].|[---.i]qni.l.ṯr[mn.art.---].|[b.yr]ḫ.riš.yn.[---].|[---.b‘]lt.bhtm.š[--.---].|[---.-]rt.l.dml[.---].|[b.yr 1106.32
at.yp‘t.b[--.---].|aliyn.b‘l[.---].|drkt k.mšl[-.---].|b riš k.aymr[.---].|ṯpṭ.nhr.yṯb[r.ḥrn.y ym.yṯbr.ḥrn].|riš k.‘ṯtrt 2.1[137].6
y.krt.ṭ‘.|bn.al.tbkn.al.|tdm.l y.al tkl.bn.|qr.‘n k.mḫ.riš k.|udm‘t.ṣḥ.aḫt k.|ṯtmnt.bt.ḥmḥ h.|d[-]n.tbkn.w tdm.l 16.1[125].27
b riš k.aymr[.---].|ṯpṭ.nhr.yṯb[r.ḥrn.y ym.yṯbr.ḥrn].|riš k.‘ṯtrt.[šm.b‘l.qdqd k.---].|[--]t.mṭ.tpln.b g[bl.šnt k.---].| 2.1[137].8
drkt k.aṯb.|an.w y‘ny.krt ṭ‘.yṯbr.|ḥrn.y bn.yṯbr.ḥrn.|riš k.‘ṯtrt.šm.b‘l.|qdqd k.tqln.b gbl.|šnt k.b ḥpn k.w t‘n.|sp 16.6[127].56
[---.--]b.|[---.r]iš k.|[---.]bn ‘n km.|[---.]alp.|[---.]ym.rbt.|[---.]b nhrm.|[3[‘NT.VI].6.2
r.brkt hm.w l kḥṯ.|zbl hm.b hm.yg‘r.b‘l.lm.ǵltm.ilm.rišt.|km l ẓr brkt km.w ln.kḥṯ.zbl km.aḥd.|ilm.t‘ny lḥt.mla 2.1[137].24
bl km.aḥd.|ilm.t‘ny lḥt.mlak.ym.t‘dt.ṯpṭ.nhr.|šu.ilm.rašt km.l ẓr.brkt km.ln.kḥṯ.|zbl km.w ank.‘ny.mlak.ym.t‘d 2.1[137].27
drt.ri[š].|‘l h.k irbym.kp.k.qṣm.|ǵrmn.kp.mhr.‘tkt.|rišt.l bmt h.šnst.|kpt.b ḥbš h.brkm.tǵl[l].|b dm.ḏmr.ḥlqm. 3[‘NT].2.12
[---.šnst.kpt.b ḥb]š h.‘tkt r[išt].|[l bmt h.---.]hy bt h t‘rb.|[---.tm]ṯḫṣ b ‘mq.|[ṯḫtṣb.b 7.1[131].2
m.lk.|hrg.ar[b‘.]ymm.bṣr.|kp.šsk k.[--].l ḥbš k.|‘tk.ri[š.]l mhr k.|w ‘p.l dr[‘].nšr k.|w rbṣ.l ǵr k.inbb.|kt ǵr k.a 13[6].7
.rbm.|l ištbm.tnn.ištml h.|mḫšt.bṯn.‘qltn.|šlyṭ.d šb‘t.rašm.|mḫšt.mdd ilm.ar[š].|ṣmt.‘gl.il.‘tk.|mḫšt.klbt.ilm išt. 3[‘NT].3.39
tmḫṣ.lim.ḫp y[m].|tṣmt.adm.ṣat.š[p]š.|tḥt h.k kdrt.ri[š].|‘l h.k irbym.kp.k.qṣm.|ǵrmn.kp.mhr.‘tkt.|rišt.l bmt 3[‘NT].2.9
.b ṣḥ]q.ymlu.lb h.|[b šmḫt.kbd.‘nt.tšyt.tḥt h.k]kdrt.riš.|[‘l h.k irbym.kp.---.k br]k.tǵll.b dm.|[ḏmr.---.]td[-.]rǵb. 7.1[131].8
rrt.|tǵll.b nr.d ‘l k.mḫṣ.aqht.|ǵzr.šrš k.b arṣ.al.|yp‘.riš.ǵly.b d.ns‘ k.|‘nt.brḥ.p ‘lm h.|‘nt.p dr.dr.‘db.uḫry mṭ yd 19[1AQHT].3.160
ṯb[.--]d h.|km trpa.hn n‘r.|d yšt.l.lṣb h ḫš‘r klb.|[w]riš.pqq.w šr h.|yšt.aḥd h.dm zt.ḫrpnt. UG5.1.2.5
[l r]iš.r‘y.y[šlm.---].|[š]lm.bnš.yš[lm.---].|[-]r.l šlmt.šl[m.---.--] 59[100].1
n hm.|nṣḥy.šrr.m[---.--]ay.|nbšr km.dnil.[--] h[.---].|riš.r[--.--]ḫ[.---]y[.---.-]nt.[š]ṣat[k.]rḥ.npš.hm.|k.iṯl.brlt n[-. 19[1AQHT].2.87
dm.l.k[-]ḫ.|ṯmnym.dd.dd.kbd.|[l].mdr[ǵ]lm.|b yrḫ[ri]šyn.|šb[‘.--]n.[k]bd.|w[.---.]qm‘t.|[---.]mdrǵlm.|[---.]md 2012.21
k.k tmḫṣ.|[ltn.bṯn.br]ḥ.tkly.|[bṯn.‘qltn.]šlyṭ.|[d šb‘t.rašm].ṯtkḥ.|[ttrp.šmm.k rks.ipd]k.|[-----]. 5[67].1.30
k tmḫṣ.ltn.bṯn.brḥ.|tkly.bṯn.‘qltn.|šlyṭ.d šb‘y.rašm.|ṯtkḥ.ttrp.šmm.k rs.|ipd k.ank.ispi.uṭm.|ḏrqm.amt 5[67].1.3
mp‘.|mlk.ugrt.|ytn.bt.anndr.|bn.ytn.bnš.|[ml]k.d.b riš.|[--.-]nt.|[l.‘b]dmlk.|[--.-]m[-]r.|[w.l.]bn h.‘d.|[‘l]m.mn 1009.7
l ri[š.---].|ypt.‘ṣ[--.---].|p šlm.[---].|bt k.b[--.--.m]|ǵy k[.---].| 58[20].1
[sp]r.bnš.ml[k.d.b] d adn[‘m].|[---].riš[.---].kt.|[y]nḥm.|ilb‘l.|‘bdyr[ḫ].|ṯtpḥ.|artn.|ybnil.|brq 1024.1.2

rišy

rišym.dt.ʻrb.|b bnš hm.|ḏmry.w.ptpṯ.ʻrb.|b.yrm.|[ily.w].ḏ 2079.1
spr šd.ri[šym].|kr[-].šdm.ʻ[--].|b gt ṯm[--] yn[.--].|[---].krm.b ypʻl. 2027.1.1
|[mi]tm.arbʻm.ṯmn.kbd.|[l.]sbrdnm.|m[i]t.l.bn.ʻẓmt.rišy.|mit.l.tlmyn.bn.ʻdy.|[---.]l.aḏddy.|[--.]l.kkln. 2095.7
rišym.qnum.|bn.ilrš.|ʻ[p]ṯn.|b[n.ʻr]my.|[--]ṯy.|bn.ǵdʻ.|bn.ʻ 2078.1
mit.ṯlṯ.mḫsrn.|ʻl.nsk.kṯṯǵlm.|arbʻm.ṯlṯ.mḫsrn.|mtbʻl.rišy.|ṯlṯm.ṯlṯ.ʻl.nsk.|arym.|alp.ṯlṯ.ʻl.|nsk.art.|ḫmš.mat.ṯlṯ.| 1137.4
ʻl.nsk.|arym.|alp.ṯlṯ.ʻl.|nsk.art.|ḫmš.mat.ṯlṯ.|ʻl.mtn.rišy. 1137.10

rišyn

[b yr]ḫ[.r]išyn.b ym.ḥdṯ.|[šmtr].uṯkl.l il.šlmm.|b [ṯlṯt].ʻšrt.yrtḥṣ.ml APP.II[173].1
b yrḫ.[rišyn.b ym.ḥdṯ].|šmtr.[uṯkl.l il.šlmm].|b ṯlṯt ʻ[šrt.yrtḥṣ.mlk 35[3].1

rišn

ʻl[--.---].|šm[---.---].|yšr[-.---].|bn.gnb[-.---].|hzpym.|rišn.[---].|bn.ʻbdy.[---].|bn.dmtn.[---].|[b]n.gʻyn.ḫr[-].|lbny 93[328].9

ru

[---.yṯ]rd h.|[---.yg]rš h.|[---.]ru.|[----] h.|[---.--]mt.|[---.--]mr.limm.|[---.]bn.ilm.mt.|[--] 6[49].6.3

rum

.limm.|w yʻn.aqht.ǵzr.adr.ṯqbm.|[d]lbnn.adr.gdm.b rumm.|adr.qrnt.b yʻlm.mtnm.|b ʻqbt.ṯr.adr.b ǵlil.qnm.|tn. 17[2AQHT].6.21
š[.-].|npš.lbun.|thw.w npš.|anḫr.b ym.|brkt.šbšt.|k rumm.hm.|ʻn.kḏd.aylt.|mt hm.ks.ym|sk.nhr hm.|šbʻ.ydt UG5.4.7
tšu knp.btlt.ʻn[t].|tšu.knp.w tr.b ʻp.|tk.aḫ šmk.mlat rumm.|w yšu.ʻn h.aliyn.bʻl.|w yšu.ʻn h.w yʻn.|w yʻn.btlt.ʻn 10[76].2.12
n.tbkyn h.|w tqbrn h.tštnn.b ḫrt.|ilm.arṣ.ṭṭbḫ.šbʻm.|rumm.k gmn.aliyn.|[b]ʻl.ṭṭbḫ.šbʻm.alpm.|[k g]mn.aliyn.bʻl. 6[62].1.19
[---.t]št.rimt.|l irt h.mšr.l.dd.aliyn.|bʻl.yd.pdry.bt.ar.|ahbt.ṭly.bt.rb 3[ʻNT].3.1
|msdt.arṣ.|sʻ.il.dqt.k amr.|sknt.k ḥwt.yman.|d b h.rumm.l rbbt. 4[51].1.44
ʻmm.b ys[mm.---].|arḫ.arḫ.[---.tld].|ibr.tld[.l bʻl].|w rum.l[rkb.ʻrpt].|tḥbq.[---].|tḥbq[.---].|w tksynn.bṯn[-.]|y[- 10[76].3.22
.|bšrt.il.bš[r.bʻ]l.|w bšr.ḥtk.dgn.|k.ibr.l bʻl[.yl]d.|w rum.l rkb.ʻrpt.|yšmḫ.aliyn.bʻl. 10[76].3.37
n m.um y.kl|y y.ytʻn.k gmrm.|mt.ʻz.bʻl.ʻz.ynghn.|k rumm.mt.ʻz.bʻl.|ʻz.ynṯkn.k bṯnm.|mt.ʻz.bʻl.ʻz.ymṣḫn.|k ls 6[49].6.18
w qṣʻt h.bm.ymn h.|idk.l ytn pnm.|tk.aḫ.šmk.mla[t.r]umm.|tšu knp.btlt.ʻn[t].|tšu.knp.w tr.b ʻp.|tk.aḫ šmk.ml 10[76].2.9
.š.npš.lbim.|thw.hm.brlt.anḫr.|b ym.hm.brk y.tkšd.|rumm.ʻn.kḏd.aylt.|hm.imt.imt.npš.blt.|ḥmr.p imt.b klt.|y 5[67].1.17
---.--]l.šir.|[---.-]tm.|[---.]yd y.|[----]y.|[---.-]lm.|[---.r]umm. 10[76].1.23

rb

bʻt.|ǵlm k.ṯmn.ḫnzr k.|ʻm k.pdry.bt.ar.|ʻm k.ṭṭly.bt.rb.idk.|pn k.al ttn.tk.ǵr.|knkny.ša.ǵr.ʻl ydm.|ḫlb.l ẓr.rḥtm 5[67].5.11
.m]at.iqnu.|argmn.nqmd.mlk.|ugrt.d ybl.l špš.|mlk.rb.bʻl h.|ks.ḫrṣ.ktn.mit.pḥm.|mit.iqni.l mlkt.|ks.ḫrṣ.ktn.m 64[118].26
---].|w l n[qmd.---].|[w]nqmd.[---].|[-.]ʻmn.šp[š.mlk.rb].|bʻl h.šlm.[w spš].|mlk.rb.bʻl h.[---].|nqmd.mlk.ugr[t.-- 64[118].11
d.[---].|[-.]ʻmn.šp[š.mlk.rb].|bʻl h.šlm.[w spš].|mlk.rb.bʻl h.[---].|nqmd.mlk.ugr[t.--].|phy.|w ṯpllm.mlk.r[b.--]. 64[118].13
w.k.rgm.špš.|mlk.rb.bʻl y.u.|ʻ[--.]mlakt.ʻbd h.|[---.]bʻl k.yḫpn.|[---.]ʻm h.u ky 1018.2
|b.[---.mlk].|rb[.bʻl y.---].|w.an[k.---].|arš[.---].|mlk.r[b.bʻ]l y.p.l.|ḥy.np[š.a]rš.|l.pn.bʻ[l y.l].pn.bʻl y.|w.urk.ym. 1018.17
d[--.]mlk.|rb.b[ʻl y.---].|[-----].|r[--.---].|b.[---.mlk].|rb[.bʻl y.---].|w.an[k.---].|arš[.---].|mlk.r[b.bʻ]l y.p.l.|ḥy.np 1018.14
n.|[---.]ʻm h.u ky.|[---.--]d k.k.tmǵy.|ml[--.--]š[.ml]k.rb.|b[ʻl y.---].|yd[--.]mlk.|rb.b[ʻl y.---].|[-----].|r[--.---].|b.[- 1018.7
k.k.tmǵy.|ml[--.--]š[.ml]k.rb.|b[ʻl y.---].|yd[--.]mlk.|rb.b[ʻl y.---].|[-----].|r[--.---].|b.[---.mlk].|rb[.bʻl y.---].|w.a 1018.10
ʻl y.|l.pn.amn.w.l.pn.|il.mṣrm.dt.tǵrn.|npš.špš.mlk.|rb.bʻl y. 1018.24
.|l irt h.mšr.l.dd.aliyn.|bʻl.yd.pdry.bt.ar.|ahbt.ṭly.bt.rb.dd.arṣy.|bt.yʻbdr.km ǵlmm.|w ʻrb n.l pʻn.ʻnt.hbr.|w ql.t 3[ʻNT].3.4
irt h.tšr.l dd.aliyn.bʻl].|[ahb]t pdr[y.bt.ar.ahbt.ṭly.bt.rb.dd].|arṣy bt.y[ʻbdr.---].|rgm l btl[t.ʻnt.ṯny.l ybmt.limm.t 7.2[130].11
.l.ṯt.mrkbtm.|inn.uṯpt.|w.ṯlṯ.ṣmdm.w.ḥrṣ.|apnt.b d.rb.ḥršm.|d.šṣa.ḥwy h. 1121.9
t.|aṯrt.ym.mṯb.|klt.knyt.|mṯb.pdry.b ar.|mẓll.ṭly.bt rb.|mṯb.arṣy.bt.yʻbdr.|ap.mṯn.rgmm.|argm k.šskn mʻ.|mg 4[51].1.18
t.aṯrt.ym.|mṯb.klt.knyt.|mṯb.pdry.bt.ar.|mẓll.ṭly.bt rb.|mṯb.arṣ.bt yʻbdr.|w yʻn lṭpn il d pid.|p ʻbd.an.ʻnn.aṯrt. 4[51].4.56
h.m]ṯb.rbt.aṯrt.|ym.mṯb.[pdr]y.bt.ar.|[mẓll.]ṭly[.bt.]rb.mṯb.|[arṣy.bt.yʻbdr.mṯb].|[klt.knyt]. 3[ʻNT.VI].5.50
bn h.m[ṯb.rbt.aṯrt.ym].|mṯb.pdr[y.bt.ar.mẓll].|ṭly.bt.r[b.mṯb.arṣy].|bt.yʻbdr[.mṯb.klt].|knyt.w tʻn[.btlt.ʻnt].|yṯb 3[ʻNT.VI].4.4
ḫss.yd.|ytr.kṯr.w ḫss.|spr.ilmlk šbny.|lmd.atn.prln.rb.|khnm rb.nqdm.|ṯʻy.nqmd.mlk ugr[t].|adn.yrgb.bʻl.ṯrm 6.6[62.2].54
l.rb.khnm.|rgm.|tḥm.[---].|yšlm[.l k.ilm].|tšlm[k.tǵr] k.|tʻ 55[18].1
rb khnm. B.1
ḫrṣn rb khnm. A.1
[---.--]l[-.---].|[---.]yplṭ[.---].|[---.--]l.rb.kzym.|[---]y.|[-----].|[-----].|[--]dt.nsk.ṯlṯ.|[ʻb]dršp.nsk.ṯl 1102.3
l.rb.|kṯkym. 1163.1
l.mlk.b[ʻl y].|r[gm].|tḥm.rb.mi[--.ʻ]bd k.|l.pʻn.bʻl y[.mrḥqtm].|šbʻ d.w.šbʻ[d.qlt].|an 2008.1.3
]bn.i[--.---].|[---].tp[--.---].|[---.a]ḥt.b d[.---].|[---.]b d.rb.[m]dlm.|[---.l i]ytlm.|[---].gmn.|[---].l.urǵṯb.|[---.]l.ʻṯr 2162.B.2
[-]m.w.ank.|k[l.]ḏrʻ hm.|[--.n]pš[.-].|w [k]l hm.b d.|rb.tmtt.lqḥt.|w.ṯṯb.ank.l hm.|w.any k.ṯt.|by.ʻky.ʻryt.|w.aḫ 2059.22
t.|likt.mṣrm.|hn dt.b.ṣr.|mtt.by.|gšm.adr.|nškḥ.w.|rb.tmtt.|lqḥ.kl.ḏrʻ.|b d a[-]m.w.ank.|k[l.]ḏrʻ hm.|[--.n]pš[. 2059.16
tr.kṯr.w ḫss.|spr.ilmlk šbny.|lmd.atn.prln.rb.|khnm rb.nqdm.|ṯʻy.nqmd.mlk ugr[t].|adn.yrgb.bʻl.ṯrmn. 6.6[62.2].55
spr.blblm.|skn uškn.|skn šbn.|skn ubrʻ.|skn ḫršbʻ.|rb.ntbtš.|[---].ʻbd.r[--].|arbʻ.k[--].|ṯlṯ.ktt. 1033.6
[.---].|[---.]dt[-.---].|[---.]ksḫ[-.--].|[---.]mnty[.-].|[---.]rb spr ḫbb.|[---.--]n.dbḥm.|[---].ʻbdssm. 49[73].2.4
rt.m[r]yn.|pǵdn.ilbʻl.krwn.lbn.ʻdn.|ḫyrn.mdʻ.|šmʻn.rb ʻšrt.kkln.ʻbd.abṣn.|šdyn.unn.dqn.|ʻbdʻnt.rb ʻšrt.mnḥm.ṯ 2011.5

nn.dqn. | ‘bd‘nt.rb ‘šrt.mnḥm.ṯb‘m.sẖr.‘zn.ilhd. | bnil.rb ‘šrt.lkn.yp‘n.ṯ[--]. | yṣḥm.b d.ubn.krwn.tǵd.[m]nḥm. | ‘pṯr 2011.8
d‘. | šm‘n.rb ‘šrt.kkln.‘bd.abṣn. | šdyn.unn.dqn. | ‘bd‘nt.rb ‘šrt.mnḥm.ṯb‘m.sẖr.‘zn.ilhd. | bnil.rb ‘šrt.lkn.yp‘n.ṯ[--]. | y 2011.7
spr.ḥpr.bnš mlk.b yrẖ iṯt[bnm]. | ršpab.rb ‘šrt.m[r]yn. | pǵḏn.ilb‘l.krwn.lbn.‘dn. | ẖyrn.md‘. | šm‘n.rb 2011.2
ṣrrt. | ṣpn.ytmr.b‘l. | bnt h.y‘n.pdry. | bt.ar.apn.ṭly. | [bt.r]b.pdr.yd‘. | [---]t.im[-]lt. | [-----]. | [---.--]rt. 3[‘NT].1.25
r.bnš.mlk. | d.b d.adn‘m. | [š]b‘.b.ḥrṯm. | [ṯ]lṯ.b.ṯǵrm. | rb qrt.aẖd. | ṯmn.ẖzr. | w.arb‘.ḥršm. | dt.tb‘ln.b.pẖn. | ṯṯtm.ẖz 1024.3.3
[---.--]y.npš[.---]. | [---.k]si h. | [---.--]y.rb.šm[.---]. 2160.3
qš. | [--]pš.šn[--]. | ṯ[-]r.b iš[-]. | b‘l h.š‘[-]rt. | ẖqr.[--.ṯq]l rb. | ṯl[ṯ.---]. | aḥt.ẖm[-.---]. | b ym.dbḥ.ṯp[-]. | aḥt.l mzy.bn[--]. 39[19].10
lkt. | [---.]bṭr.b d.mlkt. | [---].b d.mršp. | [---.m]rbṣ. | [---.r]b.ṯnnm. | [---.]asrm. | [---.--]kn. | [-----]. | [-----]. | [-----.-]l[-]. | [2015.1.5
[---].rb. | [-]lpl. | bn.asrn. | bn.šẖyn. | bn.abd‘n. | bn.ẖnqn. | bn.nmq. 1067.1
dt y.w.[---]. | tšṣḥq.hn.aṯt.l.‘bd. | šb‘t.w.nṣp.ksp. | [-]tm.rb[.--.a]ḥd. | [---.--]t.b[-]. | [---.-]y[-]. 1017.6
rb.b‘l h.[---]. | nqmd.mlk.ugr[t.--]. | phy. | w ṯpllm.mlk.r[b.--]. | mṣmt.l nqmd.[---.-]št. | hl ny.argmn.d [ybl.n]qmd. | l 64[118].16
t m. | ḥln.b q[rb.hk]l m. | al td[.pdr]y.bt ar. | [---.ṭl]y.bt.rb. | [---.m]dd.il ym. | [---.-]qlṣn.wpṯ m. | [---.]w y‘n.kṯr. | [w ẖ 4[51].6.11
tm]. | [ẖrṣ.hk]l y. | [---.]aẖ y. | [---.]aẖ y. | [----]y. | [---.]rb. | [---].ṣḥt. | [---.--]t. | [---.]ilm. | [---.--]u.yd. | [---.--]k. | [---.gp 4[51].8.41

rbil

spr.bdlm. | n‘mn. | rbil. | plsy. | ygmr. | mnṯ. | prẖ. | ‘dršp. | ršpab. | ṯnw. | abmn. | ab 1032.3
. | m[--].aḏddy. | yp‘.aḏddy. | abǵl.aḏ[ddy]. | abǵl.a[---]. | rbil.[---]. | kḏyn.[---.-]gṯ. | šmrm.a[ḏdd]y.tb[--]. | ynḥm.aḏddy. 2014.27

rbb

ṭl.yṭll. | l ǵnbm.šb‘.šnt. | yṣr k.b‘l.ṯmn.rkb. | ‘rpt.bl.ṭl.bl rbb. | bl.šr‘.thmtm.bl. | ṭbn.ql.b‘l.k tmz‘. | kst.dnil.mt.rpi. | all. 19[1AQHT].1.44
u]. | ṣbi.ng[b.w yṣi.‘dn]. | m‘[.ṣ]bu h.u[l.mad]. | ṯlṯ.mat.rbt. | hlk.l alpm.ẖḏḏ. | w l.rbt.kmyr. | aṯr.ṯn.ṯn.hlk. | aṯr.ṯlṯ.kl 14[KRT].4.179
ṣi. | ṣbu.ṣbi.ngb. | w yṣi.‘dn.m‘. | ṣbu k.ul.mad. | ṯlṯ.mat.rbt. | ẖpṯ.d bl.spr. | ṯnn.d bl.hg. | hlk.l alpm.ẖḏḏ. | w l rbt.kmy 14[KRT].2.89
trẖ.ib t‘rb m b bh | t h.w atn mhr h l a | b h.alp ksp w rbt ẖ | rṣ.išlḥ ẓhrm iq | nim.atn šd h krm[m]. | šd dd h ḥrnqm 24[77].20
ṣbṭm. | yṣq.ksp.yšl | ḥ.ẖrṣ.yṣq.ksp. | l alpm.ẖrṣ.yṣq | m.l rbbt. | yṣq-ẖym.w tbṯẖ. | kt.il.dt.rbtm. | kt.il.nbt.b ksp. | šmrgt 4[51].1.29
kd.bt ilm. | rbm. | kd l ištnm. | kd l ẖty. | maẖdh. | kd l kblbn. | kdm.mṭẖ. | 1090.2
t.rbt. | ẖpṯ.d bl.spr. | ṯnn.d bl.hg. | hlk.l alpm.ẖḏḏ. | w l rbt.kmyr. | [a]ṯr.ṯn.ṯn.hlk. | aṯr.ṯlṯ.kl hm. | yḥd.bt h.sgr. | almn 14[KRT].2.93
‘[.ṣ]bu h.u[l.mad]. | ṯlṯ.mat.rbt. | hlk.l alpm.ẖḏḏ. | w l.rbt.kmyr. | aṯr.ṯn.ṯn.hlk. | aṯr.ṯlṯ.kl hm. | aḥd.bt h.ysgr. | almn 14[KRT].4.181
[n]. | ḥš.trmmn.hk[l m]. | b tk.ṣrrt.ṣpn. | alp.šd.aẖd bt. | rbt.kmn.hkl. | w y‘n.kṯr.w ẖss. | šm‘.l aliyn b‘l. | bn.l rkb.‘rpt. 4[51].5.119
.mtḥ.ǵyrm. | idk.l ttn pnm.‘m.b‘l. | mrym.ṣpn.b alp.šd.rbt.kmn. | hlk.aẖt h.b‘l.y‘n.tdrq. | ybnt.ab h.šrḥq.aṯt.l pnn h. 3[‘NT].4.82
. | dn.almnt.yṯpṭ.ṯpṭ.ytm. | b nši ‘n h.w yphn.b alp. | šd.rbt.kmn.hlk.kṯr. | k y‘n.w y‘n.tdrq.ẖss. | hlk.qšt.ybln.hl.yš | r 17[2AQHT].5.10
. | [bt]lt.‘nt.idk.l ttn.[pnm]. | [‘m.a]qht.ǵzr.b alp.š[d]. | [rbt.]kmn.w ṣḥq.btlt.[‘nt]. | [tšu.]g h.w tṣḥ.šm‘.m[‘.l a] | [qht. 18[3AQHT].1.22
t.il.kl h]. | [kptr.]ks[u.ṯbt h.ḥkpt.arṣ.nḥlt h]. | b alp.šd.r[bt.kmn.l p‘n.kṯr]. | hbr.w ql.t[šthwy.w kbd.hwt]. | w rgm l 1[‘NT.IX].3.2
pt. | il.kl h.kptr. | ksu.ṯbt h.ḥkpt. | arṣ.nḥlt h. | b alp.šd.rbt. | kmn.l p‘n.kṯ. | hbr.w ql.tšthḥ | wy.w kbd hwt. | w rgm.l kṯ 3[‘NT.VI].6.17
t.ilm.špš. | ṣḥrrt.la. | šmm.b yd.md | d.ilm.mt.b a | lp.šd.rbt.k | mn.l p‘n.mt. | hbr.w ql. | tšthḥwy.w k | bd hwt.w rgm. | l 4[51].8.25
-].t‘tqn. | [---.-]‘b.idk. | [l ytn.pnm.tk.]in.bb.b alp ḥẓr. | [rbt.kmn.l p‘]n.‘nt. | [yhbr.w yql.yšt]ḥwyn.w y | [kbdn h.yšu. 1[‘NT.IX].2.15
.w tr.arṣ. | idk.l ttn.pnm. | ‘m.b‘l.mrym.ṣpn. | b alp.šd.rbt.kmn. | ṣḥq.btlt.‘nt.tšu. | g h.w tṣḥ.tbšr b‘l. | bšrt k.yblt.y[b 4[51].5.86
qdš. | l tphn h.aṯt.krpn. | l t‘n.aṯrt.alp. | kd.yqḥ.b ẖmr. | rbt.ymsk.b msk h. | qm.ybd.w yšr. | mṣltm.bd.n‘m. | yšr.ǵzr.ṭ 3[‘NT].1.17
h.tḥspn.m h.w trḥṣ. | ṭl.šmm.šmn.arṣ.ṭl.šm[m.t]sk h. | rbb.nsk h.kbkbm. | ttpp.anhbm.d alp.šd[.ẓu h.b ym]. | ṭl[.---] 3[‘NT].4.88
rḥṣ. | [ṭ]l.šmm.šmn.arṣ.rbb. | [r]kb ‘rpt.ṭl.šmm.tsk h. | [rb]b.nsk h.kbkbm. 3[‘NT].2.41
ṯ[.---]. | [---.]akl[.---]. | [---.-]l[-.-]hg[.---]. | [---.-]r[-.il]m.rbm.n‘l[.-]gr. | [---.]‘ṣ.b d h.ydrm[.]pi[-.]adm. | [---.]iṯ[-].yšql. UG5.8.31
k ymǵy.adn. | ilm.rbm ‘m dtn. | w yšal.mṯpṭ.yld. | w y‘ny.nn[.--]. | t‘ny.n[---.-]ṯq UG5.6.2
.tṯ‘r.l hdmm. | [t]ḥspn.m h.w trḥṣ. | [ṭ]l.šmm.šmn.arṣ.rbb. | [r]kb ‘rpt.ṭl.šmm.tsk h. | [rb]b.nsk h.kbkbm. 3[‘NT].2.39
ḥm.iṯtl. | l mnn.ilm. | tǵr k.tšlm k. | t‘zz k.alp ymm. | w rbt.šnt. | b ‘d ‘lm...gn‘. | iršt.aršt. | l aẖ y.l r‘ y.dt. | w ytnnn. | l 1019.1.5
[--].w rbb. | š[---]npš išt. | w.l.tikl w l tš[t]. 2003.1
m.a[-]ṯ[-]. | [---.--]ḥ b ym.tld[---.]b[-.]y[--.---]. | [---.il]m.rb[m.--]š[-]. | [---].nš.b [---]. | [---].tm[--.--]aṯ[.---]. | [---.]akl[.-- UG5.8.26
ylt. | mt hm.ks.ym | sk.nhr hm. | šb‘.ydt y.b ṣ‘. | [--.]šb‘.rbt. | [---.]qbṭ.ṯm. | [---.]bn.ilm. | [m]t.šmḥ.p ydd. | il[.ǵ]zr. | b [UG5.4.12
arṣ. | s‘.il.dqt.k amr. | sknt.k ḥwt.yman. | d b h.rumm.l rbbt. 4[51].1.44

rbd

h. | [---.-]ny h pdr.ttǵr. | [---.n]šr k.al ttn.l n. | [---.]tn l rbd. | [---.]b‘lt h w yn. | [---.rk]b ‘rpt. | [---.--]n.w mnu dg. | [--- 2001.2.13

rbm

.yp‘.l b‘l.ṣrt. | l rkb.‘rpt.l mẖšt.mdd. | il ym.l klt.nhr.il.rbm. | l ištbm.tnn.ištml h. | mẖšt.bṯn.‘qltn. | šlyṭ.d šb‘t.rašm. | 3[‘NT].3.36
yiẖd.b‘l.bn.aṯrt. | rbm.ymẖṣ.b ktp. | dk ym.ymẖṣ.b ṣmd. | ṣḥr mt.ymṣẖ.l arṣ. | [6[49].5.2

rb‘

kr.ṯlṯ. | ṯmn.kkr.brr. | arb‘.alpm.pḥm. | ẖmš.mat.kbd. | arb‘.alpm.iqni. | ẖmš.mat.kbd. | ṯlṯm.ẖmš kbd ktn. | ẖmš.rṭm. 1130.5
iršt.yṣḥm. | arb‘.alpm. | mitm.kbd.ṯlṯ. | arb‘.kkrm. | ṯmn.mat.kbd. | pwt. | ṯ 2051.2
ṯmn.kkr.ṯlṯ. | ṯmn.kkr.brr. | arb‘.alpm.pḥm. | ẖmš.mat.kbd. | arb‘.alpm.iqni. | ẖmš.mat.kb 1130.3
bn.lwn.ṯlṯtm.b‘lm. | bn.b‘ly.ṯlṯtm.b‘lm. | w.aḥd.ẖbṯ. | w.arb‘.aṯt. | bn.lg.ṯn.bn h. | b‘lm.w.aẖt h. | b.šrt. | šty.w.bn h. 2080.9
arb‘.‘šr.ǵzrm. | arb‘.aṯt. | pǵt.aḥt. | w.pǵy.aḥ. 2081.2
[--.]wmrkm. | bir.ẖmš. | uškn.arb‘. | ubr‘y.ṯlṯ. | ar.ṯmn ‘šr h. | mlk.arb‘. | ǵbl.ẖmš. | atlg.ẖmš ‘ 68[65].1.3
t.alp.mri. | ṯn.nšbm. | ṯmnym.tbṯẖ.alp. | uz.mrat.mlḥt. | arb‘.uzm.mrat.bq‘. | ṯlṯ.[-]ṯt.aš[‘]t.šmn.uz. | mi[t].ygb.bq‘. | a[- 1128.21
[nq]dm.dt.kn.npṣ hm. | [bn].lbn.arb‘.qšt.w.ar[b‘]. | [u]ṯpt.ql‘.w.ṯt.mr[ḥ]m. | [bn].smyy.qšt.w.u[ṯpt]. | [w.q 2047.2
nšm. | ẖmš.bnši.ṯt[---]. | ‘šr.b gt.[---]. | ṯn.‘šr.b.gt.ir[bṣ]. | arb‘.b.gt.b‘ln. | ‘št.‘šr.b.gpn. | yd.‘dnm. | arb‘.ǵzlm. | ṯn.yṣrm. 2103.6

aḥd.kbd. | arb‘m.b ḫzr. | lqḥ š‘rt. | ṯṯ ‘šr h.lqḥ. | ḫlpnt. | ṯṯ.ḥrṯm. | lqḥ.š‘rt. 2052.2
.]ksp. | [ṯ]mn.l.‘šrm[.l.b]t.‘ṯtrt. | [ṯ]lṯ.‘šr h.[b]t.ršp.gn. | arb‘.b d.b[n].ušryn. | kdm.l.urtn. | kdm.l.ilšpš. | kd.l.annṯb. | k 1088.4
[ṯ]n.prm.b ‘šrm. | arb‘.prm.b.‘š[r]m. | arb‘.b.arb‘m. | ṯṯm.[---.p]rm. | [-]l.b[--.---]. | [---].kbd. | [---].kb[1138.3
--.kb]d. | šr[-.---]. | m‘r[-.---]. | bq‘t.[---]. | šḥq[.---]. | rkby ar[b‘m]. | bir ṯ[--]. | ‘nqpat [---]. | m[--.---]. | [-----]. | k[-.---]. | [-- 2042.15
. | bn.‘my.ṯqlm. | bn.brq.ṯqlm. | bn.ḫnzr.ṯqlm. | dqn.nsk.arb‘t. | bn.ḫdyn.ṯqlm. | bn.‘bd.šḫr.ṯqlm. | bn.ḫnqn.arb‘t. | [b]n. 122[308].1.17
.nsk.arb‘t. | bn.ḫdyn.ṯqlm. | bn.‘bd.šḫr.ṯqlm. | bn.ḫnqn.arb‘t. | [b]n.ṯrk.ṯqlm. | [b]n.pdrn.ṯq[lm]. | pdy.[----]. | [i]lmlk.b 122[308].1.20
ap. | pd. | mlk.arb‘.ḥm[rm.w.arb]‘.bnšm. | ar.ḫmš.ḥmr[m.w.ḫm]š.bnšm. | atlg.ḥmr[.---.]bn 2040.3
bnšm.b.š[--]. | arb‘.bnšm.b[.---]. | ‘šrm.bnšm.[b.]‘d[--]. | arb‘.bnšm.b.ag[m]y. | arb‘.bnšm.b.ḫpty. | ṯṯ.bnšm.b.bir. | ṯṯ.b 2076.11
bn]šm.b.ǵbl. | [---.b]nšm.b.m‘r.arr. | arb‘.bnšm.b.mnt. | arb‘.bnšm.b.irbn. | ṯn.bnšm.b.y‘rt. | ṯn.bnšm.b.‘rmt. | arb‘.bnš 2076.34
rt. | ṯn.bnšm.b.‘rmt. | arb‘.bnšm.b.šrš. | ṯṯ.bnšm.b.mlk. | arb‘.bnšm.b.bṣr. | ṯn.bnšm.[b.]rqd. | ṯn.b[nšm.b.---]y. | [---].b[2076.39
ty. | ṯṯ.bnšm.b.bir. | ṯṯ.bnšm b.uḫnp. | ṯn.bnšm.b.ḫrṣb‘. | arb‘.bnšm.b.hzp. | arb‘.bnšm.b.šql. | arb‘.bnšm.b.nni. | ṯn.bnš 2076.16
m.b[.---]. | ‘šrm.bnšm.[b.]‘d[--]. | arb‘.bnšm.b.ag[m]y. | arb‘.bnšm.b.ḫpty. | ṯṯ.bnšm.b.bir. | ṯṯ.bnšm b.uḫnp. | ṯn.bnšm. 2076.12
| ṯn.bnšm.b.slḫ. | [---].bnšm.b.yny. | [--.]bnšm.b.lbnm. | arb‘.bnšm.b.ypr. | [---.]bnšm.b.šbn. | [---.b]nšm.b.šmny. | [---. 2076.22
b]nšm.b.ugrt. | [---.bn]šm.b.ǵbl. | [---.b]nšm.b.m‘r.arr. | arb‘.bnšm.b.mnt. | arb‘.bnšm.b.irbn. | ṯn.bnšm.b.y‘rt. | ṯn.bnš 2076.33
ṯn.bnšm.b.ḫrṣb‘. | arb‘.bnšm.b.hzp. | arb‘.bnšm.b.šql. | arb‘.bnšm.b.nni. | ṯn.bnšm.b.slḫ. | [---].bnšm.b.yny. | [--.]bnš 2076.18
ṯṯ.bnšm b.uḫnp. | ṯn.bnšm.b.ḫrṣb‘. | arb‘.bnšm.b.hzp. | arb‘.bnšm.b.šql. | arb‘.bnšm.b.nni. | ṯn.bnšm.b.slḫ. | [---].bnš 2076.17
. | arb‘.bnšm.b.irbn. | ṯn.bnšm.b.y‘rt. | ṯn.bnšm.b.‘rmt. | arb‘.bnšm.b.šrš. | ṯṯ.bnšm.b.mlk. | arb‘.bnšm.b.bṣr. | ṯn.bnšm. 2076.37
-]. | ṯṯ.‘šr.bnš[m.---]. | ‘šr[.bn]šm[.---]. | ṯn.bnšm.b.š[--]. | arb‘.bnšm.b[.---]. | ‘šrm.bnšm.[b.]‘d[--]. | arb‘.bnšm.b.ag[m]y. 2076.9
[r]. | pdym. | ḫmš.bnšm. | snrym. | tš‘.bnš[m]. | gb‘lym. | arb‘.b[nšm]. | ṯbqym. 79[83].17
--]. | ṯ[ṯ.bn]šm[.b.a]gmy. | ṯṯ.bn[šm.---]. | ‘šr.b[nšm.---]. | arb‘[.bnšm.---]. | ṯṯ.‘šr.bnš[m.---]. | ‘šr[.bn]šm[.---]. | ṯn.bnšm. 2076.5
bn.b‘ln.biry. | ṯlṯ.b‘lm. | w.adn hm.ṯr.w.arb‘.bnt h. | yrḫm.yd.ṯn.bn h. | b‘lm.w.ṯlṯ.n‘rm.w.bt.aḥt. | bn.l 2080.3
[---.--]š. | [---.a]rb‘m. | b‘lyn.bnš. | mlkt. | ‘šrm. | [---.--]t. 138[41].2
[---].arb[‘.d]d.š[‘rm.---]. | [--.-]rṯm š[šm]n.k[--.---]. | [---.ar]b‘.dblt.ḏr[--.---]. | [--.m]itm.nṣ.l bn[.---]. | [-]l[-.---]. | [-]ṯ.[--- 143[-].1.9
.[---]. | [----]d.n‘r.ṯ[--]d[.---]. | [---.]ṯlṯ.kṯt[.-]d.[---]. | [---.a]rb‘.dblt.m[--.---]. | [--.mi]tm nṣ.[-]ṯ[-.]gr[-.---]. | [---].arb[‘.d] 143[-].1.5
ṯlṯm.ktn. | ḫmšm.izml. | ḫmš.kbd.arb‘m. | dd.akl. | ṯṯ.‘šr h.yn. | kd.šmn.l.nr.ilm. | kdm.dǵm. | ṯṯ. 1126.3
a]rb‘.kbd. | w.[---.-]m‘t. | ṯlṯ[m.---.-]rm. | ‘šr[.---].alpm. | arb‘.ddm.l.k[-]ḫ. | ṯmnym.dd.dd.kbd. | [l].mḏr[ǵ]lm. | b yrḫ[2012.18
-.a]rb‘.dblt.m[--.---]. | [--.mi]tm nṣ.[-]ṯ[-.]gr[-.---]. | [---].arb[‘.d]d.š[‘rm.---]. | [--.-]rṯm š[šm]n.k[--.---]. | [---.ar]b‘.dblt. 143[-].1.7
.l.mit.dd.ṯn.kbd.ḥpr.bnšm.ṯmnym.dd. | l u[-]m. | b.ṯbq.arb‘m.dr‘.w.‘šr.dd.drt. | w[.a]rb‘.l.‘šrm.dd.l.yḥšr.bl.bn h. | b. 1098.10
it.dr‘.w.šb‘m.drt. | w.‘šrm.l.mit.dd.ḥpr.bnšm. | b.y‘ny.arb‘m.dr‘.w.‘šrm.drt. | w.ṯlṯm.dd.ṯṯ.kbd.ḥpr.bnšm. | b.‘nmky 1098.26
r‘.ṯṯm.drt.w.šb‘m.dd.arb‘. | kbd.ḥpr.bnšm. | b.gt.ṯrmn.arb‘m.dr‘.w.‘šrm.drt. | w.ṯlṯm.dd.ṯṯ.kbd.ḥpr.bnšm. | b.gt.ḥḏṯt 1098.20
r‘.w.‘šrm.drt. | w.ṯlṯm.dd.ṯṯ.kbd.ḥpr.bnšm. | b.gt.ḥḏṯt.arb‘m.dr‘.w.ṯlṯm.drt. | [w].šb‘m.dd.ṯn.kbd.ḥpr.bnšm. | b.nzl.‘ 1098.22
]‘ln. | ṯlṯ.mat.ṯṯm.kbd. | ṯṯm.ṯṯ.kbd.ḥpr.‘bdm. | šb‘m.drt.arb‘m.drt. | l.a[--.---]. | tgm[r.ak]l.b.gt.ḫldy. | ṯlṯ.ma[t].‘šr.kbd 2013.8
t. | [drt.ḥpr.b]nšm.w.ṯn.‘šr h.dd.l.rpš. | [---.]šb‘m.dr‘.w.arb‘m.drt.mit.dd. | [---].ḥpr.bn.šm. | [b.---.]knm.ṯṯm.l.mit.dr‘ 1098.5
| ṯlṯ.ma[t].‘šr.kbd. | šb‘ m[at].kbd.ḥpr.‘bdm. | mit[.d]rt.arb‘m.drt. | [---]m. | t[gm]r.akl.b.gt.ǵ[l]. | ṯlṯ.mat.‘šrm[.---]. | ṯ 2013.13
šr h. | aṯt.trḫ.w tb‘t. | ṯar um.tkn l h. | mṯlṯt.kṯrm.tmt. | mrb‘t.zblnm. | mḫmšt.yitsp. | ršp.nṯdṯt.ǵlm. | ym.mšb‘t hn.b š 14[KRT].1.17
ly. | yṯ‘d.ṣm[d]. | bn.liy. | ‘šrm.ṣ[md]. | ṯṯ kbd.b ḥ[--]. | w.arb‘.ḥ[mrm]. | b m[‘]rby. | ṯmn.ṣmd.[---]. | b d.b‘lsr. | yd.ṯdn.‘š 2102.1
ap. | pd. | mlk.arb‘.ḥm[rm.w.arb]‘.bnšm. | ar.ḫmš.ḥmr[m.w.ḫm]š.bnšm. | at 2040.3
.[---.bn]š. | uškn[.---].‘šr.bnšm. | ‘nqpat[.---].bnš. | ubr‘y.ar[b‘.]ḥm[r]m.w[.---.]bnšm. | ilštm‘.arb‘.ḥm[r]m.ḫmš.bnšm. 2040.20
at[.---].bnš. | ubr‘y.ar[b‘.]ḥm[r]m.w[.---.]bnšm. | ilštm‘.arb‘.ḥm[r]m.ḫmš.bnšm. | ǵr. | ary.ḥmr w.bnš. | qmy.ḥmr.w.b 2040.21
arb‘.ḥm[r.---]. | l ṯlṯ. | ṯn.l.brr[.---]. | arb‘.ḥmr[.---]. | l.pḫ[-.]w.[---]. | w.l.k[--]. | w.l.k[--]. 1139.4
arb‘.ḥm[r.---]. | l ṯlṯ. | ṯn.l.brr[.---]. | arb‘.ḥmr[.---]. | l.pḫ[-.]w.[1139.1
. | [š]b‘.b.ḥrṯm. | [ṯ]lṯ.b.ṯǵrm. | rb qrt.aḥd. | ṯmn.ḫzr. | w.arb‘.ḥršm. | dt.tb‘ln.b.pḫn. | ṯṯṯm.ḫzr.w.‘šṯ.‘šr.ḥrš. | dt.tb‘ln.b. 1024.3.5
ḫ. | ḫlpnt. | ṯṯ.ḥrṯm. | lqḥ.š‘rt. | ‘šr.ḥrš. | bhtm.lqḥ. | š‘rt. | arb‘. | ḥrš qṯn. | lqḥ š‘rt. | ṯṯ nsk.ḥdm. | lqḥ.š‘rt. 2052.11
bd.yn.d.l.ṯb. | w.arb‘m.yn.ḫlq.b.gt.sknm. | ‘šr.yn.ṭb.w.arb‘m.ḫmš.kbd. | yn.d.l.ṭb.gt.ṭbq. | mit.‘šr.kbd.yn.ṭb. | w.ṯṯm. 1084.4
gm.my.b[ilm.ydy]. | mrṣ.grš[m.zbln]. | in.b ilm.‘[ny h.yrb‘]. | yḫmš.rgm.[my.b ilm]. | ydy.mrṣ.g[ršm.zbln]. | in.b ilm 16[126].5.16
tš‘.ṯnnm. | w.arb‘.ḫsnm. | ‘šr.mrum. | w.šb‘.ḫsnm. | tš‘.‘šr. | mrynm. | ṯlṯ.‘šr. 1029.2
ṯ[--] ḫpnt. | [---] kdwṯm.[---]. | ḫmš.pld š‘rt. | ṯṯ pld pṯt. | arb‘ ḫpnt pṯt. | ḫmš ḫpnt.š‘rt. | ṯlṯ.‘šr kdwṯm. 1113.9
.kbd. | m[i]t.arb‘t.kbd. | ḫ[mš.]š‘rt. | [---.]tš‘.kbd.skm. | [arb]‘m.ḫpnt.pṯt. | [-]r.pldm.dt.š‘rt. | ṯlṯm.ṯlṯ.kbd.mṣrrt. | ‘šr.ṯn 1111.7
‘lm.kmm. | k t‘rb.‘ṯtrt.šd.bt.mlk[.---]. | ṯn.skm.šb‘.mšlt.arb‘.ḫpnt.[---]. | ḫmšm.ṯlṯ.rkb.ntn.ṯlṯ.mat.[---]. | lg.šmn.rqḥ.š UG5.9.1.19
ḫzr y.ṯn h.wspm. | atn.w ṯlṯ h.ḥrṣm. | ylk ym.w ṯn. | ṯlṯ.rb‘.ym. | aḫr.špšm.b rb‘. | ymǵy.l udm.rbt. | w udm[.ṯr]rt. | gr 14[KRT].4.208
m. | hn.ym.w ṯn.tikl. | išt.b bht m.nblat. | b hk[l] m.ṯlṯ.kb‘ ym. | tikl[.i]št.b bht m. | nbla[t.]b hkl m. | ḫmš.ṯ[d]ṯ.ym.ti 4[51].6.26
.uzr.]ilm.dnil. | [uzr.ilm.]ylḥm.uzr. | [yšqy.b]n.qdš ṯlṯ rb‘ ym. | [uzr.i]lm.dnil.uzr. | [ilm.y]lḥm.uzr.yšqy bn. | [qdš.ḫ] 17[2AQHT].1.9
| [---.r]ḫm.tld. | [---.]ḫrm.ṯn.ym. | tš[.---.]ymm.lk. | hrg.ar[b‘.]ymm.bṣr. | kp.šsk k.[--].l ḥbš k. | ‘tk.ri[š.]l mhr k. | w ‘p 13[6].5
rnt.ḥpšt. | s‘t.b nk.šibt.b bqr. | mmlat.dm.ym.w ṯn. | ṯlṯ.rb‘.ym.ymš. | ṯdṯ.ym.ḥẓ k.al.tš‘l. | qrt h.abn.yd k. | mšdpt.w h 14[KRT].3.115
nn.ṯl mrṯ.yḥrṯ.il. | hn.ym.w ṯn.tlḥmn.rpum. | tštyn.ṯlṯ.rb‘.ym.ḫmš. | ṯdṯ.ym.tlḥmn.rpum. | tštyn.bt.ikl.b pr‘. | yṣq.b i 22.2[124].22
t. | s‘t.b npk.šibt.w b | mqr.mmlat. | d[m].ym.w ṯn. | ṯlṯ.rb‘.ym. | ḫmš.ṯdṯ.ym. | mk.špšm.b šb‘. | w l.yšn.pbl. | mlk.l [qr 14[KRT].5.219
.k irby. | [t]škn.šd. | km.ḥsn.pat.mdbr. | lk.ym.w ṯn.ṯlṯ.rb‘ ym. | ḫmš.ṯdṯ.ym.mk.špšm. | b šb‘.w tmǵy.l udm. | rbm.w 14[KRT].3.106
| hn.ym.w ṯn.yšlḥm. | kṯrt.w yš[š]q.bnt.hl[l]. | snnt.ṯlṯ[.r]b‘ ym.yšl | ḥm kṯrt.w yššq. | bnt hll.snnt.ḫmš. | ṯdṯ.ym.yšlḥ 17[2AQHT].2.34
. | [---.arb]‘.yn. | [---].ṯmn.yn. | [---.-]ṯr.kdm.yn. | [-]dyn.arb‘.yn. | abškn.kdm.yn. | šbn.kdm.yn. | ‘bdiltp.ṯm[n].y[n]. | q 1085.6
.ṯlṯ.kb[d]. | [dd.--]m.šb‘.[---]. | [---].‘šr.dd[.---]. | [---]mn.arb‘m.y[n]. | b.gt.trǵnds. | tš‘.‘šr.[dd].kšmm. | ṯn.‘šr[.dd.ḫ]ṭm. 2092.14
ḫmš.‘šr.yn.ṭb. | w.tš‘m.kdm.kbd.yn.d.l.ṭb. | w.arb‘m.yn.ḫlq.b.gt.sknm. | ‘šr.yn.ṭb.w.arb‘m.ḫmš.kbd. | yn.d.l 1084.3
ṣrym. | kd.mštt.mlk. | kd.bn.amht [-]t. | w.bn.mṣrym. | arb‘m.yn. | l.ḫrd. | ḫmšm.ḫmš. | kbd.tgmr. | yn.d.nkly. 1089.11
arb‘.yn.l.mrynm.ḫ[--].kl h. | kdm.l.zn[-.---]. | kd.l.aṯr[y]m. | k 1089.1

]ʿlt. | lbnm.ʿšr.yn. | ḫlb.gngnt.ṯlṯ.y[n]. | bṣr.ʿšr.yn. | nnu arbʿ.yn. | šql ṯlṯ.yn. | šmny.kdm.yn. | šmgy.kd.yn. | hzp.tšʿ.yn. 2004.24
]. | šbʿ.yn[.---]. | mlkt[.---]. | kd.yn.l.[---]. | armwl w [--]. | arbʿ.yn.[--]. | l adrm.b[--]. | šqym. 1092.6
[---.ṯl]š.yn. | [---.a]rbʿ.yn. | [---.arb]ʿ.yn. | [---].ṯmn.yn. | [---.-]ṯr.kdm.yn. | [-]dy 1085.2
[---.ṯl]š.yn. | [---.a]rbʿ.yn. | [---.arb]ʿ.yn. | [---].ṯmn.yn. | [---.-]ṯr.kdm.yn. | [-]dyn.arbʿ.yn. | abš 1085.3
š.ḫlln.[-]. | yṯb.dnil.[l s]pr yrḫ h. | yrs.y[---.]y[--] h. | ṯlṯ.rb[ʿ.yrḫ.--]r[.--]. | yrḫm.ymǵy[.---]. | ḫ[--.]r[---]. 17[2AQHT].2.45
.ṯn.šm. | l.[---]t. | i[d.yd]bḥ.mlk.l.prgl.ṣqrn.b.gg. | ar[bʿ.]arbʿ.mṯbt.azmr.b h.š.šr[-]. | al[p.w].š.šlmm.pamt.šbʿ.klb h. | 35[3].51
mn.k dw.kr[t]. | w yʿny.ǵzr[.ilḥu]. | ṯlṯ.yrḫm.k m[rṣ]. | arbʿ.k dw.k[rt]. | mndʿ.krt.mǵ[y.---]. | w qbr.tṣr.q[br]. | tṣr.tr 16.2[125].85
ṯn.ʿšr.yn.[kps]lnm. | arbʿ.mat[.arb]ʿm.[k]bd. | d ntn.d.ksp. | arbʿ.l.ḫlby. | [---].l.bt. | arbʿ.l.kpsl 1087.2
mšm.kb[d]. | ḫmš.kbd.l.mdʿ. | b yr[ḫ.iṯtb]nm. | ṯlṯ[.mat.a]rbʿ.kbd. | w.[---.-]mʿt. | ṯlṯ[m.---.-]rm. | ʿšr[.---].alpm. | arbʿ.d 2012.14
.dd. | ḥpr.bnšm. | b.gt.knpy.mit.drʿ.ṯṯm.drt.w.šbʿm.dd.arbʿ. | kbd.ḥpr.bnšm. | b.gt.ṯrmn.arbʿm.drʿ.w.ʿšrm.drt. | w.ṯlṯ 1098.18
rd.ṯn ʿšr. | qmy.arbʿ.ʿšr. | ṣʿq.arbʿ ʿšr. | ṣʿ.ṯmn. | šḥq.ʿšrm.arbʿ.kbd. | ḫlb rpš arbʿ.ʿšr. | bqʿt ṯṯ. | irab ṯn.ʿšr. | ḥbš.ṯmn. | am 67[110].6
[---.-]kn. | [---.]ṯlṯm. | kuwṯ.ṯlṯ.kbd. | m[i]t.arbʿt.kbd. | ḫ[mš.]šʿrt. | [---.]tšʿ.kbd.skm. | [arb]ʿm.ḥpnt.pṯt. | [1111.4
.ḫmš.kbd. | yn.d.l.ṭb.gt.ṭbq. | mit.ʿšr.kbd.yn.ṭb. | w.ṯṯm.arbʿ.kbd.yn.d.l.ṭb. | b.gt.mʿrby. | ṯṯm.yn.ṭb.w.ḫmš.l.ʿšrm. | yn. 1084.7
n.d.l.ṭb.b.gnʿ[y]. | mitm.yn.ḥsp.d.nkly.b.db[ḫ.--]. | mit.arbʿm.kbd.yn.ḥsp.l.m[--]. | mit.ʿšrm.[k]bd.yn.ḥsp.l.y[--]. | ʿšr 1084.25
ym.[yn].ṭb.b.gt.š[---]. | tšʿm.[ḫ]mš[.kbd].yn.b gt[.-]n. | arbʿm.kbd.yn.ṭb.w.[--]. | ṯmn.kbd.yn.d.l.ṭb.b.gnʿ[y]. | mitm.y 1084.22
]bd.yn.ḥsp.l.y[--]. | ʿšrm.yn.ḥsp.l.ql.d.tbʿ.mṣ[r]m. | mit.arbʿm.kbd.yn.mṣb. | l.mdrǵlm. | ʿšrn ʿšr.yn.mṣb.[-]ḥ[-].l.gzz 1084.28
št. | yrmʿl. | ṣry. | iršy. | yʿdrd. | ayaḫ. | bn.aylt. | ḫmš.mat.arbʿm. | kbd.ksp.anyt. | d.ʿrb.b.anyt. | l.mlk.gbl. | w.ḫmšm.ksp 2106.10
kr. | mlk. | ṯlṯ.mat.ksp.d.šb[n]. | mit.ksp.d.ṭbq. | ṯmnym.arbʿt. | kbd.ksp. | d.nqdm. | ḫmšm.l mit. | ksp.d.mkr.ar. | arbʿ 2107.6
šr[.---]. | [ʿ]l [-]g[-.---]. | w ni[t.w.mʿṣd]. | w ḫrmṯt. | ṯlṯm.ar[bʿ]. | kbd.ksp. | ʿl.tgyn. | w ʿl.aṯt h. | ypḥ.mʿnt. | bn.lbn. 2053.18
t.kbd. | [l.]gmn.bn.usyy. | mit.ṯṯm.kbd. | l.bn.yšmʿ. | mit.arbʿm.kbd. | l.liy.bn.ʿmyn. | mit.ḫmšm.kbd. | d.škn.l.ks.ilm. 1143.11
bd. | tgmr.uz.ǵrn.arbʿ.mat. | tgmr.uz.aḫmn.arbʿ.mat. | arbʿm.kbd. | ṯlṯ.alp.ṣpr.dt.aḥd. | ḥrṯ h.aḥd.b gt.nḫl. | aḥd.b gt. 1129.7
nm. | [---]h.lbš.allm.lbnm. | [---].all.šmt. | [---].all.iqni.arbʿm.kbl. | [---].iqni.ʿšrm.ǵprt. | [---.š]pšg.iqni.mit.pṯtm. | [--- 1106.6
[.]yukl.krm.[---]. | gdn.krm.aḫ[d.--]r.krm.[---]. | ary.ʿšr.arbʿ.kbd.[---]. | [--]yy.ṯṯ.krmm.šl[-.---]. | [---.]ʿšrm.krm.[---]. | [1081.18
t.b.rḥbn. | ḫmšm.l.mitm.zt. | w.b d.krd. | ḫmšm.l.mit. | arbʿ.kbd. 1096.5
ṯ]m.ṯmn.k[bd]. | [---.yr]yt.dq[-]. | [--.ṯ]lṯm.l.mi[t]. | [---.]arbʿ.kbd. 2170.6
kd w kd. | w ʿl ym kdm. | w b ṯlṯ.kd yn w krsnm. | w b rbʿ kdm yn. | w b ḫmš kd yn. 1086.4
.zbl. | ʿšrm.yn.ṭb.w.ṯṯm.ḫmš.k[b]d. | yn.d.l.ṭb.b.gt.sǵy. | arbʿm.kdm.kbd.yn.ṭb. | w.ḫmšm.k[dm.]kbd.yn.d.l.ṭb. | b.gt.g 1084.16
.ksp. | ḫmš.mat.šmt. | b.ʿšrt.ksp. | ʿšr.ṣin.b.ṯṯt.w.kmsk. | arbʿ[.k]dwṭm.w.ṯṯ.ṯprtm. | b.ʿšr[m.]ksp. | ḫmš.kkr.ṣml. | b.ʿšrt 2100.10
rm.ṣml. | ʿšrt.ksp h. | ḫmš.kkr.qnm. | ṯlṯt.w.ṯlṯt.ksp h. | arbʿ.kkr. | algbṯ.arbʿt. | ksp h. | kkr.šʿrt. | šbʿt.ksp h. | ḫmš.mqd 1127.14
[---.]ḫ[---.]ṯmnym[.k]sp ḫmšt. | [w a]rbʿ kkr ʿl bn[.--]. | [w] ṯlṯ šmn. | [w a]r[bʿ] ksp ʿl bn ymn. | š 1103.2
iršt.yṣḥm. | arbʿ.alpm. | mitm.kbd.ṯlṯ. | arbʿ.kkrm. | ṯmn.mat.kbd. | pwt. | ṯmn.mat.pṯtm. | kkrm.alpm 2051.4
ʿšrm kk[r.---]. | mšrn.ṯlṯ.ʿš[r.kkr]. | bn.šw.šbʿ.kk[r.---]. | arbʿm.kkr.[---]. | b d.mtn.[l].šlm. 2108.4
šš[r]t.ḫrṣ.ṯqlm.kbd.ʿšrt.mzn h. | b [ar]bʿm.ksp. | b d[.ʿb]dym.ṯlṯ.kkr šʿrt. | iqn[i]m.ṯṯt.ʿšrt.ksp h. | 2100.2
rbʿt. | kbd.ksp. | d.nqdm. | ḫmšm.l mit. | ksp.d.mkr.ar. | arbʿm ksp d mkr. | atlg. | mit.ksp.d mkr. | ilštmʿ. | ʿšrm.l mit.k 2107.11
p h. | ḫmš.kkr.qnm. | ṯlṯt.w.ṯlṯt.ksp h. | arbʿ.kkr. | algbṯ.arbʿt. | ksp h. | kkr.šʿrt. | šbʿt.ksp h. | ḫmš.mqdm.dnyn. | b.ṯql. 1127.15
---]b bn[.--]. | [-]ḫ[-.---]. | [-]p[-.---.-]ny. | [-]ḫ[-.---.-]dn. | arbʿ[m.ksp.]ʿl. | il[m]l[k.a]rgnd. | uškny[.w]mit. | zt.b d hm.ri 2055.10
[.k]sp ḫmšt. | [w a]rbʿ kkr ʿl bn[.--]. | [w] ṯlṯ šmn. | [w a]r[bʿ] ksp ʿl bn ymn. | šb šr šmn [--] ṯryn. | ḫm[š]m l ʿšr ksp 1103.4
ǵdy. | w.kd.ištir.ʿm.qrt. | ʿšt.ʿšr h.šmn. | ʿmn.bn.aǵlmn. | arbʿm.ksp.ʿl.qrt. | b.šd.bn.[u]brš. | ḫmšt.ʿšrt. | b.šd.bn.[-]n. | ṯl[1083.6
[t]. | b.š[d].bn.ʿmyn. | ḫmšt. | b.[šd.--]n. | ḫ[m]št[.ʿ]šrt. | [ar]bʿm.ksp. | [---]yn. | [---.]ksp. | [---.]mit. | [-----]. 1083.15
| l špš.arn.ṯn[.ʿšr h.]mn. | ʿṣrm.ṯql.kbd[.ks].mn.ḫrṣ. | w arbʿ.ktnt.w [---]b. | [ḫm]š.mat pḥm. | [ḫm]š[.m]at.iqnu. | arg 64[118].21
kn šbn. | skn ubrʿ. | skn ḫrṣbʿ. | rb.ntbtš. | [---].ʿbd.r[--]. | arbʿ.k[--]. | ṯlṯ.ktt. 1033.8
r.yn.[kps]lnm. | arbʿ.mat[.arb]ʿm.[k]bd. | d ntn.d.ksp. | arbʿ.l.ḫlby. | [---].l.bt. | arbʿ.l.kpslnm. | kdm.b[t.]mlk. 1087.4
at[.arb]ʿm.[k]bd. | d ntn.d.ksp. | arbʿ.l.ḫlby. | [---].l.bt. | arbʿ.l.kpslnm. | kdm.b[t.]mlk. 1087.6
r.dd.drt. | w[.a]rbʿ.l.ʿšrm.dd.l.yḥšr.bl.bn h. | b.gt.mʿbr.arbʿm.l.mit.drʿ.w.ṯmnym[.drt]. | w.ʿšrm.l.mit.dd.ḥp[r.]bnšm 1098.12
ṯṯ.mat.ksp. | ḥṯbn.ybnn. | arbʿm.l.mit.šmn. | arbʿm.l.mit.tišr. | ṯṯ.ṯṯ.b [t]ql.ṯlṯt.l.ʿšrm.ksp 1127.3
ṯṯ.mat.ksp. | ḥṯbn.ybnn. | arbʿm.l.mit.šmn. | arbʿm.l.mit.tišr. | ṯṯ.ṯṯ.b [t]ql.ṯlṯt.l.ʿšrm.ksp hm. | šstm.b.šbʿm 1127.4
hbṭnm. | ṯmn. | mdrǵlm. | ṯmnym.ṯmn.kbd. | tgmr.ḫrd. | arbʿm.l.mit. | ṯn.kbd. 1031.16
]. | kd[.--].lm[d.---]. | kd[.l.]ḫzr[m.---]. | kd[.l.]ṯrtn[m]. | arbʿ l.mry[nm]. | kdm l.ḥty.[---]. | kdm l.ʿṯtr[t]. | kd l.m[d]rǵl[1091.8
rbʿ.ʿš[r.]dd.nʿr. | d.apy[.--]. | w.arb[ʿ.--]d.apy.ʿbd h. | w.mrbʿ[t.l ʿ]bdm. 2094.6
ṯmnym.dd. | l u[-]m. | b.ṭbq.arbʿm.drʿ.w.ʿšr.dd.drt. | w[.a]rbʿ.l.ʿšrm.dd.l.yḥšr.bl.bn h. | b.gt.mʿbr.arbʿm.l.mit.drʿ.w.ṯ 1098.11
š.bn.mrynm. | ʿšr.mrum.w.šbʿ.ḫsnm. | tšʿm.mdrǵlm. | arbʿ.l ʿšrm.ḫsnm. | ʿšr.hbṭnm. | ṯṯm.l.mit.ṯn.kbd. | tgmr. 1030.8
. | w.ṯlṯ.alp h.[---]. | swn.qrty.w.[b]n h[.---]. | w.alp h.w.a[r]bʿ.l.arbʿ[m.---]. | pln.ṯmry.w.ṯn.bn h.w[.---]. | ymrn.apsny 2044.7
sg]. | yky msg. | ynḥm.msg. | bn.ugr.msg. | bn.ǵlṣ msg. | arbʿ l tkṣ[-]. | nn.arspy.ms[g]. | [---.ms]g. | bn.[gr]gs.msg. | bn[. 133[-].1.10
.b.ḫmšt. | ṯprt.b.ṯlṯt. | mtyn.b.ṯṯt. | ṯn.lbšm.b.ʿšrt. | pld.b.arbʿt. | lbš.ṯn.b.ṯnt.ʿšrt. 1108.7
spr.bnš.mlk. | d.b d.prṯ. | tšʿ.l.ʿšrm. | lqḥ.ššlmt. | ṯmn.l.arbʿm. | lqḥ.šʿrt. 1025.5
bd. | [---].alpm.ḫmš.mat. | šbʿm[.t]šʿ.kbd. | tgmr.uz.ǵrn.arbʿ.mat. | tgmr.uz.aḫmn.arbʿ.mat. | arbʿm.kbd. | ṯlṯ.alp.ṣpr.d 1129.5
dl.ṯṯ.dd.šʿrm. | [---.-]hn.w.alp.kd.nbt.kd.šmn.mr. | [---.]arbʿ.mat.ḫswn.lṯḥ.aqhr. | [---.lṯḥ.]sbbyn.lṯḥ.ššmn.lṯḥ.šḫlt. | [- 142[12].3
.ym.ḥdṯ. | b.yr.pgrm. | lqḥ.bʿlmdr. | w.bn.ḫlp. | miḫd. | b.arbʿ. | mat.ḫrṣ. 1156.6
]. | bn[.---]. | bn[.---]. | w.yn[.---]. | bn.ʿdr[.---]. | ntb[t]. | b.arb[ʿ]. | mat.ḫr[ṣ]. 2007.11
pgrm. | lqḥ.bʿlmʿdr. | w bn.ḫlp. | w[--]y.d.bʿl. | miḫd.b. | arbʿ.mat. | ḫrṣ. 1155.7
alpm.arbʿ.mat.k[bd]. | mit.b d.yd[r]m. | alp ḫmš mat.kbd.d[--]. 2109.1
mnḥ.b d.ybnn. | arbʿ.mat. | l.alp.šmn. | nḥ.ṯṯ.mat. | šm[n].rqḥ. | kkrm.brdl. | mi 141[120].2
ṯn.ʿšr.yn.[kps]lnm. | arbʿ.mat[.arb]ʿm.[k]bd. | d ntn.d.ksp. | arbʿ.l.ḫlby. | [---].l.bt. | 1087.2

šb‘m[.t]š‘.kbd. | tgmr.uz.ǵrn.arb‘.mat. | tgmr.uz.aẖmn.arb‘.mat. | arb‘m.kbd. | t̲lt̲.alp.ṣpr.dt.aḥd. | ḥrt̲ h.aḥd.b gt.nẖl. 1129.6
-].ẖmšm.ḥmr.škm. | [---.t̲t̲.dd.]gdl.t̲t̲.dd.š‘rm. | [---.a]lp.arb‘.mat.tyt. | [---.kd.]nbt.k[d.]šmn.mr. | [---.l]tḥ.sb[by]n.ltḥ. 142[12].14
.b.arb‘m. | arb‘t.‘šrt.ḥrṣ. | b.t̲qlm.kbd.arb‘m. | ‘šrt.ḥrṣ.b.arb‘m. | mit.ḥršḥ.b.t̲qlm. | w.šb‘.‘šr.šmn. | d.l.yṣa.bt.mlk. | tgm 2100.18
| d.l.ṣpy. | [---.t]r hm. | [---].ššb. | [---.]tr h. | [a]rb‘.ql‘m. | arb‘.md̲rnm. | md̲rn.w.mšḫt̲. | d.mrkbt. | mlk. | mšḫt̲.w.msg. | 1122.11
n.w t̲lt̲ h.ḥrṣm. | ylk ym.w t̲n. | t̲lt̲.rb‘.ym. | aḫr.špšm.b rb‘. | ymǵy.l udm.rbt. | w udm[.tr]rt. | grnn.‘rm. | šrnn.pdrm. | 14[KRT].4.209
| [---].t̲lt̲. | [---].aḥd. | u[--].t̲n. | hz[p].t̲t̲. | ḫrṣb‘.aḥd. | ypr.arb. | m[-]qb.‘šr. | t̲n‘y.t̲lt̲. | ḫlb ‘prm.t̲n. | tmd̲y.t̲lt̲. | [--]rt.arb‘. 70[112].9
[---.--]ǵz. | [---.]qrt. | [---].at̲t. | [---.]w arb‘.n‘r[m]. | [---.a]ḫd. | [---.]t̲lt̲.at̲t. 2142.4
m. | [--.]w nṣp w t̲lt̲ spm w ‘šrm lḥ[m]. | l[.-]dt ḫnd[r]t̲ ar‘ s[p]m w ‘š[r]. | [---.]ḫndrt̲m t̲t̲ spm [w] t̲lt̲m l[ḥm]. | [---.]a 134[-].5
p]m w ‘š[r]. | [---.]ḫndrt̲m t̲t̲ spm [w] t̲lt̲m l[ḥm]. | [---.]ar‘ spm w [---]. | [---]š[.---.--]b[.---]. | [--.]sp[m.w ---.l]ḥm. 134[-].7
kqmt̲n. | [---.]klnmw. | [---.]w yky. | t̲lt̲m sp.l bnš tpnr. | arb‘.spm.l.lbnš prwsdy. | t̲t̲ spm.l bnš klnmw. | l yarš ḫswn. | 137.2[93].7
mš ‘šr.sp. | l bnš tpnr d yaḥd l g ynm. | t̲t̲ spm l tgyn. | arb‘ spm l ll[-]. | t̲n spm.l slyy. | t̲lt̲ spm l dlšpš amry. 137.2[93].13
š[t]. | abršn.‘šr[t]. | b‘ln.ẖmšt. | w.nḥl h.ẖm[š]t. | bn.unp.arb‘t. | ‘bdbn.ytrš ẖmšt. | krwn.‘šrt. | bn.ulb ẖmšt. | bn.ḥry.ẖm 1062.10
gmrš[.---]. | kd.‘l.‘bd[--]. | kd.‘l.aǵlt[n]. | t̲lt̲.‘l.a[b]m[n]. | arb‘.‘l[.--]ly. | kd.[‘l.--]ẓ. | kd.[‘l.---]. | [--.--]ẖ.bn.ag[--]. | [---.--] 1082.1.22
ik.‘m y. | ik y.aškn. | ‘ṣm.l bt.dml. | p ank.atn. | ‘ṣm.l k. | arb‘.‘ṣm. | ‘l.ar. | w.t̲lt̲. | ‘l.ubr‘y. | w.t̲n.‘l. | mlk. | w.aḥd. | ‘l atlg. 1010.9
dbḥ.t̲p[-]. | aḥt.l mzy.bn[--]. | aḥt.l mkt.ǵr. | aḥt.l ‘t̲trt. | arb‘.‘ṣrm. | gt.t̲rmn. | aḥt.slḫu. 39[19].17
py.ẖmšm. | b.bn.t̲tm.t̲lt̲m. | b.bn.agdt̲b.‘šrm. | b.bn.ibn.arb‘t.‘šrt. | b.bn.mnn.t̲t̲m. | b.rpan.bn.yyn.‘šrt. | b.yp‘r.‘šrm. | 2054.1.13
r.bnš. | yd.ytm.yd.r‘y.ḥmrm. | b.gt.gwl.t̲mn.ṣmdm. | w.arb‘.‘šr.bnš. | yd.nǵr.mdr‘.yd.š[--]m. | [b.]gt.iptl.t̲t̲.ṣmdm. | [w 2038.5
yrḫ ḫyr.b ym ḥdt̲. | alp.w š.l b‘lt bhtm. | b arb‘t ‘šrt.b‘l. | ‘rkm. | b t̲mnt.‘šrt.yr | tḫṣ.mlk.brr. | ‘lm.tzǵ.b ǵ UG5.12.A.3
‘.‘šr. | ṣ‘q.arb‘ ‘šr. | ṣ‘.t̲mn. | šḥq.‘šrm.arb‘.kbd. | ḫlb rpš arb‘.‘šr. | bq‘t t̲t̲. | irab t̲n.‘šr. | ḫbš.t̲mn. | amd̲y.arb‘.‘šr. | [-]n‘y. 67[110].7
qmḫ.d.kly.k ṣḥ.illd̲rm. | b d.zlb[n.--]. | arb‘.‘š[r.]dd.n‘r. | d.apy[.--]. | w.arb[‘.--]d.apy.‘bd h. | w.mrb‘[2094.3
arb‘.‘šr h.šd. | w.kmsk.d.iwrkl. | t̲lt̲.šd.d.bn.mlkyy. | kmsk.šd.i 1079.1
arb‘.‘šr h.šmn. | d.lqḥt.t̲lǵdy. | w.kd.ištir.‘m.qrt. | ‘št.‘šr h.šmn 1083.1
kkr.š‘rt. | b d.urtn.b.arb‘m. | arb‘t.‘šrt.ḥrṣ. | b.t̲qlm.kbd.arb‘m. | ‘šrt.ḥrṣ.b.arb‘m. | mit.ḥršḥ.b.t̲qlm. | w.šb‘.‘šr.šmn. | d. 2100.17
ml. | b.‘šrt.b d.bn.kyn. | ‘šr.kkr.š‘rt. | b d.urtn.b.arb‘m. | arb‘t.‘šrt.ḥrṣ. | b.t̲qlm.kbd.arb‘m. | ‘šrt.ḥrṣ.b.arb‘m. | mit.ḥršḥ 2100.16
.[---]. | [ẖm]šm.ksp.‘l.gd[--]. | [---].ypḥ.‘bdršp.b[--.--]. | [ar]b‘t.‘šrt.kbd[.---]. | [---.-]rwd.šmbnš[.---]. | [---].ksp.‘l.k[--]. | 1144.6
arb‘.‘šr.ǵzrm. | arb‘.at̲t. | pǵt.aḥt. | w.pǵy.aḥ. 2081.1
ḫlb ‘prm.t̲t̲. | ḫlb krd.t̲n ‘šr. | qmy.arb‘.‘šr. | ṣ‘q.arb‘ ‘šr. | ṣ‘.t̲mn. | šḥq.‘šrm.arb‘.kbd. | ḫlb rpš arb‘.‘šr. | bq‘t t̲t̲. 67[110].4
ḫlb ‘prm.t̲t̲. | ḫlb krd.t̲n ‘šr. | qmy.arb‘.‘šr. | ṣ‘q.arb‘ ‘šr. | ṣ‘.t̲mn. | šḥq.‘šrm.arb‘.kbd. | ḫlb rpš arb 67[110].3
]. | šmtr.[ut̲kl.l il.šlmm]. | b t̲lt̲t ‘[šrt.yrtḫṣ.mlk.brr]. | b arb‘[t.‘šrt.riš.argmn]. | w t̲n šm.l [b‘lt.bhtm.‘ṣrm.l inš]. | ilm. 35[3].4
| [šmtr].ut̲kl.l il.šlmm. | b [t̲lt̲t].‘šrt.yrtḫṣ.mlk. | br[r.]b a[r]b‘t.‘šrt.riš. | arg[mn.w t̲n.]šm.l b‘lt. | bhtm.‘ṣ[rm.l in]š ilm APP.II[173].4
ṣr[m] l inš. | [ilm.---].lbbmm.gdlt.‘rb špš w ḥl. | [mlk.b ar]b‘t.‘[š]rt.yrtḫṣ.mlk.brr. | [b ym.ml]at.y[ql]n.al[p]m.yrḫ.‘šr 36[9].1.10
b arb‘t.‘š[r[t]. | yrtḫṣ.mlk.b[rr]. | b ym.mlat. | tqln.alpm. | yrḫ.‘šr UG5.13.1
š[.w ḥl.mlk.w.b y] | m.ḥdt̲.t̲n šm[.---.--]t. | b yrḫ.ši[-.b ar]b‘t.‘š | rt.yr[tḫṣ.ml]k.brr. | ‘lm.š.š[--].l[--.]‘rb.šp | š.w ḥl[.ml APP.II[173].54
| ḫlb rpš arb‘.‘šr. | bq‘t t̲t̲. | irab t̲n.‘šr. | ḫbš.t̲mn. | amd̲y.arb‘.‘šr. | [-]n‘y.t̲t̲.‘šr. 67[110].11
an[y]t.mlk[.---]. | w.[t̲]lt̲.brm.[---]. | arb‘ ‘tkm[.---]. 2057.3
m. | bir.ẖmš. | uškn.arb‘. | ubr‘y.t̲lt̲. | ar.t̲mn ‘šr h. | mlk.arb‘. | ǵbl.ẖmš. | atlg.ẖmš ‘šr[h]. | ulm t̲[t̲]. | m‘rby.ẖmš. | t̲bq. 68[65].1.6
‘šr.b.gt.ir[bṣ]. | arb‘.b.gt.b‘ln. | ‘št.‘šr.b.gpn. | yd.‘dnm. | arb‘.ǵzlm. | t̲n.yṣrm. 2103.9
[t̲]n.prm.b ‘šrm. | arb‘.prm.b.‘š[r]m. | arb‘.b.arb‘m. | t̲t̲m.[---.p]rm. | [-]l.b[--.---]. 1138.2
l‘m. | ẖmš.ṣmdm.w ḥrṣ. | tryn.sšwm. | tryn.aḥd.d bnš. | arb‘.ṣmdm.apnt. | w ḥrṣ. | tš‘m.mrḥ.aḥd. | kbd. 1123.7
l t̲lt̲m. | ṣṣ ‘mlbi t̲t̲ l ‘šrm. | ṣṣ bn adty ẖmšm. | ṣṣ amtrn arb‘m. | ṣṣ iytlm mit t̲lt̲m kbd. | ṣṣ m[l]k ‘šrm. | ṣṣ abš[-] mit [‘ 2097.8
šrm. | ṣṣ bn aglby t̲lt̲[m]. | ṣṣ bn.šrš‘m.[---]. | ṣṣ mlkn‘m.a[rb‘m]. | ṣṣ mlk mit[.---]. | ṣṣ igy.ẖmšm. | ṣṣ yrpi m[it.---]. | ṣṣ 2097.15
bn.‘bdnkl.qšt.w.ql‘. | bn.znan.qšt. | bn.arz.[ar]b‘.qšt.w.arb[‘.]ql‘m. | b[n.]ad‘l.q[š]t.w.ql‘. | b[n].ilyn.qšt.w.ql‘. | šmrm. 119[321].2.45
mrkbt mlk. | d.l.ṣpy. | [---.t]r hm. | [---].ššb. | [---.]tr h. | [a]rb‘.ql‘m. | arb‘.md̲rnm. | md̲rn.w.mšḫt̲. | d.mrkbt. | mlk. | mš 1122.10
bt.kmn.hlk.kt̲r. | k y‘n.w y‘n.tdrq.ḫss. | hlk.qšt.ybln.hl.yš | rb‘.qṣ‘t.apnk.dnil. | mt.rpi.aphn.ǵzr.mt. | hrnmy.gm.l at̲t 17[2AQHT].5.12
[-----]. | [---.]abl.qšt t̲mn. | ašrb‘.qṣ‘t.w hn šb[‘]. | b ymm.apnk.dnil.mt. | rpi.a hn.ǵzr.mt. 17[2AQHT].5.3
arb‘m.qšt. | alp ḥẓm.w alp. | ntq.t̲n.ql‘m. | ẖmš.ṣmdm.w ḥrṣ. | 1123.1
[nq]dm.dt.kn.npṣ hm. | [bn].lbn.arb‘.qšt.w.ar[b‘]. | [u]t̲pt.ql‘.w.t̲t̲.mr[ḥ]m. | [bn].smyy.qšt.w.u 2047.2
.qšt.w.ql‘. | bn.‘bdnkl.qšt.w.ql‘. | bn.znan.qšt. | bn.arz.[ar]b‘.qšt.w.arb[‘.]ql‘m. | b[n.]ad‘l.q[š]t.w.ql‘. | b[n].ilyn.qšt.w 119[321].2.45
m.ḥdt̲.t̲n.šm. | l.[---]t. | i[d.yd]bḥ.mlk.l.prgl.ṣqrn.b.gg. | ar[b‘.]arb‘.mt̲bt.azmr.b h.š.šr[-]. | al[p.w].š.šlmm.pamt.šb‘.kl 35[3].51
š.kkr.ṣml. | b.‘šrt.b d.bn.kyn. | ‘šr.kkr.š‘rt. | b d.urtn.b.arb‘m. | arb‘t.‘šrt.ḥrṣ. | b.t̲qlm.kbd.arb‘m. | ‘šrt.ḥrṣ.b.arb‘m. | 2100.15
šurt l [---]. | t̲mn šurt l ar[--.---]. | t̲n šurtm l bnš [---]. | arb‘ šurt l bn[š.---]. | arb‘ šurt l q[--.---]. | t̲lt̲ šurt l bnš [---]. | t̲ 137.1[92].4
t l ar[--.---]. | t̲n šurtm l bnš [---]. | arb‘ šurt l bn[š.---]. | arb‘ šurt l q[--.---]. | t̲lt̲ šurt l bnš [---]. | t̲t̲ šurt.l bnš[.---]. | t̲n š 137.1[92].5
šurt l bnš [---]. | ẖmš kbd arb‘[.---]. | t̲t̲ šurt l tg[-.---]. | arb‘ šurt [---]. | [ẖm]šm šurt [---]. | t̲lt̲ šurt l [---]. | t̲n šurtm l [137.1[92].14
t.l bnš[.---]. | t̲n šurtm l bn[š.---]. | t̲lt̲m šurt l b[nš.---]. | arb‘ šurt [---]. | t̲t̲ šurt l bnš [---]. | ẖmš kbd arb‘[.---]. | t̲t̲ šurt l 137.1[92].10
.bnš. | qmy.ḥmr.w.bnš. | t̲bil. | ‘nmky.ḥmr.w.bnš. | rqd arb‘. | šbn aḥd. | t̲bq aḥd. | šrš aḥd. | bir aḥd. | uḫnp. | hzp t̲n. | 2040.27
arny. | w ‘l [---.]rb‘m t̲qlm.w [---] arb‘yn. | w ‘l.mnḥm.arb‘ š[mn]. | w ‘l bn a[--.-]yn t̲qlm. | [--] ksp [---] kdr [---]. | [-] 1103.9
kr. | qnm. | ‘šrm.kk[r]. | brr. | [‘]šrm.npš. | ‘šrm.zt.mm. | ‘rb‘m. | šmn.mr. 141[120].15
kd.šmn.‘l.hbm.šlmy. | kd.šmn.t̲bil. | kd.šmn.ymtšr. | arb‘.šmn.‘l.‘bdn.w.[---]. | kdm.šmn.‘l.ilršp.bn[.---]. | kd.šmn.‘l 1082.1.4
ǵbl.ẖmš. | atlg.ẖmš ‘šr[h]. | ulm t̲[t̲]. | m‘rby.ẖmš. | t̲bq.arb‘. | tkm[.---]. | uḫnp[.---]. | ušk[n.---]. | ubr[‘y.---]. | ar[.---]. | 68[65].1.11
[t̲]n.prm.b ‘šrm. | arb‘.prm.b.‘š[r]m. | arb‘.b.arb‘m. | t̲t̲m.[---.p]rm. | [-]l.b[--.---]. | [---].kbd. | [---].kb[d.---]. 1138.3
mit.t̲lt̲.mḫsrn. | ‘l.nsk.kt̲t̲ǵlm. | arb‘m.t̲lt̲.mḫsrn. | mtb‘l.rišy. | t̲lt̲m.t̲lt̲.‘l.nsk. | arym. | alp.t̲lt̲.‘l 1137.3
.altyy. | [m]it.t̲lt̲m.kbd.šmn. | [l.]abrm.mšrm. | [mi]tm.arb‘m.t̲mn.kbd. | [l.]sbrdnm. | m[i]t.l.bn.‘ẓmt.rišy. | mit.l.tlm 2095.5
t̲t̲m.t̲lt̲.kb[d]. | arb‘m.t̲p[rt]. | ksp h. | t̲mn.dd[.--]. | t̲lt̲.dd.p[--]. | šb‘t.p[--]. | tš‘t 2120.2

'šr ksp 'l bn llit. | [--]l[-.-]p 'l [---.-]b'm arny. | w 'l [---.]rb'm tqlm.w [---] arb'yn. | w 'l.mnḥm.arb' š[mn]. | w 'l bn a[- 1103.8
nt.l 'šrm.'šrt.ḫmš.kbd. | bn.ilṣdq.šb't tltt šlm. | bn.tmq.arb't tqlm šlmm. 1131.10
.---]. | 'l.pd.asr.[---.]l[.---]. | mḫlpt.w l.ytk.[d]m['t.]km. | rb't.tqlm.ttp[.---.]bm. | yd.ṣpn hm.tliy m[.--.ṣ]pn hm. | nṣḥy.š 19[1AQHT].2.83
ḫsnm. | tš'.'šr. | mrynm. | tlt.'šr.mkrm. | tlt.bn.mrynm. | arb'.trtnm. | tš'.ḫbṭnm. | tmnym.tlt.kbd. | mdrġlm. | w.šb'.'šr. 1029.9
n[-.]l ks[p.-]m. | l.mri[.--]. | tmn kbd[.--]i. | arb'm[.--]. | l apy.mr[i.--]. | [---.--]d. | [-----]. 1133.4
[--.l]bš.mtn.b.ar't. | [--.l]bš.bn.ykn'.b.ar't. | [--.l]bš.bn.grbn.b.tqlm. | [--.lb]š.bn.sgryn.b[.t]qlm. | [---. 135[330].2
[--.l]bš.mtn.b.ar't. | [--.l]bš.bn.ykn'.b.ar't. | [--.l]bš.bn.grbn.b.tqlm. | [--.lb]š. 135[330].1
spr.ḫrd.arr. | ap arb'm[.--]. | pd[.---.ḫm]šm.kb[d]. | ġb[-.---.]kbd. | m[--.---.k]bd 2042.2
-.]dyn.ḫmšt.'šrt. | [---.-]til.ḫmšt.l 'šrm. | [--.-]n.w.aḫt h.arb'm. | [--.-]dn.'šrm. | [--.-]dwn.tltm.w.šb'.alpm. | [kt]rmlk.'š 2054.2.21
.illdrm. | b d.zlb[n.--]. | arb'.'š[r.]dd.n'r. | d.apy[.--]. | w.arb['.--]d.apy.'bd h. | w.mrb'[t.l ']bdm. 2094.5
[---.']šrt. | ḫlb.ḫmšt.l.'šrm. | mril.'šrt. | glbty.arb't. | [--]tb.'šrt. 1180.4
.dd.[---]. | iwrdn.ḥ[--.---]. | w.tltm.dd.[---.]n[---.---]. | w.a[r]b'[.---].bnš[.š]dyn[.---]. | agr.[---.--]n.tn.'šr h.d[--.---]. | [--- 1098.32
[-]š[-.---]. | [-]š[-.---]. | arb['.---]. | ḫmš.[---]. | ġ[--.---]. 150[36].3
mr[.šmn.rqḥ.bt]. | mtnt.w ynt.[qrt.w tn.ḥtm]. | w bġr.arb'.[---.kdm.yn]. | prs.qmḥ.m'[--.---]. | mdbḥt.bt.i[lt.'ṣrm.l]. APP.II[173].24
r]. | šmn.rqḥ[.-]bt.mtnt[.w ynt.qrt]. | w tn ḥtm.w bġr.arb['.---]. | kdm.yn.prs.qmḥ.[---]. | mdbḥt.bt.ilt.'ṣr[m.l ṣpn.š]. 35[3].22
--.]arb'[m]. | [---.a]rb'm. | [---.tš]'m. | [---.t]š'm. | [---.--]y arb'm. | [---.]l špš tmny[m]. | [---.]dbr h l šp[š]. | [---.]dbr h l š 41[71].6
[--]n.'š[r.] | [a]rt[.a]rb'[.---]. | 'nmky.'šr.[---]. | tmry.'šr.tn.k[rmm.---]. | liy.krm. 1081.2
rb. | m[-]qb.'šr. | tn'y.tlt. | ḫlb 'prm.tn. | tmdy.tlt. | [--]rt.arb'. | [---].'šr. 70[112].14
alp ḥ.[---]. | swn.qrty.w.[b]n ḥ[.---]. | w.alp ḥ.w.a[r]b'.l.arb'[m.---]. | pln.tmry.w.tn.bn ḥ.w[.---]. | ymrn.apsny.w.att ḥ 2044.7
[-----]. | [---.]arb'[m]. | [---.a]rb'm. | [---.tš]'m. | [---.t]š'm. | [---.--]y arb'm. | [41[71].2
zp.tš'.yn. | [b]ir.'šr[.---]m ḥsp. | ḫpty.kdm[.---]. | [a]gm.arb'[.---]. | šrš.šb'.mṣb. | rqd.tlt.mṣb.w.[---]. | uḫnp.tt.mṣb. | tg 2004.31
[-----]. | [---.]arb'[m]. | [---.a]rb'm. | [---.tš]'m. | [---.t]š'm. | [---.--]y arb'm. | [---.]l špš tmn 41[71].3
l b[nš.---]. | arb' šurt [---]. | tt šurt l bnš [---]. | ḫmš kbd arb'[.---]. | tt šurt l tg[-.---]. | arb' šurt [---]. | [ḫm]šm šurt [---]. 137.1[92].12
. | tlt.k[---]. | tlt.a[--.---]. | ḫmš[.---]. | ksp[.---]. | k[--.---]. | ar[b'.---]. | tmn[.---]. | [-]r[-.---]. | w tt.[---]. | tltm[.---]. | mil[-.--- 148[96].9
-.t]lt.mat. | [---.m]itm.mqp.m[---]. | [---.tmn]ym.mgnm ar[b']. | [---.-]aḥ.mqḥ mqḥm. | [---.--]t.'šr rmġt.[--]. | [---].alp.[1145.1.3
[.---]. | ['r]gz.tlt.ṣmd[m.---]. | [m]ṣbt.ṣmdm.[---]. | [--]nr.arb'.[---]. | [--]idḫ.ṣmd[.---]. | [u]bṣ.[---]. 1179.6
]'.w[.---.m]rḥm. | [bn].ḫdmn.qšt.[w.u]tp[t].t[--]. | [---].arb'.[---]. | [---].kdl[.---.mr]ḥm.w.t[t.---]. | [---.mr]ḥm.w.t[t.--- 2047.10
[---.gd]ltm.p[--.---]. | [---.]arb't[.---]. | [---.]qdš[.---]. | [---.k]su.p[--.---]. | [---.]agn[.---]. | [- 45[45].2
']šrm[.---]. | [---.]nġr.'š[rm.---]. | [---.-]yl.'š[rm.---]. | [---.a]rb'[.---]. | [---.t]ltm[.---]. | [---.--]m.bn l[---]. | [---].bn ṣd[-.---] 149[99].5
ḥm.w.t[t.---]. | [---.mr]ḥm.w.t[t.---]. | [---].ql'[.---]. | [---.a]rb'[.---]. 2047.14
ḥd. | tbq aḥd. | šrš aḥd. | bir aḥd. | uḫnp. | hzp tn. | m'qb arb'. 2040.34

rbṣ

q]. | [ḫrṣ.]yd.mqm h. | [w 'b]d.'lm.tlt. | [ssw]m.mrkbt b trbṣ bn.amt. | [tn.b]nm.aqny. | [tn.ta]rm.amid. | [w y'n].tr.ab 14[KRT].2.56
]q. | ḫrṣ[.yd.mqm] h. | 'bd[.'lm.tlt]. | ss[wm.mrkbt]. | b[trbṣ.bn.amt]. | [qḥ.krt.šlmm]. | [šlmm.al.tṣr]. | [udm.rbt.w ud 14[KRT].5.254
]. | ḫrṣ.[yd.mqm h]. | w 'bd[.'lm.tlt]. | sswm.m[rkbt]. | b trbṣ.[bn.amt]. | q[ḥ.kr]t[.šlmm]. | š[lmm.]al.t[ṣr]. | udm[.r]bt. 14[KRT].6.273
.w yrq.ḫrṣ. | yd.mqm h.w 'bd.'lm. | tlt.sswm.mrkbt. | b trbṣ.bn.amt. | qḥ.krt.šlmm. | šlmm.w ng.mlk. | l bt y.rḥq.krt. 14[KRT].3.129
yr[q.ḫrṣ]. | yd.mqm h.w 'bd. | 'lm.tlt.sswm. | mrkbt.b trbṣ. | bn.amt.p d.[i]n. | b bt y.ttn.tn. | l y.mtt.ḥry. | n'mt.šbḥ.b 14[KRT].6.286
.w yrq.ḫrṣ. | yd.mqm h.w 'bd. | 'lm.tlt.sswm.mrkbt. | b trbṣt.bn.amt. | p d.in.b bt y.ttn. | tn.l y.mtt.ḥry. | n'mt.špḥ.bk 14[KRT].3.141
k.[--].l ḥbš k. | 'tk.ri[š.]l mhr k. | w 'p.l dr['].nšr k. | w rbṣ.l ġr k.inbb. | kt ġr k.ank.yd't. | [-]n.atn.at.mtb k[.---]. | [š] 13[6].9

rbt

hdm.ytpd.w ykrkr. | uṣb't h.yšu.g h.w y[ṣḥ]. | ik.mġyt.rbt.atr[t.y]m. | ik.atwt.qnyt.i[lm]. | rġb.rġbt.w tġt[--]. | hm.ġ 4[51].4.31
.btlt.'nt. | tmgnn.rbt[.a]trt ym. | tġzyn.qnyt.ilm. | w t'n.rbt.atrt ym. | ik.tmgnn.rbt. | atrt.ym.tġzyn. | qnyt.ilm.mgntm 4[51].3.27
ym.šm'. | l rbt.atr[t] ym.tn. | aḥd.b bn k.amlkn. | w t'n.rbt.atrt ym. | bl.nmlk.yd'.ylḥn. | w y'n.ltpn.il d pi | d dq.anm. 6.1.47[49.1.19]
m.l yrẓ. | 'm.b'l.l y'db.mrḥ. | 'm.bn.dgn.k tms m. | w 'n.rbt.atrt ym. | blt.nmlk.'ttr.'rẓ. | ymlk.'ttr.'rẓ. | apnk.'ttr.'rẓ. | y 6.1.53[49.1.25]
rt. | ary y[.ẓl].ksp.[a]trt. | k t'n.ẓl.ksp.w n[-]t. | ḫrṣ.šmḫ.rbt.a[trt]. | ym.gm.l ġlm h.k [tṣḥ]. | 'n.mktr.ap.t[---]. | dgy.rbt 4[51].2.28
. | b'l.k ḫlq.zbl.b'l. | arṣ.gm.yṣḥ il. | l rbt.atrt ym.šm'. | l rbt.atr[t] ym.tn. | aḥd.b bn k.amlkn. | w t'n.rbt.atrt ym. | bl.n 6.1.45[49.1.17]
l b'l. | km.ilm.w ḥẓr.k bn.atrt. | mtb il.mẓll.bn h. | mtb rbt.atrt.ym. | mtb.klt.knyt. | mtb.pdry.bt.ar. | mẓll.tly.bt rb. | 4[51].4.53
m.ilm.w ḥẓr]. | [k bn.at]r[t]. | m[t]b.il.mẓll. | bn h.mtb.rbt. | atrt.ym.mtb. | klt.knyt. | mtb.pdry.b ar. | mẓll.tly.bt rb. | 4[51].1.14
b'l.km.ilm.w ḥẓr]. | k bn.[atrt.mtb.il.mẓll]. | bn h.m[tb.rbt.atrt.ym]. | mtb.pdr[y.bt.ar.mẓll]. | tly.bt.r[b.mtb.arṣy]. | b 3['NT.VI].4.2
.l b'l.km.ilm. | ḥẓr.k b[n.a]trt.mtb.il. | mtll.b[n h.m]tb.rbt.atrt. | ym.mtb.[pdr]y.bt.ar. | [mẓll.]tly[.bt.]rb.mtb. | [arṣy. 3['NT.VI].5.48
.a[trt]. | ym.gm.l ġlm h.k [tṣḥ]. | 'n.mktr.ap.t[---]. | dgy.rbt.atr[t.ym]. | qḥ.rtt.b d k t[---]. | rbt.'l.ydm[.---]. | b mdd.il.y 4[51].2.31
.il.ab -.w t'n.rbt]. | atr[t.ym.šm'.l qdš]. | w am[rr.l dgy.rbt]. | atrt.ym[.mdl.'r]. | ṣmd.pḥl[.št.gpnm.dt]. | ksp.dt.yr[q.n 4[51].4.3
[i]k.mgn.rbt.atrt. | [ym].mġẓ.qnyt.ilm. | w tn.bt.l b'l.km. | [i]lm.w ḥẓr. 8[51FRAG].1
trt ym. | tġẓyn.qnyt.ilm. | w t'n.rbt.atrt ym. | ik.tmgnn.rbt. | atrt.ym.tġẓyn. | qnyt.ilm.mgntm. | tr.il.d pid.hm.ġẓtm. | 4[51].3.28
mmt.amht. | aḫr.mġy.aliyn.b'l. | mġyt.btlt.'nt. | tmgnn.rbt[.a]trt ym. | tġẓyn.qnyt.ilm. | w t'n.rbt.atrt ym. | ik.tmgnn. 4[51].3.25
d pid.hm.ġẓtm. | bny.bnwt w t'n. | btlt.'nt.nmgn. | [-]m.rbt.atrt.ym. | [nġ]ẓ.qnyt.ilm. | [---].nmgn.hwt. | [--].aliyn.b'l. | 4[51].3.34
.arṣy.bt.y'bdr. | ap.mtn.rgmm. | argm k.šskn m'. | mgn.rbt.atrt ym. | mġẓ.qnyt.ilm. | hyn.'ly.l mpḫm. | b d.ḫss.mṣbt 4[51].1.22
lbn. | lbnt.ybn.bt.l b'l. | km ilm.w ḥẓr.k bn.atrt. | w t'n.rbt.atrt ym. | rbt.ilm.l ḥkmt. | šbt.dqn k.l tsr k. | rḥntt.d[-].l ir 4[51].5.64
tr[.il.ab -.w t'n.rbt]. | atr[t.ym.šm'.l qdš]. | w am[rr.l dgy.rbt]. | atrt.ym[.mdl. 4[51].4.1
rt.ary h.k mt.aliyn. | b'l.k ḫlq.zbl.b'l. | arṣ.gm.yṣḥ il. | l rbt.atrt ym.šm'. | l rbt.atr[t] ym.tn. | aḥd.b bn k.amlkn. | w t' 6.1.44[49.1.16]
ṣ. | dm.'ṣm.hm.yd.il mlk. | yḫss k.ahbt.tr.t'rr k. | w t'n.rbt.atrt ym. | tḥm k.il.ḥkm.ḥkmt. | 'm 'lm.ḥyt.ḥẓt. | tḥm k.ml 4[51].4.40

.|[nǵ]ẓ.qnyt.ilm.|[---].nmgn.hwt.|[--].aliyn.b'l.|[--.]rbt.aṯrt.ym.|[---.]btlt.'nt.|[--.tl]ḥm.tšty.|[ilm.w tp]q.mrǵtm 4[51].3.38

.bt.l b'l.|km ilm.w ḥẓr.k bn.aṯrt.|w t'n.rbt.aṯrt ym.|rbt.ilm.l ḥkmt.|šbt.dqn k.l tsr k.|rḫntt.d[-].l irt k.|wn ap.' 4[51].5.65

.w ṯṯkl.|bnwt h.ykr.'r.d qdm.|idk.pnm.l ytn.tk aršḫ.rbt.|w aršḫ.ṯrrt.ydy.b 'ṣm.'r'r.|w b šḥt.'s.mt.'r'rm.yn'rn h. UG5.7.63

.|šlmm.w ng.mlk.|l bt y.rḥq.krt.|l ḥẓr y.al.tṣr.|udm.rbt.w udm ṯrrt.|udm.ytnt.il w ušn.|ab.adm.w ṯṯb.|mlakm.l 14[KRT].3.134

bṣ.[bn.amt].|q[ḥ.kr]t[.šlmm].|š[lmm.]al.t[ṣr].|udm[.r]bt.w u[dm].|[ṯ]rrt.udm.y[t]n[t].|il.ušn.ab[.ad]m.|rḥq.mlk 14[KRT].6.276

b[trbṣ.bn.amt].|[qḥ.krt.šlmm].|[šlmm.al.tṣr].|[udm.rbt.w udm].|[ṯrrt.udm.ytnt].|[il.w ušn.ab.adm].|[rḥq.mlk.l 14[KRT].5.257

lk ym.w ṯn.|ṯlṯ.rb'.ym.|aḫr.špšm.b rb'.|ymǵy.l udm.rbt.|w udm[.ṯr]rt.|grnn.'rm.|šrnn.pdrm.|s't.b šdm.ḥṭb.|w 14[KRT].4.210

.rb' ym.|ḫmš.ṯdṯ.ym.mk.špšm.|b šb'.w tmǵy.l udm.|rbm.w l.udm.ṯrrt.|w gr.nn.'rm.šrn.|pdrm.s't.b šdm.|ḥṭb h. 14[KRT].3.109

bl.a[ṯt y].|il.ylt.mh.ylt.yld y.šḥr.w šl[m].|šu.'db.l špš.rbt.w l kbkbm.kn[-].|yhbr.špt hm.yšq.hn.[š]pt hm.mtqtm.| 23[52].54

h.|b smkt.ṣat.npš h.|[-]mt[-].ṣba.rbt.|špš.w tgh.nyr.|rbt.w rgm.l aḫt k.|ṯtmnt.krt n.dbḥ.|dbḥ.mlk.'šr.|'šrt.qḥ.tp 16.1[125].38

]y.|[kr]t.ṯ'.'ln.bḫr.|[---].aṯt k.'l.|[---] k.yšṣi.|[---.]ḫbr.rbt.|[ḫbr.ṯrr]t.il d.|[pid.---].b anšt.|[---.]mlu.|[---.--]tm. 15[128].5.25

t[p]tḥ.rḫbt.yn.|'l h.ṯr h.tš'rb.|'l h.tš'rb.ẓby h.|ṯr.ḫbr.rbt.|ḫbr.ṯrrt.|bt.krt.tbun.|lm.mṯb[.---].|w lḥm mr.tqdm.|y 15[128].4.19

|ptḥ.[rḫ]bt.yn.|ṣḥ.šb'm.ṯr y.|ṯmnym.[ẓ]by y.|ṯr.ḫbr[.rb]t.|ḫbr[.ṯrrt].|[-]'b[-].š[--]m.|[----]r[.---]š[.--]qm.|id.u [---] 15[128].4.8

[---.--]m[.---].|[-.]rbt.ṯbt.[---].|rbt.ṯbt.ḥš[n.---].|y.arṣ.ḥšn[.---].|t'td.tkl.[---].|tkn.lbn[.---].| 5[67].3.3

[---.--]m[.---].|[-.]rbt.ṯbt.[---].|rbt.ṯbt.ḥš[n.---].|y.arṣ.ḥšn[.---].|t'td.tkl.[---].|t 5[67].3.2

p.|l alpm.ḫrṣ.yṣq|m.l rbbt.|yṣq-ḫym.w tbṯḫ.|kt.il.dt.rbtm.|kt.il.nbt.b ksp.|šmrgt.b dm.ḫrṣ.|kḥṯ.il.nḥt.|b ẓr.hd 4[51].1.31

.mkṯr.ap.t[---].|dgy.rbt.aṯr[t.ym].|qḥ.rṯt.b d k t[---].|rbt.'l.ydm[.---].|b mdd.il.y[--.---].|b ym.il.d[--.---.n]|hr.il.y[4[51].2.33

t.|al.tšt.b šdm.mm h.|b smkt.ṣat.npš h.|[-]mt[-].ṣba.rbt.|špš.w tgh.nyr.|rbt.w rgm.l aḫt k.|ṯtmnt.krt n.dbḥ.|db 16.1[125].36

[---.--]b.|[---.r]iš k.|[---.]bn 'n km.|[---.]alp.|[---.]ym.rbt.|[---.]b nhrm.|['b]r.gbl.'br.|q'l.'br.iht.|np šmm.šmšr.|l 3['NT.VI].6.5

rgbt

[---.]bn.ilm.|[m]t.šmḥ.p ydd.|il[.ǵ]zr.|b [-]dn.'.z.w.|rgbt.zbl. UG5.4.18

yḥmdn h.yrṯ y.|[---.]dmrn.l pn h yrd.|[---.]b'l.šm[.--.]rgbt yu.|[---]w yrmy[.q]rn h.|[---.-]ny h pdr.ttǵr.|[---.n]šr k 2001.2.9

rgm

[--]ty.|[---].ib'r.a[--.]ḏmr.|[---.]w mlk.w rg[m.---].|[--.rg]m.ank.[b]'r.[--]ny.|[--]n.bt k.[---.]b'[r.---].|[--]my.b d[-.-- 1002.54

.w tš'[d]n.npṣ h.|[---.]rgm.hn.[--]n.w aspt.[q]l h.|[---.rg]m.ank l[.--.--]rny.|[---.]ṯm.hw.i[--]ty.|[---].ib'r.a[--.]ḏmr. 1002.50

lk.yštal.b.hn[--].|hmt.w.anyt.hm.t'[rb].|mkr.hn d.w.rgm.ank[.--].|mlkt.ybqš.anyt.w.at[--].|w mkr n.mlk[.---]. 2008.2.12

n.|[---.a]nk.i[--.--]slm.w.yṯb.|[----.--]t.hw[-]y.h[--]r.w rgm.ank.|[---.]hdd tr[--.--]l.aṯrt y.|[--]ptm.ṣḥq.|[---.]rgm.h 1002.38

ṯḥm iwrḏr.|l iwrpḫn.|bn y.aḫ y.rgm.|ilm.tǵr k.|tšlm k.|ik y.lḥt.|spr.d likt.|'m.ṯryl.|mh y. 138.3

ṯḥm.iwrḏr.|l iwrpḫn.|bn y.aḫ y.rgm.|ilm.tǵr k.|tšlm k.|iky.lḥt.|spr.d likt.|'m.ṯryl.|mh y.r 138.3

k.'ṣ k.'bṣ k.'m y.p'n k.tls]|[m]n 'm y t[wtḥ.išd k.dm.rgm.iṯ.l y.d argmn k].|[h]wt.d aṯ[ny k.---.rgm.'ṣ].|w lḥšt.ab 7.2[130].17

smn].|'m y twtḥ.i[šd k.tk.ḫršn.-------------].|ǵr.ks.dm.r[gm.iṯ.l y.w argm k].|hwt.w aṯny k[.rgm.'ṣ.w lḥšt.abn].|tu 1['NT.IX].3.12

']ṣ k.'bṣ k.'m y.p'n k.|[tls]mn.[']m y.twtḥ.išd k.|[dm.rgm.iṯ.l y.]w argm k.hwt.|[w aṯny k.rgm.]'ṣ.w lḥšt.|[abn.rg 3['NT].4.57

ḥš k.'ṣ k.'bṣ k.|'m y.p'n k.tlsmn.'m y.|twtḥ.išd k.dm.rgm.|iṯ.l y.w argm k.|hwt.w aṯny k.rgm.|'ṣ.w lḥšt.abn.|ta 3['NT].3.17

ṯḥm[.t]lm[yn].|l ṯryl.um y.|rgm.|ugrt.tǵr k.|ugrt.tǵr k.|tšlm k.um y.|td'.ky.'rbt.|l pn. 1015.3

arḫ.td.rgm.b ǵr.|b p y.t'lgt.b lšn[y].|ǵr[.---]b.b pš y.t[--].|hwt.b'l. 2124.1

.k mtm.|tmtn.u ḫšt k.l ntn.|'tq.b d.aṯt.ab.ṣrry.|ik m.yrgm.bn.il.|krt.špḥ.lṭpn.|w qdš.u ilm.tmtn.|špḥ.lṭpn.l yḥ.| 16.1[125].20

l.ḏrdn.|b'l y.rgm.|bn.ḫrn k.|mǵy.|hbṭ.hw.|ḫrd.w.šl hw.|qr[-].|akl n.b. 2114.2

']dt.ṯpṯ.nhr.mlak.mṯḥr.yḥb[-.---.]|[---].mlak.bn.ktpm.rgm.b'l h.w y[--.---].|[---].ap.anš.zbl.b'l.šdmt.bg[--.---].|[---. 2.1[137].42

d.|ilm.p.k mtm.|'z.mid.|hm.nṯkp.|m'n k.|w.mnm.|rgm.d.tšm'.|ṯmt.w.št.|b.spr.'m y. 53[54].17

šmlšn.|w tb' ank.|'m mlakt h šm' h.|w b.'ly skn.yd' rgm h.|w ht ab y ǵm[--].|t[--.---].|ls[--.---].|ṣḥ[.---].|ky.m[- 1021.8

].|tšt.tb'[.---].|qrt.mlk[.---].|w.'l.ap.s[--.---].|b hm.w.rgm.hw.al[--].|atn.ksp.l hm.'d.|ilak.'m.mlk.|ht.lik[t.--.]ml 2008.2.6

rgm.ank.|[---.]hdd tr[--.--]l.aṯrt y.|[--]ptm.ṣḥq.|[---.]rgm.hy.[-]ḥ[-]y.ilak k.|[---.--]g k.yritn.mǵy.hy.w kn.|[---].ḥ 1002.41

.|šlm.l kb[d].awṣ.arbdd.|l kbd.š[d]m.ap.mṯn.rgmm.|argmn.lk.lk.'nn.ilm.|atm.bštm.w an.šnt.|uǵr.l rḥq.ilm.inbb 3['NT].4.76

t km.|db[ḥ.l krt.a]dn km.|'l.krt.tbun.km.|rgm.ṯ[rm.]rgm hm.|b ḏrt[.---.]krt.|[----]. 15[128].6.7

ṯḥm.ml[k.---].|l.mlk.[---].|rg[m].|hn.i[---].|ds[-.---].|t[--.---].|a[--.---].|[---].ksp.'m[.---] 2127.1.3

|[---.]škb.w m[--.]mlakt.|[---.]'l.w tš'[d]n.npṣ h.|[---.]rgm.hn.[--]n.w aspt.[q]l h.|[---.rg]m.ank l[.--.--]rny.|[---.]ṯ 1002.49

ilm.tǵr k.|tšlm k.|iky.lḥt.|spr.d likt.|'m.ṯryl.|mh y.rgmt.|w ht.aḫ y.|bn y.yšal.|ṯryl.p rgm.|l mlk.šm y.|w l h. 138.9

]at.brt.lb k.'nn.[---].|[--.]šdq.k ttn.l y.šn[.---].|[---.]bn.rgm.w yd'[.---]. 60[32].6

šṣa idn l y.|l šmn iṯr hw.|p iḫdn gnryn.|im mlkytn yrgm.|aḫnnn.|w iḫd. 1020.8

nm.šlm.|w.rgm.ṯṯb.l y.|bm.ṯy.ndr.|iṯt.'mn.mlkt.|w.rgm y.l[--].|lqt.w.pn.|mlk.nr b n. 50[117].16

--].|w ap.ht.k[--.]škn.|w.mṯnn[.---.]'mn k.|[-]štš.[---.]rgm y.|[-]wd.r[-.]pǵt.|[---.--]t.yd't.|[----.r]gm.|[---].kll h.|[- 54.1.22[13.2.7]

[--]ḏyn.w l.|[--]k b'lt bhtm[.--]tn k.|[--]y.l ihbt.yb[--].rgm y.|[---.]škb.w m[--.]mlakt.|[---.]'l.w tš'[d]n.npṣ h.|[---.] 1002.46

.'m y.p'n k.tls]|[m]n 'm y t[wtḥ.išd k.dm.rgm.iṯ.l y.d argmn k].|[h]wt.d aṯ[ny k.---.rgm.'ṣ].|w lḥšt.abn[.tant.šm 7.2[130].17

y.p'n k.|[tls]mn.[']m y.twtḥ.išd k.|[dm.rgm.iṯ.l y.]w argm k.hwt.|[w aṯny k.rgm.]'ṣ.w lḥšt.|[abn.rgm.l td]'.nš[m 3['NT].4.57

ṯḥ.i[šd k.tk.ḫršn.-------------].|ǵr.ks.dm.r[gm.iṯ.l y.w argm k].|hwt.w aṯny k[.rgm.'ṣ.w lḥšt.abn].|tunt.šmm.'m[.a 1['NT.IX].3.12

.|'m y.p'n k.tlsmn.'m y.|twtḥ.išd k.dm.rgm.|iṯ.l y.w argm k.|hwt.w aṯny k.rgm.|'ṣ.w lḥšt.abn.|tant.šmm.'m.arṣ 3['NT].3.18

.---].|[š]mm.rm.lk.prẓ kt.|[k]bkbm.ṯm.tpl k.lbnt.|[-.]rgm.k yrkt.'ṯqbm.|[---]m.'ẓpn.l pit.|m[--]m[.--]tm.w mdbḥt 13[6].14

r.|mẓll.ṯly.bt rb.|mṯb.arṣy.bt.y'bdr.|ap.mṯn.rgmm.|argm k.šskn m'.|mgn.rbt.aṯrt ym.|mǵẓ.qnyt.ilm.|hyn.'ly.l 4[51].1.21

w y'n.k[ṯr.w ḫs]s.|ṯṯb.b'l.l[hwt y].|ṯn.rgm.k[ṯr.w]ḫss.|šm'.m'.l al[iy]n b'l.|bl.ašt.ur[bt.]b bht m.| 4[51].6.3

mkt.ṣat.npš h.|[-]mt[-].ṣba.rbt.|špš.w tgh.nyr.|rbt.w rgm.l aḫt k.|ṯtmnt.krt n.dbḥ.|dbḥ.mlk.'šr.|'šrt.qḥ.tp k.b y 16.1[125].38

k.|ṯtmnt.bt.ḥmḥ h.|d[-]n.tbkn.w tdm.l y.[--].|[---].al.trgm.l aḫt k.|[---.]l [ ]dm.aḫt k.|yd't.k rḥmt.|al.tšt.b šdm. 16.1[125].31

.l arṣ.brqm. | bt.arzm.yklln h. | hm.bt.lbnt.y'msn h. | l yrgm.l aliyn b'l. | ṣḥ.ḫrn.b bhm k. | 'ḏbt.b qrb.hkl k. | tbl k.ġr 4[51].5.74
ldn.tld.[ilm.]n'mm.agzr ym. | bn.ym.ynqm.b a[p.]ḏ[d.r]gm.l il.ybl. | aṯt y.il.ylt.mh.ylt.ilmy n'mm. | agzr ym.bn ym 23[52].59
| bm.nšq.w hr.b ḥbq.ḥmḥmt.tqt[nṣn]. | tldn.šḥr.w šlm.rgm.l il.ybl.a[ṯt y]. | il.ylt.mh.ylt.yld y.šḥr.w šl[m]. | šu.'db.l 23[52].52
.rbt.k | mn.l p'n.mt. | hbr.w ql. | tšthwy.w k | bd hwt.w rgm. | l bn.ilm.mt. | ṯny.l ydd. | il.ġzr.tḥm. | aliyn.b'l. | [hw]t.al 4[51].8.29
ybl.arṣ.w pr. | 'ṣm.yraun.aliyn.b'l. | ṯt'.nn.rkb.'rpt. | tb'.rgm.l bn.ilm.mt. | ṯny.l ydd.il ġzr. | tḥm.aliyn.b'l.hwt.aliy. | q 5[67].2.8
]bd k. | l.p'n.b'l y[.mrḥqtm]. | šb' d.w.šb'[d.qlt]. | ankn.rgmt.l.b'l y. | l.špš.'lm.l.'ṯtrt. | l.'nt.l.kl.il.alṯ[y]. | nmry.mlk.'l 2008.1.6
b]t pdr[y.bt.ar.ahbt.ṭly.bt.rb.dd]. | arṣy bt.y['bdr.---]. | rgm l btl[t.'nt.ṯny.l ybmt.limm.tḥm.aliyn.b'l]. | hw[t.aliy.qr 7.2[130].13
ġlmm. | w 'rb n.l p'n.'nt.hbr. | w ql.tšthwy.kbd hyt. | w rgm.l btlt.'nt. | ṯny.l ymmt.limm. | tḥm.aliyn.b'l.hwt. | aliy.qr 3['NT].3.8
.[--].ṯtm.w.at. | nġṯ.w.ytn.hm.l k. | w.lḥt.alpm.ḫršm. | k.rgmt.l y.bly m. | alpm.aršt.l k.w.l y. | mn.bnš.d.l.i[--].'[m k]. | 2064.22
.iṯ.l y.]w argm k.hwt. | [w aṯny k.rgm.]'ṣ.w lḫšt. | [abn.rgm.l td]'.nš[m.w l t]bn. | [hmlt.a]rṣ.[tant.šmm.'m.ar]ṣ. | th 3['NT].4.59
mm.'m.arṣ. | thmt.'mn.kbkbm. | abn.brq.d l.td'.šmm. | rgm l td'.nšm.w l tbn. | hmlt.arṣ.at m.w ank. | ibġy h.b tk.ġr 3['NT].3.24
.'ṣ.w lḫšt.abn]. | tunt.šmm.'m[.arṣ.thmt.'mn.kbkbm]. | rgm.l td'.nš[m.w l tbn.hmlt.arṣ]. | at.w ank.ib[ġy h.---]. | w y' 1['NT.IX].3.15
ġt.minš.šdm l m'[rb]. | nrt.ilm.špš.mġy[t]. | pġt.l ahlm.rgm.l yṯ[pn.y] | bl.agrtn.bat.b ḏd k.[pġt]. | bat.b hlm w y'n.yṯ 19[1AQHT].4.212
g[--.---]. | [---.-]dm.mlak.ym.t'dt.ṯpṭ.nh[r.---]. | [---].an.rgmt.l ym.b'l km.ad[n km.ṯpṭ]. | [nhr.---.]hwt.gmr.hd.l wny[2.1[137].45
t.hm.iṯ[.'ẓm]. | abky.w aqbrn.ašt.b ḫrt. | i[lm.arṣ.b p h.rgm.l yṣa.b šp]t h.hwt h.knp.hrgb.b'l.ṯbr. | b'l.ṯbr.diy.hwt. 19[1AQHT].3.127
m.i[ṯ]. | 'ẓm.abky.w aqbrn h. | ašt.b ḫrt.ilm.arṣ. | b p h.rgm.l yṣa.b špt h.hwt[h]. | knp.nšrm.b'l.yṯbr. | b'l.ṯbr.diy h 19[1AQHT].3.113
. | ur.tisp k.yd.aqht.ġz[r]. | tšt k.bm.qrb m.asm. | b p h.rgm.l yṣa.b špt h[.hwt h]. | b nši 'n h.w tphn.in.[---]. | [-.]hlk. 19[1AQHT].2.75
šmt.iṯ. | 'ẓm.abky w aqbrn h.aštn. | b ḫrt.ilm.arṣ.b p h.rgm.l[yṣ]a. | b špt h.hwt h.knp.ṣml.b'[l]. | b'l.ṯbr.diy.hyt.tq[l. 19[1AQHT].3.141
t. | 'l h[wt].kṯr.w ḫss. | ṣḥq.kṯr.w ḫss. | yšu.g h.w yṣḥ. | l rgmt.l k.l ali | yn.b'l.ttbn.b'l. | l hwt y.ypṯḥ.ḫ | ln.b bht m.urb 4[51].7.23
'pr.'ẓm ny. | l b'l[-.---]. | ṯḥ.ksi.zbl.ym.w 'n.kṯr.w ḫss.l rgmt. | l k.l zbl.b'l.ṯnt.l rkb.'rpt.ht.ib k. | b'l m.ht.ib k.tmḫṣ.h 2.4[68].7
[---.d]bḥ. | t[---.id]k. | pn[m.al.ttn]. | 'm.[krt.msw]n. | w r[gm.l krt.]ṯ'. | tḥm[.pbl.mlk]. | qḥ.[ksp.w yr]q. | ḫrṣ[.yd.mqm 14[KRT].5.248
r[bt.kmn.l p'n.kṯr]. | hbr.w ql.t[šthwy.w kbd.hwt]. | w rgm l k[ṯr.w ḫss.ṯny.l hyn]. | d ḥrš.y[dm.tḥm.ṯr.il.ab k.] | hwt 1['NT.IX].3.4
d.rbt. | kmn.l p'n.kṯ. | hbr.w ql.tšth | wy.w kbd hwt. | w rgm.l kṯr. | w ḫss.ṯny.l h | yn.d ḥrš.ydm. | tḥm.al[iyn.b'l]. | h[3['NT.VI].6.21
kt. | 'm.ṯryl. | mh y.rgmt. | w ht.aḫ y. | bn y.yšal. | ṯryl.p rgm. | l mlk.šm y. | w l h.y'l m. | w h[t] aḫ y. | bn y.yšal. | ṯryl. 138.12
kt. | 'm.ṯryl. | mh y.rgmt. | w ht.aḫ y. | bn y.yšal. | ṯryl.p rgm. | l mlk.šm y. | w l h[-] y'l m. | bn y.yšal. | ṯryl.w rgm. | ṯṯb 138.12
. | [y]šlm.l k. | [il]m.tšlm k. | [tġ]r k. | [--]y.ibr[-]. | [--]wy.rgm l. | mlkt.ugrt. | [--]kt.rgmt. | [--]y.l.ilak. | [---].'m y. | [---]m 1016.8
l. | k iṯ.zbl.b'l.arṣ. | gm.yṣḥ.il.l btlt. | 'nt.šm'.l btlt.'n[t]. | rgm.l nrt.il.šp[š]. | pl.'nt.šdm.y špš. | pl.'nt.šdm.il.yšt k. | [b]'l. 6[49].3.24
-].amr. | [ṯn]y.d't hm.išt.ištm.yitmr.ḥrb.ltšt. | [--]n hm.rgm.l ṯr.ab h.il.tḥm.ym.b'l km. | [adn]km.ṯpṭ.nhr.tn.il m.d t 2.1[137].33
l.tpl.al.tšthwy.pḫr [m'd.qmm.a--.am] | r ṯny.d't km.w rgm.l ṯr.a[b.-.il.ṯny.l pḫr]. | m'd.tḥm.ym.b'l km.adn km.ṯ[pṭ. 2.1[137].16
---]. | dm.mt.aṣ[ḫ.---]. | yd.b qrb[.---]. | w lk.ilm.[---]. | w rgm.l [---]. | b mud.ṣin[.---]. | mud.ṣin[.---]. | iṯm.mui[-.---]. | d 5[67].3.21
.ydy]. | mrṣ.grš[m.zbln]. | in.b ilm.'[ny h.yrb']. | yḫmš.rgm.[my.b ilm]. | ydy.mrṣ.g[ršm.zbln]. | in.b ilm.'n[y h.]yṯdṯ. 16[126].5.17
m.[ydy.mrṣ]. | gršm.z[bln.in.b ilm]. | 'ny h.y[ṯny.yṯlṯ]. | rgm.my.b[ilm.ydy]. | mrṣ.grš[m.zbln]. | in.b ilm.'[ny h.yrb']. 16[126].5.14
lm]. | ydy.mrṣ.g[ršm.zbln]. | in.b ilm.'n[y h.]yṯdṯ. | yšb'.rgm.[my.]b ilm. | ydy.mrṣ.gršm zbln. | in.b ilm.'ny h. | w y'n. 16[126].5.20
.hn.ibm.šṣq l y. | p.l.ašt.aṯt y. | n'r y.ṯh.l pn.ib. | hn.hm.yrgm.mlk. | b'l y.tmġyy.hn. | alpm.ššwm.hnd. | w.mlk.b'l y.b 1012.30
tḥm.rgm. | mlk. | l ḥyil. | lm.tlik.'m y. | ik y.aškn. | 'ṣm.l bt.dml. | p 1010.1
aršmg.mru. | b'l.šlm.'bd. | awr.ṯġrn.'bd. | 'bd.ḫmn.šm'.rgm. | šdn.[k]bš. | šdyn.mḫ[ṣ]. | aṯry.mḫṣ. | b'ln.mḫṣ. | y[ḫ]ṣdq. 2084.12
pn. | yṣmdnn.ṣmdm.gpn.yšql.šdmt h. | km gpn. | šb' d.yrgm.'l.'d.w 'rbm.t'nyn. | w šd.šd ilm.šd aṯrt.w rḥm. | 'l.išt.š 23[52].12
---]. | w.mlk.b'l y. | lm.škn.hnk. | l 'bd h.alpm.š[šw]m. | rgmt.'ly.ṯh.lm. | l.ytn.hm.mlk.[b]'l y. | w.hn.ibm.šṣq l y. | p.l. 1012.25
tḥm.špš. | l.'mrpi.rgm. | 'm špš.kll.mid m. | šlm. | l.[--]n.špš. | ad[.']bd h.uk.škn. 2060.2
b.b hkl. | w ywsrnn.ggn h. | lk.l ab k.yṣb.lk. | l[ab]k.w rgm.'ny. | l k[rt.adn k.]ištm[']. | w tqġ[.udn.k ġz.ġzm]. | tdbr. 16.6[127].28
twtḥ.išd k. | [dm.rgm.iṯ.l y.]w argm k.hwt. | [w aṯny k.rgm.]'ṣ.w lḫšt. | [abn.rgm.l td]'.nš[m.w l t]bn. | [hmlt.a]rṣ.[ta 3['NT].4.58
. | twtḥ.išd k.dm.rgm. | iṯ.l y.w argm k. | hwt.w aṯny k.rgm. | 'ṣ.w lḫšt.abn. | tant.šmm.'m.arṣ. | thmt.'mn.kbkbm. | a 3['NT].3.19
-----]. | ġr.ks.dm.r[gm.iṯ.l y.w argm k]. | hwt.w aṯny k[.rgm.'ṣ.w lḫšt.abn]. | tunt.šmm.'m[.arṣ.thmt.'mn.kbkbm]. | rg 1['NT.IX].3.13
ḥ.išd k.dm.rgm.iṯ.l y.d argmn k]. | [h]wt.d aṯ[ny k.---.rgm.'ṣ]. | w lḫšt.abn[.tant.šmm.'m.arṣ.thmt]. | 'm kbkbm[.ab 7.2[130].18
qd y. | [--.]mt.kl.amt.w an.mtm.amt. | [ap.m]ṯn.rgmm.argm.qštm. | [----.]mhrm.ht.tṣdn.tinṯt. | [---]m.tṣḥq.'nt.w b lb 17[2AQHT].6.39
ym.ask. | šlm.l kb[d].awṣ.arbdd. | l kbd.š[d]m.ap.mṯn.rgmm. | argmn.lk.lk.'nn.ilm. | atm.bštm.w an.šnt. | uġr.l rḥq.i 3['NT].4.75
pdry.b ar. | mẓll.ṭly.bt rb. | mṯb.arṣy.bt.y'bdr. | ap.mṯn.rgmm. | argm k.šskn m'. | mgn.rbt.aṯrt ym. | mġẓ.qnyt.ilm. | h 4[51].1.20
.l ẓr.qdqd y. | [--.]mt.kl.amt.w an.mtm.amt. | [ap.m]ṯn.rgmm.argm.qštm. | [----.]mhrm.ht.tṣdn.tinṯt. | [---]m.tṣḥq.'nt 17[2AQHT].6.39
tḥm.pgn. | l.mlk.ugrt. | rgm. | yšlm.l k.[il]m. | tġr k.tšlm k. | hn ny.'m n.š[l]m. | ṯm ny 2061.3
tḥm.mlk. | l.ṯryl.um y.rgm. | yšlm.l k.ilm. | tġr k.tšlm k. | lḥt.šlm.k.lik[t]. | um y.'m y 2009.1.2
[tḥm.---]. | [l.---]. | [a]ḫt y.rgm. | [y]šlm.l k. | [il]m.tšlm k. | [tġ]r k. | [--]y.ibr[-]. | [--]wy.rg 1016.3
tḥm.iwrdr. | l.plsy. | rgm. | yšlm.l k. | l.trġds. | w.l.klby. | šm't.ḫti. | nḫtu.ht. | hm.in 53[54].3
w.k.rgm.špš. | mlk.rb.b'l y.u. | '[--.]mlakt.'bd h. | [---.]b'l k.yḫpn. | 1018.1
l.mlkt. | adt y.rgm. | tḥm.illdr. | 'bd k.. | l.p'n a[dt y]. | šb' d[.w šb' d]. | mrḥq 1014.2
[l.ml]k.[b'l y]. | rg[m]. | tḥm.wr[--]. | yšlm.[l] k. | ilm.t[ġ]r k. | tšlm k. | lm[.l.]li 2010.2
l mlkt.u[m] y. | [rg]m[.]t[ḥm]. | mlk.bn [k]. | [l].p'n.um [y]. | qlt[.l um] y. | yšl 1013.2
l.mlkt. | um y.rgm. | tḥm.mlk. | bn k. | l.p'n.um y. | qlt.l.um y. | yšlm.ilm. | tġ 50[117].2
l.mlk.ugrt. | aḫ y.rgm. | tḥm.mlk.ṣr.aḫ k. | y[š]lm.l k.ilm. | tġr k.tšlm k. | hn ny. 2059.2
l.mlk[.u]grt. | iḫ y.rgm. | [tḥ]m.m[lk.-]bl[-]. | yšlm.l[k].ilm. | tġr.tšl[m] k. | [-----]. 2159.2
.t[g]yn. | bn k. | l.p['n.adn y]. | q[lt.---]. | l.yb[nn]. | b'l y.r[gm]. | tḥm.'bd[--]. | 'bd k. | l p'n.b'l y. | ṯn id.šb' d. | mrḥqtm. 2115.2.2
l.mlk.b['l y]. | r[gm]. | tḥm.rb.mi[--.']bd k. | l.p'n.b'l y[.mrḥqtm]. | šb' d.w.š 2008.1.2
l.ybnn. | adn y. | rgm. | tḥm.t[g]yn. | bn k. | l.p['n.adn y]. | q[lt.---]. | l.yb[nn]. | b' 2115.1.3
l um y.adt ny. | rgm. | tḥm.tlmyn. | w.aḫtmlk 'bd k. | l.p'n.adt ny. | mrḥqtm. | 51[95].2

l.mlkt.|adt y.|rgm.|tḥm.tlmyn.|ʻbd k.|l.pʻn.|adt y.|šbʻ d.|w.šbʻ id.|mrḥ 52[89].3
l.mlk.bʻ[l] y.|rgm.|tḥm.tptb[ʻl].|[ʻ]bd k.|[l.p]ʻn.bʻl y.|[šbʻ] d.šbʻ [d].|[mr 2063.2
l.rb.khnm.|rgm.|tḥm.[---].|yšlm[.l k.ilm].|tšlm[k.tǵr] k.|tʻzz[k.---.]l 55[18].2
k.tšlm k.|hn ny.ʻm n.|šlm.ṯm ny.|ʻm k.mnm[.š]lm.|rgm.ṯṯ[b].|any kn.dt.|likt.mṣrm.|hn dt.b.ṣr.|mtt.by.|gšm. 2059.9
t.---.ṯn.l ʻš]|rm.pam[t.---].|š dd šmn[.gdlt.w.---].|brr.r[gm.yṯṯb.b ṯdṯ.ṯn].|l šmn.ʻ[ly h.gdlt.rgm.yṯṯb].|brr.b šbʻ[.ṣ APP.II[173].49
[.---].|ṯn.l.ʻšrm.pamt.[---].|š.dd.šmn.gdlt.w.[---.brr].|rgm.yṯṯb.b.ṯdṯ.ṯn[.--.šmn].|ʻly h.gdlt.rgm.yṯ[ṯb.brr].|b.[šb]ʻ. 35[3].45
gdlt.w.[---.brr].|rgm.yṯṯb.b.ṯdṯ.ṯn[.--.šmn].|ʻly h.gdlt.rgm.yṯ[ṯb.brr].|b.[šb]ʻ.ṣbu.[š]pš.w.ḥly[t].ʻ[r]b[.š]p[š].|w [ḥl. 35[3].46
.gdlt.w.---].|brr.r[gm.yṯṯb.b ṯdṯ.ṯn].|l šmn.ʻ[ly h.gdlt.rgm.yṯṯb].|brr.b šbʻ[.ṣbu.špš.w ḥl]|yt.ʻrb špš[.w ḥl.mlk.w.b APP.II[173].50
k.|hn ny.ʻm n.š[l]m.|ṯm ny.ʻ[m.]bn y.|mnm.[šl]m[.r]gm[.ṯṯb].|ky.lik.bn y.|lḥt.akl.ʻm y.|mid y w ǵbn y.|w.bn 2061.8
.p rgm.|l mlk.šm y.|w l h[-] yʻl m.|bn y.yšal.|ṯryl.w rgm.|ṯṯb.l aḫ k.|l adn k. 138.17
l ny.ʻm n[y].|kll.šlm.|ṯm ny.ʻm.um y.|mnm.šlm.|w.rgm.ṯṯb.l y.|bm.ṯy.ndr.|iṯt.ʻmn.mlkt.|w.rgm y.l[--].|lqt.w. 50[117].13
ʻm n[.š]lm.|w.ṯm [ny.ʻm.mlkt.u]m y.|mnm[.šlm].|w.rgm[.ṯṯb.l] y.|hl ny.ʻmn.|mlk.b.ṯy ndr.|iṯt.w.ht.|[-]sny.udr 1013.11
y.ht.ʻm[ny].|kll.šlm.ṯm ny.|ʻm.um y.mnm.šlm.|w.rgm.ṯṯb.l y.|w.mndʻ.k.ank.|aḥš.mǵy.mndʻ.|k.igr.w.u.[--].|ʻ 2009.1.9
|šbʻ d.|w.šbʻ id.|mrḥqtm.|qlt.|ʻm.adt y.|mnm.šlm.|rgm.ṯṯṯb.|l.ʻbd h. 52[89].14
ʻl y.|ṯn id.šbʻ d.|mrḥqtm.|qlt.ʻm.|bʻl y.mnm.|šlm.|[r]gm[.ṯṯb].|[l.]ʻbd[k]. 2115.2.11
.|šlm.|w.ap.ank.|nḫt.ṯm ny.|ʻm.adt ny.|mnm.šlm.|rgm.ṯṯb.|l.ʻbd k. 51[95].17
hnn.|[---.kll].šlm.|[---.ṯ]mn.ʻm k.|[m]nm.šlm.|[---.w.r]gm.ṯṯb. 2171.5
.l š[ty].ṣḥt km.|db[ḥ.l krt.a]dn km.|ʻl.krt.tbun.km.|rgm.ṯ[rm.]rgm hm.|b ḏrt[.---.]krt.|[----]. 15[128].6.7
lḥ]m.l šty.ṣḥt k[m].|[---.]brk.t[---].|[ʻl.]krt.tbkn.|[--.]rgm.ṯrm.|[--.]mtm.tbkn.|[--]t.w b lb.tqb[-].|[--]m[-].mtm.u 15[128].5.13
lk.šm y.|w l h.yʻl m.|w h[t] aḫ y.|bn y.yšal.|ṯryl.w rgm[.-].|ṯṯb.l aḫ k.|l adn k. 138.17
r.ḫ[--.---].|[--]n.bʻ[l.---].|w [--]d.[---].|idk[.-]it[.---].|trgm[.-]dk[.---].|mʻbd[.-]r[-.-]š[-.---].|w kšt.[--]šq h[.---].|bn 2158.2.3
[---.k]rgmš.|[l.m]lk.ugrt.rgm[.-]y.|[---.--]m.rgm.|[---.]šknt.|[---.--]dy. 1011.2
[m k].|l.alpm.w.l.y[n.--]t.|w.bl.bnš.hw[-.--]y.|w.k.at.trg[m.--].|w.[---]n.w.s[--].|[--]m.m[---].|[---.m]ndʻ[.--]. 2064.27
.|[tǵ]r k.|[--]y.ibr[-].|[--]wy.rgm l.|mlkt.ugrt.|[--]kt.rgmt.|[--]y.l.ilak.|[---].ʻm y.|[---]m.w.lm.|[---.]w.ʻm k.|[---] 1016.10
[---].ank.l km[.---].|l y.ank.aššu[.---.]w[.---].|w hm.at.tr[gm.---].|w.drm.ʻtr[--.---].|w ap.ht.k[--.]škn.|w.mṯnn[.---. 54.1.18[13.2.3]
k.n[--]n[.---].|kst.l[--.---].|w.hw.uy.ʻn[--.---].|l ytn.w rgm[.---].|w yrdnn.an[--.---].|[---].ank.l km[.---].|l y.ank.aš 54.1.14[13.1.11]
--.---].|u[-]šhr.nuš[-.---].|b [u]grt.w ht.a[--].|w hm.at.trg[m.---].|w sip.u hw[.---].|w ank.u šbt[--.---].|ank.n[--]n[. 54.1.8[13.1.5]
k.|[-]štš.[---.]rgm y.|[-]wd.r[-.]pǵt.|[---.--]t.ydʻt.|[----.r]gm.|[---].kll h.|[---.--]l y.|[---.--]r.|[--.]wk[--.---].|[--].lm.l 54.1.25[43.8]
|[-]r.l šlmt.šl[m.---.--]|r h.p šlmt.p šlm[.---].|bt.l bnš.trg[m.---].|l šlmt.l šlm.b[--.---]|b y.šnt.mlit.t[--.---].|ymǵy k 59[100].5
n[--.---].|rg[m.---].|nǵṯ[.---].|d.yqḥ[.---].|hm.ṯn.[---].|hn dt.[---].|[--- 2064.2
[---.k]rgmš.|[l.m]lk.ugrt.rgm[.-]y.|[---.--]m.rgm.|[---.]šknt.|[---.--]dy. 1011.3
|[---.]ṯm.hw.i[--]ty.|[---].ibʻr.a[--.]ḏmr.|[---.]w mlk.w rg[m.---].|[--.rg]m.ank.[b]ʻr.[--]ny.|[--]n.bt k.[---.]bʻ[r.---].|[1002.53
ny.ṯp[--.---].|[---.--]zn.a[--.---].|[---.--]y.ns[--.---].|[---.]trgm[.-----].|[---.]alp.p[--.---].|[--.]ht.ap[.---].|[---.]iln[--.---]. 63[26].2.2
|ʻm ny.šlm.|kll.|w mnm.|šlm ʻm.|um y.|ʻm y.ṯṯṯb.|rgm. 1015.20

rgmt

ilm.tǵr k.|tšlm k.|ik y.lḥt.|spr.d likt.|ʻm.ṯryl.|mh y.rgmt.|w ht.aḫ y.|bn y.yšal.|ṯryl.p rgm.|l mlk.šm y.|w l h[138.9

rwẓ

ilḥu.|[m]rḥ h.yiḫd.b yd.|[g]rgr h.bm.ymn.|[w]yqrb.trẓẓ h.|[---].mǵy h.w ǵlm.|[a]ḫt h.šib.yṣat.mrḥ h.|l tl.yṣb.p 16.1[125].49
ym.|bl.nmlk.ydʻ.ylḥn.|w yʻn.lṭpn.il d pi|d dq.anm.l yrẓ.|ʻm.bʻl.l yʻdb.mrḥ.|ʻm.bn.dgn.k tms m.|w ʻn.rbt.aṯrt y 6.1.50[49.1.22]

rwy

uṯryn.|[ubd]y.mrynm.|[š]d.bn.ṣnrn.b d.nrn.|[š]d.bn.rwy.b d.ydln.|[š].bn.trn.b d.ibrmḏ.|[š]d.bn.ilṯtmr.b d.tbbr. 82[300].1.9
.|w.[n]ḥl hm.|b[n.---].|bn.gzry.|bn.atyn.|bn.ttn.|bn.rwy.|bn.ʻmyn.|bdl.mrynm.|bn.ṣqn.|bn.šyn.|bn.prtn.|bn.y 113[400].3.4

rwm

br.kṯr.ṯbm.|w tšt.ʻnt.gṯr.bʻlt.mlk.bʻ|lt.drkt.bʻlt.šmm.rmm.|[bʻl]t.kpṯ.w ʻnt.di.dit.rḫpt.|[---.-]rm.aklt.ʻgl.ʻl.mšt.|[- UG5.2.1.7
yʻn.kṯr.|[w ḫss.]ṯṯb.bʻl.l hwt y.|[ḥš.]bht h.tbnn.|[ḥš.]trmm.hkl h.|y[tl]k.l lbnn.w ʻṣ h.|l[šr]yn.mḥmd.arz h.|h[n. 4[51].6.17
.hk[l.ṯpṭ].nhr.bt k.[---.]šp[-.---].|[ḥš.bh]t h.tbn[n.ḥ]š.trm[mn.hkl h.---.]bt.|[---.-]k.mnh[-.---.-]š bš[-.]t[-].ǵlm.l šdt 2.3[129].10
n[t.bnt.]bht |k.y ilm.bnt.bh[t k].a[l.tš]mḫ.|al.tšmḫ.b r[m.h]kl[k].|al.aḫd.hm.b y[--] y.[---]b[-].|b gdlt.arkt y.am[3[ʻNT.VI].5.29
|[bnt.bht]k.y ilm[.bnt.bht k.--].|[al.tšmḫ.]al.tš[mḫ.b rm.h]|[kl k.al.]aḫd hm.[---].|[---.b]gdlt.ar[kt y.am--].|[---. 18[3AQHT].1.8
š.bht m.k[ṯr].|ḥš.rmm.hk[l m].|ḥš.bht m.tbn[n].|ḥš.trmmn.hk[l m].|b tk.ṣrrt.ṣpn.|alp.šd.aḫd bt.|rbt.kmn.hkl.| 4[51].5.116
y.[w ykbdn h.---].|ṯr.il[.ab h.---].|ḥš b[ht m.tbnn.ḥš.trmmn.hkl m].|b tk.[---].|bn.[---].|a[--.---.] 1[ʻNT.IX].3.27
m].|[w]yʻn.aliy[n.bʻl].|[--]b[.---].|ḥš.bht m.k[ṯr].|ḥš.rmm.hk[l m].|ḥš.bht m.tbn[n].|ḥš.trmmn.hk[l m].|b tk.ṣrr 4[51].5.114
[r].|[---.]hrn.w[---.]tbʻ.k[ṯ]r w [ḫss.t]bn.bht zbl ym.|[trm]m.hk[l.ṯpṭ].nhr.bt k.[---.]šp[-.---].|[ḥš.bh]t h.tbn[n.ḥ]š.t 2.3[129].9
ykb[dn h.--]r y[---].|[---.k]ṯr.w ḫ[ss.t]bʻ.b[n.]bht.ym[.rm]m.hkl.ṯpṭ nh[r].|[---.]hrn.w[---.]tbʻ.k[ṯ]r w [ḫss.t]bn.bht 2.3[129].7
m.|[yqḥ.]il.mštʻltm.mštʻltm.l riš.agn.|hl h.[t]špl.hl h.trm.hl h.tṣḥ.ad ad.|w hl h.tṣḥ.um.um.tirk m.yd.il.k ym.|w 23[52].32
nbb.|kt ǵr k.ank.ydʻt.|[-]n.atn.at.mṯb k[.---].|[š]mm.rm.lk.prẓ kt.|[k]bkbm.ṯm.tpl k.lbnt.|[-.]rgm.k yrkt.ʻṯqbm. 13[6].12
-.---].|[-.]ʻl[.---].|rʻm[-.---].|mn[-.---].|hyrm.h[--.---].|yrmm h[--.---].|mlk.gbʻ h d [---].|ibr.k l hm.d l h q[--.---].|l 9[33].2.2
].|ugrt.š l ili[b.---].|rt.w ʻṣrm.l[.---].|pamt.w bt.[---].|rmm.w ʻl[y.---].|bt.il.ṯq[l.---.kbd].|w bdḥ.k[--.---].|ʻṣrm.l i[APP.II[173].41
.|h.u qšt pn hdd.b y[.----].|ʻm.b ym bʻl ysy ym[.---].|rmm.ḫnpm.mḫl[.---].|mlk.nhr.ibr[.---].|zbl bʻl.ǵlm.[---].|ṣǵ 9[33].2.8
[-----].|[---.mid.rm.]krt.|[b tk.rpi.]arṣ.|[b pḫr].qbṣ.dtn.|[w t]qrb.w ld.|bn.t 15[128].3.2
pǵ[t.---].|tld.pǵ[t.---].|tld.pǵ[t.---].|tld.p[ǵt.---].|mid.rm[.krt].|b tk.rpi.ar[ṣ].|b pḫr.qbṣ.dtn.|ṣǵrt hn.abkrn.|tbrk 15[128].3.13

m.tlḥk. | šmm.ṯtrp. | ym.ḏnbtm. | tnn.l šbm. | tšt.trks. | l mrym.l bt[.---]. | p l.tb‘[.---]. | hmlt ḫt.[---]. | l.tp[-]m.[---]. | n[- 1003.10
bat. | [---.]inšt. | [--]u.l tštql. | [---].ṭry.ap.l tlḥm. | [l]ḥm.trmmt.l tšt. | yn.tǵẓyt.špš. | rpim.tḥtk. | špš.tḥtk.ilnym. | ‘d k.i 6.6[62.2].43
l.sk.w [---] h. | ybm h.šb‘[.---]. | ǵzr.ilḥu.t[---]l. | trm.tṣr.trm[.‘]tqt. | tbky.w tšnn.[tt]n. | g h.bky.b ḥ[y k.a]b n. | nšmḫ. 16.2[125].96
.b‘l k.yṣḥ.‘n. | [gpn].w ugr.b ǵlmt. | [‘mm.]ym.bn.ẓlmt.r | [mt.pr‘]t.ibr.mnt. | [ṣḥrrm.ḥbl.‘]rpt. | [---.---.-]ḥt. | [---.---]m 4[51].7.55
. | b‘l.yṣḥ.‘n.gpn. | w ugr.bn.ǵlmt. | ‘mm ym.bn.ẓlm[t]. | rmt.pr‘t.ibr[.mnt]. | ṣḥrrm.ḥbl[.--]. | ‘rpt.tḥt.[---] | m ‘ṣrm.ḥ[- 8[51FRAG].9
ḫdm.šb‘r. | amrr.k kbkb.l pnm. | aṯr.btlt.‘nt. | w b‘l.tb‘.mrym.ṣpn. | idk.l ttn.pnm. | ‘m.il.mbk.nhrm. | qrb.apq.thmt 4[51].4.19
ḫ.btlt.‘nt.td‘ṣ. | p‘nm.w tr.arṣ. | idk.l ttn.pnm. | ‘m.b‘l.mrym.ṣpn. | b alp.šd.rbt.kmn. | ṣḥq.btlt.‘nt.tšu. | g h.w tṣḥ.tbš 4[51].5.85
pdm. | tḥt.‘nt.arṣ.ṯlṯ.mtḥ.ǵyrm. | idk.l ttn pnm.‘m.b‘l. | mrym.ṣpn.b alp.šd.rbt.kmn. | hlk.aḫt h.b‘l.y‘n.tdrq. | ybnt.ab 3[‘NT].4.82
rt.ydd.il.ǵzr. | tb‘.w l.yṯb ilm.idk. | l ytn.pnm.‘m.b‘l. | mrym.ṣpn.w y‘n. | gpn.w ugr.tḥm.bn ilm. | mt.hwt.ydd.bn.il. 5[67].1.11
y‘db.ksa.w.yṯb. | tqru.l špš.um h.špš.um.ql bl. | ‘m b‘l.mrym.ṣpn.mnt y.nṯk. | nḥš.šmrr.nḥš.‘q šr ln h. | mlḫš.abd.ln UG5.7.9
lbt.ilm išt. | klt.bt.il.ḏbb.imtḫṣ.ksp. | itrṯ.ḫrṣ.ṭrd.b‘l. | b mrym.ṣpn.mšṣṣ.[-]k‘[-]. | udn h.grš h.l ksi.mlk h. | l nḫt.l kḥṯ 3[‘NT].4.45
.--]. | l bl.sk.w [---] h. | ybm h.šb‘[.---]. | ǵzr.ilḥu.t[---]l. | trm.tṣr.trm[.‘]tqt. | tbky.w tšnn.[tt]n. | g h.bky.b ḥ[y k.a]b n. 16.2[125].96
‘.k dw.k[rt]. | mnd‘.krt.mǵ[y.---]. | w qbr.tṣr.q[br]. | tṣr.trm.tnq[--]. | km.nkyt.ṯǵr[.---]. | km.škllt.[---]. | ‘r.ym.l bl[.---] 16.2[125].88
l n‘m. | [---.]w rm ṯlbm ṯlb. | [---.-]pr l n‘m. | [---.-]mt w rm tp h. | [---.-]ḥb l n‘m. | [---.]ymǵy. | [---.]rm ṯlbm. | [---.--]m UG5.5.5
[---.]w rm tp h. | [---.-]lu mm l n‘m. | [---.]w rm ṯlbm ṯlb. | [---.-]pr l UG5.5.1
| [---.-]mt w rm tp h. | [---.-]ḥb l n‘m. | [---.]ymǵy. | [---.]rm ṯlbm. | [---.--]m. | [---.--]ḥ n‘m. UG5.5.8
[---.]w rm tp h. | [---.-]lu mm l n‘m. | [---.]w rm ṯlbm ṯlb. | [---.-]pr l n‘m. | [---.-]mt w rm tp h. | [---.-]ḥb l UG5.5.3
| [---.--]r.w ṯt pl.gdlt.[ṣ]pn.dqt. | [---.al]p ‘nt.gdlt.b ṯlṯt mrm. | [---.i]l š.b‘l š.aṯrt.š.ym š.[b‘]l knp. | [---.g]dlt.ṣpn.dqt.š 36[9].1.5

rḥ

ṯ.lk[.---]. | [--]kṯ.i[---.---]. | p.šn[-.---]. | w l ṭlb.[---]. | mit.rḥ[.---]. | ṯṭlb.a[--.---]. | yšu.g h[.---]. | i.ap.b‘[l.---]. | i.hd.d[---.- 5[67].4.3
[-]p[-]l[.---]. | k lli.[---]. | kpr.[šb‘.bnt.rḥ.gdm.w anhbm]. | w tqr[y.ǵlmm.b št.ǵr.---]. | [‘]d tš[b‘.tmt 7.2[130].3
| w ank.ib[ǵy h.---]. | [-].l y‘mdn.i[---.---]. | kpr.šb‘ bn[t.rḥ.gdm.w anhbm]. | kla[t.ṯǵ]r[t.bht.‘nt.w tqry.ǵlmm.b št.ǵr] 7.2[130].23
n[--.---.-]š[--]. | kpr.šb‘.bnt.rḥ.gdm. | w anhbm.klat.ṯǵrt. | bht.‘nt.w tqry.ǵlmm. | b št.ǵr. 3[‘NT].2.2
---]d[-]. | tnq[.---.]in[b]b.p‘r. | yd h[.--.]ṣ‘r.glgl. | a[---]m.rḥ.ḥḏ ‘[r]pt. | gl[.---.]yhpk.m[---]m. | s‘[--.]k[--]t. 13[6].34
t.npš.‘gl. | [---.-]nk.aštn.b ḫrt. | ilm.arṣ.w at.qḥ. | ‘rpt k.rḥ k.mdl k. | mṭrt k.‘m k.šb‘t. | ǵlm k.ṯmn.ḫnzr k. | ‘m k.pdry 5[67].5.7
n]. | šm‘.l dnil.[mt.rpi]. | mt.aqht.ǵzr.[šṣat]. | btlt.‘nt.k [rḥ.npš h]. | k iṯl.brlt h.[b h.p‘nm]. | ṭṭṭ.‘l[n.pn h.td‘.b ‘dn]. | ks 19[1AQHT].2.92
.‘l.udn.š[pk.km]. | šiy.dm h.km.šḫ[ṭ.l brk h]. | yṣat.km.rḥ.npš[h.km.iṯl]. | brlt h.km.qṭr.[b ap h.---]. | ‘nt.b ṣmt.mhr 18[3AQHT].4.36
. | ṯlṯ id.‘l.udn.špk.km.šiy. | dm.km.šḫṭ.l brk h.tṣi.km. | rḥ.npš h.km.iṯl.brlt h.km. | qṭr.b ap h.b ap.mhr h.ank. | l aḥ 18[3AQHT].4.25
m.dnil.[--] h[.---]. | riš.r[--.--]ḥ[.---]y[.---.-]nt.[š]ṣat[k.]rḥ.npš.hm. | k.iṯl.brlt n[-.k qṭr.b ap -]. | tmǵyn.tša.g h[m.w tṣ 19[1AQHT].2.87

rḥb

.t[b]ky k. | ab.ǵr.b‘l.ṣ[p]n.ḥlm. | qdš.nny.ḥ[l]m.adr. | ḥl.rḥb.mk[npt]. | ap.krt bn[m.il]. | špḥ.lṭpn[.w qdš]. | bkm.t‘r[b.‘ 16.2[125].109
rry. | tbky k.ab.ǵr.b‘l. | ṣpn.ḥlm.qdš. | any.ḥlm.adr.ḥl. | rḥb.mknpt.ap. | [k]rt.bnm.il.špḥ. | lṭpn.w qdš.‘l. | ab h.y‘rb.yb 16.1[125].9

rḥbn

-.ṯ]y.al.an[k.--.]il[m.--]y. | [--.m]ṣlm.pn y[.-.]tlkn. | [---.]rḥbn.hm.[-.]aṯr[.---]. | [--]šy.w ydn.b‘[l.---]n. | [--]‘.k yn.hm.l. 1002.60
b.gt.mlkt.b.rḥbn. | ḫmšm.l.mitm.zt. | w.b d.krd. | ḫmšm.l.mit. | arb‘.kbd. 1096.1

rḥbt

[--.]aḫd[.-]. | tšm‘.mṯt.[ḥ]ry. | ṯṭbḫ.šmn.[m]ri h. | t[p]tḥ.rḥbt.yn. | ‘l h.ṯr h.tš‘rb. | ‘l h.tš‘rb.ẓby h. | ṯr.ḫbr.rbt. | ḫbr.ṯrrt. 15[128].4.16
t[.yn]. | špq.ilm.kḥṯm.yn. | špq.ilht.ksat[.yn]. | špq.ilm.rḥbt yn. | špq.ilht.dkrt[.yn]. | ‘d.lḥm.šty.ilm. | w pq mrǵṯm.ṯd 4[51].6.53
aṯt h k.yṣḥ]. | šm‘[.l mṯt.ḥry]. | ṭbḫ.š[mn].mri k. | ptḥ.[rḥ]bt.yn. | ṣḥ.šb‘m.ṯr y. | ṯmnym.[ẓ]by y. | ṯr.ḫbr[.rb]t. | ḫbr[.ṯ 15[128].4.5
[-----]. | [ṯṭbḫ.šm]n.[mri h]. | [tptḥ.rḥ]bt.[yn]. | [---.]rp[.---]. | [---.ḫ]br[.---]. | bḫr[.--]t[.----]. | l mṯ 15[128].5.2
rd. | l kḥṯ.aliyn.b‘l. | w ymlk.b arṣ.il.kl h. | [---] š abn.b rḥbt. | [---] š abn.b kknt. 6.1.66[49.1.38]

rḥd

lqḥ.š‘rt. | urḫ.ln.kkrm. | w.rḥd.kd.šmn. | drt.b.kkr. | ubn.ḫṣḥ.kkr. | kkr.lqḥ.ršpy. | tmtrn. 1118.3
[--.---.]al.yns. | [---.]ysd k. | [---.--]r.dr.dr. | [---.--]y k.w rḥd. | [---]y ilm.d mlk. | y[ṯ]b.aliyn.b‘l. | yt‘dd.rkb.‘rpt. | [--].yd 4[51].3.8

rḥl

n.špš. | w pn.špš.nr. | b y.mid.w um. | tšmḫ.m ab. | w al.trḥln. | ‘tn.ḫrd.ank. | ‘m ny.šlm. | kll. | w mnm. | šlm ‘m. | um y 1015.12

rḥm

y.[--]. | [---].al.trgm.l aḫt k. | [---.]l [ ]dm.aḫt k. | yd‘t.k rḥmt. | al.tšt.b šdm.mm h. | b smkt.ṣat.npš h. | [-]mt[-].ṣba.rb 16.1[125].33
n.ilm.mt.b ḥrb. | tbq‘nn.b ḫṯr.tdry | nn.b išt.tšrpnn. | b rḥm.ttḥnn.b šd. | tdr‘nn.šir h.l tikl. | ‘ṣrm.mnt h.l tkly. | npr[6[49].2.34
r. | [---.aliy]n.b‘l. | [------.]yrḫ.zbl. | [--.kṯ]r w ḫss. | [---]n.rḥm y.ršp zbl. | [w ‘d]t.ilm.ṯlṯ h. | [ap]nk.krt.ṯ‘.‘[-]r. | [--.]b bt 15[128].2.6
[-----]. | [---.r]ḥm.tld. | [---.]ḫrm.ṯn.ym. | tš[.---.]ymm.lk. | hrg.ar[b‘.]ymm 13[6].2
‘l k.pht. | dry.b ḥrb.‘l k. | pht.šrp.b išt. | ‘l k.[pht.ṭḥ]n.b rḥ | m.‘[l k.]pht[.dr]y.b kbrt. | ‘l k.pht.[-]l[-]. | b šdm.‘l k.pht. 6[49].5.15
[----]. | w l [---]. | kd.[---]. | kd.t[---.ym.ymm]. | y‘tqn.w[rḥm.‘nt]. | tngṯ h.k lb.a[rḫ]. | l ‘gl h.k lb.ṯa[t]. | l imr h.km.lb.‘ 6[49].2.5
šmm.b yd.bn ilm.mt. | ym.ymm.y‘tqn.l ymm. | l yrḫm.rḥm.‘nt.tngṯ h. | k lb.arḫ.l ‘gl h.k lb. | ṯat.l imr h.km.lb. | ‘nt.a 6[49].2.27

rḥmy

b ḥlb.annḫ b ḫmat. | w ‘l.agn.šb‘ d m.dǵ[ṯ.---]t. | tlk m.rḥmy.w tṣd[.---]. | tḥgrn.ǵzr.n‘m.[---]. | w šm.‘rbm.yr[.---]. | 23[52].16
| šb‘ d.yrgm.‘l.‘d.w ‘rbm.t‘nyn. | w šd.šd ilm.šd aṯrt.w rḥm. | ‘l.išt.šb‘ d.ǵzrm.ṭb.[g]d.b ḥlb.annḫ b ḫmat. | w ‘l.agn.š 23[52].13
m.‘rbm.ṯn[nm]. | hlkm.b dbḥ n‘mt. | šd[.i]lm.šd.aṯrt.w rḥmy. | [---].y[ṯ]b. | [---]p.gp ym.w yṣǵd.gp..thm. | [yqḥ.]il.mš 23[52].28

rḥṣ

[--]m[.--]tm.w mdbḥt. | ḫr[.---.]ʻl.kbkbt. | nʻm.[--.-]llm.trtḥṣ. | btlt.ʻn[t].tptrʻ ṯd[h]. | limm.w tʻl.ʻm.il. | ab h.ḥpr.pʻl k. 13[6].18
ḥ.l krt. | w ǵlm.l ʻbd.il. | krt.yḫṯ.w ḥlm. | ʻbd.il.w hdrt. | yrtḥṣ.w yadm. | yrḥṣ.yd h.amt h. | uṣbʻt h.ʻd.ṯkm. | ʻrb.b ẓl.ḫ 14[KRT].3.156
[w yʻn].ṯr.ab h.il. | d[--].b bk.krt. | b dmʻ.nʻmn.ǵlm. | il.trḥṣ.w tadm. | rḥṣ[.y]d k.amt. | uṣb['t k.]ʻd[.ṯ]km. | ʻrb[.b ẓl.ḫ 14[KRT].2.62
t.l pnn h. | šṭ.alp.qdm h.mria.w tk. | pn h.tḥspn.m h.w trḥṣ. | ṭl.šmm.šmn.arṣ.ṭl.šm[m.t]sk h. | rbb.nsk h.kbkbm. | ttp 3[ʻNT].4.86
sat.ṯlḥnt. | [l]ṯlḥn.hdmm.ṯṯʻr.l hdmm. | [t]ḥspn.m h.w trḥṣ. | [ṭ]l.šmm.šmn.arṣ.rbb. | [r]kb ʻrpt.ṭl.šmm.tsk h. | [rb]b. 3[ʻNT].2.38
ʻbd.il. | krt.yḫṯ.w ḥlm. | ʻbd.il.w hdrt. | yrtḥṣ.w yadm. | yrḥṣ.yd h.amt h. | uṣbʻt h.ʻd.ṯkm. | ʻrb.b ẓl.ḫmt.lqḥ. | imr.dbḥ 14[KRT].3.157
n. | šlm.b ṣʻ.trḥṣ.yd h.bt | [l]t.ʻnt.uṣbʻt h.ybmt.limm. | [t]rḥṣ.yd h.b dm.ḏmr. | [u]ṣbʻt h.b mmʻ.mhrm. | [ṯ]ʻr.ksat.l ks 3[ʻNT].2.34
ḫṣb.bn.ṯlḥnm.ymḫ. | [b]bt.dm.ḏmr.yṣq.šmn. | šlm.b ṣʻ.trḥṣ.yd h.bt | [l]t.ʻnt.uṣbʻt h.ybmt.limm. | [t]rḥṣ.yd h.b dm.ḏ 3[ʻNT].2.32
--.---]. | [---.n]skt.nʻmn.nbl[.---]. | [--.]yṣq šmn.šlm.b ṣ[ʻ.trḥṣ]. | yd h.btlt.ʻnt.uṣbʻt[h.ybmt]. | limm.tiḫd.knr h.b yd[h. UG5.3.2.4
št.ǵr.---]. | [ʻ]d tš[bʻ.tmtḫṣ.---]. | klyn[.---]. | špk.l[---]. | trḥṣ.yd[h.---]. | [--.]yṣt ḏm[r.---]. | tšt[.r]imt.[l irt h.tšr.l dd.al 7.2[130].8
.il. | d[--].b bk.krt. | b dmʻ.nʻmn.ǵlm. | il.trḥṣ.w tadm. | rḥṣ[.y]d k.amt. | uṣb['t k.]ʻd[.ṯ]km. | ʻrb[.b ẓl.ḫmt]. | qḥ im[r.b 14[KRT].2.63
y[.km.]ilm[.w] ḫẓr[.k bn]. | [qd]š.lbum.trd.b n[p]šn y.trḥṣn.k ṯrm. | [--]b b[ht]. | [zbl.]ym.b hkl.ṯpṭ.nh[r].ytir.ṯr.il.a 2.3[129].20
[ilm.---].lbbmm.gdlt.ʻrb špš w ḥl. | [mlk.b ar]bʻt.ʻ[š]rt.yrtḥṣ.mlk.brr. | [b ym.ml]at.y[ql]n.al[p]m.yrḫ.ʻšrt. | [l bʻl.ṣ]p 36[9].1.10
b arbʻt.ʻšr[t]. | yrtḥṣ.mlk.b[rr]. | b ym.mlat. | tqln.alpm. | yrḫ.ʻšrt.l bʻ[l]. | dqt UG5.13.2
rḫ.[rišyn.b ym.ḥdṯ]. | šmtr.[uṯkl.l il.šlmm]. | b ṯlṯt ʻ[šrt.yrtḥṣ.mlk.brr]. | b arbʻ[t.ʻšrt.riš.argmn]. | w ṯn šm.l [bʻlt.bht 35[3].3
ḫ[.r]išyn.b ym.ḥdṯ. | [šmtr].uṯkl.l il.šlmm. | b [ṯlṯt].ʻšrt.yrtḥṣ.mlk. | br[r.]b a[r]bʻt.ʻšrt.riš. | arg[mn.w ṯn.]šm.l bʻlt. | b APP.II[173].3
alp.w š.l bʻlt bhtm. | b arbʻt ʻšrt.bʻl. | ʻrkm. | b ṯmnt.ʻšrt.yr | tḥṣ.mlk.brr. | ʻlm.tzǵ.b ǵb.ṣpn. | nḥkt.ksp.w ḫrṣ ṯʻ ṯn šm l UG5.12.A.5
.w.b y] | m.ḥdṯ.ṯn šm[.---.--]t. | b yrḫ.ši[-.b ar]bʻt.ʻš | rt.yr[tḥṣ.ml]k.brr. | ʻlm.š.š[--].l[--.]ʻrb.šp | š.w ḥl[.ml]k. | bn.aup[APP.II[173].55
rm.tdu.šrr. | ḥṯ m.tʻmt.[ʻ]ṯr.[k]m. | zbln.ʻl.riš h. | w ttb.trḥṣ.nn.b dʻt. | npš h.l lḥm.tpth. | brlt h.l ṯrm. | mt.dm.ḫt.šʻtq 16.6[127].10
.spu.ksm h.bt.bʻl. | [w m]nt h bt.il.ṯḥ.gg h.b ym. | [ṭi]ṭ.rḥṣ.npṣ h.b ym.rṯ. | [--.y]iḫd.il.ʻbd h.ybrk. | [dni]l mt rpi.ymr 17[2AQHT].1.34
. | spu.ksm y.bt.bʻl.[w]mn[t]. | y.bt.il.ṯḥ.gg y.b ym.ṭiṭ. | rḥṣ.npṣ y.b ym.rṯ. | dn.il.bt h.ymǵyn. | yštql.dnil.l hkl h. | ʻrb. 17[2AQHT].2.23
d.yd k.b [škrn]. | mʻms k.k šbʻt.yn.ṭ[ḫ]. | gg k.b ym.ṭiṭ.rḥṣ. | npṣ k.b ym rṯ.b uni[l]. | pnm.tšmḫ.w ʻl yṣhl pi[t]. | yprq. 17[2AQHT].2.7
mḫṣ.mḫṣ[.aḫ k]. | tkl.m[k]ly.ʻl.umt[k.--]. | d ttql.b ym.trtḥ[ṣ.--]. | [----.a]dm.tium.b ǵlp y[m.--]. | d alp šd.ẓu h.b ym. 19[1AQHT].4.203
-]. | [---.]y.mṯnt.w tḥ.ṭbt.n[--]. | [---.b]ṭnm w ttb.ʻl.bṯnt.trtḥ[ṣ.---]. | [---.t]ṯb h.aḫt.ppšr.w ppšrt[.---]. | [---.]k.drḫm.w 1001.2.5

rḥq

n.b alp.šd.rbt.kmn. | hlk.aḫt h.bʻl.yʻn.tdrq. | ybnt.ab h.šrḥq.aṯt.l pnn h. | šṭ.alp.qdm h.mria.w tk. | pn h.tḥspn.m h. 3[ʻNT].4.84
mm. | argmn.lk.lk.ʻnn.ilm. | atm.bštm.w an.šnt. | uǵr.l rḥq.ilm.inbb. | l rḥq.ilnym.ṯn.mṯpdm. | tḥt.ʻnt.arṣ.ṯlṯ.mtḥ.ǵyr 3[ʻNT].4.78
ṯr.w ḫss[.lk.lk.ʻnn.ilm.] | atm.bštm.w an[.šnt.kptr]. | l rḥq.ilm.ḥkp[t.l rḥq.ilnym]. | ṯn.mṯpdm.tḥt.[ʻnt.arṣ.ṯlṯ.mtḥ]. | 1[ʻNT.IX].3.19
[---.]n[--.---]. | [---.kpt]r.l r[ḥq.ilm.ḥkpt.l rḥq]. | [ilnym.ṯn.mṯpd]m.t[ḥt.ʻnt.arṣ.ṯlṯ.mtḥ. 2.3[129].2
[---.]n[--.---]. | [---.kpt]r.l r[ḥq.ilm.ḥkpt.l rḥq]. | [ilnym.ṯn.mṯpd]m.t[ḥt.ʻnt.arṣ.ṯlṯ.mtḥ.ǵyrm]. | [idk.]l y 2.3[129].2
.lk.ʻnn.ilm. | atm.bštm.w an.šnt. | uǵr.l rḥq.ilm.inbb. | l rḥq.ilnym.ṯn.mṯpdm. | tḥt.ʻnt.arṣ.ṯlṯ.mtḥ.ǵyrm. | idk.l ttn pn 3[ʻNT].4.79
ʻnn.ilm.] | atm.bštm.w an[.šnt.kptr]. | l rḥq.ilm.ḥkp[t.l rḥq.ilnym]. | ṯn.mṯpdm.tḥt.[ʻnt.arṣ.ṯlṯ.mtḥ]. | ǵyrm.idk.l yt[n 1[ʻNT.IX].3.19
]aliyn.bʻl. | [---.--]k.mdd il. | y[m.---.]l ṯr.qdqd h. | il[.--.]rḥq.b ǵr. | km.y[--.]ilm.b ṣpn. | ʻdr.l[ʻr].ʻrm. | ṯb.l pd[r.]pdrm. 4[51].7.5
b trbṣ.bn.amt. | qḥ.krt.šlmm. | šlmm.w ng.mlk. | l bt y.rḥq.krt. | l ḥẓr y.al.tṣr. | udm.rbt.w udm ṯrrt. | udm.ytnt.il w 14[KRT].3.132
[--]m.[---.] | gm.ṣḥ.l q[ṣ.ilm.---]. | l rḥqm.l p[-.---]. | ṣḥ.il.ytb.b[mrzḥ.---]. | bṯt.ʻllm n.[---]. | ilm.bt 1[ʻNT.X].4.3
m.rbt.w udm]. | [ṯrrt.udm.ytnt]. | [il.w ušn.ab.adm]. | [rḥq.mlk.l bt y]. | [ng.kr]t.l ḥ[ẓ]r y. | [-----]. | [---.ttbʻ]. | [mlakm 14[KRT].5.260
[.r]bt.w u[dm]. | [ṯ]rrt.udm.y[t]n[t]. | il.ušn.ab[.ad]m. | rḥq.mlk.l bt y. | n[g.]krt.l ḥẓ[r y]. | w yʻn[y.k]rt[.ṯ]ʻ. | lm.ank. 14[KRT].6.279
ny. | rgm. | ṯḥm.tlmyn. | w.aḫtmlk ʻbd k. | l.pʻn.adt ny. | mrḥqtm. | qlny.ilm. | tǵr k. | tšlm k. | hn ny.ʻm ny. | kll.mid. | šl 51[95].6
gm. | ṯḥm.illdr. | ʻbd k.. | l.pʻn a[dt y]. | šbʻ d[.w šbʻ d]. | mrḥq[tm.qlt]. | mn[m.šlm]. 1014.7
. | ṯḥm.ṯpṭb[ʻl]. | [ʻ]bd k. | [l.p]ʻn.bʻl y. | [šbʻ] d.šbʻ [d]. | [mr]ḥqtm. | qlt. | ʻbd k.b. | lwsnd. | [w] b ṣr. | ʻm.mlk. | w.ht. | ml 2063.7
m. | ṯḥm.tlmyn. | ʻbd k. | l.pʻn. | adt y. | šbʻ d. | w.šbʻ id. | mrḥqtm. | qlt. | ʻm.adt y. | mnm.šlm. | rgm.ṯṯṯb. | l.ʻbd h. 52[89].10
l y.r[gm]. | ṯḥm.ʻbd[--]. | ʻbd k. | l pʻn.bʻl y. | ṯn id.šbʻ d. | mrḥqtm. | qlt.ʻm. | bʻl y.mnm. | šlm. | [r]gm[.ṯṯṯb]. | [l.]ʻbd[k]. 2115.2.7
l.mlk.b[ʻl y]. | r[gm]. | ṯḥm.rb.mi[--.ʻ]bd k. | l.pʻn.bʻl y[.mrḥqtm]. | šbʻ d.w.šbʻ[d.qlt]. | ankn.rgmt.l.bʻl y. | l.špš.ʻlm.l.ʻ 2008.1.4
[---.a]dt y. | [---].irrṯwm.ʻbd k. | [---.a]dt y.mrḥqm. | [---].adt y.yšlm. | [---.]mlk n.amṣ. | [.---].nn. | [---.]qr 1012.3
y.bʻl.ṣ[---.-]pt h. | ql h.q[dš.ṭb]r.arṣ. | [---.]ǵrm[.t]ḫšn. | rḥq[.---.tdʻ]. | qdm ym.bmt.[nhr]. | ṯṭṯn.ib.bʻl.tiḫd. | yʻrm.šnu. 4[51].7.33
m qrt tuḫd.hm mt yʻl bnš. | bt bn bnš yqḥ ʻz. | w yḥdy mrḥqm. RS61[24.277.31]

rḥt

z. | ʻm.ǵr.ṯrmg. | ʻm.tlm.ǵṣr.arṣ. | ša.ǵr.ʻl.ydm. | ḫlb.l ẓr.rḥtm. | w rd.bt ḫpṯt. | arṣ.tspr.b y | rdm.arṣ. | idk.al.ttn. | pnm. 4[51].8.6
b.idk. | pn k.al ttn.tk.ǵr. | knkny.ša.ǵr.ʻl ydm. | ḫlb.l ẓr.rḥtm w rd. | bt ḫpṯt.arṣ.tspr b y | rdm.arṣ.w tdʻ ilm. | k mtt.yš 5[67].5.14
n. | gdy lqḥ ṣtqn gt bn ndr. | um r[-] gtn ṯṯ ḫsn l ytn. | l rḥt lqḥ ṣtqn. | bt qbṣ urt ilštmʻ dbḥ ṣtqn l. | ršp. 1154.6

rḫn

| w tʻn.rbt.aṯrt ym. | rbt.ilm.l ḥkmt. | šbt.dqn k.l tsr k. | rḫntt.d[-].l irt k. | wn ap.ʻdn.mṭr h. | bʻl.yʻdn.ʻdn.ṯkt.b glṯ. | w 4[51].5.67

rḫp

il.l ṯrm[.ʻl h]. | nšrm.trḫpn.ybṣr.[ḥbl.d] | iym.bn.nšrm.arḫp.an[k.ʻ]l. | aqht.ʻdb k.hlmn.ṯnm.qdqd. | ṯlṯ id.ʻl.udn.špk. 18[3AQHT].4.21
tʻrt h.aqht.km.ytb.l lḥ[m]. | bn.dnil.l ṯrm.ʻl h.nšr[m]. | trḫpn.ybṣr.ḥbl.diy[m.bn]. | nšrm.trḫp.ʻnt.ʻl[.aqht]. | tʻdbn h. 18[3AQHT].4.31
t y.aqht.[km.ytb]. | l lḥm.w bn.dnil.l ṯrm[.ʻl h]. | nšrm.trḫpn.ybṣr.[ḥbl.d] | iym.bn.nšrm.arḫp.an[k.ʻ]l. | aqht.ʻdb k.hl 18[3AQHT].4.20
]. | b grn.yḥrb[.---]. | yǵly.yḫsp.ib[.---]. | ʻl.bt.ab h.nšrm.trḫ[p]n. | ybṣr.ḥbl.diym. | tbky.pǵt.bm.lb. | tdmʻ.bm.kbd. | tm 19[1AQHT].1.32
il.l ṯrm.ʻl h.nšr[m]. | trḫpn.ybṣr.ḥbl.diy[m.bn]. | nšrm.trḫp.ʻnt.ʻl[.aqht]. | tʻdbn h.hlmn.ṯnm[.qdqd]. | ṯlṯ id.ʻl.udn.š[18[3AQHT].4.32
t.mlk.bʻ | lt.drkt.bʻlt.šmm.rmm. | [bʻl]t.kpṯ.w ʻnt.di.dit.rḫpt. | [---.-]rm.aklt.ʻgl.ʻl.mšt. | [---.--]r.špr.w yšt.il. | [---.--]n.i UG5.2.1.8

rṭ

b'.alpm.iqni. | ḫmš.mat.kbd. | ṯlṯm.ḫmš kbd ktn. | ḫmš.rṭm. | ḫmš.ṯnt.d ḫmšm w. | ḫmš.ṯnt.d mit. | ḫmš.ṯnt.d ṯl | ṯ ma 1130.8
'šr.ktnt. | 'šr.rṭm. | kkr[.-].ḫṭ. | mitm[.p]ttm. | ṯlṯm[.---].kst. | alp.a[bn.ṣ]rp. 1114.2
.b d.gg['t]. | b.'šrt.ksp. | ṯlṯ.uṭbm.b d.alḫn.b.'šrt[.k]sp. | rṭ.l.ql.d.ybl.prd. | b.ṯql.w.nṣp.ksp. | ṯmn.lbšm.w.mšlt. | l.udm 2101.12

rkb

t.mlk[.---]. | ṯn.skm.šb'.mšlt.arb'.ḫpnt.[---]. | ḫmšm.ṯlṯ.rkb.ntn.ṯlṯ.mat.[---]. | lg.šmn.rqḥ.šr'm.ušpǵtm.p[--.---]. | kṯ.ẓr UG5.9.1.20
.'rpt. | tmṯr.b qẓ.ṭl.yṭll. | l ǵnbm.šb'.šnt. | yṣr k.b'l.ṯmn.rkb. | 'rpt.bl.ṭl.bl rbb. | bl.šr'.thmtm.bl. | ṭbn.ql.b'l.k tmz'. | kst 19[1AQHT].1.43
t. | rbt.kmn.hkl. | w y'n.kṯr.w ḫss. | šm'.l aliyn b'l. | bn.l rkb.'rpt. | bl.ašt.urbt.b bh[t] m. | ḥln.b qrb.hkl m. | w y'n.aliy 4[51].5.122
--].b ṯlḥn y.qlt. | b ks.ištyn h. | dm.ṯn.dbḥm.šna.b'l.ṯlṯ. | rkb.'rpt.dbḥ. | bṯt.w dbḥ.w dbḥ. | dnt.w dbḥ.tdmm. | amht.k 4[51].3.18
tḥt.ksi.zbl.ym.w 'n.kṯr.w ḫss.l rgmt. | l k.l zbl.b'l.ṯnt.l rkb.'rpt.ht.ib k. | b'l m.ht.ib k.tmḫṣ.ht.tṣmt.ṣrt k. | tqḥ.mlk.'l 2.4[68].8
ys[mm.---]. | arḫ.arḫ.[---.tld]. | ibr.tld[.l b'l]. | w rum.l[rkb.'rpt]. | tḥbq.[---]. | tḥbq[.---]. | w tksynn.bṯn[-.] | y[--.]šr h. 10[76].3.22
hdmm. | [t]ḥspn.m h.w trḥṣ. | [ṭ]l.šmm.šmn.arṣ.rbb. | [r]kb 'rpt.ṭl.šmm.tsk h. | [rb]b.nsk h.kbkbm. 3['NT].2.40
m.ykly.ṭpṭ.nhr. | b šm.tg'r m.'ṯtrt.bṯ l aliyn.[b'l.] | bṯ.l rkb.'rpt.k šby n.zb[l.ym.k] | šby n.ṭpṭ.nhr.w yṣa b[.--]. | ybṯ. 2.4[68].29
u. | g h.w tṣḥ.ik.mǵy.gpn.w ugr. | mn.ib.yp'.l b'l.ṣrt. | l rkb.'rpt.l mḫšt.mdd. | il ym.l klt.nhr.il.rbm. | l ištbm.tnn.išt 3['NT].3.35
.il.bš[r.b']l. | w bšr.ḥtk.dgn. | k.ibr.l b'l[.yl]d. | w rum.l rkb.'rpt. | yšmḫ.aliyn.b'l. 10[76].3.37
rd. | k ḥrr.zt.ybl.arṣ.w pr. | 'ṣm.yraun.aliyn.b'l. | ṯt'.nn.rkb.'rpt. | tb'.rgm.l bn.ilm.mt. | tny.l ydd.il ǵzr. | ṯḥm.aliyn.b' 5[67].2.7
b'l.ṣrt.l rkb.'rpt. | [-]'n.ǵlmm.y'nyn.l ib.yp'. | l b'l.ṣrt.l rkb.'rpt. | ṯḥm.aliyn.b'l.hwt.aliy. | qrdm.qry.b arṣ.mlḥmt. | št. 3['NT].4.50
l ksi.mlk h. | l nḫt.l kḥṯ.drkt h. | mn m.ib.yp'.l b'l.ṣrt.l rkb.'rpt. | [-]'n.ǵlmm.y'nyn.l ib.yp'. | l b'l.ṣrt.l rkb.'rpt. | ṯḥm. 3['NT].4.48
.--]y k.w rḥd. | [---]y ilm.d mlk. | y[t]b.aliyn.b'l. | yt'dd.rkb.'rpt. | [--].ydd.w yqlṣn. | yqm.w ywpṯn.b tk. | p[ḫ]r.bn.ilm 4[51].3.11
| [---.]pḫr kkbm. | [---.]dr dt.šmm. | [---.al]iyn b'l. | [---].rkb.'rpt. | [---.]ǵš.l limm. | [---.]l yṯb.l arṣ. | [---].mtm. | [---.--] 10[76].1.7
-.n]šr k.al ttn.l n. | [---.]tn l rbd. | [---.]b'lt h w yn. | [---.rk]b 'rpt. | [---.--]n.w mnu dg. | [---.]l aliyn b'l. | [---].rkb 'rpt. 2001.2.15
---.rk]b 'rpt. | [---.--]n.w mnu dg. | [---.]l aliyn b'l. | [---].rkb 'rpt. 2001.2.18
r.db[ḥ]. | yṣq.b gl.ḥṯt.yn. | b gl.ḫrṣ.nbt.w 'ly. | l ẓr.mgdl.rkb. | ṯkmm.ḥmt.nša. | [y]d h.šmmh.dbḥ. | l ṯr.ab h.il.šrd. | [b' 14[KRT].4.166
.ḥṯt. | yn.b gl[.ḫ]rṣ.nbt. | 'l.l ẓr.[mg]dl. | w 'l.l ẓr.[mg]dl.rkb. | ṯkmm.ḥm[t].ša.yd k. | šmm.dbḥ.l ṯr. | ab k.il.šrd.b'l. | b 14[KRT].2.74
[---.--]ṯ[.---]. | [---.]mt[--.---]. | bk[--.--].yq[--.--]. | w [---.]rkb[.---]. | [---].d[--.---]. | b ql[.-----]. | w tštqdn[.-----]. | hm. | w 62[26].4

rkby

. | bn.krwn.b.yny.iytlm. | šgryn.ary.b.yny. | bn.yddn.b.rkby. | agyn.agny. | tqbn.mldy. 2071.7
ll.qšt.w.ql'. | ḫlb.rpš. | abmn.qšt. | ẓẓn.qšt. | dqry.qš[t]. | rkby. | bn.knn.qšt. | pbyn.qšt. | yddn.qšt.w.ql'. | š'rt. | bn.il.qšt. 119[321].2.35
ḫ[--.---.kb]d. | šr[-.---]. | m'r[-.---]. | bq't.[---]. | šḫq[.---]. | rkby ar[b'm]. | bir ṯ[--]. | 'nqpat [---]. | m[--.---]. | [-----]. | k[--.-- 2042.15
rkby. | šḫq. | ǵn. | ṣ'. | mld. | amḏy. | ḫlb'prm. | ḫpty. | [ḫr]ṣb'. | [2077.1

rkm

r.zbl.mlk. | šmm.tlak.ṭl.amr.. | bn km k bk[r.z]bl.am.. | rkm.agzrt[.--].arḫ.. | b'l.azrt.'nt.[-]ld. | kbd h.l yd' hr h.[---]d[13[6].29

rks

rḥ. | tkly.bṯn.'qltn. | šlyṭ.d šb'y.rašm. | ṯtkḥ.ttrp.šmm.k rs. | ipd k.ank.ispi.uṭm. | ḏrqm.amt m.l yrt. | b npš.bn ilm.mt. 5[67].1.4
kly. | [bṯn.'qltn.]šlyṭ. | [d šb't.rašm].ṯtkḥ. | [ttrp.šmm.k rks.ipd]k. | [-----]. 5[67].1.31
--.--]m.b km.y'n. | [---].yd'.l yd't. | [---.]tasrn.ṯr il. | [---.]rks.bn.abnm. | [---.]upqt.'rb. | [---.w ẓ]r.mtn y at zd. | [---.]t'rb 1['NT.X].5.23
m. | lšnm.tlḥk. | šmm.ttrp. | ym.ḏnbtm. | tnn.l šbm. | tšt.trks. | l mrym.l bt[.---]. | p l.tb'[.---]. | hmlt ḫt.[---]. | l.tp[-]m.[- 1003.9
.b 'n. | [---.]b km.y'n. | [---.yd'.l] yd't. | [---.t]asrn. | [---.]trks. | [---.]abnm.upqt. | [---.]l w ǵr mtn y. | [---.]rq.gb. | [---.--] 1['NT.X].5.10

rmy

n.mšt. | 'psn. | bn.ṣpr. | kmn. | bn.ršp. | tmn. | šmmn. | bn.rmy. | bn.aky. | 'bdḥmn. | bn.'dṯ. | kṯy. | bn.ḫny. | bn.ssm. | bn.ḫ 1047.12
ḫrm. | bn.qrdy. | bn.šm'n. | bn.ǵlmy. | ǵly. | bn.dnn. | bn.rmy. | dll. | mny. | krty. | bn.'bṣ. | bn.argb. | ydn. | il'nt. | bn.urt. | 2117.3.36
[---.]dmrn.l pn h yrd. | [---.]b'l.šm[.--.]rgbt yu. | [---]w yrmy[.q]rn h. | [---.-]ny h pdr.ttǵr. | [---.n]šr k.al ttn.l n. | [---. 2001.2.10

rmyy

mryn[m]. | bn.bly. | nrn. | w.nḥl h. | bn.rmyy. | bn.tlmyn. | w.nḥl h. | w.nḥl hm. | bn.ḥrm. | bn.brzn. | w 113[400].1.5
mry[n]m. | bn rmy[y]. | yšril[.---]. | anntn bn[.---]. | bn.brzn [---]. | bnil.bn.tl[- 2069.2

rmǵt

n]ym.mgnm ar[b']. | [---.-]aḥ.mqḥ mqḥm. | [---.--]t.'šr rmǵt.[--]. | [---].alp.[---].alp. | [---.-]rbd.kbd.ṯnm kbd. | [---.-]n 1145.1.5

rmṣm

[---.--]n. | [---.]rmṣm. | [---.]dyy. | [---.n]ḥl h. 2155.2

rmṣt

t.š.ršp.š.dr il w p[ḫ]r b'l. | gdlt.šlm.gdlt.w burm.[l]b. | rmṣt.ilhm.b'lm.dṯt.w kšm.ḫmš. | 'ṯr h.mlun.šnpt.ḫṣt h.b'l.ṣp 34[1].9
t.š.ršp.š.dr]. | il.w pḫr[.b'l.gdlt.šlm.gdlt]. | w burm.l[b.rmṣt.ilhm]. | b'lm.w mlu[.---.ksm]. | ṯlṯm.w m'rb[.---]. | dbḥ š APP.II[173].19
t š ršp š[.dr.il.w pḫr.b'l]. | gdlt.šlm[.gdlt.w burm.lb]. | rmṣt.ilh[m.b'lm.---]. | ksm.ṯlṯm.[---]. | d yqḥ bt[.--]r.dbḥ[.šm 35[3].18

rmš

alpm. | yrḫ.'šrt.l b'[l]. | dqtm.w ynt.qr[t]. | w mtntm.š l rmš. | w kbd.w š.l šlm kbd. | alp.w š.l b'l ṣpn. | dqt l ṣpn.šrp. UG5.13.7
.'šrt. | [l b'l.ṣ]pn.[dq]tm.w y[nt] qrt. | [w mtmt]m.[š.l] rm[š.]kbd.w š. | [l šlm.kbd.al]p.w š.[l] b'l.ṣpn. | [dqt.l.ṣpn.šrp 36[9].1.13

rmt

.b‘l k.yṣḥ.‘n. | [gpn].w ugr.b ǵlmt. | [‘mm.]ym.bn.ẓlmt.r | [mt.pr‘]t.ibr.mnt. | [ṣḥrrm.ḥbl.‘]rpt. | [---.---.-]ḥt. | [---.---]m 4[51].7.55
. | b‘l.yṣḥ.‘n.gpn. | w ugr.bn.ǵlmt. | ‘mm ym.bn.ẓlm[t]. | rmt.pr‘t.ibr[.mnt]. | ṣḥrrm.ḥbl[.--]. | ‘rpt.tḥt.[---] | m ‘ṣrm.ḥ[- 8[51FRAG].9
prgṯ. | dd.l mri. | dd.l ṯnǵly. | dd.l krwn. | dd.l ṯǵr. | dd.l rmt.r[---]. 1100.12

rn

ṣ. | ar[bdd.]l kb[d.š]dm.yšt. | [----.]b‘l.mdl h.yb‘r. | [---.]rn h.aqry. | [---.]b a[r]ṣ.mlḥmt. | ašt[.b ‘]p[r] m.ddym.ask. | šl 3['NT].4.71
š‘rt. | l.kṯrmlk.ḫpn. | l.‘bdil[m].ḫpn. | tmrtn.š‘rt. | lmd.n.rn. | [---].ḫpn. | dqn.š‘rt. | [lm]d.yrṯ. | [-.]ynḥm.ḫpn. | ṯṯ.lmd.b‘l 1117.12

rnn

ḫlb.k tgwln.šnt k. | [--.]w špt k.l tššy.hm.tqrm.l mt.b rn k. | [--]ḫp.an.arnn.ql.špš.ḥw.bṯnm.uḫd.b‘lm. | [--.a]ṯm.prṯl 1001.1.5
t k. | [--.]w špt k.l tššy.hm.tqrm.l mt.b rn k. | [--]ḫp.an.arnn.ql.špš.ḥw.bṯnm.uḫd.b‘lm. | [--.a]ṯm.prṯl.l riš h.ḥmṯ.ṯmṯ 1001.1.6

r‘

‘. | yṣq.b irt.lbnn.mk.b šb‘. | [ymm.---]k.aliyn.b‘l. | [---].r‘ h ab y. | [---.]‘[---]. 22.2[124].27
drš.w.r‘ h. | ṯrm[-].w[.r‘ h]. | [‘]ṯtr[-].w.[r‘ h]. | ḫlly[-].w.r‘[h]. | ilmškl.w.r‘[h]. | ššw[.--].w.r[‘ h]. | kr[mn.--.]w.r[‘ h]. | 2083.2.1
.r‘[h]. | ššw[.--].w.r[‘ h]. | kr[mn.--.]w.r[‘ h]. | šd.[--.w.]r[‘ h]. | ḫla[n.---]. | w lšṯr[.---]. 2083.2.5
| ǵlwš.w.r‘ h. | kdrš.w.r‘ h. | ṯrm[-].w[.r‘ h]. | [‘]ṯtr[-].w.[r‘ h]. | ḫlly[-].w.r‘[h]. | ilmškl.w.r‘[h]. | ššw[.--].w.r[‘ h]. | kr[2083.1.7
ḫrny.w.r‘ h. | klbr.w.r‘ h. | tškrǵ.w.r‘ h. | ǵlwš.w.r‘ h. | kdrš.w.r‘ h. | ṯrm[-].w[.r‘ h]. | [‘]ṯtr[-].w.[r‘ h]. | ḫlly[-].w 2083.1.4
ḫrny.w.r‘ h. | klbr.w.r‘ h. | tškrǵ.w.r‘ h. | ǵlwš.w.r‘ h. | kdrš.w.r‘ h. | ṯr 2083.1.1
].w.[r‘ h]. | ḫlly[-].w.r‘[h]. | ilmškl.w.r‘[h]. | ššw[.--].w.r[‘ h]. | kr[mn.--.]w.r[‘ h]. | šd.[--.w.]r[‘ h]. | ḫla[n.---]. | w lšṯr[. 2083.2.3
-].w[.r‘ h]. | [‘]ṯtr[-].w.[r‘ h]. | ḫlly[-].w.r‘[h]. | ilmškl.w.r‘[h]. | ššw[.--].w.r[‘ h]. | kr[mn.--.]w.r[‘ h]. | šd.[--.w.]r[‘ h]. | 2083.2.2
‘ h. | tškrǵ.w.r‘ h. | ǵlwš.w.r‘ h. | kdrš.w.r‘ h. | ṯrm[-].w[.r‘ h]. | [‘]ṯtr[-].w.[r‘ h]. | ḫlly[-].w.r‘[h]. | ilmškl.w.r‘[h]. | ššw[2083.1.6
ḫrny.w.r‘ h. | klbr.w.r‘ h. | tškrǵ.w.r‘ h. | ǵlwš.w.r‘ h. | kdrš.w.r‘ h. | ṯrm[-].w[.r‘ h]. | [‘]ṯtr[-].w.[r‘ 2083.1.3
‘lm...gn‘. | iršt.aršt. | l aḫ y.l r‘ y.dt. | w ytnnn. | l aḫ h.l r‘ h. | r‘ ‘lm. | ttn.w tn. | w l ttn. | w al ttn. | tn ks yn. | w ištn. | ‘ 1019.1.10
.r‘[h]. | ilmškl.w.r‘[h]. | ššw[.--].w.r[‘ h]. | kr[mn.--.]w.r[‘ h]. | šd.[--.w.]r[‘ h]. | ḫla[n.---]. | w lšṯr[.---]. 2083.2.4
ḫrny.w.r‘ h. | klbr.w.r‘ h. | tškrǵ.w.r‘ h. | ǵlwš.w.r‘ h. | kdrš.w.r‘ h. | ṯrm[-].w[.r‘ h]. 2083.1.2
.r‘ h. | klbr.w.r‘ h. | tškrǵ.w.r‘ h. | ǵlwš.w.r‘ h. | kdrš.w.r‘ h. | ṯrm[-].w[.r‘ h]. | [‘]ṯtr[-].w.[r‘ h]. | ḫlly[-].w.r‘[h]. | ilmš 2083.1.5
alp ymm. | w rbt.šnt. | b ‘d ‘lm...gn‘. | iršt.aršt. | l aḫ y.l r‘ y.dt. | w ytnnn. | l aḫ h.l r‘ h. | r‘ ‘lm. | ttn.w tn. | w l ttn. | w 1019.1.8
gnryn. | l mlkytn. | ḥnn y l pn mlk. | šin k itn. | r‘ y šṣa idn l y. | l šmn iṯr hw. | p iḫdn gnryn. | im mlkytn yrg 1020.5
gn‘. | iršt.aršt. | l aḫ y.l r‘ y.dt. | w ytnnn. | l aḫ h.l r‘ h. | r‘ ‘lm. | ttn.w tn. | w l ttn. | w al ttn. | tn ks yn. | w ištn. | ‘bd.prṯ 1019.1.11

r‘y

p.bn.]ḫrpn. | gmrš[.bn].mrnn. | ‘bdmlk.bn.‘myn. | agyn.r‘y. | abmlk.bn.ilrš. | iḫyn.bn.ḫryn. | [ab]ǵl.bn.gdn. | [---].bn.b 102[323].4.9
ṯn.r‘y.uzm. | sǵr.bn.ḫpsry.aḥd. | sǵr.artn.aḥd. | sǵr.‘dn.aḥd. | sǵr. 1140.1
ḥrš.anyt. | bnš.gt.gl‘d. | bnš.gt.ngr. | r‘ym. | bn.ḫri[-]. | bnš.gt.‘ttrt. | ad[-]l[-]m. | ‘šr.ksdm.yd.lmd h 1040.4
r‘ym.dt.b d.iytlm. | ḫyrn.w.šǵr h. | šǵr.bn.prsn. | agpṯr.w.šǵ[r 2072.1
mlk.‘lm.w yšt. | [--.]gṯr.w yqr.il.yṯb.b.‘ttrt. | il.ṯpṭ.b hd r‘y.d yšr.w yḏmr. | b knr.w ṯlb.b tp.w mṣltm.b m | rqdm.dšn. UG5.2.1.3
d.aṯr h].l tdd.ilnym. | [---.m]rz‘y.apnnk.yrp. | [---.]km.r‘y.ht.alk. | [---.]ṯlṯt.amǵy.l bt. | [y.---.b qrb].hkl y.w y‘n.il. | [- 21[122].1.6
[b.]gt.ṯpn.‘šr.ṣmdm. | w.ṯlṯ.‘šr.bnš. | yd.ytm.yd.r‘y.ḥmrm. | b.gt.gwl.ṯmn.ṣmdm. | w.arb‘.‘šr.bnš. | yd.nǵr.mdr 2038.3
b‘l.yṯb.k ṯbt.ǵr.hd.r[‘y]. | k mdb.b tk.ǵr h.il ṣpn.b [tk]. | ǵr.tliyt.šb‘t.brqm.[---]. | UG5.3.1.1
spr.r‘ym. | lqḥ.š‘rt. | anntn. | ‘dn. | sdwn. | mztn. | ḫyrn. | šdn. | [‘š]r 2098.1
d.sǵr h. | [---.--]r h.‘šr[m.---.‘]šrm.dd. | [---.yn.d.]nkly.l.r‘ym.šb‘m.l.mitm.dd. | [---.--]d.šb‘m.kbd.dr‘. | [---.]kbd.ddm. 1098.44
[l r]iš.r‘y.y[šlm.---]. | [š]lm.bnš.yš[lm.---]. | [-]r.l šlmt.šl[m.---.--] | r 59[100].1
| dd l krwn. | dd l [--]n. | dd l ky. | dd l ‘bdkṯr. | dd[m] l r‘y. | [--] šmḫ[.---]. | ddm gt dprnm. | l ḥršm. | ddm l ‘nqt. | dd 1101.6
dk[.---]. | m‘bd[.-]r[-.-]š[-.---]. | w kšt.[--]šq h[.---]. | bnš r‘ym.[---]. | kbdt.bnš[.---]. | šin.[---]. | b ḥlm.[---]. | pnt[.---]. 2158.2.6
.šb‘m.kbd.dr‘. | [---.]kbd.ddm.kbd[.---]. | [---.]‘m.kbd.l.r‘[ym.---]. | [---].kbd.ṯmn.kb[d.---]. 1098.47

r‘t

tk.ǵr h.il ṣpn.b [tk]. | ǵr.tliyt.šb‘t.brqm.[---]. | ṯmnt.iṣr r‘t.‘ṣ brq y. | riš h.tply.ṭly.bn.‘n h. | uz‘rt.tmll.išd h.qrn[m]. | UG5.3.1.4

rǵb

y[ṣḥ]. | ik.mǵyt.rbt.aṯr[t.y]m. | ik.atwt.qnyt.i[lm]. | rǵb.rǵbt.w tǵt[--]. | hm.ǵmu.ǵmit.w ‘s[--]. | lḥm.hm.štym.lḥ[m]. | 4[51].4.33
[mrǵ]b.yd.m[ṯkt]. | mẓma.yd.mṯkt. | ṯṯkr.[--]dn. | ‘m.krt.msw 15[128].1.1
h.w y[ṣḥ]. | ik.mǵyt.rbt.aṯr[t.y]m. | ik.atwt.qnyt.i[lm]. | rǵb.rǵbt.w tǵt[--]. | hm.ǵmu.ǵmit.w ‘s[--]. | lḥm.hm.štym.lḥ[4[51].4.33
. | [‘l h.k irbym.kp.---.k br]k.tǵll.b dm. | [ḏmr.---.]td[-.]rǵb. | [----]k. | [----] h. 7.1[131].10

rǵn

rr.nḥš.‘q šr.ln h.mlḫš. | abd.ln h.ydy.ḥmt. | b ḥrn.pnm.trǵnw.w ttkl. | bnwt h.ykr.‘r.d qdm. | idk.pnm.l ytn.tk aršḫ.r UG5.7.61

rǵṯ

ilm.rḥbt yn. | špq.ilht.dkrt[.yn]. | ‘d.lḥm.šty.ilm. | w pq mrǵtm.ṯd. | b ḥrb.mlḥt.qṣ[.m]r | i.tšty.krp[nm.y]n. | [b k]s.ḫrṣ 4[51].6.56
]rbt.aṯrt.ym. | [---.]btlt.‘nt. | [--.tl]ḥm.tšty. | [ilm.w tp]q.mrǵtm. | [ṯd.b ḥrb.m]lḥt.qṣ. | [mri.tšty.k]rpnm yn. | [b ks.ḫrṣ. 4[51].3.41
]. | yqrb.[---]. | lḥm.m[---.---]. | [‘]d.lḥm[.šty.ilm]. | w pq.mr[ǵtm.ṯd.---]. | b ḥrb.[mlḥt.qṣ.mri]. | šty.kr[pnm.yn.---]. | b 5[67].4.13

rp

[-----]. | [ṭṭbḫ.šm]n.[mri h]. | [tpṭḥ.rḥ]bt.[yn]. | [---.]rp[.---]. | [---.ḫ]br[.---]. | bḫr[.--]t[.----]. | l mṯb[.--]t[.---]. | [tqd 15[128].5.3

rpa

m. | tbky.pǵt.bm.lb. | tdm'.bm.kbd. | tmz'.kst.dnil.mt. | rpi.al.ǵzr.mt.hrnmy. | apnk.dnil.mt. | rpi.yṣly.'rpt.b | ḥm.un. 19[1AQHT].1.37
l rbb. | bl.šr'.thmtm.bl. | ṭbn.ql.b'l.k tmz'. | kst.dnil.mt.rpi. | all.ǵzr.m[t.]hr[nmy]. | gm.l bt[h.dnil.k yṣḥ]. | šm'.pǵt.ṯ 19[1AQHT].1.47
mk.b šb'.ymm. | [w]yqrb.b'l.b ḥnt h.abynt. | [d]nil.mt.rpi anḫ.ǵzr. | [mt.]hrnmy.d in.bn.l h. | km.aḫ h.w šrš.km.ary 17[2AQHT].1.18
qšt ṯmn. | ašrb'.qṣ't.w hn šb['. | b ymm.apnk.dnil.mt. | rpi.a hn.ǵzr.mt.hrnm[y]. | ytšu.yṯb.b ap.ṯǵr.tḥt. | adrm.d b gr 17[2AQHT].5.5
il.l hkl h. | 'rb.b bt h.kṯrt.bnt. | hll.snnt.apnk.dnil. | mt.rpi.ap.hn.ǵzr.mt. | hrnmy.alp.yṭbḫ.l kṯ | rt.yšlḥm.kṯrt.w y | šš 17[2AQHT].2.28
'n.tdrq.ḫss. | hlk.qšt.ybln.hl.yš | rb'.qṣ't.apnk.dnil. | mt.rpi.aphn.ǵzr.mt. | hrnmy.gm.l aṯt h.k yṣḥ. | šm'.mṯt.dnty.'d[17[2AQHT].5.14
mṣṣ[-]t[.--]. | pr'.qẓ.y[bl].šblt. | b ǵlp h.apnk.dnil. | [m]t.rpi.ap[h]n.ǵzr. | [mt.hrn]my.ytšu. | [yṯb.b ap.ṯ]ǵr[.t]ḥt. | [adr 19[1AQHT].1.20
h.tb'.kṯr. | l ahl h.hyn.tb'.l mš | knt h.apnk.dnil.m[t]. | rpi.aphn.ǵzr.m[t]. | hrnmy.qšt.yqb.[--] | rk.'l.aqht.k yq[--.---]. 17[2AQHT].5.34
[-----.apnk]. | [dnil.mt.rp]i.apn.ǵz[r]. | [mt.hrnmy.]uzr.ilm.ylḥm. | [uzr.yšqy.]bn.qd 17[2AQHT].1.2
[-----]. | [---.mid.rm.]krt. | [b tk.rpi.]arṣ. | [b pḫr].qbṣ.dtn. | [w t]qrb.w ld. | bn.tl k. | tld.pǵt.t[-- 15[128].3.3
ǵ[t.---]. | tld.pǵ[t.---]. | tld.p[ǵt.---]. | mid.rm[.krt]. | b tk.rpi.ar[ṣ]. | b pḫr.qbṣ.dtn. | ṣǵrt hn.abkrn. | tbrk.ilm.tity. | tity.i 15[128].3.14
l tdd.il[nym.---]. | mhr.b'l[.---.mhr]. | 'nt.lk b[t y.rpim.rpim.b bt y]. | aṣḥ.km.[iqra km.ilnym.b] | hkl y.aṯr[h.rpum. 22.1[123].8
[--].[-]l[--.b qr] | b hkl y.[---]. | lk bt y.r[pim.rpim.b bt y.aṣḥ]. | km.iqr[a km.ilnym.b hkl y]. | aṯr h.r[pum. 22.1[123].3
t.ṯm.ytbš.šm.il.mt m. | y'bš.brk n.šm.il.ǵzrm. | ṯm.tmq.rpu.b'l.mhr b'l. | w mhr.'nt.ṯm.yḥpn.ḥyl | y.zbl.mlk.'llm y.k 22.2[124].8
| [dni]l mt rpi.ymr.ǵzr. | [mt.hr]nmy npš.yḥ.dnil. | [mt.rp]i.brlt.ǵzr.mt hrnmy. | [---].hw.mḫ.l 'rš h.y'l. | [---].bm.nšq. 17[2AQHT].1.38
[y.---.b qrb].hkl y.w y'n.il. | [---.mrz']y.lk.bt y.rpim. | [rpim.bt y.aṣ]ḥ km.iqra km. | [ilnym.b hkl]y.aṯr h.rpum. | [l t 21[122].1.10
[---.m]rz'y.lk.bt y. | [rpim.rpim.b]t y.aṣḥ km.iqra. | [km.ilnym.b h]kl y.aṯr h.rpum. | [l t 21[122].1.2
-]m.k[---]. | [-----]. | [---]m.il[.---]. | [---]d nhr.umt. | [---.]rpat.bt. | [m]lk.itdb.d šb'. | [a]ḫm.l h.ṯmnt.bn um. | krt.ḥtk n. 14[KRT].1.7
[---.rp]um.tdbḥn. | [----.]'d.ilnym. | [---.--]l km amt m. | [---.]b w t 20[121].1.1
-.-]b[-.---]. | ['ṯ]trt w 'nt[.---]. | w b hm.tṯṯb[.--]d h. | km trpa.hn n'r. | d yšt.l.lṣb h ḫš'r klb. | [w]riš.pqq.w šr h. | yšt.a UG5.1.2.3
h. | [---.]b ḥbq h.ḥmḥmt. | [---.--] n.ylt.ḥmḥmt. | [---.mt.r]pi.w ykn.bn h. | [b bt.šrš.]b qrb.hkl h. | [nṣb.skn.i]lib h.b qd 17[2AQHT].1.43
.tšt̠ḥ | [wy.w tkbd]n h.tlšn.aqht.ǵzr. | [---.kdd.dn]il.mt.rpi.w t'n. | [btlt.'nt.tšu.g]h.w tṣḥ.hwt. | [---.]aqht.yd[--]. | [---. 17[2AQHT].6.52
. | [---].ṭry.ap.l tlḥm. | [l]ḥm.trmmt.l tšt. | yn.tǵẓyt.špš. | rpim.tḥtk. | špš.tḥtk.ilnym. | 'd k.ilm.hn.mtm. | 'd k.kṯr m.ḫb 6.6[62.2].45
m.ti[ty.l 'r hm]. | tlkn.ym.w ṯa aḫr.š[pšm.b ṯlṯ]. | mǵy.rpum.l grnt.i[lnym.l] | mṯ't.w y'n.dnil.[mt.rpi]. | yṯb.ǵzr.mt 20[121].2.6
m.tity.l] | 'r hm.tl[kn.ym.w ṯn.aḫr.špšm]. | b ṯlṯ.mǵy[.rpum.l grnt]. | i[ln]y[m].l mṯ't[.---]. | [-]m[.---]. | h.hn bn k.hn 22.1[123].25
ḫẓr h. | pẓǵm.ǵr.ybk.l aqht. | ǵzr.ydm'.l kdd.dnil. | mt.rpi.l ymm.l yrḫm. | l yrḫm.l šnt.'d. | šb't.šnt.ybk.l aq | ht.ǵzr. 19[1AQHT].4.175
im.rpim.b]t y.aṣḥ km.iqra. | [km.ilnym.b h]kl y.aṯr h.rpum. | [l tdd.aṯr h].l tdd.ilnym. | [---.m]rz'y.apnnk.yrp. | [---. 21[122].1.3
rpim.b bt y]. | aṣḥ.km.[iqra km.ilnym.b] | hkl y.aṯr[h.rpum.l tdd]. | aṯr h.l t[dd.ilnym.ṯm]. | yḥpn.ḥy[ly.zbl.mlk.'ll 22.1[123].10
t h.b bt y]. | aṣḥ.rpi[m.iqra.ilnym]. | b qrb.h[kl y.aṯr h.rpum.l] | tdd.aṯr[h.l tdd.ilnym]. | asr.mr[kbt.---]. | t'ln.l mr[22.1[123].20
.rpim.b bt y.aṣḥ]. | km.iqr[a km.ilnym.b hkl y]. | aṯr h.r[pum.l tdd.aṯr h]. | l tdd.il[nym.---]. | mhr.b'l[.---.mhr]. | 'nt.l 22.1[123].5
. | [rpim.bt y.aṣ]ḥ km.iqra km. | [ilnym.b hkl]y.aṯr h.rpum. | [l tdd.aṯr]h.l tdd.i[lnym]. | [---.]r[--.---]. | [---.yṯ]b.l ar 21[122].1.11
qṭr.b ap -]. | tmǵyn.tša.g h[m.w tṣḥn]. | šm'.l dnil.[mt.rpi]. | mt.aqht.ǵzr.[šṣat]. | btlt.'nt.k [rḥ.npš h]. | k iṯl.brlt h.[b 19[1AQHT].2.90
šnt.'d. | šb't.šnt.ybk.l aq | ht.ǵzr.yd[m'.]l kdd. | dnil.mt.r[pi.mk].b šb'. | šnt.w y'n[.dnil.mt.]rpi. | yṯb.ǵzr.m[t.hrnmy. 19[1AQHT].4.179
l iršt. | ['lm.---.--]k.l tšt k.liršt. | [---.]rpi.mlk 'lm.b 'z. | [rpu.m]lk.'lm.b ḏmr h.bl. | [---].b ḥtk h.b nmrt h.l r | [--.]arṣ.' UG5.2.2.7
['lm.---.--]k.l tšt k.l iršt. | ['lm.---.--]k.l tšt k.liršt. | [---.]rpi.mlk 'lm.b 'z. | [rpu.m]lk.'lm.b ḏmr h.bl. | [---].b ḥtk h.b n UG5.2.2.6
[---]n.yšt.rpu.mlk.'lm.w yšt. | [--.]gṯr.w yqr.il.yṯb.b.'ṯtrt. | il.ṯpṭ.b hd r' UG5.2.1.1
-.]iṯm h. | [---.y]mǵy. | [---.]dr h. | [---.-]rš.l b'l. | [---.-]ǵk.rpu mlk. | ['lm.---.--]k.l tšt k.l iršt. | ['lm.---.--]k.l tšt k.liršt. | [UG5.2.2.4
ṭ.rḥṣ.npṣ h.b ym.rṭ. | [--.y]iḫd.il.'bd h.ybrk. | [dni]l mt rpi.ymr.ǵzr. | [mt.hr]nmy npš.yḥ.dnil. | [mt.rp]i.brlt.ǵzr.mt 17[2AQHT].1.36
| [---.]dt.'l.lty. | [---.]tdbḥ.amr. | ṯmn.b qrb.hkl y.[aṯr h.rpum]. | tdd.aṯr h.tdd.iln[ym.---]. | asr.sswm.tṣmd.dg[-.---]. | t 20[121].2.1
ḫṣ.mḫṣ.aḫ y.akl[.m] | kly[.']l.umt y.w y'n[.dn] | il.mt.rpi npš tḥ[.pǵt]. | ṯ[km]t.mym.ḥspt.l š'r. | ṭl.yd't.hlk.kbkbm. 19[1AQHT].4.198
z'.kst.dnil.mt. | rpi.al.ǵzr.mt.hrnmy. | apnk.dnil.mt. | rpi.yṣly.'rpt.b | ḥm.un.yr.'rpt. | tmṭr.b qẓ.ṭl.yṭll. | l ǵnbm.šb'. 19[1AQHT].1.39
l amr.yu[ḫd.ksa.mlk h]. | nḫt.kḥṯ.d[rkt h.b bt y]. | aṣḥ.rpi[m.iqra.ilnym]. | b qrb.h[kl y.aṯr h.rpum.l] | tdd.aṯr[h.l t 22.1[123].19
[--].[-]l[--.b qr] | b hkl y.[---]. | lk bt y.r[pim.rpim.b bt y.aṣḥ]. | km.iqr[a km.ilnym.b hkl y]. | aṯr h.r 22.1[123].3
ṯr h]. | l tdd.il[nym.---]. | mhr.b'l[.---.mhr]. | 'nt.lk b[t y.rpim.rpim.b bt y]. | aṣḥ.km.[iqra km.ilnym.b] | hkl y.aṯr[h.r 22.1[123].8
[---.m]rz'y.lk.bt y. | [rpim.rpim.b]t y.aṣḥ km.iqra. | [km.ilnym.b h]kl y.aṯr h.rpu 21[122].1.2
ǵy.l bt. | [y.---.b qrb].hkl y.w y'n.il. | [---.mrz']y.lk.bt y.rpim. | [rpim.bt y.aṣ]ḥ km.iqra km. | [ilnym.b hkl]y.aṯr h.rp 21[122].1.9
ṯn.tlḥmn.rpum. | tštyn.ṯlṯ.rb'.ym.ḫmš. | ṯdṯ.ym.tlḥmn.rpum. | tštyn.bt.ikl.b pr'. | yṣq.b irt.lbnn.mk.b šb'. | [ymm.--- 22.2[124].23
išryt.'nq.smd. | lbnn.ṭl mrṯ.yḥrṯ.il. | hn.ym.w ṯn.tlḥmn.rpum. | tštyn.ṯlṯ.rb'.ym.ḫmš. | ṯdṯ.ym.tlḥmn.rpum. | tštyn.bt.i 22.2[124].21
--.]b w t'rb.sd. | [---.--]n b ym.qẓ. | [---.]ym.tlḥmn. | [---.rp]um.tštyn. | [---.]il.d 'rgzm. | [---.]dt.'l.lty. | [---.]tdbḥ.amr. | 20[121].1.7
'.]l kdd. | dnil.mt.r[pi.mk].b šb'. | šnt.w y'n[.dnil.mt.]rpi. | yṯb.ǵzr.m[t.hrnmy.y]šu. | g h.w yṣḥ.t[b'.---]. | bkyt.b hk[19[1AQHT].4.180
ṯlṯ]. | mǵy.rpum.l grnt.i[lnym.l] | mṯ't.w y'n.dnil.[mt.rpi]. | yṯb.ǵzr.mt hrnmy[.---]. | b grnt.ilm.b qrb.m[ṯ't.ilnym]. 20[121].2.7
.aṯt n.r[---]. | [---.]ḫr[-.--]. | [---.]plnt.[---]. | [---.]'mt.l ql.rpi[.---]. | [---.-]llm.abl.mṣrp k.[---]. | [---.]y.mṭnt.w tḥ.ṭbt.n[-- 1001.2.2

rpan

. | bn.ṯk. | bn.arwdn. | tmrtn. | šd'l.bn aḫyn. | m'rbym. | rpan. | abršn. | atlgy. | šršn. 95[91].7
. | w uṯpt.srdnnm. | awpn.uṯpt.ḥẓm. | w uṯpt.srdnnm. | rpan.uṯpt.srdnnm. | šb'm.uṯpt.srdnnm. | bn.aǵli.uṯpt.srdnnm 1124.6
n.ḫdmn. | [u]bdy.nqdm. | [ṯlṯ].šdm.d.n'rb.gt.npk. | [š]d.rpan.b d.klṯtb. | [š]d.ilṣy.b d.'bdym. | [ub]dy.trrm. | [šd.]bn.ṯq 82[300].2.14
.bn.agdṯb.'šrm. | b.bn.ibn.arb't.'šrt. | b.bn.mnn.ṯṯm. | b.rpan.bn.yyn.'šrt. | b.yp'r.'šrm. | b.n'mn.bn.ply.ḫmšt.l.'šrm. | 2054.1.15
dqn. | 'bd.pdr. | myṣm. | ṯgt. | w.lmd h. | yṯil. | w.lmd h. | rpan. | w.lmd h. | 'bdrpu. | w.lmd h. | 'dršp. | w.lmd h. | krwn b 1099.13

ḫmlk. | yp'n w.att h. | anntn.yṣr. | annmn.w.tlt.n'[r] h. | rpan.w.t[n.]bn h. | bn.ayln.w.tn.bn h. | yt. 2068.26
wn.ḫmšt. | bn.[-]r[-.]ḫmšt. | bn.ḥdt.'šrt. | bn.ḫnyn.'šrt. | rpan.ḫmšt. | abǵl.ḫmšt. | bn.aḫdy.'šrt. | ttn.'ṣrt. | bn.pnmn.'šrt 1062.19
[-----]. | [-]mn. | b'ly. | rpan. | 'ptrm. | bn.'bd. | šmb'l. | ykr. | bly. | tb'm. | ḥdtn. | rpty. | i 1058.4

rpiy

tn. | 'dn. | lkn. | ktr. | ubn. | dqn. | ḥttn. | [--]n. | [---]. | tsn. | rpiy. | mrtn. | tnyn. | apt. | šbn. | gbrn. | tb'm. | kyn. | b'ln. | ytršp. 1024.2.15

rpiyn

bdg. | ilyn. | bn.tan. | bn.arm. | bn.b'l.ṣdq. | bn.army. | bn.rpiyn. | bn.army. | bn.krmn. | bn.ykn. | bn.'ttrab. | uṣn[-]. | bn.a 1046.1.8

rpš

.ql'. | bn.t'ln.qš[t.w.q]l'. | 'tqbt.qšt. | [-]ll.qšt.w.ql'. | ḫlb.rpš. | abmn.qšt. | ẓẓn.qšt. | dqry.qš[t]. | rkby. | bn.knn.qšt. | pby 119[321].2.30
ubr'y. | arny. | m'r. | š'rt. | ḫlb rpš. | bq't. | šḥq. | y'by. | mḫr. 65[108].5
atn. | utly. | bn.alz. | bn ḫlm. | bn.dmr. | bn.'yn. | ubnyn. | rpš d ydy. | ǵbl. | mlk. | gwl. | rqd. | ḫlby. | 'n[q]pat. | m[']rb. | 'r 2075.20
spr.rpš d l y[dy]. | atlg. | ulm. | izly. | uḫnp. | bn sḫrn. | m'qb. | tpn. | 2075.1
ḫlb.rpš. | ẓẓn. | bn.ḥmny. | dqry. 1068.1
bšn.tlt.qšt.w.[tlt.]ql'm. | bn.army.tt.qštm.w[.]q[l']. | bn.rpš.qšt.w.ql'. | bn.ǵb.qšt. | bn.ytrm.qšt.w.ql'. | bn.'bdyrḫ.qšt. 119[321].3.23
.arb'.'šr. | ṣ'q.arb' 'šr. | ṣ'.tmn. | šḥq.'šrm.arb'.kbd. | ḫlb rpš arb'.'šr. | bq't tt. | irab tn.'šr. | ḥbš.tmn. | amdy.arb'.'šr. | [-] 67[110].7
--]dm. | [--.--]šn. | [---.--]m. | [---.--]l. | [---.--]m. | [---.ḫlb.]rp[š]. | [---.]bht[.---]. | [---.]amr[-]. | [---.']rg[z.-]. | [---.ḫl]b ṣpn. 72[-].2.1
.mit.drt.w.'šrm.l.mit. | [drt.ḥpr.b]nšm.w.tn.'šr h.dd.l.rpš. | [---.]šb'm.dr'.w.arb'm.drt.mit.dd. | [---].ḥpr.bn.šm. | [b.- 1098.4
--.]qm't. | [---.]mdrǵlm. | [---.]mdm. | [w].'šr.dd.l np[l]. | r[p]š. 2012.27

rpty

rpan. | 'ptrm. | bn.'bd. | šmb'l. | ykr. | bly. | tb'm. | ḥdtn. | rpty. | ilym. | bn.'br. | mnip'l. | amrb'l. | dqry. | tdy. | yp'b'l. | bdl 1058.12

rṣn

lrm. | [-]ral. | šdn. | [-]ǵl. | bn.b'ltǵpt. | ḥrš.btm. | ršpab. | [r]ṣn. | [a]ǵlmn. | [a]ḫyn. | [k]rwn. | [k]l[by]. | [--]tn. | [---]d. | a[ǵ] 2060.13

rq

. | [---.]trks. | [---.]abnm.upqt. | [---.]l w ǵr mtn y. | [---.]rq.gb. | [---.--]kl.tǵr.mtn h. | [---.--]b.w ym ymm. | [y'tqn.---].y 1['NT.X].5.13
šb['.]y[mm].td.išt. | b bht m.n[bl]at.b hkl m. | sb.ksp.l rqm.ḫrṣ. | nṣb.l lbnt.šmḫ. | aliyn.b'l.ht y.bnt. | dt.ksp.hkl y.dt 4[51].6.34
tn.pld.ptt[.-]r. | lpš.sgr.rq. | tt.prqt. | w.mrdt.prqt.ptt. | lbš.psm.rq. | tn.mrdt.az. | tlt.pl 1112.2
tt[.-]r. | lpš.sgr.rq. | tt.prqt. | w.mrdt.prqt.ptt. | lbš.psm.rq. | tn.mrdt.az. | tlt.pld.š'rt. | t[---].kbm. | p[---]r.aḥd. | [-----]. | 1112.5

rqd

il[štm']. | šbn. | tbq. | rqd. | uškn. | ḫbt. | [ḫlb].kr[d]. 1177.4
rqd. | bn.abdg. | ilyn. | bn.tan. | bn.arm. | bn.b'l.ṣdq. | bn.army. 1046.1.1
.dǵt hrnmy[.d k] | bkbm.'[l.---]. | [-]l h.yd 'd[.---]. | ltm.mrqdm.d š[-]l[-]. | w t'n.pǵt.tkmt.mym. | qrym.ab.dbḥ.l ilm. 19[1AQHT].4.189
t.b hd r'y.d yšr.w ydmr. | b knr.w tlb.b tp.w mṣltm.b m | rqdm.dšn.b.ḥbr.ktr.tbm. | w tšt.'nt.gtr.b'lt.mlk.b' | lt.drkt UG5.2.1.4
bn.dmr. | bn.'yn. | ubnyn. | rpš d ydy. | ǵbl. | mlk. | gwl. | rqd. | ḫlby. | 'n[q]pat. | m[']rb. | 'rm. | bn.ḫgby. | mrat. 2075.24
tlt.mat[.---.]kbd. | tt.ddm.k[--.b]rqd. | mit.tš'm.[kb]d.ddm. | b.gt.bir. 2168.2
mr w.bnš. | qmy.ḥmr.w.bnš. | tbil. | 'nmky.ḥmr.w.bnš. | rqd arb'. | šbn aḥd. | tbq aḥd. | šrš aḥd. | bir aḥd. | uḫnp. | hzp t 2040.27
qmy. | ḫlbkrd. | y'rt. | uškn. | 'nqpat. | ilštm'. | šbn. | tbq. | rqd. | šrš. | gn'y. | m'qb. | agm. | bir. | ypr. | hzp. | šql. | m'rḫ[-]. | s 2074.24
y. | m'r. | arny. | 'nqpat. | š'rt. | ubr'y. | ilštm'. | šbn. | tbq. | rqd. | [š]rš. | [-----]. | [-----]. | [-----]. | [-----]. | [-----]. | [-----]. | [ḫl]b 2058.1.18
m ḥsp. | ḫpty.kdm[.---]. | [a]gm.arb'[.---]. | šrš.šb'.mṣb. | rqd.tlt.mṣb.w.[---]. | uḫnp.tt.mṣb. | tgmr.[y]n.mṣb š[b']. | w ḥs 2004.33
.b.šrš. | tt.bnšm.b.mlk. | arb'.bnšm.b.bṣr. | tn.bnšm.[b.]rqd. | tn.b[nšm.b.---]y. | [---].b[nšm.b.--]nl. | [---.--]by. 2076.40
[-]dn[.---]. | [-]bq[.---]. | [r]qd[.---]. | šrš[.---]. | uḫnp[.---]. | [-]tn[--.---]. | km[-.---]. | lm[--. 2165.3
-]. | m'r. | arny. | ubr'y. | ilštm'. | bir. | m'qb. | uškn. | snr. | rq[d]. | [---]. | [---]. | mid[-]. | ubš. | mṣb[t]. | ḫl.y[---]. | 'rg[z]. | y'r 71[113].34

rqdy

rgs.ilštm'y. | bn.ḫran.ilštm'y. | bn.abd'n.ilštm'y. | bn.'n.rqdy. | bn.g'yn. | bn.ǵrn. | bn.agynt. | bn.abdḫr.snry. | dqn.šlm 87[64].32
ryn. | [---].bn.tyl. | annmt.nḫl h. | abmn.bn.'bd. | liy.bn.rqdy. | bn.ršp. 1036.14
spr.argmn.nskm. | rqdym. | štšm.tt mat. | ṣprn.tt mat. | dkry.tt mat. | [p]lsy.tt ma 1060.1.2
'bdyrḫ.bn.tyl. | 'bdn.w.att h.w.bn h. | gpn.bn[.a]ly. | bn.rqd[y].tbg. | iḫmlk. | yp'n w.att h. | anntn.yṣr. | annmn.w.tlt.n 2068.21

rqḥ

mlu[.---.ksm]. | tltm.w m'rb[.---]. | dbḥ šmn mr[.šmn.rqḥ.bt]. | mtnt.w ynt.[qrt.w tn.ḥtm]. | w bǵr.arb'.[---.kdm.yn APP.II[173].22
nḥ.b d.ybnn. | arb'.mat. | l.alp.šmn. | nḥ.tt.mat. | šm[n].rqḥ. | kkrm.brdl. | mit.tišrm. | tltm.almg. | ḫmšm.kkr. | qnm. | ' 141[120].5
rb'.ḫpnt.[---]. | ḫmšm.tlt.rkb.ntn.tlt.mat.[---]. | lg.šmn.rqḥ.šr'm.ušpǵtm.p[--.---]. | kt.ẓrw.kt.nbt.dnt.w [-]n[-.---]. | il. UG5.9.1.21
--]. | ksm.tltm.[---]. | d yqḥ bt[.--]r.dbḥ[.šmn.mr]. | šmn.rqḥ[.-]bt.mtnt[.w ynt.qrt]. | w tn ḥtm.w bǵr.arb['.---]. | kdm. 35[3].21
'bdrt[b.---]. | b tt 'tr tmn.r[qḥ.---]. | p bn btb[-.---]. | b ḫmt 'tr k[--.---]. | b ḫmt 'tr[.---]. | 207[57].2

rqṣ

at.aymr.aymr.mr.ym.mr.ym. | l ksi h.nhr l kḥt.drkt h.trtqṣ. | b d b'l.km.nšr b uṣb't h.hlm.qdq | d zbl ym.bn.'nm.tp 2.4[68].20
t. | ygrš.ygrš.grš ym grš ym.l ksi h. | [n]hr l kḥt drkt h.trtqṣ.b d b'l km nš | r.b uṣb't h.hlm.ktp.zbl ym.bn ydm. | [tp] 2.4[68].13
km nš | r.b uṣb't h.hlm.ktp.zbl ym.bn ydm. | [tp]t nhr.yrtqṣ.ṣmd.b d b'l.km.nšr. | b[u]ṣb't h.ylm.ktp.zbl ym.bn yd 2.4[68].15
dq | d zbl ym.bn.'nm.tpt.nhr.yprsḥ ym. | w yql.l arṣ.w trtqṣ.ṣmd.b d b'l. | [km.]nšr.b uṣb't h.ylm.qdqd.zbl. | [ym.]b 2.4[68].23

rš

t. | [m]lk.itdb.d šbʻ. | [a]ẖm.l h.ṯmnt.bn um. | krt.ḥtk n.rš. | krt.grdš.mknt. | aṯt.ṣdq h.l ypq. | mtrẖt.yšr h. | aṯt.trẖ.w t 14[KRT].1.10
lm. | ym.mšbʻt hn.b šlḥ. | ttpl.yʻn.ḥtk h. | krt yʻn.ḥtk h.rš. | mid.grdš.ṯbt h. | w b tm hn.špḥ.yitbd. | w b.pẖyr h.yrṯ. | y 14[KRT].1.22

ršy

[-----]. | [---.]ršy.[---]. | [---.-]mdr. | [---.]bty. | [---.]mrṯn.[--]. | [---.]d[.---]. 2172.2

ršp

ǵdǵd.aḏddy. | sw.aḏddy. | ildy.aḏddy. | grʻ.aḏddy. | ʻbd.ršp aḏddy. | ʻdn.bn.knn. | iwrẖz.b d.skn. | škny.aḏddy. | mšu.a 2014.35
[bʻl.w]dgn[.yi]sp.ḥmt.ʻnt.w ʻṯtrt. | [ti]sp.ḥmt.y[r]ẖ.w.ršp.yisp.ḥmt. | [ʻṯ]r.w ʻṯpr.yisp.ḥmt.ṯṯ.w kṯṯ. | [yus]p.ḥmt.m UG5.8.15
n.ugrty. | bn.tgḏn.ugrty. | tgyn.arty. | bn.nryn.arty. | bn.ršp.ary. | bn.ǵlmn ary. | bn.ḥṣbn ary. | bn.šdy ary. | bn.ktkt.mʻ 87[64].12
š. | yrẖ.š.ṣpn.š. | kṯr š ʻṯtr.š. | [ʻṯ]rt.š.šgr w iṯm š. | [---.]š.ršp.idrp.š. | [---.il.tʻ]ḏr.š. | [---.-]mt.š. | [-----]. | [-----]. | [-----]. | [- UG5.9.2.10
mrr. | ṯẖr w bd. | [k]ṯr ẖss šlm. | šlm il bt. | šlm il ẖš[t]. | ršp inšt. | [--]rm il [---]. | [---.--]m šlm [---]. UG5.7.72
q šr.yʻdb.ksa.w yṯb. | tqru.l špš.um h.špš.um.ql b.ʻm. | ršp.bbt h.mnt.nḥš.šmrr. | nḥš.ʻq šr.ln h.mlẖš.abd.ln h.ydy. | UG5.7.31
l btbt. | alp.w š šrp.alp šlmm. | l bʻl.ʻṣr l ṣpn. | npš.w.š.l ršp bbt. | [ʻ]ṣrm l h.ršp [-]m. | [---.]bqt[-]. | [b] ǵb.ršp mh bnš. UG5.12.A.11
ʻ[-]. | [--]y.l arṣ[.id]y.alt.l aḥš.idy.alt.in l y. | [--]t.bʻl.ḥẓ.ršp.b[n].km.yr.klyt h.w lb h. | [t]n.p k.b ǵr.ṯn.p k.b ẖlb.k tg 1001.1.3
.d.ntn[.d.]ksp. | [t]mn.l.ʻšrm[.l.b]t.ʻṯtrt. | [t]lṯ.ʻšr h.[b]t.ršp.gn. | arbʻ.b d.b[n].ušryn. | kdm.l.urtn. | kdm.l.ilšpš. | kd.l.a 1088.3
šm[m]. | [-----]. | [a]rṣ. | [u]šẖr[y]. | [ʻ]ṯtrt. | i[l t]ʻḏr bʻl. | ršp. | ddmš. | pẖr ilm. | ym. | uṯẖt. | knr. | mlkm. | šlm. 29[17].2.5
. | mtntm nkbd.alp.š.l il. | gdlt.ilhm.ṯkmn.w šnm dqt. | ršp.dqt.šrp w šlmm.dqtm. | [i]lh.alp w š ilhm.gdl[t.]ilhm. | [b 34[1].4
b ṯṯ ym ḥdṯ. | ḥyr.ʻrbt. | špš ṯǵr h. | ršp. | w ʻbdm tbqrn. | skn. 1162.4
liy]n.bʻl. | [------.]yrẖ.zbl. | [--.kṯ]r w ẖss. | [---]n.rḥm y.ršp zbl. | [w ʻd]t.ilm.ṯlṯ h. | [ap]nk.krt.ṯʻ.ʻ[-]r. | [--.]b bt h.yšt.ʻr 15[128].2.6
id.yph.mlk. | r[š]p.ḥgb.ap. | w[.n]pš.ksp. | w ẖrṣ.km[-]. | w.ḥ[--.-]lp. | w.š.l[-- 2005.1.2
[---]m.d.yṯ[--.]l[-]. | ršp.ḥmš.[m]šl[t]. | [--]arš[p.-]š.l[h]. | [-]ṯl[.--]š.l h. | [---]l[.--] h 2133.2
.mlk. | [-]lp.izr. | [a]rz. | k.tʻrb.ʻṯtrt.šd.bt[.m]lk. | k.tʻrbn.ršp m.bt.mlk. | ẖlu.dg. | ḥdṯm. | dbḥ.bʻl.k.tdd.bʻlt.bhtm. | b.[-] 2004.11
.w.š.l ršp bbt. | [ʻ]ṣrm l h.ršp [-]m. | [---.]bqt[-]. | [b] ǵb.ršp mh bnš. | šrp.w ṣp ẖršẖ. | ʻlm b ǵb ẖyr. | ṯmn l ṯlṯm ṣin. | š UG5.12.B.1
yr. | ṯmn l ṯlṯm ṣin. | šbʻ.alpm. | bt bʻl.ugrt.ṯn šm. | ʻlm.l ršp.mlk. | alp w.š.l bʻlt. | bwrm š.iṯtqb. | w š.nbk m w.š. | gt ml UG5.12.B.7
.yrẖ.gdlt. | gdlt.ṯrmn.gdlt.pdry.gdlt dqt. | dqt.trṯ.dqt. | [rš]p.ʻnt.ẖbly.dbḥn š[p]š pgr. | [g]dlt iltm ẖnqtm.d[q]tm. | [yr 34[1].17
lbt. | ušẖry. | ym.bʻl. | yrẖ. | kṯr. | ṯrmn. | pdry. | dqt. | trṯ. | ršp. | ʻnt ẖbly. | špš pgr. | iltm ẖnqtm. | yrẖ kty. | ygb hd. | yrgb UG5.14.A.10
w bn.bṯn.itnn y. | ytt.nḥšm.mhr k.bn bṯn. | itnn k. | aṯr ršp.ʻṯtrt. | ʻm ʻṯtrt.mr h. | mnt.nṯk.nḥš. UG5.7.TR1
mlk. | ẖlu.dg. | ḥdṯm. | dbḥ.bʻl.k.tdd.bʻlt.bhtm. | b.[-]ǵb.ršp.ṣbi. | [---.--]m. | [---.]piln. | [---].ṣmd[.---.]pd[ry]. | [-----]. | [- 2004.15
---]. | aṯrt.š.ʻnt.š.špš.š.arṣy.š.ʻṯtrt.š. | ušẖry.š.il.tʻḏr.bʻl.š.ršp.š.ddmš.š. | w šlmm.ilib.š.i[l.--]m d gbl.ṣpn.al[p]. | pẖr.ilm UG5.9.1.8
š]. | ilhm.gd[lt.ilhm.bʻl.š.aṯrt.š]. | ṯkmn.w š[nm.š.ʻnt.š.ršp.š.dr]. | il.w pẖr[.bʻl.gdlt.šlm.gdlt]. | w burm.l[b.rmṣt.ilhm APP.II[173].17
š ilhm.gdl[t.]ilhm. | [b]ʻl š.aṯrt.š.ṯkmn w šnm.š. | ʻnt.š.ršp.š.dr il w p[ẖ]r bʻl. | gdlt.šlm.gdlt.w burm.[l]b. | rmṣt.ilhm 34[1].7
]hm.[gdlt.ilhm]. | bʻ[l.š].aṯrt[.š.ṯkm]n w [šnm.š]. | ʻnt š ršp š[.dr.il.w pẖr.bʻl]. | gdlt.šlm[.gdlt.w burm.lb]. | rmṣt.ilh[35[3].16
| w b urbt.ilib š. | bʻl alp w š. | dgn.š.il tʻḏr.š. | bʻl š.ʻnt š.ršp š. | šlmm. | w šnpt.il š. | l ʻnt.ḥl š.ṯn šm. | l gṯrm.ǵṣ b šmal. UG5.13.22
.l]il.w bu[rm.---]. | ytk.gdlt.ilhm.[ṯkmn.w šnm]. | dqt.ršp.šrp.w š[lmm.dqtm]. | ilh[.a]lp.w š[.il]hm.[gdlt.ilhm]. | bʻ[35[3].13
p.l il.w bu] | [rm.---.ytk.gdlt.ilhm]. | ṯkmn.w [šnm.dqt.ršp.šrp]. | w šlmm.[dqtm.ilh.alp.w š]. | ilhm.gd[lt.ilhm.bʻl.š.a APP.II[173].14
lt.l bʻlt.bhtm]. | ʻš[rm.]l inš[.ilm.---]. | il[hm.]dqt.š[.---.rš] | [p.š]rp.w šl[mm.--.dqt]. | [i]lh.gdlt[.ilhm.gdlt.il]. | [d]qt.ṯ 35[3].28
bht[m].[ʻ]ṣrm l [inš.ilm]. | [---.]ilh[m.dqt.š.--]. | [---.--]t.r[šp.šrp.w šl] | [mm.---].dq[t.ilh.gdlt]. | n.w šnm.dqt[.---]. | [i]l APP.II[173].31
| [-----]. | ynḥm. | iḥy. | bn.mšt. | ʻpsn. | bn.ṣpr. | kmn. | bn.ršp. | tmn. | šmmn. | bn.rmy. | bn.aky. | ʻbdḥmn. | bn.ʻdṯ. | kṯy. | 1047.9
kn l h. | mṯlṯt.kṯrm.tmt. | mrbʻt.zblnm. | mẖmšt.yitsp. | ršp.nṯdṯt.ǵlm. | ym.mšbʻt hn.b šlḥ. | ttpl.yʻn.ḥtk h. | krt yʻn.ḥt 14[KRT].1.19
alp šlmm. | l bʻl.ʻṣr l ṣpn. | npš.w.š.l ršp bbt. | [ʻ]ṣrm l h.ršp [-]m. | [---.]bqt[-]. | [b] ǵb.ršp mh bnš. | šrp.w ṣp ẖršẖ. | ʻl UG5.12.A.12
tny[.--]. | sll[.--]. | mld[.--]. | yqš[.--]. | [-----]. | inš[r.---]. | ršp[.---]. | iḥy[-.--]. | iwr[--.--]. | ʻd[--.--]. | pl[--.--]. | gr[-.--]. 1074.11
ilt[.---]. | l.bʻlt[.---]. | l.il.bt[.---]. | l.ilt.[---]. | l.ḥtk[.---]. | l.ršp[.---]. | [l].ršp.[---.--]g.kbd. | [l.i]lt.qb[-.---]. | [l.a]rṣy. | [l.--]r[1004.10
t[.---]. | l.il.bt[.---]. | l.ilt.[---]. | l.ḥtk[.---]. | l.ršp[.---]. | [l].ršp.[---.--]g.kbd. | [l.i]lt.qb[-.---]. | [l.a]rṣy. | [l.--]r[-.---]. | [l.--]ḥ 1004.11
.bn.ṯyl. | annmt.nẖl h. | abmn.bn.ʻbd. | liy.bn.rqdy. | bn.ršp. 1036.15
sn l ytn. | l rḥt lqḥ ṣtqn. | bt qbṣ urt ilštmʻ dbḥ ṣtqn l. | ršp. 1154.8

ršpab

. | šǵr.sndrn.aḥd. | šǵr.adn.ṣdq.aḥd. | šǵr.irgn.aḥd. | šǵr.ršpab.aḥd. | šǵr.arwṯ.aḥd. | šǵr.bn.mǵln. | aḥd. 1140.10
. | šd.b d.ʻbdmlk. | šd.b d.yšn.ḥrš. | šd.b d.aupš. | šd.b d.ršpab.aḥ.ubn. | šd.b d.bn.uṯryn. | [ubd]y.mrynm. | [š]d.bn.ṣnr 82[300].1.5
-]ry. | [--]lim bn.brq. | [--.]qtn bn.drṣy. | [--]kn bn.pri. | [r]špab bn.pni. | [ab]mn bn.qṣy. | [ʻ]pṯrm bn.agmz. | [-]n bn.iln 2087.8
l. | brqn. | adr[dn]. | krwn. | arkḏn. | ilmn. | abškn. | ykn. | ršpab. | klyn. | ẖgbn. | ḥṯtn. | ʻbdmlk. | y[--]k. | [-----]. | pǵḏn. | [-- 1024.1.16
št.w.qlʻ. | psḥn.qšt. | bn.kmy.qšt. | bn.ilḥbn.qšt.w.q[lʻ]. | ršpab.qšt.w.qlʻ. | pdrn.qšt.w.qlʻ. | bn.pǵm[-.qšt].w.qlʻ. | nʻmn. 119[321].3.45
spr.ḥpr.bnš mlk.b yrẖ iṯt[bnm]. | ršpab.rb ʻšrt.m[r]yn. | pǵḏn.ilbʻl.krwn.lbn.ʻdn. | ẖyrn.mdʻ. | š 2011.2
nntn. | bʻlrm. | [-]ral. | šḏn. | [-]ǵl. | bn.bʻltǵpṯ. | ḥrš.btm. | ršpab. | [r]ṣn. | [a]ǵlmn. | [a]ẖyn. | [k]rwn. | [k]l[by]. | [--]ṯn. | [-- 2060.13
pr.bdlm. | nʻmn. | rbil. | plsy. | ygmr. | mnṯ. | prẖ. | ʻdršp. | ršpab. | ṯnw. | abmn. | abǵl. | bʻldn. | ypʻ. 1032.9
l.adrdn. | klyn.kkln. | ʻdmlk.tdn. | ʻzn.pǵḏn. | [a]nndn. | [r]špab. | [-]glm. 1070.8

ršpy

[--]y.w.aṯt h. | [--]r.w.aṯt h. | ʻbdyrẖ.ṯn ǵlyt h. | aršmg. | ršpy.w.aṯt h. | bn.glgl.uškny. | bn.ṯny.uškny. | mnn.w.aṯt h. | s 2068.12
. | bn.pṯḏn. | bn.nbdg. | bn.ẖgbn. | bn.tmr. | bn.prsn. | bn.ršpy. | [ʻ]bdḥgb. | [k]lby. | [-]ḥmn. | [š]pšyn. | [ʻb]dmlk. | [---]yn. 113[400].1.22
rm. | w.rḥd.kd.šmn. | drt.b.kkr. | ubn.ḥšḥ.kkr. | kkr.lqḥ.ršpy. | tmtrn.bn.pnmn. | kkr. | bn.sgttn. | kkr. | ilšpš.kkr. | bn.ḏl 1118.6
ẓbr. | bn.ṯdṯb. | bn.ʻrmn. | bn.alz. | bn.mṣrn. | bn.ʻdy. | bn.ršpy. | [---.]mn. | [--.-]sn. | [bn.-]ny. | [b]n.ẖnyn. | [bn].nbq. | [bn 115[301].2.17

ršpn

lk.bn.un[-.---].|nrn.bn.mtn[-.---].|aẖyn.bn.nbk[-.---].|ršpn.bn.b'ly[.---].|bnil.bn.yṣr[.---].|'dyn.bn.uḏr[-.---].|w.'d'. 90[314].1.11

rt

y.|bn.krwn.|bn.nǵsk.|bn.qnḏ.|bn.pity.|w.nḥl h.|bn.rt.|bn.l[--].|bn.[---].|[---.--]y.|[--.-]ḏrm.|[--.--]y.|[--.--]y.|[-- 113[400].3.19
.l.b['l.---].|[dq]t.l.ṣpn.gdlt.l[.---].|u[gr]t.š.l.[il]ib.ǵ[--.--rt].|w ['ṣrm.]l.ri[--.---].|[--]t.b'lt.bt[.---].|[md]bḥt.b.ẖmš[.--- 35[3].35
.gdlt.l b['l.--.dqt].|l ṣpn.gdlt.[l.---].|ugrt.š l ili[b.---].|rt.w 'ṣrm.l[.---].|pamt.w bt.[---].|rmm.w 'l[y.---].|bt.il.ṯq[l.- APP.II[173].39
|l ṯ[--.---].|ks[.---].|kr[pn.---].|at.š['tqt.---].|š'd[.---].|rt.[---].|'ṭr[.---].|b p.š[---].|il.p.d[---].|'rm.[di.mh.pdrm].|d 16[126].5.44

rtn

.ḥblm.alp.alp.am[-].|ṯmn.ḥblm.šb'.šb'.ma[-].|'šr.kkr.rtn.|b d.šm'y.bn.bdn. 1128.32

rtq

.y[--].|šm' k.l arẖ.w bn.[--].|limm.ql.b udn.k w[-].|k rtqt mr[.---].|k d lbšt.bir.mlak.|šmm.tmr.zbl.mlk.|šmm.tl 13[6].24

rṯ

m'ms k.k šb't.yn.ṭ[ẖ].|gg k.b ym.ṯiṭ.rḥṣ.|npṣ k.b ym rṯ.b uni[l].|pnm.tšmẖ.w 'l yṣhl pi[t].|yprq.lṣb.w yṣḥq.|p'n.l 17[2AQHT].2.8
'l.[w]mn[t].|y.bt.il.ṭẖ.gg y.b ym.ṯiṭ.|rḥṣ.npṣ y.b ym.rṯ.|dn.il.bt h.ymǵyn.|yštql.dnil.l hkl h.|'rb.b bt h.kṯrt.bnt. 17[2AQHT].2.23
'l.|[w m]nt h bt.il.ṭẖ.gg h.b ym.|[ṯi]ṭ.rḥṣ.npṣ h.b ym.rṯ.|[--.y]iẖd.il.'bd h.ybrk.|[dni]l mt rpi.ymr.ǵzr.|[mt.hr]n 17[2AQHT].1.34

rṯa

k.[---].|dl.ylkn.ḥš.b a[rṣ.---].|b 'pr.ẖbl ṭtm.[---.]|šqy.rṯa.tnm y.ytn.[ks.b yd].|krpn.b klat yd.[---].|km ll.kḥṣ.tusp 1['NT.X].4.9

rṯt

lm h.k [tṣḥ].|'n.mkṯr.ap.t[---].|dgy.rbt.aṯr[t.ym].|qḥ.rṯt.b d k t[---].|rbt.'l.ydm[.---].|b mdd.il.y[--.---].|b ym.il.d[4[51].2.32

Š

š

liyn.b'l. | w ymlk.b arṣ.il.kl h. | [---] š abn.b rḥbt. | [---] š abn.b kknt. 6.1.67[49.1.39]
'ṯtr.'rẓ.yrd. | l kḥṯ.aliyn.b'l. | w ymlk.b arṣ.il.kl h. | [---] š abn.b rḥbt. | [---] š abn.b kknt. 6.1.66[49.1.38]
ṣb[-.---]. | kṯ.aqh[r.---]. | l bn[.---]. | [ṯ]lṯ.[---]. | [---.--]yn.š.aẖ[--]. | [---.]š.nṣ[.-]al[-]. | [---.---]m[.---]. 143[-].3.1
br[-]m.[-]trmt. | lbš.w [-]tn.ušpǵt. | ẖr[-].ṯlṯt.mzn. | drk.š.alp.w ṯlṯ. | ṣin.šlm[m.]šb' pamt. | l ilm.šb['.]l kṯr. | 'lm.t'rbn. 33[5].6
tm.p[--.---]. | kṯ.ẓrw.kṯ.nbt.d̲nt.w [-]n[-.---]. | il.ẖyr.ilib.š. | arṣ w šmm.š. | il.š.kṯrt.š. | dgn.š.b'l.ḥlb alp w š. | b'l ṣpn al UG5.9.2.1
rẖ[.---]. | ṣpn.š.kṯr.š.pdry.š.ǵrm.š[.---]. | aṯrt.š.'nt.š.špš.š.arṣy.š.'ṯtrt.š. | ušẖry.š.il.t'd̲r.b'l.š.ršp.š.ddmš.š. | w šlmm.ili UG5.9.1.7
lt.[ṣ]pn.dqt. | [---.al]p 'nt.gdlt.b ṯlṯt mrm. | [---.i]l š.b'l š.aṯrt.š.ym š.[b']l knp. | [---.g]dlt.ṣpn.dqt.šrp.w [š]lmm. | [---. 36[9].1.6
w š[lmm.dqtm]. | ilh[.a]lp.w š[.il]hm.[gdlt.ilhm]. | b'[l.š].aṯrt[.š.ṯkm]n w [šnm.š]. | 'nt š ršp š[.dr.il.w pẖr.b'l]. | gdlt. 35[3].15
rp w šlmm.dqtm. | [i]lh.alp w š ilhm.gdl[t.]ilhm. | [b]'l š.aṯrt.š.ṯkmn w šnm.š. | 'nt.š.ršp.š.dr il w p[ẖ]r b'l. | gdlt.šlm. 34[1].6
.šrp]. | w šlmm.[dqtm.ilh.alp.w š]. | ilhm.gd[lt.ilhm.b'l.š.aṯrt.š]. | ṯkmn.w š[nm.š.'nt.š.ršp.š.dr]. | il.w pẖr[.b'l.gdlt.šl APP.II[173].16
pš.ṯ' w[.--.k]bdm. | [---.--]mm.ṯn.šm.w alp.l[--]n. | [---.]š.il š.b'l š.dgn š. | [---.--]r.w ṯt pl.gdlt.[ṣ]pn.dqt. | [---.al]p 'nt. 36[9].1.3
.ẓrw.kṯ.nbt.d̲nt.w [-]n[-.---]. | il.ẖyr.ilib.š. | arṣ w šmm.š. | il.š.kṯrt.š. | dgn.š.b'l.ḥlb alp w š. | b'l ṣpn alp.w.š. | ṯrty.alp. UG5.9.2.2
ry.š.ǵrm.š[.---]. | aṯrt.š.'nt.š.špš.š.arṣy.š.'ṯtrt.š. | ušẖry.š.il.t'd̲r.b'l.š.ršp.š.ddmš.š. | w šlmm.ilib.š.i[l.--]m d gbl.ṣpn.a UG5.9.1.8
| w š.pdry š.ddmš š. | w b urbt.ilib š. | b'l alp w š. | dgn.š.il t'd̲r.š. | b'l š.'nt š.ršp š. | šlmm. | w šnpt.il š. | l 'nt.ḥl š.ṯn š UG5.13.21
.'ṯtrt.š. | ušẖry.š.il.t'd̲r.b'l.š.ršp.š.ddmš.š. | w šlmm.ilib.š.i[l.--]m d gbl.ṣpn.al[p]. | pẖr.ilm.š.ym.š[.k]nr.š.[--.]'ṣrm gdl UG5.9.1.10
mn.w šnm]. | dqt.ršp.šrp.w š[lmm.dqtm]. | ilh[.a]lp.w š[.il]hm.[gdlt.ilhm]. | b'[l.š].aṯrt[.š.ṯkm]n w [šnm.š]. | 'nt š rš 35[3].14
n.w šnm dqt. | ršp.dqt.šrp w šlmm.dqtm. | [i]lh.alp w š ilhm.gdl[t.]ilhm. | [b]'l š.aṯrt.š.ṯkmn w šnm.š. | 'nt.š.ršp.š.d 34[1].5
| ṯkmn.w [šnm.dqt.ršp.šrp]. | w šlmm.[dqtm.ilh.alp.w š]. | ilhm.gd[lt.ilhm.b'l.š.aṯrt.š]. | ṯkmn.w š[nm.š.'nt.š.ršp.š.d APP.II[173].15
.ḫmš. | 'ṯr h.mlun.šnpt.ḥṣt h.b'l.ṣpn š. | [--]ṯ š.ilt.mgdl š.ilt.asrm š. | w l ll.šp. pgr.w ṯrmnm.bt mlk. | il[bt].gdlt.ušẖr 34[1].11
.dṯt.w kšm.ḫmš. | 'ṯr h.mlun.šnpt.ḥṣt h.b'l.ṣpn š. | [--]ṯ š.ilt.mgdl š.ilt.asrm š. | w l ll.šp. pgr.w ṯrmnm.bt mlk. | il[bt]. 34[1].11
bt b'l.ugrt.ṯn šm. | 'lm.l ršp.mlk. | alp w.š.l b'lt. | bwrm š.iṯtqb. | w š.nbk m w.š. | gt mlk š.'lm. | l kṯr.ṯn.'lm. | tzǵ[.---.] UG5.12.B.9
.š.kṯr.š.pdry.š.ǵrm.š[.---]. | aṯrt.š.'nt.š.špš.š.arṣy.š.'ṯtrt.š. | ušẖry.š.il.t'd̲r.b'l.š.ršp.š.ddmš.š. | w šlmm.ilib.š.i[l.--]m d UG5.9.1.7
.ṯlṯ.l.ḥlby. | b d.tlmi.b.'šrm.ḫmšt. | kbd.ksp. | kkrm.š'rt.štt.b d.gg['t]. | b.'šrt.ksp. | ṯlṯ.uṯbm.b d.alḫn.b.'šrt[.k]sp. | rṯ.l. 2101.9
rynm. | [š]d.bn.ṣnrn.b d.nrn. | [š]d.bn.rwy.b d.ydln. | [š].bn.trn.b d.ibrmd. | [š]d.bn.ilṯtmr.b d.tbbr. | [w.]šd.nḥl h.b 82[300].1.10
š. | yrẖ š.'nt ṣpn.alp. | w š.pdry š.ddmš š. | w b urbt.ilib š. | b'l alp w š. | dgn.š.il t'd̲r.š. | b'l š.'nt š.ršp š. | šlmm. | w šnp UG5.13.19
gdlt.il š.b'l š.'nt. | ṣpn.alp.w š.pdry.š. | šrp.w šlmm ilib š. | b'l ugrt š.b'l ḥlb š. | yrẖ š.'nt ṣpn.alp. | w š.pdry š.ddmš š. UG5.13.15
[-]n[-.---]. | il.ẖyr.ilib.š. | arṣ w šmm.š. | il.š.kṯrt.š. | dgn.š.b'l.ḥlb alp w š. | b'l ṣpn alp.w.š. | ṯrty.alp.w.š. | yrẖ.š.ṣpn.š. | UG5.9.2.4
š.'nt. | ṣpn.alp.w š.pdry.š. | šrp.w šlmm ilib š. | b'l ugrt š.b'l ḥlb š. | yrẖ š.'nt ṣpn.alp. | w š.pdry š.ddmš š. | w b urbt.il UG5.13.16
t. | [---.al]p 'nt.gdlt.b ṯlṯt mrm. | [---.i]l š.b'l š.aṯrt.š.ym š.[b']l knp. | [---.g]dlt.ṣpn.dqt.šrp.w [š]lmm. | [---.a]lp.l b'l.w 36[9].1.6
yr.ilib.š. | arṣ w šmm.š. | il.š.kṯrt.š. | dgn.š.b'l.ḥlb alp w š. | b'l ṣpn alp.w.š. | ṯrty.alp.w.š. | yrẖ.š.ṣpn.š. | kṯr š 'ṯtr.š. | ['ṯt UG5.9.2.4
pl.gdlt.[ṣ]pn.dqt. | [---.al]p 'nt.gdlt.b ṯlṯt mrm. | [---.i]l š.b'l š.aṯrt.š.ym š.[b']l knp. | [---.g]dlt.ṣpn.dqt.šrp.w [š]lmm. 36[9].1.6
ṯ' w[.--.k]bdm. | [---.--]mm.ṯn.šm.w alp.l[--]n. | [---.]š.il š.b'l š.dgn š. | [---.--]r.w ṯt pl.gdlt.[ṣ]pn.dqt. | [---.al]p 'nt.gdlt. 36[9].1.3
lmm. | kmm.w bbt.b'l.ugrt. | w kdm.w npš ilib. | gdlt.il š.b'l š.'nt. | ṣpn.alp.w š.pdry.š. | šrp.w šlmm ilib š. | b'l ugrt š. UG5.13.13
l]mm.kmm. | [w bbt.b'l.ugrt.]kdm.w npš. | [ilib.gdlt.il.š.b]'[l.]š.'nt ṣpn. | [---.]w [n]p[š.---]. | [---.--]t.w[.---]. | [---.--]pr 36[9].1.17
ry š.ddmš š. | w b urbt.ilib š. | b'l alp w š. | dgn.š.il t'd̲r.š. | b'l š.'nt š.ršp š. | šlmm. | w šnpt.il š. | l 'nt.ḥl š.ṯn šm. | l gṯr UG5.13.21
.l ršp.mlk. | alp w.š.l b'lt. | bwrm š.iṯtqb. | w š.nbk m w.š. | gt mlk š.'lm. | l kṯr.ṯn.'lm. | tzǵ[.---.]nšm.pr. UG5.12.B.10
pn.alp. | w š.pdry š.ddmš š. | w b urbt.ilib š. | b'l alp w š. | dgn.š.il t'd̲r.š. | b'l š.'nt š.ršp š. | šlmm. | w šnpt.il š. | l 'nt.ḥ UG5.13.20
t.d̲nt.w [-]n[-.---]. | il.ẖyr.ilib.š. | arṣ w šmm.š. | il.š.kṯrt.š. | dgn.š.b'l.ḥlb alp w š. | b'l ṣpn alp.w.š. | ṯrty.alp.w.š. | yrẖ.š. UG5.9.2.3
--.k]bdm. | [---.--]mm.ṯn.šm.w alp.l[--]n. | [---.]š.il š.b'l š.dgn š. | [---.--]r.w ṯt pl.gdlt.[ṣ]pn.dqt. | [---.al]p 'nt.gdlt.b ṯlṯ 36[9].1.3
rt.riš.argmn]. | w ṯn šm.l [b'lt.bhtm.'ṣrm.l inš]. | ilm.w š d[d.ilš.š.--.mlk]. | ytb.brr[.w mḥ-.---]. | ym.[']lm.y'[--.---]. | [- 35[3].6
t.riš. | arg[mn.w ṯn.]šm.l b'lt. | bhtm.'ṣ[rm.l in]š ilm.w š. | dd ilš.š[.---.]mlk.ytb br | r.w mḥ[--.---.]w q[--]. | ym.'lm.y[- APP.II[173].6
.[gdlt.---.dqt]. | l ṣpn.w [dqt.---.ṯn.l 'š] | rm.pam[t.---]. | š dd šmn[.gdlt.w.---]. | brr.r[gm.yṯṯb.b ṯdṯ.ṯn]. | l šmn.'[ly h.g APP.II[173].48
.g[dlt.---]. | dqt.l.ṣpn.w.dqt[.---]. | ṯn.l.'šrm.pamt.[---]. | š.dd.šmn.gdlt.w.[---.brr]. | rgm.yṯṯb.b.ṯdṯ.ṯn[.--.šmn]. | 'ly h.g 35[3].44
ilib š. | b'l ugrt š.b'l ḥlb š. | yrẖ š.'nt ṣpn.alp. | w š.pdry š.ddmš š. | w b urbt.ilib š. | b'l alp w š. | dgn.š.il t'd̲r.š. | b'l š.'n UG5.13.18
| aṯrt.š.'nt.š.špš.š.arṣy.š.'ṯtrt.š. | ušẖry.š.il.t'd̲r.b'l.š.ršp.š.ddmš.š. | w šlmm.ilib.š.i[l.--]m d gbl.ṣpn.al[p]. | pẖr.ilm.š.y UG5.9.1.8
hm.gdl[t.]ilhm. | [b]'l š.aṯrt.š.ṯkmn w šnm.š. | 'nt.š.ršp.š.dr il w p[ẖ]r b'l. | gdlt.šlm.gdlt.w burm.[l]b. | rmṣt.ilhm.b'l 34[1].7
.[gdlt.ilhm]. | b'[l.š].aṯrt[.š.ṯkm]n w [šnm.š]. | 'nt š ršp š[.dr.il.w pẖr.b'l]. | gdlt.šlm[.gdlt.w burm.lb]. | rmṣt.ilh[m.b'l 35[3].16
ilhm.gd[lt.ilhm.b'l.š.aṯrt.š]. | ṯkmn.w š[nm.š.'nt.š.ršp.š.dr]. | il.w pẖr[.b'l.gdlt.šlm.gdlt]. | w burm.l[b.rmṣt.ilhm]. | b APP.II[173].17
bt ubnyn š h d.ytn.ṣṯqn. | ṯut ṭbẖ ṣṯq[n]. | b bz 'zm ṭbẖ š[h]. | b kl ygz ḥḥ š h. 1153.4
b gt ilštm'. | bt ubnyn š h d.ytn.ṣṯqn. | ṯut ṭbẖ ṣṯq[n]. | b bz 'zm ṭbẖ š[h]. | b kl ygz 1153.2
.ṣṯqn. | ṯut ṭbẖ ṣṯq[n]. | b bz 'zm ṭbẖ š[h]. | b kl ygz ḥḥ š h. 1153.5
[---.--]ṯ.šlḥ.npš.ṯ' w[.--.k]bdm. | [---.--]mm.ṯn.šm.w alp.l[--]n. | [---.]š.il š.b'l š.dgn š. | [---.--]r.w ṯt pl.gdlt.[ṣ] 36[9].1.2
'l ugrt š.b'l ḥlb š. | yrẖ š.'nt ṣpn.alp. | w š.pdry š.ddmš š. | w b urbt.ilib š. | b'l alp w š. | dgn.š.il t'd̲r.š. | b'l š.'nt š.ršp š UG5.13.18
h.mlun.šnpt.ḥṣt h.b'l.ṣpn š. | [--]ṯ š.ilt.mgdl š.ilt.asrm š. | w l ll.šp. pgr.w ṯrmnm.bt mlk. | il[bt].gdlt.ušẖry.gdlt.ym 34[1].11
.yn.prs.qmḥ.[---]. | mdbḥt.bt.ilt.'ṣr[m.l ṣpn.š]. | l ǵlmt.š.w l [---.l yrẖ]. | gd[lt].l nkl[.gdlt.l b'lt.bhtm]. | 'š[rm.]l inš[.il 35[3].25
rs.qmḥ.m'[--.---]. | mdbḥt.bt.i[lt.'ṣrm.l]. | ṣpn š.l ǵlm[t.š.w l.---]. | l yrẖ.gdlt.l [nkl.gdlt.l b']|[lt].bht[m].[']ṣrm l [inš. APP.II[173].27
r. | [g]dlt iltm ḥnqtm.d[q]tm. | [yr]ẖ.kty gdlt.w l ǵlmt š. | [w]pamt ṯlṯm.w yrdt.[m]dbḥt. | gdlt.l b'lt bhtm.'ṣrm. | l i 34[1].19
bn.il]. | ytši.l dr.bn.il.l mpẖrt.bn.i[l.l ṯkmn.w š]nm hn š. | w šqrb.'r.mšr mšr bn.ugrt.w [npy.---.]ugr. | w npy.yman. 32[2].1.17

n.il.ytši.l d]r.bn[.il]. | [l mpẖrt.bn.il.l ṯkmn.w šnm.hn š]. | [w šqrb.š.mšr mšr.bn.ugrt.w npy.---.]w npy. | [---.w np]y 32[2].1.3
nt.š.špš.š.arṣy.š.ʿṯtrt.š. | ušẖry.š.il.tʿḏr.bʿl.š.ršp.š.ddmš.š. | w šlmm.ilib.š.i[l.--]m d gbl.ṣpn.al[p]. | pẖr.ilm.š.ym.š[.k]n UG5.9.1.8
lk. | l ušẖ[r] ẖlmṭ. | l bbt il bt. | š l ẖlmṭ. | w tr l qlḥ. | w š ḥll ydm. | b qdš il bt. | w tlḥm aṯt. | š l ilbt.šlmm. | kll ylḥm UG5.7.TR3
-.a]ṯm.prṯl.l riš h.ḥmṭ.ṯmṭ. | [--.]ydbr.ṯrmt.al m.qḥn y.š y.qḥn y. | [--.]šir.b krm.nṭṭt.dm.ʿlt.b ab y. | u---].ʿlt.b k.lk.l 1001.1.8
n.dqt. | [---.al]p ʿnt.gdlt.b ṯlṯt mrm. | [---.i]l š.bʿl š.aṯrt.š.ym š.[bʿ]l knp. | [---.g]dlt.ṣpn.dqt.šrp.w [š]lmm. | [---.a]lp.l 36[9].1.6
dmš.š. | w šlmm.ilib.š.i[l.--]m d gbl.ṣpn.al[p]. | pẖr.ilm.š.ym.š[.k]nr.š.[--.]ʿṣrm gdlt. | bʿlm.kmm.bʿlm.kmm[.bʿlm].k UG5.9.1.9
n.alp.w š.pdry.š. | šrp.w šlmm ilib š. | bʿl ugrt š.bʿl ẖlb š. | yrḫ š.ʿnt ṣpn.alp. | w š.pdry š.ddmš š. | w b urbt.ilib š. | bʿl UG5.13.16
rt.š. | dgn.š.bʿl.ẖlb alp w š. | bʿl ṣpn alp.w.š. | ṯrṯy.alp.w.š. | yrḫ.š.ṣpn.š. | kṯr š ʿṯtr.š. | [ʿṯt]rt.š.šgr w iṯm š. | [---.]š.ršp.id UG5.9.2.6
m.alp.w š[.---]. | bʿlm.alp.w š[.---]. | arṣ.w šmm.š.kṯr[t] š.yrḫ[.---]. | ṣpn.š.kṯr.š.pdry.š.ǵrm.š[.---]. | aṯrt.š.ʿnt.š.špš.š.ar UG5.9.1.5
[---.]šlm. | [---.--]š.lalit. | [---.]bt šp.š. | y[-]lm.w mlk. | ynṣl.l ṯʿy. 2005.2.6
. | w šlmm.ilib.š.i[l.--]m d gbl.ṣpn.al[p]. | pẖr.ilm.š.ym.š[.k]nr.š.[--.]ʿṣrm gdlt. | bʿlm.kmm.bʿlm.kmm[.bʿlm].kmm.b UG5.9.1.9
l.ẖlb alp w š. | bʿl ṣpn alp.w.š. | ṯrṯy.alp.w.š. | yrḫ.š.ṣpn.š. | kṯr š ʿṯtr.š. | [ʿṯt]rt.š.šgr w iṯm š. | [---.]š.ršp.idrp.š. | [---.il.tʿ UG5.9.2.7
bʿlm.alp.w š[.---]. | arṣ.w šmm.š.kṯr[t] š.yrḫ[.---]. | ṣpn.š.kṯr.š.pdry.š.ǵrm.š[.---]. | aṯrt.š.ʿnt.š.špš.š.arṣy.š.ʿṯtrt.š. | ušẖ UG5.9.1.6
.kṯ.nbt.ḏnt.w [-]n[-.---]. | il.ẖyr.ilib.š. | arṣ w šmm.š. | il.š.kṯrt.š. | dgn.š.bʿl.ẖlb alp w š. | bʿl ṣpn alp.w.š. | ṯrṯy.alp.w.š. UG5.9.2.3
---]. | bʿlm.alp.w š[.---]. | bʿlm.alp.w š[.---]. | arṣ.w šmm.š.kṯr[t] š.yrḫ[.---]. | ṣpn.š.kṯr.š.pdry.š.ǵrm.š[.---]. | aṯrt.š.ʿnt.š. UG5.9.1.5
dqt.ṯʿ.ynt.ṯʿm.dqt.ṯʿm. | mtntm nkbd.alp.š.l il. | gdlt.ilhm.ṯkmn.w šnm dqt. | ršp.dqt.šrp w šlmm.dqtm 34[1].2
[-----]. | [---.--]t.š l i[l.---]. | [--.aṯ]rt.š[.---]. | [---.]l pdr[-.---]. | ṣin aḥd h[.---]. | l ʿ 37[22].2
[--.k]mm.gdlt.l.b[ʿl.---]. | [dq]t.l.ṣpn.gdlt.l[.---]. | u[gr]t.š.l.[il]ib.ǵ[--.--rt]. | w [ʿṣrm.]l.ri[--.---]. | [--]t.bʿlt.bt[.---]. | [md] 35[3].35
k.[---]. | kmm.gdlt.l b[ʿl.--.dqt]. | l ṣpn.gdlt.[l.---]. | ugrt.š l ili[b.---]. | rt.w ʿṣrm.l[.---]. | pamt.w bt.[---]. | rmm.w ʿl[y.-- APP.II[173].38
mṭ. | w tr l qlḥ. | w š ḥll ydm. | b qdš il bt. | w tlḥm aṯt. | š l ilbt.šlmm. | kll ylḥm b h. | w l bbt šqym. | š l uẖr ẖlmṭ. | w UG5.11.9
tlḥm aṯt. | š l ilbt.šlmm. | kll ylḥm b h. | w l bbt šqym. | š l uẖr ẖlmṭ. | w tr l qlḥ. | ym aḥd. UG5.11.12
.qr[t]. | w mtntm.š l rmš. | w kbd.w š.l šlm kbd. | alp.w š.l bʿl ṣpn. | dqt l ṣpn.šrp.w šlmm. | kmm.w bbt.bʿl.ugrt. | w k UG5.13.9
rt. | [w mtmt]m.[š.l] rm[š.]kbd.w š. | [l šlm.kbd.al]p.w š.[l] bʿl.ṣpn. | [dqt.l.ṣpn.šrp].w š[l]mm.kmm. | [w bbt.bʿl.ugrt 36[9].1.14
yrḫ ḥyr.b ym ḥdṯ. | alp.w š.l bʿlt bhtm. | b arbʿt ʿšrt.bʿl. | ʿrkm. | b ṯmnt.ʿšrt.yr | tḥṣ.mlk. UG5.12.A.2
lṯt ʿ[šrt.yrtḥṣ.mlk.brr]. | b arbʿ[t.ʿšrt.riš.argmn]. | w ṯn šm.l [bʿlt.bhtm.ʿṣrm.l inš]. | ilm.w š d[d.ilš.š.--.mlk]. | yṯb.brr 35[3].5
].ʿšrt.yrtḥṣ.mlk. | br[r.]b a[r]bʿt.ʿšrt.riš. | arg[mn.w ṯn.]šm.l bʿlt. | bhtm.ʿṣ[rm.l in]š ilm.w š. | dd ilš.š[.---.]mlk.yṯb br APP.II[173].5
in. | šbʿ.alpm. | bt bʿl.ugrt.ṯn šm. | ʿlm.l ršp.mlk. | alp w.š.l bʿlt. | bwrm š.iṯtqb. | w š.nbk m w.š. | gt mlk š.ʿlm. | l kṯr.ṯn UG5.12.B.8
r | tḥṣ.mlk.brr. | ʿlm.tzǵ.b ǵb.ṣpn. | nḥkt.ksp.w ẖrṣ ṯʿ ṯn šm l btbt. | alp.w š šrp.alp šlmm. | l bʿl.ʿṣr l ṣpn. | npš.w.š.l rš UG5.12.A.8
ʿḏr.š. | bʿl š.ʿnt š.ršp š. | šlmm. | w šnpt.il š. | l ʿnt.ḥl š.ṯn šm. | l gṯrm.ǵṣ b šmal. | d alpm.w alp w š. | šrp.w šlmm kmm. UG5.13.25
id ydbḥ mlk. | l ušẖ[r] ẖlmṭ. | l bbt il bt. | š l ẖlmṭ. | w tr l qlḥ. | w š ḥll ydm. | b qdš il bt. | w tlḥm aṯt. | š UG5.7.TR3
w š. | dgn.š.il tʿḏr.š. | bʿl š.ʿnt š.ršp š. | šlmm. | w šnpt.il š. | l ʿnt.ḥl š.ṯn šm. | l gṯrm.ǵṣ b šmal. | d alpm.w alp w š. | šrp. UG5.13.24
---.]ʿṯ[trt.---]. | [-.k]su.ilt[.---]. | [ṯl]ṯ.l ʿṯtrt[.---]. | [--.]l ilt.š l ʿṯ[rt.---]. | [ʿ]ṣr.l pdr ṯṯ.ṣ[in.---]. | tšnpn.ʿlm.km[m.---]. | w.l UG5.13.24
ʿ.---]. | kdm.yn.prs.qmḥ.[---]. | mdbḥt.bt.ilt.ʿṣr[m.l ṣpn.š]. | l ǵlmt.š.w l [---.l yrḫ]. | gd[lt].l nkl[.gdlt.l bʿlt.bhtm]. | ʿš[r 38[23].4
m.yn]. | prs.qmḥ.m ʿ[--.---]. | mdbḥt.bt.i[lt.ʿṣrm.l]. | ṣpn š.l ǵlm[t.š.w l.---]. | l yrḫ.gdlt.l [nkl.gdlt.l bʿ] | [lt].bht[m].[ʿ]ṣ 35[3].24
lp w š. | šrp.w šlmm kmm. | l bʿl.ṣpn b ʿrʿr. | pamt ṯlṯm š l qrnt. | ṯlḥn.bʿlt.bhtm. | ʿlm.ʿlm.gdlt l bʿl. | ṣpn.ilbt[.---.]d[-- APP.II[173].27
ln.alpm. | yrḫ.ʿšrt.l bʿ[l]. | dqtm.w ynt.qr[t]. | w mtntm.š l rmš. | w kbd.w š.l šlm kbd. | alp.w š.l bʿl ṣpn. | dqt l ṣpn.šr UG5.13.30
.yrḫ.ʿšrt. | [l bʿl.ṣ]pn.[dq]tm.w y[nt] qrt. | [w mtmt]m.[š.l] rm[š.]kbd.w š. | [l šlm.kbd.al]p.w š.[l] bʿl.ṣpn. | [dqt.l.ṣpn UG5.13.7
m l btbt. | alp.w š šrp.alp šlmm. | l bʿl.ʿṣr l ṣpn. | npš.w.š.l ršp bbt. | [ʿ]ṣrm l h.ršp [-]m. | [---.]bqt[-]. | [b] ǵb.ršp mh b 36[9].1.13
l bʿ[l]. | dqtm.w ynt.qr[t]. | w mtntm.š l rmš. | w kbd.w š.l šlm kbd. | alp.w š.l bʿl ṣpn. | dqt l ṣpn.šrp.w šlmm. | kmm. UG5.12.A.11
]pn.[dq]tm.w y[nt] qrt. | [w mtmt]m.[š.l] rm[š.]kbd.w š. | [l šlm.kbd.al]p.w š.[l] bʿl.ṣpn. | [dqt.l.ṣpn.šrp].w š[l]mm.k UG5.13.8
-.]d[--]. | l ṣpn[.---.-]lu. | ilib[.---.b]ʿl. | ugrt[.---.--]n. | [w] š l [---]. 36[9].1.13
š]pš.w.ḥly[t].ʿ[r]b[.š]p[š]. | w [ḥl.]mlk.[w.]b.ym.ḥdṯ.ṯn.šm. | l.[---]t. | i[d.yd]bḥ.mlk.l.prgl.ṣqrn.b.gg. | ar[bʿ.]arbʿ.mṯbt 36[9].1.13
š]p.ḥgb.ap. | w[.n]pš.ksp. | w ẖrṣ.km[-]. | w.ḥ[--.-]lp. | w.š.l[--]p. | w[.---.-]nš. | i[--.---]. | w[.---]. | k[--.---]. | ṯql[.---]. UG5.13.37
r.bn[.il]. | [l mpẖrt.bn.il.l ṯkmn.w šnm.hn š]. | [w šqrb.š.mšr mšr.bn.ugrt.w npy.---.]w npy. | [---.w np]y.ugrt. | [---.u 35[3].48
ṯn šm. | ʿlm.l ršp.mlk. | alp w.š.l bʿlt. | bwrm š.iṯtqb. | w š.nbk m w.š. | gt mlk š.ʿlm. | l kṯr.ṯn.ʿlm. | tzǵ[.---.]nšm.pr. 2005.1.6
. | gpn.w ugr.tḥm.bn ilm. | mt.hwt.ydd.bn.il. | ǵzr.p np.š.npš.lbim. | thw.hm.brlt.anẖr. | b ym.hm.brk y.tkšd. | rumm. 32[2].1.4
qh[r.---]. | l bn[.---]. | [ṯ]lṯ.[---]. | [---.--]yn.š.aḫ[--]. | [---.]š.nṣ[-]al[-]. | [---.---]m[.---]. UG5.12.B.10
spr[.---]. | ybnil[.---.]kd yn.w š. | spr.m[--]. | spr d[---]b.w š. | tt.ẖmš.[---]. | skn.ul[m.---]. | [--- 5[67].1.14
| [---.-]mt.š. | [-----]. | [-----]. | [-----]. | [---.]im[-.---]. | [---.]š.s[--.---]. | [---.-]lb[.--].š[.---]. | [---.]bʿlm al[p]. 143[-].3.2
| alp w.š.l bʿlt. | bwrm š.iṯtqb. | w š.nbk m w.š. | gt mlk š.ʿlm. | l kṯr.ṯn.ʿlm. | tzǵ[.---.]nšm.pr. 1093.2
ʿlm b ǵb ẖyr. | ṯmn l ṯlṯm ṣin. | šbʿ.alpm. | bt bʿl.ugrt.ṯn šm. | ʿlm.l ršp.mlk. | alp w.š.l bʿlt. | bwrm š.iṯtqb. | w š.nbk m UG5.9.2.19
š.pdry.š. | šrp.w šlmm ilib š. | bʿl ugrt š.bʿl ẖlb š. | yrḫ š.ʿnt ṣpn.alp. | w š.pdry š.ddmš š. | w b urbt.ilib š. | bʿl alp w š UG5.12.B.11
. | kmm.w bbt.bʿl.ugrt. | w kdm.w npš ilib. | gdlt.il š.bʿl š.ʿnt. | ṣpn.alp.w š.pdry.š. | šrp.w šlmm ilib š. | bʿl ugrt š.bʿl ẖl UG5.12.B.6
mm. | [w bbt.bʿl.ugrt.]kdm.w npš. | [ilib.gdlt.il.š.b]ʿ[l.]š.ʿnt ṣpn. | [---.]w [n]p[š.---]. | [---.--]t.w[.---]. | [---.--]pr.ṯ[--.---] UG5.13.17
lp.w š[.il]hm.[gdlt.ilhm]. | bʿ[l.š].aṯrt[.š.ṯkm]n w [šnm.š]. | ʿnt š ršp š[.dr.il.w pẖr.bʿl]. | gdlt.šlm[.gdlt.w burm.lb]. | r UG5.13.13
lh.alp w š ilhm.gdl[t.]ilhm. | [b]ʿl š.aṯrt.š.ṯkmn w šnm.š. | ʿnt.š.ršp.š.dr il w p[ẖ]r bʿl. | gdlt.šlm.gdlt.w burm.[l]b. | r 36[9].1.17
.alp.w š]. | ilhm.gd[lt.ilhm.bʿl.š.aṯrt.š]. | ṯkmn.w š[nm.š.ʿnt.š.ršp.š.dr]. | il.w pẖr[.bʿl.gdlt.šlm.gdlt]. | w burm.l[b.rm 35[3].15
dmš š. | w b urbt.ilib š. | bʿl alp w š. | dgn.š.il tʿḏr.š. | bʿl š.ʿnt š.ršp š. | šlmm. | w šnpt.il š. | l ʿnt.ḥl š.ṯn šm. | l gṯrm.ǵṣ b 34[1].6
.š.kṯr[t] š.yrḫ[.---]. | ṣpn.š.kṯr.š.pdry.š.ǵrm.š[.---]. | aṯrt.š.ʿnt.š.špš.š.arṣy.š.ʿṯtrt.š. | ušẖry.š.il.tʿḏr.bʿl.š.ršp.š.ddmš.š. | APP.II[173].17
lp w š. | bʿl ṣpn alp.w.š. | ṯrṯy.alp.w.š. | yrḫ.š.ṣpn.š. | kṯr š ʿṯtr.š. | [ʿṯt]rt.š.šgr w iṯm š. | [---.]š.ršp.idrp.š. | [---.il.tʿ]ḏr.š. | UG5.13.22
]. | ṣpn.š.kṯr.š.pdry.š.ǵrm.š[.---]. | aṯrt.š.ʿnt.š.špš.š.arṣy.š.ʿṯtrt.š. | ušẖry.š.il.tʿḏr.bʿl.š.ršp.š.ddmš.š. | w šlmm.ilib.š.i[l.- UG5.9.1.7
š. | bʿl ṣpn alp.w.š. | ṯrṯy.alp.w.š. | yrḫ.š.ṣpn.š. | kṯr š ʿṯtr.š. | [ʿṯt]rt.š.šgr w iṯm š. | [---.]š.ršp.idrp.š. | [---.il.tʿ]ḏr.š. | [---.-] UG5.9.2.8
[.---]. | arṣ.w šmm.š.kṯr[t] š.yrḫ[.---]. | ṣpn.š.kṯr.š.pdry.š.ǵrm.š[.---]. | aṯrt.š.ʿnt.š.špš.š.arṣy.š.ʿṯtrt.š. | ušẖry.š.il.tʿḏr.bʿ UG5.9.1.7

šlmm ilib š. | b'l ugrt š.b'l ḫlb š. | yrḫ š.'nt ṣpn.alp. | w š.pdry š.ddmš š. | w b urbt.ilib š. | b'l alp w š. | dgn.š.il t'd̲r.š. UG5.13.18
.alp.w š[.---]. | arṣ.w šmm.š.kt̲r[t] š.yrḫ[.---]. | ṣpn.š.kt̲r.š.pdry.š.ǵrm.š[.---]. | at̲rt.š.'nt.š.špš.š.arṣy.š.'t̲trt.š. | ušḫry.š.il UG5.9.1.6
.ugrt. | w kdm.w npš ilib. | gdlt.il š.b'l š.'nt. | ṣpn.alp.w š.pdry.š. | šrp.w šlmm ilib š. | b'l ugrt š.b'l ḫlb š. | yrḫ š.'nt ṣp UG5.13.14
n.š.b'l.ḫlb alp w š. | b'l ṣpn alp.w.š. | t̲rty.alp.w.š. | yrḫ.š.ṣpn.š. | kt̲r š 't̲tr.š. | ['t̲t]rt.š.šgr w it̲m š. | [---.]š.ršp.idrp.š. | [- UG5.9.2.7
.š. | yrḫ.š.ṣpn.š. | kt̲r š 't̲tr.š. | ['t̲t]rt.š.šgr w it̲m š. | [---.]š.ršp.idrp.š. | [---.il.t']d̲r.š. | [---.-]mt.š. | [-----]. | [-----]. | [-----]. | UG5.9.2.10
[.---]. | at̲rt.š.'nt.š.špš.š.arṣy.š.'t̲trt.š. | ušḫry.š.il.t'd̲r.b'l.š.ršp.š.ddmš.š. | w šlmm.ilib.š.i[l.--]m d gbl.ṣpn.al[p]. | pḫr.il UG5.9.1.8
w š]. | ilhm.gd[lt.ilhm.b'l.š.at̲rt.š]. | t̲kmn.w š[nm.š.'nt.š.ršp.š.dr]. | il.w pḫr[.b'l.gdlt.šlm.gdlt]. | w burm.l[b.rmṣt.ilh APP.II[173].17
il]hm.[gdlt.ilhm]. | b'[l.š].at̲rt[.š.t̲km]n w [šnm.š]. | 'nt š ršp š[.dr.il.w pḫr.b'l]. | gdlt.šlm[.gdlt.w burm.lb]. | rmṣt.ilh 35[3].16
w š ilhm.gdl[t.]ilhm. | [b]'l š.at̲rt.š.t̲kmn w šnm.š. | 'nt.š.ršp.š.dr il w p[ḫ]r b'l. | gdlt.šlm.gdlt.w burm.[l]b. | rmṣt.ilh 34[1].7
š. | w b urbt.ilib š. | b'l alp w š. | dgn.š.il t'd̲r.š. | b'l š.'nt š.ršp š. | šlmm. | w šnpt.il š. | l 'nt.ḥl š.t̲n šm. | l gt̲rm.ǵṣ b šma UG5.13.22
alp.w.š. | t̲rty.alp.w.š. | yrḫ.š.ṣpn.š. | kt̲r š 't̲tr.š. | ['t̲t]rt.š.šgr w it̲m š. | [---.]š.ršp.idrp.š. | [---.il.t']d̲r.š. | [---.-]mt.š. | [--- UG5.9.2.9
d]bḥ.mlk.l.prgl.ṣqrn.b.gg. | ar[b'.]arb'.mt̲bt.azmr.b h.š.šr[-]. | al[p.w].š.šlmm.pamt.šb'.klb h. | yr[--.]mlk.ṣbu.špš.w. 35[3].51
urbt.ilib š. | b'l alp w š. | dgn.š.il t'd̲r.š. | b'l š.'nt š.ršp š. | šlmm. | w šnpt.il š. | l 'nt.ḥl š.t̲n šm. | l gt̲rm.ǵṣ b šmal. | d a UG5.13.22
l.ṣqrn.b.gg. | ar[b'.]arb'.mt̲bt.azmr.b h.š.šr[-]. | al[p.w].š.šlmm.pamt.šb'.klb h. | yr[--.]mlk.ṣbu.špš.w.ḥl.mlk. | w.[---]. 35[3].52
[t] š.yrḫ[.---]. | ṣpn.š.kt̲r.š.pdry.š.ǵrm.š[.---]. | at̲rt.š.'nt.š.špš.š.arṣy.š.'t̲trt.š. | ušḫry.š.il.t'd̲r.b'l.š.ršp.š.ddmš.š. | w šlm UG5.9.1.7
.tzǵ.b ǵb.ṣpn. | nḫkt.ksp.w ḫrṣ t̲' t̲n šm l btbt. | alp.w š šrp.alp šlmm. | l b'l.'ṣr l ṣpn. | npš.w.š.l ršp bbt. | [']ṣrm l h.r UG5.12.A.9
w kdm.w npš ilib. | gdlt.il š.b'l š.'nt. | ṣpn.alp.w š.pdry.š. | šrp.w šlmm ilib š. | b'l ugrt š.b'l ḫlb š. | yrḫ š.'nt ṣpn.alp. | UG5.13.14
š. | l 'nt.ḥl š.t̲n šm. | l gt̲rm.ǵṣ b šmal. | d alpm.w alp w š. | šrp.w šlmm kmm. | l b'l.ṣpn b 'r'r. | pamt t̲lt̲m š l qrnt. | t̲l UG5.13.27
. | dt nat. | w qrwn. | l k dbḥ. | [--]r bt [--]. | [--]bnš [--]. | š š[--]. | w [--]. | d [--]. | ypḫ[--]. | w s[--]. | [---]. | qrd ga[n.--]. | b RS61[24.277.15]
[.---.--]t. | b yrḫ.ši[-.b ar]b't.'š | rt.yr[tḥṣ.ml]k.brr. | 'lm.š.š[--].l[--.]'rb.šp | š.w ḥl[.ml]k. | bn.aup[š.--].bsbn hzpḫ t̲lt̲t. | APP.II[173].56
r[.---]. | ybnil[.---.]kd yn.w š. | spr.m[--]. | spr d[---]b.w š. | tt.ḫmš.[---]. | skn.ul[m.---]. | [---]š.[---]. | [---]y[.---]. | sk[n.--- 1093.4
w šlmm.[dqtm.ilh.alp.w š]. | ilhm.gd[lt.ilhm.b'l.š.at̲rt.š]. | t̲kmn.w š[nm.š.'nt.š.ršp.š.dr]. | il.w pḫr[.b'l.gdlt.šlm.gdlt APP.II[173].16
.dqtm]. | ilh[.a]lp.w š[.il]hm.[gdlt.ilhm]. | b'[l.š].at̲rt[.š.t̲km]n w [šnm.š]. | 'nt š ršp š[.dr.il.w pḫr.b'l]. | gdlt.šlm[.gd 35[3].15
lmm.dqtm. | [i]lh.alp.w š ilhm.gdl[t.]ilhm. | [b]'l š.at̲rt.š.t̲kmn w šnm.š. | 'nt.š.ršp.š.dr il w p[ḫ]r b'l. | gdlt.šlm.gdlt. 34[1].6
š.il t'd̲r.š. | b'l š.'nt š.ršp š. | šlmm. | w šnpt.il š. | l 'nt.ḥl š.t̲n šm. | l gt̲rm.ǵṣ b šmal. | d alpm.w alp w š. | šrp.w šlmm k UG5.13.25
mm.š. | il.š.kt̲rt.š. | dgn.š.b'l.ḫlb alp w š. | b'l ṣpn alp.w.š. | t̲rty.alp.w.š. | yrḫ.š.ṣpn.š. | kt̲r š 't̲tr.š. | ['t̲t]rt.š.šgr w it̲m š. UG5.9.2.5
mn]. | w t̲n šm.l [b'lt.bhtm.'ṣrm.l inš]. | ilm.w š d[d.ilš.š.--.mlk]. | yt̲b.brr[.w mḫ-.---]. | ym.[']lm.y'[--.---]. | [--.-]g[-.-] 35[3].6
m.ilib.š.i[l.--]m d gbl.ṣpn.al[p]. | pḫr.ilm.š.ym.š[.k]nr.š[--.]'ṣrm gdlt. | b'lm.kmm.b'lm.kmm[.b'lm].kmm.b'lm.km UG5.9.1.9
gdlt.l b'] | [lt].bht[m].[']ṣrm l [inš.ilm]. | [---.]ilh[m.dqt.š.--]. | [---.--]t.r[šp.šrp.w šl] | [mm.---].dq[t.ilh.gdlt]. | n.w šnm APP.II[173].30
-]. | [---]š.[---]. | [---]y[.---]. | sk[n.---]. | u[---.]w š. | [---].w š. | [--]b.šd.[---]. | [--]kz[--]. 1093.11
m.b'lm.dtt.w ksm.ḫmš. | 'tr h.mlun.šnpt.ḫṣt h.b'l.ṣpn š. | [--]t̲ š.ilt.mgdl š.ilt.asrm š. | w l ll.šp. pgr.w t̲rmnm.bt mlk 34[1].10
[n.---]. | il.alp.w š[.---]. | b'lm.alp.w š[.---]. | b'lm.alp.w š[.---]. | arṣ.w šmm.š.kt̲r[t] š.yrḫ[.---]. | ṣpn.š.kt̲r.š.pdry.š.ǵrm UG5.9.1.4
arṣ.w šmm.š.kt̲r[t] š.yrḫ[.---]. | ṣpn.š.kt̲r.š.pdry.š.ǵrm.š[.---]. | at̲rt.š.'nt.š.špš.š.arṣy.š.'t̲trt.š. | ušḫry.š.il.t'd̲r.b'l.š.ršp. UG5.9.1.6
pn.š. | kt̲r š 't̲tr.š. | ['t̲t]rt.š.šgr w it̲m š. | [---.]š.ršp.idrp.š. | [---.il.t']d̲r.š. | [---.-]mt.š. | [-----]. | [-----]. | [-----]. | [---.]im[-.- UG5.9.2.10
dbḥ.ṣp[n.---]. | il.alp.w š[.---]. | b'lm.alp.w š[.---]. | b'lm.alp.w š[.---]. | arṣ.w šmm.š.kt̲r[t] š.yrḫ[.---]. | ṣpn UG5.9.1.3
dbḥ.ṣp[n.---]. | il.alp.w š[.---]. | b'lm.alp.w š[.---]. | b'lm.alp.w š[.---]. | arṣ.w šmm.š.kt̲ UG5.9.1.2
n.il]. | [ytši.l dr.bn.il.l mpḫ]rt.[bn.il.l t̲kmn.w šn]m hn š. | [---.w n]py.gr[.ḥmyt.ugrt.w np]y. | [---].w n[py.---].u t̲ḫt̲i[32[2].1.9B
n.ul[m.---]. | [---]š.[---]. | [---]y[.---]. | sk[n.---]. | u[---.]w š. | [---].w š. | [--]b.šd.[---]. | [--]kz[--]. 1093.10
l il limm[.---]. | w t̲t.npš[.---]. | kbd.w [---]. | l ṣp[n.---]. | š.[---]. | w [----]. | k[--.---]. | 'n[t.---]. 40[134].12
yn.yd[-.---.]dd. | [---]n.yd.sǵ[r.---.--]k.[--]. | [---.]dd.bn.š.[---.]yd.sǵr h. | [---.--]r h.'šr[m.---.']šrm.dd. | [---.yn.d.]nkly. 1098.42
[mn.w t̲n.]šm.l b'lt. | bhtm.'ṣ[rm.l in]š ilm.w š. | dd ilš.š[.---.]mlk.yt̲b br | r.w mḫ[--.---.]w q[--]. | ym.'lm.y[---.---]. | t. APP.II[173].7
kl[.gdlt.l b'lt.bhtm]. | 'š[rm.]l inš[.ilm.---]. | il[hm.]dqt.š[.---.rš] | [p.š]rp.w šl[mm.--.dqt]. | [i]lh.gdlt[.ilhm.gdlt.il]. | [35[3].28
t̲y.alp.w.š. | yrḫ.š.ṣpn.š. | kt̲r š 't̲tr.š. | ['t̲t]rt.š.šgr w it̲m š. | [---.]š.ršp.idrp.š. | [---.il.t']d̲r.š. | [---.-]mt.š. | [-----]. | [-----]. | UG5.9.2.9
r.š. | ['t̲t]rt.š.šgr w it̲m š. | [---.]š.ršp.idrp.š. | [---.il.t']d̲r.š. | [---.-]mt.š. | [-----]. | [-----]. | [-----]. | [---.]im[-.---]. | [---.]š.s[-- UG5.9.2.11
[.w y]rḫ.l gt̲r.t̲n. | [t̲ql.ksp].t̲b.ap.w npš. | [---].bt.alp w š. | [---.--]m.l gt̲rm. | [---.]l 'nt m. | [---.--]rm.d krm. | [---].l 'nt 33[5].16
dm. | [---.--]mm.t̲n.šm.w alp.l[--]n. | [---.]š.il š.b'l š.dgn š. | [---.--]r.w t̲t pl.gdlt.[ṣ]pn.dqt. | [---.al]p 'nt.gdlt.b t̲lt̲t mrm 36[9].1.3
'[.ṣbu.špš.w ḥl] | yt.'rb špš[.w ḥl.mlk.w.b y] | m.ḥdt̲.t̲n šm[.---.--]t. | b yrḫ.ši[-.b ar]b't.'š | rt.yr[tḥṣ.ml]k.brr. | 'lm.š.š[- APP.II[173].53
---]. | [-----]. | [---.]im[-.---]. | [---.]š.s[--.---]. | [---.-]lb[.--].š[.---]. | [---.]b'lm al[p]. UG5.9.2.20
[-----]. | [---.gd]lt.[---]. | [---.d]dmš[.---]. | [---.--]b.š.[---]. | [---.yr]ḫ.š.[---]. | [---.]'[--.---]. 43[47].4
[-----]. | [---.--]t.š l i[l.---]. | [--.at̲]rt.š[.---]. | [---.]l pdr[-.---]. | ṣin aḥd h[.---]. | l 't̲trt[.---]. | 'lm.km 37[22].3
--.gd]lt.[---]. | [---.d]dmš[.---]. | [---.--]b.š.[---]. | [---.yr]ḫ.š.[---]. | [---.]'[--.---]. 43[47].5
.šgr w it̲m š. | [---.]š.ršp.idrp.š. | [---.il.t']d̲r.š. | [---.-]mt.š. | [-----]. | [-----]. | [-----]. | [---.]im[-.---]. | [---.]š.s[--.---]. | [---.-]l UG5.9.2.12

šab

.'rm.šrn. | pdrm.s't.b šdm. | ḥt̲b h.b grnt.ḥpšt. | s't.b nk.šibt.b bqr. | mmlat.dm.ym.w t̲n. | t̲lt̲.rb'.ym.ymš. | t̲dt̲.ym.ḥẓ 14[KRT].3.113
| šrnn.pdrm. | s't.b šdm.ḥt̲b. | w b grnt.ḥpšt. | s't.b npk.šibt.w b | mqr.mmlat. | d[m].ym.w t̲n. | t̲lt̲.rb'.ym. | ḫmš.t̲dt̲.y 14[KRT].5.216
m.ymn. | [w]yqrb.trẓẓ h. | [---].mǵy h.w ǵlm. | [a]ḫt h.šib.yṣat.mrḥ h. | l tl.yṣb.pn h.tǵr. | yṣu.hlm.aḫ h.tph. | [ksl]h. 16.1[125].51
šmš d[--]. | ittpq.l awl. | išttk.lm.ttkn. | štk.mlk.dn. | štk.šibt.'n. | štk.qr.bt.il. | w mṣlt.bt.ḥr[š]. 12[75].2.60

šal

ksp.l hm.'d. | ilak.'m.mlk. | ht.lik[t.--.]mlk[.--]. | w.mlk.yštal.b.hn[--]. | hmt.w.anyt.hm.t'[rb]. | mkr.hn d.w.rgm.ank[2008.2.10
m. | dt.'rb. | b.mtn.bn.ayaḫ. | b.ḫbt̲ h.ḥwt.tt h. | w.mnm.šalm. | dt.tknn. | 'l.'rbnm. | hn hmt. | tknn. | mtn.bn.'bdym. | ilr 1161.5
[---.--]d.'m y. | [--.]spr.lm.likt. | [--]y.k išal hm. | [--.'š]rm.kkr.t̲lt̲. | [--.]t̲lt̲m.kkr.t̲lt̲. | [--.]aštn.l k. | [--] 1022.3

. | [--.]ḥ[--.]d[--]t. | [---.]ḥw[t.---]. | [---.]š[--]. | w ym ym.yš | al. | w mlk.d mlk. | b ḥwt.špḥ. | l ydn.ʿbd.mlk. | d št.ʿl.ẖrd 2062.2.02

yqmṣ.w b ḥlm h. | il.yrd.b ḏhrt h. | ab adm.w yqrb. | b šal.krt.m at. | krt.k ybky. | ydmʿ.nʿmn.ǵlm. | il.mlk[.ṯ]r ab h. | 14[KRT].1.38

spr. | šal[m]. | mt[--]. 1172.2

[--]. | ʿm.špš.[---]. | nšlḥ[.---]. | [---.m]at. | [---.]mat. | š[--].išal. | ʿm k.ybl.šd. | a[--].dʿ.k. | šld.ašld. | hn.mrṯ.d.štt. | ašld b l 2009.2.3

[.l.]likt. | ši[l.š]lm y. | [ʿ]d.r[-]š. | [-]ly.l.likt. | [a]nk.[---]. | šil.[šlm y]. | [l]m.li[kt]. | [-]t.ʿ[--]. 2010.12

m.wr[--]. | yšlm.[l] k. | ilm.t[ǵ]r k. | tšlm k. | lm[.l.]likt. | ši[l.š]lm y. | [ʿ]d.r[-]š. | [-]ly.l.likt. | [a]nk.[---]. | šil.[šlm y]. | [l] 2010.8

k ymǵy.adn. | ilm.rbm ʿm dtn. | w yšal.mṯpṭ.yld. | w yʿny.nn[.--]. | tʿny.n[---.-]ṯq. | w š[--.---]. | ḥd UG5.6.3

y.yšal. | ṯryl.p rgm. | l mlk.šm y. | w l h[-] yʿl m. | bn y.yšal. | ṯryl.w rgm. | ṯṯb.l aẖ k. | l adn k. 138.16

yl.p rgm. | l mlk.šm y. | w l h.yʿl m. | w h[t] aẖ y. | bn y.yšal. | ṯryl.w rgm[.-]. | ṯṯb.l aẖ k. | l adn k. 138.16

.lḥt. | spr.d likt. | ʿm.ṯryl. | mh y.rgmt. | w ht.aẖ y. | bn y.yšal. | ṯryl.p rgm. | l mlk.šm y. | w l h[-] yʿl m. | bn y.yšal. | ṯryl 138.11

.lḥt. | spr.d likt. | ʿm.ṯryl. | mh y.rgmt. | w ht.aẖ y. | bn y.yšal. | ṯryl.p rgm. | l mlk.šm y. | w l h.yʿl m. | w h[t] aẖ y. | bn 138.11

.šḥr.[---]. | [---].al ytbʿ[.--]. | [---.]l adn.ḥwt[.--]. | [--]h.w yššil[.--]. | [---.]lp[--]. 1023.5

| t[--.---]. | ls[--.---]. | ṣḥ[.---]. | ky.m[--.---]. | w pr[--.---]. | tštil[.---]. | ʿmn.bn[.---]. 1021.15

t[--.--]ṣm k. | [-----]. | [-----.]šil. | [-----.]šilt. | [-----]. | [-----.š]ilt. | [---.--]m.lm. | [---.š]d.gṯr. | [--]ḥ[d].šd.hwt. | [--.]iḥd.šd.gṯ 55[18].12

k.tǵr] k. | tʿzz[k.---.]lm. | w t[--.--]ṣm k. | [-----]. | [-----.]šil. | [-----.]šilt. | [-----]. | [-----.š]ilt. | [---.--]m.lm. | [---.š]d.gṯr. | [55[18].9

tʿzz[k.---.]lm. | w t[--.--]ṣm k. | [-----]. | [-----.]šil. | [-----.]šilt. | [-----]. | [-----.š]ilt. | [---.--]m.lm. | [---.š]d.gṯr. | [--]ḥ[d].šd. 55[18].10

šant

l ẖmš.mrkbt.ẖmš.ʿšr h.prs. | bt.mrkbt.w l šant.ṯṯ. | l bt.ʿšrm. | bt alẖnm.ṯlṯm ṯṯ kbd. 2105.2

ši

| m ʿṣrm.ḥ[---]. | glṯ.isr[.---] | m.brt[.---]. | ymt m.[---]. | ši[.---]. | m[---.---]. 8[51FRAG].16

šib

pʿmlk. | ṯǵrm.mnḥm.klyn.ʿdršp.ǵlmn. | [a]bǵl.ṣṣn.ǵrn. | šib.mqdšt.ʿb[dml]k.ṯṯpḥ.mrṯn. | ẖḏǵlm.i[---]n.pbn.nḏbn.sbd. 2011.15

šiy

t]. | tʿdbn h.hlmn.ṯnm[.qdqd]. | ṯlṯ id.ʿl.udn.š[pk.km]. | šiy.dm h.km.šẖ[ṭ.l brk h]. | yṣat.km.rḥ.npš[h.km.iṯl]. | brlt h 18[3AQHT].4.35

.ʿ]l. | aqht.ʿdb k.hlmn.ṯnm.qdqd. | ṯlṯ id.ʿl.udn.špk.km.šiy. | dm.km.šẖṭ.l brk h.tṣi.km. | rḥ.npš h.km.iṯl.brlt h.km. | q 18[3AQHT].4.23

šim

d.brq.maẖdy. | kkr.ṯlṯ. | b d.bn.by.ar[y]. | alpm.ṯlṯ. | b d.šim.il[š]tmʿy. 1134.7

šin

gnryn. | l mlkytn. | ḥnn y l pn mlk. | šin k itn. | rʿ y šṣa idn l y. | l šmn iṯr hw. | p iẖdn gnryn. | im 1020.4

-]. | w kšt.[--]šq h[.---]. | bnš rʿym.[---]. | kbdt.bnš[.---]. | šin.[---]. | b ḥlm.[---]. | pnt[.---]. 2158.2.8

šir

h.ḥmṯ.ṯmṯ. | [--.]ydbr.ṯrmt.al m.qḥn y.š y.qḥn y. | [--.]šir.b krm.nṭṭt.dm.ʿlt.b ab y. | u---].ʿlt.b k.lk.l pn y.yrk.bʿl.[--] 1001.1.9

n.mlkyy. | kmsk.šd.iẖmn. | širm.šd.khn. | ṯlṯ.šd.w.krm.šir.d.ẖli. | širm.šd.šd.ʿšy. | w.šir.šd.krm. | d.krwn. | šir.šd.šd.ʿš 1079.6

b ẖṯr.tdry | nn.b išt.tšrpnn. | b rḥm.tṭḥnn.b šd. | tdrʿnn.šir h.l tikl. | ʿṣrm.mnt h.l tkly. | npr[m.]šir.l šir.yṣḥ. 6[49].2.35

ʿnt.hlkt.w.šnwt. | tp.aẖ.h.k.ysmsm. | tspi.šir.h.l.bl.ḥrb. | tšt.dm.h.l.bl.ks. | tpnn.ʿn.bṯy.ʿn.bṯt.tpnn. | ʿn. RS225.3

n.b šd. | tdrʿnn.šir h.l tikl. | ʿṣrm.mnt h.l tkly. | npr[m.]šir.l šir.yṣḥ. 6[49].2.37

šd. | tdrʿnn.šir h.l tikl. | ʿṣrm.mnt h.l tkly. | npr[m.]šir.l šir.yṣḥ. 6[49].2.37

w.kmsk.d.iwrkl. | ṯlṯ.šd.d.bn.mlkyy. | kmsk.šd.iẖmn. | širm.šd.khn. | ṯlṯ.šd.w.krm.šir.d.ẖli. | širm.šd.šd.ʿšy. | w.šir.šd 1079.5

d.ʿšy. | w.šir.šd.krm. | d.krwn. | šir.šd.šd.ʿšy. | d.abmn. | šir.šd.krm. | d.yrmn. | šir.[š]d.mlṯḥ.šd.ʿšy. | d.ynḥm. | tgmr.šd. 1079.12

irm.šd.khn. | ṯlṯ.šd.w.krm.šir.d.ẖli. | širm.šd.šd.ʿšy. | w.šir.šd.krm. | d.krwn. | šir.šd.šd.ʿšy. | d.abmn. | šir.šd.krm. | d.y 1079.8

[---.mr]zḥ.ʿn[.---]. | [---.]šir.šd.kr[m.---]. | [---.]l.mrzḥ.ʿn[.---]. | [---].mrzḥ.ʿn[.---]. | [---]. 2032.2

d.krwn. | šir.šd.šd.ʿšy. | d.abmn. | šir.šd.krm. | d.yrmn. | šir.[š]d.mlṯḥ.šd.ʿšy. | d.ynḥm. | tgmr.šd.ṯlṯm.šd. | w.tr[--.---]. 1079.14

krm.šir.d.ẖli. | širm.šd.šd.ʿšy. | w.šir.šd.krm. | d.krwn. | šir.šd.šd.ʿšy. | d.abmn. | šir.šd.krm. | d.yrmn. | šir.[š]d.mlṯḥ.šd 1079.10

| kmsk.šd.iẖmn. | širm.šd.khn. | ṯlṯ.šd.w.krm.šir.d.ẖli. | širm.šd.šd.ʿšy. | w.šir.šd.krm. | d.krwn. | šir.šd.šd.ʿšy. | d.abm 1079.7

--.ybmt.]limm. | [---.---]l.limm. | [---.yt]b.l arṣ. | [---.--]l.šir. | [---.-]tm. | [---.]yd y. | [----]y. | [---.-]lm. | [---.r]umm. 10[76].1.18

šurt

ṯmn ʿšr šurt l [---]. | ṯmn šurt l ar[--.---]. | ṯn šurtm l bnš [---]. | arbʿ šurt l bn[š.---]. | arb 137.1[92].2

rtm l bn[š.---]. | ṯlṯm šurt l b[nš.---]. | arbʿ šurt [---]. | ṯṯ šurt l bnš [---]. | ẖmš kbd arbʿ[.---]. | ṯṯ šurt l tg[-.---]. | arbʿ šu 137.1[92].11

bnš [---]. | ṯṯ šurt.l bnš[.---]. | ṯn šurtm l bn[š.---]. | ṯlṯm šurt l b[nš.---]. | arbʿ šurt [---]. | ṯṯ šurt l bnš [---]. | ẖmš kbd ar 137.1[92].9

ṯmn ʿšr šurt l [---]. | ṯmn šurt l ar[--.---]. | ṯn šurtm l bnš [---]. | arbʿ šurt l bn[š.---]. | arbʿ šurt l q[--.---]. | ṯlṯ 137.1[92].3

l [---]. | ṯmn šurt l ar[--.---]. | ṯn šurtm l bnš [---]. | arbʿ šurt l bn[š.---]. | arbʿ šurt l q[--.---]. | ṯlṯ šurt l bnš [---]. | ṯṯ šur 137.1[92].4

bnš [---]. | arbʿ šurt l bn[š.---]. | arbʿ šurt l q[--.---]. | ṯlṯ šurt l bnš [---]. | ṯṯ šurt.l bnš[.---]. | ṯn šurtm l bn[š.---]. | ṯlṯm š 137.1[92].6

urt l q[--.---]. | ṯlṯ šurt l bnš [---]. | ṯṯ šurt.l bnš[.---]. | ṯn šurtm l bn[š.---]. | ṯlṯm šurt l b[nš.---]. | arbʿ šurt [---]. | ṯṯ šurt 137.1[92].8

t l bn[š.---]. | arbʿ šurt l q[--.---]. | ṯlṯ šurt l bnš [---]. | ṯṯ šurt.l bnš[.---]. | ṯn šurtm l bn[š.---]. | ṯlṯm šurt l b[nš.---]. | ar 137.1[92].7

[--.---]. | ṯn šurtm l bnš [---]. | arbʿ šurt l bn[š.---]. | arbʿ šurt l q[--.---]. | ṯlṯ šurt l bnš [---]. | ṯṯ šurt.l bnš[.---]. | ṯn šurt 137.1[92].5

rbʿ šurt [---]. | ṯṯ šurt l bnš [---]. | ẖmš kbd arbʿ[.---]. | ṯṯ šurt l tg[-.---]. | arbʿ šurt [---]. | [ẖm]šm šurt [---]. | ṯlṯ šurt l [-- 137.1[92].13

ṯmn ʿšr šurt l [---]. | ṯmn šurt l ar[--.---]. | ṯn šurtm l bnš [---]. | arbʿ šu 137.1[92].1

ṯṯ šurt l tg[-.---]. | arbʿ šurt [---]. | [ẖm]šm šurt [---]. | ṯlṯ šurt l [---]. | ṯn šurtm l [---]. | [-----.]a[---]. | [---.--]ln. | [---.]kqm 137.1[92].16

].|arbʻ šurt [---].|[ḫm]šm šurt [---].|ṯlṯ šurt l [---].|ṯn šurtm l [---].|[-----.]a[---].|[---.--]ln.|[---.]kqmṯn.|[---.]klnm 137.1[92].17
l bnš [---].|ḫmš kbd arbʻ[.---].|ṯṯ šurt l tg[-.---].|arbʻ šurt [---].|[ḫm]šm šurt [---].|ṯlṯ šurt l [---].|ṯn šurtm l [---].| 137.1[92].14
š[.---].|ṯn šurtm l bn[š.---].|ṯlṯm šurt l b[nš.---].|arbʻ šurt [---].|ṯṯ šurt l bnš [---].|ḫmš kbd arbʻ[.---].|ṯṯ šurt l tg[- 137.1[92].10
d arbʻ[.---].|ṯṯ šurt l tg[-.---].|arbʻ šurt [---].|[ḫm]šm šurt [---].|ṯlṯ šurt l [---].|ṯn šurtm l [---].|[-----.]a[---].|[---.-- 137.1[92].15

šb

kkr ʻl bn[.--].|[w] ṯlṯ šmn.|[w a]r[bʻ] ksp ʻl bn ymn.|šb šr šmn [--] ṯryn.|ḫm[š]m l ʻšr ksp ʻl bn llit.|[--]l[-.-]p ʻl [- 1103.5

šbḥ

rbṣ.|bn.amt.p d.[i]n.|b bt y.ttn.tn.|l y.mṯt.ḥry.|nʻmt.šbḥ.bkr k.|d k nʻm.ʻnt.|nʻm h.km.tsm.|ʻṯtrt.tsm h.|d ʻq h.i 14[KRT].6.290

šby

ṯ.nhr.|b šm.tgʻr m.ʻṯtrt.bṯ l aliyn.[bʻl.]|bṯ.l rkb.ʻrpt.k šby n.zb[l.ym.k] |šby n.ṯpṭ.nhr.w yṣa b[.--].|ybṯ.nn.aliyn.b 2.4[68].29
.ʻṯtrt.bṯ l aliyn.[bʻl.]|bṯ.l rkb.ʻrpt.k šby n.zb[l.ym.k] |šby n.ṯpṭ.nhr.w yṣa b[.--].|ybṯ.nn.aliyn.bʻl.w [---].|ym.l mt. 2.4[68].30

šblt

.aqht.|ǵzr.tšt k.b qrb m.asm.|y.dnh.ysb.aklt h.yph.|šblt.b akt.šblt.ypʻ.|b ḥmdrt.šblt.yḫ[bq].|w ynšq.aḥl.an.šblt. 19[1AQHT].2.69
p.qšt h.l ttn.|l y.w b mt[.-]ḫ.mṣṣ[-]t[.--].|prʻ.qẓ.y[bl].šblt.|b ǵlp h.apnk.dnil.|[m]t.rpi.ap[h]n.ǵzr.|[mt.hrn]my.yt 19[1AQHT].1.18
.|y.dnh.ysb.aklt h.yph.|šblt.b akt.šblt.ypʻ.|b ḥmdrt.šblt.yḫ[bq].|w ynšq.aḥl.an.šblt.|tpʻ.b aklt.šblt.tpʻ[.b ḥm]drt 19[1AQHT].2.70
lt.b akt.šblt.ypʻ.|b ḥmdrt.šblt.yḫ[bq].|w ynšq.aḥl.an.šblt.|tpʻ.b aklt.šblt.tpʻ[.b ḥm]drt.|ur.tisp k.yd.aqht.ǵz[r].|t 19[1AQHT].2.71
ʻ.|b ḥmdrt.šblt.yḫ[bq].|w ynšq.aḥl.an.šblt.|tpʻ.b aklt.šblt.tpʻ[.b ḥm]drt.|ur.tisp k.yd.aqht.ǵz[r].|tšt k.bm.qrb m.a 19[1AQHT].2.72
r.tšt k.b qrb m.asm.|y.dnh.ysb.aklt h.yph.|šblt.b akt.šblt.ypʻ.|b ḥmdrt.šblt.yḫ[bq].|w ynšq.aḥl.an.šblt.|tpʻ.b aklt 19[1AQHT].2.69

šbm

m.tǵl[l].|b dm.ḏmr.ḥlqm.b mm[ʻ].|mhrm.mṭm.tgrš.|šbm.b ksl.qšt h.mdnt.|w hln.ʻnt.l bt h.tmǵyn.|tštql.ilt.l hkl 3[ʻNT].2.16
nm.ṯrp ym.|lšnm.tlḥk.|šmm.tṯrp.|ym.ḏnbtm.|tnn.l šbm.|tšt.trks.|l mrym.l bt[.---].|p l.tbʻ[.---].|hmlt ḫt.[---].|l 1003.8
ʻl.ṣrt.|l rkb.ʻrpt.l mḫšt.mdd.|il ym.l klt.nhr.il.rbm.|l ištbm.tnn.ištml h.|mḫšt.bṯn.ʻqltn.|šlyṭ.d šbʻt.rašm.|mḫšt. 3[ʻNT].3.37

šbn

|qmy.ḥmr.w.bnš.|ṯbil.|ʻnmky.ḥmr.w.bnš.|rqd arbʻ.|šbn aḥd.|ṯbq aḥd.|šrš aḥd.|bir aḥd.|uḫnp.|hzp ṯn.|mʻqb a 2040.28
bt šbn.|iyʻdm.w bʻl h.|ddy.|ʻmy.|iwrnr.|alnr.|maḫdt.|aby.|[107[15].1
spr.mḫṣm.|bn.ḥpṡry.b.šbn.|ilštmʻym.|y[---.]bn.ʻšq.|[---.]bn.tqy.|[---.]bn.šlmy.|[--- 1041.2
lšlm.bn.gs[-.--]r.d.ytb.b.gt.al.|ilmlk.[--]kt.[--.d.]yṯb.b.šb[n].|bn.pr[-.]d.y[ṯb.b].šlmy.|tlš.w[.n]ḥl h[.-].tgd.mrum.| 2015.2.1
dqn.|ḥṯṯn.|[--]n.|[---].|tsn.|rpiy.|mrṭn.|ṯnyn.|apṯ.|šbn.|gbrn.|ṯbʻm.|kyn.|bʻln.|ytršp.|ḥmšm.ṯmn.kbd.|tgmr. 1024.2.19
il[štmʻ].|šbn.|ṯbq.|rqd.|uškn.|ḫbt.|[ḫlb].kr[d]. 1177.2
qmṣ.|ṣʻq.|qmy.|ḫlbkrd.|yʻrt.|uškn.|ʻnqpat.|ilštmʻ.|šbn.|ṯbq.|rqd.|šrš.|gnʻy.|mʻqb.|agm.|bir.|ypr.|hzp.|šql.| 2074.22
ʻq[.---].|ḫlb.k[rd].|uškn.|ʻnqp[at].|ubrʻ[y].|ilšt[mʻ].|šbn.|ṯbq. 2146.9
yn.|[---.-]ṯr.kdm.yn.|[-]dyn.arbʻ.yn.|abškn.kdm.yn.|šbn.kdm.yn.|ʻbdiltp.ṯm[n].y[n].|qṣn.ḫ[---].|arny.[---].|aǵlt 1085.8
spr.argmnm.|ʻšrm.ksp.d mkr.|mlk.|ṯlṯ.mat.ksp.d.šb[n].|mit.ksp.d.ṯbq.|ṯmnym.arbʻt.|kbd.ksp.|d.nqdm.|ḫm 2107.4
spr.blblm.|skn uškn.|skn šbn.|skn ubrʻ.|skn ḫrṣbʻ.|rb.ntbtš.|[---].ʻbd.r[--].|arbʻ.k[--]. 1033.3
m.|[mʻ]rby.|mʻr.|arny.|ʻnqpat.|šʻrt.|ubrʻy.|ilštmʻ.|šbn.|ṯbq.|rqd.|[š]rš.|[-----].|[-----].|[-----].|[-----].|[-----].|[- 2058.1.16
--.b] d.gbʻly.|[---.b] d.ʻbdḫmn.|[---.b] d.ṯbq.|[---.b] d.šbn.|[---.b] d.ulm.|[---.b] d.ǵbl.|[---.b] d.ʻbdkṯr.|[---.b] d.ur 1052.5
ny.|[--.]bnšm.b.lbnm.|arbʻ.bnšm.b.ypr.|[---.]bnšm.b.šbn.|[---.b]nšm.b.šmny.|[---.b]nšm.b.šmngy.|[---.]bnšm.b.s 2076.23

šbny

ym.arš.w tnn.|kṯr.w ḫss.yd.|ytr.kṯr.w ḫss.|spr.ilmlk šbny.|lmd.atn.prln.rb.|khnm rb.nqdm.|ṯʻy.nqmd.mlk ugr[6.6[62.2].53
tṣḥ.hwt.|[---.]aqht.yḏ[--].|[---.--]n.ṣ[---].|[spr.ilmlk.šbny.lmd.atn.]prln. 17[2AQHT].7.1
g.|mit.ksp.d mkr.|ilštmʻ.|ʻšrm.l mit.ksp.|ʻl.bn.alkbl.šb[ny].|ʻšrm ksp.ʻl.|wrt.mtny.w ʻl.|prdny.aṯt h. 2107.16

šbʻ

ʻd.|k lbš.km.lpš.dm a[ḫ h].|km.all.dm.ary h.|k šbʻt.l šbʻm.aḫ h.ym[.--].|w ṯmnt.l ṯmnym.|šr.aḫy h.mẓa h.|w mẓ 12[75].2.49
]m.il[.---].|[---]d nhr.umt.|[---.]rpat.bt.|[m]lk.itdb.d šbʻ.|[a]ḫm.l h.ṯmnt.bn um.|krt.ḥtk n.rš.|krt.grdš.mknt.|aṯ 14[KRT].1.8
n.aliyn.bʻl.|[ṯṭ]bḫ.šbʻm.ṣin.|[k gm]n.aliyn.bʻl.|[ṭṭb]ḫ.šbʻm.aylm.|[k gmn.]aliyn.bʻl.|[ṭṭbḫ.š]bʻm.yʻlm.|[k gmn.al]i 6[62].1.24
h bnš.|šrp.w ṣp ḫršḫ.|ʻlm b ǵb ḥyr.|ṯmn l ṯlṯm ṣin.|šbʻ.alpm.|bt bʻl.ugrt.ṯn šm.|ʻlm.l ršp.mlk.|alp w.š.l bʻlt.|b UG5.12.B.5
rt.|ilm.arṣ.ṭṭbḫ.šbʻm.|rumm.k gmn.aliyn.|[b]ʻl.ṭṭbḫ.šbʻm.alpm.|[k g]mn.aliyn.bʻl.|[ṭṭ]bḫ.šbʻm.ṣin.|[k gm]n.aliy 6[62].1.20
[--.-]n.w.aḫt h.arbʻm.|[--.-]dn.ʻšrm.|[--.-]dwn.ṯlṯm.w.šbʻ.alpm.|[kt]rmlk.ʻšrm.|[--]ny.ʻšrt.trbyt.|[--.]ʻbd.ṯlṯm.|[--- 1041.2
[---.--]i[-.]a[--.---].|[---.]ilm.w ilht.dt.|[---.]šbʻ.l šbʻm.aṯr.|[---.--]ldm.dt ymtm.|[--.--]r.l ẓpn.|[---.]pn.ym.y[- 2054.2.23
dt y.|rgm.|ṯḥm.tlmyn.|ʻbd k.|l.pʻn.|adt y.|šbʻ d.|w.šbʻ id.|mrḥqtm.|qlt.|ʻm.adt y.|mnm.šlm.|rgm.ṯṯb.|l.ʻbd 25[136].3
awpn.uṯpt.ḥẓm.|w uṯpt.srdnnm.|rpan.uṯpt.srdnnm.|šbʻm.uṯpt.srdnnm.|bn.aǵli.uṯpt.srdnnm.|asrn.uṯpt.srdnnm. 52[89].9
tršp.|ḥmšm.ṯmn.kbd.|tgmr.bnš.mlk.|d.b d.adnʻm.|[š]bʻ.b.ḥrṯm.|[ṯ]lṯ.b.ṯǵrm.|rb qrt.aḥd.|ṯmn.ḫzr.|w.arbʻ.ḥrš 1124.7
[-----].|[---.]abl.qšt ṯmn.|ašrbʻ.qṣʻt.w hn šb[ʻ].|b ymm.apnk.dnil.mt.|rpi.a hn.ǵzr.mt.hrnm[y].|ytšu. 1024.3.1
.|my.hmlt.aṯr.bʻl.nrd.|b arṣ.ʻm h.trd.nrt.|ilm.špš.ʻd.tšbʻ.bk.|tšt.k yn.udmʻt.gm.|tṣḥ.l nrt.ilm.špš.|ʻms mʻ.l y.ali 17[2AQHT].5.3
.qmṣ.l[l]im.|ṣḥ.aḫ h.b bht h.a[r]y h.|b qrb hkl h.ṣḥ.|šbʻm.bn.aṯrt.|špq.ilm.krm.y[n].|špq.ilht.ḫprt[.yn].|špq.ilm 6[62].1.9
.il.|a[ṯt.tq]ḥ.y krt.aṯt.|tqḥ.bt k.ǵlmt.tšʻrb.|ḥqr k.tld.šbʻ.bnm.l k.|w ṯmn.tṯtmnm.|l k.tld.yṣb.ǵlm.|ynq.ḥlb.a[ṯ]rt 4[51].6.46
[-]p[-]l[.---].|k lli.[---].|kpr.[šbʻ.bnt.rḥ.gdm.w anhbm].|w tqr[y.ǵlmm.b št.ǵr.---].|[ʻ]d tš 15[128].2.23
.at m].|w ank.ib[ǵy h.---].|[-].l yʻmdn.i[---.---].|kpr.šbʻ bn[t.rḥ.gdm.w anhbm].|kla[t.tǵ]r[t.bht.ʻnt.w tqry.ǵlmm 7.2[130].3
7.2[130].23

n[--.---.-]š[--]. | kpr.šb‘.bnt.rḥ.gdm. | w anhbm.klat.ṯǵrt. | bht.‘nt.w tqry.ǵlmm. | 3[‘NT].2.2
ṯbt.ǵr.hd.r[‘y]. | k mdb.b tk.ǵr h.il ṣpn.b [tk]. | ǵr.tliyt.šb‘t.brqm.[---]. | ṯmnt.iṣr r‘t.‘ṣ brq y. | riš h.tply.ṯly.bn.‘n h. | UG5.3.1.3
yn.iš[ryt.-]lnr. | spr.[--]ḥ[-] k.šb‘t. | ghl.ph.ṯmnt. | nblu h.špš.ymp. | hlkt.tdr[--]. | špš.b‘d h.t 27[8].2
l.mlkt. | adt y. | rgm. | tḥm.tlmyn. | ‘bd k. | l.p‘n. | adt y. | šb‘ d. | w.šb‘ id. | mrḥqtm. | qlt. | ‘m.adt y. | mnm.šlm. | rgm.ṯṯṯ 52[89].8
]. | r[gm]. | tḥm.rb.mi[--.‘]bd k. | l.p‘n.b‘l y[.mrḥqtm]. | šb‘ d.w.šb‘[d.qlt]. | ankn.rgmt.l.b‘l y. | l.špš.‘lm.l.‘ṯtrt. | l.‘nt.l 2008.1.5
l.mlkt. | adt y.rgm. | tḥm.illdr. | ‘bd k.. | l.p‘n a[dt y]. | šb‘ d[.w šb‘ d]. | mrḥq[tm.qlt]. | mn[m.šlm]. 1014.6
bnšm.d.bu. | tš‘.dt.tq[ḥn]. | š‘rt. | šb‘ dt tqḥn. | ššlmt. 2099.4
| ‘l.išt.šb‘ d.ǵzrm.ṭb.[g]d.b ḥlb.annḫ b ḫmat. | w ‘l.agn.šb‘ d m.dǵ[t.---]t. | tlk m.rḥmy.w tṣd[.---]. | tḥgrn.ǵzr.n‘m.[--- 23[52].15
.‘l.‘d.w ‘rbm.t‘nyn. | w šd.šd ilm.šd aṯrt.w rḥm. | ‘l.išt.šb‘ d.ǵzrm.ṭb.[g]d.b ḥlb.annḫ b ḫmat. | w ‘l.agn.šb‘ d m.dǵ[t 23[52].14
]. | tḥm.rb.mi[--.‘]bd k. | l.p‘n.b‘l y[.mrḥqtm]. | šb‘ d.w.šb‘[d.qlt]. | ankn.rgmt.l.b‘l y. | l.špš.‘lm.l.‘ṯtrt. | l.‘nt.l.kl.il.alṯ 2008.1.5
brm.gpn. | yṣmdnn.ṣmdm.gpn.yšql.šdmt h. | km gpn. | šb‘ d.yrgm.‘l.‘d.w ‘rbm.t‘nyn. | w šd.šd ilm.šd aṯrt.w rḥm. | ‘l 23[52].12
| adt y.rgm. | tḥm.illdr. | ‘bd k.. | l.p‘n a[dt y]. | šb‘ d[.w šb‘ d]. | mrḥq[tm.qlt]. | mn[m.šlm]. 1014.6
[l] y. | rgm. | tḥm.ṯpṭb[‘l]. | [‘]bd k. | [l.p]‘n.b‘l y. | [šb‘] d.šb‘ [d]. | [mr]ḥqtm. | qlt. | ‘bd k.b. | lwsnd. | [w] b ṣr. | ‘m.mlk. | 2063.6
n]. | b‘l y.r[gm]. | tḥm.‘bd[--]. | ‘bd k. | l p‘n.b‘l y. | ṯn id.šb‘ d. | mrḥqtm. | qlt.‘m. | b‘l y.mnm. | šlm. | [r]gm[.ṯṯṯb]. | [l.]‘ 2115.2.6
lk.b‘[l] y. | rgm. | tḥm.ṯpṭb[‘l]. | [‘]bd k. | [l.p]‘n.b‘l y. | [šb‘] d.šb‘ [d]. | [mr]ḥqtm. | qlt. | ‘bd k.b. | lwsnd. | [w] b ṣr. | ‘m. 2063.6
gmǵ.kšmm.b.yrḫ.iṯtbnm. | šb‘m.dd.ṯn.kbd. | tgmr.ḥṭm.šb‘.ddm. | ḫmš.dd.š‘rm. | kdm.yn. | kdm.ṣmṣ. 1099.32
rt.w.ṯṯm.dd. | ḥpr.bnšm. | b.gt.knpy.mit.dr‘.ṯṯm.drt.w.šb‘m.dd.arb‘. | kbd.ḥpr.bnšm. | b.gt.ṯrmn.arb‘m.dr‘.w.‘šrm.d 1098.18
w.kd.ḥmṣ. | prš.glbm.l.bt. | tgmǵ.kšmm.b.yrḫ.iṯtbnm. | šb‘m.dd.ṯn.kbd. | tgmr.ḥṭm.šb‘.ddm. | ḫmš.dd.š‘rm. | kdm.yn. 1099.31
ṯṯ.kbd.ḥpr.bnšm. | b.gt.ḥdṯt.arb‘m.dr‘.w.ṯlṯm.drt. | [w].šb‘m.dd.ṯn.kbd.ḥpr.bnšm. | b.nzl.‘šrm.l.mit.dr‘.w.šb‘m.drt. | 1098.23
qmḫ.d.kly.b bt.skn. | l.illdrm. | ltḥ.ḫsr.b.šb‘.ddm. 2093.3
w.‘šrm.l.mit. | [drt.ḥpr.b]nšm.w.ṯn.‘šr h.dd.l.rpš. | [---.]šb‘m.dr‘.w.arb‘m.drt.mit.dd. | [---].ḥpr.bn.šm. | [b.---.]knm.ṯṯ 1098.5
[w].šb‘m.dd.ṯn.kbd.ḥpr.bnšm. | b.nzl.‘šrm.l.mit.dr‘.w.šb‘m.drt. | w.‘šrm.l.mit.dd.ḥpr.bnšm. | b.y‘ny.arb‘m.dr‘.w.‘šr 1098.24
kl.b.gt[.b]‘ln. | ṯlṯ.mat.ṯṯm.kbd. | ṯṯm.ṯṯ.kbd.ḥpr.‘bdm. | šb‘m.drt.arb‘m.drt. | l.a[--.---]. | tgm[r.ak]l.b.gt.ḫldy. | ṯlṯ.ma[2013.8
[---.---.]l.mit.dr‘.w.šb‘m.drt. | [---.ḥpr.]bnšm.w.l.ḥrš.‘rq.ṯn.‘šr h. | [---.d]r‘.w.mit. 1098.1
| b gngn h.aḥd y.d ym | lk.‘l.ilm.l ymru. | ilm.w nšm.d yšb | [‘].hmlt.arṣ.gm.l ǵ | [lm] h.b‘l k.yṣḥ.‘n. | [gpn].w ugr.b ǵl 4[51].7.51
.tmt. | mrb‘t.zblnm. | mḫmšt.yitsp. | ršp.nṯdṯt.ǵlm. | ym.mšb‘t hn.b šlḥ. | ttpl.y‘n.ḥtk h. | krt y‘n.ḥtk h.rš. | mid.grdš.ṯ 14[KRT].1.20
ṣb. | rqd.ṯlṯ.mṣb.w.[---]. | uḫnp.ṯṯ.mṣb. | tgmr.[y]n.mṣb š[b‘]. | w ḥs[p] ṯn.k[dm]. 2004.35
ym.ḥẓ k.al.tš‘l. | qrt h.abn.yd k. | mšdpt.w hn.špšm. | b šb‘.w l.yšn.pbl. | mlk.l qr.ṯigt.ibr h. | l ql.nhqt.ḥmr h. | l g‘t.al 14[KRT].3.119
. | d[m].ym.w ṯn. | ṯlṯ.rb‘.ym. | ḫmš.ṯdṯ.ym. | mk.špšm.b šb‘. | w l.yšn.pbl. | mlk.l [qr.]ṯiqt. | ibr h[.l]ql.nhqt. | ḥmr[h.l 14[KRT].5.221
dbr. | lk.ym.w ṯn.ṯlṯ.rb‘ ym. | ḫmš.ṯdṯ.ym.mk.špšm. | b šb‘.w tmǵy.l udm. | rbm.w l.udm.ṯrrt. | w gr.nn.‘rm.šrn. | pdr 14[KRT].3.108
n.b.ṯq[l]. | ḫmšm.šmt.b.ṯql. | kkr.w.[ml]tḥ.tyt.[---]. | [b]šb‘[m.w.n]ṣp.ksp. | [tgm]r.[alp.w.]ṯlṯ.mat. 2101.27
k].al[.---]. | [-]tm.iph.adt y.w.[---]. | tšṣḥq.hn.aṯt.l.‘bd. | šb‘t.w.nṣp.ksp. | [-]tm.rb[.--.a]ḥd. | [---.--]t.b[-]. | [---.-]y[-]. 1017.5
bu.ḏdm.qn[-.-]n[-.-]lt. | ql h.yš[m‘].tr.[il].ab h.[---]l. | b šb‘t.ḥdrm.[b ṯ]mn[t.ap]. | sgrt.g[-].[-]ẓ[.---] h[.---]. | ‘n.ṯk[.---] 3[‘NT.VI].5.19
d k.ašhlk.šbt[k.dmm]. | [šbt.dqn k.mm‘m.]y‘ny. | il.b šb‘t.ḥdrm.b ṯmnt. | ap.sgrt.yd‘[t k.]bt.k an[št]. | k in.b ilht.ql[3[‘NT.VI].5.34
.]aliyn.b‘l. | [ṯṭbḫ.š]b‘m.y‘lm. | [k gmn.al]iyn.b‘l. | [ṯṭbḫ.šb‘m.]ḫmrm. | [k gm]n.al[i]yn.b[‘l]. | [---]ḥ h.tšt bm.‘[--]. | [--- 6[62].1.28
šb‘.ḫdǵlm. | l.[---]mn ḫpn. | l[.--.]škn.ḫpn. | l.k[-]w.ḫpn. | l.ṣ[--] 1117.1
‘šr.ḫsnm. | n‘r.mrynm. | ḫmš. | ṯrtnm.ḫmš. | mrum.‘šr. | šb‘.ḫsnm. | mkrm. | mrynm. | ṯlṯ.‘šr. | hbṯnm. | ṯmn. | mdrǵlm. | 1031.7
‘šr.mkrm. | ḫmš.ṯrtnm. | ḫmš.bn.mrynm. | ‘šr.mrum.w.šb‘.ḫsnm. | tš‘m.mdrǵlm. | arb‘.l ‘šrm.ḫsnm. | ‘šr.hbṯnm. | ṯṯm. 1030.6
tš‘.ṯnnm. | w.arb‘.ḫsnm. | ‘šr.mrum. | w.šb‘.ḫsnm. | tš‘.‘šr. | mrynm. | ṯlṯ.‘šr.mkrm. | ṯlṯ.bn.mrynm. | ar 1029.4
| ṯlṯ.b[n.]mrynm. | ‘šr[.m]krm. | tš‘.hbṯnm. | ‘šr.mrum. | šb‘.ḫsnm. | tš‘m.ṯṯ.kbd.mdrǵlm. | ‘šrm.aḥd.kbd.ḫsnm. | ubny 1028.8
šb‘.ṯnnm.w.šb‘.ḫsnm. | ṯmn.‘šr h.mrynm. | ‘šr.mkrm. | ḫmš.ṯrtnm. | ḫmš.b 1030.1
b ym.w ndd.gzr.l zr.y‘db.u ymn. | u šmal.b p hm.w l.tšb‘n y.aṯt.itrḫ. | y bn.ašld.šu.‘db.tk.mdbr qdš. | ṯm tgrgr.l ab 23[52].64
| hm.imt.imt.npš.blt. | ḥmr.p imt.b klt. | yd y.ilḥm.hm.šb‘. | ydt y.b ṣ‘.hm.ks.ymsk. | nhr.k[--].ṣḥn.b‘l.‘m. | aḫ y.qran. 5[67].1.20
k rumm.hm. | ‘n.kdd.aylt. | mt hm.ks.ym | sk.nhr hm. | šb‘.ydt y.b ṣ‘. | [--.]šb‘.rbt. | [---.]qbṯ.ṯm. | [---.]bn.ilm. | [m]t.š UG5.4.11
ṣt h. | [dn]il.yd.ṣt h.y‘l.w yškb. | [yd.]mizrt.p yln.mk.b šb‘.ymm. | [w]yqrb.b‘l.b ḥnt h.abynt. | [d]nil.mt.rpi anḫ.ǵzr. 17[2AQHT].1.16
d]ṯ.ym.tikl. | išt.[b]bht m.nblat. | b[qrb.hk]l m.mk. | b šb[‘.]y[mm].td.išt. | b bht m.n[bl]at.b hkl m. | sb.ksp.l rqm.ḫ 4[51].6.32
š. | ṯdṯ.ym.yšlḥm.k[ṯ]rt. | w y[ššq].bnt.hll.snnt. | mk.b šb[‘.]ymm.tb‘.b bt h. | kṯrt.bnt.hll.snnt. | [-]d[-]t.n‘m y.‘rš.h[- 17[2AQHT].2.39
.tlḥmn.rpum. | tštyn.bt.ikl.b pr‘. | yṣq.b irt.lbnn.mk.b šb‘. | [ymm.---]k.aliyn.b‘l. | [---].r‘ h ab y. | [---.]‘[---]. 22.2[124].25
k.bt.[b‘l.w mnt k]. | bt il.aḥd.yd k.b [škrn]. | m‘ms k.k šb‘t.yn.ṭ[ḫ]. | gg k.b ym.ṭiṭ.rḥṣ. | npṣ k.b ym rṭ.b uni[l]. | pnm. 17[2AQHT].2.6
maḫdh. | kd l kblbn. | kdm.mṭḫ. | l.alṯy. | kd.l mrynm. | šb‘ yn. | l mrynm. | b yṯbmlk. | kdm.ǵbiš ḥry. | ḫmš yn.b d. | b 1090.10
šb‘.yn.l [---]. | ṯlṯ.l ḥr[š.---]. | ṯṯ[.l.]mštt[.---]. | ṯlṯ.l.mdr[ǵlm]. | 1091.1
ḥt. | niṣ h.grš d.‘šy.ln h. | aḥd.yd h.b škrn.m‘ms h. | [k]šb‘ yn.spu.ksm h.bt.b‘l. | [w m]nt h bt.il.ṭḫ.gg h.b ym. | [ṭi]ṭ.r 17[2AQHT].1.32
ṭbq lḥt.niṣ y.grš. | d ‘šy.ln.aḥd.yd y.b š | krn m‘ms y k šb‘t yn. | spu.ksm y.bt.b‘l.[w]mn[t]. | y.bt.il.ṭḫ.gg y.b ym.ṭiṭ. 17[2AQHT].2.20
b yrḫ.[---]. | šb‘.yn[.---]. | mlkt[.---]. | kd.yn.l.[---]. | armwl w [--]. | arb‘.yn.[1092.2
.aliyn.b‘l. | [ṯṭb]ḫ.šb‘m.aylm. | [k gmn.]aliyn.b‘l. | [ṯṭbḫ.š]b‘m.y‘lm. | [k gmn.al]iyn.b‘l. | [ṯṭbḫ.šb‘m.]ḫmrm. | [k gm]n. 6[62].1.26
. | w.ṯn.irpm.w.ṯn.trqm. | w.qpt.w.mqḥm. | w.ṯlṯm.yn šb‘.kbd d ṭbt. | w.ḫmšm.yn.d iḫ h. 1103.22
m.dd. | [---.yn.d.]nkly.l.r‘ym.šb‘m.l.mitm.dd. | [---.--]d.šb‘m.kbd.dr‘. | [---.]kbd.ddm.kbd[.---]. | [---.]‘m.kbd.l.r‘[ym.- 1098.45
ṯlṯ.mat. | šb‘m kbd. | zt.ubdym. | b mlk. 1095.2
.kbd.ḥṭm. | [-]m[-.-]‘[-.-]ag š‘rm. | [---.--]mi. | [--.]ṯṯ[m] šb‘.k[bd]. | [---]m.b.mril. 2091.8
skn.‘šrm kk[r.---]. | mšrn.ṯlṯ.‘š[r.kkr]. | bn.šw.šb‘.kk[r.---]. | arb‘m.kkr.[---]. | b d.mtn.[l].šlm. 2108.3
r[b‘.]arb‘.mṯbt.azmr.b h.š.šr[-]. | al[p.w].š.šlmm.pamt.šb‘.klb h. | yr[--.]mlk.ṣbu.špš.w.ḥl.mlk. | w.[---].ypm.w.mḫ[-- 35[3].52
t.w.ṯlṯt.ksp h. | arb‘.kkr. | algbṯ.arb‘t. | ksp h. | kkr.š‘rt. | šb‘t.ksp h. | ḫmš.mqdm.dnyn. | b.tql.dprn.aḥd. | b.tql. | ḫmšm 1127.18
[m.---]. | krm.ǵlkz.b.p[--.---]. | krm.ilyy.b.m[--.---]. | kd.šb‘.krmm.[---]. | ṯn.krm[m.i]wrǵl[.---]. | ṯn.krm.[-]myn.[---]. | 1081.25

.ṯlṯt.mzn.|drk.š.alp.w ṯlṯ.|ṣin.šlm[m.]šb‘ pamt.|l ilm.šb[‘.]l kṯr.|‘lm.t‘rbn.gṯrm.|bt.mlk.ṯql.ḫrṣ.|l špš.w yrḫ.l gṯr. 33[5].8
h.|[---.--]r h.‘šr[m.---.‘]šrm.dd.|[---.yn.d.]nkly.l.r‘ym.šb‘m.l.mitm.dd.|[---.--]d.šb‘m.kbd.dr‘.|[---.]kbd.ddm.kbd[.- 1098.44
r.|kkr.ḫmš.mat.kbd.ṯlṯ.šm[n].|alp.mitm.kbd.ṯlṯ.ḥlb.|šb‘.l.‘šrm.kkr.ṯlṯ.|d.ybl.blym. 1135.6
qpnt.‘d.|k lbš.km.lpš.dm a[ḫ h].|km.all.dm.ary h.|k šb‘t.l šb‘m.aḫ h.ym[.--].|w ṯmnt.l ṯmnym.|šr.aḫy h.mẓa h.| 12[75].2.49
[---.--]i[-.]a[--.---].|[---.]ilm.w ilht.dt.|[---.]šb‘.l šb‘m.aṯr.|[---.--]ldm.dt ymtm.|[--.--]r.l ẓpn.|[---.]pn.y 25[136].3
iyn.b‘l.|yuhb.‘glt.b dbr.prt.|b šd.šḫlmmt.škb.|‘mn h.šb‘.l šb‘m.|tš[‘]ly.ṯmn.l ṯmnym.|w [th]rn.w tldn mṯ.|al[iyn. 5[67].5.20
[---.-]grm.|[---.-]n.‘šrt.ksp.|[--.--]n.šb‘t.l ṯlṯm.|[---].šb‘t.‘šrt.|[---.-]kyn.‘šrt.|b.bn.‘sl.‘šrm.ṯqlm k 2054.1.3
rt.|mlbš.ṯrmnm.|k.yṯn.w.b.bt.|mlk.mlbš.|ytn.l hm.|šb‘.lbšm.allm.|l ušḫry.|ṯlṯ.mat.pṯtm.|l.mgmr.b.ṯlṯ.|šnt. 1107.9
ṣp.ksp.|ṯmn.lbšm.w.mšlt.|l.udmym.b.ṯmnt.‘šrt.ksp.|šb‘m.lbš.d.‘rb.bt.mlk.|b.mit.ḫmšt.kbd.ksp.|ṯlṯ.ktnt.b d.an[r 2101.16
ḫmš.bnšm[.---].|ḫḏǵlm.b d.[---].|šb‘.lmdm.b d.s[n]rn.|lmd.aḥd.b d.yr[š].|lmd.aḥd.b d.yḫ[--] 1050.3
rt.|l.a[--.---].|tgm[r.ak]l.b.gt.ḫldy.|ṯlṯ.ma[t].‘šr.kbd.|šb‘ m[at].kbd.ḫpr.‘bdm.|mit[.d]rt.arb‘m.drt.|[---]m.|t[gm] 2013.12
[--]t.ilhnm.b šnt.|[---.]šb‘.mat.š‘rt.ḫmšm.kbd.|[---.-]nd.l.mlbš.ṯrmnm.|[---]h.lbš.al 1106.2
-].šmt.ḫmšt.ḫndlt.|[---.iqn]i.l.[-]k.btbt.|[---.l.ṯrm]nm.š[b‘].mat.š‘rt.|[---.]iqnu.[---.]lbš.ṯrmnm.|[---.iqn]i.lbš.al[l.--- 1106.19
.|ṣṣ.bn.‘glt.ṯlṯm.|ṣṣ.bn.‘bd.‘šrm.|ṣṣ.bn.mṣḫ[n].‘šrm.|šb‘.mat.ṯṯm kbd. 2096.20
.qn.n‘m.‘n[m].|ṯn.ḥblm.alp.alp.am[-].|ṯmn.ḥblm.šb‘.šb‘.ma[-].|‘šr.kkr.rtn.|b d.šm‘y.bn.bdn. 1128.31
.|tšyt.k brkm.tǵll b dm.|ḏmr.ḥlqm.b mm‘.mhrm.|‘d.tšb‘.tmtḫṣ.b bt.|tḫṣb.bn.ṯlḥnm.ymḥ.|[b]bt.dm.ḏmr.yṣq.šm 3[‘NT].2.29
h.mdnt.|w hln.‘nt.l bt h.tmǵyn.|tštql.ilt.l hkl h.|w l.šb‘t.tmtḫṣ h.b ‘mq.|tḫtṣb.bn.qrtm.tṯ‘r.|ksat.l mhr.ṯ‘r.ṯlḥnt. 3[‘NT].2.19
nt.rḥ.gdm.w anhbm].|w tqr[y.ǵlmm.b št.ǵr.---].|[‘]d tš[b‘.tmtḫṣ.---].|klyn[.---].|špk.l[---].|trḥṣ.yd[h.---].|[--.]yṣ 7.2[130].5
ir.‘šr[.---]m ḥsp.|ḫpty.kdm[.---].|[a]gm.arb‘[.---].|šrš.šb‘.mṣb.|rqd.ṯlṯ.mṣb.w.[---].|uḫnp.ṯṯ.mṣb.|tgmr.[y]n.mṣb š 2004.32
.kmm.b‘lm.kmm.|k t‘rb.‘ṯtrt.šd.bt.mlk[.---].|ṯn.skm.šb‘.mšlt.arb‘.ḫpnt.[---].|ḫmšm.ṯlṯ.rkb.ntn.ṯlṯ.mat.[---].|lg.š UG5.9.1.19
‘l.|yuhb.‘glt.b dbr.prt.|b šd.šḫlmmt.škb.|‘mn h.šb‘.l šb‘m.|tš[‘]ly.ṯmn.l ṯmnym.|w [th]rn.w tldn mṯ.|al[iyn.b‘]l 5[67].5.20
šrt.|b.bn.‘sl.‘šrm.ṯqlm kbd.|b.ṯmq.ḫmšt.l.‘šrt.|b.[---].šb‘t.‘šrt.|b.bn.pdrn.‘šrm.|d.bn.šb‘l.uḫnpy.ḫmšm.|b.bn.ṯṯm. 2054.1.8
t.l.ṯrmnm.|[---].ṯlṯm.iqnu.|[---.l.]ṯrmn.mlk.|[---.]š‘rt.šb‘.‘šr h.|[---.iqn]i.l.ṯrmn.qrt.|[---.]lbš.ḫmšm.iqnu.|[---].šmt 1106.14
|arb‘.ṯrtnm.|tš‘.ḫbṯnm.|ṯmnym.ṯlṯ.kbd.|mdrǵlm.|w.šb‘.‘šr.ḫsnm.|ḫmšm.l.mit.|bnš.l.d.|yškb.l.b.bt.mlk. 1029.13
.šb‘t.‘šrt ‘šrt[.šlm.---].|ybn.ṯmnt.‘šrt ‘šrt.šlm.|‘bdyrḫ.šb‘t.‘šrt ‘šrt.šlm.|yky.‘šrt.ṯṯt šlm.‘šrt.|bn.ḫgby.ṯmnt.l ‘šrm.‘ 1131.6
m š[lm.---].|ilabn.‘šrt ṯqlm kbd.ḫmš.šl[m.---].|tlmyn.šb‘t.‘šrt ‘šrt[.šlm.---].|ybn.ṯmnt.‘šrt ‘šrt.šlm.|‘bdyrḫ.šb‘t.‘šrt 1131.4
lm.kbd.arb‘m.|‘šrt.ḫrṣ.b.arb‘m.|mit.ḫršḫ.b.ṯqlm.|w.šb‘.‘šr.šmn.|d.l.ysa.bt.mlk.|tgmr.ksp.mitm.|ḫmšm.kbd. 2100.20
[---.-]grm.|[---.-]n.‘šrt.ksp.|[--.--]n.šb‘t.l ṯlṯm.|[---].šb‘t.‘šrt.|[---.-]kyn.‘šrt.|b.bn.‘sl.‘šrm.ṯqlm kbd.|b.ṯmq.ḫmšt 2054.1.4
] h.|[---.--]mt.|[---.--]mr.limm.|[---.]bn.ilm.mt.|[--]u.šb‘t.ǵlm h.|[---].bn.ilm.mt.|p[-]n.aḫ y m.ytn.b‘l.|[s]pu y.bn 6[49].6.8
ḫrt.|ilm.arṣ.w at.qḥ.|‘rpt k.rḥ k.mdl k.|mṭrt k.‘m k.šb‘t.|ǵlm k.ṯmn.ḫnzr k.|‘m k.pdry.bt.ar.|‘m k.ṭṭly.bt.rb.id 5[67].5.8
]tn.ušpǵt.|ḫr[-].ṯlṯt.mzn.|drk.š.alp.w ṯlṯ.|ṣin.šlm[m.]šb‘ pamt.|l ilm.šb[‘.]l kṯr.|‘lm.t‘rbn.gṯrm.|bt.mlk.ṯql.ḫrṣ.|l 33[5].7
mlk.ylk.lqḥ.ilm.|aṯr.ilm.ylk.p‘nm.|mlk.p‘nm.yl[k].|šb‘.pamt.l kl hm. 33[5].26
|‘dr.l[‘r].‘rm.|ṯb.l pd[r.]pdrm.|ṯṯ.l ṯtm.aḥd.‘r.|šb‘m.šb‘.pdr.|ṯmnym.b‘l.[----].|tš‘m.b‘l.mr[-].|bt[.--]b b‘l.b qrb.| 4[51].7.10
kb[d].|arb‘m.ṯp[rt].|ksp h.|ṯmn.dd[.--].|ṯlṯ.dd.p[--].|šb‘t.p[--].|tš‘t.k[bd.---].|ḫmšt.k[bd.---].|tgmr k[--.---].|ḫmš 2120.6
].|annt[n.]w[.---].|w.ṯn.bn h.[---].|aǵltn.ypr[y.---].|w.šb‘.ṣin h[.---]. 2044.18
aliyn.|[b]‘l.ṭṭbḫ.šb‘m.alpm.|[k g]mn.aliyn.b‘l.|[ṭt]bḫ.šb‘m.ṣin.|[k gm]n.aliyn.b‘l.|[ṭtb]ḫ.šb‘m.aylm.|[k gmn.]aliy 6[62].1.22
[gm.yṯtb.b ṯdṯ.ṯn].|l šmn.‘[ly h.gdlt.rgm.yṯtb].|brr.b šb‘[.ṣbu.špš.w ḥl]|yt.‘rb špš[.w ḥl.mlk.w.b y]|m.ḥdṯ.ṯn šm[. APP.II[173].51
m.yṯtb.b.ṯdṯ.ṯn[.--.šmn].|‘ly h.gdlt.rgm.yṯ[tb.brr].|b.[šb]‘.ṣbu.[š]pš.w.ḥly[t].‘[r]b[.š]p[š].|w [ḥl.]mlk[.w.]b.ym.ḥdṯ 35[3].47
---].|w šm.‘rbm.yr[.---].|mṯbt.ilm.ṯmn.ṯ[--.--].|pamt.šb‘.|iqnu.šmt[.---].|[b]n.šrm.|iqran.ilm.n‘mm[.agzry ym.b 23[52].20
hr.il.rbm.|l ištbm.tnn.ištml h.|mḫšt.btn.‘qltn.|šlyṭ.d šb‘t.rašm.|mḫšt.mdd ilm.ar[š].|ṣmt.‘gl.il.‘tk.|mḫšt.klbt.ilm 3[‘NT].3.39
[---] k.k tmḫṣ.|[ltn.btn.br]ḥ.tkly.|[btn.‘qltn.]šlyṭ.|[d šb‘t.rašm].ṯtkḥ.|[ttrp.šmm.k rks.ipd]k.|[-----]. 5[67].1.30
k tmḫṣ.ltn.btn.brḥ.|tkly.btn.‘qltn.|šlyṭ.d šb‘y.rašm.|ṯtkḥ.ttrp.šmm.k rs.|ipd k.ank.ispi.uṭm.|ḏrqm.a 5[67].1.3
ṣrrt.ṣpn.tbkyn h.|w tqbrn h.tštnn.b ḫrt.|ilm.arṣ.ṭṭbḫ.šb‘m.|rumm.k gmn.aliyn.|[b]‘l.ṭṭbḫ.šb‘m.alpm.|[k g]mn.al 6[62].1.18
d.aylt.|mt hm.ks.ym|sk.nhr hm.|šb‘.ydt y.b ṣ‘.|[--.]šb‘.rbt.|[---.]qbṭ.ṯm.|[---.]bn.ilm.|[m]t.šmḫ.p ydd.|il[.ǵ]zr. UG5.4.12
y.b ilm].|ydy.mrṣ.g[ršm.zbln].|in.b ilm.‘n[y h.]ytdt.|yšb‘.rgm.[my.]b ilm.|ydy.mrṣ.gršm zbln.|in.b ilm.‘ny h.|w 16[126].5.20
š.‘šr.qn.n‘m.‘n[m].|ṯn.ḥblm.alp.alp.am[-].|ṯmn.ḥblm.šb‘.šb‘.ma[-].|‘šr.kkr.rtn.|b d.šm‘y.bn.bdn. 1128.31
b ṣpn.|‘dr.l[‘r].‘rm.|ṯb.l pd[r.]pdrm.|ṯṯ.l ṯtm.aḥd.‘r.|šb‘m.šb‘.pdr.|ṯmnym.b‘l.[----].|tš‘m.b‘l.mr[-].|bt[.--]b b‘l.b 4[51].7.10
|šnmtm.dbṯ[.---].|tr‘.tr‘n.a[--.---].|bnt.šdm.ṣḥr[.---].|šb‘.šnt.il.mla.[-].|w ṯmn.nqpnt.‘d.|k lbš.km.lpš.dm a[ḫ h].| 12[75].2.45
m‘.l kdd.dnil.|mt.rpi.l ymm.l yrḫm.|l yrḫm.l šnt.‘d.|šb‘t.šnt.ybk.l aq|ht.ǵzr.yd[m‘.]l kdd.|dnil.mt.r[pi.mk].b šb‘ 19[1AQHT].4.177
t hm.|w tqrb.w ld.bn.l h.|w tqrb.w ld.bnt.l h.|mk.b šb‘.šnt.|bn.krt.km hm.tdr.|ap.bnt.ḥry.|km hm.w tḫss.aṭrt. 15[128].3.22
.šnt.ybk.l aq|ht.ǵzr.yd[m‘.]l kdd.|dnil.mt.r[pi.mk].b šb‘.|šnt.w y‘n[.dnil.mt.]rpi.|ytb.ǵzr.m[t.hrnmy.y]šu.|g h.w 19[1AQHT].4.179
--].l kḥṯ.drkt h.|l [ym]m.l yrḫm.l yrḫm.|l šnt.[m]k.b šb‘.|šnt.w [--].bn.ilm.mt.|‘m.aliyn.b‘l.yšu.|g h.w yṣḥ.‘l k.b[6[49].5.8
i.yṣly.‘rpt.b |ḥm.un.yr.‘rpt.|tmṭr.b qẓ.ṭl.yṭll.|l ǵnbm.šb‘.šnt.|yṣr k.b‘l.ṯmn.rkb.|‘rpt.bl.ṭl.bl rbb.|bl.šr‘.thmtm.bl. 19[1AQHT].1.42
bn.ašld.šu.‘db.tk.mdbr qdš.|ṯm tgrgr.l abnm.w l.‘ṣm.šb‘.šnt.|tmt.ṯmn.nqpt.‘d.ilm.n‘mm.ttlkn.|šd.tṣdn.pat.mdbr 23[52].66
h.g‘r.yṯb.il.kb[-].|aṯ[rt.]il.yṯb.b mrzḥ h.|yšt[.il.y]n.‘d šb‘.trṯ.‘d škr.|il.hlk.l bt h.yštql.|l ḥṭr h.y‘msn.nn.ṯkmn.|w UG5.1.1.16
qrb|hkl [h].ṣḥ.l qṣ.ilm.tlḥmn.|ilm.w tštn.tštn y[n] ‘d šb‘.|trṯ.‘d.škr.y‘db.yrḫ.|gb h.km.[---.]yqtqt.tḥt.|ṯlḥnt.il.d y UG5.1.1.3
[---].dt.iṯ.|[---].ṯlṯ.kbd.|[---].alpm.ḫmš.mat.|šb‘m[.t]š‘.kbd.|tgmr.uz.ǵrn.arb‘.mat.|tgmr.uz.aḫmn.arb‘. 1129.4
.w tṣḥ.šm‘.m[‘.l a]|[qht.ǵ]zr.at.aḫ.w an.a[ḫt k].|[---].šb‘.ṯir k.[---].|[---.]ab y.ndt.ank[.---].|[---.--]l.mlk.tlk.b ṣd[.-- 18[3AQHT].1.25
rb‘m.l.mit.tišr.|ṯṯ.ṯṯ.b [ṯ]ql.ṯlṯt.l.‘šrm.ksp hm.|šstm.b.šb‘m.|ṯlṯ.mat.trm.b.‘šrt.|mit.adrm.b.‘šrt.|‘šr.ydt.b.‘šrt.|ḫm 1127.6
šlm.‘šrt.|bn.ḫgby.ṯmnt.l ‘šrm.‘šrt.ḫmš.kbd.|bn.ilṣdq.šb‘t ṯlṯt šlm.|bn.ṯmq.arb‘t ṯqlm šlmm. 1131.9
|ṯlṯ.mat.‘šrm[.---].|ṯmnym.drt.a[--].|drt.l.alpm[.---].|šb‘m.ṯn.kbd[.ḫpr.‘b]dm.|tg[mr.---].|[-]m.m[--.---].|[m]itm. 2013.19
šb‘.ṯnnm.w.šb‘.ḫsnm.|ṯmn.‘šr h.mrynm.|‘šr.mkrm.|ḫmš.ṯr 1030.1
|šm‘[.l mṯt.ḥry].|ṭbḫ.š[mn].mri k.|ptḥ.[rḥ]bt.yn.|ṣḥ.šb‘m.ṯr y.|ṯmnym.[z]by y.|ṯr.ḫbr[.rb]t.|ḫbr[.ṯrrt].|[-]‘b[-].š 15[128].4.6

---.]yn.l.mlkt.|[---.yrẖ.]ḫlt.šb‘.[---].mlkt.|[---.yrẖ.]gn.šb‘[.--].|[---.yrẖ.]itb.šb[‘.---].|[-----]. 1088.14
-]ẖ.|ṯmnym.dd.dd.kbd.|[l].mdr[ǵ]lm.|b yrẖ[ri]šyn.|šb[‘.--]n.[k]bd.|w[.---.]qm‘t.|[---.]mdrǵlm.|[---.]mdm.|[w].‘ 2012.22
[---.-]b‘m.|[---.b]n.yšm[‘].|[---.]mlkr[-] h.b.nṯk.|[---.]šb‘m.|[---.]ẖrg.‘šrm.|[---.]abn.ksp.ṯlṯ.|[---].bty.ksp.‘šr[t].|[- 2153.4
.|kd.l.ydn.|[---.y]rẖ.ẖyr.|[---.]yn.l.mlkt.|[---.yrẖ.]ḫlt.šb‘.[---].mlkt.|[---.yrẖ.]gn.šb‘[.--].|[---.yrẖ.]itb.šb[‘.---].|[---- 1088.13
‘r.ym.l bl[.---].|b[---.]ny[.--].|l bl.sk.w [---] h.|ybm h.šb‘[.---].|ǵzr.ilḥu.t[---]l.|trm.tṣr.trm[.‘]tqt.|tbky.w tšnn.[tt] 16.2[125].94
].|[t]lṯ kbd.yn.b [gt.---].|mit.[---].ṯlṯ.kb[d].|[dd.--]m.šb‘.[---].|[---].‘šr.dd[.---].|[---]mn.arb‘m.y[n].|b.gt.trǵnds.|t 2092.12
[---.]ṯlṯm.|[---.n]ḫl.|[---.ṯ]lṯ.mat.šb‘m[.---].|[---.--]mm.b.mṣbt[.---].|[---.ṯl]ṯ.mat.ṯmny[m.---]. 2149.3
rẖ.]ḫlt.šb‘.[---].mlkt.|[---.yrẖ.]gn.šb‘[.--].|[---.yrẖ.]itb.šb[‘.---].|[-----]. 1088.15
].|b.gt.trǵnds.|tš‘.‘šr.[dd].kšmm.|ṯn.‘šr[.dd.ḥ]ṭm.|w.šb[‘.---]. 2092.18
ary ẖmšt.|ykn‘m ẖmšt.|‘nmky ṯqlm.|[-]kt ‘šrt.|qrn šb‘t. 1176.8

šb‘l

mq.ẖmšt.l.‘šrt.|b.[---].šb‘t.‘šrt.|b.bn.pdrn.‘šrm.|d.bn.šb‘l.uẖnpy.ẖmšm.|b.bn.ṯtm.ṯlṯm.|b.bn.agdṯb.‘šrm.|b.bn.ib 2054.1.10
--].|plšb‘l.bn.n[--].|ḥy bn.dnn.ṯkt.|ilthm.bn.dnn.ṯkt.|šb‘l.bn.aly.ṯkt.|klby.bn.iḫy.ṯkt.|pss.bn.buly.ṯkt.|‘pṣpn.bn.‘ 2085.6
bdl.gt.bn.tbšn.|bn.mnyy.š‘rty.|aryn.adddy.|agptr.|šb‘l.mlky.|n‘mn.mṣry.|y‘l.kn‘ny.|gdn.bn.umy.|kn‘m.š‘rty. 91[311].5
l y.mlk[y.---].|yd.bt h.yd[.---].|ary.yd.t[--.---].|ḫtn h.šb‘l[.---].|ṯlḫny.yd[.---].|yd.ṯlṯ.kl[t h.---].|w.ṯṯm.ṣi[n.---].|tn 81[329].16
.agytn.|[---] gnym.|[--]ry.w ary.|[---]ǵrbtym.|[---.]w šb‘l.|[---.-]ym.|[---.--]ẖm.|[---.--]m.|[---]nb.w ykn.|[--]ndby 131[309].16

šbš

.mt.npš[.-].|npš.lbun.|thw.w npš.|anẖr.b ym.|brkt.šbšt.|k rumm.hm.|‘n.kdd.aylt.|mt hm.ks.ym|sk.nhr hm.| UG5.4.6

šgr

.---].|aylt tǵpy tr.‘n[.---].|b[b]r.mrḥ h.ti[ẖd.b yd h].|š[g]r h bm ymn.t[--.---].|[--.]l b‘l.‘bd[.---].|tr ab h il.ttrm[.-- 2001.1.13
lp.w.š.|ṯrty.alp.w.š.|yrẖ.š.ṣpn.š.|kṯr š ‘ṯtr.š.|[‘ṯt]rt.š.šgr w iṯm š.|[---.]š.ršp.idrp.š.|[---.il.t‘]dr.š.|[---.-]mt.š.|[----- UG5.9.2.9
lk[.---].|w lk.ilm[.---].|n‘m.ilm[.---].|šgr.mu[d.---].|šgr.mud[.---].|dm.mt.aṣ[ḥ.---].|yd.b qrb[.---].|w lk.ilm.[---]. 5[67].3.17
l[--.---].|ṯmm.w lk[.---].|w lk.ilm[.---].|n‘m.ilm[.---].|šgr.mu[d.---].|šgr.mud[.---].|dm.mt.aṣ[ḥ.---].|yd.b qrb[.---]. 5[67].3.16

šd

rm.|[šd.]bn.ṯqdy.b d.gmrd.|[š]d bn.synn.b d.gmrd.|[šd.]abyy.b d.ibrmd.|[šd.]bn.ttrn.b d.bnš.aǵlkz.|[šd.b]d.b[n 82[300].2.19
šd.snrym.dt.‘qb.|b.ayly.|šd.abršn.|šd.kkn.[bn].ubyn.|šd.bn.li[y].|šd.bn.š[--]y.|šd.bn 2026.3
|l‘q[.---].|šd.pll.b d.qrt.|š[d].anndr.b d.bdn.nḥ[l h].|[šd.]agyn.b d.kmrn.n[ḥl] h.|[š]d.nbzn.[-]l.qrt.|[š]d.agpṯr.b d 2029.8
l h.|šd knn.bn.ann.‘db.|šd.iln[-].bn.irtr.l.šḫrn.nḥl h.|šd[.ag]pṯn.b[n.]brrn.l.qrt.|šd[.--]dy.bn.brzn.|l.qrt. 2029.21
[l h].|[šd.]agyn.b d.kmrn.n[ḥl] h.|[š]d.nbzn.[-]l.qrt.|[š]d.agpṯr.b d.šḫrn.nḥl h.|šd.annmn.b d.tyn.nḥl h.|šd.pǵyn[2029.10
.bht m.tbn[n].|ḥš.trmmn.hk[l m].|b tk.ṣrrt.ṣpn.|alp.šd.aḥd bt.|rbt.kmn.hkl.|w y‘n.kṯr.w ḫss.|šm‘.l aliyn b‘l.|b 4[51].5.118
n.nḥl [h].|šd.ṯtyn[.b]n.arkšt.|l‘q[.---].|šd.pll.b d.qrt.|š[d].anndr.b d.bdn.nḥ[l h].|[šd.]agyn.b d.kmrn.n[ḥl] h.|[š] 2029.7
n[ḥl] h.|[š]d.nbzn.[-]l.qrt.|[š]d.agpṯr.b d.šḫrn.nḥl h.|šd.annmn.b d.tyn.nḥl h.|šd.pǵyn[.b] d.krmn.l.ty[n.n]ḥl h.| 2029.11
t[.b ‘]p[r] m.ddym.ask.|šlm.l kb[d].awṣ.arbdd.|l kbd.š[d]m.ap.mṯn.rgmm.|argmn.lk.lk.‘nn.ilm.|atm.bštm.w an. 3[‘NT].4.75
|km gpn.|šb‘ d.yrgm.‘l.‘d.w ‘rbm.t‘nyn.|w šd.šd ilm.šd aṯrt.w rḥm.|‘l.išt.šb‘ d.ǵzrm.ṭb.[g]d.b ḥlb.annẖ b ẖmat.| 23[52].13
ǵnbm.šlm.‘rbm.ṯn[nm].|hlkm.b dbḥ n‘mt.|šd[.i]lm.šd.aṯrt.w rḥmy.|[---].y[ṯ]b.|[---]p.gp ym.w yṣǵd.gp..thm.|[23[52].28
-].|nšlḥ[.---].|[---.m]at.|[---.]mat.|š[--].išal.|‘m k.ybl.šd.|a[--].d‘.k.|šld.ašld.|hn.mrṯ.d.štt.|ašld b ldt k. 2009.2.4
‘.‘šr h.šd.|w.kmsk.d.iwrkl.|ṯlṯ.šd.d.bn.mlkyy.|kmsk.šd.iḫmn.|širm.šd.khn.|ṯlṯ.šd.w.krm.šir.d.ḫli.|širm.šd.šd.‘šy 1079.4
.ṯlṯ.|šmny.|ḫršn.|ldn.|bn.ands.|bn.ann.|bn.‘bdpdr.|šd.iyry.l.‘bdb‘l.|šd.šmmn.l.bn.šty.|šd.bn.arws.l.bn.ḫlan.|šd 1102.17
m.ṯr.il.ab k.|hwt.lṭpn.ḥtk k.|pl.‘nt.šdm.y špš.|pl.‘nt.šdm.il.yš[t k].|b‘l.‘nt.mḥrṯ[-].|iy.aliyn.b‘l.|iy.zbl.b‘l.arṣ.|w 6[49].4.37
l btlt.‘n[t].|rgm.l nrt.il.šp[š].|pl.‘nt.šdm.y špš.|pl.‘nt.šdm.il.yšt k.|[b]‘l.‘nt.mḥrṯt.|iy.aliyn.b‘l.|iy.zbl.b‘l.arṣ.|ttb‘ 6[49].4.26
dmt h.|km gpn.|šb‘ d.yrgm.‘l.‘d.w ‘rbm.t‘nyn.|w šd.šd ilm.šd aṯrt.w rḥm.|‘l.išt.šb‘ d.ǵzrm.ṭb.[g]d.b ḥlb.annẖ b 23[52].13
[.---].|w ǵnbm.šlm.‘rbm.ṯn[nm].|hlkm.b dbḥ n‘mt.|šd[.i]lm.šd.aṯrt.w rḥmy.|[---].y[ṯ]b.|[---]p.gp ym.w yṣǵd.gp. 23[52].28
.|šd.pln.bn.tiyn.b d.ilmhr nḥl h.|šd knn.bn.ann.‘db.|šd.iln[-].bn.irtr.l.šḫrn.nḥl h.|šd[.ag]pṯn.b[n.]brrn.l.qrt.|šd[. 2029.20
.nqdm.|[ṯlṯ].šdm.d.n‘rb.gt.npk.|[š]d.rpan.b d.klttb.|[š]d.ilṣy.b d.‘bdym.|[ub]dy.trrm.|[šd.]bn.ṯqdy.b d.gmrd.|[š] 82[300].2.15
t.|šd[.-].dyn.b d.pln.nḥl h.|šd.irdyn.bn.ḫrǵš[-].l.qrt.|šd.iǵlyn.bn.kzbn.l.qr[t].|šd.pln.bn.tiyn.b d.ilmhr nḥl h.|šd 2029.17
].|šd.ṯ[r]yn.bn.tkn.b d.qrt.|šd[.-].dyn.b d.pln.nḥl h.|šd.irdyn.bn.ḫrǵš[-].l.qrt.|šd.iǵlyn.bn.kzbn.l.qr[t].|šd.pln.bn 2029.16
šd.ubdy.ilštm‘.|dt b d.skn.|šd.bn.ubr‘n b gt prn.|šd.bn.gby 1104.1
]my.|[---.]bn.[---].|[---].šd ubdy.|[---.šd] u[b]dy.|[---.]šd.ubdy.|[---.]bn.k[--.]ṯ[l]ṯm ksp b[---].|[---.]šd b‘ly.|[---.]šd 2031.5
k[--.]ṯ[l]ṯm ksp b[---].|[---.]šd b‘ly.|[---.]šd ubdy.|[---.š]d ubdy.|[---.šd] ubdy.|[---.š]d.bn.ṣin.|[---].bn.dly.|[---.]ṯṯ 2031.9
[---.--]my.|[---.]bn.[---].|[---].šd ubdy.|[---.šd] u[b]dy.|[---.]šd.ubdy.|[---.]bn.k[--.]ṯ[l]ṯm 2031.3
[---.--]my.|[---.]bn.[---].|[---].šd ubdy.|[---.šd] u[b]dy.|[---.]šd.ubdy.|[---.]bn.k[--.]ṯ[l]ṯm ksp b[---].|[--- 2031.4
bdy.|[---.]bn.k[--.]ṯ[l]ṯm ksp b[---].|[---.]šd b‘ly.|[---.]šd ubdy.|[---.š]d ubdy.|[---.šd] ubdy.|[---.š]d.bn.ṣin.|[---].b 2031.8
šd.ubdy[.---].|šd.bn.ẖb[--.---].|šd.srn[.---].|šd.y‘dr[.---].|šd. 83[85].1
b[---].|[---.]šd b‘ly.|[---.]šd ubdy.|[---.š]d ubdy.|[---.šd] ubdy.|[---.š]d.bn.ṣin.|[---].bn.dly.|[---.]tty[-.--]. 2031.10
[š]šw[.i]ryn.arr.|[š]dm.b.mlk.|[--.š]dm.b.ar.|[--.š]dm.b.ulm.|[--.š]dm.b.m‘rby.|[--.šd]m.b.ušk 2033.1.3
[š]šw[.i]ryn.arr.|[š]dm.b.mlk.|[--.š]dm.b.ar.|[--.š]dm.b.ulm.|[--.š]dm.b.m‘rby.|[--.šd]m.b.uškn.|[---.--]n.|[- 2033.1.4
.|[--.š]dm.b.ar.|[--.š]dm.b.ulm.|[--.š]dm.b.m‘rby.|[--.šd]m.b.uškn.|[---.--]n.|[---].tlmdm.|[y]bnn.ṣmdm.|ṯp[ṭ]b‘l. 2033.1.6
rdn.l bn.bly.|šd gzl.l.bn.ṭbr[n].|šd.ẖzmyn.l a[--].|ṯn šdm b uš[kn]. 2089.16
ubdy.mdm.|šd.b d.‘bdmlk.|šd.b d.yšn.ḥrš.|šd.b d.aupš.|šd.b d.ršpab.aḥ.ubn.|šd.b d.bn.uṯryn.|[ubd]y. 82[300].1.4
.b d.iwrkl.|šd.b d.klb.|šd.b d.klby.|šd.b d.iytlm.|ṯn.šdm.b d.amtrn.|šd.b d.iwrm[--].|šd.b d.yṯpr.|šd.b d.krb[-]. 2090.12

y.|šd.b d.bn.ʻyn.|ṯn.šdm.b d.klṯṯb.|šd.b d.krz[n].|ṯlṯ.šdm.b d.amtr[n].|ṯn.šdm.b d.skn.|šd.b d[.ʻb]dyrẖ.|šd.b [d.- 2090.22
md̲.|[š]d.bn.ilṯtmr.b d.tbbr.|[w.]šd.nḥl h.b d.ṯṯmd.|[š]d.b d.iwrẖṯ.|[ṯn].šdm.b d.gmrd.|[šd.]lbny.b d.tbṯṯb.|[š]d. 82[300].1.13
]d.u[--].|šd.b d.[---].|šd.b d[.---]im.|šd.b d[.bn.--]n.|šd.b d.iwrkl.|šd.b d.klb.|šd.b d.klby.|šd.b d.iytlm.|ṯn.šdm. 2090.8
d.klb.|šd.b d.klby.|šd.b d.iytlm.|ṯn.šdm.b d.amtrn.|šd.b d.iwrm[--].|šd.b d.yṯpr.|šd.b d.krb[-].|šd.b d.bn.ptd̲.|š 2090.13
[--.-]d[-.---].|[--.šd]m.b d.iyt[lm].|[šd.b]d.s[--].|š[d.b]d.u[--].|šd.b d.[---].|š 2090.2
d.b d[.bn.--]n.|šd.b d.iwrkl.|šd.b d.klb.|šd.b d.klby.|šd.b d.iytlm.|ṯn.šdm.b d.amtrn.|šd.b d.iwrm[--].|šd.b d.yṯ 2090.11
[--.-]d[-.---].|[--.šd]m.b d.iyt[lm].|[šd.b]d.s[--].|š[d.b]d.u[--].|šd.b d.[---].|šd.b d[.---]im.|šd.b d[.bn.--]n.|š 2090.4
k.|šd.b d.yšn.ḥrš.|šd.b d.aupš.|šd.b d.ršpab.aẖ.ubn.|šd.b d.bn.uṯryn.|[ubd]y.mrynm.|[š]d.bn.ṣnrn.b d.nrn.|[š]d 82[300].1.6
b[-].|šd.b d.bn.ptd̲.|šd.b d.dr.khnm.|šd.b d.bn.ʻmy.|šd.b d.bn.ʻyn.|ṯn.šdm.b d.klṯṯb.|šd.b d.krz[n].|ṯlṯ.šdm.b d. 2090.19
.yṯpr.|šd.b d.krb[-].|šd.b d.bn.ptd̲.|šd.b d.dr.khnm.|šd.b d.bn.ʻmy.|šd.b d.bn.ʻyn.|ṯn.šdm.b d.klṯṯb.|šd.b d.krz[2090.18
.amtrn.|šd.b d.iwrm[--].|šd.b d.yṯpr.|šd.b d.krb[-].|šd.b d.bn.ptd̲.|šd.b d.dr.khnm.|šd.b d.bn.ʻmy.|šd.b d.bn.ʻy 2090.16
m.|[šd.bn.-]ṯtayy.b d.ṯṯmd.|[šd.bn.-]rn.b d.ṣdqšlm.|[šd.b d.]bn.pʻṣ.|[ubdy.ʻ]šrm.|[šd.---]n.b d.brdd.|[---.--]m.|[š 82[300].1.29
rd.|[šd.]abyy.b d.ibrmd̲.|[šd.]bn.ṯṯrn.b d.bnš.aǵlkz.|[šd.b]d.b[n].tkwn.|[ubdy.md̲]rǵlm.|[šd.bn.--]n.b d.aẖny.|[š 82[300].2.21
.b]d.s[--].|š[d.b]d.u[--].|šd.b d.[---].|šd.b d[.---]im.|šd.b d[.bn.--]n.|šd.b d.iwrkl.|šd.b d.klb.|šd.b d.klby.|šd.b 2090.7
.b d.tbbr.|[w.]šd.nḥl h.b d.ṯṯmd.|[š]d.b d.iwrẖṯ.|[ṯn].šdm.b d.gmrd.|[šd.]lbny.b d.tbṯṯb.|[š]d.bn.ṯ[-]rn.b d.ʻdbml 82[300].1.14
.iwrm[--].|šd.b d.yṯpr.|šd.b d.krb[-].|šd.b d.bn.ptd̲.|šd.b d.dr.khnm.|šd.b d.bn.ʻmy.|šd.b d.bn.ʻyn.|ṯn.šdm.b d. 2090.17
ubdy.mdm.|šd.b d.ʻbdmlk.|šd.b d.yšn.ḥrš.|šd.b d.aupš.|šd.b d.ršpab.aẖ.ubn.|šd.b d.bn 82[300].1.3
y.|šd.b d.iytlm.|ṯn.šdm.b d.amtrn.|šd.b d.iwrm[--].|šd.b d.yṯpr.|šd.b d.krb[-].|šd.b d.bn.ptd̲.|šd.b d.dr.khnm.| 2090.14
d.[---].|šd.b d[.---]im.|šd.b d[.bn.--]n.|šd.b d.iwrkl.|šd.b d.klb.|šd.b d.klby.|šd.b d.iytlm.|ṯn.šdm.b d.amtrn.|š 2090.9
.brdd.|[---.--]m.|[šd.---.b d.]ṯpṯbʻl.|[šd.---.]b d.ymz.|[šd.b d].klby.psl.|[ub]dy.mri.ibrn.|[š]d.bn.bri.b d.bn.ydln.|[82[300].2.4
b d[.---]im.|šd.b d[.bn.--]n.|šd.b d.iwrkl.|šd.b d.klb.|šd.b d.klby.|šd.b d.iytlm.|ṯn.šdm.b d.amtrn.|šd.b d.iwrm[- 2090.10
d̲.|šd.b d.dr.khnm.|šd.b d.bn.ʻmy.|šd.b d.bn.ʻyn.|ṯn.šdm.b d.klṯṯb.|šd.b d.krz[n].|ṯlṯ.šdm.b d.amtr[n].|ṯn.šdm.b 2090.20
lm.|ṯn.šdm.b d.amtrn.|šd.b d.iwrm[--].|šd.b d.yṯpr.|šd.b d.krb[-].|šd.b d.bn.ptd̲.|šd.b d.dr.khnm.|šd.b d.bn.ʻm 2090.15
nm.|šd.b d.bn.ʻmy.|šd.b d.bn.ʻyn.|ṯn.šdm.b d.klṯṯb.|šd.b d.krz[n].|ṯlṯ.šdm.b d.amtr[n].|ṯn.šdm.b d.skn.|šd.b d[. 2090.21
dm.b d.klṯṯb.|šd.b d.krz[n].|ṯlṯ.šdm.b d.amtr[n].|ṯn.šdm.b d.skn.|šd.b d[.ʻb]dyrẖ.|šd.b [d.--]ṯṯb. 2090.23
[--.-]d[-.---].|[--.šd]m.b d.iyt[lm].|[šd.b]d.s[--].|š[d.b]d.u[--].|šd.b d.[---].|šd.b d[.---]im.|šd.b 2090.3
|šd.b d.krz[n].|ṯlṯ.šdm.b d.amtr[n].|ṯn.šdm.b d.skn.|šd.b d[.ʻb]dyrẖ.|šd.b [d.--]ṯṯb. 2090.24
ubdy.mdm.|šd.b d.ʻbdmlk.|šd.b d.yšn.ḥrš.|šd.b d.aupš.|šd.b d.ršpab.aẖ 82[300].1.2
y.mdm.|šd.b d.ʻbdmlk.|šd.b d.yšn.ḥrš.|šd.b d.aupš.|šd.b d.ršpab.aẖ.ubn.|šd.b d.bn.uṯryn.|[ubd]y.mrynm.|[š]d. 82[300].1.5
y.]mẖ[ṣ]m.|[šd.bn.]uzpy.b d.yšn.ḥrš.|[-----].|[-----].|[šd.b d.--]n.|[šd.b d.--]n.|[šd.b d.--]ǵl.|[šd.b d.--]pšm.šyr. 82[300].2.29
šd.bn.]uzpy.b d.yšn.ḥrš.|[-----].|[-----].|[šd.b d.--]n.|[šd.b d.--]n.|[šd.b d.--]ǵl.|[šd.b d.--]pšm.šyr. 82[300].2.30
d.yšn.ḥrš.|[-----].|[-----].|[šd.b d.--]n.|[šd.b d.--]n.|[šd.b d.--]ǵl.|[šd.b d.--]pšm.šyr. 82[300].2.31
-----].|[-----].|[šd.b d.--]n.|[šd.b d.--]n.|[šd.b d.--]ǵl.|[šd.b d.--]pšm.šyr. 82[300].2.32
lṯ.šdm.b d.amtr[n].|ṯn.šdm.b d.skn.|šd.b d[.ʻb]dyrẖ.|šd.b [d.--]ṯṯb. 2090.25
--].|[--.šd]m.b d.iyt[lm].|[šd.b]d.s[--].|š[d.b]d.u[--].|šd.b d.[---].|šd.b d[.---]im.|šd.b d[.bn.--]n.|šd.b d.iwrkl.|šd 2090.5
b d.iyt[lm].|[šd.b]d.s[--].|š[d.b]d.u[--].|šd.b d.[---].|šd.b d[.---]im.|šd.b d[.bn.--]n.|šd.b d.iwrkl.|šd.b d.klb.|šd. 2090.6
[š]šw[.i]ryn.arr.|[š]dm.b.mlk.|[--.š]dm.b.ar.|[--.š]dm.b.ulm.|[--.š]dm.b.mʻrb 2033.1.2
.arr.|[š]dm.b.mlk.|[--.š]dm.b.ar.|[--.š]dm.b.ulm.|[--.š]dm.b.mʻrby.|[--.šd]m.b.uškn.|[---.--]n.|[---].tlmdm.|[y]b 2033.1.5
[-----].|šd.prsn.l.[---].|šd.bddn.l.iytlm.|šd.bn.nbʻm.l.ṯpṯbʻl.|šd.bn mšrn.l.ilšpš.|[šd 2030.1.3
šd.bn.adn.|[b] d.armwl.|[šd].mrnn.|b d.[-]tw[-].|šd.bn[.---] 2028.1
.ann.|bn.ʻbdpdr.|šd.iyry.l.ʻbdbʻl.|šd.šmmn.l.bn.šty.|šd.bn.arws.l.bn.ẖlan.|šd.bn.ibryn.l.bn.ʻmnr. 1102.19
ry.l.ʻbdbʻl.|šd.šmmn.l.bn.šty.|šd.bn.arws.l.bn.ẖlan.|šd.bn.ibryn.l.bn.ʻmnr. 1102.20
.---.]gt.prn.|[šd.---.]gt.prn.|[š]d.bn.š[p]šn l gt pr[n].|šd bn.ilšḥr.|l.gt.mzln.|šd.gldy.|l.gt.mzln.|šd.glln.l.gt.mz[l] 1104.15
d.nrn.|[š]d.bn.rwy.b d.ydln.|[š].bn.trn.b d.ibrmd̲.|[š]d.bn.ilṯtmr.b d.tbbr.|[w.]šd.nḥl h.b d.ṯṯmd.|[š]d.b d.iwrẖ 82[300].1.11
prn.|šd.hwil.gt.prn.|šd.ḥr.gt.prn.|šd.bn.ṯbǵl.gt.prn.|šd.bn.inšr.gt.prn.|šd.[---.]gt.prn.|[šd.---.]gt.prn.|[šd.---.]gt. 1104.10
šd.ubdy.ilštmʻ.|dt b d.skn.|šd.bn.ubrʻn b gt prn.|šd.bn.gby.gt.prn.|šd.bn.kryn.gt.prn.| 1104.3
rt.|ʻšt.ʻšr h.šmn.|ʻmn.bn.aǵlmn.|arbʻm.ksp.ʻl.qrt.|b.šd.bn.[u]brš.|ẖmšt.ʻšrt.|b.šd.bn.[-]n.|ṯl[ṯt].ʻšr[t].|b.š[d].bn. 1083.7
]n.b d.aẖny.|[šd.bn.--]rt.b d.ṯpṯbʻl.|[ubdy.]mẖ[ṣ]m.|[šd.bn.]uzpy.b d.yšn.ḥrš.|[-----].|[-----].|[šd.b d.--]n.|[šd.b d 82[300].2.26
.srn[.---].|šd.yʻd̲r[.---].|šd.swr.[---].|šd.bn ppn[-.---].|šd.bn.uẖn[.---]. 83[85].7
[šd.---.]b d.ymz.|[šd.b d].klby.psl.|[ub]dy.mri.ibrn.|[š]d.bn.bri.b d.bn.ydln.|[u]bdy.ṯǵrm.|[š]d.ṯǵr.mṯpit.b d.bn.i 82[300].2.6
mrd.|[šd.]lbny.b d.tbṯṯb.|[š]d.bn.ṯ[-]rn.b d.ʻdbmlk.|[šd.]bn.brzn.b d.nwrd̲.|[šd.]bn.nḥbl.b d.ʻdbym.|[šd.b]n.qṭy. 82[300].1.17
šd.ubdy.ilštmʻ.|dt b d.skn.|šd.bn.ubrʻn b gt prn.|šd.bn.gby.gt.prn.|šd.bn.kryn.gt.prn.|šd.bn.ky.gt.prn.|šd.h 1104.4
.ml[--].|šd.b[---].|b d.[---].|šd.[---].|b d.[---].|[-----].|šd.bn.gdy.|b d.ddl. 2028.22
bn.ʻmnr.|šd.bn.krwn.l bn.ʻmyn.|šd.bn.prmn.l aẖny.|šd.bn ḥnn.l bn.adld̲n.|šd.bn.nṣdn.l bn.ʻmlbi.|šd.ṯpẖln.l bn. 2089.7
šd.ubdy[.---].|šd.bn.ẖb[--.---].|šd.srn[.---].|šd.yʻd̲r[.---].|šd.swr.[---].|šd.b 83[85].2
]bdy.ṯǵrm.|[š]d.ṯǵr.mṯpit.b d.bn.iryn.|[u]bdy.šrm.|[š]d.bn.ẖrmln.b d.bn.tnn.|[š]d.bn.ẖrmln.ṯn.b d.bn.ẖdmn.|[u 82[300].2.10
b d.bn.iryn.|[u]bdy.šrm.|[š]d.bn.ẖrmln.b d.bn.tnn.|[š]d.bn.ẖrmln.ṯn.b d.bn.ẖdmn.|[u]bdy.nqdm.|[ṯlṯ].šdm.d.nʻ 82[300].2.11
šd.bn.šty.l.bn.ṯbrn.|šd.bn.ẖtb.l bn.yʻd̲rd.|šd.gl.bʻlz.l.bn.ʻmnr.|šd.knʻm.l.bn.ʻmn 2089.2
.b d.iwrẖṯ.|[ṯn].šdm.b d.gmrd.|[šd.]lbny.b d.tbṯṯb.|[š]d.bn.ṯ[-]rn.b d.ʻdbmlk.|[šd.]bn.brzn.b d.nwrd̲.|[šd.]bn.nḥ 82[300].1.16
ddn.l.iytlm.|šd.bn.nbʻm.l.ṯpṯbʻl.|šd.bn mšrn.l.ilšpš.|[šd.bn].kbr.l.snrn.|[---.--]k.l.gmrd.|[---.--]ṯ.l.yšn.|[šd.--]ln.| 2030.1.6
ubrʻn b gt prn.|šd.bn.gby.gt.prn.|šd.bn.kryn.gt.prn.|šd.bn.ky.gt.prn.|šd.hwil.gt.prn.|šd.ḥr.gt.prn.|šd.bn.ṯbǵl.gt. 1104.6
.l bn.yʻd̲rd.|šd.gl.bʻlz.l.bn.ʻmnr.|šd.knʻm.l.bn.ʻmnr.|šd.bn.krwn.l bn.ʻmyn.|šd.bn.prmn.l aẖny.|šd.bn ḥnn.l bn.a 2089.5
|dt b d.skn.|šd.bn.ubrʻn b gt prn.|šd.bn.gby.gt.prn.|šd.bn.kryn.gt.prn.|šd.bn.ky.gt.prn.|šd.hwil.gt.prn.|šd.ḥr.g 1104.5

[---.--]ṯ.l.yšn.|[šd.--]ln.|b d.trġds.|šd.ṯ‘lb.|b d.bn.pl.|šd.bn.kt.|b d.pdy.|šd.ḫzr.|[b d].d[---]. 2030.2.5
d.snrym.dt.‘qb.|b.ayly.|šd.abršn.|šd.kkn.[bn].ubyn.|šd.bn.li[y].|šd.bn.š[--]y.|šd.bn.ṯ[---].|šd.‘dmn[.bn.]ynḥm.|š 2026.5
|šd.prsn.l.[---].|šd.bddn.l.iytlm.|šd.bn.nb‘m.l.ṯpṭb‘l.|šd.bn mšrn.l.ilšpš.|[šd.bn].kbr.l.snrn.|[---.--]k.l.gmrd.|[---.- 2030.1.5
[-----].|šd.prsn.l.[---].|šd.bddn.l.iytlm.|šd.bn.nb‘m.l.ṯpṭb‘l.|šd.bn mšrn.l.ilšpš.|[šd.bn].kbr.l.snrn.|[2030.1.4
m.|[šd.b]n.ṯpdn.b d.bn.g‘r.|[šd.b]n.ṯqrn.b d.ḫby.|[ṯn.š]d.bn.ngzḥn.b d.gmrd.|[šd.bn].pll.b d.gmrd.|[šd.bn.-]ll.b 82[300].1.23
.|[š]d.bn.ṯ[-]rn.b d.‘dbmlk.|[šd.]bn.brzn.b d.nwrḏ.|[šd.]bn.nḥbl.b d.‘dbym.|[šd.b]n.qṭy.b d.tt.|[ubd]y.mrim.|[š 82[300].1.18
bn.‘myn.|šd.bn.prmn.l aḫny.|šd.bn ḥnn.l bn.adlḏn.|šd.bn.nṣdn.l bn.‘mlbi.|šd.ṯpḫln.l bn.ġl.|w dṯn.nḥl h.l bn.pl. 2089.8
ṣy.b d.‘bdym.|[ub]dy.trrm.|[šd.]bn.ṯqdy.b d.gmrd.|[š]d bn.synn.b d.gmrd.|[šd.]abyy.b d.ibrmḏ.|[šd.]bn.ṯṯrn.b 82[300].2.18
b.šd.bn.[u]brš.|ḫmšt.‘šrt.|b.šd.bn.[-]n.|ṯl[ṯt].‘šr[t].|b.š[d].bn.‘myn.|ḫmšt.|b.[šd.--]n.|ḫ[m]št[.‘]šrt.|[ar]b‘m.ksp.| 1083.11
r.|[šd.b]n.ṯqrn.b d.ḫby.|[ṯn.š]d.bn.ngzḥn.b d.gmrd.|[šd.bn].pll.b d.gmrd.|[šd.bn.-]ll.b d.iwrḫṭ.|[šd.bn.-]nn.b d.b 82[300].1.24
.bn.ḫb[--.---].|šd.srn[.---].|šd.y‘ḏr[.---].|šd.swr.[---].|šd.bn ppn[-.---].|šd.bn.uḫn[.---]. 83[85].6
.bn.‘mnr.|šd.kn‘m.l.bn.‘mnr.|šd.bn.krwn.l bn.‘myn.|šd.bn.prmn.l aḫny.|šd.bn ḥnn.l bn.adlḏn.|šd.bn.nṣdn.l bn.‘ 2089.6
b‘ly.|[---.]šd ubdy.|[---.š]d ubdy.|[---.šd] ubdy.|[---.š]d.bn.ṣin.|[---].bn.dly.|[---.]ṯty[-.--]. 2031.11
b d.ršpab.aḫ.ubn.|šd.b d.bn.uṯryn.|[ubd]y.mrynm.|[š]d.bn.ṣnrn.b d.nrn.|[š]d.bn.rwy.b d.ydln.|[š].bn.trn.b d.ibr 82[300].1.8
lk.|[šd.]bn.brzn.b d.nwrḏ.|[šd.]bn.nḥbl.b d.‘dbym.|[šd.b]n.qṭy.b d.tt.|[ubd]y.mrim.|[šd.b]n.ṯpdn.b d.bn.g‘r.|[š 82[300].1.19
b d.bn.uṯryn.|[ubd]y.mrynm.|[š]d.bn.ṣnrn.b d.nrn.|[š]d.bn.rwy.b d.ydln.|[š].bn.trn.b d.ibrmḏ.|[š]d.bn.ilṯtmr.b 82[300].1.9
t.prn.|šd.[---.]gt.prn.|[šd.---.]gt.prn.|[šd.---.]gt.prn.|[š]d.bn.š[p]šn l gt pr[n].|šd bn.ilšḥr.|l.gt.mzln.|šd.gldy.|l.gt 1104.14
šd.bn.šty.l.bn.ṭbrn.|šd.bn.ḫtb.l bn.y‘ḏrd.|šd.gl.b‘lz.l.bn.‘mn 2089.1
qb.|b.ayly.|šd.abršn.|šd.kkn.[bn].ubyn.|šd.bn.li[y].|šd.bn.š[--]y.|šd.bn.ṯ[---].|šd.‘dmn[.bn.]ynḥm.|šd.bn.ṯmr[n. 2026.6
gmrd.|[š]d bn.synn.b d.gmrd.|[šd.]abyy.b d.ibrmḏ.|[šd.]bn.ṯṯrn.b d.bnš.aġlkz.|[šd.b]d.b[n].tkwn.|[ubdy.mḏ]rġl 82[300].2.20
t.prn.|šd.bn.ky.gt.prn.|šd.hwil.gt.prn.|šd.ḥr.gt.prn.|šd.bn.ṯbġl.gt.prn.|šd.bn.inšr.gt.prn.|šd.[---.]gt.prn.|[šd.---.] 1104.9
.li[y].|šd.bn.š[--]y.|šd.bn.ṯ[---].|šd.‘dmn[.bn.]ynḥm.|šd.bn.ṯmr[n.m]idḫy.|šd.ṯb‘m[.--]y. 2026.9
n.nḥbl.b d.‘dbym.|[šd.b]n.qṭy.b d.tt.|[ubd]y.mrim.|[šd.b]n.ṯpdn.b d.bn.g‘r.|[šd.b]n.ṯqrn.b d.ḫby.|[ṯn.š]d.bn.ngz 82[300].1.21
]d.rpan.b d.klṯtb.|[š]d.ilṣy.b d.‘bdym.|[ub]dy.trrm.|[šd.]bn.ṯqdy.b d.gmrd.|[š]d bn.synn.b d.gmrd.|[šd.]abyy.b 82[300].2.17
]n.qṭy.b d.tt.|[ubd]y.mrim.|[šd.b]n.ṯpdn.b d.bn.g‘r.|[šd.b]n.ṯqrn.b d.ḫby.|[ṯn.š]d.bn.ngzḥn.b d.gmrd.|[šd.bn].pll 82[300].1.22
d.abršn.|šd.kkn.[bn].ubyn.|šd.bn.li[y].|šd.bn.š[--]y.|šd.bn.ṯ[---].|šd.‘dmn[.bn.]ynḥm.|šd.bn.ṯmr[n.m]idḫy.|šd.ṯ 2026.7
.|[ṯn.š]d.bn.ngzḥn.b d.gmrd.|[šd.bn].pll.b d.gmrd.|[šd.bn.-]ll.b d.iwrḫṭ.|[šd.bn.-]nn.b d.bn.šmrm.|[šd.bn.-]ṯtay 82[300].1.25
ġlmn.|arb‘m.ksp.‘l.qrt.|b.šd.bn.[u]brš.|ḫmšt.‘šrt.|b.šd.bn.[-]n.|ṯl[ṯt].‘šr[t].|b.š[d].bn.‘myn.|ḫmšt.|b.[šd.--]n.|ḫ[1083.9
d.gmrd.|[šd.bn].pll.b d.gmrd.|[šd.bn.-]ll.b d.iwrḫṭ.|[šd.bn.-]nn.b d.bn.šmrm.|[šd.bn.-]ṯtayy.b d.ṯṯmd.|[šd.bn.-]r 82[300].1.26
.|[šd.bn.-]nn.b d.bn.šmrm.|[šd.bn.-]ṯtayy.b d.ṯṯmd.|[šd.bn.-]rn.b d.ṣdqšlm.|[šd.b d.]bn.p‘ṣ.|[ubdy.‘]šrm.|[šd.---] 82[300].1.28
rd.|[šd.bn.-]ll.b d.iwrḫṭ.|[šd.bn.-]nn.b d.bn.šmrm.|[šd.bn.-]ṯtayy.b d.ṯṯmd.|[šd.bn.-]rn.b d.ṣdqšlm.|[šd.b d.]bn. 82[300].1.27
.b d.bnš.aġlkz.|[šd.b]d.b[n].tkwn.|[ubdy.mḏ]rġlm.|[šd.bn.--]n.b d.aḫny.|[šd.bn.--]rt.b d.ṯpṭb‘l.|[ubdy.]mḫ[ṣ]m. 82[300].2.23
d.b[n].tkwn.|[ubdy.mḏ]rġlm.|[šd.bn.--]n.b d.aḫny.|[šd.bn.--]rt.b d.ṯpṭb‘l.|[ubdy.]mḫ[ṣ]m.|[šd.bn.]uzpy.b d.yšn. 82[300].2.24
šd.bn.adn.|[b] d.armwl.|[šd].mrnn.|b d.[-]tw[-].|šd.bn[.---].|b d.dd[--].|šd.d[---].|b d.d[---].|šd.b[---].|b d.[-- 2028.5
dy.|[---.]šd.ubdy.|[---.]bn.k[--.]ṯ[l]ṯm ksp b[---].|[---.]šd b‘ly.|[---.]šd ubdy.|[---.š]d ubdy.|[---.šd] ubdy.|[---.š]d.b 2031.7
ġl.|w dṯn.nḥl h.l bn.pl.|šd.krwn.l aḫn.|šd.‘yy.l aḫn.|šd.brdn.l bn.bly.|šd gzl.l.bn.ṭbr[n].|šd.ḫzmyn.l a[--].|ṯn šd 2089.13
.|[i]lbldn.|[p]dry.bt.mlk.|[-]lp.izr.|[a]rz.|k.t‘rb.‘ṯtrt.šd.bt[.m]lk.|k.t‘rbn.ršp m.bt.mlk.|ḫlu.dg.|ḥdṯm.|dbḫ.b‘l.k 2004.10
].kmm.b‘lm.kmm.|b‘lm.kmm.b‘lm.kmm.|k t‘rb.‘ṯtrt.šd.bt.mlk[.---].|ṯn.skm.šb‘.mšlt.arb‘.ḫpnt.[---].|ḫmšm.ṯlṯ.rk UG5.9.1.18
.[-]tw[-].|šd.bn[.---].|b d.dd[--].|šd.d[---].|b d.d[---].|šd.b[---].|b d.[---].|šd[.---].|b d[.---].|š[d.---].|b d[.---].|šd[.- 2028.9
.---].|b d[.---].|š[d.---].|b d[.---].|šd[.---].|b d.ml[--].|šd.b[---].|b d.[---].|šd.[---].|b d.[---].|[-----].|šd.bn.gdy.|b d 2028.17
n.pl.|šd.krwn.l aḫn.|šd.‘yy.l aḫn.|šd.brdn.l bn.bly.|šd gzl.l.bn.ṭbr[n].|šd.ḫzmyn.l a[--].|ṯn šdm b uš[kn]. 2089.14
šd.bn.šty.l.bn.ṭbrn.|šd.bn.ḫtb.l bn.y‘ḏrd.|šd.gl.b‘lz.l.bn.‘mnr.|šd.kn‘m.l.bn.‘mnr.|šd.bn.krwn.l bn.‘m 2089.3
prn.|[š]d.bn.š[p]šn l gt pr[n].|šd bn.ilšḥr.|l.gt.mzln.|šd.gldy.|l.gt.mzln.|šd.glln.l.gt.mz[l]n.|šd.hyabn[.l.]gt.mzln 1104.17
gt pr[n].|šd bn.ilšḥr.|l.gt.mzln.|šd.gldy.|l.gt.mzln.|šd.glln.l.gt.mz[l]n.|šd.hyabn[.l.]gt.mzln.|šd.‘bdb‘l.|l.gt.mzl 1104.19
ilt.|[---.--]m.lm.|[---.š]d.gṯr.|[--]ḫ[d].šd.hwt.|[--.]iḫd.šd.gṯr.|[w]ht.yšm‘.uḫ y.|l g y.w yhbṭ.bnš.|w ytn.ilm.b d h 55[18].16
--.]šil.|[-----.]šilt.|[-----].|[-----.š]ilt.|[---.--]m.lm.|[---.š]d.gṯr.|[--]ḫ[d].šd.hwt.|[--.]iḫd.šd.gṯr.|[w]ht.yšm‘.uḫ y.|l 55[18].14
arb‘.‘šr h.šd.|w.kmsk.d.iwrkl.|ṯlṯ.šd.d.bn.mlkyy.|kmsk.šd.iḫmn.|širm.šd.khn.|ṯlṯ.šd.w.krm.š 1079.3
.|[š]d.bn.ḫrmln.ṯn.b d.bn.ḫdmn.|[u]bdy.nqdm.|[ṯlṯ].šdm.d.n‘rb.gt.npk.|[š]d.rpan.b d.klṯtb.|[š]d.ilṣy.b d.‘bdym. 82[300].2.13
p ksp w rbt ḫ|rṣ.išlḥ ẓhrm iq|nim.atn šd h krm[m].|šd dd h ḥrnqm.w |y‘n ḫrḫb mlk qẓ [l].|n‘mn.ilm l ḫt[n].|m 24[77].23
rb.|tbq‘nn.b ḫṯr.tdry|nn.b išt.tšrpnn.|b rḥm.tṭḥnn.b šd.|tdr‘nn.šir h.l tikl.|‘ṣrm.mnt h.l tkly.|npr[m.]šir.l šir.yṣ 6[49].2.34
spr.gt.r[---].|‘šrm.l.m[it.---].|šd.dr[-.---]. 1105.3
wl.|[šd].mrnn.|b d.[-]tw[-].|šd.bn[.---].|b d.dd[--].|šd.d[---].|b d.d[---].|šd.b[---].|b d.[---].|šd[.---].|b d[.---].|š[2028.7
hr h l a|b h.alp ksp w rbt ḫ|rṣ.išlḥ ẓhrm iq|nim.atn šd h krm[m].|šd dd h ḥrnqm.w |y‘n ḫrḫb mlk qẓ [l].|n‘mn 24[77].22
.bn.gby.gt.prn.|šd.bn.kryn.gt.prn.|šd.bn.ky.gt.prn.|šd.hwil.gt.prn.|šd.ḥr.gt.prn.|šd.bn.ṯbġl.gt.prn.|šd.bn.inšr.g 1104.7
.|[-----].|[-----.š]ilt.|[---.--]m.lm.|[---.š]d.gṯr.|[--]ḫ[d].šd.hwt.|[--.]iḫd.šd.gṯr.|[w]ht.yšm‘.uḫ y.|l g y.w yhbṭ.bnš. 55[18].15
r.|l.gt.mzln.|šd.gldy.|l.gt.mzln.|šd.glln.l.gt.mz[l]n.|šd.hyabn[.l.]gt.mzln.|šd.‘bdb‘l.|l.gt.mzln. 1104.20
arb‘.‘šr h.šd.|w.kmsk.d.iwrkl.|ṯlṯ.šd.d.bn.mlkyy.|kmsk.šd.iḫmn.|šir 1079.1
.|ṯlṯ.šd.d.bn.mlkyy.|kmsk.šd.iḫmn.|širm.šd.khn.|ṯlṯ.šd.w.krm.šir.d.ḥli.|širm.šd.šd.‘šy.|w.šir.šd.krm.|d.krwn.|š 1079.6
|d.yrmn.|šir.[š]d.mltḫ.šd.‘šy.|d.ynḥm.|tgmr.šd.ṯlṯm.šd.|w.tr[--.---]. 1079.16
dm.|rbm.w l.udm.ṯrrt.|w gr.nn.‘rm.šrn.|pdrm.s‘t.b šdm.|ḥṭb h.b grnt.ḥpšt.|s‘t.b nk.šibt.b bqr.|mmlat.dm.ym. 14[KRT].3.111
udm.rbt.|w udm[.ṯr]rt.|grnn.‘rm.|šrnn.pdrm.|s‘t.b šdm.ḥṭb.|w b grnt.ḥpšt.|s‘t.b npk.šibt.w b |mqr.mmlat.|d[14[KRT].4.214
|šd.bn.kryn.gt.prn.|šd.bn.ky.gt.prn.|šd.hwil.gt.prn.|šd.ḥr.gt.prn.|šd.bn.ṯbġl.gt.prn.|šd.bn.inšr.gt.prn.|šd.[---.]g 1104.8
t.št].|[b ‘]pr[m.ddym.sk.šlm.l kbd.arṣ.arbdd].|l kbd.š[dm.ḥš k.‘ṣ k.‘bṣ k.‘m y.p‘n k.tls]|[m]n ‘m y t[wtḥ.išd k.d 7.2[130].16

lḥmt št.b ʻpr m.ddym.|sk.šlm.l kbd.arṣ.|arbdd.l kbd.šdm.|ḥš k.ʻṣ k.ʻbṣ k.|ʻm y.pʻn k.tlsmn.ʻm y.|twtḥ.išd k.dm. 3[ʻNT].3.14
mt.št b ʻp|[r m.ddym.sk.šlm].l kbd.arṣ.|[arbdd.l kbd.š]dm.ḥš k.|[ʻṣ k.ʻbṣ k.ʻm y.pʻ]n k.tlsmn.|[ʻm y.twtḥ.išd] k.t 1[ʻNT.IX].2.21
mt.|št.b ʻp[r] m.ddym.sk.šlm.|l kbd.arṣ.arbdd.l kbd.šdm.|[ḥ]š k.[ʻ]ṣ k.ʻbṣ k.ʻm y.pʻn k.|[tls]mn.[ʻ]m y.twtḥ.išd 3[ʻNT].4.54
n.|šd.ʻyy.l aẖn.|šd.brdn.l bn.bly.|šd gzl.l.bn.ṯbr[n].|šd.ẖzmyn.l a[--].|ṯn šdm b uš[kn]. 2089.15
]ln.|b d.trǵds.|šd.ṯʻlb.|b d.bn.pl.|šd.bn.kt.|b d.pdy.|šd.ẖzr.|[b d].d[---]. 2030.2.7
.ṯl.šm[m.t]sk h.|rbb.nsk h.kbkbm.|ttpp.anhbm.d alp.šd[.ẓu h.b ym].|ṯl[.---]. 3[ʻNT].4.89
l.b ym.trtḥ[ṣ.--].|[----.a]dm.tium.b ǵlp y[m.--].|d alp šd.ẓu h.b ym.t[---].|tlbš.npṣ.ǵzr.tšt.ẖ[---.b] |nšg h.ḥrb.tšt.b 19[1AQHT].4.205
ttpp.anhb[m.d alp.šd].|ẓu h.b ym[.---].|[--]rn.l [---]. 3[ʻNT].3.03
|tšu.g h.w tṣḥ.|tḥm.ṯr.il.ab k.|hwt.lṭpn.ḥtk k.|pl.ʻnt.šdm.y špš.|pl.ʻnt.šdm.il.yš[t k].|bʻl.ʻnt.mḥrṯ[-].|iy.aliyn.bʻl. 6[49].4.36
.il.l btlt.|ʻnt.šmʻ.l btlt.ʻn[t].|rgm.l nrt.il.šp[š].|pl.ʻnt.šdm.y špš.|pl.ʻnt.šdm.il.yšt k.|[b]ʻl.ʻnt.mḥrṯt.|iy.aliyn.bʻl.| 6[49].4.25
ḥrṯ[-].|iy.aliyn.bʻl.|iy.zbl.bʻl.arṣ.|w tʻn.nrt.ilm.š[p]š.|šd yn.ʻn.b qbt[.t]|bl lyt.ʻl.umt k.|w abqṯ.aliyn.bʻl.|w tʻn.btl 6[49].4.42
šd.ubdy[.---].|šd.bn.ẖb[--.---].|šd.srn[.---].|šd.yʻḏr[.---].|šd.swr.[---].|šd.bn ppn[-.---].|šd.bn.uẖn[.---]. 83[85].4
rẖ.ḥdṯ.|ybʻr.l ṯn.aṯt h.|w l nkr.mddt.|km irby.tškn.|šd.k ḥsn.pat.|mdbr.tlkn.|ym.w ṯn.aẖr.|šp[š]m.b [ṯ]lṯ.|ym[14[KRT].4.193
l ym hnd.|ʻmṯtmr.bn.|nqmpʻ.ml[k].|ugrt.ytn.|šd.kḏǵdl[.bn].|[-]š[-]y.d.b š[-]y.|[---.y]d gt h[.--].|[---.]yd.|[1008.5
sk.d.iwrkl.|ṯlṯ.šd.d.bn.mlkyy.|kmsk.šd.iẖmn.|širm.šd.khn.|ṯlṯ.šd.w.krm.šir.d.ẖli.|širm.šd.šd.ʻšy.|w.šir.šd.krm. 1079.5
šd.snrym.dt.ʻqb.|b.ayly.|šd.abršn.|šd.kkn.[bn].ubyn.|šd.bn.li[y].|šd.bn.š[--]y.|šd.bn.ṯ[---].|šd. 2026.4
ẖ.|ḥdṯ.ybʻr.l ṯn.|aṯt h.lm.nkr.|mddt h.k irby.|[t]škn.šd.|km.ḥsn.pat.mdbr.|lk.ym.w ṯn.ṯlṯ.rbʻ ym.|ẖmš.ṯdṯ.ym. 14[KRT].2.104
iǵlyn.bn.kzbn.l.qr[t].|šd.pln.bn.tiyn.b d.ilmhr nḥl h.|šd knn.bn.ann.ʻdb.|šd.iln[-].bn.irṯr.l.šẖrn.nḥl h.|šd[.ag]ptn. 2029.19
.l.bn.ṯbrn.|šd.bn.ẖtb.l bn.yʻḏrd.|šd.gl.bʻlz.l.bn.ʻmnr.|šd.knʻm.l.bn.ʻmnr.|šd.bn.krwn.l bn.ʻmyn.|šd.bn.prmn.l aẖ 2089.4
ṣdn.l bn.ʻmlbi.|šd.ṯpẖln.l bn.ǵl.|w dṯn.nḥl h.l bn.pl.|šd.krwn.l aẖn.|šd.ʻyy.l aẖn.|šd.brdn.l bn.bly.|šd gzl.l.bn.ṯb 2089.11
mn.b d.tyn.nḥl h.|šd.pǵyn[.b] d.krmn.l.ty[n.n]ḥl h.|šd.krz.[b]n.ann.ʻ[db].|šd.ṯ[r]yn.bn.tkn.b d.qrt.|šd[.-].dyn.b 2029.13
šy.|w.šir.šd.krm.|d.krwn.|šir.šd.šd.ʻšy.|d.abmn.|šir.šd.krm.|d.yrmn.|šir.[š]d.mltḥ.šd.ʻšy.|d.ynḥm.|tgmr.šd.ṯlṯ 1079.12
.šd.khn.|ṯlṯ.šd.w.krm.šir.d.ẖli.|širm.šd.šd.ʻšy.|w.šir.šd.krm.|d.krwn.|šir.šd.šd.ʻšy.|d.abmn.|šir.šd.krm.|d.yrm 1079.8
[---.mr]zḥ.ʻn[.---].|[---.]šir.šd.kr[m.---].|[---.]l.mrzḥ.ʻn[.---].|[---].mrzḥ.ʻn[.---].|[---].mr 2032.2
w ʻl.tlbš.npṣ.aṯt.[--].|ṣbi nrt.ilm.špš.[-]r[--].|pǵt.minš.šdm l mʻ[rb].|nrt.ilm.špš.mǵy[t].|pǵt.l ahlm.rgm.l yṯ[pn.y] 19[1AQHT].4.210
.nḥl h.b d.ṯtmd.|[š]d.b d.iwrẖṯ.|[ṯn].šdm.b d.gmrd.|[šd.]lbny.b d.tbṯṯb.|[š]d.bn.ṯ[-]rn.b d.ʻdbmlk.|[šd.]bn.brzn.b 82[300].1.15
ṯlṯ.|mit.ksp.ʻmn.|bn.ulbtyn.|w.kkr.ṯlṯ.|ksp.d.nkly.b.šd.|mit.ẖmšt.kbd.|[l.]gmn.bn.usyy.|mit.ṯtm.kbd.|l.bn.yšm 1143.6
m.|sb.l qṣm.arṣ.|l ksm.mhyt.ʻn.|l arṣ.m[t]r.bʻl.|w l šd.mṭr.ʻly.|nʻm.l arṣ.mṭr.bʻl.|w l šd.mṭr.ʻly.|nʻm.l ḥṭt.b gn. 16[126].3.6
|l arṣ.m[t]r.bʻl.|w l šd.mṭr.ʻly.|nʻm.l arṣ.mṭr.bʻl.|w l šd.mṭr.ʻly.|nʻm.l ḥṭt.b gn.|bm.nrt.ksmm.|ʻl.tl[-]k.ʻṭrṭrm.|n 16[126].3.8
trgm.l aẖt k.|[---.]l [ ]dm.aẖt k.|ydʻt.k rḥmt.|al.tšt.b šdm.mm h.|b smkt.ṣat.npš h.|[-]mt[-].ṣba.rbt.|špš.w tgh.n 16.1[125].34
wn.|šir.šd.šd.ʻšy.|d.abmn.|šir.šd.krm.|d.yrmn.|šir.[š]d.mltḥ.šd.ʻšy.|d.ynḥm.|tgmr.šd.ṯlṯm.šd.|w.tr[--.---]. 1079.14
arṣ.ap.|ʻnt.ttlk.w tṣd.kl.ǵr.|l kbd.arṣ.kl.gbʻ.|l [k]bd.šdm.tmǵ.l nʻm[y].|[arṣ.]dbr.ysmt.šd.|[šḥl]mmt.t[mǵ.]l bʻl. 5[67].6.28
šd.bn.adn.|[b] d.armwl.|[šd].mrnn.|b d.[-]tw[-].|šd.bn[.---].|b d.dd[--].|šd.d[---].|b 2028.3
.anndr.b d.bdn.nḥ[l h].|[šd.]agyn.b d.kmrn.n[ḥl] h.|[š]d.nbzn.[-]l.qrt.|[š]d.agpṯr.b d.šẖrn.nḥl h.|šd.annmn.b d.t 2029.9
ln.|[š].bn.trn.b d.ibrmd.|[š]d.bn.ilṯtmr.b d.tbbr.|[w.]šd.nḥl h.b d.ṯtmd.|[š]d.b d.iwrẖṯ.|[ṯn].šdm.b d.gmrd.|[šd.] 82[300].1.12
.l btlt.ʻnt.|an.itlk.w aṣd.kl.|ǵr.l kbd.arṣ.kl.gbʻ.|l kbd.šdm.npš.ẖsrt.|bn.nšm.npš.hmlt.|arṣ.mǵt.l nʻm y.arṣ.|dbr.y 6[49].2.17
spr.ubdy.art.|šd.prn.b d.agptn.nḥl h.|šd.šwn.b d.ttyn.nḥl [h].|šd.ttyn[.b]n.arkšt.|lʻq[.---].|šd.pll. 2029.3
ubdy[.---].|šd.bn.ẖb[--.---].|šd.srn[.---].|šd.yʻḏr[.---].|šd.swr.[---].|šd.bn ppn[-.---].|šd.bn.uẖn[.---]. 83[85].5
šd.snrym.dt.ʻqb.|b.ayly.|šd.abršn.|šd.kkn.[bn].ubyn.|šd.b 2026.1
šd.ubdy[.---].|šd.bn.ẖb[--.---].|šd.srn[.---].|šd.yʻḏr[.---].|šd.swr.[---].|šd.bn ppn[-.---].|šd.b 83[85].3
l.gt.mzln.|šd.glln.l.gt.mz[l]n.|šd.hyabn[.l.]gt.mzln.|šd.ʻbdbʻl.|l.gt.mzln. 1104.21
kkn.[bn].ubyn.|šd.bn.li[y].|šd.bn.š[--]y.|šd.bn.ṯ[---].|šd.ʻdmn[.bn.]ynḥm.|šd.bn.ṯmr[n.m]idẖy.|šd.ṯbʻm[.--]y. 2026.8
šd.ṯpẖln.l bn.ǵl.|w dṯn.nḥl h.l bn.pl.|šd.krwn.l aẖn.|šd.ʻyy.l aẖn.|šd.brdn.l bn.bly.|šd gzl.l.bn.ṯbr[n].|šd.ẖzmyn 2089.12
.ṯ]n.b rẖ.|m.ʻ[l k.]pht[.dr]y.b kbrt.|ʻl k.pht.[-]l[-].|b šdm.ʻl k.pht.|drʻ.b ym.tn.aḥd.|b aẖ k.ispa.w ytb.|ap.d anšt 6[49].5.18
ir.d.ẖli.|širm.šd.šd.ʻšy.|w.šir.šd.krm.|d.krwn.|šir.šd.šd.ʻšy.|d.abmn.|šir.šd.krm.|d.yrmn.|šir.[š]d.mltḥ.šd.ʻšy.|d 1079.10
d.šd.ʻšy.|d.abmn.|šir.šd.krm.|d.yrmn.|šir.[š]d.mltḥ.šd.ʻšy.|d.ynḥm.|tgmr.šd.ṯlṯm.šd.|w.tr[--.---]. 1079.14
d.iẖmn.|širm.šd.khn.|ṯlṯ.šd.w.krm.šir.d.ẖli.|širm.šd.šd.ʻšy.|w.šir.šd.krm.|d.krwn.|šir.šd.šd.ʻšy.|d.abmn.|šir.šd. 1079.7
spr šd.ri[šym].|kr[-].šdm.ʻ[--].|b gt ṯm[--] yn[.--].|[---].krm.b ypʻl.yʻdd.|[---.]kr 2027.1.2
šd.šwn.b d.ttyn.nḥl [h].|šd.ttyn[.b]n.arkšt.|lʻq[.---].|šd.pll.b d.qrt.|š[d].anndr.b d.bdn.nḥ[l h].|[šd.]agyn.b d.km 2029.6
h.|šd.irdyn.bn.ḥrǵš[-].l.qrt.|šd.iǵlyn.bn.kzbn.l.qr[t].|šd.pln.bn.tiyn.b d.ilmhr nḥl h.|šd knn.bn.ann.ʻdb.|šd.iln[-] 2029.18
.|[š]d.agpṯr.b d.šẖrn.nḥl h.|šd.annmn.b d.tyn.nḥl h.|šd.pǵyn[.b] d.krmn.l.ty[n.n]ḥl h.|šd.krz.[b]n.ann.ʻ[db].|šd. 2029.12
spr.ubdy.art.|šd.prn.b d.agptn.nḥl h.|šd.šwn.b d.ttyn.nḥl [h].|šd.ttyn[.b] 2029.2
[-----].|šd.prsn.l.[---].|šd.bddn.l.iytlm.|šd.bn.nbʻm.l.ṯpṯbʻl.|šd.bn 2030.1.2
t.|[---.--]r.špr.w yšt.il.|[---.--]n.il ǵnṯ.ʻgl il.|[---.--]d.il.šd yṣd mlk.|[---].yšt.il h.|[---.]iṯm h.|[---.y]mǵy.|[---.]dr h. UG5.2.1.12
m.w l.ʻṣm.šbʻ.šnt.|tmt.ṯmn.nqpt.ʻd.ilm.nʻmm.ttlkn.|šd.tṣdn.pat.mdbr.w ngš.hm.nǵr.|mdrʻ.w ṣḥ hm.ʻm.nǵr.mdr 23[52].68
w km.ḥrr[.---].|šnmtm.dbṯ[.---].|trʻ.trʻn.a[--.---].|bnt.šdm.ṣḥr[.---].|šbʻ.šnt.il.mla.[-].|w ṯmn.nqpnt.ʻd.|k lbš.km.l 12[75].2.44
[--.]a[--.---].|[--.-]bt.np[-.---].|[-] l šd.ql.[---.---].aṭr.|[--.]ǵrm.y[--.---.ẖ]rn.|[-]rk.ḥ[--.---.-]lk.|[-] UG5.8.3
spr šd.ri[šym].|kr[-].šdm.ʻ[--].|b gt ṯm[--] yn[.--].|[---].krm.b y 2027.1.1
.ṯlṯ.mtḥ.ǵyrm.|idk.l ttn pnm.ʻm.bʻl.|mrym.ṣpn.b alp.šd.rbt.kmn.|hlk.aẖt h.bʻl.yʻn.tdrq.|ybnt.ab h.šrḥq.aṯt.l pnn 3[ʻNT].4.82
dn.|dn.almnt.yṯpṭ.ṯpṭ.ytm.|b nši ʻn h.w yphn.b alp.|šd.rbt.kmn.hlk.kṯr.|k yʻn.w yʻn.tdrq.ḥss.|hlk.qšt.ybln.hl.yš 17[2AQHT].5.10
.[ttbʻ].|[bt]lt.ʻnt.idk.l ttn.[pnm].|[ʻm.a]qht.ǵzr.b alp.š[d].|[rbt.]kmn.w ṣḥq.btlt.[ʻnt].|[tšu.]g h.w tṣḥ.šmʻ.m[ʻ.l a] 18[3AQHT].1.21
ḥqkpt.|il.kl h.kptr.|ksu.ṯbt h.ḥkpt.|arṣ.nḥlt h.|b alp.šd.rbt.|kmn.l pʻn.kṯ.|hbr.w ql.tštḥ|wy.w kbd hwt.|w rgm. 3[ʻNT.VI].6.17
kpt.il.kl h].|[kptr.]ks[u.ṯbt h.ḥkpt.arṣ.nḥlt h].|b alp.šd.r[bt.kmn.l pʻn.kṯr].|hbr.w ql.t[štḥwy.w kbd.hwt].|w rg 1[ʻNT.IX].3.2

nrt.ilm.špš.|ṣḥrrt.la.|šmm.b yd.md|d.ilm.mt.b a|lp.šd.rbt.k|mn.l p‘n.mt.|hbr.w ql.|tštḥwy.w k|bd hwt.w rgm 4[51].8.25
‘nm.w tr.arṣ.|idk.l ttn.pnm.|‘m.b‘l.mrym.ṣpn.|b alp.šd.rbt.kmn.|ṣḥq.btlt.‘nt.tšu.|g h.w tṣḥ.tbšr b‘l.|bšrt k.yblt. 4[51].5.86
d.bn.ḫdmn.|[u]bdy.nqdm.|[ṯlṯ].šdm.d.n‘rb.gt.npk.|[š]d.rpan.b d.klṯṯb.|[š]d.ilṣy.b d.‘bdym.|[ub]dy.trrm.|[šd.]b 82[300].2.14
l.šdmt h.|km gpn.|šb‘ d.yrgm.‘l.‘d.w ‘rbm.t‘nyn.|w šd.šd ilm.šd aṯrt.w rḥm.|‘l.išt.šb‘ d.ǵzrm.ṭb.[g]d.b ḥlb.annḫ 23[52].13
.šir.d.ḫli.|širm.šd.šd.‘šy.|w.šir.šd.krm.|d.krwn.|šir.šd.šd.‘šy.|d.abmn.|šir.šd.krm.|d.yrmn.|šir.[š]d.mltḫ.šd.‘šy 1079.10
k.šd.iḫmn.|širm.šd.khn.|ṯlṯ.šd.w.krm.šir.d.ḫli.|širm.šd.šd.‘šy.|w.šir.šd.krm.|d.krwn.|šir.šd.šd.‘šy.|d.abmn.|šir. 1079.7
]l[.---.]‘d.|ksm.mhyt[.m]ǵny.|l n‘m y.arṣ.dbr.|l ysmt.šd.šḥlmmt.|mǵny.l b‘l.npl.l a|rṣ.mt.aliyn.b‘l.|ḫlq.zbl.b‘l.ar 5[67].6.7
.arṣ.kl.gb‘.|l [k]bd.šdm.tmǵ.l n‘m[y].|[arṣ.]dbr.ysmt.šd.|[šḥl]mmt.t[mǵ.]l b‘l.np[l].|[l a]rṣ[.lpš].tks.miz[rtm]. 5[67].6.29
srt.|bn.nšm.npš.hmlt.|arṣ.mǵt.l n‘m y.arṣ.|dbr.ysmt.šd.šḥlmmt.|ngš.ank.aliyn b‘l.|‘dbnn ank.imr.b p y.|k lli.b ṯ 6[49].2.20
td‘ ilm.|k mtt.yšm‘.aliyn.b‘l.|yuhb.‘glt.b dbr.prt.|b šd.šḥlmmt.škb.|‘mn h.šb‘.l šb‘m.|tš[‘]ly.ṯmn.l ṯmnym.|w [t 5[67].5.19
š]t.b ‘pr m.|ddym.ask[.šlm.]l kbd.arṣ.|ar[bdd.]l kb[d.š]dm.yšt.|[----.]b‘l.mdl h.yb‘r.|[---.]rn h.aqry.|[---.]b a[r]ṣ. 3['NT].4.69
.|ldn.|bn.ands.|bn.ann.|bn.‘bdpdr.|šd.iyry.l.‘bdb‘l.|šd.šmmn.l.bn.šty.|šd.bn.arws.l.bn.ḫlan.|šd.bn.ibryn.l.bn.‘ 1102.18
art.|šd.prn.b d.agpṯn.nḥl h.|šd.šwn.b d.ttyn.nḥl [h].|šd.ṯtyn[.b]n.arkšt.|l‘q[.---].|šd.pll.b d.qrt.|š[d].annḏr.b d.b 2029.4
.bn.ṯ[---].|šd.‘dmn[.bn.]ynḥm.|šd.bn.ṯmr[n.m]idḫy.|šd.ṯb‘m[.--]y. 2026.10
šd.krm.|d.yrmn.|šir.[š]d.mltḫ.šd.‘šy.|d.ynḥm.|tgmr.šd.ṯlṯm.šd.|w.tr[--.---]. 1079.16
.|[---.--]k.l.gmrd.|[---.--]ṯ.l.yšn.|[šd.--]ln.|b d.trǵds.|šd.ṯ‘lb.|b d.bn.pl.|šd.bn.kt.|b d.pdy.|šd.ḫzr.|[b d].d[---]. 2030.2.3
]dy.mri.ibrn.|[š]d.bn.bri.b d.bn.ydln.|[u]bdy.ṯǵrm.|[š]d.ṯǵr.mṯpit.b d.bn.iryn.|[u]bdy.šrm.|[š]d.bn.ḫrmln.b d.b 82[300].2.8
l aḫny.|šd.bn ḥnn.l bn.adlḏn.|šd.bn.nṣdn.l bn.‘mlbi.|šd.ṯpḫln.l bn.ǵl.|w dṯn.nḥl h.l bn.pl.|šd.krwn.l aḫn.|šd.‘yy. 2089.9
pǵyn[.b] d.krmn.l.ty[n.n]ḥl h.|šd.krz.[b]n.ann.‘[db].|šd.ṯ[r]yn.bn.tkn.b d.qrt.|šd[.-].dyn.b d.pln.nḥl h.|šd.irdyn. 2029.14
ḥl h.|šd.krz.[b]n.ann.‘[db].|šd.ṯ[r]yn.bn.tkn.b d.qrt.|šd[.-].dyn.b d.pln.nḥl h.|šd.irdyn.bn.ḫrǵš[-].l.qrt.|šd.iǵlyn. 2029.15
[mn.hkl h.---.]bt.|[---.-]k.mnh[-.---.-]š bš[-.]t[-].ǵlm.l šdt[.-.]ymm.|[---.]b ym.ym.y[--].yš[ ]n.ap k.‘ṯtr.dm[.---.]|[-- 2.3[129].11
|ilmškl.w.r‘[h].|ššw[.--].w.r[‘ h].|kr[mn.--.]w.r[‘ h].|šd.[--.w.]r[‘ h].|ḫla[n.---].|w lšṯr[.---]. 2083.2.5
.iln[-].bn.irṯr.l.sḫrn.nḥl h.|šd[.ag]pṯn.b[n.]brrn.l.qrt.|šd[.--]dy.bn.brzn.|l.qrt. 2029.22
š.|[šd.bn].kbr.l.snrn.|[---.--]k.l.gmrd.|[---.--]ṯ.l.yšn.|[šd.--]ln.|b d.trǵds.|šd.ṯ‘lb.|b d.bn.pl.|šd.bn.kt.|b d.pdy.|š 2030.2.1
.|b.šd.bn.[-]n.|ṯl[ṯt].‘šr[t].|b.š[d].bn.‘myn.|ḫmšt.|b.[šd.--]n.|ḫ[m]št[.‘]šrt.|[ar]b‘m.ksp.|[---]yn.|[---.]ksp.|[---.] 1083.13
rm.|[šd.---]n.b d.brdd.|[---.--]m.|[šd.---.b d.]ṯpṭb‘l.|[šd.---.]b d.ymz.|[šd.b d].klby.psl.|[ub]dy.mri.ibrn.|[š]d.bn. 82[300].2.3
.b[---].|b d.[---].|šd[.---].|b d[.---].|š[d.---].|b d[.---].|šd[.---].|b d.ml[--].|šd.b[---].|b d.[---].|šd.[---].|b d.[---].|[-- 2028.15
.]bn.p‘ṣ.|[ubdy.‘]šrm.|[šd.---]n.b d.brdd.|[---.--]m.|[šd.---.b d.]ṯpṭb‘l.|[šd.---.]b d.ymz.|[šd.b d].klby.psl.|[ub]dy 82[300].2.2
---].|b d.d[---].|šd.b[---].|b d.[---].|šd[.---].|b d[.---].|š[d.---].|b d[.---].|šd[.---].|b d.ml[--].|šd.b[---].|b d.[---].|šd 2028.13
.|b d.dd[--].|šd.d[---].|b d.d[---].|šd.b[---].|b d.[---].|šd[.---].|b d[.---].|š[d.---].|b d[.---].|šd[.---].|b d.ml[--].|šd. 2028.11
---].|b d[.---].|šd[.---].|b d.ml[--].|šd.b[---].|b d.[---].|šd.[---].|b d.[---].|[-----].|šd.bn.gdy.|b d.ddl. 2028.19
ṣ.bnš.mlk.yb‘l hm.|[---.--]t.w.ḫpn.l.azzlt.|[---.]l.‘ṯtrt.šd.|[---].yb‘lnn.|[---.--]n.b.ṯlṯ.šnt.l.nṣd.|[---.--]ršp.mlk.k.yp 1106.55
n.|šd.bn.inšr.gt.prn.|šd.[---.]gt.prn.|[šd.---.]gt.prn.|[šd.---.]gt.prn.|[š]d.bn.š[p]šn l gt pr[n].|šd bn.ilšḥr.|l.gt.mzl 1104.13
šd.bn.ṯbǵl.gt.prn.|šd.bn.inšr.gt.prn.|šd.[---.]gt.prn.|[šd.---.]gt.prn.|[šd.---.]gt.prn.|[š]d.bn.š[p]šn l gt pr[n].|šd b 1104.12
.|šd.ḥr.gt.prn.|šd.bn.ṯbǵl.gt.prn.|šd.bn.inšr.gt.prn.|šd.[---.]gt.prn.|[šd.---.]gt.prn.|[šd.---.]gt.prn.|[š]d.bn.š[p]šn 1104.11
n‘rt.|[---].qt.b[--].|[---.]kd[r].|[---.]ṯpr.|[---.]prš.|[---.]šdm.|[---.-]nm.prš.glbm.|[---.]‘gd.dqr.|[---.]ṯn.alpm.|[---.ṯ] 1142.6
-].|[---].krm.b yp‘l.y‘dd.|[---.]krm.b [-]dn.l.bn.[-]kn.|šd[.---.-]‘n.|šd[.---.-]ṣm.l.dqn.|š[d.---.--]d.pdy.|[---.dq]n.|[-- 2027.1.6
.b yp‘l.y‘dd.|[---.]krm.b [-]dn.l.bn.[-]kn.|šd[.---.-]‘n.|šd[.---.-]ṣm.l.dqn.|š[d.---.--]d.pdy.|[---.dq]n.|[---.d]qn.|[---. 2027.1.7
t.|[---].y[--.--]m.|[---.--]n.d[--.--]i.|[--]t.mdt h[.l.]‘ṯtrt.šd.|[---.-]rt.mḫṣ.bnš.mlk.yb‘l hm.|[---.--]t.w.ḫpn.l.azzlt.|[-- 1106.52
rm.b [-]dn.l.bn.[-]kn.|šd[.---.-]‘n.|šd[.---.-]ṣm.l.dqn.|š[d.---.--]d.pdy.|[---.dq]n.|[---.d]qn.|[---.--]b[.---].|[---.--]l[.- 2027.1.8
.[---].|[---]y[.---].|sk[n.---].|u[---.]w š.|[---].w š.|[--]b.šd.[---].|[--]kz[--]. 1093.12
[ḥrš].bhtm.b‘l.šd.|[---d]nil.|[a]drdn.|[---]n.|pǵḏn.|ṯṯpḥ.|ḥgbn.|šrm.|bn. 1039.1.1
šd.bn.-]rn.b d.ṣdqšlm.|[šd.b d.]bn.p‘ṣ.|[ubdy.‘]šrm.|[šd.---]n.b d.brdd.|[---.--]m.|[šd.---.b d.]ṯpṭb‘l.|[šd.---.]b d.y 82[300].1.31
n[š.mlk.---].ḫzr.lqḥ.ḥp[r].|‘št.‘šr h.bn[.---.--]ḫ.zr.|b‘l.šd. 2011.42

šdyn

ty.|artyn.ary.|brqn.ṯlḥy.|bn.aryn.|bn.lgn.|bn.b‘yn.|šdyn.|ary.|brqn.|bn.ḫlln.|bn.mṣry.|ṯmn.qšt.|w ‘šr.uṯpt.|u 118[306].9
krwn.lbn.‘dn.|ḫyrn.md‘.|šm‘n.rb ‘šrt.kkln.‘bd.abṣn.|šdyn.unn.dqn.|‘bd‘nt.rb ‘šrt.mnḥm.ṯb‘m.sḫr.‘zn.ilhd.|bnil. 2011.6
].d.yṯb.b.ilštm‘.|abmn.bn.r[---].b.syn.|bn.irṣ[-.---.]h.|šdyn.b[n.---.--]n. 2015.2.9
[---].|[---.]yn.l.m[--]m.|[---.]d.bn.[---.]l.dqn.|[---.--]‘.šdyn.l ytršn.|[---.--]ṯ.‘bd.l.kyn.|k[rm.--.]l.i[w]rtḏl.|ḥl.d[--.‘ 2027.2.8
šlm.‘bd.|awr.ṯǵrn.‘bd.|‘bd.ḫmn.šm‘.rgm.|šdn.[k]bš.|šdyn.mḫ[ṣ].|aṯry.mḫṣ.|b‘ln.mḫṣ.|y[ḥ]ṣdq.mḫṣ.|ṣp[r].ks[d]. 2084.14
l‘.|ḥd[ṯ]n.qšt.w.ql‘.|bn.bb.qšt.w[.ql]‘.|bn.aktmy.qšt.|šdyn.qšt.|bdn.qšt.w.ql‘.|bn.šmlbi.qšt.w.ql‘.|bn.yy.qšt.|ilrb. 119[321].4.11
[--]an.š[šlmt].|bnš.iwl[--.š]šlmt.|šdyn.ššlmt.|prtwn.š‘rt.|ṯṯn.š‘rt.|‘dn.š‘rt.|mnn.š‘rt.|bdn.š‘r 97[315].3
.ḥ[--.---].|w.ṯlṯm.dd.[---.]n[---.---].|w.a[r]b‘[.---].bnš[.š]dyn[.---].|agr.[---.--]n.ṯn.‘šr h.d[--.---].|[---.]ḥdṯn.‘šr.dd[.-- 1098.32

šdmy

[.---].|krm.n‘mn.b.ḫly.ull.krm.aḥ[d.---].|krm.uḫn.b.šdmy.ṯlṯ.bzl[.d]prn[.---].|aupṯ.krm.aḥd.nšpin.kr[m.]aḥd[.--- 1081.13

šdmt

lak.bn.ktpm.rgm.b‘l h.w y[--.---].|[---].ap.anš.zbl.b‘l.šdmt.bg[--.---].|[---.-]dm.mlak.ym.t‘dt.ṯpṭ.nh[r.---].|[---].an. 2.1[137].43
|ḫṭ.ulmn.yzbrnn.zbrm.gpn.|yṣmdnn.ṣmdm.gpn.yšql.šdmt h.|km gpn.|šb‘ d.yrgm.‘l.‘d.w ‘rbm.t‘nyn.|w šd.šd il 23[52].10

šdn

spr.rʻym. | lqḥ.šʻrt. | anntn. | ʻdn. | sdwn. | mztn. | ḫyrn. | šdn. | [ʻš]rm.ṯn kbd. | šǵrm. | lqḥ.ššlmt. 2098.8

šdʻl

i[l]štmʻym. | bn.ṯk. | bn.arwdn. | tmrtn. | šdʻl.bn aḫyn. | mʻrbym. | rpan. | abršn. | atlgy. | šršn. 95[91].5

šdq

-]. | [--]ṯb.ʻryt k.k qlt[.---]. | [--]at.brt.lb k.ʻnn.[---]. | [--.]šdq.k ttn.l y.šn[.---]. | [---.]bn.rgm.w ydʻ[.---]. 60[32].5

šḏn

n. | dqn. | aǵlmn. | knʻm. | aḫršp. | anntn. | bʻlrm. | [-]ral. | šḏn. | [-]ǵl. | bn.bʻltǵpṯ. | ḥrš.btm. | ršpab. | [r]ṣn. | [a]ǵlmn. | [a] 2067.1.11

šhr

ʻnt.l.kl.il.alṯ[y]. | nmry.mlk.ʻlm. | mlk n.bʻl y.ḥw[t.--]. | yšhr k.w.ʻm.ṣ[--]. | ʻš[--.---]d.lik[t.---]. | w [----]. | k[--.---]. | ʻšr 2008.1.11

šḥ

ab y. | u---].ʻlt.b k.lk.l pn y.yrk.bʻl.[--]. | [---.]ʻnt.šzrm.tštšḥ.km.ḥ[--]. | [---].ʻpr.bt k.ygr[š k.---]. | [---.]y.ḥr.ḥr.bnt.ḥ[- 1001.1.11

šḥlmmt

---.]ʻd. | ksm.mhyt[.m]ǵny. | l nʻm y.arṣ.dbr. | l ysmt.šd.šḥlmmt. | mǵny.l bʻl.npl.l a | rṣ.mt.aliyn.bʻl. | ḫlq.zbl.bʻl.arṣ. | 5[67].6.7
l.gbʻ. | l [k]bd.šdm.tmǵ.l nʻm[y]. | [arṣ.]dbr.ysmt.šd. | [šḥl]mmt.t[mǵ.]l bʻl.np[l]. | [l a]rṣ[.lpš].tks.miz[rtm]. 5[67].6.30
| bn.nšm.npš.hmlt. | arṣ.mǵt.l nʻm y.arṣ. | dbr.ysmt.šd.šḥlmmt. | ngš.ank.aliyn bʻl. | ʻdbnn ank.imr.b p y. | k lli.b ṯbr 6[49].2.20
ʻ ilm. | k mtt.yšmʻ.aliyn.bʻl. | yuhb.ʻglt.b dbr.prt. | b šd.šḥlmmt.škb. | ʻmn h.šbʻ.l šbʻm. | tš[ʻ]ly.ṯmn.l ṯmnym. | w [th] 5[67].5.19

šḥlt

at.tyt. | [---.kd.]nbt.k[d.]šmn.mr. | [---.l]tḥ.sb[by]n.ltḥ.šḥ[lt]. | [---.l]tḥ.dblt.ltḥ.ṣmqm. | [---.--]m.[ḫ]mšm.ḥmr.škm. 142[12].16
.]arbʻ.mat.ḫswn.ltḥ.aqhr. | [---.ltḥ.]sbbyn.ltḥ.ššmn.ltḥ.šḥlt. | [---.ltḥ.]ṣmqm.[t]ṯ.mat.nṣ.ṯlṯm.ʻṣr. | [---].ḫmš[m.ḥm]r.š 142[12].4

šḥq

ubrʻy. | arny. | mʻr. | šʻrt. | ḫlb rpš. | bqʻt. | šḥq. | yʻby. | mḫr. 65[108].7
ril. | ʻnmky. | ʻnqpat. | ṭbq. | hzp. | gnʻy. | mʻrby. | [ṣ]ʻq. | [š]ḥq. | nʻrm. | mḫrǵlm. | kzym. | mru.skn. | mru.ibrn. | pslm. | šr 71[113].59
.ṯṯ. | ḫlb krd.ṯn ʻšr. | qmy.arbʻ.ʻšr. | ṣʻq.arbʻ ʻšr. | ṣʻ.ṯmn. | šḥq.ʻšrm.arbʻ.kbd. | ḫlb rpš arbʻ.ʻšr. | bqʻt ṯṯ. | irab ṯn.ʻšr. | ḥbš. 67[110].6
rkby. | šḥq. | ǵn. | ṣʻ. | mld. | amḏy. | ḫlbʻprm. | ḫpty. | [ḫr]ṣbʻ. | [mʻ]rb. 2077.2
.---.k]bd. | ḫ[--.---.kb]d. | šr[-.---]. | mʻr[-.---]. | bqʻt.[---]. | šḥq[.---]. | rkby ar[bʻm]. | bir ṯ[--]. | ʻnqpat [---]. | m[--.---]. | [--- 2042.14

šḥr

[---.]l mitm.ksp. | [---.]skn. | [---.-]im.bṯd. | [---.b]šḥr.atlgn. | [---].b šḥr. | [---.]bn h. | [-]k[--]g hn.ksp. 2167.4
us]p.ḥmt.mlk.b ʻṯtrt.yisp.ḥmt. | [kṯ]r w ḫss.y[i]sp.ḥmt.šḥr.w šlm. | [yis]p.ḥmt.isp.[šp]š l hrm.ǵrpl.ʻl arṣ. | [l a]n ḥmt. UG5.8.18
ksa. | yrḫ mkty. | ṯkmn w šnm. | kṯr w ḫss. | ʻṯtr ʻṯpr. | šḥr w šlm. | ngh w srr. | ʻdw šr. | ṣdqm šr. | ḥnbn il d[n]. | [-]bd UG5.10.1.11
tldn.šḥr.w šlm.rgm.l il.ybl.a[ṯt y]. | il.ylt.mh.ylt.yld y.šḥr.w šl[m]. | šu.ʻdb.l špš.rbt.w l kbkbm.kn[-]. | yhbr.špt hm. 23[52].53
lrmn[.--]. | bm.nšq.w hr.b ḥbq.ḥmḥmt.tqt[nṣn]. | tldn.šḥr.w šlm.rgm.l il.ybl.a[ṯt y]. | il.ylt.mh.ylt.yld y.šḥr.w šl[m] 23[52].52
šr.yʻdb ksa. | w yṯb. | tqru l špš.um h.špš.um.ql bl ʻm. | šḥr.w šlm šmm h mnt.nṯk.nḥš. | šmrr.nḥš ʻq šr.ln h.mlḫš. | a UG5.7.52
k]lkl h. | [w] ytn.nn. | l.bʻln.bn. | kltn.w l. | bn h.ʻd.ʻlm. | šḥr.ʻlmt. | bnš bnšm. | l.yqḥnn.b d. | bʻln.bn.kltn. | w.b d.bn h. 1008.15
[.at.---]. | ḥmd m.[---]. | il.hr[r.---]. | kb[-.---]. | ym.[---]. | yšḥr[.---]. | yikl[.---]. | km.s[--.---]. | tš[.---]. | t[---.---]. | [-----]. | [12[75].2.13
.ksp. | [---.]skn. | [---.-]im.bṯd. | [---.b]šḥr.atlgn. | [---].b šḥr. | [---.]bn h. | [-]k[--]g hn.ksp. 2167.5
.]d arṣ. | [---.]ln. | [---.]nb hm. | [---.-]kn. | [---.]hr n.km.šḥr. | [---.y]lt n.km.qdm. | [-.k]bd n.il.ab n. | kbd k iš.tikln. | ṯd 12[75].1.7
[---.]b[--]. | [---].šḥr.[---]. | [---].al ytbʻ[.--]. | [---.]l adn.ḥwt[.--]. | [--]h.w yššil[.- 1023.2

šḥt

y k.bnm.ta[--.---]. | [b]nm.w bnt.ytn k[.---]. | [--]l.bn y.šḥt.w [---]. | [--]tt.msgr.bn k[.---]. | [--]n.tḥm.bʻl[.---]. 59[100].10
nm.l ytn.tk aršḫ.rbt. | w aršḫ.ṯrrt.ydy.b ʻṣm.ʻrʻr. | w b šḥt.ʻs.mt.ʻrʻrm.ynʻrn h. | ssnm.ysyn h.ʻdtm.yʻdyn h.yb | ltm.y UG5.7.65

šḫṭ

lmn.ṯnm[.qdqd]. | ṯlṯ id.ʻl.udn.š[pk.km]. | šiy.dm h.km.šḫ[ṭ.l brk h]. | yṣat.km.rḥ.npš[h.km.iṯl]. | brlt h.km.qṭr.[b ap 18[3AQHT].4.35
k.hlmn.ṯnm.qdqd. | ṯlṯ id.ʻl.udn.špk.km.šiy. | dm.km.šḫṭ.l brk h.tṣi.km. | rḥ.npš h.km.iṯl.brlt h.km. | qṭr.b ap h.b a 18[3AQHT].4.24

šḫyn

[---].rb. | [-]lpl. | bn.asrn. | bn.šḫyn. | bn.abdʻn. | bn.ḫnqn. | bn.nmq. | bn.amdn. | bn.špšn. 1067.4

šḫn

[---]. | npl.b mšmš[.---]. | anp n m yḥr[r.---]. | bmt n m.yšḫn.[---]. | qrn h.km.ǵb[-.---]. | hw km.ḥrr[.---]. | šnmtm.dbṭ[12[75].2.39

šḫp

]. | tḥbq.[---]. | tḥbq[.---]. | w tksynn.btn[-.] | y[--.]šr h.w šḫp h. | [--.]šḫp.ṣǵrt h. | yrk.tʻl.b ǵr. | mslmt.b ǵr.tliyt. | w tʻl.b 10[76].3.26
]. | tḥbq[.---]. | w tksynn.btn[-.] | y[--.]šr h.w šḫp h. | [--.]šḫp.ṣǵrt h. | yrk.tʻl.b ǵr. | mslmt.b ǵr.tliyt. | w tʻl.bkm.b arr. | 10[76].3.27

šḫr

bn.ḫnzr.ṯqlm.|dqn.nsk.arb‘t.|bn.ḫdyn.ṯqlm.|bn.‘bd.šḫr.ṯqlm.|bn.ḫnqn.arb‘t.|[b]n.ṯrk.ṯqlm.|[b]n.pdrn.ṯq[lm].| 122[308].1.19

šṭp

‘šr šṭpm.|b ḫmš.šmn.|‘šrm.gdy.|b ḫmš.šmn.|w ḫmš ṯ‘dt. 1097.1

šṭšm

spr.argmn.nskm.|rqdym.|šṭšm.ṯṯ mat.|ṣprn.ṯṯ mat.|ḏkry.ṯṯ mat.|[p]lsy.ṯṯ mat.|‘dn.ḫ 1060.1.3

šy

].|ṯr[--.---].|nn[-.---].|au[pš.---].|i[---.---].|pgl[--.---].|šy[.---].|bn.uḫn.|ybru.i[---].|[p]dyn.[---].|bnšm.d.b [d.---].| 2161.9

šyb

l h.[---].|[--.i]mṣḫ.nn.k imr.l arṣ.|[ašhlk].šbt h.dmm.šbt.dqn h.|[mm‘m.-]d.l ytn.bt.l b‘l.k ilm.|[w ḥẓ]r.k bn.aṯrt[3['NT.VI].5.10
.w ḥẓr.k bn.aṯrt.|w t‘n.rbt.aṯrt ym.|rbt.ilm.l ḥkmt.|šbt.dqn k.l tsr k.|rḫntt.d[-].l irt k.|wn ap.‘dn.mṭr h.|b‘l.y‘d 4[51].5.66
]gdlt.ar[kt y.am--].|[---.qdq]d k.ašhlk[.šbt k.dmm].|[šbt.dq]n k.mm‘m.w[---].|aqht.w ypltṭ k.bn[.dnil.---].|w y‘ḏ 18[3AQHT].1.12
].|b gdlt.arkt y.am[---].|qdqd k.ašhlk.šbt[k.dmm].|[šbt.dqn k.mm‘m.]y‘ny.|il.b šb‘t.ḥdrm.b ṯmnt.|ap.sgrt.yd‘[t 3['NT.VI].5.33
].|yṯb.l y.w l h.[---].|[--.i]mṣḫ.nn.k imr.l arṣ.|[ašhlk].šbt h.dmm.šbt.dqn h.|[mm‘m.-]d.l ytn.bt.l b‘l.k ilm.|[w ḥẓ 3['NT.VI].5.10
b y[--] y.[---]b[-].|b gdlt.arkt y.am[---].|qdqd k.ašhlk.šbt[k.dmm].|[šbt.dqn k.mm‘m.]y‘ny.|il.b šb‘t.ḥdrm.b ṯmn 3['NT.VI].5.32
m.[---].|[---.b]gdlt.ar[kt y.am--].|[---.qdq]d k.ašhlk[.šbt k.dmm].|[šbt.dq]n k.mm‘m.w[---].|aqht.w ypltṭ k.bn[.d 18[3AQHT].1.11

šyy

bn.šyy.|bn.ḫnzr.|bn.ydb‘l.|bn.ḥyn.|[bn].ar[-]m.|[bn].ḥrp[-].| 124[-].2.1

šyn

y.|bn.ḥrš.|[--.]kbd.|[---].|y[---].|bn.ǵlyn.|bdl.ar.|bn.šyn.|bn.ubrš.|bn.d[--]b.|abrpu.|bn.k[n]y.|bn.klyn.|bn.gm 1035.3.2
.|bn.ttn.|bn.rwy.|bn.‘myn.|bdl.mrynm.|bn.ṣqn.|bn.šyn.|bn.prtn.|bn.ypr.|mrum.|bn.‘[--]t.|bn.adty.|bn.krwn. 113[400].3.8
št.w.ql‘.|mrṯd.qšt.|ssw.qšt.|knn.qšt.|bn.ṯlln.qšt.|bn.šyn.qšt.|‘bd.qšt.|bn.ulmy.qšt.|ṯqbn.qšt.|bn.qnmlk.qšt.|ytḥ 104[316].5

šyr

]bḥ.mlk.l.prgl.ṣqrn.b.gg.|ar[b‘.]arb‘.mṯbt.azmr.b h.š.šr[-].|al[p.w].š.šlmm.pamt.šb‘.klb h.|yr[--.]mlk.ṣbu.špš.w.ḥ 35[3].51
nm.iḫ h yṯ‘r.|mšrrm.aḫt h l a|bn mznm.nkl w ib.|d ašr.ar yrḫ.w y|rḫ yar k.|[ašr ilht kṯrt bn]|t hll.snnt.bnt h|l 24[77].38
h l a|bn mznm.nkl w ib.|d ašr.ar yrḫ.w y|rḫ yar k.|[ašr ilht kṯrt bn]|t hll.snnt.bnt h|ll b‘l gml.yrdt.|b ‘rgzm.b 24[77].40
dln.|b‘ltdtt.tlgn.ytn.|b‘ltǵpṯm.krwn.ilšn.agyn.|mnn.šr.ugrt.ḏkr.yṣr.|tǵǵln.ḫmš.ddm.|[---].ḫmš.ddm.|ṯṯ.l.‘šrm.b 2011.37
b‘l.šd.|[---d]nil.|[a]drdn.|[---]n.|pǵḏn.|ṯṯpḥ.|ḥgbn.|šrm.|bn.ymil.|bn.kḏǵdl.|[-]mn.|[--]n.|[ḫr]š.qṭn.|[---]n.|[-- 1039.2.2
n.|bn.umḫ.|yky.bn.slyn.|ypln.bn.ylḥn.|‘zn.bn.mll.|šrm.|[b]n.špš[yn].|[b]n.ḫrmln.|bn.tnn.|bn.pndr.|bn.nqq.| 85[80].1.10
[---.-]ṯby[.---].|[---].abb[.---].|[---.-]k[-.-]n[-].|[---.--]m.šr.d.yṯ[b].|[---.--]y.d.ḫbṯ.sy[--].|[---.--]y.b.bt.ṯr[--]. 2134.9
‘t[h.ybmt].|limm.tiḫd.knr h.b yd[h.tšt].|rimt.l irt h.tšr.dd.al[iyn].|b‘l.ahbt. UG5.3.2.7
|km trpa.hn n‘r.|d yšt.l.lṣb h ḫš‘r klb.|[w]riš.pqq.w šr h.|yšt.aḥd h.dm zt.ḫrpnt. UG5.1.2.5
lm.w yšt.|[--.]gṯr.w yqr.il.yṯb.b.‘ṯtrt.|il.ṯpṭ.b hd r‘y.d yšr.w yḏmr.|b knr.w ṯlb.b tp.w mṣltm.b m|rqdm.dšn.b.ḥbr UG5.2.1.3
.|n‘rm.|mḫrǵlm.|kzym.|mru.skn.|mru.ibrn.|pslm.|šrm.|yṣḥm.|‘šrm.|mrum.|ṯnnm.|mqdm.|khnm.|qdšm.|n 71[113].66
|ṯmn.[---.]btlt.[‘]nt.|ṯṯb.[---.--]ša.|tlm.km[.---.]yd h.k šr.|knr.uṣb‘t h ḥrṣ.abn.|p h.tiḫd.šnt h.w akl.bqmm.|tšt ḥrṣ 19[1AQHT].1.7
-].|trḥṣ.yd[h.---].|[--.]yṣt ḏm[r.---].|tšt[.r]imt.[l irt h.tšr.l dd.aliyn.b‘l].|[ahb]t pdr[y.bt.ar.ahbt.ṭly.bt.rb.dd].|arṣ 7.2[130].10
[---.t]št.rimt.|l irt h.mšr.l.dd.aliyn.|b‘l.yd.pdry.bt.ar.|ahbt.ṭly.bt.rb.dd.arṣy.|bt 3['NT].3.2
ašr nkl w ib[.bt].|ḫrḫb.mlk qẓ ḫrḫb m|lk aǵzt.b sǵ[--.]špš.| 24[77].1
|ṯnnm.|nqdm.|khnm.|qdšm.|pslm.|mkrm.|yṣḥm.|šrm.|n‘rm.|‘bdm.|kzym.|ksdm.|[nsk].ṯlṯ.|gt.mlkym.|tmr 1026.1.11
yrḫm.|k b‘l.k yḥwy.y‘šr.ḥwy.y‘š.|r.w yšqyn h.ybd.w yšr.‘l h.|n‘m[n.w t]‘nynn.ap ank.aḥwy.|aqht[.ǵz]r.w y‘n.aq 17[2AQHT].6.31
ḫpn.d.iqni.w.šmt.|l.iyb‘l.|ṯlṯm.l.mit.š‘rt.|l.šr.‘ṯtrt.|mlbš.ṯrmnm.|k.ytn.w.b.bt.|mlk.mlbš.|ytn.l hm.|š 1107.4
r.|rbt.ymsk.b msk h.|qm.ybd.w yšr.|mṣltm.bd.n‘m.|yšr.ǵzr.ṭb.ql.|‘l.b‘l.b ṣrrt.|ṣpn.ytmr.b‘l.|bnt h.y‘n.pdry.|bt. 3['NT].1.20
rt.alp.|kd.yqḥ.b ḫmr.|rbt.ymsk.b msk h.|qm.ybd.w yšr.|mṣltm.bd.n‘m.|yšr.ǵzr.ṭb.ql.|‘l.b‘l.b ṣrrt.|ṣpn.ytmr.b‘l 3['NT].1.18
|mṯbt.ilm.ṯmn.ṯ[--.--].|pamt.šb‘.|iqnu.šmt[.---].|[b]n.šrm.|iqran.ilm.n‘mm[.agzry ym.bn]ym.|ynqm.b ap zd.aṯrt 23[52].22
dln.|[u]bdy.ṯǵrm.|[š]d.ṯǵr.mṯpit.b d.bn.iryn.|[u]bdy.šrm.|[š]d.bn.ḫrmln.b d.bn.tnn̊.|[š]d.bn.ḫrmln.ṯn.b d.bn.ḫd 82[300].2.9
šl[-].|[---]m.|[-]rm.|[-]dm.|[-]m.|[--]m.|[m]ru skn.|šrm.|[--]m.|[i]nšt. 2058.4.2
dšt.‘b[dml]k.ṯṯpḥ.mrṭn.|ḫḏǵlm.i[---]n.pbn.nḏbn.sbd.|šrm.[---].ḫpn.|ḥrš[bhtm.--]n.‘bdyrḫ.ḥdṯn.y‘r.|adb‘l[.---].ḥd 2011.17
šd.b d.--]n.|[šd.b d.--]n.|[šd.b d.--]ǵl.|[šd.b d.--]pšm.šyr. 82[300].2.32
.mr[k]bt.|[--].‘šr h[.---].|[ḫm]š.‘šr h[.---].|ḫmš.‘šr h.|šrm. 1024.4.2

šyt

m.‘bd k hwt.|[y]rš.‘m y.|mnm.iršt k.|d ḫsrt.w.ank.|aštn..l.iḫ y.|w.ap.ank.mnm.|[ḫ]s[r]t.w.uḫ y.|[y]‘msn.ṯmn.| 2065.17
n.|hlk.aḫt h.b‘l.y‘n.tdrq.|ybnt.ab h.šrḥq.aṯt.l pnn h.|št.alp.qdm h.mria.w tk.|pn h.tḥspn.m h.w trḥṣ.|ṭl.šmm.šm 3['NT].4.85
ss.|w ṯb l mspr..k tlakn.|ǵlmm.|aḫr.mǵy.kṯr.w ḫss.|št.alp.qdm h.mra.|w tk.pn h.t‘db.ksu.|w yṯṯb.l ymn.aliyn.| 4[51].5.107
‘ly.ṯh.lm.|l.ytn.hm.mlk.[b]‘l y.|w.hn.ibm.šṣq l y.|p.l.ašt.aṯt y.|n‘r y.ṯh.l pn.ib.|hn.hm.yrgm.mlk.|b‘l y.tmǵyy.hn 1012.28
].|w.yṣq[.b.ap h].|k.yiḫd[.akl.s̀sw].|št.mkš[r.grn].|w.št.ašk[rr].|w.pr.ḥḏr[t.ydk].|aḥd h.w.yṣq[.b.ap h].|k.yiḫd.a 161[56].14
ḥd h w yṣq b ap h.|[k.yiḫd akl s̀]s̀w št mkšr grn.|[w št aškrr w p]r ḥḏrt.|[-----].|[---.-]n[-].|[k yraš s̀s̀w št bln q]ṭ 160[55].11
.|dt.yrq.nqbnm.|‘db.gpn.atnt h.|yḥbq.qdš.w amrr.|yštn.aṯrt.l bmt.‘r.|l ysmsmt.bmt.pḥl.|qdš.yuḫdm.šb‘r.|amr 4[51].4.14
.yṣq[.b.ap h].|k.yiḫd.akl.s̀[s̀w].|št.nni.št.mk[št.grn].|št.irǵn.ḥmr[.ydk].|aḥd h.w.yṣq.b[.ap h].|k.yraš.s̀s̀w.[št].|bl 161[56].19
l[.---].|mǵm[ǵ.---].|w.š[t.nni.w.pr.‘bk].|w.pr[.ḥḏrt.w.št].|irǵ[n.ḥmr.ydk].|aḥd[h.w.yṣq.b.ap h].|k yr[a]š.s̀s̀[w.w. 161[56].29

.mḥmd.arz h. | h[n.l]bnn.w ‘ṣ h. | š[r]yn.mḥmd.arz h. | tšt.išt.b bht m. | nb[l]at.b hkl m. | hn.ym.w ṯn.tikl. | išt.b bht 4[51].6.22
t.urbt.b bh[t] m. | ḥln.b qrb.hkl m. | w y‘n.aliyn b‘l. | al.tšt.urbt.b[bhtm]. | [ḥln].b qrb.hk[l m]. 4[51].5.126
kl. | w y‘n.kṯr.w ḫss. | šm‘.l aliyn b‘l. | bn.l rkb.‘rpt. | bl.ašt.urbt.b bh[t] m. | ḥln.b qrb.hkl m. | w y‘n.aliyn b‘l. | al.tšt. 4[51].5.123
r[bt.]b bht m. | ḥln.b qr[b.hk]l m. | w ‘n.ali[yn.]b‘l. | al.tšt.u[rb]t.b bht m. | ḥln.b q[rb.hk]l m. | al td[.pdr]y.bt ar. | [-- 4[51].6.8
l[hwt y]. | ṯn.rgm.k[ṯr.w]ḫss. | šm‘.m‘.l al[iy]n b‘l. | bl.ašt.ur[bt.]b bht m. | ḥln.b qr[b.hk]l m. | w ‘n.ali[yn.]b‘l. | al.tš 4[51].6.5
spr ‘psm. | dt.št. | uryn. | l mlk.ugrt. 1171.2
| w yd.il.k mdb.yqḥ.il.mšt‘ltm. | mšt‘ltm.l riš.agn.yqḥ.tš.b bt h. | il.ḫṭ h.nḥt.il.ymnn.mṭ.yd h.yšu. | yr.šmm h.yr.b š 23[52].36
-.-]ṯq. | w š[--.---]. | ḥdṯ[.---.]ḥ[--]. | b bt.[-.]l bnt.q[-]. | w št.b bt.ṯap[.--]. | hy.yd h.w ym[ǵ]. | mlak k.‘m dt[n]. | lqḥ.mṯp UG5.6.9
bd[h]. | w aḥd.hm.iṯ.šmt.hm.iṯ[.‘ẓm]. | abky.w aqbrn.ašt.b ḫrt. | i[lm.arṣ.b p h.rgm.l yṣa.b šp] | t h.hwt h.knp.hrgb 19[1AQHT].3.126
.ibq‘. | kbd h.w aḥd.hm.iṯ.šmt.iṯ. | ‘ẓm.abky w aqbrn h.aštn. | b ḫrt.ilm.arṣ.b p h.rgm.l[yṣ]a. | b špt h.hwt h.knp.ṣml 19[1AQHT].3.140
hm.w] | aḥd.hm.iṯ.šmt.hm.i[ṯ]. | ‘ẓm.abky.w aqbrn h. | ašt.b ḫrt.ilm.arṣ. | b p h.rgm.l yṣa.b špt h.hwt[h]. | knp.nšrm 19[1AQHT].3.112
-.-]ip.dpr k. | [---.-]mn k.ššrt. | [---.--]t.npš.‘gl. | [---.-]nk.aštn.b ḫrt. | ilm.arṣ.w at.qḥ. | ‘rpt k.rḥ k.mdl k. | mṭrt k.‘m k. 5[67].5.5
p. | ‘nt.k tšt h.tš‘lyn h. | b ṣrrt.ṣpn.tbkyn h. | w tqbrn h.tštnn.b ḫrt. | ilm.arṣ.ṭṭbḫ.šb‘m. | rumm.k gmn.aliyn. | [b]‘l.ṭṭb 6[62].1.17
.mid. | hm.nṯkp. | m‘n k. | w.mnm. | rgm.d.tšm‘. | ṯmt.w.št. | b.spr.‘m y. 53[54].18
m.tḥm.aliyn.b‘l]. | hw[t.aliy.qrdm.qryy.b arṣ.mlḥmt.št]. | [b ‘]pr[m.ddym.sk.šlm.l kbd.arṣ.arbdd]. | l kbd.š[dm.ḥš 7.2[130].14
‘rpt. | tḥm.aliyn.b‘l.hwt.aliy. | qrdm.qry.b arṣ.mlḥmt. | št.b ‘p[r] m.ddym.sk.šlm. | l kbd.arṣ.arbdd.l kbd.šdm. | [ḥ]š 3[‘NT].4.53
mm. | tḥm.aliyn.b‘l.hwt. | aliy.qrdm.qry.b arṣ. | mlḥmt št.b ‘pr m.ddym. | sk.šlm.l kbd.arṣ. | arbdd.l kbd.šdm. | ḥš k.‘ 3[‘NT].3.12
btlt.[‘]nt.ṯṯb. | [ybmt.]limm.[a]n.aqry. | [b arṣ].mlḥmt.[aš]t.b ‘pr m. | ddym.ask[.šlm.]l kbd.arṣ. | ar[bdd.]l kb[d.š]dm 3[‘NT].4.67
.ṯḥm. | [ṯr.il.ab k.hwt.l]ṭpn.ḥtk k. | [qryy.b arṣ.mlḥ]mt.št b ‘p | [r m.ddym.sk.šlm].l kbd.arṣ. | [arbdd.l kbd.š]dm.ḥš 1[‘NT.IX].2.19
.]b‘l.mdl h.yb‘r. | [---.]rn h.aqry. | [---.]b a[r]ṣ.mlḥmt. | ašt[.b ‘]p[r] m.ddym.ask. | šlm.l kb[d].awṣ.arbdd. | l kbd.š[d] 3[‘NT].4.73
b‘l. | [ṭṭbḫ.šb‘m.]ḥmrm. | [k gm]n.al[i]yn.b[‘l]. | [---]ḥ h.tšt bm.‘[--]. | [---.]zr h.ybm.l ilm. | [id]k.l ttn.pnm.‘m. | [il.]mb 6.1.30[49.1.2]
-].al.trgm.l aḫt k. | [---.]l [ ]dm.aḫt k. | yd‘t.k rḥmt. | al.tšt.b šdm.mm h. | b smkt.ṣat.npš h. | [-]mt[-].ṣba.rbt. | špš.w t 16.1[125].34
d.ẓu h.b ym.t[---]. | tlbš.npṣ.ǵzr.tšt.ḫ[---.b] | nšg h.ḥrb.tšt.b t‘r[t h]. | w ‘l.tlbš.npṣ.aṯt.[--]. | ṣbi nrt.ilm.špš.[-]r[--]. | p 19[1AQHT].4.207
i[n.b ilht]. | qlṣ k.tb‘.bt.ḫnp.lb[k.--.ti] | ḫd.d iṯ.b kbd k.tšt.b [---]. | irt k.dṯ.ydṯ.m‘qb k.[ttb‘]. | [bt]lt.‘nt.idk.l ttn.[pnm 18[3AQHT].1.18
| dk k.kbkb[.---]. | dm.mt.aṣḫ[.---]. | ydd.b qr[b.---]. | al.ašt.b[---]. | ahpk k.l[--.---]. | ṯmm.w lk[.---]. | w lk.ilm[.---]. | n‘ 5[67].3.11
[w št aškrr w p]r ḥḏrt. | [-----]. | [---.-]n[-]. | [k yraš ššw št bln q]ṭ ydk. | [w yṣq b ap h]. | [-----]. | [-----]. | [-----]. | [---.-]r 160[55].14
št.irǵn.ḥmr[.ydk]. | aḥd h.w.yṣq.b[.ap h]. | k.yraš.ššw.[št]. | bln.qṭ.yṣq.b.a[p h]. | k yg‘r[.ššw.---]. | dprn[.---]. | dr‘.[---] 161[56].21
.ary y. | w lḥm m ‘m aḫ y.lḥm. | w št m.‘m.a[ḫ] yn. | p nšt.b‘l.[ṭ]‘n.iṭ‘n k. | [---.]ma[---] k.k tmḫṣ. | [ltn.bṯn.br]ḥ.tkly. 5[67].1.26
‘db.gpn.atnt[y]. | yšm‘.qd.w amr[r]. | mdl.‘r.ṣmd.pḥl. | št.gpnm.dt.ksp. | dt.yrq.nqbnm. | ‘db.gpn.atnt h. | yḫbq.qdš. 4[51].4.10
qdš]. | w am[rr.l dgy.rbt]. | aṯrt.ym[.mdl.‘r]. | ṣmd.pḥl[.št.gpnm.dt]. | ksp.dt.yr[q.nqbnm]. | ‘db.gpn.atnt[y]. | yšm‘.q 4[51].4.5
.my]. | ḥspt.l š‘r.ṭl.yd[‘t]. | hlk.kbkbm.mdl.‘r. | ṣmd.pḥl.št.gpn y dt ksp. | dt.yrq.nqbn y.tš[m‘]. | pǵt.ṯkmt.my.ḥspt.l[š 19[1AQHT].2.53
y.aliyn.b‘l. | tšm‘.nrt.ilm.špš. | tšu.aliyn.b‘l.l ktp. | ‘nt.k tšt h.tš‘lyn h. | b ṣrrt.ṣpn.tbkyn h. | w tqbrn h.tštnn.b ḫrt. | il 6[62].1.15
]. | l mṯb[.--]t[.---]. | [tqdm.]yd.b ṣ‘.t[šl]ḥ. | [ḥrb.b]bš[r].tštn. | [w t‘n].mṯt.ḥry. | [l lḥ]m.l šty.ṣḥt k[m]. | [---.]brk.t[---]. 15[128].5.8
m.mṯb[.---]. | w lḫm mr.tqdm. | yd.b ṣ‘.tšlḥ. | ḥrb.b bšr.tštn. | [w t]‘n.mṯt.ḥry. | [l lḥ]m.l šty.ṣḥt km. | [--.dbḥ.l]krt.b‘l 15[128].4.25
šr. | knr.uṣb‘t h ḥrṣ.abn. | p h.tiḫd.šnt h.w akl.bqmm. | tšt ḥrṣ.k lb ilnm. | w ṯn.gprm.mn gpr h.šr. | aqht.y‘n.kmr.km 19[1AQHT].1.10
n h.mks.bšr h. | tmt‘.md h.b ym.ṯn. | npyn h.b nhrm. | štt.ḫptr.l išt. | ḫbrṯ.l ẓr.pḥmm. | t‘pp.ṯr.il.d pid. | tǵẓy.bny.bn 4[51].2.8
.b ǵlp y[m.--]. | d alp šd.ẓu h.b ym.t[---]. | tlbš.npṣ.ǵzr.tšt.ḫ[---.b] | nšg h.ḥrb.tšt.b t‘r[t h]. | w ‘l.tlbš.npṣ.aṯt.[--]. | ṣbi 19[1AQHT].4.206
spr.npš.d. | ‘rb.bt.mlk. | w.b.spr.l.št. | yrm‘l. | ṣry. | iršy. | y‘ḏrd. | ayaḫ. | bn.aylt. | ḫmš.mat.arb‘m 2106.3
tp‘.b aklt.šblt.tp‘[.b ḥm]drt. | ur.tisp k.yd.aqht.ǵz[r]. | tšt k.bm.qrb m.asm. | b p h.rgm.l yṣa.b špt h[.hwt h]. | b nši ‘ 19[1AQHT].2.74
]. | ynp‘.b palt.bṣql yp‘ b yǵlm. | ur.tisp k.yd.aqht. | ǵzr.tšt k.b qrb m.asm. | y.dnh.ysb.aklt h.yph. | šblt.b akt.šblt.yp‘ 19[1AQHT].2.67
g h. | w yṣḥ.y l k.qrt.ablm. | d ‘l k.mḫṣ.aqht.ǵzr. | ‘wrt.yšt k.b‘l.l ht. | w ‘lm h.l ‘nt.p dr.dr. | ‘db.uḫry.mṭ.yd h. | dnil. 19[1AQHT].4.167
.ab k. | hwt.lṭpn.ḥtk k. | pl.‘nt.šdm.y špš. | pl.‘nt.šdm.il.yš[t k]. | b‘l.‘nt.mḥrṯ[-]. | iy.aliyn.b‘l. | iy.zbl.b‘l.arṣ. | w t‘n.nrt 6[49].4.37
[t]. | rgm.l nrt.il.šp[š]. | pl.‘nt.šdm.y špš. | pl.‘nt.šdm.il.yšt k. | [b]‘l.‘nt.mḥrṯt. | iy.aliyn.b‘l. | iy.zbl.b‘l.arṣ. | ttb‘.btlt.‘n 6[49].4.26
tir.b ḏdm.w n‘rs[.---]. | w t‘n.btlt.‘nt.ṯb.yṭp.w[---]. | l k.ašt k.km.nšr.b ḥb[š y]. | km.diy.b t‘rt y.aqht.[km.yṯb]. | l lḥm 18[3AQHT].4.17
qṭr.b ap h.b ap.mhr h.ank. | l aḥwy.tqḥ.yṭpn.mhr.št. | tštn.k nšr.b ḥbš h.km.diy. | b t‘rt h.aqht.km.yṯb.l lḥ[m]. | bn. 18[3AQHT].4.28
]. | [--.]l mlk [---]. | [---].aḫ y[.---]. | [--]q lpš[.---]. | [---] y št k[.---]. | [---.]l m[lk]. 2130.2.2
kbkbm. | bkm.tmdln.‘r. | bkm.tṣmd.pḥl.bkm. | tšu.ab h.tštnn.l[b]mt ‘r. | l ysmsm.bmt.pḥl. | y dnil.ysb.palt h. | bṣql.y 19[1AQHT].2.59
--.--]y. | w.spr.in[.-.]‘d m. | spr n.ṯhr[.--]. | aṯr.iṯ.bqṯ. | w.štn.l y. 2060.35
[--]y.k išal hm. | [--.‘š]rm.kkr.ṯlṯ. | [--.]ṯlṯm.kkr.ṯlṯ. | [--.]aštn.l k. | [--]y.kl.dbrm.hm[.--]. | [--]l.w.kl.mḫr k. | [--]tir.aštn 1022.6
tn.l k. | [--]y.kl.dbrm.hm[.--]. | [--]l.w.kl.mḫr k. | [--]tir.aštn.l [k]. | [---].kkr.ṯl[ṯ]. 1022.9
ḫṭ.il.ymnn.mṭ.yd h.yšu. | yr.šmm h.yr.b šmm.‘ṣr.yḫrṭ yšt. | l pḥm.il.aṯtm.k ypt.hm.aṯtm.tṣḥn. | y mt.mt.nḥtm.ḫṭ k. 23[52].38
tḥm b[.---]. | mrḥ h l adrt[.---]. | ttb ‘ṯtrt b ǵl[.---]. | qrẓ tšt.l šmal[.---]. | arbḫ.‘n h tšu w[.---]. | aylt tǵpy ṯr.‘n[.---]. | b[2001.1.9
.tḥm.ṯr.il.ab k.] | hwt.lṭpn[.ḥtk k.---]. | yh.kṯr.b[---]. | št.lskt.n[--.---]. | ‘db.bǵrt.ṯ[--. --]. | ḥš k.‘ṣ k.‘[bṣ k.‘m y.p‘n k.t 1[‘NT.IX].3.8
| tš‘m.b‘l.mr[-]. | bt[.--]b b‘l.b qrb. | bt.w y‘n.aliyn. | b‘l.ašt m.kṯr bn. | ym.kṯr.bnm.‘dt. | ypth.ḥln.b bht m. | urbt.b qr 4[51].7.15
. | ‘rgz[.ydk.aḥd h]. | w.yṣq[.b.ap h]. | k.yiḫd[.akl.ššw]. | št.mkš[r.grn]. | w.št.ašk[rr]. | w.pr.ḥḏr[t.ydk]. | aḥd h.w.yṣq[. 161[56].13
| [w št ‘rgz y]dk aḥd h w yṣq b ap h. | [k.yiḫd akl š]šw št mkšr grn. | [w št aškrr w p]r ḥḏrt. | [-----]. | [---.-]n[-]. | [k yr 160[55].10
.ydk]. | aḥd h.w.yṣq[.b.ap h]. | k.yiḫd.akl.š[šw]. | št.nni.št.mk[št.grn]. | št.irǵn.ḥmr[.ydk]. | aḥd h.w.yṣq.b[.ap h]. | k.y 161[56].18
w.---]. | dprn[.---]. | dr‘.[---]. | tmṯl[.---]. | mǵm[ǵ.---]. | w.š[t.nni.w.pr.‘bk]. | w.pr[.ḥḏrt.w.št]. | irǵ[n.ḥmr.ydk]. | aḥd[h. 161[56].28
.ḥḏr[t.ydk]. | aḥd h.w.yṣq[.b.ap h]. | k.yiḫd.akl.š[šw]. | št.nni.št.mk[št.grn]. | št.irǵn.ḥmr[.ydk]. | aḥd h.w.yṣq.b[.ap h 161[56].18
m.w n‘[n]. | ‘ma nkl ḫtn y.a[ḫ]r. | nkl yrḫ ytrḫ.adn h. | yšt mṣb.mznm.um h. | kp mznm.iḫ h yṯ‘r. | mšrrm.aḫt h l a | 24[77].34
m.yš | al. | w mlk.d mlk. | b ḥwt.špḥ. | l ydn.‘bd.mlk. | d št.‘l.ḫrd h. | špḥ.al.thbṭ. | ḫrd.‘ps.aḫd.kw | sgt. | ḫrd ksp.[--]r. | 2062.2.4
p zbl. | [w ‘d]t.ilm.ṯlṯ h. | [ap]nk.krt.ṯ‘.‘[-]r. | [--.]b bt h.yšt.‘rb. | [--] h.ytn.w [--]u.l ytn. | [aḫ]r.mǵy.‘[d]t.ilm. | [w]y‘n 15[128].2.9
w.y[ṣq.b.ap h]. | k.l.ḫ[ru.w.l.yṯtn.ššw]. | mss.[št.qlql.w.št]. | ‘rgz[.ydk.aḥd h]. | w.yṣq[.b.ap h]. | k.yiḫd[.akl.ššw]. | št. 161[56].9

šyt

d h w yṣq b ap h.|[k l yḫru w]l yṯtn mss št qlql.|[w št ʿrgz y]dk aḥd h w yṣq b ap h.|[k.yiḫd akl š̀]šw št mkšr gr 160[55].9
]r.|[ydk aḥd h w yṣq b ap h.|[k l yḫru w]l yṯtn mss št qlql.|[w št ʿrgz y]dk aḥd h w yṣq b ap h.|[k.yiḫd akl š̀]š̀ 160[55].8
.aḥd h].|w.y[ṣq.b.ap h].|k.l.ḫ[ru.w.l.yṯtn.š̀šw].|mss.[št.qlql.w.št].|ʿrgz[.ydk.aḥd h].|w.yṣq[.b.ap h].|k.yiḫd[.akl. 161[56].9
yd h.btlt.ʿnt.uṣbʿt[h.ybmt].|limm.tiḫd.knr h.b yd[h.tšt].|rimt.l irt h.tšr.dd.al[iyn].|bʿl.ahbt. UG5.3.2.6
yn[.---].|špk.l[---].|trḥṣ.yd[h.---].|[--.]yṣt ḏm[r.---].|tšt[.r]imt.[l irt h.tšr.l dd.aliyn.bʿl].|[ahb]t pdr[y.bt.ar.ahbt.ṭ 7.2[130].10
[---.t]št.rimt.|l irt h.mšr.l.dd.aliyn.|bʿl.yd.pdry.bt.ar.|ahbt.ṭly. 3[ʿNT].3.1
p ym.|lšnm.tlḥk.|šmm.tṯrp.|ym.ḏnbtm.|tnn.l šbm.|tšt.trks.|l mrym.l bt[.---].|p l.tbʿ[.---].|hmlt ḫt.[---].|l.tp[-] 1003.9
[--].|ʿš[--.---]d.lik[t.---].|w [----].|k[--.---].|ʿšrm[.---].|tšt.tbʿ[.---].|qrt.mlk[.---].|w.ʿl.ap.s[--.---].|b hm.w.rgm.hw. 2008.2.3
dy.ʿnt.tǵdd.kbd h.b ṣḥ]q.ymlu.lb h.|[b šmḫt.kbd.ʿnt.tšyt.tḥt h.k]kdrt.riš.|[ʿl h.k irbym.kp.---.k br]k.tǵll.b dm.|[7.1[131].8
nt.at.ʿ[l.qšt h].|tmḫṣ h.qṣʿt h.hwt.l t[ḥwy].|nʿmn.ǵzr.št.ṯrm.w[---].|ištir.b ḏdm.w nʿrs[.---].|w tʿn.btlt.ʿnt.ṯb.yṭp. 18[3AQHT].4.14
.l mt[.---].|l šrr.w tʿ[n.ʿṯtrt.---].|bʿl m.hmt.[---].|l šrr.št[.---].|b riš h.[---].|ib h.mš[--.---].|[b]n.ʿn h[.---]. 2.4[68].37
n.ib.d.b.mgšḫ.|[---.i]b.hn[.w.]ht.ank.|[---.--]š[-.--].w.ašt.|[---].amr k.|[---].k.ybt.mlk.|[---].w.ap.ank.|[---].l.ǵr.a 1012.12
pr m.|ddym.ask[.šlm.]l kbd.arṣ.|ar[bdd.]l kb[d.š]dm.yšt.|[----.]bʿl.mdl h.ybʿr.|[---.]rn h.aqry.|[---.]b a[r]ṣ.mlḥm 3[ʿNT].4.69
l hm.|w.any k.ṯt.|by.ʿky.ʿryt.|w.aḫ y.mhk.|b lb h.al.yšt. 2059.27
m.|ilak.w.at.|um y.al.tdḥṣ.|w.ap.mhkm.|b.lb k.al.|tšt. 1013.24

škb

my.]uzr.ilm.ylḥm.|[uzr.yšqy.]bn.qdš.yd.|[ṣt h.yʿl.]w yškb.yd.|[mizrt.]p ynl.hn.ym.|[w ṯn.uzr.]ilm.dnil.|[uzr.ilm 17[2AQHT].1.5
.ylḥm.|[uzr.]yšqy.bn qdš.yd.ṣt h.|[dn]il.yd.ṣt h.yʿl.w yškb.|[yd.]mizrt.p yln.mk.b šbʿ.ymm.|[w]yqrb.bʿl.b ḥnt h. 17[2AQHT].1.15
[--]k bʿlt bhtm[.--]tn k.|[--]y.l ihbt.yb[--].rgm y.|[---.]škb.w m[--.]mlakt.|[---.]ʿl.w tšʿ[d]n.npṣ h.|[---.]rgm.hn.[--] 1002.47
bd.|mḏrǵlm.|w.šbʿ.ʿšr.ḫsnm.|ḫmšm.l.mit.|bnš.l.d.|yškb.l.b.bt.mlk. 1029.16
t h.|bm.bky h.w yšn.|b dmʿ h.nhmmt.|šnt.tluan.|w yškb.nhmmt.|w yqmṣ.w b ḥlm h.|il.yrd.b ḏhrt h.|ab adm. 14[KRT].1.34
mtt.yšmʿ.aliyn.bʿl.|yuhb.ʿglt.b dbr.prt.|b šd.šḥlmmt.škb.|ʿmn h.šbʿ.l šbʿm.|tš[ʿ]ly.ṯmn.l ṯmnym.|w [th]rn.w tld 5[67].5.19
--.a]ḥd.d.sgrm.|w p[tḥ.---.]l.aḥd.adr.|[---.--]t.b[ḥd]r.mškb.|ṯl[l.---.--]ḥ.|b lṯk.bt.|[pt]ḥ.aḥd.l.bt.ʿbdm.|[ṯ]n.ptḥ m 1151.6
[---].ydm.|[---].ṯdr.|[---.]mdṯn.ipd.|[---.]m[---.]d.mškbt.|[---.--]m.|[---].ṯlḥn.|[---].ṯnn.|[---.--]b.kdr.|[---.--]m 1152.1.4
h.|arn.w mznm.|ṯn.ḫlpnm.|ṯt.mrḥm.|drb.|mrbd.|mškbt. 2050.10

škḥ

any kn.dt.|likt.mṣrm.|hn dt.b.ṣr.|mtt.by.|gšm.adr.|nškḥ.w.|rb.tmtt.|lqḥ.kl.ḏrʿ.|b d a[-]m.w.ank.|k[l.]ḏrʿ hm.| 2059.15

škm

[---.ltḥ.]ṣmqm.[ṯ]ṯ.mat.nṣ.ṯlṯm.ʿṣr.|[---].ḫmš[m.ḥm]r.škm.|[---.ṯṯ.dd.]gdl.ṯṯ.dd.šʿrm.|[---.hn.w.al]p.kd.nbt.kd.šm 142[12].6
--.-]ʿt.ltḥ.š̀šmn.|[---].ḫšwn.ṯṯ.mat.nṣ.|[---].ḫmšm.ḥmr.škm.|[---.ṯṯ.dd.]gdl.ṯṯ.dd.šʿrm.|[---.a]lp.arbʿ.mat.tyt.|[---.kd 142[12].12
.šḥ[lt].|[---.l]tḥ.dblt.ltḥ.ṣmqm.|[---.--]m.[ḫ]mšm.ḥmr.škm. 142[12].18

škn

[---].md.ʿ[ṯtr]t.|ydy.|bn.škn.|bn.mdt.|bn.ḫ[--]y.|bn.ʿ[-]y.|knʿm.|bn.yš[-]n.|bn.pd[y 1054.1.3
mn h.|bkm.yṯb.bʿl.l bht h.|u mlk.u bl mlk.|arṣ.drkt.yštkn.|dll.al.ilak.l bn.|ilm.mt.ʿdd.l ydd.|il.ǵzr.yqra.mt.|b 4[51].7.44
dʿ.|w.ap.mlk.uḏ[r].|[-]dʿ.k.iḫd.[---].|w.mlk.bʿl y.|lm.škn.hnk.|l ʿbd h.alpm.š̀[šw]m.|rgmt.ʿly.ṯh.lm.|l.ytn.hm.ml 1012.23
].|w hm.at.tr[gm.---].|w.drm.ʿtr[--.---].|w ap.ht.k[--.]škn.|w.mṯnn[.---.]ʿmn k.|[-]štš.[---.]rgm y.|[-]wd.r[-.]pǵt.|[54.1.20[13.2.5]
šbʿ.ḫḏǵlm.|l.[---]mn ḫpn.|l[.--.]škn.ḫpn.|l.k[-]w.ḫpn.|l.ṣ[--].šʿ[rt].|l.ʿdy.š[ʿ]r[t].|ṯlṯ.l.ʿd.ab[1117.3
n y.lm ṯb[t] km.|l kḥṯ.zbl k[m.a]nk.|iḥtrš.w [a]škn.|aškn.ydt.[m]rṣ gršt.|zbln.r[---].ymlu.|nʿm.[-]ṯ[-.--.]yqrṣ.|d[16[126].5.27
m.|ʿm špš.kll.mid m.|šlm.|l.[--]n.špš.|ad[.ʿ]bd h.uk.škn.|k.[---.]sglt h.hw.|w.b[.---.]uk.nǵr.|w.[---].adny.l.yḫsr. 2060.6
ʿ.|mit.arbʿm.kbd.|l.liy.bn.ʿmyn.|mit.ḫmšm.kbd.|d.škn.l.ks.ilm. 1143.14
dbḥ.mlk.ʿšr.|ʿšrt.qḥ.tp k.b yd.|[-]r[-]k.bm.ymn.|tlk.škn.ʿl.ṣrrt.|adn k.šqrb.[---].|b mgn k.w ḫrṣ.l kl.|apnk.ǵzr.il 16.1[125].43
tḥm.rgm.|mlk.|l ḥyil.|lm.tlik.ʿm y.|ik y.aškn.|ʿṣm.l bt.dml.|p ank.atn.|ʿṣm.l k.|arbʿ.ʿṣm.|ʿl.ar.|w.ṯ 1010.5
ybl.trḫ.ḥdṯ.|ybʿr.l ṯn.aṯt h.|w l nkr.mddt.|km irby.tškn.|šd.k ḥsn.pat.|mdbr.tlkn.|ym.w ṯn.aḫr.|šp[š]m.b [ṯ]lṯ. 14[KRT].4.192
yṣi.trḫ.|ḥdṯ.ybʿr.l ṯn.|aṯt h.lm.nkr.|mddt h.k irby.|[t]škn.šd.|km.ḥsn.pat.mdbr.|lk.ym.w ṯn.ṯlṯ.rbʿ ym.|ḫmš.ṯdṯ 14[KRT].2.104
id.|ṯb.bn y.lm ṯb[t] km.|l kḥṯ.zbl k[m.a]nk.|iḥtrš.w [a]škn.|aškn.ydt.[m]rṣ gršt.|zbln.r[---].ymlu.|nʿm.[-]ṯ[-.--.]y 16[126].5.26
n[.w qdš].|bkm.tʿr[b.ʿl.ab h].|tʿrb.ḥ[--].|b ṯtm.t[---].|šknt.[---].|bkym[.---].|ǵr.y[----].|ydm.[---].|apn.[---].|[--.]b[16.2[125].115
---.k]rgmš.|[l.m]lk.ugrt.rgm[.-]y.|[---.--]m.rgm.|[---.]šknt.|[---.--]dy. 1011.4
|w tštqdn[.-----].|hm.|w yḥ.mlk.|w ik m.kn.w [---].|tšknnnn[.---]. 62[26].11

škny

ʿ.aḏddy.|ʿbd.ršp aḏddy.|ʿdn.bn.knn.|iwrḫz.b d.skn.|škny.aḏddy.|mšu.aḏddy.|plsy.aḏddy.|aḫyn.|ygmr.aḏddy. 2014.38

škr

il.kb[-].|aṯ[rt.]il.yṯb.b mrzḥ h.|yšt[.il.y]n.ʿd šbʿ.trṯ.ʿd škr.|il.hlk.l bt h.yštql.|l ḥṭr h.yʿmsn.nn.ṯkmn.|w šnm.w ng UG5.1.1.16
ṯr.ṯn.ṯn.hlk.|aṯr.ṯlṯ.kl hm.|aḥd.bt h.ysgr.|almnt.škr.|tškr.zbl.ʿršm.|yšu.ʿwr.|mzl.ymzl.|w ybl.trḫ.ḥdṯ.|ybʿr.l ṯn.a 14[KRT].4.186
]ṯr.ṯn.ṯn.hlk.|aṯr.ṯlṯ.kl hm.|yḥd.bt h.sgr.|almnt.škr.|tškr.zbl.ʿršm.|yšu.ʿwr.mzl.|ymzl.w yṣi.trḫ.|ḥdṯ.ybʿr.l ṯn.|a 14[KRT].2.98
].ṣḥ.l qṣ.ilm.tlḥmn.|ilm.w tštn.tštn y[n] ʿd šbʿ.|trṯ.ʿd.škr.yʿdb.yrḫ.|gb h.km.[---.]yqṯqṭ.tḥt.|ṯlḥnt.il.d ydʿnn.|yʿdb UG5.1.1.4
pr.ḏmr.aṯr h.ṭbq.lḥt.|niṣ h.grš d.ʿšy.ln h.|aḫd.yd h.b škrn.mʿms h.|[k]šbʿ yn.spu.ksm h.bt.bʿl.|[w m]nt h bt.il.ṭḫ 17[2AQHT].1.31
ʿpr.ḏmr.aṯr[y].|ṭbq lḥt.niṣ y.grš.|d ʿšy.ln.aḫd.yd y.b š|krn mʿms y k šbʿt yn.|spu.ksm y.bt.bʿl.[w]mn[t].|y.bt.il. 17[2AQHT].2.19
y.ln k].|spu.ksm k.bt.[bʿl.w mnt k].|bt il.aḫd.yd k.b [škrn].|mʿms k.k šbʿt.yn.ṭ[ḫ].|gg k.b ym.ṭiṭ.rḥṣ.|npṣ k.b ym 17[2AQHT].2.5
r.|aṯr.ṯn.ṯn.hlk.|aṯr.ṯlṯ.kl hm.|aḥd.bt h.ysgr.|almnt.škr.|tškr.zbl.ʿršm.|yšu.ʿwr.|mzl.ymzl.|w ybl.trḫ.ḥdṯ.|ybʿr. 14[KRT].4.185

r. | [a]ṯr.ṯn.ṯn.hlk. | aṯr.ṯlṯ.kl hm. | yḥd.bt h.sgr. | almnt.škr. | tškr.zbl.ʿršm. | yšu.ʿwr.mzl. | ymzl.w yṣi.trḫ. | ḥdṯ.ybʿr.l 14[KRT].2.97

šlw

m h]. | d ʿq h.ib.iqni.ʿp[ʿp] h. | sp.ṯrml.tḫgrn.[-]dm[.-]. | ašlw.b ṣp.ʿn h. | d b ḥlm y.il.ytn. | b ḏrt y.ab.adm. | w ld.špḥ.l 14[KRT].3.149

l.ḏrdn. | bʿl y.rgm. | bn.ḫrn k. | mǵy. | hbṭ.hw. | ḫrd.w.šl hw. | qr[-]. | akl n.b.grnt. | l.bʿr. | ap.krmm. | ḫlq. | qrt n.ḫlq. | 2114.6

šlḥ

ǵlmt.k bn.qdš.]w y[--.]zbl.ym.yʿ[--.]ṯpṭ.nhr. | [-------.]yšlḥn.w yʿn ʿṯtr[.-]. 2.3[129].24

. | bt.krt.tbun. | lm.mṯb[.---]. | w lḥm mr.tqdm. | yd.b ṣʿ.tšlḥ. | ḥrb.b bšr.tštn. | [w t]ʿn.mṯt.ḥry. | [l lḥ]m.l šty.ṣḥt km. | [15[128].4.24

r[.---]. | bḫr[.--]t[.----]. | l mṯb[.--]t[.---]. | [tqdm.]yd.b ṣʿ.t[šl]ḥ. | [ḥrb.b]bš[r].tštn. | [w tʿn].mṯt.ḥry. | [l lḥ]m.l šty.ṣḥt k 15[128].5.7

.qnyt.ilm. | hyn.ʿly.l mpḫm. | b d.ḫss.mṣbṭm. | yṣq.ksp.yšl | ḥ.ḫrṣ.yṣq.ksp. | l alpm.ḫrṣ.yṣq | m.l rbbt. | yṣq-ḫym.w tbṯ 4[51].1.26

b m b bh | t h.w atn mhr h l a | b h.alp ksp w rbt ḫ | rṣ.išlḥ ẓhrm iq | nim.atn šd h krm[m]. | šd dd h ḥrnqm.w | yʿn 24[77].21

h.]w tṣḥ.šmʿ.mʿ. | [l aqht.ǵzr.i]rš.ksp.w atn k. | [ḫrṣ.w aš]lḥ k.w tn.qšt k.[l]. | [ʿnt.tq]ḥ[.q]ṣʿt k.ybmt.limm. | w yʿn.a 17[2AQHT].6.18

tlt. | ʿnt.irš ḥym.l aqht.ǵzr. | irš ḥym.w atn k.bl mt. | w ašlḥ k.links ašspr k.ʿm.bʿl. | šnt.ʿm.bn il.tspr.yrḫm. | k bʿl.k yḥwy. 17[2AQHT].6.28

.zblnm. | mḫmšt.yitsp. | ršp.nṯdṯt.ǵlm. | ym.mšbʿt hn.b šlḥ. | ttpl.yʿn.ḥtk h. | krt yʿn.ḥtk h.rš. | mid.grdš.ṯbt h. | w b t 14[KRT].1.20

. | [---]t.[ ]r. | [---.--]n. | [---] h.l ʿdb. | [---]n.yd h. | [---].bl.išlḥ. | [---] h.gm. | [l --- k.]yṣḥ. | [---]d.ʿr. | [----.-]bb. | [----.]lm y 14[KRT].5.236

dʿ.k.ank. | aḥš.mǵy.mndʿ. | k.igr.w.u.[--]. | ʿm.špš.[---]. | nšlḥ[.---]. | [---.m]at. | [---.]mat. | š[--].išal. | ʿm k.ybl.šd. | a[--]. 2009.1.14

šlyṭ

l klt.nhr.il.rbm. | l ištbm.tnn.ištml h. | mḫšt.bṯn.ʿqltn. | šlyṭ.d šbʿt.rašm. | mḫšt.mdd ilm.ar[š]. | ṣmt.ʿgl.il.ʿtk. | mḫšt.k 3[ʿNT].3.39

k tmḫṣ.ltn.bṯn.brḥ. | tkly.bṯn.ʿqltn. | šlyṭ.d šbʿy.rašm. | ṯṯkḥ.ttrp.šmm.k rs. | ipd k.ank.ispi.uṯm. | ḏ 5[67].1.3

| [---.]ma[---] k.k tmḫṣ. | [ltn.bṯn.br]ḥ.tkly. | [bṯn.ʿqltn.]šlyṭ. | [d šbʿt.rašm].ṯṯkḥ. | [ttrp.šmm.k rks.ipd]k. | [-----]. 5[67].1.29

šlm

lṯ]. | ss[wm.mrkbt]. | b[trbṣ.bn.amt]. | [qḥ.krt.šlmm]. | [šlmm.al.tṣr]. | [udm.rbt.w udm]. | [ṯrrt.udm.ytnt]. | [il.w ušn. 14[KRT].5.256

ṯ]. | sswm.m[rkbt]. | b trbṣ.[bn.amt]. | q[ḥ.kr]t[.šlmm]. | š[lmm.]al.t[ṣr]. | udm[.r]bt.w u[dm]. | [ṯ]rrt.udm.y[t]n[t]. | il. 14[KRT].6.275

mt.mlk.b ʿṯtrt.yisp.ḥmt. | [kṯ]r w ḫss.y[i]sp.ḥmt.šḥr.w šlm. | [yis]p.ḥmt.isp.[šp]š l hrm.ǵrpl.ʿl arṣ. | [l a]n ḥmt.l p[.n] UG5.8.18

t. | iyṯr.bʿl aṯt. | ptm.bʿl ššlmt. | ʿdršp.bʿl ššlmt. | ṯtrn.bʿl ššlmt. | aršwn.bʿl ššlmt. | ḥdṯn.bʿl ššlmt. | ssn.bʿl ššlmt. 1077.8

mpḫrt bn il. | ṯrmn w šnm. | il w aṯrt. | ḫnn il. | nṣbt il. | šlm il. | il ḥš il add. | bʿl ṣpn bʿl. | ugrt. | b mrḥ il. | b nit il. | b ṣ 30[107].8

yn. | atdb w ʿr. | qdš w amrr. | ṯḫr w bd. | [k]ṯr ḫss šlm. | šlm il bt. | šlm il ḥš[t]. | ršp inšt. | [--]rm il [---]. | [---.--]m šlm [UG5.7.72

ʿr. | qdš w amrr. | ṯḫr w bd. | [k]ṯr ḫss šlm. | šlm il bt. | šlm il ḥš[t]. | ršp inšt. | [--]rm il [---]. | [---.--]m šlm [---]. UG5.7.72

[--.]ab.w il[--]. | [--] šlm.šlm i[l]. | [š]lm.il.šr. | dgn.w bʿl. | ʿṯ w kmṯ. | yrḫ w ksa. | yrḫ m UG5.10.1.2

[--.]ab.w il[--]. | [--] šlm.šlm i[l]. | [š]lm.il.šr. | dgn.w bʿl. | ʿṯ w kmṯ. | yrḫ w ksa. | yrḫ mkty. | ṯkm UG5.10.1.3

pš.š.arṣy.š.ʿṯtrt.š. | ušḫry.š.il.tʿḏr.bʿl.š.ršp.š.ddmš.š. | w šlmm.ilib.š.i[l.--]m d gbl.ṣpn.al[p]. | pḫr.ilm.š.ym.š[.k]nr.š.[- UG5.9.1.10

npš ilib. | gdlt.il š.bʿl š.ʿnt. | ṣpn.alp.w š.pdry.š. | šrp.w šlmm ilib š. | bʿl ugrt š.bʿl ḫlb š. | yrḫ š.ʿnt ṣpn.alp. | w š.pdry UG5.13.15

| um y.rgm. | tḥm.mlk. | bn k. | l.pʿn.um y. | qlt.l.um y. | yšlm.ilm. | ṯǵr k.tšlm k. | hl ny.ʿm n[y]. | kll.šlm. | ṯm ny.ʿm.u 50[117].7

[yš]lm[.ilm]. | ṯǵr k[.tšlm k]. | hl ny.[---]. | w.pdr[--.---]. | tmǵyn 57[101].1

]m[.]t[ḥm]. | mlk.bn [k]. | [l].pʿn.um [y]. | qlt[.l um] y. | yšlm.il[m]. | ṯǵ[r] k.tš[lm] k. | [h]l ny.ʿm n[.š]lm. | w.ṯm [ny.ʿ 1013.6

. | šnl.bn.ṣ[q]n.š[--]. | yitṯm.w.b[--]. | yšlm. | [ʿ]šrm.ks[p].yš[lm]. | [il]ṯḥm.b d[.---]. | [---].ṯl[l]m.[---]. | [--].r[-]y[.---]. | ʿl.[- 2104.7

.-]yṯr.ur[--.---]. | [---.n]skt.nʿmn.nbl[.---]. | [--.]yṣq šmn.šlm.b ṣ[ʿ.trḥṣ]. | yd h.btlt.ʿnt.uṣbʿt[h.ybmt]. | limm.tiḫd.knr UG5.3.2.4

ṣ.b bt. | ṯḥṣb.bn.ṯlḥnm.ymḥ. | [b]bt.dm.ḏmr.yṣq.šmn. | šlm.b ṣʿ.trḥṣ.yd h.bt | [l]t.ʿnt.uṣbʿt h.ybmt.limm. | [t]rḥṣ.yd h 3[ʿNT].2.32

[b yr]ḫ[.r]išyn.b ym.ḥdṯ. | [šmtr].uṯkl.l il.šlmm. | b [ṯlṯt].ʿšrt.yrtḥṣ.mlk. | br[r].]b a[r]bʿt.ʿšrt.riš. | arg[mn APP.II[173].2

b yrḫ.[rišyn.b ym.ḥdṯ]. | šmtr.[uṯkl.l il.šlmm]. | b ṯlṯt ʿ[šrt.yrtḥṣ.mlk.brr]. | b arbʿ[t.ʿšrt.riš.argmn]. | 35[3].2

. | bn.ḥgby.ṯmnt.l ʿšrm.ʿšrt.ḥmš.kbd. | bn.ilṣdq.šbʿt ṯlṯt šlm. | bn.ṯmq.arbʿt ṯqlm šlmm. 1131.9

[--]an.š[šlmt]. | bnš.iwl[--.š]šlmt. | šdyn.ššlmt. | prtwn.šʿrt. | ṯtn.šʿrt. | 97[315].1

[l r]iš.rʿy.y[šlm.---]. | [š]lm.bnš.yš[lm.---]. | [-]r.l šlmt.šl[m.---.--] | r h.p šlmt.p šlm[. 59[100].2

.--] | r h.p šlmt.p šlm[.---]. | bt.l bnš.trg[m.---]. | l šlmt.l šlm.b[--.---] | b y.šnt.mlit.t[--.---]. | ymǵy k.bnm.ta[--.---]. | [b] 59[100].6

ṯrt.š.ṯkmn w šnm.š. | ʿnt.š.ršp.š.dr il w p[ḫ]r bʿl. | gdlt.šlm.gdlt.w burm.[l]b. | rmṣt.ilhm.bʿlm.dṯt.w kšm.ḥmš. | ʿṯr h 34[1].8

[.š.ṯkm]n w [šnm.š]. | ʿnt š ršp š[.dr.il.w pḫr.bʿl]. | gdlt.šlm[.gdlt.w burm.lb]. | rmṣt.ilh[m.bʿlm.---]. | ksm.ṯltm.[---]. | 35[3].17

rt.š]. | ṯkmn.w š[nm.š.ʿnt.š.ršp.š.dr]. | il.w pḫr[.bʿl.gdlt.šlm.gdlt]. | w burm.l[b.rmṣt.ilhm]. | bʿlm.w mlu[.---.ksm]. | ṯl APP.II[173].18

[rm.---.ytk.gdlt.ilhm]. | ṯkmn.w [šnm.dqt.ršp.šrp]. | w šlmm.[dqtm.ilh.alp.w š]. | ilhm.gd[lt.ilhm.bʿl.š.aṯrt.š]. | ṯkmn APP.II[173].15

.alp.š.l il. | gdlt.ilhm.ṯkmn.w šnm dqt. | ršp.dqt.šrp w šlmm.dqtm. | [i]lh.alp w š ilhm.gdl[t.]ilhm. | [b]ʿl š.aṯrt.š.ṯk 34[1].4

[rm.---]. | ytk.gdlt.ilhm.[ṯkmn.w šnm]. | dqt.ršp.šrp.w š[lmm.dqtm]. | ilh[.a]lp.w š[.il]hm.[gdlt.ilhm]. | bʿ[l.š].aṯrt[.š. 35[3].13

tm. | qlny.ilm. | ṯǵr k. | tšlm k. | hn ny.ʿm ny. | kll.mid. | šlm. | w.ap.ank. | nḫt.ṯm ny. | ʿm.adt ny. | mnm.šlm. | rgm.ṯṯb. 51[95].12

.ʿlm. | ṯlṯ.sswm.mrkbt. | b trbṣ.bn.amt. | qḥ.krt.šlmm. | šlmm.w ng.mlk. | l bt y.rḥq.krt. | l ḥẓr y.al.tṣr. | udm.rbt.w u 14[KRT].3.131

[qmd.---]. | [w]nqmd.[---]. | [-.]ʿmn.šp[š.mlk.rb]. | bʿl h.šlm.[w spš]. | mlk.rb.bʿl h.[---]. | nqmd.mlk.ugr[t.--]. | phy. | w 64[118].12

šlm k. | hl ny.ʿm n[y]. | kll.šlm. | ṯm ny.ʿm.um y. | mnm.šlm. | w.rgm.ṯṯb.l y. | bm.ṯy.ndr. | iṯt.ʿmn.mlkt. | w.rgm y.l[--]. 50[117].12

| [h]l ny.ʿm n[.š]lm. | w.ṯm [ny.ʿm.mlkt.u]m y. | mnm[.šlm]. | w.rgm[.ṯṯb.l] y. | hl ny.ʿmn. | mlk.b.ṯy ndr. | iṯt.w.ht. | [- 1013.10

um y.ʿm y.ht.ʿm[ny]. | kll.šlm.ṯm ny. | ʿm.um y.mnm.šlm. | w.rgm.ṯṯb.l y. | w.mndʿ.k.ank. | aḥš.mǵy.mndʿ. | k.igr.w. 2009.1.8

rbt.ilib š. | bʿl alp w š. | dgn.š.il tʿḏr.š. | bʿl š.ʿnt š.ršp š. | šlmm. | w šnpt.il š. | l ʿnt.ḥl š.ṯn šm. | l gṯrm.ǵṣ b šmal. | d alp UG5.13.23

t[.l um] y. | yšlm.il[m]. | ṯǵ[r] k.tš[lm] k. | [h]l ny.ʿm n[.š]lm. | w.ṯm [ny.ʿm.mlkt.u]m y. | mnm[.šlm]. | w.rgm[.ṯṯb.l] y 1013.8

m.bʿl ššlmt. | ʿdršp.bʿl ššlmt. | ṯtrn.bʿl ššlmt. | aršwn.bʿl ššlmt. | ḥdṯn.bʿl ššlmt. | ssn.bʿl ššlmt. 1077.9

]. | aṯry.mḫṣ. | bʿln.mḫṣ. | y[ḥ]ṣdq.mḫṣ. | ṣp[r].ks[d]. | bʿl.š[lm]. | ḫyrn[.---]. | a[--.---]. | ʿ[--.---]. | š[--.---]. | [-----]. | m[--.---] 2084.19

likt. | ši[l.š]lm y. | [ʿ]d.r[-]š. | [-]ly.l.likt. | [a]nk.[---]. | šil.[šlm y]. | [l]m.li[kt]. | [-]t.ʿ[--]. 2010.12

r[--].|yšlm.[l] k.|ilm.t[ǵ]r k.|tšlm k.|lm[.l.]likt.|ši[l.š]lm y.|[ʿ]d.r[-]š.|[-]ly.l.likt.|[a]nk.[---].|šil.[šlm y].|[l]m.li[2010.8
[.šlm.---].|ybn.ṯmnt.ʿšrt ʿšrt.šlm.|ʿbdyrḫ.šbʿt.ʿšrt ʿšrt.šlm.|yky.ʿšrt.ṯṯt šlm.ʿšrt.|bn.ḥgby.ṯmnt.l ʿšrm.ʿšrt.ḫmš.kbd 1131.6
tḥm iwrdr.|l iwrpḫn.|bn y.aḫ y.rgm.|ilm.tǵr k.|tšlm k.|ik y.lḥt.|spr.d likt.|ʿm.ṯryl.|mh y.rgmt.|w ht.aḫ y. 138.5
tḥm.iwrdr.|l iwrpḫn.|bn y.aḫ y.rgm.|ilm.tǵr k.|tšlm k.|iky.lḥt.|spr.d likt.|ʿm.ṯryl.|mh y.rgmt.|w ht.aḫ y. 138.5
[.t]lm[yn].|l ṯryl.um y.|rgm.|ugrt.tǵr k.|ugrt.tǵr k.|tšlm k.um y.|tdʿ.ky.ʿrbt.|l pn.špš.|w pn.špš.nr.|b y.mid.w 1015.6
[k].|[l].pʿn.um [y].|qlt[.l um] y.|yšlm.il[m].|tǵ[r] k.tš[lm] k.|[h]l ny.ʿm n[.š]lm.|w.ṯm [ny.ʿm.mlkt.u]m y.|mn 1013.7
.mlk.|bn k.|l.pʿn.um y.|qlt.l.um y.|yšlm.ilm.|tǵr k.tšlm k.|hl ny.ʿm n[y].|kll.šlm.|ṯm ny.ʿm.um y.|mnm.šlm.| 50[117].8
[yš]lm[.ilm].|tǵr k[.tšlm k].|hl ny.[---].|w.pdr[--.---].|tmǵyn[.---].|w.mli[.---].|[57[101].2
rt.|aḫ y.rgm.|tḥm.mlk.ṣr.aḫ k.|y[š]lm.l k.ilm.|tǵr k.tšlm k.|hn ny.ʿm n.|šlm.ṯm ny.|ʿm k.mnm[.š]lm.|rgm.ṯṯ[b 2059.5
tḥm.pgn.|l.mlk.ugrt.|rgm.|yšlm.l k.[il]m.|tǵr k.tšlm k.|hn ny.ʿm n.š[l]m.|ṯm ny.ʿ[m.]bn y.|mnm.[šl]m[.r]g 2061.5
tmlk ʿbd k.|l.pʿn.adt ny.|mrḥqtm.|qlny.ilm.|tǵr k.|tšlm k.|hn ny.ʿm ny.|kll.mid.|šlm.|w.ap.ank.|nḫt.ṯm ny.| 51[95].9
lk.|l.ṯryl.um y.rgm.|yšlm.l k.ilm.|tǵr k.tšlm k.|lḥt.šlm.k.lik[t].|um y.ʿm y.ht.ʿm[ny].|kll.šlm.ṯm ny.|ʿm.um y. 2009.1.5
tḥm.mlk.|l.ṯryl.um y.rgm.|yšlm.l k.ilm.|tǵr k.tšlm k.|lḥt.šlm.k.lik[t].|um y.ʿm y.ht.ʿm[ny].|kll.šlm.ṯm n 2009.1.4
k.[bʿl y].|rg[m].|tḥm.wr[--].|yšlm.[l] k.|ilm.t[ǵ]r k.|tšlm k.|lm[.l.]likt.|ši[l.š]lm y.|[ʿ]d.r[-]š.|[-]ly.l.likt.|[a]nk.[2010.6
l.rb.khnm.|rgm.|tḥm.[---].|yšlm[.l k.ilm].|tšlm[k.tǵr] k.|tʿzz[k.---.]lm.|w t[--.--]ṣm k.|[-----].|[-----.]š 55[18].5
[tḥm.---].|[l.---].|[a]ḫt y.rgm.|[y]šlm.l k.|[il]m.tšlm k.|[tǵ]r k.|[--]y.ibr[-].|[--]wy.rgm l.|mlkt.ugrt.|[--]kt. 1016.5
y[šlm.l k.ilm].|tǵ[r k.tšlm k].|ʿbd[.---]y.|ʿm[.---]y.|šk[--.--.]kll.|šk[--.--.]hm.|w.k 2065.2
[t]ḥm.iṯtl.|l mnn.ilm.|tǵr k.tšlm k.|tʿzz k.alp ymm.|w rbt.šnt.|b ʿd ʿlm...gnʿ.|iršt.aršt. 1019.1.3
ḫry.a[ḫ y].|w l g.p[-]r[--].|yšlm[.l k].|[i]lm[.tǵr k].|[t]š[lm k.---].|[-----].|[-----].|h[--.---].|[-----].|w [----].|w [---- 56[21].6
grt.|iḫ y.rgm.|[tḥ]m.m[lk.-]bl[-].|yšlm.l[k].ilm.|tǵr.tšl[m] k.|[-----].|[-----].|[--].bt.gb[-.--].|[--]k[-].w.špš.|[---.b] 2159.5
[l].|dqtm.w ynt.qr[t].|w mtntm.š l rmš.|w kbd.w š.l šlm kbd.|alp.w š.l bʿl ṣpn.|dqt l ṣpn.šrp.w šlmm.|kmm.w b UG5.13.8
dq]tm.w y[nt] qrt.|[w mtmt]m.[š.l] rm[š.]kbd.w š.|[l šlm.kbd.al]p.w š.[l] bʿl.ṣpn.|[dqt.l.ṣpn.šrp].w š[l]mm.kmm. 36[9].1.14
d.w um.|tšmḫ.m ab.|w al.trḥln.|ʿtn.ḫrd.ank.|ʿm ny.šlm.|kll.|w mnm.|šlm ʿm.|um y.|ʿm y.tṯṯb.|rgm. 1015.14
tr l qlḥ.|w š ḥll ydm.|b qdš il bt.|w tlḥm aṯt.|š l ilbt.šlmm.|kll ylḥm b h.|w l bbt šqym.|š l uḫr ḫlmṭ.|w tr l qlḥ UG5.11.9
kbd.w š.l šlm kbd.|alp.w š.l bʿl ṣpn.|dqt l ṣpn.šrp.w šlmm.|kmm.w bbt.bʿl.ugrt.|w kdm.w npš ilib.|gdlt.il š.bʿl UG5.13.10
.w š.|[l šlm.kbd.al]p.w š.[l] bʿl.ṣpn.|[dqt.l.ṣpn.šrp].w š[l]mm.kmm.|[w bbt.bʿl.ugrt.]kdm.w npš.|[ilib.gdlt.il.š.b]ʿ[36[9].1.15
l š.ṯn šm.|l ǵtrm.ǵṣ b šmal.|d alpm.w alp w š.|šrp.w šlmm kmm.|l bʿl.ṣpn b ʿrʿr.|pamt ṯlṯm š l qrnt.|ṯlḥn.bʿlt.bh UG5.13.28
b.ṣpn.|nḥkt.ksp.w ḫrṣ ṭʿ ṯn šm l btbt.|alp.w š šrp.alp šlmm.|l bʿl.ʿṣr l ṣpn.|npš.w.š.l ršp bbt.|[ʿ]ṣrm l h.ršp [-]m.| UG5.12.A.9
tḥm.hl[--].|l pḫry.a[ḫ y].|w l g.p[-]r[--].|yšlm[.l k].|[i]lm[.tǵr k].|[t]š[lm k.---].|[-----].|[-----].|h[--.-- 56[21].4
tḥm.pgn.|l.mlk.ugrt.|rgm.|yšlm.l k.[il]m.|tǵr k.tšlm k.|hn ny.ʿm n.š[l]m.|ṯm ny.ʿ[m.] 2061.4
l.mlk.ugrt.|aḫ y.rgm.|tḥm.mlk.ṣr.aḫ k.|y[š]lm.l k.ilm.|tǵr k.tšlm k.|hn ny.ʿm n.|šlm.ṯm ny.|ʿm k. 2059.4
y[šlm.l k.ilm].|tǵ[r k.tšlm k].|ʿbd[.---]y.|ʿm[.---]y.|šk[--.--.] 2065.1
[l.ml]k.[bʿl y].|rg[m].|tḥm.wr[--].|yšlm.[l] k.|ilm.t[ǵ]r k.|tšlm k.|lm[.l.]likt.|ši[l.š]lm y.|[ʿ]d.r 2010.4
tḥm.mlk.|l.ṯryl.um y.rgm.|yšlm.l k.ilm.|tǵr k.tšlm k.|lḥt.šlm.k.lik[t].|um y.ʿm y.ht.ʿ 2009.1.3
l.mlk[.u]grt.|iḫ y.rgm.|[tḥ]m.m[lk.-]bl[-].|yšlm.l[k].ilm.|tǵr.tšl[m] k.|[-----].|[-----].|[--].bt.gb[-.--].|[- 2159.4
[tḥm.---].|[l.---].|[a]ḫt y.rgm.|[y]šlm.l k.|[il]m.tšlm k.|[tǵ]r k.|[--]y.ibr[-].|[--]wy.rgm l.| 1016.4
l.rb.khnm.|rgm.|tḥm.[---].|yšlm[.l k.ilm].|tšlm[k.tǵr] k.|tʿzz[k.---.]lm.|w t[--.--]ṣm k. 55[18].4
tḥm.iwrdr.|l.plsy.|rgm.|yšlm.l k.|l.trǵds.|w.l.klby.|šmʿt.ḫti.|nḫtu.ht.|hm.in mm.| 53[54].4
t.aliy.|qrdm.qry.b arṣ.mlḥmt.|št.b ʿp[r] m.ddym.sk.šlm.|l kbd.arṣ.arbdd.l kbd.šdm.|[ḥ]š k.[ʿ]ṣ k.ʿbṣ k.ʿm y.pʿn 3[ʿNT].4.53
wt.|aliy.qrdm.qry.b arṣ.|mlḥmt št.b ʿpr m.ddym.|sk.šlm.l kbd.arṣ.|arbdd.l kbd.šdm.|ḥš k.ʿṣ k.ʿbṣ k.|ʿm y.pʿn k. 3[ʿNT].3.13
.aqry.|[---.]b a[r]ṣ.mlḥmt.|ašt[.b ʿ]p[r] m.ddym.ask.|šlm.l kb[d].awṣ.arbdd.|l kbd.š[d]m.ap.mṯn.rgmm.|argmn.l 3[ʿNT].4.74
]ṯpn.ḥtk k.|[qryy.b arṣ.mlḥ]mt.št b ʿp|[r m.ddym.sk.šlm].l kbd.arṣ.|[arbdd.l kbd.š]dm.ḥš k.|[ʿṣ k.ʿbṣ k.ʿm y.pʿ]n 1[ʿNT.IX].2.20
m.[a]n.aqry.|[b arṣ].mlḥmt.[aš]t.b ʿpr m.|ddym.ask[.šlm.]l kbd.arṣ.|ar[bdd.]l kb[d.š]dm.yšt.|[----.]bʿl.mdl h.ybʿr 3[ʿNT].4.68
.aliy.qrdm.qryy.b arṣ.mlḥmt.št].|[b ʿ]pr[m.ddym.sk.šlm.l kbd.arṣ.arbdd].|l kbd.š[dm.ḥš k.ʿṣ k.ʿbṣ k.ʿm y.pʿn k.t 7.2[130].15
l[m.---.--]|r h.p šlmt.p šlm[.---].|bt.l bnš.trg[m.---].|l šlmt.l šlm.b[--.---]|b y.šnt.mlit.t[--.---].|ymǵy k.bnm.ta[--.-- 59[100].6
tḥm.špš.|l.ʿmrpi.rgm.|ʿm špš.kll.mid m.|šlm.|l.[--]n.špš.|ad[.ʿ]bd h.uk.škn.|k.[---.]sglt h.hw.|w.b[.-- 2060.4
š hm.w yš[--.--]m.|lḥm.b lḥm ay.w šty.b ḫmr yn ay.|šlm.mlk.šlm.mlkt.ʿrbm m.ṯnnm.|mt.w šr.yṯb.b d h.ḫṭ.ṯkl.b 23[52].7
š[--.--]m.|lḥm.b lḥm ay.w šty.b ḫmr yn ay.|šlm.mlk.šlm.mlkt.ʿrbm m.ṯnnm.|mt.w šr.yṯb.b d h.ḫṭ.ṯkl.b d h.|ḫṭ.u 23[52].7
yrḫ mkṯy.|ṯkmn w šnm.|kṯr w ḫss.|ʿṯtr ʿṯpr.|šḥr w šlm.|ngh w srr.|ʿdw šr.|ṣdqm šr.|ḥnbn il d[n].|[-]bd w [--- UG5.10.1.11
ḥr.w šlm.rgm.l il.ybl.a[ṯt y].|il.ylt.mh.ylt.yld y.šḥr.w šl[m].|šu.ʿdb.l špš.rbt.w l kbkbm.kn[-].|yhbr.špt hm.yšq.hn 23[52].53
šp.bʿl ššlmt.|ṯtrn.bʿl ššlmt.|arświn.bʿl ššlmt.|ḥdṯn.bʿl ššlmt.|ssn.bʿl ššlmt. 1077.10
ǵrn.[---].|w.bn h.n[--.---].|ḥnil.[---].|aršmg.mru.|bʿl.šlm.ʿbd.|awr.ṯǵrn.ʿbd.|ʿbd.ḫmn.šmʿ.rgm.|šdn.[k]bš.|šdyn. 2084.10
.---].|tlmyn.šbʿt.ʿšrt ʿšrt[.šlm.---].|ybn.ṯmnt.ʿšrt ʿšrt.šlm.|ʿbdyrḫ.šbʿt.ʿšrt ʿšrt.šlm.|yky.ʿšrt.ṯṯt šlm.ʿšrt.|bn.ḥgby. 1131.5
bʿl [aṯt].|ṯṯḫ.bʿl aṯt.|ayab.bʿl aṯt.|iytr.bʿl aṯt.|ptm.bʿl ššlmt.|ʿdršp.bʿl ššlmt.|ṯtrn.bʿl ššlmt.|arświn.bʿl ššlmt.|ḥdṯn 1077.6
b.|w al.trḥln.|ʿtn.ḫrd.ank.|ʿm ny.šlm.|kll.|w mnm.|šlm ʿm.|um y.|ʿm y.tṯṯb.|rgm. 1015.17
m.b ap zd.aṯrt.[---].|špš.mṣprt dlt hm[.---].|w ǵnbm.šlm.ʿrbm.ṯn[nm].|hlkm.b dbḥ nʿmt.|šd[.i]lm.šd.aṯrt.w rḥm 23[52].26
nt.ʿšrt ʿšrt.šlm.|ʿbdyrḫ.šbʿt.ʿšrt ʿšrt.šlm.|yky.ʿšrt.ṯṯt šlm.ʿšrt.|bn.ḥgby.ṯmnt.l ʿšrm.ʿšrt.ḫmš.kbd.|bn.ilṣdq.šbʿt ṯlṯ 1131.7
-].|[-]rym.t[i]ṯṯmn.|šnl.bn.ṣ[q]n.š[--].|yiṯṯm.w.b[--].|yšlm.|[ʿ]šrm.ks[p].yš[lm].|[il]tḥm.b d[.---].|[---].ṯl[l]m.[---]. 2104.6
.---].|[š]lm.bnš.yš[lm.---].|[-]r.l šlmt.šl[m.---.--]|r h.p šlmt.p šlm[.---].|bt.l bnš.trg[m.---].|l šlmt.l šlm.b[--.---]|b y 59[100].4
ṣqrn.b.gg.|ar[bʿ.]arbʿ.mṯbt.azmr.b h.š.šr[-].|al[p.w].š.šlmm.pamt.šbʿ.klb h.|yr[--.]mlk.ṣbu.špš.w.ḥl.mlk.|w.[---].y 35[3].52
[--]an.š[šlmt].|bnš.iwl[--.š]šlmt.|šdyn.ššlmt.|prtwn.šʿrt.|ṯtn.šʿrt.|ʿdn.šʿrt.|mnn.šʿrt.|bdn.šʿrt.|ʿpṯ 97[315].3
.--].|bm.nšq.w hr.b ḥbq.ḥmḥmt.tqt[nṣn].|tldn.šḥr.w šlm.rgm.l il.ybl.a[ṯt y].|il.ylt.mh.ylt.yld y.šḥr.w šl[m].|šu.ʿ 23[52].52
.|tǵr k.tšlm k.|hn ny.ʿm n.|šlm.ṯm ny.|ʿm k.mnm[.š]lm.|rgm.ṯṯ[b].|any kn.dt.|likt.mṣrm.|hn dt.b.ṣr.|mtt.by. 2059.8

k.tšlm k.|hn ny.‘m n.š[l]m.|ṯm ny.‘[m.]bn y.|mnm.[šl]m[.r]gm[.ṯṯb].|ky.lik.bn y.|lḥt.akl.‘m y.|mid y w ǵbn y.| 2061.8
dt y.|šb‘ d.|w.šb‘ id.|mrḥqtm.|qlt.|‘m.adt y.|mnm.šlm.|rgm.tṯṯb.|l.‘bd h. 52[89].13
l p‘n.b‘l y.|ṯn id.šb‘ d.|mrḥqtm.|qlt.‘m.|b‘l y.mnm.|šlm.|[r]gm[.tṯṯb].|[l.]‘bd[k]. 2115.2.10
ll.mid.|šlm.|w.ap.ank.|nḫt.ṯm ny.|‘m.adt ny.|mnm.šlm.|rgm.ṯṯb.|l.‘bd k. 51[95].16
lbš.w [-]tn.ušpǵt.|ḫr[-].ṯlṯt.mzn.|drk.š.alp.w ṯlṯ.|ṣin.šlm[m.]šb‘ pamt.|l ilm.šb[‘.]l kṯr.|‘lm.t‘rbn.gṯrm.|bt.mlk.ṯ 33[5].7
[--]an.š[šlmt].|bnš.iwl[--.š]šlmt.|šdyn.ššlmt.|prtwn.š‘rt.|ttn.š‘rt.|‘dn.š‘rt.|mnn.š‘rt. 97[315].2
d[.‘lm.ṯlṯ].|sswm.m[rkbt].|b trbṣ.[bn.amt].|q[ḥ.kr]t[.šlmm].|š[lmm.]al.t[ṣr].|udm[.r]bt.w u[dm].|[ṯ]rrt.udm.y[t] 14[KRT].6.274
‘bd[.‘lm.ṯlṯ].|ss[wm.mrkbt].|b[trbṣ.bn.amt].|[qḥ.krt.šlmm].|[šlmm.al.tṣr].|[udm.rbt.w udm].|[ṯrrt.udm.ytnt].|[14[KRT].5.255
]ḥn tlyn.|atdb w ‘r.|qdš w amrr.|ṯḥr w bd.|[k]ṯr ḫss šlm.|šlm il bt.|šlm il ḫš[t].|ršp inšt.|[--]rm il [---].|[---.--]m UG5.7.72
[--.]ab.w il[--].|[--] šlm.šlm i[l].|[š]lm.il.šr.|dgn.w b‘l.|‘ṯ w kmṯ.|yrḫ w ksa.|yr UG5.10.1.2
h.w ‘bd.‘lm.|ṯlṯ.sswm.mrkbt.|b trbṣ.bn.amt.|qḥ.krt.šlmm.|šlmm.w ng.mlk.|l bt y.rḥq.krt.|l ḥẓr y.al.tṣr.|udm. 14[KRT].3.130
[l r]iš.r‘y.y[šlm.---].|[š]lm.bnš.yš[lm.---].|[-]r.l šlmt.šl[m.---.--]|r h.p šlmt.p šlm[.---].|bt.l bnš.trg[m.---].|l 59[100].3
ksa.|w yṯb.|tqru l špš.um h.špš.um.ql bl ‘m.|šḥr.w šlm šmm h mnt.nṯk.nḥš.|šmrr.nḥš ‘q šr.ln h.mlḫš.|abd.ln UG5.7.52
qrht.d.tššlmn.|ṯlrb h.|art.ṯn.yrḫm.|ṯlrby.yrḫ.w.ḫm[š.ym]m.|ṯlḥn 66[109].1
lt.l.um y.|yšlm.ilm.|tǵr k.tšlm k.|hl ny.‘m n[y].|kll.šlm.|ṯm ny.‘m.um y.|mnm.šlm.|w.rgm.ṯṯb.l y.|bm.ṯy.ndr. 50[117].10
k.tšlm k.|lḥt.šlm.k.lik[t].|um y.‘m y.ht.‘m[ny].|kll.šlm.ṯm ny.|‘m.um y.mnm.šlm.|w.rgm.ṯṯb.l y.|w.mnd‘.k.an 2009.1.7
.ugrt.|rgm.|yšlm.l k.[il]m.|tǵr k.tšlm k.|hn ny.‘m n.š[l]m.|ṯm ny.‘[m.]bn y.|mnm.[šl]m[.r]gm[.ṯṯb].|ky.lik.bn y 2061.6
lk.ṣr.aḫ k.|y[š]lm.l k.ilm.|tǵr k.tšlm k.|hn ny.‘m n.|šlm.ṯm ny.|‘m k.mnm[.š]lm.|rgm.ṯt[b].|any kn.dt.|likt.mṣ 2059.7
spr.bnš.mlk.|d.b d.prṯ.|tš‘.l.‘šrm.|lqḥ.ššlmt.|ṯmn.l.arb‘m.|lqḥ.š‘rt. 1025.4
aṯt.|ayab.b‘l aṯt.|iyṯr.b‘l aṯt.|ptm.b‘l ššlmt.|‘dršp.b‘l ššlmt.|ṯtrn.b‘l ššlmt.|arŝwn.b‘l ššlmt.|ḥdṯn.b‘l ššlmt.|ssn.b 1077.7
m.|[---.]l ‘nt m.|[---.--]rm.d krm.|[---].l ‘nt m.|[---.]l šlm.|[-]l[-.-]ry.ylbš.|mlk.ylk.lqḥ.ilm.|aṯr.ilm.ylk.p‘nm.|ml 33[5].21
].|‘š[rm.]l inš[.ilm.---].|il[hm.]dqt.š[.---.rš]|[p.š]rp.w šl[mm.--.dqt].|[i]lh.gdlt[.ilhm.gdlt.il].|[d]qt.ṯkmn.w [šnm. 35[3].29
l š.b‘l š.aṯrt.š.ym š.[b‘]l knp.|[---.g]dlt.ṣpn.dqt.šrp.w [š]lmm.|[---.a]lp.l b‘l.w aṯrt.‘ṣr[m] l inš.|[ilm.---].lbbmm.gdl 36[9].1.7
--.‘b]d k.|[---.--]l y.‘m.|[---.]‘m.|[---.--]y.w.lm.|[---.]il.šlm.|[---.]ank.|[---].mly. 2128.2.5
annṯb.ḫmšm.ksp ṯlṯm.šl[m.---].|iwrpzn.‘šrm ‘šrm š[lm.---].|ilabn.‘šrt ṯqlm kbd.ḫ 1131.1
annṯb.ḫmšm.ksp ṯlṯm.šl[m.---].|iwrpzn.‘šrm ‘šrm š[lm.---].|ilabn.‘šrt ṯqlm kbd.ḫmš.šl[m.---].|tlmyn.šb‘t.‘šrt ‘ 1131.2
l ri[š.---].|ypt.‘ṣ[--.---].|p šlm.[---].|bt k.b[--.--.m]|ǵy k[.---].|bt.[---]. 58[20].3
]lm.bnš.yš[lm.---].|[-]r.l šlmt.šl[m.---.--]|r h.p šlmt.p šlm[.---].|bt.l bnš.trg[m.---].|l šlmt.l šlm.b[--.---]|b y.šnt.ml 59[100].4
rm l [inš.ilm].|[---.]ilh[m.dqt.š.--].|[---.--]t.r[šp.šrp.w šl]|[mm.---].dq[t.ilh.gdlt].|n.w šnm.dqt[.---].|[i]lh[m.gd]lt.i APP.II[173].31
[---.--]y.hnn.|[---.kll].šlm.|[---.ṯ]mn.‘m k.|[m]nm.šlm.|[---.w.r]gm.ṯṯb. 2171.4
ilabn.‘šrt ṯqlm kbd.ḫmš.šl[m.---].|tlmyn.šb‘t.‘šrt ‘šrt[.šlm.---].|ybn.ṯmnt.‘šrt ‘šrt.šlm.|‘bdyrḫ.šb‘t.‘šrt ‘šrt.šlm.|yk 1131.4
t y.|[---].irrṯwm.‘bd k.|[---.a]dt y.mrḥqm.|[---].adt y.yšlm.|[---.]mlk n.amṣ.|[.---].nn.|[---.]qrt.dt.|[---.--]s‘.hn.ml 1012.4
[l r]iš.r‘y.y[šlm.---].|[š]lm.bnš.yš[lm.---].|[-]r.l šlmt.šl[m.---.--]|r h.p 59[100].1
[---].m[--].|[---.]m[--].|[---.]šlm.|[---.]šlm.|[---.]šlm.|[---.]šlm.|[---.]šlm.|[---.š]lm.|[---.š 2150.3
[---.b]n.šty.|[---.]šlm.|[---.]šlm.|[---.]šlm.|[---.]šlm.|[---.š]lm. 2151.2
[---].m[--].|[---.]m[--].|[---.]šlm.|[---.]šlm.|[---.]šlm.|[---.]šlm.|[---.]šlm.|[---.š]lm.|[---.š]lm.|[---.šl]m. 2150.5
.m[--].|[---.]m[--].|[---.]šlm.|[---.]šlm.|[---.]šlm.|[---.]šlm.|[---.]šlm.|[---.š]lm.|[---.š]lm.|[---.šl]m. 2150.6
[---].m[--].|[---.]m[--].|[---.]šlm.|[---.]šlm.|[---.]šlm.|[---.]šlm.|[---.š]lm.|[---.š]lm.|[---.š 2150.4
[---.b]n.šty.|[---.]šlm.|[---.]šlm.|[---.]šlm.|[---.]šlm.|[---.š]lm. 2151.3
-.]m[--].|[---.]šlm.|[---.]šlm.|[---.]šlm.|[---.]šlm.|[---.]šlm.|[---.š]lm.|[---.š]lm.|[---.šl]m. 2150.7
[---.b]n.šty.|[---.]šlm.|[---.]šlm.|[---.]šlm.|[---.]šlm.|[---.š]lm. 2151.4
[---.]šlm.|[---.]šlm.|[---.]šlm.|[---.]šlm.|[---.]šlm.|[---.š]lm.|[---.š]lm.|[---.šl]m. 2150.8
[---.b]n.šty.|[---.]šlm.|[---.]šlm.|[---.]šlm.|[---.]šlm.|[---.š]lm. 2151.5
[---.]šlm.|[---.]šlm.|[---.]šlm.|[---.]šlm.|[---.š]lm.|[---.š]lm.|[---.šl]m. 2150.9
|iwrpzn.‘šrm ‘šrm š[lm.---].|ilabn.‘šrt ṯqlm kbd.ḫmš.šl[m.---].|tlmyn.šb‘t.‘šrt ‘šrt[.šlm.---].|ybn.ṯmnt.‘šrt ‘šrt.šlm 1131.3
[---.--]y.hnn.|[---.kll].šlm.|[---.ṯ]mn.‘m k.|[m]nm.šlm.|[---.w.r]gm.ṯṯb. 2171.2
[l r]iš.r‘y.y[šlm.---].|[š]lm.bnš.yš[lm.---].|[-]r.l šlmt.šl[m.---.--]|r h.p šlmt.p šlm[.---].|bt.l 59[100].2
[l r]iš.r‘y.y[šlm.---].|[š]lm.bnš.yš[lm.---].|[-]r.l šlmt.šl[m.---.--]|r h.p šlmt.p šlm[.---].|bt.l bnš.trg[m.---].|l šlmt. 59[100].3
[---.]šlm.|[---.--]š.lalit.|[---.]bt šp.š.|y[-]lm.w mlk.|ynṣl.l ṯ‘y. 2005.2.4
m il bt.|šlm il ḫš[t].|ršp inšt.|[--]rm il [---].|[---.--]m šlm [---]. UG5.7.74
|sdwn.|mztn.|ḫyrn.|šdn.|[‘š]rm.ṯn kbd.|šǵrm.|lqḥ.ššlmt. 2098.11
..|l.p‘n a[dt y].|šb‘ d[.w šb‘ d].|mrḥq[tm.qlt].|mn[m.šlm]. 1014.11
kkr].|bn.šw.šb‘.kk[r.---].|arb‘m.kkr.[---].|b d.mtn.[l].šlm. 2108.5
ḏr b‘l.|ršp.|ddmš.|pḫr ilm.|ym.|uṯḫt.|knr.|mlkm.|šlm. 29[17].2.12
rt.ḫmš.kbd.|bn.ilṣdq.šb‘t ṯlṯt šlm.|bn.ṯmq.arb‘t ṯqlm šlmm. 1131.10
bnšm.d.bu.|tš‘.dt.tq[ḥn].|š‘rt.|šb‘ dt tqḥn.|ššlmt. 2099.5
trn.b‘l ššlmt.|arŝwn.b‘l ššlmt.|ḥdṯn.b‘l ššlmt.|ssn.b‘l ššlmt. 1077.11
-.b]n.šty.|[---.]šlm.|[---.]šlm.|[---.]šlm.|[---.]šlm.|[---.š]lm. 2151.6
[---.]šlm.|[---.]šlm.|[---.]šlm.|[---.š]lm.|[---.š]lm.|[---.šl]m. 2150.10

šlmy

at.|ušknym.|yp‘.alpm.|aḫ[m]lk.bn.nskn.alpm.|krw.šlmy.|alpm.|atn.bṣry.alpm.|lbnym.|ṯm[n.]alp mitm.|ilb‘l 1060.2.4
.ḫran.|bn.arŝ[w.b]ṣry.|bn.ykn.|bn.lṣn.‘rmy.|bn.b‘yn.šly.|bn.ynḥn.|bn.‘bdilm.hzpy. 99[327].2.4

|art.|ṯlḥny.|ṯlrby.|dmt.|aǵt.|w.qmnz.|slḫ.|ykn'm.|šlmy.|w.ull.|ṯmry.|qrt.|'rm.|nnu.|[--].|[---].|m'r.|arny.| 71[113].18
kd.šmn.'l.hbm.šlmy.|kd.šmn.ṯbil.|kd.šmn.ymtšr.|arb'.šmn.'l.'bdn.w.[---]. 1082.1.1
šlmym.lqḥ.akl.|yḥmn.ṯlṯ.šmn.|a[---.]kdm.|'[---]'m.kd.|a[-- 136[84].1
t.al.|ilmlk.[--]kt.[--.d.]yṯb.b.šb[n].|bn.pr[-.]d.y[ṯb.b].šlmy.|tlš.w[.n]ḥl h[.-].ṯgd.mrum.|bt.[-]b[-.-]sy[-]h.|nn[-].b[2015.2.2
qrt ṯqlm.w nṣp.|šlmy.ṯql.|ary ṯql.|ṯmry ṯql.w.nṣp.|aǵt nṣp.|dmt ṯql.|ykn'm 69[111].2
y.b.šbn.|ilštm'ym.|y[---.]bn.'šq.|[---.]bn.tqy.|[---.]bn.šlmy.|[-----].|[---].ubr'y.|[---].gwl.|[---]ady.|[---]ṣry.|miḫ[-] 1041.6
nq[pat].|glbty.|[-----].|[-----].|[-----].|[-----].|ykn'm.|šlmy.|[-----].|[-----].|q[---].|ṯ[---].|ṯl[rby].|ṯmr[y].|aǵ[t].|d 2058.2.31
b.yrml.|[---.--]n.b.yrml.|[---.--]ny.yrml.|šwn.qrty.|b.šlmy. 2119.26

šlmym

|kd.'l.šz.bn pls.|kd.'l.ynḥm.|tgrm.šmn.d.bn.kwy.|'l.šlmym.ṯmn.kbd.|ṯṯm.šmn. 1082.2.9

šlmn

n u[l]pm.|bn '[p]ty.|bn.kdgdl.|bn.smyy.|bn.lbn.|bn.šlmn.|bn.mly.|pslm.|bn.annd.|bn.gl'd.|w.nḥl h.|bn.mlky 2163.3.7
dy.|bn.g'yn.|bn.ǵrn.|bn.agynt.|bn.abdḫr.snry.|dqn.šlmn.|prdn.ndb[--].|[-]rn.ḫbty.|abmn.bn.qdmn.|n'mn.bn.' 87[64].37
]m.|[bn].smyy.qšt.w.u[ṯpt].|[w.q]l'.w.ṯt.mrḥm.|[bn].šlmn.ql'.w.ṯ[t.---].|[bn].mlṣ.qštm.w.uṯp[t].|[--.q]l'.w[.---.m] 2047.6

šm

q.špt k.ṯm.|ṯkm.bm ṯkm.aḫm.qym.il.|b lsmt.ṯm.yṯbš.šm.il.mt m.|y'bš.brk n.šm.il.ǵzrm.|ṯm.ṯmq.rpu.b'l.mhr b'l. 22.2[124].6
.aḫm.qym.il.|b lsmt.ṯm.yṯbš.šm.il.mt m.|y'bš.brk n.šm.il.ǵzrm.|ṯm.ṯmq.rpu.b'l.mhr b'l.|w mhr.'nt.ṯm.yḥpn.ḥy 22.2[124].7
ṯbr.diy hmt.tqln.|tḥt.p'n h.ybq'.kbdt hm.w[yḥd].|in.šmt.in.'ẓm.yšu.g h.|w yṣḥ.knp.nšrm.ybn.|b'l.ybn.diy hmt 19[1AQHT].3.117
l.ṯbr.diy.hwt.w yql.|tḥt.p'n h.ybq'.kbd h.w yḥd.|[i]n.šmt.in.'ẓm.yšu.g[h].|w yṣḥ.knp.hrgb.b'l.ybn.|[b]'l.ybn.diy. 19[1AQHT].3.131
'l.yṯbr.diy.|hyt.tql.tḥt.p'n y.ibq'.|kbd h.w aḥd.hm.iṯ.šmt.iṯ.|'ẓm.abky w aqbrn h.aštn.|b ḫrt.ilm.arṣ.b p h.rgm.l[19[1AQHT].3.139
.|b'l.ṯbr.diy.hyt.tq[l.tḥt].|p'n h.ybq'.kbd h.w yḥd.|iṯ.šmt.iṯ.'ẓm.w yqḥ b hm.|aqht.ybl.l qẓ.ybky.w yqbr.|yqbr.n 19[1AQHT].3.145
.l.rpš.|[---.]šb'm.dr'.w.arb'm.drt.mit.dd.|[---].ḥpr.bn.šm.|[b.---.]knm.ṯṯm.l.mit.dr'.w.mit.drt.|w[.---.]'m.l.mit.dd. 1098.6
tusp[.---].|tgr.il.bn h.ṯr[.---].|w y'n.lṭpn.il.d p[id.---].|šm.bn y.yw.ilt.[---].|w p'r.šm.ym[-.---].|t'nyn.l zn.tn[.---].| 1['NT.X].4.14
.|an.w y'ny.krt ṯ'.yṯbr.|ḥrn.y bn.yṯbr.ḥrn.|riš k.'ṯtrt.šm.b'l.|qdqd k.tqln.b gbl.|šnt k.b ḥpn k.w t'n.|spr ilmlk ṯ' 16.6[127].56
r[.---].|ṯpṭ.nhr.yṯb[r.ḥrn.y ym.yṯbr.ḥrn].|riš k.'ṯtrt.[šm.b'l.qdqd k.---].|[--]t.mṯ.tpln.b g[bl.šnt k.---].|[--]šnm.aṯt 2.1[137].8
nt h.w ydlp.tmn h.|yqṯ b'l.w yšt.ym.ykly.ṯpṭ.nhr.|b šm.tg'r m.'ṯtrt.bṯ l aliyn.[b'l.]|bṯ.l rkb.'rpt.k šby n.zb[l.ym. 2.4[68].28
.diy[.h]wt.|w yql.tḥt.p'n y.ibq'.kbd[h].|w aḥd.hm.iṯ.šmt.hm.iṯ[.'ẓm].|abky.w aqbrn.ašt.b ḫrt.|i[lm.arṣ.b p h.rg 19[1AQHT].3.125
r.diy.hmt].|tqln.tḥ p'n y.ibq['.kbd hm.w] |aḥd.hm.iṯ.šmt.hm.i[ṯ].|'ẓm.abky.w aqbrn h.|ašt.b ḫrt.ilm.arṣ.|b p h.r 19[1AQHT].3.110
yd.|ugrm.ḫl.ld.|aklm.tbrk k.|w ld 'qqm.|ilm.yp'r.|šmt hm.|b hm.qrnm.|km.ṯrm.w gbṯt.|km.ibrm.|w b hm.p 12[75].1.29
k.l tnǵṣn.pnt h.l ydlp.|tmn h.kṯr.ṣmdm.ynḥt.w yp'r.šmt hm.|šm k.at.aymr.aymr.mr.ym.mr.ym.|l ksi h.nhr l k 2.4[68].18
qḥ.mlk.'lm k.drkt.dt dr dr k.|kṯr ṣmdm.ynḥt.w yp'r.šmt hm.šm k at.|ygrš.ygrš.grš ym grš ym.l ksi h.|[n]hr l kḥ 2.4[68].11
mh y.rgmt.|w ht.aḫ y.|bn y.yšal.|tryl.p rgm.|l mlk.šm y.|w l h.y'l m.|w h[t] aḫ y.|bn y.yšal.|tryl.w rgm[.-].|ṯṯ 138.13
mh y.rgmt.|w ht.aḫ y.|bn y.yšal.|tryl.p rgm.|l mlk.šm y.|w l h[-] y'l m.|bn y.yšal.|tryl.w rgm.|ṯṯb.l aḫ k.|l ad 138.13
].|w y'n.lṭpn.il.d p[id.---].|šm.bn y.yw.ilt.[---].|w p'r.šm.ym[-.---].|t'nyn.l zn.tn[.---].|at.adn.tp'r[.---].|ank.lṭpn.il 1['NT.X].4.15
.pnt h.l ydlp.|tmn h.kṯr.ṣmdm.ynḥt.w yp'r.šmt hm.|šm k.at.aymr.aymr.mr.ym.mr.ym.|l ksi h.nhr l kḥṯ.drkt h.t 2.4[68].19
'lm k.drkt.dt dr dr k.|kṯr ṣmdm.ynḥt.w yp'r.šmt hm.šm k at.|ygrš.ygrš.grš ym grš ym.l ksi h.|[n]hr l kḥṯ drkt h 2.4[68].11
dn.tp'r[.---].|ank.lṭpn.il[.d pid.---].|'l.ydm.p'rt[.---].|šm k.mdd.i[l.---].|bt ksp y.d[--.---].|b d.aliyn b['l.---].|kd.y 1['NT.X].4.20
[šmt.n]qmp'.|[bn.nq]md.|[mlk.]ugrt.|b'l ṣdq.|skn.bt.|mlk.ṯ 1007.1
---.]b'l yḥmdn h.yrṯ y.|[---.]dmrn.l pn h yrd.|[---.]b'l.šm[.--.]rgbt yu.|[---]w yrmy[.q]rn h.|[---.-]ny h pdr.ttǵr.|[-- 2001.2.9
.'rbm.yr[.---].|mṯbt.ilm.ṯmn.ṯ[--.--].|pamt.šb'.|iqnu.šmt[.---].|[b]n.šrm.|iqran.ilm.n'mm[.agzry ym.bn]ym.|yn 23[52].21
šm [---].|kn'm.bn.[---].|plšb'l.bn.n[--].|ḥy bn.dnn.ṯkt.|ilṯḥ 2085.1
[---.--]y.npš[.---].|[---.k]si h.|[---.--]y.rb.šm[.---]. 2160.3

šmal

m.'ṣr.šmm.|w dg b ym.w ndd.gzr.l zr.y'db.u ymn.|u šmal.b p hm.w l.tšb'n y.aṯt.itrḫ.|y bn.ašld.šu.'db.tk.mdbr q 23[52].64
ršp š.|šlmm.|w šnpt.il š.|l 'nt.ḥl š.ṯn šm.|l gṯrm.ǵṣ b šmal.|d alpm.w alp w š.|šrp.w šlmm kmm.|l b'l.ṣpn b 'r'r. UG5.13.26
yd.mšḫṭ.bm.ymn.mḫṣ.ǵlmm.yš[--].|[ymn h.'n]t.tuḫd.šmal h.tuḫd.'ṯtrt.ik.m[ḫṣt.ml]|[ak.ym.t']dt.ṯpṭ.nhr.mlak.mṯ 2.1[137].40
b[.---].|mrḥ h l adrt[.---].|ṯṯb 'ṯtrt b ǵl[.---].|qrẓ tšt.l šmal[.---].|arbḫ.'n h tšu w[.---].|aylt tǵpy ṯr.'n[.---].|b[b]r. 2001.1.9

šmbnš

--].ypḫ.'bdršp.b[--.--].|[ar]b't.'šrt.kbd[.---].|[---.-]rwd.šmbnš[.---].|[---].ksp.'l.k[--].|[---.--]k.|[---.]ksp.'l.bn[.---].|[- 1144.7

šmb'l

[-----].|[-]mn.|b'ly.|rpan.|'pṯrm.|bn.'bd.|šmb'l.|ykr.|bly.|ṯb'm.|ḥdṯn.|rpty.|ilym.|bn.'br.|mnip'l.| 1058.7

šmg

y.|ypr.|ḫrṣb'.|uḫnp.|art.|[--]n.|[-----].|[-----].|nnu.|šmg.|šmn.|lbnm.|ṯrm.|bṣr.|y[--].|y[--].|snr.|midḫ.|ḥ[lym 2058.2.12

šmgy

].|bṣr.'šr.yn.|nnu arb'.yn.|šql ṯlṯ.yn.|šmny.kdm.yn.|šmgy.kd.yn.|hzp.tš'.yn.|[b]ir.'šr[.---]m ḥsp.|ḫpty.kdm[.---] 2004.27

šmḥ

un.hd. | [ʻm.ary y.---.--]p.mlḥm y. | [---.---]lt.qẓb. | [---.]šmḥ y. | [---.]tbʻ. | [---.-]nnm. 5[67].2.25
dt y.b ṣʻ. | [--.]šbʻ.rbt. | [---.]qbṭ.ṭm. | [---.]bn.ilm. | [m]t.šmḥ.p ydd. | il[.ǵ]zr. | b [-]dn.ʻ.z.w. | rgbt.zbl. UG5.4.15
wn. | dd l [--]n. | dd l ky. | dd l ʻbdkṯr. | dd[m] l rʻy. | [--] šmḥ[.---]. | ddm gt dprnm. | l ḥršm. | ddm l ʻnqt. | dd l alṯt.w l 1101.7

šmḫ

.m]t. | w tʻn.btlt.ʻn[t.bnt.]bht | k.y ilm.bnt.bh[t k].a[l.tš]mḫ. | al.tšmḫ.b r[m.h]kl[k]. | al.aḫd.hm.b y[--] y.[---]b[-]. 3[ʻNT.VI].5.28
tʻn.[btlt.ʻnt.---]. | [bnt.bht]k.y ilm[.bnt.bht k.--]. | [al.tšmḫ.]al.tš[mḫ.b rm.h] | [kl k.al.]aḫd hm.[---]. | [---.b]gdlt.ar 18[3AQHT].1.8
b bht m.n[bl]at.b hkl m. | sb.ksp.l rqm.ḫrṣ. | nṣb.l lbnt.šmḫ. | aliyn.bʻl.ht y.bnt. | dt.ksp.hkl y.dtm. | ḫrṣ.ʻdbt.bht[h.b 4[51].6.35
.mḥmd.. | ḫrṣ.w bn.bht.ksp. | w ḫrṣ.bht.ṭhrm. | iqnim.šmḫ.aliyn. | bʻl.ṣḥ.ḫrn.b bht h. | ʻḏbt.b qrb hkl h. | yblnn ǵrm. 4[51].5.97
]l. | w bšr.ḥtk.dgn. | k.ibr.l bʻl[.yl]d. | w rum.l rkb.ʻrpt. | yšmḫ.aliyn.bʻl. 10[76].3.38
.trm[.ʻ]tqt. | tbky.w tšnn.[tt]n. | g h.bky.b ḫ[y k.a]b n. | nšmḫ.b l.mt k.ngln. | k klb.[b]bt k.nʻtq. | k inr[.ap.]ḫšt k. | ap 16.2[125].99
.ʻl. | ab h.yʻrb.ybky. | w yšnn.ytn.g h. | bky.b ḫy k.ab n.ašmḫ. | b l.mt k.ngln.k klb. | b bt k.nʻtq.k inr. | ap.ḫšt k.ap.ab 16.1[125].14
ʻn.btlt.ʻn[t.bnt.]bht | k.y ilm.bnt.bh[t k].a[l.tš]mḫ. | al.tšmḫ.b r[m.h]kl[k]. | al.aḫd.hm.b y[--] y.[---]b[-]. | b gdlt.ark 3[ʻNT.VI].5.29
.ʻnt.---]. | [bnt.bht]k.y ilm[.bnt.bht k.--]. | [al.tšmḫ.]al.tš[mḫ.b rm.h] | [kl k.al.]aḫd hm.[---]. | [---.b]gdlt.ar[kt y.am 18[3AQHT].1.8
ʻl.hwt.aliy.qrdm. | bhṯ.bn.ilm.mt.ʻbd k.an. | w d ʻlm k.šmḫ.bn.ilm.mt. | [---.]g h.w aṣḥ.ik.yṣḥn. | [bʻl.ʻm.aḫ y.ik].yqr 5[67].2.20
l k.udr.ilqṣm. | w bn.bht.ksp.w ḫrṣ. | bht.ṭhrm.iqnim. | šmḫ.btlt.ʻnt.tdʻṣ. | pʻnm.w tr.arṣ. | idk.l ttn.pnm. | ʻm.bʻl.mry 4[51].5.82
l pʻn. | il.thbr.w tql. | tšṯḥwy.w tkbdn h. | tšu.g h.w tṣḥ.tšmḫ ht. | aṯrt.w bn h.ilt.w ṣb | rt.ary h.k mt.aliyn. | bʻl.k ḫlq. 6.1.39[49.1.11]
.ṭ[ḫ]. | gg k.b ym.ṭiṭ.rḥṣ. | npṣ k.b ym rṭ.b uni[l]. | pnm.tšmḫ.w ʻl yṣhl pi[t]. | yprq.lṣb.w yṣḥq. | pʻn.l hdm.ytpd.yšu. | 17[2AQHT].2.9
tʻn. | tḫtṣb.w tḥdy.ʻnt. | tǵdd.kbd h.b ṣḥq.ymlu. | lb h.b šmḫt.kbd.ʻnt. | tšyt.k brkm.tǵll b dm. | ḏmr.ḥlqm.b mmʻ.mh 3[ʻNT].2.26
n.tḫtṣb. | [w tḥdy.ʻnt.tǵdd.kbd h.b ṣḥ]q.ymlu.lb h. | [b šmḫt.kbd.ʻnt.tšyt.tḥt h.k]kdrt.riš. | [ʻl h.k irbym.kp.---.k br] 7.1[131].8
. | b ḏrt.bny.bnwt. | šmm.šmn.tmṭrn. | nḫlm.tlk.nbtm. | šmḫ.lṭpn.il.d pid. | pʻn h.l hdm.ytpd. | w yprq.lṣb w yṣḥq. | yš 6[49].3.14
y. | tdʻ.ky.ʻrbt. | l pn.špš. | w pn.špš.nr. | b y.mid.w um. | tšmḫ.m ab. | w al.trḫln. | ʻtn.ḫrd.ank. | ʻm ny.šlm. | kll. | w mn 1015.11
y.ṣ]brt. | ary y[.ẓl].ksp.[a]ṯrt. | k tʻn.ẓl.ksp.w n[-]t. | ḫrṣ.šmḫ.rbt.a[ṯrt]. | ym.gm.l ǵlm h.k [tṣḥ]. | ʻn.mkṯr.ap.t[---]. | dg 4[51].2.28

šmk

[t.r]umm. | tšu knp.btlt.ʻn[t]. | tšu.knp.w tr.b ʻp. | tk.aḫ šmk.mlat rumm. | w yšu.ʻn h.aliyn.bʻl. | w yšu.ʻn h.w yʻn. | w 10[76].2.12
ḫd.b yd h. | w qṣʻt h.bm.ymn h. | idk.l ytn pnm. | tk.aḫ.šmk.mla[t.r]umm. | tšu knp.btlt.ʻn[t]. | tšu.knp.w tr.b ʻp. | tk. 10[76].2.9

šml

blḥ. | [-----]. | w [---]. | bn.[---]. | bn.yr[--]. | bn.kṯr[t]. | bn.šml. | bn.arnbt. | qdšm. | b[-.--]t. | [---.-]l[--]. | [---.]pr[--]. | [-.a]p 2163.2.6
b.ʻrpt.l mḫšt.mdd. | il ym.l klt.nhr.il.rbm. | l ištbm.tnn.ištml h. | mḫšt.bṯn.ʻqltn. | šlyṭ.d šbʻt.rašm. | mḫšt.mdd ilm.ar[3[ʻNT].3.37

šmlbi

t.w[.ql]ʻ. | bn.aktmy.qšt. | šdyn.qšt. | bdn.qšt.w.qlʻ. | bn.šmlbi.qšt.w.qlʻ. | bn.yy.qšt. | ilrb.qšt. | bn.nmš.ṯt.qšt.w.qlʻ. | bʻl 119[321].4.13

šmlbu

. | nʻmn.bn.ʻyn.ṯkt. | ʻpṯn.bn.ilrš.ṯkt. | ilṯḥm.bn.šrn.ṯkt. | šmlbu.bn.grb.ṯkt. | šmlbu.bn.ypʻ.ṯkt. | [---.--]m. 2085.13
ʻpṯn.bn.ilrš.ṯkt. | ilṯḥm.bn.šrn.ṯkt. | šmlbu.bn.grb.ṯkt. | šmlbu.bn.ypʻ.ṯkt. | [---.--]m. 2085.14

šmlšn

.ḫbṭm. | ap ksp hm. | l yblt. | w ht.luk ʻm ml[kt]. | tǵsdb.šmlšn. | w tbʻ ank. | ʻm mlakt h šmʻ h. | w b.ʻly skn.ydʻ rgm h. 1021.5

šmm

nt.šmm.ʻm.ar]ṣ. | thmt.[ʻmn.kbkbm.abn.brq]. | d l t[dʻ.šmm.at m.w ank]. | ibǵ[y h.b tk.ǵ]r y.il.ṣpn. | b q[dš.b ǵr.nḥ]l 3[ʻNT].4.62
[.tant.šmm.ʻm.arṣ.thmt]. | ʻm kbkbm[.abn.brq.d l tdʻ.šmm.at m]. | w ank.ib[ǵy h.---]. | [-].l yʻmdn.i[---.---]. | kpr.šbʻ 7.2[130].20
ǵl[m]m[.---]. | mid.an[--.]ṣn[--]. | nrt.ilm.špš[.ṣḥrr]t. | la.šmm.b y[d.bn.ilm.m]t. | w tʻn.btlt.ʻn[t.bnt.]bht | k.y ilm.bnt. 3[ʻNT.VI].5.26
r.b p y. | k lli.b ṯbrn q y.ḫtu hw. | nrt.ilm.špš.ṣḥrrt. | la.šmm.b yd.bn ilm.mt. | ym.ymm.yʻtqn.l ymm. | l yrḫm.rḥm.ʻ 6[49].2.25
b p h. | k lli.b ṯbrn. | qn h.tḫtan. | nrt.ilm.špš. | ṣḥrrt.la. | šmm.b yd.md | d.ilm.mt.b a | lp.šd.rbt.k | mn.l pʻn.mt. | hbr.w 4[51].8.23
-----]. | [-----]. | n[----]. | bn.[---]. | bn.[---]. | bn.yk[--]. | bn.šmm. | bn.irgy. | w.nḥl h. | w.nḥl hm. | [bn].pmn. | bn.gtrn. | bn 1046.2.9
.ḫrṣ.nbt.w ʻly. | l ẓr.mgdl.rkb. | ṯkmm.ḥmt.nša. | [y]d h.šmmh.dbḥ. | l ṯr.ab h.il.šrd. | [bʻl].b dbḥ h.bn dgn. | [b m]ṣd h 14[KRT].4.168
r.[mg]dl. | w ʻl.l ẓr.[mg]dl.rkb. | ṯkmm.ḥm[t].ša.yd k. | šmm.dbḥ.l ṯr. | ab k.il.šrd.bʻl. | b dbḥ k.bn.dgn. | b mṣd k.w y 14[KRT].2.76
tʻn.pǵt.ṯkmt.mym. | qrym.ab.dbḥ.l ilm. | šʻly.dǵṯ h.b šmym. | dǵṯ.hrnmy.d kbkbm. | l tbrkn.alk brkt. | tmrn.alk.n 19[1AQHT].4.192
šspdt. | b ḥẓr y pẓǵm.ǵr.w yq. | dbḥ.ilm.yšʻly.dǵṯ h. | b šmym.dǵṯ hrnmy[.d k] | bkbm.ʻ[l.---]. | [-]l h.yd ʻd[.---]. | ltm. 19[1AQHT].4.186
gn.yqḥ.tš.b bt h. | il.ḥṭ h.nḥt.il.ymnn.mṭ.yd h.yšu. | yr.šmm h.yr.b šmm.ʻṣr.yḫrṭ yšt. | l pḥm.il.aṯtm.k ypt.hm.aṯtm. 23[52].38
. | w ytb. | tqru l špš.um h.špš.um.ql bl ʻm. | šḥr.w šlm šmm h mnt.nṯk.nḥš. | šmrr.nḥš ʻq šr.ln h.mlḫš. | abd.ln h.yd UG5.7.52
.krm ar. | [---.]h.mḥtrt.pttm. | [---.-]t h.ušpǵt tišr. | [---.šm]m h.nšat ẓl h kbkbm. | [---.]b km kbkbt k ṯn. | [---.]bʻl yḥ 2001.2.5
ynqm.b ap.ḏd.št.špt. | l arṣ.špt l šmm.w ʻrb.b p hm.ʻṣr.šmm. | w dg b ym.w ndd.gzr.l zr.yʻdb.u ymn. | u šmal.b p h 23[52].62
| rḫ l k ybrdmy.b[t.a] | b h lb[u] yʻrr.w yʻ[n]. | yrḫ nyr šmm.w nʻ[n]. | ʻma nkl ḫtn y.a[ḫ]r. | nkl yrḫ ytrḫ.adn h. | yšt 24[77].31
mm. | agzr ym.bn ym.ynqm.b ap.ḏd.št.špt. | l arṣ.špt l šmm.w ʻrb.b p hm.ʻṣr.šmm. | w dg b ym.w ndd.gzr.l zr.yʻdb. 23[52].62
um.pḥl.pḥlt.bt.abn.bt šmm w thm. | qrit.l špš.um h.špš.um.ql.bl.ʻm. | il.mbk nhrm. UG5.7.1
.ṭm.yḫpn.ḥyl | y.zbl.mlk.ʻllm y.km.tdd. | ʻnt.ṣd.tštr.ʻpt.šmm. | ṭbḫ.alpm.ap ṣin.šql.ṯrm. | w mri ilm.ʻglm.dt.šnt. | imr. 22.2[124].11
n.bṯn.brḥ. | tkly.bṯn.ʻqltn. | šlyṭ.d šbʻy.rašm. | ṯṯkḥ.ttrp.šmm.k rs. | ipd k.ank.ispi.uṭm. | ḏrqm.amt m.l yrt. | b npš.bn 5[67].1.4
n.br]ḥ.tkly. | [bṯn.ʻqltn.]šlyṭ. | [d šbʻt.rašm].ṯṯkḥ. | [ttrp.šmm.k rks.ipd]k. | [-----]. 5[67].1.31
. | ytn.ks.b d h. | krpn.b klat.yd h. | b krb.ʻẓm.ridn. | mt.šmm.ks.qdš. | l tphn h.aṯt.krpn. | l tʻn.aṯrt.alp. | kd.yqḥ.b ḫm 3[ʻNT].1.13

rtqt mr[.---]. | k d lbšt.bir.mlak. | šmm.tmr.zbl.mlk. | šmm.tlak.ṭl.amr.. | bn km k bk[r.z]bl.am.. | rkm.agzrt[.--].ar 13[6].27
.ql.b udn.k w[-]. | k rtqt mr[.---]. | k d lbšt.bir.mlak. | šmm.tmr.zbl.mlk. | šmm.tlak.ṭl.amr.. | bn km k bk[r.z]bl.am 13[6].26
--.]ym.rbt. | [---.]b nhrm. | [ʿb]r.gbl.ʿbr. | qʿl.ʿbr.iht. | np šmm.šmšr. | l dgy.aṯrt. | mǵ.l qdš.amrr. | idk.al.tnn. | pnm.tk. 3[ʿNT.VI].6.9
ḫspn.m h.w trḫṣ. | [ṭ]l.šmm.šmn.arṣ.rbb. | [r]kb ʿrpt.ṭl.šmm.tsk h. | [rb]b.nsk h.kbkbm. 3[ʿNT].2.40
ria.w tk. | pn h.tḫspn.m h.w trḫṣ. | ṭl.šmm.šmn.arṣ.ṭl.šm[m.t]sk h. | rbb.nsk h.kbkbm. | ttpp.anhbm.d alp.šd[.ẓu h. 3[ʿNT].4.87
[-----]. | yṣq.šm[n.---]. | ʿn.tr.arṣ.w šmm. | sb.l qṣm.arṣ. | l ksm.mhyt.ʿn. | l arṣ.m[ṭ]r.bʿl. | w l šd. 16[126].3.2
lḫšt. | [abn.rgm.l td]ʿ.nš[m.w l t]bn. | [hmlt.a]rṣ.[tant.šmm.ʿm.ar]ṣ. | thmt.[ʿmn.kbkbm.abn.brq]. | d l t[dʿ.šmm.at 3[ʿNT].4.60
l y.w argm k. | hwt.w aṯny k.rgm. | ʿṣ.w lḫšt.abn. | tant.šmm.ʿm.arṣ. | thmt.ʿmn.kbkbm. | abn.brq.d l.tdʿ.šmm. | rgm l 3[ʿNT].3.21
y.w argm k]. | hwt.w aṯny k[.rgm.ʿṣ.w lḫšt.abn]. | tunt.šmm.ʿm[.arṣ.thmt.ʿmn.kbkbm]. | rgm.l tdʿ.nš[m.w l tbn.hml 1[ʿNT.IX].3.14
gmn k]. | [h]wt.d aṯ[ny k.---.rgm.ʿṣ]. | w lḫšt.abn[.tant.šmm.ʿm.arṣ.thmt]. | ʿm kbkbm[.abn.brq.d l tdʿ.šmm.at m]. | 7.2[130].19
.---]. | dgn tt[--.---.-]l | ʿ.l kṯrt hl[l.sn]nt. | ylak yrḫ ny[r] šmm.ʿm. | ḫr[ḫ]b mlk qẓ.tn nkl y | rḫ ytrḫ.ib tʿrb m b bh | t h. 24[77].16
bt h. | il.ḥṭ h.nḥt.il.ymnn.mṭ.yd h.yšu. | yr.šmm h.yr.b šmm.ʿṣr.yḫrṭ yšt. | l pḥm.il.aṯtm.k ypt.hm.aṯtm.tṣḥn. | y mt. 23[52].38
y. | [---.ǵ]r.šrǵzz.ybky.km.nʿr. | [w ydmʿ.k]m.ṣǵr.špš.b šmm.tqru. | [---.]nplt.y[--].mdʿ.nplt.bšr. | [---].w tpky.k[m.]nʿ UG5.8.38
h. | [--]nn.bnt yš[--.---.-]lk. | [--]b.kmm.l k[--]. | [šp]š.b šmm.tq[ru.---.-]rt. | [---.]mn mn[-.---.--]n.nmr. | [--.]l ytk.bl[-. UG5.8.44
| tant.šmm.ʿm.arṣ. | thmt.ʿmn.kbkbm. | abn.brq.d l.tdʿ.šmm. | rgm l tdʿ.nšm.w l tbn. | hmlt.arṣ.at m.w ank. | ibǵy h. 3[ʿNT].3.23
šn.b.ḥbr.kṯr.ṭbm. | w tšt.ʿnt.gṯr.bʿlt.mlk.bʿ | lt.drkt.bʿlt.šmm.rmm. | [bʿl]t.kpṯ.w ʿnt.di.dit.rḫpt. | [---.-]rm.aklt.ʿgl.ʿl. UG5.2.1.7
l ǵr k.inbb. | kt ǵr k.ank.ydʿt. | [-]n.atn.at.mṯb k[.---]. | [š]mm.rm.lk.prẓ kt. | [k]bkbm.ṯm.tpl k.lbnt. | [-.]rgm.k yrkt.ʿ 13[6].12
-]. | kṯ.ẓrw.kṯ.nbt.dnt.w [-]n[-.---]. | il.ḫyr.ilib.š. | arṣ w šmm.š. | il.š.kṯrt.š. | dgn.š.bʿl.ḫlb alp w š. | bʿl ṣpn alp.w.š. | ṯrt UG5.9.2.2
.w š[.---]. | bʿlm.alp.w š[.---]. | bʿlm.alp.w š[.---]. | arṣ.w šmm.š.kṯr[t] š.yrḫ[.---]. | ṣpn.š.kṯr.š.pdry.š.ǵrm.š[.---]. | aṯrt.š UG5.9.1.5
. | št.alp.qdm h.mria.w tk. | pn h.tḫspn.m h.w trḫṣ. | ṭl.šmm.šmn.arṣ.ṭl.šm[m.t]sk h. | rbb.nsk h.kbkbm. | ttpp.anhb 3[ʿNT].4.87
[l]ṭlḥn.hdmm.ttʿr.l hdmm. | [t]ḫspn.m h.w trḫṣ. | [ṭ]l.šmm.šmn.arṣ.rbb. | [r]kb ʿrpt.ṭl.šmm.tsk h. | [rb]b.nsk h.kbk 3[ʿNT].2.39
.iṯ.zbl.bʿ[l.arṣ]. | b ḫlm.lṭpn.il.d pid. | b ḏrt.bny.bnwt. | šmm.šmn.tmṭrn. | nḫlm.tlk.nbtm. | w idʿ.k ḥy.aliyn.bʿl. | k iṯ. 6[49].3.6
k iṯ.zbl.bʿl.arṣ. | b ḫlm.lṭpn.il d pid. | b ḏrt.bny.bnwt. | šmm.šmn.tmṭrn. | nḫlm.tlk.nbtm. | šmḫ.lṭpn.il.d pid. | pʿn h.l 6[49].3.12
[---.]il.[---]. | [ṭṣ]un.b arṣ. | mḫnm.ṭrp ym. | lšnm.tlḥk. | šmm.ṭtrp. | ym.ḏnbtm. | tnn.l šbm. | tšt.trks. | l mrym.l bt[.---] 1003.6
pp.hrm. | [---].d l ydʿ bn il. | [---.]pḫr kkbm. | [---.]dr dt.šmm. | [---.al]iyn bʿl. | [---].rkb.ʿrpt. | [---.]ǵš.l limm. | [---.]l yṯ 10[76].1.5
.bn.ʿn h. | uzʿrt.tmll.išd h.qrn[m]. | dt.ʿl h.riš h.b glṯ.b šm[m]. | [---.i]l.ṯr.iṯ.p h.k ṯt.ǵlṯ[.--]. | [---.--] k yn.ddm.l b[--.-- UG5.3.1.7
[-----]. | [špt.l a]rṣ.špt.l šmm. | [---.l]šn.l kbkbm.yʿrb. | [bʿ]l.b kbd h.b p h yrd. | k ḫrr. 5[67].2.2
bʿlm. | [bʿ]lm. | [bʿ]lm. | [bʿ]lm. | [bʿ]lm. | [bʿl]m. | [arṣ] w šm[m]. | [-----]. | [a]rṣ. | [u]šḫr[y]. | [ʿ]ṯtrt. | i[l t]ʿḏr bʿl. | ršp. | dd 29[17].1.12

šmmlk

ly.bn[.---]. | ynḥm.bn[.---]. | gn.bn[.---]. | klby.[bn.---]. | šmmlk bn[.---]. | ʿmyn.bn.[---]. | mtbʿl.bn[.---]. | ymy.bn[.---]. | 102[322].5.9

šmmn

bn.agmz. | [-]n bn.iln. | [--]nn bn.ibm. | [-]n bn.ḫrn. | [š]mmn bn.gmz. | [yn]ḥm bn.ilmd. 2087.14
[--]kbʿl ṯṯ [mat]. | [-----]. | ilmlk ṯṯ mat. | ʿbdilm.ṯṯ mat. | šmmn.bn.ʿdš.ṯṯ mat. | ušknym. | ypʿ.alpm. | aḫ[m]lk.bn.nskn. 1060.1.12
ḥm. | iḫy. | bn.mšt. | ʿpsn. | bn.ṣpr. | kmn. | bn.ršp. | tmn. | šmmn. | bn.rmy. | bn.aky. | ʿbdḫmn. | bn.ʿdṭ. | kṭy. | bn.ḫny. | bn 1047.11
ṯlṯ.d yṣa. | b d.šmmn. | l argmn. | l nskm. | ṯmn.kkrm. | alp.kbd. | [m]itm.kbd. 147[90].2
n. | bn.ands. | bn.ann. | bn.ʿbdpdr. | šd.iyry.l.ʿbdbʿl. | šd.šmmn.l.bn.šty. | šd.bn.arws.l.bn.ḫlan. | šd.bn.ibryn.l.bn.ʿmnr 1102.18
ṣṣ mlk mit[.---]. | ṣṣ igy.ḫmšm. | ṣṣ yrpi m[it.---]. | ṣṣ bn.š[m]mn ʿ[šr.---]. | alp.ṯṯm. | kbd.mlḥt. 2097.19

šmn

zy. | ḫmš.kkr.ḥlb. | ḫmš.kkr.brr. | kkr.ḫmš.mat.kbd.ṯlṯ.šm[n]. | alp.mitm.kbd.ṯlṯ.ḥlb. | šbʿ.l.ʿšrm.kkr.ṯlṯ. | d.ybl.blym. 1135.4
lp.qdm h.mria.w tk. | pn h.tḫspn.m h.w trḫṣ. | ṭl.šmm.šmn.arṣ.ṭl.šm[m.t]sk h. | rbb.nsk h.kbkbm. | ttpp.anhbm.d al 3[ʿNT].4.87
n.hdmm.ttʿr.l hdmm. | [t]ḫspn.m h.w trḫṣ. | [ṭ]l.šmm.šmn.arṣ.rbb. | [r]kb ʿrpt.ṭl.šmm.tsk h. | [rb]b.nsk h.kbkbm. 3[ʿNT].2.39
šlmym.lqḥ.akl. | yḥmn.ṯlṯ.šmn. | a[---.]kdm. | ʿ[---]ʿm.kd. | a[----]ḥr.ṯlṯ. | y[---.bn.]kran.ḫ 136[84].2
mlkytn. | ḥnn y l pn mlk. | šin k itn. | rʿ y šṣa idn l y. | l šmn iṭr hw. | p iḫdn gnryn. | im mlkytn yrgm. | aḫnnn. | w iḫd 1020.6
alp. | uz.mrat.mlḥt. | arbʿ.uzm.mrat.bqʿ. | ṯlṯ.[-]ṯt.aš[ʿ]t.šmn.uz. | mi[t].ygb.bqʿ. | a[--].ʿṭ. | a[l]pm.alpnm. | ṯlṯ.m[a]t.art 1128.22
ṯlṯ.mat.ṯlṯm. | kbd.šmn. | l kny. | ṯmnym.šmn. | b d.adnnʿm. 1094.4
db.dgn kly. | lḥm.[b]ʿdn hm.kly. | yn.b ḥmt hm.k[l]y. | šmn.b q[bʿt hm.---]. | bt.krt.t[--]. 16[126].3.16
| yṯtn. | bn.ab[l]. | kry. | psš. | ilṯḥm. | ḥrm. | bn.bty. | ʿby. | šm[n].bn.apn. | krty. | bn.ubr. | [bn] mdḫl. | bn.sy[n]n. | bn.šrn. 2078.17
t.---.dqt]. | l ṣpn.w [dqt.---.ṯn.l ʿš] | rm.pam[t.---]. | š dd šmn[.gdlt.w.---]. | brr.r[gm.yṯtb.b ṯdṯ.ṯn]. | l šmn.ʿ[ly h.gdlt.r APP.II[173].48
t.---]. | dqt.l.ṣpn.w.dqt[.---]. | ṯn.l.ʿšrm.pamt.[---]. | š.dd.šmn.gdlt.w.[---.brr]. | rgm.yṯtb.b.ṯdṯ.ṯn[.--.šmn]. | ʿly h.gdlt.r 35[3].44
.bn.srt. | kd.ʿl.ẓrm. | kd.ʿl.šz.bn pls. | kd.ʿl.ynḥm. | tgrm.šmn.d.bn.kwy. | ʿl.šlmym.ṯmn.kbd. | ṯṯm.šmn. 1082.2.8
d.arbʿm. | ʿšrt.ḫrṣ.b.arbʿm. | mit.ḫršḫ.b.ṯqlm. | w.šbʿ.ʿšr.šmn. | d.l.yṣa.bt.mlk. | tgmr.ksp.mitm. | ḫmšm.kbd. 2100.20
arbʿ.ʿšr h.šmn. | d.lqḥt.ṯlǵdy. | w.kd.ištir.ʿm.qrt. | ʿšt.ʿšr h.šmn. | ʿmn.bn. 1083.1
mit.šmn.d.nm[-.]b d.mzy.alzy. | ḫmš.kkr.ḥlb. | ḫmš.kkr.brr. | kkr. 1135.1
lqḥ.šʿrt. | urḫ.ln.kkrm. | w.rḥd.kd.šmn. | drt.b.kkr. | ubn.ḫṣḥ.kkr. | kkr.lqḥ.ršpy. | tmtrn.bn.pnm 1118.3
ʿšr šṭpm. | b ḫmš.šmn. | ʿšrm.gdy. | b ḫmš.šmn. | w ḫmš ṯʿdt. 1097.4
. | w ʿl [---.]rbʿm ṯqlm.w [---] arbʿyn. | w ʿl.mnḥm.arbʿ š[mn]. | w ʿl bn a[--.-]yn ṯqlm. | [--] ksp [---] kdr [---]. | [-]ṯrn [1103.9
---.]ṯmnym[.k]sp ḫmšt. | [w a]rbʿ kkr ʿl bn[.--]. | [w] ṯlṯ šmn. | [w a]r[bʿ] ksp ʿl bn ymn. | šb šr šmn [--] ṯryn. | ḫm[š]m 1103.3
kd.šmn.ʿl.hbm.šlmy. | kd.šmn.ṯbil. | kd.šmn.ymtšr. | arbʿ.šmn.ʿl.ʿbdn.w.[---]. | kdm.šmn.ʿl.ilršp.bn[.-- 1082.1.3
ṯṯ.mat.ṯṯm.kbd šmn. | l.abrm.alṯyy. | [m]it.ṯlṯm.kbd.šmn. | [l.]abrm.mšrm. | [2095.1
ṯṯ.mat.ṯṯm.kbd šmn. | l.abrm.alṯyy. | [m]it.ṯlṯm.kbd.šmn. | [l.]abrm.mšrm. | [mi]tm.arbʿm.ṯmn.kbd. | [l.]sbrdnm. | 2095.3
ṯlṯ.mat.ṯlṯm. | kbd.šmn. | l kny. | ṯmnym.šmn. | b d.adnnʿm. 1094.2

ẖmšm.izml. | ẖmš.kbd.arbʿm. | dd.akl. | ṯṯ.ʿšr h.yn. | kd.šmn.l.nr.ilm. | kdm.dǵm. | ṯṯ.kdm.ztm. 1126.6
. | ẖrṣbʿ. | uẖnp. | art. | [--]n. | [-----]. | [-----]. | nnu. | šmg. | šmn. | lbnm. | trm. | bṣr. | y[--]. | y[--]. | snr. | midẖ. | ḥ[lym]. | [ẖ] 2058.2.13
l.bʿ[l.arṣ]. | b ḥlm.lṭpn.il.d pid. | b ḏrt.bny.bnwt. | šmm.šmn.tmṭrn. | nḫlm.tlk.nbtm. | w idʿ.k ḥy.aliyn.bʿl. | k iṯ.zbl.bʿl 6[49].3.6
bl.bʿl.arṣ. | b ḥlm.lṭpn.il d pid. | b ḏrt.bny.bnwt. | šmm.šmn.tmṭrn. | nḫlm.tlk.nbtm. | šmḫ.lṭpn.il.d pid. | pʿn h.l hdm. 6[49].3.12
.ilhm]. | bʿlm.w mlu[.---.ksm]. | ṯlṯm.w mʿrb[.---]. | dbḥ šmn mr[.šmn.rqḥ.bt]. | mtnt.w ynt.[qrt.w ṯn.ḥṯm]. | w bǵr.ar APP.II[173].22
ṣt.ilh[m.bʿlm.---]. | ksm.ṯlṯm.[---]. | d yqḥ bt[.--]r.dbḥ[.šmn.mr]. | šmn.rqḥ[.-]bt.mtnt[.w ynt.qrt]. | w ṯn ḥṯm.w bǵr.a 35[3].20
m. | [---.ṯṯ.dd.]gdl.ṯṯ.dd.šʿrm. | [---.hn.w.al]p.kd.nbt.kd.šmn.mr. | [---].kmn.lṯḥ.sbbyn. | [---.-]ʿt.lṯḥ.ššmn. | [---].ẖšwn.ṯ 142[12].8
dl.ṯṯ.dd.šʿrm. | [---.a]lp.arbʿ.mat.tyt. | [---.kd.]nbt.k[d.]šmn.mr. | [---.l]tḥ.sb[by]n.lṯḥ.šḥ[lt]. | [---.l]tḥ.dblt.lṯḥ.ṣmqm. 142[12].15
[---.]ṯṯ.dd.gdl.ṯṯ.dd.šʿrm. | [---.-]hn.w.alp.kd.nbt.kd.šmn.mr. | [---.]arbʿ.mat.ẖswn.lṯḥ.aqhr. | [---.lṯḥ.]sbbyn.lṯḥ.šš 142[12].2
m. | ʿšrm.kk[r]. | brr. | [ʿ]šrm.npš. | ʿšrm.zt.mm. | ʿrbʿm. | šmn.mr. 141[120].16
| id.u [---]t. | lḥn š[-]ʿ[--.]aḫd[.-]. | tšmʿ.mṯt.[ḥ]ry. | ṭbḫ.šmn.[m]ri h. | t[p]ṯḥ.rḥbt.yn. | ʿl h.ṯr h.tšʿrb. | ʿl h.tšʿrb.ẓby h. 15[128].4.15
[-----]. | [ṭbḫ.šm]n.[mri h]. | [tpṯḥ.rḥ]bt.[yn]. | [---.]rp[.---]. | [---.ẖ]br[.---]. | 15[128].5.1
p[----]. | gm.l[att h k.yṣḥ]. | šmʿ[.l mṯt.ḥry]. | ṭbḫ.š[mn].mri k. | ptḥ.[rḥ]bt.yn. | ṣḥ.šbʿm.ṯr y. | ṯmnym.[ẓ]by y. | ṯ 15[128].4.4
--.q]l.bl.tbḥ[n.l]azd.ʿr.qdm. | [---].ʿẓ q[dm.--.šp]š. | [---.šm]n.mšḥt.kṯpm.a[-]ṯ[-]. | [---.--]ḥ b ym.tld[---.]b[-.]y[--.---]. | UG5.8.23
mnḥ.b d.ybnn. | arbʿ.mat. | l.alp.šmn. | nḥ.ṯṯ.mat. | šm[n].rqḥ. | kkrm.brdl. | mit.tišrm. | ṯlṯm.al 141[120].3
.ymn. | krty. | bn.abr[-]. | yrpu. | kdn. | pʿṣ. | bn.liy. | ydʿ. | šmn. | ʿdy. | ʿnbr. | aḫrm. | bn.qrdy. | bn.šmʿn. | bn.ǵlmy. | ǵly. | 2117.1.27
n.ṯbil. | kd.šmn.ymtšr. | arbʿ.šmn.ʿl.ʿbdn.w.[---]. | kdm.šmn.ʿl.ilršp.bn[.---]. | kd.šmn.ʿl.yddn. | kd.ʿl.ššy. | kd.ʿl.nḏbn.b 1082.1.5
kd.šmn.ʿl.hbm.šlmy. | kd.šmn.ṯbil. | kd.šmn.ymtšr. | arbʿ.šmn.ʿl.ʿ 1082.1.1
arbʿ.šmn.ʿl.ʿbdn.w.[---]. | kdm.šmn.ʿl.ilršp.bn[.---]. | kd.šmn.ʿl.yddn. | kd.ʿl.ššy. | kd.ʿl.nḏbn.bn.agmn. | [k]d.ʿl.brq. | [k 1082.1.6
.šmn.ʿl.hbm.šlmy. | kd.šmn.ṯbil. | kd.šmn.ymtšr. | arbʿ.šmn.ʿl.ʿbdn.w.[---]. | kdm.šmn.ʿl.ilršp.bn[.---]. | kd.šmn.ʿl.ydd 1082.1.4
.---]. | š dd šmn[.gdlt.w.---]. | brr.r[gm.yṯṯb.b ṯdṯ.ṯn]. | l šmn.ʿ[ly h.gdlt.rgm.yṯṯb]. | brr.b šbʿ[.ṣbu.špš.w ḥl] | yt.ʿrb špš APP.II[173].50
t.[---]. | š.dd.šmn.gdlt.w.[---.brr]. | rgm.yṯṯb.b.ṯdṯ.ṯn[.--.šmn]. | ʿly h.gdlt.rgm.yṯ[ṯb.brr]. | b.[šb]ʿ.ṣbu.[š]pš.w.ḥly[t].ʿ[r 35[3].45
bʿ.ʿšr h.šmn. | d.lqḥt.ṯlǵdy. | w.kd.ištir.ʿm.qrt. | ʿšt.ʿšr h.šmn. | ʿmn.bn.aǵlmn. | arbʿm.ksp.ʿl.qrt. | b.šd.bn.[u]brš. | ẖmš 1083.4
ʿšr šṭpm. | b ẖmš.šmn. | ʿšrm.gdy. | b ẖmš.šmn. | w ẖmš ṯʿdt. 1097.2
tnt. | ẖmš.ṯnt.alpm. | ʿšrm.hbn. | ṯlṯ.mat.dd. | šʿrm. | mit.šmn. | ʿšr.kat. | ẓrw. 2102.9
ḥy[ly.zbl.mlk.ʿllm y]. | šmʿ.atm[.---]. | ym.lm.qd[.---]. | šmn.prst[.---]. | ydr.hm.ym[.---]. | ʿl amr.yu[ḫd.ksa.mlk h]. | n 22.1[123].15
ṯṯ.mat.ksp. | ḥṯbn.ybnn. | arbʿm.l.mit.šmn. | arbʿm.l.mit.tišr. | ṯṯ.ṯṯ.b [ṯ]ql.ṯlṯt.l.ʿšrm.ksp hm. | šstm. 1127.3
ʿlm.w mlu[.---.ksm]. | ṯlṯm.w mʿrb[.---]. | dbḥ šmn mr[.šmn.rqḥ.bt]. | mtnt.w ynt.[qrt.w ṯn.ḥṯm]. | w bǵr.arbʿ.[---.kd APP.II[173].22
mnḥ.b d.ybnn. | arbʿ.mat. | l.alp.šmn. | nḥ.ṯṯ.mat. | šm[n].rqḥ. | kkrm.brdl. | mit.tišrm. | ṯlṯm.almg. | ẖmšm.kkr. | 141[120].5
šlt.arbʿ.ẖpnt.[---]. | ẖmšm.ṯlṯ.rkb.ntn.ṯlṯ.mat.[---]. | lg.šmn.rqḥ.šrʿm.ušpǵtm.p[--.---]. | kṯ.ẓrw.kṯ.nbt.ḏnt.w [-]n[-.--- UG5.9.1.21
ʿlm.---]. | ksm.ṯlṯm.[---]. | d yqḥ bt[.--]r.dbḥ[.šmn.mr]. | šmn.rqḥ[.-]bt.mtnt[.w ynt.qrt]. | w ṯn ḥṯm.w bǵr.arb[ʿ.---]. | 35[3].21
. | [---.-]yṯr.ur[--.---]. | [---.n]skt.nʿmn.nbl[.---]. | [--.]yṣq šmn.šlm.b ṣ[ʿ.trḥṣ]. | yd h.btlt.ʿnt.uṣbʿt[h.ybmt]. | limm.tiḫd. UG5.3.2.4
ʿ.tmtḫṣ.b bt. | tḫṣb.bn.ṯlḥnm.ymḥ. | [b]bt.dm.ḏmr.yṣq.šmn. | šlm.b ṣʿ.trḥṣ.yd h.bt | [l]t.ʿnt.uṣbʿt h.ybmt.limm. | [t]rḥ 3[ʿNT].2.31
kd.šmn.ʿl.hbm.šlmy. | kd.šmn.ṯbil. | kd.šmn.ymtšr. | arbʿ.šmn.ʿl.ʿbdn.w.[---]. | kdm.šmn 1082.1.2
l bn[.--]. | [w] ṯlṯ šmn. | [w a]r[bʿ] ksp ʿl bn ymn. | šb šr šmn [--] ṯryn. | ẖm[š]m l ʿšr ksp ʿl bn llit. | [--]l[-.-]p ʿl [---.-]bʿ 1103.5
[-----]. | yṣq.šm[n.---]. | ʿn.tr.arṣ.w šmm. | sb.l qṣm.arṣ. | l ksm.mhyt.ʿn. | l 16[126].3.1
ynḥm. | tgrm.šmn.d.bn.kwy. | ʿl.šlmym.ṯmn.kbd. | ṯṯm.šmn. 1082.2.10

šmngy

r. | [---.]bnšm.b.šbn. | [---.b]nšm.b.šmny. | [---.b]nšm.b.šmngy. | [---.]bnšm.b.snr.mid. | [---.bn]šm.b.tkn. | [---.bn]šm.b 2076.25

šmny

k.ṯlṯ. | [ʿb]dršp.nsk.ṯlṯ. | [-]lkynt.nsk.ṯlṯ. | [-]by.nsk.ṯlṯ. | šmny. | ẖršn. | ldn. | bn.ands. | bn.ann. | bn.ʿbdpdr. | šd.iyry.l.ʿb 1102.11
lb.gngnt.ṯlṯ.y[n]. | bṣr.ʿšr.yn. | nnu arbʿ.yn. | šql ṯlṯ.yn. | šmny.kdm.yn. | šmgy.kd.yn. | hzp.tšʿ.yn. | [b]ir.ʿšr[.---]m ḥsp. 2004.26
nm. | arbʿ.bnšm.b.ypr. | [---.]bnšm.b.šbn. | [---.b]nšm.b.šmny. | [---.b]nšm.b.šmngy. | [---.]bnšm.b.snr.mid. | [---.bn]š 2076.24

šmʿ

. | [---.š]d.gṯr. | [--]ḥ[d].šd.hwt. | [--.]iḥd.šd.gṯr. | [w]ht.yšmʿ.uḫ y. | l g y.w yhbṭ.bnš. | w ytn.ilm.b d hm. | b d.iḫqm.g 55[18].17
w rd. | bt ḫpṯt.arṣ.tspr b y | rdm.arṣ.w tdʿ ilm. | k mtt.yšmʿ.aliyn.bʿl. | yuhb.ʿglt.b dbr.prt. | b šd.šḥlmmt.škb. | ʿmn 5[67].5.17
[-----]. | [-----]. | il.šmʿ.amr k.ph[-]. | k il.ḥkmt.k ṯr.lṭpn. | ṣḥ.ngr.il.ilš.il[š]. | w a 16[126].4.2
. | aṯr h.l t[dd.ilnym.ṯm]. | yḥpn.ḥy[ly.zbl.mlk.ʿllm y]. | šmʿ.atm[.---]. | ym.lm.qd[.---]. | šmn.prst[.---]. | ydr.hm.ym[.- 22.1[123].13
tzd[.--]. | pt l bšr h.dm a[--.--]ḥ. | w yn.k mtrḫt[.---]h. | šmʿ ilht kṯr[t.--]mm. | nh l yd h tzdn[.---]n. | l ad[n h.---]. | dg 24[77].11
t.luk ʿm ml[kt]. | tǵsdb.šmlšn. | w tbʿ ank. | ʿm mlakt h šmʿ h. | w b.ʿly skn.ydʿ rgm h. | w ht ab y ǵm[--]. | t[--.---]. | ls[1021.7
h. | lk.l ab k.yṣb.lk. | l[ab]k.w rgm.ʿny. | l k[rt.adn k.]ištm[ʿ]. | w tqǵ[.udn.k ǵz.ǵzm]. | tdbr.w[ǵ]rm[.ṯṯwy]. | šqlt.b 16.6[127].29
ʿ.yṣb ǵlm.ʿl. | ab h.yʿrb.yšu g h. | w yṣḥ.šmʿ mʿ.l krt. | ṯʿ.ištmʿ.w tqǵ udn. | k ǵz.ǵzm.tdbr. | w ǵrm.ṯṯwy.šqlt. | b ǵlt.yd 16.6[127].42
[--.---]. | a[--.---]. | [---].ksp.ʿm[.---]. | [---.]ilṯhm.w.[---]. | šmʿt.ḫwt[.---]. | [---].nzdt.qr[t]. | [---.]dt nzdt.m[lk]. | [---.]w.a 2127.2.3
ṯḥm.iwrḏr. | l.plsy. | rgm. | yšlm.l k. | l.trǵds. | w.l.klby. | šmʿt.ḫti. | nḫtu.ht. | hm.in mm. | nḫtu.w.lak. | ʿm y.w.yd. | ilm. 53[54].7
[t].tptrʿ td[h]. | limm.w tʿl.ʿm.il. | ab h.ḥpr.pʿl k.y[--]. | šmʿ k.l arḫ.w bn.[--]. | limm.ql.b udn.k w[-]. | k rtqt mr[.---]. 13[6].22
t.šmʿ.mʿ. | l bn.ilm.mt.ik.tmt[ḫ] | ṣ.ʿm.aliyn.bʿl. | ik.al.yšm[ʿ] k.ṯr. | il.ab k.l ysʿ.alt. | ṯbt k.l yhpk.ksa.mlk k. | l ytbr. 6[49].6.26
. | [-.yṯ]ir ṯr.il.ab k.l pn.zbl.ym.l pn[.ṯ]pṭ[.n]hr. | [ik.a]l.yšmʿ k.ṯr.[i]l.ab k.l ys[ʿ.alt.]ṯ[bt | k.l y]hpk. | [ksa.]mlk k.l yṯ 2.3[129].17
rt.ṣpn. | alp.šd.aḫd bt. | rbt.kmn.hkl. | w yʿn.kṯr.w ḫss. | šmʿ.l aliyn bʿl. | bn.l rkb.ʿrpt. | bl.ašt.urbt.b bh[t] m. | ḥln.b qr 4[51].5.121
qrn.ymn h.b anšt[.---]. | qdqd h.w yʿn.yṯpn.[mhr.št]. | šmʿ.l btlt.ʿnt.at.ʿ[l.qšt h]. | tmḫṣ h.qṣʿt h.hwt.l t[ḥwy]. | nʿmn. 18[3AQHT].4.12
š. | k ḥy.aliyn.bʿl. | k iṯ.zbl.bʿl.arṣ. | gm.yṣḥ.il.l btlt. | ʿnt.šmʿ.l btlt.ʿn[t]. | rgm.l nrt.il.šp[š]. | pl.ʿnt.šdm.y špš. | pl.ʿnt.šd 6[49].3.23
k.iṯl.brlt n[-.k qṭr.b ap -]. | tmǵyn.tša.g h[m.w tṣḥn]. | šmʿ.l dnil.[mt.rpi]. | mt.aqht.ǵzr.[šṣat]. | btlt.ʿnt.k [rḥ.npš h]. 19[1AQHT].2.90

p y.t‘lgt.b lšn[y]. | ǵr[.---]b.b pš y.t[--]. | hwt.b‘l.iš[--]. | šm‘ l y.ypš.[---]. | ḥkr[.---]. | ‘ṣr[.--.]tb[-]. | ṯat[.---]. | yn[-.---]. | i 2124.5
t.dm.ẖt.š‘tqt. | dm.lan.w ypqd. | krt.ṯ‘.yšu.g h. | w yṣḥ.šm‘.l mṯt. | ḥry.ṭbẖ.imr. | w ilḥm.mgṯ.w iṯrm. | tšm‘.mṯt.ḥry. | 16.6[127].16
p[----]. | gm.l[aṯt h k.yṣḥ]. | šm‘[.l mṯt.ḥry]. | ṭbẖ.š[mn].mri k. | ptḥ.[rḥ]bt.yn. | ṣḥ.šb‘m.ṯr 15[128].4.3
ilš.ngr.bt.b‘l. | w aṯt h.ngrt.ilht. | w y‘n.lṭpn.il d pi[d]. | šm‘.l ngr.il il[š]. | ilš.ngr bt b‘l. | w aṯt k.ngrt.il[ht]. | ‘l.l ṯkm.b 16[126].4.11
ṯr[.il.ab -.w t‘n.rbt]. | aṯr[t.ym.šm‘.l qdš]. | w am[rr.l dgy.rbt]. | aṯrt.ym[.mdl.‘r]. | ṣmd.pḥl[.š 4[51].4.2
t.aliyn. | b‘l.k ẖlq.zbl.b‘l. | arṣ.gm.yṣḥ il. | l rbt.aṯrt ym.šm‘. | l rbt.aṯr[t] ym.tn. | aḥd.b bn k.amlkn. | w t‘n.rbt.aṯrt y 6.1.44[49.1.16]
[-----]. | šm‘.l [-]mt[.-]m.l[-]ṭnm. | ‘dm.[lḥ]m.tšty. | w t‘n.mṯt ḥry. | l l 15[128].6.1
y‘n.k[ṯr.w ẖs]s. | ṯṯb.b‘l.l[hwt y]. | ṯn.rgm.k[ṯr.w]ẖss. | šm‘.m‘.l al[iy]n b‘l. | bl.ašt.ur[bt.]b bht m. | ḥln.b qr[b.hk]l m 4[51].6.4
qr. | [krpn h.-.l]arṣ.ks h.tšpk m. | [l ‘pr.tšu.g h.]w tṣḥ.šm‘.m‘. | [l aqht.ǵzr.i]rš.ksp.w atn k. | [ẖrṣ.w aš]lḥ k.w tn.qšt 17[2AQHT].6.16
b alp.š[d]. | [rbt.]kmn.w ṣḥq.btlt.[‘nt]. | [tšu.]g h.w tṣḥ.šm‘.m[‘.l a] | [qht.ǵ]zr.at.aẖ.w an.a[ẖt k]. | [---].šb‘.ṯir k.[---]. 18[3AQHT].1.23
z.b‘l.‘z.ymṣẖn. | k lsmm.mt.ql. | b‘l.ql.‘ln.špš. | tṣḥ.l mt.šm‘.m‘. | l bn.ilm.mt.ik.tmt[ẖ] | ṣ.‘m.aliyn.b‘l. | ik.al.yšm[‘] k. 6[49].6.23
t.k aṯb.an. | ytb‘.yṣb ǵlm.‘l. | ab h.y‘rb.yšu g h. | w yṣḥ.šm‘ m‘.l krt. | ṯ‘.ištm‘.w tqǵ udn. | k ǵz.ǵzm.tdbr. | w ǵrm.ṯṯw 16.6[127].41
.yrd[.--.]i[---]n.bn. | [---.-]nn.nrt.ilm.špš.tšu.g h.w t[ṣḥ.šm]‘.m‘. | [-.yṯ]ir ṯr.il.ab k.l pn.zbl.ym.l pn[.ṯ]pṭ[.n]hr. | [ik.a] 2.3[129].15
ǵt.klb. | [ṣ]pr[.apn]k. | [pb]l[.mlk.g]m.l aṯt | [h.k]y[ṣḥ.]šm‘.m‘. | [--.]‘m[.-.]aṯt y[.-]. | [---.]tḥm. | [---]t.[ ]r. | [---.--]n. | [- 14[KRT].5.229
| ḥrš yd.šlḥm.ššqy. | ilm sad.kbd.hmt.b‘l. | ḥkpt.il.kl h.tšm‘. | mṯt.dnty.t‘db.imr. | b pẖd.l npš.kṯr.w ẖss. | l brlt.hyn.d 17[2AQHT].5.21
.dnil. | mt.rpi.aphn.ǵzr.mt. | hrnmy.gm.l aṯt h.k yṣḥ. | šm‘.mṯt.dnty.‘d[b]. | imr.b pẖd.l npš.kṯr. | w ẖss.l brlt.hyn d. 17[2AQHT].5.16
. | w yṣḥ.šm‘.l mṯt. | ḥry.ṭbẖ.imr. | w ilḥm.mgṯ.w iṯrm. | tšm‘.mṯt.ḥry. | ṯṭbẖ.imr.w lḥm. | mgṯ.w yṯrm.hn.ym. | w ṯn.yṯ 16.6[127].19
. | [----]r[.---]š[.--]qm. | id.u [---]t. | lḥn š[-]‘[--.]aẖd[.-]. | tšm‘.mṯt.[ḥ]ry. | ṯṭbẖ.šmn.[m]ri h. | t[p]tḥ.rḥbt.yn. | ‘l h.ṯr h.t 15[128].4.14
yn.udm‘t.gm. | tṣḥ.l nrt.ilm.špš. | ‘ms m‘.l y.aliyn.b‘l. | tšm‘.nrt.ilm.špš. | tšu.aliyn.b‘l.l ktp. | ‘nt.k tšt h.tš‘lyn h. | b ṣr 6[62].1.13
ubn.krwn.tǵd.[m]nḥm. | ‘pṯrm.šm‘rgm.skn.qrt. | ḥgbn.šm‘.skn.qrt. | nǵr krm.‘bdadt.b‘ln.yp‘mlk. | ṯǵrm.mnḥm.klyn 2011.11
kbm.mdl.‘r. | ṣmd.pḥl.št.gpn y dt ksp. | dt.yrq.nqbn y.tš[m‘]. | pǵt.ṯkmt.my.ḥspt.l[š‘]r.ṭl. | yd‘t.hlk.kbkbm. | bkm.t 19[1AQHT].2.54
mt.rpi. | all.ǵzr.m[t.]hr[nmy]. | gm.l bt[h.dnil.k yṣḥ]. | šm‘.pǵt.ṯkmt[.my]. | ḥspt.l š‘r.ṭl.yd[‘t]. | hlk.kbkbm.mdl.‘r. | ṣ 19[1AQHT].2.50
[.št.gpnm.dt]. | ksp.dt.yr[q.nqbnm]. | ‘db.gpn.atnt[y]. | yšm‘.qd.w amr[r]. | mdl.‘r.ṣmd.pḥl. | št.gpnm.dt.ksp. | dt.yrq. 4[51].4.8
---]. | aršmg.mru. | b‘l.šlm.‘bd. | awr.ṯǵrn.‘bd. | ‘bd.ẖmn.šm‘.rgm. | sdn.[k]bs. | šdyn.mẖ[ṣ]. | aṯry.mẖṣ. | b‘ln.mẖṣ. | y[ḥ] 2084.12
.p.k mtm. | ‘z.mid. | hm.nṯkp. | m‘n k. | w.mnm. | rgm.d.tšm‘. | ṯmt.w.št. | b.spr.‘m y. 53[54].17
]š.m[l]k.ab[.šnm.]mṣr. | [t]bu.ḏdm.qn[-.-]n[-.-]lt. | ql h.yš[m‘].ṯr.[il].ab h.[---]l. | b šb‘t.ḥdrm.[b ṯ]mn[t.ap]. | sgrt.g[-]. 3[‘NT.VI].5.18

šm‘y

p.alp.am[-]. | ṯmn.ḥblm.šb‘.šb‘.ma[-]. | ‘šr.kkr.rtn. | b d.šm‘y.bn.bdn. 1128.33

šm‘n

‘ṣ. | bn.liy. | yd‘. | šmn. | ‘dy. | ‘nbr. | aẖrm. | bn.qrdy. | bn.šm‘n. | bn.ǵlmy. | ǵly. | bn.dnn. | bn.rmy. | dll. | mny. | krty. | bn. 2117.3.32
b.rb ‘šrt.m[r]yn. | pǵdn.ilb‘l.krwn.lbn.‘dn. | ẖyrn.md‘. | šm‘n.rb ‘šrt.kkln.‘bd.abṣn. | šdyn.unn.dqn. | ‘bd‘nt.rb ‘šrt.mn 2011.5

šm‘nt

.mrnn. | a[--.---.-]‘n. | ml[--.---]. | ar[--.---.--]l. | aty[n.bn.]šm‘nt. | ḥnn[.bn].pls. | abrš[p.bn.]ẖrpn. | gmrš[.bn].mrnn. | ‘b 102[323].4.4

šm‘rg

m kbd[.-] l alpm mrim. | ṯṯ ddm l ṣin mrat. | ‘šr ddm.l šm‘rgm. | ‘šr ddm.l bt. | ‘šrm.dd.l mẖṣm. | ddm l kbs. | dd l pr 1100.3

šm‘rgm

n.yp‘n.ṯ[--]. | yṣḥm.b d.ubn.krwn.tǵd.[m]nḥm. | ‘pṯrm.šm‘rgm.skn.qrt. | ḥgbn.šm‘.skn.qrt. | nǵr krm.‘bdadt.b‘ln.yp‘ 2011.10

šmrm

. | abǵl.aḏ[ddy]. | abǵl.a[---]. | rbil.[---]. | kḏyn.[---.-]gṯ. | šmrm.a[ḏdd]y.tb[--]. | ynḥm.aḏddy. | ǵdǵd.aḏddy. | sw.aḏddy 2014.29
.ssm. | bn.ẖnn. | [--]ny. | [bn].ṯrdnt. | [bn].hyadt. | [--]lt. | šmrm. | p‘ṣ.bn.byy.‘šrt. 1047.24
.arb[‘.]ql‘m. | b[n.]ad‘l.q[š]t.w.ql‘. | b[n].ilyn.qšt.w.ql‘. | šmrm.ql‘. | ubr‘y. | abmn.qšt.w.ṯn.ql‘m. | qdmn.ṯt.qštm.w.ṯlṯ. 119[321].2.48
ll.b d.gmrd. | [šd.bn.-]ll.b d.iwrẖṯ. | [šd.bn.-]nn.b d.bn.šmrm. | [šd.bn.-]ṯtayy.b d.ṯṯmd. | [šd.bn.-]rn.b d.ṣdqšlm. | [šd. 82[300].1.26
. | w nḥl h. | atn.bn.ap[s]n. | nsk.ṯlṯ. | bn.[--.]m[-]ẖr. | bn.šmrm. | ṯnnm. | [ar]swn.bn.qqln. | m[--].bn.qqln. | ‘bdil[-].bn.q 85[80].3.10
bnšm.dt.[---]. | krws.l.y[--.---]. | yp‘.l[.---]. | šmr[m.---]. | [-----]. | bn.g[r.---]. | ḏmry[.---]. | bn.pdr.l.[---]. 2122.4

šmt

.‘šrt.ksp h. | ẖmšt.ẖrṣ.bt.il. | b.ẖmšt.‘šrt.ksp. | ẖmš.mat.šmt. | b.‘šrt.ksp. | ‘šr.ṣin.b.ṯṯt.w.kmsk. | arb‘[.k]dwṯm.w.ṯt.ṯpr 2100.7
.tš‘t.ksp. | mšlt.b.ṯql.ksp. | kdwṯ.l.grgyn.b.ṯq[l]. | ẖmšm.šmt.b.ṯql. | kkr.w.[ml]tḥ.tyt.[---]. | [b]šb‘[m.w.n]ṣp.ksp. | [tg 2101.25
.‘šr h. | [---.iqn]i.l.ṯrmn.qrt. | [---.]lbš.ẖmšm.iqnu. | [---].šmt.ẖmšt.ẖndlt. | [---.iqn]i.l.[-]k.btbt. | [---.l.ṯrm]nm.š[b‘].ma 1106.17
ẖpn.d.iqni.w.šmt. | l.iyb‘l. | ṯlṯm.l.mit.š‘rt. | l.šr.‘ṯrt. | mlbš.ṯrmnm. | k.ytn. 1107.1
[---.-]nd.l.mlbš.ṯrmnm. | [---]h.lbš.allm.lbnm. | [---].all.šmt. | [---].all.iqni.arb‘m.kbl. | [---].iqni.‘šrm.ǵprt. | [---.š]pšg.i 1106.5
[---.--]mn. | [---].ḥdṯ. | [---.š]mt. | [---].y[--.--]m. | [---.--]n.d[--.--]i. | [--]t.mdt h[.l.]‘ṯtrt.šd. 1106.49

šmtr

[b yr]ẖ[.r]išyn.b ym.ḥdṯ. | [šmtr].uṯkl.l il.šlmm. | b [ṯlṯt].‘šrt.yrtḥṣ.mlk. | br[r.]b a[r]b‘t.‘š APP.II[173].2
b yrẖ.[rišyn.b ym.ḥdṯ]. | šmtr.[uṯkl.l il.šlmm]. | b ṯlṯt ‘[šrt.yrtḥṣ.mlk.brr]. | b arb‘[t.‘šrt 35[3].2

šn

t.l kḥṯ]. | drkt h[.---]. | [---.]d[--.---]. | [---].hn[.---]. | [---.]šn[.---]. | [---].pit. | [---.]qbat. | [---.]inšt. | [--]u.l tštql. | [---].ṯry. 6[49].6.38
[---.]ḥlmt.alp.šnt.w[.---]. | šntm.alp.d krr[.---]. | alp.pr.b‘l.[---]. | w prt.tkt.[---]. | šnt.[---]. 2158.1.2

mtm.dbṭ[.---].|tr‘.tr‘n.a[--.---].|bnt.šdm.ṣḥr[.---].|šb‘.šnt.il.mla.[-].|w ṯmn.nqpnt.‘d.|k lbš.km.lpš.dm a[ḫ h].|km 12[75].2.45
n k.ḥtk k.nmrt k.b tk.|ugrt.l ymt.špš.w yrḫ.|w n‘mt.šnt.il. UG5.2.2.12
‘pt.šmm.|ṭbḫ.alpm.ap ṣin.šql.ṯrm.|w mri ilm.‘glm.dt.šnt.|imr.qmṣ.llim.k ksp.|l ‘brm.zt.ḫrṣ.l ‘brm.kš.|dpr.ṯlḥn.b 22.2[124].13
l h.ṭbḫ.alpm[.ap].|ṣin.šql.ṯrm[.w]m|ria.il.‘glm.d[t].|šnt.imr.qmṣ.l[l]im.|ṣḥ.aḫ h.b bht h.a[r]y h.|b qrb hkl h.ṣḥ. 4[51].6.43
--.---].|ṭbḫ.alp[m.ap.ṣin.šql].|ṯrm.w [mri.ilm.‘glm.dt.šnt].|imr.[qmṣ.llim.---]. 1[‘NT.X].4.31
.iṯtl.|l mnn.ilm.|tǵr k.tšlm k.|t‘zz k.alp ymm.|w rbt.šnt.|b ‘d ‘lm...gn‘.|iršt.aršt.|l aḫ y.l r‘ y.dt.|w ytnnn.|l aḫ 1019.1.5
kdd.dnil.|mt.rpi.l ymm.l yrḫm.|l yrḫm.l šnt.‘d.|šb‘t.šnt.ybk.l aq|ht.ǵzr.yd[m‘.]l kdd.|dnil.mt.r[pi.mk].b šb‘.|šn 19[1AQHT].4.177
m.|w tqrb.w ld.bn.l h.|w tqrb.w ld.bnt.l h.|mk.b šb‘.šnt.|bn.krt.km hm.tdr.|ap.bnt.ḥry.|km hm.w ṯḥss.aṯrt.|nd 15[128].3.22
ybk.l aq|ht.ǵzr.yd[m‘.]l kdd.|dnil.mt.r[pi.mk].b šb‘.|šnt.w y‘n[.dnil.mt.]rpi.|ytb.ǵzr.m[t.hrnmy.y]šu.|g h.w yṣḥ. 19[1AQHT].4.180
kḥṯ.drkt h.|l [ym]m.l yrḫm.l yrḫm.|l šnt.[m]k.b šb‘.|šnt.w [--].bn.ilm.mt.|‘m.aliyn.b‘l.yšu.|g h.w yṣḥ.‘l k.b[‘]l m 6[49].5.9
[---.]ḫlmt.alp.šnt.w[.---].|šntm.alp.d krr[.---].|alp.pr.b‘l.[---].|w prt.tkt.[-- 2158.1.1
.y bn.yṯbr.ḥrn.|riš k.‘ṯtrt.šm.b‘l.|qdqd k.tqln.b gbl.|šnt k.b ḥpn k.w t‘n.|spr ilmlk ṯ‘y. 16.6[127].58
rn].|riš k.‘ṯtrt.[šm.b‘l.qdqd k.---].|[--]t.mṯ.tpln.b g[bl.šnt k.---].|[--]šnm.aṯtm.t[--.---].|[m]lakm.ylak.ym.[t‘dt.ṯpṭ. 2.1[137].9
.ḥpn.l.azzlt.|[---.]l.‘ṯtrt.šd.|[---].yb‘lnn.|[---.--]n.b.ṯlṯ.šnt.l.nṣd.|[---.--]ršp.mlk.k.ypdd.mlbš.|u---].mlk.ytn.mlbš.| 1106.57
m.qrb.apq.thmtm].|[ygly.]ḏl i[l].w ybu[.q]rš.mlk[.ab.šnm.l p‘n.il.]|[yhbr.]w yql[.y]šṯḥw[y.]w ykb[dn h.--]r y[---]. 2.3[129].5
.tk ḫrš[n.---.tk.ǵr.ks].|ygly ḏd.i[l.w ybu.qrš.mlk].|ab.šnm.l [p‘n.il.yhbr.w yql].|yšṯḥwy.[w ykbdn h.---].|ṯr.il[.ab 1[‘NT.IX].3.24
.nhrm.|qrb.apq.thmtm.|tgly.ḏd.il.w tbu.|qrš.mlk.ab.šnm.|l p‘n.il.thbr.w tql.|tšṯḥwy.w tkbd h.|hlm.il.k yphn h. 4[51].4.24
rm.qrb.|[a]pq.thmtm.tgly.ḏd.|il.w tbu.qrš..|mlk.ab.šnm.l p‘n.|il.thbr.w tql.|tšṯḥwy.w tkbdn h.|tšu.g h.w tṣḥ.tš 6.1.36[49.1.8]
hrm.|[qrb.ap]q.thmtm tgly.ḏd il.|[w tbu.qr]š.mlk.ab.šnm.|[l p‘n.il.t]hbr.w tql.tšṯḥ|[wy.w tkbd]n h.tlšn.aqht.ǵzr. 17[2AQHT].6.49
.at.|ht[.---.]špš.b‘l k.|yd‘m.l.yd‘t.|‘m y.špš.b‘l k.|šnt.šntm.lm.l.tlk.|w.lḥt.akl.ky.|likt.‘m.špš.|b‘l k.ky.akl.|b.ḫwt 2060.16
i.mlk h.|[---].l kḥṯ.drkt h.|l [ym]m.l yrḫm.l yrḫm.|l šnt.[m]k.b šb‘.|šnt.w [--].bn.ilm.mt.|‘m.aliyn.b‘l.yšu.|g h.w 6[49].5.8
šlm[.---].|bt.l bnš.trg[m.---].|l šlmt.l šlm.b[--.---]|b y.šnt.mlit.t[--.---].|ymǵy k.bnm.ta[--.---].|[b]nm.w bnt.ytn k[. 59[100].7
]b.[ap]q.|[thm]tm.tgl.ḏ[d.]i[l.]w tbu.|[qr]š.m[l]k.ab[.šnm.]mṣr.|[t]bu.ḏdm.qn[-.-]n[-.-]lt.|ql h.yš[m‘].ṯr.[il].ab h.[3[‘NT.VI].5.16
.|[qrb.apq.thmtm].|[tgly.ḏd.il.w]tb[a].|[qrš.mlk.ab.]šnm.|[tša.g hm.w tṣ]ḥ.sbn.|[---]l[.---.]‘d.|ksm.mhyt[.m]ǵny 5[67].6.2
ǵzr.ydm‘.l kdd.dnil.|mt.rpi.l ymm.l yrḫm.|l yrḫm.l šnt.‘d.|šb‘t.šnt.ybk.l aq|ht.ǵzr.yd[m‘.]l kdd.|dnil.mt.r[pi.m 19[1AQHT].4.176
.ǵzr.|irš ḥym.w atn k.bl mt.|w ašlḥ k.aššpr k.‘m.b‘l.|šnt.‘m.bn il.tspr.yrḫm.|k b‘l.k yḥwy.y‘šr.ḥwy.y‘š.|r.w yšqy 17[2AQHT].6.29
ly.‘rpt.b |ḥm.un.yr.‘rpt.|tmṭr.b qẓ.ṭl.ytll.|l ǵnbm.šb‘.šnt.|yṣr k.b‘l.ṯmn.rkb.|‘rpt.bl.ṭl.bl rbb.|bl.šr‘.thmtm.bl.|ṭb 19[1AQHT].1.42
lt h.at.|ht[.---.]špš.b‘l k.|yd‘m.l.yd‘t.|‘m y.špš.b‘l k.|šnt.šntm.lm.l.tlk.|w.lḥt.akl.ky.|likt.‘m.špš.|b‘l k.ky.akl.|b. 2060.16
ašld.šu.‘db.tk.mdbr qdš.|ṯm tgrgr.l abnm.w l.‘ṣm.šb‘.šnt.|tmt.ṯmn.nqpt.‘d.ilm.n‘mm.ttlkn.|šd.tṣdn.pat.mdbr.w 23[52].66
l.a[--]t.tšknn.|ḫmšm.l mi[t].any.|tškn[n.--]h.k[--].|w šnm[.--.]w[.--].|w ‘prm.a[--.--]n.|[--.]ḥ[--.]d[--]t.|[---.]ḥw[t.- 2062.1.6
.|šntm.alp.d krr[.---].|alp.pr.b‘l.[---].|w prt.tkt.[---].|šnt.[---].|šsw.‘ṯtrt.w šsw.‘[nt.---].|w ht.[--]k.šsw[.-]rym[.---]. 2158.1.5
[--]t.ilhnm.b šnt.|[---.]šb‘.mat.š‘rt.ḫmšm.kbd.|[---.-]nd.l.mlbš.ṯrmnm.|[- 1106.1
k.k qlt[.---].|[--]at.brt.lb k.‘nn.[---].|[--.]šdq.k ttn.l y.šn[.---].|[---.]bn.rgm.w yd‘[.---]. 60[32].5
|šb‘.lbšm.allm.|l ušḫry.|ṯlṯ.mat.pṯtm.|l.mgmr.b.ṯlṯ.|šnt. 1107.13

šna

.ilm.štt.|p[--].b ṯlḥn y.qlt.|b ks.ištyn h.|dm.ṯn.dbḥm.šna.b‘l.ṯlṯ.|rkb.‘rpt.dbḥ.|btt.w dbḥ.w dbḥ.|dnt.w dbḥ.tdm 4[51].3.17
q[.---.td‘].|qdm ym.bmt.[nhr].|tṯṯn.ib.b‘l.tiḫd.|y‘rm.šnu.hd.gpt.|ǵr.w y‘n.aliyn.|b‘l.ib.hdt.lm.tḥš.|lm.tḥš.nṯq.d 4[51].7.36

šnw

.ap.mṯn.rgmm.|argmn.lk.lk.‘nn.ilm.|atm.bštm.w an.šnt.|uǵr.l rḥq.ilm.inbb.|l rḥq.ilnym.ṯn.mṯpdm.|tḥt.‘nt.arṣ.ṯ 3[‘NT].4.77
.---].|w y‘n.kṯr.w ḫss[.lk.lk.‘nn.ilm.]|atm.bštm.w an[.šnt.kptr].|l rḥq.ilm.ḥkp[t.l rḥq.ilnym].|ṯn.mṯpdm.tḥt.[‘nt.a 1[‘NT.IX].3.18
‘nt.hlkt.w.šnwt.|tp.aḫ.h.k.ysmsm.|tspi.šir.h.l.bl.ḥrb.|tšt.dm.h.l.bl.ks. RS225.1

šnl

‘l.alpm.bnš.yd.|titṯm[n].w.‘l.[---].|[-]rym.t[i]ṯtmn.|šnl.bn.ṣ[q]n.š[--].|yiṯtm.w.b[--].|yšlm.|[‘]šrm.ks[p].yš[lm]. 2104.4

šnm

il b[n] il.|dr bn il.|mpḫrt bn il.|ṯrmn w šnm.|il w aṯrt.|ḫnn il.|nṣbt il.|šlm il.|il ḥš il add.|b‘l ṣpn 30[107].4
‘m.dqt.ṯ‘m.|mtntm nkbd.alp.š.l il.|gdlt.ilhm.ṯkmn.w šnm dqt.|ršp.dqt.šrp w šlmm.dqtm.|[i]lh.alp w š ilhm.gdl[t 34[1].3
[---].|w al[p.l]il.w bu[rm.---].|ytk.gdlt.ilhm.[ṯkmn.w šnm].|dqt.ršp.šrp.w š[lmm.dqtm].|ilh[.a]lp.w š[.il]hm.[gdlt 35[3].12
--]n[.w alp.l il.w bu]|[rm.---.ytk.gdlt.ilhm].|ṯkmn.w [šnm.dqt.ršp.šrp].|w šlmm.[dqtm.ilh.alp.w š].|ilhm.gd[lt.ilh APP.II[173].14
l[mm.--.dqt].|[i]lh.gdlt[.ilhm.gdlt.il].|[d]qt.ṯkmn.w [šnm.dqt.--].|[--]t.dqtm.[b nbk.---].|[--.k]mm.gdlt.l.b[‘l.---].| 35[3].31
-].|[---.--]t.r[šp.šrp.w šl]|[mm.---].dq[t.ilh.gdlt].|n.w šnm.dqt[.---].|[i]lh[m.gd]lt.i[l.dqt.ṯkm]|n.w šnm.dqt[.---].| APP.II[173].34
lt].|n.w šnm.dqt[.---].|[i]lh[m.gd]lt.i[l.dqt.ṯkm]|n.w šnm.dqt[.---].|bqtm.b nbk.[---].|kmm.gdlt.l b[‘l.--.dqt].|l ṣp APP.II[173].34
[t]ši.l ab.bn.il.ytši.l dr.|bn il.l mpḫrt.bn.il.l ṯkmn[.w]šnm.hn.‘r.|w.ṯb.l mspr.m[šr] mšr.bt.ugrt.w npy.gr.|ḥmyt.u 32[2].1.26
ši.l ab bn il.|ytši.l d[r.bn il.l]mpḫrt.bn il.|l ṯkm[n.w šnm.]hn ‘[r].|[---.]w npy[.---].|[---.]w npy.u[grt.---].|[---.--] 32[2].1.35
tši[.l ab.bn.il].|ytši.l dr.bn.il.l mpḫrt.bn.i[l.l ṯkmn.w š]nm hn š.|w šqrb.‘r.mšr mšr bn.ugrt.w [npy.---.]ugr.|w np 32[2].1.17
tši.l ab.bn.il.ytši.l d]r.bn[.il].|[l mpḫrt.bn.il.l ṯkmn.w šnm.hn š].|[w šqrb.š.mšr mšr.bn.ugrt.w npy.---.]w npy.|[--- 32[2].1.3
[ši.l ab.bn.il].|[ytši.l dr.bn.il.l mpḫ]rt.[bn.il.l ṯkmn.w šn]m hn š.|[---.w n]py.gr[.ḥmyt.ugrt.w np]y.|[---].w n[py.-- 32[2].1.9B
.‘d škr.|il.hlk.l bt h.yštql.|l ḥṭr h.y‘msn.nn.ṯkmn.|w šnm.w ngšnn.ḥby.|b‘l.qrnm w ḏnb.ylšn.|b ḫri h.w ṯnt h.ql. UG5.1.1.19
dgn.w b‘l.|‘ṯ w kmṯ.|yrḫ w ksa.|yrḫ mkṯy.|ṯkmn w šnm.|kṯr w ḫss.|‘ṯr ‘ṯpr.|šḥr w šlm.|ngh w srr.|‘dw šr.|ṣ UG5.10.1.8
.|[i]lh.alp w š ilhm.gdl[t.]ilhm.|[b]‘l š.aṯrt.š.ṯkmn w šnm.š.|‘nt.š.ršp.š.dr il w p[ḫ]r b‘l.|gdlt.šlm.gdlt.w burm.[l] 34[1].6
h[.a]lp.w š[.il]hm.[gdlt.ilhm].|b‘[l.š].aṯrt[.š.ṯkm]n w [šnm.š].|‘nt š ršp š[.dr.il.w pḫr.b‘l].|gdlt.šlm[.gdlt.w burm.l 35[3].15

tm.ilh.alp.w š]. | ilhm.gd[lt.ilhm.bʿl.š.aṯrt.š]. | ṯkmn.w š[nm.š.ʿnt.š.ršp.š.dr]. | il.w pẖr[.bʿl.gdlt.šlm.gdlt]. | w burm.l APP.II[173].17

šnmtm

t n m.yšẖn.[---]. | qrn h.km.ǵb[-.---]. | hw km.ḥrr[.---]. | šnmtm.dbṯ[.---]. | trʿ.trʿn.a[--.---]. | bnt.šdm.ṣḥr[.---]. | šbʿ.šnt.i 12[75].2.42

šnn

tlm.km[.---.]yd h.k šr. | knr.uṣbʿt h ḥrṣ.abn. | p h.tiḥd.šnt h.w akl.bqmm. | tšt ḥrṣ.k lb ilnm. | w ṯn.gprm.mn gpr h.š 19[1AQHT].1.9

yṯbr.bʿl.yṯbr.diy. | hmt.hm.tʿpn.ʿl.qbr.bn y. | tšẖṭann.b šnt h.qr.[mym]. | mlk.yṣm.y l km.qr.mym.d ʿ[l k]. | mẖṣ.aqht 19[1AQHT].3.151

. | [k]rt.bnm.il.špḥ. | lṯpn.w qdš.ʿl. | ab h.yʿrb.ybky. | w yšnn.ytn.g h. | bky.b ḥy k.ab n.ašmẖ. | b l.mt k.ngln.k klb. | b 16.1[125].13

h.šbʿ[.---]. | ǵzr.ilḥu.t[---]l. | trm.tṣr.trm[.ʿ]tqt. | tbky.w tšnn.[tt]n. | g h.bky.b ḥ[y k.a]b n. | nšmẖ.b l.mt k.ngln. | k kl 16.2[125].97

m.yr.klyt h.w lb h. | [ṯ]n.p k.b ǵr.ṯn.p k.b ẖlb.k tgwln.šnt k. | [--.]w špt k.l tššy.hm.tqrm.l mt.b rn k. | [--]ẖp.an.arn 1001.1.4

šns

rm.ṯn.ym. | tš[.---.]ymm.lk. | hrg.ar[bʿ.]ymm.bṣr. | kp.šsk k.[--].l ḥbš k. | ʿtk.ri[š.]l mhr k. | w ʿp.l dr[ʿ].nšr k. | w rbṣ. 13[6].6

h.k irbym.kp.k.qṣm. | ǵrmn.kp.mhr.ʿtkt. | rišt.l bmt h.šnst. | kpt.b ḥbš h.brkm.tǵl[l]. | b dm.ḏmr.ḥlqm.b mm[ʿ]. | m 3[ʿNT].2.12

[---.šnst.kpt.b ḥb]š h.ʿtkt r[išt]. | [l bmt h.---.]hy bt h tʿrb. | [---.t 7.1[131].2

šnp

ʿṯtrt[.---]. | [--.]l ilt.š l ʿṯt[rt.---]. | [ʿ]ṣr.l pdr ṯṯ.ṣ[in.---]. | tšnpn.ʿlm.km[m.---]. | w.l ll.ʿṣrm.w [---]. | kmm.w.in.ʿṣr[.---]. 38[23].6

šnpt

bʿl alp w š. | dgn.š.il tʿḏr.š. | bʿl š.ʿnt š.ršp š. | šlmm. | w šnpt.il š. | l ʿnt.ḥl š.ṯn šm. | l gṯrm.ǵṣ b šmal. | d alpm.w alp w UG5.13.24

urm.[l]b. | rmṣt.ilhm.bʿlm.dṯt.w kšm.ẖmš. | ʿṯr h.mlun.šnpt.ḥṣt h.bʿl.ṣpn š. | [--]ṯ š.ilt.mgdl š.ilt.asrm š. | w l ll.šp. pg 34[1].10

šʿd

b i[--.---]. | l ṯ[--.---]. | ks[.---]. | kr[pn.---]. | at.š[ʿtqt.---]. | šʿd[.---]. | rt.[---]. | ʿṯr[.---]. | b p.š[---]. | il.p.d[---]. | ʿrm.[di.mh. 16[126].5.43

šʿl

.y[ṯ]b. | [---]p.gp ym.w yṣǵd.gp..thm. | [yqḥ.]il.mštʿltm.mštʿltm.l riš.agn. | hl h.[t]špl.hl h.trm.hl h.tṣḥ.ad ad. | w hl h 23[52].31

k mdb.ark.yd.il.k ym. | w yd.il.k mdb.yqḥ.il.mštʿltm. | mštʿltm.l riš.agn.yqḥ.tš.b bt h. | il.ẖṭ h.nḥt.il.ymnn.mṭ.yd h. 23[52].36

y. | [---].y[ṯ]b. | [---]p.gp ym.w yṣǵd.gp..thm. | [yqḥ.]il.mštʿltm.mštʿltm.l riš.agn. | hl h.[t]špl.hl h.trm.hl h.tṣḥ.ad a 23[52].31

. | w yd il.k mdb.ark.yd.il.k ym. | w yd.il.k mdb.yqḥ.il.mštʿltm. | mštʿltm.l riš.agn.yqḥ.tš.b bt h. | il.ẖṭ h.nḥt.il.ymnn 23[52].35

šʿn

--]. | w.b.p[.--]. | apš[ny]. | b.yṣi h. | ḥwt.[---]. | alp.k[sp]. | tšʿn. | w.hm.al[-]. | l.tšʿn. | mṣrm. | tmkrn. | ypḥ.ʿbdilt. | bn.m. | 2116.12

ny]. | b.yṣi h. | ḥwt.[---]. | alp.k[sp]. | tšʿn. | w.hm.al[-]. | l.tšʿn. | mṣrm. | tmkrn. | ypḥ.ʿbdilt. | bn.m. | ypḥ.ilšlm. | bn.prqd 2116.14

šʿr

[ṯ]mnym.dd. | šʿrm.b.ṯydr. 1166.2

.w yʿn[.dn] | il.mt.rpi npš ṯḥ[.pǵt]. | ṯ[km]t.mym.ḥspt.l šʿr. | ṭl.ydʿt.hlk.kbkbm. | a[-]ḥ.hy.mẖ.tmẖṣ.mẖṣ[.aḫ k]. | tkl. 19[1AQHT].4.199

y dt ksp. | dt.yrq.nqbn y.tš[mʿ]. | pǵt.ṯkmt.my.ḥspt.l[š]r.ṭl. | ydʿt.hlk.kbkbm. | bkm.tmdln.ʿr. | bkm.tṣmd.pḥl.bkm. 19[1AQHT].2.55

y]. | gm.l bt[h.dnil.k yṣḥ]. | šmʿ.pǵt.ṯkmt[.my]. | ḥspt.l šʿr.ṭl.yd[ʿt]. | hlk.kbkbm.mdl.ʿr. | ṣmd.pḥl.št.gpn y dt ksp. | dt 19[1AQHT].2.51

ṯtbnm. | šbʿm.dd.ṯn.kbd. | tgmr.ḥṭm.šbʿ.ddm. | ẖmš.dd.šʿrm. | kdm.yn. | kdm.ṣmṣ. 1099.33

ddm.l.trbnn. | ddm.šʿrm.l.trbnn. | ddm.šʿrm.l.ẖtn. | dd.šʿrm.l.ḥmr.ḥṭb. | dd.ḥṭm.l.ẖḏǵb. | ṯṯ.ddm.l.gzzm. | kd yn.l.ẖtn 1099.24

ṯmn.ddm šʿrm.l ḥmrm. 1165.1

.kšmm.l.ẖtn. | ddm.l.trbnn. | ddm.šʿrm.l.trbnn. | ddm.šʿrm.l.ẖtn. | dd.šʿrm.l.ḥmr.ḥṭb. | dd.ḥṭm.l.ẖḏǵb. | ṯṯ.ddm.l.gzz 1099.23

rwn b.gt.nbk. | ddm.kšmm.l.ẖtn. | ddm.l.trbnn. | ddm.šʿrm.l.trbnn. | ddm.šʿrm.l.ẖtn. | dd.šʿrm.l.ḥmr.ḥṭb. | dd.ḥṭm.l. 1099.22

išr. | ẖmš.ktnt. | ẖmš.ṯnt.alpm. | ʿšrm.hbn. | ṯlṯ.mat.dd. | šʿrm. | mit.šmn. | ʿšr.kat. | ẓrw. 2102.8

[---]. | [mi]tm.ẖmšm.ẖmš.k[bd]. | [dd].kšmm.tš[.---]. | [š]ʿrm.ṯṯ.ʿ[šr]. | [dd].ḥṭm.w.ẖ[mšm]. | [ṯ]lṯ kbd.yn.b [gt.---]. | m 2092.8

.ṯṯ.mat.nṣ. | [---].ẖmšm.ḥmr.škm. | [---.ṯṯ.dd.]gdl.ṯṯ.dd.šʿrm. | [---.a]lp.arbʿ.mat.tyt. | [---.kd.]nbt.k[d.]šmn.mr. | [---.l] 142[12].13

.ṯlṯm.ʿṣr. | [---].ẖmš[m.ḥm]r.škm. | [---.ṯṯ.dd.]gdl.ṯṯ.dd.šʿrm. | [---.hn.w.al]p.kd.nbt.kd.šmn.mr. | [---].kmn.lṯḥ.sbbyn. 142[12].7

[---.]ksp dd qmḥ. | [---.]ṯlṯ dd ksmm. | [---.-]rbr dd šʿrm. | [---.]r[--.]ḥṭm. | kr[--.]tp[n]. | kkr[.---]. | kkr[.---]. | kkr[.- 2037.1.3

[---.]ṯṯ.dd.gdl.ṯṯ.dd.šʿrm. | [---.-]hn.w.alp.kd.nbt.kd.šmn.mr. | [---.]arbʿ.mat.ẖswn 142[12].1

t.m[--.---]. | [--.mi]tm nṣ.[-]ṯ[-]gr[-.---]. | [---].arb[ʿ.d]d.š[ʿrm.---]. | [--.-]rṯm š[šm]n.k[--.---]. | [---.ar]bʿ.dblt.ḏr[--.---]. 143[-].1.7

kbd. | [kš]mm. | [ʿ]š[r]m.ṯn.kbd.ḥṭm. | [-]m[-.-]ʿ[-.-]ag šʿrm. | [---.--]mi. | [--.]ṯṯ[m] šbʿ.k[bd]. | [---]m.b.mril. 2091.6

[---]t.ddm.šʿr[m.---]. | [---].mit.ẖsw.[---]. | [----]d.nʿr.ṯ[--]d[.---]. | [---.]ṯlṯ. 143[-].1.1

šʿrt

spr.rʿym. | lqḥ.šʿrt. | anntn. | ʿdn. | sdwn. | mztn. | ẖyrn. | šdn. | [ʿš]rm.ṯn kbd. | 2098.2

n.šʿrt. | ʿpṯn.šʿrt. | ʿbd.yrẖ šʿrt. | ẖbd.ṯr yṣr šʿr. | pdy.yṣr šʿrt. | atnb.ḥr. | šʿrt.šʿrt. 97[315].12

.kbd.ʿšrt.mzn h. | b [ar]bʿm.ksp. | b d[.ʿb]dym.ṯlṯ.kkr šʿrt. | iqn[i]m.ṯṯt.ʿšrt.ksp h. | ẖmšt.ẖrṣ.bt.il. | b.ẖmšt.ʿšrt.ksp. | 2100.3

h. | [-----]. | [-]bʿl. | [--]m. | [mʿ]rby. | mʿr. | arny. | ʿnqpat. | šʿrt. | ubrʿy. | ilštmʿ. | šbn. | tbq. | rqd. | [š]rš. | [-----]. | [-----]. | [--- 2058.1.13

lqḥ.šʿrt. | urẖ.ln.kkrm. | w.rḥd.kd.šmn. | drt.b.kkr. | ubn.ẖṣḥ.kkr. 1118.1

.ʿšr[m.]ksp. | ẖmš.kkr.ṣml. | b.ʿšrt.b d.bn.kyn. | ʿšr.kkr.šʿrt. | b d.urtn.b.arbʿm. | arbʿt.ʿšrt.ẖrṣ. | b.ṯqlm.kbd.arbʿm. | ʿšr 2100.14

šlmt. | šdyn.ššlmt. | prtwn.šʿrt. | ṯṯn.šʿrt. | ʿdn.šʿrt. | mnn.šʿrt. | bdn.šʿrt. | ʿpṯn.šʿrt. | ʿbd.yrẖ šʿrt. | ẖbd.ṯr yṣr šʿr. | pdy.yṣ 97[315].7

.qš[t]. | rkby. | bn.knn.qšt. | pbyn.qšt. | yddn.qšt.w.qlʿ. | šʿrt. | bn.il.qšt.w.qlʿ. | ark.qšt.w.qlʿ. | bn.ʿbdnkl.qšt.w.qlʿ. | bn.z 119[321].2.40

n.šʿrt. | ʿdn.šʿrt. | mnn.šʿrt. | bdn.šʿrt. | ʿpṯn.šʿrt. | ʿbd.yrẖ šʿrt. | ẖbd.ṯr yṣr šʿr. | pdy.yṣr šʿrt. | atnb.ḥr. | šʿrt.šʿrt. 97[315].10

ubr'y. | arny. | m'r. | š'rt. | ḫlb rpš. | bq't. | šḥq. | y'by. | mḫr. 65[108].4
| pd. | mlk. | ar. | atlg. | gb'ly. | ulm. | m'rby. | m'r. | arny. | š'rt. | ḫlbrpš. | hry. | qmṣ. | ṣ'q. | qmy. | ḫlbkrd. | y'rt. | uškn. | 'nq 2074.11
[--]t.ilhnm.b šnt. | [---.]šb'.mat.š'rt.ḫmšm.kbd. | [---.-]nd.l.mlbš.ṯrmnm. | [---]h.lbš.allm.lbn 1106.2
[---].b.ar. | špšyn[.---.]ytb.b.ar. | bn.ag[p]ṯ.ḫpṯ.d[.ytb.b].š'rt. | yly.bn.ṯrnq.[-]r.d.ytb.b.ilštm'. | ilšlm.bn.gs[-.--]r.d.ytb. 2015.1.25
.ḫpn. | l.ṣ[--].š'[rt]. | l.'dy.š[']r[t]. | ṯlṯ.l.'d.ab[ǵ]l. | l.ydln.š'rt. | l.kṯrmlk.ḫpn. | l.'bdil[m].ḫpn. | tmrtn.š'rt. | lmd.n.rn. | [- 1117.8
lm. | l.[---]mn ḫpn. | l[.--.]škn.ḫpn. | l.k[-]w.ḫpn. | l.ṣ[--].š'[rt]. | l.'dy.š[']r[t]. | ṯlṯ.l.'d.ab[ǵ]l. | l.ydln.š'rt. | l.kṯrmlk.ḫpn. 1117.5
ḫpn.d.iqni.w.šmt. | l.iyb'l. | ṯlṯm.l.mit.š'rt. | l.šr.'ṯtrt. | mlbš.ṯrmnm. | k.ytn.w.b.bt. | mlk.mlbš. | ytn.l 1107.3
l.'bdil[m].ḫpn. | tmrtn.š'rt. | lmd.n.rn. | [---].ḫpn. | dqn.š'rt. | [lm]d.yrṯ. | [-.]ynḥm.ḫpn. | ṯṯ.lmd.b'ln. | l.qḥ.ḫpnt. | ṯṯ[.-] 1117.14
[ǵ]l. | l.ydln.š'rt. | l.kṯrmlk.ḫpn. | l.'bdil[m].ḫpn. | tmrtn.š'rt. | lmd.n.rn. | [---].ḫpn. | dqn.š'rt. | [lm]d.yrṯ. | [-.]ynḥm.ḫpn 1117.11
nš.iwl[--.š]šlmt. | šdyn.ššlmt. | prtwn.š'rt. | ṯtn.š'rt. | 'dn.š'rt. | mnn.š'rt. | bdn.š'rt. | 'pṯn.š'rt. | 'bd.yrḫ š'rt. | ḫbd.ṯr yṣr š 97[315].6
nyn. | ddm.ḥ[tm].'l.šrn. | 'šrt.ksp.'l.[-]lpy. | bn.ady.kkr.š'rt. | nṯk h. | kb[d.]mn.'l.abršn. | b[n.---].kršu.nṯk h. | [---.--]m 1146.9
rtwn.š'rt. | ṯtn.š'rt. | 'dn.š'rt. | mnn.š'rt. | bdn.š'rt. | 'pṯn.š'rt. | 'bd.yrḫ š'rt. | ḫbd.ṯr yṣr š'r. | pdy.yṣr š'rt. | atnb.ḥr. | š'rt. 97[315].9
[šlmt]. | bnš.iwl[--.š]šlmt. | šdyn.ššlmt. | prtwn.š'rt. | ṯtn.š'rt. | 'dn.š'rt. | mnn.š'rt. | bdn.š'rt. | 'pṯn.š'rt. | 'bd.yrḫ š'rt. | ḫb 97[315].5
n.ššlmt. | prtwn.š'rt. | ṯtn.š'rt. | 'dn.š'rt. | mnn.š'rt. | bdn.š'rt. | 'pṯn.š'rt. | 'bd.yrḫ š'rt. | ḫbd.ṯr yṣr š'r. | pdy.yṣr š'rt. | atn 97[315].8
b'm.b ḫzr. | lqḥ š'rt. | ṯṯ 'šr h.lqḥ. | ḫlpnt. | ṯṯ.ḥrṯm. | lqḥ.š'rt. | 'šr.ḥrš. | bhtm.lqḥ. | š'rt. | arb'. | ḥrš qṯn. | lqḥ š'rt. | ṯṯ nsk. 2052.7
mnn.š'rt. | bdn.š'rt. | 'pṯn.š'rt. | 'bd.yrḫ š'rt. | ḫbd.ṯr yṣr š'r. | pdy.yṣr š'rt. | atnb.ḥr. | š'rt.š'rt. 97[315].11
r h.lqḥ. | ḫlpnt. | ṯṯ.ḥrṯm. | lqḥ.š'rt. | 'šr.ḥrš. | bhtm.lqḥ. | š'rt. | arb'. | ḥrš qṯn. | lqḥ š'rt. | ṯṯ nsk.ḥdm. | lqḥ.š'rt. 2052.10
.alp.ṯlṯ.l.ḫlby. | b d.tlmi.b.'šrm.ḫmšt. | kbd.ksp. | kkrm.š'rt.šṯt.b d.gg['t]. | b.'šrt.ksp. | ṯlṯ.uṯbm.b d.alḫn.b.'šrt[.k]sp. | 2101.9
bnšm.d.bu. | tš'.dt.tq[ḥn]. | š'rt. | šb' dt tqḥn. | ššlmt. 2099.3
. | ṯlṯt.w.ṯlṯt.ksp h. | arb'.kkr. | algbṯ.arb't. | ksp h. | kkr.š'rt. | šb't.ksp h. | ḫmš.mqdm.dnyn. | b.ṯql.dprn.aḥd. | b.ṯql. | ḫ 1127.17
-.-]qt.l.ṯrmnm. | [---].ṯlṯm.iqnu. | [---.l.]ṯrmn.mlk. | [---.]š'rt.šb'.'šr h. | [---.iqn]i.l.ṯrmn.qrt. | [---.]lbš.ḫmšm.iqnu. | [---] 1106.14
t. | 'bd.yrḫ š'rt. | ḫbd.ṯr yṣr š'r. | pdy.yṣr š'rt. | atnb.ḥr. | š'rt.š'rt. 97[315].14
[--]an.š[šlmt]. | bnš.iwl[--.š]šlmt. | šdyn.ššlmt. | prtwn.š'rt. | ṯtn.š'rt. | 'dn.š'rt. | mnn.š'rt. | bdn.š'rt. | 'pṯn.š'rt. | 'bd.yrḫ 97[315].4
| lqḥ.š'rt. | 'šr.ḥrš. | bhtm.lqḥ. | š'rt. | arb'. | ḥrš qṯn. | lqḥ š'rt. | ṯṯ nsk.ḥdm. | lqḥ.š'rt. 2052.13
aḥd.kbd. | arb'm.b ḫzr. | lqḥ š'rt. | ṯṯ 'šr h.lqḥ. | ḫlpnt. | ṯṯ.ḥrṯm. | lqḥ.š'rt. | 'šr.ḥrš. | bhtm.lq 2052.3
pld mḫ[--.---]. | ṯ[--] ḫpnt. | [---] kdwṯm.[---]. | ḫmš.pld š'rt. | ṯṯ pld pṯt. | arb' ḫpnt pṯt. | ḫmš ḫpnt.š'rt. | ṯlṯ.'šr kdwṯm. 1113.7
n ḫpn. | l[.--.]škn.ḫpn. | l.k[-]w.ḫpn. | l.ṣ[--].š'[rt]. | l.'dy.š[']r[t]. | ṯlṯ.l.'d.ab[ǵ]l. | l.ydln.š'rt. | l.kṯrmlk.ḫpn. | l.'bdil[m]. 1117.6
--]. | ḫmš.pld š'rt. | ṯṯ pld pṯt. | arb' ḫpnt pṯt. | ḫmš ḫpnt.š'rt. | ṯlṯ.'šr kdwṯm. 1113.10
š'rt. | [---.]tš'.kbd.skm. | [arb]'m.ḫpnt.pṯt. | [-]r.pldm.dt.š'rt. | ṯlṯm.ṯlṯ.kbd.mṣrrt. | 'šr.ṯn.kbd.pǵdrm. | ṯmn.mrbdt.mlk. 1111.8
.]bnšm. | m'rby.[---.--]m.ṯn[.---]. | m'r.[---]. | arny.[---]. | š'rt.ṯn[.---]. | bq't.[--].ḥ[mr.---]. | ḫlb krd.ḥ[mr.---]. | ṣ'.ḥmr.w[2040.11
qt. | w.mrdt.prqt.pṯt. | lbš.psm.rq. | ṯn.mrdt.az. | ṯlṯ.pld.š'rt. | ṯ[---].kbm. | p[---]r.aḥd. | [-----]. | [-----]. | [---.--]y. | [---.-]ṯt 1112.7
[m.---]. | w.l ll.'ṣrm.w [---]. | kmm.w.in.'ṣr[.---]. | w mit.š'rt.[-]y[-.---]. | w.kdr.w.npt t[--.---]. | w.ksp.y'db.[---]. 38[23].9
št.ḫndlt. | [---.iqn]i.l.[-]k.btbt. | [---.l.ṯrm]nm.š[b'].mat.š'rt. | [---.]iqnu.[---.]lbš.ṯrmnm. | [---.iqn]i.lbš.al[l.---]. | [---].ṯṯ. 1106.19
---]. | 'lm.kmm[.---]. | w b ṯlṯ.ṣ[in.---]. | l ll.pr[-.---]. | mit š'[rt.---]. | ptr.k[--.---]. | [-]yu[-.---]. 37[22].10
]kn. | [---.]ṯlṯm. | kuwṯ.ṯlṯ.kbd. | m[i]t.arb't.kbd. | ḫ[mš.]š'rt. | [---.]tš'.kbd.skm. | [arb]'m.ḫpnt.pṯt. | [-]r.pldm.dt.š'rt. | ṯ 1111.5
.---]. | [---.-]rt.ṯlṯm[.---]. | [--]l.ṯrmn.m[lk.---]. | [---.--]rt.š'rt[.---]. | [---.i]qni.l.ṯr[mn.art.---]. | [b.yr]ḫ.riš.yn.[---]. | [---.b' 1106.30
lk. | d.b d.prṯ. | tš'.l.'šrm. | lqḥ.ššlmt. | ṯmn.l.arb'm. | lqḥ.š'rt. 1025.6
m.lqḥ. | š'rt. | arb'. | ḥrš qṯn. | lqḥ š'rt. | ṯṯ nsk.ḥdm. | lqḥ.š'rt. 2052.15
d.mṣrrt. | 'šr.ṯn.kbd.pǵdrm. | ṯmn.mrbdt.mlk. | 'šr.pld.š'rt. 1111.12
bd.yrḫ š'rt. | ḫbd.ṯr yṣr š'r. | pdy.yṣr š'rt. | atnb.ḥr. | š'rt.š'rt. 97[315].14

š'rty

b'l.mlky. | n'mn.mṣry. | y'l.kn'ny. | gdn.bn.umy. | kn'm.š'rty. | abrpu.ubr'y. | b.gt.bn.ṯlṯ. | ild.b.gt.psḥn. 91[311].9
bdl.gt.bn.tbšn. | bn.mnyy.š'rty. | aryn.adddy. | agpṯr. | šb'l.mlky. | n'mn.mṣry. | y'l.kn'ny 91[311].2
y. | [bn].gmḥ. | [---]ty. | [b]n.ypy.gb'ly. | b[n].ḥyn. | dmn.š'rty. | bn.arwdn.ilšt'y. | bn grgs. | bn.ḥran. | bn.arš[w.b]ṣry. | b 99[327].1.7
bn.kdrn.uškny. | bn.lgn.uškny. | bn.abn.uškny. | bn.arz.š'rty. | bn.ibrd.m'rby. | ṣdqn.gb'ly. | bn.ypy.gb'ly. | bn.grgs.ilšt 87[64].25

š'ty

bn.ǵs.ḥrš.š'ty. | 'dy.bn.sl'y.gbly. | yrm.b'l.bn.kky. 2121.1

š'tqt

[m]t.dm.ḫt.š'tqt dm. | li.w ttb'.š'tqt. | bt.krt.bu.tbu. | bkt.tgly.w tbu. | nṣrt.tbu.pnm. | 'rm.tdu 16.6[127].2
ṣ.nn.b d't. | npš h.l lḥm.tptḥ. | brlt h.l ṯrm. | mt.dm.ḫt.š'tqt. | dm.lan.w ypqd. | krt.ṯ'.yšu.g h. | w yṣḥ.šm'.l mṯt. | ḥry. 16.6[127].13
[m]t.dm.ḫt.š'tqt dm. | li.w ttb'.š'tqt. | bt.krt.bu.tbu. | bkt.tgly.w tbu. | nṣrt 16.6[127].1
b i[--.---]. | l ṯ[--.---]. | ks[.---]. | kr[pn.---]. | at.š['tqt.---]. | š'd[.---]. | rt.[---]. | 'tr[.---]. | b p.š[---]. | il.p.d[---]. | ' 16[126].5.42

šp

šnpt.ḥṣt h.b'l.ṣpn š. | [--]ṯ š.ilt.mgdl š.ilt.asrm š. | w l ll.šp. pgr.w ṯrmnm.bt mlk. | il[bt].gdlt.ušḫry.gdlt.ym gdlt. | b'l 34[1].12
[---.]šlm. | [---.--]š.lalit. | [---.]bt šp.š. | y[-]lm.w mlk. | ynṣl.l ṯ'y. 2005.2.6

špḥ

n.ḥtk h. | krt y'n.ḥtk h.rš. | mid.grdš.ṯbt h. | w b tm hn.špḥ.yitbd. | w b.pḫyr h.yrṯ. | y'rb.b ḥdr h.ybky. | b ṯn.[-]gmm. 14[KRT].1.24
mlk.d mlk. | b ḥwt.špḥ. | l ydn.'bd.mlk. | d šṯ.'l.ḫrd h. | špḥ.al.thbṭ. | ḫrd.'ps.aḥd.kw | sgt. | ḫrd ksp.[--]r. | ymm.w[.---] 2062.2.5
[ṯl]ṯm.ksp.'[l]. | [b]n.bly.gb'ly. | [šp]ḥ.a[n]ntb. | w.m[--.u]škny. | [']š[r.---]t.ksp. | ['l.---]b bn[.--]. 2055.3
trbṣt.bn.amt. | p d.in.b bt y.ttn. | tn.l y.mṯt.ḥry. | n'mt.špḥ.bkr k. | d k.n'm.'nt.n'm h. | km.tsm.'ṯtrt.ts[m h]. | d 'q h.i 14[KRT].3.144

špḥ

---].|[---.]š[--].|w ym ym.yš|al.|w mlk.d mlk.|b ḥwt.špḥ.|l ydn.ʿbd.mlk.|d št.ʿl.ḫrd h.|špḥ.al.thbṭ.|ḫrd.ʿps.aḫd. 2062.2.2
šlw.b ṣp.ʿn h.|d b ḥlm y.il.ytn.|b ḏrt y.ab.adm.|w ld.špḥ.l krt.|w ǵlm.l ʿbd.il.|krt.yḫṭ.w ḥlm.|ʿbd.il.w hdrt.|yrtḥ 14[KRT].3.152
ʿp h.sp.ṯrml.|d b ḥlm y.il.ytn.|b ḏrt y.ab.adm.|w ld.špḥ.l krk|t.w ǵlm.l ʿbd.|il.ttbʿ.mlakm.|l yṯb.idk.pnm.|l ytn 14[KRT].6.298
ḫšt k.l ntn.|ʿtq.b d.aṯt.ab.ṣrry.|ik m.yrgm.bn.il.|krt.špḥ.lṭpn.|w qdš.u ilm.tmtn.|špḥ.lṭpn.l yḥ.|w yʿny.krt.ṯʿ.|b 16.1[125].21
qdš.nny.ḥ[l]m.adr.|ḥl.rḥb.mk[npt].|ap.krt bn[m.il].|špḥ.lṭpn[.w qdš].|bkm.tʿr[b.ʿl.ab h].|tʿrb.ḥ[--].|b ṯtm.t[---]. 16.2[125].111
lm.qdš.|any.ḥlm.adr.ḥl.|rḥb.mknpt.ap.|[k]rt.bnm.il.špḥ.|lṭpn.w qdš.ʿl.|ab h.yʿrb.ybky.|w yšnn.ytn.g h.|bky.b 16.1[125].10
.tmtn.|u ḫšt k.l bky.ʿtq.|b d.aṯt ab.ṣrry.|u ilm.tmtn.špḥ.|[l]ṭpn.l yḥ.t[b]ky k.|ab.ǵr.bʿl.ṣ[p]n.ḥlm.|qdš.nny.ḥ[l] 16.2[125].105
y.|ik m.yrgm.bn.il.|krt.špḥ.lṭpn.|w qdš.u ilm.tmtn.|špḥ.lṭpn.l yḥ.|w yʿny.krt.ṯʿ.|bn.al.tbkn.al.|tdm.l y.al tkl.bn 16.1[125].23

špk

.ʿnt.ʿl[.aqht].|tʿdbn h.hlmn.ṯnm[.qdqd].|ṯlṯ id.ʿl.udn.š[pk.km].|šiy.dm h.km.šḫ[ṭ.l brk h].|yṣat.km.rḥ.npš[h.km 18[3AQHT].4.34
rḫp.an[k.ʿ]l.|aqht.ʿdb k.hlmn.ṯnm.qdqd.|ṯlṯ id.ʿl.udn.špk.km.šiy.|dm.km.šḫṭ.l brk h.tṣi.km.|rḥ.npš h.km.iṯl.brlt 18[3AQHT].4.23
r[y.ǵlmm.b št.ǵr.---].|[ʿ]d tš[bʿ.tmtḫṣ.---].|klyn[.---].|špk.l[---].|trḥṣ.yd[h.---].|[--.]yṣt ḏm[r.---].|tšt[.r]imt.[l irt 7.2[130].7
b.qšt.bnt.|[---.ʿ]n h.km.bṯn.yqr.|[krpn h.-.l]arṣ.ks h.tšpk m.|[l ʿpr.tšu.g h.]w tṣḥ.šmʿ.mʿ.|[l aqht.ǵzr.i]rš.ksp.w a 17[2AQHT].6.15
-]nm[.--.]k.[--].w yḫnp[.---].|[---.]ylm.b[n.ʿ]n k.ṣmdm.špk[.---].|[---.]nt[-.]mbk kpt.w[.--].b g[--].|[---.]ḥ[--.]bnt.ṣʿṣ. 1001.1.16

špl

ǵd.gp..thm.|[yqḥ.]il.mštʿltm.mštʿltm.l riš.agn.|hl h.[t]špl.hl h.trm.hl h.tṣḥ.ad ad.|w hl h.tṣḥ.um.um.tirk m.yd.il 23[52].32

špm

.---].|w ysmm.bn.š[---].|ytnm.qrt.l ʿly[.---].|b mdbr.špm.yd[.---.---]r.|l riš hm.w yš[--.--]m.|lḥm.b lḥm ay.w šty. 23[52].4
r.|[---.--]m.ymt m.|[---].k iṯl.|[---.--]m.ʿdb.l arṣ.|[---.]špm.ʿdb.|[---].tʿtqn.|[---.-]ʿb.idk.|[l ytn.pnm.tk.]in.bb.b alp 1[ʿNT.IX].2.11

špr

kpṯ.w ʿnt.di.dit.rḫpt.|[---.-]rm.aklt.ʿgl.ʿl.mšt.|[---.--]r.špr.w yšt.il.|[---.--]n.il ǵnṯ.ʿgl il.|[---.--]d.il.šd yṣd mlk.|[---] UG5.2.1.10

špš

tḥm.špš.|l.ʿmrpi.rgm.|ʿm špš.kll.mid m.|šlm.|l.[--]n.špš.|ad[.ʿ]bd h.uk.škn.|k.[---.]sglt h.hw.|w.b[.---.]uk.nǵr.| 2060.5
yt.ʿl.umt k.|w abqṯ.aliyn.bʿl.|w tʿn.btlt.ʿnt.|an.l an.y špš.|an.l an.il.yǵr[.-].|tǵr k.š[---.---].|yštd[.---].|dr[.---].|r[6[49].4.46
|mṣmt.l nqmd.[---.-]št.|hl ny.argmn.d [ybl.n]qmd.|l špš.arn.ṯn[.ʿšr h.]mn.|ʿṣrm.ṯql.kbd[.ks].mn.ḫrṣ.|w arbʿ.ktnt 64[118].19
t.hlm.yṯq.nḥš.yšlḥm.nḥš ʿq.|š.yʿdb.ksa w yṯb.|tqru l špš.um h.špš.um.ql bl ʿm.|ṯṯ.w kmṯ.ḥryt h.mnt.nṯk.nḥš.šm UG5.7.35
.ln h.ml|ḫš.abd.ln h.ydy.ḥmt.hlm.yṯq.|w yṯb.|tqru.l špš.um h.špš.[um.q]l bl.ʿm.|yrḫ.lrgt h.mnt.nṯk.n[ḥš].šmrr.| UG5.7.25
hlm yṯq.nḥš.|yšlḥm.nḥš.ʿq šr.yʿdb ksa.|w yṯb.|tqru l špš.um h.špš.um.ql bl ʿm.|šḥr.w šlm šmm h mnt.nṯk.nḥš.|š UG5.7.51
.hlm.yṯq nḥš yšlḥm.nḥš.|ʿq.šr.yʿdb.ksa.w yṯb.|tqru l špš um h.špš um ql.bl.ʿm.|mlk.ʿṯtrt h.mnt.nṯk.nḥš.šmrr.|n UG5.7.40
.yṯq šqy.|nḥš.yšlḥm.nḥš.ʿq šr.yʿdb.|ksa.w yṯb.|tqru l špš.um h.špš.um.ql bl.|ʿm ḥrn.mṣd h.mnt.nṯk nḥš.|šmrr.n UG5.7.57
.hlm.yṯq.nḥš.yšlḥm.|nḥš.ʿq šr.yʿdb.ksa.w yṯb.|tqru l špš.um h.špš.um.ql.bl.ʿm.|ʿnt w ʿṯtrt inbb h.mnt.nṯk.|nḥš.šl UG5.7.19
.hlm.yṯq.|nḥš.yšlḥm.nḥš.ʿq šr.ydb.ksa.|w yṯb.|tqru.l špš.u h.špš.um.ql.bl.ʿm.|dgn.ttl h.mnt.nṯk.nḥš.šmrr.|nḥš.ʿq UG5.7.14
m.yṯq yṯqšqy.nḥš.yšlḥm.ʿq šr.|yʿdb.ksa.w.yṯb.|tqru.l špš.um h.špš.um.ql bl.|ʿm bʿl.mrym.ṣpn.mnt y.nṯk.|nḥš.šm UG5.7.8
.hlm.yṯq.nḥš.yšlḥm.nḥš.|ʿq šr.yʿdb.ksa.w yṯb.|tqru.l špš.um h.špš.um.ql b.ʿm.|ršp.bbt h.mnt.nḥš.šmrr.|nḥš.ʿq šr UG5.7.30
um.pḥl.pḥlt.bt.abn.bt šmm w thm.|qrit.l špš.um h.špš.um.ql.bl.ʿm.|il.mbk nhrm.b ʿdt.thmtm.|mnt. UG5.7.2
um.pḥl.pḥlt.bt.abn.bt šmm w thm.|qrit.l špš.um h.špš.um.ql.bl.ʿm.|il.mbk nhrm.b ʿdt.thmtm.|mnt.nṯk.nḥš.š UG5.7.2
šqy.nḥš.yšlḥm.ʿq šr.|yʿdb.ksa.w.yṯb.|tqru.l špš.um h.špš.um.ql bl.|ʿm bʿl.mrym.ṣpn.mnt y.nṯk.|nḥš.šmrr.nḥš.ʿq UG5.7.8
.|nḥš.yšlḥm.nḥš.ʿq šr.ydb.ksa.|w yṯb.|tqru.l špš.u h.špš.um.ql.bl.ʿm.|dgn.ttl h.mnt.nṯk.nḥš.šmrr.|nḥš.ʿq šr.ln h. UG5.7.14
nḥš.yšlḥm.nḥš.ʿq šr.yʿdb.|ksa.w yṯb.|tqru l špš.um h.špš.um.ql bl.|ʿm ḥrn.mṣd h.mnt.nṯk nḥš.|šmrr.nḥš.ʿq šr.ln UG5.7.57
.nḥš.yšlḥm.nḥš ʿq.|š.yʿdb.ksa w yṯb.|tqru l špš.um h.špš.um.ql bl ʿm.|ṯṯ.w kmṯ.ḥryt h.mnt.nṯk.nḥš.šm|rr.nḥš.ʿq UG5.7.35
š.abd.ln h.ydy.ḥmt.hlm.yṯq.|w yṯb.|tqru.l špš.um h.špš.[um.q]l bl.ʿm.|yrḫ.lrgt h.mnt.nṯk.n[ḥš].šmrr.|nḥš.ʿq šr. UG5.7.25
nḥš yšlḥm.nḥš.|ʿq.šr.yʿdb.ksa.w yṯb.|tqru l špš um h.špš um ql.bl.ʿm.|mlk.ʿṯtrt h.mnt.nṯk.nḥš.šmrr.|nḥš.ʿq šr.ln UG5.7.40
nḥš.yšlḥm.|nḥš.ʿq šr.yʿdb.ksa.w yṯb.|tqru l špš.um h.špš.um.ql.bl.ʿm.|ʿnt w ʿṯtrt inbb h.mnt.nṯk.|nḥš.šlḥm.nḥš.ʿ UG5.7.19
nḥš.yšlḥm.nḥš.|ʿq šr.yʿdb.ksa.w yṯb.|tqru.l špš.um h.špš.um.ql b.ʿm.|ršp.bbt h.mnt.nḥš.šmrr.|nḥš.ʿq šr.ln h.mlḫ UG5.7.30
ḥš.|yšlḥm.nḥš.ʿq šr.yʿdb ksa.|w yṯb.|tqru l špš.um h.špš.um.ql bl ʿm.|šḥr.w šlm šmm h mnt.nṯk.nḥš.|šmrr.nḥš ʿ UG5.7.51
.hlm.yṯq.nḥš.yšlḥm.nḥš.|ʿq šr.yʿdb.ksa.w yṯb.|tqru.l špš.um.ql bl.ʿm|kṯr.w ḫss.kptr h.mnt.nṯk.nḥš.|šmrr.nḥš.ʿq UG5.7.45
spm.|atn.w ṯlṯ h.ḫrṣm.|ylk ym.w ṯn.|ṯlṯ.rbʿ.ym.|aḫr.špšm.b rbʿ.|ymǵy.l udm.rbt.|w udm[.ṯr]rt.|grnn.ʿrm.|šrnn 14[KRT].4.209
mš.|ṯdṯ.ym.ḥẓ k.al.tšʿl.|qrt h.abn.yd k.|mšdpt.w hn.špšm.|b šbʿ.w l.yšn.pbl.|mlk.l qr.ṯigt.ibr h.|l ql.nhqt.ḥmr h 14[KRT].3.118
.mmlat.|d[m].ym.w ṯn.|ṯlṯ.rbʿ.ym.|ḫmš.ṯdṯ.ym.|mk.špšm.b šbʿ.|w l.yšn.pbl.|mlk.l [qr.]ṯiqt.|ibr h[.l]ql.nhqt.|ḥ 14[KRT].5.221
sn.pat.mdbr.|lk.ym.w ṯn.ṯlṯ.rbʿ ym.|ḫmš.ṯdṯ.ym.mk.špšm.|b šbʿ.w tmǵy.l udm.|rbm.w l.udm.ṯrrt.|w gr.nn.ʿrm. 14[KRT].3.107
.abd y.|[---.ǵ]r.šrǵzz.ybky.km.nʿr.|[w ydmʿ.k]m.ṣǵr.špš.b šmm.tqru.|[---.]nplt.y[--].mdʿ.nplt.bšr.|[---].w tpky.k[UG5.8.38
.bn]wt h.|[--]nn.bnt yš[--.---.-]lk.|[--]b.kmm.l k[--].|[šp]š.b šmm.tq[ru.---.-]rt.|[---.]mn mn[-.---.--]n.nmr.|[--.]l yt UG5.8.44
m irby.tškn.|šd.k ḥsn.pat.|mdbr.tlkn.|ym.w ṯn.aḫr.|šp[š]m.b [ṯ]lṯ.|ym[ǵy.]l qdš.|a[ṯrt.]ṣrm.w l ilt.|ṣd[yn]m.ṯm. 14[KRT].4.196
.---].|tʿln.l mrkbt hm.ti[ty.l ʿr hm].|tlkn.ym.w ṯa aḫr.š[pšm.b ṯlṯ].|mǵy.rpum.l grnt.i[lnym.l] |mṭʿt.w yʿn.dnil.[m 20[121].2.5
--].|tʿln.l mr[kbt hm.tity.l] |ʿr hm.tl[kn.ym.w ṯn.aḫr.špšm].|b ṯlṯ.mǵy[.rpum.l grnt].|i[ln]y[m].l mṭʿt[.---].|[-]m[. 22.1[123].24
zry.|bʿlytn.bn.ulb.|ytrʿm.bn.swy.|ṣḥrn.bn.qrtm.|bn.špš.bn.ibrd.|ʿpṯrm.bn.ʿbdy.|n[--.]bn.šnd.|[---].bn.[---]. 2024.5
-] k.šbʿt.|ghl.ph.ṯmnt.|nblu h.špš.ymp.|hlkt.tdr[--].|špš.bʿd h.t[--].|aṯr.aṯrm[.---].|aṯr.aṯrm[.---].|išdym.t[---].|b 27[8].6
k.yd]ʿ.l.ydʿt.|h[t.---.]l.špš.bʿl k.|ʿ[--.s]glt h.at.|ht[.---.]špš.bʿl k.|ydʿm.l.ydʿt.|ʿm y.špš.bʿl k.|šnt.šntm.lm.l.tlk.|w.l 2060.13
y.špš.bʿl k.|šnt.šntm.lm.l.tlk.|w.lḥt.akl.ky.|likt.ʿm.špš.|bʿl k.ky.akl.|b.ḥwt k.inn.|špš n.[---].|hm.al[k.--].|ytnt 2060.18
.nǵr.|w.[---].adny.l.yḫsr.|w.[ank.yd]ʿ.l.ydʿt.|h[t.---.]l.špš.bʿl k.|ʿ[--.s]glt h.at.|ht[.---.]špš.bʿl k.|ydʿm.l.ydʿt.|ʿm y. 2060.11

k.|‘[--.s]glt h.at.|ht[.---.]špš.b‘l k.|yd‘m.l.yd‘t.|‘m y.špš.b‘l k.|šnt.šntm.lm.l.tlk.|w.lḥt.akl.ky.|likt.‘m.špš.|b‘l k. 2060.15
m[-].mtm.uṣb‘[t].|[-]tr.šrk.il.|‘rb.špš.l ymǵ.|krt.ṣbia.špš.|b‘l ny.w ymlk.|[y]ṣb.‘ln.w y[-]y.|[kr]t.ṯ‘.‘ln.bḫr.|[---].a 15[128].5.19
l.yi[--.-]m[---].|b unṯ.km.špš.|d brt.kmt.|br.ṣtqšlm.|b unṯ.‘d ‘lm.|mišmn.nqmd.|ml 1001.1.19
.a]lp.l b‘l.w aṯrt.‘ṣr[m] l inš.|[ilm.---].lbbmm.gdlt.‘rb špš w ḥl.|[mlk.b ar]b‘t.‘[š]rt.yrtḥṣ.mlk.brr.|[b ym.ml]at.y[q 36[9].1.9
ḫ.ši[-.b ar]b‘t.‘š|rt.yr[tḥṣ.ml]k.brr.|‘lm.š.š[--].l[--.]‘rb.šp|š.w ḥl[.ml]k.|bn.aup[š.--].bsbn hzpḫ ṯlṯt.|kṯr[.---.--]trt ḫ APP.II[173].56
.‘[ly h.gdlt.rgm.yṯṯb].|brr.b šb‘[.ṣbu.špš.w ḥl]|yt.‘rb špš[.w ḥl.mlk.w.b y]|m.ḥdṯ.ṯn šm[.---.--]t.|b yrḫ.ši[-.b ar]b‘ APP.II[173].52
h.gdlt.rgm.yṯ[ṯb.brr].|b.[šb]‘.ṣbu.[š]pš.w.ḥly[t].‘[r]b[.š]p[š].|w [ḥl.]mlk.[w.]b.ym.ḥdṯ.ṯn.šm.|l.[---]t.|i[d.yd]bḥ.ml 35[3].47
š.šr[-].|al[p.w].š.šlmm.pamt.šb‘.klb h.|yr[--.]mlk.ṣbu.špš.w.ḥl.mlk.|w.[---].ypm.w.mḫ[--].t[ṯ]tbn.[-].|b.[--].w.km.i 35[3].53
ṯdṯ.ṯn[.--.šmn].|‘ly h.gdlt.rgm.yṯ[ṯb.brr].|b.[šb]‘.ṣbu.[š]pš.w.ḥly[t].‘[r]b[.š]p[š].|w [ḥl.]mlk.[w.]b.ym.ḥdṯ.ṯn.šm.|l. 35[3].47
.b ṯdṯ.ṯn].|l šmn.‘[ly h.gdlt.rgm.yṯṯb].|brr.b šb‘[.ṣbu.špš.w ḥl]|yt.‘rb špš[.w ḥl.mlk.w.b y]|m.ḥdṯ.ṯn šm[.---.--]t.| APP.II[173].51
]arṣ.‘z k.ḏmr k.l[-]|n k.ḥtk k.nmrt k.b tk.|ugrt.l ymt.špš.w yrḫ.|w n‘mt.šnt.il. UG5.2.2.11
š.w yrḫ.l gṯr.|ṯql.ksp.ṭb.ap w np[š].|l ‘nt h.ṯql.ḫrṣ.|l špš[.w y]rḫ.l gṯr.ṯn.|[ṯql.ksp].ṭb.ap.w npš.|[---].bt.alp w š.|[33[5].14
t.|l ilm.šb[‘.]l kṯr.|‘lm.t‘rbn.gṯrm.|bt.mlk.ṯql.ḫrṣ.|l špš.w yrḫ.l gṯr.|ṯql.ksp.ṭb.ap w np[š].|l ‘nt h.ṯql.ḫrṣ.|l špš[. 33[5].11
|ymn.|w.lmd h.|y‘ḏrn.|w.lmd h.|‘dn.|w.lmd h.|bn.špš.|[w.l]m[d h].|yṣ[---].|‘bd[--].|pr[--].|‘dr[--].|w.lm[d h]. 1049.1.11
.tšt.b šdm.mm h.|b smkt.ṣat.npš h.|[-]mt[-].ṣba.rbt.|špš.w tgh.nyr.|rbt.w rgm.l aḫt k.|ttmnt.krt n.dbḥ.|dbḥ.ml 16.1[125].37
ugrt.tǵr k.|ugrt.tǵr k.|tšlm k.um y.|td‘.ky.‘rbt.|l pn.špš.|w pn.špš.nr.|b y.mid.w um.|tšmḫ.m ab.|w al.trḫln.|‘t 1015.8
w špt k.l tššy.hm.tqrm.l mt.b rn k.|[--]ḫp.an.arnn.ql.špš.ḥw.bṭnm.uḫd.b‘lm.|[--.a]ṯm.prṯl.l riš h.ḥmṯ.ṯmṯ.|[--.]yd 1001.1.6
.l tlḥm.|[l]ḥm.trmmt.l tšt.|yn.tǵẓyt.špš.|rpim.tḥtk.|špš.tḥtk.ilnym.|‘d k.ilm.hn.mtm.|‘d k.kṯr m.ḥbr k.|w ḫss. 6.6[62.2].46
n.iš[ryt.-]lnr.|spr.[--]ḥ[-] k.šb‘t.|ghl.ph.ṯmnt.|nblu h.špš.ymp.|hlkt.tdr[--].|špš.b‘d h.t[--].|aṯr.aṯrm[.---].|aṯr.aṯr 27[8].4
šr nkl w ib[.bt].|ḫrḫb.mlk qẓ ḫrḫb m|lk aǵzt.b sǵ[--.]špš.|yrḫ ytkḥ yḫ[bq] [-].|tld bt.[--]t.ḫ[--.l k]|trt.l bnt.hll[.sn 24[77].3
tḥm.špš.|l.‘mrpi.rgm.|‘m špš.kll.mid m.|šlm.|l.[--]n.špš.|ad[.‘]bd h.uk.škn.|k.[---.]sg 2060.3
t.|[kṯ]r w ḫss.y[i]sp.ḥmt.šḥr.w šlm.|[yis]p.ḥmt.isp.[šp]š l hrm.ǵrpl.‘l arṣ.|[l a]n ḥmt.l p[.n]ṯk.abd.l p.akl ṯm.dl. UG5.8.19
bd.l p.ak[l].|[ṯm.dl.]isp.ḥ[mt.---.-]hm.yasp.ḥmt.|[---.š]pš.l [hrm.ǵrpl].‘l.arṣ.l an.|[ḥ]mt.i[l.w] ḥrn.yisp.ḥmt.|[b‘l. UG5.8.12
]p.ḫp h.ḫ[--.---.šp]š.l hrm.|[ǵrpl.]‘l.ar[ṣ.---.ḥ]mt.|[---.šp]š.l [hrm.ǵ]rpl.‘l.arṣ.|[---.]ḥmt.l p[.nṯ]k.abd.l p.ak[l].|[ṯm UG5.8.9
[-]rk.ḥ[--.---.-]lk.|[-]sr.n[--.---.]ḥrn.|[--]p.ḫp h.ḫ[--.---.šp]š.l hrm.|[ǵrpl.]‘l.ar[ṣ.---.ḥ]mt.|[---.šp]š.l [hrm.ǵ]rpl.‘l.arṣ UG5.8.7
]t.w b lb.tqb[-].|[--]m[-].mtm.uṣb‘[t].|[-]tr.šrk.il.|‘rb.špš.l ymǵ.|krt.ṣbia.špš.|b‘l ny.w ymlk.|[y]ṣb.‘ln.w y[-]y.|[k 15[128].5.18
tḥm.špš.|l.‘mrpi.rgm.|‘m špš.kll.mid m.|šlm.|l.[--]n.špš.|ad[.‘] 2060.1
.|[ḫm]š[.m]at.iqnu.|argmn.nqmd.mlk.|ugrt.d ybl.l špš.|mlk.rb.b‘l h.|ks.ḫrṣ.ktn.mit.pḥm.|mit.iqni.l mlkt.|ks. 64[118].25
--].|ik y.[---].|w l n[qmd.---].|[w]nqmd.[---].|[-.]‘mn.šp[š.mlk.rb].|b‘l h.šlm.[w spš].|mlk.rb.b‘l h.[---].|nqmd.ml 64[118].11
w.k.rgm.špš.|mlk.rb.b‘l y.u.|‘[--.]mlakt.‘bd h.|[---.]b‘l k.yḫpn.|[---.] 1018.1
urk.ym.b‘l y.|l.pn.amn.w.l.pn.|il.mṣrm.dt.tǵrn.|npš.špš.mlk.|rb.b‘l y. 1018.23
bi nrt.ilm.špš.[-]r[--].|pǵt.minš.šdm l m‘[rb].|nrt.ilm.špš.mǵy[t].|pǵt.l ahlm.rgm.l yṯ[pn.y]|bl.agrtn.bat.b ḏd k.[p 19[1AQHT].4.211
w.lḥt.akl.ky.|likt.‘m.špš.|b‘l k.ky.akl.|b.ḫwt k.inn.|špš n.[---].|hm.al[k.--].|ytnt[.---].|ṯn[.---].|w[.-----].|l[.-----]. 2060.21
|ugrt.tǵr k.|tšlm k.um y.|td‘.ky.‘rbt.|l pn.špš.|w pn.špš.nr.|b y.mid.w um.|tšmḫ.m ab.|w al.trḫln.|‘tn.ḫrd.ank. 1015.9
.|tṣḥ.l nrt.ilm.špš.|‘ms m‘.l y.aliyn.b‘l.|tšm‘.nrt.ilm.špš.|tšu.aliyn.b‘l.l ktp.|‘nt.k tšt h.tš‘lyn h.|b ṣrrt.ṣpn.tbkyn 6[62].1.13
]y.yblmm.u[---]k.yrd[.--.]i[---]n.bn.|[---.-]nn.nrt.ilm.špš.tšu.g h.w t[ṣḥ.šm]‘.m‘.|[-.yṯ]ir ṯr.il.ab k.l pn.zbl.ym.l pn 2.3[129].15
iy.zbl.b‘l.arṣ.|ttb‘.btlt.‘nt.|idk.l ttn.pnm.|‘m.nrt.ilm.špš.|tšu.g h.w tṣḥ.|tḥm.ṯr.il.ab k.|hwt.lṭpn.ḥtk k.|pl.‘nt.šd 6[49].4.32
bn dgn.|my.hmlt.aṯr.b‘l.nrd.|b arṣ.‘m h.trd.nrt.|ilm.špš.‘d.tšb‘.bk.|tšt.k yn.udm‘t.gm.|tṣḥ.l nrt.ilm.špš.|‘ms m‘. 6[62].1.9
y[.mrḥqtm].|šb‘ d.w.šb‘[d.qlt].|ankn.rgmt.l.b‘l y.|l.špš.‘lm.l.‘ṯtrt.|l.‘nt.l.kl.il.alṯ[y].|nmry.mlk.‘lm.|mlk n.b‘l y. 2008.1.7
.|ilm.špš.‘d.tšb‘.bk.|tšt.k yn.udm‘t.gm.|tṣḥ.l nrt.ilm.špš.|‘ms m‘.l y.aliyn.b‘l.|tšm‘.nrt.ilm.špš.|tšu.aliyn.b‘l.l kt 6[62].1.11
.b‘l.|yrḫ.|kṯr.|trmn.|pdry.|dqt.|trt.|ršp.|‘nt ḫbly.|špš pgr.|iltm ḫnqtm.|yrḫ kty.|ygb hd.|yrgb b‘l.|ydb il.|ya UG5.14.A.12
n.gdlt.pdry.gdlt dqt.|dqt.trt.dqt.|[rš]p.‘nt.ḫbly.dbḥn š[p]š pgr.|[g]dlt iltm ḫnqtm.d[q]tm.|[yr]ḫ.kty gdlt.w l ǵlm 34[1].17
lt.|‘nt.šm‘.l btlt.‘n[t].|rgm.l nrt.il.šp[š].|pl.‘nt.šdm.y špš.|pl.‘nt.šdm.il.yšt k.|[b]‘l.‘nt.mḥrṯt.|iy.aliyn.b‘l.|iy.zbl. 6[49].4.25
h.w tṣḥ.|tḥm.ṯr.il.ab k.|hwt.lṭpn.ḥtk k.|pl.‘nt.šdm.y špš.|pl.‘nt.šdm.il.yš[t k].|b‘l.‘nt.mḥrṯ[-].|iy.aliyn.b‘l.|iy.zbl 6[49].4.36
l.arṣ.|gm.yṣḥ.il.l btlt.|‘nt.šm‘.l btlt.‘n[t].|rgm.l nrt.il.šp[š].|pl.‘nt.šdm.y špš.|pl.‘nt.šdm.il.yšt k.|[b]‘l.‘nt.mḥrṯt.| 6[49].3.24
‘dbnn ank.imr.b p y.|k lli.b ṯbrn q y.ḫtu hw.|nrt.ilm.špš.ṣḥrrt.|la.šmm.b yd.bn ilm.mt.|ym.ymm.y‘tqn.l ymm.|l 6[49].2.24
.ṯ[--.---].|l p‘n.ǵl[m]m[.---].|mid.an[--.]ṣn[--].|nrt.ilm.špš[.ṣḥrr]t.|la.šmm.b y[d.bn.ilm.m]t.|w t‘n.btlt.‘n[t.bnt.]bh 3['NT.VI].5.25
b km.|k imr.b p ḫ.|k lli.b ṯbrn.|qn h.tḫtan.|nrt.ilm.špš.|ṣḥrrt.la.|šmm.b yd.md|d.ilm.mt.b a|lp.šd.rbt.k|mn.l 4[51].8.21
k bṯnm.|mt.‘z.b‘l.‘z.ymṣḫn.|k lsmm.mt.ql.|b‘l.ql.‘ln.špš.|tṣḥ.l mt.šm‘.m‘.|l bn.ilm.mt.ik.tmt[ḫ]|ṣ.‘m.aliyn.b‘l.|i 6[49].6.22
m.n‘mm[.agzry ym.bn]ym.|ynqm.b ap zd.aṯrt.[---].|špš.mṣprt dlt hm[.---].|w ǵnbm.šlm.‘rbm.ṯn[nm].|hlkm.b d 23[52].25
l‘.|[t]tn.qš[t].|bn.tǵdy[.qšt.]w.ql‘.|ṯty.qšt[.w.]ql‘.|bn.šp[š.]qšt.|bn.‘g[w.]qšt.w ql‘.|ḥd[t]n.qšt.w.ql‘.|bn.bb.qšt.w[. 119[321].4.6
il.ybl.a[ṯt y].|il.ylt.mh.ylt.yld y.šḥr.w šl[m].|šu.‘db.l špš.rbt.w l kbkbm.kn[-].|yhbr.špt hm.yšq.hn.[š]pt hm.mtqt 23[52].54
tšql.|[---].try.ap.l tlḥm.|[l]ḥm.trmmt.l tšt.|yn.tǵẓyt.špš.|rpim.tḥtk.|špš.tḥtk.ilnym.|‘d k.ilm.hn.mtm.|‘d k.kṯr 6.6[62.2].44
] š.yrḫ[.---].|ṣpn.š.kṯr.š.pdry.š.ǵrm.š[.---].|aṯrt.š.‘nt.š.špš.š.arṣy.š.‘ṯtrt.š.|ušḫry.š.il.t‘ḏr.b‘l.š.ršp.š.ddmš.š.|w šlm UG5.9.1.7
.‘nt.mḥrṯ[-].|iy.aliyn.b‘l.|iy.zbl.b‘l.arṣ.|w t‘n.nrt.ilm.š[p]š.|šd yn.‘n.b qbt[.t]|bl lyt.‘l.umt k.|w abqt.aliyn.b‘l.|w 6[49].4.41
q.tḥtṣb.bn.|qrytm tmḫṣ.lim.ḫp y[m].|tṣmt.adm.ṣat.š[p]š.|tḥt h.k kdrt.ri[š].|‘l h.k irbym.kp.k.qṣm.|ǵrmn.kp.m 3['NT].2.8
--.a]rb‘m.|[---.tš]‘m.|[---.t]š‘m.|[---.--]y arb‘m.|[---.]l špš ṯmny[m].|[---.]dbr h l šp[š].|[---.]dbr h l šp[š].|[---.]npṭ 41[71].7
b ṯṯ ym ḥdṯ.|ḫyr.‘rbt.|špš tǵr h.|ršp.|w ‘bdm tbqrn.|skn. 1162.3
g h.ḥrb.tšt.b t‘r[t h].|w ‘l.tlbš.npṣ.aṯt.[--].|ṣbi nrt.ilm.špš.[-]r[--].|pǵt.minš.šdm l m‘[rb].|nrt.ilm.špš.mǵy[t].|pǵt. 19[1AQHT].4.209
tǵr.tšl[m] k.|[-----].|[-----].|[--].bt.gb[-.--].|[--]k[-].w.špš.|[---.b].ṣp[n].|[---.]š[--].|[-----].|[-----].|[---.]ṯty.|[---.-]rd 2159.9
[---.]bn[.---].|[---.]bn[.---].|[---.]nḫl h.|[---.b]n.špš.|[---.b]n.mradn.|[---.m]lkym.|[---.--]d. 2137.4
š‘m.|[---.--]y arb‘m.|[---.]l špš ṯmny[m].|[---.]dbr h l šp[š].|[---.]dbr h l šp[š].|[---.]npṭry ṯ[--].|[---.--]urm.|[-----]. 41[71].8
.|[---.]l špš ṯmny[m].|[---.]dbr h l šp[š].|[---.]dbr h l šp[š].|[---.]npṭry ṯ[--].|[---.--]urm.|[-----]. 41[71].9

špš

[k.--].|ytnt[.---].|ṯn[.---].|w[.-----].|l[.-----].|h[--.---].|šp[š.---].|‘m.k[--.lḥt].|akl.yṯ[ṯb.--]pt.|ib.‘ltn.a[--.--]y.|w.spr. 2060.28
[-----].|‘m[-.---].|mǵ[-.---].|šp[š.---].|ql.[---].|w mlk[.nhš.w mlk.mg]šḫ.|‘mn.[---].|ik y. 64[118].4
y.|w.mnd‘.k.ank.|aḥš.mǵy.mnd‘.|k.igr.w.u.[--].|‘m.špš.[---].|nšlḥ[.---].|[---.m]at.|[---.]mat.|š[--].išal.|‘m k.ybl. 2009.1.13
ṯm.dl.|[---.q]l.bl.tbḥ[n.l]azd.‘r.qdm.|[---].‘ẓ q[dm.--.šp]š.|[---.šm]n.mšḥt.kṯpm.a[-]ṯ[-].|[---.--]ḥ b ym.tld[---.]b[-. UG5.8.22
akm l h.|[---.]l.bn.il.|[---.--]a.‘d h.|[---.--]rh.|[---.--]y.špš.|[---.--]h.|[---.--]th. 26[135].10
[-----.]w[.---].|[---.]l špš[.---]. 42[-].2
[---.a]rgmn.špš.|[-----].|[-----].|[-----].|[----] h.|[-----].|[-]b‘l.|[--]m.|[m‘ 2058.1.1
spr.tbṣr.|klt.bt špš. 1175.2

špšyn

aǵltn.|urtn.|annṯb.|ubn.|špšyn.|abmn.|[--]dn.|[ṯ]b‘m.|[--]mlk.|[--]ty.|mtnb‘l.|bn.n 1072.5
.|bn.abḏr.|bn.ḥrẓn.|bn.ḏqnt.|bn.gmrš.|bn.nmq.|bn.špš[yn].|bn.ar[--].|bn.gb[--].|bn.ḥn[n].|bn.gntn[-].|[--.]nqq 2023.3.14
ḫ.|yky.bn.slyn.|ypln.bn.ylḥn.|‘zn.bn.mll.|šrm.|[b]n.špš[yn].|[b]n.ḫrmln.|bn.tnn.|bn.pndr.|bn.nqq.|ḥrš.bhtm.| 85[80].1.11
spr.bnš.mlk.|d taršn.‘msn.|bṣr.abn.špšyn.|dqn.|aǵlmn.|kn‘m.|aḫršp.|anntn.|b‘lrm.|[-]ral.|š 2067.1.3
bn.pndr.|bn.nqq.|ḥrš.bhtm.|bn.izl.|bn.ibln.|bn.ilt.|špšyn.nḥl h.|n‘mn.bn.iryn.|nrn.nḥl h.|bn.ḫsn.|bn.‘bd.|[--- 85[80].2.6
.tmr.|bn.prsn.|bn.ršpy.|[‘]bdḥgb.|[k]lby.|[-]ḥmn.|[š]pšyn.|[‘b]dmlk.|[---]yn.|bn.ṭ[--].|bn.idrm.|bn.ymn.|bn.ṣ 113[400].1.26
bq‘t.|ily.qšt.w.ql‘.|bn.ḥrẓn.qšt.w.ql‘.|tgrš.qšt.w.ql‘.|špšyn.qšt.w.ql‘.|bn.ṯ‘ln.qš[t.w.q]l‘.|‘ṯqbt.qšt.|[-]ll.qšt.w.ql‘. 119[321].2.25
-].ḫbt.|[---].qmy.|[---.]qmy.|[---.--]b.|bn.t[--.---.a]ǵt.|špš[yn.---.u]br‘y.|iln.[---].|bn.[---].ar.|bn.[---].b.ar.|špšyn[.- 2015.1.20
|špš[yn.---.u]br‘y.|iln.[---].|bn.[---].ar.|bn.[---].b.ar.|špšyn[.---.]yṯb.b.ar.|bn.ag[p]ṯ.ḫpṯ.d[.yṯb.b].š‘rt.|yly.bn.ṯrnq 2015.1.24
.[bn.---]ln.|[--]dm.[bn.---]n.|b‘ly.[bn.---]n.|krr[-.---].|špš[yn.---].|[--]b[.---].|‘bd‘ṯ[tr.---].|bdil[.---].|abǵl.[---].|[.--- 102[322].1.8

špšm

spr.ḥrš.|qštipṯl.|bn.anny.|ilṣdq.|ypltn.bn iln.|špšm.nsl h.|[-----]. 1037.6

špšn

šd.[---.]gt.prn.|[šd.---.]gt.prn.|[šd.---.]gt.prn.|[š]d.bn.š[p]šn l gt pr[n].|šd bn.ilšḥr.|l.gt.mzln.|šd.gldy.|l.gt.mzln. 1104.14
n.šḫyn.|bn.abd‘n.|bn.ḫnqn.|bn.nmq.|bn.amdn.|bn.špšn. 1067.9

špt

d.aqht.ǵz[r].|tšt k.bm.qrb m.asm.|b p h.rgm.l yṣa.b špt h[.hwt h].|b nši ‘n h.w tphn.in.[---].|[-.]hlk.ǵlmm b dd 19[1AQHT].2.75
].|abky.w aqbrn.ašt.b ḫrt.|i[lm.arṣ.b p h.rgm.l yṣa.b šp]|t h.hwt h.knp.hrgb.b‘l.ṯbr.|b‘l.ṯbr.diy.hwt.w yql.|tḥt.p‘ 19[1AQHT].3.127
.abky.w aqbrn h.|ašt.b ḫrt.ilm.arṣ.|b p h.rgm.l yṣa.b špt h.hwt[h].|knp.nšrm.b‘l.yṯbr.|b‘l.ṯbr.diy hmt.tqln.|tḥt. 19[1AQHT].3.113
ky w aqbrn h.aštn.|b ḫrt.ilm.arṣ.b p h.rgm.l[yṣ]a.|b špt h.hwt h.knp.ṣml.b‘[l].|b‘l.ṯbr.diy.hyt.tq[l.tḥt].|p‘n h.yb 19[1AQHT].3.142
u.‘db.l špš.rbt.w l kbkbm.kn[-].|yhbr.špt hm.yšq.hn.[š]pt hm.mtqtm.|bm.nšq.w hr.[b]ḥbq.w ḥ[m]ḥmt.yṯb[n].|y 23[52].55
m.aṯtm.a[ṯt.il].|aṯt.il.w ‘lm h.yhbr.špt hm.yš[q].|hn.špt hm.mtqtm.mtqtm.k lrmn[.--].|bm.nšq.w hr.b ḥbq.ḥmḥ 23[52].50
y.šḥr.w šl[m].|šu.‘db.l špš.rbt.w l kbkbm.kn[-].|yhbr.špt hm.yšq.hn.[š]pt hm.mtqtm.|bm.nšq.w hr.[b]ḥbq.w ḥ[23[52].55
r.l išt.w ṣḥrt.l pḥmm.aṯtm.a[ṯt.il].|aṯt.il.w ‘lm h.yhbr.špt hm.yš[q].|hn.špt hm.mtqtm.mtqtm.k lrmn[.--].|bm.nšq 23[52].49
.b bz tdm.|lla y.‘m lẓpn i|l ḏ.pid.hn b p y sp|r hn.b špt y mn|t hn ṯlḫ h w mlg h y|ṯtqt ‘m h b q‘t.|tq‘t ‘m prbḫ 24[77].46
lb h.|[ṯ]n.p k.b ǵr.ṯn.p k.b ḫlb.k tgwln.šnt k.|[--.]w špt k.l tššy.hm.tqrm.l mt.b rn k.|[--]ḫp.an.arnn.ql.špš.ḥw.b 1001.1.5
h.hn bn k.hn[.---].|bn bn.aṯr k.hn[.---].|yd k.ṣǵr.tnšq.špt k.ṯm.|ṯkm.bm ṯkm.aḫm.qym.il.|b lsmt.ṯm.yṯbš.šm.il.m 22.2[124].4
.mh.ylt.ilmy n‘mm.|agzr ym.bn ym.ynqm.b ap.ḏd.št.špt.|l arṣ.špt l šmm.w ‘rb.b p hm.‘ṣr.šmm.|w dg b ym.w nd 23[52].61
[-----].|[špt.l a]rṣ.špt.l šmm.|[---.l]šn.l kbkbm.y‘rb.|[b‘]l.b kbd h.b 5[67].2.2
y n‘mm.|agzr ym.bn ym.ynqm.b ap.ḏd.št.špt.|l arṣ.špt l šmm.w ‘rb.b p hm.‘ṣr.šmm.|w dg b ym.w ndd.gzr.l zr. 23[52].62
[-----].|[špt.l a]rṣ.špt.l šmm.|[---.l]šn.l kbkbm.y‘rb.|[b‘]l.b kbd h.b p h yrd.|k 5[67].2.2

šqb

ǵy.npš.|[---.--]t.hd.tngṯm h.|[---.-]ḥm k b ṣpn.|[---.]išqb.aylt.|[---.--]m.b km.y‘n.|[---].yd‘.l yd‘t.|[---.]tasrn.ṯr il. 1[‘NT.X].5.19

šqy

il.ytnn.|qšt.l brk h.y‘db.|qṣ‘t.apnk.mṯt.dnty.|tšlḥm.tššqy ilm.|tsad.tkbd.hmt.b‘l.|ḥkpt il.kl h.tb‘.kṯr.|l ahl h.hy 17[2AQHT].5.29
imr.b pḫd.l npš.kṯr.|w ḫss.l brlt.hyn d.|ḥrš yd.šlḥm.ššqy.|ilm sad.kbd.hmt.b‘l.|ḥkpt.il.kl h.tšm‘.|mṯt.dnty.t‘db. 17[2AQHT].5.19
[qdš.ḫ]mš.ṯdṯ.ym.uzr.|[ilm].dnil.uzr.ilm.ylḥm.|[uzr.]yšqy.bn qdš.yd.ṣt h.|[dn]il.yd.ṣt h.y‘l.w yškb.|[yd.]mizrt.p 17[2AQHT].1.14
il.mt.rp]i.apn.ǵz[r].|[mt.hrnmy.]uzr.ilm.ylḥm.|[uzr.yšqy.]bn.qdš.yd.|[ṣt h.y‘l.]w yškb.yd.|[mizrt.]p ynl.hn.ym. 17[2AQHT].1.4
]n.qdš ṯlṯ rb‘ ym.|[uzr.i]lm.dnil.uzr.|[ilm.y]lḥm.uzr.yšqy bn.|[qdš.ḫ]mš.ṯdṯ.ym.uzr.|[ilm].dnil.uzr.ilm.ylḥm.|[u 17[2AQHT].1.11
.l h.km aḫ h.w šrš.|km.ary h.uzrm.ilm.ylḥm.|uzrm.yšqy.bn.qdš.|l tbrknn l ṯr.il ab y.|tmrnn.l bny.bnwt.|w yk 17[2AQHT].1.23
nl.hn.ym.|[w ṯn.uzr.]ilm.dnil.|[uzr.ilm.]ylḥm.uzr.|[yšqy.b]n.qdš ṯlṯ rb‘ ym.|[uzr.i]lm.dnil.uzr.|[ilm.y]lḥm.uzr. 17[2AQHT].1.9
i.ap.hn.ǵẓr.mt.|hrnmy.alp.yṭbḫ.l kṯ|rt.yšlḥm.kṯrt.w y|ššq.bnt.[hl]l.snnt.|hn.ym.w ṯn.yšlḥm.|kṯrt.w yš[š]q.bnt.h 17[2AQHT].2.30
ṯrt.w yš[š]q.bnt.hl[l].|snnt.ṯlṯ[.r]b‘ ym.yšl|ḥm kṯrt.w yššq.|bnt hll.snnt.ḫmš.|ṯdṯ.ym.yšlḥm.k[ṯ]rt.|w y[ššq].bnt.h 17[2AQHT].2.35
ṯrt.w yššq.|bnt hll.snnt.ḫmš.|ṯdṯ.ym.yšlḥm.k[ṯ]rt.|w y[ššq].bnt.hll.snnt.|mk.b šb[‘.]ymm.tb‘.b bt h.|kṯrt.bnt.hll. 17[2AQHT].2.38
ṯrt.w y|ššq.bnt.[hl]l.snnt.|hn.ym.w ṯn.yšlḥm.|kṯrt.w yš[š]q.bnt.hl[l].|snnt.ṯlṯ[.r]b‘ ym.yšl|ḥm kṯrt.w yššq.|bnt h 17[2AQHT].2.33
t.‘m.bn il.tspr.yrḫm.|k b‘l.k yḥwy.y‘šr.ḥwy.y‘š.|r.w yšqyn h.ybd.w yšr.‘l h.|n‘m[n.w t]‘nynn.ap ank.aḥwy.|aqh 17[2AQHT].6.31
h.|ybrd.ṯd.l pnw h.|b ḥrb.mlḥt.|qṣ.mri.ndd.|y‘šr.w yšqyn h.|ytn.ks.b d h.|krpn.b klat.yd h.|b krb.‘ẓm.ridn.|m 3[‘NT].1.9
n.w tšqyn.yn.qḥ.|ks.b d y.qb‘t.b ymn y[.t]q|ḥ.pǵt.w tšqyn h.tq[ḥ.ks.]b d h.|qb‘t.b ymn h.w y‘n.yṭ[p]n[.mh]r.|št. 19[1AQHT].4.217
nḥš.šmrr.nḥš.‘q šr.ln h.ml|ḫš.abd.ln h.ydy.ḥmt.hlm.ytq.|w yṯb.|tqru.l špš.um h.špš.[um.q]l bl.‘m.|yrḫ.lrgt h.m UG5.7.22
t.b ḏd k.[pǵt].|bat.b hlm w y‘n.yṭpn[.mhr].|št.qḥn.w tšqyn.yn.qḥ.|ks.b d y.qb‘t.b ymn y[.t]q|ḥ.pǵt.w tšqyn h.tq[19[1AQHT].4.215

šm l ahlm p[---.]km.|[-]bl lb h.km.bṯn.y[--.-]ah.|ṯnm.tšqy msk.hwt.tšqy[.-.]w [---].|w hn dt.yṯb.l mspr. 19[1AQHT].4.224
ḥš].šmrr.|nḥš.ʻq šr.ln h.mlḫš.abd.ln h.ydy.|ḥmt.hlm.ytq.nḥš.yšlḥm.nḥš.|ʻq šr.yʻdb.ksa.w yṯb.|tqru.l špš.um h.šp UG5.7.28
ḥš.šmrr.|nḥš.ʻq šr.ln h.mlḫš.abd.ln h.ydy.|ḥmt.hlm.ytq.nḥš.yšlḥm.nḥš ʻq.|š.yʻdb.ksa w yṯb.|tqru l špš.um h.špš UG5.7.33
|šmrr.nḥš ʻq šr.ln h.mlḫš.|abd.ln h.ydy ḥmt.hlm.ytq šqy.|nḥš.yšlḥm.nḥš.ʻq šr.yʻdb.|ksa.w yṯb.|tqru l špš.um h.š UG5.7.54
ḥš.šm|rr.nḥš.ʻq šr.ln h.mlḫš abd.ln h.|ydy.ḥmt.hlm.ytq nḥš yšlḥm.nḥš.|ʻq.šr.yʻdb.ksa.w yṯb.|tqru l špš um h.šp UG5.7.38
ḥš.šmrr.|nḥš.ʻq šr.ln h.mlḫš abd.ln h.ydy.|ḥmt.hlm.ytq.nḥš.yšlḥm.nḥš.|ʻq šr.yʻdb.ksa.w yṯb.|tqru.l špš.um.ql b UG5.7.43
ḥš.šmrr.|nḥš.ʻq šr.ln h.mlḫš.abd.ln h.|ydy.ḥmt.hlm.ytq.nḥš.yšlḥm.|nḥš.ʻq šr.yʻdb.ksa.w yṯb.|tqru l špš.um h.šp UG5.7.17
nḥš.šmrr.nḥš.ʻq šr ln h.|mlḫš.abd.ln h.ydy.ḥmt.hlm.ytq.|nḥš.yšlḥm.nḥš.ʻq šr.ydb.ksa.|w yṯb.|tqru.l špš.u h.špš. UG5.7.11
ḥš.|šmrr.nḥš.ʻq šr.ln h.mlḫš.abd.|ln h.ydy.ḥmt.hlm ytq.nḥš.|yšlḥm.nḥš.ʻq šr.yʻdb ksa.|w yṯb.|tqru l špš.um h.š UG5.7.48
šmrr.nḥš.|ʻq šr.ln h.mlḫš abd.ln h.ydy.|ḥmt.hlm.ytq ytqšqy.nḥš.yšlḥm.ʻq šr.|yʻdb.ksa.w.yṯb.|tqru.l špš.um h.špš UG5.7.6
t.bʻl k.[---].|dl.ylkn.ḥš.b a[rṣ.---].|b ʻpr.ḫbl ttm.[---.]|šqy.rṯa.tnm y.ytn.[ks.b yd].|krpn.b klat yd.[---].|km ll.kḥṣ. 1[ʻNT.X].4.9
l bt.|w tlḥm aṯt.|š l ilbt.šlmm.|kll ylḥm b h.|w l bbt šqym.|š l uḫr ḫlmṭ.|w tr l qlḥ.|ym aḥd. UG5.11.11
-.]km.|[-]bl lb h.km.bṯn.y[--.-]ah.|ṯnm.tšqy msk.hwt.tšqy[.-.]w [---].|w hn dt.yṯb.l mspr. 19[1AQHT].4.224
].|my[.---].|aṯ[t.---].|aḫ k[.---].|tr.ḫ[---].|w tṣḥ[.---].|tšqy[.---].|tr.ḥt[-.---].|w msk.tr[.---].|tqrb.aḫ[h.w tṣḥ].|lm. 16.2[125].76
d.yn.l.[---].|armwl w [--].|arbʻ.yn.[--].|l adrm.b[--].|šqym. 1092.8

šql

.tgrš.|šbm.b ksl.qšt h.mdnt.|w hln.ʻnt.l bt h.tmǵyn.|tštql.ilt.l hkl h.|w l.šbʻt.tmtḫṣ h.b ʻmq.|tḫtṣb.bn.qrtm.ttʻr.| 3[ʻNT].2.18
.gg y.b ym.ṭiṭ.|rḥṣ.npṣ y.b ym.rṯ.|dn.il.bt h.ymǵyn.|yštql.dnil.l hkl h.|ʻrb.b bt h.kṯrt.bnt.|hll.snnt.apnk.dnil.|m 17[2AQHT].2.25
h.l ʻnt.p dr.dr.|ʻdb.uḫry.mṭ.yd h.|dnil.bt h.ymǵyn.yšt|ql.dnil.l hkl h.ʻrb.b|kyt.b hkl h.mšspdt.b ḥẓr h.|pẓǵm. 19[1AQHT].4.170
t.|b ʻd h.ʻdbt.ṯlṯ.ptḥ.bt.mnt.|ptḥ.bt.w ubn.hkl.w ištql šql.|tn.km.nḥšm.yḥr.tn.km.|mhr y.w bn.bṯn.itnn y.|ytt.nḥ UG5.7.72
yṯb.b mrzḥ h.|yšt[.il.y]n.ʻd šbʻ.trṯ.ʻd škr.|il.hlk.l bt h.yštql.|l ḥṭr h.yʻmsn.nn.ṯkmn.|w šnm.w ngšnn.ḥby.|bʻl.qrn UG5.1.1.17
syn h.ʻdtm.yʻdyn h.yb|ltm.ybln h.mǵy.ḥrn.l bt h.w.|yštql.l ḥṭr h.tlu ḥt.km.nḫl.|tplg.km.plg.|bʻd h.bhtm.mnt.bʻ UG5.7.68
n.|ṯbq.|rqd.|šrš.|gnʻy.|mʻqb.|agm.|bir.|ypr.|hzp.|šql.|mʻrḫ[-].|sl[ḫ].|snr.|ʻrgz.|yknʻm.|ʻnmky.|ǵr. 2074.32
np.|ṯn.bnšm.b.ḫrṣbʻ.|arbʻ.bnšm.b.hzp.|arbʻ.bnšm.b.šql.|arbʻ.bnšm.b.nni.|ṯn.bnšm.b.slḫ.|[---].bnšm.b.yny.|[--.] 2076.17
.ʻšr.yn.|ḫlb.gngnt.ṯlṯ.y[n].|bṣr.ʻšr.yn.|nnu arbʻ.yn.|šql ṯlṯ.yn.|šmny.kdm.yn.|šmgy.kd.yn.|hzp.tšʻ.yn.|[b]ir.ʻšr[2004.25
.ʻllm y.km.tdd.|ʻnt.ṣd.tštr.ʻpt.šmm.|ṭbḫ.alpm.ap ṣin.šql.ṭrm.|w mri ilm.ʻglm.dt.šnt.|imr.qmṣ.llim.k ksp.|l ʻbrm. 22.2[124].12
k.k[--.---].|il.dbḥ.[---].|pʻr.b[--.---].|ṭbḫ.alp[m.ap.ṣin.šql].|ṭrm.w [mri.ilm.ʻglm.dt.šnt].|imr.[qmṣ.llim.---]. 1[ʻNT.X].4.30
t[h.bʻ]l.|yʻdb.hd.ʻdb[.ʻd]bt.|hkl h.ṭbḫ.alpm[.ap].|ṣin.šql.ṭrm[.w]m|ria.il.ʻglm.d[t].|šnt.imr.qmṣ.l[l]im.|ṣḥ.aḫ h. 4[51].6.41
-].|[---.]šn[.---].|[---].pit.|[---.]qbat.|[---.]inšt.|[--]u.l tštql.|[---].ṭry.ap.l tlḥm.|[l]ḥm.trmmt.l tšt.|yn.tǵẓyt.špš.|r 6.6[62.2].41

šqr

an.|[---.--]m.ank.|[---.]asrm.|[---.]dbḥm.|[---.y]rḫ.w šqr.|[---.--]b.b y[--.---].|[-----].|[-----].|[-----].|[---.]mrkbt.|[- 1002.24

šr

.ary h.|k šbʻt.l šbʻm.aḫ h.ym[.--].|w ṯmnt.l ṯmnym.|šr.aḫy h.mẓa h.|w mẓa h.šr.yly h.|b skn.sknm.b ʻdn.|ʻdnm 12[75].2.51
w akl.bqmm.|tšt ḥrṣ.k lb ilnm.|w ṯn.gprm.mn gpr h.šr.|aqht.yʻn.kmr.kmr[.--].|k apʻ.il.b gdrt.k lb.l |ḥt h.imḫṣ 19[1AQHT].1.11
kl[--].dqn[.---].|[-]ntn.artn.b d[.--]nr[.---].|ʻzn.w ymd.šr.b d ansny.|nsk.ks[p.--]mrtn.kṯrmlk.|yḥmn.aḥm[l]k.ʻbdr 2011.31
n.urt.|ydn.|qṭn.|bn.asr.|bn.ʻdy.|bn.amt[m].|myn.|šr.|bn.zql.|bn.iḫy.|bn.iytr.|bn.ʻyn.|bn.ǵzl.|bn.ṣmy.|bn.il[- 2117.2.2
[--.]ab.w il[--].|[--] šlm.šlm i[l].|[š]lm.il.šr.|dgn.w bʻl.|ʻṯ w kmṯ.|yrḫ w ksa.|yrḫ mkṭy.|ṯkmn w šn UG5.10.1.3
kb.ʻrpt].|ṯḥbq.[---].|ṯḥbq[.---].|w tksynn.btn[-].|y[--.]šr h.w šḫp h.|[--.]šḫp.ṣǵrt h.|yrk.tʻl.b ǵr.|mslmt.b ǵr.tliyt.| 10[76].3.26
|km trpa.hn nʻr.|d yšt.l.lṣb h ḫšʻr klb.|[w]riš.pqq.w šr h.|yšt.aḥd h.dm zt.ḫrpnt. UG5.1.2.5
ḫss.|ʻṯtr ʻṯpr.|šḫr w šlm.|ngh w srr.|ʻdw šr.|ṣdqm šr.|ḥnbn il d[n].|[-]bd w [---].|[--].p il[.---].|[i]l mt mr[b-].| UG5.10.1.14
.ym[.--].|w ṯmnt.l ṯmnym.|šr.aḫy h.mẓa h.|w mẓa h.šr.yly h.|b skn.sknm.b ʻdn.|ʻdnm.kn.npl.bʻl.|km ṯr.w tkms 12[75].2.52
b ḫmr yn ay.|šlm.mlk.šlm.mlkt.ʻrbm m.ṯnnm.|mt.w šr.yṯb.b d h.ḥṭ.ṯkl.b d h.|ḥṭ.ulmn.yzbrnn.zbrm.gpn.|yṣmdn 23[52].8
t.nṯk.|nḥš.šlḥm.nḥš.ʻq šr[.yʻ]db.ksa.|nḥš.šmrr.nḥš.ʻq šr.ln h.ml|ḫš.abd.ln h.ydy.ḥmt.hlm.ytq.|w yṯb.|tqru.l špš. UG5.7.21
.ql bl ʻm.|ṯṯ.w kmṯ.ḥryt h.mnt.nṯk.nḥš.šm|rr.nḥš.ʻq šr.ln h.mlḫš abd.ln h.|ydy.ḥmt.hlm.ytq nḥš yšlḥm.nḥš.|ʻq. UG5.7.37
m h.špš.um.ql b.ʻm.|ršp.bbt h.mnt.nḥš.šmrr.|nḥš.ʻq šr.ln h.mlḫš.abd.ln h.ydy.|ḥmt.hlm.ytq.nḥš.yšlḥm.nḥš ʻq.| UG5.7.32
il.mbk nhrm.b ʻdt.thmtm.|mnt.nṯk.nḥš.šmrr.nḥš.|ʻq šr.ln h.mlḫš abd.ln h.ydy.|ḥmt.hlm.ytq ytqšqy.nḥš.yšlḥm.ʻ UG5.7.5
.špš.um.ql.bl.ʻm.|dgn.ttl h.mnt.nṯk.nḥš.šmrr.|nḥš.ʻq šr.ln h.mlḫš.abd.ln h.|ydy.ḥmt.hlm.ytq.nḥš.yšlḥm.|nḥš.ʻq UG5.7.16
ql bl ʻm.|šḥr.w šlm šmm h mnt.nṯk.nḥš.|šmrr.nḥš ʻq šr.ln h.mlḫš.|abd.ln h.ydy ḥmt.hlm.ytq šqy.|nḥš.yšlḥm.nḥ UG5.7.53
pš.um.ql bl.|ʻm ḥrn.mṣd h.mnt.nṯk nḥš.|šmrr.nḥš ʻq šr.ln h.mlḫš.|abd.ln h.ydy.ḥmt.|b ḥrn.pnm.trǵnw.w ṯtkl.|b UG5.7.59
pš um ql.bl.ʻm.|mlk.ʻṯtrt h.mnt.nṯk.nḥš.šmrr.|nḥš.ʻq šr.ln h.mlḫš abd.ln h.ydy.|ḥmt.hlm.ytq.nḥš.yšlḥm.nḥš.|ʻq UG5.7.42
.[um.q]l bl.ʻm.|yrḫ.lrgt h.mnt.nṯk.n[ḥš].šmrr.|nḥš.ʻq šr.ln h.mlḫš.abd.ln h.ydy.|ḥmt.hlm.ytq.nḥš.yšlḥm.nḥš.|ʻq UG5.7.27
.ql bl.|ʻm bʻl.mrym.ṣpn.mnt y.nṯk.|nḥš.šmrr.nḥš.ʻq šr ln h.|mlḫš.abd.ln h.ydy.ḥmt.hlm.ytq.|nḥš.yšlḥm.nḥš.ʻq UG5.7.10
.ql bl.ʻm|kṯr.w ḫss.kptr h.mnt.nṯk.nḥš.|šmrr.nḥš.ʻq šr.ln h.mlḫš.abd.|ln h.ydy.ḥmt.hlm ytq.nḥš.|yšlḥm.nḥš.ʻq UG5.7.47
.mlḫš.abd.ln h.ydy.|ḥmt.hlm.ytq.nḥš.yšlḥm.nḥš ʻq.|š.yʻdb.ksa w yṯb.|tqru l špš.um h.špš.um.ql bl ʻm.|ṯṯ.w kmṯ UG5.7.34
.|mlḫš.abd.ln h.ydy.ḥmt.hlm.ytq.|nḥš.yšlḥm.nḥš.ʻq šr.ydb.ksa.|w yṯb.|tqru.l špš.u h.špš.um.ql.bl.ʻm.|dgn.ttl h. UG5.7.12
.mlḫš abd.ln h.|ydy.ḥmt.hlm.ytq nḥš yšlḥm.nḥš.|ʻq.šr.yʻdb.ksa.w yṯb.|tqru l špš um h.špš um ql.bl.ʻm.|mlk.ʻṯtr UG5.7.39
ḫš.|abd.ln h.ydy ḥmt.hlm.ytq šqy.|nḥš.yšlḥm.nḥš.ʻq šr.yʻdb.|ksa.w yṯb.|tqru l špš.um h.špš.um.ql bl.|ʻm ḥrn.m UG5.7.55
.mlḫš.abd.|ln h.ydy.ḥmt.hlm ytq.nḥš.|yšlḥm.nḥš.ʻq šr.yʻdb ksa.|w yṯb.|tqru l špš.um h.špš.um.ql bl ʻm.|šḥr.w UG5.7.49
.mlḫš.abd.ln h.|ydy.ḥmt.hlm.ytq.nḥš.yšlḥm.|nḥš.ʻq šr.yʻdb.ksa.w yṯb.|tqru l špš.um h.špš.um.ql.bl.ʻm.|ʻnt w ʻṯ UG5.7.18
lḫš abd.ln h.ydy.|ḥmt.hlm.ytq ytqšqy.nḥš.yšlḥm.ʻq šr.|yʻdb.ksa.w.yṯb.|tqru.l špš.um h.špš.um.ql bl.|ʻm bʻl.mr UG5.7.6
.mlḫš abd.ln h.ydy.|ḥmt.hlm.ytq.nḥš.yšlḥm.nḥš.|ʻq šr.yʻdb.ksa.w yṯb.|tqru.l špš.um.ql bl.ʻm|kṯr.w ḫss.kptr h. UG5.7.44

šr

.mlẖš.abd.ln h.ydy. | ḥmt.hlm.ytq.nḥš.yšlḥm.nḥš. | ‘q šr.y‘db.ksa.w ytb. | tqru.l špš.um h.špš.um.ql b.‘m. | ršp.bbt UG5.7.29
ql.bl.‘m. | ‘nt w ‘ṯtrt inbb h.mnt.nṯk. | nḥš.šlḥm.nḥš.‘q šr[.y‘]db.ksa. | nḥš.šmrr.nḥš.‘q šr.ln h.ml | ẖš.abd.ln h.ydy.ḥ UG5.7.23
b šb‘.w tmǵy.l udm. | rbm.w l.udm.ṯrrt. | w gr.nn.‘rm.šrn. | pdrm.s‘t.b šdm. | ḥṭb h.b grnt.ḥpšt. | s‘t.b nk.šibt.b bqr. 14[KRT].3.110
šm.b rb‘. | ymǵy.l udm.rbt. | w udm[.ṯr]rt. | grnn.‘rm. | šrnn.pdrm. | s‘t.b šdm.ḥṭb. | w b grnt.ḥpšt. | s‘t.b npk.šibt.w b 14[KRT].4.213
q.w hr.[b]ḥbq.w ḥ[m]ḥmt.yṯb[n]. | yspr.l ḫmš.l ṣ[---.]šr.pẖr.klat. | tqtnṣn.w tldn.tld.[ilm.]n‘mm.agzr ym. | bn.ym. 23[52].57
nm. | kṯr w ḫss. | ‘ṯtr ‘ṯtpr. | šḥr w šlm. | ngh w srr. | ‘dw šr. | ṣdqm šr. | ḥnbn il d[n]. | [-]bd w [---]. | [--].p il[.---]. | [i]l m UG5.10.1.13
r ‘l bn[.--]. | [w] ṯlṯ šmn. | [w a]r[b‘] ksp ‘l bn ymn. | šb šr šmn [--] ṯryn. | ḫm[š]m l ‘šr ksp ‘l bn llit. | [--]l[-.-]p ‘l [---.- 1103.5

šrg

t]‘nynn.ap ank.aḥwy. | aqht[.ǵz]r.w y‘n.aqht.ǵzr. | al.tšrgn.y btlt m.dm.l ǵzr. | šrg k.ẖḫm.mt.uẖryt.mh.yqḥ. | mh.y 17[2AQHT].6.34
qht[.ǵz]r.w y‘n.aqht.ǵzr. | al.tšrgn.y btlt m.dm.l ǵzr. | šrg k.ẖḫm.mt.uẖryt.mh.yqḥ. | mh.yqḥ.mt.aṯryt.spsg.ysk. | [l 17[2AQHT].6.35

šrh

ap.‘dn.mṭr h. | b‘l.y‘dn.‘dn.ṯkt.b glṯ. | w tn.ql h.b ‘rpt. | šrh.l arṣ.brqm. | bt.arzm.yklln h. | hm.bt.lbnt.y‘msn h. | l yrg 4[51].5.71

šry

dbḥt.byy.bn. | šry.l ‘ṯt. RS61[24.323.2]

šryn

]bht h.tbnn. | [ḥš.]trmm.hkl h. | y[tl]k.l lbnn.w ‘ṣ h. | l[šr]yn.mḥmd.arz h. | h[n.l]bnn.w ‘ṣ h. | š[r]yn.mḥmd.arz h. | t 4[51].6.19
lbnn.w ‘ṣ h. | l[šr]yn.mḥmd.arz h. | h[n.l]bnn.w ‘ṣ h. | š[r]yn.mḥmd.arz h. | tšt.išt.b bht m. | nb[l]at.b hkl m. | hn.y 4[51].6.21

šrk

.tbkn. | [--]t.w b lb.tqb[-]. | [--]m[-].mtm.uṣb‘[t]. | [-]tr.šrk.il. | ‘rb.špš.l ymǵ. | krt.ṣbia.špš. | b‘l ny.w ymlk. | [y]ṣb.‘ln. 15[128].5.17

šr‘

ḫpnt.[---]. | ḫmšm.ṯlṯ.rkb.ntn.ṯlṯ.mat.[---]. | lg.šmn.rqḥ.šr‘m.ušpǵtm.p[--.---]. | kṯ.ẓrw.kṯ.nbt.ḏnt.w [-]n[-.---]. | il.ḫyr. UG5.9.1.21
ǵnbm.šb‘.šnt. | yṣr k.b‘l.ṯmn.rkb. | ‘rpt.bl.ṭl.bl rbb. | bl.šr‘.thmtm.bl. | ṭbn.ql.b‘l.k tmz‘. | kst.dnil.mt.rpi. | all.ǵzr.m[t. 19[1AQHT].1.45

šrǵzz

bn.l pq ḥmt. | [---.--]n h.ḥmt.w t‘btn h.abd y. | [---.ǵ]r.šrǵzz.ybky.km.n‘r. | [w ydm‘.k]m.ṣǵr.špš.b šmm.tqru. | [---.] UG5.8.37

šrp

.tzǵ.b ǵb.ṣpn. | nḥkt.ksp.w ḫrṣ ṭ‘ ṯn šm l btbt. | alp.w š šrp.alp šlmm. | l b‘l.‘ṣr l ṣpn. | npš.w.š.l ršp bbt. | [‘]ṣrm l h.rš UG5.12.A.9
ṣpn b‘l. | ugrt. | b mrḥ il. | b nit il. | b ṣmd il. | b dṯn il. | b šrp il. | b knt il. | b ǵdyn il. | [b]n [---]. 30[107].16
yṣḥ.‘l k.b[‘]l m. | pht.qlt.‘l k.pht. | dry.b ḥrb.‘l k. | pht.šrp.b išt. | ‘l k.[pht.ṯḥ]n.b rḥ | m.‘[l k.]pht[.dr]y.b kbrt. | ‘l k.p 6[49].5.14
.b‘l.tiḫd. | bn.ilm.mt.b ḥrb. | tbq‘nn.b ḫṯr.tdry | nn.b išt.tšrpnn. | b rḥm.tṯḥnn.b šd. | tdr‘nn.šir h.l tikl. | ‘ṣrm.mnt h.l t 6[49].2.33
. | [‘]ṣrm l h.ršp [-]m. | [---.]bqt[-]. | [b] ǵb.ršp mh bnš. | šrp.w ṣp ḫršḥ. | ‘lm b ǵb ḫyr. | ṯmn l ṯlṯm ṣin. | šb‘.alpm. | bt b UG5.12.B.2
dm.w npš ilib. | gdlt.il š.b‘l š.‘nt. | ṣpn.alp.w š.pdry.š. | šrp.w šlmm ilib š. | b‘l ugrt š.b‘l ḫlb š. | yrḫ š.‘nt ṣpn.alp. | w š UG5.13.15
il.w bu[rm.---]. | ytk.gdlt.ilhm.[ṯkmn.w šnm]. | dqt.ršp.šrp.w š[lmm.dqtm]. | ilh[.a]lp.w š[.il]hm.[gdlt.ilhm]. | b‘[l.š]. 35[3].13
nkbd.alp.š.l il. | gdlt.ilhm.ṯkmn.w šnm dqt. | ršp.dqt.šrp w šlmm.dqtm. | [i]lh.alp w š ilhm.gdl[t.]ilhm. | [b]‘l š.aṯrt 34[1].4
il.w bu] | [rm.---.ytk.gdlt.ilhm]. | ṯkmn.w [šnm.dqt.ršp.šrp]. | w šlmm.[dqtm.ilh.alp.w š]. | ilhm.gd[lt.ilhm.b‘l.š.aṯrt.š APP.II[173].14
[š.]kbd.w š. | [l šlm.kbd.al]p.w š.[l] b‘l.ṣpn. | [dqt.l.ṣpn.šrp].w š[l]mm.kmm. | [w bbt.b‘l.ugrt.]kdm.w npš. | [ilib.gdlt. 36[9].1.15
mš. | w kbd.w š.l šlm kbd. | alp.w š.l b‘l ṣpn. | dqt l ṣpn.šrp.w šlmm. | kmm.w bbt.b‘l.ugrt. | w kdm.w npš ilib. | gdlt.i UG5.13.10
l ‘nt.ḥl š.ṯn šm. | l gṯrm.ǵṣ b šmal. | d alpm.w alp w š. | šrp.w šlmm kmm. | l b‘l.ṣpn b ‘r‘r. | pamt ṯlṯm š l qrnt. | ṯlḥn. UG5.13.28
t.bhtm]. | ‘š[rm.]l inš[.ilm.---]. | il[hm.]dqt.š[.---.rš] | [p.š]rp.w šl[mm.--.dqt]. | [i]lh.gdlt[.ilhm.gdlt.il]. | [d]qt.ṯkmn.w 35[3].29
. | [---.i]l š.b‘l š.aṯrt.š.ym š.[b‘]l knp. | [---.g]dlt.ṣpn.dqt.šrp.w [š]lmm. | [---.a]lp.l b‘l.w aṯrt.‘ṣr[m] l inš. | [ilm.---].lbb 36[9].1.7
].[‘]ṣrm l [inš.ilm]. | [---.]ilh[m.dqt.š.--]. | [---.--]t.r[šp.šrp.w šl] | [mm.---].dq[t.ilh.gdlt]. | n.w šnm.dqt[.---]. | [i]lh[m. APP.II[173].31

šrr

rḫ.adn h. | yšt mṣb.mznm.um h. | kp mznm.iḫ h yṯ‘r. | mšrrm.aḫt h l a | bn mznm.nkl w ib. | d ašr.ar yrḫ.w y | rḫ ya 24[77].36
.‘m y. | mid y w ǵbn y. | w.bn y.hn kt. | yškn.anyt. | ym.yšrr. | w.ak[l.---]. | [--].š[--.--]. 2061.14
‘l m.ym l[--.---]. | ḥm.l šrr.w [---]. | y‘n.ym.l mt[.---]. | l šrr.w t‘[n.‘ṯtrt.---]. | b‘l m.hmt.[---]. | l šrr.št[.---]. | b riš h.[---] 2.4[68].35
ṯ.nn.aliyn.b‘l.w [---]. | ym.l mt.b‘l m.ym l[--.---]. | ḥm.l šrr.w [---]. | y‘n.ym.l mt[.---]. | l šrr.w t‘[n.‘ṯtrt.---]. | b‘l m.hm 2.4[68].33
kt.tgly.w tbu. | nṣrt.tbu.pnm. | ‘rm.tdu.mh. | pdrm.tdu.šrr. | ḥṯ m.t‘mt.[‘]ṭr.[k]m. | zbln.‘l.riš h. | w ṯṯb.trḥṣ.nn.b d‘t. | 16.6[127].7
lm.tṭp[.---.]bm. | yd.ṣpn hm.tliy m[.--.ṣ]pn hm. | nṣḥy.šrr.m[---.--]ay. | nbšr km.dnil.[--] h[.---]. | riš.r[--.--]ḥ[.---]y[.-- 19[1AQHT].2.85
.ym.l mt[.---]. | l šrr.w t‘[n.‘ṯtrt.---]. | b‘l m.hmt.[---]. | l šrr.št[.---]. | b riš h.[---]. | ib h.mš[--.---]. | [b]n.‘n h[.---]. 2.4[68].37
‘ṭr[.---]. | b p.š[---]. | il.p.d[---]. | ‘rm.[di.mh.pdrm]. | di.š[rr.---]. | mr[ṣ.---]. | zb[ln.---]. | t[--.---]. | [-----]. 16[126].5.49

šrš

bil. | ‘nmky.ḥmr.w.bnš. | rqd arb‘. | šbn aḥd. | ṭbq aḥd. | šrš aḥd. | bir aḥd. | uḫnp. | hzp ṯn. | m‘qb arb‘. 2040.30
.gllṭky. | lbw[-].uḫ.pdm.b.y‘rt. | pǵyn.b.tpḫ. | amri[l].b.šrš. | aǵltn.b.midḫ. | [--]n.b.ayly. | [-]lyn.b.ngḫt. | [---.]b.nh[-]t. 2118.12
t. | [---.--] n.ylt.ḥmḥmt. | [---.mt.r]pi.w ykn.bn h. | [b bt.šrš.]b qrb.hkl h. | [nṣb.skn.i]lib h.b qdš. | [ztr.‘m h.l a]rṣ.mšṣ 17[2AQHT].1.44
rknn l ṯr.il ab y. | tmrnn.l bny.bnwt. | w ykn.bn h b bt.šrš.b qrb. | hkl h.nṣb.skn.ilib h.b qdš. | ztr.‘m h.l arṣ.mšṣu.qṭ 17[2AQHT].1.26
| ḫlbkrd. | y‘rt. | uškn. | ‘nqpat. | ilštm‘. | šbn. | ṭbq. | rqd. | šrš. | gn‘y. | m‘qb. | agm. | bir. | ypr. | hzp. | šql. | m‘rḫ[-]. | sl[ḫ]. | 2074.25
u.g h.w yṣḥ.y l k.mrrt. | tǵll.b nr.d ‘l k.mḥṣ.aqht. | ǵzr.šrš k.b arṣ.al. | yp‘.riš.ǵly.b d.ns‘ k. | ‘nt.brḥ.p ‘lm h. | ‘nt.p dr 19[1AQHT].3.159
.l h. | km.aḫ h.w šrš.km.ary h. | bl.iṯ.bn.l h.km aḫ h.w šrš. | km.ary h.uzrm.ilm.ylḥm. | uzrm.yšqy.bn.qdš. | l tbrknn 17[2AQHT].1.21

l.mt.rpi anẖ.ǵzr. | [mt.]hrnmy.d in.bn.l h. | km.aẖ h.w šrš.km.ary h. | bl.iṯ.bn.l h.km aẖ h.w šrš. | km.ary h.uzrm.il 17[2AQHT].1.20
. | w anẖn.w tnẖ.b irt y. | npš.k yld.bn.l y.km. | aẖ y.w šrš.km ary y. | nṣb.skn.ilib y.b qdš. | ztr.ʿm y.l ʿpr.ḏmr.aṯr[y] 17[2AQHT].2.15
šrš. | lbnm. | ẖlb.krd. | ṣʿ. | mlk. | gbʿly. | ypr. | ary. | ẓrn. | art. | ṯl 71[113].1
[b]ir.ʿšr[.---]m ḥsp. | ẖpty.kdm[.---]. | [a]gm.arbʿ[.---]. | šrš.šbʿ.mṣb. | rqd.ṯlṯ.mṣb.w.[---]. | uẖnp.ṯṯ.mṣb. | tgmr.[y]n.mṣ 2004.32
b.irbn. | ṯn.bnšm.b.yʿrt. | ṯn.bnšm.b.ʿrmt. | arbʿ.bnšm.b.šrš. | ṯṯ.bnšm.b.mlk. | arbʿ.bnšm.b.bṣr. | ṯn.bnšm.[b.]rqd. | ṯn.b 2076.37
[-]dn[.---]. | [-]bq[.---]. | [r]qd[.---]. | šrš[.---]. | uẖnp[.---]. | [-]tn[--.---]. | km[-.---]. | lm[--.---]. 2165.4
. | arny. | ʿnqpat. | šʿrt. | ubrʿy. | ilštmʿ. | šbn. | tbq. | rqd. | [š]rš. | [-----]. | [-----]. | [-----]. | [-----]. | [-----]. | [-----]. | [ẖl]bkrd. | [2058.1.19

šršy

ḥrm.b[n].ng[-]n. | atyn.š[r]šy. | ʿbdẖmn[.bn.-]bdn. | ḥṣmn.[bn.---]ln. | [--]dm.[bn.---]n 102[322].1.2

šršn

| tmrtn. | šdʿl.bn aẖyn. | mʿrbym. | rpan. | abršn. | atlgy. | šršn. 95[91].10

šršʿm

mit [ʿš]r kbd. | ṣṣ yḏrd ʿšrm. | ṣṣ bn aglby ṯlṯ[m]. | ṣṣ bn.šršʿm.[---]. | ṣṣ mlknʿm.a[rbʿm]. | ṣṣ mlk mit[.---]. | ṣṣ igy.ẖmš 2097.14

šrt

| [---].ʿgltn. | [---.]ʿgltn. | [---.šr]t.aḥt. | [---].šrt.aḥt. | [---].šrt.aḥt. | [---.]šrt.aḥt. | [---.]šrt.aḥ. | [---.]šr.aḥt. | [---].šr[t]. | [---. 2162.C.2
.brqn. | [---].skn. | [---.ʿg]ltn. | [---].ʿgltn. | [---.]ʿgltn. | [---.šr]t.aḥt. | [---].šrt.aḥt. | [---].šrt.aḥt. | [---.]šrt.aḥt. | [---.]šrt.aḥ. 2162.B.12
---.]ʿgltn. | [---.šr]t.aḥt. | [---].šrt.aḥt. | [---].šrt.aḥt. | [---.]šrt.aḥt. | [---.]šrt.aḥ. | [---.]šr.aḥt. | [---].šr[t]. | [---.k]hnm. | [---. 2162.C.3
-.šr]t.aḥt. | [---].šrt.aḥt. | [---].šrt.aḥt. | [---.]šrt.aḥt. | [---.]šrt.aḥ. | [---.]šr.aḥt. | [---].šr[t]. | [---.k]hnm. | [---.š]rt.aḥt. | [---. 2162.C.4
n. | [---.ʿg]ltn. | [---].ʿgltn. | [---.]ʿgltn. | [---.šr]t.aḥt. | [---].šrt.aḥt. | [---].šrt.aḥt. | [---.]šrt.aḥt. | [---.]šrt.aḥ. | [---.]šr.aḥt. | [- 2162.C.1
--].šrt.aḥt. | [---].šrt.aḥt. | [---.]šrt.aḥt. | [---.]šrt.aḥ. | [---.]šr.aḥt. | [---].šr[t]. | [---.k]hnm. | [---.š]rt.aḥt. | [---.šr]tm. | [---.]š 2162.C.5
t. | [---.]šrt.aḥ. | [---.]šr.aḥt. | [---].šr[t]. | [---.k]hnm. | [---.š]rt.aḥt. | [---.šr]tm. | [---.]šrtm. | [---.šrt.]aḥt. 2162.C.8
]. | [---.k]hnm. | [---.š]rt.aḥt. | [---.šr]tm. | [---.]šrtm. | [---.šrt.]aḥt. 2162.C.11
.aḥd.ẖbṯ. | w.arbʿ.aṯt. | bn.lg.ṯn.bn h. | bʿlm.w.aḥt h. | b.šrt. | šty.w.bn h. 2080.12
---].šrt.aḥt. | [---.]šrt.aḥt. | [---.]šrt.aḥ. | [---.]šr.aḥt. | [---].šr[t]. | [---.k]hnm. | [---.š]rt.aḥt. | [---.šr]tm. | [---.]šrtm. | [---.šrt 2162.C.6
. | [---].šr[t]. | [---.k]hnm. | [---.š]rt.aḥt. | [---.šr]tm. | [---.]šrtm. | [---.šrt.]aḥt. 2162.C.10
. | [---.]šr.aḥt. | [---].šr[t]. | [---.k]hnm. | [---.š]rt.aḥt. | [---.šr]tm. | [---.]šrtm. | [---.šrt.]aḥt. 2162.C.9

šš

.--]ẓ. | kd.[ʿl.---]. | [--.--]ẖ.bn.ag[--]. | [---.--]m[.---]. | [kd.]šš. | [k]d.ykn.bn.ʿbdṯrm. | kd.ʿbdil. | ṯlṯ.ʿl.bn.srt. | kd.ʿl.ẓrm. | k 1082.2.1

ššy

---]. | kdm.šmn.ʿl.ilršp.bn[.---]. | kd.šmn.ʿl.yddn. | kd.ʿl.ššy. | kd.ʿl.nḏbn.bn.agmn. | [k]d.ʿl.brq. | [kd]m.[ʿl].kṯr. | [kd]m 1082.1.7

ššmn

nṣ.[-]ṯ[-.]gr[-.---]. | [---].arb[ʿ.d]d.š[ʿrm.---]. | [--.-]rṯm š[šm]n.k[--.---]. | [---.ar]bʿ.dblt.ḏr[--.---]. | [--.m]itm.nṣ.l bn[.-- 143[-].1.8
.mr. | [---.]arbʿ.mat.ẖswn.lṯḥ.aqhr. | [---.lṯḥ.]sbbyn.lṯḥ.ššmn.lṯḥ.šḥlt. | [---.lṯḥ.]ṣmqm.[ṯ]ṯ.mat.nṣ.ṯlṯm.ʿṣr. | [---].ẖmš[142[12].4
p.kd.nbt.kd.šmn.mr. | [---].kmn.lṯḥ.sbbyn. | [---.-]ʿt.lṯḥ.ššmn. | [---].ẖswn.ṯṯ.mat.nṣ. | [---].ẖmšm.ḥmr.škm. | [---.ṯṯ.dd. 142[12].10

ššr

[---].aliyn. | [bʿl.---.-]ip.dpr k. | [---.-]mn k.ššrt. | [---.--]t.npš.ʿgl. | [---.-]nk.aštn.b ẖrt. | ilm.arṣ.w at.qḥ. | ʿr 5[67].5.3

ššrt

šš[r]t.ẖrṣ.ṯqlm.kbd.ʿšrt.mzn h. | b [ar]bʿm.ksp. | b d[.ʿb]dym.ṯ 2100.1

št

n h.tq[ḥ.ks.]b d h. | qbʿt.b ymn h.w yʿn.yṯ[p]n[.mh]r. | št.b yn.yšt.ila.il š[--.]il. | d yqny.ḏdm.yd.mẖṣt.a[qh]t.ǵ | zr.tm 19[1AQHT].4.219
. | d yqny.ḏdm.yd.mẖṣt.a[qh]t.ǵ | zr.tmẖṣ.alpm.ib.št[-]št. | ḥršm l ahlm p[---.]km. | [-]bl lb h.km.bṯn.y[--.-]ah. | tnm. 19[1AQHT].4.221
.agrtn.bat.b ḏd k.[pǵt]. | bat.b hlm w yʿn.yṯpn[.mhr]. | št.qḥn.w tšqyn.yn.qḥ. | ks.b d y.qbʿt.b ymn y[.t]q | ḥ.pǵt.w tš 19[1AQHT].4.215
.l kl.[---]. | [tt]bʿ.btlt.ʿnt[.idk.l ttn.pnm]. | ʿm.yṯpn.mhr.š[t.tšu.g h]. | w tṣḥ.yṯb.yṯp.[---]. | qrt.ablm.ablm.[qrt.zbl.yrẖ] 18[3AQHT].4.6
ḥ.gdm.w anhbm]. | kla[t.ṯǵ]r[t.bht.ʿnt.w tqry.ǵlmm.b št.ǵr]. | ap ʿnt tm[ṯḥṣ.b ʿmq.tṯḥṯṣb.bn.qrytm.tmẖṣ]. | lim ẖ[p.y 7.2[130].24
rḥ.gdm. | w anhbm.klat.ṯǵrt. | bht.ʿnt.w tqry.ǵlmm. | b št.ǵr.w hln.ʿnt.tm | ṯḥṣ.b ʿmq.tṯḥṯṣb.bn. | qrytm tmẖṣ.lim.ẖp y 3[ʿNT].2.5
---]. | kpr.[šbʿ.bnt.rḥ.gdm.w anhbm]. | w tqr[y.ǵlmm.b št.ǵr.---]. | [ʿ]d tš[bʿ.tmṯḥṣ.---]. | klyn[.---]. | špk.l[---]. | trḥṣ.yd 7.2[130].4
m. | qṭr.b ap h.b ap.mhr h.ank. | l aḥwy.tqḥ.yṯpn.mhr.št. | tštn.k nšr.b ḥbš h.km.diy. | b tʿrt h.aqht.km.yṯb.l lḥ[m]. | 18[3AQHT].4.27
-]. | b qrn.ymn h.b anšt[.---]. | qdqd h.w yʿn.yṯpn.[mhr.št]. | šmʿ.l btlt.ʿnt.at.ʿ[l.qšt h]. | tmẖṣ h.qṣʿt h.hwt.l t[ḥwy]. | n 18[3AQHT].4.11
lt.mh.ylt.ilmy nʿmm. | agzr ym.bn ym.ynqm.b ap.ḏd.št.špt. | l arṣ.špt l šmm.w ʿrb.b p hm.ʿṣr.šmm. | w dg b ym.w 23[52].61
n k. | [tlsmn.ʿm y.twt]ḥ.išd k. | [tk.ẖršn.---]r.[-]ḥm k.w št. | [---.]ẓ[--.-]rdy k. | [---.i]qnim. | [---.-]šu.b qrb. | [---].asr. | [- 1[ʿNT.IX].2.3

šty

rpa.hn nʿr. | d yšt.l.lṣb h ḥšʿr klb. | [w]riš.pqq.w šr h. | yšt.aḥd h.dm zt.ẖrpnt. UG5.1.2.6
št.il. | [---.--]n.il ǵnṯ.ʿgl il. | [---.--]d.il.šd yṣd mlk. | [---].yšt.il h. | [---.]iṯm h. | [---.y]mǵy. | [---.]dr h. | [---.-]rš.l bʿl. | [--- UG5.2.1.13
.ktp. | b il ab h.gʿr.yṯb.il.kb[-]. | at[rt.]il.yṯb.b mrzḥ h. | yšt[.il.y]n.ʿd šbʿ.trṯ.ʿd škr. | il.hlk.l bt h.yštql. | l ḥṭr h.yʿmsn. UG5.1.1.16
ʿnt.di.dit.rḥpt. | [---.-]rm.aklt.ʿgl.ʿl.mšt. | [---.-]r.špr.w yšt.il. | [---.--]n.il ǵnṯ.ʿgl il. | [---.--]d.il.šd yṣd mlk. | [---].yšt.il UG5.2.1.10
. | w tk.pn h.tʿdb.ksu. | w yṯṯb.l ymn.aliyn. | bʿl.ʿd.lḥm.št[y.ilm]. | [w]yʿn.aliy[n.bʿl]. | [--]b[.---]. | ḥš.bht m.k[ṯr]. | ḥš.r 4[51].5.110

šty

[--].aliyn.b'l. | [--.]rbt.aṯrt.ym. | [---.]btlt.'nt. | [--.tl]ḥm.tšty. | [ilm.w tp]q.mrǵṯm. | [ṯd.b ḥrb.m]lḥt.qṣ. | [mri.tšty.k]rp 4[51].3.40
sat[.yn]. | špq.ilm.rḥbt yn. | špq.ilht.dkrt[.yn]. | 'd.lḥm.šty.ilm. | w pq mrǵṯm.ṯd. | b ḥrb.mlḥt.qṣ[.m]r | i.tšty.krp[nm. 4[51].6.55
--]. | b ṯmnt.[---]. | yqrb.[---]. | lḥm.m[---.---]. | [']d.lḥm[.šty.ilm]. | w pq.mr[ǵṯm.ṯd.---]. | b ḥrb.[mlḥt.qṣ.mri]. | šty.kr[5[67].4.12
.ks.]b d h. | qb't.b ymn h.w y'n.yṯ[p]n[.mh]r. | št.b yn.yšt.ila.il š[--.]il. | d yqny.ḏdm.yd.mḫṣt.a[qh]t.ǵ | zr.tmḫṣ.alp 19[1AQHT].4.219
.yd[.---.---]r. | l riš hm.w yš[--.--]m. | lḥm.b lḥm ay.w šty.b ḫmr yn ay. | šlm.mlk.šlm.mlkt.'rbm m.ṯnnm. | mt.w šr. 23[52].6
.ǵmu.ǵmit.w 's[--]. | lḥm.hm.štym.lḥ[m]. | b ṯlḥnt.lḥm št. | b krpnm.yn.b k.ḫrṣ. | dm.'ṣm.hm.yd.il mlk. | yḫss k.ahbt. 4[51].4.36
nqdm. | bn.alṯn. | bn.dly. | bn.btry. | bn.ḫdmn. | [bn].šty. | [bn].kdgdl. | [---.-]y[-.] 2018.6
n.rpum. | tštyn.ṯlṯ.rb'.ym.ḫmš. | ṯdṯ.ym.tlḥmn.rpum. | tštyn.bt.ikl.b pr'. | yṣq.b irt.lbnn.mk.b šb'. | [ymm.---]k.aliyn 22.2[124].24
nt.hlkt.w.šnwt. | tp.aḫ.h.k.ysmsm. | tspi.šir.h.l.bl.ḥrb. | tšt.dm.h.l.bl.ks. | tpnn.'n.bty.'n.bṯt.tpnn. | 'n.mḫr.'n.pḫr.'n.ṯ RS225.4
ywpṯn.b tk. | p[ḫ]r.bn.ilm.štt. | p[--].b ṯlḥn y.qlt. | b ks.ištyn h. | dm.ṯn.dbḥm.šna.b'l.ṯlṯ. | rkb.'rpt.dbḥ. | bṯt.w dbḥ.w 4[51].3.16
.ḫbṯ. | w.arb'.aṯt. | bn.lg.ṯn.bn h. | b'lm.w.aḫt h. | b.šrt. | šty.w.bn h. 2080.13
m.hm[.iṯ.--.l]ḥm.w t[n]. | w nlḥm.hm.iṯ[.--.yn.w t]n.w nšt. | w 'n hm.nǵr mdr'[.iṯ.lḥm.---]. | iṯ.yn.d 'rb.bṯk[.---]. | mǵ 23[52].72
[-----]. | šm'.l [-]mt[.-]m.l[-]ṯnm. | 'dm.[lḥ]m.tšty. | w t'n.mṯt ḥry. | l l[ḥ]m.l š[ty].ṣḥt km. | db[ḥ.l krt.a]dn 15[128].6.2
šr. | knr.uṣb't h ḫrṣ.abn. | p h.tiḫd.šnt h.w akl.bqmm. | tšt ḫrṣ.k lb ilnm. | w ṯn.gprm.mn gpr h.šr. | aqht.y'n.kmr.km 19[1AQHT].1.10
| š[--].išal. | 'm k.ybl.šd. | a[--].d'.k. | šld.ašld. | hn.mrṯ.d.štt. | ašld b ldt k. 2009.3.1
sḥ.ym.yql. | l arṣ.tnǵṣn.pnt h.w ydlp.tmn h. | yqṭ b'l.w yšt.ym.ykly.ṯpṭ.nhr. | b šm.tg'r m.'ṯtrt.bṯ l aliyn.[b'l.] | bṯ.l rk 2.4[68].27
h.mṣd.ṣd.b qrb | hkl [h].ṣḥ.l qṣ.ilm.tlḥmn. | ilm.w tštn.tštn y[n] 'd šb'. | trṯ.'d.škr.y'db.yrḫ. | gb h.km.[---.]yqṭqṭ.tḥt. UG5.1.1.3
.]inšt. | [--]u.l tštql. | [---].ṯry.ap.l tlḥm. | [l]ḥm.trmmt.l tšt. | yn.tǵẓyt.špš. | rpim.tḥtk. | špš.tḥtk.ilnym. | 'd k.ilm.hn.m 6.6[62.2].43
.-]ǵk.rpu mlk. | ['lm.---.--]k.l tšt k.l iršt. | ['lm.---.--]k.l tšt k.liršt. | [---.]rpi.mlk 'lm.b 'z. | [rpu.m]lk.'lm.b ḏmr h.bl. | UG5.2.2.5
lt.aṯr.b'l.nrd. | b arṣ.'m h.trd.nrt. | ilm.špš.'d.tšb'.bk. | tšt.k yn.udm't.gm. | tṣḥ.l nrt.ilm.špš. | 'ms m'.l y.aliyn.b'l. | tš 6[62].1.10
-.]dr h. | [---.-]rš.l b'l. | [---.-]ǵk.rpu mlk. | ['lm.---.--]k.l tšt k.l iršt. | ['lm.---.--]k.l tšt k.liršt. | [---.]rpi.mlk 'lm.b 'z. | [r UG5.2.2.5
d.lḥm.šty.ilm. | w pq mrǵṯm.ṯd. | b ḥrb.mlḥt.qṣ[.m]r | i.tšty.krp[nm.y]n. | [b k]s.ḫrṣ.d[m.'ṣm]. | [---.--]n. | [---.---]t. | [-- 4[51].6.58
m.tšty. | [ilm.w tp]q.mrǵṯm. | [ṯd.b ḥrb.m]lḥt.qṣ. | [mri.tšty.k]rpnm yn. | [b ks.ḫrṣ.dm].'ṣm. 4[51].3.43
-.l]ḥm[.---]. | [---].ay š[---]. | [---.b ḥ]rb.mlḥ[t.qṣ]. | [mri.tšty.krpnm].yn.b ks.ḫ[rṣ]. | [dm.'ṣm.---]n.krpn.'l.[k]rpn. | [--- 17[2AQHT].6.5
[.šty.ilm]. | w pq.mr[ǵṯm.ṯd.---]. | b ḥrb.[mlḥt.qṣ.mri]. | šty.kr[pnm.yn.---]. | b ks.ḫr[ṣ.dm.'ṣm.---]. | ks.ksp[.---]. | krpn 5[67].4.15
šd.bn.šty.l.bn.ṭbrn. | šd.bn.ḫtb.l bn.y'ḏrd. | šd.gl.b'lz.l.bn.'mnr. | šd. 2089.1
rt w 'nt[.---]. | w b hm.tṯtb[.--]d h. | km trpa.hn n'r. | d yšt.l.lṣb h ḫš'r klb. | [w]riš.pqq.w šr h. | yšt.aḥd h.dm zt.ḫrp UG5.1.2.4
]. | rǵb.rǵbt.w tǵt[--]. | hm.ǵmu.ǵmit.w 's[--]. | lḥm.hm.štym.lḥ[m]. | b ṯlḥnt.lḥm št. | b krpnm.yn.b k.ḫrṣ. | dm.'ṣm.h 4[51].4.35
m. | aḫ y.qran.hd.'m.ary y. | w lḥm m 'm aḫ y.lḥm. | w št m.'m.a[ḫ] yn. | p nšt.b'l.[t]'n.iṯ'n k. | [---.]ma[---] k.k tmḫṣ. 5[67].1.25
r' h. | r' 'lm. | ttn.w tn. | w l ttn. | w al ttn. | tn ks yn. | w ištn. | 'bd.prt.ṯḥm. | qrq.pt.ḏmn. | l iṯtl. 1019.1.16
.w ṯlb.b tp.w mṣltm.b m | rqdm.dšn.b.ḥbr.kṯr.ṭbm. | w tšt.'nt.gṯr.b'lt.mlk.b' | lt.drkt.b'lt.šmm.rmm. | [b'l]t.kpṯ.w 'nt UG5.2.1.6
t. | [--].ydd.w yqlṣn. | yqm.w ywpṯn.b tk. | p[ḫ]r.bn.ilm.štt. | p[--].b ṯlḥn y.qlt. | b ks.ištyn h. | dm.ṯn.dbḥm.šna.b'l.ṯlṯ. 4[51].3.14
]m.l[-]ṯnm. | 'dm.[lḥ]m.tšty. | w t'n.mṯt ḥry. | l l[ḥ]m.l š[ty].ṣḥt km. | db[ḥ.l krt.a]dn km. | 'l.krt.tbun.km. | rgm.ṯ[rm 15[128].6.4
yd.b ṣ'.tšlḥ. | ḥrb.b bšr.tštn. | [w t]'n.mṯt.ḥry. | [l lḥ]m.l šty.ṣḥt km. | [--.dbḥ.l]krt.b'l km. 15[128].4.27
ṣ'.t[šl]ḥ. | [ḥrb.b]bš[r].tštn. | [w t'n].mṯt.ḥry. | [l lḥ]m.l šty.ṣḥt k[m]. | [---.]brk.t[---]. | ['l.]krt.tbkn. | [--.]rgm.ṯrm. | [--. 15[128].5.10
[---]n.yšt.rpu.mlk.'lm.w yšt. | [--.]gṯr.w yqr.il.yṯb.b.'ṯtrt. | il.ṯpṭ.b h UG5.2.1.1
s. | bn.ann. | bn.'bdpdr. | šd.iyry.l.'bdb'l. | šd.šmmn.l.bn.šty. | šd.bn.arws.l.bn.ḫlan. | šd.bn.ibryn.l.bn.'mnr. 1102.18
b bt h.mṣd.ṣd.b qrb | hkl [h].ṣḥ.l qṣ.ilm.tlḥmn. | ilm.w tštn.tštn y[n] 'd šb'. | trṯ.'d.škr.y'db.yrḫ. | gb h.km.[---.]yqṭqṭ UG5.1.1.3
.smd. | lbnn.ṯl mrṯ.yḫrṭ.il. | hn.ym.w ṯn.tlḥmn.rpum. | tštyn.ṯlṯ.rb'.ym.ḫmš. | ṯdṯ.ym.tlḥmn.rpum. | tštyn.bt.ikl.b pr' 22.2[124].22
[---]n.yšt.rpu.mlk.'lm.w yšt. | [--.]gṯr.w yqr.il.yṯb.b.'ṯtrt. | il.ṯpṭ.b hd r'y.d yšr.w yḏmr UG5.2.1.1
[---.b]n.šty. | [---.]šlm. | [---.]šlm. | [---.]šlm. | [---.]šlm. | [---.š]lm. 2151.1
t'rb.sd. | [---.--]n b ym.qẓ. | [---.]ym.tlḥmn. | [---.rp]um.tštyn. | [---.]il.d 'rgzm. | [---.]dt.'l.lty. | [---.]tdbḥ.amr. | ṯmn.b 20[121].1.7
.rmm. | [b'l]t.kpṯ.w 'nt.di.dit.rḥpt. | [---.-]rm.aklt.'gl.'l.mšt. | [---.--]r.špr.w yšt.il. | [---.--]n.il ǵnṯ.'gl il. | [---.--]d.il.šd UG5.2.1.9
pr m. | ddym.ask[.šlm.]l kbd.arṣ. | ar[bdd.]l kb[d.š]dm.yšt. | [----.]b'l.mdl h.yb'r. | [---.]rn h.aqry. | [---.]b a[r]ṣ.mlḥm 3['NT].4.69
[--].w rbb. | š[---]npš išt. | w.l.tikl w l tš[t]. 2003.3

štn

.ṯbil. | bn is.bn tbdn. | bn uryy. | bn abd'n. | bn prkl. | bn štn. | bn annyn. | b[n] slg. | u[--] dit. | bn p[-]n. | bn nzǵil. 101[10].11
n. | bn.ykn. | bn.'ṯtrab. | uṣn[-]. | bn.alṯn. | bn.aš[-]š. | bn.štn. | bn.ilš. | bn.tnabn. | bn.ḥṣn. | ṣprn. | bn.ašbḥ. | bn.qṯnn. | bn 1046.1.16
[b]n[.---]. | bn [-]'y. | [b]n [i]lmd. | bn [t]bdn. | bn štn. | b[n] kdn. | bn dwn. | bn ḏrn. 2088.5
[.---.]nrn. | [b]n.nmq[.---]. | [ḫm]št.ksp.'l.aṯt. | [-]ṯd[.bn.]štn. 2055.20

t

t

.]mlk.yṯb br | r.w mḫ[--.---.]w q[--]. | ym.‘lm.y[---.---]. | t.k[-]ml.[---]. | l[---].w y[nt.qrt.---]. | [---.--]n[.w alp.l il.w bu] | APP.II[173].10

tan

rqd. | bn.abdg. | ilyn. | bn.tan. | bn.arm. | bn.b‘l.ṣdq. | bn.army. | bn.rpiyn. | bn.army. | bn 1046.1.4

tant

.]‘ṣ.w lḫšt. | [abn.rgm.l td]‘.nš[m.w l t]bn. | [hmlt.a]rṣ.[tant.šmm.‘m.ar]ṣ. | thmt.[‘mn.kbkbm.abn.brq]. | d l t[d‘.šm 3[‘NT].4.60
. | iṯ.l y.w argm k. | hwt.w aṯny k.rgm. | ‘ṣ.w lḫšt.abn. | tant.šmm.‘m.arṣ. | thmt.‘mn.kbkbm. | abn.brq.d l.td‘.šmm. | r 3[‘NT].3.21
.iṯ.l y.w argm k]. | hwt.w aṯny k[.rgm.‘ṣ.w lḫšt.abn]. | tunt.šmm.‘m[.arṣ.thmt.‘mn.kbkbm]. | rgm.l td‘.nš[m.w l tbn 1[‘NT.IX].3.14
.d argmn k]. | [h]wt.d aṯ[ny k.---.rgm.‘ṣ]. | w lḫšt.abn[.tant.šmm.‘m.arṣ.thmt]. | ‘m kbkbm[.abn.brq.d l td‘.šmm.at 7.2[130].19

taršn

spr.bnš.mlk. | d taršn.‘msn. | bṣr.abn.špšyn. | dqn. | aǵlmn. | kn‘m. | aḫršp. | an 2067.1.2

tiyn

n.bn.ḫrǵš[-].l.qrt. | šd.iǵlyn.bn.kzbn.l.qr[t]. | šd.pln.bn.tiyn.b d.ilmhr nḥl h. | šd knn.bn.ann.‘db. | šd.iln[-].bn.irṯr.l.s 2029.18

tišr

ḫmšm.dd. | n‘r. | ḫmšm.tišr. | ḫmš.ktnt. | ḫmš.ṯnt.alpm. | ‘šrm.hbn. | ṯlṯ.mat.dd. | š‘rm. 2102.3
ṯ.mat.ksp. | ḥṯbn.ybnn. | arb‘m.l.mit.šmn. | arb‘m.l.mit.tišr. | ṯṯ.ṯṯ.b [ṯ]ql.ṯlṯt.l.‘šrm.ksp hm. | sstm.b.šb‘m. | ṯlṯ.mat.tr 1127.4
t. | l.alp.šmn. | nḥ.ṯṯ.mat. | šm[n].rqḥ. | kkrm.brḏl. | mit.tišrm. | ṯlṯm.almg. | ḫmšm.kkr. | qnm. | ‘šrm.kk[r]. | brr. | [‘]šr 141[120].7
[---].ab h.krm ar. | [---.]h.mḥtrt.pṯtm. | [---.-]t h.ušpǵt tišr. | [---.šm]m h.nšat ẓl h kbkbm. | [---.]b km kbkbt k ṯn. | [- 2001.2.4

tu

--.--]ḥ. | b lṯk.bt. | [pt]ḥ.aḥd.l.bt.‘bdm. | [ṯ]n.ptḥ msb.bt.tu. | w.ptḥ[.aḥ]d.mmt. | ṯṯ.pt[ḥ.---]. | ṯn.pt[ḥ.---]. | w.pt[ḥ.--]r.ṯ 1151.10

tbbr

wy.b d.ydln. | [š].bn.trn.b d.ibrmḏ. | [š]d.bn.ilṯtmr.b d.tbbr. | [w.]šd.nḥl h.b d.ṯṯmd. | [š]d.b d.iwrḫṯ. | [ṯn].šdm.b d.g 82[300].1.11

tbd

t.---]. | ‘dn.[---]. | aḫqm bir[-.---]. | kṯrmlk.ns[--.---]. | bn.tbd.ilšt[m‘y.---]. | mty.ilšt[m‘y.---]. | bn.pynq.‘nqp[a]t[y.---]. | 90[314].2.6

tbdn

w nḥl h. | bn srd.bn agmn. | bn [-]ln.bn.ṯbil. | bn is.bn tbdn. | bn uryy. | bn abd‘n. | bn prkl. | bn štn. | bn annyn. | b[n] 101[10].7
[b]n[.---]. | bn [-]‘y. | [b]n [i]lmd. | bn [t]bdn. | bn štn. | b[n] kdn. | bn dwn. | bn ḏrn. 2088.4

tbk

rnm. | mḏrn.w.mšḫṯ. | d.mrkbt. | mlk. | mšḫṯ.w.msg. | d.tbk. 1122.16

tb‘

ksp hm. | l yblt. | w ht.luk ‘m ml[kt]. | ṯǵsdb.šmlšn. | w tb‘ ank. | ‘m mlakt h šm‘ h. | w b.‘ly skn.yd‘ rgm h. | w ht ab 1021.6
.yšlḥm.k[ṯ]rt. | w y[ššq].bnt.hll.snnt. | mk.b šb[‘.]ymm.tb‘.b bt h. | kṯrt.bnt.hll.snnt. | [-]d[-]t.n‘m y.‘rš.h[--]m. | ysms 17[2AQHT].2.39
yql[.y]šṯḥw[y.]w ykb[dn h.--]r y[---]. | [---.k]ṯr.w ḫ[ss.t]b‘.b[n.]bht.ym[.rm]m.hkl.ṯpṭ nh[r]. | [---.]hrn.w[---.]tb‘.k[ṯ 2.3[129].7
‘n.lṭpn.il d p[id]. | yd‘t k.bt.k anšt.w i[n.b ilht]. | qlṣ k.tb‘.bt.ḫnp.lb[k.--.ti] | ḫd.d iṯ.b kbd k.tšt.b [---]. | irt k.ḏt.ydt. 18[3AQHT].1.17
.--.ti] | ḫd.d iṯ.b kbd k.tšt.b [---]. | irt k.ḏt.ydt.m‘qb k.[ttb‘]. | [bt]lt.‘nt.idk.l ttn.[pnm]. | [‘m.a]qht.ǵzr.b alp.š[d]. | [rb 18[3AQHT].1.19
-].yṯbr[.---]. | [---.]uṯm.ḏr[qm.---]. | [btl]t.‘nt.l kl.[---]. | [tt]b‘.btlt.‘nt[.idk.l ttn.pnm]. | ‘m.yṭpn.mhr.š[t.tšu.g h]. | w tṣ 18[3AQHT].4.5
m.il.yšt k. | [b]‘l.‘nt.mḥrṯt. | iy.aliyn.b‘l. | iy.zbl.b‘l.arṣ. | ttb‘.btlt.‘nt. | idk.l ttn.pnm. | ‘m.nrt.ilm.špš. | tšu.g h.w tṣḥ. | t 6[49].4.30
hwt.aliy. | qrdm.bhṯ.l bn.ilm mt. | ‘bd k.an.w d.‘lm k. | tb‘.w l.yṯb.ilm.idk. | l ytn.pn.‘m.bn.ilm.mt. | tk.qrt h.hmry.m 5[67].2.13
.amt m.l yrt. | b npš.bn ilm.mt.b mh | mrt.ydd.il.ǵzr. | tb‘.w l.yṯb ilm.idk. | l ytn.pnm.‘m.b‘l. | mrym.ṣpn.w y‘n. | gp 5[67].1.9
.mdw. | anšt.‘rš.zbln. | rd.l mlk.amlk. | l drkt.k aṯb.an. | ytb‘.yṣb ǵlm.‘l. | ab h.y‘rb.yšu g h. | w yṣḥ.šm‘ m‘.l krt. | ṯ‘.išt 16.6[127].39
t]b‘.b[n.]bht.ym[.rm]m.hkl.ṯpṭ nh[r]. | [---.]hrn.w[---.]tb‘.k[ṯ]r w [ḫss.t]bn.bht zbl ym. | [trm]m.hk[l.ṯpṭ].nhr.bt k.[2.3[129].8
nty. | tšlḥm.tššqy ilm. | tsad.tkbd.hmt.b‘l. | ḥkpt il.kl h.tb‘.kṯr. | l ahl h.hyn.tb‘.l mš | knt h.apnk.dnil.m[t]. | rpi.aphn. 17[2AQHT].5.31
]u.l ytn. | [aḫ]r.mǵy.‘[d]t.ilm. | [w]y‘n.aliy[n.]b‘l. | [---.]tb‘.l lṭpn. | [il.d]pid.l tbrk. | [krt.]ṯ‘.l tmr.n‘mn. | [ǵlm.]il.ks.yi 15[128].2.13
. | tsad.tkbd.hmt.b‘l. | ḥkpt il.kl h.tb‘.kṯr. | l ahl h.hyn.tb‘.l mš | knt h.apnk.dnil.m[t]. | rpi.aphn.ǵzr.m[t]. | hrnmy.qš 17[2AQHT].5.32
adm]. | [rḥq.mlk.l bt y]. | [ng.kr]t.l ḥ[ẓ]r y. | [-----]. | [---.ttb‘]. | [mlakm.l yṯb]. | [idk.pnm.l ytn]. | [‘]m[.krt.mswn h]. | t 14[KRT].6.263
ytn. | b ḏrt y.ab.adm. | w ld.špḥ.l krk | t.w ǵlm.l ‘bd. | il.ttb‘.mlakm. | l yṯb.idk.pnm. | l ytn.‘mm.pbl. | mlk.tšan. | g hm 14[KRT].6.300
[--]. | mit.‘šrm.[k]bd.yn.ḥsp.l.y[--]. | ‘šrm.yn.ḥsp.l.ql.d.tb‘.mṣ[r]m. | mit.arb‘m.kbd.yn.mṣb. | l.mḏrǵlm. | ‘šrn ‘šr.yn. 1084.27
m.[t‘dt.ṯpṭ.nhr]. | b ‘lṣ.‘lṣm.npr.š[--.---]. | uṯ.tbr.ap hm.tb‘.ǵlm[m.al.ṯṯb.idk.pnm]. | al.ttn.‘m.pḫr.m‘d.t[k.ǵr.ll.l p‘n.i 2.1[137].13
tq h.d tqyn.hmlt.tn.b‘l.[w ‘nn h]. | bn.dgn.arṯ m.pḏ h.tb‘.ǵlmm.l ṯṯb.[idk.pnm]. | l ytn.tk.ǵr.ll.‘m.phr.m‘d.ap.ilm.l 2.1[137].19
.zt.ybl.arṣ.w pr. | ‘ṣm.yraun.aliyn.b‘l. | ṯṯ‘.nn.rkb.‘rpt. | tb‘.rgm.l bn.ilm.mt. | ṯny.l ydd.il ǵzr. | ṯḥm.aliyn.b‘l.hwt.aliy 5[67].2.8
š.yuḫdm.šb‘r. | amrr.k kbkb.l pnm. | aṯr.btlt.‘nt. | w b‘l.tb‘.mrym.ṣpn. | idk.l ttn.pnm. | ‘m.il.mbk.nhrm. | qrb.apq.th 4[51].4.19
[m]t.dm.ḫt.š‘tqt dm. | li.w ttb‘.š‘tqt. | bt.krt.bu.tbu. | bkt.tgly.w tbu. | nṣrt.tbu.pnm. | ‘rm 16.6[127].2

rt.grdš.mknt. | att.ṣdq h.l ypq. | mtrḫt.yšr h. | att.trḫ.w tb‘t. | ṯar um.tkn l h. | mṯlṯt.kṯrm.tmt. | mrb‘t.zblnm. | mḫmšt 14[KRT].1.14
[---.]b[--]. | [---].šḥr.[---]. | [---].al ytb‘[.--]. | [---.]l adn.ḥwt[.--]. | [--]h.w yššil[.--]. | [---.]lp[--]. 1023.3
y‘n[.dnil.mt.]rpi. | yṯb.ǵzr.m[t.hrnmy.y]šu. | g h.w yṣḥ.t[b‘.---]. | bkyt.b hk[l]y.mšspdt. | b ḥẓr y pẓǵm.ǵr.w yq. | dbḥ 19[1AQHT].4.182
ym.ḏnbtm. | tnn.l šbm. | tšt.trks. | l mrym.l bt[.---]. | p l.tb‘[.---]. | hmlt ḫt.[---]. | l.tp[-]m.[---]. | n[-]m[.---]. 1003.11
. | ‘š[--.---]d.lik[t.---]. | w [----]. | k[--.---]. | ‘šrm[.---]. | tšt.tb‘[.---]. | qrt.mlk[.---]. | w.‘l.ap.s[--.---]. | b hm.w.rgm.hw.al[-- 2008.2.3
ry y.---.--]p.mlḥm y. | [---.---]lt.qẓb. | [---.]šmḫ y. | [---.]tb‘. | [---.-]nnm. 5[67].2.26

tbṣr

spr.tbṣr. | klt.bt špš. 1175.1

tbq

| [bn] il. | [---]ṯ. | klṯtb. | gsn. | arm[w]l. | bn.ṣdqn. | ḫlbn. | tbq.alp. 2039.17
[s]pr.bnš.mlk.d.b.tbq. | [kr]wn. | [--]n. | [q]ṣy. | ṯn.bn.iwrḫz.[n]‘rm. | yṣr[.-]qb. | w 2066.1.1
‘]rby. | m‘r. | arny. | ‘nqpat. | š‘rt. | ubr‘y. | ilštm‘. | šbn. | tbq. | rqd. | [š]rš. | [-----]. | [-----]. | [-----]. | [-----]. | [-----]. | [-----]. 2058.1.17

tbšn

bdl.gt.bn.tbšn. | bn.mnyy.š‘rty. | aryn.aḏddy. | agpṯr. | šb‘l.mlky. | n‘mn. 91[311].1
--.]dd. | bn.arwdn.dd. | mnḫm.w.kbln. | bn.ǵlm.dd. | bn.tbšn.dd. | bn.ḫran.w[.---]. | [-]n.y‘rtym. | gmm.w.bn.p[--]. | trn 131[309].7
‘. | bn.aǵlyn.ṯt.qštm[.w.ṯl]ṯ.ql‘m. | bn.‘gw.qšt.w ql‘. | bn.tbšn.ṯlṯ.qšt.w.[ṯlṯ.]ql‘m. | bn.army.ṯt.qštm.w[.]q[l‘]. | bn.rpš.q 119[321].3.21

tbtḫ

]dyt. | ṣl‘t.alp.mri. | ‘šr.bmt.alp.mri. | ṯn.nšbm. | ṯmnym.tbtḫ.alp. | uz.mrat.mlḥt. | arb‘.uzm.mrat.bq‘. | ṯlṯ.[-]ṯt.aš[‘]t.š 1128.19

tbṯṯb

d. | [š]d.b d.iwrḫṭ. | [ṯn].šdm.b d.gmrd. | [šd.]lbny.b d.tbṯṯb. | [š]d.bn.ṭ[-]rn.b d.‘dbmlk. | [šd.]bn.brzn.b d.nwrḏ. | [šd 82[300].1.15
[---.]l[.---]. | [---.]l[.---]. | [---].tbṯṯ[b.---]. | [---].bn.b[--.---]. | [---].bn.ab[--.---]. | [---.]bn.a[--.-- 2162.A.3

tg

aḏml[--.---]. | tlbr[-.---]. | isg.[---]. | ilwn.[---]. | ṯrn.d[d]. | tg d[d]. | ḥdyn.d[d]. | [-]ḏḏn.d[d]. | qtn.d[d]. | lḫsn.d[d]. | lsn.d[132[331].6

tgḏn

n.‘rm[y]. | arśw.bṣry. | arpṯr.y‘rty. | bn.ḫdyn.ugrty. | bn.tgḏn.ugrty. | tgyn.arty. | bn.nryn.arty. | bn.ršp.ary. | bn.ǵlmn 87[64].9
ly. | [mḏ]rǵlm. | [bn.]kdgdl. | [b]n.qtn. | [b]n.ǵrgn. | [b]n.tgḏn. | bn.ḫdyn. | bn.sgr. | bn.aǵltn. | bn.ktln. | bn.‘gwn. | bn.yš 104[316].9
[pš]. | bn.kdrn. | ‘rgzy.w.bn.‘dy. | bn.gmḥn.w.ḥgbt. | bn.tgḏn. | yny. | [b]n.g‘yn dd. | [-]n.dd. | [--]an dd. | [-----]. | [-----]. 131[309].29

tgyn

św.bṣry. | arpṯr.y‘rty. | bn.ḫdyn.ugrty. | bn.tgḏn.ugrty. | tgyn.arty. | bn.nryn.arty. | bn.ršp.ary. | bn.ǵlmn ary. | bn.ḥṣbn 87[64].10
l.ybnn. | adn y. | rgm. | tḥm.t[g]yn. | bn k. | l.p[‘n.adn y]. | q[lt.---]. | l.yb[nn]. | b‘l y.r[gm]. | 2115.1.4
-]. | w ni[t.w.m‘ṣd]. | w ḫrmṯt. | ṯlṯm.ar[b‘]. | kbd.ksp. | ‘l.tgyn. | w ‘l.aṯt h. | ypḥ.m‘nt. | bn.lbn. 2053.20
mḏrǵlm.dt.inn. | b d.tlmyn. | b d.gln.ary. | tgyn.y‘rty. | bn.krwn.b.yny.iytlm. | śgryn.ary.b.yny. | bn.ydd 2071.4
[--]ǵyn.b[n.---]. | krwn.b[n.---]. | tgyn.m‘[---]. | w.agpṯn[.---]. | ṯyndr[-.---]. | gt.tg[yn.---]. | pwn[. 103[334].3
swn. | ḫmš ‘šr.sp. | l bnš tpnr d yaḫd l g ynm. | ṯṯ spm l tgyn. | arb‘ spm l ll[-]. | ṯn spm.l slyy. | ṯlṯ spm l dlšpš amry. 137.2[93].12
dš. | [---].b.dmt qdš. | [---.--]n.b.anan. | [--]yl.b.bq‘t.b.gt.tgyn. | [--]in.b.trzy. | [--]yn.b.glltky. | ṯd[y]n.b.glltky. | lbw[-].u 2118.6
.b[n.---]. | tgyn.m‘[---]. | w.agpṯn[.---]. | ṯyndr[-.---]. | gt.tg[yn.---]. | pwn[.---]. 103[334].6

tgn

bn.-]nn. | [bn.-]dn. | bn.ummt. | bn.ṯb[-]. | bn.[-]r[-]. | bn.tgn. | bn.iḏrn. | mnn. | b[n].skn. | bn.p‘ṣ. | bn.ḏrm. | [bn.-]ln. | [b 124[-].6.7

tgǵln

.ytn. | b‘ltǵpṯm.krwn.ilšn.agyn. | mnn.šr.ugrt.ḏkr.yṣr. | tgǵln.ḫmš.ddm. | [---].ḫmš.ddm. | ṯṯ.l.‘šrm.bn[š.mlk.---].ḫzr.l 2011.38

tgr

.[ks.b yd]. | krpn.b klat yd.[---]. | km ll.kḥṣ.tusp[.---]. | tgr.il.bn h.ṯr[.---]. | w y‘n.lṭpn.il.d p[id.---]. | šm.bn y.yw.ilt.[- 1[‘NT.X].4.12

tgrš

klby.qšt.w.ql‘. | bq‘t. | ily.qšt.w.ql‘. | bn.ḫrẓn.qšt.w.ql‘. | tgrš.qšt.w.ql‘. | špšyn.qšt.w.ql‘. | bn.ṯ‘ln.qš[t.w.q]l‘. | ‘ṯqbt.qšt. 119[321].2.24

tgtn

w.nḥ[l h]. | bn.ẓr[-]. | mru.skn. | bn.bddn. | bn.ǵrgn. | bn.tgtn. | bn.ḥrẓn. | bn.qdšt. | bn.nṯǵ[-]. | bn.gr[--]. | bn.[---]. | bn.[- 113[400].5.9

td

li[yn.]b‘l. | al.tšt.u[rb]t.b bht m. | ḥln.b q[rb.hk]l m. | al td[.pdr]y.bt ar. | [---.ṭ]l]y.bt.rb. | [---.m]dd.il ym. | [---.-]qlṣn.w 4[51].6.10

tdgr

bǵlm.ǵlm[n]. | w.trhy.aṯt h. | w.mlky.b[n] h. | ily.mrily.tdgr. 2048.22

tdn

[---.]ṯlṯm.d.nlqḥt. | [bn.ḫ]tyn.yd.bt h. | [aǵ]ltn. | tdn.bn.ddy. | ‘bdil[.b]n ṣdqn. | bnšm.h[-]mt.ypḥm. | kbby.yd. 2045.4
‘bdyrḫ. | ubn.ḫyrn. | ybnil.adrdn. | klyn.kkln. | ‘dmlk.tdn. | ‘zn.pǵdn. | [a]nndn. | [r]špab. | [-]glm. 1070.5

yḥmn.bnil. | ‘dn.w.ildgn.ḥtbm. | tdġlm.iln.b‘[l]n.alḏy. | tdn.ṣr[--.--]t.‘zn.mtn.n[bd]g. | ḥrš qṭn[.---.]dqn.b‘ln. | ġltn.‘bd 2011.22

tdġl

b d.mlkytn. | kdrl. | slṯmg. | adrdn. | l[l]wn. | ydln. | ldn. | tdġl. | ibrkyṯ. 1034.9
n.y‘r. | adb‘l[.---].ḥdṯn.yḥmn.bnil. | ‘dn.w.ildgn.ḥtbm. | tdġlm.iln.b‘[l]n.alḏy. | tdn.ṣr[--.--]t.‘zn.mtn.n[bd]g. | ḥrš qṭn[2011.21
m. | mṣrn. | mḏrġlm. | agmy. | ‘dyn. | ‘bdb‘l. | ‘bdkṯr.‘bd. | tdġl. | b‘lṣn. | nsk.ksp. | iwrtn. | ydln. | ‘bdilm. | dqn. | nsk.ṯlṯ. | ‘b 1039.2.21

thm

.šd.aṯrt.w rḥmy. | [---].y[ṯ]b. | [---]p.gp ym.w yṣġd.gp..thm. | [yqḥ.]il.mšt‘ltm.mšt‘ltm.l riš.agn. | hl h.[t]špl.hl h.trm 23[52].30
um.pḫl.pḫlt.bt.abn.bt šmm w thm. | qrit.l špš.um h.špš.um.ql.bl.‘m. | il.mbk nhrm.b ‘dt.th UG5.7.1

thmt

bm.šb‘.šnt. | yṣr k.b‘l.ṯmn.rkb. | ‘rpt.bl.ṭl.bl rbb. | bl.šr‘.thmtm.bl. | ṭbn.ql.b‘l.k tmz‘. | kst.dnil.mt.rpi. | all.ġzr.m[t.]hr 19[1AQHT].1.45
nši.‘n h.w tphn. | [---.--]ml.ksl h.k b[r]q. | [---.]m[-]ġ[-].thmt.brq. | [---].tṣb.qšt.bnt. | [---.‘]n h.km.bṯn.yqr. | [krpn h.-. 17[2AQHT].6.12
.w tr.arṣ.idk. | [l ttn.pn]m.‘m il.mbk.nhrm. | [qrb.ap]q.thmtm tgly.ḏd il. | [w tbu.qr]š.mlk.ab.šnm. | [l p‘n.il.t]hbr.w 17[2AQHT].6.48
.a]rṣ.id[k.l ttn.p]nm. | [‘m.i]l.mbk.nhr[m.qr]b.[ap]q. | [thm]tm.tgl.ḏ[d.]i[l.]w tbu. | [qr]š.m[l]k.ab[.šnm.]mṣr. | [t]bu. 3[‘NT.VI].5.15
ḥ.ġyrm]. | [idk.]l ytn.pnm.‘m.[i]l.mbk.[nhrm.qrb.apq.thmtm]. | [ygly.]ḏl i[l].w ybu[.q]rš.mlk[.ab.šnm.l p‘n.il.] | [yh 2.3[129].4
mrym.ṣpn. | idk.l ttn.pnm. | ‘m.il.mbk.nhrm. | qrb.apq.thmtm. | tgly.ḏd.il.w tbu. | qrš.mlk.ab.šnm. | l p‘n.il.thbr.w tq 4[51].4.22
.l ilm. | [id]k.l ttn.pnm.‘m. | [il.]mbk nhrm.qrb. | [a]pq.thmtm.tgly.ḏd. | il.w tbu.qrš.. | mlk.ab.šnm.l p‘n. | il.thbr.w t 6.1.34[49.1.6]
[idk.l ttn.pnm]. | [‘m.il.mbk.nhrm]. | [qrb.apq.thmtm]. | [tgly.ḏd.il.w]tb[a]. | [qrš.mlk.ab.]šnm. | [tša.g hm. 5[67].6.01
. | qrit.l špš.um h.špš.um.ql.bl.‘m. | il.mbk nhrm.b ‘dt.thmtm. | mnt.nṯk.nḥš.šmrr.nḥš. | ‘q šr.ln h.mlḫš abd.ln h.yd UG5.7.3
wt.d aṯ[ny k.---.rgm.‘ṣ]. | w lḫšt.abn[.tant.šmm.‘m.arṣ.thmt]. | ‘m kbkbm[.abn.brq.d l td‘.šmm.at m]. | w ank.ib[ġy 7.2[130].19
m.l td]‘.nš[m.w l t]bn. | [hmlt.a]rṣ.[tant.šmm.‘m.ar]ṣ. | thmt.[‘mn.kbkbm.abn.brq]. | d l t[d‘.šmm.at m.w ank]. | ibġ[3[‘NT].4.61
| hwt.w aṯny k.rgm. | ‘ṣ.w lḫšt.abn. | tant.šmm.‘m.arṣ. | thmt.‘mn.kbkbm. | abn.brq.d l.td‘.šmm. | rgm l td‘.nšm.w l t 3[‘NT].3.22
hwt.w aṯny k[.rgm.‘ṣ.w lḫšt.abn]. | tunt.šmm.‘m[.arṣ.thmt.‘mn.kbkbm]. | rgm.l td‘.nš[m.w l tbn.hmlt.arṣ]. | at.w a 1[‘NT.IX].3.14
t ṣwd[t.---]. | tlk b mdb[r.---]. | tḥdṯn w hl[.---]. | w tglṯ thmt.‘[--.---]. | yṣi.ġl h tḥm b[.---]. | mrḥ h l adrt[.---]. | ṯṯb ‘ṯtr 2001.1.5

twyn

bn.gnb[.msg]. | bn.twyn[.msg]. | bn.‘drš[p.msg]. | pyn.yny.[msg]. | bn.mṣrn m[sg 133[-].1.2

twr

[-----]. | yṣq.šm[n.---]. | ‘n.tr.arṣ.w šmm. | sb.l qṣm.arṣ. | l ksm.mhyt.‘n. | l arṣ.m[t]r.b‘l. | 16[126].3.2
. | aṯ[t.---]. | aḫ k[.---]. | tr.ḥ[---]. | w tṣḥ[.---]. | tšqy[.---]. | tr.ḥt[-.---]. | w msk.tr[.---]. | tqrb.aḫ[h.w tṣḥ]. | lm.tb‘rn[.---]. 16.2[125].77
]. | ki[--.---]. | w ḫ[--.---]. | my[.---]. | aṯ[t.---]. | aḫ k[.---]. | tr.ḥ[---]. | w tṣḥ[.---]. | tšqy[.---]. | tr.ḥt[-.---]. | w msk.tr[.---]. | t 16.2[125].74
]. | tr.ḥ[---]. | w tṣḥ[.---]. | tšqy[.---]. | tr.ḥt[-.---]. | w msk.tr[.---]. | tqrb.aḫ[h.w tṣḥ]. | lm.tb‘rn[.---]. | mn.yrḫ.k m[rṣ.---] 16.2[125].78

tznt

ṯnt.d ṯl | ṯ mat. | ṯṯ.ṯnt.d alp | alpm.ṯlṯ ktt. | alp.brr. | kkr.tznt. | ḫmšt.kkr tyt. 1130.16

tḥm

rt h.hmry.mk.ksu. | ṯbt.ḫḫ.arṣ.nḫlt h.tša. | g hm.w tṣḥ.tḥm.aliyn. | bn.b‘l.hwt.aliy.qrdm. | bhṯ.bn.ilm.mt.‘bd k.an. | 5[67].2.17
y.w k | bd hwt.w rgm. | l bn.ilm.mt. | ṯny.l ydd. | il.ġzr.tḥm. | aliyn.b‘l. | [hw]t.aliy.q | [rdm.]bht y.bnt. | [dt.ksp.dtm]. 4[51].8.32
]. | arṣy bt.y[‘bdr.---]. | rgm l btl[t.‘nt.ṯny.l ybmt.limm.tḥm.aliyn.b‘l]. | hw[t.aliy.qrdm.qryy.b arṣ.mlḥmt.št]. | [b ‘]p 7.2[130].13
ṯt‘.nn.rkb.‘rpt. | tb‘.rgm.l bn.ilm.mt. | ṯny.l ydd.il ġzr. | tḥm.aliyn.b‘l.hwt.aliy. | qrdm.bhṯ.l bn.ilm mt. | ‘bd k.an.w d. 5[67].2.10
kbd hwt. | w rgm.l kṯr. | w ḫss.ṯny.l h | yn.d ḥrš.ydm. | tḥm.al[iyn.b‘l]. | h[wt.aliy.qrdm]. 3[‘NT.VI].6.24
kb.‘rpt. | [-]‘n.ġlmm.y‘nyn.l ib.yp‘. | l b‘l.ṣrt.l rkb.‘rpt. | tḥm.aliyn.b‘l.hwt.aliy. | qrdm.qry.b arṣ.mlḥmt. | št.b ‘p[r] m. 3[‘NT].4.51
tštḥwy.kbd hyt. | w rgm.l btlt.‘nt. | ṯny.l ymmt.limm. | tḥm.aliyn.b‘l.hwt. | aliy.qrdm.qry.b arṣ. | mlḥmt št.b ‘pr m.d 3[‘NT].3.10
tḥm iwrḏr. | l iwrpḫn. | bn y.aḫ y.rgm. | ilm.tġr k. | tšlm k. | ik 138.1
tḥm.iwrḏr. | l iwrpḫn. | bn y.aḫ y.rgm. | ilm.tġr k. | tšlm k. | ik 138.1
tḥm.iwrḏr. | l.plsy. | rgm. | yšlm.l k. | l.trġds. | w.l.klby. | šm‘t.ḫ 53[54].1
l.mlkt. | adt y.rgm. | tḥm.illdr. | ‘bd k.. | l.p‘n a[dt y]. | šb‘ d[.w šb‘ d]. | mrḥq[tm.ql 1014.3
[t]ḥm.iṯtl. | l mnn.ilm. | tġr k.tšlm k. | t‘zz k.alp ymm. | w rbt.š 1019.1.1
[t]ḥm.uṯryn[.---]. | [g]rgš ‘bdy[--]. | [--.]l mlk [---]. | [---].aḫ y[.- 2130.1.1
[r.---]. | tḥdṯn w hl[.---]. | w tglṯ thmt.‘[--.---]. | yṣi.ġl h tḥm b[.---]. | mrḥ h l adrt[.---]. | ṯṯb ‘ṯtrt b ġl[.---]. | qrẓ tšt.l š 2001.1.6
.idk. | l ytn.pnm.‘m.b‘l. | mrym.ṣpn.w y‘n. | gpn.w ugr.tḥm.bn ilm. | mt.hwt.ydd.bn.il. | ġzr.p np.š.npš.lbim. | thw.h 5[67].1.12
.---]. | [--]l.bn y.šḥt.w [---]. | [--]tt.msgr.bn k[.---]. | [--]n.tḥm.b‘l[.---]. 59[100].12
tḥm.hl[--]. | l pḫry.a[ḫ y]. | w l g.p[-]r[--]. | yšlm[.l k]. | [i]lm[.t 56[21].1
[l.ml]k.[b‘l y]. | rg[m]. | tḥm.wr[--]. | yšlm.[l] k. | ilm.t[ġ]r k. | tšlm k. | lm[.l.]likt. | ši[l. 2010.3
tḥm.ydn.‘m.mlk. | b‘l h.nġr.ḥwt k. | w l.a[--]t.tšknn. | ḫmšm.l 2062.1.1
-.am] | r ṯny.d‘t km.w rgm.l ṯr.a[b.-.il.ṯny.l pḫr]. | m‘d.tḥm.ym.b‘l km.adn km.t[pṭ.nhr]. | tn.il m.d tq h.d tqyn.hml 2.1[137].17
‘t hm.išt.ištm.yitmr.ḥrb.ltšt. | [--]n hm.rgm.l ṯr.ab h.il.tḥm.ym.b‘l km. | [adn]km.ṯpṭ.nhr.tn.il m.d tq h.d tqyn h. | [2.1[137].33
n.b ilht.ql[ṣ] k.mh.tarš[n]. | l btlt.‘nt.w t[‘]n.btlt.‘n[t]. | tḥm k.il.ḥkm.ḥkm k. | ‘m.‘lm.ḥyt.ḥẓt.tḥm k. | mlk n.aliyn.b‘l 3[‘NT.VI].5.38
m.yd.il mlk. | yḫss k.ahbt.ṯr.t‘rr k. | w t‘n.rbt.aṯrt ym. | tḥm k.il.ḥkm.ḥkmt. | ‘m ‘lm.ḥyt.ḥẓt. | tḥm k.mlk n.aliy[n.]b‘ 4[51].4.41
t‘n.rbt.aṯrt ym. | tḥm k.il.ḥkm.ḥkmt. | ‘m ‘lm.ḥyt.ḥẓt. | tḥm k.mlk n.aliy[n.]b‘l. | ṯpṭ n.w in.d ‘ln h. | klny n.q[š] h.n[4[51].4.43
t[‘]n.btlt.‘n[t]. | tḥm k.il.ḥkm.ḥkm k. | ‘m.‘lm.ḥyt.ḥẓt.tḥm k. | mlk n.aliyn.b‘l.ṯpṭ n. | in.d ‘ln h.klny y.qš h. | nbln.kl 3[‘NT.VI].5.39

tḥm

ṯb.idk.pnm.|l ytn.ʿmm.pbl.|mlk.tšan.|g hm.w tṣḥn.|tḥm.krt.ṯ[ʿ].|hwt.[n]ʿmn.[ǵlm.il]. 14[KRT].6.305
l mlkt.u[m] y.|[rg]m[.]t[ḥm].|mlk.bn [k].|[l].pʿn.um [y].|qlt[.l um] y.|yšlm.il[m]. 1013.2
l.mlkt.|um y.rgm.|tḥm.mlk.|bn k.|l.pʿn.um y.|qlt.l.um y.|yšlm.ilm.|tǵr k.tšl 50[117].3
tḥm.mlk.|l.ṯryl.um y.rgm.|yšlm.l k.ilm.|tǵr k.tšlm k.|lḥt.š 2009.1.1
l.mlk.ugrt.|aḫ y.rgm.|tḥm.mlk.ṣr.aḫ k.|y[š]lm.l k.ilm.|tǵr k.tšlm k.|hn ny.ʿm n.| 2059.3
l.mlk[.u]grt.|iḫ y.rgm.|[tḥ]m.m[lk.-]bl[-].|yšlm.l[k].ilm.|tǵr.tšl[m] k.|[-----].|[-----] 2159.3
tḥm.ml[k.---].|l.mlk.[---].|rg[m].|hn.i[---].|ds[-.---].|t[--.---] 2127.1.1
.|bn k.|l.p[ʿn.adn y].|q[lt.---].|l.yb[nn].|bʿl y.r[gm].|tḥm.ʿbd[--].|ʿbd k.|l pʿn.bʿl y.|ṯn id.šbʿ d.|mrḥqtm.|qlt.ʿm. 2115.2.3
.id]k.|pn[m.al.ttn].|ʿm.[krt.msw]n.|w r[gm.l krt.]ṯʿ.|tḥm[.pbl.mlk].|qḥ.[ksp.w yr]q.|ḫrṣ[.yd.mqm] h.|ʿbd[.ʿlm.ṯl 14[KRT].5.249
.ḥrṯ.zǵt.|klb.ṣpr.w ylak.|mlakm.l k.ʿm.krt.|mswn h.tḥm.pbl.mlk.|qḥ.ksp.w yrq.ḫrṣ.|yd.mqm h.w ʿbd.ʿlm.|ṯlṯ.s 14[KRT].3.125
.pnm.l ytn].|[ʿ]m[.krt.mswn h].|tš[an.g hm.w tṣḥn].|tḥ[m.pbl.mlk].|qḥ[.ksp.w yrq].|ḫrṣ.[yd.mqm h].|w ʿbd[.ʿl 14[KRT].6.268
tḥm.pgn.|l.mlk.ugrt.|rgm.|yšlm.l k.[il]m.|tǵr k.tšlm k.|hn 2061.1
ttn.w tn.|w l ttn.|w al ttn.|tn ks yn.|w ištn.|ʿbd.prṯ.tḥm.|qrq.pṯ.ḏmn.|l iṯtl. 1019.2.1
l.mlk.b[ʿl y].|r[gm].|tḥm.rb.mi[--.ʿ]bd k.|l.pʿn.bʿl y[.mrḥqtm].|šbʿ d.w.šbʿ[d.qlt 2008.1.3
tḥm.rgm.|mlk.|l ḥyil.|lm.tlik.ʿm y.|ik y.aškn.|ʿṣm.l bt.dm 1010.1
tḥm.špš.|l.ʿmrpi.rgm.|ʿm špš.kll.mid m.|šlm.|l.[--]n.špš.|a 2060.1
l.ybnn.|adn y.|rgm.|tḥm.t[g]yn.|bn k.|l.p[ʿn.adn y].|q[lt.---].|l.yb[nn].|bʿl y.r[g 2115.1.4
l um y.adt ny.|rgm.|tḥm.tlmyn.|w.aḫtmlk ʿbd k.|l.pʿn.adt ny.|mrḥqtm.|qlny.il 51[95].3
tḥm[.t]lm[yn].|l ṯryl.um y.|rgm.|ugrt.tǵr k.|ugrt.tǵr k.|tšl 1015.1
l.mlkt.|adt y.|rgm.|tḥm.tlmyn.|ʿbd k.|l.pʿn.|adt y.|šbʿ d.|w.šbʿ id.|mrḥqtm.| 52[89].4
l.mlk.bʿ[l] y.|rgm.|tḥm.ṯpṯbʿ[l].|[ʿ]bd k.|[l.p]ʿn.bʿl y.|[šbʿ] d.šbʿ [d].|[mr]ḥqtm 2063.3
t.|[yhbr.w yql.yšt]ḥwyn.w y|[kbdn h.yšu.g h.w y]ṣḥ.tḥm.|[ṯr.il.ab k.hwt.l]ṭpn.ḥtk k.|[qryy.b arṣ.mlḥ]mt.št b ʿp 1[ʿNT.IX].2.17
kbd.hwt].|w rgm l k[ṯr.w ḫss.ṯny.l hyn].|d ḥrš.y[dm.tḥm.ṯr.il.ab k.]|hwt.lṭpn[.ḥtk k.---].|yh.kṯr.b[---].|št.lskt.n 1[ʿNT.IX].3.5
tlt.ʿnt.|idk.l ttn.pnm.|ʿm.nrt.ilm.špš.|tšu.g h.w tṣḥ.|tḥm.ṯr.il.ab k.|hwt.lṭpn.ḥtk k.|pl.ʿnt.šdm.y špš.|pl.ʿnt.šdm. 6[49].4.34
].|d.yqḥ[.---].|hm.ṯn.[---].|hn dt.[---].|[-----].|[-----].|tḥm[.---].|l pʿn.bʿl y[.---].|qlt.|[--]t.mlk.d.y[mlk].|[--.]ʿbdyr 2064.9
[tḥm.---].|[l.---].|[a]ḫt y.rgm.|[y]šlm.l k.|[il]m.tšlm k.|[tǵ]r 1016.1
l.rb.khnm.|rgm.|tḥm.[---].|yšlm[.l k.ilm].|tšlm[k.tǵr] k.|tʿzz[k.---.]lm.|w t 55[18].3
]m.l aṯt |[h.k]y[ṣḥ.]šmʿ.mʿ.|[--.]ʿm[.-.]aṯt y[.-].|[---.]tḥm.|[---]t.[ ]r.|[---.--]n.|[---] h.l ʿdb.|[---]n.yd h.|[---].bl.išl 14[KRT].5.231

tḥr

[---.]gtn ṯṯ.|[---.]tḥr l ytn ḫs[n].|ʿbd ulm ṯn un ḫsn.|gdy lqḥ ṣtqn gt bn ndr. 1154.2

tḥt

.dnil.mt.|rpi.a hn.ǵzr.mt.hrnm[y].|ytšu.yṯb.b ap.ṯǵr.tḥt.|adrm.d b grn.ydn.|dn.almnt.yṯpṭ.ṯpṭ.ytm.|b nši ʿn h.w 17[2AQHT].5.6
m]t.rpi.ap[h]n.ǵzr.|[mt.hrn]my.ytšu.|[yṯb.b ap.ṯ]ǵr[.t]ḥt.|[adrm.d b grn.y]dn.|[dn.almnt.y]ṯpṭ.|[ṯpṭ.ytm.---] h.| 19[1AQHT].1.22
yʿdd.tḥt.bn arbn.|ʿbdil.tḥt.ilmlk.|qly.tḥt bʿln.nsk. 1053.2
yʿdd.tḥt.bn arbn.|ʿbdil.tḥt.ilmlk.|qly.tḥt bʿln.nsk. 1053.1
mlk.gbʿ h d [---].|ibr.k l hm.d l h q[--.---].|l ytn.l hm.tḥt bʿl[.---].|h.u qšt pn hdd.b y[.----].|ʿm.b ym bʿl ysy ym[. 9[33].2.5
yʿdd.tḥt.bn arbn.|ʿbdil.tḥt.ilmlk.|qly.tḥt bʿln.nsk. 1053.3
ʿnt.tǵdd.kbd h.b ṣḥ]q.ymlu.lb h.|[b šmḫt.kbd.ʿnt.tšyt.tḥt h.k]kdrt.riš.|[ʿl h.k irbym.kp.---.k br]k.tǵll.b dm.|[ḏmr 7.1[131].8
ṣb.bn.|qrytm tmḫṣ.lim.ḫp y[m].|tṣmt.adm.ṣat.š[p]š.|tḥt h.k kdrt.ri[š].|ʿl h.k irbym.kp.k.qṣm.|ǵrmn.kp.mhr.ʿtkt 3[ʿNT].2.9
nšq.|[-]htm.l arṣ.ypl.ul ny.w l.ʿpr.ʿẓm ny.|l bʿl[-.---].|tḥt.ksi.zbl.ym.w ʿn.kṯr.w ḫss.l rgmt.|l k.l zbl.bʿl.ṯnt.l rkb.ʿr 2.4[68].7
---.--]n.d[--.]bnš[.---].|[---.]idmt.n[--.]t[--].|[---.--]r.dlt.tḥt n.|[---.]dlt.|[---.b]nš.|[---.]ypʿ.|[---.]b[--]. 2158B.3
].|[---.kpt]r.l r[ḥq.ilm.ḥkpt.l rḥq].|[ilnym.ṯn.mṯpd]m.t[ḥt.ʿnt.arṣ.ṯlṯ.mtḥ.ǵyrm].|[idk.]l ytn.pnm.ʿm.[i]l.mbk.[nhr 2.3[129].3
n[.šnt.kptr].|l rḥq.ilm.ḥkp[t.l rḥq.ilnym].|ṯn.mṯpdm.tḥt.[ʿnt.arṣ.ṯlṯ.mtḥ].|ǵyrm.idk.l yt[n.pnm.ʿm.lṭpn].|il d pid. 1[ʿNT.IX].3.20
an.šnt.|uǵr.l rḥq.ilm.inbb.|l rḥq.ilnym.ṯn.mṯpdm.|tḥt.ʿnt.arṣ.ṯlṯ.mtḥ.ǵyrm.|idk.l ttn pnm.ʿm.bʿl.|mrym.ṣpn.b 3[ʿNT].4.80
p]|t h.hwt h.knp.hrgb.bʿl.ṯbr.|bʿl.ṯbr.diy.hwt.w yql.|tḥt.pʿn h.ybqʿ.kbd h.w yḥd.|[i]n.šmt.in.ʿẓm.yšu.g[h].|w yṣ 19[1AQHT].3.130
yṣ]a.|b špt h.hwt h.knp.ṣml.bʿ[l].|bʿl.ṯbr.diy.hyt.tq[l.tḥt].|pʿn h.ybqʿ.kbd h.w yḥd.|iṯ.šmt.iṯ.ʿẓm.w yqḥ b hm.|aq 19[1AQHT].3.143
t h.hwt[h].|knp.nšrm.bʿl.yṯbr.|bʿl.ṯbr.diy hmt.tqln.|tḥt.pʿn h.ybqʿ.kbdt hm.w[yḥd].|in.šmt.in.ʿẓm.yšu.g h.|w y 19[1AQHT].3.116
w l k.|[---]m.l aqry k.b ntb.pšʿ.|[---].b ntb.gan.ašql k.tḥt.|[pʿn y.a]nk.nʿmn.ʿmq.nšm.|[tdʿṣ.pʿn]m.w tr.arṣ.idk.|[l 17[2AQHT].6.44
.w yṣḥ.knp.hr[g]b.|bʿl.yṯb.bʿl.y[ṯb]r.diy[.h]wt.|w yql.tḥt.pʿn y.ibqʿ.kbd[h].|w aḥd.hm.iṯ.šmt.hm.iṯ[.ʿẓm].|abky. 19[1AQHT].3.124
|yšu.g h.w yṣḥ.knp.ṣml.|bʿl.yṯbr.bʿl.yṯbr.diy.|hyt.tql.tḥt.pʿn y.ibqʿ.|kbd h.w aḥd.hm.iṯ.šmt.iṯ.|ʿẓm.abky w aqbrn 19[1AQHT].3.138
h.]w yṣḥ[.knp.nšrm].|bʿl.yṯb.bʿl.yṯb[r.diy.hmt].|tqln.tḥ pʿn y.ibq[ʿ.kbd hm.w] |aḥd.hm.iṯ.šmt.hm.i[ṯ].|ʿẓm.abky. 19[1AQHT].3.109
n y[n] ʿd šbʿ.|trṯ.ʿd.škr.yʿdb.yrḫ.|gb h.km.[---.]yqtqt.tḥt.|ṯlḥnt.il.d ydʿnn.|yʿdb.lḥm.l h.w d l ydʿnn.|d.mṣd.|ylm UG5.1.1.5
l.d ydʿnn.|yʿdb.lḥm.l h.w d l ydʿnn.|d.mṣd.|ylmn.ḫt.tḥt.ṯlḥn.|b qrʿ.|ʿṯtrt.w ʿnt.ymǵy.|ʿṯtrt.tʿdb.nšb l h.|w ʿnt.kt UG5.1.1.8
.bn.ẓlm[t].|rmt.prʿt.ibr[.mnt].|ṣḥrrm.ḥbl[.--].|ʿrpt.tḥt.[---]|m ʿṣrm.ḥ[---].|glṯ.isr[.---]|m.brt[.---].|ymt m.[---]. 8[51FRAG].11
ṯṯ.|[ušn.yp kn.---.--]l.il.tʿḏr bʿl.|[-----.]lšnt.|[---.--]yp.tḥt.|[-----].|[---.]w npy gr.|[ḥmyt.ugrt.w npy.yman.w npy.ʿ APP.I[-].1.10

tyn

nḥl h.|šd.annmn.b d.tyn.nḥl h.|šd.pǵyn[.b] d.krmn.l.ty[n.n]ḥl h.|šd.krz.[b]n.ann.ʿ[db].|šd.ṯ[r]yn.bn.tkn.b d.qrt. 2029.12
bzn.[-]l.qrt.|[š]d.agpṯr.b d.sḫrn.nḥl h.|šd.annmn.b d.tyn.nḥl h.|šd.pǵyn[.b] d.krmn.l.ty[n.n]ḥl h.|šd.krz.[b]n.an 2029.11

tyt

kdwṯ.l.grgyn.b.ṯq[l]. | ḫmšm.šmt.b.ṯql. | kkr.w.[ml]tḥ.tyt.[---]. | [b]šb'[m.w.n]ṣp.ksp. | [tgm]r.[alp.w.]ṯlṯ.mat. 2101.26

mr.škm. | [---.ṯṯ.dd.]gdl.ṯṯ.dd.š'rm. | [---.a]lp.arb'.mat.tyt. | [---.kd.]nbt.k[d.]šmn.mr. | [---.l]tḥ.sb[by]n.ltḥ.šḥ[lt]. | [-- 142[12].14

t.ṯnt.d alp | alpm.ṯlṯ ktt. | alp.brr. | kkr.tznt. | ḫmšt.kkr tyt. 1130.17

tk

k.mla[t.r]umm. | tšu knp.btlt.'n[t]. | tšu.knp.w tr.b 'p. | tk.aḫ šmk.mlat rumm. | w yšu.'n h.aliyn.b'l. | w yšu.'n h.w y 10[76].2.12

t hn.aḫd.b yd h. | w qṣ't h.bm.ymn h. | idk.l ytn pnm. | tk.aḫ.šmk.mla[t.r]umm. | tšu knp.btlt.'n[t]. | tšu.knp.w tr.b ' 10[76].2.9

m.trǵnw.w ṯṯkl. | bnwt h.ykr.'r.d qdm. | idk.pnm.l ytn.tk aršḫ.rbt. | w aršḫ.ṯrrt.ydy.b 'ṣm.'r'r. | w b šḥt.'s.mt.'r'rm.y UG5.7.63

rṣ. | [---.]špm.'db. | [---].t'tqn. | [---.-]'b.idk. | [l ytn.pnm.tk.]in.bb.b alp ḥẓr. | [rbt.kmn.l p']n.'nt. | [yhbr.w yql.yšt]ḥw 1['NT.IX].2.14

nmrt h.l r | [--.]arṣ.'z k.ḏmr k.l[-] | n k.ḥtk k.nmrt k.b tk. | ugrt.l ymt.špš.w yrḫ. | w n'mt.šnt.il. UG5.2.2.10

[idk.al.ttn.pnm.tk.ḥkpt.il.kl h]. | [kptr.]ks[u.ṯbt h.ḥkpt.arṣ.nḥlt h]. | b alp.šd. 1['NT.IX].3.01

m.šmšr. | l dgy.aṯrt. | mǵ.l qdš.amrr. | idk.al.tnn. | pnm.tk.ḥqkpt. | il.kl h.kptr. | ksu.ṯbt h.ḥkpt. | arṣ.nḥlt h. | b alp.šd. 3['NT.VI].6.13

t.arṣ.ṯlṯ.mtḥ]. | ǵyrm.idk.l yt[n.pnm.'m.lṯpn]. | il d pid.tk ḫrš[n.---.tk.ǵr.ks]. | ygly ḏd.i[l.w ybu.qrš.mlk]. | ab.šnm.l [1['NT.IX].3.22

.ḥš k. | ['ṣ k.'bṣ k.'m y.p']n k.tlsmn. | ['m y.twtḥ.išd] k.tk.ḫršn. | [---.-]bd k.spr. | [---.-]nk. 1['NT.IX].2.23

š k.'ṣ k.'bṣ k.']m y.p[']n k. | [tlsmn.'m y.twt]ḥ.išd k. | [tk.ḫršn.---]r.[-]ḥm k.w št. | [---.]ẓ[--.-]rdy k. | [---.i]qnim. | [---. 1['NT.IX].2.3

]. | ḥš k.'ṣ k.'[bṣ k.'m y.p'n k.tlsmn]. | 'm y twtḥ.i[šd k.tk.ḫršn.-------------]. | ǵr.ks.dm.r[gm.iṯ.l y.w argm k]. | hwt.w 1['NT.IX].3.11

dmgy.amt. | aṯrt.qḥ. | ksan k.ḥdg k. | ḥtl k.w ẓi. | b aln.tk m. | b tk.mlbr. | ilšiy. | kry amt. | 'pr.'ẓm yd. | ugrm.ḫl.ld. | a 12[75].1.20

mt. | aṯrt.qḥ. | ksan k.ḥdg k. | ḥtl k.w ẓi. | b aln.tk m. | b tk.mlbr. | ilšiy. | kry amt. | 'pr.'ẓm yd. | ugrm.ḫl.ld. | aklm.tbrk 12[75].1.21

. | u šmal.b p hm.w l.tšb'n y.aṯṯ.itrḫ. | y bn.ašld.šu.'db.tk.mdbr qdš. | ṯm tgrgr.l abnm.w l.'ṣm.šb'.šnt. | tmt.ṯmn.nqp 23[52].65

n. | 'dnm.kn.npl.b'l. | km ṯr.w tkms.hd.p[.-]. | km.ibr.b tk.mšmš d[--]. | ittpq.l awl. | išttk.lm.ttkn. | štk.mlk.dn. | štk.ši 12[75].2.56

b'l.yṯb.k ṯbt.ǵr.hd.r['y]. | k mdb.b tk.ǵr h.il ṣpn.b [tk]. | ǵr.tliyt.šb't.brqm.[---]. | ṯmnt.iṣr r't.'ṣ b UG5.3.1.2

bkbm.abn.brq]. | d l t[d'.šmm.at m.w ank]. | ibǵ[y h.b tk.ǵ]r y.il.ṣpn. | b q[dš.b ǵr.nḥ]lt y. | w t['n].btlt.[']nt.ṯṯb. | [yb 3['NT].4.63

gm l td'.nšm.w l tbn. | hmlt.arṣ.at m.w ank. | ibǵy h.b tk.ǵr y.il.ṣpn. | b qdš.b ǵr.nḥlt y. | b n'm.b gb'.tliyt. | hlm.'nt.t 3['NT].3.26

r k. | 'm k.pdry.bt.ar. | 'm k.ṭṭly.bt.rb.idk. | pn k.al ttn.tk.ǵr. | knkny.ša.ǵr.'l ydm. | ḫlb.l ẓr.rḥtm w rd. | bt ḫpṯt.arṣ.t 5[67].5.12

]. | ǵyrm.idk.l yt[n.pnm.'m.lṯpn]. | il d pid.tk ḫrš[n.---.tk.ǵr.ks]. | ygly ḏd.i[l.w ybu.qrš.mlk]. | ab.šnm.l [p'n.il.yhbr. 1['NT.IX].3.22

.ap hm.tb'.ǵlm[m.al.ṯṯb.idk.pnm]. | al.ttn.'m.pḫr.m'd.t[k.ǵr.ll.l p'n.il]. | al.tpl.al.tšthwy.pḫr [m'd.qmm.a--.am] | r ṯ 2.1[137].14

]. | bn.dgn.arṯ m.pḏ h.tb'.ǵlmm.l ṯṯb.[idk.pnm]. | l ytn.tk.ǵr.ll.'m.phr.m'd.ap.ilm.l lḥ[m]. | yṯb.bn qdš.l ṯrm.b'l.qm.' 2.1[137].20

b'l.yṯb.k ṯbt.ǵr.hd.r['y]. | k mdb.b tk.ǵr h.il ṣpn.b [tk]. | ǵr.tliyt.šb't.brqm.[---]. | ṯmnt.iṣr r't.'ṣ brq y. | riš h.tply.ṭ UG5.3.1.2

'l. | yt'dd.rkb.'rpt. | [--].ydd.w yqlṣn. | yqm.w ywptn.b tk. | p[ḫ]r.bn.ilm.štt. | p[--].b ṯlḥn y.qlt. | b ks.ištyn h. | dm.ṯn. 4[51].3.13

rq. | ybnt.ab h.šrḥq.aṯt.l pnn h. | št.alp.qdm h.mria.w tk. | pn h.tḥspn.m h.w trḥṣ. | ṭl.šmm.šmn.arṣ.ṭl.šm[m.t]sk h. 3['NT].4.85

kn. | ǵlmm. | aḫr.mǵy.kṯr.w ḫss. | št.alp.qdm h.mra. | w tk.pn h.t'db.ksu. | w yṯṯb.l ymn.aliyn. | b'l.'d.lḥm.št[y.ilm]. | [4[51].5.108

mm.hk[l m]. | ḥš.bht m.tbn[n]. | ḥš.trmmn.hk[l m]. | b tk.ṣrrt.ṣpn. | alp.šd.aḫd bt. | rbt.kmn.hkl. | w y'n.kṯr.w ḫss. | š 4[51].5.117

| w rd.bt ḫpṯt. | arṣ.tspr.b y | rdm.arṣ. | idk.al.ttn. | pnm.tk.qrt h. | hmry.mk.ksu. | ṯbt h.ḫḫ.arṣ. | nḥlt h.w nǵr. | 'nn.ilm 4[51].8.11

d.'lm k. | tb'.w l.yṯb.ilm.idk. | l ytn.pn.'m.bn.ilm.mt. | tk.qrt h.hmry.mk.ksu. | ṯbt.ḫḫ.arṣ.nḥlt h.tša. | g hm.w tṣḥ.tḥ 5[67].2.15

.pǵ[t.---]. | tld.pǵ[t.---]. | tld.p[ǵt.---]. | mid.rm[.krt]. | b tk.rpi.ar[ṣ]. | b pḫr.qbṣ.dtn. | ṣǵrt hn.abkrn. | tbrk.ilm.tity. | tit 15[128].3.14

[-----]. | [---.mid.rm.]krt. | [b tk.rpi.]arṣ. | [b pḫr].qbṣ.dtn. | [w t]qrb.w ld. | bn.tl k. | tld.pǵt. 15[128].3.3

. | ṯr.il[.ab h.---]. | ḥš b[ht m.tbnn.ḥš.trmmn.hkl m]. | b tk.[---]. | bn.[---]. | a[--.---.] 1['NT.IX].3.28

tkwn

y.b d.ibrmḏ. | [šd.]bn.ṯṯrn.b d.bnš.aǵlkz. | [šd.b]d.b[n].tkwn. | [ubdy.mḏ]rǵlm. | [šd.bn.--]n.b d.aḫny. | [šd.bn.--]rt.b 82[300].2.21

tky

. | m[--.---]. | [-----]. | k[--.---]. | [-----]. | ḫmrn.'š[r.---]. | gll.tky.ṯlṯ[.---]. 2042.23

tkm

š. | atlg.ḫmš 'šr[h]. | ulm ṯ[ṯ]. | m'rby.ḫmš. | ṭbq.arb'. | tkm[.---]. | uḫnp[.---]. | ušk[n.---]. | ubr['y.---]. | ar[.---]. | mlk[.- 68[65].2.1

tkn

rmn.l.ty[n.n]ḥl h. | šd.krz.[b]n.ann.'[db]. | šd.ṯ[r]yn.bn.tkn.b d.qrt. | šd[.-].dyn.b d.pln.nḥl h. | šd.irdyn.bn.ḫrǵš[-].l.q 2029.14

t.[---]. | rbt.ṯbt.ḥš[n.---]. | y.arṣ.ḥšn[.---]. | t'td.tkl.[---]. | tkn.lbn[.---]. | dt.lbn k[.---]. | dk k.kbkb[.---]. | dm.mt.aṣḥ[.---] 5[67].3.6

ru.ibrn. | yqšm. | trrm. | kkrdnm. | yṣrm. | ktrm. | mṣlm. | tkn[m]. | ǵ[---]. | ǵm[--]. 1026.2.14

-.b]nšm.b.šmngy. | [---.]bnšm.b.snr.mid. | [---.bn]šm.b.tkn. | [---.bn]šm.b.tmrm. | [---.bn]šm.b.ṯnq. | [---.b]nšm.b.ugrt 2076.27

[by]. | [w].bn.d'm[-]. | bn.ppṯ.b[--]. | b[n.---]. | šm[-.---]. | tkn[.---]. | knn.b.ḫ[lb]. | bn mṯ.b.qmy. | n'r.b.ulm. 2046.2.3

tl

.trẓẓ h. | [---].mǵy h.w ǵlm. | [a]ḫt h.šib.yṣat.mrḥ h. | l tl.yṣb.pn h.ṯǵr. | yṣu.hlm.aḫ h.tph. | [ksl]h.l arṣ.ṯṯbr. | [---.]aḫ 16.1[125].52

tliyt

ibǵy h.b tk.ǵr y.il.ṣpn. | b qdš.b ǵr.nḥlt y. | b n'm.b gb'.tliyt. | hlm.'nt.tph.ilm.b h.p'nm. | ṭṭṭ.b'd n.ksl.ṯṯbr. | 'ln.pn h.t 3['NT].3.28

r h.w šḫp h. | [--.]šḫp.ṣǵrt h. | yrk.t'l.b ǵr. | mslmt.b ǵr.tliyt. | w t'l.bkm.b arr. | bm.arr.w b ṣpn. | b n'm.b ǵr.t[l]iyt. | q 10[76].3.29

r.tliyt. | w t'l.bkm.b arr. | bm.arr.w b ṣpn. | b n'm.b ǵr.t[l]iyt. | ql.l b'l.ttnn. | bšrt.il.bš[r.b']l. | w bšr.ḥtk.dgn. | k.ibr.l 10[76].3.32

ṯb.k ṯbt.ǵr.hd.r['y]. | k mdb.b tk.ǵr h.il ṣpn.b [tk]. | ǵr.tliyt.šb't.brqm.[---]. | ṯmnt.iṣr r't.'ṣ brq y. | riš h.tply.ṭly.bn.'n UG5.3.1.3

tlby

w.[---].|ity[.---].|tlby[.---].|ir[--.---].|pndyn[.---].|w.idṯ[-.---].|b.gt.b[n.---].|y 1078.3

tlgn

.aẖm[l]k.ʿbdrpu.adn.ṯ[--].|bdn.qln.mtn.ydln.|bʿltdtt.tlgn.ytn.|bʿltǵpṯm.krwn.ilšn.agyn.|mnn.šr.ugrt.ḏkr.yṣr.|tg 2011.35

tldn

tldn.|ṯrkn.|kli.|plǵn.|apsny.|ʿrb[.---].|w.b.p[.--].|aps[ny]. 2116.1
t[n.---].|ipṯn[.---].|ybni[l.---].|ikrn[.---].|tlmyn[.---].|tldn[.---].|annḏr[.---].|[-]m[--.---]. 106[332].8

tlyn

lk [---].|kbd d ilgb[-].|mrmnmn.|brrn aryn.|a[-]ḥn tlyn.|atdb w ʿr.|qdš w amrr.|ṯḫr w bd.|[k]ṯr ḫss šlm.|šlm i UG5.7.71

tlm

idk.al.ttn.pnm.|ʿm.ǵr.trǵzz.|ʿm.ǵr.ṯrmg.|ʿm.tlm.ǵṣr.arṣ.|ša.ǵr.ʿl.ydm.|ḫlb.l ẓr.rḥtm.|w rd.bt ḫpṯt.|arṣ.t 4[51].8.4

tlmi

at.brr.|b.ṯmnym.ksp.ṯlṯt.kbd.|ḫmš.alp.ṯlṯ.l.ḫlby.|b d.tlmi.b.ʿšrm.ḫmšt.|kbd.ksp.|kkrm.šʿrt.štt.b d.gg[ʿt].|b.ʿšrt.k 2101.7
]r.bn.psḫn.|alṯy.|sǵr.npr.|bn.ḫty.|ṯn.bnš ibrḏr.|bnš tlmi.|sǵr.ḫryn.|ʿdn.w sǵr h.|bn.ḥgbn. 2082.7

tlmu

qrṭym.mddbʿl.|kdn.zlyy.|krwn.arty.|tlmu.zlyy.|pdu.qmnzy.|bdl.qrṭy.|trgn.bn.tǵḥ.|aupš.qmnzy 89[312].4
[-]y[-.---].|iwr[--.---].|iwr[--.---].|tlmu[.---].|gngn[.---].|nwr[--.---].|sg[---.---].|[-]s[-.---]. 2138.4

tlmyn

mḏrǵlm.dt.inn.|b d.tlmyn.|b d.gln.ary.|tgyn.yʿrty.|bn.krwn.b.yny.iytlm.|sgry 2071.2
miḫdy[m].|bn.ḥgb[n].|bn.ulbt[-].|ḏkry[-].|bn.tlm[yn].|bn.yʿdd.|bn.idly[-].|bn.ʿbd[--].|bn.ṣd[qn]. 2017.5
bʿm.ṯmn.kbd.|[l.]sbrdnm.|m[i]t.l.bn.ʿẓmt.rišy.|mit.l.tlmyn.bn.ʿdy.|[---.]l.aḏddy.|[--.]l.kkln. 2095.8
l um y.adt ny.|rgm.|ṯḥm.tlmyn.|w.aḫtmlk ʿbd k.|l.pʿn.adt ny.|mrḥqtm.|qlny.ilm.|t 51[95].3
mryn[m].|bn.bly.|nrn.|w.nḥl h.|bn.rmyy.|bn.tlmyn.|w.nḥl h.|w.nḥl hm.|bn.ḥrm.|bn.brzn.|w.nḥl h.|bn 113[400].1.6
ṯḥm[.t]lm[yn].|l ṯryl.um y.|rgm.|ugrt.tǵr k.|ugrt.tǵr k.|tšlm k.u 1015.1
l.mlkt.|adt y.|rgm.|ṯḥm.tlmyn.|ʿbd k.|l.pʿn.|adt y.|šbʿ d.|w.šbʿ id.|mrḥqtm.|qlt.|ʿ 52[89].4
ṣṣ.bn.ilyn.ṯlṯm.|ṣṣ.bn.kzn.ṯlṯm.|ṣṣ.bn.tlmyn.ʿšrm.|ṣṣ.bn.krwn.ʿš[rm].|ṣṣ.bn.iršyn.[---].|[ṣṣ].bn.ilbʿ 2096.3
šrm ʿšrm š[lm.---].|ilabn.ʿšrt ṯqlm kbd.ḫmš.šl[m.---].|tlmyn.šbʿt.ʿšrt ʿšrt[.šlm.---].|ybn.ṯmnt.ʿšrt ʿšrt.šlm.|ʿbdyrḫ.š 1131.4
.qlʿ.|gtn.qšt.|pmn.ṯt.qšt.w.qlʿ.|bn.zry.q[š]t.w.qlʿ.|bn.tlmyn.ṯt.qštm.w.qlʿ.|bn.ysd.qšt.|[ǵ]mrm.|ilgn.qšt.|abršp.q 104[316].9
yn[.---].|annt[n.---].|ipṯn[.---].|ybni[l.---].|ikrn[.---].|tlmyn[.---].|tldn[.---].|annḏr[.---].|[-]m[--.---]. 106[332].7

tlš

.mrm.tqrṣn.|il.yẓḥq.bm.|lb.w ygmḏ.bm kbd.|ẓi.at.l tlš.|amt.yrḫ.|l dmgy.amt.|aṯrt.qḥ.|ksan k.ḥdg k.|ḥtl k.w ẓ 12[75].1.14
[---].|[---].|[---].|bn[.---]y.|yr[---].|ḫdyn.|grgš.|b[n.]tlš.|dmr.|mkrm.|ʿzn.|yplṭ.|ʿbdmlk.|ynḥm.|aḏddn.|mtn.| 1035.3.22
lmlk.[--]kt.[--.d.]yṯb.b.šb[n].|bn.pr[-.]d.y[ṯb.b].šlmy.|tlš.w[.n]ḥl h[.-].tgd.mrum.|bt.[-]b[-.-]sy[-]h.|nn[-].b[n].py[- 2015.2.3

tlšn

.|[iw]ryn.|[--.w.n]ḥl h.|[-]ibln.|bn.nḏbn.|bn.ʿbl.|bn.tlšn.|bn.sln.|w nḥl h. 1063.13

tmy

.w.ṯn.qlʿm.|ulšn.ṯt.qšm.w.qlʿ.|bn.mlʿn.qšt.w.qlʿ.|bn.tmy.qšt.w.qlʿ.|ʿky.qšt.|ʿbdlbit.qšt.|kṯy.qšt.w.qlʿ.|bn.ḫršn.q 119[321].3.36

tmyn

|mnn.bn.gṯtn.kdm.|ynḥm.bn[.-]r[-]t.ṯlṯ.|plwn.kdm.|tmyn.bn.ubrš.kd. 136[84].12

tmm

ttpl.yʿn.ḥtk h.|krt yʿn.ḥtk h.rš.|mid.grdš.ṯbt h.|w b tm hn.špḥ.yitbd.|w b.pḫyr h.yrṯ.|yʿrb.b ḥdr h.ybky.|b ṯn.[- 14[KRT].1.24
ug[r.---].|ʿnt[.---].|tmm l bt[.---].|b[ʿ]l.ugr[t.---].|w ʿṣrm[.---].|ṣlyh šr[-.---].|[ṯ] 40[134].3
šu.ʿdb.tk.mdbr qdš.|ṯm tgrgr.l abnm.w l.ʿṣm.šbʿ.šnt.|tmt.ṯmn.nqpt.ʿd.ilm.nʿmm.ttlkn.|šd.tṣdn.pat.mdbr.w ngš.h 23[52].67

tmn

m.bn ydm.ṯpṭ.|nhr.ʿz.ym.l ymk.l tnǵṣn.pnt h.l ydlp.|tmn h.kṯr.ṣmdm.ynḥt.w ypʿr.šmt hm.|šm k.at.aymr.aymr. 2.4[68].18
.ʿnm.ṯpṭ.nhr.yprsḥ.ym.yql.|l arṣ.tnǵṣn.pnt h.w ydlp.tmn h.|yqṯ bʿl.w yšt.ym.ykly.ṯpṭ.nhr.|b šm.tgʿr m.ʿṯtrt.bṯ l 2.4[68].26
mšm ḫmš kbd.|ṣṣ ubn ḫmš ʿšr h.|ṣṣ ʿmyd ḫmšm.|ṣṣ tmn.ḫmšm.|[ṣṣ] ʿmtḏl ṯlṯm.|ṣṣ ʿmlbi ṯt l ʿšrm.|ṣṣ bn adty ḫ 2097.4
-].|ynḥm.|iḫy.|bn.mšt.|ʿpsn.|bn.ṣpr.|kmn.|bn.ršp.|tmn.|šmmn.|bn.rmy.|bn.aky.|ʿbdḫmn.|bn.ʿdṯ.|kṯy.|bn.ḫ 1047.10

tmr

bn.arwṭ.|bn.ṯbtnq.|bn.pṭḏn.|bn.nbdg.|bn.ḥgbn.|bn.tmr.|bn.prsn.|bn.ršpy.|[ʿ]bdḥgb.|[k]lby.|[-]ḥmn.|[š]pšyn. 113[400].1.20

tmry

m.|nʿrm.|ʿbdm.|kzym.|ksdm.|[nsk].ṯlṯ.|gt.mlkym.|tmrym.|ṯnqym.|ṯǵrm.|mru.skn.|mru.ibrn.|yqšm.|trrm.| 1026.2.3

tmrm

|[---.]bnšm.b.snr.mid.|[---.bn]šm.b.tkn.|[---.bn]šm.b.tmrm.|[---.bn]šm.b.ṯnq.|[---.b]nšm.b.ugrt.|[---.bn]šm.b.ġbl. 2076.28

tmrtn

i[l]štm‘ym.|bn.ṯk.|bn.arwdn.|tmrtn.|šd‘l.bn aẖyn.|m‘rbym.|rpan.|abršn.|atlgy.|šršn. 95[91].4
l.‘d.ab[ġ]l.|l.ydln.š‘rt.|l.kṯrmlk.ẖpn.|l.‘bdil[m].ẖpn.|tmrtn.š‘rt.|lmd.n.rn.|[---].ẖpn.|dqn.š‘rt.|[lm]d.yrṯ.|[-.]ynḥ 1117.11

tmtrn

.rḥd.kd.šmn.|drt.b.kkr.|ubn.ẖṣẖ.kkr.|kkr.lqḥ.ršpy.|tmtrn.bn.pnmn.|kkr.|bn.sgṯtn.|kkr.|ilšpš.kkr.|bn.ḏltn.|k 1118.7

tmtṯb

kr[.---].|kkr[.---].|k[kr.---].|k[kr.---].|[---.-]krr.|[---.]tmtṯb.|[---.-]dy.|[---.]‘dyin.|[---.]‘bdẖ[-]m. 2037.2.6

tmṯl

qṯ.yṣq.b.a[p h].|k yg‘r[.ššw.---].|dprn[.---].|dr‘.[---].|tmṯl[.---].|mġm[ġ.---].|w.š[t.nni.w.pr.‘bk].|w.pr[.ḥdrt.w.št] 161[56].26

tnabn

.‘ṯtrab.|uṣn[-].|bn.alṯn.|bn.aš[-]š.|bn.štn.|bn.ilš.|bn.tnabn.|bn.ḥṣn.|ṣprn.|bn.ašbḥ.|bn.qṭnn.|bn.ġlmn.|[bn].ṣw 1046.1.18

tny

k[---].|‘bd.[---].|mtn[.---].|ṯdpṯn[.--].|tny[.--].|sll[.--].|mld[.--].|yqš[.--].|[-----].|inš[r.---].|ršp[.--- 1074.5
---].mṣrm[.---].|[---.--]n mkr[.---].|[---].ank.[---].|[---.]tny.[---].|[---.]mlk[.---].|[---.--]m.‘[--.---]. 2126.7

tnm

---].|dl.ylkn.ḥš.b a[rṣ.---].|b ‘pr.ẖbl ṭtm.[---.]|šqy.rṯa.tnm y.ytn.[ks.b yd].|krpn.b klat yd.[---].|km ll.kḥṣ.tusp[.--- 1[‘NT.X].4.9

tnn

lḥn.|‘zn.bn.mll.|šrm.|[b]n.špš[yn].|[b]n.ẖrmln.|bn.tnn.|bn.pndr.|bn.nqq.|ḥrš.bhtm.|bn.izl.|bn.ibln.|bn.ilt.|š 85[80].1.13
[k.ym]ẖṣ.b‘l m[.--]y.tnn.w ygl.w ynsk.‘[-].|[--]y.l arṣ[.id]y.alt.l aḥš.idy.alt.in l y. 1001.1.1
.hn.mtm.|‘d k.kṯr m.ḥbr k.|w ẖss.d‘t k.|b ym.arš.w tnn.|kṯr.w ẖss.yd.|ytr.kṯr.w ẖss.|spr.ilmlk šbny.|lmd.atn. 6.6[62.2].50
ṣ.|mẖnm.ṯrp ym.|lšnm.tlḥk.|šmm.tṯrp.|ym.ḏnbtm.|tnn.l šbm.|tšt.trks.|l mrym.l bt[.---].|p l.tb‘[.---].|hmlt ẖt.[- 1003.8
mṯpit.b d.bn.iryn.|[u]bdy.šrm.|[š]d.bn.ẖrmln.b d.bn.tnn.|[š]d.bn.ẖrmln.ṯn.b d.bn.ẖdmn.|[u]bdy.nqdm.|[ṯlṯ].šd 82[300].2.10
l rkb.‘rpt.l mẖšt.mdd.|il ym.l klt.nhr.il.rbm.|l ištbm.tnn.ištml h.|mẖšt.bṯn.‘qltn.|šlyṭ.d šb‘t.rašm.|mẖšt.mdd il 3[‘NT].3.37
--].ymlu.|n‘m.[-]ṯ[-.--.]yqrṣ.|d[-] b pẖ[-.--.]mẖt.|[---.]tnn.|[---.]tnn. 16[126].5.31
n‘m.[-]ṯ[-.--.]yqrṣ.|d[-] b pẖ[-.--.]mẖt.|[---.]tnn.|[---.]tnn. 16[126].5.32

tnq

[.--].arẖ..|b‘l.azrt.‘nt.[-]ld.|kbd h.l yd‘ hr h.[---]d[-].|tnq[.---.]in[b]b.p‘r.|yd h[.--.]ṣ‘r.glgl.|a[---]m.rḥ.ẖd ‘[r]pt.|g 13[6].32

tsn

[--]ntn.|‘dn.|lkn.|ktr.|ubn.|dqn.|ḥttn.|[--]n.|[---].|tsn.|rpiy.|mrṯn.|ṯnyn.|apṯ.|šbn.|gbrn.|ṯb‘m.|kyn.|b‘ln.| 1024.2.14

t‘d

l.šnt k.---].|[--]šnm.aṯtm.t[--.---].|[m]lakm.ylak.ym.[t‘dt.ṯpṭ.nhr].|b ‘lṣ.‘lṣm.npr.š[--.---].|uṭ.ṯbr.ap hm.tb‘.ġlm[m 2.1[137].11
hm.l ẓr.brkt hm.ln.kḥṯ.zbl hm.|aẖr.tmġyn.mlak ym.t‘dt.ṯpṭ.nhr.l p‘n.il.|[l t]pl.l tšṯḥwy.pẖr.m‘d.qmm.a[--].amr. 2.1[137].30
n h.‘n]t.tuẖd.šmal h.tuẖd.‘ṯtrt.ik.m[ẖṣt.ml]|[ak.ym.t‘]dt.ṯpṭ.nhr.mlak.mṯḥr.yẖb[-.---.]|[---].mlak.bn.ktpm.rgm. 2.1[137].41
t km.l ẓr.brkt km.ln.kḥṯ.|zbl km.w ank.‘ny.mlak.ym.t‘dt.ṯpṭ.nhr.|tšu ilm rašt hm.l ẓr.brkt hm.ln.kḥṯ.zbl hm.|aẖ 2.1[137].28
brkt km.w ln.kḥṯ.zbl km.aḥd.|ilm.t‘ny lḥt.mlak.ym.t‘dt.ṯpṭ.nhr.|šu.ilm.rašt km.l ẓr.brkt km.ln.kḥṯ.|zbl km.w a 2.1[137].26
qdš.l ṯrm.b‘l.qm.‘l.il.hlm.|ilm.tph hm.tphn.mlak.ym.t‘dt.ṯpṭ[.nhr].|t[ġ]ly.hlm.rišt hm.l ẓr.brkt hm.w l kḥṯ.|zbl h 2.1[137].22
[---].ap.anš.zbl.b‘l.šdmt.bg[--.---].|[---.-]dm.mlak.ym.t‘dt.ṯpṭ.nh[r.---].|[---].an.rgmt.l ym.b‘l km.ad[n km.ṯpṭ].|[n 2.1[137].44

t‘ḏr

.|[arṣ] w šm[m].|[-----].|[a]rṣ.|[u]šẖr[y].|[‘]ṯtrt.|i[l t]‘ḏr b‘l.|ršp.|ddmš.|pẖr ilm.|ym.|uṯẖt.|knr.|mlkm.|šlm. 29[17].2.4
š.ġrm.š[.---].|aṯrt.š.‘nt.š.špš.š.arṣy.š.‘ṯtrt.š.|ušẖry.š.il.t‘ḏr.b‘l.š.ršp.š.ddmš.š.|w šlmm.ilib.š.i[l.--]m d gbl.ṣpn.al[p] UG5.9.1.8
kn.u b qṣrt.npšt kn.u b qṭ]t tqṭṭ.|[ušn.yp kn.---.--]l.il.t‘ḏr b‘l.|[-----.]lšnt.|[---.--]yp.tḥt.|[-----].|[---.]w npy gr.|[ḥ APP.I[-].1.8
.---.--]y.|[---.np]y nqmd.|[---.]pẖr.|[-----].|[-----].|[---.t‘ḏ]r b‘l.|[-----].|[-----].|[---.--]r.|[---.]npy.|[---.ušn.yp kn.ul APP.I[-].2.7
š.pdry š.ddmš š.|w b urbt.ilib š.|b‘l alp w š.|dgn.š.il t‘ḏr.š.|b‘l š.‘nt š.ršp š.|šlmm.|w šnpt.il š.|l ‘nt.ḥl š.ṯn šm.|l UG5.13.21
r š ‘ṯtr.š.|[‘ṯ]rt.š.šgr w iṯm š.|[---.]š.ršp.idrp.š.|[---.il.t‘]ḏr.š.|[---.-]mt.š.|[-----].|[-----].|[-----].|[---.]im[-.---].|[---.] UG5.9.2.11

t‘lgt

arẖ.td.rgm.b ġr.|b p y.t‘lgt.b lšn[y].|ġr[.---]b.b pš y.t[--].|hwt.b‘l.iš[--].|šm‘ l y.yp 2124.2

t‘mt

tbu.|nṣrt.tbu.pnm.|‘rm.tdu.mh.|pdrm.tdu.šrr.|ẖṭ m.t‘mt.[‘]ṭr.[k]m.|zbln.‘l.riš h.|w ṯṯb.trḥṣ.nn.b d‘t.|npš h.l lḥ 16.6[127].8

t‘r

w b[--.---].|ilib[.---].|alp.[---].|ili[b.---].|t‘r[.---].|dq[t.---].|nb[--.---]. 44[44].5

t'rt

aḥwy.tqḥ.yṯpn.mhr.št.|tštn.k nšr.b ḥbš h.km.diy.|b t'rt h.aqht.km.ytb.l lḥ[m].|bn.dnil.l ṯrm.'l h.nšr[m].|trḫpn. 18[3AQHT].4.29

h.b ym.t[---].|tlbš.npṣ.ġzr.tšt.ḫ[---.b] |nšg h.ḥrb.tšt.b t'r[t h].|w 'l.tlbš.npṣ.aṯt.[--].|ṣbi nrt.ilm.špš.[-]r[--].|pġt.mi 19[1AQHT].4.207

t.ṯb.yṯp.w[---].|l k.ašt k.km.nšr.b ḥb[š y].|km.diy.b t'rt y.aqht.[km.yṯb].|l lḥm.w bn.dnil.l ṯrm[.'l h].|nšrm.trḫp 18[3AQHT].4.18

tġd

.ilhd.|bnil.rb 'šrt.lkn.yp'n.ṯ[--].|yṣḥm.b d.ubn.krwn.tġd.[m]nḥm.|'pṯrm.šm'rgm.skn.qrt.|ḥgbn.šm'.skn.qrt.|nġr 2011.9

tġḏ

l.ib.hdt.lm.tḥš.|lm.tḥš.nṯq.dmrn.|'n.b'l.qdm.yd h.|k tġḏ.arz.b ymn h.|bkm.yṯb.b'l.l bht h.|u mlk.u bl mlk.|arṣ. 4[51].7.41

tġh

rwn.arty.|tlmu.zlyy.|pdu.qmnzy.|bdl.qrṯy.|trgn.bn.tġh.|aupš.qmnzy.|ṯrry.mṣbty.|prn.nġṯy.|ṯrḏn.zlyy. 89[312].7

tġyn

[-----].|bn.t[--.---].|agmy[.---].|bn.dlq[-.---].|tġyn.bn.ubn.ṯql[m].|yšn.ḥrš.mrkbt.ṯq[lm].|bn.p'ṣ.ṯqlm.|mṣ 122[308].1.5

tġpṯ

l.|[-]mn.|[--]n.|[ḥr]š.qṭn.|[---]n.|[-----].|[--]dd.|[b']l.tġpṯm.|[k]rwn.|ḥrš.mrkbt.|mnḥm.|mṣrn.|mḏrġlm.|agmy 1039.2.11

tġpṯn

[---.]ybnn.|[---.]mlkn'm.|[---.]tġpṯn.|[--.]ubln.|[--.-]ḫ[-].|[--.-]s[-]n.|[--.-]nyn.|[---].[-]ġṯyn 123[326].1.3

tp

.|[---.]w rm ṯlbm ṯlb.|[---.-]pr l n'm.|[---.-]mt w rm tp h.|[---.-]ḥb l n'm.|[---.]ymġy.|[---.]rm ṯlbm.|[---.--]m.|[- UG5.5.5

[---.]w rm tp h.|[---.-]lu mm l n'm.|[---.]w rm ṯlbm ṯlb.|[---.-]pr l n'm. UG5.5.1

ṯb.b.'ṯtrt.|il.ṯpṯ.b hd r'y.d yšr.w yḏmr.|b knr.w ṯlb.b tp.w mṣltm.b m|rqdm.dšn.b.ḥbr.kṯr.ṭbm.|w tšt.'nt.gṯr.b'lt. UG5.2.1.4

w rgm.l aḫt k.|ṯtmnt.krt n.dbḥ.|dbḥ.mlk.'šr.|'šrt.qḥ.tp k.b yd.|[-]r[-]k.bm.ymn.|tlk.škn.'l.ṣrrt.|adn k.šqrb.[---]. 16.1[125].41

tpḥ

lltky.|ṯd[y]n.b.glltky.|lbw[-].uḫ.pdm.b.y'rt.|pġyn.b.tpḥ.|amri[l].b.šrš.|aġltn.b.midḫ.|[--]n.b.ayly.|[-]lyn.b.nġḥt 2118.11

b grnt.ilm.b qrb.m[ṯ't.ilnym].|d tit.yspi.spu.q[--.---].|tpḥ.ṭṣr.shr[.---].|mr[.---]. 20[121].2.11

tpn

lṯ dd ksmm.|[---.-]rbr dd š'rm.|[---.]r[--.]ḥṭm.|kr[--.]tp[n].|kkr[.---].|kkr[.---].|kkr[.---].|kkr[.---].|k[kr.---].|k[k 2037.1.5

tpnr

|ṯṯ spm.l bnš klnmw.|l yarš ḫswn.|ḫmš 'šr.sp.|l bnš tpnr d yaḫd l g ynm.|ṯṯ spm l tgyn.|arb' spm l ll[-].|ṯn spm 137.2[93].11

ḥm.|mit.iqni.l uṯryn.|ks.ksp.ktn.mit.pḥm.|mit.iqni.l tpnr.|[ks.ksp.kt]n.mit.pḥ[m].|[mit.iqni.l]ḫbrtn[r].|[ks.ksp. 64[118].32

.|[---.]kqmṯn.|[---.]klnmw.|[---.]w yky.|ṯlṯm sp.l bnš tpnr.|arb'.spm.l.lbnš prwsdy.|ṯṯ spm.l bnš klnmw.|l yarš ḫ 137.2[93].6

tpp

ttpp.anhb[m.d alp.šd].|ẓu h.b ym[.---].|[--]rn.l [---]. 3['NT].3.03

.|ṭl.šmm.šmn.arṣ.ṭl.šm[m.t]sk h.|rbb.nsk h.kbkbm.|ttpp.anhbm.d alp.šd[.ẓu h.b ym].|ṭl[.---]. 3['NT].4.89

tqy

ṣm.|bn.ḫpṡry.b.šbn.|ilštm'ym.|y[---.]bn.'šq.|[---.]bn.tqy.|[---.]bn.šlmy.|[-----].|[---].ubr'y.|[---].gwl.|[---]ady.|[- 1041.5

tqn

n.|gmrt.ṯlmyn.|'bdnt.|bdy.ḥrš arkd.|blšš lmd.|ḥṯṯn.tqn.|ydd.idṯn.|šġr.ilgdn. 1045.11

tr

ṯlṯ mrkb[t].|ṣpyt b ḫrṣ[.w] ṣmdm trm.d [ṣ]py.|w.trm.aḥdm.|ṣpym.|ṯlṯ mrkbt mlk.|d.l.ṣpy.|[---.t]r hm.|[---]. 1122.3

.|ṯṯ.ṯṯ.b [t]ql.ṯlṯt.l.'šrm.ksp hm.|šstm.b.šb'm.|ṯlṯ.mat.trm.b.'šrt.|mit.adrm.b.'šrt.|'šr.ydt.b.'šrt.|ḫmš.kkrm.ṣml.|' 1127.7

ṯlṯ mrkb[t].|ṣpyt b ḫrṣ[.w] ṣmdm trm.d [ṣ]py.|w.trm.aḥdm.|ṣpym.|ṯlṯ mrkbt mlk.|d.l.ṣpy.|[1122.2

.|ṯlṯ mrkbt mlk.|d.l.ṣpy.|[---.t]r hm.|[---].ššb.|[---.]tr h.|[a]rb'.ql'm.|arb'.mḏrnm.|mḏrn.w.mšḫṭ.|d.mrkbt.|m 1122.9

py.|w.trm.aḥdm.|ṣpym.|ṯlṯ mrkbt mlk.|d.l.ṣpy.|[---.t]r hm.|[---].ššb.|[---.]tr h.|[a]rb'.ql'm.|arb'.mḏrnm.|mḏrn 1122.7

mn.mrkbt.dt.|'rb.bt.mlk.|yd.apnt hn.|yd.ḥẓ hn.|yd.tr hn.|w.l.ṯt.mrkbtm.|inn.uṯpt.|w.ṯlṯ.ṣmdm.w.ḥrṣ.|apnt.b 1121.5

id ydbḥ mlk.|l ušḫ[r] ḫlmṭ.|l bbt il bt.|š l ḫlmṭ.|w tr l qlḥ.|w š ḥll ydm.|b qdš il bt.|w tlḥm aṯt.|š l ilbt.šlmm. UG5.7.TR3

.šlmm.|kll ylḥm b h.|w l bbt šqym.|š l uḫr ḫlmṭ.|w tr l qlḥ.|ym aḥd. UG5.11.13

[---].in ḥẓm.l hm.|[---.--]ḏn.|mrkbt.mtrt.|ngršp.|ngġln.|ilṯḥm.|b'lṣdq. 1125.2.1

tran

mṣry.d.'rb.b.unṯ.|bn.qrrn.mḏrġl.|bn.tran.mḏrġl|bn.ilh.mḏrġl|špšyn.b.ulm.|bn.qṭn.b.ulm.|bn.g 2046.1.3

trbyt

[--.-]dwn.ṯlṯm.w.šb'.alpm.|[kṯ]rmlk.'šrm.|[--]ny.'šrt.trbyt.|[--.]'bd.ṯlṯm.|[---].ṯlṯm.|[--.p]ndyn.ṯlṯm. 2054.2.25

trbnn

.gt.nbk.|ddm.kšmm.l.ḫtn.|ddm.l.trbnn.|ddm.š'rm.l.trbnn.|ddm.š'rm.l.ḫtn.|dd.š'rm.l.ḥmr.ḥṭb.|dd.ḥṭm.l.ḫdǵb. 1099.22
.|w.lmd h.|krwn b.gt.nbk.|ddm.kšmm.l.ḫtn.|ddm.l.trbnn.|ddm.š'rm.l.trbnn.|ddm.š'rm.l.ḫtn.|dd.š'rm.l.ḥmr.ḥ 1099.21

trgn

.zlyy.|krwn.arty.|tlmu.zlyy.|pdu.qmnzy.|bdl.qrṭy.|trgn.bn.tǵh.|aupš.qmnzy.|ṯrry.mṣbty.|prn.nǵṯy.|ṯrḏn.zlyy 89[312].7

trdn

.i[--].|'d[--].|ild[--].|bn.qṣn.|'lpy.|kṭy.|bn.ẓmn.|bn.trdn.|ypq.|'bd.|qrḥ.|abšr.|bn.bdn.|ḏmry.|bn.pndr.|bn.aḫ 2117.2.24

trhy

.ḫm[š.---].|[n]it.krk.m'ṣ[d.---].|b.ḫrbǵlm.ǵlm[n].|w.trhy.aṯt h.|w.mlky.b[n] h.|ily.mrily.tdgr. 2048.20

trzy

t qdš.|[---.--]n.b.anan.|[--]yl.b.bq't.b.gt.tgyn.|[--]in.b.trzy.|[--]yn.b.glltky.|ṯd[y]n.b.glltky.|lbw[-].uḫ.pdm.b.y'rt. 2118.7

trḫ

.|yrḫ nyr šmm.w n'[n].|'ma nkl ḫtn y.a[ḫ]r.|nkl yrḫ ytrḫ.adn h.|yšt mṣb.mznm.um h.|kp mznm.iḫ h yṯ'r.|mšrr 24[77].33
.|ylak yrḫ ny[r] šmm.'m.|ḫr[ḫ]b mlk qẓ.tn nkl y|rḫ ytrḫ.ib t'rb m b bh|t h.w atn mhr h l a|b h.alp ksp w rbt ḫ 24[77].18
.rš.|krt.grdš.mknt.|aṯt.ṣdq h.l ypq.|mtrḫt.yšr h.|aṯt.trḫ.w tb't.|ṯar um.tkn l h.|mṯlṯt.kṯrm.tmt.|mrb't.zblnm.| 14[KRT].1.14
.|almnt.škr.|tškr.zbl.'ršm.|yšu.'wr.mzl.|ymzl.w yṣi.trḫ.|ḥdṯ.yb'r.l ṯn.|aṯt h.lm.nkr.|mddt h.k irby.|[t]škn.šd.| 14[KRT].2.100
almnt.škr.|tškr.zbl.'ršm.|yšu.'wr.|mzl.ymzl.|w ybl.trḫ.ḥdṯ.|yb'r.l ṯn.aṯt h.|w l nkr.mddt.|km irby.tškn.|šd.k 14[KRT].4.189
d.gzr.l zr.y'db.u ymn.|u šmal.b p hm.w l.tšb'n y.aṯt.itrḫ.|y bn.ašld.šu.'db.tk.mdbr qdš.|ṯm tgrgr.l abnm.w l.'ṣm 23[52].64
n um.|krt.ḥtk n.rš.|krt.grdš.mknt.|aṯt.ṣdq h.l ypq.|mtrḫt.yšr h.|aṯt.trḫ.w tb't.|ṯar um.tkn l h.|mṯlṯt.kṯrm.tmt. 14[KRT].1.13
[n].|m.b'l trḫ pdry b[t h].|aqrb k ab h b'[l].|yǵtr.'ṯtr t|rḫ l k ybrdmy.b[t.a]|b h lb[u] y'rr.w y'[n].|yrḫ nyr šmm. 24[77].28
nqm.w |y'n ḫrḫb mlk qẓ [l].|n'mn.ilm l ḫt[n].|m.b'l trḫ pdry b[t h].|aqrb k ab h b'[l].|yǵtr.'ṯtr t|rḫ l k ybrdmy. 24[77].26
.|'n ha l yd h.tzd[.--].|pt l bšr h.dm a[--.--]ḥ.|w yn.k mtrḫt[.---]h.|šm' ilht kṯr[t.--]mm.|nh l yd h tzdn[.---]n.|l 24[77].10

trn

.|[š]d.bn.ṣnrn.b d.nrn.|[š]d.bn.rwy.b d.ydln.|[š].bn.trn.b d.ibrmḏ.|[š]d.bn.ilṯtmr.b d.tbbr.|[w.]šd.nḥl h.b d.ṯṯm 82[300].1.10
n.dd.|bn.ḫran.w[.---].|[-]n.y'rtym.|gmm.w.bn.p[--].|trn.w.p[-]y.|bn.b'yn.w.agytn.|[---] gnym.|[--]ry.w ary.|[--- 131[309].11

tr'

h.km.ǵb[-.---].|hw km.ḥrr[.---].|šnmtm.dbṭ[.---].|tr'.tr'n.a[--.---].|bnt.šdm.ṣḥr[.---].|šb'.šnt.il.mla.[-].|w ṯmn.nq 12[75].2.43
rn h.km.ǵb[-.---].|hw km.ḥrr[.---].|šnmtm.dbṭ[.---].|tr'.tr'n.a[--.---].|bnt.šdm.ṣḥr[.---].|šb'.šnt.il.mla.[-].|w ṯmn. 12[75].2.43

trǵds

tḥm.iwrḏr.|l.plsy.|rgm.|yšlm.l k.|l.trǵds.|w.l.klby.|šm't.ḫti.|nḫtu.ht.|hm.in mm.|nḫtu.w.lak. 53[54].5
r.l.snrn.|[---.--]k.l.gmrd.|[---.--]ṯ.l.yšn.|[šd.--]ln.|b d.trǵds.|šd.ṯ'lb.|b d.bn.pl.|šd.bn.kt.|b d.pdy.|šd.ḫzr.|[b d].d 2030.2.2
t h.b.bt.alḫn.|[aṯt.w.]pǵt.aḥt.b.bt.tt.|[aṯt.w.]bt h.b.bt.trǵds.|[---.]aṯt.adrt.w.pǵt.a[ḥt.b.bt.---].|[---.']šrm.npš.b.bt.[- 80[119].27

trǵzz

idk.al.ttn.pnm.|'m.ǵr.trǵzz.|'m.ǵr.ṯrmg.|'m.tlm.ǵṣr.arṣ.|ša.ǵr.'l.ydm.|ḫlb.l ẓr.rḥ 4[51].8.2

trǵnds

m.šb'.[---].|[---].'šr.dd[.---].|[---]mn.arb'm.y[n].|b.gt.trǵnds.|tš'.'šr.[dd].kšmm.|ṯn.'šr[.dd.ḥ]ṭm.|w.šb['.---]. 2092.15

trǵt

[---.]ydm ym.|[---.]ydm nhr.|[---.]trǵt.|[---.]h aḫd[.--].|[---.]iln[-.---].|[---.--]ḫ[.---].|[---.]dt[-.-- 49[73].1.3

trp

ḫṣ.ltn.bṯn.brḥ.|tkly.bṯn.'qltn.|šlyṭ.d šb'y.rašm.|ṯṯkḥ.ttrp.šmm.k rs.|ipd k.ank.ispi.uṭm.|ḏrqm.amt m.l yrt.|b np 5[67].1.4
n.bṯn.br]ḥ.tkly.|[bṯn.'qltn.]šlyṭ.|[d šb't.rašm].ṯṯkḥ.|[ttrp.šmm.k rks.ipd]k.|[-----]. 5[67].1.31

trq

spl ṯlṯ.mat.|w mmskn.|w.ṯt.mqrtm.|w.ṯn.irpm.w.ṯn.trqm.|w.qpt.w.mqḥm.|w.ṯlṯm.yn šb'.kbd d ṯbṭ.|w.ḫmšm.y 1103.20

trr

]b[dm].|'šrm.|inšt.|mdm.|gt.mlkym.|yqšm.|kbšm.|trrm.|khnm.|kzym.|yṣrm.|mru.ibrn.|mru.skn.|nsk.ksp| 74[115].8
|tmrym.|ṯnqym.|ṯǵrm.|mru.skn.|mru.ibrn.|yqšm.|trrm.|kkrdnm.|yṣrm.|ktrm.|mṣlm.|tkn[m].|ǵ[---].|ǵm[--] 1026.2.9
npk.|[š]d.rpan.b d.klṯtb.|[š]d.ilṣy.b d.'bdym.|[ub]dy.trrm.|[šd.]bn.ṯqdy.b d.gmrd.|[š]d bn.synn.b d.gmrd.|[šd.]a 82[300].2.16

trtn

.ḥgbn.'dn.ynḥm[.---].|ḥrš.mrkbt.'zn.[b]'ln.ṯb[--.-]nb.trtn.|[---]mm.klby.kl[--].dqn[.---].|[-]ntn.artn.b d[.--]nr[.---] 2011.28

trṯ

.|b'l gdlt.yrḫ.gdlt.|gdlt.ṯrmn.gdlt.pdry.gdlt dqt.|dqt.trṯ.dqt.|[rš]p.'nt.ḫbly.dbḥn š[p]š pgr.|[g]dlt iltm ḫnqtm.d[34[1].16
'r.ytb.il.kb[-].|aṯ[rt.]il.ytb.b mrzḥ h.|yšt[.il.y]n.'d šb'.trṯ.'d škr.|il.hlk.l bt h.yštql.|l ḥṭr h.y'msn.nn.ṯkmn.|w šnm UG5.1.1.16
hkl [h].ṣḥ.l qṣ.ilm.tlḥmn.|ilm.w tštn.tštn y[n] 'd šb'.|trṯ.'d.škr.y'db.yrḫ.|gb h.km.[---.]yqṭqṭ.tḥt.|ṯlḥnt.il.d yd'nn. UG5.1.1.4

trṯ

ilbt. | ušḫry. | ym.bʻl. | yrḫ. | kṯr. | ṯrmn. | pdry. | dqt. | trṯ. | ršp. | ʻnt ḫbly. | špš pgr. | iltm ḫnqtm. | yrḫ kṯy. | ygb hd. | UG5.14.A.9
ks.ḫ[rṣ]. | [dm.ʻṣm.---]n.krpn.ʻl.[k]rpn. | [---.]ym.w tʻl.trṯ. | [---].yn.ʻšy l ḥbš. | [---.]ḥtn.qn.yṣbt. | [---.--]m.b nši.ʻn h. 17[2AQHT].6.7

tš

[-----]. | [---.r]ḥm.tld. | [---.]ḫrm.ṯn.ym. | tš[.---.]ymm.lk. | hrg.ar[bʻ.]ymm.bṣr. | kp.šsk k.[--].l ḥbš k. | ʻ 13[6].4
kb[-.---]. | ym.[---]. | yšḥr[.---]. | yikl[.---]. | km.s[--.---]. | tš[.---]. | t[---.---]. | [-----]. | [-----]. | b [----]. | w [----]. | bʻl.[---]. | i 12[75].2.16

tškrǵ

ḫrny.w.rʻ h. | klbr.w.rʻ h. | tškrǵ.w.rʻ h. | ǵlwš.w.rʻ h. | kdrš.w.rʻ h. | ṯrm[-].w[.rʻ h]. | [ʻ]ṯtr 2083.1.3

tšʻ

| ṣbu.any[t]. | bn abdḥ[r]. | pdym. | ḫmš.bnšm. | snrym. | tšʻ.bnš[m]. | gbʻlym. | arbʻ.b[nšm]. | ṯbqym. 79[83].15
khnm.tšʻ. | bnšm.w.ḥmr. | qdšm.tšʻ. | bnšm.w.ḥmr. 77[63].1
khnm.tšʻ. | bnšm.w.ḥmr. | qdšm.tšʻ. | bnšm.w.ḥmr. 77[63].3
drm. | ṯṯ.l ṯṯm.aḫd.ʻr. | šbʻm.šbʻ.pdr. | ṯmnym.bʻl.[----]. | tšʻm.bʻl.mr[-]. | bt[.--]b bʻl.b qrb. | bt.w yʻn.aliyn. | bʻl.ašt m.k 4[51].7.12
bnšm.d.bu. | tšʻ.dt.tq[ḥn]. | šʻrt. | šbʻ dt tqḥn. | ššlmt. 2099.2
ṯlṯm.dd[.---]. | b.gt.ṣb[-.---]. | mit.ʻšr.[---.]dd[.--]. | tšʻ.dd.ḥ[ṭm.w].ḫm[šm]. | kdm.kbd.yn.b.gt.[---]. | [mi]tm.ḫmš 2092.4
| w.ʻšrm.l.mit.dd.ḥp[r.]bnšm. | b.gt.ǵl.ʻšrm.l.mit.drʻ.w.tšʻm.drt. | [w].ṯmnym.l.mit.dd.ḥpr.bnšm. | b.gt.alḫb.ṯṯm.drʻ. 1098.14
.mrynm. | ḫmš.[tr]tnm. | ṯlṯ.b[n.]mrynm. | ʻšr[.m]krm. | tšʻ.hbṭnm. | ʻšr.mrum. | šbʻ.ḫsnm. | tšʻm.ṯṯ.kbd.mdrǵlm. | ʻšrm 1028.6
r. | mrynm. | ṯlṯ.ʻšr.mkrm. | ṯlṯ.bn.mrynm. | arbʻ.trtnm. | tšʻ.ḫbṭnm. | ṯmnym.ṯlṯ.kbd. | mdrǵlm. | w.šbʻ.ʻšr.ḫsnm. | ḫmš 1029.10
[.kbd.yn].d.l[.ṭb].b.gt.ipṯl. | ṯmnym.[yn].ṭb.b.gt.š[---]. | tšʻm.[ḫ]mš[.kbd].yn.b gt[.-]n. | arbʻm.kbd.yn.ṭb.w.[--]. | ṯmn. 1084.21
arbʻ.yn. | šql ṯlṯ.yn. | šmny.kdm.yn. | šmgy.kd.yn. | hzp.tšʻ.yn. | [b]ir.ʻšr[.---]m ḥsp. | ḫpty.kdm[.---]. | [a]gm.arbʻ[.---]. 2004.28
b.b.ulm. | mit.yn.ṭb.w.ṯṯm.ṯṯ.kbd. | yn.d.l.ṭb.b.gt.ḥdṯt. | tšʻm.yn.d.l.ṭb.b.zbl. | ʻšrm.yn.ṭb.w.ṯṯm.ḫmš.k[b]d. | yn.d.l.ṭb. 1084.13
[---].dt.iṯ. | [---].ṯlṯ.kbd. | [---].alpm.ḫmš.mat. | šbʻm[.t]šʻ.kbd. | tgmr.uz.ǵrn.arbʻ.mat. | tgmr.uz.aḫmn.arbʻ.mat. | ar 1129.4
ṯlṯ.mat[.---.]kbd. | ṯṯ.ddm.k[--.b]rqd. | mit.tšʻm.[kb]d.ddm. | b.gt.bir. 2168.3
.yn.ṭb. | w.ḫmšm.k[dm.]kbd.yn.d.l.ṭb. | b.gt.gwl. | ṯlṯm.tšʻ[.kbd.yn].d.l[.ṭb].b.gt.ipṯl. | ṯmnym.[yn].ṭb.b.gt.š[---]. | tšʻ 1084.19
ṯlṯm. | kuwṯ.ṯlṯ.kbd. | m[i]t.arbʻt.kbd. | ḫ[mš.]šʻrt. | [---.]tšʻ.kbd.skm. | [arb]ʻm.ḫpnt.pṯt. | [-]r.pldm.dt.šʻrt. | ṯlṯm.ṯlṯ.kb 1111.6
ʻm.ṯp[rt]. | ksp h. | ṯmn.dd[.--]. | ṯlṯ.dd.p[--]. | šbʻt.p[--]. | tšʻt.k[bd.---]. | ḫmšt.k[bd.---]. | tgmr k[--.---]. | ḫmšm a[--.---]. 2120.7
ḫmš.ʻšr.yn.ṭb. | w.tšʻm.kdm.kbd.yn.d.l.ṭb. | w.arbʻm.yn.ḫlq.b.gt.sknm. | ʻšr.yn.ṭ 1084.2
r[ṣ.]b.ṯmnt.ksp. | ʻšrt.ksp.b.alp.[b d].bn.[---]. | tšʻ.ṣin.b.tšʻt.ksp. | mšlt.b.ṯql.ksp. | kdwṯ.l.grgyn.b.ṯq[l]. | ḫmšm.šmt.b. 2101.22
spr.bnš.mlk. | d.b d.prṯ. | tšʻ.l.ʻšrm. | lqḥ.ššlmt. | ṯmn.l.arbʻm. | lqḥ.šʻrt. 1025.3
ḫmš.ṯrtnm. | ḫmš.bn.mrynm. | ʻšr.mrum.w.šbʻ.ḫsnm. | tšʻm.mdrǵlm. | arbʻ.l ʻšrm.ḫsnm. | ʻšr.hbṭnm. | ṯṯm.l.mit.ṯn.kb 1030.7
ryn.ššwm. | ṯryn.aḥd.d bnš. | arbʻ.ṣmdm.apnt. | w ḥrṣ. | tšʻm.mrḫ.aḥd. | kbd. 1123.9
]. | ʻšr sp.m[ry-.---]. | ṯṯ sp.mry[-.---]. | ʻšr sp.m[ry-.---]. | tšʻm s[p.---]. | tšʻ[m.sp.---]. | ṯṯ[.---]. 139[310].12
-.---]. | ṯṯ sp.mry[-.---]. | ʻšr sp.m[ry-.---]. | tšʻm s[p.---]. | tšʻ[m.sp.---]. | ṯṯ[.---]. 139[310].13
ṣb[u.anyt]. | ʻdn. | ṭbq[ym]. | mʻq[bym]. | tšʻ.ʻ[šr.bnš]. | ǵr.ṯ[--.---]. | ṣbu.any[t]. | bn.kṭan. | ǵr.tšʻ[.ʻšr.b]nš 79[83].5
m]. | tšʻ.ʻ[šr.bnš]. | ǵr.ṯ[--.---]. | ṣbu.any[t]. | bn.kṭan. | ǵr.tšʻ[.ʻšr.b]nš. | ṣbu.any[t]. | bn abdḥ[r]. | pdym. | ḫmš.bnšm. | sn 79[83].9
--]. | [---].ʻšr.dd[.---]. | [---]mn.arbʻm.y[n]. | b.gt.trǵnds. | tšʻ.ʻšr.[dd].kšmm. | ṯn.ʻšr[.dd.ḥ]ṭm. | w.šb[ʻ.---]. 2092.16
spr.ḥpr.bt.k[--]. | tšʻ.ʻšr h.dd.l.b[t.--]. | ḫmš.ddm.l.ḫtyt. | ṯlṯm.dd.kšmn.l.gzzm. 1099.2
tšʻ.ṯnnm. | w.arbʻ.ḥsnm. | ʻšr.mrum. | w.šbʻ.ḫsnm. | tšʻ.ʻšr. | mrynm. | ṯlṯ.ʻšr.mkrm. | ṯlṯ.bn.mrynm. | arbʻ.ṯrtnm. | tš 1029.5
]m.y[d].š[--]. | [-]lm.b d.r[-]m.l[-]m. | ṯṯ.ʻšr.ṣ[mdm]. | w.tšʻ.ʻ[šr.--]m.ḥr[š]. | [---].ḥr[š.---]. | [---.ṯ]lṯ.[---.]dpm. | [---.]bnš 2038.11
ilm[.---]. | tšʻ.ʻš[r.---]. | bn ʻdr[.---]. | ḫmš ʻl.bn[.---]. | ḫmš ʻl rʻl[-]. | ḫmš ʻl 2034.2.2
. | ṯqlm.ḫr[ṣ.]b.ṯmnt.ksp. | ʻšrt.ksp.b.alp.[b d].bn.[---]. | tšʻ.ṣin.b.tšʻt.ksp. | mšlt.b.ṯql.ksp. | kdwṯ.l.grgyn.b.ṯq[l]. | ḫmš 2101.22
w.]ṯlṯm.ṣin. | anndr.yknʻmy. | w.aṯt h.w.bn h. | w.alp.w.tš[ʻ.]ṣin. 1080.17
tšʻ.ṣmdm. | ṯlṯm.b d. | ibrtlm. | w.pat.aḫt. | in.b hm. 1141.1
rynm. | ʻšr[.m]krm. | tšʻ.hbṭnm. | ʻšr.mrum. | šbʻ.ḫsnm. | tšʻm.ṯṯ.kbd.mdrǵlm. | ʻšrm.aḥd.kbd.ḫsnm. | ubnyn. | ṯṯm[.l.] 1028.9
tšʻ.ṯnnm. | w.arbʻ.ḫsnm. | ʻšr.mrum. | w.šbʻ.ḫsnm. | tšʻ.ʻšr. | mr 1029.1
d.yn.b.gt.[---]. | [mi]tm.ḫmšm.ḫmš.k[bd]. | [dd].kšmm.tšʻ[.---]. | [š]ʻrm.ṯṯ.ʻ[šr]. | [dd].ḥṭm.w.ḫ[mšm]. | [t]lṯ kbd.yn.b [2092.7
[-----]. | [---.]arbʻ[m]. | [---.a]rbʻm. | [---.tš]ʻm. | [---.t]šʻm. | [---.--]y arbʻm. | [---.]l špš ṯmny[m]. | [---.]d 41[71].4
[-----]. | [---.]arbʻ[m]. | [---.a]rbʻm. | [---.tš]ʻm. | [---.t]šʻm. | [---.--]y arbʻm. | [---.]l špš ṯmny[m]. | [---.]dbr h l šp[š] 41[71].5
ṯṯm.[---.p]rm. | [-]l.b[--.---]. | [---].kbd. | [---].kb[d.---]. | [t]šʻm. 1138.8

tt

.bt.rpi[--]. | [aṯt.]w.bt h.b.bt.alḫn. | [aṯt.w.]pǵt.aḥt.b.bt.tt. | [aṯt.w.]bt h.b.bt.trǵds. | [---.]aṯt.adrt.w.pǵt.a[ḥt.b.bt.---]. | 80[119].26
n.b d.nwrd. | [šd.]bn.nḥbl.b d.ʻdbym. | [šd.b]n.qty.b d.tt. | [ubd]y.mrim. | [šd.b]n.ṯpdn.b d.bn.gʻr. | [šd.b]n.ṯqrn.b d. 82[300].1.19
alpm.pḥm.ḫm[š].mat.kbd. | b d.tt.w.ṯlṯ.ktnt.b dm.tt. | w.ṯmnt.ksp.hn. | ktn.d.ṣr.pḥm.b h.w.ṯq 1110.2
alpm.pḥm.ḫm[š].mat.kbd. | b d.tt.w.ṯlṯ.ktnt.b dm.tt. | w.ṯmnt.ksp.hn. | ktn.d.ṣr.pḥm.b h.w.ṯqlm. | ksp h.mitm.p 1110.2
---]. | ybnil[.---.]kd yn.w š. | spr.m[--]. | spr d[---]b.w š. | tt.ḫmš.[---]. | skn.ul[m.---]. | [---]š.[---]. | [---]y[.---]. | sk[n.---]. | 1093.5

ttḫ

ilk.r[--]. | aršm.bʻl [aṯt]. | ttḫ.bʻl aṯt. | ayab.bʻl aṯt. | iyṯr.bʻl aṯt. | ptm.bʻl ššlmt. | ʻdršp.bʻl 1077.3

ttyn

spr.ubdy.art. | šd.prn.b d.agpṯn.nḥl h. | šd.šwn.b d.ttyn.nḥl [h]. | šd.ttyn[.b]n.arkšt. | lʻq[.---]. | šd.pll.b d.qrt. | š[d 2029.3

ttl

.ydb.ksa. | w yṯb. | tqru.l špš.u h.špš.um.ql.bl.ʻm. | dgn.ttl h.mnt.nṯk.nḥš.šmrr. | nḥš.ʻq šr.ln h.mlḫš.abd.ln h. | ydy.ḥ UG5.7.15

ttn

.nḥl hm. | w.[n]ḥl hm. | b[n.---]. | bn.gzry. | bn.atyn. | bn.ttn. | bn.rwy. | bn.ʻmyn. | bdl.mrynm. | bn.ṣqn. | bn.šyn. | bn.pr 113[400].3.3
dt. | bn.ḫ[--]y. | bn.ʻ[-]y. | knʻm. | bn.yš[-]n. | bn.pd[y]. | ttn. | md.ʻtt[rt]. | kṯkt. | bn.ṯtn[--]. | [m]d.m[--]. | [b]n.annḏ[r]. | 1054.1.10
[.--]l[-]. | ʻbdy[rḫ].bn.gṯtn. | yrmn.bn.ʻn. | krwn.nḥl h. | ttn.[n]ḥl h. | bn.b[r]zn. | [---.-]ḫn. 85[80].4.11
rn.qšt.w.qlʻ. | bn.pǵm[-.qšt].w.qlʻ. | nʻmn.q[št.w.]qlʻ. | [t]tn.qš[t]. | bn.ṯǵdy[.qšt.]w.qlʻ. | ṯty.qšt[.w.]qlʻ. | bn.šp[š.]qšt. | 119[321].4.3
| nṣṣn.qšt. | mʻr. | [ʻ]dyn.ṯt.qštm.w.qlʻ. | [-]lrš.qšt.w.qlʻ. | t[t]n.qšt.w.qlʻ. | u[l]n.qšt.w.qlʻ. | yʻrn.qšt.w.qlʻ. | klby.qšt.w.ql 119[321].2.16

ttǵl

ʻd[rš]p. | pqr. | ṯǵr. | ttǵl. | ṯn.yṣḥm. | slṯmg. | kdrl. | wql. | adrdn. | prn. | ʻbdil. | ušy.š 1069.4

tṯb

.hmlt.tn.bʻl.[w ʻnn h]. | bn.dgn.arṯ m.pḏ h.tbʻ.ǵlmm.l ṯṯb.[idk.pnm]. | l ytn.tk.ǵr.ll.ʻm.phr.mʻd.ap.ilm.l lḥ[m]. | yṯb. 2.1[137].19

tṯyn

. | šd.prn.b d.agpṯn.nḥl h. | šd.šwn.b d.ttyn.nḥl [h]. | šd.ṯṯyn[.b]n.arkšt. | lʻq[.---]. | šd.pll.b d.qrt. | š[d].annḏr.b d.bdn. 2029.4

tṯkn

b ym ḥdṯ. | b.yrḫ.pgrm. | lqḥ.iwrpzn. | argḏḏ. | ṯṯkn. | ybrk. | ntbt. | b.mitm. | ʻšrm. | kbd.ḫrṣ. 2006.5

tṯmd

.b d.ibrmḏ. | [š]d.bn.ilṯtmr.b d.tbbr. | [w.]šd.nḥl h.b d.ṯṯmd. | [š]d.b d.iwrḫṯ. | [ṯn].šdm.b d.gmrd. | [šd.]lbny.b d.tbtṯ 82[300].1.12
d.iwrḫṯ. | [šd.bn.-]nn.b d.bn.šmrm. | [šd.bn.-]ṯtayy.b d.ṯṯmd. | [šd.bn.-]rn.b d.ṣdqšlm. | [šd.b d.]bn.pʻṣ. | [ubdy.ʻ]šrm. 82[300].1.27

tṯn

. | bn.ḫnyn.ʻšrt. | rpan.ḫmšt. | abǵl.ḫmšt. | bn.aḫdy.ʻšrt. | ṯṯn.ʻṣrt. | bn.pnmn.ʻšrt. | ʻbdadt.ḫmšt. | abmn.ilštmʻy.ḫmš[t]. | 1062.22
n.š[šlmt]. | bnš.iwl[--.š]šlmt. | šdyn.ššlmt. | prtwn.šʻrt. | ṯṯn.šʻrt. | ʻdn.šʻrt. | mnn.šʻrt. | bdn.šʻrt. | ʻpṯn.šʻrt. | ʻbd.yrḫ šʻrt. 97[315].5

tṯp

.asr.[---.]l[.---]. | mḫlpt.w l.ytk.[d]m[ʻt.]km. | rbʻt.ṯqlm.ṯtp[.---.]bm. | yd.ṣpn hm.tliy m[.--.ṣ]pn hm. | nṣḥy.šrr.m[---.- 19[1AQHT].2.83

tṯrn

[š]d bn.synn.b d.gmrd. | [šd.]abyy.b d.ibrmḏ. | [šd.]bn.ṯṯrn.b d.bnš.aǵlkz. | [šd.b]d.b[n].tkwn. | [ubdy.mḏ]rǵlm. | [šd 82[300].2.20

ṯ

ṯag

ẖmš.ṯdṯ.ym.|mk.špšm.b šb‘.|w l.yšn.pbl.|mlk.l [qr.]ṯiqt.|ibr h[.l]ql.nhqt.|ḥmr[h.l g‘t.]alp.|ḥrṯ[.l z]ǵt.klb.|[ṣ]p 14[KRT].5.223

.yd k.|mšdpt.w hn.špšm.|b šb‘.w l.yšn.pbl.|mlk.l qr.ṯigt.ibr h.|l ql.nhqt.ḥmr h.|l g‘t.alp.ḥrṯ.zǵt.|klb.ṣpr.w ylak. 14[KRT].3.120

ṯap

w š[--.---].|ḥdṯ[.---.]ḫ[--].|b bt.[-.]l bnt.q[-].|w št.b bt.ṯap[.--].|hy.yd h.w ym[ǵ].|mlak k.‘m dt[n].|lqḥ.mṯpṭ.|w y‘ UG5.6.9

ṯar

š.mknt.|aṯt.ṣdq h.l ypq.|mtrẖt.yšr h.|aṯt.trẖ.w tb‘t.|ṯar um.tkn l h.|mṯlṯt.kṯrm.tmt.|mrb‘t.zblnm.|mẖmšt.yitsp 14[KRT].1.15

tṣḥ.šm‘.m[‘.l a]|[qht.ǵ]zr.at.aẖ.w an.a[ẖt k].|[---].šb‘.ṯir k.[---].|[---.]ab y.ndt.ank[.---].|[---.--]l.mlk.tlk.b ṣd[.---].| 18[3AQHT].1.25

ṯlṯ.|[ssw]m.mrkbt b trbṣ bn.amt.|[tn.b]nm.aqny.|[tn.ṯa]rm.amid.|[w y‘n].ṯr.ab h.il.|d[--].b bk.krt.|b dm‘.n‘mn.ǵ 14[KRT].2.58

n y.trḥṣn.k ṯrm.|[--]b b[ht].|[zbl.]ym.b hkl.ṯpṭ.nh[r].yṯir.ṯr.il.ab h l pn[.zb]l y[m].|[l pn.ṯp]ṭ[.nhr.]mlkt.[--]pm.l 2.3[129].21

-]n.bn.|[---.-]nn.nrt.ilm.špš.tšu.g h.w t[ṣḥ.šm]‘.m‘.|[-.yṯ]ir ṯr.il.ab k.l pn.zbl.ym.l pn[.ṯ]pṭ[.n]hr.|[ik.a]l.yšm‘ k.ṯr.[2.3[129].16

ṯat

b gt ilštm‘.|bt ubnyn š h d.ytn.ṣtqn.|ṯut ṭbẖ ṣtq[n].|b bz ‘zm ṭbẖ š[h].|b kl ygz ẖẖ š h. 1153.3

m].|y‘tqn.w[rḥm.‘nt].|tngṯ h.k lb.a[rẖ].|l ‘gl h.k lb.ṯa[t].|l imr h.km.lb.‘n[t].|aṯr.b‘l.tiẖd.m[t].|b sin.lpš.tšṣq[n 6[49].2.7

.l ymm.|l yrẖm.rḥm.‘nt.tngṯ h.|k lb.arẖ.l ‘gl h.k lb.|ṯat.l imr h.km.lb.|‘nt.aṯr.b‘l.tiẖd.|bn.ilm.mt.b ḥrb.|tbq‘nn. 6[49].2.29

wt.b‘l.iš[--].|šm‘ l y.ypš.[---].|ḥkr[.---].|‘ṣr[.--.]tb[-].|ṯat[.---].|yn[-.---].|i[--.---]. 2124.8

ṯiṭ

‘ yn.spu.ksm h.bt.b‘l.|[w m]nt h bt.il.ṭẖ.gg h.b ym.|[ṯi]ṭ.rḥṣ.npṣ h.b ym.rṯ.|[--.y]iẖd.il.‘bd h.ybrk.|[dni]l mt rpi. 17[2AQHT].1.34

t yn.|spu.ksm y.bt.b‘l.[w]mn[t].|y.bt.il.ṭẖ.gg y.b ym.ṯiṭ.|rḥṣ.npṣ y.b ym.rṯ.|dn.il.bt h.ymǵyn.|yštql.dnil.l hkl h. 17[2AQHT].2.22

.aẖd.yd k.b [škrn].|m‘ms k.k šb‘t.yn.ṭ[ẖ].|gg k.b ym.ṯiṭ.rḥṣ.|npṣ k.b ym rṯ.b uni[l].|pnm.tšmẖ.w ‘l yṣhl pi[t].|yp 17[2AQHT].2.7

ṯbil

n yṣmẖ.bn.ṯrn w nḥl h.|bn srd.bn agmn.|bn [-]ln.bn.ṯbil.|bn is.bn tbdn.|bn uryy.|bn abd‘n.|bn prkl.|bn štn.|b 101[10].6

bdlḥn[-].|bn.mqwṭ.|bn.bsn.|bn.inr[-].|bn.ṯbil.|bn.iryn.|ṯtl.|bn.nṣdn.|bn.ydln.|[bn].‘dy.|[bn].ilyn. 1071.5

kd.šmn.‘l.hbm.šlmy.|kd.šmn.ṯbil.|kd.šmn.ymtšr.|arb‘.šmn.‘l.‘bdn.w.[---].|kdm.šmn.‘l.ilr 1082.1.2

]m.ẖmš.bnšm.|ǵr.|ary.ḥmr w.bnš.|qmy.ḥmr.w.bnš.|ṯbil.|‘nmky.ḥmr.w.bnš.|rqd arb‘.|šbn aḥd.|ṭbq aḥd.|šrš aḥ 2040.25

d ṯbil.|‘ṯtrt ṣwd[t.---].|tlk b mdb[r.---].|tḥdṯn w hl[.---].|w tgl 2001.1.1

ln[.---].|bn.pndr[.---].|bn.idr[-.---].|bn.ḥdn[-.---].|bn.ṯbi[l.---]. 2070.2.8

ṯbg

bn.ṯyl.|‘bdn.w.aṯt h.w.bn h.|gpn.bn[.a]ly.|bn.rqd[y].ṯbg.|iẖmlk.|yp‘n w.aṯt h.|anntn.yṣr.|annmn.w.ṯlṯ.n‘[r] h.| 2068.21

ṯbṭ

pm.w.ṯn.trqm.|w.qpt.w.mqḥm.|w.ṯlṯm.yn šb‘.kbd d ṯbṭ.|w.ẖmšm.yn.d iẖ h. 1103.22

ṯbln

nm].|[b‘]l.[---].|mr[--.---].|hm.[---].|kmrṯn[.---].|bn.ṯbln[.---].|bn.pndr[.---].|bn.idr[-.---].|bn.ḥdn[-.---].|bn.ṯbi[l 2070.2.4

ṯb‘m

[-]mn.|b‘ly.|rpan.|‘pṯrm.|bn.‘bd.|šmb‘l.|ykr.|bly.|ṯb‘m.|ḥdṯn.|rpty.|ilym.|bn.‘br.|mnip‘l.|amrb‘l.|dqry.|ṯd 1058.10

nš hm.|ḏmry.w.pṯpṯ.‘rb.|b.yrm.|[ily.w].ḏmry.‘rb.|b.ṯb‘m.|ydn.bn.ilrpi.|w.ṯb‘m.‘rb.b.‘[d]n.|ḏmry.bn.yrm.|‘rb.b 2079.6

[--]n.|[---].|tsn.|rpiy.|mrṭn.|ṯnyn.|apṯ.|šbn.|gbrn.|ṯb‘m.|kyn.|b‘ln.|ytršp.|ḥmšm.ṯmn.kbd.|tgmr.bnš.mlk.|d. 1024.2.21

t.kkln.‘bd.absn.|šdyn.unn.dqn.|‘bd‘nt.rb ‘šrt.mnḥm.ṯb‘m.sẖr.‘zn.ilhd.|bnil.rb ‘šrt.lkn.yp‘n.ṯ[--].|yṣḥm.b d.ubn. 2011.7

b.|b.yrm.|[ily.w].ḏmry.‘rb.|b.ṯb‘m.|ydn.bn.ilrpi.|w.ṯb‘m.‘rb.b.‘[d]n.|ḏmry.bn.yrm.|‘rb.b.ad‘y. 2079.8

.ṯ[---].|šd.‘dmn[.bn.]ynḥm.|šd.bn.ṯmr[n.m]idẖy.|šd.ṯb‘m[.--]y. 2026.10

aǵltn.|urtn.|annṯb.|ubn.|špšyn.|abmn.|[--]dn.|[ṯ]b‘m.|[--]mlk.|[--]ty.|mtnb‘l.|bn.ndbn.|bn irgn. 1072.8

ṯb‘nq

idrm.|bn.grgš.|bn.bly.|bn.apṯ.|bn.ysd.|bn.pl[-].|bn.ṯb‘nq.|brqd.|bnn.|kbln.ṣ[md].|bn gmrt.|bn.il.ṣm[d].|bn a 2113.14

ṯbǵl

šd.bn.ky.gt.prn.|šd.hwil.gt.prn.|šd.ḥr.gt.prn.|šd.bn.ṯbǵl.gt.prn.|šd.bn.inšr.gt.prn.|šd.[---.]gt.prn.|[šd.---.]gt.prn 1104.9

ṯbq

d.š[--]mlk.|[---.b] d.gb‘ly.|[---.b] d.‘bdẖmn.|[---.b] d.ṯbq.|[---.b] d.šbn.|[---.b] d.ulm.|[---.b] d.ǵbl.|[---.b] d.‘bdkṯ 1052.4

ṯbr

akm.ylak.ym.[t‘dt.ṯpṭ.nhr].|b ‘lṣ.‘lṣm.npr.š[--.---].|uṭ.ṯbr.ap hm.tb‘.ǵlm[m.al.ṯṯb.idk.pnm].|al.ttn.‘m.pẖr.m‘d.t[k. 2.1[137].13

p]t.|ql h.qdš.b[‘l.y]tn.|yṯny.b‘l.ṣ[---.-]pt h.|ql h.q[dš.ṯb]r.arṣ.|[---.]ǵrm[.t]ẖšn.|rḥq[.---.td‘].|qdm ym.bmt.[nhr]. 4[51].7.31

i[lm.arṣ.b p h.rgm.l yṣa.b šp]|t h.hwt h.knp.hrgb.b‘l.ṯbr.|b‘l.ṯbr.diy.hwt.w yql.|tḥt.p‘n h.ybq‘.kbd h.w yḥd.|[i]n 19[1AQHT].3.128

n. | yḥd.hrgb.ab.nšrm. | yšu.g h.w yṣḥ.knp.hr[g]b. | b'l.yṯb.b'l.y[ṯb]r.diy[.h]wt. | w yql.tḥt.p'n y.ibq'.kbd[h]. | w aḥd 19[1AQHT].3.123
]yphn.yḥd.ṣml.um.nšrm. | yšu.g h.w yṣḥ.knp.ṣml. | b'l.yṯbr.b'l.yṯbr.diy. | hyt.tql.tḥt.p'n y.ibq'. | kbd h.w aḥd.hm.iṯ. 19[1AQHT].3.137
.nn.b mdgt.b knk[-]. | w yšu.g h.w yṣḥ.knp.nšrm. | b'l.yṯbr.b'l.yṯbr.diy. | hmt.hm.t'pn.'l.qbr.bn y. | tšḫṭann.b šnt h. 19[1AQHT].3.149
yḥd]. | b 'rpt[.nšrm.yšu]. | [g h.]w yṣḥ[.knp.nšrm]. | b'l.yṯb.b'l.yṯb[r.diy.hmt]. | tqln.tḥ p'n y.ibq['.kbd hm.w] | aḥd.h 19[1AQHT].3.108
m.arṣ. | b p h.rgm.l yṣa.b špt h.hwt[h]. | knp.nšrm.b'l.yṯbr. | b'l.ṯbr.diy hmt.tqln. | tḥt.p'n h.ybq'.kbdt hm.w[yḥd]. 19[1AQHT].3.114
.hrgb.ab.nšrm. | yšu.g h.w yṣḥ.knp.hr[g]b. | b'l.yṯb.b'l.y[ṯb]r.diy[.h]wt. | w yql.tḥt.p'n y.ibq'.kbd[h]. | w aḥd.hm.iṯ. 19[1AQHT].3.123
.b p h.rgm.l yṣa.b šp] | t h.hwt h.knp.hrgb.b'l.ṯbr. | b'l.ṯbr.diy.hwt.w yql. | tḥt.p'n h.ybq'.kbd h.w yḥd. | [i]n.šmt.in.' 19[1AQHT].3.129
rṣ.b p h.rgm.l[yṣ]a. | b špt h.hwt h.knp.ṣml.b'[l]. | b'l.ṯbr.diy.hyt.tq[l.tḥt]. | p'n h.ybq'.kbd h.w yḥd. | iṯ.šmt.iṯ.'ẓm. 19[1AQHT].3.143
ḥd.ṣml.um.nšrm. | yšu.g h.w yṣḥ.knp.ṣml. | b'l.yṯbr.b'l.yṯbr.diy. | hyt.tql.tḥt.p'n y.ibq'. | kbd h.w aḥd.hm.iṯ.šmt.iṯ. | ' 19[1AQHT].3.137
dgt.b knk[-]. | w yšu.g h.w yṣḥ.knp.nšrm. | b'l.yṯbr.b'l.yṯbr.diy. | hmt.hm.t'pn.'l.qbr.bn y. | tšḫṭann.b šnt h.qr.[mym 19[1AQHT].3.149
'rpt[.nšrm.yšu]. | [g h.]w yṣḥ[.knp.nšrm]. | b'l.yṯb.b'l.yṯb[r.diy.hmt]. | tqln.tḥ p'n y.ibq['.kbd hm.w] | aḥd.hm.iṯ.š 19[1AQHT].3.108
p h.rgm.l yṣa.b špt h.hwt[h]. | knp.nšrm.b'l.yṯbr. | b'l.ṯbr.diy hmt.tqln. | tḥt.p'n h.ybq'.kbdt hm.w[yḥd]. | in.šmt.i 19[1AQHT].3.115
'rš.zbln.rd.l mlk. | amlk.l drkt k.aṯb. | an.w y'ny.krt ṯ'.yṯbr. | ḥrn.y bn.yṯbr.ḥrn. | riš k.'ṯtrt.šm.b'l. | qdqd k.tqln.b gb 16.6[127].54
.b'l[.---]. | drkt k.mšl[-.---]. | b riš k.aymr[.---]. | ṯpṭ.nhr.yṯb[r.ḥrn.y ym.yṯbr.ḥrn]. | riš k.'ṯtrt.[šm.b'l.qdqd k.---]. | [--] 2.1[137].7
.mšl[-.---]. | b riš k.aymr[.---]. | ṯpṭ.nhr.yṯb[r.ḥrn.y ym.yṯbr.ḥrn]. | riš k.'ṯtrt.[šm.b'l.qdqd k.---]. | [--]t.mṭ.tpln.b g[bl. 2.1[137].7
k. | amlk.l drkt k.aṯb. | an.w y'ny.krt ṯ'.yṯbr. | ḥrn.y bn.yṯbr.ḥrn. | riš k.'ṯtrt.šm.b'l. | qdqd k.tqln.b gbl. | šnt k.b ḥpn 16.6[127].55
' k.ṯr.[i]l.ab k.l ys'.[alt.]ṯ[bt | k.l y]hpk. | [ksa.]mlk k.l yṯbr.ḫṭ.mṯpṭ k.w y'n[.'ṯtr].dm[-]k[-]. | [--]ḥ.b y.ṯr.il.ab y.ank. 2.3[129].18
šm['] k.ṯr. | il.ab k.l ys'.alt. | ṯbt k.l yhpk.ksa.mlk k. | l yṯbr.ḫṭ.mṯpṭ k. | yru.bn ilm t.ṯt'.y | dd.il.ǵzr.y'r.mt. | b ql h.y[6[49].6.29
si y.w pr[']. | [---].pr'.ank.[---]. | [---.]ank.nši[.---]. | [---.ṯ]br.ḫss.[---]. | [---.--]št.b [---]. | [---.--]b. | [---.--]k. | [---.--]an. | [1002.16
]. | k iṯl.brlt h.[b h.p'nm]. | ṭṭṭ.'l[n.pn h.td'.b 'dn]. | ksl.y[ṯbr.yǵṣ.pnt.ksl h]. | anš.[dt.ẓr h.yšu.g h]. | w yṣ[ḥ.---]. | mḫṣ 19[1AQHT].2.95
m.b gb'.tliyt. | hlm.'nt.tph.ilm.b h.p'nm. | ṭṭṭ.b'd n.ksl.ṯṯbr. | 'ln.pn h.td'.tǵṣ.pnt. | ksl h.anš.dt.ẓr h.tšu. | g h.w tṣḥ.ik 3['NT].3.30
tlt. | 'nt.tdrq.ybmt. | [limm].b h.p'nm. | [ṭṭṭ.b ']dn.ksl. | [ṯṯbr.'ln.p]n h.td['']. | tǵṣ[.pnt.ks]l h. | anš.dt.ẓr.[h]. | tšu.g h.w 4[51].2.18
al. | tqrb.l bn.ilm. | mt.al.y'db km. | k imr.b p h. | k lli.b ṯbrn. | qn h.tḫtan. | nrt.ilm.špš. | ṣḥrrt.la. | šmm.b yd.md | d.il 4[51].8.19
mmt. | ngš.ank.aliyn b'l. | 'dbnn ank.imr.b p y. | k lli.b ṯbrn q y.ḫtu hw. | nrt.ilm.špš.ṣḥrrt. | la.šmm.b yd.bn ilm.mt. 6[49].2.23
[l a]q[h]t. | [t]krb.[---.]l qrb.mym. | tql.[---.]lb.tt[b]r. | qšt[.---]r.y[t]br. | ṯmn.[---.]btlt.[']nt. | ttb.[---.--]ša. | tl 19[1AQHT].1.3
]t. | [t]krb.[---.]l qrb.mym. | tql.[---.]lb.tt[b]r. | qšt[.---]r.y[t]br. | ṯmn.[---.]btlt.[']nt. | ttb.[---.--]ša. | tlm.km[.---.]yd h.k 19[1AQHT].1.4
ḥ h. | l tl.yṣb.pn h.ṯǵr. | yṣu.hlm.aḫ h.tph. | [ksl]h.l arṣ.ṯṯbr. | [---.]aḫ h.tbky. | [--.m]rṣ.mlk. | [---.]krt.adn k. | [w y'ny. 16.1[125].54
[---.]ps[.---]. | [---].yṯbr[.---]. | [---.]uṭm.ḏr[qm.---]. | [btl]t.'nt.l kl.[---]. | [tt]b'.btlt 18[3AQHT].4.2

ṯbry

n.a[--]. | bn.iy[--]. | bn.ḥ[---]. | bn.plš. | bn.ubr. | bn.'pṯb. | ṯbry. | bn.ymn. | krty. | bn.abr[-]. | yrpu. | kdn. | p'ṣ. | bn.liy. | yd' 2117.1.18

ṯbrn

.[---]. | [-----]. | bn[---]. | bn.mlkyy. | bn.atn. | bn.bly. | bn.ṯbrn. | bn.ḥgby. | bn.pity. | bn.slgyn. | 'zn.bn.mlk. | bn.alṯn. | bn 115[301].2.4

ṯbš

r.tnšq.špt k.ṯm. | ṯkm.bm ṯkm.aḫm.qym.il. | b lsmt.ṯm.yṯbš.šm.il.mt m. | y'bš.brk n.šm.il.ǵzrm. | ṯm.ṯmq.rpu.b'l.mh 22.2[124].6

ṯbtnq

n. | w.nḥl h. | bn.adldn. | bn.šbl. | bn.ḫnzr. | bn.arwṯ. | bn.ṯbtnq. | bn.pṯdn. | bn.nbdg. | bn.ḥgbn. | bn.tmr. | bn.prsn. | bn.r 113[400].1.16

ṯgbr

d. | [---]yb'.b'l.ḫr[-]. | pqr.yḥd. | bn.ktmn.ṯǵr.hk[l]. | bn.ṯgbr.ṯǵr.hk[l]. | bn.ydln. | bn.ktmn. 1056.9

ṯgd

. | bn.ṯ'y. | w.nḥl h. | w.nḥl hm. | bn.nqly. | bn.snrn. | bn.ṯgd. | bn.d[-]n. | bn.amdn. | bn.ṯmrn. | bn.pzny. | bn.mglb. | bn.[105[86].3
]yṯb.b.šb[n]. | bn.pr[-.]d.y[ṯb.b].šlmy. | tlš.w[.n]ḥl h[.-].ṯgd.mrum. | bt.[-]b[-.-]sy[-]h. | nn[-].b[n].py[-.d.]yṯb.b.gt.aǵld 2015.2.3

ṯgmi

b yrḫ.mgm[r.---]. | yṣu.ḫlpn[.---]. | ṯlṯ.dt.p[--.---]. | dt.ṯgmi.[---]. | b d [---]t.[---]. 1159.4

ṯgrb

[--]. | bn[.---]. | [-----]. | bn kr[k]. | bn ḫtyn. | w nḥl h. | bn ṯgrb. | bn ṯdnyn. | bn pbn. 2016.3.5

ṯgt

| ṯlṯm.dd.kšmn.l.gzzm. | yyn. | ṣdqn. | 'bd.pdr. | myṣm. | ṯgt. | w.lmd h. | yṯil. | w.lmd h. | rpan. | w.lmd h. | 'bdrpu. | w.l 1099.9

ṯd

šrm. | iqran.ilm.n'mm[.agzry ym.bn]ym. | ynqm.b ap zd.aṯrt.[---]. | špš.mṣprt dlt hm[.---]. | w ǵnbm.šlm.'rbm.ṯn[n 23[52].24
yn. | špq.ilht.dkrt[.yn]. | 'd.lḥm.šty.ilm. | w pq mrǵtm.ṯd. | b ḥrb.mlḫt.qṣ[.m]r | i.tšty.krp[nm.y]n. | [b k]s.ḫrṣ.d[m.'ṣ 4[51].6.56
m. | [---.]btlt.'nt. | [--.tl]ḥm.tšty. | [ilm.w tp]q.mrǵtm. | [ṯd.b ḥrb.m]lḫt.qṣ. | [mri.tšty.k]rpnm yn. | [b ks.ḫrṣ.dm].'ṣm. 4[51].3.42
w ṯmn.tṯtmnm. | l k.tld.yṣb.ǵlm. | ynq.ḥlb.a[ṯ]rt. | mṣṣ.ṯd.btlt.['nt]. | mšnq.[---]. 15[128].2.27
t. | ḫr[.---.]'l.kbkbt. | n'm.[--.-]llm.trtḥṣ. | btlt.'n[t].tptr' ṯd[h]. | limm.w t'l.'m.il. | ab h.ḥpr.p'l k.y[--]. | šm' k.l arḫ.w 13[6].19
i[yn]. | b'l.sid.zbl.b'l. | arṣ.qm.yt'r. | w yšlḥmn h. | ybrd.ṯd.l pnw h. | b ḥrb.mlḥt. | qṣ.mri.ndd. | y'šr.w yšqyn h. | ytn.k 3['NT].1.6
[---.y]lt n.km.qdm. | [-.k]bd n.il.ab n. | kbd k iš.tikln. | ṯd n.km.mrm.tqrṣn. | il.yẓḥq.bm. | lb.w ygmd.bm kbd. | ẓi.at. 12[75].1.11
.w tldn.tld.[ilm.]n'mm.agzr ym. | bn.ym.ynqm.b a[p.]ḏ[d.r]gm.l il.ybl. | aṯt y.il.ylt.mh.ylt.ilmy n'mm. | agzr ym.bn 23[52].59
.il.ylt.mh.ylt.ilmy n'mm. | agzr ym.bn ym.ynqm.b ap.ḏd.št.špt. | l arṣ.špt l šmm.w 'rb.b p hm.'ṣr.šmm. | w dg b ym 23[52].61

---]. | lḥm.m[---.---]. | [ʻ]d.lḥm[.šty.ilm]. | w pq.mr[ǵṯm.ṯd.---]. | b ḥrb.[mlḥt.qṣ.mri]. | šty.kr[pnm.yn.---]. | b ks.ḫr[ṣ.d 5[67].4.13

ṯdy

. | ḥdṯn. | rpty. | ilym. | bn.ʻbr. | mnipʻl. | amrbʻl. | dqry. | ṯdy. | ypʻbʻl. | bdlm. | bn.pḏ[-]. | bn.[---]. 1058.18

ṯdyn

| [--]yl.b.bqʻt.b.gt.tgyn. | [--]in.b.trzy. | [--]yn.b.glltky. | ṯd[y]n.b.glltky. | lbw[-].uḫ.pdm.b.yʻrt. | pǵyn.b.tpḥ. | amri[l]. 2118.9

ṯdn

rbʻ.ḥ[mrm]. | b m[ʻ]rby. | ṯmn.ṣmd.[---]. | b d.bʻlsr. | yd.ṯdn.ʻšr. | [ḥ]mrm. | ddm.l.ybr[k]. | bdmr.prs.l.u[-]m[-]. | ṯmn.l. 2102.5

ṯdnyn

---]. | [-----]. | bn kr[k]. | bn ḫtyn. | w nḥl h. | bn ṯgrb. | bn ṯdnyn. | bn pbn. 2016.3.6
n. | [----.-]mn. | [---.--]m.mṣl. | [---].prš.ḥtm. | ṯlṯ[.---].bn.ṯdnyn. | ddm.ḥ[ṯm].ʻl.šrn. | ʻšrt.ksp.ʻl.[-]lpy. | bn.ady.kkr.šʻrt. 1146.6

ṯdpṯn

k[---]. | ʻbd.[---]. | mtn[.---]. | ṯdpṯn[.--]. | tny[.--]. | sll[.--]. | mld[.--]. | yqš[.--]. | [-----]. | inš[r.- 1074.4

ṯdr

[---].ydm. | [---].ṯdr. | [---.]mdṯn.ipd. | [---.]m[---.]d.mškbt. | [---.--]m. | [---].ṯlḥ 1152.1.2

ṯdṯ

m.y[--.]ilm.b ṣpn. | ʻdr.l[ʻr].ʻrm. | ṯb.l pd[r.]pdrm. | ṯṯ.l ṯṯm.aḫd.ʻr. | šbʻm.šbʻ.pdr. | ṯmnym.bʻl.[----]. | ṯšʻm.bʻl.mr[-]. | 4[51].7.9
mnm. | [---.iqn]i.lbš.al[l.---]. | [---].ṯṯ.lbš[.---]. | [---.]kbd.ṯṯ.i[qnu.---]. | [---.]ǵprt.ʻš[r.---]. | [---.p]ṯtm.l.ip[--.---]. | [---.]ksl 1106.23
ʻšr. | ṣʻ.ṯmn. | šḫq.ʻšrm.arbʻ.kbd. | ḫlb rpš arbʻ.ʻšr. | bqʻt ṯṯ. | irab ṯn.ʻšr. | ḥbš.ṯmn. | amḏy.arbʻ.ʻšr. | [-]nʻy.ṯṯ.ʻšr. 67[110].8
ṯlṯm. | b.bn.agdṯb.ʻšrm. | b.bn.ibn.arbʻt.ʻšrt. | b.bn.mnn.ṯṯm. | b.rpan.bn.yyn.ʻšrt. | b.ypʻr.ʻšrm. | b.nʻmn.bn.ply.ḫmšt.l. 2054.1.14
sp. | ḥṯbn.ybnn. | arbʻm.l.mit.šmn. | arbʻm.l.mit.tišr. | ṯṯ.ṯṯ.b [ṯ]ql.ṯlṯt.l.ʻšrm.ksp hm. | šstm.b.šbʻm. | ṯlṯ.mat.trm.b.ʻšrt. 1127.5
[sp]r.k[--]. | ṯ[ṯ.bn]šm[.b.a]gmy. | ṯṯ.bn[šm.---]. | ʻšr.b[nšm.---]. | arbʻ[.bnš 2076.2
bʻ.bnšm.b.ag[m]y. | arbʻ.bnšm.b.ḫpty. | ṯṯ.bnšm.b.bir. | ṯṯ.bnšm b.uḫnp. | ṯn.bnšm.b.ḫrṣbʻ. | arbʻ.bnšm.b.hzp. | arbʻ.b 2076.14
m.[b.]ʻd[--]. | arbʻ.bnšm.b.ag[m]y. | arbʻ.bnšm.b.ḫpty. | ṯṯ.bnšm.b.bir. | ṯṯ.bnšm b.uḫnp. | ṯn.bnšm.b.ḫrṣbʻ. | arbʻ.bnšm 2076.13
n. | ṯn.bnšm.b.yʻrt. | ṯn.bnšm.b.ʻrmt. | arbʻ.bnšm.b.šrš. | ṯṯ.bnšm.b.mlk. | arbʻ.bnšm.b.bṣr. | ṯn.bnšm.[b.]rqd. | ṯn.b[nšm 2076.38
[sp]r.k[--]. | ṯ[ṯ.bn]šm[.b.a]gmy. | ṯṯ.bn[šm.---]. | ʻšr.b[nšm.---]. | arbʻ[.bnšm.---]. | ṯṯ.ʻšr.bnš[m.--- 2076.3
l.ar[ṣ.---]. | [---.--]g.irb[-.---]. | [---.-]rd.pn.[---]. | [---.--]r.ṯṯ d.[---]. | [---.--]r.[---]. 2157.6
[---.]ṯṯ.dd.gdl.ṯṯ.dd.šʻrm. | [---.-]hn.w.alp.kd.nbt.kd.šmn.mr. | [---. 142[12].1
qm.[ṯ]ṯ.mat.nṣ.ṯlṯm.ʻṣr. | [---].ḫmš[m.ḥm]r.škm. | [---.ṯṯ.dd.]gdl.ṯṯ.dd.šʻrm. | [---.hn.w.al]p.kd.nbt.kd.šmn.mr. | [---] 142[12].7
šmn. | [---].ḫšwn.ṯṯ.mat.nṣ. | [---].ḫmšm.ḥmr.škm. | [---.ṯṯ.dd.]gdl.ṯṯ.dd.šʻrm. | [---.a]lp.arbʻ.mat.tyt. | [---.kd.]nbt.k[d. 142[12].13
| b[yrḫ.---]. | [---.]prš. | [-----]. | l.mšḫ[.---]. | ʻšr.d[d.---]. | ṯṯm.dd.dd[.---]. | l.mdrǵlm[.---]. | ṯlṯ.mat.ḫmšm.kb[d]. | ḫmš.k 2012.9
.l.mit.dd.ḥpr.bnšm. | b.gt.alḫb.ṯṯm.drʻ.w.ḫmšm.drt.w.ṯṯm.dd. | ḥpr.bnšm. | b.gt.knpy.mit.drʻ.ṯṯm.drt.w.šbʻm.dd.ar 1098.16
ṯlṯ.mat[.---.]kbd. | ṯṯ.ddm.k[--.b]rqd. | mit.ṯšʻm.[kb]d.ddm. | b.gt.bir. 2168.2
ddm.šʻrm.l.ḫtn. | dd.šʻrm.l.ḥmr.ḥṭb. | dd.ḥṭm.l.ḫdǵb. | ṯṯ.ddm.l.gzzm. | kd yn.l.ḫtn.w.kd.ḥmṣ.w.[lt]ḥ.ʻšdm. | kd yn.l. 1099.26
ʻšrm ddm kbd[.-] l alpm mrim. | ṯṯ ddm l ṣin mrat. | ʻšr ddm.l šmʻrgm. | ʻšr ddm.l bt. | ʻšrm.dd 1100.2
.ḫšwn.ṯṯ.mat.nṣ. | [---].ḫmšm.ḥmr.škm. | [---.ṯṯ.dd.]gdl.ṯṯ.dd.šʻrm. | [---.a]lp.arbʻ.mat.tyt. | [---.kd.]nbt.k[d.]šmn.mr. | 142[12].13
at.nṣ.ṯlṯm.ʻṣr. | [---].ḫmš[m.ḥm]r.škm. | [---.ṯṯ.dd.]gdl.ṯṯ.dd.šʻrm. | [---.hn.w.al]p.kd.nbt.kd.šmn.mr. | [---].kmn.lṯḥ.s 142[12].7
[---.]ṯṯ.dd.gdl.ṯṯ.dd.šʻrm. | [---.-]hn.w.alp.kd.nbt.kd.šmn.mr. | [---.]arbʻ.mat 142[12].1
w.ṯšʻm.drt. | [w].ṯmnym.l.mit.dd.ḥpr.bnšm. | b.gt.alḫb.ṯṯm.drʻ.w.ḫmšm.drt.w.ṯṯm.dd. | ḥpr.bnšm. | b.gt.knpy.mit.dr 1098.16
w.ḫmšm.drt.w.ṯṯm.dd. | ḥpr.bnšm. | b.gt.knpy.mit.drʻ.ṯṯm.drt.w.šbʻm.dd.arbʻ. | kbd.ḥpr.bnšm. | b.gt.ṯrmn.arbʻm.dr 1098.18
ʻmm. | ytn.l.ʻbdyrḫ. | w.mlk.z[--.--]n.ššwm. | nʻmm.[--].ṯṯm.w.at. | nǵṯ.w.ytn.hm.l k. | w.lḥt.alpm.ḫrṯm. | k.rgmt.l y.b 2064.19
. | b.ḫmšt.ʻšrt.ksp. | ḫmš.mat.šmt. | b.ʻšrt.ksp. | ʻšr.ṣin.b.ṯṯt.w.kmsk. | arbʻ[.k]dwṭm.w.ṯṯ.ṯprtm. | b.ʻšr[m.]ksp. | ḫmš.k 2100.9
aḫd.kbd. | arbʻm.b ḫzr. | lqḥ šʻrt. | ṯṯ ʻšr h.lqḥ. | ḫlpnt. | ṯṯ.ḥrṯm. | lqḥ.šʻrt. | ʻšr.ḥrš. | bhtm.lqḥ. | šʻrt. | arbʻ. | ḥrš qṭn. | lq 2052.6
b[--.]l[-.]mat[.-]y. | ḫmšm[.--]i. | ṯlṯ m[at] ḫswn. | ṯlṯ ṯ[-].ṯṯ ḥ[--]. 140[98].10
t.tbʻln.b.pḫn. | ṯṯtm.ḫzr.w.ʻšt.ʻšr.ḥrš. | dt.tbʻln.b.ugrt. | ṯṯtm.ḫzr. | dt.tbʻln. | b.gt.ḥršm. | ṯn.ḥršm. | [-]nbkm. | ṯn.ḥršm. 1024.3.9
. | rb qrt.aḫd. | ṯmn.ḫzr. | w.arbʻ.ḥršm. | dt.tbʻln.b.pḫn. | ṯṯtm.ḫzr.w.ʻšt.ʻšr.ḥrš. | dt.tbʻln.b.ugrt. | ṯṯtm.ḫzr. | dt.tbʻln. | b. 1024.3.7
ḫlb ʻprm.ṯṯ. | ḫlb krd.ṯn ʻšr. | qmy.arbʻ.ʻšr. | ṣʻq.arbʻ ʻšr. | ṣʻ.ṯmn. | šḫq.ʻšr 67[110].1
yn.d.l.ṭb.b.gt.ḥdṯt. | ṯšʻm.yn.d.l.ṭb.b.zbl. | ʻšrm.yn.ṭb.w.ṯṯm.ḫmš.k[b]d. | yn.d.l.ṭb.b.gt.šǵy. | arbʻm.kdm.kbd.yn.ṭb. | w 1084.14
ulm ṯn un ḫsn. | gdy lqḥ ṣtqn gt bn ndr. | um r[-] gtn ṯṯ ḫsn l ytn. | l rḥt lqḥ ṣtqn. | bt qbṣ urt ilštmʻ dbḥ ṣtqn l. | ršp 1154.5
qb. | b.gwl.ṯmn.ḫrmṯt.[nit]. | krk.mʻṣd.mqb. | [b] gt.iptl.ṯṯ.ḫrmṯ[t.nit]. | [k]rk.mʻṣd.mqb. | [b.g]t.bir.ʻš[r.---]. | [---].krk. 2048.13
[---].ṯlṯ. | [---].ṯmn. | [---].ṯlṯ. | [---].aḫd. | u[--].ṯn. | hz[p].ṯṯ. | ḫrṣbʻ.aḫd. | ypr.arb. | m[-]qb.ʻšr. | ṯnʻy.ṯlṯ. | ḫlb ʻprm.ṯn. | t 70[112].7
.ṯlṯ.kbʻ ym. | tikl[.i]št.b bht m. | nbla[t.]b hkl m. | ḫmš.ṯ[d]ṯ.ym.tikl. | išt.[b]bht m.nblat. | b[qrb.hk]l m.mk. | b šb[ʻ. 4[51].6.29
zr.i]lm.dnil.uzr. | [ilm.y]lḥm.uzr.yšqy bn. | [qdš.ḫ]mš.ṯdṯ.ym.uzr. | [ilm].dnil.uzr.ilm.ylḥm. | [uzr.]yšqy.bn qdš.yd.ṣ 17[2AQHT].1.12
b ṯṯ ym ḥdṯ. | ḫyr.ʻrbt. | špš ṯǵr h. | ršp. | w ʻbdm tbqrn. | skn. 1162.1
nk.šibt.b bqr. | mmlat.dm.ym.w ṯn. | ṯlṯ.rbʻ.ym.ymš. | ṯdṯ.ym.ḥẓ k.al.ṯšʻl. | qrt h.abn.yd k. | mšdpt.w hn.špšm. | b šb 14[KRT].3.116
nt.ṯlṯ[.r]bʻ ym.yšl | ḥm kṯrt.w yššq. | bnt hll.snnt.ḫmš. | ṯdṯ.ym.yšlḥm.k[ṯ]rt. | w y[ššq].bnt.hll.snnt. | mk.b šb[ʻ.]ymm 17[2AQHT].2.37
rṯ.il. | hn.ym.w ṯn.tlḥmn.rpum. | ṯštyn.ṯlṯ.rbʻ.ym.ḫmš. | ṯdṯ.ym.tlḥmn.rpum. | ṯštyn.bt.ikl.b prʻ. | yṣq.b irt.lbnn.mk.b 22.2[124].23
bt.w b | mqr.mmlat. | d[m].ym.w ṯn. | ṯlṯ.rbʻ.ym. | ḫmš.ṯdṯ.ym. | mk.špšm.b šbʻ. | w l.yšn.pbl. | mlk.l [qr.]ṯiqt. | ibr h[.l 14[KRT].5.220
n.šd. | km.ḥsn.pat.mdbr. | lk.ym.w ṯn.ṯlṯ.rbʻ ym. | ḫmš.ṯdṯ.ym.mk.špšm. | b šbʻ.w tmǵy.l udm. | rbm.w l.udm.ṯrrt. | 14[KRT].3.107

.ʿšr.kbd.yn.ṭb. | w.ṯṯm.arbʿ.kbd.yn.d.l.ṭb. | b.gt.mʿrby. | ṯṯm.yn.ṭb.w.ẖmš.l.ʿšrm. | yn.d.l.ṭb.b.ulm. | mit.yn.ṭb.w.ṯṯm.ṯṯ 1084.9
gt.ʿdb. | akl.l qryt. | ḥṭt.l bt.ẖbr. | yip.lḥm.d ẖmš. | mǵd.ṯdṯ.yrẖm. | ʿdn.ngb.w yṣi. | ṣbu.ṣbi.ngb. | w yṣi.ʿdn.mʿ. | ṣbu k. 14[KRT].2.84
gt.ʿdb.akl.l qryt. | ḥṭt.l bt.ẖbr. | yip.lḥm.d ẖmš. | [mǵ]d.ṯdṯ.yr[ẖm]. | ʿdn.ngb.w [yṣi.ṣbu]. | ṣbi.ng[b.w yṣi.ʿdn]. | mʿ[.ṣ] 14[KRT].4.175
.il.ṣm[d]. | bn abbly. | yṯʿd.ṣm[d]. | bn.liy. | ʿšrm.ṣ[md]. | ṯṯ kbd.b ẖ[--]. | w.arbʿ.ḥ[mrm]. | b m[ʿ]rby. | ṯmn.ṣmd.[---]. | b 2113.24
pr.bnšm. | b.gt.ṯrmn.arbʿm.drʿ.w.ʿšrm.drt. | w.ṯlṯm.dd.ṯṯ.kbd.ḥpr.bnšm. | b.gt.ḥdṯt.arbʿm.drʿ.w.ṯlṯm.drt. | [w].šbʿm. 1098.21
d.ḥpr.bnšm. | b.yʿny.arbʿm.drʿ.w.ʿšrm.drt. | w.ṯlṯm.dd.ṯṯ.kbd.ḥpr.bnšm. | b.ʿnmky.ʿšrm.drʿ[.---.d]rt. | w.ṯn.ʿšr h.dd.[1098.27
nym.drt. | tgmr.akl.b.gt[.b]ʿln. | ṯlṯ.mat.ṯṯm.kbd. | ṯṯm.ṯṯ.kbd.ḥpr.ʿbdm. | šbʿm.drt.arbʿm.drt. | l.a[--.---]. | tgm[r.ak]l. 2013.7
n.ṭb.w.ẖmš.l.ʿšrm. | yn.d.l.ṭb.b.ulm. | mit.yn.ṭb.w.ṯṯm.ṯṯ.kbd. | yn.d.l.ṭb.b.gt.ḥdṯt. | tšʿm.yn.d.l.ṭb.b.zbl. | ʿšrm.yn.ṭb. 1084.11
mšq.mlkt. | mitm.ṯṯm. | kbd.ks[p]. | ksp. | ṯmnym. | ẖrṣ. 1157.2
sp.d.nkly.b.šd. | mit.ẖmšt.kbd. | [l.]gmn.bn.usyy. | mit.ṯṯm.kbd. | l.bn.yšmʿ. | mit.arbʿm.kbd. | l.liy.bn.ʿmyn. | mit.ẖm 1143.9
. | ʿšr[.m]krm. | tšʿ.hbṭnm. | ʿšr.mrum. | šbʿ.ẖsnm. | tšʿm.ṯṯ.kbd.mḏrǵlm. | ʿšrm.aḥd.kbd.ẖsnm. | ubnyn. | ṯṯm[.l.]mit.ṯlṯ 1028.9
y.ẖmšm. | ṣṣ yrpi m[it.---]. | ṣṣ bn.š[m]mn ʿ[šr.---]. | alp.ṯṯm. | kbd.mlḥt. 2097.20
ṯṯ.mat.ṯṯm.kbd šmn. | l.abrm.alṯyy. | [m]it.ṯlṯm.kbd.šmn. | [l.]abrm. 2095.1
. | mitm.drt.ṯmnym.drt. | tgmr.akl.b.gt[.b]ʿln. | ṯlṯ.mat.ṯṯm.kbd. | ṯṯm.ṯṯ.kbd.ḥpr.ʿbdm. | šbʿm.drt.arbʿm.drt. | l.a[--.-- 2013.6
h.prs. | bt.mrkbt.w l šant.ṯṯ. | l bt.ʿšrm. | bt alẖnm.ṯlṯm ṯṯ kbd. 2105.4
ʿglt.ṯlṯm. | ṣṣ.bn.ʿbd.ʿšrm. | ṣṣ.bn.mṣẖ[n].ʿšrm. | šbʿ.mat.ṯṯm kbd. 2096.20
ʿm. | dd.akl. | ṯṯ.ʿšr h.yn. | kd.šmn.l.nr.ilm. | kdm.dǵm. | ṯṯ.kdm.ztm. 1126.8
w.aḥd. | ʿl atlg. | w l.ʿṣm. | tspr. | nrn.al.tud | ad.at.l hm. | ṯṯm.ksp. 1010.21
[.---]. | mgdly.ǵlpṯr.ṯn.krmm.w.ṯlṯ.ub[dym.---]. | qmnz.ṯṯ.krm.yknʿm.ṯmn.krm[.---]. | krm.nʿmn.b.ẖly.ull.krm.aẖ[d.- 1081.11
.krm.aẖ[d.--]r.krm.[---]. | ary.ʿšr.arbʿ.kbd.[---]. | [--]yy.ṯṯ.krmm.šl[-.---]. | [---.]ʿšrm.krm.[---]. | [ṯ]lrby.ʿšr.ṯn.kb[d.---]. 1081.19
-]. | [---.]ʿšrm.krm.[---]. | [ṯ]lrby.ʿšr.ṯn.kb[d.---]. | ẖmrm.ṯṯ.krm[m.---]. | krm.ǵlkz.b.p[--.---]. | krm.ilyy.b.m[--.---]. | kd. 1081.22
l ẖmš.mrkbt.ẖmš.ʿšr h.prs. | bt.mrkbt.w l šant.ṯṯ. | l bt.ʿšrm. | bt alẖnm.ṯlṯm ṯṯ kbd. 2105.2
.drʿ.w.arbʿm.drt.mit.dd. | [---].ḥpr.bn.šm. | [b.---.]knm.ṯṯm.l.mit.drʿ.w.mit.drt. | w[.---.]ʿm.l.mit.dd.ṯn.kbd.ḥpr.bnš 1098.7
. | tšʿm.ṯṯ.kbd.mḏrǵlm. | ʿšrm.aḥd.kbd.ẖsnm. | ubnyn. | ṯṯm[.l.]mit.ṯlṯ. | kbd[.tg]mr.bnš. | l.b.bt.mlk. 1028.12
ʿ.ẖsnm. | tšʿm.mḏrǵlm. | arbʿ.l ʿšrm.ẖsnm. | ʿšr.hbṭnm. | ṯṯm.l.mit.ṯn.kbd. | tgmr. 1030.10
šbʿ.yn.l [---]. | ṯlṯ.l ẖr[š.---]. | ṯṯ[.l.]mšṯt[.---]. | ṯlṯ.l.mḏr[ǵlm]. | kd[.--].lm[d.---]. | kd[.l.]ẖzr[1091.3
nn.šr.ugrt.ḏkr.yṣr. | tǵǵln.ẖmš.ddm. | [---].ẖmš.ddm. | ṯṯ.l.ʿšrm.bn[š.mlk.---].ẖzr.lqḥ.ẖp[r]. | ʿšt.ʿšr h.bn[.---.--]ẖ.zr. | 2011.40
ʿmyd ẖmšm. | ṣṣ ṯmn.ẖmšm. | [ṣṣ] ʿmṯdl ṯlṯm. | ṣṣ ʿmlbi ṯṯ l ʿšrm. | ṣṣ bn adty ẖmšm. | ṣṣ amtrn arbʿm. | ṣṣ iytlm mit ṯl 2097.6
r. | km.y[--.]ilm.b ṣpn. | ʿdr.l[ʿr].ʿrm. | ṭb.l pd[r.]pdrm. | ṯṯ.l ṯṯm.aḥd.ʿr. | šbʿm.šbʿ.pdr. | ṯmnym.bʿl.[----]. | tšʿm.bʿl.mr[- 4[51].7.9
| [---.]iqnu.[---.]lbš.ṯrmnm. | [---.iqn]i.lbš.al[l.---]. | [---].ṯṯ.lbš[.---]. | [---.]kbd.ṯṯ.i[qnu.---]. | [---.]ǵprt.ʿš[r.---]. | [---.p]ṯṯ 1106.22
[-]b[-.---.--]| r ṯṯm lḥm. | l[.-]ry ṯlṯ spm w ʿšr lḥm. | [--.]w nṣp w ṯlṯ spm w ʿš 134[-].2
.n.rn. | [---].ẖpn. | dqn.šʿrt. | [lm]d.yrṯ. | [-.]ynẖm.ẖpn. | ṯṯ.lmd.bʿln. | l.qḥ.ẖpnt. | ṯṯ[.-]l.md.ʿṯtr[t]. | l.qḥ.ẖpnt. 1117.17
t]. | [-----]. | ilmlk ṯṯ mat. | ʿbdilm.ṯṯ mat. | šmmn.bn.ʿdš.ṯṯ mat. | ušknym. | ypʿ.alpm. | aẖ[m]lk.bn.nskn.alpm. | krw.šl 1060.1.12
| ẖmš.kkrm.alp kb[d]. | ṯlṯ.l.nskm.birtym. | b d.urtn.w.ṯṯ.mat.brr. | b.ṯmnym.ksp.ṯlṯt.kbd. | ẖmš.alp.ṯlṯ.l.ẖlby. | b d.tl 2101.4
spr.argmn.nskm. | rqdym. | šṭšm.ṯṯ mat. | ṣprn.ṯṯ mat. | ḏkry.ṯṯ mat. | [p]lsy.ṯṯ mat. | ʿdn.ẖmš [m]at. | [--]kbʿl 1060.1.4
ʿšrm.kkr.kkrm. | alp.ṯṯ.mat.kbd. 2111.2
ṯṯ.mat.ksp. | ḥṭbn.ybnn. | arbʿm.l.mit.šmn. | arbʿm.l.mit.tišr. | 1127.1
qhr. | [---.ltḥ.]sbbyn.ltḥ.ššmn.ltḥ.šḥlt. | [---.ltḥ.]ṣmqm.[ṯ]t.mat.nṣ.ṯlṯm.ʿṣr. | [---].ẖmš[m.ḥm]r.škm. | [---.ṯṯ.dd.]gdl.ṯṯ. 142[12].5
r. | [---].kmn.ltḥ.sbbyn. | [---.-]ʿt.ltḥ.ššmn. | [---].ẖšwn.ṯṯ.mat.nṣ. | [---].ẖmšm.ḥmr.škm. | [---.ṯṯ.dd.]gdl.ṯṯ.dd.šʿrm. | [142[12].11
ṯ mat. | ʿdn.ẖmš [m]at. | [--]kbʿl ṯṯ [mat]. | [-----]. | ilmlk ṯṯ mat. | ʿbdilm.ṯṯ mat. | šmmn.bn.ʿdš.ṯṯ mat. | ušknym. | ypʿ.a 1060.1.10
qdym. | šṭšm.ṯṯ mat. | ṣprn.ṯṯ mat. | ḏkry.ṯṯ mat. | [p]lsy.ṯṯ mat. | ʿdn.ẖmš [m]at. | [--]kbʿl ṯṯ [mat]. | [-----]. | ilmlk ṯṯ ma 1060.1.6
rgmn.nskm. | rqdym. | šṭšm.ṯṯ mat. | ṣprn.ṯṯ mat. | ḏkry.ṯṯ mat. | [p]lsy.ṯṯ mat. | ʿdn.ẖmš [m]at. | [--]kbʿl ṯṯ [mat]. | [---- 1060.1.5
spr.argmn.nskm. | rqdym. | šṭšm.ṯṯ mat. | ṣprn.ṯṯ mat. | ḏkry.ṯṯ mat. | [p]lsy.ṯṯ mat. | ʿdn.ẖmš [1060.1.3
[m]at. | [--]kbʿl ṯṯ [mat]. | [-----]. | ilmlk ṯṯ mat. | ʿbdilm.ṯṯ mat. | šmmn.bn.ʿdš.ṯṯ mat. | ušknym. | ypʿ.alpm. | aẖ[m]lk.b 1060.1.11
mnḥ.b d.ybnn. | arbʿ.mat. | l.alp.šmn. | nḥ.ṯṯ.mat. | šm[n].rqḥ. | kkrm.brḏl. | mit.tišrm. | ṯlṯm.almg. | ẖmš 141[120].4
ṯṯ.mat.ṯṯm.kbd šmn. | l.abrm.alṯyy. | [m]it.ṯlṯm.kbd.šmn. | [l.] 2095.1
. | ḏkry.ṯṯ mat. | [p]lsy.ṯṯ mat. | ʿdn.ẖmš [m]at. | [--]kbʿl ṯṯ [mat]. | [-----]. | ilmlk ṯṯ mat. | ʿbdilm.ṯṯ mat. | šmmn.bn.ʿdš. 1060.1.8
| ilbʿl ẖmš m[at]. | ʿdn.ẖmš.mat. | bn.[-]d.alp. | bn.[-]pn.ṯṯ mat. 1060.2.12
b.atlg.ṯlṯ.ẖrmṯt.ṯṯm. | mẖrhn.nit.mit.krk.mit. | mʿṣd.ẖmšm.mqb.[ʿ]šrm. | b.ul 2048.1
.ṯmn ʿšr h. | mlk.arbʿ. | ǵbl.ẖmš. | atlg.ẖmš ʿšr[h]. | ulm ṯ[ṯ]. | mʿrby.ẖmš. | ṭbq.arbʿ. | tkm[.---]. | uẖnp[.---]. | ušk[n.---]. 68[65].1.9
]gm.arbʿ[.---]. | šrš.šbʿ.mṣb. | rqd.ṯlṯ.mṣb.w.[---]. | uẖnp.ṯṯ.mṣb. | tgmr.[y]n.mṣb š[bʿ]. | w ḥs[p] ṯn.k[dm]. 2004.34
t. | yd.llẖ hm. | w.ṯlṯ.l.ʿšrm. | ẖpnt.ššwm.ṯn. | pddm.w.d.ṯṯ. | [mr]kbt.w.ẖrṣ. 2049.8
šʿrt. | ʿšr.ẖrš. | bhtm.lqḥ. | šʿrt. | arbʿ. | ẖrš qṭn. | lqḥ šʿrt. | ṯṯ nsk.ḥdm. | lqḥ.šʿrt. 2052.14
lḥ[m]. | l[.-]dt ẖnd[r]t arʿ s[p]m w ʿš[r]. | [---.]ẖndrtm ṯṯ spm [w] ṯlṯm l[ḥm]. | [---.]arʿ spm w [---]. | [---]š[.---.--]b[.-- 134[-].6
| [--]l.ṯṯm sp[m.---]. | [p]drn.ẖm[š.---]. | l bn ẖdnr[.---]. | ṯṯm sp.km[-.---]. | ʿšrm.sp[.---]. | ʿšr sp.m[ry-.---]. | ʿšr sp.m[ry- 139[310].6
.]w yky. | ṯlṯm sp.l bnš tpnr. | arbʿ.spm.l.lbnš prwsdy. | ṯṯ spm.l bnš klnmw. | l yarš ẖswn. | ẖmš ʿšr.sp. | l bnš tpnr d 137.2[93].8
l yarš ẖswn. | ẖmš ʿšr.sp. | l bnš tpnr d yaẖd l g ynm. | ṯṯ spm l tgyn. | arbʿ spm l ll[-]. | ṯn spm.l slyy. | ṯlṯ spm l dlšpš 137.2[93].12
.---]. | ʿšrm.sp[.---]. | ʿšr sp.m[ry-.---]. | ʿšr sp.m[ry-.---]. | ṯṯ sp.mry[-.---]. | ʿšr sp.m[ry-.---]. | tšʿm s[p.---]. | tšʿ[m.sp.---]. 139[310].10
[---.]mr[y-.---]. | [--]sp.mr[y-.---]. | [--]l.ṯṯm sp[m.---]. | [p]drn.ẖm[š.---]. | l bn ẖdnr[.---]. | ṯṯm sp.km[- 139[310].3
ʿmn.bn.ply.ẖmšt.l.ʿšrm. | b.gdn.bn.uss.ʿšrm. | b.ʿdn.bn.ṯṯ.ʿšrt. | b.bn.qrdmn.ṯlṯm. | b.bṣmn[.bn].ẖrtn.ʿ[--]. | b.t[--.---] h 2054.1.19
a]gmy. | ṯṯ.bn[šm.---]. | ʿšr.b[nšm.---]. | arbʿ[.bnšm.---]. | ṯṯ.ʿšr.bnš[m.---]. | ʿšr[.bn]šm[.---]. | ṯn.bnšm.b.š[--]. | arbʿ.bnš 2076.6
[mi]tm.ẖmšm.ẖmš.k[bd]. | [dd].kšmm.tšʿ[.---]. | [š]ʿrm.ṯṯ.ʿ[šr]. | [dd].ḥtm.w.ẖ[mšm]. | [ṯ]lṯ kbd.yn.b [gt.---]. | mit.[---] 2092.8
rhn.nit.mit.krk.mit. | mʿṣd.ẖmšm.mqb.[ʿ]šrm. | b.ulm.ṯṯ.ʿšr h.ẖrmṯt. | ṯṯ.nitm.ṯn.mʿṣdm.ṯn.mqbm. | krk.aḥt. | b.sǵy. 2048.4

ṯlṯm.ktn. | ḫmšm.izml. | ḫmš.kbd.arbʻm. | dd.akl. | ṯṯ.ʻšr h.yn. | kd.šmn.l.nr.ilm. | kdm.dǵm. | ṯṯ.kdm.ztm. 1126.5
aḥd.kbd. | arbʻm.b ḫzr. | lqḥ šʻrt. | ṯṯ ʻšr h.lqḥ. | ḫlpnt. | ṯṯ.ḥrṯm. | lqḥ.šʻrt. | ʻšr.ḥrš. | bhtm.lqḥ. | šʻr 2052.4
ṯnnm.ṯṯ. | ʻšr.ḫsnm. | nʻr.mrynm. | ḫmš. | ṯrtnm.ḫmš. | mrum.ʻšr. | šbʻ. 1031.1
n h. | b [ar]bʻm.ksp. | b d[.ʻb]dym.ṯlṯ.kkr šʻrt. | iqn[i]m.ṯṯṯ.ʻšrt.ksp h. | ḫmšt.ḫrṣ.bt.il. | b.ḫmšt.ʻšrt.ksp. | ḫmš.mat.šmt 2100.4
dm. | [w.ʻ]šr.bn[š]m.y[d].š[--]. | [-]lm.b d.r[-]m.l[-]m. | ṯṯ.ʻšr.ṣ[mdm]. | w.tšʻ.ʻ[šr.--]m.ḥr[š]. | [---].ḥr[š.---]. | [---.ṯ]lṯ.[-- 2038.10
ʻbdrṯ[b.---]. | b ṯṯ ʻṯr ṯmn.r[qḥ.---]. | p bn btb[-.---]. | b ḫmṯ ʻṯr k[--.---]. | b ḫm 207[57].2
r. | bqʻt ṯṯ. | irab ṯn.ʻšr. | ḥbš.ṯmn. | amdy.arbʻ.ʻšr. | [-]nʻy.ṯṯ.ʻšr. 67[110].12
p[n.---]. | ap[n.---]. | ap[n.---]. | ap[n.---]. | tgmr[.---]ṯm. | ṯṯ.ʻ[--.---]. 152[-].8
l h. | mṯlṯt.kṯrm.tmt. | mrbʻt.zblnm. | mḫmšt.yitsp. | ršp.nṯdṯt.ǵlm. | ym.mšbʻt hn.b šlḥ. | ttpl.yʻn.ḥtk h. | krt yʻn.ḥtk h. 14[KRT].1.19
ḥ[--.---]. | ṯ[--] ḫpnt. | [---] kdwṯm.[---]. | ḫmš.pld šʻrt. | ṯṯ pld pṯt. | arbʻ ḫpnt pṯt. | ḫmš ḫpnt.šʻrt. | ṯlṯ.ʻšr kdwṯm. 1113.8
[-]k[-.---]. | ar[--.---]. | yrt.[---]. | ṯṯ.prš[.---]. | bn.ʻmyn[.---]. 2152.6
ḥd.l.bt.ʻbdm. | [ṯ]n.ptḥ msb.bt.tu. | w.ptḥ[.aḥ]d.mmt. | ṯṯ.pt[ḥ.---]. | ṯn.pt[ḥ.---]. | w.pt[ḥ.--]r.ṯǵr. | ṯmn.ḥlnm. | ṯt.ṯḫ[-- 1151.12
[.---]. | [ṯl]ṯ.l ʻṯrt[.---]. | [--.]l ilt.š l ʻṯ[rt.---]. | [ʻ]ṣr.l pdr ṯṯ.ṣ[in.---]. | tšnpn.ʻlm.km[m.---]. | w.l ll.ʻṣrm.w [---]. | kmm.w 38[23].5
-]. | ḫtn h.šbʻl[.---]. | ṯlḫny.yd[.---]. | yd.ṯlṯ.kl[t h.---]. | w.ṯṯm.ṣi[n.---]. | ṯn[--]. | agyn.[---]. | [w].ṯn.[---]. 81[329].19
m. | w.arbʻ.ʻšr.bnš. | yd.nǵr.mdrʻ.yd.š[--]m. | [b.]gt.iptl.ṯṯ.ṣmdm. | [w.ʻ]šr.bn[š]m.y[d].š[--]. | [-]lm.b d.r[-]m.l[-]m. | ṯṯ. 2038.7
rbʻm.ḫmš.kbd. | yn.d.l.ṭb.gt.ṭbq. | mit.ʻšr.kbd.yn.ṭb. | w.ṯṯm.arbʻ.kbd.yn.d.l.ṭb. | b.gt.mʻrby. | ṯṯm.yn.ṭb.w.ḫmš.l.ʻšrm. 1084.7
šurtm l bn[š.---]. | ṯlṯm šurt l b[nš.---]. | arbʻ šurt [---]. | ṯṯ šurt l bnš [---]. | ḫmš kbd arbʻ[.---]. | ṯṯ šurt l tg[-.---]. | arbʻ 137.1[92].11
urt l bn[š.---]. | arbʻ šurt l q[--.---]. | ṯlṯ šurt l bnš [---]. | ṯṯ šurt.l bnš[.---]. | ṯn šurtm l bn[š.---]. | ṯlṯm šurt l b[nš.---]. | 137.1[92].7
| arbʻ šurt [---]. | ṯṯ šurt l bnš [---]. | ḫmš kbd arbʻ[.---]. | ṯṯ šurt l tg[-.---]. | arbʻ šurt [---]. | [ḫm]šm šurt [---]. | ṯlṯ šurt l 137.1[92].13
r]m.ṯn.kbd.ḥtm. | [-]m[-.-]ʻ[-.-]ag šʻrm. | [---.--]mi. | [--.]ṯṯ[m] šbʻ.k[bd]. | [---]m.b.mril. 2091.8
m.[my.b ilm]. | ydy.mrṣ.g[ršm.zbln]. | in.b ilm.ʻn[y h.]ytdṯ. | yšbʻ.rgm.[my.]b ilm. | ydy.mrṣ.gršm zbln. | in.b ilm.ʻny 16[126].5.19
n.ṯmnt.ʻšrt ʻšrt.šlm. | ʻbdyrḫ.šbʻt.ʻšrt ʻšrt.šlm. | yky.ʻšrt.ṯṯṯ šlm.ʻšrt. | bn.ḥgby.ṯmnt.l ʻšrm.ʻšrt.ḫmš.kbd. | bn.ilṣdq.šbʻt 1131.7
d.ʻl.ynḫm. | tgrm.šmn.d.bn.kwy. | ʻl.šlmym.ṯmn.kbd. | ṯṯm.šmn. 1082.2.10
.ksp. | ḥtbn.ybnn. | arbʻm.l.mit.šmn. | arbʻm.l.mit.tišr. | ṯṯ.ṯṯ.b [ṯ]ql.ṯlṯt.l.ʻšrm.ksp hm. | sstm.b.šbʻm. | ṯlṯ.mat.trm.b.ʻš 1127.5
rt.ṯmnym.drt. | tgmr.akl.b.gt[.b]ʻln. | ṯlṯ.mat.ṯṯm.kbd. | ṯṯm.ṯṯ.kbd.ḥpr.ʻbdm. | šbʻm.drt.arbʻm.drt. | l.a[--.---]. | tgm[r. 2013.7
ṯm.yn.ṭb.w.ḫmš.l.ʻšrm. | yn.d.l.ṭb.b.ulm. | mit.yn.ṭb.w.ṯṯm.ṯṯ.kbd. | yn.d.l.ṭb.b.gt.ḥdṯt. | tšʻm.yn.d.l.ṭb.b.zbl. | ʻšrm.y 1084.11
ṯṯm.ṯlṯ.kb[d]. | arbʻm.ṯp[rt]. | ksp h. | ṯmn.dd[.--]. | ṯlṯ.dd.p[--]. 2120.1
[---].yryt. | [---.a]drt. | [--.ṯṯ]m.ṯmn.k[bd]. | [---.yr]yt.dq[-]. | [--.ṯ]lṯm.l.mi[t]. | [---.]arbʻ. 2170.3
rm.pam[t.---]. | š dd šmn[.gdlt.w.---]. | brr.r[gm.yṯṯb.b ṯdṯ.ṯn]. | l šmn.ʻ[ly h.gdlt.rgm.yṯṯb]. | brr.b šbʻ[.ṣbu.špš.w ḥl] APP.II[173].49
lbš.aḥd. | b.ʻšrt. | w.ṯn.b.ḫmšt. | ṯprt.b.ṯlṯt. | mṯyn.b.ṯṯt. | ṯn.lbšm.b.ʻšrt. | pld.b.arbʻt. | lbš.ṯn.b.ṯnt.ʻšrt. 1108.5
šrm.pamt.[---]. | š.dd.šmn.gdlt.w.[---.brr]. | rgm.yṯṯb.b.ṯdṯ.ṯn[.--.šmn]. | ʻly h.gdlt.rgm.yṯ[ṯb.brr]. | b.[šb]ʻ.ṣbu.[š]pš.w 35[3].45
m]. | ṯn mq[pm]. | ulṯ.ṯl[ṯ]. | krk.kly[.--]. | ḫmš.mr[kbt]. | ṯṯ [-]az[-]. | ʻšṯ[--.---]. | irg[mn.---]. | krk[.---]. 2056.10
rt. | [lm]d.yrṯ. | [-.]ynḫm.ḫpn. | ṯṯ.lmd.b ʻln. | l.qḥ.ḫpnt. | ṯṯ[.-]l.md.ʻṯr[t]. | l.qḥ.ḫpnt. 1117.19
n.[---]m.ṣ[-]n. | [b].bn.ay[--.---].l.ʻšrm. | [-]gp[.---.]ʻrny.ṯṯm. | [---.]dyn.ḫmšt.ʻšrt. | [---.-]til.ḫmšt.l ʻšrm. | [--.-]n.w.aḫṯ 2054.2.18
--.]ḫgbn.kbs.ks[p]. | [---].dmrd.bn.ḥrmn. | [---.-]ǵn.ksp.ṯṯṯ. | [---.]ygry.ṯlṯm.ksp.b[--]. 2153.11
[ṯ]n.prm.b ʻšrm. | arbʻ.prm.b.ʻš[r]m. | arbʻ.b.arbʻm. | ṯṯm.[---.p]rm. | [-]l.b[--.---]. | [---].kbd. | [---].kb[d.---]. | [t]šʻm. 1138.4
[---.]gtn ṯṯ. | [---.]ṯḥr l ytn ḥs[n]. | ʻbd ulm ṯn un ḫsn. | gdy lqḥ ṣṭqn gt 1154.1
| ksp[.---]. | k[--.---]. | ar[bʻ.---]. | ṯmn[.---]. | [-]r[-.---]. | w ṯṯ.[---]. | ṯlṯm[.---]. | mil[-.---]. 148[96].12
ry[-.---]. | ʻšr sp.m[ry-.---]. | tšʻm s[p.---]. | tšʻ[m.sp.---]. | ṯṯ[.---]. 139[310].14

ṯdṯb

y. | bn.slgyn. | ʻzn.bn.mlk. | bn.alṯn. | bn.ṯmyr. | ẓbr. | bn.ṯdṯb. | bn.ʻrmn. | bn.alz. | bn.mṣrn. | bn.ʻdy. | bn.ršpy. | [---.]mn. 115[301].2.12

ṯdyy

ṯt[rt]. | kṯkt. | bn.ṯtn[--]. | [m]d.m[--]. | [b]n.annd[r]. | bn.ṯdyy. | bn.grbn. | [--.]ully. | [--]ṯiy. 1054.2.3

ṯh

k.bʻl y.bnš. | bnny.ʻmn. | mlakty.hnd. | ylak ʻm y. | w.tʻl.ṯh.hn. | [a]lpm.ššwm. | [---].w.ṭb. 1012.37
.hm.mlk.[b]ʻl y. | w.hn.ibm.šṣq l y. | p.l.ašt.aṯt y. | nʻr y.ṯh.l pn.ib. | hn.hm.yrgm.mlk. | bʻl y.tmǵyy.hn. | alpm.ššwm.h 1012.29
lk.bʻl y. | lm.škn.hnk. | l ʻbd h.alpm.š[šw]m. | rgmt.ʻly.ṯh.lm. | l.ytn.hm.mlk.[b]ʻl y. | w.hn.ibm.šṣq l y. | p.l.ašt.aṯt y. 1012.25

ṯwb

k. | [---.--]r.dr.dr. | [---.--]y k.w rḥd. | [---]y ilm.d mlk. | y[ṯ]b.aliyn.bʻl. | ytʻdd.rkb.ʻrpt. | [--].ydd.w yqlṣn. | yqm.w yw 4[51].3.10
m k. | hn ny.ʻm n. | šlm.ṯm ny. | ʻm k.mnm[.š]lm. | rgm.ṯṯ[b]. | any kn.dt. | likt.mṣrm. | hn dt.b.ṣr. | mtt.by. | gšm.adr. | 2059.9
.]drʻ hm. | [--.n]pš[.-]. | w [k]l hm.b d. | rb.tmtt.lqḥt. | w.ṯṯb.ank.l hm. | w.any k.ṯt. | by.ʻky.ʻryt. | w.aḫ y.mhk. | b lb h.a 2059.23
-]. | [---].mr[--.]ydm[.---]. | [---.]mṯbt.ilm.w.b.[---]. | [---.]ṯṯbn.ilm.w.[---]. | [---.]w.ksu.bʻlt.b[htm.---]. | [---.]il.bt.gdlt.[- 47[33].6
n.l ʻš] | rm.pam[t.---]. | š dd šmn[.gdlt.w.---]. | brr.r[gm.yṯṯb.b ṯdṯ.ṯn]. | l šmn.ʻ[ly h.gdlt.rgm.yṯṯb]. | brr.b šbʻ[.ṣbu.špš APP.II[173].49
. | ṯn.l.ʻšrm.pamt.[---]. | š.dd.šmn.gdlt.w.[---.brr]. | rgm.yṯṯb.b.ṯdṯ.ṯn[.--.šmn]. | ʻly h.gdlt.rgm.yṯ[ṯb.brr]. | b.[šb]ʻ.ṣbu.[35[3].45
nṯq.dmrn. | ʻn.bʻl.qdm.yd h. | k tǵd.arz.b ymn h. | bkm.yṯb.bʻl.l bht h. | u mlk.u bl mlk. | arṣ.drkt.yštkn. | dll.al.ilak.l 4[51].7.42
]dd.il ym. | [---.-]qlṣn.wpṯ m. | [---.]w yʻn.kṯr. | [w ḫss.]ṯṯb.bʻl.l hwt y. | [ḥš.]bht h.tbnn. | [ḥš.]trmm.hkl h. | y[tl]k.l lb 4[51].6.15
| ṣḥq.kṯr.w ḫss. | yšu.g h.w yṣḥ. | l rgmt.l k.l ali | yn.bʻl.ṯṯbn.bʻl. | l hwt y.yptḥ.ḥ | ln.b bht m.urbt. | b qrb.hk[l m.yp]t 4[51].7.24
w yʻn.k[ṯr.w ḫs]s. | ṯṯb.bʻl.l[hwt y]. | ṯn.rgm.k[ṯr.w]ḫss. | šmʻ.mʻ.l al[iy]n bʻl. | bl. 4[51].6.2
w.[---.brr]. | rgm.yṯṯb.b.ṯdṯ.ṯn[.--.šmn]. | ʻly h.gdlt.rgm.yṯ[ṯb.brr]. | b.[šb]ʻ.ṣbu.[š]pš.w.ḥly[t].ʻ[r]b[.š]p[š]. | w [ḥl.]mlk 35[3].46
.w.---]. | brr.r[gm.yṯṯb.b ṯdṯ.ṯn]. | l šmn.ʻ[ly h.gdlt.rgm.yṯṯb]. | brr.b šbʻ[.ṣbu.špš.w ḥl] | yt.ʻrb špš[.w ḥl.mlk.w.b y] | APP.II[173].50

šm.l bʿlt. | bhtm.ʿṣ[rm.l in]š ilm.w š. | dd ilš.š[.---.]mlk.yṯb br | r.w mḫ[--.---.]w q[--]. | ym.ʿlm.y[---.---]. | t.k[-]ml.[---] APP.II[173].7
š[.---]. | [-.]kbd.w.db[ḥ.---]. | [--].aṯrt.ʿṣr[m.l inš.ilm]. | [t]ṯb.mdbḥ.bʿl.g[dlt.---]. | dqt.l.ṣpn.w.dqt[.---]. | ṯn.l.ʿšrm.pam 35[3].41
---]. | bt.il.ṯq[l.---.kbd]. | w bdḥ.k[--.---]. | ʿṣrm.l i[nš.ilm.ṯb.md] | bḥ.bʿl.[gdlt.---.dqt]. | l ṣpn.w [dqt.---.ṯn.l ʿš] | rm.pam APP.II[173].44
ll.snnt. | [-]d[-]t.nʿm y.ʿrš.h[--]m. | ysmsmt.ʿrš.ḫlln.[-]. | yṯb.dnil.[l s]pr yrḫ h. | yrs.y[---.]y[--] h. | ṯlṯ.rb[ʿ.yrḫ.--]r[.--]. | 17[2AQHT].2.43
h. | l[q]ḥt. | [--]km.ʿm.mlk. | [b]ǵl hm.w.iblbl hm. | w.b.ṯb h.[---]. | spr ḥ[--.---]. | w.ʿm[.---]. | yqḥ[.---]. | w.n[--.---]. 2129.11
-]. | [--.n]pš.ttn[.---]. | [---.]ydʿt.k[---]. | [---].w hm. | [--]y.ṯb y.w [---]. | [---.]bnš.[---]. 61[-].5
b tk.ǵ]r y.il.ṣpn. | b q[dš.b ǵr.nḥ]lt y. | w t[ʿn].btlt.[ʿ]nt.ṯṯb. | [ybmt.]limm.[a]n.aqry. | [b arṣ].mlḥmt.[aš]t.b ʿpr m. | d 3[ʿNT].4.65
.št.ṯrm.w[---]. | ištir.b ddm.w nʿrs[.---]. | w tʿn.btlt.ʿnt.ṯb.ytp.w[---]. | l k.ašt k.km.nšr.b ḥb[š y]. | km.diy.b tʿrt y.aq 18[3AQHT].4.16
n ny.ʿm n.š[l]m. | ṯm ny.ʿ[m.]bn y. | mnm.[šl]m[.r]gm[.ṯṯb]. | ky.lik.bn y. | lḥt.akl.ʿm y. | mid y w ǵbn y. | w.bn y.hn k 2061.8
. | iwrkl.mit. | ksp.b y[d]. | birtym. | [un]ṯ inn. | l [h]m ʿd ṯṯtbn. | ksp.iwrkl. | w ṯb.l unṯ hm. 1006.17
. | w l h.yʿl m. | w h[t] aḫ y. | bn y.yšal. | ṯryl.w rgm[.-]. | ṯṯb.l aḫ k. | l adn k. 138.18
. | l mlk.šm y. | w l h[-] yʿl m. | bn y.yšal. | ṯryl.w rgm. | ṯṯb.l aḫ k. | l adn k. 138.18
. | [---.al]iyn bʿl. | [---].rkb.ʿrpt. | [---.]ǵš.l limm. | [---.]l yṯb.l arṣ. | [---].mtm. | [---.--]d mhr.ur. | [---.]yḥnnn. | [---.--]t.y 10[76].1.9
tn. | [---.btlt.]ʿnt. | [---.ybmt.]limm. | [---.---]l.limm. | [---.yṯ]b.l arṣ. | [---.--]l.šir. | [---.-]tm. | [---.]yd y. | [----]y. | [---.-]lm 10[76].1.17
d]. | birtym. | [un]ṯ inn. | l [h]m ʿd ṯṯtbn. | ksp.iwrkl. | w ṯb.l unṯ hm. 1006.19
.ʿm n[y]. | kll.šlm. | ṯm ny.ʿm.um y. | mnm.šlm. | w.rgm.ṯṯb.l y. | bm.ṯy.ndr. | iṯt.ʿmn.mlkt. | w.rgm y.l[--]. | lqt.w.pn. | 50[117].13
.š]lm. | w.ṯm [ny.ʿm.mlkt.u]m y. | mnm[.šlm]. | w.rgm[.ṯṯb.l] y. | hl ny.ʿmn. | mlk.b.ṯy ndr. | iṯt.w.ht. | [-]sny.udr h. | w. 1013.11
t.ʿm[ny]. | kll.šlm.ṯm ny. | ʿm.um y.mnm.šlm. | w.rgm.ṯṯb.l y. | w.mndʿ.k.ank. | aḥš.mǵy.mndʿ. | k.igr.w.u.[--]. | ʿm.šp 2009.1.9
.mṯb.klt]. | knyt.w tʿn[.btlt.ʿnt]. | yṯb l y.ṯr.il[.ab y.---]. | yṯb.l y.w l h.[---]. | [--.i]mṣḫ.nn.k imr.l arṣ. | [ašhlk].šbt h.dm 3[ʿNT.VI].4.8
nṯt. | [---]m.tṣḥq.ʿnt.w b lb.tqny. | [---.]ṯb l y.l aqht.ǵzr.ṯb l y w l k. | [---]m.l aqry k.b ntb.pšʿ. | [---].b ntb.gan.ašql k.t 17[2AQHT].6.42
mhrm.ht.tṣdn.tinṯt. | [---]m.tṣḥq.ʿnt.w b lb.tqny. | [---.]ṯb l y.l aqht.ǵzr.ṯb l y w l k. | [---]m.l aqry k.b ntb.pšʿ. | [---].b 17[2AQHT].6.42
.mṯb.arṣy]. | bt.yʿbdr[.mṯb.klt]. | knyt.w tʿn[.btlt.ʿnt]. | yṯb l y.ṯr.il[.ab y.---]. | yṯb.l y.w l h.[---]. | [--.i]mṣḫ.nn.k imr.l 3[ʿNT.VI].4.7
.---]. | [---.t]ṯb h.aḫt.ppšr.w ppšrt[.---]. | [---.]k.drḥm.w aṯb.l ntbt.k.ʿṣm l t[--]. | [---.]drk.brḥ.arṣ.lk pn h.yrk.bʿ[l]. | [-- 1001.2.7
gbʿm lḥmd.ḫrṣ. | yblnn.udr.ilqṣm. | yak.l kṯr.w ḫss. | w ṯb l mspr..k tlakn. | ǵlmm. | aḥr.mǵy.kṯr.w ḫss. | št.alp.qdm h 4[51].5.104
ytši.l dr. | bn il.l mpḫrt.bn.il.l ṯkmn[.w]šnm.hn.ʿr. | w.ṯb.l mspr.m[šr] mšr.bt.ugrt.w npy.gr. | ḥmyt.ugrt.w [np]y.nṯ 32[2].1.27
.y[--.-]ah. | ṯnm.tšqy msk.hwt.tšqy[.-.]w [---]. | w hn dt.yṯb.l mspr. 19[1AQHT].5.1
d. | w.šbʿ id. | mrḥqtm. | qlt. | ʿm.adt y. | mnm.šlm. | rgm.ṯṯṯb. | l.ʿbd h. 52[89].14
n id.šbʿ d. | mrḥqtm. | qlt.ʿm. | bʿl y.mnm. | šlm. | [r]gm[.ṯṯb]. | [l.]ʿbd[k]. 2115.2.11
. | w.ap.ank. | nḫt.ṯm ny. | ʿm.adt ny. | mnm.šlm. | rgm.ṯṯb. | l.ʿbd k. 51[95].17
h. | il[.--.]rḥq.b ǵr. | km.y[--.]ilm.b ṣpn. | ʿdr.l[ʿr].ʿrm. | ṯb.l pd[r.]pdrm. | ṯṯ.l ṯṯm.aḥd.ʿr. | šbʿm.šbʿ.pdr. | ṯmnym.bʿl.[- 4[51].7.8
. | udm.rbt.w udm ṯrrt. | udm.ytnt.il w ušn. | ab.adm.w ṯṯb. | mlakm.l h.lm.ank. | ksp.w yrq.ḫrṣ. | yd.mqm h.w ʿbd. | ʿl 14[KRT].3.136
n.[š]pt hm.mtqtm. | bm.nšq.w hr.[b]ḥbq.w ḥ[m]ḥmt.yṯb[n]. | yspr.l ḫmš.l ṣ[---.]šr.pḫr.klat. | tqtnṣn.w tldn.tld.[il 23[52].56
.mṣrp k.[---]. | [---.]y.mṯnt.w th.ṯbt.n[--]. | [---.b]ṯnm w ṯṯb.ʿl.bṯnt.trtḥ[ṣ.---]. | [---.t]ṯb h.aḫt.ppšr.w ppšrt[.---]. | [---.]k 1001.2.5
.mt. | p[-]n.aḫ y m.ytn.bʿl. | [s]pu y.bn m.um y.kly y. | yṯb.ʿm.bʿl.ṣrrt. | ṣpn.yšu g h.w yṣḥ. | aḫ y m.ytnt.bʿl. | spu y.b 6[49].6.12
r.ṯṯb. | ʿn.pḫr.l.pḫr.ṯṯb. | ʿn.mḫr.l.mḫr.ṯṯb. | ʿn.bṯy.l.bṯy.ṯṯb. | ʿn.bṯt.l.bṯt.ṯṯb. RS225.10
ʿn.ṯǵr. | ʿn.ṯǵr.l.ṯǵr.ṯṯb. | ʿn.pḫr.l.pḫr.ṯṯb. | ʿn.mḫr.l.mḫr.ṯṯb. | ʿn.bṯy.l.bṯy.ṯṯb. | ʿn.bṯt.l.bṯt.ṯṯb. RS225.9
n. | ʿn.mḫr.ʿn.pḫr.ʿn.ṯǵr. | ʿn.ṯǵr.l.ṯǵr.ṯṯb. | ʿn.pḫr.l.pḫr.ṯṯb. | ʿn.mḫr.l.mḫr.ṯṯb. | ʿn.bṯy.l.bṯy.ṯṯb. | ʿn.bṯt.l.bṯt.ṯṯb. RS225.8
n.ʿn.bṯy.ʿn.bṯt.tpnn. | ʿn.mḫr.ʿn.pḫr.ʿn.ṯǵr. | ʿn.ṯǵr.l.ṯǵr.ṯṯb. | ʿn.pḫr.l.pḫr.ṯṯb. | ʿn.mḫr.l.mḫr.ṯṯb. | ʿn.bṯy.l.bṯy.ṯṯb. | ʿn. RS225.7
thmt.ʿ[--.---]. | yṣi.ǵl h ṯḥm b[.---]. | mrḫ h l adrt[.---]. | ṯṯb ʿṯtrt b ǵl[.---]. | qrẓ tšt.l šmal[.---]. | arbḫ.ʿn h tšu w[.---]. | 2001.1.8
kdd. | dnil.mt.r[pi.mk].b šbʿ. | šnt.w yʿn[.dnil.mt.]rpi. | yṯb.ǵzr.m[t.hrnmy.y]šu. | g h.w yṣḥ.ṯ[bʿ.---]. | bkyt.b hk[l]y. 19[1AQHT].4.181
mǵy.rpum.l grnt.i[lnym.l] | mṯʿ.w yʿn.dnil.[mt.rpi]. | yṯb.ǵzr.mt hrnmy[.---]. | b grnt.ilm.b qrb.m[ṯʿ.ilnym]. | d tit. 20[121].2.8
.ank. | ʿm ny.šlm. | kll. | w mnm. | šlm ʿm. | um y. | ʿm y.ṯṯb. | rgm. 1015.19
. | pdrm.tdu.šrr. | ḥṯ m.tʿmt.[ʿ]ṯr.[k]m. | zbln.ʿl.riš h. | w ṯṯb.trḥṣ.nn.b dʿt. | npš h.l lḥm.tpth. | brlt h.l ṯrm. | mt.dm.ḫt. 16.6[127].10
h. | yr[--.]mlk.ṣbu.špš.w.ḥl.mlk. | w.[---].ypm.w.mḫ[--].t[ṯ]tbn.[-]. | b.[--].w.km.iṯ.y[--.]šqm.yd[-]. 35[3].54
trt.tṣdn.[---]. | [---.-]b[-.---]. | [ʿ]ṯrt w ʿnt[.---]. | w b hm.ṯṯtb[.--]d h. | km trpa.hn nʿr. | d yšt.l.lṣb h ḫšʿr klb. | [w]riš.p UG5.1.2.2
w[.-----]. | l[.-----]. | h[--.---]. | šp[š.---]. | ʿm.k[--.lḥt]. | akl.yṯ[ṯb.--]pt. | ib.ʿltn.a[--.--]y. | w.spr.in[.-.]ʿd m. | spr n.ṯḫr[.--]. 2060.30
tql.[---.]lb.ṯṯ[b]r. | qšt[.---]r.y[ṯ]br. | ṯmn.[---.]btlt.[ʿ]nt. | ṯṯb.[---.--]ša. | tlm.km[.---.]yd h.k šr. | knr.uṣbʿt h ḫrṣ.abn. | p 19[1AQHT].1.6
[---.kll].šlm. | [---.ṯ]mn.ʿm k. | [m]nm.šlm. | [---.w.r]gm.ṯṯb. 2171.5
ḫr.ṯṯb. | ʿn.mḫr.l.mḫr.ṯṯb. | ʿn.bṯy.l.bṯy.ṯṯb. | ʿn.bṯt.l.bṯt.ṯṯb. RS225.11
ty.hnd. | ylak ʿm y. | w.tʿl.ṯh.hn. | [a]lpm.ššwm. | [---].w.ṯb. 1012.39

ṯwy

[k]l hm.b d. | rb.tmtt.lqḥt. | w.ṯṯb.ank.l hm. | w.any k.ṯt. | by.ʿky.ʿryt. | w.aḫ y.mhk. | b lb h.al.yšt. 2059.24
ʿ mʿ.l krt. | ṯʿ.ištmʿ.w tqǵ udn. | k ǵz.ǵzm.tdbr. | w ǵrm.ṯṯwy.šqlt. | b ǵlt.yd k.l tdn. | dn.almnt.l ṯṯpṭ. | ṯpṭ qṣr.npš.l td 16.6[127].44
.adn k.]ištm[ʿ]. | w tqǵ[.udn.k ǵz.ǵzm]. | tdbr.w[ǵ]rm[.ṯṯwy]. | šqlt.b ǵlt.yd k. | l tdn.dn.almnt. | l ṯṯpṭ.ṯpṭ.qṣr.npš. | k 16.6[127].31

ṯwl

l.ʿṯtrt.abdr. | l.dml. | l.ilt[.-]pn. | l.uš[ḫr]y. | [---.-]mrn. | l ṯwl. | [--]d[--]. 1001.1.14

ṯḫr

mn. | brrn aryn. | a[-]ḥn tlyn. | atdb w ʿr. | qdš w amrr. | ṯḫr w bd. | [k]ṯr ḫss šlm. | šlm il bt. | šlm il ḫš[t]. | ršp inšt. | [--] UG5.7.71

ṯṯ

ṯn.pld.pṯt[.-]r. | lpš.sgr.rq. | ṯṯ.prqt. | w.mrdt.prqt.pṯt. | lbš.psm.rq. | ṯn.mrdt.az. | ṯlṯ.pld.š‘ 1112.3

ṯy

[--]my.b d[-.--]y.[---]. | [---.]‘m.w hm[.--]yt.w.[---]. | [---.ṯ]y.al.an[k.--.]il[m.--]y. | [--.m]ṣlm.pn y[.-.]tlkn. | [---.]rḫbn.h 1002.58
]m y. | mnm[.šlm]. | w.rgm[.ṯṯb.l] y. | hl ny.‘mn. | mlk.b.ṯy ndr. | iṯt.w.ht. | [-]sny.uḏr h. | w.hm.ḫt. | ‘l.w.likt. | ‘m k.w.h 1013.13
l.šlm. | ṯm ny.‘m.um y. | mnm.šlm. | w.rgm.ṯṯb.l y. | bm.ṯy.ndr. | iṯt.‘mn.mlkt. | w.rgm y.l[--]. | lqt.w.pn. | mlk.nr b n. 50[117].14

ṯydr

[ṯ]mnym.dd. | š‘rm.b.ṯydr. 1166.2

ṯyl

. | [---]bln. | [---]dy. | [---.n]ḥl h. | [---].bn.mryn. | [---].bn.ṯyl. | annmt.nḥl h. | abmn.bn.‘bd. | liy.bn.rqdy. | bn.ršp. 1036.11
.w.aṯt h. | slmu.ḫrš.mrkbt. | bnšm.dt.l.mlk. | ‘bdyrḫ.bn.ṯyl. | ‘bdn.w.aṯt h.w.bn h. | gpn.bn[.a]ly. | bn.rqd[y].ṯbg. | iḫml 2068.18

ṯyn

‘myn. | bn aṯtyy. | bn ḫlp. | bn.ẓll. | bn ydy. | bn lzn. | bn.ṯyn. | bn g‘r. | bn.prtn. | bn ḫnn. | b[n.-]n. | bn.ṣṣb. | bn.b‘ltn ḫlq 2016.1.15
w šnm.w ngšnn.ḥby. | b‘l.qrnm w ḏnb.ylšn. | b ḫri h.w ṯnt h.ql.il.[--]. | il.k yrdm.arṣ.‘nt. | w ‘ṯtrt.ṣdn.[---]. | [---.-]b[-. UG5.1.1.21
w ṯ[qd m]r. | [ydk aḥd h w yṣq b ap h. | [k l yḫru w]l yṯtn mss št qlql. | [w št ‘rgz y]dk aḥd h w yṣq b ap h. | [k.yiḫ 160[55].8
. | w.ṯ[qd.mr.ydk.aḥd h]. | w.y[ṣq.b.ap h]. | k.l.ḫ[ru.w.l.yṯtn.ššw]. | mss.[št.qlql.w.št]. | ‘rgz[.ydk.aḥd h]. | w.yṣq[.b.ap 161[56].8

ṯk

šb‘t.ḥdrm.[b ṯ]mn[t.ap]. | sgrt.g[-].[-]ẓ[.---] h[.---]. | ‘n.ṯk[.---]. | ‘ln.ṯ[--.---]. | l p‘n.ǵl[m]m[.---]. | mid.an[--.]ṣn[--]. | n 3[‘NT.VI].5.21
i[l]štm‘ym. | bn.ṯk. | bn.arwdn. | tmrtn. | šd‘l.bn aḫyn. | m‘rbym. | rpan. | abršn. 95[91].2

ṯkḥ

[--].yṯkḥ.w yiḫd.b qrb[.-]. | [--.t]ṯkḥ.w tiḫd.b uš[k.--]. | [-.b]‘l.yabd.l alp. | [---.bt]lt.‘nt. | [---]q 11[132].1.2
[--].yṯkḥ.w yiḫd.b qrb[.-]. | [--.t]ṯkḥ.w tiḫd.b uš[k.--]. | [-.b]‘l.yab 11[132].1.1
b[.bt]. | ḫrḫb.mlk qẓ ḫrḫb m | lk aǵzt.b sǵ[--.]špš. | yrḫ yṯkḥ yḥ[bq] [-]. | tld bt.[--]t.ḫ[--.l k] | ṯrt.l bnt.hll[.snnt]. | hl ǵ 24[77].4
ḫṣ. | [ltn.bṯn.br]ḥ.tkly. | [bṯn.‘qltn.]šlyṭ. | [d šb‘t.rašm].ṯṯkḥ. | [ttrp.šmm.k rks.ipd]k. | [-----]. 5[67].1.30
k tmḫṣ.ltn.bṯn.brḥ. | tkly.bṯn.‘qltn. | šlyṭ.d šb‘y.rašm. | ṯṯkḥ.ttrp.šmm.k rs. | ipd k.ank.ispi.uṭm. | ḏrqm.amt m.l yrt. 5[67].1.4

ṯkl

lm.mlk.šlm.mlkt.‘rbm m.ṯnnm. | mt.w šr.yṯb.b d h.ḫṭ.ṯkl.b d h. | ḫṭ.ulmn.yzbrnn.zbrm.gpn. | yṣmdnn.ṣmdm.gpn.y 23[52].8
šr.ln h.mlḫš. | abd.ln h.ydy.ḥmt. | b ḥrn.pnm.trǵnw.w ṯṯkl. | bnwt h.ykr.‘r.d qdm. | idk.pnm.l ytn.tk aršḫ.rbt. | w arš UG5.7.61
km.r[--]. | amr.[---]. | ḫṭ.ṯk[l.---]. | [-]l[--.---]. 2002.3

ṯkm

bn bn.aṯr k.hn[.---]. | yd k.ṣǵr.tnšq.špt k.ṯm. | ṯkm.bm ṯkm.aḫm.qym.il. | b lsmt.ṯm.yṭbš.šm.il.mt m. | y‘bš.brk n.šm 22.2[124].5
hn[.---]. | bn bn.aṯr k.hn[.---]. | yd k.ṣǵr.tnšq.špt k.ṯm. | ṯkm.bm ṯkm.aḫm.qym.il. | b lsmt.ṯm.yṭbš.šm.il.mt m. | y‘bš. 22.2[124].5
šm‘.l ngr.il il[š]. | ilš.ngr bt b‘l. | w aṯt k.ngrt.il[ht]. | ‘l.l ṯkm.bnw n. | l nḫnpt.mšpy. | ṯlṯ.kmm.ṯrr y. | [---.]l ǵr.gm.ṣḥ. | 16[126].4.14
]. | yṣq.b gl.ḥtt.yn. | b gl.ḫrṣ.nbt.w ‘ly. | l ẓr.mgdl.rkb. | ṯkmm.ḥmt.nša. | [y]d h.šmmh.dbḥ. | l ṯr.ab h.il.šrd. | [b‘l].b d 14[KRT].4.167
yn.b gl[.ḫ]rṣ.nbt. | ‘l.l ẓr.[mg]dl. | w ‘l.l ẓr.[mg]dl.rkb. | ṯkmm.ḥm[t].ša.yd k. | šmm.dbḥ.l ṯr. | ab k.il.šrd.b‘l. | b dbḥ k 14[KRT].2.75
all.ǵzr.m[t.]hr[nmy]. | gm.l bt[h.dnil.k yṣḥ]. | šm‘.pǵt.ṯkmt[.my]. | ḥspt.l š‘r.ṭl.yd[‘t]. | hlk.kbkbm.mdl.‘r. | ṣmd.pḥl. 19[1AQHT].2.50
[.m] | kly[.‘]l.umt y.w y‘n[.dn] | il.mt.rpi npš ṯḥ[.pǵt]. | ṯ[km]t.mym.ḥspt.l š‘r. | ṭl.yd‘t.hlk.kbkbm. | a[-]ḥ.hy.mḫ.tmḫ 19[1AQHT].4.199
. | ṣmd.pḥl.št.gpn y dt ksp. | dt.yrq.nqbn y.tš[m‘]. | pǵt.ṯkmt.my.ḥspt.l[š‘]r.ṭl. | yd‘t.hlk.kbkbm. | bkm.tmdln.‘r. | bk 19[1AQHT].2.55
--]. | [-]l h.yd ‘d[.---]. | ltm.mrqdm.d š[-]l[-]. | w t‘n.pǵt.ṯkmt.mym. | qrym.ab.dbḥ.l ilm. | š‘ly.dǵt h.b šmym. | dǵt.hrn 19[1AQHT].4.190
n.ǵlm. | il.trḥṣ.w tadm. | rḥṣ[.y]d k.amt. | uṣb[‘t k.]‘d[.ṯ]km. | ‘rb[.b ẓl.ḫmt]. | qḥ im[r.b yd k]. | imr.d[bḥ.bm].ymn. | 14[KRT].2.64
l.w hdrt. | yrtḥṣ.w yadm. | yrḥṣ.yd h.amt h. | uṣb‘t h.‘d.ṯkm. | ‘rb.b ẓl.ḫmt.lqḥ. | imr.dbḥ.b yd h. | lla.klatnm. | klt.lḥm 14[KRT].3.158

ṯkmn

il b[n] il. | dr bn il. | mpḫrt bn il. | ṯrmn w šnm. | il w aṯrt. | ḫnn il. | nṣbt il. | šlm il. | il ḥš il add. | 30[107].4
t.ṯ‘.ynt.ṯ‘m.dqt.ṯ‘m. | mtntm nkbd.alp.š.l il. | gdlt.ilhm.ṯkmn.w šnm dqt. | ršp.dqt.šrp w šlmm.dqtm. | [i]lh.alp w š il 34[1].3
[t.q]rt.y[---]. | w al[p.l]il.w bu[rm.---]. | ytk.gdlt.ilhm.[ṯkmn.w šnm]. | dqt.ršp.šrp.w š[lmm.dqtm]. | ilh[.a]lp.w š[.il] 35[3].12
.---]. | [---.--]n[.w alp.l il.w bu] | [rm.---.ytk.gdlt.ilhm]. | ṯkmn.w [šnm.dqt.ršp.šrp]. | w šlmm.[dqtm.ilh.alp.w š]. | ilh APP.II[173].14
p.š]rp.w šl[mm.--.dqt]. | [i]lh.gdlt[.ilhm.gdlt.il]. | [d]qt.ṯkmn.w [šnm.dqt.--]. | [--]t.dqtm.[b nbk.---]. | [--.k]mm.gdlt.l 35[3].31
dq[t.ilh.gdlt]. | n.w šnm.dqt[.---]. | [i]lh[m.gd]lt.i[l.dqt.ṯkm] | n.w šnm.dqt[.---]. | bqtm.b nbk.[---]. | kmm.gdlt.l b[‘l.- APP.II[173].33
.nkt.nkt.y[t]ši.l ab.bn.il.ytši.l dr. | bn il.l mpḫrt.bn.il.l ṯkmn[.w]šnm.hn.‘r. | w.ṯb.l mspr.m[šr] mšr.bt.ugrt.w npy.g 32[2].1.26
kt.nk]t.ytši.l ab bn il. | ytši.l d[r.bn il.l]mpḫrt.bn il. | l ṯkm[n.w šnm.]hn ‘[r]. | [---.]w npy[.---]. | [---.]w npy.u[grt.--- 32[2].1.35
kt.n[k]t.ytši[.l ab.bn.il]. | ytši.l dr.bn.il.l mpḫrt.bn.i[l.l ṯkmn.w š]nm hn š. | w šqrb.‘r.mšr mšr bn.ugrt.w [npy.---.]u 32[2].1.17
kt.nkt.ytši.l ab.bn.il.ytši.l d]r.bn[.il]. | [l mpḫrt.bn.il.l ṯkmn.w šnm.hn š]. | [w šqrb.š.mšr mšr.bn.ugrt.w npy.---.]w 32[2].1.3
t.nkt.]yt[ši.l ab.bn.il]. | [ytši.l dr.bn.il.l mpḫ]rt.[bn.il.l ṯkmn.w šn]m hn š. | [---.w n]py.gr[.ḥmyt.ugrt.w np]y. | [---]. 32[2].1.9B
.‘d šb‘.trṯ.‘d škr. | il.hlk.l bt h.yštql. | l ḥṭr h.y‘msn.nn.ṯkmn. | w šnm.w ngšnn.ḥby. | b‘l.qrnm w ḏnb.ylšn. | b ḫri h. UG5.1.1.18
lm.il.šr. | dgn.w b‘l. | ‘ṯ w kmṯ. | yrḫ w ksa. | yrḫ mkty. | ṯkmn w šnm. | kṯr w ḫss. | ‘ṯtr ‘ṯtpr. | šḥr w šlm. | ngh w srr. | ‘ UG5.10.1.8
.dqtm]. | ilh[.a]lp.w š[.il]hm.[gdlt.ilhm]. | b‘[l.š].aṯrt[.š.ṯkm]n w [šnm.š]. | ‘nt š ršp š[.dr.il.w pḫr.b‘l]. | gdlt.šlm[.gdlt 35[3].15
m.dqtm. | [i]lh.alp w š ilhm.gdl[t.]ilhm. | [b]‘l š.aṯrt.š.ṯkmn w šnm.š. | ‘nt.š.ršp.š.dr il w p[ḫ]r b‘l. | gdlt.šlm.gdlt.w 34[1].6

lmm.[dqtm.ilh.alp.w š].|ilhm.gd[lt.ilhm.bʿl.š.aṯrt.š].|ṯkmn.w š[nm.š.ʿnt.š.ršp.š.dr].|il.w pẖr[.bʿl.gdlt.šlm.gdlt].| APP.II[173].17

ṯkn

alnr.|maẖdt.|aby.|[-----].|[-]nt.|ydn.|mnn.w bn h.|ṯkn. 107[15].13

ṯkp

.|nẖtu.w.lak.|ʿm y.w.yd.|ilm.p.k mtm.|ʿz.mid.|hm.nṯkp.|mʿn k.|w.mnm.|rgm.d.tšmʿ.|ṯmt.w.št.|b.spr.ʿm y. 53[54].14

ṯkr

[mrǵ]b.yd.m[ṯkt].|mẓma.yd.mṯkt.|tṯkr.[--]dn.|ʿm.krt.mswn h.|arẖ.tzǵ.l ʿgl h.|bn.ẖpṯ.l umht 15[128].1.3

ṯkt

šm [---].|knʿm.bn.[---].|pls̀bʿl.bn.n[--].|ḥy bn.dnn.ṯkt.|ilṯḥm.bn.dnn.ṯkt.|šbʿl.bn.aly.ṯkt.|klby.bn.iẖy.ṯkt.|ps̀s̀. 2085.4
y.ṯkt.|ʿpṣpn.bn.ʿdy.ṯkt.|nʿmn.bn.ʿyn.ṯkt.|ʿpṯn.bn.ilrš.ṯkt.|ilṯḥm.bn.s̀rn.ṯkt.|šmlbu.bn.grb.ṯkt.|šmlbu.bn.ypʿ.ṯkt.| 2085.11
sr k.|rẖntt.d[-].l irt k.|wn ap.ʿdn.mṭr h.|bʿl.yʿdn.ʿdn.ṯkt.b glṯ.|w tn.ql h.b ʿrpt.|šrh.l arṣ.brqm.|bt.arzm.yklln h. 4[51].5.69
anyt.miẖd[t].|br.ṯpṯbʿ[l.---].|br.dmty[.---].|ṯkt.ydln[.---].|ṯkt.ṯryn[.---].|br.ʿbdm[lk.---].|wry[.---].|ṯkt[. 84[319].1.4
n.n[--].|ḥy bn.dnn.ṯkt.|ilṯḥm.bn.dnn.ṯkt.|šbʿl.bn.aly.ṯkt.|klby.bn.iẖy.ṯkt.|ps̀s̀.bn.buly.ṯkt.|ʿpṣpn.bn.ʿdy.ṯkt.|nʿm 2085.6
ly.ṯkt.|klby.bn.iẖy.ṯkt.|ps̀s̀.bn.buly.ṯkt.|ʿpṣpn.bn.ʿdy.ṯkt.|nʿmn.bn.ʿyn.ṯkt.|ʿpṯn.bn.ilrš.ṯkt.|ilṯḥm.bn.s̀rn.ṯkt.|šml 2085.9
dnn.ṯkt.|šbʿl.bn.aly.ṯkt.|klby.bn.iẖy.ṯkt.|ps̀s̀.bn.buly.ṯkt.|ʿpṣpn.bn.ʿdy.ṯkt.|nʿmn.bn.ʿyn.ṯkt.|ʿpṯn.bn.ilrš.ṯkt.|ilṯḥ 2085.8
y.ṯkt.|ps̀s̀.bn.buly.ṯkt.|ʿpṣpn.bn.ʿdy.ṯkt.|nʿmn.bn.ʿyn.ṯkt.|ʿpṯn.bn.ilrš.ṯkt.|ilṯḥm.bn.s̀rn.ṯkt.|šmlbu.bn.grb.ṯkt.|š 2085.10
n.ṯkt.|ilṯḥm.bn.dnn.ṯkt.|šbʿl.bn.aly.ṯkt.|klby.bn.iẖy.ṯkt.|ps̀s̀.bn.buly.ṯkt.|ʿpṣpn.bn.ʿdy.ṯkt.|nʿmn.bn.ʿyn.ṯkt.|ʿpṯ 2085.7
bn.[---].|pls̀bʿl.bn.n[--].|ḥy bn.dnn.ṯkt.|ilṯḥm.bn.dnn.ṯkt.|šbʿl.bn.aly.ṯkt.|klby.bn.iẖy.ṯkt.|ps̀s̀.bn.buly.ṯkt.|ʿpṣpn. 2085.5
y.ṯkt.|nʿmn.bn.ʿyn.ṯkt.|ʿpṯn.bn.ilrš.ṯkt.|ilṯḥm.bn.s̀rn.ṯkt.|šmlbu.bn.grb.ṯkt.|šmlbu.bn.ypʿ.ṯkt.|[---.--]m. 2085.12
.ṯkt.|ʿpṯn.bn.ilrš.ṯkt.|ilṯḥm.bn.s̀rn.ṯkt.|šmlbu.bn.grb.ṯkt.|šmlbu.bn.ypʿ.ṯkt.|[---.--]m. 2085.13
.miẖd[t].|br.ṯpṯbʿ[l.---].|br.dmty[.---].|ṯkt.ydln[.---].|ṯkt.ṯryn[.---].|br.ʿbdm[lk.---].|wry[.---].|ṯkt[.---].|ṯk[t.---].| 84[319].1.5
-].|ṯkt.ṯryn[.---].|br.ʿbdm[lk.---].|wry[.---].|ṯkt[.---].|ṯk[t.---].|br[.---].|br[.---].|br[.---].|br[.---].|br[.---].|br[.---]. 84[319].1.9
t.ydln[.---].|ṯkt.ṯryn[.---].|br.ʿbdm[lk.---].|wry[.---].|ṯkt[.---].|ṯk[t.---].|br[.---].|br[.---].|br[.---].|br[.---].|br[.---]. 84[319].1.8
t.|ilṯḥm.bn.s̀rn.ṯkt.|šmlbu.bn.grb.ṯkt.|šmlbu.bn.ypʿ.ṯkt.|[---.--]m. 2085.14

ṯlb

r.il.yṯb.b.ʿṯtrt.|il.ṯpṭ.b hd rʿy.d yšr.w ydmr.|b knr.w ṯlb.b tp.w mṣltm.b m|rqdm.dšn.b.ḥbr.kṯr.ṭbm.|w tšt.ʿnt.gṯr UG5.2.1.4
[---.]w rm tp h.|[---.-]lu mm l nʿm.|[---.]w rm ṯlbm ṯlb.|[---.-]pr l nʿm.|[---.-]mt w rm tp h.|[---.-]ḥb l nʿm.|[---. UG5.5.3
-.-]mt w rm tp h.|[---.-]ḥb l nʿm.|[---.]ymǵy.|[---.]rm ṯlbm.|[---.--]m.|[---.--]ḥ nʿm. UG5.5.8

ṯlbm

[---.]w rm tp h.|[---.-]lu mm l nʿm.|[---.]w rm ṯlbm ṯlb.|[---.-]pr l nʿm.|[---.-]mt w rm tp h.|[---.-]ḥb l nʿm. UG5.5.3

ṯlḥy

ḏrǵlm.d inn.|msgm.l hm.|pʿṣ.ẖbty.|artyn.ary.|brqn.ṯlḥy.|bn.aryn.|bn.lgn.|bn.bʿyn.|šdyn.|ary.|brqn.|bn.ẖlln. 118[306].5

ṯlḥn

] ʿd šbʿ.|trṯ.ʿd.škr.yʿdb.yrẖ.|gb h.km.[---.]yqṭqṭ.tḥt.|ṯlḥnt.il.d ydʿnn.|yʿdb.lḥm.l h.w d l ydʿnn.|d.mṣd.|ylmn.ẖṭ. UG5.1.1.6
r.hdm.id.|d prša.b br.|nʿl.il.d qblbl.|ʿln.ybl hm.ẖrṣ.|ṯlḥn.il.d mla.|mnm.dbbm.d |msdt.arṣ.|sʿ.il.dqt.k amr.|skn 4[51].1.39
šnt.|imr.qmṣ.llim.k ksp.|l ʿbrm.zt.ẖrṣ.l ʿbrm.kš.|dpr.ṯlḥn.b qʿl.b qʿl.|mlkm.hn.ym.yṣq.yn.ṯmk.|mrṯ.yn.srnm.yn. 22.2[124].16
dʿnn.|yʿdb.lḥm.l h.w d l ydʿnn.|d.mṣd.|ylmn.ẖṭ.tḥt.ṯlḥn.|b qrʿ.|ʿṯtrt.w ʿnt.ymǵy.|ʿṯtrt.tʿdb.nšb l h.|w ʿnt.ktp.b UG5.1.1.8
---.--]n [ṯ]lḥn.|[---.ṯ]lḥ[n].|[---.--ṯ]lḥn.|[---.]ṯlḥn.|[---.]ṯlḥn.|bn adty ṯlḥn.bn qrwl ṯlḥn. 98[11].35
[---.ṯ]lḥ[n].|[---.--ṯ]lḥn.|[---.]ṯlḥn.|[---.]ṯlḥn.|bn adty ṯlḥn.bn qrwl ṯlḥn. 98[11].36
rp.w šlmm kmm.|l bʿl.ṣpn b ʿrʿr.|pamt ṯlṯm š l qrnt.|ṯlḥn.bʿlt.bhtm.|ʿlm.ʿlm.gdlt l bʿl.|ṣpn.ilbt[.---.]d[--].|l ṣpn[.- UG5.13.31
r.|[u]ṣbʿt h.b mmʿ.mhrm.|[t]ʿr.ksat.l ksat.ṯlḥnt.|[l]ṯlḥn.hdmm.ttʿr.l hdmm.|[t]ḥspn.m h.w trḥṣ.|[ṭ]l.šmm.šmn 3[ʿNT].2.37
yqlṣn.|yqm.w ywpṯn.b tk.|p[ẖ]r.bn.ilm.štt.|p[--].b ṯlḥn y.qlt.|b ks.ištyn h.|dm.ṯn.dbḥm.šna.bʿl.ṯlṯ.|rkb.ʿrpt.db 4[51].3.15
ḏmr.ḥlqm.b mmʿ.mhrm.|ʿd.tšbʿ.tmtẖṣ.b bt.|tẖṣb.bn.ṯlḥnm.ymḥ.|[b]bt.dm.ḏmr.yṣq.šmn.|šlm.b ṣʿ.trḥṣ.yd h.bt| 3[ʿNT].2.30
šbʿt.tmtẖṣ h.b ʿmq.|tẖtṣb.bn.qrtm.ttʿr.|ksat.l mhr.ṯʿr.ṯlḥnt.|l ṣbim.hdmm.l ǵzrm.|mid.tmtẖṣn.w tʿn.|tẖtṣb.w tḥd 3[ʿNT].2.21
-.]hy bt h tʿrb.|[---.tm]tẖṣ b ʿmq.|[tẖtṣb.bn.qrtm.ttʿr.ṯlḥnt.]l ṣbim.|[hdmm.l ǵzrm.mid.tmtẖṣn.w t]ʿn.tẖtṣb.|[w t 7.1[131].5
h.b dm.ḏmr.|[u]ṣbʿt h.b mmʿ.mhrm.|[t]ʿr.ksat.l ksat.ṯlḥnt.|[l]ṯlḥn.hdmm.ttʿr.l hdmm.|[t]ḥspn.m h.w trḥṣ.|[ṭ]l. 3[ʿNT].2.36
ǵt[--].|hm.ǵmu.ǵmit.w ʿs[--].|lḥm.hm.štym.lḥ[m].|b ṯlḥnt.lḥm št.|b krpnm.yn.b k.ẖrṣ.|dm.ʿṣm.hm.yd.il mlk.|y 4[51].4.36
ag[--].|ẖp[--].|mʿq[b].|ar[--].|ẓr[n].|ṯlḥ[n].|ṯlr[by].|qm[--].|šl[--].|a[---].|d[---].|q[---].|ʿm[--].| 2147.6
-].|d.b d.a[--.---].|w.b d.b[--.---].|udbr[.---].|ʿrš[.---].|ṯl[ḥn.---].|a[--.---].|ṯn[.---].|ptr[-.---].|yp[-.---].|b[--.---]. 1120.6
-]n ṯlḥn.|[---.--]n [ṯ]lḥn.|[---.ṯ]lḥ[n].|[---.--ṯ]lḥn.|[---.]ṯlḥn.|[---.]ṯlḥn.|bn adty ṯlḥn.bn qrwl ṯlḥn. 98[11].34
[---.ṯ]lḥn.|[---.ṯ]lḥn.|[---.ṯ]lḥn.|[---.--]t.ṯlḥn.|[---.]ṯlḥn.|[---.]ṯlḥn.|[---.--ṯ]lḥn.|[---.--ṯ]lḥn.|[---.--ṯ]lḥ 98[11].4
.]ṯlḥn.|[---.]ṯlḥn.|[---.]ṯlḥn.|[---.]ṯlḥn.|[---.]ṯlḥn.|[---.]ṯlḥn.|[---.]ṯlḥn.|[---.]ṯlḥn.|[---.]ṯlḥn.|[---.]ṯlḥn.|[---.]ṯlḥn.|[- 98[11].22
lḥn.|[---.--ṯ]lḥn.|[---.]ṯlḥn.|[---.]ṯlḥn.|[---.]ṯlḥn.|[---.]ṯlḥn.|[---.]ṯlḥn.|[---.]ṯlḥn.|[---.]ṯlḥn.|[---.]ṯlḥn.|[---.]ṯlḥn.|[- 98[11].19
.]ṯlḥn.|[---.]ṯlḥn.|[---.]ṯlḥn.|[---.]ṯlḥn.|[---.]ṯlḥn.|[---.]ṯlḥn.|[---.]ṯlḥn.|[---.]ṯlḥn.|[---.]ṯlḥn.|[---.]ṯlḥn.|[---.--ṯ]lḥn.| 98[11].23
ṯ]lḥn.|[---.--]n ṯlḥn.|[---.--]n [ṯ]lḥn.|[---.ṯ]lḥ[n].|[---.--ṯ]lḥn.|[---.]ṯlḥn.|[---.]ṯlḥn.|bn adty ṯlḥn.bn qrwl ṯlḥn. 98[11].33
.|[---.--ṯ]lḥn.|[---.--ṯ]lḥn.|[---.--ṯ]lḥn.|[---.]ṯlḥn.|[---.]ṯlḥn.|[---.]ṯlḥn.|[---.]ṯlḥn.|[---.]ṯlḥn.|[---.]ṯlḥn.|[---.]ṯlḥn.|[- 98[11].17
[---.--ṯ]lḥn.|[---.--ṯ]lḥn.|[---.--ṯ]lḥn.|[---.--ṯ]lḥn.|[---.--ṯ]lḥn.|[---.]ṯlḥn.|[---.]ṯlḥn.|[---.]ṯlḥn.|[---.]ṯlḥn.|[---.]ṯlḥn.|[98[11].15
n.|[---.--ṯ]lḥn.|[---.--ṯ]lḥn.|[---.]ṯlḥn.|[---.]ṯlḥn.|[---.]ṯlḥn.|[---.]ṯlḥn.|[---.]ṯlḥn.|[---.]ṯlḥn.|[---.]ṯlḥn.|[---.]ṯlḥn.|[- 98[11].18

ṯlḥn

.]ṯlḥn. | [---.]ṯlḥn. | [---.]ṯlḥn. | [---.]ṯlḥn. | [---.]ṯlḥn. | [---.]ṯlḥn. | [---.]ṯlḥn. | [---.]ṯlḥn. | [---.]ṯlḥn. | [---.--ṯ]lḥn. | [---.--]n [ṯ] 98[11].24
.]ṯlḥn. | [---.]ṯlḥn. | [---.]ṯlḥn. | [---.]ṯlḥn. | [---.]ṯlḥn. | [---.]ṯlḥn. | [---.]ṯlḥn. | [---.]ṯlḥn. | [---.--ṯ]lḥn. | [---.--]n [ṯ]lḥn. | [---.-- 98[11].25
[---.ṯ]lḥn. | [---.ṯ]lḥn. | [---.ṯ]lḥn. | [---.--]t.ṯlḥn. | [---.]ṯlḥn. | [---.]ṯlḥ 98[11].1
| [---.--ṯ]lḥn. | [---.--ṯ]lḥn. | [---.--ṯ]lḥn. | [---.--ṯ]lḥn. | [---.]ṯlḥn. | [---.]ṯlḥn. | [---.]ṯlḥn. | [---.]ṯlḥn. | [---.]ṯlḥn. | [---.]ṯlḥn. | [- 98[11].16
ṯ]lḥn. | [---.]ṯlḥn. | [---.]ṯlḥn. | [---.]ṯlḥn. | [---.]ṯlḥn. | [---.]ṯlḥn. | [---.]ṯlḥn. | [---.]ṯlḥn. | [---.]ṯlḥn. | [---.]ṯlḥn. | [---.]ṯlḥn. | [- 98[11].20
.]ṯlḥn. | [---.]ṯlḥn. | [---.]ṯlḥn. | [---.]ṯlḥn. | [---.]ṯlḥn. | [---.]ṯlḥn. | [---.]ṯlḥn. | [---.]ṯlḥn. | [---.]ṯlḥn. | [---.]ṯlḥn. | [---.]ṯlḥn. | [- 98[11].21
[---.ṯ]lḥn. | [---.ṯ]lḥn. | [---.ṯ]lḥn. | [---.--]t.ṯlḥn. | [---.]ṯlḥn. | [---.]ṯlḥn. | [---.--ṯ]l 98[11].2
.]ṯlḥn. | [---.]ṯlḥn. | [---.]ṯlḥn. | [---.]ṯlḥn. | [---.]ṯlḥn. | [---.]ṯlḥn. | [---.]ṯlḥn. | [---.--ṯ]lḥn. | [---.--]n [ṯ]lḥn. | [---.--]n ṯlḥn. | [- 98[11].26
n. | [---.--ṯ]lḥn. | [---.--]n [ṯ]lḥn. | [---.--]n ṯlḥn. | [---.--]n [ṯ]lḥn. | [---.ṯ]lḥ[n]. | [---.--ṯ]lḥn. | [---.]ṯlḥn. | [---.]ṯlḥn. | bn adty 98[11].31
[---.ṯ]lḥn. | [---.ṯ]lḥn. | [---.ṯ]lḥn. | [---.--]t.ṯlḥn. | [---.]ṯlḥn. | [---.]ṯlḥn. | [---.--ṯ]lḥn. | [---.--ṯ]lḥn. | [---.--ṯ]lḥn. | [---.--ṯ]l 98[11].5
r. | [---.]mdṯn.ipd. | [---.]m[---.]d.mškbt. | [---.--]m. | [---].ṯlḥn. | [---].ṯnn. | [---.--]b.kdr. | [---.--]m n‘rt. | [---].qt.b[--]. | [--- 1152.1.6
.]ṯlḥn. | [---.]ṯlḥn. | [---.--ṯ]lḥn. | [---.--]n [ṯ]lḥn. | [---.--]n ṯlḥn. | [---.--]n [ṯ]lḥn. | [---.ṯ]lḥ[n]. | [---.--ṯ]lḥn. | [---.]ṯlḥn. | [---. 98[11].30
| [---.]ṯlḥn. | [---.]ṯlḥn. | [---.]ṯlḥn. | [---.--ṯ]lḥn. | [---.--]n [ṯ]lḥn. | [---.--]n ṯlḥn. | [---.--]n [ṯ]lḥn. | [---.ṯ]lḥ[n]. | [---.--ṯ]lḥn. 98[11].29
ṯlḥn. | [---.]ṯlḥn. | [---.]ṯlḥn. | [---.]ṯlḥn. | [---.]ṯlḥn. | [---.--ṯ]lḥn. | [---.--]n [ṯ]lḥn. | [---.--]n ṯlḥn. | [---.--]n [ṯ]lḥn. | [---.ṯ]lḥ[98[11].28
[---.ṯ]lḥn. | [---.ṯ]lḥn. | [---.ṯ]lḥn. | [---.--]t.ṯlḥn. | [---.]ṯlḥn. | [---.]ṯlḥn. | [---.--ṯ]lḥn. | [---.--ṯ] 98[11].3
[---.--ṯ]lḥn. | [---.--ṯ]lḥn. | [---.--ṯ]lḥn. | [---.--ṯ]lḥn. | [---.--ṯ]lḥn. | [---.--ṯ]lḥn. | [---.]ṯlḥn. | [---.]ṯlḥn. | [---.]ṯlḥn. | [---.]ṯlḥn. 98[11].14
ḥn. | [---.--]n [ṯ]lḥn. | [---.--]n ṯlḥn. | [---.--]n [ṯ]lḥn. | [---.ṯ]lḥ[n]. | [---.--ṯ]lḥn. | [---.]ṯlḥn. | [---.]ṯlḥn. | bn adty ṯlḥn.bn qr 98[11].32
.]ṯlḥn. | [---.]ṯlḥn. | [---.]ṯlḥn. | [---.]ṯlḥn. | [---.]ṯlḥn. | [---.]ṯlḥn. | [---.--ṯ]lḥn. | [---.--]n [ṯ]lḥn. | [---.--]n ṯlḥn. | [---.--]n [ṯ]lḥ 98[11].27
n. | [---.]ṯlḥn. | [---.]ṯlḥn. | [---.--ṯ]lḥn. | [---.--ṯ]lḥn. | [---.--ṯ]lḥn. | [---.--ṯ]lḥn. | [---.--ṯ]lḥn. | [---.--ṯ]lḥn. | [---.--ṯ]lḥn. | [---.- 98[11].9
[---.--ṯ]lḥn. | [---.--ṯ]lḥn. | [---.--ṯ]lḥn. | [---.--ṯ]lḥn. | [---.--ṯ]lḥn. | [---.--ṯ]lḥn. | [---.--ṯ]lḥn. | [---.]ṯlḥn. | [---.]ṯlḥn. | [---.]ṯlḥ 98[11].13
ḥn. | [---.ṯ]lḥn. | [---.ṯ]lḥn. | [---.--]t.ṯlḥn. | [---.]ṯlḥn. | [---.]ṯlḥn. | [---.--ṯ]lḥn. | [---.--ṯ]lḥn. | [---.--ṯ]lḥn. | [---.--ṯ]lḥn. | [---.-- 98[11].6
[---.--ṯ]lḥn. | [---.--ṯ]lḥn. | [---.--ṯ]lḥn. | [---.--ṯ]lḥn. | [---.--ṯ]lḥn. | [---.--ṯ]lḥn. | [---.--ṯ]lḥn. | [---.--ṯ]lḥn. | [---.]ṯlḥn. | [---.]ṯl 98[11].12
. | [---.--]t.ṯlḥn. | [---.]ṯlḥn. | [---.]ṯlḥn. | [---.--ṯ]lḥn. | [---.--ṯ]lḥn. | [---.--ṯ]lḥn. | [---.--ṯ]lḥn. | [---.--ṯ]lḥn. | [---.--ṯ]lḥn. | [---.- 98[11].8
[---.--ṯ]lḥn. | [---.--ṯ]lḥn. | [---.--ṯ]lḥn. | [---.--ṯ]lḥn. | [---.--ṯ]lḥn. | [---.--ṯ]lḥn. | [---.--ṯ]lḥn. | [---.--ṯ]lḥn. | [---.--ṯ]lḥn. | [---.] 98[11].11
. | [---.]ṯlḥn. | [---.--ṯ]lḥn. | [---.--ṯ]lḥn. | [---.--ṯ]lḥn. | [---.--ṯ]lḥn. | [---.--ṯ]lḥn. | [---.--ṯ]lḥn. | [---.--ṯ]lḥn. | [---.--ṯ]lḥn. | [---.- 98[11].10
n. | [---.ṯ]lḥn. | [---.--]t.ṯlḥn. | [---.]ṯlḥn. | [---.]ṯlḥn. | [---.--ṯ]lḥn. | [---.--ṯ]lḥn. | [---.--ṯ]lḥn. | [---.--ṯ]lḥn. | [---.--ṯ]lḥn. | [---.- 98[11].7
---.--ṯ]lḥn. | [---.]ṯlḥn. | [---.]ṯlḥn. | bn adty ṯlḥn.bn qrwl ṯlḥn. 98[11].36

ṯlḥny

y. | bn.ḥṣbn ary. | bn.ŝdy ary. | bn.ktkt.m‘qby. | bn.[---.]ṯlḥny. | b[n.---.ub]r‘y. | [bn.---.ubr]‘y. | b[n.---]. | bn[.---.ušk]ny 87[64].17
.---]. | yd.bt h.yd[.---]. | ary.yd.t[--.---]. | ḫtn h.šb‘l[.---]. | ṯlḥny.yd[.---]. | yd.ṯlṯ.kl[t h.---]. | w.ṯṯm.ṣi[n.---]. | tn[--]. | agyn 81[329].17
šlmn. | ṯlrb h. | art.ṯn.yrḫm. | ṯlrby.yrḫ.w.ḫm[š.ym]m. | ṯlḥny.yrḫ.w.ḫm[š.ymm]. | ẓrn.yrḫ.w.ḫmš.y[m]m. | mrat.ḫmš 66[109].5
| lbnm. | ḫlb.krd. | ṣ‘. | mlk. | gb‘ly. | ypr. | ary. | ẓrn. | art. | ṯlḥny. | ṯlrby. | dmt. | aǵt. | w.qmnz. | slḫ. | ykn‘m. | šlmy. | w.ull. 71[113].11

ṯlḫ

y.‘m lẓpn i | l ḏ.pid.hn b p y sp | r hn.b špt y mn | t hn ṯlḫ h w mlg h y | ṯtqt ‘m h b q‘t. | tq‘t ‘m prbḫṯ. | dmqt ṣǵrt kṯ 24[77].47

ṯlṭ

n‘ny. | gdn.bn.umy. | kn‘m.š‘rty. | abrpu.ubr‘y. | b.gt.bn.ṯlṭ. | ilḏ.b.gt.psḥn. 91[311].11
n.ṯt.qštm.w.ṯlṯ.ql‘m. | bn.ṣdqil.ṯt.qštm.w.ṯn.ql‘m. | bn.ṯlṭ.ṯ[lṯ.]qšt.w.ṯn.ql‘m. | qṣn.ṯt.qštm.w.ql‘. | bn.gṯrn.q[š]t. | bn. 119[321].3.5

ṯll

.d.sgrm. | w p[ṯḥ.---.]l.aḥd.adr. | [---.--]t.b[ḥd]r.mškb. | ṯl[l.---.--]ḥ. | b lṯk.bt. | [pt]ḥ.aḥd.l.bt.‘bdm. | [ṯ]n.ptḥ msb.bt.tu 1151.7

ṯlln

m. | bn.qṭn.qšt.w.ql‘. | mrṯd.qšt. | ssw.qšt. | knn.qšt. | bn.ṯlln.qšt. | bn.šyn.qšt. | ‘bd.qšt. | bn.ulmy.qšt. | ṯqbn.qšt. | bn.qn 119[316].4

ṯllt

n mn[-.---.--]n.nmr. | [--.]l ytk.bl[-.---.]m[--.]hwt. | [---].ṯllt.khn[m.---.]k p‘n. | [---.--]y.yd.nšy.[---.--]š.l mdb. | [---] h. UG5.8.47

ṯlǵḏy

arb‘.‘šr h.šmn. | d.lqḥt.ṯlǵḏy. | w.kd.ištir.‘m.qrt. | ‘št.‘šr h.šmn. | ‘mn.bn.aǵlmn. | arb‘ 1083.2

ṯlrb

qrht.d.tššlmn. | ṯlrb h. | art.ṯn.yrḫm. | ṯlrby.yrḫ.w.ḫm[š.ym]m. | ṯlḥny.yrḫ.w. 66[109].2

ṯlrby

ḫlb.krd. | ṣ‘. | mlk. | gb‘ly. | ypr. | ary. | ẓrn. | art. | ṯlḥny. | ṯlrby. | dmt. | aǵt. | w.qmnz. | slḫ. | ykn‘m. | šlmy. | w.ull. | ṯmry. 71[113].12
qrht.d.tššlmn. | ṯlrb h. | art.ṯn.yrḫm. | ṯlrby.yrḫ.w.ḫm[š.ym]m. | ṯlḥny.yrḫ.w.ḫm[š.ymm]. | ẓrn.yrḫ. 66[109].4
bd.[---]. | [--]yy.ṯṯ.krmm.šl[-.---]. | [---.]‘šrm.krm.[---]. | [ṯ]lrby.‘šr.ṯn.kb[d.---]. | ḫmrm.ṯṯ.krm[m.---]. | krm.ǵlkz.b.p[--. 1081.21
ag[--]. | ḫp[--]. | m‘q[b]. | ar[--]. | ẓr[n]. | ṯlḥ[n]. | ṯlr[by]. | qm[--]. | šl[--]. | a[---]. | d[---]. | q[---]. | ‘m[--]. | ar[--]. | y 2147.7
-]. | [-----]. | ykn‘m. | šlmy. | [-----]. | [-----]. | q[---]. | ṭ[---]. | ṯl[rby]. | ṯmr[y]. | aǵ[t]. | dm[t]. | šl[-]. | [---]m. | [-]rm. | [-]dm. | [2058.2.36

ṯlš

[---.ṯl]š.yn. | [---.a]rb‘.yn. | [---.arb]‘.yn. | [---].ṯmn.yn. | [---.-]ṯr.kd 1085.1

t̲lty

[---]y. | [---.]w.nḥl h. | bn ksln.t̲lt̲ḫ. | bn yṣmḫ.bn.t̲rn w nḥl h. | bn srd.bn agmn. | bn [-]ln.bn. 101[10].3

t̲lt̲

mit.ʿ[šr.---]. | [t̲]lt̲.abd[.---]. | [---.]anyt[.---]. | [-----]. | ʿšrm.l.umdym. | ʿšr.l.ktl 2110.2
.--]gbn. | [---.a]bṣdq. | [---.--]š. | [---.ṣ]dq. | tgmr. | yṣḥm. | t̲lt̲m. | aḥd. | kbd. | bnš.mlk. 1055.2.3
.šmn. | nḥ.t̲t̲.mat. | šm[n].rqḥ. | kkrm.brd̲l. | mit.tišrm. | t̲lt̲m.almg. | ḫmšm.kkr. | qnm. | ʿšrm.kk[r]. | brr. | [ʿ]šrm.npš. | ʿ 141[120].8
.[---]. | am[-]n.[---]. | w.a[t̲t̲] h.[---]. | ḫd̲mtn.t̲n[.---]. | w.t̲lt̲.alp h.[---]. | swn.qrty.w.[b]n h[.---]. | w.alp h.w.a[r]bʿ.l.arb 2044.5
z.ǵrn.arbʿ.mat. | tgmr.uz.aḫmn.arbʿ.mat. | arbʿm.kbd. | t̲lt̲.alp.ṣpr.dt.aḥd. | ḥrt̲ h.aḥd.b gt.nḥl. | aḥd.b gt.knpy.w.aḥd. 1129.8
| [at̲]t.b.bt.t̲pt̲bʿl. | [---.]n[--.md]rǵlm. | [---.]b.bt[.---]l. | [t̲]lt̲.at̲t.adrt.w.t̲lt̲.ǵzr[m]. | w.ḫmš.nʿrt.b.bt.sk[n]. | t̲t.at̲tm.adr 80[119].16
[---.]qrt. | [---].at̲t. | [---.]w arbʿ.nʿr[m]. | [---.a]ḥd. | [---.]t̲lt̲.at̲t. 2142.6
[--.]wmrkm. | bir.ḫmš. | uškn.arbʿ. | ubrʿy.t̲lt̲. | ar.t̲mn ʿšr h. | mlk.arbʿ. | ǵbl.ḫmš. | atlg.ḫmš ʿšr[h]. | ulm 68[65].1.4
alp[.---]. | mat[.---]. | ḫrṣ[.---]. | t̲lt̲.k[---]. | t̲lt̲.a[--.---]. | ḫmš[.---]. | ksp[.---]. | k[--.---]. | ar[bʿ.---]. | t̲mn[.--- 148[96].5
]. | nšrm.trḫp.ʿnt.ʿl[.aqht]. | tʿdbn h.hlmn.t̲nm[.qdqd]. | t̲lt̲ id.ʿl.udn.š[pk.km]. | šiy.dm h.km.šḫ[t̲.l brk h]. | yṣat.km.r 18[3AQHT].4.34
.bn.nšrm.arḫp.an[k.ʿ]l. | aqht.ʿdb k.hlmn.t̲nm.qdqd. | t̲lt̲ id.ʿl.udn.špk.km.šiy. | dm.km.šḥt̲.l brk h.tṣi.km. | rḥ.npš h 18[3AQHT].4.23
lmm b dd y.yṣ[--]. | [-.]yṣa.w l.yṣa.hlm.[t̲nm]. | [q]dqd.t̲lt̲ id.ʿl.ud[n]. | [---.-]sr.pdm.riš h[m.---]. | ʿl.pd.asr.[---.]l[.---]. 19[1AQHT].2.79
skn.t̲lt̲m. | iytlm.t̲lt̲m. | ḫyml.t̲lt̲m. | ǵlkz.t̲lt̲m. | mlknʿm.ʿšrm. | mrʿ 1116.1
b t̲lt̲. | ilmlk.ʿšr.ṣin. | mlknʿm.ʿšr. | bn.adty.ʿšr. | [ṣ]dqšlm ḫmš. | k 2039.1
l.t̲n.ḫpn[.---]. | [---].aḥd.ḫmš.am[--.---]. | [---.--]m.qmṣ.t̲lt̲m.i[qnu.---]. | [b.yr]ḫ.mgmr.mš[--.---]. | [---].iqnu.ḫmš[.---]. 1106.37
slm. | [---].pwt.t̲lt̲.mat.abn.ṣrp. | [---.-]qt.l.t̲rmnm. | [---].t̲lt̲m.iqnu. | [---.l.]t̲rmn.mlk. | [---.]šʿrt.šbʿ.ʿšr h. | [---.iqn]i.l.t̲r 1106.12
ubdym.l mlkt.b.ʿnmky[.---]. | mgdly.ǵlptr.t̲n.krmm.w.t̲lt̲.ub[dym.---]. | qmnz.t̲t̲.krm.yknʿm.t̲mn.krm[.---]. | krm.nʿ 1081.10
.ḫmšt. | kbd.ksp. | kkrm.šʿrt.štt.b d.gg[ʿt]. | b.ʿšrt.ksp. | t̲lt̲.uṭbm.b d.alḫn.b.ʿšrt[.k]sp. | rt̲.l.ql.d.ybl.prd. | b.t̲ql.w.nṣp. 2101.11
t. | b.bn.pdrn.ʿšrm. | d.bn.šbʿl.uḫnpy.ḫmšm. | b.bn.t̲tm.t̲lt̲m. | b.bn.agdt̲b.ʿšrm. | b.bn.ibn.arbʿt.ʿšrt. | b.bn.mnn.t̲t̲m. | 2054.1.11
rm. | b.gdn.bn.uss.ʿšrm. | b.ʿdn.bn.t̲t̲.ʿšrt. | b.bn.qrdmn.t̲lt̲m. | b.bṣmn[.bn].ḥrtn.ʿ[--]. | b.t[--.---] h.[---]. | [-----]. | [--]ly. 2054.1.20
tšʿ.ṣmdm. | t̲lt̲m.b d. | ibrtlm. | w.pat.aḥt. | in.b hm. 1141.2
spr.irgmn. | t̲lt̲.ḫmš.alpm. | b d.brq.maḫdy. | kkr.t̲lt̲. | b d.bn.by.ar[y]. | alpm.t̲lt̲. | b d.šim.il[š]tmʿy. 1134.4
lpm. | b d.brq.maḫdy. | kkr.t̲lt̲. | b d.bn.by.ar[y]. | alpm.t̲lt̲. | b d.šim.il[š]tmʿy. 1134.6
mn.kbd. | tgmr.bnš.mlk. | d.b d.adnʿm. | [š]bʿ.b.ḥrt̲m. | [t̲]lt̲.b.t̲ǵrm. | rb qrt.aḥd. | t̲mn.ḫzr. | w.arbʿ.ḥršm. | dt.tbʿln.b.p 1024.3.2
| krm.nʿmn.b.ḫly.ull.krm.aḫ[d.---]. | krm.uḫn.b.šdmy.t̲lt̲.bzl[.d]prn[.---]. | aupt̲.krm.aḥd.nšpin.kr[m.]aḥd[.---]. | dm 1081.13
y.lḥm.w dqn[.t̲tlt̲]. | qn.d̲rʿ h.t̲ḥrt̲.km.gn. | ap lb.k ʿmq.t̲t̲lt̲.bmt. | bʿl.mt.my.lim.bn dgn. | my.hmlt.at̲r.bʿl.nrd. | b arṣ. 6[62].1.5
hdy.lḥm.w dqn. | yt̲lt̲.qn.d̲rʿ h.yḥrt̲. | k gn.ap lb.k ʿmq.yt̲lt̲. | bmt.yšu.g h.w yṣḥ. | bʿl.mt.my.lim.bn. | dgn.my.hmlt.at̲ 5[67].6.21
ḫmš.t̲nnm.ʿšr.ḫsnm. | t̲lt̲.ʿšr.mrynm. | ḫmš.[tr]tnm. | t̲lt̲.b[n.]mrynm. | ʿšr[.m]krm. | tšʿ.hbt̲nm. | ʿšr.mrum. | šbʿ.ḫsn 1028.4
r.mrum. | w.šbʿ.ḫsnm. | tšʿ.ʿšr. | mrynm. | t̲lt̲.ʿšr.mkrm. | t̲lt̲.bn.mrynm. | arbʿ.t̲rtnm. | tšʿ.ḫbt̲nm. | t̲mnym.t̲lt̲.kbd. | md̲r 1029.8
].mṣrn. | [a]ršwn. | ʿb[d]. | w nḥl h. | atn.bn.ap[s]n. | nsk.t̲lt̲. | bn.[--.]m[-]ḫr. | bn.šmrm. | t̲nnm. | [ar]swn.bn.qqln. | m[-- 85[80].3.8
mḫsrn.d.[--.]uškny m. | brq.t̲lt̲.[mat.t̲]lt̲. | bsn.mi[t.--]. | ar[--.---]. | k[--.---]. 1136.2
. | yrḫm.yd.t̲n.bn h. | bʿlm.w.t̲lt̲.nʿrm.w.bt.aḥt. | bn.lwn.t̲lt̲tm.bʿlm. | bn.bʿly.t̲lt̲tm.bʿlm. | w.aḥd.ḫbt̲. | w.arbʿ.at̲t. | bn.l 2080.6
bn.bʿln.biry. | t̲lt̲.bʿlm. | w.adn hm.t̲r.w.arbʿ.bnt h. | yrḫm.yd.t̲n.bn h. | bʿlm. 2080.2
bʿlm.w.t̲lt̲.nʿrm.w.bt.aḥt. | bn.lwn.t̲lt̲tm.bʿlm. | bn.bʿly.t̲lt̲tm.bʿlm. | w.aḥd.ḫbt̲. | w.arbʿ.at̲t. | bn.lg.t̲n.bn h. | bʿlm.w.a 2080.7
an[y]t.mlk[.---]. | w.[t̲]lt̲.brm.[---]. | arbʿ ʿtkm[.---]. 2057.2
bmlk. | kdm.ǵbiš ḫry. | ḫmš yn.b d. | bḥ mlkt. | b mdrʿ. | t̲lt̲ bt.il | ann. | kd.bt.ilann. 1090.17
krm. | yṣḥm. | šrm. | nʿrm. | ʿbdm. | kzym. | ksdm. | [nsk].t̲lt̲. | gt.mlkym. | tmrym. | t̲nqym. | t̲ǵrm. | mru.skn. | mru.ibrn. 1026.2.1
d.t̲nm kbd. | [---.-]nnm t̲rm. | [---.]t̲lt̲ kbd.ṣin. | [---.--]a.t̲[l]t̲.d.a[--]. | [---].mrn. | [---.]bn pnt̲bl. | [---.-]py w.bn h. 1145.1.10
at.kbd.t̲lt̲.šm[n]. | alp.mitm.kbd.t̲lt̲.ḥlb. | šbʿ.l.ʿšrm.kkr.t̲lt̲. | d.ybl.blym. 1135.6
t̲lt̲.d yṣa. | b d.šmmn. | l argmn. | l nskm. | t̲mn.kkrm. | alp.kbd 147[90].1
[---.]t̲lt̲m.d.nlqḥt. | [bn.ḫ]tyn.yd.bt h. | [aǵ]ltn. | tdn.bn.ddy. | ʿbdil[2045.1
b yrḫ.mgm[r.---]. | yṣu.ḫlpn[.---]. | t̲lt̲.dt.p[--.---]. | dt.tgmi.[---]. | b d [---]t.[---]. 1159.3
pr.ḥpr.bt.k[--]. | tšʿ.ʿšr h.dd.l.b[t.--]. | ḫmš.ddm.l.ḫtyt. | t̲lt̲m.dd.kšmn.l.gzzm. | yyn. | ṣdqn. | ʿbd.pdr. | myṣm. | t̲gt. | w.l 1099.4
[---.]ksp dd qmḥ. | [---.]t̲lt̲ dd ksmm. | [---.-]rbr dd šʿrm. | [---.]r[--.]ḫtm. | kr[--.]tp[n]. 2037.1.2
t̲t̲m.t̲lt̲.kb[d]. | arbʿm.t̲p[rt]. | ksp h. | t̲mn.dd[.--]. | t̲lt̲.dd.p[--]. | šbʿt.p[--]. | tšʿt.k[bd.---]. | ḫmšt.k[bd.---]. | tgmr k 2120.5
ʿ. | kbd.ḥpr.bnšm. | b.gt.t̲rmn.arbʿm.drʿ.w.ʿšrm.drt. | w.t̲lt̲m.dd.t̲t̲.kbd.ḥpr.bnšm. | b.gt.ḥdt̲t.arbʿm.drʿ.w.t̲lt̲m.drt. | [1098.21
.l.mit.dd.ḥpr.bnšm. | b.yʿny.arbʿm.drʿ.w.ʿšrm.drt. | w.t̲lt̲m.dd.t̲t̲.kbd.ḥpr.bnšm. | b.ʿnmky.ʿšrm.drʿ[.---.d]rt. | w.t̲n.ʿš 1098.27
t̲lt̲m.dd[.---]. | b.gt.ṣb[-.---]. | mit.ʿšr.[---.]dd[.--]. | tšʿ.dd.ḥ[t̲m. 2092.1
rm.drʿ[.---.d]rt. | w.t̲n.ʿšr h.dd.[---]. | iwrd̲n.ḥ[--.---]. | w.t̲lt̲m.dd.[---.]n[---.---]. | w.a[r]bʿ[.---].bnš[.š]dyn[.---]. | agr.[---. 1098.31
t. | w.t̲lt̲m.dd.t̲t̲.kbd.ḥpr.bnšm. | b.gt.ḥdt̲t.arbʿm.drʿ.w.t̲lt̲m.drt. | [w].šbʿm.dd.t̲n.kbd.ḥpr.bnšm. | b.nzl.ʿšrm.l.mit.drʿ 1098.22
.zbl. | [--.kt̲]r w ḫss. | [---]n.rḥm y.ršp zbl. | [w ʿd]t.ilm.t̲lt̲ h. | [ap]nk.krt.t̲ʿ.ʿ[-]r. | [--.]b bt h.yšt.ʿrb. | [--] h.ytn.w [--]u 15[128].2.7
m.ḥry.bt y. | iqḥ.ašʿrb.ǵlmt. | ḥzr y.t̲n h.wspm. | atn.w t̲lt̲ h.ḫrṣm. | ylk ym.w t̲n. | t̲lt̲.rbʿ.ym. | aḫr.špšm.b rbʿ. | ymǵy. 14[KRT].4.206
w y[---]. | bʿd[.---]. | yatr[.---]. | b d k.[---]. | t̲nnt h[.---]. | t̲lt̲t h[.-.w yʿn]. | ltpn.[il.d pid.my]. | b ilm.[ydy.mrṣ]. | gršm.z 16[126].5.9
l bt[.---]. | b[ʿ]l.ugr[t.---]. | w ʿṣrm[.---]. | ṣlyh šr[-.---]. | [t̲]lt̲m.w b[--.---]. | l il limm[.---]. | w t̲t.npš[.---]. | kbd.w [---]. | l 40[134].7
ḫnqtm.d[q]tm. | [yr]ḫ.kty gdlt.w l ǵlmt š. | [w]pamt t̲lt̲m.w yrdt.[m]dbḥt. | gdlt.l bʿlt bhtm.ʿṣrm. | l inš ilm. 34[1].20
gdlt]. | w burm.l[b.rmṣt.ilhm]. | bʿlm.w mlu[.---.ksm]. | t̲lt̲m.w mʿrb[.---]. | dbḥ šmn mr[.šmn.rqḥ.bt]. | mtnt.w ynt.[q APP.II[173].21
l ʿšrm. | [--.-]n.w.aḫt h.arbʿm. | [--.-]dn.ʿšrm. | [--.-]dwn.t̲lt̲m.w.šbʿ.alpm. | [kt̲]rmlk.ʿšrm. | [--]ny.ʿšrt.trbyt. | [--.]ʿbd.t̲lt̲ 2054.2.23
dt.b.ʿšrt. | ḫmš.kkrm.ṣml. | ʿšrt.ksp h. | ḫmš.kkr.qnm. | t̲lt̲t.w.t̲lt̲t.ksp h. | arbʿ.kkr. | algbt̲.arbʿt. | ksp h. | kkr.šʿrt. | šbʿt 1127.13
š.kkr.brr. | kkr.ḫmš.mat.kbd.t̲lt̲.šm[n]. | alp.mitm.kbd.t̲lt̲.ḥlb. | šbʿ.l.ʿšrm.kkr.t̲lt̲. | d.ybl.blym. 1135.5

skn.ṯlṯm.|iytlm.ṯlṯm.|ḫyml.ṯlṯm.|ǵlkz.ṯlṯm.|mlkn'm.'šrm.|mr'm.'šrm.|'ml 1116.2
--].ṯn.|hz[p].ṯṯ.|ḫrṣb'.aḥd.|ypr.arb.|m[-]qb.'šr.|ṯn'y.ṯlṯ.|ḫlb 'prm.ṯn.|tmḏy.ṯlṯ.|[--]rt.arb'.|[---].'šr. 70[112].11
spr.irgmn.|ṯlṯ.ḫmš.alpm.|b d.brq.maḫdy.|kkr.ṯlṯ.|b d.bn.by.ar[y].|alp 1134.2
.pḥm.|ḫmš.mat.kbd.|arb'.alpm.iqni.|ḫmš.mat.kbd.|ṯlṯm.ḫmš kbd ktn.|ḫmš.rṯm.|ḫmš.ṯnt.d ḫmšm w.|ḫmš.ṯnt. 1130.7
b.atlg.ṯlṯ.ḫrmṯt.ṯṯm.|mḫrhn.nit.mit.krk.mit.|m'ṣd.ḫmšm.mqb.[']š 2048.1
.---.]pd[ry].|[-----].|[---.b]'lt.|lbnm.'šr.yn.|ḫlb.gngnt.ṯlṯ.y[n].|bṣr.'šr.yn.|nnu arb'.yn.|šql ṯlṯ.yn.|šmny.kdm.yn.| 2004.22
.ṯt.mqrtm.|w.ṯn.irpm.w.ṯn.trqm.|w.qpt.w.mqḥm.|w.ṯlṯm.yn šb'.kbd d ṯbṯ.|w.ḫmšm.yn.d iḫ h. 1103.22
r.yn.|ḫlb.gngnt.ṯlṯ.y[n].|bṣr.'šr.yn.|nnu arb'.yn.|šql ṯlṯ.yn.|šmny.kdm.yn.|šmgy.kd.yn.|hzp.tš'.yn.|[b]ir.'šr[.--- 2004.25
n.yrḫ.k m[rṣ.---].|mn.k dw.kr[t].|w y'ny.ǵzr[.ilḥu].|ṯlṯ.yrḫm.k m[rṣ].|arb'.k dw.k[rt].|mnd'.krt.mǵ[y.---].|w qb 16.2[125].84
akl.|yḥmn.ṯlṯ.šmn.|a[---.]kdm.|'[---]'m.kd.|a[----]ḫr.ṯlṯ.|y[---.bn.]kran.ḫmš.|'[---].kd.|amry.kdm.|mnn.bn.gṯtn. 136[84].5
bd.mḏrǵlm.|'šrm.aḥd.kbd.ḫsnm.|ubnyn.|ṯṯm[.l.]mit.ṯlṯ.|kbd[.tg]mr.bnš.|l.b.bt.mlk. 1028.12
|[dd].ḥṭm.w.ḫ[mšm].|[ṯ]lṯ kbd.yn.b [gt.---].|mit.[---].ṯlṯ.kb[d].|[dd.--]m.šb'.[---].|[---].'šr.dd[.---].|[---]mn.arb'm. 2092.11
.l.nskm.birtym.|b d.urtn.w.ṯṯ.mat.brr.|b.ṯmnym.ksp.ṯlṯt.kbd.|ḫmš.alp.ṯlṯ.l.ḫlby.|b d.tlmi.b.'šrm.ḫmšt.|kbd.ksp. 2101.5
.kšmm.tš'[.---].|[š]'rm.ṯṯ.'[šr].|[dd].ḥṭm.w.ḫ[mšm].|[ṯ]lṯ kbd.yn.b [gt.---].|mit.[---].ṯlṯ.kb[d].|[dd.--]m.šb'.[---].|[- 2092.10
[---.-]kn.|[---.]ṯlṯm.|kuwṯ.ṯlṯ.kbd.|m[i]t.arb't.kbd.|ḫ[mš.]š'rt.|[---.]tš'.kbd.skm.|[arb] 1111.3
krm.|ṯlṯ.bn.mrynm.|arb'.ṯrtnm.|tš'.ḫbṯnm.|ṯmnym.ṯlṯ.kbd.|mḏrǵlm.|w.šb'.'šr.ḫsnm.|ḫmšm.l.mit.|bnš.l.d.|yš 1029.11
š'.kbd.skm.|[arb]'m.ḫpnt.pṯt.|[-]r.pldm.dt.š'rt.|ṯlṯm.ṯlṯ.kbd.mṣrrt.|'šr.ṯn.kbd.pǵdrm.|ṯmn.mrbdt.mlk.|'šr.pld.š' 1111.9
---].alp.|[---.-]rbd.kbd.ṯnm kbd.|[---.-]nnm ṯrm.|[---.]ṯlṯ kbd.ṣin.|[---.--]a.ṯ[l]ṯ.d.a[--].|[---].mrn.|[---.]bn pnṯbl.|[- 1145.1.9
rm.|ṣṣ bn adty ḫmšm.|ṣṣ amtrn arb'm.|ṣṣ iytlm mit ṯlṯm kbd.|ṣṣ m[l]k 'šrm.|ṣṣ abš[-] mit ['š]r kbd.|ṣṣ yḏrd 'šr 2097.9
ṯṯm.ṯlṯ.kb[d].|arb'm.ṯp[rt].|ksp h.|ṯmn.dd[.--].|ṯlṯ.dd.p[--].|šb' 2120.1
ṯṯ.mat.ṯṯm.kbd šmn.|l.abrm.alṯyy.|[m]it.ṯlṯm.kbd.šmn.|[l.]abrm.mšrm.|[mi]tm.arb'm.ṯmn.kbd.|[l.] 2095.3
ṯlṯ.mat.ṯlṯm.|kbd.šmn.|l kny.|ṯmnym.šmn.|b d.adnn'm. 1094.1
[---].dt.iṯ.|[---].ṯlṯ.kbd.|[---].alpm.ḫmš.mat.|šb'm[.t]š'.kbd.|tgmr.uz.ǵrn.ar 1129.2
[-] ym.pr' d nkly yn kd w kd.|w 'l ym kdm.|w b ṯlṯ.kd yn w krsnm.|w b rb' kdm yn.|w b ḫmš kd yn. 1086.3
[---.-]kn.|[---.]ṯlṯm.|kuwṯ.ṯlṯ.kbd.|m[i]t.arb't.kbd.|ḫ[mš.]š'rt.|[---.]tš'.kbd 1111.2
ḫrṣ.ṯqlm.kbd.'šrt.mzn h.|b [ar]b'm.ksp.|b d[.'b]dym.ṯlṯ.kkr š'rt.|iqn[i]m.ṯṯt.'šrt.ksp h.|ḫmšt.ḫrṣ.bt.il.|b.ḫmšt.'šr 2100.3
[--.]spr.lm.likt.|[--]y.k išal hm.|[--.'š]rm.kkr.ṯlṯ.|[--.]ṯlṯm.kkr.ṯlṯ.|[--.]aštn.l k.|[--]y.kl.dbrm.hm[.--].|[--]l.w.kl.m 1022.5
rbt.|hlk.l alpm.ḫḏd.|w l.rbt.kmyr.|aṯr.ṯn.ṯn.hlk.|aṯr.ṯlṯ.kl hm.|aḥd.bt h.ysgr.|almnt.škr.|tškr.zbl.'ršm.|yšu.'wr. 14[KRT].4.183
g.|hlk.l alpm.ḫḏd.|w l rbt.kmyr.|[a]ṯr.ṯn.ṯn.hlk.|aṯr.ṯlṯ.kl hm.|yḥd.bt h.sgr.|almnt.škr.|tškr.zbl.'ršm.|yšu.'wr. 14[KRT].2.95
mḏrǵlm.d.b.i[-]'lt.mlk.|arsw.|dqn.|ṯlṯ.klbm.|ḫmn.|[---.-]rsd.|bn[.-]pṯ.|bn kdrn.|awldn.|arsw 86[305].4
--].|ary.yd.ṯ[--.---].|ḫtn h.šb'l[.---].|ṯlḥny.yd[.---].|yd.ṯlṯ.kl[t h.---].|w.ṯṯm.ṣi[n.---].|ṯn[--].|agyn.[---].|[w].ṯn.[---]. 81[329].18
'l.|w aṯt k.ngrt.il[ht].|'l.l ṯkm.bnw n.|l nḫnpt.mšpy.|ṯlṯ.kmm.ṯrr y.|[---.]l ǵr.gm.ṣḥ.|[---.]r[-]m. 16[126].4.16
s[p].|[---].ḏmrd.bn.ḫrmn.|[---.-]ǵn.ksp.ṯṯt.|[---.]ygry.ṯlṯm.ksp.b[--]. 2153.12
.šd ubdy.|[---.šd] u[b]dy.|[---.]šd.ubdy.|[---.]bn.k[--.]ṯ[l]ṯm ksp b[---].|[---.]šd b'ly.|[---.]šd ubdy.|[---.š]d ubdy.|[2031.6
].ṣdqn.|w.kkrm.ṯlṯ.|mit.ksp.'mn.|bn.ulbtyn.|w.kkr.ṯlṯ.|ksp.d.nkly.b.šd.|mit.ḫmšt.kbd.|[l.]gmn.bn.usyy.|mit.ṯṯ 1143.5
šrt.|ḫmš.kkrm.ṣml.|'šrt.ksp h.|ḫmš.kkr.qnm.|ṯlṯt.w.ṯlṯt.ksp h.|arb'.kkr.|algbṯ.arb't.|ksp h.|kkr.š'rt.|šb't.ksp h 1127.13
[ṯl]ṯm.ksp.'[l].|[b]n.bly.gb'ly.|[šp]ḥ.a[n]nṯb.|w.m[--.u]škny. 2055.1
[.---].|ḫmš 'š[r].|kkr.ṯ[lṯ].|ṯt hrt[m].|ṯn mq[pm].|ulṯ.ṯl[ṯ].|krk.kly[.--].|ḫmš.mr[kbt].|ṯṯ [-]az[-].|'šṯ[--.---].|irg[m 2056.7
aḫ[d.---].|krm.ubdy.b d.ǵ[--.---].|krm.pyn.arty[.---].|ṯlṯ.krm.ubdym.l mlkt.b.'nmky[.---].|mgdly.ǵlpṯr.ṯn.krmm. 1081.9
'šrt.ksp.|šb'm.lbš.d.'rb.bt.mlk.|b.mit.ḫmšt.kbd.ksp.|ṯlṯ.ktnt.b d.an[r]my.|b.'šrt.ksp.b.a[--].|ṯqlm.ḫr[ṣ.]b.ṯmnt.ks 2101.18
alpm.pḥm.ḫm[š].mat.kbd.|b d.tt.w.ṯlṯ.ktnt.b dm.tt.|w.ṯmnt.ksp.hn.|ktn.d.ṣr.pḥm.b h.w.ṯqlm.| 1110.2
ṯlṯm.ktn.|ḫmšm.izml.|ḫmš.kbd.arb'm.|dd.akl.|ṯṯ.'šr h.yn. 1126.1
ḫmš.ṯnt.d mit.|ḫmš.ṯnt.d ṯl|ṯ mat.|ṯt.ṯnt.d alp|alpm.ṯlṯ ktt.|alp.brr.|kkr.tznt.|ḫmšt.kkr tyt. 1130.14
n ubr'.|skn ḫršb'.|rb.ntbtš.|[---].'bd.r[--].|arb'.k[--].|ṯlṯ.ktt. 1033.9
[m.---].|[---].mit.ḫsw.[---].|[----]d.n'r.ṯ[--]d[.---].|[---.]ṯlṯ.kṯt[.-]d.[---].|[---.a]rb'.dblt.m[--.---].|[--.mi]tm nṣ.[-]ṯ[-.]g 143[-].1.4
h.l ypq.|mtrḫt.yšr h.|aṯt.trḫ.w tb't.|ṯar um.tkn l h.|mṯlṯt.kṯrm.tmt.|mrb't.zblnm.|mḫmšt.yitsp.|ršp.nṯdṯt.ǵlm. 14[KRT].1.16
.š[--].l[--.]'rb.šp|š.w ḥl[.ml]k.|bn.aup[š.--].bsbn hzpḫ ṯlṯt.|kṯr[.---.--]trt ḫmšt.bn gda[.-.]mḏ'.|kl[--.---.]ṯmnt.[--.]w APP.II[173].58
alp[.---].|mat[.---].|ḫrṣ[.---].|ṯlṯ.k[---].|ṯlṯ.a[--.---].|ḫmš[.---].|ksp[.---].|k[--.---].|ar[b'.---] 148[96].4
šb'.yn.l [---].|ṯlṯ.l ḥr[š.---].|ṯṯ[.l.]mšṯt[.---].|ṯlṯ.l.mḏr[ǵlm].|kd[.--].lm[d.-- 1091.2
d.urtn.w.ṯṯ.mat.brr.|b.ṯmnym.ksp.ṯlṯt.kbd.|ḫmš.alp.ṯlṯ.l.ḫlby.|b d.tlmi.b.'šrm.ḫmšt.|kbd.ksp.|kkrm.š'rt.šṯt.b d. 2101.6
ḫpn.d.iqni.w.šmt.|l.iyb'l.|ṯlṯm.l.mit.š'rt.|l.šr.'ṯrt.|mlbš.ṯrmnm.|k.yṯn.w.b.bt.|mlk.m 1107.3
yt.|[---.a]drt.|[--.ṯṯ]m.ṯmn.k[bd].|[---.yr]yt.dq[-].|[--.ṯ]lṯm.l.mi[t].|[---.]arb'.kbd. 2170.5
šb'.yn.l [---].|ṯlṯ.l ḥr[š.---].|ṯṯ[.l.]mšṯt[.---].|ṯlṯ.l.mḏr[ǵlm].|kd[.--].lm[d.---].|kd[.l.]ḫzr[m.---].|kd[.l.]ṯrt 1091.4
spr.ḥṯbn.sbrdnm.|ḫmš.kkrm.alp kb[d].|ṯlṯ.l.nskm.birtym.|b d.urtn.w.ṯṯ.mat.brr.|b.ṯmnym.ksp.ṯlṯt. 2101.3
[.--.]škn.ḫpn.|l.k[-]w.ḫpn.|l.ṣ[--].š'[rt].|l.'dy.š[']r[t].|ṯlṯ.l.'d.ab[ǵ]l.|l.ydln.š'rt.|l.kṯrmlk.ḫpn.|l.'bdil[m].ḫpn.|tm 1117.7
.|w.ṯn.'šr h.ḫpnt.|[s]šwm.amtm.'kyt.|yd.llḫ hm.|w.ṯlṯ.l.'šrm.|ḫpnt.sšwm.ṯn.|pddm.w.d.ṯṯ.|[mr]kbt.w.ḥrṣ. 2049.6
ybnn.|arb'm.l.mit.šmn.|arb'm.l.mit.tišr.|ṯṯ.ṯṯ.b [ṯ]ql.ṯlṯt.l.'šrm.ksp hm.|sstm.b.šb'm.|ṯlṯ.mat.trm.b.'šrt.|mit.adr 1127.5
[---.]'ṯ[rt.---].|[-.k]su.ilt[.---].|[ṯl]ṯ.l 'ṯrt[.---].|[--.]l ilt.š l 'ṯt[rt.---].|[']ṣr.l pdr ṯṯ.ṣ[in.---].|tš 38[23].3
]dt ḫnd[r]ṯ ar' s[p]m w 'š[r].|[---.]ḫndrṯm ṯt spm [w] ṯlṯm l[ḥm].|[---.]ar' spm w [---].|[---]š[.---.--]b[.---].|[--.]sp[134[-].6
.b d.s[n]rn.|lmd.aḥd.b d.yr[š].|lmd.aḥd.b d.yḫ[--].|ṯlṯ.lmdm.b d.nḫ[--].|lmd.aḥd.b d.ar[--].|ṯlṯ.lmdm.b d.[---].| 1050.6
.b d.yḫ[--].|ṯlṯ.lmdm.b d.nḫ[--].|lmd.aḥd.b d.ar[--].|ṯlṯ.lmdm.b d.[---].|ṯlṯ.lmdm.b d.[---]. 1050.8
m.b d.nḫ[--].|lmd.aḥd.b d.ar[--].|ṯlṯ.lmdm.b d.[---].|ṯlṯ.lmdm.b d.[---]. 1050.9
t.|[---.š]pšg.iqni.mit.pṯtm.|[---].mitm.kslm.|[---].pwt.ṯlṯ.mat.abn.ṣrp.|[---.-]qt.l.ṯrmnm.|[---].ṯlṯm.iqnu.|[---.l.]ṯr 1106.10

aš[ʿ]t.šmn.uz. | mi[t].ygb.bqʿ. | a[--].ʿṭ. | a[l]pm.alpnm. | ṯlṯ.m[a]t.art.ḥkpt. | mit.dnn. | mitm.iqnu. | ḫmš.ʿšr.qn.nʿm.ʿn[1128.26
nʿr. | ḫmšm.tišr. | ḫmš.ktnt. | ḫmš.ṯnt.alpm. | ʿšrm.hbn. | ṯlṯ.mat.dd. | šʿrm. | mit.šmn. | ʿšr.kat. | ẓrw. 2102.7
šm [-]t ṯlṯ ty[--]. | bn.grgš. | w.npṣ bt ṯn.ṯlṯ mat. | w spl ṯlṯ.mat. | w mmskn. | w.ṯt.mqrtm. | w.ṯn.irpm.w.ṯn.trqm. | w.q 1103.17
šq krsnm. | ḫmšm [-]t ṯlṯ ty[--]. | bn.grgš. | w.npṣ bt ṯn.ṯlṯ mat. | w spl ṯlṯ.mat. | w mmskn. | w.ṯt.mqrtm. | w.ṯn.irpm. 1103.16
šḫ[.---]. | ʿšr.d[d.---]. | ṯtm.dd.dd[.---]. | l.mdrǵlm[.---]. | ṯlṯ.mat.ḫmšm.kb[d]. | ḫmš.kbd.l.mdʿ. | b yr[ḫ.iṯtb]nm. | ṯlṯ[.m 2012.11
-]. | w blḫ br[-]m p[-]. | b[--.]l[-.]mat[.-]y. | ḫmšm[.--]i. | ṯlṯ m[at] ḫswn. | ṯlṯ ṯ[-].ṯt ḥ[--]. 140[98].9
spr.argmnm. | ʿšrm.ksp.d mkr. | mlk. | ṯlṯ.mat.ksp.d.šb[n]. | mit.ksp.d.ṭbq. | ṯmnym.arbʿt. | kbd.ksp. | 2107.4
| šbʿm.drt.arbʿm.drt. | l.a[--.---]. | tgm[r.ak]l.b.gt.ḫldy. | ṯlṯ.ma[t].ʿšr.kbd. | šbʿ m[at].kbd.ḥpr.ʿbdm. | mit[.d]rt.arbʿm. 2013.11
m. | mit[.d]rt.arbʿm.drt. | [---]m. | t[gm]r.akl.b.gt.ǵ[l]. | ṯlṯ.mat.ʿšrm[.---]. | ṯmnym.drt.a[--]. | drt.l.alpm[.---]. | šbʿm.ṯn 2013.16
w.b.bt. | mlk.mlbš. | ytn.l hm. | šbʿ.lbšm.allm. | l ušḫry. | ṯlṯ.mat.pṯtm. | l.mgmr.b.ṯlṯ. | šnt. 1107.11
[yṣi.ṣbu]. | ṣbi.ng[b.w yṣi.ʿdn]. | mʿ[.ṣ]bu h.u[l.mad]. | ṯlṯ.mat.rbt. | hlk.l alpm.ḫdd. | w l.rbt.kmyr. | aṯr.ṯn.ṯn.hlk. | aṯ 14[KRT].4.179
ngb.w yṣi. | ṣbu.ṣbi.ngb. | w yṣi.ʿdn.mʿ. | ṣbu k.ul.mad. | ṯlṯ.mat.rbt. | ḫpṯ.d bl.spr. | ṯnn.d bl.hg. | hlk.l alpm.ḫdd. | w l 14[KRT].2.89
lṯ.mat.ḫmšm.kb[d]. | ḫmš.kbd.l.mdʿ. | b yr[ḫ.iṯtb]nm. | ṯlṯ[.mat.a]rbʿ.kbd. | w.[---.-]mʿt. | ṯlṯ[m.---.-]rm. | ʿšr[.---].alpm 2012.14
ṯlṯ.mat. | šbʿm kbd. | zt.ubdym. | b mlk. 1095.1
[---.]ṯlṯm. | [---.n]ḥl. | [---.ṯ]lṯ.mat.šbʿm[.---]. | [---.--]mm.b.mṣbt[.---]. | [---.ṯl]ṯ.mat.ṯmn 2149.3
mit.tišr. | ṯt.ṯt.b [ṯ]ql.ṯlṯt.l.ʿšrm.ksp hm. | šstm.b.šbʿm. | ṯlṯ.mat.trm.b.ʿšrt. | mit.adrm.b.ʿšrt. | ʿšr.ydt.b.ʿšrt. | ḫmš.kkr 1127.7
]r.ʿbdm. | mitm.drt.ṯmnym.drt. | tgmr.akl.b.gt[.b]ʿln. | ṯlṯ.mat.ṯtm.kbd. | ṯtm.ṯt.kbd.ḥpr.ʿbdm. | šbʿm.drt.arbʿm.drt. | 2013.6
mḫsrn.d.[--.]uškny. | brq.ṯlṯ.[mat.ṯ]lṯ. | bsn.mi[t.--]. | ar[--.---]. | k[--.---]. 1136.2
ṯlṯ.mat.ṯlṯm. | kbd.šmn. | l kny. | ṯmnym.šmn. | b d.adnʿm. 1094.1
l. | [---.ṯ]lṯ.mat.šbʿm[.---]. | [---.--]mm.b.mṣbt[.---]. | [---.ṯl]ṯ.mat.ṯmny[m.---]. 2149.5
.rṯm. | ḫmš.ṯnt.d ḫmšm w. | ḫmš.ṯnt.d mit. | ḫmš.ṯnt.d ṯl | ṯ mat. | ṯt.ṯnt.d alp | alpm.ṯlṯ ktt. | alp.brr. | kkr.tznt. | ḫmšt. 1130.11
ṯlṯ.mat[.---.]kbd. | ṯt.ddm.k[--.b]rqd. | mit.tšʿm.[kb]d.ddm. | 2168.1
--]. | ṯn.skm.šbʿ.mšlt.arbʿ.ḫpnt.[---]. | ḫmšm.ṯlṯ.rkb.ntn.ṯlṯ.mat.[---]. | lg.šmn.rqḥ.šrʿm.ušpǵtm.p[--.---]. | kṯ.ẓrw.kṯ.nb UG5.9.1.20
[---.ṯ]lṯ.mat. | [---.m]itm.mqp.m[---]. | [---.ṯmn]ym.mgnm ar[bʿ]. | 1145.1.1
ṯlṯ.mat.[---]. | ṯmnt.k[---]. 1149.1
.dr[t.---]. | [ʿš]r.[k]bd[.---]. | [a]lpm[.---]. | tg[m]r.[---]. | ṯlṯ ma[t.---]. | ṯmnym[.---]. | [ṯ]mny[m.---]. | [-]r[-.---]. | [--]m.l. 2013.26
.---]. | [---.]ǵprt.ʿš[r.---]. | [---.p]ṯtm.l.ip[--.---]. | [---.]ksl.ṯlṯ.m[at.---]. | [---].abn.ṣr[p.---]. | [---.-]rt.ṯlṯm[.---]. | [--]l.ṯrmn. 1106.26
.[ml]tḥ.tyt.[---]. | [b]šbʿ[m.w.n]ṣp.ksp. | [tgm]r.[alp.w.]ṯlṯ.mat. 2101.28
mitm.ksp.ʿmn.b[n].ṣdqn. | w.kkrm.ṯlṯ. | mit.ksp.ʿmn. | bn.ulbtyn. | w.kkr.ṯlṯ. | ksp.d.nkly.b.šd. | mi 1143.2
r.[--].bt ilm. | kbr[-]m.[-]trmt. | lbš.w [-]tn.ušpǵt. | ḫr[-].ṯlṯt.mzn. | drk.š.alp.w ṯlṯ. | ṣin.šlm[m.]šbʿ pamt. | l ilm.šb[ʿ.]l 33[5].5
mit.ṯlṯ.mḫsrn. | ʿl.nsk.kṯtǵlm. | arbʿm.ṯlṯ.mḫsrn. | mtbʿl.rišy. | ṯlṯm.ṯlṯ.ʿl.nsk. | arym. | alp.ṯlṯ.ʿl. | nsk. 1137.3
mit.ṯlṯ.mḫsrn. | ʿl.nsk.kṯtǵlm. | arbʿm.ṯlṯ.mḫsrn. | mtbʿl.rišy. | ṯlṯm 1137.1
skn.ṯlṯm. | iytlm.ṯlṯm. | ḥyml.ṯlṯm. | ǵlkz.ṯlṯm. | mlknʿm.ʿšrm. | mrʿm.ʿšrm. | ʿmlbu.ʿšrm. | ʿmtdl.ʿšrm. | y 1116.4
nym. | [---.m]rzʿy.apnnk.yrp. | [---.]km.rʿy.ht.alk. | [---.]ṯlṯt.amǵy.l bt. | [y.---.b qrb].hkl y.w yʿn.il. | [---.mrzʿ]y.lk.bt y 21[122].1.7
n. | šd.k ḥsn.pat. | mdbr.ṯlkn. | ym.w ṯn.aḥr. | šp[š]m.b [ṯ]lṯ. | ym[ǵy.]l qdš. | a[ṯrt.]ṣrm.w l ilt. | ṣd[yn]m.ṯm. | yd[r.k]rt 14[KRT].4.196
mr[kbt hm.tity.l] | ʿr hm.ṯl[kn.ym.w ṯn.aḥr.špšm]. | b ṯlṯ.mǵy[.rpum.l grnt]. | i[ln]y[m].l mṯʿt[.---]. | [-]m[.---]. | h.hn 22.1[123].25
.l mrkbt hm.ti[ty.l ʿr hm]. | ṯlkn.ym.w ṯa aḥr.š[pšm.b ṯlṯ]. | mǵy.rpum.l grnt.i[lnym.l] | mṯʿt.w yʿn.dnil.[mt.rpi]. | y 20[121].2.5
p. | ḫpty.kdm[.---]. | [a]gm.arbʿ[.---]. | šrš.šbʿ.mṣb. | rqd.ṯlṯ.mṣb.w.[---]. | uḫnp.ṯt.mṣb. | tgmr.[y]n.mṣb š[bʿ]. | w ḥs[p] ṯ 2004.33
yt b ḫrṣ[.w] ṣmdm trm.d [ṣ]py. | w.trm.aḥdm. | ṣpym. | ṯlṯ mrkbt mlk. | d.l.ṣpy. | [---.t]r hm. | [---].ššb. | [---.]tr h. | [a]r 1122.5
ṯlṯ mrkb[t]. | ṣpyt b ḫrṣ[.w] ṣmdm trm.d [ṣ]py. | w.trm.aḥdm 1122.1
.l r[ḥq.ilm.ḥkpt.l rḥq]. | [ilnym.ṯn.mṯpd]m.ṯ[ḥt.ʿnt.arṣ.ṯlṯ.mtḥ.ǵyrm]. | [idk.]l ytn.pnm.ʿm.[i]l.mbk.[nhrm.qrb.apq.t 2.3[129].3
ǵr.l rḥq.ilm.inbb. | l rḥq.ilnym.ṯn.mṯpdm. | tḥt.ʿnt.arṣ.ṯlṯ.mtḥ.ǵyrm. | idk.l ttn pnm.ʿm.bʿl. | mrym.ṣpn.b alp.šd.rbt. 3[ʿNT].4.80
. | l rḥq.ilm.ḥkp[t.l rḥq.ilnym]. | ṯn.mṯpdm.tḥt.[ʿnt.arṣ.ṯlṯ.mtḥ]. | ǵyrm.idk.l yt[n.pnm.ʿm.lṭpn]. | il d pid.tk ḫrš[n.---. 1[ʿNT.IX].3.20
lbš.aḥd. | b.ʿšrt. | w.ṯn.b.ḫmšt. | tprt.b.ṯlṯt. | mṯyn.b.ṯṯt. | ṯn.lbšm.b.ʿšrt. | pld.b.arbʿt. | lbš.ṯn.b.ṯnt.ʿšrt 1108.4
d[y].ṭbg. | iḫmlk. | ypʿn w.aṯt h. | anntn.yṣr. | annmn.w.ṯlṯ.nʿ[r] h. | rpan.w.ṯ[n.]bn h. | bn.ayln.w.ṯn.bn h. | yt. 2068.25
w.adn hm.ṯr.w.arbʿ.bnt h. | yrḫm.yd.ṯn.bn h. | bʿlm.w.ṯlṯ.nʿrm.w.bt.aḥt. | bn.lwn.ṯlṯtm.bʿlm. | bn.bʿly.ṯlṯtm.bʿlm. | w 2080.5
m.l h.lm.ank. | ksp.w yrq.ḫrṣ. | yd.mqm h.w ʿbd. | ʿlm.ṯlṯ.sswm.mrkbt. | b trbṣt.bn.amt. | p d.in.b bt y.ttn. | tn.l y.mṯ 14[KRT].3.140
m.pbl.mlk. | qḥ.ksp.w yrq.ḫrṣ. | yd.mqm h.w ʿbd.ʿlm. | ṯlṯ.sswm.mrkbt. | b trbṣ.bn.amt. | qḥ.krt.šlmm. | šlmm.w ng. 14[KRT].3.128
.pbl.mlk]. | qḥ.[ksp.w yr]q. | ḫrṣ[.yd.mqm] h. | ʿbd[.ʿlm.ṯlṯ]. | ss[wm.mrkbt]. | b[trbṣ.bn.amt]. | [qḥ.krt.šlmm]. | [šlmm 14[KRT].5.252
l.mlk]. | qḥ[.ksp.w yrq]. | ḫrṣ.[yd.mqm h]. | w ʿbd[.ʿlm.ṯlṯ]. | sswm.m[rkbt]. | b trbṣ.[bn.amt]. | q[ḥ.kr]t[.šlmm]. | š[lm 14[KRT].6.271
[.ṯ]ʿ. | lm.ank.ksp. | w yr[q.ḫrṣ]. | yd.mqm h.w ʿbd. | ʿlm.ṯlṯ.sswm. | mrkbt.b trbṣ. | bn.amt.p d.[i]n. | b bt y.ttn.tn. | l y. 14[KRT].6.285
-.lm]. | [ank.ksp.w yrq]. | [ḫrṣ.]yd.mqm h. | [w ʿb]d.ʿlm.ṯlṯ. | [ssw]m.mrkbt b trbṣ bn.amt. | [tn.b]nm.aqny. | [tn.ṯa]rm 14[KRT].2.55
--] | r ṯtm lḥm. | l[.-]ry ṯlṯ spm w ʿšr lḥm. | [--.]w nṣp w ṯlṯ spm w ʿšrm lḥ[m]. | l[.-]dt ḫnd[r]ṯ arʿ s[p]m w ʿš[r]. | [---.] 134[-].4
[-]b[-.---.--] | r ṯtm lḥm. | l[.-]ry ṯlṯ spm w ʿšr lḥm. | [--.]w nṣp w ṯlṯ spm w ʿšrm lḥ[m]. | l[.-]d 134[-].3
---]. | [---.--]ln. | [---.]kqmṯn. | [---.]klnmw. | [---.]w yky. | ṯlṯm sp.l bnš tpnr. | arbʿ.spm.l.lbnš prwsdy. | ṯt spm.l bnš kln 137.2[93].6
g ynm. | ṯt spm l tgyn. | arbʿ spm l ll[-]. | ṯn spm.l slyy. | ṯlṯ spm l dlšpš amry. 137.2[93].15
tdǵl. | bʿlṣn. | nsk.ksp. | iwrtn. | ydln. | ʿbdilm. | dqn. | nsk.ṯlṯ. | ʿbdadt. | bṣmn.spr. 1039.2.28
--]. | [---.--]l.rb.kzym. | [---]y. | [-----]. | [-----]. | [--]dt.nsk.ṯlṯ. | [ʿb]dršp.nsk.ṯlṯ. | [-]lkynt.nsk.ṯlṯ. | [-]by.nsk.ṯlṯ. | šmny. | ḫ 1102.7
d.ʿl.[---]. | ṯlṯ.ʿl.gmrš[.---]. | kd.ʿl.ʿbd[--]. | kd.ʿl.aǵlt[n]. | ṯlṯ.ʿl.a[b]m[n]. | arbʿ.ʿl[.--]ly. | kd.[ʿl.--]ẓ. | kd.[ʿl.---]. | [--.--]ḫ.b 1082.1.21
| ʿṣm.l bt.dml. | p ank.atn. | ʿṣm.l k. | arbʿ.ʿṣm. | ʿl.ar. | w.ṯlṯ. | ʿl.ubrʿy. | w.ṯn.ʿl. | mlk. | w.aḥd. | ʿl atlg. | w l.ʿṣm. | tspr. | nr 1010.11
[---.--]m[.---]. | [kd.]šš. | [k]d.ykn.bn.ʿbdtrm. | kd.ʿbdil. | ṯlṯ.ʿl.bn.srt. | kd.ʿl.ẓrm. | kd.ʿl.šz.bn pls. | kd.ʿl.ynḥm. | tgrm.š 1082.2.4
.---]. | [kd.]ʿ[l.---]. | [k]d.ʿl[.---]. | [k]d.ʿl.[---]. | kd.ʿl.[---]. | ṯlṯ.ʿl.gmrš[.---]. | kd.ʿl.ʿbd[--]. | kd.ʿl.aǵlt[n]. | ṯlṯ.ʿl.a[b]m[n]. | a 1082.1.18
y. | ṯlṯm.ṯlṯ.ʿl.nsk. | arym. | alp.ṯlṯ.ʿl. | nsk.art. | ḫmš.mat.ṯlṯ. | ʿl.mtn.rišy. 1137.9
rn. | ʿl.nsk.kṯtǵlm. | arbʿm.ṯlṯ.mḫsrn. | mtbʿl.rišy. | ṯlṯm.ṯlṯ.ʿl.nsk. | arym. | alp.ṯlṯ.ʿl. | nsk.art. | ḫmš.mat.ṯlṯ. | ʿl.mtn.rišy 1137.5

b'm.ṯlṯ.mḫsrn.|mtb'l.rišy.|ṯlṯm.ṯlṯ.'l.nsk.|arym.|alp.ṯlṯ.'l.|nsk.art.|ḫmš.mat.ṯlṯ.|'l.mtn.rišy. 1137.7
[---.']ṣrm.|[--]ṯpḥ b'l.|[ṯl]ṯ.'ṣrm.|[w]b'lt btm.|[---.--]ṣn.l.dgn.|[---.--]m.|[---].pi[--.- 39[19].3
ḥ.]sbbyn.lṯḥ.ššmn.lṯḥ.šḥlt.|[---.lṯḥ.]ṣmqm.[ṯ]ṯ.mat.nṣ.ṯlṯm.'ṣr.|[---].ḫmš[m.ḥm]r.škm.|[---.ṯṯ.dd.]gdl.ṯṯ.dd.š'rm.|[142[12].5
m.ksp.'l.qrt.|b.šd.bn.[u]brš.|ḫmšt.'šrt.|b.šd.bn.[-]n.|ṯl[ṯt].'šr[t].|b.š[d].bn.'myn.|ḫmšt.|b.[šd.--]n.|ḫ[m]št[.']šrt. 1083.10
[b.]gt.ṯpn.'šr.ṣmdm.|w.ṯlṯ.'šr.bnš.|yd.ytm.yd.r'y.ḥmrm.|b.gt.gwl.ṯmn.ṣmdm.|w.ar 2038.2
[--].d.ntn[.d.]ksp.|[ṯ]mn.l.'šrm[.l.b]t.'ṯtrt.|[ṯ]lṯ.'šr h.[b]t.ršp.gn.|arb'.b d.b[n].ušryn.|kdm.l.urtn.|kdm. 1088.3
[---.ṯ]lṯ.'š[r h.---].|d bnšm.yd.grbs hm.|w.ṯn.'šr h.ḫpnt.|[š]šwm 2049.1
.|ṯrtnm.ḫmš.|mrum.'šr.|šb'.ḫsnm.|mkrm.|mrynm.|ṯlṯ.'šr.|hbṭnm.|ṯmn.|mdrġlm.|ṯmnym.ṯmn.kbd.|tgmr.ḫrd. 1031.10
mš.pld š'rt.|ṯṯ pld pṯt.|arb' ḫpnt pṯt.|ḫmš ḫpnt.š'rt.|ṯlṯ.'šr kdwṯm. 1113.11
skn.'šrm kk[r.---].|mšrn.ṯlṯ.'š[r.kkr].|bn.šw.šb'.kk[r.---].|arb'm.kkr.[---].|b d.mtn.[l] 2108.2
.arb'.ḫsnm.|'šr.mrum.|w.šb'.ḫsnm.|tš'.'šr.|mrynm.|ṯlṯ.'šr.mkrm.|ṯlṯ.bn.mrynm.|arb'.ṯrtnm.|tš'.ḫbṭnm.|ṯmny 1029.7
ḫmš.ṯnnm.'šr.ḫsnm.|ṯlṯ.'šr.mrynm.|ḫmš.[ṯr]tnm.|ṯlṯ.b[n.]mrynm.|'šr[.m]krm.|t 1028.2
[b yr]ḫ[.r]išyn.b ym.ḥdṯ.|[šmtr].uṯkl.l il.šlmm.|b [ṯlṯt].'šrt.yrtḥṣ.mlk.|br[r.]b a[r]b't.'šrt.riš.|arg[mn.w ṯn.]šm. APP.II[173].3
b yrḫ.[rišyn.b ym.ḥdṯ].|šmtr.[uṯkl.l il.šlmm].|b ṯlṯt '[šrt.yrtḥṣ.mlk.brr].|b arb'[t.'šrt.riš.argmn].|w ṯn šm.l [35[3].3
'l.|[---.]n[--.md]rġlm.|[---.]b.bt[.---]l.|[ṯ]lṯ.aṯt.adrt.w.ṯlṯ.ġzr[m].|w.ḫmš.n'rt.b.bt.sk[n].|ṯt.aṯtm.adrtm.w.pġt.w ġz 80[119].16
skn.ṯlṯm.|iytlm.ṯlṯm.|ḫyml.ṯlṯm.|ġlkz.ṯlṯm.|mlkn'm.'šrm.|mr'm.'šrm.|'mlbu.'šrm.|'m 1116.3
.|ṯṯ.prqt.|w.mrdt.prqt.pṯt.|lbš.psm.rq.|ṯn.mrdt.az.|ṯlṯ.pld.š'rt.|ṯ[---].kbm.|p[---]r.aḥd.|[-----].|[-----].|[---.--]y.| 1112.7
.kd.|amry.kdm.|mnn.bn.gttn.kdm.|ynḥm.bn[.-]r[-]t.ṯlṯ.|plwn.kdm.|tmyn.bn.ubrš.kd. 136[84].10
šm.|b.gt.ġl.|[-.]nġr.mdr'.|[-].nġr.[--]m.|[--.]psl.qšt.|[ṯl]ṯ.psl.ḥẓm.|[---.ḥ]rš.mr[k]bt.|[--].'šr h[.---].|[ḫm]š.'šr h[.-- 1024.3.19
.km.plg.|b'd h.bhtm.mnt.b'd h.bhtm.sgrt.|b'd h.'dbt.ṯlṯ.ptḥ.bt.mnt.|ptḥ.bt.w ubn.hkl.w ištql šql.|tn.km.nḥšm.y UG5.7.71
by[.---].|swn.qrty.w[.aṯt h].|[w].bn h.w.ṯn.alpm.|[w.]ṯlṯm.ṣin.|anndr.ykn'my.|w.aṯt h.w.bn h.|w.alp.w.tš['.]ṣin. 1080.14
] ġb.ršp mh bnš.|šrp.w ṣp ḫršḫ.|'lm b ġb ḫyr.|ṯmn l ṯlṯm ṣin.|šb'.alpm.|bt b'l.ugrt.ṯn šm.|'lm.l ršp.mlk.|alp w.š UG5.12.B.4
-]trmt.|lbš.w [-]tn.ušpġt.|ḫr[-].ṯlṯt.mzn.|drk.š.alp.w ṯlṯ.|ṣin.šlm[m.]šb' pamt.|l ilm.šb['.]l kṯr.|'lm.t'rbn.gṯrm.|b 33[5].6
-.---].|ṣin aḥd h[.---].|l 'ṯtrt[.---].|'lm.kmm[.---].|w b ṯlṯ.ṣ[in.---].|l ll.pr[-.---].|mit š'[rt.---].|ptr.k[--.---].|[-]yu[-.-- 37[22].8
ṯlṯ.ṣmdm.|b.nḫry.|ṣmdm.b.ṯp[--].|aḥdm.b.gm[--]. 144[317].1
dnn.ṯlṯ.ṣmdm.|bn.'mnr.|bn.kmn.|bn.ibyn.|bn.mryn.ṣmd.w.ḥrṣ 2113.1
hn.|yd.ḥẓ hn.|yd.tr hn.|w.l.ṯt.mrkbtm.|inn.uṯpt.|w.ṯlṯ.ṣmdm.w.ḥrṣ.|apnt.b d.rb.ḥršm.|d.šṣa.ḥwy h. 1121.8
[.---].|[ul]l.aḥdm.w[.---].|[m'q]b.aḥdm.w[.---].|['r]gz.ṯlṯ.ṣmd[m.---].|[m]ṣbt.ṣmdm.[---].|[--]nr.arb'.[---].|[--]idḫ.ṣ 1179.4
].|apnm.l.bn[.---].|apnm.l.[b]n[.---].|apnm.l.bn[.---].|ṯlṯ.ṣmdm[.---].|mṣ[r]n[.---]. 145[318].9
ṣṣ.bn.ilyn.ṯlṯm.|ṣṣ.bn.kzn.ṯlṯm.|ṣṣ.bn.tlmyn.'šrm.|ṣṣ.bn.krwn.'š[rm]. 2096.1
-.---].|[ṣṣ].bn.npr.ḫmšm.|ṣṣ.bn.adldn.ṯlṯm.|ṣṣ.bn.'glt.ṯlṯm.|ṣṣ.bn.'bd.'šrm.|ṣṣ.bn.mṣḫ[n].'šrm.|šb'.mat.ṯṯm kbd. 2096.17
--].|[ṣṣ].b[n].ṣd[-.---].|[ṣṣ].bn.npr.ḫmšm.|ṣṣ.bn.adldn.ṯlṯm.|ṣṣ.bn.'glt.ṯlṯm.|ṣṣ.bn.'bd.'šrm.|ṣṣ.bn.mṣḫ[n].'šrm.|šb 2096.16
rm.|ṣṣ.bn.krwn.'š[rm].|ṣṣ.bn.iršyn.[---].|[ṣṣ].bn.ilb'l.ṯl[ṯ]m.|ṣṣ.bn.ptdn.[--]m.|ṣṣ.[bn].gyn.[---].|[-----].|[-----].|[-- 2096.6
rm.|ṣṣ abš[-] mit ['š]r kbd.|ṣṣ ydrd 'šrm.|ṣṣ bn aglby ṯlṯ[m].|ṣṣ bn.šrš'm.[---].|ṣṣ mlkn'm.a[rb'm].|ṣṣ mlk mit[.--- 2097.13
ṣṣ.bn.ilyn.ṯlṯm.|ṣṣ.bn.kzn.ṯlṯm.|ṣṣ.bn.tlmyn.'šrm.|ṣṣ.bn.krwn.'š[rm].|ṣṣ.bn.iršyn.[---]. 2096.2
ḫmš 'šr h.|ṣṣ 'myd ḫmšm.|ṣṣ tmn.ḫmšm.|[ṣṣ] 'mtdl ṯlṯm.|ṣṣ 'mlbi ṯt l 'šrm.|ṣṣ bn adty ḫmšm.|ṣṣ amtrn arb'm. 2097.5
štm[.w.ṯl]ṯ.ql'm.|bn.'gw.qšt.w ql'.|bn.tbšn.ṯlṯ.qšt.w.[ṯlṯ.]ql'm.|bn.army.ṯt.qštm.w[.]q[l'].|bn.rpš.qšt.w.ql'.|bn.ġb 119[321].3.21
l.qšt.|bn.[ḫ]dptr.ṯt.qštm.[w].ql'.|bn.aġlyn.ṯt.qštm[.w.ṯl]ṯ.ql'm.|bn.'gw.qšt.w ql'.|bn.tbšn.ṯlṯ.qšt.w.[ṯlṯ.]ql'm.|bn.a 119[321].3.19
rm.ql'.|ubr'y.|abmn.qšt.w.ṯn.ql'm.|qdmn.ṯt.qštm.w.ṯlṯ.ql'm.|bn.ṣdqil.ṯt.qštm.w.ṯn.ql'm.|bn.ṯlṯ.ṯ[lṯ.]qšt.w.ṯn.ql' 119[321].3.3
dmt ṯlṯ.|qmnz ṯql.|zlyy ṯql.|ary ḫmšt.|ykn'm ḫmšt.|'nmky ṯql 1176.1
mizrtm.ġr.b abn.|ydy.psltm.b y'r.|yhdy.lḥm.w dqn.|ytlṯ.qn.ḏr' h.yḥrṯ.|k gn.ap lb.k 'mq.ytlṯ.|bmt.yšu.g h.w yṣḥ 5[67].6.20
l b'l.|ġr.b ab.td[.ps]ltm[.b y'r].|thdy.lḥm.w dqn[.ttlṯ].|qn.ḏr' h.tḥrṯ.km.gn.|ap lb.k 'mq.ttlṯ.bmt.|b'l.mt.my.l 6[62].1.3
.aġlyn.ṯt.qštm[.w.ṯl]ṯ.ql'm.|bn.'gw.qšt.w ql'.|bn.tbšn.ṯlṯ.qšt.w.[ṯlṯ.]ql'm.|bn.army.ṯt.qštm.w[.]q[l'].|bn.rpš.qšt.w. 119[321].3.21
ṯt.qštm.w.ṯlṯ.ql'm.|bn.ṣdqil.ṯt.qštm.w.ṯn.ql'm.|bn.ṯlṯ.ṯ[lṯ.]qšt.w.ṯn.ql'm.|qṣn.ṯt.qštm.w.ql'.|bn.gṯrn.q[š]t.|bn.ḫdi. 119[321].3.5
t.|ḥẓr y.ṯn h.wspm.|atn.w ṯlṯ h.ḥrṣm.|ylk ym.w ṯn.|ṯlṯ.rb'.ym.|aḫr.špšm.b rb'.|ymġy.l udm.rbt.|w udm[.ṯr]rt.| 14[KRT].4.208
hkl m.|hn.ym.w ṯn.tikl.|išt.b bht m.nblat.|b hk[l] m.ṯlṯ.kb' ym.|tikl[.i]št.b bht m.|nbla[t.]b hkl m.|ḫmš.ṯ[d]ṯ.y 4[51].6.26
ṯn.uzr.]ilm.dnil.|[uzr.ilm.]ylḥm.uzr.|[yšqy.b]n.qdš ṯlṯ rb' ym.|[uzr.i]lm.dnil.uzr.|[ilm.y]lḥm.uzr.yšqy bn.|[qdš 17[2AQHT].1.9
b grnt.ḥpšt.|s't.b nk.šibt.b bqr.|mmlat.dm.ym.w ṯn.|ṯlṯ.rb'.ym.ymš.|ṯdṯ.ym.ḥẓ k.al.tš'l.|qrt h.abn.yd k.|mšdpt. 14[KRT].3.115
t h.k irby.|[t]škn.šd.|km.ḥsn.pat.mdbr.|lk.ym.w ṯn.ṯlṯ.rb' ym.|ḫmš.ṯdṯ.ym.mk.špšm.|b šb'.w tmġy.l udm.|rbm 14[KRT].3.106
pšt.|s't.b npk.šibt.w b |mqr.mmlat.|d[m].ym.w ṯn.|ṯlṯ.rb'.ym.|ḫmš.ṯdṯ.ym.|mk.špšm.b šb'.|w l.yšn.pbl.|mlk.l 14[KRT].5.219
.|lbnn.ṯl mrt.yḥrṯ.il.|hn.ym.w ṯn.tlḥmn.rpum.|tštyn.ṯlṯ.rb'.ym.ḫmš.|ṯdṯ.ym.tlḥmn.rpum.|tštyn.bt.ikl.b pr'.|yṣq. 22.2[124].22
nnt.|hn.ym.w ṯn.yšlḥm.|kṯrt.w yš[š]q.bnt.hl[l].|snnt.ṯlṯ[.r]b' ym.yšl|ḥm kṯrt.w yššq.|bnt hll.snnt.ḫmš.|ṯdṯ.ym.y 17[2AQHT].2.34
t.'rš.ḫlln.[-].|ytb.dnil.[l s]pr yrḫ h.|yrs.y[---.]y[--] h.|ṯlṯ.rb['.yrḫ.--]r[.--].|yrḫm.ymġy[.---].|ḫ[--.]r[---]. 17[2AQHT].2.45
].|[']šr[.---].|[']l [-]g[-.---].|w ni[t.w.m'ṣd].|w ḫrmṯt.|ṯlṯm.ar[b'].|kbd.ksp.|'l.tgyn.|w 'l.aṯt h.|ypḥ.m'nt.|bn.lbn. 2053.18
iršt.yṣḥm.|arb'.alpm.|mitm.kbd.ṯlṯ.|arb'.kkrm.|ṯmn.mat.kbd.|pwt.|ṯmn.mat.pṯtm.|kkrm.a 2051.3
].|b ilm.[ydy.mrṣ].|gršm.z[bln.in.b ilm].|'ny h.y[ṯny.ytlṯ].|rgm.my.b[ilm.ydy].|mrṣ.grš[m.zbln].|in.b ilm.'[ny h 16[126].5.13
n š.|[---.--]r.w ṯt pl.gdlt.[ṣ]pn.dqt.|[---.al]p 'nt.gdlt.b ṯlṯt mrm.|[---.i]l š.b'l š.aṯrt.š.ym š.[b']l knp.|[---.g]dlt.ṣpn.d 36[9].1.5
d.bt.mlk[.---].|ṯn.skm.šb'.mšlt.arb'.ḫpnt.[---].|ḫmšm.ṯlṯ.rkb.ntn.ṯlṯ.mat.[---].|lg.šmn.rqḥ.šr'm.ušpġtm.p[--.---].|k UG5.9.1.20
.|p[--].b ṯlḥn y.qlt.|b ks.ištyn h.|dm.ṯn.dbḥm.šna.b'l.ṯlṯ.|rkb.'rpt.dbḥ.|bṯt.w dbḥ.w dbḥ.|dnt.w dbḥ.tdmm.|amh 4[51].3.17
.w alp w š.|šrp.w šlmm kmm.|l b'l.ṣpn b 'r'r.|pamt ṯlṯm š l qrnt.|ṯlḥn.b'lt.bhtm.|'lm.'lm.gdlt l b'l.|ṣpn.ilbt[.---. UG5.13.30
urt l bnš [---].|ṯṯ šurt.l bnš[.---].|ṯn šurtm l bn[š.---].|ṯlṯm šurt l b[nš.---].|arb' šurt [---].|ṯṯ šurt l bnš [---].|ḫmš k 137.1[92].9
m l bnš [---].|arb' šurt l bn[š.---].|arb' šurt l q[--.---].|ṯlṯ šurt l bnš [---].|ṯṯ šurt.l bnš[.---].|ṯn šurtm l bn[š.---].|ṯlṯ 137.1[92].6
].|ṯṯ šurt l tg[-.---].|arb' šurt [---].|[ḫm]šm šurt [---].|ṯlṯ šurt l [---].|ṯn šurtm l [---].|[-----.]a[---].|[---.--]ln.|[---.]k 137.1[92].16

ʿmy. | šd.b d.bn.ʿyn. | ṯn.šdm.b d.klṯṯb. | šd.b d.krz[n]. | ṯlṯ.šdm.b d.amtr[n]. | ṯn.šdm.b d.skn. | šd.b d[.ʿb]dyrḫ. | šd.b 2090.22
arbʿ.ʿšr h.šd. | w.kmsk.d.iwrkl. | ṯlṯ.šd.d.bn.mlkyy. | kmsk.šd.iḫmn. | širm.šd.khn. | ṯlṯ.šd.w.kr 1079.3
.tnn. | [š]d.bn.ḫrmln.ṯn.b d.bn.ḫdmn. | [u]bdy.nqdm. | [ṯlṯ].šdm.d.nʿrb.gt.npk. | [š]d.rpan.b d.klṯṯb. | [š]d.ilṣy.b d.ʿbd 82[300].2.13
rkl. | ṯlṯ.šd.d.bn.mlkyy. | kmsk.šd.iḫmn. | širm.šd.khn. | ṯlṯ.šd.w.krm.šir.d.ḫli. | širm.šd.šd.ʿšy. | w.šir.šd.krm. | d.krwn 1079.6
krm. | d.yrmn. | šir.[š]d.mlṯḥ.šd.ʿšy. | d.ynḥm. | tgmr.šd.ṯlṯm.šd. | w.tr[--.---]. 1079.16
.ʿšrt. | bn.ḫgby.ṯmnt.l ʿšrm.ʿšrt.ḫmš.kbd. | bn.ilṣdq.šbʿt ṯlṯt šlm. | bn.ṯmq.arbʿt ṯqlm šlmm. 1131.9
annṯb.ḫmšm.ksp ṯlṯm.šl[m.---]. | iwrpzn.ʿšrm ʿšrm š[lm.---]. | ilabn.ʿšrt ṯqlm k 1131.1
.alzy. | ḫmš.kkr.ḥlb. | ḫmš.kkr.brr. | kkr.ḫmš.mat.kbd.ṯlṯ.šm[n]. | alp.mitm.kbd.ṯlṯ.ḥlb. | šbʿ.l.ʿšrm.kkr.ṯlṯ. | d.ybl.bly 1135.4
šlmym.lqḥ.akl. | yḥmn.ṯlṯ.šmn. | a[---.]kdm. | ʿ[---]ʿm.kd. | a[----]ḥr.ṯlṯ. | y[---.bn.]kran 136[84].2
]ḫ[---.]ṯmnym[.k]sp ḫmšt. | [w a]rbʿ kkr ʿl bn[.--]. | [w] ṯlṯ šmn. | [w a]r[bʿ] ksp ʿl bn ymn. | šb šr šmn [--] ṯryn. | ḫm[š 1103.3
dt.nsk.ṯlṯ. | [ʿb]dršp.nsk.ṯlṯ. | [-]lkynt.nsk.ṯlṯ. | [-]by.nsk.ṯlṯ. | šmny. | ḫršn. | ldn. | bn.ands. | bn.ann. | bn.ʿbdpdr. | šd.iyry 1102.10
t.w.ḫpn.l.azzlt. | [---.]l.ʿṯtrt.šd. | [---].ybʿlnn. | [---.--]n.b.ṯlṯ.šnt.l.nṣd. | [---.--]ršp.mlk.k.ypdd.mlbš. | u---].mlk.ytn.mlb 1106.57
hm. | šbʿ.lbšm.allm. | l ušḫry. | ṯlṯ.mat.pṯtm. | l.mgmr.b.ṯlṯ. | šnt. 1107.12
-]. | [-]ṯrn [k]sp [-]al[.-]r[-]. | [--]dšq krsnm. | ḫmšm [-]t ṯlṯ ty[--]. | bn.grgš. | w.npṣ bt ṯn.ṯlṯ mat. | w spl ṯlṯ.mat. | w m 1103.14
.kbd.yn.ṭb. | w.ḫmšm.k[dm.]kbd.yn.d.l.ṭb. | b.gt.gwl. | ṯlṯm.tšʿ[.kbd.yn].d.l[.ṭb].b.gt.ipṯl. | ṯmnym.[yn].ṭb.b.gt.š[---]. 1084.19
š.ʿšr h.prs. | bt.mrkbt.w l šant.ṯṯ. | l bt.ʿšrm. | bt alḫnm.ṯlṯm ṯṯ kbd. 2105.4
[---.]tšʿ.kbd.skm. | [arb]ʿm.ḫpnt.pṯt. | [-]r.pldm.dt.šʿrt. | ṯlṯm.ṯlṯ.kbd.mṣrrt. | ʿšr.ṯn.kbd.pǵdrm. | ṯmn.mrbdt.mlk. | ʿšr. 1111.9
ṯ.mḫsrn. | ʿl.nsk.kṯṯǵlm. | arbʿm.ṯlṯ.mḫsrn. | mtbʿl.rišy. | ṯlṯm.ṯlṯ.ʿl.nsk. | arym. | alp.ṯlṯ.ʿl. | nsk.art. | ḫmš.mat.ṯlṯ. | ʿl.mt 1137.5
ṯmn.kkr.ṯlṯ. | ṯmn.kkr.brr. | arbʿ.alpm.pḥm. | ḫmš.mat.kbd. | arbʿ.alpm 1130.1
any.al[ty]. | d b atlg[.---]. | ḫmš ʿš[r]. | kkr.ṯ[lṯ]. | ṯṯ hrt[m]. | ṯn mq[pm]. | ulṯ.ṯl[ṯ]. | krk.kly[.--]. | ḫmš.mr[2056.4
arbʿ.ḥm[r.---]. | l ṯlṯ. | ṯn.l.brr[.---]. | arbʿ.ḥmr[.---]. | l.pḥ[-.]w.[---]. | w.l.k[--]. | w 1139.2
d.b.ṯqlm. | lbš.aḥd.b.ṯqlm. | ḫpn.pṯtm.b ʿšr. | tgmr.ksp.ṯlṯm. | ṯqlm.kbd. 1115.5
p[-]. | b[--.]l[-.]mat[.-]y. | ḫmšm[.--]i. | ṯlṯ m[at] ḫswn. | ṯlṯ ṯ[-].ṯṯ ḥ[--]. 140[98].10
]. | [-----]. | [--]dt.nsk.ṯlṯ. | [ʿb]dršp.nsk.ṯlṯ. | [-]lkynt.nsk.ṯlṯ. | [-]by.nsk.ṯlṯ. | šmny. | ḫršn. | ldn. | bn.ands. | bn.ann. | bn.ʿ 1102.9
ym. | [---]y. | [-----]. | [-----]. | [--]dt.nsk.ṯlṯ. | [ʿb]dršp.nsk.ṯlṯ. | [-]lkynt.nsk.ṯlṯ. | [-]by.nsk.ṯlṯ. | šmny. | ḫršn. | ldn. | bn.and 1102.8
ṯmnym.tbṯḫ.alp. | uz.mrat.mlḥt. | arbʿ.uzm.mrat.bqʿ. | ṯlṯ.[-]ṯt.aš[ʿ]t.šmn.uz. | mi[t].ygb.bqʿ. | a[--].ʿṭ. | a[l]pm.alpnm. 1128.22
. | [kṯ]rmlk.ʿšrm. | [--]ny.ʿšrt.trbyt. | [--.]ʿbd.ṯlṯm. | [---].ṯlṯm. | [--.p]ndyn.ṯlṯm. 2054.2.27
m.likt. | [--]y.k išal hm. | [--.ʿš]rm.kkr.ṯlṯ. | [--.]ṯlṯm.kkr.ṯlṯ. | [--.]aštn.l k. | [--]y.kl.dbrm.hm[.--]. | [--]l.w.kl.mḫr k. | [-- 1022.5
d.ʿm y. | [--.]spr.lm.likt. | [--]y.k išal hm. | [--.ʿš]rm.kkr.ṯlṯ. | [--.]ṯlṯm.kkr.ṯlṯ. | [--.]aštn.l k. | [--]y.kl.dbrm.hm[.--]. | [--] 1022.4
ḥd. | ypr.arb. | m[-]qb.ʿšr. | ṯnʿy.ṯlṯ. | ḥlb ʿprm.ṯn. | tmdy.ṯlṯ. | [--]rt.arbʿ. | [---].ʿšr. 70[112].13
[---].ʿšr. | [---].ṯlṯ. | [---].ṯmn. | [---].ṯlṯ. | [---].aḥd. | u[--].ṯn. | hz[p].ṯṯ. | ḫrṣbʿ.aḥd. | ypr.arb. | m[-]qb 70[112].4
[--]pš.šn[--]. | ṯ[-]r.b iš[-]. | bʿl h.šʿ[-]rt. | ḫqr.[--.ṯq]l rb. | ṯl[ṯ.---]. | aḥt.ḫm[-.---]. | b ym.dbḥ.ṯp[-]. | aḥt.l mzy.bn[--]. | aḥ 39[19].11
y. | [-----.]yn. | [----.-]mn. | [---.--]m.mṣl. | [---].prš.ḥtm. | ṯlṯ[.---].bn.ṯdnyn. | ddm.ḥ[ṯm].ʿl.šrn. | ʿšrt.ksp.ʿl.[-]lpy. | bn.ad 1146.6
kr[-] h.b.nṯk. | [---.]šbʿm. | [---.]ḥrg.ʿšrm. | [---.]abn.ksp.ṯlṯ. | [---].bty.ksp.ʿšr[t]. | [---.-]mbʿl.[---].ʿšrt. | [---.]ḥgbn.kbs.ks 2153.6
gdlt.šlm[.gdlt.w burm.lb]. | rmṣt.ilh[m.bʿlm.---]. | ksm.ṯlṯm.[---]. | d yqḥ bt[.--]r.dbḥ[.šmn.mr]. | šmn.rqḥ[.-]bt.mtnt[35[3].19
ṯṯ.ʿšr.ṣ[mdm]. | w.ṯšʿ.ʿ[šr.--]m.ḥr[š]. | [---].ḥr[š.---]. | [---.ṯ]lṯ.[---.]dpm. | [---.]bnšn. | [---.ḫ]mš.ṣmd.alpm. | [---.bn]šm. | [2038.13
[-----]. | [-----]. | ḥd[-.---]. | ṯlṯm.[---]. | ksn.[---]. | u[--.---]. | [-----]. | a[--.---]. 155[-].4
ʿṣr.ktnt. | ʿšr.rṭm. | kkr[.-].ḫt. | mitm[.p]ṯtm. | ṯlṯm[.---].kst. | alp.a[bn.ṣ]rp. 1114.5
]. | k[--.---]. | ar[bʿ.---]. | ṯmn[.---]. | [-]r[-.---]. | w ṯṯ.[---]. | ṯlṯm[.---]. | mil[-.---]. 148[96].13
[---.]ṯlṯm. | [---.n]ḥl. | [---.ṯ]lṯ.mat.šbʿm[.---]. | [---.--]mm.b.mṣbt[.-- 2149.1
[-]k[-.---]. | [-]rn[.---]. | [-----]. | yt[--.---]. | ṯl[ṯ.---]. | ṯl[ṯ.---]. | ʿnmk[.---]. | yknʿm[.---]. | qm[n]z[---]. | šl[-.---]. | ar[--. 1181.6
[---.-]grm. | [---.-]n.ʿšrt.ksp. | [--.--]n.šbʿt.l ṯlṯm. | [---].šbʿt.ʿšrt. | [---.-]kyn.ʿšrt. | b.bn.ʿsl.ʿšrm.ṯqlm kbd. | 2054.1.3
.w.šbʿ.alpm. | [kṯ]rmlk.ʿšrm. | [--]ny.ʿšrt.trbyt. | [--.]ʿbd.ṯlṯm. | [---].ṯlṯm. | [--.p]ndyn.ṯlṯm. 2054.2.26
[-]k[-.---]. | [-]rn[.---]. | [-----]. | yt[--.---]. | ṯl[ṯ.---]. | ṯl[ṯ.---]. | ʿnmk[.---]. | yknʿm[.---]. | qm[n]z[---]. | šl[-.-- 1181.5
[---].ʿšr. | [---].ṯlṯ. | [---].ṯmn. | [---].ṯlṯ. | [---].aḥd. | u[--].ṯn. | hz[p].ṯṯ. | ḫrṣbʿ.aḥ 70[112].2
[---.]npṣ ṯlṯ. | [---.-]kṣ. 154[-].1
dʿ. | b yr[ḫ.iṯtb]nm. | ṯlṯ[.mat.a]rbʿ.kbd. | w.[---.-]mʿt. | ṯlṯ[m.---.-]rm. | ʿšr[.---].alpm. | arbʿ.ddm.l.k[-]ḫ. | ṯmnym.dd.d 2012.16
[--]. | yšlm. | [ʿ]šrm.ks[p].yš[lm]. | [il]ṯhm.b d[.---]. | [---].ṯl[l]m.[---]. | [--.]r[-]y[.---]. | ʿl.[--]l[-] h. | ʿdn.[---]. | d.u[--.---]. 2104.9
-.---]. | [---.]ksl.ṯlṯ.m[at.---]. | [---].abn.ṣr[p.---]. | [---.-]rt.ṯlṯm[.---]. | [--]l.trmn.m[lk.---]. | [---.--]rt.šʿrt[.---]. | [---.i]qni.l. 1106.28
[-.---]. | [---.--]mn.mi[t.---]. | [---.ṯm]nym[.---]. | [---.-]dn.ṯlṯ[m.---]. | [---].mitm[.---]. | [---.--]m.mšrn[.---]. 149[99].11
ṯ[--.---]. | [-----]. | [---.--]lk[.---]. | [---.--]g.tuṣl[-.---]. | [---].ṯlṯ.[---]. | [---.]tʿr[-.---]. 36[9].2.6
l[-.---]. | [-]ṯ.[---]. | mṣb[-.---]. | kṯ.aqh[r.---]. | l bn[.---]. | [ṯ]lṯ.[---]. | [---.--]yn.š.aḫ[--]. | [---.]š.nṣ[.-]al[-]. | [---.---]m[.---]. 143[-].2.6
.]nǵr.ʿš[rm.---]. | [---.-]yl.ʿš[rm.---]. | [---.a]rbʿ[.---]. | [---.ṯ]lṯm[.---]. | [---.--]m.bn l[---]. | [---].bn ṣd[-.---]. | [---.--]mn.mi 149[99].6
da[.-.]mdʿ. | kl[--.---.]ṯmnt.[--.]w[.---]. | [-]m[.---.]ṣpiry[.ṯ]lṯt[.---]. APP.II[173].61
[--.---]. | [-----]. | k[--.---]. | [-----]. | ḫmrn.ʿš[r.---]. | gll.tky.ṯlṯ[.---]. 2042.23
.hm[.--]. | [--]l.w.kl.mḫr k. | [--]tir.aštn.l [k]. | [---].kkr.ṯl[ṯ]. 1022.10
| [--]ny.ʿšrt.trbyt. | [--.]ʿbd.ṯlṯm. | [---].ṯlṯm. | [--.p]ndyn.ṯlṯm. 2054.2.28

ṯm

l[b]nm. | nnu. | ʿrm. | bṣr. | mʿr. | ḫlby. | mṣbt. | snr. | ṯm. | ubš. | glbt. | mi[d]ḫ. | mr[i]l. | ḫlb. | šld. | ʿrgz. | [-----]. 2041.9
m.w l.tšbʿn y.aṯt.itrḫ. | y bn.ašld.šu.ʿdb.tk.mdbr qdš. | ṯm tgrgr.l abnm.w l.ʿṣm.šbʿ.šnt. | tmt.ṯmn.nqpt.ʿd.ilm.nʿmm 23[52].66
k.b. | lwsnd. | [w] b ṣr. | ʿm.mlk. | w.ht. | mlk.syr. | ns.w.ṯm. | ydbḥ. | mlǵ[.---]. | w.m[--.--]y. | y[--.---]. 2063.15
š.l [hrm.ǵ]rpl.ʿl.arṣ. | [---.]ḥmt.l p[.nt]k.abd.l p.ak[l]. | [ṯm.dl.]isp.ḥ[mt.---.-]hm.yasp.ḥmt. | [---.š]pš.l [hrm.ǵrpl].ʿl.a UG5.8.11
[šp]š l hrm.ǵrpl.ʿl arṣ. | [l a]n ḥmt.l p[.n]ṯk.abd.l p.akl ṯm.dl. | [---.q]l.bl.tbḥ[n.l]azd.ʿr.qdm. | [---].ʿẓ q[dm.--.šp]š. | [UG5.8.20

ṯm

.hn.[--]n.w aspt.[q]l h. | [---.rg]m.ank l[.--.--]rny. | [---.]ṯm.hw.i[--]ty. | [---].ib‘r.a[--.]ḏmr. | [---.]w mlk.w rg[m.---]. | [1002.51
štn..l.iẖ y. | w.ap.ank.mnm. | [ẖ]s[r]t.w.uẖ y. | [y]‘msn.ṯmn. | w.[u]ẖ y.al yb‘rn. 2065.20
lnym.b] | hkl y.aṯr[h.rpum.l tdd]. | aṯr h.l t[dd.ilnym.ṯm]. | yḥpn.ḥy[ly.zbl.mlk.‘llm y]. | šm‘.atm[.---]. | ym.lm.qd[. 22.1[123].11
rk n.šm.il.ǵzrm. | ṯm.ṯmq.rpu.b‘l.mhr b‘l. | w mhr.‘nt.ṯm.yḥpn.ḥyl | y.zbl.mlk.‘llm y.km.tdd. | ‘nt.ṣd.tštr.‘pt.šmm. | 22.2[124].9
--].w b ym.mnẖ l abd.b ym.irtm.m[--]. | [ṯpṭ].nhr.tl‘m.ṯm.ḥrbm.its.anšq. | [-]htm.l arṣ.ypl.ul ny.w l.‘pr.‘ẓm ny. | l b‘ 2.4[68].4
š]m.b [ṯ]lṯ. | ym[ǵy.]l qdš. | a[ṯrt.]ṣrm.w l ilt. | ṣd[yn]m.ṯm. | yd[r.k]rt.ṯ‘. | i.iṯt.aṯrt.ṣrm. | w ilt.ṣdynm. | hm.ḥry.bt y. | i 14[KRT].4.199
. | tšlm k. | hn ny.‘m ny. | kll.mid. | šlm. | w.ap.ank. | nẖt.ṯm ny. | ‘m.adt ny. | mnm.šlm. | rgm.ṯṯb. | l.‘bd k. 51[95].14
m y. | yšlm.ilm. | tǵr k.tšlm k. | hl ny.‘m n[y]. | kll.šlm. | ṯm ny.‘m.um y. | mnm.šlm. | w.rgm.ṯṯb.l y. | bm.ṯy.ndr. | iṯt.‘ 50[117].11
lm k. | lḥt.šlm.k.lik[t]. | um y.‘m y.ht.‘m[ny]. | kll.šlm.ṯm ny. | ‘m.um y.mnm.šlm. | w.rgm.ṯṯb.l y. | w.mnd‘.k.ank. | a 2009.1.7
rgm. | yšlm.l k.[il]m. | tǵr k.tšlm k. | hn ny.‘m n.š[l]m. | ṯm ny.‘[m.]bn y. | mnm.[šl]m[.r]gm[.ṯṯb]. | ky.lik.bn y. | lḥt.a 2061.7
r.aẖ k. | y[š]lm.l k.ilm. | tǵr k.tšlm k. | hn ny.‘m n. | šlm.ṯm ny. | ‘m k.mnm[.š]lm. | rgm.ṯṯ[b]. | any kn.dt. | likt.mṣrm. | 2059.7
y. | yšlm.il[m]. | tǵ[r] k.tš[lm] k. | [h]l ny.‘m n[.š]lm. | w.ṯm [ny.‘m.mlkt.u]m y. | mnm[.šlm]. | w.rgm[.ṯṯb.l] y. | hl ny.‘ 1013.9
[-]n.atn.at.mṯb k[.---]. | [š]mm.rm.lk.prẓ kt. | [k]bkbm.ṯm.tpl k.lbnt. | [-.]rgm.k yrkt.‘ṯqbm. | [---]m.‘ẓpn.l pit. | m[--] 13[6].13
.ṣǵr.tnšq.špt k.ṯm. | ṯkm.bm ṯkm.aẖm.qym.il. | b lsmt.ṯm.yṯbš.šm.il.mt m. | y‘bš.brk n.šm.il.ǵzrm. | ṯm.ṯmq.rpu.b‘l. 22.2[124].6
n k.hn[.---]. | bn bn.aṯr k.hn[.---]. | yd k.ṣǵr.tnšq.špt k.ṯm. | ṯkm.bm ṯkm.aẖm.qym.il. | b lsmt.ṯm.yṯbš.šm.il.mt m. | 22.2[124].4
l. | b lsmt.ṯm.yṯbš.šm.il.mt m. | y‘bš.brk n.šm.il.ǵzrm. | ṯm.ṯmq.rpu.b‘l.mhr b‘l. | w mhr.‘nt.ṯm.yḥpn.ḥyl | y.zbl.mlk.‘ 22.2[124].8
s.ym | sk.nhr hm. | šb‘.ydt y.b ṣ‘. | [--.]šb‘.rbt. | [---.]qbṯ.ṯm. | [---.]bn.ilm. | [m]t.šmḥ.p ydd. | il[.ǵ]zr. | b [-]dn.‘.z.w. | rg UG5.4.13

ṯmgdl

.alp.w ṯmn.ṣin. | [-]dln.qmnzy.w.a[ṯt h]. | wšṯn.bn h. | ṯmgdl.ykn‘my.w.aṯt h. | w.bn h.w.alp.aḥ[d]. | aǵltn.[--]y.w[.a 1080.5

ṯmyr

n.ḥgby. | bn.pity. | bn.slgyn. | ‘zn.bn.mlk. | bn.alṯn. | bn.ṯmyr. | ẓbr. | bn.ṯdṯb. | bn.‘rmn. | bn.alz. | bn.mṣrn. | bn.‘dy. | bn 115[301].2.10

ṯmk

ṣ.l ‘brm.kš. | dpr.ṯlḥn.b q‘l.b q‘l. | mlkm.hn.ym.yṣq.yn.ṯmk. | mrṯ.yn.srnm.yn.bld. | ǵll.yn.išryt.‘nq.smd. | lbnn.ṭl mrṯ 22.2[124].17

ṯmm

ḥ[.---]. | ydd.b qr[b.---]. | al.ašt.b[---]. | ahpk k.l[--.---]. | ṯmm.w lk[.---]. | w lk.ilm[.---]. | n‘m.ilm[.---]. | šgr.mu[d.---]. | 5[67].3.13
---]. | iṯm.mui[-.---]. | dm.mt.aṣ[ḥ.---]. | ydd.b qr[b.---]. | ṯmm.w lk[.---]. | [--]ṯ.lk[.---]. | [--]kṯ.i[---.---]. | p.šn[-.---]. | w l 5[67].3.27

ṯmn

skn.alpm. | krw.šlmy. | alpm. | atn.bṣry.alpm. | lbnym. | ṯm[n.]alp mitm. | ilb‘l ẖmš m[at]. | ‘dn.ẖmš.mat. | bn.[-]d.alp. 1060.2.8
m.arb‘.kbd. | ẖlb rpš arb‘.‘šr. | bq‘t ṯṯ. | irab ṯn.‘šr. | ḥbš.ṯmn. | amḏy.arb‘.‘šr. | [-]n‘y.ṯṯ.‘šr. 67[110].10
-]n[-.-]lt. | ql h.yš[m‘].ṯr.[il].ab h.[---]l. | b šb‘t.ḥdrm.[b ṯ]mn[t.ap]. | sgrt.g[-].[-]ẓ[.---] h[.---]. | ‘n.ṯk[.---]. | ‘ln.ṯ[--.---]. 3[‘NT.VI].5.19
t[k.dmm]. | [šbt.dqn k.mm‘m.]y‘ny. | il.b šb‘t.ḥdrm.b ṯmnt. | ap.sgrt.yd‘[t k.]bt.k an[št]. | k in.b ilht.ql[ṣ] k.mh.tarš 3[‘NT.VI].5.34
k mdb.b tk.ǵr h.il ṣpn.b [tk]. | ǵr.tliyt.šb‘t.brqm.[---]. | ṯmnt.iṣr r‘t.‘ṣ brq y. | riš h.tply.ṭly.bn.‘n h. | uz‘rt.tmll.išd h.q UG5.3.1.4
.tštyn. | [---.]il.d ‘rgzm. | [---.]dt.‘l.lty. | [---.]tdbḥ.amr. | ṯmn.b qrb.hkl y.[aṯr h.rpum]. | tdd.aṯr h.tdd.iln[ym.---]. | asr 20[121].2.1
]d nhr.umt. | [---.]rpat.bt. | [m]lk.itdb.d šb‘. | [a]ẖm.l h.ṯmnt.bn um. | krt.ḥtk n.rš. | krt.grdš.mknt. | aṯt.ṣdq h.l ypq. | 14[KRT].1.9
].‘rm. | ṯb.l pd[r.]pdrm. | ṯṯ.l ṯṯm.aẖd.‘r. | šb‘m.šb‘.pdr. | ṯmnym.b‘l.[----]. | tš‘m.b‘l.mr[-]. | bt[.--]b b‘l.b qrb. | bt.w y‘n. 4[51].7.11
]m‘t. | ṯlṯ[m.---.-]rm. | ‘šr[.---].alpm. | arb‘.ddm.l.k[-]ẖ. | ṯmnym.dd.dd.kbd. | [l].mḏr[ǵ]lm. | b yrẖ[ri]šyn. | šb[‘.--]n.[k 2012.19
it.dr‘.w.mit.drt. | w[.---.]‘m.l.mit.dd.ṯn.kbd.ḥpr.bnšm.ṯmnym.dd. | l u[-]m. | b.ṭbq.arb‘m.dr‘.w.‘šr.dd.drt. | w[.a]rb‘.l 1098.8
[ṯ]mnym.dd. | š‘rm.b.ṯydr. 1166.1
ṯmn.ddm š‘rm.l ḥmrm. 1165.1
ṯṯm.ṯlṯ.kb[d]. | arb‘m.ṯp[rt]. | ksp h. | ṯmn.dd[.--]. | ṯlṯ.dd.p[--]. | šb‘t.p[--]. | tš‘t.k[bd.---]. | ẖmšt.k[bd 2120.4
.drt. | [---]m. | t[gm]r.akl.b.gt.ǵ[l]. | ṯlṯ.mat.‘šrm[.---]. | ṯmnym.drt.a[--]. | drt.l.alpm[.---]. | šb‘m.ṯn.kbd[.ḥpr.‘b]dm. | 2013.17
.akl.b.g[t.b]ir.alp. | [‘]šrm.l.mit.ḥ[p]r.‘bdm. | mitm.drt.ṯmnym.drt. | tgmr.akl.b.gt[.b]‘ln. | ṯlṯ.mat.ṯṯm.kbd. | ṯṯm.ṯṯ.k 2013.4
.l.‘šrm.dd.l.yḥšr.bl.bn h. | b.gt.m‘br.arb‘m.l.mit.dr‘.w.ṯmnym[.drt]. | w.‘šrm.l.mit.dd.ḥp[r.]bnšm. | b.gt.ǵl.‘šrm.l.mi 1098.12
prt. | b šd.šḥlmmt.škb. | ‘mn h.šb‘.l šb‘m. | tš[‘]ly.ṯmn.l ṯmnym. | w [th]rn.w tldn mṯ. | al[iyn.b‘]l šlbšn. | i[---.---.--]l h. 5[67].5.21
.iqnu. | ẖmš.‘šr.qn.n‘m.‘n[m]. | ṯn.ḥblm.alp.alp.am[-]. | ṯmn.ḥblm.šb‘.šb‘.ma[-]. | ‘šr.kkr.rtn. | b d.šm‘y.bn.bdn. 1128.31
[.aḥ]d.mmt. | ṯṯ.pt[ḥ.---]. | ṯn.pt[ḥ.---]. | w.pt[ḥ.--]r.ṯǵr. | ṯmn.ḥlnm. | ṯṯ.ṯẖ[--].l.mtm. 1151.15
d.b d.adn‘m. | [š]b‘.b.ḥrṯm. | [ṯ]lṯ.b.ṯǵrm. | rb qrt.aẖd. | ṯmn.ẖzr. | w.arb‘.ḥršm. | dt.tb‘ln.b.pẖn. | ṯṯṯm.ẖzr.w.‘št.‘šr.ḥr 1024.3.4
ṣ.w at.qḥ. | ‘rpt k.rḥ k.mdl k. | mṭrt k.‘m k.šb‘t. | ǵlm k.ṯmn.ẖnzr k. | ‘m k.pdry.bt.ar. | ‘m k.ṭṭly.bt.rb.idk. | pn k.al tt 5[67].5.9
qb. | b.gt.‘mq.ẖmš.ẖrmṯt.n[it]. | krk.m‘ṣd.mqb. | b.gwl.ṯmn.ẖrmṯt.[nit]. | krk.m‘ṣd.mqb. | [b] gt.ipṯl.ṯṯ.ẖrmṯ[t.nit]. | [2048.11
mšq.mlkt. | mitm.ṯṯm. | kbd.ks[p]. | ksp. | ṯmnym. | ẖrṣ. 1157.5
.ḥry]. | ṭbẖ.š[mn].mri k. | ptḥ.[rḥ]bt.yn. | ṣḥ.šb‘m.ṯr y. | ṯmnym.[ẓ]by y. | ṯr.ẖbr[.rb]t. | ẖbr[.ṯrrt]. | [-]‘b[-].š[--]m. | [---- 15[128].4.7
n.d.l.ṭb. | b.gt.gwl. | ṯlṯm.tš‘[.kbd.yn].d.l[.ṭb].b.gt.ipṯl. | ṯmnym.[yn].ṭb.b.gt.š[---]. | tš‘m.[ẖ]mš[.kbd].yn.b gt[.-]n. | ar 1084.20
[-]dyn.arb‘.yn. | abškn.kdm.yn. | šbn.kdm.yn. | ‘bdiltp.ṯm[n].y[n]. | qṣn.ẖ[---]. | arny.[---]. | aǵltn.ẖmš[.yn]. 1085.9
[---.ṯl]š.yn. | [---.a]rb‘.yn. | [---.arb]‘.yn. | [---].ṯmn.yn. | [---.-]ṯr.kdm.yn. | [-]dyn.arb‘.yn. | abškn.kdm.yn. | š 1085.4
yn. | apṯ. | šbn. | gbrn. | ṯb‘m. | kyn. | b‘ln. | ytršp. | ḥmšm.ṯmn.kbd. | tgmr.bnš.mlk. | d.b d.adn‘m. | [š]b‘.b.ḥrṯm. | [ṯ]lṯ.b. 1024.2.25
rm. | mrynm. | ṯlṯ.‘šr. | hbṭnm. | ṯmn. | mḏrǵlm. | ṯmnym.ṯmn.kbd. | tgmr.ẖrd. | arb‘m.l.mit. | ṯn.kbd. 1031.14
‘m.[ẖ]mš[.kbd].yn.b gt[.-]n. | arb‘m.kbd.yn.ṭb.w.[--]. | ṯmn.kbd.yn.d.l.ṭb.b.gn‘[y]. | mitm.yn.ḥsp.d.nkly.b.db[ḥ.--]. | 1084.23
. | [m]it.ṯlṯm.kbd.šmn. | [l.]abrm.mšrm. | [mi]tm.arb‘m.ṯmn.kbd. | [l.]sbrdnm. | m[i]t.l.bn.‘ẓmt.rišy. | mit.l.tlmyn.bn.‘ 2095.5
z.bn pls. | kd.‘l.ynḥm. | tgrm.šmn.d.bn.kwy. | ‘l.šlmym.ṯmn.kbd. | ṯṯm.šmn. 1082.2.9
n[-.]l ks[p.-]m. | l.mri[.--]. | ṯmn kbd[.--]i. | arb‘m[.--]. | l apy.mr[i.--]. | [---.--]d. | [-----]. 1133.3

[---].yryt. | [---.a]drt. | [--.ṯṯ]m.ṯmn.k[bd]. | [---.yr]yt.dq[-]. | [--.ṯ]lṯm.l.mi[t]. | [---.]arbʿ.kbd. 2170.3
kbd.ddm.kbd[.---]. | [---.]ʿm.kbd.l.rʿ[ym.---]. | [---].kbd.ṯmn.kb[d.---]. 1098.48
ṯlṯ.d yṣa. | b d.šmmn. | l argmn. | l nskm. | ṯmn.kkrm. | alp.kbd. | [m]itm.kbd. 147[90].5
ṯmn.kkr.ṯlṯ. | ṯmn.kkr.brr. | arbʿ.alpm.pḥm. | ḫmš.mat.kbd. | arbʿ.alpm.iqni 1130.2
ṯmn.kkr.ṯlṯ. | ṯmn.kkr.brr. | arbʿ.alpm.pḥm. | ḫmš.mat.kbd. | a 1130.1
pm.pḥm.ḫm[š].mat.kbd. | b d.tt.w.ṯlṯ.ktnt.b dm.tt. | w.ṯmnt.ksp.hn. | ktn.d.ṣr.pḥm.b h.w.ṯqlm. | ksp h.mitm.pḥm.b 1110.3
[---.]ḫ[---.]ṯmnym[.k]sp ḫmšt. | [w a]rbʿ kkr ʿl bn[.--]. | [w] ṯlṯ šmn. | [w 1103.1
. | ṯlṯ.ktnt.b d.an[r]my. | b.ʿšrt.ksp.b.a[--]. | ṯqlm.ḫr[ṣ.]b.ṯmnt.ksp. | ʿšrt.ksp.b.alp.[b d].bn.[---]. | tšʿ.ṣin.b.tšʿt.ksp. | mšl 2101.20
lp kb[d]. | ṯlṯ.l.nskm.birtym. | b d.urtn.w.ṯṯ.mat.brr. | b.ṯmnym.ksp.ṯlṯt.kbd. | ḫmš.alp.ṯlṯ.l.ḫlby. | b d.tlmi.b.ʿšrm.ḫm 2101.5
lpṯr.ṯn.krmm.w.ṯlṯ.ub[dym.---]. | qmnz.ṯṯ.krm.yknʿm.ṯmn.krm[.---]. | krm.nʿmn.b.ḫly.ull.krm.aḫ[d.---]. | krm.uḫn. 1081.11
ṯlṯ.mat.[---]. | ṯmnt.k[---]. 1149.2
tt. | tqḥ.bt k.ǵlmt.tšʿrb. | ḥqr k.tld.šbʿ.bnm.l k. | w ṯmn.ṯṯmnm. | l k.tld.yṣb.ǵlm. | ynq.ḥlb.a[ṯ]rt. | mṣṣ.ṯd.btlt.[ʿnt]. | 15[128].2.24
dd.ḥp[r.]bnšm. | b.gt.ǵl.ʿšrm.l.mit.drʿ.w.tšʿm.drt. | [w].ṯmnym.l.mit.dd.ḥpr.bnšm. | b.gt.alḫb.ṯṯm.drʿ.w.ḫmšm.drt.w 1098.15
ṯdn.ʿšr. | [ḥ]mrm. | ddm.l.ybr[k]. | bdmr.prs.l.u[-]m[-]. | ṯmn.l.ʿšrm. | dmd.b d.mry[n]m. 2102.9
[--].d.ntn[.d.]ksp. | [ṯ]mn.l.ʿšrm[.l.b]t.ʿṯtrt. | [ṯ]lṯ.ʿšr h.[b]t.ršp.gn. | arbʿ.b d.b[n].u 1088.2
bdyrḫ.šbʿt.ʿšrt ʿšrt.šlm. | yky.ʿšrt.ṯṯt šlm.ʿšrt. | bn.ḥgby.ṯmnt.l ʿšrm.ʿšrt.ḫmš.kbd. | bn.ilṣdq.šbʿt ṯlṯt šlm. | bn.ṯmq.arb 1131.8
spr.bnš.mlk. | d.b d.prṭ. | tšʿ.l.ʿšrm. | lqḥ.ššlmt. | ṯmn.l.arbʿm. | lqḥ.šʿrt. 1025.5
[-]. | [b] ǵb.ršp mh bnš. | šrp.w ṣp ḫršḥ. | ʿlm b ǵb ḥyr. | ṯmn l ṯlṯm ṣin. | šbʿ.alpm. | bt bʿl.ugrt.ṯn šm. | ʿlm.l ršp.mlk. | UG5.12.B.4
b dbr.prt. | b šd.šḥlmmt.škb. | ʿmn h.šbʿ.l šbʿm. | tš[ʿ]ly.ṯmn.l ṯmnym. | w [th]rn.w tldn mṯ. | al[iyn.bʿ]l šlbšn. | i[---.--- 5[67].5.21
[ḫ h]. | km.all.dm.ary h. | k šbʿt.l šbʿm.aḫ h.ym[.--]. | w ṯmnt.l ṯmnym. | šr.aḫy h.mẓa h. | w mẓa h.šr.yly h. | b skn.sk 12[75].2.50
.alḫn.b.ʿšrt[.k]sp. | rṭ.l.ql.d.ybl.prd. | b.ṯql.w.nṣp.ksp. | ṯmn.lbšm.w.mšlt. | l.udmym.b.ṯmnt.ʿšrt.ksp. | šbʿm.lbš.d.ʿrb. 2101.14
iršt.yṣḥm. | arbʿ.alpm. | mitm.kbd.ṯlṯ. | arbʿ.kkrm. | ṯmn.mat.kbd. | pwt. | ṯmn.mat.pṯṯm. | kkrm.alpm. | ḫmš.mat. 2051.5
lpm. | mitm.kbd.ṯlṯ. | arbʿ.kkrm. | ṯmn.mat.kbd. | pwt. | ṯmn.mat.pṯṯm. | kkrm.alpm. | ḫmš.mat.kbd. | abn.ṣrp. 2051.7
[---.ṯ]lṯ.mat. | [---.m]itm.mqp.m[---]. | [---.ṯmn]ym.mgnm ar[bʿ]. | [---.-]aḥ.mqḥ mqḥm. | [---.--]t.ʿšr rmǵ 1145.1.3
rum.ʿšr. | šbʿ.ḫsnm. | mkrm. | mrynm. | ṯlṯ.ʿšr. | hbṯnm. | ṯmn. | mdrǵlm. | ṯmnym.ṯmn.kbd. | tgmr.ḥrd. | arbʿm.l.mit. | ṯ 1031.12
.pldm.dt.šʿrt. | ṯlṯm.ṯlṯ.kbd.mṣrrt. | ʿšr.ṯn.kbd.pǵdrm. | ṯmn.mrbdt.mlk. | ʿšr.pld.šʿrt. 1111.11
ṯmn.mrkbt.dt. | ʿrb.bt.mlk. | yd.apnt hn. | yd.ḥẓ hn. | yd.tr hn. 1121.1
yn.iš[ryt.-]lnr. | spr.[--]ḥ[-] k.šbʿt. | ghl.ph.ṯmnt. | nblu h.špš.ymp. | hlkt.tdr[--]. | špš.bʿd h.t[--]. | aṯr.aṯr 27[8].3
b.tk.mdbr qdš. | ṯm tgrgr.l abnm.w l.ʿṣm.šbʿ.šnt. | tmt.ṯmn.nqpt.ʿd.ilm.nʿmm.ttlkn. | šd.tṣdn.pat.mdbr.w ngš.hm.n 23[52].67
ʿ.trʿn.a[--.---]. | bnt.šdm.ṣḥr[.---]. | šbʿ.šnt.il.mla.[-]. | w ṯmn.nqpnt.ʿd. | k lbš.km.lpš.dm a[ḫ h]. | km.all.dm.ary h. | k 12[75].2.46
[---.--]y.hnn. | [---.kll].šlm. | [---.ṯ]mn.ʿm k. | [m]nm.šlm. | [---.w.r]gm.ṯṯb. 2171.3
[--.]wmrkm. | bir.ḫmš. | uškn.arbʿ. | ubrʿy.ṯlṯ. | ar.ṯmn ʿšr h. | mlk.arbʿ. | ǵbl.ḫmš. | atlg.ḫmš ʿšr[h]. | ulm ṯ[ṯ]. | m 68[65].1.5
šbʿ.ṯnnm.w.šbʿ.ḫsnm. | ṯmn.ʿšr h.mrynm. | ʿšr.mkrm. | ḫmš.ṯrtnm. | ḫmš.bn.mrynm. 1030.2
.prd. | b.ṯql.w.nṣp.ksp. | ṯmn.lbšm.w.mšlt. | l.udmym.b.ṯmnt.ʿšrt.ksp. | šbʿm.lbš.d.ʿrb.bt.mlk. | b.mit.ḫmšt.kbd.ksp. | ṯ 2101.15
kbd.ḫmš.šl[m.---]. | tlmyn.šbʿt.ʿšrt ʿšrt[.šlm.---]. | ybn.ṯmnt.ʿšrt ʿšrt.šlm. | ʿbdyrḫ.šbʿt.ʿšrt ʿšrt.šlm. | yky.ʿšrt.ṯṯt šlm.ʿ 1131.5
ym ḥdṯ. | alp.w š.l bʿlt bhtm. | b arbʿt ʿšrt.bʿl. | ʿrkm. | b ṯmnt.ʿšrt.yr | tṯṣ.mlk.brr. | ʿlm.tzǵ.b ǵb.ṣpn. | nḥkt.ksp.w ḫrṣ UG5.12.A.5
ṯmn ʿšr šurt l [---]. | ṯmn šurt l ar[--.---]. | ṯn šurtm l bnš [---]. 137.1[92].1
.ṯlṯt. | mṯyn.b.ṯṯt. | ṯn.lbšm.b.ʿšrt. | pld.b.arbʿt. | lbš.ṯn.b.ṯnt.ʿšrt. 1108.8
[-]ḏmu.apsty.b[--]. | w.bn h.w aṯt h.w.alp.w ṯmn.ṣin. | [-]dln.qmnzy.w.a[ṯt h]. | wšṯn.bn h. | ṯmgdl.yknʿmy 1080.2
.ṣmdm. | w.ṯlṯ.ʿšr.bnš. | yd.ytm.yd.rʿy.ḥmrm. | b.gt.gwl.ṯmn.ṣmdm. | w.arbʿ.ʿšr.bnš. | yd.ngr.mdrʿ.yd.š[--]m. | [b.]gt.ip 2038.4
m.ṣ[md]. | ṯṯ kbd.b ḥ[--]. | w.arbʿ.ḥ[mrm]. | b m[ʿ]rby. | ṯmn.ṣmd.[---]. | b d.bʿlsr. | yd.ṯdn.ʿšr. | [ḥ]mrm. | ddm.l.ybr[k]. 2102.2
n.lgn. | bn.bʿyn. | šdyn. | ary. | brqn. | bn.ḫlln. | bn.mṣry. | ṯmn.qšt. | w ʿšr.uṯpt. | upšt irš[-]. 118[306].14
ksp.d mkr. | mlk. | ṯlṯ.mat.ksp.d.šb[n]. | mit.ksp.d.ṯbq. | ṯmnym.arbʿt. | kbd.ksp. | d.nqdm. | ḫmšm.l mit. | ksp.d.mkr.a 2107.6
[-----]. | [---.]abl.qšt ṯmn. | ašrbʿ.qṣʿt.w hn šb[ʿ]. | b ymm.apnk.dnil.mt. | rpi.a hn.ǵ 17[2AQHT].5.2
un.yr.ʿrpt. | tmṭr.b qẓ.ṭl.yṭll. | l ǵnbm.šbʿ.šnt. | yṣr k.bʿl.ṯmn.rkb. | ʿrpt.bl.ṭl.bl rbb. | bl.šrʿ.thmtm.bl. | ṭbn.ql.bʿl.k tmzʿ 19[1AQHT].1.43
ʿbdrṯ[b.---]. | b ṯṯ ʿtr ṯmn.r[qḥ.---]. | p bn btb[-.---]. | b ḫmṯ ʿtr k[--.---]. | b ḫmṯ ʿtr[. 207[57].2
ṯmn ʿšr šurt l [---]. | ṯmn šurt l ar[--.---]. | ṯn šurtm l bnš [---]. | arbʿ šurt l bn[š.---] 137.1[92].2
ʿprm.ṯṯ. | ḫlb krd.ṯn ʿšr. | qmy.arbʿ.ʿšr. | ṣʿq.arbʿ ʿšr. | ṣʿ.ṯmn. | šḥq.ʿšrm.arbʿ.kbd. | ḫlb rpš arbʿ.ʿšr. | bqʿt ṯṯ. | irab ṯn.ʿšr 67[110].5
ṯlṯ.mat.ṯlṯm. | kbd.šmn. | l kny. | ṯmnym.šmn. | b d.adnnʿm. 1094.4
m.all.dm.ary h. | k šbʿt.l šbʿm.aḫ h.ym[.--]. | w ṯmnt.l ṯmnym. | šr.aḫy h.mẓa h. | w mẓa h.šr.yly h. | b skn.sknm.b ʿ 12[75].2.50
[m.---.-]dyt. | ṣlʿt.alp.mri. | ʿšr.bmt.alp.mri. | ṯn.nšbm. | ṯmnym.tbṯḫ.alp. | uz.mrat.mlḥt. | arbʿ.uzm.mrat.bqʿ. | ṯlṯ.[-]ṯt 1128.19
ṯlṯ.ʿšr.mkrm. | ṯlṯ.bn.mrynm. | arbʿ.ṯrtnm. | tšʿ.ḫbṯnm. | ṯmnym.ṯlṯ.kbd. | mdrǵlm. | w.šbʿ.ʿšr.ḫsnm. | ḫmšm.l.mit. | bnš 1029.11
m. | mkrm. | mrynm. | ṯlṯ.ʿšr. | hbṯnm. | ṯmn. | mdrǵlm. | ṯmnym.ṯmn.kbd. | tgmr.ḥrd. | arbʿm.l.mit. | ṯn.kbd. 1031.14
krt.aṯt. | tqḥ.bt k.ǵlmt.tšʿrb. | ḥqr k.tld.šbʿ.bnm.l k. | w ṯmn.ṯṯmnm. | l k.tld.yṣb.ǵlm. | ynq.ḥlb.a[ṯ]rt. | mṣṣ.ṯd.btlt.[ʿn 15[128].2.24
-]. | ṯḥgrn.ǵzr.nʿm.[---]. | w šm.ʿrbm.yr[.---]. | mṯbt.ilm.ṯmn.ṯ[--.---]. | pamt.šbʿ. | iqnu.šmt[.---]. | [b]n.šrm. | iqran.ilm.n 23[52].19
zpḫ ṯlṯt. | kṯr[.---.--]trt ḫmšt.bn gda[.-.]mḏʿ. | kl[--.---.]ṯmnt.[--.]w[.---]. | [-]m[.---.]ṣpiry[.ṯ]lṯt[.---]. APP.II[173].60
b.[---.]l qrb.mym. | tql.[---.]lb.tt[b]r. | qšt[.---]r.y[t]br. | ṯmn.[---.]btlt.[ʿ]nt. | ttb.[---.--]ša. | tlm.km[.---.]yd h.k šr. | knr 19[1AQHT].1.5
rbʿm. | [---.tš]ʿm. | [---.t]šʿm. | [---.--]y arbʿm. | [---.]l špš ṯmny[m]. | [---.]dbr h l šp[š]. | [---.]dbr h l šp[š]. | [---.]npṯry ṯ[41[71].7
.g h[.---]. | i.ap.bʿ[l.---]. | i.hd.d[---.---]. | ynpʿ.bʿ[l.---]. | b ṯmnt.[---]. | yqrb.[---]. | lḥm.m[---.---]. | [ʿ]d.lḥm[.šty.ilm]. | w 5[67].4.9
[---].ʿšr. | [---].ṯlṯ. | [---].ṯmn. | [---].ṯlṯ. | [---].aḥd. | u[--].ṯn. | hz[p].ṯṯ. | ḫrṣbʿ.aḥd. | ypr.a 70[112].3
]r.[k]bd[.---]. | [a]lpm[.---]. | tg[m]r.[---]. | ṯlṯ ma[t.---]. | ṯmnym[.---]. | [ṯ]mny[m.---]. | [-]r[-.---]. | [--]m.l.[---]. | a[---.---] 2013.27
. | ṯlṯ.a[--.---]. | ḫmš[.---]. | ksp[.---]. | k[--.---]. | ar[bʿ.---]. | ṯmn[.---]. | [-]r[-.---]. | w ṯṯ.[---]. | ṯlṯm[.---]. | mil[-.---]. 148[96].10
[a]lpm[.---]. | tg[m]r.[---]. | ṯlṯ ma[t.---]. | ṯmnym[.---]. | [ṯ]mny[m.---]. | [-]r[-.---]. | [--]m.l.[---]. | a[---.---]. | ʿšrm.drt[.--- 2013.28

[---]t ṯm[n.---]. | [--]l ḫmš[.---]. | [----.]ḫmš[.---]. | [--.-]rn.ʻrbt[.---]. | [151[25].1
]m.bn l[---]. | [---].bn ṣd[-.---]. | [---.--]mn.mi[t.---]. | [---.ṯm]nym[.---]. | [---.-]dn.ṯlṯ[m.---]. | [---].mitm[.---]. | [---.--]m. 149[99].10
[--]l ḫmš[.---]. | [----.]ḫmš[.---]. | [--.-]rn.ʻrbt[.---]. | [---].ṯmnym[.---]. | [---.--]p.mit[.---]. 151[25].5
lṯ.mat.šbʻm[.---]. | [---.--]mm.b.mṣbt[.---]. | [---.ṯl]ṯ.mat.ṯmny[m.---]. 2149.5
bn ʻṭl.[---]. | ypḫ knʻm[.---]. | aḫmn bt[.---]. | b ḫmṯ ʻṯr ṯmn[.---]. 207[57].11

ṯmq

[-----]. | [bn.]ibln. | ysd. | bn.ṯmq. | bn.agmn. | bn.uṣb. | bn.yzg. | bn.anntn. | bn.kwn. | ǵmšd. 115[301].4.3
| [--]šmyn. | [w.]nḫl h. | bn.qṣn. | bn.ksln. | bn.ṣrym. | bn.ṯmq. | bn.ntp. | bn.mlk. | bn.ṭʻ[-]. | bn.km[-]. | bn.r[--]. | [bn.]ʻ[-- 1073.1.8
]. | [b]n.[---]. | bn.a[--]. | bn.ml[k]. | bn.glyn. | bn.ʻdr. | bn.ṯmq. | bn.ntp. | bn.ʻgrt. 1057.20
---].šbʻt.ʻšrt. | [---.-]kyn.ʻšrt. | b.bn.ʻsl.ʻšrm.ṯqlm kbd. | b.ṯmq.ḫmšt.l.ʻšrt. | b.[---].šbʻt.ʻšrt. | b.bn.pdrn.ʻšrm. | d.bn.šbʻl.u 2054.1.7
y.ṯmnt.l ʻšrm.ʻšrt.ḫmš.kbd. | bn.ilṣdq.šbʻt ṯlṯt šlm. | bn.ṯmq.arbʻt ṯqlm šlmm. 1131.10
lsmt.ṯm.yṯbš.šm.il.mt m. | yʻbš.brk n.šm.il.ǵzrm. | ṯm.ṯmq.rpu.bʻl.mhr bʻl. | w mhr.ʻnt.ṯm.yḥpn.ḥyl | y.zbl.mlk.ʻllm 22.2[124].8

ṯmr

yknʻm[.---]. | qm[n]z[---]. | šl[-.---]. | ar[--.---]. | qrt[.---]. | ṯm[r.---]. | dm[t.---]. | gl[bt.---]. | al[-.---]. 1181.13

ṯmry

]. | yknʻm. | šlmy. | [-----]. | [-----]. | q[---]. | ṯ[---]. | ṯl[rby]. | ṯmr[y]. | aǵ[t]. | dm[t]. | šl[-]. | [---]m. | [-]rm. | [-]dm. | [-]m. | [--] 2058.2.37
qrty.w.[b]n h[.---]. | w.alp h.w.a[r]bʻ.l.arbʻ[m.---]. | pln.ṯmry.w.ṯn.bn h.w[.---]. | ymrn.apsny.w.aṯt h..b[n.---]. | prd.m 2044.8
tn bn.agyn. | ullym.bn.abynm. | antn.bn.iwr[n]r. | pwn.ṯmry. | ksyn.bn.lḫsn. | [-]kyn.ṯmry. 94[313].8
[--]n.ʻš[r.] | [a]rt[.a]rbʻ[.---]. | ʻnmky.ʻšr.[---]. | ṯmry.ʻšr.ṯn.k[rmm.---]. | liy.krm.aḥd[.---]. | ʻbdmlk.krm.aḥ[d. 1081.4
lrby. | dmt. | aǵt. | w.qmnz. | slḫ. | yknʻm. | šlmy. | w.ull. | ṯmry. | qrt. | ʻrm. | nnu. | [--]. | [---]. | mʻr. | arny. | ubrʻy. | ilštmʻ. | 71[113].20
qrt ṯqlm.w nṣp. | šlmy.ṯql. | ary ṯql. | ṯmry ṯql.w.nṣp. | aǵt nṣp. | dmt ṯql. | yknʻm ṯql. 69[111].4
. | antn.bn.iwr[n]r. | pwn.ṯmry. | ksyn.bn.lḫsn. | [-]kyn.ṯmry. 94[313].10

ṯmrn

. | bn.nqly. | bn.snrn. | bn.ṯgd. | bn.d[-]n. | bn.amdn. | bn.ṯmrn. | bn.pzny. | bn.mglb. | bn.[--]b. | bn.[---]. | bn.[---]. 113[400].6.30
šd.bn.š[--]y. | šd.bn.ṯ[---]. | šd.ʻdmn[.bn.]ynḥm. | šd.bn.ṯmr[n.m]idḫy. | šd.ṯbʻm[.--]y. 2026.9

ṯmt

tm. | ʻz.mid. | hm.nṯkp. | mʻn k. | w.mnm. | rgm.d.tšmʻ. | ṯmt.w.št. | b.spr.ʻm y. 53[54].18

ṯnw

. | nʻmn. | rbil. | plsy. | ygmr. | mnṯ. | prḫ. | ʻdršp. | ršpab. | ṯnw. | abmn. | abǵl. | bʻldn. | ypʻ. 1032.10

ṯny

ddt. | km irby.tškn. | šd.k ḥsn.pat. | mdbr.tlkn. | ym.w ṯn.aḫr. | šp[š]m.b [ṯ]lṯ. | ym[ǵy.]l qdš. | a[ṯrt.]ṣrm.w l ilt. | ṣd[y 14[KRT].4.195
d.dg[-.---]. | tʻln.l mrkbt hm.ti[ty.l ʻr hm]. | tlkn.ym.w ṯa aḫr.š[pšm.b ṯlṯ]. | mǵy.rpum.l grnt.i[lnym.l] | mṭʻt.w yʻn. 20[121].2.5
r[kbt.---]. | tʻln.l mr[kbt hm.tity.l] | ʻr hm.tl[kn.ym.w ṯn.aḫr.špšm]. | b ṯlṯ.mǵy[.rpum.l grnt]. | i[ln]y[m].l mṭʻt[.---]. 22.1[123].24
md.arz h. | tšt.išt.b bht m. | nb[l]at.b hkl m. | hn.ym.w ṯn.tikl. | išt.b bht m.nblat. | b hk[l] m.ṯlṯ.kbʻ ym. | tikl[.i]št.b b 4[51].6.24
--]. | [--]d mʻqby[.---]. | swn.qrty.w[.aṯt h]. | [w].bn h.w.ṯn.alpm. | [w.]ṯlṯm.ṣin. | anndr.yknʻmy. | w.aṯt h.w.bn h. | w.al 1080.13
ḫmšm.dd. | nʻr. | ḫmšm.tišr. | ḫmš.ktnt. | ḫmš.ṯnt.alpm. | ʻšrm.hbn. | ṯlṯ.mat.dd. | šʻrm. | mit.šmn. | ʻšr.kat. | ẓr 2102.5
prš. | [---.]šdm. | [---.-]nm.prš.glbm. | [---.]ʻgd.dqr. | [---.]ṯn.alpm. | [---.ṯ]n alpm. | [---.--]r[.ʻ]šr.ṣin. | [---.]klkl. 1142.8
. | [---.-]nm.prš.glbm. | [---.]ʻgd.dqr. | [---.]ṯn.alpm. | [---.ṯ]n alpm. | [---.--]r[.ʻ]šr.ṣin. | [---.]klkl. 1142.8
ṯṯ. | ḫrṣbʻ.aḥd. | ypr.arb. | m[-]qb.ʻšr. | ṯnʻy.ṯlṯ. | ḫlb ʻprm.ṯn. | tmdy.ṯlṯ. | [--]rt.arbʻ. | [---].ʻšr. 70[112].12
ṯb. | aṯt.w.ṯn.bn h.b.bt.iwwpzn. | aṯt.w.pǵt.b.bt.ydrm. | ṯṯ.aṯtm.adrtm.w.pǵt.aḥt.b[.bt.---]. | aṯt.w ṯn.nʻrm.b.bt.ilsk. | a 80[119].7
-]l. | [ṯ]lṯ.aṯt.adrt.w.ṯlṯ.ǵzr[m]. | w.ḫmš.nʻrt.b.bt.sk[n]. | ṯṯ.aṯtm.adrtm.w.pǵt.w ǵzr[.aḥd.b.bt.---]. | aṯt.w.ṯṯ.pǵtm.w.ǵ 80[119].18
r.zbl.ʻršm. | yšu.ʻwr. | mzl.ymzl. | w ybl.trḫ.ḥdṯ. | ybʻr.l ṯn.aṯt h. | w l nkr.mddt. | km irby.tškn. | šd.k ḥsn.pat. | mdbr. 14[KRT].4.190
škr.zbl.ʻršm. | yšu.ʻwr.mzl. | ymzl.w yṣi.trḫ. | ḥdṯ.ybʻr.l ṯn. | aṯt h.lm.nkr. | mddt h.k irby. | [t]škn.šd. | km.ḥsn.pat.md 14[KRT].2.101
.b.bt.ilsk. | aṯt.ad[r]t.b.bt.armwl. | aṯt.aḥt.b.bt.iwrpzn. | ṯṯ.aṯtm.w.pǵt.aḥt.b bt.[-]r[-]. | [aṯ]t.b.bt.aupš. | [aṯ]t.b.bt.ṯpṭbʻ 80[119].11
ǵzr[.aḥd.b.bt.---]. | aṯt.w.ṯṯ.pǵtm.w.ǵzr.aḥd.b.[bt.---]. | ṯṯ.aṯtm.w.pǵt.w.ǵzr.aḥd.b.[bt.---]. | aṯt.w.bn h.w.pǵt.aḥt.b.bt 80[119].20
l.yb[nn]. | bʻl y.r[gm]. | ṯḥm.ʻbd[--]. | ʻbd k. | l pʻn.bʻl y. | ṯn id.šbʻ d. | mrḥqtm. | qlt.ʻm. | bʻl y.mnm. | šlm. | [r]gm[.ṯṯṯb]. 2115.2.6
gkbr. | [---] y.ʻm k. | [-]ṯn.l.stn. | [--.]d.nʻm.lbš k. | [-]dm.ṯn id. | [--]m.d.l.nʻmm. | [lm.]l.likt.ʻm y. | [---.]ʻbd.ank. | [---.ʻb] 2128.1.5
ṯn.ṯlṯ mat. | w spl ṯlṯ.mat. | w mmskn. | w.ṯṯ.mqrtm. | w.ṯn.irpm.w.ṯn.trqm. | w.qpt.w.mqḥm. | w.ṯlṯm.yn šbʻ.kbd d ṯb 1103.20
dš.yd. | [ṣt h.yʻl.]w yškb.yd. | [mizrt.]p ynl.hn.ym. | [w ṯn.uzr.]ilm.dnil. | [uzr.ilm.]ylḥm.uzr. | [yšqy.b]n.qdš ṯlṯ rbʻ y 17[2AQHT].1.7
[---.]gtn ṯṯ. | [---.]ṯḥr l ytn ḫs[n]. | ʻbd ulm ṯn un ḫsn. | gdy lqḥ šṭqn gt bn ndr. | um r[-] gtn ṯṯ ḫsn l ytn. 1154.3
rḫ.ṯn ǵlyt h. | aršmg. | ršpy.w.aṯt h. | bn.glgl.uškny. | bn.ṯny.uškny. | mnn.w.aṯt h. | slmu.ḥrš.mrkbt. | bnšm.dt.l.mlk. | ʻ 2068.14
ṯn.b gt.mzln. | ṯn.b ulm. | abmn.b gt.mʻrb. | atn. | ḫryn. | bn.ʻnt. | llwn. | agdṯb. 1061.2
lmk. | ʻdršp. | bn.knn. | pdyn. | bn.aṯtl.ṯn. | kdln.akdṯb. | ṯn.b gt yknʻm. 1061.22
ṯn.b gt.mzln. | ṯn.b ulm. | abmn.b gt.mʻrb. | atn. | ḫryn. | bn.ʻnt 1061.1
lbš.aḥd. | b.ʻšrt. | w.ṯn.b.ḫmšt. | ṯprt.b.ṯlṯt. | mṯyn.b.ṯṯt. | ṯn.lbšm.b.ʻšrt. | pld.b.arbʻ 1108.3
u]bdy.šrm. | [š]d.bn.ḫrmln.b d.bn.tnn. | [š]d.bn.ḫrmln.ṯn.b d.bn.ḫdmn. | [u]bdy.nqdm. | [ṯlṯ].šdm.d.nʻrb.gt.npk. | [š] 82[300].2.11
prt.b.ṯlṯt. | mṯyn.b.ṯṯt. | ṯn.lbšm.b.ʻšrt. | pld.b.arbʻt. | lbš.ṯn.b.ṯnt.ʻšrt. 1108.8
[s]pr.bnš.mlk.d.b.tbq. | [kr]wn. | [--]n. | [q]ṣy. | ṯn.bn.iwrḫz.[n]ʻrm. | yṣr[.-]qb. | w.ṯn.bnš.iytlm. | w.ʻšrm.ṣmd. 2066.2.4

|anntn bn[.---].|bn.brzn [---].|bnil.bn.tl[--].|bn.brzn.ṯn.|bn.išb'l[.---].|bn.s[---].|dnn.[bn.---].|bn[.--]'nt. 2069.7

.gg.|[ǵz]r.aḥd.b.bt.nwrḏ.|[aṯ]t.adrt.b.bt.artṯb.|aṯt.w.ṯn.bn h.b.bt.iwwpzn.|aṯt.w.pǵt.b.bt.ydrm.|ṯt.aṯtm.adrtm.w 80[119].5

p'n w.aṯt h.|anntn.yṣr.|annmn.w.ṯlṯ.n'[r] h.|rpan.w.ṯ[n.]bn h.|bn.ayln.w.ṯn.bn h.|yt. 2068.26

lm.|bn.b'ly.ṯlṯtm.b'lm.|w.aḥd.ḫbṯ.|w.arb'.aṯt.|bn.lg.ṯn.bn h.|b'lm.w.aḫt h.|b.šrt.|šty.w.bn h. 2080.10

n.biry.|ṯlṯ.b'lm.|w.adn hm.ṯr.w.arb'.bnt h.|yrḫm.yd.ṯn.bn h.|b'lm.w.ṯlṯ.n'rm.w.bt.aḥt.|bn.lwn.ṯlṯtm.b'lm.|bn.b' 2080.4

ry.---].|klt h.[---].|ṯty.ary.m[--.---].|nrn.arny[.---].|w.ṯn.bn h.w.b[---.---].|b tn[--.---].|swn.qrty[.---].|uḫ h.w.'šr[.- 81[329].6

b]n h[.---].|w.alp h.w.a[r]b'.l.arb'[m.---].|pln.ṯmry.w.ṯn.bn h.w[.---].|ymrn.apsny.w.aṯt h..b[n.---].|prd.m'qby[.w 2044.8

ṯr.|[']bdyrḫ.|[b]n.gg't.|[']dy.|armwl.|uwaḫ.|ypln.w.ṯn.bn h.|ydln.|anr[my].|mld.|krmp[y].|bṣmn. 2086.8

ṣr.|annmn.w.ṯlṯ.n'[r] h.|rpan.w.ṯ[n.]bn h.|bn.ayln.w.ṯn.bn h.|yt. 2068.27

n h.w aṯt h.w.alp.w ṯmn.ṣin.|[-]dln.qmnzy.w.a[ṯt h].|wšṯn.bn h.|ṯmgdl.ykn'my.w.aṯt h.|w.bn h.w.alp.aḥ[d].|aǵl 1080.4

.|w.ṯn[.bn h.---].|iwrm[-.]b[n.---].|annt[n.]w[.---].|w.ṯn.bn h.[---].|aǵltn.ypr[y.---].|w.šb'.ṣin h[.---]. 2044.16

w.---.a]ṯt h[.---].|prṯ.mgd[ly.---.]aṯ[t h].|'dyn[.---].|w.ṯn[.bn h.---].|iwrm[-.]b[n.---].|annt[n.]w[.---].|w.ṯn.bn h.[-- 2044.13

---].'tgrm.|[---.-]ṣbm.|[---.]nrn.m'ry.|[---.--]r.|[---.]w.ṯn.bn h.|[---.b]t h.'tgrm. 2043.11

ltn.[--]y.w[.aṯt h].|w.bn h.w.alp.w.[---].|[-]ln.[---].|w.ṯn.bn [h.---].|[--]d m'qby[.---].|swn.qrty.w[.aṯt h].|[w].bn h 1080.10

ṯn.bn.klby.|bn.iyṯr.|[']bdyrḫ.|[b]n.gg't.|[']dy.|armwl.|uw 2086.1

[s]ǵr.bn.bdn.|[sǵ]r.bn.psḥn.|alṯy.|sǵr.npr.|bn.ḫty.|ṯn.bnš ibrḏr.|bnš tlmi.|sǵr.ḫryn.|'dn.w sǵr h.|bn.ḥgbn. 2082.6

r]wn.|[--]n.|[q]ṣy.|ṯn.bn.iwrḫz.[n]'rm.|yṣr[.-]qb.|w.ṯn.bnš.iytlm.|w.'šrm.ṣmd.alpm. 2066.2.6

.|arb'.bnšm.b.ḫpty.|ṯṯ.bnšm.b.bir.|ṯṯ.bnšm b.uḫnp.|ṯn.bnšm.b.ḫrṣb'.|arb'.bnšm.b.hzp.|arb'.bnšm.b.šql.|arb'.b 2076.15

]nšm.b.m'r.arr.|arb'.bnšm.b.mnt.|arb'.bnšm.b.irbn.|ṯn.bnšm.b.y'rt.|ṯn.bnšm.b.'rmt.|arb'.bnšm.b.šrš.|ṯṯ.bnšm.b 2076.35

arb'.bnšm.b.hzp.|arb'.bnšm.b.šql.|arb'.bnšm.b.nni.|ṯn.bnšm.b.slḫ.|[---].bnšm.b.yny.|[--.]bnšm.b.lbnm.|arb'.bn 2076.19

arb'.bnšm.b.mnt.|arb'.bnšm.b.irbn.|ṯn.bnšm.b.y'rt.|ṯn.bnšm.b.'rmt.|arb'.bnšm.b.šrš.|ṯṯ.bnšm.b.mlk.|arb'.bnš 2076.36

t.|arb'.bnšm.b.šrš.|ṯṯ.bnšm.b.mlk.|arb'.bnšm.b.bṣr.|ṯn.bnšm.[b.]rqd.|ṯn.b[nšm.b.---]y.|[---].b[nšm.b.--]nl.|[---.-- 2076.40

-].|arb'[.bnšm.---].|ṯṯ.'šr.bnš[m.---].|'šr[.bn]šm[.---].|ṯn.bnšm.b.š[--].|arb'.bnšm.b[.---].|'šrm.bnšm.[b.]'d[--].|arb 2076.8

š.|ṯṯ.bnšm.b.mlk.|arb'.bnšm.b.bṣr.|ṯn.bnšm.[b.]rqd.|ṯn.b[nšm.b.---]y.|[---].b[nšm.b.--]nl.|[---.--]by. 2076.41

.aḥd.b.[bt.---].|aṯt.w.bn h.w.pǵt.aḥt.b.bt.m[--].|aṯt.w.ṯt.bt h.b.bt.ḫḏmrd.|aṯt.w.ṯn.ǵzrm.b.bt.ṣdqš[lm].|[a]ṯt.aḥt.b 80[119].22

qrb.hk[l m.yp]tḥ.|b'l.b dqt[.'rp]t.|ql h.qdš.b['l.y]tn.|yṯny.b'l.ṣ[---.-]pt h.|ql h.q[dš.ṭb]r.arṣ.|[---.]ǵrm[.t]ḫšn.|rḥq 4[51].7.30

bn.|p h.tiḫd.šnt h.w akl.bqmm.|tšt ḥrṣ.k lb ilnm.|w ṯn.gprm.mn gpr h.šr.|aqht.y'n.kmr.kmr[.--].|k ap'.il.b gdrt 19[1AQHT].1.11

|p[ḫ]r.bn.ilm.štt.|p[--].b ṯlḥn y.qlt.|b ks.ištyn h.|dm.ṯn.dbḥm.šna.b'l.ṯlṯ.|rkb.'rpt.dbḥ.|bṯt.w dbḥ.w dbḥ.|dnt.w 4[51].3.17

spr.'rbnm.|dt.'rb.|b.mtn.bn.ayaḫ.|b.ḫbṯ h.ḥwt.ṯt h.|w.mnm.šalm.|dt.tknn.|'l.'rbnm.|hn hmt.|tknn.|mtn. 1161.4

m.|w ilt.ṣdynm.|hm.ḥry.bt y.|iqḥ.aš'rb.ǵlmt.|ḥẓr y.ṯn h.wspm.|atn.w ṯlṯ h.ḫrṣm.|ylk ym.w ṯn.|ṯlṯ.rb'.ym.|aḫr. 14[KRT].4.205

---].|'r[.---].|w y[---].|b'd[.---].|yaṯr[.---].|b d k.[---].|ṯnnt h[.---].|ṯlṯt h[.-.w y'n].|lṭpn.[il.d pid.my].|b ilm.[ydy. 16[126].5.8

[---].'šr.|[---].ṯlṯ.|[---].ṯmn.|[---].ṯlṯ.|[---].aḥd.|u[--].ṯn.|hz[p].ṯṯ.|ḫrṣb'.aḥd.|ypr.arb.|m[-]qb.'šr.|ṯn'y.ṯlṯ.|ḫlb ' 70[112].6

d].|ṯlṯ.mat.rbt.|hlk.l alpm.ḫḏḏ.|w l.rbt.kmyr.|aṯr.ṯn.ṯn.hlk.|aṯr.ṯlṯ.kl hm.|aḥd.bt h.ysgr.|almnt.škr.|tškr.zbl.'rš 14[KRT].4.182

.|ṯnn.d bl.hg.|hlk.l alpm.ḫḏḏ.|w l rbt.kmyr.|[a]ṯr.ṯn.ṯn.hlk.|aṯr.ṯlṯ.kl hm.|yḥd.bt h.sgr.|almnt.škr.|tškr.zbl.'rš 14[KRT].2.94

any.al[ṯy].|d b atlg[.---].|ḫmš 'š[r].|kkr.ṯ[lṯ].|ṯt hrt[m].|ṯn mq[pm].|ulṯ.ṯl[t].|krk.kly[.--].|ḫmš.mr[kbt].| 2056.5

t.ḥkpt.|mit.dnn.|mitm.iqnu.|ḫmš.'šr.qn.n'm.'n[m].|ṯn.ḥblm.alp.alp.am[-].|ṯmn.ḥblm.šb'.šb'.ma[-].|'šr.kkr.rtn. 1128.30

t.|ṯṯtm.ḫzr.|dt.tb'ln.|b.gt.ḥršm.|ṯn.ḥršm.|[-]nbkm.|ṯn.ḥršm.|b.gt.ǵl.|[-.]nǵr.mdr'.|[-].nǵr[.--]m.|[-.-]psl.qšt.|[ṯl 1024.3.14

r.ḥrš.|dt.tb'ln.b.ugrt.|ṯṯtm.ḫzr.|dt.tb'ln.|b.gt.ḥršm.|ṯn.ḥršm.|[-]nbkm.|ṯn.ḥršm.|b.gt.ǵl.|[-.]nǵr.mdr'.|[-].nǵr[.- 1024.3.12

-]r.dbḥ[.šmn.mr].|šmn.rqḥ[.-]bt.mtnt[.w ynt.qrt].|w ṯn ḥṯm.w bǵr.arb['.---].|kdm.yn.prs.qmḥ.[---].|mdbḥt.bt.ilt. 35[3].22

b[.---].|dbḥ šmn mr[.šmn.rqḥ.bt].|mtnt.w ynt.[qrt.w ṯn.ḥṯm].|w bǵr.arb'.[---.kdm.yn].|prs.qmḥ.m'[--.---].|mdbḥ APP.II[173].23

ṯn.ḫ[---].pgam.|ṯn[.---.b]n.mlk.|ṯ[n.---.]gpn.|[-----].|[---.--]b 1150.1

m.ṯn.kst.|spl.mšlt.w.mqḥm.|w md h.|arn.w mznm.|ṯn.ḫlpnm.|ṯt.mrḥm.|drb.|mrbd.|mškbt. 2050.6

ṯn pǵn.[-]dr|m.ṯn kndwm adrm.|w knd pnṯ.dq.|ṯn ḫpnm.ṯn pldm ǵlmm.|kpld.b[-.-]r[--].|w blḫ br[-]m p[-]. 140[98].4

---.b']lt.bhtm.š[--.---].|[---.-]rt.l.dml[.---].|[b.yrḫ].nql.ṯn.ḫpn[.---].|[---].aḥd.ḫmš.am[--.---].|[---.--]m.qmṣ.ṯlṯm.i[q 1106.35

spr.npṣ.krw.|ṯt.ḫṭrm.ṯn.kst.|spl.mšlt.w.mqḥm.|w md h.|arn.w mznm.|ṯ 2050.2

nhr.l p'n.il.|[l t]pl.l tštḥwy.pḫr.m'd.qmm.a[--].amr.|[ṯn]y.d't hm.išt.ištm.yitmr.ḥrb.ltšt.|[--]n hm.rgm.l ṯr.ab h.il. 2.1[137].32

r.ll.l p'n.il].|al.tpl.al.tštḥwy.pḫr [m'd.qmm.a--.am]|r ṯny.d't km.w rgm.l ṯr.a[b.-.il.ṯny.l pḫr].|m'd.tḥm.ym.b'l k 2.1[137].16

[-----].|[---.r]ḥm.tld.|[---.]ḫrm.ṯn.ym.|tš[.---.]ymm.lk.|hrg.ar[b'.]ymm.bṣr.|kp.šsk k.[--].l 13[6].3

'd[rš]p.|pqr.|ṯǵr.|ttǵl.|ṯn.yṣḥm.|slṯmg.|kdrl.|wql.|adrdn.|prn.|'bdil.|ušy.šbn[-]. 1069.5

ṣ].|arb'.b.gt.b'ln.|'št.'šr.b.gpn.|yd.'dnm.|arb'.ǵzlm.|ṯn.yṣrm. 2103.10

qrht.d.tššlmn.|ṯlrb h.|art.ṯn.yrḫm.|ṯlrby.yrḫ.w.ḫm[š.ym]m.|ṯlḥny.yrḫ.w.ḫm[š.ymm] 66[109].3

m'.mṯt.ḥry.|ṯṭbḫ.imr.w lḥm.|mgṯ.w yṯrm.hn.ym.|w ṯn.yṯb.krt.l 'd h.|yṯb.l ksi mlk.|l nḫt.l kḥṯ.drkt.|ap.yṣb.yṯb. 16.6[127].22

.[']m y.twtḥ.išd k.|[dm.rgm.iṯ.l y.]w argm k.hwt.|[w aṯny k.rgm.]'ṣ.w lḫšt.|[abn.rgm.l td]'.nš[m.w l t]bn.|[hmlt. 3['NT].4.58

n.'m y.|twtḥ.išd k.dm.rgm.|iṯ.l y.w argm k.|hwt.w aṯny k.rgm.|'ṣ.w lḫšt.abn.|tant.šmm.'m.arṣ.|thmt.'mn.kbk 3['NT].3.19

.------------].|ǵr.ks.dm.r[gm.iṯ.l y.w argm k].|hwt.w aṯny k[.rgm.'ṣ.w lḫšt.abn].|tunt.šmm.'m[.arṣ.thmt.'mn.kbk 1['NT.IX].3.13

n 'm y t[wtḥ.išd k.dm.rgm.iṯ.l y.d argmn k].|[h]wt.d aṯ[ny k.---.rgm.'ṣ].|w lḫšt.abn[.tant.šmm.'m.arṣ.thmt].|'m 7.2[130].18

ṣ.|prs̀.glbm.l.bt.|tgmǵ.ks̀mm.b.yrḫ.iṯtbnm.|šb'm.dd.ṯn.kbd.|tgmr.ḥṭm.šb'.ddm.|ḫmš.dd.š'rm.|kdm.yn.|kdm.ṣ 1099.31

š'm.mḏrǵlm.|arb'.l 'šrm.ḫsnm.|'šr.hbṭnm.|ṯṯm.l.mit.ṯn.kbd.|tgmr. 1030.10

.|ks̀mm.b.mṣbt.|mit.'šrm.ṯn kbd.|[ks̀]mm.|[']š[r]m.ṯn.kbd.ḥṭm.|[-]m[-.-]'[-.-]ag š'rm.|[---.--]mi.|[--.]ṯt[m] šb'.k 2091.5

r.bnšm.|b.gt.ḥḏṯt.arb'm.dr'.w.ṯlṯm.drt.|[w].šb'm.dd.ṯn.kbd.ḥpr.bnšm.|b.nzl.'šrm.l.mit.dr'.w.šb'm.drt.|w.'šrm.l. 1098.23

.---.]knm.ṯṯm.l.mit.dr'.w.mit.drt.|w[.---.]'m.l.mit.dd.ṯn.kbd.ḥpr.bnšm.ṯmnym.dd.|l u[-]m.|b.ṭbq.arb'm.dr'.w.'šr. 1098.8

at.'šrm[.---].|ṯmnym.drt.a[--].|drt.l.alpm[.---].|šb'm.ṯn.kbd[.ḥpr.'b]dm.|tg[mr.---].|[-]m.m[--.---].|[m]itm.dr[t.-- 2013.19

mitm.'šr kbd.|ks̀mm.b.mṣbt.|mit.'šrm.ṯn kbd.|[ks̀]mm.|[']š[r]m.ṯn.kbd.ḥṭm.|[-]m[-.-]'[-.-]ag š'rm. 2091.3

ḥ.š‘rt. | anntn. | ‘dn. | sdwn. | mztn. | ḫyrn. | šdn. | [‘š]rm.ṯn kbd. | s̀ǵrm. | lqḥ.ššlmt. 2098.9
‘m.ḫpnt.pṯt. | [-]r.pldm.dt.š‘rt. | ṯlṯm.ṯlṯ.kbd.mṣrrt. | ‘šr.ṯn.kbd.pǵdrm. | ṯmn.mrbdt.mlk. | ‘šr.pld.š‘rt. 1111.10
--]yy.ṯṯ.krmm.šl[-.---]. | [---.]‘šrm.krm.[---]. | [ṯ]lrby.‘šr.ṯn.kb[d.---]. | ḫmrm.ṯṯ.krm[m.---]. | krm.ǵlkz.b.p[--.---]. | krm 1081.21
[---.--]t.‘šr rmǵt.[--]. | [---].alp.[---].alp. | [---.-]rbd.kbd.ṯnm kbd. | [---.-]nnm ṯrm. | [---.]ṯlṯ kbd.ṣin. | [---.--]a.ṯ[l]ṯ.d.a[- 1145.1.7
| mḏrǵlm. | ṯmnym.ṯmn.kbd. | tgmr.ḫrd. | arb‘m.l.mit. | ṯn.kbd. 1031.17
b.w.[---]. | uḫnp.ṯṯ.mṣb. | tgmr.[y]n.mṣb š[b‘]. | w ḥs[p] ṯn.k[dm]. 2004.36
[i]wryn. | ḫbsn. | ulmk. | ‘dršp. | bn.knn. | pdyn. | bn.aṯtl.ṯn. | kdln.akdṯb. | ṯn.b gt ykn‘m. 1061.20
ṯn pǵn.[-]dr | m.ṯn kndwm adrm. | w knd pnṯ.dq. | ṯn ḫpnm.ṯn pldm ǵlmm. | 140[98].2
l]ḫbrtn[r]. | [ks.ksp.ktn.mit.pḥ]m. | [mit.iqni.l ḫbrtn]r ṯn. | [ks.ksp.ktn.mit.pḥm]. | [mit.iqn]i.l skl.[--]. | [---.m]it pḥ 64[118].36
spr.npṣ.krw. | ṯt.ḫṯrm.ṯn.kst. | spl.mšlt.w.mqḥm. | w md h. | arn.w mznm. | ṯn.ḫlpn 2050.2
z.b.p[--.---]. | krm.ilyy.b.m[--.---]. | kd.šb‘.krmm.[---]. | ṯn.krm[m.i]wrǵl[.---]. | ṯn.krm.[-]myn.[---]. | ṯn.krm[.---]. | kr 1081.26
--]. | ṯlṯ.krm.ubdym.l mlkt.b.‘nmky[.---]. | mgdly.ǵlpṯr.ṯn.krmm.w.ṯlṯ.ub[dym.---]. | qmnz.ṯṯ.krm.ykn‘m.ṯmn.krm[.- 1081.10
b.m[--.---]. | kd.šb‘.krmm.[---]. | ṯn.krm[m.i]wrǵl[.---]. | ṯn.krm.[-]myn.[---]. | ṯn.krm[.---]. | krm.[---]. | [--].kr[m.---]. | 1081.27
mm.[---]. | ṯn.krm[m.i]wrǵl[.---]. | ṯn.krm.[-]myn.[---]. | ṯn.krm[.---]. | krm.[---]. | [--].kr[m.---]. | ar[--.---]. | yp[-.---]. | ḫ 1081.28
[--]n.‘š[r.] | [a]rt[.a]rb‘[.---]. | ‘nmky.‘šr.[---]. | ṯmry.‘šr.ṯn.k[rmm.---]. | liy.krm.aḥd[.---]. | ‘bdmlk.krm.aḥ[d.---]. | kr 1081.4
n.d.ṣr.pḥm.b h.w.ṯqlm. | ksp h.mitm.pḥm.b d.skn. | w.ṯt.ktnm.ḫmšt.w.nṣp.ksp.hn. 1110.6
arb‘.ḥm[r.---]. | l ṯlṯ. | ṯn.l.brr[.---]. | arb‘.ḥmr[.---]. | l.pḥ[-.]w.[---]. | w.l.k[--]. | w.l.k[1139.3
r]. | hbr.w ql.t[štḥwy.w kbd.hwt]. | w rgm l k[ṯr.w ḫss.ṯny.l hyn]. | d ḥrš.y[dm.tḥm.ṯr.il.ab k.] | hwt.lṭpn[.ḥtk k.---]. 1['NT.IX].3.4
kṯ. | hbr.w ql.tštḥ | wy.w kbd hwt. | w rgm.l kṯr. | w ḫss.ṯny.l h | yn.d ḥrš.ydm. | tḥm.al[iyn.b‘l]. | h[wt.aliy.qrdm]. 3['NT.VI].6.22
.l p‘n.‘nt.hbr. | w ql.tštḥwy.kbd hyt. | w rgm.l btlt.‘nt. | ṯny.l ymmt.limm. | tḥm.aliyn.b‘l.hwt. | aliy.qrdm.qry.b arṣ. | 3['NT].3.9
.ahbt.ṭly.bt.rb.dd]. | arṣy bt.y[‘bdr.---]. | rgm l btl[t.‘nt.ṯny.l ybmt.limm.tḥm.aliyn.b‘l]. | hw[t.aliy.qrdm.qryy.b arṣ. 7.2[130].13
yraun.aliyn.b‘l. | ṯt‘.nn.rkb.‘rpt. | tb‘.rgm.l bn.ilm.mt. | ṯny.l ydd.il ǵzr. | tḥm.aliyn.b‘l.hwt.aliy. | qrdm.bhṯ.l bn.ilm 5[67].2.9
. | hbr.w ql. | tštḥwy.w k | bd hwt.w rgm. | l bn.ilm.mt. | ṯny.l ydd. | il.ǵzr.tḥm. | aliyn.b‘l. | [hw]t.aliy.q | [rdm.]bht y.b 4[51].8.31
.ilm]. | [ṯ]ṯb.mdbḥ.b‘l.g[dlt.---]. | dqt.l.ṣpn.w.dqt[.---]. | ṯn.l.‘šrm.pamt.[---]. | š.dd.šmn.gdlt.w.[---.brr]. | rgm.yṯṯb.b.ṯ 35[3].43
l i[nš.ilm.ṯb.md] | bḥ.b‘l.[gdlt.---.dqt]. | l ṣpn.w [dqt.---.ṯn.l ‘š] | rm.pam[t.---]. | š dd šmn[.gdlt.w.---]. | brr.r[gm.yṯṯb. APP.II[173].46
ḫr [m‘d.qmm.a--.am] | r ṯny.d‘t km.w rgm.l ṯr.a[b.-.il.ṯny.l pḫr]. | m‘d.tḥm.ym.b‘l km.adn km.ṯ[pṭ.nhr]. | tn.il m.d 2.1[137].16
---]. | tḥt.ksi.zbl.ym.w ‘n.kṯr.w ḫss.l rgmt. | l k.l zbl.b‘l.ṯnt.l rkb.‘rpt.ht.ib k. | b‘l m.ht.ib k.tmḫṣ.ht.tṣmt.ṣrt k. | tqḥ. 2.4[68].8
pam[t.---]. | š dd šmn[.gdlt.w.---]. | brr.r[gm.yṯṯb.b ṯdṯ.ṯn]. | l šmn.‘[ly h.gdlt.rgm.yṯṯb]. | brr.b šb‘[.ṣbu.špš.w ḥl] | yt. APP.II[173].49
lbš.aḥd. | b.‘šrt. | w.ṯn.b.ḫmšt. | ṯprt.b.ṯlṯt. | mṯyn.b.ṯṯt. | ṯn.lbšm.b.‘šrt. | pld.b.arb‘t. | lbš.ṯn.b.ṯnt.‘šrt. 1108.6
ḫ.l kṯ | rt.yšlḥm.kṯrt.w y | ššq.bnt.[hl]l.snnt. | hn.ym.w ṯn.yšlḥm. | kṯrt.w yš[š]q.bnt.hl[l]. | snnt.ṯlṯ[.r]b‘ ym.yšl | ḥm 17[2AQHT].2.32
d. | ǵll.yn.išryt.‘nq.smd. | lbnn.ṭl mrṯ.yḥrṯ.il. | hn.ym.w ṯn.tlḥmn.rpum. | tštyn.ṯlṯ.rb‘.ym.ḫmš. | ṯdṯ.ym.tlḥmn.rpum. 22.2[124].21
]pṯ. | bn kdrn. | awldn. | arswn.y‘r[ty.--]. | bn.ugr. | gny. | ṯn.mdm. 86[305].13
‘ṣd.ḫmšm.mqb.[‘]šrm. | b.ulm.ṯṯ.‘šr h.ḫrmṯt. | ṯt.nitm.ṯn.m‘ṣdm.ṯn.mqbm. | krk.aḥt. | b.sǵy.ḫmš.ḫrmṯt.nit. | krk.m‘ṣ 2048.5
rb‘. | šbn aḥd. | ṭbq aḥd. | šrš aḥd. | bir aḥd. | uḫnp. | hzp ṯn. | m‘qb arb‘. 2040.33
.mqb.[‘]šrm. | b.ulm.ṯṯ.‘šr h.ḫrmṯt. | ṯt.nitm.ṯn.m‘ṣdm.ṯn.mqbm. | krk.aḥt. | b.sǵy.ḫmš.ḫrmṯt.nit. | krk.m‘ṣd.mqb. | b. 2048.5
.al[ṯy]. | d b atlg[.---]. | ḫmš ‘š[r]. | kkr.ṯ[lṯ]. | ṯt hrt[m]. | ṯn mq[pm]. | ulṯ.ṯl[t]. | krk.kly[.--]. | ḫmš.mr[kbt]. | ṯṯ [-]az[-]. 2056.6
gš. | w.npṣ bt ṯn.ṯlṯ mat. | w spl ṯlṯ.mat. | w mmskn. | w.ṯt.mqrtm. | w.ṯn.irpm.w.ṯn.trqm. | w.qpt.w.mqḥm. | w.ṯlṯm.y 1103.19
]r. | lpš.sgr.rq. | ṯṯ.prqt. | w.mrdt.prqt.pṯt. | lbš.psm.rq. | ṯn.mrdt.az. | ṯlṯ.pld.š‘rt. | ṯ[---].kbm. | p[---]r.aḥd. | [-----]. | [---- 1112.6
dt.kn.npṣ hm. | [bn].lbn.arb‘.qšt.w.ar[b‘]. | [u]ṯpt.ql‘.w.ṯt.mr[ḥ]m. | [bn].smyy.qšt.w.u[ṯpt]. | [w.q]l‘.w.ṯt.mrḥm. | [bn 2047.3
t.ql‘.w.ṯt.mr[ḥ]m. | [bn].smyy.qšt.w.u[ṯpt]. | [w.q]l‘.w.ṯt.mrḥm. | [bn].šlmn.ql‘.w.ṯ[t.---]. | [bn].mlṣ.qštm.w.uṯp[t]. | [2047.5
pl.mšlt.w.mqḥm. | w md h. | arn.w mznm. | ṯn.ḫlpnm. | ṯt.mrḥm. | drb. | mrbd. | mškbt. 2050.7
.dt. | ‘rb.bt.mlk. | yd.apnt hn. | yd.ḥẓ hn. | yd.tr hn. | w.l.ṯt.mrkbtm. | inn.uṯpt. | w.ṯlṯ.ṣmdm.w.ḥrṣ. | apnt.b d.rb.ḥršm. 1121.6
.mit. | m‘ṣd.ḫmšm.mqb.[‘]šrm. | b.ulm.ṯṯ.‘šr h.ḫrmṯt. | ṯt.nitm.ṯn.m‘ṣdm.ṯn.mqbm. | krk.aḥt. | b.sǵy.ḫmš.ḫrmṯt.nit. | 2048.5
r h.w ilt.p[--]. | w tšu.g h.w [tṣḥ]. | ph m‘.ap.k[rt.--]. | u ṯn.ndr[.---]. | apr.[---]. | [-----]. 15[128].3.29
t.b.bt.ydrm. | ṯt.aṯtm.adrtm.w.pǵt.aḥt.b[.bt.---]. | aṯt.w ṯn.n‘rm.b.bt.ilsk. | aṯt.ad[r]t.b.bt.armwl. | aṯt.aḥt.b.bt.iwrpzn 80[119].8
plk.qlt.b ymn h. | npyn h.mks.bšr h. | tmt‘.md h.b ym.ṯn. | npyn h.b nhrm. | štt.ḫptr.l išt. | ḫbrṯ.l ẓr.pḥmm. | t‘pp.ṯr.i 4[51].2.6
--]. | ṣlyh šr[-.---]. | [ṯ]lṯm.w b[--.---]. | l il limm[.---]. | w ṯt.npš[.---]. | kbd.w [---]. | l ṣp[n.---]. | š.[---]. | w [----]. | k[--.---]. 40[134].9
-]r. | mit.lḥ[m.---.-]dyt. | ṣl‘t.alp.mri. | ‘šr.bmt.alp.mri. | ṯn.nšbm. | ṯmnym.tbtḫ.alp. | uz.mrat.mlḥt. | arb‘.uzm.mrat.b 1128.18
m. | b‘lm.kmm.b‘lm.kmm. | k t‘rb.‘ṯtrt.šd.bt.mlk[.---]. | ṯn.skm.šb‘.mšlt.arb‘.ḫpnt.[---]. | ḫmšm.ṯlṯ.rkb.ntn.ṯlṯ.mat.[-- UG5.9.1.19
r.w.s̀ǵ[r h]. | ṯ‘ln. | mztn.w.s̀ǵr [h]. | s̀ǵr.plṭ. | s[d]rn [w].ṯn.s̀ǵr h. | [---.]w.s̀ǵr h. | [---.]w.s̀ǵr h. | [---.]krwn. | [---].ḫzmy 2072.8
tpnr d yaḫd l g ynm. | ṯṯ spm l tgyn. | arb‘ spm l ll[-]. | ṯn spm.l slyy. | ṯlṯ spm l dlšpš amry. 137.2[93].14
p ank.atn. | ‘ṣm.l k. | arb‘.‘ṣm. | ‘l.ar. | w.ṯlṯ. | ‘l.ubr‘y. | w.ṯn.‘l. | mlk. | w.aḥd. | ‘l atlg. | w l.‘ṣm. | tspr. | nrn.al.tud | ad.at.l 1010.13
‘lt. | bwrm š.iṯtqb. | w š.nbk m w.š. | gt mlk š.‘lm. | l kṯr.ṯn.‘lm. | tzǵ[.---.]nšm.pr. UG5.12.B.12
bt.alpm. | ‘šr.bnšm. | ḫmš.bnši.ṯt[---]. | ‘šr.b gt.[---]. | ṯn.‘šr.b.gt.ir[bṣ]. | arb‘.b.gt.b‘ln. | ‘št.‘šr.b.gpn. | yd.‘dnm. | arb‘ 2103.5
. | [---]mn.arb‘m.y[n]. | b.gt.trǵnds. | tš‘.‘šr.[dd].ks̀mm. | ṯn.‘šr[.dd.ḥ]ṭm. | w.šb[‘.---]. 2092.17
h. | [---.d]r‘.w.mit.drt.w.‘šrm.l.mit. | [drt.ḥpr.b]nšm.w.ṯn.‘šr h.dd.l.rpš. | [---.]šb‘m.dr‘.w.arb‘m.drt.mit.dd. | [---].ḥpr 1098.4
m.dd.ṯṯ.kbd.ḥpr.bnšm. | b.‘nmky.‘šrm.dr‘[.---.d]rt. | w.ṯn.‘šr h.dd.[---]. | iwrḏn.ḥ[--.---]. | w.ṯlṯm.dd.[---.]n[---.---]. | w. 1098.29
-.]n[---.---]. | w.a[r]b‘[.---].bnš[.š]dyn[.---]. | agr.[---.--]n.ṯn.‘šr h.d[--.---]. | [---.]ḥdṯn.‘šr.dd[.---]. | [---.]yd.sǵr[.---.--]r h. 1098.33
[---.ṯ]lṯ.‘š[r h.---]. | d bnšm.yd.grbs hm. | w.ṯn.‘šr h.ḫpnt. | [s̀]s̀wm.amtm.‘kyt. | yd.llḫ hm. | w.ṯlṯ.l.‘šrm. | 2049.3
l nqmd.[---.-]št. | hl ny.argmn.d [ybl.n]qmd. | l špš.arn.ṯn[.‘šr h.]mn. | ‘ṣrm.ṯql.kbd[.ks].mn.ḫrṣ. | w arb‘.ktnt.w [---] 64[118].19
--.---.]l.mit.dr‘.w.šb‘m.drt. | [---.ḥpr.]bnšm.w.l.ḥrš.‘rq.ṯn.‘šr h. | [---.d]r‘.w.mit.drt.w.‘šrm.l.mit. | [drt.ḥpr.b]nšm.w.ṯ 1098.2
mn. | šḥq.‘šrm.arb‘.kbd. | ḫlb rpš arb‘.‘šr. | bq‘t ṯṯ. | irab ṯn.‘šr. | ḥbš.ṯmn. | amḏy.arb‘.‘šr. | [-]n‘y.ṯṯ.‘šr. 67[110].9
ṯn.‘šr.yn.[kps]lnm. | arb‘.mat[.arb]‘m.[k]bd. | d ntn.d.ksp. | ar 1087.1

ḫlb ʻprm.ṯṯ. | ḫlb krd.ṯn ʻšr. | qmy.arbʻ.ʻšr. | ṣʻq.arbʻ ʻšr. | ṣʻ.ṯmn. | šḥq.ʻšrm.arbʻ.kbd. 67[110].2
w.pǵt.aḥt.b.bt.m[--]. | aṯt.w.ṯt.bt h.b.bt.ḫdmrd. | aṯt.w.ṯn.ǵzrm.b.bt.ṣdqš[lm]. | [a]ṯt.aḥt.b.bt.rpi[--]. | [aṯt.]w.bt h.b.b 80[119].23
h. | [--]an.w.aṯt h. | [--]y.w.aṯt h. | [--]r.w.aṯt h. | ʻbdyrḫ.ṯn ǵlyt h. | aršmg. | ršpy.w.aṯt h. | bn.glgl.uškny. | bn.ṯny.uškn 2068.10
.qrn[m]. | dt.ʻl h.riš h.b glṯ.b šm[m]. | [---.i]l.ṯr.iṯ.p h.k ṯt.ǵlṯ[.--]. | [---.--] k yn.ddm.l b[--.---]. | [---.-]yt š[--.---]. | [---.] UG5.3.1.8
[--]t.bʻl.ḫẓ.ršp.b[n].km.yr.klyt h.w lb h. | [ṯ]n.p k.b ǵr.ṯn.p k.b ḫlb.k tgwln.šnt k. | [--.]w špt k.l tššy.hm.tqrm.l mt. 1001.1.4
y.alt.in l y. | [--]t.bʻl.ḫẓ.ršp.b[n].km.yr.klyt h.w lb h. | [ṯ]n.p k.b ǵr.ṯn.p k.b ḫlb.k tgwln.šnt k. | [--.]w špt k.l tššy.h 1001.1.4
šwm.amtm.ʻkyt. | yd.llḫ hm. | w.ṯlṯ.l.ʻšrm. | ḫpnt.ššwm.ṯn. | pddm.w.d.ṯṯ. | [mr]kbt.w.ḫrṣ. 2049.7
m.ṯn.šm.w alp.l[--]n. | [---.]š.il š.bʻl š.dgn š. | [---.--]r.w ṯt pl.gdlt.[ṣ]pn.dqt. | [---.al]p ʻnt.gdlt.b ṯlṯt mrm. | [---.i]l š.bʻl 36[9].1.4
[-----]. | ʻšr[.---]. | ud[-.---]. | ṯn pld mḫ[--.---]. | ṯ[--] ḫpnt. | [---] kdwṯm.[---]. | ḫmš.pld šʻrt. 1113.4
n.[-]dr | m.ṯn kndwm adrm. | w knd pnṯ.dq. | ṯn ḫpnm.ṯn pldm ǵlmm. | kpld.b[-.-]r[--]. | w blḫ br[-]m p[-]. | b[--.]l[-.] 140[98].4
ṯn.pld.pṯt[.-]r. | lpš.sgr.rq. | ṯṯ.prqt. | w.mrdt.prqt.pṯt. | lbš.ps 1112.1
ṯn pǵn.[-]dr | m.ṯn kndwm adrm. | w knd pnṯ.dq. | ṯn ḫpnm.ṯ 140[98].1
k[n]. | ṯt.aṯtm.adrtm.w.pǵt.w ǵzr[.aḥd.b.bt.---]. | aṯt.w.ṯt.pǵtm.w.ǵzr.aḥd.b.[bt.---]. | ṯt.aṯtm.w.pǵt.w.ǵzr.aḥd.b.[bt.- 80[119].19
[ṯ]n.prm.b ʻšrm. | arbʻ.prm.b.ʻš[r]m. | arbʻ.b.arbʻm. | ṯṯm.[---.p] 1138.1
d]r.mškb. | ṯl[l.---.--]ḫ. | b lṯk.bt. | [pt]ḥ.aḥd.l.bt.ʻbdm. | [ṯ]n.ptḥ msb.bt.tu. | w.ptḥ[.aḥ]d.mmt. | ṯṯ.pt[ḥ.---]. | ṯn.pt[ḥ.--- 1151.10
. | [ṯ]n.ptḥ msb.bt.tu. | w.ptḥ[.aḥ]d.mmt. | ṯṯ.pt[ḥ.---]. | ṯn.pt[ḥ.---]. | w.pt[ḥ.--]r.ṯǵr. | ṯmn.ḫlnm. | ṯṯ.ṯḫ[--].l.mtm. 1151.13
ṯn.ṣbrm. | b.uškn. | ṣbr.aḥd. | b.ar. | ṣbr.aḥd. | b.mlk. | ṣbr.aḥd. | 2073.1
.[ḫbl.d] | iym.bn.nšrm.arḫp.an[k.ʻ]l. | aqht.ʻdb k.hlmn.ṯnm.qdqd. | ṯlṯ id.ʻl.udn.špk.km.šiy. | dm.km.šḫṭ.l brk h.tṣi.k 18[3AQHT].4.22
ḫbl.diy[m.bn]. | nšrm.trḫp.ʻnt.ʻl[.aqht]. | tʻdbn h.hlmn.ṯnm[.qdqd]. | ṯlṯ id.ʻl.udn.š[pk.km]. | šiy.dm h.km.šḫ[ṭ.l brk 18[3AQHT].4.33
.[---]. | [-.]hlk.ǵlmm b dd y.yṣ[--]. | [-.]yṣa.w l.yṣa.hlm.[ṯnm]. | [q]dqd.ṯlṯ id.ʻl.ud[n]. | [---.-]sr.pdm.riš h[m.---]. | ʻl.pd. 19[1AQHT].2.78
. | qṣn.ṯt.qštm.w.qlʻ. | bn.gṯrn.q[š]t. | bn.ḫdi.ṯt.qštm.w.ṯn.qlʻm. | ildgn.qšt. | bn.yʻrn.ṯt.qštm w.qlʻ. | bn.ḥṣn.qšt.w.qlʻ. | 119[321].3.8
q]lʻ. | bn.bdn.qšt. | bn.pls.qšt. | ǵmrm. | [-]lhd.ṯt.qštm.w.ṯn.qlʻm. | ulšn.ṯt.qšm.w.qlʻ. | bn.mlʻn.qšt.w.qlʻ. | bn.tmy.qšt.w 119[321].3.33
n.qlʻm. | qdmn.ṯt.qštm.w.ṯlṯ.qlʻm. | bn.ṣdqil.ṯt.qštm.w.ṯn.qlʻm. | bn.ṯlṯ.ṯ[lṯ.]qšt.w.ṯn.qlʻm. | qṣn.ṯt.qštm.w.qlʻ. | bn.gṯr 119[321].3.4
bn.[-]q.qšt.w.qlʻ. | gb[l]n.qšt.w.qlʻ. | bn.[-]bl.ṯt.qštm.w.ṯn.qlʻm. | bn.[-]rkṯ.ṯt.qštm.w.qlʻ. | bn.ṯʻl.qšt. | bn.[ḫ]dpṯr.ṯt.qšt 119[321].3.15
arbʻm.qšt. | alp ḥẓm.w alp. | nṯq.ṯn.qlʻm. | ḫmš.ṣmdm.w ḫrṣ. | ṯryn.ššwm. | ṯryn.aḥd.d bnš. | ar 1123.3
[u]lm. | mṯpṯ.ṯt.qštm.w.ṯn.q[l]ʻm. | kmrṯn.ṯt.qštm.ṯn.[q]lʻm. | ǵdyn.qšt.w.qlʻ. | bn.gzl. 119[321].1.2
[u]lm. | mṯpṯ.ṯt.qštm.w.ṯn.q[l]ʻm. | kmrṯn.ṯt.qštm.ṯn.[q]lʻm. | ǵdyn.qšt.w.qlʻ. | bn.gzl.qšt.w.qlʻ. | [---]n.qšt. | ilhd. 119[321].1.3
lʻ. | b[n].ilyn.qšt.w.qlʻ. | šmrm.qlʻ. | ubrʻy. | abmn.qšt.w.ṯn.qlʻm. | qdmn.ṯt.qštm.w.ṯlṯ.qlʻm. | bn.ṣdqil.ṯt.qštm.w.ṯn.qlʻ 119[321].3.2
ṯlṯ.qlʻm. | bn.ṣdqil.ṯt.qštm.w.ṯn.qlʻm. | bn.ṯlṯ.ṯ[lṯ.]qšt.w.ṯn.qlʻm. | qṣn.ṯt.qštm.w.qlʻ. | bn.gṯrn.q[š]t. | bn.ḫdi.ṯt.qštm.w. 119[321].3.5
.qlʻm. | bn.[-]rkṯ.ṯt.qštm.w.qlʻ. | bn.ṯʻl.qšt. | bn.[ḫ]dpṯr.ṯt.qštm.[w].qlʻ. | bn.aǵlyn.ṯt.qštm[.w.ṯl]ṯ.qlʻm. | bn.ʻgw.qšt.w 119[321].3.18
dqil.ṯt.qštm.w.ṯn.qlʻm. | bn.ṯlṯ.ṯ[lṯ.]qšt.w.ṯn.qlʻm. | qṣn.ṯt.qštm.w.qlʻ. | bn.gṯrn.q[š]t. | bn.ḫdi.ṯt.qštm.w.ṯn.qlʻm. | ildg 119[321].3.6
nʻmn.ṯt.qštm.w.qlʻ. | gln.ṯt.qštm.w.qlʻ. | gtn.qšt. | pmn.ṯt.qšt.w.qlʻ. | bn.zry.q[š]t.w.qlʻ. | bn.tlmyn.ṯt.qštm.w.qlʻ. | bn. 104[316].9
n.q[š]t. | bn.ḫdi.ṯt.qštm.w.ṯn.qlʻm. | ildgn.qšt. | bn.yʻrn.ṯt.qštm w.qlʻ. | bn.ḥṣn.qšt.w.qlʻ. | bn.gdn.ṯt.qštm.w.qlʻ. | bn.[- 119[321].3.10
n.qšt. | pmn.ṯt.qšt.w.qlʻ. | bn.zry.q[š]t.w.qlʻ. | bn.tlmyn.ṯt.qštm.w.qlʻ. | bn.ysd.qšt. | [ǵ]mrm. | ilgn.qšt. | abršp.qšt. | ssg 104[316].9
št. | bn.pls.qšt. | ǵmrm. | [-]lhd.ṯt.qštm.w.ṯn.qlʻm. | ulšn.ṯt.qšm.w.qlʻ. | bn.mlʻn.qšt.w.qlʻ. | bn.tmy.qšt.w.qlʻ. | ʻky.qšt. | ʻ 119[321].3.34
n.ʻgw.qšt.w qlʻ. | bn.tbšn.ṯlṯ.qšt.w.[ṯlṯ.]qlʻm. | bn.army.ṯt.qštm.w[.]q[lʻ]. | bn.rpš.qšt.w.qlʻ. | bn.ǵb.qšt. | bn.ytrm.qšt. 119[321].3.22
gb[l]n.qšt.w.qlʻ. | bn.[-]bl.ṯt.qštm.w.ṯn.qlʻm. | bn.[-]rkṯ.ṯt.qštm.w.qlʻ. | bn.ṯʻl.qšt. | bn.[ḫ]dpṯr.ṯt.qštm.[w].qlʻ. | bn.aǵly 119[321].3.16
.qšt. | bn.yʻrn.ṯt.qštm w.qlʻ. | bn.ḥṣn.qšt.w.qlʻ. | bn.gdn.ṯt.qštm.w.qlʻ. | bn.[-]q.qšt.w.qlʻ. | gb[l]n.qšt.w.qlʻ. | bn.[-]bl.ṯt. 119[321].3.12
.qlʻ. | bn.šmlbi.qšt.w.qlʻ. | bn.yy.qšt. | ilrb.qšt. | bn.nmš.ṯt.qšt.w.qlʻ. | bʻl.qšt.w.qlʻ. 119[321].4.16
qšt. | bn.qnmlk.qšt. | ytḫm.qšt. | grp.qšt. | mʻrby. | nʻmn.ṯt.qštm.w.qlʻ. | gln.ṯt.qštm.w.qlʻ. | gtn.qšt. | pmn.ṯt.qšt.w.qlʻ. | 104[316].9
. | ytḫm.qšt. | grp.qšt. | mʻrby. | nʻmn.ṯt.qštm.w.qlʻ. | gln.ṯt.qštm.w.qlʻ. | gtn.qšt. | pmn.ṯt.qšt.w.qlʻ. | bn.zry.q[š]t.w.qlʻ. 104[316].9
n.blẓn.qšt.w.qlʻ. | gbʻ.qšt.w.qlʻ. | nṣṣn.qšt. | mʻr. | [ʻ]dyn.ṯt.qštm.w.qlʻ. | [-]lrš.qšt.w.qlʻ. | ṯ[ṯ]n.qšt.w.qlʻ. | u[l]n.qšt.w.qlʻ 119[321].2.14
.qlʻ. | bn.ṯʻl.qšt. | bn.[ḫ]dpṯr.ṯt.qštm.[w].qlʻ. | bn.aǵlyn.ṯt.qštm[.w.ṯl]ṯ.qlʻm. | bn.ʻgw.qšt.w qlʻ. | bn.tbšn.ṯlṯ.qšt.w.[ṯlṯ. 119[321].3.19
.w.qlʻ. | šmrm.qlʻ. | ubrʻy. | abmn.qšt.w.ṯn.qlʻm. | qdmn.ṯt.qštm.w.ṯlṯ.qlʻm. | bn.ṣdqil.ṯt.qštm.w.ṯn.qlʻm. | bn.ṯlṯ.ṯ[lṯ.]q 119[321].3.3
t.w.ṯn.qlʻm. | qṣn.ṯt.qštm.w.qlʻ. | bn.gṯrn.q[š]t. | bn.ḫdi.ṯt.qštm.w.ṯn.qlʻm. | ildgn.qšt. | bn.yʻrn.ṯt.qštm w.qlʻ. | bn.ḥṣn. 119[321].3.8
yn.qšt.w[.q]lʻ. | bn.bdn.qšt. | bn.pls.qšt. | ǵmrm. | [-]lhd.ṯt.qštm.w.ṯn.qlʻm. | ulšn.ṯt.qšm.w.qlʻ. | bn.mlʻn.qšt.w.qlʻ. | bn. 119[321].3.33
mn.qšt.w.ṯn.qlʻm. | qdmn.ṯt.qštm.w.ṯlṯ.qlʻm. | bn.ṣdqil.ṯt.qštm.w.ṯn.qlʻm. | bn.ṯlṯ.ṯ[lṯ.]qšt.w.ṯn.qlʻm. | qṣn.ṯt.qštm.w. 119[321].3.4
tm.w.qlʻ. | bn.[-]q.qšt.w.qlʻ. | gb[l]n.qšt.w.qlʻ. | bn.[-]bl.ṯt.qštm.w.ṯn.qlʻm. | bn.[-]rkṯ.ṯt.qštm.w.qlʻ. | bn.ṯʻl.qšt. | bn.[ḫ] 119[321].3.15
[u]lm. | mṯpṯ.ṯt.qštm.w.ṯn.q[l]ʻm. | kmrṯn.ṯt.qštm.ṯn.[q]lʻm. | ǵdyn.qšt.w.ql 119[321].1.2
[u]lm. | mṯpṯ.ṯt.qštm.w.ṯn.q[l]ʻm. | kmrṯn.ṯt.qštm.ṯn.[q]lʻm. | ǵdyn.qšt.w.qlʻ. | bn.gzl.qšt.w.qlʻ. | [---]n.qš 119[321].1.3
w yʻn.k[ṯr.w ḫs]s. | ṯtb.bʻl.l[hwt y]. | ṯn.rgm.k[ṯr.w]ḫss. | šmʻ.mʻ.l al[iy]n bʻl. | bl.ašt.ur[bt.]b bht 4[51].6.3
m.ddym.ask. | šlm.l kb[d].awṣ.arbdd. | l kbd.š[d]m.ap.mṯn.rgmm. | argmn.lk.lk.ʻnn.ilm. | atm.bštm.w an.šnt. | uǵr.l 3[ʻNT].4.75
mṯb.pdry.b ar. | mẓll.ṭly.bt rb. | mṯb.arṣy.bt.yʻbdr. | ap.mṯn.rgmm. | argm k.šskn mʻ. | mgn.rbt.aṯrt ym. | mǵẓ.qnyt.il 4[51].1.20
iš.ḥrṣ.l ẓr.qdqd y. | [--.]mt.kl.amt.w an.mtm.amt. | [ap.m]ṯn.rgmm.argm.qštm. | [----.]mhrm.ht.tṣdn.tinṯt. | [---]m.tṣ 17[2AQHT].6.39
ṯn.rʻy.uzm. | sǵr.bn.ḫpsry.aḥd. | sǵr.artn.aḥd. | sǵr.ʻdn.aḥd. | s 1140.1
[---.--]ṯ.slḫ.npš.ṯʻ w[.--.k]bdm. | [---.--]mm.ṯn.šm.w alp.l[--]n. | [---.]š.il š.bʻl š.dgn š. | [---.--]r.w ṯt pl.gdlt 36[9].1.2
b ṯlṯt ʻ[šrt.yrthṣ.mlk.brr]. | b arbʻ[t.ʻšrt.riš.argmn]. | w ṯn šm.l [bʻlt.bhtm.ʻṣrm.l inš]. | ilm.w š d[d.ilš.š.--.mlk]. | yṯb. 35[3].5
[ṯlṯt].ʻšrt.yrthṣ.mlk. | br[r.]b a[r]bʻt.ʻšrt.riš. | arg[mn.w ṯn.]šm.l bʻlt. | bhtm.ʻṣ[rm.l in]š ilm.w š. | dd ilš.š[.---.]mlk.yṯ APP.II[173].5
t.yr | ṯḥṣ.mlk.brr. | ʻlm.tzǵ.b ǵb.ṣpn. | nḥkt.ksp.w ḫrṣ ṯʻ ṯn šm l btbt. | alp.w š šrp.alp šlmm. | l bʻl.ʻṣr l ṣpn. | npš.w.š.l UG5.12.A.8
il tʻḏr.š. | bʻl š.ʻnt š.ršp š. | šlmm. | w šnpt.il š. | l ʻnt.ḫl š.ṯn šm. | l gtrm.ǵṣ b šmal. | d alpm.w alp w š. | šrp.w šlmm k UG5.13.25
u.[š]pš.w.ḥly[t].ʻ[r]b[.š]p[š]. | w [ḥl.]mlk.[w.]b.ym.ḥdṯ.ṯn.šm. | l.[---]t. | i[d.yd]bḥ.mlk.l.prgl.ṣqrn.b.gg. | ar[bʻ.]arbʻ.m 35[3].48
. | ʻlm b ǵb ḫyr. | ṯmn l ṯlṯm ṣin. | šbʻ.alpm. | bt bʻl.ugrt.ṯn šm. | ʻlm.l ršp.mlk. | alp w.š.l bʻlt. | bwrm š.iṯtqb. | w š.nbk UG5.12.B.6
šbʻ[.ṣbu.špš.w ḥl] | yt.ʻrb špš[.w ḥl.mlk.w.b y] | m.ḥdṯ.ṯn šm[.---.--]t. | b yrḫ.ši[-.b ar]bʻt.ʻš | rt.yr[ṯḥṣ.ml]k.brr. | ʻlm.š APP.II[173].53

ṯny

ṯmn ‘šr šurt l [---].|ṯmn šurt l ar[--.---].|ṯn šurtm l bnš [---].|arb‘ šurt l bn[š.---].|arb‘ šurt l q[--.---]. 137.1[92].3
‘ šurt l q[--.---].|ṯlṯ šurt l bnš [---].|ṯṯ šurt.l bnš[.---].|ṯn šurtm l bn[š.---].|ṯlṯm šurt l b[nš.---].|arb‘ šurt [---].|ṯṯ š 137.1[92].8
.---].|arb‘ šurt [---].|[ḫm]šm šurt [---].|ṯlṯ šurt l [---].|ṯn šurtm l [---].|[-----.]a[---].|[---.--]ln.|[---.]kqmṭn.|[---.]kln 137.1[92].17
d.brdn.l bn.bly.|šd gzl.l.bn.ṭbr[n].|šd.ḫzmyn.l a[--].|ṯn šdm b uš[kn]. 2089.16
|šd.b d.iwrkl.|šd.b d.klb.|šd.b d.klby.|šd.b d.iytlm.|ṯn.šdm.b d.amtrn.|šd.b d.iwrm[--].|šd.b d.yṯpr.|šd.b d.krb[2090.12
tmr.b d.tbbr.|[w.]šd.nḥl h.b d.ṯṯmd.|[š]d.b d.iwrḫṭ.|[ṯn].šdm.b d.gmrd.|[šd.]lbny.b d.tbṯṯb.|[š]d.bn.ṭ[-]rn.b d.‘db 82[300].1.14
.pṭḏ.|šd.b d.dr.khnm.|šd.b d.bn.‘my.|šd.b d.bn.‘yn.|ṯn.šdm.b d.klṯṯb.|šd.b d.krz[n].|ṯlṯ.šdm.b d.amtr[n].|ṯn.šd 2090.20
n.šdm.b d.klṯṯb.|šd.b d.krz[n].|ṯlṯ.šdm.b d.amtr[n].|ṯn.šdm.b d.skn.|šd.b d[.‘b]dyrḫ.|šd.b [d.--]ṯṯb. 2090.23
rim.|[šd.b]n.ṯpdn.b d.bn.g‘r.|[šd.b]n.ṯqrn.b d.ḫby.|[ṯn.š]d.bn.ngzḥn.b d.gmrd.|[šd.bn].pll.b d.gmrd.|[šd.bn.-]ll. 82[300].1.23
t.|ḥršm l ahlm p[---.]km.|[-]bl lb h.km.bṯn.y[--.-]ah.|ṯnm.tšqy msk.hwt.tšqy[.-.]w [---].|w hn dt.yṯb.l mspr. 19[1AQHT].4.224
|ṯṯ.pt[ḥ.---].|ṯn.pt[ḥ.---].|w.pt[ḥ.--]r.ṯǵr.|ṯmn.ḥlnm.|ṯṯ.ṯḫ[--].l.mtm. 1151.16
w spl ṯlṯ.mat.|w mmskn.|w.ṯṯ.mqrtm.|w.ṯn.irpm.w.ṯn.trqm.|w.qpt.w.mqḥm.|w.ṯlṯm.yn šb‘.kbd d ṭbṭ.|w.ḫmš 1103.20
il].|špḥ.lṭpn[.w qdš].|bkm.t‘r[b.‘l.ab h].|t‘rb.ḥ[--].|b ṯtm.t[---].|šknt.[---].|bkym[.---].|ǵr.y[----].|ydm.[---].|apn.[16.2[125].114
--]dšq krsnm.|ḫmšm [-]t ṯlṯ ty[--].|bn.grgš.|w.npṣ bt ṯn.ṯlṯ mat.|w spl ṯlṯ.mat.|w mmskn.|w.ṯt.mqrtm.|w.ṯn.irp 1103.16
.ǵlmt.|ḥẓr y.ṯn h.wspm.|atn.w ṯlṯ h.ḫrṣm.|ylk ym.w ṯn.|ṯlṯ.rb‘.ym.|aḫr.špšm.b rb‘.|ymǵy.l udm.rbt.|w udm[.ṯr 14[KRT].4.207
b h.b grnt.ḥpšt.|s‘t.b nk.šibt.b bqr.|mmlat.dm.ym.w ṯn.|ṯlṯ.rb‘.ym.ymš.|ṯdṯ.ym.ḥẓ k.al.tš‘l.|qrt h.abn.yd k.|mš 14[KRT].3.114
rnt.ḥpšt.|s‘t.b npk.šibt.w b |mqr.mmlat.|d[m].ym.w ṯn.|ṯlṯ.rb‘.ym.|ḫmš.ṯdṯ.ym.|mk.špšm.b šb‘.|w l.yšn.pbl.|m 14[KRT].5.218
ddt h.k irby.|[t]škn.šd.|km.ḥsn.pat.mdbr.|lk.ym.w ṯn.ṯlṯ.rb‘ ym.|ḫmš.ṯdṯ.ym.mk.špšm.|b šb‘.w tmǵy.l udm.|r 14[KRT].3.106
id.my].|b ilm.[ydy.mrṣ].|gršm.z[bln.in.b ilm].|‘ny h.y[ṯny.yṯlṯ].|rgm.my.b[ilm.ydy].|mrṣ.grš[m.zbln].|in.b ilm. 16[126].5.13
ad].|ṯlṯ.mat.rbt.|hlk.l alpm.ḫḏḏ.|w l.rbt.kmyr.|aṯr.ṯn.ṯn.hlk.|aṯr.ṯlṯ.kl hm.|aḥd.bt h.ysgr.|almnt.škr.|tškr.zbl. 14[KRT].4.182
pr.|ṯnn.d bl.hg.|hlk.l alpm.ḫḏḏ.|w l rbt.kmyr.|[a]ṯr.ṯn.ṯn.hlk.|aṯr.ṯlṯ.kl hm.|yḥd.bt h.sgr.|almnt.škr.|tškr.zbl.‘ 14[KRT].2.94
š.ṯnt.d ḫmšm w.|ḫmš.ṯnt.d mit.|ḫmš.ṯnt.d ṯl|ṯ mat.|ṯt.ṯnt.d alp|alpm.ṯlṯ ktt.|alp.brr.|kkr.tznt.|ḫmšt.kkr tyt. 1130.13
[---.]n[--.---].|[---.kpt]r.l r[ḥq.ilm.ḥkpt.l rḥq].|[ilnym.ṯn.mṯpd]m.t[ḥt.‘nt.arṣ.ṯlṯ.mtḥ.ǵyrm].|[idk.]l ytn.pnm.‘m.[i] 2.3[129].3
|atm.bštm.w an.šnt.|uǵr.l rḥq.ilm.inbb.|l rḥq.ilnym.ṯn.mṯpdm.|tḥt.‘nt.arṣ.ṯlṯ.mtḥ.ǵyrm.|idk.l ttn pnm.‘m.b‘l.| 3[‘NT].4.79
.bštm.w an[.šnt.kptr].|l rḥq.ilm.ḥkp[t.l rḥq.ilnym].|ṯn.mṯpdm.tḥt.[‘nt.arṣ.ṯlṯ.mtḥ].|ǵyrm.idk.l yt[n.pnm.‘m.lṭp 1[‘NT.IX].3.20
mt.|b.‘šrt.ksp.|‘šr.ṣin.b.ṯṯt.w.kmsk.|arb‘[.k]dwṯm.w.ṯt.ṯprtm.|b.‘šr[m.]ksp.|ḫmš.kkr.ṣml.|b.‘šrt.b d.bn.kyn.|‘šr. 2100.10
l.ksp.ṭb.ap w np[š].|l ‘nt h.ṯql.ḫrṣ.|l špš[.w y]rḫ.l gṯr.ṯn.|[ṯql.ksp].ṭb.ap.w npš.|[---].bt.alp w š.|[---.--]m.l gṯrm.|[33[5].14
hn.špḥ.yitbd.|w b.pḫyr h.yrṯ.|y‘rb.b ḥdr h.ybky.|b ṯn.[-]gmm.w ydm‘.|tntkn.udm‘t h.|km.ṯqlm.arṣ h.|km ḫm 14[KRT].1.27
.pamt.[---].|š.dd.šmn.gdlt.w.[---.brr].|rgm.yṯṯb.b.ṯdṯ.ṯn[.--.šmn].|‘ly h.gdlt.rgm.yṯ[ṯb.brr].|b.[šb]‘.ṣbu.[š]pš.w.ḥly 35[3].45
[---.]ṯn[.--].|[---.-]dym.ṯn[.--].|[---.--]y.ṯn[.--].|[---.]ṯn[.--]. 129[-].3
[---.]ṯn[.--].|[---.-]dym.ṯn[.--].|[---.--]y.ṯn[.--].|[---.]ṯn[.--]. 129[-].1
[---.]ṯn[.--].|[---.-]dym.ṯn[.--].|[---.--]y.ṯn[.--].|[---.]ṯn[.--]. 129[-].2
[---.]ṯn[.--].|[---.-]dym.ṯn[.--].|[---.--]y.ṯn[.--].|[---.]ṯn[.--]. 129[-].4
ṯn.ḥ[---].pgam.|ṯn[.---.b]n.mlk.|ṯ[n.---.]gpn.|[-----].|[---.--]b.|b[--.---.b]n.‘m 1150.2
yy.qšt.w.u[ṯpt].|[w.q]l‘.w.ṯt.mrḥm.|[bn].šlmn.ql‘.w.ṯ[t.---].|[bn].mlṣ.qštm.w.uṯp[t].|[--.q]l‘.w[.---.m]rḥm.|[bn]. 2047.6
šm.|atlg.ḥmr[.---.]bnšm.|gb‘ly.ḥmr š[--.b]nšm.|ulm.ṯn.[---.]bnšm.|m‘rby.[---.--]m.ṯn[.---].|m‘r.[---].|arny.[---].| 2040.7
išr.|[---.šm]m h.nšat ẓl h kbkbm.|[---.]b km kbkbt k ṯn.|[---.]b‘l yḥmdn h.yrṯ y.|[---.]dmrn.l pn h yrd.|[---.]b‘l.š 2001.2.6
šm.|m‘rby.[---.--]m.ṯn[.---].|m‘r.[---].|arny.[---].|š‘rt.ṯn[.---].|bq‘t.[--].ḥ[mr.---].|ḫlb krd.ḥ[mr.---].|ṣ‘.ḥmr.w[.---]. 2040.11
ṯn.ḥ[---].pgam.|ṯn[.---.b]n.mlk.|ṯ[n.---.]gpn.|[-----].|[---.--]b.|b[--.---.b]n.‘my. 1150.3
n[--.---].|rg[m.---].|nǵṯ[.---].|d.yqḥ[.---].|hm.ṯn.[---].|hn dt.[---].|[-----].|[-----].|tḥm[.---].|l p‘n.b‘l y[.---]. 2064.5
yd.[---].|am[-]n.[---].|w.a[ṯt] h.[---].|ḫḏmtn.ṯn[.---].|w.ṯlṯ.alp h.[---].|swn.qrty.w.[b]n h[.---].|w.alp h.w. 2044.4
.akl.|b.ḥwt k.inn.|špš n.[---].|hm.al[k.--].|ytnt[.---].|ṯn[.---].|w[.-----].|l[.-----].|h[--.---].|šp[š.---].|‘m.k[--.lḥt].|a 2060.24
ly.ḥmr š[--.b]nšm.|ulm.ṯn.[---.]bnšm.|m‘rby.[---.--]m.ṯn[.---].|m‘r.[---].|arny.[---].|š‘rt.ṯn[.---].|bq‘t.[--].ḥ[mr.---]. 2040.8
---].|b ks.ḫr[ṣ.dm.‘ṣm.---].|ks.ksp[.---].|krpn.[---].|w ṯṯn.[---].|t‘l.tr[-.---].|bt.il.li[mm.---].|‘l.ḥbš.[---].|mn.lik.[--- 5[67].4.19
.b d.b[--.---].|udbr[.---].|‘rš[.---].|ṯl[ḥn.---].|a[--.---].|ṯn[.---].|ptr[-.---].|yp[-.---].|b[--.---]. 1120.8
.[w.u]ṯp[t].ṯ[--].|[---].arb‘.[---].|[---].kdl[.---.mr]ḥm.w.ṯ[t.---].|[---.mr]ḥm.w.ṯ[t.---].|[---].ql‘[.---].|[---.a]rb‘[.---]. 2047.11
rb‘.[---].|[---].kdl[.---.mr]ḥm.w.ṯ[t.---].|[---.mr]ḥm.w.ṯ[t.---].|[---].ql‘[.---].|[---.a]rb‘[.---]. 2047.12
.ṯlṯ.kl[t h.---].|w.ṯṯm.ṣi[n.---].|tn[--].|agyn.[---].|[w].ṯn.[---]. 81[329].22
[-----].|[---.]‘l.ṯny[.---]|[---.]pḫyr.bt h.[---].|[ḫm]šm.ksp.‘l.gd[--].|[---].ypḥ 1144.2

ṯnyn

|ktr.|ubn.|dqn.|ḥṯṯn.|[--]n.|[---].|tsn.|rpiy.|mrṭn.|ṯnyn.|apṯ.|šbn.|gbrn.|ṯb‘m.|kyn.|b‘ln.|ytršp.|ḥmšm.ṯmn. 1024.2.17

ṯnn

h.|atn.bn.ap[s]n.|nsk.ṯlṯ.|bn.[--.]m[-]ḫr.|bn.šmrm.|ṯnnm.|[ar]swn.bn.qqln.|m[--].bn.qqln.|‘bdil[-].bn.qqln.|liy 85[80].4.1
ṯnnm.|bn.qqln.|w.nḥl h.|w.nḥl h.|bn.šml[-].|bn.brzn.|bn. 116[303].1
yṣi.‘dn.m‘.|ṣbu k.ul.mad.|ṯlṯ.mat.rbt.|ḫpṯ.d bl.spr.|ṯnn.d bl.hg.|hlk.l alpm.ḫḏḏ.|w l rbt.kmyr.|[a]ṯr.ṯn.ṯn.hlk.| 14[KRT].2.91
d.aṯrt.[---].|špš.mṣprt dlt hm[.---].|w ǵnbm.šlm.‘rbm.ṯn[nm].|hlkm.b dbḥ n‘mt.|šd[.i]lm.šd.aṯrt.w rḥmy.|[---].y[23[52].26
tš‘.ṯnnm.|w.arb‘.ḫsnm.|‘šr.mrum.|w.šb‘.ḫsnm.|tš‘.‘šr.|mryn 1029.1
šb‘.ṯnnm.w.šb‘.ḫsnm.|ṯmn.‘šr h.mrynm.|‘šr.mkrm.|ḫmš.ṯrtn 1030.1
ḥm ay.w šty.b ḫmr yn ay.|šlm.mlk.šlm.mlkt.‘rbm m.ṯnnm.|mt.w šr.yṯb.b d h.ḫṭ.ṯkl.b d h.|ḫṭ.ulmn.yzbrnn.zbrm 23[52].7
mrynm.|mrum.|‘šrm.|ṯnnm.|nq[dm].|kh[nm].|inšt. 2019.4
ru.skn.|mru.ibrn.|pslm.|šrm.|yṣḥm.|‘šrm.|mrum.|ṯnnm.|mqdm.|khnm.|qdšm.|nsk.ksp.|mkrm. 71[113].70

mrynm. | mrum. | ʻšrm. | ṯnnm. | nqdm. | khnm. | qdšm. | pslm. | mkrm. | yṣḥm. | šrm. | nʻ 1026.1.4
ḫmš.ṯnnm.ʻšr.ḫsnm. | ṯlṯ.ʻšr.mrynm. | ḫmš.[ṯr]tnm. | ṯlṯ.b[n.]mryn 1028.1
tnnm.ṯṯ. | ʻšr.ḫsnm. | nʻr.mrynm. | ḫmš. | ṯrtnm.ḫmš. | mrum.ʻš 1031.1
| [---.]bṯr.b d.mlkt. | [---].b d.mršp. | [---.m]rbṣ. | [---.r]b.ṯnnm. | [---.]asrm. | [---.--]kn. | [-----]. | [-----]. | [-----.-]l[-]. | [----- 2015.1.5
ṯn.ipd. | [---.]m[---.]d.mškbt. | [---.--]m. | [---].ṯlḥn. | [---].ṯnn. | [---.--]b.kdr. | [---.--]m nʻrt. | [---].qt.b[--]. | [---.]kd[r]. | [-- 1142.1

ṯnʻy

d. | u[--].ṯn. | hz[p].ṯṯ. | ḫrṣbʻ.aḥd. | ypr.arb. | m[-]qb.ʻšr. | ṯnʻy.ṯlṯ. | ḫlb ʻprm.ṯn. | tmdy.ṯlṯ. | [--]rt.arbʻ. | [---].ʻšr. 70[112].11

ṯnǵly

rm.dd.l mḫṣm. | ddm l kbs. | dd l prgṭ. | dd.l mri. | dd.l ṯnǵly. | dd.l krwn. | dd.l ṯǵr. | dd.l rmt.r[---]. 1100.9

ṯnǵrn

ay[.---]. | [a]rš[mg.---]. | urt[n.---]. | ʻdn[.---]. | bqrt[.---]. | ṯnǵrn.[---]. | w.bn h.n[--.---]. | ḥnil.[---]. | aršmg.mru. | bʻl.šlm.ʻ 2084.6

ṯnq

d. | [---.bn]šm.b.tkn. | [---.bn]šm.b.tmrm. | [---.bn]šm.b.ṯnq. | [---.b]nšm.b.ugrt. | [---.bn]šm.b.ǵbl. | [---.b]nšm.b.mʻr.ar 2076.29

ṯnqy

. | ʻbdm. | kzym. | ksdm. | [nsk].ṯlṯ. | gt.mlkym. | tmrym. | ṯnqym. | ṯǵrm. | mru.skn. | mru.ibrn. | yqšm. | trrm. | kkrdnm. | 1026.2.4

ṯnr

n]. | [bn].ǵr[--]. | d.b[n.---]. | d.bn.[---]. | d.bn.š[--]. | d.bn.ṯn[r]. | d.kmry. 2164.B.4

ṯnt

nt.d ḫmšm w. | ḫmš.ṯnt.d mit. | ḫmš.ṯnt.d ṯl | ṯ mat. | ṯṯ.ṯnt.d alp | alpm.ṯlṯ ktt. | alp.brr. | kkr.tznt. | ḫmšt.kkr tyt. 1130.13
ni. | ḫmš.mat.kbd. | ṯlṯm.ḫmš kbd ktn. | ḫmš.rṭm. | ḫmš.ṯnt.d ḫmšm w. | ḫmš.ṯnt.d mit. | ḫmš.ṯnt.d ṯl | ṯ mat. | ṯṯ.ṯnt.d 1130.9
m.ḫmš kbd ktn. | ḫmš.rṭm. | ḫmš.ṯnt.d ḫmšm w. | ḫmš.ṯnt.d mit. | ḫmš.ṯnt.d ṯl | ṯ mat. | ṯṯ.ṯnt.d alp | alpm.ṯlṯ ktt. | alp 1130.10
. | ḫmš.rṭm. | ḫmš.ṯnt.d ḫmšm w. | ḫmš.ṯnt.d mit. | ḫmš.ṯnt.d ṯl | ṯ mat. | ṯṯ.ṯnt.d alp | alpm.ṯlṯ ktt. | alp.brr. | kkr.tznt. | 1130.11

ṯʻ

[ǵy.]l qdš. | a[ṯrt.]ṣrm.w l ilt. | ṣd[yn]m.ṯm. | yd[r.k]rt.ṯʻ. | i.iṯt.aṯrt.ṣrm. | w ilt.ṣdynm. | hm.ḥry.bt y. | iqḥ.ašʻrb.ǵlmt. 14[KRT].4.200
ḥ.lṯpn. | w qdš.u ilm.tmtn. | špḥ.lṭpn.l yḥ. | w yʻny.krt.ṯʻ. | bn.al.tbkn.al. | tdm.l y.al tkl.bn. | qr.ʻn k.mḫ.riš k. | udmʻt 16.1[125].24
m. | l ytn.ʻmm.pbl. | mlk.tšan. | g hm.w tṣḥn. | tḥm.krt.ṯ[ʻ]. | hwt.[n]ʻmn.[ǵlm.il]. 14[KRT].6.305
]yʻn.aliy[n.]bʻl. | [---.]tbʻ.l lṭpn. | [il.d]pid.l tbrk. | [krt.]ṯʻ.l tmr.nʻmn. | [ǵlm.]il.ks.yiḫd. | [il.b]yd.krpn.bm. | [ymn.]br 15[128].2.15
d]m. | rḥq.mlk.l bt y. | n[g.]krt.l ḥẓ[r y]. | w yʻn[y.k]rt[.ṯ]ʻ. | lm.ank.ksp. | w yr[q.ḫrṣ]. | yd.mqm h.w ʻbd. | ʻlm.ṯlṯ.ssw 14[KRT].6.281
yd.krpn.bm. | [ymn.]brkm.ybrk. | [ʻbd h.]ybrk.il.krt. | [ṯʻ.ymr]m.nʻm[n.]ǵlm.il. | a[ṯt.tq]ḥ.y krt.aṯt. | tqḥ.bt k.ǵlmt.tš 15[128].2.20
ḥ. | brlt h.l ṯrm. | mt.dm.ḫt.šʻtqt. | dm.lan.w ypqd. | krt.ṯʻ.yšu.g h. | w yṣḥ.šmʻ.l mṯt. | ḥry.ṭbḫ.imr. | w ilḥm.mgṯ.w iṯr 16.6[127].15
. | krt.ṣbia.špš. | bʻl ny.w ymlk. | [y]ṣb.ʻln.w y[-]y. | [kr]t.ṯʻ.ʻln.bḫr. | [---].aṯt k.ʻl. | [---] k.yšṣi. | [---.]ḫbr.rbt. | [ḫbr.ṯrr]t.i 15[128].5.22
ss. | [---]n.rḥm y.ršp zbl. | [w ʻd]t.ilm.ṯlṯ h. | [ap]nk.krt.ṯʻ.ʻ[-]r. | [--.]b bt h.yšt.ʻrb. | [--] h.ytn.w [--]u.l ytn. | [aḫ]r.mǵy 15[128].2.8
tbʻ.yṣb ǵlm.ʻl. | ab h.yʻrb.yšu g h. | w yṣḥ.šmʻ mʻ.l krt. | ṯʻ.ištmʻ.w tqǵ udn. | k ǵz.ǵzm.tdbr. | w ǵrm.ṯṯwy.šqlt. | b ǵlt.y 16.6[127].42
[---.id]k. | pn[m.al.ttn]. | ʻm.[krt.msw]n. | w r[gm.l krt.]ṯʻ. | tḥm[.pbl.mlk]. | qḥ.[ksp.w yr]q. | ḫrṣ[.yd.mqm] h. | ʻbd[.ʻl 14[KRT].5.248
t. | ʻrš.zbln.rd.l mlk. | amlk.l drkt k.aṯb. | an.w yʻny.krt ṯʻ.ytbr. | ḥrn.y bn.ytbr.ḥrn. | riš k.ʻṯtrt.šm.bʻl. | qdqd k.tqln.b 16.6[127].54
šrt.yr | tḥṣ.mlk.brr. | ʻlm.tzǵ.b ǵb.ṣpn. | nḥkt.ksp.w ḫrṣ ṯʻ ṯn šm l btbt. | alp.w š šrp.alp šlmm. | l bʻl.ʻṣr l ṣpn. | npš.w.š UG5.12.A.8
ʻgl h. | bn.ḫpṯ.l umht hm. | k tnḥn.udmm. | w yʻny.krt.ṯʻ. 15[128].1.8

ṯʻd

ʻšr šṭpm. | b ḫmš.šmn. | ʻšrm.gdy. | b ḫmš.šmn. | w ḫmš ṯʻdt. 1097.5

ṯʻy

.mglb. | bn.ntp. | ʻmyn.bn ǵḥpn. | bn.kbln. | bn.bly. | bn.ṯʻy. | bn.nṣdn. | klby. 104[316].7
b qṣ]rt.npš kn.u b qṭt. | tqṭṭn.ušn y[p kn.l dbḥm.]w l ṯʻ dbḥ n. | ndbḫ.hw.ṯʻ n[ṯʻy.hw.nkt.nk]t.ytši.l ab bn il. | ytši.l 32[2].1.32
b q[ṣ]rt.npš km.u b qṭt.tqṭṭ. | ušn yp km.l d[b]ḥm.w l.ṯʻ.dbḥ n.ndbḥ.hw.ṯʻ | nṯʻy. | hw.nkt.nkt.y[t]ši.l ab.bn.il.ytši.l 32[2].1.24
kn.u b [q]ṣrt.npš[kn.u b qṭt]. | tqṭṭn u tḥṭin.l bḥm.w l ṯʻ.d[bḥ n.ndbḥ]. | hw.ṯʻ.nṯʻy.hw.nkt.n[k]t.ytši[.l ab.bn.il]. | yt 32[2].1.15
km.u b qṣrt.npš km.u b qṭt]. | [tqṭṭ.u tḥṭu.l dbḥm.w l.ṯʻ.dbḥ n.ndb]ḥ. | [hw.ṯʻ.nṯʻy.hw.nkt.nkt.]yt[ši.l ab.bn.il]. | [yt 32[2].1.9
dqt.ṯʻ.ynt.ṯʻm.dqt.ṯʻm. | mtntm nkbd.alp.š.l il. | gdlt.ilhm.ṯkmn.w šnm 34[1].1
t. | tqṭṭn.ušn y[p kn.l dbḥm.]w l ṯʻ dbḥ n. | ndbḥ.hw.ṯʻ n[ṯʻy.hw.nkt.nk]t.ytši.l ab bn il. | ytši.l d[r.bn il.l]mpḫrt.bn i 32[2].1.33
b qṭt]. | [tqṭṭ.u tḥṭu.l dbḥm.w l.ṯʻ.dbḥ n.ndb]ḥ. | [hw.ṯʻ.nṯʻy.hw.nkt.nkt.]yt[ši.l ab.bn.il]. | [ytši.l dr.bn.il.l mpḫ]rt.[b 32[2].1.9A
ṭt.tqṭṭ. | ušn yp km.l d[b]ḥm.w l.ṯʻ.dbḥ n.ndbḥ.hw.ṯʻ | nṯʻy. | hw.nkt.nkt.y[t]ši.l ab.bn.il.ytši.l dr. | bn il.l mpḫrt.bn.i
b qṭt]. | tqṭṭn u tḥṭin.l bḥm.w l ṯʻ.d[bḥ n.ndbḥ]. | hw.ṯʻ.nṯʻy.hw.nkt.n[k]t.ytši[.l ab.bn.il]. | ytši.l dr.bn.il.l mpḫrt.bn.i 32[2].1.16
[---.hw.ṯʻ.nṯʻ]y. | [hw.nkt.nkt.ytši.l ab.bn.il.ytši.l d]r.bn.[il]. | [l mpḫrt. 32[2].1.1
dl.mdrǵlm. | bn.mmy. | bn.ḫnyn. | bn.knn. | khnm. | bn.ṯʻy. | w.nḥl h. | w.nḥl hm. | bn.nqly. | bn.snrn. | bn.ṯgd. | bn.d[-] 104[316].9
[---.--]ṯ.slḫ.npš.ṯʻ w[.--.k]bdm. | [---.--]mm.ṯn.šm.w alp.l[--]n. | [---.]š.il š.bʻl š 36[9].1.1
dqt.ṯʻ.ynt.ṯʻm.dqt.ṯʻm. | mtntm nkbd.alp.š.l il. | gdlt.ilhm.ṯkmn.w 34[1].1
dqt.ṯʻ.ynt.ṯʻm.dqt.ṯʻm. | mtntm nkbd.alp.š.l il. | gdlt.ilhm.ṯkmn.w šnm dqt. | ršp 34[1].1
s. | spr.ilmlk šbny. | lmd.atn.prln.rb. | khnm rb.nqdm. | ṯʻy.nqmd.mlk ugr[t]. | adn.yrgb.bʻl.ṯrmn. 6.6[62.2].56
[spr.ilmlk.ṯʻ]y.nqmd.mlk.ugrt. 4[51].9.1

ṯ‘y

u b qṯṯ]. | tqṯṯn u ṯḫṯin.l bḥm.w l ṯ‘.d[bḥ n.ndbḥ]. | hw.ṯ‘.nṯ‘y.hw.nkt.n[k]t.ytši[.l ab.bn.il]. | ytši.l dr.bn.il.l mpḫrt.b 32[2].1.16
u b qṯṯ]. | [tqṯṯ.u ṯḫṯu.l dbḥm.w l.ṯ‘.dbḥ n.ndb]ḥ. | [hw.ṯ‘.nṯ‘y.hw.nkt.nkt.]yt[ši.l ab.bn.il]. | [ytši.l dr.bn.il.l mpḫ]rt.[32[2].1.9A
b qṯt.tqṯṯ. | ušn yp km.l d[b]ḥm.w l.ṯ‘.dbḥ n.ndbḥ.hw.ṯ‘ | nṯ‘y. | hw.nkt.nkt.y[t]ši.l ab.bn.il.ytši.l dr. | bn il.l mpḫrt. 32[2].1.24
[---.hw.ṯ‘.nṯ‘]y. | [hw.nkt.nkt.ytši.l ab.bn.il.ytši.l d]r.bn[.il]. | [l mpḫr 32[2].1.1
qṯt. | tqṯṯn.ušn y[p kn.l dbḥm.]w l ṯ‘ dbḥ n. | ndbḥ.hw.ṯ‘ n[ṯ‘y.hw.nkt.nk]t.ytši.l ab bn il. | ytši.l d[r.bn il.l]mpḫrt.b 32[2].1.33
‘l. | qdqd k.tqln.b gbl. | šnt k.b ḥpn k.w t‘n. | spr ilmlk ṯ‘y. 16[127]EDGE
]šlm. | [---.--]š.lalit. | [---.]bt šp.š. | y[-]lm.w mlk. | ynṣl.l ṯ‘y. 2005.2.8

ṯ‘l

n.[-]bl.ṯt.qštm.w.ṯn.ql‘m. | bn.[-]rkṯ.ṯt.qštm.w.ql‘. | bn.ṯ‘l.qšt. | bn.[ḫ]dpṯr.ṯt.qštm.[w].ql‘. | bn.aǵlyn.ṯt.qštm[.w.ṯl]ṯ.q 119[321].3.17

ṯ‘lb

---.--]k.l.gmrd. | [---.--]ṯ.l.yšn. | [šd.--]ln. | b d.trǵds. | šd.ṯ‘lb. | b d.bn.pl. | šd.bn.kt. | b d.pdy. | šd.ḫzr. | [b d].d[---]. 2030.2.3

ṯ‘ln

d.iytlm. | ḫyrn.w.šǵr h. | šǵr.bn.prsn. | agpṯr.w.šǵ[r h]. | ṯ‘ln. | mztn.w.šǵr [h]. | šǵr.plṭ. | s[d]rn [w].ṯn.šǵr h. | [---.]w.šǵ 2072.5
bn.ḥrẓn.qšt.w.ql‘. | tgrš.qšt.w.ql‘. | špšyn.qšt.w.ql‘. | bn.ṯ‘ln.qš[t.w.q]l‘. | ‘ṯqbt.qšt. | [-]ll.qšt.w.ql‘. | ḫlb.rpš. | abmn.qšt. 119[321].2.26

ṯ‘r

al.ṯǵl[.---]. | prdmn.‘bd.ali[yn]. | b‘l.sid.zbl.b‘l. | arṣ.qm.yṯ‘r. | w yšlḥmn h. | ybrd.ṯd.l pnw h. | b ḥrb.mlḥt. | qṣ.mri.nd 3['NT].1.4
m. | [t]rḥṣ.yd h.b dm.ḏmr. | [u]ṣb‘t h.b mm‘.mhrm. | [ṯ]‘r.ksat.l ksat.ṯlḥnt. | [l]ṯlḥn.hdmm.ṯṯ‘r.l hdmm. | [t]ḥspn.m 3['NT].2.36
tql.ilt.l hkl h. | w l.šb‘t.tmtḫṣ h.b ‘mq. | tḫtṣb.bn.qrtm.ṯṯ‘r. | ksat.l mhr.ṯ‘r.ṯlḥnt. | l ṣbim.hdmm.l ǵzrm. | mid.tmtḫṣn 3['NT].2.20
.b mm‘.mhrm. | [ṯ]‘r.ksat.l ksat.ṯlḥnt. | [l]ṯlḥn.hdmm.ṯṯ‘r.l hdmm. | [t]ḥspn.m h.w trḥṣ. | [ṭ]l.šmm.šmn.arṣ.rbb. | [r] 3['NT].2.37
rḫ ytrḫ.adn h. | yšt mṣb.mznm.um h. | kp mznm.iḫ h yṯ‘r. | mšrrm.aḫt h l a | bn mznm.nkl w ib. | d ašr.ar yrḫ.w y | 24[77].35
l.šb‘t.tmtḫṣ h.b ‘mq. | tḫtṣb.bn.qrtm.ṯṯ‘r. | ksat.l mhr.ṯ‘r.ṯlḥnt. | l ṣbim.hdmm.l ǵzrm. | mid.tmtḫṣn.w t‘n. | tḫtṣb.w 3['NT].2.21
h.---.]hy bt h t‘rb. | [---.tm]tḫṣ b ‘mq. | [tḫtṣb.bn.qrtm.ṯṯ‘r.ṯlḥnt.]l ṣbim. | [hdmm.l ǵzrm.mid.tmtḫṣn.w t]‘n.tḫtṣb. | [7.1[131].5

ṯǵdy

bn.pǵm[-.qšt].w.ql‘. | n‘mn.q[št.w.]ql‘. | [t]ṯn.qš[t]. | bn.ṯǵdy[.qšt.]w.ql‘. | ṯṯy.qšt[.w.]ql‘. | bn.šp[š.]qšt. | bn.‘g[w.]qšt. 119[321].4.4

ṯǵr

rt.w ‘nt.ymǵy. | ‘ṯtrt.t‘db.nšb l h. | w ‘nt.ktp.b hm.yg‘r.ṯǵr. | bt.il.pn.l mgr lb.t‘dbn. | nšb.l inr.t‘dbn.ktp. | b il ab h.g‘r UG5.1.1.11
‘mdn.i[---.---]. | kpr.šb‘ bn[t.rḥ.gdm.w anhbm]. | kla[t.ṯǵ]r[t.bht.‘nt.w tqry.ǵlmm.b št.ǵr]. | ap ‘nt tm[tḫṣ.b ‘mq.tḫtṣ 7.2[130].24
n[--.---.-]š[--]. | kpr.šb‘.bnt.rḥ.gdm. | w anhbm.klat.ṯǵrt. | bht.‘nt.w tqry.ǵlmm. | b št.ǵr.w hln.‘nt.tm | tḫṣ.b ‘mq.t 3['NT].2.3
kbs. | dd l prgṭ. | dd.l mri. | dd.l ṯnǵly. | dd.l krwn. | dd.l ṯǵr. | dd.l rmt.r[---]. 1100.11
b ṯṯ ym ḥdṯ. | ḫyr.‘rbt. | špš ṯǵr h. | ršp. | w ‘bdm tbqrn. | skn. 1162.3
---]yb‘.b‘l.ḫr[-]. | pqr.yḥd. | bn.ktmn.ṯǵr.hk[l]. | bn.ṯgbr.ṯǵr.hk[l]. | bn.ydln. | bn.ktmn. 1056.9
[-----]. | [---.-]bd. | [---]yb‘.b‘l.ḫr[-]. | pqr.yḥd. | bn.ktmn.ṯǵr.hk[l]. | bn.ṯgbr.ṯǵr.hk[l]. | bn.ydln. | bn.ktmn. 1056.8
-].mǵy h.w ǵlm. | [a]ḫt h.šib.yṣat.mrḥ h. | l tl.yṣb.pn h.ṯǵr. | yṣu.hlm.aḫ h.tph. | [ksl]h.l arṣ.ṯṯbr. | [---.]aḫ h.tbky. | [-- 16.1[125].52
l.ks. | tpnn.‘n.bṯy.‘n.bṯt.tpnn. | ‘n.mḫr.‘n.pḫr.‘n.ṯǵr. | ‘n.ṯǵr.l.ṯǵr.ṯṯb. | ‘n.pḫr.l.pḫr.ṯṯb. | ‘n.mḫr.l.mḫr.ṯṯb. | ‘n.bṯy.l.bṯy. RS225.7
]qmp‘. | [bn.nq]md. | [mlk.]ugrt. | b‘l ṣdq. | skn.bt. | mlk.ṯǵr. | [m]lk.bny. | [--].lb.mlk. | [---.]ṣmḫ. 1007.6
.qrt. | ḥgbn.šm‘.skn.qrt. | nǵr krm.‘bdadt.b‘ln.yp‘mlk. | ṯǵrm.mnḥm.klyn.‘dršp.ǵlmn. | [a]bǵl.ṣṣn.ǵrn. | šib.mqdšt.‘b[2011.13
kzym. | ksdm. | [nsk].ṯlṯ. | gt.mlkym. | tmrym. | ṯnqym. | ṯǵrm. | mru.skn. | mru.ibrn. | yqšm. | trrm. | kkrdnm. | yṣrm. | k 1026.2.5
.mri.ibrn. | [š]d.bn.bri.b d.bn.ydln. | [u]bdy.ṯǵrm. | [š]d.ṯǵr.mṯpit.b d.bn.iryn. | [u]bdy.šrm. | [š]d.bn.ḫrmln.b d.bn.tn 82[300].2.8
m.h.l.bl.ks. | tpnn.‘n.bṯy.‘n.bṯt.tpnn. | ‘n.mḫr.‘n.pḫr.‘n.ṯǵr. | ‘n.ṯǵr.l.ṯǵr.ṯṯb. | ‘n.pḫr.l.pḫr.ṯṯb. | ‘n.mḫr.l.mḫr.ṯṯb. | ‘n.b RS225.6
bd. | tgmr.bnš.mlk. | d.b d.adn‘m. | [š]b‘.b.ḥrṯm. | [ṯ]lṯ.b.ṯǵrm. | rb qrt.aḥd. | ṯmn.ḫzr. | w.arb‘.ḥršm. | dt.tb‘ln.b.pḫn. | ṯṯ 1024.3.2
psl. | [ub]dy.mri.ibrn. | [š]d.bn.bri.b d.bn.ydln. | [u]bdy.ṯǵrm. | [š]d.ṯǵr.mṯpit.b d.bn.iryn. | [u]bdy.šrm. | [š]d.bn.ḫrml 82[300].2.7
pnk.dnil.mt. | rpi.a hn.ǵzr.mt.hrnm[y]. | ytšu.ytb.b ap.ṯǵr.ṯḥt. | adrm.d b grn.ydn. | dn.almnt.yṯpṭ.ṯpṭ.ytm. | b nši ‘n 17[2AQHT].5.6
nil. | [m]t.rpi.ap[h]n.ǵzr. | [mt.hrn]my.ytšu. | [ytb.b ap.ṯ]ǵr[.ṯ]ḥt. | [adrm.d b grn.y]dn. | [dn.almnt.y]ṯpṭ. | [ṯpṭ.ytm.-- 19[1AQHT].1.22
‘d[rš]p. | pqr. | ṯǵr. | ṯṯǵl. | ṯn.yṣḥm. | slṯmg. | kdrl. | wql. | adrdn. | prn. | ‘bdil. | u 1069.3
tpnn.‘n.bṯy.‘n.bṯt.tpnn. | ‘n.mḫr.‘n.pḫr.‘n.ṯǵr. | ‘n.ṯǵr.l.ṯǵr.ṯṯb. | ‘n.pḫr.l.pḫr.ṯṯb. | ‘n.mḫr.l.mḫr.ṯṯb. | ‘n.bṯy.l.bṯy.ṯṯb. | RS225.7
.ptḥ[.aḥ]d.mmt. | ṯṯ.pt[ḥ.---]. | ṯn.pt[ḥ.---]. | w.pt[ḥ.--]r.ṯǵr. | ṯmn.ḥlnm. | ṯṯ.ṯḫ[--].l.mtm. 1151.14
t.mǵ[y.---]. | w qbr.ṯṣr.q[br]. | ṯṣr.trm.ṯnq[--]. | km.nkyt.ṯǵr[.---]. | km.škllt.[---]. | ‘r.ym.l bl[.---]. | b[---.]ny[.--]. | l bl.sk. 16.2[125].89

ṯǵrn

n h.n[--.---]. | ḥnil.[---]. | aršmg.mru. | b‘l.šlm.‘bd. | awr.ṯǵrn.‘bd. | ‘bd.ḫmn.šm‘.rgm. | šdn.[k]bš. | šdyn.mḫ[ṣ]. | aṯry.m 2084.11

ṯpd

d h. | hlm.il.k yphn h. | yprq.lṣb.w yṣḥq. | p‘n h.l hdm.yṯpd.w ykrkr. | uṣb‘t h.yšu.g h.w y[ṣḥ]. | ik.mǵyt.rbt.aṯr[t.y] 4[51].4.29
ṭrn. | nḫlm.tlk.nbtm. | šmḫ.lṭpn.il.d pid. | p‘n h.l hdm.yṯpd. | w yprq.lṣb w yṣḥq. | yšu.g h.w yṣḥ. | aṯbn.ank.w anḫn. 6[49].3.15
nm.tšmḫ.w ‘l yṣhl pi[t]. | yprq.lṣb.w yṣḥq. | p‘n.l hdm.yṯpd.yšu. | g h.w yṣḥ.aṯbn.ank. | w anḫn.w tnḫ.b irt y. | npš.k 17[2AQHT].2.11
štm.w an[.šnt.kptr]. | l rḥq.ilm.ḥkp[t.l rḥq.ilnym]. | ṯn.mṯpdm.ṯḥt.[‘nt.arṣ.ṯlṯ.mtḥ]. | ǵyrm.idk.l yt[n.pnm.‘m.lṭpn]. | 1['NT.IX].3.20
tm.bštm.w an.šnt. | uǵr.l rḥq.ilm.inbb. | l rḥq.ilnym.ṯn.mṯpdm. | ṯḥt.‘nt.arṣ.ṯlṯ.mtḥ.ǵyrm. | idk.l ttn pnm.‘m.b‘l. | mr 3['NT].4.79
-.]n[--.---]. | [---.kpt]r.l r[ḥq.ilm.ḥkpt.l rḥq]. | [ilnym.ṯn.mṯpd]m.t[ḥt.‘nt.arṣ.ṯlṯ.mtḥ.ǵyrm]. | [idk.]l ytn.pnm.‘m.[i]l. 2.3[129].3

ṯpdn

.b d.‘dbym. | [šd.b]n.qṭy.b d.tt. | [ubd]y.mrim. | [šd.b]n.ṯpdn.b d.bn.g‘r. | [šd.b]n.ṯqrn.b d.ḫby. | [ṯn.š]d.bn.ngzḥn.b d. 82[300].1.21

n.lṯḥ. | ykn.lṯḥ. | ḥgbn.lṯḥ. | spr.mkrm. | bn.sl‘n.prs. | bn.ṯpdn.lṯḥ. | bn.urm.lṯḥ. 1059.8

r. | [bn.p]rn. | [bn.a]nny. | [---]n. | bn.kbln. | bn.pdy. | bn.ṯpdn. 1075.2.3

ṯpḫln

ny. | šd.bn ḥnn.l bn.adlḏn. | šd.bn.nṣdn.l bn.‘mlbi. | šd.ṯpḫln.l bn.ǵl. | w dṯn.nḫl h.l bn.pl. | šd.krwn.l aḫn. | šd.‘yy.l a 2089.9

ṯpṭ

.yšt.rpu.mlk.‘lm.w yšt. | [--.]gṯr.w yqr.il.yṯb.b.‘ṯtrt. | il.ṯpṭ.b hd r‘y.d yšr.w yḏmr. | b knr.w ṯlb.b tp.w mṣltm.b m | r UG5.2.1.3

b bt.ṭap[.--]. | hy.yd h.w ym[ǵ]. | mlak k.‘m dt[n]. | lqḥ.mṯpṭ. | w y‘ny.nn. | dtn.bt n.mḫ[-]. | l dg.w [-]kl. | w aṯr.hn.mr UG5.6.12

k ymǵy.adn. | ilm.rbm ‘m dtn. | w yšal.mṯpṭ.yld. | w y‘ny.nn[.--]. | t‘ny.n[---.-]ṯq. | w š[--.---]. | ḥdṯ[.--- UG5.6.3

u.yṯb.b ap.ṯǵr.ṯḥt. | adrm.d b grn.ydn. | dn.almnt.yṯpṭ.ṯpṭ.ytm. | b nši ‘n h.w yphn.b alp. | šd.rbt.kmn.hlk.kṯr. | k y‘n 17[2AQHT].5.8

ap.ṯ]ǵr[.t]ḥt. | [adrm.d b grn.y]dn. | [dn.almnt.y]ṯpṭ. | [ṯpṭ.ytm.---] h. | [---.---]n. | [-----]. | hlk.[---.b n]ši. | ‘n h.w tphn. 19[1AQHT].1.25

]l.ab k.l ys‘.[alt.]ṯ[bt | k.l y]hpk. | [ksa.]mlk k.l ytbr.ḫṭ.mṯpṭ k.w y‘n[.‘ṯtr].dm[-]k[-]. | [--]ḫ.b y.ṯr.il.ab y.ank.in.bt[.l] 2.3[129].18

.ṯr. | il.ab k.l ys‘.alt. | ṯbt k.l yhpk.ksa.mlk k. | l ytbr.ḫṭ.mṯpṭ k. | yru.bn ilm t.ṯt‘.y | dd.il.ǵzr.y‘r.mt. | b ql h.y[---.---]. | 6[49].6.29

il.ḥkm.ḥkm k. | ‘m.‘lm.ḥyt.ḥẓt.ṯḥm k. | mlk n.aliyn.b‘l.ṯpṭ n. | in.d ‘ln h.klny y.qš h. | nbln.klny y.nbl.ks h. | any.l yṣ 3[‘NT.VI].5.40

ḥkm.ḥkmt. | ‘m ‘lm.ḥyt.ḥẓt. | ṯḥm k.mlk n.aliy[n.]b‘l. | ṯpṭ n.w in.d ‘ln h. | klny n.q[š] h.n[bln]. | klny n[.n]bl.ks h. | [4[51].4.44

g h.w t[ṣḥ.šm]‘.m‘. | [-.yṯ]ir ṯr.il.ab k.l pn.zbl.ym.l pn[.ṯ]pṭ[.n]hr. | [ik.a]l.yšm‘ k.ṯr.[i]l.ab k.l ys‘.[alt.]ṯ[bt | k.l y]hpk 2.3[129].16

t k.---]. | [--]šnm.aṯtm.t[--.---]. | [m]lakm.ylak.ym.[t‘dt.ṯpṭ.nhr]. | b ‘lṣ.‘lṣm.npr.š[--.---]. | uṯ.ṯbr.ap hm.tb‘.ǵlm[m.al.t 2.1[137].11

arṣ.tngṣn.pnt h.w ydlp.tmn h. | yqṯ b‘l.w yšt.ym.ykly.ṯpṭ.nhr. | b šm.tg‘r m.‘ṯtrt.bṯ l aliyn.[b‘l.] | bṯ.l rkb.‘rpt.k šby 2.4[68].27

.w[---.]tb‘.k[ṯ]r w [ḫss.t]bn.bht zbl ym. | [trm]m.hk[l.ṯpṭ].nhr.bt k.[---.]šp[-.---]. | [ḥš.bh]t h.tbn[n.ḥ]š.trm[mn.hkl 2.3[129].9

bṯ l aliyn.[b‘l.] | bṯ.l rkb.‘rpt.k šby n.zb[l.ym.k] | šby n.ṯpṭ.nhr.w yṣa b[.--]. | ybṯ.nn.aliyn.b‘l.w [---]. | ym.l mt.b‘l m. 2.4[68].30

t. | [--]n hm.rgm.l ṯr.ab h.il.ṯḥm.ym.b‘l km. | [adn]km.ṯpṭ.nhr.tn.il m.d tq h.d tqyn h. | [hml]t.tn.b‘l.w ‘nn h.bn.dg 2.1[137].34

m.l ṯr.a[b.-.il.ṯny.l pḫr]. | m‘d.ṯḥm.ym.b‘l km.adn km.ṯ[pṭ.nhr]. | tn.il m.d tq h.d tqyn.hmlt.tn.b‘l.[w ‘nn h]. | bn.dg 2.1[137].17

.l ẓr.brkt hm.ln.kḥṯ.zbl hm. | aḫr.tmǵyn.mlak ym.t‘dt.ṯpṭ.nhr.l p‘n.il. | [l t]pl.l tštḥwy.pḫr.m‘d.qmm.a[--].amr. | [ṯn 2.1[137].30

p.amr[--]. | [---].w b ym.mnḫ l abd.b ym.irtm.m[--]. | [ṯpṭ].nhr.tl‘m.ṯm.ḥrbm.its.anšq. | [-]htm.l arṣ.ypl.ul ny.w l.‘p 2.4[68].4

.‘n]t.tuḫd.šmal h.tuḫd.‘ṯtrt.ik.m[ḫṣt.ml] | [ak.ym.t‘]dt.ṯpṭ.nhr.mlak.mṯḫr.yḥb[-.---.] | [---].mlak.bn.ktpm.rgm.b‘l h. 2.1[137].41

m.b hkl.ṯpṭ.nh[r].yṯir.ṯr.il.ab h l pn[.zb]l y[m]. | [l pn.ṯp]ṭ[.nhr.]mlkt.[--]pm.l mlkt.wn.in.aṯt. | [l]k.k[m.ilm]. | [w ǵ 2.3[129].22

.l ẓr.brkt km.ln.kḥṯ. | zbl km.w ank.‘ny.mlak.ym.t‘dt.ṯpṭ.nhr. | tšu ilm rašt hm.l ẓr.brkt hm.ln.kḥṯ.zbl hm. | aḫr.t 2.1[137].28

t km.w ln.kḥṯ.zbl km.aḥd. | ilm.t‘ny lḥt.mlak.ym.t‘dt.ṯpṭ.nhr. | šu.ilm.rašt km.l ẓr.brkt km.ln.kḥṯ. | zbl km.w ank.‘ 2.1[137].26

d.b d b‘l.km.nšr. | b[u]šb‘t h.ylm.ktp.zbl ym.bn ydm.ṯpṭ. | nhr.‘z.ym.l ymk.l tngṣn.pnt h.l ydlp. | tmn h.kṯr.ṣmdm. 2.4[68].16

l trm.b‘l.qm.‘l.il.hlm. | ilm.tph hm.tphn.mlak.ym.t‘dt.ṯpṭ[.nhr]. | t[ǵ]ly.hlm.rišt hm.l ẓr.brkt hm.w l kḥṯ. | zbl hm.b 2.1[137].22

ṣ. | b d b‘l.km.nšr b uṣb‘t h.hlm.qdq | d zbl ym.bn.‘nm.ṯpṭ.nhr.yprsḥ ym. | w yql.l arṣ.w trtqṣ.ṣmd.b d b‘l. | [km.]nšr 2.4[68].22

d b‘l. | [km.]nšr.b uṣb‘t h.ylm.qdqd.zbl. | [ym.]bn.‘nm.ṯpṭ.nhr.yprsḥ.ym.yql. | l arṣ.tngṣn.pnt h.w ydlp.tmn h. | yqṯ 2.4[68].25

ṣ.b d b‘l km nš | r.b uṣb‘t h.hlm.ktp.zbl ym.bn ydm. | [ṯp]ṭ nhr.yrtqṣ.ṣmd.b d b‘l.km.nšr. | b[u]ṣb‘t h.ylm.ktp.zbl y 2.4[68].15

rd.b n[p]šn y.trḫṣn.k ṯrm. | [--]b b[ht]. | [zbl.]ym.b hkl.ṯpṭ.nh[r].yṯir.ṯr.il.ab h l pn[.zb]l y[m]. | [l pn.ṯp]ṭ[.nhr.]mlkt. 2.3[129].21

]. | aliyn.b‘l[.---]. | drkt k.mšl[-.---]. | b riš k.aymr[.---]. | ṯpṭ.nhr.ytb[r.ḥrn.y ym.ytbr.ḥrn]. | riš k.‘ṯtrt.[šm.b‘l.qdqd k.- 2.1[137].7

.t‘dt.ṯpṭ.nh[r.---]. | [---].an.rgmt.l ym.b‘l km.ad[n km.ṯpṭ]. | [nhr.---.]hwt.gmr.hd.l wny[-.---]. | [---.]iyr h.g[-.]thbr[.- 2.1[137].45

--]r y[---]. | [---.k]ṯr.w ḫ[ss.t]b‘.b[n.]bht.ym[.rm]m.hkl.ṯpṭ nh[r]. | [---.]hrn.w[---.]tb‘.k[ṯ]r w [ḫss.t]bn.bht zbl ym. | [2.3[129].7

.ap.anš.zbl.b‘l.šdmt.bg[--.---]. | [---.-]dm.mlak.ym.t‘dt.ṯpṭ.nh[r.---]. | [---].an.rgmt.l ym.b‘l km.ad[n km.ṯpṭ]. | [nhr.-- 2.1[137].44

l]k.k[m.ilm]. | [w ǵlmt.k bn.qdš.]w y[--.]zbl.ym.y‘[--.]ṯpṭ.nhr. | [-------.]yšlḥn.w y‘n ‘ṯtr[.-]. 2.3[129].23

[ǵ]rm[.ṯṯwy]. | šqlt.b ǵlt.yd k. | l tdn.dn.almnt. | l ṯṯpṭ.ṯpṭ.qṣr.npš. | km.aḫt.‘rš.mdw. | anšt.‘rš.zbln. | rd.l mlk.amlk. 16.6[127].34

. | w ǵrm.ṯṯwy.šqlt. | b ǵlt.yd k.l tdn. | dn.almnt.l ṯṯpṭ. | ṯpṭ qṣr.npš.l tdy. | ṯšm.‘l.dl.l pn k. | l tšlḥm.ytm.b‘d. | ksl k.al 16.6[127].47

. | ytšu.yṯb.b ap.ṯǵr.ṯḥt. | adrm.d b grn.ydn. | dn.almnt.yṯpṭ.ṯpṭ.ytm. | b nši ‘n h.w yphn.b alp. | šd.rbt.kmn.hlk.kṯr. | 17[2AQHT].5.8

. | [yṯb.b ap.ṯ]ǵr[.t]ḥt. | [adrm.d b grn.y]dn. | [dn.almnt.y]ṯpṭ. | [ṯpṭ.ytm.---] h. | [---.---]n. | [-----]. | hlk.[---.b n]ši. | ‘n h. 19[1AQHT].1.24

br.w[ǵ]rm[.ṯṯwy]. | šqlt.b ǵlt.yd k. | l tdn.dn.almnt. | l ṯṯpṭ.ṯpṭ.qṣr.npš. | km.aḫt.‘rš.mdw. | anšt.‘rš.zbln. | rd.l mlk.a 16.6[127].34

.tdbr. | w ǵrm.ṯṯwy.šqlt. | b ǵlt.yd k.l tdn. | dn.almnt.l ṯṯpṭ. | ṯpṭ qṣr.npš.l tdy. | ṯšm.‘l.dl.l pn k. | l tšlḥm.ytm.b‘d. | ks 16.6[127].46

ṯpṭb‘l

ubdy.mḏ]rǵlm. | [šd.bn.--]n.b d.aḫny. | [šd.bn.--]rt.b d.ṯpṭb‘l. | [ubdy.]mḫ[ṣ]m. | [šd.bn.]uzpy.b d.yšn.ḥrš. | [-----]. | [-- 82[300].2.24

l.mlk.b‘[l] y. | rgm. | ṯḥm.ṯpṭb[‘l]. | [‘]bd k. | [l.p]‘n.b‘l y. | [šb‘] d.šb‘ [d]. | [mr]ḥqtm. | qlt 2063.3

-.šd]m.b.uškn. | [---.--]n. | [---].tlmdm. | [y]bnn.ṣmdm. | ṯp[ṭ]b‘l.ṣmdm. | [---.ṣ]mdm.w.ḥrṣ. | [---].aḥdm. | [iwr]pzn.aḥd 2033.2.4

[-----]. | šd.prsn.l.[---]. | šd.bddn.l.iytlm. | šd.bn.nb‘m.l.ṯpṭb‘l. | šd.bn mšrn.l.ilšpš. | [šd.bn].kbr.l.snrn. | [---.--]k.l.gmr 2030.1.4

[ubdy.‘]šrm. | [šd.---]n.b d.brdd. | [---.--]m. | [šd.---.b d.]ṯpṭb‘l. | [šd.---.]b d.ymz. | [šd.b d].klby.psl. | [ub]dy.mri.ibrn. | 82[300].2.2

anyt.miḫd[t]. | br.ṯpṭb‘[l.---]. | br.dmty[.---]. | ṯkt.ydln[.---]. | ṯkt.ṯryn[.---]. | br.‘b 84[319].1.2

spr.[---]. | ṯpṭb[‘l.---]. | mb[--.---]. | gmr[.---]. | [---]. 92[302].2

.aṯtm.w.pǵt.aḥt.b bt.[-]r[-]. | [aṯ]t.b.bt.aupš. | [aṯ]t.b.bt.ṯpṭb‘l. | [---.]n[--.mḏ]rǵlm. | [---.]b.bt[.---]l. | [ṯ]lṯ.aṯt.adrt.w.ṯlṯ 80[119].13

ṯpllm

spš]. | mlk.rb.b‘l h.[---]. | nqmd.mlk.ugr[t.--]. | phy. | w ṯpllm.mlk.r[b.--]. | mṣmt.l nqmd.[---.-]št. | hl ny.argmn.d [yb 64[118].16

ṯpn

pš d l y[dy]. | atlg. | ulm. | izly. | uḫnp. | bn sḫrn. | m'qb. | ṯpn. | m'r. | lbnm. | nḫl. | y'ny. | atn. | utly. | bn.alz. | bn ḫlm. | bn 2075.8
[b.]gt.ṯpn.'šr.ṣmdm. | w.ṯlṯ.'šr.bnš. | yd.ytm.yd.r'y.ḥmrm. | b.gt.gwl 2038.1

ṯpr

.--]b.kdr. | [---.--]m n'rt. | [---].qt.b[--]. | [---.]kd[r]. | [---.]ṯpr. | [---.]prš. | [---.]šdm. | [---.-]nm.prš.glbm. | [---.]'gd.dqr. | [- 1142.4

ṯprt

t. | b.'šrt.ksp. | 'šr.ṣin.b.ṯṯt.w.kmsk. | arb'[.k]dwṯm.w.ṯt.ṯprtm. | b.'šr[m.]ksp. | ḫmš.kkr.ṣml. | b.'šrt.b d.bn.kyn. | 'šr.k 2100.10
lbš.aḥd. | b.'šrt. | w.ṯn.b.ḫmšt. | ṯprt.b.ṯlṯt. | mṯyn.b.ṯṯt. | ṯn.lbšm.b.'šrt. | pld.b.arb't. | lbš.ṯn.b.ṯ 1108.4
ṯṯm.ṯlṯ.kb[d]. | arb'm.ṯp[rt]. | ksp h. | ṯmn.dd[.--]. | ṯlṯ.dd.p[--]. | šb't.p[--]. | tš't.k[bd. 2120.2

ṯṣr

nt.ilm.b qrb.m[ṯ't.ilnym]. | d tit.yspi.spu.q[--.---]. | tpḥ.ṯṣr.shr[.---]. | mr[.---]. 20[121].2.11

ṯqb

.[l]. | ['nt.tq]ḫ[.q]ṣ't k.ybmt.limm. | w y'n.aqht.ġzr.adr.ṯqbm. | [d]lbnn.adr.gdm.b rumm. | adr.qrnt.b y'lm.mtnm. | b 17[2AQHT].6.20

ṯqbn

ytlm. | šgryn.ary.b.yny. | bn.yddn.b.rkby. | agyn.agny. | ṯqbn.mldy. 2071.9
n.qšt. | bn.ṯlln.qšt. | bn.šyn.qšt. | 'bd.qšt. | bn.ulmy.qšt. | ṯqbn.qšt. | bn.qnmlk.qšt. | ytḥm.qšt. | grp.qšt. | m'rby. | n'mn.ṯ 104[316].5

ṯqd

'rgz.ydk]. | a[ḥd h.w.yṣq.b.ap h]. | k.[ḫr.ššw.ḫndrṯ]. | w.ṯ[qd.mr.ydk.aḥd h]. | w.y[ṣq.b.ap h]. | k.l.ḫ[ru.w.l.yṯtn.ššw]. | 161[56].6
'rgz]. | [ydk aḥ]d h w yṣq b ap h. | [k ḫr]ššw ḫndrṯ w ṯ[qd m]r. | [ydk aḥd h w yṣq b ap h. | [k l yḫru w]l yṯtn mss 160[55].6

ṯqdy

.b d.klṯtb. | [š]d.ilṣy.b d.'bdym. | [ub]dy.trrm. | [šd.]bn.ṯqdy.b d.gmrd. | [š]d bn.synn.b d.gmrd. | [šd.]abyy.b d.ibrm 82[300].2.17

ṯql

dmt ṯlṯ. | qmnz ṯql. | zlyy ṯql. | ary ḫmšt. | ykn'm ḫmšt. | 'nmky ṯqlm. | [-]kt 'šrt. | qrn šb 1176.3
qrt ṯqlm.w nṣp. | šlmy.ṯql. | ary ṯql. | ṯmry ṯql.w.nṣp. | aġt nṣp. | dmt ṯql. | ykn'm ṯql. 69[111].2
dr h.ybky. | b ṯn.[-]gmm.w ydm'. | tntkn.udm't h. | km.ṯqlm.arṣ h. | km ḫmšt.mṯt h. | bm.bky h.w yšn. | b dm' h.nhm 14[KRT].1.29
. | mṣrn.ḥrš.mrkbt.ṯqlm. | 'pṯn.ḥrš.qṭn.ṯqlm. | bn.pġdn.ṯqlm. | bn.b'ln.ṯqlm. | 'bdyrḫ.nqd.ṯqlm. | bt.sgld.ṯqlm. | bn.'m 122[308].1.10
n.b'ln.ṯqlm. | 'bdyrḫ.nqd.ṯqlm. | bt.sgld.ṯqlm. | bn.'my.ṯqlm. | bn.brq.ṯqlm. | bn.ḫnzr.ṯqlm. | dqn.nsk.arb't. | bn.ḫdyn. 122[308].1.14
'bdyrḫ.nqd.ṯqlm. | bt.sgld.ṯqlm. | bn.'my.ṯqlm. | bn.brq.ṯqlm. | bn.ḫnzr.ṯqlm. | dqn.nsk.arb't. | bn.ḫdyn.ṯqlm. | bn.'bd. 122[308].1.15
ḫnzr.ṯqlm. | dqn.nsk.arb't. | bn.ḫdyn.ṯqlm. | bn.'bd.šḫr.ṯqlm. | bn.ḫnqn.arb't. | [b]n.ṯrk.ṯqlm. | [b]n.pdrn.ṯq[lm]. | pdy. 122[308].1.19
bn.brq.ṯqlm. | bn.ḫnzr.ṯqlm. | dqn.nsk.arb't. | bn.ḫdyn.ṯqlm. | bn.'bd.šḫr.ṯqlm. | bn.ḫnqn.arb't. | [b]n.ṯrk.ṯqlm. | [b]n. 122[308].1.18
.pġdn.ṯqlm. | bn.b'ln.ṯqlm. | 'bdyrḫ.nqd.ṯqlm. | bt.sgld.ṯqlm. | bn.'my.ṯqlm. | bn.brq.ṯqlm. | bn.ḫnzr.ṯqlm. | dqn.nsk.a 122[308].1.13
ḫdyn.ṯqlm. | bn.'bd.šḫr.ṯqlm. | bn.ḫnqn.arb't. | [b]n.ṯrk.ṯqlm. | [b]n.pdrn.ṯq[lm]. | pdy.[----]. | [i]lmlk.bn.[---]. | [--]'[-.-- 122[308].1.21
--]. | bn.dlq[-.---]. | tġyn.bn.ubn.ṯql[m]. | yšn.ḥrš.mrkbt.ṯq[lm]. | bn.p'ṣ.ṯqlm. | mṣrn.ḥrš.mrkbt.ṯqlm. | 'pṯn.ḥrš.qṭn.ṯql 122[308].1.6
m]. | bn.p'ṣ.ṯqlm. | mṣrn.ḥrš.mrkbt.ṯqlm. | 'pṯn.ḥrš.qṭn.ṯqlm. | bn.pġdn.ṯqlm. | bn.b'ln.ṯqlm. | 'bdyrḫ.nqd.ṯqlm. | bt.sg 122[308].1.9
š.qṭn.ṯqlm. | bn.pġdn.ṯqlm. | bn.b'ln.ṯqlm. | 'bdyrḫ.nqd.ṯqlm. | bt.sgld.ṯqlm. | bn.'my.ṯqlm. | bn.brq.ṯqlm. | bn.ḫnzr.ṯql 122[308].1.12
b't. | ksp h. | kkr.š'rt. | šb't.ksp h. | ḫmš.mqdm.dnyn. | b.ṯql.dprn.aḥd. | b.ṯql. | ḫmšm.'rgz.b.ḫmšt. 1127.20
. | bt.sgld.ṯqlm. | bn.'my.ṯqlm. | bn.brq.ṯqlm. | bn.ḫnzr.ṯqlm. | dqn.nsk.arb't. | bn.ḫdyn.ṯqlm. | bn.'bd.šḫr.ṯqlm. | bn.ḫ 122[308].1.16
qrt ṯqlm.w nṣp. | šlmy.ṯql. | ary ṯql. | ṯmry ṯql.w.nṣp. | aġt nṣp. | dmt ṯql. | ykn'm ṯql. 69[111].4
sp. | ṯlṯ.uṭbm.b d.alḫn.b.'šrt[.k]sp. | rṭ.l.ql.d.ybl.prd. | b.ṯql.w.nṣp.ksp. | ṯmn.lbšm.w.mšlt. | l.udmym.b.ṯmnt.'šrt.ksp. 2101.13
qrt ṯqlm.w nṣp. | šlmy.ṯql. | ary ṯql. | ṯmry ṯql.w.nṣp. | aġt nṣp. | d 69[111].1
.ḥrṣ. | b.ṯqlm.kbd.arb'm. | 'šrt.ḥrṣ.b.arb'm. | mit.ḥršḫ.b.ṯqlm. | w.šb'.'šr.šmn. | d.l.yṣa.bt.mlk. | tgmr.ksp.mitm. | ḫmš 2100.19
p 'l bn llit. | [--]l[-.-]p 'l [---.-]b'm arny. | w 'l [---.]rb'm ṯqlm.w [---] arb'yn. | w 'l.mnḥm.arb' š[mn]. | w 'l bn a[--.-]yn 1103.8
dmt ṯlṯ. | qmnz ṯql. | zlyy ṯql. | ary ḫmšt. | ykn'm ḫmšt. | 'nmky ṯqlm. | [-]kt 'šr 1176.2
'rt. | šb't.ksp h. | ḫmš.mqdm.dnyn. | b.ṯql.dprn.aḥd. | b.ṯql. | ḫmšm.'rgz.b.ḫmšt. 1127.21
---]. | tš'.ṣin.b.tš't.ksp. | mšlt.b.ṯql.ksp. | kdwṯ.l.grgyn.b.ṯq[l]. | ḫmšm.šmt.b.ṯql. | kkr.w.[ml]tḥ.tyt.[---]. | [b]šb'[m.w.n 2101.24
[-----]. | [ḫ]pn.aḥd.b.ṯqlm. | lbš.aḥd.b.ṯqlm. | ḫpn.pṯtm.b 'šr. | tgmr.ksp.ṯlṯm. | ṯqlm.kbd. 1115.3
mšt.kbd.ksp. | ṯlṯ.ktnt.b d.an[r]my. | b.'šrt.ksp.b.a[--]. | ṯqlm.ḫr[ṣ.]b.ṯmnt.ksp. | 'šrt.ksp.b.alp.[b d].bn.[---]. | tš'.ṣin.b. 2101.20
m.]šb' pamt. | l ilm.šb['.]l kṯr. | 'lm.t'rbn.gtrm. | bt.mlk.ṯql.ḫrṣ. | l špš.w yrḫ.l gtr. | ṯql.ksp.ṭb.ap w np[š]. | l 'nt h.ṯql.ḫ 33[5].10
l.ḫrṣ. | l špš.w yrḫ.l gtr. | ṯql.ksp.ṭb.ap w np[š]. | l 'nt h.ṯql.ḫrṣ. | l špš[.w y]rḫ.l gtr.ṯn. | [ṯql.ksp].ṭb.ap.w npš. | [---].bt. 33[5].13
ṣp. | šlmy.ṯql. | ary ṯql. | ṯmry ṯql.w.nṣp. | aġt nṣp. | dmt ṯql. | ykn'm ṯql. 69[111].6
-]. | bn.ṯ[--.---]. | agmy[.---]. | bn.dlq[-.---]. | tġyn.bn.ubn.ṯql[m]. | yšn.ḥrš.mrkbt.ṯq[lm]. | bn.p'ṣ.ṯqlm. | mṣrn.ḥrš.mrkb 122[308].1.5
šb't.l ṯlṯm. | [---].šb't.'šrt. | [---.-]kyn.'šrt. | b.bn.'sl.'šrm.ṯqlm kbd. | b.ṯmq.ḫmšt.l.'šrt. | b.[---].šb't.'šrt. | b.bn.pdrn.'šr 2054.1.6
ṯlṯm.šl[m.---]. | iwrpzn.'šrm 'šrm š[lm.---]. | ilabn.'šrt ṯqlm kbd.ḫmš.šl[m.---]. | tlmyn.šb't.'šrt 'šrt[.šlm.---]. | ybn.ṯ 1131.3
y.argmn.d [ybl.n]qmd. | l špš.arn.ṯn[.'šr h.]mn. | 'ṣrm.ṯql.kbd[.ks].mn.ḫrṣ. | w arb'.ktnt.w [---]b. | [ḫm]š.mat pḥm. | 64[118].20
šš[r]t.ḫrṣ.ṯqlm.kbd.'šrt.mzn h. | b [ar]b'm.ksp. | b d['.'b]dym.ṯlṯ.kkr š'rt 2100.1
.kyn. | 'šr.kkr.š'rt. | b d.urtn.b.arb'm. | arb't.'šrt.ḫrṣ. | b.ṯqlm.kbd.arb'm. | 'šrt.ḫrṣ.b.arb'm. | mit.ḥršḫ.b.ṯqlm. | w.šb'.'š 2100.17
lm. | lbš.aḥd.b.ṯqlm. | ḫpn.pṯtm.b 'šr. | tgmr.ksp.ṯlṯm. | ṯqlm.kbd. 1115.6
p. | mšlt.b.ṯql.ksp. | kdwṯ.l.grgyn.b.ṯq[l]. | ḫmšm.šmt.b.ṯql. | kkr.w.[ml]tḥ.tyt.[---]. | [b]šb'[m.w.n]ṣp.ksp. | [tgm]r.[al 2101.25

ṯlṯ.ktnt.b dm.tt. | w.ṯmnt.ksp.hn. | ktn.d.ṣr.pḥm.b h.w.ṯqlm. | ksp h.mitm.pḥm.b d.skn. | w.ṯt.ktnm.ḫmšt.w.nṣp.ksp. 1110.4
ṯr. | ʻlm.tʻrbn.gṯrm. | bt.mlk.ṯql.ḫrṣ. | l špš.w yrḫ.l gṯr. | ṯql.ksp.ṯb.ap w np[š]. | l ʻnt h.ṯql.ḫrṣ. | l špš[.w y]rḫ.l gṯr.ṯn. | 33[5].12
.ṯb.ap w np[š]. | l ʻnt h.ṯql.ḫrṣ. | l špš[.w y]rḫ.l gṯr.ṯn. | [ṯql.ksp].ṯb.ap.w npš. | [---].bt.alp w š. | [---.--]m.l gṯrm. | [---.]l 33[5].15
| ʻšrt.ksp.b.alp.[b d].bn.[---]. | tšʻ.ṣin.b.tšʻt.ksp. | mšlt.b.ṯql.ksp. | kdwṯ.l.grgyn.b.ṯq[l]. | ḫmšm.šmt.b.ṯql. | kkr.w.[ml]t 2101.23
[-----]. | [ḫ]pn.aḥd.b.ṯqlm. | lbš.aḥd.b.ṯqlm. | ḫpn.pṯtm.b ʻšr. | tgmr.ksp.ṯlṯm. | ṯqlm 1115.2
-]. | tǵyn.bn.ubn.ṯql[m]. | yšn.ḥrš.mrkbt.ṯq[lm]. | bn.pʻṣ.ṯqlm. | mṣrn.ḥrš.mrkbt.ṯqlm. | ʻpṯn.ḥrš.qṭn.ṯqlm. | bn.pǵdn.ṯq 122[308].1.7
rkbt.ṯqlm. | ʻpṯn.ḥrš.qṭn.ṯqlm. | bn.pǵdn.ṯqlm. | bn.bʻln.ṯqlm. | ʻbdyrḫ.nqd.ṯqlm. | bt.sgld.ṯqlm. | bn.ʻmy.ṯqlm. | bn.brq 122[308].1.11
| yšn.ḥrš.mrkbt.ṯq[lm]. | bn.pʻṣ.ṯqlm. | mṣrn.ḥrš.mrkbt.ṯqlm. | ʻpṯn.ḥrš.qṭn.ṯqlm. | bn.pǵdn.ṯqlm. | bn.bʻln.ṯqlm. | ʻbdy 122[308].1.8
d.šḫr.ṯqlm. | bn.ḫnqn.arbʻt. | [b]n.ṯrk.ṯqlm. | [b]n.pdrn.ṯq[lm]. | pdy.[----]. | [i]lmlk.bn.[---]. | [--]ʻ[-.---]. | [---.k]kr. | [---- 122[308].1.22
[--.-]qš. | [--]pš.šn[--]. | ṯ[-]r.b iš[-]. | bʻl h.š[-]rt. | ḫqr.[--.ṯq]l rb. | ṯl[ṯ.---]. | aḥt.ḫm[-.---]. | b ym.dbḥ.ṯp[-]. | aḥt.l mzy.b 39[19].10
rm.ʻšrt.ḫmš.kbd. | bn.ilṣdq.šbʻt ṯlṯt šlm. | bn.ṯmq.arbʻt ṯqlm šlmm. 1131.10
| ʻl.pd.asr.[---.]l[.---]. | mḫlpt.w l.ytk.[d]m[ʻt.]km. | rbʻt.ṯqlm.ṯtp[.---.]bm. | yd.ṣpn hm.tliy m[.--.ṣ]pn hm. | nṣḥy.šrr. 19[1AQHT].2.83
ṯbn.ybnn. | arbʻm.l.mit.šmn. | arbʻm.l.mit.tišr. | ṯt.ṯt.b [ṯ]ql.ṯlṯt.l.ʻšrm.ksp hm. | šstm.b.šbʻm. | ṯlṯ.mat.trm.b.ʻšrt. | mit 1127.5
qrt ṯqlm.w nṣp. | šlmy.ṯql. | ary ṯql. | ṯmry ṯql.w.nṣp. | aǵt nṣp. | dmt ṯql. | yknʻm ṯql. 69[111].3
| qmnz ṯql. | zlyy ṯql. | ary ḫmšt. | yknʻm ḫmšt. | ʻnmky ṯqlm. | [-]kt ʻšrt. | qrn šbʻt. 1176.6
[---] arbʻyn. | w ʻl.mnḥm.arbʻ š[mn]. | w ʻl bn a[--.-]yn ṯqlm. | [--] ksp [---] kdr [---]. | [-]ṯrn [k]sp [-]al[.-]r[-]. | [--]dšq 1103.10
š.mtn.b.arʻt. | [--.l]bš.bn.yknʻ.b.arʻt. | [--.l]bš.bn.grbn.b.ṯqlm. | [--.lb]š.bn.sgryn.b[.ṯ]qlm. | [---.]bn.ully.b.ṯ[qlm]. | [---.] 135[330].3
rbn.b.ṯqlm. | [--.lb]š.bn.sgryn.b[.ṯ]qlm. | [---.]bn.ully.b.ṯ[qlm]. | [---.]bn.anndy.b[.---]. | [---.]bn.pd[--.---]. 135[330].5
nʻ.b.arʻt. | [--.l]bš.bn.grbn.b.ṯqlm. | [--.lb]š.bn.sgryn.b[.ṯ]qlm. | [---.]bn.ully.b.ṯ[qlm]. | [---.]bn.anndy.b[.---]. | [---.]bn. 135[330].4
.w ʻṣrm.l[.---]. | pamt.w bt.[---]. | rmm.w ʻl[y.---]. | bt.il.ṯq[l.---.kbd]. | w bdḥ.k[--.---]. | ʻṣrm.l i[nš.ilm.ṯb.md]| bḥ.bʻl.[APP.II[173].42
.-]lp. | w.š.l[--]p. | w[.--.-]nš. | i[--.---]. | w[.---]. | k[--.---]. | ṯql[.---]. 2005.1.11
l. | ary ṯql. | ṯmry ṯql.w.nṣp. | aǵt nṣp. | dmt ṯql. | yknʻm ṯql. 69[111].7

ṯqrn

d.tt. | [ubd]y.mrim. | [šd.b]n.ṯpdn.b d.bn.gʻr. | [šd.b]n.ṯqrn.b d.ḫby. | [ṯn.š]d.bn.ngzḥn.b d.gmrd. | [šd.bn].pll.b d.g 82[300].1.22

ṯr

| b šal.krt.m at. | krt.k ybky. | ydmʻ.nʻmn.ǵlm. | il.mlk[.ṯ]r ab h. | yarš.hm.drk[t]. | k ab.adm. | [-----]. 14[KRT].1.41
rbṣ bn.amt. | [ṯn.b]nm.aqny. | [ṯn.ṯa]rm.amid. | [w yʻn].ṯr.ab h.il. | d[--].b bk.krt. | b dmʻ.nʻmn.ǵlm. | il.ṯrḥṣ.w tadm. | 14[KRT].2.59
| l zr.mgdl.rkb. | ṯkmm.ḥmt.nša. | [y]d h.šmmh.dbḥ. | l ṯr.ab h.il.šrd. | [bʻl].b dbḥ h.bn dgn. | [b m]ṣd h.yrd.krt. | [l g] 14[KRT].4.169
h. | [hml]t.ṯn.bʻl.w ʻnn h.bn.dgn.arṯ m.pd h. | [w yʻn.]ṯr.ab h.il.ʻbd k.bʻl.y ym m.ʻbd k.bʻl. | [--.--]m.bn.dgn.a[s]r k 2.1[137].36
. | [ṯn]y.dʻt hm.išt.ištm.yitmr.ḥrb.ltšt. | [--]n hm.rgm.l ṯr.ab h.il.ṯḥm.ym.bʻl km. | [adn]km.ṯpṭ.nhr.tn.il m.d tq h.d 2.1[137].33
d.b yd h]. | š[g]r h bm ymn.t[--.---]. | [--.]l bʻl.ʻbd[.---]. | ṯr ab h il.ṯtrm[.---]. | tšlḥm yrḫ.ggn[.---]. | k[.---.ḫ]mš.ḫssm[.- 2001.1.15
ʻl.l zr.[mg]dl.rkb. | ṯkmm.ḥm[t].ša.yd k. | šmm.dbḥ.l ṯr. | ab k.il.šrd.bʻl. | b dbḥ k.bn.dgn. | b mṣd k.w yrd. | krt.l gg 14[KRT].2.76
l.tšṯḥwy.pḫr [mʻd.qmm.a--.am]] | r ṯny.dʻt km.w rgm.l ṯr.a[b.-.il.ṯny.l pḫr]. | mʻd.ṯḥm.ym.bʻl km.adn km.ṯ[pṭ.nhr]. | 2.1[137].16
nn.adr.gdm.b rumm. | adr.qrnt.b yʻlm.mtnm. | b ʻqbt.ṯr.adr.b ǵlil.qnm. | tn.l kṯr.w ḫss.ybʻl.qšt l ʻnt. | qṣʻt.l ybmt.li 17[2AQHT].6.23
[-----]. | [---.--]y. | [-----]. | [any.l yṣ]ḥ.ṯr. | [il.ab h.i]l.mlk. | [d yknn h.yṣ]ḥ.aṯ | [rt.w bn h.]ilt. | [w ṣbr 4[51].1.4
n.d ʻln h.klny y.qš h. | nbln.klny y.nbl.ks h. | any.l yṣḥ.ṯr.il.ab h.il. | mlk.d yknn h.yṣḥ.aṯrt. | w bn h.ilt.w ṣbrt.arḫ h. 3[ʻNT.VI].5.43
. | klny n.q[š] h.n[bln]. | klny n[.n]bl.ks h. | [an]y.l yṣḥ.ṯr il.ab h. | [i]l.mlk.d yknn h.yṣḥ. | aṯrt.w bn h.ilt.w ṣbrt. | ary 4[51].4.47
trḥṣn.k ṯrm. | [--]b b[ht]. | [zbl.]ym.b hkl.ṯpṭ.nh[r].yṯir.ṯr.il.ab h l pn[.zb]l y[m]. | [l pn.ṯp]ṭ[.nhr.]mlkt.[--]pm.l mlkt 2.3[129].21
b.šnm.l [pʻn.il.yhbr.w yql]. | yšṯḥwy.[w ykbdn h.---]. | ṯr.il[.ab h.---]. | ḥš b[ht m.tbnn.ḥš.trmmn.hkl m]. | b tk.[---]. | 1[ʻNT.IX].3.26
.ab[.šnm.]mṣr. | [t]bu.ddm.qn[-.-]n[-.-]lt. | ql h.yš[mʻ].ṯr.[il].ab h.[---]l. | b šbʻt.ḥdrm.[b ṯ]mn[t.ap]. | sgrt.g[-].[-]ẓ[.-- 3[ʻNT.VI].5.18
lk k.l ytbr.ḫṭ.mṯpṭ k.w yʻn[.ʻṯtr].dm[-]k[-]. | [--]ḥ.b y.ṯr.il.ab y.ank.in.bt[.l] y[.km.]ilm[.w] ḥẓr[.k bn]. | [qd]š.lbum 2.3[129].19
.ary h.uzrm.ilm.ylḥm. | uzrm.yšqy.bn.qdš. | l tbrknn l ṯr.il ab y. | tmrnn.l bny.bnwt. | w ykn.bn h b bt.šrš.b qrb. | hk 17[2AQHT].1.24
rṣy]. | bt.yʻbdr[.mṯb.klt]. | knyt.w tʻn[.btlt.ʻnt]. | yṯb l y.ṯr.il[.ab y.---]. | yṯb.l y.w l h.[---]. | [--.i]mṣḫ.nn.k imr.l arṣ. | [a 3[ʻNT.VI].4.7
hwt]. | w rgm l k[ṯr.w ḫss.ṯny.l hyn]. | d ḥrš.y[dm.ṯḥm.ṯr.il.ab k.] | hwt.lṭpn[.ḥtk k.---]. | yh.kṯr.b[---]. | šṭ.lskt.n[--.--- 1[ʻNT.IX].3.5
r.w yql.yšt]ḥwyn.w y | [kbdn h.yšu.g h.w y]ṣḥ.ṯḥm. | [ṯr.il.ab k.hwt.l]ṭpn.ḥtk k. | [qryy.b arṣ.mlḥ]mt.št b ʻp | [r m.d 1[ʻNT.IX].2.18
t. | idk.l ttn.pnm. | ʻm.nrt.ilm.špš. | tšu.g h.w tṣḥ. | ṯḥm.ṯr.il.ab k. | hwt.lṭpn.ḥtk k. | pl.ʻnt.šdm.y špš. | pl.ʻnt.šdm.il.yš 6[49].4.34
ʻ. | l bn.ilm.mt.ik.tmt[ḫ] | ṣ.ʻm.aliyn.bʻl. | ik.al.yšm[ʻ] k.ṯr. | il.ab k.l ysʻ.alt. | ṯbt k.l yhpk.ksa.mlk k. | l ytbr.ḫṭ.mṯpṭ k 6[49].6.26
r ṯr.il.ab k.l pn.zbl.ym.l pn[.ṯ]pṭ[.n]hr. | [ik.a]l.yšmʻ k.ṯr.[i]l.ab k.l ysʻ.[alt.]ṯ[bt | k.l y]hpk. | [ksa.]mlk k.l ytbr.ḫṭ.m 2.3[129].17
. | [---.-]nn.nrt.ilm.špš.tšu.g h.w t[ṣḥ.šm]ʻ.mʻ. | [-.yṯ]ir ṯr.il.ab k.l pn.zbl.ym.l pn[.ṯ]pṭ[.n]hr. | [ik.a]l.yšmʻ k.ṯr.[i]l.ab 2.3[129].16
ṯr[.il.ab -.w tʻn.rbt]. | aṯr[t.ym.šmʻ.l qdš]. | w am[rr.l dgy.rbt] 4[51].4.1
ym. | ik.tmgnn.rbt. | aṯrt.ym.tǵẓyn. | qnyt.ilm.mgntm. | ṯr.il.d pid.hm.ǵẓtm. | bny.bnwt w tʻn. | btlt.ʻnt.nmgn. | [-]m.r 4[51].3.31
npyn h.b nhrm. | štt.ḫptr.l išt. | ḫbrṯ.l zr.pḥmm. | tʻpp.ṯr.il.d pid. | tǵẓy.bny.bnwt. | b nši.ʻn h.w tphn. | hlk.bʻl.aṯtrt. | 4[51].2.10
b.aylt. | [---.--]m.b km.yʻn. | [---].ydʻ.l ydʻt. | [---.]tasrn.ṯr il. | [---.]rks.bn.abnm. | [---.]upqt.ʻrb. | [---.w ẓ]r.mtn y at z 1[ʻNT.X].5.22
.tmll.išd h.qrn[m]. | dt.ʻl h.riš h.b glṯ.b šm[m]. | [---.i]l.ṯr.iṯ.p h.k ṯt.ǵlt[.--]. | [---.--] k yn.ddm.l b[--.---]. | [---.-]yt š[--. UG5.3.1.8
šmʻ.mtt.[ḥ]ry. | ṯṯbḫ.šmn.[m]ri h. | t[p]tḥ.rḥbt.yn. | ʻl h.ṯr h.tšʻrb. | ʻl h.tšʻrb.ẓby h. | ṯr.ḫbr.rbt. | ḫbr.ṯrrt. | bt.krt.tbun. 15[128].4.17
k k. | w ld ʻqqm. | ilm.ypʻr. | šmt hm. | b hm.qrnm. | km.ṯrm.w gbṯt. | km.ibrm. | w b hm.pn.bʻl. | bʻl.ytlk.w yṣd. | yḥ pa 12[75].1.31
a h.šr.yly h. | b skn.sknm.b ʻdn. | ʻdnm.kn.npl.bʻl. | km ṯr.w tkms.hd.p[-]. | km.ibr.b tk.mšmš d[--]. | ittpq.l awl. | išt 12[75].2.55
.bʻ]l. | yʻdb.hd.ʻdb[.ʻd]bt. | hkl h.ṯbḫ.alpm[.ap]. | ṣin.šql.ṯrm[.w]m | ria.il.ʻglm.d[t]. | šnt.imr.qmṣ.l[l]im. | ṣḥ.aḫ h.b bh 4[51].6.41
-.---]. | il.dbḥ.[---]. | pʻr.b[--.---]. | ṯbḫ.alp[m.ap.ṣin.šql]. | ṯrm.w [mri.ilm.ʻglm.dt.šnt]. | imr.[qmṣ.llim.---]. 1[ʻNT.X].4.31
m y.km.tdd. | ʻnt.ṣd.tštr.ʻpt.šmm. | ṯbḫ.alpm.ap ṣin.šql.ṯrm. | w mri ilm.ʻglm.dt.šnt. | imr.qmṣ.llim.k ksp. | l ʻbrm.zt. 22.2[124].12
bn.bʻln.biry. | ṯlṯ.bʻlm. | w.adn hm.ṯr.w.arbʻ.bnt h. | yrḫm.yd.ṯn.bn h. | bʻlm.w.ṯlṯ.nʻrm.w.bt.aḥt. 2080.3

ṯr

.at.ʻ[l.qšt h]. | tmḫṣ h.qṣʻt h.hwt.l t[ḥwy]. | nʻmn.ǵzr.št.ṯrm.w[---]. | ištir.b ddm.w nʻrs[.---]. | w tʻn.btlt.ʻnt.ṯb.yṯp.w[18[3AQHT].4.14
]ri h. | t[p]ṯḥ.rḥbt.yn. | ʻl h.ṯr h.tšʻrb. | ʻl h.tšʻrb.ẓby h. | ṯr.ḫbr.rbt. | ḫbr.ṯrrt. | bt.krt.tbun. | lm.mṯb[.---]. | w lḥm mr.tq 15[128].4.19
.mri k. | pṯḥ.[rḥ]bt.yn. | ṣḥ.šbʻm.ṯr y. | ṯmnym.[ẓ]by y. | ṯr.ḫbr[.rb]t. | ḫbr[.ṯrrt]. | [-]ʻb[-].š[--]m. | [----]r[.---]š[.--]qm. | i 15[128].4.8
.l mṯt.ḥry]. | ṭbḫ.š[mn].mri k. | pṯḥ.[rḥ]bt.yn. | ṣḥ.šbʻm.ṯr y. | ṯmnym.[ẓ]by y. | ṯr.ḫbr[.rb]t. | ḫbr[.ṯrrt]. | [-]ʻb[-].š[--]m. 15[128].4.6
.šʻrt. | mnn.šʻrt. | bdn.šʻrt. | ʻpṯn.šʻrt. | ʻbd.yrḫ šʻrt. | ḫbd.ṯr yṣr šʻr. | pdy.yṣr šʻrt. | atnb.ḥr. | šʻrt.šʻrt. 97[315].11
tmt[.---]. | [---.]k.w ṯṯ[--.---]. | [---.]k.w ṯ[--.---]. | [---.]k ṯrm.l p[--.---]. | [---.]l.[--.]rlg[-.---]. | [---.]bn.w [---]. | [---.--]ṯ.k 2125.9
[-----]. | [-----]. | il.šmʻ.amr k.ph[.-]. | k il.ḥkmt.k ṯr.lṭpn. | ṣḥ.ngr.il.ilš.il[š]. | w aṯt h.ngrt[.i]lht. | kḥṣ.k mʻr[.---]. 16[126].4.3
]. | qrẓ tšt.l šmal[.---]. | arbḫ.ʻn h tšu w[.---]. | aylt tǵpy ṯr.ʻn[.---]. | b[b]r.mrḫ h.ti[ḫd.b yd h]. | š[g]r h bm ymn.t[--.-- 2001.1.11
rpnm.yn.b k.ḫrṣ. | dm.ʻṣm.hm.yd.il mlk. | yḫss k.ahbt.ṯr.tʻrr k. | w tʻn.rbt.aṯrt ym. | ṯḥm k.il.ḥkm.ḥkmt. | ʻm ʻlm.ḥyt 4[51].4.39
.i]qnim.[--]. | [---.]aliyn.bʻl. | [---.--]k.mdd il. | y[m.---.]l ṯr.qdqd h. | il[.--.]rḥq.b ǵr. | km.y[--.]ilm.b ṣpn. | ʻdr.l[ʻr].ʻrm. 4[51].7.4
ty].ṣḥt km. | db[ḥ.l krt.a]dn km. | ʻl.krt.tbun.km. | rgm.ṯ[rm.]rgm hm. | b drt[.---.]krt. | [----]. 15[128].6.7
.l šty.ṣḥt k[m]. | [---.]brk.t[---]. | [ʻl.]krt.tbkn. | [--.]rgm.ṯrm. | [--.]mtm.tbkn. | [--]t.w b lb.tqb[-]. | [--]m[-].mtm.uṣbʻ[t] 15[128].5.13
ilm[.w] ḥẓr[.k bn]. | [qd]š.lbum.trd.b n[p]šn y.trḥṣn.k ṯrm. | [--]b b[ht]. | [zbl.]ym.b hkl.ṯpṭ.nh[r].yṯir.ṯr.il.ab h l pn[2.3[129].20
[-----]. | [------.]ṯr. | [---.aliy]n.bʻl. | [------.]yrḫ.zbl. | [--.kt]r w ḫss. | [---]n.rḥm 15[128].2.2
| krpn.b klat yd.[---]. | km ll.kḥṣ.tusp[.---]. | tgr.il.bn h.ṯr[.---]. | w yʻn.lṭpn.il.d p[id.---]. | šm.bn y.yw.ilt.[---]. | w pʻr.š 1[ʻNT.X].4.12
| [---].alp.[---].alp. | [---.-]rbd.kbd.ṯnm kbd. | [---.-]nnm ṯrm. | [---.]ṯlṯ kbd.ṣin. | [---.--]a.ṯ[l]ṯ.d.a[--]. | [---].mrn. | [---.]b 1145.1.8

ṯrin

ksdm. | ṣdqn. | nwrdr. | ṯrin. | ʻdršp. | pqr. | agbṯr. | ʻbd. | ksd. 1044.4

ṯrdnt

. | bn.ʻdṯ. | kṯy. | bn.ḫny. | bn.ssm. | bn.ḫnn. | [--]ny. | [bn].ṯrdnt. | [bn].hyadt. | [--]lt. | šmrm. | pʻṣ.bn.byy.ʻšrt. 1047.21

ṯrdn

y. | trgn.bn.tǵḥ. | aupš.qmnzy. | ṯrry.mṣbty. | prn.nǵṯy. | ṯrdn.zlyy. 89[312].11

ṯryl

ṯḥm[.t]lm[yn]. | l ṯryl.um y. | rgm. | ugrt.tǵr k. | ugrt.tǵr k. | tšlm k.um y. | tdʻ.k 1015.2
ṯḥm.mlk. | l.ṯryl.um y.rgm. | yšlm.l k.ilm. | tǵr k.tšlm k. | lḥt.šlm.k.lik[t]. | 2009.1.2
l. | ṯryl.p rgm. | l mlk.šm y. | w l h[-] yʻl m. | bn y.yšal. | ṯryl.w rgm. | ṯṯb.l aḫ k. | l adn k. 138.17
gm. | l mlk.šm y. | w l h.yʻl m. | w h[t] aḫ y. | bn y.yšal. | ṯryl.w rgm[.-]. | ṯṯb.l aḫ k. | l adn k. 138.17
.aḫ y.rgm. | ilm.tǵr k. | tšlm k. | iky.lḥt. | spr.d likt. | ʻm.ṯryl. | mh y.rgmt. | w ht.aḫ y. | bn y.yšal. | ṯryl.p rgm. | l mlk.š 138.8
.aḫ y.rgm. | ilm.tǵr k. | tšlm k. | ik y.lḥt. | spr.d likt. | ʻm.ṯryl. | mh y.rgmt. | w ht.aḫ y. | bn y.yšal. | ṯryl.p rgm. | l mlk.š 138.8
pr.d likt. | ʻm.ṯryl. | mh y.rgmt. | w ht.aḫ y. | bn y.yšal. | ṯryl.p rgm. | l mlk.šm y. | w l h[-] yʻl m. | bn y.yšal. | ṯryl.w rg 138.12
pr.d likt. | ʻm.ṯryl. | mh y.rgmt. | w ht.aḫ y. | bn y.yšal. | ṯryl.p rgm. | l mlk.šm y. | w l h.yʻl m. | w h[t] aḫ y. | bn y.yšal. 138.12

ṯryn

.w alp. | nṯq.ṯn.qlʻm. | ḫmš.ṣmdm.w ḥrṣ. | ṯryn.ššwm. | ṯryn.aḥd.d bnš. | arbʻ.ṣmdm.apnt. | w ḥrṣ. | tšʻm.mrḥ.aḥd. | kb 1123.6
.nḥl h. | w.nḥl hm. | [bn].pmn. | bn.gṯrn. | bn.arpḫn. | bn.ṯryn. | bn.dll. | bn.ḫswn. | mrynm. | ʻzn. | ḥyn. | ʻmyn. | ilyn. | yr 1046.3.30
n[.b] d.krmn.l.ty[n.n]ḥl h. | šd.krz.[b]n.ann.ʻ[db]. | šd.ṯ[r]yn.bn.tkn.b d.qrt. | šd[.-].dyn.b d.pln.nḥl h. | šd.irdyn.bn. 2029.14
[sp]r.akl[.---].ṯryn. | [tg]mr.akl.b.g[t.b]ir.alp. | [ʻ]šrm.l.mit.ḥ[p]r.ʻbdm. | mit 2013.1
| [w] ṯlṯ šmn. | [w a]r[bʻ] ksp ʻl bn ymn. | šb šr šmn [--] ṯryn. | ḫm[š]m l ʻšr ksp ʻl bn llit. | [--]l[-.-]p ʻl [---.-]bʻm arny. 1103.5
.qšt. | alp ḥẓm.w alp. | nṯq.ṯn.qlʻm. | ḫmš.ṣmdm.w ḥrṣ. | ṯryn.ššwm. | ṯryn.aḥd.d bnš. | arbʻ.ṣmdm.apnt. | w ḥrṣ. | tšʻm. 1123.5
ḫd[t]. | br.ṯpṭbʻ[l.---]. | br.dmty[.---]. | ṯkt.ydln[.---]. | ṯkt.ṯryn[.---]. | br.ʻbdm[lk.---]. | wry[.---]. | ṯkt[.---]. | ṯk[t.---]. | br[.- 84[319].1.5

ṯrk

bn.ḫdyn.ṯqlm. | bn.ʻbd.šḫr.ṯqlm. | bn.ḫnqn.arbʻt. | [b]n.ṯrk.ṯqlm. | [b]n.pdrn.ṯq[lm]. | pdy.[----]. | [i]lmlk.bn.[---]. | [--]ʻ 122[308].1.21

ṯrkn

tldn. | ṯrkn. | kli. | plǵn. | apšny. | ʻrb[.---]. | w.b.p[.--]. | apš[ny]. | b.yṣi 2116.2

ṯrm

nm.uḫd.bʻlm. | [--.a]ṯm.prṯl.l riš h.ḥmṯ.ṯmṯ. | [--.]ydbr.ṯrmt.al m.qḥn y.š y.qḥn y. | [--.]šir.b krm.nṭṭt.dm.ʻlt.b ab y. 1001.1.8
l ytn.tk.ǵr.ll.ʻm.phr.mʻd.ap.ilm.l lḥ[m]. | yṯb.bn qdš.l ṯrm.bʻl.qm.ʻl.il.hlm. | ilm.tph hm.tphn.mlak.ym.tʻdt.ṯpṭ[.nh 2.1[137].21
p. | art. | [--]n. | [-----]. | [-----]. | nnu. | šmg. | šmn. | lbnm. | ṯrm. | bṣr. | y[--]. | y[--]. | snr. | midḫ. | ḫ[lym]. | [ḫ]lby. | ʻr. | ʻnq[2058.2.15
.mgṯ.w iṯrm. | ṯšmʻ.mṯt.ḥry. | ṭṭbḫ.imr.w lḥm. | mgṯ.w yṯrm.hn.ym. | w ṯn.yṯb.krt.l ʻd h. | yṯb.l ksi mlk. | l nḫt.l kḥṯ. 16.6[127].21
l.riš h. | w ṯṯb.trḥṣ.nn.b dʻt. | npš h.l lḥm.tpṯḥ. | brlt h.l ṯrm. | mt.dm.ḫt.šʻtqt. | dm.lan.w ypqd. | krt.ṯʻ.yšu.g h. | w yṣḥ 16.6[127].12
ḥbš h.km.diy. | b tʻrt h.aqht.km.yṯb.l lḥ[m]. | bn.dnil.l ṯrm.ʻl h.nšr[m]. | trḫpn.ybṣr.ḥbl.diy[m.bn]. | nšrm.trḫp.ʻnt.ʻl[18[3AQHT].4.30
š y]. | km.diy.b tʻrt y.aqht.[km.yṯb]. | l lḥm.w bn.dnil.l ṯrm[.ʻl h]. | nšrm.trḫpn.ybṣr.[ḥbl.d] | iym.bn.nšrm.arḫp.an[k. 18[3AQHT].4.19
šu.g h. | w yṣḥ.šmʻ.l mṯt. | ḥry.ṭbḫ.imr. | w ilḥm.mgṯ.w iṯrm. | ṯšmʻ.mṯt.ḥry. | ṭṭbḫ.imr.w lḥm. | mgṯ.w yṯrm.hn.ym. | 16.6[127].18
. | š[g]r h bm ymn.t[--.---]. | [--.]l bʻl.ʻbd[.---]. | ṯr ab h il.ṯṯrm[.---]. | tšlḥm yrḫ.ggn[.---]. | k[.---.ḫ]mš.ḫssm[.---]. | [---.-- 2001.1.15

ṯrmg

idk.al.ttn.pnm. | ʻm.ǵr.trǵzz. | ʻm.ǵr.ṯrmg. | ʻm.tlm.ǵṣr.arṣ. | ša.ǵr.ʻl.ydm. | ḫlb.l ẓr.rḥtm. | w rd.bt 4[51].8.3

ṯrml

.|n‘m h.km.tsm.|‘ṯtrt.tsm h.|d ‘q h.ib.iqni.|‘p‘p h.sp.ṯrml.|d b ḥlm y.il.ytn.|b ḏrt y.ab.adm.|w ld.šph.l krk|t.w 14[KRT].6.295
‘m h.|km.tsm.‘ṯtrt.ts[m h].|d ‘q h.ib.iqni.‘p[‘p] h.|sp.ṯrml.tḥgrn.[-]dm[.-].|ašlw.b ṣp.‘n h.|d b ḥlm y.il.ytn.|b ḏrt 14[KRT].3.148

ṯrmn

t.aḫd.|ḥrṯ h.aḫd.b gt.nḫl.|aḫd.b gt.knpy.w.aḫd.b gt.ṯrmn.|aḫd.alp.idṯn.d aḫd.b.‘nqpat.|[aḫd.al]p.d aǵlmn.|[d a 1129.10
t.l mzy.bn[--].|aḫt.l mkt.ǵr.|aḫt.l ‘ṯtrt.|arb‘.‘ṣrm.|gt.ṯrmn.|aḫt.slḫu. 39[19].18
---].|[--]l.ṯrmn.m[lk.---].|[---.--]rt.š‘rt[.---].|[---.i]qni.l.ṯr[mn.art.---].|[b.yr]ḫ.riš.yn.[---].|[---.b‘]lt.bhtm.š[--.---].|[- 1106.31
il[bt].gdlt.ušḫry.gdlt.ym gdlt.|b‘l gdlt.yrḫ.gdlt.|gdlt.ṯrmn.gdlt.pdry.gdlt dqt.|dqt.trṯ.dqt.|[rš]p.‘nt.ḫbly.dbḥn š[34[1].15
dbḥ klyrḫ.|ndr.|dbḥ.|dt nat.|w ytnt.|ṯrmn w.|dbḥ kl.|kl ykly.|dbḥ k.sprt.|dt nat.|w qrwn.|l k RS61[24.277.6]
.d.iqni.w.šmt.|l.iyb‘l.|ṯlṯm.l.mit.š‘rt.|l.šr.‘ṯtrt.|mlbš.ṯrmnm.|k.ytn.w.b.bt.|mlk.mlbš.|ytn.l hm.|šb‘.lbšm.allm.| 1107.5
mat.abn.ṣrp.|[---.-]qt.l.ṯrmnm.|[---].ṯlṯm.iqnu.|[---.l.]ṯrmn.mlk.|[---.]š‘rt.šb‘.‘šr h.|[---.iqn]i.l.ṯrmn.qrt.|[---.]lbš.ḫ 1106.13
lṯ.m[at.---].|[---].abn.ṣr[p.---].|[---.-]rt.ṯlṯm[.---].|[--]l.ṯrmn.m[lk.---].|[---.--]rt.š‘rt[.---].|[---.i]qni.l.ṯr[mn.art.---].| 1106.29
ilbt.|ušḫry.|ym.b‘l.|yrḫ.|kṯr.|ṯrmn.|pdry.|dqt.|trṯ.|ršp.|‘nt ḫbly.|špš pgr.|iltm ḫnqtm.| UG5.14.A.6
.iqnu.|[---.l.]ṯrmn.mlk.|[---.]š‘rt.šb‘.‘šr h.|[---.iqn]i.l.ṯrmn.qrt.|[---.]lbš.ḫmšm.iqnu.|[---].šmt.ḫmšt.ḫndlt.|[---.iq 1106.15
.mit.dr‘.ṯṯm.drt.w.šb‘m.dd.arb‘.|kbd.ḥpr.bnšm.|b.gt.ṯrmn.arb‘m.dr‘.w.‘šrm.drt.|w.ṯlṯm.dd.ṯṯ.kbd.ḥpr.bnšm.|b.g 1098.20
iqnu.|[---].šmt.ḫmšt.ḫndlt.|[---.iqn]i.l.[-]k.btbt.|[---.l.ṯrm]nm.š[b‘].mat.š‘rt.|[---.]iqnu.[---.]lbš.ṯrmnm.|[---.iqn]i.l 1106.19
k.btbt.|[---.l.ṯrm]nm.š[b‘].mat.š‘rt.|[---.]iqnu.[---.]lbš.ṯrmnm.|[---.iqn]i.lbš.al[l.---].|[---].ṯṯ.lbš[.---].|[---.]kbd.ṯṯ.i[q 1106.20
|[---].mitm.kslm.|[---].pwt.ṯlṯ.mat.abn.ṣrp.|[---.-]qt.l.ṯrmnm.|[---].ṯlṯm.iqnu.|[---.l.]ṯrmn.mlk.|[---.]š‘rt.šb‘.‘šr h. 1106.11
m.b šnt.|[---.]šb‘.mat.š‘rt.ḫmšm.kbd.|[---.-]nd.l.mlbš.ṯrmnm.|[---]h.lbš.allm.lbnm.|[---].all.šmt.|[---].all.iqni.arb‘ 1106.3
.|khnm rb.nqdm.|ṯ‘y.nqmd.mlk ugr[t].|adn.yrgb.b‘l.ṯrmn. 6.6[62.2].57

ṯrmnm

.b‘l.ṣpn š.|[--]ṯ š.ilt.mgdl š.ilt.asrm š.|w l ll.šp. pgr.w ṯrmnm.bt mlk.|il[bt].gdlt.ušḫry.gdlt.ym gdlt.|b‘l gdlt.yrḫ.g 34[1].12

ṯrn

y.|b‘l.bt.pdy.|b‘l.bt.nqly.|b‘l.bt.‘lr.|b‘l.bt.ssl.|b‘l.bt.ṯrn.|b‘l.bt.ktmn.|b‘l.bt.ndbd.|[--].ṣnr.|[b‘l].bt.bsn.|[-----].| 31[14].7
aḏml[--.---].|tlbr[-.---].|isg.[---].|ilwn.[---].|ṯrn.d[d].|tg d[d].|ḥdyn.d[d].|[-]ḏdn.d[d].|qṭn.d[d].|lḥsn.d[132[331].5
[---]y.|[---.]w.nḥl h.|bn ksln.ṯlṯh.|bn yṣmḫ.bn.ṯrn w nḥl h.|bn srd.bn agmn.|bn [-]ln.bn.ṯbil.|bn is.bn tbd 101[10].4
|b[-.--]t.|[---.-]l[--].|[---.]pr[--].|[-.a]pln.|bn.mzt.|bn.ṯrn.|w.nḥl h.|[--.-]hs.|[--.--]nyn.|[-----].|[-----].|bn.‘dy.|w. 2163.2.14
wryn.|n‘mn.|[-----].|b gt.yny.|agtṯp.|bn.‘nt.|ǵzldn.|ṯrn.|ḫdbṯ.|[-]ḥl.aǵltn.|[-]n.|[-]mṯ.|[--.]bn.[‘]zn.|[--]yn. 1043.14

ṯrnq

šyn[.---.]yṯb.b.ar.|bn.ag[p]ṯ.ḫpṯ.d[.yṯb.b].š‘rt.|yly.bn.ṯrnq.[-]r.d.yṯb.b.ilštm‘.|ilšlm.bn.gs[-.--]r.d.yṯb.b.gt.al.|ilml 2015.1.26

ṯrp

il.[---].|[tṣ]un.b arṣ.|mḫnm.ṯrp ym.|lšnm.tlḥk.|šmm.ṯtrp.|ym.ḏnbtm.|tnn.l šbm.|tšt.trks.|l mrym.l bt[.---].|p l. 1003.6
[--]r.[---].|[---.]il.[---].|[tṣ]un.b arṣ.|mḫnm.ṯrp ym.|lšnm.tlḥk.|šmm.ṯtrp.|ym.ḏnbtm.|tnn.l šbm.|tšt.tr 1003.4

ṯrr

‘.‘ln.bḫr.|[---].aṯt k.‘l.|[---] k.yšṣi.|[---.]ḫbr.rbt.|[ḫbr.ṯrr]t.il d.|[pid.---].b anšt.|[---.]mlu.|[---.--]tm. 15[128].5.26
ḥ.kr]t[.šlmm].|š[lmm.]al.t[ṣr].|udm[.r]bt.w u[dm].|[ṯ]rrt.udm.y[t]n[t].|il.ušn.ab[.ad]m.|rḥq.mlk.l bt y.|n[g.]krt 14[KRT].6.277
g.mlk.|l bt y.rḥq.krt.|l ḥẓr y.al.tṣr.|udm.rbt.w udm ṯrrt.|udm.ytnt.il w ušn.|ab.adm.w ṯṯb.|mlakm.l h.lm.ank.| 14[KRT].3.134
].|[qḥ.krt.šlmm].|[šlmm.al.tṣr].|[udm.rbt.w udm].|[ṯrrt.udm.ytnt].|[il.w ušn.ab.adm].|[rḥq.mlk.l bt y].|[ng.kr] 14[KRT].5.258
bt.yn.|‘l h.ṯr h.tš‘rb.|‘l h.tš‘rb.ẓby h.|ṯr.ḫbr.rbt.|ḫbr.ṯrrt.|bt.krt.tbun.|lm.mṯb[.---].|w lḥm mr.tqdm.|yd.b ṣ‘.tšl 15[128].4.20
ṯlṯ.rb‘.ym.|aḫr.špšm.b rb‘.|ymǵy.l udm.rbt.|w udm[.ṯr]rt.|grnn.‘rm.|šrnn.pdrm.|s‘t.b šdm.ḥṭb.|w b grnt.ḥpšt.| 14[KRT].4.211
.ṯdṯ.ym.mk.špšm.|b šb‘.w tmǵy.l udm.|rbm.w l.udm.ṯrrt.|w gr.nn.‘rm.šrn.|pdrm.s‘t.b šdm.|ḥṭb h.b grnt.ḥpšt.|s 14[KRT].3.109
k.ngrt.il[ht].|‘l.l ṯkm.bnw n.|l nḫnpt.mšpy.|ṯlṯ.kmm.ṯrr y.|[---.]l ǵr.gm.ṣḥ.|[---.]r[-]m. 16[126].4.16
t h.ykr.‘r.d qdm.|idk.pnm.l ytn.tk aršḫ.rbt.|w aršḫ.ṯrrt.ydy.b ‘ṣm.‘r‘r.|w b šḥt.‘s.mt.‘r‘rm.yn‘rn h.|ssnm.ysyn UG5.7.64
.yn.|ṣḥ.šb‘m.ṯr y.|ṯmnym.[ẓ]by y.|ṯr.ḫbr[.rb]t.|ḫbr[.ṯrrt].|[-]‘b[-].š[--]m.|[----]r[.---]š[.--]qm.|id.u [---]t.|lḥn š[-]‘ 15[128].4.9

ṯrry

y.|pdu.qmnzy.|bdl.qrty.|trgn.bn.ṯǵḥ.|aupš.qmnzy.|ṯrry.mṣbty.|prn.nǵṯy.|ṯrdn.zlyy. 89[312].9

ṯrtn

nnm.w.šb‘.ḫsnm.|ṯmn.‘šr h.mrynm.|‘šr.mkrm.|ḫmš.ṯrtnm.|ḫmš.bn.mrynm.|‘šr.mrum.w.šb‘.ḫsnm.|tš‘m.mḏrǵl 1030.4
ṯnnm.ṯṯ.|‘šr.ḫsnm.|n‘r.mrynm.|ḫmš.|ṯrtnm.ḫmš.|mrum.‘šr.|šb‘.ḫsnm.|mkrm.|mrynm.|ṯlṯ.‘šr.| 1031.5
.mḏr[ǵlm].|kd[.--].lm[d.---].|kd[.l.]ḫzr[m.---].|kd[.l.]ṯrtn[m].|arb‘ l.mry[nm].|kdm l.ḫty.[---].|kdm l.‘ṯtr[t].|kd l 1091.7
.|tš‘.‘šr.|mrynm.|ṯlṯ.‘šr.mkrm.|ṯlṯ.bn.mrynm.|arb‘.ṯrtnm.|tš‘.ḫbṭnm.|ṯmnym.ṯlṯ.kbd.|mḏrǵlm.|w.šb‘.‘šr.ḫsn 1029.9
ḫmš.ṯnnm.‘šr.ḫsnm.|ṯlṯ.‘šr.mrynm.|ḫmš.[ṯr]tnm.|ṯlṯ.b[n.]mrynm.|‘šr[.m]krm.|tš‘.hbṭnm.|‘šr.mrum. 1028.3

ṯrṯy

.š.|il.š.kṯrt.š.|dgn.š.b‘l.ḫlb alp w š.|b‘l ṣpn alp.w.š.|ṯrṯy.alp.w.š.|yrḫ.š.ṣpn.š.|kṯr š ‘ṯtr.š.|[‘ṯ]rt.š.šgr w iṯm š.|[- UG5.9.2.6

ṯšm

.|b ǵlt.yd k.l tdn.|dn.almnt.l ttpṭ.|ṯpṭ qṣr.npš.l tdy.|ṯšm.ʻl.dl.l pn k.|l tšlḥm.ytm.bʻd.|ksl k.almnt.km.|aḫt.ʻrš.m 16.6[127].48

ṯty

ḥdd.ar[y.---].|bʻlsip.a[ry.---].|klt h.[---].|ṯty.ary.m[--.---].|nrn.arny[.---].|w.ṯn.bn h.w.b[---.---].|b tn[81[329].4
---]nb.w ykn.|[--]ndbym.|[ʻ]rmy.w snry.|[b]n.sdy.bn.ṯty.|bn.ḥyn.bn.ǵlm.|bn.yyn.w.bn.au[pš].|bn.kdrn.|ʻrgzy.w 131[309].23
[-].w.špš.|[---.b].ṣp[n].|[---.]š[--].|[-----].|[-----].|[---.]ṯty.|[---.-]rd y.|[---.]bʻl.|[---].plz.|[---.-]tt k.|[---.]mlk. 2159.14

ṯtm

ʻt.ʻšrt.|b.bn.pdrn.ʻšrm.|d.bn.šbʻl.uḫnpy.ḫmšm.|b.bn.ṯtm.ṯlṯm.|b.bn.agdṯb.ʻšrm.|b.bn.ibn.arbʻt.ʻšrt.|b.bn.mnn.ṯṯ 2054.1.11

ṯtmnt

|tdm.l y.al tkl.bn.|qr.ʻn k.mḫ.riš k.|udmʻt.ṣḥ.aḫt k.|ṯtmnt.bt.ḥmḥ h.|d[-]n.tbkn.w tdm.l y.[--].|[---].al.trgm.l aḫ 16.1[125].29
.|[-]mt[-].ṣba.rbt.|špš.w tgh.nyr.|rbt.w rgm.l aḫt k.|ṯtmnt.krt n.dbḥ.|dbḥ.mlk.ʻšr.|ʻšrt.qḥ.tp k.b yd.|[-]r[-]k.b 16.1[125].39

ṯtʻ

bt k.l yhpk.ksa.mlk k.|l yṯbr.ḫṭ.mṯpṭ k.|yru.bn ilm t.ṯtʻ.y|dd.il.ǵzr.yʻr.mt.|b ql h.y[---.---].|bʻl.yṯṯbn[.l ksi].|mlk 6[49].6.30
p h yrd.|k ḥrr.zt.ybl.arṣ.w pr.|ʻṣm.yraun.aliyn.bʻl.|ṯtʻ.nn.rkb.ʻrpt.|tbʻ.rgm.l bn.ilm.mt.|ṯny.l ydd.il ǵzr.|tḥm.a 5[67].2.7

ṯtq

ḏ.pid.hn b p y sp|r hn.b špt y mn|t hn ṯlḫ h w mlg h y|ṯtqt ʻm h b qʻt.|tqʻt ʻm prbḫṯ.|dmqt ṣǵrt kṯrt. 24[77].47

ṯtrn

ab.bʻl aṯt.|iyṯr.bʻl aṯt.|ptm.bʻl ššlmt.|ʻdršp.bʻl ššlmt.|ṯtrn.bʻl ššlmt.|arŝwn.bʻl ššlmt.|ḥdṯn.bʻl ššlmt.|ssn.bʻl ššlmt 1077.8

ṯṯw

ar[.---].|ʻṯtr[.---].|bn.[---].|yly[.---].|ykn[.---].|rp[--].|ṯṯw.[---].|[---.ʻ]šrm.ṣmd.ŝŝw. 2131.11

ṯṯy

lʻ.|nʻmn.q[št.w.]qlʻ.|[t]tn.qš[t].|bn.ṯǵḏy[.qšt.]w.qlʻ.|ṯṯy.qšt[.w.]qlʻ.|bn.šp[š.]qšt.|bn.ʻg[w.]qšt.w qlʻ.|ḥd[ṯ]n.qšt. 119[321].4.5

ṯṯl

n[-].|bn.mqwṭ.|bn.bsn.|bn.inr[-].|bn.ṯbil.|bn.iryn.|ṯṯl.|bn.nṣdn.|bn.ydln.|[bn].ʻdy.|[bn].ilyn. 1071.7

ṯṯpḥ

d adn[ʻm].|[---].riš[.---].kt.|[y]nḥm.|ilbʻl.|ʻbdyr[ḫ].|ṯṯpḥ.|artn.|ybnil.|brqn.|adr[dn].|krwn.|arkḏn.|ilmn.|abš 1024.1.6
[ḥrš].bhtm.bʻl.šd.|[---d]nil.|[a]drdn.|[---]n.|pǵḏn.|ṯṯpḥ.|ḥgbn.|šrm.|bn.ymil.|bn.kḏǵdl.|[-]mn.|[--]n.|[ḥr]š.q 1039.1.25
.klyn.ʻdršp.ǵlmn.|[a]bǵl.ṣṣn.ǵrn.|šib.mqdšt.ʻb[dml]k.ṯṯpḥ.mrṭn.|ḫḏǵlm.i[---]n.pbn.nḏbn.sbd.|šrm.[---].ḫpn.|ḥrš[2011.15

Index